Mills College Library
WITHDRAWN

The Europa World Year Book 1989

The Europa World Year Book 1989

VOLUME I

PART ONE INTERNATIONAL ORGANIZATIONS
PART TWO AFGHANISTAN–JORDAN

EUROPA PUBLICATIONS LIMITED

First published 1926

© **Europa Publications Limited 1989**
18 Bedford Square, London, WC1B 3JN, England

All rights reserved. No part of this
publication may be photocopied, recorded,
or otherwise reproduced, stored in a retrieval
system or transmitted in any form or by any
electronic or mechanical means without the
prior permission of the copyright owner.

Australia and New Zealand
James Bennett (Collaroy) Pty Ltd, 4 Collaroy Street,
Collaroy, NSW 2097, Australia

India
UBS Publishers' Distributors Ltd,
POB 7015, 5 Ansari Road, New Delhi 110002

Japan
Maruzen Co Ltd, POB 5050, Tokyo International 100-31

ISBN 0-946653-49-6
ISSN 0956-2273
Library of Congress Catalog Card Number 59-2942

Printed and bound in England by
Staples Printers Rochester Limited, Love Lane, Rochester, Kent.

FOREWORD

THE EUROPA WORLD YEAR BOOK (formerly THE EUROPA YEAR BOOK: A WORLD SURVEY) was first published in 1926. Since 1960 it has appeared in annual two-volume editions, and has become established as an authoritative reference work, providing a wealth of detailed information on the political, economic and commercial institutions of the world.

Volume I contains international organizations and the first part of the alphabetical survey of countries of the world, from Afghanistan to Jordan. Volume II contains countries from Kampuchea to Zimbabwe.

Readers are referred to our six regional books, THE MIDDLE EAST AND NORTH AFRICA, AFRICA SOUTH OF THE SAHARA, THE FAR EAST AND AUSTRALASIA, SOUTH AMERICA, CENTRAL AMERICA AND THE CARIBBEAN, WESTERN EUROPE and THE USA AND CANADA (forthcoming), for additional information on the geography, history and economy of these areas.

The information is revised annually by a variety of methods, including direct mailing to all the institutions listed. Many other sources are used, such as national statistical offices, government departments and diplomatic missions. The editors thank the innumerable individuals and organizations throughout the world whose generous co-operation in providing current information for this edition is invaluable in presenting the most accurate and up-to-date material available, and acknowledge particular indebtedness for material from the following publications: the United Nations' *Demographic Yearbook*, *Statistical Yearbook* and *Industrial Statistics Yearbook*; the Food and Agriculture Organization of the United Nations' *Production Yearbook*, *Yearbook of Fishery Statistics* and *Yearbook of Forest Products*; and *The Military Balance 1988–1989*, published by the International Institute for Strategic Studies, 23 Tavistock Street, London, WC2E 7NQ.

February 1989.

CONTENTS

Abbreviations	Page xi
International Comparisons	xiv
Late Information	xix

PART ONE
International Organizations*

The United Nations	3
Members	3
Permanent Missions	4
Observers	6
Information Centres	6
Budget	8
Charter of the United Nations	9
Secretariat	17
General Assembly	18
Security Council	19
Economic and Social Council—ECOSOC	19
Trusteeship Council	20
International Court of Justice	20
United Nations Training and Research Institutes	22
United Nations Regional Commissions	24
Economic Commission for Europe—ECE	24
Economic and Social Commission for Asia and the Pacific—ESCAP	25
Economic Commission for Latin America and the Caribbean—ECLAC	27
Economic Commission for Africa—ECA	28
Economic and Social Commission for Western Asia—ESCWA	31
Other United Nations Bodies	33
International Sea-Bed Authority	33
Office of the United Nations Disaster Relief Co-Ordinator—UNDRO	34
United Nations Centre for Human Settlements—UNCHS (Habitat)	35
United Nations Children's Fund—UNICEF	36
United Nations Conference on Trade and Development—UNCTAD	37
United Nations Development Programme—UNDP	38
United Nations Environment Programme—UNEP	40
United Nations High Commissioner for Refugees—UNHCR	42
United Nations Observer Missions and Peace-keeping Forces	44
United Nations Population Fund—UNFPA	46
United Nations Relief and Works Agency for Palestine Refugees in the Near East—UNRWA	47
World Food Council—WFC	Page 48
World Food Programme—WFP	49
Membership of the United Nations and its Specialized Agencies	50
Specialized Agencies within the UN System	53
Food and Agriculture Organization—FAO	53
General Agreement on Tariffs and Trade—GATT	56
International Atomic Energy Agency—IAEA	58
International Bank for Reconstruction and Development—IBRD (World Bank)	60
International Development Association—IDA	64
International Finance Corporation—IFC	65
Multilateral Investment Guarantee Agency—MIGA	66
International Civil Aviation Organization—ICAO	66
International Fund for Agricultural Development—IFAD	68
International Labour Organisation—ILO	69
International Maritime Organization—IMO	71
International Monetary Fund—IMF	72
International Telecommunication Union—ITU	76
United Nations Educational, Scientific and Cultural Organization—UNESCO	77
United Nations Industrial Development Organization—UNIDO	79
Universal Postal Union—UPU	80
World Health Organization—WHO	81
World Intellectual Property Organization—WIPO	84
World Meteorological Organization—WMO	85
African Development Bank—ADB	88
Andean Group	90
ANZUS	92
Arab Bank for Economic Development in Africa—BADEA	93
Arab Fund for Economic and Social Development—AFESD	95
Arab Monetary Fund	96
Asian Development Bank—ADB	98
Association of South East Asian Nations—ASEAN	101
Bank for International Settlements—BIS	104
Caribbean Community and Common Market—CARICOM	106
Central American Common Market—CACM	108
The Colombo Plan for Co-operative Economic and Social Development in Asia and the Pacific	110
The Commonwealth	111
Communauté Economique de l'Afrique de l'Ouest—CEAO	119
Conseil de l'Entente	121
Co-operation Council for the Arab States of the Gulf	122
Council for Mutual Economic Assistance—CMEA	124
Council of Arab Economic Unity	126
Council of Europe	128

---

* A complete Index of International Organizations is to be found on p. 1514.

CONTENTS

	Page
Economic Community of West African States—ECOWAS	132
The European Communities	134
European Free Trade Association—EFTA	152
The Franc Zone	154
Inter-American Development Bank—IDB	156
Intergovernmental Committee for Migration—ICM	158
International Bank for Economic Co-operation—IBEC	159
International Chamber of Commerce—ICC	160
International Confederation of Free Trade Unions—ICFTU	162
International Investment Bank	164
International Olympic Committee	165
International Red Cross	166
International Committee of the Red Cross	166
League of Red Cross and Red Crescent Societies	167
Islamic Development Bank	168
Latin American Integration Association—LAIA	170
League of Arab States	171
Nordic Council	176
Nordic Council of Ministers	177
North Atlantic Treaty Organisation—NATO	179
Organisation for Economic Co-operation and Development—OECD	182
International Energy Agency	184
OECD Nuclear Energy Agency—NEA	184
Organization of African Unity—OAU	186
Organization of American States—OAS	190
Organization of Arab Petroleum Exporting Countries—OAPEC	193
Organization of the Islamic Conference—OIC	194
Organization of the Petroleum Exporting Countries—OPEC	196
OPEC Fund for International Development	199
South Pacific Commission—SPC	201
South Pacific Forum	203
South Pacific Bureau for Economic Co-operation—SPEC	203
Southern African Development Co-ordination Conference—SADCC	205
Warsaw Treaty of Friendship, Co-operation and Mutual Assistance—The Warsaw Pact	207
Western European Union—WEU	208
World Confederation of Labour—WCL	209
World Council of Churches—WCC	210
World Federation of Trade Unions—WFTU	211
Other International Organizations	213

PART TWO

Afghanistan–Jordan

Afghanistan	277
Albania	292
Algeria	304
Andorra	322
Angola	325
Antarctica	339
Antigua and Barbuda	341

	Page
Argentina	347
Australia	369
Australian External Territories:	394
Christmas Island	394
Cocos (Keeling) Islands	394
Norfolk Island	395
Other Territories	396
Austria	398
The Bahamas	416
Bahrain	423
Bangladesh	432
Barbados	450
Belgium	457
Belize	479
Benin	486
Bhutan	497
Bolivia	505
Botswana	520
Brazil	531
Brunei	558
Bulgaria	564
Burkina Faso	581
Burma	592
Burundi	605
Cameroon	614
Canada	628
Cape Verde	658
The Central African Republic	664
Chad	674
Chile	684
China, People's Republic	702
China (Taiwan)	728
Colombia	742
The Comoros	760
The Congo	766
Costa Rica	777
Côte d'Ivoire	789
Cuba	803
Cyprus	819
Czechoslovakia	835
Denmark	854
Danish External Territories:	875
Faeroe Islands	875
Greenland	877
Djibouti	881
Dominica	887
The Dominican Republic	893
Ecuador	906
Egypt	922
El Salvador	944
Equatorial Guinea	958
Ethiopia	964
Fiji	977
Finland	985
Finnish External Territory:	1005
Åland Islands	1005
France	1007
French Overseas Possessions:	1051

CONTENTS

	Page		Page
Overseas Departments:	1051	Guinea-Bissau	1224
French Guiana	1051	Guyana	1230
Guadeloupe	1054	Haiti	1239
Martinique	1058	Honduras	1249
Réunion	1062	Hungary	1261
Overseas Collectivités Territoriales:	1066	Iceland	1282
Mayotte	1066	India	1291
Saint Pierre and Miquelon	1068	Indonesia	1328
Overseas Territories:	1071	Iran	1347
French Polynesia	1071	Iraq	1366
French Southern and Antarctic Territories	1075	Ireland	1383
New Caledonia	1076	Israel	1401
Wallis and Futuna Islands	1081	Italy	1422
Gabon	1083	The Ivory Coast—see Côte d'Ivoire	
The Gambia	1095	Jamaica	1454
German Democratic Republic	1101	Japan	1467
Federal Republic of Germany	1122	Jordan	1499
Ghana	1163		
Greece	1177	**Index of International Organizations**	1514
Grenada	1194		
Guatemala	1201	An Index of Territories is to be found at the end of Volume II.	
Guinea	1215		

ABBREVIATIONS

AB	Aktiebolag (Joint Stock Company)
Abog.	Abogado (Lawyer)
Acad.	Academician; Academy
ACT	Australian Capital Territory
ADB	African Development Bank; Asian Development Bank
Adm.	Admiral
admin.	administration
AG	Aktiengesellschaft (Joint Stock Company)
a.i.	ad interim
AID	(US) Agency for International Development
AIDS	Acquired Immunodeficiency Syndrome
Al.	Aleja (Alley, Avenue)
Ala	Alabama
ALADI	Asociación Latino-Americana de Integración
Alt.	Alternate
Alta	Alberta
AM	Amplitude Modulation
amalg.	amalgamated
AP	Andhra Pradesh
Apdo	Apartado (Post Box)
approx.	approximately
Apt	Apartment
Ariz	Arizona
Ark	Arkansas
A/S	Aktieselskab (Joint Stock Company)
ASEAN	Association of South East Asian Nations
assen	association
assoc.	associate
asst	assistant
Aug.	August
auth.	authorized
Ave	Avenue
Avda	Avenida (Avenue)
Avv.	Avvocato (Lawyer)
BC	British Columbia
Bd	Board
Bd, Bld, Blv., Blvd	Boulevard
b/d	barrels per day
Bhd	Berhad (Public Limited Company)
Bldg	Building
BP	Boîte postale (Post Box)
br.(s)	branch(es)
Brig.	Brigadier
Bt	Baronet
bte	boîte (box)
bul.	bulvar (boulevard)
C	Centigrade
c.	circa; cuadra(s) (block(s))
CACM	Central American Common Market
Cad.	Caddesi (Street)
Calif	California
cap.	capital
Capt.	Captain
CARICOM	Caribbean Community
CB	Companion of (the Order of) the Bath
CBE	Commander of (the Order of) the British Empire
CCL	Caribbean Congress of Labour
Cdre	Commodore
Cen.	Central
CEO	Chief Executive Officer
CFA	Communauté Financière Africaine; Co-opération Financière en Afrique centrale
CFP	Communauté française du Pacifique; Comptoirs français du Pacifique
CH	Companion of Honour
Chair.	Chairman/woman
CI	Channel Islands
Cia	Companhia
Cía	Compañía
Cie	Compagnie
c.i.f.	cost, insurance and freight
C-in-C	Commander-in-Chief
circ.	circulation
cm	centimetre(s)
CMEA	Council for Mutual Economic Assistance
Cnr	Corner
Co	Company; County
Col	Colonel
Col.	Colonia
Colo	Colorado
Comm.	Commission; Commendatore
Commdr	Commander
Commdt	Commandant
Commr	Commissioner
Confed.	Confederation
Conn	Connecticut
Cont.	Contador (Accountant)
Corpn	Corporation
CP	Case Postale; Caixa Postal; Casella Postale (Post Box); Communist Party
CPSU	Communist Party of the Soviet Union
Cres.	Crescent
CSTAL	Confederación Sindical de los Trabajadores de América Latina
CTCA	Confederación de Trabajadores Centro-americanos
Cttee	Committee
cu	cubic
cwt	hundredweight
DC	District of Columbia; Distrito Central
DDR	Deutsche Democratische Republik (German Democratic Republic)
DE	Departamento Estatal
Dec.	December
Del	Delaware
Del.	Delegación
Dem.	Democratic; Democrat
Dep.	Deputy
dep.	deposits
Dept	Department
devt	development
DF	Distrito Federal
Diag.	Diagonal
Dir	Director
Div.	Division(al)
DM	Deutsche Mark
DN	Distrito Nacional
Doc.	Docent
Dott.	Dottore
Dr	Doctor
Dr.	Drive
Dra	Doctora
dr.(e)	drachma(e)
Drs	Doctorandus
dwt	dead weight tons
E	East; Eastern
ECA	(United Nations) Economic Commission for Africa
ECE	(United Nations) Economic Commission for Europe
ECLAC	(United Nations) Economic Commission for Latin America and the Caribbean
Econ.	Economist; Economics
ECOSOC	(United Nations) Economic and Social Council
ECOWAS	Economic Community of West African States
ECU	European Currency Unit
ECWA	(United Nations) Economic Commission for Western Asia
Edif.	Edificio (Building)
edn	edition
EEC	European Economic Community
EFTA	European Free Trade Association
e.g.	exempli gratia (for example)
eKv	electron kilovolt
eMv	electron megavolt
Eng.	Engineer; Engineering
Esc.	Escuela; Escudos; Escritorio

ABBREVIATIONS

ESCAP	(United Nations) Economic and Social Commission for Asia and the Pacific
esq.	esquina (corner)
est.	established; estimate; estimated
etc.	et cetera
eV	eingetragener Verein
excl.	excluding
exec.	executive
Ext.	Extension
F	Fahrenheit
f.	founded
FAO	Food and Agriculture Organization
Feb.	February
Fed.	Federation; Federal
Fla	Florida
FM	frequency modulation
fmrly	formerly
f.o.b.	free on board
Fr	Father
Fr.	Franc
FRG	Federal Republic of Germany
Fri.	Friday
ft	foot (feet)
g	gram(s)
Ga	Georgia
GATT	General Agreement on Tariffs and Trade
GBE	Knight (or Dame) Grand Cross of (the Order of) the British Empire
GCMG	Knight Grand Cross of (the Order of) St Michael and St George
GDP	gross domestic product
GDR	German Democratic Republic
Gen.	General
GeV	giga electron volts
GmbH	Gesellschaft mit beschränkter Haftung (Limited Liability Company)
GNP	gross national product
Gov.	Governor
Govt	Government
grt	gross registered tons
GWh	gigawatt hours
ha	hectares
HE	His (or Her) Eminence; His (or Her) Excellency
hf	hlutafelag (Company Limited)
hl	hectolitre(s)
HM	His (or Her) Majesty
Hon.	Honorary (or Honourable)
hp	horsepower
HQ	Headquarters
HRH	His (or Her) Royal Highness
IBRD	International Bank for Reconstruction and Development (World Bank)
ICC	International Chamber of Commerce
ICFTU	International Confederation of Free Trade Unions
IDA	International Development Association
IDB	Inter-American Development Bank
i.e.	id est (that is to say)
Ill	Illinois
ILO	International Labour Organisation
IMF	International Monetary Fund
in (ins)	inch (inches)
Inc, Incorp., Incd	Incorporated
incl.	including
Ind	Indiana
Ind.	Independent
INF	Intermediate-Range Nuclear Forces
Ing.	Engineer
Insp.	Inspector
Int.	International
Inzå.	Engineer
irreg.	irregular
Is	Islands
ISIC	International Standard Industrial Classification
Jan.	January
Jnr	Junior
Jr	Jonkheer (Netherlands); Junior
Jt	Joint
Kans	Kansas
KBE	Knight Commander of (the Order of) the British Empire
KCMG	Knight Commander of (the Order of) St Michael and St George
kg	kilogram(s)
KG	Knight of (the Order of) the Garter; Kommandit Gesellschaft (Limited Partnership)
kHz	kilohertz
KK	Kaien Kaisha (Limited Company)
km	kilometre(s)
kv.	kvartal (apartment block)
kW	kilowatt(s)
kWh	kilowatt hours
Ky	Kentucky
La	Louisiana
lb	pound(s)
Lic.	Licenciado
Licda	Licenciada
LNG	liquefied natural gas
LPG	liquefied petroleum gas
Lt, Lieut	Lieutenant
Ltd	Limited
m	metre(s)
m.	million
Maj.	Major
Man	Manitoba
Man.	Manager; managing
March.	Marchese
Mass	Massachusetts
MBE	Member of (the Order of) the British Empire
mbH	mit beschränkter Haftung (with limited liability)
Mc/s	megacycles per second
Md	Maryland
Me	Maine
mem.	member
MEP	Member of the European Parliament
MEV	mega electron volts
mfrs	manufacturers
Mgr	Monseigneur; Monsignor
MHz	megahertz
Mich	Michigan
Mil.	Military
Minn	Minnesota
Miss	Mississippi
Mlle	Mademoiselle
mm	millimetre(s)
Mme	Madame
Mo	Missouri
Mon.	Monday
Mont	Montana
MP	Member of Parliament; Madhya Pradesh
MSS	Manuscripts
MW	megawatt(s); medium wave
MWh	megawatt hour(s)
N	North; Northern
n.a.	not available
nab.	naberezhnaya (embankment, quai)
nám.	náměstí (square)
Nat.	National
NATO	North Atlantic Treaty Organization
NB	New Brunswick
NC	North Carolina
NCO	Non-Commissioned Officer
ND	North Dakota
Neb	Nebraska
Nev	Nevada
Nfld	Newfoundland
NH	New Hampshire
NJ	New Jersey
NM	New Mexico
NMP	net material product
no	número (number)
no.	number
Nov.	November
nr	near
nrt	net registered tons
NS	Nova Scotia
NSW	New South Wales
NV	Naamloze Vennootschap (Limited Company)
NY	New York
NZ	New Zealand
OAPEC	Organization of Arab Petroleum Exporting Countries

ABBREVIATIONS

OAS	Organization of American States
OAU	Organization of African Unity
OBE	Officer of (the Order of) the British Empire
OCAM	Organisation Commune Africaine et Mauricienne
Oct.	October
OECD	Organisation for Economic Co-operation and Development
OECS	Organization of East Caribbean States
Of.	Oficina (Office)
OIC	Organization of the Islamic Conference
Okla	Oklahoma
Ont	Ontario
OPEC	Organization of Petroleum Exporting Countries
opp.	opposite
Ore	Oregon
Org.	Organization
ORIT	Organización Regional Interamericana de Trabajadores
p.	page
p.a.	per annum
Pa	Pennsylvania
Parl.	Parliament(ary)
PC	Privy Counsellor
per.	pereulok (lane, alley)
Perm. Rep.	Permanent Representative
PK	Post Box (Turkish)
pl.	platz; place; ploshchad (square)
PLC	Public Limited Company
PLO	Palestine Liberation Organization
PMB	Private Mail Bag
POB	Post Office Box
Pr.	prospekt (avenue)
Pres.	President
Prin.	Principal
Prof.	Professor
Propr	Proprietor
Prov.	Province; Provincial; Provinciale (Dutch)
PT	Perseroan Tarbates (Limited Company)
Pte	Private
Pty	Proprietary
p.u.	paid up
publ.	publication; published
Publr	Publisher
Pvt.	Private
QC	Queen's Counsel
Qld	Queensland
Qué	Québec
q.v.	quod vide (to which refer)
Rag.	Ragioniere (Accountant)
Rd	Road
R(s)	rupee(s)
reg., regd	register; registered
reorg.	reorganized
Rep.	Republic; Republican; Representative
Repub.	Republic
res	reserve(s)
retd	retired
Rev.	Reverend
RI	Rhode Island
RJ	Rio de Janeiro
Rm	Room
ro-ro	roll-on roll-off
Rp.(s)	rupiah(s)
RSFSR	Russian Soviet Federative Socialist Republic
RSR	Republica Socialistă România (Socialist Republic of Romania)
Rt	Right
S	South; Southern; San
SA	Société Anonyme, Sociedad Anónima (Limited Company); South Australia
SADCC	Southern African Development Co-ordination Conference
SARL	Sociedade Anônima de Responsabilidade Limitada (Joint Stock Company of Limited Liability)
Sask	Saskatchewan
Sat.	Saturday
SC	South Carolina
SD	South Dakota
Sdn Bhd	Sendirian Berhad (Private Limited Company)
SDR(s)	Special Drawing Right(s)
Sec.	Secretary
Secr.	Secretariat
Sen.	Senior; Senator
Sept.	September
SER	Sua Eccellenza Reverendissima (His Eminence)
SFRY	Socialist Federal Republic of Yugoslavia
SITC	Standard International Trade Classification
SJ	Society of Jesus
Soc.	Society
Sok.	Sokak (Street)
SP	São Paulo
SpA	Società per Azioni (Joint Stock Company)
Sq.	Square
sq	square (in measurements)
Sr	Senior; Señor
Sra	Señora
Srl	Società a Responsabilità Limitata (Limited Company)
SSR	Soviet Socialist Republic
St	Saint; Street
Sta	Santa
Ste	Sainte
subs.	subscriptions; subscribed
Sun.	Sunday
Supt	Superintendent
Tas	Tasmania
TD	Teachta Dála (Member of Parliament)
tech., techn.	technical
tel.	telephone
Tenn	Tennessee
Tex	Texas
Thur.	Thursday
Treas.	Treasurer
Tue.	Tuesday
TV	television
t/yr	tons per year
u.	utca (street)
u/a	unit of account
UAE	United Arab Emirates
UDEAC	Union Douanière et Economique de l'Afrique Centrale
UEE	Unidade Económica Estatal
UK	United Kingdom
ul.	ulitsa (street)
UN	United Nations
UNCTAD	United Nations Conference on Trade and Development
UNDP	United Nations Development Programme
UNESCO	United Nations Educational, Scientific and Cultural Organization
UNHCR	United Nations High Commissioner for Refugees
Univ.	University
UNRWA	United Nations Relief and Works Agency for Palestine Refugees in the Near East
UP	Uttar Pradesh
USA	United States of America
USAID	United States Agency for International Development
USSR	Union of Soviet Socialist Republics
Va	Virginia
VAT	Value Added Tax
VEB	Volkseigener Betrieb (Public Company)
Ven.	Venerable
VHF	Very High Frequency
Vic	Victoria
viz.	videlicet (namely)
Vn	Veien (Street)
vol.(s)	volume(s)
Vt	Vermont
W	West; Western
WA	Western Australia
Wash	Washington (State)
WCL	World Confederation of Labour
Wed.	Wednesday
WFTU	World Federation of Trade Unions
WHO	World Health Organization
Wis	Wisconsin
W Va	West Virginia
Wy	Wyoming
yr	year

INTERNATIONAL COMPARISONS

The following table provides a general comparison of area, population, life expectancy and gross national product for every independent state (excluding the Vatican City) and every other territory with more than 25,000 inhabitants (excluding the Gaza Strip). An attempt has been made to provide comparable information under each heading, and the figures in the table refer to the latest period for which uniform data are available in each category.

Area figures refer to total area, including inland water. Unless otherwise indicated, population figures are mid-year estimates. Most of the data refer to *de facto* population (persons actually present in the area), though some are estimates of *de jure* population (persons normally resident). Figures for life expectancy are estimates, prepared in the Population Division of the United Nations, of the average number of years of life remaining to a new-born child if subject to the mortality conditions (recorded or assumed) of the period 1980–85. It should be stressed that the figures refer to the average life expectancy *at birth* for both sexes. In many developing countries mortality rates are high during the first few years of life, but persons who survive infancy have a life expectancy much greater than the average at birth. It is also noteworthy that in all developed countries the life expectancy of females is greater than that of males.

Figures for gross national product (GNP) may be taken as indicators of the comparative sizes of the various national economies, while data on GNP per head facilitate international comparisons of average levels of economic activity. Owing to variations in price levels and the unequal distribution of income, a figure for GNP per head is only an approximate measure of a country's wealth or poverty, and should not be regarded as a reliable indicator of the relative standard of living in each country. Sources are quoted at the end of the tables, but it must be stressed that the data on total GNP and on GNP per head are, to a considerable extent, estimates, and may be used only as a general guide. In particular, a wide margin of error may be expected in estimates for centrally planned economies, and in figures for GNP per head of less than $300, where the subsistence sector is unusually important and the degree of precision tends to decrease as the ratio of subsistence production to total GNP increases. Figures refer to GNP at market prices, converted to US dollars, with GNP per head usually rounded to the nearest $10. The conversion factor from national currencies to US dollars is the average of exchange rates for three consecutive years, e.g. for 1987 the base period is 1985–87. Data on GNP per head are based on World Bank figures for population, which may differ from figures shown elsewhere in the tables.

Country	Area (sq km)	Mid-1987 population ('000)	Mid-1987 population density (per sq km)	Average population increase, 1980–87 (% per year)	Life expectancy at birth, 1980–85 (years)	1987 Gross national product ($ million)	1987 GNP per head ($)
Afghanistan[1, 2, 3, 4]	652,090	18,614	29	2.6	37.0	2,290	160
Albania[4]	28,748	3,083	107	2.1	70.9	1,930	740
Algeria[3, 5]	2,381,741	22,971	9.6	3.2	60.1	63,560	2,760
American Samoa[2, 3]	195	36	185	1.8	n.a.	190	5,410
Andorra	467	48	103	4.6	n.a.	n.a.	n.a.
Angola[6]	1,246,700	9,226*	7.4	2.6	42.0	3,320	470
Antigua and Barbuda[2, 3]	440	76	173	0.2	n.a.	211	2,570
Argentina	2,766,889	31,497	11	1.6	69.7	74,490	2,370
Aruba[2, 7, 8]	193	60	311	n.a.	n.a.	n.a.	n.a.
Australia[9]	7,682,300	16,249	2.1	1.4	75.0	176,301	10,900
Austria	83,855	7,576	90	0.1	73.0	90,484	11,970
Bahamas	13,878	240	17	1.9	n.a.	2,488	10,320
Bahrain[10, 11]	678	430	634	3.3	69.2	3,670	8,530
Bangladesh	143,998	102,563	712	2.1	47.8	17,408	160
Barbados	430	254	591	n.a.	72.7	1,358	5,330
Belgium[3, 12]	30,519	9,859	323	0.0	73.5	112,009	11,360
Belize[2, 3]	22,965	171	7.4	2.8	n.a.	219	1,250
Benin	112,622	4,304	38	3.2	44.0	1,315	300
Bermuda[8, 11, 13, 14]	53	68	1,279	1.5	n.a.	1,143	20,410
Bhutan[15]	47,000	1,165	25	n.a.	45.9	201	150
Bolivia	1,098,581	6,797	6.2	2.8	50.7	4,150	570
Botswana[10]	581,730	1,169	2.0	3.7	54.5	1,175	1,030
Brazil[16]	8,511,965	141,452	17	2.2	63.4	314,642	2,020
Brunei[8, 11, 17]	5,765	233	40	3.4	n.a.	3,571	15,390
Bulgaria[6]	110,912	8,970	81	0.2	71.6	37,390	4,150
Burkina Faso[18]	274,200	7,747	28	n.a.	45.2	1,426	170
Burma[2, 11, 19]	676,552	39,411	58	2.3	57.5	7,450	200
Burundi	27,834	4,920	177	2.7	46.5	1,205	240
Cameroon[10]	475,442	10,822	23	3.2	50.9	10,441	960
Canada	9,976,139	25,652	2.6	0.9	75.7	390,052	15,080
Cape Verde[20, 21]	4,033	334	83	2.4	59.0	170	500
Central African Republic[2, 3]	622,984	2,740	4.4	2.9	43.0	912	330
Chad	1,284,000	5,268*	4.1	2.4	43.0	805	150
Channel Islands[19, 22]	195	136	697	1.0	n.a.	1,350	10,390
Chile	756,945	12,536	17	1.7	69.7	16,468	1,310
China, People's Republic[3, 23, 24]	9,571,300	1,057,210	110	1.2	67.8	319,780	300
China (Taiwan)[17, 25, 26]	36,000	19,564	543	1.5	68.2	97,208	4,969
Colombia[27, 28]	1,138,914	27,867	24	1.8	63.6	36,027	1,220
Comoros[23, 29, 30]	2,235	484	217	4.2	50.0	160	380
Congo[31, 32]	342,000	1,909	5.6	3.5	46.5	1,761	880
Costa Rica[20, 33]	51,100	2,489	49	2.3	73.0	4,299	1,590
Côte d'Ivoire[34, 35]	322,463	9,300	29	4.1	50.5	8,262	750
Cuba[4, 36]	110,861	10,288	93	1.0	73.4	12,330	1,270

See notes on page xvii

(continued opposite)

INTERNATIONAL COMPARISONS

(continued)

Country	Area (sq km)	Mid-1987 population ('000)	Mid-1987 population density (per sq km)	Average population increase, 1980-87 (% per year)	Life expectancy at birth, 1980-85 (years)	1987 Gross national product ($ million)	1987 GNP per head ($)
Cyprus	9,251	680	74	1.2	74.0	3,532	5,210
Czechoslovakia[6]	127,905	15,573	122	0.2	71.0	89,260	5,820
Denmark	43,092	5,127	119	0.0	74.5	76,640	15,010
Djibouti[2, 3, 37]	23,200	456	20	4.2	n.a.	180	480
Dominica[38, 39, 40]	751	83	111	2.9	69.1	115	1,440
Dominican Republic[2, 3]	48,734	6,416	132	2.8	62.6	4,930	730
East Timor[21, 41, 42, 43, 44]	14,874	631	42	2.6	39.9	100	150
Ecuador[45]	283,561	9,923	35	2.9	64.3	10,333	1,040
Egypt[46, 47]	1,001,449	48,205	48	2.4	58.1	36,028	710
El Salvador	21,041	5,009	238	1.5	64.8	4,220	850
Equatorial Guinea[37, 48]	28,051	300	11	n.a.	44.0	62	180
Ethiopia	1,221,900	46,184	38	n.a.	40.9	5,537	120
Faeroe Islands[11, 49]	1,399	47	34	1.3	73.9	549	11,930
Fiji[47, 50]	18,274	715	39	2.0	68.9	1,091	1,510
Finland	338,145	4,932	15	0.4	73.8	71,084	14,370
France	543,965	55,632	102	0.5	74.5	714,994	12,860
French Guiana[2, 3, 51]	90,000	86	1.0	4.0	n.a.	210	3,230
French Polynesia[17, 22, 52, 53, 54]	4,000	170	43	3.0	56.7	1,370	7,840
Gabon[20]	267,667	1,206	4.5	n.a.	49.0	2,890	2,750
Gambia[55, 56]	11,295	688	61	3.4	35.0	177	220
German Democratic Republic[6]	108,333	16,641	154	−0.1	72.1	120,940	7,180
Germany, Federal Republic[57]	248,709	61,171	246	−0.1	73.7	879,630	14,460
Ghana[58, 59]	238,537	12,206	51	2.6	52.0	5,328	390
Gibraltar[19, 22, 23]	5.5	29	5,303	0.3	n.a.	130	4,370
Greece[2, 3]	131,957	9,966	76	0.6	74.0	43,557	4,350
Greenland[8, 11]	2,175,600	54	0.02	1.1	n.a.	465	8,780
Grenada[10, 40]	344	98*	285	1.6	69.1	134	1,340
Guadeloupe[2, 3, 17, 22]	1,705	334	196	0.4	72.4	1,100	3,300
Guam[22, 60]	541	126	233	2.4	68.0	670	5,470
Guatemala	108,889	8,438	77	2.9	59.0	6,839	940
Guinea[22, 61]	245,857	4,533	18	n.a.	40.2	1,940	320
Guinea-Bissau[62]	36,125	810	22	n.a.	43.0	152	170
Guyana[20, 21]	214,969	790	3.7	0.8	68.2	310	380
Haiti[36]	27,750	5,438	196	1.5	52.7	2,221	360
Honduras	112,088	4,656	42	3.4	59.9	3,627	780
Hong Kong[17]	1,071	5,613	5,241	1.5	75.5	45,280	8,260
Hungary[63]	93,033	10,613	114	−0.1	70.3	23,757	2,240
Iceland	103,000	246	2.4	1.1	76.8	4,083	16,670
India[64]	3,287,590	781,374	238	2.1	55.4	241,305	300
Indonesia[21, 41, 42]	1,904,569	163,416	86	2.1	53.5	76,766	450
Iran[2, 3, 65]	1,648,000	49,765	30	4.0	57.3	69,170	2,060
Iraq[6, 66, 67]	438,317	14,110	32	3.2	62.4	39,500	3,020
Ireland[68]	70,283	3,543	50	0.6	73.0	21,761	6,030
Isle of Man[19, 22, 69]	572	64	112	−0.1	n.a.	380	5,910
Israel[70]	20,770	4,369	210	1.7	74.4	29,803	6,810
Italy	301,279	57,355	190	0.2	74.5	596,995	10,420
Jamaica[23, 71]	10,990	2,346	213	1.0	73.0	2,256	960
Japan	377,815	122,091	323	0.6	76.9	1,925,614	15,770
Jordan[72]	97,740	3,790*	39	3.8	63.7	4,370	1,540
Kampuchea[43, 73]	181,035	7,683*	42	2.6	43.4	570	70
Kenya[2, 3]	580,367	21,163	36	4.0	52.9	7,500	340
Kiribati[60, 74, 75]	861	64	74	2.0	68.0	32	480
Korea, Democratic People's Republic[4]	120,538	21,389*	177	2.5	67.7	17,040	1,000
Korea, Republic	99,222	42,082	424	1.4	67.7	112,947	2,690
Kuwait	17,818	1,873	105	4.6	71.6	27,324	14,870
Laos[76]	236,800	3,585	15	n.a.	49.7	590	160
Lebanon[43, 77]	10,400	2,762*	266	0.5	65.0	3,290	1,070
Lesotho	30,355	1,619	53	2.7	49.3	591	360
Liberia	111,369	2,349	21	3.5	49.0	1,030	440
Libya[33, 78]	1,759,540	3,637	2.1	4.5	58.3	22,326	5,500
Liechtenstein[19, 23]	160	27	171	1.0	n.a.	n.a.	n.a.
Luxembourg[19, 23]	2,586	370	143	0.2	70.8	5,805	15,860
Macau[10, 51]	16	429	26,800	7.2	n.a.	810	2,710
Madagascar[20, 79]	587,041	9,985	17	2.8	49.6	2,172	200
Malawi[80, 81]	118,484	7,983	67	3.7	45.0	1,223	160
Malaysia	329,749	16,528	50	2.6	66.8	29,556	1,800
Maldives[2, 8, 82]	298	189	634	3.3	n.a.	58	300
Mali[83, 84]	1,240,192	7,620	6.1	1.7	42.0	1,576	200
Malta[85]	316	344	1,089	0.5	71.7	1,444	4,010
Martinique[17, 22, 36]	1,102	334	303	0.4	73.2	1,400	4,280
Mauritania[86, 87]	1,025,520	1,339	1.3	n.a.	44.0	816	440
Mauritius	2,040	1,040	510	1.2	66.7	1,524	1,470
Mexico[10]	1,958,201	81,163	41	2.2	65.7	149,395	1,820

See notes on page xvii

(continued overleaf)

INTERNATIONAL COMPARISONS
(continued)

Country	Area (sq km)	Mid-1987 population ('000)	Mid-1987 population density (per sq km)	Average population increase, 1980–87 (% per year)	Life expectancy at birth, 1980–85 (years)	1987 Gross national product ($ million)	1987 GNP per head ($)
Monaco[88,89]	2.0	27	13,878	1.1	n.a.	n.a.	n.a.
Mongolia[3,4,90]	1,565,000	1,966	1.3	2.6	62.0	1,100	700
Morocco[36,86]	446,550	23,306*	52	2.7	58.3	14,213	620
Mozambique[91]	801,590	14,458	18	2.6	45.3	2,135	150
Namibia[11,92]	824,292	1,705*	2.1	3.2	48.2	1,150	1,020
Nauru[60,93]	21	7	345	n.a.	68.0	n.a.	n.a.
Nepal[19,94]	140,797	17,131	122	2.7	45.9	2,836	160
Netherlands	40,844	14,661	359	0.5	76.0	173,357	11,860
Netherlands Antilles[7,22,95]	800	172	215	n.a.	n.a.	1,610	6,110
New Caledonia[2,3,17,22,54]	19,103	154	8.1	1.7	65.9	860	5,760
New Zealand[19,96]	269,057	3,307	12	0.8	73.8	27,131	8,230
Nicaragua[2,3]	130,000	3,384	26	3.6	59.8	2,959	830
Niger[62]	1,267,000	5,686	4.5	n.a.	42.5	1,898	280
Nigeria[97]	923,768	101,907*	110	3.4	48.5	39,533	370
Norway	323,878	4,187	13	0.3	76.0	71,420	17,110
Oman	212,457	1,334*	6.3	4.4	52.3	7,768	5,780
Pacific Islands (Trust Territory)[34,60,98,99]	1,779	142	80	2.4	68.0	160	1,100
Pakistan[1,100]	796,095	102,238	128	3.1	50.0	36,211	350
Panama	77,082	2,274	30	2.2	71.0	5,128	2,240
Papua New Guinea	462,840	3,480	7.5	2.3	51.9	2,555	730
Paraguay	406,752	3,922	9.6	3.2	65.1	3,923	1,000
Peru[16]	1,285,216	20,727	16	2.6	58.6	29,682	1,430
Philippines	300,000	57,356	191	2.5	61.9	34,638	590
Poland[63]	312,683	37,664	120	0.8	71.2	72,439	1,920
Portugal	92,072	10,350	112	0.8	71.7	29,555	2,890
Puerto Rico	8,897	3,291	370	0.4	74.0	18,472	5,520
Qatar[101]	11,000	369	34	n.a.	67.6	4,129	12,360
Réunion[11,17]	2,510	565	225	1.5	69.7	2,120	3,940
Romania[2,3,37,63]	237,500	22,823	96	0.5	70.2	57,030	2,540
Rwanda[21,102]	26,338	6,274	238	3.6	46.5	2,008	310
Saint Christopher and Nevis[2]	261	44	169	n.a.	n.a.	80	1,700
Saint Lucia[2,3,40]	622	140	225	2.0	69.1	196	1,370
Saint Vincent and the Grenadines[2,3,40]	388	111	286	1.3	69.1	121	1,070
San Marino[84]	61	23	374	1.6	n.a.	n.a.	n.a.
São Tomé and Príncipe[20,79]	964	108	112	2.9	n.a.	32	280
Saudi Arabia[11,103]	2,149,690	13,612	6.3	5.3	60.9	83,270	6,930
Senegal[104,105]	196,722	6,397	33	2.9	43.3	3,545	510
Seychelles[8]	308	66	214	0.7	n.a.	210	3,180
Sierra Leone	71,740	3,849*	54	2.4	34.0	1,172	300
Singapore	623	2,613	4,197	1.1	71.8	20,717	7,940
Solomon Islands[47,54]	27,556	290	11	3.5	41.1	123	420
Somalia	637,657	6,859*	11	3.6	40.9	1,656	290
South Africa[92]	1,221,037	33,016*	27	2.2	53.5	62,926	1,890
Spain[106]	504,782	38,832	77	0.5	74.3	233,417	6,010
Spanish North Africa[43,44,106,107,108]	32	129	4,041	−0.2	n.a.	90	720
Sri Lanka	65,610	16,361	249	1.5	68.4	6,560	400
Sudan[109]	2,505,813	20,564	8.2	n.a.	47.7	7,646	330
Suriname[38,105]	163,265	389	2.4	2.2	68.0	972	2,360
Swaziland[47,110]	17,364	676	39	3.2	48.5	496	700
Sweden	440,945	8,399	19	0.2	76.3	131,142	15,690
Switzerland	41,293	6,538	158	0.5	76.1	138,163	21,250
Syria	185,180	10,969	59	3.4	62.6	20,421	1,820
Tanzania[111]	945,087	23,217	25	3.2	51.0	5,202	220
Thailand	513,115	53,605	104	2.0	62.7	44,785	840
Togo[112]	56,785	2,747	48	n.a.	50.5	963	300
Tonga[54,113]	748	97	130	0.9	55.2	72	720
Trinidad and Tobago[20,21]	5,130	1,181	230	1.8	68.7	5,130	4,220
Tunisia[2,3]	163,610	7,465	46	2.6	60.6	9,019	1,210
Turkey[21,114]	779,452	50,664	65	2.5	61.6	63,463	1,200
Tuvalu[37,60,115]	25	7	292	n.a.	68.0	5	680
Uganda[1,116,117]	235,880	13,225	56	3.4	49.0	4,086	260
USSR[6]	22,402,200	283,100	13	0.9	70.9	1,212,030	4,550
United Arab Emirates[34,98]	83,600	1,206	14	5.9	67.6	22,827	15,680
United Kingdom	244,103	56,891	233	0.1	73.7	592,946	10,430
USA	9,372,614	243,773	26	1.0	74.3	4,486,176	18,430
US Virgin Islands[11,17,104,105]	342	108	316	2.7	n.a.	1,074	9,760
Uruguay[118]	177,414	3,058	17	0.5	70.3	6,556	2,180
Vanuatu[37,54]	12,190	145	12	3.4	44.6	40	350
Venezuela[16]	912,050	18,272	20	2.8	69.0	48,241	3,230
Viet-Nam[65]	332,559	62,808*	189	2.3	58.8	7,750	160
Western Sahara[86,116,117]	266,000	165	0.6	8.9	n.a.	n.a.	n.a.
Western Samoa[8,104,105]	2,831	159	56	0.5	n.a.	93	560

See notes on opposite page

(continued opposite)

INTERNATIONAL COMPARISONS

(continued)

Country	Area (sq km)	Mid-1987 population ('000)	Mid-1987 population density (per sq km)	Average population increase, 1980-87 (% per year)	Life expectancy at birth, 1980-85 (years)	1987 Gross national product ($ million)	1987 GNP per head ($)
Yemen Arab Republic[119]	195,000	9,274	48	n.a.	48.4	4,918	580
Yemen, People's Democratic Republic	332,968	2,438	7.3	3.1	48.4	956	420
Yugoslavia	255,804	23,411	92	0.7	70.7	57,985	2,480
Zaire	2,345,409	32,461	14	n.a.	50.0	5,287	160
Zambia[20]	752,614	6,725	8.9	n.a.	51.3	1,696	240
Zimbabwe	390,580	8,640	22	2.9	55.8	5,265	590

* United Nations estimate.

[1] Figures for population and increase rate assume stable growth and take no account of inward or outward migration.

[2] Figures for population and density refer to mid-1986.

[3] The population increase rate refers to 1980-86.

[4] Figures for GNP refer to 1978 and are estimated on a 1977-79 base period.

[5] Figures for population and density refer to the census of April 1987.

[6] Figures for GNP are provisional data for 1980 and are estimated on a 1978-80 base period.

[7] Aruba, listed separately, was part of the Netherlands Antilles prior to 1 January 1986. Data relating to life expectancy and GNP for the Netherlands Antilles include Aruba.

[8] Although no estimates are available of 1980-85 life expectancy for both sexes, the UN *Demographic Yearbook* includes separate figures of life expectancy for males and females at another date.

[9] Figure for life expectancy includes Australian dependencies: Christmas Island, the Cocos (Keeling) Islands and Norfolk Island.

[10] The population increase rate refers to 1981-87.

[11] Figures for GNP refer to 1986 and are estimated on a 1984-86 base period.

[12] Figures for population and density refer to 1 January 1986.

[13] Figures for population and density refer to the census of 12 May 1980.

[14] The population increase rate refers to 1970-80.

[15] Figures for population and density refer to mid-1980.

[16] Population figures exclude Indian jungle inhabitants.

[17] Figures for GNP refer to estimates of gross domestic product.

[18] Figures for population and density refer to the census of 10-20 December 1985.

[19] The population increase rate refers to 1981-86.

[20] Figures for population and density refer to mid-1985.

[21] The population increase rate refers to 1980-85.

[22] Figures for GNP refer to 1985 and are estimated on a 1983-85 base period.

[23] Figures for population and density refer to 31 December 1986.

[24] The figure for life expectancy refers to the whole of China, including Taiwan.

[25] The estimate of life expectancy refers to 1965-70.

[26] Figures for GNP are in terms of current 1987 prices, rather than on a 1985-87 base period.

[27] Figures for population and density refer to the census of 15 October 1985.

[28] The population increase rate refers to 1973-85.

[29] Except for GNP, figures include the island of Mayotte, which has remained under French administration since the Comoros became independent in July 1975.

[30] The population increase rate refers to 1973-86.

[31] Figures for population and density refer to the census of 22 December 1984.

[32] The population increase rate refers to 1974-84.

[33] The population increase rate refers to 1973-84.

[34] Figures for population and density refer to mid-1983.

[35] The population increase rate refers to 1979-83.

[36] The population increase rate refers to 1982-87.

[37] Figures for GNP refer to 1981 and are estimated on a 1979-81 base period.

[38] Figures for population and density refer to 31 December 1984.

[39] The population increase rate refers to 1981-84.

[40] The figure for life expectancy is the average for the Windward Islands (Dominica, Grenada, Saint Lucia and Saint Vincent and the Grenadines).

[41] East (formerly Portuguese) Timor, listed separately, was incorporated into Indonesia on 17 July 1976. Figures for Indonesia, except the data on GNP, exclude East Timor.

[42] Figures for population and density refer to 31 October 1985.

[43] Figures for GNP refer to 1974.

[44] Figures for GNP are estimated on a 1973-75 base period.

[45] Population figures exclude nomadic Indian tribes.

[46] Figures for population and density refer to the census of 17-18 November 1986.

[47] The population increase rate refers to 1976-86.

[48] Figures for population and density refer to 1 January 1983.

[49] The figure for life expectancy is the 1965-70 average for the Faeroe Islands and Iceland.

[50] Figures for population and density refer to the census of 31 August 1986.

[51] Figures for GNP refer to 1982 and are estimated on a 1980-82 base period.

[52] Figures for population and density refer to 1 January 1985.

[53] The population increase rate refers to 1977-83.

[54] The estimate of life expectancy refers to 1965.

[55] Figures for population and density refer to the census of 15 April 1983.

[56] The population increase rate refers to 1973-83.

[57] Figures include data for West Berlin.

[58] Figures for population and density refer to the census of 11 March 1984.

[59] The population increase rate refers to 1970-84.

[60] The figure for life expectancy is the average for Micronesia.

[61] Figures for population and density refer to the census of 4-17 February 1983.

[62] Figures for population and density refer to mid-1981.

[63] Figures for the GNP of Hungary, Poland and Romania are not comparable with those of other centrally planned economies.

[64] Figures include the Indian-held part of the disputed territory of Jammu and Kashmir.

[65] Figures for GNP refer to 1976 and are estimated on a 1975-77 base period.

[66] Figures for population and density refer to October 1982.

[67] The population increase rate refers to 1979-82.

[68] Figures for population and density refer to 15 April 1987.

[69] Figures for population and density refer to the census of 6 April 1986.

[70] Including East Jerusalem, annexed from Jordan in 1967. Population figures also include Israeli residents in other territories under military occupation.

[71] The population increase rate refers to 1970-82.

[72] Figures for GNP relate to the East Bank region only.

[73] Figures for GNP are estimated on a 1972-74 base period.

[74] Figures for population and density refer to the census of 9-10 May 1985.

[75] The population increase rate refers to 1978-85.

INTERNATIONAL COMPARISONS

[76] Figures for population and density refer to the census of 1 March 1985.

[77] Figures for GNP are estimated on a 1974–76 base period.

[78] Figures for population and density refer to the census of 31 July 1984.

[79] The population increase rate refers to 1981–85.

[80] Figures for population and density refer to the census of 1–21 September 1987.

[81] The population increase rate refers to 1977–87.

[82] The population increase rate refers to 1977–85.

[83] Figures for population and density refer to the census of 1–14 April 1987.

[84] The population increase rate refers to 1976–87.

[85] The population increase rate refers to 1967–85.

[86] Western (formerly Spanish) Sahara, listed separately, was partitioned in 1976 between Mauritania and Morocco. Mauritania withdrew in August 1979, when Morocco annexed the former Mauritanian area. Figures for the area, life expectancy and GNP of these countries exclude their respective portions of the territory.

[87] Figures for population and density refer to the census of 1 January 1977.

[88] Figures for population and density refer to the census of 4 March 1982.

[89] The population increase rate refers to 1975–82.

[90] Figures for population and density refer to 1 January 1987.

[91] Figures for population and density refer to 1 August 1987.

[92] The area and population of Walvis Bay, an integral part of South Africa, are included with Namibia.

[93] Figures for population and density refer to the census of 22 January 1977.

[94] Figures for population and density refer to 22 June 1986.

[95] Figures for population and density refer to the census of 1 February 1981.

[96] Figures for population and density refer to the census of 4 March 1986.

[97] Population estimates are UN projections which assume stable growth and take no account of the effect of civil disturbances.

[98] The population increase rate refers to 1980–83.

[99] Figures for GNP refer to 1984 and are estimated on a 1982–84 base period.

[100] Figures exclude the disputed territory of Jammu and Kashmir (total area 222,802 sq km, of which 83,807 sq km is held by Pakistan).

[101] Figures for population and density refer to the census of 16 March 1986.

[102] Figures for population and density refer to 31 December 1985.

[103] The population increase rate refers to 1974–87.

[104] Figures for population and density refer to mid-1984.

[105] The population increase rate refers to 1980–84.

[106] Data for Spanish North Africa (Ceuta and Melilla) are also included with the figures for Spain.

[107] Figures for population and density refer to the census of 1 March 1981.

[108] The population increase rate refers to 1970–81.

[109] Figures for population and density refer to the census of 1 February 1983.

[110] Figures for population and density refer to the census of 25 August 1986.

[111] Figures for GNP refer to mainland Tanzania only, excluding Zanzibar (population 606,000 at mid-1987).

[112] Figures for population and density refer to mid-1982.

[113] The population increase rate refers to 1976–85.

[114] Figures for population and density refer to the census of 20 October 1985.

[115] Figures for population and density refer to the census of May 1979.

[116] Figures for population and density refer to mid-1979.

[117] The population increase rate refers to 1975–79.

[118] The population increase rate refers to 1975–85.

[119] Figures for population and density refer to the census of 1 February 1986, including nationals living abroad.

Principal Sources: Population estimates taken from the United Nations *Population and Vital Statistics Report* (quarterly); figures for area taken from the United Nations *Demographic Yearbook 1986*; data on life expectancy taken mainly from *World Population Prospects: Estimates and Projections as Assessed in 1984* (UN Population Studies, No. 98); estimates of gross national product and GNP per head taken from *The World Bank Atlas* (International Bank for Reconstruction and Development, 1988).

LATE INFORMATION

UNITED NATIONS (p. 17)
Director-General for Development and International Economic Co-operation: ANTOINE BLANCA (France) (from 15 February 1989).

INTERNATIONAL COURT OF JUSTICE (p. 20)
Judge NAGENDRA SINGH died in December 1988.

UNITED NATIONS OBSERVER MISSIONS AND PEACE-KEEPING FORCES (p. 44)
United Nations Angola Verification Mission: established by the UN Security Council in December 1988 to supervise the withdrawal of Cuban troops from Angola by July 1991; comprises 70 military officers and 20 civilians. Chief Military Observer Brig. PERICLES FERREIRA GOMES (Brazil).

United Nations Transition Assistance Group—UNTAG: to be deployed in Namibia from 1 April 1989; peace-keeping force of 4,650 men to supervise Namibia's transition to independence.

INTERNATIONAL LABOUR ORGANISATION (p. 69)
Director-General: MICHEL HANSENNE (Belgium) (from 27 February 1989).

ECONOMIC COMMUNITY OF WEST AFRICAN STATES (p. 132)
Executive Secretary: ABBAS BUNDU (Sierra Leone) (from 1 January 1989).

COMMISSION OF THE EUROPEAN COMMUNITIES (p. 139)
Members of the Commission
(with their responsibilities; effective from 6 January 1989)

President: JACQUES DELORS (France): Secretariat-General; Legal Service; Spokesman's Service; Joint Interpreting and Conference Service; Security Office; Monetary Affairs.

FRANS ANDRIESSEN (Netherlands): External Relations; Trade Policy.

HENNING CHRISTOPHERSEN (Denmark): Economic and Financial Affairs; Structural Funds.

MANUEL MARÍN (Spain): Co-operation and Development; Fisheries.

FILIPPO MARIA PANDOLFI (Italy): Science; Research and Development; Telecommunications; Information Technology.

MARTIN BANGEMANN (FRG): Internal Market; Industrial Affairs; Relations with the European Parliament.

Sir LEON BRITTAN (UK): Competition Policy; Financial Institutions.

CARLO RIPA DI MENA (Italy): Environment; Nuclear Safety.

ANTÓNIO CARDOSO E CUNHA (Portugal): Energy; Tourism; Small and Medium-sized Businesses.

ABEL MATUTES (Spain): Mediterranean Policy; Relations with Latin America; North-South Relations.

PETER SCHMIDHÜBER (FRG): Budget; Financial Control.

CHRISTIANE SCRIVENER (France): Taxation and Customs Union; Social Security.

BRUCE MILLAN (UK): Regional Policy.

JEAN DONDELINGER (Luxembourg): Cultural Affairs; Audiovisual Affairs; Information; Citizens' Europe; Publications.

RAY McSHARRY (Ireland): Agriculture and Rural Development.

KAREL VAN MIERT (Belgium): Transport; Credit and Investment; Consumer Affairs.

VASSO PAPANDREOU (Greece): Employment; Industrial Relations; Social Affairs; Education and Training.

ORGANIZATION OF THE ISLAMIC CONFERENCE (p. 194)
Secretary-General: HAMID AL-GABID (Niger) (from 1 January 1989).

WARSAW PACT (p. 207)
Commander-in-Chief, Joint Command of the Armed Forces: Army Gen. PYOTR GEORGIEVICH LUSHEV (appointed February 1989).

AFGHANISTAN (p. 286)
Government Changes
(February 1989)

Prime Minister: (vacant).
Minister of Commerce: BORHANODDIN GHIASI.
Minister of Civil Aviation: SHER JAN MAZDURYAR.
Minister of Light Industries and Foodstuffs: ABDOLLAH BAHAR.
Minister of Education and Training: KHODAYDAD BASHARMAL.
Minister of Higher and Vocational Education: MOHAMMAD ESMAIL DANESH.
Minister of Public Health: SAYED AMIR ZARA.
Minister of Returnees' Affairs: SAYED EKRAM PAYGIR.
Minister of Islamic Affairs and Endowment: ABDOL GHAFUR BAHER.
Minister without Portfolio: Dr NUR AHMAD BARETS.

Following the declaration of a state of emergency on 18 February 1989, a 20-member Supreme Military Council for the Defence of the Homeland was established. The Council, which was led by President Najibullah and was composed of ministers, Politburo members and high-ranking military figures, assumed full responsibility for the country's economic, political and military policies. In accordance with the law regarding the state of emergency, the legislative power vested in the Meli Shura (National Assembly) was transferred to the Council of Ministers.

ALBANIA (p. 299)
(February 1989)
Government Changes
Council of Ministers

Deputy Chairman and Minister of Agriculture: PALI MISKA.
Deputy Chairman and Chairman of the State Control Commission: MANUSH MYFTIU.
Deputy Chairman and Minister of Internal Affairs: SIMON STEFANI.

(BESNIK BEKTESHI, HEKURAN ISAI and VANGJEL ÇERRAVA ceased to be Deputy Chairmen of the Council of Ministers.)

Minister of Industry and Mining and Acting Minister of Energy: BESNIK BEKTESHI.
Minister of Transport: HAJREDIN ÇELIKU.
Minister, General Secretary of the Council of Ministers: ENVER HALILI.

Political Organizations (p. 300)
Partia e Punës e Shqipërisë (Party of Labour of Albania): HAJREDIN ÇELIKU and SIMON STEFANI were relieved of their posts as Secretaries of the Central Committee. HEKURAN ISAI was elected a Central Committee Secretary.

ALGERIA (p. 314–p. 315)
On 22 December 1988 BEN DJEDID CHADLI was re-elected for a third term as President of Algeria. Chadli was the sole candidate and received 81.2% of votes cast.

On 23 February 1989 the Algerian electorate overwhelmingly endorsed constitutional amendments permitting the creation of political associations independent of the FLN, guaranteeing the right to strike, and removing all references to socialism from the Constitution.

ANGOLA (p. 334)
Government Changes
(January 1989)

Minister of State for the Productive Sphere, Minister of Petroleum and Energy: ZEFERINO CASSA YOMBO.
Minister of External Relations: Lt-Col PEDRO DE CASTRO DOS SANTOS VAN-DÚNEM (LOY).

(February 1989)

Minister of Youth and Sport: JOSÉ CARLOS MOÇO.
Minister of Industry, Trade and Tourism: DOMINGO DAS CHAGAS SIMÕES RANGEL.

LATE INFORMATION

AUSTRIA (p. 406–p. 407)
Government and Nationalrat Changes

In January 1989 the Minister of the Interior, KARL BLECHA (SPÖ), resigned, following allegations of his involvement in an insurance scandal, and was replaced by Dr FRANZ LÖSCHNAK (SPÖ), the former Minister of the Federal Chancellery (Health and Public Service). Dr LÖSCHNAK was replaced by Ing. HARALD ETTL (SPÖ).

In February 1989 LEOPOLD GRATZ was replaced as President of the Nationalrat by RUDOLF PÖDER. Also in February, the Minister of Employment and Social Affairs, ALFRED DALLINGER (SPÖ), was killed in an air crash.

THE BAHAMAS (p. 419)
Government Changes
(January 1989)

Minister of Foreign Affairs: CHARLES CARTER.
Attorney-General: SEAN MCWEENEY.
Minister of Consumer Affairs: BERNARD NOTTAGE.
Deputy Prime Minister CLEMENT MAYNARD retained his portfolio of Tourism, and PAUL ADDERLEY remained Minister of Education.

BRAZIL (p.542–p. 543)
Government Changes
(January 1989)

Minister of Health: SEIGO SUZUKI.
Minister of Education: CARLOS SANT'ANNA.
Minister of Mines and Energy: VICENTE FIALHO.
Minister of Justice: OSCAR DIAS CORREIA.

BURMA (p. 601)
Government Changes
(February 1989)

Minister of Energy and of Mines: Rear-Adm. MAUNG MAUNG KHIN.
Minister of Transport and Communications and of Labour and Social Welfare: Maj.-Gen. TIN TUN.
Minister of Construction and of Co-operatives: Brig.-Gen. AUNG YE KYAW.
Minister of Livestock Breeding and Fisheries and of Agriculture and Forests: Maj.-Gen. CHIT SWE.
Minister of Planning and Finance and of Trade: Col ABEL.
Minister of Health and of Education: Dr PE THEIN.

CANADA (p. 637)
Government Changes
(January 1989)

The following government changes were announced on 30 January 1989:

Minister of Public Works and Minister responsible for the Atlantic Canada Opportunities Agency: ELMER MACINTOSH MACKAY.
Minister of Energy, Mines and Resources: ARTHUR JACOB EPP.
President of the Treasury Board: ROBERT R. DE COTRET.
Minister of National Health and Welfare: HENRY PERRIN BEATTY.
Minister of Regional Industrial Expansion and Minister of State (Science and Technology): HARVIE ANDRE.
Minister of National Revenue: OTTO JOHN JELINEK.
Minister of Western Economic Diversification and Minister of State (Grains and Oilseeds): CHARLES JAMES MAYER.
Minister of National Defence: WILLIAM HUNTER MCKNIGHT.
Minister of Communications: MARCEL MASSE.
Secretary of State for Canada and Minister of State (Multiculturalism and Citizenship): GERRY WEINER.
Minister of Justice and Attorney-General, and Government Leader in the House of Commons: DOUGLAS GRINSLADE LEWIS.
Minister of the Environment: LUCIEN BOUCHARD.
Minister of Labour: JEAN CORBEIL.
Minister of Veterans' Affairs: GERALD STAIRS MERRITHEW.
Minister of Supply and Services: PAUL WYATT DICK.
Minister of Indian Affairs and Northern Development: PIERRE H. CADIEUX.
Minister of Consumer and Corporate Affairs: BERNARD VALCOURT.
Solicitor-General and Minister of State (Agriculture): PIERRE BLAIS.
Minister of State (Forestry): FRANK OBERLE.
Leader of the Government in the Senate and Minister of State (Federal-Provincial Relations): LOWELL MURRAY.
Minister of State (Youth), Minister of State (Fitness and Amateur Sport) and Deputy Leader of the Government in the House of Commons: JEAN J. CHAREST.
Minister of State (Small Businesses and Tourism): THOMAS HOCKIN.
Minister of State (Privatization and Regulatory Affairs): JOHN HORTON MCDERMID.
Associate Minister of National Defence: MARY COLLINS.
Minister of State (Housing): ALAN REDWAY.
Minister of State (Science and Technology): WILLIAM WINEGARD.
Minister of State (Indian Affairs and Northern Development): KIM CAMPBELL.
Minister of State (Finance): GILLES LOISELLE.

Provincial Legislatures—Newfoundland and Labrador (p. 638)

Following Premier A. BRIAN PECKFORD's announcement of his resignation, elections were to be held in March 1989.

CHAD (p. 681)
Government Changes
(March 1989)

Minister of Agriculture: GOUARA LASSOU.
Minister of Foreign Affairs: ACHEIKH IBN OUMAR.

COLOMBIA (p. 751)
Government Changes
(February 1989)

Minister of Government (Interior): RAÚL OREJUELA BUENO.
Minister of Labour and Social Security: MARÍA TERESA FORERO DE SAADE.
Minister of Public Health: EDUARDO DÍAZ URIBE.
Minister of Communications: CARLOS LEMOS SIMMONS.
Minister of Public Works and Transportation: PRISCILA CEBALLOS ORDÓÑEZ.

FRANCE (p. 1027)
Government Changes
(February 1989)

Minister of State for the Civil Service and Administrative Reform: MICHEL DURAFOUR (UDF/Rad).
Minister of Equipment, Housing, Transport and the Sea: MICHEL DELEBARRE (PS).

IRAQ (p. 1375)

The Minister of Defence, Gen. ADNAN KHAIRALLAH, was dismissed in March 1989.

PART ONE
International Organizations

THE UNITED NATIONS

Address: United Nations Plaza, New York, NY 10017, USA.
Telephone: (212) 963-1234.

The United Nations was founded in 1945 to maintain international peace and security and to develop international co-operation in economic, social, cultural and humanitarian problems.

The United Nations was a name devised by President Franklin D. Roosevelt of the United States. It was first used in the Declaration by United Nations of 1 January 1942, when representatives of 26 nations pledged their governments to continue fighting together against the Axis powers.

The United Nations Charter (see p. 9) was drawn up by the representatives of 50 countries at the United Nations Conference on International Organization, which met at San Francisco from 25 April to 26 June 1945. The representatives deliberated on the basis of proposals worked out by representatives of China, the USSR, the United Kingdom and the United States at Dumbarton Oaks in August–October 1944. The Charter was signed on 26 June 1945. Poland, not represented at the Conference, signed it later but nevertheless became one of the original 51 members.

The United Nations officially came into existence on 24 October 1945, when the Charter had been ratified by China, France, the USSR, the United Kingdom and the United States, and by a majority of other signatories. United Nations Day is now celebrated annually on 24 October.

Membership

MEMBERS OF THE UNITED NATIONS

(with assessments for percentage contributions to the UN budget for 1986, 1987 and 1988, and year of admission)

Country	%	Year
Afghanistan	0.01	1946
Albania	0.01	1955
Algeria	0.14	1962
Angola	0.01	1976
Antigua and Barbuda	0.01	1981
Argentina	0.62	1945
Australia	1.66	1945
Austria	0.74	1955
Bahamas	0.01	1973
Bahrain	0.02	1971
Bangladesh	0.02	1974
Barbados	0.01	1966
Belgium	1.18	1945
Belize	0.01	1981
Benin	0.01	1960
Bhutan	0.01	1971
Bolivia	0.01	1945
Botswana	0.01	1966
Brazil	1.40	1945
Brunei	0.04	1984
Bulgaria	0.16	1955
Burkina Faso	0.01	1960
Burma	0.01	1948
Burundi	0.01	1962
Byelorussian SSR[1]	0.34	1945
Cameroon	0.01	1960
Canada	3.06	1945
Cape Verde	0.01	1975
Central African Republic	0.01	1960
Chad	0.01	1960
Chile	0.07	1945
China, People's Republic[2]	0.79	1945
Colombia	0.13	1945
Comoros	0.01	1975
Congo	0.01	1960
Costa Rica	0.02	1945
Côte d'Ivoire	0.02	1960
Cuba	0.09	1945
Cyprus	0.02	1960
Czechoslovakia	0.70	1945
Denmark	0.72	1945
Djibouti	0.01	1977
Dominica	0.01	1978
Dominican Republic	0.03	1945
Ecuador	0.03	1945
Egypt	0.07	1945
El Salvador	0.01	1945
Equatorial Guinea	0.01	1968
Ethiopia	0.01	1945
Fiji	0.01	1970
Finland	0.50	1955
France	6.37	1945
Gabon	0.03	1960
The Gambia	0.01	1965
German Democratic Republic	1.33	1973
Germany, Federal Republic	8.26	1973
Ghana	0.01	1957
Greece	0.44	1945
Grenada	0.01	1974
Guatemala	0.02	1945
Guinea	0.01	1958
Guinea-Bissau	0.01	1974
Guyana	0.01	1966
Haiti	0.01	1945
Honduras	0.01	1945
Hungary	0.22	1955
Iceland	0.03	1946
India	0.35	1945
Indonesia	0.14	1950
Iran	0.63	1945
Iraq	0.12	1945
Ireland	0.18	1955
Israel	0.22	1949
Italy	3.79	1955
Jamaica	0.02	1962
Japan	10.84	1956
Jordan	0.01	1955
Kampuchea	0.01	1955
Kenya	0.01	1963
Kuwait	0.29	1963
Laos	0.01	1955
Lebanon	0.01	1945
Lesotho	0.01	1966
Liberia	0.01	1945
Libya	0.26	1955
Luxembourg	0.05	1945
Madagascar	0.01	1960
Malawi	0.01	1964
Malaysia	0.10	1957
Maldives	0.01	1965
Mali	0.01	1960
Malta	0.01	1964
Mauritania	0.01	1961
Mauritius	0.01	1968
Mexico	0.89	1945
Mongolia	0.01	1961
Morocco	0.05	1956
Mozambique	0.01	1975
Nepal	0.01	1955
Netherlands	1.74	1945
New Zealand	0.24	1945
Nicaragua	0.01	1945
Niger	0.01	1960
Nigeria	0.19	1960
Norway	0.54	1945
Oman	0.02	1971
Pakistan	0.06	1947
Panama	0.02	1945
Papua New Guinea	0.01	1975
Paraguay	0.02	1945
Peru	0.07	1945
Philippines	0.10	1945
Poland	0.64	1945
Portugal	0.18	1955
Qatar	0.04	1971
Romania	0.19	1955
Rwanda	0.01	1962
Saint Christopher and Nevis	0.01	1983
Saint Lucia	0.01	1979
Saint Vincent and the Grenadines	0.01	1980
São Tomé and Príncipe	0.01	1975
Saudi Arabia	0.97	1945

INTERNATIONAL ORGANIZATIONS

United Nations

Senegal	0.01	1960
Seychelles	0.01	1976
Sierra Leone	0.01	1961
Singapore	0.10	1965
Solomon Islands	0.01	1978
Somalia	0.01	1960
South Africa	0.44	1945
Spain	2.03	1955
Sri Lanka	0.01	1955
Sudan	0.01	1956
Suriname	0.01	1975
Swaziland	0.01	1968
Sweden	1.25	1946
Syria	0.04	1945
Tanzania[3]	0.01	1961
Thailand	0.09	1946
Togo	0.01	1960
Trinidad and Tobago	0.04	1962
Tunisia	0.03	1956
Turkey	0.34	1945
Uganda	0.01	1962
Ukrainian SSR[1]	1.28	1945
USSR	10.20	1945
United Arab Emirates	0.18	1971
United Kingdom	4.86	1945
USA	25.00	1945
Uruguay	0.04	1945
Vanuatu	0.01	1981
Venezuela	0.60	1945
Viet-Nam	0.01	1977
Western Samoa	0.01	1976
Yemen Arab Republic	0.01	1947
Yemen, People's Democratic Republic	0.01	1967
Yugoslavia	0.46	1945
Zaire	0.01	1960
Zambia	0.01	1964
Zimbabwe	0.02	1980

Total Membership: 159 (October 1988)

[1] The Byelorussian SSR and the Ukrainian SSR are integral parts of the USSR and not independent countries, but they have separate UN membership.
[2] From 1945 until 1971 the Chinese seat was occupied by the Republic of China (confined to Taiwan since 1949).
[3] Tanganyika was a member of the United Nations from December 1961 and Zanzibar was a member from December 1963. From April 1964, the United Republic of Tanganyika and Zanzibar continued as a single member, changing its name to United Republic of Tanzania in November 1964.

SOVEREIGN COUNTRIES NOT IN THE UNITED NATIONS
(October 1988)

Andorra	Monaco
China (Taiwan)	Nauru
Kiribati	San Marino
Democratic People's Republic of Korea	Switzerland
	Tonga
Republic of Korea	Tuvalu
Liechtenstein	Vatican City (Holy See)

Diplomatic Representation

MEMBER STATES' PERMANENT MISSIONS TO THE UNITED NATIONS
(with Permanent Representatives—September 1988)

Afghanistan: 866 United Nations Plaza, Suite 520, New York, NY 10017; tel. (212) 754-1191; SHAH MUHAMMAD DOST.

Albania: 320 East 79th St, New York, NY 10021; tel. (212) 249-2059; BASHKIM PITARKA.

Algeria: 15 East 47th St, New York, NY 10017; tel. (212) 750-1960; HOCINE DJOUDI.

Angola: 747 Third Ave, 18th Floor, New York, NY 10017; tel. (212) 752-4612; MANUEL PEDRO PACAVIRA.

Antigua and Barbuda: 610 Fifth Ave, Suite 311, New York, NY 10020; tel. (212) 541-4117; LLOYDSTONE JACOBS.

Argentina: 1 United Nations Plaza, 25th Floor, New York, NY 10017; tel. (212) 688-6300; Dr MARCELO DELPECH.

Australia: 1 Dag Hammarskjöld Plaza, 885 Second Ave, 16th Floor, New York, NY 10017; tel. (212) 421-6910; RICHARD A. WOOLCOTT.

Austria: 809 United Nations Plaza, 7th Floor, New York, NY 10017; tel. (212) 949-1840; PETER HOHENFELLNER.

Bahamas: 767 Third Ave, 9th Floor, New York, NY 10017; tel. (212) 421-6925; Dr DAVIDSON L. HEPBURN.

Bahrain: 2 United Nations Plaza, 25th Floor, New York, NY 10017; tel. (212) 223-6200; KARIM EBRAHIM AL-SHAKAR.

Bangladesh: 821 United Nations Plaza, 8th Floor, New York, NY 10017; tel. (212) 867-3434; B. A. SIDDIKY.

Barbados: 800 Second Ave, 18th Floor, New York, NY 10017; tel. (212) 867-8431; Dame RUTH NITA BARROW.

Belgium: 809 United Nations Plaza, 2nd Floor, New York, NY 10017; tel. (212) 599-5250; PAUL NOTERDAEME.

Belize: 801 Second Ave, Suite 401-02, New York, NY 10017; tel. (212) 599-0233; KENNETH E. TILLETT.

Benin: 4 East 73rd St, New York, NY 10021; tel. (212) 249-6014; GRATIEN TONAKPON CAPO-CHICHI.

Bhutan: 2 United Nations Plaza, 27th Floor, New York, NY 10017; tel. (212) 826-1919; JIGMI YOSER THINLEY.

Bolivia: 211 East 43rd St, 8th Floor (Room 802), New York, NY 10017; tel. (212) 682-8132; HUGO NAVAJAS-MOGRO.

Botswana: 103 East 37th St, New York, NY 10016; tel. (212) 889-2277; LEGWAILA JOSEPH LEGWAILA.

Brazil: 747 Third Ave, 9th Floor, New York, NY 10017; tel. (212) 832-6868; PAULO NOGUEIRA-BATISTA.

Brunei: 866 United Nations Plaza, Room 248, New York, NY 10017; tel. (212) 838-1600; Awang Haji JAYA BIN ABDUL LATIF.

Bulgaria: 11 East 84th St, New York, NY 10028; tel. (212) 737-4790; ALEXANDER STREZOV.

Burkina Faso: 115 East 73rd St, New York, NY 10021; tel. (212) 288-7515; MICHEL MONVEL DAH.

Burma: 10 East 77th St, New York, NY 10021; tel. (212) 535-1310; MAUNG MAUNG GYI.

Burundi: 201 East 42nd St, 28th Floor, New York, NY 10017; tel. (212) 687-1180; JONATHAS NIYUNGEKO.

Byelorussian Soviet Socialist Republic: 136 East 67th St, New York, NY 10021; tel. (212) 535-3420; LEV I. MAKSIMOV.

Cameroon: 22 East 73rd St, New York, NY 10021; tel. (212) 794-2295; PAUL BAMELA ENGO.

Canada: 866 United Nations Plaza, Suite 250, New York, NY 10017; tel. (212) 751-5600; YVES FORTIER.

Cape Verde: 27 East 69th St, New York, NY 10021; tel. (212) 472-0333; HUMBERTO BETTENCOURT SANTOS.

Central African Republic: 386 Park Ave South, Room 1614, New York, NY 10016; tel. (212) 689-6195; MICHEL GBEZERA-BRIA.

Chad: 211 East 43rd St, Suite 1703, New York, NY 10017; tel. (212) 986-0980; MAHAMAT ALI ADOUM.

Chile: 809 United Nations Plaza, 4th Floor, New York, NY 10017; tel. (212) 687-7547; PEDRO DAZA.

China, People's Republic: 155 West 66th St, New York, NY 10023; tel. (212) 787-3838; LI LUYE.

Colombia: 140 East 57th St, 5th Floor, New York, NY 10022; tel. (212) 355-7776; Dr ENRIQUE PEÑALOSA.

Comoros: 336 East 45th St, New York, NY 10017; tel. (212) 972-8010; AMINI ALI MOUMIN.

Congo: 14 East 65th St, New York, NY 10021; tel. (212) 744-7840; Dr MARTIN ADOUKI.

Costa Rica: 211 East 43rd St, Room 903, New York, NY 10017; tel. (212) 986-6373; Dr CARLOS JOSÉ GUTIÉRREZ.

Côte d'Ivoire: 117 East 55th St, New York, NY 10022; tel. (212) 988-3930; AMARA ESSY.

Cuba: 315 Lexington Ave and 38th St, New York, NY 10016; tel. (212) 689-7215; OSCAR ORAMAS-OLIVA.

Cyprus: 13 East 40th St, New York, NY 10016; tel. (212) 481-6023; CONSTANTINE MOUSHOUTAS.

Czechoslovakia: 1109–1111 Madison Ave, New York, NY 10028; tel. (212) 535-8814; EVŽEN ZÁPOTOCKÝ.

Democratic Kampuchea: (see Kampuchea).

Democratic Yemen: (see Yemen, People's Democratic Republic).

Denmark: 2 United Nations Plaza, 26th Floor, New York, NY 10017; tel. (212) 308-7009; OLE BIERRING.

Djibouti: 866 United Nations Plaza, Suite 4011, New York, NY 10017; tel. (212) 753-3163; ROBLE OLHAYE.

Dominica: 41 East 42nd St, Suite 315, New York, NY 10017; tel. (212) 791-1872; FRANKLIN ANDREW BARON.

Dominican Republic: 144 East 44th St, 4th Floor, New York, NY 10017; tel. (212) 867-0833; JUAN ARÍSTIDES TAVERAS-GUZMÁN.

Ecuador: 820 Second Ave, 15th Floor, New York, NY 10017; tel. (212) 986-6670; CARLOS TOBAR-ZALDUMBIDE.

INTERNATIONAL ORGANIZATIONS United Nations

Egypt: 36 East 67th St, New York, NY 10021; tel. (212) 879-6300; ABDEL HADIM BADAWI.
El Salvador: 46 Park Ave, New York, NY 10016; tel. (212) 679-1616; ROBERTO MEZA.
Equatorial Guinea: 801 Second Ave, Room 1403, New York, NY 10017; tel. (212) 599-1523.
Ethiopia: 866 United Nations Plaza, Room 560, New York, NY 10017; tel. (212) 421-1830; TESFAYE TADESSE.
Fiji: 1 United Nations Plaza, 26th Floor, New York, NY 10017; tel. (212) 355-7316; WINSTON THOMPSON.
Finland: 866 United Nations Plaza, 2nd Floor, New York, NY 10017; tel. (212) 355-2100; Dr KEIJO KORHONEN.
France: 1 Dag Hammarskjöld Plaza, 245 East 47th St, New York, NY 10017; tel. (212) 308-5700; PIERRE-LOUIS BLANC.
Gabon: 18 East 41st St, 6th Floor, New York, NY 10017; tel. (212) 686-9720; LAURENT-MARIE BIFFOT.
The Gambia: 19 East 47th St, New York, NY 10017; tel. (212) 752-6213; OUSMAN AHMADU SALLAH.
German Democratic Republic: 58 Park Ave, New York, NY 10016; tel. (212) 686-2596; SIEGFRIED ZACHMANN.
Germany, Federal Republic: 600 Third Ave, 41st Floor, New York, NY 10016; tel. (212) 949-9200; ALEXANDER Count YORK VON WARTENBURG.
Ghana: 19 East 47th St, New York, NY 10017; tel. (212) 832-1300; JAMES VICTOR GBEHO.
Greece: 733 Third Ave, 23rd Floor, New York, NY 10017; tel. (212) 490-6060; CONSTANTINE ZEPOS.
Grenada: 820 Second Ave, New York, NY 10017; tel. (212) 599-0301; Dr LAMUEL A. STANISLAUS.
Guatemala: 57 Park Ave, New York, NY 10016; tel. (212) 679-4760; FERNANDO ANDRADE-DÍAZ DURÁN.
Guinea: 1 United Nations Plaza, 26th Floor, New York, NY 10017; tel. (212) 486-9170; MOHAMED TRAORE.
Guinea-Bissau: 211 East 43rd St, Room 604, New York, NY 10017; tel. (212) 661-3977; ALFREDO LOPES CABRAL.
Guyana: 622 Third Ave, 35th Floor, New York, NY 10017; tel. (212) 953-0930; SAMUEL R. INSANALLY.
Haiti: 801 Second Ave, Room 300, New York, NY 10017; tel. (212) 370-4840; YVES L. AUGUSTE.
Honduras: 866 United Nations Plaza, Suite 509, New York, NY 10017; tel. (212) 752-3370; JORGE RAMÓN HERNÁNDEZ ALCERRO.
Hungary: 10 East 75th St, New York, NY 10021; tel. (212) 535-8660; FERENC ESZTERGALYOS.
Iceland: 370 Lexington Ave, 5th Floor, New York, NY 10017; tel. (212) 686-4100; HANS G. ANDERSEN.
India: 866 United Nations Plaza, Suite 505, New York, NY 10017; tel. (212) 751-0900; CHINMAYA RAJANINATH GHAREKHAN.
Indonesia: 325 East 38th St, New York, NY 10016; tel. (212) 972-8333; NANA S. SUTRESNA.
Iran: 622 Third Ave, 34th Floor, New York, NY 10017; tel. (212) 687-2020; MUHAMMAD JA'AFAR MAHALLATI.
Iraq: 14 East 79th St, New York, NY 10017; tel. (212) 737-4434; ISMAT TAHA KITTANI.
Ireland: 1 Dag Hammarskjöld Plaza, 885 Second Ave, 19th Floor, New York, NY 10017; tel. (212) 421-6934; ROBERT McDONAGH.
Israel: 800 Second Ave, New York, NY 10017; tel. (212) 351-5200; BENJAMIN NETANYAHU.
Italy: 2 United Nations Plaza, 24th Floor, New York, NY 10017; tel. (212) 486-9191; MAURIZIO BUCCI.
Jamaica: 866 Second Ave, 15th Floor, 2 Dag Hammarskjöld Plaza, New York, NY 10017; tel. (212) 688-7040; LLOYD M. H. BARNETT.
Japan: 866 United Nations Plaza, 2nd Floor, New York, NY 10017; tel. (212) 223-4300; HIDEO KAGAMI.
Jordan: 866 United Nations Plaza, Room 550–552, New York, NY 10017; tel. (212) 752-0135; ABDULLAH SALAH.
Kampuchea: 747 Third Ave, 8th Floor, New York, NY 10017; tel. (212) 888-6646; PRASITH THIOUNN.*
Kenya: 866 United Nations Plaza, Room 486, New York, NY 10017; tel. (212) 421-4740; RAPHAEL MULI KIILU.
Kuwait: 321 East 44th St, New York, NY 10017; tel. (212) 973-4300; MOHAMMAD A. ABULHASAN.
Laos: 820 Second Ave, Suite 400, New York, NY 10017; tel. (212) 986-0227.

Lebanon: 866 United Nations Plaza, Room 531–533, New York, NY 10017; tel. (212) 355-5460; RACHID FAKHOURY.
Lesotho: 866 United Nations Plaza, Suite 580, New York, NY 10017; tel. (212) 421-7543.
Liberia: 820 Second Ave, 4th Floor, New York, NY 10017; tel. (212) 687-1033; SYLVESTER JARRETT.
Libya: 309-315 East 48th St, New York, NY 10017; tel. (212) 752-5775; Dr ALI A. TREIKI.
Luxembourg: 801 Second Ave, New York, NY 10017; tel. (212) 370-9850; JEAN FEYDER.
Madagascar: 801 Second Ave, Suite 404, New York, NY 10017; tel. (212) 986-9491; BLAISE RABETAFIKA.
Malawi: 600 Third Ave, 30th Floor, New York, NY 10016; tel. (212) 949-0180; TIMON SAM MANGWAZU.
Malaysia: 140 East 45th St, 43rd Floor, New York, NY 10017; tel. (212) 986-6310; RAZALI ISMAILI.
Maldives: 820 Second Ave, Suite 800C, New York, NY 10017; tel. (212) 599-6195; HUSSEIN MANIKFAN.
Mali: 111 East 69th St, New York, NY 10021; tel. (212) 737-4150; NOUMOU DIAKITE.
Malta: 249 East 35th St, New York, NY 10016; tel. (212) 725-2345; Dr ALEXANDER BORG OLIVIER.
Mauritania: 9 East 77th St, New York, NY 10021; tel. (212) 737-7780; MOHAMED MAHJOUB OULD BOYE.
Mauritius: 211 East 43rd St, 15th Floor, New York, NY 10017; tel. (212) 949-0190; Dr SATTEEANUND PEERTHUM.
Mexico: 2 United Nations Plaza, 28th Floor, New York, NY 10017; tel. (212) 752-0220; MARIO MOYA-PALENCIA.
Mongolia: 6 East 77th St, New York, NY 10021; tel. (212) 861-9460; GENDENGIIN NYAMDOO.
Morocco: 767 Third Ave, 30th Floor, New York, NY 10017; tel. (212) 421-1580; DRISS SLAOUI.
Mozambique: 70 East 79th St, New York, NY 10021; tel. (212) 517-4550; MANUEL DOS SANTOS.
Nepal: 820 Second Ave, Suite 202, New York, NY 10017; tel. (212) 370-4188; JAI PRATAP RANA.
Netherlands: 711 Third Ave, 9th Floor, New York, NY 10017; tel. (212) 697-5547; ADRIAAN JACOBOVITS DE SZEGED.
New Zealand: 1 United Nations Plaza, 25th Floor, New York, NY 10017; tel. (212) 826-1960; DAVID KEITH McDOWELL.
Nicaragua: 820 Second Ave, 8th Floor, New York, NY 10017; tel. (212) 490-7997.
Niger: 417 East 50th St, New York, NY 10022; tel. (212) 421-3260; Col MOUMOUNI DJERMAKOYE.
Nigeria: 733 Third Ave, 15th Floor, New York, NY 10017; tel. (212) 953-9130; Maj.-Gen. JOSEPH GARBA.
Norway: 825 Third Ave, 18th Floor, New York, NY 10022; tel. (212) 421-0280; TOM ERIC VRAALSEN.
Oman: 866 United Nations Plaza, Suite 540, New York, NY 10017; tel. (212) 355-3505; SALIM BIN MUHAMMAD AL-KHUSSAIBY.
Pakistan: 8 East 65th St, New York, NY 10021; tel. (212) 879-8600; S. SHAH NAWAZ.
Panama: 866 United Nations Plaza, Room 544–545, New York, NY 10017; tel. (212) 421-5420; Dr JORGE E. RITTER.
Papua New Guinea: 100 East 42nd St, Room 1005, New York, NY 10017; tel. (212) 682-6447; RENAGI RENAGI LOHIA.
Paraguay: 211 East 43rd St, Room 1206, New York, NY 10017; tel. (212) 687-3490; ALFREDO CAÑETE.
Peru: 820 Second Ave, Suite 1600, New York, NY 10017; tel. (212) 687-3336; CARLOS ALZAMORA.
Philippines: 556 Fifth Ave, 5th Floor, New York, NY 10036; tel. (212) 764-1300; EMMANUEL PELAEZ.
Poland: 9 East 66th St, New York, NY 10021; tel. (212) 744-2506; EUGENIUSZ NOWORYTA.
Portugal: 777 Third Ave, 27th Floor, New York, NY 10017; tel. (212) 759-9444; JOÃO UVA DE MATOS PROENÇA.
Qatar: 747 Third Ave, 22nd Floor, New York, NY 10017; tel. (212) 486-9335; HAMAD ABDELAZIZ AL-KAWARI.
Romania: 573-577 Third Ave, New York, NY 10016; tel. (212) 682-3273; PETRE TANASIE.
Rwanda: 124 East 39th St, New York, NY 10016; tel. (212) 696-0644; CÉLESTIN KABANDA.
Saint Christopher and Nevis: 414 East 75th St, 5th Floor, New York, NY 10021; tel. (212) 535-1234; Dr WILLIAM HERBERT.
Saint Lucia: 41 East 42nd St, Suite 315, New York, NY 10017; tel. (212) 697-9360; Dr JOSEPH EDSEL EDMUNDS.
Saint Vincent and the Grenadines: 801 Second Ave, 21st Floor, New York, NY 10017; tel. (212) 687-4490; JONATHAN C. PETERS.

* Representing the government of Democratic Kampuchea, overthrown in January 1979. The People's Republic of Kampuchea, which succeeded the deposed regime, has not been recognized by the United Nations.

INTERNATIONAL ORGANIZATIONS

United Nations

São Tomé and Príncipe: 801 Second Ave, Suite 1504, New York, NY 10017; tel. (212) 697-4211; Joaquim Rafael Branco.
Saudi Arabia: 405 Lexington Ave, 56th Floor, New York, NY 10017; tel. (212) 697-4830; Samir Shihabi.
Senegal: 238 East 68th St, New York, NY 10021; tel. (212) 517-9030; Absa Claude Diallo.
Seychelles: 820 Second Ave, Suite 203, New York, NY 10017; tel. (212) 687-9766.
Sierra Leone: 57 East 64th St, New York, NY 10021; tel. (212) 570-0030; Dr Tom Obaleh Kargbo.
Singapore: 2 United Nations Plaza, 25th Floor, New York, NY 10017; tel. (212) 826-0840; Kishore Mahbubani.
Solomon Islands: 820 Second Ave, Suite 800A, New York, NY 10017; tel. (212) 599-6193; Francis Joseph Saemala.
Somalia: 425 East 61st St, Suite 703, New York, NY 10021; tel. (212) 688-9410; Abdillahi Said Osman.
South Africa: 326 East 48th St, New York, NY 10017; tel. (212) 371-8154; Albert Leslie Manley.
Spain: 809 United Nations Plaza, 6th Floor, New York, NY 10017; tel. (212) 661-1050; Francisco Villar y Ortiz de Urdía.
Sri Lanka: 630 Third Ave, 20th Floor, New York, NY 10017; tel. (212) 986-7040; Daya Perera.
Sudan: 210 East 49th St, New York, NY 10017; tel. (212) 421-2680; Amin M. Abdoun.
Suriname: 1 United Nations Plaza, 26th Floor, New York, NY 10017; tel. (212) 826-0660.
Swaziland: 866 United Nations Plaza, Suite 420, New York, NY 10017; tel. (212) 371-8910; Dr Timothy L. L. Dlamini.
Sweden: 825 Third Ave, 39th Floor, New York, NY 10022; tel. (212) 751-5900; Jan K. Eliasson.
Syria: 820 Second Ave, 10th Floor, New York, NY 10017; tel. (212) 661-1313; Ahmad Fathi al-Masri.
Tanzania: 205 East 42nd St, 13th Floor, New York, NY 10017; tel. (212) 972-9160; Dr Wilbert K. Chagula.
Thailand: 628 Second Ave, New York, NY 10016; tel. (212) 689-1004; Nitya Pibulsonggram.
Togo: 112 East 40th St, New York, NY 10016; tel. (212) 490-3455; Koffi Adjoyi.
Trinidad and Tobago: 675 Third Ave, New York, NY 10017; tel. (212) 697-7620; D. H. N. Alleyne.
Tunisia: 405 Lexington Ave, 65th Floor, New York, NY 10174; tel. (212) 557-3344; Ahmed Ghezal.
Turkey: 821 United Nations Plaza, 11th Floor, New York, NY 10017; tel. (212) 949-0150; İlter Türkmen.
Uganda: 336 East 45th St, New York, NY 10017; tel. (212) 949-0110; Wanume Kibedi.
Ukrainian Soviet Socialist Republic: 136 East 67th St, New York, NY 10021; tel. (212) 535-3418; Guennadi I. Oudovenko.
USSR: 136 East 67th St, New York, NY 10021; tel. (212) 861-4900; Aleksandr Belonogov.
United Arab Emirates: 747 Third Ave, 36th Floor, New York, NY 10017; tel. (212) 371-0480; Muhammad Hussain al-Shaali.
United Kingdom: 845 Third Ave, 10th Floor, New York, NY 10022; tel. (212) 752-8586; Sir Crispin Tickell.
United Republic of Tanzania: (see Tanzania).
USA: 799 United Nations Plaza, New York, NY 10017; tel. (212) 415-4000; Vernon A. Walters.
Uruguay: 747 Third Ave, 37th Floor, New York, NY 10017; tel. (212) 752-8240; Dr Felipe Héctor Paolillo.
Vanuatu: 411 West 148th St, New York, NY 10031; tel. (212) 926-3311; Nikenike Vurobaravu.
Venezuela: 335 East 46th St, New York, NY 10017; tel. (212) 557-2055; Dr Andrés Aguilar.
Viet-Nam: 20 Waterside Plaza (Lobby), New York, NY 10010; tel. (212) 679-3779.
Western Samoa: 820 Second Ave, Suite 800D, 8th Floor, New York, NY 10017; tel. (212) 599-6196; Maiava Iulai Toma.
Yemen Arab Republic: 747 Third Ave, 8th Floor, New York, NY 10017; tel. (212) 355-1730; Salem Basendwah.
Yemen, People's Democratic Republic: 413 East 51st St, New York, NY 10022; tel. (212) 752-3066; Abdalla Saleh al-Ashtal.
Yugoslavia: 854 Fifth Ave, New York, NY 10021; tel. (212) 879-8700; Dragoslav Pejić.
Zaire: 767 Third Ave, 25th Floor, New York, NY 10017; tel. (212) 754-1966; Bagbeni Adeito Nzengeya.
Zambia: 237 East 52nd St, New York, NY 10022; tel. (212) 758-1110; Peter Dingiswaye Zuze.
Zimbabwe: 19 East 47th St, New York, NY 10017; tel. (212) 980-9511; Dr Isack S. G. Mudenge.

OBSERVERS

Non-member states, inter-governmental and other organizations which have received an invitation to participate in the sessions and the work of the General Assembly as Observers, maintaining permanent offices at the UN.

Non-member states

Holy See: 20 East 72nd St, New York, NY 10021; tel. (212) 734-2900; The Most Rev. Mgr Renato Raffaele Martino.
Korea, Democratic People's Republic: 225 East 86th St, New York, NY 10028; tel. (212) 722-3536; Pak Gil Yon.
Korea, Republic: 866 United Nations Plaza, Suite 300, New York, NY 10017; tel. (212) 371-1280; Dr Keun Park.
Monaco: 845 Third Ave, 2nd Floor, New York, NY 10022; tel. (212) 759-5227; John Dubé.
San Marino: 745 Fifth Ave, Suite 1219, New York, NY 10151; tel. (212) 688-9806; Gian Nicola Filippi-Balestra.
Switzerland: 757 Third Ave, 21st Floor, New York, NY 10017; tel. (212) 421-1480; Dieter Chenaux-Repond.

Inter-governmental organizations*

Asian-African Legal Consultative Committee: 404 East 66th St, New York, NY 10021; tel. (212) 734-7608; K. Bhagwat-Singh.
European Community: 3 Dag Hammarskjöld Plaza, 12th Floor, 305 East 47th St, New York, NY 10017; tel. (212) 371-3804; the Observer is the Permanent Representative to the UN of the country currently exercising the Presidency of the Council of Ministers of the Community.
League of Arab States: 747 Third Ave, 35th Floor, New York, NY 10017; tel. (212) 838-8700; Dr Clovis Maksoud.
Organization of African Unity: 346 East 50th St, New York, NY 10022; tel. (212) 319-5490; Oumara Garba Youssoufou.
Organization of the Islamic Conference: 130 East 40th St, 5th Floor, New York, NY 10016; tel. (212) 883-0140.

* The following inter-governmental organizations have a standing invitation to participate as Observers, but do not maintain permanent offices at the United Nations:
    African, Caribbean and Pacific Group of States.
    Agency for Cultural and Technical Co-operation.
    Commonwealth Secretariat.
    Organization of American States.
    Sistema Económica Latinoamericana.

The Council for Mutual Economic Assistance (CMEA–COMECON) is represented by the Permanent Mission of the country currently holding the Presidency of the CMEA.

Other organizations

Palestine Liberation Organization: 115 East 65th St, New York, NY 10021; tel. (212) 288-8500; Zuhdi Labib Terzi.
South West Africa People's Organisation of Namibia: 801 Second Ave, Room 1401, New York, NY 10017; tel. (212) 557-2450; Helmut Angula.

United Nations Information Centres

Afghanistan: POB 5; Shah Mahmoud Ghazi Watt, Kabul.
Algeria: POB 823; 19 ave Chahid el-Ouali Mustapha Sayed, Algiers.
Argentina: Junín 1940, 1° piso, 1113 Buenos Aires (also covers Uruguay).
Australia: GPO Box 4045; 44 Market St, Sydney, NSW 2001 (also covers Fiji, Kiribati, Nauru, New Zealand, Tonga, Tuvalu, Vanuatu and Western Samoa).
Austria: POB 500; Vienna International Centre, Wagramerstrasse 5, 1220 Vienna (also covers the Federal Republic of Germany and Hungary).
Bahrain: POB 26004; King Faisal Rd, Gufool, Manama (also covers Qatar and the United Arab Emirates).
Bangladesh: POB 3658; House 12, Rd 6, Dhanmandi, Dhaka 1205.
Belgium: 108 rue d'Arlon, 1040 Brussels (also covers Luxembourg and the Netherlands).
Bolivia: POB 686; Edif. Naciones Unidas, Plaza Isabel la Católica, Ex-Clínica Santa Isabel, Planta Baja, La Paz.
Brazil: Palacio Itamaraty, Avda Marechal Floriano 196, Rio de Janeiro.

INTERNATIONAL ORGANIZATIONS   *United Nations*

Burkina Faso: POB 135; 218 rue de la Gare, Secteur no 3, Ouagadougou (also covers Chad, Mali and Niger).
Burma: POB 230; 28A Manawhari Rd, Rangoon.
Burundi: POB 2160; ave de la Poste 7, place de l'Indépendance, Bujumbura.
Cameroon: POB 836; Immeuble Kamden, rue Joseph Clère, Yaoundé (also covers the Central African Republic and Gabon).
Chile: Edif. Naciones Unidas, Avda Dag Hammarskjöld, Casilla 179-D, Santiago.
Colombia: Apdo Aéreo 058964; Calle 72, No. 12-65, Piso 2, Bogotá 2 (also covers Ecuador and Venezuela).
Congo: POB 465; ave Pointe-Hollandaise, Quartier Mpila, Brazzaville.
Czechoslovakia: Panská 5, 110 00 Prague 1 (also covers the German Democratic Republic).
Denmark: 37 H. C. Andersen Blvd, 1553 Copenhagen V (also covers Finland, Iceland, Norway and Sweden).
Egypt: POB 262; 1 Osiris St, Tagher Bldg, Garden City, Cairo (also covers Saudi Arabia and the Yemen Arab Republic).
El Salvador: Apdo 2157; 87 Avda Norte, Colonia Escalón, San Salvador.
Ethiopia: POB 3001; Africa Hall, Addis Ababa.
France: 1 rue Miollis, 75732 Paris Cedex 15.
Ghana: POB 2339; Liberia and Nassar Rds, Accra (also covers Sierra Leone).
Greece: 36 Amalia Ave, 105 58 Athens (also covers Cyprus and Israel).
India: 55 Lodi Estate, New Delhi 110003 (also covers Bhutan).
Indonesia: Gedung Dewan Pers, 5th Floor, 32-34 Jalan Kebon Sirih, Jakarta.
Iran: POB 1555; Gandhi Ave, 43 St No. 3, Teheran.
Iraq: POB 27; Amiríya, Airport St, Baghdad.
Italy: Palazzetto Venezia, Piazza San Marco 50, Rome (also covers the Holy See and Malta).
Japan: Shin Aoyama Bldg Nishika, 22nd Floor, 1-1 Minami Aoyama 1-chome, Minato-ku, Tokyo 107 (also covers the Trust Territory of the Pacific Islands).
Kenya: POB 34135; United Nations Office, Gigiri, Nairobi (also covers Seychelles and Uganda).
Lebanon: POB 4656; Apt No 1, Fakhoury Bldg, Montée Bain Militaire, Beirut (also covers Jordan, Kuwait and Syria).
Lesotho: POB 301; Corner Kingsway and Hilton Rds, opposite Sanlam Centre, Maseru 100.
Liberia: POB 274; LBDI Bldg, Tubman Blvd, Monrovia.
Libya: POB 286; Muzaffar Al Aftas St, Hay El-Andalous, Tripoli.
Madagascar: POB 1348; 22 rue Rainitovo, Antsahavola, Antananarivo.
Mexico: Presidente Mazaryk 29, 7° piso, México 11570, DF (also covers Cuba and the Dominican Republic).
Morocco: 'Casier ONU', Angle Charia Moulay Ibnouzaid et Zankat Roundanat No. 6, Rabat.
Nepal: POB 107; Pulchowk, Patan, Kathmandu.
Nicaragua: POB 3260; Bolonia, de Plaza España, 2 cuadros abajo, Managua.
Nigeria: POB 1068; 17 Kingsway Rd, Ikoyi, Lagos.
Pakistan: POB 1107; House No. 26, 88th St, Ramna 16/3, Islamabad.
Panama: POB 6-9083, El Dorado; Urbanización Obarrio, Calle 54 y Avda Tercera Sur, Edif. No. 17, Panama City.
Paraguay: Casilla de Correo 1107, Asunción.
Peru: Apdo 14-0199; Mariscal Blas Cerdeña 450, San Isidro, Lima.
Philippines: POB 7285 (ADC); NEDA Bldg, Ground Floor, 106 Amorsolo St, Legaspi Village, Makati, Metro Manila (also covers Papua New Guinea and Solomon Islands).
Portugal: Rua Latina Coelho No. 1, Edif. Aviz, Bloco A1, 10°, 1000 Lisbon.
Romania: POB 1-701; 16 Aurel Vlaicu St, Bucharest.
Senegal: POB 154; 9 allées Robert Delmas, Dakar (also covers Cape Verde, Côte d'Ivoire, The Gambia, Guinea, Guinea-Bissau and Mauritania).
Spain: POB 3400, 28080; Avda General Perón 32-1°, 28020 Madrid.
Sri Lanka: POB 1505; 202-204 Bauddhaloka Mawatha, Colombo 7.
Sudan: POB 1992; Al Qasr Ave, St No. 15, Block No. 3, House No. 3, Khartoum East (also covers Somalia).
Switzerland: Palais des Nations, 1211 Geneva 10 (also covers Bulgaria and Poland).
Tanzania: POB 9224; Matasalamat Bldg, Samora Machel Ave, Dar es Salaam.
Thailand: United Nations Bldg, Rajadamnern Ave, Bangkok 10200 (also covers Kampuchea, Laos, Malaysia, Singapore and Viet-Nam).
Togo: POB 911; 107 blvd de 13 janvier, Lomé (also covers Benin).
Trinidad and Tobago: POB 130; 15 Keate St, Port of Spain (also covers Antigua and Barbuda, the Bahamas, Barbados, Belize, Dominica, Grenada, Guyana, Jamaica, the Netherlands Antilles, Saint Christopher and Nevis, Saint Lucia, Saint Vincent and the Grenadines and Suriname).
Tunisia: POB 863; 61 blvd Bab Benat, Tunis.
Turkey: PK 407; 197 Atatürk Bulvarı, Ankara.
USSR: 4/16 Ulitsa Lunacharskogo, Moscow 121002 (also covers the Byelorussian SSR and the Ukrainian SSR).
United Kingdom: 20 Buckingham Gate, London, SW1E 6LB (also covers Ireland).
USA: 1889 F St, NW, Washington, DC 20006.
Yugoslavia: POB 157; Svetozara Markovica 58, Belgrade (also covers Albania).
Zaire: POB 7248: Bâtiment Deuxième République, blvd du 30 juin, Kinshasa.
Zambia: POB 32905; Profound House, Ground Floor, Cairo Rd, Kabwe Roundabout, Lusaka (also covers Botswana, Malawi and Swaziland).
Zimbabwe: POB 4408; Dolphin House, 23 Moffat St/Union Ave, Harare.

United Nations Publications

The UN Chronicle (quarterly).
United Nations Documents Index (quarterly).
Current Bibliographical Information (monthly).
Monthly Bulletin of Statistics.
Population and Vital Statistics Report (monthly).
Objective: Justice (2 a year).
Bulletin on Narcotics (quarterly).
CTC Reporter (Centre on Transnational Corporations; 3 a year).
Documents (of the General Assembly; the Security Council; the Economic and Social Council; the Trusteeship Commission; the International Law Commission).
Other UN publications are listed in the chapters dealing with the agencies concerned.

Finance

The United Nations Budget is mainly financed by contributions from member states (in the proportions shown on pp. 3–4). In 1986 and 1987 there was a serious financial crisis, as a result of arrears in payments by some members. The USA (which was due to pay some 25% of the 1986-87 budget), withheld part of its contributions, demanding financial reforms and the introduction of 'weighted' voting (in proportion to members' contributions) on budgetary matters. An 18-member panel of experts was established in December 1985 to review UN administration and finance. Its report was presented to the UN Secretary-General in August 1986, and the recommendations were approved by the General Assembly later in the year. The reforms were to include: a limit on the number of UN conferences to be held each year; a reduction in numbers of staff (by 15% at lower levels and by 25% at the most senior levels), together with a restructuring of the principal administrative departments; a reduction in the volume of documents produced by the UN; and more efficient collaboration between UN agencies. The most important innovation was made in response to demands by the principal contributors to the UN budget (including both the USA and the USSR) for greater control over spending: from 1990 the budget was to be drafted by the 21-member Committee for Programme and Co-ordination (expanded to 34 members in 1987), and to be adopted by consensus, giving the major contributors a power of veto for the first time (although the budget would still be subject to approval by the General Assembly). In September 1988 the US Government, expressing its satisfaction with the reforms, authorized the immediate payment of $144m. and the eventual payment of $520m. in current and overdue contributions.

INTERNATIONAL ORGANIZATIONS
United Nations

TWO-YEAR BUDGET OF THE UNITED NATIONS (US dollars)

	1986–87*	1988–89†
Overall policy-making, direction and co-ordination	46,148,900	44,932,900
Political and Security Council affairs, peace-keeping activities	94,625,400	89,892,700
Political affairs, trusteeship and decolonization	30,677,700	31,824,500
Policy-making organs (economic and social activities)	2,666,400	2,040,600
Office of the Director-General for Development and International Economic Co-operation	3,813,400	3,840,100
Regional Commissions Liaison Office	705,000	641,000
Department of International Economic and Social Affairs	55,783,500	40,280,500
Activities on global social development issues	—	12,007,100
Department of Technical Co-operation for Development	20,611,300	19,922,900
Office of Secretariat Services for Economic and Social Matters	4,405,300	—
Transnational corporations	10,178,700	9,529,200
Economic Commission for Europe	30,942,500	35,797,400
Economic and Social Commission for Asia and the Pacific	34,840,400	33,483,000
Economic Commission for Latin America and the Caribbean	39,284,200	43,069,900
Economic Commission for Africa	46,063,300	44,234,600
Economic and Social Commission for Western Asia	32,722,900	32,599,900
United Nations Conference on Trade and Development	69,278,100	78,936,000
International Trade Centre	11,010,000	12,242,800
Centre for Science and Technology for Development	4,224,800	3,971,300
United Nations Environment Programme	10,117,100	10,651,100
United Nations Centre for Human Settlements (Habitat)	8,364,900	8,356,100
International drug control	7,158,100	8,750,200
Office of the United Nations High Commissioner for Refugees	36,701,400	39,444,400
Office of the United Nations Disaster Relief Co-ordinator	6,418,300	7,289,400
Human rights	14,078,100	17,008,800
Regular programme of technical co-operation	28,325,900	32,346,100
International Court of Justice	11,485,600	12,527,700
Legal activities	16,282,100	16,706,000
Public information	76,182,700	77,001,700
Administration and management	338,469,800	377,150,000
Conference and library services	310,763,500	333,779,200
United Nations bond issue	16,788,400	3,520,800
Staff assessment	261,259,800	266,605,900
Construction, alteration, improvement and major maintenance of premises	30,823,100	19,202,500
Grant to United Nations Institute for Training and Research	600,000	—
Grand total	**1,711,801,200**	**1,769,586,300**

* Budget approved December 1985 and revised December 1986 and December 1987.
† Budget approved December 1987.

Charter of the United Nations

We the peoples of the United Nations determined

to save succeeding generations from the scourge of war, which twice in our lifetime has brought untold sorrow to mankind, and

to reaffirm faith in fundamental human rights, in the dignity and worth of the human person, in the equal rights of men and women and of nations large and small, and

to establish conditions under which justice and respect for the obligations arising from treaties and other sources of international law can be maintained, and

to promote social progress and better standards of life in larger freedom,

And for these ends

to practise tolerance and live together in peace with one another as good neighbours, and

to unite our strength to maintain international peace and security, and

to ensure, by the acceptance of principles and the institution of methods, that armed force shall not be used, save in the common interest, and

to employ international machinery for the promotion of the economic and social advancement of all peoples,

Have resolved to combine our efforts to accomplish these aims.

Accordingly, our respective Governments, through representatives assembled in the city of San Francisco, who have exhibited their full powers found to be in good and due form, have agreed to the present Charter of the United Nations and do hereby establish an international organization to be known as the United Nations.

I. PURPOSES AND PRINCIPLES

Article 1

The Purposes of the United Nations are:

1. To maintain international peace and security, and to that end: to take effective collective measures for the prevention and removal of threats to the peace, and for the suppression of acts of aggression or other breaches of the peace, and to bring about by peaceful means, and in conformity with the principles of justice and international law, adjustment or settlement of international disputes or situations which might lead to a breach of the peace:

2. To develop friendly relations among nations based on respect for the principle of equal rights and self-determination of peoples, and to take other appropriate measures to strengthen universal peace;

3. To achieve international co-operation in solving international problems of an economic, social, cultural, or humanitarian character, and in promoting and encouraging respect for human rights and for fundamental freedoms for all without distinction as to race, sex, language, or religion; and

4. To be a centre for harmonizing the accusations of nations in the attainment of these common ends.

Article 2

The Organization and its Members, in pursuit of the Purposes stated in Article 1, shall act in accordance with the following Principles.

1. The Organization is based on the principle of the sovereign equality of all its Members.

2. All Members, in order to ensure to all of them the rights and benefits resulting from membership, shall fulfil in good faith the obligations assumed by them in accordance with the present Charter.

3. All Members shall settle their international disputes by peaceful means in such a manner that international peace and security, and justice, are not endangered.

4. All Members shall refrain in their international relations from the threat or use of force against the territorial integrity or political independence of any state, or in any manner inconsistent with the Purposes of the United Nations.

5. All Members shall give the United Nations every assistance in any action it takes in accordance with the present Charter, and shall refrain from giving assistance to any state against which the United Nations is taking preventive or enforcement action.

6. The Organization shall ensure that states which are not Members of the United Nations act in accordance with these Principles so far as may be necessary for the maintenance of international peace and security.

7. Nothing contained in the present Charter shall authorize the United Nations to intervene in matters which are essentially within the domestic jurisdiction of any state or shall require the Members to submit such matters to settlement under the present Charter; but this principle shall not prejudice the application of enforcement measures under Chapter VII.

II. MEMBERSHIP

Article 3

The original Members of the United Nations shall be the states which, having participated in the United Nations Conference on International Organization at San Francisco, or having previously signed the Declaration by United Nations of January 1, 1942, sign the present Charter and ratify it in accordance with Article 110.

Article 4

1. Membership in the United Nations is open to all other peace-loving states which accept the obligations contained in the present Charter and, in the judgement of the Organization, are able and willing to carry out these obligations.

2. The admission of any such state to membership in the United Nations will be effected by a decision of the General Assembly upon the recommendation of the Security Council.

Article 5

A member of the United Nations against which preventive or enforcement action has been taken by the Security Council may be suspended from the exercise of the rights and privileges of membership by the General Assembly upon the recommendation of the Security Council. The exercise of these rights and privileges may be restored by the Security Council.

Article 6

A Member of the United Nations which has persistently violated the Principles contained in the present Charter may be expelled from the Organization by the General Assembly upon the recommendation of the Security Council.

III. ORGANS

Article 7

1. There are established as the principal organs of the United Nations: a General Assembly, a Security Council, an Economic and Social Council, a Trusteeship Council, an International Court of Justice, and a Secretariat.

2. Such subsidiary organs as may be found necessary may be established in accordance with the present Charter.

Article 8

The United Nations shall place no restrictions on the eligibility of men and women to participate in any capacity and under conditions of equality in its principal and subsidiary organs.

IV. THE GENERAL ASSEMBLY

Composition

Article 9

1. The General Assembly shall consist of all the Members of the United Nations.

2. Each Member shall have not more than five representatives in the General Assembly.

Functions and Powers

Article 10

The General Assembly may discuss any questions or any matters within the scope of the present Charter or relating to the powers and functions of any organs provided for in the present Charter, and, except as provided in Article 12, may make recommendations to the Members of the United Nations or to the Security Council or to both on any such questions or matters.

Article 11

1. The General Assembly may consider the general principles of co-operation in the maintenance of international peace and security, including the principles governing disarmament and the regulation of armaments, and may make recommendations with regard to such principles to the Members or to the Security Council or to both.

2. The General Assembly may discuss any questions relating to the maintenance of international peace and security brought before it by any Member of the United Nations, or by the Security Council, or by a state which is not a Member of the United Nations in accordance with Article 35, paragraph 2, and, except as provided in Article 12, may make recommendations with regard to any such question to the state or states concerned or to the Security Council or both. Any such question on which action is necessary shall be referred to the Security Council by the General Assembly either before or after discussion.

3. The General Assembly may call the attention of the Security Council to situations which are likely to endanger international peace and security.

4. The powers of the General Assembly set forth in this Article shall not limit the general scope of Article 10.

Article 12

1. While the Security Council is exercising in respect of any dispute or situation the functions assigned to it in the present Charter, the General Assembly shall not make any recommendations with regard to that dispute or situation unless the Security Council so requests.

2. The Secretary-General, with the consent of the Security Council, shall notify the General Assembly at each session of any matters relative to the maintenance of international peace and security which are being dealt with by the Security Council and shall similarly notify the General Assembly, or the Members of the United Nations if the General Assembly is not in session, immediately the Security Council ceases to deal with such matters.

Article 13

1. The General Assembly shall initiate studies and make recommendations for the purpose of:

(a) promoting international co-operation in the political field and encouraging the progressive development of international law and its codification;

(b) promoting international co-operation in the economic, social, cultural, educational, and health fields, and assisting in the realization of human rights and fundamental freedoms for all without distinction as to race, sex, language, or religion.

2. The further responsibilities, functions and powers of the General Assembly with respect to matters mentioned in paragraph 1(b) above are set forth in Chapters IX and X.

Article 14

Subject to the provision of Article 12, the General Assembly may recommend measures for the peaceful adjustment of any situation, regardless of origin, which it deems likely to impair the general welfare or friendly relations among nations, including situations resulting from a violation of the provisions of the present Charter setting forth the Purposes and Principles of the United Nations.

Article 15

1. The General Assembly shall receive and consider annual and special reports from the Security Council; these reports shall include an account of the measures that the Security Council has decided upon or taken to maintain international peace and security.

2. The General Assembly shall receive and consider reports from the other organs of the United Nations.

Article 16

The General Assembly shall perform such functions with respect to the international trusteeship system as are assigned to it under Chapters XII and XIII, including the approval of the trusteeship agreements for areas not designated as strategic.

Article 17

1. The General Assembly shall consider and approve the budget of the Organization.

2. The expenses of the Organization shall be borne by the Members as apportioned by the General Assembly.

3. The General Assembly shall consider and approve any financial and budgetary arrangements with specialized agencies referred to in Article 57 and shall examine the administrative budgets of such specialized agencies with a view to making recommendations to the agencies concerned.

Voting

Article 18

1. Each Member of the General Assembly shall have one vote.

2. Decisions of the General Assembly on important questions shall be made by a two-thirds majority of the members present and voting. These questions shall include: recommendations with respect to the maintenance of international peace and security, the election of the non-permanent Members of the Security Council, the election of the Members of the Economic and Social Council, the election of Members of the Trusteeship Council in accordance with paragraph 1(c) of Article 86, the admission of new Members to the United Nations, the suspension of the rights and privileges of membership, the expulsion of Members, questions relating to the operation of the trusteeship system, and budgetary questions.

3. Decisions on other questions, including the determination of additional categories of questions to be decided by a two-thirds majority, shall be made by a majority of the members present and voting.

Article 19

A Member of the United Nations which is in arrears in the payment of its financial contributions to the Organization shall have no vote in the General Assembly if the amount of its arrears equals or exceeds the amount of the contributions due from it for the preceding two full years. The General Assembly may, nevertheless, permit such a Member to vote if it is satisfied that the failure to pay is due to conditions beyond the control of the Member.

Procedure

Article 20

The General Assembly shall meet in regular annual sessions and in such special sessions as occasion may require. Special sessions shall be convoked by the Secretary-General at the request of the Security Council or of a majority of the members of the United Nations.

Article 21

The General Assembly shall adopt its own rules of procedure. It shall elect its President for each session.

Article 22

The General Assembly may establish such subsidiary organs as it deems necessary for the performance of its functions.

V. THE SECURITY COUNCIL
Composition

Article 23

1. The Security Council shall consist of 11 Members of the United Nations. The Republic of China, France, the Union of Soviet Socialist Republics, the United Kingdom of Great Britain and Northern Ireland, and the United States of America shall be permanent members of the Security Council. The General Assembly shall elect six other Members of the United Nations to be non-permanent members of the Security Council, due regard being specially paid, in the first instance to the contribution of Members of the United Nations to the maintenance of international peace and security and to the other purposes of the Organization, and also to equitable geographical distribution.

2. The non-permanent members of the Security Council shall be elected for a term of two years. In the first election of the non-permanent members, however, three shall be chosen for a term of one year. A retiring member shall not be eligible for immediate re-election.

3. Each member of the Security Council shall have one representative.

Functions and Powers

Article 24

1. In order to ensure prompt and effective action by the United Nations, its Members confer on the Security Council primary responsibility for the maintenance of international peace and security, and agree that in carrying out its duties under this responsibility the Security Council acts on their behalf.

2. In discharging these duties the Security Council shall act in accordance with the Purposes and Principles of the United Nations. The specific powers granted to the Security Council for the discharge of these duties are laid down in Chapters VI, VII, VIII and XII.

3. The Security Council shall submit annual and, when necessary, special reports to the General Assembly for its consideration.

Article 25

The Members of the United Nations agree to accept and carry out the decisions of the Security Council in accordance with the present Charter.

Article 26

In order to promote the establishment and maintenance of international peace and security with the least diversion for armaments of the world's human and economic resources, the Security Council shall be responsible for formulating, with the assistance of the Military Staff Committee referred to in Article 47, plans to be submitted to the Members of the United Nations for the establishment of a system for the regulation of armaments.

Voting

Article 27

1. Each member of the Security Council shall have one vote.
2. Decisions of the Security Council on procedural matters shall be made by an affirmative vote of seven members.
3. Decisions of the Security Council on all other matters shall be made by an affirmative vote of seven members including the concurring votes of the permanent members; provided that, in decisions under Chapter VI, and under paragraph 3 of Article 52, a party to a dispute shall abstain from voting.

Procedure

Article 28

1. The Security Council shall be so organized as to be able to function continuously. Each member of the Security Council shall for this purpose be represented at all times at the seat of the Organization.
2. The Security Council shall hold periodic meetings at which each of its members may, if it so desires, be represented by a member of the government or by some other specially designated representative.
3. The Security Council may hold meetings at such places other than the seat of the Organization as in its judgment will best facilitate its work.

Article 29

The Security Council may establish such subsidiary organs as it deems necessary for the performance of its functions.

Article 30

The Security Council shall adopt its own rules of procedure, including the method of selecting its President.

Article 31

Any Member of the United Nations which is not a member of the Security Council may participate, without vote, in the discussion of any question brought before the Security Council whenever the latter considers that the interests of that Member are specially affected.

Article 32

Any Member of the United Nations which is not a member of the Security Council or any state which is not a Member of the United Nations, if it is a party to a dispute under consideration by the Security Council, shall be invited to participate, without vote, in the discussion relating to the dispute. The Security Council shall lay down such conditions as it deems just for the participation of a state which is not a Member of the United Nations.

VI. PACIFIC SETTLEMENT OF DISPUTES

Article 33

1. The parties to any dispute, the continuance of which is likely to endanger the maintenance of international peace and security, shall, first of all, seek a solution by negotiation, enquiry, mediation, conciliation, arbitration, judicial settlement, resort to regional agencies or arrangements, or other peaceful means of their own choice.
2. The Security Council shall, when it deems necessary, call upon the parties to settle their disputes by such means.

Article 34

The Security Council may investigate any dispute, or any situation which might lead to international friction or give rise to a dispute, in order to determine whether the continuance of the dispute or situation is likely to endanger the maintenance of international peace and security.

Article 35

1. Any Member of the United Nations may bring any dispute, or any situation of the nature referred to in Article 34, to the attention of the Security Council or of the General Assembly.
2. A state which is not a Member of the United Nations may bring to the attention of the Security Council or of the General Assembly any dispute to which it is a party if it accepts in advance, for the purposes of the dispute, the obligations of pacific settlement provided in the present Charter.
3. The proceedings of the General Assembly in respect of matters brought to its attention under this Article will be subject to the provisions of Articles 11 and 12.

Article 36

1. The Security Council may, at any stage of a dispute of the nature referred to in Article 33 or of a situation of like nature, recommend appropriate procedures or methods of adjustment.
2. The Security Council should take into consideration any procedures for the settlement of the dispute which have already been adopted by the parties.
3. In making recommendations under this Article the Security Council should also take into consideration that legal disputes should as a general rule be referred by the parties to the International Court of Justice in accordance with the provisions of the statute of the Court.

Article 37

1. Should the parties to a dispute of the nature referred to in Article 33, fail to settle it by the means indicated in that Article, they shall refer it to the Security Council.
2. If the Security Council deems that the continuance of the dispute is in fact likely to endanger the maintenance of international peace and security, it shall decide whether to take action under Article 36 or to recommend such terms of settlement as it may consider appropriate.

Article 38

Without prejudice to the provisions of Articles 33 to 37, the Security Council may, if all the parties to any dispute so request, make recommendations to the parties with a view to a pacific settlement of the dispute.

VII. ACTION WITH RESPECT TO THREATS TO THE PEACE, BREACHES OF THE PEACE, AND ACTS OF AGGRESSION

Article 39

The Security Council shall determine the existence of any threat to the peace, breach of the peace, or act of aggression and shall make recommendations, or decide what measures shall be taken in accordance with Articles 41 and 42, to maintain or restore international peace and security.

Article 40

In order to prevent an aggravation of the situation, the Security Council may, before making the recommendations or deciding upon the measures provided for in Article 39, call upon the parties concerned to comply with such provisional measures as it deems necessary or desirable. Such provisional measures shall be without prejudice to the rights, claims, or position of the parties concerned. The Security Council shall duly take account of failure to comply with such provisional measures.

Article 41

The Security Council may decide what measures not involving the use of armed force are to be employed to give effect to its decisions, and it may call upon the Members of the United Nations to apply such measures. These may include complete or partial interruption of economic relations and of rail, sea, air, postal, telegraphic, radio, and other means of communication, and the severance of diplomatic relations.

Article 42

Should the Security Council consider that measures provided for in Article 41 would be inadequate or have proved to be inadequate, it may take such action by air, sea, or land forces as may be necessary to maintain or restore international peace and security. Such action may include demonstrations, blockade, and other operations by air, sea, or land forces of Members of the United Nations.

Article 43

1. All Members of the United Nations, in order to contribute to the maintenance of international peace and security, undertake to make available to the Security Council, on its call and in accordance with a special agreement or agreements, armed forces, assistance, and facilities, including rights of passage, necessary for the purpose of maintaining international peace and security.
2. Such agreement or agreements shall govern the numbers and types of forces, their degree of readiness and general location, and the nature of the facilities and assistance to be provided.
3. The agreement or agreements shall be negotiated as soon as possible on the initiative of the Security Council. They shall be concluded between the Security Council and Members or between the Security Council and groups of Members and shall be subject to ratification by the signatory states in accordance with their respective constitutional processes.

Article 44

When the Security Council has decided to use force it shall, before calling upon a Member not represented on it to provide armed forces in fulfilment of the obligations assumed under Article 43, invite that Member, if the Member so desires, to participate in the decisions of the Security Council concerning the employment of contingents of that Member's armed forces.

Article 45

In order to enable the United Nations to take urgent military measures, Members shall hold immediately available national air-force contingents for combined international enforcement action. The strength and degree of readiness of these contingents and plans for their combined action shall be determined, within the limits laid down in the special agreement and agreements referred to in Article 43, by the Security Council with the assistance of the Military Staff Committee.

Article 46

Plans for the application of armed force shall be made by the Security Council with the assistance of the Military Staff Committee.

Article 47

1. There shall be established a Military Staff Committee to advise and assist the Security Council on all questions relating to the Security Council's military requirements for the maintenance of international peace and security, the employment and command of forces placed at its disposal, the regulation of armaments, and possible disarmament.
2. The Military Staff Committee shall consist of the Chiefs of Staff of the permanent members of the Security Council or their representatives. Any Member of the United Nations not permanently represented on the Committee shall be invited by the Committee to be associated with it when the efficient discharge of the Committee's responsibilities requires the participation of that Member in its work.
3. The Military Staff Committee shall be responsible under the Security Council for the strategic direction of any armed forces placed at the disposal of the Security Council. Questions relating to the command of such forces shall be worked out subsequently.
4. The Military Staff Committee, with the authorization of the Security Council and after consultation with appropriate regional agencies, may establish regional sub-committees.

Article 48

1. The action required to carry out the decisions of the Security Council for the maintenance of international peace and security shall be taken by all the Members of the United Nations or by some of them, as the Security Council may determine.
2. Such decisions shall be carried out by the Members of the United Nations directly and through their action in the appropriate international agencies of which they are members.

Article 49

The Members of the United Nations shall join in affording mutual assistance in carrying out the measures decided upon by the Security Council.

Article 50

If preventive or enforcement measures against any state are taken by the Security Council, any other state, whether a Member of the United Nations or not, which finds itself confronted with special economic problems arising from the carrying out of those measures shall have the right to consult the Security Council with regard to a solution of those problems.

Article 51

Nothing in the present Charter shall impair the inherent right of individual or collective self-defence if an armed attack occurs against a Member of the United Nations, until the Security Council has taken measures necessary to maintain international peace and security. Measures taken by Members in the exercise of this right of self-defence shall be immediately reported to the Security Council and shall not in any way affect the authority and responsibility of the Security Council under the present Charter to take at any time such action as it deems necessary in order to maintain or restore international peace and security.

VIII. REGIONAL ARRANGEMENTS

Article 52

1. Nothing in the present Charter precludes the existence of regional arrangements or agencies for dealing with such matters relating to the maintenance of international peace and security as are appropriate for regional action, provided that such arrangements or agencies and their activities are consistent with the Purposes and Principles of the United Nations.

2. The Members of the United Nations entering into such arrangements or constituting such agencies shall make every effort to achieve pacific settlement of local disputes through such regional agencies before referring them to the Security Council.
3. The Security Council shall encourage the development of pacific settlement of local disputes through such regional arrangements or by such regional agencies either on the initiative of the states concerned or by reference from the Security Council.
4. This Article in no way impairs the application of Articles 34 and 35.

Article 53

1. The Security Council shall, where appropriate, utilize such regional arrangements or agencies for enforcement action under its authority. But no enforcement action shall be taken under regional arrangements or by regional agencies without the authorization of the Security Council, with the exception of measures against any enemy state, as defined in paragraph 2 of this Article, provided for pursuant to Article 107 or in regional arrangements directed against renewal of aggressive policy on the part of any such state, until such time as the Organization may, on request of the Governments concerned, be charged with the responsibility for preventing further aggression by such a state.
2. The term enemy state as used in paragraph 1 of this Article applies to any state which during the Second World War has been an enemy of any signatory of the present Charter.

Article 54

The Security Council shall at all times be kept fully informed of activities undertaken or in contemplation under regional arrangements or by regional agencies for the maintenance of international peace and security.

IX. INTERNATIONAL ECONOMIC AND SOCIAL CO-OPERATION

Article 55

With a view to the creation of conditions of stability and well-being which are necessary for peaceful and friendly relations among nations based on respect for the principle of equal rights and self-determination of peoples, the United Nations shall promote:

(a) higher standards of living, full employment, and conditions of economic and social progress and development;

(b) solutions of international economic, social, health, and related problems; and international cultural and educational co-operation; and

(c) universal respect for, and observance of, human rights and fundamental freedoms for all without distinction as to race, sex, language, or religion.

Article 56

All Members pledge themselves to take joint and separate action in co-operation with the Organization for the achievement of the purposes set forth in Article 55.

Article 57

1. The various specialized agencies, established by intergovernmental agreement and having wide international responsibilities, as defined in their basic instruments, in economic, social, cultural, educational, health, and related fields, shall be brought into relationship with the United Nations in accordance with the provisions of Article 63.
2. Such agencies thus brought into relationship with the United Nations are hereinafter referred to as specialized agencies.

Article 58

The Organization shall make recommendations for the co-ordination of the policies and activities of the specialized agencies.

Article 59

The Organization shall, where appropriate, initiate negotiations among the states concerned for the creation of any new specialized agencies required for the accomplishment of the purposes set forth in Article 55.

Article 60

Responsibility for the discharge of the functions of the Organization set forth in this Chapter shall be vested in the General Assembly and, under the authority of the General Assembly, in the Economic and Social Council, which shall have for this purpose the powers set forth in Chapter X.

X. THE ECONOMIC AND SOCIAL COUNCIL
Composition

Article 61

1. The Economic and Social Council shall consist of 18 Members of the United Nations elected by the General Assembly.

2. Subject to the provisions of paragraph 3, six members of the Economic and Social Council shall be elected each year for a term of three years. A retiring member shall be eligible for immediate re-election.

3. At the first election, 18 members of the Economic and Social Council shall be chosen. The term of office of six members so chosen shall expire at the end of one year, and of six other members at the end of two years, in accordance with arrangements made by the General Assembly.

4. Each member of the Economic and Social Council shall have one representative.

Functions and Powers

Article 62

1. The Economic and Social Council may make or initiate studies and reports with respect to international economic, social, cultural, educational, health, and related matters and may make recommendations with respect to any such matters to the General Assembly, to the Members of the United Nations, and to the specialized agencies concerned.

2. It may make recommendations for the purpose of promoting respect for, and observance of, human rights and fundamental freedoms for all.

3. It may prepare draft conventions for submission to the General Assembly, with respect to matters falling within its competence.

4. It may call, in accordance with the rules prescribed by the United Nations, international conferences on matters falling within its competence.

Article 63

1. The Economic and Social Council may enter into agreements with any of the agencies referred to in Article 57, defining the terms on which the agency concerned shall be brought into relationship with the United Nations. Such agreements shall be subject to approval by the General Assembly.

2. It may co-ordinate the activities of the specialized agencies through consultation with and recommendations to such agencies and through recommendations to the General Assembly and to the Members of the United Nations

Article 64

1. The Economic and Social Council may take appropriate steps to obtain regular reports from the specialized agencies. It may make arrangements with the Members of the United Nations and with specialized agencies to obtain reports on the steps taken to give effect to its own recommendations and to recommendations on matters falling within its competence made by the General Assembly.

2. It may communicate its observations on these reports to the General Assembly.

Article 65

The Economic and Social Council may furnish information to the Security Council and shall assist the Security Council upon its request.

Article 66

1. The Economic and Social Council shall perform such functions as fall within its competence in connection with the carrying out of the recommendations of the General Assembly.

2. It may, with the approval of the General Assembly, perform services at the request of Members of the United Nations and at the request of specialized agencies.

3. It shall perform such other functions as are specified elsewhere in the present Charter or as may be assigned to it by the General Assembly.

Voting

Article 67

1. Each member of the Economic and Social Council shall have one vote.

2. Decisions of the Economic and Social Council shall be made by a majority of the members present and voting.

Procedure

Article 68

The Economic and Social Council shall set up commissions in economic and social fields and for the promotion of human rights, and such other commissions as may be required for the performance of its functions.

Article 69

The Economic and Social Council shall invite any Member of the United Nations to participate, without vote, in its deliberations on any matter of particular concern to that Member.

Article 70

The Economic and Social Council may make arrangements for representatives of the specialized agencies to participate, without vote, in its deliberations and in those of the commissions established by it, and for its representatives to participate in the deliberations of the specialized agencies.

Article 71

The Economic and Social Council may make suitable arrangements for consultation with non-governmental organizations which are concerned with matters within its competence. Such arrangements may be made with international organizations and, where appropriate, with national organizations after consultation with the Member of the United Nations concerned.

Article 72

1. The Economic and Social Council shall adopt its own rules of procedure, including the method of selecting its President.

2. The Economic and Social Council shall meet as required in accordance with its rules, which shall include provision for the convening of meetings on the request of a majority of its members.

XI. NON-SELF-GOVERNING TERRITORIES

Article 73

Members of the United Nations which have or assume responsibilities for the administration of territories whose peoples have not yet attained a full measure of self-government recognize the principle that the interests of the inhabitants of these territories are paramount, and accept as a sacred trust the obligation to promote to the utmost, within the system of international peace and security established by the present Charter, the well-being of the inhabitants of these territories, and, to this end:

   (a) to ensure, with due respect for the culture of the peoples concerned, their political, economic, social, and educational advancement, their just treatment, and their protection against abuses;

   (b) to develop self-government, to take due account of the political aspirations of the peoples, and to assist them in the progressive development of their free political institutions, according to the particular circumstances of each territory and its peoples and their varying stages of advancement;

   (c) to further international peace and security;

   (d) to promote constructive measures of development, to encourage research, and to co-operate with one another and, when and where appropriate, with specialized international bodies with a view to the practical achievement of the social, economic, and scientific purposes set forth in this Article; and

   (e) to transmit regularly to the Secretary-General for information purposes, subject to such limitations as security and constitutional considerations may require, statistical and other information of a technical nature relating to economic, social, and educational conditions in the territories for which they are respectively responsible other than those territories to which Chapters XII and XIII apply.

Article 74

Members of the United Nations also agree that their policy in respect of the territories to which this Chapter applies, no less than in respect of their metropolitan areas, must be based on the general principles of good-neighbourliness, due account being taken of the interests and well-being of the rest of the world, in social, economic, and commercial matters.

XII. INTERNATIONAL TRUSTEESHIP SYSTEM

Article 75

The United Nations shall establish under its authority an international trusteeship system for the administration and supervision of such territories as may be placed thereunder by subsequent individual agreements. These territories are hereinafter referred to as trust territories.

Article 76

The basic objectives of the trusteeship system, in accordance with the Purposes of the United Nations laid down in Article 1 of the present Charter, shall be:

   (a) to further international peace and security;

   (b) to promote the political, economic, social, and educational advancement of the inhabitants of the trust territories, and their progressive development towards self-government or independence as may be appropriate to the particular circumstances of each territory and its peoples and the freely expressed wishes of the peoples concerned, and as may be provided by the terms of each trusteeship agreement;

(c) to encourage respect for human rights and for fundamental freedoms for all without distinction as to race, sex, language, or religion, and to encourage recognition of the interdependence of the peoples of the world; and

(d) to ensure equal treatment in social, economic, and commercial matters for all Members of the United Nations and their nationals, and also equal treatment for the latter in the administration of justice, without prejudice to the attainment of the foregoing objectives and subject to the provisions of Article 80.

Article 77

1. The trusteeship system shall apply to such territories in the following categories as may be placed thereunder by means of trusteeship agreements.

(a) territories now held under mandate;

(b) territories which may be detached from enemy states as a result of the Second World War; and

(c) territories voluntarily placed under the system by states responsible for their administration.

2. It will be a matter for subsequent agreement as to which territories in the foregoing categories will be brought under the trusteeship system and upon what terms.

Article 78

The trusteeship system shall not apply to territories which have become Members of the United Nations, relationship among which shall be based on respect for the principle of sovereign equality.

Article 79

The terms of trusteeship for each territory to be placed under the trusteeship system, including any alteration or amendment, shall be agreed upon by the states directly concerned, including the mandatory power in the case of territories held under mandate by a Member of the United Nations, and shall be approved as provided for in Articles 83 and 85.

Article 80

1. Except as may be agreed upon in individual trusteeship agreements, made under Articles 77, 79, and 81, placing each territory under the trusteeship system, and until such agreements have been concluded, nothing in this Chapter shall be construed in or of itself to alter in any manner the rights whatsoever of any states or any peoples or the terms of existing international instruments to which Members of the United Nations may respectively be parties.

2. Paragraph 1 of this Article shall not be interpreted as giving grounds for delay or postponement of the negotiation and conclusion of agreements for placing mandated and other territories under the trusteeship system as provided for in Article 77.

Article 81

The trusteeship agreement shall in each case include the terms under which the trust territory will be administered and designate the authority which will exercise the administration of the trust territory. Such authority, hereinafter called the administering authority, may be one or more states or the Organization itself.

Article 82

There may be designated, in any trusteeship agreement, a strategic area or areas which may include part or all of the trust territory to which the agreement applies, without prejudice to any special agreement or agreements made under Article 43.

Article 83

1. All functions of the United Nations relating to strategic areas, including the approval of the terms of the trusteeship agreements and of their alteration or amendment, shall be exercised by the Security Council.

2. The basic objectives set forth in Article 76 shall be applicable to the people of each strategic area.

3. The Security Council shall, subject to the provisions of the trusteeship agreements and without prejudice to security considerations, avail itself of the assistance of the Trusteeship Council to perform those functions of the United Nations under the trusteeship system relating to political, economic, social, and educational matters in the strategic areas.

Article 84

It shall be the duty of the administering authority to ensure that the trust territory shall play its part in the maintenance of international peace and security. To this end the administering authority may make use of volunteer forces, facilities, and assistance from the trust territory in carrying out the obligations towards the Security Council undertaken in this regard by the administering authority, as well as for local defence and the maintenance of law and order within the trust territory.

Article 85

1. The functions of the United Nations with regard to trusteeship agreements for all areas not designated as strategic, including the approval of the terms of the trusteeship agreements and of their alteration or amendment, shall be exercised by the General Assembly.

2. The Trusteeship Council, operating under the authority of the General Assembly, shall assist the General Assembly in carrying out these functions.

XIII. THE TRUSTEESHIP COUNCIL

Composition

Article 86

1. The Trusteeship Council shall consist of the following Members of the United Nations:

(a) those Members administering trust territories:

(b) such of those Members mentioned by name in Article 23 as are not administering trust territories; and

(c) as many other Members elected for three-year terms by the General Assembly as may be necessary to ensure that the total number of members of the Trusteeship Council is equally divided between those Members of the United Nations which administer trust territories and those which do not.

2. Each member of the Trusteeship Council shall designate one specially qualified person to represent it therein.

Functions and Powers

Article 87

The General Assembly and, under its authority, the Trusteeship Council, in carrying out their functions, may:

(a) consider reports submitted by the administering authority;

(b) accept petitions and examine them in consultation with the administering authority;

(c) provide for periodic visits to the respective trust territories at times agreed upon with the administering authority; and

(d) take these and other actions in conformity with the terms of the trusteeship agreements.

Article 88

The Trusteeship Council shall formulate a questionnaire on the political, economic, social, and educational advancement of the inhabitants of each trust territory, and the administering authority for each trust territory within the competence of the General Assembly shall make an annual report to the General Assembly upon the basis of such questionnaire.

Voting

Article 89

1. Each member of the Trusteeship Council shall have one vote.

2. Decisions of the Trusteeship Council shall be made by a majority of the members present and voting.

Procedure

Article 90

1. The Trusteeship Council shall adopt its own rules of procedure, including the method of selecting its President.

2. The Trusteeship Council shall meet as required in accordance with its rules, which shall include provision for the convening of meetings on the request of a majority of its members.

Article 91

The Trusteeship Council shall, when appropriate, avail itself of the assistance of the Economic and Social Council and of the specialized agencies in regard to matters with which they are respectively concerned.

XIV. THE INTERNATIONAL COURT OF JUSTICE

Article 92

The International Court of Justice shall be the principal judicial organ of the United Nations. It shall function in accordance with the annexed Statute, which is based upon the Statute of the Permanent Court of International Justice and forms an integral part of the present Charter.

Article 93

1. All Members of the United Nations are *ipso facto* parties to the Statute of the International Court of Justice.

2. A state which is not a Member of the United Nations may

become a party to the Statute of the International Court of Justice on condition to be determined in each case by the General Assembly upon the recommendation of the Security Council.

Article 94

1. Each Member of the United Nations undertakes to comply with the decision of the International Court of Justice in any case to which it is a party.

2. If any party to a case fails to perform the obligations incumbent upon it under a judgment rendered by the Court, the other party may have recourse to the Security Council, which may, if it deems necessary, make recommendations or decide upon measures to be taken to give effect to the judgment.

Article 95

Nothing in the present Charter shall prevent Members of the United Nations from entrusting the solution of their differences to other tribunals by virtue of agreements already in existence or which may be concluded in the future.

Article 96

1. The General Assembly or the Security Council may request the International Court of Justice to give an advisory opinion on any legal question.

2. Other organs of the United Nations and specialized agencies, which may at any time be so authorized by the General Assembly, may also request advisory opinions of the Court on legal questions arising within the scope of their activities.

XV. THE SECRETARIAT

Article 97

The Secretariat shall comprise a Secretary-General and such staff as the Organization may require. The Secretary-General shall be appointed by the General Assembly upon the recommendation of the Security Council. He shall be the chief administrative officer of the Organization.

Article 98

The Secretary-General shall act in that capacity in all meetings of the General Assembly, of the Security Council, of the Economic and Social Council, and of the Trusteeship Council, and shall perform such other functions as are entrusted to him by these organs. The Secretary-General shall make an annual report to the General Assembly on the work of the Organization.

Article 99

The Secretary-General may bring to the attention of the Security Council any matter which in his opinion may threaten the maintenance of international peace and security.

Article 100

1. In the performance of their duties the Secretary-General and the staff shall not seek or receive instructions from any government or from any other authority external to the Organization. They shall refrain from any action which might reflect on their position as international officials responsible only to the Organization.

2. Each Member of the United Nations undertakes to respect the exclusively international character of the responsibilities of the Secretary-General and the staff and not to seek to influence them in the discharge of their responsibilities.

Article 101

1. The staff shall be appointed by the Secretary-General under regulations established by the General Assembly.

2. Appropriate staffs shall be permanently assigned to the Economic and Social Council, the Trusteeship Council, and, as required, to other organs of the United Nations. These staffs shall form a part of the Secretariat.

3. The paramount consideration in the employment of the staff and in the determination of the conditions of service shall be the necessity of securing the highest standards of efficiency, competence, and integrity. Due regard shall be paid to the importance of recruiting the staff on as wide a geographical basis as possible.

XVI. MISCELLANEOUS PROVISIONS

Article 102

1. Every treaty and every international agreement entered into by any Member of the United Nations after the present Charter comes into force shall as soon as possible be registered with the Secretariat and published by it.

2. No party to any such treaty or international agreement which has not been registered in accordance with the provisions of paragraph 1 of this Article may invoke that treaty or agreement before any organ of the United Nations.

Article 103

In the event of a conflict between the obligations of the Members of the United Nations under the present Charter and their obligations under any other international agreement, their obligations under the present Charter shall prevail.

Article 104

The Organization shall enjoy in the territory of each of its Members such legal capacity as may be necessary for the exercise of its functions and the fulfilment of its purposes.

Article 105

1. The Organization shall enjoy in the territory of each of its Members such privileges and immunities as are necessary for the fulfilment of its purposes.

2. Representatives of the Members of the United Nations and officials of the Organization shall similarly enjoy such privileges and immunities as are necessary for the independent exercise of their functions in connection with the Organization.

3. The General Assembly may make recommendations with a view to determining the details of the application of paragraphs 1 and 2 of this Article or may propose conventions to the Members of the United Nations for this purpose.

XVII. TRANSITIONAL SECURITY ARRANGEMENTS

Article 106

Pending the coming into force of such special agreements referred to in Article 43 as in the opinion of the Security Council enable it to begin the exercise of its responsibilities under Article 42, the parties to the Four-Nation Declaration signed at Moscow, October 30, 1943, and France, shall, in accordance with the provisions of paragraph 5 of that Declaration, consult with one another and as occasion requires with other Members of the United Nations with a view to such joint action on behalf of the Organization as may be necessary for the purpose of maintaining international peace and security.

Article 107

Nothing in the present Charter shall invalidate or preclude action, in relation to any state which during the Second World War has been an enemy of any signatory to the present Charter, taken or authorized as a result of that war by the Governments having responsibility for such action.

XVIII. AMENDMENTS

Article 108

Amendments to the present Charter shall come into force for all Members of the United Nations when they have been adopted by a vote of two-thirds of the members of the General Assembly and ratified in accordance with their respective constitutional processes by two-thirds of the Members of the United Nations, including all the permanent members of the Security Council.

Article 109

1. A General Conference of the Members of the United Nations for the purpose of reviewing the present Charter may be held at a date and place to be fixed by a two-thirds vote of the members of the General Assembly and by a vote of any seven members of the Security Council. Each Member of the United Nations shall have one vote in the conference.

2. Any alteration of the present Charter recommended by a two-thirds vote of the conference shall take effect when ratified in accordance with their respective constitutional processes by two-thirds of the Members of the United Nations including all the permanent members of the Security Council.

3. If such a conference has not been held before the tenth annual session of the General Assembly following the coming into force of the present Charter, the proposal to call such a conference shall be placed on the agenda of that session of the General Assembly, and the conference shall be held if so decided by a majority vote of the members of the General Assembly and by a vote of any seven members of the Security Council.

XIX. RATIFICATION AND SIGNATURE

Article 110

1. The present Charter shall be ratified by the signatory states in accordance with their respective constitutional processes.

2. The ratifications shall be deposited with the Government of the United States of America, which shall notify all the signatory states of each deposit as well as the Secretary-General of the Organization when he has been appointed.

3. The present Charter shall come into force upon the deposit of ratifications by the Republic of China, France, the Union of Soviet

Socialist Republics, the United Kingdom of Great Britain and Northern Ireland, and the United States of America, and by a majority of the other signatory states. A protocol of the ratifications deposited shall thereupon be drawn up by the Government of the United States of America which shall communicate copies thereof to all the signatory states.

4. The states signatory to the present Charter which ratify it after it has come into force will become original Members of the United Nations on the date of the deposit of their respective ratifications.

Article 111

The present Charter, of which the Chinese, French, Russian, English, and Spanish texts are equally authentic, shall remain deposited in the archives of the Government of the United States of America. Duly certified copies thereof shall be transmitted by that Government to the Governments of the other signatory states.

IN FAITH WHEREOF the representatives of the Governments of the United Nations have signed the present Charter.

DONE at the city of San Francisco the twenty-sixth day of June, one thousand nine hundred and forty-five.

Amendments

The following amendments to Articles 23 and 27 of the Charter came into force in August 1965.

Article 23

1. The Security Council shall consist of 15 Members of the United Nations. The Republic of China, France, the Union of Soviet Socialist Republics, the United Kingdom of Great Britain and Northern Ireland, and the United States of America shall be permanent members of the Security Council. The General Assembly shall elect 10 other Members of the United Nations to be non-permanent members of the Security Council, due regard being specially paid, in the first instance to the contribution of Members of the United Nations to the maintenance of international peace and security and to the other purposes of the Organization, and also to equitable geographical distribution.

2. The non-permanent members of the Security Council shall be elected for a term of two years. In the first election of the non-permanent members after the increase of the membership of the Security Council from 11 to 15, two of the four additional members shall be chosen for a term of one year. A retiring member shall not be eligible for immediate re-election.

3. Each member of the Security Council shall have one representative.

Article 27

1. Each member of the Security Council shall have one vote.

2. Decisions of the Security Council on procedural matters shall be made by an affirmative vote of nine members.

3. Decisions of the Security Council on all other matters shall be made by an affirmative vote of nine members including the concurring votes of the permanent members; provided that, in decisions under Chapter VI and under paragraph 3 of Article 52, a party to a dispute shall abstain from voting.

The following amendments to Article 61 of the Charter came into force in September 1973.

Article 61

1. The Economic and Social Council shall consist of 54 Members of the United Nations elected by the General Assembly.

2. Subject to the provisions of paragraph 3, 18 members of the Economic and Social Council shall be elected each year for a term of three years. A retiring member shall be eligible for immediate re-election.

3. At the first election after the increase in the membership of the Economic and Social Council from 27 to 54 members, in addition to the members elected in place of the nine members whose term of office expires at the end of that year, 27 additional members shall be elected. Of these 27 additional members, the term of office of nine members so elected shall expire at the end of one year, and of nine other members at the end of two years, in accordance with arrangements made by the General Assembly.

4. Each member of the Economic and Social Council shall have one representative.

The following amendment to Paragraph 1 of Article 109 of the Charter came into force in June 1968.

Article 109

1. A General Conference of the Members of the United Nations for the purpose of reviewing the present Charter may be held at a date and place to be fixed by a two-thirds vote of the members of the General Assembly and by a vote of any nine members of the Security Council. Each Member of the United Nations shall have one vote in the conference.

INTERNATIONAL ORGANIZATIONS   *United Nations*

Secretariat

SECRETARY-GENERAL

The Secretary-General is the UN's chief administrative officer, elected for a five-year term by the General Assembly on the recommendation of the Security Council. He acts in that capacity at all meetings of the General Assembly, the Security Council, the Economic and Social Council, and the Trusteeship Council, and performs such other functions as are entrusted to him by those organs. He is required to submit an annual report to the General Assembly and may bring to the attention of the Security Council any matter which in his opinion may threaten international peace. (See Charter, p. 15.)

Secretary-General: JAVIER PÉREZ DE CUÉLLAR (Peru) (1982–91).

HEADQUARTERS STAFF
(October 1988)

Office of the Director-General for Development and International Economic Co-operation
Director-General: JEAN L. RIPERT (France).

Executive Office of the Secretary-General
Chef de Cabinet: VIRENDRA DAYAL (India).

Office of the Under-Secretaries-General for Special Political Affairs
Under-Secretaries-General: MARRACK I. GOULDING (United Kingdom), ALVARO DE SOTO (Peru).

Office for Research and the Collection of Information
Assistant Secretary-General: JAMES O. C. JONAH (Sierra Leone).

Department for Political and General Assembly Affairs and Secretariat Services
Under-Secretary-General: JOSEPH VERNER REED (USA).

Office of Legal Affairs
Under-Secretary-General, The Legal Counsel: CARL-AUGUST FLEISCHHAUER (FRG).

Department of Political and Security Council Affairs
Under-Secretary-General: VASILIY S. SAFRONCHUK (USSR).

Department for Disarmament Affairs
Under-Secretary-General: YASUSHI AKASHI (Japan).

Department for Special Political Questions, Regional Co-operation, Decolonization and Trusteeship
Under-Secretary-General: ABDULRAHIM A. FARAH (Somalia).

Department of International Economic and Social Affairs
Under-Secretary-General: RAFEEUDDIN AHMED (Pakistan).

Department of Technical Co-operation for Development
Under-Secretary-General: XIE QIMEI (People's Republic of China).

Department of Administration and Management
Under-Secretary-General: MARTTI AHTISAARI (Finland).

Office of Programme Planning, Budget and Finance
Assistant Secretary-General, Controller: L. M. GÓMEZ (Argentina).

Office of Human Resources Management
Assistant Secretary-General: KOFI A. ANNAN (Ghana).

Office of General Services
Assistant Secretary-General: J. RICHARD FORAN (Canada).

Department of Conference Services
Under-Secretary-General: EUGENIUSZ WYZNER (Poland).

Department of Public Information
Under-Secretary-General: THÉRÈSE PAQUET-SEVIGNY (Canada).

Office of the United Nations Commissioner for Namibia
Assistant Secretary-General, Commissioner for Namibia: BERNT CARLSSON (Sweden).

Office of the Special Representative of the Secretary-General for Namibia
Under-Secretary-General: MARTTI AHTISAARI (Finland).

Office for Ocean Affairs and the Law of the Sea
Under-Secretary-General, Special Representative of the Secretary-General for the Law of the Sea: SATYA N. NANDAN (Fiji).

United Nations Centre against Apartheid
Assistant Secretary-General: SOTIRIOS MOUSOURIS (Greece).

The chief administrative staff of the UN Regional Commissions and of all the subsidiary organs of the UN are also members of the Secretariat staff and are listed in the appropriate chapters. The Secretariat staff also includes a number of special missions and special appointments, including some of senior rank. In 1986 and 1987 there were reductions in the number of staff, as a result of budgetary restrictions.

On 31 December 1987 the total number of staff of the Secretariat holding appointments continuing for a year or more was 13,663 (compared with 15,701 two years previously—a 13% decrease), including those serving away from the headquarters. This comprised 3,802 professional and higher-level staff and 8,699 in the General Service, Field Service and other categories.

On 31 December 1987 the total number of staff in the whole United Nations system (including the specialized agencies) was 25,589 (compared with 27,304 two years previously—a 6% decrease). This comprised 6,314 professional and higher-level staff and 16,855 in the General Service and other categories.

GENEVA OFFICE

Address: Palais des Nations, 1211 Geneva 10, Switzerland.
Telephone: (022) 310211.
Director-General: Under-Sec.-Gen. JAN MARTENSON (Sweden)

VIENNA OFFICE

Address: Vienna International Centre, POB 500, 1400 Vienna, Austria.
Director-General: Under-Sec.-Gen. MARGARET JOAN ANSTEE (United Kingdom).

UN CONFERENCES, 1987–88

UN Conference for the Promotion of International Co-operation in the Peaceful Uses of Nuclear Energy: Geneva, March–April 1987.
International Conference on Drug Abuse and Illicit Trafficking: Vienna, June 1987.
UN Conference on Trade and Development (seventh session): Geneva, July 1987.
International Conference on the Relationship Between Disarmament and Development: New York, August–September, 1987.
Review Conference on the International Code of Conduct for Liner Conferences: Geneva, October–November 1988.
Plenipotentiary Conference to adopt a Convention against Illicit Trafficking in Narcotic Drugs and Psychotropic Substances: Vienna, November–December 1988.

General Assembly

The General Assembly was established as a principal organ of the United Nations under the UN Charter (see p. 9). It first met on 10 January 1946. It is the main deliberative organ of the United Nations, and the only one composed of representatives of all the UN member states. Each delegation consists of not more than five representatives and five alternates, with as many advisers as may be required. The Assembly meets regularly for three months each year, and special sessions may also be held. It has specific responsibility for electing the Secretary-General and members of other UN councils and organs, and for approving the UN budget and the assessments for financial contributions by member states. It is also empowered to make recommendations (but not binding decisions) on questions of international security and co-operation.

After the election of its President and other officers, the Assembly opens its general debate, a three-week period during which the head of each delegation makes a formal statement of his or her government's views on major world issues. The Assembly then begins examination of the principal items on its agenda: it acts directly on a few agenda items, but most business is handled by the seven Main Committees (listed below), which study and debate each item and present draft resolutions to the Assembly. After a review of the report of each Main Committee, the Assembly formally approves or rejects the Committee's recommendations. On designated 'important questions', such as recommendations on international peace and security, the admission of new members to the United Nations, or budgetary questions, a two-thirds majority is needed for adoption of a resolution. Other questions may be decided by a simple majority. In the Assembly, each member has one vote. Voting in the Assembly is sometimes replaced by an effort to find consensus among member states, in order to strengthen support for the Assembly's decisions: the President consults delegations in private to find out whether they are willing to agree to adoption of a resolution without a vote; if they are, the President can declare that a resolution has been so adopted.

Special sessions of the Assembly may also be held to discuss issues which require particular attention. By 1988 there had been 15 such sessions, on issues which included the problems of Palestine, Namibia, the African economic situation, and disarmament. Nine 'emergency special sessions' had also been held to discuss situations on which the UN Security Council had been unable to reach a decision: the Middle East (1958 and 1967), Hungary (1956), Suez (1956), the Congo (1960), Afghanistan (1980), Palestine (1980), Namibia (1981) and the occupied Arab territories (1982).

President of 43rd Session (from September 1988): DANTE CAPUTO (Argentina).

MAIN COMMITTEES

There are seven Main Committees, on which all members have a right to be represented. The first six were appointed in 1946. An *ad hoc* Political Committee was first established in November 1948 and re-established annually until November 1956, when it was made permanent and renamed Special Political Committee.

First Committee: Disarmament and Related International Security Questions.
Special Political Committee.
Second Committee: Economic and Financial.
Third Committee: Social, Humanitarian and Cultural.
Fourth Committee: Decolonization.
Fifth Committee: Administrative and Budgetary.
Sixth Committee: Legal.

OTHER SESSIONAL COMMITTEES

General Committee: f. 1946; composed of 29 members, including the Assembly President, the 21 Vice-Presidents and the Chairmen of the seven Main Committees.
Credentials Committee: f. 1946; composed of nine members elected at each Assembly session.

POLITICAL AND SECURITY MATTERS

Special Committee on Peace-keeping Operations: f. 1965; 33 appointed members.

Disarmament Commission: f. 1978 (replacing body f. 1952); composed of all UN members.
UN Scientific Committee on the Effects of Atomic Radiation: f. 1955; 20 members.
UN Scientific Advisory Committee: f. 1954 under different title; seven members.
Committee on the Peaceful Uses of Outer Space: f. 1959; 53 members; has a Legal Sub-Committee and a Scientific and Technical Sub-Committee.
Special Committee against Apartheid: f. 1962; 18 members.
Committee of Trustees of the UN Trust Fund for South Africa: f. 1965; five members.
Ad Hoc Committee on the Indian Ocean: f. 1972; 48 members.
Ad Hoc Committee on the Implementation of the Collective Security Provisions of the Charter of the United Nations: f. 1983.
Committee on the Exercise of the Inalienable Rights of the Palestinian People: f. 1975; 23 members.

TRUST TERRITORY AND COLONIAL QUESTIONS

UN Council for Namibia: f. 1967 as UN Council for South West Africa; changed name in 1968; 31 members.
Special Committee on the Implementation of the Declaration on Decolonization: f. 1961; 24 members.
Advisory Committee on the UN Educational and Training Programme for Southern Africa: f. 1968; 13 members.

DEVELOPMENT

Intergovernmental Committee on Science and Technology for Development: f. 1980; open to all states.
Committee on the Development and Utilization of New and Renewable Sources of Energy: f. 1983; open to all states.
United Nations Environment Programme (UNEP) Governing Council: f. 1972; 58 members.
World Food Council: f. 1974; 36 members.

LEGAL QUESTIONS

International Law Commission: f. 1947; 34 members elected for a five-year term; originally established in 1946 as the Committee on the Progressive Development of International Law and its Codification.
Advisory Committee on the UN Programme of Assistance in Teaching, Study, Dissemination and Wider Appreciation of International Law: f. 1965; 13 members.
UN Commission on International Trade Law: f. 1966; 36 members.
Special Committee on the Charter of the United Nations and on the Strengthening of the Role of the Organization: f. 1975; 47 members.
Special Committee on Enhancing the Effectiveness of the Principle of Non-Use of Force in International Relations: f. 1977; 35 members.
Committee against Torture: f. 1987; 10 members.

ADMINISTRATIVE AND FINANCIAL QUESTIONS

Advisory Committee on Administrative and Budgetary Questions: f. 1946; 16 members appointed for three-year terms.
Committee on Contributions: f. 1946; 18 members appointed for three-year terms.
International Civil Service Commission: f. 1948; 15 members appointed for four-year terms.
Committee on Information: f. 1978, formerly the Committee to review UN Policies and Activities; 69 members.

There is also a Board of Auditors, Investments Committee, UN Administrative Tribunal, Committee on Applications for Review of Administrative Tribunal Judgments, UN Joint Staff Pension Board, Joint Inspection Unit, UN Staff Pension Committee and Committee on Conferences.

Security Council

The Security Council was established as a principal organ under the United Nations Charter; its first meeting was held on 17 January 1946. Its task is to promote international peace and security in all parts of the world. (See Charter, p. 10.)

MEMBERS

Permanent members:
People's Republic of China, France, USSR, United Kingdom, USA.
The remaining 10 members are normally elected by the General Assembly for two-year periods (five countries from Africa and Asia, two from Latin America, one from socialist Eastern Europe, and two from Western Europe and others).

ORGANIZATION

The Security Council has the right to investigate any dispute or situation which might lead to friction between two or more countries, and such disputes or situations may be brought to the Council's attention either by one of its members, by any member state, by the General Assembly, by the Secretary-General or even, under certain conditions, by a state which is not a member of the United Nations.

The Council has the right to recommend ways and means of peaceful settlement and, in certain circumstances, the actual terms of settlement. In the event of a threat to or breach of international peace or an act of aggression, the Council has powers to take 'enforcement' measures in order to restore international peace and security. These include severance of communications and of economic and diplomatic relations and, if required, action by air, land and sea forces.

All members of the United Nations are pledged by the Charter to make available to the Security Council, on its call and in accordance with special agreements, the armed forces, assistance and facilities necessary to maintain international peace and security. These agreements, however, have not yet been concluded.

The Council is organized to be able to function continuously. The Presidency of the Council is held monthly in turn by the member states in English alphabetical order. Each member of the Council has one vote. On procedural matters decisions are made by the affirmative vote of any nine members. For decisions on other matters the required nine affirmative votes must include the votes of the five permanent members. This is the rule of 'great power unanimity' popularly known as the 'veto' privilege. In practice, an abstention by one of the permanent members is not regarded as a veto. Any member, whether permanent or non-permanent, must abstain from voting in any decision concerning the pacific settlement of a dispute to which it is a party.

The Council held 49 meetings in 1987. Of these, 26 were devoted to the situation in South Africa and related questions, including the situation in Namibia and Angola's complaint of South African aggression; 11 to the Middle East and related questions, including the situation in the occupied Arab territories, the United Nations Interim Force in Lebanon (UNIFIL) and the UN Disengagement Observer Force (UNDOF); five to the election of members to the International Court of Justice; two to the application of the Republic of Nauru to become a party to the Statute of the International Court of Justice; two to the extension of the mandate of the UN Peace-keeping Force in Cyprus (UNFICYP); and two to the war between Iran and Iraq. One of the Council's meetings was held in private to adopt its report to the General Assembly.

SUBSIDIARY BODIES

Military Staff Committee: Consists of the Chiefs of Staff (or their representatives) of the five permanent members of the Security Council: assists the Council on all military questions.
(See also UN Observer Mission and Peace-keeping Forces.)

STANDING COMMITTEES

There are three standing committees, each composed of representatives of all Council members: Committee of Experts (to examine provisional rules of procedure and other matters); Committee on Council Meetings Away from Headquarters; Committee on the Admission of New Members.

Economic and Social Council—ECOSOC

ECOSOC promotes world co-operation on economic, social, cultural and humanitarian problems. (See Charter, p. 12.)

MEMBERS

Fifty-four members are elected by the General Assembly for three-year terms: 18 are elected each year. Membership is allotted by regions as follows: Africa 14 members, Western Europe and others 13, Asia 11, Latin America 10, Eastern Europe 6.

ORGANIZATION

The Council, normally meeting twice a year in New York and Geneva, is mainly a central policy-making and co-ordinating organ. It has a co-ordinating function between the UN and the specialized agencies, and also makes consultative arrangements with approved voluntary or non-governmental organizations which work within the sphere of its activities. The Council has functional and regional commissions to carry out much of its detailed work.

SESSIONAL COMMITTEES

Each sessional committee comprises the 54 members of the Council: there is a First (Economic) Committee, a Second (Social) Committee and a Third (Programme and Co-ordination) Committee.

FUNCTIONAL COMMISSIONS

Statistical Commission: Standardizes terminology and procedure in statistics and promotes the development of national statistics; 24 members.

Population Commission: Advises the Council on population matters and their relation to socio-economic conditions; 27 members.

Commission for Social Development: Plans social development programmes; 32 members.

Commission on Human Rights: Seeks greater respect for the basic rights of man, the prevention of discrimination and the protection of minorities; reviews specific instances of human rights violation, provides policy guidance; works on declarations, conventions and other instruments of international law; 43 members. There is a Sub-Commission on Prevention of Discrimination and Protection of Minorities.

Commission on the Status of Women: Aims at equality of political, economic and social rights for women; 32 members.

Commission on Narcotic Drugs: Mainly concerned in combating illicit traffic; 40 members. There is a Sub-Commission on Illicit Drug Traffic and Related Matters in the Near and Middle East.

COMMITTEES AND SUBSIDIARY BODIES

Committee for Programme and Co-ordination: f. 1962.
Committee on Non-Governmental Organizations: f. 1946.
Committee on Negotiations with Intergovernmental Agencies: f. 1946.
Committee for Development Planning: f. 1965.
Committee on Natural Resources: f. 1970.
Committee on Crime Prevention and Control: f. 1972.
Commission on Transnational Corporations: f. 1974.
Commission on Human Settlements: f. 1977.

REGIONAL COMMISSIONS
(see pp. 24–32)

Economic Commission for Europe—ECE.

Economic and Social Commission for Asia and the Pacific—ESCAP.

Economic Commission for Latin America and the Caribbean—ECLAC.

INTERNATIONAL ORGANIZATIONS

Economic Commission for Africa—ECA.
Economic and Social Commission for Western Asia—ESCWA.

RELATED BODIES

UNICEF Executive Board: 41 members, elected by ECOSOC (see p. 36).
UNHCR Executive Committee: 41 members, elected by ECOSOC (see p. 42).

UNDP Governing Council: 48 members, elected by ECOSOC (see p. 38).
Committee on Food Aid Policies and Programmes: one-half of the 30 members are elected by ECOSOC, one-half by FAO; governing body of the World Food Programme (see p. 49).
International Narcotics Control Board: f. 1964; 13 members.
Board of Trustees of the International Research and Training Institute for Women (INSTRAW): 11 members.

The Trusteeship Council

The Trusteeship Council has supervised United Nations Trust Territories through the administering authorities to promote the political, economic, social and educational advancement of the inhabitants towards self-government or independence. (See Charter, p. 14.)

MEMBERS

The Council consists of member states administering Trust Territories, permanent members of the Security Council which do not administer Trust Territories, and other non-administering countries elected by the Assembly for three-year terms.

Administering Country:
United States

Other Countries:
China, People's Republic*
France
USSR
United Kingdom

* China does not participate in the work of the Council.

ORGANIZATION

The Council generally meets once a year, in May–June. Each member has one vote, and decisions are made by a simple majority of the members present and voting. A new President is elected at the beginning of the Council's regular session each year.

By 1988 the only territory remaining under United Nations trusteeship was the Trust Territory of the Pacific Islands, now comprising only the Republic of Palau, part of the archipelago of the Caroline Islands. The Northern Mariana Islands, formerly the Marianas District of the Trust Territory, became a Commonwealth territory of the USA in January 1978, although it remained legally part of the area covered by the Trusteeship Agreement. The Trust Territory of the Pacific Islands has been designated a strategic area, and the supervisory functions of the United Nations are, in its case, exercised by the Trusteeship Council under the authority of the Security Council.

The Constitution of the Marshall Islands entered into force on 1 May 1979. The Constitution of the Federated States of Micronesia, four districts of the Caroline Islands, entered into force on 10 May 1979. A referendum held in July 1979 in the Palau district approved a proposed local constitution, and in January 1981 it became the Republic of Palau. With the entries into force of the Constitutions, the High Commissioner, the chief executive of the Trust Territory, retained only the authority necessary to carry out the obligations of the USA under the Trusteeship and other agreements. In October and November 1980 agreements were initialled providing for the future self-government of the islands under compacts of 'free association' with the USA, subject to approval by the US Congress and by plebiscite in the islands (conducted in Palau, the Marshall Islands and the Federated States of Micronesia in 1983, and again in Palau in 1986 and 1987), after which the agreements were to be submitted to the UN for formal termination of the trusteeship agreements.

In May 1986, the USA requested termination of the Trusteeship. The Trusteeship Council stated that it considered that the USA had satisfactorily discharged its obligations under the Trusteeship Agreement and that it was appropriate for that Agreement to be terminated upon entry into force of the Compact of Free Association for the Federated States of Micronesia, the Marshall Islands and Palau, and the Commonwealth Covenant in respect of the Northern Mariana Islands. The Compact with the Marshall Islands entered into force on 21 October 1986; the Compact with the Federated States and the Commonwealth Covenant entered into force on 3 November 1986. In a plebiscite held in Palau in August 1987 the Compact with Palau received the number of votes necessary to complete the ratification process. In April 1988, however, the Supreme Court of Palau declared the result of the plebiscite to be invalid. Because it is a 'strategic area', any alteration of the status of Micronesia must be exercised by the Security Council.

High Commissioner: JANET MCCOY.

International Court of Justice

Address: Peace Palace, 2517 KJ The Hague, Netherlands.
Telephone: (070) 92-44-41.
Telex: 32323.

Set up in 1945, the Court is the principal judicial organ of the UN. All members of the UN, and also Switzerland, Liechtenstein and San Marino, are parties to the Statute of the Court. (See Charter, p. 14.)

THE JUDGES

(October 1988; in order of precedence)

	Term Ends*
President: JOSÉ MARÍA RUDA (Argentina)	1991
Vice-President: KÉBA MBAYE (Senegal)	1991
Judges:	
NAGENDRA SINGH (India)	1991
MANFRED LACHS (Poland)	1994
TASLIM OLAWALE ELIAS (Nigeria)	1994
SHIGERU ODA (Japan)	1994
ROBERTO AGO (Italy)	1997
STEPHEN M. SCHWEBEL (USA)	1997
Sir ROBERT JENNINGS (United Kingdom)	1991
MOHAMMED BEDJAOUI (Algeria)	1997
NI ZHENGYU (People's Republic of China)	1994
JENS EVENSEN (Norway)	1994
NIKOLAI K. TARASSOV (USSR)	1997
GILBERT GUILLAUME (France)	1991
MOHAMED SHAHABUDDEEN (Guyana)	1997

* Each term ends on 5 February of the year indicated.

The Court is composed of 15 judges, each of a different nationality, elected with an absolute majority by both the General Assembly and the Security Council. Representation of the main forms of civilization and the different legal systems of the world are borne

INTERNATIONAL ORGANIZATIONS
United Nations

in mind in their election. Candidates are nominated by national panels of jurists.

The judges are elected for nine years and may be re-elected; elections for five seats are held every three years. The Court elects its President and Vice-President for each three-year period. Members may not have any political, administrative, or other professional occupation, and may not sit in any case with which they have been otherwise connected than as a judge of the Court. For the purposes of a case, each side—consisting of one or more States—may, unless the Bench already includes a judge with a corresponding nationality, choose a person from outside the Court to sit as a judge on terms of equality with the Members. Judicial decisions are taken by a majority of the judges present, subject to a quorum of nine Members. The President has a casting vote.

FUNCTIONS

The International Court of Justice operates in accordance with a Statute which is an integral part of the UN Charter. Only States may be parties in cases before the Court; those not parties to the Statute may have access in certain circumstances and under conditions laid down by the Security Council.

The Jurisdiction of the Court comprises:

1. All cases which the parties refer to it jointly by special agreement (indicated in the list below by a stroke between the names of the parties).

2. All matters concerning which a treaty or convention in force provides for reference to the Court. About 700 bilateral or multilateral agreements make such provision. Among the more noteworthy: Treaty of Peace with Japan (1951), European Convention for Peaceful Settlement of Disputes (1957), Single Convention on Narcotic Drugs (1961), Protocol relating to the Status of Refugees (1967), Hague Convention on the Suppression of the Unlawful Seizure of Aircraft (1970).

3. Legal disputes between States which have recognized the jurisdiction of the Court as compulsory for specified classes of dispute. Declarations by the following 46 States accepting the compulsory jurisdiction of the Court are in force: Australia, Austria, Barbados, Belgium, Botswana, Canada, Colombia, Costa Rica, Denmark, the Dominican Republic, Egypt, El Salvador, Finland, The Gambia, Haiti, Honduras, India, Japan, Kampuchea, Kenya, Liberia, Liechtenstein, Luxembourg, Malawi, Malta, Mauritius, Mexico, the Netherlands, New Zealand, Nicaragua, Nigeria, Norway, Pakistan, Panama, the Philippines, Portugal, Senegal, Somalia, Sudan, Swaziland, Sweden, Switzerland, Togo, Uganda, the United Kingdom and Uruguay.

Disputes as to whether the Court has jurisdiction are settled by the Court.

Judgments are without appeal, but are binding only for the particular case and between the parties. States appearing before the Court undertake to comply with its Judgment. If a party to a case fails to do so, the other party may apply to the Security Council, which may make recommendations or decide upon measures to give effect to the Judgment.

Advisory opinions on legal questions may be requested by the General Assembly, the Security Council or, if so authorized by the Assembly, other United Nations organs or specialized agencies.

Rules of Court governing procedure are made by the Court under a power conferred by the Statute.

CONSIDERED CASES

Judgments

By September 1988, 58 cases had been referred to the Court by States. Some were removed from the list as a result of settlement or discontinuance, or on the grounds of a lack of basis for jurisdiction. Cases which have been the subject of a Judgment by the Court include: Corfu Channel (United Kingdom v. Albania); Fisheries (United Kingdom v. Norway); Asylum (Colombia/Peru), Haya de la Torre (Colombia v. Peru); Rights of Nationals of the United States of America in Morocco (France v. United States); Ambatielos (Greece v. United Kingdom); Anglo-Iranian Oil Co. (United Kingdom v. Iran); Minquiers and Ecrehos (France/United Kingdom); Nottebohm (Liechtenstein v. Guatemala); Monetary Gold Removed from Rome in 1943 (Italy v. France, United Kingdom and United States); Certain Norwegian Loans (France v. Norway); Right of Passage over Indian Territory (Portugal v. India); Application of the Convention of 1902 Governing the Guardianship of Infants (Netherlands v. Sweden); Interhandel (Switzerland v. United States); Sovereignty over Certain Frontier Land (Belgium/Netherlands); Arbitral Award made by the King of Spain on 23 December 1906 (Honduras v. Nicaragua); Temple of Preah Vihear (Cambodia v. Thailand); South West Africa (Ethiopia and Liberia v. South Africa); Northern Cameroons (Cameroon v. United Kingdom); Barcelona Traction, Light and Power Co, Ltd (New Application: 1962) (Belgium v. Spain); North Sea Continental Shelf (Federal Republic of Germany/Denmark and Netherlands); Appeal relating to the Jurisdiction of the ICAO Council (India v. Pakistan); Fisheries Jurisdiction (United Kingdom v. Iceland; Federal Republic of Germany v. Iceland); Nuclear Tests (Australia v. France; New Zealand v. France); Aegean Sea Continental Shelf (Greece v. Turkey); United States Diplomatic and Consular Staff in Teheran (USA v. Iran); Continental Shelf (Tunisia/Libya); Delimitation of the Maritime Boundary in the Gulf of Maine Area (Canada/USA); Continental Shelf (Libya/Malta); Application for revision and interpretation of the Judgment of 24 February 1982 in the case concerning the Continental Shelf (Tunisia v. Libya); Military and Paramilitary Activities in and against Nicaragua (Nicaragua v. USA); Frontier Dispute (Burkina Faso/Mali); Delimitation of Maritime Boundary (Denmark v. Norway).

The cases under consideration in 1988 concerned: Border and Transborder Armed Actions (Nicaragua v. Honduras); Elettronica Sicula SpA (USA v. Italy); Land, Island and Maritime Frontier Dispute (El Salvador/Honduras).

Advisory Opinions

Advisory Opinions on the following matters have been given by the Court at the request of the United Nations General Assembly or an organ thereof: Condition of Admission of a State to Membership in the United Nations; Competence of the General Assembly for the Admission of a State to the United Nations; Reparation for Injuries Suffered in the Service of the United Nations; Interpretation of the Peace Treaties with Bulgaria, Hungary and Romania; International Status of South West Africa; Voting Procedure on Questions relating to Reports and Petitions concerning the Territory of South West Africa; Admissibility of Hearings of Petitioners by the Committee on South West Africa; Reservations to the Convention on the Prevention and Punishment of the Crime of Genocide; Effect of Awards of Compensation Made by the United Nations Administrative Tribunal (UNAT); Certain Expenses of the United Nations; Western Sahara; Application for Review of UNAT Judgment No. 158; Application for Review of UNAT Judgment No. 273; Application for Review of UNAT Judgment No. 333; Applicability of the Obligation to Arbitrate under Section 21 of the United Nations Headquarters Agreement of 26 June 1947 (relating to the closure of the Observer Mission to the United Nations maintained by the Palestine Liberation Organization).

One Advisory Opinion has been given at the request of the Security Council: Legal Consequences for States of the continued presence of South Africa in Namibia (South West Africa) notwithstanding Security Council resolution 276 (1970).

The Court has also, at the request of UNESCO, given an Advisory Opinion on Judgments of the Administrative Tribunal of the ILO upon Complaints made against UNESCO and, at the request of IMCO, on the Constitution of the Maritime Safety Committee of the Inter-Governmental Maritime Consultative Organization.

In December 1980 the Court gave the World Health Organization an advisory opinion concerning the Interpretation of the Agreement of 25 March 1951 between WHO and Egypt.

FINANCE

The budget for the two years 1988–89 amounted to US $12,527,700, financed entirely by the United Nations.

PUBLICATIONS

Reports (Judgments, Opinions and Orders): series.

Pleadings (Written Pleadings and Statements, Oral Proceedings, Correspondence): series.

Yearbook (published in 3rd quarter each year).

Bibliography (annually).

Catalogue (irregular).

Acts and Documents, No. 4 (contains Statute and Rules of the Court, the Resolution concerning its internal judicial practice and other documents).

United Nations Training and Research Institutes

UNITED NATIONS INSTITUTE FOR DISARMAMENT RESEARCH—UNIDIR

Address: Palais des Nations, 1211 Geneva 10, Switzerland.
Telephone: (022) 346011.
Telex: 289696.

UNIDIR is an autonomous institution within the United Nations. It was established by the General Assembly in 1980 and its statute became effective on 1 January 1985. Its purpose is to undertake independent research on disarmament and related problems, particularly international security issues, in order to provide the international community with more diversified and complete data and to assist negotiations on disarmament.

Research projects are conducted within the Institute, or commissioned to individual experts or research organizations. For some major studies, multinational groups of experts are established. There is a fellowship programme to enable scholars from developing countries to conduct research at the Institute.

In 1988/89 the Institute's work programme included the following studies: national security concepts; security in the Third World; disarmament and outer space; technical aspects of the verification of arms control; analysis of confidence and security-building measures; disarmament and development. A pilot project on a computer data base was started in 1986, and a survey of disarmament research being conducted by governments and institutes was begun in 1988. The following meetings were planned for 1988 and 1989: Conference of Research Institutes (1988); Conference of African Research Institutes (1989); Conference on Conventional Disarmament in Europe (1989); Symposium on Defensive Strategies, Defence Postures and Disarmament (1989).

The Insitute's budget for 1988 amounted to US $1m. It is financed mainly by voluntary contributions from governments and public or private organizations. A contribution to the costs of the Director and staff may be provided from the UN regular budget.
Director: JAYANTHA DHANAPALA.
Publications: *UNIDIR Newsletter* (quarterly); studies.

UNITED NATIONS INSTITUTE FOR TRAINING AND RESEARCH—UNITAR

Address: 801 United Nations Plaza, New York, NY 10017, USA.

UNITAR was established in 1965 as an autonomous body within the United Nations to improve, by means of training and research, the effectiveness of the United Nations, in particular the maintenance of peace and security and the promotion of economic and social development.

Training is given at various levels, with particular attention given to the needs of officials from developing countries. The Institute organizes seminars and short courses for delegates to the UN, including new delegates to the General Assembly and new members of permanent missions, and briefing seminars on issues currently before the UN, such as international economic development and international negotiations. Courses are also held for officials other than diplomats, e.g. training in the modernization of public administration, the management of public enterprises and finance. UNITAR has also organized special programmes at the request of member states, including courses on basic diplomacy and multinational co-operation.

UNITAR's research is divided between those studies which focus on the short- and medium-term needs of the UN, and those dealing with longer-term trends. Since 1966 the Institute has published many studies on peace and security, international organization and development, and the first of a series of studies on the effectiveness of various parts of the UN system and aspects of regional co-operation (including case studies of the Economic and Social Council, the International Law Commission and the Law of the Sea Conference, which have been debated by the General Assembly).

The 'Project on the Future' includes studies and conferences on two broad themes: (a) policy choices related to the creation of a new international economic order, and (b) the meaning of physical limits and supply constraints in energy and natural resources. A major project on Technology, Domestic Distribution and North-South Relations is to prepare a new model of economic growth relevant to the social and economic circumstances of the developing countries. Conferences have been organized dealing with aspects of energy, including two on small-scale resources and two on heavy crude and tar sands.

UNITAR's grant from the UN regular budget was reduced from US $1,500,000 for the two years 1984–85 to $600,000 for 1986–87.
Executive Director: MICHEL DOO KINGUÉ (Cameroon).

UNITED NATIONS INTERNATIONAL RESEARCH AND TRAINING INSTITUTE FOR THE ADVANCEMENT OF WOMEN—INSTRAW

Address: POB 21747, Santo Domingo, Dominican Republic.
Telephone: 685-2111.
Telex: 326-4280.

The Institute was established in 1979 as an autonomous institution within the United Nations, to encourage the advancement of women and their integration in the development process at all levels.

INSTRAW provides training in the compiling of statistics related to women and their role in development, and conducts research on measuring women's contribution to household income and national economies. Other studies include 'Women and the World Economy' and sectoral issues, e.g. women, water and sanitation; women and food security. There is a network of 'focal points' in 21 countries. INSTRAW has an annual budget of about US $2.5m.
Director: DUNJA PASTIZZI-FERENCIC.
Publications: *INSTRAW News* (3 a year); studies.

UNITED NATIONS RESEARCH INSTITUTE FOR SOCIAL DEVELOPMENT—UNRISD

Address: Palais des Nations, 1211 Geneva 10, Switzerland.
Telephone: (022) 988400.
Telex: 289696.

UNRISD was established in 1964 as an autonomous body within the United Nations, to conduct research into problems and policies of social and economic development during different phases of economic growth.

The Institute focuses its research on the social implications of global questions that are a major concern of the United Nations and of governments and on what can be done, locally and nationally and by the international community, to speed the achievement of development goals. It believes, however, that this can be accomplished most effectively by first identifying and analysing the impact on different social groups of dominant social processes at the national and local levels. What must be analysed are the social structures and the social forces associated with these processes, the practical policy alternatives in each situation and the social forces that might sustain these alternatives. Studies need to be carried out in a wide variety of ecological and institutional settings. Only then can analyses and generalizations be attempted at inter-country levels. The task is further complicated by the fact that there are seldom simple relationships among different social systems and subsystems.

From the late 1970s onwards three major themes (livelihood, participation and development policy) were given prominence in UNRISD's research, through two principal projects: Food Systems and Society (studying the impact of the 'Green Revolution', and aiming at a better understanding of the extent and causes of food insecurity), and Popular Participation (studying less-privileged social groups and their organized efforts to increase their control over resources and institutions). In 1986 the Board of UNRISD reviewed the Institute's research interests and approved a new medium-term programme for 1988–89, involving research in the following areas:

Adjustment, Livelihood and Power: the Social Impact of the Economic Crisis. This project was to assess the impact of the prolonged economic crisis that affected a large number of developing countries in the 1980s, investigating the origins of the crisis, survival strategies of vulnerable groups, and the impact of the crisis on economic structure and organization, and on social movements and balance of political power.

Food Policy in the World Recession. This project was to study the socio-economic and political implications of reforms in food pricing and marketing of the type implemented in many developing countries during the 1980s.

Refugees, Returnees and Local Society in Developing Countries:

Interaction and Livelihood. This project was to study the impact of refugees on the living conditions of host populations, and the reintegration of refugees returning to their country of origin, looking particularly at how government and international policies and programmes affect this process.

Research Data Bank and Trend Analysis: Work was to continue on updating the Institute's data bank of 18 development indicators for 122 countries.

It was also agreed in 1986 that UNRISD should be associated with a series of research projects in Strategies for the Future of Africa, co-sponsored by the United Nations University and the Third World Forum.

The Institute is supported by voluntary grants from governments, and also receives financing from other UN organizations, and from various other national and international agencies. Estimated income and expenditure for 1988 was US $1.8m.

There are seven full-time professional researchers and a number of consultants and collaborators, particularly in the developing countries.

Director: DHARAM GHAI (Kenya).

Publications: *Research Notes* (annually), studies.

UNITED NATIONS UNIVERSITY

Address: Toho Seimei Building, 15-1, Shibuya 2-chome, Shibuya-ku, Tokyo 150, Japan.

Telephone: (81) (3) 499-2811.

Telex: 25442.

The University is sponsored jointly by the United Nations and UNESCO. It is an autonomous institution within the United Nations, guaranteed academic freedom by a charter approved by the General Assembly in 1973. The University is not traditional in the sense of having students or awarding degrees, but works through networks of collaborating institutions and individuals. It had 38 Associated Institutions in 1988. Initially, the University's activities were concentrated in the areas of hunger, human and social development, and use and management of natural resources. In 1988 work was being undertaken in the following areas of study: Peace, Development and Democracy; The Global Economy; Global Life Support Systems; Alternative Rural-Urban Configurations; Science, Technology and Global Learning. In 1984 the UNU established the World Institute of Development Economics Research in Helsinki, Finland, and in 1987 it was announced that an Institute for Natural Resources in Africa was to be established in Côte d'Ivoire.

By the end of 1987 UNU fellowships had enabled almost 1,000 scholars and scientists from 90 countries to engage in postgraduate training and research.

Rector: Prof. HEITOR GURGULINO DE SOUZA.

Chairman of Council: Dr JUSTIN THORENS.

UNIVERSITY FOR PEACE

Address: Apdo postal 199, 1.250 Escazú, Costa Rica.

Telephone: 49-10-72.

Telex: 2331.

The University for Peace was established by the United Nations in 1980 to conduct research on disarmament, mediation, the resolution of conflicts and the relationship between peace and economic development.

Rector: ADOLFO PÉREZ ESQUIVEL.

Publication: *Carta Informativa*.

UNITED NATIONS REGIONAL COMMISSIONS

Economic Commission for Europe—ECE

Address: Palais des Nations, 1211 Geneva 10, Switzerland.
Telephone: (022) 346011.
Telex: 289696.

The UN Economic Commission for Europe was established in 1947. Representatives of all European countries (including Cyprus and Turkey) and of the USA and Canada study the economic, environmental and technological problems of the region and recommend courses of action.

MEMBERS

Albania	Italy
Austria	Luxembourg
Belgium	Malta
Bulgaria	Netherlands
Byelorussian SSR	Norway
Canada	Poland
Cyprus	Portugal
Czechoslovakia	Romania
Denmark	Spain
Finland	Sweden
France	Switzerland
German Democratic Republic	Turkey
Federal Republic of Germany	Ukrainian SSR
Greece	USSR
Hungary	United Kingdom
Iceland	USA
Ireland	Yugoslavia

Organization
(October 1988)

COMMISSION

ECE, with ECAFE (now ESCAP), was the earliest of the five regional economic commissions set up by the UN Economic and Social Council. The Commission holds an annual plenary session and meetings of subsidiary bodies are convened throughout the year.

President: ERCUMENT YAVUZALP (Turkey).

SECRETARIAT

The Secretariat services the meetings of the Commission and its subsidiary bodies and publishes periodic surveys and reviews, including a number of specialized statistical bulletins on coal, timber, steel, chemicals, housing and building, electric power, gas, general energy and transport (see list of publications below). It maintains close and regular liaison with the United Nations Secretariat in New York, with the secretariats of the other UN regional commissions, and with the UN Specialized Agencies. The Executive Secretary also carries out secretarial functions for the executive body of the 1979 Convention on Long-range Transboundary Air Pollution and its protocols. The ECE Secretariat also services the ECOSOC Committee of Experts on the Transport of Dangerous Goods.

Executive Secretary: GERALD HINTEREGGER (Austria).

Activities

The principal topics in the ECE work programme are: environmental protection; scientific and technical co-operation; energy; transport policies; trade and industrial co-operation between eastern and western Europe; and economic projections. Work is carried out by the principal subsidiary bodies listed below, assisted by sub-committees, working parties and meetings of experts.

Committee on Agricultural Problems: Reviews agricultural developments in the region and conditions in major commodity markets; elaborates commercial quality standards for perishable produce in international trade, and deals with a wide range of economic and technical problems relating to the production and marketing of crop and animal products. Mechanization of agriculture, questions of agrarian structure, farm rationalization and management, and regional developments, are studied and discussed in joint FAO/ECE working parties.

Timber Committee: Regularly reviews markets for softwoods, hardwoods, wood-based panels and industrial wood raw material; analyses medium- and long-term prospects for timber; keeps under review developments in forest industries, including environmental and energy-related aspects. Subsidiary bodies run jointly with the FAO deal with forest techniques and worker-training and with forest economics and statistics.

Coal Committee: Concentrates on problems of production (underground and open-cast), upgrading, conversion, trade (including world trade) and use; studies related research and development activities; analyses market developments; exchanges information on policies; undertakes demand projections.

Committee on Electric Power: Analyses the electric power situation and its prospects, studies the planning and operation of large power systems, as well as particular aspects of hydroelectric, thermal and nuclear generation, international interconnections, the efficient use of electricity, and the relation between electricity and the environment.

Committee on Gas: Deals with gas resources, the economic and technical aspects of the production, transport and utilization of gas, natural and manufactured as well as liquefied petroleum gases; monitors trade in gas, and forecasts demand.

Committee on Housing, Building and Planning: Reviews trends and policies in the field of human settlements. Undertakes studies and organizes seminars on housing, building and planning issues. Promotes international co-operation in the field of urban and regional research. Also promotes international harmonization of building regulations and standards. Human settlements problems of southern Europe receive special consideration.

Inland Transport Committee: Covers road, rail and inland water transport, customs, contracts, transport of dangerous and perishable goods, equipment, statistics, tariffs, river law, road transport regime and road traffic accidents, construction of vehicles and passenger transport services by road. A number of international agreements are in force following their adoption through ECE.

Steel Committee: Annually reviews trends in the European and world markets, changes in price policy, growth of capacity supply factors and future prospects. Also studies long-term economic and technological problems.

Committee on the Development of Trade: Serves as a forum for studying means of expanding and diversifying trade among European countries, as well as with countries in other regions, and for drawing up recommendations on how to achieve these ends. Analyses trends, problems and prospects in intra-European trade, notably east-west trade; explores means of removing or reducing obstacles to the development of trade; promotes new or improved methods of trading by means of marketing, industrial co-operation, standardization, contractual guides, and the facilitation of international trade procedures.

Conference of European Statisticians: Promotes improvement of national statistics and their international comparability in economic, social, demographic and environmental fields; facilitates exchange of information between European countries. A joint study group is held with the FAO on food and agriculture statistics.

Senior Economic Advisers to ECE Governments: Brings together high-level governmental experts for an exchange of views and experience on current, medium- and long-term economic development; organizes groups of experts, joint research projects and seminars on selected issues of common interest; a major project (near to completion in 1988) is the Overall Economic Perspective of the ECE region to the year 2000.

Chemical Industry Committee: Regularly reviews the market of chemical products and their raw materials in Europe, USA and elsewhere. Compiles annual statistics on production of and trade in chemical products. Carries out studies on special problems arising in connection with the development of the chemical industry.

Senior Advisers to ECE Governments on Science and Technology: Keeps under review developments in the sphere of science and technology. Major activities are: review and analysis of national scientific and technological policies; evaluation of research and development; innovation policies; technological forecasting; transfer of technology, including licensing procedures; study of selected issues, such as biotechnology and economic development; new

INTERNATIONAL ORGANIZATIONS

United Nations (Regional Commissions)

sources of energy and prediction of earthquakes; and assessment of medium- and long-term perspectives in science and technology.

Senior Advisers to ECE Governments on Environmental Problems and Water: Exchanges experience and information on problems of environmental protection and improvement, in particular those of a transboundary nature; surveys and assesses the state of the environment in the region; develops a long-term strategy for environmental protection and rational use of natural resources in member countries; promotes the protection of flora, fauna and their habitats in the region; promotes the application of environmental technology; promotes the development of intergovernmental agreements and other forms of international arrangements dealing with environmental problems.

Reviews major trends and policies with regard to the conservation and development of water resources, particularly where international co-operation is required. Studies problems relating to the rational use of water resources. Also studies selected problems of water pollution control and of governmental policy related to the formulation and administration of water management plans.

There are working groups on environmental impact assessment, on air pollution problems, on low- and non-waste technology and re-utilization and recycling of wastes.

Senior Advisers to ECE Governments on Energy: Exchanges information on general energy problems, including energy resources and national policies; work programme comprises programmes, policies and prospects; demand and supply; trade and co-operation; conservation.

BUDGET

ECE's budget for the two years 1988–89 was US $35.8m.

PUBLICATIONS

ECE Annual Report.
Economic Bulletin for Europe.
Economic Survey of Europe.
Prices of Agricultural Products and Selected Inputs in Europe and North America—Annual ECE/FAO Price Review.
Agricultural Trade in Europe.
Review of the Agricultural Situation in Europe.
Timber Bulletin for Europe.
ECE Timber Committee Yearbook.
Annual Forest Products Market Review.
Annual Review of the Chemical Industry.
Annual Review of Engineering Industries and Automation.
Annual Bulletin of Coal Statistics for Europe.
Annual Bulletin of Electrical Energy Statistics for Europe.
Annual Bulletin of General Energy Statistics for Europe.
Annual Bulletin of Gas Statistics for Europe.
Annual Bulletin of Housing and Building Statistics for Europe.
Annual Bulletin of Steel Statistics for Europe.
Annual Bulletin of Trade in Chemical Products.
Annual Bulletin of Transport Statistics for Europe.
Statistics of Road Traffic Accidents in Europe.
Bulletin of Statistics on World Trade in Engineering Products.
The Steel Market.
Series of studies on air pollution, water, the environment, trade facilitation, industrial co-operation and energy.
Reports, proceedings of meetings, technical documents, etc.

Economic and Social Commission for Asia and the Pacific—ESCAP

Address: United Nations Bldg, Rajadamnern Ave, Bangkok 2, Thailand.
Telephone: 2829161.
Telex: 82392.

The Commission was founded in 1947 to encourage the economic and social development of Asia and the Far East; it was originally known as the Economic Commission for Asia and the Far East (ECAFE). The title ESCAP, which replaced ECAFE, was adopted after a reorganization in 1974.

MEMBERS

Afghanistan	Japan	Philippines
Australia	Kampuchea	Singapore
Bangladesh	Korea, Republic	Solomon Islands
Bhutan	Laos	Sri Lanka
Brunei	Malaysia	Thailand
Burma	Maldives	Tonga
China, People's Republic	Mongolia	Tuvalu
	Nauru	USSR
Fiji	Nepal	United Kingdom
France	Netherlands	USA
India	New Zealand	Vanuatu
Indonesia	Pakistan	Viet-Nam
Iran	Papua New Guinea	Western Samoa

ASSOCIATE MEMBERS

Cook Islands	Marshall Islands	Northern Mariana Islands
Guam	Federated States of Micronesia	Palau
Hong Kong	Niue	
Kiribati		

Organization

(October 1988)

COMMISSION

The Commission meets annually at ministerial level to examine the region's problems, to review progress, to establish priorities and to launch new projects.

Committees of officials dealing with the specific areas of work listed below meet annually or every two years; *ad hoc* conferences may also be held on subjects not otherwise covered.

SECRETARIAT

Executive Secretary: S. A. M. S. KIBRIA (Bangladesh).
Deputy Executive Secretary: KOJI NAKAGAWA.
Chief, Programme Co-ordination and Monitoring Office: SEIKO TAKAHASHI.

The secretariat includes the Programme Co-ordination and Monitoring Office, the Information Service and three specialized units: the ESCAP/CTC Joint Unit on Transnational Corporations (working with the UN Centre for Transnational Corporations), the Inter-agency Committee and Task Force on Integrated Rural Development (comprising specialists from ESCAP and nine UN agencies), and the Environmental Co-ordinating Unit (run jointly with the UN Environment Programme). ESCAP's work is covered by 12 Divisions: Administration; Agriculture; Development Planning; Industry, Human Settlements and Technology; International Trade; Natural Resources; Population; Shipping, Ports and Inland Waterways; Social Development; Statistics; Transport, Communications and Tourism; and Technical Co-operation.

PACIFIC OFFICE

Pacific Operations Centre: Port Vila, Vanuatu; f. 1984 by merging the ESCAP Pacific Liaison Office (Nauru) and the UN Development Advisory Team (Fiji).

Activities

ESCAP acts as a UN regional centre, providing the only intergovernmental forum for the whole of Asia and the Pacific, and executing a wide range of development programmes through technical assistance, advisory services to governments, research, training and information.

AGRICULTURE

ESCAP's Agriculture Division carries out programmes aimed at helping farming communities to improve their livelihood and to increase the production of food. It collects and disseminates information through a quarterly bulletin, and also issues periodicals on agro-chemicals and fertilizers. It provides training in farm broadcasting and in the safe use of pesticides. In co-operation with other UN agencies (especially FAO and ILO) it assists low-income farmers and the landless, by introducing innovative credit schemes, and organizing groups of landless workers and co-operatives. A Fertilizer Advisory, Development and Information Network for Asia and the Pacific is run in co-operation with UNIDO and FAO. ESCAP also monitors the effects of weather on certain crops, enabling prediction of food shortages.

Regional Co-ordination Centre for Research and Development of Coarse Grains, Pulses, Roots and Tuber Crops: Jalan Merdeka 99, Bogor 16111, Indonesia; tel. (0251) 26290; telex 48369; f. 1981 to provide technical services for research on the production of and trade in these crops in the humid tropics of Asia and the Pacific. Publ. *Palawija News* (quarterly). Dir SHIRO OKABE.

DEVELOPMENT PLANNING

This division undertakes research and provides information on and technical assistance for regional planning. It publishes studies on specific development issues, together with an annual Economic and Social Survey of the region. In 1987 its research programme included issues relating to external debt, trade in primary commodities, foreign investment and public finance. Two special sub-programmes cover the least-developed countries of the region and the Pacific islands.

INDUSTRY, HUMAN SETTLEMENTS AND TECHNOLOGY

In co-operation with the UN Industrial Development Organization (UNIDO), ESCAP provides support for industrial development, through industrial reviews of developing countries, studies on policy reorientation, investment promotion, advisory services, information and training. It carries out feasibility studies for the establishment of industries away from metropolitan areas, and promotes 'catalyst' industries in the least-developed countries of the region. It encourages foreign investment and provides tax advice.

Asian and Pacific Centre for Transfer of Technology: 49 Palace Rd, POB 115, Bangalore 560052, India; tel. 76931; tel. 845-2719; f. 1977 to assist countries of the ESCAP region in technology development and transfer. Dir M. NAWAZ SHARIF. Publs *Asia Pacific Tech Monitor* (every 2 months), monographs, proceedings.

Regional Network for Agricultural Machinery: c/o UNDP, POB 7285 ADC, Pasay City, Metro Manila, Philippines; tel. 3470; telex 72222250; f. 1977 to promote the local manufacture of agricultural machinery, to increase agricultural output and productivity, and to improve the working conditions and income of farmers; assists members to develop and demonstrate tools and machines. Mems: 10 participating countries. Project Man. Dr ZIA UR RAHMAN. Publs *RNAM Newsletter* (3 a year), technical bulletins.

INTERNATIONAL TRADE

The International Trade Division organizes inter-governmental meetings for trade negotiations and the formulation of measures for expanding trade. It provides training and advisory services in export promotion and market development. It conducts programmes for the promotion of trade in manufactured goods, regional joint ventures, and the development of human resources. ESCAP has helped to establish a number of regional groups linking producers of coconuts, jute, rubber and other commodities. Technical assistance is given to land-locked and remote island countries of the region for the improvement of transport facilities.

MARINE RESOURCES

The ESCAP Programme on Marine Affairs (established in 1986) helps member countries to benefit under the UN Convention on the Law of the Sea (1982) which established 'exclusive economic zones' for coastal states: ESCAP advises on the planning of policies and legislation, and offers training in the assessment and exploitation of marine resources.

NATURAL RESOURCES

ESCAP assists the countries of the region to benefit from their mineral resources, by encouraging exploration and assessment of land and marine areas, conducting studies of mineral commodities, promoting interdisciplinary research, sponsoring technical co-operation, and stressing the environmental impact of the exploitation of these resources.

ESCAP's Regional Energy Development Programme encourages co-operation in the planning and management of energy programmes, the efficient use of energy and development of new sources of energy, with special emphasis on augmenting rural energy supplies. There is also a special Pacific Energy Development Programme. ESCAP assists countries in the efficient use of fossil energy supplies, and sponsors the investigation of new and renewable energy sources in the region. It provides a regional network of information and advisory services on solar, wind and biomass energy.

ESCAP's Regional Remote Sensing Programme promotes advanced techniques in compiling and analysing remote-sensing data, gathered by aircraft and satellites, for use in agriculture, forestry, and exploration for mineral and water resources. Special training was provided during the period 1985–87 for about 50 trainees annually. A special programme provides training and other assistance for the planning of human settlements, taking into account geological and hydrological features.

The development of water resources through national water plans (covering irrigation, drinking-water supply and sanitation, hydroelectric power, and control of flood and storm damage) also forms part of the work of this division.

ESCAP/WMO Typhoon Committee: c/o UNDP, POB 7285 ADC, Pasay City, Metro Manila, Philippines; tel. 922-8055; telex 42021; f. 1968; an intergovernmental body sponsored by ESCAP and WMO for mitigation of typhoon damage. It aims at establishing efficient typhoon and flood warning systems through improved meteorological and telecommunication facilities. Other activities include promotion of disaster preparedness, training of personnel and co-ordination of research. The committee's programme is supported from national resources and also by UNDP and other international and bilateral assistance. Mems: People's Republic of China, Hong Kong, Japan, Kampuchea, Republic of Korea, Laos, Malaysia, the Philippines, Thailand, Viet-Nam. Co-ordinator of Secretariat: Dr ROMAN L. KINTANAR.

WMO/ESCAP Panel on Tropical Cyclones: Technical Support Unit, c/o Dept of Meteorology, Colombo, Sri Lanka; tel. 93943; f. 1973 to mitigate damage caused by tropical cyclones in the Bay of Bengal and the Arabian Sea; mems: Bangladesh, Burma, India, Maldives, Pakistan, Sri Lanka, Thailand.

POPULATION

The region's high density of population means that population control has an important place in development planning. ESCAP makes comparative demographic studies of individual member countries, and reviews national family-planning programmes. ESCAP co-ordinates a population information network for the region, and member governments receive advice on demography and family planning. Much of ESCAP's work in this field is funded by the UN Population Fund (UNFPA).

SHIPPING, PORTS AND INLAND WATERWAYS

ESCAP aims to help developing maritime members to adopt up-to-date technology in shipping, ports and inland waterways. Programme activities include regular reviews of developments in this field; compilation of statistics; guidelines for maritime legislation; the expansion of container transport; maintaining an information system on ports management; promotion of the interests of maritime transport users; and rehabilitation of inland waterways.

SOCIAL DEVELOPMENT

ESCAP's social development programme aims to encourage participation in development by disadvantaged groups, namely the disabled, women, the young and the old. ESCAP attempts to increase the self-reliance of women by providing a regional women's information network for the sharing of expertise, and provides advice for policy-makers in the area of women's participation in development. In 1986 ESCAP began a programme of assistance for member governments on improving national programmes for disability prevention and the rehabilitation of disabled persons.

STATISTICS

Recognizing the importance of statistical data in drawing up and evaluating development programmes, ESCAP undertakes periodical reviews of national statistical systems, provides training and advisory services, and organizes technical meetings. A major objective is to develop national statistical services in the region. Particular emphasis is placed on household surveys as a means of compiling demographic information. ESCAP also collects and publishes a wide range of statistical information on the Asia-Pacific region.

Statistical Institute for Asia and the Pacific: Akasaka POB 13, Tokyo 107–91, Japan; tel. (03) 357-8351; telex 32217; f. 1970; trains government statisticians; prepares teaching materials, provides facilities for special studies and research of a statistical nature, assists in the development of statistical education and training at all levels in national and sub-regional centres. Dir S. A. MEEGAMA.

INTERNATIONAL ORGANIZATIONS   *United Nations (Regional Commissions)*

TRANSPORT AND COMMUNICATIONS

At the 40th session of ESCAP, delegates agreed to designate the period 1985–94 as the Transport Decade for Asia and the Pacific, owing to the vital part played by transport improvements in the process of development.

Intergovernmental meetings of road experts are regularly held by ESCAP to discuss road transport. The Asian Highway Network Project comprises a network of 65,000 km of roads in 15 countries; ESCAP publishes maps of the network and reports on its development. In 1983 a study of potential standardization of vehicle safety requirements was undertaken. ESCAP also publishes manuals on labour-intensive rural road construction and maintenance, and conducts training courses for officials in charge of roadworks.

ESCAP gives technical assistance to member countries for modernizing railways. An Asia-Pacific Railway Co-operation Group was established by transport ministers in 1983. Studies have been made by ESCAP on container transport by rail in selected countries, and on the feasibility of the electrification of railways in Thailand.

ESCAP also assists member countries in matters relating to integrated transport planning, urban transport, the environmental impact of transport planning, and the facilitation of international traffic.

FINANCE

For the two-year period 1988–89 ESCAP's regular budget, an appropriation from the UN budget, was US $33.5m. The regular budget is supplemented annually by funds from various sources for technical assistance.

PUBLICATIONS

Economic and Social Survey of Asia and the Pacific (annually).
Small Industry Bulletin for Asia and the Pacific.
Industry and Technology Development News for Asia and the Pacific.
Transport and Communications Bulletin for Asia and the Pacific.
Review of Developments in Shipping, Ports and Inland Waterways.
Agricultural Information Development Bulletin (quarterly).
Agro-chemicals News in Brief (quarterly).
Fertilizer Trade Information (monthly).
Economic Bulletin (2 a year).
Development Papers (occasional).
Atlas of Stratigraphy.
Atlas of Mineral Resources of the ESCAP Region.
ESCAP Energy News.
Electric Power in Asia and the Pacific (2 a year).
Water Resources Journal.
Confluence (water resources newsletter).
Asia-Pacific Population Journal.
Statistical Yearbook for Asia and the Pacific.
Quarterly Bulletin of Statistics for Asia and the Pacific.
Sample Surveys in the ESCAP Region (annually).
Bibliographies; trade profiles; commodity prices; statistics.

Economic Commission for Latin America and the Caribbean—ECLAC

Address: Edif. Naciones Unidas, Avda Dag Hammarskjöld, Casilla 179D, Santiago, Chile.
Telephone: 485051.
Telex: 340925.

The UN Economic Commission for Latin America was founded in 1948 to co-ordinate policies for the promotion of economic development in the Latin American region. In 1984 the title 'Economic Commission for Latin America and the Caribbean' was adopted.

MEMBERS

Antigua and Barbuda
Argentina
Bahamas
Barbados
Belize
Bolivia
Brazil
Canada
Chile
Colombia
Costa Rica
Cuba
Dominica
Dominican Republic
Ecuador
El Salvador
France
Grenada
Guatemala
Guyana
Haiti
Honduras
Jamaica
Mexico
Netherlands
Nicaragua
Panama
Paraguay
Peru
Portugal
Saint Christopher and Nevis
Saint Lucia
Saint Vincent and the Grenadines
Spain
Suriname
Trinidad and Tobago
United Kingdom
USA
Uruguay
Venezuela

ASSOCIATE MEMBERS

British Virgin Islands
Montserrat
Netherlands Antilles
United States Virgin Islands

Organization
(October 1988)

COMMISSION

The Commission normally meets every two years in one of the Latin American capitals. It has established permanent bodies with various sub-committees:
Committee of the Whole.

Central American Economic Co-operation Committee: sub-committees on trade; statistical co-ordination; transport; housing, building and planning; electric power; industrial initiatives; and agricultural development.
Committee of High-Level Government Experts.
Caribbean Development and Co-operation Committee.

SECRETARIAT

The Executive Secretariat comprises the Executive Secretary; Deputy Executive Secretaries for Economic and Social Development and for Co-operation and Support Services; the Programme Planning and Co-ordination Office; the Secretary of the Commission, with a conference service unit; and the UN Information Service.

There is a library, a computer centre, and a service for producing documents and publications. In addition, work in specific fields is carried out by divisions of the Secretariat as indicated below under 'Activities'.

There is a sub-regional Office in Mexico, a sub-regional Headquarters for the Caribbean, and offices in Bogotá, Brasília, Buenos Aires, Montevideo and Washington.

Executive Secretary: GERT ROSENTHAL (Guatemala).

Activities

ECLAC collaborates with regional governments in the investigation and analysis of regional and national economic problems, and provides guidance in the formulation of development plans. Many of its activities are undertaken in co-operation with other UN agencies. Under the programme headings listed below, ECLAC conducts: research; analysis; publication of information; provision of technical assistance; participation in seminars and conferences; training courses; and co-operation with national, regional and international organizations.

Development Issues and Policies
Energy
Environment (Joint ECLAC/UNEP Development and Environment Unit)
Food and Agriculture (Joint ECLAC/FAO Agriculture Division)
Human Settlements (Joint ECLAC/UNCHS Human Settlements Unit)

INTERNATIONAL ORGANIZATIONS

Industrial Development
International Trade and Development Financing
Natural Resources
Population (see CELADE below)
Science and Technology
Social Development and Humanitarian Affairs
Statistics
Transnational Corporations
Transport

In April 1986 the Commission discussed international development strategy and the economic prospects for Latin America and the Caribbean during the remainder of the 1980s; the region's external debt; and policies for the stabilization, adjustment and reactivation of regional economies. The meeting decided to hold a special conference, which took place in January 1987, to discuss national and international strategies for the region's economic recovery and development. A regional conference on poverty was held in August 1988.

Latin American and Caribbean Institute for Economic and Social Planning—ILPES: Edif. Naciones Unidas, Avda Dag Hammarskjöld, Casilla 179D, Santiago, Chile; f. 1962; undertakes research and provides training and advisory services; encourages co-operation among the planning services of the region. Dir ALFREDO COSTA-FILHO.

Latin American Demographic Centre—CELADE: Alonso de Córdova 3107, Casilla 91, Santiago, Chile; f. 1957, became an integral part of the Commission in 1975; assists governments in forming population policies; provides demographic estimates and projections, documentation, data processing and training.

BUDGET

ECLAC's share of the UN budget for the two years 1988–89 was US $43m. In addition, voluntary extrabudgetary contributions are received.

PUBLICATIONS

Revista de la CEPALC (Spanish and English, 3 a year).
Economic Survey of Latin America (Spanish and English, annually).
Boletín de planificación (2–3 a year).
Temas de planificación (3 a year).
PLANINDEX (2 a year).
Boletín demográfico (2 a year).
DOCPAL Resúmenes (population studies, 2 a year).
Notas de Población (3 a year).
Boletín del Banco de Datos (annually).
Statistical Yearbook for Latin America (Spanish and English, annually).
CEPALCINDEX (2 a year).
Studies, reports, bibliographical bulletins.

Economic Commission for Africa—ECA

Address: Africa Hall, POB 3001, Addis Ababa, Ethiopia.
Telephone: 447200.
Telex: 976 21029.

The UN Economic Commission for Africa was founded in 1958 by a resolution of ECOSOC to initiate and take part in measures for facilitating Africa's economic development.

MEMBERS

Algeria	Madagascar
Angola	Malawi
Benin	Mali
Botswana	Mauritania
Burkina Faso	Mauritius
Burundi	Morocco
Cameroon	Mozambique
Cape Verde	Niger
Central African Republic	Nigeria
Chad	Rwanda
Comoros	Sao Tomé and Príncipe
Congo	Senegal
Côte d'Ivoire	Seychelles
Djibouti	Sierra Leone
Egypt	Somalia
Equatorial Guinea	South Africa*
Ethiopia	Sudan
Gabon	Swaziland
The Gambia	Tanzania
Ghana	Togo
Guinea	Tunisia
Guinea-Bissau	Uganda
Kenya	Zaire
Lesotho	Zambia
Liberia	Zimbabwe
Libya	

* Suspended since 1965.

Organization
(October 1988)

COMMISSION

The Commission may only act with the agreement of the government of the country concerned. It is also empowered to make recommendations on any matter within its competence directly to the government of the member or associate member concerned, to governments admitted in a consultative capacity, and to the UN Specialized Agencies. The Commission is required to submit for prior consideration by ECOSOC any of its proposals for actions that would be likely to have important effects on the international economy.

CONFERENCE OF MINISTERS

The Conference is attended by Ministers responsible for economic or financial affairs, planning and development of governments of Member States, and is the main deliberative body of the Commission. It meets annually. A Technical Preparatory Committee of the Whole, representing all Member States, was established in 1979 to deal with matters submitted for the consideration of the Conference.

The Commission's responsibility to promote concerted action for the economic and social development of Africa is vested primarily in the Conference, which considers matters of general policy and the priorities to be assigned to the Commission's programmes, considers inter-African and international economic policy and makes recommendations to Member States in connection with such matters. It reviews the course of programmes being implemented in the preceding year and examines and approves the programmes proposed for the next.

OTHER POLICY-MAKING BODIES

Conference of African Ministers of Finance.

Conference of African Ministers of Industry.

Conference of African Ministers of Social Affairs.

Conference of African Ministers of Trade.

Conference of African Ministers of Transport, Communications and Planning.

Conference of Ministers Responsible for Human Resources Planning Development and Utilization.

Conference of Ministers of Finance.

Councils of Ministers of the MULPOCs (see below).

SECRETARIAT

The Secretariat provides the services necessary for the meeting of the Conference of Ministers and the meetings of the Commission's subsidiary bodies, carries out the resolutions and implements the programmes adopted there.

The Headquarters of the Secretariat is in Addis Ababa, Ethiopia. It comprises a Cabinet Office and 11 Divisions.

INTERNATIONAL ORGANIZATIONS

United Nations (Regional Commissions)

Cabinet Office of the Executive Secretary:
　Policy and Programme Co-ordination Office
　Economic Co-operation Office
　Office of the Secretary of the Commission
　Technical Assistance Co-ordination and Operations Office
　Information Service
　Pan-African Documentation and Information Service (PADIS)
　African Training and Research Centre for Women
　Security and Safety Unit

Divisions:
　Socio-Economic Research and Planning
　International Trade and Finance
　Joint ECA/FAO Agriculture
　Joint ECA/UNIDO Industry
　Social Development, Environment and Human Settlements
　Natural Resources
　Transport, Communications and Tourism
　Public Administration, Management and Manpower
　Statistics
　Population
　Administration and Conference Services

Executive Secretary: ADEBAYO ADEDEJI (Nigeria).

Subsidiary Bodies

Joint Conference of African Planners, Statisticians and Demographers.
Intergovernmental Committee of Experts for Science and Technology Development.
Intergovernmental Regional Committee on Human Settlements and Environment.
Follow-up Committee on Industrialization in Africa.
Intergovernmental Committee of Experts of African Least-Developed Countries.
Conference of Ministers of African Least-Developed Countries.

Regional Operational Centres

Multinational Programming and Operational Centres (MULPOC) act as 'field agents' for the implementation of regional development programmes. The Centres are located in Yaoundé, Cameroon (serving central Africa), Gisenyi, Rwanda (Great Lakes Community), Lusaka, Zambia (east and southern Africa), Niamey, Niger (west Africa) and Tangier, Morocco (north Africa). Each centre holds regular ministerial meetings.

Activities

The Commission's 1984–89 work programme is largely derived from the 'Development Strategy for Africa for the United Nations' Third Development Decade', which was drawn up by the ECA Conference of Ministers and approved by the OAU summit conference in 1979. The plan for the implementation of this strategy, known as the Lagos Plan of Action, was adopted by the OAU in 1980: it envisaged the economic integration of the continent (an 'African Common Market') by the end of the century. The Commission's work is also based on the UN Programme of Action for African Economic Recovery and Development (1986–90) and on the 'Strategies for the Advancement of Women' adopted in 1985 by the conference held in Nairobi to mark the end of the UN Decade for Women.

POLICY AND PROGRAMME CO-ORDINATION

The Policy and Programme Co-ordination Office assists the Executive Secretary in directing the Commission's work programme. It submits proposals on African development to the policy-making bodies of the UN and OAU, and co-ordinates the ECA side of the ECA/OAU Intersecretariat Committee and other inter-agency committees. It services the annual conference of ministers, and attempts to ensure that policy decisions are reflected in the planning of ECA activities. It prepares reports for the evaluation of programme performance.

SOCIO-ECONOMIC RESEARCH AND PLANNING

Monitoring economic and social trends in the African region and studying the development problems concerning it are among the fundamental tasks of the Commission. The annual Survey of Economic and Social Conditions in Africa analyses past trends and prospects. Studies of specific issues are also carried out at the request of member States of the Commission.

The Commission gives assistance to governments in general economic analysis, in fiscal, financial and monetary issues and in planning. Studies on planning are carried out in the Secretariat in order to provide African planning departments with better tools. A current project is to develop short-term forecasting techniques suitable to the needs and means of African countries, particularly for least-developed, land-locked and island countries which have a much lower income level than other countries and which are faced with heavier constraints than others.

The Conference of African Planners, Statisticians and Demographers, which is held every two years, provides an important opportunity for African governments to exchange views and experiences, to obtain information on new techniques and to discuss the most appropriate approaches to development problems.

STATISTICS

The Statistics Division of ECA, which comprises four sections (General Economic Statistics, Demographic and Social Statistics, Censuses and Surveys Advisory Service and International Trade and Related Statistics) promotes the development and co-ordination of national statistical services in the region and the improvement and comparability of statistical data. It prepares documents to assist in the improvement of statistical methodology and undertakes the collection, evaluation and dissemination of statistical information. Since 1978 ECA's efforts in the field of statistics have been concentrated in five main areas:

(i) The African Household Survey Capability Programme (AHSCP), which aims at helping African countries in the collection and analysis of integrated demographic, social and economic data on households and household members on a continuing basis;

(ii) The Statistical Training Programme for Africa (STPA), which aims to make the region self-sufficient in statistical personnel at all levels;

(iii) The Statistical Data Base, part of the Pan-African Documentation and Information Service (PADIS), which provides on-line statistical information to users;

(iv) The Regional Advisory Service in Demographic Statistics (RASDS), which provides technical advisory services for population censuses, demographic surveys and civil registration; and

(v) The National Accounts Capability Programme (NACP), which aims at improving economic statistics generally by building up a capability in each country for the collection, processing and analysis of economic data.

POPULATION

ECA assists its member states in (i) population data collection and data processing, which is done by the Statistics Division of the Commission; (ii) analysis of demographic data obtained from censuses or surveys: this assistance is given by the Population Division; (iii) training demographers at the Regional Institute for Population Studies (RIPS) in Accra (Ghana) and at the Institut de formation et de recherche démographiques (IFORD) in Yaoundé (Cameroon); (iv) formulation of population policies and integrating population variables in development planning, through advisory missions and through the organization of national seminars on population and development; and (v) dissemination of information through its *Newsletter*, *Demographic Handbook for Africa*, the *African Population Studies* series and other publications. The Commission conducts studies on population dynamics and their relationship to development.

The Lagos Plan of Action called for greater integration of population variables in development planning, bearing in mind the expected doubling of the African population between 1975 and 2000 and the impact of this on economic planning and development. It appealed to member states to attach importance to (a) the analysis of demographic data from censuses and demographic surveys and (b) training of nationals of ECA member states in demographic data collection and analysis.

The second African Population Conference was held in Arusha, Tanzania, in January 1984; it adopted 93 recommendations for the future management of the regional population. The Fourth Joint Conference of African Planners, Statisticians and Demographers was held in March 1986. The Population Information Network for Africa (POPIN-Africa) began operations in January 1984.

TRANSPORT AND COMMUNICATIONS

For the United Nations Transport and Communications Decade in Africa (UNTACDA), a comprehensive programme was adopted by ECA for the period 1978–88, to encourage the formation of efficient and reliable transport and communications links among all African countries.

The programme included the construction of the following trans-African roads: Lagos–Mombasa (6,300 km); Dakar–N'Djamena (4,600 km); Nouakchott–Lagos (4,600 km); Cairo–Gaborone (9,027 km); and Algiers–Lagos, the Trans-Saharan Highway (5,929 km). The programme also envisaged uniform road traffic regulations, signs, signals and a highway code.

The UNTACDA programme aimed to enable inter-connection of some African railway networks, extension of some into the land-locked countries, modernization of track and rolling stock and the introduction of uniform operating and training procedures. Efforts were also made to establish the manufacturing of spare parts and components in Africa.

The programme aimed to strengthen international and coastal shipping in Africa through the pooling of resources on a subregional basis, the rationalization of sailing schedules, port modernization, and the establishment of joint training and repair facilities in the continent. ECA assisted in the formation of the Port Management Associations of West and Central Africa and of Eastern and Southern Africa.

In the air transport subsector, the programme aimed to introduce a four-zone air-route grid system covering the entire region, development of a regional air navigational plan, joint acquisition of aircraft and equipment, establishment of joint maintenance and repair facilities, establishment of regional and sub-regional training institutions and the harmonization of tariffs and charges within the region.

ECA and the International Telecommunication Union (ITU) collaborate with the OAU in assisting member states towards completion of the Pan-African Telecommunication network (PAN-AFTEL). Projects on low-cost broadcasting systems have also been undertaken, in collaboration with UNESCO. In 1986 funds were secured for a feasibility study for a Regional Satellite Communications System.

The Pan-African Documentation and Information Service (PADIS) was established in 1980. The main objectives of PADIS are: to provide access to numerical and other information on African social, economic, scientific and technological development issues; to assist African countries in their efforts to develop national information handling capabilities; to establish teledata-transmission linkages within and beyond Africa; and to design sound technical specifications, norms and standards to minimize technical barriers in the exchange of information.

SOCIAL DEVELOPMENT, ENVIRONMENT AND HUMAN SETTLEMENTS

The Social Development, Environment and Human Settlements Division undertakes studies, produces technical publications and organizes meetings. It provides advisory services to member states on formulating policies relating to overall social development, integrated rural development, youth and social welfare, and housing. It co-ordinates environmental activities in Africa with UNEP and other agencies.

In January 1980 the African Centre for Applied Research and Training in Social Development (ACARTSOD) was inaugurated in Tripoli, Libya, to provide training of high-level personnel required for research and development programmes, and to organize seminars and conduct research.

AGRICULTURE

Major emphasis continues to be laid on the problem of attaining self-sufficiency in food. The Regional Food Plan for Africa, prepared by ECA in collaboration with FAO, was adopted by the African ministers of agriculture in 1978. ECA has undertaken the implementation of the Regional Food Plan along with the various intergovernmental organizations working in Africa. During 1984-86 its work fell into three main categories: (i) agricultural planning, including the conservation of forest and land resources; (ii) promotion of integrated rural development, particularly institution-building, agricultural research and livestock improvement; (iii) marketing of produce, with emphasis on prevention of food losses and providing incentives for increasing food production. In 1986, as part of the UN Programme of Action for African Economic Recovery, ECA drew up strategies for improving Africa's preparedness to meet emergencies without losing sight of the need for long-term development; it emphasized agricultural planning, forestry, integrated rural development, inter-country co-operation in the production of fish and livestock, and the development of food security systems.

INDUSTRY

The UN Industrial Development Decade for Africa covers the years 1980-90. The fifth conference of African ministers of industry (1979), sponsored jointly by the ECA, OAU and UNIDO, gave priority to five basic industries: food and agro-industry; building materials and construction; engineering; basic metals; chemicals. It initiated plans for the setting-up of African multinational corporations in these areas. The preparatory phase of the Decade (1982-84) was for reviewing and adjusting the industrial plans of a number of African countries in order to lay the foundation for self-sustained industrial development in the ensuing years. The economic crisis aggravated by drought and famine during 1983-85 meant that African countries were forced to use their foreign exchange earnings for food imports rather than for industrial investment. The Decade's aim that Africa should produce at least 1.4% of world industrial production by the year 1990 could not therefore be achieved.

The African Industrial Development Fund was established in 1979 to provide resources for pre-investment activities for developing industrial projects, especially multinational ones. The African Regional Centre for Engineering Design and Manufacturing (Ibadan, Nigeria) was established in 1980.

SCIENCE AND TECHNOLOGY

ECA activities in this field concentrate on the development of training facilities and on promoting regional co-operation. The African Regional Centre for Technology (Dakar, Senegal) became operational in 1980, aiming to assist African countries in the development of indigenous technologies, the improvement of negotiating capabilities for imported technologies and related areas. In 1986 and 1987 the Secretariat organized a meeting of experts on production of school science equipment for the region; working-group meetings on science and technology for north and southern Africa; advisory missions on scientific research to Burundi, Rwanda and Zaire; and on metal-working technology to Tanzania; and training for African officials involved in the acquisition of foreign technology. Work on a Rural Technology Demonstration Centre, in Dakar, Senegal, began in 1986.

NATURAL RESOURCES

The Eastern and Southern African Mineral Resources Development Centre at Dodoma, Tanzania, provides information on the development of mineral resources, practical courses in geology and mining, advisory services, pre-feasibility studies and specialized laboratory services; in 1986 it had six member states. A similar Central African multinational centre was established in 1983 at Brazzaville, Congo, and had eight member states by 1986. The second Regional Conference on the Development and Utilization of Mineral Resources, held in 1985, adopted a programme of action including surveys of raw materials for fertilizers, small-scale mining, intra-African trade in minerals, and drawing up national and regional policies for exploitation of minerals, particularly aluminium, copper and phosphates.

Two Regional Centres, for Services in Surveying, Mapping and Remote Sensing (Nairobi, Kenya) and for Training in Aerospace Surveys (Ile-Ife, Nigeria), provide specialized services for an inventory of natural resources. Standardized specifications for basic topographical mapping in Africa were drawn up in 1985. In 1988 three ground stations (in Burkina Faso, Kenya and Zaire) were being planned to receive signals from US and European remote-sensing satellites and process the data received on mineral, land and water resources. Two ECA-sponsored organizations were amalgamated in 1987 to form the African Organization for Cartography and Remote Sensing. In 1988 the Conference of Ministers approved the establishment of an African Centre of Meteorological Applications for Development.

Member states are assisted in the assessment and use of water resources, and the development of river-basins common to more than one country. A programme of activities for marine development was begun in 1983, with particular reference to the effects of the United Nations Convention on the Law of the Sea (adopted in 1982), and the subsequent establishment of 'exclusive economic zones' for coastal states.

ENERGY

Assistance is given in the development of energy resources, in planning and efficient utilization. A study of African coal resources began in 1984. Investigations are being made on development and use of non-conventional sources of energy including solar, geothermal and biogas energy. Maps of the primary energy resources of Africa were updated and published in 1984, and work on an atlas of energy resources continued. A study on the prospects of nuclear energy in Africa was completed in 1985. The African Regional Centre for Solar Energy, in Bujumbura, Burundi, was to be inaugurated in 1989.

INTERNATIONAL TRADE AND FINANCE

In its efforts to meet its mandate and the goals set out in the Lagos Plan of Action, ECA assists African countries in expanding trade among themselves and with other regions of the world and in promoting financial and monetary co-operation. ECA attempts to ensure that African countries should participate effectively in current international negotiations. To this end, assistance has been provided to member states in negotiations under UNCTAD and GATT; in the annual conferences of the IMF and IBRD; in negotiations with the European Community; and in meetings related to economic co-operation among developing countries. Studies have been prepared on problems and prospects likely to arise for the African region from the implementation of the Common Fund Agreement; the Generalized System of Trade Preferences; the impacts of exchange rate fluctuations on the economies of African countries; and on long-term implications of different debt arrangements for African economies. Other studies have also been undertaken on prospects for expansion of African trade with Arab, Latin American and European socialist countries.

The expansion of trade within Africa is constrained by the low level of industrial production, and by the strong emphasis on commodity trade. ECA encourages the diversification of production and the expansion of domestic trade structures, within regional economic groupings. ECA was instrumental in the establishment of the Preferential Trade Area for Eastern and Southern Africa (1983) and of the Economic Community of Central African States (1985). In West Africa, assistance has been provided to harmonize the trade liberalization programmes of the Economic Community of West African States (ECOWAS), the Communauté économique de l'Afrique de l'ouest (CEAO) and the Mano River Union.

ECA encouraged the founding in 1974 of the Association of African Trade Promotion Organizations, based in Morocco, and the establishment in 1984 of the Federation of African Chambers of Commerce, based in Egypt. In 1982 experts from central banks and ministries of finance adopted draft guidelines for the establishment of an African Monetary Fund, together with draft terms of reference for a feasibility study on the establishment of the Fund. A second meeting, held in 1985, agreed that the Fund's initial authorized capital should be US $2,000m., of which $750m. should be paid during the first five years, with participation of up to $250m. by non-African members.

As part of its programme on trade expansion, the activities of ECA in the field of transnational corporations (TNC) have included the preparation of several studies on transnational corporations, e.g. (during 1987) on the role of joint ventures in Mauritius, the transfer of technology in the Algerian petrochemicals industry, and the impact of the TNC on social development (the promotion of baby-food).

In June 1987 ECA organized an international conference on African economic recovery, held in Abuja, Nigeria, which discussed the region's heavy external debts and the need for more favourable trading conditions for African commodities.

PUBLIC ADMINISTRATION, MANAGEMENT AND MANPOWER

The Public Administration, Management and Manpower Division aims to assist governments and public corporations in, for example, budgeting and financial management; planning of human resources; and administration of fellowships and scholarships. It conducts studies and analyses and provides advisory services and training programmes in public administration.

The Division services the Conference of Ministers Responsible for Human Resources, Planning, Development and Utilization and meetings of various African professional bodies, and supports regional and sub-regional institutions such as the African Institute for Higher Technical Training and Research in Nairobi, Kenya, and the Eastern and Southern African Management Institute in Arusha, Tanzania.

BUDGET

ECA's share of the UN budget for the two years 1988–89 was US $44.2m.

PUBLICATIONS

Report of the Executive Secretary (every 2 years).

African Statistical Yearbook.

Foreign Trade Statistics for Africa series.
   Direction of Trade (quarterly).
   Summary Table (annually).

Statistical Information Bulletin for Africa (annually).

Statistical Newsletter (2 a year).

Directory of African Statisticians (every 2 years).

African Socio-Economic Indicators (every 2 years).

Focus on African Industry (2 a year).

Survey of Economic Conditions in Africa (annually).

Survey of Economic Conditions in Africa (annually).

African Directory of Demographers (irregular).

African Population Newsletter (quarterly).

African Population Studies Series (irregular).

Demographic Handbook for Africa (irregular).

African Trade (quarterly).

Bulletin of ECA-sponsored Institutions (annually).

Rural Progress (quarterly).

Economic and Social Commission for Western Asia—ESCWA

Address: Amiriyah, POB 27, Baghdad, Iraq.

Telephone: 5569400-49.

Telex: 213468.

The UN Economic Commission for Western Asia was established in 1974 by a resolution of the UN Economic and Social Council (ECOSOC), to provide facilities of a wider scope for those countries previously served by the UN Economic and Social Office in Beirut (UNESOB). The name 'Economic and Social Commission for Western Asia' (ESCWA) was adopted in 1985.

MEMBERS

Bahrain
Egypt
Iraq
Jordan
Kuwait
Lebanon
Oman
Palestine Liberation
   Organization (PLO)
Qatar
Saudi Arabia
Syria
United Arab Emirates
Yemen Arab Republic
Yemen, People's Democratic
   Republic

Organization

(October 1988)

COMMISSION

The sessions of the Commission (held annually until 1987, and every two years from 1987 onwards) are attended by representatives of member states, of UN bodies and specialized agencies, of regional and intergovernmental organizations, and of other states attending as observers.

SECRETARIAT

In 1982 the Commission established its permanent headquarters in Baghdad, Iraq.

Divisions:
   Development Planning
   Joint ESCWA/FAO Agriculture
   Joint ESCWA/UNIDO Industry
   Administration

Natural Resources, Science and Technology
Human Settlements
Transport, Communications and Tourism
Social Development and Population
Statistics
Technical Co-operation
Programme Planning and Co-ordination
Environmental Co-ordination
Information

Executive Secretary: (vacant).

Activities

ESCWA undertakes or sponsors studies of economic and technological problems of the region, collects and disseminates information, and provides advisory services.

ESCWA's development plans for the 1980s comprised the following points: making the best use of natural resources; strengthening the regional economy so as to reduce dependence on external sources, such as food imports, and to cut trade imbalances; planned use of petroleum energy; development of human resources; regulation of the movement of workers between countries; integration of women in development.

Owing to limits on recruitment imposed by the budgetary crisis affecting the United Nations, one-third of ESCWA's professional posts were vacant at the beginning of 1987, and the Commission's work programme for 1986–87 was curtailed accordingly.

Much of ESCWA's work is carried out in co-operation with other UN bodies. It conducts industrial studies for individual countries in conjunction with UNIDO. It co-operates with FAO in regional planning, food security and management of agricultural resources; in 1983–84, for example, a joint mission was undertaken with FAO and UNDP to Egypt, Iraq, Kuwait and Saudi Arabia, to assess training needs in agricultural planning and project analysis. UNDP supports ESCWA's work on household surveys in western Asia and the Arab Planning Institute in Kuwait. Work is also undertaken with UNFPA in population programmes, with ILO in statistical surveys on labour, with UNCTAD in development planning and maritime transport training, and with UNEP in integrating environmental considerations (particularly control of desertification) into development programmes.

The programme of work and priorities comprises studies of various technical and socio-economic problems, particularly those demanding inter-country and sub-regional co-operation. The main areas are:

food and agriculture;

development planning (particularly in the least-developed countries in the region);

human settlement (particularly housing finance and city management);

industrial development (appraisal of potential, co-ordination of policies);

international trade (identification of intra-regional trade and integration opportunities);

labour, management and employment (making the best use of available manpower, development of required skills);

natural resources (energy planning, minerals and water development);

science and technology (problems of dependence on imported technology; training of manpower);

social development (welfare, participation in development, training and planning);

statistics (improvement of procedures, adopting uniform standards);

transport, communications and tourism (multinational shipping enterprises, railway networks, road construction and maintenance, and tourism development);

transnational corporations.

BUDGET

ESCWA's share of the UN budget for the two years 1988–89 was US $32.6m.

PUBLICATIONS

Agriculture and Development (annually).

Population Bulletin (2 a year).

Studies on Development Problems in Selected Countries of the Middle East (annually).

Statistical Abstract (annually).

Survey of Economic and Social Developments in the ESCWA Region (annually).

External Trade Bulletin.

National Accounts Studies.

Reports and studies.

OTHER UNITED NATIONS BODIES

International Sea-Bed Authority

The Authority is to be established one year after the United Nations Convention on the Law of the Sea, adopted in 1982, has been ratified by 60 countries. The seat of the Authority is to be in Kingston, Jamaica.

Organization
(October 1988)

ASSEMBLY
The Assembly is to be the supreme organ of the Authority, consisting of representatives of all parties to the Convention, and will establish policies, approve the budget and elect council members.

COUNCIL
The Council will be elected by the Assembly, and is to consist of 36 members, of whom 18 are to be elected from four 'major interest groups'—the four states who are the largest investors in sea-bed minerals, the four major importers of sea-bed minerals, the four major land-based exporters of the same minerals, and six developing countries representing special interests—while 18 are to be elected on a general basis, but ensuring that all regions of the world are represented. The Council is to decide on the most important questions by consensus rather than by voting.

OTHER ORGANS
The Council is to be assisted by an Economic Planning Commission, which will review supply, demand and pricing of sea-bed minerals and monitor the effects of sea-bed production on land-based mining concerns; and by a Legal and Technical Commission which will supervise sea-bed activities. Each Commission is to have 15 members, elected by the Council with regard for equitable geographical distribution and the representation of special interests. The Sea-Bed Disputes Chamber of the International Tribunal for the Law of the Sea will adjudicate on disputes with respect to activities.

PREPARATORY COMMISSION
Address: Office for Ocean Affairs and the Law of the Sea, United Nations Plaza, New York, NY 10017, USA.

Special Representative of the Secretary-General for the Law of the Sea: SATYA N. NANDAN (Fiji).

The Preparatory Commission, which first met in 1983 and held its sixth session in March/April 1988, was formed to set up the different organs of the Authority pending the entering into force of the Convention. It is also to act as an executive body when registering the applications of pioneer investors.

The Law of the Sea Convention

The third UN Conference on the Law of the Sea (UNCLOS) began its work in 1973, with the aim of regulating maritime activities by defining zones and boundaries, ensuring fair exploitation of resources, and providing machinery for settlement of disputes. Negotiations, involving over 160 countries, continued until 1982, having been delayed in 1981 when the newly elected US Government decided to review its policy. The UN Convention on the Law of the Sea was finally adopted by UNCLOS in April 1982; 130 states voted in its favour, while the USA, Israel, Turkey and Venezuela voted against, and there were 17 abstentions including the Federal Republic of Germany, the USSR and the United Kingdom. The Convention was opened for signing in December for a two-year period: by 1987 159 states had signed, but the USA, the United Kingdom, and the Federal Republic of Germany refused to sign, and by March 1988 only 35 states had ratified the Convention, which requires 60 ratifications before it can come into force. The main provisions of the Convention are as follows:

Coastal states are allowed sovereignty over their territorial waters of up to 12 miles in breadth; foreign vessels are to be allowed 'innocent passage' through these waters.

Ships and aircraft of all states are allowed 'transit passage' through straits used for international navigation.

Archipelagic states (composed of islands) have sovereignty over a sea area enclosed by straight lines drawn between the outermost points of the islands.

Coastal states have sovereign rights in a 200-mile exclusive economic zone with respect to natural resources and certain economic activities, and rights over the adjacent continental shelf up to 350 miles from the shore under specified circumstances.

All states have freedom of navigation, overflight, scientific research and fishing on the high seas, but must co-operate in measures to conserve living resources.

A 'parallel system' is to be established for exploiting the international sea-bed, where all activities are to be supervised by the International Sea-Bed Authority. The Authority will conduct its own mining operations and also contract with private and state ventures to give them mining rights.

States are bound to control pollution and co-operate in forming preventive rules, and incur penalties for failing to combat pollution.

Marine scientific research in the zones under national jurisdiction is subject to the prior consent of the coastal state, but consent may be denied only under specific circumstances.

States must submit disputes on the application and interpretation of the Convention to a compulsory procedure entailing decisions binding on all parties. An International Tribunal for the Law of the Sea is to be established.

The objections of the USA and other industrialized nations which have refused to support the Convention concern the provisions for exploitation of the international ocean bed, and particularly the minerals to be found there (chiefly manganese, cobalt, copper and nickel), envisaged as the 'common heritage of mankind'. It is argued that those countries which possess adequate technology for deep-sea mining would be insufficiently represented in the new Authority; the operations of private mining consortia, according to the objectors, would be unacceptably limited by the stipulations that their technology should be shared with a supranational mining enterprise, and that production should be limited in order to protect land-based producers.

Office of the United Nations Disaster Relief Co-ordinator—UNDRO

Address: Palais des Nations, 1211 Geneva 10, Switzerland.
Telephone: (022) 346011.
Telex: 28148.

UNDRO was established in 1972 to mobilize and co-ordinate international emergency relief to disaster-stricken areas, and to cooperate in promoting disaster preparedness and prevention.

Organization
(October 1988)

DISASTER RELIEF CO-ORDINATOR
In March 1972 a Disaster Relief Co-ordinator was appointed, at Under-Secretary-General level, to report directly to the UN Secretary-General. UNDRO is a separate entity within the UN Secretariat and consists of a Relief Co-ordination and Preparedness Branch and a Prevention and Support Services Branch.
Co-ordinator: M'Hamed Essaafi (Tunisia).

FIELD ORGANIZATION
UNDRO is represented in developing countries by the Resident Representatives of UNDP (q.v.). UNDRO also has a Liaison Office at UN headquarters in New York.
Liaison Office: Room 2935A, United Nations, New York, NY 10017; tel. (212) 754-5704; telex 421852.

Activities

The Co-ordinator's mandate derives from a number of General Assembly resolutions on assistance in case of natural disaster and other disaster situations. The Office has four main functions: relief co-ordination; disaster preparedness; disaster prevention; and the provision of public information, data processing services and communications. UNDRO has also entered into agreements (Memoranda of Understanding) with other UN agencies, defining areas and means of co-operation, in order to strengthen the collective response of the United Nations system to disasters.

RELIEF CO-ORDINATION
The Office aims to ensure that, in case of natural or other disaster, all emergency relief activities are mobilized and co-ordinated so as to supply the needs of the disaster-stricken country in a timely and effective manner. UNDRO provides 24-hour monitoring of natural disasters and emergency situations as they occur. Once a disaster situation calling for international assistance is recognized and a request from the government of the affected country is received, the UNDP Resident Representative, often assisted by an UNDRO relief co-ordination officer, reviews the damage and the immediate relief needs with the competent local authorities, and communicates the findings to UNDRO headquarters. The extent and the compound nature of disasters often calls for an assessment by specialists in various spheres, and multi-agency missions are organized in which representatives of specialized agencies and other organizations take part. Close co-operation is maintained with the other organizations of the UN system and with other intergovernmental and non-governmental organizations. UNDRO places emphasis on obtaining and disseminating all relevant information in good time, so as to avoid waste or misuse of resources, and to determine the timing of the response. During the two years 1986-87 UNDRO was involved, in varying degrees, in 110 disaster situations, of which a considerable number were of a long-standing nature, requiring UNDRO assistance over a lengthy period. The more complex situations often require concerted relief programmes whereby bilateral donors, the United Nations system and other agencies provide assistance to the stricken population. During 1986-87 major disasters requiring UNDRO involvement included cyclonic storms and floods in Bangladesh, the release of toxic gas from Lake Nyos in Cameroon, an earthquake in El Salvador, floods in Bolivia, Haiti and Peru, drought in Ethiopia and Sudan, armed conflict and floods in Lebanon, cyclones in Madagascar, the Solomon Islands and Vanuatu, drought and armed conflict in Mozambique, a tsunami (tidal wave) in the Maldives, civil strife in the People's Democratic Republic of Yemen, and a widespread plague of locusts in Africa.

DISASTER PREPAREDNESS AND PREVENTION
UNDRO promotes the integration of human and material resources and of different skills and disciplines into an effective national system of readiness, in order to minimize the loss of lives and the damage when a disaster strikes.

Disaster preparedness advisory missions are usually undertaken by consultants recruited by UNDRO, who advise governments on the best methods of improving their organization to deal with all kinds of disasters, and not just those which arise from natural causes. The recommendations of these missions sometimes call for specific projects to be carried out, and if these cannot be funded by the government then UNDRO may be asked to seek the necessary financing from donors. Preparedness organizations naturally need trained personnel, and UNDRO arranges or takes part in many seminars for disaster managers and others concerned in relief work, in the preparation and issue of warnings, and in the application of new technologies to disaster work generally. UNDRO is also engaged in attempts to remove obstacles to the rapid delivery of international relief, and this requires willingness by donors as well as by potential recipients to streamline procedures and to waive normal legal requirements for the movement of relief goods and personnel.

In the area of disaster prevention UNDRO is engaged in the development and application of techniques of vulnerability analysis, and in promoting the use of legislation, land-use planning and other inexpensive methods of reducing or eliminating disaster risks. UNDRO is also engaged, jointly with other UN agencies, in attempts to reduce both the hazards created by industrial activities and the effects of industrial accidents.

In 1986-87 some 30 projects for disaster prevention and preparedness, both national and regional, were in various stages of implementation: for example, the Seismic Risk Reduction Project in the Balkans area of eastern Europe, the Co-operative Project for Seismic Risk Reduction in the Mediterranean Region, the Pan-Caribbean Disaster Preparedness and Prevention Project, and a seminar on earthquake prediction. A disaster mitigation programme for the Pacific area was being prepared during this period, together with a regional prevention and preparedness programme for Latin America. National projects were co-ordinated in Egypt, Haiti, Indonesia, Madagascar, Nepal and Niger.

In 1986 UNDRO established a warehouse in Pisa, Italy, which stocks relief supplies ready for shipment anywhere in the world.

In 1988, following a decision by the UN General Assembly to designate the 1990s as the International Decade for Natural Disaster Reduction, UNDRO was host to the first meetings of an inter-agency working group and a group of experts preparing for the Decade, and was to provide a secretariat for the Decade.

PUBLIC INFORMATION, DATA PROCESSING AND COMMUNICATIONS
As well as issuing the publications listed below, UNDRO maintains a reference library and a data processing and communications unit. There is a large and comprehensive data base of disaster-related information, also available to other organizations. A computer-based information network for internal disaster management, UNDRONET, is also accessible to any individual or organization actively engaged in disaster management. UNDRONET provides an electronic mail service, a bulletin board and access to data bases, and is connected to all other UN information networks.

FINANCE
The amount allocated to UNDRO in the regular budget of the UN for the two years 1984-85 was US $4.8m., and UNDRO's share for 1986-87 amounted to $6m. In 1986-87 voluntary contributions to cover operational and administrative costs amounted to $2.2m., and a further $21m. was channelled through UNDRO for relief and technical assistance.

As a co-ordinating Office, UNDRO is not itself regarded as a principal source of relief assistance, although the Co-ordinator has the authority to make a contribution from the regular budget not exceeding $50,000 for any one disaster (and not exceeding in total $360,000 in one year) to meet immediate needs, e.g. for medicines, food or the transport of life-saving equipment. The Co-ordinator is also empowered to receive contributions in kind or in cash to be used for providing relief supplies. However, the greater part of the international assistance provided goes direct to the country concerned, and it is normally expected that the amount and nature of these contributions will be based upon the information given in UNDRO 'situation reports' which are sent by telex to donor sources and other interested organizations throughout the world. During the two years 1986–87 emergency relief accounted for by UNDRO exceeded $1,400m.

PUBLICATIONS

Annual Report to the UN General Assembly.
UNDRO News (6 a year).
Disaster News in Brief (annually).

Disaster Prevention and Mitigation: a Compendium of Current Knowledge (12 vols).
Guidelines for Disaster Prevention (3 vols).
Shelter after Disaster: Guidelines for Assistance.
Volcanic Emergency Management.
Disasters and the Disabled.

Technical papers, case reports, Disaster Assessment Mission reports.

United Nations Centre for Human Settlements—UNCHS (Habitat)

Address: POB 30030, Nairobi, Kenya.
Telephone: 333930/520600.
Telex: 22996.

UNCHS (Habitat) was established in October 1978 to service the intergovernmental Commission on Human Settlements, and to serve as a focus for human settlements activities in the UN system.

Organization
(October 1988)

UN COMMISSION ON HUMAN SETTLEMENTS

The Commission (see ECOSOC, p. 19) is the governing body of UNCHS. It meets annually and has 58 members, serving for four years. Sixteen members are from Africa, 13 from Asia, six from Eastern European Socialist countries, 10 from Latin America and 13 from Western Europe and other countries.

CENTRE FOR HUMAN SETTLEMENTS

The Centre's work covers technical co-operation, research and development (incorporating settlement planning and policies, shelter and community services, construction and infrastructure), training and information, audio-visual and documentation. Other units include the Office of the Executive Director and the Division of Administration. The Habitat and Human Settlements Foundation (HHSF) serves as the financial arm of the Centre.

The Executive Director oversees the work of the Centre, which is to service the Commission on Human Settlements and to implement its resolutions; to ensure the integration and co-ordination of technical co-operation, research and the exchange and dissemination of information; and to execute human settlements projects funded by the United Nations Development Programme (UNDP), funds-in-trust or other contributions.

Executive Director: Dr ARCOT RAMACHANDRAN.

Activities

UNCHS (Habitat) assists governments in activities related to human settlements. It supports and conducts research, provides technical co-operation and disseminates information, under the eight sub-programmes listed below. At the end of 1987 activities included 178 technical co-operation projects in 87 countries, with project budgets exceeding US $18m. for 1987; of these, 68 were in Africa, 42 in Latin America and the Caribbean, 39 in Asia and the Pacific, 16 in western Asia and 10 in Europe.

UNCHS also conducts research and training and organizes meetings of experts. Advisory services are provided to governments on building materials and methods, financing procedures, and the application of advanced technology to human settlements planning. UNCHS runs an informal network of human settlements planners who use microcomputers.

UNCHS acted as the secretariat for the International Year of Shelter for the Homeless (1987), which was intended to persuade governments to adopt practical solutions to the shelter needs of disadvantaged people. In October of that year it published the Global Report on Human Settlements, an analysis of world-wide and regional developments over the past 10 years. In 1988 the Commission on Human Settlements approved a Global Shelter Strategy to the year 2000.

Settlement Policies and Strategies

This sub-programme aims to identify high-priority settlements policy issues and to prepare guidelines for formulating and implementing national policies.

Settlements Planning

UNCHS promotes the use of effective methods of settlements planning in both urban and rural areas. In 1986–87 the main emphasis was on forecasting settlements trends and prospects, and on the planning and development of rural settlements. During 1986 training courses in community participation were in operation in Bolivia, Sri Lanka and Zambia.

Shelter and Community Services

This sub-programme assists in improving conditions and services for low-income settlements in urban and rural areas, by upgrading squatter settlements, rehabilitating inner-city slums and supporting co-operative housing: community participation is seen as an essential part of this work.

Development of the Indigenous Construction Sector

Work under this sub-programme concentrates on increasing the capacity of the construction sector to meet demand. Reports being prepared during 1986 covered earth construction; planning of the construction industry using indigenous methods; reformulation of building acts, regulations and codes in African countries; and the use of selected indigenous building materials with potential for wide application in developing countries. Manuals were being prepared on lime, stone construction and earth construction.

Low-cost Infrastructure for Human Settlements

UNCHS encourages the development of appropriate infrastructure. In 1985–86 reports were published on traffic in low-income urban settlements and on low-cost vehicles, and the Centre was in the process of preparing guidelines for legislation on water supply and sanitation; a design manual on shallow sewerage; and guidelines for the operation of low-cost water supply and sanitation systems. It published reports on the use of solar energy, and on natural forces in the design of buildings, and studies on energy-efficient housing.

Land

This sub-programme promotes effective government measures for developing land for human settlements, essentially through evaluating regulations on land use, analysing methods of land acquisition and allocation, and collecting data on land use.

Mobilization of Finance

This sub-programme aims to mobilize financial resources for the development of human settlements. Particular emphasis is placed on monitoring the performance of human settlements finance institutions, the role of non-conventional finance mechanisms and support to community-based institutions.

Human Settlements Institutions and Management

UNCHS helps to establish or strengthen institutions and management capabilities through case studies, guidelines and training.

FINANCE

The amount allocated to the Centre in the UN budget for the two years 1988–89 was US $8.4m., and extra-budgetary resources were expected to amount to $40m., while contributions to the HHSF were expected to total $6m.

PUBLICATIONS

UNCHS Habitat News (3 a year).

Shelter Bulletin (3 a year).

Technical reports and studies, occasional papers, bibliographies, directories.

United Nations Children's Fund—UNICEF

Address: 3 United Nations Plaza, New York, NY 10017, USA.
Telephone: (212) 326-7000.
Telex: 175989.

UNICEF was established in 1946 by the General Assembly as the UN International Children's Emergency Fund, to meet the emergency needs of children in post-war Europe and China. In 1950 its mandate was changed to respond to the needs of children in developing countries. In 1953 the General Assembly decided that UNICEF should continue its work, as a permanent arm of the UN system, with an emphasis on programmes giving long-term benefits to children everywhere, particularly those in developing countries who are in the greatest need.

Organization
(October 1988)

EXECUTIVE BOARD

The governing body of UNICEF meets once a year to establish policy, review programmes and commit funds. Membership comprises 41 governments from all regions, elected in rotation for a three-year term by ECOSOC.

SECRETARIAT

The Executive Director of UNICEF is appointed by the UN Secretary-General in consultation with the Executive Board. The administration of UNICEF and the appointment and direction of staff are the responsibility of the Executive Director, under policy directives laid down by the Executive Board, and under a broad authority delegated to the Executive Director by the Secretary-General. UNICEF has a network of country and regional offices serving 119 countries in the developing world; these offices are supported by partner national committees and other voluntary agencies.

Executive Director: JAMES P. GRANT (USA).

MAJOR UNICEF OFFICES

Europe: Palais des Nations, 1211 Geneva 10, Switzerland.
Eastern and Southern Africa: POB 44145, Nairobi, Kenya.
Middle East and North Africa: POB 811721, Amman, Jordan.
Central and West Africa: BP 443, Abidjan 04, Côte d'Ivoire.
The Americas and Caribbean: Apdo Aéreo 7555, Bogotá, Colombia.
East Asia and Pakistan: POB 2-154, Bangkok 10200, Thailand.
South Central Asia: UNICEF House, 73 Lodi Estate, New Delhi 110003, India.
Australia and New Zealand: GPO Box 4045, Sydney, NSW 2001, Australia.
Japan: c/o UN Information Centre, 22nd Floor, Shin Aoyama Bldg, Nishikan, 1-1, Minami-Aoyama 1-chome, Minato-ku, Tokyo 107, Japan.

NATIONAL COMMITTEES

There are 34 National Committees, mostly in industrialized countries, whose volunteer members raise money through various activities, including the sale of greetings cards; the Committees also undertake advocacy efforts within their own societies and act as focal points of local support for governmental fund-raising.

Activities

UNICEF's efforts for the 1980s concentrate on the drastic reduction of infant mortality rates through an attack on the principal causes of preventable death and disease, using community-based health and other first-level services and drawing on a wide variety of national and community organizations for support in mobilizing the necessary human and financial resources. In 1986 UNICEF was working with the governments of 119 developing countries by assisting in the development, administration and evaluation of services benefiting children; delivery of technical supplies, equipment and other aid for extending those services; and providing funds to strengthen training of national personnel. UNICEF facilitates the exchange of programming experience among developing countries, and encourages governments to undertake a regular review of the situation of their children and to incorporate a national policy for children in their comprehensive development plans. UNICEF provides assistance on the basis of mutually agreed priorities for children in collaboration with the governments concerned. Priority is given by UNICEF to aiding children in the lower-income groups in the least-developed countries.

Community participation is the key element of the 'basic services' approach adopted by UNICEF in 1975. This approach emphasizes meeting the basic needs of children through community involvement in the planning and running of services. By mobilizing community energies, drawing on local skills through simple training, and the use of relevant and available technology, a great deal can be done to improve maternal and child care, introduce safe water supplies and sanitation, expand primary and non-formal education, including nutrition education for mothers and children, improve the household production of nutritious foods and improve the situation of women, particularly through training and support for income-generating activities.

Economic stringency in the 1980s sharpened the search for innovative, low-cost solutions to development problems. Alternative approaches to tackling such major problems of child health and nutrition as immunizable diseases, diarrhoeal dehydration and others have made possible a virtual revolution in child survival and development, with a substantial reduction of death and disease. Since 1982 UNICEF has advocated a concerted international effort to make this potential a reality, focusing on: (a) immunizable, child-killing diseases such as measles, diphtheria, tuberculosis, whooping cough, tetanus and poliomyelitis; (b) diarrhoeal disease; (c) early detection of malnutrition through growth monitoring; (d) promotion of breast-feeding and proper weaning; (e) female education; and (f) birth spacing. The new approaches depend crucially upon community participation and therefore build upon the community-based services strategy which UNICEF has been advocating and supporting since 1975. An allied dimension is social mobilization, by which community organizations and other groups and sectors of society involve themselves in broad, mutually-reinforcing efforts, often on a nation-wide basis. This approach is exemplified by a number of recent immunization campaigns, such as those undertaken by Bolivia, Brazil, Burkina Faso, Colombia, the Dominican Republic, Mozambique, Nigeria and Turkey, among others. By 1987 78 countries had committed themselves to the UN goal of universal child immunization by 1990.

In several crucial health areas, new medical technologies have substantially improved the chances of success. In particular, the development of a simple mixture of salt plus sugar or cereal starch in water (oral rehydration therapy) has revolutionized family and community-level treatment of diarrhoeal dehydration, one of the leading causes of death for infants and young children.

UNICEF estimated that about 1.5m. child deaths were being averted each year during the mid-1980s by oral rehydration therapy and immunization. Sustained efforts of this kind against the major killers of children, it was felt, could reduce child death and disability by 50% in much of the developing world by the early 1990s.

In emergency relief and rehabilitation, UNICEF works closely with other UN agencies (as well as with numerous non-governmental organizations); in 1986 it provided about US $33m. worth of assistance to 15 countries affected by disasters. Aid was in the form of shelter materials, medicaments, water supply equipment, food supplements, and the support or strengthening of essential services. UNICEF supports the initiative of the UN Secretary-General, aimed at mobilizing extra resources for the victims of drought, famine and conflict in the African continent. In Lebanon, where a significant role has been undertaken since 1974, UNICEF is continuing to co-operate in a major UN programme of rehabilitation.

FINANCE

UNICEF's work is accomplished with voluntary contributions from both governments and non-governmental sources. Total income in 1986 came to US $463m. Income from governments and inter-governmental organizations accounted for 75% of this.

UNICEF's income is divided between contributions for general resources and contributions for specific purposes or emergencies. General resources are the funds available to fulfil commitments for co-operation in country programmes approved by the Executive Board, and to meet administrative and programme support expenditures. They include contributions from governments, the net income from greetings cards sales, funds contributed by the public (mainly through National Committees) and other income. These funds amounted to $299m. in 1986. Contributions for specific purposes are those sought by UNICEF from governments and intergovernmental organizations as supplementary funds to support projects for which general resources are insufficient, or for relief and rehabilitation programmes in emergency situations. Supplementary funding in 1986 amounted to $164m.

UNICEF PROGRAMME EXPENDITURE BY SECTOR
(1986)

	Cost (US $ million)
Basic health (including family planning)	119.4
Water supply	58.2
Nutrition	17.1
Community and family-based services for children	16.1
Formal and non-formal education	30.7
Planning and project support	52.3
Emergency relief	32.1
Total	325.9

PUBLICATIONS

State of the World's Children (annually, in English, French, Spanish and Arabic).
UNICEF Annual Report (summarizes UNICEF policies and programmes; in English, French and Spanish).
Facts about UNICEF (annually, in English, French and Spanish).
Les Carnets de l'Enfance/Assignment Children (concerned with planning development for women, children and youth; in English and French).

United Nations Conference on Trade and Development—UNCTAD

Address: Palais des Nations, 1211 Geneva 10, Switzerland.
Telephone: (022) 346011.
Telex: 289696.

UNCTAD was established by the UN General Assembly as one of its permanent organs in December 1964. Its role is to promote international trade, particularly that of developing countries, with a view to accelerating economic development. It is the principal instrument of the General Assembly for deliberation and negotiation in the field of international trade and related issues of international economic cooperation.

Organization
(October 1988)

CONFERENCE
The Conference is held every four years in different capitals of member states. Seventh session: Geneva, Switzerland, July 1987.
Secretary-General: KENNETH DADZIE (Ghana).
Deputy Secretaries-General: YVES BERTHELOT (France), DIOGO DE GASPAR (Brazil).

TRADE AND DEVELOPMENT BOARD
Between Conferences, the continuing work of the organization is carried out by the Trade and Development Board together with its various committees and subsidiary bodies.

MAIN COMMITTEES
The Board has six main committees: on commodities, manufactures, invisibles and financing related to trade, shipping, technology, and economic co-operation among developing countries; there is also a special committee on preferences.

COMMODITY CONFERENCES
UNCTAD has primary responsibility within the United Nations system for the negotiation and renegotiation of international commodity agreements. For this purpose, it convenes commodity conferences as required.

Activities

UNCTAD's concern covers the entire spectrum of policies in both developed and developing countries which influence the external trade and payments and economic progress of developing countries.

UNCTAD's efforts to strengthen the commodity sector in developing countries are carried out through the Integrated Programme for Commodities (IPC), adopted by the Conference in 1976. Through international agreements by both consuming and producing countries on individual commodities (some of which already existed before the Programme's inception, e.g. agreements on cocoa, coffee, sugar, wheat, olive oil and tin), the IPC aims to stabilize prices by the use of 'buffer stocks' and/or export quotas, and to improve the productivity and competitiveness of the developing exporters. Under the IPC, three international commodity agreements have so far been concluded: on rubber (entered into force in April 1982), jute and jute products (January 1984) and tropical timber (April 1985). Renegotiation of existing agreements due for renewal also takes place under the IPC, e.g. the negotiations on sugar which took place, unsuccessfully, in 1984. (See also the section on Other International Organizations—Commodities.)

A report by the UNCTAD Secretariat in 1985, however, showed that the commodity agreements had in many respects failed to achieve their aims: although the agreements on coffee, wheat, tin and rubber had so far been relatively successful in stabilizing prices, the agreements on cocoa and sugar had virtually collapsed, and little progress had been made in the longer-term objectives of improving developing countries' export earnings and competitiveness and enabling them to cope with falls in demand. The report argued that the success of such agreements depended on a high degree of participation by both producers and consumers, suggesting that the cocoa agreement had failed owing to the absence of the USA and the Ivory Coast (the largest consumer and producer respectively) while the non-participation of the USA and the European Community had led to the failure of the sugar agreement. The collapse of the International Tin Agreement in October 1985 cast further doubt on the efficacy of the commodity agreements.

Another important component of the IPC is the Common Fund for Commodities, with capital of US $470m. to support buffer stocks, together with voluntary contributions of about $255m., intended for longer-term purposes such as research, market promotion and conservation of resources. The Fund's articles of agreement were adopted in 1980. For it to become operational, ratification by countries that would contribute at least two-thirds of the capital was necessary: this was not achieved until July 1988.

Another major concern of UNCTAD is the expansion and diversification of the export trade of developing countries in manufactured and semi-manufactured products, chiefly through the Generalized System of Preferences, under which manufactured goods that are exported by developing countries receive preferential tariff treatment by developed countries. A comprehensive review of the system was to take place in 1990. In 1980 UNCTAD adopted a set of rules for the control of restrictive business practices that adversely affect international trade: these rules were reviewed by a special conference in November 1985. UNCTAD also has a mandate to review problems of protectionism and structural adjustment, and the secretariat has established a comprehensive database on trade measures.

In the area of finance, UNCTAD is intended to give particular attention to the debt problems of developing countries, and has negotiated measures of debt relief for the poorer of these countries, together with a set of guidelines for dealing with future debt problems before they reach a critical stage.

UNCTAD also seeks to help developing countries to increase their participation in world shipping. It negotiated the Convention on a Code of Conduct for Liner Conferences, which entered into force in 1983, and in 1985 it was studying the problems of securing for developing countries a greater share in the bulk cargo sector. Another UNCTAD initiative led to the adoption in 1980 of the UN Convention on International Multimodal Transport of Goods, which establishes a single liability regime for the carriage of goods entailing more than one mode of transport. In 1984–85 UNCTAD serviced the UN Conference on Conditions for the Registration of Ships, which drew up an agreement on ownership and manning of open-registry ships (flying 'flags of convenience'). The Convention on Registration of Ships was adopted in 1986, subject to ratification by a minimum of 40 countries, representing at least one-quarter of the world's shipping.

UNCTAD's work also covers the transfer of technology to developing countries. The sixth session of the UN Conference on an International Code of Conduct on the Transfer of Technology, in June 1985, failed to reach agreement and referred the issue to the UN General Assembly.

Through technical assistance activities, studies and the arrangement of bilateral consultations, UNCTAD seeks to promote trade between developing countries and the socialist countries of eastern Europe. It also supports programmes of economic co-operation between developing countries themselves. In 1981 it serviced the UN Conference on the Least Developed Countries, which adopted the 'Substantial New Programme of Action' for the 1980s for the 36 poorest countries; a mid-term review of this programme was carried out by UNCTAD in October 1985. In its 1986 annual report, UNCTAD analysed the effect of the developed countries' deflationary policies on commodity prices and on the developing economies, and called for the developed countries to adopt co-ordinated fiscal and monetary measures in order to stimulate the world economy. UNCTAD also proposed measures (based on domestic bankruptcy legislation in the USA) to deal with the international debt crisis, allowing debtor countries to rebuild their debt-servicing capacity.

At the 1987 session of UNCTAD, developing countries failed to persuade the developed countries to increase debt relief or to reduce interest rates, but the Conference agreed on the need for flexibility in the rescheduling of debts, so that the medium-term economic plans of debtor governments were not imperilled by the short-term austerity measures imposed by creditors. The Conference also agreed on the importance of reducing restrictive trade practices through the current round of negotiations under the General Agreement on Tariffs and Trade (q.v.). In 1988 UNCTAD proposed (in its annual *Trade and Development Report*) that at least 30% of debts owed to commercial banks by the 15 most heavily indebted countries (principally Argentina, Brazil and Mexico) should be written off.

The International Trade Centre in Geneva is operated jointly by GATT and UNCTAD.

FINANCE

The budget approved by the UN General Assembly for the two-year period 1988–89 was US $78.9m.

PUBLICATIONS

UNCTAD Bulletin (monthly).
Trade and Development (annually).
Trade and Development Report (annually).
Handbook of International Trade and Development Statistics (annually).
Monthly Commodity Price Bulletin.
Guide to UNCTAD Publications (monthly).
Reports.

United Nations Development Programme—UNDP

Address: One United Nations Plaza, New York, NY 10017, USA.
Telephone: (212) 906-5000.

The Programme was established in 1965 by the General Assembly to help the developing countries increase the wealth-producing capabilities of their natural and human resources.

Organization
(October 1988)

The UNDP is responsible to the UN General Assembly, to which it reports through ECOSOC.

GOVERNING COUNCIL

The Council, which meets annually, is the policy-making body of UNDP, and comprises representatives of 48 countries; 27 seats are filled by developing countries and 21 by economically more advanced countries; one-third of the membership changes each year.

SECRETARIAT

Administrator: WILLIAM H. DRAPER (USA).

REGIONAL BUREAUX

Headed by assistant administrators, the regional bureaux share the responsibility for implementing the programme with the Administrator's office. Within certain limitations, large-scale projects may be approved and funding allocated by the Administrator, and smaller-scale projects by the Resident Representatives, based in 112 countries.

The four regional bureaux, all at the Secretariat in New York, cover: Africa; Asia and the Pacific; the Arab states and Europe; and Latin America and the Caribbean; there is also a Division for Global and Interregional Projects.

FIELD OFFICES

In almost every country receiving UNDP assistance there is a Country Office, headed by the UNDP Resident Representative, who co-ordinates all UN technical assistance, advises the government on formulating the country programme, sees that field activities are carried out, and acts as the leader of the UN team of experts working in the country. Resident Representatives are normally designated as co-ordinators for all UN operational development activities; the field offices function as the primary presence of the UN in most developing countries.

EXECUTING AGENCIES

The following act as executing agencies or otherwise participate in the work of UNDP: the UN Department of Technical Co-operation for Development, the International Trade Centre and 26 of the UN agencies and organizations, three regional development banks, five regional economic commissions and the Arab Fund for Economic and Social Development. An Inter-Agency Task Force co-ordinates the activities of participating agencies.

Activities

As the world's largest source of grant technical assistance in developing countries, UNDP works with more than 150 governments and 36 international agencies for faster economic growth and better standards of living throughout the world. Agriculture (including forestry and fisheries) is the largest component of UNDP activities, accounting for about 21% of project expenditure in 1987 (see table). Most of the work is carried out in the field by the United Nations and its agencies, or by the government of the country concerned.

Assistance is mostly non-monetary, comprising the provision of experts' services, consultancies, equipment, and fellowships for advanced study abroad. In 1987 about 45% of spending on projects was for the services of experts, 24% was for equipment, 12% was for training, and the remainder was for other costs, such as maintenance of equipment. Many projects are designed to continue with national resources once UNDP assistance comes to an end.

Project work covers five main areas: locating, assessing and activating latent natural resources and other development assets; stimulating capital investment to help realize these possibilities; support for professional and vocational training; expansion of scientific research and applied technology; and strengthening of national and regional development planning.

Countries receiving UNDP assistance are allocated an indicative planning figure (IPF) for a five-year period. The IPF represents the approximate total funding that a country can expect to receive, based on a formula taking per caput GNP and other criteria into account. In partnership with UNDP's Country Offices, governments calculate their technical assistance requirements on the basis of this formula. Activities covering more than one country are developed by UNDP's Division for Global and Interregional Projects, in consultation with the relevant national and regional institutions.

In UNDP's Fourth Programming Cycle (1987-91), 80% of the resources available was to be devoted to the poorest developing countries, with per caput GNP of US $750 or less; within this group, countries with per caput GNP of less than $375 were to receive particular attention. For 1987-91 UNDP drew up 152 country programmes of medium-term technical assistance.

During 1986 UNDP created a Division for Women and Development, to ensure that women should play a greater part in UNDP-supported activities, and a Division for Non-Governmental Organizations, to encourage a more effective partnership with such organizations in development work. In the same year a system for providing short-term advisory services was initiated.

UNDP supports the Caribbean Project Development Facility (established in 1981) and the Africa Project Development Facility (established in 1986), which are administered by the International Finance Corporation (q.v.), and which aim to encourage private investment in these regions.

UNDP also takes part in emergency relief operations with UNDRO and other agencies. During 1986 it approved 27 relief projects.

FINANCE

The Development Programme is financed by the voluntary contributions of members of the United Nations and the Programme's participating Agencies. Voluntary pledges from member governments amounted to US $1,113.3m. for 1987 (including pledges to funds administered by UNDP, and co-financing of projects). Total expenditure in 1987 was estimated at $1,050m., of which $680m. was for field programmes (see table below) and the remainder was for planning, management and co-ordination by UNDP's headquarters staff and field offices, and project implementation services by 29 executing agencies.

UNDP EXPENDITURE BY SECTOR (1987)

	Estimated cost (US $ m. equivalent)
Agriculture, forestry and fisheries	141.5
General development, policies and planning	120.0
Natural resources	71.5
Industry	86.5
Transport and communication	72.0
Employment	30.5
Science and technology	39.5
Education	31.0
Health	33.5
Population, human settlements, humanitarian aid	32.0
Total (incl. other)	680.0

UNDP EXENDITURE BY REGION (1987)

	Estimated expenditure (US $ million)
Asia and the Pacific	249.0
Africa	235.0
Latin America and Caribbean	101.5
Arab states and Europe	70.0
Interregional and global	24.5
Total	680.0

PUBLICATIONS

Mini Report (annually: summary of Administrator's Report).
Co-operation South (quarterly).
World Development (6 a year).
Decade Watch (quarterly, on International Drinking Water Supply and Sanitation Decade).

Affiliated Organizations

UNITED NATIONS CAPITAL DEVELOPMENT FUND—UNCDF

The Fund was established in 1966 and became fully operational in 1974. It assists developing countries by supplementing existing sources of capital assistance, through grants and loans on concessionary terms. Rapid assistance is available to governments for small-scale projects directly and immediately benefiting the low-income groups who have not benefited from earlier development efforts. Assistance may be given to any of the member states of the UN system, and is not necessarily limited to specific projects. The Fund is mainly used for the benefit of the least-developed countries. In 1987 UNCDF approved a total of US $59m. in assistance for 59 projects. Voluntary contributions pledged for 1987 amounted to $32m.

Examples of projects financed by UNCDF include: creation of 'revolving funds' for village co-operatives to obtain supplies of seeds and fertilizers; credit for low-cost housing or small businesses; provision of facilities for irrigation, drinking-water and food storage; construction of roads, schools and health centres; and reafforestation of land.

UNITED NATIONS DEVELOPMENT FUND FOR WOMEN

This Fund (formerly the Voluntary Fund for the UN Decade for Women) became an associated fund of UNDP in 1985. Its purpose is to involve women in development and to support innovative activities benefiting women in all regions, e.g. small-scale group enterprises to raise incomes, and training in work-saving and fuel-conserving technologies. Pledges for 1987 totalled $4.8m.

UNITED NATIONS FUND FOR SCIENCE AND TECHNOLOGY FOR DEVELOPMENT—UNFSTD

UNFSTD was established in 1982 to help developing countries acquire the capacity to formulate science and technology policies linked to their development goals. Training and the exchange of information are also undertaken. In 1987 UNFSTD received $778,397 in contributions.

UNITED NATIONS REVOLVING FUND FOR NATURAL RESOURCES EXPLORATION—RFNRE

The RFNRE was established in 1974 to provide risk capital to finance exploration for natural resources (particularly minerals) in developing countries and, when discoveries are made, to help to attract investment. The revolving character of the Fund, which distinguishes it from most other UN system technical co-operation programmes, lies in the undertaking of contributing governments to make replenishment contributions to the Fund when the projects it finances lead to commercial production.

Contributions pledged to the Fund amounted to $2.7m. for 1987.

UNITED NATIONS SUDANO-SAHELIAN OFFICE—UNSO

UNSO's dual responsibility is to help eight countries of the Sahel region (members of the CILSS, q.v.) to carry out their medium- and long-term programmes for recovery from drought; and to assist them, along with 11 other Sudano-Sahelian and adjacent countries, in implementing the Plan of Action to Combat Desertification. Activities include planting improved crop strains; setting up food storage facilities; establishing agricultural implement workshops; developing transport and communications; agrometeorological and hydrological services; forest conservation and expansion; water resources management; sand dune fixation; and the development of alternative systems for energy production and overall policy planning. Voluntary contributions pledged for 1987 amounted to $6.8m., and other income (from trust funds and cost-sharing) was $13.9m.

UN Sahelian Regional Office: BP 366, ave Dimdolobsom, Ouagadougou, Burkina Faso; tel. 367-81; telex 5262; Chief WALLY N'DOW.

UNITED NATIONS VOLUNTEERS—UNV

The United Nations Volunteers is an important source of urgently needed middle-level skills for the UN development system supplied at modest cost, particularly in the least-developed countries. Volunteers expand the scope of UNDP project activities by supplementing the work of international and host country experts and by extending the influence of projects to local community levels. One of the most important parts of its work is the support of technical co-operation within and among the developing countries by encouraging volunteers from the countries themselves and by forming regional exchange teams made up of such volunteers. UNV is also engaged in a variety of activities to increase youth participation in development and to promote the involvement of domestic development services.

In 1987 1,269 volunteers from both developed and developing nations were serving in more than 90 countries.

OTHER FUNDS

Other special funds include the International Initiative against Avoidable Disablement; the Trust Fund for Assistance to Refugee-related Development Projects in Africa; the Trust Fund to Combat Poverty and Hunger in Africa; the Partners in Development Fund to support local non-governmental organizations; the Special Fund for Landlocked Developing Countries; and the Energy Account, which works with the World Bank to carry out energy sector assessments in developing countries. UNDP also gives assistance to national liberation movements in southern Africa for training in technical skills, agriculture and health.

United Nations Environment Programme—UNEP

Address: POB 30552, Nairobi, Kenya.
Telephone: 333930.
Telex: 22068.

The United Nations Environment Programme was established in 1972 by the UN General Assembly following recommendations of the 1972 UN Conference on the Human Environment, in Stockholm, Sweden, to encourage international co-operation in matters relating to the human environment.

Organization
(October 1988)

GOVERNING COUNCIL

The main function of the Governing Council, which meets every two years, is to provide general policy guidelines for the direction and co-ordination of environmental programmes within the UN system. It comprises representatives of 58 states, elected by the UN General Assembly on a rotating basis.

SECRETARIAT

The Secretariat serves as a focal point for environmental action within the UN system.
Executive Director: MOSTAFA K. TOLBA (Egypt).

REGIONAL OFFICES

Europe: Pavillon du Petit Saconnex, 16 ave Jean Trembley, 1209 Geneva, Switzerland; tel. (022) 999400; telex 28877.
Asia and the Pacific: UN Bldg, 10th Floor, Rajadamnern Ave, Bangkok 10200, Thailand; tel. 2829161; telex 82392.
Latin America and the Caribbean: Presidente Mazaryk 29, Ap. Postal 6-718, México 5, DF, Mexico; tel. 2501555; telex 01771055.
West Asia: 1083 Road No 425, Jufair 342, Manama, Bahrain; tel. 729040; telex 8337.
Africa: UNEP Headquarters (see above).
Liaison Office: UNDC Two Bldg, Room 0803, 2 United Nations Plaza, New York, NY 10017, USA; tel. (212) 754-8139; telex 420544.

Activities

UNEP aims to maintain a constant watch on the changing state of the environment; to analyse the trends; to assess the problems using a wide range of data and techniques; and to promote projects leading to environmentally sound development. It plays a catalytic and co-ordinating role within and beyond the UN system. During 1986, 88 UNEP projects were being implemented in co-operation with other UN agencies, particularly FAO, UNESCO and WHO. About 40 intergovernmental organizations outside the UN system have official observer status on UNEP's Governing Council, and, through the Environment Liaison Centre in Nairobi, UNEP is linked to over 6,000 non-governmental bodies concerned with the environment.

ENVIRONMENT AND DEVELOPMENT

UNEP encourages the integration of environmental considerations in development planning; in 1986, for example, it convened a conference of experts in Canberra (Australia) and 'workshops' in New Delhi (India) and Beijing (People's Republic of China), on the economics of dry-land degradation and rehabilitation; assisted the Government of Cyprus in analysis of local needs and environmentally sound planning; co-operated with the World Bank in developing guidelines on how to introduce considerations of environmental resources into national income accounting; and worked with the Government of Jamaica on planning improved management of river-basins. Training courses for those involved in planning are also provided. In 1985 UNEP (with the OAU and ECA) convened the first African Ministerial Conference on the Environment, and in 1986 a similar conference was held for government ministers from the Arab states.

UNEP makes comparative assessments of the environmental impact of different energy sources, and encourages the development of new and renewable sources of energy. Work on the more efficient use of fuel-wood was being undertaken in Bolivia, Brazil and Kenya during 1986, and a meeting of experts was held to discuss energy conservation in western Asia.

UNEP draws up and reviews international environmental law. It administers the Convention on International Trade in Endangered Species of Wild Fauna and Flora (to which 95 states were parties at the end of 1986). It also organizes working groups of experts to develop legal guidelines and principles on, for example, the protection of the earth's ozone layer, management of hazardous wastes, and marine pollution. UNEP also provides technical assistance for drawing up national legislation.

UNEP draws up guidelines on environmentally sound industrial development, and provides information and training for plant managers and government decision makers in this field. Annual consultations are held with UNIDO, and during 1986 UNEP, the World Bank and WHO prepared a manual on the safe disposal of hazardous wastes.

ENVIRONMENTAL AWARENESS

UNEP encourages the inclusion of environmental issues in education. The joint UNEP/UNESCO International Programme in Environmental Education, launched in 1976, includes the training of teachers, publications and technical assistance to governments. UNEP also provides environmental training components for use in ILO management programmes, and supports regional networks of environmental training institutions.

UNEP provides information through its publications (see below), and press releases. A News and Data team was established in 1986 to provide information for the news media and to establish a data base.

ENVIRONMENTAL ASSESSMENT

UNEP's environmental assessment programme, known as Earthwatch, aims to study the interaction between man and the environment, provide early warning of potential environmental hazards, and determine the state of natural resources. The Global Environment Monitoring System (GEMS), which began in 1975, collects data on the following topics: renewable resources; climate; health hazards; long-range transport of pollutants; integrated monitoring of pollutants and ecosystems; and oceans. In September 1988 UNEP and WHO held a meeting of experts to discuss reports on the findings of long-term GEMS studies on air pollution, water pollution and food contamination by chemicals. To convert the data collected into information usable by decision-makers, a global resource information data-base (GRID) was set up in 1985. The INFOTERRA programme forms a network of 129 national 'focal points' for the exchange of environmental information, including the annual compilation of a Directory of Sources.

UNEP conducts research on the 'outer limits' of tolerance of the biosphere and its subsystems to the demands made on it by human activities, and undertakes climate impact studies (e.g. assessing the effect of carbon dioxide emission on climate—the 'greenhouse effect'— and developing the use of data derived from satellites). In 1985 a study was completed on the effects of chlorofluorocarbon emissions on the layer of ozone in the earth's atmosphere, warning that serious climatic changes were likely to result if governments did not limit such emissions. Following the adoption in 1985 of the Vienna Convention for the Protection of the Ozone Layer, UNEP began a programme of legal and technical activities, with the aim of securing agreement on a protocol to the Convention that would impose legal limits on the emission of chloro-fluorocarbons. Agreement was reached by 24 nations in September 1987, subject to ratification by individual governments.

In 1988, following a conference held in February, a treaty was being drafted to govern the transport and disposal of hazardous wastes, with the aim of preventing the 'dumping' of wastes from industrialized countries in countries that have no processing facilities.

OCEANS

UNEP co-operates with other agencies in assessing marine pollution, chiefly through its regional seas programme: by the end of 1986 action plans had been adopted in nine regions (the Mediterranean; the seas around Kuwait; the Caribbean; the West and Central African region; the East African region; the East Asian region; the Red Sea and the Gulf of Aden; the South Pacific; and the South-East Pacific), and regional conventions had been signed by member states in six of these regions. With FAO, a joint Plan of Action for the Conservation, Management and Utilization of Marine Mammals was drawn up in 1984.

WATER AND LAND ECOSYSTEMS

UNEP supports research and training in the management of inland water resources and the protection of fresh-water ecosystems. It monitors and attempts to combat topsoil erosion, the destruction of tropical forests and the misuse of agricultural pesticides. It collaborates with the International Union for the Conservation of Nature and Natural Resources (IUCN, q.v.) in the protection of endangered species and habitats, and provides a secretariat for the Ecosystem Conservation Group (consisting of UNEP, FAO, UNESCO and IUCN), which sends expert missions to help prepare national conservation strategies. UNEP supports a number of projects which collect and conserve plant and animal genetic resources, including a 'gene bank' for crops and trees, and also supports six regional Microbiological Resources Centres which undertake training and research in this field.

DESERTIFICATION CONTROL

UNEP co-ordinates the UN Plan of Action to Combat Desertification (begun in 1978), which is particularly active in the Sudano-Sahelian region. Individual countries are assisted in formulating plans of action, including the planting of shrubs and trees, and prevention of the encroachment of sand-dunes. In 1986 and 1987 UNEP assisted in the formation of regional networks of non-governmental organizations engaged in anti-desertification activities, in Africa, Latin America and Asia and the Pacific.

HEALTH AND HUMAN SETTLEMENTS

UNEP promotes increased awareness of environmental health problems, particularly those caused by chemical contamination and the side-effects of pesticides. It maintains the International Register of Potentially Toxic Chemicals, and provides guidance on chemical hazards and waste management. UNEP collaborates with other UN agencies, especially UNCHS, in combating deteriorating environmental standards in towns; in 1986 it completed work on guidelines for the control of environmental pollution in human settlements of developing countries, and took part in preparations for the International Year of Shelter for the Homeless (1987).

FINANCE

UNEP derives its finances from the regular budget of the United Nations (from which US $10.1m. was allotted to it for the two years 1986–87), and from voluntary contributions to the Environment Fund, which amounted to about $28m. in 1986 (with a further $2.3m. in contributions outstanding as at 31 March 1987). For 1988–89 UNEP's allocation from the UN budget was $10.7m.

ENVIRONMENT FUND: COMMITMENTS FOR PROGRAMME ACTIVITIES, 1986

Purpose	Commitments (US dollars)
Environment and development	1,970,546
Environmental awareness	3,130,398
'Earthwatch'	4,017,680
Oceans	2,507,702
Water	626,663
Terrestrial ecosystems	2,256,010
Desertification	1,375,269
Health and human settlements	2,191,592
Arms race and the environment	121,656
Regional and technical co-operation	1,956,748
Fund programme reserve	488,708
Total	20,642,972

GEOGRAPHICAL DISTRIBUTION OF FUND EXPENDITURE, 1986

Region	Amount (US dollars)
Africa	1,432,071
Asia	1,357,452
Latin America	863,267
North America	9,928
Europe	105,320
Inter-regional	1,193,383
Global	10,548,531
Total	15,509,377

PUBLICATIONS

Annual Report of the Executive Director.

State of the Environment Report (annually).

UNEP News (every 2 months).

Desertification Control Bulletin (2 a year).

Industry and Environment Bulletin (quarterly).

INFOterra Bulletin (quarterly).

INFOterra International Directory of Sources.

IRPTC Bulletin (3 a year: on toxic chemicals).

Ozone Layer Bulletin (annually).

The Siren (quarterly, on regional seas programme).

Catalogue of Publications (annually).

Studies, reports, legal texts, technical guidelines, etc.

United Nations High Commissioner for Refugees— UNHCR

Address: Palais des Nations, 1211 Geneva 10, Switzerland.
Telephone: (022) 398111.
Telex: 27492.

The Office of the High Commissioner was established in 1951 to provide international protection for refugees and to seek permanent solutions to their problems.

Organization
(October 1988)

HIGH COMMISSIONER

The High Commissioner is elected by the United Nations General Assembly on the nomination of the Secretary-General, and is responsible to the General Assembly and to the UN Economic and Social Council (ECOSOC).

High Commissioner: JEAN-PIERRE HOCKÉ (Switzerland).
Deputy High Commissioner: ARTHUR E. DEWEY (USA).

EXECUTIVE COMMITTEE

The Executive Committee of the High Commissioner's Programme, established by ECOSOC, gives the High Commissioner policy directives in respect of material assistance programmes and advice at his request in the field of international protection. It meets once a year, usually at Geneva. It includes representatives of 43 states, both members and non-members of the UN.

ADMINISTRATION

Headquarters includes the High Commissioner's Office, the Division of Refugee Law and Doctrine, and five Regional Bureaux (Africa; Asia and Oceania; Europe and North America; Latin America and the Caribbean; South-West Asia, the Middle East and North Africa). In 1988 the High Commissioner had more than 100 field offices, covering 128 countries.

Activities

The competence of the High Commissioner extends to any person who, owing to well-founded fear of being persecuted for reasons of race, religion, nationality or political opinion, is outside the country of his or her nationality and is unable or, owing to such fear or for reasons other than personal convenience, remains unwilling to accept the protection of that country; or who, not having a nationality and being outside the country of his or her former habitual residence, is unable or, owing to such fear or for reasons other than personal convenience, is unwilling to return to it. Refugees meeting these criteria are entitled to the protection of the Office of the High Commissioner irrespective of their geographical location. Refugees who are assisted by other United Nations agencies, or who have the same rights or obligations as nationals of their country of residence, are outside the mandate of UNHCR.

INTERNATIONAL PROTECTION

As laid down in the Statute of the Office, one of the two primary functions of UNHCR is to extend international protection to refugees. In the exercise of this function, UNHCR seeks to ensure that refugees and asylum-seekers are protected against *refoulement* (forcible return), that they receive asylum, and that they are treated according to internationally recognized standards of treatment. UNHCR pursues these objectives by a variety of means which include promoting the conclusion and ratification by states of international conventions for the protection of refugees.

The most comprehensive instrument concerning refugees which has been elaborated at the international level is the 1951 United Nations Convention relating to the Status of Refugees. This Convention, the scope of which was extended by a Protocol adopted in 1967, defines the rights and duties of refugees and contains provisions dealing with a variety of matters which affect the day-to-day lives of refugees. The application of the 1951 United Nations Refugee Convention and the 1967 Protocol is supervised by UNHCR. Important provisions for the treatment of refugees are also contained in a number of instruments adopted at the regional level. These include the OAU Convention of 1969 Governing the Specific Aspects of Refugee Problems, the European Agreement on the Abolition of Visas for Refugees, and the 1969 American Convention on Human Rights.

UNHCR has actively encouraged States to accede to the 1951 United Nations Refugee Convention and the 1967 Protocol: 103 States had accepted either or both of these basic refugee instruments by July 1987. An increasing number of states have also adopted domestic legislation and/or administrative measures to implement the international instruments, particularly in the field of procedures for the determination of refugee status. Such measures provide an important guarantee that refugees will be accorded the standards of treatment which have been internationally established for their benefit.

A continuing concern of UNHCR has been to ensure that States scrupulously observe the fundamental principle of *non-refoulement* according to which no-one may be forcibly returned to a territory where he or she has reason to fear persecution. While this principle is now widely reflected in the practice of States, violations still occur. UNHCR has also continued to promote the adoption of liberal practices of asylum by States, so that refugees and asylum seekers are granted admission, at least on a temporary basis. Major problems have arisen in regard to violation of the physical safety of refugees as a result of piracy, abduction and armed attack. UNHCR has urged the international community to find solutions to these problems as a matter of priority. In 1981 the High Commissioner launched an anti-piracy campaign in the Gulf of Thailand. The campaign was continued in subsequent years, but in 1986 15% of boats carrying refugees arriving in Malaysia and Thailand had been attacked by pirates, with 18 people reported killed, 64 abducted and 143 missing. UNHCR has also attempted to deal with the problem of military attacks on refugee camps in southern Africa and elsewhere, by formulating and encouraging the acceptance of a set of principles to ensure the safety of refugees.

MATERIAL ASSISTANCE TO REFUGEES

Emergency relief is provided to refugees when food supplies, medical aid or other forms of assistance are required on a large scale at short notice. Other members of the UN system, as well as inter-governmental and non-governmental organizations, co-operate closely with UNHCR in this field.

Even in the more stable refugee situations, UNHCR is often called upon to provide material assistance beyond the initial emergency phase, while permanent solutions are being sought. This assistance can take various forms, including the provision of food, shelter, medical care and essential supplies. Also covered in many instances are basic services, including education and counselling. Whenever possible, measures of this kind are accompanied by efforts to encourage maximum levels of self-reliance among the refugee population.

As far as possible, assistance is geared towards the identification and implementation of durable solutions to refugee problems—this being the second statutory responsibility of UNHCR. Such solutions generally take one of three forms: voluntary repatriation, local integration or resettlement in another country. Where voluntary repatriation is feasible, the Office assists refugees to overcome obstacles preventing their return to their country of origin. This may be done through negotiations with governments involved, or by providing funds either for the physical movement of refugees or for the rehabilitation of returnees once back in their own country.

When voluntary repatriation is not feasible, efforts are made to assist refugees to integrate locally and to become self-supporting in their countries of asylum. In Europe, this has generally been done either by granting loans to refugees, or by assisting them, through vocational training or in other ways, to learn a skill and to set themselves up in gainful occupations. One major form of assistance to help refugees re-establish themselves outside camps is the provision of housing.

In contrast to the situation in Europe, the majority of refugees in Africa, and some of those in Asia, are assisted through local settlement in agriculture. In Africa, the consolidation of refugee settlements frequently requires close co-operation between UNHCR and other members of the UN system which provide development assistance to the areas affected. The problem of needy individual refugees in search of employment or educational opportunities in urban areas of Africa, and who are mainly without agricultural skills, also claims special attention. Assistance is provided through special refugee counselling services, in some cases in co-operation with the OAU Bureau for African Refugees.

In cases where resettlement through emigration is the only viable solution to a refugee problem, UNHCR negotiates with governments in an endeavour to obtain suitable resettlement opportunities, to encourage liberalization of admission criteria and to draw up special immigration schemes.

ASIA AND THE MIDDLE EAST

Since 1975 UNHCR assistance activities in the Far East and Australasia have been dominated by the problems of refugees and displaced persons in and from the Indo-Chinese peninsula: Laotians, Kampucheans and Vietnamese, needing both immediate assistance in the countries of temporary asylum to which they had fled, and help in finding a place of permanent resettlement. Between 1975 and 1985 UNHCR provided assistance to over 570,000 refugees in Thailand, at a cost of US $376m.; in 1981, however, departures began to outnumber arrivals. The total number of refugee arrivals in South-East Asian countries of temporary asylum fell from 119,402 in 1980 to 99,168 in 1981. By September 1986 over 1.1m. Indo-Chinese refugees had been resettled, chiefly in the USA (638,752, a figure which does not include some 130,000 persons who arrived in the USA in 1975), the People's Republic of China (262,873), France (103,390), Canada (106,447) and Australia (103,639). During the first six months of 1987 28,562 refugees left the region for resettlement abroad. At the end of June 1987 142,429 refugees still remained in camps, however, awaiting resettlement; of these 118,374 were in Thailand, 7,838 in Hong Kong and 8,439 in Malaysia. A special programme, launched in 1980, continued to assist about 400,000 Kampucheans who had returned to their homeland from Thailand, Viet-Nam and Laos.

In May 1979 UNHCR and Viet-Nam signed a 'memorandum of understanding' on the orderly departure of persons wishing to leave: under the Orderly Departure Programme which resulted, 119,470 persons had left Viet-Nam by the end of January 1987. During the first six months of 1987 7,594 Vietnamese left the country under the programme. In 1988 the increasing difficulty of finding resettlement places for refugees led to the adoption of stricter policies of deterrence by countries of first asylum, particularly Thailand and Hong Kong, on the grounds that many of those arriving were fleeing for economic reasons rather than for political ones, and were therefore not 'genuine' refugees. At a meeting sponsored by UNHCR, held in Geneva in May 1988, Viet-Nam did not reject (as it had done previously) the possibility of allowing repatriation of 'economic' refugees.

In Papua New Guinea there were 1,225 refugees from the Indonesian province of Irian Jaya at the beginning of 1984, and this number increased to 10,500 by mid-1986.

As a result of events in Afghanistan, almost 1m. refugees crossed into the North-West Frontier and Baluchistan provinces of Pakistan between January 1979 and mid-1980. In 1987 UNHCR assistance was being extended to over 2.4m. beneficiaries in 340 refugee villages, and covered immediate relief assistance, health care, education, vocational training and the promotion of income-generating and self-help programmes, in collaboration with the World Food Programme, the International Labour Organisation and the World Bank. The UNHCR budget allocated $78.8m. to Pakistan in 1986, and an estimated $82.3m. in 1987. UNHCR also provided assistance for Afghan refugees in Iran, who were estimated to number 2.2m. In April 1988 the Afghan and Pakistani Governments signed an agreement on the withdrawal of Soviet troops from Afghanistan and on the subsequent voluntary repatriation of Afghan refugees. UNHCR was to participate in the programme of repatriation, which was to be organized by a special United Nations co-ordinating office.

UNHCR co-ordinates humanitarian assistance for Sahrawis in the Tindouf area of Algeria; there were 167,000 registered refugees in Algeria at mid-1987, and UNHCR expenditure in Algeria for that year was estimated at US $4m.

In 1987 UNHCR allocations for the relief and rehabilitation of displaced persons in Lebanon (estimated to number 100,000 families) amounted to about $350,000.

AFRICA

The total number of refugees and displaced persons in Africa (including North Africa) increased from about 1m. in 1975 to over 5m. in 1980: the main groups had fled from Ethiopia to Djibouti, Somalia and Sudan, from Chad to Cameroon and Nigeria, from Burundi to Tanzania and from Uganda to Zaire.

In April 1981 the first International Conference on Assistance to Refugees in Africa (ICARA) was held, with the object of focusing public attention on the plight of refugees in Africa, mobilizing additional resources for refugee programmes there, and strengthening the economic capacity of countries affected by large influxes of refugees. A total of US $566.9m. was pledged by donor governments as a result of the conference: the original target had been $1,150m. A second conference (ICARA II) was held in July 1984, with the particular aim of helping host countries, themselves poor, to cope with large numbers of refugees. During 1983 a team of UN experts visited 14 countries at the invitation of the governments, evaluating proposed projects relating to refugees and returnees, and a list of 128 projects, requiring a total of $362m., was drawn up for presentation to ICARA II. The projects include improvement of transport and energy supplies; development of agriculture; education and training; health; water supplies; and social development, such as the organization of handicrafts. By the end of the Conference one-third of the necessary funds had been pledged.

In November and December 1984 the High Commissioner launched special appeals for $24.8m., and for over 12,000 metric tons of cereals, to meet the urgent additional needs of refugees and returnees in Africa caused by drought, food shortages and

REFUGEES OF CONCERN TO UNHCR*
(1 January 1987 unless otherwise stated)

Host Country	Number of registered refugees
Africa†	
Algeria	167,000
Angola	92,200
Burundi	267,500
Djibouti	16,700
Ethiopia	132,400
Malawi	100,000
Rwanda	19,400
Somalia	700,000
South Africa	150,000
Sudan	974,000
Swaziland	12,100
Tanzania	220,300
Uganda	144,000
Zaire	301,000
Zambia	138,300
Zimbabwe	65,200
Asia and the Pacific	
Australia	85,900
China, People's Republic	285,500
Iran	2,600,000
Malaysia	99,000
Pakistan	2,882,000
Papua New Guinea	10,100
Philippines	13,700
Thailand	119,900
Viet-Nam	25,000
Latin America	
Argentina	14,000
Costa Rica	31,200
Guatemala	12,000
Honduras	68,000
Mexico	175,000
Nicaragua	8,200
Europe and North America	
Austria	18,500
Belgium	35,900
Canada	353,000
France	180,300
Federal Republic of Germany	140,300
Italy	15,500
Netherlands	16,000
Norway	13,200
Sweden	120,000
Switzerland	30,100
United Kingdom	100,000
USA	1,000,000

* The table shows only those countries where more than 10,000 refugees were present. The figures do not include Palestine refugees, who come under the care of UNRWA (q.v.), nor non-registered refugees (e.g. Ethiopians living in Somalia outside official refugee camps), nor returnees and persons displaced within their own country (e.g. in Ethiopia, Kampuchea, Uganda, Zaire and Zimbabwe). Most figures are based on government estimates.

† Figures for Africa as of 1 June 1987.

insecurity. UNHCR established emergency programmes in Ethiopia, Somalia and Sudan, and for limited periods in the Central African Republic and Djibouti. By the end of 1985 the situation had improved, but UNHCR continued to provide relief assistance for Sudanese refugees in Ethiopia, for Ethiopian refugees in Somalia, and for refugees from Ethiopia, Uganda and Chad in Sudan. As a result of favourable rains, emergency programmes in Ethiopia, Somalia and Sudan were phased out in early 1987. There were, however, new influxes of Sudanese refugees into Ethiopia during 1986 and early 1987. UNHCR provided assistance for large numbers of refugees who were able to return home in 1986 and 1987, to Chad (mostly from the Central African Republic and Sudan), to Ethiopia (mostly from Djibouti, Somalia and Sudan) and to Uganda (mostly from Sudan). In 1987, owing to the security crisis in Mozambique, there was massive movement of Mozambican refugees into neighbouring countries: by early 1988 there were an estimated 800,000 Mozambican refugees, mostly in Malawi. During the first half of 1988 there was a new influx of refugees from Sudan into Ethiopia (numbering more than 300,000), and in June and July 100,000 refugees from Somalia also entered Ethiopia. In July UNHCR issued an appeal for $42m. to assist newly-arrived refugees in Ethiopia and Malawi. In September an appeal was also issued for $4.7m. to assist 55,000 refugees from Burundi who had fled to Rwanda after tribal massacres.

CENTRAL AND SOUTH AMERICA

The total refugee population of Central America and the Caribbean in June 1987 was about 312,000, of whom 118,400 were receiving UNHCR assistance. The largest refugee population was in Mexico (about 175,000 refugees, mostly from El Salvador and Guatemala), followed by Honduras (68,000, mostly from Nicaragua and El Salvador). During 1987 UNHCR continued to provide emergency relief to newly-arrived groups of refugees, and to implement self-sufficiency programmes, including, in some Central American countries, 'active refugee centres' which aim to combine a degree of agricultural self-sufficiency with increasing access for refugees to the local economy and labour market. In the 18 months to mid-1987 about 11,000 Central American refugees returned voluntarily to their countries of origin.

UNHCR also provides assistance for numbers of refugees in South America (particularly Chileans and Uruguayans). At the end of 1986 there were about 14,000 refugees in Argentina (of whom 4,260 were receiving UNHCR assistance) and over 12,000 in other countries of the region.

EUROPE AND NORTH AMERICA

UNHCR's material assistance activities in Europe are limited in scale as assistance is, in most cases, provided by governments and private organizations. At the beginning of 1987 there were about 670,000 refugees in Europe. During 1986 204,000 people requested asylum in European countries, compared with 170,000 in 1985.

Canada and the USA are major countries of resettlement for refugees: Canada admitted 18,000 refugees in 1986, while the USA admitted 62,500 in the 12 months to September 1986. UNHCR provides counselling and legal services for asylum-seekers in these countries.

Finance

UNHCR administrative expenditure is financed under the United Nations Regular Budget, under which it was allocated US $36.7m. for the two years 1986–87. Material assistance programmes are financed from voluntary contributions made by governments and also from non-governmental sources. Revised allocations for General Programmes in 1986 amounted to $281m., and estimates for 1987 were $348m. In addition, UNHCR undertakes a number of Special Programmes, as requested by the UN General Assembly, the Secretary-General of the UN or a member state, to assist returnees and, in some cases, displaced persons. In 1986 funds for Special Programmes amounted to $159.6m., and the estimate for 1987 was $75.3m.

UNHCR Expenditure by Region (US $'000)

	1986	1987 estimates
Africa	193,551.6	153,943.6
Asia and Oceania	73,353.4	69,225.1
Europe and North America	16,889.1	19,595.4
Latin America and the Caribbean	38,397.7	36,101.6
South West Asia, North Africa and the Middle East*	97,486.6	102,299.7
Headquarters programmes, global and regional projects	37,020.9	58,573.5
Total	456,699.3	439,738.9

* Including Pakistan.

PUBLICATIONS

Refugees (monthly, in English and French).
UNHCR Handbook for Emergencies.
Refugee Abstracts.
Press releases, reports.

United Nations Observer Missions and Peace-keeping Forces

Address: Office of the Under-Secretary-General for Special Political Affairs, United Nations, New York, NY 10017, USA.

United Nations peace-keeping operations have been conceived as instruments of conflict control. Each operation has been established with a specific mandate. The UN has used these operations, with the consent of the parties involved in various conflicts, to maintain peaceful conditions, without prejudice to the parties, in order to facilitate the search for political settlements through peaceful means such as mediation and the good offices of the Secretary-General. United Nations peace-keeping operations fall into two categories: peace-keeping forces and observer missions.

Peace-keeping forces are composed of contingents of armed troops made available by member states. These forces assist in preventing the recurrence of fighting, restoring and maintaining law and order, and promoting a return to normal conditions. To this end, peace-keeping forces are authorized as necessary to undertake negotiations, persuasion, observation and fact-finding. They run patrols and interpose physically between the opposing parties. They must at all times maintain complete impartiality and avoid any action that might affect the claims or positions of the parties. Peace-keeping forces are armed but are permitted to use their weapons only in self-defence.

Military observer missions are composed of unarmed officers made available, on the Secretary-General's request, by member states. A mission's function is to observe and report to the Secretary-General (who in turn informs the UN Security Council) on the maintenance of a cease-fire, to investigate violations and to do what it can to improve the situation.

UNITED NATIONS TRUCE SUPERVISION ORGANIZATION—UNTSO

Headquarters: Government House, Jerusalem.

Set up in 1948 to supervise the truce called for by the Security Council in Palestine. The authorized strength of UNTSO in 1988 was 298 military observers from 17 countries.

Chief of Staff: Lt-Gen. MARTIN VADSET (Norway).

ACTIVITIES

UNTSO was established initially to supervise the truce called by the Security Council in May 1948 and has assisted in the application of the 1949 Armistice Agreements. Its activities have changed over the years in response to developments in the Middle East and in accordance with the relevant resolutions of the Security Council.

UNTSO observers have been available at short notice to form the nucleus of other peace-keeping operations. UNTSO observers assist the UN peace-keeping forces in the Middle East (see below), UNIFIL as a separate group and UNDOF as an integral part of the force. In addition, a small group of observers remains in the

INTERNATIONAL ORGANIZATIONS   *United Nations (Other Bodies)*

Sinai region of Egypt to maintain a UN presence. There are also small detachments of observers in Beirut, Lebanon and Amman, Jordan.

FINANCE

UNTSO expenditures are covered by the regular budget of the United Nations. For the biennial period 1988–89, a sum of US $41,373,000 was appropriated by the General Assembly.

UNITED NATIONS DISENGAGEMENT OBSERVER FORCE—UNDOF

Headquarters: Damascus, Syria.

Established for an initial period of six months by a Security Council resolution in May 1974, following the signature in Geneva of a disengagement agreement between Syrian and Israeli forces. The mandate has since been extended by successive resolutions. In May 1988 the Force comprised about 1,360 troops from Austria, Canada, Finland and Poland, and seven military observers detailed from UNTSO.

Commander: Maj.-Gen. ADOLF RADAUER (Austria).

ACTIVITIES

The initial task of the Force was to take over territory evacuated in stages by the Israeli troops, in accordance with the disengagement agreement, to hand over territory to Syrian troops, and to establish an area of separation on the Golan Heights.

UNDOF continues to man the area of separation, from which Syrian and Israeli forces are excluded; it carries out inspections of the areas of limited armaments and forces, and it uses its best efforts to maintain the ceasefire. The area of separation has been placed under Syrian civil administration.

FINANCE

In December 1987 the UN General Assembly authorized the Secretary-General to enter into commitments for UNDOF at a rate not to exceed US $2.9m. per month for the period from 1 June to 30 November 1988.

UNITED NATIONS INTERIM FORCE IN LEBANON—UNIFIL

Headquarters: Naqoura, Lebanon.

Set up in March 1978 by Security Council resolution, for a six-month period, subsequently extended by successive resolutions. In May 1988 the Force comprised about 5,900 troops from nine countries. A group of some 70 UNTSO military observers assists UNIFIL in the performance of its tasks. They form the Observer Group, Lebanon.

Commander: Maj.-Gen. LARS-ERIK WAHLGREN (Sweden).

ACTIVITIES

The mandate of the force is to confirm the withdrawal of Israeli forces, to restore international peace and security and to assist the Government of Lebanon in ensuring the return of its effective authority in southern Lebanon. In June 1982, after the invasion of Lebanon by Israel, UNIFIL was also given the interim task of extending protection and humanitarian assistance to the population of the area.

FINANCE

In December 1987, the General Assembly authorized the Secretary-General to enter into commitments for UNIFIL at a rate not to exceed US $11.6m. per month for the 12 months from 1 February 1988. Owing to the failure of some states (notably the USA, whose Senate described UNIFIL in October 1987 as an 'ineffective and symbolic force') to pay their assessed contributions, UNIFIL had an accumulated financial shortfall of more than $300m. by the end of 1987.

UNITED NATIONS PEACE-KEEPING FORCE IN CYPRUS—UNFICYP

Headquarters: POB 1642, Nicosia, Cyprus.

Set up in March 1964 by Security Council resolution, for a three-month period, subsequently extended by successive resolutions. In May 1988 the Force comprised some 2,090 military personnel, and 35 civilian police, from eight countries.

Special Representative of the Secretary-General: OSCAR CAMILION (Argentina).

Commander: Maj.-Gen. GÜNTHER G. GREINDL (Austria).

ACTIVITIES

UNFICYP was established to prevent a recurrence of fighting between the Greek and Turkish Cypriot communities, and to contribute to the maintenance of law and order and a return to normal conditions. The Force controls a 180-km buffer zone, established (following the Turkish intervention in 1974) between the cease-fire lines of the Turkish forces and the Cyprus National Guard. It is also responsible for ensuring that the status quo along the two cease-fire lines is maintained, and it provides security for civilians of both communities who live or work in the area between the lines. The United Nations High Commissioner for Refugees (q.v.) acts as co-ordinator of UN humanitarian assistance for Cyprus.

FINANCE

The estimated cost to the United Nations of maintaining the Force during the six months from 15 June 1988 was US $12.6m., to be covered entirely by voluntary contributions; additional costs were to be absorbed by the countries contributing troops. In February 1988 the UN Secretary-General appealed for an increase in voluntary contributions to meet an accumulated deficit of $166m.

UNITED NATIONS GOOD OFFICES MISSION IN AFGHANISTAN AND PAKISTAN—UNGOMAP

Headquarters: Kabul, Afghanistan, and Islamabad, Pakistan.

Established in April 1988 to monitor the withdrawal of Soviet troops from Afghanistan, as stipulated in the peace agreements signed in Geneva in that month. The mission was to comprise some 50 military officers from 10 countries.

Officer-in-charge: Maj.-Gen. RAULI HELMINEN (Finland).

UNITED NATIONS IRAN-IRAQ MILITARY OBSERVER GROUP—UNIIMOG

Headquarters: Baghdad, Iraq and Teheran, Iran.

Established in August 1988 by the Security Council, for a period of six months, following the announcement of a cease-fire in the war between Iran and Iraq. UNIIMOG was to comprise some 350 officers from 26 countries, plus military and civilian support staff. The Group's principal tasks were to monitor the two sides' compliance with the cease-fire, to supervise the withdrawal of troops to internationally-recognized boundaries, and to obtain the agreement of the parties to other arrangements which, pending a comprehensive settlement, might help to reduce tension and build confidence between them.

Commander: Maj.-Gen. SLAVKO JOVIĆ (Yugoslavia).

United Nations Population Fund—UNFPA

Address: 220 East 42nd St, New York, NY 10017, USA.
Telephone: (212) 963-1234.

Created in 1967 as the Trust Fund for Population Activities, the UN Fund for Population Activities (UNFPA) was established as a Fund of the UN General Assembly in 1972 and was made a subsidiary organ of the UN General Assembly in 1979, with the UNDP Governing Council designated as its governing body. In 1987 UNFPA's name was changed to the United Nations Population Fund (retaining the same acronym).

Organization
(October 1988)

EXECUTIVE DIRECTOR

The Executive Director, who has the rank of Under-Secretary-General of the UN, is responsible for the overall direction of the Fund, working closely with governments, United Nations bodies and agencies, regional groups, and non-governmental organizations to ensure the most effective programming and use of resources in population activities.

Executive Director: Dr NAFIS SADIK (Pakistan).
Deputy Executive Director: TATSURO KUNUGI.

EXECUTING AGENCIES

In most projects assistance is extended through member organizations of the UN system; ultimate responsibility for execution of projects lies with recipient governments, using the services of the UN organizations as required. The Fund may also call on the services of non-governmental organizations in this role and sometimes it acts as its own executing agency.

FIELD ORGANIZATION

UNFPA Deputy Representatives and Senior Advisers on Population, attached to the offices of the UNDP Resident Representatives, assist governments in formulating requests for aid and co-ordinate the work of the executing agencies in any given country or area.

Activities

At the end of 1987 UNFPA was providing assistance for 2,756 projects, of which 882 were in Africa, 735 in Asia and the Pacific, 431 in Latin America and the Caribbean, 362 in the Arab states and Europe, 187 inter-regional, and 159 global. UNFPA approved 376 new projects during 1987, at a total cost of US $32.6m. Many UNFPA-supported projects are executed by other UN agencies, notably WHO, UNESCO and ILO, or by the government of the country concerned. 'Needs assessment missions' were undertaken to six countries to assist governments in drawing up or reviewing population programmes.

Priority programme areas are as follows:

1. Family planning. In 1987 54.8% of total programme expenditure allocations were for family planning, concentrating on extending acceptance of family planning and expanding the delivery of services to rural and marginal urban areas. The emphasis is on combining family planning services with maternal and child health care. UNFPA also supports research into contraceptives and training in contraceptive technology.

2. Information, education and communication. This accounted for 14% of total programme allocations in 1987. UNFPA assists broadcasting, poster campaigns and itinerant drama groups which convey family planning information, and supports school education programmes.

3. Basic data collection. This accounted for 7.9% of programme expenditure in 1987. UNFPA provides assistance and training for carrying out censuses and demographic surveys.

4. Utilization of population data and research for policy formulation and development planning. This accounted for 18.5% of programme expenditure in 1987. UNFPA provides assistance for analysis of demographic and socio-economic data, and for research on population trends and policies. It supports a programme of fellowships in demographic analysis, data processing and cartography.

UNFPA also has special programmes on women, population and development, on youth, on ageing, and on AIDS, involving national and regional seminars and training programmes. It produces publications (see below) and audio-visual aids, promotes conferences, and encourages wider coverage of population issues in the media.

FINANCE

Total expenditure in 1987 (provisional) was $140.6m. (compared with $132m. in 1986): this included $74.6m. for country programmes and $32.6m. for inter-country programmes. UNFPA's income in 1987 (provisional) totalled $156.7m., compared with $140m. in 1986. The USA, the largest traditional donor, pledged no funds to UNFPA for 1986 or 1987 (in protest at the Fund's support for the 'one child per family' policy of the People's Republic of China), but the shortfall was largely compensated for by other donors.

Project expenditure:
allocations by region, 1987 (US $ million)

Africa south of the Sahara	30.4
Arab states	13.1
Asia and the Pacific	53.5
Latin America and the Caribbean	17.3
Europe	1.4
Inter-regional	16.6
Global	1.4
Total	133.7

PUBLICATIONS

Annual Report.

State of World Population Report (annually).

Population (newsletter, monthly in Arabic, English, French and Spanish).

Populi (quarterly).

Inventory of Population Projects in Developing Countries Around the World (annually).

Guide to Sources of International Population Assistance (every 3 years).

Reports and reference works.

INTERNATIONAL ORGANIZATIONS — United Nations (Other Bodies)

United Nations Relief and Works Agency for Palestine Refugees in the Near East—UNRWA

Addresses: (Vienna): POB 700, 1400 Vienna, Austria; (Amman): POB 484, Amman, Jordan.
Telephone (Vienna): (0222) 2631-4530.
Telex (Vienna): 135310.

UNRWA began operations in 1950 to provide relief, health, education and welfare services for Palestine refugees in the Near East.

Organization
(October 1988)

UNRWA employs an international staff of 125 and 17,600 local staff, mainly Palestine refugees. The Commissioner-General is assisted by an Advisory Commission consisting of representatives of the governments of:

Belgium, Jordan, Turkey
Egypt, Lebanon, United Kingdom
France, Syria, USA
Japan

Commissioner-General: GIORGIO GIACOMELLI (Italy).

REGIONAL OFFICES

Gaza Strip: UNRWA Field Office, POB 61, Gaza.
Jordan: UNRWA Field Office, POB 484, Amman.
West Bank: UNRWA Field Office, POB 19149, Jerusalem.
Lebanon: UNRWA Field Office, POB 947, Beirut.
Syria: UNRWA Field Office, POB 4313, Damascus.
Egypt: UNRWA Liaison Office, 2 Dar-esh-Shifa St, Garden City, POB 277, Cairo.
United States: UNRWA Liaison Office, Room DC 2-0550, United Nations, New York, NY 10017.

Activities

SERVICES FOR PALESTINE REFUGEES

Since 1950, UNRWA has provided relief, health and education services for the needy among the Palestine refugees in Lebanon, Syria, Jordan, the West Bank and the Gaza Strip. For UNRWA's purposes, a Palestine refugee is one whose normal residence was in Palestine for a minimum of two years before the 1948 conflict and who, as a result of the Arab–Israeli hostilities, lost his home and means of livelihood. To be eligible for assistance, a refugee must reside in one of the 'host' countries in which UNRWA operates and be in need. A refugee's children and grandchildren who fulfil certain criteria are also eligible for UNRWA assistance. At 30 June 1987, the registered refugee population numbered 2,201,123 (about half the estimated total number of Palestinians), living in five areas administered by four governments. There were 766,973 registered refugees (plus about 52,000 unregistered) living in 61 camps, while the remaining refugees have settled in the towns and villages already existing.

UNRWA's activities fall into the categories of education and training; health services; and relief and welfare services.

Education (under the technical supervision of UNESCO) took up about two-thirds of UNRWA's budget for 1987. In the 1987/88 school year there were 349,321 pupils in 633 UNRWA schools (83 schools in Lebanon, 111 in Syria, 195 in Jordan, 98 on the West Bank and 146 in the Gaza Strip) and 10,100 teachers. At three-quarters of the schools, morning and afternoon shifts are held in order to accommodate more pupils. UNRWA also runs eight vocational and teacher-training centres with 4,754 places. UNRWA awarded 397 scholarships for study at Arab universities in 1987/88.

Health services accounted for about 20% of UNRWA expenditure in 1987. There are 2,964 medical staff posts, 98 health units, 86 specialist clinics and laboratories, and 93 mother and child health clinics; over 5m. visits by patients are made each year to UNRWA medical units. UNRWA also runs a supplementary feeding programme, mainly for children, to combat malnutrition: there are 92 feeding centres. Technical supervision for the health programme is provided by WHO.

Relief services (which accounted for 10% of UNRWA expenditure in 1987) comprise the distribution of food rations, the provision of emergency shelter and the organization of welfare programmes for about 120,000 of the poorest refugees.

AID TO DISPLACED PERSONS

After the renewal of Arab–Israeli hostilities in the Middle East in June 1967, hundreds of thousands of people fled from the fighting and Israeli-occupied areas to east Jordan, Syria and Egypt. UNRWA provided emergency relief for displaced refugees and was additionally empowered by a UN General Assembly resolution to provide 'humanitarian assistance, as far as practicable, on an emergency basis and as a temporary measure' for those persons other than Palestine refugees who were newly displaced and in urgent need. In practice, UNRWA has lacked the funds to aid the other displaced persons and the main burden of supporting them has fallen on the Arab governments concerned. The Agency, as requested by the Government of Jordan in 1967 and on that Government's behalf, distributes rations to displaced persons in Jordan who are not registered refugees of 1948.

With the agreement of the Israeli Government, UNRWA has continued to provide assistance for registered refugees living in the Israeli-occupied territories of the West Bank and the Gaza Strip.

RECENT EMERGENCIES

Beginning with the 1975–1976 civil war, Palestine refugees and UNRWA's services have been adversely affected by the continuing disturbances in Lebanon. UNRWA launched an emergency relief programme following the Israeli invasion of the south in March 1978, which caused the temporary evacuation of most of the 60,000 refugees living there and the flight of 17,000 refugees in other parts of the country.

In 1979 UNRWA again launched an emergency appeal for aid to southern Lebanon because of continuing Israeli and other attacks. In 1981 civil strife and Israeli attacks disrupted UNRWA activities. The education programme was hardest hit, with up to 50 school days lost in some schools during the 1980/81 school year.

The Israeli invasion of June 1982 meant that over 150,000 persons were displaced, necessitating an emergency relief programme costing US $52m. Many UNRWA schools, clinics and offices were destroyed or damaged. The emergency programme was extended to spring 1984 and an appeal for $13m. was made to provide funds for reconstruction of UNRWA facilities, refugee shelters and refugee camp infrastructure.

During the first half of 1985 UNRWA organized two emergency relief operations in Lebanon, providing food and medical care for 40,000 displaced refugees during factional fighting in the Sidon area in March and April, and emergency assistance to 35,000 displaced refugees when refugee camps in Beirut were besieged in May and June. Two similar emergency operations were also mounted in the first half of 1986. UNRWA also provides cash grants to refugees whose homes have been damaged or destroyed in the fighting. In late 1986 and early 1987 UNRWA faced another emergency in Lebanon. Three camps in Beirut and Tyre were besieged for some months, and 48,000 refugees were displaced. In February 1987 the Agency launched an emergency appeal for $20.6m. to finance emergency relief and repair of thousands of refugee homes, and a number of Agency schools, clinics and other installations. By mid-1988, $15m. had been collected.

Meanwhile, UNRWA faced increasing problems in the Israeli-occupied territories of the West Bank and the Gaza Strip, where unrest broke out in December 1987. In the next six months, more than 200 Palestinians, including many registered refugees, were killed, and thousands were injured. Schools in the West Bank were closed for the first four months of 1988, and UNRWA services in both territories were frequently interrupted as curfews were imposed on camps. UNRWA began an appeal which raised US $26m. in financial and material assistance for the refugees in the two territories by June 1988.

FINANCE

For the most part, UNRWA's income is made up of voluntary contributions, almost entirely from governments, the remainder being provided by voluntary agencies, business corporations and private sources. Much of UNRWA's budget is used to pay its educational and medical staff. However, the cost of 125 international staff is funded by the UN, WHO and UNESCO, and a further nine international staff are paid from UNRWA's budget.

Contributions dropped from $190.6m. in 1980 to about $174m. in

1985, despite UNRWA's rising expenses. Planned expenditure for 1985 had to be cut by $43m., through deferral of pay and cost-of-living increases to 12,000 field staff, a cut in overhead costs and supplies and cuts in construction, maintenance and the purchase of new equipment. Austerity measures continued during 1986, but the Agency was able to find the funds for most programmes, although construction plans were not fully funded. UNRWA's financial situation subsequently improved, and in June 1988 the budget for 1988 (amounting to $216.4m.) was almost fully funded.

STATISTICS

Refugees Registered with UNRWA (30 June 1987)

	Refugees in camps	Refugees not in camps	Total registered refugees
Jordan	208,716	636,826	845,542*
West Bank	94,824	278,762	373,586†
Gaza Strip	244,416	200,981	445,397
Lebanon	143,809	134,800	278,609
Syria	75,208	182,781	257,989‡
Total	766,973	1,434,150	2,201,123

* Including refugees displaced from the West Bank and the Gaza Strip in 1967. These totalled 375,738 at 30 June 1987.
† Figure includes 4,961 refugees displaced from Gaza Strip.
‡ Figure includes 32,236 refugees displaced in 1967.

Displaced Persons

Apart from the Palestine refugees of 1948 who are registered with UNRWA and who are UNRWA's main concern (see table above), considerable numbers of people have, since 1967, been displaced within the UNRWA areas of operations, and others have had to leave these areas. According to government estimates, there were 210,000 displaced persons in Jordan and 125,000 in Syria in June 1987.

UNRWA Schools (1987/88)

	Number of schools	Number of teachers	Number of pupils
Jordan	195	3,701	134,601
West Bank	98	1,314	39,895
Gaza Strip	146	2,514	88,816
Lebanon	83	1,024	33,433*
Syria	111	1,548	52,576
Total	633	10,101	349,321

* Estimate.

PUBLICATIONS

Annual Report of the Commissioner-General of UNRWA.
UNRWA—a Survey of United Nations Assistance to Palestine Refugees (every 2 years).
Palestine Refugees Today—the UNRWA Newsletter (quarterly).
UNRWA Report (quarterly).
A Brief History: 1950–82.
UNRWA: Past, Present and Future.
Catalogues of publications and audio-visual materials.

World Food Council—WFC

Address: Via delle Terme di Caracalla, 00100 Rome, Italy.
Telephone: 57971.
Telex: 610181.

The World Food Council was created in December 1974 by the UN General Assembly, upon the specific recommendation of the World Food Conference held in November 1974. It aims to stimulate governments and the international community to adopt the necessary policies and programmes required to alleviate world hunger and improve the global food system.

Organization

(October 1988)

COUNCIL

The Council meets annually and consists of ministers representing 36 member states, elected by the UN General Assembly: one-third retire each year. Membership is drawn from regional groups in the following proportions: nine from Africa, eight from Asia, seven from Latin America, four from the socialist states of Eastern Europe, and eight from Western Europe and North America.

SECRETARIAT

With the help of various multilateral and bilateral organizations and research institutions, the Secretariat reviews the current world food situation and recommends to the Council appropriate policy changes designed to improve food production and nutritional well-being, particularly in the developing countries.

Executive Director: GERALD I. TRANT (Canada).

Activities

The Council reviews problems and recommends actions; it co-ordinates the activities of the UN in relation to food problems, and co-operates with regional bodies to formulate and follow up the approved policies.

The Council concentrates on promoting the international political consensus necessary (1) to increase food production in the developing countries, most notably in sub-Saharan Africa; (2) to improve national and international food security measures through policies that link food production, agricultural trade and nutritional concerns; (3) to assure the greater effectiveness of food aid; and (4) to reduce barriers to trade in agricultural commodities between developed and developing countries.

At the 13th session of the Council, held in Beijing, the People's Republic of China, in June 1987, the ministers noted that, although total food production had increased since the 1974 World Food Conference, the number of undernourished people in the world had risen. They stated that hunger is often not caused by scarcity of food, but rather by lack of access to food: reduced economic activity, falling national incomes and net capital outflows, and programmes aiming to bring about stabilization and adjustment, had led in many countries to significant reductions in purchasing power, growing unemployment, and rising food prices. In their discussion of 'South-South' co-operation the ministers recognized the will of the developing countries to work together, particularly in food and agriculture, and recommended four priority areas for attention in such co-operation: food production; institution-building, including training and enhancement of management capability; development of agro-industries; and trade.

The Council considered the impact of international trade and related national policies on food and development, and concluded that growing protectionism, the decline in commodity prices, the deterioration in the terms of trade, and limited access to markets had had a negative impact on international agricultural trade, and impeded the efforts of developing countries to overcome hunger and malnutrition. The Council urged the OECD member countries to avoid excessive market support for agricultural products, and requested that food surpluses should be used to assist the developing countries.

At its 14th session, held in Nicosia, Cyprus, in May 1988, the Council noted that food consumption per person had decreased further in all developing regions in 1987, while the living conditions of the poorest people had continued to deteriorate. It requested a joint effort by all countries and international agencies to improve the nutritional levels of low-income groups during periods of economic adjustment. The Council decided to launch the 'Cyprus Initiative against Hunger in the World' in an attempt to balance access to food, by asking countries with a food surplus to contribute part of their over-production to nations that are short of food; developed nations without a surplus would be asked to contribute cash, while food-deficit nations would be asked to deploy domestic resources in order to bring maximum benefit to the poor and hungry. The Council also discussed sustainable food security, with reference to a report by the UN Environment Programme on the ecological stress caused by increasing food cultivation on marginal lands.

FOOD PRODUCTION

In 1979 a system of 'food strategies' was launched, whereby individual developing countries, in collaboration with a particular developed country or institution, were to prepare overall food plans so as to enable a more co-ordinated approach and the best use of aid: strategies would include consideration of such issues as the stimulation of production by price incentives; improvement of marketing and distribution infrastructure; the effect of exchange rates on production; research on higher-yielding crops; improved supply of fertilizers and pesticides; land-holding reforms; and the supply of credit to small farmers. By 1987 more than 50 developing countries had adopted such a scheme, with assistance from developed countries, the World Bank, FAO, ILO, IFAD, UNDP, the African Development Bank and the Inter-American Development Bank.

At the 1984 Council meeting ministers agreed to give priority to African food problems and to undertake a review of the implementation of national food sector plans and policies in Africa. The agreed work programme also included reviews of the effectiveness of systems whereby food is delivered to the poor; of resources requirements and priorities; and of the progress made in GATT, UNCTAD and other institutions pertaining to the liberalization of international trade.

FOOD SECURITY

In July 1980 a new Food Aid Convention entered into force, increasing the guaranteed minimum level of food aid from grain-exporting countries to developing countries in need from 4.2 to 7.6m. tons a year, which was, however, still short of the 10m. minimum recommended by the WFC. The 1985 Council called for a clearer distinction between food aid and the disposal of highly subsidized surpluses, which has disruptive effects on markets and production incentives; it criticized the 'dumping' of surplus cereals by industrialized countries.

At successive Council meetings, ministers have discussed the international agricultural problems caused by the farm policies of the major grain exporters, such as the European Community and the USA, which subsidize both the production and export of major cereal crops. These subsidies have not only proved costly to taxpayers, but also create a major disincentive to domestic cereal producers in the developing countries because of the artificially low price of internationally-traded cereals.

World Food Programme—WFP

Address: Via Cristoforo Colombo 426, 00145 Rome, Italy.
Telex: 626675.

WFP, the food aid arm of the United Nations, became operational in 1963. It aims to stimulate economic and social development through food aid and to provide emergency relief.

Organization
(October 1988)

COMMITTEE ON FOOD AID POLICIES AND PROGRAMMES (CFA)

The Committee has 30 members: 15 elected by the UN Economic and Social Council (ECOSOC, q.v.) and 15 by FAO.

SECRETARIAT

Executive Director: JAMES INGRAM (Australia).

Activities

Member governments make voluntary contributions of commodities, cash, and services (particularly shipping) to WFP, which uses the food to support economic and social development projects in the developing countries. The food is supplied, for example, as an incentive in development self-help schemes, as part wages in labour-intensive projects of many kinds, particularly in the rural economy, but also in the industrial field, and in support of institutional feeding schemes where the emphasis is mainly on enabling the beneficiaries to have an adequate and balanced diet. One of the criteria for WFP aid to projects is that the recipient country can continue them after the aid has ceased. Priority is given to low-income, food-deficit countries and to vulnerable groups such as pregnant women and children.

WFP also provides emergency food aid for victims of natural and man-made disasters, chiefly from the International Emergency Food Reserve, which it manages. In 1987 donors pledged US $195.5m. to the Reserve, and the target of 500,000 metric tons of cereals was exceeded.

By the end of December 1987, 1,437 projects in 115 countries had been approved since the beginning of the Programme's operations, at a total cost to WFP of $8,559m. In addition, 936 emergency operations had been undertaken in 106 countries at a total cost to the Programme of $2,192m.

In 1987 311 projects, valued at $3,541.9m., were operational in 86 countries. By the end of the year, pledges in food aid and cash for the two years 1987–88 amounted to $1,323.5m. A total of $532m. was committed to development projects in 1987; of this, over 80% was for low-income, food-deficit countries. In value terms, 48% of development commitments went to agricultural and rural development projects, while the remaining 52% was invested in human resource development, including food for vulnerable groups and primary schools. Examples of projects supported by WFP food aid in 1987 were: tree-planting in the People's Republic of China and India; rebuilding railways in Ghana; rural development in Haiti; rehabilitation of the sisal industry in Tanzania; training in handicrafts for women in Syria; and fishing co-operatives in the People's Democratic Republic of Yemen.

In 1987 WFP also committed $271.3m. to provide emergency food aid to an estimated 15m. people. More than two-thirds of this was for refugees. The largest continuing beneficiary groups of refugees were in Pakistan and Somalia. About 27% of emergency assistance was for victims of drought.

PUBLICATION

World Food Programme Journal (every 2 months).

INTERNATIONAL ORGANIZATIONS   United Nations (Membership)

Membership of the United Nations and its Specialized Agencies

	UN	IAEA	IBRD	IDA	IFC	IMF	FAO	IFAD[4]	GATT	IMO[5]	ICAO[6]	ILO[7]	ITU[8]	UNESCO[9]	UNIDO	UPU[10]	WHO[11]	WMO[12]	WIPO
Afghanistan	x	x	x	x	x	x	x	x			x	x	x	x	x	x	x	x	
Albania	x	x					x							x	x	x	x	x	
Algeria[1]	x	x	x	x		x	x	x		x	x	x	x	x	x	x	x	x	x
Angola[1]	x						x	x		x	x	x	x	x	x	x	x	x	x
Antigua and Barbuda	x		x		x	x	x	x	x	x	x	x	x	x		x	x		
Argentina	x	x	x	x	x	x	x	x	x	x	x	x	x	x	x	x	x	x	x
Australia	x	x	x	x	x	x	x	x	x	x	x	x	x	x	x	x	x	x	x
Austria	x	x	x	x	x	x	x	x	x	x	x	x	x	x	x	x	x	x	x
Bahamas[1]	x		x		x	x	x			x	x	x	x	x		x	x	x	
Bahrain[1]	x		x			x	x			x	x	x	x	x		x	x		
Bangladesh	x	x	x	x	x	x	x	x		x	x	x	x	x	x	x	x	x	x
Barbados	x		x		x	x	x		x	x	x	x	x	x		x	x	x	x
Belgium	x	x	x	x	x	x	x	x	x	x	x	x	x	x	x	x	x	x	x
Belize	x		x	x	x	x	x	x			x		x	x	x	x	x		
Benin	x		x	x	x	x	x	x	x		x	x	x	x	x	x	x	x	x
Bhutan	x		x	x		x	x	x						x	x	x	x		
Bolivia	x	x	x	x	x	x	x	x		x	x	x	x	x	x	x	x	x	x
Botswana	x		x	x	x	x	x	x	x		x	x	x	x		x	x	x	
Brazil	x	x	x	x	x	x	x	x	x	x	x	x	x	x	x	x	x	x	x
Brunei[1]	x									x	x		x			x	x		
Bulgaria	x	x					x			x	x	x	x	x	x	x	x	x	x
Burkina Faso	x		x	x	x	x	x	x	x		x	x	x	x	x	x	x	x	x
Burma	x	x	x	x	x	x	x		x	x	x	x	x	x	x	x	x	x	
Burundi	x		x	x	x	x	x	x			x	x	x	x	x	x	x	x	x
Byelorussian SSR	x	x									x	x	x	x	x	x	x	x	x
Cameroon	x	x	x	x	x	x	x	x	x	x	x	x	x	x	x	x	x	x	x
Canada	x	x	x	x	x	x	x	x	x	x	x	x	x	x	x	x	x	x	x
Cape Verde[1]	x		x	x		x	x	x		x	x	x	x	x	x	x	x	x	x
Central African Republic	x		x	x	x	x	x	x			x	x	x	x	x	x	x	x	x
Chad	x		x	x	x	x	x	x	x		x	x	x	x	x	x	x	x	x
Chile	x	x	x	x	x	x	x	x	x	x	x	x	x	x	x	x	x	x	x
China, People's Republic	x	x	x	x	x	x	x	x		x	x	x	x	x	x	x	x	x	x
Colombia	x	x	x	x	x	x	x	x		x	x	x	x	x	x	x	x	x	x
Comoros	x		x	x		x	x	x			x	x	x	x	x	x	x		
Congo	x		x	x	x	x	x	x		x	x	x	x	x	x	x	x	x	x
Costa Rica	x	x	x	x	x	x	x	x		x	x	x	x	x	x	x	x	x	x
Côte d'Ivoire	x	x	x	x	x	x	x	x	x	x	x	x	x	x	x	x	x	x	x
Cuba	x	x					x		x	x	x	x	x	x	x	x	x	x	x
Cyprus	x	x	x	x	x	x	x	x	x	x	x	x	x	x	x	x	x	x	x
Czechoslovakia	x	x					x		x	x	x	x	x	x	x	x	x	x	x
Denmark	x	x	x	x	x	x	x	x	x	x	x	x	x	x	x	x	x	x	x
Djibouti	x		x	x	x	x	x	x			x	x	x	x		x	x	x	
Dominica[1]	x		x	x	x	x	x		x		x		x	x	x	x	x		
Dominican Republic	x	x	x	x	x	x	x	x		x	x	x	x	x	x	x	x	x	x
Ecuador	x	x	x	x	x	x	x	x		x	x	x	x	x	x	x	x	x	x
Egypt	x	x	x	x	x	x	x	x	x	x	x	x	x	x	x	x	x	x	x
El Salvador	x	x	x	x	x	x	x	x		x	x	x	x	x	x	x	x	x	x
Equatorial Guinea[1]	x		x	x	x	x	x	x			x	x	x	x	x	x	x		
Ethiopia	x	x	x	x	x	x	x	x		x	x	x	x	x	x	x	x	x	x
Fiji[1]	x		x	x	x	x	x	x		x	x	x	x	x		x	x	x	x
Finland	x	x	x	x	x	x	x	x	x	x	x	x	x	x	x	x	x	x	x
France	x	x	x	x	x	x	x	x	x	x	x	x	x	x	x	x	x	x	x
Gabon	x	x	x	x	x	x	x	x		x	x	x	x	x	x	x	x	x	x
The Gambia	x		x	x	x	x	x	x	x		x	x	x	x		x	x	x	
German Democratic Republic	x	x								x		x	x	x	x	x	x	x	x
Germany, Federal Republic	x	x	x	x	x	x	x	x	x	x	x	x	x	x	x	x	x	x	x
Ghana	x	x	x	x	x	x	x	x	x	x	x	x	x	x	x	x	x	x	x
Greece	x	x	x	x	x	x	x	x	x	x	x	x	x	x	x	x	x	x	x
Grenada[1]	x		x	x	x	x	x				x		x	x	x	x	x		
Guatemala	x	x	x	x	x	x	x	x		x	x	x	x	x	x	x	x	x	x
Guinea	x		x	x	x	x	x	x			x	x	x	x	x	x	x	x	x
Guinea-Bissau[1]	x		x	x		x	x	x			x	x	x	x	x	x	x	x	
Guyana	x		x	x	x	x	x	x	x		x	x	x	x	x	x	x	x	x
Haiti	x	x	x	x	x	x	x	x	x	x	x	x	x	x	x	x	x	x	x
Honduras	x		x	x	x	x	x	x		x	x	x	x	x	x	x	x	x	x
Hungary	x	x					x		x	x	x	x	x	x	x	x	x	x	x
Iceland	x	x	x	x		x	x		x	x	x	x	x	x	x	x	x	x	x
India	x	x	x	x	x	x	x	x	x	x	x	x	x	x	x	x	x	x	x
Indonesia	x	x	x	x	x	x	x	x		x	x	x	x	x	x	x	x	x	x
Iran	x	x	x	x	x	x	x			x	x	x	x	x	x	x	x	x	

continued

INTERNATIONAL ORGANIZATIONS

United Nations (Membership)

	UN	IAEA	IBRD	IDA	IFC	IMF	FAO	IFAD[4]	GATT	IMO[5]	ICAO[6]	ILO[7]	ITU[8]	UNESCO[9]	UNIDO	UPU[10]	WHO[11]	WMO[12]	WIPO
Iraq	x	x	x	x	x	x	x	x		x	x	x	x	x	x	x	x	x	x
Ireland	x	x	x	x	x	x	x	x	x	x	x	x	x	x	x	x	x	x	x
Israel	x	x	x	x	x	x	x		x	x	x	x	x	x	x	x	x	x	x
Italy	x	x	x	x	x	x	x	x	x	x	x	x	x	x	x	x	x	x	x
Jamaica	x	x	x			x	x	x	x	x	x	x	x	x	x	x	x	x	x
Japan	x	x	x	x	x	x	x	x	x	x	x	x	x	x	x	x	x	x	x
Jordan	x	x	x	x	x	x	x	x		x	x	x	x	x	x	x	x	x	x
Kampuchea[1]	x		x	x	x	x	x			x	x	x	x	x		x	x	x	
Kenya	x	x	x	x	x	x	x	x	x	x	x	x	x	x	x	x	x	x	x
Kiribati[1]			x	x	x						x		x			x	x		
Korea, Democratic People's Republic		x					x	x		x			x	x	x	x	x	x	x
Korea, Republic		x	x	x	x	x	x	x		x	x		x	x	x	x	x	x	x
Kuwait	x	x	x	x	x	x	x	x	x	x	x	x	x	x	x	x	x	x	x
Laos	x		x	x		x	x	x			x	x	x	x	x	x	x	x	
Lebanon	x	x	x		x	x	x		x	x	x	x	x	x	x	x	x	x	x
Lesotho	x		x	x	x	x	x	x	x		x	x	x	x	x	x	x	x	
Liberia	x		x	x	x	x	x	x		x	x	x	x	x	x	x	x	x	
Libya	x	x	x	x	x	x	x	x		x	x	x	x	x	x	x	x	x	x
Liechtenstein		x											x			x			x
Luxembourg	x	x	x	x	x	x	x	x	x		x	x	x	x	x	x	x	x	x
Madagascar	x	x	x	x	x	x	x	x		x	x	x	x	x	x	x	x	x	x
Malawi	x		x	x	x	x	x	x	x		x	x	x	x	x	x	x	x	
Malaysia	x	x	x	x	x	x	x	x	x	x	x	x	x	x	x	x	x	x	
Maldives	x		x	x	x	x	x	x		x	x		x	x	x	x	x	x	x
Mali[1]	x	x	x	x	x	x	x	x			x	x	x	x	x	x	x	x	
Malta	x		x			x	x		x	x	x	x	x	x	x	x	x	x	x
Mauritania	x		x	x	x	x	x	x		x	x	x	x	x	x	x	x	x	
Mauritius	x		x	x	x	x	x	x	x	x	x	x	x	x	x	x	x	x	x
Mexico	x	x	x	x	x	x	x	x		x	x	x	x	x	x	x	x	x	x
Monaco		x									x		x	x		x	x	x	x
Mongolia	x	x					x					x	x	x	x	x	x	x	x
Morocco	x	x	x	x	x	x	x	x	x	x	x	x	x	x	x	x	x	x	x
Mozambique[1]	x		x	x	x	x	x	x		x	x	x	x	x	x	x	x	x	
Nauru										x		x	x			x	x		
Nepal	x		x	x	x	x	x	x			x	x	x	x	x	x	x	x	
Netherlands	x	x	x	x	x	x	x	x	x	x	x	x	x	x	x	x	x	x	x
New Zealand	x	x	x	x	x	x	x	x	x	x	x	x	x	x	x	x	x	x	x
Nicaragua	x	x	x	x	x	x	x	x	x		x	x	x	x	x	x	x	x	x
Niger	x	x	x	x	x	x	x	x			x	x	x	x	x	x	x	x	x
Nigeria	x	x	x	x	x	x	x	x	x	x	x	x	x	x	x	x	x	x	x
Norway	x	x	x	x	x	x	x	x	x	x	x	x	x	x	x	x	x	x	x
Oman	x		x	x	x	x	x	x		x	x	x	x	x	x	x	x	x	
Pakistan	x	x	x	x	x	x	x	x	x	x	x	x	x	x	x	x	x	x	x
Panama	x	x	x	x	x	x	x	x		x	x	x	x	x	x	x	x	x	x
Papua New Guinea[1]	x		x	x	x	x	x	x		x	x	x	x	x	x	x	x	x	
Paraguay	x		x	x	x	x	x	x			x	x	x	x	x	x	x	x	x
Peru	x	x	x	x	x	x	x	x	x	x	x	x	x	x	x	x	x	x	x
Philippines	x	x	x	x	x	x	x	x	x	x	x	x	x	x	x	x	x	x	x
Poland	x	x	x	x		x	x		x	x	x	x	x	x	x	x	x	x	x
Portugal	x	x	x		x	x	x		x	x	x	x	x	x	x	x	x	x	x
Qatar[1]	x	x	x			x	x	x		x	x	x	x	x	x	x	x	x	x
Romania	x	x	x			x	x		x	x	x	x	x	x	x	x	x	x	x
Rwanda	x		x	x	x	x	x	x			x	x	x	x	x	x	x	x	x
Saint Christopher and Nevis[1]	x		x	x		x	x	x						x	x	x	x		
Saint Lucia[1]	x		x	x	x		x	x			x			x	x	x	x		
Saint Vincent and the Grenadines[1]	x					x	x	x		x	x			x	x	x	x		
San Marino										x		x	x	x		x	x		
São Tomé and Príncipe[1]	x		x	x		x	x	x			x	x	x	x	x	x	x	x	
Saudi Arabia	x	x	x	x	x	x	x	x		x	x	x	x	x	x	x	x	x	x
Senegal	x	x	x	x	x	x	x	x	x	x	x	x	x	x	x	x	x	x	x
Seychelles[1]	x		x	x	x	x	x	x			x	x	x	x	x	x	x	x	
Sierra Leone	x		x	x	x	x	x	x	x	x	x	x	x	x	x	x	x	x	
Singapore	x	x	x	x	x	x	x		x	x	x	x	x		x	x	x	x	
Solomon Islands[1]	x		x	x	x	x	x	x		x	x		x		x	x	x		
Somalia	x		x	x	x	x	x		x	x	x	x	x	x	x	x	x	x	x
South Africa[2]	x	x	x	x	x	x			x	x	x		x			x	x	x	x
Spain	x	x	x	x	x	x	x	x	x	x	x	x	x	x	x	x	x	x	x
Sri Lanka	x	x	x	x	x	x	x	x	x	x	x	x	x	x	x	x	x	x	x
Sudan	x	x	x	x	x	x	x	x		x	x	x	x	x	x	x	x	x	x
Suriname	x		x			x	x	x		x	x	x	x	x	x	x	x	x	
Swaziland[1]	x		x	x	x	x	x	x			x	x	x	x	x	x	x	x	
Sweden	x	x	x	x	x	x	x	x	x	x	x	x	x	x	x	x	x	x	x
Switzerland		x					x	x		x	x	x	x	x	x	x	x	x	x
Syria	x	x	x	x		x	x	x		x	x	x	x	x	x	x	x	x	x
Tanzania	x	x	x	x	x	x	x	x		x	x	x	x	x	x	x	x	x	x

continued

INTERNATIONAL ORGANIZATIONS — United Nations (Membership)

	UN	IAEA	IBRD	IDA	IFC	IMF	FAO	IFAD[4]	GATT	IMO[5]	ICAO[6]	ILO[7]	ITU[8]	UNESCO[9]	UNIDO	UPU[10]	WHO[11]	WMO[12]	WIPO
Thailand	x	x	x	x	x	x	x	x	x	x	x	x	x	x	x	x	x	x	
Togo	x		x	x	x	x	x	x	x	x	x	x	x	x	x	x	x	x	x
Tonga[1]			x		x	x	x	x		x			x	x	x	x	x		
Trinidad and Tobago	x		x	x	x	x	x	x	x	x	x	x	x	x	x	x	x	x	x
Tunisia[3]	x	x	x	x	x	x	x	x	x	x	x	x	x	x	x	x	x	x	x
Turkey	x	x	x	x	x	x	x	x	x	x	x	x	x	x	x	x	x	x	x
Tuvalu[1]														x					
Uganda	x	x	x	x	x	x	x	x	x		x	x	x	x	x	x	x	x	x
Ukrainian SSR	x	x									x	x	x	x	x	x	x	x	x
USSR	x	x								x	x	x	x	x	x	x	x	x	x
United Arab Emirates[1]	x	x	x	x	x	x	x	x		x	x	x	x	x	x	x	x	x	x
United Kingdom	x	x	x	x	x	x	x	x	x	x	x	x	x		x	x	x	x	x
USA	x	x	x	x	x	x	x	x	x	x	x	x	x		x	x	x	x	x
Uruguay	x	x	x			x	x	x	x	x	x	x	x	x	x	x	x	x	x
Vanuatu	x				x	x	x			x	x		x			x	x	x	
Vatican City		x											x		x				x
Venezuela	x	x	x		x	x	x	x		x	x	x	x	x	x	x	x	x	x
Viet-Nam	x	x		x		x	x	x		x	x	x	x	x	x	x	x	x	x
Western Samoa	x		x	x	x	x	x							x			x		
Yemen Arab Republic	x		x	x	x	x	x	x			x	x	x	x	x	x	x	x	x
Yemen, People's Democratic Republic[1]	x		x	x		x	x			x	x	x	x	x	x	x	x		
Yugoslavia	x	x	x	x	x	x	x	x	x	x	x	x	x	x	x	x	x	x	x
Zaire	x	x	x	x	x	x	x	x	x	x	x	x	x	x	x	x	x	x	x
Zambia[1]	x	x	x	x	x	x	x	x	x		x	x	x	x	x	x	x	x	x
Zimbabwe	x	x	x	x	x	x	x	x	x		x	x	x	x	x	x	x	x	x

[1] Countries to whose territories GATT has been applied and which now, as independent states, maintain a *de facto* application of the GATT pending final decisions as to their future commercial policy.
[2] Suspended from WMO April 1975.
[3] Acceded provisionally to GATT.
[4] For a breakdown of IFAD members by category, see p. 68.
[5] Hong Kong is an associate member of IMO.
[6] The Cook Islands and the Marshall Islands are members of ICAO.
[7] Namibia (South West Africa) is a full member of ILO.
[8] Members also include British Overseas Territories, French Overseas Territories, Macau, United States Territories and Namibia (South West Africa).
[9] Namibia (South West Africa) is also a member of UNESCO.
[10] Members also include British Overseas Territories, French Overseas Territories, Macau, the Netherlands Antilles and United States Territories.
[11] The Cook Islands is a member of WHO and Namibia (South West Africa) is an associate member.
[12] Members also include British Caribbean Territories, French Polynesia, Hong Kong, the Netherlands Antilles and New Caledonia, all of which maintain their own meteorological service.

SPECIALIZED AGENCIES WITHIN THE UN SYSTEM

Food and Agriculture Organization—FAO

Address: Via delle Terme di Caracalla, 00100 Rome, Italy.
Telephone: 57971.
Telex: 610181.

FAO, the first specialized agency of the UN to be founded after World War II, was established in Quebec, Canada, in October 1945. The Organization fights malnutrition and hunger and serves as a co-ordinating agency for development programmes in the whole range of food and agriculture, including forestry and fisheries. It helps developing countries to promote educational and training facilities and institution-building.

MEMBERS

158 members: see Table on pp. 50–52.

Organization
(October 1988)

CONFERENCE

The governing body is the FAO Conference of member nations. It meets every two years, formulates policy, determines the Organization's programme and budget on a biennial basis, and elects new members. It also elects the Director-General of the Secretariat and the Independent Chairman of the Council. Every other year, FAO also holds conferences in each of its five regions (the Near East, Asia and the Pacific, Africa, Latin America and the Caribbean, and Europe).

COUNCIL

The FAO Council is composed of representatives of 49 member nations, elected by the Conference for staggered three-year terms. It is the interim governing body of FAO between sessions of the Conference. The most important standing Committees of the Council are: the Finance and Programme Committees, the Committee on Commodity Problems, the Committee on Fisheries, the Committee on Agriculture and the Committee on Forestry.

SECRETARIAT

The total number of staff at FAO headquarters at the end of 1986 was 3,475, while staff in field, regional and country offices numbered 3,099; there were also 38 associate experts at headquarters and 252 in field, regional and country offices. Work is supervised by the following Departments: Administration and Finance; General Affairs and Information; Economic and Social Policy; Agriculture; Forestry; Fisheries; and Development.

Director-General (1976–92): EDOUARD SAOUMA (Lebanon).
Deputy Director-General: (vacant).

REGIONAL OFFICES

Africa: UN Agency Building, North Maxwell Rd, POB 1628, Accra, Ghana; tel. 666851; telex 2139; Regional Rep. T. TAKA.
Asia and the Pacific: Maliwan Mansion, Phra Atit Rd, Bangkok 2, Thailand; tel. 2817844; telex 82815; Regional Rep. SURGIT SINGH PURI.
Europe: Via delle Terme di Caracalla, 00100 Rome, Italy; tel. 57971; telex 610181; Regional Rep. ALESSANDRO BOZZINI.
Latin America and the Caribbean: Avenida Santa Maria 6700, Casilla 10095, Santiago, Chile; tel. 462061; telex 228 8056; Regional Rep. MARIO E. JALIL.
Near East: Via delle Terme di Caracalla, 00100 Rome, Italy; tel. 57971; telex 610181; Regional Rep. S. JUMA.

LIAISON OFFICES

North America: Suite 300, 1001 22nd St, NW, Washington, DC 20437, USA; telex 64255; Dir R. A. SORENSON.
United Nations: Suite DC1-1125, 1 United Nations Plaza, New York, NY 10017, USA; tel. (212) 754-6036; telex 236350; Rep. GABRIEL S. SAAB.

Activities

FAO published its fifth World Food Survey in 1985. It showed that during the 1970s, for the first time on record, the proportion of the world's population recorded as undernourished fell (from 19% to 15%). But with increasing populations, the estimated total number of undernourished people increased by about 10m.; by the most conservative criteria, there were at least 335m. undernourished people in the world in 1980.

FAO aims to raise levels of nutrition and standards of living, by improving the production and distribution of food and other commodities derived from farms, fisheries and forests. Its work falls into four basic categories: analysis and dissemination of information; advising governments on policy and planning; promoting consultations and co-operation among member countries; and providing technical advice and assistance.

AGRICULTURE

About one third of FAO's Field Programme expenditure is devoted to increasing crop production, through demonstrating techniques that will enable small farmers to increase production, particularly of staple foods and oil crops, without high risk of failure. Governments are advised on the conservation of genetic resources, on improving the supply of seeds and on crop protection.

Cereal and food legume production continue to be a primary focus of FAO's activities, with emphasis on demonstrations at the farm level. During 1986, for example, FAO assisted in promoting the production of under-exploited traditional food crops, such as cassava, yams, breadfruit, sweet potato and plantains, through training sessions for agricultural extension staff and pilot projects for small farmers. It was also involved in the preparation of large-scale regional programmes to promote these crops: a programme for nine African countries (costing US $4.5m.), and another for 12 Pacific island states began in 1987. Through the International Rice Commission FAO promotes the development of the world's most important single food crop. Particular attention is given to methods of integrating rice cultivation with other produce—allowing farmers with little land to produce more rice and, for example, fish, small animals, or mushrooms. FAO also gives considerable help to horticulture and to livestock production, with the aim of raising standards of nutrition as well as increasing the availability of staple foods. Despite the emphasis on Africa (see below), FAO programmes do not overlook the needs of the rest of the developing world: during 1987 FAO was operating 652 projects in Asia, 353 in the Near East, 335 in Latin America and the Caribbean, and 1,145 in Africa.

Plant protection and animal health programmes form an important part of FAO's work as farming methods become more intensive, and pests more resistant to control methods. At the FAO conference in November 1985 the member nations approved an International Code of Conduct on the Distribution and Use of Pesticides. FAO has also been developing and introducing new weed-control techniques, which require less labour and enable poor farming families to cultivate larger areas than is possible with traditional methods. In 1986 FAO set up an emergency centre for operations to counter the threat to much of Africa posed by enormous numbers of five separate species of grasshoppers and locusts, and the campaign continued in 1987 and 1988. At the beginning of 1988 FAO reported that the infestation affecting north and west Africa was the worst for 30 years. An emergency programme to spray pesticides in the insects' principal breeding areas (Chad, Mali and Niger) was initiated in April, and in September FAO estimated that some 6.5m. hectares of land (mainly in Chad, Niger and Sudan) would need to be sprayed before the end of the year, in order to prevent even more serious infestation in 1989.

In mid-1986, FAO presented a major study *African Agriculture: the Next 25 Years*. This study examined the reasons for the widening gap between population growth and food production throughout much of that continent—highlighted by the disastrous drought years in the first half of the 1980s. It concluded that if current agricultural conditions were to continue, many countries would need to import massive quantities of food (far beyond the capacities of their economies) to feed the populations predicted for the year 2010. However, with changes in development policies and external economic conditions, food production could be raised to the level where only a handful of countries could neither grow nor import enough food, and would need to rely on food aid.

Following the study, FAO's Plan of Action for African Agriculture was adopted by 49 countries at the 14th Regional Conference for Africa in September 1986; it calls for changes in agricultural policies to give greater priority to food production by concentrating on measures to conserve the environment; and by providing small-scale producers with the inputs (including improved seeds, fertilizers, pesticides, and access to credit) needed for increased production, improving incentives (for example with more favourable pricing policies), together with the development of the institutions and infrastructure required to support increased production. The plan also emphasizes the importance of increased assistance from the industrialized countries—especially making use of their vast overcapacity in many areas—and on the vital importance of creating international trade conditions that no longer hinder the economic development of African countries.

FISHERIES

In 1979 FAO began a special programme to help developing countries to adjust to the imposition of exclusive economic zones (EEZs) which extend the jurisdiction of coastal states over the waters up to 200 nautical miles (370 km) offshore. It also runs a Fisheries Law Advisory Programme, enabling neighbouring states, for example, to harmonize legislation and provide uniform conditions of access to foreign fleets. FAO's work on fisheries development concentrates on small-scale fisheries and aquaculture, such as a programme for developing artisanal fisheries in the countries with a coastline on the Bay of Bengal (from 1979). It also supports projects for improving the processing and transport of fish so as to avoid wastage. In 1984 FAO held the first World Conference on Fisheries Management and Development, which approved five 'action programmes' on planning and management, small-scale fisheries, aquaculture, trade in fish and fish products, and promoting the role of fisheries in alleviating under-nutrition.

FORESTRY

FAO emphasizes the importance of tropical forests in the provision of food, wood for energy, shelter and employment for millions of people, as well as their role in the conservation of soil and water, and attempts to prevent their destruction. Following the first comprehensive study of the world's tropical forest resources, undertaken by FAO and UNEP, the Forest Resources Information System came into operation in 1983. In 1985 FAO introduced a Tropical Forestry Action Plan, which outlines priority action in five major areas: forestry in land use; forest-based industrial development; fuelwood and energy; conservation of tropical forest ecosystems; and the development of institutions. An international conference on tropical forestry was jointly organized by FAO in July 1987, and in October an international seminar on wood-based energy was held to discuss the planning of national programmes for the use of fuel-wood.

PROCESSING AND MARKETING

Conservative estimates suggest that at least 10% of all food harvested is lost before it can be consumed. FAO helps reduce immediate post-harvest losses, with the introduction of improved processing methods and storage systems. It also advises on the distribution and marketing of agricultural produce and on the selection and preparation of foods for optimum nutrition. Many of these activities form part of wider rural development projects. For many developing countries, agricultural products are the main source of foreign earnings, but the terms under which they are traded often favour the industrialized countries. FAO's long-standing Committee on Commodity Problems agreed at its 55th session in 1985 that all efforts should be made to eliminate export subsidies and other related practices, as well as protectionist measures which curb access to international markets.

FOOD SECURITY

FAO's food security policy aims to encourage the production of adequate food supplies, to maximize stability in the flow of supplies, and to ensure access on the part of those who need them. The Global Information and Early Warning System monitors the world food situation and identifies countries threatened by shortages to guide potential donors. The Food Security Assistance Scheme, established in 1976, aims to help developing countries in strengthening their food security by setting up food reserves and by developing national and regional early warning systems. In 1985 the FAO Conference approved a World Food Security Compact, requesting that governments and organizations should direct their efforts to satisfying the inalienable right of all people, at all times, to the food they need.

FAO INVESTMENT CENTRE

The Investment Centre was established in 1964 to help countries prepare viable investment projects that will attract external financing. By the end of 1986 it had channelled US $31,000m. for 667 projects. The World Bank is the single most important financing institution for investment projects prepared by FAO. Joint activities with regional development banks have increased during the 1980s, along with support for national development banks and co-operation with various Arab funds.

EMERGENCY RELIEF

The Office for Special Relief Operations (OSRO) was set up in 1973 to cope with the disastrous drought in the Sahel in that year. In 1975 the office was expanded to handle such emergencies globally. As well as providing emergency aid, OSRO aims to rehabilitate agricultural production following disasters. Jointly with the United Nations, FAO is responsible for the World Food Programme (q.v.) which provides emergency food supplies, and food aid in support of development projects.

INFORMATION AND RESEARCH

FAO issues regular statistical reports, commodity studies, and technical manuals in local languages (see list of publications below).

General and specialized computerized data bases co-ordinated by FAO contain information on every area of food and agriculture; the Current Agricultural Research Information System (CARIS), for example, enables over 70 countries to exchange information on current research; other systems provide information on agricultural sciences and technology (AGRIS), commodities (ICS), fisheries (ASFIS and FISHDAB) and forest resources (FORIS).

FAO's Research and Technology Development Division helps to co-ordinate members' agricultural research. Missions to review and plan research are sent to member countries.

FAO Councils and Commissions

(Based at the Rome headquarters unless otherwise indicated.)

African Commission on Agricultural Statistics: c/o FAO Regional Office for Africa, POB 1628, Accra, Ghana: f. 1961 to advise member countries on the development and standardization of food and agricultural statistics. Mems: 37 states.

African Forestry Commission: f. 1959 to advise on the formulation of forest policy and to review and co-ordinate its implementation on a regional level; to exchange information and advise on technical problems. Mems: 41 states.

Asia and Pacific Commission on Agricultural Statistics: c/o FAO Regional Office, Maliwan Mansion, Phra Atit Rd, Bangkok 2, Thailand; f. 1962 to review the state of food and agricultural statistics in the region and to advise member countries on the development and standardization of agricultural statistics. Mems: 23 states.

Asia and Pacific Plant Protection Commission: c/o FAO Regional Office, Maliwan Mansion, Phra Atit Rd, Bangkok 2, Thailand; f. 1956 (new title 1983) to strengthen international co-operation in plant protection to prevent the introduction and spread of destructive plant diseases and pests. Mems: 27 states.

Asia-Pacific Forestry Commission: f. 1949 to advise on the formulation of forest policy, and review and co-ordinate its implementation throughout the region; to exchange information and advise on technical problems. Mems: 24 states.

Caribbean Plant Protection Commission: f. 1967 to preserve the existing plant resources of the area. Mems: 21 states.

Commission for Controlling the Desert Locust in the Eastern Region of its distribution area in South West Asia: f. 1964 to carry out all possible measures to control plagues of the desert locust in the region. Mems: Afghanistan, India, Iran, Pakistan.

Commission for Controlling the Desert Locust in the Near East: f. 1965 to carry out all possible measures to control plagues of the desert locust within the Middle East and to reduce crop damage. Mems: 14 states.

Commission for Controlling the Desert Locust in North-West Africa: f. 1971 to promote research on control of the desert locust in NW Africa. Mems: 4 states.

INTERNATIONAL ORGANIZATIONS

United Nations (Specialized Agencies)

Commission for Inland Fisheries of Latin America: f. 1976 to promote, co-ordinate and assist national and regional fishery and limnological surveys and programmes of research and development leading to the rational utilization of inland fishery resources. Mems: 20 states.

Commission on African Animal Trypanosomiasis: f. 1979 to develop and implement programmes to combat this disease. Mems: 39 states.

Commission on Fertilizers: f. 1973 to provide guidance on the effective distribution and use of fertilizers. Mems: 83 states.

Commission on Plant Genetic Resources: f. 1983 to provide advice on programmes dealing with crop improvement through plant genetic resources. Mems: 77 states.

European Commission for the Control of Foot-and-Mouth Disease: f. 1953 to promote national and international action for the control of the disease in Europe and its final eradication. Mems: 25 states.

European Commission on Agriculture: f. 1949 to encourage and facilitate action and co-operation in technological agricultural problems among member states and between international organizations concerned with agricultural technology in Europe; to make recommendations on all matters within its technical and geographical competence. Mems: 29 states.

European Forestry Commission: f. 1947 to advise on the formulation of forest policy and to review and co-ordinate its implementation on a regional level; to exchange information and to make recommendations. Mems: 28 states.

European Inland Fisheries Advisory Commission: f. 1957 to promote improvements in inland fisheries and to advise member Governments and FAO on inland fishery matters. Mems: 25 states.

FAO Regional Commission on Farm Management for Asia and the Far East: c/o FAO Regional Office, Maliwan Mansion, Phra Atit Rd, Bangkok 2, Thailand; f. 1959 to stimulate and co-ordinate farm management research and extension activities and to serve as a clearing-house for the exchange of information and experience among the member countries in the region.

FAO/WHO Codex Alimentarius Commission: f. 1962 to make proposals for the co-ordination of all international food standards work and to publish a code of international food standards. Mems: 130 states.

General Fisheries Council for the Mediterranean—GFCM: f. 1952 to develop aquatic resources, to encourage and co-ordinate research in the fishing and allied industries, to assemble and publish information, and to recommend the standardization of equipment, techniques and nomenclature. Mems: 19 states.

Indian Ocean Fishery Commission: c/o FAO Regional Office, Maliwan Mansion, Phra Atit Rd, Bangkok 2, Thailand; f. 1967 to promote national programmes, research and development activities, and to examine management problems. Mems: 41 states.

Indo-Pacific Fishery Commission: c/o FAO Regional Office, Maliwan Mansion, Phra Atit Rd, Bangkok 2, Thailand; f. 1948 to develop fisheries, encourage and co-ordinate research, disseminate information, recommend projects to governments, propose standards in technique and nomenclature. Mems: 19 states.

International Poplar Commission: f. 1947 to study scientific, technical, social and economic aspects of poplar and willow cultivation; to promote the exchange of ideas and material between research workers, producers and users; to arrange joint research programmes, congresses, study tours; to make recommendations to the FAO Conference and to National Poplar Commissions. Mems: 32 states.

International Rice Commission: f. 1948 to promote national and international action on production, conservation, distribution and consumption of rice, except matters relating to international trade. Meetings: Sessions of the IRC are held every four years and its three technical working parties every two years. Mems: 54 states.

Joint FAO/WHO/OAU Regional Food and Nutrition Commission for Africa: c/o FAO Regional Office for Africa, POB 1628, Accra, Ghana; f. 1962 to provide liaison in matters pertaining to food and nutrition, and to review food and nutrition problems in Africa. Mems: 43 states.

Latin American Forestry Commission: f. 1948 to advise on formulation of forest policy and review and co-ordinate its implementation throughout the region; to exchange information and advise on technical problems. Mems: 29 states.

Near East Forestry Commission: f. 1953 to advise on formulation of forest policy and review and co-ordinate its implementation throughout the region; to exchange information and advise on technical problems. Mems: 21 states.

Near East Regional Commission on Agriculture: f. 1983 to conduct periodic reviews of agricultural problems in the region; to promote policies and regional and national programmes for improving production of crops and livestock; to expand agricultural services and research; to promote the transfer of technology and regional technical co-operation; and to provide guidance on training and manpower development. Mems: 18 states.

Near East Regional Economic and Social Policy Commission: f. 1983 to review developments relating to food, agriculture and food security; to recommend policies on agrarian reform and rural development; to review and exchange information on food and nutrition policies and on agricultural planning; and to compile statistics. Mems: 19 states.

North American Forestry Commission: f. 1959 to advise on the formulation and co-ordination of national forest policies; to exchange information and to advise on technical problems. Mems: Canada, Mexico, USA.

Regional Animal Production and Health Commission for Asia, the Far East and the South-West Pacific: c/o FAO Regional Office, Maliwan Mansion, Phra Atit Rd, Bangkok 2, Thailand; f. 1973 to promote livestock development in general, and national and international research and action with respect to animal health and husbandry problems in the region. Mems: 14 states.

Regional Commission on Food Security for Asia and the Pacific: c/o FAO Regional Office, Maliwan Mansion, Phra Atit Rd, Bangkok 2, Thailand; f. 1982 to review regional food security; to assist member states in preparing programmes for strengthening food security and for dealing with acute food shortages; and to encourage technical co-operation. Mems: 17 states.

Regional Commission on Land and Water Use in the Near East: f. 1967 to review the current situation with regard to land and water use in the region; to identify the main problems concerning the development of land and water resources which require research and study and to consider other related matters. Mems: 22 states.

Regional Fisheries Advisory Commission for the Southwest Atlantic: f. 1961 to advise FAO on fisheries in the South-west Atlantic area, to advise member countries on the administration and rational exploitation of marine and inland resources; to assist in the collection and dissemination of data, in training, and to promote liaison and co-operation. Mems: Argentina, Brazil, Uruguay.

Western Central Atlantic Fishery Commission: f. 1973 to assist international co-operation for the conservation, development and utilization of the living resources, especially shrimps, of the Western Central Atlantic. Mems: 28 states.

FINANCE

The Regular Programme Budget for the two years 1986–87 amounted to US $437m. The Regular Programme, which is financed by contributions from member governments, covers the cost of the FAO's Secretariat, its Technical Co-operation Programme and part of the cost of several special action programmes. The budget for 1988–89 amounted to $492m. In November 1987 it was reported that arrears in payments by member countries amounted to some $100m., of which about $67m. was owed by the USA. The delay in payment was partly attributed to the dissatisfaction expressed by some member countries at lack of consultation in FAO's budgetary procedures.

Advice and assistance in the field is provided through the Field Programme, funded largely from external sources such as the UNDP and various trust funds provided by donor governments. Owing to a reduction in funds available from UNDP, its share of FAO's Field Programme costs was 41% in 1986, compared with 87% in 1972. This fall was partly offset by an increase in financing by trust funds, which amounted to US $151m. in 1986 (about 48% of Field Programme costs). The total Field Programme expenditure in 1986 exceeded $315m.

FAO FIELD PROGRAMMES BY REGION, 1986

Region	Number of projects	Number of staff	Expenditure in 1986 (US $ million)
Africa	1,041	1,382	137.8
Asia and the Pacific	614	726	71.5
Latin America and the Caribbean	307	440	23.6
Near East	354	578	51.4
Europe	75	51	4.4
Global/inter-regional	115	89	26.4
World Total	**2,248**	**3,177**	**315.1**

INTERNATIONAL ORGANIZATIONS United Nations (Specialized Agencies)

FAO PUBLICATIONS
Quarterly Bulletin of Statistics.
Food Outlook (monthly).
Production Yearbook.
Yearbook of Fishery Statistics.
Yearbook of Forest Products.
The State of Food and Agriculture (annually).
Food and Agricultural Legislation.
Commodity reviews; studies; manuals.

General Agreement on Tariffs and Trade—GATT

Address: Centre William Rappard, 154 rue de Lausanne, 1211 Geneva 21, Switzerland.
Telephone: (022) 395111.
Telex: 28 787.

GATT was established in 1948 as a multilateral treaty aiming to liberalize world trade and place it on a secure basis.

CONTRACTING PARTIES TO GATT
In October 1988 there were 96 contracting parties (including Hong Kong, which became a member in its own right in 1986); one state has acceded provisionally to GATT and a further 28 in practice apply the rules of GATT to their commercial policy: see Table on pp. 50–52.

Organization
(October 1988)

SESSIONS
The sessions of contracting parties are usually held annually, in Geneva. The session is the highest body of GATT. Decisions are generally arrived at by consensus, not by vote. On the rare occasions that voting takes place, each contracting party (member country) has one vote. Most decisions by vote are taken by simple majority; but a two-thirds majority, with the majority comprising more than half the member countries, is needed for 'waivers': authorizations, in particular cases, to depart from specific obligations under the General Agreement. Outside the sessions, votes may be taken by postal ballot.

COUNCIL OF REPRESENTATIVES
Meets as necessary (generally about 10 times a year) to deal with urgent and routine matters arising between sessions of contracting parties and to supervise the work of committees and working groups.

SECRETARIAT
The secretariat, numbering about 400 people, consists of experts in trade policy and economics and an administrative staff (including translators and interpreters). It prepares and runs the sessions of contracting parties and services the work of the Council and of the committees, working groups and panels of independent experts. It is also responsible for organizing multilateral trade negotiations held within the framework of GATT.
Director-General: ARTHUR DUNKEL (Switzerland).
Deputy Directors-General: MADAN MATHUR (India), CHARLES CARLISLE (USA).

COMMITTEES AND WORKING PARTIES
Standing committees or councils exist to direct GATT work on trade and development issues; to carry on trade negotiations among developing countries; to examine the situation of countries using trade restrictions to protect their balance of payments; to supervise implementation of the various Tokyo Round agreements; to supervise the Arrangement Regarding International Trade in Textiles (Multi-fibre Arrangement); and to deal with budget, financial and administrative questions.

A Consultative Group of Eighteen, consisting of high-level representatives with responsibility for trade policy in their countries, was established in 1975. It meets at least once a year.

Working parties (ad hoc committees) are set up to deal with current questions, such as requests for accession to GATT; verification that agreements concluded by member countries are in conformity with GATT; or studies of issues on which the member countries will later wish to take a joint decision. Panels of independent experts are often set up to investigate disputes and report their conclusions to the Council. Twelve trade disputes were under consideration by the Council in 1987.

INTERNATIONAL TRADE CENTRE
Address: 54–56 rue de Montbrillant, 1202 Geneva, Switzerland.
Telephone: (022) 34 60 21.
Telex: 289052.

Established by GATT in 1964, the Centre has been jointly operated since 1968 by GATT and the UN (the latter through UNCTAD). It assists developing countries to formulate and implement trade promotion programmes, provides information and advice on export markets and marketing techniques, helps to develop export promotion and marketing institutions and services, and trains national personnel. In 1984 it became an executing agency of the UN Development Programme (UNDP, q.v.), directly responsible for carrying out UNDP-financed projects related to trade promotion.
Executive Director: GÖRAN M. ENGBLOM (Sweden).

The Agreement

GATT is based on a few fundamental principles. First, as directed in the famous 'most-favoured-nation' clause, trade must be conducted on the basis of non-discrimination: all contracting parties are bound to grant to each other treatment as favourable as they give to any country in the application and administration of import and export duties and charges. Exceptions—principally for customs unions and free trade areas and for measures in favour of and among developing countries (see Tokyo Round 'framework' agreements below)—are granted only subject to strict rules.

Second, protection should be given to domestic industry essentially through the customs tariff. The aim of this rule is to make the extent of protection clear and to make competition possible.

Third, a stable and predictable basis for trade is provided by the binding of the tariff levels negotiated among the contracting parties. These bound items are listed for each country in tariff schedules which form an integral part of the General Agreement. A return to higher tariffs is discouraged by the requirement that any increases are compensated for; consequently this provision is invoked rarely.

Consultation, to avoid damage to the trading interests of contracting parties, is another fundamental principle of GATT. Members are able to call on GATT for a fair settlement of cases in which they think their rights under the General Agreement are being withheld or compromised by other members.

There are 'waiver' procedures whereby a country may, when its economic or trade circumstances so warrant, seek a derogation from a particular GATT obligation or obligations. There are also escape provisions for emergency action against imports in certain defined circumstances.

The trade problems of developing countries receive special attention in GATT. In 1965 a new chapter on Trade and Development was added to the General Agreement; a key provision is that developing countries should not be expected to offer reciprocity in negotiations with developed countries. GATT members have also relaxed the most-favoured-nation rule to accommodate the Generalized System of Preferences by developed for developing countries and to allow an exchange of preferential tariff reductions among developing countries. (See UNCTAD.)

Finally, GATT offers a framework within which negotiations are held for the reduction of tariffs and other barriers to trade and a structure for putting the results of such negotiations into a legal instrument.

INTERNATIONAL ORGANIZATIONS — United Nations (Specialized Agencies)

Activities

Much of GATT's regular work consists of consultations and negotiations on specific trade problems affecting individual commodities or member countries.

From time to time, major multilateral trade negotiations also take place under GATT auspices. There have been seven rounds of such negotiations: in 1947 (in Geneva), in 1949 (Annecy, France), 1951 (Torquay, England), 1956 (Geneva), 1960–61 (Geneva, the 'Dillon Round'), 1964–67 (Geneva, the 'Kennedy Round'), and 1973–79 (Geneva, the 'Tokyo Round', so called because the negotiations were launched at a ministerial meeting in the Japanese capital in 1973). A further round began at Punta del Este, Uruguay, in September 1986 (see below).

Ninety-nine countries participated in the Tokyo Round. In November 1979 the negotiations were concluded with agreements covering: an improved legal framework for the conduct of world trade (which includes recognition of tariff and non-tariff treatment in favour of and among developing countries as a permanent legal feature of the world trading system); non-tariff measures (subsidies and countervailing duties; technical barriers to trade; government procurement; customs valuation; import licensing procedures; and a revision of the 1967 GATT anti-dumping code); bovine meat; dairy products; tropical products; and an agreement on free trade in civil aircraft. The agreements contain provisions for special and more favourable treatment for developing countries.

Participating countries also agreed to reduce tariffs on thousands of industrial and agricultural products, for the most part by annual cuts over a period of seven years beginning on 1 January 1980. By the beginning of 1987 all contracting parties had implemented the final tariff cuts negotiated in the Tokyo Round: cuts worth some US $300,000m. had reduced the average level of industrial tariffs in the developed countries by 34% (from 7.0% to 4.7%).

The agreements providing an improved framework for the conduct of world trade took effect in November 1979. The other agreements took effect on 1 January 1980, except for those covering government procurement and customs valuation, which took effect on 1 January 1981, and the concessions on tropical products which began as early as 1977. Committees were established to supervise implementation of the agreements.

A new work programme was established in November 1979, giving priority to full implementation of the Tokyo Round agreements, future trade liberalization and further efforts to assist the trade of developing countries; the Committee on Trade and Development is largely responsible for these efforts, and its role was strengthened in the work programme. Two new sub-committees were established in 1981: one to examine any new protective measures taken by developed countries against imports from developing countries, and the other to consider the trade problems of the least-developed countries.

A considerable proportion of world trade in textiles and clothing is carried out by the 39 signatories participating in the Arrangement Regarding International Trade in Textiles (Multi-fibre Arrangement), which entered into force in January 1974 under GATT auspices for a period of four years. Its aim was to allow the major importers (the USA, Japan and the European Community) to reorganize their textile industries in the face of low-cost production by developing countries. Under the Arrangement all fibres, fabrics and garments are divided into categories, and within each category bilateral agreements are negotiated between suppliers and importers for every product that is likely to cause disruption in the importer's domestic textile industry. In December 1977 the signatory Governments of the Arrangement decided to extend it for four years, and at the end of 1981 the Arrangement was extended for a further period of four years and seven months, from 1 January 1982 to 31 July 1986. Although many developing countries demanded that the Arrangement should be abolished and that trade in textiles should be covered by normal GATT procedures, a new Arrangement was agreed with effect from 1 August 1986, for five years. A negotiating group on textiles and clothing was established in 1987 under the Uruguay Round of negotiations (see below).

The 1982 session of contracting parties was held in Geneva in November and included a ministerial-level meeting (the first for nine years), attended by some 70 ministers from the GATT member countries, who adopted a joint declaration, affirming their commitment against protectionism and calling for a renewed consensus in support of the GATT. The declaration also set out a programme of work covering many aspects of trade policy, with emphasis on the following aims: to identify the means of bringing agriculture more fully into the multilateral trading system; to revise the GATT rules on emergency 'safeguard' action against imports; to identify and examine quantitative restrictions and other non-tariff barriers and to consider their possible elimination or liberalization; to review the implementation of GATT rules relating to developing countries; to examine the scope for trade liberalization in textiles and clothing; to look at problems affecting trade in certain natural resource products; and to review the operation of the Tokyo Round agreements and arrangements. Reports on much of this work were presented to the session of contracting parties in November 1984, and it was subsequently continued.

During 1985 and 1986 preparations were made for a new round of multilateral trade negotiations. Many developing countries opposed the USA's proposal that the agenda should include liberalizing trade in services (such as tourism, banking and insurance), an area not previously covered by GATT, but eventually a compromise was reached whereby negotiations on services were to be conducted by a separate committee, supervised by GATT but outside its legal framework. Proposals by the USA and others to discuss distortion of agricultural trade by export subsidies and farm support policies were adopted, despite opposition from the European Community. The negotiations were also to cover textiles; tropical products; tariffs; non-tariff measures; barriers to foreign investment; and 'piracy' of intellectual property (counterfeiting and copyright violations). The Uruguay Round began in September 1986 and was expected to be completed in four years. Participants agreed that during the course of the negotiations they would observe a 'standstill' in measures that restrict or distort trade, and a 'rollback' or phasing-out of existing trade practices that were inconsistent with GATT rules. The progress of negotiations was, however, delayed by a dispute over the best method of supervising the 'standstill' and 'rollback' undertakings; there was also disagreement on the timetable for negotiations on agricultural trade. At the end of January 1987, however, agreement was reached on the programme for the negotiations, which were to be conducted by 14 groups dealing with aspects of trade in goods (and by the separate group discussing trade in services). During 1987 105 countries and territories were participating in the negotiations. One of the earliest results of the Uruguay Round was expected to be an agreement on the removal of trade restrictions affecting imports of tropical products from developing countries: this was expected to be approved by ministers before the end of 1988.

FINANCE

Payments are based on each member's share of the total trade between members. The budget for 1988 amounted to 61.4m. Swiss francs.

PUBLICATIONS

(available in English, French and Spanish editions).

International Trade (annual report on the main developments in international trade).

GATT Activities (annual).

GATT Focus (newsletter, 10 a year).

Basic Instruments and Selected Documents series. Annual supplements record the formal decisions of the Members, important committee papers, etc. Volume IV gives the current text of the General Agreement.

GATT Studies in International Trade (occasional series of staff papers).

GATT: What it is, What it does.

The Tokyo Round of Multilateral Trade Negotiations. A two-volume report by the Director-General. Copies of the multilateral agreements concluded in the Tokyo Round are also available.

International Atomic Energy Agency—IAEA

Address: POB 100, Wagramerstrasse 5, 1400 Vienna, Austria.
Telephone: (0222) 2360.
Telex: 1-12645.

The International Atomic Energy Agency (IAEA) is an intergovernmental organization, established in 1957 in accordance with a decision of the General Assembly of the United Nations. Although it is autonomous, the IAEA is administratively a member of the United Nations, and reports on its activities once a year to the UN General Assembly. Its main objectives are to enlarge the contribution of atomic energy to peace, health and prosperity throughout the world and to ensure, so far as it is able, that assistance provided by it or at its request or under its supervision or control is not used in such a way as to further any military purpose.

MEMBERS

113 members: see Table on pp. 50-52.

Organization

(October 1988)

GENERAL CONFERENCE

The Conference, comprising representatives of all 113 member states, convenes each year for general debate on the Agency's policy, budget and programme. It elects members to the Board of Governors, and approves the appointment of the Director-General; it admits new member states.

BOARD OF GOVERNORS

The Board of Governors consists of 35 member states: 22 elected by the General Conference for two-year periods and 13 designated by the Board from among member states which are advanced in nuclear technology. It is the principal policy-making body of the Agency and is responsible to the General Conference. Under its own authority, the Board approves all safeguards agreements, important projects and safety standards.

SECRETARIAT

The Secretariat, comprising about 2,000 staff, is headed by the Director-General, who is assisted by five Deputy Directors-General. The Secretariat is divided into five departments: Technical Co-operation; Nuclear Energy and Safety; Research and Isotopes; Safeguards; Administration. The Director-General is also advised on scientific and technical matters by a Scientific Advisory Committee, comprising 15 distinguished scientists having a wide variety of expertise. A Standing Advisory Group on Safeguards Implementation advises the Director-General on technical aspects of safeguards.

Director-General: HANS BLIX (Sweden).

Activities

The IAEA's functions can be divided into two main categories: technical co-operation (assisting research on and practical application of atomic energy for peaceful uses); and safeguards (ensuring that special fissionable and other materials, services, equipment and information made available by the Agency or at its request or under its supervision are not used for any military purpose).

TECHNICAL CO-OPERATION AND TRAINING

In 1987 technical co-operation provided by the IAEA exceeded $46m. for 962 projects. More than 80 countries received technical co-operation in the form of expert services, equipment and training. The IAEA held 64 training courses during the year, and trained 945 people through its fellowship programme. More than 1,800 expert assignments were made, to provide specialized help on specific nuclear applications.

FOOD AND AGRICULTURE

In co-operation with FAO (q.v.), the Agency conducts programmes of applied research on the use of radiation and isotopes in six main fields: efficiency in the use of water and fertilizers; improvement of food crops by induced mutations; eradication or control of destructive insects by the introduction of sterilized insects; improvement of livestock nutrition and health; studies on improving efficacy and reducing residues of pesticides, and increasing utilization of agricultural wastes; and food preservation by irradiation. In 1987 assistance to member states was provided through 64 research contracts and agreements and 70 technical co-operation projects.

LIFE SCIENCES

In co-operation with the World Health Organization (WHO, q.v.), IAEA promotes the use of nuclear techniques in medicine, biology and health-related environmental research, provides training, and conducts research on techniques for improving the accuracy of radiation dosimetry.

The IAEA/WHO Network of Secondary Standard Dosimetry Laboratories (SSDLs) comprised 50 member laboratories in 1987. The Agency's Dosimetry Laboratory performs dose inter-comparisons for both SSDLs and radiotherapy centres. In 1987 the number of radiotherapy hospitals participating in the cobalt-60 postal dose inter-comparison service being conducted by the Agency and WHO rose to about 140. The IAEA undertakes maintenance plans for nuclear laboratories; national programmes of quality control for nuclear medicine instruments; quality control of radioimmunoassay techniques; radiation sterilization of medical supplies; and improvement of cancer therapy.

PHYSICAL SCIENCES AND LABORATORIES

The Agency's programme in physical sciences includes industrial applications of isotopes and radiation technology; application of nuclear techniques to mineral exploration and exploitation; radiopharmaceuticals; and hydrology, involving the use of isotope techniques for assessment of water resources. Nuclear data services are provided, and training is given for nuclear scientists from developing countries. The IAEA Laboratory at Seibersdorf, Austria, supports the Agency's research, radio-isotope and safeguards programmes, while the Safeguards Analytical Laboratory, in Vienna, analyses nuclear fuel-cycle samples collected by IAEA safeguards inspectors. The International Laboratory of Marine Radioactivity, in Monaco, studies radionuclides and other ocean pollutants. From 1979 onwards the European Community, Japan, the USA and the USSR worked as partners on the International Tokamak Reactor (INTOR) for controlled fusion. In 1987 the four agreed to begin a conceptual design study for an international thermonuclear experimental reactor (ITER) as a continuation of work on INTOR.

NUCLEAR POWER

At the end of 1987 there were 417 nuclear power plants in operation throughout the world, with a total capacity of 297,927 MW. These plants accounted for more than 16% of total electrical energy generated during the year. The Agency helps developing member states to introduce nuclear-powered electricity-generating plants through assistance with planning, feasibility studies, surveys of manpower and infrastructure, and safety measures. It publishes books on numerous aspects of nuclear power, and provides training courses on safety in nuclear power plants and other topics. An energy data bank collects and disseminates information on nuclear technology, and a power-reactor information system monitors the technical performance of nuclear power plants.

RADIOACTIVE WASTE MANAGEMENT

During 1987 there was a shift of emphasis in the Agency's waste management programme towards the increased provision of practical help to member states in the management of radioactive waste. The Waste Management Advisory Programme (WAMAP) was established and carried out four missions in 1987, while 13 were requested by member states for 1988.

NUCLEAR SAFETY

The IAEA's nuclear safety programme encourages international co-operation in the exchange of information, promoting implementation of its safety standards and providing advisory safety services. It includes the IAEA Incident Reporting System; an emergency preparedness programme; operational safety review teams; and a safety research co-ordination programme.

The revised edition of the Basic Safety Standards for Radiation Protection (IAEA Safety Series No. 9) was published in 1982. The Nuclear Safety Standards programme, initiated in 1974 with five codes of practice and more than 60 safety guides, was reviewed in 1987, and revised in the light of members' comments.

In 1982, to provide member states with advice on achieving and maintaining a high level of safety in the operation of nuclear power plants, the Agency established operational safety review teams, which will visit a power plant on request. In 1987 10 such missions visited seven countries. Co-ordinated research programmes establish risk criteria for the nuclear fuel cycle and identify cost-effective means to reduce risks in energy systems. The International Nuclear Safety Advisory Group (INSAG) met for the first time in March 1985: it comprises 13 experts from nuclear safety licensing authorities, nuclear industry and research, and aims to provide a forum for exchange of information and to identify important current safety issues.

During 1987 there were 94 technical co-operation projects under way in the field of radiation protection. Missions visited six countries to assist with radiation protection.

Following the serious accident at the Chernobyl nuclear power plant in the Ukraine, in April 1986, the IAEA convened a series of meetings to consider the implications of the disaster and ways of improving the response to such emergencies. Two conventions were drawn up and entered into force in October: the first commits parties to provide early notification and information about nuclear accidents with possible trans-boundary effects (it had 30 parties in August 1988); and the second commits parties to endeavour to provide assistance in the event of a nuclear accident (it had 25 parties in August 1988).

DISSEMINATION OF INFORMATION

The International Nuclear Information System (INIS) provides a computerized indexing and abstracting service. Information on the peaceful uses of atomic energy is collected by member states and international organizations and sent to the IAEA for processing and dissemination (see list of publications below). IAEA also co-operates with the FAO in an information system for agriculture (AGRIS). The IAEA Nuclear Data Section provides cost-free data centre services and co-operates with other national and regional nuclear and atomic data centres in the systematic worldwide collection, compilation, dissemination and exchange of nuclear reaction data, nuclear structure and decay data, and atomic and molecular data for fusion.

SAFEGUARDS

The Treaty on the Non-Proliferation of Nuclear Weapons (NPT), which entered into force in 1970, requires each non-nuclear-weapon state (one which had not manufactured and exploded a nuclear weapon or other nuclear explosive device prior to 1 January 1967) Party to the Treaty to conclude a safeguards agreement with the IAEA. Under such an agreement the State undertakes to accept IAEA safeguards on all nuclear material in all its peaceful nuclear activities for the purpose of verifying that such material is not diverted to nuclear weapons or other nuclear explosive devices. By the end of 1987 137 states had ratified and acceded to the Treaty, but 52 non-nuclear-weapon states had not complied, within the prescribed time-limit, with their obligations under the Treaty regarding the conclusion of the relevant safeguards agreement with the Agency.

Two nuclear-weapon states, the United Kingdom and the USA, both Party to the NPT, concluded safeguards agreements with the Agency (in 1978 and 1980 respectively) that permit the application of IAEA safeguards to all their nuclear activities, excluding those with 'direct national significance'. A third nuclear-weapon state, France, concluded a similar agreement in 1981 under which it accepts IAEA safeguards on nuclear material in facilities to be designated by France. In February 1985 an agreement was signed by the IAEA and the USSR on the application of IAEA safeguards to certain peaceful nuclear installations in the USSR.

The Treaty for the prohibition of Nuclear Weapons in Latin America (Tlatelolco Treaty) entered into force in 1968, aiming to create a zone free of nuclear weapons in Latin America. The IAEA administers full applications of safeguards in relation to the Treaty. In addition, the IAEA applies safeguards in 10 states under agreements other than those in connection with the NPT and the Tlatelolco Treaty.

In 1987 2,133 inspections were carried out under safeguards agreements at 631 nuclear installations in 52 non-nuclear-weapon states and four nuclear-weapon states. Some 320 automatic photographic and television surveillance systems operated in the field, and 12,500 seals applied to nuclear material were detached and subsequently verified. About 1,340 samples of uranium and plutonium were analysed.

INTERNATIONAL CENTRE FOR THEORETICAL PHYSICS

The Centre, in Trieste, Italy, brings together scientists from the developed and the developing countries. With support from the Italian government, the Centre has been operated jointly by the IAEA and UNESCO since 1970. Each year it offers seminars followed by a research workshop, as well as short topical seminars, training courses, symposia and panels. Independent research is also carried out. The programme concentrates on solid-state physics, high-energy and elementary particle physics, physics of nuclear structure and reactions, applicable mathematics and, to a lesser extent, on physics of the earth and the environment, physics of energy, biophysics, microprocessors and physics of technology.

NUCLEAR FUEL CYCLE

The Agency promotes the exchange of information between Member States on technical, safety, environmental, and economic aspects of nuclear fuel cycle technology, including uranium prospecting and the treatment and disposal of radioactive waste; it provides assistance to Member States in the planning, implementation and operation of nuclear fuel cycle facilities and assists in the development of advanced nuclear fuel cycle technology. Every two years, in collaboration with the OECD, the Agency prepares estimates of world uranium resources, demand and production.

BUDGET

The Agency is financed by regular and voluntary contributions from member states.

The regular budget for 1987 was about US $145.9m., and the target for voluntary contributions to finance the IAEA technical assistance programme in 1987 was $34m. A regular budget of $151m. was approved for 1988, and the target for voluntary contributions was $38m.

PUBLICATIONS

Annual Report.
Nuclear Safety Review (annually).
IAEA Newsbriefs (monthly).
IAEA News Features.
IAEA Bulletin (quarterly).
Nuclear Fusion (monthly).
Meetings on Atomic Energy (quarterly).
Technical Directories.
Panel Proceedings Series.
Safety Series.
Legal Series.
Technical Reports Series.
INIS Atomindex (bibliography, 2 a month).
INIS Reference Series.
Publications Catalogue (annually).

INTERNATIONAL ORGANIZATIONS *United Nations (Specialized Agencies)*

International Bank for Reconstruction and Development—IBRD (World Bank)

Address: 1818 H St, NW, Washington, DC 20433, USA.
Telephone: (202) 477-1234.
Telex: 248423.

The IBRD was established on 27 December 1945. Initially it was concerned with post-war reconstruction in Europe; since then its aim has been to assist the economic development of member nations by making loans where private capital is not available on reasonable terms to finance productive investments. Loans are made either direct to governments, or to private enterprise with the guarantee of their governments. The IBRD has three affiliates, the International Development Association (IDA, q.v.), the International Finance Corporation (IFC, q.v.) and the Multilateral Investment Guarantee Agency (MIGA, q.v.). The 'World Bank', as it is commonly known, comprises the IBRD and IDA.

MEMBERS

There are 151 members: see Table on pp. 50-52. Only members of the International Monetary Fund (IMF, q.v.) may be considered for membership in the Bank. Subscriptions to the capital stock of the Bank are based on each member's quota in the IMF, which is designed to reflect the country's relative economic strength. Voting rights are related to shareholdings.

Organization
(October 1988)

Officers and staff of the IBRD serve concurrently as officers and staff in the International Development Association (IDA). The Bank has offices in New York, Paris, Geneva and Tokyo; regional missions in Nairobi (for eastern and southern Africa), Abidjan (for western Africa) and Bangkok; and resident missions in 40 countries.

BOARD OF GOVERNORS

The Board of Governors consists of one Governor appointed by each member nation. Typically, a Governor is the country's finance minister, central bank governor, or a minister or an official of comparable rank. The Board normally meets once a year.

EXECUTIVE DIRECTORS

With the exception of certain powers specifically reserved to them by the Articles of Agreement, the Governors of the Bank have delegated their powers for the conduct of the general operations of the Bank to a Board of Executive Directors that performs its duties on a full-time basis at the Bank's headquarters. There are 22 Executive Directors; each Director selects an Alternate. Five Directors are appointed by the five members having the largest number of shares of capital stock, and the rest are elected by the Governors representing the other members. The President of the Bank is Chairman of the Board.

The Executive Directors fulfil dual responsibilities. First, they represent the interests of their country or groups of countries. Second, they exercise their authority as delegated by the Governors in overseeing the policies of the Bank and evaluating completed projects. Since the Bank operates on the basis of consensus (formal votes are rare), this dual role involves frequent communication and consultations with governments so as to reflect accurately their views in Board discussions.

The Directors consider and decide on the loan and credit proposals made by the President. They are also responsible for presentation to the Board of Governors at its Annual Meetings of an audit of accounts, an administrative budget, the *Annual Report* on the operations and policies of the World Bank, and any other matter that, in their judgement, requires submission to the Board of Governors. Matters may be submitted to the Governors at the Annual Meetings or at any time between Annual Meetings.

OFFICERS

President and Chairman of Executive Directors: BARBER B. CONABLE.
Senior Vice-President, Policy, Planning, Research: W. DAVID HOPPER.
Senior Vice-President, Operations: MOEEN A. QURESHI.
Senior Vice-President, Finance: ERNEST STERN.
Senior Vice-President, Administration: WILLI A. WAPENHANS.

OFFICES

New York Office and World Bank Mission to the United Nations: 747 Third Ave (26th Floor), New York, NY 10017, USA; Special Rep. to UN G. DAVID LOOS.
European Office: 66 ave d'Iéna, 75116 Paris, France; Dir (vacant).
Regional Mission in Eastern Africa: POB 30577; Reinsurance Plaza, Taifa Rd, Nairobi, Kenya; Dir PETER EIGEN.
Regional Mission in Western Africa: BP 1850; Corner Booker Washington and Jacques AKA Sts, Abidjan 01, Côte d'Ivoire; Chief ELKYN CHAPARRO.
Regional Mission in Thailand: Udom Vidhya Bldg, 956 Rama IV Rd, Sala Daeng, Bangkok 10500, Thailand; Chief PHILIPPE AMEZ.

Activities

FINANCIAL OPERATIONS

The Bank's capital is derived from members' subscriptions to capital shares, the calculation of which is based on their quotas in the International Monetary Fund (q.v.). In April 1988 the Board of Governors approved an increase of about 80% in the Bank's authorized capital, to US $171,000m. On 30 June 1988 the total subscribed capital of the Bank was US $91,436m. of which the paid-in portion is 9%; the remainder is subject to call if required to meet the Bank's obligations. Most of the Bank's lendable funds come from its borrowing, on commercial terms, in world capital markets, and also from its retained earnings and the flow of repayments on its loans. Bank loans carry a variable interest rate, rather than a rate fixed at the time of borrowing.

IBRD loans are usually for a period of 20 years or less. Loans are made to governments, or must be guaranteed by the government concerned, and are normally made for projects likely to offer a commercially viable rate of return. In 1980 the Bank introduced structural adjustment lending, which (instead of financing specific projects) supports programmes and changes necessary to 'modify the structure of an economy so that it can restore or maintain its growth and viability in its balance of payments over the medium term'.

The IBRD and IDA together made new lending and investment commitments totalling $19,221m. during the year ending 30 June 1988, compared with $17,674m. in the previous year. During the year, the IBRD alone approved 118 loans to 37 countries totalling $14,762m., compared with $14,188m. in the previous year, the largest borrowers being Brazil, India, Indonesia and Mexico (see table). Disbursements by the IBRD in the year ending 30 June 1988 amounted to $11,636m., compared with $11,383m. in the previous year. In the year ending 30 June 1988 19.9% of IBRD loans were for agriculture and rural developments, 15.1% for energy projects, 14.3% for transport and 14.0% for industry. (For details of IDA operations, see separate chapter on IDA.)

The Bank's operations were supported by borrowings in international capital markets, which totalled $10,832m. in the year ending 30 June 1988 ($9,321m. in the previous year). During the year ending 30 June 1986 the Bank made a record profit of $1,243m., owing largely to its low borrowing costs and the high rates of return on its liquid assets portfolio; in 1986/87 net income fell to $1,113m., and in 1987/88 it was $1,004m.

In July 1985 a Special Facility for Sub-Saharan Africa became effective for a three-year period, with funds of $1,250m., to finance structural adjustment, sectoral reform programmes and rehabilitation, on the same concessional terms as IDA (q.v.). In December 1987 a Regional Project Facility for sub-Saharan Africa was established by the World Bank, jointly with UNDP and the African Development Bank, to enable governments to assist the poor people most likely to be adversely affected by economic adjustment programmes.

In 1987 the Bank established a 'poverty task force' to strengthen the Bank's work in alleviating poverty. It also undertook to conduct more extensive analysis of the social effects of economic adjustment programmes. The importance of environmental protection also received greater emphasis than in the past, and in 1987/88 a central environment department and four regional environment units were established to examine the environmental impact of development projects. During the year the Bank also undertook research and operations designed to enhance the role of women in development.

INTERNATIONAL ORGANIZATIONS

United Nations (Specialized Agencies)

EXECUTIVE DIRECTORS AND THEIR VOTING POWER (June 1988)

Executive Director	Casting Votes of	IBRD Total votes	IBRD % of total	IDA Total votes	IDA % of total
Appointed:					
ROBERT B. KEATING	USA	148,957	18.93	1,057,107	18.22
MITSUKAZU ISHIKAWA	Japan	52,876	6.72	537,655	9.27
GERHARD BOEHMER	Federal Republic of Germany	40,882	5.20	414,497	7.14
HÉLÈNE PLOIX	France	39,197	4.98	227,465	3.92
FRANK CASSELL	United Kingdom	39,197	4.98	358,528	6.18
Elected:					
FRANK POTTER (Canada)	Antigua and Barbuda*, Bahamas*, Barbados*, Belize, Canada, Dominica, Grenada, Guyana, Ireland, Jamaica*, Saint Christopher and Nevis, Saint Lucia, Saint Vincent and the Grenadines	36,587	4.65	258,570	4.46
MERCEDES RUBIO (Spain)	Costa Rica, El Salvador, Guatemala, Honduras, Mexico, Nicaragua, Panama, Spain, Suriname*, Venezuela*	36,435	4.63	157,587	2.72
JACQUES DE GROOTE	Austria, Belgium, Hungary, Luxembourg, Turkey	32,871	4.18	203,167	3.50
MOURAD BENACHENHOU (Algeria)	Afghanistan, Algeria, Ghana, Iran, Libya, Morocco, Tunisia, People's Democratic Republic of Yemen	29,990	3.81	114,652	1.98
C. R. KRISHNASWAMY RAO SAHIB (India)	Bangladesh, Bhutan, India, Sri Lanka	29,941	3.80	258,624	4.46
FAWZI HAMAD AL-SULTAN (Kuwait)	Bahrain*, Egypt, Iraq, Jordan, Kuwait, Lebanon, Maldives, Oman, Pakistan, Qatar*, Syrian Arab Republic, United Arab Emirates, Yemen Arab Republic	29,593	3.76	242,231	4.18
PAUL ARLMAN (Netherlands)	Cyprus, Israel, Netherlands, Romania*, Yugoslavia	28,749	3.65	182,775	3.15
C. ULRIK HAXTHAUSEN (Denmark)	Denmark, Finland, Iceland, Norway, Sweden	26,519	3.37	291,456	5.02
MITIKU JEMBERE (Ethiopia)	Botswana, Burundi, Ethiopia, The Gambia, Guinea, Kenya, Lesotho, Liberia, Malawi, Mozambique, Nigeria, Seychelles*, Sierra Leone, Sudan, Swaziland, Tanzania, Trinidad and Tobago, Uganda, Zambia, Zimbabwe	25,540	3.25	215,893	3.72
MARIO DRAGHI (Italy)	Greece, Italy, Malta*, Portugal*	25,454	3.23	166,150	2.86
XU NAIJIONG (China)	People's Republic of China	25,392	3.23	117,316	2.02
JOBARAH E. SURAISRY (Saudi Arabia)	Saudi Arabia	25,390	3.23	155,193	2.68
MURRAY A. SHERWIN (New Zealand)	Australia, Kiribati, Republic of Korea, New Zealand, Papua New Guinea, Solomon Islands, Vanuatu, Western Samoa	24,861	3.16	151,765	2.62
PEDRO SAMPAIO MALAN (Brazil)	Brazil, Colombia, Dominican Republic, Ecuador, Haiti, Philippines	23,912	3.04	179,402	3.09
MOHD RAMLI WAJIB (Malaysia)	Burma, Fiji, Indonesia, Laos, Malaysia, Nepal, Singapore*, Thailand, Tonga, Viet-Nam	22,544	2.86	187,667	3.23
FÉLIX ALBERTO CAMARASA (Argentina)	Argentina, Bolivia, Chile, Paraguay, Peru, Uruguay*	21,035	2.67	129,051	2.22
ANDRÉ MILONGO (Congo)	Benin, Burkina Faso, Cameroon, Cape Verde, Central African Republic, Chad, Comoros, Congo, Côte d'Ivoire, Djibouti, Equatorial Guinea, Gabon, Guinea-Bissau, Madagascar, Mali, Mauritania, Mauritius, Niger, Rwanda, São Tomé and Príncipe, Senegal, Somalia, Togo, Zaire	21,013	2.67	194,568	3.35

* Members of IBRD only (not IDA).

Note: Democratic Kampuchea (464 votes in IBRD and 7,826 in IDA), Poland (499 votes in IBRD and 6,670 votes in IDA) and South Africa (7,805 votes in IBRD and 19,760 in IDA) did not participate in the 1986 regular election of Executive Directors.

TECHNICAL ASSISTANCE

The provision of technical assistance to member countries has become a major component of Bank activities. The economic, sector and project analysis undertaken by the Bank in the normal course of its operations is the vehicle for considerable technical assistance. In addition, project loans and credits may include funds earmarked specifically for feasibility studies, resource surveys, management or planning advice, and training. During the calendar year 1987, technical assistance components of loans amounted to $1,022.3m. In addition, 16 free-standing technical assistance loans were approved, amounting to $146.6m.

The Bank serves as an executing agency for projects financed by the UN Development Programme. At the end of 1987 the number in progress was 149, with a total allocation of $223.9m.

Technical assistance (usually reimbursable) is also extended to countries that do not need Bank financial support, e.g. for training and transfer of technology.

ECONOMIC RESEARCH AND STUDIES

The Bank's research, carried out by its own research staff, is intended to provide a source of policy advice to members, and to encourage the development of indigenous research. The principal areas of research are: economic adjustment and growth; the problems of highly-indebted countries; the development of sub-Saharan Africa; alleviating poverty; the role of women in economic development; preservation of the environment; and the private sector's contribution to development.

CO-OPERATION WITH OTHER ORGANIZATIONS

The Bank co-operates closely with other UN bodies through consultations, meetings, and joint activities; co-operation with UNDP

INTERNATIONAL ORGANIZATIONS

United Nations (Specialized Agencies)

and WHO, in their programmes to improve health, nutrition and sanitation, is especially important. It collaborates with the IMF in implementing economic adjustment programmes in developing countries. The Bank holds regular consultations with the European Community and OECD on development issues, and the Bank-NGO Committee provides an annual forum for discussion with non-governmental organizations (NGOs). The Bank chairs meetings of donor governments and organizations for the co-ordination of aid to particular countries.

The Bank conducts co-financing and aid co-ordination projects with official aid agencies, export credit institutions, and commercial banks. During the year ending 30 June 1988 a total of 96 IBRD and IDA projects involved co-financers' contributions amounting to $6,621m. In 1983 the Bank announced the introduction of a set of new co-financing instruments designed to increase the participation of commercial banks in project loans. In 1987/88 commercial co-financing under these instruments amounted to $952m.

EVALUATION

The Bank's Operations Evaluation Department studies and publishes the results of projects after a loan has been fully disbursed, so as to identify problems and possible improvements in future activities. Internal auditing is also carried out, to monitor the effectiveness of the Bank's management.

IBRD INSTITUTIONS

Economic Development Institute—EDI: founded in 1955. Training is provided for government officials at the middle and upper levels of responsibility who are concerned with development programmes and projects. Courses are in national economic management and project analysis. The EDI has become one of the most important of the Bank's activities in technical assistance. In its overseas courses, the aim is to build up local capability to conduct projects courses in future. The Institute also produces training materials, and administers the World Bank Graduate Scholarship Programme (funded by the Government of Japan), which awarded 59 scholarships for post-graduate development studies in the 1988/89 academic year. In the year ending 30 June 1988 88 courses and seminars were held, mostly abroad. Dir CHRISTOPHER R. WILLOUGHBY.

Consultative Group for International Agricultural Research—CGIAR: founded in 1971 under the sponsorship of the World Bank, FAO and UNDP. The Bank is chairman of the group (which includes governments, private foundations and multilateral development agencies) and provides its secretariat. The group was formed to raise financial support for international agricultural research work for improving crops and animal production in the developing countries. The group supports 13 research centres; donations for the year ending 30 June 1987 amounted to $201m. (of which the Bank provided $30m.). Exec. Sec. CURTIS FARRAR.

International Centre for Settlement of Investment Disputes—ICSID: founded in 1966 under the Convention of the Settlement of Investment Disputes between States and Nationals of Other States. The Convention was designed to encourage the growth of private foreign investment for economic development, by creating the possibility, always subject to the consent of both parties, for a Contracting State and a foreign investor who is a national of another Contracting State to settle any legal dispute that might arise out of such an investment by conciliation and/or arbitration before an impartial, international forum. The governing body of the Centre is its Administrative Council, composed of one representative of each Contracting State, all of whom have equal voting power. The President of the World Bank is (ex officio) the non-voting Chairman of the Administrative Council.

By the end of June 1988, 90 states had signed and ratified the Convention. At mid-1988 there were nine disputes before the Centre. Sec.-Gen. IBRAHIM F. I. SHIHATA.

PUBLICATIONS

World Bank Catalog of Publications.
World Bank News (weekly).
World Bank Annual Report.
World Development Report (annually).
World Bank Economic Review (3 a year).
World Bank Research Observer.
Research News (quarterly).
World Bank Atlas (annually).
Abstracts of Current Studies: The World Bank Research Program (annually).
Annual Review of Project Performance Results.
Staff Working Papers.
ICSID Annual Report.
ICSID Review—Foreign Investment Law Journal (2 a year).

World Bank Statistics

LENDING OPERATIONS, BY PURPOSE
(year ending 30 June 1988; US $ million)

	IBRD	IDA
Agriculture and rural development	2,932.1	1,561.8
Development finance companies	1,490.1	222.5
Education	654.9	209.1
Energy	1,908.0	98.9
Industry	2,062.7	161.9
Non-project	1,020.0	667.0
Population, health and nutrition	109.0	195.9
Small-scale enterprises	493.0	20.0
Technical assistance	15.2	80.5
Telecommunications	36.0	—
Transportation	2,117.2	525.3
Urban development	1,108.5	607.8
Water supply and sewerage	490.3	45.0
Total	**14,762.0**	**4,458.7**

IBRD INCOME AND EXPENDITURE
(US $'000, year ending 30 June 1988)

Revenue	
Income from loans:	
Interest	6,534,718
Commitment charges	262,676
Income from investments	1,719,673
Other income	31,928
Total income	**8,548,995**

Expenditure	
Interest on borrowings	6,399,871
Amortization of issuance costs	191,269
Administrative expenses	475,845
Provision for loan losses	421,477
Other financial expenses	3,687
Total	**7,492,149**
Operating income	**1,056,846**
Contributions to special programmes	52,616
Net income	**1,004,230**

INTERNATIONAL ORGANIZATIONS — United Nations (Specialized Agencies)

IBRD LOANS AND IDA CREDITS APPROVED, BY REGION (1 July 1987–30 June 1988)

	IBRD Loans[1]		IDA Credits[1]		Total[1]	
	Number[2]	US $ m.	Number[2]	US $ m.	Number[2]	US $ m.
Africa:						
Benin	—	—	1	21.0	1	21.0
Burkina Faso	—	—	1	17.9	1	17.9
Burundi	—	—	5	153.5	5	153.5
Cameroon	1	103.0	—	—	1	103.0
Cape Verde	—	—	1	4.2	1	4.2
Central African Republic	—	—	3	73.0	3	73.0
Chad	—	—	3	78.4	3	78.4
Congo	2	85.2	—	—	2	85.2
Côte d'Ivoire	1	57.4	—	—	1	57.4
Ethiopia	—	—	2	103.0	2	103.0
Gabon	1	50.0	—	—	1	50.0
Ghana	—	—	6	261.1	6	261.1
Guinea	—	—	4	148.7	4	148.7
Guinea-Bissau	—	—	2	14.0	2	14.0
Kenya	—	—	3	133.8	3	133.8
Lesotho	—	—	2	36.4	2	36.4
Madagascar	—	—	4	180.5	4	180.5
Malawi	—	—	3	89.3	3	89.3
Mali	—	—	3	89.3	3	89.3
Mauritania	—	—	1	10.0	1	10.0
Mauritius	1	10.0	—	—	1	10.0
Mozambique	—	—	2	85.9	2	85.9
Niger	—	—	3	46.3	3	46.3
Nigeria	3	342.8	—	—	3	342.8
Senegal	—	—	4	129.6	4	129.6
Somalia	—	—	2	18.0	2	18.0
Sudan	—	—	3	139.7	3	139.7
Tanzania	—	—	1	60.0	1	60.0
Togo	—	—	4	111.6	4	111.6
Uganda	—	—	4	142.4	4	142.4
Zaire	—	—	2	56.0	2	56.0
Zimbabwe	2	76.7	—	—	2	76.7
Total	11	725.1	69	2,203.6	80	2,928.7
Asia						
Bangladesh	—	—	5	227.8	5	227.8
Bhutan	—	—	2	5.3	2	5.3
Burma	—	—	1	63.0	1	63.0
China	10	1,053.7	4	639.9	14	1,693.6
Fiji	1	23.4	—	—	1	23.4
India	8	2,255.0	2	717.2	10	2,972.2
Indonesia	10	1,375.3	—	—	10	1,375.3
Korea, Republic	3	196.0	—	—	3	196.0
Laos	—	—	1	14.1	1	14.1
Malaysia	3	170.2	—	—	3	170.2
Nepal	—	—	3	71.2	3	71.2
Philippines	4	505.0	—	—	4	505.0
Sri Lanka	—	—	5	179.5	5	179.5
Thailand	3	173.0	—	—	3	173.0
Total	42	5,751.6	23	1,918.0	65	7,669.6
Europe, Middle East, North Africa						
Algeria	4	391.0	—	—	4	391.0
Cyprus	2	65.0	—	—	2	65.0
Hungary	3	320.0	—	—	3	320.0
Jordan	3	107.0	—	—	3	107.0
Morocco	3	338.0	—	—	3	338.0
Pakistan	3	277.4	2	189.5	5	466.9
Portugal	2	92.0	—	—	2	92.0
Tunisia	5	291.0	—	—	5	291.0
Turkey	4	1,063.9	—	—	4	1,063.9
Yemen Arab Republic	—	—	2	35.6	2	35.6
Yugoslavia	2	188.0	—	—	2	188.0
Total	31	3,133.3	4	225.1	35	3,358.4
Latin America and the Caribbean						
Argentina	3	626.5	—	—	3	626.5
Belize	2	13.4	—	—	2	13.4
Bolivia	—	—	3	112.0	3	112.0
Brazil	9	1,359.5	—	—	9	1,359.5
Chile	1	250.0	—	—	1	250.0
Colombia	3	465.0	—	—	3	465.0
Dominican Republic	1	105.0	—	—	1	105.0
Ecuador	2	160.0	—	—	2	160.0
El Salvador	1	65.0	—	—	1	65.0
Guatemala	1	29.0	—	—	1	29.0
Jamaica	2	26.3	—	—	2	26.3
Mexico	8	2,030.0	—	—	8	2,030.0
Uruguay	1	22.3	—	—	1	22.3
Total	34	5,152.0	3	112.0	37	5,264.0
Grand total	118	14,762.0	99	4,458.7	217	19,220.7

[1] Supplements are included in amounts, but are not counted as separate lending operations.
[2] Joint IBRD/IDA operations are counted only once, as Bank operations.

INTERNATIONAL ORGANIZATIONS   United Nations (Specialized Agencies)

IBRD OPERATIONS AND RESOURCES, 1979–88 (years ending 30 June)

	1978/79	1979/80	1980/81	1981/82	1982/83	1983/84	1984/85	1985/86	1986/87	1987/88
Amounts in US $ m.										
Loans approved*	6,989	7,644	8,809	10,330	11,138	11,947	11,356	13,179	14,188	14,762
Disbursements†	3,602	4,363	5,063	6,326	6,817	8,580	8,645	8,263	11,383	11,636
Total income	2,425	2,800	2,999	3,372	4,232	4,655	5,529	6,815	7,689	8,549
Net income	407	588	610	598	752	600	1,137	1,243	1,113	1,004
General reserve	2,205	2,600	2,567	2,772	3,052	3,337	3,586	4,896	6,284	7,242
New borrowings	5,085	5,173	5,069	8,521	10,292	9,831	11,086	10,609	9,321	10,832
Subscribed capital	37,429	39,959	36,614	43,165	52,089	56,011	58,846	77,526	85,231	91,436
Operations, Countries										
Operations approved	142	144	140	150	136	129	131	131	127	118
Recipient countries	44	48	50	43	43	43	44	41	39	37
Member countries	134	135	139	142	144	146	148	150	151	151
Higher-level staff	2,361	2,463	2,552	2,689	2,703	2,735	2,805	3,617‡	3,843	3,556

* Excludes loans to IFC of $100m. in 1980/81, $390m. in 1981/82, $145m. in 1982/83, $100m. in 1983/84, $400m. in 1984/85, $150m. in 1985/86, $200m. in 1986/87 and $200m. in 1987/88.
† Excludes disbursements on loans to IFC.
‡ Increase reflects a change in job-grading structure.
Source: *World Bank Annual Report 1988.*

International Development Association—IDA

Address: 1818 H Street, NW, Washington, DC 20433, USA.
Telephone: (202) 477-1234.

The International Development Association began operations in November 1960. Affiliated to the IBRD (see above), IDA advances capital to the poorer developing member countries on more flexible terms than those offered by the IBRD.

MEMBERS
137 members: see Table on pp. 50–52.

Organization

Officers and staff of the IBRD serve concurrently as officers and staff of IDA.
President and Chairman of Executive Directors: BARBER B. CONABLE (ex officio).

Activities

IDA assistance is aimed at the poorer developing countries (i.e. those with a per caput GNP of less than US $791 in 1983 dollars). Under IDA lending conditions, credits can be extended to countries which, for balance of payments reasons, could not assume the burden of repayment required for IBRD loans. Terms are more favourable than those provided by the IBRD; credits are for a period of 50 years, with a grace period of 10 years, and no interest charges.

IDA's total resources, consisting of members' subscriptions and supplementary resources (additional subscriptions and contributions) amounted to US $48,665m. on 30 June 1988. Resources are replenished periodically by contributions from the more affluent member countries. Owing to a decision by the government of the USA to cut its annual contributions by 20% to $750m., a total of $9,000m. was made available for the seventh replenishment (covering the period 1984–87), compared with the IDA target figure of $16,000m., and the previous three-year replenishment amounting to $12,000m. Supplementary funding of $1,200m. was provided by developed countries (excluding the USA). Negotiations on an eighth replenishment of $12,400m. were concluded in 1986.

During the year ending 30 June 1988, 35% of IDA assistance approved was for agriculture and rural development, 14% for urban development and 12% for transport. About 49% of assistance was for Africa and 43% was for Asia (chiefly India, the People's Republic of China and Bangladesh) (see tables on pp. 62–63).

IDA OPERATIONS AND RESOURCES, 1979–88 (years ending 30 June)

	1978/79	1979/80	1980/81	1981/82	1982/83	1983/84	1984/85	1985/86	1986/87	1987/88
Amounts in US $ m.										
Credit amounts	3,022	3,838	3,482	2,686	3,341	3,575	3,028	3,140	3,486	4,459
Disbursements	1,222	1,411	1,878	2,067	2,596	2,524	2,491	3,155	3,088	3,397
Usable resources, cumulative	19,661	20,773	22,331	25,280	27,967	30,910	33,295	39,167	43,614	48,665
Operations, Countries										
Operations approved*	105	103	106	97	107	106	105	97	108	99
Recipient countries	43	40	40	42	44	43	45	37	39	36
Member countries	121	121	125	130	131	131	133	134	135	137

*Joint IBRD/IDA operations are counted only once, as IBRD operations.
Source: *World Bank Annual Report 1988.*

INTERNATIONAL ORGANIZATIONS   United Nations (Specialized Agencies)

International Finance Corporation—IFC

Address: 1818 H Street, NW, Washington, DC 20433, USA.
Telephone: (202) 477-1234.
Telex: 440098.

IFC was founded in 1956 as an affiliate of the World Bank to encourage the growth of productive private enterprise in its member countries, particularly in the less-developed areas.

MEMBERS

133 members: see Table on pp. 50–52.

Organization

(October 1988)

IFC is a separate legal entity in the World Bank Group. Executive Directors of the World Bank also serve as Directors of IFC. The President of the World Bank is ex-officio Chairman of the IFC Board of Directors, which has appointed him President of IFC. Subject to his overall supervision, the day-to-day operations of IFC are conducted by its staff under the direction of the Executive Vice-President. In June 1988 IFC had 523 members of staff.

PRINCIPAL OFFICERS

President: BARBER B. CONABLE.
Executive Vice-President: Sir WILLIAM RYRIE.

REGIONAL MISSIONS

East Asia: c/o Central Bank of the Philippines, Manila, Philippines: tel. 59-99-35; telex 40541; Dir RICHARD L. RANKEN.
Eastern and Southern Africa: Reinsurance Plaza, 5th Floor, Taifa Rd, POB 30577, Nairobi, Kenya; tel. 24726; telex 22022; Dir ERNEST M. KEPPER.
Middle East: 5 El Falah St, Mohandessin, Giza, Cairo, Egypt; tel. 347-3739; telex 93110; Dir JOHN H. STEWART.
North Africa: 30 ave des FAR, Casablanca, Morocco; tel. 312-888; telex 22606; Dir SAMI HADDAD.
Western Africa: BP 1850, Corner of Booker Washington and Jacques AKA Sts, Abidjan 01, Côte d'Ivoire; tel. 44-32-44; telex 28132; Dir HUNG D. NGUYEN.

There are also offices in France, India, Indonesia, Japan, Morocco, Nigeria, Thailand, Turkey and the United Kingdom.

Activities

IFC functions as follows:

1. In association with private investors, invests without government guarantee in productive private enterprises of economic priority in member countries where sufficient private capital is not available on reasonable terms.
2. Stimulates the international flow of private capital to developing countries.
3. Encourages the development of local capital markets.
4. Invests in and gives technical help to development finance companies, and assists other institutions which also support economic development and follow policies generally consistent with those of IFC.
5. Commits limited amounts of funds for promotional purposes, to help bring development enterprises into being.
6. Revolves its portfolio by sales of its investments to other investors.

IFC's authorized capital is US $1,300m., following the authorization of $650m. in new shares in 1985. At 30 June 1988 paid-in capital was $850.2m. The World Bank is the principal source of borrowed funds, but IFC also borrows from private capital markets, which provided the equivalent of $595.4m. in the financial year ending 30 June 1988. IFC's net income increased to $100.6m. in 1987/88, compared with $53.8m. in the previous year.

In the year ending 30 June 1988 investments approved by IFC amounted to $1,270m. for 95 projects (compared with $920m. for 92 projects in the previous year). Of the total approved, about 83% was for loans and 17% was for equity or equity-like investments. Participation by other investors brought the total amount invested in these projects to $5,010m.: in other words, for every $1 that IFC agreed to invest, other investors were to invest more than $4. Disbursements for IFC's account amounted to $762m. (compared with $328m. in the previous year).

Projects approved during the year were located in 40 countries; one was regional and one world-wide in scope. The largest proportion of investment finance was allocated to Latin America (49%); Asia received 24%, Europe and the Middle East 16% and Africa (including Morocco and Tunisia) 11%. About 22% of IFC's investment was in countries with a per caput annual income of less than $805. The Corporation invested in a wide variety of business and financial institutions in the following sectors: capital markets and financial services; agriculture; mining; telecommunications; tourism; and various types of manufacturing, including cement, chemicals, electronics, food-processing, wood and paper, shipbuilding, and textiles.

IFC's five-year programme for 1985–89 included four major objectives: to provide technical and financial assistance to firms which, although otherwise sound, are faced with severe market and financial difficulties and must re-structure their businesses; to give increased attention to high-priority development projects in low-income countries, especially in agriculture and agro-industry; to increase investment in petroleum and gas exploration and development; and to expand its activities in Africa south of the Sahara. Real net investment was expected to expand by about 7% per year during the period. During 1986/87 the Board made certain adjustments to the programme: restructuring activities were to be intensified; more attention was to be given to special services of an innovative nature in sub-Saharan Africa; and the energy exploration and development initiative was to be revised in response to changing market needs and opportunities. During the year IFC also adopted new approaches to loan funding that bring to borrowers advantages arising from developments in international financial markets. IFC's clients were in future to have access to some of the new financial instruments and techniques actively in use in the industrialized countries, but seldom offered to the private sector of the developing countries.

IFC also undertakes technical assistance for attracting foreign investment, the creation of new enterprises and the restructuring of existing ones, often in co-operation with the UN Development Programme (UNDP). IFC acts as the executing agency of the Caribbean Project Development Facility, established by UNDP in 1981 to raise funds for new investment in the Caribbean. In 1987/88 the Facility completed 18 project proposals. In 1986 IFC, in co-operation with UNDP and the African Development Bank, launched the Africa Project Development Facility (APDF). IFC manages the Facility, which consists of two teams of experts based in Nairobi, Kenya (covering eastern and southern Africa) and in Abidjan, Côte d'Ivoire (covering western and central Africa). The APDF aims to support the private sector of African countries by helping African entrepreneurs to develop sound investment projects (small and medium-sized businesses) and to find financing for them. During 1987/88 APDF secured financing for about 25 projects and feasibility studies were being undertaken for about 100 more, mostly in the agro-industrial sector. The Emerging Markets Growth Fund (EMGF) was initiated in 1987 to invest in publicly listed shares in certain developing countries, and a similar fund, the Emerging Markets Investment Fund (directed mainly towards Japanese investors) was established in 1988. The technique known as Guaranteed Recovery of Investment Principal (GRIP) was introduced during 1986/87, as a means of sharing the risks with foreign equity investors in certain cases. Preparatory work was carried out in 1987 on a new facility (the African Management Services Company) which is to help find qualified senior executives from around the world to work with African companies, assist in the training of local managers, and provide supporting services. In July 1988 IFC announced that it was to establish the African Enterprise Fund, with capital of $60m., to provide financial and non-financial assistance directly to small and medium-sized enterprises. The Fund was expected to support 100 projects over an initial three-year period.

PUBLICATION

Annual Report.

IFC OPERATIONS AND RESOURCES, 1984–88 (fiscal years ending 30 June)

	1984	1985	1986	1987	1988
Approved investments					
Number of projects	62	75	85	92	95
Number of countries	37	38	39	41	40
Amount (gross US $ million)	696	937	1,156	920	1,270
Total project costs* (US $ million)	2,473	2,768	3,588	4,343	5,010
Disbursements (IFC's own account)	238	266	325	328	762
Resources and income (US $ million)					
Borrowings	582	825	1,223	1,581	2,047
Paid-in capital	544	546	602	722	850
Accumulated earnings	230	258	284	338	438
Net income	26.3	28.3	25.4	53.8	100.6

* Including investment mobilized from other sources.

Multilateral Investment Guarantee Agency—MIGA

Address: 1818 H Street, NW, Washington, DC 20433, USA.
Telephone: (202) 477-1234.
Telex: 440098.

MIGA was founded in 1988 as an affiliate of the World Bank, to encourage the flow of investments for productive purposes among its member countries, especially developing countries.

MEMBERS

By mid-1988 MIGA had 42 member countries. Membership is open to all nations that are members of the World Bank, and Switzerland.

Organization
(October 1988)

MIGA is legally and financially separate from the World Bank. It is supervised by a Board of Directors.
President: BARBER B. CONABLE.
Executive Vice-President: YOSHIO TERASAWA.

Activities

MIGA's purpose is to guarantee eligible investments against losses resulting from non-commercial risks, under four main categories:

transfer risk resulting from host government restrictions on currency conversion and transfer;

risk of loss resulting from legislative or administrative actions of the host government;

repudiation by the host government of contracts with investors in cases in which the investor has no access to a competent forum;

the risk of armed conflict and civil unrest.

MIGA also provides technical assistance and undertakes research and promotional activities.

The convention establishing MIGA took effect in April 1988. Authorized capital was US $1,082m. By 30 June the convention had been signed by 15 Category One (capital-exporting) countries and by 55 Category Two (capital-importing) countries, and had been ratified by 42 countries.

International Civil Aviation Organization—ICAO

Address: 1000 Sherbrooke St West, Montreal, PQ H3A 2R2, Canada.
Telephone: (514) 285-8219.
Telex: 05-24513.

The Convention on International Civil Aviation was signed in Chicago in 1944. As a result ICAO was founded in 1947 to develop the techniques of international air navigation and to help in the planning and improvement of international air transport.

MEMBERS
159 members: see Table on pp. 50–52.

Organization
(October 1988)

ASSEMBLY

Composed of representatives of all member states, the Assembly is the organization's legislative body and meets at least once in three years. It reviews the work of the organization, sets out the work programme for the next three years, approves the budget and determines members' contributions.

COUNCIL

Composed of representatives of 33 member states, elected by the Assembly. It is the executive body, and establishes and supervises subsidiary technical committees and makes recommendations to member governments; meets in virtually continuous session; elects the President, appoints the Secretary-General, and administers the finances of the organization. The functions of the Council are:

to adopt international standards and recommended practices and incorporate them as annexes to the Convention on International Civil Aviation;

to arbitrate between member states on matters concerning aviation and implementation of the Convention;

to investigate any situation which presents avoidable obstacles to development of international air navigation;

to take whatever steps are necessary to maintain safety and regularity of operation of international air transport;

to provide technical assistance to the developing countries under the UN Development Programme and other assistance programmes.

President of the Council: Dr ASSAD KOTAITE (Lebanon).
Secretary-General: Dr SHIVINDER SINGH SIDHU (India).

INTERNATIONAL ORGANIZATIONS   *United Nations (Specialized Agencies)*

AIR NAVIGATION COMMISSION
The Commission comprises 15 members.
President: C. COSTANTINI.

STANDING COMMITTEES
These include the Air Transport Committee, the Committee on Joint Support of Air Navigation Services, the Finance Committee, the Legal Committee, the Committee on Unlawful Interference, and the Edward Warner Award Committee.

REGIONAL OFFICES
Western and Central Africa: BP 2356, Dakar, Senegal.
Eastern and Southern Africa: POB 46294, Nairobi, Kenya.
Asia and Pacific: POB 614, Bangkok, Thailand.
Europe: 3 bis, Villa Emile-Bergerat, 92522 Neuilly-sur-Seine Cedex, France.
Middle East: 16 Hassan Sabri, Zamalek, Cairo, Egypt.
North America, Central America and the Caribbean: Apartado Postal 5-377, CP 11590, México 5, DF, Mexico.
South America: Apartado 4127, Lima 100, Peru.

Activities
ICAO aims to ensure the safe and orderly growth of civil aviation; to encourage skills in aircraft design and operation; to improve airways, airports and air navigation; to prevent the waste of resources in unreasonable competition; to safeguard the rights of each contracting party to operate international air transport; and to prevent discriminatory practices.

ICAO SPECIFICATIONS
These are contained in annexes to the Chicago Convention, and in three sets of Procedures for Air Navigation Services (PANS Documents). The specifications are periodically revised in keeping with developments in technology and changing requirements. The 18 annexes to the Convention include personnel licensing, rules relating to the conduct of flights, meteorological services, aeronautical charts, air-ground communications, safety specifications, identification, air traffic control, rescue services, environmental protection, security and the transporting of dangerous goods. Technical Manuals and Circulars are issued to facilitate implementation.

ICAO REGIONAL PLANS
These set out the technical requirements for air navigation facilities in the nine ICAO regions; Regional Offices offer assistance (see addresses above). Because of growth in air traffic and changes in the pattern of air routes, the Plans are periodically amended.

EUROPEAN AIR NAVIGATION PLANNING GROUP
Reviews current problems and the need for changes in the air navigation facilities in the European Region.

ICAO PROJECTS
Studies of current problems aiming to apply new technology, including: airworthiness of aircraft, all-weather navigation, aircraft separation, obstacle clearances, noise abatement, operation of aircraft and carriage by air of dangerous goods, automated data interchange systems, aviation security and use of space technology in air navigation.

ENVIRONMENT
International standards and guidelines for noise certification of aircraft and international provisions for the regulation of aircraft engine emissions have been adopted and published in Annex 16 to the Chicago Convention.

AIR TRANSPORT
Continuing functions include preparation of regional air transport development studies; studies on international air transport fares and rates; review of the economic situation of airports and route facilities; development of guidance material on civil aviation forecasting and planning; collection and publication of statistics; facilitation of passenger and freight clearance formalities; and multilateral financing of certain air navigation facilities.

TECHNICAL ASSISTANCE BUREAU
The Bureau assists developing countries in the execution of various projects. At least US $50.6m. was to be spent on assistance in 1988.

LEGAL COMMITTEE
The general work programme of the Committee in 1988 included the following subjects: the UN Convention on the Law of the Sea and its implications for the application of the Chicago Convention, its annexes and other international air law instruments; the liability of air traffic control agencies; study of the status of the instruments of the 'Warsaw System'; the institutional and legal aspects of future air navigation systems; the legal aspects of global air-ground communications; and preparation of a draft instrument on the interception of civil aircraft.

FINANCE
Total ICAO net budget appropriations for 1987 were US $30.8m., and for 1988 were $32.1m.

PUBLICATIONS
Catalogue of ICAO Publications.
ICAO Bulletin (monthly, in English, French and Spanish; quarterly digest in Russian).
Digest of Statistics.
Minutes and Documents of the Legal Committee.
Lexicon of terms.
The 18 Annexes to the Convention.
Procedures for Air Navigation Services.
ICAO Training Manual.
Regional Air Navigation Plans.
Aircraft Accident Digest.

INTERNATIONAL ORGANIZATIONS United Nations (Specialized Agencies)

International Fund for Agricultural Development—IFAD

Address: Via del Serafico 107, 00142 Rome, Italy.
Telephone: 54591.
Telex: 620330.

Following a decision by the 1974 UN World Food Conference, IFAD was established in 1976 to fund rural development programmes specifically aimed at the poorest of the world's people. It began operations in December 1977.

MEMBERS

143 members: see Table on pp. 50–52.

Category I	Category II	Category III
Australia	Algeria	111 developing countries
Austria	Gabon	
Belgium	Indonesia	
Canada	Iran	
Denmark	Iraq	
Finland	Kuwait	
France	Libya	
Germany, Federal Republic	Nigeria	
	Qatar	
Ireland	Saudi Arabia	
Italy	United Arab Emirates	
Japan	Venezuela	
Luxembourg		
Netherlands		
New Zealand		
Norway		
Spain		
Sweden		
Switzerland		
United Kingdom		
USA		

Organization

(October 1988)

GOVERNING COUNCIL

Each member state is represented in the Governing Council by a Governor and an Alternate. There are three categories of members: industrialized countries (OECD members) forming Category I; petroleum-exporting developing countries (OPEC members) forming Category II; recipient developing countries (Category III). Categories I and II *shall* contribute to the resources of the Fund while Category III *may* do so. All the powers of the Fund are vested in the Governing Council. It may, however, delegate certain powers to the Executive Board. Sessions are held annually with special sessions as required. The Governing Council elects the President of the Fund by a two-thirds majority for a four-year term. He is eligible for re-election. The President is also the Chairman of the Executive Board.

EXECUTIVE BOARD

Consists of 18 members and 17 alternates, elected by the Governing Council, one-third by each category of membership. Members serve for three years. The Executive Board is responsible for the conduct and general operation of IFAD and approves loans and grants for projects; it meets three or four times a year.

The total number of votes in the Governing Council and the Executive Board is 1,800, distributed equally between the three categories of membership. Thus two-thirds of the votes lie with the developing countries (Categories II and III) which will therefore have a major influence on the investment decisions of the Fund. At the same time two-thirds of the votes are held by donor countries (Categories I and II).

President and Chairman of Executive Board: IDRISS JAZAIRY.

DEPARTMENTS

IFAD has three main administrative departments: the Economic and Planning Department (with Divisions for Planning and Economic Analysis, Policy Review, and Monitoring and Evaluation); the Project Management Department (with four regional Divisions, a Loan Implementation Unit and a Technical Advisory Unit); and the General Affairs Department. In 1988 IFAD had 190 regular staff, of whom about 40% were in executive or technical positions.

Activities

The Fund's objective is to mobilize additional resources to be made available on concessional terms for agricultural development in developing member states. IFAD provides financing primarily for projects designed to improve food production systems and to strengthen related policies and institutions within the framework of national priorities and strategies. In allocating resources IFAD is guided by: the need to increase food production in the poorest food-deficit countries; the potential for increasing food production in other developing countries; and the importance of improving the nutritional level of the poorest populations in developing countries and the conditions of their lives. Particular emphasis is placed on assistance to rural women.

IFAD is empowered to make both grants and loans. Under its Agreement, grants are limited to 12.5% of the resources committed in any one financial year. There are three kinds of loan: highly concessional loans, which carry no interest but have an annual service charge of 1% and a maturity period of 50 years, including a grace period of 10 years; intermediate term loans, which have an annual interest rate of 4% and a maturity period of 20 years, including a grace period of five years; and ordinary term loans which have an interest rate of 8% and a maturity period of 15–18 years, including a grace period of three years. To avoid duplication of work, the administration of loans, for the purposes of disbursements and supervision of project implementation, is entrusted to competent international financial institutions, with the Fund retaining an active interest. In order to increase the impact of its lending resources on food production, the Fund seeks as much as possible to attract other external donors and beneficiary governments as co-financiers of its projects.

In 1985 IFAD launched a Special Programme for Sub-Saharan Africa, aiming to spend $300m. over the next three years on improving food production and water conservation in Africa, in addition to operations in the region carried out under its regular programme.

Between 1978 and the end of 1987 the Fund approved loans for 220 projects in 89 countries, and 262 technical assistance grants, at a cost of about SDR 2,167.5m. (US $2,529.2m.) from its own resources. IFAD's investment represented 23.9% of total project costs, while 34.4% was provided by other external donors and 41.7% by domestic sources. During 1978–87, 67% of loans were in the highly concessional category.

In 1987 IFAD approved total loans (including those under the Special Programme for Sub-Saharan Africa) amounting to SDR 164.6m. (The average value of the SDR—Special Drawing Right—in 1987 was US $1.29307.) Of this total, 55% was for sub-Saharan Africa, 27% for Asia, 17% for Latin America and 1% for the Near East and North Africa. Technical assistance grants amounting to SDR 10.8m. (for research, training and project preparation) were also made, bringing the total financial assistance approved to SDR 175.4m. This represented an increase over the total of SDR 124.9m. approved in 1986, but was still considerably less than the annual average of SDR 280m. approved in 1979–83 (reflecting a reduction in IFAD's resources: see Finance, below). Loan disbursements during 1987 amounted to SDR 163.9m.

IFAD's development projects usually include a number of components, such as infrastructure (e.g. improvement of water supplies, small-scale irrigation and road construction); input supply (e.g. improved seeds, fertilizers and pesticides); institutional support (e.g. research, training and extension services); and producer incentives (e.g. pricing and marketing improvements). IFAD also attempts to enable the landless to acquire income-generating assets: by increasing the supply of loanable funds for the rural poor, it seeks to free them from dependence on the unorganized and exploitative capital market and to generate productive activities. An example is IFAD's support for the Grameen Bank in Bangladesh, which at the beginning of 1987 was handling 215,000 small loans (70% of which were to women) and had a credit recovery rate of 99%.

In addition to its regular efforts to identify projects and programmes, IFAD organizes special programming missions to certain selected countries to undertake a comprehensive review of the constraints affecting the rural poor, and to help countries to design strategies for the removal of these constraints. Based on the recommendations of these missions, a number of projects have been identified or prepared. In general, these projects tend to focus on institutional improvements at the national and local level to direct inputs and services to small farmers and the landless rural poor. During 1987 five such missions were undertaken (to

Ecuador, Ghana, Nepal, the Philippines and the Yemen Arab Republic). Monitoring and evaluation missions are also sent to check the progress of projects.

PROJECTS APPROVED BY IFAD IN 1987

Region and Country	Loan Amount (SDR million)
Africa south of the Sahara	41.80
Benin	7.95
Cape Verde	4.35
Ethiopia	4.50
Malawi	4.95
Togo	4.90
Zaire	6.05
Zambia	9.10
Asia	44.60
India	9.25
Indonesia	10.60
Laos	3.50
Nepal	4.75
Pakistan	8.70
Thailand	7.80
Latin America and the Caribbean	27.40
Bolivia	4.20
Colombia	7.15
Dominican Republic	6.10
Honduras	4.85
Jamaica	5.10
Near East and North Africa	2.00
Yemen Arab Republic	2.00
Total (regular programmes)	115.80
Special Programme for Sub-Saharan Africa	48.80
Burkina Faso	7.00
Guinea-Bissau	3.50
Mozambique	11.85
Niger	10.25
Uganda	9.10
Zambia	7.10
Total loans	164.60
Technical assistance grants	10.84
Total operations in 1987	175.44

FINANCE

The total initial resources pledged by members, valued as at 31 December 1981, amounted to US $1,015m. In 1982 agreement was reached on the first replenishment of the Fund's resources. Member countries offered to provide contributions totalling about US $1,100m. for the period 1981–83 (later extended to 1984). This comprised $620m. (56%) from the developed (Category I) countries, $450m. (41%) from petroleum-exporting developing (Category II) countries and $30m. (3%) from other developing (Category III) countries. Together with the carrying-over of available resources, this would have enabled the Fund to undertake an operational programme of about $1,350m. during 1981–84. However, actual payments (particularly those of the USA) were slower than expected. As a result, the size of IFAD's lending operations decreased from 1982 until 1986.

Negotiations on a second replenishment for 1985–87 began in July 1983, and continued until January 1986, when members finally agreed on a replenishment of $460m. This was to be supplemented by an extra $300m. for a Special Programme for Sub-Saharan Africa: by April 1988 the amount required for this Programme had been fully pledged by donor countries.

PUBLICATION

Annual Report.

International Labour Organisation—ILO

Address: 4 route des Morillons, 1211 Geneva 22, Switzerland.
Telephone: (022) 996111.
Telex: 22 271.

ILO was founded in 1919 to work for social justice as a basis for lasting peace. It carries out this mandate by promoting decent living standards, satisfactory conditions of work and pay and adequate employment opportunities. Methods of action include the creation of international labour standards; the provision of technical co-operation services; and research and publications on social and labour matters. In 1946, the Organisation became a specialized agency associated with the UN. It was awarded the Nobel Peace Prize in 1969.

MEMBERS

150 members: see Table on pp. 50–52.

Organization

(October 1988)

INTERNATIONAL LABOUR CONFERENCE

The supreme deliberative body of ILO, the Conference normally meets annually in Geneva, with a session devoted to maritime questions when necessary; it is attended by about 2,000 delegates, advisers and observers. National delegations are composed of two government delegates, one employers' delegate and one workers' delegate. Non-governmental delegates can speak and vote independently of the views of their government. Conference elects the Governing Body and adopts the Budget and International Labour Conventions and Recommendations.

The President and Vice-Presidents hold office for the term of the Conference only.

GOVERNING BODY

ILO's executive council; normally meets three or four times a year in Geneva to decide policy and programmes. Composed of 28 Government members, 14 employers' members and 14 workers' members. Ten seats are reserved for 'states of chief industrial importance': Brazil, the People's Republic of China, France, the Federal Republic of Germany, India, Italy, Japan, the USSR, the United Kingdom and the USA. The remaining 18 are elected from other countries every three years. Employers' and workers' members are elected as individuals, not as national candidates.

Chairman (1988/89): NATHANAËL G. MENSAH (Benin).
Employers' Vice-Chairman: JEAN-JACQUES OECHSLIN (France).
Workers' Vice-Chairman: GERD MUHR (Federal Republic of Germany).

INTERNATIONAL LABOUR OFFICE

The International Labour Office is the Organisation's secretariat, operational headquarters and publishing house. It is staffed in Geneva and in the field by about 1,900 people of some 110 nationalities. Operations are decentralized to regional, area and branch offices in nearly 40 countries.

Director-General: FRANCIS BLANCHARD (France).

INTERNATIONAL ORGANIZATIONS   United Nations (Specialized Agencies)

REGIONAL OFFICES
Regional Office for Africa: POB 2788, Addis Ababa, Ethiopia.
Regional Office for the Americas: Apdo Postal 3638, Lima 1, Peru.
Regional Office for Arab States: ILO, 4 route des Morillons, 1211 Geneva 22, Switzerland.
Regional Office for Asia and the Pacific: POB 1759, Bangkok 2, Thailand.

Activities

INTERNATIONAL LABOUR CONFERENCE

72nd session: June 1986. Adopted a Convention and Recommendation on safety in the use of asbestos. General discussions were held on youth and unemployment, and on the promotion of small- and medium-sized enterprises. The session also adopted amendments to the Constitution, reforming the structure of ILO.

73rd session: June 1987. Held first discussions on employment promotion and social security, and on safety and health in construction, with a view to the adoption of standards on these themes in 1988.

74th session (maritime): Sept.-Oct. 1987. Adopted a Convention and Recommendation on seafarers' welfare at sea and in port, a Convention on social security protection for seafarers, a Convention on health protection and medical care, and a revised Convention and Recommendation on repatriation.

75th session: June 1988. Adopted a Convention and Recommendation on employment promotion and protection against unemployment, and a Convention and Recommendation on safety and health in construction. The session began the two-year process of updating standards relating to indigenous and tribal populations.

INTERNATIONAL LABOUR STANDARDS

One of the ILO's primary functions is the adoption by the International Labour Conference of Conventions and Recommendations setting minimum labour standards. Through ratification by member states, Conventions create binding obligations to put their provisions into effect. Recommendations provide guidance as to policy and practice. A total of 168 Conventions and 176 Recommendations have been adopted, ranging over a wide field of social and labour matters, including basic human rights such as freedom of association, abolition of forced labour and elimination of discrimination in employment. Together they form the International Labour Code. By July 1988 more than 5,300 ratifications of the Conventions had been registered by member states.

TECHNICAL CO-OPERATION

Technical co-operation continues to be a major ILO activity. Over US $112m. from all sources, including the United Nations Development Programme, was spent in 1987 for the promotion of employment, the development of human resources and social institutions, and the improvement of living and working conditions. Of the total figure, 44.7%. was provided by UNDP, 37.2% by bilateral aid agencies in trust fund arrangements, and 6.1% by the UN Population Fund, the ILO regular budget contributing 12%.

WORLD EMPLOYMENT PROGRAMME

The employment objective has been incorporated by the United Nations as a key policy factor in the Second United Nations Development Decade. The ILO has the role of catalyst in bringing employment considerations to the fore in the activities of all agencies within the UN system, and for this purpose launched the World Employment Programme.

The aim of the programme is to assist decision makers in identifying and putting into effect specific employment-promoting development policies. This is accomplished through comprehensive employment strategy missions and exploratory country employment missions; through regional employment teams for Africa, Asia and Latin America and the Caribbean; and through country employment teams.

The programme also includes research activities which cover eight major project areas: technology and employment, income distribution and employment, population and employment, education and training and employment, rural employment, promotion, urbanization and employment, trade expansion and employment, and emergency employment schemes.

MEETINGS

Among meetings held during 1988, in addition to the regular International Labour Conference and Governing Body sessions, were the 12th session of the Coal Mines Committee, a tripartite Conference on Action against Apartheid, and a session of the Committee on Conditions of Work in the Fishing Industry. Due to be held later in the year were the 10th session of the Chemical Industries Committee, the fourth session of the Joint Committee on the Public Service, the seventh African Regional Conference, and the 12th session of the Metal Trades Committee.

INTERNATIONAL INSTITUTE FOR LABOUR STUDIES

Established in 1960 and based at the ILO's Geneva headquarters, the Institute is an advanced educational and research institution dealing with social and labour policy, and brings together international experts representing employers, management, workers and government interests. Activities include international and regional study courses, and are financed by grants and an Endowment Fund to which governments and other bodies contribute.

INTERNATIONAL CENTRE FOR ADVANCED TECHNICAL AND VOCATIONAL TRAINING

Address: Via Ventimiglia 201, 10127 Turin, Italy.

The Centre became operational in 1965. It provides programmes for directors in charge of technical and vocational institutions, training officers, senior and middle-level managers in private and public enterprises, trade union leaders, and technicians, primarily from the developing regions of the world. The ILO Director-General is Chairman of the Board of the Centre.

FINANCE

The net expenditure budget for the two years 1988–89 was US $357m.

PUBLICATIONS

(in English, French and Spanish unless otherwise indicated)

International Labour Review (6 a year).
Official Bulletin (3 a year).
Legislative Series (selected labour and social security laws and regulations; 2 a year).
Bulletin of Labour Statistics (quarterly).
Social and Labour Bulletin (quarterly).
Year Book of Labour Statistics.
International studies, surveys, works of practical guidance or reference on questions of social policy, manpower, industrial relations, working conditions, social security, training, management development, etc.
Training and Development Abstracts (a service providing digests of articles, laws, reports on vocational guidance and training and management development).
Reports for the annual sessions of the International Labour Conference, etc. (in English, French, German, Russian, Spanish).
ILO-Information (bulletin issued in Arabic, Danish, English, Finnish, French, German, Japanese, Norwegian, Russian, Spanish, Swedish and Urdu).

INTERNATIONAL ORGANIZATIONS   *United Nations (Specialized Agencies)*

International Maritime Organization—IMO

Address: 4 Albert Embankment, London, SE1 7SR, England.
Telephone: (01) 735-7611.
Telex: 23588.

The Inter-Governmental Maritime Consultative Organization (IMCO) began operations in 1959, as a specialized agency of the UN to facilitate co-operation among governments on technical matters affecting international shipping. Its main functions are the achievement of safe and efficient navigation, and the control of pollution caused by ships and craft operating in the marine environment. IMCO became IMO in 1982.

MEMBERS

132 members and one associate member: see Table on pp. 50–52.

Organization

(October 1988)

ASSEMBLY

The Assembly consists of delegates from all member countries, who each have one vote. Associate members and observers from other governments and the international agencies are also present. Regular sessions are held every two years. The Assembly is responsible for the election of members to the Council and to the Maritime Safety Committee. It considers reports from all subsidiary bodies and decides the action to be taken on them; it votes the agency's budget and determines the work programme and financial policy.

The Assembly also recommends to members measures to promote maritime safety and to prevent and control maritime pollution from ships.

COUNCIL

The Council is the governing body of the Organization between the biennial sessions of the Assembly. Its members, representatives of 32 states, are elected by the Assembly for a term of two years. The Council appoints the Secretary-General; transmits reports by the subsidiary bodies, including the Maritime Safety Committee, to the Assembly and reports on the work of the Organization generally; submits budget estimates and financial statements with comments and recommendations to the Assembly. The Council normally meets twice a year.

Chairman: W. A. O'NEIL (Canada).

Facilitation Committee: Constituted by the Council in May 1972 as a subsidiary body, this Committee deals with measures to facilitate maritime travel and transport and matters arising from the 1965 Facilitation Convention. Membership open to all IMO member states.

MARITIME SAFETY COMMITTEE

The Maritime Safety Committee is open to all IMO members. The Committee meets at least once a year and submits proposals to the Assembly on technical matters affecting shipping, including prevention of marine pollution.

Sub-Committees:

Bulk Chemicals.
Containers and Cargoes.
Carriage of Dangerous Goods.
Fire Protection.
Life-Saving, Search and Rescue.
Radiocommunications.
Safety of Navigation.
Standards of Training and Watchkeeping.
Ship Design and Equipment.
Stability and Load Lines and Fishing Vessel Safety.

LEGAL COMMITTEE

Established by the Council in June 1967 to deal initially with problems connected with the loss of the tanker *Torrey Canyon*, and subsequently with any legal problems laid before IMO. Membership open to all IMO Member States.

MARINE ENVIRONMENT PROTECTION COMMITTEE

Established by the eighth Assembly (1973) to co-ordinate IMO's work on the prevention and control of marine pollution from ships, and to assist IMO in its consultations with other UN bodies, and with international organizations and expert bodies in the field of marine pollution. Membership is open to all IMO members.

TECHNICAL CO-OPERATION COMMITTEE

Constituted by the Council in May 1972, this Committee evaluates the implementation of UN Development Programme projects for which IMO is executing agency and generally reviews IMO's technical assistance programmes. Its membership is open to all IMO member states.

SECRETARIAT

The Secretariat consists of the Secretary-General and a staff appointed by the Secretary-General and recruited on as wide a geographical basis as possible.

Secretary-General: C. P. SRIVASTAVA (India).

Divisions of the Secretariat:

Maritime Safety
Navigation (Sub-Division)
Technology (Sub-Division)
Marine Environment
Legal Affairs and External Relations
Administrative
Conference
Technical Co-operation

Activities

In addition to the work of its committees and sub-committees, the organization works in connection with the following Conventions, of which it is the depository:

International Convention for the Prevention of Pollution of the Sea by Oil, 1954. IMO has taken over administration from the United Kingdom.

Convention on Facilitation of International Maritime Traffic, 1965. Came into force in March 1967.

International Convention on Load Lines, 1966. Came into force in July 1968.

International Convention on Tonnage Measurement of Ships, 1969. Convention embodies a universal system for measuring ships' tonnage. Came into force in 1982.

International Convention relating to Intervention on the High Seas in Cases of Oil Pollution Casualties, 1969. Came into force in May 1975.

International Convention on Civil Liability for Oil Pollution Damage, 1969. Came into force in June 1975.

Intenational Convention on the Establishment of an International Fund for Compensation for Oil Pollution Damage, 1971. Came into force in October 1978.

Convention on the International Regulations for Preventing Collisions at Sea, 1972. Came into force in July 1977.

International Convention for Safe Containers, 1972. Came into force in September 1977.

International Convention on the Prevention of Pollution from Ships, 1973 (as modified by the Protocol of 1978). Came into force in October 1983.

International Convention for Safety of Life at Sea, 1974. Came into force in May 1980. A Protocol drawn up in 1978 came into force in May 1981.

Athens Convention relating to the Carriage of Passengers and their Luggage by Sea, 1974. Came into force in April 1987.

Convention on the International Maritime Satellite Organization, 1976. Came into force in July 1979.

Convention on Limitation of Liability for Maritime Claims, 1976. Came into force in December 1986.

International Convention for the Safety of Fishing Vessels, Torremolinos, 1977. Will come into force 12 months after 15 countries whose combined fishing fleets constitute 50% of world fishing fleets of 24 metres in length and over have become parties.

International Convention on Standards of Training, Certification and Watchkeeping for Seafarers, 1978. Came into force in April 1984.

International Convention on Maritime Search and Rescue, 1979. Came into force in June 1985.

An international convention against terrorism at sea was adopted in 1988.

BUDGET

Contributions are received from the member states. The budget appropriation for 1988–89 was £19.1m.

PUBLICATIONS

IMO News (quarterly, English and French).

Numerous specialized publications, including international conventions of which IMO is depositary.

INTERNATIONAL ORGANIZATIONS   United Nations (Specialized Agencies)

International Monetary Fund—IMF

Address: 700 19th St, NW, Washington, DC 20431, USA.
Telephone: (202) 477-7000.

The IMF was established at the same time as the World Bank in December 1945, to promote international monetary co-operation, to facilitate the expansion and balanced growth of international trade and to promote stability in foreign exchange.

MEMBERS

151 members: see Table on pp. 50–52.

Organization

(October 1988)

Managing Director: MICHEL CAMDESSUS (France).
Deputy Managing Director: RICHARD D. ERB (USA).

BOARD OF GOVERNORS

The highest authority of the Fund is exercised by the Board of Governors, on which each member country is represented by a Governor and an Alternate Governor. Normally the Board of Governors meets once a year, but the Governors may take votes by mail or other means between annual meetings. The Board of Governors has delegated many of its powers to the Executive Directors. However, the conditions governing the admission of new members, adjustment of quotas, election of Executive Directors, as well as certain other important powers remain the sole responsibility of the Board of Governors. The voting power of each member in the Board of Governors is related to its quota in the Fund (see p. 74).

The Interim Committee of the Board of Governors, established in 1974, usually meets twice a year. It comprises 22 members, representing the same countries or groups of countries as those on the Board of Executive Directors (see below). It reviews the international monetary system and advises the Board of Governors.

The Development Committee (the Joint Ministerial Committee of the Boards of Governors of the World Bank and the IMF on the Transfer of Real Resources to Developing Countries) was also set up in 1974, with a structure similar to that of the Interim Committee, to review development policy issues and financing requirements.

BOARD OF EXECUTIVE DIRECTORS

(see Table overleaf)

The 22-member Board of Executive Directors, responsible for the day-to-day operations of the Fund, is in continuous session in Washington, under the chairmanship of the Fund's Managing Director. The USA, the United Kingdom, the Federal Republic of Germany, France, Japan and Saudi Arabia each appoint one Executive Director, while 15 of the remaining Executive Directors are

BOARD OF EXECUTIVE DIRECTORS (November 1988)

Director	Casting Votes of	Total Votes	%
Appointed:			
CHARLES H. DALLARA	USA	179,433	19.14
FRANK CASSELL	United Kingdom	62,190	6.63
GÜNTER GROSCHE	Federal Republic of Germany	54,287	5.79
HÉLÈNE PLOIX	France	45,078	4.81
KOJI YAMAZAKI	Japan	42,483	4.53
YUSUF A. NIMATALLAH	Saudi Arabia	32,274	3.44
Elected:			
LEONOR FILARDO (Venezuela)	Costa Rica, El Salvador, Guatemala, Honduras, Mexico, Nicaragua, Spain, Venezuela	44,401	4.74
G. A. POSTHUMUS (Netherlands)	Cyprus, Israel, Netherlands, Romania, Yugoslavia	40,425	4.31
JACQUES DE GROOTE (Belgium)	Austria, Belgium, Hungary, Luxembourg, Turkey	40,178	4.29
MOHAMED FINAISH (Libya)	Bahrain, Egypt, Iraq, Jordan, Kuwait, Lebanon, Libya, Maldives, Oman, Pakistan, Qatar, Somalia, Syria, United Arab Emirates, Yemen Arab Republic, People's Democratic Republic of Yemen	39,526	4.22
MARCEL MASSÉ (Canada)	Antigua and Barbuda, Bahamas, Barbados, Belize, Canada, Dominica, Grenada, Ireland, Jamaica, Saint Christopher and Nevis, Saint Lucia, Saint Vincent and the Grenadines	38,709	4.13
SALVATORE ZECCHINI (Italy)	Greece, Italy, Malta, Portugal	38,307	4.09
C. R. RYE (Australia)	Australia, Kiribati, Republic of Korea, New Zealand, Papua New Guinea, Philippines, Seychelles, Solomon Islands, Vanuatu, Western Samoa	33,254	3.55
JORGEN OVI (Denmark)	Denmark, Finland, Iceland, Norway, Sweden	32,338	3.45
BIMAL JALAN (India)	Bangladesh, Bhutan, India, Sri Lanka	28,208	3.01
ALEXANDRE KAFKA (Brazil)	Brazil, Colombia, Dominican Republic, Ecuador, Guyana, Haiti, Panama, Suriname, Trinidad and Tobago	27,582	2.94
JULIUS EMMANUEL ISMAEL (Indonesia)	Burma, Fiji, Indonesia, Laos, Malaysia, Nepal, Singapore, Thailand, Tonga, Viet-Nam	27,094	2.89
EL TAYEB EL KOGALI (Sudan)	Botswana, Burundi, Ethiopia, The Gambia, Kenya, Lesotho, Liberia, Malawi, Mozambique, Nigeria, Sierra Leone, Sudan, Swaziland, Tanzania, Uganda, Zambia, Zimbabwe	26,738	2.85
DAI QIANDING	People's Republic of China	24,159	2.58
ERNESTO FELDMAN (Argentina)	Argentina, Bolivia, Chile, Paraguay, Peru, Uruguay	23,373	2.49
MOHAMMED REZA GHAZIMI (Iran)	Afghanistan, Algeria, Ghana, Iran, Morocco, Tunisia	21,691	2.31
MAWAKANI SAMBA (Zaire)	Benin, Burkina Faso, Cameroon, Cape Verde, Central African Republic, Chad, Comoros, Congo, Côte d'Ivoire, Djibouti, Equatorial Guinea, Gabon, Guinea, Guinea-Bissau, Madagascar, Mali, Mauritania, Mauritius, Niger, Rwanda, São Tomé and Príncipe, Senegal, Togo, Zaire	18,940	2.02

Note: Votes in the General Department and the SDR Department total 937,625, including the votes of Kampuchea, Poland and South Africa, which did not participate in the 1986 and 1988 Regular Elections of Executive Directors. The number of votes in the Executive Board is 920,668.

elected by groups of member countries with similar interests; there is also a Director from the People's Republic of China. As in the Board of Governors, the voting power of each member is related to its quota in the Fund, but in practice the Executive Directors operate by consensus.

The Managing Director of the Fund serves as head of its staff, which is organized into departments by function and area. On 30 April 1987 the Fund staff comprised 1,667 people from 101 countries.

Activities

The purposes of the IMF, as set out in the Articles of Agreement, are:

(i) To promote international monetary co-operation through a permanent institution which provides the machinery for consultation and collaboration on monetary problems.

(ii) To facilitate the expansion and balanced growth of international trade, and to contribute thereby to the promotion and maintenance of high levels of employment and real income and to the development of members' productive resources.

(iii) To promote exchange stability, to maintain orderly exchange arrangements among members, and to avoid competitive exchange depreciation.

(iv) To assist in the establishment of a multilateral system of payments in respect of current transactions between members and in the elimination of foreign exchange restrictions which hamper the growth of trade.

(v) To give confidence to members by making the general resources of the Fund temporarily available to them, under adequate safeguards, thus providing them with the opportunity to correct maladjustments in their balance of payments, without resorting to measures destructive of national or international prosperity.

(vi) In accordance with the above, to shorten the duration of and lessen the degree of disequilibrium in the international balances of payments of members.

In joining the Fund, each country agrees to co-operate with the above objectives, and the Fund monitors members' compliance by holding an annual consultation with each country, in order to survey the country's exchange rate policies and determine its need for assistance.

SPECIAL DRAWING RIGHTS

The special drawing right (SDR) was introduced in 1970 as a substitute for gold in international payments: it is intended eventually to become the principal reserve asset in the international monetary system. SDRs are allocated to members in proportion to their quotas. Originally SDR 9,300m. were allocated, and further allocations of approximately SDR 4,000m. each were made in 1979, 1980 and 1981, bringing the total of SDRs in existence to SDR 21,300m. or about 5% of international non-gold reserves.

From 1974 to 1980 the SDR was valued on the basis of the market exchange rate for a basket of 16 currencies, belonging to the members with the largest exports of goods and services; since 1981 it has been based on the currencies of the five largest exporters (France, the Federal Republic of Germany, Japan, the United Kingdom and the USA). The average value of the SDR in 1987 was US $1.29307.

The Second Amendment to the Articles of Agreement (1978) altered and expanded the possible uses of the SDR in transactions with other participants. 'Other holders' of the SDRs have the same degree of freedom as Fund members to buy and sell SDRs and to receive or use them in loans, pledges, swaps, donations or settlement of financial obligations. In September 1988 there were 16 'other holders': the African Development Bank and the African Development Fund, the Andean Reserve Fund, the Arab Monetary Fund, the Asian Development Bank, the Bank of Central African States, the Bank for International Settlements, the Central Bank of West African States, the East African Development Bank, the Eastern Caribbean Central Bank, the International Bank for Reconstruction and Development and the International Development Association, the International Fund for Agricultural Development, the Islamic Development Bank, the Nordic Investment Bank and the Swiss National Bank.

QUOTAS

Each member is assigned a quota related to its national income, monetary reserves, trade balance and other economic indicators. A member's subscription is equal to its quota and is payable partly in SDRs and partly in its own currency. The quota approximately determines a member's voting power, the amount of foreign exchange it may purchase from the Fund, and its allocation of SDRs.

Quotas are reviewed at intervals of not more than five years, to take into account the state of the world economy and members' different rates of development. General increases were made in 1959, 1966, 1970, 1978 and 1980, while special increases were made for the People's Republic of China in April 1980, for a group of 11 members in December 1980, and for Saudi Arabia in April 1981. The eighth general review of quotas resulted in March 1983 in an agreement to raise quotas by 47.5% to SDR 90,035m., subject to approval by national legislatures. The early review (two years ahead of schedule) was considered necessary in view of the debt crisis afflicting some member states. By April 1984 all of the 142 members that had consented to increases in quotas had completed payments of their subscriptions, raising the total of IMF quotas to SDR 89,236.3m. At 31 July 1988 total quotas in the Fund amounted to SDR 89,987.6m. (see table below). The Executive Board was to submit proposals for a ninth general review of quotas by April 1989.

RESOURCES

Members' subscriptions form the basic resource of the IMF. They are supplemented by borrowing. Under the General Arrangements to Borrow (GAB), established in 1962, the 'Group of Ten' industrialized nations (Belgium, Canada, France, the Federal Republic of Germany, Italy, Japan, the Netherlands, Sweden, the United Kingdom and the USA) and Switzerland (not a member of the IMF, but a full participant in the GAB from April 1984) undertake to lend the Fund up to SDR 17,000m. in their own currencies, so as to help meet the balance-of-payments requirements of any member of the group, or to meet requests to the Fund from countries with balance-of-payments problems that could threaten the stability of the international monetary system. In July 1983 the Fund entered into an agreement with Saudi Arabia, in association with the GAB, making available SDR 1,500m., and other borrowing arrangements were completed in 1984 with the BIS, the Saudi Arabian Monetary Agency, Belgium and Japan, making available a further SDR 6,000m. In December 1986 another borrowing arrangement with Japan made available SDR 3,000m.

As part of the effort to reduce the monetary role of gold, a third of the Fund's gold holdings was sold between 1976 and 1980: one-half of this amount was sold at public auction for the benefit of developing member states. Of the resulting US $4,640m., part was allotted to the 104 eligible members according to their quotas, and part was put into a Trust Fund making low-interest loans. By the time the Trust Fund was wound up in April 1981 it had disbursed $3,560m. Repayments of Trust Fund loans are used to make further concessionary loans, for example under the structural adjustment facility described below.

DRAWING ARRANGEMENTS

Exchange transactions within the Fund take the form of members' purchases (i.e. drawings) from the Fund of the currencies of other members for the equivalent amounts of their own currencies. Fund resources are available to eligible members on an essentially short-term and revolving basis to provide members with temporary assistance to contribute to the solution of their payments problems. Before making a purchase, a member must show that its balance of payments or reserve position make the purchase necessary. Apart from this requirement, reserve tranche purchases (i.e. purchases that do not bring the Fund's holdings of the member's currency to a level above its quota) are permitted unconditionally.

With further purchases, however, the Fund's policy of 'conditionality' means that a member requesting assistance must agree to adjust its economic policies, as stipulated by the IMF. All requests other than for use of the reserve tranche are examined by the Executive Board to determine whether the proposed use would be consistent with the Fund's policies, and a member must discuss its proposed adjustment programme (including fiscal, monetary, exchange and trade policies) with IMF staff. Purchases outside the reserve tranche are made in four credit tranches, each equivalent to 25% of the member's quota; a member must reverse the transaction by repurchasing its own currency (with SDRs or currencies specified by the Fund) within a specified time. A credit tranche purchase is usually made under a 'stand-by arrangement' with the Fund, or under the extended Fund facility. A stand-by arrangement is normally of one or two years' duration, and the member can make drawings on the Fund up to a specified amount without further review of its performance and policies; repayment must be made within three-and-a-quarter to five years. An extended arrangement is normally of three years' duration, and the member must submit detailed economic programmes and progress reports for each year; repayment must be made within four-and-a-half to 10 years. A member whose payments imbalance is large in relation to its quota may make use of temporary facilities established by the Fund using borrowed resources, namely the

INTERNATIONAL ORGANIZATIONS

United Nations (Specialized Agencies)

'enlarged access policy' established in 1981, which helps to finance stand-by and extended arrangements for such a member, up to a limit of between 90% and 110% of the member's quota annually.

In addition, there are special-purpose arrangements, all of which are subject to the member's co-operation with the Fund to find an appropriate solution to its difficulties. The buffer stock financing facility (established in 1969) enables members to pay their contributions to the buffer stocks which are intended to stabilize primary commodity markets. Members may draw up to 45% of their quota for this purpose. In August 1988 the Fund established the compensatory and contingency financing facility (CCFF), which replaced and expanded the former compensatory financing facility, established in 1963. The CCFF provides compensation to members whose export earnings are reduced owing to circumstances beyond their control, or who are affected by excess costs of cereal imports. Contingency financing is provided to help members maintain their efforts at economic adjustment even when affected by a sharp increase in interest rates or other externally-derived difficulties.

In March 1986 the Fund established a structural adjustment facility (SAF) to provide balance of payments assistance on concessional terms to low-income developing countries. The facility was to be funded with about SDR 2,700m., expected to become available during 1985-91 from repayments of Trust Fund loans. SAF loans carry an interest rate of 0.5%, repayable within 10 years, including a five-and-a-half-year grace period. The member concerned may draw up to 63.5% of its quota over three years, and must develop a three-year adjustment programme (with assistance given jointly by staff of the Fund and of the World Bank) to restore sustainable economic growth. At mid-1988 62 countries were eligible for assistance under the SAF (but two, the People's Republic of China and India, had indicated that they would not avail themselves of the facility, thus enlarging the amount available for other countries). By August 1988 27 countries had three-year arrangements under the SAF, for a total amount of SDR 1,400m.

In December 1987 the Fund established an Enhanced Structural Adjustment Facility (ESAF), which was to provide new resources of SDR 6,000m. (in addition to SDR 2,200m. as yet undisbursed under the SAF), to assist the adjustment efforts of, in particular, heavily-indebted countries. Maximum access was to be set at 250% of the member's quota, and conditions for repayment were to be similar to those imposed under the SAF.

During the year ending 30 April 1987 eight members made reserve tranche purchases, totalling SDR 516m. Credit tranche purchases were made by 36 members and amounted to SDR 2,325m., (of which SDR 752m. was financed from borrowed resources under the enlarged access policy). Stand-by arrangements were approved for 22 members and totalled SDR 4,118m., while total purchases under the extended facility were SDR 250m. Under the compensatory financing facility purchases of SDR 593m. were made. No purchases were made under the buffer stock financing facility. Total purchases during the year amounted to SDR 3,685m., compared with SDR 4,101m. in 1985/86, SDR 6,289m. in 1984/85 and SDR 11,518m. in 1983/84. Repurchases during the year ending 30 April 1987 came to SDR 6,169m., compared with SDR 4,289m. in the previous year.

TECHNICAL ASSISTANCE

This is provided by special missions or resident representatives who advise members on every aspect of economic management. The Central Banking Department and the Fiscal Affairs Department are particularly involved in technical assistance. The IMF Institute, founded in 1964, trains officials from member countries in financial analysis and policy, balance of payments methodology and public finance: it also gives assistance to national and regional training centres.

PUBLICATIONS

Annual Report.

Annual Report on Exchange Arrangements and Exchange Restrictions.

International Financial Statistics (monthly and annually).

Balance of Payments Statistics (monthly and annually).

Government Finance Statistics Yearbook.

Direction of Trade Statistics (monthly and annually).

IMF Survey (2 a month).

Finance and Development (quarterly, published jointly with the World Bank).

Staff Papers (quarterly economic journal).

International Capital Markets (annually).

World Economic Outlook (annually).

Occasional papers, publications brochure.

Statistics

QUOTAS

	Quotas (31 July 1988; million SDRs)	% of total
Afghanistan	86.7	0.10
Algeria	623.1	0.69
Antigua and Barbuda	5.0	0.01
Argentina	1,113.0	1.24
Australia	1,619.2	1.80
Austria	775.6	0.86
Bahamas	66.4	0.07
Bahrain	48.9	0.05
Bangladesh	287.5	0.32
Barbados	34.1	0.04
Belgium	2,080.4	2.31
Belize	9.5	0.01
Benin	31.3	0.03
Bhutan	2.5	0.002
Bolivia	90.7	0.10
Botswana	22.1	0.02
Brazil	1,461.3	1.62
Burkina Faso	31.6	0.04
Burma	137.0	0.15
Burundi	42.7	0.05
Cameroon	92.7	0.10
Canada	2,941.0	3.27
Cape Verde	4.5	0.01
Central African Republic	30.4	0.03
Chad	30.6	0.03
Chile	440.5	0.49
China, People's Republic	2,390.9	2.66
Colombia	394.2	0.44
Comoros	4.5	0.01
Congo	37.3	0.04
Costa Rica	84.1	0.09
Côte d'Ivoire	165.5	0.18
Cyprus	69.7	0.08
Denmark	711.0	0.79
Djibouti	8.0	0.01
Dominica	4.0	0.004
Dominican Republic	112.1	0.12
Ecuador	150.7	0.17
Egypt	463.4	0.51
El Salvador	89.0	0.10
Equatorial Guinea	18.4	0.02
Ethiopia	70.6	0.08
Fiji	36.5	0.04
Finland	574.9	0.64
France	4,482.8	4.98
Gabon	73.1	0.08
The Gambia	17.1	0.02
Germany, Federal Republic	5,403.7	6.00
Ghana	204.5	0.23
Greece	399.9	0.44
Grenada	6.0	0.01
Guatemala	108.0	0.12
Guinea	57.9	0.06
Guinea-Bissau	7.5	0.01
Guyana	49.2	0.05
Haiti	44.1	0.05
Honduras	67.8	0.08
Hungary	530.7	0.59
Iceland	59.6	0.07
India	2,207.7	2.45
Indonesia	1,009.7	1.12
Iran	660.0	0.73
Iraq	504.0	0.56
Ireland	343.4	0.38
Israel	446.6	0.50
Italy	2,909.1	3.23
Jamaica	145.5	0.16
Japan	4,223.3	4.69
Jordan	73.9	0.08
Kampuchea	25.0	0.03
Kenya	142.0	0.16
Kiribati	2.5	0.002
Korea, Republic	462.8	0.51
Kuwait	635.3	0.71
Laos	29.3	0.03
Lebanon	78.7	0.09

INTERNATIONAL ORGANIZATIONS — United Nations (Specialized Agencies)

	Quotas (31 July 1988; million SDRs)	% of total		Quotas (31 July 1988; million SDRs)	% of total
Lesotho	15.1	0.02	Seychelles	3.0	0.003
Liberia	71.3	0.08	Sierra Leone	57.9	0.06
Libya	515.7	0.57	Singapore	92.4	0.10
Luxembourg	77.0	0.09	Solomon Islands	5.0	0.01
Madagascar	66.4	0.07	Somalia	44.2	0.05
Malawi	37.2	0.04	South Africa	915.7	1.02
Malaysia	550.6	0.61	Spain	1,286.0	1.43
Maldives	2.0	0.002	Sri Lanka	223.1	0.25
Mali	50.8	0.06	Sudan	169.7	0.19
Malta	45.1	0.05	Suriname	49.3	0.05
Mauritania	33.9	0.04	Swaziland	24.7	0.03
Mauritius	53.6	0.06	Sweden	1,064.3	1.18
Mexico	1,165.5	1.30	Syria	139.1	0.15
Morocco	306.6	0.34	Tanzania	107.0	0.12
Mozambique	61.0	0.07	Thailand	386.6	0.43
Nepal	37.3	0.04	Togo	38.4	0.04
Netherlands	2,264.8	2.52	Tonga	3.2	50.003
New Zealand	461.6	0.51	Trinidad and Tobago	170.1	0.19
Nicaragua	68.2	0.08	Tunisia	138.2	0.15
Niger	33.7	0.04	Turkey	429.1	0.48
Nigeria	849.5	0.94	Uganda	99.6	0.11
Norway	699.0	0.78	United Arab Emirates	202.6	0.23
Oman	63.1	0.07	United Kingdom	6,194.0	6.88
Pakistan	546.3	0.61	USA	17,918.3	19.91
Panama	102.2	0.11	Uruguay	163.8	0.18
Papua New Guinea	65.9	0.07	Vanuatu	9.0	0.01
Paraguay	48.4	0.05	Venezuela	1,371.5	1.52
Peru	330.9	0.37	Viet-Nam	176.8	0.20
Philippines	440.4	0.49	Western Samoa	6.0	0.01
Poland	680.0	0.76	Yemen Arab Republic	43.3	0.05
Portugal	376.6	0.42	Yemen, People's Democratic Republic	77.2	0.09
Qatar	114.9	0.13	Yugoslavia	613.0	0.68
Romania	523.4	0.58	Zaire	291.0	0.32
Rwanda	43.8	0.05	Zambia	270.3	0.30
Saint Christopher and Nevis	4.5	0.01	Zimbabwe	191.0	0.21
Saint Lucia	7.5	0.01	**Total**	**89,987.55**	**100.0***
Saint Vincent and the Grenadines	4.0	0.004			
São Tomé and Príncipe	4.0	0.004			
Saudi Arabia	3,202.4	3.56			
Senegal	85.1	0.09			

* The sum of the individual percentage shares differs from 100.0 because of rounding.

TRANSACTIONS (SDR million, year ending 30 April)

Type of Transaction	1981	1982	1983	1984	1985	1986	1987
Total purchases	4,860	8,041	11,392	11,518	6,289	4,101	3,685
Reserve tranche	474	1,080	1,134	1,354	229	160	517
Credit tranches	2,682	2,748	3,703	4,164	2,768	2,841	2,325
Buffer stock financing facility	—	—	352	102	—	—	—
Compensatory financing facility	784	1,635	3,740	1,180	1,248	601	593
Extended Fund facility	920	2,578	2,463	4,718	2,044	498	250
Total repurchases	2,811	1,894	1,547	2,015	2,730	4,274	6,162
Outstanding Fund credit	9,545	14,802	23,590	31,742	34,973	34,640	31,646
Outstanding borrowings	4,323	6,773	10,952	13,791	14,203	14,556	12,700§
In connection with oil facility	1,528	526	18	—	—	—	—
Under General Arrangements to Borrow	777	777	777	—	—	—	—
Supplementary financing facility	2,018	4,112	6,037	6,915	6,239	5,038	3,381
Under policy on enlarged access	—	1,358	4,120	6,876	7,964	9,518	9,304
Holdings of the General Resources Account at end of year*							
Usable currencies†	23,000	17,000	14,400	32,900	37,300	34,400	37,300
SDRs	5,445	5,456	4,335	6,437	4,616	2,722	1,960
Gold‡	3,620	3,620	3,620	3,620	3,620	3,620	3,620
Reserve tranche positions of members at end of year	13,125	15,621	20,592	27,415	28,290	26,087	24,025

* Total excludes Fund's gold holdings.
† 'Usable currencies' are those that are available to the Fund for net sales through the operational budget, except for those currencies held by the Fund in excess of quota. Since the Second Amendment became effective on 1 April 1978, the criterion for including currencies for net sales is that the members concerned have a balance-of-payments and reserve position that the Fund considers 'sufficiently strong' for that purpose.
‡ Valued at SDR 35 per troy ounce (0.888671 g of fine gold per SDR).
§ Includes SDR 15m. under borrowing agreement with Japan.
Source: *International Monetary Fund Annual Report 1987*.

INTERNATIONAL ORGANIZATIONS   United Nations (Specialized Agencies)

International Telecommunication Union—ITU

Address: Place des Nations, 1211 Geneva 20, Switzerland.
Telephone: (022) 995111.
Telex: 421 000.

Founded in 1865, ITU became a Specialized Agency of the UN in 1947. It acts to encourage world co-operation in the use of telecommunication, to promote technical development and to harmonize national policies in the field.

MEMBERS
164 members: see Table on pp. 50–52.

Organization
(October 1988)

PLENIPOTENTIARY CONFERENCE
The supreme organ of ITU; meets about every five years. Each member has one vote at the Conference, whose main tasks are to approve budget policy and accounts, to negotiate with other international organizations, and generally direct policy. The 1989 Conference (May/June) was to be held in Nice, France.

WORLD ADMINISTRATIVE CONFERENCES
The Administrative Telegraph and Telephone Conference revises telegraph and telephone regulations. The World Administrative Radio Conference revises radio regulations and reviews the activities of the International Frequency Registration Board. World Administrative Conferences meet at irregular intervals according to technical needs, and there may also be regional Administrative Conferences held *ad hoc*.

ADMINISTRATIVE COUNCIL
The Administrative Council meets annually in Geneva and is composed of 41 members elected by the Plenipotentiary Conference.

The Council helps the implementation of the Convention's provisions, and executes the decisions of the Plenipotentiary Conference and, where appropriate, the decisions of the conferences and meetings of the Union. It conducts relations with other international organizations, and approves the annual budget.

GENERAL SECRETARIAT
The Secretary-General is elected by the Plenipotentiary Conference, and is responsible to it for the General Secretariat's work, and for the Union's administrative and financial services. The General Secretariat's staff totals 425; the working languages are English, French and Spanish.
Secretary-General: RICHARD E. BUTLER (Australia).

Convention
The International Telecommunication Convention is the definitive convention of the Union, member countries being those who signed it in 1932 or acceded to it later. Since 1932 it has been superseded by new versions at successive plenipotentiary conferences.

The Convention deals with the structure of the Union, the application of its own provisions and regulations, relations with the United Nations and other organizations, and special rules for radio.

TELEGRAPH AND TELEPHONE REGULATIONS
The Telegraph and Telephone Regulations were adopted during the 1973 Geneva Telegraph and Telephone Conference. They deal with problems of telegraph and telephone rates and tariffs among ITU member countries. These two Regulations lay down the general principles to be observed in the international telegraph and telephone service. Their provisions are applied to both wire and wireless telegraph and telephone communications in so far as the Radio Regulations and the Additional Radio Regulations do not provide otherwise.

RADIO REGULATIONS
The Radio Regulations include general rules for the assignment and use of frequencies and—the most important part of the Regulations—a Table of Frequency Allocations between 10 kHz and 275 GHz to the various radio services: broadcasting, television, radio astronomy, navigation aid, point-to-point service, maritime mobile, amateur, etc. Chapter III deals with the duties of the International Frequency Registration Board. The Regulations governing measures against interference follow. Subsequently, there are administrative provisions for stations (secrecy, licences, identification, service documents, inspection of mobile stations).

Chapters VI and VII are concerned with personnel and working conditions in the mobile services, and Chapter VIII with radio assistance in life saving. The last two chapters deal with radiotelegrams and radiotelephone calls and miscellaneous stations and services. Partial revisions of the Radio Regulations are in force for Space Services (1965 and 1973), the Aeronautical Mobile Services (1967 and 1978), the Maritime Mobile Service (1969 and 1974), Broadcasting (1975), and Broadcasting–Satellite Service (1977).

A 10-week World Administrative Radio Conference (WARC) was held in 1979 to undertake the most complete revision of the radio spectrum allocation to be made since 1959. The results of this conference were expected to govern the planning and operation of radio communication services (radio navigation, broadcasting, mobile radio and satellites) for the rest of the century. Partial revisions were also made subsequently by regional administrative radio conferences. The 1984 WARC agreed on a plan to make more high-frequency broadcasting channels available through the use of 'single sideband' transmissions, although developing member countries opposed this method because it requires new equipment. The Conference also agreed to monitor the deliberate 'jamming' of broadcasts.

The first session of the WARC on the use of the geostationary-satellite orbit and the planning of space services using it opened in August 1985, and the second session began in August 1988. The objective of the Conference was to guarantee in practice, for all countries, equitable access to the geostationary-satellite orbit and to the frequency bands allocated to the space services using it.

Activities

INTERNATIONAL FREQUENCY REGISTRATION BOARD—IFRB
IFRB records assignments of radio frequencies and provides technical advice to enable members of the Union to operate as many radio channels as possible in overcrowded parts of the radio spectrum. It also investigates cases of harmful interference and makes recommendations for their solution.
Chairman: W. H. BELLCHAMBERS (United Kingdom).

INTERNATIONAL TELEGRAPH AND TELEPHONE CONSULTATIVE COMMITTEE—CCITT
CCITT is currently organizing 18 study groups covering transmission problems, operation and tariffs, maintenance, electromagnetic dangers, protection of equipment, definitions, vocabulary and symbols, apparatus, local connecting lines, facsimile and photo-telegraphy, quality of transmission, specifications, telegraph and telex switching, telephone signalling and switching and planning the development of an international network. It has its own telephony laboratory.
Director: T. IRMER (Federal Republic of Germany).

INTERNATIONAL RADIO CONSULTATIVE COMMITTEE—CCIR
The work of CCIR is done by 11 study groups covering spectrum utilization and monitoring; space research and radio astronomy services; fixed services below about 30 MHz; fixed services using satellites; propagation in non-ionized media; ionospheric propagation; standard frequency and time-signal services; mobile services; fixed services using radio-relay systems; sound broadcasting service; television broadcasting service. The television study group is working on the following matters: television recording, television standards for both black and white and colour transmission, ratio of the wanted to unwanted signal in television, reduction of band width, conversion of a television signal from one standard to another, estimates of the quality of television pictures, etc.
Director: RICHARD C. KIRBY (USA).

PLAN COMMITTEES
The Plan Committees are joint CCIR/CCITT committees responsible for preparing plans setting out circuit and routing requirements

INTERNATIONAL ORGANIZATIONS

United Nations (Specialized Agencies)

for international telecommunications and for giving estimates of the growth of international traffic. They comprise a World Plan Committee and four regional committees, for Africa, for Latin America, for Asia and Oceania and for Europe and the Mediterranean Basin.

TECHNICAL CO-OPERATION

ITU's programme of technical co-operation in developing countries is carried out within the framework of UNDP (q.v.). In 1987, 590 experts were on mission, 1,081 fellows were undergoing training abroad and US $6.5m. worth of equipment was delivered. The total cost of this assistance amounted to $27.5m.

The three main objectives of ITU's activity in the field of technical co-operation are: (*a*) promoting the development of regional telecommunication networks in Africa, Asia and Latin America; (*b*) strengthening telecommunications technical and administrative services in developing countries; and (*c*) developing the human resources required for telecommunications. A Center for Telecommunications Development was established in Geneva in 1986.

Assistance is also provided by ITU in the specialized fields of telephony, telegraphy, radio-communications, frequency management, satellite communications, planning, organization, administration and management.

INFORMATION

ITU issues numerous technical and statistical publications (see below) and maintains a library and archives.

FINANCE

The total 1988 budget amounted to 106m. Swiss francs (compared with $107m. in 1987).

PUBLICATIONS

List of Publications (2 a year).
Telecommunication Journal (monthly).
Conventions, statistics, technical documents and manuals, conference documents.

United Nations Educational, Scientific and Cultural Organization—UNESCO

Address: 7 place de Fontenoy, 75700 Paris.
Telephone: (1) 45-68-10-00.
Telex: 204461.

UNESCO was established in 1946 'for the purpose of advancing, through the educational, scientific and cultural relations of the peoples of the world, the objectives of international peace and the common welfare of mankind'.

MEMBERS

158 members: see Table on pp. 50–52.

Organization

(October 1988)

GENERAL CONFERENCE

The supreme governing body of the Organization, the Conference meets in ordinary session once in two years and is composed of representatives of the member states.

EXECUTIVE BOARD

The Board, comprising 50 members, prepares the programme to be submitted to the Conference and supervises its execution; it meets twice or sometimes three times a year.
President (1988–89): JOSÉ ISRAEL VARGAS (Brazil).

SECRETARIAT

Director-General: FEDERICO MAYOR ZARAGOZA (Spain).
Director of the Executive Office: LUIS MARQUES (Spain).

CO-OPERATING BODIES

In accordance with UNESCO's Constitution, national Commissions have been set up in most member states. These help to integrate work within the member states and the work of UNESCO.

UNESCO REGIONAL OFFICES

Africa

Regional Office for Education in Africa: BP 3311, Dakar, Senegal; Dir BABA HAIDARA.
Regional Office for Science and Technology for Africa: POB 30592, Nairobi, Kenya; tel. 333930; telex 22275; Dir Dr M. S. NTAMILA.

Latin America and the Caribbean

Regional Centre for Higher Education in Latin America and the Caribbean (CRESALC): Altos de Sebucan, Avda Los Chorros/Cruce, Calle Acueducto, Edificio Asovincar, Apdo 62090, Caracas 1060, Venezuela.
Regional Office for Culture in Latin America and the Caribbean: Calzada 551, esq. a D, Vedado, Apdo 4158, Havana, Cuba; tel. 32-7741; telex 51-2154.

Regional Office for Education in Latin America and the Caribbean: POB 3187, Santiago, Chile; tel. 223-5582; telex 340258.
Regional Office for Science and Technology for Latin America and the Caribbean: 1320 Bulevar Artigas, Casilla 859, Montevideo, Uruguay; tel. 41.18.07; telex 22340; Dir Dr GUSTAVO MALEK.

Asia and the Pacific

Office for the Pacific States: POB 5766, Matautu, Apia, Western Samoa; tel. 24276; telex 209; Chief of Mission F. L. HIGGINSON.
Principal Regional Office for Asia and the Pacific (including the Asian Centre for Educational Innovation for Development): 920 Sukhumvit Rd, POB 1425, Bangkok 10501, Thailand; tel. 391-0577; telex 20591; Dir Dr M. MAKAGIANSAR.
Regional Office for Book Development in Asia and the Pacific: POB 8950, Karachi 75400, Pakistan; tel. 416428; telex 25044.
Regional Office for Science and Technology for South and Central Asia: UNESCO House, 15 Jor Bagh, New Delhi 110003, India; tel. 618092; telex 31-65896; Dir Dr M. P. DERKATCH.
Regional Office for Science and Technology for South-East Asia: UN Building (2nd Floor), Jl. Thamrin 14, Tromol Pos 273/JKT, Jakarta, Indonesia; tel. 321308; telex 44178.

Arab States and Europe

European Centre for Higher Education (CEPES): Palatul Kretulescu, Stirbei Voda 39, Bucharest, Romania; tel. 159956; telex 11658.
Regional Office for Education in the Arab States: 7 place de Fontenoy, 75700 Paris, France.
Regional Office for Science and Technology in the Arab States: POB 950492, Amman, Jordan; tel. 606559; telex 24357; Dir Dr OSMAN ABAYAZID.

Activities

UNESCO's activities, which take three main forms as outlined below, are funded through a regular budget provided by member states and also through other sources, particularly UNDP. UNESCO co-operates with many other UN agencies and international non-governmental organizations.

International Intellectual Co-operation: UNESCO assists the interchange of experience, knowledge and ideas through a world network of specialists. Apart from the work of its professional staff, UNESCO co-operates regularly with the national associations and international federations of scientists, artists, writers and educators, some of which it helped to establish. UNESCO convenes conferences and meetings, and co-ordinates international scientific efforts; it helps to standardize procedures of documentation and provides clearing house services; it offers fellowships; and it publishes a wide range of specialized works, including source books and works of reference. UNESCO promotes various international agreements, including the International Copyright Convention and the World Cultural and National Heritage Convention, which member states are invited to accept.

Operational Assistance: UNESCO has established missions which advise governments, particularly in the developing member countries, in the planning of projects; and it appoints experts to assist in carrying them out. The projects are concerned with the teaching of functional literacy to workers in development undertakings; teacher training; establishing of libraries and documentation centres; provision of training for journalists, radio, television and film workers; improvement of scientific and technical education; training of planners in cultural development; and the international exchange of persons and information.

Promotion of Peace: UNESCO organizes various research efforts on racial problems, and is particularly concerned with prevention of discrimination in education, and improving access for women to education. It also promotes studies and research on conflicts and peace, violence and obstacles to disarmament, and the role of international law and organizations in building peace. It is stressed that human rights, peace and disarmament cannot be dealt with separately, as the observance of human rights is a prerequisite to peace and vice versa.

In 1984 the government of the USA (which had been due to provide about 25% of UNESCO's budget for the two years 1984–85) withdrew from the organization, alleging inefficiency, financial mismanagement and political bias against Western countries. The United Kingdom and Singapore also withdrew from UNESCO at the end of 1985.

EDUCATION

UNESCO's most important activities are in the sphere of education, particularly the spread of literacy, adult education, and the encouragement of universal primary education. It places special emphasis on the attainment of education by women and the handicapped, and on literacy as an integral part of rural development. During the two years 1986–87 this sector was allocated US $71m. from the organization's regular budget of $307m.

Each year expert missions are sent to member states on request to advise on all matters concerning education. In 1987 UNESCO provided about 5,000 fellowships and travel grants. In these forms of assistance priority is given to the rural regions of developing member countries.

Examples of activities include: co-operation with UNRWA (q.v.) to provide schooling for Palestinian refugee children; educational assistance for African refugees; preparation of a major scheme to eradicate illiteracy in Latin America and the Caribbean by the year 2000; studies on the establishment of regional industries to provide educational equipment; and about 90 teacher-training schemes. The International Institute for Educational Planning and the International Bureau of Education (q.v.) carry out training, research and the exchange of information on aspects of education.

NATURAL SCIENCES AND TECHNOLOGY

UNESCO's science and technology programme was allocated US $49m. from the organization's regular budget of $307m. for 1986–87. While the main emphasis in UNESCO's work in science and technology is on harnessing these to development, and above all on meeting the needs of developing countries, the Organization is also active in promoting and fostering collaborative international projects among the highly industrialized countries. UNESCO's activities can be divided into three levels: international, regional and sub-regional, and national.

At the international level, UNESCO has over the years set up various forms of intergovernmental co-operation concerned with the environmental sciences and research on natural resources. Examples of these are the Man and Biosphere Programme (MAB) which by 1988 had undertaken 1,000 programmes in 100 countries, involving local people in solving practical problems of environmental resource management in such areas as arid lands, humid tropical zones, mountain ecosystems, urban systems, etc.; the International Geological Correlation Programme (IGCP), run jointly with the International Union of Geological Sciences (q.v.); the International Hydrological Programme (IHP), dealing with the scientific aspects of water resources assessment and management; and the Intergovernmental Oceanographic Commission (q.v.) which promotes scientific investigation into the nature and resources of the oceans through the concerted action of its member states. Another programme, the Intergovernmental Informatics Programme, encourages co-operation between developed and developing countries in computer sciences. In the basic sciences, UNESCO helps promote international and regional co-operation in close collaboration with the world scientific communities, with which it maintains close co-operative links particularly through its support to ICSU and member unions. Major disciplinary programmes are promoted in the fields of physics (including support to the International Centre for Theoretical Physics), the chemical sciences, life sciences, including applied microbiology, mathematics, informatics and new sources of energy.

At the regional and sub-regional level, UNESCO develops co-operative scientific and technological research programmes through organization and support of scientific meetings and contacts with research institutions, and the establishment or strengthening of co-operative networks; the African Network of Scientific and Technological Institutions, for example, was launched in 1980 at UNESCO's Nairobi Regional Office, to encourage collaboration among these institutions, and in 1982 a regional network of engineering institutions was established in the Middle East. Periodically, regional ministerial conferences are organized on science and technology policy and on the application of science and technology to development. A second conference of ministers responsible for the application of science and technology to development in Africa was held in July 1987. More specialized regional and sub-regional meetings are also organized.

At the national level, UNESCO assists member states, upon request, in policy-making and planning in the field of science and technology generally, and by organizing training and research programmes in basic sciences, engineering sciences and environmental sciences, particularly work relevant to development, such as projects concerning the use of small-scale energy sources for rural and dispersed populations. In 1983 a two-year programme was set up to assist the teaching of the natural sciences in universities in the developing countries, through grants for the production of low-cost laboratory equipment and teaching materials, and training courses for university teachers and laboratory technicians.

SOCIAL SCIENCES

The social and human sciences programme aims to encourage the development of the social sciences throughout the world by strengthening national and regional institutions, the conceptual development of the social sciences, training, the exchange and diffusion of information, and co-operation with international non-governmental organizations. The programme was allocated US $14m. from UNESCO's 1986–87 budget of $307m.

The activities concerning human rights and peace include two major programmes: the elimination of prejudice, intolerance, racism and apartheid; and a programme for peace, international understanding, human rights and the rights of peoples.

CULTURE

UNESCO's cultural heritage programme was allocated US $19m. from the organization's budget of $307m. for 1986–87. The programme is in three parts: activities designed to foster the worldwide application of three international conventions that aim to protect and conserve cultural property; international safeguarding campaigns to help member states to conserve and restore monuments and sites (in 1988 there were 22 such campaigns in progress); and the training of museum managers and conservationists and promotion of public awareness of the cultural heritage.

UNESCO's World Heritage Programme, launched in 1978, aims to protect landmarks of outstanding universal value, in accordance with the 1972 UNESCO Convention Concerning the Protection of the World Cultural and Natural Heritage, by providing financial aid for restoration, technical assistance, training and management planning. By September 1988 the 'World Heritage List' comprised 288 sites in more than 60 countries. UNESCO has participated in the restoration of the Buddhist temple at Borobudur, Indonesia (1973–83), the re-siting of the temples of Abu Simbel, Egypt, preliminary work on preserving the ancient city of Moenjodaro, Pakistan, and many other conservation projects.

The seventh volume of an eight-volume history of Africa was published in 1985, and in 1988 work was also in progress on histories of Latin America, the Caribbean and the civilizations of Central Asia, and on a six-volume publication on Islamic culture. A 10-year programme for the collection and safeguarding of the non-physical heritage (oral traditions, music, dance, medicine, etc.) was begun in 1988. UNESCO encourages the translation and publication of literary works, publishes albums of art, and produces records, audiovisual programmes and travelling art exhibitions. It supports the development of book publishing and distribution and the training of editors and managers in publishing. UNESCO is active in preparing and encouraging the enforcement of international legislation on copyright.

COMMUNICATION

UNESCO's programme aims at fostering a free flow of information among individuals, communities and countries, The international movement of persons and circulation of materials are promoted through measures for the reduction of obstacles of a legislative, administrative or economic nature. The communication programme received US $13m. in the 1986–87 budget.

Assistance is provided to member states in the formulation of national communication policies, and a series of regional inter-governmental conferences on this subject has been organized since

INTERNATIONAL ORGANIZATIONS

1976. UNESCO also promotes research in the field of communication.

At the General Conference in October 1980 a 'New World Information and Communication Order' (NWICO) (including plans for an international code of journalistic ethics and for the 'licensing' of journalists) was approved, in spite of objections from the United Kingdom and USA; those in favour of NWICO argued that established agencies and commercial interests had too much control over news and information, while their opponents maintained that the new proposals infringed press freedom. Following the approval of NWICO, the Intergovernmental Programme for the Development of Communication (IPDC) was established, under which UNESCO executes a number of programmes both in individual countries and at the regional and sub-regional levels, to provide advisory services and help advance professional training in communication skills. Projects included the Pan-African News Agency, a regional training centre for the Arab states, a Latin American information service and, in Asia, a network of information exchange and a 'bank' of films and television programmes. Two international projects were also planned: a study on the role of satellites in the exchange of information, and a project on rural communications.

FINANCE

UNESCO's Regular Programme budget for the two years 1984–85 was US $374.4m.; for 1986–87 it was $307m., and for 1988–89 it was $350.4m. Extra-budgetary funds were expected to amount to $213m. in 1988–89.

PUBLICATIONS

(mostly in English, French and Spanish editions; Arabic, Chinese and Russian versions are also available in many cases)

UNESCO Courier (monthly, in 35 languages).
UNESCO News (fortnightly).
Copyright Bulletin (quarterly).
Museum (quarterly).
Impact of Science on Society (quarterly).
International Social Science Journal (quarterly).
Nature and Resources (quarterly review of the Man and Biosphere programme, the International Hydrological Programme and the International Geological Correlation Programme).
Prospects (quarterly review on education).
International Marine Science Newsletter (quarterly).
Books, statistics, scientific maps and atlases.

INTERNATIONAL INSTITUTE FOR EDUCATIONAL PLANNING—IIEP

Address: 7-9 rue Eugène Delacroix, 75116 Paris, France.
Telephone: (1) 45-04-28-22.
Telex: 620074.

United Nations (Specialized Agencies)

The Institute was established by UNESCO in 1963 to serve as a world centre for advanced training and research in educational planning. Its purpose is to help all member states of UNESCO in their social and economic development efforts, by enlarging the fund of knowledge about educational planning and the supply of competent experts in this field.

Legally and administratively a part of UNESCO, the Institute is autonomous, and its policies and programme are controlled by its own Governing Board, under special statutes voted by the General Conference of UNESCO.

Chairman of Governing Board: Prof. MALCOLM S. ADISESHIAH.
Director: JACQUES HALLAK.

INTERNATIONAL BUREAU OF EDUCATION—IBE

Address: POB 199, 1211 Geneva 20, Switzerland.
Telephone: (022) 981455.
Telex: 22644.

Founded in 1925, the IBE became an intergovernmental organization in 1929 and was incorporated into UNESCO in 1969 as an international centre of comparative education. Through its International Educational Reporting Service (IERS) the Bureau provides information on developments and innovations in education; it has a library of 100,000 volumes, with 215,000 research reports on microfiche. It publishes a quarterly bulletin and newsletter, and various reference works. The Council of the IBE is composed of representatives of 24 Member States designated by the General Conference of UNESCO. The International Conference on Education is held every two years or so: its 40th session (1986) discussed improvement of secondary education, and the 41st session (1989) was to discuss diversification of post-secondary education in relation to employment.

INTERGOVERNMENTAL COMMITTEE FOR PHYSICAL EDUCATION AND SPORT—ICPES

Address: 7 place de Fontenoy, 75700 Paris.

Established by UNESCO in 1978 to serve as a permanent intergovernmental body in the field of physical education and sport.

The Committee is composed of 30 representatives of member states of UNESCO, elected by the General Conference.

Among its many activities aimed at further development of physical education and sport throughout the world, the Committee is responsible for supervising the planning and implementation of UNESCO's programme of activities in physical education and sport, promoting international co-operation in this area and facilitating the adoption and implementation of an International Charter of physical education and sport.

United Nations Industrial Development Organization—UNIDO

Address: POB 300, 1400 Vienna, Austria.
Telephone: (01) 26 310.
Telex: 135612.

UNIDO began operations in 1967, as an autonomous organization within the UN Secretariat, and became a specialized agency of the UN on 1 January 1986. Its objective is to promote industrial development in developing countries, so as to help in the establishment of a new international economic order.

MEMBERS

152 members: see Table on pp. 50–52.

Organization

(October 1988)

GENERAL CONFERENCE

The General Conference meets every two years and consists of representatives of all member states. It is the chief policy-making body of the Organization.

INDUSTRIAL DEVELOPMENT BOARD

The Board consists of 53 members elected by the General Conference for a three-year period: 33 members are from developing countries, 15 from developed market-economy countries, and five from countries with centrally-planned economies.

PROGRAMME AND BUDGET COMMITTEE

The Committee consists of 27 members, elected by the General Conference for a two-year term.

SECRETARIAT

At the beginning of 1988 there were 1,286 staff members in the UNIDO Secretariat. The Secretariat comprises the office of the Director-General and five departments, each headed by a Deputy Director-General: Programme and Project Development; Industrial Operations; Industrial Promotion, Consultations and Technology; External Relations, Public Information, Language and Documentation Services; and Administration.

Director-General: DOMINGO L. SIAZON, Jr.

INTERNATIONAL ORGANIZATIONS

United Nations (Specialized Agencies)

FIELD REPRESENTATION

UNIDO's Senior Industrial Development Field Advisers work in developing countries, in collaboration with the Resident Representatives of UNDP. In 1987 there were 31 such advisers, and 87 Junior Professional Officers. A total of 1,904 experts were engaged in field work.

Activities

Activities cover macro-economic and micro-economic aspects of industrial development. At macro-economic level, questions are considered concerning the formulation of industrial development policies, planning, programming, surveys, infrastructure and structure, and institutional services to industry. At micro-economic level, assistance is provided in problems of pre-feasibility and feasibility of industry or plant, investment and financing, production and productivity, product development and design, technology and techniques, management, marketing, quality and research.

Technical assistance is provided on request to developing countries through governments, industries or other bodies. Such assistance usually consists of expert services, but can also include supply of equipment or fellowships for training. During 1987 UNIDO's technical assistance activities included support for the cement industry in Nigeria and the Yemen Arab Republic, for a national agency for investment promotion in Senegal, and for manufacture of carbon fibres in the Republic of Korea. International 'workshops' were held on cement, lime and related industries; on hazardous waste management, industrial safety and emergency planning; on national instrumentation policies; and on production of essential and non-essential drugs in African countries; a study tour of the Caribbean for industrial managers from the Pacific islands was also held. Studies were published on industrial development in Botswana, the Central African Republic, Colombia, the Congo, Ghana, the Republic of Korea, Malawi, and the Caribbean region.

The Secretariat provides contacts between industrialized and developing countries and identifies possibilities for the solution of specific problems in developing countries. The Industrial and Technological Information Bank provides information on technologies developed or adapted for developing countries.

There are Investment Promotion Offices in Cologne, Milan, Paris, Seoul, Tokyo, Vienna, Warsaw, Washington and Zürich to publicize investment opportunities and provide information to investors. UNIDO also co-sponsors (with the governments concerned) investment promotion meetings in a particular country or region, identifying projects and bringing together potential investors. During 1987 'Investment Forums' were held in Dhaka, Bangladesh; Bangkok, Thailand; Cairo, Egypt; and Jakarta, Indonesia.

The System of Consultations, introduced in 1977, is designed to help developing countries increase their share of total world production as much as possible. During 1987 Consultations were held on the fisheries industry, the training of industrial manpower, the pharmaceuticals industry and the non-ferrous metals industry. These meetings are attended by representatives of government, labour, industry, consumer interests and financial institutions, who examine prospects and targets for the growth of production of the commodity concerned in both developed and developing countries.

UNIDO assisted in establishing the International Centre for Genetic Engineering and Biotechnology, based in Trieste (Italy) and New Delhi (India), and linked with national centres. The Centre began an interim programme of work in 1988.

During 1987 UNIDO awarded 1,532 fellowships (1,598 in 1986). A total of 73 group training programmes were carried out, and training was provided for 1,262 nationals of developing countries through fellowships, group training programmes and workshops in factories, study tours and as counterparts attached to field projects.

In 1987 UNIDO carried out 1,822 projects at a cost of $97.7m., of which 42.8% was for expert personnel, 25% for equipment and 14.9% for training and fellowships.

UNIDO project expenditure (1987)

Purpose	Amount (US $ million)
Chemical industries	24.6
Engineering industries	14.4
Agro-industries	9.4
Metallurgical industries	8.6
Institutional infrastructure	10.6
Industrial training	14.5
Feasibility studies	5.5
Industrial planning	5.9
Industrial management and rehabilitation	4.0

FINANCE

During 1986 and 1987 UNIDO was obliged to reduce its expenditure, owing to arrears in payments of members' contributions, and to the depreciation of the US dollar against the Austrian schilling. In 1986–87 the Organization received only $89.8m. of the $115.8m. in contributions originally assessed for its regular budget for the two-year period. The regular budget for the two years 1988–89 amounted to $116.6m. (a decline of 3.2% in real terms from the level of the 1986–87 budget). An operational budget of $34.2m. was approved for 1988–89. The UN Industrial Development Fund is used by UNIDO to finance development projects which fall outside the usual systems of multilateral funding. In 1987 the Industrial Development Board appealed for an increase in contributions to the Fund to a level of $50m. annually.

PUBLICATIONS

Annual Report.
UNIDO Newsletter (monthly).
Industrial Development Survey (annually).
Handbook of Industrial Statistics (annually).
Guide to Information Sources (about 6 a year).
Transfer of Technology Series (6 to 8 a year).
Guide to Training Opportunities for Industrial Development (annually).
Manual for the Preparation of Industrial Feasibility Studies (10 languages).

Numerous working papers and reports (listed in *UNIDO Newsletter* as they appear).

Universal Postal Union—UPU

Address: Case postale, 3000 Berne 15, Switzerland.
Telephone: (031) 432211.
Telex: 912761.

The General Postal Union was founded by the Treaty of Berne (1874), beginning operations in July 1875. Three years later its name was changed to the Universal Postal Union. In 1948 UPU became a Specialized Agency of the UN.

MEMBERS

169 members: see Table on pp. 50–52.

Organization

(October 1988)

CONGRESS

The supreme body of the Union is Congress, which meets every five years. Its duties are legislative and consist mainly of revision of the Acts (see below). The 19th Congress was held in Hamburg, Federal Republic of Germany, in 1984, and the 20th was to be held in Washington, DC, USA, in 1989.

EXECUTIVE COUNCIL

Between Congresses, an Executive Council, created by the Paris Congress, 1947, meets annually at Berne. It is composed of 40 member countries of the Union elected by Congress on the basis of an equitable geographical distribution. It ensures continuity of the Union's work in the interval between Congresses, supervises the activities of the International Bureau, undertakes studies, draws up proposals, and makes recommendations to the Congress. It is responsible for encouraging, supervising and co-ordinating international co-operation in the form of postal technical assistance and vocational training.

CONSULTATIVE COUNCIL FOR POSTAL STUDIES

At the Ottawa Congress, 1957, a Consultative Committee for Postal Studies was established, which, at the Tokyo Congress,

INTERNATIONAL ORGANIZATIONS

United Nations (Specialized Agencies)

1969, became the Consultative Council for Postal Studies (CCPS). Its 35 member countries meet annually, generally at Berne. It is responsible for organizing studies of major problems affecting postal administrations in all UPU member countries, in the technical operations and economic fields and in the sphere of technical co-operation. The CCPS also provides information and opinions on these matters, and examines teaching and training problems arising in the new and developing countries.

INTERNATIONAL BUREAU

The day-to-day administrative work of UPU is executed through the International Bureau, stationed at Berne. It serves as an instrument of liaison, information and consultation for the postal administration of the member countries, provides secretarial services for UPU bodies, promotes technical assistance and organizes conferences.

Director-General of the International Bureau: A. C. BOTTO DE BARROS (Brazil).

Activities

The essential principles of the Union are the following:
1. Formation of one single postal territory.
2. Unification of postal charges and weight steps.
3. Non-sharing of postage paid for ordinary letters between the sender country and the country of destination.
4. Guarantee of freedom of transit.
5. Settlement of disputes by arbitration.
6. Establishment of a central office under the name of the International Bureau paid for by all members.
7. Periodical meeting of Congress.
8. Promotion of the development of international postal services and postal technical assistance to Union members.

The common rules applicable to the international postal service and to the letter-post provisions are contained in the Universal Postal Convention and its Detailed Regulations. Owing to their importance in the postal field and their historical value, these two Acts, together with the Constitution and the General Regulations, constitute the compulsory Acts of the Union. It is therefore not possible to be a member country of the Union without being a party to these Acts and applying their provisions.

The activities of the international postal service, other than letter mail, are governed by Special Agreements. These are binding only for the countries which have acceded to them. There are eight such Agreements:

1. Agreement concerning Insured Letters and Boxes.
2. Agreement concerning Postal Parcels.
3. Agreement concerning Postal Money Orders and Postal Travellers' Cheques.
4. Agreement concerning Giro Transfers.
5. Agreement concerning Cash on Delivery Items.
6. Agreement concerning the Collection of Bills.
7. Agreement concerning the International Savings Bank Service.
8. Agreement concerning Subscriptions to Newspapers and Periodicals.

FINANCE

The Executive Council fixed 22.5m. Swiss francs as the maximum figure for annual gross expenditure in the year 1988. Members are listed in eight classes setting out the proportion they should pay.

PUBLICATIONS

Union Postale (quarterly, in French, German, English, Arabic, Chinese, Spanish and Russian).

Other UPU publications are listed in *Liste des publications du Bureau international*; all are in French, some also in English, Arabic and Spanish.

World Health Organization—WHO

Address: Avenue Appia, 1211 Geneva 27, Switzerland.
Telephone: (022) 912111.
Telex: 27821.

WHO was established in 1948 as the central agency directing international health work. Of its many activities, the most important single aspect is technical co-operation with national health administrations, particularly in the developing countries.

MEMBERS

166 members: see Table on pp. 50–52.

Organization

(October 1988)

WORLD HEALTH ASSEMBLY

The Assembly usually meets in Geneva, once a year; it is responsible for policy making, and the biennial programme and budget; appoints the Director-General, admits new members and reviews budget contributions.

EXECUTIVE BOARD

The Board is composed of 31 health experts designated by, but not representing, their governments; they serve for three years, and the World Health Assembly elects 10 or 11 member states each year to the Board. It meets at least twice a year to review the Director-General's programme, which it forwards to the Assembly with any recommendations that seem necessary. It advises on questions referred to it by the Assembly and is responsible for putting into effect the decisions and policies of the Assembly. It is also empowered to take emergency measures in case of epidemics or disasters.

SECRETARIAT

Director-General: Dr HIROSHI NAKAJIMA (Japan).
Deputy Director-General: Dr MOHAMED ABDELMOUMÈNE (Algeria).

Assistant Directors-General: Dr HU CHING-LI (People's Republic of China), WARREN W. FURTH (USA), Dr JEAN-PAUL JARDEL (France), Dr TAGUIR BEKTIMIROV (USSR).

Administrative Divisions and Programmes:
Office of Research Promotion and Development.
Special Programme of Research, Development and Research Training in Human Reproduction.
Programme for External Coordination.
Division of Noncommunicable Diseases.
Health and Biomedical Information Programme.
Parasitic Diseases Programme.
Pharmaceuticals.
Division of Health Manpower Development.
Special Programme for Research and Training in Tropical Diseases.
Expanded Programme on Immunization.
Division of Budget and Finance.
Health for all Strategy Coordination.
Division of Environmental Health.
Action Programme on Essential Drugs.
Division of Information Systems Support.
Global Programme on AIDS.
Diarrhoeal Diseases Control.
Division of Personnel and General Services.
Malaria Action Programme.
Division of Family Health.
Staff Development and Training.
Internal Audit.
Division of Mental Health.
Division of Vector Biology and Control.
Division of Strengthening of Health Services.
Division of Communicable Diseases.
Division of Epidemiological Surveillance and Health Situation and Trend Assessment.
Managerial Process for National Health Development.
Division of Diagnostic, Therapeutic and Rehabilitative Technology.

REGIONAL OFFICES

Each of WHO's six geographical regions has its own organization consisting of a regional committee representing the member states and associate members in the region concerned, and a regional office staffed by experts in various fields of health.

Africa: POB 6, Brazzaville, Congo; tel. 813860; telex 5217; Prof. GOTTLIEB LOBE MONEKOSSO.

Americas: Pan-American Sanitary Bureau, 525 23rd St, NW, Washington, DC 20037, USA; tel. (202) 861-3200; telex 248338; Dir Dr CARLYLE GUERRA DE MACEDO.

Eastern Mediterranean: POB 1517, Alexandria 21511, Egypt; tel. (02) 4830090; telex 54028; Dir Dr HUSSEIN ABDUL-RAZZAQ GEZAIRY.

Europe: 8 Scherfigsvej, 2100 Copenhagen Ø, Denmark; tel. (01) 29-01-11; telex 15348; Dir Dr Jo ERIK ASVALL.

South-East Asia: Indraprastha Estate, Mahatma Gandhi Rd, New Delhi 110002, India; tel. (11) 3317804; telex 3165095; Dir Dr U KO KO.

Western Pacific: POB 2932, Manila 2801, Philippines; tel. (02) 5218421; telex 27652; Dir (vacant).

Activities

WHO's objective is stated in the constitution as 'the attainment by all peoples of the highest possible level of health'.

It acts as the central authority directing international health work, and establishes relations with professional groups and government health authorities on that basis.

It supports, on request from member states, programmes to control or eradicate disease, train health workers best suited to local needs and strengthen national health systems. Aid is provided in emergencies and natural disasters.

A global programme of collaborative research and exchange of scientific information is carried out in co-operation with leading national institutions (numbering 911 in 1988). Particular stress is laid on the widespread communicable diseases of the tropics, and the countries directly concerned are assisted in developing their research capabilities.

It keeps communicable diseases under constant surveillance, promotes the exchange of prompt and accurate information, and administers the International Health Regulations. It sets standards for the quality control of drugs, vaccines and other substances affecting health.

It collects and disseminates health data and carries out statistical analyses and comparative studies in such diseases as cancer, heart disease and mental illness.

It receives reports on drugs observed to have shown adverse reactions in any country, and transmits the information to other member states. All available information on effects on human health of the pollutants in the environment is critically reviewed and published.

Co-operation among scientists and professional groups is encouraged, and the organization may propose international conventions and agreements. It assists in developing an informed public opinion on matters of health.

HEALTH FOR ALL

In May 1981 the 34th World Health Assembly adopted a Global Strategy in support of 'Health for all by the year 2000', or the attainment by all citizens of the world of a level of health that will permit them to lead a socially and economically productive life. Almost all members indicated a high level of commitment to this goal, and guiding principles for national, regional and global plans of action were prepared, in response to the UN General Assembly resolution concerning health as an integral part of development. Primary health care is seen as the key to 'Health for all', with the following as minimum requirements:

Safe water in the home or within 15 minutes' walking distance, and adequate sanitary facilities in the home or immediate vicinity;

Immunization against diphtheria, pertussis (whooping cough), tetanus, poliomyelitis, measles and tuberculosis;

Local health care, including availability of at least 20 essential drugs, within one hour's travel;

Trained personnel to attend childbirth, and to care for pregnant mothers and children up to at least one year old.

The Seventh General Programme of Work for the period 1984–89, approved in 1982, comprised activities supporting the 'Health for All' strategy outlined above.

DISEASE PREVENTION AND CONTROL

One of WHO's major achievements was the eradication of smallpox, which, following a massive international campaign of vaccination and surveillance, begun in 1958 and intensified in 1967, was declared to have been achieved in 1977. In 1988 the World Health Assembly declared its commitment to the similar eradication of poliomyelitis by the year 2000.

WHO's Expanded Programme on Immunization (EPI), launched in 1974, aims to provide immunization for all children by 1990 against six diseases which constitute a major cause of death and disability in the developing countries: diphtheria, pertussis (whooping cough), tetanus, poliomyelitis, measles and tuberculosis. In 1988 it was estimated that 50% of the world's children were being immunized against these diseases, compared with 5% 10 years previously, and that the EPI was preventing more than 1m. infant deaths annually. The programme costs WHO some US $8m. annually. An essential requirement is the 'cold chain' providing special containers and refrigerators for the transport of vaccines in tropical climates; WHO has developed appropriate equipment and training manuals for this purpose, and by 1985 about 18,000 health workers had attended its special training courses.

In 1984 a new vaccine development programme was launched to complement the EPI, by co-ordinating research on new vaccines and improving vaccine distribution systems, technical support and the transfer of technology.

Since 1960 WHO's Division of Vector Biology and Control has maintained a programme for the control of vector-borne diseases such as malaria, African trypanosomiasis (sleeping-sickness), American trypanosomiasis (Chagas disease), onchocerciasis (river-blindness), filiariases, dengue and dengue haemorrhagic fever—all of which are transmitted by insects—and schistosomiasis (bilharzia), transmitted by a water-snail. WHO evaluates the insecticides developed to control these vectors, and also conducts research on biological control, using the natural enemies of the vectors, such as larva-eating fish. It also encourages the environmental management of potential breeding-grounds for vectors. The programme aimed to establish, by 1989, national vector control strategies in at least 50% of the countries affected. A special programme for research and training in tropical diseases, sponsored jointly by WHO, UNDP and the World Bank, was set up in 1975, and by 1986 it comprised a worldwide network of about 4,000 scientists, working on the development of vaccines, new drugs, diagnostic kits, non-chemical insecticides and other methods of control. The programme aims to strengthen research institutions in developing countries, and to encourage participation by scientists from the countries most affected.

WHO helped in preparations for the UN International Drinking Water Supply and Sanitation Decade (1981–90) by participating in regional and national meetings to plan strategies for the Decade and by drawing up new guidelines for drinking water quality. In 1987 a review of progress showed that despite some major achievements (provision of access to clean water for some 300m. people since the beginning of the Decade), by 1990, owing to the expected growth in population, there were likely to be more people without access to clean water and sanitation than at the beginning of the decade, particularly in rural areas. WHO's Diarrhoeal Diseases Control Programme encourages national programmes based on improved hygienic practices and the use of simple oral rehydration therapy to prevent infant deaths.

WHO's Global Programme on AIDS (Acquired Immunodeficiency Syndrome) began in 1987. At mid-1988 more than 94,000 cases of AIDS had been officially reported to WHO by 138 countries, while the total number of cases was believed to be about 150,000, and the number of people infected with the human immunodeficiency virus (HIV), which causes AIDS, was estimated at between 5m. and 10m. The aims of WHO's Global Programme are to prevent HIV transmission, to care for HIV-infected people, and to unify national and international efforts against AIDS. In March 1988 WHO formed an 'alliance' with UNDP, aiming to expand the struggle against AIDS by using UNDP's already existing network of resident representatives and development programmes. WHO supports national AIDS control plans, which (in the absence of a vaccine) stress education and information as vital in stopping the spread of the HIV. Programmes also include funds for training medical personnel; improving facilities for screening and protecting blood supplies; epidemiological surveillance; and establishing or expanding laboratory facilities for diagnosing AIDS and treatment facilities for AIDS patients. WHO's Global Programme on AIDS required an estimated $66m. in funding for 1988.

NUTRITION

WHO collaborates with FAO, the World Food Programme and other UN agencies to ensure that health needs are included in their nutrition programmes. A joint WHO/UNICEF Nutrition Support Programme was active in 17 countries in 1987, assisting long-term national nutrition plans. Jointly with FAO, WHO establishes food standards (through the FAO/WHO Codex Alimentarius Commission) and evaluates food additives for safety.

In May 1981 the International Code of Marketing of Breastmilk Substitutes was adopted by the World Health Assembly, aiming to provide safe and adequate nutrition for infants by promoting

DRUGS

The WHO Action Programme on Essential Drugs and Vaccines aims to prevent the inappropriate and excessive prescription of drugs and to ensure the availability of a selected number of safe and effective drugs and vaccines of acceptable quality and at low cost, in support of primary health care. WHO maintains and regularly revises a Model List of Essential Drugs, numbering 250 substances that will treat over 80% of the health problems of a given population, and should be available in adequate quantities at all times, in the appropriate dosage forms.

WHO is also active in monitoring and controlling drug abuse. Guidelines for member states on the assessment of drug abuse problems were prepared in 1986, together with a manual for primary health care workers in drug dependence and alcohol-related problems.

DISASTER RELIEF

Who acts as the 'health arm' of disaster relief carried out within the UN system, particularly by UNDP, UNDRO and UNICEF (q.v.). It works in close co-operation with the UN High Commissioner for Refugees, appointing joint health co-ordinators and providing technical advice, for example in listing essential drugs needed for refugee camps.

WORLD HEALTH DAY

World Health Day is held on 7 April every year, and is used to promote awareness of a particular health topic. In 1988 the theme was 'Health for All—All for Health'. This day was also designated as the world's first 'No Tobacco Day'.

ASSOCIATED AGENCY

International Agency for Research on Cancer: 150 Cours Albert Thomas, 69372 Lyon Cedex 08, France. Established in 1965 as a self-governing body within the framework of WHO, the Agency organizes international research on cancer. It has its own laboratories and runs a programme of research on the environmental factors causing cancer. Members: Australia, Belgium, Canada, France, Federal Republic of Germany, Italy, Japan, Netherlands, Sweden, USSR, United Kingdom, USA.

Director: Dr LORENZO TOMATIS (Italy).

FINANCE

WHO's regular budget is provided by assessment of member states and associate members. An additional fund for specific projects is provided by voluntary contributions from members and other sources. Funds are received from the UN Development Programme for particular projects and from UNFPA for appropriate programmes.

Total budget appropriations for the two years 1986–87 amounted to US $554m., but delays in the payment of government contributions meant that implementation of the budget had to be reduced by $35m. The budget for 1988–89 amounted to $633.98m., representing a slight decrease from the previous biennial total in real terms.

WHO Budget appropriations by region, 1986–87

Region	Amount (US dollars)	% of total budget
Africa	101,164,000	18.26
Americas	58,076,000	10.48
South-East Asia	69,873,000	12.62
Europe	36,503,000	6.59
Eastern Mediterranean	62,405,000	11.26
Western Pacific	51,288,000	9.26
Global and inter-regional	167,689,100	30.27
World Health Assembly & Executive Board	7,001,900	1.26
Total	554,000,000	100.00

Budget appropriations by purpose, 1986–87

Purpose	Amount (US dollars)	% of total budget
Direction, co-ordination and management	64,450,700	11.63
Health system infrastructure	180,705,500	32.62
Health science and technology—health promotion and care	102,513,300	18.51
Health science and technology—disease prevention and control	85,377,400	15.41
Programme support	120,953,100	21.83
Total	554,000,000	100.00

PUBLICATIONS

Full catalogue of publications supplied free on request.

World Health (10 a year in English, French, Portuguese, Russian and Spanish; quarterly in Arabic and Farsi).

Technical Report Series.

Public Health Papers.

Monograph Series (technical guides on specific subjects serving as textbooks for the postgraduate worker).

Bulletin of WHO (6 a year).

Official Records.

Weekly Epidemiological Record.

World Health Statistics Report (quarterly).

World Health Statistics Annual.

International Digest of Health Legislation (quarterly).

Reports on the World Health Situation: (approximately every 6 years) the sixth report (January 1981) covers the period 1973–77.

World Health Forum (quarterly, in Arabic, Chinese, English, French, Russian and Spanish).

World Intellectual Property Organization—WIPO

Address: 34 chemin des Colombettes, 1211 Geneva 20, Switzerland.
Telephone: (022) 730-9111.
Telex: 412912.

WIPO was established by a Convention signed in Stockholm in 1967, which came into force in 1970. It became a specialized agency of the UN in December 1974.

MEMBERS

121 members: see Table on pp. 50-52.

Organization

(October 1988)

INTERNATIONAL BUREAU

The secretariat of WIPO and the Unions which it administers (see below). It is controlled by the member states in the General Assembly and Conference of WIPO, and in the separate Assemblies and Conferences of Representatives held by its constituent Unions. The Paris and Berne Unions elect Executive Committees from among their members and the joint membership of these two Committees constitutes the Co-ordination Committee of WIPO.

The International Bureau prepares the meetings of the various bodies of WIPO and the Unions, mainly through the provision of reports and working documents. It organizes the meetings, and sees that the decisions are communicated to all concerned, and, as far as possible, that they are carried out.

The International Bureau carries out projects and initiates new ones to promote international co-operation in the field of intellectual property. It acts as an information service and publishes reviews. It is also the depositary of most of the treaties administered by WIPO.

Director General: Dr ARPAD BOGSCH (USA).
Deputy Directors General: SHAHID ALIKHAN, LEV KOSTIKOV, ALFONS SCHÄFERS.

Activities

WIPO is responsible for promoting the protection of intellectual property throughout the world. Intellectual property comprises two principal branches: industrial property (patents and other rights in technological inventions, rights in trademarks, industrial designs, appellations of origin, etc.) and copyright and neighbouring rights (in literary, musical and artistic works, in films and records, etc.).

WIPO administers various international treaties, of which the most important are the Paris Convention for the Protection of Industrial Property (1883) and the Berne Convention for the Protection of Literary and Artistic Works (1886). WIPO carries out a programme of activities in the field of intellectual property, in order to promote creative intellectual activity and to facilitate the transfer of technology, especially to and among developing countries.

CO-OPERATION WITH DEVELOPING COUNTRIES

In the field of industrial property, the main objectives of WIPO's co-operation with developing countries are: to encourage and increase, in quantity and quality, the creation of patentable inventions by their own nationals and in their own enterprises, and thereby to increase the degree of their technological self-reliance; to improve the conditions of acquisition of foreign patented technology; to increase the competitiveness of developing countries in international trade through better protection of the trademarks and service marks of relevance in such trade; and to facilitate access by developing countries to the technological information contained in patent documents. In order to achieve these objectives, most developing countries need to create or modernize domestic legislation and governmental institutions; to accede to international treaties; to employ more specialists in government, in industry and in the legal professions; and to acquire more patent documents and better methods of analysing their contents.

These activities are supervised by the WIPO Permanent Committee for Development Co-operation Related to Industrial Property, membership of which is voluntary and carries no financial obligation with it. By September 1988, 102 States were members of the Permanent Committee.

In the field of copyright, the main objectives of WIPO's co-operation with developing countries are: to encourage and increase the creation of literary and artistic works by their own nationals, and thereby to maintain their national culture in their own languages and/or corresponding to their own ethnic and social traditions and aspirations; and to improve the conditions of acquisition of the right to use or enjoy the literary and artistic works in which copyright is owned by foreigners. In order to achieve these objectives, most developing countries are in need of creating or modernizing domestic legislation and institutions, acceding to international treaties and having more specialists, all in the field of copyright.

Most of these development co-operation activities are kept under review by the WIPO Permanent Committee for Development Co-operation Related to Copyright and Neighbouring Rights, membership of which is voluntary and carries no financial obligation with it. By September 1988, this Committee had 82 States as members.

In both industrial property and copyright, WIPO's development co-operation consists mainly of advice, training and the furnishing of documents and equipment. The advice is given by the staff of WIPO, experts chosen by WIPO or international meetings called by WIPO. The training is individual (on-the-job) or collective (courses, seminars and workshops).

LEGAL AND TECHNICAL

Revision of treaties; revision of classifications of goods and services; preparation for entry into force of new treaties, and for other possible new international instruments.

WIPO Permanent Committee on Industrial Property Information: composed of representatives of 72 states; encourages co-operation between national and regional industrial property offices in all matters concerning documentation and information on industrial property.

International Patent Documentation Centre—INPADOC: Vienna, Austria; f. 1972; computer storage of bibliographic data on patent documents; access to the data is given to patent offices, industry and research and development institutions.

SERVICES

International registration of trademarks: operating since 1893; by September 1988 over 604,600 registrations and renewals of trademarks had been made, of which nearly 11,000 were made during the first eight months of 1988; publ. *Les Marques internationales* (monthly).

International deposit of industrial designs: operating since 1928; by September 1988 over 87,000 deposits had been made, of which about 1,700 were made during the first eight months of 1988; publ. *International Designs Bulletin* (monthly).

International registration of appellations of origin: operating since 1966; by September 1988 over 725 appellations had been registered; publ. *Les Appellations d'origine* (irreg.).

International applications for patents: operating since 1978; by September 1988 over 58,000 record copies of international applications for patents under the Patent Co-operation Treaty (PCT) had been received.

THE UNIONS

International Union for the Protection of Industrial Property (Paris Convention): the treaty was signed in Paris in 1883; there were 99 member states in September 1988. Member states must accord to nationals and residents of other member states the same advantages under their laws relating to the protection of inventions, trademarks and other subjects of industrial property as they accord to their own nationals.

The treaty contains provisions concerning the conditions under which a state may license the use of a patent in its territory; for example, that the owner of the patent does not exploit it to unfair advantage in that country.

Diplomatic conferences were held in 1980, 1981, 1982 and 1984, for the revision of the Paris Convention, with the particular aim of meeting the needs of developing countries. The fourth Consultative Meeting on the revision took place in September 1987.

International Union for the Protection of Literary and Artistic Works (Berne Union): the treaty was signed in Berne in 1886 and last revised in 1971; there were 76 member states in September 1987. Member states must accord the same protection to the copyright of nationals of other member states as to their own. The treaty also prescribes minimum standards of protection, for

INTERNATIONAL ORGANIZATIONS   United Nations (Specialized Agencies)

example, that copyright protection generally continues throughout the author's life and for 50 years after. It includes special provision for the developing countries.

OTHER AGREEMENTS

Signatories of the agreements form unions similar to those described above.

International Protection of Industrial Property:
Madrid Agreement of 14 April 1891, for the Repression of False or Deceptive Indications of Source on Goods.
Madrid Agreement of 14 April 1891, Concerning the International Registration of Marks.
The Hague Agreement of 6 November 1925, Concerning the International Deposit of Industrial Designs.
Nice Agreement of 15 June 1957, Concerning the International Classification of Goods and Services for the Purposes of the Registration of Marks.
Lisbon Agreement of 31 October 1958, for the Protection of Appellations of Origin and their International Registration.
Locarno Agreement of 8 October 1968, Establishing an International Classification for Industrial Designs.
Patent Co-operation Treaty of 19 June 1970 (PCT).
Strasbourg Agreement of 24 March 1971, Concerning the International Patent Classification (IPC).
Vienna Agreement of 12 June 1973, Establishing an International Classification of the Figurative Elements of Marks.
Budapest Treaty of 28 April 1977, on the International Recognition of the Deposit of Micro-organisms for the Purposes of Patent Procedure.

Nairobi Treaty of 26 September 1981, on the Protection of the Olympic Symbol.

Special International Protection of the Rights of Performers, Producers of Phonograms and Broadcasting Organizations ('Neighbouring Rights'):
Rome Convention, 26 October 1961, for the Protection of Performers, Producers of Phonograms and Broadcasting Organizations.
Geneva Convention, 29 October 1971, for the Protection of Producers of Phonograms against Unauthorized Duplication of their Phonograms.
Brussels Convention, 21 May 1974, Relating to the Distribution of Programme-carrying Signals Transmitted by Satellite.

FINANCE

The budget for the two years 1986–87 was about 100m. Swiss francs, and that for 1988–89 amounted to 107m. Swiss francs.

PUBLICATIONS

Copyright (monthly in English and French).
Industrial Property (monthly in English and French).
International Designs Bulletin (monthly in English and French).
Les marques internationales (monthly in French).
Newsletter (irregular in Arabic, English, French, Portuguese, Russian and Spanish).
PCT Gazette (fortnightly in English and French).
Les appellations d'origine (irregular in French).
Intellectual Property in Asia and the Pacific (quarterly in English).

World Meteorological Organization—WMO

Address: Case postale 5, 1211 Geneva 20, Switzerland.
Telephone: (022) 346400.
Telex: 23260.

The WMO started activities and was recognized as a Specialized Agency of the UN in 1951, aiming to improve the exchange of weather information and its applications.

MEMBERS

160 members, of which one is suspended; see Table on pp. 50–52.

Organization
(October 1988)

WORLD METEOROLOGICAL CONGRESS

The supreme organ of the Organization, the Congress is convened every four years and represents all members; it adopts regulations, approves policy, programme and budget. Tenth session: May 1987.

EXECUTIVE COMMITTEE

The Committee has 36 members and meets at least yearly to prepare studies and recommendations for the Congress; it supervises the implementation of Congress resolutions and regulations, informs members on technical matters and offers advice.

SECRETARIAT

The secretariat acts as an administrative, documentary and information centre; undertakes special technical studies; produces publications; organizes meetings of WMO constituent bodies; acts as a link between the meteorological and hydrometeorological services of the world, and provides information for the general public. In December 1986 there were 291 staff members in Geneva and in two regional offices, together with 44 experts and 28 local staff employed in Technical Assistance projects in 23 countries.
Secretary-General: Prof. G. O. P. OBASI (Nigeria).

REGIONAL ASSOCIATIONS

Members are grouped in six Regional Associations (Africa, Asia, Europe, North and Central America, South America and South-West Pacific), whose task is to co-ordinate meteorological activity within their regions and to examine questions referred to them by the Executive Committee. Sessions are held at least once every four years.

TECHNICAL COMMISSIONS

The Technical Commissions are composed of experts nominated by the members of the Organization. Sessions are held at least once every four years. The Commissions cover the following areas:
Basic Systems
Climatology
Instruments and Methods of Observation
Atmospheric Sciences
Aeronautical Meteorology
Agricultural Meteorology
Hydrology
Marine Meteorology

Activities

WORLD WEATHER WATCH PROGRAMME

Combining facilities and services provided by the members, the Programme's primary purpose is to make available meteorological and related geophysical and environmental information enabling them to maintain efficient meteorological services. Facilities in regions outside any national territory (outer space, ocean areas and Antarctica) are maintained by members on a voluntary basis.
Global Observing System: Simultaneous observations are made by 9,500 land stations. Meteorological information is also received from 3,000 aircraft, 7,400 ships, 300 fixed and drifting buoys, 200 background pollution monitoring stations and a number of polar orbiting and geostationary meteorological satellites. About 150 members operate some 300 ground stations equipped to receive picture transmissions from the satellites.
Global Data Processing System: consists of world meteorological centres (WMCs) at Melbourne (Australia), Moscow (USSR) and Washington, DC (USA), 26 regional meteorological centres (RMCs) and national meteorological centres. The WMCs and RMCs provide analyses, forecasts and warnings for exchange on the Global Telecommunications System. Some centres concentrate on the monitoring and forecasting of special weather phenomena, such as tropical cyclones, monsoons, droughts, etc., which have a major impact on human safety and national economies. These analyses and forecasts are designed to assist the members in making local and specialized forecasts.
Global Telecommunication System: consists of (a) the Main Telecommunication Network (MTN), (b) the regional telecommunication

INTERNATIONAL ORGANIZATIONS

United Nations (Specialized Agencies)

networks, and (c) the national telecommunication networks. The system operates through 160 national meteorological centres, 30 Regional Telecommunications Hubs and three World Meteorological Centres.

Executive Council Working Group on Antarctic Meteorology: The Executive Council Working Group on Antarctic Meteorology co-ordinates WMO activities related to the Antarctic, in particular the surface and upper-air observing programme, plans the regular exchange of observational data and products needed for operational and research purposes, studies problems related to instruments and methods of observation peculiar to the Antarctic and develops appropriate regional coding practices. It maintains active contacts with scientific bodies dealing with Antarctic research and co-operates with relevant WMO constituent bodies with regard to aspects of Antarctic meteorology.

Executive Council Panel of Experts on Satellites: co-ordinates WMO's satellite-related activities, examines and records plans for new satellites and satellite operations in member countries and promotes the use of satellite data in WMO programmes. It makes appropriate recommendations to WMO bodies and considers ways in which the processing and distribution of information from satellites may best meet the needs of the members.

Tropical Cyclone Programme: established in response to UN General Assembly Resolution 2733 (XXV), aims at the development of national and regionally co-ordinated systems to ensure that the loss of life and damage caused by tropical cyclones are reduced to a minimum. The programme operates through general and regional components, the latter conducted principally by five regional tropical cyclone bodies, to improve warning systems and for collaboration with other international organizations in activities related to disaster preparedness.

WORLD CLIMATE PROGRAMME

Adopted by the Eighth World Meteorological Congress (1979), the World Climate Programme (WCP) comprises the following components: World Climate Data Programme (WCDP), World Climate Applications Programme (WCAP), World Climate Impact Studies Programme (WCIP), World Climate Research Programme (WCRP). The objectives of the WCP are: to use existing climate information to improve economic and social planning; to improve the understanding of climate processes through research, so as to determine the predictability of climate and the extent of man's influence on it; and to detect and warn governments of impending climate variations or changes, either natural or man-made, which may significantly affect critical human activities.

Co-ordination of the overall Programme is the responsibility of the WMO, along with direct management of the WCDP and WCAP. The UN Environment Programme (q.v.) has accepted responsibility for the WCIP, while the WCRP is a joint effort between WMO and the International Council of Scientific Unions (ICSU, q.v.). Other organizations involved in the Programme include UNESCO, FAO, WHO, IFAD and the Consultative Group for International Agricultural Research.

World Climate Data Programme: aims to make available reliable climate data, through four main projects: the Climate Data Information Service; transfer of technology in the use of computer-based climate data; the Climate Monitoring System; and the Data Rescue Project.

World Climate Applications Programme: promotes applications of climate knowledge in the areas of food production, water, energy (especially solar and wind energy), urban planning and building, and human health.

World Climate Research Programme: organized jointly with the International Council of Scientific Unions, to determine to what extent climate can be predicted, and the extent of man's influence on climate. Its three specific objectives are: establishing the physical basis for weather predictions over time ranges of one to two months; understanding the variability of the global climate over periods of several years; and studying the long-term variations and the response of climate to natural or man-made influence over periods of several decades. Studies include: the effect of cloudiness on the radiation balance; the effect of ground water storage and vegetation on evaporation; and the effects of oceanic circulation changes on the global atmosphere.

World Climate Impact Studies Programme: aims to make reliable estimates of the socio-economic impact of climate changes, and to assist in forming national policies accordingly. It concentrates on: study of the impact of climate variations on national food systems; assessment of the impact of man's activities on the climate, especially through increasing the amount of carbon dioxide and other radiatively active gases in the atmosphere; and developing the methodology of climate impact assessments.

RESEARCH AND DEVELOPMENT PROGRAMME

This major programme aims to help members to implement research projects; to disseminate relevant scientific information; to draw the attention of members to outstanding research problems of major importance; and to encourage and help members to incorporate the results of research into operational forecasting or other appropriate techniques, particularly when such changes of procedure require international co-ordination and agreement.

Weather Prediction Research Programmes: The programmes assist members in exchanging the results of research on weather prediction, organize international conferences, and publish technical reports and progress reports on numerical weather prediction, in order to improve members' weather services. The Programme on Short- and Medium-Range Weather Prediction Research aims at strengthening members' research in short- and medium-range weather forecasting, including local forecasting techniques. The main objective of the Programme on Long-Range Forecasting Research is to improve the level of members' capabilities in monthly and seasonal weather forecasting.

Tropical Meteorology Research Programme: aims at the promotion and co-ordination of members' research efforts into such important problems as monsoons, tropical cyclones, droughts in the arid zones of the tropics, rain-producing tropical weather systems, and the interaction between tropical and mid-latitude weather systems. This should lead to a better understanding of tropical systems and forecasting, and thus be of economic benefit to tropical countries.

Cloud Physics and Weather Modification Programme: encourages scientific research on weather modification, based on cloud physics, particularly rain-making and hail suppression. It provides information on world-wide weather modification projects, and guidance in the design and evaluation of experiments.

Environmental Pollution Monitoring and Research Programme: The projects under this programme deal mainly with the organization of global, standardized observations of substances and parameters (e.g. carbon dioxide, precipitation chemistry, and aerosols) which have or may have a long-term effect on the state of the environment and on climate. The Background Air Pollution Monitoring Network involves 91 countries. WMO is responsible for the meteorological part of the ECE Co-operative Programme for the Monitoring and Evaluation of the Long-range Transmission of Air Pollutants in Europe, and has organized two Meteorological Synthesizing Centres. It implements the Global Ozone Research and Monitoring Project.

The programme also includes atmospheric chemistry studies (e.g. on ozone and acidifying deposition) and the furthering of integrated environmental monitoring. The UN Environment Programme has been providing support to many projects under this programme.

APPLICATIONS OF METEOROLOGY PROGRAMME

Services to ocean activities: Supervised by the Commission for Marine Meteorology, international arrangements are made for the provision of marine meteorological and other related geophysical information, including sea ice and wave information, to shipping, fishing operations and other marine activities; the preparation of marine climatological information is also arranged internationally for multiple applications. Close collaboration is maintained with the Intergovernmental Oceanographic Commission to undertake joint programmes in ocean services and oceanic research.

Applications to aviation: to contribute to the safety and efficiency of civil aviation, the Commission for Aeronautical Meteorology supervises the applications projects; close collaboration is maintained with ICAO (q.v.), particularly in the development of joint regulatory material.

Applications to agriculture: the study of weather and climate as they affect agriculture, the selection of crops and their protection from disease and deterioration in storage, soil conservation, phenology and physiology of crops and farm animals; the Commission for Agricultural Meteorology supervises the applications projects and also advises the Secretary-General in his efforts to co-ordinate activities in support of food production. There are also special activities in agrometeorology to monitor and combat drought and desertification and to apply climate information in agricultural planning; close co-operation is maintained with the UN Environment Programme.

HYDROLOGY AND WATER RESOURCES PROGRAMME

This major programme concentrates on promoting world-wide co-operation in the evaluation of water resources and the development of hydrological networks and services, including data collection and processing, hydrological forecasting and warnings and the supply of meteorological and hydrological data for design purposes. The three components of the programme are:

Operational Hydrology Programme: Planned and executed under the auspices of the Commission of Hydrology, this Programme deals with all aspects of hydrological data, including instruments, methods of observation and transmission, systems of forecasting and their application to water resources projects. The regional implementation of this Programme is the responsibility of the WMO Regional Associations.

Hydrological Operational Multipurpose Subprogramme: consists of the organized transfer of hydrological technology used in network design, observations, collection, processing and storage of data and hydrological modelling. Manuals of procedures and general guidance, descriptions of equipment and computer software are produced.

Applications and Services to Water Resources: directed towards achieving the targets of various water-dependent sectors, it also contributes to WMO projects which have important hydrological aspects, such as those in the Tropical Cyclone and World Climate programmes.

Co-operation with Water-Related Programmes of other International Organizations: includes participation in the International Hydrological Programme of UNESCO, joint activities with other UN agencies, and participation in regional projects concerned with large international river basins such as the Rhine and the Danube.

EDUCATION AND TRAINING PROGRAMME

Activities include surveys of personnel training requirements, the development of appropriate training programmes, the establishment and improvement of regional training centres, the organization of training courses, seminars and conferences and the preparation of training materials. The Programme also arranges individual training programmes and the provision of fellowships. There are about 500 trainees in any one year. About 230 fellowships are awarded annually. Advice is given on training facilities, and there is a library of training materials for meteorological and related instruction. The focal point of WMO's education and training activities is the Panel of Experts on Education and Training set up by the Executive Council.

TECHNICAL CO-OPERATION PROGRAMME

United Nations Development Programme: WMO provides assistance in the development of national meteorological and hydrological services, in the application of meteorological and hydrological data to national economic development, and in the training of personnel. Assistance in the form of expert missions, fellowships and equipment was provided to 118 countries in 1986 at a cost of US $12.5m., financed by UNDP.

Voluntary Co-operation Programme: WMO assists members in implementing the World Weather Watch Programme to develop an integrated observing and forecasting system. Member governments contribute equipment, services and fellowships for training. In 1986, 30 projects were completed and a further 109 were in progress under this programme.

WMO also carries out assistance projects under Trust Fund arrangements, financed by national authorities, either for activities in their own country or in a beneficiary country. Six such projects, at a cost of $1.9m., were in progress in 1986.

Financial support from WMO's regular budget for fellowships, group training, technical conferences and study tours amounted to $1m. in 1986.

CO-OPERATION WITH OTHER BODIES

As a Specialized Agency of the UN, WMO is actively involved in the activities of the UN system. In addition, WMO has concluded a number of formal agreements and working arrangements with international organizations both within and outside the UN system, at the inter-governmental and non-governmental level. As a result, WMO participates in major international conferences convened under the auspices of the United Nations or other organizations.

FINANCE

WMO is financed by contributions from members on a proportional scale of assessment. The budget for 1988-91 was 170m. Swiss francs. Outside this budget, WMO implements a number of projects as executing agency for the UNDP or else under trust-fund arrangements.

PUBLICATIONS

Annual Report.

WMO Bulletin (quarterly in English, French, Russian and Spanish).

Reports, technical notes and training publications.

AFRICAN DEVELOPMENT BANK—ADB

Address: 01 BP 1387, Abidjan 01, Côte d'Ivoire.
Telephone: 32-07-11.
Telex: 23717.

Established in August 1963, the Bank began operations in July 1966.

AFRICAN MEMBERS

Algeria	Libya
Angola	Madagascar
Benin	Malawi
Botswana	Mali
Burkina Faso	Mauritania
Burundi	Mauritius
Cameroon	Morocco
Cape Verde	Mozambique
Central African Republic	Niger
Chad	Nigeria
Comoros	Rwanda
Congo	São Tomé and Príncipe
Côte d'Ivoire	Senegal
Djibouti	Seychelles
Egypt	Sierra Leone
Equatorial Guinea	Somalia
Ethiopia	Sudan
Gabon	Swaziland
The Gambia	Tanzania
Ghana	Togo
Guinea	Tunisia
Guinea-Bissau	Uganda
Kenya	Zaire
Lesotho	Zambia
Liberia	Zimbabwe

There are also 25 non-African members.

Organization
(October 1988)

BOARD OF GOVERNORS

The highest policy-making body of the Bank. Each member country nominates one Governor, usually its Minister of Finance and Economic Affairs, and an alternate Governor. The Board meets once a year. It elects the Board of Directors and the President.

BOARD OF DIRECTORS

The Board consists of 18 members (of whom six are non-African and hold 36.57% of the voting power) elected by the Board of Governors for a term of three years; it is responsible for the general operations of the Bank. It holds ordinary meetings twice a month.

OFFICERS

The President is responsible for the organization and the day-to-day operations of the Bank under guidance of the Board of Directors. The President is elected for a five-year term and serves as the Chairman of the Board of Directors. He is assisted by five Vice-Presidents, elected for a three-year term by the Board of Directors on his recommendation.

During 1986 the Bank's organization was restructured, in preparation for the expected increase in capital (see below) and the resultant expansion of operations. Activities were divided into three sections (for eastern, western and central Africa) and a separate department for disbursements was created, while greater emphasis was to be placed on the evaluation of projects. During the year offices were opened in Conakry (Guinea), Addis Ababa (Ethiopia) and Rabat (Morocco).

Executive President and Chairman of Board of Directors: BABACAR N' DIAYE (Senegal).
Secretary-General: KOFI DEI-ANANG (Ghana).

FINANCIAL STRUCTURE

The Bank uses a unit of account (UA) which is equivalent to one United States dollar before the devaluation of 1971.

The capital stock of the Bank was at first exclusively open for subscription by African countries, with each member's subscription consisting of an equal number of paid-up and callable shares. In 1978, however, the Governors agreed to open the capital stock of the Bank to subscription by non-regional states on the basis of nine principles aimed at maintaining the African character of the institution. The decision was finally ratified in May 1982, and the participation of non-regional countries became effective on 30 December. It was agreed that African members should still hold two-thirds of the share capital, that all loan operations should be restricted to African members, and that the Bank's President should always be an African national. In 1986 a special committee established by the Board of Governors approved an increase in the Bank's authorized capital from UA 5,400m. (US $6,500m.) to UA 16,200m. ($19,600m.) (with paid-up capital as a proportion of the whole to be reduced from 25% to 6¼%). This took effect from June 1987.

Activities

The ADB Group of development financing institutions comprises the African Development Fund (ADF) and the Nigeria Trust Fund (NTF), which provide concessional loans, and the African Development Bank itself.

At the end of 1986 total loan approvals by the ADB Group since the beginning of its operations amounted to US $8,440m. In 1986 the Group approved loans of $1,640m., compared with $1,154m. in 1985. Co-financing amounting to $2,032m. was arranged with a number of other organizations and governments. Disbursement of loans during 1986 rose to $672m. from $531m. in 1985 and $288m. in 1984: this increase was attributed to efforts made during the year to strengthen dialogue with borrowers, and especially with officials responsible for the execution of projects. During 1985 and 1986 the Group increased its emphasis on: use of agricultural lines of credit; help for countries affected by drought; and the inclusion of environmental considerations in its operations. Priority was given to rehabilitation projects in all sectors.

In 1987 loans approved by the Group as a whole amounted to $2,141m. Of this total, the largest share (43%) was for agriculture, while transport and industrial projects received some 13% each, and public utilities 7%. Non-project lending received greater emphasis than in the past, with loans allocated to Congo, Guinea-Bissau and São Tomé and Príncipe to support their economic adjustment policies, and a major loan of $255m. (the largest in the Bank's history) to Nigeria for export promotion. During 1987 disbursements by the Group amounted to $934.3m.

The Bank also provides technical assistance in the form of experts' services, pre-investment studies, and staff training; much of this assistance is financed through bilateral aid funds contributed by developed member states.

AFRICAN DEVELOPMENT BANK (ADB)

The Bank makes loans at a variable annual interest rate (7.33% in 1987), plus commission and commitment fees of 1% each. Loan approvals increased from $1,034m. in 1986 to $1,356m. in 1987, while disbursements increased from $380m. in 1986 to $563m. in 1987. About 46% of loans approved were for North African countries (Algeria, Morocco and Tunisia). The capital increase approved in 1986 (see above) was to support a programme of lending amounting to $6,050m. in 1987-91.

AFRICAN DEVELOPMENT FUND (ADF)

The Fund commenced operations in 1973. It grants interest-free loans to African countries for projects with repayment over 50 years (including a 10-year grace period) and with a service charge of 0.75% per annum. Grants for project feasibility studies are made to the poorest countries.

In 1986 loans were approved totalling $585m., and disbursements came to $282m. In 1987 the Fund approved loans amounting to $766.1m. In November donor countries agreed on a fifth replenishment of the Fund's resources, amounting to $2,700m. for 1988-90. In future 85% of available resources were to be reserved for the poorest countries (those with annual GDP per caput of less than $510, at 1985 prices).

NIGERIA TRUST FUND (NTF)

The Agreement establishing the Nigeria Trust Fund was signed in February 1976 by the Bank and the Government of Nigeria. It came into force in April. The Fund is administered by the Bank and its loans are granted for up to 25 years, including grace periods of up to five years, and carry 0.75% commitment charges and 4% interest charges. The loans are intended to provide financing for projects in co-operation with other lending institutions.

By the end of 1985 the Fund had approved 29 loans, amounting to $127m., of which 34% was for transport projects. During 1985 only one loan was approved, amounting to $5.5m. (compared with three loans totalling $15.6m. in 1984). In 1986 the Fund approved four loans amounting to $20m.

ASSOCIATED INSTITUTIONS

The ADB actively participated in the setting-up of four associated institutions:

Africa Reinsurance Corporation—Africa-Re: 60/52 Broad St, PMB 12765, Lagos, Nigeria; f. 1977; started operations in 1978; its purpose is to foster the development of the insurance and reinsurance industry in Africa and to promote the growth of national and regional underwriting capacities. Africa-Re has an authorized capital of US $15m., of which the African Development Bank holds 10%. There are nine Directors, one appointed by the Bank. Gen. Man. E. ZAFU.

Association of African Development Finance Institutions—AADFI: c/o ADB, 01 BP 1387, Abidjan 01, Côte d'Ivoire; tel. 32-07-11; telex 23717; f. 1975; aims to promote co-operation among the development banks of the region in matters relating to development ideas, project design and financing. Mems: 130 institutions. Dir HENRY ANDREWS.

Shelter-Afrique (Société pour l'habitat et le logement territorial en Afrique): Mamlaka Rd, POB 41479, Nairobi, Kenya; tel. 722305; telex 25355; f. 1982 to finance housing in ADB member countries. Share capital is US $300m., held by 29 African countries, the ADB, Africa-Re and the Commonwealth Development Corporation. Dir EBENEZER OLUSEYI LUFADEJU.

Société internationale financière pour les investissements et le développement en Afrique—SIFIDA: 8C ave de Champel, BP 396, 1211 Geneva 12, Switzerland; tel. (022) 476000; telex 422047; f. 1970; holding company which aims to promote the establishment and growth of productive enterprises in Africa. It finances industrial projects, organizes syndicated loans, project identification and development, and export finance. At the end of 1985 SIFIDA was engaged in 87 operations in 28 African countries. Its shareholders include the ADB, IFC and about 130 financial, industrial and commercial institutions in the USA, Europe and Asia. Initial authorized share capital was US $50m., subscribed capital $18.7m. Chair. DEREK C. PEY; Man. Dir PHILIPPE SÉCHAUD.

PUBLICATIONS

Annual Report.

ADB News (monthly).

Quarterly Statement.

Basic Information (2 a year).

Statistical Handbook (annually).

Summaries of operations in each member country.

ANDEAN GROUP
(ACUERDO DE CARTAGENA)

Address: Avda Paseo de la República 3895, Casilla 18-1177, Lima 27, Peru.
Telephone: 414212.
Telex: 20104.

The organization, officially known as the Acuerdo de Cartagena (from the Cartagena Agreement which established it in 1969) and also known as the Grupo Andino (Andean Group) or the Pacto Andino (Andean Pact), aims to accelerate the harmonious development of the member states through economic and social integration. The group covers an area of 4,710,000 sq km, with about 80m. inhabitants.

MEMBERS

Bolivia   Colombia   Ecuador   Peru   Venezuela

Chile withdrew from the Group in January 1977.

Organization
(October 1988)

COMMISSION

This is the supreme authority of the Group, consisting of a plenipotentiary representative from each member country. Each country has the presidency in turn. The Commission is assisted by two Consultative Councils, each comprising four representatives from each country, elected respectively by national employers' organizations and by trades unions.

ANDEAN COUNCIL

The Council consists of the ministers of foreign affairs of the member countries, meeting annually or whenever it is considered necessary, to formulate a common external policy and to co-ordinate the process of integration.

JUNTA

Technical body which ensures that the Agreement is implemented and that the Commission's decisions are complied with. It submits proposals to the Commission for facilitating the fulfilment of the Agreement. Members are appointed for a three-year term. They supervise technical officials assigned to the following Departments: External Relations, Agricultural Development, Press Office, Economic Policy, Physical Integration, Programme of Assistance to Bolivia, Industrial Development, Programme Planning, Legal Affairs, Technology.

Members: JAIME SALAZAR MONTOYA (Colombia), PEDRO LUIS ECHEVERRÍA MONAGAS (Venezuela).

PARLIAMENT

Parlamento Andino: Sede del Congreso Nacional, Bogotá, Colombia; f. 1979; comprises five members from each country, and meets in each capital city in turn; makes recommendations on regional policy. Pres. HUMBERTO PELÁEZ; Exec. Sec. MILOS ALCALAY.

COURT OF JUSTICE

Tribunal de Justicia del Acuerdo de Cartagena: Calle Roca 450, Apdo Postal 9054 Suc. 7, Quito, Ecuador; tel. 529-990; telex 21263; f. 1979, began operating in 1984; its function is to resolve disputes and interpret legislation. It comprises five judges, one from each member country, appointed for a renewable period of six years. The Presidency is assumed annually by each judge in turn. Judges: Dr GALO PICO MANTILLA (Ecuador), Dr IVÁN GABALDÓN MÁRQUEZ (Venezuela), Dr HUGO POPPE ENTRAMBASAGUAS (Bolivia), Dr NICOLÁS DE PIEROLA Y BALTA (Peru), Dr FERNANDO URIBE RESTREPO (Colombia).

RESERVE FUND

Fondo Andina de Reservas: Carrera 13, No. 27-47, 10°, Bogotá, Colombia; tel. 285811; f. 1978 to support the balance of payments of member countries, provide credit, guarantee loans, and contribute to the harmonization of monetary and financial policies. In 1984 it began operating in the foreign exchange market. It is administered by an Assembly of the ministers of finance and economy of the member countries, and a Board of Directors comprising the presidents of the central banks of member states. In October 1985 it was decided that the Fund's capital should be expanded from US $100m. to $500m. In 1988 the admission of other Latin American countries, to create the Fondo Latinoamericano de Reservas, was approved. Exec. Pres. GUILLERMO CASTAÑEDA MUNGI (Peru).

DEVELOPMENT CORPORATION

Corporación Andina de Fomento: Torre Central, Avda Luis Roche, Altamira, Pisos 5°–10°, Apdo 5086, Caracas, Venezuela; tel. 284 2221; telex 22587; f. 1968, began operations in 1970; aims to encourage the integration of the Andean countries by specialization and an equitable distribution of investments. It conducts research to identify investment opportunities, and prepares the resulting investment projects; gives technical and financial assistance; and attracts internal and external credit. Authorized capital: US $1,000m., subscribed by the member states; shares worth about $200m. were to be offered to non-regional countries in 1986, and in 1987 it was announced that shares would also be offered to banks and other private organizations. The Board of Directors comprises representatives of each country at ministerial level. Exec. Pres. JOSÉ C. CARDENAS (Ecuador).

Activities

At a three-day summit meeting held at Cartagena, Colombia, in May 1979, the Presidents of the five member countries signed the 'Mandate of Cartagena', which called for greater economic and political co-operation in the 1980s, including the establishment of more sub-regional development programmes (especially in industry).

The operations of the Group have frequently been hindered by political problems: Bolivia threatened to withdraw in September 1980 following criticism of its Government by other members of the group, while Ecuador also suspended its membership temporarily at the beginning of 1981, following border disputes with Peru. In 1983 the Presidents of the five member states reaffirmed their commitment to regional integration, particularly in agriculture, trade, industry, finance, science and technology, physical integration, and aid to Bolivia and Ecuador.

In May 1987 representatives of member countries signed the Quito Protocol, modifying the Cartagena Agreement. The protocol included a relaxation of the strict rules that had formerly been imposed on foreign investors in the region (see below). It came into force in May 1988.

TRADE

Trade between members amounted to US $1,400m. in 1980, or about 4.5% of their foreign trade, compared with $111m. (2.5%) between the same countries in 1970. Trade within the group increased by about 37% annually between 1978 and 1980. Tariff reduction on manufactured goods traded between Colombia, Peru and Venezuela was almost complete by 1980, although agreement on a common external tariff had not yet been made. A council for customs affairs met for the first time in January 1982, aiming to harmonize national legislation within the group. Owing to the world recession trade within the group fell by some 40% during 1983. In response the Junta undertook schemes to promote exports and to establish a barter system.

In December 1983 an agreement was signed with the European Community, to eliminate obstacles in trade between the two regions and to develop co-operation programmes. The first joint meeting under the agreement was to be held in December 1987.

In December 1984 the member states launched a new common currency, the Andean peso, aiming to reduce dependence on the US dollar and to increase regional trade. The new currency was to be backed by special contributions to the Fondo Andina de Reservas amounting to $80m., and was to be 'pegged' to the US dollar, taking the form of financial drafts rather than notes and coins.

In May 1986 a new formula for trade among member countries was agreed, in order to restrict the number of products exempted from trade liberalization measures: under the new agreement each country could retain trade restrictions on up to 40 'sensitive' products.

INDUSTRY

Negotiations began in 1970 for the formulation of joint industrial programmes, particularly in the petrochemicals, metal-working and motor vehicle industries, but disagreements over the allocation of different plants, and the choice of foreign manufacturers for co-operation, prevented progress and by 1984 the more ambitious schemes had been abandoned. Instead, emphasis was to be placed on assisting small- and medium-sized industries, particularly in the agro-industrial and electronics sectors, in co-operation with national industrial organizations.

From 1971, in accordance with a Commission directive (Decision 24), foreign investors were required to transfer 51% of their shares to local investors within 15 years, in order to qualify for the preferential trade arrangements. Transfers were to be completed by 1989 for Colombia, Peru and Venezuela, and by 1994 for Bolivia and Ecuador. Foreign-owned companies were not to repatriate dividends of more than 14% (later raised to 20%), except with approval of the Commission, on pain of disqualification from preferential tariffs. In addition, foreign investors were forbidden to participate in transport undertakings, public utilities, banking and insurance, and were not to engage in activities already adequately covered by existing national enterprises. In early 1985 individual Pact members began to liberalize these laws, recognizing that the Group's policy, by deterring foreign investors, had contributed to its collective foreign debt of some US $70,000m., and in February 1986 ministers discussed a relaxation of the 'Decision 24' rules for foreign investors.

The Quito Protocol, modifying the Cartagena Agreement, was signed by members in May 1987 and entered into force one year later. It finally annulled Decision 24, and replaced it with Decision 220, allowing greater freedom for individual countries to establish their own rules on foreign investment. Each government was to decide which sectors were to be closed to foreign participation, and the period within which foreign investors must transfer a majority shareholding to local investors was extended to 30 years (37 years in Bolivia and Ecuador).

A further directive (Decision 169), in force since 1982, covers the formation of 'Empresas Multinacionales Andinas' (multinational enterprises) with capital from two or more member countries and non-member countries. At the end of 1985 there were 11 such enterprises (six in industry and the rest in agro-industry, trade, transport and construction).

AGRICULTURE

The Andean Agricultural Development Programme was formulated at a meeting of the Ministers of Agriculture held in Quito, Ecuador, in 1976. Twenty-two resolutions aimed at integrating the Andean agricultural sector were approved there. In 1984 the Andean Food Security System was created to develop the agrarian sector, replace imports progressively with local produce, and improve rural living conditions.

TRANSPORT AND COMMUNICATIONS

The first meeting of Andean Group transport ministers was held in March 1982, and adopted a plan of action for improving road and maritime transport. In 1983 the Commission drew up a plan to assist Bolivia by giving attention to its problems as a landlocked country, particularly through improving roads connecting it with the rest of the region and with the Pacific. Studies on the improvement of regional posts and telecommunications were under way in 1984, and a scheme for attracting tourists to the region was drawn up.

Asociación de Empresas Estatales de Telecomunicaciones: Avda Coruña 2669 y González Suárez, Casilla 6042, Quito, Ecuador; tel. 547-572; undertakes improvements of the postal and telecommunications systems in the region. Sec.-Gen. Jaime Aguilera Blanco.

SOCIAL DEVELOPMENT

Three Secretariats co-ordinate activities in social development and welfare:

Health: Trinidad Morán 1404, Lince, Casilla 5170, Lima 100, Peru; tel. 403324; telex 21444; Exec. Sec. Dr Hugo Urquieta Morales.

Labour Affairs: Luis Felipe Borja y Ponce s/n, Edif. Géminis, 9°, Casilla 601 A, Quito, Ecuador; tel. 545 374; Exec. Sec. Washington Barriga López.

Education, Science and Culture: Carrera 19, No 80-64, Apdo Aéreo 53465, Bogotá, Colombia; tel. 256-0221; telex 45569. Exec. Sec. Hernando Ochoa Núñez.

ANZUS

Address: c/o Dept of Foreign Affairs, Canberra, ACT 2600, Australia.

The ANZUS Security Treaty was signed in San Francisco in September 1951 and ratified in April 1952 to co-ordinate partners' efforts for collective defence for the preservation of peace and security in the Pacific area.

MEMBERS

Australia   New Zealand   USA

Organization
(October 1988)

ANZUS COUNCIL

The ANZUS Council is the main consultative organ of the ANZUS Treaty, consisting of the Ministers of Foreign Affairs (or their deputies), of the three signatory powers. Until 1985 meetings were held annually, rotating between capitals. Talks between officials, and other forms of practical co-operation, were held more frequently. The Council meetings were also attended by a military officer representing each country. These officers also met separately, and it was their function to advise the Council on military co-operation.

Following a dispute in 1985 over access by the United States forces to New Zealand ports and airfields (see below), meetings of the full ANZUS Council ceased, and instead ministerial talks were held annually between Australia and the USA, without New Zealand, under ANZUS auspices. For the time being ANZUS continued to govern security relations between Australia and the USA, and between Australia and New Zealand; security relations between New Zealand and the USA were the only aspect of the treaty to be suspended. The Australian Government expressed the hope that at some time in the future a change in policy by New Zealand would allow a return to full trilateral co-operation.

ANZUS has no permanent staff or secretariat, and costs are borne by the Government in whose territory meetings are held.

The instruments of ratification are deposited with the Government of Australia in Canberra.

Activities

Military co-operation among the ANZUS partners includes the exchange of technical information and strategic intelligence, together with a programme of exercises, exchanges and visits involving their armed forces, in particular naval visits to one another's ports. Defence co-operation programmes are also arranged on a bilateral basis with other countries of the region.

Following the election of a Labour Government in New Zealand in July 1984, New Zealand refused to allow visits by US naval vessels carrying nuclear weapons, and this led to the cancellation of joint ANZUS military exercises planned for March and October 1985. In August 1986 the USA formally announced the suspension of its security commitment to New Zealand under ANZUS. Instead of the annual ANZUS Council meetings, bilateral talks were subsequently held every year between Australia and the USA. Free access to Australian ports for US naval vessels continued.

Security Treaty

The treaty itself is brief, containing only 11 articles. Like the NATO treaty upon which it was based, the ANZUS Treaty is largely a declaratory document which is not drafted in precise and detailed legal terms.

In the words of the preamble to the treaty, the purposes of the signatory powers are: 'to strengthen the fabric of peace in the Pacific Area'; 'to declare publicly and formally their sense of unity, so that no potential aggressor could be under the illusion that any of them stand alone in the Pacific Area'; 'to co-ordinate further their efforts for collective defence for the preservation of peace and security pending the development of a more comprehensive system of regional security in the Pacific Area'.

The Parties to the treaty undertake to 'consult together whenever in the opinion of any of them, the territorial integrity, political independence or security of any of the parties is threatened in the Pacific' (Article 3). Each Party is bound to act to meet the common danger according to its constitutional processes, since each Party recognizes that an armed attack on any of the Parties would be dangerous to its own peace and safety (Article 4).

An armed attack in the terms of the treaty includes an armed attack on the metropolitan territory of any of the Parties, or on the island territories under its jurisdiction in the Pacific, or on its armed forces, public vessels or aircraft in the Pacific.

An armed attack and all measures taken as a result thereof shall be immediately reported to the Security Council of the UN. These measures are to be terminated when the Security Council has taken the measures necessary to restore and maintain international peace and security (Article 4).

ARAB BANK FOR ECONOMIC DEVELOPMENT IN AFRICA
(BANQUE ARABE POUR LE DÉVELOPPEMENT ÉCONOMIQUE EN AFRIQUE—BADEA)

Address: Sayed Abdar-Rahman el-Mahdi Ave, POB 2640, Khartoum, Sudan.
Telephone: 73646, 73709.
Telex: 22248, 22739.

The Bank was created by the Arab League at the Sixth Arab Summit Conference in Algiers, November 1973. Operations began in early 1975. The purpose of the Bank is to contribute to Africa's economic development by providing all or part of the financing required for development projects and by supplying technical assistance to African countries.

MEMBERS

Subscribing countries: all members of the Arab League except Djibouti, Somalia, the Yemen Arab Republic and the People's Democratic Republic of Yemen. Egypt's membership was suspended in April 1979, but restored in April 1988.

Recipient countries: all member countries of the Organization of African Unity except the member countries of the Arab League. A total of 41 countries are eligible for BADEA aid.

Organization
(October 1988)

BOARD OF GOVERNORS

The Board of Governors, the highest authority of the Bank, is composed of finance ministers of Arab League member states; it meets annually, examines the Bank's activities in the preceding past year and provides the resources required for the tasks assigned to it in the coming year. Only the Board of Governors has the power to increase the Bank's capital.

BOARD OF DIRECTORS

The Board meets four times a year to make recommendations concerning policy to the Board of Governors and supervises the implementation of their decisions; performs all the executive functions of the Bank. The Board comprises a chairman, appointed by the Board of Governors for a five-year term, and 11 other members. Countries with 200 or more shares each have a permanent seat on the Board (Algeria, Iraq, Kuwait, Libya, Qatar, Saudi Arabia and the United Arab Emirates); appointments to the remaining four seats are made by the Governors for a four-year term.

Chairman: AHMAD ABDALLAH AL-AKEIL (Saudi Arabia).
Director-General: AHMAD AL-HARTI AL-OUARDI (Morocco).

SUBSCRIPTIONS TO CAPITAL STOCK
(US $ million at 31 December 1987)

Algeria	42.6	Oman	15.6
Bahrain	2.1	Palestine	2.1
Egypt	2.1	Qatar	85.2
Iraq	149.1	Saudi Arabia	255.6
Jordan	2.1	Sudan	2.1
Kuwait	156.2	Syria	1.4
Lebanon	7.1	Tunisia	8.9
Libya	170.4	United Arab Emirates	127.8
Mauritania	2.1		
Morocco	15.6	**Total**	**1,048.3**

Paid-up capital: US $1,045.5m.

Activities

BADEA aid consists mainly of loans on concessional terms for development projects, not exceeding US $10m. (exceptionally $15m.) or 40% of the total cost of each project (80% for loans of under $5m.). Technical assistance (e.g. pre-investment studies, training and assistance for institutions) is also provided, and Arab investment in Africa is encouraged.

The Special Arab Assistance Fund for Africa (SAAFA), established in 1972 to provide loans for Africa, was integrated with BADEA in 1977 after disbursing aid to the total of $214,244,000 to 32 African countries.

By December 1987 BADEA had approved loans and grants amounting to US $828.8m. (or $1,043.1m. when SAAFA operations are included) involving 114 projects, seven lines of credit, 41 grants for technical assistance and 14 special emergency aid operations, for a total of 39 African countries. Most projects are co-financed with other organizations or countries, chiefly Arab or predominantly Arab aid organizations (including the OPEC Fund and the Islamic Development Bank), western industrialized countries, the World Bank and the African Development Bank. Total disbursements to the end of 1987 (including SAAFA loans) amounted to $652m., or about 62.5% of total commitments. In regional terms, $452.2m. of total aid approved (up to the end of 1987) went to West Africa and $374.2m. to East Africa.

The sectoral distribution of aid is determined by development priorities adopted by the African countries themselves. The average distribution has been weighted in favour of projects for infrastructural development, which received 49.7% of total aid up to the end of 1987. The commitments to agriculture, industrial and energy development projects in 1975–87 were 25.8%, 13.3% and 9.3% respectively.

In 1987 US $70.7m. was allocated for 11 projects and seven technical assistance operations. Projects for which loans were approved in that year were: petroleum storage facilities in the Comoros ($1.8m.); feeder roads in Botswana ($6.1m.); completion of a road ($1.2m.) and construction of a sewerage network ($6.5m.) in Burundi; industrial fisheries in Cape Verde ($4.0m.); abattoirs and cold storage facilities in Zimbabwe ($9.2m.); cocoa rehabilitation in Ghana ($10m.); road construction in Lesotho ($10m.); energy in Madagascar ($5.4m.); and road maintenance ($8.2m.) and poultry development ($6.8m.) in Uganda.

LOANS APPROVED BY BADEA*
(US $ million cumulative to 31 December 1987)

Angola	32.4	Madagascar	36.8
Benin	38.7	Mali	39.7
Botswana	33.0	Mauritius	12.7
Burkina Faso	33.3	Mozambique	55.0
Burundi	35.9	Niger	35.9
Cameroon	31.9	Rwanda	35.8
Cape Verde	28.2	São Tomé and Príncipe	20.7
Central African Republic	13.2	Senegal	41.0
Chad	10.7	Seychelles	6.1
Comoros	27.7	Sierra Leone	25.1
Congo	33.8	Swaziland	4.2
Côte d'Ivoire	3.3	Tanzania	34.2
Equatorial Guinea	8.0	Togo	8.6
Ethiopia	14.7	Uganda	45.2
Ghana	46.8	Zaire	22.4
Guinea	35.5	Zambia	47.7
Guinea-Bissau	22.2	Zimbabwe	37.3
Kenya	30.4	Unspecified	9.7
Lesotho	25.6		
Liberia	10.6	**Total**	**1,043.1**

Grants totalling US $4.964m. were made for a telecommunications study (1983), technical assistance (1984 and 1986), and exceptional aid to Sudan (1985). A line of credit of $5m. was opened for the Banque des états de l'Afrique centrale (1978), and another for the Banque ouest-africaine de développement (1984), to help finance small and medium-sized industries.

* Including grants made by the Special Arab Assistance Fund for Africa before 1977, totalling $214.2m.

TOTAL BADEA COMMITMENTS BY SECTOR
(US $ million)

Sector	1987	1975–87
Infrastructure	34.0	412.2
Roads	25.5	217.1
Railways	—	24.3
Maritime and river transport	—	45.6
Air transport	—	37.1
Telecommunications	—	19.4
Water supply	6.7	19.8
Dams, bridges and public services	1.8	48.9
Agriculture	30.6	213.5
Rural development	0.3	76.6
Food production	10.0	41.1
Livestock	7.0	19.6
Fishing	4.0	38.8
Agro-industry	9.2	39.4
Forestry development	—	8.0
Industry	—	110.5
Building materials industry	—	51.2
Chemical industry	—	30.0
Small and medium-sized industry	—	34.2
Textile industry	—	4.7
Energy infrastructure and electric power	5.4	76.2
Special programme (emergency aid)	—	14.6
Technical assistance	0.6	1.9
Human resources	—	0.1
Support for institutions	0.6	1.8
Total	70.7	828.8

PUBLICATIONS

Annual Report.
Co-operation for Development (quarterly).
Studies on Afro-Arab Co-operation.

ARAB FUND FOR ECONOMIC AND SOCIAL DEVELOPMENT—AFESD

Address: POB 21923, Safat, 13080 Kuwait.
Telephone: 2451580.
Telex: 22153.

Established in 1968 by the Economic Council of the Arab League, the Fund began its operations in 1973. It participates in the financing of economic and social development projects in the Arab states.

MEMBERSHIP

Twenty-one countries and the Palestine Liberation Organization (see table of subscriptions below).

Organization
(October 1988)

BOARD OF GOVERNORS

The Board of Governors consists of a Governor and an Alternate Governor appointed by each member of the Fund. The Board of Governors is considered as the General Assembly of the Fund, and has all powers.

BOARD OF DIRECTORS

The Board of Directors is composed of six Directors elected by the Board of Governors from among Arab citizens of recognized experience and competence. They are elected for a renewable term of two years.

The Board of Directors is charged with all the activities of the Fund and exercises the powers delegated to it by the Board of Governors.

Director-General and Chairman of the Board of Directors: ABD AL-LATIF YOUSUF AL-HAMAD.

FINANCIAL STRUCTURE

The authorized capital at commencement of operations in April 1973 was 100m. Kuwaiti dinars (KD). In 1982 the capital was increased to KD 800m., divided into 80,000 shares having a value of KD 10,000 each. At the end of 1987 subscribed capital was KD 694.8m. (see table below), and paid-up capital was KD 644.2m.

SUBSCRIPTIONS (KD million)*

Country	Amount	Country	Amount
Algeria	64.78	Palestine Liberation Organization	1.10
Bahrain	2.16	Qatar	6.75
Djibouti	0.20	Saudi Arabia	159.07
Egypt†	21.75	Somalia	0.21
Iraq	31.76	Sudan	11.06
Jordan	17.30	Syria	24.0
Kuwait	169.70	Tunisia	6.16
Lebanon	2.0	United Arab Emirates	28.00
Libya	59.85	Yemen Arab Republic	4.25
Mauritania	0.82	Yemen, People's Democratic Republic	0.20
Morocco	16.0		
Oman	17.28	**Total**	**644.22**

* 100 Kuwaiti dinars = US $368.32 (December 1987).
† In April 1979 all aid to and economic relations with Egypt were suspended, but finance for projects already in progress continued. In April 1988 Egypt was reported to have been reintegrated into the Fund.

Activities

The Fund participates in the financing of economic and social development projects in the Arab states and countries by:

1. Financing economic projects of an investment character by means of loans granted on easy terms to governments, and to public or private organizations and institutions, giving preference to economic projects of interest specifically to Arab peoples, and to joint Arab projects.

2. Encouraging, directly or indirectly, the investment of public and private capital in such a manner as to ensure the development and growth of the Arab economy.

3. Providing technical expertise and assistance in the various fields of economic development.

The Fund co-operates with other Arab organizations such as the Arab Monetary Fund, the League of Arab States and OAPEC in preparing regional studies and conferences, and acts as the secretariat of the Co-ordination Group of Arab National and Regional Development Institutions.

By the end of 1987 the Fund had made 208 loans for 161 projects in 17 countries, since the beginning of its operations. The total value of these loans was KD 888.1m. Disbursements amounted to KD 454.1m. by the end of 1987.

During 1987 the Fund approved 18 loans totalling KD 106.3m. for 18 projects (see table below). Agricultural projects received by far the largest share of lending (37.1%). Disbursements of loans during the year amounted to KD 48.4m.

Technical assistance grants reached KD 17.2m. by the end of 1987. During 1987, 36 new grants were approved, totalling KD 3.8m., of which nine were for feasibility studies; other grants were for institutions, agricultural research, training in planning and statistics, and conferences.

LOANS BY SECTOR, 1987

Sector	Amount (KD million)	%
Agriculture (incl. fisheries)	39.5	37.1
Transport and telecommunications	26.5	25.0
Electrical power	18.0	16.9
Water and sewerage	20.0	18.8
Mining and industry	2.3	2.2
Total	**106.3**	**100.0**

LOANS BY COUNTRY, 1987

Country	Project	Amount (KD million)
Bahrain	Roads	5.50
Djibouti	Communications development	0.40
Iraq	Agricultural credit	8.00
Jordan	Thermal power station	7.00
Mauritania	Development credit	1.00
	Iron ore production	1.30
Morocco	Dam and agricultural development	15.0
Oman	Desalination and power	6.00
Sudan	National power grid	8.50
	Water supply	10.00
Syria	Irrigation	15.00
	Power station	2.50
Tunisia	Road development	7.00
	Fishery port	1.30
Yemen Arab Republic	Road improvement	6.80
Yemen, People's Democratic Republic	Water supply	4.00
	Road maintenance	5.50
	Fisheries	1.50
Total		**106.30**

ARAB MONETARY FUND

Address: POB 2818, Abu Dhabi, United Arab Emirates.
Telephone: 215000.
Telex: 22989.

The Agreement establishing the Arab Monetary Fund was approved by the Economic Council of Arab States in Rabat, Morocco, in April 1976 and entered into force on 2 February 1977.

MEMBERS

Algeria	Palestine Liberation Organization
Bahrain	Qatar
Egypt*	Saudi Arabia
Iraq	Somalia
Jordan	Sudan
Kuwait	Syria
Lebanon	Tunisia
Libya	United Arab Emirates
Mauritania	Yemen Arab Republic
Morocco	Yemen, People's Democratic Republic
Oman	

* Egypt's membership was suspended in April 1979, but resumed in April 1988.

Organization
(October 1988)

BOARD OF GOVERNORS

The Board of Governors is the highest authority of the Arab Monetary Fund. It formulates policies on Arab economic integration and liberalization of trade among member states. With certain exceptions, it may delegate to the Board of Executive Directors any of its powers. The Board of Governors is composed of a governor and a deputy governor appointed by each member state for a term of five years. It meets at least once a year; meetings may also be convened at the request of half the members, or of members holding half of the total voting power.

BOARD OF EXECUTIVE DIRECTORS

The Board of Executive Directors exercises all powers vested in it by the Board of Governors and may delegate to the Managing Director such powers as it deems fit. It is composed of the Managing Director and eight non-resident directors elected by the Board of Governors. Each director holds office for three years and may be re-elected.

MANAGING DIRECTOR

The Managing Director of the Fund is appointed by the Board of Governors for a renewable five-year term, and serves as Chairman of the Board of Executive Directors.

The Managing Director supervises a Committee on Loans and a Committee on Investments to make recommendations on loan and investment policies to the Board of Executive Directors, and is required to submit an Annual Report to the Board of Governors.

Managing Director (1987–92): Dr ABDULLAH AL-KUWAIZ.

FINANCE

The Arab Accounting Dinar (AAD) is a unit of account equivalent to 3 IMF Special Drawing Rights (The average value of the SDR in 1987 was US $1.29307.)

Each member paid, in convertible currencies, 5% of the value of its shares at the time of its ratification of the Agreement and another 20% when the Agreement entered into force. In addition, each member paid 2% of the value of its shares in its national currency regardless of whether it is convertible. The second 25% of the capital was to be subscribed by the end of September 1979, bringing the total paid-up capital in convertible currencies to AAD 131.5m. (SDR 394.5m.). An increase in requests for loans led to a resolution by the Board of Governors in April 1981, giving members the option of paying the balance of their subscribed capital. This payment became obligatory in July 1981, when total approved loans exceeded 50% of the already paid-up capital in convertible currencies. In April 1983 the authorized capital of the Fund was increased from AAD 288m. to AAD 600m. The new capital stock comprised 12,000 shares, each having the value of AAD 50,000. The increase was to be paid (in convertible currencies) over five years by annual instalments, equally divided. At the end of 1987 total paid-up capital was AAD 290.2m.

CAPITAL SUBSCRIPTIONS
(million Arab Accounting Dinars, 31 December 1987)

Member	Authorized capital	Paid-up capital	Shares
Algeria	60.00	38.00	1,200
Bahrain	9.00	5.00	180
Egypt	60.00	6.75	1,200
Iraq	60.00	38.00	1,200
Jordan	11.00	5.40	220
Kuwait	60.00	32.00	1,200
Lebanon	13.00	5.00	260
Libya	30.00	13.44	600
Mauritania	9.00	5.00	180
Morocco	35.00	15.00	700
Oman	9.00	5.00	180
Palestine Liberation Organization	4.00	—	80
Qatar	24.00	10.00	480
Saudi Arabia	90.00	48.40	1,800
Somalia	9.00	4.00	180
Sudan	25.00	10.00	500
Syria	20.00	7.20	400
Tunisia	15.00	7.00	300
United Arab Emirates	36.00	19.20	720
Yemen Arab Republic	12.00	10.80	240
Yemen, People's Democratic Republic	9.00	5.00	180
Total	**600.00**	**290.19**	**12,000**

Activities

The creation of the Arab Monetary Fund was seen as a step towards the goal of Arab economic integration. It assists member states in balance of payments difficulties, and also has a broad range of aims.

The Articles of Agreement define the Fund's aims as follows:

(a) to correct disequilibria in the balance of payments of member states;

(b) to promote the stability of exchange rates among Arab currencies, the realization of their mutual convertibility, and the removal of restrictions on current payments between member states;

(c) to establish policies and modes of monetary co-operation to speed up Arab economic integration and economic development in the member states;

(d) to tender advice on the investment of member states' financial resources in foreign markets, whenever called upon to do so;

(e) to promote the development of Arab financial markets;

(f) to promote the use of the Arab dinar as a unit of account and to pave the way for the creation of a unified Arab currency;

(g) to co-ordinate the positions of member states in dealing with international monetary and economic problems; and

(h) to provide a mechanism for the settlement of current payments between member states in order to promote trade among them.

The Arab Monetary Fund functions both as a fund and a bank. It is empowered:

(a) to provide short- and medium-term loans to finance balance of payments deficits of member states;

INTERNATIONAL ORGANIZATIONS

Arab Monetary Fund

(*b*) to issue guarantees to member states to strengthen their borrowing capabilities;

(*c*) to act as intermediary in the issuance of loans in Arab and international markets for the account of member states and under their guarantees;

(*d*) to co-ordinate the monetary policies of member states;

(*e*) to manage any funds placed under its charge by member states;

(*f*) to hold periodic consultations with member states on their economic conditions; and

(*g*) to provide technical assistance to banking and monetary institutions in member states.

Loans are intended to finance an overall balance of payments deficit and a member may draw up to 75% of its paid-up subscription, in convertible currencies, for this purpose unconditionally (automatic loans). A member may, however, obtain loans in excess of this limit, subject to agreement with the Fund on a programme aimed at reducing its balance of payments deficit (ordinary and extended loans, equivalent to 175% and 225% of its quota respectively). A country receiving no extended loans is entitled to a loan under the Inter-Arab Trade Facility (introduced in 1981) of up to 100% of its quota. In addition, a member has the right to borrow up to 100% of its paid-up capital in order to cope with an unexpected deficit in its balance of payments resulting from a decrease in its exports of goods and services or a large increase in its imports of agricultural products following a poor harvest (compensatory loans). Over the period 1978–87, 67 loans were extended to nine member countries.

Automatic and compensatory loans are repayable within three years, while ordinary and extended loans are repayable within five and seven years respectively, and trade facility loans within four years. Loans are granted at concessionary and uniform rates of interest which increase with the length of the period of the loan.

At the end of 1987 total approved loans amounted to AAD 358,188,000, of which AAD 347,972,500 had been disbursed and AAD 190,522,179 repaid.

The Fund's lending declined from AAD 85m. in 1983 to AAD 18.5m. in 1984, but increased to AAD 51m. in 1985, comprising nine loans to five member states. In 1986 the Fund extended 11 loans amounting to AAD 33.9m., and in 1987 it approved three loans totalling AAD 29.1m.

LOANS APPROVED, 1987

Type of loan	Borrower	Amount (AAD '000)
Ordinary	Yemen Arab Republic	7,050
Inter-Arab Trade Facility	Iraq	18,260
	Tunisia	3,450
Total		29,120

LOANS APPROVED, 1977–87

Type of loan	Number of loans	Amount (AAD '000)
Automatic	40	149,708
Extended	7	78,830
Ordinary	5	32,320
Compensatory	7	58,280
Inter-Arab Trade Facility	8	39,050
Total	67	358,188

The Fund also undertakes studies and surveys on inter-Arab trade; provides technical assistance, in the form of training courses or placements for trainees, seminars, and expert advisory services; and co-operates with other regional organizations by participating in meetings.

PUBLICATIONS

Annual Report.
Arab Countries: Selected Economic Indicators.
Cross Rates of Currencies of Arab Countries.
Foreign Trade of Arab Countries.
Foreign Trade of Members of the Arab Common Market.
Foreign Trade of Members of the Arab Gulf Co-operation Council.
Joint Arab Economic Report (annually).
Money and Credit in Arab Countries.
National Accounts of Arab Countries.
Balance of Payments Statistics for Arab Countries.
Reports on commodity structure (by value and quantity) of member countries' imports from and exports to other Arab countries.

ASIAN DEVELOPMENT BANK—ADB

Address: 2330 Roxas Blvd, 1300 Metro Manila, Philippines; POB 789, 1099 Manila, Philippines.
Telephone: 8344444; (632) 7113851 (international calls).
Telex: 23103.

The Bank commenced operations in December 1966; its aims are to raise funds from private and public sources for development purposes in the region, to assist member states in co-ordinating economic policies, and to give technical assistance in development projects.

MEMBERS

There are 32 member countries within the ESCAP region and 15 others (see list of subscriptions below).

Organization
(October 1988)

BOARD OF GOVERNORS

All powers of the Bank are vested in the Board which may delegate its powers to the Board of Directors except in such matters as admission of new members, changes in the Bank's authorized capital stock, election of Directors and President, amendment of the Charter. One Governor and one Alternate Governor are appointed by each member country. The Board meets at least once a year.

BOARD OF DIRECTORS

The Board of Directors is responsible for general direction of operations and exercises all powers delegated by the Board of Governors, which elects it. Of the 12 Directors, eight represent constituency groups of member countries within the ESCAP region (with about 65% of the voting power) and four represent the rest of the member countries. Each Director serves for two years and may be re-elected. The President of the Bank, though not a Director, is Chairman of the Board.

Chairman of Board of Directors and President: MASAO FUJIOKA (Japan).

Vice-Presidents: IN YONG CHUNG (Republic of Korea); S. STANLEY KATZ (USA); GÜNTHER SCHULZ (Federal Republic of Germany).

ADMINISTRATION

There were 1,605 Bank staff from 39 countries on 31 December 1987.

Departments: Programs (East and West), Agriculture (East and West), Infrastructure (including an Environment Unit), Industry and Development Banks, Budget, Personnel and Management Systems, Controller's, Treasurer's.

Offices: President, Secretary, General Counsel, Development Policy, Central Projects Services, Administrative Services, Special Projects, Economics, Information, Computer Services, Internal Auditor, Post-Evaluation, Bangladesh Resident Office, Indonesia Resident Office and Regional Office for the South Pacific.

Secretary: ARUN B. ADARKAR (India).

General Counsel: CHUN PYO JHONG (Republic of Korea).

South Pacific Regional Office: Pilioko House, Kumul Highway, POB 127, Port Vila, Vanuatu; tel. 3300; telex 1082.

FINANCIAL STRUCTURE

The Bank's ordinary capital resources (which are used for loans to the more advanced developing countries in the region) are held and used entirely separately from its Special Funds resources (see below). A third General Capital Increase, of 105%, was authorized in April 1983.

At 31 December 1987 the position of subscriptions to the capital stock was as follows: Authorized US $22,987m.; Subscribed $22,770m.; Paid-in $2,752m.

The Bank also borrows funds from the world capital markets. Total borrowings during 1986 amounted to the equivalent of $813m., decreasing to $537m. in 1987.

In July 1986 the Bank abolished the system of fixed lending rates, under which ordinary operations loans had carried interest rates fixed at the time of loan commitment for the entire life of the loan. Under the new system the lending rate is adjusted every six months, to take into account changing conditions in international financial markets.

SUBSCRIPTIONS AND VOTING POWER
(31 December 1987)

Country	Total subscriptions to capital stock (US $'000)	Voting power (% of total)
Regional:		
Afghanistan	16,953	0.485
Australia	1,452,282	5.528
Bangladesh	256,267	1.326
Bhutan	1,561	0.431
Burma	136,688	0.906
China, People's Republic	1,617,272	6.108
Cook Islands	667	0.428
Fiji	17,066	0.485
Hong Kong	136,688	0.906
India	1,588,970	6.008
Indonesia	1,366,879	5.228
Japan	3,417,197	12.432
Kampuchea	12,413	0.469
Kiribati	1,007	0.429
Korea, Republic	1,264,352	4.868
Laos	3,490	0.438
Malaysia	683,439	2.827
Maldives	1,007	0.429
Nepal	36,899	0.555
New Zealand	385,450	1.780
Pakistan	546,752	2.346
Papua New Guinea	23,550	0.508
Philippines	597,994	2.527
Singapore	85,403	0.726
Solomon Islands	1,674	0.431
Sri Lanka	145,555	0.937
Taiwan	273,376	1.386
Thailand	341,713	1.626
Tonga	1,007	0.429
Vanuatu	1,674	0.431
Viet-Nam	85,659	0.726
Western Samoa	823	0.428
Sub-total	14,501,727	64.567
Non-regional:		
Austria	85,403	0.726
Belgium	85,403	0.726
Canada	1,312,871	5.038
Denmark	85,403	0.726
Finland	85,403	0.726
France	584,176	2.478
Germany, Fed. Repub.	1,085,758	4.240
Italy	453,617	2.019
Netherlands	257,444	1.330
Norway	85,403	0.726
Spain	85,403	0.726
Sweden	34,162	0.546
Switzerland	146,477	0.940
United Kingdom	512,576	2.226
USA	3,368,466	12.260
Sub-total	8,267,965	35.433
Total	22,769,692	100.000

SPECIAL FUNDS

The Asian Development Fund (ADF) was established in 1974 in order to provide a systematic mechanism for mobilizing and administering resources for the Bank to lend on concessionary terms to the least-developed member countries. Administration of the earlier Special Funds—the Multi-Purpose Special Fund (MPSF) and the Agricultural Special Fund (ASF)—had been complicated by the fact that contributions of individual donors had been made voluntarily at the initiative of the countries concerned and were frequently tied to procurement in those countries.

Successive replenishments of the Fund's resources amounted to $809m. for the period 1976–78, $2,150m. for 1979–82, and $3,214m. for 1983–86. A further replenishment (ADF V) was approved in 1986, and came into effect in May 1987, providing $3,600m. for the four years 1987-90.

The Bank provides technical assistance grants from its Technical Assistance Special Fund. By the end of 1987, direct voluntary contributions to this fund amounted to $84m., of which $81.9m. had been used by the Bank.

Activities

Loans by the Bank are usually aimed at specific projects, resulting in the creation of real physical assets. In responding to requests from member governments for loans, the Bank's staff assesses the financial and economic viability of projects and the way in which they fit into the economic framework and priorities of development of the country concerned.

In 1987 the Bank approved 48 loans, amounting to US $2,438.5m., (compared with a total of $2,004m. in 1986 and a peak of $2,234.3m. in 1984). Loans from ordinary capital resources totalled $1,480.9m., while loans from the ADF amounted to $957.6m. The Bank also approved eight equity investments totalling $22.8m. Co-financing by other institutions amounted to $498m. Disbursements of loans during 1987 amounted to $1,232m., an increase of 20% over the previous year's total. In 1986 there was a negative net transfer of ordinary capital resources to developing member countries, amounting to $129m.; this increased to $359.5m. in 1987. In other words, the Bank was receiving more in repayments and interest than it was paying out in loans (although this was not the case with ADF loans).

During 1987 the transport and communications sector received the largest share of loans approved (33%): these included finance for road improvements and maintenence in Bangladesh, Indonesia, the Republic of Korea, Laos and Sri Lanka, railways in India, and port improvements in India, the Philippines, Solomon Islands and Vanuatu. The industry and non-fuel minerals sector received 26%, agriculture and agro-industry 22% and energy 14%.

Loans and grants for technical assistance (e.g. project preparation, consultant services and training) amounted to $143m. for 158 projects in 1987. The Bank's Post-Evaluation Office prepares reports on completed projects, in order to assess achievements and problems.

In 1985 the Bank decided to expand its assistance to the private sector. It was decided that a government guarantee would no longer be necessary for providing loans to private enterprises, and that the Bank would increase its support for financial institutions and capital markets and, where appropriate, give assistance for the privatization of public sector enterprises. During 1987 the Bank approved three loans to private-sector companies without government guarantees, totalling $20.5m.

BANK ACTIVITIES BY SECTOR

Sector	Loan Approvals (US $ million)			
	1987		1968–87	
	Amount	%	Amount	%
Agriculture and agro-industry.	528.99	21.69	6,705.55	30.71
Energy	331.70	13.60	5,218.85	23.90
Industry and non-fuel minerals	645.50	26.47	3,102.34	14.21
Transport and communications	793.85	32.56	3,340.44	15.30
Social infrastructure	135.70	5.57	3,264.90	14.96
Multi-sector	2.75	0.11	200.41	0.92
Total	**2,438.49**	**100.00**	**21,832.49**	**100.00**

LENDING ACTIVITIES BY COUNTRY (US $ million)

Country	Loans approved in 1987			Cumulative 1968–87			
	Ordinary Capital	ADF	Total	Ordinary Capital	ADF	Total	%
Afghanistan	—	—	—	—	95.10	95.10	0.44
Bangladesh	—	265.70	265.70	11.40	2,181.29	2,192.69	10.04
Bhutan	—	3.30	3.30	—	27.98	27.98	0.13
Burma	—	—	—	6.60	524.26	530.86	2.43
China, People's Republic	133.30	—	133.30	133.30	—	133.30	0.61
Cook Islands	—	2.75	2.75	—	5.25	5.25	0.02
Fiji	—	—	—	60.50	—	60.50	0.28
Hong Kong	—	—	—	101.50	—	101.50	0.47
India	393.60	—	393.60	643.60	—	643.60	2.95
Indonesia	441.00	135.00	576.00	4,051.80	297.28	4,349.08	19.92
Kampuchea (Cambodia)	—	—	—	—	1.67	1.67	0.01
Kiribati	—	—	—	—	3.00	3.00	0.01
Korea, Republic	133.20	—	133.20	2,199.03	3.70	2,202.73	10.09
Laos	—	34.50	34.50	—	106.64	106.64	0.49
Malaysia	82.30	—	82.30	1,361.64	3.30	1,364.94	6.25
Maldives	—	6.10	6.10	—	9.48	9.48	0.04
Nepal	—	91.29	91.29	2.00	638.86	640.86	2.94
Pakistan	249.00	292.60	541.60	1,689.17	2,080.45	3,769.62	17.27
Papua New Guinea	5.00	5.00	10.00	142.25	140.34	282.59	1.29
Philippines	43.50	—	43.50	2,342.04	129.30	2,471.34	11.32
Singapore	—	—	—	178.08	3.00	181.08	0.83
Solomon Islands	—	9.30	9.30	—	38.11	38.11	0.17
Sri Lanka	—	106.30	106.30	14.13	660.63	674.76	3.09
Taiwan	—	—	—	100.39	—	100.39	0.46
Thailand	—	—	—	1,656.25	72.10	1,728.35	7.92
Tonga	—	—	—	—	11.25	11.25	0.05
Vanuatu	—	5.75	5.75	—	10.85	10.85	0.05
Viet-Nam	—	—	—	3.93	40.67	44.60	0.20
Western Samoa	—	—	—	—	50.37	50.37	0.23
Total	**1,480.90**	**957.59**	**2,438.49**	**14,697.61**	**7,134.88**	**21,832.49**	**100.00**

Source: *ADB Annual Report 1987.*

INTERNATIONAL ORGANIZATIONS

Asian Development Bank

In 1987 the Bank adopted a policy of lending in support of programmes of sectoral adjustment, not limited to specific projects; such lending was not to exceed 15% of total Bank lending. In December the first such loan was approved, providing $150m. to Indonesia for the promotion of exports other than petroleum.

The Bank co-operates with other international organizations active in the region, particularly the World Bank group and UNDP, and participates in meetings of aid donors for developing member countries.

BUDGET

Internal administrative expenses amounted to US $89.5m. in 1987, and were expected to come to $98.4m. in 1988. Services to member countries financed from the Bank's own resources (e.g. project preparation and advisory services) totalled $26m. in 1987.

PUBLICATIONS

Annual Report.
ADB Quarterly Review.
Summary of Proceedings (Annual Meeting of the Board of Governors).
Regional Studies and Reports, Occasional Papers, Sector Papers, Economic Staff Papers.
Key Indicators of Developing Member Countries of ADB (annually).
Asian Development Review (2 a year).
Operational Information on Proposed Projects (monthly).
Project Profiles for Potential Co-financing (quarterly).

ASSOCIATION OF SOUTH EAST ASIAN NATIONS—ASEAN

Address: Jalan Sisingamangaraja, POB 2072, Jakarta, Indonesia.
Telephone: 712272.
Telex: 47214.

ASEAN was established in August 1967 at Bangkok, Thailand, to accelerate economic progress and to increase the stability of the South-East Asian region.

MEMBERS

Brunei	Malaysia	Singapore
Indonesia	Philippines	Thailand

Organization

(October 1988)

SUMMIT MEETING

The highest authority of ASEAN, bringing together the Heads of Government of member countries. The first meeting was held in Bali, Indonesia, in February 1976; the second in Kuala Lumpur, Malaysia, in August 1977. A third summit meeting was held in Manila, the Philippines, in December 1987.

MINISTERIAL CONFERENCES

The ministers of foreign affairs of member states meet annually in each member country in turn. Ministers of economic affairs also meet about once a year, to direct ASEAN economic co-operation, and other ministers meet when necessary. Ministerial meetings are serviced by the committees described below.

STANDING COMMITTEE

The Standing Committee normally meets every two months. It consists of the minister of foreign affairs of the host country and ambassadors of the other five.

SECRETARIATS

A permanent secretariat was established in Jakarta, Indonesia, in 1976 to form a central co-ordinating body. The post of Secretary-General rotates among the member countries in alphabetical order every three years. In each member country day-to-day work is co-ordinated by an ASEAN national secretariat.

Secretary-General: RODERICK YONG YIN FATT (Brunei).

COMMITTEES

Economic co-operation is directed by ministers of economic affairs through five Committees, on Food, Agriculture and Forestry; Finance and Banking; Industry, Minerals and Energy; Transport and Communications; and Trade and Tourism.

Other ministerial meetings are serviced by the following three Committees: Culture and Information; Science and Technology; and Social Development.

These committees are serviced by a network of subsidiary technical bodies comprising sub-committees, expert groups, ad-hoc working groups, working parties, etc.

To support the conduct of relations with other countries and international organizations, ASEAN committees (composed of heads of diplomatic missions) have been established in 10 foreign capitals: those of Australia, Belgium, Canada, France, the Federal Republic of Germany, Japan, New Zealand, Switzerland, the United Kingdom and the USA.

Activities

ASEAN was established in 1967 with the signing of the ASEAN Declaration, otherwise known as the Bangkok Declaration, by the ministers of foreign affairs of Indonesia, Malaysia, the Philippines, Singapore and Thailand. Brunei joined the organization in January 1984, shortly after attaining independence. The ASEAN Declaration sets out the objectives of the organization as follows:

(i) To accelerate economic growth, social progress and cultural development in the region through joint endeavours in the spirit of equality and partnership in order to strengthen the foundation for a prosperous and peaceful community of South East Asian nations;

(ii) To promote regional peace and stability through abiding respect for justice and the rule of law in the relationship among countries of the region and adherence to the principles of the United Nations Charter;

(iii) To promote active collaboration and mutual assistance on matters of common interest in the economic, social, cultural, technical, scientific and administrative fields;

(iv) To provide assistance to each other in the form of training and research facilities in the educational, professional, technical and administrative spheres;

(v) To collaborate more effectively for the greater utilization of their agriculture and industries, the expansion of their trade, including the study of the problems of international commodity trade, the improvement of their transportation and communication facilities and the raising of the living standards of their people;

(vi) To promote South-East Asian studies; and

(vii) To maintain close and beneficial co-operation with existing international and regional organizations with similar aims and purposes, and explore all avenues for even closer co-operation among themselves.

ASEAN's first summit meeting was held at Denpasar, Bali, Indonesia, in February 1976. Two major documents were signed:

Treaty of Amity and Co-operation, laying down principles of mutual respect for the independence and sovereignty of all nations; non-interference in the internal affairs of one another; settlement of disputes by peaceful means; and effective co-operation among the five countries. (Amended in 1987 by a Protocol which would allow other states within and outside the region to accede to the Treaty.)

Declaration of Concord, giving guidelines for action in economic, social and cultural relations, including: the maintenance of political stability; the establishment of a 'Zone of Peace, Freedom and Stability'; the promotion of social justice and improvement of living standards; mutual assistance in the event of natural disasters; and co-operation in economic development.

EXTERNAL RELATIONS

The European Community: In March 1980 a co-operation agreement was signed between ASEAN and the EEC, following a joint ministerial conference. The agreement, which entered into force on 1 October, provided for the strengthening of existing trade links and increased co-operation in the scientific and agricultural spheres. A joint co-operation committee met in Manila in November (and annually thereafter); it drew up a programme of scientific and technological co-operation, approved measures to promote contacts between industrialists from the two regions, and agreed on the financing of ASEAN regional projects by the Community. An ASEAN-EEC Business Council was launched in December 1983 to provide a forum for businessmen from the two regions and to identify joint projects. The first meeting of ministers of economic affairs from ASEAN and EEC member countries took place in October 1985, and agreed to encourage European investment in the ASEAN region (then estimated at 13% of total foreign investment, compared with 28% for Japanese investment and 17% for the USA). In 1986 a joint group of experts on trade was set up, to examine problems of access to ASEAN markets and similar matters, and in 1987 joint investment committees were established in all the ASEAN capital cities. In 1988 it was agreed that a joint management centre should be established in Brunei.

Japan: The ASEAN-Japan Forum was established in 1977 to discuss matters of mutual concern in trade, investment, technology transfer and development assistance. In 1981 the Japanese Government approved yen-based credits worth $870m. for Indonesia, Malaysia, the Philippines and Thailand. Further support was offered in 1983 in the form of increased financial aid for Indonesia, Malaysia and Thailand and a scheme for renovating industrial installations originally built with Japanese assistance. Discussions were also held concerning Japanese restrictions on imports of ASEAN agricultural produce: Thailand and the Philippines in particular expressed concern over their trade deficit with Japan. Tariff cuts on certain ASEAN exports were made by Japan in 1985, but ASEAN members continued to criticize Japan's attitude and called for Japan to import more manufactured products rather than raw materials. In 1987 Japan established an 'ASEAN Fund' of about $2,000m. for assistance to ASEAN members, particularly in industrial development.

Other countries: ASEAN holds regular 'Dialogues' on trade and other matters with a number of countries, and receives assistance for various development projects. Under the ASEAN-Australia Economic Co-operation Programme, Australia gives financial support for ASEAN activities, including (in 1987) training in water quality management, prevention of drug abuse, and development education. A joint Business Council was set up in 1980. New Zealand has given technical and financial assistance in forestry development, dairy technology, veterinary management and legal aid training. The USA gives assistance for the development of small and medium-sized businesses and other projects, and supports a Center for Technology Exchange. ASEAN-Canada co-operation projects include fisheries technology, a joint programme to reduce post-harvest crop losses, and a forest seed centre.

Indo-China: The question of relations with the new communist governments in Indo-China was prominent at the Bali summit in February 1976. The documents signed at the summit made clear that ASEAN countries wished to form a zone of peace, freedom and neutrality, a concept adopted by ASEAN in 1971, and would respect the independence and sovereignty of all nations. ASEAN was to be an economic and diplomatic forum, with no question of a military alliance. Diplomatic relations with the communist governments were established in 1976. In 1978 the hostilities between Viet-Nam, Kampuchea and the People's Republic of China caused both Viet-Nam and China to seek closer ties with ASEAN and to negotiate with ASEAN as a group, not in bilateral terms. Fears of Viet-Nam's military ambitions, stirred by the invasion of Kampuchea in December 1978, and the severe strain placed on the ASEAN countries by the exodus of refugees from Viet-Nam, however, caused ASEAN to reassess its relations with Viet-Nam, which it accused of trying to destabilize South-East Asia, and to seek new ways of establishing peace. At the 12th meeting of ministers of foreign affairs in June 1979 grave concern was expressed over the thousands of displaced persons from Indo-China, and the delegates deplored the fact that Viet-Nam had not taken effective measures to stop the exodus. The ASEAN Foreign Ministers also reiterated their support for the right of the Kampuchean people to self-determination. In July 1981 the United Nations held a conference on Kampuchea, sponsored by ASEAN: the ASEAN countries proposed a coalition of the three main factions in Kampuchea, the withdrawal of Vietnamese troops, and elections supervised by the UN (see chapter on Viet-Nam). ASEAN made it clear that it would not, as a group, supply arms to any faction.

In September 1983 ASEAN issued an 'Appeal for Kampuchean Independence', in which it called for phased withdrawals of Vietnamese troops, supervised by a peace-keeping force, and for safe areas to be established for Kampuchean refugee camps; these actions were seen as the first steps in a comprehensive political settlement. This appeal was rejected by Viet-Nam in October.

In February 1985 a meeting of ASEAN ministers of foreign affairs, repeating their previous demands for Vietnamese withdrawal from Kampuchea, also called for military aid from foreign countries to the anti-Vietnamese coalition in Kampuchea. In July ASEAN proposed 'proximity' talks to be held (through an intermediary) between Viet-Nam and the Kampuchean coalition, but Viet-Nam refused to take part. In July 1988 an 'informal' meeting was held at Bogor, Indonesia, between representatives of Viet-Nam, Laos, ASEAN and the Kampuchean factions, to discuss a possible political settlement in Kampuchea and further discussions were held in October. In July ASEAN officials also took part in discussions with the Vietnamese Government on the voluntary repatriation of Vietnamese refugees who had fled to ASEAN countries.

INDUSTRY

In 1976 ASEAN ministers agreed to set up five equity-sharing medium-sized industries; a 60% share of each was to be owned by the host country, and the remaining 40% by the other four members. The projects originally comprised the manufacture of diesel engines in Singapore, urea for fertilizers in Indonesia and Malaysia, superphosphates in the Philippines, and soda ash in Thailand. In 1978 the text of the Basic Agreement on ASEAN Industrial Projects was agreed. By 1982, however, only the urea projects in Indonesia and Malaysia were ready to be implemented. The Indonesian project had its ASEAN company incorporated in March 1979 and was inaugurated in January 1984, with an annual production capacity of 570,000 metric tons. The Malaysian project, with an annual production capacity of 495,000 tons of urea and 330,000 tons of ammonia, began operations in 1985. The Singapore diesel engine project was abandoned and an alternative scheme, the establishment of a hepatitis vaccine plant, was approved in 1984, but was also abandoned in 1987. The Thai soda ash project was also abandoned in 1985 owing to falling demand, and the Philippine superphosphates scheme proved not to be feasible and was abandoned in favour of a copper fabrication project.

In July 1980 ASEAN representatives agreed to set up their first joint private banking institution, the ASEAN Finance Corporation, to provide financing for industrial projects of benefit to the region. The Corporation had an initial capital of US $47m.

The ASEAN Industrial Complementation programme, begun in 1981, encourages member countries to produce complementary products in specific industrial sectors for preferential exchange among themselves, for example components to be used in the automobile industry. The establishment of ASEAN Industrial Joint Ventures was approved in 1983. This scheme, initiated by ASEAN chambers of commerce and industry, aims to set up projects with at least 51% participation (reduced to 40% in 1987) by private sector companies from two or more ASEAN member states; the resultant products would receive preferential treatment (tariff reductions of 75%, increased to 90% in 1987) from the participating countries, and, after four years, preferential treatment from other member states. By August 1988 15 joint projects had been approved, including the manufacture of vehicle components and security paper (for banknotes), production of potash, feldspar and quartz, and meat processing. The ASEAN Finance Corporation (see above) plays an important part in evaluating and financing such projects.

TRADE

A Basic Agreement on the Establishment of ASEAN Preferential Trade Arrangements was concluded in 1977. This was not intended to lead directly to the formation of a free trade zone. The Philippines, Thailand and Singapore have been in favour of trade liberalization, and early in 1977 they concluded bilateral agreements for 10% tariff cuts on a wide range of items traded between themselves. Indonesia, on the other hand, has been opposed to trade liberalization, taking the view that its own economy is of a type that would be bound to suffer under free trade. The ASEAN agreement therefore provided for negotiations to lead to the introduction of preferences product by product. In July 1980 it was decided that all imports with trade values of less than US $50,000 (as recorded in the trade statistics for 1978) should have the existing tariff reduced by 20%, bringing the number of items under the preferential trading arrangements to over 6,000. A system of 'across-the-board' tariff cuts of 20%–25% was adopted in 1982 to replace the 'product-by-product' approach. An import value ceiling of US $1m. for these cuts, imposed in January, was raised to $2.5m. in May and to $10m. in November. Tariff cuts of 50% were approved in November for certain non-food products. In February 1985 the 'across-the-board' tariff cut was raised to 25% (instead of 20%–25% as previously). Although by mid-1987 almost 19,000 items were included on the list of products granted preferential import tariff rates, most of these items were insignificant in regional trade. Because individual countries are permitted to exclude any 'sensitive' products from preferential import tariffs, the system only covered about 5% of trade between the members. In December 1987 the meeting of ASEAN heads of government resolved to reduce such exclusions to a maximum of 10% of the number of items traded and to a maximum of 50% of the value of trade, over the next five years (seven years for Indonesia and the Philippines).

FINANCE AND BANKING

In 1987 heads of government agreed to accelerate regional co-operation in this field, in order to support intra-ASEAN trade and investment; they adopted measures to increase the role of ASEAN currencies in regional trade, to assist negotiations on the avoidance of double taxation, and to improve the efficiency of tax and customs administrators. An ASEAN Reinsurance Corporation was to be established in 1988, with initial authorized capital of US $10m.

AGRICULTURE

The ASEAN Agricultural Development Planning Centre was set up in 1981 to conduct research and training and to draw up regional production plans.

An emergency grain reserve agreement was signed in 1979. During the year an emergency reserve of 50,000 tons of rice was established, available to any member country at three days' notice. Other areas of co-operation include: a Plant Quarantine Training Institute; an Agricultural Development Planning Centre; a Forest Tree Seed Centre; and a post-harvest programme for conserving grain. An ASEAN centre for training and research in poultry diseases was opened in 1988.

In October 1983 a ministerial agreement on fisheries co-operation was concluded, providing for the joint management of fish resources, the sharing of technology, and co-operation in marketing. An agreement on the co-ordination and development of aquaculture was signed in 1987.

The first ASEAN Forestry Congress was held in October 1983 to discuss the state of the regional timber industry and the problems of forest depletion. In January 1985 it was announced that an ASEAN Institute for Forest Management was to be set up in Malaysia, with assistance from Canada.

ENERGY

In 1983 a ministerial meeting on energy co-operation resulted in the formation of a Committee on Energy Co-operation, the commissioning of a study on coal power development, a scheme for petroleum sharing, and 10 co-operative projects. In 1986 member states signed an agreement on regional sharing of petroleum supplies in the event of an emergency.

TRANSPORT AND COMMUNICATIONS

Joint transport projects being undertaken in 1988 included the Pan Borneo Highway (linking Brunei with Indonesia and Malaysia), and improvement of roads and ferry links. An agreement on the mutual recognition of driving licences came into effect in 1988. Four centres for training in civil aviation were in operation in 1988, and two more were to be opened in 1989. In 1987 heads of government agreed to promote shipping links among member states and to investigate the feasibility of joint facilities for shipping companies.

JOINT RESEARCH AND TECHNOLOGY

The ASEAN Committee on Science and Technology has co-ordinated the Protein Project, investigating low-cost alternative sources of protein; research in food technology and the management of food waste materials; completion of a Climatic Atlas and Regional Compendium of Climatic Statistics; a nature conservation scheme; and non-conventional energy research. The ASEAN–US Center for Technology Exchange (based in New York, with a regional office in Kuala Lumpur, Malaysia) was opened in November 1984. The first ASEAN Science and Technology Week was held in 1986, and the second was to be held in January 1989. In 1987 heads of government adopted a programme of action for regional co-operation in biotechnology, materials science, microelectronics and new sources of energy; the programme was also to include the establishment of regional research networks. In 1987 the principle of 'sustainable development' was adopted by heads of government, and an environment programme for 1988–92 was also adopted.

EDUCATION

Under the ASEAN Development Education Programme five projects (financed by Australia) have been set up: Special Education; Education Management Information System; Teacher Education Reform; Work-oriented Education; Test Development. A National Agency of Development Education has been set up in each country.

SOCIAL DEVELOPMENT

Activities include a Population Programme to co-ordinate demographic research; co-operation against drug abuse; mutual assistance in natural disasters; collaboration in health and nutrition programmes; technical co-operation in the production of pharmaceuticals; a youth programme; and a women's programme. A ministerial-level conference on drug abuse and illicit trafficking was held in June 1987.

TOURISM

An ASEAN Tourism Forum is held annually to assist in co-ordinating the region's tourism industry. In 1986 ASEAN ministers of foreign affairs approved the establishment of a Tourism Promotion Centre, to be situated in Kuala Lumpur, Malaysia. In 1987 it was decided that 1992 should be designated 'Visit ASEAN year'.

CULTURE

Joint cultural activities being undertaken in 1988 included: preparation of an ASEAN literary anthology; archaeological excavations; studies of children's rhymes and chants, and of traditional games and sports; and exchanges of librarians. In 1987 an ASEAN Performing Arts Festival and an ASEAN Song Festival were held in Brunei and Singapore respectively, and a Theatre Festival was held in the Philippines in 1988. ASEAN finances seminars for journalists and news agencies, and operates a News Exchange.

PUBLICATIONS

Annual Report of the ASEAN Standing Committee.

ASEAN Newsletter (every 2 months).

ASEAN Journal on Science and Technology for Development (2 a year).

Information Series and *Documents Series*.

BANK FOR INTERNATIONAL SETTLEMENTS—BIS

Address: Centralbahnplatz 2, 4002 Basel, Switzerland.
Telephone: (061) 208111.
Telex: 962487.

The Bank for International Settlements was founded pursuant to the Hague Agreements of 1930 to promote co-operation among national central banks and to provide additional facilities for international financial operations.

Organization

(October 1988)

GENERAL MEETING

The General Meeting is held annually. The right of representation and of voting is exercised, in proportion to the number of shares subscribed in each country, by the central banks (or the financial institutions acting in their stead) of the following countries: Australia, Austria, Belgium, Bulgaria, Canada, Czechoslovakia, Denmark, Finland, France, the Federal Republic of Germany, Greece, Hungary, Iceland, Ireland, Italy, Japan, the Netherlands, Norway, Poland, Portugal, Romania, South Africa, Spain, Sweden, Switzerland, Turkey, the United Kingdom, the USA and Yugoslavia (i.e. 24 European countries and five others).

BOARD OF DIRECTORS

The Board of Directors is responsible for the conduct of the Bank's operations at the highest level, and comprises the Governors in office of the central banks of Belgium, France, the Federal Republic of Germany, Italy and the United Kingdom, each of whom appoints another member of the same nationality. The USA does not occupy the two seats to which it is entitled. The statutes also provide for the election to the Board of not more than nine Governors of other member central banks: those of the Netherlands, Sweden and Switzerland are also members of the Board.

Chairman of the Board and President of the Bank: Dr W. F. DUISENBERG (Netherlands).

Vice-Chairman: Lord RICHARDSON OF DUNTISBOURNE (United Kingdom).

CHIEF EXECUTIVE OFFICER

General Manager: Prof. Dr ALEXANDRE LAMFALUSSY (Belgium).
The Bank has a staff of about 330 employees.

Activities

The BIS is a financial institution whose special role is to promote the co-operation of central banks, and to fulfil the function of a 'central banks' bank'. Although it has the legal form of a company limited by shares, it is an international organization governed by international law, and enjoys special privileges and immunities in keeping with its role (a Headquarters Agreement was concluded with Switzerland in 1987). The participating central banks were originally given the option of subscribing to the shares themselves or arranging for their subscription in their own countries: thus the BIS also has some private shareholders, but they have no right of participation in the General Meeting and 85% of the total share capital is in the hands of central banks.

FINANCE

The authorized capital of the Bank is 1,500m. gold francs, divided into 600,000 shares of 2,500 gold francs each.

Statement of Account*
(In gold francs; units of 0.29032258 . . . gram of fine gold—Art. 4 of the Statutes; 30 June 1988)

Assets		%
Gold	4,964,636,598	12.9
Cash on hand and on sight a/c with banks	17,213,896	0.1
Treasury bills	2,132,545,609	5.6
Time deposits and advances	27,375,584,919	71.3
Securities at term	3,856,404,854	10.1
Miscellaneous	13,519,239	0.0
Total	**38,359,905,115**	**100.0**

Liabilities		%
Authorized cap.: 1,500,000,000		
Issued cap.: 1,182,812,500		
viz. 473,125 shares of which 25% paid up	295,703,125	0.8
Reserves	1,039,483,397	2.7
Deposits (gold)	4,472,605,801	11.6
Deposits (currencies)	31,553,290,566	82.3
Staff pension scheme	107,935,439	0.3
Miscellaneous	859,949,735	2.2
Dividend payable on 1 July 1988	30,937,052	0.1
Total	**38,359,905,115**	**100.0**

* Assets and liabilities in US dollars are converted at US $208 per fine ounce of gold (equivalent to 1 gold franc = US $1.94149 . . .) and all other items in currencies on the basis of market rates against the US dollar.

BANKING OPERATIONS

The BIS assists central banks in managing and investing their monetary reserves: in 1988 about 80 central banks from all over the world had deposits with the BIS, which managed more than 10% of world foreign exchange reserves.

The BIS uses the funds deposited with it partly for lending to central banks. Its credit transactions may take the form of swaps against gold; covered credits secured by means of a pledge of gold or marketable short-term securities; credits against gold or currency deposits of the same amount and for the same duration held with the BIS; unsecured credits in the form of advances or deposits; or standby credits, which in individual instances are backed by guarantees given by member central banks. In addition, the Bank undertakes operations in foreign exchange and in gold, both with central banks and with the markets.

In late 1982, faced with the increasingly critical debt situation of some Latin American countries and the resultant threat to the viability of the international financial system, the BIS granted comparatively large-scale loans to central banks that did not number among its shareholders: the central banks of Argentina, Brazil and Mexico were granted bridging loans pending the disbursement of balance-of-payments credits extended by the IMF. These facilities amounted to almost US $3,000m., all of which had been repaid by the end of 1983. The Bank subsequently made similar loans, but with decreasing frequency. During 1986 financial assistance was arranged for the Mexican central bank (a facility of $1,600m., of which the BIS contributed $400m.) and the Nigerian central bank (a facility of $250m., of which the BIS contributed $176m.). In March 1987 a bridging facility was arranged for the central bank of Argentina (amounting to $500m., of which the BIS contributed $275m.).

Between 1981 and 1984 the BIS provided a facility of SDR 675m. to the IMF to enable the latter to anticipate the availability of cash resulting from the eighth review of IMF quotas. In April 1984 the BIS concluded an agreement with the IMF to provide a credit of SDR 2,505m. in order to cover the 'commitment gap' in connection with the policy of enlarged access to the IMF.

The BIS also engages in traditional types of investment: funds not required for lending to central banks are placed in the market as deposits with commercial banks and purchases of short-term negotiable paper, including Treasury bills. Such operations constitute a major part of the Bank's business.

Because the central banks' monetary reserves must be available at short notice, they can only be placed with the BIS at short term, for fixed periods and with clearly defined repayment terms. The BIS has to match its assets to the maturity structure and nature of its commitments, and must therefore conduct its business with special regard to maintaining a high degree of liquidity.

The Bank's operations must be in conformity with the monetary policy of the central banks of the countries concerned. It is not permitted to make advances to governments or to open current accounts in their name. Real estate transactions are also excluded.

INTERNATIONAL MONETARY CO-OPERATION

Governors of central banks meet for regular discussions at the BIS to co-ordinate international monetary policy and ensure orderly conditions on the international financial markets. There is close co-operation with the IMF and, since its membership includes central banks of eastern European countries, the BIS also provides a forum for contacts between East and West.

The BIS provides the secretariat for the Committee of Governors of the EEC Central Banks and for the Board of Governors of the European Monetary Co-operation Fund.

A Euro-currency Standing Committee was set up at the BIS in 1971 to provide the central bank Governors of the 'Group of Ten' industrialized countries (see p. 73) and Switzerland with information concerning the monetary policy aspects of the Euro-currency markets. Since 1982 it has provided a regular critical survey of the entire international credit system.

In 1974 the Governors of central banks of the Group of Ten and Switzerland set up the Committee on Banking Regulations and Supervisory Practices (whose secretariat is provided by the BIS) to co-ordinate banking supervision at the international level. The Committee pools information on banking supervisory regulations and surveillance systems, including the supervision of banks' foreign currency business, identifies possible danger areas and proposes measures to safeguard the banks' solvency and liquidity.

The Bank also organizes and provides the secretariat for periodic meetings of experts, such as the Group of Computer Experts, the Group of Experts on Payment Systems and the Group of Experts on Monetary and Economic Data Bank Questions, which aims to develop a data bank service for the central banks of the Group of Ten countries and the BIS.

RESEARCH

The Bank's Monetary and Economic Department conducts research, particularly into monetary questions; collects and publishes data on international banking developments; and organizes a data bank for central banks. The BIS Annual Report provides an independent analysis of monetary and economic developments. Statistics on international banking and on external indebtedness are also published regularly.

AGENCY AND TRUSTEE FUNCTIONS

The BIS acts as an agent for the European Monetary Co-operation Fund, conducting operations in connection with the working of the European Monetary System (EMS) and with borrowing and lending by the European Community. In 1986 the Bank assumed the functions of agent in a private international clearing and settlement system for bank deposits denominated in European Currency Units (ECUs). The Bank also acts as trustee for certain international governmental loans.

PUBLICATIONS

Annual Report.

Quarterly press release on international banking developments; half-yearly reports (jointly with the OECD) on external indebtedness.

CARIBBEAN COMMUNITY AND COMMON MARKET—CARICOM

Address: Bank of Guyana Building, POB 10827, Georgetown, Guyana.
Telephone: 02-69281.
Telex: 2263.

CARICOM was formed by the Treaty of Chaguaramas in 1973 as a movement towards unity in the Caribbean; it replaced the Caribbean Free Trade Association (CARIFTA), founded in 1965.

MEMBERS

Antigua and Barbuda
Bahamas
Barbados
Belize
Dominica
Grenada
Guyana
Jamaica
Montserrat
Saint Christopher and Nevis
Saint Lucia
Saint Vincent and the Grenadines
Trinidad and Tobago

OBSERVERS

Dominican Republic
Haiti
Suriname

Organization
(October 1988)

HEADS OF GOVERNMENT CONFERENCE

The Conference is the final authority of the Community and determines policy. It is responsible for the conclusion of treaties on behalf of the Community and for entering into relationships between the Community and international organizations and states. The Conference is also responsible for making the financial arrangements to meet the expenses of the Community, but has delegated this function to the Common Market Council. Decisions of the Conference are generally taken unanimously. Heads of Government met in November 1982 (the first meeting for seven years) and thereafter annually.

COMMON MARKET COUNCIL

The principal organ of the Common Market, the Council consists of a Minister of Government designated by each member state. It is responsible for the development and smooth running of the Common Market, and for the settlement of any problems arising out of its functioning. However, the Conference may issue directives to the Council. The Council generally takes decisions unanimously.

INSTITUTIONS

There are several institutions of the Caribbean Community responsible for formulating policies and supervising co-operation in services such as education, health, labour matters and foreign policy. Each member state is represented on each institution by a Minister of Government. These institutions are the Conference of Ministers Responsible for Health and the Standing Committees of Ministers Responsible (respectively) for Education; Labour; Foreign Affairs; Finance; Agriculture; Industry; Transport; Energy, Mines and Natural Resources; and Science and Technology.

The Dominican Republic, Haiti and Suriname enjoy observer status in the Community's institutions in the areas of agriculture, education, health and labour. Further co-operation with these countries is pursued through Joint Technical Groups.

SECRETARIAT

The Secretariat is organized into five divisions: Trade and Agriculture; Economics and Industry; Functional Co-operation; General Services and Administration; Office of the Legal Counsel. At the end of 1986 there were 153 permanent staff and 27 project staff. The functions of the Secretariat are: to service meetings of the Community and of its Institutions or Committees; to take appropriate follow-up action on decisions made at such meetings; to carry out studies on questions of economic and functional co-operation relating to the region as a whole; to provide services to member states at their request in respect of matters relating to the achievement of the objectives of the Community.

Secretary-General: RODERICK RAINFORD (Jamaica).
Deputy Secretary-General: LOUIS A. WILTSHIRE (Trinidad and Tobago).

Activities

CO-ORDINATION OF FOREIGN POLICY

The Community's Standing Committee of ministers responsible for foreign affairs meets at least twice a year. Activities for the co-ordination of foreign policy include: strengthening of member states' position in international organizations; joint diplomatic action on issues of particular interest to the Caribbean; and the evaluation of the Community's relations with third countries and organizations, together with joint co-operation arrangements.

ECONOMIC CO-OPERATION

The Caribbean Community's main field of activity is economic integration, by means of a Caribbean Common Market which replaced the former Caribbean Free Trade Association (CARIFTA). The Secretariat and the Caribbean Development Bank carry out research on the best means of facing economic difficulties, and meetings of the Chief Executives of commercial banks and of central bank officials are also held with the aim of strengthening regional co-operation.

The economic difficulties of member states have hindered the development of intra-regional trade, which accounted for 10.2% of imports in 1985, falling to 7.5% in 1986, when their value was less than half the 1981 level. The value of Community trade fell from US $555m. in 1982 to about $290m. in 1986. Among the reasons for this decline were currency fluctuations within the region, import-licensing measures taken by individual members (notably Trinidad and Tobago), and the collapse in 1983 of the Community's trade payments facility, the Multilateral Clearing Facility (MCF) after it had exceeded its credit limit. Another problem is the difficulty of applying the CARICOM Rules of Origin, which attempt to verify that imported goods genuinely come from within the community; the garment industry is particularly affected by illegal imports. At the annual Conference held in June/July 1987, the heads of government agreed to dismantle all obstacles to trade within CARICOM by October 1988. This was implemented as planned, but a three-year period was permitted during which certain products from the OECS states would be allowed protection. The value of trade within the Community increased to $317m. in 1987, and was expected to increase further as a result of the removal of restrictions.

In July 1984 heads of government agreed to establish a common external tariff on certain products, such as steel, cement and fertilizers. They also issued the 'Nassau Understanding' calling for structural adjustment in the economies of the region, including measures to expand production and reduce imports. The revised target date for the implementation of the common external tariff was January 1989. In July 1986 the Conference agreed to establish a trade credit facility to replace the defunct MCF, in the form of a Caribbean Export Bank, based in Barbados, which was to begin operations in early 1988, with initial equity of US $17m.; it was envisaged that the Bank would provide pre-shipment financing for a maximum of two years, and post-shipment financing for up to five years, covering most of the region's exports, except for well-established ones such as sugar, bananas and bauxite. However, the beginning of operations was delayed owing to difficulty in attracting finance from external donors, and in July 1988 it was announced that the establishment of the bank had been postponed for the time being. Instead, it was proposed by the CARICOM Conference that an export credit facility should be established within the Caribbean Development Bank.

INDUSTRY AND ENERGY

The CARICOM industrial programme aims to promote the development of joint ventures in exporting industries (particularly the woodwork, furniture, ceramics and foundry industries) through an 'Enterprise Regime' (awaiting ratification by member governments in 1988). Work on an Investors' Guide for each member state was completed in 1984. CARICOM's Export Development

Council gives training and consultancy services to regional manufacturers. The first regional manufacturers' exhibition (CARIMEX) was held in 1985, and the second was to be held in 1988. A Regional Exporters' Directory was due to be completed in 1988. By 1987 the 'pilot phase' of the Caribbean Trade Information System (CARTIS) had compiled computer data-bases covering country and product profiles, trade statistics, trade opportunities, institutions and bibliographical information; 'on-line' links were to be established with national trade centres of CARICOM members, and a shipping data system was also to be set up.

The Secretariat is active in setting up a National Standards Bureau in each member country to harmonize technical standards, and supervises the metrication of weights and measures.

The CARICOM Alternative Energy Systems Project provides training, assesses energy needs and conducts energy audits.

TRANSPORT

The West Indies Shipping Corporation (WISCO) forms the official carrier in the region, and in 1983 a special CARICOM committee was formed to encourage co-operation between WISCO and the national shipping lines. A Caribbean Confederation of Shippers' Councils represents the interests of regional exporters and importers. A feasibility study on the establishment of a single air carrier service for the Eastern Caribbean was undertaken in 1987.

AGRICULTURE

In 1985 the New Marketing Arrangements for Primary Agricultural Products and Livestock were instituted, with the aim of increasing the flow of agricultural commodities within the region. The Regional Agricultural Sector Programme for 1987–91 gives targets for crop and livestock production, fisheries and forestry, and also covers marketing, research, training and agricultural finance. A computer-based Caribbean Agricultural Marketing Information System was being prepared in 1987. The Caribbean Agricultural Research and Development Institute (CARDI), founded in 1975, devises and transfers appropriate technology for small-scale farmers, and provides training and advisory services. The Caribbean Food Corporation, established in 1976, implements joint-venture projects with investors from the private and public sectors; at the end of August 1987 there were 26 projects under way.

HEALTH AND EDUCATION

In 1986 CARICOM and the Pan-American Health Organization launched 'Caribbean Co-operation in Health' with projects to be undertaken in six main areas: environmental protection, including the control of disease-bearing pests; development of human resources; chronic non-communicable diseases and accidents; strengthening health systems; food and nutrition; maternal and child health care, and population activities.

CARICOM educational programmes have included the improvement of reading in schools through assistance for teacher-training; and ensuring the availability of low-cost educational material throughout the region. A survey of the facilities for technical and vocational training was being undertaken in 1987.

ASSOCIATE INSTITUTIONS

Caribbean Development Bank: POB 408, Wildey, St Michael, Barbados; tel. (809) 42 61152; telex 2287; f. 1969 to stimulate regional economic growth through support for agriculture, industry, transport, tourism and education; cap. US $400m. (Dec. 1988). In 1987 loan approvals totalled $40m. and disbursements $53m. Mems: CARICOM states, plus Canada, Colombia, the Federal Republic of Germany, Italy, Mexico, Venezuela, the United Kingdom, Anguilla, the British Virgin Islands, the Cayman Islands, and the Turks and Caicos Islands. Pres. NEVILLE NICHOLLS.

Organisation of Eastern Caribbean States—OECS: POB 179, The Morne, Castries, Saint Lucia; tel. 22537; Economic Affairs Secretariat: POB 822, St John's, Antigua; f. 1981 by the seven states which formerly belonged to the West Indies Associated States (f. 1966). Principal institutions are: the Authority of Heads of Government (the supreme policy-making body), the Foreign Affairs Committee, the Defence and Security Committee, and the Economic Affairs Committee. A treaty forming the Eastern Caribbean Central Bank was signed by the seven members in July 1983. Mems: Antigua and Barbuda, Dominica, Grenada, Montserrat, Saint Christopher and Nevis, Saint Lucia and Saint Vincent and the Grenadines; assoc. mem.: the British Virgin Islands. Dir-Gen. Dr VAUGHAN A. LEWIS.

Other Associate Institutions of CARICOM, in accordance with its constitution, are: the Caribbean Examinations Council, the Caribbean Meteorological Institute, the Council of Legal Education, the West Indies Shipping Corporation, the University of Guyana and the University of the West Indies.

CENTRAL AMERICAN COMMON MARKET—CACM

(MERCADO COMÚN CENTROAMERICANO)

Address: 4a Avda 10-25, Zona 14, Apdo 1237, Guatemala City, Guatemala.
Telephone: 682151.
Telex: 5676.

CACM was established by the Organization of Central American States (ODECA, q.v.) under the General Treaty of Central American Economic Integration (Tratado General de Integración Económica Centroamericana) signed in Managua on 15 December 1960. It was ratified by all countries by September 1963.

MEMBERS

Costa Rica	El Salvador	Nicaragua
Guatemala	Honduras	

Organization

(October 1988)

MINISTERIAL MEETINGS

The organization's policy is formulated by regular meetings of Ministers and Vice-Ministers of Central American Integration; meetings of other ministers, and of Presidents of Central Banks, also play an important part.

PERMANENT SECRETARIAT

Secretaría Permanente del Tratado General de Integración Económica Centroamericana—SIECA: supervises the correct implementation of the legal instruments of economic integration, carries out relevant studies at the request of the Common Market authorities, and arranges the meetings of the main bodies. There are departments of: industry; agriculture; taxes and tariffs; physical integration; commercial policy; statistics; economic and social programmes; finance and administration; and science and technology.
Secretary-General: Marco Antonio Villamar Contreras.

Activities

The General Treaty envisaged the eventual liberalization of intra-regional trade and the establishment of a free-trade area and a customs union. Economic integration in the region, however, has been hampered by ideological differences between governments, difficulties in internal supply, protectionist measures by overseas markets, external and intra-regional debts, adverse rates of exchange and high interest rates.

By 1969, 95% of customs items had been awarded free-trade status; the remaining 5% consisted of goods covered by international agreements and other special arrangements. In 1970, however, following a dispute with El Salvador, Honduras reintroduced duties on imports from other CACM countries; trade between El Salvador and Honduras was not resumed until 1982, and Honduras' trade with the other members continued to be governed by bilateral agreements. Regular meetings of senior customs officials aim to increase co-operation, to develop a uniform terminology, and to recommend revisions of customs legislation. CACM member-countries also aim to pursue a common policy in respect of international trade agreements on commodities, raw materials and staples. SIECA participates in meetings with other regional organizations (such as SELA and ECLAC, q.v.) and represents the region at meetings of international organizations, such as UNCTAD.

Little headway has been made in industrial integration, mainly because of the continuing heavy external dependence of the region's economies. Under the Convention for Fiscal Incentives for Industrial Development, which came into operation in 1969, a wide range of tax benefits are applied to various categories of industries in the region, to encourage productivity. SIECA carries out studies on the industrial sector, compiles statistics, and provides information to member governments. It also analyses energy consumption in the region and gives assistance to governments in drawing up energy plans, aiming to reduce dependence on imported petroleum.

A co-ordinating commission supervises the marketing of four basic crops (maize, rice, beans and sorghum), recording and forecasting production figures and recommending minimum guarantee prices. Information on other crops is also compiled. A permanent commission for agricultural research and extension services monitors and co-ordinates regional projects in this field.

SIECA gives technical assistance to governments in improving their transport systems. In March 1983 regional Ministers of Transport agreed to establish in each country, in collaboration with existing bodies, a mechanism for encouraging regional co-operation in transport and related matters.

An agreement to establish a Central American Monetary Union was signed in 1964, with the eventual aim of establishing a common currency (the Central American peso, at par with the US dollar) and aligning foreign exchange and monetary policies. The Central American Monetary Council, comprising the Presidents of the member states' Central Banks, meets regularly to consider monetary policy and financial affairs. A Fund for Monetary Stabilization, founded in 1969 by the Central Banks of member states, provides short-term financial assistance to members facing temporary balance-of-payments difficulties.

In 1971 the Secretariat began work on a new integration model for the region and a draft treaty for a Central American Economic and Social Community was finalized in March 1976. It provided for the establishment of new top-level administrative organizations and a number of regional institutions, for a free-trade area, a customs union, and common industrial policies similar to those contained in the 1960 General Treaty. It also called for the harmonization of fiscal and financial policies, the establishment of a monetary union and the enactment of common programmes for social and economic development. Member states' legislatures, however, failed to ratify the new treaty, and CACM's achievements remained limited.

Trade within the region increased in value from US $33m. in 1960 to $1,129m. in 1980, but subsequently diminished every year, amounting to less than $411m. in 1986. This decline was due to a number of factors: low prices for the region's main export commodities, and heavy external debts, both resulting in a severe shortage of foreign exchange; and intra-regional trade 'freezes' provoked by trade debts amounting to $700m. at mid-1986 (Guatemala and Costa Rica being the chief creditors, and Nicaragua and El Salvador the main debtors). In January 1986 a new CACM tariff and customs agreement came into effect, imposing standard import duties for the whole region (aimed at discouraging the import of non-essential goods from outside the region), and a uniform tariff nomenclature. Honduras, however, continued to insist on bilateral tariff agreements with other member countries. In July CACM members agreed on a new payments mechanism for mutual trade, based on the Derecho de Importación Centroamericano (DICA—Central American Import Right), a voucher issued by central banks and used as currency to avoid using scarce US dollars. Trade between member countries increased to $484m. in 1987.

An agreement with the European Community was signed in November 1985, providing for economic co-operation and EEC aid for the region.

PUBLICATIONS

Carta Informativa (monthly).
Anuario Estadístico Centroamericano de Comercio Exterior.
Cuadernos de la SIECA (2 a year).

Institutions

FINANCE

Banco Centroamericano de Integración Económica—BCIE (Central American Bank for Economic Integration): Apdo Postal 772, Tegucigalpa, Honduras; tel. 222805; f. 1960 to promote the economic integration and balanced economic development of member countries; finances public and private development projects, particularly those related to industrialization and infrastructure. By June 1986 cumulative lending amounted to US $1,731m., mainly for roads, hydroelectricity projects, housing and telecommunications. Authorized capital was increased from $200m. to $600m. in January 1982. Exec. Pres. Rolando Ramírez Paniagua. Publs *Annual Report, Revista de la Integración.*

Consejo Monetario Centroamericano: Apdo 5438, San José, Costa

Rica; formed by the presidents of CACM central banks, to co-ordinate monetary policies. Sec.-Gen. OLIVIER CASTRO. Publs *Boletín Estadístico* (annualy), *Balanza de Pagos* (annually).

TRADE AND INDUSTRY

Federación de Cámaras de Comercio del Istmo Centroamericano (Federation of Central American Chambers of Commerce): Avda Cuba 33A-18, Apdo 74, Panamá 1, Panama; tel. 25-0833; telex 2434; f. 1961; for planning and co-ordinating industrial and commercial interchanges. Pres. ENRIQUE HEINEMAN.

Federación de Cámaras y Asociaciones Industriales Centroamericanas—FECAICA (Federation of Industrial Chambers and Associations in Central America): Edif. Cámara de Industria de Guatemala, Ruta 6 No. 9-21, Zona 4, POB 214, Guatemala City; established in 1959 by the Chambers of Commerce and Industry of the CACM countries to promote commerce and industry, principally by interchange of information.

Instituto Centroamericano de Administración de Empresas (Central American Institute for Business Administration): Apdo 2485, Managua, Nicaragua; tel. 58403; telex 2360; Apdo 960, 4050 Alajuela, Costa Rica; tel. 41 22 55; telex 7040; f. 1964; provides postgraduate programme in business administration; executive training programmes; management research and consulting; libraries of 52,000 vols. Dean Dr MELVYN COPEN.

Instituto Centroamericano de Investigación y Tecnología Industrial (Central American Research Institute for Industry): Apdo Postal 1552, Avda La Reforma 4-47, Zona 10, Guatemala City; tel. 310631; telex 5312; f. 1956 by the five Central American Republics, with assistance from the United Nations, to provide technical advisory services to regional governments and private enterprise. Acting Dir W. LUDWIG INGRAM (Nicaragua).

PUBLIC ADMINISTRATION

Instituto Centroamericano de Administración Pública (Central American Institute of Public Administration): Apdo 10.025, San José, Costa Rica; tel. 223133; telex 2180; f. 1954 by the five Central American Republics and the United Nations, with later participation by Panama. The Institute aims to train the region's public servants, provide technical assistance and carry out research leading to reforms in public administration. Dir CARLOS CORDERO D' AUBUISSON.

EDUCATION AND HEALTH

Confederación Universitaria Centroamericana (Central American University Confederation): Apdo 37, Universidad de Costa Rica, San José, Costa Rica; tel. 252744; telex 3011; f. 1948 to guarantee academic, administrative and economic autonomy for universities and to encourage regional integration of higher education; Council of 14 mems. Mems.: seven universities, in Costa Rica (two), El Salvador, Guatemala, Honduras, Nicaragua and Panama. Sec.-Gen. Dr RODRIGO FERNÁNDEZ (Costa Rica). Publs *Estudios Sociales Centroamericanas* (quarterly), *Estadísticas Universitarias* (2 a year), *Cuadernos de Investigación* (monthly), *Carta Informativa de la Secretaría General* (monthly).

Instituto de Nutrición de Centro América y Panamá—INCAP (Institute of Nutrition of Central America and Panama): Apdo 1188, Carretera Roosevelt, Zona 11, 01901 Guatemala City, Guatemala; tel. 723762; telex 5696; f. 1949 to promote the development of nutritional sciences and their application and to strengthen the technical capacity of member countries to solve problems of food and nutrition; provides training and technical assistance for nutrition education and planning; conducts research. Divisions: agricultural and food sciences; nutrition and health; food and nutrition planning. Maintains library (including about 600 periodicals). Administered by the Pan American Health Organization (PAHO) and the World Health Organization. Mems: CACM mems and Panama. Dir Dr LUIS OCTAVIO ANGEL. Publs *Boletín PROPAG* (quarterly), *Boletín ASI* (quarterly), annual report, compilations.

TRANSPORT AND COMMUNICATIONS

Comisión Técnica de las Telecomunicaciones de Centroamerica—COMTELCA (Technical Commission for Telecommunications in Central America): Apdo 1793, Tegucigalpa, Honduras; tel. 32-9527; telex 1235; f. 1966 to co-ordinate and improve the regional telecommunications network; Dir RAFAEL LEMUS.

Corporación Centroamericana de Servicios de Navegación Aérea—COCESNA (Central American Air Navigation Service Corporation): Apdo 660, Tegucigalpa, Honduras; tel. 331141; telex 1411; f. 1960; Gen. Man. FERNANDO A. CASTILLO R.

THE COLOMBO PLAN FOR CO-OPERATIVE ECONOMIC AND SOCIAL DEVELOPMENT IN ASIA AND THE PACIFIC

Address: 12 Melbourne Ave, POB 596, Colombo 4, Sri Lanka.
Telephone: 581813.
Telex: 21537.

Founded by seven Commonwealth countries in 1950 (as the Colombo Plan for Co-operative Economic Development in South and South-East Asia), the Colombo Plan was subsequently joined by more countries in Asia and the Pacific as well as the USA and Japan. The purpose of the Plan is to make a collective international effort to encourage the economic and social development of member countries in the Asia and Pacific region.

MEMBERS

Afghanistan
Australia
Bangladesh
Bhutan
Burma
Canada
Fiji
India
Indonesia
Iran
Japan
Kampuchea
Korea, Republic
Laos
Malaysia
Maldives
Nepal
New Zealand
Pakistan
Papua New Guinea
Philippines
Singapore
Sri Lanka
Thailand
United Kingdom
USA

Organization
(October 1988)

CONSULTATIVE COMMITTEE
The Committee is the principal policy-making and deliberative body of the Colombo Plan, consisting of ministers representing member governments. It meets every two years in a member country. It reviews the progress of member countries, discusses how available resources can best be used for development, and exchanges views on specific development issues.

COLOMBO PLAN COUNCIL
The Council consists of the heads of member countries' diplomatic missions in Colombo, who meet several times a year to identify development issues of current interest for consideration by the Consultative Committee, and gives guidance for the functioning of the Colombo Plan Bureau and the Drug Advisory Programme.

COLOMBO PLAN BUREAU
The only permanent institution of the Plan, with its headquarters in Colombo, the Bureau services meetings of the Council, carries out research, arranges seminars and workshops and maintains a record of aid flows among member countries.
Director: GILBERT SHEINBAUM (USA).

Activities

The basic principles and policies governing assistance under the Plan are agreed upon by ministers at the meetings of the Consultative Committee. Specific aid programmes are then negotiated bilaterally on a government-to-government basis, within the framework of the policies adopted. There is no centralized programming, nor a common fund to finance national development projects.

CAPITAL AID
Capital aid under the Plan takes the form of grants and concessional loans for national projects, mainly from six developed countries to the developing member countries of the Plan. It covers many aspects of social and economic development, including projects in agriculture, industry, communications, energy and education.

ASSISTANCE PROVIDED IN 1986

Donor country	US $ million
Australia	383.6
Canada	269.9
Japan	2,695.6
New Zealand	8.8
United Kingdom	433.8
USA	1,224.0
Total	**5,015.7**

TECHNICAL CO-OPERATION
Under the Technical Co-operation programme experts and volunteers are provided, training fellowships are awarded and equipment for training and research is supplied, to assist recipient countries in agriculture, fisheries, industry, planning, education, health, and many other aspects of economic and social development. Examples of projects being undertaken in 1986 included the following (the donor country is indicated in parentheses): equipment, specialist advisers and training for the modernization and expansion of the Animal Diseases Research Institute in Indonesia (Australia); research into the eradication of aflatoxins in poultry feeds and pest control to improve cotton yields in Pakistan (United Kingdom); 75 projects addressing long-term issues of population control, job creation and participation of women in development in Bangladesh (Canada); advisory services to the Royal Bhutan Polytechnic to improve its civil engineering course (Japan); introduction of sheep-farming for smallholders in the highlands of Papua New Guinea (New Zealand).

During 1986, 19,522 students and trainees received training, and 12,794 experts and volunteers were engaged under technical assistance programmes. The total value of technical co-operation disbursements in 1986 amounted to $746m.

The largest number of fellowship awards (9,699) during 1986 was provided by Japan. Among recipients, Indonesia was the chief beneficiary, receiving 3,486 awards; the other main recipients were India, Thailand, Malaysia, the Philippines and the Republic of Korea. Of the total of 10,306 experts financed in 1986, Japan provided 6,091 and the USA 2,589. Indonesia received the largest number of experts (2,094).

A major objective of the Colombo Plan is to foster economic and technical co-operation among developing member countries themselves. During 1986 developing member countries (principally India and the Republic of Korea) financed 107 experts, 1,067 students and 1,807 trainees. Their technical co-operation expenditure during the year amounted to $20.5m.

DRUG ADVISORY PROGRAMME
The programme was launched in 1973 to help develop co-operative schemes to eliminate the causes and ameliorate the effects of drug abuse in member states. Seminars are held in member countries to inform governments and the public and to help organize remedial measures. Assistance is given in training narcotics officials in all aspects of drug abuse prevention by means of exchanges, fellowships, study, training and observation. Member countries are helped in establishing narcotics control offices or boards, revising legislation on narcotics, improving law enforcement, treatment, rehabilitation and prevention education, and in improving public understanding of these matters by the use of mass media, workshops and seminars.

TRAINING COLLEGE
Colombo Plan Staff College for Technician Education: POB 7500, Airmail Distribution Center, MIA D3120, Philippines; tel. 673-1925; f. 1974 as a specialized institution of the Colombo Plan, funded by contributions from member governments; trains staff for the education of technicians, conducts conferences and research, and provides advisory services. Dir Dr ROBERT MCCAIG (Australia). Publs *Annual Report*, *Newsletter* (quarterly).

PUBLICATIONS

The Colombo Plan Newsletter (quarterly).

Proceedings and Conclusions of the Consultative Committee (every 2 years).

Annual Report of the Colombo Plan Council.

The Colombo Plan Brochure.

Development Perspectives: Country Issues Papers by Member Governments to the Consultative Committee (every 2 years).

THE COMMONWEALTH

Address: Marlborough House, Pall Mall, London, SW1Y 5HX, England.
Telephone: (01) 839-3411.
Telex: 27678.

The Commonwealth is a voluntary association of independent states, comprising about one-quarter of the world's population. It includes the United Kingdom and most of its former dependencies, and former dependencies of Australia and New Zealand (themselves Commonwealth countries).

The evolution of the Commonwealth began with the introduction of self-government in Canada in the 1840s; Australia, New Zealand and South Africa became independent before the first world war. At the Imperial Conference of 1926 the United Kingdom and the four Dominions, as they were then called, were described as 'autonomous communities within the British Empire, equal in status', and this change was enacted into law by the Statute of Westminster, in 1931.

The modern Commonwealth began with the entry of India and Pakistan in 1947, and of Sri Lanka (then Ceylon) in 1948. In 1950 India became a republic, and the Commonwealth Heads of Government then decided that allegiance to the same monarch need not be a condition of membership. This was a precedent for a number of other members (see Heads of State and Heads of Government, below).

MEMBERS*

Antigua and Barbuda	Mauritius
Australia	Nauru†
Bahamas	New Zealand
Bangladesh	Nigeria
Barbados	Papua New Guinea
Belize	Saint Christopher and Nevis
Botswana	Saint Lucia
Brunei	Saint Vincent and the Grenadines
Canada	Seychelles
Cyprus	Sierra Leone
Dominica	Singapore
The Gambia	Solomon Islands
Ghana	Sri Lanka
Grenada	Swaziland
Guyana	Tanzania
India	Tonga
Jamaica	Trinidad and Tobago
Kenya	Tuvalu†
Kiribati	Uganda
Lesotho	United Kingdom
Malawi	Vanuatu
Malaysia	Western Samoa
Maldives	Zambia
Malta	Zimbabwe

* Ireland, South Africa and Pakistan withdrew from the Commonwealth in 1949, 1961 and 1972 respectively. In October 1987 Fiji's membership was declared to have lapsed (following the proclamation of a republic there).
† Nauru and Tuvalu are special members of the Commonwealth; they have the right to participate in functional activities but are not represented at Meetings of Heads of Government.

Dependencies and Associated States

Australia:
  Australian Antarctic Territory
  Christmas Island
  Cocos (Keeling) Islands
  Coral Sea Islands Territory
  Heard and McDonald Islands
  Norfolk Island
New Zealand:
  Cook Islands
  Niue
  Ross Dependency
  Tokelau
United Kingdom:
  Anguilla
  Bermuda
  British Antarctic Territory
  British Indian Ocean Territory
  British Virgin Islands
  Cayman Islands
  Channel Islands
  Falkland Islands
  Gibraltar
  Hong Kong
  Isle of Man
  Montserrat
  Pitcairn Islands
  St Helena
    Ascension
    Tristan da Cunha
  South Georgia and South Sandwich Islands
  Turks and Caicos Islands

HEADS OF STATE AND HEADS OF GOVERNMENT

In November 1988, 22 member countries were monarchies and 26 were republics. All Commonwealth countries accept Queen Elizabeth II as the symbol of the free association of the independent member nations and as such the Head of the Commonwealth. Of the 26 republics, the offices of Head of State and Head of Government were combined in 19: Bangladesh, Botswana, Cyprus, The Gambia, Ghana, Guyana, Kenya, Kiribati, Malawi, Maldives, Nauru, Nigeria, Seychelles, Sierra Leone, Sri Lanka, Tanzania, Uganda, Zambia and Zimbabwe. The two offices were separated in the remaining seven: Dominica, India, Malta, Singapore, Trinidad and Tobago, Vanuatu and Western Samoa.

Of the monarchies, the Queen is Head of State of the United Kingdom and of 16 others, in each of which she is represented by a Governor-General: Antigua and Barbuda, Australia, the Bahamas, Barbados, Belize, Canada, Grenada, Jamaica, Mauritius, New Zealand, Papua New Guinea, Saint Christopher and Nevis, Saint Lucia, Saint Vincent and the Grenadines, Solomon Islands and Tuvalu. Brunei, Lesotho, Malaysia, Swaziland and Tonga are also monarchies, where the traditional monarch is Head of State.

The Governors-General are appointed by the Queen on the advice of the Prime Ministers of the country concerned. They are wholly independent of the Government of the United Kingdom.

HIGH COMMISSIONERS

Governments of member countries are represented in other Commonwealth countries by High Commissioners, who have a status equivalent to that of Ambassadors.

Organization
(October 1988)

The Commonwealth is not a federation: there is no central government nor are there any rigid contractual obligations such as bind members of the United Nations.

The Commonwealth has no written constitution but its members subscribe to the ideals of the Declaration of Commonwealth Principles (see below) unanimously approved by a meeting of Heads of Government in Singapore in 1971. Members also approved the 1977 statement on apartheid in sport (the Gleneagles Agreement); the 1979 Lusaka Declaration on Racism and Racial Prejudice; the 1981 Melbourne Declaration on relations between developed and developing countries; the 1983 New Delhi Statement on Economic Action; the 1983 Goa Declaration on International Security; the 1985 Nassau Declaration on World Order; the 1987 Vancouver Declaration on World Trade, and the Okanagan Statement and Programme of Action on Southern Africa (1987).

MEETINGS OF HEADS OF GOVERNMENT

Meetings are private and informal and operate not by voting but by consensus. The emphasis is on consultation and exchange of views for co-operation. A communiqué is issued at the end of every meeting. Meetings are held every two years in different capitals in the Commonwealth. The 1987 meeting was held in Vancouver, Canada, and the 1989 meeting was to be held in Kuala Lumpur, Malaysia.

OTHER CONSULTATIONS

Meetings at ministerial and official level are also held regularly. Since 1959 Finance Ministers have met in a Commonwealth country in the week prior to the annual meetings of the IMF and the World Bank. Education Ministers usually meet about every three years. Ministers of Health and of Employment and Labour hold annual meetings, and the Commonwealth Youth Affairs Council, at ministerial level, meets every two years.

Senior officials—Cabinet Secretaries, Permanent Secretaries to Heads of Government and others—meet regularly in the year between meetings of Heads of Government to provide continuity and to exchange views on various developments.

COMMONWEALTH SECRETARIAT

The Secretariat, established by Commonwealth Heads of Government in 1965, operates as an international organization at the service of all Commonwealth countries. It organizes consultations between governments and runs programmes of co-operation. Meetings of heads of government, ministers and senior officials decide these programmes and provide overall direction.

The Secretariat is headed by a Secretary-General (elected by Heads of Government), with two Deputy Secretaries-General and two Assistant Secretaries-General. One Deputy is responsible for political affairs (divisions of international affairs, legal affairs, information, and administration and conference services), the other for economic affairs (divisions of economic affairs, export market development, and food production and rural development). One Assistant Secretary-General is responsible for the Human Resource Development Group (education, training, management, medical, women's and youth programmes) and the science division, the other for the Commonwealth Fund for Technical Co-operation (CFTC).

Secretary-General: Sir SHRIDATH S. RAMPHAL (Guyana).
Deputy Secretary-General (Political): Chief EMEKA C. ANYAOKU (Nigeria).
Deputy Secretary-General (Economic): PETER UNWIN (UK) (from January 1989).
Assistant Secretaries-General: WILLIAM MONTGOMERY (Canada), MANMOHAN MALHOUTRA (India).
Director, Administration Division: Tunku ABDUL AZIZ (Malaysia).
Director, Information Division: PATSY ROBERTSON (Jamaica).

BUDGET

The Secretariat's budget for 1987/88 was £6,543,315, and the budget for 1988/89 was £6,792,610. Member governments meet the cost of the Secretariat through subscriptions on a scale related to income and population, similar to the scale for contributions to the United Nations.

Activities

INTERNATIONAL AFFAIRS

The most publicized achievement of the 1979 Lusaka meeting of Heads of Government was the nine-point plan to direct Zimbabwe-Rhodesia towards internationally recognized independence, formulated by a group of leaders—from Australia, Jamaica, Nigeria, Tanzania, the United Kingdom and Zambia, together with the Commonwealth Secretary-General—and endorsed at a special session of all heads of delegation. The leaders issued the Lusaka Declaration on Racism and Racial Prejudice as a formal expression of their abhorrence of all forms of racist policy. A proposal for a Commonwealth role in upholding human rights was welcomed in principle and was to be further studied.

At their 1981 meeting in Melbourne, the Heads of Government issued the Melbourne Declaration in which they asserted that the current 'gross inequality of wealth and opportunity' was a 'fundamental source of tension and instability in the world', and declared their common resolve 'to end the present impasse; to advance the dialogue between developing and developed countries; to infuse an increased sense of urgency and direction into the resolution of these common problems of mankind'. The meeting confirmed the Commonwealth's commitment to independence for Namibia, and condemned South Africa's attempts to destabilize neighbouring states.

In November 1983 the Heads of Government, meeting in New Delhi, issued the Goa Declaration on International Security 'in the context of heightened tensions and a continuing build-up of nuclear arsenals' threatening the future of civilization. The leaders called for 'a concerted effort . . . to restore constructive dialogue to the conduct of East-West relations', for the cessation of the nuclear arms race, and for funds released by disarmament to be used in world development. More specifically, the leaders expressed concern at the vulnerability of small states to external attack and interference in their affairs, and requested the Secretary-General to undertake a study of the special needs of such states. The Secretary-General subsequently established a Commonwealth Consultative Group for this purpose, to report to the 1985 meeting of Heads of Government. The New Delhi meeting also decided that the Commonwealth (in co-operation with the United Nations) should undertake to disseminate accurate information about South African apartheid.

In October 1985 Heads of Government, meeting at Nassau, Bahamas, issued the Nassau Declaration on World Order, reaffirming Commonwealth commitment to the United Nations, to international co-operation for development and to the eventual elimination of nuclear weapons. The same meeting issued the Commonwealth Accord on Southern Africa, calling on the South African authorities to dismantle apartheid and open dialogue with a view to establishing a representative government. The meeting also established a Commonwealth 'Eminent Persons Group'. It visited South Africa in February and March 1986 and attempted unsuccessfully to establish a dialogue between the South African Government and opposition leaders. In August the heads of government of seven Commonwealth countries (Australia, the Bahamas, Canada, India, the United Kingdom, Zambia and Zimbabwe) met to consider the Group's report, and (with the exception of the United Kingdom) agreed to adopt a series of measures to exert economic pressure on the South African Government, and to encourage other countries to adopt such measures. These included bans on the following: air links with South Africa; new investment or reinvestment of profits earned in South Africa; imports of agricultural produce from South Africa; government assistance to, investment in, and trade with, South Africa; government contracts with majority-owned South African companies; promotion of tourist visits to South Africa; new bank loans to South Africa; imports of uranium, coal, iron and steel from South Africa.

In October 1987 Heads of Government, meeting at Vancouver, Canada, issued the Okanagan Statement and Programme of Action on Southern Africa, to strengthen the Commonwealth effort to end apartheid and bring about political freedom in South Africa. They also established the Commonwealth Committee of Foreign Ministers on Southern Africa, comprising the ministers of foreign affairs of Australia, Canada, Guyana, India, Nigeria, Tanzania, Zambia and Zimbabwe. The Committee is to provide high-level impetus and guidance in furtherance of the objectives of the Statement. The Vancover meeting also issued the Vancouver Declaration on World Trade, condemning protectionism and reaffirming their commitment to work for a durable and just world trading system. They pledged to work to strengthen the General Agreement on Tariffs and Trade (GATT), and gave their support to the Uruguay Round of multilateral trade negotiations (begun in 1986).

International Affairs Division: assists consultation among member governments on international and Commonwealth matters of common interest. In association with host governments, it organizes the meetings of Heads of Government and senior officials. Since 1978 the Division has organized and serviced Commonwealth regional Heads of Government meetings for the Asia-Pacific region (CHOGRM): these meetings discuss regional political trends and establish programmes of co-operation in trade, energy, industry, agriculture and maritime issues. The Division services committees and special groups set up by Heads of Government dealing with political matters, such as the Commonwealth Committee on Southern Africa through which governments have worked to help Zimbabwe to independence and continue to do so for Namibia; and the Commonwealth Committee on Cyprus. It serviced the Commonwealth observer groups at the pre-independence elections in Zimbabwe and the 1980 elections in Uganda. The Secretariat has observer status at the United Nations, and manages an office in New York to enable small states, which would otherwise be unable to afford facilities there, to maintain a presence at the United Nations. The Division monitors political developments in the Commonwealth and international progress in such matters as disarmament, the concerns of small states, dismantling of apartheid and the Law of the Sea. It also undertakes research on matters of common interest to member governments, and reports back to them. The Division is involved in diplomatic training and consular co-operation. A Unit for the Promotion of Human Rights in the Commonwealth was established within the Division in 1985.

Director: MAX GAYLARD (Australia).

LAW

Legal Division: services the meetings of law ministers and attorneys-general. It runs a Commonwealth commercial crime service, administers training programmes for legislative draftsmen, and assists co-operation and exchange of information on law reform, taxation policy, extradition, the reciprocal enforcement of judgments, the Commonwealth Scheme for Mutual Assistance in Criminal Matters, the scheme for the Transfer of Convicted Offenders within the Commonwealth, and other legal matters. It liaises with the Commonwealth Magistrates' Association, the Commonwealth Legal Education Association, the Commonwealth Lawyers' Association, the Commonwealth Association of Legislative Counsel, and with other international organizations. It also provides in-house legal advice for the Secretariat, and helps to prepare the triennial Commonwealth Law Conference for the practising profession. The 1986 Conference, involving about 2,000 delegates, was held in Jamaica. The quarterly *Commonwealth Law Bulletin* reports on legal developments in and beyond the Commonwealth.

Director: JEREMY D. POPE (New Zealand).

INTERNATIONAL ORGANIZATIONS

The Commonwealth

ECONOMIC CO-OPERATION

Economic Affairs Division: forms the focus for Secretariat activities in the economic sphere. It organizes and services the regular meetings of Commonwealth ministers of finance, and of labour and employment, and assists in servicing the biennial meetings of Heads of Government. It engages in research and analysis on economic issues of interest to member governments; organizes seminars and conferences of government officials and experts; and publishes regular bulletins on commodities, international development policies, capital markets, regional co-operation and on basic statistics of small countries. The Division initiated a major programme of technical assistance to enable developing Commonwealth countries to participate in the Uruguay Round of multilateral trade negotiations (begun in 1986). The Division also services expert groups commissioned by governments. Such groups have reported on, among other things, protectionism; obstacles to the North-South negotiating process; reform of the international financial and trading system; the debt crisis; management of technological change; the special needs of small states; and youth unemployment. In early 1988 the Division was servicing two expert groups dealing with the implications of climatic change for development, and the impact of structural adjustment of national economies on women.

Director: Dr BISHNODAT PERSAUD (Barbados).

Export Market Development Division: assists governments to improve foreign exchange earnings through identification and exploration of export markets, using trade promotion events such as export business intensification programmes, buyer-seller meetings, integrated marketing programmes and contact promotion programmes. It gives advice on setting up export institutions and promoting exports, and organizes conferences and seminars. The Division is financed by the CFTC.

Director: ARVIND G. BARVE (Kenya).

Food Production and Rural Development Division: offers expert technical advice in food production and rural development. It derives its mandate from meetings of ministers of agriculture. Priority is given to policy advice and questions of planning and management, including agricultural diversification; food strategies; food security; provision of support services to small-scale farmers; technology transfer; development of livestock and fisheries; and conservation of natural resources to enable sustainable development. The division is financed by the CFTC.

Director: JOSHUA K. MUTHAMA (Kenya).

HUMAN RESOURCES

Human Resource Development Group (HRDG): set up in 1983, brings together six previously separate programmes (see below) whose primary purpose is the development of human resources in Commonwealth countries. The group encourages increased inter-programme collaboration and more multi-disciplinary activity, with greater emphasis on operational projects in the field. The group aims to assist member countries in a number of important areas of human resource development and the upgrading of professional skills.

Assistant Secretary-General, HRDG: MANMOHAN MALHOUTRA (India).

The **Education Programme** arranges specialist seminars and co-operative projects and commissions studies in areas identified by education ministers, whose three-yearly meetings it also services. Its present areas of emphasis include Commonwealth student mobility and co-operation in higher education, distance teaching and new technologies in education, education and work, education in small states and education in science and technology.

The **Fellowships and Training Programme** (financed by the CFTC) provides awards, finds training places and arranges training attachments and study visits. Applicants must be nominated by their governments. In 1987/88 the Programme supported over 3,000 trainees. The majority of trainees are at middle management and technician level and most training is provided in developing countries. The Programme has established distance education units for Namibians and South Africans (in Lusaka, Zambia and Dar es Salaam, Tanzania, respectively), and a Nassau Fellowship Scheme, for South Africans who are victims of apartheid, was begun in 1986. Awards for practical training attachments are provided under the Commonwealth Industrial Training and Experience Programme.

The **Management Development Programme** (financed by the CFTC) assists governments (particularly those of small states) in improving public management systems and practice, through seminars, training programmes, consultations, project studies and publications; it provides opportunities for policy-makers to share their experience, and acts as a clearing-house for information. A *Directory of Commonwealth Training in Public Administration* is published, together with research results and case studies.

The **Health Programme,** guided by the meetings of Commonwealth health ministers, assists governments to strengthen their health services. It supports the work of regional health organizations, undertakes studies and provides advisory services at the request of governments.

The **Women and Development Programme** supports the efforts of governments to enhance women's participation in and benefits from development through training, policy analysis, research, and consultancies on issues such as employment and income, health, agriculture, education and violence against women. In 1988 the Programme serviced a group of experts studying the effect of structural adjustment on women in developing countries.

The **Commonwealth Youth Programme,** funded through separate contributions from governments, seeks to promote the involvement of young people in the economic and social development of their countries. It provides policy advice for governments and operates regional training programmes for youth workers and policy-makers through its centres in Africa, Asia, the Caribbean and Pacific. It conducts a Youth Study Fellowship scheme, a Youth Project Fund, a Youth Exchange Programme (in the Caribbean), and a Youth Service Awards Scheme, holds conferences and seminars, carries out research and disseminates information.

SCIENCE

Science Division: provides the secretariat of the Commonwealth Science Council of 34 governments; organizes regional and global programmes to enhance the scientific and technological capabilities of member countries, through co-operative research, training and the exchange of information. Work is carried out in the areas of energy, water and mineral resources, biological resources, environmental planning, agriculture, industrial support, and science management and organization.

Science Adviser: Dr G. THYAGARAJAN (India).

TECHNICAL CO-OPERATION

Commonwealth Fund for Technical Co-operation: financed by voluntary subscriptions from all member governments, provides technical assistance to developing Commonwealth countries. It provides consultancy and advisory services, assigns experts to work in member countries, and finances specialized training. The CFTC also funds the Fellowships and Training Programme (see under Human Resources). CFTC expenditure during the year ending 30 June 1989 was expected to be £23.2m. The number of experts on long-term assignments was 160 in September 1988, with about 50 more experts on assignments of less than six months' duration.

The **General Technical Assistance Division** of the CFTC supplies experts and consultants and commissions specialist studies. Each year it provides governments with more than 200 experts in law, finance, planning, agriculture, industry, communications, education and other areas.

The CFTC's **Technical Assistance Group** is an in-house consultancy providing governments with assistance (including financial, legal and policy advice) in negotiations on natural resources and other investment projects, maritime boundary delimitation and fisheries, macroeconomic policies, computer systems and debt management.

The **Industrial Development Unit** of the CFTC assists governments in the development and implementation of industrial projects. During 1987/88 more than 190 projects were assisted, chiefly food-processing, agricultural inputs, light engineering and minerals; assistance includes investment planning and project design, entrepreneurial development, transfer of technology, and upgrading enterprises.

CFTC Managing Director: WILLIAM MONTGOMERY (Canada).

SELECTED PUBLICATIONS

The Commonwealth Today (revised every 2 years).
The Commonwealth Factbook.
Report of the Commonwealth Secretary-General (every 2 years).
Commonwealth Currents (every 2 months).
Commonwealth Organisations (directory).
Notes on the Commonwealth (series of reference leaflets).
Commonwealth Youth Programme Youth News Service (quarterly).
International Development Policies (quarterly).
Meat and Dairy Products (2 a year).
Fruit and Tropical Products (2 a year).

Hides and Skins (2 a year).
Tobacco Quarterly.
Wool Quarterly.
Wool Statistics (annually).
Science and Technology News.
Numerous reports, studies and papers.

Commonwealth Organizations
(In England, unless otherwise stated)

AGRICULTURE AND FORESTRY

CAB International (CABI): Wallingford, Oxon, OX10 8DE, England; tel. (0491) 32111; telex 847964; f. 1929; formerly Commonwealth Agricultural Bureaux; consists of four Institutes, 11 Bureaux and a development services unit, under the control of an Executive Council comprising representatives from member countries which contribute to its funds. Its functions are to provide:

(i) a world information service for agricultural scientists and other professional workers in the same and allied fields;

(ii) a biological control service; and

(iii) a pest and disease identification service.

Each Institute and Bureau is concerned with its own particular branch of agricultural science and acts as an effective clearing house for the collection, collation and dissemination of information of value to research workers. The information, compiled from worldwide literature is published in 26 main journals, 21 specialist journals and several serial publications which have a monthly circulation of 32,000 in 150 countries.

Annotated bibliographies provide information on specific topics, and review articles, books, maps and monographs are also issued. The CABI Abstracts database is accessible online through the following retrieval services: DIALOG (USA), BRS (USA), CAN/OLE (Canada), ESA-IRS (Italy), DIMDI (Federal Republic of Germany), and JICST (Japan); many organizations provide SDI services from CABI tapes.

In addition, Institutes of Entomology, Mycology and Parasitology provide identification and taxonomic services and the Institute of Biological Control undertakes field work in biological control throughout the world. Dir-Gen. D. MENTZ.

CABI Bureau of Agricultural Economics: Wallingford, Oxon, OX10 8DE; tel. (0491) 32111; telex 847964; f. 1966; provides an information service on agricultural economics and business, rural sociology, rural development in low-income countries, rural extension, education and training, tourism, leisure and recreation. Man. Editor MARGOT BELLAMY. Publs *World Agricultural Economics and Rural Sociology Abstracts* (monthly), *Rural Development Abstracts* (quarterly), *Rural Extension, Education and Training Abstracts* (2 a year), *Leisure, Recreation and Tourism Abstracts* (quarterly), *LRTA Word List*, bibliographies and articles.

CABI Bureau of Animal Breeding and Genetics: Wallingford, Oxon, OX10 8DE; tel. (0491) 32111; telex 847964; f. 1929 for the collection and abstracting of the world's literature on the breeding and the genetics of animals, and for the dissemination of this information throughout the world. Man. Editor J. D. TURTON. Publs *Animal Breeding Abstracts* (monthly), *Poultry Abstracts* (monthly).

CABI Bureau of Crop Protection: Wallingford, Oxon, OX10 8DE; tel. (0491) 32111; f. 1987 for the collection and abstracting of world scientific literature on crop protection, including the biology and control of weeds, insects and other pests, plant nematodes, pathogenic fungi, bacteria and viruses. Man. Editor Dr P. R. SCOTT. Publs. *Review of Plant Pathology, Review of Applied Entomology, Weed Abstracts, Helminthological Abstracts*, bibliographies.

CABI Bureau of Dairy Science and Technology: Wallingford, Oxon, OX10 8DE; tel. (0491) 32111; telex 847964; f. 1938 for the collection, collation, and distribution of scientific and technological information on dairy husbandry, milk and milk products, and the economics, physiology, microbiology, chemistry and physics of dairying for the benefit of research workers, teachers, advisory officers, etc. Man. Editor P. D. WILSON. Publs *Dairy Science Abstracts* (monthly).

CABI Bureau of Horticulture and Plantation Crops: Wallingford, Oxon, OX10 8DE; tel. (0491) 32111; telex 847964; f. 1929. Man. Editor Dr K. K. S. BHAT. Publs *Horticultural Abstracts, Ornamental Horticulture, Cotton and Tropical Fibres Abstracts, Sorghum and Millets Abstracts, Tropical Oil Seeds Abstracts* (all monthly).

CABI Bureau of Nutrition: Wallingford, Oxon, OX10 8DE; tel. (0491) 32111; telex 847964; f. 1929 to collect and abstract the world's literature in the field of human and animal nutrition, and to disseminate this information world-wide. Man. Editor (vacant). Publs *Nutrition Abstracts and Reviews: Series A—Human and Experimental* (monthly), *Series B—Livestock Feeds and Feeding* (monthly).

CABI Bureau of Pastures and Field Crops: Wallingford, Oxon, OX10 8DE; tel. (0491) 32111; telex 847964; f. 1929; publishes abstracts compiled from the world's scientific literature on grasses and grasslands, herbage plants, rangelands and annual field crops, and produces annotated bibliographies on selected subjects within its scope. Man. Editor P. WIGHTMAN. Publs *Herbage Abstracts, Field Crop Abstracts, Crop Physiology Abstracts, Potato Abstracts, Rice Abstracts, Seed Abstracts, Soyabean Abstracts* (all monthly), *Faba Bean Abstracts* (quarterly), *Lentil Abstracts* (annually), and occasional publications.

CABI Bureau of Plant Breeding and Genetics: Wallingford, Oxon, OX10 8DE; tel. (0491) 32111; telex 847964; f. 1929 to abstract and review current world literature on the breeding and genetics of plants of economic importance and to maintain an information service on all these subjects. Man. Editor RAY WATKINS. Publs *Plant Breeding Abstracts* (monthly), *Maize Abstracts* (every 2 months), *Wheat, Barley and Triticale Abstracts* (every 2 months).

CABI Bureau of Soils: Wallingford, Oxon, OX10 8DE; tel. (0491) 32111; telex 847964; f. 1929 for the collection and dissemination of information from the world scientific literature on all aspects of soils, the use of fertilizers, and the relationship between plants and soils, particularly plant nutrition. Man. Editor B. BUTTERS. Publs *Soils and Fertilizers* (monthly), *Irrigation and Drainage Abstracts* (quarterly), series of technical communications (occasional).

CABI Forestry Bureau: Wallingford, Oxon, OX10 8DE; tel. (0491) 32111; telex 847964; f. 1938 for the collection and abstracting of the world's literature on forestry, forest products and their utilization, and for the dissemination of this information throughout the world. Man. Editor K. BECKER. Publs *Forestry Abstracts* (monthly), *Forest Products Abstracts* (monthly), *COM Catalogue* (quarterly, cumulative), *Annotated Bibliography* (occasional), textbooks.

CABI Institute of Biological Control: Silwood Park, Buckhurst Rd, Ascot, Berks, SL5 7TA; tel. (0990) 28426; telex 847964; f. 1927 as the Farnham House Laboratory of the Imperial Institute of Entomology; transferred to Canada 1940 and to Trinidad 1962; since 1983 its main research and administrative centre has been in the United Kingdom; its purpose is the biological control of injurious insects and noxious weeds, and the collection and distribution throughout the world of beneficial organisms with which to attack the pests. Dir D. J. GREATHEAD. Publs *A Catalogue of the Parasites and Predators of Insect Pests, Technical Communications, Biocontrol News and Information* (quarterly).

CABI Institute of Entomology: 56 Queen's Gate, London, SW7 5JR; tel. (01) 584-0067; telex 93121-02251; f. 1913 for the collection, co-ordination and dissemination of all information concerning injurious and useful insects and other arthropods; undertakes identifications; organizes international training courses and workshops on applied taxonomy of insects and mites. Dir K. M. HARRIS. Publs *Bulletin of Entomological Research* (quarterly), *Review of Applied Entomology* (monthly); *Distribution Maps of Pests* (18 a year), bibliographies and monographs.

CABI Institute of Parasitology: 395A Hatfield Rd, St Albans, Herts, AL4 0XU; tel. (0727) 33151; telex 847964; f. 1929; collates world research literature on helminth parasites of animals, on nematode parasites of plants and on parasitic protozoans with reference particularly to those of economic importance; also provides advisory services and conducts identification and taxonomic research. Dir R. MULLER. Publs *Helminthological Abstracts: Series A—Animal and Human Helminthology* (monthly); *Protozoological Abstracts* (monthly).

CABI Mycological Institute: Ferry Lane, Kew, Surrey, TW9 3AF; tel. (01) 940-4086; telex 265871; f. 1920 for the collection and dissemination of information on the fungal, bacterial, virus and physiological disorders of plants; on fungal diseases of man and animals; and on the taxonomy of fungi; undertakes identifications of micro-fungi and plant pathogenic bacteria from all over the world; incorporates national collection of fungus cultures and a biodeterioration centre; consultancy services, especially in industrial mycology and surveys on plant disease; holds training courses. Dir D. L. HAWKSWORTH. Publs *Biodeterioration Abstracts* (quarterly), *Distribution Maps of Plant Diseases* (42 a year), *Index of Fungi* (2 a year), *Mycological Papers* (irregular), *Phytopathological Papers* (irregular), *Descriptions of Pathogenic Fungi and Bacteria* (4 sets a year), *Bibliography of*

INTERNATIONAL ORGANIZATIONS

The Commonwealth

Systematic Mycology (2 a year), *Systema Ascomycetum* (2 a year), books on mycology and plant pathology.

Commonwealth Forestry Association: c/o Oxford Forestry Institute, South Parks Rd, Oxford, OX1 3RB; tel. (0865) 275072; telex 83147; f. 1921; produces, collects and circulates information relating to forestry and the commercial utilization of forest products and provides a means of communications in the Commonwealth and other interested countries. Mems: 1,500. Chair. R. T. BRADLEY. Publs *Commonwealth Forestry Review* (quarterly), *Commonwealth Forestry Handbook*.

Standing Committee on Commonwealth Forestry: Forestry Commission, 231 Corstorphine Rd, Edinburgh, EH12 7AT, Scotland; tel. (031) 334-0303; telex 727879; f. 1923 to provide continuity between Conferences, and to provide a forum for discussion on any forestry matters of common interest to member governments which may be brought to the Committee's notice by any member country or organization; mems about 50. Sec. A. MCCABE. Publs *Newsletter*, reports and papers.

COMMONWEALTH STUDIES

Institute of Commonwealth Studies: 27–28 Russell Sq., London, WC1B 5DS; tel. (01) 580-5876; f. 1949 to promote advanced study of the Commonwealth; provides a library and meeting place for postgraduate students and academic staff engaged in research in this field. Incorporates the Sir Robert Menzies Centre for Australian Studies. Dir SHULA MARKS; Publs *Annual Report, Commonwealth Papers* (series), *Collected Seminar Papers*.

COMMUNICATIONS

Commonwealth Air Transport Council: 2 Marsham St, Room S5/05A, London, SW1P 3EB; tel. (01) 276-5436; telex 22221; f. 1945 to keep under review the development of Commonwealth civil air transport. Meetings every three years. Mems: governments of Commonwealth Countries and British Dependent Territories. Sec. Miss P. BRAUNTON. Publs *Commonwealth Air Transport Review* (3 a year), *Commonwealth Air Transport Electronics News* (2 a year), *Selected R & D Abstracts* (2 a year), *Civil Aviation Training Facilities in Commonwealth Countries* (every 3 years).

Commonwealth Telecommunications Organization: 28 Haymarket, London, SW1Y 4SR; tel. (01) 930-5511; telex 27328; f. 1967 to enhance the development of international telecommunications in Commonwealth countries through financial and technical collaborative arrangements. Gen. Sec. GRAHAM H. CUNNOLD.

EDUCATION

Association of Commonwealth Universities: John Foster House, 36 Gordon Sq., London, WC1H 0PF; tel. (01) 387-8572; f. 1913; holds quinquennial Congresses and other meetings in intervening years; publishes factual information about Commonwealth universities and access to them; acts as a general information centre and provides an advisory service for the filling of university teaching staff appointments overseas; supplies secretariats for the Commonwealth Scholarship Commission in the United Kingdom and the Marshall Aid Commemoration Commission; administers Senior Travelling Fellowships for academics with administrative roles, Administrative Travelling Fellowships for registrars, etc., the Overseas Development Administration Shared Scholarship Scheme, the Third World Academic Exchange Programme, the THES Third World Academic Exchange Fellowship and (for medical students) the Commonwealth Foundation, Edward Boyle and Lennox-Boyd electives bursaries schemes. Mems: 331 universities in 29 countries or regions. Sec.-Gen. Dr A. CHRISTODOULOU. Publs include *Commonwealth Universities Yearbook, Commonwealth University Situation Reports, ACU Bulletin of Current Documentation, British Universities' Guide to Graduate Study, University Entrance: the Official Guide, Awards for Commonwealth University Academic Staff, Scholarships Guide for Commonwealth Postgraduate Students, Financial Aid for First Degree Study at Commonwealth Universities, Grants for Study Visits by University Administrators and Librarians, Research Opportunities in Commonwealth Developing Countries, Higher Education in the United Kingdom* (handbook), *Study Abroad* (series of student information papers), *Who's Who of Commonwealth University Vice-Chancellors, Presidents and Rectors*.

Commonwealth Association of Science, Technology and Mathematics Educators—CASTME: c/o Education Programme, HRDG, Commonwealth Secretariat, Marlborough House, Pall Mall, London, SW1Y 5HX; tel. (01) 839-3411; telex 27678; f. 1974; special emphasis is given to the social significance of education in these subjects. Organizes an Awards Scheme to promote effective teaching and learning in these subjects, and biennial regional seminars. Pres. Dr MAURICE GOLDSMITH; Hon. Sec. E. APEA. Publ. *CASTME Journal* (quarterly).

Commonwealth Council for Educational Administration: c/o Faculty of Education, University of New England, Armidale, NSW 2351, Australia; tel. (067) 732543; telex 66050; f. 1970; aims to foster links among educational administrators; holds annual national conferences and biennial regional conferences, as well as visits and seminars. Mems: 23 affiliated groups representing 5,000 persons. Pres. Prof. MEREDYDD HUGHES; Exec. Dir JOHN WEEKS. Publs *Newsletter* (quarterly), *Studies in Educational Administration* (quarterly), *Directory of Courses*, reports.

League for the Exchange of Commonwealth Teachers: Seymour Mews House, 26-37 Seymour Mews, London, W1H 9PE; tel. (01) 486-2849; f. 1901; promotes educational exchanges for a period of one year between teachers in Australia, the Bahamas, Barbados, Bermuda, Canada, India, Jamaica, Kenya, New Zealand and Trinidad and Tobago. Exec. Sec. PATRICIA SWAIN. Publ. *Annual Report*.

HEALTH

Commonwealth Medical Association: c/o BMA House, Tavistock Sq., London, WC1H 9JP; tel. (01) 387-4499; telex 265929; f. 1962 to promote within the Commonwealth the interests of the medical and allied sciences; meetings of its Council are held every two years. Mems: Medical Associations in 31 countries. Sec. Dr J. D. J. HAVARD (UK). Publ. *Bulletin* (quarterly).

Commonwealth Pharmaceutical Association: 1 Lambeth High St, London, SE1 7JN; tel. (01) 735-9141; telex 265871; f. 1969 to promote the interests of pharmaceutical sciences and the profession of pharmacy in the Commonwealth; to maintain high professional standards, encourage links between members and the creation of national associations; and to facilitate the dissemination of information. Holds conferences (every four years) and regional meetings. Mems: 35 pharmaceutical associations. Sec. RAYMOND DICKINSON (UK). Publ. *Quarterly Newsletter*.

Commonwealth Society for the Deaf: 105 Gower St, London, WC1E 6AH; tel. (01) 631-5311; promotes the health, education and general welfare of the deaf in developing Commonwealth countries; encourages and assists the development of educational facilities, the training of teachers of the deaf, and the provision of support for parents of deaf children; assists volunteer workers to find posts abroad; provides audiological equipment and encourages the establishment of maintenance services for such equipment; conducts research into the causes and prevention of deafness. Admin. Sec. Miss E. LUBIENSKA (UK). Publs *Annual Report, Research Report*.

Royal Commonwealth Society for the Blind: Commonwealth House, Haywards Heath, Sussex, RH16 3AZ; tel. (0444) 412424; telex 87167; f. 1950 to prevent blindness and to promote the education, employment and welfare of the 15m. blind people in the Commonwealth countries of Africa, Asia, the Caribbean, and the Pacific. The Society conducts the largest non-governmental international programme of its kind for the restoration of sight. Chair. Sir FRANK MILLS; Dir A. W. JOHNS. Publs *Annual Report, Horizons* (newsletter).

INFORMATION AND THE MEDIA

Commonwealth Broadcasting Association: Broadcasting House, London, W1A 1AA; tel. (01) 580-4468, ext. 6023; telex 265781; f. 1945; General Conferences are held every two years. Mems: 55 national public service broadcasting organizations in 51 Commonwealth countries. Sec.-Gen. ALVA CLARKE. Publs *COMBROAD* (quarterly), *CBA Handbook* (updated every 2 years).

Commonwealth Institute: Kensington High St, London, W8 6NQ; tel. (01) 603-4535; f. 1887 as the Imperial Institute; a centre for public information and educational services, the Institute houses a permanent exhibition designed to express countries of the modern Commonwealth in visual terms, art galleries showing contemporary works of art, a library and resource centre of more than 40,000 vols and audiovisual materials, and an Arts Centre with a continuous programme of dance, drama, music and films. Dir JAMES PORTER.

Commonwealth Institute, Scotland: 8 Rutland Sq., Edinburgh, EH1 2AS, Scotland; tel. (031) 229-6668. Dir C. G. CARROL.

Commonwealth Journalists' Association: Castle House, 25 Castlereagh St, London, W1H 5YR; tel. (01) 262-1054; f. 1978 to improve standards of journalism, and provide training and conferences. Pres. DEREK INGRAM; Sec. LAWRIE BREEN.

Commonwealth Press Union (Association of Commonwealth Newspapers): Studio House, Hen and Chickens Court, 184 Fleet St, London, EC4A 2DU; tel. (01) 242-1056; telex 936565; f. 1959 to promote the welfare of the Commonwealth press by defending its freedom, providing training and working for improved reporting and transmitting facilities; organizes annual conferences. Mems: over 500 newspapers, news agencies, periodicals in 31 countries. Pres. Lord ROTHERMERE; Chair. of Council LYLE TURNBULL; Dir JAYANATH C. RAJEPAKSE. Publs *CPU Quarterly, Annual Report*.

LAW

Commonwealth Lawyers' Association: c/o The Law Society, 113 Chancery Lane, London, WC2A 1PL; tel. (01) 242-1222; telex 261203; f. 1983 (fmrly the Commonwealth Legal Bureau); seeks to maintain and promote the rule of law throughout the Commonwealth, by ensuring that the people of the Commonwealth are served by an independent and efficient legal profession; assists in organizing the triennial Commonwealth law conferences. Pres. Lt-Col H. ST C. WHITEHORNE; Exec. Sec. H. C. ADAMSON. Publ. *Commonwealth Lawyer* (2 a year).

Commonwealth Legal Advisory Service: c/o British Institute of International and Comparative Law, Charles Clore House, 17 Russell Sq., London, WC1B 5DR; tel. (01) 636-5802; financed by the British Institute and by contributions from the Commonwealth Governments; besides operating the advisory service, the British Institute prepares surveys and organizes lectures, study courses and conferences. Dir ROGER ROSE. Publ. *ICLQ, Bulletin of Legal Developments*.

Commonwealth Legal Education Association: Legal Division, Commonwealth Secretariat, Marlborough House, Pall Mall, London, SW1Y 5HX; tel. (01) 839-3411; f. 1971; to promote contacts and exchanges; to provide information. Hon. Sec. JEREMY POPE. Publs *Commonwealth Legal Education Newsletter, List of Schools of Law in the Commonwealth* (every 2 years), *Compendium of Post-Graduate Law Courses in the Commonwealth*, occasional papers and reports.

Commonwealth Magistrates' Association: 28 Fitzroy Sq., London, W1P 6DD; tel. (01) 387-4889; telex 937400; f. 1970 to advance the administration of the law by promoting the independence of the judiciary, to further education in law and crime prevention and to disseminate information; conferences and study tours; corporate membership for associations of the judiciary or courts of limited jurisdiction; associate membership for individuals. Pres. ANDREAS LOIZOU; Sec. Dr J. S. BUCHANAN. Publs *Commonwealth Judicial Journal* (2 a year), Reports.

PARLIAMENTARY AFFAIRS

Commonwealth Parliamentary Association: 7 Old Palace Yard, London, SW1P 3JY; tel. (01) 799-1460; telex 911569; f. 1911 to promote understanding and co-operation between Commonwealth parliamentarians; organization: Executive Committee of 25 Members of Parliament responsible to annual General Assembly; 115 branches throughout the Commonwealth; holds annual Commonwealth Parliamentary Conferences and seminars, and also regional conferences and seminars; 34th Conference, Canberra, Australia, 1988. Sec.-Gen. DAVID TONKIN. Publs *The Parliamentarian* (quarterly), newsletters and reports.

PROFESSIONAL AND INDUSTRIAL RELATIONS

Commonwealth Association of Architects: The Building Centre, 26 Store St, London, WC1E 7BT; tel. (01) 636-8276; telex 22914; f. 1964; an association of 31 societies of architects in various Commonwealth countries. Objects: to facilitate the reciprocal recognition of professional qualifications through a Commonwealth Board of Architectural Education; to provide a clearing house for information on architectural practice, and to encourage collaboration. Plenary Conferences every two years; regional Conferences have also been held. Sec. GEORGE WILSON. Publs *Handbook, Architectural Education in the Commonwealth, Issues in Architectural Practice, List of Recognised Schools of Architecture*, Conference Reports, low-cost textbooks, slide-tape programmes and manuals.

Commonwealth Foundation: Marlborough House, Pall Mall, London, SW1Y 5HY; tel. (01) 930-3783; f. 1966 to administer a fund to promote closer professional co-operation within the Commonwealth (reconstituted as an international organization 1983). The Foundation is an autonomous body assisting professionals from Commonwealth countries to visit other Commonwealth countries to attend conferences and undertake advisory and study visits and training attachments. Also supports Commonwealth professional associations and professional centres; runs short-term fellowship schemes to promote Commonwealth understanding, mid-career training, health, the media and culture; and makes grants to encourage exchange of information; facilitates the establishment of units in each Commonwealth country for liaison between non-governmental organizations and the Commonwealth. Funds are provided by 43 Commonwealth governments on an agreed basis: in 1988 £1.2m. was available for grant-making. Chair. ROBERT STANFIELD (Canada); Dir 'INOKE FALETAU (Tonga).

Commonwealth Trade Union Council: c/o TUC, Congress House, 23–28 Great Russell St, London, WC1B 3LS; tel. (01) 636-4030; telex 266006; f. 1979 to promote the interests of workers in the Commonwealth and encourage the development of trades unions in developing countries of the Commonwealth; provides assistance for training. Dir PAT QUINN (UK).

SCIENCE AND TECHNOLOGY

Commonwealth Advisory Aeronautical Research Council: Room 9145, St Christopher House, Southwark St, London, SE1 0TD; tel. (01) 921-1355; f. 1946; encourages and co-ordinates aeronautical research throughout the Commonwealth. Sec. R. D. HILLARY.

Commonwealth Engineers' Council: c/o Institution of Civil Engineers, 1–7 Great George St, London, SW1P 3AA; tel. (01) 222-7722; telex 935637; f. 1946; the Conference meets every 2 years to provide an opportunity for Presidents and Secretaries of Engineering Institutions of Commonwealth countries to exchange views on collaboration; there is a standing committee on engineering education and training; organizes seminars on related topics; last meeting held in Montréal, Canada, 1987. Sec. J. C. McKENZIE.

Commonwealth Geological Surveys Consultative Group: c/o Commonwealth Science Council, CSC Earth Services Programme, Marlborough House, Pall Mall, London, SW1Y 5HX; tel. (01) 839-3411; telex 27678; f. 1948 (as the Commonwealth Committee on Mineral Resources and Geology) to promote collaboration in geological, geochemical, geophysical and remote sensing techniques and the exchange of information. Publ. *Earth Sciences Newsletter*.

SPORT

Commonwealth Games Federation: 197 Knightsbridge, London, SW7 1RZ; tel. (01) 225-5555; telex 919156; the Games were first held in 1930 and are now held every four years; participation is limited to amateur teams representing the member countries of the Commonwealth; held in Edinburgh, Scotland, in 1986, and to be held in Auckland, New Zealand, in 1990. Mems: 64 affiliated bodies. Chair. PETER HEATLY; Hon. Sec. DAVID DIXON.

YOUTH

Commonwealth Youth Exchange Council: 18 Fleet St, London, EC4Y 1AA; tel. (01) 353-3901; f. 1970; promotes contact between groups of young people of the United Kingdom and other Commonwealth countries by means of educational exchange visits, provides information for organizers and allocates grants; 177 member organizations. Dir V. S. G. CRAGGS. Publs *Contact* (handbook), *Exchange* (newsletter).

Duke of Edinburgh's Award Scheme: 5 Prince of Wales Terrace, London, W8 5PG; tel. (01) 938-4545; telex 923753; f. 1956; offers a programme of leisure activities for young people, comprising service, expeditions, sport and skills, operating in over 40 countries (not confined to the Commonwealth). Dir Maj.-Gen. MICHAEL F. HOBBS; International Sec.-Gen. DAVID NEWING. Publs *Award World* (3 a year), handbooks and guides.

MISCELLANEOUS

British Commonwealth Ex-services League: 48 Pall Mall, London, SW1Y 5JG; tel. (01) 930-8131, ext. 263; links the ex-service organizations in the Commonwealth, assists ex-servicemen of the Crown and their dependants; holds triennial conferences. Sec.-Gen. Brig. M. J. DOYLE. Publ. *Triennial Report*.

Commonwealth Countries League: 14 Thistleworth Close, Isleworth, Middx, TW7 4QQ; tel. (01) 568-9868; f. 1925 to secure equal opportunities and status between men and women in the Commonwealth, and the social and political education of women, to act as a link between Commonwealth women's organizations, and to promote and finance secondary education of disadvantaged girls of high ability in their own countries, through the CCL Educational Fund; holds meetings with speakers and an annual Conference, organizes the annual Commonwealth Fair for fund-raising; individual mems and affiliated socs in the Commonwealth. Sec.-Gen. SHEILA O'REILLY. Publ. *CCL Newsletter* (3 a year).

Commonwealth War Graves Commission: 2 Marlow Rd, Maidenhead, Berks, SL6 7DX; tel. (0628) 34221; telex 847526; f. 1917 (as Imperial War Graves Commission); provides for the marking and permanent care of the graves of members of the Commonwealth Forces who died during the wars of 1914–18 and 1939–45; maintains over 1m. graves in some 140 countries and commemorates by name on memorials more than 750,000 who have no known grave or who were cremated. Mems: Australia, Canada, India, New Zealand, South Africa, United Kingdom. Pres. HRH The Duke of KENT; Dir-Gen. Sir ARTHUR HOCKADAY.

Joint Commonwealth Societies' Council: c/o Victoria League for Commonwealth Friendship, 18 Northumberland Ave, London, WC2N 5BJ; tel. (01) 930-1671; co-ordinates the activities of recognized societies promoting mutual understanding in the Commonwealth; mems: 13 unofficial Commonwealth organizations and four official bodies. Secs Mrs SYLVIA BARNETT, Sir MICHAEL SCOTT.

Royal Commonwealth Society: 18 Northumberland Ave, London, WC2N 5BJ; tel. (01) 930-6733; to promote knowledge and understanding among the people of the Commonwealth; branches in principal Commonwealth countries; has full residential club facilities, lectures and library. Sec.-Gen. (vacant). Publs *Newsletter* (3 a year), *Library Notes,* conference reports.

Royal Over-Seas League: Over-Seas House, Park Place, St James's St, London, SW1A 1LR; tel. (01) 408-0214; telex 268995; f. 1910 to promote friendship and understanding in the Commonwealth; membership is open to all British subjects and Commonwealth citizens. Dir-Gen. Capt. J. B. RUMBLE. Publ. *Overseas* (quarterly).

Victoria League for Commonwealth Friendship: 18 Northumberland Ave, London, WC2N 5BJ; tel. (01) 930-1671; f. 1901 to further personal friendship among Commonwealth peoples; about 41,000 mems. Pres. HRH Princess MARGARET, Countess of Snowdon; Chair. Sir ZELMAN COWEN; Sec. Mrs SYLVIA BARNETT.

Declaration of Commonwealth Principles

Agreed by the Commonwealth Heads of Government Meeting at Singapore, 22 January 1971.

The Commonwealth of Nations is a voluntary association of independent sovereign states, each responsible for its own policies, consulting and co-operating in the common interests of their peoples and in the promotion of international understanding and world peace.

Members of the Commonwealth come from territories in the six continents and five oceans, include peoples of different races, languages and religions, and display every stage of economic development from poor developing nations to wealthy industrialized nations. They encompass a rich variety of cultures, traditions and institutions.

Membership of the Commonwealth is compatible with the freedom of member-governments to be non-aligned or to belong to any other grouping, association or alliance. Within this diversity all members of the Commonwealth hold certain principles in common. It is by pursuing these principles that the Commonwealth can continue to influence international society for the benefit of mankind.

We believe that international peace and order are essential to the security and prosperity of mankind; we therefore support the United Nations and seek to strengthen its influence for peace in the world, and its efforts to remove the causes of tension between nations.

We believe in the liberty of the individual, in equal rights for all citizens regardless of race, colour, creed or political belief, and in their inalienable right to participate by means of free and democratic political processes in framing the society in which they live. We therefore strive to promote in each of our countries those representative institutions and guarantees for personal freedom under the law that are our common heritage.

We recognize racial prejudice as a dangerous sickness threatening the healthy development of the human race and racial discrimination as an unmitigated evil of society. Each of us will vigorously combat this evil within our own nation.

No country will afford to regimes which practise racial discrimination assistance which in its own judgment directly contributes to the pursuit or consolidation of this evil policy. We oppose all forms of colonial domination and racial oppression and are committed to the principles of human dignity and equality.

We will therefore use all our efforts to foster human equality and dignity everywhere, and to further the principles of self-determination and non-racialism.

We believe that the wide disparities in wealth now existing between different sections of mankind are too great to be tolerated. They also create world tensions. Our aim is their progressive removal. We therefore seek to use our efforts to overcome poverty, ignorance and disease, in raising standards of life and achieving a more equitable international society.

To this end our aim is to achieve the freest possible flow of international trade on terms fair and equitable to all, taking into account the special requirements of the developing countries, and to encourage the flow of adequate resources, including governmental and private resources, to the developing countries, bearing in mind the importance of doing this in a true spirit of partnership and of establishing for this purpose in the developing countries conditions which are conducive to sustained investment and growth.

We believe that international co-operation is essential to remove the causes of war, promote tolerance, combat injustice, and secure development among the peoples of the world. We are convinced that the Commonwealth is one of the most fruitful associations for these purposes.

In pursuing these principles the members of the Commonwealth believe that they can provide a constructive example of the multi-national approach which is vital to peace and progress in the modern world. The association is based on consultation, discussion and co-operation.

In rejecting coercion as an instrument of policy they recognize that the security of each member state from external aggression is a matter of concern to all members. It provides many channels for continuing exchanges of knowledge and views on professional, cultural, economic, legal and political issues among member states.

These relationships we intend to foster and extend, for we believe that our multi-national association can expand human understanding and understanding among nations, assist in the elimination of discrimination based on differences of race, colour or creed, maintain and strengthen personal liberty, contribute to the enrichment of life for all, and provide a powerful influence for peace among nations.

The Gleneagles Agreement on Sporting Contacts with South Africa

In 1977 Commonwealth Heads of Government, meeting at Gleneagles in Scotland, reached the following agreement on discouraging sporting links with South Africa:

They were conscious that sport is an important means of developing and fostering understanding between the people, and especially between the young people, of all countries. . . .

Mindful of these and other considerations, they accepted it as the urgent duty of each of their Governments vigorously to combat the evil of apartheid by withholding any form of support for, and by taking every practical step to discourage contact or competition by their nationals with sporting organizations, teams or sportsmen from South Africa or from any other country where sports are organized on the basis of race, colour or ethnic origin.

They fully acknowledged that it was for each Government to determine in accordance with its law the methods by which it might best discharge these commitments. But they recognized that the effective fulfilment of their commitments was essential to the harmonious development of Commonwealth sport hereafter. . . .

Heads of Government specially welcomed the belief, unanimously expressed at their Meeting, that in the light of their consultations and accord there were unlikely to be future sporting contacts of any significance between Commonwealth countries or their nationals and South Africa while that country continues to pursue the detestable policy of apartheid. . . .

The Lusaka Declaration on Racism and Racial Prejudice

The Declaration, adopted by Heads of Government in 1979, includes the following statements:

United in our desire to rid the world of the evils of racism and racial prejudice, we proclaim our faith in the inherent dignity and worth of the human person and declare that:

   (i) the peoples of the Commonwealth have the right to live freely in dignity and equality, without any distinction or exclusion based on race, colour, sex, descent, or national or ethnic origin;
   (ii) while everyone is free to retain diversity in his or her culture and lifestyle this diversity does not justify the perpetuation of racial prejudice or racially discriminatory practices;
   (iii) everyone has the right to equality before the law and equal justice under the law; and
   (iv) everyone has the right to effective remedies and protection against any form of discrimination based on the grounds of race, colour, sex, descent, or national or ethnic origin.

We reject as inhuman and intolerable all policies designed to perpetuate apartheid, racial segregation or other policies based on theories that racial groups are or may be inherently superior or inferior.

We reaffirm that it is the duty of all the peoples of the Commonwealth to work together for the total eradication of the infamous policy of apartheid which is internationally recognized as a crime against the conscience and dignity of mankind and the very existence of which is an affront to humanity.

We agree that everyone has the right to protection against acts of incitement to racial hatred and discrimination, whether committed by individuals, groups or other organizations. . . .

Inspired by the principles of freedom and equality which characterise our association, we accept the solemn duty of working together to eliminate racism and racial prejudice. This duty involves the acceptance of the principle that positive measures may be required to advance the elimination of racism, including assistance to those struggling to rid themselves and their environment of the practice.

Being aware that legislation alone cannot eliminate racism and racial prejudice, we endorse the need to initiate public information and education policies designed to promote understanding, tolerance, respect and friendship among peoples and racial groups. . . .

We note that racism and racial prejudice, wherever they occur, are significant factors contributing to tension between nations and thus inhibit peaceful progress and development. We believe that the goal of the eradication of racism stands as a critical priority for governments of the Commonwealth committed as they are to the promotion of the ideals of peaceful and happy lives for their people.

COMMUNAUTÉ ÉCONOMIQUE DE L'AFRIQUE DE L'OUEST—CEAO

(WEST AFRICAN ECONOMIC COMMUNITY)

Address: rue Agostino Neto, BP 643, Ouagadougou, Burkina Faso.
Telephone: 33-22-32.
Telex: 5212.
Established in January 1974 to replace the West African Customs Union (UDEAO).

MEMBERS

Benin	Mali	Niger
Burkina Faso	Mauritania	Senegal
Côte d'Ivoire		

Observers: Guinea, Togo.

Organization
(October 1988)

CONFERENCE OF HEADS OF STATE
The Conference of Heads of State is the supreme organ of the Community. Until 1987 it was held at least once a year in one of the member states, and its President is the Head of State of the host country. Decisions of the Conference must be unanimous. It appoints the officers of the Community. In 1987 it was announced that the conference would take place every two years in future.
President (1987–89): Brig.-Gen. MATHIEU KEREKOU (Benin).

COUNCIL OF MINISTERS
The Council of Ministers meets at least twice a year, usually at the seat of the Community. Each member state is represented by its Minister of Finance or a member of government, according to the subject under discussion. Decisions are taken unanimously.

GENERAL SECRETARIAT
The Secretariat is responsible for carrying out decisions of the Conference of Heads of State and the Council of Ministers. It comprises four main departments: trade; rural development; industrial development; administration and finance. The Secretary-General is appointed for a four-year term.
Secretary-General: MAMADOU HAIDARA (Mali).

Activities

The Community has three main areas of activity: trade, regional economic co-operation and economic integration through Community projects.

TRADE
Three categories of produce are traded within the Community:
  Non-manufactured, crude products may be imported and exported within the Community without import taxes, paying only internal taxes.
  Traditional handicrafts are to be exempted from import taxes, and subject to the payment of internal taxes only, according to an agreement in June 1979.
  Industrial products of member states, when exported to other member states, may benefit from the special preferential system based on the Regional Co-operation Tax (see below), which replaces the import taxes of the separate states. Certain products remain subject to special agreements.

In 1981 total community imports from non-member countries amounted to 1,200,000m. francs CFA, while intra-community trade was worth 90,000m. francs CFA, of which 29% was subject to preferential agreements (chiefly textiles, food products and chemicals).

In 1984 a three-year programme was begun, aiming to harmonize customs procedure and the codification of merchandise, and to establish a common tariff for imports from outside the community. Other projects included the improvement of statistical data; commercial training (through, for example, regional seminars on marketing and exporting); and the establishment of a Centre Régional d'Information et de Documentation Commerciale. In 1984 the Conference of Heads of State adopted a convention harmonizing rates of taxation for nationals of member states, and in 1985 the first part of a common investment code was completed.

RURAL AND INDUSTRIAL DEVELOPMENT
Proposals for regional rural development projects approved in 1984 and under way in 1985 comprised the establishment of a seed-production centre in Baguinéda, Mali, of an agricultural training centre in Ouagadougou, Burkina Faso, and of rural savings banks. Studies were also being made for a programme of industrial co-operation (particularly in the production of fertilizers, glass and metals); the harmonization of national investment laws; co-operation in traditional medicine; development of regional tourism; setting up a community shipping line; a regional transport plan; and a programme of agricultural and veterinary research. A five-year plan (1988–92) for transport and communications was adopted by regional ministers of transport in 1987, and a study was commissioned on the access of land-locked states to the sea.

ECONOMIC INTEGRATION
In 1978, 1982 and 1983 the conferences of Heads of State approved the formation of common programmes and institutions, at a cost of over 60,000m. francs CFA, to be financed by a number of donors (notably the African Development Bank and African Development Fund, BADEA, the Islamic Development Bank, the World Bank, the OPEC Fund, France, the Federal Republic of Germany and Kuwait). The projects comprised: a rural water programme throughout the region, to provide 2,634 village wells at a cost of some 23,000m. francs CFA; a regional solar energy centre in Bamako, Mali, to be completed in late 1986 (8,146m. francs CFA); a corporation for the manufacture of railway rolling-stock, to be based in Burkina Faso and Senegal; a centre for higher studies in management, opened in Dakar, Senegal in 1985 (2,217m. francs CFA); a college of geology and mining, to be constructed in Niamey, Niger, by 1987 (11,046m. francs CFA); a college for textile studies in Ségou, Mali, construction of which began in 1986 (5,002m. francs CFA); a community fisheries company, based in Mauritania (17,136m. francs CFA); and two centres for research and training in fisheries, in Mauritania and Côte d'Ivoire.

In 1983 a total of 800m. francs CFA was allotted to member states affected by drought, and in 1984 a second rural waterworks programme was approved, to provide a further 500 village wells and boreholes in each of the member states.

REGIONAL CO-OPERATION TAX
Industrial products manufactured in the West African Economic Community may benefit from a special preferential system when exported to the other member states. This system involves the substitution for customs duties and taxes of a sole tax called Regional Co-operation Tax. The main purpose of the tax is to encourage exchanges within the Community; it is always lower than the ones payable in the member states. The tax came into force on 1 January 1976: by mid-1985 it had been applied to 428 products or groups of products from 253 enterprises, of which 127 were from Côte d'Ivoire and 75 from Senegal. Trade in these products increased sevenfold from 4,500m. francs CFA in 1976 to 32,000m. in 1984.

COMMUNITY DEVELOPMENT FUND—FCD
The Fund is financed by member states according to their respective shares in the trade of industrial products within the Community. The sum is decided annually, at the Conference of Heads of State, in relation to the revenue from the Regional Co-operation Tax. It compensates for certain types of trade loss and finances economic development projects. The Fund's budget for 1985 amounted to 10,571m. francs CFA. Members' difficulties in paying their subscriptions, however, have severely hampered the Fund's activities: by June 1985 overdue contributions amounted to 15,333m. francs CFA.

SOLIDARITY AND INTERVENTION FUND
Fonds de Solidarité et d'Intervention pour le Développement—FOSIDEC (Solidarity and Intervention Fund): BP 2529, Ouagadougou, Burkina Faso; tel. 33-47-94; telex 5205; f. 1977 to contribute to regional equilibrium by granting and guaranteeing loans, financing studies and granting subsidies. The Fund's initial capital was 5,000m. francs CFA. By June 1985 the Fund's total interventions

amounted to 26,267.6m. francs CFA, of which 49.5% was for industrial projects, 32.3% for water development and 14.4% for agriculture and agro-industry. In November 1984 the Fund's director was dismissed, and in April 1986 he was convicted (together with a former secretary-general of the CEAO) of the embezzlement of 6,400m. francs CFA.

CO-OPERATION AGREEMENTS

An agreement of non-aggression and mutual co-operation was signed by the member countries in June 1977, and an agreement on free circulation and the right to establish residence was signed in October 1978. Agreements to exchange information on economic development, to co-ordinate general studies and finance joint projects had been signed with 19 other international and regional organizations by the end of 1985.

PUBLICATIONS

Rapport annuel (annually).

Intégration africaine (2 a year).

CONSEIL DE L'ENTENTE
(ENTENTE COUNCIL)

Address: Fonds d'Entraide et de Garantie des Emprunts, 01 BP 3734, Abidjan 01, Côte d'Ivoire.
Telephone: 33-28-35.
Telex: 23558.

The Conseil de l'Entente, founded in 1959, is a political and economic association of four states which were formerly part of French West Africa, and Togo, which joined in 1966. It gives priority to economic co-ordination in member states.

MEMBERS
Benin   Burkina Faso   Côte d'Ivoire   Niger   Togo

Organization
(October 1988)

THE COUNCIL
The Council consists of the Heads of State and the ministers concerned with the items on the agenda of particular meetings.

The Council meets annually, the place rotating each year between the member states, and is chaired by the President of the host country. Secretariat services are provided by the Secretariat of the Mutual Aid and Guarantee Fund. Extraordinary meetings may be held at the request of two or more members.

FONDS D'ENTRAIDE ET DE GARANTIE DES EMPRUNTS
The Mutual Aid and Loan Guarantee Fund is responsible for carrying out the economic projects decided on by the Council. Its Management Committee, comprising three representatives of each member state, meets twice a year, and a small group of professional advisers assists development institutions in member countries in the preparation of projects and the presentation of requests for aid. Financial resources comprise annual contributions from member states, subsidies and grants (mainly from the French Government), and investment returns and commissions from guarantee operations. At the end of 1987 the Fund's capital amounted to 14,172m. francs CFA.

Administrative Secretary: PAUL KAYA.

Activities

The Entente Council, through the Mutual Aid and Loan Guarantee Fund, aims to promote economic development in the region; to assist in preparing specific projects and to mobilize funds from other sources; to act as a guarantee fund to encourage investments in the region; and to encourage trade and investment between the member states. It is empowered to finance the reduction of interest rates and the extension of maturity periods of foreign loans to member countries.

Between 1978 and 1980 the Fund initiated eight agricultural projects for improving and rehabilitating crop production, at a cost of 9,000m. francs CFA, and seven projects for the development of livestock, at a cost of 3,000m. francs CFA. In 1987 the Fund began a five-year programme of agricultural projects, one in each of the five member countries, with emphasis on training and organizing farmers and modernizing methods of production. The programme was expected to cost 5,000m. francs CFA.

Between 1983 and 1985 a programme of hydraulics was undertaken in four of the five member countries, providing 1,475 wells and 1,641 pumps at a cost of 6,330m. francs CFA. The second phase of the programme, under way in 1987, envisaged the provision of a further 2,000 wells.

The Fund's programme of assistance to industry, begun in 1972 with financial aid from the USA, had led to the creation or expansion of 821 small and medium-sized enterprises by the end of 1987. In 1987 assistance amounting to 82m. francs CFA was given to 127 enterprises. Studies on industrial standardization were undertaken in 1985, and identified the following priorities: training for industrial inspectors, the creation of a standards bureau (particularly for food products and building materials), a system for standardizing electrical equipment, and safety regulations for public buildings. The first project to be undertaken in this field, providing training in quality control, was under way in 1987. Preliminary studies on joint production of agricultural machinery were undertaken in 1986 and 1987.

The Fund also supports two centres (in Niamey, Niger, and Ouagadougou, Burkina Faso) for the training of motor mechanics and drivers of heavy goods vehicles; research into new sources of energy (particularly the exploitation of biogas and the use of vegetable waste as fuel); conducting energy 'audits' for transport companies, factories and public buildings and recommending economies; the building of hotels and encouragement of tourism; and support for national schools of administration and technical training.

Loans guaranteed by the Fund included assistance for extension of the port of Lomé, Togo, in 1981 (1,276m. francs CFA), for building a telecommunications station in Benin in 1982 (1,000m. francs CFA), for the development of coffee and cotton cultivation in Togo in 1983 (6,750m. francs CFA), and for a hydroelectric scheme to benefit Benin and Togo (4,300m. francs CFA).

The Fund's budget for 1988 anticipated expenditure of 1,277m. francs CFA (compared with 1,217m. francs CFA in 1987 and 1,244m. francs CFA in 1986). Assistance from France amounted to 544m. francs CFA in 1987.

PUBLICATIONS
Entente Africaine (quarterly).
Rapport d'activité (annually).

ASSOCIATED ORGANIZATION
Communauté économique du bétail et de la viande du Conseil de l'Entente (Livestock and Meat Economic Community of the Entente Council): BP 638, Ouagadougou, Burkina Faso; f. 1970 to promote the production, processing and marketing of livestock and meat; negotiates between members and with third countries on technical and financial co-operation and co-ordinated legislation; attempts to co-ordinate measures to combat drought and cattle disease. Budget (1987): 105.4m. francs CFA. Mems: states belonging to the Conseil de l'Entente. Sec. Dr ALOUA MOUSSA.

CO-OPERATION COUNCIL FOR THE ARAB STATES OF THE GULF

Address: POB 7153, Riyadh 11462, Saudi Arabia.
Telephone: 482-7777.
Telex: 403635.

More generally known as the Gulf Co-operation Council (GCC), the organization was established on 25 May 1981 by six Arab states.

MEMBERS

Bahrain	Oman	Saudi Arabia
Kuwait	Qatar	United Arab Emirates

Organization
(October 1988)

SUPREME COUNCIL

The Supreme Council comprises the heads of member states, meeting annually in ordinary session, and in emergency session if demanded by two or more members. The Presidency of the Council is undertaken by each state in turn, in alphabetical order. The Supreme Council draws up the overall policy of the organization; it discusses recommendations and laws presented to it by the Ministerial Council and the Secretariat General in preparation for endorsement. A body for resolving disputes is also to be attached to and formed by the Supreme Council.

MINISTERIAL COUNCIL

The Ministerial Council consists of the foreign ministers of member states, meeting every three months, and in emergency session if demanded by two or more members. It prepares for the meetings of the Supreme Council, and draws up policies, recommendations, studies and projects aimed at developing co-operation and co-ordination among member states in various spheres.

SECRETARIAT GENERAL

The Secretariat assists member states in implementing recommendations by the Supreme and Ministerial Councils, and prepares reports and studies, budgets and accounts. The Secretary-General is appointed by the Supreme Council, upon the recommendation of the Ministerial Council, for a renewable three-year term. All member states contribute in equal proportions towards the budget of the Secretariat, which amounted to US $27m. for 1985/86.

Secretary-General: ABDULLAH YACOUB BISHARA (Kuwait).
Assistant Secretary-General for Political Affairs: SAIF BIN HASHIL AL-MASKERY (Oman).
Assistant Secretary-General for Economic Affairs: Dr ABDULLAH AL-KUWAIZ (Saudi Arabia).

Activities

The Council was set up following a series of meetings of foreign ministers of the states concerned, culminating in an agreement on the basic details of its constitution on 10 March 1981. The Constitution was signed by the six heads of state on 25 May. It describes the organization as providing 'the means for realizing co-ordination, integration and co-operation' in all economic, social and cultural affairs. A series of ministerial meetings subsequently began to put the proposals into effect.

ECONOMIC CO-OPERATION

In June 1981 Gulf finance ministers drew up an economic co-operation agreement covering investment, petroleum, the abolition of customs duties, harmonization of banking regulations and financial and monetary co-ordination. In November 1982 Heads of State approved the formation of a Gulf Investment Corporation with capital of US $2,100m., to be based in Kuwait (see below). Customs duties on domestic products of the Gulf states were abolished in March 1983, and new regulations allowing free movement of workers and vehicles between member states were also introduced. A common minimum customs levy on foreign imports was imposed from September 1983. In 1985 unified patent legislation was discussed, to deal with the increasing problem of counterfeit goods in the region. In February 1987 the governors of the member states' central banks agreed in principle to co-ordinate their rates of exchange, and this was approved by the Supreme Council in November of that year, but disagreement remained over whether to link the Gulf currencies to the US dollar, the SDR or a 'basket' of other currencies.

TRADE

In 1982 a ministerial committee was formed to co-ordinate trade development in the region. A feasibility study was commissioned on the establishment of strategic food reserves for the member states, and the joint purchase of rice was undertaken. In November 1986 the Supreme Council approved a measure whereby citizens of GCC member states were enabled to undertake certain retail trade activities in any other member state, with effect from 1 March 1987. The ministerial committee in charge of trade also forms the board of directors of the GCC Standards and Metrology Organization, which approves minimum standards for goods produced in or imported to the region: by mid-1988 99 Gulf standards had been approved. A joint trade exhibition is held annually.

INDUSTRY

In 1985, following a series of meetings of the GCC ministers of industry, the Supreme Council endorsed a common industrial strategy for the GCC states. It approved regulations stipulating that priority should be given to imports of GCC industrial products. During 1987 and 1988 studies were being undertaken on the joint development of small and medium-sized industries in the region and on the joint manufacture of spare parts for petroleum refineries. In December 1987 the Supreme Council discussed a system for regulating regional industry in order to avoid duplication. Under the proposed system, member states would have to obtain approval from the GCC Secretariat for any major new industrial project. During 1988 unified legislation was being prepared on the investment of foreign capital in the GCC states.

AGRICULTURE

In January 1983 ministers of agriculture met to draw up a unified agricultural policy, which was endorsed by the Supreme Council in November 1985. Between 1983 and 1987 ministers also approved proposals for harmonizing legislation relating to water conservation, veterinary vaccines, insecticides, fertilizers, fisheries and seeds. Studies on the establishment of two joint veterinary laboratories (for diagnosis of virus diseases and for production of vaccines), and on agricultural and veterinary quarantine, have also been undertaken. In 1987 two private Saudi Arabian companies were designated as official GCC producers of seed and poultry.

TRANSPORT AND COMMUNICATIONS

During 1985 feasibility studies were being undertaken on new rail and road links between member states, and on the establishment of a joint coastal transport company. In December it was announced that implementation of a scheme to build a 1,700-km railway to link all the member states and Iraq (and thereby the European railway network) had been postponed, owing to its high cost (estimated at US $4,000m.). In January 1986 ministers agreed to establish a joint telecommunications network.

ENERGY

In 1982 a ministerial committee was established to co-ordinate hydrocarbons policies and prices. Sub-committees were also formed to exchange information on marketing and prices; to discuss the development of the hydrocarbons refining industry; to examine domestic energy consumption and subsidies; to co-ordinate training by national oil companies; and to co-ordinate exploration for minerals. Specific studies were undertaken on the expansion of hydrocarbons refining in Oman, and on the building of a pipeline from the Gulf oilfields to the coast of Oman, which would mean that petroleum no longer had to be carried by sea through the Strait of Hormuz. In 1982 ministers also adopted a petroleum security plan to safeguard individual members against a halt in their production, to form a stockpile of petroleum products, and to organize a boycott of any non-member country when appropriate. A unified policy on the acquisition of technology was also approved. Feasibility studies on the integration of member states' electricity networks to form a regional power grid were commissioned in March 1983, and the scheme was approved by ministers of energy in September 1986. Financing for the project was still being discussed in 1987. In December 1987 the Supreme Council adopted a plan whereby a member state whose petroleum production was disrupted could 'borrow' petroleum from other members, in order to fulfil its export obligations.

REGIONAL SECURITY

Although no mention of defence or security was made in the original constitution, the summit meeting which ratified the constitution also issued a statement rejecting any foreign military presence in the region. The Supreme Council meeting in November 1981 agreed to include defence co-operation in the activities of the organization: as a result, defence ministers met in January 1982 to discuss a common security policy, including a joint air defence system and standardization of weapons. Ground forces of the member states held a joint military exercise in October 1983, followed by naval and air exercises in 1984. In November 1984 member states agreed to form a joint defence force for rapid deployment against external aggression, comprising units from the armed forces of each country under a central command.

In 1981 the Council jointly endorsed the Saudi Arabian 'Fahd Plan' (see under Arab League) for peace in the Middle East. Between 1982 and 1986 the Council made repeated offers to mediate in the war between Iraq (supported by the member states individually) and Iran. In November 1986 the Supreme Council reiterated its demands that Iran should agree to submit to mediation in the conflict, and urged Iran to stop its attacks on merchant shipping in the Gulf. In July 1987 GCC ministers of foreign affairs approved the UN Security Council resolution (No. 598) which recommended that Iran and Iraq should settle their conflict through negotiation, and they offered their support to the UN Secretary-General in his efforts to mediate. In October (following an Iranian missile attack on Kuwait) GCC ministers of foreign affairs issued a statement declaring that aggression against one member state was regarded as aggression against them all. In December the Supreme Council studied a report by ministers of defence on protecting vessels and coastal installations against Iranian attacks, and approved a joint pact on regional co-operation in matters of security. The meeting issued a statement regretting Iran's 'procrastination' in implementing the UN Security Council resolution No. 598.

EXTERNAL RELATIONS

In 1984 and 1985 representatives of the GCC and the European Community discussed access to European markets by GCC petrochemical products (with reference to tariffs that were imposed on GCC petrochemicals by the EEC in June 1984). In June 1988 an agreement was signed by GCC and EEC ministers on economic co-operation: the EEC agreed to assist the GCC states in developing their agriculture and industry. Negotiations were to take place subsequently on trade liberalization and in particular on the reduction of tariffs imposed by the EEC on petrochemical imports: it was expected, however, that a full free-trade agreement would be opposed by some EEC member governments, who were apprehensive that this would adversely affect the European petrochemicals industry.

INVESTMENT CORPORATION

Gulf Investment Corporation: POB 3402, Safat 13035, Kuwait; tel. 2431911; telex 23146; f. 1983 by the six member states of the GCC, each contributing US $350m. of the total capital of $2,100m.; paid-up capital $540m., total assets $1,311.2m. (Dec. 1986); investment chiefly in the Gulf region, financing industrial projects (including pharmaceuticals, chemicals, steel wire, aircraft engineering, aluminium, dairy produce and chicken-breeding). By the end of 1987 about 90 proposed projects had been reviewed, and 11 (with equity participation by the Corporation amounting to $60m.) had been approved. Chair. IBRAHIM ABD AL-KARIM (Bahrain); Chief Exec. Dr KHALED AL-FAYEZ.

COUNCIL FOR MUTUAL ECONOMIC ASSISTANCE—CMEA

Address: Prospekt Kalinina 56, Moscow 121205, USSR.
Telephone: (095) 290-91-11.
Telex: 411141.

The CMEA (sometimes known as COMECON) was founded in 1949 to assist the economic development of its member states through the sharing of resources and the co-ordination of efforts.

MEMBERS

Bulgaria	German Democratic Republic	Poland
Cuba	Hungary	Romania
Czechoslovakia	Mongolia	USSR
		Viet-Nam

Albania ceased to participate in the activities of the Council at the end of 1961. The Mongolian People's Republic was admitted in 1962, the Republic of Cuba in 1972 and the Socialist Republic of Viet-Nam in 1978.

OBSERVERS

In accordance with Article XI of the Charter, the Council may invite participation of non-member countries in the work of its organs, or in spheres agreed by arrangement with the relevant countries. Afghanistan, Angola, Ethiopia, Laos, Mozambique, Nicaragua and the People's Democratic Republic of Yemen participate as observers in the work of certain CMEA organs. In 1964 an agreement was concluded whereby Yugoslavia can participate in certain defined spheres of the Council's activity.

Organization
(October 1988)

MEETING OF HEADS OF STATE

A summit meeting of heads of state of member countries (the first since 1969) was held in June 1984, and another took place in November 1986.

COUNCIL

The Council meets once a year in the capital of each member state in turn, all members being represented, usually by heads of government. It examines the reports of the Executive Committee, discusses economic, scientific and technical co-operation and determines the main directions of activities.

EXECUTIVE COMMITTEE

The Executive Committee, the chief executive organ of the CMEA, is composed of the representatives of the member states at the level of deputy heads of government. It meets at least once every three months to examine proposals from member states, the Permanent Commissions and the Secretariat. It guides all co-ordinating work, in agreement with the decisions of the Session of the Council. The Chair is taken in turn by representatives of each country.

COMMITTEES

The CMEA has committees for co-operation in the following areas: planning; science and technology; machine-building; electronics; agro-industry; external economic relations; fuel and raw materials.

PERMANENT COMMISSIONS

There are Permanent Commissions on co-operation in the areas of: statistics; electricity and nuclear power engineering; the chemical industry; metallurgy; light industry; transport; standardization; communications and postal services; environmental protection; monetary and financial matters; and legal matters.

CONFERENCES

Certain conferences are established in the CMEA structure as permanent representative bodies. These include conferences of heads of water management bodies; ministers of internal trade; heads of agencies for inventions; legal experts; heads of pricing agencies; heads of state labour organizations; representatives of freight organizations and shipowners' organizations.

SECRETARIAT

Secretary of Council: VYACHESLAV VLADIMIROVICH SYCHEV (USSR).
Deputy Secretaries: M. MARINOV (Bulgaria), K. BORCH (German Democratic Republic), I. SZIGETI (Hungary), D. ZAGASBALDAN (Mongolia), S. ZAWODZINSKI (Poland), I. RĂTOI (Romania).

Activities

The CMEA aims to unite and co-ordinate the efforts of the member countries in order to improve the development of socialist economic integration; to achieve more rapid economic and technical progress in these countries, and particularly a higher level of industrialization in countries where this is lacking; to achieve a steady growth of labour productivity; to work gradually towards a balanced level of development in the different regions, and a steady increase in standards of living in the member states.

Trade is one of the most important forms of economic co-operation between member states of CMEA. Trade between member states was planned by yearly agreements until 1951 and thereafter by long-term bilateral and multilateral trade agreements linked to the development plans of the member countries. In 1985 trade between member countries comprised about 60% of their foreign trade, which is wholly state-controlled.

In 1971 the Council adopted the 'Comprehensive Programme for Further Extension and Improvement of Co-operation and the Development of Socialist Economic Integration among CMEA Countries'. Reviewing the first 10 years of this programme in 1981, the Council noted that CMEA industrial production had increased by 84% during the period, and trade among members by over 300%. In 1979 the Council adopted long-term specific programmes for energy, fuel, raw materials, agriculture, food production, machine-building and transport for the period up to 1990.

The national five-year economic plans of member states are co-ordinated by the CMEA secretariat, in consultation with national planning offices. The original emphasis on mutual trade has shifted to co-operation in production, involving specialization, joint ventures and the standardization of equipment and components, supervised by the various Permanent Commissions listed above. A number of joint organizations (listed on the following page) co-ordinate members' planning in various branches of industry and transport.

The CMEA's long-term programme on fuels and energy provides for joint power engineering projects and supply networks, with particular emphasis on the development of nuclear and solar power and the reduction of petroleum consumption.

In industry, the programme for the 1980s gave special attention to the electronics industry and the standardization of electronic components. A major plan for the introduction of robots in industry was agreed in 1982. Member countries also co-operate in attempts to protect the environment from pollution caused by industry (especially the chemicals industry). In December 1985 the Council adopted a 'Comprehensive Programme for the Scientific and Technical Progress of the CMEA Countries to the Year 2000', covering electronics, industrial automation (robotics), development of new industrial materials and computer technology, biotechnology, and nuclear energy. A new organization, Interrobot, was established to co-ordinate industrial automation.

Agricultural co-operation emphasizes the improved availability and nutritional quality of food supplies, through higher-yielding crop varieties, more extensive use of fertilizers, and collaboration in producing up-to-date equipment for processing foodstuffs.

Problems in co-operation have included the lack of a convertible currency for trade between member nations, and the cumbersome procedures of state trading organizations. There were disagreements over the pricing of food and petroleum during 1983 and 1984: although the USSR agreed to raise the prices it pays for imports of food from other members, chiefly Bulgaria, Hungary and Romania (the first increase for 10 years), this was offset by the high price of petroleum exports to them from the USSR. The USSR also expressed dissatisfaction with the quality of goods imported from its partners.

In 1988 a reorganization of the CMEA's administrative structure took place, involving the amalgamation of a number of existing bodies and the creation of new ones (notably a Committee for

INTERNATIONAL ORGANIZATIONS

Council for Mutual Economic Assistance

External Economic Relations, and a Permanent Commission for Environmental Protection). In July the Council discussed economic reforms and the need to stimulate trade between members and to improve production-sharing. The creation of a convertible currency was supported by all the members except the German Democratic Republic and Romania. The meeting approved special programmes of assistance for Cuba, Mongolia and Viet-Nam.

EXTERNAL RELATIONS

In accordance with an agreement concluded in 1964, Yugoslavia participates in the work of some CMEA bodies: areas of co-operation include foreign trade, monetary and financial matters, scientific and technological co-operation, metallurgy and engineering. Between 1973 and 1988 Finland signed 120 multilateral and bilateral agreements and protocols with the CMEA, including agreements on co-operation in engineering, timber production, petroleum and gas, environmental protection and transport. Other co-operation agreements were signed with Iraq (1975), Mexico (1975), Nicaragua (1983), Mozambique (1985), Angola (1986), Ethiopia (1986), the People's Democratic Republic of Yemen (1986) and Afghanistan (1987). Special commissions meet regularly to discuss and organize co-operation with each of these countries. At the beginning of 1984 there were over 300 industrial co-operation projects in developing countries, particularly India. The CMEA has observer status at the United Nations, and co-operates with numerous UN and other international bodies. In June 1985 CMEA leaders agreed to propose the establishment of official links with the European Community, and formal relations were established in June 1988.

TRADE TOTALS WITHIN CMEA (million roubles)

	1950	1960	1970	1980
Bulgaria	199	872	2,570	9,623
Cuba	n.a.	192	1,355	5,541
Czechoslovakia	695	2,150	4,329	13,252
German Democratic Republic	570	2,679	5,709	16,122
Hungary	356	1,037	2,669	10,303
Mongolia	64	127	176	616
Poland	685	1,437	4,067	13,211
Romania	342	821	1,689	5,714
USSR	1,679	5,343	12,284	45,777
Total	4,525	14,338	33,493	120,159

International Economic Bodies established by CMEA member countries

INDUSTRIAL ORGANIZATIONS

Assofoto: 2 Smolenskii per. 1/4, Moscow, USSR; f. 1973; photo-chemical industry; joint planning; co-operation in all stages of the reproduction process. Mems: German Democratic Republic, USSR.

Central Control Administration of the United Power Grids of European CMEA Member Countries (CCA): Jungmannova 29, 111 32 Prague 1, Czechoslovakia; f. 1962. Mems: seven countries.

Computers: ul. Chaikovskogo 11, Moscow, USSR; f. 1969; computer engineering, establishment of standardized computer technology; joint planning of international industrial complex. Mems: nine countries.

Interatomenergo: ul. Kitaiskii proezd 7, Moscow, USSR; f. 1973; nuclear power plant construction; co-ordination of research, development and production; specialization and co-operation of production; mutual support in planning and training. Mems: eight countries.

Interatominstrument: ul. Chocimska 28, 00-791 Warsaw, Poland; nuclear-technical apparatus construction; co-operation in research, production and sales, industrial co-ordination. Mems: six countries.

Interchim: Thälmannplatz 5, PSF 726, Halle 4020, German Democratic Republic; tel. 38401; telex 4322; f. 1970; branches of chemical industry. Specialization and co-operation in production; co-ordination of production plans. Mems: eight countries. Dir J. SCHNEIDER.

Interchimvolokno: Piaţa Rosetti, Sector 1, Bucharest, Romania; f. 1974; organizes and co-ordinates research and production in the chemical fibres industry, promotes the development of trade and co-ordinates the supply of raw materials and equipment.

Interelektro: ul. 1 Smolenskaya 7, Moscow, USSR; f. 1973; selected branches of electrotechnology; joint planning and prognostics; specialization and co-operation of production; scientific and technical co-operation; co-ordination of mutual goods supplies. Mems: eight countries.

Intermetall: Cházár András ul. 9, 1146 Budapest, Hungary; f. 1964; ferrous metallurgy; specialization and co-operation in production; assortment exchange. Mems: six countries.

Interoceanmetall: Szczecin, Poland; f. 1987 to undertake sea-bed mining. Mems: seven countries.

Interrobot: f. 1985; for co-ordination of industrial automation. Mems: six countries.

Intertextilmash: ul. Shchepkina 49, Moscow, USSR; f. 1973; selected branches of textile machinery construction; co-ordination of research, development and production; specialization and co-operation in production, research, development, construction, sales and service. Mems: seven countries.

Organization for Co-operation in the Roller-Bearings Industry: ul. Senatorska 13/15, Warsaw, Poland; tel. 261546; telex 813489; f. 1964; co-ordinates production of anti-friction roller-bearings for use in engineering; carries out research into standardization and improvements in design and equipment. Mems: eight countries.

JOINT RESEARCH INSTITUTES AND ASSOCIATIONS

Interetalonpribor: Ezdakov per, Moscow, USSR; f. 1972; measurement technology, joint research, development and production of measuring apparatus. Mems: seven countries.

Interkosmos: Leninskii prospekt 14, Moscow, USSR; f. 1970; research. Mems: 10 countries.

International Centre for Scientific and Technological Information: ul. Kuusinena 21b, Moscow, USSR; f. 1969; develops methods and technical aspects of information work, provides an information service for participating countries. Mems: 10 countries.

TRANSPORT ORGANIZATIONS

International Shipowners Association: Sieroszewskiego 7, 81-376 Gdynia, Poland; tel. 210974; telex 54250; f. 1970; members co-operate in technical, operational, documentary and legal matters concerning maritime traffic. Mems: four national associations and five shipping companies from nine countries. Pres. J. IVOVIĆ; Sec.-Gen. A. I. FROLOV.

Interport: 70-464 Szczecin, ul. Armii Czerwonej 37, Poland; f. 1973; co-ordination and rationalization of seaport capacities. Mems: German Democratic Republic, Poland.

OPW: ul. Italska 37, Prague, Czechoslovakia; f. 1963; railway freight transport. Mems: seven countries.

Ship-chartering Co-ordination Bureau: Prospekt Kalinina 56, Moscow, USSR; telex 411159; f. 1952; co-operation in rationalizing maritime freight. Mems: nine countries.

CURRENCY AND CREDIT ORGANIZATIONS

See chapters on the International Bank for Economic Co-operation and the International Investment Bank.

PUBLICATIONS

Statistical Yearbook.
Survey of CMEA Activities (annually).
Economic Co-operation of the CMEA Member Countries (monthly in Russian; quarterly in English and Spanish).
Press Bulletin.
International Agricultural Journal.
Books (between 10 and 15 a year) and press releases.

COUNCIL OF ARAB ECONOMIC UNITY

Address: POB 925100, Amman, Jordan.
Telephone: 664326-9.
Telex: 21900.
The first meeting of the Council was held in 1964.

MEMBERS

Egypt*
Iraq
Jordan
Kuwait
Libya
Mauritania
Palestine Liberation Organization
Somalia
Sudan
Syria
United Arab Emirates
Yemen Arab Republic
Yemen, People's Democratic Republic

* Egypt's membership is suspended.

Organization
(October 1988)

COUNCIL

The Council consists of representatives of member states, usually ministers of economy, finance and trade. It meets twice a year; meetings are chaired by the representative of each country for one year.

GENERAL SECRETARIAT

Entrusted with the implementation and follow-up of the Council's decisions and with proposing work plans, including efforts to encourage participation by member states in the Arab Economic Unity Agreement. The Secretariat also conducts research and publishes studies on Arab economic problems and on the effects of major world economic trends.
Secretary-General: HASAN IBRAHIM.
Assistant Secretary-General: Dr HASSAN GHARIEBH.

COMMITTEES

There are seven standing committees: preparatory, follow-up and Arab Common Market Development; Permanent Delegates; budget; economic planning; fiscal and monetary matters; customs and trade planning and co-ordination; statistics. There are also seven 'ad hoc' committees, including meetings of experts on tariffs, trade promotion and trade legislation.

STATISTICAL BUREAU

Arab Central Bureau of Statistics and Documentation: established in 1976 to co-ordinate the activities of Arab national statistical offices and regional organizations; provides training, technical assistance and documentary services. Dir ANWAR A. KHALIL.

Activities

A five-year work plan for the General Secretariat in 1986–90 was approved in December 1985. Like the previous five-year plan, it included the co-ordination of measures leading to a customs union subject to a unified administration; market and commodity studies; unification of statistical terminology and methods of data collection; studies for the formation of new joint Arab companies and federations; formulation of specific programmes for agricultural and industrial co-ordination and for improving road and railway networks.

ARAB COMMON MARKET

Members: Iraq, Jordan, Libya, Mauritania, Syria and the People's Democratic Republic of Yemen (Egypt's membership is suspended).

Based on a resolution passed by the Council in August 1964; its implementation is supervised by the Council and does not constitute a separate organization. Customs duties and other taxes on trade between the member countries were eliminated in annual stages, the process being completed in 1971. The second stage was to be the adoption of a full customs union, and ultimately all restrictions on trade between the member countries, including quotas, and restrictions on residence, employment and transport, were to be abolished. In practice, however, the trading of national products has not been freed from all monetary, quantitative and administrative restrictions.

Between 1978 and 1988, the following measures were undertaken by the Council for the development of the Arab Common Market:

Introduction of flexible membership conditions for the least developed Arab states (Mauritania, Somalia, Sudan, People's Democratic Republic of Yemen, Yemen Arab Republic).

Approval in principle of a fund to compensate the least developed countries for financial losses incurred as a result of joining the Arab Common Market.

Approval of legal, technical and administrative preparations for unification of tariffs levied on products imported from non-member countries.

Formation of a committee of ministerial deputies to deal with problems in the application of market rulings and to promote the organization's activities.

Preparation of an integrated programme aimed at enhancing trade between member states.

MULTILATERAL AGREEMENTS

The Council has initiated the following multilateral agreements aimed at achieving economic unity:

Agreement on Basic Levels of Social Insurance.

Agreement on Reciprocity in Social Insurance Systems.

Agreement on Labour Mobility.

Agreement on Organization of Transit Trade.

Agreement on Avoidance of Double Taxation and Elimination of Tax Evasion.

Agreement on Co-operation in Collection of Taxes.

Agreement on Capital Investment and Mobility.

Agreement on Settlement of Investment Disputes between Host Arab Countries and Citizens of Other Countries.

JOINT VENTURES

A number of multilateral organizations in industry and agriculture have been formed on the principle that faster development and economies of scale may be achieved by combining the efforts of member states. In industries that are new to the member countries, Arab Joint Companies are formed, while existing industries are co-ordinated by the setting up of Arab Specialized Unions. The unions are for closer co-operation on problems of production and marketing, and to help companies deal as a group in international markets. The companies are intended to be self-supporting on a purely commercial basis; they may issue shares to citizens of the participating countries. The joint ventures are:

Arab Joint Companies (cap. = capital; figures in Kuwaiti dinars unless otherwise stated):

Arab Company for Drug Industries and Medical Appliances: POB 925161, Amman, Jordan; cap. 60m.

Arab Company for Industrial Investment: POB 2154, Baghdad, Iraq; cap. 150m.

Arab Company for Livestock Development: POB 5305, Damascus, Syria; tel. 66 60 37; telex 11376; cap. 60m.

Arab Mining Company: POB 20198, Amman, Jordan; telex 21169; cap. 120m.

Specialized Arab Unions and Federations:

Arab Co-operative Federation: POB 57640, Baghdad, Iraq; telex 2685.

Arab Federation for Cement and Building Materials: POB 9015, Damascus, Syria.

Arab Federation of Chemical Fertilizers Producers: POB 23696, Kuwait.

Arab Federation of Engineering Industries: POB 509, Baghdad, Iraq; tel. 776 11 01; telex 2724.

Arab Federation of Leather Industries: POB 2188, Damascus, Syria.

Arab Federation of Paper Industries: POB 5456, Baghdad, Iraq.

Arab Federation of Shipping Industries: POB 1161, Baghdad, Iraq.

Arab Federation of Textile Industries: POB 620, Damascus, Syria.

INTERNATIONAL ORGANIZATIONS

Arab Seaports Federation: Basrah, Iraq.
Arab Sugar Federation: POB 195, Khartoum, Sudan.
Arab Union of Fish Producers: POB 15064, Baghdad, Iraq; tel. 55 11 261.
Arab Union of Food Industries: POB 13025, Baghdad, Iraq.
Arab Union of Land Transport: POB 926324, Amman, Jordan.
Arab Union of Pharmaceutical Manufacturers and Medical Appliance Manufacturers: POB 1124, Amman, Jordan; tel. 665320; telex 21528.
Arab Union of Railways: POB 6599, Aleppo, Syria; tel. 220302; telex 331009.

PUBLICATIONS

Economic Report of the General Secretary (2 a year).
Progress Report (2 a year).

Council of Arab Economic Unity

Arab Economic Unity Bulletin (2 a year).
Statistical Yearbook for Arab Countries.
Economic Indicators for Arab Countries (annually).
Annual Bulletin for Arab Countries' Foreign Trade Statistics.
Yearbook for Intra-Arab Trade Statistics.
Yearbook of National Accounts for Arab Countries.
Demographic Yearbook for Arab Countries.
Annual Bulletin for Official Exchange Rates of Arab Currencies.
Annual Bibliography.
Guide to Studies prepared by Secretariat.

THE COUNCIL OF EUROPE

Address: BP 431, R6-67006 Strasbourg Cedex, France.
Telephone: (88) 61-49-61.
Telex: 870943.

The Council was founded in May 1949 to achieve a greater unity between its members, to facilitate their economic and social progress and to uphold the principles of parliamentary democracy. Membership has risen from the original 10 to 22.

MEMBERS

Austria	Luxembourg
Belgium	Malta
Cyprus	Netherlands
Denmark	Norway
France	Portugal
Federal Republic of Germany	San Marino
	Spain
Greece	Sweden
Iceland	Switzerland
Ireland	Turkey
Italy	United Kingdom
Liechtenstein	

San Marino was admitted as a member in October 1988. Finland also applied for membership in 1988.

Organization
(October 1988)

COMMITTEE OF MINISTERS

The Committee consists of the Ministers of Foreign Affairs of all member states; it decides with binding effect all matters of internal organization, makes recommendations to governments and may also draw up conventions and agreements; it also discusses matters of political concern, such as East-West and North-South relations, United Nations activities, the protection of human rights and prevention of terrorism. It usually meets in April/May and November each year.

CONFERENCES OF SPECIALIZED MINISTERS

There are 19 Conferences of specialized ministers, meeting regularly for intergovernmental co-operation in various fields.

MINISTERS' DEPUTIES

Senior diplomats are accredited to the Council as permanent representatives of their governments, and deal with most of the routine work at monthly meetings. Any decision reached by the Deputies has the same force as one adopted by the Ministers.

PARLIAMENTARY ASSEMBLY

President: LOUIS JUNG (France).
Chairman of the Socialist Group: KARL AHRENS (FRG).
Chairman of the Christian Democrat Group: ADOLFO SARTI (Italy).
Chairman of the European Democratic (Conservative) Group: ANDERS BJÖRCK (Sweden).
Chairman of the Liberal Democratic and Reformers' Group: BJØRN ELMQUIST (Denmark).
Chairman of the Group of Communists and Allies: CARLOS CARVALHAS (Portugal).

Members are elected or appointed by their national parliaments from among the members thereof; political parties in each delegation follow the proportion of their strength in the national parliament. Members do not represent their governments; they are spokesmen for public opinion. The Assembly has 170 members: 18 each for France, the Federal Republic of Germany, Italy and the United Kingdom; 12 each for Spain and Turkey; seven each for Belgium, Greece, the Netherlands and Portugal; six each for Austria, Sweden and Switzerland; five each for Denmark and Norway; four for Ireland; three each for Cyprus, Iceland, Luxembourg and Malta; and two for Liechtenstein.

The Assembly meets in ordinary session once a year for not more than a month. The session is usually divided into three parts held in January–February, April–May and September–October. The Assembly may submit recommendations to the Committee of Ministers, pass resolutions, discuss reports and any matters of common European interest. It is also a consultative body to the Committee of Ministers, and elects the Secretary-General, the Deputy Secretary-General, the Clerk of the Assembly and the members of the European Court of Human Rights.

Standing Committee: Represents the Assembly when it is not in session, and may adopt Recommendations to the Committee of Ministers and Resolutions on behalf of the Assembly. Consists of the President, Vice-Presidents, Chairmen of the Ordinary Committees and a number of ordinary members. Meets at least three times a year (once in 'mini' session).

Ordinary Committees: political, economic and development, social and health, legal, culture and education, science and technology, environment, regional planning and local authorities, rules of procedure, agriculture, relations with European non-member countries, parliamentary and public relations, migration, refugees and demography, budget and intergovernmental work programme.

SECRETARIAT

Secretary-General: MARCELINO OREJA AGUIRRE (Spain).
Deputy Secretary-General: GAETANO ADINOLFI (Italy).
Clerk of the Parliamentary Assembly: HEINRICH KLEBES (FRG).

Activities

In an effort to harmonize national laws, to put the citizens of member countries on an equal footing and to pool certain resources and facilities, the Council has concluded a number of Conventions and Agreements covering particular aspects of European co-operation. By June 1988 a total of 129 treaties had been concluded, of which 21 had not yet come into force.

HUMAN RIGHTS

The promotion and development of human rights is one of the major tasks of the Council of Europe. All member states are parties to the European Convention for the Protection of Human Rights and Fundamental Freedoms of 1950. A steering committee for human rights prepares new protocols to the Convention, and declarations of the Committee of Ministers; it also conducts a human rights education and information programme. The first ministerial conference on human rights was held in March 1985.

European Commission of Human Rights

The Commission has 21 members. It is competent to examine complaints made either by a contracting party, or in certain cases, by an individual, non-governmental organization or group of individuals, that the European Convention for the Protection of Human Rights and Fundamental Freedoms has been violated by one or more of the contracting parties. If the Commission decides to admit the application, it then ascertains the full facts of the case and places itself at the disposal of the parties in order to try and reach a friendly settlement. If no settlement is reached, the Commission sends a report to the Committee of Ministers in which it states an opinion as to whether there has been a violation of the Convention. It is then for the Committee of Ministers or, if the case is referred to it, the Court to decide whether or not a violation has taken place. By the end of 1987 over 13,400 human rights applications had been lodged.

President: Prof. CARL AAGE NØRGAARD (Denmark).
First Vice-President: Prof. Dr JOCHEN A. FROWEIN (FRG).
Second Vice-President: Prof. STEPHAN TRECHSEL (Switzerland).
Secretary: HANS-CHRISTIAN KRÜGER (FRG).

European Court of Human Rights

The Court comprises 21 judges. It may deal with a case only after the Commission has acknowledged the failure of efforts for a friendly settlement. The following may bring a case before the Court, provided that the High Contracting Party or Parties concerned have accepted its compulsory jurisdiction or, failing that, with the consent of the High Contracting Party or Parties concerned: the Commission, a High Contracting Party whose national is alleged to be a victim, a High Contracting Party which referred the case to the Commission, and a High Contracting Party against which the complaint has been lodged. In the event of dispute as to whether the Court has jurisdiction, the matter is settled by the Court. The judgment of the Court is final. The Court may, in certain circumstances, give advisory opinions at the request of the Committee of Ministers.

President: ROLV RYSSDAL (Norway).
Vice-President: JOHN J. CREMONA (Malta).
Registrar: MARC-ANDRÉ EISSEN (France).

MASS MEDIA

In 1982 the Committee of Ministers adopted a Declaration on the freedom of expression and information, which forms the basis for the Council of Europe's mass media activities. Activities in the media field are carried out by a steering committee of governmental experts and cover all aspects of mass communication—legal, political, cultural, economic, social and technical—notably as far as current developments relating to broadcasting are concerned.

At the first European ministerial conference on mass media policy (December 1986) the participating states agreed on concerted actions with a view to promoting a coherent mass media policy in Europe. The Ministers also affirmed the importance they attached to the Council of Europe as the 'most suitable institution in Europe' for the elaboration of such a policy.

From 1984 onwards, the Committee of Ministers adopted a number of recommendations concerning principles on television advertising (in particular when it is transmitted by satellite), use of satellite capacity for television and sound radio, promotion of audio-visual production, copyright aspects of television by satellite and cable, private copying of videograms and phonograms, and audio-visual piracy.

In early 1987 the Committee of Ministers instructed its Steering Committee on the Mass Media (CDMM) to draw up a European Convention on transfrontier television. The Draft Convention establishes a framework for the transfrontier circulation of television programme services. It guarantees freedom of reception as well as the principle of non-restriction of the retransmission of services conforming to minimum standards embodied in it.

The CDMM was also responsible for preparing the second European ministerial conference on mass media policy (November 1988). During 1988 its committee of experts on media policy was considering measures to promote European audio-visual works and the committee of legal experts in the media field was conducting work on copyright issues arising in relation to reprographic techniques and especially to direct broadcasting satellites, fixed satellite services and cable distribution of television programmes.

SOCIAL WELFARE

The European Social Charter, in force since 1965, is now applied in Austria, Cyprus, Denmark, France, the Federal Republic of Germany, Greece, Iceland, Ireland, Italy, the Netherlands, Norway, Spain, Sweden and the United Kingdom; it lays down the rights and principles which are the basis of the Council's social policy, and guarantees a number of social and economic rights to the citizen, including the right to work, the right to form workers' organizations, the right to social security and social assistance, the right of the family to protection and the right of migrant workers to protection and assistance. In May 1988 the Charter was completed by an Additional Protocol which extends these rights.

The European Code of Social Security and its Protocol entered into force in 1968; by 1988 the Code and Protocol had been ratified by Belgium, the Federal Republic of Germany, Luxembourg, the Netherlands, Norway, Portugal and Sweden, while the Code alone had been ratified by Denmark, France, Greece, Ireland, Italy, Switzerland, Turkey and the United Kingdom. These instruments set minimum standards for medical care and the following benefits: sickness, old-age, unemployment, employment injury, family, maternity, invalidity and survivor's benefit. In 1987 a revision of these instruments, aiming to provide higher standards and greater flexibility, was submitted to the Parliamentary Assembly.

The European Convention on Social Security, in force since 1977, now applies in Austria, Belgium, Luxembourg, the Netherlands, Portugal, Spain and Turkey; most of the provisions apply automatically, while others are subject to the conclusion of additional multilateral or bilateral agreements. The Convention is concerned with establishing equality of treatment for nationals of member states and with ensuring the granting and maintenance of social security rights by such means as the adding together of insurance periods completed in more than one state; two interim agreements are also in force, which will progressively be superseded by the Convention.

A number of resolutions passed by the Committee of Ministers give guidance for intergovernmental action on particular aspects of social policy, welfare or labour law. Eight states are co-operating in drawing up common standards on the protection of safety and health at work.

The Council of Europe operates a fellowships scheme for the benefit of personnel in the social services drawn from the member countries, and an annual research fellowships programme, in which a group of specialists investigates a subject chosen by the Social Committee.

HEALTH

Through a series of expert committees, the Council aims at ensuring constant co-operation in Europe in a variety of health-related fields: e.g., promotion of education for health, evaluation of programmes for the prevention of diseases, assessment and implementation of new methods of treatment and techniques, adaptation of training curricula for health personnel. It strives to formulate cost-effective policies in order to contain the rising costs of health care.

A programme of Medical Fellowships enables members of the health professions to study new techniques and participate in co-ordinated research programmes. Availability of blood and blood products (also of very rare groups) has been ensured through European Agreements and a network of co-operating transfusion centres. Advances in this field and in histocompatibility are continuously assessed by expert committees.

Twelve states co-operate in establishing common standards regarding the use of pesticides, food additives, flavouring substances, and plastic materials that come into contact with food. They also deal with adverse effects of pharmaceutical and cosmetic products, of residues of veterinary drugs in food of animal origin, and of wood protection products.

Thirteen states co-operate in establishing a coherent policy on the rehabilitation of disabled people, aiming to allow such people the greatest possible degree of independence, equality and participation. Assistance is given in the assessment of national legislation in this field.

In the co-operation group to combat drug abuse and illicit drug trafficking (Pompidou Group), 19 states work together at ministerial level to counteract drug abuse. The Group follows a multi-disciplinary approach embracing in particular legislation, law enforcement, prevention, treatment, rehabilitation and data collection.

The European Agreement on the restriction of the use of certain detergents in washing and cleaning products entered into force in 1971 (amended by a protocol, 1984). There are 10 parties to the Agreement.

The Convention on the Elaboration of a European Pharmacopoeia (establishing standards for medicinal substances) entered into force in May 1974: 18 state are parties to the Convention and one observer state, WHO and the EEC participate in the meetings. Publication of a second edition began in 1980: it covered about 700 substances by 1988.

POPULATION

The European Population Committee, an intergovernmental committee of scientists and government officials engaged in demography, monitors and analyses population trends in member states and informs governments and the public of developments that may require political action. It compiles an annual review of demographic developments and publishes the results of studies of particular aspects of population, for example the implications of declining fertility, the changing age structure of European populations, the labour market, new patterns of family and life-style, and the demographic consequences of migration. Seminars and conferences are held; a Population Conference is planned for 1992.

MIGRANT WORKERS AND REFUGEES

In May 1977 the Committee of Ministers adopted the European Convention on the Legal Status of Migrant Workers. The Committee also made a number of recommendations to governments on the reunion of migrant workers' families; clandestine immigration; social and economic repercussions on migrant workers of economic recessions and crises; migrant women; integration of migrant workers returning to their countries of origin.

Language classes for migrant workers and special experimental classes for their children are sponsored. Vocational training grants are awarded to student-instructors and instructor-trainees.

The Council of Europe Resettlement Fund was created in 1956 to make loans for the resettlement of refugees or those made homeless by natural disasters, and to assist in job creation, vocational training and health education schemes. In 1988 19 countries were members of the Fund and the loans granted since the Fund's inception amounted to about US $7,436m.

LEGAL MATTERS

The European Committee on Legal Co-operation supervises the work programme for international, administrative, civil and commercial law. Specialized committees of legal experts work under its direction. There are also committees concerned with the movement of persons, refugees and bio-ethics. Numerous conventions have been adopted, on matters which include: foreign liabilities; information on foreign law; consular functions; bearer securities; state immunity; motorists' liability; adoption; nationality; animal protection; mutual aid in administrative matters; custody of children; data protection. Conferences of ministers of justice of member states, although not formally under the Council of Europe, make proposals for the Council's work programme.

CRIME

The European Committee on Crime Problems has prepared conventions on such matters as extradition, mutual assistance, recognition and enforcement of foreign judgments, the transfer of proceedings, the suppression of terrorism, the transfer of prisoners and the compensation to be paid to victims of violent crime. A number of resolutions on various questions relating to penal law, penology and criminology have been adopted by the Committee of Ministers.

The Criminological Scientific Council is composed of specialists in law, psychology, sociology and related sciences. It advises the European Committee on Crime Problems and the conferences of directors of criminological research institutes.

Penological matters are examined by the directors of prison administrations whose resolutions and conclusions serve as guidelines to the member States for the penal policy to be adopted. A Committee on Co-operation in Prison Affairs prepared new European Prison Rules in 1987 and was examining alternatives to imprisonment in 1988.

EDUCATION AND CULTURE

The Council for Cultural Co-operation implements the educational and cultural programme which gives priority to primary education, human rights education in schools, education and cultural development of migrants, modern language teaching, reform and development of tertiary education, adult education and social development, cultural development policies at regional and local level, evaluation of national cultural policies, and action to promote reading, poetry and translation. It administers the Cultural Fund which was established to promote and finance educational and cultural activities in accordance with the statute of the Council of Europe. Mems: member states and other signatories of the Cultural Convention, namely Finland and the Holy See. The Parliamentary Assembly is also represented. Other activities include the European Schools Day Competition, and the management of the European Documentation and Information System in Education (EUDISED).

The Council also organizes Council of Europe Higher Education scholarships, teacher-training courses and bursaries, and European Art Exhibitions.

Secretariat services are provided by the Council of Europe for the standing conference of European ministers of education. Sessions are held every two years. The conference of European ministers responsible for cultural affairs is held every three years.

YOUTH

The European Youth Centre (EYC) is equipped with audio-visual workshops, reading and conference rooms; provides about 40 residential courses a year for youth leaders, on European affairs, problems of modern society, the role of youth, and techniques of leading and organizing youth movements. About 1,500 people can be accommodated annually. A notable feature of the EYC, which it shares with the European Youth Foundation, is its decision-making structure, by which decisions on its programme and general policy matters are taken by a Governing Board composed of an equal number of youth organizations and government representatives. A European Youth Week was organized by the EYC in 1985, involving more than 600 young people, and symposia were subsequently held on such topics as youth exchanges, challenges to democracy and North-South interdependence.

The European Youth Foundation (EYF) aims to provide financial assistance to European activities of non-governmental youth organizations and began operations in 1973. Since that time more than 100 organizations have received financial aid for carrying out international activities held in all member countries of the Council of Europe. The total number of young people taking part in meetings supported by the Foundation amounted to about 78,000 by 1988, coming from more than 30 countries. More than 87m. French francs have been distributed.

The European Steering Committee for Intergovernmental Co-operation in the Youth Field conducts research in youth-related matters and prepares for ministerial conferences.

SPORT

The Committee for the Development of Sport, founded in November 1977, has the same membership as the Council for Cultural Co-operation (see above) and administers the Sports Fund. Its activities concentrate on the implementation of the European Sport for All Charter (1975); the role of sport in society (e.g. medical, political, ethical and educational aspects); the practice of sport (activities, special projects, etc.); the diffusion of sports information and co-ordination of sports research. The Committee is also responsible for preparing the conference of European ministers responsible for sport. In 1984 the conference adopted an Anti-Doping Charter for Sport, and in 1985 it adopted the European Convention on Spectator Violence and Misbehaviour at Sports Events. A Charter on Sport for Disabled Persons was adopted in 1986.

ENVIRONMENT

The Steering Committee for the Conservation and Management of the Environment and Natural Habitats, founded in 1962, prepares policy recommendations and promotes co-operation in all environmental questions. It introduced a European Water Charter in 1968, a Soil Charter in 1974 and a Charter on Invertebrates in 1986. The Committee awards the European Diploma for protection of areas of European significance, supervises a network of biogenetic reserves, and maintains 'red lists' of threatened animals and plants.

The fifth ministerial conference on the environment was held in 1987, and discussed the protection and management of the natural heritage, the drafting of a European Conservation Strategy and of a Convention on Soil Protection. Sixteen member states, two non-members and the European Community have ratified a Convention on the Conservation of European Wildlife and Natural Habitats, which entered into force in June 1982 and gives total protection to 119 species of plants, 55 mammals, 294 birds, 34 reptiles, 17 amphibians, 115 freshwater fishes, 81 invertebrates and their habitats. A European Campaign for the Countryside was to be undertaken in 1987–88, attempting to reconcile development with conservation.

LOCAL GOVERNMENT AND REGIONAL PLANNING

The standing conference of local and regional authorities in Europe was created in 1957 as a representative assembly of regions and municipalities of the member states of the Council of Europe; since April 1976 annual sessions have been chiefly concerned with local government matters, regional planning, regional problems, protection of the environment, town and country planning and social and cultural affairs. Ad hoc conferences and public hearings are also held.

The Steering Committee on Regional and Municipal Matters was set up in 1970 as a forum for senior officials from ministries of local government, for the exchange of experience between national governments, and for a common approach to the development of the national structures and legislature. The committee has stressed the value of strengthening local government, and adapting it to changing requirements, as well as to the increasing contacts between all European countries. It publishes an information bulletin and studies on local and regional authorities.

Secretariat services for the conference of European ministers responsible for local government are provided by the Council of Europe. The seventh conference was held in 1986, discussing local finance and foreign workers. The seventh conference of ministers responsible for regional planning was held in 1985.

MONUMENTS AND SITES

The Steering Committee for Integrated Conservation of the Historic Heritage maintains contact between authorities in charge of historic buildings and encourages public interest. A third conference of ministers responsible for conservation of the architectural heritage was to be held in 1989/90.

A Convention for the Conservation of the Architectural Heritage of Europe entered into force in 1987, and had been ratified by five states at mid-1988.

EXTERNAL RELATIONS

Agreements providing for co-operation and exchange of documents and observers have been concluded with the United Nations and its Agencies, and with most of the European inter-governmental organizations and the Organization of American States. Particularly close relations exist with the European Community, OECD, EFTA and Western European Union.

Israel is represented in the Parliamentary Assembly by an observer, and certain European and other non-member countries have been invited to participate in or send observers to certain meetings of technical committees and specialized conferences.

Relations with non-member states, other organizations and non-governmental organizations are co-ordinated within the Secretariat by the Directorate of Political Affairs.

In 1988 the Council of Europe organized a Campaign on North-South Interdependence and Solidarity, to raise public awareness of global interdependence.

FINANCE

The ordinary budget for 1988 was 415m. French francs, of which France, the Federal Republic of Germany, Italy and the United Kingdom each contributed 16.71%; other states make smaller contributions.

PUBLICATIONS

Forum (quarterly, in English, French, German and Italian).
Catalogue of Publications (annually).

ECONOMIC COMMUNITY OF WEST AFRICAN STATES—ECOWAS

Address: 6 King George V Rd, PMB 12745, Lagos, Nigeria.
Telephone: 636841.
Telex: 22633.

The Treaty of Lagos, establishing ECOWAS, was signed in May 1975 by 15 states, with the object of promoting trade, co-operation and self-reliance in West Africa. Outstanding protocols bringing certain key features of the Treaty into effect were ratified in November 1976. Cape Verde joined in 1977.

MEMBERS

Benin
Burkina Faso
Cape Verde
Côte d'Ivoire
The Gambia
Ghana
Guinea
Guinea-Bissau
Liberia
Mali
Mauritania
Niger
Nigeria
Senegal
Sierra Leone
Togo

Organization
(October 1988)

CONFERENCE OF HEADS OF STATE AND GOVERNMENT

The Conference, the highest authority of ECOWAS, meets once a year. The Chairman is drawn from the member states in turn.

COUNCIL OF MINISTERS

The Council consists of two representatives from each country; a chairman is drawn from each country in turn. It meets twice a year, and is responsible for the running of the Community.

TRIBUNAL

The treaty provides for a Community Tribunal, whose composition and competence are determined by the Authority of Heads of State and Government; it interprets the provisions of the treaty and settles disputes between member states that are referred to it.

EXECUTIVE SECRETARIAT

The Headquarters of the Executive Secretariat is in Lagos. There was a staff of about 240 in 1986. The Executive Secretary is elected for a four-year term, which may be renewed once only. The Secretariat's operational budget for 1988 was US $7m.
Executive Secretary: (vacant).

SPECIALIZED COMMISSIONS

There are five commissions:
 (i) Trade, Customs, Immigration, Monetary and Payments;
 (ii) Industry, Agriculture and Natural Resources;
 (iii) Transport, Communications and Energy;
 (iv) Social and Cultural Affairs;
 (v) Administration and finance.

FUND FOR CO-OPERATION, COMPENSATION AND DEVELOPMENT

Address: ave du 24 janvier, Lomé, Togo.
Telex: 5339.

The Fund is administered by a Board of Directors. The chief executive of the Fund is the Managing Director, who holds office for a renewable term of four years. There is a staff of 50. The authorized capital of the Fund was raised from US $90m. to $360m. in 1986. The Fund's first loan was approved in November 1982, amounting to $12.5m. for the initial phase of a telecommunications improvement scheme involving seven member states (see below). By the end of 1985 loans (totalling $6m.) had also been approved for the construction of bridges in Benin and a major highway in Liberia; grants amounting to $665,221 had been approved for Liberia, Mali and Togo, for feasibility studies on the proposed Trans-West African Highway. Grants were also made to finance studies by the Secretariat on energy and monetary affairs. The Fund's investment budget for 1986 amounted to $25.7m. In 1988 agreements were reached with the African Development Bank and the Islamic Development Bank on the co-financing of projects and joint training of staff, and it was agreed that the Fund should be opened to non-regional participants.
Managing Director: MAHANTA FALL (Senegal).

Activities

ECOWAS aims to promote co-operation and development in economic, social and cultural activity, particularly in the fields for which specialized commissions (see above) are appointed, to raise the standard of living of the people of the member countries, increase and maintain economic stability, improve relations among member countries and contribute to the progress and development of Africa.

The treaty provides for compensation for states whose import duties are reduced through trade liberalization and contains a clause permitting safeguard measures in favour of any country affected by economic disturbances through the application of the treaty.

The treaty also contains a commitment to abolish all obstacles to the free movement of people, services and capital, and to promote: harmonization of agricultural policies; common projects in marketing, research and the agriculturally based industries; joint development of economic and industrial policies and elimination of disparities in levels of development; and common monetary policies.

Lack of success in many of ECOWAS' aims has been attributed to the existence of numerous other intergovernmental organizations in the region (such as the francophone CEAO and the Mano River Union, q.v.), and to member governments' lack of commitment, shown by their reluctance to implement policies at the national level, their failure to provide the agreed financial resources, and the absence of national links with the Secretariat.

CUSTOMS UNION

Elimination of tariffs and other obstructions to trade among member states, and the establishment of a common external tariff, are planned over a transitional period of 15 years. At the 1978 Conference of Heads of State and Government it was decided that from 28 May 1979 no member state might increase its customs tariff on goods from another member. This was regarded as the first step towards the abolition of customs duties within the Community. During the first two years import duties on intra-community trade were to be maintained, and then eliminated in phases over the next eight years. Quotas and other restrictions of equivalent effect were to be abolished in the first 10 years. In the remaining five years all differences between external customs tariffs were to be abolished.

The 1980 Conference of Heads of State and Government decided to establish a free trade area for unprocessed agricultural products and handicrafts from May 1981. Tariffs on industrial products made by specified community enterprises were also to be abolished from that date, but implementation was delayed by difficulties in defining the enterprises. An eight-year timetable for liberalizing trade in industrial products was established: the more developed members (Ghana, Côte d'Ivoire, Nigeria and Senegal) were to eliminate barriers more quickly than the less developed. A compensation procedure for loss of revenue among the less advanced states resulting from trade liberalization was also adopted.

The 1983 Conference of Heads of State and Government decided to initiate studies on the formation of a single ECOWAS monetary zone. The Governors of member states' central banks met in September to examine the project. In the same year a programme was approved for the establishment of a computer unit (ASYCUDA) in Lomé, to process customs and trade statistics and to calculate the loss of revenue resulting from the liberalization of intra-community trade.

TRAVEL, TRANSPORT AND COMMUNICATIONS

At the 1979 Conference of Heads of State a Protocol was signed relating to free circulation of the region's citizens and to rights of residence and establishment. The first provision (the right of entry without a visa) came into force in July 1980, following ratification by eight members. The second provision, allowing unlimited rights of residence, was signed in 1986 (although Nigeria indicated that

of residence, was signed in 1986 (although Nigeria indicated that unskilled workers and certain categories of professionals would not be allowed to stay for an indefinite period); by mid-1987 however, only one country (Senegal) had ratified the protocol on rights of residence.

The Conference also adopted a programme for the improvement and extension of the internal and interstate telecommunications network, 'Intelcom', estimated to cost US $60m. In June 1983 equipment supply contracts were awarded to French and Federal German companies for the first phase of the programme, comprising the construction of microwave telephone, telex and television links between Ghana and Burkina Faso, Benin and Burkina Faso, Nigeria and Niger, and Mali and Côte d'Ivoire. Contracts for part of the second phase, financed by the European Investment Bank, were awarded in 1985.

A programme for the development of regional transport was adopted by the 1980 Conference. It includes the harmonization of road signs and laws and the construction of new road and rail links between member states. A regional motor insurance ('Brown Card') scheme was launched in July 1984, and a revised regional road map was being drawn up in collaboration with the UN Economic Commission for Africa. In April 1988 a meeting of donor organizations, led by the World Bank, agreed to provide finance amounting to US $276m. for constructing and improving roads in the region.

A feasibility study on the establishment of an ECOWAS shipping line was completed in 1984, and a programme on air traffic safety was begun with the co-operation of the International Civil Aviation Organization. In 1986 a data bank was established to monitor traffic in West African ports, with the aim of improving efficiency.

ECONOMIC DEVELOPMENT

ECOWAS undertook a critical appraisal of economic conditions in member states in 1979 and 1980 to provide information for development planning. The Nigerian Institute of Social and Economic Research co-ordinated the survey, and other institutions and universities were called upon to take part. In September 1978 a meeting of Customs and Statistics Experts was convened in Lagos to consider the problem of different standards and measures in the region; this led to the adoption of a common customs and statistical nomenclature and a code of standards and definitions.

Pre-feasibility studies on the establishment of a private regional investment bank were undertaken by the ECOWAS Secretariat in 1984. The creation of the bank (to be known as Eco-Bank Transnational Inc, based in Lomé, Togo) was approved by heads of state and government in November. It opened in March 1988. ECOWAS has a 10% share in the bank. The ECOWAS Reinsurance Corporation (Eco-Re) was expected to begin operations in 1989.

The West African Industrial Forum, sponsored by ECOWAS, is held every two years to promote regional industrial investment. The seventh Forum was held in Dakar, Senegal, in December 1986, with assistance from the European Community and UNIDO.

In 1987 ECOWAS launched an Economic Recovery Programme (ERP) for 1988-91. The ERP originally envisaged expenditure of US $920m. (later increased to $1,670m.) for 136 regional projects, of which 64 were concerned with rural development, 21 with transport improvements and 23 with industry. By December 54 projects were described as ready for execution, while 66 were at the stage of feasibility studies, and 16 still awaited funding.

DEFENCE

At the third Conference of Heads of State and Government a protocol of non-aggression was signed. Thirteen members signed a protocol on mutual defence assistance at the 1981 Conference. A mutual defence force and defence council were planned.

ENERGY

The 1981 Conference agreed on a work programme for energy development, involving a regional analysis of energy use and plans for increasing efficiency and finding alternative sources. The creation of an Energy Resources Development Fund was approved in 1982. In October 1983 it was announced that (in co-operation with UNESCO) a regional information centre and data base was to be set up in Dakar, Senegal, to disseminate information on renewable energy. In 1987 plans were announced for the construction of an ECOWAS refinery, to supply refined petroleum products for the region.

AGRICULTURE

An Agricultural Development Strategy was adopted in 1982, aiming at sub-regional self-sufficiency by the year 2000. The strategy included plans for selecting seeds and cattle species, and called for solidarity among member states during international commodity negotiations. Seven seed selection and multiplication centres and eight livestock-breeding centres were designated in 1984. In 1988 it was announced that ECOWAS was to establish a cattle-ranch in southern Mali, over an area of 18,000 ha, to breed cattle for distribution in the ECOWAS region. A tsetse-fly control programme was also to be undertaken.

The years 1983-93 were designated as an ECOWAS tree-planting decade by the 1982 Conference.

SOCIAL PROGRAMME

Four organizations have been established within ECOWAS by the Executive Secretariat: the Organization of Trade Unions of West Africa, which held its first meeting in 1984; the West African Youth Association; the West African Universities' Association; and the West Africa Women's Association (whose statutes were approved by a meeting of ministers of social affairs in May 1987). Regional sports competitions are held annually.

TOURISM

In March 1987 regional ministers of tourism met for the first time and agreed to integrate policies on the development of tourism and to exchange information.

ENVIRONMENT

The 1988 Conference adopted a resolution condemning the dumping of nuclear and industrial waste in Africa by countries outside the region. All members agreed to promulgate domestic legislation prohibiting such dumping.

THE EUROPEAN COMMUNITIES

No final decision has been made on a headquarters for the Communities. Meetings of the principal organs take place in Brussels, Luxembourg and Strasbourg.

The European Coal and Steel Community (ECSC) was created by a treaty signed in Paris on 18 April 1951 (effective from 25 July 1952) to pool the coal and steel production of the six original members (see below). It was seen as a first step towards a united Europe. The European Economic Community (EEC) and European Atomic Energy Community (Euratom) were established by separate treaties signed in Rome on 25 March 1957 (effective from 1 January 1958), the former to create a Common Market and to approximate economic policies, the latter to promote growth in nuclear industries. The common institutions of the three Communities were established by a treaty signed in Brussels on 8 April 1965 (effective from 1 July 1967). Political union is regarded as the ultimate aim of the Communities. Increasingly the three institutions are being regarded as a single entity, the European Community, and since 1967 they have been supervised by a single Commission (see p. 139).

MEMBERS

Belgium*
Denmark
France*
Federal Republic of Germany*
Greece
Ireland
Italy*
Luxembourg*
Netherlands*
Portugal
Spain
United Kingdom

* Original members. Denmark, Ireland and the United Kingdom joined on 1 January 1973, and Greece on 1 January 1981. In a referendum held in February 1982, the inhabitants of Greenland voted to end their membership of the Community, entered into when under full Danish rule. Greenland's withdrawal took effect from 1 February 1985. Portugal and Spain became members on 1 January 1986.

PERMANENT REPRESENTATIVES OF MEMBER STATES

Belgium: 62 Belliardstraat, 1040 Brussels; tel. (02) 230-99-00; P. DE SCHOUTHEETE.

Denmark: 73 rue d'Arlon, 1040 Brussels; tel. (02) 233-08-11; JAKOB E. LARSEN.

France: 37–40 blvd du Régent, 1000 Brussels; tel. (02) 513-64-45; telex 21265; PHILIPPE LOUET.

Federal Republic of Germany: 64 rue Royale, 1000 Brussels; tel. (02) 513-45-00; telex 21745; WERNER UNGERER.

Greece: 71 ave de Cortenberg, 1040 Brussels; tel. (02) 735-80-85; CONSTANTINOS LYBEROPOULOS.

Ireland: 5 ave Galilée, bte 22, 1030 Brussels; tel. (02) 218-06-05; telex 26730; JOHN CAMPBELL.

Italy: 74 rue de la Loi, 1040 Brussels; tel. (02) 230-81-70; telex 01121462; PIETRO CALAMIA.

Luxembourg: 73 ave de Cortenberg, 1040 Brussels; tel. (02) 735-20-60; telex 21707; JOSEPH WEYLAND.

Netherlands: 46 ave des Arts, 1040 Brussels; tel. (02) 513-77-75; telex 26125; P. C. NIEMAN.

Portugal: 11-13 rue Marie-Thérèse, 1000 Brussels; tel. (02) 211-12-11; LEONARDO C. DE ZAFFIRI DUARTE MATHIAS.

Spain: 52 blvd du Régent, 1000 Brussels; tel. (02) 509-86-11; CARLOS WESTENDORP Y CABEZA.

United Kingdom: 6 rond-point Robert Schumann, 1040 Brussels; tel. (02) 230-62-05; telex 24312; Sir DAVID HANNAY.

PERMANENT MISSIONS TO THE EUROPEAN COMMUNITIES, WITH AMBASSADORS
(October 1988)

Afghanistan: 32 ave Raphaël, 75016 Paris, France; tel. (1) 45-27-66-09; Chargé d'affaires: ABDULLAH KESHTMAND.

Algeria: 209 ave Molière, 1060 Brussels; tel. (02) 343-50-78; SIDAHMED GHOZALI.

Angola: 182 rue Franz Merjay, 1180 Brussels; tel. (02) 344-49-80.

Antigua and Barbuda: 15 Thayer St, London, W1, England; tel. (01) 486-7073; telex 8814503.

Argentina: 225 ave Louise (7e étage), 1050 Brussels; tel. (02) 648-93-71; telex 23079; LUIS RAMIRO ALFONSÍN.

Australia: 6/8 rue Guimard, 1040 Brussels; tel. (02) 231-05-00; telex 21834; PETER C. J. CURTIS.

Austria: 35–36 ave des Klauwaerts, 1050 Brussels; tel. (02) 649-00-83; telex 21407; WOLFGANG WOLTE.

Bahamas: 10 Chesterfield St, London, W1X 8AH, England; tel. (01) 408-4488; telex 892617.

Bangladesh: 29–31 rue Jacques Jordaens, 1050 Brussels; tel. (02) 640-55-00; telex 63189; MOHAMMED MOHSIN.

Barbados: 14 ave Lloyd George, 1050 Brussels; tel. (02) 648-12-28; telex 63926; RASHID ORLANDO MARVILLE.

Belize: 15 Thayer St, London, W1, England; tel. (01) 486-8381; telex 8814503; Sir EDNEY CAIN.

Benin: 5 ave de l'Observatoire, 1180 Brussels; tel. (02) 374-91-91; telex 24568; MAMADOU TAÏROU DJAOUGA.

Bhutan: 17–19 chemin Champs-d'Amier, 1209 Geneva, Switzerland; tel. (022) 987971; TOBGYE S. DORJI.

Bolivia: 176 ave Louise, 1050 Brussels; tel. (02) 647-27-18; telex 63494; AUGUSTO CUADROS SÁNCHEZ.

Botswana: 169 ave de Tervuren, 1040 Brussels; tel. (02) 735-61-10; telex 22849; ERNEST SIPHO MPOFU.

Brazil: 350 ave Louise (6e étage), 1050 Brussels; tel. (02) 640-20-40; GERALDO EGIDIO DA COSTA HOLANDA CAVALCANTI.

Burkina Faso: 16 place Guy d'Arezzo, 1060 Brussels; tel. (02) 345-99-11; AMADÉ OUEDRAOGO.

Burma: 5300 Bonn, Schumannstrasse 112, Federal Republic of Germany; tel. (0228) 21 00 91; telex 8869560; U MAUNG MAUNG THAN TUN.

Burundi: 46 square Marie-Louise, 1040 Brussels; tel. (02) 230-45-35; telex 23572; ASTÈRE NZISABIRA.

Cameroon: 131 ave Brugmann, 1060 Brussels; tel. (02) 345-18-70; telex 24117; SIMONE MAIRIE.

Canada: 2 ave de Tervuren, 1040 Brussels; tel. (02) 735-91-25; DANIEL MOLGAT.

Cape Verde: 44 Koninginnegracht, 2514 AK The Hague, Netherlands; tel. (070) 46-96-23; telex 34321; MONTEIRO DA FONSECA.

Central African Republic: 416 blvd Lambermont, 1030 Brussels; tel. (02) 242-28-80; telex 0222 493; JOSÉ-MARIE PEHOUA.

Chad: 52 blvd Lambermont, 1030 Brussels; tel. (02) 215-19-75; ABDOULAYE LAMANA.

Chile: 326 ave Louise, Boîte 22 (5e étage), 1050 Brussels; tel. (02) 649-94-83; telex 61442; DIEGO VALENZUELA RODRÍGUEZ.

China, People's Republic: 445 ave de Tervuren, 1150 Brussels; tel. (02) 771-58-57; LIU SHAN.

Colombia: 44 rue Van Eyck (2e étage), 1050 Brussels; tel. (02) 649-56-79; telex 25254; RAFAEL RIVAS POSADA.

Comoros: 15 rue de la Néva, 75008 Paris, France; tel. (1) 47-63-81-78; telex 642390; ALI MLAHAILI.

Congo: 16 ave F. D. Roosevelt, 1050 Brussels; tel. (02) 648-38-56; telex 23677; AMBROISE GAMBOUELE.

Costa Rica: 437 ave Louise (6 étage), 1050 Brussels; tel. (02) 640-55-41; DANIEL RATTÓN-THIERY.

Côte d'Ivoire: 234 ave F. D. Roosevelt, 1050 Brussels; tel. (02) 672-23-57; CHARLES VALY TUHO.

Cyprus: 83–85 rue de la Loi, 1040 Brussels; tel. (02) 230-12-95; ANGELOS ANGELIDES.

Djibouti: 26 rue Emile Ménier, 75116 Paris, France; tel. (1) 47-27-49-22.

Dominica: 12 rue des Bollandistes, 1040 Brussels; tel. (02) 733-43-28; CHARLES SAVARIN.

Dominican Republic: 2 rue Georges-Ville, 75116 Paris, France; tel. (1) 45-01-88-81.

Ecuador: 70 chaussée de Charleroi, 1060 Brussels; tel. (02) 537-91-30; DIEGO PAREDES-PEÑA.

Egypt: 44 ave Léo Errera, 1180 Brussels; tel. (02) 345-52-53; FAWZI MOHAMED EL IBRACHY.

El Salvador: 3 blvd Saint-Michel, 1040 Brussels; tel. (02) 733-04-85; FRANCISCO A. SOLER.

Equatorial Guinea: 6 rue Alfred de Vigny, 75008 Paris, France; tel. 47-66-44-33; FAUSTINO NGUEMA ESONO AFONG.

INTERNATIONAL ORGANIZATIONS

European Communities

Ethiopia: 32 blvd Saint-Michel, 1040 Brussels; tel. (02) 733-49-29.

Fiji: 66 ave de Cortenberg (7e étage, boîte 7), 1040 Brussels; tel. (02) 736-90-50; telex 26934; KALIOPATE TAVOLA.

Finland: 489 ave Louise, 1050 Brussels; tel. (02) 648-84-84; telex 23099; LEIF BLOMQVIST.

Gabon: 112 ave Winston Churchill, 1180 Brussels; tel. (02) 343-00-55; MARCEL ODONGUI-BONNARD.

The Gambia: 126 ave F. D. Roosevelt, 1050 Brussels; tel. (02) 640-10-49; telex 24344; ABDULLAH M. K. BOJANG.

Ghana: 44 rue Gachard, 1050 Brussels; tel. (02) 649-01-63; JOSEPH AHWA LARYEA.

Grenada: 24 ave des Arts, 1040 Brussels; tel. (02) 230-62-65; telex 64015; OSWALD M. GIBBS.

Guatemala: 53 blvd Général Wahis, 1030 Brussels; tel. (02) 736-03-40; telex 25130; ALEXEY DE SYNEGUB.

Guinea: 75 ave Roger Vandendriessche, 1150 Brussels; tel. (02) 771-01-26; IBRAHIM SYLLA.

Guinea-Bissau: 70 ave F. D. Roosevelt, 1050 Brussels; tel. (02) 647-08-90; telex 63631; BUBACAR TURÉ.

Guyana: 21–22 ave des Arts, 1040 Brussels; tel. (02) 230-60-65; telex 26180; JAMES HENRY E. MATHESON.

Haiti: 160A ave Louise, 1050 Brussels; tel. (02) 649-73-81.

Holy See: 5–9 ave des Franciscains, 1150 Brussels; tel. (02) 762-20-05; Apostolic Nuncio: Mgr ANGELO PEDRONI.

Honduras: 3 ave des Gaulois (5e étage), 1040 Brussels; tel. (02) 734-00-00; MANUEL LÓPEZ LUNA.

Iceland: 5 rue Archimède, 1040 Brussels; tel. (02) 231-03-95; telex 29459; EINAR BENEDIKTSSON.

India: 217 chaussée de Vleurgat, 1050 Brussels; tel. (02) 640-91-40; NARENDRAKUMAR PANNALALJI JAIN.

Indonesia: 294 ave de Tervuren, 1150 Brussels; tel. (02) 771-20-12; ATMONO SURYO.

Iran: 415 ave de Tervuren, 1150 Brussels; tel. (02) 762-37-45; ALIREZA SALARI.

Iraq: 131 ave de la Floride, 1180 Brussels; tel. (02) 374-59-91; Dr ZAID HWAISHAN HAIDAR.

Israel: 40 ave de l'Observatoire, 1180 Brussels; tel. (02) 374-90-80; AVRAHAM PRIMOR.

Jamaica: 83–85 rue de la Loi, 1040 Brussels: tel. (02) 230-11-70; LESLIE ARMON WILSON.

Japan: 58 ave des Arts (7e étage), 1040 Brussels; tel. (02) 513-92-00; MUNEOKI DATE.

Jordan: 104 ave F. D. Roosevelt, 1050 Brussels; tel. (02) 640-77-55; telex 62513; HASAN ABU NIMAH.

Kenya: 1–5 ave de la Joyeuse Entrée, 1040 Brussels; tel. (02) 230-30-65.

Korea, Republic: 3 ave Hamoir, 1180 Brussels; tel. (02) 375-39-80; telex 24668; CHONG HA YOO.

Kuwait: 43 ave F. D. Roosevelt, 1050 Brussels; tel. (02) 647-79-50.

Laos: 74 ave Raymond Poincaré, 75116 Paris, France; tel. 45-53-70-47; telex 610711; THONGSAY BODHISANE.

Lebanon: 2 rue Guillaume Stocq, 1050 Brussels; tel. (02) 649-94-60; telex 22547; SAID AL-ASSAAD.

Lesotho: 66 ave de Cortenberg, 1040 Brussels; tel. (02) 736-39-76.

Liberia: 55 ave F. D. Roosevelt, 1050 Brussels; tel. (02) 640-84-46; telex 61384.

Libya: 28 ave Victoria, 1050 Brussels; tel. (02) 649-21-12; telex 23398.

Madagascar: 276 ave de Tervuren, 1150 Brussels; tel. (02) 770-17-26; CHRISTIAN RÉMI RICHARD.

Malawi: 15 rue de la Loi, 1040 Brussels; tel. (02) 231-09-80; telex 24128; LAWRENCE P. ANTHONY.

Malaysia: 414A ave de Tervuren, 1150 Brussels; tel. (02) 762-67-67; telex 26396; Dato NOOR ADLAN BIN YAHAYAUDDIN.

Maldives: 212 East 47th St, New York, NY 10017, USA; tel. (212) 688-07-76; telex 960945; MOHAMED MUSTHAFA HUSSAIN.

Mali: 487 ave Molière, 1060 Brussels; tel. (02) 345-74-32; telex 22508; LAMINE KEITA.

Malta: 44 rue Jules Lejeune, 1060 Brussels; tel. (02) 343-01-95; telex 26616; JOSEPH LICARI.

Mauritania: 1 rue Paul Lauters, 1050 Brussels; tel. (02) 640-76-75; telex 26034; ELY OULD ALLAF.

Mauritius: 68 rue des Bollandistes, 1040 Brussels; tel. (02) 733-99-88; RAYMOND CHASLE.

Mexico: 6 rue Paul Emile Janson, 1050 Brussels; tel. (02) 648-26-71; telex 22355; ALFREDO DEL MAZO GONZÁLEZ.

Morocco: 29 blvd Saint-Michel, 1040 Brussels; tel. (02) 736-11-00; telex 21233; ABDELMALEK CHERKAOUI.

Mozambique: 97 blvd St Michel, 1040 Brussels; tel. (02) 736-25-64; telex 65478; FRANCES VITORIA VELHO RODRIGUES.

Nepal: 53 Bonn-Bad Godesberg, Im Hag 15, Federal Republic of Germany; tel. (0228) 34-30-97; SIMHA PRATAP SHAH.

New Zealand: 47–48 blvd du Régent, 1000 Brussels; tel. (02) 512-10-40; telex 22025; GERARD FRANCIS THOMPSON.

Nicaragua: 255 chaussée de Vleurgat, 1050 Brussels; tel. (02) 345-19-25; telex 63553; GIOVANNI DELGADO CAMPOS.

Niger: 78 ave F. D. Roosevelt, 1050 Brussels; tel. (02) 648-61-40; telex 22857; YACOUBA SANDI.

Nigeria: 288 bis ave de Tervuren, 1150 Brussels; tel. (02) 762-52-00; telex 22435; JOSHUA O. B. IROHA.

Norway: 17 rue Archimède, 1040 Brussels; tel. (02) 230-78-65; telex 21071; CHRISTIAN BERG-NIELSEN.

Oman: 50 ave d'Iéna, 75116 Paris, France; tel. (1) 47-23-01-63; telex 613765; MUNIR BIN ABDULNABI BIN YOUSUF MAKKI.

Pakistan: 57 ave Delleurs, 1170 Brussels; tel. (02) 673-80-07; telex 61816; MUNIR AKRAM.

Panama: 8 blvd Brand Whitlock, 1040 Brussels; tel. (02) 733-97-98; telex 25169.

Papua New Guinea: 17–19 ave Montoyer, 1040 Brussels; tel. (02) 512-31-26; telex 62249.

Paraguay: 42 ave de Saturne, 1180 Brussels; tel. (02) 374-87-48; telex 26535; DIDO FLORENTIN-BAGADO.

Peru: 179 ave de Tervuren, 1150 Brussels; tel. (02) 733-33-19; JULIO EGO-AGUIRRE-ALVAREZ.

Philippines: 299 ave Molière, 1060 Brussels; tel. (02) 343-68-32.

Qatar: 37 ave F. D. Roosevelt, 1050 Brussels; tel. (02) 640-29-00; telex 63754; ABDULRAHMAN ABDULLAH AL-WOHAIBI.

Rwanda: 1 ave des Fleurs, 1150 Brussels; tel. (02) 763-07-21; telex 26653; ILDÉPHONSE MUNYESHYAKA.

Saint Lucia: 10 Kensington Court, London, W8, England; tel. (01) 937-9522.

Saint Vincent and the Grenadines: 10 Kensington Court, London W8, England; tel. (01) 937-9522; ALAN RICHARD GUNN.

San Marino: 44 ave Brugmann, 1060 Brussels; tel. (02) 344-60-67; ADALMIRO BARTOLINI.

São Tomé and Príncipe: 42 ave Brugmann, 1060 Brussels; tel. (02) 347-53-75; telex 65313; MARIA MANUELA MARGARIDO.

Saudi Arabia: 45 ave F. D. Roosevelt, 1050 Brussels; tel. (02) 649-57-25; IBRAHIM SALEH BAKR.

Senegal: 196 ave F. D. Roosevelt, 1050 Brussels; tel. (02) 672-90-51.

Seychelles: 53 bis rue François Ier, 75008 Paris, France; tel. (1) 47-23-98-11; telex 649634; GEORGES PAYET.

Sierra Leone: 410 ave de Tervuren, 1150 Brussels; tel. (02) 771-00-52; telex 63624; MARIAN JUDITH TANNER KAMARA.

Singapore: 198 ave F. D. Roosevelt, 1050 Brussels; tel. (02) 660-30-98; FRANCIS YEO TENG YANG.

Somalia: 66 ave F. D. Roosevelt, 1050 Brussels; tel. (02) 640-16-69; telex 24807; SAID HAGI MOHAMOUD FARAH.

South Africa: 26 rue de la Loi, 1040 Brussels; tel. (02) 231-17-25; BHADRA GALU RANCHOD.

Sri Lanka: 21–22 ave des Arts, 1040 Brussels; tel. (02) 230-48-90; ANTHONY WIRATUNGA.

Sudan: 124 ave F. D. Roosevelt, 1050 Brussels; tel. (02) 647-51-59; FAROUK A. RAHMAN A. EISA.

Suriname: 379 ave Louise, 1050 Brussels; tel. (02) 640-11-72; FRANKLIN JULIAN LEEFLANG.

Swaziland: 71 rue Joseph II (5e étage), 1040 Brussels; tel. (02) 230-00-44.

Sweden: 6 rond-point Robert Schumann, 1040 Brussels; tel. (02) 237-01-11; telex 26126; STIG BRATTSTRÖM.

Switzerland: 53 rue d'Arlon, 1040 Brussels; tel. (02) 230-14-90; telex 21660; BÉNÉDICT DE TSCHARNER.

Syria: 3 ave F. D. Roosevelt, 1050 Brussels; tel. (02) 648-01-35.

Tanzania: 363 ave Louise, 1050 Brussels; tel. (02) 640-65-00; telex 63616; SIMON M. M. MBILINYI.

Thailand: 2 square du Val de la Cambre, 1050 Brussels; tel. (02) 640-68-10; telex 63510.

Togo: 264 ave de Tervuren, 1150 Brussels; tel. (02) 770-17-91; EKOUÉ ASSIONGBON.

Tonga: New Zealand House (12th floor), Haymarket, London, SW1Y 4TE, England; tel. (01) 839-3287; telex 8954094; SIAOSI TAIMANI'AHO.

INTERNATIONAL ORGANIZATIONS

European Communities

Trinidad and Tobago: 14 ave de la Faisanderie, 1150 Brussels; tel. (02) 762-94-00; telex 23539.

Tunisia: 278 ave de Tervuren, 1150 Brussels; tel. (02) 771-73-94; MOHAMED MEGDICHE.

Turkey: 4 rue Montoyer, 1040 Brussels; tel. (02) 513-28-34; OZDEM SANBERK.

Uganda: 317 ave de Tervuren, 1150 Brussels; tel. (02) 762-58-25; telex 62814.

United Arab Emirates: 73 ave F. D. Roosevelt, 1050 Brussels; tel. (02) 640-60-00.

USA: 40 blvd du Régent, 1000 Brussels; tel. (02) 513-44-50; ALFRED HUGH KINGON.

Uruguay: 437 ave Louise, 1050 Brussels; tel. (02) 649-46-26; telex 24663; MIGUEL J. BERTHET.

Venezuela: 5 square Vergote, 1200 Brussels; tel. (02) 736-10-23; telex 61742; ROMÁN ROJAS-CABOT.

Western Samoa: 95 ave F. D. Roosevelt, 1050 Brussels; tel. (02) 660-84-54; telex 25657; FEESAGO SIAOSI FEPULEA'I.

Yemen Arab Republic: Surinamestraat 9, 2585 GC The Hague, Netherlands; tel. (070) 65-39-36; telex 33290; MOHAMMED ABDUL REHMAN AL-ROBAEE.

Yugoslavia: 11 ave Emile de Mot, 1050 Brussels; tel. (02) 649-83-49; telex 26156; JOZEF KOROSEC.

Zaire: 30 rue Marie de Bourgogne, 1040 Brussels; tel. (02) 513-66-10.

Zambia: 469 ave Molière, 1060 Brussels; tel. (02) 343-56-49; telex 63102; KOPEMBE NSINGO.

Zimbabwe: 21-22 ave des Arts, 1040 Brussels; tel. (02) 230-85-35.

Source: Directorate-General for External Relations.

Summary of the Treaty establishing the European Economic Community (Treaty of Rome)

(effective from 1 January 1958)

PART I. PRINCIPLES

The aim of the Community is, by establishing a Common Market and progressively approximating the economic policies of the member states, to promote throughout the Community a harmonious development of economic activities, a continuous and balanced expansion, an increased stability, an accelerated raising of the standard of living and closer relations between its member states. With these aims in view, the activities of the Community will include:

(a) the elimination between member states of customs duties and of quantitative restrictions in regard to the importation and exportation of goods, as well as of all other measures with equivalent effect;

(b) the establishment of a common customs tariff and a common commercial policy towards third countries;

(c) the abolition between member states of the obstacles to the free movement of persons, services and capital;

(d) the inauguration of a common agricultural policy;

(e) the inauguration of a common transport policy;

(f) the establishment of a system ensuring that competition shall not be distorted in the Common Market;

(g) the application of procedures that will make it possible to co-ordinate the economic policies of member states and to remedy disequilibria in their balance of payments;

(h) the approximation of their respective municipal law to the extent necessary for the functioning of the Common Market;

(i) the creation of a European Social Fund in order to improve the possibilities of employment for workers and to contribute to the raising of their standard of living;

(j) the establishment of a European Investment Bank intended to facilitate the economic expansion of the Community through the creation of new resources; and

(k) the association of overseas countries and territories with the Community with a view to increasing trade and to pursuing jointly their effort toward economic and social development.

Member states, acting in close collaboration with the institutions of the Community, shall co-ordinate their respective economic policies to the extent that is necessary to attain the objectives of the Treaty; the institutions of the Community shall take care not to prejudice the internal and external financial stability of the member states. Within the field of application of the Treaty and without prejudice to certain special provisions which it contains, any discrimination on the grounds of nationality shall be hereby prohibited.

The Common Market shall be progressively established in the course of a transitional period of 12 years. This transitional period shall be divided into three stages of four years each.

PART II. BASES OF THE COMMUNITY

Free Movement of Goods

Member states shall refrain from introducing between themselves any new import or export customs duties, or charges with equivalent effect, and from increasing such duties or charges as they apply in their commercial relations with each other. Member states shall progressively abolish between themselves all import and export customs duties, charges with an equivalent effect, and also customs duties of a fiscal nature. Independently of these provisions, any member state may, in the course of the transitional period, suspend in whole or in part the collection of import duties applied by it to products imported from other member states, or may carry out the foreseen reductions more rapidly than laid down in the Treaty if its general economic situation and the situation of the sector so concerned permit.

A common customs tariff shall be established, which, subject to certain conditions (especially with regard to the Italian tariff), shall be at the level of the arithmetical average of the duties applied in the four customs territories (i.e. France, Germany, Italy and Benelux) covered by the Community. This customs tariff shall be applied in its entirety not later than at the date of the expiry of the transitional period. Member states may follow an independent accelerating process similar to that allowed for reduction of inter-Community customs duties.

Member states shall refrain from introducing between themselves any new quantitative restrictions or measures with equivalent effect, and existing restrictions and measures shall be abolished not later than at the end of the first stage of the transitional period. These provisions shall not be an obstacle to prohibitions or restrictions in respect of importation, exportation or transit which are justified on grounds of public morality, health or safety, the protection of human or animal life or health, the preservation of plant life, the protection of national treasures of artistic, historic or archaeological value or the protection of industrial and commercial property. Such prohibitions or restrictions shall not, however, constitute either a means of arbitrary discrimination or a disguised restriction on trade between member states. Member states shall progressively adjust any state monopolies of a commercial character in such a manner as will ensure the exclusion, at the end of the transitional period, of all discrimination between the nationals of member states in regard to conditions of supply and marketing of goods. These provisions shall apply to any body by means of which a member state shall *de jure* or *de facto* either directly or indirectly, control or appreciably influence importation or exportation between member states, and also to monopolies assigned by the state. In the case of a commercial monopoly which is accompanied by regulations designed to facilitate the marketing or the valorisation of agricultural products, it should be ensured that in the application of these provisions equivalent guarantees are provided in respect of the employment and standard of living of the producers concerned.

The obligations incumbent on member states shall be binding only to such extent as they are compatible with existing international agreements.

Agriculture

The Common Market shall extend to agriculture and trade in agricultural products. The common agricultural policy shall have as its objectives:

(a) the increase of agricultural productivity by developing technical progress and by ensuring the rational development of agricultural production and the optimum utilization of the factors of production, particularly labour;

(b) the ensurance thereby of a fair standard of living for the agricultural population;

(c) the stabilization of markets;

(d) regular supplies;

(e) reasonable prices in supplies to consumers.

Due account must be taken of the particular character of agricultural activities, arising from the social structure of agriculture and from structural and natural disparities between the various agricultural regions; of the need to make the appropriate adjustments gradually; and of the fact that in member states agriculture constitutes a sector which is closely linked with the economy as a whole. With a view to developing a common agricultural policy during the transitional period and the establishment of it not later than at the end of the period, a common organization of agricultural markets shall be effected.

Free Movement of Persons, Services and Capital

Workers: The free movement of workers shall be ensured within the Community not later than at the date of the expiry of the transitional period, involving the abolition of any discrimination based on nationality between workers of the member states as regards employment, remuneration and other working conditions. This shall include the right to accept offers of employment actually made, to move about freely for this purpose within the territory of the member states, to stay in any member state in order to carry on an employment in conformity with the legislative and administrative provisions governing the employment of the workers of that state, and to live, on conditions which shall be the subject of implementing regulations laid down by the Commission, in the territory of a member state after having been employed there. (These provisions do not apply to employment in the public administration.)

In the field of social security, the Council shall adopt the measures necessary to effect the free movement of workers, in particular, by introducing a system which permits an assurance to be given to migrant workers and their beneficiaries that, for the purposes of qualifying for and retaining the rights to benefits and of the calculation of these benefits, all periods taken into consideration by the respective municipal law of the countries concerned shall be added together, and that these benefits will be paid to persons resident in the territories of the member states.

Right of Establishment: Restrictions on the freedom of establishment of nationals of a member state in the territory of another member state shall be progressively abolished during the transitional period, nor may any new restrictions of a similar character be introduced. Such progressive abolition shall also extend to restrictions on the setting up of agencies, branches or subsidiaries. Freedom of establishment shall include the right to engage in and carry on non-wage-earning activities and also to set up and manage enterprises and companies under the conditions laid down by the law of the country of establishment for its own nationals, subject to the provisions of this Treaty relating to capital.

Services: Restrictions on the free supply of services within the Community shall be progressively abolished in the course of the transitional period in respect of nationals of member states who are established in a state of the Community other than that of the person to whom the services are supplied; no new restrictions of a similar character may be introduced. The Council, acting by a unanimous vote on a proposal of the Commission, may extend the benefit of these provisions to cover services supplied by nationals of any third country who are established within the Community.

Particular services involved are activities of an industrial or artisan character and those of the liberal professions.

Capital: Member states shall during the transitional period progressively abolish between themselves restrictions on the movement of capital belonging to persons resident in the member states, and also any discriminatory treatment based on the nationality or place of residence of the parties or on the place in which such capital is invested. Current payments connected with movements of capital between member states shall be freed from all restrictions not later than at the end of the first stage of the transitional period.

Member states shall endeavour to avoid introducing within the Community any new exchange restrictions which affect the movement of capital and current payments connected with such movements, and making existing rules more restrictive.

Transport

With a view to establishing a common transport policy, the Council of Ministers shall, acting on a proposal of the Commission and after consulting the Economic and Social Committee and the European Parliament, lay down common rules applicable to international transport effected from or to the territory of a member state or crossing the territory of one or more member states, conditions for the admission of non-resident carriers to national transport services within a member state and any other appropriate provisions. Until these have been enacted and unless the Council of Ministers gives its unanimous consent, no member state shall apply the various provisions governing this subject at the date of the entry into force of this Treaty in such a way as to make them less favourable, in their direct or indirect effect, for carriers of other member states by comparison with its own national carriers.

Any discrimination which consists in the application by a carrier, in respect of the same goods conveyed in the same circumstances, of transport rates and conditions which differ on the ground of the country of origin or destination of the goods carried, shall be abolished in the traffic of the Community not later than at the end of the second stage of the transitional period.

A Committee with consultative status, composed of experts appointed by the governments of the member states, shall be established and attached to the Commission, without prejudice to the competence of the transport section of the Economic and Social Committee.

PART III. POLICY OF THE COMMUNITY

Common Rules

Enterprises: The following practices by enterprises are prohibited: the direct or indirect fixing of purchase or selling prices or of any other trading conditions; the limitation of control of production, markets, technical development of investment; market-sharing or the sharing of sources of supply; the application to parties to transactions of unequal terms in respect of equivalent supplies, thereby placing them at a competitive disadvantage; the subjection of the conclusion of a contract to the acceptance by a party of additional supplies which, either by their nature or according to commercial usage, have no connection with the subject of such contract. The provisions may be declared inapplicable if the agreements neither impose on the enterprises concerned any restrictions not indispensable to the attainment of improved production, distribution or technical progress, nor enable enterprises to eliminate competition in respect of a substantial proportion of the goods concerned.

Dumping: If, in the course of the transitional period, the Commission, at the request of a member state or of any other interested party, finds that dumping practices exist within the Common Market, it shall issue recommendations to the originator of such practices with a view to bringing them to an end. Where such practices continue, the Commission shall authorise the member state injured to take protective measures of which the Commission shall determine the conditions and particulars.

Re-importation within the Community shall be free of all customs duties, quantitative restrictions or measures with equivalent effect.

Aid granted by States: Any aid granted by a member state or granted by means of state resources which is contrary to the purposes of the treaty is forbidden. The following shall be deemed to be compatible with the Common Market:

(a) aids of a social character granted without discrimination to individual consumers;

(b) aids intended to remedy damage caused by natural calamities or other extraordinary events;

(c) aids granted to the economy of certain regions of the Federal German Republic affected by the division of Germany, to the extent that they are necessary to compensate for the economic disadvantages caused by the division.

The following may be deemed to be compatible with the Common Market:

(a) aids intended to promote the economic development of regions where the standard of living is abnormally low or where there exists serious under-employment;

(b) aids intended to promote the execution of important projects of common European interest or to remedy a serious economic disturbance of the economy of a member state;

(c) aids intended to facilitate the development of certain activities or of certain economic regions, provided that such aids do not change trading conditions to such a degree as would be contrary to the common interest;

(d) such other categories of aids as may be specified by a decision of the Council of Ministers acting on a proposal of the Commission.

The Commission is charged to examine constantly all systems of aids existing in the member states, and may require any member state to abolish or modify any aid which it finds to be in conflict with the principles of the Common Market.

Fiscal Provisions: A member state shall not impose, directly or indirectly, on the products of other member states, any internal charges of any kind in excess of those applied directly or indirectly to like domestic products. Furthermore, a member state shall not impose on the product of other member states any internal charges of such a nature as to afford indirect protection to other productions. Member states shall, not later than at the beginning of the second stage of the transitional period, abolish or amend any provisions existing at the date of the entry into force of the Treaty which are contrary to these rules. Products exported to any member state may not benefit from any drawback on internal charges in excess of those charges imposed directly or indirectly on them. Subject to these conditions, any member states which levy a turnover tax calculated by a cumulative multi-stage system may, in the case of internal charges imposed by them on imported products or of drawbacks granted by them on exported products, establish average rates for specific products or groups of products.

Approximation of Laws: The Council, acting by means of a unanimous vote on a proposal of the Commission, shall issue directives for the approximation of such legislative and administrative provisions of the member states as have a direct incidence on the establishment or functioning of the Common Market. The European Parliament and the Economic and Social Committee shall be consulted concerning any directives whose implementation in one or more of the member states would involve amendment of legislative provisions.

Economic Policy

Balance of Payments: Member states are charged to co-ordinate their economic policies in order that each may ensure the equilibrium of their overall balances of payments and maintain confidence in their currency, together with a high level of employment and stability of prices. In order to promote this co-ordination a Monetary Committee is established.

Each member state engages itself to treat its policy with regard to exchange rates as a matter of common interest. Where a member state is in difficulties or seriously threatened with dificulties as regards its balance of payments as a result either of overall disequilibrium of the balance of payments or of the kinds of currency at its disposal, and where such difficulties are likely, in particular, to prejudice the functioning of the Common Market or the progressive establishment of the common commercial policy, the Commission shall examine the situation and indicate the measures which it recommends to the state concerned to adopt; if this action proves insufficient to overcome the difficulties, the Commission shall, after consulting the Monetary Committee, recommend to the Council of Ministers the granting of mutual assistance. This mutual assistance may take the form of:

(a) concerted action in regard to any other international organization to which the member states may have recourse;

(b) any measures necessary to avoid diversions of commercial traffic where the state in difficulty maintains or re-establishes quantitative restrictions with regard to third countries;

(c) the granting of limited credits by other member states, subject to their agreement.

Furthermore, during the transitional period, mutual assistance may also take the form of special reductions in customs duties or enlargements of quotas. If the mutual assistance recommended by the Commission is not granted by the Council, or if the mutual assistance granted and the measures taken prove insufficient, the Commission shall authorise the state in difficulties to take measures of safeguard, of which the Commission shall determine the conditions and particulars. In the case of a sudden balance-of-payments crisis, any member state may take immediate provisional measures of safeguard, which must be submitted to the consideration of the Commission as soon as possible. On the basis of an opinion of the Commission and after consulting the Monetary Committee, the Council may decide that the state concerned shall amend, suspend or abolish such measures.

Commercial Policy: Member states shall co-ordinate their commercial relations with third countries in such a way as to bring about, not later than at the expiry of the transitional period, the conditions necessary to the implementation of a common policy in the matter of external trade. After the expiry of the transitional period, the common commercial policy shall be based on uniform principles, particularly in regard to tariff amendments, the conclusion of tariff or trade agreements, the alignment of measures of liberalisation, export policy and protective commercial measures, including measures to be taken in cases of dumping or subsidies. The Commission will be authorised to conduct negotiations with third countries. As from the end of the transitional period, member states shall, in respect of all matters of particular interest in regard to the Common Market, within the framework of any international organizations of an economic character, only proceed by way of common action. The Commission shall for this purpose submit to the Council of Ministers proposals concerning the scope and implementation of such common action. During the transitional period, member states shall consult with each other with a view to concerting their action and, as far as possible, adopting a uniform attitude.

Social Policy

Social Provisions: Without prejudice to the other provisions of the Treaty and in conformity with its general objectives, it shall be the aim of the Commission to promote close collaboration between member states in the social field, particularly in matters relating to employment, labour legislation and working conditions, occupational and continuation training, social security, protection against occupational accidents and diseases, industrial hygiene, the law as to trade unions and collective bargaining between employers and workers.

Each member state shall in the course of the first stage of the transitional period ensure and subsequently maintain the application of the principle of equal pay for men and women.

The European Social Fund: See p. 143.

The European Investment Bank: See p. 142.

PART IV. OVERSEAS COUNTRIES AND TERRITORIES

The member states agree to bring into association with the Community the non-European countries and territories which have special relations with Belgium, France, Italy and the Netherlands in order to promote the economic and social development of these countries and territories and to establish close economic relations between them and the Community as a whole.

Member states shall, in their commercial exchanges with the countries and territories, apply the same rules which they apply among themselves pursuant to the Treaty. Each country or territory shall apply to its commercial exchanges with member states and with other countries and territories the same rules which it applied in respect of the European state with which it has special relations. Member states shall contribute to the investments required by the progressive development of these countries and territories.

Customs duties on trade between member states and the countries and territories are to be progressively abolished according to the same timetable as for trade between the member states themselves. The countries and territories may, however, levy customs duties which correspond to the needs of their development and to the requirements of their industrialisation or which, being of a fiscal nature, have the object of contributing to their budgets.

(The Convention implementing these provisions is concluded for a period of five years only from the date of entry into force of the Treaty.)

PART V. INSTITUTIONS OF THE COMMUNITY

Provisions Governing Institutions

For the achievement of their aims and under the conditions provided for in the Treaty, the Council and the Commission shall adopt regulations and directives, make decisions and formulate recommendations or opinions. Regulations shall have a general application and shall be binding in every respect and directly applicable in each member state. Directives shall bind any member state to which they are addressed, as to the result to be achieved, while leaving to domestic agencies a competence as to form and means. Decisions shall be binding in every respect for the addressees named therein. Recommendations and opinions shall have no binding force.

Financial Provisions

Estimates shall be drawn up for each financial year for all revenues and expenditures of the Community and shall be shown in the budget.

The revenues of the budget shall comprise the financial contributions of member states assessed by reference to a fixed scale.

The Commission shall implement the budget on its own responsibility and within the limits of the appropriations made. The Council of Ministers shall:

(a) lay down the financial regulations specifying, in particular, the procedure to be adopted for establishing and implementing the budget, and for rendering and auditing accounts;

(b) determine the methods and procedure whereby the contributions by member states shall be made available to the Commission; and

(c) establish rules concerning the responsibility of pay-commissioners and accountants and arrange for the relevant supervision.

PART VI. GENERAL AND FINAL PROVISIONS

Member states shall, in so far as is necessary, engage in negotiations with each other with a view to ensuring for the benefit of their nationals:

(a) the protection of persons as well as the enjoyment and protection of rights under the conditions granted by each state to its own nationals;

(b) the elimination of double taxation within the Community;

(c) the mutual recognition of companies, the maintenance of their legal personality in cases where the registered office is transferred from one country to another, and the possibility for companies subject to the municipal law of different member states to form mergers; and

(d) the simplification of the formalities governing the reciprocal recognition and execution of judicial decisions and arbitral awards.

Within a period of three years after the date of the entry into

INTERNATIONAL ORGANIZATIONS
European Communities

force of the Treaty, member states shall treat nationals of other member states in the same manner, as regards financial participation by such nationals in the capital of companies, as they treat their own nationals, without prejudice to the application of the other provisions of the Treaty.

The Treaty shall in no way prejudice the system existing in member states in respect of property.

The provisions of the Treaty shall not detract from the following rules:

(a) no member state shall be obliged to supply information the disclosure of which it considers contrary to the essential interests of its security.

(b) any member state may take the measures which it considers necessary for the protection of the essential interests of its security, and which are connected with the production of or the trade in arms, ammunition and war material; such measures shall not, however, prejudice conditions of competition in the Common Market in respect of products not intended for specifically military purposes.

The list of products to which (b) applies shall be determined by the Council in the course of the first year after the date of entry into force of the Treaty. The list may be subsequently amended by the unanimous vote of the Council on a proposal of the Commission.

Member states shall consult one another for the purpose of enacting in common the necessary provisions to prevent the functioning of the Common Market from being affected by measures which a member state may be called upon to take in case of serious internal disturbances affecting public order, in case of war or in order to carry out undertakings into which it has entered for the purpose of maintaining peace and international security.

In the course of the transitional period, where there are serious difficulties which are likely to persist in any sector of economic activity or difficulties which may seriously impair the economic situation in any region, any member state may ask for authorization to take measures of safeguard in order to restore the situation and adapt the sector concerned to the Common Market economy.

The provisions of the Treaty shall not affect those of the Treaty establishing the European Coal and Steel Community, nor those of the Treaty establishing the European Atomic Energy Community; nor shall they be an obstacle to the existence or completion of regional unions between Belgium and Luxembourg, and between Belgium, Luxembourg and the Netherlands, in so far as the objectives of these regional unions are not achieved by the application of this Treaty.

The government of any member state of the Commission may submit to the Council proposals for the revision of the Treaty.

Any European state may apply to become a member of the Community.

The Community may conclude with a third country, a union of states or an international organization agreements creating an association embodying reciprocal rights and obligations, joint actions and special procedures.

The Treaty is concluded for an unlimited period.

OTHER TREATIES

The following additional treaties have been signed by the members of the European Communities:

Treaty Instituting a Single Council and a Single Commission of the European Communities: signed in Brussels on 8 April 1965 by the six original members.

Treaty Modifying Certain Budgetary Arrangements of the European Communities and of the Treaty Instituting a Single Council and a Single Commission of the European Communities: signed in Luxembourg on 22 April 1970 by the six original members.

Treaty Concerning the Accession of the Kingdom of Denmark, Ireland, the Kingdom of Norway and the United Kingdom of Great Britain to the European Economic Community and the European Atomic Energy Community: signed in Brussels on 22 January 1972 (amended on 1 January 1973, owing to the non-accession of Norway).

Treaty of Accession of the Hellenic Republic to the European Economic Community and to the European Atomic Energy Community: signed in Athens on 28 May 1979.

Treaty of Accession of the Portuguese Republic and the Kingdom of Spain to the European Economic Community and to the European Atomic Energy Community: signed in Lisbon and Madrid on 12 June 1985.

(Accession of new members to the European Coal and Steel Community is enacted separately, by a Decision of the Council of the European Communities.)

THE SINGLE EUROPEAN ACT

On 1 July 1987 amendments to the Treaty of Rome, in the form of the 'Single European Act', came into effect, following ratification by all the member states. The Act contained provisions which aimed to complete by 1992 the creation of a single Community market—'an area without internal frontiers in which the free movement of goods, persons, services and capital is ensured'. Other provisions increased Community co-operation in research and technology, social policy (particularly the improvement of working conditions), economic and social cohesion (reduction of disparities between regions), environmental protection, creation of economic and monetary union, and foreign policy. It allowed the Council of Ministers to take decisions by a qualified majority vote on matters which previously, under the Treaty of Rome, had required unanimity: this applied principally to matters relating to the establishment of the internal market (see below under the heading Council of Ministers). The Act increased the powers of the European Parliament to delay and amend legislation, although the Council retained final decision-making powers. The Act also provided for the establishment of a secretariat for European political co-operation on matters of foreign policy.

Community Institutions

Originally each of the Communities had its own Commission (High Authority in the case of the ECSC) and Council, but a treaty transferring the powers of these bodies to a single Commission and a single Council came into effect in 1967.

COMMISSION OF THE EUROPEAN COMMUNITIES

Address: 200 rue de la Loi, 1049 Brussels, Belgium.
Telephone: (02) 235-11-11.
Telex: 21877.

MEMBERS OF THE COMMISSION*
(with their responsibilities: October 1988)

President: JACQUES DELORS (France): Secretariat-General; Legal Service; Spokesman's Service; Joint Interpreting and Conference Service; Security Office; Monetary Affairs.

Vice-Presidents:

LORENZO NATALI (Italy): Co-operation and Development.

KARL-HEINZ NARJES (Federal Republic of Germany): Industrial Affairs; Information Technology; Science and Research; Joint Research Centre.

FRANS ANDRIESSEN (Netherlands): Agriculture; Forestry.

Lord (ARTHUR) COCKFIELD (United Kingdom): Internal Market; Customs Union; Taxation; Financial Institutions.

HENNING CHRISTOPHERSEN (Denmark): Budget; Financial Control; Personnel and Administration.

MANUEL MARÍN (Spain): Social Affairs and Employment; Education and Training.

Other members:

CLAUDE CHEYSSON (France): Mediterranean Policy; North-South Relations.

PETER SCHMIDTHUBER (Federal Republic of Germany): Economic Affairs; Regional Policy; Statistical Office.

GRIGORIS VARFIS (Greece): Co-ordination of Structural Instruments; Consumer Protection.

WILLY DE CLERCQ (Belgium): External Relations and Trade Policy.

NICOLAS MOSAR (Luxembourg): Energy; Euratom Supply Agency; Publications Office.

STANLEY CLINTON DAVIS (United Kingdom): Environment; Nuclear Safety; Transport.

CARLO RIPA DE MEANA (Italy): Institutional Questions; Matters concerning a Citizen's Europe; Information and Communication; Culture; Tourism.

PETER D. SUTHERLAND (Ireland): Competition; Relations with European Parliament.

ANTÓNIO CARDOSO E CUNHA (Portugal): Fisheries.

ABEL MATUTES (Spain): Credit; Investments; Financial Instruments; Small and Medium-Sized Businesses.

* A number of new members of the Commission were appointed in 1988, to take office from January 1989 (see Late Information).

The functions of the Commission are fourfold: to ensure the application of the provisions of the Treaties and of the provisions enacted by the institutions of the Communities in pursuance thereof; to formulate recommendations or opinions in matters which are the subject of the Treaties, where the latter expressly so provides or where the Commission considers it necessary; to dispose, under the conditions laid down in the Treaties, of a power of decision of its own and to participate in the preparation of acts of the Council of Ministers and of the European Parliament; and to exercise the competence conferred on it by the Council of Ministers for the implementation of the rules laid down by the latter.

The Commission may not include more than two members having the nationality of the same state; the number of members of the Commission may be amended by a unanimous vote of the Council of Ministers. In the performance of their duties, the members of the Commission are forbidden to seek or accept instructions from any Government or other body, or to engage in any other paid or unpaid professional activity.

The members of the Commission are appointed by the Governments of the member states acting in common agreement for a renewable term of four years; the President and Vice-Presidents are appointed for renewable terms of two years. Any member of the Commission, if he no longer fulfils the conditions required for the performance of his duties, or if he commits a serious offence, may be declared removed from office by the Court of Justice. The Court may furthermore, on the petition of the Council of Ministers or of the Commission itself, provisionally suspend any member of the Commission from his duties.

ADMINISTRATION

Offices are at the address of the European Commission: 200 rue de la Loi, 1049 Brussels, Belgium; tel. (02) 235-11-11; telex 21877 (unless otherwise stated).

Secretariat-General of the Commission: Sec.-Gen. DAVID WILLIAMSON.

Legal Service: Dir-Gen. JEAN-LOUIS DEWOST.

Spokesman's Service: CLAUS-DIETER EHLERMANN.

Joint Interpreting and Conference Service: Dir-Gen. RENÉE VAN HOOF.

Statistical Office: Bâtiment Jean Monnet, rue Alcide de Gasperi, 2920 Luxembourg; tel. 430-11; telex 3423; Dir-Gen. YVES FRANCHET.

Directorates-General:

I **(External Relations):** Dir-Gen. HORST KRENZLER.

II **(Economic and Financial Affairs):** Dir-Gen. ANTONIO MARIA COSTA.

III **(Internal Market and Industrial Affairs):** Dir-Gen. FERNAND BRAUN.

IV **(Competition):** Dir-Gen. MANFRED CASPARI.

V **(Employment, Social Affairs and Education):** Dir-Gen. JEAN DEGIMBE.

VI **(Agriculture):** Dir-Gen. GUY LEGRAS.

VII **(Transport):** Dir-Gen. EDUARDO PEÑA ABIZANDA.

VIII **(Development):** Dir-Gen. DIETER FRISCH.

IX **(Personnel and Administration):** Dir-Gen. RICHARD HAY.

X **(Information, Communication and Culture):** Dir-Gen. (vacant).

XI **(Environment, Consumer Protection and Nuclear Safety):** Dir-Gen. LAURENS JAN BRINKHORST.

XII **(Science, Research and Development):** Dir-Gen. PAOLO FASELLA.

  Joint Research Centre: Dir-Gen. JEAN-PIERRE CONTZEN.

XIII **(Telecommunications, Information and Innovation):** Dir-Gen. MICHEL CARPENTIER.

XIV **(Fisheries):** Dir-Gen. EAMONN GALLAGHER.

XV **(Financial Institutions and Company Law):** Dir-Gen. GEOFFREY FITCHEW.

XVI **(Regional Policy):** Dir-Gen. ENEKO LANDABURU.

XVII **(Energy):** Dir-Gen. CONSTANTINOS MANIATOPOULOS.

XVIII **(Credit and Investments):** Bâtiment Jean Monnet, rue Alcide de Gasperi, 2920 Luxembourg-Kirchberg; tel. 430-11; telex 3423; Dir-Gen. ENRICO CIOFFI.

XIX **(Budgets):** Dir-Gen. JEAN-CLAUDE MOREL.

XX **(Financial Control):** Dir-Gen. GIOVANNI RAVASIO.

XXI **(Customs Union and Indirect Taxation):** Dir-Gen. EMILIO RUI VILAR.

XXII **(Co-ordination of Structural Instruments):** Dir-Gen. KAJ BARLEBO-LARSEN.

Euratom Supply Agency: Dir-Gen. GEORG VON KLITZING.

Security Office: Dir PIETER DE HAAN.

THE EUROPEAN COUNCIL

The Heads of State or of Government of the member countries meet at least twice a year, in the capital of the member state which currently exercises the presidency of the Council of Ministers, or in Brussels.

Until 1975 summit meetings were held at rather less frequent intervals and were often required to take decisions which came to be regarded as the major guidelines for the development of the Community.

In answer to the evident need for more frequent consultation at the highest level it was decided at the summit meeting in Paris in December 1974 to hold the meetings on a regular basis. The Council discusses matters relating to the Community and matters handled by the 'Political Co-operation' system (under which the Foreign Ministers of the member states meet at least four times a year to co-ordinate foreign policy).

COUNCIL OF MINISTERS OF THE EUROPEAN COMMUNITIES

Address: 170 rue de la Loi, 1049 Brussels, Belgium.

The Council of Ministers has the double responsibility of ensuring the co-ordination of the general economic policies of the member states and of taking the decisions necessary for carrying out the Treaties.

The Council is composed of representatives of the member states, each Government delegating to it one of its members, according to the subject to be discussed. The Councils of foreign affairs, economics and finance and agriculture normally meet once a month. About 60 Council sessions are held each year. The office of President is exercised for a term of six months by each member of the Council in rotation according to the alphabetical order of the member states. Meetings of the Council are called by the President acting on his or her own initiative or at the request of a member or of the Commission.

The Treaty of Rome prescribed three types of voting: simple majority, qualified majority and unanimity. Where conclusions require a qualified majority, the votes of its members are weighted as follows: France, Federal Republic of Germany, Italy and the United Kingdom 10; Spain 8; Belgium, Greece, the Netherlands and Portugal 5; Denmark and Ireland 3; Luxembourg 2 (Total 76). Majorities are required for the adoption of any conclusions as follows: 54 votes in cases where the Treaty requires a previous proposal of the Commission, or 54 votes including a favourable vote by more than half the members in all other cases. It was declared at a meeting of the Council of Ministers in 1966 that when decisions affecting very important national interests were at stake, discussions should be continued for a reasonable length of time, so that mutually acceptable solutions could be found, giving each member what amounted to a right of veto. Amendments to the Treaty of Rome, effective from July 1987 (following ratification by national legislatures), restricted the right of 'veto', and were expected to speed up the development of a genuine common market: they allowed proposals relating to the dismantling of barriers to the free movement of goods, persons, services and capital to be approved by a majority vote in the Council, rather than by a unanimous vote. Unanimity would still be required, however, for certain areas, including harmonization of indirect taxes, legislation on health and safety, veterinary controls, and environmental protection; individual states would also retain control over immigration rules, prevention of terrorism and drug-trafficking.

The amendments also introduced a 'co-operation procedure' whereby a proposal adopted by a qualified majority in the Council must be submitted to the European Parliament for approval: if the Parliament rejects the Council's common position, unanimity shall be required for the Council to act on a second reading, and if the Parliament suggests amendments, the Commission must re-examine the proposal and forward it to the Council again.

PERMANENT REPRESENTATIVES

Preparation and co-ordination of the Council's work is entrusted to a Committee of Permanent Representatives (COREPER), meeting in Brussels, consisting of the ambassadors of the member countries to the Communities, and aided by committees of national civil servants.

SECRETARIAT

The General Secretariat of the Council has a staff of about 1,600, who service the Council and COREPER.

Secretary-General: NIELS ERSBØLL (Denmark).

INTERNATIONAL ORGANIZATIONS   *European Communities*

EUROPEAN PARLIAMENT

Address: Centre Européen, Plateau de Kirchberg, BP 2929, Luxembourg.
Telephone: 43001.

PRESIDENT AND MEMBERS
(October 1988)

President: Lord PLUMB (United Kingdom).
Members: 518 members, apportioned as follows: France, the Federal Republic of Germany, Italy and the United Kingdom 81 members each; Spain 60; the Netherlands 25; Belgium, Greece and Portugal 24 each; Denmark 16; Ireland 15; Luxembourg 6. Members are elected by direct universal suffrage by the citizens of the member states. Members sit in the Chamber in political, not national, groups.

Political Groupings

	Distribution of seats (October 1988)
Socialist Group	165
European People's Party (Christian-Democratic Group)	114
European Democratic Group	66
Communist and Allies Group	48
Liberal and Democratic Reformist Group	45
European Democratic Alliance*	29
Rainbow Group	20
Group of the European Right	16
Non-affiliated	15
Total	**518**

* Formerly Group of European Progressive Democrats.

The tasks of the European Parliament are: advising on legislation, scrutinizing the Community budget and exercising a measure of democratic control over the executive organs of the European Communities, the Commission and the Council. It has the power to dismiss the Commission by a vote of censure. An increase in parliamentary powers was brought about by the amendments to the Treaty of Rome, known as the Single European Act, which were adopted in 1986 and which entered into force on 1 July 1987: in certain circumstances where the Council of Ministers normally adopts legislation through majority voting, a co-operation procedure involving a second parliamentary reading comes into force should the Council not wish to accept Parliament's amendments. Community agreements with third countries now require parliamentary approval. The reforms fell far short of demands by members of Parliament for full powers of joint decision-making.

Parliament has an annual session, divided into about 12 one-week meetings, normally held in Strasbourg. The session opens with the March meeting. Committees normally meet in Brussels.

The budgetary powers of Parliament (which, with the Council, forms the Budgetary Authority of the Communities) were increased to their present status by a treaty of 22 July 1975. Under this treaty, it can amend non-agricultural spending and reject the draft budget, acting by a majority of its members and two-thirds of the votes cast.

The Parliament is run by a Bureau comprising the President, and 14 vice-presidents elected from its members by secret ballot to serve for 2½ years. Parliament has 18 specialized committees, which deliberate on proposals for legislation put forward by the Commission before Parliament's final opinion is delivered by a resolution in plenary session.

There are Standing Committees on Political Affairs; Agriculture, Fisheries and Food; Budgets; Budgetary Control; Economic and Monetary Affairs and Industrial Policy; Energy, Research and Technology; External Economic Relations; Legal Affairs and Citizens' Rights; Social Affairs and Employment; Regional Policy and Planning; Transport; Environment, Public Health and Consumer Protection; Youth, Culture, Education, Information and Sport; Development and Co-operation; Rules of Procedure, the Verification of Credentials and Immunities; Institutional Affairs; Petitions; Women's Rights.

The first direct elections to the European Parliament took place in June 1979. The directly elected Parliament met for the first time in July 1979. The second elections were held from 14–17 June 1984 (with separate elections held in Portugal and Spain in 1987, following the accession of these two countries to the Community), and the third elections were due to be held on 15–18 June 1989.

COURT OF JUSTICE OF THE EUROPEAN COMMUNITIES

Address: 2925 Luxembourg.
Telephone: 4303-1.
Telex: 2510.

The task of the Court of Justice is to ensure the observance of law in the interpretation and application of the Treaties setting up the three Communities, and in implementing regulations issued by the Council or the Commission. The 13 Judges and the six Advocates General are appointed for renewable six-year terms by the Governments of the member states. The President of the Court is elected by the Judges from among their number for a renewable term of three years. The majority of cases, including all those of major importance, are dealt with by a full bench of 13 judges. The remainder are dealt with by one of the six chambers, each of which consists of a President of Chamber and two or four judges. The Court has jurisdiction to award damages. It may review the legality of acts (other than recommendations or opinions) of the Council or the Commission and is competent to give judgment on actions by a member state, the Council or the Commission on grounds of lack of competence, of infringement of an essential procedural requirement, of infringement of a Treaty or of any legal rule relating to its application, or of misuse of power. Any natural or legal person may, under the same conditions, appeal against a decision addressed to him or against a decision which, although in the form of a regulation or decision addressed to another person, is of direct and individual concern to him.

The Court is also empowered to hear certain other cases concerning the contractual and non-contractual liability of the Communities and disputes between member states in connection with the objects of the Treaties. It also gives preliminary rulings at the request of national courts on the interpretation of the Treaties, of Community legislation, and of the Brussels Convention on Jurisdiction and the Enforcement of Judgments in Civil and Commercial Matters. During 1987 395 new cases were brought before the Court, of which 144 were cases referred to it for preliminary rulings by the national courts of the member states. In the same period 208 judgments and interim orders were delivered.

Composition of the Court (in order of precedence, October 1988)
Judge O. DUE, President.
Judge T. KOOPMANS (President of the Fourth and Sixth Chambers).
Judge R. JOLIET (President of the First and Fifth Chambers).
Judge T. F. O'HIGGINS (President of the Second Chamber).
Judge F. GREVISSE (President of the Third Chamber).
First Advocate General J. MISCHO.
Sir GORDON SLYNN, Judge.
Judge G. F. MANCINI.
Judge C. N. KAKOURIS.
Advocate General C. O. LENZ.
Advocate General M. DARMON.
Judge F. A. SCHOCKWEILER.
Judge J. C. MOITINHO DE ALMEIDA.
Judge G. C. RODRÍGUEZ IGLESIAS.
Judge M. DIEZ DE VELASCO.
Judge M. ZULEEG.
Advocate General W. VAN GERVEN.
Advocate General F. JACOBS.
Advocate General G. TESAURO.
J.-G. GIRAUD (Registrar).

COURT OF AUDITORS OF THE EUROPEAN COMMUNITIES

Address: 12 rue Alcide de Gasperi, 1615 Luxembourg.
Telephone: 4398-1.
Telex: 3512.

The Court of Auditors was created by a Treaty which came into force on 1 July 1977. It is the body responsible for the external audit of the resources managed by the three Communities. It consists of 12 Members who are appointed for six-year terms by unanimous decision of the Council of Ministers, after consultation with the European Parliament. The Members elect the President from among their number for a term of three years.

The Court is organized and acts as a corporate body. It adopts its decisions by a majority of its Members. Each Member, however, has a direct responsibility to audit certain Community sectors.

The Court examines the accounts of all expenditure and revenue of the European Communities and of any body created by them in so far as the relevant constituent instrument does not preclude such examination. It examines whether all revenue has been received and all expenditure incurred in a lawful and regular manner and whether the financial management has been sound. The audit is based on records, and if necessary is performed on the spot in the institutions of the Communities and in the member states. In the member states the audit is carried out in liaison with the national audit bodies. The Court draws up an annual report after the close of each financial year. It may also, at any time, submit observations on specific questions and deliver opinions at the request of one of the institutions of the Communities. It assists the Assembly and the Council in exercising their powers of control over the implementation of the budget, and gives its prior opinion on the financial regulations, on the methods and procedure whereby the budgetary revenue is made available to the Commission, and on the laying-down of rules concerning the responsibility of authorizing officers and accounting officers and concerning appropriate arrangements for inspection.

President: MARCEL MART (Luxembourg).

First Group: RICHIE RYAN (Ireland), CHARLES J. CAREY (United Kingdom), KELD BRIXTOFTE (Denmark), FERNAND HEBETTE (Belgium).

Second Group: ALDO ANGIOI (Italy), PIERRE LELONG (France), ANDRÉ J. MIDDELHOEK (Netherlands), JOSEP SUBIRATS (Spain).

Third Group: MARCEL MART (Luxembourg), LOTHAR HAASE (Federal Republic of Germany), STERGIOS VALLAS (Greece), CARLOS MANUEL BOTELHEIRO MORENO (Portugal).

EUROPEAN INVESTMENT BANK

Address: 100 blvd Konrad Adenauer, 2950 Luxembourg.

Telephone: 4379-1.

Telex: 3530.

Board of Governors: One Minister (usually the Finance Minister) from each member state.

Board of Directors: Three directors and two alternates each come from France, the Federal Republic of Germany, Italy and the United Kingdom; two directors come from Spain and one from Portugal, and both countries have a joint alternate; one director each comes from Belgium, Luxembourg and the Netherlands, who jointly have one alternate; Denmark, Greece and Ireland each have one director and jointly one alternate. The Commission of the European Communities has one director and one alternate.

Management Committee:

President: ERNST-GÜNTHER BRÖDER (FRG).

Vice-Presidents: C. RICHARD ROSS (UK), LUCIO IZZO (Italy), ALAIN PRATE (France), M. ARNEDO ORBAÑOS (Spain), ERLING JØRGENSEN (Denmark), LUDOVICUS MEULEMANS (Belgium).

The European Investment Bank (EIB) was created in 1958 by the six founder member states of the European Economic Community. The capital subscribed by the 12 member states stands at 28,800m. ECUs, of which 9.01% is paid-in or to be paid-in (see table). The bulk of the EIB's resources, however, comes from borrowings, principally public or private bond issues on capital markets inside and outside the Community. In 1987 the Bank borrowed 5,593m. ECUs, compared with 6,786m. in 1986.

The EIB's principal task is laid down in Article 130 of the Treaty: working on a non-profit basis, the Bank makes or guarantees loans for investment projects which contribute to the balanced and steady development of the common market. Throughout the Bank's history, priority has been given to financing investment projects which further regional development. The EIB also finances projects of common interest to several member countries, or the Community as a whole, particularly projects which meet the Community's energy objectives and large infrastructure projects, and gives support to industrial modernization and conversion. During the 1980s, the Bank increased its lending for investments in environmental protection and the development and introduction of advanced technology.

Lending within the Community totalled 7,450m. ECUs in 1987, compared with 7,071m. ECUs in 1986. In 1987 26.2% of financing within the Community was for energy production, transmission and supply; 39.5% was for infrastructure (transport, communications, water supply); and 34.3% was for industry, services and agriculture.

The EIB plays a major part in the implementation of the Community's development policy. The Bank has financed projects in 12 countries in the Mediterranean region and 66 African, Caribbean and Pacific (ACP) countries, signatories to the Lomé Convention (q.v.). During 1987 it made available 42.7m. ECUs in the Mediterranean countries and 349m. ECUs in the ACP states.

In 1978 the New Community Instrument for Borrowing and Lending (NCI) was set up to raise funds for financing structural investment projects to reflect the Community's priorities, particularly for energy, industrial conversion and infrastructure. Funds are deposited with the European Investment Bank. Loans granted under the NCI amounted to 447m. ECUs in 1987, of which 87% was for investment in small and medium-sized businesses. Total loans granted since 1979 came to 5,910.5m. ECUs, of which Italy was the largest recipient with 50%.

CAPITAL STRUCTURE
(as from 1 January 1986, in ECUs)

	Subscribed	Paid-in	%
France	5,508,725,000	497,529,375	19.127
Federal Republic of Germany	5,508,725,000	497,529,375	19.127
Italy	5,508,725,000	497,529,375	19.127
United Kingdom	5,508,725,000	497,529,375	19.127
Spain	2,024,928,000	181,333,940	7.031
Belgium	1,526,980,000	136,742,250	5.302
Netherlands	1,526,980,000	136,742,250	5.302
Denmark	773,154,000	69,236,550	2.684
Greece	414,190,000	37,091,750	1.438
Portugal	266,922,000	23,903,086	0.927
Ireland	193,288,000	17,309,100	0.671
Luxembourg	38,658,000	3,461,850	0.134
Total	28,800,000,000	2,595,938,276	100.000

FINANCING PROVIDED (million ECUs)

Recipient	1987 Amount	1987 %	1983–87 Amount	1983–87 %
Community				
Belgium	37.1	0.5	193.6	0.6
Denmark	315.3	4.2	1,565.1	4.8
France	1,006.5	13.5	4,971.6	15.2
Federal Republic of Germany	276.5	3.7	1,096.2	3.4
Greece	164.8	2.2	1,635.9	5.0
Ireland	178.6	2.4	1,093.2	3.3
Italy	3,112.2	41.8	14,760.7	45.2
Luxembourg	1.6	—	36.2	0.1
Netherlands	18.0	0.2	185.3	0.6
Portugal	389.9	5.2	580.2[1]	1.8
Spain	707.4	9.5	1,116.7[1]	3.4
United Kingdom	1,133.7	15.2	5,259.2	16.1
Non-member countries	108.7	1.5	183.7	0.5
Sub-total	7,450.4	100.0	32,677.7[3]	100.0
Outside the Community				
from the Bank's own resources	188.8		2,195.5	
from budgetary resources	203.3		510.1	
Sub-total	392.1		2,705.6	
Total	7,842.5		35,383.3	

[1] Excluding pre-accession aid (Portugal 725m. ECUs; Spain 550m. ECUs).
[2] Loans granted for energy projects in Austria, Norway and Tunisia but of direct importance to the Community.
[3] Including loans granted from the resources of the New Community Instrument for borrowing and lending, i.e. a total of 4,105m. ECUs in 1983–87, of which 388m. was for investments in Denmark, 1,065.5m. for France, 181.2m. for Greece, 195.1m. for Ireland, 1,844.4m. for Italy, 39.8m. for Portugal, 183.0m. for Spain and 208m. for the United Kingdom.

SPECIAL FUNDS

The European Agricultural Guidance and Guarantee Fund, the European Regional Development Fund and the European Social Fund are part of the General Budget and are financed by the Community's own resources.

INTERNATIONAL ORGANIZATIONS   *European Communities*

EUROPEAN AGRICULTURAL GUIDANCE AND GUARANTEE FUND

Created in 1962, the European Agricultural Guidance and Guarantee Fund (or FEOGA as it is known after its French initials) is administered by the Commission. The Guidance Section contributes credits towards the structural reform of agriculture. Proposed appropriations for payments under this section in the 1989 preliminary draft budget amounted to 1,567m. ECUs. The Guarantee Section, under which a large proportion of the Community's budget is spent, intervenes to regularize the internal market, and provides export refunds which compensate for the difference between Community and world market prices. Guarantee appropriations for 1987 amounted to 22,960.8m. ECUs (61.3% of the total budget); for 1988 the amount was 27,500m. ECUs and the preliminary draft budget for 1989 envisaged spending of 28,190m. ECUs.

EUROPEAN REGIONAL DEVELOPMENT FUND

Payments began in 1975. The Fund is intended to compensate for the unequal rate of development in different regions of the Community, by encouraging investment and improving infrastructure in 'problem regions'. Initially, funds were spent entirely according to a system of national quotas, but in 1979 an additional non-quota section was adopted, allowing the financing of specific Community measures to aid, for example, frontier areas or different areas affected by the same problem. In 1984 agreement was reached on a revision of the Fund, whereby a larger proportion (up to 15%) could be allocated to supra-national programmes, initiated by the Commission but subject to a veto by the governments concerned. In addition, more flexible national quotas were drawn up, with upper and lower limits. In 1987 the Fund made commitments of 3,533m. ECUs and payments of 2,444m. ECUs.

EUROPEAN SOCIAL FUND

The Fund was established in 1960, with the aim of improving employment opportunities by assisting training and workers' mobility. From 1972 there was a new emphasis on job creation schemes as well as on training. Under new rules approved in 1983 the Fund was to increase its aid for the employment of young people, reserving 75% of its resources for this purpose, while a guaranteed minimum of 40% was to be spent in the Community's poorest regions. Areas of high unemployment and industrial decline were also to be given priority, while about 5% of aid was to be used for pilot projects experimenting with new training methods, job creation schemes, or job-sharing projects.

Appropriations for commitments by the Fund in 1987 amounted to 3,150m. ECUs, of which about 21% was for Italy, 19% for the United Kingdom and 14% for Spain. From 1986 stricter rules were applied for selection of suitable schemes, but in 1987 eligible applications still exceeded available resources by over 63%.

CONSULTATIVE BODIES

ECONOMIC AND SOCIAL COMMITTEE—ECOSOC

Address: 2 rue Ravenstein, 1000 Brussels.
Telephone: (02) 519-90-11.
Telex: 25 983.

The Committee is advisory and is consulted by the Council of Ministers or by the Commission of the European Communities, particularly with regard to agriculture, free movement of workers, harmonization of laws and transport, as well as legislation adopted under the Euratom Treaty. In addition, the Committee has the power to deliver opinions on its own initiative.

The Committee has 189 members representing economic and social fields, 24 each from France, the Federal Republic of Germany, Italy and the United Kingdom, 21 from Spain, 12 each from Belgium, Greece, the Netherlands and Portugal, nine from Denmark and Ireland, and six from Luxembourg. One-third represent each side of industry and one-third the general economic interest. The Committee is appointed for a renewable term of four years by the unanimous vote of the Council of Ministers of the European Communities. Members are appointed in their personal capacity and are not bound by any mandatory instructions.

President: ALFONS MARGOT.
Secretary-General: JACQUES MOREAU.

ECSC CONSULTATIVE COMMITTEE

The Committee is advisory and is attached to the Commission. Its members are appointed by the Council of Ministers for two years and are not bound by any mandate from the organizations that designated them in the first place.

There are 84 members representing, in equal proportions, producers, workers and consumers and dealers in the coal and steel industries.

AGRICULTURAL ADVISORY COMMITTEES

There is one Committee for the organization of the market of each sector; two for dealing with social questions in agriculture; and one for structures.

In addition to the consultative bodies listed above there are several hundred special interest groups representing every type of interest within the Community. All these hold unofficial talks with the Commission.

Activities of the Community

AGRICULTURE

Co-operation in the Community is at its most highly-organized in the area of agriculture. The objectives of the Common Agricultural Policy (CAP) are described in the Treaty of Rome (see p. 136). The markets for agricultural products have been progressively organized following three basic principles: (i) unity of the market (products must be able to circulate freely within the Community and markets must be organized according to common rules); (ii) Community preference (products must be protected from low-cost imports and from fluctuations on the world market); (iii) common financial responsibility (the European Agricultural Guidance and Guarantee Fund, described on this page, finances, through its Guarantee Section, all public expenditure intervention, storage costs, marketing subsidies and export rebates, and, through its Guidance Section, the improvement of farms and facilities).

Monetary compensation amounts (MCAs) are added or deducted in agricultural exchanges between member states to take account of fluctuations between the reference rate of exchange (the 'green' currencies) and the real rate. Thus a subsidy is paid to the supplier in a country whose currency has appreciated against a reference rate of exchange, and a tax is paid by the supplier where the currency has depreciated or not appreciated as much. In practice, however, the MCA system has led to wide variations in prices within the Community, and has proved disadvantageous to any country which is a net food exporter with a weak currency. In 1984 it was decided that the system should eventually be phased out, thereby restoring a single market.

Agricultural prices are, in theory, fixed each year at a common level for the community as a whole, taking into account the rate of inflation and the need to discourage surplus production of certain commodities. Export subsidies are paid to enable farmers to sell produce at the lower world market prices without loss. These subsidies account for some 50% of agricultural spending, and have attracted criticism from other producers, particularly the USA.

An intervention price has been established for sugar, certain cereals, dairy produce, beef, veal and sheep-meat: when market prices fall below this level the Community intervenes, and buys a certain quantity which is then stored until prices recover. Expanding production has led to food surpluses, costly to maintain, particularly in dairy produce, beef, cereals and wine. In 1982 production guarantee thresholds, already existing for sugar, were extended to dairy products, cereals, colza and processed tomatoes: once these thresholds are passed, producers do not receive the full guaranteed EEC prices, and have to share the cost of disposing of surpluses.

Agriculture is by far the largest item on the Community budget, accounting for over two-thirds of annual expenditure, mainly for supporting prices. In 1984 ministers of agriculture adopted proposals for adapting the CAP so as to limit the burden on the Community budget and make the agricultural sector more responsive to the level of supply and demand. They agreed to eliminate the system of MCAs, in phases (see above). Lower milk production quotas were to be imposed in most countries. The guaranteed prices for most agricultural products were 'frozen' between 1984 and 1987, with adjustments in the 'green' currencies being made to alleviate the effect on producers. As a result of the imposition of quotas, milk production decreased slightly, but consumption also fell, and by 1986 surplus dairy produce had reached record levels, despite the Community's efforts to dispose of surplus butter by selling it cheaply within and outside Europe, and to use skimmed milk powder as animal feed. In 1986 and 1987 further reductions in milk production quotas were imposed, and by mid-1988 surpluses of dairy produce had been considerably reduced.

In February 1988 the Council agreed upon budgetary reforms which included a legally-enforceable 'ceiling' on agricultural expenditure. The annual rate of increase in spending on agricultural guarantees was not to exceed 74% of the year's increase in the Community's gross national product. Existing 'stabilizers' on agricultural production were extended: a guarantee threshold of 160m. metric tons per year was imposed for cereals for the period 1988–92, with any excess production being penalized by a cut of 3% in the guaranteed intervention price for the ensuing year.

Guarantee thresholds were also imposed on oilseeds and protein feed crops, while subsequent meetings of ministers of agriculture imposed similar 'stabilizers' on production of wine, sugar, fruit and vegetables, tobacco, olive oil, cotton and sheep-meat. The system of milk production quotas was extended until 1992. The Council meeting in February also agreed to adopt a 'set-aside' scheme whereby farmers would be compensated for withdrawing land from cultivation. In June ministers of agriculture agreed once again to a virtual 'freeze' of guaranteed prices for 1988/89.

FISHERIES

The Common Fisheries Policy (CFP) came into effect in January 1983 after seven years of negotiations, particularly over the problem of access to fishing-grounds. In 1973 a 10-year agreement had been reached, whereby member states could have exclusive access to waters up to six nautical miles (11.1 km) or in some cases 12 miles from their shores; 'historic rights' were reserved in certain cases for foreign fishermen who had traditionally fished within a country's waters. In 1977 the Community set up a 200-mile (370-km) fishing zone around its coastline (excluding the Mediterranean) within which all members would have access to fishing. The 1983 agreement confirmed the 200-mile zone and allowed exclusive national zones of six miles with access between six and 12 miles from the shore for other countries according to specified 'historic rights'. Rules furthering conservation (e.g. standards for fishing tackle) are imposed under the policy, with checks by a Community fisheries inspectorate. Total allowable catches are fixed annually by species, divided into national quotas. During 1985 negotiations on fishing quotas for Portugal and Spain were successfully concluded, enabling them to participate in the CFP after their accession to the Community in January 1986.

The organization of fish marketing involves common rules on quality and packing, and a system of guide prices established annually by the Council of Ministers. Fish are withdrawn from the market if prices fall too far below the guide price, and compensation may then be paid to the fishermen. As with agricultural produce, export subsidies are paid to enable the export of fish onto the lower-priced world market, and import levies are imposed to prevent competition from low-priced imports.

The Community supports re-structuring of the fishing industry by offering grants for equipment and building. A three-year plan, beginning in 1983 and involving expenditure of 250m. ECUs, supported capacity reduction (scrapping or laying-up of fishing-vessels), the exploration and development of new grounds and the modernization of existing facilities.

Agreements have been signed with other countries (Norway, Sweden, Canada and the USA) allowing reciprocal fishing rights and other advantages, and with some African countries which receive assistance in building up their fishing industries in return for allowing EEC boats to fish in their waters. Following the withdrawal of Greenland from the Community in February 1985, Community vessels retained fishing rights in Greenland waters, in exchange for financial compensation under a 10-year agreement.

SCIENCE AND TECHNOLOGY

In September 1981 the Commission brought together under a single Directorate-General all the departments responsible for scientific research, and proposed the formation of a common research and development policy, aiming to make the most of national potential, with emphasis on industrial and agricultural applications. In July 1983 the Council approved a programme for scientific research and technological development during the period 1984–87, involving total expenditure originally estimated at 3,750m. ECUs, and covering: promotion of industrial and agricultural competitiveness; improving the management of raw materials (including recycling and substitution); improving management of energy resources and reducing energy dependence; reinforcing development aid; improving living and working conditions; and improving the efficacy of the Community's scientific and technical potential. In the amendments to the Treaty of Rome, effective from July 1987, a section on research and technology was included for the first time, defining the extent of Community co-operation and introducing new decision-making structures. In 1987 the Council adopted a programme of research and technological development for 1987–91, with a budget of 5,396m. ECUs. The programme was divided into eight areas: quality of life (health; radiation protection; environment); towards a common market and an information and communications society (information technology, telecommunications, services); modernization of industrial sectors (manufacturing industry, advanced materials, raw materials and recycling, technical standards); exploitation of biological resources (biotechnology, agro-industry, agricultural resources); energy (nuclear safety; controlled thermonuclear fusion; non-nuclear energy and rational use of energy); science and technology for development; exploitation of the sea-bed and use of marine resources (marine science; fisheries); and improvement of European co-operation (human resources; joint use of major installations; forecasting, assessment and statistics, dissemination of research results).

Of the planned expenditure on scientific and technical research for the 1984–87 period, over 47% was allotted to energy research (see separate section below). The Community's Joint Research Centre (JRC) has establishments at Ispra (Italy), Geel (Belgium), Karlsruhe (Federal Republic of Germany) and Petten (Netherlands). Its 1984–87 work programme (with a budget of 700m. ECUs and a staff complement of 2,260) comprised joint research activities chiefly in energy (nuclear fusion, fission and non-nuclear energy sources) and also in industrial technologies and environmental problems.

Another major area of research is information technology: in November 1982 the Council approved a series of pilot projects preparing for the 10-year European Strategic Research Programme in Information Technology (ESPRIT), which concentrates on five key areas: advanced micro-electronics; software technology; advanced information processing; office automation; and computer integrated manufacturing. The programme, launched in 1984, is financed half by the EEC and half by research institutes, universities and industrial companies. At the end of 1987 there were 227 ESPRIT projects under way, involving almost 3,000 scientists and engineers.

In 1987 the Council agreed on the main phase of a joint programme for 1987–91 of research and development in advanced communications technology in Europe (RACE), aiming to establish an integrated broad-band telecommunications network.

The Community also supports biotechnological research, aiming to promote the use of modern biology in agriculture and industry. The 1985–89 biotechnology programme involved 93 transnational joint research projects.

A second research project on forecasting and assessment in science and technology (FAST) took place in 1983–87, with a budget of 8.5m. ECUs: its work covered the effects of new technology on work and employment; the development of renewable natural resources; technological change in the service industries; and new industrial systems, particularly in the communications and food industries. A third FAST programme was envisaged for 1988–92.

An experimental project was approved by the Council in June 1983 to encourage joint scientific research, for example in pharmaco-biology, solid state physics, optics, combustion, photometry/photoacoustics, interface phenomena and climatology. The means of stimulating joint research include grants, twinning laboratories in different countries, developing specific multinational projects and encouraging the mobility of research workers. The project proved successful and led to a four-year programme (1985–88) for stimulating joint research, with an appropriation of 60m. ECUs. The Community also co-operates with non-member countries in specific research projects, for example (in 1986) on marine navigation (with Finland, Norway and Sweden), on thrombosis (with Switzerland), and on plant culture (with five non-Community countries). In 1985 the Commission and 18 European countries (including the members of the Community as individuals) adopted the draft charter for the EUREKA programme of research in advanced technology. By June 1988 214 EUREKA projects had been approved.

The Direct Information Access Network (Euronet DIANE), inaugurated in 1980, comprises more than 750 data bases and banks, managed by national posts and telecommunications administrations and easily accessible to individuals or organizations seeking information on thousands of scientific, medical, technological or economic topics.

ENERGY

The treaty setting up the European Atomic Energy Community (Euratom) came into force on 1 January 1958, to encourage the growth of the nuclear energy industry in the Community through conducting research, providing access to information, supplying nuclear fuels, building reactors, and establishing common laws and procedures for the nuclear industry. A common market for nuclear materials was introduced in 1959, and there is a common insurance scheme against nuclear risks. The Commission is empowered to make loans on behalf of Euratom to finance investment in nuclear power stations and the enrichment of fissile materials. Loans made during 1987 amounted to 313.7m. ECUs for five firms, bringing the total since 1977 (when such operations began) to 2,753.1m. ECUs. An agreement with the International Atomic Energy Authority entered into force in 1977, to facilitate co-operation in research on nuclear safeguards and controls.

Activities are also undertaken in other fields of energy, and the Commission has consistently urged the formation of an effective overall energy policy. Energy objectives for the decade to 1995 were adopted by the Council in 1986: they aimed to restrict the Community's reliance on petroleum to 40% of energy consumption, and to keep net petroleum imports at less than 30% of energy consumption; to improve energy efficiency by at least 20%; to

INTERNATIONAL ORGANIZATIONS

European Communities

reduce the proportion of electricity generated using petroleum to less than 15%; and to increase the use of new and renewable energy sources.

The Joint Research Centre's 1984-87 programme included research on nuclear fusion (particularly safety and waste processing), fission and non-nuclear energy resources. In 1985 the Council adopted a programme of research in non-nuclear energy for 1985-88, with funding of 175m. ECUs.

The Joint European Torus (JET) is an experimental thermonuclear machine designed to pioneer new processes of nuclear fusion, using the 'Tokamak' system of magnetic confinement to heat gases to very high temperatures and bring about the fusion of tritium and deuterium nuclei. Sweden and Switzerland are also members of the JET project. Since 1974 work has been proceeding at Culham in the United Kingdom, and the project was formally inaugurated in April 1984. In 1982 a five-year programme of research in the field of controlled thermonuclear fusion was established (revised and continued for the period 1985-89 when the Commission's financial contribution was set at 690m. ECUs). The programme also includes preparation of the Next European Torus (NET), the intermediate stage in the development of a demonstration reactor: work on possible alternative methods of nuclear fusion is also being undertaken. In 1987 negotiations began with representatives of Japan, the USSR and the USA on the possible joint construction of an International Thermonuclear Experimental Reactor (ITER).

INDUSTRY

Industrial co-operation was the earliest activity of the Community, or more accurately of the European Coal and Steel Community (ECSC). The treaty establishing the ECSC came into force in July 1952, and by the end of 1954 nearly all barriers to trade in coal, coke, steel, pig-iron and scrap iron had been removed. The Community fixes prices and supervises production levels, and assists investment and redevelopment programmes by granting loans, from funds raised on the capital market (see below).

In other sectors the Community has less influence, although the European Commission has to approve state aid to industry by Community members, and forbids measures which might result in unfair competition. Community aid is given to certain sectors. Steel, textiles and shipbuilding have been given particular attention as areas with special difficulties.

'Anti-crisis' measures for the steel industry, first adopted in 1977 in the face of a fall in world demand and a 50% price slump between 1974 and 1977, were renewed in December 1979, mainly consisting of minimum price rules, guide prices and arrangements with 17 major steel-exporting countries. In October 1980 the Council agreed to proclaim a state of 'manifest crisis' in the steel industry, enabling compulsory production quotas to be imposed so as to maintain price levels. In 1981 a new aid code for the steel industry was introduced, ensuring that assistance is granted only to firms implementing a restructuring programme which will reduce their capacity and restore their competitiveness and financial viability. By late 1985 the industry had lost 30m. metric tons of annual production capacity. In July ministers of industry agreed to phase out state aids to steel and production quotas by the end of 1988. Stricter controls on state aid to the coal industry were also envisaged over the same period. The quota system for steel production was abolished on 30 June 1988, despite continuing overproduction.

Through redeployment loans and non-reimbursable aid for re-training, the Community has attempted to compensate for the loss of about 350,000 jobs in the steel industry between 1974 and 1984. During 1987 the Community made loans of 969.3m. ECUs to the coal and steel industries for investment in job-creation projects (66%), conversion in areas affected by the restructuring of the steel industry (31%) and subsidized housing (3%).

The European textile and clothing industry has been affected by overseas competition: 15% of the Community's textile firms closed between 1973 and 1980, with an average loss of 115,000 jobs per year during that period. The Community participates in the Multi-fibre Arrangement (see GATT, p. 56), to limit imports from low-cost suppliers overseas. The European Regional Development Fund gives particular support to regions where textiles formerly provided a large proportion of industrial employment, while the European Social Fund also assists in retraining workers. An Information Centre on Textiles and Clothing was set up in 1981 to provide economic and statistical details of production levels, stocks and consumption.

In the Community's shipyards, production fell by 50% in 1976-80, while the workforce was reduced by 40%. In 1981 the Council adopted the fifth directive on aid to shipbuilding, providing a framework for aid in reorganizing the industry and increasing efficiency, while discouraging any increase in capacity; this directive was extended until the end of 1986, after which the Council adopted a sixth directive, involving rigorous curbs on state aids to ship-building. A programme of assistance to shipbuilding workers for the period 1987-90 (worth 350m. ECUs) was announced in 1987.

The Commission has made a number of proposals on a joint strategy for developing the information technology industry in Europe, particularly in view of the superiority of Japan and the USA in the market for advanced electronic circuits. The ESPRIT research programme (see under Science and Technology) aims to build the technological foundations for a fully competitive European industry. In 1985 the Council adopted a programme of basic research in industrial technologies (BRITE), with Community funding of 125m. ECUs for 1985-88, aiming to develop new methods for the benefit of existing industries, such as aeronautics, chemicals, textiles and metalworking. A research programme on raw materials and advanced materials was also undertaken for 1986-89.

Harmonization of national company law to form a common legal structure is continuing: by the end of 1986 10 directives (concerning disclosure of information, company capital, internal mergers, the accounts of companies and of financial institutions, division of companies and the qualification of auditors) had been adopted, and others on cross-frontier mergers of public limited liability companies and the qualification of auditors) had been adopted, and others on cross-frontier mergers of public limited liability companies, on take-over bids, on participation in management by workers, and on company taxation were being considered in 1987 and 1988. The Community Patent Convention, providing for the issue of a Community patent valid for all members, was signed in 1975, subject to ratification by all member states. A Community Trade Mark Office was to be in operation by 1990. By the end of 1987 the Council had adopted 189 directives on the removal of technical barriers to trade with regard to industrial products. worth more than 5m. ECUs were to be offered for tender throughout the Community.

The Business Co-operation Centre, created by the Commission in 1973, supplies information to businesses and introduces businesses from different countries wishing to co-operate or form links. It gives particular attention to small and medium-sized concerns, and to companies in applicant countries wishing to acquaint themselves with the Community market. In 1986 the Council adopted an action programme for small and medium-sized enterprises, including simplified tax procedures and easier access to capital. A network of 39 Centres for European Business Information (aimed particularly at small businesses) began work in 1987.

TRANSPORT

The establishment of a common transport policy is stipulated in the EEC Treaty (see p. 137), with the aim of gradually standardizing national regulations which hinder the free movement of traffic within the Community, such as the varying safety and licensing rules, diverse restrictions on the size of lorries, and frontier-crossing formalities. Although by 1983 some progress had been made (for example in fixing rates for carriage of goods between states, harmonizing safety regulations such as the control of hours worked by drivers, standardizing the beginning of 'summer time', and reducing frontier delays) large-scale co-operation had not been achieved, and in that year the President of the European Parliament brought an action against the Council before the European Court of Justice for failure to implement the common transport policy: at this time over 40 Commission proposals on transport were still before the Council. In May 1985 the Court ruled that the Council had indeed failed to carry out its obligations: no penalty, however, could be imposed by the Court, and it emphasized that member states must agree on a common policy according to their own timetable.

Revised proposals for a common policy for inland transport, issued by the Commission in February 1983, included: co-operation in removing physical and legislative obstacles to a unified railway network; creation of Community authorizations for specific types of road transport; adjustment of national taxation systems for commercial vehicles; a permanent pricing system for international road haulage; harmonization of national scrapping schemes to reduce surplus capacity on inland waterways; negotiations with non-member countries such as Yugoslavia and Austria on transit and combined services; and the establishment of a Community system for paying infrastructure costs. In 1986 transport ministers agreed on a system of Community-wide permits for commercial vehicles, to allow easier crossing of frontiers. In June 1988 they agreed to abolish existing quotas for road-haulage firms by 1993, thus deregulating transport of goods by road.

In 1984 and 1985 the Commission also made proposals on the development of a Community air transport policy (to apply only to flights within the Community and aiming to produce a more flexible system, with greater scope for competition and more moderate fares). In April 1986 the European Court of Justice confirmed that the Community's rules on competition applied to air transport, and the Commission subsequently threatened to begin legal proceedings against European airlines operating a price-fixing 'cartel'. In 1987 ministers of transport reached an agreement on the liberalization of air transport, which included the deregulation of air fares and of route-sharing.

During 1985 the Commission also made proposals for maritime transport (including co-ordinated action against restrictive practices by other countries, preventing EEC vessels from having free access to cargoes; and freedom for any company to provide sea transport services throughout the Community).

In 1988 the Commission proposed a five-year transport infrastructure programme (already approved in principle by the Council) whereby support would be given from Community funds for projects deemed to be of European importance, such as improvement of road and rail links with Portugal and Spain and with Scandinavia, and the Channel tunnel between France and the United Kingdom.

EDUCATION AND CULTURE

The postgraduate European University Institute was founded in Florence in 1972, with departments of history and civilization, economics, law, and political and social sciences; it had about 180 students in 1987. In June 1980 the Council approved the following recommendations by the Commission: intensification of modern language teaching; promotion of the study of the European Community in schools; development of a common policy on the admission of higher-education students from other member states; equality of education and vocational training for girls.

In September 1980 an educational information network known as EURYDICE began operations, with a central unit in Brussels and national units providing data on the widely varying systems of education within member states. In 1987 the Council adopted a European Action Scheme for the Mobility of University Students (ERASMUS), which aimed to make grants enabling 25,000 university students to spend a study period in another Community country during 1987–89, at a cost of 85m. ECUs.

In 1985 the Council approved a programme of education and training for technology (COMETT), comprising a network of university/industry training partnerships and exchange schemes, to be undertaken in 1987–89, with a budget of 45m. ECUs.

Although it has no common cultural policy as such, the Community has given practical help for cultural activities. Grants are given to young musicians and cultural workers, and to conservation and restoration centres. A programme of sponsoring translations of works from member states began in 1982 with 20 titles. In 1985 the Community sponsored a 'European Music Year' jointly with the Council of Europe. Under the Community's programme for conserving the European architectural heritage, 30 projects were approved in 1988.

SOCIAL POLICY

The Single European Act, which entered into force in 1987, added to the original EEC Treaty articles which emphasized the need for 'economic and social cohesion' in the Community and the reduction of disparities between the various regions, principally through the existing 'structural funds'—the European Regional Development Fund, the European Social fund, and the Guidance Section of the European Agricultural Guidance and Guarantee Fund (for details of these funds see p. 143). In February 1988 the Council declared that Community operations through the structural funds, the European Investment Bank and other financial instruments should have five priority objectives:

(i) Promoting the development and structural adjustment of the less-developed regions;
(ii) Converting the regions, frontier regions or parts of regions seriously affected by industrial decline;
(iii) Combating long-term unemployment (which affected some 12% of the Community's labour force in 1987, with considerable regional variations);
(iv) Providing employment for young people;
(v) With a view to the reform of the common agricultural policy: speeding up the adjustment of agricultural structures and promoting the development of rural areas.

The Council agreed that appropriations for commitments for the structural funds should increase from 7,700m. ECUs in 1988 to 12,900m. ECUs in 1992 (at 1988 prices).

A number of Community directives have been adopted on equal rights for women in pay, access to employment and social security, and the Commission has undertaken legal proceedings against several member states before the European Court of Justice for infringements. In 1982 the Council adopted the Community Action Programme on the Promotion of Equal Opportunities for Women (1982–85), involving concrete action by national governments (including positive discrimination where necessary) in combating unemployment among women; bringing about equal treatment for men and women in occupational social schemes (e.g. sick pay and pensions) and in self-employed occupations, including agriculture; and legislation on parental leave. A second programme (1986–90) was aproved in 1986 to encourage more effective action by member states. In 1987 the Commission adopted a programme to improve the working and living conditions of workers and reduce accidents and occupational diseases.

CONSUMER PROTECTION

The Community's second five-year Consumer Protection Programme was approved by the Council in 1981, based on the same principles as those of the first programme (protection of health and safety, with procedures for withdrawal of goods from the market; standardization of rules for food additives and packaging; rules for machines and equipment; authorization procedures for new products). The second programme also included measures for monitoring the quality and durability of products, improving after-sale service, legal remedies for unsatisfactory goods and services, and the encouragement of consumer associations. The Consumers' Consultative Committee, established in 1973, represents European consumers' organizations, and gives opinions on consumer matters. In 1983 the Council approved a proposal for a Community system for the rapid exchange of information whenever a particular consumer product is found to present an immediate risk to consumers. In 1986 it adopted directives on permitted levels of pesticide residues in food, and on rules for consumer credit, and in 1987 it adopted a directive on the approximation of the laws of member states concerning products which, appearing to be other than they are, endanger the health or safety of consumers.

ENVIRONMENT POLICY

The second environment Action Programme (1977–81) laid down the following principles for action: reduction of pollution and nuisance, protection of natural resources, organization of relevant research and participation in international efforts to improve the environment. A third Action Programme (1982–86) laid greater emphasis on prevention, and included the introduction of environmental impact assessment in all forms of planning, improved monitoring techniques and co-operation with developing countries. A fourth Action Programme (1987–92) was adopted in 1986, aiming to make environmental protection an integral part of economic and social policies.

By 1987 over 60 directives had been adopted, obliging member states to make regulations on air and water pollution (e.g. 'acid rain' and lead emissions from vehicles), the transport of toxic waste, waste treatment, noise abatement and the protection of natural resources. In 1985 the Community (and a number of individual member states) signed an international agreement, the Vienna Convention for the Protection of the Ozone Layer, and in 1987 the Community signed a protocol to the treaty, controlling the production of chlorofluorocarbons.

In 1981 the Council adopted a five-year programme (1981–85) for environmental research done on a shared-cost basis by various scientific institutions; the programme included measurements of pollutants, development of 'clean technologies', and climatology. The programme for 1986–90 comprised research on environmental protection, climatology and natural hazards, and technological hazards.

FINANCIAL SERVICES

A directive on Community banking, adopted in 1977, laid down common prudential criteria for the establishment and operation of banks in member states. A second banking directive, proposed by the Commission in 1988, aimed to create a single community licence for banking, whereby the authorization initially given to a bank by its country of origin is automatically valid for the whole Community: in other words, a bank established in one member country can open branches in any other.

Proposals on the liberalization of non-life insurance, giving insurance companies from one member state free access to customers in other member states without having to establish a base there, were also approved by the Council in 1987.

ECONOMIC AND MONETARY UNION

A report on the economic situation is presented annually by the Commission, analysing recent developments and short- and medium-term prospects. Economic policy guidelines for the following year are adopted annually by the Council.

The following objectives for the end of 1973 were agreed by the Council in 1971, as the first of three stages towards European economic and monetary union:

the narrowing of exchange rate margins to 2.25%;

creation of a medium-term pool of reserves;

co-ordination of short- and medium-term economic and budgetary policies;

a joint position on international monetary issues;

harmonization of taxes;

creation of the European Monetary Co-operation Fund;
creation of the European Regional Development Fund.

The narrowing of exchange margins (the 'snake') came into effect in 1972; but Denmark, France, Ireland, Italy and the United Kingdom later floated their currencies, with only Denmark permanently returning to the arrangement. Sweden and Norway also linked their currencies to the 'snake'; but Sweden withdrew from the arrangement in August 1977, and Norway withdrew in December 1978.

The European Monetary System (EMS) came into force in March 1979, with the aim of creating closer monetary co-operation leading to a zone of monetary stability in Europe. All the Community members except the United Kingdom joined the EMS; Greece did not join on acceding to the Community in 1981, but did so in July 1985, though without participating in the exchange rate mechanism described below. Portugal and Spain joined the EMS in 1987, again without participating in the exchange rate mechanism. The system works by fixing for each currency a central rate in European Currency Units (ECUs, see below), which are based on a 'basket' of national currencies identical to those used to calculate the European unit of account (EUA). A reference rate in relation to other currencies is fixed for each currency, with established fluctuation margins (6% for the Italian lira, 2.25% for others); Central Banks of the participating states intervene when the agreed margin is likely to be exceeded. Each member places 20% of its gold reserves and dollar reserves respectively into the European Monetary Co-operation Fund, and receives a supply of ECUs to regulate Central Bank interventions. Short- and medium-term credit facilities are given to support the balance of payments of member countries. The EMS is put under strain by the wide fluctuations in the exchange rates of non-Community currencies and by the differences in economic development among members, which led to 11 realignments of currencies between the system's inception and mid-1987. The absence of the pound sterling from the exchange rate mechanism is regarded by the Commission as hindering the EMS from achieving its full potential. In June 1985 measures were adopted by the governors of the Community's central banks, aiming to strengthen the EMS by expanding the use of the ECU, e.g. by allowing international monetary institutions and the central banks of non-member countries to become 'other holders' of ECUs.

Freedom of capital movements and the creation of a uniform financial area were regarded as vital for the completion of the internal market by 1992. In 1987, as part of the liberalization of the flow of capital, a Council directive came into force, whereby member states were obliged to remove restrictions on three categories of transactions: long-term credits related to commercial transactions; acquisition of securities; and the admission of securities to capital markets. Portugal and Spain were allowed extra time to comply (until the end of 1992 and 1990 respectively), while temporary protective measures were applied for Greece, Ireland and Italy. In November the Commission proposed further measures that would lead to full liberalization of capital movements: removal of restrictions on short-term capital movements (covering investments in short-term securities, current and deposit accounts, and financial loans and credits); liberalization of capital movements to and from countries outside the Community; and establishment of a body providing medium-term financial support to Community countries having balance-of-payments difficulties. In June 1988 the Council agreed to remove all barriers to capital movement by 1990 (1992 for Ireland and Spain, and 1995 for Greece and Portugal): members of the Community were, however, to be allowed to impose emergency controls in the event of a balance-of-payments crisis. The Commission was asked to study ways of preventing tax frauds that might occur as a result of such liberalization.

In September 1988 a committee (comprising the governors of member countries' central banks, two representatives of the European Commission and three outside experts) was established to discuss European monetary union.

The European Currency Unit

With the creation of the European Monetary System (EMS) a new monetary unit, the European Currency Unit (ECU) was adopted. Its value and composition were identical to those of the European Unit of Account (EUA) already used in the administrative fields of the Community. The ECU is a composite monetary unit, in which the relative value of each currency is determined by the gross national product and the volume of trade of each country. In September 1984 the Greek drachma was incorporated for the first time, and the amounts of other currencies were altered. The composition of the ECU thus became (with previous amounts in brackets):

3.71 Belgian francs (3.66)
0.219 Danish krone (0.217)
1.31 French francs (1.15)
0.719 Deutsche Mark (0.828)
1.15 Greek drachmae
0.00871 Irish pound (0.00759)
140 Italian lire (109)
0.14 Luxembourg franc (0.14)
0.256 Netherlands guilder (0.286)
0.0878 pound sterling (0.0885).

The rate of the ECU in terms of any currency is equal to the sum of the equivalents in that currency of the amounts of each of the above currencies.

The ECU, which has been assigned the function of the unit of account used by the European Monetary Co-operation Fund, is also used:

as the denominator for the exchange rate mechanism;

as the basis for the divergence indicator;

as the denominator for operations in both the intervention and the credit mechanisms;

as a means of settlement between monetary authorities of the European Community.

From April 1979 onwards the ECU has also been used as the unit of account for the purposes of the common agricultural policy. Since 1981 it has replaced the EUA in the general budget of the Community; the activities of the European Development Fund under the Lomé Convention; the balance sheets and loan operations of the European Investment Bank; and the activities of the European Coal and Steel Community. It is now the only unit of account used in the Community.

The ECU's value in national currencies is calculated and published daily. Its value on 31 October 1988 was US $1.17102.

External Relations

Although there is no single Community institution dealing with foreign affairs, the Community acts as a single entity in many aspects of international affairs. It has diplomatic relations in its own right with over 100 countries (see p. 134), and with international organizations, and participates as a body in international conferences on trade and development and the 'North-South dialogue'. It has observer status at the United Nations.

Under the Single European Act, which came into force on 1 July 1987 (amending the Treaty of Rome), it was laid down formally for the first time that member states should inform and consult each other on foreign policy matters (as was already, in practice, often the case) and a secretariat was to be established to assist the Presidency in preparing and implementing the activities of European political co-operation and in administrative matters.

Agreements have been signed with numerous countries and groups of countries, allowing for co-operation in trade and other matters. The Community is also a party to 37 International Conventions (in 17 of these to the exclusion of the individual member states).

EUROPE

Association agreements, intended to lead to customs union or possible accession, were signed between the Community and Greece (1961), Turkey (1963), Malta (1970) and Cyprus (1972). The agreements established free access to the Community market for most industrial products and tariff reductions for most agricultural products. Annexed are financial protocols under which the Community provides concessional finance to these countries. Aid to Turkey (which had originally been allocated 600m. ECUs for the period 1981–86) was suspended owing to the violation of human rights there following the coup in 1980. With a view to the progressive normalization of relations with Turkey, a meeting with Turkish government ministers (the first for six years) was held in October 1986. In April 1987 Turkey applied for membership of the Community, but it was not expected to be admitted for many years. In 1987 an agreement was concluded with Cyprus, setting out the details for the progressive establishment of a customs union over a 15-year period.

Trade negotiations with the CMEA (mainly Eastern European) countries were proposed by the Community in 1974, but progress over the ensuing decade was largely confined to sectoral agreements on textiles, steel and certain agricultural products with Bulgaria, Czechoslovakia, Hungary, Poland and Romania. A proposal for talks leading to closer co-operation with the Community was made by the CMEA in June 1985; in 1986 discussions were opened with several of the European CMEA countries and with the CMEA itself on the normalization of relations and the possibility of more far-reaching agreements. In 1988 agreement was reached on the establishment of diplomatic relations between the Community and most of the East European countries, including the USSR, and on official relations between the Community and the CMEA. A trade and co-operation agreement was concluded with Hungary, and negotiations were held on agreements with the USSR and other European CMEA members.

A co-operation agreement was also signed with Yugoslavia in 1980 (but not ratified until April 1983), allowing tariff-free imports (with 'ceilings' for a number of sensitive items) and Community loans of 200m. ECUs over five years. In 1987 a new financial protocol, providing loans of 550m. ECUs over six years, was concluded. At the same time the trade agreement was renewed, with improvements in the conditions of access to the Community market for certain Yugoslav industrial and agricultural products.

The members of EFTA (Austria, Finland, Iceland, Norway, Sweden and Switzerland) each have bilateral Free Trade Agreements with the EEC and the ECSC. The agreements mainly concern the industrial sector. Free trade was introduced by the immediate abolition of quantitative restrictions and the elimination of tariffs in stages. For certain 'sensitive' industrial products, which could have had a disruptive effect on the Community market, the transition period was longer. Customs duties for the majority of products were abolished in July 1977. On 1 January 1984 the last tariff barriers were eliminated, thus establishing full free trade for industrial products. It was expected that Austria would make a formal application to join the Community in 1989.

THE MIDDLE EAST

Co-operation agreements came into force with Israel in 1975, with the Maghreb countries (Algeria, Morocco and Tunisia) in 1976 and with the Mashreq countries (Egypt, Jordan, Lebanon and Syria) in 1977, covering free access to the Community market for industrial products, customs preferences for certain agricultural products, and financial aid in the form of grants and loans from the European Investment Bank. In order to ensure that the enlargement of the Community would not have an adverse effect on the traditional agricultural exports of these countries to the Community (mainly citrus fruit, wines and olive oil), protocols to the agreements were concluded with most of these countries in 1987, containing provisions designed to ensure that traditional trade patterns are maintained. A non-preferential co-operation agreement was negotiated with the Yemen Arab Republic in 1984. In July 1987 Morocco applied to join the Community, but its application was rejected on the grounds that it is not a European country.

Three protocols were concluded in 1987 on assistance to Israel for the period 1987–91, and on modification of the co-operation agreement with Israel to take into account the accession of Portugal and Spain to the Community; however, approval of these protocols was delayed by the European Parliament until October 1988, as a protest against Israel's response to unrest in the occupied territories of the West Bank and the Gaza Strip.

In 1984 discussions began with the Gulf Co-operation Council (GCC) on the possibility of concluding a comprehensive co-operation agreement covering trade, energy and industrial matters. During 1984–87 talks took place in particular on access to European markets for GCC refined petroleum products, after tariffs were imposed by the EEC in 1984 on certain petrochemicals from the region. In June 1988 an agreement was signed with the countries of the GCC, providing for co-operation in industry, energy, technology and other fields. Both sides agreed to start discussions with a view to concluding a second agreement, designed to expand and liberalize trade between the parties. Contacts with the Arab world in general take place within the framework of the 'Euro-Arab Dialogue', established in 1973 to provide a forum for discussion of economic issues through working groups on specific topics.

LATIN AMERICA

A non-preferential trade agreement was signed with Uruguay in 1974 and economic and commercial co-operation agreements with Mexico in 1975 and Brazil in 1980. A five-year co-operation agreement with the members of the Central American Common Market and with Panama entered into force in 1987, as did a similar agreement with the member countries of the Andean Group.

ASIA AND AUSTRALASIA

Non-preferential co-operation agreements were signed with the EEC by India (1973 and 1981), Bangladesh (1976), Sri Lanka (1975) and Pakistan (1976 and 1986). A trade agreement was signed with the People's Republic of China in 1978, and renewed and expanded in May 1985. A co-operation agreement was signed with the countries of the Association of South East Asian Nations (ASEAN) in 1980.

Textiles exports by Asian countries have caused concern in the EEC owing to the depressed state of its own textiles industry. During 1982 bilateral negotiations were held under the Multi-Fibre Arrangement (see GATT, p. 56) with Asian producers, notably Hong Kong, the Republic of Korea and Macau, which, together with Taiwan (not a party to the Multi-Fibre Arrangement) account for some 40% of EEC textile imports. Agreements were eventually reached involving cuts in clothing quotas of between 8% and 10% for the four dominant countries, 'anti-surge' clauses to prevent flooding of European markets, and measures to be imposed in the event of fraud. In 1986 new bilateral negotiations were held and agreements were reached with the principal Asian textile exporters, for the period 1987–91: in most cases a slight increase in quotas was permitted by the EEC.

Numerous discussions have been held since 1981 on the Community's increasing trade deficit with Japan. The Community has requested in particular a greater opening of the Japanese market to European goods and moderation in Japanese exports of certain sensitive products. Between 1981 and 1985 the Japanese Government announced seven series of external economic measures in order to improve access to the Japanese market. Moderation of exports of certain products to the Community was exercised between 1983 and 1985, but in June 1985 and December 1986 European heads of government repeated their concern at the continuing trade deficit with Japan, amounting to some US $20,000m. in 1986, and at the failure of the Japanese market to accept more European exports. In May 1987 the Community adopted 'anti-dumping' measures, including tariffs of up to 100%, to prevent the diversion to Europe of Japanese products originally intended for the USA, where import restrictions had been imposed on Japanese goods. In June rules were adopted by the Community (principally affecting Japan), imposing duties on the imported components of products assembled within the EEC by non-EEC firms.

Regular consultations are held with Australia at ministerial level. Australia has repeatedly criticized the Community's agricultural export subsidies and their effect on Australia's own agriculture. In 1986 Australia received assurances that the Community would not extend its export subsidies to markets in the Far East, and talks were to be held on improving access to the European market for Australian beef. An agreement was reached in 1988 on maintaining the Community's imports of butter from New Zealand, despite the surplus of dairy produce within the Community.

CANADA AND THE USA

A framework agreement for commercial and economic co-operation between the Community and Canada was signed in Ottawa in July 1976, the Community's first non-preferential co-operation agreement concerned not only with trade promotion but also with wide-ranging economic co-operation.

A number of specific agreements have been concluded between the Community and the USA: a co-operation agreement on the peaceful use of atomic energy entered into force in 1959, and agreements on environmental matters and on fisheries came into force in 1974 and 1984 respectively.

The USA has frequently criticized Community policy, in particular the Common Agricultural Policy, which it sees as creating unfair competition for American exports by its system of export refunds and preferential agreements: in 1985, for example, the USA raised its import duties on European pasta products, as a retaliatory measure, alleging that Community agreements with Mediterranean producers of citrus fruit discriminated against US citrus exports. An agreement on Mediterranean preferences and on citrus fruit was reached in August 1986, and an interim settlement on pasta in August 1987. A similar criticism has been levelled at Community subsidies to the steel industry. In October 1982 the Community and the USA concluded an Arrangement relating to the export of steel products to the USA, but disputes continued over certain categories of steel products of which Community exports to the USA trebled between 1981 and 1984. In October 1985 an agreement was reached on Community exports of steel to the USA for the period to September 1989, covering carbon steels, speciality steel and pipes and tubes. In September 1986 the agreement was extended to cover Community exports of semi-finished steel products.

GENERALIZED PREFERENCES

In July 1971 the Community introduced a scheme of generalized preferences (GSP) in favour of developing countries: in 1986 the list of beneficiaries covered 128 independent states and 22 dependent territories. In line with objectives agreed by UNCTAD (see p. 37), the scheme provides for duty-free entry of all otherwise dutiable manufactured and semi-manufactured industrial products, including textiles—but subject in certain circumstances to preferential limits. Preferences, usually in the form of a tariff reduction, are also offered on some 360 agricultural products. In 1980 the Council agreed to the extension of the scheme for a second decade (1981–90): at the same time it adopted an operational framework for industrial products, which gives individual preferential limits based on the degree of competitiveness of the developing country concerned. Since 1977 the Community has progressively liberalized GSP access for the least-developed countries (numbering 38 under the United Nations definition) by according them duty-free entry on all products and by exempting them from virtually all preferential limits.

INTERNATIONAL ORGANIZATIONS

European Communities

OVERSEAS AID

The main channel for Community aid to developing countries is the Lomé Convention (see below), but technical and financial aid, and assistance for refugees, training, trade promotion and co-operation in industry, energy, science and technology (about 400m. ECUs in 1987) is also given to about 30 non-associated countries, mainly in Asia and Latin America. During 1987 food aid worth about 600m. ECUs was provided for developing countries. Assistance of about 60m. ECUs was also granted through non-governmental organizations, in the form of co-financing for projects.

THE LOMÉ CONVENTION

The First Lomé Convention (Lomé I), which came into force on 1 April 1976, replaced the Yaoundé Conventions and the Arusha Agreement (under which some of the former overseas possessions of France and the United Kingdom retained privileged access to the European market, together with financial assistance). Lomé I was designed to provide a new framework of co-operation, taking into account the varying needs of developing countries. The Second Lomé Convention came into force on 1 January 1981. The Third Lomé Convention was signed in December 1984, and came into force on 1 March 1985. In October 1988 66 African, Caribbean and Pacific (ACP) states were parties to the Convention.

ACP-EEC INSTITUTIONS

Council of Ministers: one Minister from each signatory state; one Co-chairman from each of the two groups; meets annually.

Committee of Ambassadors: one Ambassador from each signatory state; Chairmanship alternates between the two groups; meets at least every six months.

Joint Assembly: EEC and ACP are equally represented; attended by delegates of the ACP countries and members of the European Parliament; one Co-chairman from each of the two groups; meets twice a year.

Centre for the Development of Industry: 28 rue de l'Industrie, 1040 Brussels, Belgium; tel. 513-41-00; telex 61427; f. 1977 to encourage investment in the ACP states by providing contracts and advice, holding promotion meetings, and helping to finance feasibility studies; Dir Dr ISAAC ADEDAYO AKINRELE.

Technical Centre for Agricultural and Rural Co-operation: Postbus 380, 6700 AJ Wageningen, Netherlands; tel. (08380) 20484; telex 20577; Dir ASSOUMOU MBA.

ACP INSTITUTIONS

ACP Council of Ministers.

ACP Committee of Ambassadors.

ACP Secretariat: ACP House, ave Georges Henri, Brussels, Belgium; Sec.-Gen. EDWIN W. CARRINGTON.

THE ACP STATES

Angola	Madagascar
Antigua and Barbuda	Malawi
Bahamas	Mali
Barbados	Mauritania
Belize	Mauritius
Benin	Mozambique
Botswana	Niger
Burkina Faso	Nigeria
Burundi	Papua New Guinea
Cameroon	Rwanda
Cape Verde	Saint Christopher and Nevis
Central African Republic	Saint Lucia
Chad	Saint Vincent and the Grenadines
Comoros	São Tomé and Príncipe
Congo	Senegal
Côte d'Ivoire	Seychelles
Djibouti	Sierra Leone
Dominica	Solomon Islands
Equatorial Guinea	Somalia
Ethiopia	Sudan
Fiji	Suriname
Gabon	Swaziland
The Gambia	Tanzania
Ghana	Togo
Grenada	Tonga
Guinea	Trinidad and Tobago
Guinea-Bissau	Tuvalu
Guyana	Uganda
Jamaica	Vanuatu
Kenya	Western Samoa
Kiribati	Zaire
Lesotho	Zambia
Liberia	Zimbabwe

FUNCTIONS

Under the First Lomé Convention the Community committed 3,052.4m. ECUs for aid and investment in developing countries. Provision was made for over 99% of ACP (mainly agricultural) exports to enter the EEC market duty free, while certain products which compete directly with Community agriculture, such as sugar, were given preferential treatment but not free access. The Stabex (Stabilization of Export Earnings) scheme was designed to help developing countries to withstand fluctuations in the price of their agricultural products, by paying compensation for lost export earnings. The Convention also provided for Community funds to help finance projects in ACP countries through grants and loans from the European Development Fund and also from the European Investment Bank (q.v.).

The Second Lomé Convention, which came into force on 1 January 1981, to run until 28 February 1985, envisaged Community expenditure of 5,530m. ECUs: it extended some of the provisions of Lomé I, and introduced new fields of co-operation. One of the most important innovations was a scheme (Sysmin), similar to Stabex, to safeguard exports of mineral products. Other chapters concerned new rules on investment protection, migrant labour, fishing, sea transport, co-operation in energy policy and agricultural development, and procedures to speed the administration of aid. Negotiations for a Third Lomé Convention began in October 1983. The ACP states expressed dissatisfaction with the current arrangements, particularly the inadequacy of Stabex funds (which had been unable to cover more than 50% of the amounts requested during 1979-83) and the presence of non-tariff barriers which restricted their access to European markets.

The Third Lomé Convention, which came into force on 1 March 1985 (trade provisions) and 1 May 1986 (aid), and was due to expire on 28 February 1990, made commitments of 8,500m. ECUs, including loans of 1,100m. ECUs from the European Investment Bank. Innovations included an emphasis on agriculture and fisheries, and measures to combat desertification; assistance for rehabilitating existing industries or sectoral improvements, rather than new individual capital projects; improvements in the efficiency of the Stabex system (now covering a list of 48 agricultural products) and of Sysmin; simplification of the rules of origin of products exported to the EEC; an undertaking to promote private investment; co-operation in transport and communications, particularly shipping; cultural and social co-operation; restructuring of emergency aid, and more efficient procedures for technical and financial assistance.

Negotiations for a fourth convention began in October 1988.

COMMITMENTS MADE UNDER THE LOMÉ CONVENTION
(million ECUs)*

	1987	1976–87
Development of production	1,249.00	4,377.48
Industrialization	320.05	1,640.10
Tourism	−0.75	31.53
Rural production	886.43	2,660.05
Specific campaign	43.80	45.80
Economic infrastructure, transport and communications	510.71	1,977.67
Social development	124.21	1,164.00
Education and training	47.55	566.17
Health	43.17	194.53
Hydraulics, environment	33.49	403.30
Trade promotion	27.43	116.74
Rehabilitation	−0.05	99.95
Emergency aid	22.16	365.84
Stabex	269.04	1,364.63
AIDS	35.00	35.00
Refugees	0.86	0.86
Other	10.25	221.88
Total	**2,249.14**	**9,274.05**

* Estimated.

Source: Directorate-General for Development.

Finance

THE COMMUNITY BUDGET

Until 1970 the Community's revenue was derived from financial contributions by member states, based on their gross national product (GNP). In 1970 the Commission was empowered to begin raising money from 'own resources': member states were to collect on the Community's behalf levies on the imports of agricultural produce, and customs duties on products covered by the common customs tariff. A proportion (not to exceed 1%) of revenue gained from value-added tax (VAT) on goods and services was to be transferred to the Community. The creation of new own resources required approval by the national legislatures.

The replacement of financial contributions by revenue from own resources did not take place on 1 January 1975, as planned, and only in 1980 did all members transfer VAT own resources to the Community budget. Between 1981 and 1986 Greece was allowed to defer application of the common VAT system and to pay a financial contribution based on GNP. Portugal was to be allowed to do the same for three years from 1 January 1986, while Spain was to pay VAT own resources from that date.

Under this system it proved possible for an unfair proportion of the budget to be paid by certain countries, particularly in view of the large amount allocated to agriculture, to the disadvantage of those countries with a relatively small agricultural sector, such as the United Kingdom. In 1980 the Council adopted a three-year plan to reduce the British contribution to the budget by making refunds in the form of special investments to benefit disadvantaged areas, and in 1984 the Council reached the 'Fontainebleau Agreement' on the amount of compensation to be granted to the United Kingdom, to reduce its contribution to the Community budget: a lump-sum of 1,000m. ECUs was to be paid in 1985, while in subsequent years the United Kingdom was to receive 66% of the difference between what it paid in VAT and what it received from the Community budget. Agreement was also reached on the creation of new resources by raising the VAT 'ceiling' from 1% to 1.4%, and on future budgetary and financial discipline (including curbs on agricultural spending). The budgets for 1983 and 1984 envisaged the exhaustion of almost all the available own resources, and supplementary budgets (mostly for agricultural spending) were required.

The draft budget for 1985 was rejected in December 1984 by the European Parliament, on the grounds that it was not sufficient for a 12-month period. As a result, expenditure during the first half of 1985 had to be calculated in 'provisional twelfths'—monthly payments each equivalent to one-twelfth of the previous year's expenditure. A budget for 1985 was finally approved by Parliament in June.

It was hoped that the raising of the VAT 'ceiling' to 1.4%, with effect from 1 January 1986, would increase revenue sufficiently to avoid a recurrence of the budget crises of previous years. In the event, however, the 1986 budget was the subject of a complex dispute. In December 1985 the European Parliament rejected the budget approved by the Council of Ministers, on the grounds that it failed to meet legal commitments to the Community's regional and social funds and to the new members, Portugal and Spain:

Parliament approved a new budget, which was then adopted by the Commission. In July, however, the European Court of Justice declared this budget illegal, ruling that Parliament had exceeded its powers by approving a budget without the approval of the Council of Ministers. Another budget for 1986 was then drawn up urgently, and approved by both the Council and Parliament: it comprised commitments of 36,267m. ECUs and payments of 35,125m. ECUs (see footnote to table of Budget Expenditure)—considerably more than the amounts previously disputed. This increase had become necessary for three principal reasons: the ever-increasing cost of the Common Agricultural Policy, particularly the growth in export subsidies as a result of the falling value of the US dollar against the ECU; the backlog of commitments to the social and regional funds; and the budget rebate owed to the United Kingdom, which was higher than originally calculated.

The same problems affected negotiations for the 1987 budget, which began in July 1986: technological research and overseas aid were the principal targets for spending cuts, and, as in 1986, agricultural market support absorbed over 60% of proposed expenditure. The budget was not accepted by Parliament (which demanded higher non-agricultural spending) until February 1987: appropriations for payments amounted to 36,313m. ECUs, and appropriations for commitments totalled 37,415m. ECUs. Controversy continued during the year over methods of financing overspending, projected at 5,000m. ECUs: the principal expedients adopted involved paying farming subsidies in arrears, rather than in advance, and withholding the percentage of customs duties to be paid back to member states for administrative costs. In October 1987 a fresh budgetary crisis arose when ministers of finance failed to agree on a figure for expenditure in the draft budget for 1988: the United Kingdom objected on the grounds that proposed expenditure would again greatly exceed income, while Greece and Spain demanded that more assistance should be given to the southern member states. In February 1988 the Community's heads of government agreed to implement budgetary reforms. Total expenditure for each year was to be limited (by 1992) to 1.2% of member countries' total annual GNP (or more precisely 1.2% for payments and 1.3% for commitments). A 'fourth resource' was to be added to the existing sources of income (agricultural import levies, customs duties and VAT), namely contributions based on each country's GNP. The assessment base for VAT was not to exceed 55% of GNP. It was hoped that, by linking member states' payments more closely to their GNP, contributions to the budget would be more fairly distributed among the richer and poorer countries. Overall income was also expected to rise, because VAT does not apply to government expenditure, investment and certain

BUDGET EXPENDITURE (ECUs)

	Appropriations for payments*		Appropriations for commitments*	
	1988	1989 (preliminary draft)	1988	1989 (preliminary draft)
Administration				
Expenditure concerning personnel	899,318,353	1,006,379,000	899,318,353	1,006,379,000
Buildings, equipment and miscellaneous expenditure	246,500,900	286,097,500	246,500,900	286,097,500
Expenditure resulting from special functions	125,563,642	133,136,548	125,563,642	133,136,548
Total	1,271,382,895	1,425,613,048	1,271,382,895	1,425,613,048
Operations				
Agricultural market guarantee	27,500,000,000	28,190,000,000	27,500,000,000	28,190,000,000
Guidance (agricultural structures)	1,222,006,000	1,567,000,000	1,201,566,000	1,599,000,000
Fisheries	281,046,000	395,600,000	337,066,000	361,100,000
Regional development and transport	3,201,410,000	4,325,450,000	4,006,310,000	4,946,550,000
Operations in the social sector	2,845,276,600	3,273,755,000	3,119,486,600	3,688,255,000
Energy, technology, research, nuclear safeguards, information market and innovation	1,153,598,800	1,479,217,600	1,360,363,800	1,773,677,600
Repayments and aid to member states	3,774,370,074	2,993,050,496	3,774,370,074	2,993,050,496
Co-operation with developing countries	870,497,900	1,084,907,000	1,072,797,900	1,303,207,000
Other expenditure	1,005,000,000	1,005,000,000	1,005,000,000	1,005,000,000
Operations—Total	41,853,205,374	44,313,980,096	43,376,960,374	45,859,840,096
Commission—Total	43,124,588,269	45,739,593,144	44,648,343,269	47,285,453,144
Other institutions	695,808,255	736,165,134	695,808,255	736,165,134
Grand total	43,820,396,524	46,475,758,278	45,344,151,524	48,021,618,278

* Appropriations for payments cover the expenditure needed to honour commitments entered into during the current budget year or previous years and falling due in the current budget year. Appropriations for commitments cover the total cost, during the current budget year, of the legal obligations entered into for operations to be carried out over a number of years. In any given budget year the totals for these two types of appropriation normally differ, since commitments appropriations are required ahead of the matching payment appropriations.

INTERNATIONAL ORGANIZATIONS

European Communities

MEMBER STATES' CONTRIBUTIONS

Country	Contribution for 1988 (forecast) (million ECUs)	% of total
Belgium	1,880.1	4.4
Denmark	965.0	2.2
France	9,332.6	21.7
Federal Republic of Germany	11,677.3	27.2
Greece	422.5	1.0
Ireland	328.2	0.8
Italy	6,771.8	15.7
Luxembourg	83.6	0.2
Netherlands	2,775.1	6.5
Portugal	432.5	1.0
Spain	3,158.0	7.3
United Kingdom	5,182.4	12.0

services, and contributions based on VAT are therefore less than those based on total GNP. Production 'ceilings' were set for cereals and other crops (see under Agriculture) and the annual increase in spending on agricultural guarantees was not to exceed 74% of the annual growth rate of the Community GNP. A monetary reserve was to be established to compensate for distortions in spending on agricultural guarantees caused by fluctuations in exchange rates. Commitment appropriations for structural funds (for assistance to the less-developed areas of the Community) were to be doubled by 1993. The United Kingdom was to continue to receive a budget rebate.

REVENUE (million ECUs)

Source of revenue	1988 (provisional)	1989 (forecast)
Agricultural levies	1,435	1,337
Sugar levies	1,386	1,359
Customs duties	8,595	9,315
VAT	23,207	26,184
Additional resource*	8,049	7,882
Surpluses available	850	—
Miscellaneous revenue	257	275
Total	**43,779**	**46,352**

* Based on GNP.

PUBLICATIONS*

General Report on the Activities of the European Communities (annually).
Bulletin of the European Communities (11 a year).
The Courier (every 2 months, on ACP-EEC affairs).
European Economy (quarterly, with supplements).
Publications of the European Communities (quarterly).
Information sheets, background reports and statistical documents.

* Most publications are available in all the official languages of the Community. They are obtainable from the Office for Official Publications of the European Communities, 5 rue du Commerce, 2985 Luxembourg; tel. 49 00 81; telex 1324.

EUROPEAN FREE TRADE ASSOCIATION—EFTA

Address: 9-11 rue de Varembé, 1211 Geneva 20, Switzerland.
Telephone: (022) 349000.
Telex: 22660.

Established in 1960, EFTA aims to bring about free trade in industrial goods and an expansion of trade in agricultural goods between its member countries, and to contribute to the liberalization and expansion of world trade.

MEMBERS

Austria   Iceland   Sweden
Finland   Norway   Switzerland

Three founder members subsequently left EFTA and joined the European Community: Denmark (1973), the United Kingdom (1973) and Portugal (1986). Finland, formerly an associate member of EFTA, became a full member on 1 January 1986.

Organization
(October 1988)

COUNCIL

Council delegations are led by Ministers (normally twice a year) or by the Heads of National Delegations (usually every other week). The Chair is held for six months by each country in turn.

Heads of Permanent Delegations:
Austria: F. Ceska
Finland: O. Mennander
Iceland: S. Gunnlaugsson
Norway: M. Huslid
Sweden: L. Anell
Switzerland: W. Rossier

EFTA STANDING COMMITTEES

Committee of Trade Experts.
Committee of Origin and Customs Experts.
Committee on Technical Barriers to Trade.
Group of Legal Experts.
Economic Committee.
Consultative Committee.
Committee of Members of Parliament of the EFTA Countries.
Budget Committee.
Economic Development Committee.
Committee on Agriculture and Fisheries.

SECRETARIAT

Secretary-General: Georg Reich (Austria).
Deputy Secretary-General: Berndt Olof Johansson (Finland).

Activities

EFTA unites in one free trade area the markets of its member countries, as a means of working towards a sustained growth in economic activity and a continuous improvement in living standards in EFTA countries, and of contributing to the growth of world trade.

The creation of a single market including all the countries in Western Europe was the ultimate objective of EFTA when it was created in 1960. Its first target, the creation of free trade in industrial goods between its members, was achieved by the end of 1966.

Each of the members is also linked with the European Community, through agreements which established free trade in most industrial goods between them from 1 July 1977. The last restrictions on free industrial trade were abolished from 1 January 1984. In April of that year ministers from all EFTA and EEC member countries agreed on general guidelines for developing the EFTA-EEC relationship. Their Declaration (known as the Luxembourg Declaration) recommended intensified efforts to promote the free movement of goods between their countries, and closer co-operation in a number of other fields, including research and development. In 1987 the European Community accounted for 61% of EFTA's imports and for 55% of EFTA's exports.

In 1976, while Portugal was a member, EFTA set up the Industrial Development Fund for Portugal to assist the development of the Portuguese economy and in particular the modernization or creation of small and medium-sized industries. Although Portugal left EFTA at the end of 1985 to join the European Community, EFTA decided to maintain the Fund in operation to the end of the 25-year period originally foreseen. The Joint EFTA-Yugoslavia Committee, established in 1978, aims to expand trade and industrial co-operation with Yugoslavia.

EFTA's main tasks are to ensure the efficient working of free trade between its members; to use the framework of EFTA for consultations or co-ordination between members on matters connected with their free trade agreements with the European Community, which to a large extent are identical; and to implement the Luxembourg Declaration. It also encourages co-operation between its members, not only in trade matters but also in other economic questions, particularly those which are dealt with by large international organizations: EFTA countries, each of them relatively small, often have similar interests which can be furthered by their mutual support.

EFTA TRADE, 1987
Imports, c.i.f. (US $ million)

	EFTA	EEC	USA	Japan	Eastern Europe	Rest of world	World
Importing Country:							
Austria	2,555.6	22,223.5	1,131.3	1,423.7	2,212.2	3,128.0	32,674.2
Finland	3,643.3	8,789.6	1,041.5	1,406.2	3,270.1	1,716.8	19,867.6
Iceland	326.7	823.8	112.8	129.5	91.5	97.1	1,581.5
Norway	5,901.9	11,207.0	1,454.7	1,287.5	444.7	2,288.9	22,584.8
Sweden	6,648.5	23,284.8	2,811.2	2,433.5	1,647.5	3,819.2	40,644.7
Switzerland	3,576.9	36,514.1	2,697.1	2,321.7	718.7	4,781.0	50,609.5
Total EFTA	22,653.0	102,842.8	9,248.6	9,002.1	8,384.8	15,831.1	167,962.3

INTERNATIONAL ORGANIZATIONS — European Free Trade Association

Exports, f.o.b. (US $ million)

	EFTA	EEC	USA	Japan	Eastern Europe	Rest of world	World
Exporting Country:							
Austria	3,024.6	17,224.4	967.7	316.4	2,447.5	3,190.5	27,171.0
Finland	4,525.5	8,341.5	1,030.0	280.3	3,370.7	2,511.3	20,059.4
Iceland	113.1	788.6	251.2	107.2	65.1	49.9	1,375.1
Norway	3,260.7	13,809.9	1,222.5	265.7	221.6	2,679.0	21,459.4
Sweden	9,215.6	22,663.1	4,794.0	653.1	914.7	6,206.1	44,446.7
Switzerland	3,352.7	25,361.1	4,003.6	1,735.1	1,490.4	9,544.2	45,487.2
Total EFTA	23,492.2	88,188.6	12,269.0	3,357.8	8,510.0	24,181.1	159,998.8

EFTA trade with the European Community, 1987

	Imports		Exports		Trade balance (US $ million)
	Value in US $ million	% of total imports	Value in US $ million	% of total exports	
Austria	22,223.5	68.0	17,224.4	63.4	−4,999.1
Finland	8,789.6	44.2	8,341.5	41.6	−448.1
Iceland	823.8	52.1	788.6	57.3	−35.2
Norway	11,207.0	49.6	13,809.9	64.4	2,602.9
Sweden	23,284.8	57.3	22,663.1	51.0	−621.7
Switzerland	36,514.1	72.1	25,361.1	55.8	−11,153.0
Total EFTA	102,842.8	61.2	88,188.6	55.1	−14,654.2

FINANCE

Net budget for 1988/89: 16.4m. Swiss francs. The basis for contributions, determined by reference to the GNP at factor cost of the EFTA countries, was as follows: Austria 17.03%, Finland 13.66%, Iceland 1.68%, Norway 14%, Sweden 25.13%, Switzerland 28.5%.

PUBLICATIONS

EFTA Bulletin (4 a year).
EFTA Annual Report.
Annual Report of EFTA Industrial Development Fund for Portugal.

THE FRANC ZONE

Address: Direction Générale des Services Etrangers (Service des Relations avec la Zone Franc), Banque de France, 39 rue Croix-des-Petits-Champs, BP 140-01, Paris Cedex 01, France.
Telephone: (1) 42-92-31-46.
Telex: 220932.

MEMBERS

Benin	Equatorial Guinea
Burkina Faso	French Republic*
Cameroon	Gabon
Central African Republic	Mali
Chad	Niger
Comoros	Senegal
Congo	Togo
Côte d'Ivoire	

* Metropolitan France, Mayotte, St Pierre and Miquelon and the Overseas Departments and Territories.

The Franc Zone embraces all those countries and groups of countries whose currencies are linked with the French franc at a fixed rate of exchange and who agree to hold their reserves mainly in the form of French francs and to effect their exchange on the Paris market. Each of these countries or groups of countries has its own central issuing Bank and its currency is freely convertible into French francs. This monetary union is based on agreements concluded between France and each country or group of countries.

Apart from Guinea and Mauritania, all of the countries that formerly comprised French West and Equatorial Africa are members of the Franc Zone. The former West and Equatorial African territories are still grouped within the currency areas that existed before independence, each group having its own currency issued by a central bank.

Mali withdrew from the Franc Zone in 1962, setting up its own currency, the Mali franc, and its own issuing Bank. Mali rejoined the Franc Zone in 1968, and the Mali franc returned to full convertibility with the French franc: agreement was reached on the establishment of a central issuing bank, jointly administered by France and Mali, until Mali rejoined UMOA (see below) in 1984.

A number of states left the Franc Zone during the period 1958–73: Guinea, Tunisia, Morocco, Algeria, Mauritania and Madagascar.

The Comoros, formerly a French Overseas Territory, did not join the Franc Zone on achieving independence in 1975. However, francs CFA were used as the currency of the new state and the Institut d'émission des Comores continued to function as a Franc Zone organization. In 1976 the Comoros formally assumed membership. In July 1981 the Banque centrale des Comores replaced the Institut d'émission des Comores, establishing its own currency, the Comoros franc.

Equatorial Guinea, a former Spanish colony, joined the Franc Zone in January 1985.

WEST AFRICA

Union monétaire ouest-africaine—UMOA (West African Monetary Union): established by Treaty of November 1973, entered into force 1974; comprises Benin, Burkina Faso, Côte d'Ivoire, Niger, Senegal (all parts of former French West Africa) and Togo; Mali, which left the Union in 1962 after creating its own currency, rejoined in June 1984.

Banque centrale des états de l'Afrique de l'ouest—BCEAO: ave du Barachois, BP 3108, Dakar, Senegal; tel. 21 16 15; telex 21815; f. 1955 under the title 'Institut d'émission de l'AOF et du Togo' and re-created under present title by a treaty between the West African states and a convention with France in 1962, both of which were modified in 1973; central bank of issue for the members of UMOA; capital 39,368m. francs CFA (Sept. 1987). Gov. ALASSANE D. OUATTARA (Côte d'Ivoire); Dep. Gov. BOUBACAR AMADOU HAMA (Burkina Faso); Sec.-Gen. JACQUES DIOUF. Publs *Annual Report, Notes d'Information et Statistiques* (monthly).

Banque ouest-africaine de développement—BOAD: BP 1172, Lomé, Togo; tel. 21-42-44; telex 5289; f. 1973 by heads of member states of UMOA, to promote the balanced development of member states and the economic integration of West Africa; capital (authorized) 100,000m. francs CFA, (subscribed) 73,500m. francs CFA. Mems: Benin, Burkina Faso, Côte d'Ivoire, Mali, Niger, Senegal, Togo. Pres. ABOU BAKAR BABA-MOUSSA; Vice-Pres. HAROUNA BEMBELLO; Sec.-Gen. (vacant). Publ. *Rapport Annuel*.

CENTRAL AFRICA

Union douanière et économique de l'Afrique centrale—UDEAC (Customs and Economic Union of Central Africa): BP 969, Bangui, Central African Republic; tel. 61-09-22; telex 5254; established by the Brazzaville Treaty in 1964 (revised in 1974); comprises: Cameroon, Central African Republic, Congo, Equatorial Guinea and Gabon; Chad left the Union in 1968, retaining observer status until it rejoined in December 1984. As well as forming a customs union, with free trade between members and a common external tariff for imports from other countries, UDEAC has a common code for investment policy and a Solidarity Fund to counteract regional disparities of wealth and economic development. Plans for four community industrial projects were drawn up in 1977: a petrochemicals complex in Gabon, a chemical complex in Congo, a pharmaceuticals laboratory and watchmaking factory in the Central African Republic, and an aluminium plant in Cameroon, none of which was under way by 1988. UDEAC co-sponsored the Central African Industrial Forum, held in December 1985 and December 1987, aiming to promote industrial investment by the European Community and other industrialized nations. Budget (1988) 2,000m. francs CFA. Sec.-Gen. AMBROISE FOALEM (Cameroon).

At the summit meeting in December 1981, UDEAC leaders agreed in principle to form an economic community of Central African states (Communauté économique des états d'Afrique centrale—CEEAC), to include UDEAC members and Burundi, Rwanda, São Tomé and Príncipe and Zaire. CEEAC (q.v.) began operations in 1985.

Banque des états de l'Afrique centrale: BP 1917, Yaoundé, Cameroon; f. 1973 as the central bank of issue of Cameroon, the Central African Republic, Chad, Congo, Equatorial Guinea and Gabon; cap. 36,000m. francs CFA, res 138,794m. francs CFA (Nov. 1987). Gov. CASIMIR OYE MBA (Gabon); Vice-Gov. JEAN-EDOUARD SATHOUD (Congo). Publs *Rapport annuel, Etudes et statistiques* (monthly).

Banque de développement des états de l'Afrique centrale: BP 1177, Brazzaville, Congo; tel. 81 02 12; telex 5306; f. 1976; capital 41,880m. francs CFA (June 1986); non-African shareholders comprise govts of France, the Federal Republic of Germany and Kuwait; Dir-Gen. CÉLESTIN LEROY GAOMBALET.

CENTRAL ISSUING BANKS

Banque des états de l'Afrique centrale: see above.

Banque centrale des états de l'Afrique de l'ouest: see above.

Banque centrale des Comores: BP 405, Moroni, Comoros; tel. 73-10-02; telex 213; f. 1981; Dir-Gen. MOHAMED HALIFA.

Institut d'émission des départements d'outre-mer: Cité du Retiro, 35/37 rue Boissy d'Anglas, 75379 Paris Cedex 08, France; tel. 40-06-41-41; issuing authority for the French Overseas Departments and the French Overseas Collectivité Territoriale of St Pierre and Miquelon; Pres. JACQUES WAITZENEGGER; Dir-Gen. YVES ROLAND-BILLECART.

Institut d'émission d'outre-mer: Cité du Retiro, 35/37 rue Boissy d'Anglas, 75379 Paris Cedex 08, France; tel. 40-06-41-41; issuing authority for the French Overseas Territories and the French Overseas Collectivité Territoriale of Mayotte; Pres. JACQUES WAITZENEGGER; Dir-Gen. YVES ROLAND-BILLECART.

Banque de France: 1 rue de la Vrillière, Paris, France; f. 1800; issuing authority for Metropolitan France; Gov. J. DE LAROSIÈRE; Dep. Govs JACQUES WAITZENEGGER, PHILIPPE LAGAYETTE.

EXCHANGE REGULATIONS

Currencies of the Franc Zone are freely convertible into the French franc at a fixed rate, through 'Operations Accounts' established by agreements concluded between the French Treasury and the individual issuing Banks. It is backed fully by the French Treasury, which also provides the issuing Banks with overdraft facilities.

The monetary reserves of the CFA countries are normally held in French francs in the French Treasury. However, the Banque centrale des états de l'Afrique de l'ouest and the Banque des états de l'Afrique centrale are authorized to hold up to 35% of their foreign exchange holdings in currencies other than the franc.

Exchange is effected on the Paris market. Part of the reserves earned by richer members can be used to offset the deficits incurred by poorer countries.

Regulations drawn up in 1967 provided for the free convertibility of currency with that of countries outside the Franc Zone. Restrictions were removed on the import and export of CFA banknotes, although some capital transfers are subject to approval by the governments concerned.

When the French government instituted exchange control to protect the French franc following the May 1968 crisis, other Franc Zone countries were obliged to take similar action in order to maintain free convertibility within the Franc Zone. The franc CFA was devalued following devaluation of the French franc in August 1969. Since March 1973 the French authorities have ceased to maintain the franc–US dollar rate within previously agreed margins, and, as a result, the value of the franc CFA has fluctuated on foreign exchange markets in line with the French franc.

CURRENCIES OF THE FRANC ZONE

French franc (= 100 centimes): used in Metropolitan France, in the Overseas Departments of Guadeloupe, French Guiana, Martinique, Réunion, and in the Overseas Collectivités Territoriales of St Pierre and Miquelon and Mayotte.

1 franc CFA=2 French centimes. CFA stands for Communauté financière africaine in the West African area and for Coopération financière en Afrique centrale in the Central African area. Used in the monetary areas of West and Central Africa respectively.

1 Comoros franc=2 French centimes. Used in the Comoros, where it replaced the franc CFA in 1981.

1 franc CFP=5.5 French centimes. CFP stands for Comptoirs français du Pacifique. Used in New Caledonia, French Polynesia and the Wallis and Futuna Islands.

French Economic Aid

France's ties with the African Franc Zone countries involve not only monetary arrangements, but also include comprehensive French assistance in the forms of budget support, foreign aid, technical assistance and subsidies on commodity exports.

Official French financial aid and technical assistance to developing countries is administered by the following agencies:

Fonds d'aide et de coopération—FAC: 20 rue Monsieur, 75007 Paris, France; in 1959 FAC took over from FIDES (Fonds d'investissement pour le développement économique et social) the administration of subsidies and loans from the French government to the former French African states. FAC is administered by the Ministry of Co-operation, which allocates budgetary funds to it.

Caisse centrale de coopération économique—CCCE: Cité du Retiro, 35/37 rue Boissy d'Anglas, 75379 Paris Cedex 08, France; tel. (1) 40-06-31-31; telex 212632; f. 1941, and given present name in 1958. French development bank which lends monet to member states and former member states of the Franc Zone and several other states, and executes the financial operations of the FAC. Loans for Franc Zone countries approved in 1986 totalled 3,010m. French francs; Dir-Gen. YVES ROLAND-BILLECART.

INTER-AMERICAN DEVELOPMENT BANK—IDB

Address: 1300 New York Ave, NW, Washington, DC 20577, USA.

The Bank was founded in 1959 to promote the individual and collective development of regional developing member countries through the financing of economic and social development projects and the provision of technical assistance; helps to implement the objectives of the Inter-American system. Membership was increased in 1976 and 1977 to include countries in other world regions.

MEMBERS

Argentina	Finland	Norway
Austria	France	Panama
Bahamas	Germany, Federal	Paraguay
Barbados	Republic	Peru
Belgium	Guatemala	Portugal
Bolivia	Guyana	Spain
Brazil	Haiti	Suriname
Canada	Honduras	Sweden
Chile	Israel	Switzerland
Colombia	Italy	Trinidad and Tobago
Costa Rica	Jamaica	United Kingdom
Denmark	Japan	USA
Dominican Republic	Mexico	Uruguay
Ecuador	Netherlands	Venezuela
El Salvador	Nicaragua	Yugoslavia

Organization
(October 1988)

BOARD OF GOVERNORS

All the powers of the Bank are vested in a Board of Governors, consisting of one Governor and one alternate appointed by each member country. The Board meets annually, with special meetings when necessary.

BOARD OF EXECUTIVE DIRECTORS

There are 12 executive directors and 12 alternates. Each Director is elected by a group of two or more countries, except the Directors representing Canada and the USA. The USA holds 34.5% of votes on the Board, proportional to its contribution to the Bank's capital.

ADMINISTRATION

The Bank has eight departments: operations; finance; economic and social development; project analysis; legal affairs; plans and programmes; administrative; and secretariat. There are External Relations, Controller's and Auditor General's Offices, an External Review and Evaluation Office, and field offices in 23 countries. At the end of 1987 there were 1,800 Bank staff, of whom 535 were serving in field offices.

President: ENRIQUE V. IGLESIAS (Uruguay).
Executive Vice-President: JAMES W. CONROW (USA).

Activities

Loans are made to governments, and to public and private entities for specific economic and social development projects. These loans are repayable in the currencies lent and their terms range from 15 to 40 years. Total lending by the Bank at the end of 1987 amounted to US $39,691m. During 1987 the Bank approved 43 loans, totalling $2,361m., compared with 63 loans totalling $3,037m. in 1986. Disbursements during the year came to $1,919m. The decline in lending was attributed to the stagnation of the Latin American economy as a whole, making it difficult for governments to pay their share of project costs.

The subscribed ordinary capital stock, including inter-regional capital, which was merged into it in 1987, totalled $34,486m. at the end of 1987, of which $2,674m. is paid-in and $31,812m. is callable. The callable capital constitutes, in effect, a guarantee of the securities which the Bank issues in the capital markets in order to increase its resources available for lending. Replenishments are made every four years: the sixth replenishment, agreed in 1983, raised the authorized capital to $35,000m. During 1987 and 1988 agreement on a seventh replenishment of the Bank's capital was delayed by the US Government's demands for a restructuring of lending policies. Previously, a simple majority of directors' votes was sufficient to ensure the approval of a loan; developing member countries had nearly 54% of the voting power. The USA now proposed that a 65% majority should be necessary, thus giving the USA and Canada combined a virtual power of veto. The US Government also criticized the Bank's policy of lending mostly for specific projects, rather than in support of economic adjustment programmes.

The Fund for Special Operations enables the Bank to make concessional loans for economic and social projects where circumstances call for special treatment, such as lower interest rates and longer repayment terms than those applied to loans from the ordinary resources. Under the Sixth Replenishment (1983) the Fund received only $703m., compared with $1,750m. four years previously. During 1987 the Fund made 12 loans totalling $346m.

Several donor countries have placed sums under the Bank's administration for assistance to Latin America, outside the framework of the Ordinary Resources and the Bank's Special Operations. These include the United States Social Progress Trust Fund (set up in 1961), which had made loans amounting to $538m. by the end of 1987; the Venezuelan Trust Fund (set up in 1975), which had made loans totalling $725m. by the end of 1987; and other funds administered on behalf of Argentina, Canada, Norway, Sweden, Switzerland, the United Kingdom and the Vatican. Total cumulative lending from all these funds amounted to $1,369m. at the end of 1987. In October 1988 the Spanish Government agreed to establish a $500m. special fund at the IDB, together with a $150m. compensation account to subsidize interest rates and thereby allow the approval of concessional loans.

Loans to the 'productive sectors' (agriculture and fisheries, industry and mining, and tourism) accounted for 28% of the Bank's total lending in 1987; physical infrastructure (energy, transport and communications) for 41.4%; social infrastructure (health, education, science and urban development) for 27%; and other sectors (including export financing and pre-investment studies) for 3.6%.

A special programme provides financing for small projects run by, for example, co-operatives or local producers' associations, which would normally fail to obtain credit from conventional sources: the beneficiaries are low-income farmers, small-scale entrepreneurs and craftsmen. During 1987 19 projects were financed at a cost of $8.5m.

The Bank provides grants and technical co-operation for the countries of the region. Such assistance amounted to $46.8m. in 1987.

In March 1986 the charter of the Inter-American Investment Corporation (IIC), an affiliate of the Bank, entered into force, with the aim of promoting private-sector investment in the region (particularly in small- and medium-sized industries).

Distribution of loans (US $ million)

Sector	1987	%	1961–87	%
Productive Sectors				
Agriculture and fisheries	562	23.8	8,476	21.3
Industry and mining	100	4.2	6,187	15.6
Tourism	—	—	547	1.3
Physical Infrastructure				
Energy	631	26.7	10,973	27.6
Transportation and communications	347	14.7	5,141	13.0
Social Infrastructure				
Environmental and public health	434	18.4	3,739	9.4
Education, science and technology	75	3.2	1,695	4.3
Urban development	128	5.4	1,604	4.0
Other				
Export financing	80	3.4	788	2.0
Preinvestment	—	—	378	1.0
Other	4	0.2	163	0.5
Total	2,361	100.0	36,691	100.0

INTERNATIONAL ORGANIZATIONS

Inter-American Development Bank

Cumulative lending, 1961–87 (US $ million; net of cancellations and exchange adjustments)

Country	Total amount	Ordinary capital	Fund for special operations	Funds in administration
Argentina	4,264.4	3,696.0	519.4	49.0
Bahamas	6.0	4.0	—	2.0
Barbados	147.7	86.3	43.2	18.2
Bolivia	1,261.9	556.8	651.5	53.6
Brazil	6,580.7	5,253.0	1,195.8	131.9
Chile	3,205.0	2,958.5	203.3	43.2
Colombia	3,856.4	3,150.8	642.9	62.7
Costa Rica	1,120.8	686.1	355.9	78.8
Dominican Republic	910.8	306.4	535.4	69.0
Ecuador	2,304.1	1,414.3	800.0	89.8
El Salvador	987.5	313.0	567.8	106.7
Guatemala	1,166.2	574.4	531.0	60.8
Guyana	232.9	107.6	119.3	6.0
Haiti	295.1	—	287.1	8.0
Honduras	940.2	285.4	597.6	57.2
Jamaica	599.4	345.2	178.6	75.6
Mexico	5,185.0	4,575.8	574.2	35.0
Nicaragua	472.2	100.4	317.6	54.2
Panama	881.0	561.4	283.0	36.6
Paraguay	602.7	190.6	399.4	12.7
Peru	1,747.7	1,129.7	431.7	186.3
Suriname	21.9	18.9	3.0	—
Trinidad and Tobago	82.4	55.0	25.4	2.0
Uruguay	729.2	582.7	104.7	41.8
Venezuela	1,264.3	1,090.0	101.4	72.9
Regional	825.0	615.6	194.7	14.7
Total	39,690.5	28,657.9	9,663.9	1,368.7

Total loans by country (US $ million)

Country	1985	1986	1987
Argentina	108.9	516.3	13.1
Barbados	21.7	20.9	0.6
Bolivia	—	140.4	89.7
Brazil	395.3	428.8	369.9
Chile	522.5	359.8	—
Colombia	413.3	87.0	546.6
Costa Rica	6.0	179.9	112.8
Dominican Republic	146.2	140.0	0.4
Ecuador	274.4	272.7	263.5
El Salvador	26.2	25.2	169.3
Guatemala	192.0	65.8	43.8
Guyana	58.5	—	6.7
Haiti	24.7	56.5	—
Honduras	69.8	122.9	1.5
Jamaica	30.1	59.3	57.4
Mexico	401.5	327.9	164.1
Panama	52.8	98.4	16.7
Paraguay	—	—	32.1
Peru	14.5	19.2	85.9
Suriname	8.0	6.0	7.8
Trinidad and Tobago	25.6	36.8	1.0
Uruguay	21.6	73.2	153.2
Venezuela	238.0	—	225.0
Regional	9.6	—	—
Total	3,061.2	3,037.0	2,361.1

AFFILIATED INSTITUTIONS

Instituto para la Integración de América Latina (Institute for Latin American Integration): Esmeralda 130, 16°, Casilla de Correo 39, Sucursal 1, Buenos Aires, Argentina; f.1964 as a permanent department of the Inter-American Development Bank. Its functions are: to study the regional integration process; to carry out research into problems which the integration movement poses for individual countries; to organize training courses and seminars; to conduct, at the request of member countries, preliminary studies on joint development schemes and on economic integration alternatives available to individual countries; to provide advisory services to the Bank and to other public and private institutions; to offer courses on the economic, political, social, institutional, legal, scientific and technological aspects of regional integration. Dir EDUARDO ZALDUENDO.

Inter-American Investment Corporation—IIC: f. 1986 as an affiliate of the Inter-American Development Bank, to promote private-sector investment in the region. The IIC's initial capital stock was to be US $200m., of which 55% was contributed by developing member nations, 25.5% by the USA, and the remainder by non-regional members. Emphasis is placed on investment in small and medium-sized enterprises. Gen. Man. GUNTHER H. MULLER.

PUBLICATIONS

Integración Latinoamericana (monthly).
Annual Report (annually, in English and Spanish).
The Process of Integration in Latin America (monthly, in English and Spanish).

INTERGOVERNMENTAL COMMITTEE FOR MIGRATION—ICM

Address: 17 route des Morillons, POB 71, 1211 Geneva 19, Switzerland.
Telephone: (022) 980066.
Telex: 22155.

Founded on 5 December 1951, ICM is a non-political and humanitarian organization with a predominantly operational mandate, which includes the handling of orderly and planned migration to meet specific needs of emigration and immigration countries; and the processing and movement of refugees, displaced persons and other individuals in need of international migration services to countries offering them resettlement opportunities.

MEMBERS

Argentina	Ecuador	Nicaragua
Australia	El Salvador	Norway
Austria	Germany,	Panama
Belgium	Federal Republic	Paraguay
Bolivia	Greece	Peru
Chile	Guatemala	Portugal
Colombia	Honduras	Switzerland
Costa Rica	Israel	Thailand
Cyprus	Italy	USA
Denmark	Kenya	Uruguay
Dominican	Luxembourg	Venezuela
Republic	Netherlands	

Eighteen other States have observer status: Belize, Brazil, Canada, Cape Verde, Egypt, France, Guinea-Bissau, Holy See, Japan, Republic of Korea, Malta, Mexico, Philippines, San Marino, Spain, Sweden, Turkey, United Kingdom.

Organization
(October 1988)

ICM is governed by a Council which is composed of representatives of all member governments, and has the responsibility for making final decisions on policy, programmes and financing. An Executive Committee of nine member governments elected by the Council prepares the work of the Council and makes recommendations on the basis of reports from the Sub-Committee on Budget and Finance and the Sub-Committee on the Co-ordination of Transport.

Director General: JAMES N. PURCELL (USA).
Deputy Director General: HÉCTOR CHARRY SAMPER (Colombia) (from 1 January 1989).

Activities

Upon request from member governments, ICM arranges the organized transfer of migrants, refugees, displaced persons and other individuals in need of international migration services. This includes (for refugees) processing, medical services to respond to entry requirements in resettlement countries, and language and cultural orientation courses; and (for migrants) counselling, recruitment, selection, processing in country of origin, reception, placement and integration assistance in the receiving country, and language courses. ICM co-ordinates its refugee activities with the UN High Commissioner for Refugees (q.v.) and with governmental and non-governmental organizations.

ICM's programmes of 'Migration for Development' aim at contributing towards alleviating economic and social problems through recruitment and selection of high-level workers and professionals to fill positions in priority sectors of the economy in developing countries for which qualified persons are not available locally (particularly in Latin America and Africa). These programmes comprise Selective Migration and Integrated Experts—to provide highly qualified professionals and technicians; Return of Talent—to facilitate the return of qualified nationals to their home countries or region after they have acquired skills and experience in industrialized countries; and Horizontal Co-operation in the field of qualified human resources, through the exchange of governmental experts and the intraregional transfer of professionals and technicians. During 1983-87 536 qualified African nationals returned to Africa from industrialized countries under these programmes, and in 1987 2,289 professionals, technicians and highly-skilled workers were transferred to Latin America. A pilot project to assign experts to Malaysia and the Philippines was under way in 1987.

ICM provides advisory services and carries out studies to assist member governments in the formation and implementation of their migration policy, legislation and administration.

International Seminars are organized by ICM on international migration issues. These ICM Seminars serve as a forum for exchange of information and ideas among member and observer governments, governmental and non-governmental organizations, with a view to devising practical recommendations to current migration problems.

A number of UN agencies, 10 international governmental and 23 non-governmental organizations co-operate in the programmes which ICM carries out within the framework of the policies of its member governments.

During 1987 ICM handled 125,245 people (including 116,500 refugees), bringing to 3,884,002 the total number of persons resettled in 126 new home countries since the organization began operations in 1952. In 1987 the largest group of refugees resettled by ICM comprised Indochinese refugees from countries of asylum in south-east Asia (58,362). ICM arranges the movement of persons emigrating directly from Viet-Nam under the 'Orderly Departure Programme' (12,672 in 1987). During the year, ICM assisted in the resettlement or repatriation of 13,270 Latin American refugees and displaced people; 40,500 Eastern Europeans; 3,158 African and Middle Eastern refugees; and 5,095 refugees in Pakistan (mainly Afghan nationals). ICM assisted 3,200 Portuguese who obtained immigration opportunities abroad. Some 10,000 people were also assisted in resettlement or repatriation through programmes for asylum-seekers in Belgium and the Federal Republic of Germany.

FINANCE

The ICM budget for 1987 amounted to US $100,780,550, of which $89,280,550 (financed by voluntary contributions) was for operations, the principal item of expenditure ($47,639,550) being for assistance to refugees in Asia. The projected budget for 1988 was $105,683,650.

PUBLICATIONS

Monthly Dispatch.
International Migration (quarterly).
ICM Latin American Migration Journal (3 a year).

INTERNATIONAL BANK FOR ECONOMIC CO-OPERATION—IBEC

Address: 15 Kuznetski Most, 103031 Moscow, USSR.
Telephone: 925-16-88.
Telex: 411391.

The Bank was founded in October 1963 with eight member countries, and commenced operations in January 1964 to assist in the economic co-operation and development of member countries (see also CMEA, p. 124, and International Investment Bank, p. 164).

MEMBERS

Bulgaria	German Democratic Republic	Poland
Cuba*	Hungary	Romania
Czechoslovakia	Mongolia	USSR
		Viet-Nam*

* Cuba joined the Bank in 1974, and Viet-Nam in 1977.

Organization

(October 1988)

THE COUNCIL

The Council is composed of representatives of all member countries. Each country has one vote irrespective of its share in the capital of the Bank. The Council considers and decides questions of policy, determining the general policy of the Bank and the orientation of the development of its activities. It meets about twice a year. Representatives of the central banks of Afghanistan, Ethiopia, Finland, Laos, Mozambique, the People's Democratic Republic of Yemen and Yugoslavia attend spring meetings (at which the Annual Report and balance sheet are approved) as observers.

THE BOARD

The Board is the executive body subordinate to the Council; there is one permanent representative from each of the member states.
Chairman: V. S. KHOKHLOV (USSR).

Activities

The Bank acts as the central institution of the CMEA member countries for credit and settlements. Its main purpose is to effect multilateral settlements in the collective currency of its members, the transferable rouble (TR), and to grant credits in TRs to the authorized banks of the member countries and to international economic organizations. Favourable credit conditions are granted to Cuba, Mongolia and Viet-Nam. Settlements in the collective currency include trade-related and non-commercial payments. The Bank also carries out credit and other transactions in convertible currencies with members and non-member countries.

The total volume of the Bank's operations grew by 12.2% in 1987 to reach 668,900m. TR; operations in transferable roubles totalled 321,100m. TR. At 31 December 1987 the balance total of the IBEC amounted to 6,383m. TR, compared with 5,922m. TR one year previously.

During 1986 the volume of settlements among member countries channelled through the IBEC was 222,200m. TR, compared with the previous year's total of 221,100m. TR. The volume of trade-related settlements, accounting for 94% of the total, met the targets of the authorized banks. Settlements on non-commercial operations increased by 13.4% over the previous year. Credits extended by the IBEC to the banks of member countries amounted to 15,900m. TR, compared with 18,000m. TR in 1986.

CAPITAL (31 December 1987; million transferable roubles)

	Authorized	Paid-up
Bulgaria	17.0	12.9
Cuba	4.4	3.3
Czechoslovakia	45.0	34.0
German Democratic Republic	55.0	41.6
Hungary	21.0	15.9
Mongolia	3.0	1.7
Poland	27.0	20.4
Romania	16.0	12.1
USSR	116.0	87.7
Viet-Nam	0.9	0.7
Total	**305.3**	**230.3**

BALANCE SHEET (31 December; transferable roubles)

Assets	1986	1987
Monetary funds	1,177,065,032	1,280,333,059
Current accounts and cash on hand	5,940,626	14,870,901
Time deposits	1,171,124,406	1,265,462,158
Credits granted	4,693,278,800	5,044,832,233
Property of the Bank	822,478	832,514
Other assets	50,403,927	57,174,465
Total	**5,921,570,237**	**6,383,172,271**

Liabilities	1986	1987
Capital funds of the Bank	447,282,872	457,692,499
Capital paid up	230,316,560	230,316,560
Reserve capital	216,966,312	227,375,939
Deposits	4,868,019,301	5,314,869,702
Current accounts	227,772,205	654,226,275
Time deposits	4,640,247,096	4,660,643,427
Credits received	504,276,604	500,082,658
Other liabilities	79,618,017	82,627,810
Net profit	22,373,443	27,899,602
Total	**5,921,570,237**	**6,383,172,271**

INTERNATIONAL CHAMBER OF COMMERCE—ICC

Address: 38 Cours Albert 1er, 75008 Paris, France.
Telephone: 45-62-34-56.
Telex: 650770.

The ICC was founded in 1919 to promote free trade and private enterprise, provide practical services and represent business interests at governmental and inter-governmental levels.

MEMBERS

At the end of 1987 membership consisted of about 5,364 individual corporations and 1,701 organizations (mainly trade and industrial organizations and chambers of commerce). In the following 60 countries National Committees or Councils have been formed to co-ordinate certain functions at the national level, while the ICC is also represented in 50 other countries and territories.

Argentina	Indonesia	Senegal
Australia	Iran	Singapore
Austria	Ireland	South Africa
Belgium	Israel	Spain
Brazil	Italy	Sri Lanka
Burkina Faso	Ivory Coast	Sweden
Cameroon	Japan	Switzerland
Canada	Jordan	Syria
Colombia	Republic of Korea	Taiwan
Cyprus	Kuwait	Thailand
Denmark	Lebanon	Togo
Ecuador	Luxembourg	Tunisia
Egypt	Madagascar	Turkey
Finland	Mexico	United Kingdom
France	Morocco	USA
Gabon	Netherlands	Uruguay
Federal Republic of Germany	Nigeria	Venezuela
	Norway	Yugoslavia
Greece	Pakistan	Zaire
Iceland	Portugal	
India	Saudi Arabia	

Organization

(October 1988)

COUNCIL

The Council is the governing body of the organization. It is composed of members nominated by the National Committees and meets twice a year.
President: THEOPHILO DE AZEREDO SANTOS (Brazil).
Vice-President: PETER WALLENBERG (Sweden).

EXECUTIVE BOARD

The Executive Board consists of 12–15 members appointed by the Council on the recommendation of the President and six ex-officio members. Members serve for a three-year term, one-third of the members retiring at the end of each year. It ensures close direction of ICC activities and meets four times a year.

INTERNATIONAL SECRETARIAT

The ICC secretariat is based at International Headquarters in Paris, with additional offices maintained in Geneva and New York principally for liaison with the United Nations and its agencies.
Secretary-General: HANS KÖNIG.
First Director: MARIE C. PSIMÈNOS.

NATIONAL COMMITTEES AND GROUPS

Each affiliate is composed of leading business organizations and individual companies. It has its own secretariat, monitors issues of concern to its national constituents, and draws public and government attention to ICC policies.

CONGRESS

The ICC's supreme assembly, to which all member companies and organizations are invited to send senior representatives. Congresses are held every three years, in a different place on each occasion, with up to 2,000 participants. The 29th Congress was held in New Delhi, India, in February 1987, and the 30th Congress was due to be held in Hamburg, Federal Republic of Germany, in June 1990.

CONFERENCE

Conferences with about 250 participants take place in non-Congress years. The eighth Conference was held in Istanbul, Turkey, in September 1988.

Activities

The various Commissions of the ICC (listed below) are composed of practising businessmen and experts from all sectors of economic life, nominated by National Committees. ICC recommendations must be adopted by a Commission following consultation with National Committees, and then approved by the Council or Executive Board, before they can be regarded as official ICC policies. Meetings of Commissions are generally held twice a year. Working Parties are frequently constituted by Commissions to undertake specific projects and report back to their parent body. Officers of Commissions, and specialized Working Parties, often meet in the intervals between Commission sessions. The Commissions produce a wide array of specific codes and guidelines of direct use to the world business community; draw up statements and initiatives for presentation to governments and international bodies; and comment constructively and in detail on proposed actions by inter-governmental organizations that are likely to affect business.

ICC works closely with the United Nations and its various organizations. The ICC-UN, GATT Economic Consultative Committee, for example, brings together ICC members and the heads of UN economic organizations and the OECD for annual discussions on the world economy. The Commission on International Trade Policy campaigns against protectionism in world trade and in support of the General Agreement on Tariffs and Trade (GATT, q.v.), and ensures that ICC views are represented in the multilateral trade negotiations which take place under GATT auspices. The ICC also works closely with the European Community, commenting on EEC directives and making recommendations on, for example, tax harmonization and laws relating to competition.

ICC plays a part in combating international crime connected with commerce. The ICC International Maritime Bureau combats maritime fraud, for example insurance fraud and the theft of cargoes. The ICC Counterfeiting Intelligence Bureau was established in 1985 to investigate counterfeiting in trade-marked goods, copyrights and industrial designs. Commercial disputes are submitted to the ICC Court of Arbitration: during 1987 285 new cases were registered and 149 partial or final awards were made, together with 17 awards made with the consent of the parties.

Policy and Technical Commissions:

Commission on International Trade Policy
Commission on International Monetary Relations
Commission on Multinational Enterprises and International Investments
Commission on Industrial Property
Commission on Taxation
Commission on Law and Practices Relating to Competition
Commission on Insurance
Commission on Marketing
Commission on Energy
Commission on Environment
Commission on Computing, Telecommunications and Information Policy
Commission on Sea Transport
Commission on Air Transport
Commission on Trade Regulations and Procedures
Commission on International Commercial Practice
Commission on Banking Technique and Practice
Commission on International Arbitration
East-West Committee

Bodies for the Settlement of Disputes:

Court of Arbitration
International Centre for Technical Expertise
International Maritime Arbitration Organization

Other Bodies:
ICC-UN, GATT Economic Consultative Committee
International Bureau of Chambers of Commerce
ICC International Maritime Bureau
ICC Counterfeiting Intelligence Bureau
ICC Centre for Maritime Co-operation
ICC Institute of International Business Law and Practice
ICC International Environmental Bureau
ICC Corporate Security Services

FINANCE

The International Chamber of Commerce is a private organization financed partly by contributions from National Committees and other members, according to the economic importance of the country which each represents, and partly by revenue from fees for various services and from sales of publications. The operating budget for 1987 was about 55m. French francs.

PUBLICATIONS

Annual Report.
Handbook.
IGO Monitor
ICC Contact
Numerous publications on general and technical business and trade-related subjects.

INTERNATIONAL CONFEDERATION OF FREE TRADE UNIONS—ICFTU

Address: 37-41 rue Montagne aux Herbes Potagères, 1000 Brussels, Belgium.
Telephone: (02) 217-80-85.
Telex: 26785.

ICFTU was founded in 1949 by trade union federations which had withdrawn from the World Federation of Trade Unions (see p. 211). It aims to promote the interests of working people and to secure recognition of workers' organizations as free bargaining agents; to reduce the gap between rich and poor; and to defend fundamental human and trade union rights. See also the World Confederation of Labour (p. 209).

MEMBERS

141 organizations in 97 countries with 87m. members (January 1988).

Organization
(October 1988)

WORLD CONGRESS

The Congress, the highest authority of ICFTU, normally meets every four years. The 14th Congress was held in Melbourne, Australia, in March 1988.

Delegations from national federations vary in size according to membership. The Congress examines past activities, maps out future plans, elects the Executive Board and the General Secretary, considers the functioning of the regional machinery, examines financial reports and social, economic and political situations. It works through plenary sessions and through technical committees which report to the plenary sessions.

EXECUTIVE BOARD

The Board meets twice a year, for about three days, usually at Brussels, or at the Congress venue; it consists of 37 members elected by Congress and nominated by areas of the world. The General Secretary is an ex-officio member. After each Congress the Board elects a President and at least seven Vice-Presidents.

The Board considers administrative questions; hears reports from field representatives, missions, regional organizations and affiliates, and makes resultant decisions; and discusses finances, applications for affiliation, and problems affecting world labour. It elects a sub-committee of nine to deal with urgent matters between Board meetings.

President: P. P. NARAYANAN (Malaysia).

PERMANENT COMMITTEES

Finance and General Purposes Committee. Administers the General Fund made up of affiliation fees and the International Solidarity Fund constituting additional voluntary contributions.
Economic and Social Committee.
Education Policy Committee.
Women's Committee.
ICFTU/ITS Working Group on Young Workers' Questions.
ICFTU/ITS Working Party on Multinational Corporations.
Working Group on International Trade and Monetary Questions.

SECRETARIAT

The headquarters staff numbers 97, comprising some 25 different nationalities.

The six departments are: Economic and Social Policy; Education; Administration; Finance; Press, Publications and Communications; Programme Administration and Co-ordination. There are also Regional Desks and a Women's Bureau.

General Secretary: JOHN VANDERVEKEN.

BRANCH OFFICES

ICFTU Geneva Office: 27-29 rue de la Coulouvrenière, 1204 Geneva, Switzerland.

ICFTU United Nations Office: Room 304, 104 East 40th St, New York, NY 10016, USA.

There are also Permanent Representatives accredited to FAO (Rome) and to UNIDO (Vienna).

REGIONAL ORGANIZATIONS

ICFTU African Regional Organization—AFRO: c/o Liberia Federation of Labour Unions, POB 415, Monrovia, Liberia; Sec. KANDEH YILLA (Sierra Leone).

Inter-American Regional Organization of Workers—ORIT: POB 7039, 06000 México, DF, Mexico; tel. 566-7024; telex 1771699; Pres. A. MADARIAGA; Gen. Sec. LUIS ANDERSON.

ICFTU Asian and Pacific Regional Organization—APRO: Trade Union House, Shenton Way, Singapore 0106; tel. 2226555; telex 24543; Pres. T. USAMI; Gen. Sec. V. S. MATHUR.

There is a Liaison Office in Indonesia and Field Representatives in Brazil, Kenya, Lesotho, Thailand and Papua New Guinea. In addition, a number of Project Planners for development co-operation travel in different countries.

FINANCE

Affiliated federations pay a standard fee of 5,132 Belgian francs (1988), or its equivalent in other currencies, per 1,000 members per annum, which covers the establishment and routine activities of the ICFTU headquarters in Brussels.

An International Solidarity Fund was set up in 1956 to assist unions in developing countries, and workers and trade unionists victimized by repressive political measures. It provides legal assistance and supports educational activities. In cases of major natural disasters affecting workers token relief aid is granted.

PUBLICATIONS

Free Labour World (official journal, fortnightly).
Economic and Social Bulletin (quarterly).
World Economic Review (annually).
Survey of Violations of Trade Union Rights (annually).
Occupational Health and Safety Bulletin.

All these periodicals are issued in English, French, German and Spanish. In addition Congress reports and numerous other publications on labour, economic and trade union training have been published in various languages.

Associated International Trade Secretariats

International Federation of Building and Woodworkers: 27-29 rue de la Coulouvrenière, 1204 Geneva; tel. (022) 211611; telex 428577; f. 1934. Mems: national unions with a membership of 3m. workers. Organization: Congress, Executive Committee. Pres. KONRAD CARL (FRG); Sec.-Gen. J. LÖFBLAD (Sweden). Publs *Bulletin* (quarterly).

International Federation of Chemical, Energy and General Workers' Unions—ICEF: 109 ave Emile de Béco, 1050 Brussels, Belgium; tel. (02) 647-02-35; telex 20847; f. 1907. Mems: 189 national unions covering 6m. people in 59 countries. Holds Congress (every four years). Pres. NILS KRISTOFFERSON (Sweden); Gen. Sec. MICHAEL BOGGS. Publs *Bulletin* (quarterly), *ICEF Info* (monthly), reports.

International Federation of Commercial, Clerical, Professional and Technical Employees—FIET: 15 ave de Balexert, 1219 Châtelaine-Geneva, Switzerland; tel. (022) 962733; telex 418736; f. 1904. Mems: 304 national unions of non-manual workers comprising 9m. people in 96 countries. Holds World Congresses (every four years); has seven trade sections (for bank workers, insurance workers, workers in social insurance and health care, commercial workers, salaried employees in industry, hairdressers and workers in property services), regional organizations for Europe, Western Hemisphere, Asia and Africa. Pres. BENGT LLOYD (Sweden); Sec.-Gen. HERIBERT MAIER (Austria). Publs *FIET INFO* (monthly in English, French, German and Spanish), Press service, *Studies*.

International Federation of Free Teachers' Unions: Herengracht 54-56, 1015 BN Amsterdam, Netherlands; tel. (020) 24 90

72; telex 17118; f. 1951. Mems: 75 national organizations of teachers' trade unions covering 6.5m. members in 53 countries. Holds Congress (every four years). Pres. A. SHANKER (USA); Gen. Sec. FRED VAN LEEUWEN (Netherlands). Publs *Fortnightly Bulletin, Workers in Education* (4–6 a year in English, French and Spanish).

International Federation of Journalists: IPC, blvd Charlemagne 1, Bte 5, 1041 Brussels, Belgium; tel. (02) 238-09-51; telex 61275; f. 1952 to link national unions of professional journalists dedicated to the freedom of the press, to defend the rights of journalists, and to raise professional standards; it conducts surveys, assists in trade union training programmes, organizes seminars and provides information; it arranges fact-finding missions in countries where press freedom is under pressure, and issues protests against the persecution and detention of journalists and the censorship of the mass media. Mems: 44 unions in 37 countries, comprising 150,000 individuals. Pres. MIA DOORNAERT (Belgium); Gen. Sec. AIDAN WHITE (United Kingdom).

International Federation of Plantation, Agricultural and Allied Workers: 17 rue Necker, 1201 Geneva, Switzerland; tel. (022) 313105; telex 28775; f. 1959. Mems: unions covering approx. 6m. workers. Holds Congress (every six years). Pres P. P. NARAYANAN (Malaysia); Gen. Sec. BÖRJE SVENSSON (Sweden). Publ. *News* (monthly).

International Graphical Federation: Monbijoustrasse 73, 3007 Berne, Switzerland; tel. (31) 45-99-20; telex 913274; f. 1949. Mems: 45 national organizations in 37 countries, covering 790,000 individuals. Holds: Congress (every three years). Pres. ERWIN FERLEMANN (FRG); Gen. Sec. ALFRED KAUFMANN (Switzerland). Publs *Journal of the IGF* (2 a year), reports.

International Metalworkers' Federation: Route des Acacias 54 bis, 1227 Geneva, Switzerland; tel. (022) 436150; telex 423298; f. 1893. Mems: national organizations covering 14m. workers in 70 countries. Holds Congress (every four years); has seven regional offices; six industrial departments; World Company Councils for unions in multinational corporations. Pres. F. STEINKUHLER (FRG); Gen. Sec. HERMAN REBHAN (USA). Publ. *IMF News* (every 2 weeks, seven languages).

International Secretariat for Arts, Mass Media and Entertainment Trade Unions: 15 ave de Balexert, 1219 Châtelaine-Geneva, Switzerland; tel. (022) 962733; telex 418736; f. 1965; Pres. WALTER BACHER; Sec.-Gen. IRENE ROBADEY.

International Textile, Garment and Leather Workers' Federation: rue Joseph Stevens 8, 1000 Brussels, Belgium; tel. (02) 512-26-06; f. 1970. Mems: 160 unions covering over 5m. workers in 75 countries. Pres. B. KELLER (FRG); Gen. Sec. NEIL KEARNEY (Ireland).

International Transport Workers' Federation: 133–135 Great Suffolk St, London, SE1 1PD, England; tel. (01) 403-2733; telex 8811397; f. 1896. Mems: national trade unions covering 4.5m. workers in 90 countries. Holds Congress (every four years); has eight Industrial Sections. Pres. JIM HUNTER (Canada); Gen. Sec. HAROLD LEWIS (UK). Publ. *ITF News* (monthly), special bulletins.

International Union of Food and Allied Workers' Associations: 8 rampe du Pont-Rouge, 1213 Petit-Lancy, Switzerland; tel. (022) 93-22-33; telex 429292; f. 1920. Mems: national organizations covering about 2.1m workers in 62 countries. Holds Congress (every four years). Pres. G. DÖDING (FRG); Gen. Sec. DAN GALLIN (Switzerland). Publs monthly bulletins, reports, brochures.

Miners' International Federation: 8 rue Joseph Stevens, 1000 Brussels, Belgium; tel. (02) 511-35-43; f. 1890. Mems: 34 national unions covering over 1.4m. miners in 31 countries. Holds Congress (every four years). Pres. A. STENDALEN (Sweden); Gen. Sec. J. OLYSLAEGERS (Belgium).

Postal, Telegraph and Telephone International: 36 ave du Lignon, 1219 Geneva, Switzerland; tel. (022) 96-83-11; f. 1920. Mems: national trade unions covering 3,924,319 workers in 93 countries. Holds Congress (every four years). Pres. AKIRA YAMAGISHI (Japan); Gen. Sec. S. NEDZYNSKI. Publs *PTTI News* (six languages, monthly), *PTTI Studies* (four languages, quarterly).

Public Services International: 45 ave Voltaire, 01210 Ferney-Voltaire, France; tel. 50-40-64-64; telex 390559; f. 1907; Mems: 250 unions and professional associations covering over 11m. workers in 80 countries. Holds Congress (every four years). Pres. VICTOR GOTBAUM (USA); Gen. Sec. HANS ENGELBERTS (Netherlands). Publs *INFO* (10 a year), *Focus*, specialized reports.

Universal Alliance of Diamond Workers: Lange Kievitstraat 57 (Bus 1), 2018 Antwerp, Belgium; tel. (03) 232-91-51; f. 1905. Mems: 10,100 in six countries. Pres. J. MEIJNIKMAN (Netherlands); Gen. Sec. C. DENISSE (Belgium).

INTERNATIONAL INVESTMENT BANK

Address: 17 Presnensky Val, Moscow 123557, USSR.
Telephone: 253-80-24.
Telex: 411358.

Established by an intergovernmental Agreement of the members of the Council for Mutual Economic Assistance (see p. 124) in 1970, the Bank commenced operations on 1 January 1971.

MEMBERS

Bulgaria	German Democratic Republic	Poland
Cuba	Hungary	Romania
Czechoslovakia	Mongolia	USSR
		Viet-Nam

Organization
(October 1988)

COUNCIL

The Council of the Bank is the highest authority and consists of representatives of all the member countries. Each member country, irrespective of the amount of its quota, has one vote in the Council. Major decisions require a unanimous vote. The Council meets as often as necessary but not less than twice a year.

BOARD

The Board is the executive body of the Bank and consists of a Chairman and three Deputies appointed by the Council. Its task is to supervise the Bank's activities in accordance with the Agreement, the Statutes of the Bank and the decisions of the Council.

Chairman: ALBERT N. BELICHENKO (USSR).

Activities

Under Article II of the Agreement on the Establishment of the International Investment Bank the fundamental task of the Bank is to grant long-term and medium-term credits for projects connected with the international socialist division of labour, specialization and co-operation in production, expenditure for expansion of raw materials and fuel resources in the members' collective interest, for the construction of enterprises of mutual concern to member countries in other branches of the economy, for the construction of projects for the development of the national economies of member countries and for other purposes established by the Council. Credits are granted for a period of up to 15 years, and may be granted to:

(i) banks, economic organizations and enterprises of member countries;
(ii) international economic organizations and enterprises of member countries;
(iii) banks and economic organizations of other countries.

The Bank may:

(i) form reserve capital and create its own special funds;
(ii) attract funds in collective currency (transferable roubles), in national currencies of interested countries and in convertible currency;
(iii) issue interest-bearing bond loans placed on international capital markets;
(iv) place surplus funds with other banks, buy and sell currency, gold and securities, grant guarantees and conduct other banking operations;
(v) co-operate with the Council for Mutual Economic Assistance, the International Bank for Economic Co-operation (q.v.) and other economic organizations of the member countries of the Bank;
(vi) make contact and establish business relations with international and other financial and credit institutions as well as with banks;
(vii) conclude international agreements and the like, as well as making business transactions within its competence.

In 1974, a Special Fund was formed for financing programmes of economic and technical assistance to developing countries.

By the end of 1987 the Bank had authorized credits for 111 projects, with a total estimated value of more than 20,000m. transferable roubles. The largest proportion of credits granted between 1971 and the end of 1987 was for the energy and fuel sector (63%), while 28% was for machine-building and metal-working (including electrical engineering and electronics). During 1987 credits were approved for: expansion and modernization of a combine producing electrical tools in Bulgaria, modernization of plants producing printing systems, shock-absorbers and brakes, and food-industry machinery in Poland; Czechoslovak equipment for a Soviet iron-ore mining complex; cement production and kenaf processing in Viet-Nam; construction of a nuclear power station in Cuba; washing-machine production in the German Democratic Republic; and equipment for a chemical plant in Czechoslovakia.

AUTHORIZED CAPITAL
(million transferable roubles as at 1 January 1988)

Country	Amount
Bulgaria	85.1
Cuba	15.7
Czechoslovakia	129.9
German Democratic Republic	176.1
Hungary	83.7
Mongolia	4.5
Poland	121.4
Romania	52.6
USSR	399.3
Viet-Nam	3.0
Total	**1,071.3**

STATEMENT OF ACCOUNT (transferable roubles)

Assets	As at 1 January 1988
Cash, balance on current accounts and time deposits with banks	1,025,456,258
Settlements on replenishment of paid-up portion of authorized capital	99,986,667
Credits disbursed	1,520,950,906
Bank building and other property	21,885,620
Other assets	51,445,790
Total	**2,719,725,241**

Liabilities	As at 1 January 1988
Authorized capital	1,071,300,000
Paid-up portion	489,243,333
Settlements on replenishment of paid-up portion of authorized capital	99,986,667
Reserve capital	186,494,198
Special Fund	34,635,704
Credits and time deposits received	1,816,831,787
Bank premises construction fund and amortization	20,426,407
Other liabilities	45,896,786
Net income	26,210,359
Total	**2,719,725,241**

INTERNATIONAL OLYMPIC COMMITTEE

Address: Château de Vidy, 1007 Lausanne, Switzerland.
Telephone: 253271.
Telex: 454024.

The International Olympic Committee was founded in 1894 to ensure the regular celebration of the Olympic Games.

Organization
(October 1988)

INTERNATIONAL OLYMPIC COMMITTEE

The International Olympic Committee (IOC) is a non-governmental international organization comprising 91 members, who are representatives of the IOC in their countries and not their countries' delegates to the IOC. The members meet in session at least once a year.

The IOC is the final authority on all questions concerning the Olympic Games and the Olympic movement. There are 167 recognized National Olympic Committees, which are the sole authorities responsible for the representation of their respective countries at the Olympic Games. The IOC may give recognition to International Federations which undertake to adhere to the Olympic Charter, and which govern sports that comply with the IOC's criteria.

EXECUTIVE BOARD

The session of the IOC delegates to the Executive Board the authority to manage the IOC's affairs. The President of the Board is elected for an eight-year term, and is eligible for re-election for successive terms of four years. The Vice-Presidents are elected for four-year terms, and may be re-elected after a minimum interval of four years. Members of the Board are elected to hold office for four years.

President: JUAN ANTONIO SAMARANCH (Spain).
First Vice-President: BERTHOLD BEITZ (FRG).
Second Vice-President: Prince ALEXANDRE DE MÉRODE (Belgium).
Third Vice-President: RICHARD W. POUND (Canada).
Members of the Board:
Major SYLVIO DE MAGALHÃES PADILHA (Brazil).
Judge KÉBA MBAYE (Senegal).
HE ZHENLIANG (People's Republic of China).
MARC HODLER (Switzerland).
KEVAN GOSPER (Australia).
VITALY SMIRNOV (USSR).
CHIHARU IGAYA (Japan).

ADMINISTRATION

The administration of the IOC is under the authority of the Administrator and the Secretary-General, who are appointed by the Executive Board.
Administrator: RAYMOND GAFNER.
General Secretary: FRANÇOISE ZWEIFEL.

Activities

According to Rule 1 of the Olympic Charter, the aims of the Olympic movement are:

to promote the development of those physical and moral qualities which are the basis of sport,

to educate young people through sport in a spirit of better understanding between each other and of friendship, thereby helping to build a better and more peaceful world,

to spread the Olympic principles throughout the world, thereby creating international goodwill,

to bring together the athletes of the world in the great four-yearly sport festival, the Olympic Games.

THE GAMES OF THE OLYMPIAD

The Olympic Games take place during the first year of the Olympiad (period of four years) which they are to celebrate. They are the exclusive property of the IOC, which entrusts their organization to a host city seven years in advance.

1896	Athens	1952	Helsinki
1900	Paris	1956	Melbourne
1904	St Louis	1960	Rome
1908	London	1964	Tokyo
1912	Stockholm	1968	Mexico City
1920	Antwerp	1972	Munich
1924	Paris	1976	Montreal
1928	Amsterdam	1980	Moscow
1932	Los Angeles	1984	Los Angeles
1936	Berlin	1988	Seoul
1948	London	1992	Barcelona

The programme of the Games must include at least 15 of the total number of Olympic sports (sports governed by recognized International Federations and admitted to the Olympic programme by decision of the IOC at least six years before the Games). The Olympic summer sports are: archery, athletics, badminton (from 1992), basketball, boxing, canoeing, cycling, equestrian sports, fencing, football, gymnastics, handball, field hockey, judo, modern pentathlon, rowing, shooting, swimming, table tennis, tennis, volleyball, water polo, weight-lifting, wrestling, yachting.

OLYMPIC WINTER GAMES

The Olympic Winter Games comprise competitions in sports practised on snow and ice. From 1994 onwards, they are to be held in the second calendar year following that in which the Games of the Olympiad take place.

1924	Chamonix	1968	Grenoble
1928	St Moritz	1972	Sapporo
1932	Lake Placid	1976	Innsbruck
1936	Garmisch-Partenkirchen	1980	Lake Placid
1948	St Moritz	1984	Sarajevo
1952	Oslo	1988	Calgary
1956	Cortina d'Ampezzo	1992	Albertville
1960	Squaw Valley	1994	Lillehammer
1964	Innsbruck		

The Winter Games may include skiing, skating, ice hockey, bobsleigh, luge and biathlon.

THE INTERNATIONAL RED CROSS

The International Red Cross is a world-wide independent humanitarian organization, comprising two bodies working at an international level: one in time of armed conflict, the International Committee of the Red Cross (ICRC), founded in 1863; and the other in peace time, the League of Red Cross and Red Crescent Societies (LRCS), founded in 1919, and 146 National Red Cross and Red Crescent Societies working mainly at national level.

Organization

INTERNATIONAL CONFERENCE

The supreme deliberative body of the International Red Cross, the Conference comprises delegations from the ICRC, the League and the National Societies, and of representatives of States Parties to the Geneva Conventions (see below). The Conference's function is to determine the general policy of the Red Cross movement and to ensure unity in the work of the various bodies. It usually meets every four years, and is hosted by the National Society of the country in which it is held.

STANDING COMMISSION

The Commission meets twice a year in ordinary session, to coordinate the work of the ICRC and the League, and to prepare for the next International Conference. It is formed of two members from the ICRC, two from the League, and five elected by the Conference.

OTHER MEETINGS

The three Presidents of the Standing Commission, the ICRC and the League meet as a rule every six months, or as necessary. At least once a month a meeting is held between representatives of the ICRC and of the League.

Principles of the Red Cross

Humanity. The Red Cross endeavours to prevent and alleviate human suffering wherever it may be found, to protect life and health and to ensure respect for the human being.

Impartiality. It makes no discrimination as to nationality, race, religious beliefs, class or political opinions.

Neutrality. The Red Cross may not take sides in hostilities or engage in controversies of a political, racial, religious or ideological nature.

Independence. The National Societies, while auxiliaries in the humanitarian services of their governments and subject to national laws, must retain their autonomy so that they may always be able to act in accordance with Red Cross principles.

Voluntary Service. The Red Cross is a voluntary relief organization, not prompted by desire for gain.

Unity. There must be only one Red Cross Society in any one country, open to all.

Universality. The Red Cross is a world-wide organization in which all National Societies have equal status and share equal responsibilities and duties.

International Committee of the Red Cross—ICRC

Address: 17 avenue de la Paix, 1202 Geneva, Switzerland.
Telephone: (022) 346001.
Telex: 22269.

Organization
(October 1988)

INTERNATIONAL COMMITTEE

The ICRC is an independent institution of a private character. It is exclusively composed of Swiss nationals. Members are co-opted, and their total number may not exceed 25. The international character of the ICRC is based on its mission and not on its composition.

President: CORNELIO SOMMARUGA.
Vice-Presidents: MAURICE AUBERT, DENISE BINDSCHEDLER-ROBERT.

EXECUTIVE COUNCIL

The Executive Council meets weekly.
President: CORNELIO SOMMARUGA.
Members: MAURICE AUBERT, RICHARD PESTALOZZI, ATHOS GALLINO, RUDOLF JÄCKLI, PIERRE KELLER, ANDRÉ GHELFI.

DIRECTORATE

The Directorate is responsible for administration, in accordance with decisions taken by the International Committee, the Executive Council and the President. It was restructured in 1988 and comprises six departments: operations; operational support; principles and law and relations with the movement; finance and administration; human resources; communications. The ICRC employed about 3,600 people at mid-1988, of whom more than 80% were working in the field among its 44 delegations.
Director-General: (vacant).

Activities

The International Committee of the Red Cross was founded in 1863, in Geneva, by Henry Dunant and four of his friends. The original purpose of the Committee was to assist wounded soldiers on the battlefield. The present activities of the ICRC consist in giving legal protection and material assistance to military and civilian victims of wars (international wars, internal strife and disturbances).

The ICRC promoted the foundation in each country of the world of National Committees of the Red Cross, which later became the National Societies of the Red Cross (and National Societies of the Red Crescent in Islamic countries).

As well as providing medical aid and emergency food supplies in many countries, the ICRC plays an important part in inspecting prison conditions and in tracing missing persons. Examples of its activities include the following:

Africa: assistance for detainees and their families in southern Africa; food and medical aid in Angola, Chad, Ethiopia, Mozambique, Sudan and other countries; programmes for the rehabilitation of the disabled in several countries.

Latin America: relief activities, medical aid, visits to detainees, and a campaign to disseminate humanitarian principles in an attempt to protect non-combatants from violence.

Asia: medical assistance in Kampuchea and Thailand, visits to detainees in Afghanistan, Indonesia, Malaysia, the Philippines and Thailand; dealing with enquiries about missing relatives among refugees from Viet-Nam and Kampuchea; medical assistance programme for Afghan refugees in Pakistan; assistance in Timor.

Middle East: emergency action in Lebanon, providing medical supplies and evacuating the wounded and refugees; visits to prisoner-of-war camps in Iran and Iraq, and repatriation of prisoners following the cease-fire in the war between Iran and Iraq in 1988; exchanges of war-wounded.

THE GENEVA CONVENTIONS

In 1864, one year after its foundation, the ICRC submitted to the states called to a Diplomatic Conference in Geneva a draft international treaty for 'the Amelioration of the Condition of the Wounded in Armies in the Field'. This treaty was adopted and signed by twelve states, which thereby bind themselves to respect as neutral wounded soldiers and those assisting them. This was the first Geneva Convention.

With the development of technology and weapons, the introduction of new means of waging war, and the manifestation of certain phenomena (the great number of prisoners of war during World War I; the enormous number of displaced persons and refugees during World War II; the internationalization of internal conflicts in recent years) the necessity was felt of having other international treaties to protect new categories of war victims. The ICRC, for over 120 years now, has been the leader of a movement to improve and complement international humanitarian law.

There are now four Geneva Conventions, adopted on 12 August 1949: I—to protect wounded and sick in armed forces on land, as well as medical personnel; II—to protect the same categories of people at sea, as well as the shipwrecked; III—concerning the treatment of prisoners of war; IV—for the protection of civilians in time of war; and there are two Additional Protocols of 8 June 1977, for the protection of victims in international armed conflicts (Protocol I) and in non-international armed conflicts (Protocol II).

In October 1988, 165 states were parties to the Geneva Conventions; 76 were parties to Protocol I and 67 to Protocol II.

FINANCE

The ICRC's work is financed by a voluntary annual grant from governments parties to the Geneva Conventions, voluntary contributions from National Red Cross Societies and by gifts and legacies from private people. The ICRC's various budgets for 1988 amounted to some 500m. Swiss francs.

PERIODICALS AND PUBLICATIONS

International Review of the Red Cross (every 2 months, Arabic, French, English and Spanish editions; short edition *Extracts* in German).

ICRC Bulletin (monthly, French, English, Spanish and German editions).

Annual Report (editions in Arabic, English, French, German and Spanish).

The Geneva Conventions: texts and commentaries.

The Protocols Additional.

Various publications on humanitarian law and subjects of Red Cross interest.

League of Red Cross and Red Crescent Societies—LORCS

Address: 17 Chemin des Crêts, Petit-Saconnex, Case Postale 372, 1211 Geneva 19, Switzerland.
Telephone: (022) 345580.
Telex: 22555.

The League was founded in 1919. It is the world federation of all Red Cross and Red Crescent Societies. The general aim of the League is to inspire, encourage, facilitate and promote at all times all forms of humanitarian activities by the National Societies, with a view to the prevention and alleviation of human suffering, and thereby contribute to the maintenance and promotion of peace in the world.

MEMBERS

National Red Cross and Red Crescent Societies in 146 countries in October 1988, with an aggregate youth and adult membership of over 250m.

Organization
(October 1988)

GENERAL ASSEMBLY

The General Assembly is the highest authority of the League and meets every two years in commission sessions (for development, disaster relief, health and community services, and youth) and plenary sessions. It is composed of representatives from all National Societies that are members of the League.
President: Dr MARIO VILLARROEL LANDER (Venezuela).

EXECUTIVE COUNCIL

The Council, which meets every six months, is composed of the President of the League, nine Vice-Presidents and 16 National Societies elected by the Assembly. Its functions include the implementation of decisions of the General Assembly; it also has powers to act between meetings of the Assembly.

ASSEMBLY AND FINANCE COMMISSIONS

Development Commission.
Disaster Relief Commission.
Health and Community Services Commission.
Youth Commision.
Finance Commission.
Permanent Scale of Contributions Commission.

The Advisory Commissions meet, in principle, once every two years, at the same time as the General Assembly. Members are elected by the Assembly under a system that ensures each Society a seat on one Commission. The Finance Commission, which has seven members, meets twice a year, and the Permanent Scale of Contributions Commission, also with seven members, meets annually.

SECRETARIAT

Secretary General: PÄR STENBÄCK (Finland).
Treasurer-General: AL-MEHDI BENNOUNA (Morocco).

Activities

RELIEF

The Secretariat assumes the statutory responsibilities of the League in the field of relief to victims of natural disasters, refugees and civilian populations who may be displaced or exposed to abnormal hardship. This activity has three main aspects:

(i) Relief Operations: for the co-ordination of relief operations on the international level and execution by the National Society of the stricken country or by the League itself;

(ii) Supply, Logistics and Warehouses: for the co-ordination and purchase, transport and warehousing of relief supplies;

(iii) Disaster Preparedness: for co-ordination of assistance to National Societies situated in disaster-prone areas in the study and execution of practical measures calculated to prevent disasters and diminish their effects.

SERVICES TO NATIONAL SOCIETIES

The Secretariat promotes and co-ordinates assistance to National Societies in developing their basic structure and their services to the community. The Secretariat is equipped to advise Societies in the fields of health, social welfare, information, nursing, first aid and training; and the operation of blood programmes. It also promotes the establishment and development of educational and service programmes for children and youth.

The League maintains close relations with many inter-governmental organizations, the United Nations and its Specialized Agencies, and with non-governmental organizations, and represents member Societies in the international field.

FINANCE

The permanent secretariat of the League is financed by the contributions of Member Societies on a pro-rata basis. Each relief action is financed by separate, voluntary contributions, and development programme projects are also financed on a voluntary basis.

PUBLICATIONS

(in English, French and Spanish; the *Annual Review* and *Weekly News* also appear in Arabic)

Annual Review.
Red Cross Red Crescent (quarterly).
Weekly News.
Transfusion International (quarterly).

ISLAMIC DEVELOPMENT BANK

Address: POB 5925, Jeddah 21432, Saudi Arabia.
Telephone: 6361400.
Telex: 601137.

An international financial institution established following a conference of finance ministers of member countries of the Organization of the Islamic Conference (q.v.), held in Jeddah in December 1973. Its aim is to encourage economic development and social progress of member countries and Muslim communities, in accordance with the principles of the Islamic Shari'a (sacred law). The Bank formally opened in October 1975.

MEMBERS

There are 44 members (see table of subscriptions below).

Organization
(October 1988)

BOARD OF GOVERNORS

Each member country is represented by a governor, usually its Finance Minister, or an alternate. The Board of Governors is the Supreme Authority of the Bank, and meets annually.

BOARD OF EXECUTIVE DIRECTORS

The Board consists of 11 members, five of whom are appointed by the four largest subscribers to the capital stock of the Bank; the remaining six are elected by Governors representing the other subscribers. Members of the Board of Executive Directors are elected for three-year terms. The Board is responsible for the direction of the general operations of the Bank.

President of the Bank and Chairman of the Board of Executive Directors: Dr AHMAD MUHAMMAD ALI (Saudi Arabia).

FINANCIAL STRUCTURE

The authorized capital of the Bank is 2,000m. Islamic Dinars divided into 200,000 shares having a value of 10,000 Islamic Dinars each. The Islamic Dinar (ID) is the Bank's unit of account and is equivalent to the value of one Special Drawing Right of the IMF (SDR 1 = US $1.29313 at the end of August 1987).

At 24 August 1987 subscribed capital amounted to ID 1,958.37m., and paid-up capital was ID 1,602.12m.

SUBSCRIPTIONS (million Islamic Dinars, as at 24 August 1987)

Afghanistan	2.5	Morocco	12.6
Algeria	63.1	Niger	6.3
Bahrain	7.0	Oman	7.0
Bangladesh	25.0	Pakistan	63.1
Benin	2.5	Palestine Liberation Organization	5.0
Brunei	6.3		
Burkina Faso	6.3		
Cameroon	6.3	Qatar	50.0
Chad	2.5	Saudi Arabia	506.37
Comoros	2.5	Senegal	6.3
Djibouti	2.5	Sierra Leone	2.5
Egypt	25.0	Somalia	2.5
Gabon	7.5	Sudan	25.2
The Gambia	2.5	Syria	2.5
Guinea	6.3	Tunisia	5.0
Guinea-Bissau	6.3	Turkey	160.0
Indonesia	63.1	Uganda	6.3
Iraq	25.2	United Arab Emirates	194.7
Jordan	10.1		
Kuwait	252.2	Yemen Arab Republic	6.3
Lebanon	2.5		
Libya	315.3	Yemen, People's Democratic Republic	6.3
Malaysia	40.4		
Maldives	2.5		
Mali	2.5	**Total**	**1,958.37**
Mauritania	2.5		

Activities

The Bank adheres to the Islamic principle forbidding usury, and does not grant loans or credits for interest. Instead, its methods of financing are: provision of interest-free loans (with a service fee) mainly for infrastructural projects which are expected to have a marked impact on long-term socio-economic development; provision of technical assistance (e.g. for feasibility studies); equity participation in industrial and agro-industrial projects; leasing operations, involving the leasing of equipment such as ships, and instalment sale financing; and profit-sharing operations. Funds not immediately needed for projects are used for foreign trade financing, particularly for importing commodities to be used in development (i.e. raw materials and intermediate industrial goods, rather than consumer goods); priority is given to the import of goods from other member countries (see table). In addition, the Special Assistance Account provides emergency aid and other assistance, with particular emphasis on education in Islamic communities in non-member countries.

By August 1987 the Bank had approved a total of ID 1,565.3m. for project financing and technical assistance, and a total of ID 4,354.8m. for foreign trade financing. During the Islamic year 1407, from 5 September 1986 to 24 August 1987, the Bank approved a total of ID 587.3m. for 101 operations (excluding those covered by the Special Assistance Account), compared with ID 740.7m. for 93 projects in the previous year. The decrease reflected restrictions on borrowing imposed on some member countries by their economic difficulties. Of financing approved in the year to 24 August 1987 (excluding the Special Assistance Account), 23% was for ordinary operations and 77% for foreign trade financing.

The Bank approved 11 interest-free loans in the year ending 24 August 1987, amounting to ID 36.08m. (compared with seven loans of ID 28.27m. in the previous year). These loans supported the following projects: reconstruction of Cotonou port, Benin; petroleum storage in the Comoros; road-building in The Gambia and the Yemen Arab Republic; primary education in rural areas of Guinea; building schools in Maldives and Niger; a dam in Morocco;

Operations approved, 5 September 1986–24 August 1987

Type of operation	Number of operations	Total amount (milllion Islamic Dinars)
Ordinary operations	48	134.22
Project financing	24	128.16
Loan	11	36.08
Equity	1	0.75
Leasing	1*	10.00
Profit-sharing	—	—
Instalment sales	11	81.34
Technical assistance	24	6.06
Foreign trade financing	53	453.03
Operations financed from the Special Assistance Account	12	9.12
Total	**113**	**596.44**

* A combined equity and leasing operation.

Project financing and technical assistance by sector, 5 September 1986–24 August 1987

Sector	Amount (million Islamic Dinars)	%
Agriculture	25.77	19.2
Industry and mining	19.51	14.6
Transport and communications	36.06	26.9
Utilities	30.91	23.0
Social services	11.22	8.4
Other	10.75	8.0
Total	**134.22**	**100.0**

railway improvements in Pakistan; rice-growing in Senegal; and the Middle East Technical University, Turkey. During the same year the Bank approved only one equity project and one combined line of equity and leasing. Instalment sale financing was approved for 11 projects and amounted to ID 81.34m.

The Bank approved 24 technical assistance operations during the year, amounting to ID 6.06m., of which about 38% was in the form of grants.

Nineteen member countries are among the world's least-developed countries (as designated by the United Nations). During the year 67.5% of loan financing was directed to these countries.

Foreign trade financing approved during the year amounted to ID 453.03m. for 53 operations in 12 member countries: of this amount 49% was for imports of crude petroleum, 28% for intermediate industrial goods, and 6% for vegetable oil.

Under the Bank's Special Assistance Account, 12 operations were approved during the year, amounting to ID 9.12m., mostly for Islamic education centres. Implementation of a special programme of emergency aid to Sahelian member countries suffering from drought (approved two years previously, at a cost of ID 49m.) continued during the year. The Bank's scholarships programme sponsored 223 students from 16 countries during the year to 24 August 1987. The Bank also undertakes the distribution of meat sacrificed by Muslim pilgrims: during the year meat from 478,994 head of sheep was distributed to the needy in 19 member countries.

Disbursements during the year ending 24 August 1987 totalled ID 523.92m. (compared with ID 557.16m. in the previous year). Of this total ID 89m. was for project financing and technical assistance, and ID 427.83m. was for foreign trade financing, while ID 7.1m. was provided from the Special Assistance Account.

RESEARCH AND TRAINING INSTITUTE

Islamic Research and Training Institute: POB 9201, Jeddah 21413, Saudi Arabia; tel. 6361400; telex 601407; f. 1982 for research enabling economic, financial and banking activities to conform to Islamic law, and to provide training for staff involved in development activities in the Bank's member countries.

PUBLICATION

Annual Report.

LATIN AMERICAN INTEGRATION ASSOCIATION—LAIA

(ASOCIACIÓN LATINOAMERICANA DE INTEGRACIÓN—ALADI)

Address: Cebollatí 1461, Casilla 577, Montevideo, Uruguay.
Telephone: 40 11 21-28.
Telex: 26944.

The Latin American Integration Association was established in August 1980 to replace the Latin American Free Trade Association, set up in February 1960.

MEMBERS

Argentina	Colombia	Peru
Bolivia	Ecuador	Uruguay
Brazil	Mexico	Venezuela
Chile	Paraguay	

Observers: Costa Rica, Cuba, Dominican Republic, El Salvador, Guatemala, Honduras, Italy, Nicaragua, Panama, Portugal and Spain; also the UN Economic Commission for Latin America and the Caribbean (ECLAC), the UN Development Programme (UNDP), the Inter-American Development Bank and the Organization of American States.

Organization
(October 1988)

COUNCIL OF MINISTERS

The Council of Ministers of Foreign Affairs is responsible for the adoption of the Association's policies. It meets when convened by the Committee of Representatives.

EVALUATION AND CONVERGENCE CONFERENCE

The Conference, comprising plenipotentiaries of the member governments, assesses the Association's progress and encourages negotiations betwen members. It meets when convened by the Committee of Representatives.

COMMITTEE OF REPRESENTATIVES

The Committee, the permanent political body of the Association, comprises a permanent and a deputy representative from each member country, and, by mid-1988, 15 permanent observers (see above). Its task is to ensure the correct implementation of the Treaty and its supplementary regulations. There are six auxiliary bodies:

Council for Financial and Monetary Affairs: comprises the Presidents of member states' central banks, who examine all aspects of financial, monetary and exchange co-operation.
Advisory Commission on Financial and Monetary Affairs.
Meeting of Directors of National Customs Administrations.
Council on Transport for Trade Facilitation.
Advisory Council for Export Financing.
Tourism Council.

SECRETARIAT

The Secretariat is the technical body of the Association; it submits proposals for action, carries out research and follows the progress of activities. The Secretary-General is appointed for a three-year term.

Secretary-General: NORBERTO BERTAINA (Argentina).
Deputy Secretaries-General: JAIME QUIJANDRÍA (Peru), RENÉ JORDÁN (Bolivia).

Activities

The Latin American Free Trade Association (LAFTA) was an intergovernmental organization, created by the Treaty of Montevideo in February 1960 with the object of increasing trade between the Contracting Parties and of promoting regional integration, thus contributing to the economic and social development of the member countries. The Treaty provided for the gradual establishment of a free trade area, which would form the basis for a Latin American Common Market. Reduction of tariff and other trade barriers was to be carried out gradually up to 1980.

This scheme, however, made little progress. By 1980 only 14% of annual trade among members could be attributed to LAFTA agreements, and it was the richest states which were receiving most benefit. In June 1980 it was decided that LAFTA should be replaced by a less ambitious and more flexible organization, the Latin American Integration Association (LAIA), established by the 1980 Montevideo Treaty, which came into force in March 1981, and was fully ratified in March 1982. Instead of across-the-board tariff cuts, the Treaty envisaged an area of economic preferences, comprising a regional tariff preference for goods originating in member states (in effect from 1 July 1984) and regional and partial scope agreements (on economic complementation, trade promotion, trade in agricultural goods, scientific and technical co-operation, the environment, tourism, and other matters), taking into account the different stages of development of the members, and with no definite timetable for the establishment of a full common market.

The members of LAIA are divided into three categories: most developed (Argentina, Brazil and Mexico); intermediate (Chile, Colombia, Peru, Uruguay and Venezuela); and least developed (Bolivia, Ecuador and Paraguay), enjoying a special preferential system. By the end of 1983 the transition from LAFTA to LAIA had been completed with the renegotiation of over 23,000 tariff cuts granted among the partners from 1962 onwards. During 1981 the value of exports within LAIA accounted for 13% of member countries' total exports; the proportion fell to 8.1% in 1985, and stood at 11.6% in 1986 and 10.3% in 1987.

Certain LAFTA institutions were retained and adapted by LAIA, e.g. the Reciprocal Payments and Credits Agreement (1965, modified in 1982) and the Multilateral Credit Agreement to Alleviate Temporary Shortages of Liquidity, known as the Santo Domingo Agreement (1969, extended in 1981 to include mechanisms for counteracting global balance-of-payments difficulties and for assisting in times of natural disaster).

A feature of LAIA is its 'outward' projection, allowing for multilateral links or agreements with Latin American non-member countries or integration organizations. Likewise, the Treaty contemplates partial agreements with other developing countries or economic groups outside the continent.

By mid-1988 the following agreements had entered into force: 34 renegotiation agreements (concerning the former LAFTA tariff cuts); 23 trade agreements (mostly on the basis of former LAFTA industrial complementation pacts); 11 economic complementation agreements; one agricultural agreement; one agreement on tourism; 18 agreements with Latin American non-member countries; three regional market-opening agreements in favour of the least developed members; an agreement on the regional tariff preference; and a regional agreement for the recovery and expansion of intra-LAIA trade. A new system of tariff nomenclature was adopted from 1 January 1986 as a basis for common trade negotiations.

The Secretariat convenes meetings of entrepreneurs in various private industrial sectors, to encourage regional trade and co-operation. There were 15 such meetings in 1987, and 22 were planned for 1988.

A regional round of negotiations was launched by LAIA members in April 1986, aiming to develop a renewed preferential trade and payments system in the region, open to the participation of Latin American non-member countries. The agenda comprised four main fields of negotiation: trade expansion and regulation; co-operation and economic complementarity; payments and export financing; and preferential measures for the less-developed members. In early 1987 multilateral programmes were approved for the elimination of non-tariff barriers, the recovery and expansion of intra-LAIA trade and for alleviating trade imbalances between partners; new rules on origin and safeguards were also approved.

PUBLICATIONS

Síntesis ALADI (monthly, in Spanish).

Newsletter (6 a year, in English).

Ambito Empresarial (monthly for entrepreneurs, in Portuguese and Spanish).

Reports, studies, texts of agreements, and trade statistics.

LEAGUE OF ARAB STATES

Address: 37 avenue Khereddine Pacha, Tunis, Tunisia.
Telephone: 890 100.
Telex: 13241.

The League of Arab States (more generally known as the Arab League) is a voluntary association of sovereign Arab states designed to strengthen the close ties linking them and to co-ordinate their policies and activities and direct them towards the common good of all the Arab countries. It was founded in March 1945 (see Pact of the League, p. 174).

MEMBERS

Algeria	Palestine†
Bahrain	Qatar
Djibouti	Saudi Arabia
Egypt*	Somalia
Iraq	Sudan
Jordan	Syria
Kuwait	Tunisia
Lebanon	United Arab Emirates
Libya	Yemen Arab Republic
Mauritania	Yemen, People's Democratic Republic
Morocco	
Oman	

* In March 1979 Egypt's membership of the Arab League was suspended, and it was decided to make Tunis the temporary headquarters of the League, its Secretariat and its permanent committees.
† Palestine is considered an independent state, as explained in the Charter Annex on Palestine, and therefore a full member of the League.

Organization
(October 1988)

COUNCIL

The supreme organ of the Arab League. Consists of representatives of the 21 member states, each of which has one vote, and a representative for Palestine. Unanimous decisions of the Council shall be binding upon all member states of the League; majority decisions shall be binding only on those states which have accepted them.

The Council may, if necessary, hold an extraordinary session at the request of two member states. Invitations to all sessions are extended by the Secretary-General. The ordinary sessions are presided over by representatives of the member states in turn.

Sixteen committees are attached to the Council:

Political Committee: studies political questions and reports to the Council meetings concerned with them. All member states are members of the Committee. It represents the Council in dealing with critical political matters when the Council is meeting. Usually composed of the foreign ministers.

Cultural Committee: in charge of following up the activities of the Cultural Department and the cultural affairs within the scope of the secretariat; co-ordinates the activities of the general secretariat and the various cultural bodies in member states.

Economic Committee: complemented by the Economic Council since 1953.

Communications Committee: supervises land, sea and air communications, together with weather forecasts and postal matters.

Social Committee: supports co-operation in such matters as family and child welfare.

Legal Committee: an extension of the Nationality and Passports Committee abolished in 1947; studies and legally formulates draft agreements, bills, regulations and official documents.

Arab Oil Experts Committee: for study of oil affairs; also investigates methods to prevent the smuggling of Arab oil into Israel; and for co-ordination of oil policies in general.

Information Committee: studies information projects, suggests plans and carries out the policies decided by the Council of Information Ministers.

Health Committee: for co-operation in health affairs.

Human Rights Committee: studies subjects concerning human rights, particularly violations by Israel; collaborates with the Information and Cultural Committees.

Permanent Committee for Administrative and Financial Affairs.

Permanent Committee for Meteorology.

Committee of Arab Experts on Co-operation.

Arab Women's Committee.

Organization of Youth Welfare.

Conference of Liaison Officers: co-ordinates trade activities among commercial attachés of various Arab embassies abroad.

The Arab League maintains a permanent office at the United Nations in New York, and has observer status at the UN General Assembly.

GENERAL SECRETARIAT

The administrative and financial offices of the League. The Secretariat carries out the decisions of the Council, and provides financial and administrative services for the personnel of the League. There are a number of departments: economic, political, legal, cultural, social and labour affairs, petroleum, finance, Palestine, health, information, communications, protocol. The most recently formed department deals with African affairs.

The Secretary-General is appointed by the League Council by a two-thirds majority of the member states, for a five-year term. He appoints the assistant Secretaries-General and principal officials, with the approval of the Council. He has the rank of ambassador, and the assistant Secretaries-General have the rank of ministers plenipotentiary.

Secretary General: CHEDLI KLIBI (Tunisia).
Assistant Secretaries-General:

Arab Affairs: ASAAD AL-ASSAAD (Lebanon).

Economic Affairs: Dr ABD AL-HASSAN ZALZALAH (Iraq).

Political, Financial and Administrative Affairs: ADNAN OMRAN (Syria).

Legal Affairs and Palestine Affairs: Dr MUHAMMAD AL-FARRA (Jordan).

Special Affairs: LAKHDAR AL-IBRAHIMI (Algeria).

Social and Cultural Affairs, Technical Assistance Fund: MAHDHI MUSTAFA AL-HADI (Sudan).

DEFENCE AND ECONOMIC CO-OPERATION

Groups established under the Treaty of Joint Defence and Economic Co-operation, concluded in 1950 to complement the Charter of the League.

Arab Unified Military Command: f. 1964 to co-ordinate military policies for the liberation of Palestine.

Economic Council: to compare and co-ordinate the economic policies of the member states; the Council is composed of ministers of economic affairs or their deputies. Decisions are taken by majority vote. The first meeting was held in 1953.

Joint Defence Council: supervises implementation of those aspects of the treaty concerned with common defence. Composed of foreign and defence ministers; decisions by a two-thirds majority vote of members are binding on all.

Permanent Military Commission: established 1950; composed of representatives of army general staffs; main purpose: to draw up plans of joint defence for submission to the Joint Defence Council.

ARAB DETERRENT FORCE

Set up in June 1976 by the Arab League Council to supervise successive attempts to cease hostilities in Lebanon, and afterwards to maintain the peace. The mandate of the Force has been successively renewed. The Arab League Summit Conference in October 1976 agreed that costs were to be paid in the following percentage contributions: Saudi Arabia and Kuwait 20% each, United Arab Emirates 15%, Qatar 10% and other Arab states 35%.

OTHER INSTITUTIONS OF THE COUNCIL

Other bodies established by resolutions adopted by the Council of the League:

INTERNATIONAL ORGANIZATIONS
League of Arab States

Academy of Arab Music: POB 6150, Baghdad, Iraq; tel. 552 15 37; Sec.-Gen. MUNIR BASHIR.

Administrative Tribunal of the Arab League: f. 1964; began operations 1966.

Special Bureau for Boycotting Israel: POB 437, Damascus, Syria.

SPECIALIZED ORGANIZATIONS

All member states of the Arab League are also members of the Specialized Agencies, which constitute an integral part of the Arab League. (See also chapters on the Arab Bank for Economic Development in Africa, the Arab Fund for Economic and Social Development, the Arab Monetary Fund, the Council of Arab Economic Unity and the Organization of Arab Petroleum Exporting Countries.)

Arab Academy of Maritime Transport: POB 1552, Sharjah, United Arab Emirates; tel. 358866; telex 68167; f. 1975. Dir-Gen. MUSTAFA WAJIH TAYARA.

Arab Centre for the Study of Arid Zones and Dry Lands (ACSAD): POB 2440, Damascus, Syria; tel. 755713; telex 412697; f. 1971 to conduct regional research and development programmes related to water and soil resources, plant and animal production, agro-meteorology, and socio-economic studies of arid zones. The Centre holds conferences and training courses and encourages the exchange of information by Arab scientists. Dir-Gen. MUHAMMAD EL-KHASH.

Arab Civil Aviation Council: POB 4410, 17 Al-Nasr St, Rabat, Morocco; tel. 74178; telex 32817; created 1965, began operations 1967; aims to develop the principles, techniques and economics of air transport in the Arab world; to co-operate with the International Civil Aviation Organization and to attempt to standardize laws and technical terms; also deals with Arab air rates. Pres. N. AL-KHANI. Publs *Air Transport Activities in Arab Countries, Lexicon of Civil Aviation Terminology* (Arabic); *Unified Air Law for Arab States* (Arabic and English).

Arab Fund for Technical Assistance to African and Arab Countries—AFTAAAC: 37 ave Khereddine Pacha, Tunis, Tunisia; tel. 890 100; telex 13242; f. 1975 to provide technical assistance for development projects by providing African and Arab experts, grants for scholarships and training, and finance for technical studies. Exec. Sec. MAHDI MUSTAFA AL-HADI.

Arab Industrial Development Organization: POB 3156, Al-Sa'adoun, Baghdad, Iraq; tel. 7184655; telex 2823; f. 1980; conducts sectoral studies on the situation and prospects of Arab industry, assists national industrial surveys, and provides consultation and training services. Dir-Gen. HATEM ABD AR-RASHEED. Publs *Bulletin, Journal of Arab Industrial Development* (in Arabic), reports and studies.

Arab Labour Organization: Sa'adoun Ave, POB 3237, Baghdad, Iraq; tel. 96191; telex 212746; established in 1965 for co-operation between member states in labour problems; unification of labour legislation and general conditions of work wherever possible; research; technical assistance; social insurance; training, etc.; the organization has a tripartite structure: governments, employers and workers. Dir-Gen. HASHEMI AL-BANANI. Publs *Bulletin* (monthly), *Arab Labour Review* (quarterly).

Arab League Educational, Cultural and Scientific Organization—ALECSO: BP 1120, ave Mohamed V, Tunis, Tunisia; tel. 784-466; telex 13825; f. 1970 to promote and co-ordinate educational, cultural and scientific activities in the Arab region. Dir-Gen. Dr MOHEDDINE SABER. Publs *Arab Journal of Language Studies, Arab Journal of Information, Arab Journal of Educational Research, Arab Journal of Culture, Arab Journal of Science, Arab Educational Statistical Bulletin, Yearbook of Science, Yearbook of Arab Culture.*

Arab Organization for Agricultural Development: 4 El Jamea St, POB 474, Khartoum, Sudan; tel. 78760; telex 22554; f. 1970 to contribute to co-operation in agricultural activities, and in the development of natural and human resources for agriculture; compiles data, conducts studies, training and food security programmes; has regional offices in eight countries; includes Arab Forestry and Pastures Institute, Syria. Dir-Gen. Dr HASSAN FAHMI JUMAH.

Arab Organization for Standardization and Metrology: POB 926161, Amman, Jordan; tel. 663834; telex 22463; began activity in 1968 to co-ordinate standards and metrology in the Arab states, and standardize methods of analysis and testing of products; sponsors seminars and training courses in standardization, metrology, and quality control; has 33 technical committees in 18 Arab countries; runs an Arab Centre for Information and Documentation; assists in the establishment of national bodies and collaborates with international standards activities. Sec.-Gen. Dr MAHDI H. HNOOSH. Publs *Annual Report* (Arabic and English), *Standardization* (10 a year, Arabic, English and French).

Arab Organization of Administrative Sciences: POB 17159, Amman, Jordan; tel. 814118; telex 21594; f. 1969 to improve Arab administrative systems, develop Arab administrative organizations and enhance the capabilities of Arab civil servants, through training, consultancy research and documentation. Dir-Gen. Dr NASSIR AL-SAIGH. Publs *Arab Journal of Administration* (quarterly), research series.

Arab Postal Union: POB 7999, Dubai, United Arab Emirates; tel. 690508; telex 46284; f. 1952; aims to establish more strict postal relations between the Arab countries than those laid down by the Universal Postal Union, to pursue the development and modernization of postal services in member countries. Sec.-Gen. HUSSEIN AL-HAMDANI. Publ. *Review* (quarterly).

Arab Satellite Communication Organization—ASCO: POB 1038, Riyadh, Saudi Arabia; tel. 464 6666; telex 201300; plans ARABSAT project, under which the first satellite was launched in February 1985, for the improvement of telephone, telex, data transmission and radio and television in Arab countries. Dir-Gen. ABD AL-KADER BAIRI.

Arab States Broadcasting Union—ASBU: POB 65, 17 rue el-Mensoura, el-Mensah 4, Tunis 1014, Tunisia; tel. 238 044; telex 13398; f. 1969 to promote Arab fraternity, co-ordinate and study broadcasting subjects, to exchange expertise and technical co-operation in broadcasting; conducts training and audience research. Mems: 21 Arab radio and TV stations and six foreign associates. Sec.-Gen. ABDALLAH CHAKROUN. Publ. *ASBU Review* (every 2 months).

Arab Telecommunications Union: POB 2397, Baghdad, Iraq; tel. 776-1713; telex 212007; f. 1953 to co-ordinate and develop telecommunications between the 21 member countries; to exchange technical aid and encourage research. Sec.-Gen. ABDUL JABBAR HASSAN KHALAF IBRAHIM AL-ANI. Publs *Economic and Technical Studies; Arab Telecommunications Union Journal* (quarterly).

Council of Arab Ministers of the Interior: POB 490, Hashad, Tunis, Tunisia; tel. 237320; telex 14887; f. 1983 to reinforce internal security and combat crime; Sec.-Gen. Dr AKRAM NASHA'T.

Arab Bureau for Narcotics: POB 17225, Amman, Jordan; tel. 813012; telex 21020; f. 1961 to supervise anti-drug campaigns and co-ordinate efforts to prevent the illegal production and smuggling of drugs.

Arab Bureau for Prevention of Crime: POB 5687, Baghdad, Iraq.

Arab Bureau of Criminal Police: Immeuble Union Sportive, ave Mayssaloume, Damascus, Syria.

Inter-Arab Investment Guarantee Corporation: POB 23568, Safat 13096, Kuwait; tel. 2542011; telex 22562-46312; f. 1975; insures Arab investors for non-commercial risks, and export credits for commercial and non-commercial risks; authorized capital 25m. Kuwaiti dinars (Dec. 1987). Mems: 22 Arab governments. Dir-Gen. MAMOUN I. HASSAN. Publ. *News Bulletin* (monthly), *Arab Investment Climate Report* (annually).

External Relations

ARAB LEAGUE OFFICES AND INFORMATION CENTRES ABROAD

Set up by the Arab League to co-ordinate work at all levels among Arab embassies abroad.

Argentina: Avda 3 de Febrero 1358, 1426 Buenos Aires.

Austria: Grimmelshausengasse 12, 1030 Vienna.

Belgium: 106 ave Franklin D. Roosevelt, 1050 Brussels.

Brazil: Shis-Qi 15, Conj. 7, Casa 23, 71600 Brasília, DF.

Canada: 170 Laurier Ave West, Suite 709, Ottawa K1P 5VP.

Ethiopia: POB 5768, Addis Ababa.

France: 114 blvd Malesherbes, 75017 Paris.

Federal Republic of Germany: Friedrich Wilhelm Str. 2A, 5300 Bonn 1.

Greece: 10 Antheon St, Palaio Psychico, Athens.

India: 61 Golf Links, New Delhi 110003.

Italy: Piazzale delle Belle Arti 6, 00196 Rome.

Japan: 1-1-12 Moto Asabu, Minato-ku, Tokyo 106.

Kenya: POB 30770, Nairobi.

Mexico: Monte Altai 524, Lomas de Chapultepec, 11000 México, DF.

Netherlands: Lange Voorhout 12, 2514 ED The Hague.

Senegal: 41 rue el-Hadji Amadou, Assane Ndoye, Dakar.

Switzerland: 9 rue du Valais, 1202 Geneva.

United Kingdom: 52 Green St, London W1Y 3RH.

INTERNATIONAL ORGANIZATIONS   *League of Arab States*

USA: 747 Third Ave, New York, NY 10017; 1100 17th St, NW, Suite 901, Washington, DC 20036; and in Chicago, Dallas and San Francisco.

Record of Events

1945 Pact of the Arab League signed, March.

1946 Cultural Treaty signed.

1950 Joint Defence and Economic Co-operation Treaty.

1952 Agreements on extradition, writs and letters of request, nationality of Arabs outside their country of origin.

1953 Formation of Economic Council.
Convention on the privileges and immunities of the League.

1954 Nationality Agreement.

1956 Agreement on the adoption of a Common Tariff Nomenclature.
Sudan joined Arab League.

1961 Kuwait joined League.
Syrian Arab Republic rejoined League as independent member.

1962 Arab Economic Unity Agreement.

1964 First Summit Conference of Arab kings and presidents, Cairo, January.
First session of the Council of Arab information ministers, Cairo, March.
First meeting of Economic Unity Council, June. Arab Common Market approved by Arab Economic Unity Council, August.
Second Summit Conference welcomed establishment of Palestine Liberation Organization (PLO), September.
First Conference of Arab ministers of communications, Beirut, November.

1965 Arab Common Market established, January.

1969 Fifth Summit Conference, Rabat. Call for mobilization of all Arab Nations against Israel.

1971 Bahrain, Qatar and Oman admitted to Arab League, September.

1973 Mauritania admitted to Arab League, December.

1974 Somalia admitted to Arab League, February.

1977 Djibouti admitted to membership, September.
Tripoli Declaration, December. Decision of Algeria, Iraq, Libya and Yemen PDR to boycott League meetings in Egypt in response to President Sadat's visit to Israel.

1978 69th meeting of Arab League Council in Cairo, March, boycotted by 'rejectionist' states. Resolutions calling for an emergency summit to settle differences within the League and for the establishment of an Arab Solidarity Committee to be chaired by President Nimeri of Sudan. All members except Egypt were present at a Council meeting in Baghdad in November. A number of resolutions were adopted to be taken should Egypt sign a peace treaty with Israel of which the three principal ones were: diplomatic rupture with Egypt, transfer of the League's headquarters from Cairo, and the economic boycott of Sadat's Government.

1979 Council meeting in Baghdad, March: various resolutions were adopted of which the main points were: to withdraw Arab ambassadors from Egypt; to recommend severance of political and diplomatic relations with Egypt; to suspend Egypt's membership of the League on the date of the signing of the peace treaty with Israel; to make the city of Tunis the temporary HQ of the League, its Secretariat, ministerial councils and permanent technical committees; to condemn United States' policy regarding its role in concluding the Camp David agreements and the peace treaty; to halt all bank loans, deposits, guarantees or facilities, as well as all financial or technical contributions and aid to Egypt; to prohibit trade exchanges with the Egyptian state and with private establishments dealing with Israel.

1980 Meeting of Arab foreign and economic ministers (as the Arab Economic and Social Council), Amman, July. An Iraqi plan for investment of at least $10,000m. over 10 years, to aid development in poorer Arab states (particularly Djibouti, Mauritania, Somalia, Sudan and the two Yemens), was discussed. The November Summit Conference in Amman was boycotted by the Palestine Liberation Organization, Algeria, Lebanon, Libya, Syria and the People's Democratic Republic of Yemen, maintaining that the conference should have been postponed because of the serious differences in the Arab world over the Iran-Iraq war and the approach to negotiations on Israel. The Summit Conference agreed to set up a $5,000m. fund for the benefit of poorer Arab states, with Iraq, Kuwait, Qatar, Saudi Arabia and the United Arab Emirates as donors: assistance was to take the form of 20-year development loans, and the fund was to be administered by the Arab Fund for Social and Economic Development (q.v.). The conference also approved a wider 'Strategy for Joint Arab Economic Action', covering pan-Arab development planning up to the year 2000.

1981 In March the Council of Ministers set up a conciliation mission to try to improve relations between Morocco and Mauritania.
Extraordinary meeting of Arab foreign ministers in May (on Lebanon), and June (following the Israeli attack on an Iraqi nuclear reactor).
Twelfth Summit Conference, Fez, Morocco, November. The meeting was suspended after a few hours, following disagreement over a Saudi Arabian proposal known as the Fahd Plan, which includes not only the Arab demands on behalf of the Palestinians, as approved by the UN General Assembly, but also an implied *de facto* recognition of Israel.

1982 In February the conference of Arab ministers set up a ministerial commission to consider retaliatory measures against states supporting Israel.
Second Arab Energy Conference held in Qatar, March.
Twelfth Summit Conference reconvened, Fez, September: peace plan, similar to the Fahd Plan mentioned above, adopted. The plan demanded Israel's withdrawal from territories occupied in 1967, and removal of Israeli settlements in these areas; freedom of worship for all religions in the sacred places; the right of the Palestinian people to self-determination, under the leadership of the Palestine Liberation Organization; temporary UN supervision for the West Bank and the Gaza Strip; the creation of an independent Palestinian state, with Jerusalem as its capital; and a guarantee of peace for all the states of the region by the UN Security Council. An Arab League delegation, led by King Hussein of Jordan, subsequently visited Washington, Paris, Moscow and Beijing seeking support for the peace plan.

1983 The summit meeting due to be held in November was postponed owing to members' differences of opinion concerning Syria's opposition to Yasser Arafat's chairmanship of the PLO, and Syrian support of Iran in the war against Iraq.

1984 In March an emergency meeting established an Arab League committee to encourage international efforts to bring about a negotiated settlement of the Iran-Iraq war. In May ministers of foreign affairs adopted a resolution calling on Iran to stop attacking non-belligerent ships and installations in the Gulf region: similar attacks by Iraq were not mentioned.

1985 The Third Arab Energy Conference, sponsored by the Arab League and OAPEC, was held in Algeria in May. In August an emergency Summit Conference was boycotted by Algeria, Lebanon, Libya, Syria and the People's Democratic Republic of Yemen, while of the other 16 members only nine were represented by their heads of state. The conference reaffirmed its support for the peace plan adopted in 1982 (see above), but was non-committal on proposals made by Jordan and the Palestine Liberation Organization, envisaging eventual talks with Israel on Palestinian rights. Two commissions were set up to mediate in disagreements between Arab states (between Jordan and Syria, Iraq and Syria, Iraq and Libya, and Libya and the PLO).

1986 Proposals to hold an emergency summit meeting in May, in response to the US bombing of Libyan cities in April, were unsuccessful. In July King Hassan of Morocco announced that he was resigning as chairman of the next League Summit Conference (for which no date had yet been fixed), after criticism by several Arab leaders of his meeting with the Israeli Prime Minister earlier that month. In August it was announced that more than one-half of the League's members were in arrears with their contributions to the annual budget of some US $30m., and that a financial crisis was imminent. A ministerial meeting held in October condemned any attempt at direct negotiation with Israel, and reiterated that an international conference convened by the United Nations would be the only acceptable means of bringing about a peaceful settlement in the Middle East. In December a special ministerial committee was created to attempt to stop the fighting for control of the Palestinian refugee camps in Lebanon between Palestinian guerrillas and the Shi'ite Amal militia.

1987 In April the Council demanded that Iran should accept a settlement of the conflict with Iraq by peaceful means, in compliance with the UN Charter. In August the Council agreed on a resolution criticizing Iran for persisting in its hostilities against Iraq and for making threats against the Gulf states, and hinted that a break in member states' diplomatic relations with Iran might take place. An extraordinary Summit Conference was held in November, mainly to discuss the war between Iran and Iraq. Contrary to expectations, the participants (including President Assad of Syria) unanimously agreed on a statement expressing support for Iraq in its defence of its legitimate rights, and condemning Iran for its aggression against Iraq and for its procrastination in accepting the UN Security Council resolution No. 598 of July 1987, which had recommended a cease-fire in the Iran-Iraq war and negotiations on a settlement of the conflict. The meeting also stated that the resumption of diplomatic relations with Egypt was a matter to be decided by individual states.

1988 In June a Summit Conference was held in Algiers to discuss the seven-month uprising by Palestinians in Israeli-occupied territories. The meeting agreed to provide finance for the PLO to continue the uprising. It reiterated the Arab League's demand for an international conference, attended by the PLO, to seek to bring about a peaceful settlement in the Middle East (thereby implicitly rejecting recent proposals by the US Government for a conference that would exclude the PLO). At the conference, the leaders of Algeria, Libya. Mauritania, Morocco and Tunisia met informally to discuss the formation of a Maghreb regional grouping.

PUBLICATIONS

Sh'oun Arabiyya (Journal of Arab Affairs, monthly).
Information Bulletin (Arabic and English).
Bulletins of treaties and agreements concluded among the member states.
New York Office: *Arab World* (monthly), and *News and Views*.
Geneva Office: *Le Monde Arabe* (monthly), and *Nouvelles du Monde Arabe* (weekly).
Buenos Aires Office: *Arabia Review* (monthly).
Paris Office: *Actualités Arabes* (fortnightly).
Brasília Office: *Oriente Arabe* (monthly).
Rome Office: *Rassegna del Mondo Arabo* (monthly).
London Office: *The Arab* (monthly).
New Delhi Office: *Al Arab* (monthly).
Bonn Office: *Arabische Korrespondenz* (fortnightly).
Ottawa Office: *Spotlight on the Arab World* (fortnightly), *The Arab Case* (monthly).

The Pact of the League of Arab States

(22 March 1945)

Article 1. The League of Arab States is composed of the independent Arab States which have signed this Pact.

Any independent Arab state has the right to become a member of the League. If it desires to do so, it shall submit a request which will be deposited with the Permanent Secretariat-General and submitted to the Council at the first meeting held after submission of the request.

Article 2. The League has as its purpose the strengthening of the relations between the member states; the co-ordination of their policies in order to achieve co-operation between them and to safeguard their independence and sovereignty; and a general concern with the affairs and interests of the Arab countries. It has also as its purpose the close co-operation of the member states, with due regard to the organization and circumstances of each state, on the following matters:

(a) Economic and financial affairs, including commercial relations, customs, currency, and questions of agriculture and industry.
(b) Communications: this includes railways, roads, aviation, navigation, telegraphs and posts.
(c) Cultural affairs.
(d) Nationality, passports, visas, execution of judgments, and extradition of criminals.
(e) Social affairs.
(f) Health problems.

Article 3. The League shall possess a Council composed of the representatives of the member states of the League; each state shall have a single vote, irrespective of the number of its representatives.

It shall be the task of the Council to achieve the realization of the objectives of the League and to supervise the execution of agreements which the member states have concluded on the questions enumerated in the preceding article, or on any other questions.

It likewise shall be the Council's task to decide upon the means by which the League is to co-operate with the international bodies to be created in the future in order to guarantee security and peace and regulate economic and social relations.

Article 4. For each of the questions listed in Article 2 there shall be set up a special committee in which the member states of the League shall be represented. These committees shall be charged with the task of laying down the principles and extent of co-operation. Such principles shall be formulated as draft agreements, to be presented to the Council for examination preparatory to their submission to the aforesaid states.

Representatives of the other Arab countries may take part in the work of the aforesaid committees. The Council shall determine the conditions under which these representatives may be permitted to participate and the rules governing such representation.

Article 5. Any resort to force in order to resolve disputes arising between two or more member states of the League is prohibited. If there should rise among them a difference which does not concern a state's independence, sovereignty, or territorial integrity, and if the parties to the dispute have recourse to the Council for the settlement of this difference, the decision of the Council shall then be enforceable and obligatory.

In such a case, the states between whom the difference has arisen shall not participate in the deliberations and decisions of the Council.

The Council shall mediate in all differences which threaten to lead to war between two member states, or a member state and a third state, with a view to bringing about their reconciliation.

Decisions of arbitration and mediation shall be taken by majority vote.

Article 6. In case of aggression or threat of aggression by one state against a member state, the state which has been attacked or threatened with aggression may demand the immediate convocation of the Council.

The Council shall by unanimous decision determine the measures necessary to repulse the aggression. If the aggressor is a member state, its vote shall not be counted in determining unanimity.

If, as a result of the attack, the government of the state attacked finds itself unable to communicate with the Council, that state's representative in the Council shall have the right to request the convocation of the Council for the purpose indicated in the foregoing paragraph. In the event that this representative is unable to communicate with the Council, any member state of the League shall have the right to request the convocation of the Council.

Article 7. Unanimous decisions of the Council shall be binding upon all member states of the League; majority decisions shall be binding only upon those states which have accepted them.

In either case the decisions of the Council shall be enforced in each member state according to its respective basic laws.

Article 8. Each member state shall respect the systems of government established in the other member states and regard them as exclusive concerns of those states. Each shall pledge to abstain from any action calculated to change established systems of government.

Article 9. States of the League which desire to establish closer co-operation and stronger bonds than are provided by this Pact may conclude agreements to that end.

Treaties and agreements already concluded or to be concluded in the future between a member state and another state shall not be binding or restrictive upon other members.

Article 10. The permanent seat of the League of Arab States is established in Cairo. The Council may, however, assemble at any other place it may designate.

Article 11. The Council of the League shall convene in ordinary session twice a year, in March and in September. It shall convene in extraordinary session upon the request of two member states of the League whenever the need arises.

Article 12. The League shall have a permanent Secretariat-General which shall consist of a Secretary-General, Assistant Secretaries, and an appropriate number of officials.

The Council of the League shall appoint the Secretary-General by a majority of two-thirds of the states of the League. The Secretary-General, with the approval of the Council, shall appoint the Assistant Secretaries and the principal officials of the League.

The Council of the League shall establish an administrative

regulation for the functions of the Secretariat-General and matters relating to the Staff.

The Secretary-General shall have the rank of Ambassador and the Assistant Secretaries that of Ministers Plenipotentiary.

Article 13. The Secretary-General shall prepare the draft of the budget of the League and shall submit it to the Council for approval before the beginning of each fiscal year.

The Council shall fix the share of the expenses to be borne by each state of the League. This share may be reconsidered if necessary.

Article 14. The members of the Council of the League as well as the members of the committees and the officials who are to be designated in the administrative regulation shall enjoy diplomatic privileges and immunity when engaged in the exercise of their functions.

The building occupied by the organs of the League shall be inviolable.

Article 15. The first meeting of the Council shall be convened at the invitation of the head of the Egyptian Government. Thereafter it shall be convened at the invitation of the Secretary-General.

The representatives of the member states of the League shall alternately assume the presidency of the Council at each of its ordinary sessions.

Article 16. Except in cases specifically indicated in this Pact, a majority vote of the Council shall be sufficient to make enforceable decisions on the following matters:

(*a*) Matters relating to personnel.

(*b*) Adoption of the budget of the League.

(*c*) Establishment of the administrative regulations for the Council, the Committees, and the Secretariat-General.

(*d*) Decisions to adjourn the sessions.

Article 17. Each member state of the League shall deposit with the Secretariat-General one copy of every treaty or agreement concluded or to be concluded in the future between itself and another member state of the League or a third state.

Article 18. (deals with withdrawal).

Article 19. (deals with amendment).

Article 20. (deals with ratification).

ANNEX REGARDING PALESTINE

Since the termination of the last great war the rule of the Ottoman Empire over the Arab countries, among them Palestine, which has become detached from that Empire, has come to an end. She has come to be autonomous, not subordinate to any other state.

The Treaty of Lausanne proclaimed that her future was to be settled by the parties concerned.

However, even though she was as yet unable to control her own affairs, the Covenant of the League (of Nations) in 1919 made provision for a regime based upon recognition of her independence.

Her international existence and independence in the legal sense cannot, therefore, be questioned, any more than could the independence of the Arab countries.

Although the outward manifestations of this independence have remained obscured for reasons beyond her control, this should not be allowed to interfere with her participation in the work of the Council of the League.

The states signatory to the Pact of the Arab League are therefore of the opinion that, considering the special circumstances of Palestine and until that country can effectively exercise its independence, the Council of the League should take charge of the selection of an Arab representative from Palestine to take part in its work.

ANNEX REGARDING CO-OPERATION WITH COUNTRIES WHICH ARE NOT MEMBERS OF THE COUNCIL OF THE LEAGUE

Whereas the member states of the League will have to deal in the Council as well as in the committees with matters which will benefit and affect the Arab world at large;

And whereas the Council has to take into account the aspirations of the Arab countries which are not members of the Council and has to work toward their realization;

Now therefore, it particularly behoves the states signatory to the Pact of the Arab League to enjoin the Council of the League, when considering the admission of those countries to participation in the committees referred to in the Pact, that it should do its utmost to co-operate with them, and furthermore, that it should spare no effort to learn their needs and understand their aspirations and hopes; and that it should work thenceforth for their best interests and the safeguarding of the future with all the political means at its disposal.

NORDIC COUNCIL

Address: Tyrgatan 7, Box 19506, 10432 Stockholm, Sweden.
Telephone: (08) 14-34-20.
Telex: 12 867.

The Nordic Council was founded in 1952 for co-operation between the Nordic parliaments and governments. The four original members were Denmark, Iceland, Norway and Sweden; Finland joined in 1955, and the Faeroe Islands and Åland Islands were granted representation in 1970 within the Danish and Finnish delegations respectively. Greenland had separate representation within the Danish delegation from 1984. Co-operation was first regulated by a Statute, and subsequently by the Helsinki Treaty of 1962. The Nordic region has a population of about 23 million.

MEMBERS

Denmark (with the autonomous territories of the Faeroe Islands and Greenland)
Finland (with the autonomous territory of the Åland Islands)
Iceland
Norway
Sweden

Organization
(October 1988)

COUNCIL

The Nordic Council is not a supranational parliament, but a place where representatives of all the Nordic parliaments take decisions guiding Nordic co-operation. The Nordic Council of Ministers (see next page) represents the governments of the Nordic countries when decisions are to be implemented.

The Council convenes annually in a plenary session of about one week's duration. Following an introductory general debate, the Session considers proposals put forward by Council members, by the Council of Ministers or national governments. The Session also follows up the outcome of past decisions and the work of the various Nordic institutions.

The Council comprises 87 members, elected annually by and from the parliaments of the respective countries (Denmark 16 members; Faeroes 2; Greenland 2; Finland 18; Åland 2; Iceland 7; Norway 20; Sweden 20). The various parties are proportionately represented in accordance with their representation in the national parliaments.

The Council initiates and follows up co-operative efforts among the Nordic countries. It does this by issuing recommendations and statements of position to the Council of Ministers and the respective governments. The recommendations of the Council, which express political judgements and opinions with solid foundations in the Nordic parliaments, generally result in the taking of measures on the part of Councils of Ministers of the national governments in question.

The session of the Council held in March 1988 dealt with 44 members' proposals and 10 proposals by the Council of Ministers. Topics covered in members' proposals included Nordic co-operation in the following: urban traffic problems; merchant shipping; improvement of postal services; alcohol and drug abuse; strengthening European environmental co-operation; waste management; marine pollution; a proposed Nordic nuclear-free zone; adult education; and harmonization of laws relating to marriage and to companies. The proposals submitted by the Council of Ministers included programmes of co-operation in biotechnology, in development assistance, in food standards and in health and social services; 'action plans' for road safety and cultural co-operation; establishment of a Nordic Industry Centre in Oslo; permanent status for the Nordic Project Fund and for the Nordic Investment Bank's regional loan facility; and the establishment of a Nordic Development Fund for concessional loans to developing countries.

STANDING COMMITTEES

Council members are assigned to six Standing Committees (Economic; Legal; Communications; Cultural; Social and Environmental; and Budget and Control Committees). The first five Committees prepare business to be put before the Council during the annual Session. The Budget and Control Committee co-ordinates consideration by the other Committees of ministers' budget proposals, and supervises activities funded by the Council of Ministers.

PRESIDIUM

The Presidium of the Council, in which all five countries have two parliamentary representatives, is the supreme executive body of the Council. It directs the Council's day-to-day work between the annual sessions.
President (1988/1989): JAN P. SYSE (Norway).

SECRETARIATS

Each delegation to the Nordic Council has a secretariat at its national parliament. The secretaries of the six standing committees are attached to the secretariat of the Presidium in Stockholm.
Secretary of the Presidium: GERHARD AF SCHULTÉN (Finland).

PUBLICATIONS

Yearbook of Nordic Statistics (in English and Swedish).
Nordiska Samarbetsorgan (list of all Nordic institutions, with their names in English).
Nordisk Kontakt.
Books and pamphlets on Nordic co-operation; summaries of Council sessions.

NORDIC COUNCIL OF MINISTERS

Address: Store Strandstraede 18, 1255 Copenhagen K, Denmark.
Telephone: (01) 11-47-11.
Telex: 15544.

The Governments of Denmark, Finland, Iceland, Norway and Sweden co-operate through the Nordic Council of Ministers. This co-operation is regulated by the Treaty of Co-operation between Denmark, Finland, Iceland, Norway and Sweden of 1962 (amended in 1971, 1979, 1983 and 1985) and the Treaty between Denmark, Finland, Iceland, Norway and Sweden concerning cultural co-operation of 1971 (amended in 1983 and 1985). The Prime Ministers and the Ministers of Defence and Foreign Affairs do not meet within the Nordic Council of Ministers. The Prime Ministers, however, meet once a year on an informal basis with the Ministers of Nordic Co-operation.

MEMBERS

Denmark	Iceland	Norway
Finland		Sweden

Organization
(October 1988)

COUNCIL OF MINISTERS

The Nordic Council of Ministers holds formal and informal meetings and is attended by ministers with responsibility for the subject under discussion. Each member state also appoints a minister in its own cabinet as Minister for Nordic Co-operation.

Decisions of the Council of Ministers must be unanimous, except for procedural questions, which may be decided by a simple majority of those voting. Abstention constitutes no obstacle to a decision. Decisions are binding on the individual countries, provided that no parliamentary approval is necessary under the constitution of any of the countries. If such approval is necessary, the Council of Ministers must be so informed before its decision.

Meetings are concerned with: agreements and treaties, guidelines for national legislation, recommendations from the Nordic Council, financing joint studies, setting up Nordic institutions.

The Council of Ministers reports each year to the Nordic Council on progress in all co-operation between member states as well as on future plans.

SECRETARIAT

The Office of the Secretary-General deals with co-ordination and legal matters.
There are Divisions for:
1. Budget and administration;
2. Cultural and educational co-operation;
3. Research, advanced education, computer technology, protection of the environment, energy;
4. Labour market questions, occupational environment, social policy and health care, equality;
5. Finance and monetary policy, industry, housing, trade and development aid;
6. Regional policy, transport, communications, tourism, farming, forestry, fishing and consumer questions;
7. Information.

Secretary-General: FRIDTJOV CLEMET.

COMMITTEES

Committee of Ministers' Deputies: for final preparation of material for the meetings of Ministers of Nordic Co-operation.
Committees of Senior Civil Servants: prepare the meetings of the Council of Ministers and conduct research at its request. There are a number of sub-committees. The Committees of Senior Civil Servants cover the subjects listed under the Secretariat (above).

Activities

ECONOMIC CO-OPERATION

Economic co-operation is undertaken in the following areas; investments in infrastructure; measures on training and employment; elimination of trade barriers; liberalization of capital movements; research and development; export promotion; taxes and other levies; and regional policy. During 1988 a new economic plan of action was being drawn up for the four year 1989–92. The national administrations for overseas development have carried out several projects as a group, and consult with one another frequently.

Nordic Investment Bank: founded under an agreement of December 1975 to provide finance and guarantees for the implementation of investment projects and exports; authorized and subscribed capital 800m. IMF Special Drawing Rights. The main sectors of the Bank's activities are energy, metal and wood-processing industries (including petroleum extraction) and manufacturing. By December 1985 the Bank had granted 341 loans totalling 1,713m. SDRs. In 1982 a scheme for financing investments in developing countries was established.

Nordic Industrial Fund: f. 1973 with a capital of 10m. Swedish kronor, to be increased in stages to 50m. Makes grants, subsidies and loans for industrial research and development projects of interest to more than one member country.

Nordic Economic Research Council: f. 1980 to promote research and analysis on Nordic economic interdependence particularly with regard to economic stabilization policies.

NORDTEST: f. 1973 as an inter-Nordic agency for technical testing and standardization; collaborates with the Nordic Committee on Building Regulations.

Nordic Project Fund: f. 1982 to strengthen the international competitiveness of Nordic exporting companies, and to promote industrial co-operation.

COMMUNICATIONS AND TRANSPORT

A Nordic agreement for transport and communications entered into force in 1973. The main areas of co-operation have been road research, urban transport, transport in sparsely populated areas, transport for the disabled and road safety. Earlier agreements cover co-operation in post and telecommunications. Passports are not required for travel by Nordic citizens within the region.

LABOUR MARKET

Since 1954 a free labour market has been in force between Denmark, Finland, Norway and Sweden. By 1980 more than one million people had moved across the frontiers in Scandinavia. There is a joint centre for labour market training at Övertorneå in Sweden.

ENVIRONMENT

The Nordic Convention on the protection of the environment was signed in 1974, entering into force in October 1976. The member states undertake to harmonize regulations for protecting the environment, and to assess certain measures affecting neighbouring countries.

The coastal states have also signed a Convention on the Marine Environment of the Baltic, which entered into force in May 1980; special agreements have been concluded between Denmark and Sweden on pollution in the Öresund, and between Finland and Sweden on pollution in the Gulf of Bothnia.

NORDFORSK (Scandinavian Council for Applied Research) has a special secretariat for environmental research in Helsinki.

The Nordic Institute for Advanced Studies on Occupational Environment was established in 1982.

ENERGY

Co-operation within the sector includes studies of energy saving, the use of coal, the introduction of new and renewable sources of energy, and the use of petroleum and gas. There is a special committee for atomic energy. A common authority for electricity supply (NORDEL) was set up in 1963.

CONSUMER AFFAIRS

The main areas of co-operation are in consumer legislation, information on goods and services, consumer education and general questions of consumer policy.

FOOD AND NUTRITION

Co-operation in this sector began in 1982, and includes projects in food legislation, diet and nutrition, toxicology, risk evaluation and food controls.

LAW

The five countries have similar legal systems and tend towards uniformity in legislation and interpretation of law. Much of the preparatory committee work within the national administrations on new legislation involves consultation with the neighbour countries.

Citizens of one Nordic country working in another are in many respects given the status of nationals. In all the Nordic countries they already have the right to vote in local elections in the country of residence. The changing of citizenship from one Nordic country to another has been simplified.

There are special extradition facilities between the countries and further stages towards co-operation between the police and the courts have been recommended.

There is a permanent Council for Criminology, a Nordic Institute for Maritime Law in Oslo and a permanent committee for Penalty Law.

REGIONAL POLICY

Under a joint programme agreed in 1986, regional policy gives priority to cross-border co-operation for development in nine areas, with most financial support allotted to the 'Northern Cap' area (the northern provinces of Finland, Norway and Sweden) and the Western Nordic area (Greenland, the Faeroes and Iceland).

SOCIAL WELFARE AND HEALTH

Under the Convention on Social Security, 1955 (renewed in 1981), Nordic citizens have the same rights, benefits and obligations in each Nordic country. In 1974 a new agreement was made on arrangements for sickness, pregnancy and childbirth when temporarily in another Nordic country. Uniform provisions exist concerning basic pension and supplementary pension benefits when moving from one Nordic country to another.

In 1981 an agreement was concluded for doctors, dentists, nurses and pharmacists on the standards of competence required for obtaining work in other Nordic countries.

Institutions:
Nordic School of Public Health, Gothenburg, Sweden;
Scandinavian Institute of Dental Materials, Oslo;
Nordic Council on Medicines, Uppsala, Sweden;
Nordic Council on Alcohol and Drug Research, Helsinki;
Nordic Committee on Disability, Stockholm.

Other Permanent Bodies:
Scandiatransplant, under Nordic Committee on Kidney Transplantation, Århus, Denmark;
Nordic Medico-Statistical Committee, Copenhagen;
Nordic Committee of Social Security Statistics, Helsinki.

EDUCATIONAL AND SCIENTIFIC CO-OPERATION

Education: Nordic co-operation in the educational field includes the objective content and means of education, the structure of the educational system and pedagogical development work.

Priority is given to:
1. Secondary education, adult education and vocational training.
2. Projects relevant for all levels of the educational system such as the teaching of Nordic languages and pedagogical research and development.

Joint projects include:
Nordic Co-operation in Adult Education
Nordic Educational Courses
Nordic Folk Academy
Nordic School of Journalism
Nordic Language Secretariat
Nordic Language and Information Centre
Nordic Federation for Medical Education
Nordic School of Nutritional and Textile Sciences
Nordic School Co-operation

Research: Nordic co-operation in research comprises information on research activities and research findings, joint research projects, joint research institutions, the methods and means in research policy, the organizational structure of research and a co-ordination of the national research programmes.

Much of the research co-operation activities at the more permanent joint research institutions consists of establishing science contacts in the Nordic areas by means of grants, visiting lecturers, courses and symposia.

The research institutions and research bodies listed below receive continuous financial support via the Nordic cultural budget. In many cases, these joint Nordic institutions ensure a high international standard that would otherwise have been difficult to maintain at a purely national level.

Nordic Accelerator Committee
Nordic Council for Arctic Medical Research
Scandinavian Institute of Asian Studies
Nordic Documentation Centre for Mass Communication Research
Nordic Committee on East European Studies
Nordic Council for Ecology
Nordic Institute of Folklore
Nordic Geoexcursions to Iceland
Nordic Co-operation Committee for International Politics
Nordic Council for Marine Biology
Scandinavian Institute of Maritime Law
Nordic Council for Physical Oceanography
Nordic Institute for Studies in Urban and Regional Planning
Nordic Research Courses
Nordic Research Grants
Nordic Research Symposia
Nordic Association for Research on Latin America
Nordic Council for Scientific Information and Research Libraries
Nordic Summer University
Nordic Institute for Theoretical Atomic Physics
Nordic Volcanological Institute
Nordic Council for Co-operation in Silvicultural Research
Nordic Gene Bank
Nordic Research Policy Council

Cultural activities: Cultural co-operation is concerned with artistic and other cultural exchange between the Nordic countries; activities relating to libraries, museums, radio, television, and film; promotion of activities within organizations with general cultural aims, including youth and sports organizations; the improvement of conditions for the creative and performing arts; and encouragement for artists and cultural workers.

Joint projects include:
Nordic Co-operation among Adult Education Organizations
Nordic Amateur Theatre Council
Nordic Art Association
Nordic Arts Centre
Nordic Co-operation in Athletics
Nordic Council Literature Prize
Nordic Council Music Prize
Nordic Film Seminars
Nordic House in Reykjavík
Nordic House in the Faeroe Islands
Nordic Music Co-operation
Nordic Sami Institute
Nordic Theatre Committee
Nordic Writers' Courses
Nordic Youth Co-operation Committee
Nordic Literature Committee

NORDIC CULTURAL FUND

The Nordic Cultural Fund was founded in 1966 to promote cultural co-operation by making grants for Nordic cultural projects within the region. A Board of 10 members (meeting four times a year) administers and distributes the resources of the Fund and supervises its activities. Five of the members are appointed by the Nordic Council and five by the Nordic Council of Ministers (of culture and education), for a period of two years. The Fund is located within and administered by the Secretariat of the Nordic Council of Ministers. It considers applications for assistance for research, education and general cultural activities; grants may also be made for disseminating information concerning Nordic culture within and outside the region. In 1987 the Fund was allotted 11m. Danish kroner.

FINANCE

Joint expenses are divided according to an agreed scale in proportion to the relative national product of the member countries. The 1988 budget of the Nordic Council of Ministers amounted to 565m. Danish kroner, of which Sweden was to contribute 37.3%, Norway 21.5%, Denmark 20.0%, Finland 20.3% and Iceland 0.9%. Various forms of co-operation are financed directly from the national budgets.

NORTH ATLANTIC TREATY ORGANISATION—NATO

Address: 1110 Brussels, Belgium.
Telephone: (02) 241-00-40.
Telex: 23867.

NATO was founded in 1949 by the North Atlantic Treaty as an international collective defence organization linking a group of European states with the USA and Canada. Member countries agree to treat an armed attack on any one of them as an attack against all.

MEMBERS*

Belgium	Greece	Portugal
Canada	Iceland	Spain
Denmark	Italy	Turkey
France	Luxembourg	United Kingdom
Federal Republic of Germany	Netherlands	USA
	Norway	

* France withdrew from the integrated military structure of NATO in 1966 although remaining a member of the Atlantic Alliance. Following the Turkish invasion of Cyprus in 1974, Greece also announced a partial withdrawal from the integrated military structure of NATO; it re-joined in October 1980. Spain joined NATO in May 1982.

Organization
(October 1988)

NORTH ATLANTIC COUNCIL

The highest authority of the alliance, composed of representatives of the 16 member states. It meets at the level of Permanent Representatives, ministers of foreign affairs, or heads of state and government. Ministerial meetings are held at least twice a year. At the level of Permanent Representatives the Council meets at least once a week.

The Secretary General of NATO is chairman of the Council. Annually, the minister of foreign affairs of a member state is nominated honorary President, following the English alphabetical order of countries.

Decisions are taken by common consent and not by majority vote. The Council is a forum for wide consultation between member governments on major issues, including political, military, economic and other subjects. It also gives political guidance to the military authorities.

PERMANENT REPRESENTATIVES

Belgium: PROSPER THUYSBAERT
Canada: GORDON SCOTT SMITH
Denmark: OTTO ROSE BORCH
France: GABRIEL ROBIN
Federal Republic of Germany: NIELS HANSEN
Greece: CHRISTOS ZACHARAKIS
Iceland: EINAR BENEDIKTSSON
Italy: FRANCESCO PAOLO FULCI
Luxembourg: GUY DE MUYSER
Netherlands: J. G. N. DE HOOP SCHEFFER
Norway: EIVINN BERG
Portugal: ANTÓNIO VAZ PEREIRA
Spain: JAIME DE OJEDA
Turkey: OSMAN OLÇAY
United Kingdom: MICHAEL ALEXANDER
USA: ALTON G. KEEL Jr

DEFENCE PLANNING COMMITTEE

The Committee, in which decisions are taken on matters relating specifically to defence, comprises representatives of all the member countries except France. It is the highest forum for discussion of military policy. Like the Council it meets in both ministerial and Permanent Representative sessions. Ministerial meetings of the Committee are attended by ministers of defence.

NUCLEAR PLANNING GROUP

The Group meets regularly at the level of Permanent Representatives, and twice yearly with ministers of defence; 14 countries participate.

OTHER COMMITTEES

There are also committees for political affairs, economics, armaments, defence review, science, infrastructure, logistics, communications, civil emergency planning, information and cultural relations, and civil and military budgets. The Committee on the Challenges of Modern Society examines methods of improving allied co-operation in creating a better environment. In addition other committees deal with specialized subjects such as NATO pipelines, European air space co-ordination, etc.

INTERNATIONAL SECRETARIAT

The Secretary General is Chairman of the North Atlantic Council, the Defence Planning Committee, the Nuclear Planning Group, and the Committee on the Challenges of Modern Society. He is the head of the International Secretariat, with staff drawn from the member countries. He proposes items for NATO consultation and is generally responsible for promoting consultation and co-operation in accordance with the provisions of the North Atlantic Treaty. He is empowered to offer his help informally in cases of disputes between member countries, to facilitate procedures for settlement.

Secretary General: MANFRED WÖRNER (FRG).
Deputy Secretary General: MARCELLO GUIDI (Italy).

There is an Assistant Secretary General for each of the divisions listed below.

PRINCIPAL DIVISIONS

Division of Political Affairs: maintains political liaison with national delegations and international organizations. Prepares reports on political subjects for the Secretary General and the Council. Asst Sec. Gen. Dr HENNING WEGENER (FRG).

Division of Defence Planning and Policy: studies all matters concerning the defence of the Alliance, especially any with economic implications for defence, and also the overall financial aspects of the defence efforts of each country. Asst Sec. Gen. MICHAEL LEGGE (UK).

Division of Defence Support: promotes the most efficient use of the Allies' resources in the production of military equipment and studies its standardization. Asst Sec. Gen. MACK FRANCIS MATTINGLY (USA).

Division of Infrastructure, Logistics and Civil Emergency Planning: supervises the technical and financial aspects of the infrastructure programme. Co-ordinates the operational aspects of the Council's activities, crisis management plans and arrangements. Provides guidance, co-ordination and support to the activities of all NATO committees or bodies active in the field of consumer logistics. Asst Sec. Gen. C. M. E. DE LAAT DE KANTER (Netherlands).

Division of Scientific and Environmental Affairs: advises the Secretary-General on scientific matters of interest to NATO. Responsible for promoting and administering scientific exchange programmes between member countries, research fellowships, advanced study institutes and special programmes of support for the scientific and technological development of less-advanced member countries. Asst Sec. Gen. JACQUES DUCUING (France).

Military Organization

MILITARY COMMITTEE

Composed of the allied Chiefs-of-Staff, or their representatives, of all member countries except France: the highest military authority in NATO. Meets at least twice a year at Chiefs-of-Staff level and remains in permanent session with Permanent Military Representatives. It is responsible for making recommendations to the Council and Defence Planning Committee on military matters and for supplying guidance on military questions to Supreme Allied Commanders and subordinate military authorities.

France maintains a Military Mission to the Military Committee for regular consultation.

President: Gen. P. D. MANSON (Canada).
Chairman: Gen. WOLFGANG ALTENBURG (FRG).
Deputy Chairman: Lt-Gen. R. D. BECKEL (USA).

INTERNATIONAL MILITARY STAFF
Director: Lt-Gen. CORRADO MELILLO (Italy).

COMMANDS
European Command: Casteau, Belgium—Supreme Headquarters Allied Powers Europe—SHAPE. Supreme Allied Commander Europe—SACEUR: Gen. JOHN R. GALVIN (USA).

Atlantic Ocean Command: Norfolk, Virginia, USA. Supreme Allied Commander Atlantic—SACLANT: Admiral FRANK B. KELSO (USA).

Channel Command: Northwood, England. Allied Commander-in-Chief Channel—CINCHAN: Vice-Admiral Sir JULIAN J. R. OSWALD (UK).

Activities

The NATO Alliance maintains military preparedness with the aim of preventing war. It provides for consultation on all relevant political problems, draws up joint defence plans, organizes the necessary infrastructure and arranges for joint training and exercises.

NATO aims to maintain sufficient forces to preserve the military balance with the countries of the Warsaw Pact (q.v.) and to provide a credible deterrent against aggression. NATO forces comprise three elements: conventional forces; intermediate and short-range nuclear forces; and the strategic nuclear forces of the United Kingdom and the USA.

Each year member countries take part in a Defence Review designed to assess their contribution to the common defence in relation to their respective capabilities and constraints. Allied defence policy is reviewed periodically by ministers of defence.

Political consultations are regarded as a vital and permanent feature of the Alliance. Discussion of East-West relations and of arms reduction plays a particularly important role in the decision-making process. The North Atlantic Council is the principal forum for such consultations, and is directly involved in a management capacity in the negotiations on Mutual and Balanced Force Reductions in Central Europe, which began in 1973.

Co-operation in science and technology is undertaken under the Science Fellowships Programme, the Advanced Study Institutes Programme and the Research Grants Programme. A Science for Stability Programme was established in 1980 to help Greece, Portugal and Turkey develop their scientific and technological capabilities.

NATO AGENCIES

1. Civilian production and logistics organizations responsible to the Council:

Central European Operating Agency—CEOA: Versailles, France; f. 1957 to supervise the integrated military pipeline network in Central Europe; eight member nations.

Nato Airborne Early Warning and Control Programme Management Organisation—NAPMO: Brunssum, Netherlands; f. 1978 to manage the procurement aspects of the NATO Airborne Early Warning and Control System.

NATO Communications and Information Systems Organisation—NACISO: Brussels, Belgium; f. 1985 by expansion of NATO Integrated Communications System Organisation; supervises planning and implementation of an integrated voice, telegraph and data communications system, to improve the Alliance's capability for crisis management and for the command and control of NATO forces.

NATO European Fighter Aircraft Development, Production and Logistics Management Organisation—NEFMO: Munich, Federal Republic of Germany; f. 1987; mems: Federal Republic of Germany, Italy, Spain, UK.

NATO HAWK Management Office: Rueil-Malmaison, France; f. 1959 to supervise the multinational production of the HAWK surface-to-air missile system in Europe; now gives logistic support to HAWK units and has started a European Limited Improvement Programme; seven nations participate.

NATO Maintenance and Supply Agency—NAMSA: Luxembourg; f. 1958; supplies spare parts and logistic support for a number of jointly-used weapon systems, missiles and electronic systems; all member nations except Iceland participate.

NATO MRCA Development and Production Management Organisation—NAMMO: Munich, Federal Republic of Germany; f. 1969 to supervise development and production of the Multi-Role Combat Aircraft project; mems: Federal Republic of Germany, Italy, UK.

2. Responsible to the Military Committee:

Advisory Group for Aerospace Research and Development—AGARD: Neuilly-sur-Seine, France; f. 1952; brings together aerospace scientists from member countries for exchange of information and research co-operation; provides scientific and technical advice for the Military Committee, for other NATO bodies and for member nations.

Allied Communications Security Agency—ACSA: Brussels, Belgium; f. 1953.

Allied Data Systems Interoperability Agency—ADSIA: Brussels, Belgium; f. 1979 to improve interoperability within the NATO Command, Control and Information Systems.

Allied Long Lines Agency—ALLA: Brussels, Belgium; f. 1951 to formulate policies to meet the long lines communications requirements of NATO.

Allied Naval Communications Agency—ANCA: London, England; f. 1951 to establish reliable communications for maritime operations.

Allied Radio Frequency Agency—ARFA: Brussels, Belgium; f. 1951 to establish policies concerned with military use of the radio frequency spectrum.

Allied Tactical Communications Agency—ATCA: Brussels, Belgium; f. 1972 to establish policies concerned with tactical communications for land and air operations.

Military Agency for Standardization—MAS: Brussels, Belgium; f. 1951 to improve military standardization of equipment for NATO forces.

NATO Defense College—NADEFCOL: Rome, Italy; f. 1951 to train officials for posts in NATO organizations or in national ministries.

3. Responsible to Supreme Allied Commander Atlantic (SACLANT):

SACLANT Anti-submarine Warfare Research Centre—SACLANTCEN: La Spezia, Italy; f. 1962 for research in submarine detection and oceanographic problems.

4. Responsible to Supreme Allied Commander Europe (SACEUR):

SHAPE Technical Centre—STC: The Hague, Netherlands; f. 1960 to provide scientific and technical advice, originally on the formation of an integrated air defence system, subsequently on a broader programme covering force capability and structure; command and control; communications.

NATO MILITARY FORCES
(number of military personnel, '000)

	1985	1986	1987 estimates
Belgium	107	107	110
Denmark	29	28	29
France	563	558	559
Germany, Federal Republic	495	495	495
Greece	201	201	202
Italy	531	529	534
Luxembourg	1	1	1
Netherlands	103	106	107
Norway	36	38	38
Portugal	102	101	103
Turkey	814	860	916
United Kingdom	334	331	327
Total Europe	3,316	3,355	3,421
Canada	83	85	86
United States	2,244	2,260	2,275
Total NATO	5,643	5,700	5,782

Iceland has no armed forces. Data for Spain are not provided by NATO: the Spanish armed forces numbered 325,000 at mid-1987, according to *The Military Balance* (International Institute for Strategic Studies).

FINANCE

As NATO is an international, not a supra-national, organization, its member countries themselves decide the amount to be devoted to their defence effort and the form which the latter will assume. Thus, the aim of NATO's defence planning is to develop realistic military plans for the defence of the alliance at reasonable cost. Under the annual Defence Planning review, political, military and economic factors are considered in relation to strategy, force requirements and available resources. The procedure for the co-ordination of military plans and defence expenditures rests on the detailed and comparative analysis of the capabilities of member countries. All installations for the use of international forces are financed under a common-funded infrastructure programme.

INTERNATIONAL ORGANIZATIONS

North Atlantic Treaty Organisation

TOTAL DEFENCE EXPENDITURE (Current Prices)

	Unit (million)	1985	1986	1987 (forecast)
Belgium	B. Francs	144,183	152,079	154,703
Canada	Can. $	10,332	10,971	11,403
Denmark	D. Kroner	13,344	13,333	14,547
France	Francs	186,715	197,110	207,552
Germany, Federal Republic[1]	DM	58,650	60,131	61,551
Greece	Drachmae	321,981	338,465	402,459
Italy	'000 Lire	18,584	20,071	21,797
Luxembourg	L. Francs	2,265	2,390	2,824
Netherlands	Guilders	12,901	13,035	13,174
Norway	N. Kroner	15,446	16,034	17,736
Portugal	Escudos	111,375	139,972	159,889
Turkey	Liras	1,234,547	1,867,990	2,476,869
United Kingdom	£ Sterling	18,352	18,639	19,387
USA	US $	258,165	281,102	288,433
Total Europe[2]	US $	88,742	115,658	131,735
Total North America	US $	265,731	288,997	296,817
Total NATO[2]	US $	354,473	404,656	428,552

Figures are based on NATO definitions of defence expenditure. Data for Spain are not available.

[1] Excluding expenditure for Berlin, forecast to be 16,081m. DM in 1987.

[2] Totals based on currency exchange rates in force during the years concerned.

PUBLICATIONS

(in English and French, with some editions in other languages)

NATO Review (6 a year in English, French, Danish, Dutch, German, Italian and Spanish; quarterly editions in Greek, Norwegian, Portuguese and Turkish; annual edition in Icelandic).

NATO Facts and Figures. A major reference book giving a detailed description of the historical, operational and structural aspects of NATO.

NATO Basic Documents.

NATO Final Communiqués.

NATO and the Warsaw Pact Force Comparisons.

NATO Handbook.

Economic and scientific publications.

ORGANISATION FOR ECONOMIC CO-OPERATION AND DEVELOPMENT—OECD

Address: 2 rue André-Pascal, 75775 Paris Cedex 16, France.
Telephone: (1) 45-24-82-00.
Telex: 620160.

OECD was founded in 1961, replacing the Organisation for European Economic Co-operation (OEEC) which had been set up in 1948 in connection with the Marshall Plan. It constitutes a forum where representatives of the governments of the industrialized democracies discuss and attempt to co-ordinate their economic and social policies.

MEMBERS

Australia
Austria
Belgium
Canada
Denmark
Finland
France
Federal Republic of Germany
Greece
Iceland
Ireland
Italy
Japan
Luxembourg
Netherlands
New Zealand
Norway
Portugal
Spain
Sweden
Switzerland
Turkey
United Kingdom
USA

Yugoslavia participates in the work of OECD with a special status. The Commission of the European Communities also takes part in the Organisation's work.

Organization

(October 1988)

COUNCIL

The governing body of OECD is the Council on which each member country is represented. The Council meets from time to time (usually once a year) at the level of government ministers, and regularly at official level, when it comprises the heads of Permanent Delegations to OECD (diplomatic missions headed by ambassadors). It is responsible for all questions of general policy and may establish subsidiary bodies as required to achieve the aims of the Organisation. Decisions and recommendations of the Council are adopted by mutual agreement of all its members. The Chairman of the Council at ministerial level is a member of government from the country elected to the chairmanship for that year. The Chairman of the Council at official level is the Secretary-General.

Heads of Permanent Delegations (with ambassadorial rank):

Australia: ED VISBORD
Austria: GEORG LENNKH
Belgium: JUAN CASSIER
Canada: MICHAEL BERRY
Denmark: HENRIK NETTERSTRØM
Finland: WILHELM BREITENSTEIN
France: MARC BONNEFOUS
Germany, Federal Republic: KLAUS MEYER
Greece: DIMITRIS KOULOURIANOS
Iceland: HARALDUR KRÖYER
Ireland: TADHG O'SULLIVAN
Italy: LUIGI FONTANA GIUSTI
Japan: HISASHI OWADA
Luxembourg: PIERRE WURTH
Netherlands: A. G. O. SMITSENDONK
New Zealand: JUDITH TROTTER
Norway: THORVALD MOE
Portugal: FERNANDO DOS SANTOS MARTINS
Spain: JOSÉ ANTONIO LÓPEZ ZATÓN
Sweden: BO KJELLEN
Switzerland: ERIC ROETHLISBERGER
Turkey: MUSTAFA ASULA
United Kingdom: J. W. D. GRAY
USA: DENIS LAMB

Participants with Special Status:

Yugoslavia: TOMISLAV JANKOVIĆ
Commission of the European Communities: RAYMOND PHAN VAN PHI

EXECUTIVE COMMITTEE

Each year the Council designates 14 of its members to form the Executive Committee which prepares the work of the Council. It is also called upon to carry out specific tasks where necessary. Apart from its regular meetings, the Committee meets occasionally in special sessions attended by senior government officials.

SECRETARIAT

The Council, the committees and other bodies in OECD are assisted by an independent international secretariat headed by the Secretary-General.
Secretary-General: JEAN-CLAUDE PAYE (France).
Deputy Secretary-General: PIERRE VINDE (Sweden).

AUTONOMOUS AND SEMI-AUTONOMOUS BODIES

International Energy Agency (see p. 184).
Nuclear Energy Agency (see p. 184).
Development Centre: f. 1962; includes all member countries except New Zealand. Pres. LOUIS EMMERIJ (see also under Development Co-operation, next page).
Centre for Educational Research and Innovation: includes all member countries and Yugoslavia. Dir J. R. GASS (UK) (see also under Manpower, Social Affairs and Education, next page).

Activities

The greater part of the work of OECD, which covers all aspects of economic and social policy, is prepared and carried out in about 200 specialized bodies (Committees, Working Parties, etc.); all members are normally represented on these bodies, except on those of a restricted nature. Participants are usually civil servants coming either from the capitals of member states or from the Permanent Delegations to OECD. The main bodies are:

Economic Policy Committee
Economic and Development Review Committee
Environment Committee
Group on Urban Affairs
Development Assistance Committee
Technical Co-operation Committee
Trade Committee
Payments Committee
Committee on Capital Movements and Invisible Transactions
Committee on International Investment and Multinational Enterprises
Committee on Financial Markets
Committee on Fiscal Affairs
Committee on Competition Law and Policy
Committee on Consumer Policy
Tourism Committee
Maritime Transport Committee
Committee for Agriculture
Fisheries Committee
Committee for Scientific and Technological Policy
Committee for Information, Computer and Communications Policy
Education Committee
Industry Committee
Steel Committee
Committee for Energy Policy
Manpower and Social Affairs Committee
Steering Committee of the Programme of Co-operation in the Field of Road Research
Steering Committee of the Programme on Educational Building
High Level Group on Commodities
Group on North-South Economic Issues

ECONOMIC POLICY

The main organ for the consideration and direction of economic policy among the member countries is the Economic Policy Committee, which comprises governments' chief economic advisors and central bankers, and meets two or three times a year to review the economic and financial situation and policies of member countries. It has several working parties and groups, the most important of which are Working Party No. 1 on Macro-Economic and

INTERNATIONAL ORGANIZATIONS

OECD

Structural Policy Analysis, Working Party No. 3 on Policies for the Promotion of Better International Payments Equilibrium and the Working Group on Short-Term Economic Prospects.

The Economic and Development Review Committee is responsible for the annual examination of the economic situation of each member country. Usually, a report is issued each year on each country, after an examination carried out by a panel of representatives of a number of other member countries; this process of mutual examination, has been extended also to other branches of the Organisation's work (agriculture, manpower and social affairs, scientific policy and development aid efforts).

ENERGY

Work in the field of energy includes co-ordination of members' energy policies, assessment of short-, medium- and long-term energy prospects; a long-term programme of energy conservation, development of alternative energy sources and energy research and development; a system of information on the international oil and energy markets; and improvement of relations between oil-producing and oil-consuming countries. This work is carried out in OECD's International Energy Agency (IEA: see below), an autonomous body in which 21 member countries of OECD and the Commission of the European Communities participate, as well as within the context of OECD as a whole under the Committee for Energy Policy. Co-operation in the development of nuclear power is undertaken by the Nuclear Energy Agency (see below).

DEVELOPMENT CO-OPERATION

The Development Assistance Committee (DAC) consists of representatives of the main OECD capital-exporting countries; it discusses methods for making national resources available for assisting countries and areas in the process of economic development anywhere in the world, and for expanding and improving the flow of development assistance and other long-term funds.

The Group on North-South Economic Issues deals with the wide range of subjects involved in economic relationships between OECD countries and developing countries. It is particularly concerned with the treatment of these issues in the various fora of international economic discussion, such as UNCTAD.

A Technical Co-operation Committee has the task of drawing up and supervising the programmes of technical assistance arranged for the benefit of member countries, or areas of member countries, in the process of development.

The OECD Development Centre (a semi-autonomous body) was set up in 1962 for the collection and dissemination of information in the field of economic development, research into development problems and the training of specialists both from the industrialized and developing countries.

INTERNATIONAL TRADE

The activities of the Trade Committee are aimed at maintaining the degree of trade liberalization achieved, avoiding the emergence of new trade barriers, and improving further the liberalization of trade on a multilateral and non-discriminatory basis. These activities include examination of issues concerning trade relations among member countries as well as relations with non-member countries, in particular developing countries. The existing procedures allow, inter alia, any member country to obtain prompt consideration and discussions by the Trade Committee of trade measures taken by another member country which adversely affect its own interests.

The task of the High-Level Group on Commodities is to find a more active and broader approach to commodity problems, notably with a view to contributing to a greater stability in the markets.

FINANCIAL AND FISCAL AFFAIRS

The progressive abolition of obstacles to the international flow of services and capital is the responsibility of various OECD Committees. The Committee on Capital Movements and Invisible Transactions watches over the implementation of the Codes of Liberalization of Invisible Transactions and of Capital Movements. The Committee on International Investment and Multinational Enterprises prepared a Code of Behaviour (called 'Guidelines') for multinational enterprises, recommended to them by all member governments; the Committee is to follow up the implementation of these guidelines in order to improve the effectiveness of co-operation among member countries in international investment and multinational enterprises. Other specialized committees have been set up to deal with financial markets, fiscal matters, competition law and policy, tourism, maritime transport, consumer policy, etc.

FOOD, AGRICULTURE AND FISHERIES

The Committee for Agriculture reviews major developments in agricultural policies, deals with the adaptation of agriculture to changing economic conditions, elaborates forecasts of production and market prospects, holds consultations on import and export practices and assesses implications of world developments in food and agriculture for member countries' policies. A separate Fisheries Committee carries out similar tasks in its own sector.

ENVIRONMENT

The Environment Committee is responsible for the economic and policy aspects of OECD's work in this field. The Committee is assisted by various Sector Groups. Its work has led to agreements adopted by member countries setting out guiding principles on the international trade aspects of environment policies (e.g. the 'Polluter pays' principle), and on trans-frontier movements of hazardous waste. A special Chemicals Programme promotes co-operation and mutual assistance in controlling the 80,000 chemicals on the commercial market. The Committee also deals with policies for air and water management, noise abatement, trans-frontier pollution, etc.

Urban problems in OECD countries are dealt with by a Group on Urban Affairs, covering economic, social and administrative issues in cities, as well as ecological aspects of the built-up environment.

SCIENCE, TECHNOLOGY AND INDUSTRY

The Committee for Scientific and Technological Policy is responsible for encouraging co-operation among member countries in scientific and technological policies with a view to contributing to the achievement of their economic and social aims.

The Committee for Information, Computer and Communications Policy is to examine policy issues arising from the development and application of technologies in the field of information, computer and communications systems and services, including the impact of such issues on the economy and on society in general.

The Steel Committee, enables governments, consistent with general economic policies, to act promptly to cope with crisis situations, to keep steel trade as unrestricted and undistorted as possible and to facilitate the necessary structural adjustment of the industry.

The Industry Committee has overall responsibility for all aspects of the Organisation's work in the field of industry which require co-operation and confrontation among member governments.

MANPOWER, SOCIAL AFFAIRS AND EDUCATION

The Manpower and Social Affairs Committee is concerned with the development of manpower and selective employment policies to ensure the utilization of manpower at the highest possible level and to improve the quality and flexibility of working life as well as the integration of social policies. Its work includes such aspects as the role of women in the economy, industrial relations, intra-European migration movements and the development of social indicators.

The Committee for Education relates educational planning to educational policy and evaluates the implications of policy for the allocation and use of resources. The Committee reviews educational trends, develops statistics and indicators and analyses policies for greater equality of educational opportunity, new options for youth and learning opportunities for adults. Together, the Manpower and Education Committees seek to provide for greater integration of manpower and educational policy.

The OECD's Centre for Educational Research and Innovation (CERI) promotes the development of research activities in education together with experiments of an advanced nature designed to test innovations in educational systems and to stimulate research and development. Yugoslavia is also a member.

RELATIONS WITH OTHER INTERNATIONAL ORGANIZATIONS

Under a Protocol signed at the same time as the OECD Convention, the Commission of the European Communities generally takes part in the work of OECD. EFTA may also send representatives to OECD meetings. Formal relations exist with a number of other international organizations, including the ILO, FAO, IMF, IBRD, UNCTAD, IAEA and the Council of Europe. Only a very few non-governmental organizations have been granted consultative status, notably the Business and Industry Advisory Committee to OECD (BIAC) and the Trade Union Advisory Committee to OECD (TUAC).

PUBLICATIONS

News from OECD (monthly).

The OECD Observer (every 2 months).

Activities of OECD (Secretary-General's Annual Report).

Main Economic Indicators (monthly).

The OECD Economic Outlook (2 a year).

INTERNATIONAL ORGANIZATIONS

Economic Surveys by OECD (annually for each country).
OECD Employment Outlook (annually).
Foreign Trade Statistics (monthly).
Financial Statistics (24 a year).
National Accounts (annually).
Development Assistance Efforts and Policies (annually).

OECD Nuclear Energy Agency

Tourism Policy and International Tourism.
Oil and Gas Statistics (quarterly).
Energy Balances (annually).

Numerous specialized reports, books and statistics on economic and social subjects (about 130 titles a year, both in English and French) are also published.

International Energy Agency

Address: 2 rue André Pascal, 75775 Paris Cedex 16, France.

The Agency was set up by the Council of OECD in 1974 to develop co-operation on energy questions among participating countries.

MEMBERS

Australia	Ireland	Spain
Austria	Italy	Sweden
Belgium	Japan	Switzerland
Canada	Luxembourg	Turkey
Denmark	Netherlands	United
Federal Republic of	New Zealand	Kingdom
Germany	Norway	USA
Greece	Portugal	

The Commission of the European Communities is also represented.

Activities

The Agreement on an International Energy Programme was signed in November 1974 and formally entered into force in January 1976. The Programme commits the participating countries of the International Energy Agency to share oil in emergencies, to strengthen their long-term co-operation in order to reduce dependence on oil imports, to increase the availability of information on the oil market and to develop relations with the oil-producing and other oil-consuming countries.

The emergency oil-sharing plan has been established and the IEA ensures that the necessary technical information and facilities are in place so that it can be readily used in the event of a reduction in oil supplies.

The IEA Long-Term Co-operation Programme is designed to strengthen the security of energy supplies and promote stability in world energy markets. It provides for co-operative efforts to conserve energy, to accelerate the development of alternative energy sources by means of both specific and general measures, to step up research and development of new energy technologies and to remove legislative and administrative obstacles to increased energy supplies. Regular reviews of member countries' efforts in the fields of energy conservation and accelerated development of alternative energy sources assess the effectiveness of national programmes in relation to the objectives of the Agency.

The Agency has developed an extensive system of information and consultation on the oil market with a view to obtaining a better idea of probable future developments in the oil market. Another function of the Agency is to develop a long-term co-operative relationship among oil-producing and consuming countries.

GOVERNING BOARD

Composed of ministers or senior officials of the member governments. Decisions may be taken by a weighted majority on a number of specified subjects, particularly concerning emergency measures and the emergency reserve commitment; a simple weighted majority is required for procedural decisions and decisions implementing specific obligations in the agreement. Unanimity is required only if new obligations, not already specified in the agreement, are to be undertaken.

The Governing Board is assisted by four Standing Groups and a high-level Committee, dealing respectively with emergency questions; long-term co-operation; oil market; relations with producer and other consumer countries; and energy research and development.

There is also a Coal and an Oil Industry Advisory Board, composed of industrial executives.

SECRETARIAT

Executive Director: HELGA STEEG (FRG).
Deputy Executive Director: J. WALLACE HOPKINS (USA).

OECD Nuclear Energy Agency—NEA

Address: 38 boulevard Suchet, 75016 Paris, France.
Telephone: (1) 45-24-82-00.
Telex: 630668.

The NEA was established in 1958 to further the peaceful uses of nuclear energy. Originally a European agency, it has since admitted four of the five OECD members outside Europe.

MEMBERS

All members of OECD except New Zealand.

Organization

(October 1988)

STEERING COMMITTEE FOR NUCLEAR ENERGY

Chairman: RICHARD KENNEDY (USA).

SECRETARIAT

Director-General: Dr KUNIHIKO UEMATSU.
Deputy Director-General: PIERRE STROHL (France).
Deputy Director (Science and Development): SUMIO HORIUCHI.
Deputy Director (Safety and Regulation): KLAUS STADIE.

MAIN COMMITTEES

Committee for Technical and Economic Studies on Nuclear Energy Development and the Fuel Cycle;
Committee on the Safety of Nuclear Installations;
Committee on Radiation Protection and Public Health;
Radioactive Waste Management Committee;
NEA Nuclear Data Committee (NEANDC);
NEA Committee on Reactor Physics (NEACRP);
Group of Governmental Experts on Third Party Liability in the Field of Nuclear Energy.

Activities

The main purpose of the Agency is to promote international co-operation within the OECD area for the development and application of nuclear power for peaceful purposes through international research and development projects and exchange of scientific and technical experience and information. The Agency also maintains a continual survey with the co-operation of other organizations, notably the International Atomic Energy Agency (IAEA, q.v.), of world uranium resources, production and demand, and of economic and technical aspects of the nuclear fuel cycle.

A major part of the Agency's work is devoted to the safety and regulation of nuclear power, including co-operative studies and projects related to the prevention of nuclear accidents and the long-term safety of radioactive waste disposal systems.

JOINT PROJECTS

Halden Project: Halden, Norway; experimental boiling heavy water reactor, which became an OECD project in 1958. From 1964, under successive agreements with participating countries, the reactor has been used for long-term testing of water reactor fuels and for research into automatic computer-based control of nuclear power stations. Nuclear energy research institutions and authorities in 10 countries support the project.

OECD Loft Project: this international safety research programme, launched in 1983, is designed to provide data for developing and verifying nuclear safety computer programmes, for identifying important reactor accident phenomena experimentally, and for providing information on the operator/plant interface, using the Loss-of-Fluid Test Facility at the Idaho National Engineering Laboratory in the USA. Ten countries are members of this project.

Co-operative Programme on Three Mile Island: a multinational programme (established in 1986) which examines samples taken from the Three Mile Island nuclear reactor in Pennsylvania, USA (following the accident which took place there in 1979) and develops computer codes for analysis of severe accidents. The objective of this programme is to contribute to a better understanding of the accident, in particular of the sequence of events and the behaviour of fission products. Eleven countries participate in the programme.

International Stripa Project: set up in early 1980, this project is conducting experiments in an abandoned iron mine in Sweden, on the use of hard crystalline rock for isolating nuclear waste. Nine countries participate in the project.

Incident Reporting System: introduced in 1980 to exchange experience in operating nuclear power plants in OECD member countries and to improve nuclear safety by facilitating feedback of this experience to nuclear regulatory authorities, utilities and manufacturers.

Chemical Thermodynamic Data Base: the objective of this project, set up in 1983, is to compile fundamental chemical thermodynamic data which permit the quantification of mass transfers in chemical reactions occurring in ground water and in water-rock reactions. Such data can be used in geochemical modelling of waste disposal systems performance assessments to predict the concentration of radioelements under various conditions.

Alligator Rivers Analogue Project: an international research project, established in 1988 to gain further insight into the long-term physical and chemical processes likely to influence the transport of radionuclides through rock masses. Research involves the study of geochemical and hydrogeological processes acting upon the Koongarra uranium ore deposit in Australia, which may resemble those processes acting upon high-level radioactive waste disposal facility.

Decommissioning of Nuclear Installations: this co-operative programme, set up in 1985, provides for an exchange of scientific and technical information to develop the operational experience and data base needed for the future decommissioning of large nuclear power plants. Nine countries are participating in this programme.

COMMON SERVICE

NEA Data Bank: Saclay, France; set up in 1978 in succession to the Computer Programme Library and the Neutron Data Compilation Centre, the Data Bank allows the 16 participating countries to share large computer programmes used in reactor calculations, and nuclear data applications. It also operates as one of a worldwide network of four nuclear data centres.

FINANCE

The Agency's budget for 1987 amounted to 56.7m. French francs.

PUBLICATIONS

Annual Report.
NEA Newsletter (2 a year).
Nuclear Law Bulletin (2 a year).
Summary of Nuclear Power and Fuel Cycle Data for the OECD area (annually).
Reports and proceedings.

ORGANIZATION OF AFRICAN UNITY—OAU

Address: POB 3243, Addis Ababa, Ethiopia.
Telephone: 157700.

The Organization was founded in 1963 to promote unity and solidarity among African states.

FORMATION

There were various attempts at establishing an inter-African organization before the OAU Charter was drawn up. In November 1958 Ghana and Guinea (later joined by Mali) drafted a Charter which was to form the basis of a Union of African States. In January 1961 a conference was held at Casablanca, attended by the Heads of State of Ghana, Guinea, Mali, Morocco, and representatives of Libya and of the provisional government of the Algerian Republic (GPRA). Tunisia, Nigeria, Liberia and Togo declined the invitation to attend. An African Charter was adopted and it was decided to set up an African Military Command and an African Common Market.

Between October 1960 and March 1961 three conferences were held by French-speaking African countries, at Abidjan, Brazzaville and Yaoundé. None of the 12 countries which attended these meetings had been present at the Casablanca Conference. These conferences led eventually to the signing in September 1961, at Tananarive, of a charter establishing the Union africaine et malgache, later the Organisation commune africaine et mauricienne (OCAM).

In May 1961 a conference was held at Monrovia, Liberia, attended by the Heads of State or representatives of 19 countries: Cameroon, Central African Republic, Chad, Congo Republic (ex-French), Côte d'Ivoire, Dahomey, Ethiopia, Gabon, Liberia, Madagascar, Mauritania, Niger, Nigeria, Senegal, Sierra Leone, Somalia, Togo, Tunisia and Upper Volta. They met again (with the exception of Tunisia and with the addition of the ex-Belgian Congo Republic) in January 1962 at Lagos, Nigeria, and set up a permanent secretariat and a standing committee of finance ministers, and accepted a draft charter for an Organization of Inter-African and Malagasy States.

It was the Conference of Addis Ababa, held in 1963, which finally brought together African states despite the regional, political and linguistic differences which divided them. The Foreign Ministers of 32 African states attended the Preparatory Meeting held in May: Algeria, Burundi, Cameroon, Central African Republic, Chad, Congo (Brazzaville) (now the Congo), Congo (Léopoldville) (now Zaire), Côte d'Ivoire, Dahomey (now Benin), Ethiopia, Gabon, Ghana, Guinea, Liberia, Libya, Madagascar, Mali, Mauritania, Morocco, Niger, Nigeria, Rwanda, Senegal, Sierra Leone, Somalia, Sudan, Tanganyika (now Tanzania), Togo, Tunisia, Uganda, the United Arab Republic (Egypt) and Upper Volta (now Burkina Faso).

Organization of African States; (ii) co-operation among African states in the following fields: economic and social; education, culture and science; collective defence; (iii) decolonization; (iv) apartheid and racial discrimination; (v) effects of economic grouping on the economic development of Africa; (vi) disarmament; (vii) creation of a Permanent Conciliation Commission; and (viii) Africa and the United Nations.

The Heads of State Conference which opened on 23 May drew up the Charter of the Organization of African Unity, which was then signed by the heads of 30 states on 25 May 1963. The Charter was essentially functional and reflected a compromise between the concept of a loose association of states favoured by the Monrovia Group and the federal idea supported by the Casablanca Group, and in particular by Ghana.

SUMMARY OF OAU CHARTER

Article I. Establishment of the Organization of African Unity. The Organization to include continental African states, Madagascar, and other islands surrounding Africa.

Article II. Aims of the OAU:

1. To promote unity and solidarity among African states.

2. To intensify and co-ordinate efforts to improve living standards in Africa.

3. To defend sovereignty, territorial integrity and independence of African states.

4. To eradicate all forms of colonialism from Africa.

5. To promote international co-operation in keeping with the Charter of the United Nations.

Article III. Member states adhere to the principles of sovereignty, non-interference in internal affairs of member states, respect for territorial integrity, peaceful settlement of disputes, condemnation of political subversion, dedication to the emancipation of dependent African territories, and international non-alignment.

Article IV. Each independent sovereign African state shall be entitled to become a member of the Organization.

Article V. All member states shall have equal rights and duties.

Article VI. All member states shall observe scrupulously the principles laid down in Article III.

Article VII. Establishment of the Assembly of Heads of State and Government, the Council of Ministers, the General Secretariat, and the Commission of Mediation, Conciliation and Arbitration.

Articles VIII–XI. The Assembly of Heads of State and Government co-ordinates policies and reviews the structure of the Organization.

Articles XII–XV. The Council of Ministers shall prepare conferences of the Assembly, and co-ordinate inter-African co-operation. All resolutions shall be by simple majority.

Articles XVI–XVIII. The General Secretariat. The Administrative Secretary-General and his staff shall not seek or receive instructions from any government or other authority external to the Organization. They are international officials responsible only to the Organization.

Article XIX. Commission of Mediation, Conciliation and Arbitration. A separate protocol concerning the composition and nature of this Commission shall be regarded as an integral part of the Charter.

Articles XX–XXII. Specialized Commissions shall be established, composed of Ministers or other officials designated by Member Governments. Their regulations shall be laid down by the Council of Ministers.

Article XXIII. The Budget shall be prepared by the Secretary-General and approved by the Council of Ministers. Contributions shall be in accordance with the scale of assessment of the United Nations. No Member shall pay more than 20% of the total yearly amount.

Article XXIV. Texts of the Charter in African languages, English and French shall be equally authentic. Instruments of ratification shall be deposited with the Government of Ethiopia.

Article XXV. The Charter shall come into force on receipt by the Government of Ethiopia of the instruments of ratification of two-thirds of the signatory states.

Article XXVI. The Charter shall be registered with the Secretariat of the United Nations.

Article XXVII. Questions of interpretation shall be settled by a two-thirds majority vote in the Assembly of Heads of State and Government.

Article XXVIII. Admission of new independent African states to the Organization shall be decided by a simple majority of the Member States.

Articles XXIX–XXXIII. The working languages of the Organization shall be African languages, English and French. The Secretary-General may accept gifts and bequests to the Organization, subject to the approval of the Council of Ministers. The Council of Ministers shall establish privileges and immunities to be accorded to the personnel of the Secretariat in the territories of Member States. A State wishing to withdraw from the Organization must give a year's written notice to the Secretariat. The Charter may only be amended after consideration by all Member States and by a two-thirds majority vote of the Assembly of Heads of State and Government. Such amendments will come into force one year after submission.

INTERNATIONAL ORGANIZATIONS

Organization of African Unity

MEMBERS*

Algeria
Angola
Benin
Botswana
Burkina Faso
Burundi
Cameroon
Cape Verde
Central African Republic
Chad
The Comoros
Congo
Côte d'Ivoire
Djibouti
Egypt
Equatorial Guinea
Ethiopia
Gabon
The Gambia
Ghana
Guinea
Guinea-Bissau
Kenya
Lesotho
Liberia
Libya
Madagascar
Malawi
Mali
Mauritania
Mauritius
Mozambique
Niger
Nigeria
Rwanda
São Tomé and Príncipe
Senegal
Seychelles
Sierra Leone
Somalia
Sudan
Swaziland
Tanzania
Togo
Tunisia
Uganda
Zaire
Zambia
Zimbabwe

* The Sahrawi Arab Democratic Republic (Western Sahara) was admitted to the OAU in February 1982, following recognition by 26 of the 50 members, but its membership was disputed by Morocco and other states which claimed that a two-thirds majority was needed to admit a state whose existence was in question. Morocco withdrew from the OAU with effect from November 1985.

Organization
(October 1988)

ASSEMBLY OF HEADS OF STATE

The Assembly of Heads of State and Government meets annually to co-ordinate policies of African states. Resolutions are passed by a two-thirds majority, procedural matters by a simple majority. A chairman is elected at each meeting from among the members, to hold office for one year.

Chairman (1988/89): Gen MOUSSA TRAORÉ (Mali).

COUNCIL OF MINISTERS

Consists of Foreign and/or other Ministers and meets twice a year, with provision for extraordinary sessions. Each session elects its own Chairman. Prepares meetings of, and is responsible to, the Assembly of Heads of State.

GENERAL SECRETARIAT

The permanent headquarters of the organization. It carries out functions assigned to it in the Charter of the OAU and by other agreements and treaties made between member states. Departments: Political; Finance; Education, Science, Culture and Social Affairs; Economic Development and Co-operation; Administration and Conferences. The Secretary-General is elected for a four-year term by the Assembly of Heads of State.

Secretary-General: IDE OUMAROU (Niger).

ARBITRATION COMMISSION

Commission of Mediation, Conciliation and Arbitration: Addis Ababa; f. 1964; consists of 21 members elected by the Assembly of Heads of State for a five-year term; no state may have more than one member; has a Bureau consisting of a President and two Vice-Presidents, who shall not be eligible for re-election. Its task is to hear and settle disputes between member states by peaceful means.

SPECIALIZED COMMISSIONS

There are specialized commissions for economic, social, transport and communications affairs; education, science, culture and health; defence; human rights; and labour.

LIBERATION COMMITTEE

Co-ordinating Committee for the Liberation Movements of Africa: Dar es Salaam, Tanzania; f. 1963; to provide financial and military aid to nationalist movements in dependent countries; regional offices in Maputo, Mozambique, Lusaka, Zambia, and Luanda, Angola.

Executive Secretary: Col HASHIM MBITA (Tanzania).

BUDGET

Member states contribute in accordance with their United Nations assessment. No member state is assessed for an amount exceeding 20% of the yearly regular budget of the Organization. The 1986/87 budget amounted to US $25.3m., and the budget for 1987/88 was estimated at $23.2m. The budget for 1988/89 was estimated at $25.03m. Arrears in payments of contributions by members were reported to amount to $45m. at the beginning of 1988.

Principal Events, 1980–88

1980

May	An economic summit meeting resolved to take steps towards establishment of an African Common Market by year 2000; adopted 'Lagos Plan of Action' to this end.
July	The 17th Assembly of Heads of State postponed a decision on admitting the Sahrawi Arab Democratic Republic (SADR), proclaimed by the Frente Popular para la Liberación de Sakiet el Hamra y Río de Oro, known as the Frente Polisario (Polisario Front) in Western Sahara (the former Spanish Sahara, claimed by Morocco), after Morocco threatened to leave the OAU if admission were granted.
Sept.	The OAU committee on Western Sahara announced a six-point ceasefire plan, to include a referendum organized by the OAU with assistance from the UN.

1981

Jan.	A conference on Chad and Libya condemned the proposed merger of the two countries, demanded the withdrawal of all foreign forces from Chad and decided to send an African force to maintain peace there and supervise elections. A meeting of Ministers of Justice approved an African Charter on Human and People's Rights which (subject to ratification by a majority of OAU members) would establish a Commission to investigate violations of human rights.
Feb.	Ministers of foreign affairs supported proposals for an intensified guerrilla war in Namibia and mandatory economic sanctions against South Africa to persuade the South African Government to negotiate on Namibian independence.
June	At the 18th Assembly of Heads of State, Morocco agreed to hold a referendum in Western Sahara. A ministerial committee was created to investigate the Nigeria-Cameroon border dispute.
Nov.	The first members of the OAU peace-keeping force (from Nigeria, Senegal and Zaire) arrived in Chad to replace the Libyan troops previously supporting the Government against opposition forces.

1982

Feb.	The OAU committee on Chad established a timetable for ceasefire, negotiations, a provisional constitution and elections in Chad, and announced that the OAU peace-keeping force's mandate would cease at the end of June. The committee on Western Sahara empowered Pres. Moi of Kenya to conduct negotiations for a ceasefire between Morocco and the Polisario Front. At a meeting of Ministers of Foreign Affairs, the admission of a representative of the SADR led to a walk-out by 19 countries.
March–April	Ordinary OAU business was disrupted because boycotts by opponents and supporters of Polisario meant that three ministerial meetings were without a quorum of members. Discussions by a special group representing nine countries failed to solve the deadlock.
Aug.	The 19th Assembly of Heads of State, due to be held in Tripoli, Libya, failed to achieve a quorum when 19 states boycotted the meeting owing to the dispute over the admission of the SADR. A five-member committee was set up to try to convene another summit before the end of the year.
Nov.	A second attempt to hold the 19th Assembly of Heads of State in Tripoli was abandoned after a dispute over the representation of Chad: the Libyan leader, Col Gaddafi, and others opposed the presence of Pres. Hissène Habré in favour of the former Pres. Goukouni Oueddei, leading to a boycott by representatives of 14 moderate states.

1983

June	The 19th Assembly of Heads of State met in Addis Ababa:

SADR representatives agreed not to attend, in order to avoid a boycott of the meeting by their opponents. The Assembly again called for a referendum in Western Sahara and for direct negotiations between Morocco and the SADR.

1984

Jan. The OAU-sponsored talks between the rival factions in Chad, held in Addis Ababa, broke down without result, chiefly owing to the refusal of Pres. Habré to attend.

March The council of ministers of foreign affairs discussed cumulative budgetary arrears amounting to over US $34m.: less than one-third of contributions due for the 1983/84 period had been paid. The SADR delegation again agreed not to attend the meeting, but declared that they would be present at the next Assembly of Heads of State.

May The 20th Assembly, due to be held in Guinea in May, was postponed following the death in March of Pres. Sekou Touré.

Nov. The 20th Assembly was held in Addis Ababa. Nigeria became the 30th OAU member to recognize the Sahrawi Arab Democratic Republic. A delegation from the SADR was admitted to the Assembly, and Morocco immediately announced its resignation from the OAU (to take effect after one year); only Zaire supported Morocco by withdrawing from the meeting. The Assembly concentrated on economic matters, discussing Africa's balance-of-payments problems, debts and the drought affecting many countries. An emergency fund was set up to combat the effects of drought, with initial contributions of US $10m. each from Algeria and Libya.

1985

July The 21st Assembly of Heads of State was held in Addis Ababa, and again discussed mainly economic issues. It resulted in the Addis Ababa Declaration, in which member countries reiterated their commitment to the Lagos Plan of Action (see under 1980) and adopted a priority programme for the next five years, emphasizing the rehabilitation of African agriculture: they agreed to increase agriculture's share of public investment to between 20% and 25% by the year 1989. The meeting also expressed concern at Africa's heavy external debt (expected to total over US $170,000m. by the end of 1985) and called for a special conference of creditors and borrowers to seek a solution to the problem, and for an increase in concessional financial resources. The Assembly also agreed on the appointment of a new Secretary-General. A special emergency fund was created by the Assembly to combat drought and famine in Africa.

1986

May At a special session of the UN General Assembly on the economic problems of Africa, the OAU (represented by its Chairman) presented a programme, prepared jointly with the UN Economic Commission for Africa, calling for debt relief and an increase in assistance for agricultural investment.

July The 22nd Assembly of Heads of State called for comprehensive economic sanctions against South Africa, and strongly criticized the governments of the United Kingdom and the USA for opposing sanctions. Among other resolutions the Assembly condemned outside interference in Angola; called upon France to return the island of Mayotte to the Comoros; and resolved to continue efforts (led by the OAU Chairman) to bring about reconciliation in Chad. A council of 'wise men', comprising former African heads of state, was established to mediate, when necessary, in disputes between member countries. The Assembly reiterated its call for an international conference on Africa's foreign debt.

1987

Feb. The OAU Chairman, President Sassou-Nguessou of the Congo, undertook a tour of Europe to discuss the possibility of a negotiated settlement in Chad; the political situation in South Africa; and African debt.

July The Assembly of Heads of State reiterated its demands that Western countries should impose economic sanctions on South Africa. It renewed the mandate of the special OAU committee which had been attempting to resolve the dispute between Chad and Libya. It also discussed the spread of the disease AIDS in Africa; and approved the establishment of an African commission on human rights, now that the African Charter on Human and People's Rights (approved in 1981) had been ratified by a majority of member states.

Nov. A summit meeting on the subject of Africa's external debt (now estimated to total US $200,000m.) was held in Addis Ababa (but was attended by only 10 heads of state and government). The meeting issued a statement requesting the conversion of past bilateral loans into grants, a 10-year suspension of debt-service payments, reduction of interest rates and the lengthening of debt-maturity periods. It asked that creditors should observe the principle that debt-servicing should not exceed a 'reasonable and bearable' percentage of the debtor country's export earnings. A 'contact group' was established to enlist support for an international conference on African debt.

1988

May The Assembly of Heads of State recognized that no conference on debt was likely to be held until 1989, owing to the reluctance of creditors to participate. It condemned the links with South Africa still maintained by some African countries, and protested at the recently-reported unauthorized disposal of toxic waste in Africa by industrial companies from outside the continent.

Specialized Agencies

African Bureau for Educational Sciences: BP 14, Kisangani, Zaire.

African Civil Aviation Commission—AFCAC: 15 blvd de la République, BP 2356, Dakar, Senegal; telex 61182; f. 1969 to encourage co-operation in all civil aviation activities; promotes co-ordination and better utilization and development of African air transport systems and the standardization of aircraft, flight equipment and training programmes for pilots and mechanics; organizes working groups and seminars, and compiles statistics. Pres. VASSIRIKI SAVANE (Côte d'Ivoire); Sec. EDOUARD LOMBOLOU.

International Scientific Council for Trypanosomiasis Research and Control: Joint Secretariat, OAU/STRC, PM Bag 2359, Lagos, Nigeria; tel. 633289; telex 22199; f. 1949 to review the work on tsetse and trypanosomiasis problems carried out by organizations and workers concerned in laboratories and in the field; to stimulate further research and discussion and to promote co-ordination between research workers and organizations in the different countries in Africa, and to provide a regular opportunity for the discussion of particular problems and for the exposition of new experiments and discoveries. Exec. Sec. Prof. A. OLUFEMI WILLIAMS; Publ. Proceedings of ISCTR Conferences.

Organization of African Trade Union Unity—OATUU: POB M386, Accra, Ghana; tel. 74531; f. 1973 as a single continental trade union organization, independent of international trade union organizations; has affiliates from all African trade unions. Congress, composed of four delegates from all affiliated trade union centres, meets at least every four years as supreme policy-making body; General Council, composed of one representative from all affiliated trade unions, meets annually to implement Congress decisions and to approve annual budget. Mems: trade union movements in 50 independent African countries, including trade unions within the liberation movements; in February 1986, however, 28 countries formed a separate group, alleging financial mismanagement by OATUU officials. Sec.-Gen. HASSAN SUNMONU (Nigeria). Publ. *Voice of African Workers*.

Pan-African News Agency—PANA: BP 4056, Dakar, Senegal; tel. 22 61 20; telex 3261 3307; regional headquarters in Khartoum, Sudan; Lusaka, Zambia; Kinshasa, Zaire; Lagos, Nigeria; Tripoli, Libya; began operations in May 1983; receives information from national news agencies and circulates news in English and French. Dir AUGUSTE MPASSI-MUBA (Congo).

Pan-African Postal Union: POB 6026, Arusha, Tanzania; tel. 3910; telex 42096; f. 1980; Admin. Council representing 16 countries elected on regional basis. Sec.-Gen. COMLANVI AMOUSSOU (Togo).

Pan-African Telecommunications Union—PATU: BP 8634, Kinshasa, Zaire; tel. 22175; telex 21049; f. 1977 for co-ordination of telecommunications development. Sec.-Gen. RAJABU MABULA YUSUF.

Scientific, Technical and Research Commission—OAUSTRC: Nigerian Ports Authority Bldg, PMB 2359, Marina, Lagos, Nigeria; tel. 633289; telex 22199; f. 1965 to succeed the Commission for Technical Co-operation in Africa (f. 1954). Supervises the Inter-African Bureau for Animal Resources (Nairobi, Kenya), the Inter-African Bureau for Soils (Bangui, Central African Republic) and the Inter-African Phytosanitary Commission (Yaoundé, Cameroon) and several joint research projects (see also International Scientific Council on Trypanosomiasis Research and Control, above); a centre for Fertilizer Development was to be established in 1988. The Commission provides training in agricultural management, and conducts pest control programmes. Exec. Sec. Prof. A. OLUFEMI WILLIAMS.

Supreme Council for Sports in Africa: BP 1363, Yaoundé, Cameroon; tel. 22-27-11; telex 8295. Sec.-Gen. AMADOU LAMINE BA.

Union of African Railways: BP 687, Kinshasa, Zaire; tel. 23861; telex 21258 ZR; f. 1972 to standardize, expand, co-ordinate and improve members' railway services; the ultimate aim is to link all systems; main organs: General Assembly, Executive Board, General Secretariat, five technical cttees. Mems in 30 African countries. Pres. TOM MMARI; Sec.-Gen. ROBERT GEBE NKANA (Malawi).

ORGANIZATION OF AMERICAN STATES—OAS

Address: 1889 F St, NW, Washington, DC 20006, USA.
Telephone: (202) 458-3000.
Telex: 440118.

The OAS was founded at Bogotá, Colombia, in 1948 (succeeding the International Union of American Republics, founded in 1890) to foster peace, security, mutual understanding and co-operation among the nations of the Western Hemisphere.

MEMBERS

Antigua and Barbuda
Argentina
Bahamas
Barbados
Bolivia
Brazil
Chile
Colombia
Costa Rica
Cuba*
Dominica
Dominican Republic
Ecuador
El Salvador
Grenada
Guatemala
Haiti
Honduras
Jamaica
Mexico
Nicaragua
Panama
Paraguay
Peru
Saint Christopher and Nevis
Saint Lucia
Saint Vincent and the Grenadines
Suriname
Trinidad and Tobago
USA
Uruguay
Venezuela

Permanent Observers: Algeria, Austria, Belgium, Canada, Cyprus, Egypt, Equatorial Guinea, Finland, France, the Federal Republic of Germany, Greece, Guyana, the Holy See, Israel, Italy, Japan, the Republic of Korea, Morocco, the Netherlands, Pakistan, Portugal, Saudi Arabia, Spain and Switzerland.

* The Cuban Government was suspended from OAS activities in 1962.

Organization
(October 1988)

GENERAL ASSEMBLY

The Assembly meets annually and can also hold special sessions when convoked by the Permanent Council. Supreme organ of the OAS, it decides general action and policy.

MEETINGS OF CONSULTATION OF MINISTERS OF FOREIGN AFFAIRS

Meetings are held to consider problems of an urgent nature and of common interest to member states; they may be held at the request of any member state.

PERMANENT COUNCIL

The Council meets regularly throughout the year at OAS headquarters. It is composed of one representative of each member state with the rank of ambassador; each government may accredit alternate representatives and advisers and when necessary appoint an interim representative. The office of Chairman is held in turn by each of the representatives, following alphabetical order according to the names of the countries in Spanish. The Vice-Chairman is determined in the same way, following reverse alphabetical order. Their terms of office are three months.

The Council acts as an Organ of Consultation and oversees the maintenance of friendly relations between members. It supervises the work of the OAS and promotes co-operation with a variety of other international bodies including the United Nations. The official languages are English, French, Portuguese and Spanish.

INTER-AMERICAN ECONOMIC AND SOCIAL COUNCIL

The Council holds annual meetings of expert representatives and of ministers of finance and economy. Its aim is to promote co-operation among the countries of the region, in order to accelerate economic and social development. The permanent executive committee of the Council provides technical assistance.
Executive Secretary: (vacant).

INTER-AMERICAN COUNCIL FOR EDUCATION, SCIENCE AND CULTURE

The Council is composed of one representative from each member state, appointed by the respective governments; it meets annually at the level of ministers of education. Its principal purpose is to promote friendly relations and mutual understanding between the peoples of the Americas through educational, scientific and cultural co-operation and exchange between member states.

The council has a permanent executive committee and three committees in charge of carrying out regional development programmes in the fields of education, science and technology, and culture.
Executive Secretary: ENRIQUE MARTÍN DEL CAMPO (Mexico).

INTER-AMERICAN JURIDICAL COMMITTEE

Address: Rua Senador Vergueiro 81, Rio de Janeiro, RJ, Brazil; tel. 225-1361. Composed of 11 jurists, nationals of different member states, elected for a period of four years with the possibility of re-election once. Equitable geographical distribution is sought as far as possible, and a proportion of members are replaced each year. The Committee's purpose is to serve as an advisory body to the Organization on juridical matters; to promote the progressive development and codification of international law and to study juridical problems related to the integration of the developing countries in the hemisphere, and in so far as may appear desirable, the possibility of attaining uniformity in legislation. Meetings are held twice a year for about four weeks. Special meetings can also be called. The Committee has prepared numerous studies, reports and draft conventions on legal topics.

INTER-AMERICAN COMMISSION ON HUMAN RIGHTS

The Commission was established in 1960 and comprises seven members. It promotes the observance and protection of human rights in the member states of the OAS; it examines and reports on the human rights situation in member countries, and provides consultative services.

INTER-AMERICAN COURT OF HUMAN RIGHTS

Based in San José, Costa Rica, the Court was established in 1978, as an autonomous judicial institution whose purpose is to apply and interpret the American Convention on Human Rights (which entered into force in 1978 and had been ratified by 19 OAS member states by the end of June 1987). The Court comprises seven jurists from OAS member states.

GENERAL SECRETARIAT

The central and permanent organ of the Organization, carries out the duties entrusted to it by the General Assembly, Meetings of Consultation of Ministers of Foreign Affairs and the Councils.
Secretary-General: JOÃO CLEMENTE BAENA SOARES (Brazil).
Assistant Secretary-General: VAL MCCOMIE (Barbados).

Record of Events

1826	First Congress of American States, convened by Simón Bolívar at Panama City. The Treaty of Perpetual Union, League and Confederation was signed by Colombia, the United Provinces of Central America, Peru, and Mexico.
1889–90	First International Conference of American States (Washington) founded the International Union of American Republics and established a central office, the Commercial Bureau, the purpose of which was the 'prompt collection and distribution of commercial information'.
1910	Fourth Conference (Buenos Aires) changed the organization's name to Union of American Republics. The name of its principal organ was changed from Commercial Bureau to Pan American Union.
1923	Fifth Conference (Santiago, Chile) changed the title to Union of Republics of the American Continent, with the Pan American Union as its permanent organ.

1928	Sixth Conference (Havana): the Governing Board and Pan American Union were prohibited from exercising political functions.
1945	Inter-American Conference on Problems of War and Peace: Mexico City. The Act of Chapultepec established a system of Continental Security for the American States.
1947	The Inter-American Treaty of Reciprocal Assistance set up a joint security pact for the defence of the Western Hemisphere against attack from outside and for internal security.
1948	Ninth Conference (Bogotá). Member Governments signed the Charter of the Organization of American States.
1954	The OAS adopted the Declaration of Solidarity for the Preservation of the Political Integrity of the American States against the Intervention of International Communism.
1959	An Act was passed by 21 American States to establish the Inter-American Development Bank (q.v.).
1960	A committee was established to co-ordinate the activities of the OAS, the Inter-American Development Bank and the UN Economic Commission for Latin America (ECLA).
1962	Cuba was suspended from the OAS, which supported the USA in its demand for the removal of missile bases in Cuba.
1964	The OAS mediated in dispute between USA and Panama, and voted for sanctions against Cuba by 15 votes to 4 (Bolivia, Chile, Mexico and Uruguay).
1965	An Inter-American Peace Force was created in reaction to events in the Dominican Republic.
1967	A treaty for the establishment of a Latin American nuclear-free zone was signed in Mexico City. In April a regional summit conference agreed to create a Latin American Common Market based on existing integration systems LAFTA and CACM.
1969	El Salvador and Honduras called on the OAS to investigate alleged violation of human rights of Salvadoreans in Honduras. A committee was sent to investigate after fighting broke out. Observers from OAS member nations supervised cease-fire and exchange of prisoners.
1970	Entry into force of the Protocol of Buenos Aires, establishing the General Assembly as the highest body of the OAS, replacing the Inter-American Conferences, and the three Councils as its main organs. The General Assembly held two special sessions to establish the new system and to discuss other current problems, in particular kidnapping and extortion.
1971	First regular Session of the General Assembly of the OAS at San José, Costa Rica, in April.
1976	Sixth General Assembly; chief resolutions concerned human rights, the US Trade Act of 1974 and transnational enterprises. It also resolved to hold a Special Assembly to review matters concerning inter-American co-operation for development. The Assembly proclaimed a Decade of Women 1976–85: Equality, Development and Peace. Honduras and El Salvador signed the Act of Managua to end a series of border incidents between them.
1977	The Seventh General Assembly was held in Grenada, a new member state. The delegations adopted four resolutions on human rights and a resolution condemning terrorist activities in the hemisphere and in the world. The financial problems of many of the countries, caused by the energy crisis and their less-than-satisfactory positions in international trade, was a matter of continuing concern. 1978 was declared Inter-American Rural Youth Year.
1978	The Eighth General Assembly was held in Washington, DC; resolutions included one calling for member states to co-operate with the Inter-American Commission on Human Rights in on-site inspections, and another recommending the establishment of an Inter-American Court of Human Rights in San José, Costa Rica. In view of the USA's announced intention to reduce its quota, the Permanent Council received a mandate to develop a new formula to finance the OAS programme budget. Funds were authorized for purchase of new OAS headquarters under construction in Washington, DC.
1979	The Inter-American Court of Human Rights was formally established in San José, Costa Rica, its members installed, and the statutes governing its operation were adopted.
1980	The Permanent Council met in July and passed a resolution condemning the military coup in Bolivia and deploring the interruption of the return to democracy there. In November the Tenth General Assembly named Argentina, Chile, El Salvador, Haiti, Paraguay and Uruguay as countries of special concern with regard to human rights violations (but avoided condemning them outright after Argentina threatened to withdraw from the organization if this was done).
1981	In February Ministers of Foreign Affairs called on Ecuador and Peru to stop military operations in their border area: both countries agreed to a cease-fire monitored by a committee composed of representatives of Argentina, Brazil, Chile and the USA.
1982	In May the Ministers of Foreign Affairs called on Argentina and the United Kingdom to cease hostilities over the Falkland (Malvinas) Islands and to resume negotiations for a peaceful settlement of the conflict, taking into account Argentina's 'rights of sovereignty' and the interests of the islanders.
1984	In November the General Assembly discussed the political crisis in Central America and the increasing foreign debts incurred by Latin American countries; it agreed to attempt to 'revitalize' the OAS during the next year, so that the Organization could play a more effective part in solving regional problems.
1985	In December amendments to the OAS Charter were adopted by the General Assembly (subject to ratification by two-thirds of the member states, which was expected to take several years). The amendments increased the executive powers of the OAS Secretary-General, who would henceforth be allowed to take the initiative in bringing before the Permanent Council matters that 'might threaten the peace and security of the hemisphere or the development of the member states', something which previously only a member country had been permitted to do. The OAS also gained greater powers of mediation through an amendment allowing the Permanent Council to try to resolve a dispute between members, whether or not all the parties concerned had (as previously stipulated) agreed to take the matter before the OAS.
1986	In November the General Assembly passed a resolution expressing 'strong concern' over the United Kingdom's decision, in the previous month, to establish an exclusive 'conservation and management zone' extending for 150 nautical miles around the Falkland Islands. The Assembly also expressed its support for the negotiations conducted by the Contadora Group (q.v.) with the aim of bringing about peace in Central America.
1987	Following the signing in August of the 'Esquipulas II' agreement (in which the heads of government of Costa Rica, El Salvador, Guatemala, Honduras and Nicaragua agreed to implement a cease-fire between government forces and rebel groups, an amnesty for rebels, and democratic political processes) the Secretary-General of the OAS was invited to serve as a member of the international commission which was established to oversee compliance with the agreement.
1988	The OAS Secretary-General was invited to witness negotiations held in March between the Nicaraguan Government and rebel forces, and, following the signing of a cease-fire agreement with effect from 1 April, he continued to serve as a member of the verification commission established by the agreement.

FINANCE

The total funds managed by the OAS in 1987 amounted to US $85m. in quotas and contributions of the member states, together with counterpart contributions from them, and additional contributions from Permanent Observers and other organizations. Serious arrears in members' payments were reported in 1987, and a 'financial crisis' was reported at mid-1988, with a deficit of $20m. expected by the end of the year.

PUBLICATIONS
(in English and Spanish)

Catalog of Publications (annually).
Américas (6 a year).

Annual Report.
Ciencia Interamericana (quarterly).
La Educación (quarterly).
Statistical Bulletin (quarterly).
Numerous cultural, legal and scientific reports and studies.

SPECIALIZED ORGANIZATIONS OF THE OAS

Inter-American Children's Institute: Avda 8 de Octubre 2904, Montevideo, Uruguay; tel. 80 14 12; f. 1927 to achieve better health, education, social legislation, social services and statistics. Dir-Gen. EUGENIA M. ZAMONA (Costa Rica). Publ. *Boletín*.

Inter-American Commission of Women: General Secretariat of the OAS, 1889 F St, NW, Washington, DC 20006, USA; tel. (202) 458-6084; f. 1928 for the extension of civil, political, economic, social and cultural rights for women. Chair. SARA NAVAS DE SIEFER (Chile).

Inter-American Indian Institute: Avda Insurgentes Sur 1690, Col. Florida, México 01030, DF, Mexico; tel. 660-0007; f. 1940 to direct research for the better understanding of Indian groups and the solution of their educational, economic and social problems; provides technical assistance for programmes of Indian community development and trains personnel. Dir OSCAR ARZE QUINTANILLA; Sec. ARTURO MORENO. Publs *América Indígena* (quarterly), *Anuario Indigenista*, *Indian News of the Americas*, *Noticias Indigenistas de América* (every 4 months).

Inter-American Institute for Co-operation on Agriculture: Apdo 55–2200 Coronado, San José, Costa Rica; tel. 290222; telex 21441; f. 1942 (as the Inter-American Institute of Agricultural Sciences: new name 1980); supports the efforts of member states to improve agricultural development and rural well-being; encourages co-operation between regional organizations, and provides a forum for the exchange of experience. Dir Dr MARTÍN E. PIÑEIRO (Argentina).

Pan American Health Organization: 525 23rd St, NW, Washington, DC 20037, USA; tel. (202) 861-3200; co-ordinates regional efforts to improve health; maintains close relations with national health organizations and serves as the Regional Office for the Americas of the World Health Organization. Dir Dr CARLYLE GUERRA DE MACEDO (Brazil).

Pan-American Institute of Geography and History: Ex-Arzobispado 29, 11860 México, DF, Mexico; tel. 5151910; has four Commissions: Commission on Cartography (México, DF); Commission on Geography (Quebec, Canada); Commission on History (Caracas, Venezuela); Commission on Geophysics (Lima, Peru). Each Commission promotes and conducts studies in the appropriate fields, provides training and promotes co-operation among interested organizations. Sec.-Gen. LEOPOLDO RODRÍGUEZ (Argentina). Publs *Boletín Aéreo*, *Revista Cartográfica*, *Revista Geográfica*, *Revista de Historia de América*, *Boletín de Antropología Americana*, *Revista Geofísica*, *Folklore Americano*.

ASSOCIATED ORGANIZATIONS

Inter-American Defense Board: 2600 16th St, NW, Washington, DC 20441, USA; tel. (202) 939-6600; works in liaison with member governments to plan the common defence of the western hemisphere; operates the Inter-American Defense College. Chair. Lieut-Gen. JOHN L. BALLANTYNE (USA).

Inter-American Nuclear Energy Commission: General Secretariat of the OAS, 17th St and Constitution Ave, NW, Washington, DC 20006, USA; tel. (202) 458-3369; telex 64128; f. 1959 to assist member countries in developing and co-ordinating nuclear energy research; organizes periodic conferences and gives fellowships and financial assistance to research institutions. Exec. Sec. MIGUEL LAUFER (Venezuela).

ORGANIZATION OF ARAB PETROLEUM EXPORTING COUNTRIES—OAPEC

Address: POB 20501, Safat, 13066 Kuwait.
Telephone: 2448200.
Telex: 22166.

OAPEC was established in 1968 to safeguard the interests of members and to determine ways and means for their co-operation in various forms of economic activity in the petroleum industry.

MEMBERS*

Algeria	Kuwait	Syria
Bahrain	Libya	United Arab Emirates
Egypt	Qatar	
Iraq	Saudi Arabia	

* Egypt's membership was suspended from 17 April 1979. Tunisia ceased to be a member from 1 January 1987.

Organization
(October 1988)

MINISTERIAL COUNCIL

The Council consists normally of the ministers of petroleum of the member states, and forms the supreme authority of the Organization, responsible for drawing up its general policy, directing its activities and laying down its governing rules. It meets twice yearly as a minimum requirement and may hold extraordinary sessions. Chairmanship is on an annual rotation basis.

EXECUTIVE BUREAU

Assists the Council to direct the management of the Organization, approves staff regulations, reviews the budget, and refers it to the Council, considers matters relating to the Organization's agreements and activities and draws up the agenda for the Council. The Bureau comprises one senior official from each member state. Chairmanship is by rotation. The Bureau normally convenes twice a year before meetings of the Ministerial Council.

SECRETARIAT

Secretary-General: (vacant).
Acting Secretary-General: ABDELAZIZ ALWATTARI (Iraq).

Besides the Office of the Secretary-General, there are four departments: Financial, Administrative Affairs, Information and Library. The Arab Centre for Energy Studies, established in 1983, comprises the Technical Affairs and Economics Departments.

JUDICIAL TRIBUNAL

The Tribunal comprises nine judges from Arab countries. Its task is to settle differences in interpretation and application of the OAPEC Agreement, arising between members and also between OAPEC and its affiliates; disputes among member countries on oil activities falling within OAPEC's jurisdiction and not under the sovereignty of member countries; and disputes that the Council of Ministers decides to submit to the Tribunal.
President: FARES AL-WEGEYAN.

Activities

OAPEC co-ordinates different aspects of the Arab petroleum industry through the joint undertakings described below. It co-operates with the League of Arab States and other Arab organizations, and attempts to link petroleum research institutes in the Arab states. It organizes or participates in conferences and seminars, many of which are held in co-operation with non-Arab organizations; examples include the Fifth Arab Conference on Mineral Resources and the fourth triennial Arab Energy Conference (1988); and seminars on new techniques in petroleum production, on the integration of the Arab petrochemical industry and on financing petroleum projects (1985 and 1986). One of the principal features of OAPEC's 1987–91 programme of activities was the promotion of inter-Arab trade in petroleum products and petrochemicals.

OAPEC provides training in technical matters and in documentation and information. It holds an annual Training Programme on the Fundamentals of the Oil and Gas Industry, for about 70 trainees at middle management level. It also holds a training programme every two years for specialists in information on petroleum (e.g. from news agencies, the press and government ministries). The General Secretariat also conducts technical and feasibility studies and carries out market reviews. It provides information through a library, data base and the publications listed below.

At the end of 1986 it was reported that members' arrears in contributions to OAPEC's budget amounted to about US $14m. The budget for 1988 was about $4.5m., compared with the 1987 budget of $7.3m.

JOINTLY SPONSORED UNDERTAKINGS

Arab Engineering Company—AREC: POB 898, Abu Dhabi; f. 1981 to give support to national engineering firms by providing Arab experts, organizing a common operational base and supervising the training of Arab engineers. Authorized capital $20m.; subscribed capital $12m.

Arab Maritime Petroleum Transport Company—AMPTC: POB 22525, Safat, 13086 Kuwait; tel. 2411815; telex 23175; f. 1973 to undertake transport of crude oil, gas, refined products and petrochemicals, and thus to increase Arab participation in the tanker transport industry; capital (authorized and subscribed) $500m. Chair. RASHID AWEIDAH ATH-THANI; Man.-Dir SULEIMAN AL-BASSAM.

Arab Petroleum Investments Corporation—APICORP: POB 448, Dhahran Airport 31932, Saudi Arabia; tel. 864-74-00; telex 870068; f. 1975 to finance investments in petroleum and petrochemicals projects and related industries in the Arab world and in developing countries, with priority being given to Arab joint ventures. Projects financed include gas liquefaction plants, petrochemicals, tankers, oil refineries and fertilizers. Authorized capital: US $1,200m.; subscribed capital: $400m. Shareholders: Kuwait, Saudi Arabia and United Arab Emirates (17% each), Libya (15%), Iraq and Qatar (10% each), Algeria (5%), Bahrain, Egypt and Syria (3% each). Chair. JAMAL HASSAN JAWA; Gen.-Man. Dr NUREDDIN FARRAG.

Arab Petroleum Services Company—APSC: POB 12925, Tripoli, Libya; tel. 45861; telex 20405; f. 1977 to provide petroleum services through the establishment of companies specializing in various activities, and to train specialized personnel. Authorized capital: 100m. Libyan dinars; subscribed capital: 15m. Libyan dinars. Chair. AYYAD AD-DALY; Gen.-Man. ISMAIL AL-KORAITLI.

Arab Drilling and Workover Company: POB 680, Tripoli, Libya; f. 1980 as a subsidiary of APSC; subscribed capital: 12m. Libyan dinars; Gen. Man. MUHAMMAD AHMAD ATTIGA.

Arab Geophysical Exploration Services Company: POB 12925, Tripoli, Libya; tel. 38700; telex 20405; f. 1985.

Arab Logging Company: POB 6225, Baghdad, Iraq; tel. 5411125; telex 213688; f. 1983 to test stratigraphic measuring instruments.

Arab Petroleum Training Institute: POB 6037, Al-Tajeyat, Baghdad, Iraq; f. 1979; tel. 5234100; telex 212728; Dir BARAK SAID YEHYA.

Arab Shipbuilding and Repair Yard Company—ASRY: POB 50110, Manama, Bahrain; tel. 671111; telex 8455; f. 1974 to undertake repairs and servicing of vessels; operates a dry dock in Bahrain. Capital (authorized and subscribed) $340m. Chair. Sheikh DAIJ BIN KHALIFAH AL-KHALIFAH; Gen.-Man. ANTÓNIO MACHADO LOPES.

PUBLICATIONS

Secretary-General's Annual Report (Arabic and English editions).
Oil and Arab Cooperation (quarterly, Arabic).
OAPEC Monthly Bulletin (Arabic and English).
Energy Bibliography (annually, Arabic and English).
Energy Resources Monitor (quarterly, Arabic).
OAPEC Library Index of Periodical Articles (every 2 months, Arabic and English).
Current Awareness (every 2 months).
Papers, studies, conference proceedings.

ORGANIZATION OF THE ISLAMIC CONFERENCE—OIC

Address: Kilo 6, Mecca Rd, POB 178, Jeddah, Saudi Arabia.
Telephone: 6873880.
Telex: 401366.

The Organization was established in May 1971, following a summit meeting of Muslim heads of state at Rabat, Morocco, in September 1969, and the Islamic Foreign Ministers' Conference in Jeddah in March 1970, and in Karachi, Pakistan in December 1970.

MEMBERS

Afghanistan*
Algeria
Bahrain
Bangladesh
Benin
Brunei
Burkina Faso
Cameroon
Chad
The Comoros
Djibouti
Egypt*
Gabon
The Gambia
Guinea
Guinea-Bissau
Indonesia
Iran
Iraq
Jordan
Kuwait
Lebanon
Libya
Malaysia
Maldives
Mali
Mauritania
Morocco
Niger
Nigeria
Oman
Pakistan
Palestine Liberation Organization
Qatar
Saudi Arabia
Senegal
Sierra Leone
Somalia
Sudan
Syria
Tunisia
Turkey
Uganda
United Arab Emirates
Yemen Arab Republic
Yemen, People's Democratic Republic

* Egypt's membership was suspended in May 1979 and restored in March 1984. Afghanistan's membership was suspended in January 1980.

Note: Observer status has been granted to the 'Turkish Federated State of Cyprus' (which declared independence as the 'Turkish Republic of Northern Cyprus' in November 1983).

Organization

(October 1988)

SUMMIT CONFERENCES

The supreme body of the Organization is the Conference of Heads of State, which met in 1969 at Rabat, Morocco, in 1974 at Lahore, Pakistan, and in January 1981 at Mecca, Saudi Arabia, when it was decided that summit conferences would be held every three years in future. Fifth Conference: Kuwait, January 1987.

CONFERENCES OF FOREIGN MINISTERS

Conferences take place annually, to consider the means for implementing the general policy of the Organization. An extraordinary session was held for the first time in January 1980 to discuss the situation in Afghanistan: further extraordinary sessions were held in July, September and October.

SECRETARIAT

The executive organ of the Organization, headed by a Secretary-General and four Assistant Secretaries-General.

Secretary-General: SAYED SHARIF ED-DIN PIRZADA.

SPECIALIZED COMMITTEES

Al-Quds Committee: f. 1975 to implement the resolutions of the Islamic Conference on the status of Jerusalem (Al-Quds); since 1979 it has met at the level of foreign ministers, under the chairmanship of King Hassan II of Morocco.

Islamic Commission for Economic, Cultural and Social Affairs: f. 1976.

Permanent Finance Committee.

Standing Committee for Scientific and Technical Co-operation: f. 1981.

Standing Committee for Economic and Trade Co-operation: f. 1981.

Standing Committee for Information and Cultural Affairs: f. 1981.

Activities

The Organization's aims, as set out in the Charter adopted in 1972 are:

(i) To promote Islamic solidarity among member states;

(ii) To consolidate co-operation among member states in the economic, social, cultural, scientific and other vital fields, and to arrange consultations among member states belonging to international organizations;

(iii) To endeavour to eliminate racial segregation and discrimination and to eradicate colonialism in all its forms;

(iv) To take necessary measures to support international peace and security founded on justice;

(v) To co-ordinate all efforts for the safeguard of the Holy Places and support of the struggle of the people of Palestine, and help them to regain their rights and liberate their land;

(vi) To strengthen the struggle of all Muslim people with a view to safeguarding their dignity, independence and national rights; and

(vii) To create a suitable atmosphere for the promotion of co-operation and understanding among member states and other countries.

The first summit conference of Islamic leaders (representing 24 states) took place in 1969 following the burning of the Al Aqsa Mosque in Jerusalem. At this conference it was decided that Islamic governments should 'consult together with a view to promoting close co-operation and mutual assistance in the economic, scientific, cultural and spiritual fields, inspired by the immortal teachings of Islam'. Thereafter the foreign ministers of the countries concerned met annually, and adopted the Charter of the Organization of the Islamic Conference in 1972.

At the second Islamic summit conference (Lahore, Pakistan, 1974), the Islamic Solidarity Fund was established, together with a committee of representatives which later evolved into the Islamic Commission for Economic, Social and Cultural Affairs. Subsequently, numerous other subsidiary bodies have been set up (see below).

ECONOMIC CO-OPERATION

A general agreement for economic, technical and commercial co-operation came into force in 1981, providing for the establishment of joint investment projects and trade co-ordination. This was followed by an agreement on promotion, protection and guarantee of investments among member states. A plan of action to strengthen economic co-operation was adopted at the third Islamic summit conference in 1981, aiming to promote collective self-reliance and the development of joint ventures in all sectors. In April 1983 the Islamic Reinsurance Corporation was launched by the OIC with authorized capital of US $200m.

A meeting of ministers of industry was held in February 1982, and agreed to promote industrial co-operation, including joint ventures in agricultural machinery, engineering and other basic industries.

CULTURAL CO-OPERATION

The Organization supports education in Muslim communities throughout the world, and, through the Islamic Solidarity Fund, has helped to establish Islamic universities in Niger, Uganda and Malaysia. It organizes seminars on various aspects of Islam, and encourages dialogue with the other monotheistic religions. Support is given to publications on Islam both in Muslim and Western countries.

HUMANITARIAN ASSISTANCE

Assistance is given to Muslim communities affected by wars and natural disasters, in co-operation with UN organizations, particularly UNHCR. The countries of the Sahel region (Burkina Faso, Cape Verde, Chad, The Gambia, Guinea, Guinea-Bissau, Mali,

Mauritania, Niger and Senegal) receive particular attention as victims of drought.

POLITICAL CO-OPERATION

The Organization is also active at a political level. From the beginning it called for vacation of Arab territories by Israel, recognition of the rights of Palestinians and of the Palestine Liberation Organization as their sole legitimate representative, and the restoration of Jerusalem to Arab rule. The 1981 summit conference called for a *jihad* (holy war—though not necessarily in a military sense) 'for the liberation of Jerusalem and the occupied territories'; this was to include an Islamic economic boycott of Israel.

The first extraordinary Conference of Foreign Ministers was held in Islamabad, Pakistan, in January 1980. The member states called for the immediate and unconditional withdrawal of Soviet troops from Afghanistan and suspended Afghanistan's membership of the organization. The Conference also reaffirmed the importance of the Iranian Islamic Republic's sovereignty, territorial integrity and political independence, and adopted a resolution opposing any foreign pressures exerted on Islamic countries in general and Iran in particular. The Conference further asked members not to participate in the 1980 Olympics unless the Soviet troops had withdrawn from Afghanistan; and adopted a resolution condemning armed aggression against Somalia and denouncing the presence of military forces of the USSR and some of its allies in the Horn of Africa.

In May 1980 a special committee was set up to conduct consultations on Afghanistan. Mediation in the Gulf war between Iran and Iraq was also attempted: an Islamic Peace Committee, headed by the Secretary-General of the Organization, was established in September 1980 and suggested a cease-fire supervised by an observer force of troops drawn from Islamic countries, but the terms were rejected by the protagonists.

The third Islamic summit conference (Mecca, Saudi Arabia, January 1981) repeated the demand for Soviet withdrawal from Afghanistan and affirmed Afghanistan's political independence. It also decided to continue attempts at mediation between Iran and Iraq.

In 1982 Islamic foreign ministers decided to set up Islamic offices for boycotting Israel and for military co-operation with the Palestine Liberation Organization. The OIC endorsed the peace plan proposed by the League of Arab States.

The 1984 summit conference agreed to reinstate Egypt as a member of the Organization, although the resolution was opposed by seven states.

The fourth summit conference, held in Kuwait in January 1987, again discussed the continuing Iran-Iraq war, and agreed that the Islamic Peace Committee should attempt to prevent the sale of military equipment to the parties in the conflict. The conference also discussed the conflicts in Chad and Lebanon, and requested the holding of a United Nations conference to define international terrorism, as opposed to legitimate fighting for freedom. The conference also approved proposals for joint development of modern technology, and for improving scientific and technical skills in the less-developed Islamic countries.

SUBSIDIARY ORGANS

Al-Quds Fund: f. 1976.

International Commission for the Islamic Heritage: f. 1980.

International Islamic Law Commission: f. 1982.

Islamic Centre for the Development of Trade: Complexe Commerciale des Habous, ave des FAR, BP 13545, Casablanca, Morocco; tel. 31 49 74; telex 22026; opened 1983 to encourage regular commercial contacts, harmonize policies and promote investments among OIC members.

Islamic Centre for Technical and Vocational Training and Research: KB Bazar, Joydebpur, Gazipur Dist., Dhaka, Bangladesh; tel. 390154; telex 642739; f. 1979 to provide skilled technicians and instructors in mechanical, electrical, electronic and chemical technology, and to conduct research; expected to begin operations in 1986, with 650 students, later to increase to 1,150. Dir Dr RAFIQ ED-DIN AHMAD.

Islamic Commission for the International Crescent: f. 1980.

Islamic Foundation for Science, Technology and Development—IFSTAD: POB 9833, Jeddah 21423, Saudi Arabia; tel. 6322273; telex 604081; f. 1981 to promote co-operation in science and technology within the Islamic world. Dir-Gen. (vacant).

Islamic Jurisprudence Academy: f. 1982.

Islamic Solidarity Fund: c/o OIC Secretariat, POB 178, Jeddah, Saudi Arabia; f. 1974 to meet the needs of Islamic communities by providing emergency aid and the wherewithal to build mosques, Islamic centres, hospitals, schools and universities. Exec. Dir HASSAN M. DAOUD.

Research Centre for Islamic History, Art and Culture: POB 24, Beşiktaş 80700, Istanbul, Turkey; tel. 1605988; telex 26484; f. 1979; library of 22,000 vols; Dir-Gen. E. IHSANOĞLU. Publ. *Newsletter* (3 a year).

Statistical, Economic and Social Research and Training Centre for the Islamic Countries: Attar Sok. 4, GOP, Ankara, Turkey; tel. 1286105; telex 43163; f. 1978; Dir Dr ŞADI CINDORUK.

OTHER INSTITUTIONS WITHIN THE OIC SYSTEM

International Islamic News Agency: Prince Fahd St, POB 5054, Jeddah, Saudi Arabia; f. 1972. Dir-Gen. AHMAD FARRAG.

Islamic Capitals Organization: c/o Mayor of Mecca, Mecca, Saudi Arabia; f. 1978.

Islamic Chamber of Commerce, Industry and Commodity Exchange: POB 3831; Clifton Road, Karachi, Pakistan; tel. 530535; telex 25533; f. 1979. Pres. Sheikh ISMAIL ABU DAWOOD; Sec.-Gen. ALIOUNE DAT. Publ. *Quarterly Information Bulletin*.

Islamic Development Bank (q.v.).

Islamic Educational, Scientific and Cultural Organization: BP 755, Agdal, Rabat, Morocco; tel. 724-33; telex 326-45; f. 1982. Dir-Gen. ABD AL-HADI BOUTALEB. Publs *ISESCO Bulletin* (quarterly), *Islam Today* (annually), *ISESCO Triennial*.

Islamic States Broadcasting Organization: c/o Pakistan Broadcasting Corpn, Broadcasting House, Islamabad, Pakistan; tel. 829021; telex 5816; f. 1975. Sec.-Gen. AHMAD FARRAJ.

At the summit conference in January 1981 it was decided that an Islamic Court of Justice should be established to adjudicate in disputes between Muslim countries. Experts met in January 1983 to draw up a constitution for the court. In 1987 it was decided that an Islamic Institute of Agriculture was to be established in Dakar, Senegal, by 1990.

ORGANIZATION OF THE PETROLEUM EXPORTING COUNTRIES—OPEC

Address: Obere Donaustrasse 93, 1020 Vienna, Austria.
Telephone: (0222) 26-55-11.
Telex: 134474.

OPEC was established in 1960 to link countries whose main source of export earnings is petroleum; it aims to unify and co-ordinate members' petroleum policies and to safeguard their interests generally. The OPEC Fund for International Development is described on p. 199.

MEMBERS*

Algeria	Iraq	Saudi Arabia
Ecuador	Kuwait	United Arab
Gabon	Libya	Emirates
Indonesia	Nigeria	Venezuela
Iran	Qatar	

* OPEC's share of world petroleum production was 32.6% in 1986, increasing from 29% in 1985 (compared with 45% in 1980 and a peak of 55.5% in 1973). At the end of 1986 OPEC members were estimated to possess 67.9% of the world's known reserves of crude petroleum, and 32.8% of known reserves of natural gas.

Organization
(October 1988)

CONFERENCE

The Conference is the supreme authority of the Organization, responsible for the formulation of its general policy. It consists of representatives of member countries, who examine reports and recommendations submitted by the Board of Governors. It approves the appointment of Governors from each country and elects the Chairman of the Board of Governors. It works on the unanimity principle, and meets at least twice a year.

THE BOARD OF GOVERNORS

The Board directs the management of the Organization; it implements resolutions of the Conference and draws up an annual budget. It consists of one governor for each member country, and meets at least twice a year.

THE ECONOMIC COMMISSION

A specialized body operating within the framework of the Secretariat, with a view to assisting the Organization in promoting stability in international oil prices at equitable levels; consists of a board, national representatives and a commission staff; the Board meets at least twice a year.

SECRETARIAT

Office of the Secretary-General: Provides the Secretary-General with executive assistance in carrying out contacts with governments, organizations and delegations, in matters of protocol and in the preparation for and co-ordination of meetings.
Secretary-General: Dr Subroto (Indonesia).
Deputy Secretary-General: Dr Fadhil J. al-Chalabi (Iraq).
Energy Studies Department: Conducts a continuous programme for research in energy and related matters; monitors, forecasts and analyses developments in the energy and petrochemical industries; and the evaluation of hydrocarbons and products and their non-energy uses.
Economics and Finance Department: Analyses economic and financial issues of significant interest; in particular those related to international financial and monetary matters, and to the international petroleum industry.
Data Services Department:
  Computer Section: Maintains and expands information services to support the research activities of the Secretariat and those of member countries.
  Statistics Section: Collects, collates and analyses statistical information from both primary and secondary sources.
Personnel and Administration Department: Responsible for all organization methods, provision of administrative services for all meetings, personnel matters, budgets accounting and internal control.
Public Information Department: Responsible for a central public relations programme; production and distribution of publications, films, slides and tapes; and communication of OPEC objectives and decisions to the world at large.
Legal Office: Undertakes special and other in-house legal studies and reports to ascertain where the best interests of the Organization and member countries lie.

OPEC NEWS AGENCY

Founded 1980 to provide information on OPEC to about 80 countries and counteract inaccurate reporting by some other sources: covers member countries' petroleum and energy issues; activities of the OPEC Secretariat; co-operation with other developing countries; news on oil companies; technical and policy information on the upstream and downstream sectors of the industry; energy supply and demand; and economic and social development in member countries.

Record of Events

1960 The first OPEC Conference was held in Baghdad in September, attended by representatives from Iran, Iraq, Kuwait, Saudi Arabia and Venezuela.

1961 Second Conference, Caracas, January. Qatar was admitted to membership; a Board of Governors was formed and statutes agreed.

1962 Fourth Conference, Geneva, April and June. Protests were addressed to oil companies against price cuts introduced in August 1960. Indonesia and Libya were admitted to membership.

1965 In July the Conference reached agreement on a two-year joint production programme, implemented from 1965 to 1967, to limit annual growth in output to secure adequate prices.

1967 Abu Dhabi was admitted to membership.

1968 Fifteenth Conference (extraordinary), Beirut, January. OPEC accepted an offer of elimination of discounts submitted by oil companies following negotiations in November 1967.

1969 Algeria was admitted to membership.

1970 Twenty-first Conference, Caracas, December. Tax on income of oil companies was raised to 55%.

1971 A five-year agreement was concluded in February between the six producing countries in the Gulf and 23 international oil companies (Teheran Agreement).
Twenty-fourth Conference, Vienna, July. Nigeria was admitted to membership.

1972 In January oil companies agreed to adjust oil revenues of the largest producers after changes in currency exchange rates (Geneva Agreement).

1973 Agreement with companies was reached under which posted prices of crude oil were raised by 11.9% and a mechanism was installed to make monthly adjustments to prices in future (Second Geneva Agreement).
Negotiations with oil companies on revision of the Teheran Agreement broke down in October and the Gulf states unilaterally declared 70% increases in posted prices, from $3.01 to $5.11 per barrel.
Thirty-sixth Conference, Teheran, December. The posted price was to increase by nearly 130%, from $5.11 to $11.65 per barrel, from 1 January 1974. Ecuador was admitted to full membership and Gabon became an associate member.

1974 As a result of Saudi opposition to the December price increase, prices were held at current level for first quarter (and subsequently for the remainder of 1974). Abu Dhabi's membership was transferred to the United Arab Emirates.
A meeting in June increased royalties charged to oil companies from 12.5% to 14.5% in all member states except Saudi Arabia.
A meeting in September increased governmental take by about 3.5% through further increases in royalties on equity crude to 16.67% and in taxes to 65.65%, except in Saudi Arabia.

INTERNATIONAL ORGANIZATIONS   *Organization of the Petroleum Exporting Countries*

1975 OPEC's first summit conference was held in Algiers in March. Gabon was admitted to full membership.

A ministerial meeting in September agreed to raise prices by 10% for the period until June 1976.

1976 The OPEC Special Fund for International Development was created in May.

In December, a general 15% rise in basic prices was proposed and supported by 11 member states. This was to take place in two stages: a 10% rise as of 1 January 1977, and a further 5% rise as of 1 July 1977. However, Saudi Arabia and the United Arab Emirates decided to raise their prices by 5% only.

1977 Following an earlier waiver by nine members of the 5% second stage of the price rise agreed at Doha, Saudi Arabia and the United Arab Emirates announced in July that they would both raise their prices by 5%. As a result, a single level of prices throughout the organization was restored.

Because of continued disagreements between the 'moderates', led by Saudi Arabia and Iran, and the 'radicals', led by Algeria, Libya and Iraq, the year's second Conference at Caracas, December, was unable to settle on an increase in prices.

1978 In May a ministerial committee from six member states was established to draw up long-term pricing and production strategy. Production ceilings of members were lowered.

Fifty-first Conference, Geneva, June. Price levels were to remain stable until the end of 1978. A committee of experts, chaired by Kuwait, met in July to consider ways of compensating for the effects of the depreciation of the US dollar.

In December 1978 it was decided to raise prices by instalments of 5%, 3.8%, 2.3% and 2.7%. These would bring a rise of 14.5% over nine months, but an average increase of 10% for 1979.

1979 At an extraordinary meeting in Geneva at the end of March it was decided to raise prices by 9%. Many members maintained surcharges they had imposed in February after Iranian exports were halted.

In June the Conference agreed minimum and maximum prices which seemed likely to add between 15% and 20% to import bills of consumer countries.

The December Conference recommended replenishment of the OPEC Fund and agreed in principle to convert the Fund into a development agency with its own legal personality. An OPEC News Agency was to be set up, based at the Secretariat.

1980 In June the Conference decided to set the price for a marker crude at US $32.00 per barrel, and that the value differentials which could be added above this ceiling (on account of quality and geographical location) should not exceed $5.00 per barrel.

It was decided to begin studies on the feasibility of an OPEC Institute of Higher Education, for technological research and training.

The planned OPEC summit meeting in Baghdad in November was postponed indefinitely because of the Iran–Iraq war, but the scheduled price-fixing meeting of petroleum ministers went ahead in Bali in December, with both Iranians and Iraqis present. A ceiling price of US $41.00 per barrel was fixed for premium crudes.

1981 In May attempts to achieve price reunification were made, but Saudi Arabia refused to increase its $32.00 per barrel price unless the higher prices charged by other countries were lowered. Most of the other OPEC countries agreed to cut production by 10% so as to reduce the surplus. An emergency meeting in Geneva in August again failed to unify prices, although Saudi Arabia agreed to reduce production by 1m. barrels per day, with the level of output to be reviewed monthly.

In October OPEC countries agreed to increase the Saudi marker price by 6% to $34 per barrel, with a ceiling price of $38 per barrel. This price structure was intended to remain in force until the end of 1982. Saudi Arabia also announced that it would keep its production below 8.5m.b/d.

1982 The continuing world oil glut (resulting from a fall in demand to a predicted 46m. b/d in 1982, compared with 52m. in 1979) forced prices below the official mark of $34 per barrel in some producer countries. In March an emergency meeting of petroleum ministers was held in Vienna and agreed (for the first time in OPEC's history) to defend the Organization's price structure by imposing an overall production ceiling of 18m. b/d, effectively 17.5m. b/d with Saudi Arabia's separate announcement of a cut to 7m. b/d in its own production. Measures were taken to support Nigerian prices following a slump in production.

In December the Conference agreed to limit OPEC production to 18.5m. b/d in 1983 (representing about one-third of total world production) but postponed the allocation of national quotas pending consultations among the respective governments.

1983 In January an emergency meeting of petroleum ministers, fearing a collapse in world oil prices, decided to reduce the production ceiling to 17.5m. b/d (itself several million b/d above actual current output) but failed to agree on individual production quotas or on adjustments to the differentials in prices charged for the high-quality crude petroleum produced by Algeria, Libya and Nigeria compared with that produced by the Gulf States.

In February Nigeria cut its prices to $30 per barrel, following a collapse in its production. To avoid a 'price war' OPEC set the official price of marker crude at $29 per barrel, and agreed to maintain existing differentials among the various OPEC crudes at the level agreed on in March 1982, with the temporary exception that the differentials for Nigerian crudes should be $1 more than the price of the marker crude. It also agreed to maintain the production ceiling of 17.5m. b/d and allocated quotas for each member country except Saudi Arabia, which was to act as a 'swing producer' to supply the balancing quantities to meet market requirements. It called on member countries to avoid giving discounts in any form, and to refrain from 'dumping' petroleum products into the world oil market at prices which would endanger the crude oil pricing structure. The official marker price and production ceiling were maintained throughout the year, although actual production by members was believed to be in excess of 18m. b/d at the end of the year. Despite demands for revised quotas by some countries, and Iran's attempt to restore the marker price to $34 per barrel, the meeting agreed to maintain the existing production and pricing agreement as the policy most likely to restore stability to the world petroleum market.

1984 The production ceiling of 17.5m. b/d and the official price of $29 per barrel were maintained until October, when the production ceiling was lowered to 16m. b/d. In December price differentials for light (more expensive) and heavy (cheaper) crudes were slightly altered in an attempt to counteract price-cutting by non-OPEC producers, particularly Norway and the United Kingdom. An auditing commission was set up to monitor members' adherence to production limits.

1985 In January members (except Algeria, Iran and Libya) effectively abandoned the marker price system: the price of Arabian light crude (the former marker price) was lowered to $28 per barrel, and price differentials between the cheapest and most expensive grades were cut from $4 to $2.40; this system was also adopted by Iran in February.

During the year production in excess of quotas by OPEC members, unofficial discounts and barter deals by members, and price cuts by non-members (such as Mexico, which had hitherto kept its prices in line with those of OPEC) contributed to a weakening of the market. Saudi Arabia indicated that it was not prepared to continue cutting its own output, to make up for others' increases, in an attempt to support world prices. In July, 10 members agreed to small price cuts of $0.50 and $0.20 per barrel respectively for heavy and medium crudes. Ecuador, Gabon and Iraq demanded larger production quotas, and when, in October, discussion of the redistribution of quotas was postponed, Ecuador announced that it was 'temporarily' leaving OPEC, the first member country to do so. In December ministers of petroleum of OPEC member states resolved to 'secure and defend for OPEC a fair share in the world market consistent with the income necessary for member countries' development'. A special committee was established to determine what OPEC's share of the world market should be, and how it should be defended in the face of falling prices and the steady production levels maintained by some non-members.

1986 During the first half of the year prices dropped to below $10 per barrel. In April ministers from 10 member states agreed to set OPEC production at 16.7m. b/d for the third quarter of 1986 and at 17.3m. b/d for the fourth quarter. Algeria, Iran and Libya dissented, arguing that production should be reduced to 14.5m. b/d and 16.8m. b/d respectively for those periods, in order to restore prices. Discussions were also held with non-member countries (Angola, Egypt, Malaysia, Mexico and Oman), which agreed to co-operate in limiting production. However, requests by OPEC that the United Kingdom should reduce its petroleum production levels continued to be rejected by the British Government.

In August all members, with the exception of Iraq (which demanded to be allowed the same quota as Iran and, when this was denied it, refused to be a party to the agreement), agreed upon a return to production quotas, with the aim of cutting production to 14.8m. b/d (about 16.8m. b/d including Iraq's production) for the ensuing two months. This measure resulted in an increase in prices to about $15 per barrel, and in October the agreement was extended until the end of the year, with a slight increase in collective output to 15m. b/d (excluding Iraq's production). In December members (with the exception of Iraq) agreed to return to a fixed pricing system at a level of $18 per barrel as the OPEC reference price, with effect from 1 February 1987 (following a one-month phase-out period on existing contracts). It was also agreed that, in order to support the reference price, cuts in production should be made: OPEC's total production for the first and second quarters of 1987 was not to exceed 15.8m. b/d.

1987 At their meeting in June ministers noted that the agreement reached in the previous December had succeeded in stabilizing prices, despite the fact that production was believed to have exceeded the agreed limit during the first half of the year. The Conference decided that production during the third and fourth quarters of the year should be limited to 16.6m. b/d (including Iraq's production). It established a committee of three heads of delegations to visit member countries, to motivate them to comply with the agreement, while another group of five heads of delegations undertook to seek the co-operation of non-member producers. During the third and fourth quarters, however, total production was reported to be at least 1m. b/d above the agreed level. In December ministers decided to extend the existing agreement for the first half of 1988, although Iraq, once more, refused to participate.

1988 By March petroleum prices had fallen below $15 per barrel. In April non-OPEC producers offered to reduce the volume of their petroleum exports by 5% if OPEC members would do the same. Saudi Arabia, however, refused to accept further reductions in production, saying that existing quotas should first be more strictly enforced. In June the previous production limit (15.06m. b/d, excluding Iraq's production) was again renewed for six months, in the hope that increasing demand would be sufficient to raise prices. By October, however, petroleum prices were below $12 per barrel. OPEC members (excluding Iraq) were estimated to be producing about 21m. b/d. In November a new agreement was reached, limiting total production (including that of Iraq) to 18.5m. b/d, with effect from 1 January 1989. Iran and Iraq finally agreed to accept identical quotas. It was hoped that the agreement would raise prices to $18 per barrel.

FINANCE

The budget for 1987 was: 221.6m. Austrian schillings, and that for 1988 amounted to 236.8m. schillings.

PUBLICATIONS

OPEC Bulletin (monthly).
OPEC Review (quarterly).
Annual Report.
Selected Documents of the International Petroleum Industry.
Annual Statistical Bulletin.
Facts and Figures.
OPEC Information Booklet.
OPEC at a Glance.
OPEC Official Resolutions and Press Releases.

OPEC FUND FOR INTERNATIONAL DEVELOPMENT

Address: POB 995, 1011 Vienna, Austria.
Telephone: (0222) 51-56-40.
Telex: 1-31734.
The Fund was established by OPEC member countries in 1976.

MEMBERS
Member countries of OPEC (q.v.).

Organization
(October 1988)

ADMINISTRATION
The Fund is administered by a Ministerial Council and a Governing Board. Each member country is represented on the Council by its minister of finance. The Board consists of one representative and one alternate for each member country.

Chairman, Ministerial Council: HECTOR HURTADO (Venezuela).
Chairman, Governing Board: OSAMAH FAQUIH (Saudi Arabia).
Director-General of the Fund: YESUFU SEYYID ABDULAI (Nigeria).

FINANCIAL STRUCTURE
The resources of the Fund, whose unit of account is the US dollar, consist of contributions by OPEC member countries, and income received from operations or otherwise accruing to the Fund.

The initial endowment of the Fund amounted to US $800m. Its resources have been replenished three times, and have been further increased by the profits accruing to seven OPEC member countries through the sales of gold held by the International Monetary Fund. The pledged contributions to the OPEC Fund amounted to US $3,435m. at the end of 1987, and paid-in contributions totalled $2,658m.

Activities

The OPEC Fund for International Development is a multilateral agency for financial co-operation and assistance. Its objective is to reinforce financial co-operation between OPEC member countries and other developing countries through the provision of financial support to the latter on appropriate terms, to assist them in their economic and social development. The Fund was conceived as a collective financial facility which would consolidate the assistance extended by its member countries; its resources are additional to those already made available through other bilateral and multilateral aid agencies of OPEC members. It is empowered to:

(*a*) Provide concessional loans for balance-of-payments support;

(*b*) Provide concessional loans for the implementation of development projects and programmes;

(*c*) Make contributions and/or provide loans to eligible international agencies; and

(*d*) Finance technical assistance and research through grants.

The eligible beneficiaries of the Fund's assistance are the governments of developing countries other than OPEC member countries, and international development agencies whose beneficiaries are developing countries. The Fund gives priority to the countries with the lowest income.

The Fund may undertake technical, economic and financial appraisal of a project submitted to it, or entrust such an appraisal to an appropriate international development agency, the executing national agency of a member country, or any other qualified agency. Most projects financed by the Fund have been co-financed by other development finance agencies. In each such case, one of the co-financing agencies may be appointed to administer the Fund's loan in association with its own. This practice has enabled the Fund to extend its lending activities to 89 countries over a short period of time and in a simple way, avoiding duplication and complications. As its experience grew, the Fund increasingly resorted to parallel, rather than joint financing, taking up separate project components to be financed according to its rules and policies. In addition, it has started to finance some projects completely on its own. These new trends necessitated the issuance in 1982 of guidelines for the procurement of goods and services under the Fund's loans, allowing for a margin of preference for goods and services of local origin or originating in other developing countries: the general principle of competitive bidding is, however, followed by the Fund. The loans are not tied to procurement from Fund member countries or from any other countries. The margin of preference for goods and services obtainable in developing countries is allowed on the request of the borrower and within defined limits.

By 1987 the Fund had implemented seven lending programmes; the eighth lending programme, covering the period 1988–89, was approved in 1987. Besides extending loans for project and programme financing and balance of payments support, the Fund also undertakes other operations, including grants in support of technical assistance and other activities (mainly research), and financial contributions to other international institutions.

By the end of December 1987 the number of loans extended by the Fund was 448, totalling US $2,136.3m., of which 254 loans were for project financing, 185 for balance-of-payments support and nine for programme financing. Over 75% of the amount committed had been disbursed.

Direct loans are supplemented by grants to support technical assistance, food aid and research. By the end of December 1987, 213 grants, amounting to $209.9m., had been extended, including $83.6m. to the Common Fund for Commodities, and a special contribution of $20m. to the International Fund for Agricultural Development (IFAD). In addition, the Fund had contributed $971.9m. to other international institutions by the end of 1987, comprising OPEC members' contributions to the resources of IFAD, and irrevocable transfers in the name of its members to the IMF Trust Fund.

During the year ending 31 December 1987, the Fund's total commitments amounted to $140.7m., of which 79% was for project financing. The largest proportion of project loans ($32.35m., or 29%) was for the transport sector, financing road improvements in Bangladesh, Guatemala, Honduras, Rwanda, the Yemen Arab Republic and the People's Democratic Republic of Yemen, and airport improvements in Maldives and Zambia. Loans amounting to $27.4m. (25% of the total) were approved for agriculture, including irrigation schemes in Burkina Faso, Ethiopia, Morocco and Thailand, rehabilitation of the cocoa and cotton sectors respectively in São Tomé and Príncipe and Tanzania, and increasing agricultural production in Bolivia. Education projects received 22% of the total ($24.9m.), for technical education and vocational training in Angola, Bangladesh, Botswana and the Philippines, primary education in Guinea and secondary schools in Niger. Two lines of credit, amounting to $14m., were extended to the national development banks of India and Uganda. The remaining loans were for a health project in Pakistan ($8m.) and a thermal power project in Jordan ($5m.). In 1987, eight balance-of-payments support loans were also approved, amounting to $26.4m., for seven African countries and Nicaragua. Grants made for technical assistance and research amounted to $2.7m.

OPEC FUND COMMITMENTS AND DISBURSEMENTS
(1987, US $ million).

	Commitments	Disbursements
Lending operations:	138.050	75.072
Project financing	111.650	62.740
Balance of payments support	26.400	5.500
Programme financing	—	6.832
Grant Programme	2.653	3.400
Technical assistance	2.463	3.180
Research and other intellectual activities	0.190	0.220
Total	140.703	78.472

INTERNATIONAL ORGANIZATIONS

Project loans approved in 1987 (US $ million)

Region and country	Loans approved
Africa	
Angola	1.000
Botswana	3.000
Burkina Faso	4.300
Ethiopia	4.000
Guinea	3.500
Morocco	6.400
Niger	4.900
Rwanda	3.500
São Tomé and Príncipe	1.100
Tanzania	6.600
Uganda	6.000
Zambia	5.000
Total	49.300
Asia and the Middle East	
Bangladesh	14.000
India	8.000
Jordan	5.000
Maldives	2.000
Pakistan	8.000
Philippines	6.500
Thailand	3.000
Yemen Arab Republic	4.350
Yemen, People's Democratic Republic	2.000
Total	52.850
Latin America and the Caribbean	
Bolivia	2.000
Guatemala	4.000
Honduras	3.500
Total	9.500
Grand Total	111.650

OPEC Fund for International Development

PUBLICATIONS

Annual Report.
OPEC Fund Newsletter (3 a year).
OPEC Aid and OPEC Aid Institutions—A Profile (annually).
Occasional books and papers.

SOUTH PACIFIC COMMISSION—SPC

Address: BP D5, Nouméa Cedex, New Caledonia.
Telephone: 26-20-00.
Telex: 3139.

The Commission was established by an agreement signed in Canberra, Australia, by the governments of Australia, France, the Netherlands, New Zealand, the United Kingdom and the USA, in February 1947, effective from July 1948. (The Netherlands withdrew from the Commission in 1962, when it ceased to administer the former colony of Dutch New Guinea, now Irian Jaya, part of Indonesia.) The Commission provides technical advice, training and assistance in economic, social and cultural development to the countries of the region. It serves a population of about 5m. people, scattered over some 30m. sq km., over 98% of which is sea.

MEMBERS

American Samoa	Northern Mariana Islands
Australia	Palau
Cook Islands	Papua New Guinea
Federated States of Micronesia	Pitcairn Islands
Fiji	Solomon Islands
France	Tokelau
French Polynesia	Tonga
Guam	Tuvalu
Kiribati	United Kingdom
Marshall Islands	USA
Nauru	Vanuatu
New Caledonia	Wallis and Futuna Islands
New Zealand	Western Samoa
Niue	

Organization

(October 1988)

SOUTH PACIFIC CONFERENCE

The Conference is held annually and since 1974 has combined the former South Pacific Conference, attended by delegates from the countries and territories within the Commission's area of action, and the former Commission Session, attended by representatives of the participating governments. Each government and territorial administration has the right to send a representative and alternates to the Conference and each representative (or alternate) has the right to cast one vote on behalf of the government or territorial administration which he or she represents.

The Conference is the supreme decision-making body of the Commission; it examines and adopts the Commission's work programme and budget for the coming year, and discusses any other matters within the competence of the Commission.

COMMITTEE OF REPRESENTATIVES OF GOVERNMENTS AND ADMINISTRATIONS

This Committee comprises representatives of all 27 member states and territories, having equal voting rights, and was formed in 1983 to replace the former Committee of Representatives (of only 13 members) and the Planning and Evaluation Committee. It meets annually, before the annual South Pacific Conference: it recommends the administrative budget, evaluates the effectiveness of the past year's work programme, examines the draft budget and work programme presented by the Secretary-General, and nominates the principal officers of the Commission.

SECRETARIAT

Since November 1976 the Secretariat has had a Management Committee which has a supervisory and advisory role over all Commission activities. Committee members are the Principal Officers of the Commission. The Secretary-General is the chief executive officer of the Commission. The Commission has about 140 staff members

Secretary-General: PALAUNI TUIASOSOPO (American Samoa).
Director of Programmes: JON JONASSEN (Cook Islands).
Deputy Director of Programmes: HÉLÈNE COURTE (New Caledonia).

Activities

Each territory has its own programme of development activities. The Commission's role is advisory and consultative: it assists these programmes by bringing people together for discussion and study, by research into some of the problems common to the region, by providing expert advice and assistance and by disseminating technical information.

The 16th South Pacific Conference adopted a recommendation by the 1976 Review Committee that the Commission should carry out the following specific activities:

(i) rural development;

(ii) youth and community development;

(iii) *ad hoc* expert consultancies;

(iv) cultural exchanges (in arts, sports and education);

(v) training facilitation; and

(vi) assessment and development of marine resources and research;

and that special consideration should be given to projects and grants-in-aid which do not necessarily fall within these specific activities, but which respond to pressing regional or sub-regional needs or to the expressed needs of the smaller Pacific countries. The work programme subsequently adopted by the South Pacific Conference was developed in response to these guidelines, and gives priority to projects in the following areas:

FOOD AND MATERIALS

The Commission's tropical agriculture programme aims to develop subsistence and commercial agriculture, in order to reduce dependence on imports and to increase exports. The objective of the plant protection programme is to assist governments in investigating and controlling diseases, pests and weeds affecting crops. Two staff members, the Tropical Agriculturist and the Plant Protection Officer, travel in the region providing information and advice, and organize publications, training courses and workshops.

MARINE RESOURCES

This programme aims to increase fisheries production in accordance with national planning objectives, and to improve the technical expertise of national fisheries administrations, in subsistence, artisanal, commercial and international fishing. The Commission's fisheries programme, headed by a Fisheries Co-ordinator, comprises five main projects: the Tuna and Billfish Assessment Programme (which monitors catches and analyses data to provide a basis for sustainable benefits from tuna resources); the Inshore Fisheries Research Project; the Deep Sea Fisheries Development Project (which employs four roving master fishermen, developing and evaluating new, simple types of fishing gear and providing training); the Fish Handling and Processing Project (providing training and advice, for example in refrigeration techniques); and the Regional Fisheries Training Project.

RURAL MANAGEMENT AND TECHNOLOGY

The projects under this programme seek to ensure that the development of resources for the benefit of the people shall be in harmony with the unique environmental quality of the region. Activities include surveys of resources; environmental assessments and monitoring; preparation of associated management plans and standards; and the use of appropriate technology in energy and rural development, health and sanitation, employment and water supplies.

The Commission serves as the implementing agency for the South Pacific Regional Environment Programme (SPREP): ESCAP, the UN Environment Programme and the South Pacific Bureau for Economic Co-operation are also represented in the co-ordinating group. SPREP undertakes research, monitoring, education and the provision of information on the sustainable management of land, sea and air resources. Major projects include: watershed management, monitoring and controlling the quality of inland and coastal water, tropical coastal ecosystems, oceanography, and the use and misuse of pesticides.

In November 1986 the Commission was host to a conference at which representatives of 16 countries adopted the Convention for the Protection of the Natural Resources and Environment of the

South Pacific Region, to 'prevent, reduce and control pollution' in the region (with a specific prohibition of the dumping of radioactive waste at sea). The Convention was to enter into force following ratification by 10 signatories (only two had ratified it by the end of 1987).

The aim of the Rural Health, Sanitation and Water Supply Programme is to provide information, instruction and assistance for the improvement of sanitary conditions in rural communities. The Rural Technology Programme aims to provide technical assistance, advice and pilot projects on alternative energy sources: projects, in villages and rural areas, make use of solar and wind energy for the production of electricity, and of wind energy for mechanical water pumping. The overall objective of the Rural Development Programme is to assist in improving the quality of life in the rural areas and outer islands of the region, by helping to integrate the rural development activities of member countries.

COMMUNITY AND EDUCATION SERVICES

The Commission employs a Health Education Officer, a Nutritionist and an Epidemiologist, who travel in the region, visiting health and community institutions, helping to organize surveys and analyse data, and giving advice on possible improvements. Educational materials, such as leaflets on nutritious foods, are published. Regional training courses in drug identification and drug concealment methods are held.

The SPC Community Education Training Centre at Narere, Fiji, provides training in the form of 10-month courses for about 30 community-work students annually. Mobile training units also provide short courses in community development and youth work. The Commission's Youth Development Officer assists national youth programmes. The Pacific Women's Resource Bureau aims to link regional and national women's organizations and to assist governments, on request, in bringing about the active participation of women in national development efforts.

The SPC Regional Media Centre in Fiji conducts regular workshops and training courses in radio, video, photography, graphic arts, printing and other audio-visual communications media.

SOCIO-ECONOMIC STATISTICAL SERVICES

The Statistics Section assists governments and administrations in the region to develop the range of socio-economic statistics produced, to improve their quality, and to encourage the use of such data in planning. It fosters co-operation between national statistical agencies, and issues regional reports and other publications. SPC training courses on statistical operations and procedures, at basic and intermediate levels, are held regularly in different places. The Population Section assists in conducting censuses and population surveys, and in the analysis and application of population data. Training in demographic data collection and application is also given. A project on Migration, Employment and Development in the South Pacific was begun in 1981 in collaboration with the International Labour Organisation (ILO), to collect and analyse data.

The Economic Section provides advisory services of a technical nature in economic development planning, marketing and price stabilization, and holds annual or biennial training courses on planning techniques, project analysis, farm management and negotiations with overseas interests. The Section also compiles and publishes relevant economic data. A Regional Conference of Development Planners is held every two years.

CULTURAL CONSERVATION AND EXCHANGE

The Commission supports cultural development and conservation. It organizes meetings of the Council of Pacific Arts and provides assistance for the Festival of Pacific Arts: the fourth Festival was held in Tahiti (French Polynesia) in December 1984, and the fifth was to be held in Australia in 1988.

INFORMATION

The Commission issues publications (see below) and provides a library, computer processing services, and interpreting and translating services.

AWARDS AND GRANTS

The Commission provides awards and grants for the services of experts and specialists; applied research and field work; and inter-country study visits.

FINANCE

Contributions to the regular budget of the Commission are made by member governments and administrations, according to a formula based on per caput income, in the following proportions: Australia 33.3%, USA 16.8%, New Zealand 16.1%, France 13.9%, United Kingdom 12.2%, others 7.7%. In addition to projects funded from the regular budget, the Commission carries out activities funded by special voluntary contributions from governments, international organizations and other sources. Assessed and extra-budgetary contributions for 1987 amounted to about 1,000m. francs CFP, of which extra-budgetary contributions represented about one-half.

PUBLICATIONS

SPC Publications Catalogue.

Library Accessions List.

Annual Report.

Report of the South Pacific Conference.

Pacific Impact (quarterly).

SPELT News.

Fisheries Newsletter.

Youthlink.

Women's Newsletter.

Cultural Newsletter.

Plant Protection News.

Health Information (monthly).

Technical publications, statistical bulletins, advisory leaflets and reports.

SOUTH PACIFIC FORUM

c/o SPEC (see below)

MEMBERS

Australia	New Zealand
Cook Islands	Niue
Fiji	Papua New Guinea
Kiribati	Solomon Islands
Marshall Islands	Tonga
Federated States of Micronesia	Tuvalu
	Vanuatu
Nauru	Western Samoa

The South Pacific Forum is the gathering of Heads of Government of the independent and self-governing states of the South Pacific. Its first meeting was held on 5 August 1971, in Wellington, New Zealand. It provides an opportunity for informal discussions to be held on a wide range of common issues and problems and meets annually or when issues require urgent attention. The Forum has no written constitution or international agreement governing its activities nor any formal rules relating to its purpose, membership or conduct of meeting. Decisions are always reached by consensus, it never having been found necessary or desirable to vote formally on issues.

The 14th Forum was held in August 1983 in Canberra, Australia. It adopted a resolution calling on France to grant greater political and administrative autonomy to the French Overseas Territory of New Caledonia, and to establish a timetable for the territory's independence. The Forum reiterated that it would continue to condemn nuclear testing by France or by any other country in the South Pacific region, and to oppose the dumping of nuclear waste there; it commended the Australian initiative in reviving the concept of a nuclear-free zone in the region and undertook to continue consultations on the matter.

The 15th Forum, held in August 1984 in Tuvalu, commissioned a group of experts to draw up a treaty for establishing a nuclear-free zone, to be presented at the next year's meeting. It also discussed the question of independence for New Caledonia, and agreed that there was a risk of serious violence in the territory if France refused to grant it independence before 1989; the Forum decided, however, not to bring the matter before the United Nations Special Committee on Decolonization, as requested by the government of Vanuatu.

The 16th Forum was held in August 1985 in Rarotonga, Cook Islands. It adopted a treaty declaring a nuclear-free zone in the South Pacific and prohibiting the possession, testing and use of nuclear weapons in the region (which would come into force following ratification by eight member states). France, the United Kingdom, the USA, the People's Republic of China and the USSR were invited to sign protocols committing them to support the treaty. The Forum also reaffirmed its support for self-determination in New Caledonia, and set up a group to observe developments there. The SPARTECA agreement (see below) was discussed, and its scope was widened.

The 17th Forum, held in August 1986 in Suva, Fiji, agreed unanimously to bring the question of New Caledonia before the UN Special Committee on Decolonization, on the grounds that the French Government which had taken office earlier that year appeared to be committed to retaining New Caledonia as a French territory. Five countries declared that they were ready to ratify the 1985 treaty on a nuclear-free zone, which had so far been ratified by only four members. The Forum also approved an amendment in the protocols to be offered to the non-regional powers for signature: this would allow the signatories to withdraw if unforeseen circumstances made it necessary for their national interest. The meeting expressed concern over the lack of progress in negotiations with the USA over fishing rights in the region.

The treaty on the South Pacific nuclear-free zone came into effect in December 1986, following ratification by eight states. In the same month the USSR signed the protocols in support of the treaty, and the People's Republic of China did so in February 1987; the other three major nuclear powers, however, intimated that they did not intend to adhere to the treaty.

The 18th Forum, held in May 1987 in Apia, Western Samoa, took place earlier in the year than usual, in anticipation of the referendum on independence due to be held in New Caledonia. The meeting denounced the referendum as 'divisive and futile' on the grounds that the voting procedure to be followed favoured the European settlers in New Caledonia, and recommended that a UN-sponsored referendum should be held instead. The Forum also expressed grave concern over the military coup which had taken place in Fiji earlier that month, and offered to send a mission to Fiji to assist in establishing an acceptable government there. The Forum welcomed the signing of a Multilateral Fisheries Treaty with the USA in April 1987, and strongly condemned the illegal fishing activities of United States and other foreign vessels in the region. It was decided that a Committee on Regional Institutional Arrangements should be established to examine ways to increase international recognition of the Forum, and to examine the concept of a single regional organization.

The 19th Forum, held in September 1988 in Tonga, discussed the threat posed to low-lying island countries by the predicted rise in sea-level caused by heating of the earth's atmosphere as a result of pollution (the 'greenhouse effect'). The Forum agreed to establish a network of stations to monitor climatic change in the Pacific region. The meeting also discussed the establishment of a regional telecommunications network (to be based on a satellite station in Sydney, Australia), and agreed to seek multilateral (rather than bilateral) negotiations with Japan on fishing rights in the Pacific.

South Pacific Bureau for Economic Co-operation—SPEC

Address: GPO Box 856, Suva, Fiji.
Telephone: 312600.
Telex: 2229.

SPEC was established by an agreement signed on 17 April 1973, at the third meeting of the South Pacific Forum in Apia, Western Samoa.

Organization*

(October 1988)

COMMITTEE

The Committee is the Bureau's executive board. It comprises representatives and senior officials from all member countries. It meets twice a year, immediately before the meetings of the South Pacific Forum and at the end of the year, to discuss in detail the Bureau's work programme and annual budget.

SECRETARIAT

The Secretariat carries out the day-to-day activities of the Bureau. It is headed by a Director, with an executive staff of 25 drawn from the member countries. It is responsible for the administration of the South Pacific Forum.

Director: HENRY FATI NAISALI.

* At the 19th Forum, held in September 1988, it was decided that SPEC should be renamed the South Pacific Forum Secretariat.

Activities

The Bureau was set up as a result of proposals for establishing a 'Trade Bureau' which were put forward at the second meeting of the South Pacific Forum in 1972. Its aim is to facilitate continuing co-operation and consultation between members on trade, economic development, transport, tourism and other related matters. In 1974 the Bureau absorbed the functions of the Pacific Islands Producers' Association (PIPA).

SPEC's trade activities cover trade promotion, the identification and development of export-oriented industries, and the negotiation of export opportunities. Following a study of trade relations and industrial development in the South Pacific, SPEC co-ordinated and assisted island countries in negotiating the South Pacific Regional Trade and Economic Co-operation Agreement (SPARTECA) which came into force in 1981, aiming to redress the trade deficit of the South Pacific countries with Australia and New Zealand. It is a non-reciprocal trade agreement under which Australia and New Zealand offer duty-free and unrestricted access or concessional access for specified products originating from the developing island member countries of the Forum. In August 1985 Australia agreed to further liberalization of trade by abolishing (from the beginning of 1987) duties and quotas on all Pacific products except steel, cars, sugar, footwear and garments. SPEC has also undertaken an investigation into the prospects for closer economic co-operation between members, market surveys in Japan and the USA, and surveys on regional industry, the harmonization of industrial incentives, possibilities of bulk purchasing and regional crop insurance. It provides support for national trade promotion and trade information services, and in 1984 presided over the formation of the Pacific Islands Association of Chambers of Commerce, to promote contacts between organizations in the private sector.

Regional transport forms an important part of SPEC's activities. A Regional Shipping Council was set up by the Forum in 1974, and a Regional Civil Aviation Council and Advisory Committee in 1976. In 1984 these bodies undertook a regional transport survey, to compile a comprehensive data base on transport in the region. SPEC established the Pacific Forum Line and the Association of South Pacific Airlines (see below), and is involved in formulating regional maritime standards and in supervising wage rates and working conditions for seamen. In 1986 the South Pacific Maritime Development Programme was established. Its initial work programme comprised assistance for regional maritime training, and for the development of regional maritime administrations and legislation; and approaches to international aid donors for capital-intensive projects, including the possible replacement of domestic fleets in the region.

Since 1973 SPEC has acted as the co-ordinating agency for telecommunications work undertaken in the region by UNDP and other agencies. In 1983 the 14th South Pacific Forum approved the establishment of the South Pacific Telecommunications Development Programme, to be conducted over the next decade.

In 1981 the Forum decided that SPEC should assume the role of overall regional energy co-ordinator, and a SPEC Energy Unit was formed in 1982: its work includes research on alternative energy sources, financed by the European Community.

Since 1981 SPEC has acted as the secretariat to the Pacific Group Council of ACP states receiving assistance from the European Community under the Lomé Convention (q.v.). It also manages a regional disaster relief fund and a Fellowship Scheme to provide in-service training in island member countries for about 25 candidates per year, financed by Australia, New Zealand and the Commonwealth Fund for Technical Co-operation. With funds from UNDP, SPEC recruits specialists to carry out short-term advisory services in the islands of the region. A Pacific Regional Advisory Service was established in 1981, to maintain a register of locally-available skills and to co-ordinate the transfer of these skills from one member to another, through the exchange of advisers and consultants. SPEC participates in the South Pacific Regional Environment Programme (SPREP) with the South Pacific Commission.

BUDGET

The Governments of Australia and New Zealand each contribute one-third of the annual budget and the remaining third is equally shared by the other member Governments. Total estimated revenue for 1988 was $F 1,759,093, an increase of about 46% over the 1987 budget of $F 1,203,881. Extra-budgetary funding during 1987 was estimated at $F 1,920,885, and for 1988 it was estimated at $F 3,832,800.

Associated and Affiliated Organizations

Association of South Pacific Airlines—ASPA: POB 9817, Nadi Airport, Nadi, Fiji; tel. 73526; telex 5139; f. 1979 at a meeting of airlines in the South Pacific, convened by SPEC, to promote co-operation among the member airlines for the development of regular, safe and economical commercial aviation within, to and from the South Pacific. Mems: 19 regional airlines, three associates. Chair. ANDREW DRYSDALE; Sec.-Gen. GEORGE E. FAKTAUFON.

Pacific Forum Line: POB 796, Apia, Western Samoa; f. 1977 as a joint venture by 10 South Pacific countries, to provide shipping services to meet the special requirements of the region; operates three container vessels and one general cargo vessel; conducts shipping agency services in Fiji, New Zealand and Western Samoa, and stevedoring in Western Samoa. Chair. D. TUFUI; CEO W. J. MACLENNAN.

South Pacific Forum Fisheries Agency—FFA: POB 629, Honiara, Solomon Islands; tel. (677) 21-124; telex 66336; f. 1978 by the South Pacific Forum to promote co-operation in fisheries among coastal states in the region; polices an Exclusive Economic Zone within 370 km (200 nautical miles) of the coastlines of member states; signed a five-year agreement with the USA in April 1987, allowing fishing rights to the US fishing fleet in exchange for payments amounting to US $60m. Dir P. A. MULLER.

South Pacific Trade Commission: 225 Clarence St, Sydney, NSW 2000, Australia; tel. 290-2833; telex 70342; opened 1979 to identify and develop markets in Australia for exports from the Pacific islands; funded by the Australian govt. Trade Commr WILLIAM T. MCCABE.

PUBLICATIONS

Annual Report.
SPEC Directory of Aid Agencies.
SPARTECA (guide for Pacific island exporters).
SPEC Series for Trade and Investment in the South Pacific.
Reports of Forum and Bureau meetings.

SOUTHERN AFRICAN DEVELOPMENT CO-ORDINATION CONFERENCE—SADCC

Address: Private Bag 0095, Gaborone, Botswana.
Telephone: 51863.
Telex: 2555.

The first Conference was held at Arusha, Tanzania, in July 1979, to harmonize development plans and to reduce the region's economic dependence on South Africa.

MEMBERS

Angola	Malawi	Tanzania
Botswana	Mozambique	Zambia
Lesotho	Swaziland	Zimbabwe

Organization
(October 1988)

SUMMIT MEETING
The Meeting is held annually and is attended by heads of state and government or their representatives.

COUNCIL OF MINISTERS
Representatives of SADCC member countries at ministerial level meet at least twice a year; in addition, special meetings are held to co-ordinate regional policy in a particular field by, for example, ministers of energy and ministers of transport.

CONFERENCES ON CO-OPERATION
A conference with SADCC's 'international co-operating partners' (donor governments and international agencies) is held annually to review progress in the various sectors of the SADCC programme and to present new projects requiring assistance.

SECRETARIAT
Executive Secretary: Dr SIMBARASHE MAKONI (Zimbabwe).

SECTORAL CO-ORDINATION OFFICES
Southern Africa Transport and Communications Commission (SATCC): c/o Dr S. Bhatt, CP 2677, Maputo, Mozambique; tel. 20246; telex 6597.
Energy Sector Technical and Administrative Unit: c/o Carvalho Simões, CP 172, Luanda, Angola; tel. 23382; telex 3170.
Agricultural Research and Animal Disease Control: c/o M. Mokone, Ministry of Agriculture, Private Bag 003, Gaborone, Botswana; tel. 51171; telex 2414.
Tourism: Lesotho Tourist Board, POB 1378, Maseru, Lesotho; tel. 323760; telex 4820.
Soil and Water Conservation and Utilisation: c/o B. Leleka, Ministry of Agriculture and Marketing, POB 24, Maseru 100, Lesotho; tel. 22741; telex 4330.
Fisheries, Wildlife and Forestry: c/o B. Ndisale, Ministry of Forestry and Natural Resources, Private Bag 350, Lilongwe 3, Malawi; tel. 731322; telex 4465.
Manpower Development: c/o V. E. Sikhondze, Dept of Economic Planning and Statistics, POB 602, Mbabane, Swaziland; tel. 43765; telex 2109.
Trade and Industrial Co-ordination Division: c/o A. T. Pallangyo, Ministry of Industries, POB 9503, Dar es Salaam, Tanzania; tel. 22775; telex 41686.
Mining: c/o K. Nyirenda, Ministry of Mines, POB 31969, Lusaka, Zambia; tel. 211220; telex 45970.
Food Security Technical and Administrative Unit: c/o K. Dhliwayo, Ministry of Agriculture, Private Bag 7701, Causeway, Harare, Zimbabwe; tel. 706081; telex 2455.

Activities

In July 1979 the first Southern African Development Co-ordination Conference was attended by delegations from Angola, Botswana, Mozambique, Tanzania and Zambia, with representatives from donor governments and international agencies; the group was later joined by Lesotho, Malawi, Swaziland and Zimbabwe. In April 1980 a regional economic summit conference was held in Lusaka, Zambia, and the Lusaka Declaration, a statement of strategy entitled 'Southern Africa: Towards Economic Liberation', was approved, together with a programme of action allotting specific studies and tasks to member governments (see list of co-ordinating offices, above). The members aimed to reduce their dependence on South Africa for rail and air links and port facilities, imports of raw materials and manufactured goods, and the supply of electric power. In 1985, however, an SADCC report noted that since 1980 the region had become still more dependent on South Africa for its trade outlets, and the 1986 summit meeting, although it recommended the adoption of economic sanctions against South Africa, failed to establish a timetable for doing so.

In July 1987 it was announced that so far US $2,500m. of the $6,000m. required for SADCC projects had been secured. At the donors' conference held in January 1988, a further $1,000m. was pledged.

TRANSPORT AND COMMUNICATIONS

Transport is seen as the most important area to be developed, on the grounds that, as the Lusaka Declaration noted, 'The dominance of the Republic of South Africa has been reinforced by its transport system. Without the establishment of an adequate regional transport and communications system, other areas of co-operation become impractical'. Priority was to be given to the improvement of road and railway services into Mozambique, so that the land-locked countries of the region could transport their goods through Mozambican ports instead of South African ones.

Rehabilitation of the railway between Malawi and Beira on the coast of Mozambique was under way in 1982, while work on the line from Malawi to the port of Nacala in Mozambique began in 1983. Other proposed railway projects include improvement of lines and equipment in Angola and Botswana, between Mozambique and Swaziland, and between Tanzania and Zambia. In early 1988 plans were announced for a 10-year rehabilitation plan (to cost $575m.) for the Benguela railway, leading to the port of Lobito in Angola, and for the second phase of the rehabilitation of the Limpopo railway, running from Zimbabwe to Maputo, Mozambique.

Port facilities are to be improved at Luanda in Angola, Beira, Maputo and Nacala in Mozambique, and Dar es Salaam, Tanzania. There are plans for the rehabilitation and upgrading of roads throughout the region, and, in particular, work on the main roads connecting Mozambique with Swaziland (to begin in 1986) and with Zimbabwe, and on the road between Tanzania and Zambia. Civil aviation projects include a new airport at Maseru, Lesotho, completed in 1985, and improvements of major airports in Mozambique, Swaziland, Zambia and Zimbabwe, together with studies on the joint use of maintenance facilities, on regional airworthiness certification and aviation legislation, and on navigational aids. Work on a satellite earth station in Swaziland had been completed by 1984, while two more, in Angola and Zimbabwe, were being constructed, and microwave communications links are planned throughout the region.

In August 1986 the total cost of the 150 projects planned for this sector was estimated at US $2,991m. By that date $1,093m. of this amount had been secured, and a further $256m. was under negotiation. The number of fully-financed projects was 27, and partial financing had been agreed for another 29 projects.

ENERGY

The energy programme consists of 75 projects, with total funding requirements of US $300m. (as at May 1988). By that date 38 projects had been fully funded. Funding secured amounted to $143m. The main areas of work comprised: a study on regional self-sufficiency in the supply of petroleum products; exploitation of the region's coal resources; development of hydroelectric power, and the linking of national electricity grids (Botswana-Zimbabwe, Botswana-Zambia, Mozambique-Swaziland and Zimbabwe-Mozambique); and new and renewable sources of energy, including pilot projects in solar energy and wind-power and the developing of integrated energy systems for villages.

TRADE, INDUSTRY AND MINING

In the industry sector 53 projects were being planned in August 1986, at a total cost of $1,619m. together with 37 feasibility studies.

At that date US $450m. of funding had been secured and $30m. was under negotiation. Projects include production of textiles, salt, pesticides, cement, machine tools, mining equipment, farming equipment, railway rolling-stock, pharmaceuticals and baby-foods. During 1985 a group of experts was established to co-ordinate standardization and quality control. An investment guide was to be issued in 1986, to encourage the mobilization of capital from private and public sources, and in 1987 a study of member states' investment regulations was undertaken with a view to harmonizing them.

In 1986 it was announced that, as well as attempting to improve the region's physical infrastructure, SADCC would also place more emphasis on increasing the production of goods and on stimulating intra-regional trade, which accounted for only about 5% of the members' total external trade. A trade promotion programme was approved in 1986: it included the possible formation of a regional export credit facility. The annual co-operation conference held in February 1987 was attended by about 120 representatives of private-sector businesses, and it was hoped that this would stimulate private investment in the region.

At the end of August 1986, planned mining projects required financing of $2m., of which $1.4m. had been secured. Studies on the manufacturing of mining machinery and spare parts, repairing and reconditioning facilities, and the development of a regional iron and steel industry had been completed by that date, and studies on the availability of skilled manpower, small-scale mining and a geological inventory were being undertaken.

MANPOWER

SADCC aims to meet the region's requirements in skilled manpower by providing training in the following categories: high-level managerial personnel; high- and medium-level technicians; artisans; and instructors. In August 1986 the funding required for manpower projects was US $34.2m., of which $7m. had been secured and $19.1m. was under negotiation.

FOOD AND AGRICULTURE

At the end of August 1986 the total cost of projects in this sector was US $506.9m., of which $230.6m. had been secured. Priority is given to regional food security and to self-sufficiency in basic foods. During 1986 work was under way on a regional early warning system for anticipating food shortages, and an inventory of agricultural resources. In 1988 a regional food reserve (to consist of 356,000 metric tons of maize) was under discussion. Improvement of livestock production and the control of animal diseases also form an important part of the work in this sector. The Southern African Centre for Co-operation in Agricultural Research (SACCAR), in Gaborone, Botswana, began operations in 1985. It co-ordinates national research systems and operates a small research grants programme. Its three initial programmes covered sorghum and millet improvement, grain legume improvement, and land and water management. Other agricultural projects undertaken by SADCC include inland fisheries, wildlife protection, and forestry.

SADCC PROJECT FINANCING BY SECTOR (US $ million, August 1986)

Sector	Total cost	Funding secured	Funding under negotiation
Agriculture	506.86	230.62	44.07
Agricultural research	40.8	30.62	—
Fisheries	6.66	5.77	0.88
Food security	299.42	100.73	23.45
Forestry	35.79	25.92	6.0
Livestock production and animal disease control	116.75	65.34	13.33
Soil and water conservation and land utilization	2.56	2.24	0.33
Wildlife	4.88	—	0.08
Energy	237.07	69.56	—
Industry	1,619.25	449.85	29.62
Manpower	34.19	6.91	19.08
Mining	2.04	1.4	0.54
Tourism	0.15	0.15	—
Transport and communications	2,991.55	1,092.95	255.5
Total	5,391.04	1,851.42	348.81

PUBLICATIONS

Annual Progress Report.
SADCC Energy Bulletin.
SACCAR Newsletter.
Soil and Water Conservation and Land Utilization Newsletter.

THE WARSAW TREATY OF FRIENDSHIP, CO-OPERATION AND MUTUAL ASSISTANCE— THE WARSAW PACT

Headquarters of the Joint Command: Moscow, USSR.

The Warsaw Treaty of Friendship, Co-operation and Mutual Assistance (the Warsaw Pact) was signed in Warsaw in May 1955. It was automatically extended for a further 10 years in June 1975, and renewed, before its expiry, for a further period of 20 years (with an option to extend it for a further 10 years) in April 1985: the terms of the treaty were unchanged. The treaty is supplemented by an interlocking system of treaties between the member countries. Albania, one of the original signatories, ceased to participate in 1961 and formally withdrew from the Treaty in 1968.

MEMBERS

Bulgaria
Czechoslovakia
German Democratic Republic
Hungary
Poland
Romania
USSR

Organization
(October 1988)

POLITICAL CONSULTATIVE COMMITTEE (PCC)

The PCC was intended to meet not less than twice a year but, in fact, there have been fewer meetings: between 1972 and 1985 meetings took place in alternate years. Following the renewal of the Warsaw Treaty in April 1985, however, the PCC met annually. The place of meeting rotates among the member countries and individual sessions are chaired by the leaders of the delegations in turn. Delegations of member states are normally led by the General Secretary of the Party, supported by the Head of Government, Ministers for Foreign Affairs and Defence and others. Meetings are normally attended by the Commander-in-Chief, Warsaw Pact Joint Armed Forces. Summit meetings of leaders of Pact countries (not formally described as PCC meetings) also take place from time to time.

COMMITTEE OF DEFENCE MINISTERS

The Committee was established by the PCC in 1969, as part of a reorganization of the Treaty's military structure; it meets annually. Each member country provides the Chairman and the venue in turn. Meetings receive a report from the Commander-in-Chief of the Armed Forces.

MILITARY COUNCIL

Established by the PCC in 1969, the Council comprises national Chiefs of Staff or Deputy Ministers of Defence, with status of Deputy Commanders-in-Chief of the Warsaw Pact Joint Armed Forces. It normally meets twice a year, in each member country in turn, under the Chairmanship of the Commander-in-Chief of the Joint Armed Forces. The autumn meeting of the Military Council is usually combined with a general conference of national Force Commanders.

TECHNICAL COMMITTEE OF THE JOINT ARMED FORCES

The Technical Committee was established in 1969.
Chairman: Lt-Gen. P. A. MAMCHUR.

COMMITTEE OF FOREIGN MINISTERS

The Committee was established by the PCC in 1976 as a permanent organ parallel to the Committee of Defence Ministers. It meets in each member country in turn.

JOINT SECRETARIAT

The Secretariat was formally established in Moscow in 1956, and reinstituted in 1976, after a period of inactivity.

JOINT COMMAND OF THE ARMED FORCES

Set up in 1955 under the general supervision of the PCC.
Commander-in-Chief: Marshal VIKTOR G. KULIKOV (USSR).
Chief of Staff and First Deputy Commander-in-Chief: Army Gen. ANATOLY I. GRIBKOV (USSR).
Deputy Commanders-in-Chief: The members of the Military Council.

COMBINED GENERAL STAFF

Composed of representatives of the seven member states with headquarters in Moscow. Services meetings of the Committee of Defence Ministers and of the Military Council. Plans and evaluates manoeuvres and exercises of Warsaw Pact Joint Armed Forces.

WARSAW PACT FORCES (June 1988)

	Army	Navy	Air Force	Total regular forces
Bulgaria	115,000	8,800	34,000	157,800
Czechoslovakia	145,000	—	52,000	197,000
German Democratic Republic	120,000	15,000	37,000	172,000
Hungary	77,000	—	22,000	99,000
Poland	230,000	19,000	92,000	406,000*
Romania	140,000	7,500	32,000	179,500
USSR	1,900,000	458,000	444,000	5,096,000†

* The total includes 65,000 territorial defence troops.
† The total includes strategic nuclear forces (298,000), air defence troops (520,000), and about 1,476,000 railway, construction, labour and civil defence troops, but excludes paramilitary forces numbering 570,000 (internal security, border guards, etc.).

Source: International Institute of Strategic Studies, *The Military Balance 1988–1989*.

WESTERN EUROPEAN UNION—WEU

Address: 9 Grosvenor Place, London, SW1X 7HL, England.
Telephone: (01) 235-5351.

Based on the Brussels Treaty of 1948, Western European Union was set up in 1955. Member States seek to harmonize their views on security and defence questions.

MEMBERS

Belgium
France
Federal Republic of Germany
Italy
Luxembourg
Netherlands
Portugal*
Spain*
United Kingdom

* Membership to be ratified by national legislatures in 1989.

Organization
(October 1988)

COUNCIL

The Council of Western European Union consists of the ministers of foreign affairs and of defence of the seven member countries, or the Ambassadors resident in London and an Under-Secretary of the British Foreign and Commonwealth Office. As supreme authority of WEU, it is responsible for formulating policy and issuing directives to the Secretary-General and the Agencies for Security Questions (see below). The Council meets twice a year at ministerial level, and at permanent (ambassadorial) level as often as required (usually twice a month). Each country holds the Presidency of the Council for one year, beginning on 1 July.

SECRETARIAT-GENERAL

Secretary-General: ALFRED CAHEN (Belgium).
Deputy Secretary-General: H. HOLZHEIMER (FRG).

AGENCIES FOR SECURITY QUESTIONS

Address: 43 ave du Président Wilson, 75775 Paris Cedex 16, France.

Agency for the Study of Arms Control and Disarmament Questions.
Agency for the Study of Security and Defence Questions.
Agency for the Development of Co-operation in the Field of Armaments.

ASSEMBLY

Address: 43 ave du Président Wilson, 75775 Paris Cedex 16, France.

The Assembly of Western European Union consists of the delegates of the member countries to the Parliamentary Assembly of the Council of Europe. It meets twice a year in Paris. The Assembly considers defence policy in Western Europe, besides other matters concerning member states in common, and may make recommendations or transmit opinions to the Council, to national parliaments, governments and international organizations. An annual report is presented to the Assembly by the Council.

President: CHARLES GOERENS (Luxembourg).
Clerk: GEORGES MOULIAS (France).

PERMANENT COMMITTEES OF THE ASSEMBLY

There are permanent committees on: Defence Questions and Armaments; General Affairs; Scientific Questions; Budgetary Affairs and Administration; Rules of Procedure and Privileges; and Parliamentary and Public Relations.

Activities

The Brussels Treaty was signed in 1948 by Belgium, France, Luxembourg, the Netherlands and the United Kingdom. It foresaw the potential for international co-operation in Western Europe and provided for collective defence and collaboration in economic, social and cultural activities. Within this framework, NATO and the Council of Europe (see chapters) were formed in 1949.

On the collapse in 1954 of plans for a European Defence Community, a nine-power conference was convened in London to try to reach a new agreement. This conference's decisions were embodied in a series of formal agreements drawn up by a ministerial conference held in Paris in October 1954. The agreements entailed: arrangements for the Brussels Treaty to be strengthened and modified to include the Federal Republic of Germany and Italy, the ending of the occupation regime in the Federal Republic of Germany, and the invitation to the latter to join NATO. These agreements were ratified on 6 May 1955, on which date the seven-power Western European Union came into being.

The new organization was given the task of settling the future of the Saar region. Under a Franco-German agreement of October 1954, the Saar was to have a European statute within the framework of WEU, subject to approval by referendum. In October 1955 the Saar population voted against the statute and expressed the wish for incorporation in the Federal Republic of Germany. Political and economic incorporation were achieved in January 1957 and July 1959 respectively.

The modified Brussels Treaty provided for a system of co-operation in social and cultural affairs, and these activities were transferred in June 1960 to the Council of Europe.

Between 1963 and 1970, while negotiations for the United Kingdom's accession to the EEC were suspended, the WEU Council invited the Commission of the EEC to participate in meetings on European economic affairs. These were discontinued in 1970 on the re-opening of negotiations which led to the Treaty of Accession in January 1972.

A meeting of ministers of defence and of foreign affairs, held in Rome in October 1984, agreed to 'reactivate' WEU by restructuring its organization and by holding more frequent ministerial meetings, in order to harmonize members' views on defence questions, arms control and disarmament, developments in East-West relations, Europe's contribution to the Atlantic alliance, and European armaments co-operation.

At its meeting in April 1987 the Council discussed recent proposals made by the USSR concerning reductions in nuclear weapons. WEU expressed its commitment to the abolition of the USA's long-range intermediate nuclear forces in Europe, but the meeting did not reach agreement on the abolition of shorter-range intermediate nuclear forces.

In October 1987 the Council adopted a 'Platform on European Security Interests', declaring its intention to develop a 'more cohesive European defence identitiy', while affirming that 'the substantial presence of US conventional and nuclear forces plays an irreplaceable part in the defence of Europe'. The document also resolved to improve consultations and extend co-ordination in defence and security matters, and to use existing resources more effectively by expanding bilateral and regional military co-operation.

In November 1988 Portugal and Spain were admitted to membership of WEU (subject to approval by the legislatures of member states, a process which was expected to be concluded by April 1989).

PUBLICATIONS

Assembly of Western European Union: Texts adopted and Brief Account of the Session (2 a year).
Annual Report of the Council.
Assembly documents and reports.

WORLD CONFEDERATION OF LABOUR—WCL

Address: 33 rue de Trèves, 1040 Brussels, Belgium.
Telephone: (02) 230-62-95.
Telex: 26966.
Founded in 1920 as the International Federation of Christian Trade Unions (IFCTU); reconstituted under present title in 1968. (See also the International Confederation of Free Trade Unions and the World Federation of Trade Unions.)

MEMBERS
Affiliated national federations and trade union internationals; about 15,000,000 members in 78 countries.

Organization
(October 1988)

CONGRESS
The supreme and legislative authority. The most recent meeting was held in October 1985 in Baden, Austria. Congress consists of delegates from national confederations and trade internationals. Delegates have votes according to the size of their organization. Congress receives official reports, elects the Executive Board, considers the future programme and any proposals.

CONFEDERAL BOARD
The Board meets annually, and consists of 34 members (including 15 representatives of national confederations and nine representatives of trade internationals) elected by Congress from among its members for four-year terms. It issues executive directions and instructions to the Secretariat.

SECRETARIAT-GENERAL
Secretary-General: JAN KULAKOWSKI (Belgium).

REGIONAL OFFICES
Latin America: Latin-American Confederation of Workers, Apdo 6681, Caracas 1010, Venezuela. Sec.-Gen. EMILIO MASPERO.
Asia: BATU, POB 163, Manila, Philippines. Pres. J. TAN.
North America: c/o National Alliance of Postal and Federal Employees, 1628 11th St, NW, Washington, DC 20001, USA.

INTERNATIONAL INSTITUTES OF TRADE UNION STUDIES
Africa: Fondation panafricaine pour le développement économique, social et culturel (Fopadesc), Lomé, Togo.
Asia: Batu Social Institute, Manila, Philippines.
Latin America:
Instituto Andino de Estudios Sociales, Lima, Peru.
Instituto Centro-Americano de Estudios Sociales (ICAES), San José, Costa Rica.
Instituto de Formación del Caribe, Willemstad, Curaçao, Netherlands Antilles.
Instituto del Cono Sur (INCASUR), Buenos Aires, Argentina.
Universidad de Trabajadores de América Latina (UTAL).

FINANCE
Income is derived from affiliation dues, contributions, donations and capital interest.

PUBLICATIONS
Labor Press and Information Bulletin (8 a year; in English, French, German, Dutch and Spanish).
Flash (in English, French, German, Dutch and Spanish).
Reports of Congresses; Study Documents.

International Trade Federations

International Federation of Textile and Clothing Workers: 27 Koning Albertlaan, Ghent, Belgium; f. 1901. Mems: unions covering 400,000 workers in 19 countries. Organization: Congress (every two years), Bureau, Secretariat. Pres. L. FRURU (Belgium); Sec. C. PAUWELS (Belgium). Publ. *Intervetex* (quarterly).

International Federation of Trade Unions of Employees in Public Service—INFEDOP: 33 rue de Trèves, 1040 Brussels, Belgium; tel. (02) 230-60-90; f. 1922. Mems: national federations of workers in public service, covering 4m. workers. Organization: World Congress (at least every five years), World Confederal Board (meets every year), six Trade Groups, Secretariat. Pres. A. HENGCHEN (Belgium); Sec.-Gen. JOS DE CEULAER (Belgium). Publ. *Labor Professional Action* (6 a year).

INFEDOP has four regional organizations:
EUROFEDOP: 33 rue de Trèves, 1040 Brussels, Belgium.
CLASEP: Apartado 6681, Caracas 101, Venezuela.
CLTC: Apartado 4456, Caracas 101, Venezuela.
ASIAFEDOP: POB 163, Manila, Philippines.

International Federation of Trade Unions of Transport Workers—FIOST: 33 rue de Trèves, 1040 Brussels, Belgium; tel. (02) 230-60-90; telex 26966; f. 1921. Mems: national federations in 28 countries covering 600,000 workers. Organization: Congress (every four years), Committee (meets twice a year), Executive Board. Pres. JOHN JANSSENS (Belgium); Sec.-Gen. ALFRED GOSSELIN (Belgium). Publ. *Labor* (6 a year).

World Confederation of Teachers: 33 rue de Trèves, 1040 Brussels, Belgium; tel. (02) 230-60-90; telex 26966; f. 1963. Mems: national federations of unions concerned with teaching. Organization: Congress (every four years), Council (at least once a year), Steering Committee. Pres. L. VAN BENEDEN; Sec.-Gen. R. DENIS (Belgium).

World Federation of Agriculture and Food Workers: 31 rue de Trèves, 1040 Brussels, Belgium; tel. (02) 230-60-90; f. 1982 (merger of former World Federation of Agricultural Workers and World Federation of Workers in the Food, Drink, Tobacco and Hotel Industries). Mems: national federations covering 2,800,000 workers in 38 countries. Organization: Congress (every five years), World Board, Daily Management Board. Pres. O. SEMEREL (Netherlands Antilles); Sec. E. VERVLIET (Belgium). Publ. *Labor* (10 a year).

World Federation of Building and Woodworkers Unions: 31 rue de Trèves, 1040 Brussels, Belgium; f. 1936. Mems: national federations covering 2,438,000 workers in several countries. Organization: Congress, Bureau, Permanent Secretariat. Pres. (vacant); Sec. G. DE LANGE (Netherlands). Publ. *Bulletin*.

World Federation of Clerical Workers: 1 Beggaardenstraat, 2000 Antwerp, Belgium; f. 1921. Mems: national federations of unions and professional associations covering 400,000 workers in 11 countries. Organization: Congress (every two years), Council, Executive Bureau, Secretariat. Sec.-Gen. M. GEERTS (Belgium). Publ. *Revue* (every 2 years).

World Federation of Industry Workers: 33 rue de Trèves, 1040 Brussels, Belgium; f. 1985. Mems: regional and national federations covering about 500,000 workers in 30 countries. Organization: Congress (every five years), World Board (every year), Executive Committee, six World Trade Councils. Pres. C. DE SCHRIJVER (Belgium); Sec.-Gen. E. MOLANO (Colombia). Publ. *Labor*.

WORLD COUNCIL OF CHURCHES—WCC

Address: 150 route de Ferney, POB 66, 1211 Geneva 20, Switzerland.
Telephone: (022) 916111.
Telex: 23423.
The Council was founded in 1948 to promote co-operation between Christian Churches and to prepare for a clearer manifestation of the unity of the Church.

MEMBERS

There are 306 member Churches in over 100 countries, of which 30 are associate members. Chief denominations: Anglican, Baptist, Congregational, Lutheran, Methodist, Moravian, Old Catholic, Orthodox, Presbyterian, Reformed and Society of Friends. The Roman Catholic Church is not a member but sends official observers to meetings.

Organization
(October 1988)

ASSEMBLY

The governing body of the World Council, consisting of delegates of the member Churches, it meets every six or seven years to frame policy and consider some main theme. The sixth Assembly was held at Vancouver, Canada, in 1983.
Presidium: Dame R. Nita Barrow (Barbados), Dr Marga Buehrig (Switzerland), Metropolitan Paulos Mar Gregorios (India), Bishop Johannes Hempel (GDR), Patriarch Ignatios IV (Syria), Most Rev. W. P. Khotso Makhulu (Botswana), Very Rev. Dr Lois Wilson (Canada).

CENTRAL COMMITTEE

Appointed by the Assembly to carry out its policies and decisions, the Committee consists of 150 members chosen from Assembly delegates. It meets annually.
Moderator: Rev. Dr Heinz Joachim Held (FRG).
Vice-Moderators: Metropolitan Chrystostomos of Myra (Turkey), Dr Sylvia Talbot (USA).

EXECUTIVE COMMITTEE

Consists of the Presidents, the Officers and 16 members chosen by the Central Committee from its membership to prepare its agenda, expedite its decisions and supervise the work of the Council between meetings of the Central Committee. Meets every six months.

GENERAL SECRETARIAT

The General Secretariat implements the policies laid down by the WCC, and co-ordinates the work programme units described below. It includes a Communication Department, a Finance Department and a Library, and supervises the work of the Ecumenical Institute at Bossey, Switzerland, which provides training in ecumenical leadership.
General Secretary: Rev. Dr Emilio Castro (Uruguay).

Activities

The work of the WCC is carried out by three programme units:

FAITH AND WITNESS

This unit studies the theological questions which divide the churches (producing, for example, recent statements on baptism, the Eucharist and the ministry) and the problems facing the Church in the modern world; it assists the Christian community in sharing information and resources for mission and evangelism; and conducts dialogues with people of non-Christian faiths.

JUSTICE AND SERVICE

The mandate of the unit on Justice and Service is 'to assist the churches in combating poverty, injustice and oppression and to facilitate ecumenical co-operation in service to human need and in promoting freedom, justice, peace, human dignity and world community.' The five sub-units reflect these tasks: Commission on Inter-Church Aid, Refugee and World Service (CICARWS), Commission of the Churches in International Affairs (CCIA), Programme to Combat Racism (PCR), Commission on the Churches' Participation in Development (CCPD) and Christian Medical Commission (CMC). Unit-wide programme priorities are covered by the Programme on Justice, Peace and the Integrity of Creation. The Human Rights Resources Office for Latin America assists many programmes and initiatives in Latin Amercia and the Caribbean, in close consultation with the local churches, in the area of human rights.

EDUCATION AND RENEWAL

This unit aims to increase participation by women, young people and lay people generally in the activities of the Church and of society; to serve theological education institutions and stimulate new developments in Christian education; and to help make the ecumenical movement a reality at parish level.

FINANCE

The WCC's budget for 1987 amounted to 41.2m. Swiss francs, and that for 1988 was 39.4m. Swiss francs. The main contributors are the churches and their agencies, with funds for certain projects contributed by other organizations. Of total income in 1988, about 41% was allotted to the Justice and Service Unit, 13% to the Faith and Witness Unit, and 16% to the Education and Renewal Unit; the General Secretariat, Communication Department, Governing Bodies, administrative services and Library together account for 25%; and an allocation to the Ecumenical Institute, Bossey, 5%.

PUBLICATIONS

Catalogue of periodicals, books and audio-visuals.
One World (monthly).
Ecumenical Review (quarterly).
International Review of Mission (quarterly).
Ecumenical Press Service (weekly).

WORLD FEDERATION OF TRADE UNIONS—WFTU

Address: Vinohradská 10, 12147 Prague 2, Czechoslovakia.
Telephone: (2) 353565.
Telex: 121525.

The Federation was founded in 1945, on a world-wide basis. A number of members withdrew from the Federation in 1949 to set up the International Confederation of Free Trade Unions (see p. 162). (See also the World Confederation of Labour, p. 209.)

MEMBERS
There are 94 affiliated national federations in 82 countries, with 214m. members.

Organization
(October 1988)

WORLD TRADE UNION CONGRESS
The Congress meets every four years. The size of the delegations is based on the total membership of national federations. The Congress is also open to participation by non-affiliated organizations. The 11th Congress, held in East Berlin in September 1986, was attended by 1,014 delegates, observers and guests.

The Congress reviews WFTU's work, endorses reports from the executives, and elects the General Council and Bureau.

GENERAL COUNCIL
The General Council meets once a year and comprises members and deputies, representing 82 countries and 11 Trade Unions Internationals, and elected by Congress from nominees of national federations. Every affiliated organization has one member and one deputy member.

The Council receives reports from the Bureau, approves the budget, plans the Congress agenda, and elects the General Secretary and Secretariat officers.

BUREAU
President: SÁNDOR GASPAR (Hungary).
Vice-Presidents: ERNEST BOATSWAIN (Australia), INDRAJIT GUPTA (India), ELIAS EL-HABR (Lebanon), KAREL HOFFMANN (Czechoslovakia), HENRI KRASUCKI (France), B. LUVSATSEREN (Mongolia), IZZEDINE NASSER (Syria), VALENTIN PACHO (Peru), STEPAN A. SHALAYEV (USSR), TADESSE TAMERAT (Ethiopia), ROBERTO VEIGA (Cuba), ROMAIN VILON GUEZO (Benin), MIROSLAV ZAVADIL (Czechoslovakia), ANDREAS ZIARTIDES (Cyprus).

The Bureau, which has 40 members, meets twice a year and conducts most of the executive work of WFTU.

SECRETARIAT
The Secretariat consists of the General Secretary and eight secretaries. It is appointed by the General Council and is responsible for economic and social affairs, national trade union liaison, press and information, the Trade Unions Internationals, women's affairs, solidarity activities, education, administration and finance.
General Secretary: IBRAHIM ZAKARIA.

BUDGET
Income is derived from affiliation dues, which are based on the number of members in each trade union federation.

PUBLICATIONS
World Trade Union Movement (monthly; published in 10 languages).
Flashes from the Trade Unions (weekly; published in five languages).

Trade Unions Internationals
The following autonomous Trade Unions Internationals are associated with WFTU:

Trade Unions International of Agricultural, Forestry and Plantation Workers: Bolshaya Serpouklovskaya 44, 113093 Moscow, USSR; f. 1949. Mems: 106 unions grouping over 70m. workers in 66 countries. Pres. A. KYRIACOU (Cyprus); Sec.-Gen. ANDRÉ HEMMERLÉ (France). Publ. *Bulletin* (every 2 months in Arabic, French, Spanish, English and Russian).

Trade Unions International of Chemical, Oil and Allied Workers (ICPS): 1415 Budapest, Hungary; f. 1950. Mems: about 13m., grouped in 100 unions in 54 countries; Industrial Commissions for Oil, Chemicals, Rubber, Paper-board and Glass/Pottery. Pres. FERENC DAJKA (Hungary); Gen. Sec. ALAIN COVET (France). Publs *Information Bulletin*, *Information Sheet* (French, English, Spanish, Russian, German, Arabic, Japanese).

Trade Unions International of Food, Tobacco, Hotel and Allied Industries Workers: 6th September St 4, Sofia 1000, Bulgaria; tel. 88-02-51; telex 23410; f. 1949. Mems: 94 unions grouping 21m. individuals in 54 countries. Pres. FREDDY HUCK (France); Gen. Sec. LUIS MARTELL ROSA (Cuba). Publ. *News Bulletin*.

Trade Unions International of Metal Workers: POB 158, Pouchkinskaya 5/6, Moscow 109003, USSR; tel. (095) 230-21-23; telex 411370; f. 1949. Mems: 62 unions grouping 22.5m. workers from 43 countries. Pres. REINHARD SOMMER (GDR); Secs V. GOSHCHINSKI (USSR), J. ROMERO (Colombia). Publ. *Informations, Bulletin*.

Trade Unions International of Public and Allied Employees: 1086 Berlin, Französische Str. 47, German Democratic Republic; tel. 2292662; f. 1949. Mems: 35.6m. in 143 unions in 51 countries. Branch Commissions: State, Municipal, Postal and Telecommunications, Health, Banks and Insurance. Pres. ALAIN POUCHOL (France); Gen. Sec. JOCHEN MEINEL (GDR). Publs *Public Services* (in English, French and Spanish), *Information Bulletin* (in seven languages).

Trade Unions International of Textile, Clothing, Leather and Fur Workers: Opletalova 57, 110 00 Prague 1, Czechoslovakia; f. 1949. Mems: 12m. workers in 71 organizations in 58 countries. Pres. GILBERTO MORALES (Colombia); Sec.-Gen. JAN HÜBNER (Czechoslovakia). Publ. *Information Courier*.

Trade Unions International of Transport Workers: Váci u. 73, 1139 Budapest, Hungary; tel. 209-601; telex 225861; f. 1949. Mems: 173 unions grouping 20m. workers from 72 countries. Pres. G. LANOUE (France); Gen. Sec. K. C. MATHEW (India). Publs *Bulletin* (monthly, in English, French, Russian and Spanish), *Journal* (quarterly, in English, French and Spanish).

Trade Unions International of Workers in Commerce: Opletalova 57, 110 00 Prague I, Czechoslovakia; f. 1959. Mems: 70 national federations in 61 countries, grouping 23m. members. Pres. JANOS VAS (Hungary); Sec.-Gen. ALVARO VILLAMARÍN (Colombia).

Trade Unions International of Workers in Energy: 36/40 ul. Kopernika, 00-924 Warsaw, Poland; tel. 264316; telex 816913; f. 1949. Mems: 30 unions with 7.5m. mems. in 28 countries. Pres. FRANÇOIS DUTEIL (France); Gen. Sec. MIECZYSŁAW JUREK (Poland). Publ. *Information Bulletin*.

Trade Unions International of Workers of the Building, Wood and Building Materials Industries: Box 281, Helsinki 10, Finland; tel. 693-10-50; f. 1949. Mems: 78 unions in 60 countries, grouping 17m. workers. Pres. LOTHAR LINDNER (GDR); Sec.-Gen. MAURI PERÄ (Finland). Publ. bulletin in seven languages.

World Federation of Teachers' Unions: 1110 Berlin, Wilhelm-Wolff-Str. 21, Postfach 176, German Democratic Republic; tel. 4800591; telex 115037; f. 1946. Mems: 132 national unions of teachers and educational and scientific workers in 85 countries, representing over 25m. individuals. Pres. LESTURUGE ARIYAWANSA (Sri Lanka); Gen. Sec. GERARD MONTANT (France). Publs *Teachers of the World* (quarterly, in English, French, German and Spanish), *International Teachers' News* (8 a year, in seven languages), reports and papers.

OTHER INTERNATIONAL ORGANIZATIONS

Agriculture, Food, Forestry and Fisheries	page 215	Religion	page 245
Aid and Development	218	Science	248
Arts and Culture	220	Social Sciences and Humanistic Studies	254
Commodities	223	Social Welfare	257
Economics and Finance	225	Sport and Recreations	260
Education	227	Technology	261
Government and Politics	230	Tourism	265
Industrial and Professional Relations	233	Trade and Industry	266
Law	235	Transport	270
Medicine and Health	237	Youth and Students	272
Posts and Telecommunications	243		
Press, Radio and Television	244	**Index at end of volume**	

OTHER INTERNATIONAL ORGANIZATIONS

Agriculture, Food, Forestry and Fisheries

(For organizations concerned with agricultural commodities, see Commodities, p. 223)

African Timber Organization: BP 1077, Libreville, Gabon; tel. (241) 732928; telex 5620; f. 1976 to enable members to study and co-ordinate ways of influencing prices of wood and wood products by ensuring a continuous flow of information on forestry matters; to harmonize commercial policies and carry out industrial and technical research. Mems: Angola, Cameroon, Central African Republic, Congo, Côte d'Ivoire, Equatorial Guinea, Gabon, Ghana, Liberia, Tanzania, São Tomé and Príncipe, Zaire. Sec.-Gen. GAHURANYI TANGANIKA.

Asian Vegetable Research and Development Center: POB 42, Shanhua, Tainan 74199, Taiwan; tel. (06) 5837801; telex 73560; f. 1971 to improve diet and standard of living of rural populations in the humid tropics by increased production of vegetable crops through the breeding of better varieties and the development of improved cultural methods; research programme includes plant breeding, plant pathology, plant physiology, soil science, entomology, crop management, cropping systems and chemistry; the Centre has an experimental farm, laboratories, gene-bank, greenhouses, library and weather station and provides training for research and production specialists in tropical vegetables. Mems: Australia, France, Federal Republic of Germany, Japan, the Republic of Korea, the Philippines, Taiwan, Thailand and the USA. Dir-Gen. Dr G. A. MARLOWE; Deputy Dir-Gen. PAUL M. H. SUN. Publs *Annual Report, Newsletter, Technical Bulletin, CENTERPOINT*, crop research reports, scientific papers.

Association for the Advancement of Agricultural Science in Africa—AAASA: POB 30087, Addis Ababa, Ethiopia; f. 1968 to promote the development and application of agricultural sciences and the exchange of ideas; to encourage Africans to enter training; holds several seminars each year in different African countries. Mems: individual agronomists, research institutes, organizations in the agricultural sciences in Africa. Sec.-Gen. Prof. M. EL-FOULY (acting). Publs *Journal* (2 a year), *Newsletter* (quarterly).

Caribbean Food and Nutrition Institute: Jamaica Centre, UWI Campus, POB 140, Kingston 7, Jamaica; tel. (809) 927-1540; Trinidad Centre, UWI Campus, St. Augustine, Trinidad; tel. 66 31544; f. 1967 to serve the governments and people of the region and to act as a catalyst among persons and organizations concerned with food and nutrition through research and field investigations, training in nutrition, dissemination of information, advisory services and production of educational material. Mems: all English-speaking Caribbean territories, including the mainland countries of Belize and Guyana. Dir Dr ADELINE WYNANTE PATTERSON. Publs *Cajanus* (quarterly), *Nyam News* (monthly), educational material.

Collaborative International Pesticides Analytical Council Ltd.—CIPAC: c/o Plantenziektenkundige Dienst, Postbus 9102, 6700 HC Wageningen, Netherlands; tel. 8370 96420; telex 45163; f. 1957 to organize international collaborative work on methods of analysis for pesticides used in crop protection. Mems: individuals in 15 countries and corresponding mems. in 19 countries. Chair. Dr H. P. BOSSHARDT (Switzerland); Sec. Dr A. MARTIJN (Netherlands).

Common Organization for the Control of Desert Locust and Bird Pests—OCLALAV: BP 1066, Dakar, Senegal; f. 1965 to destroy insect pests, in particular the desert locust, and grain-eating birds, in particular the quelea-quelea, and to sponsor related research projects; co-operates with the International African Migratory Locust Organization (see below). Mems: Benin, Burkina Faso, Cameroon, Chad, Côte d'Ivoire, The Gambia, Mali, Mauritania, Niger, Senegal. Dir-Gen. ABDULLAHI OULD SOUEÏD AHMED.

Dairy Society International—DSI: 7185 Ruritan Drive, Chambersburg, Pa 17201, USA; tel. (717) 375-4392; f. 1946 to foster the extension of dairy and dairy industrial enterprise internationally through an interchange and dissemination of scientific, technological, economic, dietary and other relevant information; organizer and sponsor of the first World Congress for Milk Utilization. Mems: in 50 countries. Pres. JAMES E. CLICK (USA); Man. Dir G. W. WEIGOLD (USA). Publs *DSI Report to Members, DSI Bulletin, Market Frontier News, Dairy Situation Review*.

Desert Locust Control Organization for Eastern Africa: POB 4255, Addis Ababa, Ethiopia; tel. 18 14 75; f. 1962 to promote most effective control of desert locust in the region and to carry out research into the locust's environment and behaviour, and pesticides residue analysis; assists member states in the monitoring and extermination of other migratory pests such as the quelea-quelea (grain-eating birds), the army worm and the tsetse fly; bases at Asmara and Dire Dawa (Ethiopia), Mogadishu and Hargeisa (Somalia), Nairobi (Kenya), Khartoum (Sudan), Arusha (Tanzania) and Djibouti. Mems: Djibouti, Ethiopia, Kenya, Somalia, Sudan, Tanzania and Uganda. Dir-Gen. HOSEA KAYUMBO. Publs *Desert Locust Situation Reports* (monthly), *Annual Report*.

European and Mediterranean Plant Protection Organization: 1 rue Le Nôtre, 75016 Paris, France; tel. (1) 45-20-77-94; telex 614148; f. 1951, present name adopted in 1955; aims to promote international co-operation in plant protection research and in preventing the introduction and spread of pests and diseases of plants and plant products. Mems: governments of 34 countries and territories. Chair. H. PAG; Dir-Gen. I. M. SMITH. Publs *EPPO Bulletin, Data Sheets on Quarantine Organisms, Guidelines for the Biological Evaluation of Pesticides, Crop Growth Stage Keys, Summary of the Phytosanitary Regulations of EPPO Member Countries, Reporting Service*.

European Association for Animal Production (Fédération européenne de zootechnie): Corso Trieste 67, 00198 Rome, Italy; tel. (06) 8840785; f. 1949 to help improve the conditions of animal production and meet consumer demand; holds annual meetings; Mems: associations in 31 member countries. Pres. A. ROOS (Sweden); Sec.-Gen. Prof. Dr J. BOYAZOGLU. Publ. *Livestock Production Science* (12 a year).

European Association for Research on Plant Breeding—EUCARPIA: c/o POB 128, 6700 AC Wageningen, Netherlands; f. 1956 to promote scientific and technical co-operation in the plant breeding field. Mems: 1,075 individuals, 80 corporate mems; 12 sections and several working groups. Pres. Prof. Dr G. RÖBBELEN (Federal Republic of Germany); Sec. M. MESKEN. Publ. *Bulletin*.

European Confederation of Agriculture: CP 87, 5200 Brugg, Aargau, Switzerland; tel. (056) 413177; telex 825110; f. 1889 as International Confederation, re-formed in 1948 as European Confederation; represents the interests of European agriculture in the international field; social security for independent farmers and foresters in the member countries. Mems: 436 ordinary and 43 advisory mems. from 20 countries. Pres. HEINRICH ORSINI-ROSENBERG (Austria); Gen. Sec. WILLY STRAUB. Publs *CEA Dialog, Rapport sur le marché international du lait et des produits laitiers* (quarterly).

European Grassland Federation: c/o Dr W. H. Prins, POB 30003, 9750 RA Haren, Netherlands; tel. (050) 337315; telex 53990; f. 1963 to facilitate and maintain liaison between European grassland organizations and to promote the interchange of scientific and practical knowledge and experience; a general meeting is held every two or three years (1990 in Czechoslovakia) and symposia at other times. Mems: 21 organizations and three individuals from 24 countries. Pres. Dr N. GABORCIK; Federation Sec. Dr W. H. PRINS.

European Livestock and Meat Trade Union: 81a rue de la Loi, 1040 Brussels, Belgium; tel. (02) 230-46-03; telex 64685; f. 1952 to study problems of the European livestock and meat trade and inform members of all legislation affecting it, and to act as an international arbitration commission; conducts research on agricultural markets, quality of livestock, and veterinary regulations. Mems: national organizations in Austria, Belgium, Denmark, France, Federal Republic of Germany, Greece, Ireland, Italy, Luxembourg, Netherlands, Portugal, Spain, Sweden and Switzerland; and the European Association of Livestock Markets. Pres. F. BERTOLAZZI; Sec.-Gen. J.-L. MERIAUX.

Inter-American Association of Agricultural Librarians and Documentalists (Asociación Interamericana de Bibliotecarios y Documentalistas Agrícolas—AIBDA): CP 7170, Turrialba, Costa Rica; tel. 566431; telex 8005; f. 1953 to promote professional improvement of its members through technical publications and meetings, and to promote improvement of library services in agricultural sciences. Mems: about 700 in 30 countries. Pres. NITZIA BARRANTES DE CEBALLOS; Exec. Sec. ANA MARÍA PAZ DE ERICKSON. Publs *Boletín Informativo* (quarterly), *Boletín Especial* (irregular), *Proceedings of Inter-American Meetings of AIBDA* (every

3 years), *Revista AIBDA* (2 a year), *Páginas de Contenido: Ciencias de la Información* (quarterly), *AIBDA Actualidades* (quarterly), *Guía para Bibliotecas Agrícolas*.

Inter-American Tropical Tuna Commission—IATTC: c/o Scripps Institution of Oceanography, La Jolla, Calif 92093, USA; tel. (619) 546-7100; telex 697115; f. 1950; investigates the biology of the tunas of the eastern Pacific Ocean to determine the effects of fishing and natural factors on stocks; recommends appropriate conservation measures to maintain stocks at levels which will afford maximum sustainable catches; attempts to maintain a high level of tuna production, and also to maintain porpoise stocks and avoid the needless killing of porpoise by tuna-fishers. Mems: France, Japan, Nicaragua, Panama, USA. Dir JAMES JOSEPH. Publs *Bulletin* (irregular), *Annual Report*.

International Association for Cereal Science and Technology: Wiener Strasse 22A, POB 77, 2320 Schwechat, Austria; tel. (0222) 77-72-02; telex 133316; f. 1955 (as the International Association for Cereal Chemistry; name changed 1984) to standardize the methods of testing and analysing cereals and cereal products. Mems: 33 member states. Sec.-Gen. Dr Dipl. Ing. H. GLATTES (Austria).

International Association for Vegetation Science: 3400 Göttingen, Wilhelm-Weber-Str. 2, Federal Republic of Germany; tel. (0551) 395700; f. 1938. Mems: 540 from 39 countries. Chair. Prof. Dr S. PIGNATTI; Sec. Prof. Dr H. DIERSCHKE. Publs *Phytocoenologia, Vegetatio*.

International Association of Agricultural Economists: 1211 West 22nd St, Oak Brook, Ill 60521, USA; f. 1929 to foster development of the sciences of agricultural economics and further the application of the results of economic investigation in agricultural processes and the improvement of economic and social conditions relating to agricultural and rural life. Mems: 1,544 from 88 countries. Pres. MICHEL PETIT (France); Sec. and Treas. R. J. HILDRETH (USA).

International Association of Agricultural Librarians and Documentalists: c/o Drs J. van der Burg, PUDOC, PO Box 4, 6700 AA Wageningen, Netherlands; telex 45015; f. 1955 to promote agricultural library science and documentation, and the professional interests of agricultural librarians and documentalists; affiliated to the International Federation of Library Associations and to the Fédération Internationale de Documentation. Mems: 600 in 80 countries. Pres. E. MANN (UK); Sec.-Treas. Drs J. VAN DER BURG (Netherlands). Publs *Quarterly Bulletin, Current Agricultural Serials* (2 vols.), *Primer for Agricultural Libraries, IAALD News*.

International Association of Horticultural Producers: Bezuidenhoutseweg 153, 361, 2501 BE The Hague, Netherlands; tel. (070) 81-46-31; telex 31 406; f. 1948; represents the common interests of commercial horticultural producers in the international field by frequent meetings, regular publications, press-notices, resolutions and addresses to governments and international authorities; authorizes international horticultural exhibitions. Mems: national associations in 24 countries. Pres. R. MATHIS; Gen. Sec. Drs J. B. M. ROTTEVEEL. Publ. *Yearbook of International Horticultural Statistics*.

International Bee Research Association: 18 North Rd, Cardiff, CF1 3DY, Wales; tel. (0222) 372409; telex 23152; f. 1949 to further and co-ordinate research on bees, etc. (including pollination) in all countries. Mems: 1,200 in 130 countries. Dir DAVID A. FRANCIS. Publs *Bee World* (quarterly), *Apicultural Abstracts* (quarterly), *Journal of Apicultural Research* (quarterly).

International Centre for Advanced Mediterranean Agronomic Studies: 11 rue Newton, 75116 Paris, France; postgraduate centre provides a supplementary technical, economic and social education for graduates of agriculture, forestry, veterinary sciences and economics in Mediterranean countries; examines the international problems posed by agricultural development; participates in research; attached agronomic institutes in Bari (Italy), Chania (Greece), Montpellier (France) and Zaragoza (Spain). Mems: Algeria, Egypt, France, Greece, Italy, Lebanon, Morocco, Portugal, Spain, Tunisia, Turkey, Yugoslavia. Sec.-Gen. RAYMOND FÉVRIER.

International Centre for Tropical Agriculture (Centro Internacional de Agricultura Tropical): Apdo Aéreo 6713, Cali, Colombia; tel. 57-3-675050; telex 05769; f. 1969 to accelerate agricultural and economic development and to increase agricultural productivity in the tropics; research and training focuses on production problems of the lowland tropics concentrating on field beans, cassava, rice and tropical pastures. Dir-Gen. Dr JOHN L. NICKEL. Publs *Annual Report*, catalogue of publications.

International Commission for Agricultural and Food Industries: 35 rue du Général Foy, 75008 Paris, France; tel. (1) 42-93-19-24; f. 1934 to study scientific, technical and economic questions related to the food and agricultural industries in various countries, to co-ordinate investigations in these areas and to assemble and distribute relevant documentation for these industries (the information centre is managed by CDIUPA, Le Noyer Lambert, 91305 Massy, France); to organize yearly international congresses for agricultural and food industries. Pres. GÓMEZ NAVARRO; Gen. Sec. GUY DARDENNE (France). Publs *Comptes Rendus des Congrès Internationaux des Industries Agricoles*, Reports of Symposia, Calendar of international meetings related to food industries, List of international organizations associated with food industries.

International Commission for the Conservation of Atlantic Tunas: Calle Príncipe de Vergara 17, 28001 Madrid, Spain; tel. 431 03 29; telex 46330; f. 1969 to promote the conservation and rational exploitation of tuna resources in the Atlantic Ocean and adjacent seas. Exec. Sec. O. RODRÍGUEZ MARTÍN.

International Commission for the Southeast Atlantic Fisheries: Paseo de la Habana 65, 28036 Madrid, Spain; tel. 458 8766; telex 45533; f. 1971 under the Convention for the Conservation of the Living Resources of the Southeast Atlantic; monitors fish stocks and determines quotas. Mems: 17 countries. Chair. Capt. K. N. GAYDAROV (Bulgaria); Exec. Sec. R. LAGARDE.

International Commission of Sugar Technology: 1 Aandorenstraat, 3300 Tienen, Belgium; f. 1948 to organize meetings with a view to discussing past investigations and promoting scientific and technical research work. Pres. of Scientific Cttee. G. MANTOVANI (Italy); Gen. Sec. R. PIECK (Belgium).

International Committee for Recording the Productivity of Milk Animals: Corso Trieste 67, 00198 Rome, Italy; tel. (06) 8840785; f. 1951 to extend and improve the work of milk recording, standardize methods; 26th session, Norway, July 1988. Mems: in 26 countries. Pres. P. CATTIN-VIDAL (France); Sec.-Gen. Prof. Dr J. BOYAZOGLU.

International Crops Research Institute for the Semi-Arid Tropics—ICRISAT: Patancheru, Andhra Pradesh 502 324, India; tel. 224016; telex 0422-203; f. 1972 as world centre for genetic improvement of sorghum, pearl millet, pigeonpea, chickpea and groundnut, and for research on the management of resources in the world's semi-arid tropics; research covers all physical and socio-economic aspects of improving farming systems on unirrigated land. Dir LESLIE D. SWINDALE (New Zealand). Publs *Annual Report, Research Highlights, At ICRISAT* (quarterly), *Sorghum and Millet Information Center Newsletter* (3 a year), *International Chickpea Newsletter* (2 a year).

International Dairy Federation: 41 Square Vergote, 1040 Brussels, Belgium; tel. (02) 733-98-88; telex 63818; f. 1903 to link all dairy associations in order to encourage the solution of scientific, technical and economic problems affecting the dairy industry. Mems: national committees in 35 countries. Sec.-Gen. P. F. J. STAAL (Netherlands). Publs *Annual Bulletin, IDF News, Mastitis Newsletter, Packaging News*, standards for sampling and analysis.

International Federation of Agricultural Producers—IFAP: 21 rue Chaptal, 75009 Paris, France; tel. (1) 45-26-05-53; telex 281210; f. 1946 to represent, in the international field, the interests of agricultural producers; to exchange information and ideas and help develop understanding of world problems and their effects upon agricultural producers; to encourage efficiency of production, processing, and marketing of agricultural commodities; holds conference every two years. National farmers' organizations and agricultural co-operatives of 51 countries are represented in the Federation. Pres. GLEN FLATEN (Canada); Sec.-Gen. D. KING. Publs *IFAP Newsletter* (monthly), *World Agriculture/IFAP News* (quarterly), *Farming for Development* (quarterly), *IFAP Tropical Commodity Newsletter* (monthly), *Proceedings of General Conferences*.

International Federation of Beekeepers' Associations—APIMONDIA: Corso Vittorio Emanuele 101, 00186 Rome, Italy; tel. (6) 65121; telex 612533; f. 1949; collects and brings up to date documentation concerning international beekeeping; studies the particular problems of beekeeping through its permanent committees; organizes international congresses, seminars, symposia and meetings; stimulates research into new techniques for more economical results; co-operates with other international organizations interested in beekeeping, in particular with FAO. Mems: 80 associations from 68 countries. Pres. BORNECK RAYMOND; Sec.-Gen. Dr SILVESTRO CANNAMELA. Publ. *Apiacta* (quarterly, in English, French, German, Russian and Spanish).

International Hop Growers' Convention: c/o Institut za hmeljarstvo in pivovarstvo, 63310 Žalec, Yugoslavia; tel. (063) 711221; telex 33 514; f. 1950 to act as a centre for the collection of data on hop production, and to conduct scientific, technical and economic commissions. Mems: national associations in Australia, Belgium, Czechoslovakia, France, German Democratic Republic, Federal Republic of Germany, Hungary, Poland, Spain, United Kingdom, USA and Yugoslavia. Pres. GEORGE W. SIGNOROTTI (USA); Gen. Sec. ALOJZ ČETINA (Yugoslavia). Publ. *Hopfen-Rundschau* (fortnightly).

OTHER INTERNATIONAL ORGANIZATIONS   *Agriculture, Food, Forestry and Fisheries*

International Institute for Sugar Beet Research: 47 rue Montoyer, 1040 Brussels, Belgium; tel. (02) 509-15-33; telex 21287; f. 1931 to promote research and exchange of information, by organizing meetings and study groups. Mems: 517 in 33 countries. Pres. of the Admin. Council M. MARTENS; Sec.-Gen. L. WEICKMANS. Publ. *IIRB Winter Congress Proceedings*.

International Institute of Tropical Agriculture—IITA: Oyo Rd, PMB 5320, Ibadan, Nigeria; tel. 400300; telex 31417; f. 1967; principal financing arranged by the Consultative Group on International Agricultural Research (CGIAR), co-ordinated by the IBRD. The four main research programmes comprise farming systems, grain legume improvement, cereal improvement and root and tuber improvement; training programme for researchers in tropical agriculture; library of 35,000 vols. Dir LAURENCE D. STIFEL. Publs *Annual Report*, technical bulletins, research reports.

International Laboratory for Research on Animal Diseases—ILRAD: POB 30709, Nairobi, Kenya; tel. 592311; telex 22040; f. 1973, became operational 1976; support provided by 14 countries, UNDP, the EEC, the Rockefeller Foundation and the World Bank; research programmes on the development of control procedures for trypanosomiasis and theileriosis; training programme for researchers in animal disease control as well as technical and other staff; regular seminars, conferences; specialized library. Dir-Gen. Dr A. R. GRAY. Publs *Annual Report, ILRAD Report*.

International Livestock Centre for Africa—ILCA: POB 5689, Addis Ababa, Ethiopia; tel. 183215; telex 21207; f. 1974; an international research centre supported by and financed largely through the Consultative Group on International Agricultural Research of the IBRD; a multidisciplinary research, information and training institute concerned with livestock and agricultural production systems, particularly the productivity of ruminants and the pastoral resources of Africa, and the interdependence of crop and livestock production; also stimulates and reinforces national research programmes. Dir-Gen. JOHN WALSH. Publs *ILCA Bulletin, ILCA Newsletter*, research reports, bibliographies.

International Maize and Wheat Improvement Centre—CIMMYT: Apdo. Postal 6-641, 06600 México, DF, Mexico; tel. (905) 7613311; telex 177 2023; assists developing countries in increasing production of maize, wheat and triticale, primarily through improved germ-plasm. Dir-Gen. Dr DONALD WINKELMANN.

International North Pacific Fisheries Commission: 6640 N.W. Marine Drive, Vancouver, British Columbia, V6T 1X2, Canada; tel. (604) 228-1128; f. 1953. Mems: Canada, Japan and USA. Publs *Annual Report, Bulletin and Statistical Yearbook*.

International Organization for Biological Control of Noxious Animals and Plants: Institut für Phytomedizin, Swiss Federal Institute of Technology (ETH), 8092 Zürich, Switzerland; tel. (01) 2563921; telex 53178; f. 1955 to promote and co-ordinate research on the more effective biological control of harmful insects and plants; re-organized in 1971 as a central council with world-wide affiliations and largely autonomous regional sections in different parts of the world: the West Palaearctic (Europe, North Africa, the Middle East), the Western Hemisphere, South-East Asia, Pacific Region and Tropical Africa. Pres. Dr J. COULSON (USA); Sec.-Gen. Dr J.-P. AESCHLIMANN (Switzerland). Publs *Entomophaga* (quarterly), *Newsletter*.

International Organization of Citrus Virologists: c/o Dr H. D. Ohr, Dept of Plant Pathology, University of California, Riverside, Calif 92521, USA; tel. (714) 787-4140; f. 1957 to promote research on citrus virus diseases at international level by standardizing diagnostic techniques and exchanging information relating to these diseases and their control. Mems: 250. Chair. Dr LUIS NAVARRO; Sec.-Treas. Dr H. D. OHR.

International Red Locust Control Organization for Central and Southern Africa: POB 240252, Ndola, Zambia; tel. 612433; telex 30072; f. 1971 as successor to International Red Locust Control Service, to control red locust populations in recognized outbreak areas. Mems: nine countries. Dir Dr SAUL MOOBOLA. Publs *Annual Report, Quarterly Report* and scientific reports.

International Regional Organization of Plant Protection and Animal Health (Organismo Internacional Regional de Sanidad Agropecuaria—OIRSA): Edif. Carbonell 2, Carretera a Santa Tecla, San Salvador, El Salvador; tel. 232391; telex (0373) 20746; f. 1953 for the prevention of the introduction of animal and plant pests and diseases unknown in the region; research, control and eradication programmes of the principal pests present in agriculture; technical assistance and advice to the ministries of agriculture and livestock of member countries; education and qualification of personnel. Mems: Costa Rica, Dominican Republic, El Salvador, Guatemala, Honduras, Mexico, Nicaragua, Panama. Exec. Dir Ing. RAFAEL GARCÍA BESNÉ.

International Rice Research Institute—IRRI: POB 933, Manila, Philippines; tel. 888-351; telex 45365; f. 1960; conducts a comprehensive basic research programme on the rice plant and its management with the objective of increasing the quantity and quality of rice; maintains a library to collect and provide access to the world's technical rice literature; publishes and disseminates research results; conducts regional rice research projects in co-operation with scientists in rice-producing countries; offers a resident training programme in rice research methods and techniques for staff members of organizations concerned with rice; organizes international conferences and symposia. Dir-Gen. KLAUS LAMPE. Publs *Annual Report, IRRI Reporter, The International Bibliography of Rice Research, International Rice Research Newsletter, IRRI Research Paper Series, Research Highlights*.

International Seed Testing Association: Reckenholz, POB 412, 8046 Zürich, Switzerland; tel. (01) 3713133; f. 1906 (reconstituted 1924) to promote uniformity and accurate methods of seed testing and evaluation in order to facilitate efficiency in production, processing, distribution and utilization of seeds; organizes triennial conventions, meetings, workshops, symposia and training courses. Mems: 60 countries. Pres. A. B. EDNIE (Canada); Hon. Sec. Treas. Dr C. ANSELME (France). Publs *Seed Science and Technology* (3 a year), *ISTA News Bulletin* (quarterly).

International Sericultural Commission: 25 quai Jean-Jacques Rousseau, 69350 La Mulatière, France; tel. 78-50-41-98; f. 1948 to encourage the development of silk production. Library of 8,000 vols. Mems: governments of Brazil, Egypt, France, India, Japan, Lebanon, Madagascar, Mauritius, Philippines, Romania, Thailand, Tunisia. Sec.-Gen. Dr H. BOUVIER (France). Publ. *Sericologia* (quarterly).

International Service for National Agricultural Research—ISNAR: POB 93375, 2509 AJ The Hague, Netherlands; tel. (070) 49-61-00; telex 33746; f. 1980 by the Consultative Group on International Agricultural Research (q.v.) to strengthen national agricultural research systems in developing countries; to link these systems to sources of technical assistance and co-operation. Chair. HENRI CARSALADE; Dir-Gen. ALEXANDER VON DER OSTEN.

International Society for Horticultural Science: Dreijenplein 4, 6703 BC Wageningen, Netherlands; tel. (08370) 21747; telex 45760; f. 1959 to co-operate in the research field. Mems: 50 member-countries, 265 organizations, 2,800 individuals. Pres. Prof. Dr F. SCARAMUZZI (Italy); Sec.-Gen. and Treas. Ir. H. H. VAN DER BORG (Netherlands). Publs *Chronica Horticulturae* (4 a year), *Acta Horticulturae, Scientia Horticulturae* (monthly), *Horticultural Research International*.

International Society for Soilless Culture—ISOSC: POB 52, 6700 AB Wageningen, Netherlands; tel. (08370) 13809; f. 1955 as International Working Group on Soilless Culture, to promote world-wide distribution and co-ordination of research, advisory services, and practical application of soilless culture; international congress held every four years. Mems: 433 from 67 countries. Pres. Prof. Dr FRANZ PENNINGSFELD; Sec.-Gen. Ing. Agr. ABRAM A. STEINER. Publs *Bibliography on Hydroponics, Soilless Culture* (2 a year).

International Society of Soil Science: c/o POB 353, 6700 AJ Wageningen, Netherlands; tel. (08370) 19063; telex 45888; f. 1924. Mems: 8,000 individuals and associations in 135 countries. Pres. Prof. Dr A. TANAKA (Japan); Sec.-Gen. Dr W. G. SOMBROEK (Netherlands). Publ. *Bulletin* (2 a year).

International Union of Forestry Research Organizations—IUFRO: 1131 Vienna, Schönbrunn-Tirolergarten, Austria; tel. (01) 82-01-51; f. 1890/92. Mems: 600 organizations in 100 countries, more than 15,000 individual mems. Pres. Prof. R. E. BUCKMAN (USA); Sec. HEINRICH SCHMUTZENHOFER (Austria). Publs *Annual Report, IUFRO News* (quarterly), scientific papers.

International Veterinary Association for Animal Production: c/o Sociedad Veterinaria de Zootecnia, Isabel la Católica 12, 4° izq., 28013 Madrid, Spain; tel. 2471838; holds world congresses on livestock genetics, animal feeding and zootechnology. Mems: about 1,400 veterinary specialists. Pres of Exec. Cttee Prof. A. DE VUYST (Belgium); Sec.-Gen. Prof. Dr CARLOS LUIS DE CUENCA (Spain). Publs *Zootecnia* (4 a year).

Northwest Atlantic Fisheries Organization: POB 638, Dartmouth, Nova Scotia, B2Y 3Y9, Canada; tel. 469-9105; telex 019-31475; f. 1979 (formerly International Commission for the Northwest Atlantic Fisheries); aims at optimum use, management and conservation of resources, promotes research and compiles statistics. Pres. F. HARTUNG; Exec. Sec. J. C. E. CARDOSO. Publs *Annual Report, Statistical Bulletin, Journal of Northwest Atlantic Fishery Science, Scientific Council Reports, Scientific Council Studies, Sampling Yearbook, Proceedings, List of Fishing Vessels*.

World Association for Animal Production: Corso Trieste 67, 00198 Rome, Italy; tel. (06) 8840785; f. 1965; holds world conference on animal production every five years; encourages, sponsors and participates in regional meetings, seminars and symposia. Pres.

Prof. Dr R. BLAIZ (Canada); Sec.-Gen. Prof. Dr J. BOYAZOGLU. Publ. *News Items* (2 a year).

World Association of Veterinary Food-Hygienists: Institut für Veterinärmedizin des Bundesgesundheitsamtes, Postfach 330013, 1000 Berlin 33, Federal Republic of Germany; tel. (030) 83082705; telex 184016; f. 1955 to promote hygienic food control and discuss research. Mems: 36 member countries. Pres. Prof. Dr D. GROSSKLAUS (FRG); Sec. Treas. Dr P. TEUFEL.

World Association of Veterinary Microbiologists, Immunologists and Specialists in Infectious Diseases: Ecole Nationale Vétérinaire d'Alfort, 7 ave du Général de Gaulle, 94704 Maisons-Alfort Cedex, France; f. 1967 to facilitate international contacts in the fields of microbiology, immunology and animal infectious diseases. Pres. Prof. CH. PILET (France). Publs *Comparative Immunology, Microbiology and Infectious Diseases*.

World Ploughing Organization—WPO: Whiteclose, Longtown, Carlisle, Cumbria, CA6 5TY, England; tel. (0228) 791153; f. 1952 to promote World Ploughing Contest in a different country each year, to improve techniques and promote better understanding of soil cultivation practices through research and practical demonstrations. Affiliates in 26 countries. Gen. Sec. ALFRED HALL. Publs *WPO Handbook* (annual), *WPO Bulletin of News and Information* (irregular).

World's Poultry Science Association: Institut für Kleintierzucht, Postfach 280, 3100 Celle, Dörnbergstr. 25/27, Federal Republic of Germany; tel. (05141) 31031; f. 1912 to exchange knowledge in the industry, to encourage research and teaching, to publish information relating to production and marketing problems; to promote World Poultry Congresses and co-operate with governments. Mems: individuals in 95 countries, branches in 40 countries. Pres. KRISTER EKLUND (Finland); Sec. Prof. ROSE-MARIE WEGNER (FRG). Publ. *The World Poultry Science Journal* (3 a year).

World Veterinary Association: c/o Prof. Dr C. L. De Cuenca, Isabel la Católica 12, 28013 Madrid, Spain; tel. 247 18 38; telex 22762; f. 1959 as a continuation of the International Veterinary Congresses; first Congress 1863. Mems: organizations in 72 countries and 18 organizations of veterinary specialists as associate members. Pres. Dr J. F. FIGUEROA (Peru); Sec.-Treas. Prof. Dr CARLOS L. DE CUENCA. Publs *WVA Informative Bulletin, World Catalogue of Veterinary Films*.

Aid and Development

African Training and Research Centre in Administration for Development (Centre africain de formation et de recherches administratives pour le développement—CAFRAD): Pavillon International de Tanger, BP 310, Tanger, Morocco; tel. 36430; telex 33664; f. 1964 by agreement between Morocco and UNESCO, final agreement signed by 33 African states; undertakes research into administrative problems in Africa, documentation of results, provision of a consultation service for governments and organizations; holds frequent seminars; aided by UNESCO and the UN Development Programme. Mems: 27 African countries. Pres. ABDERRAHIM BANABDELJALAL; Dir-Gen. TSHIANDA KASADI BASUEBABU. Publs *Cahiers Africains d'Administration Publique* (4 a year), *Administrative Information Sources* (quarterly, also in French), *CAFRAD News* (3 a year, in English, French and Arabic).

Afro-Asian Housing Organization—AAHO: POB 523, 30 26th July St, Cairo, Egypt; tel. 752-757; f. 1965 to promote co-operation between African and Asian countries in housing, reconstruction, physical planning and related matters. Sec.-Gen. HASSAN M. HASSAN (Egypt).

Afro-Asian Rural Reconstruction Organization—AARRO: C/117-118, Defence Colony, New Delhi 110024, India; tel. 621175; f. 1962 to act as a catalyst for co-operative restructuring of rural life in Africa and Asia; to explore collectively opportunities for co-ordination of efforts for promoting welfare and eradicating hunger, thirst, disease, illiteracy and poverty amongst the rural people; and to assist the formation of organizations of farmers and other rural people. Activities include collaborative research on development issues, training; assistance in forming organizations of farmers and other rural people; the exchange of information; international conferences and seminars; and awarding 98 individual training fellowships at six institutes in Egypt, India, Japan, the Republic of Korea and Taiwan. Mems: 12 African, 13 Asian countries and the Central Union of Agricultural Co-operatives, Japan. Sec.-Gen. B. C. GANGOPADHYAY. Publ. *Rural Reconstruction* (2 a year), *AARRO Newsletter* (2 a year).

Agence de coopération culturelle et technique: 13 quai André Citroën, 75015 Paris, France: tel. (1) 45-75-62-41; telex 2011916; f. 1970, Niamey, Niger, to exchange knowledge of the cultures of French-speaking countries, to provide technical assistance, to assist relations between member countries. Technical and financial assistance has been given to projects in every member country, mainly to aid rural people. Mems: 30 countries, mainly African; associates: Cameroon, Egypt, Guinea-Bissau, Laos, Mauritania, Morocco; participants: Saint Lucia and the Canadian provinces of Quebec and New Brunswick. Sec.-Gen. PAUL OKUMBA D'OKOUATSEGUE (Gabon). Publ. *Agecoop Liaison* (monthly).

Arab Authority for Agricultural Investment and Development—AAAID: POB 2102, Khartoum, Sudan; tel. 41423; telex 24041; f. 1976 to accelerate agricultural development in the Arab world and to ensure food security; activities began in Sudan owing to its great unexplored agricultural potential; by the end of 1985 seven companies had been launched in Sudan, covering dairy products, vegetable oils, starch and glucose, poultry, fruit and vegetables, sugar, sesame, sorghum and soya beans; capital US $512m. (Dec. 1986), of which $326m. was paid-in. Mems: Algeria, Egypt, Iraq, Kuwait, Mauritania, Morocco, Qatar, Saudi Arabia, Somalia, Sudan, Syria, Tunisia, United Arab Emirates. Pres. Dr HUSSAIN YOUSEF AL-ANI.

Arab Gulf Programme for the United Nations Development Organizations—AGFUND: POB 18371, Riyadh 11415, Saudi Arabia; tel. 4416240; telex 404071; f. 1981 to provide grants for projects carried out by United Nations organizations and co-ordinate assistance by the nations of the Gulf; between 1981 and July 1987 AGFUND committed a total of US $163.7m. for the benefit of 115 countries. Contributions to AGFUND stood at US $207.8m. in July 1987. Pres. HRH Prince TALAL IBN ABDUL AZIZ AL-SAUD.

Association of Development Financing Institutions in Asia and the Pacific: c/o Private Development Corporation of the Philippines, PDCP Building, Ayala Ave, Makati, Manila, Philippines; tel. 816-16-72; telex 45022; f. 1976 to promote the interest and economic development of the respective countries of its member-institutions, and the Asia-Pacific region as a whole, through development financing. Mems: 49 ordinary (national), seven special (national and international) mems and 15 associate (regional) (national) and two co-operating (national) mems. Chair. Management Cttee S. S. NADKARNI (India).

BAM International (Frères des Hommes): 45 bis rue de la Glacière, 75013 Paris, France; tel. (1) 47-07-00-00; f. 1965 to support local partners helping the under-privileged to have more control of their own development, to recruit qualified European volunteers to work on development and health projects in Asia, Africa and South America, and to increase public awareness of the Third World in Europe. Affiliated organizations in Belgium, Italy, Luxembourg and the United Kingdom. Mems: approx. 1,000. Pres. JEAN ALLAIN. Publ. *Newsletter* (4 a year).

Caritas Internationalis (International Confederation of Catholic Organizations for charitable and social action): Palazzo San Calisto, 00120 Città del Vaticano; tel. 6987197; telex 504/2014; f. 1950 to study problems arising from poverty, their causes and possible solutions; national member organizations undertake assistance and development activities. The Confederation co-ordinates emergency relief and development projects, and represents members at international level. Mems: 120 national organizations. Pres. Cardinal ALEXANDRE DO NASCIMENTO (Angola); Sec.-Gen. Dr GERHARD MEIER (Switzerland). Publs *Intercaritas* (quarterly), leaflets, monographs.

Club of Dakar: 4 ave Hoche, 75008 Paris, France; tel. (1) 42-67-16-00; f. 1974; an informal international forum for dialogue and development research, particularly concerned with Africa. Mems: 200 administrators, industrial executives, scientists and bankers from many industrialized and developing countries. Pres. AMADOU SEYDOU; Dir E. GUILLON.

Club of the Sahel (Club du Sahel): c/o OECD, 2 rue André Pascal, 75775 Paris, France; tel. (1) 45-24-90-22; telex 620160; f. 1976; an informal forum of donor countries and member states of the permanent Inter-State Committee on Drought Control in the Sahel—CILSS (q.v.), for promoting the co-ordination of long-term policies and programmes in key development sectors affecting food production and drought control in the nine member countries of the CILSS; formed by the CILSS in association with the OECD. The Club collects information, conducts studies and helps to mobilize resources for the development of the Sahel region in agriculture livestock, cereals pricing policy, ecology, forestry and village water supplies.

Communauté Economique des Etats de l'Afrique Centrale—CEEAC (Economic Community of Central African States): BP 2112, Libreville, Gabon; f. 1983; operational 1 January 1985; aims to promote co-operation between member states by abolishing trade restrictions, establishing a common external customs tariff, linking commercial banks, and setting up a development fund, over a period of 12 years. Budget (1988): US $3.6m. Membership comprises the states belonging to UDEAC (q.v.) and five others: Burundi, Cameroon, Central African Republic, Chad, Congo, Equatorial Guinea, Gabon, Rwanda, São Tomé and Príncipe and Zaire; Angola has observer status. Sec.-Gen. Prof. LUNDA-BULULU.

OTHER INTERNATIONAL ORGANIZATIONS *Aid and Development*

Conference of Regions in North-West Europe: POB 107, 8000 Bruges 1, Belgium; f. 1955 to co-ordinate regional studies with a view to planned development in the area between the North Sea, the Ruhr, Rhine Valley and Boulogne; also compiles cartographical documents. Mems: individual scholars and representatives of planning offices in Belgium, France, Federal Republic of Germany, Luxembourg, Netherlands and the United Kingdom. Pres. Sir JACK STEWART-CLARKE (UK); Sec.-Gen. Prof. I. B. F. KORMOSS (Belgium).

Council of American Development Foundations—SOLIDARIOS: Frank Feliz Miranda 21, POB 620, Santo Domingo, Dominican Republic; tel. (809) 567-7725; telex 0597; f. 1972; exchanges information and experience, arranges technical assistance, raises funds to organize training programmes and scholarships; administers development fund to finance programmes carried out by members through a guarantee programme; provides consultancy services. Member foundations provide technical and financial assistance to low-income groups for rural, housing and handicraft projects. Mems: 28 institutional mems in 14 Latin American and Caribbean countries. Pres. SILVESTRE ALONSO; Sec.-Gen. ENRIQUE A. FERNÁNDEZ P. Publ. *Solidarios* (quarterly), *Annual Report*.

Economic Co-operation Organization—ECO: 5 Hejab Ave, Blvd Keshavarz, POB 14155-6176, Teheran, Iran; tel. 658045; telex 213774; f. 1964 (as Regional Co-operation for Development, renamed 1985), a tripartite arrangement aiming at closer co-operation in economic infrastructure, industry, banking, trade, education, science and agriculture; the introduction of a preferential trade system was announced in July 1987. Mems: Iran, Pakistan, Turkey. Sec.-Gen. ALI REZA SALARI (Iran).

Food Aid Committee: c/o International Wheat Council, Haymarket House, 28 Haymarket, London, SW1Y 4SS, England; tel. (01) 930-4128; telex 916128; f. 1967; responsible for administration of the Food Aid Convention (1986), a constituent element of the International Wheat Agreement. The 22 donor members are pledged to supply 7.5m. metric tons of grain annually to developing countries, mostly as gifts: in practice aid has exceeded 10m. tons annually. Publ. *Report on shipments* (annually).

Gambia River Basin Development Organization—OMVG: BP 2353, Région du Cap Vert, Dakar, Senegal; tel. 21-16-48; f. 1978 by Senegal and The Gambia; Guinea joined in 1981 and Guinea-Bissau in 1983. Plans include the construction of dams on the 1,100-km river at Balingho, The Gambia, and Kekreti, Senegal, to provide irrigation and hydroelectricity, at a cost of about US $400m.; feasibility studies were undertaken in 1984, and a meeting of heads of state in January 1985 agreed to seek funding for the project, but by late 1988 no progress towards beginning construction of the dams had been reported. High Commissioner MALICK JOHN.

Indian Ocean Commission—IOC: permanent secretariat not yet established; f. 1982 to promote regional co-operation, particularly in economic development; principal projects under way in 1987 (at a cost of 4,000m. francs CFA) comprised tuna-fishing development and the development of new and renewable energy systems, with assistance principally from the European Community; tariff reduction is also envisaged. The first annual IOC trade fair was to be held in Réunion in 1989. Mems: Comoros, France (representing the French Overseas Department of Réunion), Madagascar, Mauritius and Seychelles.

Inter-American Planning Society (Sociedad Interamericana de Planificación—SIAP): Apdo postal 27-716, 06760 México, DF, Mexico; f. 1956 to promote development of comprehensive planning as a continuous and co-ordinated process at all levels. Mems: 55 institutions and 2,460 individuals in 25 countries. Pres. Arq. HERMES MARROQUÍN (Guatemala); Exec. Sec. LUIS E. CAMACHO (Colombia). Publs *Correo Informativo* (quarterly), *Inter-American Journal of Planning* (quarterly).

Intergovernmental Authority on Drought and Development—IGADD: BP 2653, Djibouti; f. 1986 by six drought-affected states to co-ordinate measures to combat the effects of drought and desertification; donor countries meeting in March 1987 agreed to provide technical and financial support for 63 projects in the region. Mems: Djibouti, Ethiopia, Kenya, Somalia, Sudan, Uganda. Exec. Sec. MAKONNEN KEBRET (Ethiopia).

International Co-operation for Development and Solidarity—CIDSE: 1-2 ave des Arts, 1040 Brussels, Belgium; tel. (02) 219-00-80; telex 64208; f. 1967 to study the means of rendering more effective the co-operation amongst member organizations in the field of socio-economic development aid; to promote the creation of new organizations in both developed and developing countries, the co-ordination of its members, development aid projects and programmes by means of a computerized central registration of all development projects introduced to the affiliated organizations. Mems: Catholic agencies in 13 countries. Pres. JULIAN FILOCHOWSKI (UK); Sec.-Gen. PATRICE ROBINEAU.

Lake Chad Basin Commission: Maroua, Chad; tel. 30 34; telex 5250; f. 1964 to encourage co-operation in developing the Lake Chad region by attracting financial and technical assistance for research; the 1986-91 programme emphasizes anti-desertification measures and improvements in road and railway links between member countries; proposed operating budget (1988) 455.5m. francs CFA; capital budget 500m. francs CFA. Mems: Cameroon, Chad, Niger and Nigeria.

Latin American Association of Development Financing Institutions (Asociación Latinoamericana de Instituciones Financieros de Desarrollo—ALIDE): POB 3988, Lima 100, Peru; tel. 422400; telex 21037; f. 1968 to promote co-operation among regional development financing bodies. Mems: about 180 financing institutions and development organizations in 30 countries. Pres. Dr RICARDO AVELLANEDA; Sec.-Gen. CARLOS GARATEA YORI. Publs *Memoria anual, Directorio Latinoamericano de Instituciones Financieras de Desarrollo, Boletín Informativo, ALIDE Noticias*.

Latin American Economic System (Sistema Económico Latinoamericano—SELA): Apdo 17035, El Conde, Caracas 1010, Venezuela; tel. 9514233; telex 23508; f. 1975 by the Panama Convention; aims to accelerate the economic and social development of its members through intra-regional co-operation, and to provide a permanent system of consultation and co-ordination in economic and social matters. The Latin American Council meets annually at ministerial level; there are also Action Committees and a Permanent Secretariat. The following organizations have also been created within SELA:

Trade Information and Foreign Trade Support Programme;
Latin American Tourism Training Institute;
Latin American Housing and Human Settlements Development Organization;
Latin American Multinational Fertilizer Marketing Enterprise;
Latin American Features Agency;
Latin American Fisheries Development Organization;
Latin American Shipping Organization;
Latin American Commission for Science and Technology.

Perm. Sec. CARLOS PÉREZ DE CASTILLO.

Liptako-Gourma Integrated Development Authority: POB 619, route de Fada, N'Gourma, Burkina Faso; f. 1972; scope of activities includes water infrastructure, telecommunications and construction of roads and railways; in 1986 undertook study on development of water resources in the basin of the Niger river (for hydroelectricity and irrigation). Budget (1988) 161.4m. francs CFA. Mems: Burkina Faso, Mali, Niger. Sec.-Gen. SILIMANE GANOU (Niger).

Mano River Union: Private Post Bag 113, Freetown, Sierra Leone; f. 1973 to establish a customs and economic union between member states to improve living standards. A common external tariff was instituted in April 1977. Intra-union free trade was officially introduced in May 1981, as the first stage in progress towards a customs union. An industrial development unit was set up in 1980 to identify projects and encourage investment. Construction of a Freetown–Monrovia road and other road projects are planned. Feasibility studies for a hydroelectric scheme were completed in 1983. Joint institutes have been set up to provide training in posts and telecommunications, forestry, marine activities and customs, excise and trade. Decisions are taken at meetings of a Joint Ministerial Cttee formed by the economic and finance ministers of member states. Mems: Guinea, Liberia, Sierra Leone. Sec.-Gen. Dr ABDOULAYE DIALLO (Guinea).

Niger Basin Authority (Autorité du bassin du Niger): BP 729, Niamey, Niger; f. 1964 (as River Niger Commission; name changed 1980) to harmonize national programmes concerned with the River Niger Basin and to execute an integrated development plan; activities comprise: statistics; navigation regulation; hydrological forecasting; environmental control; infrastructure and agro-pastoral development; and arranging assistance for these projects; in 1986 the Authority's activities were reported to be suspended owing to shortage of funds. Budget (1986): 285m. francs CFA. Mems: Benin, Burkina Faso, Cameroon, Chad, Côte d'Ivoire, Mali, Niger, Nigeria. Exec. Sec. IBRAHIM SORY BALDE (Guinea). Publ. *Bulletin*.

Organization for the Development of the Senegal River (Organisation pour la Mise en Valeur du Fleuve Sénégal—OMVS): 46 rue Carnot, BP 3152, Dakar, Senegal; tel. 22-36-79; telex 670; f. 1972 to use the Senegal river for hydroelectricity, irrigation and navigation. The Djama dam in Senegal (completed in 1986) provides a barrage to prevent salt water from moving upstream, and the Manantali dam in Mali (completed in 1988) is intended to provide a reservoir for irrigation of about 400,000 ha of land and (eventually) for production of hydroelectricity and provision of year-round navigation for ocean-going vessels. Mems: Mali, Mauritania, Senegal; the admission of Guinea was approved in principle by heads of state of the member countries in 1987. High Commr AHMED MOHAMED AG HAMANI (Mali); Sec.-Gen. FOUNÉKÉ KEITA (Mali).

Organization for the Management and Development of the Kagera River Basin (Organisation pour l'aménagement et le développement du bassin de la rivière Kagera): BP 297, Kigali, Rwanda; tel. 84665; telex 0909 22567; f. 1978; for joint development and management of resources, including the construction of an 80-MW hydroelectric dam at Rusumo Falls, on the Rwanda-Tanzania border (for which final engineering studies were under review in 1987), and a 2,000-km railway network between the four member countries (for which the final study was completed in 1983); contracts for a telecommunications network between member states (financed by US $16m. from the African Development Bank) were being negotiated in 1988. Budget (1988) $2.3m. Mems: Burundi, Rwanda, Tanzania and Uganda. Exec. Sec. GRÉGOIRE BANYI-YEZAKO.

Pacific Basin Economic Council: Industry House, Barton, Canberra, Australia; tel. (062) 732311; telex 62733; f. 1967; a businessmen's organization composed of the representatives of business circles of Australia, Canada, Japan, Republic of Korea, New Zealand, Taiwan, USA and the countries of the Pacific Basin, which co-operates with government and international institutions in the overall economic development of the Pacific Area and the advancement of the livelihood of the population; promotes economic collaboration among the member countries and co-operates with the developing countries in their effort to achieve self-sustaining economic growth; holds annual International General Meeting. Chair. W. G. KENT (Australia); Dir-Gen. M. J. OVERLAND.

Pan-African Institute for Development—PAID: BP 4056, Douala, Cameroon; tel. 42-43-35; telex 6048; f. 1964 to train rural development officers from Africa at intermediate and senior levels; emphasis in education is given to: women in development; promotion of small and medium-sized enterprises; involvement of local populations in development; staff training for national centres; preparation of projects for regional co-operation; consultation, applied research, local project support and specialized training. There are four regional institutes: Central Africa (Douala), Sahel (Ouagadougou, Burkina Faso) (French-speaking), West Africa (Buéa, Cameroon), Eastern and Southern Africa (Kabwe, Zambia) (English-speaking). Sec.-Gen. Prof. A. C. MONDJANAGNI. Publs *Newsletter* (3 a year), *PAID Report* (2 a year).

Pan American Development Foundation—PADF: 1889 F St, NW, Washington, DC 20006, USA; tel. (202) 458-6153; telex 64128; f. 1962 to improve the quality of life of low-income groups in Latin America and the Caribbean through providing low-interest credit for small-scale entrepreneurs, vocational training, improved health care, agricultural development and reforestation, and to strengthen the ability of the private sector in the region to participate in development activities; provides emergency disaster relief and reconstruction assistance. Chair. JOÃO CLEMENTE BAENA SOARES; Pres. LEVEO V. SÁNCHEZ; Exec. Dir MARVIN WEISSMAN. Publ. *PADF Newsletter* (3 a year).

Permanent Inter-State Committee on Drought Control in the Sahel—CILSS: POB 7049, Ouagadougou, Burkina Faso; f. 1973; works in co-operation with UN Sudano-Sahelian Office (UNSO, q.v.); aims to combat the effects of chronic drought in the Sahel region (where the deficit in grain production was estimated at 1.7m. metric tons for 1988), by improving irrigation and food production, halting deforestation and creating food reserves. Budget (1987): 444.5m. francs CFA. Mems: Burkina Faso, Cape Verde, Chad, The Gambia, Guinea-Bissau, Mali, Mauritania, Niger, Senegal. Exec. Sec. BRAH MAHAMANE (Niger).

Population Council: 1 Dag Hammarskjöld Plaza, New York, NY 10017, USA; tel. (212) 644-1300; telex 234722; f. 1952; conducts research in human reproductive biomedicine, the development of contraceptive methods, and social science useful to the understanding of public policy issues; disseminates information and publications. Three regional offices, in Mexico City, Bangkok and Cairo. Chair. ROBERT H. EBERT; Pres. GEORGE ZEIDENSTEIN. Publs *Studies in Family Planning* (every 2 months), *Population and Development Review* (quarterly).

Preferential Trade Area for Eastern and Southern African States—PTA: POB 30051, Lusaka, Zambia; tel. 219880; telex 40127; f. 1981 with the aim of improving commercial and economic co-operation in the region, and ultimately to form a common market and economic community; began operations in July 1984 with the announcement of tariff reductions for six categories of goods traded between members; the Reserve Bank of Zimbabwe acts as a clearing house for transactions for goods and services within the PTA, enabling member states to conduct multilateral trade in their own currencies. Meetings of manufacturers and chambers of commerce are held, and the second PTA trade fair took place in 1988. A PTA development bank (based in Bujumbura, Burundi) began operations in 1987, with initial capital of US $400m. Mems: Burundi, the Comoros, Djibouti, Ethiopia, Kenya, Lesotho, Malawi, Mauritius, Rwanda, Somalia, Swaziland, Tanzania, Uganda, Zambia, Zimbabwe. Sec.-Gen. BAX NOMVETE.

Society for International Development: Palazzo Civiltà del Lavoro, EUR, 00144 Rome, Italy; telex 616484; f. 1957 to provide a forum for an exchange of ideas, facts and experience among persons concerned with the problems of economic and social development in both developed and developing countries. Mems: 10,000 (90 brs in 75 countries). Pres. ENRIQUE IGLESIAS; Exec. Dir HENNY HELMICH. Publs *Development* (quarterly), *Compass* (quarterly).

South Asian Association for Regional Co-operation—SAARC: GPO Box 4222, Kathmandu, Nepal; tel. 216350; telex 2561; f. 1985 by the leaders of seven South Asian nations, to accelerate economic growth, social progress and cultural development, and to strengthen collective self-reliance. There are 11 agreed areas of co-operation: agriculture and forestry; health and population; meteorology; rural development; telecommunications; transport; science and technology; postal services; sports, arts and culture; women in development; drug-trafficking and abuse. Other schemes include the South Asian Broadcasting Programme, SAARC Documentation Centre, SAARC fellowships and scholarships, a youth volunteers' programme and organized tourism. A regional convention on the suppression of terrorism, and an agreement on establishing a food security reserve, were signed in 1987. Studies were under way in 1988 on natural disasters, protection of the environment, intra-regional trade expansion, and joint ventures in agriculture, industry and energy. The SAARC charter stipulates that decisions should be made unanimously, and that 'bilateral and contentious issues' should not be discussed; meetings of heads of governments are to be held annually, and ministers of foreign affairs are to meet at least twice a year. Mems: Bangladesh, Bhutan, India, Maldives, Nepal, Pakistan and Sri Lanka. Sec.-Gen. ABUL AHSAN.

Vienna Institute for Development (Wiener Institut für Entwicklungsfragen): Vienna 1010, Kärntner Str. 25, Austria; tel. (01) 521681; telex 112035; f. 1964 to publicize problems and achievements of developing countries, to encourage industrialized countries to increase aid; research programmes. Mems from 20 countries. Dir ARNE HASELBACH.

World University Service—WUS: 5 chemin des Iris, 1216 Geneva, Switzerland; tel. (022) 988711; telex 27273; f. 1920; links students, faculty and administrators in post-secondary institutions concerned with economic and social development, and seeks to protect their academic freedom and autonomy; seeks to extend technical, personal and financial resources of post-secondary institutions to under-developed areas and communities; provides scholarships at university level for refugees from South Africa, Namibia and Latin America and supports informal education projects for women in these areas; the principle is to assist people to improve and develop their own communities. WUS is independent and is governed by an assembly of national committees. Pres. HUGO MIRANDA (Chile); Gen. Sec. NIGEL HARTLEY (UK). Publs *WUS Activities*, *WUS News*, Reports on conferences and research.

Arts and Culture

Europa Nostra: 9 Buckingham Gate, London, SW1E 6JP, England; tel. (01) 821-1171; f. 1963 as an international federation of non-governmental associations for the protection of Europe's natural and cultural heritage; has consultative status with the Council of Europe. Mems: c. 200 associations; associated corporate membership open to all European local authorities. Pres. HENRI J. DE KOSTER (Netherlands); Hon. Sec.-Gen. Dr MAURICE LINDSAY (UK).

European Association of Conservatoires, Music Academies and Music High Schools: Place Neuve, 1204 Geneva, Switzerland; f. 1953 to establish and foster contacts and exchanges between members. Mems: 100. Sec.-Gen. CLAUDE VIALA.

European Cultural Centre (Centre Européen de la Culture): Villa Moynier, 122 rue de Lausanne, 1211 Geneva 21, Switzerland; tel. (022) 322803; telex 289917; f. 1950 to contribute to the unity of Europe by encouraging cultural pursuits, providing a meeting place, and conducting research in the various fields of European Studies; holds conferences on European subjects, European documentation and archives. Groups the Secretariats of the European Association of Music Festivals and the Association of Institutes of European Studies. Pres. JACQUES FREYMOND (Switzerland); Sec.-Gen. GÉRARD DE PUYMÈGE. Publ. *Cadmos* (quarterly).

European Society of Culture: S. Marco 2516, 30124 Venice, Italy; tel. (041) 5230210; f. 1950 to unite artists, poets, scientists, philosophers and others through mutual interests and friendship in order to safeguard and improve the conditions required for creative activity; library of 10,000 volumes. Mems: 2,000. Pres. Prof. GIUSEPPE GALASSO (Italy); Gen. Sec. Dott. MICHELLE CAMPAGNOLO-BOUVIER.

Inter-American Music Council (Consejo Interamericano de Música—CIDEM): 1889 F St, NW, 510-B, Washington, DC 20006, USA; tel. (202) 458-3706; telex 64128; f. 1956 to promote the

OTHER INTERNATIONAL ORGANIZATIONS — Arts and Culture

exchange of works, performances and information in all fields of music, to study problems relative to music education, to encourage activity in the field of musicology, to promote folklore research and music creation, to establish distribution centres for music material of the composers of the Americas, etc. Mems: national music societies of 30 American countries. Sec.-Gen. EFRAIN PAESKY.

Interfilm (International Interchurch Film Centre): POB 515, 1200 AM Hilversum, Netherlands; tel. (035) 17645; f. 1955 to promote film criticism and film education; ecumenical, associated with the World Council of Churches; makes awards and recommendations at international film festivals, holds study conferences. Mems: organizations in 40 countries. Pres. Dr AMAL DIBO (Lebanon); Gen. Sec. Dr JAN HES (Netherlands). Publ. *Interfilm Information* (quarterly).

International Association of Art (Painting-Sculpture-Graphic Art) (Association internationale des arts plastiques—Peinture, Sculpture, Arts Graphiques): Maison de l'UNESCO, 1 rue Miollis, 75015 Paris, France; f. 1954. Mems: 81 national committees. Sec.-Gen. CRISTINA RUBALCAVA (Mexico).

International Association of Art Critics: 9 rue Berryer, 75008 Paris, France; tel. (1) 42-56-17-53; f. 1949 to increase co-operation in plastic arts, promote international cultural exchanges and protect the interests of members. Mems: 3,000, in 53 countries. Pres. BÉLGICA RODRÍGUEZ (Venezuela); Sec.-Gen. HÉLÈNE LASALLE.

International Association of Bibliophiles: Bibliothèque nationale, 58 rue Richelieu, 75084 Paris Cedex 02, France; f. 1963 to create contacts between bibliophiles and to encourage book-collecting in different countries; to organize or encourage congresses, meetings, exhibitions, the award of scholarships, the publication of a bulletin, yearbooks, and works of reference or bibliography. Mems: 500. Pres. ANTHONY R. A. HOBSON (UK); Sec.-Gen. ANTOINE CORON (France). Publ. *Le Bulletin du Bibliophile*.

International Association of Literary Critics: 38 rue du Faubourg St-Jacques, 75015 Paris, France; f. 1969; organizes congresses. Pres. ROBERT ANDRÉ. Publ. *Revue* (2 a year).

International Association of Museums of Arms and Military History—IAMAM: Bayerisches Armeemuseum, 8070 Ingolstadt, Neues Schloss, Paradeplatz 4, Federal Republic of Germany; tel. (0841) 35067; f. 1957; links museums and other scientific institutions with public collections of arms and armour and military equipment, uniforms, etc.; triennial conferences and occasional specialist symposia. Mems: 252 institutions in 50 countries. Pres. BENGT HOLMQUIST (Sweden); Sec.-Gen. Dr ERNST AICHNER (FRG). Publs *Repertory of Museums of Arms and Military History*, *Triennial Report*, *Glossarium Armorum*, reports on symposia.

International Board on Books for Young People—IBBY: Nonnenweg 12, Postfach, 4003 Basel, Switzerland; tel. (061) 232917; telex 727925; f. 1953 to support and link bodies in all countries connected with children's book work; to encourage the distribution of good children's books; to promote scientific investigation into problems of juvenile books; to organize educational aid for developing countries; presents the Hans Christian Andersen Award every two years to a living author and a living illustrator whose work is an outstanding contribution to juvenile literature, and the Rising Sun Prize annually to an organization which has made a significant contribution to children's literature; sponsors International Children's Book Day (2 April). Mems: national sections and individuals in 60 countries. Pres. Dr DUŠAN ROLL (Czechoslovakia); Sec. LEENA MAISSEN. Publs *Bookbird* (quarterly, in English), *Congress Papers*, *IBBY Honour List* (every 2 years); special bibliographies.

International Centre for the Study of the Preservation and Restoration of Cultural Property—ICCROM: Via di San Michele 13, 00153 Rome, Italy; tel. 580 9021; telex 613114; f. 1959; assembles documents on preservation and restoration of cultural property; stimulates research and proffers advice in this domain; organizes missions of experts; undertakes training of specialists and organizes regular courses on (i) Architectural Conservation; (ii) Conservation of Mural Paintings; (iii) Scientific Principles of Conservation; (iv) Preventive Conservation in Museums; (v) Conservation of Paper. Mems: 79 countries. Dir Prof. ANDRZEJ TOMASZEWSKI. Publ. *Newsletter* (annually, English and French).

International Centre of Films for Children and Young People—ICFCYP: 9 rue Bargue, 75015 Paris, France; f. 1957; a clearing house of information about: entertainment films (cinema and television) for children and young people, influence of films on the young, and regulations in force for the protection and education of young people; promotes production and distribution of suitable films and their appreciation; to this end it encourages the setting up of National Centres. Mems: 33 full mems (National Centres), 23 associated organizations. Pres. PREDRAG GOLUBOVIĆ (Yugoslavia); Dir MONIQUE GRÉGOIRE. Publ. *Young Cinema International*.

International Committee for the Diffusion of Arts and Literature through the Cinema (Comité international pour la diffusion des arts et des lettres par le cinéma—CIDALC): 24 blvd Poissonnière, 75009 Paris, France; tel. (1) 42-46-65-36; f. 1930 to promote the creation and release of educational, cultural and documentary films and other films of educational value in order to contribute to closer understanding between peoples; awards medals and prizes for films of exceptional merit. Mems: national committees in 25 countries. Pres. JEAN-PIERRE FOUCAULT (France); Sec.-Gen. MARIO VERDONE (Italy). Publ. *Annuaire CIDALC*.

International Comparative Literature Association: c/o L. Metzger, Dept of English, Emory University, Atlanta, Ga 30322, USA; f. 1954 to work for the development of the comparative study of literature in modern languages. Member societies and individuals in 58 countries. Sec. LORE METZGER. Publ. *ICLA Bulletin*.

International Confederation of Societies of Authors and Composers—World Congress of Authors and Composers: 11 rue Keppler, 75116 Paris, France; tel. (1) 45-53-59-37; f. 1926 to protect the rights of authors and composers; documentation centre. Mems: 99 member societies from 49 countries. Pres. EDGAR FAURE (France); Sec.-Gen. JEAN-ALEXIS ZIEGLER.

International Council of Graphic Design Associations: POB 398, London, W11 4UG, England; tel. (01) 603-8494; f. 1963; aims to raise standards of graphic design, to exchange information, and to organize exhibitions and congresses. Mems: 53 associations in 33 countries. Pres. NIKO SPELBRINK (Netherlands). Publs *Newsletter* (quarterly), *Graphic Design World Views*.

International Council of Museums—ICOM: Maison de l'UNESCO, 1 rue Miollis, 75732 Paris Cedex 15, France; tel. (1) 47-34-05-00; f. 1946 to further international co-operation among museums and to advance museum interests; maintains with UNESCO the most extensive museum documentation centre in the world. Mems: 8,000 individuals and institutions from 114 countries. Pres. G. LEWIS (UK); Sec.-Gen. P. CARDON (USA). Publ. *ICOM News—Nouvelles de l'ICOM* (quarterly).

International Council on Monuments and Sites—ICOMOS: 75 rue du Temple, 75003 Paris, France; tel. (1) 42-77-35-76; telex 240918; f. 1965 to promote the study and preservation of monuments and sites; to arouse and cultivate the interest of public authorities, and people of every country in their monuments and sites and in their cultural heritage; to liaise between public authorities, departments, institutions and individuals interested in the preservation and study of monuments and sites; to disseminate the results of research into the problems, technical, social and administrative, connected with the conservation of the architectural heritage, and of centres of historic interest; holds triennial General Assembly and Symposium. Mems: 3,500; 13 International Committees, 66 National Committees. Pres. ROBERTO DI STEFANO (Italy); Sec.-Gen. HELMUT STELZER (GDR). Publ. *ICOMOS Information* (quarterly).

International Federation for Theatre Research: 14 Woronzow Rd, London, NW8 6QE, England; f. 1955 by 21 countries at the International Conference on Theatre History, London. Chair. Prof. W. GREISENEGGER; Joint Secs-Gen. Prof. J.-C. GODIN, ERIC ALEXANDER. Publ. *Theatre Research International* (in association with Oxford University Press) (3 a year).

International Federation of Film Archives: c/o B. van der Elst, 70 Coudenberg, 1000 Brussels, Belgium; tel. (02) 511-13-90; telex 26146; f. 1938 to encourage the creation of archives in all countries for the collection and conservation of the film heritage of each land; to facilitate co-operation and exchanges between these film archives; to promote public interest in the art of the cinema; to aid research in this field and to compile new documentation; conducts research; publishes manuals, etc.; holds annual congresses. Mems in 55 countries. Pres. ANNA-LENA WIBOM (Sweden); Sec.-Gen. GUIDO CINCOTTI (Italy).

International Federation of Film Producers' Associations: 33 ave des Champs-Elysées, 75008 Paris, France; tel. (1) 42-25-62-14; f. 1933 to represent film production internationally, to defend its general interests and promote its development, to study all cultural, legal, economic, technical and social problems of interest to the activity of film production. Mems: national associations in 21 countries. Pres. FRANCO CRISTALDI (Italy); Sec.-Gen. ALPHONSE BRISSON (France).

International Institute for Children's Literature and Reading Research (Internationales Institut für Jugendliteratur und Leseforschung): 1040 Vienna, Mayerhofgasse 6, Austria; tel. (01) 65-03-59; f. 1965 as an international documentation, research and advisory centre of juvenile literature and reading; maintains specialized library; arranges conferences and exhibitions; compiles recommendation lists. Mems: individual and group members in 28 countries. Pres. Dr HERMANN LEIN; Dir Dr LUCIA BINDER. Publs *Bookbird* (quarterly in co-operation with the International Board on Books for Young People), *1000 & 1 Buch* (quarterly in co-operation with the Austrian Children's Book Club), *Schriften zur Jugendlektüre, PA-Kontakte* (published irregularly).

International Institute for Conservation of Historic and Artistic Works: 6 Buckingham St., London, WC2N 6BA, England; tel. (01) 839-5975; f. 1950. Mems: 3,000 individual, 450 institutional members. Pres. S. P. SACK; Sec.-Gen. Prof. H. W. M. HODGES. Publs *Studies in Conservation* (quarterly), *Art and Archaeology Technical Abstracts—IIC* (2 a year).

International Institute of Iberoamerican Literature: 1312 C.L., University of Pittsburgh, Pa 15260, USA; f. 1938 to advance the study of Iberoamerican literature, and intensify cultural relations among the peoples of the Americas. Mems: scholars and artists in 35 countries. Exec. Dir ALFREDO ROGGIANO. Publs *Revista Iberoamericana, Memorias.*

International Liaison Centre for Cinema and Television Schools (Centre international de liaison des écoles de cinéma et de télévision): 8 rue Thérésienne, 1000 Brussels, Belgium; tel. (02) 512-32-36; f. 1955 to co-ordinate teaching standards and to develop plans for creation of cultural, artistic, teaching and technical relations between mems. Pres. COLIN YOUNG (UK); Sec.-Gen. RAYMOND RAVAR (Belgium).

International Music Council—IMC: Maison de l'UNESCO, 1 rue Miollis, 75732 Paris Cedex 15, France; tel. (1) 45-68-25-50; telex 204461; f. 1949 to foster the exchange of musicians, music (written and recorded), and information between countries and cultures; to support contemporary composers and young professional musicians. Mems: 23 international non-governmental organizations, national committees in 65 countries. Pres. LUPWISHI MBUYAMBA (Zaire); Sec.-Gen. CAMILLE SWINNEN (Belgium); Exec. Sec. GUY HUOT.

Members of IMC include:

European Association of Music Festivals: 122 rue de Lausanne, 1211 Geneva 21, Switzerland; tel. (022) 322803; telex 289917; f. 1951; aims to maintain high artistic standards and the representative character of music festivals; holds annual General Assembly. Mems: 48 regularly-held music festivals in 23 European countries, Israel and Japan. Pres. TASSILO NEKOLA (Austria). Publs *Season* (annually), *Festivals* (annually).

International Association of Music Libraries, Archives and Documentation Centres—IAML: Svenskt Musikhistoriskt Arkiv, Box 16326, 10326 Stockholm, Sweden; f. 1951. Mems: 1,830 institutions and individuals in 38 countries. Pres. MARIA CALDERISI BRYCE (Canada); Sec.-Gen. V. HEINTZ (Sweden). Publ. *Fontes artis musicae* (every 4 months).

International Council for Traditional Music: Dept of Music, Columbia University, New York, NY 10027; tel. (212) 678-0332; telex 220094; f. 1947 (as International Folk Music Council) to further the study, practice, documentation, preservation and dissemination of traditional music of all countries; conferences held every two years. Mems: 1,100. Pres. Dr ERICH STOCKMANN (German Democratic Republic); Sec.-Gen. Prof. DIETER CHRISTENSEN (USA). Publs *Yearbook for Traditional Music, Bulletin* (2 a year), *Directory of Traditional Music.*

International Federation of 'Jeunesses Musicales': Palais des Beaux-Arts, 10 rue Royale, 1000 Brussels, Belgium; tel. (02) 513-97-74; telex 61825; f. 1945 to promote the development of musical appreciation among young people, to encourage the creation of new societies and to ensure co-operation between national societies. Mems: organizations in 40 countries. Sec.-Gen. ALEXANDER SCHISCHLIK.

International Federation of Musicians: Hofackerstrasse 7, 8032 Zürich, Switzerland; tel. (01) 556611; f. 1948 to promote and protect the interests of musicians in affiliated unions; promotes international exchange of musicians. Mems: 34 unions totalling 331,765 individuals in 34 countries. Pres. JOHN MORTON (UK); Gen. Sec. YVONNE BURCKHARDT (Switzerland).

International Institute for Comparative Music Studies and Documentation (Internationales Institut für Vergleichende Musikstudien und Dokumentation); 1000 Berlin 33, Winklerstrasse 20; tel. (030) 8262853; telex 182875; f. 1963; supported by the City of Berlin to study practical means of integrating the musical achievements of extra-European cultures into world culture and of helping the preservation of authentic traditional music. Mems from 20 countries. Dir MAX PETER BAUMANN; Gen. Sec. MICHAEL JENNE. Publs *Unesco Anthology of the Orient, Unesco Anthology of African Music, Musical Sources, Musical Atlas* (record series), books, etc., *The World of Music* (quarterly).

International Jazz Federation: 13 Foulser Rd., London, SW17 8UE, England; tel. (01) 767-2213; f. 1969 to promote the knowledge and appreciation of jazz throughout the world; arranges jazz education conferences and competitions for young jazz groups; encourages co-operation among national societies.

Mems: 16 national organizations. Pres. CHARLES ALEXANDER (UK). Publ. *Jazz Forum* (6 a year).

International Music Centre (Internationales Musikzentrum—IMZ): 1030 Vienna, Lothringerstr. 20, Austria; tel. (01) 72-57-95; telex 753-11745; f. 1961 for the study and dissemination of music through the technical media (film, television, radio, gramophone); co-operates with other international organizations such as EBU and OIRT; organizes congresses, seminars and screenings on music in the audio-visual media; courses and competitions to strengthen the relationship between performing artists and the audio-visual media. Mems: 85 ordinary mems and 30 associate mems in 33 countries, including 50 broadcasting organizations. Pres. LUBOMIR CIZEK (Czechoslovakia); Sec.-Gen. WILFRIED SCHEIB (Austria); Exec. Sec. ERIC MARINITSCH. Publs *IMZ Report, UNESCO Catalogue, IMZ Bulletin* (10 a year in English, French and German).

International Society for Contemporary Music: c/o Nordwall, Södermannagatan 18, 116 23 Stockholm, Sweden; tel. (8) 41-35-10; f. 1922 to promote the development of contemporary music and to organize annual World Music Days. Member organizations in 33 countries. Pres. ZYGMUNT KRAUZE (Poland); Sec.-Gen. TRYGVE NORDWALL.

World Federation of International Music Competitions: 104 rue de Carouge, 1205 Geneva, Switzerland; tel. (022) 213620; f. 1957 to co-ordinate the arrangements for affiliated competitions, to exchange experience, etc.; a General Assembly is held every April. Mems: 82. Pres. ROBERT DUNAND; Sec.-Gen. JACQUES HALDENWARG.

International PEN (A World Association of Writers): 38 King St, London, WC2E 8JT, England; f. 1921 to promote co-operation between writers. There are 87 centres throughout the world, with total membership about 9,000. International Pres. FRANCIS KING; International Sec. ALEXANDRE BLOKH. Publs *The Survival and Encouragement of Literature*, International PEN anthologies, *PEN International* (in English and French, with the assistance of UNESCO).

International Theatre Institute—ITI: Maison de l'UNESCO, 1 rue Miollis, 75015 Paris, France; tel. (1) 45-68-26-50; f. 1948 to facilitate cultural exchanges and international understanding in the domain of the theatre; conferences, publications, etc. Mems: 74 member nations, each with an ITI national centre. Pres. MARTHA COIGNEY (USA); Sec.-Gen. ANDRÉ-LOUIS PERINETTI.

International Typographic Association: 4142 Münchenstein, Gutenbergstrasse 1, Switzerland; tel. (061) 468820; f. 1957 to co-ordinate the ideas of those whose profession or interests have to do with the art of typography and to obtain effective international legislation to protect type designs. Mems: 400. Pres. MARTIN FEHLE.

Royal Asiatic Society of Great Britain and Ireland: 60 Queen's Gardens, London, W2; f. 1823 for the study of history and cultures of the East. Mems: c. 1,000, branch societies in Asia. Pres. F. F. STEELE; Dir Dr D. J. DUNCANSON; Sec. L. COLLINS. Publ. *Journal* (2 a year).

Society of African Culture: 18 rue des Ecoles, 75005 Paris, France; tel. (1) 43-54-57-69; telex 200891; f. 1956 to create unity and friendship among scholars in Africa for the encouragement of their own cultures and the development of a universal culture. Mems: from 45 countries. Pres. AIMÉ CÉSAIRE; Sec.-Gen. CHRISTIANE YANDÉ DIOP. Publ. *Présence Africaine* (quarterly).

United Towns Organization: 2 rue de Logelbach, 75017 Paris, France; tel. (1) 47-66-75-10; telex 644569; f. 1957 by Le Monde Bilingue (f. 1951); since 1960 has specialized in twinning towns in developed areas with those in less developed areas; aims to set up permanent links between towns throughout the world, leading to social, cultural, economic and other exchanges favouring world peace, understanding and development; encourages the spread of bilingualism. The Organization has consultative status with the UN, UNESCO, UNICEF and the Council of Europe. Mems: 3,500 towns throughout the world. World Pres. PIERRE MAUROY; Sec.-Gen. HUBERT LESIRE-OGREL. Publs *Cités Unies* (quarterly, French, English and Spanish), *United Towns Newsletter* (quarterly, English), *Cités Unies Informations* (monthly), *Notiziario* (quarterly), *Mitteilungsblatt* (quarterly), quarterly newsletter in Arabic, *Index of International Relations of Towns of World.*

World Crafts Council: POB 2045, 1012 Copenhagen K, Denmark; tel. (01) 15-75-14; telex 16600; f. 1964; aims to strengthen the status of crafts as a vital part of cultural life, to link craftsmen around the world, and to foster wider recognition of their work. Mems: national organizations in more than 80 countries. Pres. ANDERS CLASON (Sweden); Sec.-Gen. JOHN VEDEL-RIEPER (Denmark). Publs *Annual Report, Craft International Newsletter* (quarterly).

World Union of French Speakers (Union mondiale des voix françaises): BP 56-05, 75222 Paris Cedex 05, France; f. 1960;

OTHER INTERNATIONAL ORGANIZATIONS   Arts and Culture, Commodities

cultural exchange in the French language by records, tape recordings, etc. Mems: 1,000. Pres. B. LABONDE; Sec.-Gen. A. REGUS. Publ. *Via Vox Contact.*

Commodities

African Groundnut Council: Trade Fair Complex, Badagry Expressway Km 15, POB 3025, Lagos, Nigeria; tel. 880982; telex 21366; f. 1964 to advise producing countries on marketing policies. Mems: The Gambia, Mali, Niger, Nigeria, Senegal, Sudan. Chair. M. M. JALLOW (The Gambia); Exec. Sec. MOUR MAMADOU SAMB (Senegal).

African Petroleum Producers' Association: c/o Nigerian National Petroleum Corpn, PMB 12701, Ikoyi, Lagos, Nigeria; f. 1986 by African petroleum-producing countries to reinforce co-operation among regional producers and to stabilize prices. Mems: Algeria, Angola, Benin, Cameroon, Congo, Gabon, Libya, Nigeria.

Asian and Pacific Coconut Community: POB 343, 3rd Floor, Wisma Bakrie Bldg, Jalan H. R. Rasuna Said Kav. Bl., Kuningan, Jak-Selatan 10002, Indonesia; tel. 510073; telex 62863; f. 1969 to promote, co-ordinate, and harmonize all activities of the coconut industry towards better production, processing, marketing and research. Mems: India, Indonesia, Malaysia, Papua New Guinea, the Philippines, Solomon Islands, Sri Lanka, Thailand, Vanuatu, Western Samoa; assoc. mems: Federated States of Micronesia, Palau. Exec. Dir P. G. PUNCHIHEWA. Publs. *COCOMUNITY* (every 2 weeks, with quarterly supplement), *CORD* (2 a year), *Statistical Yearbook.*

Association of Iron Ore Exporting Countries—APEF: Le Château, 14 chemin Auguste Vilbert, 1218 Grand Saconnex, Geneva, Switzerland; tel. (022) 982955; telex 289443; f. 1975 to collect and disseminate information on iron ore. Mems: nine countries. Sec.-Gen. L. ROIGART.

Association of Natural Rubber Producing Countries—ANRPC: Natural Rubber Bldg, 148 Jalan Ampang, 40450 Kuala Lumpur, Malaysia; tel. 481735; telex 30953; f. 1970 to co-ordinate the production and marketing of natural rubber, to promote technical co-operation amongst members and to bring about fair and stable prices for natural rubber. A joint regional marketing system has been agreed in principle. Seminars and meetings on technical and statistical subjects are held. Mems: India, Indonesia, Malaysia, Papua New Guinea, Singapore, Sri Lanka and Thailand. Sec.-Gen. (vacant). Publs *Quarterly Statistical Bulletin.*

Association of Tin Producing Countries (ATPC): Wisma Yeng Chong, 2nd Floor, Jalan Punchank, Kuala Lumpur, Malaysia; f. 1983; allocates export quotas to tin-producing countries, in order to reduce surplus stocks and support prices. Mems: Australia, Bolivia, Indonesia, Malaysia, Nigeria, Thailand and Zaire. Sec.-Gen. VICTOR SIAHAAN (Indonesia).

Cadmium Association: 34 Berkeley Square, London, W1X 6AJ, England; tel. (01) 499-8425; telex 261286; f. 1976; covers all aspects of the use of cadmium; an affiliate of the Zinc Development Association (q.v.); includes almost all companies concerned with the production of cadmium except in North America, where close liaison is kept with the Cadmium Council. Chair. K. A. HEWITT (UK); Chief Exec. F. D. WARD (UK).

Cocoa Producers' Alliance: POB 1718, Western House, 8-10 Broad St, Lagos, Nigeria; tel. 635506; telex 21311; f. 1962 to exchange technical and scientific information; to discuss problems of mutual concern to producers; to ensure adequate supplies at remunerative prices; to promote consumption. Mems: Brazil, Cameroon, Côte d'Ivoire, Dominican Republic, Ecuador, Gabon, Ghana, Mexico, Nigeria, São Tomé and Príncipe, Togo and Trinidad and Tobago. Sec.-Gen. DJEUMO SILAS KAMGA.

European Aluminium Association: 4000 Dusseldorf 1, Königsallee 30, POB 1207, Federal Republic of Germany; tel. (0211) 80871; telex 8587407; f. 1981 to encourage studies, research and technical co-operation, to make representations to international bodies and to assist national associations in dealing with national authorities. Mems: individual producers of primary aluminium, 14 national groups for wrought producers, the Organization of European Aluminium Smelters, representing producers of secondary aluminium and the European Aluminium Foil Association, representing foil rollers and converters. Chair. G. Y. KERVERN (France); Sec.-Gen. F. OOSTLAND.

European Association for the Trade in Jute Products: Adriaan Goekooplaan 5, 2517 JX The Hague, Netherlands; tel. (070) 54-68-11; telex 31440; f. 1970 to maintain contacts between national associations and carry out scientific research; to exchange information and to represent the interests of the trade. Mems: enterprises in Belgium, Denmark, France, Federal Republic of Germany, Netherlands, Spain, Switzerland, United Kingdom. Sec.-Gen. L. ANTONINI (Netherlands).

European Committee of Sugar Manufacturers: 45 ave Montaigne, 75008 Paris, France; tel. (1) 47-23-68-25; telex 280401; f. 1954 to collect statistics and information, conduct research and promote co-operation between national organizations. Mems: national associations in Austria, Belgium, Denmark, Finland, France, Federal Republic of Germany, Greece, Ireland, Italy, Netherlands, Spain, Sweden, Switzerland, United Kingdom. Pres. O. ADRIAENSEN; Dir-Gen. M. DE LA FOREST DIVONNE.

Group of Latin American and Caribbean Sugar Exporting Countries—GEPLACEA: Ejército Nacional 373, 1°, 11520 México DF, Mexico; tel. 250-75-66; telex 1771042; f. 1974 to serve as a forum of consultation on the production and sale of sugar; to contribute to the adoption of agreed positions at international meetings on sugar; to exchange scientific and technical knowledge on agriculture and the sugar industry; to consider the co-ordination of the various branches of sugar processing; to co-ordinate policies of action in order to achieve fair and remunerative prices. Mems: 22 Latin American and Caribbean countries and the Philippines. Exec. Sec. EDUARDO LATORRE (Dominican Republic).

Inter-African Coffee Organization—IACO: BP V210, Abidjan, Côte d'Ivoire; tel. 32 61 31; telex 22406; f. 1960. Mems: 25 coffee-producing countries in Africa. Pres. O. MUNYARADZI (Zimbabwe); Sec.-Gen. AREGA WORKU (Ethiopia). Publs *African Coffee* (quarterly), *Directory of African Exporters* (every 2 years).

Intergovernmental Council of Copper Exporting Countries (Conseil intergouvernemental des pays exportateurs de cuivre—CIPEC): 39 rue de la Bienfaisance, 75008 Paris, France; tel. (1) 42-25-00-24; telex 649077; f. 1967 to co-ordinate research and information policies among the members. Mems: Chile, Peru, Zaire, Zambia. Assoc. mems: Australia, Indonesia, Papua New Guinea and Yugoslavia. Sec.-Gen. WINDSOR K. NKOWANI. Publ. *CIPEC Quarterly Review.*

International Bauxite Association: 36 Trafalgar Rd, POB 551, Kingston 5, Jamaica; tel. 92-64535; telex 2428; f. 1974 to promote the development of the bauxite industry, to co-ordinate policies of the producing countries and to ensure a fair price for exports of bauxite and its products. Mems: Australia, Ghana, Guinea, Guyana, India, Indonesia, Jamaica, Sierra Leone, Suriname, Yugoslavia. Sec.-Gen. IBRAHIMA BAH (Guinea). Publ. *Quarterly Review.*

International Cocoa Organization—ICCO: 22 Berners St, London, W1P 3DB, England; tel. (01) 637-3211; telex 28173; f. 1973 under the first International Cocoa Agreement, 1972 (renewed in 1975 and 1980; the fourth agreement entered into force in January 1987). ICCO supervises the implementation of the agreement, and provides member governments with conference facilities and up-to-date information on the world cocoa economy and the operation of the agreement. Mems: 18 exporting countries which account for over 90% of world cocoa exports, and 22 importing countries which account for over 66% of world cocoa imports. (The USA is not a member.) Chair. K. N. OWUSU (Ghana); Exec. Dir E. KOUAMÉ (Côte d'Ivoire); Buffer Stock Manager J. PLAMBECK (FRG). Publs *Quarterly Bulletin of Cocoa Statistics, Annual Report*, studies on the world cocoa economy.

International Coffee Organization: 22 Berners St, London, W1P 4DD, England; tel. (01) 580-8591; telex 267659; f. 1963 under the International Coffee Agreement, 1962, which was renegotiated in 1968, 1976 and 1983; aims to achieve a reasonable balance between supply and demand on a basis which will assure adequate supplies at fair prices to consumers and expanding markets in remunerative prices to producers; resumption of coffee export quotas (suspended in February 1986) was agreed in October 1987. Mems: 50 exporting countries accounting for over 99% of world coffee exports, and 24 importing countries accounting for approximately 90% of world imports. Chair. of Council TOMMY JOHANSSON (Sweden); Exec. Dir ALEXANDRE F. BELTRÃO.

International Confederation of European Sugar Beet Growers: 29 rue du Général Foy, 75008 Paris, France; tel. (1) 42-94-41-00; telex 640241; f. 1925 to act as a centre for the co-ordination and dissemination of information about beet sugar production and the industry; to represent the interests of sugar beet growers at an international level. Member associations in Austria, Belgium, Denmark, Finland, France, Federal Republic of Germany, Greece, Ireland, Italy, Netherlands, Spain, Sweden, Switzerland, United Kingdom. Pres. F. GHAYE (Belgium); Sec.-Gen. H. CHAVANES (France).

International Cotton Advisory Committee: 1901 Pennsylvania Ave, NW, Suite 201, Washington, DC 20006, USA; tel. (202) 463-6660; telex 701517; f. 1939 to keep in touch with developments affecting the world cotton situation; to collect and disseminate statistics; to suggest to the governments represented any measures for the furtherance of international collaboration in maintaining and developing a sound world cotton economy. Mems: 45 countries. Exec. Dir Dr L. H. SHAW. Publs *Cotton—Review of the World Situation, Cotton—World Statistics.*

OTHER INTERNATIONAL ORGANIZATIONS — *Commodities*

International Institute for Cotton: Suite 627, 1511 K St NW, Washington, DC 20005, USA; tel. (202) 347-4220; f. 1966 to increase world consumption of raw cotton and cotton products through utilization research, market research, sales promotion, education and public relations; to form a link between cotton exporting countries and the main importers. Mems: nine countries. Pres. Dr SHAILENDRA K. AGNIHOTRI (India); Exec. Dir PETER PEREIRA (UK); Sec. HARPAL LUTHER (India).

International Jute Organization: 95A Rd No 4, Banani, POB 6073, Gulshan, Dhaka, Bangladesh; tel. 412146; telex 642792; f. 1984 in accordance with an agreement made by 48 producing and consuming countries in 1982, under the auspices of UNCTAD; aims to improve the jute economy by research and development projects, market promotion and cost reduction. Mems: five exporting and 27 importing countries. Exec. Dir H. SINGH.

International Lead and Zinc Study Group: Metro House, 58 St James's St, London, SW1A 1LD, England; tel. (01) 499-9373; telex 299819; f. 1959, for intergovernmental consultation on world trade in lead and zinc; conducts studies and provides information on trends in supply and demand. Standing committee usually meets in spring in London, and the study group and all committees in October in Geneva. Mems: 31 countries. Chair. G. WITTUR (Canada); Sec.-Gen. R. W. BOEHNKE. Publs *Lead and Zinc Statistics* (monthly), reports of studies.

International Natural Rubber Organization—INRO: 12th Floor, MUI Plaza, Jalan P. Ramlee, POB 10374, 50712 Kuala Lumpur, Malaysia; tel. 486466; telex 31570; f. 1980 to stabilize natural rubber prices by operating a buffer stock, and to seek to ensure an adequate supply, under the International Natural Rubber Agreement (1979), which entered into force in April 1982, and was extended for two years in 1985; a new agreement was adopted in March 1987 and was expected to come into force before the end of 1988. Mems: 26 importing countries (including the European Community) and seven exporting countries (principally Indonesia, Malaysia, and Thailand). Exec. Dir PANG SOEPARTO.

International Olive Oil Council: Juan Bravo 10, 2°–3°, 28006 Madrid, Spain; tel. 5640568; telex 48197; f. 1959 to administer the International Agreement on Olive Oil and Table Olives, the objectives of which are as follows: to promote international co-operation in connection with problems of the world economy for olive products; to prevent the occurrence of any unfair competition in the world olive products trade; to encourage the production and consumption of, and international trade in, olive products, and to reduce the disadvantages due to fluctuations of supplies on the market. Mems: of the 1986 Agreement (Fourth Agreement): four mainly producing countries, two mainly importing countries, and the European Economic Community. Dir FAUSTO LUCHETTI. Publs *Information Sheet of the IOOC* (fortnightly, French and Spanish), *OLIVAE* (5 a year, in English, French, Italian and Spanish), *National Policies for Olive Products* (annually).

International Pepper Community: 3rd Floor, Wisma Bakrie, Jalan H. R. Rasuna Said, Kav. B1, Kuningan, Jakarta 12920, Indonesia; tel. 510192; telex 62218; f. 1972 for promoting pepper and co-ordinating activities relating to the pepper economy; mems: Brazil, India, Indonesia, Malaysia. Dir A. G. NASUTION.

International Rubber Study Group: 7 Albemarle St, London, W1X 3HF; tel. (01) 629-1603; telex 895 1293; f. 1944 to provide a forum for the discussion of problems affecting synthetic and natural rubber and to provide statistical and other general information on rubber. Mems: 27 governments. Sec.-Gen. Dr B. C. SEKHAR. Publs *Rubber Statistical Bulletin* (monthly), *International Rubber Digest* (monthly), *Proceedings of Group Meetings and Assemblies*, *Records of International Rubber Forums* (annually), *World Rubber Statistics Handbook*.

International Silk Association: 20 rue Joseph Serlin, 69001 Lyon, France; tel. 78-39-18-41; telex 330949; f. 1949 to promote closer collaboration between all branches of the silk industry and trade, develop the consumption of silk and foster scientific research; collects and disseminates information and statistics relating to the trade and industry; organizes triennial Congresses. Mems: employers' and technical organizations in 36 countries. Pres. MARIO BOSELLI (Italy); Gen. Sec. R. CURRIE. Publs *ISA Newsletter* (monthly), standards, trade rules, etc.

International Sugar Organization: 28 Haymarket, London, SW1Y 4SP, England; tel. (01) 930-3666; telex 24143; administers the International Sugar Agreement (1988–90); the agreement does not include measures for stabilizing markets. Mems: 35 exporting countries and nine importing countries. Exec. Dir ALFREDO A. RICART; Sec. (vacant). Publs *Sugar Year Book*, *Monthly Statistical Bulletin*, *Annual Report*, *World Sugar Economy, Structure and Policies*.

International Tea Committee Ltd: Sir John Lyon House, 5 High Timber St, London, EC4V 3NH, England; tel. (01) 248-4672; telex 887911; f. 1933 to administer the International Tea Agreement; now serves as a statistical and information centre; in 1979 membership was extended to include consuming countries. Producer Mems: national tea boards of Bangladesh, India, Indonesia, Kenya, Malawi, Sri Lanka, Zimbabwe; Consumer Mems: United Kingdom Tea Association, Tea Association of the USA Inc., Comité Européen du Thé, The Australian Tea and Coffee Traders' Association and the Tea Council of Canada; Assoc. Mems: Netherlands and UK ministries of agriculture. Chair. A. C. DAVIES; Vice-Chair. W. J. EDGE; Sec. Mrs N. C. CARNEGIE-BROWN. Publs *Bulletin of Statistics* (annually), *Statistical Summary* (monthly).

International Tea Promotion Association: POB 20064, Tea Board of Kenya, Nairobi, Kenya; tel. 220241; telex 987-22190; f. 1979. Mems: eight countries (Bangladesh, Indonesia, Kenya, Malawi, Mauritius, Mozambique, Tanzania, and Uganda), accounting for about 35% of world exports of black tea. Chair. GEORGE M. KIMANI; Liaison Officer NGOIMA WA MWAURA. Publ. *International Tea Journal* (annually).

International Tin Council: Haymarket House, 1 Oxendon St, London, SW1Y 4EQ, England; tel. (01) 930-0451; telex 918939; f. 1956; the Sixth International Tin Agreement (1982–87) was intended to achieve a long-term balance between world production and consumption of tin and to prevent excessive fluctuations in the price of tin. Under the Agreement the Council was to set floor and ceiling prices, operate a buffer stock and regulate tin exports from producing members. In 1985 a crisis arose in the tin market when the world production (including that by non-members of the ITC, notably Brazil and the People's Republic of China) greatly exceeded demand, and the ITC was obliged to protect the price of tin by buying up the surplus, thereby incurring heavy debts. In October the ITC was no longer able to buy surplus stocks, and trading in tin on the London Metal Exchange was suspended. Negotiations with creditors continued during 1986, and legal proceedings were undertaken by a number of creditors, owing to the refusal of some member governments to meet the ITC's debts. The Sixth Agreement was extended for two years from July 1987, but the ITC's activities (apart from participating in legal proceedings) were to be confined to statistical work and research. Mems: governments of 22 countries (of which six are producers), and the EEC. Exec. Chair. PETER LAI; Sec. I. A. J. CRAWLEY.

International Tropical Timber Organization: Sangyo Boeki Centre Bldg, 2 Yamashita-cho, Naka-ku, Yokohama 231, Japan; tel. 671-7045; telex 3822480; f. 1985 under the International Tropical Timber Agreement; aims to assist timber-producing countries in forest management, replenishment and timber processing, to gather information and promote research; no provision is made for price stabilization. Mems: 41 producing and consuming countries. Exec. Dir FREEZAILAH BIN CHE YEOM (Malaysia).

International Tungsten Industry Association: 280 Earls Court Rd, London, SW5 9AS, England; tel. (01) 373-7413; telex 889077; f. 1988 (fmrly Primary Tungsten Asscn, f. 1975); promotes use of tungsten, collates statistics, prepares market reports, monitors health and environmental issues. Mems: 66. Pres. O. HEDEBRANT; Sec. M. R. P. MABY. Publ. *Bulletin* (quarterly).

International Vine and Wine Office: 11 rue Roquépine, 75008 Paris, France; tel. (1) 42-65-04-16; telex 281196; f. 1924 to study all the scientific, technical, economic and human problems concerning the vine and its products; to spread knowledge by means of its publications; to assist contacts between researchers and establish international research programmes. Mems: 33 countries. Dir ROBERT TINLOT. Publs *Bulletin de l'OIV* (every 2 months), *Lexique de la Vigne et du Vin*, *Recueil des méthodes internationales d'analyse des vins*, *Code international des Pratiques oenologiques*, *Codex oenologique international*, numerous scientific publications.

International Wheat Council: Haymarket House, 28 Haymarket, London, SW1Y 4SS, England; tel. (01) 930-4128; telex 916128; f. 1949; responsible for the administration of the Wheat Trade Convention of the International Wheat Agreement, 1986; aims to further international co-operation in all aspects of trade in wheat and other grains, to promote international trade in grains, and to secure the freest possible flow of this trade in the interests of members, particularly developing member countries; and to contribute to the stability of the international grain market; acts as forum for consultations between members, and provides comprehensive information on the international grain market and factors affecting it. Mems: 48 countries and the EEC. Exec. Dir. J. H. PAROTTE. Publs *World Wheat Statistics* (annually), *Record of Operations* (annually), *Market Report* (monthly), *Annual Report*, *Secretariat Papers* (occasional).

International Wool Secretariat: Wool House, 6 Carlton Gardens, London, SW1Y 5AE; tel. (01) 930-7300; telex 263926; f. 1937 to expand the use and usefulness of wool through promotion and research. Financed by Australia, New Zealand, South Africa and Uruguay, it has an international policy of promoting wool irrespective of the country of origin. A non-trading organization, IWS has branches in over 30 countries and Technical Offices in Italy, Japan, Netherlands, United Kingdom and the USA. Man. Dir J. McPHEE.

International Wool Study Group: Ashdown House, 123 Victoria St, London, SW1E 6RB, England; tel. (01) 215-6215; telex 8813148; f. 1946 to collect and collate statistics relating to world supply of and demand for wool; to review developments and to consider possible solutions to problems and difficulties unlikely to be resolved in the ordinary course of world trade in wool. Mems: 14 countries. Sec.-Gen. M. T. DUNN.

Lead Development Association: 34 Berkeley Square, London, W1X 6AJ, England; tel. (01) 499-8422; telex 261286; f. 1954; provides authoritative information on the use of lead and its compounds; maintains a library and abstracting service in collaboration with the Zinc Development Association (see below). Financed by lead producers and users in the United Kingdom, Europe and elsewhere. Chair. A. E. J. YELLAND (UK); Chief Exec. F. D. WARD (UK).

Mutual Assistance of the Latin American Government Oil Companies (Asistencia Recíproca Petrolera Estatal Latinoamericana—ARPEL): Javier de Viana 2345, Montevideo, Uruguay; tel. 406993; telex 22560; f. 1965 to study and recommend the implementation of mutually beneficial agreements among members in order to promote technical and economic development; to further Latin-American integration; to promote the interchange of technical assistance and information; to plan congresses, lectures, and meetings concerning the oil industry. Mems: state enterprises in Argentina, Bolivia, Brazil, Chile, Colombia, Costa Rica, Ecuador, Jamaica, Mexico, Paraguay, Peru, Suriname, Trinidad and Tobago, Uruguay, Venezuela. Sec.-Gen. HÉCTOR J. FIORIOLI. Publs *Boletín Informativo, Boletín Técnico ARPEL.*

Sugar Association of the Caribbean (Inc.): POB 719C, Bridgetown, Barbados; f. 1942. Mems: six national associations. Chair. H. B. DAVIS; Sec. D. H. A. JOHNSON. Publs *SAC Handbook, SAC Annual Report, Proceedings of Meetings of WI Sugar Technologists.*

Union of Banana-Exporting Countries—UPEB: Apdo 4273, Panamá 5, Panama; tel. 636266; telex 2568; f. 1974 as an intergovernmental agency to further the banana industry; mems: Colombia, Costa Rica, Dominican Republic, Guatemala, Nicaragua, Panama, Venezuela. Exec. Dir HAROLDO RODAS. Publs *Informe Mensual UPEB, Boletín Mensual de Estadísticas, BIBLIOBAN* (annually), bibliographies.

West Africa Rice Development Association—WARDA: 01 BP 2551 Bouaké 01, Côte d'Ivoire; tel. 63-21-29; telex 69138; f. 1970, aiming to make West Africa self-sufficient in rice; has three regional research stations in Côte d'Ivoire, Senegal and Sierra Leone; assists in rural development projects and operates regional training centre in Liberia and courses in member countries; budget (1987) US $4.5m.; funded by member countries, donor governments, UN agencies, the EEC and other organizations. Mems: Benin, Burkina Faso, Chad, Côte d'Ivoire, The Gambia, Ghana, Guinea, Guinea-Bissau, Liberia, Mali, Mauritania, Niger, Nigeria, Senegal, Sierra Leone, and Togo. Dir.-Gen. Dr EUGENE ROBERT TERRY (Sierra Leone). Publs technical reports.

West Indian Sea Island Cotton Association (Inc.): c/o Barbados Agricultural Development Corporation, Fairy Valley, Christ Church, Barbados. Pres. E. LEROY WARD; Sec. MICHAEL I. EDGHILL.

World Federation of Diamond Bourses: 62 Pelikaanstraat, 2018 Antwerp, Belgium; tel. (03) 232-76-55; telex 73314; f. 1947 to protect the interests of affiliated organizations and their individual members and to settle or arbitrate in disputes. Mems: 20 in 12 countries. Pres. E. GOLDSTEIN (UK); Sec.-Gen. PH. BLONDIN (Belgium).

World Gold Council: 1 rue de la Rôtisserie, 1204 Geneva, Switzerland; tel. (022) 219666; telex 428471; f. 1986 to link the world's principal producers of gold and to promote the sale of gold. Chair. GORDON PARKER; CEO E. M. HOOD.

Zinc Development Association: 34 Berkeley Square, London, W1X 6AJ, England; tel. (01) 499-6636; telex 261286; provides authoritative advice on the uses of zinc, its alloys and its compounds; maintains a library and abstracting service in collaboration with the Lead Development Association (q.v.). Affiliates are: Zinc Alloy Die Casters Association, Galvanizers' Association and Zinc Pigment Development Association. Financed by zinc producers and users in the United Kingdom, Europe and elsewhere. Chair. L. HENNIKER-HEATON (UK); Chief Exec. F. D. WARD (UK).

Economics and Finance

African Centre for Monetary Studies: 15 blvd Franklin Roosevelt, BP 1791, Dakar, Senegal; tel. 21-38-21; telex 61256; began operations 1978; aims to promote better understanding of banking and monetary matters; to study monetary problems of African countries and the effect on them of international monetary developments; seeks to enable African countries to co-ordinate strategies in international monetary affairs. Established as an organ of the Association of African Central Banks (AACB) as a result of a decision by the OAU Heads of State and Government. Mems: all mems of AACB (q.v.).

Arab Bankers Association: 1/2 Hanover St, London, W1R 9WB; tel. (01) 629-5423; telex 297338; f. 1980 to co-ordinate interests of Arab bankers, improve relations with other countries, prepare studies for development projects in the Arab world, administer a code for arbitration between financial institutions, and provide training for Arab bankers. Mems: 400. Chair. HIKMAT S. NASHASHIBI; Gen. Man. GHAYTH ARMANAZI.

Asian Clearing Union—ACU: c/o Central Bank of the Islamic Republic of Iran, POB 11365/8531, Teheran, Iran; tel. 237677; telex 213120; f. 1974 to provide clearing arrangements to economize on the use of foreign exchange and promote the use of domestic currencies in trade transactions among developing countries; part of ESCAP's Asian trade expansion programme; the Central Bank of Iran is the Union's agent. Mems: Bangladesh, Burma, India, Iran, Nepal, Pakistan, Sri Lanka. Gen.-Man. HASSAN GOLRIZ. Publs *Annual Report, Newsletter* (monthly).

Asian Reinsurance Corporation: Sinthon Bldg, 6th Floor, 132 Wireless Rd, Lumpini, Bangkok 10500, Thailand; tel. 250-1476; telex 87231; f. 1979 by ESCAP with UNCTAD, to operate as a professional reinsurer, giving priority in retrocessions to national insurance and reinsurance markets of member countries, and as a development organization providing technical assistance to national markets; cap. (auth.) US $15m., (p.u) US $4.5m. Mems: Afghanistan, Bangladesh, Bhutan, the People's Republic of China, India, the Republic of Korea, the Philippines, Sri Lanka, Thailand. Gen. Man. M. S. WIJENAIKE.

Association of African Central Banks: 15 blvd Franklin Roosevelt, BP 1791, Dakar, Senegal; tel. 21-38-21; telex 61256; f. 1968 to promote contacts in the monetary and financial sphere in order to increase co-operation and trade among member states; to strengthen monetary and financial stability on the African continent. Mems: 33 African central banks representing 44 states.

Association of African Tax Administrators: c/o ECA, POB 3001, Addis Ababa, Ethiopia; f. 1980 to promote co-operation in the field of taxation policy, legislation and administration among African countries. Mems: 20 states. Chair. ABDERREZAG NAILI-DOUAOUDA (Algeria).

Association of European Institutes of Economic Research (Association d'instituts européens de conjoncture économique): 3 place Montesquieu, BP 4, 1348 Louvain-la-Neuve, Belgium; tel. (10) 43-41-52; f. 1955; provides a means of contact between member institutes; organizes two meetings yearly, in the spring and autumn, at which discussions are held, on the economic situation and on a special theoretical subject. Mems: 40 institutes in 20 European countries. Admin. Sec. PAUL OLBRECHTS.

Association of International Bond Dealers: Postfach, 8033 Zürich, Switzerland; tel. (01) 3634222; telex 815812; f. 1969 for discussion of questions relating to the international securities markets, to issue rules governing their functions, and to maintain a close liaison between the primary and secondary markets. Mems: 881 banks and major financial institutions in 38 countries. Chair. ARTHUR SCHMIEGELOW (Denmark); Sec.-Gen. JOHN WOLTERS (Switzerland). Publs *International Bond Manual,* daily Eurobond listing, electronic price information, weekly Eurobond guide, yield book, reports, etc.

Benelux Economic Union: 39 rue de la Régence, 1000 Brussels, Belgium; tel. (02) 519-38-11; telex 61540; f. 1960 to bring about the economic union of Belgium, Luxembourg and the Netherlands; structure comprises: the Committee of Ministers; the Council, consisting of one chairman from each country and the presidents of the eight Committees, on foreign economic relations, monetary and financial matters, industry and commerce, agriculture, food and fisheries, customs and taxation, transport, social affairs and movement of persons; the Court of Justice; the Consultative Inter-Parliamentary Council; the Economic and Social Advisory Council; and the Secretariat-General. Sec.-Gen. Drs E. D. J. KRUIJTBOSCH (Netherlands), M. R. WORMERINGER-BERNA (Luxembourg). Publs *Benelux-Info* (occasional), *Benelux Review* (quarterly), *Benelux Textes de Base.*

Centre for Latin American Monetary Studies (Centro de Estudios Monetarios Latinoamericanos): Durango 54, Col. Roma, Del. Cuauhtémoc, 06700 México, DF, Mexico; tel. 533-03-00; telex 1771229; f. 1952; organizes technical training programmes on monetary policy, development finance, etc., applied research programmes on monetary and central banking policies and procedures, regional meetings of banking officials. Mems: 29 associated members (Central Banks of Latin America and the Caribbean), 22 co-operating members (development agencies, regional financial agencies and non-Latin American Central Banks). Dir JORGE GONZÁLEZ DEL VALLE. Publs *Bulletin* (every 2 months), *Monetaria* (quarterly).

Econometric Society: Dept of Economics, Northwestern University, Evanston, Ill 60208, USA; tel. (312) 491-3615; f. 1930 to promote studies that aim at a unification of the theoretical-quantitative and the empirical-quantitative approach to economic problems. Mems: 6,000. Exec. Dir and Sec. JULIE P. GORDON. Publ. *Econometrica* (6 a year).

Economic Community of the Great Lakes Countries (Communauté économique des pays des Grands Lacs—CEPGL): POB 58, Gisenyi, Rwanda; telex 602; f. 1976; main organs: annual Conference of Heads of State, Council of Ministers of Foreign Affairs, Permanent Executive Secretariat, Consultative Commission, three Specialized Technical Commissions. There are four specialized agencies: a development bank, the Banque de Développement des Etats des Grands Lacs (BDEGL) at Goma, Zaire; an energy centre at Bujumbura, Burundi; the Institute of Agronomic and Zootechnical Research, Gitega, Burundi; and a regional electricity company (SINELAC) at Bukavu, Zaire. A five-year plan (1987–91) was adopted in 1986, requiring financing of about US $3.87m. for agricultural, industrial and energy projects. Mems: Burundi, Rwanda, Zaire. Exec. Sec. ANTOINE NDUWAYO (Burundi). Publs *Grands Lacs* (quarterly review), and an annual journal.

Eurofinas: 267 ave de Tervuren, bte 10, 1150 Brussels, Belgium; tel. (02) 771-21-08; telex 63804; f. 1959 to study the development of instalment credit financing in Europe, to collate and publish instalment credit statistics, to promote research into instalment credit practice; mems: finance houses and professional associations in Austria, Belgium, Finland, France, Federal Republic of Germany, Ireland, Italy, Netherlands, Norway, Spain, Sweden, Switzerland and United Kingdom. Chair. PAUL HAEGEL (France); Sec.-Gen. MARC BAERT. Publs *Eurofinas Newsletter* (monthly), *Study Reports*.

European Federation of Financial Analysts Societies: c/o SAFE, 41 ave de l'Opéra, 75002 Paris, France; tel. (1) 47-63-12-13; telex 280392; f. 1962 to co-ordinate the activities of all European associations of financial analysts. Mems: 5,283 in 13 societies. Pres. A. LAVIOLETTE; Sec.-Gen. J.-G. DE WAEL.

European Financial Management and Marketing Association: 16 rue d'Aguesseau, 75008 Paris, France; tel. (1) 47-42-52-72; telex 280288; f. 1971 to link financial institutions by organizing seminars, conferences and training sessions and an annual World Convention, and by providing documentation services. Mems: over 700 European financial institutions. Pres. ROBERT AMOS; Sec.-Gen. LOUIS LENGRAND. Publ. *Newsletter*.

European Insurance Committee: 3 bis rue de la Chaussée d'Antin, 75009 Paris, France; tel. (1) 48-24-66-00; telex 281829; f. 1953. Mems: national insurance associations of 18 western European countries. Pres. M. R. SLOAN (UK); Sec.-Gen. F. LOHEAC (France).

European Venture Capital Association: 11F clos du Parnasse, 1040 Brussels, Belgium; tel. (02) 513-74-39; telex 23379; f. 1983 to link venture capital companies within the European Community and to encourage joint investment projects, particularly in support of small and medium-sized businesses; holds annual convention, seminars. Mems: 120 (corporate and individual), and 65 associate mems, in 21 countries. Sec.-Gen. YVES FASSIN.

Inter-American Institute of Capital Markets: Apdo 1766, Caracas 1010-A, Venezuela; f. 1977 under the joint sponsorship of the OAS and the Venezuelan Government, to assist member countries in the development of their capital markets; organizes international conferences. Mems: 28 countries. Pres. BERNARDO PAUL. Publ. *Boletín Bibliográfico*.

International Accounting Standards Committee—IASC: 41 Kingsway, London, WC2B 6YU, England; tel. (01) 240-8781; telex 295177; f. 1973 to formulate and publish in the public interest standards to be observed in the presentation of financial statements and to promote worldwide acceptance and observance, and to work for the improvement and harmonization of regulations, accounting standards and procedures relating to the presentation of financial statements. Mems: over 90 accounting bodies representing 900,000 accountants in 70 countries. Chair. GEORGES BARTHES DE RUYTER; Sec.-Gen. DAVID H. CAIRNS. Publs *Statements of International Accounting Standards*, *Exposure Drafts*, *IASC News* (4 a year), *Discussion Papers*.

International Association for Research in Income and Wealth: POB 1962, Yale Station, New Haven, Conn 06520, USA; tel. (203) 436-6866; f. 1947 to further research in the general field of national income and wealth and related topics by the organization of periodic conferences and by other means. Mems: approx. 350. Chair. T. P. HILL (UK); Exec. Sec. RICHARD RUGGLES (USA). Publ. *Review of Income and Wealth* (quarterly).

International Association of Islamic Banks: POB 4992, Jeddah, Saudi Arabia; branches in Cairo, Egypt (POB 2838), and Karachi, Pakistan (POB 541); f. 1977 to link Islamic banks, which do not deal at interest but work on the principle of participation: activities include training and research. Chair. Prince MOHAMED AL-FAISAL AL-SAUD; Sec.-Gen. Dr AHMED AL-NAGGAR.

International Bureau of Fiscal Documentation: 'Muiderpoort', Sarphatistraat 124, POB 20237, 1000 HE Amsterdam, Netherlands; tel. (020) 267726; telex 13217; f. 1938 to supply information on fiscal law and its application; library on international taxation. Pres. A. NOOTEBOOM; Man. Dir H. M. A. L. HAMAEKERS. Publs *Bulletin for International Fiscal Documentation*, *European Taxation*, *Supplementary Service to European Taxation* (all monthly), *Tax News Service* (fortnightly); studies, data bases.

International Centre for Local Credit: Koninginnegracht 2, 2514 AA The Hague, Netherlands; f. 1958 to promote local authority credit by gathering, exchanging and distributing information and advice on member institutions and on local authority credit and related subjects; studies important subjects in the field of local authority credit. Mems: 21 financial institutions in 15 countries. Pres. F. NARMON (Belgium); Sec.-Gen. W. GRIFFIOEN (The Netherlands). Publs *Bulletin*, *Newsletter*, special reports.

International Economic Association: 23 rue Campagne Première, 75014 Paris, France; tel. (1) 43-27-91-44; telex 240 918; f. 1949 to promote international collaboration for the advancement of economic knowledge and develop personal contacts between economists, and to encourage provision of means for the dissemination of economic knowledge. Member associations in 59 countries. Pres. Prof. AMARTYA SEN (India); Sec.-Gen. Prof. JEAN-PAUL FITOUSSI (France).

International Federation of Accountants: 540 Madison Ave, New York, NY 10022, USA; tel. (212) 486-2446; telex 640428; f. 1977 to develop a co-ordinated worldwide accounting profession with harmonized standards. Mems: 100 accountancy bodies in 74 countries. Pres. ROBERT L. MAY (USA); Exec. Dir ROBERT SEMPIER (USA).

International Federation of Stock Exchanges: 22 blvd de Courcelles, 75017 Paris, France; tel. (1) 47-63-17-60; telex 642720; f. 1961 to promote among its members a co-operation that is not detrimental to the traditional relations which some of them may maintain with stock exchanges of third countries; represents its members at international organizations. Mems: 15 European and 18 other stock exchanges. Pres. Baron B. F. VAN ITTERSUM; Sec.-Gen. Mrs JEANNE ABBEY.

International Fiscal Association: c/o Erasmus University, Woudestein, POB 1738, Burg. Oudlaan 50, 3000 DR Rotterdam, Netherlands; tel. (010) 452-59-57; telex 24421; f. 1938 to study international and comparative public finance and fiscal law, especially taxation; holds annual congresses. Mems in over 80 countries and national branches in 35 countries. Pres. RICHARD M. HAMMER (USA); Sec.-Gen. Prof. Dr J. H. CHRISTIAANSE (Netherlands). Publs *Cahiers de Droit Fiscal International*, *Yearbook of the International Fiscal Association*, *IFA Congress Seminar Series*.

International Institute of Public Finance: University of the Saar, 6600 Saarbrücken 11, Federal Republic of Germany; f. 1937; a private scientific organization aiming to establish contacts between people of every nationality, whose main or supplementary activity consists in the study of public finance; holds one meeting a year devoted to a certain scientific subject. Acting Pres. VICTOR HALBERSTADT (Netherlands).

International Savings Banks Institute: 1–3 rue Albert Gos, 1206 Geneva, Switzerland; tel. (022) 477466; telex 428702; f. 1925 to act as an intelligence and liaison centre for savings banks. Mems: 119 savings banks and savings banks associations in 74 countries. Pres. AKE JANSON (Sweden); Gen. Man. J. M. PESANT (France). Publs (in English, French and German) *Savings Banks International* (quarterly), *International Information* (monthly), *International Savings Banks Directory*, *Savings Banks Foreign Business Directory*.

International Union of Building Societies and Savings Associations: 3 Savile Row, London, W1X 1AF, England; tel. (01) 437-0655; telex 24538; f. 1914 to foster world-wide interest in savings and home-ownership and co-operation among members; to encourage comparative study of methods and practice in housing finance; to encourage appropriate legislation on housing finance. Sec.-Gen. MARK BOLEAT. Publs *Housing Finance International* (quarterly), *Directory* (every 2 years), *International Housing Finance Factbook* (every 2 years), *IUBSSA Newsletter* (3 a year).

Latin American Banking Federation (Federación Latino-americana de Bancos—FELABAN): Apdo Aéreo 091959, Bogotá, DE8, Colombia; tel. 2560875; telex 45548; f. 1965 to co-ordinate efforts towards a wide and accelerated economic development in Latin American countries. Mems: 18 Latin American national banking associations. Pres. of Board Dr LEONIDAS ORTEGA TRUJILLO; Sec.-Gen. Dra MARICIELO GLEN DE TOBÓN (Colombia).

OTHER INTERNATIONAL ORGANIZATIONS

Economics and Finance, Education

Pacific Economic Co-operation Conference: no permanent secretariat; f. 1980; annual meetings of business representatives, academic staff and government officials, to discuss regional economic matters; standing committee of 17 mems, including mems from the ASEAN states, Australia, Canada, the People's Republic of China, Japan, the Republic of Korea, New Zealand, the Pacific islands, Taiwan and the USA; 1989 Conference to be held in Wellington, New Zealand (November).

West African Clearing House: PMB 218, Freetown, Sierra Leone; tel. 24485; telex 3368; f. 1975; administers transactions between its nine member central banks in order to promote local trade and currency transactions. Mems: Banque Centrale des Etats de l'Afrique de l'Ouest (serving Benin, Burkina Faso, Côte d'Ivoire, Mali, Niger, Senegal, Togo) and the central banks of The Gambia, Ghana, Guinea, Guinea-Bissau, Liberia, Mauritania, Nigeria and Sierra Leone. Exec. Sec. CHRIS E. NEMEDIA (Nigeria).

World Council of Credit Unions—WOCCU: POB 391, 5810 Mineral Point Rd, Madison, WI 53701, USA; tel. (608) 231-7130; telex 467918; f. 1970 to link credit unions and similar co-operative financial institutions and assist them in expanding and improving their services; provides technical and financial assistance to credit union associations in developing countries. Mems: 43,000 credit unions in 76 countries. Pres. G. A. CHARBONNEAU. Publs *WOCCU Statistical Report and Directory* (annually), *World Reporter* (quarterly), *Credit Union Technical Reporter* (quarterly).

Education

African Association for Literacy and Adult Education: POB 72511/50768, Finance House, 6th Floor, Loita St, Nairobi, Kenya; tel. 331512; telex 23240; f. 1984, combining the former African Adult Education Association and the AFROLIT Society (both f. 1968); aims to promote adult education and literacy in Africa, to study the problems involved, and to allow the exchange of information; holds Conference every three years. Mems: 21 national education associations and 267 institutions. Chair. Dr ANTHONY SETSABI (Lesotho); Sec.-Gen. PAUL WANGOOLA (Uganda). Publs *AALAE Newsletter* (2 a year, French and English), *Journal* (2 a year).

Association for Childhood Education International: 11141 Georgia Ave, Suite 200, Wheaton, Md 20902, USA; tel. (301) 942-2443; f. 1892 to work for the education of children (from infancy through early adolescence) by promoting desirable conditions in schools, raising the standard of teaching, co-operating with all groups concerned with children, informing the public of the needs of children. Mems: 12,000. Pres. VERL SHORT; Exec. Dir A. GILSON BROWN. Publs *Childhood Education* (5 a year), *ACEI Exchange Newsletter* (6 a year), *Journal of Research in Childhood Education* (2 a year), leaflets on current educational subjects (3 a year).

Association of African Universities: POB 5744, Accra North, Ghana; tel. 63670; telex 2284; f. 1967 to promote exchanges, contact and co-operation among African university institutions and to collect and disseminate information on research and higher education in Africa. Mems: 92 university institutions. Pres. Prof. DONALD E. U. EKONG (Nigeria); Sec.-Gen. Prof. DONALD EKONG (Nigeria). Publs *AAU Newsletter* (quarterly), *Directory of African Universities* (every 2 years).

Association of Arab Universities: POB 401, Jubeyha, Amman, Jordan; tel. 845131; telex 23855; f. 1964. Mems: 61 universities. Sec.-Gen. Dr MOHAMMAD F. DOGHAIM. Publs *Bulletin* (annually in Arabic and English), *Directory of Arab Universities*, *Directory of Teaching Staff of Arab Universities*.

Association of Caribbean Universities and Research Institutes: POB 11532, Caparra Heights Station, San Juan, Puerto Rico 00922; tel. (809) 720-4381; f. 1968 to foster contact and collaboration between member universities and institutes; conferences, meetings, seminars, etc.; circulation of information through newsletters, bulletins; facilitates co-operation and the pooling of resources in research; encourages exchange of staff and students. Mems: 46. Sec.-Gen. Dr THOMAS MATHEWS. Publ. *Caribbean Educational Bulletin* (quarterly).

Association of Institutes for European Studies (Association des Instituts d'Etudes Européennes—AIEE): 122 rue de Lausanne, 1202 Geneva, Switzerland; tel. (022) 322803; f. 1951, to co-ordinate activities of member institutes in teaching and research, exchange information, provide a centre for documentation. Mems: 32 institutes in nine countries. Pres. Prof. E. CEREXHE (Belgium); Sec.-Gen. Prof. DUSAN SIDJANSKI. Publ. *Bulletin intérieur* (2 a month).

Association of Partially or Wholly French-Language Universities (Association des universités partiellement ou entièrement de langue française—AUPELF): Université de Montréal, BP 6128, Montreal, Canada H3C 3J7; tel. (514) 343-6630; telex 055-60955; f. 1961; aims: documentation, co-ordination, co-operation, exchange.

Mems: 188, and 331 assoc. mems. Pres. BAKARY TOURÉ; Sec.-Gen. MAURICE-ETIENNE BEUTLER. Publs *Perspectives universitaires* (2 a year), *Idées* (irregular), *Universités* (quarterly).

Association of South-East Asian Institutions of Higher Learning—ASAIHL: Secretariat, Ratasastra Bldg, Chulalongkorn University, Henri Dunant Rd, Bangkok 10500, Thailand; tel. 251 6966; telex 72432; f. 1956 to promote the economic, cultural and social welfare of the people of South-East Asia by means of educational co-operation and research programmes. Mems: 100 university institutions in 11 countries. Pres. Dr SUJUDI (Indonesia); Exec. Sec. Dr NINNAT OLANVORAVUTH. Publs *Newsletter*, *Handbook*.

Catholic International Education Office: 60 rue des Eburons, 1040 Brussels, Belgium; tel. (02) 230-72-52; f. 1952 for the study of the problems of Catholic education throughout the world; co-ordination of the activities of members; and representation of Catholic education at international bodies. Mems: 84 countries, 16 assoc. mems, 13 collaborating mems, 5 corresponding mems. Pres. Mgr J. MEYERS (acting); Sec.-Gen. PAULUS ADAMS, FSC. Publs *OIEC Bulletin* (every 2 months in English, French and Spanish), *L'éducation sociale des jeunes à l'école* (French and Spanish), *Aujourd'hui l'école et l'audiovisuel*, *Les organisations internationales catholiques d'enseignement*.

Catholic International Federation for Physical and Sports Education: 5 rue Cernuschi, 75017 Paris, France; tel. (1) 47-66-03-23; f. 1911 to group Catholic associations for physical education and sport of different countries and to develop the principles and precepts of Christian morality by fostering meetings, study and international co-operation. Mems: 14 affiliated national federations representing about 2.5m. members. Pres. Dr J. FINDER (Austria); Sec.-Gen. ROBERT PRINGARBE (France).

Centre for Research and Documentation on International Language Problems: Nieuwe Binnenweg 176, 3015 BJ Rotterdam, Netherlands; tel. (010) 436-10-44; telex 23721; f. 1952 by Universala Esperanto-Asocio (renamed 1969); encourages and disseminates information about research on language problems in international relations; sponsors seminars on Esperanto studies. Dirs D. BLANKE, P. DASGUPTO, B. GOLDEN, U. LINS, J. POOL, E. SHERWOOD, E. SYMOENS, H. TONKIN. Publ. *Newsletter* (irregular).

Comparative Education Society in Europe: 51 rue de la Concorde, 1050 Brussels, Belgium; f. 1961 to promote teaching and research in comparative and international education; the Society organizes conferences and promotes literature. Mems in 39 countries. Pres. Prof. H. VAN DAELE (Belgium). Publs *Proceedings*, *Newsletter* (quarterly).

European Association of Teachers: AEDE, 1049 Bournens, Switzerland; tel. (022) 447750; f. 1956 to develop understanding of European civilization and of European problems and to instruct students in this understanding. Mems in Austria, Belgium, France, Federal Republic of Germany, Greece, Italy, Luxembourg, Portugal, Spain, Switzerland, United Kingdom. Pres. P. VANBERGEN (Belgium); Sec.-Gen. S. MOSER (Switzerland). Publs *Documents pour l'enseignement*, *Education for Europe*, 9 national newsletters.

European Bureau of Adult Education: Nieuweweg 4, POB 367, 3800 AJ Amersfoort, Netherlands; tel. (33) 631114; f. 1953 as a clearing-house and centre of co-operation for all groups concerned with adult education in Europe. Mems: 150 in 18 countries. Pres. A. K. STOCK (UK); Sec., Dir W. BAX. Publs *Conference Reports*, *Directory of Adult Education Organisations in Europe*, *Newsletter*, *Survey of Adult Education Legislation*, *Glossary of Terms*.

European Cultural Foundation: Jan van Goyenkade 5, 1075 HN Amsterdam, Netherlands; tel. (20) 760222; telex 18710; f. 1954 as a non-governmental organization, supported by private sources, to promote activities of mutual interest to European countries, concerning basic values, culture, education, environment, international affairs, communications media, social issues, or the problems of European society in general (excluding strictly scientific or medical subjects); national committees in 16 countries; has established a transnational network of eight institutes and centres: European Institute of Education and Social Policy, Paris (with Erasmus Bureau, Brussels); Institute for European Environmental Policy, Bonn (branch offices in London, Brussels and Paris); European Co-operation Fund, Brussels; European Centre for Environmental Communication, Paris; European Centre for Work and Society, Maastricht; EURYDICE Central Unit (the Education Information Network of the European Community), Brussels; European Institute for the Media, Manchester. A grants programme, for projects involving at least three European countries, is also conducted. Pres. HRH Princess MARGRIET of the Netherlands; Sec.-Gen. R. GEORIS. Publs *Annual Report*, *Newsletter* (2 a year).

European Federation for Catholic Adult Education: Kapuzinerstrasse 84, 4020 Linz, Austria; tel. (0732) 27-44-41; f. 1963 to

OTHER INTERNATIONAL ORGANIZATIONS

strengthen international contact between members, to assist international research and practical projects in adult education; to help communications between its members and other international bodies; holds conference every two years. Pres. Dr WALTER SUK (Austria).

European Foundation for Management Development: 40 rue Washington, 1050 Brussels, Belgium; tel. (02) 648-03-85; telex 65080; f. 1971 through merger of European Association of Management Training Centres and International University Contact for Management Education; aims to help improve the quality of management development within the economic, social and cultural context of Europe and in harmony with its overall needs. Mems: more than 550 institutions and individuals. Pres. Baron ANTOINE BEKAERT; Dir-Gen. WILLIAM A. G. BRADDICK. Publs *International Management Development* (quarterly), *IMD Bulletin* (every 2 months), *Documentation on Books, Cases and other teaching Material in Management* (every 2 months).

European Union of Arabic and Islamic Scholars: Duque de Medinaceli 6, 28014 Madrid, Spain; tel. 4292017; f. 1960 to organize congresses of Arabic and Islamic Studies; congresses are held every two years. Mems: about 200. Sec. Dr MANUELA MARIN (Spain).

Graduate Institute of International Studies (Institut universitaire de hautes études internationales): POB 36, 132 rue de Lausanne, Geneva, Switzerland; tel. (022) 311730; telex 412151; f. 1927 to establish a centre for advanced studies in international relations of the present day, juridical, historical, political, economic and social. Library of 120,000 vols. Dir Prof. LUCIUS CAFLISCH; Sec.-Gen. J.-C. FRACHEBOURG.

Inter-American Centre for Research and Documentation on Vocational Training (Centro Interamericano de Investigación y Documentación sobre Formación Profesional—CINTERFOR): Avda Uruguay 1238, Casilla de correo 1761, Montevideo, Uruguay; tel. 98 65 71; telex 6521; f. 1964 by the International Labour Organisation (q.v.) for mutual help among the Latin American and Caribbean countries in planning vocational training; services are provided in documentation, research, exchange of experience; holds seminars and courses. Dir JOÃO CARLOS ALEXIM. Publs *Bulletin* (4 a year), *Documentation* (2 a year), *Bibliographical Series, Studies, Monographs and Abstracts*.

Inter-American Confederation for Catholic Education (Confederación Interamericana de Educación Católica): Calle 78 No 12-16 (ofna 101), Apdo Aéreo 90036, Bogotá 8 DE, Colombia; tel. 255-3676; f. 1945 to defend and extend the principles and rules of Catholic education, freedom of education, and human rights; organizes congress every three years. Pres. CÉSAR BLONDET SABROSO; Sec.-Gen. MARIO IANTORNO. Publs *Educación Hoy: Perspectivas Latinoamericanas* (every 3 months), *Colección CENTRAL, Colección RADIAR, Colección Textos*.

International Association for Educational and Vocational Guidance—IAEVG: Dept of Economic Development, Gloucester House, Chichester St, Belfast, BT1 4RA, Northern Ireland; tel. (0232) 321200; f. 1951 to contribute to the development of vocational guidance and promote contact between persons associated with it. Mems: 40,000 from 60 countries. Pres. Prof. WILLIAM C. BINGHAM (USA); Sec.-Gen. KATHLEEN M. V. HALL (UK). Publ. *Bulletin* (2 a year), *Newsletter* (3 a year).

International Association for Educational and Vocational Information: 20 rue de l'Estrapade, 75005 Paris, France; f. 1956 to facilitate co-operation between national organizations concerned with supplying information to university and college students and secondary pupils and their parents. Mems: national organizations in 50 countries. Pres. C. VIMONT (France); Sec.-Gen. J. L. C. BOUVIER (Belgium); Dir L. TODOROV. Publ. *Informations universitaires et professionnelles internationales* (quarterly).

International Association for the Development of Documentation, Libraries and Archives in Africa: BP 375, Dakar, Senegal; f. 1957 to organize and develop documentation and archives in all African countries. Sec.-Gen. ZACHEUS SUNDAY ALI (Nigeria).

International Association of Colleges of Physical Education: Institut Supérieur d'Education Physique, Université de Liège au Sart Tilman, 4000 Liège, Belgium; tel. (041) 56-38-90; telex 41397; f. 1962; organizes congresses, exchanges, and research in physical education. Mems: institutions in 43 countries. Sec.-Gen. Dr MAURICE PIERON.

International Association of Papyrologists: Fondation Egyptologique Reine Elisabeth, Parc du Cinquantenaire 10, 1040 Brussels, Belgium; f. 1947; Mems: about 500. Pres. Prof. ORSOLINA MONTEVECCHI (Italy); Sec. Prof. JEAN BINGEN (Belgium).

International Association of Universities—IAU/International Universities Bureau—IUB: 1 rue Miollis, 75732 Paris Cedex 15, France; tel. (1) 45-68-25-45; telex 250615; f. 1950 to allow co-operation at the international level among universities and other institutions of higher education; provides information and

Education

maintains a Documentation Centre; conducts research programme on issues concerning higher education. Ninth General Conference, University of Helsinki, Finland, 1990. Budget: approximately US $800,000 each year. Mems: over 800 universities and institutions of higher education in 123 countries; assoc. mems: eight international university organizations. Pres. JUSTIN THORENS; Sec.-Gen. FRANZ EBERHARD. Publs *Higher Education Policy* (quarterly), *International Handbook of Universities* (every 2 years), *World List of Universities* (every 2 years).

International Association of University Professors and Lecturers—IAUPL: 18 rue du Docteur Roux, 75015 Paris, France; tel. (1) 47-83-31-65; f. 1945 for the development of academic fraternity amongst university teachers and research workers; the protection of independence and freedom of teaching and research; the furtherance of the interests of all university teachers; and the consideration of academic problems. Mems: federations in 18 countries. Hon. Sec.-Gen. Dr L. P. LAPRÉVOTE. Publ. *Communication*.

International Baccalaureate Office—IBO: Route des Morillons 15, Grand Saconnex 1218, Geneva, Switzerland; tel. (022) 910274; telex 265871; f. 1967 to plan curricula and an international university entrance examination, the International Baccalaureate, recognized by major universities in Europe, North and South America, Africa, Middle East and Australia; provides international board of examiners. Mems: 350 participating schools. Chair. of Council Dr PIET GATHIER (Netherlands); Dir-Gen. ROGER M. PEEL.

International Congress of African Studies: c/o Yusuf Fadhil Hassan, Vice-Chancellor, University of Khartoum, POB 321, Khartoum, Sudan; tel. 75100; f. 1962 to encourage co-operation and research in African studies. Sec.-Gen. Prof. SAYID H. HURREIZ.

International Council for Adult Education: 720 Bathurst St, Suite 500, Toronto, Ont, Canada M5S 2R4; tel. (416) 588-1211; telex 06-986766; f. 1973 to promote adult education and thereby further economic and social development; undertakes research and training; organizes seminars, the exchange of information, and co-operative publishing; General Assembly meets every three years. Mems: six regional organizations and national associations in 71 countries. Pres. Dame NITA BARROW; Sec.-Gen. BUDD HALL. Publ. *Convergence*.

International Council for Distance Education: PB 2100 Grunerlokka, 0505 Oslo 5, Norway; f. 1938 (name changed 1982); furthers distance (correspondence) education by promoting research, encouraging regional links, providing information and organizing conferences. Mems: 120 institutions, 600 individuals in 50 countries. Pres. Dr DAVID STEWART (UK); Sec.-Gen. REIDAR ROLL (Norway).

International Federation for Parent Education: 1 ave Léon Journault, 92311 Sèvres Cedex, France; tel. (1) 45-34-75-27; f. 1964 to gather in congresses and colloquia experts from different scientific fields and those responsible for family education in their own countries and to encourage the establishment of family education where it does not exist. Mems: 120. Pres. JEAN AUBA (France). Publs *Quarterly Bulletin, Child International Review*.

International Federation of Catholic Universities: 78A rue de Sèvres, 75341 Paris Cedex 07, France; tel. (1) 42-73-36-25; f. 1948; to ensure a strong bond of mutual assistance among all Catholic universities in the search for truth; to help to solve problems of growth and development, and to co-operate with other international organizations. Mems: 172 in 36 countries. Pres. M. MICHEL FALISE (France); Sec.-Gen. LUCIEN MICHAUD (Canada). Publs *Quarterly Newsletter*.

International Federation of 'Ecole Moderne' Movements: 24 ave des Armes, BP 109, 06322 Cannes-la-Bocca Cedex, France; tel. 93-47-96-11; f. 1957 to bring into contact associations devoted to the improvement of school organization and to work for the adoption of techniques advocated by C. Freinet; conducts courses for teachers, promotes interschool exchange of correspondence and magazines. Mems: associations of teachers in 40 countries. Pres. HENRY LANDROIT. Publs *L'Educateur* (2 a month), *Art Enfantin* (bi-monthly), *Bibliothèque de Travail Sonore, Bibliothèque de l'Ecole Moderne, Bibliothèque de Travail* (bi-monthly), *Bibliothèque de Travail Junior* (monthly), *Bibliothèque de Travail Second degré, La Multilettre*.

International Federation of Library Associations and Institutions—IFLA: c/o Royal Library, POB 95312, 2509 CH The Hague, Netherlands; tel. (70) 140884; telex 34402; f. 1927 to promote international co-operation in librarianship and bibliography. Mems: 181 associations, representing 123 countries, 1,040 institutions and individual members. Pres. Dr HANS-PETER GEH; Sec.-Gen. Dr PAUL NAUTA. Publs *IFLA Annual, IFLA Directory, IFLA Journal, International Cataloguing and Bibliographic Control* (quarterly), *IFLA Professional Reports*.

International Federation of Organisations for School Correspondence and Exchange: 29 rue d'Ulm, 75230 Paris Cedex 05, France; tel. (1) 43-45-37-21; f. 1929 to contribute to the knowledge of foreign languages and civilizations and to bring together young people of all nations by furthering international scholastic exchanges including correspondence, individual and group visits to foreign countries, individual accommodation with families, placements in international holiday camps, etc. Mems: comprises 78 national bureaux of scholastic correspondence and exchange in 36 countries. Pres. A. H. MALE (UK); Gen. Sec. A. ELMARY (France).

International Federation of Physical Education: 4 Cleevecroft Ave, Bishops Cleeve, Cheltenham, GL52 4JZ, England; f. 1923; studies physical education on scientific, pedagogic and aesthetic bases in order to stimulate health, harmonious development or preservation, healthy recreation, and the best adaptation of the individual to the general needs of social life; organizes international congresses and courses. Mems: from 112 countries. Pres. JOHN C. ANDREWS. Publ. *FIEP Bulletin* (quarterly in Arabic, French, English, Portuguese and Spanish).

International Federation of Secondary Teachers: 7 rue de Villersexel, 75007 Paris, France; tel. (1) 47-05-65-06; f. 1912 to contribute to the progress of secondary education. Mems: 47 associations with 850,000 members in 30 countries. Gen. Sec. LOUIS WEBER. Publs *Newsletter* (quarterly), *International Bulletin* (2 a year).

International Federation of Teachers' Associations: 3 rue de La Rochefoucauld, 75009 Paris, France; tel. (1) 48-74-58-44; f. 1926 to raise the level of popular education and improve teaching methods; to protect interests of teachers; to promote international understanding. Mems: 43 national associations. Pres. FERD MILBERT (Luxembourg); Sec.-Gen. JEAN-BERNARD GICQUEL (France). Publs *Feuilles d'Informations* (9 or 10 a year), *FIAI-IFTA-Informations* (2 a year).

International Federation of Teachers of Modern Languages: Seestrasse 247, 8038 Zürich, Switzerland; tel. (01) 4825040; telex 815250; f. 1931; holds meetings on every aspect of foreign-language teaching; has consultative status with UNESCO. Mems: 33 national and regional language associations and six international unilingual associations (teachers of English, French, German, Italian and Spanish). Pres. EDWARD M. BATLEY; Sec.-Gen. GYÖRGY SZÉPE. Publ. *FIPLV World News* (quarterly in English, French and Spanish).

International Federation of University Women: 37 Quai Wilson, 1201 Geneva, Switzerland; tel. (022) 7312380; f. 1919 to promote understanding and friendship among university women of the world; to encourage international co-operation; to further the development of education; to represent university women in international organizations; to encourage the full application of members' skills to the problems which arise at all levels of public life. Affiliates: 50 national associations with over 230,000 mems. Pres. Dr RITVA-LIISA KARVETTI (Finland); Exec. Sec. D. DAVIES (UK). Publs *The Newsletter* (annually), *Communiqué* (annually), triennial report.

International Federation of Workers' Educational Associations: Histadrut, 93 Arlosoroff St, Tel Aviv 61002, Israel; tel. 03-262335; telex 342488; f. 1947 to promote co-operation between national non-governmental bodies concerned with workers' education, through clearing-house services, exchange of information, publications, international seminars, conferences, summer schools, etc. Pres. Prof. KURT PROKOP (Austria); Sec.-Gen. DAVID FARAN-FRANKFURTER (Israel).

International Institute for Adult Literacy Methods: POB 13145-654, Teheran, Iran; f. 1968 by UNESCO and the government of Iran; a clearing-house for information on activities concerning literacy in various countries; carries out comparative studies of the methods, media and techniques used in literacy programmes; maintains documentation service and library on literacy; arranges seminars. Dir Dr HASSAN SADOGH VANINI.

International Institute of Philosophy—IIP (Institut international de philosophie—IIP): 8 rue Jean-Calvin, 75005 Paris, France; tel. (1) 43-36-39-11; f. 1937 to clarify fundamental issues of contemporary philosophy in annual meetings and to promote mutual understanding among thinkers of different backgrounds and traditions; a maximum of 115 members are elected, chosen from all countries and representing different tendencies. Mems: 105 in 36 countries. Pres. DAVID PEARS (UK); Sec.-Gen. Y. BELAVAL (France). Publs *Bibliography of Philosophy* (quarterly), *Proceedings* of annual meetings, *Chroniques, Philosophy and World Community* (series).

International Institute of Public Administration: 2 ave de l'Observatoire, Paris 6e; tel. (1) 43-26-49-00; telex 270229; f. 1967; trains high-ranking civil servants from abroad; administrative, economic, financial and diplomatic programmes; Africa, Latin America, Asia, Europe and Near East departments; research department, library of 80,000 vols; Documentation Centre. Dir M. FRANC. Publs *Revue française d'administration publique* (quarterly), *L'année administrative* (annually).

International Montessori Association: Koninginneweg 161, 1075 CN Amsterdam, Netherlands; tel. (20) 798932; f. 1929 to propagate the ideals and educational methods of Dr Maria Montessori, co-operate with organizations which strive to promote peace and human rights, and to improve systems of education; organizes training courses for teachers, and international congresses connected with education; creates training centres and new national Montessori Associations. Pres. G. J. PORTIELJE; Organizing Sec. J. DEN ENGELSMAN. Publ. *Communications* (quarterly).

International Reading Association: 800 Barksdale Rd, POB 8139, Newark, Del 19714-8139, USA; tel. (302) 731-1600; telex 5106002813; f. 1956 to improve the quality of reading instruction at all levels, to promote the habit of lifelong reading, and to develop every reader's proficiency. Mems: 80,000 in 90 countries. Pres. PATRICIA KOPPMAN. Publs *The Reading Teacher* (9 a year), *Journal of Reading* (8 a year), *Reading Research Quarterly*, *Lectura y Vida* (quarterly in Spanish), *Reading Today* (6 a year).

International Schools Association—ISA: CIC CASE 20, 1211 Geneva 20, Switzerland; f. 1951 to co-ordinate work in international schools and promote their development; member schools maintain the highest standards and accept pupils of all nationalities, irrespective of race and creed. ISA carries out curriculum research; convenes annual conferences on problems of curriculum and educational reform; organizes occasional teachers' training workshops and specialist seminars; has consultative status with UNESCO, UNEP, UNICEF and ECOSOC. Mems: 80 schools throughout the world. Pres. ROBERT BELLE-ISLE. Publs *Education Bulletin* (2 a year), *ISA Magazine* (annually), *Conference Report* (annually), curriculum studies (occasional).

International Society for Business Education: Bureau Permanent, Rédaction de la Revue Félix Schmidt, 1052 Le Mont sur Lausanne, Switzerland; f. 1901 to organize international courses and congresses on business education; 2,200 mems, national organizations and individuals in 15 countries. Pres. CHRISTIAN THIERSTEIN (Switzerland); Dir Prof. FELIX SCHMID (Switzerland). Publ. *International Review for Business Education*.

International Society for Education through Art: c/o NSEAD, 7A High St, Corsham, Wilts, SN13 0ES, England; tel. (0249) 714825; f. 1951 to unite art teachers throughout the world, to exchange information and to co-ordinate research into art education; organizes international congresses and exhibitions of children's art. Pres. Prof. ELLIOT EISNER (USA); Sec. JOHN STEERS. Publ. *INSEA News*.

International Society for Music Education: 14 Bedford Sq., London, WC1B 3JG; tel. (01) 636-5400; f. 1953 to organize international conferences, seminars and publications on matters pertaining to music education; acts as advisory body to UNESCO in matters of music education. Mems: national committees and individuals in 58 countries. Pres. KATALIN FORRAI (Hungary); Sec.-Gen. RONALD SMITH (UK). Publ. *ISME Yearbook and Journal*.

International Society for the Study of Medieval Philosophy: Collège Thomas More, 1348 Louvain-la-Neuve, Belgium; tel. (010) 47-48-07; telex 59037; f. 1958 to promote the study of medieval thought and the collaboration between individuals and institutions concerned in this field; organizes international congresses. Mems: 511. Pres. Prof. TULLIO GREGORY (Italy); Sec. Dr JACQUELINE HAMESSE (Belgium). Publ. *Bulletin de Philosophie Médiévale* (annually).

International Youth Library (Internationale Jugendbibliothek): 8000 Munich 60, Schloss Blutenburg, Federal Republic of Germany; tel. (089) 8112028; f. 1948, since 1953 an associated project of UNESCO, to promote the international exchange of children's literature and to provide study opportunities for specialists in children's books. Maintains a library of over 460,000 volumes in about 120 languages. Dir of the Library Board Dr ANDREAS BODE. Publs *The White Ravens, IJB Bulletin, IJB Report,* catalogues.

League of European Research Libraries—LIBER: Universitätsbibliothek Graz, 8010 Graz, Universitätsplatz 3, Austria; tel. (0316) 380-3101; telex 03-11662; f. 1971 to establish close collaboration between the general research libraries of Europe, and national and university libraries in particular; and to help in finding practical ways of improving the quality of the services these libraries provide. Mems: 180. Pres. FRANZ KROLLER. Publs *LIBER Bulletin* (2 a year), *LIBER News Sheet* (2 or 3 a year).

Organization for Museums, Monuments and Sites in Africa: Centre for Museum Studies, PMB 2031, Jos, Nigeria; f. 1975 to foster the collection, study and conservation of the natural and cultural heritage of Africa; co-operation between member countries through seminars, workshops, conferences, etc., exchange of personnel, training facilities. Mems from 30 countries. Pres. Dr J. M. ESSOMBA (Cameroon); Sec.-Gen. KWASI MYLES.

Organization of Ibero-American States for Education, Science and Culture (Organización de Estados Iberoamericanos para la Educación, la Ciencia y la Cultura): Ciudad Universitaría, 28040 Madrid, Spain; tel. 449 69 54; telex 48422; f. 1949 (as the Ibero-American Bureau of Education); provides information on education, science and culture; encourages exchanges and organizes training courses; the General Assembly (at ministerial level) meets every four years. Mems: governments of 20 countries. Sec.-Gen. SIMÓN ROMERO LOZANO. Publs *Educación—Noticias de Educación, Ciencia y Cultura Iberoamericana* (every 2 months), *Sumarios de Revistas de Educación* (2 a year), studies.

Organization of the Catholic Universities of Latin America (Organización de Universidades Católicas de América Latina—ODUCAL): c/o Rev. Dr A. N. Fosbery, Univ. del Norte Santo Tomas de Aquino, 9 de Julio 165, CP 4000, San Miguel de Tucuman, Argentina; f. 1953 to assist the social, economic and cultural development of Latin America through the promotion of Catholic higher education in the continent. Mems: 24 Catholic universities in Argentina, Brazil, Chile, Colombia, Dominican Republic, Ecuador, Mexico, Nicaragua, Paraguay, Peru, Puerto Rico and Venezuela. Pres. Rev. Dr ANNIBAL ERNESZT FOSBERY (Argentina); Publs *Anuario; Sapientia; Universitas.*

Regional Centre for Adult Education and Functional Literacy in Latin America (Centro Regional de Educación de Adultos y Alfabetización Funcional para América Latina): Quinta Eréndira s/n, Pátzcuaro, Michoacán, Mexico; tel. 20005; f. 1951 by UNESCO and OAS to encourage literacy and rural development through adult education and co-operative research; library of 60,000 vols. Dir Dr LUIS G. BENAVIDES ILIZALITURRI. Publ. *Retablos de Papel, Cuadernos del CREFAL.*

Southeast Asian Ministers of Education Organization —SEAMEO: Darakarn Bldg, 920 Sukhumvit Rd, Bangkok 10110, Thailand; tel. 391 0144; f. 1965 to promote co-operation among the Southeast Asian nations through education, science and culture, and to advance the mutual knowledge and understanding of the peoples in Southeast Asia. Mems: Brunei, Indonesia, Kampuchea, Laos, Malaysia, the Philippines, Singapore and Thailand; Assoc. mems: Australia, Canada, France and New Zealand. Pres. Prof. Dr FUAD HASSAN (Indonesia); Dir Prof. Dr JAKUB ISMAN. Publs *SEAMEO Quarterly.*

Standing Conference of Rectors, Presidents and Vice-Chancellors of the European Universities (Conférence permanente des recteurs, présidents et vice-chanceliers des universités européennes—CRE): 10 rue du Conseil Général, 1211 Geneva 4, Switzerland; tel. (022) 292644; telex 428380; f. 1959; holds two conferences a year, a General Assembly every five years, and special seminars. Mems: 370 university heads in 23 countries. Pres. Prof. CARMINE ROMANZI; Sec.-Gen. Dr ANDRIS BARBLAN; Asst Sec.-Gen. ALISON M. DE PUYMÈGE. Publ. *CRE-action* (4 a year).

Union of Latin American Universities (Unión de Universidades de América Latina—UDUAL): Edificio UDUAL, Apdo postal 70-232, Ciudad Universitaria, Del. Coyoacán, 04510 México, DF, Mexico; tel. 548-9786; telex 1777429; f. 1949 to further the improvement of university association, to organize the interchange of professors, students, research fellows and graduates and generally encourage good relations between the Latin American universities; arranges conferences, conducts statistical research; centre for university documentation. Mems: 151 universities. Pres. Dr JORGE CARPIZO (Mexico); Sec.-Gen. Dr JOSÉ LUIS SOBERANES. Publs *Universidades* (annually), *Gaceta UDUAL* (quarterly), *Censo* (every 2 years).

Universal Esperanto Association: Nieuwe Binnenweg 176, 3015 BJ Rotterdam, Netherlands; tel. (010) 4361044; telex 23721; f. 1908 to assist the spread of the international language, Esperanto, and to facilitate the practical use of the language. Mems: 45 affiliated national associations and 43,642 individuals in 104 countries. Pres. Dr HUMPHREY TONKIN (USA); Gen. Sec. Dr FLORÁ SZABÓ-FELSÖ (Hungary). Publs *Esperanto* (monthly), *Kontakto* (every 2 months), *Jarlibro* (yearbook), *Esperanto Documents.*

World Association for Educational Research: Rijksuniversiteit Gent, Pedagogisch Laboratorium, 1 Henri Dunantlaan, 9000 Ghent, Belgium; tel. (91) 25-41-00; f. 1953, present title adopted 1977; aims to encourage research in educational sciences by organizing congress, issuing publications, the exchange of information, etc. Member societies and individual members in 50 countries. Pres. Prof. Dr ARTURO DE LA ORDÉN (Spain); Gen. Sec. Prof. Dr M.-L. VAN HERREWEGHE (Belgium). Publ. *Communicationes* (2 a year).

World Confederation of Organizations of the Teaching Profession: 5 ave du Moulin, 1110 Morges, Vaud, Switzerland; tel. (021) 8017467; telex 458 219; f. 1952 to foster a conception of education directed toward the promotion of international understanding and goodwill; to improve teaching methods, educational organization and the training of teachers to equip them better to serve the interests of youth; to defend the rights and the material and moral interests of the teaching profession; to promote closer relationships between teachers in different countries. Mems: 162 national teachers' associations in 110 countries. Pres. JOSEPH O. ITOTOH; Sec.-Gen. ROBERT HARRIS. Publs *WCOTP Biennial Report* (in English, French, Spanish), *Echo* (quarterly, in English, French, Spanish, Japanese, Chinese and German).

World Education Fellowship: 33 Kinnaird Ave, London, W4 3SH, England; tel. (01) 994-7258; f. 1921 to promote education for international understanding, and the exchange and practice of ideas together with research into progressive educational theories and methods. Sections and groups in 20 countries. Pres. Mrs MADHURI R. SHAH; Chair. Prof. NORMAN GRAVES; Sec. Mrs R. CROMMELIN. Publ. *The New Era in Education* (3 a year).

World Union of Catholic Teachers (Union Mondiale des Enseignants Catholiques—UMEC): Piazza San Calisto 16, 00120 Città del Vaticano; tel. 698-7286; f. 1951. Objects: (1) on the national level, the Union encourages the grouping of Catholic teachers for the greater effectiveness of the Catholic school, distributes documentation on Catholic doctrine with regard to education, and facilitates personal contacts through congresses, seminars, etc.; (2) on the international level, the Union is a member of the Conference of International Catholic Organizations, and has consultative status with UNESCO and other UN agencies, and with the Council of Europe and other non-governmental organizations. Mems: 63 organizations in 56 countries. Pres. HARRY MELLON; Sec.-Gen. GIUSEPPE CICOLINI. Publ. *Nouvelles de l'UMEC.*

Government and Politics

African Association for Public Administration and Management: POB 60087, Addis Ababa, Ethiopia; tel. 150389; telex 21029; f. 1971 to provide senior officials with opportunities for exchanging ideas and experience, to promote the study of professional techniques and encourage research in particular African administrative problems. Mems: over 500 corporate and individual. Pres WILLIAM N. WAMALWA; Sec.-Gen. GELASE MUTAHABA. Publs *Newsletter* (quarterly), *Annual Seminar Report,* studies.

Afro-Asian Peoples' Solidarity Organization—AAPSO: 89 Abdel Aziz Al-Saoud St, Manial, Cairo, Egypt; tel. 843066; telex 92627; f. 1957; acts among and for the peoples of Africa and Asia in their struggle for genuine independence, sovereignty, socio-economic development, peace and disarmament; sixth Congress held in 1984 (the first since 1972). Mems: 82 national committees and 10 affiliated European organizations. Pres. Dr MOURAD GHALEB; Sec.-Gen. NOURI ABDAR-RAZZAK (Iraq). Publ. *Socio-Economic Development and Progress* (quarterly).

Agency for the Prohibition of Nuclear Weapons in Latin America (Organismo para la Proscripción de las Armas Nucleares en la América Latina—OPANAL): Temístocles 78, Col. Polanco, CP 11560, México, DF, Mexico; tel. 250-62-22; f. 1969 to administer the Treaty for the Prohibition of Nuclear Weapons in Latin America (Treaty of Tlatelolco), 1967; to ensure the absence of all nuclear weapons in the application zone of the Treaty; to provide protection against possible nuclear attacks on the zone; to contribute to the movement against proliferation of nuclear weapons; to promote general and complete disarmament; to prohibit all testing, use, manufacture, acquisition, storage, installation and any form of possession, by any means, of nuclear weapons. Mems: 23 states which have fully ratified the Treaty. The Treaty has two additional Protocols; the first signed and ratified by the UK, the Netherlands and the USA, and signed by France; the second signed and ratified by China, the USA, France, the UK and the USSR. Sec.-Gen. Dr ANTONIO STEMPEL PARÍS (Venezuela).

Association of Secretaries General of Parliaments: c/o Committee Office, House of Commons, London, SW1, England; f. 1938; studies the law, practice and working methods of different Parliaments and proposes measures for improving those methods and for securing co-operation between the services of different Parliaments; operates as a consultative body to the Inter-Parliamentary Union (q.v.), and assists the Union on subjects within the scope of the Association. Mems: about 125, representing about 60 countries. Pres. Sir KENNETH BRADSHAW (UK); Joint Sec. A. R. KENNON (UK). Publ. *Constitutional and Parliamentary Information* (quarterly).

Atlantic Treaty Association: 185 rue de la Pompe, 75116 Paris, France; tel. (1) 45-53-28-80; f. 1954 to inform public opinion on the North Atlantic Alliance and to promote the solidarity of the peoples of the North Atlantic; holds annual assemblies, seminars, study conferences for teachers and young politicians. Mems: national associations in the 16 member countries of NATO (q.v.). Chair. FRANCIS PYM; Sec.-Gen. JEAN BELIARD (France).

Celtic League: 24 St Germains Place, Peel, Isle of Man; f. 1961 to foster co-operation between the six Celtic nations (Ireland, Scotland, Man, Wales, Cornwall and Brittany), especially those who are actively working for political autonomy by non-violent means; campaigns politically on issues affecting the Celtic countries; monitors military activity in the Celtic countries; co-operates with national cultural organizations to promote the languages and culture of the Celts. Mems: approx. 1,400 individuals in the Celtic communities and elsewhere. Chair. D. BERESFORD ELLIS; Gen. Sec. D. FEAR. Publ. *Carn* (quarterly).

Christian Democrat International: 16 rue de la Victoire, Boîte 1, 1060 Brussels, Belgium; tel. (02) 537-13-22; telex 61118; f.1961; to serve as a platform for the co-operation of political parties of Christian Social inspiration. Mems: parties in 21 countries. Sec.-Gen. LUÍS HERRERA-CAMPINS. Publ. *CD-Info* (quarterly, in six languages).

Confederation of Socialist Parties of the European Community: 13 rue Belliard, 1040 Brussels, Belgium; tel. (02) 234-29-76; telex 62184; f. 1974; affiliated to the Socialist International (q.v.). Mems: 14 parties, and seven with observer status. Chair. JOOP DEN UYL (Netherlands); Sec.-Gen. MAURO GIALLOMBARDO (Italy).

Contadora Group: c/o Secretariat for Foreign Affairs, Avda Constituyentes 161, 7°, 11850 México, DF, Mexico; tel. 2775470; telex 1763478; comprises representatives of Colombia, Mexico, Panama and Venezuela, with a 'support group' representing Argentina, Brazil, Peru and Uruguay; first met January 1983 on the island of Contadora, Panama, to seek a peaceful solution to conflict in the countries of Central America (Costa Rica, El Salvador, Guatemala, Honduras and Nicaragua) through negotiating the withdrawal of external and irregular military forces and the holding of democratic elections. In September 1984 the Group submitted a draft agreement, the 'Acta de Contadora para la paz y la cooperación en Centroamérica', to the Central American countries. Subsequent discussion failed to resolve questions of arms control and demilitarization in the region, and in 1986 the June deadline for signing a regional peace treaty passed without agreement, although a summit meeting of Central American leaders, held in May, agreed to establish a Central American parliament. In August 1987 the Group expressed support for the 'Esquipulas II' peace plan for Central America proposed by the President of Costa Rica, Oscar Arias. (See chapters on the countries concerned.)

Eastern Regional Organization for Public Administration—EROPA: Rizal Hall, Padre Faura St, Manila, Philippines; tel. 596378; f. 1960 to promote regional co-operation in improving knowledge, systems and practices of governmental administration to help accelerate economic and social development; organizes regional conferences, seminars, special studies, surveys and training programmes. There are three regional centres: Training Centre (New Delhi), Local Government Centre (Tokyo), Development Management Centre (Seoul). Mems: 13 countries, 86 organizations, 256 individuals. Chair. PATRICIA ST TOMAS (Philippines); Sec.-Gen. RAUL P. DE GUZMAN (Philippines). Publs *EROPA Bulletin* (quarterly), *EROPA Journal*.

European Movement: 66 rue de Trèves, 1040 Brussels, Belgium; tel. (02) 230-08-51; f. 1947 by a liaison committee of representatives from European organizations, to study the political, economic and technical problems of a European Union and suggest how they can be solved; to inform and lead public opinion in the promotion of integration. Conferences have led to the creation of the Council of Europe, College of Europe, etc. Mems: European movements and national councils in Austria, Belgium, Denmark, France, Federal Republic of Germany, Greece, Ireland, Italy, Luxembourg, Malta, Netherlands, Norway, Spain, Sweden, Switzerland, United Kingdom and several international social and economic organizations. Pres. ENRIQUE BARÓN CRESPO (Spain); Sec.-Gen. J. H. C. MOLENAAR (Netherlands).

European Union of Women—EUW: Nymphenburger Str 64, 8000 Munich, Federal Republic of Germany; f. 1955 to increase the influence of women in the political and civic life of their country and of Europe. Mems: 16 member countries. Chair. URSULA SCHLEICHER. Publ. *Bulletin* (biennial).

European Young Christian Democrats—EYCD: 16 rue de la Victoire, 1060 Brussels, Belgium; tel. (02) 537-41-47; telex 63885; f. 1947; holds monthly seminars and meetings for young political leaders; conducts training in international political matters. Mems: 20 organizations in 18 European countries, Pres. ANDREA DE GUTTRY (Italy); Sec.-Gen. MARC BERTRAND (Belgium). Publ. *Newsletter* (monthly), *CD-Future* (quarterly).

Group of Eight: f. 1987 at a meeting in Acapulco, Mexico, of eight Latin American government leaders, who agreed to establish a 'permanent mechanism for joint political action'. The group discussed, in particular, the region's foreign debt, and demanded a reduction in interest rates and a limit on debt-service payments. Mems: Argentina, Brazil, Colombia, Mexico, Panama, Peru, Uruguay and Venezuela.

Hansard Society for Parliamentary Government: 16 Gower St, London, WC1E 6DP, England; tel. (01) 323-1131; f. 1944 to promote political education and research and the informed discussion of all aspects of modern parliamentary government. Dir MARY GOUDIE. Publ. *Parliamentary Affairs—A Journal of Comparative Politics* (quarterly), reports and teaching aids.

Inter-African Socialists and Democrats: c/o RCD, blvd 9 avril 1938, Tunis, Tunisia; f. 1981 (as Inter-African Socialist Organization; name changed 1988). Chair. ABDOU DIOUF (Senegal); Sec.-Gen. HEDI BACCOUCHE (Tunisia).

International Alliance of Women: 1st Floor, Jebb Wing, Regent's College, Inner Circle, Regent's Park, London, NW1 9NS, England; tel. (01) 487-7437; f. 1904 to obtain equality for women in all fields and to encourage women to take up their responsibilities; to join in international activities. Mems: 75 national affiliates in 65 countries. Pres. Mrs OLIVE BLOOMER. Publ. *International Women's News* (quarterly).

International Association of Educators for World Peace: POB 3282, Mastin Lake Station, Huntsville, Alabama 35810, USA; tel. (205) 534-5501; f. 1969 to develop the kind of education which will contribute to the promotion of peaceful relations at personal, community and international levels, to communicate and clarify controversial views in order to achieve maximum understanding and to help put into practice the Universal Declaration of Human Rights. Mems: 17,500 in 52 countries. Pres. Prof. NORMAN MARCUS (UK); Exec. Vice-Pres. Dr CHARLES MERCIECA (USA); Sec.-Gen. Dr GEORGE VAIDEANU (Romania). Publs *Peace Progress* (annually), *IAEWP Newsletter* (quarterly), *Peace Education* (2 a year).

International Commission for the History of Representative and Parliamentary Institutions: c/o M. S. Corciulo, Via A. Baldassarri 25, 00139 Rome, Italy; tel. (06) 8125156; f. 1936. Mems: 300 individuals in 31 countries. Pres. S. MASTELLONE (Italy); Sec. M. S. CORCIULO (Italy). Publs *Parliaments, Estates and Representation*; many monographs.

International Democrat Union: 48 Westminster Palace Gardens, Artillery Row, London, SW1P 1RR, England; tel. (01) 222-0847; telex 8955242; f. 1983; group of centre-right political parties; holds conference every six months. Mems: 28 political parties within and outside Europe. Exec. Sec. SCOTT HAMILTON.

International Federation of Resistance Movements: 1021 Vienna II, Alliiertenstrasse 2-4/5, Austria; tel. (01) 247135; f. 1951; supports the medical and social welfare of former victims of fascism; works for peace, disarmament and human rights, against fascism and neo-fascism; has consultative status at UN Economic and Social Council and UNESCO. Mems: 72 national organizations in 27 European countries and in Israel. Pres. ARIALDO BANFI (Italy); Sec.-Gen. ALIX LHOTE (France). Publs *Résistance Unie—Service d'Information* (5 a year, in French and German), *Cahier d'informations médicales, sociales et juridiques* (in French and German).

International Institute for Peace: 1040 Vienna, Mollwaldplatz 4, Austria; f. 1957; studies the possibilities, principles and forms of peaceful co-existence and co-operation between the two social world systems. Mems: individuals and corporate bodies invited by the executive board. Pres. Dr GEORG FUCHS (Austria); Vice-Pres. Prof. Dr RAIMO VÄYRYNEN (Finland), Prof. Dr OLEG BYKOV (USSR). Publ. *Peace and the Sciences* (in English and German).

International Institute for Strategic Studies: 23 Tavistock St, London, WC2E 7NQ, England; tel. (01) 379-7676; telex 265871; f. 1958; concerned with the study of the role of force in international relations, including problems of international strategy, disarmament and arms control, peace-keeping and intervention, defence economics, etc.; is independent of any government. Mems: 3,000. Dir FRANÇOIS HEISBOURG. Publs *Survival* (every 2 months), *The Military Balance* (annually), *Strategic Survey* (annually), *Adelphi Papers* (10 a year), *Studies in International Security* (occasional).

International League for Human Rights: 432 Park Avenue South, 11th Floor, New York, NY 10016, USA; tel. (212) 684-1221; f. 1942 to implement political, civil, social, economic and cultural rights contained in the Universal Declaration of Human Rights adopted by the United Nations and to support and protect defenders of human rights world-wide. Maintains consultative relations with UN, ILO, UNESCO and the Council of Europe. Mems: individuals, national affiliates and correspondents throughout the world. Exec. Dir FELICE D. GAER. Publs *Review*, *Human Rights Bulletin*, human rights reports.

International Peace Bureau: 41 rue de Zürich, 1200 Geneva, Switzerland; tel. (022) 316429; telex 289712; f. 1892; promotes international co-operation for general and complete disarmament and the non-violent solution of international conflicts; the Bureau was awarded the Nobel Peace Prize in 1910. Mems: international organizations, national peace councils or other federations co-ordinating peace movements in their respective countries, national and local organizations, totalling 75 organizations with a total affiliated membership of about 30 million. Pres. BRUCE KENT; Sec.-Gen. RAINER SANTI. Publs *Geneva Monitor* (every 2 months), *IPB Geneva News*.

International Political Science Association: c/o University of Ottawa, Ottawa, Ontario K1N 6N5, Canada; tel. (613) 564-5818; telex 053-3338; f. 1949; aims to promote the development of political science. Mems: 39 national associations, 105 institutions, 1,200 individual mems. Pres. KINHIDE MUSHAKOJI (Japan); Sec.-Gen.

JOHN E. TRENT (Canada). Publs *Newsletter* (3 a year), *Information Supplement* (annually), *International Political Science Abstracts* (bi-monthly), *International Political Science Review* (quarterly), *Advances in Political Science* (annually).

International Union of Local Authorities: Wassenaarseweg 41, 2596 CG The Hague, Netherlands; tel. (070) 244032; telex 30510; f. 1913 to promote local government, improve local administration and encourage popular participation in public affairs. Functions include organization of conferences, seminars, and biennial international congress; servicing of specialized committees (municipal insurance, wholesale markets, European affairs, technical); research projects; comparative courses for local government officials, primarily from developing countries; development of inter-municipal relations to provide a link between local authorities of all countries; maintenance of a permanent office for the collection and distribution of information on municipal affairs. Members in over 65 countries. Pres. LARS ERIC ERICSSON (Sweden); Sec.-Gen. JACEK ZAPASNIK. Publs *Local Government* (monthly newsletter), *Bibliographia* (every 2 months), *Planning and Administration* (2 a year).

International Union of Young Christian Democrats—IUYCD: Via del Plebiscito 107, 00186 Rome, Italy; tel. 6784535; telex 611356; f. 1962. Mems: 54 national organizations. Pres. GUILLERMO YUNGE (Chile); Sec.-Gen. FILIPPO LOMBARDI (Switzerland). Publs *Information* (monthly), *Documents* (quarterly).

Inter-Parliamentary Union: place du Petit-Saconnex, CP 438, 1211 Geneva 19, Switzerland; tel. (022) 344150; telex 289784; f. 1889 to promote personal contacts among the members of the world's parliaments, with a view to the firm establishment and development of representative institutions and to advancing international peace and co-operation; holds two conferences annually, bringing together national groups of MPs to study political, economic, social and cultural problems; there are four Committees comprising representatives of all national groups. The Union operates an International Centre for Parliamentary Documentation, and co-ordinates a technical co-operation programme to help strengthen the infrastructures of legislatures in developing countries. Budget (1989) 5.9m. Swiss francs. Mems: 110 Inter-Parliamentary Groups. Assoc. Mem.: the European Parliament. Pres. of Inter-Parliamentary Council DAOUDA SOW (Senegal); Sec.-Gen. PIERRE CORNILLON (France). Publs. *Inter-Parliamentary Bulletin* (quarterly), *World Directory of Parliaments* (annually), *Chronicle of Parliamentary Elections and Developments* (annually), *Parliaments of the World: A Reference Compendium*.

Inuit Circumpolar Conference: Box 204, Godthåb, Greenland; tel. 23632; telex 90671; f. 1977 to protect the indigenous culture, environment and rights of the Inuit people (Eskimoes), and to encourage co-operation among the Inuit; conferences held every three years. Mems: Inuit communities in Canada, Greenland and Alaska. Pres. HANS-PAVIA ROSING.

Jewish Agency for Israel: POB 91920, Jerusalem, Israel; f. 1929 as an instrument through which world Jewry could build up a national home. It is now the executive arm of the World Zionist Organization. Mems: Zionist federations in 45 countries. Exec. Chair. LEON DULZIN; Sec.-Gen. HARRY M. ROSEN. Publs *Israel Digest* (weekly), *Economic Horizons* (monthly in USA), *Folk und Zion* (monthly in Yiddish).

Latin American Parliament (Parlamento Latinoamericano): c/o Cámara de Diputados, Buenos Aires, Argentina; f. 1965; permanent democratic institution, representative of all existing political trends within the national legislative bodies of Latin America; aims to promote the movement towards economic, political and cultural integration of the Latin American republics, and to uphold human rights, peace and security. Sec.-Gen. ANDRÉS TOWNSEND EZCURRA (Peru). Publs *Acuerdos, Resoluciones de las Asambleas Ordinarias* (annually), *Revista del Parlamento Latinoamericano* (annually); statements and agreements.

Liberal International: 1 Whitehall Place, London, SW1A 2HE, England; tel. (01) 839-5905; telex 8956551; f. 1947 to bring together people of liberal ideas and principles all over the world and to secure international co-operation amongst the political parties which accept the Manifesto (1947), the Liberal Declaration of Oxford (1967) and the Appeal of Rome (1981), and are affiliated to the International. Pres. Senator GIOVANNI MALAGODI (Italy); Exec. Vice-Pres. URS SCHÖTTLI (Switzerland).

Non-aligned Movement: Co-ordination Bureau, ul. Kneza Miloša 24, 11000 Belgrade, Yugoslavia; f. 1961 by a meeting of 25 Heads of State, aiming to link countries which refuse to adhere to the main East-West military and political blocs; co-ordination bureau established in 1973; works for the establishment of a new international economic order, and especially for better terms for countries producing raw materials; maintains special funds for agricultural development, improvement of food production and the financing of buffer stocks; 'South-South Commission' promotes co-operation between developing countries. Ninth summit conference: Belgrade, Yugoslavia, 1989. Mems: 101 (including the Palestine Liberation Organization and the South-West Africa People's Organisation).

North Atlantic Assembly: 3 place du Petit Sablon, Brussels, Belgium; tel. (02) 513-28-65; telex 24809; f. 1955 as the NATO Parliamentarians' Conference; name changed 1966; the inter-parliamentary assembly of the North Atlantic Alliance; holds two plenary sessions a year and meetings of committees (Political, Military, Economic, Scientific and Technical, Civilian Affairs, Special Committee on NATO Strategy and Arms Control) where North Americans and Europeans examine the problems confronting the Alliance. Pres. T. FRINKING (Netherlands); Sec.-Gen. PETER CORTERIER (FRG). Publs *North Atlantic Assembly News*, *Bulletin*.

Open Door International (for the Economic Emancipation of the Woman Worker); 16 rue Américaine, 1050 Brussels, Belgium; tel. (02) 537-67-61; f. 1929 to obtain equal rights and opportunities for women in the whole field of work. Mems in 10 countries. Pres. ESTHER HODGE (UK); Hon. Sec. ADÈLE HAUWEL (Belgium).

Organization of Central American States (Organización de Estados Centroamericanos—ODECA): 81 Avda Norte 520, Colonia Escalón, San Salvador, El Salvador; f. 1951 to strengthen unity in Central America, settle disputes, provide mutual assistance and promote economic, social and cultural development through joint action. Mems: Costa Rica, El Salvador, Guatemala, Honduras, Nicaragua. Gen. Sec. RICARDO JUÁREZ MÁRQUEZ (Guatemala).

Organization of Solidarity of the Peoples of Africa, Asia and Latin America (Organización de Solidaridad de los Pueblos de Africa, Asia y América Latina—OSPAAAL): Apdo 4224, Havana 10400, Cuba; tel. 30-5520; telex 512259; f. 1966 at the first Conference of Solidarity of the Peoples of Africa, Asia and Latin America, to unite, co-ordinate and encourage national liberation movements in the three continents, to oppose foreign intervention in the affairs of sovereign states, colonial and neo-colonial practices, and to fight against racialism and all forms of racial discrimination; favours the establishment of a new international economic order. Mems: revolutionary organizations in 82 countries. Sec.-Gen. Dr RENÉ ANILLO CAPOTE. Publ. *Tricontinental* (every 2 months, in English, French and Spanish).

Organization of the Cooperatives of America (Organización de las Cooperativas de América): Carrera 11, No 79-19 (302), Apdo Postal 241263, Bogotá, DE, Colombia; tel. 2552867; telex 45103; f. 1963 for improving socio-economic, cultural and moral conditions through the use of the co-operatives system; works in every country of the continent; regional offices sponsor plans of activities based on the most pressing needs and special conditions of individual countries. Mems: 7,000. Pres. Dr ARMANDO TOVAR PARADA; Exec. Sec. CARLOS JULIO PINEDA. Publ. *Cooperative America* (every 4 months, in Spanish).

Parliamentary Association for Euro-Arab Co-operation: 33–35 ave d'Auderghem, 1040 Brussels, Belgium; tel. (02) 231-13-00; f. 1974 as an association of more than 650 parliamentarians of all parties from the national parliaments of the 21 Council of Europe countries and from the European Parliament, to promote friendship and co-operation between Europe and the Arab World; Executive Committee holds joint meetings with Arab Parliamentary Union; represented in Council of Europe, Western European Union and European Parliament, and has observer status with the UN (ECOSOC) and the Inter-Parliamentary Union; works for the progress of the Euro-Arab Dialogue and a settlement in the Middle East which takes into account the national rights of the Palestinian people. Joint Chair. MICHELE ACHILLI (Italy), MICHAEL LANIGAN (Ireland); Sec.-Gen. HANS-PETER KOTTHAUS.

Socialist International: Maritime House, Old Town, Clapham, London, SW4 0JW, England; tel. (01) 627-4449; telex 261735; f. 1864; the world's oldest and largest association of political parties, grouping democratic socialist, labour and social democratic parties from every continent; provides a forum for political action, policy discussion and the exchange of ideas; works with many international organizations and trades unions (particularly members of ICFTU, q.v.); holds Congress every three years; the Council meets twice a year, and regular conferences and meetings of party leaders are also held; committees and councils on a variety of subjects and in different regions meet frequently. Mems: 47 full member parties and 23 consultative parties in 59 countries. There are three fraternal organizations (see below) and nine associated organizations, including: the Asia-Pacific Socialist Organization; the Confederation of Socialist Parties of the European Community (q.v.); and the International Federation of the Socialist and Democratic Press (q.v.). Pres. WILLY BRANDT (FRG); Gen. Sec. PENTTI VAANANEN; Publ. *Socialist Affairs* (quarterly).

International Falcon Movement—Socialist Educational International: 13 place du Samedi, 1000 Brussels, Belgium; tel. (02) 217-97-86; f. 1924 to promote international understanding, develop a sense of social responsibility and to prepare children and adolescents for democratic life. The Movement has consultative status with ECOSOC, UNESCO and Council of Europe and co-operates with several institutions concerned with children, youth and education. Mems: about 1m.; 62 co-operating organizations in all countries. Pres. NIC NILLSON (Sweden); Sec.-Gen. JACQUI COTTYN (Belgium). Publs *IFM-SEI Bulletin* (quarterly in English, French, German, Spanish, Finnish and Swedish), *IFM-SEI Documents* (in the same languages).

International Union of Socialist Youth: 1070 Vienna, Neustiftgasse 3, Austria; f. 1946 to educate young people in the principles of free and democratic socialism and further the co-operation of democratic socialist youth organizations; conducts international meetings, symposia, etc. Mems: 75 youth and student organizations in 56 countries. Pres. JOAN CALABUIG; Gen. Sec. RICARD TORRELL. Publ. *IUSY Newsletter*.

Socialist International Women: Maritime House, Old Town, Clapham, London, SW4 0JW, England; tel. (01) 627-4449; telex 261735; f. 1955 to strengthen relations between its members, to exchange experience and views, to promote the understanding among women of the aims of democratic socialism, to promote programmes to oppose any discrimination in society and to work for human rights in general and for development and peace. Mems: 57 organizations. Pres. ANITA GRADIN; Gen. Sec. MARÍA RODRÍGUEZ-JONAS. Publ. *Bulletin* (quarterly).

Stockholm International Peace Research Institute—SIPRI: Pipers väg 28, 171 73 Solna, Sweden; tel. 46 8 559700; f. 1966; studies relate to disarmament and arms control, e.g. the implications of new weapon technology, production and transfer of arms, military expenditure, etc. About 55 staff mems, half of whom are research workers. Dir Dr WALTHER STÜTZLE (FRG); Chair. Dr INGA THORSSON (Sweden). Publs *SIPRI Yearbook*, *Monographs*, and research reports.

Trilateral Commission: 345 East 46th St, New York, NY 10017, USA; tel. (212) 661-1180; telex 650-252-5637; (also offices in Paris and Tokyo); f. 1973 by private citizens of Western Europe, Japan and North America, to encourage closer co-operation among these regions on matters of common concern; by analysis of major issues the Commission seeks to improve public understanding of such problems, to develop and support proposals for handling them jointly, and to nurture the habit of working together in the 'trilateral' area. The Commission issues 'task force' reports on such subjects as monetary affairs, political co-operation, trade issues, the energy crisis and reform of international institutions. Mems: about 300 individuals eminent in academic life, industry, finance, labour, etc.; those currently engaged as senior government officials are excluded. Chairmen DAVID ROCKEFELLER, GEORGES BERTHOIN, ISAMU YAMASHITA; Dirs CHARLES B. HECK, PAUL REVAY, TADASHI YAMAMOTO. Publs Task Force Reports, Triangle Papers.

War Resisters' International: 55 Dawes St, London, SE17 1EL, England; tel. (01) 703-7189; f. 1921; encourages refusal to participate in or support wars or military service, collaborates with peace and non-violent social change movements. Mems: approx. 200,000. Chair. NARAYAN DESAI; Secs HOWARD CLARK, VERONICA KELLY. Publs *Newsletter* (6 a year in English).

Women's International Democratic Federation: 1080 Berlin, Unter den Linden 13, German Democratic Republic; f. 1945 to unite women regardless of nationality, race, religion and political opinion, so that they may work together to win and defend their rights as citizens, mothers and workers, to protect children and to ensure peace and progress, democracy and national independence. Structure: Congress, Council, Bureau, Secretariat and Finance Control Commission. Mems: 138 organizations in 124 countries as well as individual mems. Pres. FREDA BROWN (Australia); Sec.-Gen. MIRJAM VIRE-TUOMINEN (Finland). Publs *Women of the Whole World* (quarterly in 6 languages), *Documents and Information*, *News in Brief*, *Women in Action* (4 languages).

World Association for World Federation: Leliegracht 21, 1016 GR Amsterdam, Netherlands; tel. (020) 227502; f. 1947 to achieve a just world order through a strengthened United Nations; to acquire for the UN the authority to make and enforce laws for peaceful settlement of disputes, to govern the high seas and outer space, and to raise revenue under limited taxing powers; to establish better international co-operation in areas of environment, development and disarmament. Mems: 25,000 in 20 countries. Pres. Dr J. F. LEDDY. Publs *World Federalist News* (quarterly).

World Council of Indigenous Peoples: 555 King Edward Ave, Ottawa, Ontario K1N 6N5, Canada; tel. (613) 230-9030; telex 0533338; f. 1975 to promote the rights of indigenous peoples and to support their cultural, social and economic development. The organization is divided into five regions: North, South and Central America, Pacific-Asia and Scandinavia. Pres. DONALD ROJAS MAROTO. Publ. *WCIP Newsletter* (4-6 a year).

World Disarmament Campaign: 45-47 Blythe St, London, E2 6LX, England; tel. (01) 729-2523; f. 1980 to encourage governments to take positive and decisive action to end the arms race, acting on the four main commitments called for in the Final Document of the UN's First Special Session on Disarmament; aims to mobilize people of every country in a demand for multilateral disarmament, and to encourage consideration of alternatives to the nuclear deterrent for ensuring world security. Chair. Dr FRANK BARNABY, Dr TONY HART.

World Federation of United Nations Associations—WFUNA: c/o Palais des Nations, 1211 Geneva 10, Switzerland; tel. (022) 330730; telex 289696; f. 1946 to encourage popular interest and participation in United Nations programmes, discussion of the role and future of the UN, and education for international understanding. Plenary Assembly meets every two years; WFUNA founded International Youth and Student Movement for the United Nations (q.v.); has consultative status with ECOSOC and UNESCO and consultative relations with other Specialized Agencies. Mems in 67 countries. Pres. MAURICE F. STRONG (Canada); Chair. Exec. Cttee MURLI M. AGARWAL (India); Sec.-Gen. Dr MAREK HAGMAJER (Poland). Publ. *WFUNA Bulletin* (quarterly).

World Peace Council: Lönnrotinkatu 25A/VI, SF 00180 Helsinki 18, Finland; tel. 649004; telex 121680; f. 1950 at the Second World Peace Congress, Warsaw. Principles: the prevention of nuclear war; the peaceful co-existence of the various socio-economic systems in the world; settlement of differences between nations by negotiation and agreement; complete disarmament; elimination of colonialism and racial discrimination; respect for the right of peoples to sovereignty and independence; status as a non-governmental organization with UN, UNESCO, UNCTAD, UNIDO, ILO. Mems: Representatives of c. 2,500 political parties and national organizations from 141 countries, and of 30 international organizations; Presidential Committee of 228 mems elected by the Council. Sec.-Gen. ROMESH CHANDRA. Publs *New Perspectives* (every 2 months), *Peace Courier* (monthly).

Industrial and Professional Relations

See also the chapters on ICFTU, WCL and WFTU.

Arab Federation of Petroleum, Mining and Chemicals Workers: POB 1905, Tripoli, Libya; f. 1961; runs the Arab Petroleum Institute for Labour Studies, Cairo. Mems: 18 affiliated unions in 12 countries. Sec.-Gen. ANWAR ASHMAWI MOHAMED (Egypt). Publs *Arab Petroleum* (monthly), specialized publications and statistics.

Association for Systems Management: 24587 Bagley Rd, Cleveland, Ohio 44138, USA; tel. (216) 243-6900; f. 1947; an international professional organization for the advancement and self-renewal of management information systems analysis throughout business and industry. Mems: 10,000 in 35 countries. Pres. JAMES T. HERLIKY; Exec. Dir RICHARD L. IRWIN. Publ. *Journal of Systems Management*.

Caribbean Congress of Labour: Room 405, Norman Centre, Broad St, Bridgetown, Barbados; tel. 429-5517; f. 1960 to fight for the recognition of trade union organizations; to build and strengthen the ties between the Free Trade Unions of the Caribbean and the rest of the world; to support the work of ICFTU (q.v.); to encourage the formation of national groupings and centres. Mems: 26 in 17 countries. Pres. LEONARD ARCHER (Bahamas); Sec.-Treas. KERTIST AUGUSTUS (Dominica).

European Association for Personnel Management: 29 ave Hoche, 75008, Paris, France; f. 1962 to disseminate knowledge and information concerning the personnel function of management, to establish and maintain professional standards, to define the specific nature of personnel management within industry, commerce and the public services, and to assist in the development of national associations. Mems: 14 national associations. Sec.-Gen. R. JOUFFRET.

European Civil Service Federation: 200 rue de la Loi, 1049 Brussels, Belgium; tel. (02) 235-11-11; telex 21877; f. 1962 to foster the idea of a European civil service of staff of international organizations operating in Western Europe or pursuing regional objectives; upholds the interests of civil service members. Pres. HELMUT MUELLERS; Sec. MARINA IJDENBERG. Publ. *Eurechos*.

European Federation of Conference Towns: 40 rue Washington, 1050 Brussels, Belgium; tel. (02) 452-98-30; telex 20429; lays down standards for conference towns; provides advice and assistance to its members and other organizations holding conferences in Europe; undertakes publicity and propaganda for promotional purposes; helps conference towns to set up national centres. Perm. Sec. RITA DE LANDTSHEER.

European Industrial Research Management Association—

EIRMA: 38 cours Albert 1, 75008 Paris, France; tel. (1) 42-25-60-44; telex 643 908; f. 1966 under auspices of the OECD (q.v.); a permanent body in which European science-based firms meet to discuss and study industrial research policy and management and take joint action in trying to solve problems in this field. Mems: 150 in 15 countries. Pres. H.-J. HELLER; Gen. Sec. Dr R. SCHULZ. Publs *Annual Report, Conference Reports, Working Group Reports.*

European Trade Union Confederation: 37 rue Montagne aux Herbes Potagères, 1000 Brussels, Belgium; tel. (02) 218-31-00; telex 62241; f. 1973; comprises 36 national trade union confederations in 21 western European countries, representing over 43m. workers; holds congress every three years. Gen. Sec. MATHIAS HINTERSCHEID.

Federation of International Civil Servants' Associations: Palais des Nations, 1211 Geneva 10, Switzerland; tel. (022) 988400; telex 289696; f. 1952 to co-ordinate policies and activities of member associations, to represent staff interests before inter-agency and legislative organs of the UN and to promote the development of an international civil service. Mems: 26 associations consisting of staff of UN organizations, 18 consultative associations and four inter-organizational Federations with observer status. Pres. FRANCOISE SALA. Publs *Annual Report, FICSA News.*

Graphical International Federation: Valeriusplein 30, 1075 BJ Amsterdam, Netherlands; tel. (020) 71-32-79; telex 18695; f. 1925. Mems: national federations in 15 countries, covering 100,000 workers. Pres. L. VAN HAUDT (Belgium); Sec.-Gen. R. E. VAN KESTEREN (Netherlands).

International Association of Conference Interpreters: 10 ave de Sécheron, 1202 Geneva, Switzerland; tel. (022) 313323; f. 1953 to represent professional conference interpreters, ensure the highest possible standards and protect the legitimate interests of members. Establishes criteria designed to improve the standards of training and recognizes schools meeting the required standards. Has consultative status with the UN and several of its agencies. Mems: 1,800 in 53 countries. Pres. GISELA SIEBOURG (FRG); Vice-Pres. MONIQUE DUCROUX (Switzerland). Publs *Code of Professional Conduct, Yearbook* (listing interpreters), etc.

International Association of Conference Translators: 15 route des Morillons, 1218 Le Grand-Saconnex, Geneva, Switzerland; tel. (022) 910666; f. 1962; aims to examine problems of revisers, translators, précis writers and editors working for international conferences and organizations, to protect the interests of those in the profession and help maintain high standards; establishes links with international organizations and conference organizers. Mems: 460 in 17 countries. Pres. SHEILA HALL (UK). Publ. *Directory.*

International Association of Crafts and Small and Medium-Sized Enterprises—IACME: Schwarztorstrasse 26, 3007 Berne, Switzerland; tel. (031) 257785; telex 912947; f. 1947 to defend undertakings and the freedom of enterprise within private economy, to develop training, to encourage the creation of national organizations of independent enterprises and promote international collaboration, to represent the common interests of members and to institute exchange of ideas and information. Mems: organizations in 26 countries which also belong to one of the international organic federations composing the IACME: International Federation of Master Craftsmen (IFC), International Federation of Small and Medium-Sized Industrial Enterprises (IFSMI) and International Federation of Small and Medium-Sized Commercial Enterprises (IFSMC). Chair. PAUL SCHNITKER; Gen. Sec. BALZ HORBER.

International Association of Medical Laboratory Technologists: c/o SLF/SSF, Ostermalmsgatan 19, 114 26 Stockholm, Sweden; f. 1954 to afford opportunities for meetings and communication between medical laboratory technologists, to raise training standards and to standardize training in different countries in order to facilitate free exchange of labour; holds international congress every second year. Mems: 60,000 in 37 countries. Exec. Dir MARGARETTA HAAG. Publ. *MedTecInternational* (2 a year).

International Association of Mutual Insurance Companies: 114 rue La Boétie, 75008 Paris, France; tel. (1) 42-25-84-86; f. 1964 for the establishment of good relations between its members and the protection of the general interests of private insurance based on the principle of mutuality. Mems: over 250 in 25 countries. Pres. A. TORP-PEDERSEN (Denmark); Sec.-Gen. A. TEMPELAERE (France). Publs *Mutuality* (2 a year), *AISAM dictionary, Newsletter* (3 a year).

International Confederation of Executive and Professional Staffs (Confédération internationale des cadres): 30 rue de Gramont, 75002 Paris, France; telex 215116; f. 1950 to improve the material and moral status of executive staffs. Mems: national organizations in Belgium, Denmark, France, Federal Republic of Germany, Italy, Luxembourg, Monaco, Netherlands, Portugal, Spain, UK, and international professional federations for chemistry and allied industries (FICCIA), mines (FICM), transport (FICT), metallurgical industries (FIEM), agriculture (FIDCA) and insurance (AECA). Pres. Dr FAUSTO D'ELIA (Italy); Sec.-Gen. JEAN DE SANTIS (France). Publ. *Cadres.*

International European Construction Federation: 9 rue La Pérouse, 75116 Paris, France; tel. (1) 47-20-80-74; telex 613456; f. 1905. Mems: 25 national employers' organizations in 18 countries. Pres. PAUL WILLEMEN (Belgium); Sec.-Gen. ERIC LEPAGE (France). Publ. *L'Enreprise Européenne.*

International Federation of Actors: 31A Thayer St, London, W1M 5LH, England; tel. (01) 487-4699; f. 1952. Mems: actors' unions totalling 200,000 individuals in 43 countries. Pres. PETER HEINZ KERSTEN (Austria); Sec.-Gen. ROLF REMBE.

International Federation of Air Line Pilots' Associations: Interpilot House, 116 High St, Egham, Surrey, TW20 9HQ, England; tel. (0784) 37361; telex 8951918; f. 1948 to aid in the establishment of fair conditions of employment; to contribute towards safety within the industry; to provide an international basis for rapid and accurate evaluation of technical and industrial aspects of the profession. Mems: 72 associations, 60,000 pilots. Pres. Capt. R. H. J. SMITH; Exec. Administrator T. V. MIDDLETON.

International Federation of Business and Professional Women: Studio 16, Cloisters Business Centre, 8 Battersea Park Rd, London, SW8 4BG, England; tel. (01) 738-8323; f. 1930 to promote interests of business and professional women and secure combined action by them. Mems: national federations and associate clubs totalling more than 200,000 mems in 67 countries. Pres. TUULIKKI JUUSELA; Gen. Sec. MARIANNE HASLEGRAVE. Publ. *Widening Horizons* (quarterly).

International Industrial Relations Association: c/o International Labour Office, 1211 Geneva 22, Switzerland; tel. (022) 996841; telex 22271; f. 1966 to encourage development of national associations of specialists, facilitate the spread of information, organize conferences, and to promote internationally planned research, through study groups and regional meetings. Mems: 26 associations, 44 institutions and 850 individuals. Pres. Prof. Dr ROGER BLANPAIN; Sec. Dr A. GLADSTONE. Publs *IIRA Bulletin* (3 a year).

International Organization of Employers—IOE: 28 chemin de Joinville, 1216 Cointrin/Geneva, Switzerland; tel. (022) 981616; telex 28 92 95; f. 1920, reorganized 1948; aims to represent the interests of private employers, to defend free enterprise, to maintain contacts in labour matters; has consultative status with the UN Economic and Social Council and the International Labour Organisation. General Council meets annually; there is an Executive Committee and a General Secretariat. Mems: 99 federations in 95 countries. Sec.-Gen. RAPHAEL LAGASSE (Belgium). Publ. *Information Bulletin* (monthly).

International Organization of Experts—ORDINEX: 163 rue Saint-Honoré, 75001 Paris, France; tel. (1) 42-60-54-41; f. 1961 to establish co-operation between experts on an international level. Mems: 2,400. Pres.-Gen. AHMED GHALMI (Algeria). Publ. *General Yearbook.*

International Public Relations Association—IPRA: Case Postale 126, 1211 Geneva 20, Switzerland; tel. (022) 910550; telex 289817; f. 1955 to provide for an exchange of ideas, technical knowledge and professional experience among those engaged in international public relations, and to foster the highest standards of professional competence. Mems: over 800 in 60 countries. Pres. ANAND AKERKAR (India); Sec.-Gen. ROGER HAYES. Publs *Newsletter* (6 a year), *International Public Relations Review* (4 a year).

International Society of City and Regional Planners—ISoCaRP: Mauritskade 23, 2514 HD The Hague, Netherlands; tel. (70) 46 26 54; f. 1965 to promote better planning practice through the exchange of knowledge. Mems: 398 in 49 countries. Pres. K. O. SCHMID (Switzerland); Sec.-Gen. H. W. STRUBEN (Netherlands). Publ. *News Bulletin* (2 a year).

International Union of Architects: 51 rue Raynouard, 75016 Paris, France; tel. (1) 45-24-36-88; telex 614 855; f. 1948; 16th Congress: Brighton, 1987. Mems: 81 countries. Pres. ROD HACKNEY (UK); Sec.-Gen. NILS CARLSON. Publ. *Bulletin d'informations* (monthly).

Latin American Farmworkers Federation (Federación Campesina Latinoamericana): Apdo 1422, Caracas 1010A, Venezuela; tel. (032) 712005; telex 29873; f. 1961 to represent the interests of farmworkers in Latin America and to fight for their active participation in the social, economic, cultural, technical and scientific aspects of life in that area. Mems: national unions in 28 countries and territories. Sec.-Gen. I. LASSO. Publ. *Boletín Luchemos* (quarterly).

Nordic Federation of Factory Workers' Unions (Nordiska Fabriksarbetarefederationen): Box 1114, 111 81 Stockholm, Sweden; f. 1901 to promote collaboration between affiliates in Denmark, Finland, Iceland, Norway and Sweden; supports sister unions economically and in other ways in labour market conflicts.

Mems: 400,000 in 13 unions. Pres. UNO EKBERG (Sweden); Sec. NILS KRISTOFFERSON (Sweden).

World Federation of Scientific Workers: 6 Endsleigh St, London, WC1H 0DX, England; tel. (01) 387-5096; f. 1946 to improve the position of science and scientists, to assist in promoting international scientific co-operation and to promote the use of science for beneficial ends; studies and publicizes problems of general, nuclear, biological and chemical disarmament; surveys the position and activities of scientists. Member organizations in 35 countries, totalling over 300,000 mems. Sec.-Gen. R. A. BIRD (UK). Publ. *Scientific World* (quarterly in English, Esperanto, German and Russian).

World Movement of Christian Workers—WMCW: 90 rue des Palais, 1210 Brussels, Belgium; tel. (02) 216-56-96; f. 1961 to unite national movements which advance the spiritual and collective well-being of workers; general assembly every four years. Mems: 49 affiliated movements in 42 countries. Sec.-Gen. LUC VOS. Publ. *Infor-WMCW*.

World Union of Liberal Professions (Union mondiale des professions libérales): 28 rue Hamelin, 75116 Paris, France; tel. (1) 47-23-00-02; f. 1987 to represent and link members of the liberal professions. Mems: 22 national organizations. Pres. ALAIN TINAYRE.

Law

Asian-African Legal Consultative Committee: 27 Ring Rd, Lajpat Nagar-IV, New Delhi 110024, India; tel. 6415280; f. 1956 to consider legal problems referred to it by member countries and to be a forum for Afro-Asian co-operation in international law and economic relations; provides background material for conferences, prepares standard/model contract forms suited to the needs of the region; promotes arbitration as a means of settling international commercial disputes; trains officers of member states; has permanent UN observer status. Mems: 40 states. Pres. TAN BOON TEIK (Singapore); Sec.-Gen. FRANK X. NJENGA (Kenya).

Consultative Committee of the Bars and Law Societies of the European Community—CCBE: 40 rue Washington, 1050 Brussels, Belgium; tel. (02) 640-42-74; telex 65080; f. 1960 to ensure liaison between the bars and law societies of the member countries as between these and the European Community authorities (Parliament, Economic and Social Committee, Court and Commission). Mems: 12 delegations, and observers from Austria, Norway, Sweden and Switzerland. Pres. JØRGEN GRØNBORG (Denmark); Sec.-Gen. JEAN-RÉGNIER THYS (Belgium).

Hague Conference on Private International Law: Javastraat 2C, 2585 AM The Hague, Netherlands; tel (070) 633303; telex 33383; f. 1893 to work for the unification of the rules of private international law, Permanent Bureau f. 1955. Mems: 23 European and 13 other countries. Sec.-Gen. Dr G. A. L. DROZ.

Institute of International Law (Institut de droit international): 22 ave William Favre, 1207 Geneva, Switzerland; tel. (022) 360772; f. 1873 to promote the development of international law by endeavouring to formulate general principles in accordance with civilized ethical standards, and by giving assistance to genuine attempts at the gradual and progressive codification of international law. Mems: limited to 132 members and associates from all over the world. Sec.-Gen. NICOLAS VALTICOS (Greece). Publ. *Annuaire de l'Institut de Droit international*.

Inter-American Bar Association: 1889 F St, NW, Suite 450, Washington, DC 20006–4499, USA; tel. (202) 789-2747; telex 64128; f. 1940 to promote the rule of law and to establish and maintain relations between associations and organizations of lawyers in the Americas. Mems: 90 associations and 3,500 individuals in 27 countries. Sec.-Gen. JOHN O. DAHLGREN (USA). Publs *Newsletter* (quarterly), *Conference Proceedings*.

Intergovernmental Copyright Committee: Copyright Division, UNESCO, 7 place de Fontenoy, 75700 Paris, France; tel. (1) 45-68-10-00; established to study the problems concerning the application and operation of the Universal Copyright Convention and to make preparations for periodic revisions of this Convention. Mems: 18 states. Chair. SALAH ABADA.

International Association for the Protection of Industrial Property: Bleicherweg 58, Postfach, 8027 Zürich 27, Switzerland; tel. (01) 2041212; telex 815656; f. 1897 to encourage legislation regarding the international protection of industrial property and the development and extension of international conventions, and to make comparative studies of existing legislation with a view to its improvement and unification; holds triennial congress. Mems: 6,400 (national and regional groups and individual mems) in 96 countries. Exec. Pres. TEARTSE SCHAPER (Netherlands); Sec.-Gen. ALFRED BRINER (Switzerland).

International Association of Democratic Lawyers: 263 ave Albert, 1180 Brussels, Belgium; tel. (02) 345-14-71; f. 1946 to facilitate contacts and exchange between lawyers, to encourage study of legal science and international law and support the democratic principles favourable to maintenance of peace and co-operation between nations; conducts research on banning atomic weapons, on labour law, private international law, agrarian law, etc.; consultative status with UN. Mems: in 96 countries. Pres. JOË NORDMANN (France); Sec.-Gen. AMAR BENTOUMI (Algeria). Publs *International Review of Contemporary Law*, in French, English and Spanish (every 6 months).

International Association of Juvenile and Family Court Magistrates: Tribunal pour Enfants, Palais de Justice, 75055 Paris, France; f. 1928 to consider questions concerning child welfare legislation and to encourage research in the field of juvenile courts and delinquency. Activities: international congress, study groups and regional meetings. Pres. A. BARBOSA (Portugal); Gen.-Sec. LUCIEN BEAULIEU (Canada).

International Association of Law Libraries: c/o The Law School Library, University of Chicago, 1121 East 60th St, Chicago, Ill 60637, USA; tel. (312) 702-9599; f. 1959 to encourage and facilitate the work of librarians and others concerned with the bibliographic processing and administration of legal materials. Mems: 600 from more than 50 countries (personal and institutional). Pres. ADOLF SPRUDZS (USA); Sec. TIMOTHY KEARLEY (USA). Publ. *International Journal of Legal Information* (3 a year), *The IALL Messenger* (irregular).

International Association of Legal Sciences (Association internationale des sciences juridiques): c/o CISS, 1 rue Miollis, 75015 Paris, France; tel. (1) 45-68-25-59; f. 1950 to promote the mutual knowledge and understanding of nations and the increase of learning by encouraging throughout the world the study of foreign legal systems and the use of the comparative method in legal science. Governed by a president and an executive bureau of 10 members known as the International Committee of Comparative Law. National committees in 47 countries. Sponsored by UNESCO. Pres. Prof. W. LORENZ (FRG); Sec.-Gen. Dr S. FRIEDMAN (France).

International Association of Penal Law: Güntersstalstrasse 73, 7800 Freiburg i. Br., Federal Republic of Germany; tel. (0761) 7081217; f. 1924 to establish collaboration between those from different countries who are working in penal law, studying criminology, and promoting the theoretical and practical development of an international penal law. Mems: 1,500. Pres. H.-H. JESCHECK. Publ. *Revue Internationale de Droit Pénal* (bi-annual).

International Bar Association: 2 Harewood Place, Hanover Sq., London, W1R 9HB, England; tel. (01) 629-1206; telex 8812664; f. 1947; a non-political federation of national bar associations and law societies; aims to discuss problems of professional organization and status; to advance the science of jurisprudence; to promote uniformity and definition in appropriate fields of law; to promote administration of justice under law among peoples of the world; to promote in their legal aspects the principles and aims of the United Nations. Mems: 109 member organizations in 66 countries, 11,000 individual members in 129 countries. Pres. W. REECE SMITH (USA); Exec. Dir Mrs MADELEINE MAY (UK); Sec.-Gen. ANTHONY F. SMITH (Australia). Publs *International Business Lawyer* (11 a year), *International Bar News* (6 a year), *International Legal Practitioner* (quarterly), *Journal of Energy and Natural Resources Law* (quarterly).

International Commission of Jurists: POB 120, 109 route de Chêne, 1224 Chêne-Bougeries, Geneva, Switzerland; f. 1952 to strengthen the Rule of Law in its practical manifestations and to defend it by mobilizing world legal opinion; has consultative status with UN, UNESCO and the Council of Europe. There are 59 sections in 49 countries. Pres. ANDRÉS AGUILAR MAWDSLEY (Venezuela); Sec.-Gen. NIALL MACDERMOT. Publs *The Rule of Law and Human Rights, The Review, ICJ Newsletter, Bulletin of the Centre for the Independence of Judges and Lawyers (CIJL)*, special reports.

International Commission on Civil Status: Faculté de Droit et des Sciences politiques, place d'Athènes, 67084 Strasbourg Cedex, France; f. 1950 for the establishment and presentation of legislative documentation relating to the rights of individuals, and research on means of simplifying the judicial and technical administration concerning civil status. Mems: governments of Austria, Belgium, France, the Federal Republic of Germany, Greece, Italy, Luxembourg, Netherlands, Portugal, Spain, Switzerland, Turkey. Pres. H. DELVAUX (Luxembourg); Sec.-Gen. J. M. BISCHOFF (France).

International Copyright Society: 1000 Berlin 15, Kurfürstendamm 35, Federal Republic of Germany; tel. (030) 8815423; telex 183881; f. 1954 to enquire scientifically into the natural rights of the author and to put the knowledge obtained to practical application all over the world, in particular in the field of legislation. Mems: 446 individuals and 52 corresponding organizations and personalities. Pres. Prof. Dr ERICH SCHULZE; Gen. Sec. VERA MOVSESSIAN. Publs *Schriftenreihe* (61 vols), *Yearbook*.

OTHER INTERNATIONAL ORGANIZATIONS

International Council of Environmental Law: 5300 Bonn, Adenauerallee 214, Federal Republic of Germany; tel. (0228) 2692-240; f. 1969 to exchange information and expertise on legal, administrative and policy aspects of environmental questions. Exec. Governors Dr WOLFGANG BURHENNE, Dr NAGENDRA SINGH. Publs *Directory, References, Environmental Policy and Law.*

International Criminal Police Organization—INTERPOL: POB 205, 26 rue Armengaud, 92210 Saint Cloud, France; tel. (1) 46-02-55-50; telex 270658; f. 1923, reconstituted 1946; aims to promote and ensure the widest possible mutual assistance between police forces within the limits of laws existing in different countries, to establish and develop all institutions likely to contribute to the prevention and suppression of ordinary law crimes; co-ordinates activities of police authorities of member states in international affairs, centralizes records and information regarding international criminals; operates a radio network of 70 stations. The General Assembly is held annually. Mems: official bodies of 138 countries. Pres. IVAN BARBOT (France); Sec.-Gen. R. E. KENDALL. Publs *International Criminal Police Review* (6 a year), *Counterfeits and Forgeries, International Crime Statistics.*

International Customs Tariffs Bureau: 38 rue de l'Association, 1000 Brussels, Belgium; tel. (02) 516-87-74; the executive instrument of the International Union for the Publication of Customs Tariffs; f. 1890, to translate and publish all customs tariffs in five languages—English, French, German, Italian, Spanish. Mems: 76. Pres. F. ROELANTS (Belgium); Dir BERNARD DENNE. Publs *International Customs Journal, Annual Report.*

International Development Law Institute: Via Paolo Frisi 23, 00197 Rome, Italy; tel. 872008; telex 622381; f. 1983 to strengthen the lawyer's role in solving development problems, by offering training and technical assistance to legal advisers and contract negotiators from developing countries; the 1988 training programme includes seminars on international business transactions and courses for development lawyers; provides specially-designed training 'workshops' for particular countries on request. Dir L. MICHAEL HAGER.

International Federation for European Law—FIDE: POB 14, 55102 Kalamaria, Thessaloniki, Greece; tel. (031) 473403; telex 412976; f. 1961 to advance studies on European law among members of the European Community by co-ordinating activities of member societies and by organizing conferences every two years. Mems: 12 national associations. Pres. P. D. DAGTOGLOU.

International Federation of Senior Police Officers: 4400 Münster, Feldkamp 4, Postfach 480 164, Federal Republic of Germany; tel. (02501) 7171; f. 1950 to unite policemen of different nationalities, adopting the general principle that prevention should prevail over repression, and that the citizen should be convinced of the protective role of the police; seeks to develop methods, and studies problems of traffic police. Set up International Centre of Crime and Accident Prevention, 1976. Mems: 16 national groups and individuals of 48 different nationalities. Pres. HERMAN BERGER (Norway); Vice-Pres. Dr HUBERT HOLLER (Austria), Col WARICHET (Belgium); Sec.-Gen. G. KRATZ (FRG). Publ. *International Police Information* (every 3 months, French, German and English).

International Institute for the Unification of Private Law—UNIDROIT: Via Panisperna 28, 00184 Rome, Italy; tel. (06) 6783189; telex 623166; f. 1926 to undertake studies of comparative law, to prepare for the establishment of uniform legislation, to prepare drafts of international agreements on private law and to organize conferences and publish works on such subjects; holds international congresses on private law and meetings of organizations concerned with the unification of law; library of 215,000 vols. Mems: governments of 52 countries. Pres. RICCARDO MONACO (Italy); Sec.-Gen. MALCOLM EVANS (UK). Publs *Uniform Law Review* (2 a year), *Digest of Legal Activities of International Organizations, News Bulletin* (quarterly), etc.

International Institute of Space Law—IISL: 3–5 rue Mario Nikis, 75015 Paris, France; f. 1959 at the XI Congress of the International Astronautical Federation; organizes annual Space Law colloquium; studies juridical and sociological aspects of astronautics and makes awards. Mems: individuals from many countries elected for life. Pres. I. DIEDERICKS-VERSCHOOR (Netherlands). Publs *Proceedings of Annual Colloquium on Space Law, Survey of Teaching of Space Law in the World.*

International Juridical Institute: Permanent Office for the Supply of International Legal Information, 't Hoenstraat 5, 2596 HX The Hague, Netherlands; tel. (070) 460974; f. 1918 to supply information on any matter of international interest, not being of a secret nature, respecting international, municipal and foreign law and the application thereof. Pres. C. D. VAN BOESCHOTEN; Sec. C. J. VAN RIJN VAN ALKEMADE; Dir A. L. G. A. STILLE.

International Law Association: 3 Paper Buildings, The Temple, London, EC4Y 7EU, England; tel. (01) 353-2904; f. 1873 for the study and advancement of international law, public and private; the promotion of international understanding and goodwill. Mems: 4,000 in 40 regional branches. Pres. Dr THOK-KYU LIMB (Republic of Korea); Chair. Exec. Council Prof. C. J. OLMSTEAD (USA); Sec.-Gen. BRUCE MAULEVERER.

International Maritime Committee (Comité Maritime International): 203 Mechelsesteenweg, 2018 Antwerp, Belgium; tel. (03) 218-48-87; telex 31653; f. 1897 to contribute to the unification of maritime law by means of conferences, publications, etc. and to encourage the creation of national associations; work includes drafting of conventions on collisions at sea, salvage and assistance at sea, limitation of shipowners' liability, maritime mortgages, etc. Mems: national associations in 48 countries. Pres. FRANCESCO BERLINGIERI (Italy); Secs-Gen. JAN RAMBERG (Exec.), HENRI VOET (Admin. and Treas.). Publs *CMI Newsletter, Year Book.*

International Nuclear Law Association: 29 sq. de Meeûs, 1040 Brussels, Belgium; f. 1972 to promote international studies of legal problems related to the peaceful use of nuclear energy, particularly the protection of man and the environment; holds conference every two years. Mems: 450 in 30 countries. Pres. F. VANDENABEELE (Belgium); Sec.-Gen. FERNAND LACROIX (Belgium).

International Penal and Penitentiary Foundation: c/o Dr K. Hobe, Bundesministerium der Justiz, Postfach 20 0365, 5300 Bonn 2, Federal Republic of Germany; tel. (0228) 584226; telex 8869679; f. 1951 to encourage studies in the field of prevention of crime and treatment of delinquents. Mems in 20 countries (membership limited to three people from each country) and corresponding mems. Pres. HELGE RÖSTAD (Norway); Sec.-Gen. KONRAD HOBE (FRG).

International Police Association—IPA: Postbus 100, 3970 AC Driebergen, Netherlands; f. 1950 to exchange professional information, create ties of friendship between all sections of police service, organize group travel, studies, etc. Mems: 210,000. Sec. T. A. LEENDERS. Publs *Police World* (quarterly), *International Bibliography of the Police, Annual Scholarship Report, Youth Gatherings, Police and Public, Police Participation in the Council of Europe.*

International Society for Labour Law and Social Security: ILO, Case 500, 1211 Geneva 22, Switzerland; f. 1958 to encourage collaboration between specialists; holds World Congress every three years as well as irregular regional congresses (Europe, Asia and Americas). Mems: 1,000 in 60 countries. Pres. Prof. L. NAGY (Hungary); Sec.-Gen. J.-M. SERVAIS (Belgium).

International Union of Latin Notaries (Unión Internacional del Notariado Latino): Via Senato 37, 20121 Milan, Italy; f. 1948 to study and standardize notarial legislation and promote the progress and stability and advancement of the Latin notarial system. Mems: organizations and individuals in 39 countries. Sec. DIANE CARLO LAURINI. Publ. *Revista Internacional del Notariado* (quarterly).

International Union of Lawyers: 18 ave Charles de Gaulle, 92200 Neuilly, France; tel. (1) 47-38-13-11; telex 620101; f. 1927 to promote the independence and freedom of lawyers, and defend their ethical and material interests on an international level; to contribute to the development of international order based on law. Mems: 55 associations in 41 countries. Publs *Bulletin* (quarterly).

Law Association for Asia and the Pacific—Lawasia: 10th Floor, 170 Phillip St, Sydney, NSW 2000, Australia; tel. (02) 221-2970; telex 73063; f. 1966 to promote the administration of justice, the protection of human rights and the maintenance of the rule of law within the region, to advance the standard of legal education, to promote uniformity within the region in appropriate fields of law and to advance the interests of the legal profession. Mems: 52 asscns in 21 countries; 2,000 individual mems. Pres. G. T. S. SIDHU (Malaysia); Sec.-Gen. Dr D. H. GEDDES. Publs *Lawasia* (annual journal), *Lawasia Human Rights Bulletin, Lawasia Newsletter, Lawasia Human Rights Newsletter.*

Permanent Court of Arbitration: Carnegieplein 2, 2517 KJ The Hague, Netherlands; tel. (070) 469680; f. by the Convention for the Pacific Settlement of International Disputes (1899, 1907) to enable immediate recourse to be made to arbitration for international disputes which cannot be settled by diplomacy, to facilitate the solution of disputes by international inquiry and conciliation commissions. Mems: governments of 76 countries. Sec.-Gen. JACOB VAREKAMP (Netherlands).

Society of Comparative Legislation: 28 rue Saint-Guillaume, 75007 Paris, France; tel. (1) 45-44-44-67; f. 1869 to study and compare laws of different countries, and to investigate practical means of improving the various branches of legislation. Mems: 1,700 in 48 countries. Pres. JACQUES BOUTET (France); Sec.-Gen. XAVIER BLANC-JOUVAN (France). Publs *Revue Internationale de Droit Comparé* (quarterly), *Journées de la Société de Législation comparée* (annually).

Union of Arab Jurists: POB 6026, Al-Mansour, Baghdad, Iraq; tel. 5375820; telex 21-2661; f. 1975 to facilitate contacts between

Arab lawyers, to safeguard the Arab legislative and judicial heritage; to encourage the study of Islamic jurisprudence; and to defend human rights. Mems: 16 bar associations in 16 countries and individual mems. Sec.-Gen. SHEBIB LAZIM AL-MALIKI. Publ. *Al-Hukuki al-Arabi* (Arab Law).

Union of International Associations: 40 rue Washington, 1050 Brussels, Belgium; tel. (02) 640-41-09; telex 65080; f. 1907, present title adopted 1910. Aims: to serve as a documentation centre on international organizations, to undertake and promote research into the phenomenon of 'organization' and into the legal, administrative and technical problems common to international organizations, to publicize their work and to encourage mutual contacts. Mems: 200 in 54 countries. Pres. F. A. CASADIO (Italy); Sec.-Gen. JACQUES RAEYMAECKERS (Belgium). Publs *Transnational Associations* (6 a year), *International Congress Calendar* (quarterly), *Yearbook of International Organizations, International Organization Participation* (annually), *Global Action Network* (annually), *Encyclopedia of World Problems and Human Potential, Documents for the Study of International Non-Governmental Relations, International Congress Science Series.*

World Peace through Law Center—WPTLC: Suite 800, 1000 Connecticut Ave, NW, Washington, DC 20036, USA; tel. (202) 466-5428; telex 440456; f. 1963; promotes the continued development of international law and legal maintenance of world order; holds biennial world conferences, World Law Day, demonstration trials; organizes research programmes. Mems: lawyers, jurists and legal scholars in 155 countries. Pres. CHARLES S. RHYNE; Exec. Vice-Pres. MARGARETHA M. HENNEBERRY (USA). Publs *The World Jurist* (English, every 2 months), Research Reports, *Law and Judicial Systems of Nations*, 3rd revised edn (directory), *World Legal Directory* (biennial), *Law and Computer Technology* (quarterly), *World Law Review* Vols I-V (World Conference Proceedings), *The Chief Justices and Judges of the Supreme Courts of Nations* (directory), etc.

World Association of Center Associates: f. 1979.

World Association of Judges—WAJ: f. 1966 to advance the administration of judicial justice through co-operation and communication among ranking jurists of all countries. Pres. Dr T. O. ELIAS; Sec.-Gen. Dr KARL-GEORG ZIERLEIN.

World Association of Law Professors—WALP: f. 1975 to improve scholarship and education in dealing with matters related to international law; Chair. Z. ALEKSIC, J. N. HAZARD; Sec.-Gen. V. P. NANDA.

World Association of Lawyers—WAL: f. 1975 to develop international law and improve lawyers' effectiveness in dealing with it; Pres. CURT FREIHERR VON STACKLEBERG; Sec.-Gen. YVONNE TOLMAN-GUILLARD.

Medicine and Health

Council for International Organisations of Medical Sciences—CIOMS: c/o WHO, ave Appia, 1211 Geneva 27, Switzerland; tel. (022) 913406; telex 27821; f. 1949; general assembly every three years. Mems: 90 organizations. Pres. Prof F. VILARDELL; Exec. Sec. Dr Z. BANKOWSKI. Publs *Calendar of International and Regional Congresses* (annual), *Proceedings of CIOMS, Round Table Conferences, International Nomenclature of Diseases.*

MEMBERS OF CIOMS

Members of CIOMS include the following:

International Academy of Legal and Social Medicine: c/o 49A ave Nicolai, BP 8, 4802 Verviers, Belgium; tel. (087) 22-21-98; f. 1938; holds an international Congress and General Assembly every three years, and interim meetings. Mems in 50 countries. Exec. Sec. ELIZABETH FRANCSON. Publs *Newsletter* (3 a year), *Acta* (annually).

International Agency for the Prevention of Blindness: c/o Dr V. Clemmesen, Chr. Winthers Vej 28, 4700 Naestved, Denmark; f. 1975 to collaborate with the World Health Organization and other UN organizations in promoting and co-ordinating global action for the prevention of blindness, with emphasis on the major blinding diseases of the developing world. Operates through national committees in 64 countries and regional organizations in eight areas. Pres. CARL KUPFER; Sec. Dr VIGGO CLEMMESEN. Publ. *IAPB Newsletter* (2 a year).

International Association for the Study of the Liver: c/o J. Bircher, 3400 Göttingen, Robert-Koch-Str. 40, Federal Republic of Germany; f. 1958; Pres. LAWRIE POWELL; Sec. J. BIRCHER.

International Association of Allergology and Clinical Immunology: 611 East Wells St, Milwaukee, WI 53202, USA; tel. (414) 276-6445; f. 1945 to further work in the educational, research and practical medical aspects of allergic and immunological diseases. Mems: 40 national societies. Pres. Prof. J. CHARPIN (France); Sec.-Gen. Dr O. L. FRICK (USA); Exec. Sec. R. IBER (USA).

International Association of Gerontology: Duke University Medical Center, Box 2948, Durham, NC 27710, USA; tel. (919) 684-3416; telex 802829; f. 1950 to promote research and training in all fields of gerontology and to protect interests of gerontologic societies and institutions. Mems: 49 national societies and groups in 46 countries. Pres. Dr E. W. BUSSE (USA); Sec. Prof. Dr G. MADDOX (USA).

International College of Surgeons: 1516 N. Lake Shore Drive, Chicago, Ill 60610, USA; tel. (312) 642-3555; telex 324629; f. 1935, as a world-wide institution for the advancement of the art and science of surgery, to create a common bond among the surgeons of all nations and promote the highest standards of surgery without regard to nationality, creed, or colour; sends teams of surgeons to developing countries to teach local surgeons; organizes research and scholarship programme and International Surgical Congresses; maintains the International Museum of Surgical Science in Chicago. Mems: about 15,000 in 100 countries. Pres. Prof. GIUSEPPE PEZZUOLI; Corporate Sec. Dr ANDREW G. SHARF; International Sec.-Gen. Dr F. C. OTTATI. Publ. *International Surgery* (quarterly).

International Dental Federation: 64 Wimpole St, London, W1M 8AL, England; tel. (01) 935-7852; telex 25247; f. 1900. Mems: 83 national dental associations in 77 countries and 15 affiliates. Pres. Dr C. H. WILLIAMS (USA); Exec. Dir Dr J. E. AHLBERG (Sweden). Publs *International Dental Journal* (quarterly) and *Newsletter* (every 2 months).

International Diabetes Federation: 40 rue Washington, 1050 Brussels, Belgium; tel. (02) 647-44-14; telex 65080; f. 1949 to help in the collection and dissemination of information regarding diabetes and to improve the welfare of people suffering from that disease. Mems: associations in 76 countries. Pres. Prof J. J. HOET (Belgium); Sec. N. STIELS (Belgium). Publ. *IDF News Bulletin* (quarterly).

International Epidemiological Association—IEA: c/o Dr A. Aromaa, Research Institute for Social Security, Social Insurance Institution, PO Box 78, 00381 Helsinki, Finland; tel. (90) 4343560; telex 122375; f. 1954. Mems: 1,700. Pres. and Chair. Dr WALTER W. HOLLAND; Sec. Dr ARPO AROMAA. Publ. *International Journal of Epidemiology* (quarterly).

International Federation of Oto-Rhino-Laryngological Societies: 91-12 Fruithoflaan, 2600 Antwerp, Belgium; tel. (32-3) 440-20-21; f. 1965; Congresses every four years. Pres. J. R. CHANDLER (USA); Exec. Dir Prof. J. MARQUET (Belgium). Publ. *IFOS Newsletter* (6 a year).

International Federation of Physical Medicine and Rehabilitation: Mount Sinai Hospital, Dept of Rehabilitation Medicine, 600 University Ave, Toronto, Canada M5G 1X5; f. 1952 to link national societies, organize conferences and disseminate information to developing countries. Last conference: Israel, 1984. Pres. Dr C. M. GODFREY; Sec. Dr J. JIMÉNEZ.

International Federation of Societies for Electroencephalography and Clinical Neurophysiology: c/o Dr B. W. Ongerboer de Visser, Department of Clinical Neurophysiology, Academic Medical Centre, Meibergdreef 9, 1105 AZ Amsterdam, Netherlands; tel. (020) 5663415; telex 11944; f. 1949 to attain the highest level of knowledge in the field of electro-encephalography and clinical neurophysiology in all the countries of the world. Mems: 45 organizations. Pres. Prof. J. E. DESMEDT (Belgium); Sec. Dr B. W. ONGERBOER DE VISSER (Netherlands). Publ. *The EEG Journal* (monthly), *Evoked Potentials* (every 2 months).

International League Against Rheumatism: Hôpital Cochin, 27 rue du Faubourg St Jacques, 75014 Paris, France; tel. (1) 42-34-18-15; f. 1927 to promote international co-operation for the study and control of rheumatic diseases; to encourage the foundation of national leagues against rheumatism; to organize regular international congresses and to act as a connecting link between national leagues and international organizations. Pres. Prof. JACQUES VILLIAUMEY (France); Sec. Prof. C. J. MENKES (France). Publs *Annals of the Rheumatic Diseases* (in England), *Revue du Rhumatisme* (in France), *Reumatismo* (in Italy), *Arthritis and Rheumatism* (USA), etc.

International Leprosy Association: Salur 532 591, Vizianagaram District, Andhra Pradesh, India; f. 1931 to promote international co-operation in work on leprosy, from which about 15m. people in the world are suffering. Thirteenth Congress, The Hague, 1988. Pres. Prof. M. F. LECHAT (Belgium); Sec. Dr R. H. THANGARAJ (India). Publ. *International Journal of Leprosy and Other Mycobacterial Diseases* (quarterly).

International Pediatric Association: Château de Longchamp, Carrefour de Longchamp, Bois de Boulogne, 75016 Paris, France; tel. (1) 45-27-15-90; telex 648379; f. 1912; holds triennial congresses and regional meetings. Mems: 100 national paediatric societies, associations or academies in 96 countries. Pres. Prof. NIILO HALLMAN (Finland); Exec. Dir Prof. IHSAN DOGRAMACI (Turkey). Publ. *Bulletin* (quarterly).

International Rhinologic Society: c/o Dr Drumheller, 1515 Pacific Ave, Everett, Washington 98201, USA; f. 1985; holds congress every four years. Pres. T. AZUARA; Sec. Dr G. DRUMHELLER. Publ. *Journal of International Rhinology*.

International Society and Federation of Cardiology: CP 117, 1211 Geneva 12, Switzerland; tel. (022) 476755; f. 1978 through merger of the International Society of Cardiology and the International Cardiology Federation; aims to promote the study, prevention and relief of the cardiovascular diseases through scientific and public education programme and the exchange of materials between its affiliated societies and foundations and with other agencies having related interests. Official relations with WHO. Organizes World Congresses every four years. Pres. Dr M. R. GARCÍA-PALMIERI (Puerto Rico); Sec. Dr E. G. OLSEN; Exec. Sec. M. B. DE FIGUEIREDO. Publ. *Heartbeat* (quarterly).

International Society of Audiology: 330–332 Gray's Inn Rd, London, WC1X 8EE, England; tel. (01) 837-8855, ext. 4321; f. 1962. Mems: 300 individuals. Pres. Prof. W. NIEMEYER (FRG); Gen. Sec. R. HINCHCLIFFE. Publ. *Audiology* (every 2 months).

International Society of Criminology: 4 rue de Mondovi, 75001 Paris, France; tel. (1) 42-61-80-22; f. 1934 to promote the development of the sciences in their application to the criminal phenomenon. Mems: in 63 countries. Sec.-Gen. GEORGES PICCA. Publ. *Annales internationales de Criminologie* (2 a year).

International Society of Geographical Pathology—ISGP: c/o Dr R. Cooke, Pathology Dept, Herston Rd, Brisbane 4029, Australia; tel. (07) 253 8030; telex 40871; f. 1931 to study the relations between diseases and the geographical environments in which they occur. Mems: national and regional committees in 42 countries. Sec.-Gen. Dr ROBIN A. COOKE.

International Society of Internal Medicine: Dept. of Medicine, Regionalspital, 4900 Langenthal, Switzerland; tel. (063) 293131; f. 1948 to encourage research and education in internal medicine. Mems: 35 national societies, 3,000 individuals in 57 countries. Congresses: Brussels 1988, Stockholm 1990. Pres. Prof. M. SANGIORGI (Italy); Sec. Dr ROLF A. STREULI (Switzerland).

International Society of Psychosomatic Obstetrics and Gynaecology: c/o Prof. E. V. van Hall, Dept of Obstetrics and Gynaecology, University Hospital, Rijnsburgerweg 10, 2333 AA Leiden, Netherlands; tel. (071) 263332. Pres. Dr LORRAINE DENNERSTEIN (Australia); Sec.-Gen. Prof. EYLARD VAN HALL (Netherlands).

International Union against Cancer: 3 rue du Conseil Général, 1205 Geneva, Switzerland; tel. (022) 201811; telex 429724; f. 1933 to promote on an international level the campaign against cancer in its research, therapeutic and preventive aspects; organizes International Cancer Congress every four years; administers the American Cancer Society Eleanor Roosevelt International Cancer Fellowships, the International Cancer Research Technology Transfer Project and the Yamagiwa-Yoshida Memorial International Cancer Study Grants; conducts worldwide programmes of campaign orgnization and public education, detection and diagnosis, epidemiology and prevention, etc. Mems: voluntary national organizations, private or public cancer research and treatment organizations and institutes and governmental agencies in 82 countries. Pres. Dr C. G. SCHMIDT (FRG); Sec.-Gen. Dr G. P. MURPHY (USA). Publs *International Cancer News* (quarterly), *International Journal of Cancer* (monthly), *International Calendar of Meetings on Cancer*, technical reports and monographs.

International Union against Tuberculosis and Lung Disease: 68 blvd St Michel, 75006 Paris, France; tel. (1) 46-33-08-30; f. 1920 to co-ordinate the efforts of anti-tuberculosis and respiratory disease associations, to mobilize public interest, to assist control programmes and research around the world, to collaborate with governments and the WHO, to promote conferences. Mems: associations in 118 countries, numerous individual mems. Pres. Dr J. SWOMLEY; Chair. Exec. Cttee Dr M. A. BLEIKER; Exec. Dir Dr ANNIK ROUILLON. Publ. *Bulletin* (in English, French and Spanish; incl. conference proceedings).

International Union for Health Education: 15/21 rue de l'Ecole de Médecine, 75270 Paris Cedex 06, France; tel. (1) 43-26-72-28; f. 1951; provides an international network for the exchange of practical information on developments in health education; promotes research into effective methods and techniques in health education and encourages professional training in health education for health workers, teachers, social workers and others; holds regional and world conferences. Mems: in 75 countries. Pres. DENNIS TOLSMA (USA). Publ. *HYGIE-International Journal of Health Education* (quarterly).

International Union of Therapeutics: c/o Prof. A. A. Pradalier, Hôpital Rothschild, 33 blvd de Picpus, 75571 Paris Cedex 12, France; tel. (1) 43-41-72-72; f. 1934; international congresses every other year. Mems: 500 from 22 countries. Pres. Prof. J. DRY; Gen. Sec. Prof. A. PRADALIER.

Latin American Association of National Academies of Medicine: Calle 60A, No-5-29, Bogotá 2, Colombia; tel. 2-493122; f. 1967. Mems: nine national Academies. Pres. Dr CARLOS LANFRANCO LA HOZ (Peru); Sec. Dr ALBERTO CÁRDENAS-ESCOVAR (Colombia).

Medical Women's International Association: 5000 Cologne 41, Herbert-Levin-Strasse 5, Federal Republic of Germany; tel. (221) 4004235; telex 08882161; f. 1919 to facilitate contacts between medical women and to encourage their co-operation in matters connected with international health problems. Mems: national associations in 39 countries, and individuals. Pres. Prof. FERNANDA DE BENEDETTI VENTURINI (Italy); Sec.-Gen. CAROLYN MOTZEL (FRG).

World Association of Societies of (Anatomic and Clinical) Pathology—WASP: c/o Prof. T. Kawai, Jichi Medical School, Minami-Kawachi-machi, Tochigi 32904, Japan; f. 1947 to link national societies and to co-ordinate their scientific and technical means of action; and to promote the development of anatomic and clinical pathology, especially by convening conferences, congresses and meetings, and by the interchange of publications and personnel. Membership: 45 national associations. Pres. Dr. H. LOMMEL (FRG); Sec. Prof. T. KAWAI. Publ. *Newsletter* (quarterly).

World Federation of Associations of Clinical Toxicology Centres and Poison Control Centres: c/o Prof. L. Roche, 150 cours Albert-Thomas, 69372 Lyon Cedex 2, France; tel. 78-74-16-74. Pres. Prof. F. OEHME; Sec. Prof. L. ROCHE.

World Federation of Associations of Paediatric Surgeons: c/o Prof. J. Boix-Ochoa, Clinica Infantil 'Vall d'Hebrón', Departemento de Cirugía Pediátrica, Valle de Hebrón, s/n, Barcelona 08035, Spain; f. 1974. Mems: 50 associations. Pres. J. R. PYNEYRO; Sec. Prof. J. BOIX-OCHOA.

World Federation of Neurology: Dept of Neurology, Bowman Gray School of Medicine, Winston-Salem, NC 27103, USA; tel. (919) 748-2336; telex 806449; f. 1955 as International Neurological Congress, present title adopted 1957. Aims to assemble at the same time and place members of various congresses associated with neurology, and organize co-operation of neurological researchers. Organizes Congress every four years. Mems: 12,000 in 68 countries. Pres. RICHARD L. MASLAND (USA); Sec.-Treas. JAMES F. TOOLE (USA). Publs *Journal of the Neurological Sciences*, *Acta Neuropathologica*, *World Neurology*.

World Federation of Societies of Anaesthesiologists—WFSA: Pantai Medical Centre, 59100 Kuala Lumpur, Malaysia; tel. (03) 7575077; telex 32234; f. 1955 to make available the highest standards of anaesthesia to all peoples of the world. Mems: 82 national societies. Pres. Dr JOHN S. M. ZORAB (UK); Sec. Dr SAYWAN LIM (Malaysia). Publ. *Newsletter* (2 a year), *Annual Report*, *Lectures in Anaesthesiology* (2 a year), *Career Guide*.

World Medical Association: 28 ave des Alpes, 01210 Ferney-Voltaire, France; tel. (50) 40-75-75; telex 385755; f. 1947 to achieve the highest international standards in all aspects of medical practice, to promote closer ties among doctors and national medical associations by personal contact and all other means, to study problems confronting the medical profession and to present its views to appropriate bodies. Structure: annual General Assembly and Council (meets twice a year). Mems: 43 national medical associations. Pres. Dr H. L. THOMPSON (Australia); Sec.-Gen. Dr ANDRÉ WYNEN (Belgium). Publ. *The World Medical Journal* (6 a year).

World Organization of Gastroenterology: Department of Medicine, Royal Infirmary, Edinburgh EH3 9YW, Scotland; tel. (031) 229-2477; telex 727442; f. 1935. Mems in 73 countries. Sec.-Gen. Prof. IAN A. D. BOUCHIER (UK).

World Psychiatric Association: Dept of Psychiatry, Kommunehospitalet, 1399 Copenhagen K, Denmark; tel. (1) 938500, ext. 3390; f. 1961 for the exchange of information concerning the problems of mental illness and the strengthening of relations between psychiatrists in all countries; organizes World Psychiatric Congresses and regional and inter-regional scientific meetings. Mems: 72 societies totalling 65,000 psychiatrists. Sec.-Gen. Prof. FINI SCHULSINGER (Denmark).

ASSOCIATE MEMBERS OF CIOMS

Asia Pacific Academy of Ophthalmology: Dept of Ophthalmology, Juntendo University School of Medicine, 3-1-3 Hongo Bunkyo-ku, Tokyo 113, Japan; tel. 03-813-3111 (ext. 3354); f. 1956; holds congress every two years (12th congress: Seoul, Republic of Korea, 1989). Pres. Prof. R. K. TAMIN RADJAMIN; Sec.-Gen. Dr AKIRA NAKAJIMA (Japan).

Association for Paediatric Education in Europe: Juliana Children's Hospital, POB 60604, 2506 LP The Hague, Netherlands; f.

OTHER INTERNATIONAL ORGANIZATIONS — Medicine and Health

1970 to encourage improvements and promote research in paediatric education. Mems: 70 in 20 European countries. Pres. Mrs O. NEYZI (Turkey); Sec. Dr M. LOURDES LEVY (Portugal).

International Association of Hydatid Disease: Florida 460, 1005 Buenos Aires, Argentina; tel. 322-3431; telex 23414; f. 1941. Mems: 500 in 40 countries. Pres. Dr DINORAH CASTIGLIONI TULA (Uruguay); Sec.-Gen. Prof. Dr RAUL MARTÍN MENDY (Argentina). Publ. *Archivos Internacionales de la Hidatidosis* (every 4 years), *Boletín de Hidatidosis* (quarterly).

International Association of Medicine and Biology of the Environment: c/o 115 rue de la Pompe, 75116 Paris, France; tel. (1) 45-53-45-04; telex 614584; f. 1972 with assistance from the UN Environment Programme; aims to contribute to the solution of problems caused by human influence on the environment; structure includes 13 technical commissions. Mems: individuals and organizations in 71 countries. Hon. Pres. Prof. R. DUBOS; Pres. Dr R. ABBOU.

International Committee of Military Medicine and Pharmacy: 79 rue Saint-Laurent, 4000 Liège, Belgium; tel. (41) 22-21-83; f. 1921. Mems: official delegates from 91 countries. Pres. Maj.-Gen. A. HUBER (Switzerland); Sec.-Gen. Lt.-Col Dr M. COOLS (Belgium). Publ. *Revue Internationale des Services de Santé des Forces Armées* (quarterly).

International Congress on Tropical Medicine and Malaria: c/o Prof. M. Miller, Faculty of Medicine, University of Calgary, Calgary T2N 1N4, Canada; to work towards the solution of the problems concerning malaria and tropical diseases. Sec. Prof. MAX MILLER.

International Council for Laboratory Animal Science: POB 6, 70211 Kuopio 10, Finland; f. 1976. Pres. S. ERICHSEN (Norway); Sec.-Gen. O. HÄNNINEN (Finland).

International Federation of Clinical Chemistry: c/o Dr R. K. Vihko, Dept of Clinical Chemistry, University of Oulu, 90220 Oulu 22, Finland; tel. (981) 254464; telex 32305; f. 1952. Mems: 52 national societies (about 22,000 individuals). Pres. Dr D. S. YOUNG (USA); Sec. Dr. R. K. VIHKO (Finland). Publs *News* (3 a year), *Annual Report*.

International Medical Society of Paraplegia: National Spinal Injuries Centre, Stoke Mandeville Hospital, Aylesbury, Bucks, HP21 8AL, England; tel. (0296) 84111. Pres. Prof. R. E. CARTER (USA); Sec. I. NUSEIBEH.

International Society of Neuropathology: c/o Dr S. Ludwin, Dept of Pathology, Queen's University, Kingston, Ontario K7L 3N6, Canada. Pres. Dr H. DEF. WEBSTER; Sec.-Gen. Dr S. LUDWIN.

Transplantation Society: c/o Dr R. Ferguson, Dept of Surgery, Means Hall, Ohio State University Medical School, Columbus, Ohio 43210, USA. Pres. Dr J. RICHARD BATCHELOR; Secs Prof. R. F. M. WOOD, Dr RONALD FERGUSON (USA).

OTHER ORGANIZATIONS

Aerospace Medical Association: 320 Henry St, Alexandria, Va 22314, USA; tel. (703) 739-2240; f. 1929 as Aero Medical Association; to advance the science and art of aviation and space medicine; to establish and maintain co-operation between medical and allied sciences concerned with aerospace medicine; to promote, protect, and maintain safety in aviation and astronautics. Mems: individual, constituent and corporate in 75 countries. Pres. DANIEL B. LESTAGE (USA); Exec. Vice-Pres. RUFUS R. HESSBERG (USA). Publ. *Aviation Space and Environmental Medicine* (monthly).

Asian-Pacific Dental Federation: 841 Mountbatten Rd, Singapore 1543; tel. 3453125; telex 34189; f. 1955 to establish closer relationship among dental associations in Asian and Pacific countries and to encourage research, with particular emphasis on dental health in the region; holds congress every two years. Mems: 16 national associations. Sec.-Gen. Dr OLIVER HENNEDIGE. Publ. *APDF/APRO Newsletter* (3 a year).

Association of National European and Mediterranean Societies of Gastro-enterology—ASNEMGE: Lange Lozanastraat 222, 2018 Antwerp, Belgium; tel. (03) 238-01-85; f. 1947 to facilitate the exchange of ideas between gastro-enterologists and disseminate knowledge; organizes International Congress of Gastroenterology every four years. Mems in 30 countries, national societies and sections of national medical societies. Pres. Prof. Dr J. M. CARRILHO-RIBEIRO (Portugal); Sec. Dr L. O. STANDAERT (Belgium).

Balkan Medical Union: 1 rue Gabriel Peri, 70148 Bucharest, Romania; tel. 16-78-46; f. 1932; studies medical problems, particularly ailments specific to the Balkan region, to promote a regional programme of public health; enables exchange of information between doctors in the region; organizes research programmes and congresses. Mems: doctors and specialists from Albania, Bulgaria, Cyprus, Greece, Romania, Turkey and Yugoslavia. Pres. Dr M. POPESCU BUZEU (Romania); Sec.-Gen. Dr P. FIRU (Romania). Publs *Archives de l'union médicale Balkanique* (6 a year), *Bulletin de l'union médicale Balkanique* (6 a year), *Annuaire, Bulletin de l'Entente Médicale Méditerranéenne* (annually).

European Association for Cancer Research: c/o Dr M. R. Price, Cancer Research Campaign Laboratories, University of Nottingham, University Park, Nottingham, NG7 2RD, UK; tel. (0602) 484848 (ext. 3401); f. 1968 to facilitate contact between cancer research workers and to organize scientific meetings in Europe. Mems: over 1,300 in 40 countries in and outside Europe. Pres. Prof. Dr P. BANNASCH (FRG); Sec. Dr M. R. PRICE (UK).

European Association for Health Information and Libraries: 60 rue de la Concorde, 1050 Brussels, Belgium; f. 1987; serves professionals in health information and libraries of the member states of the Council of Europe; holds regular conferences of medical librarians. Pres. M. WALCKIERS (Belgium); Sec. D. WRIGHT (UK). Publ. *Newsletter*.

European Association for the Study of Diabetes: Auf'm Hennekamp 32, 4000 Dusseldorf 1, Federal Republic of Germany; tel. (0211) 316738; f. 1965 to support research in the field of diabetes, to promote the rapid diffusion of acquired knowledge and its application; holds annual scientific meetings within Europe. Mems: 2,360 in 62 countries, not confined to Europe. Pres. Prof. P. FREYCHET (France); Exec. Dir Dr VIKTOR JOERGENS. Publ. *Diabetologia* (12 a year).

European Association of Internal Medicine: Clinique Médicale B, 1 place de l'Hôpital, 67091 Strasbourg, France; tel. 88-16-12-50; f. 1969 to promote internal medicine from the ethical, scientific and professional points of view; to bring together European internists; to organize meetings, etc. Mems: 400 in 20 European countries. Pres. Prof. E. COCHE (Belgium); Sec. Prof J. F. BLICKLE (France). Publ. *European Journal of Internal Medicine*.

European Association of Radiology: c/o P. Delorme, Hôpital Pellegrin, Place Amélie Raba-Léon, 33076 Bordeaux, France; tel. (56) 96-83-83; f. 1962 to develop and co-ordinate the efforts of radiologists in Europe by promoting radiology in both biology and medicine, studying its problems, developing professional training and establishing contact between radiologists and professional, scientific and industrial organizations. Mems: national associations in 25 countries. Sec.-Gen. Pr. G. DELORME.

European Association of Social Medicine: Via dei Mille 34, 10123 Turin, Italy; f. 1953 to provide co-operation between national associations of preventive medicine and public health. Mems: associations in 10 countries. Pres. Prof. Dr FERNANDO LUIGI PETRILLI (Italy); Sec.-Gen. Prof. Dr ENRICO BELLI (Italy).

European Brain and Behaviour Society: c/o G. Mohn, Univ.-Augenklinik, 7400 Tübingen, Schleichstr. 12, Federal Republic of Germany; tel. (07071) 293734; holds two conferences a year. Pres. Prof. M. JEANNEROD; Sec. Dr G. MOHN.

European Committee for the Protection of the Population against the Hazards of Chronic Toxicity—EUROTOX: Faculté des Sciences Pharmaceutiques et Biologiques, Laboratoire de Toxicologie et d'Hygiène Industrielle, 4 ave de l'Observatoire, Paris 6e, France; tel. (1) 43-26-71-22; f. 1957; studies risks of long-term build-up of toxicity. Gen. Sec. Prof. R. TRUHAUT (France).

European Healthcare Management Association: 1 Carlton Villas, Shelbourne Rd, Dublin 4, Ireland; tel. 689642; f. 1966 to promote collaboration between European countries in the organization and development of training programmes in hospital and health services administration; to encourage studies and research. Mems: 74 (corporate) in 21 countries, and 28 associate mems. Pres. Prof. Dr H. VAN ANDEL; Dir PHILIP C. BERMAN; Publ. *Newsletter* (quarterly), *Directory* (every 2 years).

European League against Rheumatism: Promenadengasse 18, Zürich, Switzerland; tel. (01) 252-48-66; f. 1947 to co-ordinate research and treatment of rheumatic complaints, conducted by national societies; holds annual symposia, and congress every four years. Mems in 32 countries. Exec. Sec. F. WYSS. Publ. *Bulletin*.

European Organization for Caries Research—ORCA: c/o Dr C. Robinson, Dept of Oral Biology, School of Dentistry, University of Leeds, Leeds, LS2 9LU, England; tel. (0532) 440111, ext. 298; f. 1953 to promote and undertake research on dental health, encourage international contacts, and make the public aware of the importance of care of the teeth. Mems: research workers in 23 countries. Pres. Prof. J. A. WEATHERELL (UK); Sec.-Gen. Dr C. ROBINSON (UK).

European Orthodontic Society: Flat 31, 49 Hallam St, London, W1N 5LL, England; tel. (01) 935-2795; f. 1907 to advance the science of orthodontics and its relations with the collateral arts and sciences. Mems: 1,559 in 48 countries. Sec. Prof. J. MOSS. Publ. *European Journal of Orthodontics* (quarterly).

European Society for Comparative Endocrinology: c/o Prof. A. de Loof, Zoologisch Instituut, 59 Naamsestraat, 3000 Leuven,

OTHER INTERNATIONAL ORGANIZATIONS

Belgium; tel. (16) 28-39-12; f. 1965 to promote interdisciplinary exchange between scientists engaged in various aspects of comparative endocrinology; sponsors a conference every two years. Mems: 320 in 30 countries. Pres. Prof. Dr Y. FONTAINE; Sec. Prof. A. DE LOOF.

European Union of Medical Specialists: 20 ave de la Couronne, Brussels 1050, Belgium; tel. (02) 649-21-47; f. 1958 to safeguard the interests of medical specialists. Mems: two representatives each from Belgium, Denmark, France, Federal Republic of Germany, Greece, Ireland, Italy, Luxembourg, Netherlands, Portugal, Spain and UK. Pres. Dr A. KUTTNER (FRG); Sec.-Gen. Dr G. DES MAREZ (Belgium).

Eurotransplant Foundation: c/o University Hospital, Leiden 2333 AA, Netherlands; tel. (071) 268008; telex 39266; f. 1967; co-ordinates the exchange of organs for transplants in the Federal Republic of Germany, Austria, Belgium, the Netherlands; keeps register of almost 8,000 patients with all necessary information for matching with suitable donors in the shortest possible time; organizes transport of the organ and the transplantation; collaboration with similar organizations in Western and Eastern Europe. Chair. Prof. Dr J. J. VAN ROOD; Dir Drs B. COHEN.

Federation of French-Language Obstetricians and Gynaecologists (Fédération des gynécologues et obstetriciens de langue française): Clinique Baudelocque, 123 blvd de Port-Royal, 75674 Paris Cedex 14, France; tel. (1) 42-34-11-40; f. 1920 for the scientific study of phenomena having reference to obstetrics, gynaecology and reproduction in general. Mems: 1,500 in 50 countries. Pres. Prof. C. SUREAU (France); Gen. Sec. Prof. J. R. ZORN (France). Publ. *Journal de Gynécologie Obstétrique et Biologie de la Reproduction* (8 a year).

Federation of the European Dental Industry: 5000 Cologne 1, Pipinstrasse 16, Federal Republic of Germany; tel. (0221) 215993; telex 8882226; f. 1957 to promote the interests of the dental industry. Mems: national associations in Austria, Denmark, France, the Federal Republic of Germany, Italy, the Netherlands, Sweden, Switzerland and the United Kingdom. Pres. and Chair. A. D'HOLLOSY (Netherlands).

Federation of World Health Foundations: Ave Appia, 1211 Geneva 27, Switzerland; f. 1967 to co-ordinate the work of the members and to maintain relations between them and the World Health Organization. The General Council of representatives of the member foundations is assisted by a steering committee. The Federation examines projects to be considered by the foundations, seeks to establish new foundations, provides advice and training. Mems: 10 national health foundations which have entered into formal agreement with WHO, in Canada, Hong Kong, Indonesia, Ireland, Philippines, Sri Lanka, Switzerland, USA. Pres., CEO MILTON P. SIEGEL.

General Association of Municipal Health and Technical Experts: 9 rue de Phalsbourg, 75017 Paris, France; tel. (1) 42-27-38-91; f. 1905 to study all questions related to urban and rural health—the control of preventable diseases, disinfection, distribution and purification of drinking water, construction of drains, sewage, collection and disposal of household refuse, etc. Mems in 35 countries. Pres. F. OZANNE (France); Sec.-Gen. M. BRÈS (France). Publ. *TSM-Techniques, Sciences, Méthodes* (monthly).

Inter-American Association of Sanitary and Environmental Engineering: Av. Beira-Mar 216, 13° andar, 20021 Rio de Janeiro, RJ Brazil; tel. (21) 210-3221; telex 21 31902; f. 1948 to establish uniform health standards in water supply and sanitation. Mems: 24 countries. Publ. *Revista Ingeniería Sanitaria* (quarterly).

Inter-American Society of Cardiology (Sociedad Interamericana de Cardiología): Instituto Nacional de Cardiología Ignacio Chávez de México, Juan Badiano 1, Tlalpan, DF, Mexico 14080; tel. (905) 573-29-11; f. 1944 to stimulate the development of cardiology. Mems: 22,000 in 23 countries. Pres. (1985–89) Dr BERNARDO BOSKIS; Sec.-Treas. Dr EDUARDO SALAZAR.

International Academy of Aviation and Space Medicine: 224 place Air Canada, Montreal, PQ H2Z 1X5, Canada; tel. (514) 879-7511; f. 1955; to facilitate international co-operation in research and teaching in the fields of aviation and space medicine. Mems: in 40 countries. Sec.-Gen. Dr ANTOINE SAINT-PIERRE.

International Academy of Cytology: 1050 chemin Ste-Foy, Québec, Que., Canada G1S 4L8; tel. (418) 682-8033; f. 1957 to foster and facilitate international exchange of knowledge and information on specialized problems of clinical cytology and to stimulate research in clinical cytology; to standardize terminology. Mems: 1,975. Pres. ALEXANDER MEISELS; Sec.-Treas. CLAUDE GOMPEL. Publ. *Acta Cytologica*.

International Anatomical Congress: Prof. L. J. A. DiDio, Dept of Anatomy, Medical College of Ohio, CS 10008 Toledo, OH 43699, USA; f. 1903; runs congresses for anatomists from all over the world to discuss research, teaching methods and terminology in the fields of gross and microscopical anatomy, histology, cytology, etc. Pres. Prof. L. J. A. DiDio (USA); Sec.-Gen. Prof. J. A. E. PINA (Portugal).

International Association for Child and Adolescent Psychiatry and Allied Professions: Tirilvej 8, 0875 Oslo, Norway; f. 1948 to promote scientific research in the field of child psychiatry by collaboration with allied professions. Mems: national associations and individuals in 36 countries. Sec.-Gen. MÅFRID FLEKKØY. Publ. *International Yearbook of Child Psychiatry*.

International Association for Dental Research: 1111 14th St, NW, Suite 1000, Washington, DC 20005, USA; tel. (202) 898-1050; f. 1920 to encourage research in dentistry and related fields, and to further the communication of the results of such research by publication and by annual meetings; triennial conferences and divisional meetings are also held. Pres. WILLIAM D. McHUGH; Exec. Dir Dr J. A. GRAY.

International Association of Agricultural Medicine and Rural Health: Saku Central Hôspital, 197 Usuda-machi, Minamisaku-Gun, Nagano 384-03, Japan; f. 1961 to study the problems of medicine in agriculture in all countries and to prevent the diseases caused by the conditions of work in agriculture. Mems: 405. Pres. Prof. J. TÉNYI (Hungary); Sec.-Gen. Prof. TOSHIKAZU WAKATSUKI (Japan).

International Association of Applied Psychology: Montessorilaan 3, Nijmegen 6525 HR, Netherlands; tel. (080) 51-26-39; f. 1920, present title adopted in 1955; aims to establish contacts between those carrying out scientific work on applied psychology, to promote research and the adoption of measures contributing to this work. Mems: 3,000 in 90 countries. Pres. Prof. C. LEVY-LEBOYER (France); Sec.-Gen. and Treas. Prof. CH. J. DE WOLFF (Netherlands). Publ. *Applied Psychology: An International Review* (quarterly).

International Association of Asthmology—INTERASMA: c/o Prof. F. Michel, ave du Major Flandre, 34059, Montpellier, France; f. 1954 to advance medical knowledge of bronchial asthma and allied disorders. Mems: 1,100 in 54 countries. Pres. Prof. A. OEHLING (Spain); Sec.-Gen. Prof. F. MICHEL (France). Publ. *Allergologia et Immunopathologia* (every 2 months).

International Association of Catholic Health Care Institutions: Piazza San Calisto 16, 00153 Rome, Italy; f. 1951 (as International Catholic Confederation of Hospitals); organizes regular international and regional congresses. Mems: 17 national organizations.

International Association of Group Psychotherapy: Viale San Gimignano 10, 20146 Milan, Italy; tel. (02) 4154072; f. 1954; holds congresses every three years. Mems: 500 individuals in 30 countries; 20 organizations in 10 countries. Pres. GRETE A. LEUTZ (FRG); Sec.-Treas. GIOVANNI BORIA (Italy). Publ. *Newsletter*.

International Association of Logopedics and Phoniatrics: 6 ave de la Gare, 1003 Lausanne, Switzerland; f. 1924 to promote standards of training and research in human communication disorders in all countries, to establish information centres and communicate with kindred organizations. Mems: 400 individuals and 50 societies from 31 countries. Pres. Dr ANDRÉ MULLER; Gen. Sec. M. DE MONTFORT. Publ. *Folia Phoniatrica* (6 a year).

International Association of Oral and Maxillofacial Surgeons: c/o Dept of Oral and Maxillofacial Surgery, Guy's Hospital, London, SE1 9RT, England; tel. (01) 378-6918; f. 1963 to advance the science and art of oral surgery. Mems: 2,000. Pres. Prof. Dr W. SCHILLI (FRG); Sec.-Gen. Prof. D. E. POSWILLO (UK). Publs *International Journal of Oral Surgery* (every 2 months), *Newsletter* (every 6 months).

International Brain Research Organization—IBRO: 51 blvd de Montmorency, 75016 Paris, France; f. 1958 to further all aspects of brain research. Mems: 35 corporate and 19,500 individual. Pres. Prof. D. P. PURPURA (USA); Sec.-Gen. Dr D. OTTOSON. Publs *IBRO News, Neuroscience* (bi-monthly), *IBRO Membership Directory*.

International Bronchoesophagological Society: Mayo Clinic, Scottsdale, Ariz 65258, USA; f. 1951 to promote by all means the progress of bronchoesophagology and to provide a forum for discussion among broncho-esophagologists of various specialities; holds congress every three years. Mems: 500 in 49 countries. Exec. Sec. Dr DAVID SANDERSON.

International Bureau for Epilepsy: 118 East Hamilton Ave, Englewood, NJ 07631, USA; f. 1961; the national branches of the International League against Epilepsy (q.v.) are members of the Bureau; to collect and disseminate information about social and medical care for epileptics, to organize international and regional meetings; to advise and answer questions on social aspects of epilepsy. Mems: in 26 countries. Sec.-Gen. Dr RICHARD L. MASLAND. Publ. *Newsletter* (quarterly).

International Cell Research Organization: c/o UNESCO, 7 place de Fontenoy, 75700 Paris, France; f. 1962 to create, encourage and promote co-operation between scientists of different disciplines throughout the world for the advancement of fundamental knowledge of the cell, normal and abnormal; organizes every year six to eight international laboratory courses on modern topics of cell and molecular biology and biotechnology for young research scientists in important research centres all over the world. Mems: 400. Chair. Prof. L. ERNSTER (Sweden); Exec. Sec. Prof. G. N. COHEN (France).

International Chiropractors' Association: 1901 L St, NW, Suite 800, Washington, DC, USA; tel. (202) 659-6476; f. 1926 to promote advancement of the art and science of chiropractic. Mems: 7,000 individuals in addition to affiliated associations. Pres. FRED BARGE; Sec.-Treas. ANDREW WYMORE. Publs *International Review of Chiropractic* (every 2 months), *ICA Today* (every 2 months).

International Commission for Optics: Blackett Laboratory, Imperial College, London, SW7 2BZ, England; tel. (01) 589-5111; telex 929484; f. 1948 to contribute to the progress of theoretical and instrumental optics, to assist in research and to promote international agreement on specifications; Gen. Assembly every three years. Mems: national committees in 33 countries. Pres. Prof. J. W. GOODMAN (USA); Sec.-Gen. Prof. J. C. DAINTY (UK). Publs *ICO Bulletin*.

International Commission on Occupational Health: 10 ave Jules-Crosnier, 1206 Geneva, Switzerland; tel. (022) 476184; f. 1906 (present name 1985) to study and prevent pathological conditions arising from industrial work; arranges congresses on occupational medicine and the protection of workers' health; provides information for public authorities and learned societies. Mems: 1,200 from 75 countries. Pres. Dr ROBERT MURRAY (UK); Sec.-Treas. Prof. LUIGI PARMEGGIANI (Italy). Publ. *Newsletter* (quarterly).

International Commission on Radiological Protection—ICRP: POB 35, Didcot, OX11 0RJ, England; f. 1928 to provide technical guidance and promote international co-operation in the field of radiation protection; committees on Radiation Effects, Secondary Limits, Protection in Medicine, and the application of recommendations. Mems: about 70. Chair. Dr D. BENINSON (Argentina); Scientific Sec. Dr H. SMITH (UK). Publ. *Annals of the ICRP*.

International Committee of Catholic Nurses: Palazzo San Calisto, Piazza San Calisto 16, 00153 Rome, Italy; f. 1933 to group professional catholic nursing associations; to represent Christian thought in the general professional field at international level; to co-operate in the general development of the profession and to promote social welfare. Mems: 49 full, 20 corresponding mems. Pres. RICHARD LAI PONG CHONG; Gen. Sec. LILIANA FIORI. Publs *Nouvelles/News/Nachrichten* (every 4 months).

International Council for Physical Fitness Research—ICPFR: Dept of Pediatrics, McMaster University, Hamilton, Ont L8N 3Z5, Canada; f. 1964 to construct international standardized physical fitness tests, to obtain information on world standards of physical fitness, to promote comparative studies and to encourage health and physical fitness in all countries through the exchange of scientific knowledge. Mems: in 25 countries. Pres. Prof. O. BAR-OR.

International Council of Nurses—ICN: 3 place Jean-Marteau, 1201 Geneva, Switzerland; tel. (022) 312960; f. 1899 to provide a medium through which national associations of nurses may share their common interests, working together to develop the contribution of nursing to the promotion of the health of people and the care of the sick. Quadrennial congresses are held in different countries. Mems: 101 national nurses' associations. Pres. NELLY GARZÓN (Colombia); Exec. Dir CONSTANCE HOLLERAN. Publ. *The International Nursing Review* (6 a year, in English).

International Cystic Fibrosis (Mucoviscidosis) Association: 3 Lecky St, London, SW7 3QP, England; tel. (01) 373-8300; f. 1964 to disseminate current information on cystic fibrosis in those areas of the world where the disease occurs and to stimulate the work of scientific and medical researchers attempting to discover its cure. Conducts annual medical symposia. Mems: 26 national organizations. Pres. MARTIN WEIBEL (Switzerland); Sec. ROBERT JOHNSON (UK).

International Federation for Hygiene, Preventive Medicine and Social Medicine: Via Salaria 237, 00199 Rome, Italy; tel. 8457928; f. 1951. Eleventh Conference: Madrid, Spain, September 1986. Mems: national associations and individual members in 74 countries. Pres. Prof. Dr G. A. CANAPERIA (Italy); Sec.-Gen. Dr ERNST MUSIL (Austria). Publ. *Bulletin*.

International Federation for Medical and Biological Engineering: National Research Council of Canada, Bldg M-50, Ottawa, Ont. K1A 0R8, Canada; tel. (613) 993-1686; telex 053-4134; f. 1959. Mems: national associations in 30 countries. Sec.-Gen. OREST Z. ROY (Canada).

International Federation for Medical Psychotherapy: Box 26, Vinderen, Oslo 3, Norway; tel. (02) 146190; f. 1946 to further research and teaching of psychotherapy, to organize international congresses. Mems: 3,200 psychotherapists from 24 countries, 36 societies. Pres. Dr FINN MAGNUSSEN (Norway); Sec.-Gen. Dr TRULS-EIRIK MOGSTAD (Norway). Publ. *Psychotherapy and Psychosomatics*.

International Federation of Fertility Societies: Michaelisstrasse 16, 2300 Kiel 1, Federal Republic of Germany; tel. (0431) 5972040. Pres. Prof. Dr KURT SEMM.

International Federation of Gynecology and Obstetrics: 27 Sussex Place, Regent's Park, London, NW1 4RG, England; tel. (01) 723-2951; f. 1954; assists and contributes to research in gynaecology and obstetrics; aims to facilitate the exchange of information and perfect methods of teaching; organizes international congresses. Membership: national societies in 86 countries. Pres. of Bureau Prof. S. RATNAM (Singapore); Sec.-Gen. Prof. D. V. I. FAIRWEATHER (UK). Publ. *Journal*.

International Federation of Multiple Sclerosis Societies: 3/9 Heddon St, London, W1R 7LE, England; tel. (01) 734-9120; f. 1965 to co-ordinate and further the work of 31 national multiple sclerosis organizations throughout the world, to stimulate and encourage scientific research in this and related neurological diseases, to aid member societies in helping individuals who are in any way disabled as a result of these diseases, to collect and disseminate information and to provide counsel and active help in furthering the development of voluntary national multiple sclerosis organizations. Pres. WILLIAM P. BENTON; Sec.-Gen. JOSEPH M. AGUAYO. Publs *Federation Update* (quarterly), *Annual Report*.

International Federation of Ophthalmological Societies: c/o Prof. A. Deutman, Institute of Ophthalmology, University of Nijmegen, 16 Philips van Leijden laan, 6525 EX Nijmegen, Netherlands; tel. (080) 513138; f. 1953; holds international congress every four years. Pres. Prof. A. E. MAUMENEE (USA); Sec. Prof. A. DEUTMAN.

International Federation of Pharmaceutical Manufacturers Associations—IFPMA: 67 rue St Jean, 1201 Geneva, Switzerland; tel. (022) 326317; telex 27042; f. 1968 for the exchange of information and international co-operation in all questions of interest to the pharmaceutical industry, particularly in the field of health legislation, science and research in order to contribute to the advancement of the health and welfare of the peoples of the world; development of ethical principles and practices and co-operation with national and international organizations, governmental and non-governmental. Mems: the pharmaceutical manufacturers associations of the EEC, EFTA, Latin America, Australia, Canada, Hong Kong, India, Israel, Japan, Kenya, Republic of Korea, Malaysia, New Zealand, Pakistan, the Philippines, Singapore, South Africa, Spain, Sri Lanka, Thailand, Turkey and the USA. Pres. P. JOLY; Exec. Vice-Pres. Dr RICHARD B. ARNOLD.

International Federation of Surgical Colleges: c/o Prof. W. A. L. MacGowan, Royal College of Surgeons in Ireland, 123 St Stephen's Green, Dublin 2, Ireland; tel. 780200; telex 30795; f. 1958 to encourage high standards of surgery and surgical training; co-operates closely with the World Health Organization in compiling standard lists of surgical requirements in developing countries and evaluating surgical manpower. Mems: colleges or associations in 35 countries, and 210 individual associates. Pres. Dr ROBERT B. SALTER (Canada); Sec. Prof. W. A. L. MACGOWAN (Ireland).

International Federation of Thermalism and Climatism: 16 rue de l'Estrapade, 75005 Paris, France; tel. (1) 43-25-11-85; telex 203187; f. 1947. Mems in 26 countries. Pres. Dr G. EBRARD; Gen. Sec. M. VITU.

International Guild of Dispensing Opticians: 40 Portland Place, London, W1N 4BA, England; tel. (01) 637-2507; f. 1951 to promote the science of, and to maintain and advance standards and effect co-operation in optical dispensing. Central Sec. A. P. D. WESTHEAD (UK).

International Hospital Federation: 2 St Andrew's Place, London, NW1 4LB, England; tel. (01) 935-9487; f. 1947 for information exchange and education in hospital and health service matters; represents institutional health care in discussions with WHO; conducts conferences and courses on management and policy issues. Mems in five categories: national hospital and health service organizations, professional associations, regional organizations and individual hospitals; individual mems; professional and industrial mems; honorary mems. Pres. Prof. Dr T. TOLLOCZKO (Poland); Dir-Gen. Dr E. N. PICKERING. Publ. *Yearbook, Journal, Newsletter*.

International League against Epilepsy: c/o Dr F. E. Dreifuss, University of Virginia Medical Center, Charlottesville, Va 22903, USA; tel. (804) 924-5669; f. 1910 to link national professional associations and to encourage research, including classification and anti-epileptic drugs; collaborates with the International Bureau for Epilepsy (q.v.) and with WHO. Mems: 33 associations. Pres. F. E. DREIFUSS (USA); Sec.-Gen. H. MEINARDI (Netherlands).

International Medical Association for the Study of Living Conditions and Health: Institute of Nutrition, blvd D. Nestorov 15, 1431 Sofia, Bulgaria; tel. 58 101 707; f. 1951 to co-ordinate research

OTHER INTERNATIONAL ORGANIZATIONS — Medicine and Health

in a wide range of subjects relating to living, working and environmental conditions which favour man's healthy physical and moral development; holds international congresses. Mems: doctors in 35 countries. Pres. Prof. T. TASHEV (Bulgaria). Publ. *Acta Medica et Sociologica*, congress and conference reports.

International Narcotics Control Board—INCB: 1400 Vienna, POB 500, Austria; tel. 26310; telex 135612; f. 1961 to supervise the implementation of the Drug Control Treaties by governments. Mems: 13 individuals. Pres. SAHIBZADA RAOOF ALI KHAN; Sec. ABDELAZIZ BAHI (Tunisia). Publ. *Annual Report* (with two statistical supplements).

International Optometric and Optical League: 10 Knaresborough Place, London, SW5 0TG, England; tel. (01) 370-4765; f. 1927 to co-ordinate efforts to provide a good standard of ophthalmic optical (optometric) care throughout the world; the League is active in providing a forum for exchange of ideas between different countries; a large part of its work is concerned with optometric education, and advice upon standards of qualification. The League also interests itself in legislation in relation to optometry throughout the world. Mems: 61 optometric organizations in 49 countries. Pres. G. B. HOLMES; Sec. D. A. LEASON. Publs *Interoptics* (6 a year).

International Organization for Medical Physics: c/o Prof. C. G. Orton, Gershenson Radiation Oncology Center, Harper Hospital, 3990 John R. St, Detroit, Mich 48201, USA; tel. (313) 745-2489; f. 1963 to organize international co-operation in medical physics, to promote communication between the various branches of medical physics and allied subjects, to contribute to the advancement of medical physics in all its aspects and to advise on the formation of national organizations. Mems: national organizations of medical physics in 40 countries. Pres. Prof. JOHN R. CUNNINGHAM (Canada); Sec.-Gen. Prof. COLIN G. ORTON (USA). Publ. *Medical Physics World*.

International Pharmaceutical Federation: Alexanderstraat 11, 2514 JL The Hague, Netherlands; tel. (70) 63-19-25; telex 32781; f. 1912 to promote the development of pharmacy both as a profession and as an applied science; holds Assembly of Pharmacists every two years, International Congress every year. Mems: 69 national pharmaceutical organizations in 53 countries, 75 associate collective mems, 3,650 individuals. Dir L. FÉLIX-FAURE. Publ. *International Pharmacy Journal* (every 2 months).

International Psycho-Analytical Association: Broomhills, Woodside Lane, London, N12 8UD, England; tel. (01) 446-8324; f. 1908 to hold meetings to define and promulgate the theory and teaching of psychoanalysis, to act as a forum for scientific discussions, to control and regulate training and to contribute to the interdisciplinary area which is common to the behavioural sciences. Mems: 6,700. Pres. ROBERT S. WALLERSTEIN (USA); Sec. EDWARD M. WEINSHEL (USA). Publs *Bulletin, Newsletter*.

International Rehabilitation Medicine Association: c/o Prof. M. Grabois, Dept of Physical Medicine, Baylor College of Medicine, 1333 Moursund Ave, Houston, Texas 77030, USA; tel. (713) 799-5090; f. 1968. Mems: 1,160 in 59 countries. Pres. TYRONE REYES (Philippines); Sec. Prof. M. GRABOIS (USA). Publ. *Journal of International Rehabilitation Medicine* (quarterly).

International Society for Cardiovascular Surgery: 13 Elm St, POB 1565, Manchester, MA 01944-0865, USA; tel. (617) 927-8330; telex 940103; f. 1950 to stimulate research in the diagnosis and therapy of cardiovascular diseases and to exchange ideas on an international basis. Sec.-Gen. JAMES A. DEWEESE (USA). Publ. *Journal of Cardiovascular Surgery*.

International Society for Mental Imagery Techniques: 12 rue St Julien-le-Pauvre, 75005 Paris, France; tel. (1) 46-33-52-47; f. 1968; a group of research workers, technicians and psychotherapists using oneirism techniques under waking conditions, with the belief that a healing action cannot be dissociated from the restoration of creativity. Mems: in 17 countries. Pres. Dr ANDRÉ VIREL (France); Sec. PHILIPPE GROSBOIS (France).

International Society for Research on Civilization Diseases and Environment: 61 rue E. Bouilliot, Bte 11, 1060 Brussels, Belgium; tel. (02) 343-97-48; f. 1972 to study environmental conditions, non-transmissive diseases and occupational medicine; holds annual congress and one or two workshops a year. Mems: associations and individuals in 61 countries. Pres. Dr S. KLEIN (Belgium); Dirs of Scientific Council Prof. M. CLOAREC (France), Prof. H. WRBA (Austria). Publ. *Newsletter*.

International Society of Art and Psychopathology: Centre Hospitalier St Anne, 100 rue de la Santé, 75014 Paris, France; tel. (1) 45-89-55-21; f. 1959 to bring together the various specialists interested in the problems of expression and artistic activities in connection with psychiatric, sociological and psychological research, as well as in the use of methods applied to other fields than that of mental illness. Mems: 625. Pres. Prof. VOLMAT (France); Sec.-Gen. Dr C. WIART (France).

International Society of Blood Transfusion: BP 100, 91943 Les Ulis Cedex, France; tel. (1) 69-07-20-40; telex 603218; f. 1937. Mems: about 1,600 in 89 countries. Pres. G. ARCHER (Australia); Sec.-Gen. M. GARRETTA. Publ. *Vox Sanguinis*.

International Society of Developmental Biologists: Institut d'Embryologie, CNRS, 49 bis ave de la Belle Gabrielle, 94736 Nogent sur Marne, France; tel. (1) 48-73-60-90; f. 1911 as International Institute of Embryology. Objects: to promote the study of developmental biology and to promote international co-operation among the investigators in this field; the Hubrecht Laboratory is an International Research Laboratory for descriptive and experimental embryology, and has a Central Embryological Library and Collection of slides and material. Mems: 850 in 33 countries. Sec. Prof. N. LE DOUARIN. Publ. *Cell Differentiation*.

International Society of Lymphology: 1501 North Campbell Ave, Tucson, Ariz 85724, USA; tel. (602) 626-6118; f. 1966 to further progress in lymphology through personal contact and exchange of ideas among members. Mems: 400 in 43 countries. Pres. M. FÖLDI (FRG); Sec.-Gen. M. H. WITTE (USA). Publ. *Lymphology* (quarterly).

International Society of Orthopaedic Surgery and Traumatology: 40 rue Washington, 1050 Brussels, Belgium; tel. (02) 648-68-23; telex 65080; f. 1929; congresses are convened every three years. Mems: 74 countries, 2,500 individuals. Pres. Sir DENNIS PATERSON (Australia); Sec.-Gen. JACQUES WAGNER (Belgium). Publ. *International Orthopaedics* (quarterly).

International Society of Radiology: Dept of Medical Radiology, University Hospital, 8091 Zürich, Switzerland; f. 1953 to promote diagnostic radiology and radiation oncology through its International Commissions on Radiation Units and Measurements, on Radiation Protection, on Radiological Education and on Rules and Regulations; organizes quadrennial International Congress of Radiology; collaborates with the World Health Organization. Mems: 63 national radiological societies. Sec. W. A. FUCHS.

International Society of Surgery: Hauptstrasse 63, PO Box, 4153 Reinach BL 1, Switzerland; tel. (061) 767036; f. 1902; organizes congresses: 33rd World Congress of Surgery, Toronto, Canada, 1989. Mems: 3,500. Sec.-Gen. Prof. MARTIN ALLGOWER. Publ. *World Journal of Surgery* (every 2 months).

International Society of Urology: 9 blvd du Temple, 75003 Paris, France; tel. (1) 42-78-40-09; f. 1921; congress every three years. Mems: 1,500 in 84 countries. Sec.-Gen. ALAIN JARDIN (France).

Middle East Neurosurgical Society: c/o Dr Fuad S. Haddad, Neurosurgical Department, American University Medical Centre, POB 113-6044, Beirut, Lebanon; tel. 347348; telex 20801; f. 1958 to promote clinical advances and scientific research among its members and to spread knowledge of neurosurgery and related fields among all members of the medical profession in the Middle East. Mems: 684 in nine countries. Pres. Dr STAMATIS COMNINOS; Hon. Sec. Dr FUAD S. HADDAD.

Organization for Co-ordination and Co-operation in the Fight against Endemic Diseases (Organisation de coordination et de coopération pour la lutte contre les grandes endémies—OCCGE): BP 153, Bobo-Dioulasso, Burkina Faso; tel. 98-28-75; f. 1960. Mems: governments of Benin, Burkina Faso, Côte d'Ivoire, Mali, Mauritania, Niger, Senegal, Togo; assoc. mem: France. Sec.-Gen. Dr EMMANUEL AKINOCHO. Publs *Rapport Technique, Revue d'épidémiologie et de santé publique* (3 a year).

Research centres:

Centre de Recherches sur les Méningites et les Schistosomiases: BP 10 887, Niamey, Niger.

Centre Muraz: BP 153, Bobo-Dioulasso, Burkina Faso; tel. 98-18-72; telex 8260; f. 1939; multi-discipline research centre with special interest in epidemiology. Dir Dr CHARLES DOUCHET.

Institut de Léprologie E. Marchoux: BP 251, Bamako, Mali; tel. 22-51-31; telex 1200; Dir MAX NEBOUT.

Institut d'Ophtalmologie Tropicale Africaine: BP 248, Bamako, Mali; Dir PIERRE VINGTAIN.

Institut Pierre Richet: BP 1500, Bouaké, Côte d'Ivoire; tel. 63-37-46; research on trypanosomiasis and onchocerciasis; Dir JEAN-PIERRE EDUZAN.

Office de Recherches sur l'Alimentation et la Nutrition Africaine: BP 2089, Dakar, Senegal; tel. 22-58-92; Dir Dr MAKHTAR N'DIAYE.

Offices are also based in Cotonou, Benin, (entomology), Lomé, Togo (nutrition), Nouakchott, Mauritania (tuberculosis), and Bafoulabé, Mali (onchocerciasis).

Organization for Co-ordination in the Fight against Endemic Diseases in Central Africa (Organisation de coordination pour la lutte contre les endémies en Afrique Centrale—OCEAC): BP 288,

Yaoundé, Cameroon; tel. 23-22-32; telex 8411; f. 1965 to standardize methods of controlling endemic diseases, to co-ordinate national action, and to negotiate programmes of assistance and training on a regional scale. Mems: Cameroon, Central African Republic, Chad, Congo, Equatorial Guinea, Gabon. Pres. SISSINIO MBANA NSORO MBANA; Sec.-Gen. Dr DANIEL KOUKA BEMBA. Publs *EPI—Notes* (quarterly), *Bulletin de Liaison et de Documentation* (quarterly).

Pan-American Association of Ophthalmology: 1301 South Bowen Rd, Suite 365, Arlington, Texas 76013, USA; tel. (817) 265-2831; f. 1940 to promote friendship and dissemination of scientific information among the profession throughout the Western Hemisphere. Mems: national ophthalmological societies in 22 countries. Pres. Dr BRADLEY R. STRAATSMA (USA); Exec. Dir Dr FRANCISCO CONTRERAS (Peru).

Pan-American Medical Association (Asociación Médica Panamericana): 222 Kent Terrace, West Palm Beach, Fla 33407, USA; f. 1925; holds inter-American congresses, conducts seminars and grants post-graduate scholarships. Mems: 5,500 in 31 countries. Dir-Gen. JOSEPH J. ELLER.

Pan-Pacific Surgical Association: POB 553, Honolulu, Hawaii 96809, USA; f. 1929 to bring together surgeons to exchange scientific knowledge relating to surgery and medicine, and to promote the improvement and standardization of hospitals and their services and facilities; congresses are held every two years. Mems: 2,716 regular, associate and senior mems from 44 countries. Chair. WILLIAM J. YARBROUGH.

Rehabilitation International: 25 East 21st St, New York, NY 10010, USA; tel. (212) 420-1500; telex 66125; f. 1922 to advance the welfare of the disabled through the exchange of information and research on equipment and methods of assistance; organizes international conferences and co-operates with UN agencies and other international organizations. Mems: national organizations in 80 countries. Pres. OTTO GEIECKER; Sec.-Gen. SUSAN R. HAMMERMAN. Publs *International Rehabilitation Review* (3 a year), *International Journal of Rehabilitation Research* (quarterly), *Rehabilitación* (2 a year).

Society of French-speaking Neuro-Surgeons (Société de neurochirurgie de langue française): Hôpital Neurologique, 59 blvd Pinel, BP Lyon-Montchat, 69394 Lyon Cedex 3, France; tel. 72-35-72-35; f. 1949; holds annual convention and congress. Mems: 600 in numerous countries. Pres. M. HURTH (France); Sec. G. FISCHER (France). Publ. *Neuro-Chirurgie* (6 a year).

Transnational Association of Acupuncture and Taoist Medicine: 48 ave Kléber, 75116 Paris, France; tel. (1) 47-27-05-95; f. 1963 to develop and promote knowledge of acupuncture in the world. Mems: national societies and individuals in 70 countries. Pres. Dr J. C. DE TYMOWSKI; Sec.-Gen. J. DE KERGUENEC. Publ. *Ecomédecine* (monthly).

World Confederation for Physical Therapy: 16–19 Eastcastle St, London, W1N 7PA, England; tel. (01) 637-2104; f. 1951 to encourage improved standards of physical therapy in training and practice; to promote exchange of information between nations; to assist the development of informed public opinion regarding physical therapy. Mems: 48 organizations. Sec.-Gen. Miss M. H. O'HARE. Publs *Newsletter* (2 a year), *Programmes of Physical Therapy Education*.

World Federation for Medical Education: c/o Medical School, University of Edinburgh, Teviot Place, Edinburgh, EH8 9AG, Scotland; tel. (031) 226-3125; telex 727442; f. 1972; promotes and integrates medical education world-wide; links regional and international associations. Pres. Prof. H. J. WALTON.

World Federation for Mental Health: 1021 Prince St, Alexandria, Va 22314, USA; tel. (703) 684-7722; f. 1948 to promote among all people and nations the highest possible standard of mental health in the broadest biological, medical, educational, and social aspects; to work with ECOSOC, UNESCO, the World Health Organization, and other agencies of the United Nations, in so far as they promote mental health; to help other voluntary associations in the improvement of mental health services; and to further the establishment of better human relations. Mems: 96 associations in 41 countries and five trans-national associations. Pres. Dr GAMAL ABOU EL AZAYEM (Egypt); Dir-Gen. Dr EUGENE B. BRODY; Deputy Sec.-Gen. RICHARD HUNTER. Publs *Newsletter* (5 a year).

World Federation of Neurosurgical Societies: c/o Dr H. A. D. Walder, Bergweg 12, 6523 MD Nijmegen, Netherlands; tel. (80) 231146; f. 1957 to assist the development of neurosurgery and to help the formation of associations; to assist the exchange of information and to encourage research. Mems: 57 societies representing 56 countries. Pres. Prof. W. KEMP CLARK; Sec. Dr H. ALPHONS D. WALDER.

World Federation of Occupational Therapists: University of Western Ontario, Occupational Therapy Dept, Health Sciences Bldg, London, Ontario, Canada N6A 5C1; tel. (519) 661-2179; f. 1952 to further the rehabilitation of the physically and mentally disabled by promoting the development of occupational therapy in all countries; to facilitate the exchange of information and publications; to promote research in occupational therapy; international congresses are held every four years. Mems: national professional associations in 36 countries, with total membership of approximately 36,000. Pres. JOANNA BARKER (Australia)); Hon. Sec.-Treas. BARBARA POSTHUMA (Canada). Publs *Bulletin* (2 a year).

World Federation of Public Health Associations: c/o Dr W. McBeath, Director of International Health Programs, American Public Health Asscn, 1015 15th St, NW, Washington, DC 20005, USA; tel. (202) 789-5691; f. 1967. Mems: 45 national public health associations. Exec. Sec. Dr WILLIAM H. MCBEATH (USA). Publs *Salubritas* (newsletter in English, French and Spanish), *WFPHA News* (in English), and occasional technical papers.

Posts and Telecommunications

African Posts and Telecommunications Union: ave Patrice Lumumba, BP 44, Brazzaville, Congo; tel. 812778; telex 5212; f. 1961 to improve postal and telecommunication services between member administrations. Mems: 12 countries. Sec.-Gen. M. SIMPORE.

Asia-Pacific Telecommunity: No. 12/49, Soi 5, Chaengwattana Rd, Thungsonghong, Bangkaen, Bangkok 10210, Thailand; tel. 573-6891; f. 1979 to cover all matters relating to telecommunications in the region. Mems: Afghanistan, Australia, Bangladesh, Brunei, Burma, the People's Republic of China, India, Indonesia, Iran, Japan, the Republic of Korea, Malaysia, Maldives, Nauru, Nepal, Pakistan, the Philippines, Singapore, Sri Lanka, Thailand, Viet-Nam; assoc. mem: Hong Kong; two affiliated mems in the Republic of Korea, two in Hong Kong, two in Japan, and five in the Philippines. Exec. Dir CHAO THONGMA.

Asian-Pacific Postal Union: Post Office Bldg, Manila, Philippines 2801; tel. 47-07-60; f. 1962 to extend, facilitate and improve the postal relations between the member countries and to promote co-operation in the field of postal services. Mems: 20 countries. Dir ANGELITO T. BANAYO. Publs *Annual Report*, *Exchange Program of Postal Officials*, *Newsletter*.

European Conference of Postal and Telecommunications Administrations: Dept of Trade and Industry, Telecommunications and Posts Division, Kingsgate House, 66-74 Victoria St, London, SW1E 6SW, England; tel. (01) 215-8149; telex 936069; f. 1959 to strengthen relations between member administrations and to harmonize and improve their technical services; set up Eurodata Foundation, for research and publishing. Mems: 26 countries. Publ. *Bulletin*.

European Telecommunications Satellite Organization—EUTELSAT: Tour Maine Montparnasse, 33 ave du Maine, 75755 Paris Cedex, France; tel. (1) 45-38-47-47; telex 203823; f. 1977 to develop and operate the European satellite telecommunications system. Mems: 26 national telecommunications administrations. Dir-Gen. ANDREA CARUSO.

International Maritime Satellite Organization—INMARSAT: 40 Melton St, London, NW1 2EQ, England; tel. (01) 387-9089; telex 297201; f. 1979 to provide (from February 1982) global communications for shipping via satellites on a commercial basis; satellites in geo-stationary orbit over the Atlantic, Indian and Pacific Oceans provide telephone, telex, facsimile, telegram, low to high speed data services and distress and safety communications for ships of all nations and structures such as oil rigs; in 1985 the operating agreement was amended to include aeronautical communications, and in 1988 amendments were being considered which would allow provision of global land-mobile communications. Organs: Assembly of all Parties to the Convention (every 2 years); council of representatives of 22 national telecommunications administrations; executive Directorate. Mems: 54 countries. Chair. of Council H. NAGATA (Japan); Dir-Gen. OLOF LUNDBERG (Sweden). Publ. *Ocean Voice* (quarterly), *Aeronautical Satellite News* (quarterly), *Transat* (quarterly).

International Telecommunications Satellite Organization—INTELSAT: 3400 International Drive, NW, Washington, DC 20008-3098, USA; tel. (202) 944-6800; telex 892707; f. 1964 to establish a global commercial satellite communications system. Assembly of Parties attended by representatives of member governments, meets every two years to consider policy and long-term aims and matters of interest to members as sovereign states. Meeting of Signatories to the Operating Agreement held annually. Sixteen INTELSAT satellites in synchronous orbit provide a global communications service; there are 212 earth stations carrying international commercial traffic and 14 facilities for performing specialized tracking, telemetry, command and monitoring (TTC & M). INTELSAT provides two-thirds of the world's overseas traffic through 70,000 units. Mems: 110 governments. Dir-Gen. DEAN BURCH.

OTHER INTERNATIONAL ORGANIZATIONS

Pacific Telecommunications Council: 1110 University Ave, Suite 308, Honolulu, HI 96826; tel. (808) 941-3789; telex 7430550; f. 1980 to promote the development, understanding and beneficial use of telecommunications throughout the Pacific region; provides forum for users and providers of communications services; sponsors annual conference and seminars. Exec. Dir RICHARD J. BARBER. Publ. *Journal* (quarterly).

Postal Union of the Americas and Spain (Unión Postal de las Américas y España): Calle Cebollatí 1468/70, Casilla de Correos 20.042, Montevideo, Uruguay; tel. 400070; telex 22073; f. 1911 to extend, facilitate and study the postal relationships of member countries. Mems: 24 countries. Sec.-Gen. Ing. PEDRO MIGUEL CABERO (Argentina).

Press, Radio and Television

Asia-Pacific Broadcasting Union—ABU: POB 1164, Jalan Pantai Bahru, 59700 Kuala Lumpur, Malaysia; tel. 2743592; telex 32227; f. 1964 to assist in the development of radio and television in the Asia/Pacific area, particularly in its use for educational purposes. Mems: 37 full, 11 additional and 25 associates. Pres. BEVERLEY WAKEM (New Zealand); Sec.-Gen. HUGH LEONARD. Publs *ABU News* (every 2 months), *ABU Technical Review* (every 2 months).

Association for the Promotion of the International Circulation of the Press—DISTRIPRESS: 8002 Zürich, Beethovenstrasse 20, Switzerland; tel. (01) 2024121; telex 815591; f. 1955 to assist in the promotion of the freedom of the press throughout the world, supporting and aiding UNESCO in promoting the free flow of ideas. Organizes meetings of publishers and distributors of newspapers, periodicals and paperback books, to promote the exchange of information and experience among members. Mems: 441. Pres. ALAN FRASER (UK); Man. Dr ARNOLD E. KAULICH (Switzerland). Publs *Distripress News, Distripress Letter*.

Association of European Journalists: Kastanienweg 26, 5300 Bonn 2, Federal Republic of Germany; tel. (0228) 324381; f. 1963 to participate actively in the development of a European consciousness; to promote deeper knowledge of European problems and secure appreciation by the general public of the work of European institutions; and to facilitate members' access to sources of European information. Mems: 1,500 individuals and national associations in 12 countries. Sec.-Gen. GUENTHER WAGENLEHNER.

Association of French-Language Television Services (Communauté des télévisions francophones): c/o Radio-Télévision Suisse Romande, 20 quai Ernest Ansermet, 1211 Geneva 8, Switzerland; f. 1964 to promote programme exchanges, joint ventures, exchange of information relating to television production and programming. Mems: French-language television organizations in France, Belgium, Switzerland, Monaco, Luxembourg and Canada. Pres. PIERRE DESROCHES (Canada); Gen. Sec. HENRI BUJARD (Switzerland).

Broadcasting Organizations of Non-aligned Countries—BONAC: Jugoslavenska Radiotelevizija, General Ždanova 28, 11000 Belgrade, Yugoslavia; tel. (011) 332271; telex 11469; f. 1977 to ensure an equitable, objective and comprehensive flow of information through broadcasting; assists in training of broadcasters, maintains programme bank, and organizes radio and TV festival and competition; General Conference held every three years; Secretariat moves to the broadcasting organization of host country. Mems: in 101 countries. Chair. DEMETRIOS KYPRIANOU; Sec. RADMILA MIHAILOVIĆ.

Community of French-Language Radio Broadcasters (Communauté des radios publiques de langue française): c/o Société Nationale de Radiodiffusion, 116 ave Président Kennedy, 75016 Paris, France; tel. (1) 42-30-27-41; telex 200002; f. 1955 for the diffusion of French culture through the co-operation of Programme Directors in France, Belgium, Switzerland and Canada; holds annual competition. Gen. Sec. M. GÉRALD CAZAUBON (France).

Confederation of ASEAN Journalists: Gedung Dewan Pers, Lantai 4, Jalan Kebonsirih 34, Jakarta, 10110 Indonesia; f. 1975 for journalists of South-East Asia. Exec. Sec. DIA'FAR H. ASSEGAFF. Publs *CAJ Newsletter* (quarterly), *CAJ Year Book*.

European Alliance of Press Agencies: c/o ANSA, Via della Dataria 94, 00187 Rome; tel. 67741; telex 610242; f. 1957 to assist co-operation among members and to study and protect their common interests; annual assembly. Mems in 24 countries. Sec.-Gen. ARRIGO ACCORNERO.

European Broadcasting Union—EBU: Ancienne-Route 17A, CP 67, 1218 Grand-Saconnex, Geneva, Switzerland; tel. (022) 7987766; telex 415700; f. 1950 in succession to the International Broadcasting Union; a professional association of broadcasting organizations, supporting the interests of members and assisting the development of broadcasting in all its forms; activities include the Eurovision news and programme exchanges (linking 33 television services in 26 countries). General Assembly meets annually, Admin. Council composed of 15 members meets twice a year; there are four standing committees (Legal, Technical, Television Programme and Radio Programme). Mems: 100 active (European) and associate in 72 countries. Pres. (1987-88) ALBERT SCHARF (FRG); Sec.-Gen. Dr R. DE KALBERMATTEN (Switzerland). Publs *EBU Review* (monthly in English and French).

Inca-Fiej Research Association: Washingtonplatz 1, 6100 Darmstadt, Federal Republic of Germany; tel. (6151) 70050; telex 0419273; f. 1961 to develop methods, machines and techniques for the newspaper industry; to evaluate standard specifications for raw materials for use in newspaper production; to investigate economy and quality improvements for newspaper printing and publishing. Mems: 762 newspapers, 67 suppliers. Pres. ODD RØNNESTAD (Norway); Man. Dir Dr F. W. BURKHARDT. Publ. *Newspaper Techniques* (in English, French and German).

Inter-American Press Association (Sociedad Interamericana de Prensa): 2911 NW 39th St, Miami, Fla 33142, USA; tel. (305) 634-2465; telex 522873; f. 1942 to guard the freedom of the press in the Americas; to promote and maintain the dignity, rights and responsibilities of the profession of journalism; to foster a wider knowledge and greater interchange among the peoples of the Americas. Mems: 1,400. Exec. Dir W. P. WILLIAMSON, Jr. Publ. *IAPA News* (monthly in English and Spanish).

International Alliance of Distribution by Cable: 1 blvd Anspach, boîte 28, 1000 Brussels, Belgium; tel. (02) 211-94-49; telex 11473; f. 1955 to encourage the development of distribution by cable and defend its interests; to ensure exchange of documentation and carry out research on relevant technical and legal questions. Mems: 17 organizations in 11 countries. Pres. M. DE SUTTER; Sec.-Gen. G. MOREAU.

International Association of Broadcasting (Asociación Internacional de Radiodifusión—AIR): 25 de Mayo 520, Montevideo, Uruguay; tel. 95-8141; telex 23225; f. 1946 to preserve free and private radio broadcasting; to promote co-operation between the corporations and public authorities; to defend freedom of expression. Mems: national associations of broadcasters. Pres. LUIZ EDUARDO BORGERTH; Sec. Dr OSCAR MARIA GARIBALDI (Argentina). Publ. *La Gaceta de AIR* (every 2 months).

International Association of Sound Archives: c/o J.-C. Hayoz, Radio DRS, Studio Bern, Phonothek, Schwarztorstr. 21, 3000 Berne 14, Switzerland; tel. (031) 469111; telex 911833; f. 1969; involved in the preservation and exchange of sound recordings, and in developing recording techniques; holds annual conference. Mems: institutions in 42 countries, and 10 international and regional organizations. Pres. HELEN HARRISON (UK); Sec.-Gen. J.-CLAUDE HAYOZ (Switzerland). Publ. *Phonographic Bulletin* (3 a year).

International Catholic Union of the Press (Union catholique internationale de la presse—UCIP): 37-39 rue de Vermont, Case Postale 197, 1211 Geneva 20, Switzerland; tel. (022) 340017; f. 1927 to link all Catholics who influence public opinion through the press, to inspire a high standard of professional conscience and to represent the interest of the Catholic press at international organizations. Mems: International Federation of Catholic Press Agencies, International Federation of Catholic Journalists, International Federation of Catholic Dailies and Periodicals, International Catholic Association of Teachers in Information and Communication, International Federation of Church Press Associations, UCIP Africa, UCIP Asia, UCIP Latin America. Sec.-Gen. Rev. BRUNO HOLTZ (Switzerland). Publ. *UCIP-Informations*.

International Council of French-speaking Radio and Television Organizations: (Conseil international des radios-télévisions d'expression française): 23 rue Gourgas, 1205 Geneva, Switzerland; tel. (022) 281211; telex 428274; f. 1978 to establish links between French-speaking radio and television organizations. Mems: 42 organizations. Pres. ROBERT STEPHANE (Belgium); Sec.-Gen. RENÉ SCHENKER (Switzerland).

International Federation of Newspaper Publishers—FIEJ: 6 rue du Faubourg Poissonnière, 75010 Paris, France; tel. (1) 45-23-38-88; telex 290513; f. 1948 to defend the freedom of the press, to safeguard the ethical and economic interests of newspapers and to study all questions of interest to newspapers at international level. Mems: national organizations in 30 countries, individual publishers in five others, and 13 news agencies. Pres. GIOVANNI GIOVANNINI (Italy); Sec.-Gen. JAN J. NOUWEN.

International Federation of Press Cutting Agencies: Streulistrasse 19, POB 8030 Zürich, Switzerland; tel. (01) 2524937; telex 816543; f. 1953 to improve the standing of the profession, prevent infringements, illegal practices and unfair competition; and to develop business and friendly relations among press cuttings agencies throughout the world. Mems: 62 agencies. Pres. LAURENCE D'ARAINON (France); Gen. Sec. Dr DIETER HENNE (Switzerland).

International Federation of the Cinematographic Press—

OTHER INTERNATIONAL ORGANIZATIONS

FIPRESCI: 1000 Munich 40, Schleissheimer Str. 83, Federal Republic of Germany; tel. (089) 182303; telex 214674; f. 1930 to develop the cinematographic press and promote cinema as an art; organizes international meetings and juries in film festivals. Mems: national organizations or corresponding members in 45 countries. Pres. MARCEL MARTIN (France); Sec.-Gen. KLAUS EDER (FRG).

International Federation of the Periodical Press: Suite 19, Grosvenor Gardens House, 35–37 Grosvenor Gardens, London, SW1W 0BS, England; tel. (01) 828-1366; telex 24224; f. 1925 to protect and promote the material and moral interests of the periodical press, facilitate contacts between members and develop the free exchange of ideas and information. Mems: 104 national associations and publishing companies in 31 countries. Pres. M. GILL (UK); Dir R. WHARMBY (UK).

International Federation of the Socialist and Democratic Press: Foro Bonaparte 24, 20101 Milan, Italy; tel. (02) 8050105; f. 1953 to promote co-operation between editors and publishers of socialist newspapers; affiliated to the Socialist International (q.v.). Mems: about 100. Sec. UMBERTO GIOVINE.

International Film and Television Council: 1 rue Miollis, 75732 Paris Cedex 15, France; f. 1958 to arrange meetings and co-operation generally. Mems: 36 international film and television organizations. Pres. Prof. ENRICO FULCHIGNONI; Dir MARIO VERDONE. Publ. *IFTC Newsletter*.

International Institute of Communications: Tavistock House South, Tavistock Sq., London, WC1H 9LF, England; tel. (01) 388-0671; telex 24578; f. 1969 (as the International Broadcast Institute) to link all working in the field of communications, including policy makers, broadcasters, industrialists and engineers; holds local, regional and international meetings, undertakes and sponsors research and gathers information. Mems: over 80 corporate and institutional. Pres. BRIAN QUINN (UK); Exec. Dir JOHN HAWKINS.

International Maritime Radio Committee: Southbank House, Black Prince Rd, London, SE1 7SJ, England; tel. (01) 587-1245; telex 295555; f. 1928 to study and develop means of improving marine wireless communications and radio aids to marine navigation. Mems: 52 organizations and companies operating wireless stations on vessels of the Merchant Marine and fishing boats of practically all the maritime nations of the world. Pres. G. G. HILL (UK); Sec.-Gen. and Chair. of Technical Cttee Commdr C. C. WAKE-WALKER (UK); Admin. Sec. Miss J. CASTANHETA (Belgium).

International Organization of Journalists: Pařížská 9, 110 01 Prague 1, Czechoslovakia; tel. 2328015; telex 122631; f. 1946 to defend the freedom of the press and of journalists and to promote their material welfare. Activities include the maintenance of international training centres and international recreation centres for journalists. Consultative status with UN (ECOSOC) and UNESCO. Mems: national organizations and individuals in 120 countries. Chair. KAARLE NORDENSTRENG (Finland); Sec.-Gen. DUŠAN ULČÁK (Czechoslovakia). Publs *The Democratic Journalist* (monthly in English, French, Russian and Spanish), *Interpressgrafik* (quarterly), *Interpressmagazin* (every 2 months), *IOJ Newsletter* (2 a month, in Arabic, English, French, German, Russian and Spanish).

International Press Institute—IPI: Dilke House, Malet St, London, WC1E 7JA, England; tel. (01) 636-0703; telex 25950; f. 1951 as a non-governmental association of editors, publishers and news broadcasters who support the principles of a free and responsible press; activities: defence of press freedom, regional meetings of members, programme to train staff of Asian newspapers, research and library and press centre; annual general assembly. Mems: 1,700 from 62 countries. Pres. ENRIQUE ZILERI (Peru); Dir PETER GALLINER (UK). Publ. *IPI Report* (monthly).

International Press Telecommunications Council: Studio House, 184 Fleet St, London, EC4, England; tel. (01) 405-2608; f. 1965 to safeguard and promote the interests of the Press on all matters relating to telecommunications; keeps its members informed of current and future telecommunications developments. The Council meets once a year and maintains five committees. Mems: 26 press associations, newspapers and news agencies. Chair. JOSEPH P. RAWLEY; Dir OLIVER G. ROBINSON. Publ. *IPTC News* (3 a year).

International Radio and Television Organization (OIRT): ul. Skokanská 169 56 Prague 6, Czechoslovakia; tel. 341371; telex 122144; f. 1946 as the International Broadcasting Organization in succession to Union internationale de radiodiffusion; present name adopted 1959; links broadcasting and television services in member countries and exchanges information on technical developments and programmes; includes Technical Commission (with five study groups), Radio Programme Commission (with six specialized groups), Television Programme Commission and Intervision Council; Technical Centre; Intervision network to link members' television services; holds general assembly every two years. Mems: broadcasting organizations from Afghanistan, Algeria, Bulgaria, Byelorussian SSR, Cuba, Czechoslovakia, Egypt, Estonian SSR, Finland, German Democratic Republic, Hungary, Iraq, Kampuchea, Democratic People's Republic of Korea, Laos, Latvian SSR, Lithuanian SSR, Mali, Moldavian SSR, Mongolia, Nicaragua, Poland, Romania, Sudan, Ukrainian SSR, USSR, Viet-Nam, People's Democratic Republic of Yemen. Sec.-Gen. Dr GENNADIJ CODR.

Latin-American Catholic Press Union: CP 90023, 25600 Petropolis, Brazil; tel. (0242) 435112; f. 1959 to co-ordinate, promote and improve the Catholic press in Latin America. Mems: national groups and local associations in Latin America. Pres. CLARENCIO NEOTTI (Brazil); Sec. PEDRO GILBERTO GOMES (Brazil).

Organization of Asia-Pacific News Agencies—OANA: c/o Press Trust of India, 4 Parliament St, New Delhi 110001, India; tel. 385848; telex 031-66400; f. 1961 to promote co-operation in professional matters and mutual exchange of news, features, etc. among the news agencies of Asia and the Pacific via the Asia-Pacific News Network (ANN). Mems: Anadolu Ajansi (Turkey), Antara (Indonesia), APP (Pakistan), Bakhtar Information Agency (Afghanistan), BERNAMA (Malaysia), BSS (Bangladesh), ENA (Bangladesh), Hindustan Samachar (India), IRNA (Iran), KCNA (Korea, Democratic People's Republic), KPL (Laos), Kyodo (Japan), Lankapuvath (Sri Lanka), Montsame (Mongolia), PNA (Philippines), PPI (Pakistan), PTI (India), RSS (Nepal), Samachar Bharati (India), TASS (USSR), TNA (Thailand), UNI (India), Viet-Nam News Agency, Yonhap (Republic of Korea), Xinhua (People's Republic of China). Pres. P. UNNIKRISHNAN (India); Sec.-Gen. P. K. BANDYOPADHYAY (India).

Press Foundation of Asia: POB 1843, 1500 Roxas Blvd, Manila, Philippines; tel. 598633; telex 27674; f. 1967; an independent, non-profit making organization governed by its newspaper members; acts as a professional forum for about 200 newspapers in Asia; aims to reduce cost of newspapers to potential readers, to improve editorial and management techniques through research and training programmes and to encourage the growth of the Asian press; operates *Depthnews* feature service. Mems: 200 newspapers. Chair. KIM SANG MAN (Republic of Korea); Dir-Gen. MOCHTAR LUBIS (Indonesia). Publ. *Pressasia* (quarterly), *Asian Women and Children* (quarterly), *Environment Folio* (quarterly).

Union of National Radio and Television Organizations of Africa—URTNA: 101 rue Carnot, BP 3237, Dakar, Senegal; tel. 21-59-70; telex 650; f. 1962; co-ordinates radio and television services, including monitoring and frequency allocation, the exchange of information and coverage of national and international events among African countries; maintains programme exchange centre (Nairobi, Kenya), technical centre (Bamako, Mali) and a centre for rural radio studies (Ouagadougou, Burkina Faso); in 1988 URTNA decided to establish a centre for the exchange of television news in Algiers, Algeria. Mems: 44 organizations and eight associate members. Sec.-Gen. KASSAYE DEMENA (Ethiopia). Publs *URTNA Review* (English and French, 2 a year), *Family Health and Communication Bulletin* (monthly), reports.

World Association for Christian Communication—WACC: 357 Kennington Lane, London, SE11 5QY, England; tel. (01) 582-9139; telex 8812669; f. 1975; works among churches, church-related organizations and individuals to promote more effective use of all forms of media (including radio, television, newspapers, books, film, cassettes, dance, drama etc.) for proclaiming the Christian gospel, particularly with reference to ethical and social issues. Mems in 61 countries. Pres. WILLIAM F. FORE; Gen.-Sec. CARLOS A. VALLE. Publs *Action* newsletter (10 a year), *Media Development* (quarterly).

Religion

Agudath Israel World Organisation: Hacherut Sq, POB 326, Jerusalem 91002, Israel; tel. 384357; f. 1912 to help solve the problems facing Jewish people all over the world in the spirit of the Jewish tradition; holds World Rabbinical Council (every five years), and an annual Central Council comprising 100 mems nominated by affiliated organizations; has consultative status with UN (ECOSOC) and UNESCO. Mems: over 500,000 in 25 countries. Sec.-Gen. A. HIRSCH (Jerusalem). Publs *Hamodia* (Jerusalem daily newspaper), *Jewish Tribune* (London, weekly), *Jewish Observer* (New York, monthly), *La Voz Judia* (Buenos Aires, monthly), *Jüdische Stimme* (Zürich, monthly).

All Africa Conference of Churches—AACC: Waiyaki Way, POB 14205, Nairobi, Kenya; tel. 61166; telex 22175; f. 1958; an organ of co-operation and continuing fellowship among Protestant, Orthodox and Independent churches and Christian Councils in Africa. Mems: 118 churches and 20 associated councils in 38 African countries. Pres. Archbishop DESMOND TUTU (South Africa); Gen. Sec. Rev. JOSÉ CHIPENDA (Angola). Publ. *The African Challenge* (quarterly).

Alliance Israélite Universelle; 45 rue La Bruyère, 75425 Paris Cedex 09, France; tel. (1) 42-80-35-00; f. 1860 to work for the

OTHER INTERNATIONAL ORGANIZATIONS

Religion

emancipation and moral progress of the Jews; maintains 39 schools in the Mediterranean area; library of 100,000 vols. Mems: 12,000 in 20 countries. Pres. ADY STEG; Dir JACQUES LEVY (France). Publs *Cahiers de l'Alliance Israélite Universelle* (2 a year) in French, *The Alliance Review* in English, *Les Nouveaux Cahiers* (quarterly) in French.

Bahá'í International Community: Bahá'í World Centre, POB 155, 31 001 Haifa, Israel; tel. (04) 672433; telex 46626; f. 1844 in Persia to promote the unity of mankind and world peace through the teachings of the Bahá'í religion, including the equality of men and women and the elimination of all forms of prejudice; maintains schools for children and adults worldwide, and maintains educational and cultural radio stations in the USA and Latin America; has 25 publishing trusts throughout the world; consultative status with UN (ECOSOC) and UNICEF. Governing body: Universal House of Justice (nine mems elected by 148 National Spiritual Assemblies). Mems: in 118,000 centres (166 countries). Sec.-Gen. DONALD BARRETT (USA). Publs *Bahá'í World*, *La Pensée Bahá'ie* (quarterly), *World Order* (quarterly), *Opinioni Bahá'í* (quarterly).

Baptist World Alliance: 6733 Curran St, McLean, Va 22101, USA; tel. (703) 790-8980; f. 1905 as an association of national Baptist conventions and unions; 15th World Congress, Los Angeles, 1985. Mems in 144 countries. Pres. Dr G. NOEL VOSE (Australia); Gen. Sec. Dr GERHARD CLAAS. Publ. *The Baptist World* (11 a year).

Caribbean Conference of Churches: POB 616, Bridgetown, Barbados; tel. (809) 427-2681; telex 2335; f. 1973; holds Assembly every five years; conducts study and research programmes and supports education and community development projects. Mems: 34 churches. Sec.-Gen. Rev. ALLAN F. KIRTON.

Christian Conference of Asia: Fifth Floor, 57 Peking Rd, Kowloon, Hong Kong; tel. 3-680205; telex 37618; f. 1959 to promote co-operation and joint study in matters of common concern among the Churches of the region and to encourage interaction with other regional Conferences and the World Council of Churches. Mems: 110 churches and national councils of churches. Gen. Sec. Rev. PARK SANG JUNG. Publ. *CCA News* (monthly).

Christian Peace Conference: 111 21 Prague 1, Jungmannova 9, Czechoslovakia; tel. 2360289; telex 123363; f. 1958 as an international movement of theologians, clergy and laymen, aiming to bring Christendom to recognize its share of guilt in both world wars and to dedicate itself to the service of friendship, reconciliation and peaceful co-operation of nations, to concentrate on united action for peace, and to co-ordinate peace groups in individual churches and facilitate their effective participation in the peaceful development of society. It works through regional committees and member churches in many countries. Pres. Bishop Dr KÁROLY TÓTH (Reformed Church of Hungary); Gen. Sec. Rev. LUBOMÍR MIŘEJOVSKÝ (Evangelical Church of Czech Brethren). Publs *Christian Peace Conference* (quarterly in English and German), *CPC News Bulletin* (2 a month in English and German), occasional *Study Volume* and *Summary of Information* (in French and Spanish), *News from the UN* (monthly, in English).

Conference of European Churches—CEC: 150 route de Ferney, 1211 Geneva 20, Switzerland; tel. (022) 916111; telex 23423; f. 1957 to provide a meeting-place for European churches from East and West and for members and non-members of the World Council of Churches; conferences every few years (latest: Stirling, 1986). Mems: 120 Protestant, Anglican and Orthodox churches in 27 European countries. Pres. Metropolitan ALEKSI of Leningrad; Gen. Sec. JEAN FISCHER. Publ. *CEC News*.

Conference of International Catholic Organizations: 37-39 rue de Vermont, Geneva, Switzerland; f. 1927 to encourage collaboration and agreement between the different Catholic international organizations in their common interests, and to contribute to international understanding; organizes international assemblies and meetings to study specific problems. Permanent commissions deal with human rights, the new international economic order, social problems, the family health, education, etc. Mems: 30 Catholic international organizations. Administrator RUDI RUEGG (Switzerland).

Consultative Council of Jewish Organizations—CCJO: Woburn House, Upper Woburn Place, London, WC1H 0EP, England; f. 1946 to co-operate and consult with the UN and other international bodies directly concerned with human rights and to defend the cultural, political and religious rights of Jews throughout the world. The CCJO has consultative status with the UN, UNESCO, UNICEF and the Council of Europe. Mems: Jewish organizations with over 46,000 mems. Sec.-Gen. MOSES MOSKOWITZ (USA).

European Baptist Federation: Laerdalsgade 7, 2300 Copenhagen S, Denmark; tel. (01) 590904; f. 1949 to promote fellowship and co-operation among Baptists in Europe; to further the aims and objects of the Baptist World Alliance; to stimulate and co-ordinate evangelism in Europe; to provide for consultation and planning of missionary work in Europe and elsewhere in the world. Mems: Baptist Unions in 23 European countries. Pres. Dr VASILE TALPOS; Sec.-Treas. Dr KNUD WÜMPELMANN.

Evangelical Alliance: 186 Kennington Park Rd, London, SE11 4BT, England; tel. (01) 582-0228; f. 1846 to promote Christian unity and co-operation, religious freedom and evangelization; affiliated to the European Evangelical Alliance and the World Evangelical Fellowship. Gen. Dir CLIVE CALVER. Publs *Idea* (quarterly).

Friends (Quakers) World Committee for Consultation: Drayton House, 30 Gordon St, London, WC1H 0AX, England; tel. (01) 388-0497; f. 1937 to encourage and strengthen the spiritual life within the Religious Society of Friends; to help Friends to a better understanding of their vocation in the world; to promote consultation among Friends of all countries; representation at the United Nations as a non-governmental organization. Mems: appointed representatives and individuals from 56 countries. Gen. Sec. VAL FERGUSON. Publs *Friends World News* (2 a year), *Calendar of Yearly Meetings* (annually), *Finding Friends around the World* (handbook), *Quaker Information Network* (6 a year).

General Anthroposophical Society: The Goetheanum, 4143 Dornach, Switzerland; f. 1923 by Rudolf Steiner to study spiritual science and its application to art, education, medicine, agriculture, and other spheres of life. There are branches in practically all countries. Pres MANFRED SCHMIDT-BRABANT; Lending Library: Rudolf Steiner Library, 38 Museum St, London, WC1, England. Publ. *Das Goetheanum* (weekly).

International Association for Religious Freedom—IARF: 6000 Frankfurt 70, Dreieichstr. 59, Federal Republic of Germany; tel. (69) 617367; f. 1900 as a world community of religions, subscribing to the principle of openness; conducts intercultural encounters, inter-religious dialogues, a social service network and development programme. Regional conferences and triennial congress. Mems: 50 groups in 21 countries. Pres. Rev. Dr EUGENE PICKETT (USA); Gen. Sec. Rev. DIETHER GEHRMANN (FRG). Publ. *IARF World* (2 a year).

International Association of Buddhist Studies: c/o Prof. Lewis Lancaster, Dept of Oriental Languages, University of California, Berkeley, Calif 94720, USA; tel. (415) 642-3480; f. 1976; holds international conference every two years; supports studies of Buddhist literature. Gen. Sec. LUIS GOMEZ. Publ. *Journal* (2 a year).

International Bible Reading Association; Robert Denholm House, Nutfield, Redhill, Surrey, RH1 4HW, England; tel. (073) 782-2411; f. 1882 to encourage reading and study of the Bible. Total membership over 250,000. Gen. Sec. Rev. SIMON OXLEY. Publs Bible readings and notes, prayer-books.

International Council of Christians and Jews: 6148 Heppenheim, Werlestrasse 2, Postfach 305, Federal Republic of Germany; f. 1955 to promote mutual respect and co-operation; holds annual international colloquium, seminars, meetings for young people. Mems: national councils in 19 countries. Chair. Sir SIGMUND STERNBERG; Sec.-Gen. Dr JACOBUS SCHONEVELD.

International Council of Jewish Women: 19 rue de Téhéran, 75008 Paris, France; tel. (1) 46-24-78-34; telex 612874; f. 1912 to promote friendly relations and understanding among Jewish women throughout the world; exchanges information on community welfare activities, promotes volunteer leadership, sponsors field work in social welfare and fosters Jewish education. It has consultative status with UN (ECOSOC), UNICEF, UNESCO and Council of Europe. Mems: affiliates totalling over 1 million members in 35 countries. Pres. STELLA ROZAN (France); Sec. JANINE GDALIA (France). Publ. *Newsletter* (2 a year, English and Spanish).

International Fellowship of Reconciliation: Spoorstraat 38-40, 1815 BK Alkmaar, Netherlands; tel. (72) 123014; f. 1919; a transnational inter-religious movement committed to non-violence as a principle of life and to forming a world community of peace and liberation. Branches in 30 countries. Pres. DIANA FRANCIS (UK); Gen. Sec. DAVID C. ATWOOD. Publ. *Reconciliation International* (5 a year).

International Humanist and Ethical Union: Oudkerkof 11, 3512 Utrecht, Netherlands; tel. (30) 31-21-55; f. 1952 to bring into association all those interested in promoting ethical and scientific humanism. Mems: national organizations and individuals in 51 countries. Pres Prof. Dr P. KURTZ (USA), Prof. Dr S. STOJANOVIĆ (Yugoslavia), Dr R. A. P. TIELMAN (Netherlands). Publ. *International Humanist* (quarterly).

International Organization for the Study of the Old Testament: c/o 34 Gough Way, Cambridge, CB3 9LN, England; f. 1950. Holds triennial congresses (next congress: Leuven, 1989). Pres. C. BREKELMANS (Belgium); Sec. Prof. J. A. EMERTON (UK). Publ. *Vetus Testamentum* (quarterly).

Islamic Council of Europe: 16 Grosvenor Crescent, London, SW1X 7EP, England; tel. (01) 235-9832; telex 894240; f. 1973 as a co-ordinating body for Islamic centres and organizations in Europe; an autonomous Council collaborating with the Islamic Secretariat

OTHER INTERNATIONAL ORGANIZATIONS
Religion

and other Islamic organizations; aims to develop a better understanding of Islam and Muslim culture in the West. Sec.-Gen. SALEM AZZAM.

Latin American Council of Churches (Consejo Latinoamericano de Iglesias—CLAI): Casilla 85-22, Av. Patria 640 y Amazonas, Of. 1001, Quito, Ecuador; tel. 561-539; telex 21150; f. 1982. Mems: 94 churches in 19 countries, and seven associated organizations. Pres. Bishop FEDERICO J. PAGURA; Gen. Sec. Rev. FELIPE ADOLF.

Latin American Episcopal Council: Apartado Aéreo 5278, Bogotá, Colombia; tel. 2357044; telex 41388; f. 1955 to study the problems of the Church in Latin America; to co-ordinate Church activities. Mems: the Episcopal Conferences of Central and South America and the Caribbean. Pres. Most Rev. DARÍO CASTRILLÓN (Colombia).

Lutheran World Federation: 150 route de Ferney, 1211 Geneva 20, Switzerland; tel. (022) 916111; telex 23423; f. 1947; confederation of 105 Lutheran Churches of 87 countries. Current activities: interchurch aid; relief work in various areas of the globe; service to refugees including resettlement; aid to missions; theological research, conferences and exchanges; scholarship aid in various fields of church life; inter-confessional dialogue with Roman Catholic, Reformed, Anglican and Orthodox churches; religious communications projects and international news and information services; eighth Assembly, Brazil, 1990. Pres. Dr JOHANNES HANSELMANN; Gen. Sec. Rev. Dr GUNNAR JOHAN STAALSETT (Norway). Publs *Lutheran World Information* (English and German, weekly and monthly editions), *LWF Report* and *LWF Documentation* (English and German, 6 a year).

Middle East Council of Churches: POB 4529, 1 Petrarhi St, Limassol, Cyprus; tel. 26022; telex 5378; f. 1974. Mems: 19 churches. Pres. Catholicos KAREKIN II, Patriarch IGNATIOS IV, Rt Rev. SAMIR KAFITY; Gen. Sec. GABRIEL HABIB.

Moral Re-Armament: Mountain House, Caux, 1824 Vaud, Switzerland; tel. (021) 9634821; other international centres at Panchgani, India, Petropolis, Brazil, London and Tirley Garth, UK, and Gweru, Zimbabwe; f. 1921; aims: a new social order for better human relations and the elimination of political, industrial and racial antagonism. Legally incorporated bodies in 20 countries. Pres. GERHARD GROB; Sec. HEINRICH KARRER. Publs *Changer* (French, monthly), *For a Change* (English, monthly), *Caux Information* (German, monthly).

Muslim World League (Rabitat al-Alam al-Islami): POB 537, Mecca al-Mukarramah, Mecca, Saudia Arabia; tel. 025 363995; f. 1962 to advance Islamic unity and solidarity; provides financial assistance for Islamic education, medical care and relief work; has 30 offices throughout the world. Sec.-Gen. Dr ABDULLAH OMAR NASSEEF. Publs *Majalla Rabitat al-Alam al Islami* (monthly, Arabic), *Akhbar al-Alam al Islami* (weekly, Arabic), *Journal* (monthly, English).

Pacific Council of Churches: POB 208, 4 Thurston St, Suva, Fiji; tel. 311335; f. 1966. Mems: 17 churches, four councils and associations. Chair. Rt Rev. JABEZ L. BRYCE; Gen. Sec. Rev. BAITEKE NABETARI.

Opus Dei (Prelature of the Holy Cross and Opus Dei): Viale Bruno Buozzi 73, 00197 Rome, Italy; tel. 870562; f. 1928 by Mgr Escrivá de Balaguer to spread, at every level of society, a profound awakening of consciences to the universal calling to sanctity and apostolate in the course of members' own professional work. Mems: 74,370 laymen and 1,350 priests. Prelate Mgr ALVARO DEL PORTILLO.

Pacific Conference of Churches: POB 208, 4 Thurston St, Suva, Fiji; tel. 302332; f. 1961. Mems: 26 churches, councils and associations; holds assembly every five years. Chair. Rt Rev. LESLIE BOSETO; Gen. Sec. Rev. SIONE K. F. MOTU'AHALA. Publ. *PCC News* (quarterly).

Pax Romana International Catholic Movement for Intellectual and Cultural Affairs—ICMICA; and International Movement of Catholic Students—IMCS: 1 route de Jura, BP 1062, 1701 Fribourg, Switzerland; tel. (037) 262649; f. 1921 (IMCS), 1947 (ICMICA), to encourage in members an awareness of their responsibilities as men and Christians in the student and intellectual milieux; to promote contacts between students and graduates throughout the world and co-ordinate the contribution of Catholic intellectual circles to international life. Mems: 80 student and 60 intellectual organizations in 80 countries. ICMICA—Pres. WILLIAM NEVILLE (Australia); Gen. Sec. VICTOR KARUNAN (India); IMCS—Pres. CARLES TORNER; Sec.-Gen. ETIENNE BISIMWA. Publ. *Convergence* (every 2 months).

Salvation Army: International HQ, 101 Queen Victoria St, London, EC4P 4EP, England; tel. (01) 236-5222; telex 8954847; f. 1865 to spread the Christian gospel; emphasis is placed on the need for personal discipleship, and to make its evangelism effective it adopts a quasi-military form of organization. Social, medical and educational work is also performed in the 89 countries where the Army operates. Gen. EVA BURROWS; Chief of Staff Commissioner RON COX; Chancellor Commissioner PETER HAWKINS. Publs: 132 periodicals in 31 languages.

Soroptimist International: 87 Glisson Rd, Cambridge, CB1 2HG, England; tel. (0223) 311833; f. 1921 to maintain high ethical standards in business, the professions, and other aspects of life; to strive for human rights for all people and, in particular, to advance the status of women; to develop friendship and unity among Soroptimists of all countries; to contribute to international understanding and universal friendship. Mems: 87,000 in 2,605 clubs in 85 countries and territories. International Pres. MARILYNN K. HOFSTETTER (USA); Exec. Officer DOREEN ASTLEY (UK). Publ. *International Soroptimist* (quarterly).

Theosophical Society: Adyar, Madras 600 020, India; tel. (044) 412815; f. 1875; aims at universal brotherhood, without distinction of race, creed, sex, caste or colour; study of comparative religion, philosophy and science; investigation of unexplained laws of nature and powers latent in man. Mems: 35,000 in 70 countries. Pres. RADHA S. BURNIER; Sec. CONRAD JAMIESON. Publs *The Theosophist* (monthly), *Adyar News Letter* (quarterly), *Brahmavidya* (annually).

United Bible Societies: 7th Floor, Reading Bridge House, Reading, RG1 8PJ, England; f. 1946. Mems: 78 Bible Societies and 32 Bible Society Offices at work throughout the world. Pres. Rev. Dr OSWALD C. J. HOFFMANN (USA); Gen. Sec. Rev. Dr CIRILO RIGOS. Publs *United Bible Societies Bulletin, Technical and Practical Papers on Translation* (both quarterly), *Prayer Booklet* (annually), *World Report* (monthly).

United Lodge of Theosophists: Theosophy Hall, 40 New Marine Lines, Bombay 400020, India; tel. 299024; f. 1929 to form the nucleus of a Universal Brotherhood of Humanity, without distinction of race, creed, sex, caste or colour; Mems: 22 lodges in nine countries. Publs *Theosophy, The Theosophical Movement* (monthly), *The Aryan Path* (bi-monthly), *Bulletin* (quarterly).

Watch Tower Bible and Tract Society: 25 Columbia Heights, Brooklyn, New York, NY 11201, USA; tel. (718) 625-3600; f. 1881; 95 branches; serves as legal agency for Jehovah's Witnesses, whose membership is 3m. Pres. FREDERICK W. FRANZ; Sec. and Treas. LYMAN SWINGLE. Publs *The Watchtower* (2 a month, in 103 languages), *Awake!* (2 a month, in 53 languages).

World Alliance of Reformed Churches (Presbyterian and Congregational): 150 route de Ferney, 1211 Geneva 20, Switzerland; tel. (022) 916111; telex 23423; f. 1970 by merger of WARC (Presbyterian) (f. 1875) with International Congregational Council (f. 1891) to promote fellowship among Reformed, Presbyterian and Congregational churches. Mems: 164 churches in 81 countries. Gen. Sec. Prof. MILAN OPOCENSKY (Czechoslovakia). Publs *Reformed World* (quarterly), *Reformed Perspectives* (monthly, in four languages).

World Conference on Religion and Peace: 14 chemin Auguste-Vilbert, 1218 Grand Saconnex, Geneva, Switzerland; tel. (022) 985162; f. 1970 to co-ordinate education and action of various world religions for world peace and justice. Mems: religious organizations and individuals in 50 countries. Pres. Dr INAMULLAH KHAN; Sec.-Gen. Dr JOHN B. TAYLOR. Publ. *Religion for Peace* (quarterly newsletter).

World Congress of Faiths: 28 Powis Gdns, London, W11 1JG, England; tel. (01) 727-2607; f. 1936 to promote a spirit of fellowship among mankind through religion, to bring together people of all nationalities, backgrounds and creeds, to encourage the study and understanding of world faiths, and to promote welfare and peace. Mems: about 500. Pres. Rev. Dr EDWARD CARPENTER; Chair. Prof. KEITH WARD. Publs *World Faith Insight, Interfaith News* (3 a year).

World Federation of Christian Life Communities: Borgo S. Spirito 8, Casella Postale 6139, 00195 Rome, Italy; tel. (06) 6868079; f. 1953 as World Federation of the Sodalities of our Lady (first group founded 1563) as a lay movement (based on the teachings of Ignatius Loyola) to integrate Christian faith and daily living. Mems: groups in 55 countries representing about 100,000 individuals. Pres. BRENDAN MCLOUGHLIN (Ireland); Exec. Sec. JOSÉ REYES (Chile). Publ. *Progressio* (every 2 months in English, French, Spanish).

World Fellowship of Buddhists: 33 Sukhumvit Rd, (between Soi 1 and Soi 3), Bangkok 10110, Thailand; f. 1950 to promote practice, teaching and philosophy of Buddhism; holds annual General Congress; has 94 regional centres in 37 countries. Pres. SANYA DHARMASAKTI; Hon. Gen. Sec. PRASERT RUANGSKUL. Publ. *WFB Review* (quarterly).

World Jewish Congress: 501 Madison Ave, New York, NY 10022, USA; tel. (212) 755-5770; f. 1936; a voluntary association of representative Jewish communities and organizations throughout the world, aiming to foster the unity of the Jewish people and to ensure the continuity and development of their heritage. Mems: Jewish communities in 63 countries. Pres. EDGAR M. BRONFMAN;

OTHER INTERNATIONAL ORGANIZATIONS Religion, Science

Sec.-Gen. ISRAEL SINGER. Publs *Patterns of Prejudice* (quarterly, London), *Gesher* (Hebrew quarterly, Israel), *Christian Jewish Relations* (quarterly, London), *Boletín Informativo OJI* (fortnightly, Buenos Aires).

World Methodist Council: International Headquarters, POB 518, Lake Junaluska, NC 28745, USA; tel. (704) 456-9432; f. 1881 to deepen the fellowship of the Methodist peoples, to encourage evangelism, to foster Methodist participation in the ecumenical movement, and to promote the unity of Methodist witness and service. Mems: 64 Church bodies in 90 countries, comprising 25m. individuals. Chair. Bishop LAWI IMATHIU (Kenya); Gen. Sec. JOE HALE (USA). Publ. *World Parish* (6 a year).

World Sephardi Federation: 13 rue Marignac, 1206 Geneva, Switzerland; tel. (022) 473313; telex 427569; f. 1951 to strengthen the unity of Jewry and Judaism among Sephardi and Oriental Jews, to defend and foster religious and cultural activities of all Sephardi and Oriental Jewish communities and preserve their spiritual heritage, to provide moral and material assistance where necessary and to co-operate with other similar organizations. Mems: 50 communities and organizations in 33 countries. Pres. Sec.-Gen. SHIMON DERY.

World Student Christian Federation: 5 route des Morillons, Grand-Saconnex, 1218 Geneva, Switzerland; tel. (022) 988953; f. 1895 to proclaim Jesus Christ as Lord and Saviour in the academic community, and to present students with the claims of the Christian faith over their whole life. Gen. Assembly every four years. Mems: 67 national Student Christian Movements, and 34 national correspondents. Chair. Bishop POULOSE MAR POULOSE (India); Sec.-Gen. CHRISTINE LEDGER (Australia), MANUEL QUINTERO (Cuba).

World Union for Progressive Judaism: 838 Fifth Ave, New York, NY 10021, USA; tel. (212) 249-0100; f. 1926; promotes and co-ordinates efforts of Reform, Liberal and Progressive congregations throughout the world; supports new congregations; assigns and employs rabbis; sponsors seminaries and schools; organizes international conferences; maintains a youth section. Mems: organizations and individuals in 23 countries. Exec. Dir Rabbi RICHARD G. HIRSCH (Israel). Publs *AMMI* (quarterly), *Telem* (monthly in Hebrew), *International Conference Reports, European Judaism* (bi-annual).

World Union of Catholic Women's Organisations: 20 rue Notre-Dame-des-Champs, 75006 Paris, France; tel. (1) 45-44-27-65; f. 1910 to promote and co-ordinate the contribution of Catholic women in international life, in social, civic, cultural and religious matters. Mems: 30,000,000. Pres.-Gen. M. T. VAN HETEREN-HOGENHUIS (Netherlands); Sec.-Gen. GERALDINE MACCARTHY. Publ. *Newsletter* (quarterly in four languages).

Science

International Council of Scientific Unions—ICSU: 51 blvd de Montmorency, 75016 Paris, France; tel. (1) 45-25-03-29; telex 630 553; f. 1919 as International Research Council; present name adopted 1931; new statutes adopted 1984; to co-ordinate international co-operation in theoretical and applied sciences and to promote national scientific research through the intermediary of affiliated national organizations; General Assembly of representatives of national and scientific members meets every two years to formulate policy. The following committees have been established: Scientific Cttee on Antarctic Research, Scientific Cttee on Oceanic Research, Cttee on Space Research, ICSU-UATI Co-ordinating Cttee on Water Research, Scientific Cttee on Solar-Terrestrial Physics, Cttee on Science and Technology in Developing Countries, Cttee on Data for Science and Technology, Cttee on the Teaching of Science, Scientific Cttee on Problems of the Environment, Cttee on Genetic Experimentation, Cttee on Biotechnology and Special Cttee on International Geosphere-Biosphere Programme. The following services and Inter-Union Committees and Commissions have been established: Federation of Astronomical and Geophysical Services, Inter-Union Commission on Frequency Allocations for Radio Astronomy and Space Science, Inter-Union Commission on Radio Meteorology, Inter-Union Commission on Spectroscopy, Inter-Union Commission on Lithosphere and Inter-Union Commission on the Application of Science to Agriculture, Fisheries and Aquaculture. National mems: academies or research councils in 74 countries; Scientific mems and assocs: 20 international unions (see below) and 26 scientific associates. Pres. Prof. M. G. K. MENON (India); Sec.-Gen. L. ERNSTER (Sweden); Exec. Sec. F. W. G. BAKER (UK). Publs *ICSU Yearbook, ICSU Newsletter* (quarterly).

UNIONS FEDERATED TO THE ICSU

International Astronomical Union: Institut d'Astrophysique, Université de Liège, 5 ave de Cointe, 4200 Cointe-Ougrée, Belgium; tel. 52-99-80; telex 41264; f. 1919 to facilitate co-operation between the astronomers of various countries and to further the study of astronomy in all its branches; last General Assembly was held in 1985 in Delhi, India. Mems: organizations in 51 countries, and over 6,000 individual mems. Pres. J. SAHADE (Argentina); Gen. Sec. Dr J.-P. SWINGS (Belgium). Publs *IAU Information Bulletin* (2 a year).

International Geographical Union—IGU: Dept of Geography, University of Alberta, Edmonton, Alberta, T6G 2H4, Canada; tel. (403) 432-3329; telex 037-2979; f. 1922 to encourage the study of problems relating to geography, to promote and co-ordinate research requiring international co-operation, and to organize international congresses and commissions. Mems: 78 regular mem. countries, 10 associates. Pres. Prof. PETER SCOTT (Australia); Sec.-Gen. Prof. L. A. KOSINSKI (Canada). Publs *IGU Bulletin* (1–2 a year), *Circular Letter, congress proceedings*.

International Mathematical Union: c/o Dept of Mathematics, Hallituskatu 15, 00100 Helsinki, Finland; tel. (3580) 191-2883; telex 124690; f. 1952 to support and assist the International Congress of Mathematicians and other international scientific meetings or conferences; to encourage and support other international mathematical activities considered likely to contribute to the development of mathematical science—pure, applied or educational. Mems: 52 countries. Pres. Prof. L. FADDEEV; Sec.-Gen. Prof. O. LEHTO.

International Union for Pure and Applied Biophysics: Institute of Biophysics, Medical University, 7643 Pécs, Hungary; tel. (72) 14017; telex 12311; f. 1961 to organize international co-operation in biophysics and promote communication between biophysics and allied subjects, to encourage national co-operation between biophysical societies, and to contribute to the advancement of biophysical knowledge. Mems: 41 adhering bodies. Pres. Prof. L. D. PEACHEY (USA); Sec.-Gen. Prof. J. TIGYI (Hungary). Publ. *Quarterly Reviews of Biophysics*.

International Union of Biochemistry: Dept of Biochemistry, Duke University Medical Center, POB 3711, Durham, NC 27710, USA; tel. (919) 684-5326; telex 802829; f. 1955 to sponsor the International Congresses of Biochemistry, to co-ordinate research and discussion, to organize co-operation between the societies of biochemistry, to promote high standards of biochemistry throughout the world and to contribute to the advancement of biochemistry in all its international aspects. Mems: 51 bodies. Pres. Dr E. C. SLATER (UK); Sec.-Gen. Dr R. L. HILL (USA).

International Union of Biological Sciences: 51 blvd de Montmorency, 75016 Paris, France; tel. (1) 45-25-00-09; telex 630553; f. 1919. Mems: 67 scientific bodies. Exec. Sec. Dr T. YOUNES. Publ. *Biology International* (2 a year, plus special issues).

International Union of Crystallography: c/o Dr J. N. King, 5 Abbey Sq., Chester, CH1 2HU, England; tel. 42878; f. 1947 to facilitate international standardization of methods, of units, of nomenclature and of symbols used in crystallography; and to form a focus for the relations of crystallography to other sciences. Mems in 34 countries. Pres. Prof. M. NARDELLI (Italy); Gen. Sec. Prof. A. HORDVIK (Norway); Exec. Sec. Dr J. N. KING. Publs *Acta Crystallographica, Journal of Applied Crystallography* (bi-monthly), *Structure Reports* (2 volumes a year), *International Tables for Crystallography, Molecular Structures and Dimensions, World Directory of Crystallographers, Index of Crystallographic Supplies, Crystallographic Book List, Bibliographies, World List of Crystallographic Computer Programs*.

International Union of Geodesy and Geophysics—IUGG: Observatoire Royal de Belgique, 3 ave Circulaire, 1180 Brussels, Belgium; tel. (02) 375-24-84; telex 21565; f. 1919; federation of seven associations representing Geodesy, Seismology and Physics of the Earth's Interior, Physical Sciences of the Ocean, Volcanology and Chemistry of the Earth's Interior, Scientific Hydrology, Meteorology and Atmospheric Physics, Geomagnetism and Aeronomy, which meet at the General Assemblies of the Union. In addition, there are Joint Committees of the various associations either among themselves or with other unions. The Union organizes scientific meetings and also sponsors various permanent services, to collect, analyse and publish geophysical data. Mems: in 78 countries. Pres. Prof. V. KEILIS-BOROK (USSR); Gen. Sec. Prof. P. MELCHIOR (Belgium). Publs *IUGG Chronicle* (6 a year), *Geodetic Bulletin* (quarterly), *International Bibliography of Geodesy* (irregular), *International Seismological Summary* (yearly), *Bulletin Volcanologique* (2 a year), *Bulletin mensuel du Bureau Central Sismologique* (monthly), *Bulletin de l'Association Internationale d'Hydrologie Scientifique* (quarterly), *International Bibliography of Hydrology, Catalogue des Volcans Actifs* (both irregular).

International Union of Geological Sciences—IUGS: Leiv Erikssons vei 39, POB 3006, 7002 Trondheim, Norway; tel. (7) 92-15-00; telex 55417; f. 1961 to encourage the study of geoscientific problems, facilitate international and inter-disciplinary co-operation in geology and related sciences, and support the quadrennial International Geological Congress. IUGS organizes international meetings and co-sponsors joint programmes, including the International Geological Correlation Programme (with UNESCO). Mems from 95 countries. Pres. Prof. Dr E. SEIBOLD (FRG) (acting); Sec.-Gen. Prof. R. SINDING-LARSEN (Norway).

International Union of Immunological Societies: 9650 Rockville Pike, Bethesda, Md 20814, USA; tel. (301) 530-7178; holds triennial international congress. Mems: national societies in 39 countries. Pres. G. V. NOSSAL (Australia); Sec.-Gen. H. METZGER (USA).

International Union of Microbiological Societies—IUMS: Dept of Biochemistry and Genetics, Catherine Cookson Bldg, Framlington Place, Newcastle-upon-Tyne, NE2 4HH, England; tel. (091) 232-8511; telex 53654; f. 1930. Mems: 94 national microbiological societies. Pres. Prof. K. ARIMA (Japan); Sec.-Gen. Prof. S. W. GLOVER. Publs *Microbiological Sciences* (monthly), *International Journal of Systematic Bacteriology* (quarterly), *Intervirology* (monthly), *International Journal of Food Microbiology* (every 2 months), *Advances in Microbial Ecology* (annually), *Journal of Biological Standardization* (quarterly).

International Union of Nutritional Sciences: c/o Dept of Human Nutrition, Agricultural University, POB 8129, 6700 EV Wageningen, Netherlands; tel. (08370) 82589; telex 45015; f. 1946 to promote international co-operation in the scientific study of nutrition and its applications, to encourage research and exchange of scientific information by holding international congresses and issuing publications. Mems: 60 organizations. Pres. Prof. M. GABR (Egypt); Sec.-Gen. Prof. J. G. A. J. HAUTVAST (Netherlands). Publs *IUNS Directory, Newsletter*.

International Union of Pharmacology: Laboratoire de Pharmacologie, UCL 7350, 73 ave E. Mounier, 1200 Brussels, Belgium; tel. (02) 764-73-50; f. 1963 to promote international co-ordination of research, discussion and publication in the field of pharmacology, including clinical pharmacology, drug metabolism and toxicology; co-operates with WHO in all matters concerning drugs and drug research; holds international congresses. Mems: national and regional societies in 50 countries. Pres. C. DOLLÉRY (UK); Sec.-Gen. T. GODFRAIND (Belgium). Publ. *TIPS (Trends in Pharmacological Sciences)*.

International Union of Physiological Sciences: c/o Prof. R. Naquet, Laboratoire de Physiologie Nerveuse, CNRS, ave de la Terrasse, 91190 Gif-sur-Yvette, France; tel. (1) 69-07-61-45; telex 691137; f. 1955. Mems: 48 national and six assoc. mems. Pres. Sir ANDREW HUXLEY (UK); Sec.-Gen. Prof. R. NAQUET.

International Union of Psychological Science: c/o Prof. K. Pawlik, Psychologisches Institut I, Von-Melle-Park II, 2000 Hamburg 13, Federal Republic of Germany; tel. (040) 4123-4723; f. 1951 to contribute to the development of intellectual exchange and scientific relations between psychologists of different countries. Mems: national societies in 48 countries. Pres. Prof. WAYNE H. HOLTZMAN (USA); Sec.-Gen. Prof. KURT PAWLIK (FRG). Publs *International Journal of Psychology* (quarterly), *International Directory of Psychologists* (irregular).

International Union of Pure and Applied Biophysics: Institute of Biophysics, Medical University, 7643 Pécs, Hungary; tel. (72) 14017; f. 1961 to promote international co-operation in biophysics. Mems: national societies in 41 countries. Pres. L. D. PEACHEY (USA); Sec.-Gen. J. TIGYI (Hungary). Publ. *Quarterly Review of Biophysics*.

International Union of Pure and Applied Chemistry—IUPAC: Bank Court Chambers, 2-3 Pound Way, Cowley Centre, Oxford, OX4 3YF, England; tel. (0865) 747744; telex 83220; f. 1919 to organize permanent co-operation between chemical associations in the member countries, to study topics of international importance requiring regulation, standardization or codification, to co-operate with other international organizations in the field of chemistry and to contribute to the advancement of all aspects of chemistry. Biennial General Assembly. Mems: in 43 countries. Pres. Prof. V. A. KOPTYUG (USSR); Sec.-Gen. Prof. T. S. WEST (UK). Publs *Chemistry International* (bi-monthly), *Pure and Applied Chemistry* (monthly).

International Union of Pure and Applied Physics: Chalmers University of Technology, 412 96 Göteborg, Sweden; tel. (031) 63-18-83; telex 2369; f. 1922 to promote and encourage international co-operation in physics. Mems: in 45 countries. Pres. Prof. L. KERWIN (Canada); Sec.-Gen. JAN S. NILSSON (Sweden).

International Union of Radio Science: c/o Observatoire Royal de Belgique, 3 ave Circulaire, 1180 Brussels, Belgium; tel. (02) 374-13-08; f. 1919 to encourage and organize scientific research in radio science, particularly where international co-operation is required; and to promote the development of uniform methods of measurement and standardized measuring instruments on an international basis, to stimulate and co-ordinate studies of the scientific aspects of telecommunications using electro-magnetic waves, guided and unguided. There are 40 national committees. Pres. A. L. CULLEN (UK); Sec.-Gen. Prof. J. VAN BLADEL (Belgium). Publs *URSI Information Bulletin, Review of Radio Science*.

International Union of the History and Philosophy of Science: Division of the History of Science: Dept of Philosophy, McGill University, 855 Sherbrooke West, Montreal H3A 2T7, Canada; tel. (514) 398-6057; telex 05268510; Division of the History of Logic, Methodology and Philosophy of Science: Dept of Philosophy, University of Turku, 20500 Turku 50, Finland; f. 1954 to promote research into the history and philosophy of science. There are 34 national committees. DHS Council (Montreal): Pres. Prof. P. GALLUZZI (Italy); Sec. W. SHEA (Canada). DLMPS Council: Pres. Prof. JONATHAN COHEN (UK); Sec. R. HILPINEN (Finland).

International Union of Theoretical and Applied Mechanics: Institute B of Mechanics, University of Stuttgart, 7000 Stuttgart 80, Federal Republic of Germany; telex 7255445; f. 1947 to form a link bween persons and organizations engaged in scientific work (theoretical or experimental) in mechanics or in related sciences; to organize international congresses of theoretical and applied mechanics, through a standing Congress Committee, and to organize other international meetings for subjects falling within this field; and to engage in other activities meant to promote the development of mechanics as a science. Mems: from 37 countries. Pres. Sir JAMES LIGHTHILL (UK); Sec. Prof. W. SCHIEHLEN (FRG). Publ. *Annual Report*.

OTHER ORGANIZATIONS

Association for the Taxonomic Study of the Flora of Tropical Africa: Institut für Allgemeine Botanik und Botanischer Garten, 2000 Hamburg 52, Ohnhorststr. 18, Federal Republic of Germany; tel. (040) 8222397; telex 214732; f. 1950 to facilitate co-operation and liaison between botanists engaged in the study of the flora of Tropical Africa; maintains a library in Brussels. Mems: about 800 botanists in 70 countries. Sec.-Gen. Prof. Dr H.-D. IHLENFELDT. Publs *Bulletin* (annual), *Proceedings*.

Association of African Geological Surveys: c/o CIFEG, 103 rue de Lille, 75007 Paris, France; tel. (1) 45-50-32-22; f. 1929 to synthesize the geological knowledge of Africa and neighbouring countries and encourage research in geological and allied sciences; affiliated to the International Union of Geological Sciences (q.v.). Mems: about 60 (Official Geological Surveys, public and private organizations). Pres. G. O. KESSE (Ghana); Sec.-Gen. M. BENSAÏD (Morocco). Publs *African Geology*, maps and studies.

Association of European Atomic Forums—FORATOM: 1 St Alban's St, London, SW1Y 4SL, England; tel. (01) 930-6888; telex 264476; f. 1960; holds periodical conferences. Mems: atomic 'forums' in Austria, Belgium, Finland, France, Federal Republic of Germany, Italy, Luxembourg, Netherlands, Norway, Spain, Sweden, Switzerland, United Kingdom. Pres. RÉMY CARLE; Sec. Gen. JIM CORNER.

Association of Geoscientists for International Development—AGID: c/o Dr T. Thanasuthipitak, Asian Institute of Technology, POB 2754, Bangkok 10501, Thailand; tel. 529-0100-13, ext. 2528; telex 84276; f. 1974 to encourage communication between those interested in the application of the geosciences to international development; to give priority to the developing countries in these matters; to organize meetings and publish information; affiliated to the International Union of Geological Sciences (q.v.). Mems: in 97 countries (individuals, and 44 institutions). Sec.-Treas. Dr THEERAPONGS THANASUTHIPITAK (Thailand).

Biometric Society: Dept of Applied Statistics, University of Reading, Whiteknights, POB 217, Reading, RG6 2AN, England; tel. (0734) 875123, ext. 450; telex 847813; f. 1947 for the advancement of quantitative biological science through the development of quantitative theories and the application, development and dissemination of effective mathematical and statistical techniques; the Society has 14 regional organizations and 5 national groups, is affiliated with the International Statistical Institute and the World Health Organization, and constitutes the Section of Biometry of the International Union of Biological Sciences (q.v.). Mems: over 6,000 in more than 60 countries. Pres. Prof. G. H. FREEMAN (UK); Sec. Prof. R. MEAD (UK). Publ. *Biometrics* (quarterly).

Charles Darwin Foundation for the Galapagos Isles: c/o Juan Black, Casilla 38-91, Quito, Ecuador; f. 1959 to support and administer research at a station authorized by the Government of Ecuador, with primary emphasis on ecology and conservation; to protect the wildlife of the Galapagos Islands; and to encourage scientific education. Pres. Dr CRAIG MACFARLAND (USA); Sec.-Gen. JUAN BLACK. Publs *Noticias de Galapágos* (twice a year), *Annual Report*.

Council for the International Congresses of Entomology: c/o CSIRO Division of Entomology, POB 1700, Canberra City, Australia; f. 1910 to act as a link between quadrennial congresses and to arrange the venue for each congress; the committee is also the entomology section of the International Union of Biological

Sciences (q.v.). Chair. Dr R. GALUN (Israel); Sec. Dr M. J. WHITTEN (Australia). Publ. *Proceedings* (after each Congress).

European Association of Exploration Geophysicists: Wassenaarseweg 22, 2596 CH The Hague, Netherlands; tel. (70) 45-36-88; telex 33480; f. 1951 to facilitate contacts between exploration geophysicists, disseminate information to members, arrange annual meetings, technical exhibitions, and courses. Mems 4,000, and 905 subscribers in 90 countries throughout the world. Treas./Sec. D. G. CANE (UK). Publs *Geophysical Prospecting* (9 a year), *First Break* (monthly), *Tidal Gravity Corrections* (annually).

European Association of Veterinary Anatomists: 3000 Hannover 1, Bischofsholer Damm 15, Federal Republic of Germany; f. 1964 to provide opportunities for meetings for the advancement of studies in veterinary anatomy. Mems: 195 in 30 countries. Pres. Prof. A. KING (UK); Gen. Sec. Prof. R. SCHWARZ (FRG).

European Atomic Energy Society: UKAEA, 11 Charles II St, London, SW1Y 4QP; f. 1954 to encourage co-operation in atomic energy research. Mems: national atomic energy commissions in Austria, Belgium, Denmark, Finland, France, Federal Republic of Germany, Greece, Italy, Netherlands, Norway, Portugal, Spain, Sweden, Switzerland, United Kingdom. Pres. Prof. J. VEIGA SIMAO; Exec. Vice-Pres. R. N. SIMEONE.

European Molecular Biology Organization—EMBO: 6900 Heidelberg 1, Postfach 1022.40, Federal Republic of Germany; tel. (6221) 383031; telex 461613; f. 1964 to promote collaboration in the field of molecular biology; to establish fellowships for training and research; to establish a European Laboratory of Molecular Biology where a majority of the disciplines comprising the subject will be represented. Mems: approximately 650. Chair. Prof. M. BIRNSTIEL (Austria); Sec.-Gen. Prof. G. SCHATZ (Switzerland); Exec. Sec. Dr J. TOOZE (FRG). Publ. *EMBO Journal* (13 a year).

European Organization for Nuclear Research—CERN: European Laboratory for Particle Physics, 1211 Geneva 23, Switzerland; tel. (022) 836111; telex 41900; f. 1954 to provide for collaboration among European states in nuclear research of a pure scientific and fundamental character; the work of CERN is for peaceful purposes only and concerns subnuclear, high-energy and elementary particle physics; it is not concerned with the development of nuclear reactors or fusion devices. Council comprises two representatives of each member state. Major experimental facilities: Synchro-Cyclotron (of 600 MeV), Proton Synchrotron (of 25-28 GeV), and Super Proton Synchrotron (of 450 GeV). A large electron-positron ring (of 50 GeV per beam) is due to be completed in 1989. Budget (1988) 793m. Swiss francs. Mems: Austria, Belgium, Denmark, France, Federal Republic of Germany, Greece, Italy, Netherlands, Norway, Portugal, Spain, Sweden, Switzerland, United Kingdom; Observers: Poland, Turkey, Yugoslavia. Pres. of Council Dr J. REMBSER (FRG); Dir-Gen. Prof. CARLO RUBBIA (Italy). Publs *CERN Courier* (monthly), *Annual Report*, *Scientific Reports*.

European Space Agency—ESA: 8-10 rue Mario Nikis, 75738 Paris Cedex 15, France; tel. (1) 42-73-76-54; telex 202746; f. 1975 to promote co-operation among European states in space research and technology and their application for peaceful purposes. Council composed of representatives of member states is the governing body. The Agency runs ESTEC (European Space Research and Technology Centre), ESOC (European Space Operations Centre) and ESRIN (Space Documentation Centre). The Agency's 'Ariane' programme (begun in 1979) develops rockets to launch satellites for telecommunications, meteorology and other scientific and industrial purposes. In 1987 member governments approved a programme to include a new type of Ariane launcher, a manned space-shuttle (Hermes), and collaboration with the USA on a manned space-station. Mems: Austria, Belgium, Denmark, France, Federal Republic of Germany, Ireland, Italy, Netherlands, Norway, Spain, Sweden, Switzerland, United Kingdom; associated states: Canada, Finland. Chair. Dr H. GRAGE (Denmark); Dir-Gen. REIMAR LÜST. Publs *Annual Report*, *ESA Bulletin*, *ESA Journal*.

European-Mediterranean Seismological Centre: 5 rue René Descartes, 67084 Strasbourg Cedex, France; tel. 88-41-63-69; telex 890 826; f. 1976 for rapid determination of seismic hypocentres in the region; maintains data base. Mems: institutions in 14 countries. Sec.-Gen. J. BONNIN. Publ. monthly list of preliminary hypocentral determinations.

Federation of Arab Scientific Research Councils: POB 13027, Baghdad, Iraq; tel. 5381090; telex 212466; f. 1976 to encourage co-operation in scientific research, to promote the establishment of new institutions and plan joint regional research projects. Mems: national science bodies in 15 countries. Sec.-Gen. MUHAMMAD O. KHIDIR. Publs *Journal*, *Newsletter*.

Federation of Asian Scientific Academies and Societies —FASAS: c/o Indian National Science Academy, Bahadur Shah Zafar Marg, New Delhi 110002, India; tel. 331-0717; telex 3161835; f. 1984 to stimulate regional co-operation and promote national and regional self-reliance in science and technology, by organizing meetings, training and research programmes and encouraging the exchange of scientists and of scientific information. Mems: national scientific academies and societies from Afghanistan, Bangladesh, the People's Republic of China, India, the Republic of Korea, Malaysia, Nepal, Pakistan, the Philippines, Singapore, Sri Lanka and Thailand. Pres. Prof. A. K. SHARMA (India); Sec. Dr S. RADHAKRISHNA (India).

Federation of European Biochemical Societies: c/o Prof. G. Dirheimer, 15 rue René-Descartes, 67084 Strasbourg Cedex, France; tel. 88-41-70-00; telex 880492; f. 1964 to promote the science of biochemistry through meetings of European biochemists, provision of fellowships and advanced courses and issuing publications. Mems: 40,000 in 27 societies. Chair. Prof. V. TURK; Sec.-Gen. Prof. G. DIRHEIMER. Publs *European Journal of Biochemistry*, *FEBS Letters*, *FEBS Bulletin*.

Foundation for International Scientific Co-ordination (Fondation 'Pour la science', Centre international de synthèse): 12 rue Colbert, 75002 Paris, France; tel. (1) 42-97-50-68; f. 1924. Dir JACQUES ROGER. Publs *Revue de Synthèse*, *Revue d'Histoire des Sciences*, *Semaines de Synthèse*, *L'Évolution de l'Humanité*.

Intergovernmental Oceanographic Commission: UNESCO, 7 place de Fontenoy, 75700 Paris, France; tel. (1) 45-68-39-83; telex 204461; f. 1960 to promote scientific investigation with a view to learning more about the nature and resources of the oceans through the concerted action of its members. Mems: 117 governments. Chair. Prof. ULF LIE (Norway); Sec. MARIO RUIVO. Publs *IOC Technical series* (irregular), *IOC Manuals* and *Guides* (irregular).

International Academy of Astronautics—IAA: 3-5 rue Mario-Nikis, BP 62, 75722 Paris Cedex 15, France; tel. (1) 45-67-49-66; f. 1960 at the XI Congress of the International Astronautical Federation; holds scientific meetings and makes scientific studies and reports, awards and prizes; maintains committees on numerous aspects of space science and Scientific-Legal Liaison Committees. Mems: 515 mems and 284 corresponding mems from 44 countries. Pres. GEORGE E. MUELLER; Dir Dr THEODORE VON KARMAN. Publs *Acta Astronautica* (monthly).

International Association for Earthquake Engineering: Kenchiku Kaikan, 3rd Floor, 5-26-20, Shiba, Minato-ku, Tokyo 108, Japan; f. 1963 to promote international co-operation among scientists and engineers in the field of earthquake engineering through exchange of knowledge, ideas and results of research and practical experience. Mems: 38 countries. Pres. GIUSEPPE GRANDORI (Italy).

International Association for Ecology—INTECOL: Institute of Ecology, University of Georgia, Athens, GA 30602, USA; tel. (404) 542-2968; telex 8107543908; f. 1967 to provide opportunities for communication between ecologists; to co-operate with organizations and individuals having related aims and interests; to encourage studies in the different fields of ecology; affiliated to the International Union of Biological Sciences (q.v.). Mems: 35 national and international ecological societies, and 1,000 individuals. Pres. F. GOLLEY (USA); Sec.-Gen. P. MAYCOCK (Canada).

International Association for Mathematical Geology: c/o Prof. J. C. Davis, US Geological Society, National Center 920, Reston, Va 22092, USA; f. 1968 for the preparation and elaboration of mathematical models of geological processes; the introduction of mathematical methods in geological sciences and technology; assistance in the development of mathematical investigation in geological sciences; the organization of international collaboration in mathematical geology through various forums and publications; educational programmes for mathematical geology; affiliated to the International Union of Geological Sciences (q.v.). Mems: c. 800. Pres. Prof. J. C. DAVIS (USA); Sec.-Gen. Dr R. B. MCCAMMON (USA). Publs *Journal of the International Association for Mathematical Geology* (8 a year), *Computers and Geosciences* (4 a year), *Newsletter* (quarterly).

International Association for Mathematics and Computers in Simulation: c/o Institut Montefiore, Bâtiment B28, Sart Tilman, 4000 Liège, Belgium; tel. (41) 56-17-10; f. 1955 to further the study of mathematical tools and computer software and hardware, analogue, digital or hybrid computers for simulation of soft or hard systems. Mems: 1,100 and 27 assoc. mems. Pres. R. VICHNEVETSKY (USA); Sec. J. ROBERT (Belgium). Publs *Mathematics and Computers in Simulation* (6 a year), *Applied Numerical Mathematics* (6 a year).

International Association for the Physical Sciences of the Ocean—IAPSO: POB 1161, Del Mar, Ca 92014-1161, USA; f. 1919 to promote the study of scientific problems relating to the oceans and interactions occurring at its boundaries, chiefly in so far as such study may be carried out by the aid of mathematics, physics and chemistry; to initiate, facilitate and co-ordinate research; to provide for discussion, comparison and publication; affiliated to the International Union of Geodesy and Geophysics (q.v.). Mems: 71 member states. Pres. Prof. JAMES J. O'BRIEN (USA); Sec.-Gen. Dr

OTHER INTERNATIONAL ORGANIZATIONS

ROBERT E. STEVENSON (USA). Publs *Publications Scientifiques* (irregular).

International Association for Plant Physiology—IAPP: c/o Dr D. Graham, Food Research Laboratories, CSIRO, POB 52, North Ryde, NSW, Australia 2113; tel. (02) 887-8333; telex 23407; f. 1955 to promote the development of plant physiology at the international level through congresses, symposia and workshops, by maintaining communication with national societies and by encouraging interaction between plant physiologists in developing and developed countries; affiliated to the International Union of Biological Sciences (q.v.). Pres. Prof. Dr H. ZIEGLER; Sec.-Treas. Dr D. GRAHAM.

International Association for Plant Taxonomy: Botanisches Museum, Königin Luisestr. 6–8, 1000 Berlin 33, Federal Republic of Germany; tel. (030) 8300-6132; f. 1950 to promote the development of plant taxonomy and encourage contacts between people and institutes interested in this work; affiliated to the International Union of Biological Sciences (q.v.). Mems: institutes and individuals in 85 countries. Pres. F. A. STAFLEN (Netherlands); Sec.-Gen. W. GREUTER (FRG). Publs *Taxon* (quarterly), *Regnum vegetabile* (irregular).

International Association of Biological Standardization: Biostandards, CP 229, 1211 Geneva 4, Switzerland; telex 421859; f. 1955 to connect producers and controllers of immunological products (sera, vaccines, etc.) for the study and the development of methods of standardization; supports international organizations in their efforts to solve problems of standardization. Mems: 650. Pres. IRENE BATTY (UK); Sec.-Gen. D. GAUDRY (France). Publs *Newsletter* (2 a year), *Journal of Biological Standardization* (quarterly).

International Association of Botanic Gardens: c/o Dr B. Morley, Botanic Gardens of Adelaide, North Terrace, Adelaide, SA 5000, Australia; tel. (08) 228-2311; f. 1954 to promote co-operation between scientific collections of living plants, including the exchange of information and specimens; to promote the study of the taxonomy of cultivated plants; and to encourage the conservation of rare plants and their habitats; affiliated to the International Union of Biological Sciences (q.v.). Pres. Prof. PETER ASHTON (USA); Sec. Dr BRIAN D. MORLEY (Australia).

International Association of Geodesy: 140 rue de Grenelle, 75700 Paris, France; tel. (1) 45-50-34-95; telex 204989; f. 1922 to promote the study of all scientific problems of geodesy and encourage geodetic research; to promote and co-ordinate international co-operation in this field; to publish results; affiliated to the International Union of Geodesy and Geophysics (q.v.). Mems: national committees in 73 countries. Pres. I. I. MUELLER (USA); Sec.-Gen. M. LOUIS (France); Asst. Sec.-Gen. C. BOUCHER (France). Publs *Bulletin géodésique, Travaux de l'AIG, Bibliographie géodésique internationale*.

International Association of Geomagnetism and Aeronomy—IAGA: Physics Dept, Aberdeen University, Aberdeen, AB9 2UE, Scotland; tel. (0224) 574585; telex 73458; f. 1919 for the study of questions relating to geomagnetism and aeronomy and the encouragement of research; holds General and Scientific Assemblies every four years; affiliated to the International Union of Geodesy and Geophysics (IUGG, q.v.). Mems: the countries which adhere to the IUGG. Pres. R. E. GENDRIN (France); Sec.-Gen. M. GADSDEN (UK). Publs *IAGA Bulletin* (including annual *Geomagnetic Data*), *IAGA News* (annually).

International Association of Hydrological Sciences: Committee for Hydrological Research TNO, POB 297, 2501 BD The Hague, Netherlands; tel. (070) 49-65-37; telex 31660; f. 1922 to promote co-operation in the study of hydrology and water resources. Pres. VIT KLEMEŠ (Canada); Sec.-Gen. H. C. COLENBRANDER. Publs *Journal* (every 2 months), *Newsletter* (3 a year).

International Association of Meteorology and Atmospheric Physics—IAMAP: Institute for Meteorology and Geophysics, University of Innsbruck, 6020 Innsbruck, Austria; f. 1919; permanent commissions on atmospheric ozone, radiation, atmospheric chemistry and global pollution, dynamic meteorology, polar meteorology, cloud physics, climate, atmospheric electricity, planetary atmospheres and their evolution, and meteorology of the upper atmosphere; general assemblies held once every four years; special assemblies held once between general assemblies; affiliated to the International Union of Geodesy and Geophysics (q.v.). Pres. Dr G. B. TUCKER (Australia); Sec.-Gen. Prof. M. KUHN (Austria).

International Association of Photobiology: c/o Rex M. Tyrrell, Institut Suisse de Recherches Expérimentales sur le Cancer, 1066 Epalinges, Lausanne, Switzerland; tel. (021) 333061; telex 26156; f. 1928; stimulation of scientific research concerning the physics, chemistry and climatology of non-ionizing radiations (ultra-violet, visible and infra-red) in relation to their biological efffects and their applications in biology and medicine; 18 national committees represented; affiliated to the International Union of Biological Sciences (q.v.). International Congresses held every four years. Pres. Prof. K. K. ROHATGI-MUKHERJEE; Sec.-Gen. Dr R. M. TYRRELL (Switzerland).

International Association of Sedimentologists: c/o Dr F. Surlyk, Geological Survey of Greenland, Oster Voldgade 10, 1350 Copenhagen K, Denmark; f. 1952; affiliated to the International Union of Geological Sciences (q.v.). Mems: 2,100. Pres. Prof. H. FUCHTBAUER (FRG); Gen. Sec. Dr FINN SURLYK (Denmark). Publ. *Sedimentology* (every 2 months).

International Association of Theoretical and Applied Limnology (Societas Internationalis Limnologiae): Dept of Biology, University of Michigan, Ann Arbor, Mich. 48109, USA; f. 1922; study of physical, chemical and biological phenomena of lakes and rivers; affiliated to the International Union of Biological Sciences (q.v.). Mems: about 3,200. Pres. D. G. FREY (USA); Gen. Sec. and Treas. ROBERT G. WETZEL (USA).

International Association of Volcanology and Chemistry of the Earth's Interior—IAVCEI: c/o Institut Mineralogie, Ruhr Universität Bochum, 4630 Bochum, Federal Republic of Germany; tel. (0234) 7003520; telex 0825-860; f. 1919 to examine scientifically all aspects of volcanology; affiliated to the International Union of Geodesy and Geophysics (q.v.). Pres. S. ARAMAKI; Sec.-Gen. H.-U. SCHMINKE (FRG). Publs *Bulletin of Volcanology, Catalogue of the Active Volcanoes of the World, Newsletter*.

International Association of Wood Anatomists: c/o Institute of Systematic Botany, University of Utrecht, Netherlands; tel. 030-532643; f. 1931 for the purpose of study, documentation and exchange of information on the structure of wood. Mems: 500 in 61 countries. Exec. Sec. B. J. H. TER WELLE. Publ. *IAWA Bulletin*.

International Association on Water Pollution Research and Control: 1 Queen Anne's Gate, London, SW1H 9BT, England; tel. (01) 222-3848; telex 918518; f. 1965 to encourage international communication, co-operative effort, and a maximum exchange of information on water quality management; to sponsor conferences every two years; to publish research reports. Mems: 43 national, 280 corporate and 1,703 individuals. Pres. Prof. P. HARREMOES; Exec. Dir A. MILBURN. Publs *Water Research* (monthly), *Water Science and Technology* (12 a year), *Water Quality International* (quarterly), *Yearbook*.

International Astronautical Federation—IAF: 3–5 rue Mario-Nikis, 75015 Paris, France; tel. (1) 45-67-42-60; telex 205917; f. 1950 to foster the development of astronautics for peaceful purposes at national and international levels. The IAF has created the International Academy of Astronautics (IAA) and the International Institute of Space Law (IISL). Mems: 93 national astronautical societies in 37 countries. Pres. J. ORTNER (Austria); Exec. Sec. M. CLAUDIN.

International Botanical Congress: c/o Prof. K. Iwatsuki, Botanical Gardens, University of Tokyo, Hakusan 3-7-1, Bunkyo-ku, Tokyo 112, Japan; tel. (03) 814-2625; f. 1864 to inform botanists of recent progress in the plant sciences; the Nomenclature Section of the Congress attempts to provide a uniform terminology and methodology for the naming of plants; other Divisions deal with developmental, metabolic, structural, systematic and evolutionary, ecological botany; genetics and plant breeding; next Congress: Tokyo, 1993; affiliated to the International Union of Biological Sciences (q.v.). Sec. Prof. K. IWATSUKI.

International Bureau of Weights and Measures: Pavillon de Breteuil, 92312 Sèvres Cedex, France; tel. 45-34-00-51; telex 201067; f. 1875 for the international unification of physical measures; establishment of fundamental standards and of scales of the principal physical dimensions; preservation of the international prototypes; determination of national standards; precision measurements in physics. Mems: 47 states. Pres. D. KIND (FRG); Sec. J. DE BOER (Netherlands); Dir T. J. QUINN (UK).

International Cartographic Association: 24 Strickland Rd, Mt Pleasant, Western Australia 6153, Australia; tel. (09) 364-5380; telex 95791; f. 1959 for the advancement, instigation and co-ordination of cartographic research involving co-operation between different nations. Particularly concerned with furtherance of training in cartography, study of source material, compilation, graphic design, drawing, scribing and reproduction techniques of maps; organizes international conferences, symposia, meetings, exhibitions. Mems: 64 nations. Sec.-Treas. DON PEARCE (Australia). Publs *ICA Newsletter* (2 a year).

International Centre of Insect Physiology and Ecology: POB 30772, Nairobi, Kenya; tel. 43081; telex 22053; f. 1970 to increase food production by undertaking research on pests of major crops, vectors of livestock diseases, and insect carriers of human diseases critical to tropical rural health; and to increase the capacity of developing countries in pest management research and its application, by training scientists and technologists; field stations in

OTHER INTERNATIONAL ORGANIZATIONS

Kenya and the Philippines. Dir Prof. THOMAS R. ODHIAMBO (Kenya). Publs *Insect Science and its Application* (quarterly), *Annual Report, DUDU* (quarterly).

International Commission for Physics Education: c/o Dept of Physics, Ohio State University, 174 West 18th Ave, Columbus, OH 43210-1106, USA; tel. (614) 422-6959; telex 810482 1715; f. 1960 to encourage and develop international collaboration in the improvement and extension of the methods and scope of physics education at all levels; collaborates with UNESCO and organizes international conferences. Mems: appointed triennially by the International Union of Pure and Applied Physics. Chair. Prof. R. U. SEXL (Austria); Sec. E. L. JOSSEM (USA).

International Commission for Plant-Bee Relationships: c/o Dr S. N. Holm, Royal Veterinary and Agricultural University, Department of Crop Husbandry, Experimental Station, Hojbakkegaard, 2630 Taastrup, Denmark; f. 1950 to promote research and its application in the field of bee botany, and collect and spread information; to organize meetings, etc., and collaborate with scientific organizations; affiliated to the International Union of Biological Sciences (q.v.). Mems: 175 in 34 countries. Pres. Dr S. N. HOLM; Sec. J. N. TASEI.

International Commission for the Scientific Exploration of the Mediterranean Sea (Commission internationale pour l'exploration scientifique de la mer Méditerranée—CIESM): 16 blvd de Suisse, 98030 Monaco Cedex; tel. (93) 30-38-79; f. 1919 for scientific exploration of the Mediterranean Sea; includes 12 scientific committees. Mems: 1,650 scientists, 17 member countries. Pres. SAS The Prince RAINIER III of MONACO; Sec.-Gen. Cdt. J. Y. COUSTEAU (France).

International Commission on Glass: c/o Institut National du Verre, 10 blvd Defontaine, 6000 Charleroi, Belgium; tel. (071) 31-00-41; telex 51430; f. 1950 to organize and co-ordinate research in glass and allied products and to promote scientific co-operation through exchange of information and the holding of congresses. Mems: 24 organizations. Treas. P. VAN DE PUTTE.

International Commission on Radiation Units and Measurements—ICRU: 7910 Woodmont Ave, Suite 800, Bethesda, Md 20814, USA; tel. (301) 657-2652; f. 1925 to develop internationally acceptable recommendations regarding: (1) quantities and units of radiation and radioactivity, (2) procedures suitable for the measurement and application of these quantities in clinical radiology and radiobiology, (3) physical data needed in the application of these procedures. Makes recommendations on quantities and units for radiation protection (see below, International Radiation Protection Association). Mems: from about 18 countries. Chair. A. ALLISY; Sec. R. S. CASWELL; Exec. Sec. W. R. NEY. Publs *Reports*.

International Commission on Zoological Nomenclature: c/o British Museum (Natural History), Cromwell Rd, London, SW7 5BD, England; tel. (01) 938-9387; f. 1895; has judicial powers to determine all matters relating to the interpretation of the International Code of Zoological Nomenclature and also plenary powers to suspend the operation of the Code where the strict application of the Code would lead to confusion and instability of nomenclature; the Commission is responsible also for maintaining and developing the Official Lists and Official Indexes of Names in Zoology; affiliated to the International Union of Biological Sciences (q.v.). Pres. W. D. L. RIDE (Australia); Exec. Sec. Dr P. K. TUBBS (UK). Publs *International Code of Zoological Nomenclature, Bulletin of Zoological Nomenclature*, official lists and indexes.

International Council for Bird Preservation: 32 Cambridge Rd, Girton, CB3 0PJ, England; tel. (0223) 277318; telex 818794; f. 1922; determines status of bird species throughout the world and compiles data on all endangered species; identifies conservation problems and priorities; initiates and co-ordinates conservation projects and international conventions. Representatives in 42 countries; national sections in 63 countries. Pres. Dr R. W. PETERSON (USA); Dir Dr CHRISTOPH IMBODEN (UK). Publs *Bulletin, ICBP/IUCN Bird Red Data Book, World Birdwatch*, technical publications, study reports.

International Council for Scientific and Technical Information: 51 blvd de Montmorency, 75016 Paris, France; tel. (1) 45 25 65 92; telex 630553; f. 1984; aims to increase accessibility to scientific and technical information; fosters communication and interaction among all participants in the information transfer chain. Mems: 45 organizations. Pres. J. MICHEL (France); Exec. Sec. M. ORFUS (France).

International Council for the Exploration of the Sea —ICES: Palaegade 2-4, 1261, Copenhagen K, Denmark; tel. (01) 15-42-25; telex 22498; f. 1902 to encourage concerted biological and hydrographical investigations for the promotion of a planned exploitation of the resources of the Atlantic Ocean and its adjacent seas, and primarily the North Atlantic; library of 15,000 vols. Membership: governments of 18 countries. Gen. Sec. B. B. PARRISH. Publs *Journal du Conseil, Bulletin Statistique, ICES Oceanographic Data Lists and Inventories, Co-operative Research Reports, Fiches d'Identification du Plancton, Fiches d'Identification des Maladies et Parasites des Poissons, Crustacés et Mollusques*.

International Council of Psychologists: 4805 Regent St, Madison, WI 53705, USA; tel. (608) 238-5373; f. 1959 to advance psychology and the application of its findings throughout the world; holds annual conventions. Mems: 1,800 qualified psychologists. Sec.-Gen. PATRICIA CAUTLEY. Publs. *International Psychologist* (quarterly).

International Council of the Aeronautical Sciences: c/o Royal Aeronautical Society, 4 Hamilton Place, London, W1V 0BQ, England; f.1957 to encourage free interchange of information on all phases of mechanical flight; holds biennial Congresses. Mems: national associations in 28 countries. Pres. B. LASCHKA (FRG); Exec. Sec. A. D. YOUNG (UK).

International Earth Rotation Service: National Astronomical Observatory, Division of Earth Rotation, Mizusawa-shi, Iwateken, 023 Japan; f. 1988 (fmrly International Polar Motion Service); maintained by the International Astronomical Union and the International Union of Geodesy and Geophysics; defines and maintains terrestrial and celestial reference systems; determines earth orientation parameters (terrestrial and celestial co-ordinates of the pole and universal time) connecting these systems; organizes collection, analysis and dissemination of data. Dir Prof. K. YOKOYAMA.

International Federation of Cell Biology: c/o Dr A. Zimmerman, Dept of Zoology, University of Toronto, 25 Harbord St, Toronto M5S 1A1, Canada; f. 1972 to foster international co-operation, and organize conferences. Sec.-Gen. Dr A. ZIMMERMAN. Publs *Cell Biology International* (monthly), reports.

International Federation of Operational Research Societies: c/o IMSOR, Bldg 321, Technical University of Denmark, 2800 Lyngby, Denmark; tel. (2) 881433; telex 37529; f. 1959 for development of operational research as a unified science and its advancement in all nations of the world. Mems: about 30,000 individuals, 35 national societies, six kindred societies. Pres. Prof. WILLIAM PIERSKALLA (USA); Sec. Mrs HELLE WELLING. Publs *International Abstracts in Operational Research, IFORS Bulletin*.

International Federation of Scientific Editors' Associations: BioSciences Information Service, 2100 Arch St, Philadelphia, Pa 19103, USA; tel. (215) 587-4815; telex 831739; f. 1978; links associations of editors in different branches of science; recommends standards and practices for manuscript preparation; co-operates with secondary sources in facilitating information retrieval. Pres. J. WATSON (Canada); Sec.-Gen. E. M. ZIPF (USA).

International Federation of Societies for Electron Microscopy: Dept of Cell Biology, Institute of Anatomy, University of Aarhus, Aarhus, Denmark; f. 1955. Mems: representative organizations of 40 countries. Pres. Prof. G. THOMAS (USA); Gen.-Sec. Prof. A. MAUNSBACH (Denmark).

International Food Information Service: Editorial Office, Lane End House, Shinfield, Reading, RG2 9BB, England; tel. (0734) 883895; telex 847204; f. 1968 by the Gesellschaft für Information und Dokumentation (Frankfurt), the Institute of Food Technologists (Chicago), the Commonwealth Agricultural Bureaux (now CAB International) and the Centrum voor Landbouwpublikaties en Landbouwdocumentates for the collection and dissemination of scientific and technological information on foods and their processing. Joint Man. Dirs H. BROOKES, Dr U. SCHÜTZSACK. Publ. *Food Science and Technology Abstracts* (monthly).

International Foundation of the High-Altitude Research Stations Jungfraujoch and Gornergrat: Sidlerstrasse 5, 3012 Berne, Switzerland; tel. (031) 654052; telex 912643; f. 1931; international research centre which enables scientists from many scientific fields to carry out experiments at high altitudes. Eight countries contribute to support the station: Austria, Belgium, France, Federal Republic of Germany, Italy, Switzerland, United Kingdom. Pres. Prof. H. DEBRUNNER.

International Glaciological Society: Lensfield Rd, Cambridge, CB2 1ER, England; tel. (0223) 355974; f. 1936 to stimulate interest in and encourage research into the scientific and technical problems of snow and ice in all countries. Mems: 850 in 33 countries. Pres. Dr S. C. COLBECK (USA); Sec.-Gen. H. RICHARDSON. Publs *Journal of Glaciology* (3 a year), *Ice* (News Bulletin—3 a year), *Annals of Glaciology*.

International Group of Scientific, Technical and Medical Publishers: Keizersgracht 462, 1016 GE Amsterdam, Netherlands; tel. (020) 22-52-14; f. 1969 to deal with problems of international copyright protection and assist publishers and authors in disseminating scientific information by both conventional and advanced methods; holds seminars and study groups. Sec. PAUL NIJHOFF ASSER. Publs *STM Newsletter, STM Copyright Bulletin, STM Innovations Bulletin*.

International Hibernation Society: 300 Dean Drive, Rockville, Md 20851, USA; f. 1960 for exchange of information on mammalian

OTHER INTERNATIONAL ORGANIZATIONS

hibernation. Mems: 147 in 14 countries. Exec. Sec. RICHARD C. SIMMONDS (USA). Publ. *Newsletter* (fortnightly).

International Hydrographic Organization: ave Président J. F. Kennedy, BP 445, Monte Carlo, 98011 Monaco Cedex; tel. (93) 506587; telex 479164; f. 1921 to link the hydrographic offices of its member governments and co-ordinate their work with a view to rendering navigation easier and safer on all the seas of the world; to obtain as far as possible uniformity in charts and hydrographic documents; to encourage the adoption of the best methods of conducting hydrographic surveys and improvements in the theory and practice of the science of hydrography, and to encourage surveying in those parts of the world where accurate charts are lacking; to extend and facilitate the application of oceanographic knowledge for the benefit of navigators and specialists in marine sciences; to render advice and assistance to developing countries upon request, facilitating their application for financial aid from the UNDP for creation or extension of their hydrographic capabilities; to fulfil the role of world data centre for bathymetry; provides computerized Tidal Constituent Data Bank. Next conference: 1992. Mems: 57 states. Directing Committee: Pres. Rear Adm. Sir DAVID W. HASLAM (UK); Dirs Rear Adm. A. CIVETTA (Italy), A. J. KERR (Canada). Publs *International Hydrographic Review* (2 a year), *International Hydrographic Bulletin* (monthly), *IHO Yearbook*.

International Institute of Refrigeration: 177 blvd Malesherbes, 75017 Paris, France; tel. (1) 42-27-32-35; telex 643269; f. 1908 to further the development of the science and practice of refrigeration on a world-wide scale; to investigate, discuss and recommend any aspects leading to improvements in the field of refrigeration; maintains FRIGINTER data-base. Mems: 57 national organizations and 800 associates. Dir A. GAC (France). Publs *Bulletin* (every 2 months), *International Journal of Refrigeration* (every 2 months).

International Mineralogical Association: Institute of Mineralogy, University of Marburg, 3550 Marburg, Federal Republic of Germany; tel. 28-5617; telex 482372; f. 1958 to further international co-operation in the science of mineralogy; affiliated to the International Union of Geological Sciences (q.v.). Mems: national societies in 31 countries. Sec. Prof. S. S. HAFNER.

International Organisation of Legal Metrology: 11 rue Turgot, 75009 Paris, France; tel. (1) 48-78-12-82; telex 215463; f. 1955 to serve as documentation and information centre on the verification, checking, construction and use of measuring instruments, to determine characteristics and standards to which measuring instruments must conform for their use to be recommended internationally, and to determine the general principles of legal metrology. Mems: governments of 50 countries. Dir B. ATHANÉ (France). Publ. *Bulletin* (quarterly).

International Palaeontological Association: US Geological Survey, E-305 Natural History Museum, Smithsonian Institution, Washington, DC 20560, USA; tel. (202) 343-3523; telex 264729; f. 1933; affiliated to the International Union of Geological Sciences and the International Union of Biological Sciences (q.v.). Pres. Prof. A. J. BOUCOT (USA); Sec.-Gen. Dr W. A. OLIVER, Jr (USA). Publs *Lethaia* (quarterly), *Directory*.

International Peat Society: Unioninkatu 40B, 00170 Helsinki, Finland; tel. 358-0-1924340; f. 1968 to encourage co-operation in the study and use of mires, peatlands, peat and related material, through international meetings, research groups and the exchange of information. Mems: 14 National Cttees, 225 research institutes and other organizations, and 500 individuals from 41 countries. Pres. Dr Y. PESSI (Finland); Sec.-Gen. V. KONDRATIEV (USSR). Publs *IPS Bulletin* (annually), *International Peat Journal* (annually).

International Phonetic Association—IPA: Dept of Linguistics and Phonetics, University of Leeds, LS2 9JT, England; f. 1886 to promote the scientific study of phonetics and its applications. Mems: 800. Sec. P. J. ROACH (UK). Publ. *Journal* (2 a year).

International Phycological Society: c/o Dept of Biology, Dalhousie University, Halifax, NS, Canada B3H 4J1; tel. (902) 424-2168; telex 921863; f. 1961 to promote the study of algae, the distribution of information, and international co-operation in this field. Mems: about 1,000. Sec. A. R. O. CHAPMAN (Canada). Publ. *Phycologia* (quarterly).

International Primatological Society: c/o Dr G. Epple, 3500 Market St, Philadelphia, Pa 19104, USA; f. 1964 to promote primatological science in all fields. Mems: about 900. Pres. Dr JOHN P. HEARN (UK); Sec.-Gen. Dr GISELA EPPLE (FRG).

International Radiation Protection Association—IRPA: 10 rue Poussin, 75016 Paris, France; tel. (1) 42-88-08-24; f. 1966 to unite in an international scientific society, individuals and societies throughout the world concerned with protection against ionizing radiations and allied effects, and to be representative of doctors, health physicists, radiological protection officers and others engaged in radiological protection, radiation safety, nuclear safety, legal, medical and veterinary aspects and in radiation research and other allied activities. Mems: 12,000 in 32 countries. Pres. M. W. CARTER (USA); Dir GILBERT BRESSON (France). Publ. *IRPA Bulletin*.

International Society for General Semantics: POB 2469, San Francisco, Calif 94126, USA; f. 1943 to advance knowledge of and inquiry into non-Aristotelian systems and general semantics. Mems: 3,000 individuals in 28 countries. Pres. MARY MORAIN (USA); Exec. Dir RUSSELL JOYNER (USA).

International Society for Human and Animal Mycology—ISHAM: c/o C. de Vroey, Laboratory for Mycology, Institute of Tropical Medicine, 155 Nationalestraat, 2000 Antwerp, Belgium; tel. (03) 238-58-80; telex 31648; f. 1954 to pursue the study of fungi pathogenic for man and animals; holds congresses (1991 Congress: Montreal, Canada). Mems: 820 from 71 countries. Pres. D. W. R. MACKENZIE; Gen. Sec. C. DE VROEY. Publ. *Journal of Medical and Veterinary Mycology* (6 a year).

International Society for Rock Mechanics: c/o Laboratório Nacional de Engenharia Civil, 101 Av. do Brasil, 1799 Lisboa Codex, Portugal; tel. (1) 882131; telex 16760; f. 1962 to encourage and co-ordinate international co-operation in the science of rock mechanics; to assist individuals and local organizations to form national bodies primarily interested in rock mechanics; to maintain liaison with other organizations that represent sciences of interest to the Society, including geology, geophysics, soil mechanics, mining engineering, petroleum engineering and civil engineering. The Society organizes international meetings and encourages the publication of the results of research in rock mechanics. Mems: c. 6,000. Pres. Dr JOHN FRANKLIN; Sec.-Gen. JOSÉ G. CHARRUA GRAÇA. Publ. *News* (quarterly).

International Society for Stereology: c/o Dr T. Mattfeldt, Institute of Pathology, 6900 Heidelberg, Im Neuenheimer Feld 220/221, Federal Republic of Germany; tel. (06221) 562624; f. 1961; an interdisciplinary society gathering scientists from metallurgy, geology, mineralogy and biology to exchange ideas on three-dimensional interpretation of two-dimensional samples (sections, projections) of their material by means of stereological principles; seventh Congress: Caen, France 1987. Mems: 450. Pres. JEAN-LOUIS CHERMANT; Sec. Dr TORSTEN MATTFELDT.

International Society for Tropical Ecology: c/o Botany Dept, Banaras Hindu University, Varanasi, 221005 India; f. 1956 to promote and develop the science of ecology in the tropics in the service of man; to publish a journal to aid ecologists in the tropics in communication of their findings; and to hold symposia from time to time to summarize the state of knowledge in particular or general fields of tropical ecology. Mems: 500. Sec. Dr K. C. MISRA (India); Editor Prof. J. S. SINGH. Publ. *Tropical Ecology* (2 a year).

International Society of Biometeorology: 440 Witikonerstrasse, 8053 Zürich, Switzerland; f. 1956 to unite all biometeorologists working in the fields of agricultural, botanical, cosmic, entomological, forest, human, medical, veterinarian, zoological and other branches of biometeorology. Mems: 450 individuals, nationals of 46 countries. Pres. Prof. B. NEWMAN (USA); Sec. Dr B. P. PRIMAULT (Switzerland). Publ. *International Journal of Biometeorology* (quarterly).

International Translations Centre: Schuttersveld 2, 2611 WE Delft, Netherlands; tel. (015) 142242; telex 38104; f. 1961 as the European Translations Centre, by the OECD; an international clearing house for scientific and technical translations prepared from all languages into Western languages; over 200 organizations regularly send notifications of translations to the Centre, or deposit a copy; through the World Translations Index over 290,000 translations are made available. Chair. Dr D. WOOD (UK); Dir M. RISSEEUW (Netherlands). Publs *World Translations Index* (10 a year, annual cumulative edition), *WTI Database*, *Journals in Translation* (irregular).

International Union for Conservation of Nature and Natural Resources—IUCN: 1196 Gland, Switzerland; tel. (022) 647181; telex 22618; f. 1948 to promote the conservation of natural resources by the scientific monitoring of their conditions, by determining scientific priorities for conservation, mobilizing the scientific and professional resources to investigate the most serious conservation problems and recommend solutions to them, developing programmes to protect and sustain the most important and threatened species and eco-systems and assisting governments to devise and carry out conservation projects; maintains a conservation library and documentation centre and units for monitoring traffic in wildlife. Mems: governments of 61 countries, 128 government agencies, 383 national and 33 international non-governmental organizations and 29 affiliates. Pres. Dr MONKUMBU K. SWAMINATHAN (India); Dir-Gen. Dr MARTIN W. HOLDGATE (UK). Publs *IUCN Bulletin* (every 3 months) incl. annual report, *Red Data Book* (on mammals, plants, invertebrates, amphibians and reptiles), *World Conservation Strategy*, *United Nations List of National Parks and Protected Areas*, Environmental Policy and Law Papers.

OTHER INTERNATIONAL ORGANIZATIONS

International Union for Quaternary Research—INQUA: Institut für Grundbau und Bodenmechanik, ETH-Hönggerberg, 8093 Zürich, Switzerland; tel. (01) 3772521; telex 823474; f. 1928 to co-ordinate research on the quaternary geological era throughout the world. Pres. N. W. RUTTER (Canada); Sec. C. SCHLÜCHTER (Switzerland).

International Union of Food Science and Technology: c/o National Food Centre, Dunsinea, Castleknock, Dublin 15, Ireland; tel. (01) 303222; telex 31947; f. 1970; sponsors international symposia and congresses. Mems; 46 national groups. Pres. E. VON SYDOW (Sweden); Sec.-Gen. D. E. HOOD (Ireland). Publ. *IUFOST Newsletter* (2 a year).

International Waterfowl and Wetlands Research Bureau: Slimbridge, Glos, GL2 7BX, England; tel. (045 389) 624; telex 437145; f. 1954 to stimulate and co-ordinate research on and conservation of waterfowl and their wetland habitats, particularly through the Ramsar Convention; co-ordinates research by institutes and individuals (professional and amateur) throughout the world; alerts governments and organizations when wetlands are threatened. Mems: 38 countries. Dir Dr MIKE MOSER. Publ. *Information Letter*.

Joint Institute for Nuclear Research: POB 79, 101000 Moscow, USSR; tel. (095) 226-22-29; telex 7521; f. 1956 to promote the development of nuclear research among member countries; Committee of Government Plenipotentiaries meets annually to determine future policy and finance; Institute includes research laboratories for: Nuclear Problems, High Energies, Theoretical Physics, Neutron Physics, Nuclear Reactions, Computing and Automation, New Methods of Acceleration. Mems: Bulgaria, Cuba, Czechoslovakia, German Democratic Republic, Hungary, Democratic People's Republic of Korea, Mongolia, Poland, Romania, USSR, Viet-Nam. Chair. Scientific Council and Dir Academician N. N. BOGOLUBOV (USSR); Admin. Dir V. L. KARPOVSKY.

Nordic Society for Cell Biology (Nordisk Forening for Celleforskning): c/o Prof. Nils Björkman, Dept of Anatomy, Royal Veterinary and Agricultural College, Bülowsvej 13, 1870 Frederiksberg C, Denmark; tel. (01) 351788; f. 1960 to promote contact between cell biologists through symposia and a congress every two years. Mems: 150 in Denmark, Finland, Iceland, Norway, Sweden. Chair. OLLE HEBY (Sweden); Sec. Dr V. DANTZER (Denmark).

Pacific Science Association: POB 17801, Honolulu, Hawaii 96817; tel. (808) 847-3511; f. 1920 to promote co-operation in the study of scientific problems relating to the Pacific region, more particularly those affecting the prosperity and well-being of Pacific peoples; sponsors Pacific Science Congresses and Inter-Congresses. Mems: institutional representatives from 35 areas, scientific societies, individual scientists. Sixth Inter-Congress, Chile, 1989; 17th Congress, Hawaii, 1991. Pres. Dr D. D. DUCKWORTH; Gen. Sec. BRENDA BISHOP. Publ. *Information Bulletin* (3–4 a year).

Pugwash Conferences on Science and World Affairs: 63A Great Russell St, London, WC1B 3BG; tel. (01) 405 6661; f. 1957 to organize international conferences of scientists to discuss problems arising from development of science, particularly the dangers to mankind from weapons of mass destruction. Mems: national Pugwash groups in 38 countries. Sec.-Gen. Dr MARTIN M. KAPLAN. Publ. *Pugwash Newsletter* (quarterly).

Unitas Malacologica (Malacological Union): Dr E. Gittenberger, Rijksmuseum van Natuurlijke Historie, POB 9517, 2300 RA Leiden, Netherlands; tel. (071) 14-38-44; f. 1962 to further the study of molluscs; affiliated to the International Union of Biological Sciences (q.v.); holds triennial congress. Mems: 310 in over 30 countries. Pres. Dr C. MEIER-BROOK (FRG); Sec. Dr E. GITTENBERGER. Publ. *UM Newsletter* (annually).

World Organization of Systems and Cybernetics —WOGSC: c/o Prof. R. Vallée, 2 rue de Vouillé, 75015 Paris, France; tel. (1) 45-33-62-46; f. 1969 to act as clearing-house for all societies concerned with cybernetics and allied subjects, to aim for the recognition of cybernetics as a fundamental science, to organize and sponsor international exhibitions of automation and computer equipment, congresses and symposia, and to promote and co-ordinate research in general systems and cybernetics. Mems: national and international societies in 42 countries. Dir-Gen. Prof. R. VALLÉE (France). Publs *International Journal of Cybernetics and Systems (Kybernetes), International Journal of Information, Education and Research (Robotica)*.

World Wide Fund for Nature—WWF: World Conservation Centre, ave du Mont-Blanc, 1196 Gland, Switzerland; tel. (022) 647181; telex 419618; f. 1961 (as World Wildlife Fund) to conserve the world's flora, fauna and natural resources and environment; to attract moral and financial support for safeguarding the living world and to convert such support into action based on scientific priorities. Mems: 23 national organizations, two associates, and individuals. Pres. HRH The Prince PHILIP, Duke of EDINBURGH;

Science, Social Sciences and Humanistic Studies

Dir-Gen. CH. DE HAES. Publs *Conservation Yearbook* (every 2 years), *The New Road* (quarterly), *WWF News* (every 2 months).

Social Sciences and Humanistic Studies

International Council for Philosophy and Humanistic Studies—ICPHS: Maison de l'UNESCO, 1 rue Miollis, 75732 Paris Cedex 15, France; tel. (1) 45-68-26-85; f. 1949 under the auspices of UNESCO to encourage respect for cultural autonomy by the comparative study of civilization and to contribute towards international understanding through a better knowledge of man; to develop international co-operation in philosophy, humanistic and kindred studies and to encourage the setting up of international organizations; to promote the dissemination of information in these fields; to sponsor works of learning, etc. Mems: organizations (see below) representing 145 countries. Pres. J. BIAŁOSTOCKI (Poland); Sec.-Gen. J. D'ORMESSON (France). Publs *Bulletin of Information* (biennially), *Diogenes* (quarterly).

UNIONS FEDERATED TO THE ICPHS

International Academic Union: Palais des Academies, 1 rue Ducale, 1000 Brussels, Belgium; tel. (02) 512-60-79; f. 1919 to promote international co-operation through collective research in philology, archaeology, history and social sciences. Mems: academic institutions in 35 countries. Pres. S. A. WURM (Australia); Sec. PHILIPPE ROBERTS-JONES.

International Association for the History of Religions: c/o Philipps-Universität, FG Religionswissenschaft, Liebigstrasse 37, 3550 Marburg, Federal Republic of Germany; f. 1950 to promote international collaboration of scholars, to organize congresses and to stimulate the production of works. Mems: 24 countries. Pres. A. SCHIMMEL; Sec.-Gen. MICHAEL PYE.

International Committee for Historical Sciences: 28 rue Guynemer, 75006 Paris, France; f. 1926 to work for the advancement of historical sciences by means of international co-ordination; 10 internal commissions; an international congress is held every five years. Mems: 47 national committees and 24 affiliated international organizations. Sec.-Gen. HÉLÈNE AHRWEILER. Publs *Bulletin d'Information du CISH, Bibliographie internationale des sciences historiques*.

International Committee on the History of Art: 1 rue du Simplon, 1700 Fribourg, Switzerland; f. 1900 by the 12th International Congress on the History of Art, for collaboration in the scientific study of the history of art. International congress every five years, and two colloquia between congresses. Mems: National Committees in 31 countries. Pres. Prof. IRVING LAVIN (USA); Sec. Prof. A. A. SCHMID (Switzerland). Publs *Répertoire d'Art et d'Archéologie* (quarterly), *Corpus international des vitraux, Bulletin du CIHA*.

International Federation of Modern Languages and Literatures: c/o D. A. Wells, Dept of German, Birkbeck College, Malet St, London, WC1E 7HX; tel. (01) 631-6103; f. 1928 to establish permanent contact between historians of literature, to develop or perfect facilities for their work and to promote the study of the history of modern literature. Congress every three years. Mems: 20 associations, with individual mems in 98 countries. Sec.-Gen. D. A. WELLS (UK).

International Federation of Philosophical Societies: c/o E. Agazzi, Séminaire de Philosophie, Université, 1700 Fribourg, Switzerland; f. 1948 under the auspices of UNESCO, to encourage international co-operation in the field of philosophy; holds World Congress of Philosophy every five years. Mems: 112 societies from 47 countries; 27 international societies. Pres. EVANDRO AGAZZI (Switzerland); Sec.-Gen. IOANNA KUCURADI (Turkey). Publs *International Bibliography of Philosophy, Chroniques de Philosophie, Contemporary Philosophy, Philosophical Problems Today*.

International Federation of Societies of Classical Studies: c/o Prof. F. Paschoud, 6 chemin aux Folies, 1293 Bellevue, Switzerland; tel. (022) 742656; f. 1948 under the auspices of UNESCO. Mems: 61 societies in 35 countries. Pres. Prof. E. GABBA (Italy); Sec. Prof. F. PASCHOUD (Switzerland). Publs *L'Année Philologique*, other bibliographies, dictionaries, reference works, *Thesaurus linguae Latinae*.

International Union for Oriental and Asian Studies: 77 quai du Port-au-Fouarre, 94100 Saint Maur, France; f. 1951 by the 22nd International Congress of Orientalists under the auspices of UNESCO, to promote contacts between orientalists throughout the world, and to organize congresses, research and publications. Mems: in 64 countries. Pres. R. N. DANDEKAR (India); Sec.-Gen. LOUIS BAZIN (France). Publs Four oriental bibliographies, *Philologiae Turcicae Fundamenta, Materialien zum Sumerischen Lexikon, Sanskrit Dictionary, Corpus Inscriptionum Iranicarum, Linguistic Atlas of Iran, Matériels des parlers iraniens, Turcica*.

OTHER INTERNATIONAL ORGANIZATIONS   *Social Sciences and Humanistic Studies*

International Union of Anthropological and Ethnological Sciences: c/o Prof. E. Sunderland, University College of North Wales, Bangor, Gwynedd, LL57 2DG, Wales; tel. (0248) 351151, ext. 2000; telex 61100; f. 1948 under the auspices of UNESCO; has 17 international research commissions. Mems: institutions and individuals in 100 countries. Pres. Prof. Dr LOURDES ARIZPE (Mexico); Sec.-Gen. Prof. E. SUNDERLAND (UK). Publs *IUAES Newsletter* (3 a year), *Anthropological Index* (4 a year).

International Union of Prehistoric and Protohistoric Sciences: c/o Prof. J. Nenquin, Séminaire d'archéologie de l'Université de Gand, Blandijnberg 2, 9000 Ghent, Belgium; tel. (91) 25-75-71; f. 1931 to promote congresses and scientific work in the fields of pre- and proto-history. Mems: 120 countries. Pres. Prof. J. EVANS (UK); Sec.-Gen. Prof. JACQUES NENQUIN (Belgium).

Permanent International Committee of Linguists: Dr Kuyperlaan 11, 2215 NE Voorhout, Netherlands; tel. (02522) 11852; f. 1928 to further linguistic research, to co-ordinate activities undertaken for the advancement of linguistics, and to make the results of linguistic research known internationally; holds Congress every five years. Mems: 47 national and two international linguistic organizations. Pres. R. H. ROBINS (UK); Sec.-Gen. E. M. UHLENBECK (Netherlands). Publs *Linguistic Bibliography* (annually).

OTHER ORGANIZATIONS

Arab Towns Organization: PO Box 4954, Safat 13050, Kuwait; tel. 2435540; telex 46390; f. 1967 to help Arab towns in solving problems, preserving the natural environment and cultural heritage; runs a fund to provide loans on concessional terms for needy members, and an Institute for Urban Development (AUDI) based in Riyadh, Saudi Arabia; provides training courses for officials of Arab municipalities and holds seminars on urban development and other relevant subjects; offers awards for preservation of Arabic architecture. Mems: 350 towns. Dir-Gen. TALEB T. AT-TAHER; Sec.-Gen. ABD AL-AZIZ Y. AL-ADASANI. Publ. *Al-Madinah Al-Arabiyah* (every 2 months).

Association for the Study of the World Refugee Problem—AWR: Piazzale di Porta Pia 121, 00198 Rome, Italy; tel. 22424; f. 1961 to promote and co-ordinate scholarly research on refugee problems. Mems: 475 in 19 countries. Pres. FRANCO FOSCHI (Italy); Sec.-Gen. ALDO CLEMENTE (Italy). Publ. *AWR Bulletin* (quarterly) in English, French, Italian and German; treatises on refugee problems (17 vols).

Council for the Development of Economic and Social Research in Africa: BP 3304, Dakar, Senegal; tel. 230211; telex 3339; f. 1973; provides conferences, working groups and information services. Mems: research institutes and university faculties in all African countries. Exec. Sec. THANDIKA MKANDAWIRE. Publs *Africa Development* (quarterly), *Codesria Bulletin* (quarterly).

Eastern Regional Organisation for Planning and Housing: 4 Jalan Tangsi, Kuala Lumpur, Malaysia; f. 1958 to promote and co-ordinate the study and practice of housing and regional town and country planning. Offices in Japan, India and Indonesia. Mems: 71 organizations and 160 individuals in 13 countries. Sec.-Gen. C. S. CHANDRASEKHARA (India). Publs *EAROPH News and Notes* (monthly), *Town and Country Planning* (bibliography).

English-Speaking Union of the Commonwealth: Dartmouth House, 37 Charles St, Berkeley Square, London, W1X 8AB, England; tel. (01) 493-3328; f. 1918 to promote international understanding between Britain, the Commonwealth, the United States and Europe, in conjunction with the ESU of the USA. Mems: 70,000 (incl. USA). Chair. Lord PYM; Dir-Gen. Rear-Adm. RICHARD HEASLIP. Publ. *Concord*.

European Association for Population Studies: POB 11676, 2502 AR The Hague, Netherlands; tel. (070) 469482; telex 31138; f. 1983 to conduct research and provide information on European population problems; organizes conferences, seminars and workshops. Mems: demographers from 29 countries. Sec.-Treas. Prof. GUILLAUME WUNSCH. Publ. *European Journal of Population/Revue Européenne de Démographie* (quarterly).

European Co-ordination Centre for Research and Documentation in Social Sciences: POB 974, 1011 Vienna, Grünangergasse 2, Austria; tel. (0222) 52-43-33; telex 112035; f. 1963 for promotion of contacts between East and West European countries in all areas of social sciences. Activities include co-ordination of international comparative research projects; training of social scientists in problems of international research; organization of conferences; exchange of information and documentation; administered by a Board of Directors (20 social scientists from East and West) and a permanent secretariat in Vienna. Pres. ØRJAR ØYEN (Norway); Dir F. CHARVAT (Czechoslovakia). Publs *Vienna Centre Newsletter*, *ECSSID Bulletin*.

European Society for Rural Sociology: c/o Prof. H. Newby, University of Essex, Colchester CO4 35Q, England; f. 1957 to further research in, and co-ordination of, rural sociology and provide a centre for documentation of information. Mems: 360 individuals, institutions and associations in 21 European countries and 16 countries outside Europe. Chair. Prof. H. NEWBY (UK); Sec. H. J. BECKER (FRG). Publ. *Sociologia Ruralis* (quarterly).

Experiment in International Living: POB 595, Putney, Vermont 05346, USA; tel. (802) 387-4210; telex 6503490251; a non-profit educational and cultural exchange institution; f. 1932 to create mutual understanding and respect among people of different nations, as a means of furthering peace. Mems: over 100,000; national offices in 38 countries. Sec.-Gen. ROBIN BITTERS.

Institute for International Sociological Research: 35 Am Urbacher Wall (90), POB 100705, 5000 Cologne 1, Federal Republic of Germany; tel. (0221) 486019; f. 1964; diplomatic and international affairs, social and political sciences, moral and behavioural sciences, arts and literature. Mems: 132 Life Fellows, 44 Assoc. Fellows; 14 research centres; affiliated institutes: Academy of Diplomacy and International Affairs, International Academy of Social and Moral Sciences, Arts and Letters. Pres., Chair. Exec. Cttee and Dir-Gen. Consul Dr EDWARD S. ELLENBERG. Publs *Diplomatic Observer* (monthly), *Newsletter*, *Bulletin* (quarterly), *Annual Report*, etc.

International African Institute: 10 Portugal St, London, WC2A 2HD, England; tel. (01) 831-3068; f. 1926 to promote the study of African peoples, their languages, cultures and social life in their traditional and modern settings; international seminar programme brings together scholars from Africa and elsewhere; links scholars so as to facilitate research projects, especially in the social sciences. Mems: 1,500 in 97 countries. Chair. Prof. WILLIAM A. SHACK; Dir Prof. PETER LLOYD. Publs *Africa*, *Ethnographic Survey*, *International African Library* (monograph series), *International African Seminar Series*.

International Association for Mass Communication Research: c/o Prof. J. D. Halloran, Centre for Mass Communication Research, Univ. of Leicester, 104 Regent Rd, Leicester, LE1 7LT, UK; tel. (0533) 523864; f. 1957 to stimulate interest in mass communication research and the dissemination of information about research and research needs, to improve communication practice, policy and research and training for journalism, to provide a forum for researchers and others involved in mass communication to meet and exchange information. Mems: over 1,000 in 65 countries. Pres. JAMES D. HALLORAN; Sec.-Gen. T. SZECSKO (Hungary).

International Association of Applied Linguistics: c/o Dr M. Spoelders, Seminarie en Laboratorium voor Pedagogiek, 1 Henri Dunantlaan, 9000 Ghent, Belgium; tel. (091) 25-41-00; telex 12754; f. 1964; organizes seminars on applied linguistics, and a World Congress every three years (1990 Congress: Thessaloniki, Greece). Mems: associations in 37 countries. Pres. Prof. Dr ALBERT VALDMAN (USA); Sec.-Gen. Prof. Dr MARC SPOELDERS (Belgium). Publs *AILA Review* (annually), *AILA News* (quarterly).

International Association of Documentalists and Information Officers—IAD: 74 rue des Saints-Pères, Paris 7e, France; f. 1962 to serve the professional interests of documentalists and to work on the problems of documentation at an international level. Mems: approx. 700. Gen. Sec. Dr JACQUES SAMAIN. Publ. *Monthly News*.

International Association of Metropolitan City Libraries —INTAMEL: Dienst Openbare Bibliotheek, Bilderdijkstraat 1-3, 2513 CM The Hague, Netherlands; tel. (070) 469235; f. 1967. Pres. C. B. COOKE (USA); Sec. W. M. RENES (Netherlands).

International Committee for Social Sciences Information and Documentation: c/o Prof. J. Meyriat, 27 rue Saint-Guillaume, 75007 Paris, France; tel. (1) 42-60-39-60; telex 201002; f. 1950 to collect and disseminate information on documentation services in social sciences, help improve documentation, advise societies on problems of documentation and to draw up rules likely to improve the presentation of all documents. Members from international associations specializing in social sciences or in documentation, and from other specialized fields. Sec.-Gen. JEAN MEYRIAT (France). Publs *International Bibliography of the Social Sciences* (annually), *Confluence* (surveys of research; irregular), occasional reports, etc.

International Council on Archives: 60 rue des Francs-Bourgeois, 75003 Paris, France; tel. (1) 42-77-11-30; f. 1948. Mems: 720 from 125 countries. Pres. HANS BOOMS (FRG); Exec. Sec. CHARLES KECSKEMETI (France). Publs *Archivum* (annually), *ICA Bulletin* (2 a year).

International Ergonomics Association: c/o H. W. Hendrick, College of Systems Science, University of Denver, Denver, Colo 80208, USA; tel. (303) 871-2621; f. 1957 to bring together organizations and persons interested in the scientific study of human work and its environment; to establish international contacts among those specializing in this field, co-operate with employers' associations and trade unions in order to encourage the practical application of ergonomic sciences in industries, and promote scientific research in this field. Mems: 17 federated societies. Pres. ILKKA KUORINKA

(Finland); Sec.-Gen. Hal W. Hendrick (USA). Publ. *Ergonomics* (monthly).

International Federation for Housing and Planning: Wassenaarseweg 43, 2596 CG The Hague, Netherlands; tel. (070) 24-45-57; telex 31578; f. 1913 to study and promote the improvement of housing, the theory and practice of town planning inclusive of the creation of new agglomerations and the planning of territories at regional, national and international levels. Mems: 400 organizations and 500 individuals in 65 countries. Pres. Prof. R. Radović (Yugoslavia); Sec.-Gen. J. H. Léons (Netherlands). Publs *Prospect* (quarterly).

International Federation of Institutes for Socio-religious Research: 1/21 place Montesquieu, Bte 21, 1348 Louvain-la-neuve, Belgium; f. 1958; federates centres engaged in undertaking scientific research in order to analyse and discover the social and religious phenomena at work in contemporary society. Mems: institutes in 26 countries. Pres. V. Cosmao (France); Vice-Pres. Canon Fr. Houtart (Belgium); Sec.-Gen. F. Dassetto (Italy). Publ. *Social Compass (International Review of Sociology of Religion)* (4 a year, in English and French).

International Federation of Social Science Organizations: Forskningssekretariatet, Holmens Kanal 7, 1060 Copenhagen, Denmark; f. 1979 to succeed the Conference of National Social Science Councils and Analogous Bodies (f. 1975) to further the exchange of information, experience and ideas among its member organizations, to contribute to the more effective organizations of research and teaching and to institution-building in the social sciences, and to facilitate co-operation and enlist mutual assistance in the planning and evaluation of programmes of major importance to members. Mems: 31 organizations. Pres. W. Kalweit; Sec.-Gen. Prof. T. Fujii. Publs *Newsletter, International Directory of Social Science Organizations*.

International Federation of Vexillological Associations: Box 580, Winchester, Mass 01890, USA; tel. (617) 729-9410; f. 1967 to promote through its member organizations the scientific study of the history and symbolism of flags, and especially to hold International Congresses every two years and sanction international standards for scientific flag study. Mems: 21 associations in 15 countries. Pres. Rev. Hugh Boudin (Belgium); Sec.-Gen. Dr Whitney Smith (USA). Publs *Recueil* (every 2 years), *The Flag Bulletin* (every 2 months), *Info FIAV* (every 4 months).

International Institute for Ligurian Studies: Museo Bicknell, via Romana 39 bis, 18012 Bordighera, Italy; tel. (0184) 263601; f. 1947 to conduct research on ancient monuments and regional traditions in the north-west arc of the Mediterranean (France and Italy). Library of 55,000 vols. Mems: in France, Italy, Spain, Switzerland. Dir Dott Francisca Pallarés (Italy).

International Institute of Administrative Sciences: 1 rue Defacqz, Bte 11, 1050 Brussels, Belgium; tel. (02) 538-91-65; telex 65933; f. 1930 for comparative examination of administrative experience in the various countries; research and programmes for improving administrative law and practices and for technical assistance; library of 10,000 vols; consultative status with UN and UNESCO; international congresses. Mems: 51 mem. states, 37 national sections, 39 corporate and individual members. Pres. Muhammad al-Tawail (Saudi Arabia); Dir.-Gen. Carlos Almada (Mexico). Publs *International Review of Administrative Sciences* (quarterly), *Interadmin* (3 a year), *Infoadmin* (2 a year).

International Institute of Sociology: c/o E. Borgatta, Dept of Sociology, DK40, University of Washington, Seattle, Wash 98195, USA; f. 1893 to enable sociologists to meet and study sociological questions. Mems: 300, representing 45 countries. Pres. Edgar Borgatta (USA); Gen. Sec. Alan Hedley. Publ. *Revue Internationale de Sociologie*.

International Numismatic Commission: Oslo University Coin Collection, Frederiksgate 2, Oslo 1, Norway; tel. (2) 41-63-00; f. 1936; enables co-operation between scholars studying coins and medals. Mems: numismatic organizations in 35 countries. Pres. K. Skaare (Norway); Sec. R. Weiller (Luxembourg).

International Peace Academy: 777 United Nations Plaza, New York, NY 10017, USA; tel. (212) 949-8480; telex 6503307142; f. 1967 to educate government officials in the procedures needed for conflict resolution, peace-keeping, mediation and negotiation, through international training seminars and publications; off-the-record meetings are also conducted to gain complete understanding of a specific conflict. Chair. Maj.-Gen. Indar Jit Rikhye (retd) (India); Exec. Dir Thomas Weiss. Publ. *Annual Report*.

International Peace Research Association: c/o IUPERJ/SBI, Rua Paulino Fernandes 32, CEP 22270, Rio de Janeiro, RJ, Brazil; tel. (021) 286-6197; telex (021) 37842; f. 1964 to increase research on world peace and to ensure its scientific quality; to promote the establishment of new research institutions and develop contacts and co-operation between scholars from different parts of the world and different disciplines interested in peace research. Mems: 71 corporate mems in 28 countries, four scientific associations, and 572 individuals in 61 countries. Sec.-Gen. Clovis Brigagão (Brazil). Publs *International Peace Research Newsletter* (4 a year).

International Social Science Council—ISSC: Maison de l'UNESCO, 1 rue Miollis, Paris 75015, France; tel. (1) 45-68-25-58; f. 1952; since 1973 a federation of the organizations listed below. Aims: the advancement of the social sciences throughout the world and their application to the major problems of the world; the spread of co-operation at an international level between specialists in the social sciences. ISSC has a Standing Committee for Conceptual and Terminological Analysis (COCTA, established in co-operation with IPSA and ISA); and Issue Groups on Peace and on Technological Change; also created the European Co-ordination Centre for Research and Documentation in the Social Sciences, in Vienna. Pres. C. Mendes (Brazil); Sec.-Gen. L. I. Ramallo (Spain).

Associations Federated to the ISSC

(details of these organizations will be found under their appropriate category elsewhere in the International Organizations section)

International Association of Legal Sciences (p. 235).
International Economic Association (p. 226).
International Federation of Social Science Organizations (p. 256).
International Geographical Union (p. 248).
International Institute of Administrative Sciences (p. 256).
International Law Association (p. 236).
International Peace Research Association (p. 256).
International Political Science Association (p. 231).
International Sociological Association (p. 256).
International Studies Association (p. 256).
International Union for the Scientific Study of Population (p. 256).
International Union of Anthropological and Ethnological Sciences (p. 255).
International Union of Psychological Science (p. 249).
World Association for Public Opinion Research (p. 257).
World Federation for Mental Health (p. 243).

International Society of Social Defence: 28 rue Saint-Guillaume, 75007 Paris, France; f. 1945 to combat crime, to protect society and to prevent citizens from being tempted to commit criminal actions. Mems in 34 countries. Pres. Simone Rozes (France); Sec.-Gen. A. Beria di Argentine (Italy). Publs *Cahiers de défense sociale, Bulletin de la Société internationale de défense sociale* (annually).

International Sociological Association: Calle Pinar 25, 28006 Madrid, Spain; tel. 2617483; f. 1949 to promote sociological knowledge, facilitate contacts between sociologists, encourage the dissemination and exchange of information and facilities and stimulate research; has 42 research committees on various aspects of sociology; holds World Congresses every four years (12th Congress: Madrid, Spain, 1990). Pres. Margaret Archer (UK); Exec. Sec. Izabela Barlinska. Publs *Current Sociology* (3 a year), *International Sociology* (4 a year), *Sage Studies in International Sociology* (based on World Congress).

International Statistical Institute: Prinses Beatrixlaan 428, 2270 AZ Voorburg, Netherlands; tel. (70) 694341; telex 32260; f. 1885; devoted to the development and improvement of statistical methods and their application throughout the world; administers among others a statistical education centre in Calcutta in co-operation with UNESCO and the Indian Statistical Institute; executes international research programmes. Mems: 1,404 ordinary mems; 171 ex-officio mems; 42 affiliated organizations. Pres. I. P. Fellegi; Dir Permanent Office C. Jarque. Publs *Bulletin of the International Statistical Institute* (proceedings of biennial sessions), *International Statistical Review* (3 a year), *Statistical Education Newsletter* (3 a year), *Short Book Reviews* (3 a year), *Statistical Theory and Method Abstracts* (quarterly), *International Statistical Information* (newsletter, 3 a year), *Directories* (annually).

International Studies Association: c/o Dr W. Welsh, James F. Byrnes International Center, University of South Carolina, Columbia, SC 29208, USA; tel. (803) 777-2933; f. 1959; links those whose professional concerns extend beyond their own national boundaries (government officials, representatives of business and industry, and scholars). Exec. Dir Dr William A. Welsh. Publs *International Studies Quarterly, ISA Newsletter*.

International Union for the Scientific Study of Population: 34 rue des Augustins, 4000 Liège, Belgium; tel. (041) 22-40-80; telex 42648; f. 1928 to advance the progress of quantitative and qualitative demography as a science. Mems: 1,800 in 114 countries. Pres. W. Brass (UK); Sec.-Gen. G. Tapinos (France). Publs. *IUSSP Newsletter*.

Mensa International: 15 The Ivories, 6–8 Northampton St, London, N1 2HY; tel. (01) 226-6891; f. 1946 to identify and foster intelligence for the benefit of humanity. Members are individuals who score in a recognized intelligence test higher than 98% of people in general: there are 85,000 mems world-wide. Pres. Chair. DAVID SCHULMAN (Ireland); Exec. Dir E. J. VINCENT (UK). Publ. *Mensa Journal International* (monthly).

Third World Forum: BP 3501, Dakar, Senegal; f. 1973 to link social scientists and others from the developing countries, to discuss alternative development policies and encourage research. Regional offices in Egypt, Mexico, Senegal and Sri Lanka. Mems: individuals in more than 50 countries. Dir SAMIR AMIN.

World Association for Public Opinion Research: c/o The Roper Centre, POB 440, Storrs, CT 06268-0440, USA; f. 1947 to establish and promote contacts between persons in the field of survey research on opinions, attitudes and behaviour of people in the various countries of the world; to further the use of objective, scientific survey research in national and international affairs. Mems: 430 from 57 countries. Exec. Sec. EVERETT C. LADD. Publ. *WAPOR Newsletter* (quarterly).

World Society of Ekistics: c/o Athens Centre of Ekistics, 24 Strat. Syndesmou St, 106 73 Athens, Greece; tel. 3623-216; telex 215227; f. 1965; aims to promote knowledge and ideas concerning ekistics through research, publications and conferences; to recognize the benefits and necessity of an inter-disciplinary approach to the needs of human settlements. Pres. GERALD B. DIX; Sec.-Gen. P. PSOMOPOULOS.

World Union of Catholic Philosophical Societies: c/o Prof. G. F. McLean, School of Philosophy, Catholic University of America, Washington, DC 20064, USA; tel. (202) 635-5636; f. 1948. Mems: societies and individuals in 44 countries. Pres. Prof. JEAN LADRIÈRE (Belgium); Sec.-Gen. Prof. GEORGE F. MCLEAN (USA). Publ. *Circulaires* (1 or 2 issues a year).

Social Welfare

Aid to Displaced Persons and its European Villages: 35 rue du Marché, 5200 Huy, Belgium; tel. (085) 21-34-81; f. 1957 to carry on and develop work begun by the Belgian association Aid to Displaced Persons; aims to provide material and moral aid for refugees; European Villages established at Aachen, Bregenz, Augsburg, Berchem-Ste-Agathe, Spiesen, Euskirchen, Wuppertal as centres for refugees. Pres. J. EECKHOUT (Belgium).

Amnesty International: 1 Easton St, London, WC1X 8DJ, England; tel. (01) 833-1771; telex 28502; f. 1961; an independent worldwide movement working impartially for the release of all prisoners of conscience, fair and prompt trials for all political prisoners, and the abolition of torture and the death penalty; financed by donations. Mems: 3,700 local groups in 60 countries. Chair. FRANCA SCIUTO (Italy); Sec.-Gen. IAN MARTIN (UK). Publs *Newsletter* (monthly), *Annual Report*.

Anti-Slavery Society for the Protection of Human Rights: 180 Brixton Rd, London, SW9 6AT, England; tel. (01) 582-4040; f. 1839 to eradicate slavery and forced labour in all their forms, to promote the well-being of indigenous peoples, and to protect human rights in accordance with the Universal Declaration of Human Rights, 1948. Mems: 900 members in 30 countries. Chair. MICHAEL HARRIS; Dir R. P.H. DAVIES. Publs *Annual Report, Anti-Slavery Reporter* (annually) and special reports on research.

Associated Country Women of the World: Vincent House, Vincent Square, London, SW1P 2NB; tel. (01) 834-8635; f. 1930 to aid the economic and social development of countrywomen and home-makers of all nations; to promote study of an interest in home-making, housing, health, education, and aspects of food and agriculture. Mems: approx. 9m. Pres. Dr E. MCLEAN; Gen. Sec. JENNIFER PEARCE. Publ. *The Countrywoman* (quarterly).

Association Internationale de la Mutualité (International Association for Mutual Benefit Societies): 8–10 rue de Hesse, 1204 Geneva, Switzerland; tel. (022) 214528; f. 1947 to propagate and develop mutual benefits funds in all countries. Mems: national and regional institutions in 14 countries. Pres. ROBERT VAN DEN HEUVEL (Belgium); Sec.-Gen. RENÉ-NOËL BESSI.

Association of Social Work Education in Africa: POB 1176, Addis Ababa, Ethiopia; tel. 126827; f. 1971 to promote teaching and research in social development, to improve standards of institutions in this field, to exchange information and experience. Mems: schools of social work, community development training centres, other institutions and centres; 53 training institutions and 140 social work educators in 32 African countries, 22 non-African assoc. mems. in Europe and North America. Exec. Sec. AREGA YIMAN. Publs *Journal for Social Work Education in Africa*.

Aviation sans frontières—ASF: Brussels National Airport, Bldg 2, LC 142, 1930 Zaventem, Belgium; tel. (02) 722-35-35; telex 22569; f. 1980 to make available the resources of the aviation industry to humanitarian organizations, for carrying supplies and equipment at minimum cost, both on long-distance flights and locally. Mems: about 200 pilots and other airline staff. Pres. JEAN-LUC STORDER; Man. YVON LEPEZ.

Catholic International Union for Social Service: 111 rue de la Poste, 1030 Brussels, Belgium; tel. (02) 217-29-87; f. 1925 to develop social service on the basis of Christian doctrine; to unite Catholic social schools and social workers' associations in all countries to promote their foundation; to represent at the international level the Catholic viewpoint as it affects social service. Mems: 172 schools of social service, 26 associations of social workers, 52 individual members. Exec. Sec. ALEXANDRE CARLSON. Publs *Service Social dans le monde* (quarterly), *News Bulletin*, *Bulletin de Liaison*, *Boletín de Noticias* (quarterly).

Co-ordinating Committee for International Voluntary Service—CCIVS: Maison de l'UNESCO, 1 rue Miollis, 75015 Paris, France; tel. (1) 45-68-27-31; f. 1948; acts as an information centre and co-ordinating body for voluntary service organizations all over the world. Affiliated mems: 110 organizations. Dir C. BARBE. Publs *News from CCIVS* (4 a year), handbook, directories.

EIRENE—International Christian Service for Peace: 5450 Neuwied 1, Engerser Str. 74B, Federal Republic of Germany; f. 1957; works in North Africa, Asia and Latin America (professional training, apprenticeship programmes, agricultural work and co-operatives), Europe and the USA (volunteer programmes in co-operation with peace groups). Gen. Sec. JOSEF FREISE.

European Federation for the Welfare of the Elderly—EURAG: 8010 Graz, Schmiedg. 26 (Amtshaus), Austria; tel. (0316) 7038-3008; f. 1962 for the exchange of experience among member associations; practical co-operation among member organizations to achieve their objectives in the field of ageing; representation of the interests of members before international organizations; promotion of understanding and co-operation in matters of social welfare; to draw attention to the problems of old age. Mems: organizations in 25 countries. Pres. NELLA M. BERTO (Italy); Sec.-Gen. EDUARD PUMPERNIG (Austria). Publs. (in English, French, German and Italian) *EURAG Newsletter* (quarterly), *EURAG Information* (monthly).

Federation of Asian Women's Associations—FAWA: Centro Escolar University, 9 Mendiola St, San Miguel, Manila, Philippines; tel. 741-04-46; f. 1959 to provide closer relations, and bring about joint efforts among Asians, particularly among the women, through mutual appreciation of cultural, moral and socio-economic values. Mems: 415,000. Pres. Dr H. SJAMSINOOR ADNOES; Sec. Mrs NICOLASA J. TRIA TIRONA (Philippines). Publ. *FAWA News Bulletin* (every 3 months).

Inter-American Conference on Social Security (Comité Permanente Interamericano de Seguridad Social): Apdo postal 99089, CP 10100 México 20, DF, Mexico; tel. 595-01-07; telex 1775793; f. 1942 to facilitate and develop co-operation between social security administrations and institutions in the American states; 14th General Assembly, 1986. Mems: governments and social security institutions in 20 countries. Pres. Lic. RICARDO GARCÍA SAINZ (Mexico); Sec.-Gen. E. RABASA GAMBOA (Mexico). Publs *Seguridad Social, Boletín Informativo*.

International Abolitionist Federation: 47 rue de Rivoli, 75001 Paris, France; tel. (1) 45-08-97-52; f. 1875 for the abolition of the organization and exploitation of the prostitution of others and the regulation of prostitution by public authorities; holds international congress every three years; consultative status with UN (ECOSOC). Affiliated organizations in 21 countries. Corresponding mems in 60 countries. Pres. ANIMA BASAK (Austria); Gen. Sec. MARIE-RENÉE JAMET (France). Publs *Revue abolitionniste* (2 a year).

International Association against Noise: Hirschenplatz 7, 6004 Lucerne, Switzerland; tel. (041) 513013; f. 1959 to promote noise-control at an international level; to promote co-operation and the exchange of experience and prepare supranational measures; issues information, carries out research, organizes conferences, and assists national anti-noise associations. Mems: 17, and three associate mems. Pres. JUDITH LANG; Sec. Dr WILLY AECHERLI (Switzerland).

International Association for Children's International Summer Villages: Mea House, Ellison Place, Newcastle upon Tyne, England; f. 1950 to conduct International Camps for children and young people between the ages of 11 and 18. Mems: c. 15,000. International Pres. RUTH LUND; Sec.-Gen. JOSEPH G. BANKS. Publ. *CISV News* (3 a year).

International Association for Suicide Prevention: 1811 Trousdale Drive, Burlingame, Calif 94010, USA; tel. (415) 877-5604; f. 1960 to establish an organization where individuals and agencies of various disciplines and professions from different countries can find a common platform for interchange of acquired experience, literature and information about suicide; disseminates information;

arranges special training; encourages and carries out research; organizes the Biannual International Congress for Suicide Prevention. Mems: 730 individuals and societies, in 42 countries of all continents. Vice-Pres. CHARLOTTE P. ROSS (USA). Publ. *Crisis* (2 a year).

International Association for Education to a Life without Drugs (Internationaler Verband für Erziehung zu suchtmittelfreiem Leben—IVES): Lyshoj 6, 6300 Graasten, Denmark; f. 1954 (as the International Association for Temperance Education) to promote international co-operation in education on the dangers of alcohol and drugs; collection and distribution of information on drugs; maintains regular contact with national and international organizations active in these fields; holds conferences. Mems: 17,000 in seven countries. Pres. WILLY STUBER; Sec. JÜRGEN KLAHN.

International Association of Schools of Social Work: 1210 Vienna, Freytaggasse 32, Austria; tel. (0222) 38-74-79; f. 1929 to provide international leadership and encourage high standards in social work education. Mems: 450 schools of social work in 70 countries, and 23 associations of schools. Sec.-Gen. VERA MEHTA (India). Publs *International Social Work* (quarterly), *Directory of Members, IASSW News*.

International Association of Workers for Troubled Children and Youth: 66 chaussée d'Antin, 75009 Paris, France; f. 1951 to promote the profession of specialized social workers for maladjusted children; to provide a centre of information about child welfare and encourage co-operation between the members; 1990 Congress: USA. Mems: national and regional public or private associations from 19 countries and individual members in many other countries. Pres. DANIEL DUPIED (France); Sec.-Gen. BRUNO NEFF (France).

International Catholic Migration Commission: CP 96, 37–39 rue de Vermont, 1211 Geneva 20, Switzerland; tel. (022) 334150; telex 28100; f. 1951; offers migration aid programmes to those who are not in a position to secure by themselves their resettlement elsewhere; grants interest-free travel loans; assists refugees on a worldwide basis, helping with all social and technical problems. Sub-committees dealing with Europe and Latin America. Mems: in 76 countries. Pres. EDWARD DE BRANDT; Sec.-Gen. Dr ANDRÉ N. VAN CHAU (USA). Publs *Migrations, Migration News, Menschen Unterwegs, ICMC Newsletter*.

International Children's Centre (Centre international de l'enfance): Château de Longchamp, carrefour de Longchamp, Bois de Boulogne, 75016 Paris, France; tel. (1) 45-20-79-92; telex 648379; f. 1949 to improve the health and well-being of children and families, especially in developing countries; financed by the French Government and other sources; three departments: Education and Training (organizing courses, seminars and working groups all over the world), Communicable Diseases and Immunization (developing immunization techniques), Information (documentation centre, publications and bibliographical data base), and External Relations Office. Pres. of Admin. Council Prof. PIERRE ROYER; Dir-Gen. JEAN BROUSTE. Publs *Adolescents, Sport, enfant et adolescent, Children in the Tropics*.

International Christian Federation for the Prevention of Alcoholism and Drug Addiction: 27 Tavistock Sq., London, WC1H 9HH, England; tel. (01) 387-8413; f. 1960, reconstituted 1980 to promote worldwide education and remedial work through the churches, to co-ordinate Christian concern about alcohol and drug abuse, in co-operation with WHO. Chair. Bishop JAMES K. MATHEWS (USA); Gen. Sec. Rev. J. KENNETH LAWTON (UK).

International Civil Defence Organisation: 10–12 chemin Surville, 1213 Petit-Lancy-Geneva, Switzerland; tel. (022) 7934433; telex 423786; f. 1931, present statutes in force 1972; aims to intensify and co-ordinate on a world-wide scale the development and improvement of organization, means and techniques for preventing and reducing the consequences of natural disasters in peacetime or of the use of weapons in time of conflict. Sec.-Gen. SADOK ZNAÏDI (Tunisia). Publs *International Civil Defence Review* (quarterly, in English, French, Spanish and Arabic).

International Commission for the Prevention of Alcoholism and Drug Dependence: 6830 Laurel St, NW, Washington, DC 20012, USA; tel. (202) 722-6729; telex 440186; f. 1953 to encourage scientific research on intoxication by alcohol, its physiological, mental and moral effects on the individual, and its effect on the community; seventh World Congress, Brisbane, Australia, 1988. Mems: individuals in 90 countries. Exec. Dir ERNEST H. J. STEED. Publ. *ICPA Quarterly*.

International Commission for the Protection of the Rhine against Pollution: 5400 Koblenz, Hohenzollernstrasse 18, POB 309, Federal Republic of Germany; tel. (0261) 12495; telex 862499; f. 1950 to prepare and commission research to establish the nature of the pollution of the Rhine; to propose measures of protection to the signatory governments. Mems: 23 delegates from France, Federal Republic of Germany, Luxembourg, the Netherlands, Switzerland and the EEC. Pres. Dr R. PEDROLI; Sec. J. M. GOPPEL. Publ. *Annual Report*.

International Council of Voluntary Agencies: 13 rue Gautier, 1201 Geneva, Switzerland; tel. (022) 326600; telex 22891; f. 1962 to provide a forum for voluntary humanitarian and development agencies. Mems: 79 non-governmental organizations. Chair. FRANK JUDD; Exec. Dir ANTHONY J. KOZLOWSKI. Publs *ICVA News* (10 a year, English, French and Spanish), *NGO Management* (quarterly in English and French).

International Council of Women: c/o 13 rue Caumartin, 75009 Paris, France; tel. (1) 47-42-19-40; f. 1888 to bring together in international affiliation National Councils of Women from all continents for consultation and joint action in order to promote equal rights for men and women and the integration of women in development and in decision-making; has consultative status with ECOSOC (UN); 13 standing committees. Mems: 75 national councils. Pres. Dr SOOKJA HONG; Sec.-Gen. Mrs JACQUELINE BARBET-MASSIN.

International Council on Alcohol and Addictions: CP 189, 1001 Lausanne, Switzerland; tel. (021) 209865; telex 450666; f. 1907; consultative status with UN (ECOSOC), and official relations with WHO; organizes training courses, congresses, symposia and seminars in different countries. Mems: affiliated organizations in 62 countries, as well as individual members. Pres. STEIN BERG (Norway); Dir ARCHER TONGUE (UK). Publs *ICAA News* (quarterly), *Alcoholism* (2 a year), *Drug and Alcohol Dependence* (bi-monthly).

International Council on Disability: c/o Rehabilitation International, 25 East 21st St, New York, NY 10010, USA; tel. (212) 420-1500; telex 66125; f. 1953 to assist the UN and its specialized agencies to develop a well co-ordinated international programme for rehabilitation of the handicapped. Mems: 66 organizations. Chair. NORMAN ACTON.

International Council on Jewish Social and Welfare Services: 75 rue de Lyon, 1211 Geneva 13, Switzerland; tel. (022) 449000; telex 23163; f. 1961; functions include the exchange of views and information among member agencies concerning the problems of Jewish social and welfare services including medical care, old age, welfare, child care, rehabilitation, technical assistance, vocational training, agricultural and other resettlement, economic assistance, refugees, migration, integration and related problems; representation of views to governments and international organizations. Mems: six national and international organizations. Pres. K. D. RUBENS; Exec. Sec. L. LEIBERG.

International Council on Social Welfare: 1060 Vienna, Koestlergasse 1/29, Austria; tel. (022) 587-81-64; f. 1928 to provide an international forum for the discussion of social work and related issues; to promote interest in social welfare; holds international conference every two years; provides documentation and information services. Mems: 68 countries, 23 international organizations. Pres. KHUNYING A. MEESOOK (Thailand); Sec.-Gen. INGRID GELINEK (Austria). Publs *International Social Work* (quarterly), *ICSW Newsletter* (quarterly).

International Dachau Committee: 65 rue de Haerne, 1040 Brussels, Belgium; f. 1958 to perpetuate the memory of the political prisoners of Dachau; to manifest the friendship and solidarity of former prisoners whatever their beliefs or nationality; to maintain the ideals of their resistance, liberty, tolerance and respect for persons and nations; and to maintain the former concentration camp at Dachau as a museum and international memorial. Pres. Dr A. GUERISSE; Sec.-Gen. GEORGES-VALÉRY WALRAEVE. Publ. *Bulletin Officiel du Comité International de Dachau* (2 a year).

International Federation of Blue Cross Societies: CP 271, 1211 Geneva 25, Switzerland; tel. (022) 472088; telex 428088; f. 1877 to aid the victims of intemperance and drug addicts; and to take part in the general movement against alcoholism. Pres. Dr HANS SCHAFFNER (Switzerland); Gen. Sec. ERIC ZIEHLI.

International Federation of Disabled Workers and Civilian Handicapped: c/o Reichsbund, 5300 Bonn 2, Beethovenallee 56–58, Federal Republic of Germany; tel. (0228) 363071; telex 885557; f. 1953 to bring together representatives of the disabled and handicapped into an international non-political organization under the guidance of the disabled themselves; to promote greater opportunities for the disabled; to create rehabilitation centres; to act as a co-ordinating body for all similar national organizations. Consultative member of ECOSOC, official relations with ILO, WHO and UNESCO. Mems: national groups from Austria, Czechoslovakia, Denmark, Finland, France, German Federal Republic, Hungary, Iceland, Italy, Netherlands, Norway, Poland, Spain, Sweden, Switzerland, Yugoslavia. Pres. HERMANN MEYER (FRG); Gen. Sec. MARIJA ŠTIGLIC (FRG). Publs *Bulletin, Nouvelles*.

International Federation of Educative Communities: Rämistrasse 27, 8001 Zürich, Switzerland; tel. (01) 470247; f. 1948 under the auspices of UNESCO; consultative status with ECOSOC,

Social Welfare

UNICEF and UNESCO. Objects: to co-ordinate the work of national associations, and to promote children's communities. Mems: national associations from 18 European countries, Israel, Canada and the USA. Pres. Prof. Dr HEINRICH TUGGENER (Switzerland); Gen. Sec. Dr FRANZ ZÜSLI-NISCOSI (Switzerland). Publs *Etudes Pédagogiques, Documents, Recherches et Témoignages*.

International Federation of Human Rights: 6 rue J.-C. Amat, 1202 Geneva, Switzerland; tel. (022) 313332; f. 1922 to uphold the principles of justice, liberty and equality; conducts missions of enquiry, makes protests and representations to governments concerning violations of human rights. Mems: national leagues in 36 countries and territories. Pres. DANIEL JACOBY. Publ. *Lettre* (weekly).

International Federation of Social Workers—IFSW: 33 rue de l'Athénée, 1206 Geneva, Switzerland; tel. (022) 471236; f. 1928 as International Permanent Secretariat of Social Workers; present name adopted 1950; aims to promote social work as a profession through international co-operation concerning standards, training, ethics and working conditions; represents the profession at international meetings; assists in welfare programmes sponsored by international organizations. Mems: national associations in 50 countries. Pres. Prof. GAYLE G. JAMES (Canada); Sec.-Gen. ANDREW M. APOSTOL (Switzerland).

International Fellowship of Former Scouts and Guides—IFOFSAG: 9 rue du Champ de Mars, bte 14, 1050 Brussels, Belgium; tel. (02) 511-46-95; f. 1953 to help former scouts and guides to keep alive the spirit of the Scout and Guide Promise and Laws in their own lives; to bring that spirit into the communities in which they live and work; to establish liaison and co-operation between national organizations for former scouts and guides; to encourage the founding of an organization in any country where no such organization exists; to promote friendship amongst former scouts and guides throughout the world. Mems: 56,000 in 33 member states. Chair. of Council ULLA MEDIN; Sec.-Gen. NAÏC PIRARD. Publ. *The Fellowship Bulletin* (quarterly).

International League of Societies for Persons with Mental Handicap: 248 ave Louise, bte 17, 1050 Brussels, Belgium; tel. (02) 647-61-80; f. 1960 to promote the interests of the mentally handicapped without regard to nationality, race or creed, furthers co-operation between national bodies, organizes congresses. Consultative status with UNESCO, UNICEF, official relations with WHO, ILO, ECOSOC, the Council of Europe and other organizations. Mems: 113 in 76 countries (incl. 53 national associations and 60 affiliates) and four associate (regional) mems. Pres. ELOISA G. E. DE LORENZO (Uruguay); Sec.-Gen. V. WAHLSTRÖM (Sweden).

International Lifeboat Federation: c/o Royal National Lifeboat Institution, West Quay Rd, Poole, Dorset, BH15 1HZ, England; tel. (0202) 671133; telex 41328; f. 1924; conferences held at four-yearly intervals; next Conference: Norway, 1991. Sec. RAY KIPLING. Publ. *Lifeboat International*.

International Planned Parenthood Federation—IPPF: Regent's College, Inner Circle, Regent's Park, London, NW1 4NS, England; tel. (01) 486-0741; telex 919573; f. 1952; aims to initiate and support family planning services throughout the world, and to increase understanding of population problems; offers technical assistance and training; collaborates with other international organizations and provides information on all aspects of family planning; annual budget of US $60m. (1987). Mems: independent family planning associations in 123 countries. Pres. Mrs AVABAI WADIA; Sec.-Gen. Dr HALFDAN MAHLER. Publs *People* (quarterly, in English and French), *Medical Bulletin* (every 2 months, in English, French and Spanish), *Research in Reproduction* (quarterly), publications list.

International Prisoners Aid Association: c/o Dr Ali, Department of Sociology, University of Louisville, Louisville, Ky 40292, USA; tel. (502) 588-6836; f. 1950; to improve prisoners' aid services for rehabilitation of the individual and protection of society. Mems: national federations in 29 countries. Pres. Dr WOLFGANG DOLEISCH (Austria); Exec. Dir Dr BADR-EL-DIN ALI. Publ. *Newsletter* (3 a year).

International Social Security Association: Case Postale No. 1, 1211 Geneva 22, Switzerland; telex 22271; f. 1927 to promote the development of social security through the improvement of techniques and administration. Mems: 312 institutions in 125 countries. Pres. JÉRÔME DEJARDIN (Belgium); Sec.-Gen. VLADIMIR RYS (UK). Publs *International Social Security Review* (quarterly, English, French, German, Spanish), *Estudios de la Seguridad Social* (irregular), *World Bibliography of Social Security* (2 a year, English, French, Spanish, German), *African News Sheet* (English and French), *Asian News Sheet, Caribbean News Sheet, Social Security Documentation* (African, Asian, European and American series), *Current Research in Social Security* (2 a year, English, French, German and Spanish), *ISSA News* (2 a year).

International Social Service: 32 quai du Seujet, 1201 Geneva, Switzerland; tel. (022) 317454; telex 289283; f. 1921 to aid families and individuals whose problems require services beyond the boundaries of the country in which they live and where the solution of these problems depends upon co-ordinated action on the part of social workers in two or more countries; to study from an international standpoint the conditions and consequences of emigration in their effect on individual, family, and social life. Operates on a non-sectarian and non-political basis. Mems: branches in 14 countries, two affiliated offices, and correspondents in some 100 other countries. Pres. Sir CLIVE BOSSOM (UK); Sec.-Gen. MARCELLE L. BRISSON (Canada).

International Union of Family Organisations: 28 place Saint-Georges, 75009 Paris, France; tel. (1) 48-78-07-59; f. 1947 to bring together all organizations throughout the world which are working for family welfare; conducts permanent commissions on standards of living, housing, marriage guidance, work groups on family movements, rural families, etc.; there are five regional organizations: the Pan-African Family Organisation (Dakar, Senegal), the Arab Family Organisation (Tunis, Tunisia), the Asian Union of Family Organisations (New Delhi, India), the European regional organization (Vienna, Austria) and the Latin American Secretariat (Bogotá, Colombia). Mems: national associations, groups and governmental departments in 55 countries. Pres. MARIA TERESA DA COSTA MACEDO (Portugal); Sec.-Gen. ANDRÉ RAUGET (France).

International Union of Societies for the Aid of Mental Health: Croix Marine, 39 rue Charles Monselet, 33000 Bordeaux, France; tel. 56-81-60-05; f. 1964 to group national societies and committees whose aim is to help mentally handicapped or maladjusted people. Gen. Pres Mme DELAUNAY, Prof. CARAVEDO; Gen. Sec. Dr DEMANGEAT.

International Union of Tenants: Box 7514, 10392 Stockholm, Sweden; tel. (08) 24-63-50; f. 1955 to achieve a fruitful measure of collaboration which will help safeguard the interests of tenants. Mems: national tenant organizations in 13 European countries and Tanzania. Chair. LARS ANDERSTIG; Sec. NIC NILSSON. Publ. *IUT International Information* (quarterly).

International Workers' Aid (Entraide Ouvrière Internationale): 5300 Bonn, Oppelner Strasse 130, Federal Republic of Germany; tel. (0228) 66850; telex 8869654; f. 1950 to support welfare services for youth (especially the unemployed), the elderly and disadvantaged groups, to assist refugees and displaced persons, to take action as a relief organization in cases of catastrophes or political disturbances and to work for social justice and human solidarity. Members in Austria, Belgium, Denmark, France, Federal Republic of Germany, Israel, Italy, Luxembourg, Norway, Portugal, Spain, Switzerland, United Kingdom. Pres. HERMANN BUSCHFORT (FRG); Sec.-Gen. RICHARD HAAR.

Inter-University European Institute on Social Welfare—IEISW: 179 rue de Débarcadène, 6001 Marcinelle, Belgium; tel. (71) 36-62-73; f. 1970 to promote, carry out and publicize scientific research on social welfare and community work. Chair. Board of Dirs JACQUES HOCHEPIED (Belgium); Gen. Sec. P. ROZEN (Belgium). Publ. *COMM*.

Lions Clubs International: 300 West 22nd St, Oak Brook, Ill 60570-0001, USA; tel. (312) 571-5466; telex 297236; f. 1917 to foster understanding among people of the world; to promote principles of good government and citizenship; and an interest in civic, cultural, social and moral welfare; to encourage service-minded people to serve their community without financial reward. Mems: 1.36m. with over 39,000 clubs in 163 countries and geographic areas. Exec. Admin. MARK C. LUKAS. Publ. *The Lion* (10 a year, in 18 languages).

Médecins sans frontières—MSF: 8 rue Saint Sabin, 75011 Paris, France; tel. (1) 40-21-29-29; telex 214360; f. 1971; composed of physicians and other members of the medical profession; aims to provide medical assistance to victims of war and natural disasters, and medium-term programmes of nutrition, immunization, sanitation, public health, and rehabilitation of hospitals and dispensaries. Mems: 3,000 in France, groups in other European countries. Pres. Dr RONY BRAUMAN; Dir-Gen. Dr FRANCIS CHARHON.

Pan-Pacific and South East Asia Women's Association—PPSEAWA: 2234 New Petchburi Rd, Bangkok 10310, Thailand; f. 1928 to strengthen the bonds of peace by fostering better understanding and friendship among women of all Pacific and South-East Asian areas, and to promote co-operation among women of these regions for the study and improvement of social conditions; holds international conference every three years. Pres. KHUNYING SUMALEE CHARTIKAVANIJ. Publ. *PPSEAWA Bulletin*.

Rotary International: 1560 Sherman Ave, Evanston, Ill 60201, USA; tel. (312) 866-3000; telex 724465; f. 1905 to foster the ideal of service as a basis of worthy enterprise, to promote high ethical standards in business and professions and to further international understanding, goodwill and peace. Mems: over 1,060,000 in 23,800 Rotary Clubs in 162 countries and regions. Pres. HUGH ARCHER (from July 1989); Gen. Sec. PHILIP H. LINDSEY (USA). Publs *The Rotarian* (monthly, English), *Revista Rotaria* (bi-monthly, Spanish).

Service Civil International—SCI: 28 Venusstraat, 2000 Antwerp, Belgium; tel. (03) 233-63-95; f. 1920 to promote peace and understanding through voluntary service projects (work-camps, local groups, long-term community development projects and education). Mems: 10,000 in 22 countries; projects in 20 countries. Pres. NIGEL WATT. Publ. *Action* (quarterly).

Society of Saint Vincent de Paul: 5 rue du Pré-aux-Clercs, Paris 7e, France; tel. (1) 42-61-50-25; telex 240918; f. 1833 to conduct charitable activities such as child care, youth work, work with immigrants, adult literacy programmes, residential care for the sick, handicapped and elderly, social counselling and work with prisoners and the unemployed—all conducted through personal contact. Mems: over 800,000 in 110 countries. Pres. AMIN A. DE TARRAZI; Sec.-Gen. COLETTE GLANDIÈRES. Publ. *Vincenpaul* (monthly, in French, English and Spanish).

World Blind Union: 58 ave Bosquet, 75007 Paris, France; tel. (1) 45-55-67-54; telex 206471; f. 1984 (amalgamating the World Council for the Welfare of the Blind and the International Federation of the Blind) to work for the prevention of blindness and the welfare of blind and visually-impaired people; encourages development of braille, talking book programmes and other media for the blind; rehabilitation, training and employment; prevention and cure of blindness in co-operation with the International Agency for the Prevention of Blindness; co-ordinates aid to the blind in developing countries; conducts studies on technical, social and educational matters, maintains the Louis Braille birth-place as an international museum. Mems in 106 countries. Pres. A. M. AL-GHANIM (Saudi Arabia); Sec.-Gen. PEDRO ZURITA (Spain). Publs *World Blind* (quarterly, in English, English Braille, French, Spanish).

World Federation of the Deaf—WFD: 120 via Gregorio VII, 00165, Rome, Italy; tel. (06) 6377041; f. 1951 for the social rehabilitation of the deaf and the fight against deafness; aims to promote and exchange information; to facilitate the union and federation of national associations; organize international meetings and protect the rights of the deaf. Mems: 72 member countries. Pres. Dr Y. ANDERSSON; Sec.-Gen. Dr C. MAGAROTTO (Italy). Publ. *The Voice of Silence* (quarterly).

World ORT Union: ORT House, Sumpter Close, Finchley Rd, POB 346, London, NW3 5HR, England; tel. (01) 431-1333; telex 8953281; f. 1880 for the development of industrial, agricultural and artisan work among the Jews, training and generally improving the economic situation; conducts vocational training programmes for adolescents and adults, including instructors' and teachers' education and apprenticeship training in more than 40 countries, including technical assistance programmes in co-operation with interested governments. Mems: committees in 30 countries. Dir-Gen. JOSEPH HARMATZ. Publs *Annual Report, Yearbook, Technical and Pedagogical Bulletin, ORT data, ORT Magazine*.

World Society for the Protection of Animals: 106 Jermyn St, London, SW1Y 6EE, England; tel. (01) 839-3026; f. 1981, incorporating the World Federation for the Protection of Animals (f. 1950) and the International Society for the Protection of Animals (f. 1959); promotes animal welfare and conservation by humane education; disseminates literature to encourage humane management and slaughter of food animals, control of domestic and wild animal communities. Dir-Gen. T. H. SCOTT (UK).

World Veterans Federation: 16 rue Hamelin, 75116 Paris, France; tel. (1) 47-04-33-00; telex 643253; f. 1950 to maintain international peace and security by the application of the San Francisco Charter and helping to implement the Universal Declaration of Human Rights and related international conventions, to defend the spiritual and material interests of war veterans and war victims. It promotes practical international co-operation in disarmament, human rights problems, economic development, rehabilitation of the handicapped, accessibility of the man-made environment, legislation concerning war veterans and war victims, and development of international humanitarian law; in 1986 established International Socio-Medical Centre (Oslo, Norway) for psycho-medical problems resulting from stress. Regional committees for Africa, Asia and the Pacific, and Europe; consultative status with UN (ECOSOC), with several UN specialized agencies and the Council of Europe. Mems: national organizations in 53 countries, representing more than 20,000,000 war veterans and war victims. Pres. W. Ch. J. M. VAN LANSCHOT (Netherlands); Sec.-Gen. SERGE WOURGAFT (France). Publs special studies (disarmament, human rights, rehabilitation).

Zonta International: 557 W. Randolph St, Chicago, Ill 60606, USA; telex 19020; f. 1919; executive women's service organization; international and community service projects, educational and cultural needs. Mems: 35,000 in 50 countries. Pres. RUTH F. WALKER (USA); Exec. Dir VALERIE LEVITAN. Publ. *The Zontian* (quarterly).

Sport and Recreations

Arab Sports Confederation: POB 6040, Riyadh, Saudi Arabia; tel. 482-3215; telex 404760; f. 1976 to encourage regional co-operation in sport. Mems: 22 national Olympic Committees, 26 Arab sports federations. Pres. Prince FAISAL BIN FAHD ABD AL-AZIZ; Sec.-Gen. OTHMAN M. AS-SAAD.

Fédération Aéronautique Internationale (International Aeronautical Federation): 6 rue Galilee, 75782 Paris Cedex 16, France; tel. (1) 47-20-91-85; telex 611580; f. 1905 to encourage all aeronautical sports; organizes world championships and makes rules through technical committees; endorses world aeronautical and astronautical records. Mems: in 79 countries. Pres. G. A. PETER LLOYD; Dir Dr CENEK KEPAK. Publs *Annual Bulletin, FAI News* (2 a year).

General Association of International Sports Federations—GAISF: 7 blvd de Suisse, Monte Carlo, Monaco; tel. (93) 507413; telex 479459; f. 1967 to act as a forum for the exchange of ideas and discussion of common problems in sport; to collect and circulate information; to provide secretarial and translation services; and to co-ordinate the main international competitions. Mems: 71 international sports organizations; Pres. Dr UN YONG KIM; Sec.-Gen. LUC NIGGLI (Monaco). Publs *Calendar of International Sports Competitions* (2 a year), *GAISF News* (monthly, in English and French).

International Amateur Athletic Federation: 3 Hans Crescent, Knightsbridge, London, SW1X 0LN, England; tel. (01) 581-8771; telex 296859; f. 1912 to ensure co-operation and fairness among members, and to combat discrimination in athletics; to affiliate national governing bodies, to compile athletic competition rules and to organize championships at all levels; to settle disputes between members, and to conduct a programme of development for members who need coaching, judging courses, etc., and to frame regulations for the establishment of World, Olympic and other athletic records. Mems: 179 countries. Pres. P. NEBIOLO (Italy); Gen. Sec. J. B. HOLT (UK). Publs *IAAF Handbook* (English and French editions; biennial); *IAAF Magazine/Newsletter* (6 a year each in English and French); *New Studies in Athletics* (quarterly).

International Amateur Boxing Association: 1137 Berlin, Postamt Volkradstrasse, Post-Iagernd, German Democratic Republic; tel. 2293413; telex 115149; f. 1946 as the world body controlling amateur boxing for the Olympic Games, continental, regional and international championships and tournaments in every part of the world. Mems: 137 nations. Pres. Prof. A. CHOWDHRY (Pakistan); Sec.-Gen. KARL-HEINZ WEHR (GDR). Publ. *World Amateur Boxing* (quarterly).

International Amateur Radio Union: POB AAA, Newington, CT 06111, USA; tel. (203) 666-1541; telex 6502155052; f. 1925 to link national amateur radio societies and represent the interests of two-way amateur radio communication. Mems: 126 national amateur radio societies. Pres. RICHARD L. BALDWIN; Sec. DAVID SUMNER.

International Amateur Swimming Federation (Fédération internationale de natation amateur—FINA): 208-3540 West 41st Ave, Vancouver, BC, V6N 3E6, Canada; tel. (604) 263-4144; telex 04508534; f. 1908 to promote amateur swimming and swimming sports internationally; to administer rules for swimming sports, for competitions and for establishing records; to arbitrate in disputes between members; to secure guarantees that members travelling to FINA international events will not be denied visas by the countries concerned. Mems: 120 countries. Pres. MUSTAPHA LARFAOUI (Algeria); Sec. ROSS WALES (USA). Publs *Handbook* (every 4 years), *FINA News* (monthly).

International Amateur Wrestling Federation: 3 ave Ruchonnet, 1003 Lausanne, Switzerland; tel. (021) 228426; telex 455958; f. 1912 to encourage the development of amateur wrestling and promote the sport in countries where it is not yet practised; to further friendly relations between all members; to oppose any form of political, racial or religious discrimination. Mems: 111 federations. Pres. MILAN ERCEGAN; Sec.-Gen. MICHEL DUSSON. Publs *News Bulletin, Theory and Practice of Wrestling*.

International Council for Health, Physical Education, and Recreation: 1900 Association Drive, Reston, VA 22091, USA; f. 1958 by the World Confederation of Organizations of the Teaching Profession; f. as separate organization in 1959 to encourage the development of programmes in health, physical education, and recreation throughout the world.

International Cricket Conference: Lord's Cricket Ground, London, NW8 8QN, England; f. 1909 (as Imperial Cricket Conference; name changed 1965) to discuss aspects of the game at the international level. Annual conference; seven full and 18 associate mems. Sec. Lt-Col J. R. STEPHENSON.

OTHER INTERNATIONAL ORGANIZATIONS

International Cycling Union: 6 rue Amat, 1202 Geneva, Switzerland; tel. (022) 322914; telex 27196; f. 1900 to develop, regulate and control all forms of cycling as a sport. Mems: 128 federations. Pres. LUIS PUIG; Gen. Sec. MICHAL JEKIEL. Publs *Le Monde Cycliste Magazine* (4 a year), *International Calendar* (annually).

International Federation of Association Football (Fédération internationale de football association—FIFA): Hitzigweg 11, POB 85, 8030 Zürich, Switzerland; tel. (01) 555400; telex 817240; f. 1904 to promote the game of association football and foster friendly relations among players and national associations; to control football and uphold the laws of the game as laid down by the International Football Association Board; to prevent discrimination of any kind between players; and to provide arbitration in any disputes between national associations; organizes World Cup competition every four years. Mems: 166 national associations, six regional confederations. Pres. Dr JOÃO HAVELANGE (Brazil); Gen. Sec. J. S. BLATTER (Switzerland). Publs. *FIFA News, FIFA Magazine* (quarterly) (both in English, French, Spanish and German).

International Federation of Park and Recreation Administration—IFPRA: The Grotto, Lower Basildon, Reading, Berkshire, RG8 9NE, England; tel. (0491) 873558; f. 1957 to provide a world centre where members of government departments, local authorities, and all organizations concerned with recreational services can discuss relevant matters. Mems: 225 in 34 countries. Pres. ROGER K. BROWN (USA); Gen. Sec. LAWRENCE A. HOLMES.

International Gymnastic Federation: CP 405, 3250 Lyss, Switzerland; tel. (032) 841960; telex 934961; f. 1881 to promote the exchange of official documents and publications on gymnastics; to set up a procedure for invitations among members; and to organize international competitions. Associations pursuing political or religious aims are not recognized, and professionals are banned from competitions. Mems: 100 affiliated federations. Pres. YURI TITOV (USSR); Gen. Sec. MAX BANGERTER (Switzerland). Publ. *Bulletin* (4 a year).

International Hockey Federation: Boîte 5, 1 ave des Arts, 1040 Brussels, Belgium; tel. (02) 219-45-37; telex 63393; f. 1924 to fix the rules of outdoor and indoor hockey for all affiliated national associations; to control the game of hockey and indoor hockey; to control the organization of international tournaments, such as the Olympic Games and the World Cup. Mems: 101 national associations. Pres. ETIENNE GLICHITCH (France); Sec.-Gen. JUAN ANGEL CALZADO DE CASTRO. Publ. *World Hockey* (quarterly).

International Judo Federation: 106 Berlin, PSF 380, German Democratic Republic; tel. 2291633; telex 112137; f. 1949 to promote cordial and friendly relations between members; to protect the interests of Judo throughout the world; to organize the separate Senior, Junior and Women's World Championships every two years and organize the Judo events of the Olympic Games; to develop and spread the techniques and spirit of Judo throughout the world. Pres. SARKIS KALOGHLIAN; Sec.-Gen. HEINZ KEMPA.

International Philatelic Federation: Zollikerstrasse 128, 8008 Zürich, Switzerland; tel. (01) 553839; f. 1926 to promote philately internationally. Pres. L. DVORACEK; Sec.-Gen. M. L. HEIRI.

International Rowing Federation (Fédération internationale des Sociétés d'Aviron—FISA): CP 352, 2001 Neuchâtel, Switzerland; tel. (38) 257222; telex 931102; f. 1892 to establish contacts between oarsmen in all countries and to draw up racing rules. Mems: national organizations in 65 countries. Pres. THOMAS KELLER; Sec.-Gen. DENIS OSWALD.

International Shooting Union: 8000 Munich 2, Bavariaring 21, Federal Republic of Germany; tel. (089) 531012; telex 5216792; f. 1907 to promote and guide the development of the amateur shooting sports; to organize World Championships; to control the organization of continental and regional championships; to supervise the shooting events of the Olympic and Continental Games under the auspices of the International Olympic Committee. Mems: in 113 countries. Pres. OLEGARIO VÁZQUEZ-RAÑA (Mexico); Sec.-Gen. HORST G. SCHREIBER (FRG). Publ. *UIT Journal, International Shooting Sport* (6 a year).

International Skating Union: Promenade 73, 7270 Davos-Platz, Switzerland; tel. (083) 37577; telex 853123; f. 1892; holds regular conferences. Mems: 47 skating organizations in 37 countries. Pres. OLAF POULSEN; Sec.-Gen. BEAT HÄSLER.

International Ski Federation: Worbstrasse 210, 3073 Guemligen bei Bern, Switzerland; tel. (31) 525815; telex 911109; f. 1924 to further the sport of skiing, to create and maintain friendly relations between the member associations; to prevent discrimination in skiing matters on racial, religious or political grounds; to organize World Ski Championships and regional championships and, as supreme international skiing authority, to establish the international competition calendar and rules for all ski competitions approved by the FIS, and to arbitrate in any disputes. Mems: 62 national ski associations. Pres. MARC HODLER (Switzerland); Gen. Sec. GIAN-FRANCO KASPER (Switzerland). Publ. *FIS Bulletin* (4 times a year).

Sport and Recreations, Technology

International Table Tennis Federation: 53 London Rd, St Leonards-on-Sea, East Sussex, TN37 6AY, England; tel. (0424) 721414; telex 95277. Pres. ICHIRO OGIMURA; Sec.-Gen. TONY BROOKS.

International Tennis Federation: Palliser Rd, Barons Court, London, W14 9EN, England; tel. (01) 381-8060; telex 919253; f. 1913 to govern the game of tennis throughout the world and promote its teaching; to preserve its independence of outside authority; to produce the Rules of Tennis, to promote the Davis Cup Competition for men, the Federation Cup for women, seven cups for veterans and the World Youth Cup for players of 16 years old and under; to organize tournaments. Mems: 88 full and 59 associate. Pres. PHILIPPE CHATRIER (France). Publs *World of Tennis* (annually), *President's Newsletter* (monthly), *ITF News* (quarterly).

International Weightlifting Federation: PF 614, 1374 Budapest, Hungary; tel. 311162; telex 227553; f. 1905 to control international weightlifting; to set up technical rules and to train referees; to supervise World Championships, Olympic Games, regional games and international contests of all kinds; to supervise the activities of national and continental federations; to register world records. Mems: in 128 countries. Pres. GOTTFRIED SCHÖDL (Austria); Gen. Sec. TAMÁS AJAN (Hungary). Publs *IWF Constitution and Rules* (every 4 years), *World Weightlifting* (quarterly).

International Yacht Racing Union: 60 Knightsbridge, London, SW1X 7JX, England; tel. (01) 235-6221; telex 915487; f. 1907; establishes and amends international yacht racing rules, organizes the Olympic Yachting Regatta and other championships. Mems: 93 national yachting authorities. Pres. PETER TALLBERG; Exec. Dir MIKE EVANS.

World Bridge Federation: 56 route de Vandoeuvres, 1253 Geneva, Switzerland; tel. (022) 501541; telex 422887; f. 1958 to promote the game of contract bridge throughout the world, federate national bridge associations in all countries, conduct bridge associations in all countries, conduct world championships competitions, establish standard bridge laws. Mems: 81 countries. Pres. DENIS HOWARD (Australia); Sec. ERNESTO D'ORSI (Brazil). Publ. *World Bridge News* (quarterly).

World Chess Federation: Abendweg 1, 6006 Lucerne, Switzerland; tel. (041) 513378; telex 862845; f. 1924; controls chess competitions of world importance and awards international chess titles. Pres. FLORENCIO CAMPOMANES (Philippines); Asst Gen. Sec. CASTO ABUNDO (Philippines).

World Underwater Federation: 47 rue du Commerce, 75015 Paris, France; tel. (1) 45-75-42-75; telex 205734; f. 1959 to develop underwater activities; to form bodies to instruct in the techniques of underwater diving; to perfect existing equipment and encourage inventions and to experiment with newly marketed products, suggesting possible improvements; to organize international competitions. Mems: 72 countries. Pres. PIERRE PERRAUD (France); Gen. Sec. MARCEL BIBAS (France). Publs *International Year Book of CMAS, Bulletin News* (every 3 months).

Technology

Union of International Technical Associations (Union des associations techniques internationales—UATI): UNESCO House, Room S1.27, 1 rue Miollis, 75015 Paris, France; tel. (1) 45-66-94-10; telex 204461; f. 1951 under the auspices of UNESCO to co-ordinate activities of member organizations and represent their interests; helps to arrange international congresses and the publication of technical material. Mems: 30 organizations. Chair. ROGER GINOCCHIO (France); Sec.-Gen. PIERRE PECOUX. Publ. *Bulletin* (quarterly).

MEMBER ORGANIZATIONS

Members of UATI include the following:

International Association for Hydraulic Research: c/o Delft Hydraulics Laboratory, Rotterdamseweg 185, POB 177, 2600 MH Delft, Netherlands; tel. (015) 569353; f. 1935; holds biennial congresses. Mems: 2,300 individual, 280 corporate. Sec. J. E. PRINS (Netherlands). Publs *Directory of Hydraulic Research Institutes and Laboratories, Journal of Hydraulic Research*

International Association of Lighthouse Authorities: 13 rue Yvon Villarceau, 75116 Paris, France; tel. (1) 45-00-38-60; telex 610 480; f. 1957; holds technical conference every five years; working groups study special problems and formulate technical recommendations, guidelines and manuals. Mems in 80 countries. Sec.-Gen. PIERRE BELLIER (France). Publs *Bulletin* (quarterly), technical dictionary (in English, French, German and Spanish).

International Bridge, Tunnel and Turnpike Association: 2120 L

OTHER INTERNATIONAL ORGANIZATIONS

Technology

St, NW, Suite 305, Washington, DC 20037, USA; tel. (202) 659-4620; telex 275445; f. 1932. Exec. Dir. Neil D. Schuster. Publ. *Tollways* (monthly).

International Commission of Agricultural Engineering: 17–21 rue de Javel, 75015 Paris, France; tel. (1) 45-77-75-78; f. 1930. Mems: associations from 26 countries, individual mems from six countries. Pres. Prof. Lehoczky (Hungary); Sec.-Gen. M. Carlier (France). Publs *Yearbook*, technical reports.

International Commission on Irrigation and Drainage: 48 Nyaya Marg, Chanakyapuri, New Delhi 110021, India; tel. (11) 301 68 37; telex 031-65920; f. 1950; holds triennial congresses. Mems: 72 national committees. Pres. Othman Lahlou (Morocco); Sec.-Gen. Dr K. K. Framji (India). Publs *Bulletin* (2 a year), *Bibliography* (annually), *World Irrigation*, *Multilingual Technical Dictionary*, *World Flood Control*, technical books.

International Commission on Large Dams: 151 blvd Haussmann, 75008 Paris, France; tel. (1) 40-42-67-33; telex 641320; f. 1928; holds triennial congresses. Mems in 78 countries. Pres. J. A. Veltrop (USA); Sec.-Gen. J. Cotillon. Publs *Technical Bulletin*, *World Register of Dams*, *World Register of Mine and Industrial Wastes*, *Technical Dictionary on Dams*, studies.

International Committee of Foundry Technical Associations: Walchestrasse 27, Case Postale 7190, 8023 Zürich, Switzerland; tel. (01) 3613060; telex 56669. Pres. M. Grandpierre; Sec. M. J. Gerster.

International Federation for the Theory of Machines and Mechanisms: Dolejskova 5, Prague 8, Czechoslovakia. Pres. G. Bianchi; Sec.-Gen. L. Pust.

International Federation of Automatic Control—IFAC: 2361 Laxenburg, Schlossplatz 12, Austria; tel. (02236) 71447; telex 79248; f. 1957 to serve those concerned with the theory and application of automatic control and systems engineering. Mems: 42 national associations. Pres. B. Tamm; Sec. G. Hencsey. Publs *Automatica* (bi-monthly), *Newsletter*.

International Federation of Industrial Energy Consumers: Rhône-Poulenc SA, 25 quai Paul-Doumer, 92408 Courbevoie Cedex, France; tel. (1) 47-68-16-98. Pres. Gerhard Stein; Sec.-Gen. A. Mongon.

International Fertilizer Industry Association: 28 rue Marbeuf, 75008 Paris, France; tel. (1) 42-25-27-07; telex 640481. Pres. Dr G. P. Giusti; Sec.-Gen. K. L. C. Windridge.

International Gas Union: c/o Swissgas, Grütlistrasse 44, POB 658, Zürich, Switzerland; tel. (01) 2028075; telex 58527; f. 1931 to study all aspects and problems of the gas industry with a view to promoting international co-operation and the general improvement of the industry. Mems: national organizations in 46 countries. Pres. H. Richter (GDR); Sec.-Gen. J. P. Lauper (Switzerland).

International Institute of Welding: 11/12 Pall Mall, London, SW1Y 5LU, England; tel. (01) 925-0082; telex 81183; f. 1948. Mems: 50 societies in 37 countries. Pres. R. V. Salkin (Belgium); Sec.-Gen. P. D. Boyd (UK). Publs *Welding in the World* (7 a year).

International Institution for Production Engineering Research: 10 rue Mansart, 75009 Paris, France; tel. (1) 45-26-21-80; telex 281029; f. 1951 to promote by scientific research the study of the mechanical processing of all solid materials including checks on efficiency and quality of work. Mems: 143 active, 133 associate, 75 corresponding, in 38 countries. Pres. Prof. P. A. McKeown; Sec.-Gen. R. Geslot. Publ. *Annals*.

International Measurement Confederation: POB 457, 1371 Budapest 5, Hungary; tel. (36 1) 531 562; telex 225792. Pres. G. Toumanoff; Sec.-Gen. T. Kemeny.

International Society for Soil Mechanics and Foundation Engineering: Engineering Dept, Trumpington St, Cambridge, CB2 1PZ, England; tel. (0223) 355020; telex 81239; f. 1936 to promote international co-operation among scientists and engineers in the field of geotechnics and its engineering applications; maintains 24 technical committees; holds quadrennial international conference, and regional conferences. Mems: 16,000 individuals, 58 national societies. Pres. Prof. B. B. Broms; Gen. Sec. Dr R. Parry. Publs *Newsletter* (quarterly), *Lexicon of Soil Mechanics Terms* (in eight languages).

International Solid Wastes and Public Cleansing Association: Vester Farimagsgade 29, 1606 Copenhagen V, Denmark; tel. (01) 15-65-65. Pres. J. A. Den Dulk (Netherlands); Sec.-Gen. Jeanne Møller (Denmark).

International Union for Electro-heat: Tour Atlantique, 92080 Paris-la-Défense Cedex 6; tel. (1) 47-78-99-34; telex 615739; f. 1953, present title adopted 1957. Aims to study all questions relative to electro-heat, except commercial questions; links national groups and organizes international congresses on electro-heat. Mems: national committees and titular members in 24 countries. Pres. M. Setterwall (Sweden); Gen. Sec. A. Dailliet (Belgium).

International Union of Air Pollution Prevention Associations: 136 North St, Brighton, BN1 1RG, England; tel. (0273) 26313. Pres. L. A. Clarenburg; Dir-Gen. J. Langston.

International Union of Producers and Distributors of Electrical Energy: 39 ave de Friedland, 75008 Paris, France; tel. (1) 40-42-37-08; telex 644471; f. 1925 for study of all questions relating to the production, transmission and distribution of electrical energy. Mems: 42 countries. Pres. Christophe Babaiantz; Sec.-Gen. Georges Lucenet.

International Union of Testing and Research Laboratories for Materials and Structures: 12 rue Brancion, 75015 Paris, France; tel. (1) 45-39-22-33; telex 250071; f. 1947 for the exchange of information and the promotion of co-operation on experimental research concerning structures and materials, for the study of research methods with a view to improvement and standardization. Mems: laboratories and individuals in 73 countries. Pres. I. Dunstan (UK); Sec.-Gen. M. Fickelson (France). Publ. *Materials and Structures—Testing and Research* (bi-monthly).

Permanent International Association of Navigation Congresses—PIANC: 155 rue de la Loi, 1040 Brussels, Belgium; tel. (02) 733-96-70; f. 1885, present form adopted 1902; fosters progress in the construction, maintenance and operation of inland and maritime waterways, of inland and maritime ports and of coastal areas; publishes information in this field, undertakes studies, organizes international and national meetings. Congresses are held every four years. Mems: 40 governments, 2,786 others. Pres. Ir. R. de Paepe; Sec.-Gen. H. Vandervelden. Publs *Bulletin* (quarterly), *Illustrated Technical Dictionary* (in 6 languages).

Permanent International Association of Road Congresses: 27 rue Guénégaud, 75006 Paris, France; tel. (1) 46-33-71-90; f. 1909 to promote the construction, improvement, maintenance, use and economic development of roads; organizes technical committees and study sessions. Mems: governments, public bodies, organizations and private individuals in 70 countries. Pres. M. E. Balaguer (Spain); Sec.-Gen. M. B. Fauveau (France). Publs *Bulletin*, *Technical Dictionary*.

World Energy Conference: 34 St James's St, London, SW1A 1HD, England; tel. (01) 930-3966; telex 264707; f. 1924 to link all branches of energy and resources technology and maintain liaison between world experts; holds congresses every three years. Mems: 77 committees. Pres. M. Boiteux (France); Sec.-Gen. I. D. Lindsay (UK). Publs energy supply and demand projections, resources surveys, technical assessments, reports.

OTHER ORGANIZATIONS

African Organization of Cartography and Remote Sensing: BP 102, Hussein Dey, Algiers, Algeria; tel. 77-79-34; telex 65474; f. 1988 by amalgamation of African Association of Cartography and African Council for Remote Sensing; aims to encourage the development of cartography and of remote sensing by satellites; organizes conferences and other meetings, promotes establishment of training institutions; the ECA has set up two centres, one in Kenya for cartographic services and one in Nigeria for training. Mems: principal cartographic services of African countries. Sec.-Gen. Dr Chedly Fezzani.

African Regional Centre for Technology: Ave Cheikh Anta Diop, BP 2435, Dakar, Senegal; tel. 22-77-11; telex 3282; f. 1980 to encourage the development of indigenous technology and to improve the terms of access to imported technology; assists the establishment of national centres. Dir D. Babatunde Thomas. Publs *African Technodevelopment*, *Alert Africa*, directories of institutions.

Bureau International de la Récupération: 13 place du Samedi, 1000 Brussels, Belgium; tel. (02) 217-82-51; telex 61965; f. 1948 as the world federation of the reclamation and recycling industries, to promote international trade in scrap iron and steel, non-ferrous metals, paper, textiles, plastics and rubber. Mems: associations and individuals in 46 countries. Sec.-Gen. Francis Veys.

European Builders of Internal Combustion Engines and Electric Locomotives: 12 rue Bixio, 75007 Paris, France; tel. (1) 47-05-36-62; telex 270105; f. 1953 as an information centre on economic and technical matters relating to the production, distribution and consumption of locomotives throughout the world. Mems: 27 full, 12 associates in 12 countries. Chair. B. G. Sephton; Gen. Del. J.-L. Burckhardt.

European Computer Manufacturers Association—ECMA: 114 rue de Rhône, 1204 Geneva, Switzerland; tel. (022) 353634; telex 22288; f. 1961 to study and develop, in co-operation with the appropriate national and international organizations, as a scientific endeavour and in the general interest, methods and procedures in order to facilitate and standardize the use of data processing systems; and to promulgate various standards applicable to the functional design and use of data processing equipment. Mems: 30 ordinary and 12 associate. Sec.-Gen. D. Hekimi. Publ. *ECMA Standards*.

OTHER INTERNATIONAL ORGANIZATIONS — Technology

European Convention for Constructional Steelwork: 32/36 ave des Ombrages, bte 20, 1200 Brussels, Belgium; tel. (02) 762-04-29; f. 1955 for the consideration of problems involved in metallic construction. Member organizations in Austria, Belgium, Denmark, Finland, France, Federal Republic of Germany, Italy, Japan, Luxembourg, Netherlands, Norway, Spain, Sweden, Switzerland, United Kingdom, USA, Yugoslavia.

European Federation of Chemical Engineering: c/o Institution of Chemical Engineers, Geo. E. Davis Bldg, 165–171 Railway Terrace, Rugby, Warwickshire, CV21 3HQ, England; tel. (0788) 78214; telex 311780; f. 1953 to encourage co-operation in Europe between non-profit-making scientific and technical societies for the advancement of chemical engineering and its application in the process industries. Mems: 56 societies in 22 European countries; 12 corresponding societies in other countries.

European Federation of Corrosion: 1 Carlton House Terrace, London, SW1Y 5DB, England; tel. (01) 839-4071; telex 8814813; f. 1955 to encourage co-operation in research on corrosion and methods of combating it. Member societies in 20 countries. Hon. Secs R. MAS (France), DIETER BEHRENS (FRG), R. B. WOOD (UK).

European Federation of National Associations of Engineers: 4 rue de la Mission Marchand, 75016 Paris, France; tel. (1) 42-24-91-43; f. 1951 to strengthen cultural and professional links and exchange information among members; to study problems of training engineers and recognizing and protecting their status; and to organize periodical congresses. Mems: 1m. in 20 national engineers' associations. Pres. A. J. THOR; Sec.-Gen. M. GUERIN (France). Publ. *FEANI Letter*.

European Organization for Civil Aviation Electronics—EUROCAE: 11 rue Hamelin, 75783 Paris Cedex 16, France; tel. (1) 45-05-71-88; telex 611045; f. 1963; studies and advises on problems related to the application of electronics and electronic equipment to aeronautics and assists international bodies in the establishment of international standards. Mems: 61. Pres. B. DUBOIS; Chair. B. PERRET.

Eurospace: 16 bis ave Bosquet, 75007 Paris, France; tel. (1) 45-55-83-53; telex 270716; f. 1961; an association of European aerospace industrial companies, banks, press organizations and national associations for promoting space activity in the fields of telecommunication, television, aeronautical, maritime, meteorological, educational and press usage satellites, as well as launchers (conventional and recoverable). The Association carries out studies on the legal, economic, technical and financial aspects. It enjoys consultative status with UNESCO and the Council of Europe; acts as an industrial adviser to the European Space Agency. Mems (direct or associate) in the following countries: Belgium, Denmark, Finland, France, Federal Republic of Germany, Italy, Netherlands, Norway, Spain, Sweden, Switzerland, United Kingdom. Pres. JEAN DELORME; Sec.-Gen. YVES DEMERLIAC; Tech. Sec. REX TURNER.

Federation of Technical and Scientific Organizations of the Socialist Countries—FENTO: c/o MTESZ, 1055 Budapest, Kossuth Lajos tér 6-8, Hungary; tel. 533-333; telex 225792; f. 1962. Pres. JENŐ FOCK; Gen. Sec. JÁNOS TÓTH.

Inter-African Committee for Hydraulic Studies—CIEH: BP 369, Ouagadougou, Burkina Faso; tel. 33-34-76; telex 5266; f. 1960 to ensure co-operation in hydrology, hydrogeology, climatology, urban sanitation and other water sciences, through exchange of information and co-ordination of research and other projects; administrative budget (1986/87): 110m. francs CFA; investment budget 400m. francs CFA. Mems: 13 African countries. Sec.-Gen. ABDOU HASSANE. Publs *Bulletin de Liaison technique* (quarterly), research studies.

Intergovernmental Bureau for Informatics: POB 10253, Viale Civiltà del Lavoro, 00144 Rome, Italy; tel. (396) 5916041; telex 612065; f. 1969, replacing the International Computation Centre; present title adopted in 1974; the only international organization in the field of informatics with intergovernmental status; aims to promote the development and knowledge of informatics; an advisory body, helping member countries to establish national policies in informatics and to execute technical projects. Structure: General Assembly (every two years) and Executive Council. Mems: 36 countries. Dir-Gen. Prof. F. A. BERNASCONI. Publs *Agora* (quarterly), *IBI Newsletter* (every 2 months).

International Association for Bridge and Structural Engineering: ETH—Hönggerberg, 8093 Zürich, Switzerland; tel. (01) 3772647; telex 822 186; f. 1929 to promote the interchange of knowledge and research work results concerning bridge and structural engineering and to foster co-operation among those connected with this work. Mems: 3,000 government departments, local authorities, universities, institutes, firms and individuals in 70 countries. Pres. Prof. H. VON GUNTEN (Switzerland); Exec. Dir A. GOLAY. Publs *IABSE Periodica* (quarterly), *Congress Report*, *IABSE Report*, *Structural Engineering Documents*.

International Association for Cybernetics: c/o P. Dricot, Palais des Expositions, place André Rijckmans, 5000 Namur, Belgium; tel. (081) 22-22-09; f. 1957 to ensure liaison between research workers engaged in various sectors of cybernetics, to promote the development of the science and of its applications and to disseminate information about it. Mems: firms and individuals in 42 countries. Sec.-Gen. PIERRE DRICOT. Publs *Cybernetica* (quarterly).

International Association of Rolling Stock Builders: 12 rue Bixio, 75007 Paris, France; tel. (1) 47-05-36-62; telex 270105; f. 1934; an information centre on economic and technical questions relating to the production, distribution and consumption of railway rolling stock throughout the world. Mems: 52 firms in 12 countries. Chair. C. BERNSTEIN; Gen. Del. J.-L. BURCKHARDT.

International Association of Technological University Libraries: c/o Radcliffe Science Library, University of Oxford, Parks Rd, Oxford, OX1 3QP, England; tel. (0865) 272820; telex 83656; f. 1955 to promote co-operation between member libraries and stimulate research on library problems. Mems: about 175 university libraries in 39 countries. Pres. Dr D. F. SHAW (UK); Sec. Dr N. FJÄLLBRANT (Sweden). Publ. *IATUL Quarterly*.

International Cargo Handling Co-ordination Association—ICHCA: Unit 4.15, 71 Bondway, London, SW8 1SH, England; tel. (01) 793-1022; telex 261106; f. 1952. Mems: in 90 countries. Pres. W. BOLITHO (Australia); Sec.-Gen. JOHN T. WARBURTON. Publs *Cargo Systems International* (monthly), *Cargo Handling Abstracts* (quarterly), *Biennial Report*, *Who's Who in Cargo Handling* (annually), *International Cargo Handling* (annual buyers' guide).

International Colour Association: c/o Dr J. Walraven, Institute for Perception TNO, POB 23, 3769 ZG Soesterberg, Netherlands; tel. (034) 63-62-11; f. 1967 to encourage research in colour in all its aspects, disseminate the knowledge gained from this research and promote its application to the solution of problems in the fields of science, art and industry; holds international congresses and symposia. Mems: organizations in 21 countries. Pres. Dr H. TERSTIEGE (FRG); Sec. Dr J. WALRAVEN (Netherlands).

International Commission on Illumination: Kegelgasse 27, 1030 Vienna, Austria; tel. (01) 75-31-87; telex 111151; f. 1900 as International Commission on Photometry, present name 1913; aims to provide an international forum for all matters relating to the science and art of light and lighting; to exchange information; to develop and publish international standards, and to provide guidance in their application. Mems: 38 national committees and five individuals. Exec. Sec. J. SCHANDA. Publs standards, technical reports, *CIE Journal*.

International Committee on Aeronautical Fatigue—ICAF: c/o Prof. J. Schijve, Dept of Aerospace Engineering, THD, Kluyverweg 1, 2629 HS Delft, Netherlands; tel. (15) 781341; telex 38151; f. 1951 for collaboration on fatigue of aeronautical structures among aeronautical bodies and laboratories by means of exchange of documents and by organizing periodical conferences. Mems: national centres in 13 countries. Sec. Prof. J. SCHIJVE (Netherlands).

International Conference on Large High-Voltage Electric Systems: 112 blvd Haussmann, 75008 Paris, France; tel. (1) 45-22-65-12; telex 650445; f. 1921 to facilitate and promote the exchange of technical knowledge and information between all countries in the general field of electrical generation and transmission at high voltages; holds general sessions (every two years), symposia. Mems: 3,500 in 79 countries. Pres. W. S. WHITE, Jr (USA); Sec.-Gen. G. LEROY (France). Publ. *Electra* (every 2 months).

International Copper Research Association, Inc: 708 Third Ave, New York, NY 10017, USA; tel. (212) 697-9355; telex 62934; f. 1960; non-profit association financed by the copper mining industry; sponsors and directs research at laboratories, institutes and universities throughout the world. Mems: companies in 13 countries. Pres. WILLIAM H. DRESHER.

International Council for Building Research, Studies and Documentation—CIB: POB 20704, Weena 704, 3001 JA Rotterdam, Netherlands; tel. (010) 411-02-40; telex 22530; f. 1953 to encourage and facilitate co-operation in building research, studies and documentation in all aspects. Mems: governmental and industrial organizations and qualified individuals in 70 countries. Pres. P. CHEMILLIER (France); Gen. Sec. GY. SEBESTYEN. Publs *Information Bulletin* (bi-monthly), *Building Research and Practice* (bi-monthly).

International Electrotechnical Commission—IEC: 3 rue de Varembé, POB 131, 1211 Geneva 20, Switzerland; tel. (022) 340150; telex 28872; f. 1906 as the authority for world standards for electrical and electronic engineering: its standards are used as the basis for regional and national standards, and are used in preparing specifications for international trade. Mems: national committees representing all branches of electrical and electronic activities in 40 countries. Gen.-Sec. C. J. STANFORD. Publs *International Standards and Reports*, *IEC Bulletin*, *Annual Report*, *Report on Activities*, *Catalogue of Publications*.

OTHER INTERNATIONAL ORGANIZATIONS — Technology

International Special Committee on Radio Interference: British Electrotechnical Committee, British Standards Institution, 2 Park St, London, W1A 2BS, England; tel. (01) 629-9000; telex 266933; f. 1934; special committee of the IEC to promote international agreement on the protection of radio reception from interference by equipment other than authorized transmitters; recommends limits of such interference and specifies equipment and methods of measurement; determines requirements for immunity of sound and TV broadcasting receivers from interference and the impact of safety regulations on interference suppression. Mems: national committees of IEC and seven other international organizations. Sec. M. H. LOCKTON.

International Federation for Information and Documentation: POB 90402, 2509 LK The Hague, Netherlands; tel. (070) 14-06-71; f. 1895 to promote, through international co-operation, research in and development of documentation; study committees for: universal decimal classification; research on the theoretical basis of information; classification research; linguistics in documentation; information for industry; education and training; terminology of information and documentation; patent information and documentation; social sciences documentation; Broad system of ordering; informetrics; information systems and network design and management; study of user needs; regional commissions for Latin America, Asia and Oceania. Mems: 69 national, two international, some 270 affiliates. Pres. M. W. HILL; Sec.-Gen. STELLA KEENAN. Publs *International Forum on Information and Documentation* (quarterly), *FID News Bulletin* (monthly), *R & D Projects in Documentation and Librarianship* (bi-monthly), *FID/ET Newsletter on Education and Training Programmes for Information Personnel* (quarterly), monographs.

International Federation for Information Processing: 16 place Longemalle, 1204 Geneva, Switzerland; tel. (022) 282649; telex 428472; f. 1960 to promote information science and technology; to stimulate research, development and application of information processing in science and human activities; to further the dissemination and exchange of information on information processing; to encourage education in information processing; to advance international co-operation in the field of information processing. Mems: 46 national organizations representing 60 countries. Pres. A. W. GOLDSWORTHY (Australia).

International Federation of Airworthiness—IFA: 58 Whiteheath Ave, Ruislip, Middx, HA4 7PW, England; tel. (0895) 672504; telex 8951771; f. 1964 to provide a forum for the exchange of international experience in maintenance, design and operations; holds annual conference; awards international aviation scholarship annually. Mems: 91, comprising nine aircraft engineering and allied organizations, 35 airlines, 16 airworthiness authorities, 21 aerospace manufacturing companies, seven societies of aeronautical engineers, and the Flight Safety Foundation (USA). Pres. Sir JOHN DENT (UK); Exec. Dir K. J. ANDERSON (UK). Publ. *IFA News* (quarterly).

International Federation of Automotive Engineering Societies: Steinacherstrasse 59, 8308 Ober-Illnau, Zürich, Switzerland; f. 1947 to promote the technical development of mechanical transport engineering and research; congresses every two years. Mems: national organizations in 19 countries. Sec.-Gen. W. LEMMENMEYER. Publ. *Bulletin*.

International Federation of Consulting Engineers: 13c ave du Temple, POB 86, 1000 Lausanne 12, Switzerland; tel. (021) 335003; telex 454698; f. 1913 to encourage international co-operation and the setting up of standards for consulting engineers. Mems: national associations in 50 countries, comprising some 26,000 individual members. Pres. S. E. FRICK-MEIJER.

International Federation of Hospital Engineering: 69 Evans Lane, Kidlington, Oxford, OX5 2JA, England; f. 1970 to promote internationally the standards of hospital engineering and to provide for the interchange of knowledge and ideas. Mems: 50. Gen. Sec. BASIL HERMON.

International Information Management Congress: 345 Woodcliff Drive, Fairport, NY 14450, USA; tel. (716) 383-8330; telex 6714921; f. 1962 (as the International Micrographic Congress) to promote co-operation in document-based information management; to provide an international clearing-house for information, exchange publications and encourage the establishment of international standards; to promote international product exhibitions, seminars and conventions. Mems: 36 associations, 116 regular and 700 affiliate mems from 64 countries. Exec. Dir GEORGE D. HOFFMANN (USA). Publ. *IMC Journal* (every 2 months).

International Institute of Seismology and Earthquake Engineering: Building Research Institute, Ministry of Construction, 1 Tatehara, Oho-machi, Tsukuba-gun, Ibaraki Pref., Japan; tel. 0298 64-2151; telex 3652560; f. 1962 to work on seismology and earthquake engineering for the purpose of reducing earthquake damage in the world; trains seismologists and earthquake engineers from the seismic countries and undertakes surveys, research, guidance and analysis of information on earthquakes and related matters. Mems: 51 countries. Dir M. HIROSAWA.

International Iron and Steel Institute—IISI: 120 rue Col Bourg, 1140 Brussels, Belgium; tel. (02) 375-90-75; telex 22639; f. 1967 to promote the welfare and interest of the world's steel industries; to undertake research in all aspects of steel industries; to serve as a forum for exchange of knowledge and discussion of problems relating to steel industries; to collect, disseminate and maintain statistics and information; to serve as a liaison body between international and national steel organizations. Mems: in 44 countries. Chair. D. M. RODERICK; Sec.-Gen. LENHARD J. HOLSCHUH.

International Organization for Standardization: POB 56, 1 rue de Varembé, 1211 Geneva 20, Switzerland; tel. (022) 412205; telex 412205; f. 1947 to reach international agreement on industrial and commercial standards. Mems: national standards institutions of 90 countries. Pres. I. YAMASHITA; Sec.-Gen. LAWRENCE D. EICHER. Publs *ISO International Standards*, *ISO Memento* (annually), *ISO Catalogue* (annually), *ISO Bulletin* (monthly).

International Research Group on Wood Preservation: Drottning Kristinas väg 47c, 114 28 Stockholm, Sweden; tel. (08) 10 14 53; telex 14375; f. 1965 as Wood Preservation Group by OECD; independent since 1969; consists of five working groups and 17 sub-groups; holds plenary annual meeting. Mems: 345 in 55 countries. Pres. Dr JOHN A. BUTCHER (New Zealand); Sec.-Gen. JÖRAN JERMER (Sweden). Publs technical documents and books, *Annual Report*.

International Rubber Research and Development Board—IRRDB: Chapel Building, Brickendonbury, Hertford, SG13 8NP, England; tel. (0992) 584966; telex 817449; f. 1937. Mems: 15 research institutes. Sec. P. W. ALLEN.

International Society for Photogrammetry and Remote Sensing: c/o Institute of Industrial Science, University of Tokyo, 7–22 Roppongi, Minato-ku, Tokyo, Japan; tel. (03) 4026231, ext. 2560; telex 720242; f. 1910; holds congress every four years, and technical symposia. Mems: 81 countries. Pres. K. TORLEGÅRD (Sweden); Sec.-Gen. S. MURAI (Japan). Publs *International Archives of Photogrammetry and Remote Sensing*, *Photogrammetria*.

International Solar Energy Society: POB 52, National Science Centre, 191 Royal Parade, Parkville, Melbourne, Victoria 3052, Australia; tel. (03) 211-7557; telex 154087; f. 1954 to foster science and technology relating to the applications of solar energy, to encourage research and development, to promote education and to gather, compile and disseminate information in this field; holds international conferences. Mems: 3,600 in 95 countries. Pres. Dr C. CORVI; Sec.-Treas. W. R. READ (Australia). Publs *Journal* (monthly), *Newsletter* (quarterly), *Sunworld* (quarterly).

International Tin Research Institute: Kingston Lane, Uxbridge, Middx, UB8 3PJ, England; tel. (0895) 72406; telex 265451; f. 1932 to develop world consumption of tin; engages in scientific research, technical development and aims to spread knowledge of tin throughout the world by publishing research articles, issuing handbooks, giving lectures and demonstrations, and taking part in exhibitions and trade fairs. Dir B. T. K. BARRY. Publs *Annual Report*, *Tin and its Uses* (quarterly, in English, French, German, Japanese, Italian and Spanish), various studies and reports.

International Union for Vacuum Science, Technique and Applications: c/o Prof. Dr T. E. Madey, Rutgers University, Serin Physics Laboratory, POB 849, Piscataway, NJ 08855, USA; tel. (201) 932-2501; telex 703528; f. 1958; collaborates with the International Standards Organization in defining and adopting technical standards; holds triennial International Vacuum Congress and International Conference on Solid Surfaces; regulates the Welch Foundation for postgraduate research in vacuum science and technology; scientific divisions for surface science, applied surface science, thin film physics, vacuum science, electronic materials and processes, fusion technology and vacuum metallurgy. Mems: organizations in 26 countries. Pres. Prof. Dr H. JAHRREISS (FRG); Sec.-Gen. Prof. Dr THEODORE E. MADEY (USA). Publs *News Bulletin* (every 2 months).

International Union of Heat Distributors: Bahnhofplatz 3, 8023 Zürich, Switzerland; tel. (01) 2113635; telex 814002; f. 1954 to study the various problems concerning the development and distribution of heat for all purposes by means of pipes laid underground. The Union assembles the results of research and tests and puts statistical information at the disposal of the members; holds conference every two years. Mems: 150 companies in 16 countries. Pres. Dr K. FRIEDRICH (Austria); Sec. Dr E. KEPPLER (Switzerland). Publ. *Bulletin* (quarterly).

International Union of Metal: Seestrasse 105, 8002 Zürich, Switzerland; tel. (01) 2017376; telex 57644; f. 1954 for liaison between national bodies to exchange documentation and study common problems. Mems: national federations from Austria, Belgium, Federal Republic of Germany, Luxembourg, Netherlands, Sweden,

OTHER INTERNATIONAL ORGANIZATIONS

Switzerland. Pres. FRANÇOIS BICHEL (Luxembourg); Sec. HANS-JÖRG FEDERER (Switzerland).

International Water Resources Association: 205 North Mathews St, Urbana, Ill 61801 USA; tel. (217) 333-0536; telex 5101011969; f. 1972 to promote collaboration in and support for international water resources programmes; holds conferences; conducts training in water resources management. Pres. PETER J. REYNOLDS (Canada); Sec.-Gen. GLENN E. STOUT (USA). Publs *Water International* (quarterly), *Frontiers in Hydrology*.

International Water Supply Association: 1 Queen Anne's Gate, London, SW1H 9BT, England; tel. (01) 222-8111; telex 918518; f. 1947 to co-ordinate technical, legal and administrative aspects of public water supply; congresses held every two years. Mems: national organizations, water authorities and individuals in 107 countries. Pres. W. H. RICHARDSON; Sec.-Gen. L. R. BAYS (UK). Publs *Aqua* (6 a year), *Water Supply* (quarterly).

Latin-American Energy Organization (Organización Latino-americana de Energía—OLADE): Av. Occidental, OLADE Bldg, Sector San Carlos, POB 6413 CCI, Quito, Ecuador; tel. 538-122; f. 1973 to act as an instrument of co-operation in using and conserving the energy resources of the region. Mems: 26 Latin-American and Caribbean countries. Exec. Sec. AUGUSTO TANDAZO BORRERO (Ecuador). Publ. *Revista Energética*.

Latin-American Iron and Steel Institute: Dario Urzua 1994, Casilla 16065, Santiago 9, Chile; tel. 2237581; telex 340348; f. 1959 to help achieve the harmonious development of iron and steel production, manufacture and marketing in Latin America; conducts economic surveys on the steel sector; organizes technical conventions and meetings; disseminates industrial processes suited to regional conditions; prepares and maintains statistics on production, end uses, prices, etc., of raw materials and steel products within this area. Mems: 91, and 92 associates. Chair. CARLOS A. MAGLIANO; Sec.-Gen. ANÍBAL GÓMEZ. Publs *Siderurgia Latinoamericana* (monthly), *Statistical Year Book, Directory of Latin American Iron and Steel Companies* (every 2 years).

Regional Centre for Services in Surveying, Mapping and Remote Sensing: POB 18118, Nairobi, Kenya; tel. 803320; telex 25258; f. 1975 to provide services in the professional techniques of map-making, and the application of satellites and remote sensing in resource analysis and development planning; to undertake research and provide advisory services to African governments. Mems: 11 signatory and 11 non-signatory governments. Dir-Gen. B. A. SIKILO.

Regional Centre for Training in Aerial Surveys: PMB 5545, Ile-Ife, Nigeria; tel. (234) 2225; telex 34257; f. 1972 for training, research and advisory services; administered by the ECA; bilingual in English and French. Mems: eight governments. Dir Prof. O. AYENI.

World Association of Industrial and Technological Research Organizations—WAITRO: c/o Jutland Technological Institute, Teknologiparken, 8000 Aarhus C, Denmark; tel. (06) 14-24-00; telex 68722; f. 1970 by the UN Industrial Development Organization to encourage co-operation in industrial and technological research, through financial assistance for training and joint activities, arranging international seminars, and allowing the exchange of information; has consultative status with the UN and co-operates closely with UNIDO, UNDP and UNESCO. Mems: about 70 research institutes in 43 countries. Sec.-Gen. S. O. STORM. Publs *Communique* (quarterly).

World Bureau of Metal Statistics: 27A High St, Ware, Herts, SG12 9BA, England; tel. (0920) 61274; telex 817746; f. 1949; statistics of production, consumption, stocks, prices and international trade in copper, lead, zinc, tin, nickel, aluminium and several other minor metals. Gen. Man. J. L. T. DAVIES. Publs *World Metal Statistics* (monthly).

World Federation of Engineering Organizations—WFEO: c/o C. Herselin, 19 rue Blanche, 75009 Paris, France; tel. (1) 45-26-34-82; telex 650594; f. 1968 to advance engineering as a profession in the interests of the world community; to foster co-operation between engineering organizations throughout the world; to undertake special projects through co-operation between members and in co-operation with other international bodies. Mems: 80 national, five international. Pres. S. BEN JEMAA (Tunisia); Sec.-Gen. C. HERSELIN (France).

World Petroleum Congresses: 61 New Cavendish St, London, W1M 8AR, England; tel. (01) 636-1004; telex 264380; f. 1933 to provide an international congress every four years, as a management forum for petroleum economics, science and technology; executive board represents 16 member countries. Pres. Dr KLAUS L. MAI (USA); Sec.-Gen. D. C. PAYNE (UK).

Technology, Tourism

Tourism

Alliance Internationale de Tourisme: 2 quai Gustave Ador, 1207 Geneva, Switzerland; tel. (022) 352727; telex 413103; f. 1898, present title adopted 1919; aims to study all questions relating to international touring and to suggest reforms, to encourage the development of tourism and all matters concerning the motorist, traffic management, road safety, consumer protection and to defend the interests of touring associations. Mems: 130 associations totalling over 70m. members in 87 countries. Pres. B. R. LUNN (Australia); Sec.-Gen. J. WARD (UK).

Arab Tourism Organization: POB 2354, Amman, Jordan; tel. 30340; telex 21471; f. 1954. Mems: national tourist organizations of 21 Arab countries, and four associate members in the private sector. Sec.-Gen. Dr ABDUL RAHMAN ABU RABAH (Jordan). Publs *Arab Tourism Magazine* (every 2 months), *Bulletin* (monthly), studies.

Caribbean Tourism Association—CTA: 20 East 46th St, New York, NY 10017, USA; tel. (212) 682-0435; telex 666916; f. 1951 to encourage tourism in the Caribbean region; to become Caribbean Tourism Organization (based in Barbados) in 1989. Mems: 26 Caribbean governments and 400 allied mems. Dir-Gen. MARKLY WILSON.

East Asia Travel Association: c/o Japan National Tourist Organization, 2-10-1 Yurakucho, Chiyoda-ku, Tokyo, Japan; tel. (03) 216-2905; telex 24132; f. 1966 to promote tourism in the East Asian region, encourage and facilitate the flow of tourists to that region from other parts of the world, and to develop regional tourist industries by close collaboration among members. Mems: six national tourist organizations, seven airlines and two travel associations. Pres. DHARMNOON PRACHUABMOH (Thailand); Sec.-Gen. TETSUYA SATO (Japan).

European Motel Federation—EMF: Jutfaseweg 206, 3522 HS Utrecht, Netherlands; tel. (030) 892282; telex 47009; f. 1956 to represent the interests of European motel-owners. Mems: 133. Sec. H. J. KLOOSTERHUIS (Netherlands).

European Travel Commission: 2 rue Linois, 75015 Paris, France; tel. (1) 45-75-62-16; telex 270974; f. 1948 to promote tourism in and to Europe, particularly from the United States, Canada, Japan, Australia and Latin America, to foster co-operation and the exchange of information, to organize research. Mems: national tourist organizations of 23 European countries. Exec. Dir ROBERT HOLLIER (France); Sec. E. P. KEARNEY.

International Academy of Tourism: 4 rue des Iris, 98000 Monte-Carlo, Monaco; tel. 93-30-97-68; f. 1951 to develop the cultural and humanistic aspects of international tourism and to establish an accepted vocabulary for tourism. Mems: 117. Pres. TIMOTHY O'DRISCOLL; Chancellor LOUIS NAGEL. Publs *Revue, Dictionnaire Touristique International*.

International Association of Scientific Experts in Tourism: Varnbüelstrasse 19, 9000 St Gallen, Switzerland; tel. (071) 302530; telex 77425; f. 1949 to encourage scientific activity by its members; to support tourist institutions of a scientific nature; to organize conventions. Mems: 345 from 40 countries. Pres. Prof. Dr CLAUDE KASPAR (Switzerland); Gen. Sec. Dr HANSPETER SCHMIDHAUSER (Switzerland). Publ. *The Tourist Review* (quarterly).

International Congress and Convention Association: Concertgebouwplein 27, POB 5343, 1007 AH Amsterdam, Netherlands; tel. (020) 664-74-21; telex 11629; f. 1963 to establish worldwide co-operation between all involved in organizing congresses, conventions and exhibitions (including travel agents, airlines, hotels, congress centres and professional congress organizers). Mems: 400 in 70 countries. Sec.-Gen. DICK OUWEHAND. Publ. *TW/ICCA News* (every 2 months).

International Federation of Popular Travel Organizations: Tour Maine Montparnasse, 33 ave du Maine, 75755 Paris Cedex 15, France; tel. (1) 45-38-28-28; telex 260938; f. 1950. Mems: 23 organizations. Pres. ANDRÉ GUIGNAND (France); Sec.-Gen. FLORENCE FOUQUIER (France).

International Federation of Tourist Centres: Brennerstrasse 30, 4820 Bad Ischl, Austria; f. 1949. Mems: Austria, Belgium, France, Federal Republic of Germany, Finland, Italy, Liechtenstein, Netherlands, Norway, Sweden, Switzerland, United Kingdom. Pres. Dr ALDO DEBENE (Austria); Sec.-Gen. KONRAD BERTHOLD (Liechtenstein).

International Ho-Re-Ca: Gotthardstrasse 61, 8027 Zürich, Switzerland; tel. (01) 2012611; f. 1949 to bring together national associations of hotel, restaurant and café proprietors to further the interests of the trade, international tourism, etc. Mems: 29 national organizations. Pres. JOCHEN KOEPP (FRG); Gen. Sec. Dr XAVER FREI (Switzerland).

International Hotel Association: 80 rue de la Roquette, 75544 Paris Cedex 11, France; tel. (1) 47-00-84-57; telex 216410; f. 1946 to link internationally national hotel associations and hotels active in international tourism; to consider all questions of interest to the international hotel industry; to assist in the employment of qualified hotel staff and the exchange of students; to distribute information. Mems: 90 national hotel associations, 220 restaurants, 240 affiliate mems, 95 national and international chains, and 3,600 hotels. Pres. PETER BALAS (USA); Gen. Sec. RAYMOND K. FENELON (UK). Publs *Hotels and Restaurants International* (monthly), *International Hotel Guide* (annually), *Directory of Travel Agencies* (annually), *Opportunities Newsletter* (6 a year), *Dialogue* (every 2 months).

Latin-American Confederation of Tourist Organizations: Viamonte 640, 8°, 1053 Buenos Aires, Argentina; tel. 392-4003; telex 23385; f. 1957 to link Latin American national associations of travel agents and their members with other tourist bodies around the world. Mems: in 19 countries and affiliate mems in 70 countries. Pres. GUILLERMO SALABRIA; Sec.-Gen. CARLOS A. PATRANI; Publs *Revista COTAL* (monthly), *Aqui-Cotal Newsletter*.

Pacific Asia Travel Association—PATA: 1 Montgomery St, Suite 1750, San Francisco, Calif 94104, USA; tel. (415) 986-4646; f. 1951 for the promotion of travel to and between the countries and islands of the Pacific; regional offices in Singapore and Sydney; holds annual conference, seminars. Mems: governments, carriers, travel agents, tour operators and hotels in 68 countries and territories. Exec. Vice-Pres. KENNETH L. CHAMBERLAIN. Publs *Pacific Travel News* (monthly).

Universal Federation of Travel Agents' Associations—UFTAA: 1 rue Defacqz, 1050 Brussels, Belgium; tel. (02) 537-03-20; telex 61808; f. 1966 to unite travel agents associations, to represent the interests of travel agents at the international level, to help in international legal differences; issues literature on travel, etc. Mems: national associations of travel agencies in 81 countries. Sec.-Gen. (vacant).

World Association of Travel Agencies: 37 Quai Wilson, 1201 Geneva, Switzerland; tel. (022) 314760; telex 22447; f. 1949 to foster the development of tourism, to help the rational organization of tourism in all countries, to collect and disseminate information and to participate in all commercial and financial operations which will foster the development of tourism. Individual travel agencies may use the services of the world-wide network of 250 members. Pres. URS BAUER (Switzerland); Sec.-Gen. HERVÉ CHOISY (Switzerland).

World Tourism Organization: Calle Capitán Haya 42, 28020 Madrid, Spain; tel. 5710628; telex 42188; f. 1975 to promote travel and tourism; undertakes technical co-operation, and the protection of tourists and tourist facilities; provides training and information (including statistics). There are six regional commissions and a General Assembly is held every two years. Mems: governments of 108 countries; also four associate members, one observer, and 151 affiliated tourism organizations. Sec.-Gen. WILLIBALD PAHR.

Trade and Industry

African Regional Organization for Standardization: POB 57363, Nairobi, Kenya; tel. 24561; telex 22097; f. 1977 to promote standardization, quality control, certification and metrology in the African region, formulate regional standards, and co-ordinate participation in international standardization activities. Mems: 23 states. Sec.-Gen. ZAWDU FELLEKE.

Arab Iron and Steel Union—AISU: BP 4, Cheraga, Algiers, Algeria; tel. 78 15 78; telex 63158; f. 1972 to develop commercial and technical aspects of Arab steel production by helping member associations to commercialize their production in Arab markets, guaranteeing them high quality materials and intermediary products, informing them of recent developments in the industry and organizing training sessions. Mems: 71 producers in 14 Arab countries. Gen. Sec. MUHAMMAD LAID LACHGAR. Publs *Arab Steel Review* (monthly), *Information Bulletin* (2 a month), *Directory* (annually).

Asian Productivity Organization: 4-14 Akasaka, 8-chome, Minato-ku, Tokyo 107, Japan; tel. (03) 4087221; f. 1961 to strengthen the productivity movement in the Asian region and disseminate technical knowledge. Mems: 17 countries. Sec.-Gen. NAGAO YOSHIDA. Publs *APO News* (monthly), *Annual Report*.

Association of African Trade Promotion Organizations—AATPO: BP 23, Tangier, Morocco; tel. 41687; telex 33695; f. 1975 under the auspices of the OAU and the ECA to foster regular contact between African states in trade matters and to assist in the harmonization of their commercial policies in order to promote intra-African trade; conducts research and training; organizes meetings and trade information missions. Mems: 26 states. Sec.-Gen. Dr FAROUK SHAKWEER. Publs *FLASH: African Trade* (monthly), *Directory of Trade Information Sources in Africa*, *Directory of State Trading Organizations*, *Directory of Importers and Exporters of Food Products in Africa*.

Association of European Chambers of Commerce (EUROCHAMBERS): 5 rue Archimède, 1040 Brussels, Belgium; tel. (02) 231-07-15; telex 25315; f. 1958 to promote the exchange of experience and information among its members and to bring their joint opinions to the attention of the institutions of the European Community; conducts studies and seminars. Mems: associations in the EEC member states; seven associate and corresponding mems; Pres. H. PATTBERG (FRG); Sec.-Gen. H. J. VON BÜLOW (FRG).

Committee for European Construction Equipment—CECE: 22–26 Dingwall Rd, Croydon, Surrey, CR9 2PL, England; tel. (01) 688-4422; telex 9419625; f. 1959 to further contact between manufacturers, to improve market conditions and productivity and to conduct research into techniques. Mems: representatives from Belgium, Finland, France, Federal Republic of Germany, Italy, Sweden, United Kingdom. Pres. H.-D. VON BERNUTH (FRG); Sec.-Gen. D. BARRELL (UK).

Committee of European Foundry Associations: 2 rue de Bassano, 75783 Paris Cedex 16, France; tel. (1) 47-23-55-50; telex 620617; f. 1953 to safeguard the common interests of European foundry industries; to collect and exchange information. Mems: associations in 13 countries. Pres. M. BECCARIA (Italy); Sec.-Gen. J. P. BURDEAU.

Confederation of Asia-Pacific Chambers of Commerce and Industry: 10th Floor, 122 Tunhua North Rd, Taipei 10590, Taiwan; tel. 7163016; telex 11144; f. 1966; holds biennial conferences to examine regional co-operation; undertakes liaison with governments in the promotion of laws conducive to regional co-operation; serves as a centre for compiling and disseminating trade and business information; encourages contacts between businesses; conducts training and research. Mems: national chambers of commerce and industry of Australia, Hong Kong, India, Indonesia, Japan, Republic of Korea, New Zealand, the Philippines, Sri Lanka, Taiwan and Thailand; also affiliate, associate and special mems. Dir-Gen. JOHNSON C. YEN.

Confederation of European Soft Drinks Associations—CESDA: 51 ave Général de Gaulle, 1050 Brussels, Belgium; tel. (02) 649-12-86; f. 1961 to promote co-operation among the national associations of soft drinks manufacturers on all industrial and commercial matters, to stimulate the sales and consumption of soft drinks, to deal with matters of interest to all member-associations and to represent the common interests of member-associations and authorities; holds a congress every two years. Pres. R. DELVILLE; Gen. Sec. P. E. FOSSEPREZ.

Confederation of International Contractors' Associations: 9 rue Lapérouse, 75116 Paris, France; tel. (1) 47-20-80-74, telex 613456; f. 1974 to promote co-operation and the exchange of information among building contractors' federations. Mems: four international associations (Europe, Asia and the Western Pacific, North America and Latin America). Pres. RICHARD E. HALL; Sec.-Gen. ERIC LEPAGE.

Co-ordinating Committee for Multilateral Export Controls—COCOM: 58 bis rue de la Boétie, 75008 Paris, France; f. 1949; aims to prevent the transfer of military technology to communist countries, by controlling the sale of strategically important goods by Western exporters. Mems: governments belonging to NATO (with the exception of Iceland) and Japan.

Customs Co-operation Council: 26–38 rue de l'Industrie, 1040 Brussels, Belgium; tel. (02) 513-99-00; telex 61597; f. 1950 to study all questions relating to co-operation in customs matters, and examine technical aspects, bearing in mind economic factors, of customs systems with a view to attaining uniformity; preparation of conventions and recommendations; ensuring uniform interpretation and application of customs conventions (e.g. on valuation and tariff nomenclature), and conciliatory action in case of dispute; circulation of information and advice regarding Customs regulations and procedures and co-operation with other international organizations. Mems: governments of 104 countries or territories. Chair. B. ERIKSSON (Sweden); Sec.-Gen. G. R. DICKERSON (USA). Publs *Bulletin* (annually), *CCC News*.

Economic Research Committee of the Gas Industry: 4 ave Palmerston, 1040 Brussels, Belgium. Mem. organizations in Austria, Belgium, Denmark, Federal Republic of Germany, France, Ireland, Italy, Netherlands, Spain, Sweden, Switzerland, United Kingdom. Pres. R. G. HAVAUX (Belgium); Gen. Sec. L. BLOM (Belgium).

European Association of Advertising Agencies: 28 ave du Barbeau, 1160 Brussels, Belgium; f. 1960 to maintain and to raise the standards of service to advertisers of all European advertising agencies, and to strive towards uniformity in fields where this would be of benefit; to serve the interests of all agency members in Europe. Mems: 16 national advertising agency associations and 23 multinational agency groups. Pres. DAVID CAMPBELL-HARRIS; Sec.-Gen. RONALD BEATSON. Publ. *Bulletin*.

OTHER INTERNATIONAL ORGANIZATIONS — Trade and Industry

European Association of Manufacturers of Radiators—EURORAD: Walchestrasse 27, 8023 Zürich, Switzerland; f. 1966 to represent the national associations of manufacturers of radiators made of steel and cast iron, intended to be attached to central heating plants and which convey heat by natural convection and radiation without the need for casing. Mems: in 12 countries. Pres. G. VANDENSCHRIECK (Belgium); Gen. Sec. K. EGLI (Switzerland).

European Association of National Productivity Centres: 60 rue de la Concorde, 1050 Brussels, Belgium; tel. (02) 511-71-00; f. 1966 to enable members to pool knowledge about their policies and activities, specifically as regards the relative importance of various productivity factors, and the ensuing economic and social consequences; co-operation with the OECD, UN bodies and Asian productivity centres. Mems: 18 European, North American and Australasian centres. Pres. ZOLTAN ROMAN; Sec.-Gen. A. C. HUBERT. Publs *EPI* (quarterly), *EUROproductivity* (monthly), *Annual Report*.

European Brewery Convention: POB 510, 2380 BB Zoeterwoude, Netherlands; tel. (071) 814047; telex 39390; f. 1947, present name adopted 1948; aims to promote scientific co-ordination in brewing. Mems: national associations in Austria, Belgium, Denmark, Finland, France, Federal Republic of Germany, Italy, Luxembourg, Netherlands, Norway, Portugal, Spain, Sweden, Switzerland, United Kingdom. Pres. T. M. ENARI (Finland); Sec.-Gen. Mrs M. VAN WIJNGAARDEN (Netherlands).

European Ceramic Association: 44 rue Copernic, 75116 Paris, France; tel. (1) 45-00-18-56; telex 611913; f. 1948 to improve techniques of the industry and promote use all of types of ceramics. Mems: national organizations in Austria, Belgium, Denmark, Finland, France, Federal Republic of Germany, Greece, Italy, Luxembourg, Netherlands, Norway, Portugal, Spain, Sweden, Switzerland, United Kingdom. Pres. HELMUT LEHMANN (FRG); Sec. ROBERT BOUCHET (France).

European Committee for Standardization (Comité européen de normalisation—CEN): 2 rue Bréderode, Bte 5, 1000 Brussels, Belgium; tel. (02) 513-55-64; telex 26257; f. 1961 to promote European standardization and provide the CEN conformity certification marking system and the CEN system of mutual recognition of test and inspection results, so as to eliminate obstacles caused by technical requirements in order to facilitate the exchange of goods and services. Mems: 16 national standards bodies. Sec.-Gen. EVANGELOS VARDAKAS.

European Committee of Associations of Manufacturers of Agricultural Machinery: 19 rue Jacques Bingen, 75017 Paris, France; tel. (1) 47-66-02-20; telex 640362; f. 1959 to study economic and technical problems, to protect members' interests and to disseminate information. Mems: Austria, Belgium, Denmark, Finland, France, Federal Republic of Germany, Italy, Netherlands, Spain, Sweden, Switzerland, United Kingdom. Pres. R. PACKO (Belgium); Sec.-Gen. R. PICARD (France).

European Committee of Paint, Printing Ink and Artists' Colours Manufacturers' Associations: 49 square Marie Louise, 1040 Brussels, Belgium; tel. (02) 230-78-09; telex 23167; f. 1951 to study questions relating to paint and printing ink industries, to take or recommend measures for their development and interests, to exchange information. Mems: national associations in 16 European countries. Pres. B. BENEDINI (Italy); Gen. Sec. H.-A. LENTZE (Belgium).

European Committee of Textile Machinery Manufacturers: Kirchenweg 4, Postfach, 8032 Zürich, Switzerland; telex 816519; f. 1952; organizes international textile machinery exhibitions. Mems: organizations in Belgium, France, Federal Republic of Germany, Italy, Netherlands, Spain, Switzerland, United Kingdom. Pres. E. G. SMALLEY (UK); Sec. Dr J. MERMOD (Switzerland).

European Confederation of Iron and Steel Industries—EUROFER: 5 square de Meeûs, Bte 9, 1040 Brussels, Belgium; tel. (02) 512-98-30; telex 62112; f. 1976 as a confederation of national federations or companies in the steel industries of member states of the European Coal and Steel Community to foster co-operation between the member federations and to represent their common interests to the EEC and other international organizations. Mems: Belgium, Denmark, France, Federal Republic of Germany, Ireland, Italy, Luxembourg, Netherlands, Portugal, Spain, United Kingdom. Dir-Gen. H.-G. VORWERK.

European Confederation of Woodworking Industries: 109–111 rue Royale, 1000 Brussels, Belgium; tel. (02) 217-63-65; telex 64143; f. 1952 to act as a liaison between national organizations, to undertake research and to defend the interests of the industry. Mems: national federations in 13 European countries and European sectoral organizations in woodworking. Pres. M. ROUGIER (France); Sec.-Gen. Dr G. VAN STEERTEGEM.

European Council of Chemical Manufacturers' Federations: 250 ave Louise, bte 71, 1050 Brussels, Belgium; tel. (02) 640-20-95; telex 62444; represents and defends the interests of the chemical industry relating to legal and trade policy, internal market, environmental and technical matters; liaises with intergovernmental organizations. Mems: 15 national federations and 34 major Europe-based companies. Dir.-Gen. Drs H. H. LEVER.

European Federation of Associations of Insulation Enterprises: 10 rue du Débarcadère, 75852 Paris Cedex 17, France; tel. (1) 40-55-13-70; telex 644044; f. 1970; groups the organizations in Europe representing insulation firms including thermal insulation, soundproofing and fire-proofing insulation; aims to facilitate contacts between member associations, to study any problems of interest to the profession, to safeguard the interests of the profession and represent it in international forums. Mems: professional organizations in 15 European countries. Chair. W. B. MACMILLAN; Vice-Chair. J. EPAILLY, T. WREDE.

European Federation of Handling Industries: POB 179, Kirchenweg 4, 8032 Zürich, Switzerland; tel. (01) 478400; telex 816519; f. 1953 to facilitate contact between members of the profession, conduct research, standardize methods of calculation and construction and promote standardized safety regulations. Mems: organizations in 13 European countries. Sec. E. HORAT (Switzerland).

European Federation of Management Consultants' Associations: 3 rue Léon Bonnat, 75016 Paris, France; tel. (1) 45-24-43-53; telex 612938; f. 1960 to bring management consultants together and promote a high standard of professional competence in all European countries concerned, by encouraging discussions of, and research into, problems of common professional interest. Mems: 15 associations. Gen. Sec. E. LABOUREAU.

European Federation of Associations of Particle Board Manufacturers: 63 Giessen, Wilhelmstrasse 25, Federal Republic of Germany; telex 482877; f. 1958 to develop and encourage international co-operation in the particle board industry. Pres. T. BOJSEN-MØLLER (Denmark); Sec.-Gen. A. KRIER (FRG). Publs *Annual Report*, technical documents.

European Federation of Plywood Industry: 30 ave Marceau, 75008 Paris, France; f. 1957 to organize joint research between members of the industry at international level. Mems: associations in eight European countries. Pres. B. HAUSMANN (FRG); Sec.-Gen. PIERRE LAPEYRE.

European Federation of Productivity Services: c/o Sveriges Rationaliseringsförbund SRF, Tjärhovsgatan 8A, 11621 Stockholm, Sweden; tel. (8) 249225; telex 8106304; f. 1961 to promote throughout Europe the application of productivity services; to promote and support the development of the practice and techniques of industrial and commercial productivity and efficiency; and to provide a contact network for the exchange of information and ideas. Mems: 14, and three corresponding organizations. Pres. W. HELMS; Exec. Sec. K. HELMRICH.

European Federation of Tile and Brick Manufacturers: Obstgartenstrasse 28, 8035 Zürich, Switzerland; f. 1952 to co-ordinate research between members of the industry, improve technical knowledge, encourage professional training. Mems: associations in Austria, Belgium, Denmark, Finland, France, Federal Republic of Germany, Ireland, Italy, Netherlands, Norway, Spain, Sweden, Switzerland, United Kingdom. Chair. C. KOREVAAR.

European Furniture Manufacturers Federation: 15 rue de l'Association, 1000 Brussels, Belgium; tel. (02) 218-18-89; telex 61933; f. 1950 to determine and support general interests of the European furniture industry, facilitate contacts between members of the industry, and to support the Federation's decisions internally and internationally. Mems: organizations in Belgium, Denmark, France, Federal Republic of Germany, Italy, Norway, Spain, Sweden, Switzerland, United Kingdom, Yugoslavia. Pres. R. RODRÍGUEZ; Sec.-Gen. B. DE TURCK.

European General Galvanizers Association: c/o Zinc Development Association, 34 Berkeley Square, London, W1X 6AJ, England; tel. (01) 499-6636; telex 261286; f. 1955 to promote co-operation between members of the industry, especially in improving processes and finding new uses for galvanized products; maintains a film and photographic section and library. Mems: associations in Austria, Belgium, Denmark, Finland, France, Federal Republic of Germany, Italy, Netherlands, Norway, Portugal, Spain, Sweden, Switzerland, United Kingdom. Pres. A. MOHRENSCHILDT (Italy).

European Glass Container Manufacturers' Committee: Northumberland Rd, Sheffield, S10 2UA, England; tel. (0742) 686201; telex 547591; f. 1951 to facilitate contacts between members of the industry, inform them of legislation regarding it. Mems: representatives from 15 European countries. Sec. D. K. BARLOW (UK).

European Organization for Quality—EOQC: POB 2613, 3001 Berne, Switzerland; tel. (031) 216111; telex 912110; f. 1956 to encourage the use and application of quality control with the intent to improve quality, reduce costs and increase productivity; organizes annual congresses for the exchange of information, documentation, etc. Member organizations in all European countries.

OTHER INTERNATIONAL ORGANIZATIONS

Trade and Industry

Pres. Prof. JOHN A. GOLDSMITH; Sec. M. CONRAD (Switzerland). Publs *Quality* (quarterly), *Glossary, Sampling Books, Specifications Guide, Quality Survey in Automotive Industry, Reliability Book*.

European Packaging Federation: c/o Nederlands Verpakkingscentrum NVC, Postbus 164, 2800 Gouda, Netherlands; f. 1953 to encourage the exchange of information between national packaging institutes and to promote technical and economic progress. Mems: organizations in Austria, Belgium, Denmark, Finland, France, Federal Republic of Germany, Hungary, Italy, Netherlands, Poland, Spain, Sweden, Switzerland, United Kingdom. Sec.-Gen. GERT SCHAAP (Netherlands).

European Patent Office—EPO: 8000 Munich 2, Erhardtstrasse 27, Federal Republic of Germany; tel. (089) 2399; telex 523656; f. 1977 to grant European patents according to the Munich convention of 1973; conducts searches and examination of patent applications. Mems: Austria, Belgium, France, Federal Republic of Germany, Greece, Italy, Liechtenstein, Luxembourg, Netherlands, Spain, Sweden, Switzerland, United Kingdom. Pres. P. BRAENDLI (Switzerland); Chair. Admin. Council Prof. O. LEBERL (Austria). Publs *Annual Report, Official Journal* (monthly), *European Patent Bulletin, European Patent Applications, Granted Patents*.

European Society for Opinion and Marketing Research—ESOMAR: J. J. Viottastraat 29, 1071 JP Amsterdam, Netherlands; tel. (020) 64-21-41; telex 18535; f. 1948 to further professional interests and encourage high technical standards. Mems: about 2,100 in 45 countries. Pres. BRYAN A. BATES (UK); Dir FERNANDA MONTI (Netherlands). Publs *European Research* (4 a year), *Newsbrief* (6 a year), *Marketing Research in Europe* (annually).

European Union of Coachbuilders: 46 Woluwedal, bte 14, 1200 Brussels, Belgium; tel. (02) 771-17-42; f. 1948 to promote research on questions affecting the industry, exchange information, and establish a common policy for the industry. Mems: national federations in Belgium, France, Federal Republic of Germany, Italy, Luxembourg, Netherlands, Switzerland, United Kingdom. Pres. G. BAETEN (Belgium); Sec.-Gen. KRIS BOSTOEN (Belgium).

General Union of Chambers of Commerce, Industry and Agriculture for Arab Countries: POB 11-2837, Beirut, Lebanon; tel. 814269; telex 20347; f. 1951 to foster Arab economic collaboration, to increase and improve production and to facilitate the exchange of technical information in Arab countries. Mems: Chambers of Commerce, Industry and Agriculture in 22 Arab countries. Gen. Sec. BURHAN DAJANI. Publ. *Arab Economic Report* (Arabic and English).

Gulf Organization for Industrial Consulting: POB 5114, Doha, Qatar; tel. 831234; telex 4619; f. 1976 by seven Gulf Arab states to pool industrial expertise and encourage joint development of projects. Sec.-Gen. Dr ABDULLAH AL-MOAJIL (Saudi Arabia). Publs *Arab Gulf Industry* (quarterly), *Bulletin* (monthly), *Gulf Industrial Focus* (every 2 months), *Annual Report*.

Inter-American Commercial Arbitration Commission: 1889 F St, NW, Room 440-C, Washington, DC 20006, USA; tel. (202) 789-3444; telex 64128; f. 1934 to establish an inter-American system of arbitration for the settlement of commercial disputes by means of tribunals. Mems: national committees, commercial firms and individuals in 22 countries. Dir CHARLES R. NORBERG.

International Advertising Association Inc: 342 Madison Ave, Suite 2000, New York, NY 10017, USA; tel. (212) 557-1133; telex 983-0455; f. 1938 to raise the general level of advertising and marketing efficiency throughout the world; to promote the concept of freer trade and facilitate the interchange of ideas, experience and information. Mems: 2,700. Pres. CLAY S. TIMON (USA); Exec. Dir MARY W. COVINGTON (USA). Publs *IAA Membership Directory and Annual Report, International Advertiser Magazine*.

International Association for Business Research and Corporate Development: Gainsford House, 115 Station Rd, West Wickham, Kent, BR4 0PX, England; tel. (01) 777-9200; telex 8951165; f. 1965 to facilitate contacts between researchers; holds annual conferences and seminars; main specialist divisions: European chemical marketing research; European technological forecasting; paper and related industries; industrial materials; automotive; textiles; methodology. Mems: 700. Pres. DAVID A. CLARK (France); Gen. Sec. A. L. WADDAMS.

International Association of Buying Groups: 5000 Cologne 1, Lindenstr. 20, Federal Republic of Germany; tel. (0221) 219456; f. 1951 for research, documentation and compilation of statistics; holds congress every three years. Mems: 80 buying groups in 12 countries. Sec.-Gen. Dr GÜNTER OLESCH.

International Association of Chain Stores: 61 quai d'Orsay, Paris 7e, France; tel. (1) 47-05-48-43; telex 206387; f. 1953; links general merchandise and food retail companies and their suppliers; organizes annual congress and symposia to exchange ideas on trends, techniques and practices, and to improve professional standards and consumer service. Mems: 500 companies in 30 countries. Chair. HELMUT NANZ; CEO ETIENNE LAURENT. Publ. *CIES Communication* (2 a year).

International Association of Congress Centres (Association internationale des palais de Congrès—AIPC): c/o Muzejski prostor, Jezuitski trg 4, POB 19, 41000 Zagreb, Yugoslavia; tel. (041) 433-722; telex 22398; f. 1958 to unite conference centres fulfilling certain criteria, to study the administration and technical problems of international conferences, to promote a common commercial policy and co-ordinate all elements of conferences. Mems: 73 from 29 countries. Pres. MATTHIAS FUCHS; Sec.-Gen. RADOVAN VOLMUT (Yugoslavia). Publ. list of principal conferences of the world (3 a year).

International Association of Department Stores: 72 blvd Haussmann, 75008 Paris, France; tel. (1) 43-87-25-80; f. 1928 to conduct research, exchange information and statistics on management, organization and technical problems; centre of documentation. Mems: large-scale retail enterprises in Andorra, Belgium, Denmark, Finland, France, Federal Republic of Germany, Italy, Netherlands, Norway, Spain, Sweden, United Kingdom; associate mem. in Japan. Pres. GEORGES MEYER (France); Gen. Sec. E. KALDEREN (Sweden). Publ. *Retail News Letter* (monthly).

International Association of Electrical Contractors: 5 rue Hamelin, 75116 Paris, France; tel. (1) 47-27-97-49; telex 620 993. Pres. KARL F. HAAS.

International Association of Insurance and Reinsurance Intermediaries: 47 rue d'Alsace, 75010 Paris France; tel. (1) 46-07-04-40; telex 250303; f. 1937. Mems: 41 associations from 29 countries, representing approx. 250,000 brokers and agents. Dir HARALD KRAUSS. Publ. *Lettre* (5 a year).

International Association of Scholarly Publishers: c/o Edvard Aslaksen, Universitetsforlaget, POB 2959 Toyen, 0608 Oslo 6, Norway; tel. (2) 677600; telex 71896; f. 1972 for the exchange of information and experience on scholarly and academic publishing by universities and others; assists in the transfer of publishing skills to developing countries. Mems: 139 in 40 countries. Pres. EDVARD ASLAKSEN (Norway); Sec.-Gen. DOROTHY J. ANTHONY (USA). Publs *IASP Newsletter* (every 2 months), *International Directory of Scholarly Publishers*.

International Association of Textile Dyers and Printers: Reedham House, 31 King St West, Manchester, M3 2PF, England; tel. (061) 834-7871; telex 666737; f. 1967 to defend and promote the interests of members in international affairs and to provide a forum for discussion of matters of mutual interest. Mems: national trade associations representing dyers and printers in nine countries. Pres. Dr ANDREAS RHOMBERG (Austria); Sec.-Gen. BARRY G. HAZEL (UK).

International Booksellers Federation—IBF: 1010 Vienna, Grünangergasse 4, Austria; tel. (0222) 512-15-35; f. 1956 to promote the booktrade and the exchange of information and to protect the interests of booksellers when dealing with other international organizations; special committees deal with questions of postage, resale price maintenance, book market research, advertising, customs and tariffs, the problems of young booksellers, etc.; consultative relationship with UNESCO. Mems: 200 in 26 countries. Pres. PETER MEILI; Sec.-Gen. Dr GERHARD PROSSER. Publs *IBF-bulletin* (4 a year), *Booksellers International*.

International Bureau for the Standardization of Man-Made Fibres: Lautengartenstrasse 12, 4010 Basel, Switzerland; tel. 236250; telex 964331; f. 1928 to examine and establish rules for the standardization, classification and naming of various categories of man-made fibres. Mems: 62. Sec.-Gen. Dr H. L. SARASIN.

International Confederation for Printing and Allied Industries—INTERGRAF: 18 square Marie-Louise, bte 25, 1040 Brussels, Belgium; tel. (02) 230-86-46; telex 64393; f. 1983 (formerly EUROGRAF, f. 1975) to defend the common interests of the printing and allied interests in member countries. Mems: federations in 15 countries. Pres. W. J. PRICE; Sec.-Gen. GEOFFREY WILSON.

International Confederation of Art Dealers: 1 bis rue Clément Marot, 75008 Paris, France; f. 1936 to co-ordinate the work of associations of dealers in works of art and paintings and to contribute to artistic and economic expansion. Mems: associations in 14 countries. Pres. EMILE BOURGEY (France).

International Confederation of the Butchers' and Delicatessen Trade: Steinwiesstrasse 59, 8028 Zürich, Switzerland; tel. (01) 2527766; f. 1946 to safeguard common interests. Sec.-Gen. Dr H. GERBER.

International Co-operative Alliance—ICA: 15 route des Morillons, 1218 Grand-Saconnex, Geneva, Switzerland; tel. (022) 984121; telex 27935; f. 1895 for the pursuit of co-operative aims: regional offices in India, Tanzania and Côte d'Ivoire; Congress meets every four years; 13 auxiliary committees exist for the sharing of technical expertise by co-operative organizations in the following fields: agriculture, banking, fisheries, consumer affairs, wholesale distribution, housing, insurance, women's participation and industrial and artisanal co-operatives; annual budget about £500,000 obtained from subscriptions. Mems: 500m. individuals in 705,640 co-operative societies. Pres. LARS MARCUS (Sweden); Dir R. BEASLEY (USA). Publs *Review of International Co-operation* (quarterly).

International Council of Shopping Centres: 665 Fifth Ave, New York, NY 10022, USA; tel. (212) 421-8181; telex 128185; f. 1957 as a trade association for the shopping centre industry, to promote professional standards of performance in the development, construction, financing, leasing and management of shopping centres throughout the world; organizes training courses; gives awards for new centres. Exec. Vice-Pres. JOHN T. RIORDAN.

International Council of Societies of Industrial Design—ICSID: Kluuvikatu 1D, 00100 Helsinki, Finland; tel. (90) 626661; telex 124723; f. 1957 to encourage the development of high standards in the practice of industrial design; to improve and expand the contribution of industrial design throughout the world. Mems: in 38 countries. Pres. ROBERT I. BLAICH (Netherlands); CEO KAARINA POHTO. Publ. *ICSID News* (5 or 6 a year).

International Council of Tanners: 192 High St, Lewes, East Sussex, BN7 2NP, England; tel. (0273) 472149; telex 21505; f. 1926 to study all questions relating to the leather industry and maintain contact with national associations. Mems: national tanners' organizations in 35 countries. Pres. PERTTI HELLEMAA (Finland); Sec. G. G. REAKS (UK).

International Exhibitions Bureau: 56 ave Victor Hugo, Paris 16e, France; tel. (1) 45-00-38-63; f. 1928, revised by Protocol 1972, for the authorization and registration of international exhibitions falling under the 1928 Convention. Mems: 45 states. Pres. JACQUES SOL-ROLLAND; Sec.-Gen. MARIE-HÉLÈNE DEFRENE.

International Federation for Household Maintenance Products: 49 sq. Marie-Louise, 1040 Brussels, Belgium; tel. (02) 230-40-90; telex 23167; f. 1967 to promote in all fields the manufacture and use of a wide range of cleaning products, polishes, bleaches, disinfectants and insecticides, to develop the exchange of statistical information and to study technical, scientific, economic and social problems of interest to its members. Mems: in 10 countries. Pres. G. F. BISCHOFF; Sec. P. COSTA (Belgium).

International Federation of Associations of Specialists in Occupational Safety and Hygiene: Verhagenstraat 36, 9000 Ghent, Belgium; tel. (091) 22-30-23; f. 1952 (as European Federation of Associations of Engineers and Heads of Industrial Safety Services); promotes the prevention of accidents at work and of occupational illnesses; provides information exchange, training and education programmes, and international conferences. Pres. A. DE BOCK.

International Federation of Associations of Textile Chemists and Colourists—IFATCC: 4133 Pratteln, Postfach 93, Switzerland; f. 1930 for liaison on professional matters between members; and the furtherance of scientific and technical collaboration in the development of the textile finishing industry and the colouring of materials. Mems: in 13 countries. Pres. Dr W. KRUCKER (Switzerland); Sec. Dr PIERRE ALBRECHT (Switzerland).

International Federation of Grocers' Associations—IFGA: Falkenplatz 1, 3001 Berne, Switzerland; tel. (031) 237646; f. 1927; initiates special studies and works to further the interests of members having special regard to new conditions resulting from European integration and developments in consuming and distribution. Mems: 500,000. Sec.-Gen. PETER SCHUETZ (Switzerland).

International Federation of Phonogram and Videogram Producers: 54 Regent St, London, W1R 5PJ, England; tel. (01) 434-3521; telex 919044; f. 1933; association of the worldwide sound and music video recording industry, making representations to governments and international bodies and generally defending the interests of its members. Mems: 890 in 62 countries. Pres. NESUHI ERTEGUN; Dir-Gen. I. D. THOMAS.

International Fragrance Association—IFRA: 8 rue Charles-Humbert, 1205 Geneva, Switzerland; tel. (022) 213548; telex 428354; f. 1973 to collect and study scientific data on fragrance materials and to make recommendations on their safe use. Mems: national Associations in 14 countries. Pres. HORST F. W. GEBERDING; Sec.-Gen. F. GRUNDSCHOBER.

International Fur Trade Federation: 69 Cannon St, London, EC4N 5AB, England; tel. (01) 248-4444; telex 888941; f. 1949 to promote and organize joint action by fur trade organizations for promoting, developing and protecting trade in furskins and/or processing thereof. Mems: 32 organizations in 29 countries. Pres. J. E. POSER (USA); Sec. J. KRAUSE.

International Group of National Associations of Manufacturers of Agrochemical Products: 79A ave Albert Lancaster, 1180 Brussels, Belgium; tel. (02) 375-68-60; telex 62120; f. 1967 to encourage the rational use of chemicals in agriculture, the harmonization of national and international legislation, and the respect of industrial property rights; encourages research on chemical residues and toxicology. Mems: associations in 20 countries. Dir-Gen. HANS G. VAN LOEPER.

International Organization for Motor Trades and Repairs: Veraartlaan 12, 2288 GM Rijswijk, Netherlands; tel. (70) 907222; telex 31296; f. 1947 to collect and disseminate information about all aspects of the trade; to hold meetings and congresses. Mems: 36 associations in 26 countries. Pres. J. A. WILLIAMS (UK); Gen. Sec. J. A. HOEKZEMA (Netherlands). Publ. *Newsletter*.

International Organization of Consumers' Unions—IOCU: Emmastraat 9, 2595 EG The Hague, Netherlands; tel. (070) 47-63-31; telex 33561; f. 1960; links consumer groups worldwide through information networks and international seminars; supports new consumer groups and represents consumers' interests at the international level. Mems: 170 national associations in 58 countries. Dir-Gen. (vacant). Publs *IOCU Newsletter* (10 a year), *Consumer Currents* (10 a year).

International Organization of Motor Manufacturers: 4 rue de Berri, 75008 Paris; tel. (1) 43-59-00-13; telex 290012; f. 1919 to co-ordinate and further the interests of the automobile industry, to promote the study of economic and other matters affecting automobile construction; to control automobile manufacturers' participation in international exhibitions in Europe. Full mems: manufacturers' associations of 15 European countries, Japan and the USA. Assoc. mems: three importers' associations. Corresponding mems: five automobile associations. Pres. S. PININFARINA (Italy); Gen. Sec. J. M. MULLER. Publ. *Yearbook of the World's Motor Industry*.

International Organization of the Flavour Industry—IOFI: 8 rue Charles-Humbert, 1205 Geneva, Switzerland; tel. (022) 213548; telex 428354; f. 1969 to support and promote the flavour industry; active in the fields of safety evaluation and regulation of flavouring substances. Mems: national associations in 21 countries. Pres. F. RIJKENS; Sec.-Gen. F. GRUNDSCHOBER. Publs *Documentation Bulletin* (monthly), *Information Letters*, *Code of Practice*.

International Publishers' Association: 3 ave de Miremont, 1206 Geneva, Switzerland; tel. (022) 463018; telex 421883; f. 1896 to defend the freedom of publishers, promote their interests and foster international co-operation; helps the international trade in books and music, works on international copyright, and translation rights. Mems: 48 professional book publishers' organizations in 43 countries and music publishers' associations in 20 countries. Pres. ANDREW NEILLY; Sec.-Gen. J. ALEXIS KOUTCHOUMOW.

International Rayon and Synthetic Fibres Committee: 29 rue de Courcelles, Paris 8e, France; tel. (1) 45-63-87-10; telex 650931; f. 1950 to improve the quality and use of rayon and man-made fibres and of products made from fibres. Mems: national associations and individual producers in 17 countries. Pres. Dr G. METZ (FRG); Dir-Gen. Prof. J. L. JUVET.

International Shopfitting Organisation: Schmelzbergstr. 56, 8044 Zürich, Switzerland; tel. (01) 473540; telex 816207; f. 1959 to promote friendship and interchange of ideas between individuals and firms concerned with the common interests of shopfitting. Mems: companies in 16 countries. Pres. J. RABEY; Sec. O. MALZ.

International Textile Manufacturers Federation—ITMF: Am Schanzengraben 29, Postfach, 8039 Zürich, Switzerland; tel. (01) 2017800; telex 56798; f. 1904, present title adopted 1978. Aims to protect and promote the interests of its members, to disseminate information, and encourage co-operation. Mems: national textile trade associations in 44 countries. Pres. M. MANGALDAS (India); Dir Dr HERWIG STROLZ (Austria). Publs *Newsletter*, *State of Trade Report* (quarterly), statistics.

International Union of Marine Insurance: Aeschengraben 21, 4002 Basel, Switzerland; f. 1873 to collect and distribute information on marine insurance on a world-wide basis. Mems: 50 associations. Pres. A. W. KAMP; Gen. Sec. E. BURCKHARDT.

International Whaling Commission: The Red House, Station Rd, Histon, Cambridge, CB4 4NP, England; tel. (022 023) 3971; telex 817960; f. 1946 under the International Convention for the Regulation of Whaling, for the conservation of the world whale stocks; aims to review the regulations covering the operations of whaling; to encourage research relating to whales and whaling, to collect and analyse statistical information and to study and disseminate information concerning methods of increasing whale stocks; a ban on commercial whaling was passed by the Commission in July 1982, to take effect three years subsequently (although, in some cases, a phased reduction of commercial operations was not completed until 1988). An assessment of the effects on whale stocks of this ban was to be completed by 1990, when modifications were to be considered. Mems: governments of 38 countries. Chair. S. IRBERGER (Sweden); Sec. Dr R. GAMBELL. Publ. *Annual Report*.

International Wool Textile Organisation: 165 Queen Victoria St, London, EC4 4DD, England; tel. (01) 788-8876; f. 1929 to link wool textile organizations in member-countries and represent their

OTHER INTERNATIONAL ORGANIZATIONS — Trade and Industry, Transport

interests; holds annual International Wool Conference. Mems: in 28 countries. Pres. JEAN-MARIE SEGARD (France); Sec.-Gen. W. H. LAKIN (UK).

International Wrought Copper Council: 6 Bathurst St, Sussex Sq., London, W2 2SD, England; tel. (01) 723-7465; telex 23556; f. 1953 to bind together and represent the copper fabricating industries in the member countries, and to represent the views of copper consumers to raw material producers; organizes specialist activities on technical work, development of copper and uses, accident prevention. Mems: 15 national groups representing non-ferrous metals industries in all West European countries, Australia and Japan. Chair. Dr J. M. BUTLER; Sec. S. N. PAYTON.

Liaison Organization of the European Engineering Industries: 99 rue de Stassart, 1050 Brussels, Belgium; tel. (02) 511-34-84; telex 21078; f. 1954 to provide a permanent liaison between the mechanical, electrical and electronic engineering, and metalworking industries of member countries. Mems: 23 trade associations in 15 West European countries. Pres. FRANK BOTTRUP (Denmark); Sec.-Gen. TREVOR GAY.

Union of Industrial and Employers' Confederations of Europe—UNICE: 40 rue Joseph II, 1040 Brussels, Belgium; tel. (02) 237-65-11; telex 26013; aims to ensure that European Community policy-making takes account of the views of industry; committees and working groups work out joint positions in the various fields of interest to industry and submit them to the Community institutions concerned. The Council of Presidents (of member federations) lays down general policy; the Executive Committee (of Directors-General of member federations) is the managing body; and the Committee of Permanent Delegates, consisting of federation representatives in Brussels, ensures permanent liaison with members. Mems: 17 industrial and employers' federations from the EEC member states, and 16 federations from non-Community countries. Pres. KARL-GUSTAF RATJEN; Sec.-Gen. ZYGMUNT TYSZKIEWICZ. Publ. *Report* (every 2 months).

Union of International Fairs: 35 bis, rue Jouffroy, 75017 Paris, France; tel. (1) 42-67-99-12; telex 644097; f. 1925 to increase co-operation between international fairs, safeguard their interests and extend their operations; holds annual congress. The Union has defined the conditions to be fulfilled to qualify as an international fair, and is concerned with the standards of the fairs. It studies improvements which could be made in the conditions of the fairs and organizes training seminars. Mems: 140 organizers, 66 general fairs and 326 specialized exhibitions. Pres. Prof. CARLO G. BERTO-LOTTI (Italy); Sec.-Gen. GERDA MARQUARDT (France).

World Council of Management—CIOS: c/o RKW, 6236 Eschborn, Düsseldorfstr. 40, POB 5867, Federal Republic of Germany; tel. (06196) 495366; telex 4072755; f. 1926 to promote the understanding of the principles and the practice of the methods of modern management; to organize conferences, congresses and seminars on management; to exchange information on management techniques; to promote training programmes. Mems: national organizations in 45 countries. Pres. ARNO MOCK (FRG); Sec. HERBERT MÜLLER (FRG). Publ. *Newsletter*.

World Federation of Advertisers: 54 rue des Colonies, Bte 13, 1000 Brussels; tel. (02) 219-06-98; telex 63801; f. 1953; promotes and studies advertising and its related problems. Mems: associations in 33 countries and 21 international companies. Dir P. P. DE WIN.

World Packaging Organisation: 42 ave de Versailles, 75016 Paris, France; tel. (1) 42-88-29-74; telex 648838; f. 1967 to provide a forum for the exchange of knowledge of packaging technology and, in general, to create conditions for the conservation, preservation and distribution of world food production; holds annual congress and competition. Mems: Asian, North American, Latin American and European packaging federations. Pres. PIERRE SCHMIT (France); Gen. Sec. PIERRE J. LOUIS (France).

World Trade Centers Association: One World Trade Center, Suite 7701, New York, NY 10048, USA; tel. (212) 313-4600; telex 285472; f. 1968 to promote trade through the establishment of world trade centres, including education facilities, information services and exhibition facilities. Mems: trade centres, chambers of commerce and other organizations in 53 countries. Pres. GUY F. TOZZOLI; Chair. TADAYOSHI YAMADA. Publs *WTCA News* (monthly), *World Traders* (quarterly).

Transport

African Airlines Association: POB 20116, Nairobi, Kenya; tel. 502645; f. 1968 to give African air companies expert advice in technical, financial, juridical and market matters; to improve communications in Africa; to represent the mem. airlines; and to develop manpower resources. Mems: 35 national carriers. Sec.-Gen. Capt. FRANK OKYNE.

Arab Air Carriers' Organization—AACO: POB 130468, Chouran, Beirut, Lebanon; tel. 861294; telex 22370; f. 1965 to co-ordinate and promote co-operation in the activities of Arab airline companies. Mems: 18 Arab air carriers. Pres. Air Maj.-Gen. ADNAN AL-JABI (Syria); Sec.-Gen. ADLI DAJANI.

Arab Union of Railways: POB 6599, Aleppo, Syria; tel. 220302; telex 331009; f. 1979 to stimulate co-operation between railways in Arab countries, and to co-ordinate the interconnection of Arab railways with each other and with international railways; holds Symposium every two years. Mems: 16, comprising railways of Algeria, Iraq, Jordan, Lebanon, Morocco, Sudan, Syria, Tunisia; construction companies in Morocco, Tunisia and Syria; the Arab Union of Land Transport; and the Palestine Liberation Organization. Gen. Sec. MOURHAF SABOUNI. Publs *Al Sikak Al Arabie* (Arab Railways, quarterly), *Statistics of Arab Railways* (annually), *Glossary of Railway Terms* (Arabic, English, French and German).

Association of European Airlines: 350 ave Louise, Bte 4, 1050 Brussels, Belgium; tel. (02) 640-31-75; telex 22918; f. 1954 to carry out research on political, commercial, economic and technical aspects of air transport; maintains statistical data bank. Mems: 21 airlines. Pres. J. DE LENCASTRE (Portugal); Sec.-Gen. KARL-HEINZ NEUMEISTER.

Baltic and International Maritime Council—BIMCO: 19 Kristianiagade, 2100 Copenhagen, Denmark; tel. (01) 26-30-00; telex 19086; f. 1905 to unite shipowners and other persons and organizations connected with the industry. Mems: in 104 countries, representing nearly 50% of world merchant tonnage. Pres. Dr HELMUT SOHMEN; Sec.-Gen. TORBEN C. SKAANILD.

Central Commission for the Navigation of the Rhine: Palais du Rhin, 67082 Strasbourg Cedex, France; tel. (88) 32-35-84; f. 1815 to ensure free movement of traffic and standard river facilities to ships of all nations; draws up navigational rules, standardizes customs regulations, arbitrates in disputes involving river traffic, approves plans for river maintenance work; there is an administrative centre for social security for boatmen, and a tripartite commission for labour conditions. Mems: Belgium, France, Federal Republic of Germany, Netherlands, Switzerland, United Kingdom. Pres. M. HÖYNCK; Sec.-Gen. R. DOERFLINGER (France).

Central Office for International Carriage by Rail: Thunplatz, 3006 Berne, Switzerland; tel. (031) 431762; telex 912063; f. 1893; maintains and publishes lists of lines on which international carriage is undertaken; circulates communications from the contracting States and railways to other States and railways; publishes information on behalf of international transport services; undertakes conciliation, gives an advisory opinion or assists in arbitration on disputes arising between railways; examines requests for the amendment of the Conventions concerning International Carriage by Rail, and convenes conferences. Mems: 34 states. Dir-Gen. PETER TRACHSEL. Publ. *Bulletin des Transports Internationaux ferroviaires* (every 2 months, in French and German).

Danube Commission: Benczúr utca 25, 1068 Budapest, Hungary; tel. 228-083; f. 1948 to supervise facilities for shipping on the Danube; holds annual sessions; approves projects for river maintenance, supervises a uniform system of traffic regulations on the whole navigable portion of the Danube. Mems: seven countries on the Danube. Pres. V. KOTZEV (Bulgaria); Sec. F. SCHMID (Austria). Publs *Basic Regulations for Navigation on the Danube, Hydrological Yearbook, Statistical Yearbook*.

European Civil Aviation Conference—ECAC: 3 bis Villa Emile-Bergerat, 92522 Neuilly-sur-Seine Cedex, France; tel. (1) 46-37-96-96; telex 610075; f. 1955 to review the development of European air transport with the object of promoting the co-ordination, the better utilization, and the orderly development of such air transport, and to consider any special problem that might arise in this field. Mems: 22 European states. Pres. DETLEF WINTER; Sec. EDWARD HUDSON.

European Conference of Ministers of Transport—ECMT: 19 rue Franqueville, 75775 Paris Cedex 16, France; tel. (1) 45-24-82-00; telex 611040; f. 1953 to achieve the maximum use and most rational development of European inland transport. Council of Ministers of Transport meets twice yearly; Committee of Deputy Ministers meets six times a year and is assisted by Subsidiary Bodies concerned with; General Transport Policy, Railways, Roads, Inland Waterways, Investment, Road and Traffic Signs and Signals, Urban Safety and Economic Research. Mems: 19 European countries; Associate Mems: Australia, Canada, Japan, USA. Chair. A. CABALLERO (Spain); Sec.-Gen. Dr J. C. TERLOUW.

European Organisation for the Safety of Air Navigation—EUROCONTROL: 72 rue de la Loi, 1040 Brussels, Belgium; tel. (02) 233-02-11; telex 21173; f. 1963 to strengthen co-operation among member states in matters of air navigation. Permanent Commission is governing body, consisting of two representatives from each member state, who are the Ministers responsible for civil and military aviation; there are four Directorates: Operations (incl. Central Data Bank), Engineering, Personnel and Finance, and

OTHER INTERNATIONAL ORGANIZATIONS — Transport

General Secretariat. The EUROCONTROL External Services comprise the Eurocontrol Experimental Centre, the EUROCONTROL Institute of Air Navigation Services, the Central Route Charges Office and the Upper Area Control Centre at Maastricht, Netherlands. Budget (1988) 199.24m. ECUs. Mems: Belgium, France, Federal Republic of Germany, Greece, Ireland, Luxembourg, Netherlands, Portugal, United Kingdom. Pres. Perm. Commission Lord BRABAZON OF TARA (UK); Pres. Cttee of Management GEORGES VERHOEVEN (Belgium); Dir-Gen. KEITH MACK (UK).

European Passenger Train Time-Table Conference: Direction générale des chemins de fer fédéraux suisses, Hochschulstrasse 6, 3030 Berne, Switzerland; tel. (031) 601111; telex 991121; f. 1923 to arrange international passenger connections by rail and water and to help obtain easing of customs and passport control at frontier stations. Mems: rail and steamship companies and administrations, representatives of governments and other organizations in 25 countries. Administered by the Directorate of the Swiss Federal Railways.

European Railway Wagon Pool—EUROP: SNCB, Département Transport, 85 rue de France, 1070 Brussels, Belgium; tel. (02) 525-41-30; telex 21526; f. 1953 for the common use of wagons put into the pool by member railways. Mems: nine national railway administrations. Managing railway: Belgian Railways. Pres. J. DEKEMPENEER.

Institute of Air Transport: 103 rue La Boétie, 75008 Paris, France; tel. (1) 43-59-38-68; telex 642584; f. 1945 to serve as an international centre of research on economic, technical and policy aspects of air transport, and on the economy and sociology of transport and tourism; acts as economic and technical consultant in carrying out research requested by members on specific subjects; maintains a data bank, a library and a consultation and advice service; organizes training courses on air transport economics. Mems: organizations involved in air transport, production and equipment, universities, banks, insurance companies, private individuals and government agencies in 79 different countries. Pres. HENRI SAUVAN; Dir-Gen. JACQUES PAVAUX. Publs in French and English, *ITA Magazine* (every 2 months), *ITA Newsletter* (2 a month).

International Air Transport Association—IATA: POB 160, 26 chemin de Joinville, 1216 Cointrin-Geneva, Switzerland; tel. (022) 983366; telex 23391; f. 1945 to promote safe, regular and economic air transport, to foster air commerce and to provide a means of international air transport collaboration. Fields of activity: finance (through IATA Clearing House for international accounts), technical problems, air traffic fares and documentation, international law on conditions of contract and carriage, documentation and information research and international co-operation. Exec. Cttee of 25 members, assisted by Financial, Legal, Technical and Traffic Cttees; Tariff Co-ordinating Conferences on fares and rates meet regularly; there are Traffic Service Offices in Montreal and Singapore; Regional Technical Offices for Africa in Nairobi and Dakar, Europe in Geneva, Middle East, North Atlantic/North America in London, South America/Caribbean in Rio de Janeiro and South East Asia/Pacific in Bangkok. Mems: 172 companies. Dir-Gen. GÜNTER ESER; Corporate Sec. Mrs H. AUBRY.

International Association for the Rhine Vessels Register—IVR: Koningin Emmaplein 6, 3016 AA Rotterdam (POB 23210, 3001 KE Rotterdam), Netherlands; tel. (010) 4361133; telex 22600; f. 1947 for the classification of Rhine ships, the organization and publication of a Rhine ships register and for the unification of general average rules, etc. Mems: shipowners and associations, insurers and associations, shipbuilding engineers, average adjusters and others interested in Rhine traffic. Dir J. W. THISSEN.

International Association of Ports and Harbors: Kotohira-Kaikan Bldg, 2-8 Toranomon 1-chome, Minato-ku, Tokyo 105, Japan; tel. (03) 591-4261; telex 02222516; f. 1955 to increase the efficiency of ports and harbours through the dissemination of information relative to the fields of port organization, management, administration, operation, development and promotion; to encourage the growth of water-borne commerce. Mems: 359 in 78 states. Pres. WONG HUNG KHIM (Singapore); Sec.-Gen. HIROSHI KUSAKA (Japan). Publs *Ports and Harbors* (10 a year), *Membership Directory* (annually), *Proceedings of Conference*.

International Automobile Federation: 8 place de la Concorde, 75008 Paris, France; tel. (1) 42-65-99-51; telex 290442; f. 1904 to develop international automobile sport and motor touring. Represented at UN (ECOSOC), Council of Europe and EEC. Mems: 107 national automobile clubs or associations in 95 countries. Pres. JEAN-MARIE BALESTRE; Sec.-Gen. J. J. FREVILLE.

International Chamber of Shipping: 30/32 St. Mary Axe, London, EC3A 8ET, England; tel. (01) 283-2922; telex 884008; f. 1921 to co-ordinate the views of the international shipping industry on matters of common interest, notably in the technical and legal fields of shipping operations. Mems: national associations representative of free enterprise shipowners in 34 countries, covering 50% of world merchant shipping. Sec.-Gen. J. C. S. HORROCKS.

International Civil Airports Association—ICAA: Bâtiment 226, Orly Sud 103, 94396 Orly Aérogare Cedex, France; tel. (1) 49-75-44-70; telex 261120; f. 1962 to develop relations and co-operation among civil airports throughout the world and promote the interests of air transport in general. Mems: 250 from 90 countries and territories. Pres. CLIFTON A. MOORE (USA); Dir-Gen. JACQUES BLOCK (France). Publs *ICAA INFO*, *ICAA News*.

International Container Bureau: 14 rue Jean Rey, 75015 Paris, France; tel. (1) 47-34-68-13; telex 270835; f. 1933 to group representatives of all means of transport and activities concerning containers, to promote combined door-to-door transport by the successive use of several means of transport; to examine and bring into effect administrative, technical and customs advances and to centralize data on behalf of its members. Mems: 800. Pres. C. SEIDELMANN. Publs *Containers* (quarterly), *Container Bulletin*.

International Federation of Freight Forwarders' Associations: Baumackerstr. 24, POB 8493, 8050 Zürich, Switzerland; f. 1926 to protect and represent its members at international level. Mems: 60 organizations and 1,400 associate members in 130 countries. Pres. A. N. PARIKH; Sec.-Gen. Dr F. GYSSENS; Dir-Gen. K. JAGERS-BACKER. Publ. *FIATA News* (quarterly).

International Rail Transport Committee: Direction générale des chemins de fer fédéraux suisses, Service juridique, 43 Mittelstrasse, 3030 Berne, Switzerland; tel. (031) 602565; telex 691212; f. 1902 for the development of international law relating to railway transport on the basis of the Convention concerning International Carriage by Rail and its Appendices, and for the adoption of standard rules on other questions relating to international transport law. Mems: 300 transport undertakings in 34 countries Pres. M. LATSCHA (Switzerland); Sec. M. BERTHERIN (Switzerland).

International Railway Congress Association: 85 rue de France, 1070 Brussels, Belgium; tel. (02) 522-62-83; f. 1885 to facilitate the progress and development of railways by holding periodical congresses and by issuing publications. Mems: governments, railway administrations and national or international organizations. Pres. E. FLACHET; Sec.-Gen. L. VERBERCKT. Publs *Rail International* (monthly in French, German, Russian and English).

International Road Federation—IRF: 525 School St, SW, Washington, DC 20024, USA; tel. (202) 554-2106; telex 44036; f. 1948 to encourage the development and improvement of highways and highway transportation; organizes World Highway Conferences. Mems: 68 national road associations and 500 individual firms and industrial associations. *Geneva:* Chair. JEAN CLOUET; Dir-Gen. E. CARRON DE LA CARRIÈRE; *Washington:* Chair. WILLIAM G. MULLIGAN; Pres. W. J. WILSON. Publs *World Road Statistics* (annually, Geneva), *Routes du Monde* (8 a year), *World Highways* (9 a year), *IRF Directory of World Road Administrators* (Geneva/Washington).

International Road Safety: 75 rue de Mamer, 8081 Luxembourg-Bertrange; tel. 31 83 41; telex 2338; f. 1959 for exchange of ideas and material on road safety; organizes international action; assists non-member countries; consultative status at UN and Council of Europe. Mems: 58 national organizations. Pres. L. NILLES. Publ. quarterly liaison bulletin.

International Road Transport Union—IRU: Centre International, 3 rue de Varembé, BP 44, 1202 Geneva, Switzerland; tel. (022) 341330; telex 27107; f. 1948 to study all problems of road transport, to promote unification and simplification of regulations relating to road transport, and to develop the use of road transport for passengers and goods. Mems: 120 national federations for road transport and interested groups, in 52 countries. Sec.-Gen. P. GROENENDIJK.

International Shipping Federation Ltd: 30/32 St Mary Axe, London, EC3A 8ET, England; tel. (01) 283-2922; telex 884008; f. 1909 to consider all personnel questions affecting the interests of shipowners; responsible for Shipowners' Group at conferences of the International Labour Organisation. Mems: national shipowners' organizations in 28 countries. Pres. J. B. HUTCHISON (UK); Dir J. LUSTED; Sec. D. A. DEARSLEY.

International Union for Inland Navigation: 7 quai du Général Koenig, 67085 Strasbourg Cedex, France; tel. 88-36-28-44; f. 1952 to promote the interests of inland waterways carriers before all international organizations. Mems: national waterways organizations of Belgium, France, Federal Republic of Germany, Italy, Luxembourg, Netherlands, Switzerland, United Kingdom. Pres. P. DE PROOST (Belgium); Sec. M. RUSCHER (France). Publs annual and occasional reports.

International Union of Public Transport: 19 ave de l'Uruguay, 1050 Brussels, Belgium; tel. (02) 673-33-25; telex 63916; f. 1885 to study all problems connected with the urban and regional public passenger transport industry. Mems: 400 public transport systems in 68 countries, 251 contractors and services and 904 personal members. Pres. I. BÄCKSTRÖM (Sweden); Sec.-Gen. PIERRE

LACONTE. Publs *Review* (quarterly), *Biblio-Index* (quarterly), Compendium of Statistics.

International Union of Railways: 14 rue Jean-Rey, 75015 Paris, France; tel. (1) 42-73-01-20; telex 270835; f. 1922 for the harmonization of railway operations; compiles information concerning economic, management and technical aspects of railways. Mems: 84 railways. Chair. R. GOHLKE; Sec.-Gen. J. BOULEY. Publs *Rail International*, jointly with the International Railway Congress Association (IRCA) (monthly, in English, French and German), *International Railway Statistics* (annually, in English, French and German), Annual Report.

Northern Shipowners' Defence Club (Nordisk Skibsrederforening): Kristinelundv. 22, POB 3033 El., 0207 Oslo 2, Norway; f. 1889 to assist members in disputes over contracts, taking the necessary legal steps on behalf of members and bearing the cost of such claims. Members are mainly Finnish, Swedish and Norwegian and some non-Scandinavian shipowners, representing about 1,500 ships and drilling rigs with gross tonnage of about 37 million. Man. Dir NICHOLAS HAMBRO; Chair. FRIDTJOF LORENTZEN. Publ. *A Law Report of Scandinavian Maritime Cases* (annually), and a quarterly members' periodical.

Organisation for the Collaboration of Railways: Hozà 63-67, 00681 Warsaw, Poland; tel. 21 61 54; f. 1956 for the development of international traffic and technical and scientific co-operation in the sphere of railway and road traffic. Conference of Ministers of member countries meets annually. Mems: ministries of transport of the People's Republic of China, Cuba, Democratic People's Republic of Korea, Mongolia, Viet-Nam, Albania, Bulgaria, Czechoslovakia, German Democratic Republic, Hungary, Poland, Romania and USSR. Chair. Dr RYSZARD STAWROWSKI (Poland). Publ. *O.S.SH.D. Journal* (bi-monthly; in Chinese, German and Russian).

Orient Airlines Association: POB 161 MCPO, Makati, Metro Manila, Philippines; tel. 8190151; f. 1967; member carriers exchange information and plan the development of the industry within the region by means of research, technical, security, data processing and marketing committees. Mems: Air New Zealand, Air Niugini, All Nippon Airways, Cathay Pacific Airways Ltd, China Airlines, Japan Air Lines, Korean Air, Malaysian Airline System, Philippine Airlines, Qantas Airways Ltd, Singapore Airlines, Royal Brunei Airlines and Thai Airways International. Sec.-Gen. MICHAEL C. HEWITT. Publs *MIC Monthly Bulletin*, *Annual Report*, *Operating Manual*.

Pan American Railway Congress Association (Asociación del Congreso Panamericano de Ferrocarriles): Av. 9 de Julio 1925, 13°, 1332 Buenos Aires, Argentina; tel. 38 4625; telex 22507; f. 1907; present title adopted 1941; aims to promote the development and progress of railways in the American continent; holds Congresses every three years. Mems: government representatives, railway enterprises and individuals in 21 countries. Pres. JUAN CARLOS DE MARCHI (Argentina); Gen. Sec. CAYETANO MARLETTA RAINIERI (Argentina). Publ. *Technical Bulletin* (every 2 months).

Union of European Railway Industries: 12 rue Bixio, 75007 Paris, France; tel. (1) 47-05-36-62; telex 270105; f. 1975 as a union of associations which represent companies concerned in the manufacture of railway equipment in Europe, in order to represent their collective interests towards all European and international organizations concerned. Chair. M. O. J. BRONCHART; Sec.-Gen. J. L. BURCKHARDT.

Union of European Railway Road Services: Direction générale de la Société Nationale des Chemins de Fer Français (SNCF), 88 rue Saint-Lazare, 75436 Paris, France; f. 1950/1951; runs the EUROPABUS international railway road services, an international network of scheduled coach services covering 100,000 km. Mems: railway administrations in Austria, Belgium, Denmark, France, Federal Republic of Germany, Greece, Hungary, Italy, Luxembourg, Netherlands, Norway, Portugal, Spain, Sweden, Switzerland and the United Kingdom. Pres. LOUIS LACOSTE (France); Sec.-Gen. (vacant).

World Airlines Clubs Association: c/o IATA, Suite 3050, 2000 Peel St, Montreal, Quebec, Canada H3A 2R4; f. 1966; holds a General Assembly annually, regional meetings, international events and sports tournaments. Mems: 98 clubs in 42 countries. Pres. DAVID LARKIN (UK); Man. JOSEPH LEDWOS. Publs *WACA World*, *WACA Contact*, *WACA World News*, annual report.

Youth and Students

Asian Students' Association: 511 Nathan Rd, 1/F, Kowloon, Hong Kong; tel. 880515; telex 52988; f. 1969 to help in the solution of local and regional problems; to assist in promotion of an Asian identity; to promote programmes of common benefit to member organizations; since 1972 the organization has opposed all forms of colonialism or foreign intervention in Asia; activities: Conference, Seminars, Workshops. There are Student Commissions for Economics, Education, Students' Rights, Women's Affairs, and a Nuclear-Free and Independent Pacific. Mems: 14 national or regional student unions, 12 associate co-operating mems. Co-Secs. EMMANUEL CALONZO, BOONTHAN T. VERAWONGSE. Publ. *Asian Student News*.

Council of European National Youth Committees—CENYC: 8 ave des Courses, 1050 Brussels, Belgium; f. 1963 to further the consciousness of European youth and to represent the European National Co-ordinating Committees of youth work vis-à-vis European institutions. Activities include research on youth problems in Europe; projects, seminars, study groups, study tours; the Council provides a forum for the exchange of information, experiences and ideas between members, and represents European youth organizations in relations with other regions; has observer status with the Council of Europe and UNESCO. Mems: national committees in 16 countries. Sec.-Gen. RACHEL KYTE (UK). Publ. *CENYC Contact* (quarterly).

Council on International Educational Exchange: 205 East 42nd St, New York, NY 10017, USA; tel. (212) 661-1414; f. 1947; issues International Student Identity Card entitling holders to discounts and to accommodation in student hostels and restaurants; arranges passage on intra-European student flights and trans-Atlantic transport; offers students short-term unskilled jobs in Europe and New Zealand for full-time US university students, and similar work programmes in the USA for students from participating countries in Europe and New Zealand; provides low-cost accommodation in New York City; co-ordinates summer programmes in the USA for foreign students and teachers; sponsors conferences on educational exchange; publications list overseas programmes for high school and college students, sources of information on independent student travel abroad and describe transport and student travel services. Mems: 186 student organizations. Exec. Dir JACK EGLE. Publs include *Annual Report*, *Work, Study, Travel Abroad: The Whole World Handbook*, *Campus Update* (monthly).

International Association for the Exchange of Students for Technical Experience—IAESTE: Instituto Superior Técnico, Av. Rovisco Pais, 1096 Lisbon Codex, Portugal; tel. 890844; telex 63423; f. 1948. Mems: 50 national committees. Gen. Sec. Prof. BERNARDO J. HEROLD. Publ. *Annual Report*.

International Association of Dental Students: 64 Wimpole St, London, W1M 8AL, England; f. 1951 to represent dental students and their opinions internationally, to promote dental student exchanges and international congresses. Mems: 20,000 students in 19 countries (and 15,000 corresponding mems). Pres. S. SMITH (UK); Sec.-Gen. JILL ADAM (UK). Publ. *IADS Newsletter* (3 a year).

International Association of Students in Economics and Management: 40 rue Washington, POB 10, 1050 Brussels, Belgium; tel. (02) 648-88-03; telex 65080; f. 1948 to contribute to the development of member countries through international education programmes, e.g. trainee exchanges, seminars, conferences and study tours. Mems: 40,000 from 560 universities in 67 countries. Pres. MATTHEW DE VILLIERS. Publs *Compendium*, *Annual Report*, *Linkletter*, *Programmes Manual*.

International Federation of Medical Students Associations: 1090 Vienna, Liechtensteinstr. 13, Austria; tel. (022) 31-55-66; telex 116706; f. 1951 to study and promote the professional interests of medical students throughout the world; to improve medical education, and arrange international exchanges and projects in primary health care. Mems: national associations in 65 countries, corresponding mems in 34 countries. Sec.-Gen. KLEOPATRA ORMOS. Publ. *Intermedica*.

International Pharmaceutical Students' Federation: Alexanderstraat 11, 2514 JL The Hague, Netherlands; tel. (070) 63-19-25; f. 1949 to study and promote the interests of pharmaceutical students and to encourage international co-operation. Mems: 27 national organizations and 17 local associations. Pres. RUI DOS SANTOS IVO; Sec.-Gen. ILAN KREISER. Publ. *IPSF News Bulletin* (3 a year).

International Union of Students: POB 58, 17 November St, 110 01 Prague 01, Czechoslovakia; tel. 231 28 12; telex 122858; f. 1946 to defend the rights and interests of students and strive for peace, disarmament, the eradication of illiteracy and of all forms of discrimination; activities include conferences, meetings, solidarity campaigns, relief projects, award of 300 scholarships, travel and exchange, sports events, cultural projects. Mems: 109 organizations from 105 countries. Pres. MIROSLAV ŠTĚPÁN (Czechoslovakia); Gen. Sec. GIORGOS MICHAELIDES (Cyprus). Publs *World Student News* (monthly), *News Service* (fortnightly), *Young Cinema and Theatre* (quarterly), *DE—Democratization of Education* (quarterly), regional bulletins and newsletters.

International Young Christian Workers: 11 rue Plantin, 1070

Brussels, Belgium; tel. (02) 521-69-83; f. 1945, on the inspiration of the Priest-Cardinal Joseph Cardijn; aims to educate young workers to take on present and future responsibilities in their commitment to the working class, and to confront all the situations which prevent them from fulfilling themselves. Pres. FÉLIX OLLARVES SÁNCHEZ (Venezuela); Sec.-Gen. GLYNN CLOETE (South Africa).

International Youth and Student Movement for the United Nations—ISMUN: c/o Palais des Nations, 1211 Geneva 10, Switzerland; tel. (022) 330861; f. 1948 by the World Federation of United Nations Associations, independent since 1949; an international non-governmental organization of students and young people dedicated especially to supporting the principles embodied in the United Nations Charter and Universal Declaration of Human Rights; encourages constructive action in building economic, social and cultural equality and in working for national independence, social justice and human rights on a worldwide scale; regional offices in Austria, France, Ghana, Panama and the USA. Mems: associations in 53 countries. Sec.-Gen. JUAN CARLOS GIACOSA. Publs *ISMUN Newsletter* (monthly).

International Youth Hostel Federation: 9 Guessens Rd, Welwyn Garden City, Herts., AL8 6QW, England; tel. (0707) 324170; telex 298784; f. 1932; facilitates international travel by members of the various youth hostel associations and advises and helps in the formation of youth hostel associations in all countries where no such organizations exist; records over 34m. overnight stays annually in 5,000 youth hostels. Mems: 57 national associations with 4m. individual members; 13 associated national organizations. Pres. OTTO WIRTHENSOHN (FRG); Sec.-Gen. DENNIS LEWIS (Canada). Publs *Annual Report, Guidebook on World Hostels* (annually), *Manual, Monthly News Bulletin, Phrase Book*.

Jaycees International: 400 University Drive (POB 140-577), Coral Gables, Fla 33134-0577, USA; tel. (305) 446-7608; telex 441084; f. 1944 to encourage and advance international understanding and goodwill. Jaycee organizations throughout the world provide young people with opportunities for leadership training, promoting goodwill through international fellowship, solving civic problems by arousing civic consciousness and discussing social, economic and cultural questions. Mems: over 400,000 in 80 countries. Pres. PHILLIP R. BERRY; Sec.-Gen. W. DANIEL LAMEY. Publs *Leader* (annually, in English, Spanish, French, Japanese, Korean and Chinese), *Leader-Extra* (quarterly).

Latin American Confederation of Young Men's Christian Associations (Confederación Latinoamericana de Asociaciones Cristianas de Jóvenes): Casilla 172, Montevideo, Uruguay; tel. 49-71-94; telex 23106; f. 1914 to unite the Young Men's Christian Associations of the continent; to secure the moral, spiritual, intellectual, social and physical development of young men; to strengthen the work of the Associations and to sponsor the establishment of new Associations. Mems: affiliated YMCAs in 14 countries, with over 500,000 individuals. Pres. RAÚL BEATI (Argentina); Gen. Sec. EDGARDO CROVETTO (Peru). Publs *Articulos Técnicos, Revista Trimestral, Informes Internacionales*.

Pan-African Youth Movement (Mouvement pan-africain de la jeunesse): 19 rue Debbih Chérif, BP 72, Plateau Saulière, Algiers, Algeria; tel. 57-19-78; telex 61244; f. 1962; promotes political independence and the economic, social and cultural development of Africa; serves as the voice of African youth in regional and international forums. Mems: over 40 organizations. Sec.-Gen. HAMADOUN IBRAHIM ISSEBERE. Publ. *MPJ News* (quarterly).

World Alliance of Young Men's Christian Associations: 37 quai Wilson, 1201 Geneva; tel. (022) 323100; telex 27332; f. 1855 to unite the National Alliances of Young Men's Christian Associations throughout the world. Mems: national alliances and related associations in 97 countries. Pres. ALEJANDRO VASSILAQUI; Sec.-Gen. LEE SOO-MIN. Publ. *World Communique* (quarterly).

World Association of Girl Guides and Girl Scouts: Olave Centre, 12c Lyndhurst Rd, London, NW3 5PQ, England; tel. (01) 794-1181; f. 1928 to promote unity of purpose and common understanding in the fundamental principles of the Girl Guide and Girl Scout Movement throughout the world and to encourage friendship amongst girls of all nations within frontiers and beyond; World Conference meets every three years. Mems: about 8m. individuals in 112 organizations. Chair. World Cttee ODILE BONTE; Dir World Bureau ELLEN CLARK; Publs *Triennial Report, Trefoil Round the World, Newsletter*.

World Council of Young Men's Service Clubs: c/o J. Bennett, Polton Rd, Loanhead, EH20 9DB, Scotland; tel. (031) 440-1236; telex 727285; f. 1946 to provide a means of exchange of information and news for furthering international understanding and co-operation, to facilitate the extension of young men's service clubs, and to create in young men a sense of civic responsibility. Mems: 4,000 clubs (about 100,000 individuals) in 76 countries. Gen. Sec. JOHN B. BENNETT.

World Federation of Democratic Youth—WFDY: POB 147, 1389 Budapest, Hungary; tel. 154-095; telex 22-7197; f. 1945 to strive for peace and disarmament and joint action by democratic and progressive youth movements in support of national independence, democracy, social progress and youth rights; to support liberation struggles in Asia, Africa and Latin America; and to work for a new and more just international economic order; 12th Assembly, Budapest, Hungary, November 1986. Mems: 270 organizations in 115 countries. Pres. WALID MASRI (Lebanon); Gen. Sec. VILMOS CSERVENY (Hungary). Publs *WFDY News* (fortnightly, in English, French and Spanish), *World Youth* (monthly, in English, French and Spanish).

World Organization of the Scout Movement: Case Postale 241, 1211 Geneva 4, Switzerland; tel. (022) 204233; telex 428139; f. 1922 to promote unity and understanding of scouting throughout the world; to develop good citizenship among young people by forming their characters for service, co-operation and leadership; to provide aid and advice to members and potential member associations. The World Scout Bureau (Geneva) has regional offices in Costa Rica, Egypt, Kenya, the Philippines and Switzerland. Mems: over 16m. in 150 countries and territories. Sec.-Gen. Dr JACQUES MOREILLON (Switzerland). Publs *World Scouting News* (monthly), *Triennial Report*.

World Union of Jewish Students: POB 7914, 91077 Jerusalem, Israel; tel. 02-637482; telex 25615; f. 1924; organization for national student bodies concerned with educational and political matters, where possible in co-operation with non-Jewish student organizations, UNESCO, etc.; divided into six regions; organizes Congress every three years. Mems: 35 national unions representing over 700,000 students. Chair. YOSEF I. ABRAMOWITZ; Exec. Dir DANIEL YOSSEF (UK). Publs *Shofar, WUJS Report*.

World Young Women's Christian Association—World YWCA: 37 quai Wilson, 1201 Geneva, Switzerland; tel. (022) 323100; f. 1894 for the linking together of national YWCAs in 88 countries for their mutual help and development and the initiation of work in countries where the Association does not yet exist; works for international understanding, for improved social and economic conditions and for basic human rights for all people. Pres. JEWEL GRAHAM; Gen. Sec. ELAINE H. GREIF. Publs *Annual Report, Programme of International Co-operation, Programme Material, Common Concern*.

Youth for Development and Co-operation—YDC: Leliegracht 21, 1016 GR Amsterdam, Netherlands; tel. (020) 261993; works for a new international order fulfilling the conditions for responsible use and fair distribution of the world's resources, full realization of human rights, and decentralization of decision-making; seminars, exhibitions and campaigns on the problems of the Third World (development, environment), and important problems dealt with by the UN and specialized agencies (food, population, law of the seas, etc.). Mems: 37 organizations. Chair. J. R. MOLINA. Publs *FLASH* (every 2 months), *Progress Report* (bi-monthly), *LLDCs—Campaign Newsletter* (quarterly).

PART TWO

Afghanistan–Jordan

AFGHANISTAN

Introductory Survey

Location, Climate, Language, Religion, Flag, Capital

The Republic of Afghanistan is a land-locked country in south-western Asia. Its neighbours are the USSR to the north, Iran to the west, the People's Republic of China to the north-east and Pakistan to the east and south. The climate varies sharply between the highlands and lowlands; the temperature in the south-west in summer reaches 48.8°C (120°F), but in the winter, in the Hindu Kush mountains of the north-east, it falls to −26°C (−15°F). Of the many languages spoken in Afghanistan, the principal two are Pashtu and Dari (a dialect of Persian). The majority of Afghans are Muslims of the Sunni sect; there are also minority groups of Hindus, Sikhs and Jews. The national flag has three equal horizontal stripes, of red, black and green, with a superimposed emblem of an open book under a candle, surrounded by stylized heads of grain. The capital is Kabul.

Recent History

The last King of Afghanistan, Muhammad Zahir Shah, reigned from 1933 to 1973. His country was neutral during both World Wars and became a staunch advocate of non-alignment. In 1953 the King's cousin, Lt-Gen. Sardar Mohammad Daud Khan, became Prime Minister and, securing aid from the USSR, initiated a series of economic plans for the modernization of the country. In 1963 Gen. Daud resigned and Dr Mohammad Yusuf became the first Prime Minister not of royal birth. He introduced a new democratic constitution which combined western ideas with Islamic religious and political beliefs, but the King never allowed political parties to operate. Afghanistan made little progress under the succeeding Prime Ministers.

In July 1973, while King Zahir was in Italy, the monarchy was overthrown by a coup, in which the main figure was the former Prime Minister, Gen. Daud. The 1964 constitution was abolished and Afghanistan was declared a republic. Daud renounced his royal titles and took office as Head of State, Prime Minister and Minister of Foreign Affairs and Defence.

A Loya Jirgah (National Assembly), appointed from among notable elders by provincial governors, was convened in January 1977 and adopted a new constitution, providing for presidential government and a one-party state. Daud was elected to continue as President for six years and the Assembly was then dissolved. In March 1977 President Daud formed a new civilian government, nominally ending military rule. However, during 1977 there was growing discontent with Daud, especially within the armed forces, and in April 1978 a coup, known (from the month) as the 'Saur Revolution', ousted the President, who was killed with several members of his family.

Nur Mohammad Taraki, imprisoned leader of the formerly banned People's Democratic Party of Afghanistan (PDPA), was released and installed as President of the Revolutionary Council and Prime Minister. The country was renamed the Democratic Republic of Afghanistan, the year-old constitution was abolished and no political parties other than the communist PDPA were allowed to function. Afghanistan's already close relations with the USSR were further strengthened. However, opposition to the new regime led to armed insurrection, particularly by fiercely traditionalist Muslim rebel tribesmen (known, collectively, as the Mujaheddin), in almost all provinces, and the flight of thousands of refugees to Pakistan and Iran. In spite of purges of the army and civil service, Taraki's position became increasingly insecure, and in September 1979 he was ousted by Hafizullah Amin, who had been Deputy Prime Minister and Minister of Foreign Affairs since March. Amin's imposition of rigorous communist policies was unsuccessful and unpopular. In December 1979 he was removed and killed in a coup that was supported by the entry into Afghanistan of about 80,000 combat troops from the USSR. This incursion by Soviet armed forces into a traditionally non-aligned neighbouring country aroused world-wide condemnation. Babrak Karmal, a former Deputy Prime Minister under Taraki, was installed as the new Head of State, having been flown into Kabul by a Soviet aircraft from virtual exile in Eastern Europe.

Riots, strikes and inter-factional strife and purges continued into 1980 and 1981. President Karmal centralized his authority by reorganizing government departments within the Prime Minister's Office in July 1980. Sultan Ali Keshtmand, hitherto a Deputy Prime Minister, replaced Karmal as Prime Minister in June 1981. In the hope of strengthening the position of Karmal's Parcham ('Flag') faction of the PDPA over the Khalq ('Masses') faction of the party, the Revolutionary Council and the Politburo were enlarged. In the same month the regime launched the long-awaited National Fatherland Front (NFF), incorporating the PDPA and other organizations, with the aim of promoting national unity. Neither measure appeared to be achieving its aim, so the Council of Ministers was reshuffled again in August and September 1982, further strengthening Karmal's Parcham faction. At its 12th plenum in July 1983, the PDPA Central Committee elected 10 new full members and 16 new alternate members, nearly all of them Parcham supporters. However, the PDPA regime continued to fail to win widespread popular support. As a result, the Government attempted to broaden the base of its support: in April 1985 it summoned a Loya Jirgah (National Assembly), comprising indirectly-elected tribal elders, who ratified a new constitution for Afghanistan; a non-PDPA member was appointed chairman of the NFF in May 1985; elections were held between August 1985 and March/April 1986 for new local government organs (it was claimed that 60% of those elected were non-party members), and several non-party members were appointed to high-ranking government posts between December 1985 and February 1986.

In May 1986, however, Dr Najibullah Ahmadzai (the former head of the state security service, KHAD) succeeded Karmal as General Secretary of the PDPA. Karmal was allowed to retain the lesser post of President of the Revolutionary Council. In the same month Dr Najibullah (like Karmal, a member of the Parcham faction) announced the formation of a collective leadership comprising himself, Karmal and Prime Minister Keshtmand. In November 1986, however, Karmal was relieved of all party and government posts. Muhammad Chamkani, formerly First Vice-President (and a non-PDPA member), became Acting President of the Revolutionary Council, pending the introduction of a new constitution and the establishment of a permanent legislature.

In December 1986 an extraordinary plenum of the PDPA Central Committee approved a policy of national reconciliation, which involved a unilateral cease-fire for six months from 15 January 1987, negotiations with opposition groups, and the formation of a coalition government of national unity. On 3 January 1987 a Supreme Extraordinary Commission for National Reconciliation, led by Abd ar-Rahim Hatif (the Chairman of the National Committee of the NFF), was formed to conduct the negotiations. The NFF was renamed the National Front (NF), and became a separate organization from the PDPA. The new policy of reconciliation won some support from former opponents, but the seven-party opposition alliance (Ittehad-i-Islami Afghan Mujaheddin, Islamic Unity of Afghan Mujaheddin—IUAM) refused to observe the cease-fire or to participate in negotiations, while continuing to demand a complete and unconditional Soviet withdrawal.

In July 1987, as part of the process of national reconciliation, several important developments occurred: a law permitting the formation of other political parties (according to certain provisions) was introduced; a six-month extension of the cease-fire was announced; Dr Najibullah announced that the PDPA would be prepared to share power with representatives of opposition groups in the event of the formation of a coalition government of national unity; and the draft of a new constitution was approved by the Presidium of the Revolutionary Council. The main innovations to be incorporated in this draft constitution were: the formation of a multi-party political system, under the auspices of the NF; the formation of a bicameral legislature, called the Meli Shura (National Assembly), which was composed of a Sena (Senate) and a Wolasi Jirgah (House of Representatives); the granting of a permanent constitutional status to the PDPA; the bestowal of unlimited power on the President, who was to hold office for seven years; and the change in the name of the country from the Democratic Republic to the Republic of Afghanistan. A Loya Jirgah ratified the new Constitution in November, and a third six-month extension of the cease-fire was announced.

A further round of local elections throughout the country began in August 1987. A considerable number of those elected were reported to be non-PDPA members. On 30 September Dr Najibullah was unanimously elected as President of the Revolutionary Council, and Haji Muhammad Chamkani resumed his former post as First Vice-President. In order to strengthen his position, Dr Najibullah ousted all the remaining supporters of the former President, Babrak Karmal, from the Central Committee and Politburo of the PDPA in October, a few days before opening the second nation-wide PDPA conference in Kabul. In November a Loya Jirgah unanimously elected Dr Najibullah as President of the country.

In April 1988 elections were held to both houses of the new National Assembly, which replaced the Revolutionary Council. Although the elections were boycotted by the Mujaheddin, the Government left vacant 50 of the 234 seats in the House of Representatives, and a small number of seats in the Senate, in the hope that the guerrillas would abandon their armed struggle and present their own representatives to participate in the new administration. The PDPA itself won only 46 seats in the House of Representatives, but was guaranteed support from the NF, which gained 45, and from the various newly-recognized left-wing parties, which won a total of 24 seats. In May Dr Muhammad Hasan Sharq (a non-PDPA member and a Deputy Prime Minister since June 1987) replaced Sultan Ali Keshtmand as Prime Minister, and in June a new Council of Ministers was appointed.

Fighting between the Mujaheddin and Afghan army units had begun in the eastern provinces after the 1978 coup and was aggravated by the implementation of social and economic reforms by the new administrations. The Afghan army relied heavily upon Soviet military aid in the form of weapons, equipment and expertise, but morale and resources were severely affected by defections to the rebels' ranks: numbers fell from about 80,000 men in 1978 to about 40,000 in 1985. A vigorous recruitment drive and stricter conscription regulations, implemented by Dr Najibullah in June 1986, failed to increase the size of the Afghan army by any great extent, and the defections continued.

In 1984–88 the guerrilla groups, which had been poorly armed at first, received ever-increasing support (both military and financial) from abroad, notably from the USA (which began to supply them with sophisticated anti-aircraft weapons in 1986), the United Kingdom and the People's Republic of China. Despite the Government's decision to seal the border with Pakistan, announced in September 1985, and the strong presence of Soviet forces there, foreign weapons continued to reach the guerrillas via Pakistan. Many of the guerrillas are now based in the North-West Frontier Province of Pakistan (notably in the provincial capital, Peshawar). A major effort has been made by the Government to enlist the support of border tribes by offering important concessions, financial inducements and guns in return for their support. A frontier tribal jirgah (assembly), held in September 1985, decided to establish anti-Mujaheddin militias on both sides of the Pakistan border. From 1985 the fighting intensified, especially in areas close to the border between Afghanistan and Pakistan. There were many violations of the border, involving shelling, bombing and incursions into neighbouring airspace. The general pattern of the war, however, remained the same: the regime held the main towns and a few strategic bases, and relied on bombing of both military and civilian targets, and occasional attacks in force, together with conciliatory measures such as the provision of funds for local development, while the rebel forces dominated rural areas and could cause serious disruption.

With the civil war came famine in parts of Afghanistan, and there was a mass movement of population from the countryside to Kabul (whose population increased from about 750,000 in 1978 to 1,287,000, according to a municipal census, in late 1986), and of refugees to Pakistan and Iran. In mid-1988 a UNHCR estimate assessed the number of Afghan refugees in Pakistan at 3.15m., and the number in Iran at 2.35m.

From 1980, extensive international negotiations took place to try to achieve the complete withdrawal of Soviet forces. The UN General Assembly demanded the withdrawal of foreign troops in nine successive resolutions between 1980 and 1987. Between June 1982 and September 1987, seven rounds of indirect talks, the last in several phases, took place between the Afghan and Pakistani Ministers of Foreign Affairs in Geneva, under the auspices of the UN. In October 1986 the USSR made a token withdrawal of six regiments (6,000–8,000 men) from Afghanistan. As a result of the discussions in Geneva, an agreement was finally signed on 14 April 1988. The Geneva accords consisted of five documents: detailed undertakings by Afghanistan and Pakistan, relating to non-intervention and non-interference in each other's affairs; international guarantees of Afghan neutrality (with the USA and the USSR as the principal guarantors); arrangements for the voluntary and safe return of Afghan refugees from Pakistan and Iran; a document linking the preceding documents with a timetable for a Soviet withdrawal; and the establishment of a UN monitoring force, to be known as the United Nations Good Offices Mission in Afghanistan and Pakistan (UNGOMAP) and to be based in Kabul and Islamabad, which was to monitor both the Soviet troop departures and the return of the refugees. The withdrawal of Soviet troops (who numbered 100,000, according to Soviet figures, or 115,000, according to Western sources) commenced on 15 May. As agreed, one-half of the Soviet troops had reportedly withdrawn by 15 August, and the remainder were to leave by 15 February 1989.

Neither the Mujaheddin nor Iran played any role in the formulation of the Geneva accords, and, in spite of protests by Pakistan, the accords did not incorporate an agreement regarding the composition of an interim coalition government in Afghanistan, or the 'symmetrical' cessation of Soviet aid to Najibullah's regime and US aid to the Mujaheddin. Therefore, despite the withdrawal of the Soviet troops, the supply of weapons to both sides was not stopped, and the fighting continued. Pakistan repeatedly denied accusations, made by the Afghan and Soviet Governments, that it had violated the accords by continuing to harbour Afghan guerrillas and to act as a conduit for arms supplies to the latter from various sympathizers. Despite the sudden death of the Pakistani President, Gen. Zia ul-Haq (who had been one of the Mujaheddin's staunchest allies), in August, neither Pakistan's nor the USA's support for the guerrillas' cause showed any sign of faltering. In November, however, the USSR temporarily suspended its withdrawal from Afghanistan, while expressing hope that the February deadline for a complete withdrawal would still be attained, and substantially increased its supply of powerful ballistic missiles to the Afghan army. Its reasons for these actions were that the flow of weapons from Pakistan to the Mujaheddin had allegedly increased and that, consequently, the guerrillas' attacks on important cities (including Kabul and Qandahar) and on the retreating Soviet troops had become more unremitting and serious. At the end of the month, Soviet officials held direct talks with representatives of the Mujaheddin in Peshawar, Pakistan, the first such meeting since the start of the 10-year conflict. The two sides reportedly discussed the release of Soviet troops taken prisoner by the guerrillas. High-level discussions, regarding various aspects of the Afghanistan crisis, were held in early December in Saudi Arabia between Prof. Burhanuddin Rabbani, the current Chairman of the IUAM, and Yuliy Vorontsov, who had recently been appointed Soviet ambassador to Afghanistan (while retaining his post as First Deputy Minister of Foreign Affairs).

Government

In November 1987 a new Constitution was ratified by a Loya Jirgah. A new bicameral legislature, called the Meli Shura (National Assembly), was formed to replace the Revolutionary Council. The National Assembly is composed of a 192-member Sena (Senate) and a 234-member Wolasi Jirgah (House of Representatives). A small number of seats in the Senate and 50 seats in the House of Representatives have been reserved for members of the opposition. The President is elected by a majority vote of the Loya Jirgah for a term of seven years. The President appoints the Prime Minister, who, in turn, appoints the members of the Council of Ministers. The 31 provinces of Afghanistan are each administered by an appointed governor.

Defence

Every able-bodied Afghan male (excepting religious scholars and preachers) between the ages of 15 and 55 years has to serve three years or more in the army (up to five years for

AFGHANISTAN

non-combatants), which was estimated to number 55,000 men in June 1988, but conscription is difficult to enforce and desertions are frequent. Equipment and training are provided largely by the USSR, which in December 1988 had an estimated 50,000–70,000 troops stationed in Afghanistan (compared with an estimated 115,000 in early 1988). The Afghan air force, which numbered 5,000, is equipped with supersonic jet aircraft. Paramilitary forces include a gendarmerie of 30,000, a state security service (KHAD), a border guard and numerous regional militias; police security forces come under the Ministry of the Interior (gendarmerie) and the Ministry of State Security (KHAD). A company of guards was formed to defend the capital city in 1988.

Economic Affairs

Afghanistan is essentially a tribal society, and in 1982 about 2.6m. of its people were nomadic. Agriculture, which provided employment for an estimated 78% of the settled labour force in 1980, was the mainstay of the economy, prior to the major development of natural gas in the 1980s, and accounted for 50% of export earnings and for 63% of gross domestic product (GDP) in 1981/82. Principal agricultural exports include livestock, wool and cotton, fresh and dried fruits, processed hides and skins and medicinal herbs. The formation of farm cooperatives was officially encouraged, and, according to the Government, they numbered 544 (with a total cultivated area of 127,000 ha) in 1987. In May 1987 the Government raised the upper limit for the amount of land that can be owned by private landowners and the clergy to 100 *jeribs* (20 ha). Afghanistan is self-sufficient in food in years of normal output. According to government figures, Afghanistan's annual production of wheat remained stable at 2.8m.–2.9m. metric tons in 1980–86. However, shortages of food became a serious problem in 1981 and 1982, as Soviet troops destroyed crops in their efforts to curb the activities of anti-government rebels, who themselves were engaged in fighting rather than farming. Regular agricultural production has also been disrupted by the scarcity of fertilizers and new seed and by the damage done to many irrigation systems. Since the beginning of the conflict, it has been estimated that about one-third of total farms have been abandoned, and large areas of arable land have been destroyed. The Government claimed that the volume of agricultural production increased by 0.7% in 1987/88. An external source, however, estimated that, by 1988, total food production had fallen to around 45% of the level prevailing prior to the Soviet invasion, the number of livestock had declined drastically, and Afghanistan had to import 500,000 tons of wheat annually from the USSR. Following the commencement of the Soviet withdrawal in May 1988, the UN was greatly concerned that the expected return of thousands of Afghan refugees might result in serious food shortages and, possibly, widespread famine.

The country is well-endowed with minerals: natural gas (with estimated reserves of over 100,000m. cu m), coal, salt, lapis lazuli, barite and talc are extracted. In May 1980 a new complex for the extraction and purification of gas became operational at Jarquduq, with an annual capacity of 2,000m. cu m. Gas exports to the USSR totalled 2,400m. cu m in 1983/84, according to government figures, and rose to 2,600m. cu m (about 97% of the total annual production) in 1985/86. Natural gas is Afghanistan's major export commodity and, according to IMF figures, it provided about 47% of the total income from exports in 1986/87. The most promising recent discovery is that of 1,700m. metric tons of high-grade iron ore at Hajigak, although the high altitude of the site was expected to cause problems in exploiting the deposit. According to official plans, other mineral deposits, such as petroleum and copper (estimated total reserves 4.7m. tons), are to be exploited with the help of foreign aid. A copper mining and smelting project has been initiated near Kabul; when completed, this could give Afghanistan a 2% share of world copper production. Afghanistan's first steel smelter (built with Soviet technical and financial assistance) started functioning at the Jangalak factory complex in April 1987. Energy plans include the development of two small oilfields in the north of the country, which, when fully operational, should satisfy Afghanistan's total needs for petroleum products. Such products have been imported at special low prices from Iran and the USSR, but it is planned to increase internal sources of energy by establishing hydro- and thermal electric power stations. Hydroelectricity constitutes about 80% of energy resources. The first hydroelectric power station to be built since 1978 began operating in October 1983 at Asadabad. The large Sarobi II hydroelectric dam on the Kabul River was due to be completed by 1988. In 1987 a Czechoslovak company signed a contract to supply equipment for the reconstruction of the hard coal-mines in the north of the country. The aim is to increase annual production of hard coal to 180,000 tons. Coal production, centred at Pwul-e-Khumri, was expected to reach 150,000 tons in 1986/87.

Afghanistan's major manufacturing industries include cotton textiles, chemical fertilizers, leather and plastic goods. The output of cotton textiles in 1980/81, however, was 43.3m. metres, which was insufficient to satisfy domestic demand, and by 1981/82 it had fallen to 26.5m. metres, but by 1985/86 output had risen to 45m. metres. However, cotton exports, according to IMF figures, declined from US $22.4m. in 1984/85 to $9.8m. in 1986/87. In 1987 the Government introduced a number of incentives for cotton farmers, including tax exemption and transport allowances. Since the Soviet intervention in 1979, Afghanistan has become increasingly dependent for its industrial progress upon the USSR and other Eastern bloc countries. Two new cement factories (including a second factory at Ghowri, which is being built with Czechoslovak assistance) are due to be completed by 1990, and are expected to have a combined annual production capacity of 510,000 tons. Official sources claimed that the volume of industrial output increased by 3.5% in 1987. According to government figures, income from industrial production totalled Afs 37,000m. in 1986/87 (equivalent to 23.8% of GDP), with the handicraft sector accounting for Afs 15,000m. (1.3% more than in 1985/86), and the private sector contributing Afs 4,370m. (11.8%). During 1981–85 the annual rate of inflation remained at about 20%. In January 1986 the Government announced a Five-Year Economic and Social Development Plan (March 1986–March 1991), involving proposed expenditure of Afs 115,000m. ($2,300m.). The Government admitted that spending on such a scale would necessitate a large amount of external assistance. The main emphasis of the Plan was on improving the infrastructure and on increasing investment in industry (which employed only 12% of the working population in 1979). Of the Plan objectives included, the extraction of gas condensate was to rise to 6,000 tons annually, and coal output was to double to 370,000 tons per year by 1991; a new petroleum refinery was to be constructed in Jawzjan Province; new irrigation systems were to be constructed (at the cost of Afs 5,200m.) throughout the country; a Soviet-assisted project to connect Kabul and adjacent provinces to the Soviet power grid by 1991; the Industrial Development Bank was to provide Afs 2,660m. to promote the handicraft industry; a unified banking system was to be established, and private businessmen and local merchants were to be encouraged under a government-sponsored system of 'state capitalism'. (The private sector accounted for 74% of gross national product (GNP) in 1985.) The economy, which, according to government figures, had expanded by less than 2% annually since 1980, was projected to grow by 25% over the Plan period. Gross industrial production was scheduled to increase by 28% between 1986 and 1991, agricultural production by 14%–16%, domestic trade by 150%, and foreign trade by 17%. In May 1986 the Economic Consultative Council, the body responsible for economic planning, was restructured. According to government figures, the total GNP in 1986/87 amounted to US $3,156m., an increase of 5.2%, compared with 1985/86, and GNP per head stood at $155–$160. Despite the Government's policy of national reconciliation, which was introduced in December 1986, and the Soviet withdrawal, which commenced in May 1988, the economy, as a whole, showed no real signs of improvement, and the ambitious targets of the Plan appeared highly unlikely to be attained.

As well as carpets and rugs, Afghanistan exports fruit and vegetables to Pakistan and India, natural gas and ginned cotton to the USSR (its principal trading partner), oil-cake to Iran and Pakistan and karakul to the European fur markets. Imports include wheat, buses, machinery and petroleum products from the USSR. According to government figures, the two main exporters to Afghanistan in 1983/84 were the USSR (62.2%) and Japan (13.1%); principal importers of Afghanistan goods in 1983/84 were the USSR (55.0%, compared with 35.1% in 1978/79) and Pakistan (16.2%). In 1986/87 total exports, according to IMF figures (which differ substantially from government figures), were worth $551.9m., and imports amounted to $1,403.5m. The trade deficit thus increased to

AFGHANISTAN

$851.6m., compared with $637.4m. in 1985/86 (exports $556.8m., imports $1,194.2m.). According to government figures, the Eastern bloc countries accounted for 68% (USSR 60%) of the total foreign trade turnover (imports plus exports) in 1986/87. Over the five-year period March 1986–March 1991, the total value of trade between Afghanistan and other countries was expected to amount to only US $5,000m., compared with $43,000m. in the period 1981–85.

Owing to the backwardness of the economy and continuing civil strife, the Government has had difficulty in raising revenue. About 50% of domestic revenue comes from indirect taxes and only 10% from direct taxes. Revenue from natural gas is the next largest contributor, totalling 21% in 1979 and 34% in 1980. Aid from Western countries and OPEC members declined from about US $100m. per year in the late 1970s to $23.2m. in 1981. Since 1980 Afghanistan has received foreign aid chiefly from the USSR. Project aid from the USSR in the year to March 1986 totalled US $110m., 73.3% of the total. In 1981 the two countries concluded a mutual trade agreement for the period 1981–85, whereby Afghanistan was to supply the USSR with raw materials, natural gas and food products in return for industrial equipment and machinery. During this period, Soviet trade with Afghanistan was reported to have increased by almost 300%. A further five-year agreement, under which bilateral trade was to expand by 30%, was signed in 1986. In 1987 the Government estimated that financial contributions from the USSR constituted 40% of the country's civilian budget. In 1988/89 the USSR and other member countries of the Council for Mutual Economic Assistance (CMEA, see p. 124) were to contribute 97% (USSR 81%) of foreign aid to Afghanistan, which totalled an estimated US $223.3m., an increase of 14.5% compared with 1987/88. In June 1988 the UN launched an appeal to raise US $1,160m. towards the implementation of a large-scale, 18-month, programme for reconstruction and rehabilitation in Afghanistan. In October the USSR pledged to contribute $600m. in humanitarian aid.

Social Welfare

Workers and employees are entitled to free hospital treatment. Most private companies have their own doctor and hospitals. Disabled people are looked after in social welfare centres in the provincial capitals. In 1982 Afghanistan had 68 hospital establishments, with a total of 4,837 beds, and there were 1,160 physicians working in the government health service. Serious damage was reported to have been caused to hospital facilities by the disturbances from 1980 onwards. The estimated average life expectancy at birth in 1980–85 had fallen by two years from the 1970 figure to 36 years, the lowest in Asia. Between 1980 and 1985, according to UN estimates, there were 194 deaths of children under 12 months old for every 1,000 live births, the highest infant mortality rate in Asia. In 1980 only 20% of the urban population and 3% of the rural population had access to safe water supplies. The average daily intake of calories per person had fallen to 1,775, also the lowest in Asia, although this had risen to 2,280 in 1982, according to government figures. In 1982/83 estimated expenditure on social services was Afs 2,315m., about 20% of the ordinary budget. In 1988 government officials assessed the combined total of medical centres and hospitals at 196 and physicians at 1,931.

Education

Primary education, which is officially compulsory, begins at seven years of age and lasts for eight years. Secondary education, beginning at 15 years of age, lasts for a further four years. As a proportion of the school-age population, the total enrolment at primary and secondary schools declined from 29% (boys 46%; girls 11%) in 1981 to only 15% (boys 20%; girls 9%) in 1985. Enrolment at primary schools declined from 1,198,286 in 1981 to 449,948 in 1982, rising to 580,499 in 1985. Primary enrolment in 1985 included an estimated 15% of children in the relevant age-group (boys 20%; girls 10%).

In September 1982 the Government announced a plan to eradicate illiteracy by 1990. Afghanistan has one of the highest levels of adult illiteracy in Asia, with an average rate of 76.3% (males 61.1%; females 92.2%) in 1985, according to estimates by UNESCO. In 1987 the Government claimed that there were more than 20,000 literacy courses, attended by a total of about 400,000 students, throughout Afghanistan. According to the Government, about 857,000 pupils were studying at 1,348 schools in September 1988, compared with 700,544 pupils at 1,236 schools in 1986. Since 1979 higher education has been disrupted by the departure of many teaching staff from Afghanistan. In 1987 an estimated 15,000 Afghan students and trainees were receiving education at establishments in the USSR. In 1988 there were eight vocational colleges, 15 technical colleges and five universities (including an Islamic university in Kabul) in Afghanistan.

Public Holidays

The Afghan year 1368 runs from 21 March 1989 to 20 March 1990, and the year 1369 runs from 21 March 1990 to 20 March 1991.

1989: 21 March (Nau-roz: New Year's Day, Iranian calendar), 7 April* (first day of Ramadan), 27 April (Revolution Day), 1 May (Workers' Day), 7 May* (Id al-Fitr, end of Ramadan), 14 July* (Id al-Adha, Feast of the Sacrifice), 13 August* (Ashura, Martyrdom of Iman Husayn), 18 August (Independence Day), 13 October* (Roze-Maulud, Birth of Prophet Muhammad).

1990: 21 March (Nau-roz: New Year's Day, Iranian calendar), 28 March* (first day of Ramadan), 27 April (Revolution Day and Id al-Fitr, end of Ramadan*), 1 May (Workers' Day), 4 July* (Id al-Adha, Feast of the Sacrifice), 2 August* (Ashura, Martyrdom of Iman Husayn), 18 August (Independence Day), 2 October* (Roze-Maulud, Birth of Prophet Muhammad).

* These holidays are dependent on the Islamic lunar calendar and may vary by one or two days from the dates given.

Weights and Measures

The metric system has been officially adopted but traditional weights are still used. One 'seer' equals 16 lb (7.3 kg).

Statistical Survey

Source (unless otherwise stated): Central Statistics Office, Kabul.

Area and Population

AREA, POPULATION AND DENSITY

Area (sq km)	652,225*
Population (census results) 23 June 1979†	
Males	6,712,377
Females	6,338,981
Total	13,051,358
Population (official estimates at mid-year)‡	
1984	17,672,000
1985	18,136,000
1986	18,614,000
Density (per sq km) at mid-1986	28.5

* 251,773 sq miles.
† Figures exclude nomadic population, estimated to total 2,500,000. The census data also exclude an adjustment for underenumeration, estimated to have been 5% for the urban population and 10% for the rural population.
‡ These data include estimates for nomadic population (2,734,000 in 1983), but take no account of emigration by refugees. Assuming an average net outflow of 260,000 persons per year in 1980–85, the UN Population Division has estimated Afghanistan's total mid-year population (in '000) as: 16,128 in 1984; 16,519 in 1985; 17,193 in 1986 (Source: UN, *World Population Prospects: Estimates and Projections as Assessed in 1984*). In 1988, according to UNHCR estimates, the total Afghan refugee population numbered 5.5m., of whom 3.15m. were living in Pakistan and 2.35m. in Iran.

PROVINCES (estimates, March 1982)*

	Area (sq km)	Population	Density (per sq km)	Capital (with population)
Kabul	4,585	1,517,909	331.1	Kabul (1,036,407)
Kapesa†	1,871	262,039	140.1	Mahmudraki (1,262)
Parwan	9,399	527,987	56.2	Sharikar (25,117)
Wardag†	9,023	300,796	33.3	Maidanshar (2,153)
Loghar†	4,652	226,234	48.6	Baraiki Barak (1,164)
Ghazni	23,378	676,416	28.9	Ghazni (31,985)
Paktia	9,581	506,264	52.8	Gardiz (10,040)
Nangarhar	7,616	781,619	102.6	Jalalabad (57,824)
Laghman	7,210	325,010	45.0	Mehterlam (4,191)
Kunar	10,479	261,604	25.0	Asadabad (2,196)
Badakhshan	47,403	520,620	10.9	Faizabad (9,564)
Takhar	12,376	543,818	43.9	Talukan (20,947)
Baghlan	17,109	516,921	30.2	Baghlan (41,240)
Kunduz	7,827	582,600	74.4	Kunduz (57,112)
Samangan	15,465	273,864	17.7	Aibak (5,191)
Balkh	12,593	609,590	48.4	Mazar-i-Sharif (110,367)
Jawzjan	25,553	615,877	24.1	Shiberghan (19,969)
Fariab	22,279	609,703	27.3	Maymana (40,212)
Badghis	21,858	244,346	11.2	Kalainow (5,614)
Herat	61,315	808,224	13.2	Herat (150,497)
Farah	47,788	245,474	5.1	Farah (19,761)
Neemroze	41,356	108,418	2.6	Zarang (6,809)
Helmand	61,829	541,508	8.8	Lashkargha (22,707)
Qandahar	47,676	597,954	12.5	Qandahar (191,345)
Zabul	17,293	187,612	10.8	Qalat (6,251)
Uruzgan	29,295	464,556	15.5	Terincot (3,534)
Ghor	38,666	353,494	9.1	Cheghcheran (3,126)
Bamian	17,414	280,859	16.1	Bamian (7,732)
Paktika	19,336	256,470	13.3	Sheran (1,469)
Total	652,225	13,747,786	21.1	

* Population figures refer to settled inhabitants only, excluding kuchies (nomads), estimated at 2,600,000 for the whole country.
† Formed in 1981.

Note: Two new provinces, named Sar-e Pol and Nurestan, were formed in April 1988 and July 1988 respectively, bringing the total number of provinces in Afghanistan to 31.

PRINCIPAL TOWNS (estimated population at March 1982)

Kabul (capital)	1,036,407	Kunduz	57,112
Qandahar	191,345	Baghlan	41,240
Herat	150,497	Maymana	40,212
Mazar-i-Sharif	110,367	Pul-i-Khomri	32,695
Jalalabad	57,824	Ghazni	31,985

BIRTHS AND DEATHS

1979 (demographic survey): Live births 627,619 (birth rate 48.1 per 1,000); Deaths 290,974 (death rate 22.3 per 1,000).

ECONOMICALLY ACTIVE POPULATION* (ISIC Major Divisions, persons aged 8 years and over, 1979 census)

	Males	Females	Total
Agriculture, hunting, forestry and fishing	2,358,821	10,660	2,369,481
Mining and quarrying	57,492	1,847	59,339
Manufacturing	170,908	252,465	423,373
Electricity, gas and water	11,078	276	11,354
Construction	50,670	416	51,086
Wholesale and retail trade	135,242	2,618	137,860
Transport, storage and communications	65,376	867	66,243
Other services	716,511	32,834	749,345
Total	3,566,098	301,983	3,868,081

* Figures refer to settled population only and exclude 77,510 persons seeking work for the first time (66,057 males; 11,453 females).

Agriculture

PRINCIPAL CROPS ('000 metric tons)

	1984	1985	1986
Wheat	2,850	2,750	2,500*
Rice (paddy)	480	475	454†
Barley	333	330	300*
Maize	799	810	750*
Millet	38	38*	38*
Potatoes	320*	330*	330*
Pulses	38*	38*	40*
Sesame seed	30†	28†	28*
Cottonseed	44†	44†	44*
Cotton (lint)	22†	22†	22*
Watermelons	6*	6*	6*
Melons	120*	120*	120*
Grapes	510*	510*	512*
Sugar cane	70*	70*	70*
Sugar beets	20*	20*	20*
Plums	36*	37*	37*
Oranges	24*	24*	24*
Apricots	36*	37*	37*

* FAO estimate.   † Unofficial figure.
Source: FAO, *Production Yearbook*.

AFGHANISTAN

LIVESTOCK
(FAO estimates, '000 head, year ending 30 September)

	1984	1985	1986
Horses	410	410	410
Mules	30	30	30
Asses	1,250	1,250	1,250
Cattle	3,750	3,750	3,750
Camels	270	270	270
Sheep	20,000	20,000	20,000
Goats	3,000	3,000	3,000

Poultry (FAO estimates, million): 7 in 1984; 7 in 1985; 7 in 1986.
Source: FAO, *Production Yearbook*.

LIVESTOCK PRODUCTS (FAO estimates, '000 metric tons)

	1984	1985	1986
Beef and veal	68	68	68
Mutton and lamb	133	133	133
Goats' meat	26	26	26
Poultry meat	13	13	13
Other meat	12	12	12
Cows' milk	600	610	610
Sheep's milk	245	245	245
Goats' milk	55	55	55
Cheese	10.2	10.2	10.2
Butter and ghee	12.6	12.7	12.7
Hen eggs	14.2	14.2	14.2
Honey	3.0	3.0	3.0
Wool:			
greasy	23.5	23.5	23.5
clean	13.5	13.5	13.5
Cattle hides	11.2	11.2	11.2
Sheep skins	20.8	20.8	20.8
Goat skins	3.9	3.9	3.9

Source: FAO, *Production Yearbook*.

Forestry

ROUNDWOOD REMOVALS
(FAO estimates, '000 cu m, excluding bark)

	1984	1985	1986
Sawlogs, veneer logs and logs for sleepers*	856	856	856
Other industrial wood	677	681	715
Fuel wood	4,887	4,915	5,159
Total	6,420	6,452	6,730

* Assumed to be unchanged from 1976.
Source: FAO, *Yearbook of Forest Products*.

SAWNWOOD PRODUCTION (FAO estimates, '000 cu m)

	1974	1975	1976
Total (incl. boxboards)	410	330	400

1977-86: Annual production as in 1976 (FAO estimates).
Source: FAO, *Yearbook of Forest Products*.

Fishing

1964-86: Total catch 1,500 metric tons each year (FAO estimate).

Mining
('000 metric tons, unless otherwise indicated)

	1983	1984	1985
Hard coal	145	148	151
Salt (unrefined)*	52	53	51
Gypsum (crude)	10	8	8
Natural gas (petajoules)	99	106	111

* Production during 12 months beginning 21 March of year stated.
Source: UN, *Industrial Statistics Yearbook*.

Industry

SELECTED PRODUCTS (year ending 20 March, '000 metric tons, unless otherwise indicated)

	1983/84	1984/85	1985/86
Margarine	2.1	2.7	3.6
Vegetable oil	2	1	3
Wheat flour†	136	154	173
Wine ('000 hectolitres)†	256	262	264
Soft drinks ('000 hectolitres)	7,000	7,300	7,600
Woven cotton fabrics (million metres)	38	45	45
Woven woollen fabrics (million metres)*	0.5	0.5	0.4
Blankets ('000)†	67	62	23
Carpets and rugs ('000 sq metres)†	17	18	20
Footwear—excl. rubber ('000 pairs)†	297	344	380
Rubber footwear ('000 pairs)†	2,600	2,400	2,400
Nitrogenous fertilizers‡	48	50	48
Cement	130	112	127
Electric energy (million kWh)†	1,025	1,045	1,060

* Provisional.   † Production in calendar years 1983, 1984 and 1985.
‡ Production in terms of nitrogen in year ending 30 June (Source: FAO).
Source: UN, *Industrial Statistics Yearbook*.

Finance

CURRENCY AND EXCHANGE RATES

Monetary Units
  100 puls (puli) = 2 krans = 1 afghani (Af).

Denominations
  Coins: 25 and 50 puls: 1, 2, and 5 afghanis.
  Notes: 10, 20, 50, 100, 500 and 1,000 afghanis.

Sterling and Dollar Equivalents (30 September 1988)
  £1 sterling = 85.56 afghanis;
  US $1 = 50.60 afghanis;
  1,000 afghanis = £11.69 = $19.76.

Exchange Rate
  The official rate has been maintained at US $1 = 50.60 afghanis since September 1981.

AFGHANISTAN

BUDGET (million afghanis, year ending 21 September)

Revenue	1977/78	1978/79	1979/80
Direct taxes	2,428	2,535	2,461
Indirect taxes	6,830	6,913	4,794
Revenue from monopolies and other enterprises	1,316	1,192	1,407
Natural gas revenue	1,510	2,637	3,874
Revenue from other property and services	2,357	1,954	2,456
Other revenue	480	1,224	796
Total revenue	14,921	16,455	15,788

Expenditure	1977/78	1978/79	1979/80
Administration	1,255	1,690	4,218
Defence, security	2,656	3,007	6,294
Social services	2,538	3,186	3,279
Economic services	870	985	1,092
Total ministries	7,319	8,868	14,883
Foreign debt service	2,087	2,493	1,029
Subsidies (exchange, etc.)	2,532	1,024	870
Total ordinary	11,938	12,385	16,782
Development budget	5,200	6,845	5,374

1980/81 (estimates in million afghanis): Revenue: internal sources 23,478, grants-in-aid from USSR 1,735, loans and project assistance 8,546, total revenue 33,759; Expenditure: ministries' allocation 19,213, development budget 14,546, total expenditure 33,759.

In January 1986 the Government announced a Five-Year Economic and Social Development Plan (March 1986–91), involving proposed expenditure of Afs 115,000m. ($2,300m.).

BANK OF AFGHANISTAN RESERVES*
(US $ million at December)

	1985	1986	1987
IMF special drawing rights	13.64	13.99	14.91
Reserve position in IMF	5.29	5.92	6.87
Foreign exchange	276.27	238.61	257.90
Total	295.21	258.52	279.68

* Figures exclude gold reserves, totalling 965,000 troy ounces since 1980. Assuming a gold price of 12,850 afghanis per ounce, these reserves were officially valued at US $245.06 million in December 1985 and December 1986.

Source: IMF, *International Financial Statistics*.

MONEY SUPPLY (million afghanis at 21 December)

	1984	1985	1986
Currency outside banks	58,716	64,390	71,402
Private sector deposits at Bank of Afghanistan	5,561	7,212	8,006
Demand deposits at commercial banks	2,946	3,705	4,127

Source: IMF, *International Financial Statistics*.

COST OF LIVING
(retail price index, excluding rent; base: 1980 = 100)

	1983	1984	1985
All items	107.7	116.0	126.6

Source: IMF, *International Financial Statistics*.

NATIONAL ACCOUNTS
('000 million afghanis at 1978 prices, year ending 20 March)
Net Material Product (NMP)* by Economic Activity

	1983/84	1984/85	1985/86†
Agriculture, hunting, forestry and fishing	65.8	65.4	65.1
Mining and quarrying			
Manufacturing	14.9	15.3	16.3
Electricity, gas and water			
Construction	3.6	3.9	4.0
Trade, restaurants and hotels	9.2	10.1	10.2
Transport, storage and communications	3.4	3.7	3.1
Other services	1.7	1.8	1.7
Total	98.6	100.2	100.4

* Defined as the total net value of goods and 'productive' services, including turnover taxes, produced by the economy. This excludes economic activities not contributing directly to material production, such as public administration, defence and personal and professional services.
† Figures are provisional. Revised total (in '000 million afghanis) is 99.9.

1986/87 ('000 million afghanis at 1978 prices): NMP 104.0.

BALANCE OF PAYMENTS (US $ million)

	1984	1985	1986
Merchandise exports f.o.b.	787.7	628.2	537.0
Merchandise imports f.o.b.	−1,204.7	−921.4	−1,141.5
Trade balance	−417.0	−293.2	−604.5
Exports of services	53.8	69.2	72.3
Imports of services	−214.7	−162.7	−215.5
Balance on goods and services	−577.9	−386.7	−747.7
Unrequited transfers (net)	127.3	143.7	191.3
Current balance	−450.6	−243.0	−556.4
Long-term capital (net)	57.0	77.6	225.7
Short-term capital (net)	256.2	224.3	293.4
Net errors and omissions	202.7		
Total (net monetary movements)	65.3	58.9	−37.3
Valuation changes (net)	−11.3	7.6	0.6
Changes in reserves	54.0	66.5	−36.7

Source: IMF, *International Financial Statistics*.

AFGHANISTAN

External Trade

PRINCIPAL COMMODITIES
(US $ '000, year ending 20 March)

Imports c.i.f.	1980/81	1981/82	1983/84*
Wheat	798	18,100	38,251
Sugar	40,833	50,328	25,200
Tea	28,369	n.a.	23,855
Cigarettes	5,114	7,219	12,755
Vegetable oil	17,320	26,332	30,481
Drugs	4,497	4,195	3,768
Soaps	9,991	17,256	8,039
Tyres and tubes	16,766	12,764	28,823
Textile yarn and thread	16,800	24,586	n.a.
Cotton fabrics	873	6,319	n.a.
Rayon fabrics	6,879	9,498	n.a.
Other textile goods	52,546	49,036	n.a.
Vehicles and spare parts	89,852	141,062	n.a.
Petroleum products	124,000	112,093	n.a.
Footwear (new)	2,058	5,275	5,317
Bicycles	2,042	488	1,952
Matches	1,171	1,542	1,793
Sewing machines	140	285	266
Electric and non-electric machines	2,333	765	n.a.
Chemical materials	7,464	6,636	n.a.
Agricultural tractors	1	8,280	n.a.
Fertilizers	8,325	3,300	3,904
Used clothes	2,523	1,875	5,334
Television receivers	5,391	3,241	10,139
Other items	106,662	92,307	n.a.
Total	**551,748**	**622,416**	**846,022**

* Figures for 1982/83 are not available.

Total imports c.i.f. (US $ '000, year ending 20 March): 1,389,500 in 1984/85; 1,194,200 in 1985/86; 1,403,500 in 1986/87 (Source: IMF, *International Financial Statistics*).

Exports f.o.b.	1980/81	1981/82	1983/84*
Fresh fruit	39,762	50,544	66,374
Dried fruit	169,478	174,933	191,971
Hides and skins	14,491	11,711	15,547
Karakul fur skins	33,299	18,845	9,592
Oil-seeds	6,412	2,031	3,888
Wool and other animal hair	12,308	23,364	25,380
Cotton	39,650	22,566	10,175
Casings	5,369	4,617	3,336
Medicinal herbs and caraway seeds	4,206	11,511	16,524
Natural gas	233,128	272,589	305,276
Carpets and rugs	103,590	72,680	50,361
Other commodities	43,551	28,901	30,155
Total	**705,244**	**694,292**	**728,579**

* Figures for 1982/83 are not available.

1984/85 (US $ '000, year ending 20 March): Fruit and nuts 181,900; Karakul fur skins 9,200; Natural gas 314,300; Wool 26,100; Carpets 42,200; Cotton 22,400; Total (incl. others) 632,900.
1985/86 (US $ '000, year ending 20 March): Fruit and nuts 120,000; Karakul fur skins 10,500; Natural gas 309,400; Wool 22,500; Carpets 58,400; Cotton 19,200; Total (incl. others) 556,800.
1986/87 (US $ '000, year ending 20 March): Fruit and nuts 134,900; Karakul fur skins 10,500; Natural gas 259,600; Wool 14,600; Carpets 39,500; Cotton 9,800; Total (incl. others) 551,900 (Source: IMF, *International Financial Statistics*).

PRINCIPAL TRADING PARTNERS (US $ '000)

Imports	1980/81	1981/82	1983/84*
Germany, Federal Republic	16,959	16,779	17,076
Hong Kong	18,586	27,386	n.a.
India	20,572	17,024	28,985
Japan	98,207	76,670	111,061
Pakistan	14,895	11,737	14,882
USSR	290,496	365,000	526,319
USA	14,216	7,156	8,721
Total (incl. others)	**551,748**	**622,416**	**846,022**

* Figures for 1982/83 are not available.

Exports	1980/81	1981/82	1983/84*
Czechoslovakia	14,585	12,088	4,836
Germany, Federal Republic	51,513	41,801	26,130
India	54,746	43,212	84,212
Pakistan	52,101	61,249	118,080
Saudi Arabia	21,188	19,214	n.a.
USSR	417,872	412,635	400,756
United Kingdom	51,844	36,340	25,137
Total (incl. others)	**705,244**	**694,292**	**728,579**

* Figures for 1982/83 are not available.

Transport

ROAD TRAFFIC (motor vehicles in use)

	1979/80	1980/81	1981/82
Passenger cars	34,192	34,080	34,908
Commercial vehicles	27,555	28,714	30,800

CIVIL AVIATION (year ending 20 March)

	1979/80	1980/81	1981/82
Kilometres flown ('000)	3,765	3,012	2,071
Passengers carried	104,000	86,199	69,364
Passenger-km ('000)	238,068	173,855	164,455
Freight ton-km ('000)	19,084	21,366	21,032
Cargo and mail	6,000	7,070	7,752

Tourism

INTERNATIONAL TOURIST ARRIVALS BY COUNTRY

	1978	1979	1980
Australia	3,070	967	28
France	4,781	1,153	234
Germany, Federal Republic	7,496	1,817	258
India	9,744	4,350	992
Pakistan	23,663	10,126	2,466
United Kingdom	9,102	1,850	128
USA	6,389	1,039	79
Others	27,744	8,902	2,438
Total	**91,989**	**30,204**	**6,623**

1981: Total tourist arrivals 9,200.

Receipts from tourism (US $ million): 28 in 1978; 7 in 1979; 1 in 1980.

AFGHANISTAN

Communications Media

Telephones in use: 23,680 in 1979/80. Radio receivers in use: an estimated 135,000 in 1986. Television receivers in use: an estimated 12,800 in 1986.

Education

(1985)

	Teachers	Pupils
Pre-primary	873	17,000
Elementary	15,881	580,499
Secondary*	5,715	105,032

* Figures refer to general education only, excluding vocational training (teachers 1,262 in 1980; pupils 12,410 in 1980; 14,532 in 1981).

Higher education (1982): Universities, etc.: 1,212 teachers, 13,611 students; Other institutions: 512 teachers, 6,041 students.

Source: UNESCO, *Statistical Yearbook*.

Directory

The Constitution

Immediately after the coup of 27 April 1978 (the Saur Revolution), the 1977 Constitution was abolished. Both Nur Muhammad Taraki (Head of State from April 1978 to September 1979) and his successor, Hafizullah Amin (September–December 1979), promised to introduce new constitutions, but these leaders were removed from power before any drafts had been prepared by special commissions which they had appointed. On 21 April 1980 the Revolutionary Council ratified the Basic Principles of the Democratic Republic of Afghanistan. These were superseded by a new constitution ratified in April 1985. Another new constitution was ratified by a meeting of the Loya Jirgah (National Assembly), held on 29–30 November 1987. The following is a summary of the 1987 Constitution:

GENERAL PROVISIONS

The fundamental duty of the State is to defend the independence, national sovereignty and territorial integrity of the Republic of Afghanistan. National sovereignty belongs to the people.

Foreign policy is based on the principle of peaceful co-existence and active and positive non-alignment. Friendship and co-operation are to be strengthened with all countries, particularly neighbouring and Islamic ones. Afghanistan abides by the UN Charter and the Universal Declaration of Human Rights and supports the struggle against colonialism, imperialism, Zionism, racism and fascism. Afghanistan favours disarmament and the prevention of proliferation of nuclear and chemical weapons. War propaganda is prohibited.

Islam is the religion of Afghanistan and no law shall run counter to the principles of Islam.

Political parties are allowed to be formed, under the auspices of the National Front, providing that their policies and activities are in accordance with the provisions of the Constitution.

Pashtu and Dari are the official languages.

The capital is Kabul.

The State shall follow the policy of understanding and co-operation between all nationalities, clans and tribes within the country to ensure equality and the rapid development of backward regions.

The family constitutes the basic unit of society. The State shall adopt necessary measures to ensure the health of mothers and children.

The State protects all forms of legal property, including private property. The State guarantees the right of ownership of land. The hereditary right to property shall be guaranteed according to Islamic law.

The State shall develop and strengthen both the State sector (particularly co-operatives) and the private sector of the economy. Domestic and foreign trade are directed and regulated by the State, in accordance with the interests of the people.

RIGHTS AND DUTIES OF THE PEOPLE

All subjects of Afghanistan are equal before the law. The following rights are guaranteed: the right to life and security, to complain to the appropriate government organs, to participate in the political sphere, to freedom of speech and thought, to hold peaceful demonstrations and strikes, to work, to free education, to protection of health and social welfare, to scientific, technical and cultural activities, to freedom of movement both within Afghanistan and abroad, to observe the religious rites of Islam and of other religions, to security of residence and privacy of communication and correspondence, and to liberty and human dignity.

In criminal cases, an accused person is considered innocent until guilt is recognized by the court. Nobody may be arrested, detained or punished except in accordance with the law.

Every citizen is bound to observe the Constitution and the laws of the Republic of Afghanistan, to pay taxes and duties to the state in accordance with the provisions of the law, and to undertake military service, when and as required.

LOYA JIRGAH

This is the highest manifestation of the will of the people of Afghanistan. It is composed of: members of the Meli Shura (National Assembly), 10 deputies of the people from each province and equivalent administrative unit, the governors of each province and the mayor of Kabul, the Council of Ministers, the Chief Justice and his deputies and judges of the Supreme Court, the Attorney-General and his deputies, the Constitution Council, the executive board of the National Front, and a maximum of 50 people appointed by the President on the basis of the recommendation of the secretariat of the National Front.

The Loya Jirgah is empowered: to approve and amend the Constitution; to elect the President and to accept the resignation of the President; to consent to the declaration of war and armistice; and to adopt decisions on major questions regarding the destiny of the country. The Loya Jirgah shall be summoned, opened and chaired by the President. Sessions of the Loya Jirgah require a minimum attendance of two-thirds of the members. Decisions shall be adopted by a majority vote. In the event of the dissolution of the Wolasi Jirgah (House of Representatives), its members shall retain their membership of the Loya Jirgah until a new Wolasi Jirgah is elected. Elections to the Loya Jirgah shall be regulated by law and the procedure laid down by the Loya Jirgah itself.

THE PRESIDENT

The President is the Head of State and shall be elected by a majority vote of the Loya Jirgah for a term of seven years. No person can be elected as President for more than two terms. The President is accountable, and shall report, to the Loya Jirgah. The Loya Jirgah shall be convened to elect a new President 30 days before the end of the term of office of the outgoing President. Any Muslim citizen of the Republic of Afghanistan who is more than 40 years of age can be elected as President.

The President shall exercise the following executive powers: the supreme command of the armed forces; the ratification of the resolutions of the Meli Shura; the appointment of the Prime Minister; the approval of the appointment of ministers, judges and army officials; the granting of citizenship and the commuting of punishment; the power to call a referendum, to proclaim a state of emergency, and to declare war (with the consent of the Loya Jirgah).

In the event of the President being unable to perform his duties, the presidential functions and powers shall be entrusted to the first Vice-President. In the event of the death or resignation of the President, the first Vice-President shall ask the Loya Jirgah to elect a new President within one month. In the event of resignation, the President shall submit his resignation directly to the Loya Jirgah.

AFGHANISTAN

MELI SHURA

The Meli Shura (National Assembly) is the highest legislative organ of the Republic of Afghanistan. It consists of two houses: the Wolasi Jirgah (House of Representatives) and the Sena (Senate). Members of the Wolasi Jirgah (representatives) are elected from electoral constituencies for a legislative term of five years. Members of the Sena (senators) are elected and appointed in the following manner: two people from each province and equivalent administrative unit are elected for a period of five years; two people from each provincial council and equivalent councils are elected by the council for a period of three years; and the remaining one-third of senators are appointed by the President for a period of three years.

The Meli Shura is vested with the authority: to approve, amend and repeal laws and legislative decrees, and to present them to the President for his signature; to interpret laws; to ratify and annul international treaties; to approve socio-economic development plans and to endorse the Government's reports on their execution; to approve the state budget and to evaluate the Government's report on its execution; to establish and make changes to administrative units; to establish and abolish ministries and equivalent organs; to appoint and remove Vice-Presidents, on the recommendation of the President; and to endorse the establishment of relations with foreign countries and international organizations. The Wolasi Jirgah also has the power to approve a vote of confidence or no confidence in the Council of Ministers or one of its members.

At its first session, the Wolasi Jirgah elects, from among its members, an executive committee, composed of a chairman, two deputy chairmen and two secretaries, for the whole term of the legislature. The Sena elects, from among its members, an executive committee, composed of a chairman for a term of five years, and two deputy chairmen and two secretaries for a term of one year.

Ordinary sessions of the Meli Shura are held twice a year and do not normally last longer than three months. An extraordinary session can be held at the request of the President, the chairman of either house, or one-fifth of the members of each house. The houses of the Meli Shura can hold separate or joint sessions. Sessions require a minimum attendance of two-thirds of the members of each house and decisions shall be adopted by a majority vote. Sessions are open, unless the houses decide to meet in closed sessions.

The following authorities have the right to propose the introduction, amendment or repeal of a law in either house of the Meli Shura: the President, the standing commissions of the Meli Shura, at least one-tenth of the membership of each house, the Council of Ministers, the Supreme Court, the office of the Attorney-General, the executive board of the National Front, and the High Council of Ulema and Clergy.

If the decision of one house is rejected by the other, a joint committee, consisting of an equal number of members from both houses, shall be formed. If the joint committee fails to resolve differences, the matter shall be discussed in a joint session of the Meli Shura, and a decision reached by a majority vote. The decisions that are made by the Meli Shura are enforced after being signed by the President.

After consulting the chairman of the Wolasi Jirgah, the chairman of the Sena, the Prime Minister and the Chief Justice, the President can declare the dissolution of the Wolasi Jirgah, stating his justification for doing so. Re-elections shall be held within 30 days of the dissolution.

COUNCIL OF MINISTERS

The Council of Ministers is composed of: a Prime Minister, deputy Prime Ministers, Ministers, and presidents of central organs, which are equivalent to ministries. The Council of Ministers is appointed by the Prime Minister. It is empowered: to formulate and implement domestic and foreign policies; to formulate economic development plans and state budgets; and to ensure public order.

The term of office of the Council of Ministers shall expire at the end of the legislative term of the Wolasi Jirgah.

THE JUDICIARY

(See section on the Judicial System.)

THE CONSTITUTION COUNCIL

The responsibilities of this body are: to evaluate and ensure the conformity of laws, legislative decrees and international treaties with the Constitution; and to give legal and judicial advice to the President on constitutional matters. The Constitution Council is composed of a chairman, a deputy chairman and eight members, who are appointed by the President for a term of six years.

LOCAL ADMINISTRATIVE ORGANS

For the purposes of local administration, the Republic of Afghanistan is divided into provinces, divisions, districts, cities, sub-districts, precincts and villages. Each administrative unit has a local council, with an executive committee headed by governors, mayors, village chiefs, sub-district administrators, and heads of precincts. The term of office of local councils is three years.

FINAL PROVISIONS

Amendments to the Constitution shall be made by the Loya Jirgah. Any amendment shall be on the proposal of the President, or on the proposal of one-third and the approval of two-thirds of the members of the Meli Shura. Amendment to the Constitution during a state of emergency is not allowed.

The Government

HEAD OF STATE

President: Dr Najibullah Ahmadzai (took office 30 November 1987).

Vice-Presidents: Abd ar-Rahim Hatif, Lt-Gen. Muhammad Rafi, Abd al-Hamid Mohtat, Dr Abd al-Wahed Sorabi.

COUNCIL OF MINISTERS
(December 1988)

Prime Minister: Dr Muhammad Hasan Sharq.
Deputy Prime Ministers: Sayed Amanoddin Amin, Muhammad Sarwar Mangal, Mahbubollah Koshani.
Minister of Finance: Hamidollah Tarzi.
Minister of the Interior: Maj.-Gen. Muhammad Aslam Watanjar.
Minister of Defence: Lt-Gen. Shahnawaz Tanay.
Minister of Foreign Affairs: Abd al-Wakil.
Minister of State Security: Lt-Gen. Ghulam Faruq Yaqubi.
Minister of Justice: Muhammad Bashir Baghlani.
Minister of Commerce: Muhammad Khan Jalalar.
Minister of Planning: Soltan Hosayn.
Minister of Islamic Affairs and Endowment: I. Rashid (acting).
Minister of Higher and Vocational Education: Nur Ahmad Barets.
Minister of Public Health: Dr Abd al-Fatah Najm.
Minister of Agriculture and Land Reform: Eng. Muhammad Ghofran.
Minister of Border Affairs: Suleiman La'eq.
Minister of Returnees' Affairs: Abd al-Ghafar.
Minister of Education and Training: Prof. Gholam Rasul.
Minister of Civil Aviation: Pacha Gol Wafadar.
Minister of Transport: Muhammad Aziz.
Minister of Mines and Industries: Muhammad Eshaq Kawa.
Minister of Water and Electricity: Prof. Ras Muhammad Paktin.
Minister of Construction Affairs: Nazar Muhammad.
Minister of Communications: (vacant).
Minister of Revival and Rural Development: Muhammad Asef Zaher.
Minister of Light Industries and Foodstuffs: Dost Muhammad Fazl.
Minister of Information and Culture: Bashir Ahmad Roygar.

MINISTRIES

Office of the Council of Ministers: Shar Rahi Sedarat, Kabul; tel. (93) 26926.

Office of the Prime Minister: Shar Rahi Sedarat, Kabul; tel. (93) 26926.

Ministry of Agriculture and Land Reform: Jamal Mina, Kabul; tel. (93) 41151.

Ministry of Border Affairs: Shah Mahmud Ghazi Ave, Kabul; tel. (93) 21793.

Ministry of Civil Aviation: POB 165, Ansari Wat, Kabul; tel. (93) 21015.

Ministry of Commerce: Darulaman Wat, Kabul; tel. (93) 41041; telex 34.

Ministry of Communications: Puli Bagh-i-Omomi, Kabul; tel. (93) 21341; telex 297.

Ministry of Construction Affairs: Micro-Rayon, Kabul; tel. (93) 63701.

AFGHANISTAN

Ministry of Defence: Darulaman Wat, Kabul; tel. (93) 41232.
Ministry of Education: Shar Rahi Malek Asghar, Kabul; tel. (93) 25151.
Ministry of Energy: Micro-Rayon, Kabul; tel. (93) 25109.
Ministry of Finance: Shar Rahi Pashtunistan, Kabul; tel. (93) 26041.
Ministry of Foreign Affairs: Shah Mahmud Ghazi St, Shar-i-Nau, Kabul; tel. (93) 25441.
Ministry of Higher and Vocational Education: Jamal Mina, Kabul; tel. (93) 40041.
Ministry of the Interior: Shar-i-Nau, Kabul; tel. (93) 32441.
Ministry of Justice: Shar Rahi Pashtunistan, Kabul; tel. (93) 23404.
Ministry of Light Industries and Foodstuffs: Ansari Wat, Kabul; tel. (93) 41551.
Ministry of Mines and Industries: Shar Rahi Pashtunistan, Kabul; tel. (93) 25841.
Ministry of Planning: Shar-i-Nau, Kabul; tel. (93) 21273.
Ministry of Public Health: Micro-Rayon, Kabul; tel. (93) 40851.
Ministry of State Security: Kabul.
Ministry of Transport: Ansari Wat, Kabul; tel. (93) 25541.
Ministry of Water Resources Development and Irrigation: Darulaman Wat, Kabul; tel. (93) 40743.

POLITBURO OF THE CENTRAL COMMITTEE OF THE PEOPLE'S DEMOCRATIC PARTY OF AFGHANISTAN

General Secretary: Dr NAJIBULLAH.
Full Members: SULTAN ALI KESHTMAND, NUR AHMAD NUR, Lt-Gen. MUHAMMAD RAFI, Maj.-Gen. MUHAMMAD ASLAM WATANJAR, Lt-Gen. GHULAM FARUQ YAQUBI, ABD AL-WAKIL, SULEIMAN LA'EQ, Lt-Gen. SAYED MUHAMMAD GULABZOI, NAJMUDDIN KAWIANI, NIAZ MUHAMMAD MOHMAND, HAYDAR MASUD.
Candidate Members: Lt-Gen. NAZAR MUHAMMAD, FARID AHMAD MAZDAK, Lt-Gen. SHAHNAWAZ TANAI, MIR SAHEB KARWAL.

Legislature

MELI SHURA
(National Assembly)

The Meli Shura, which was established in 1987 and replaced the Revolutionary Council, is composed of two houses: the Wolasi Jirgah (House of Representatives) and the Sena (Senate). Elections were held to both houses in April 1988.

Wolasi Jirgah

Representatives are elected for five years. Of the total 234 seats, 184 were contested in the general election in April 1988. The remaining 50 seats were reserved for members of the opposition.
Chairman: Dr KHALIL AHMAD ABAWI.

Sena

The Sena comprises 192 members. One-third of its members are elected for five years, one-third are elected for three years, and one-third are appointed for three years. At the general election in 1988, 115 senators were elected, while the majority of the remaining 77 seats were filled by senators appointed by the President. A small number of seats were reserved for members of the opposition.
Chairman: Dr MAHMUD HABIBI.

Political Organizations

Jamiyat-e Demokrati Khalq-e Afghanistan (People's Democratic Party of Afghanistan—PDPA): Kabul; f. 1965, split 1967; refounded 1976, when the Khalq (Masses) Party and its splinter Parcham (Flag) Party reunited and absorbed the Musawat Party; communist; 205,000 mems; cen. cttee of 140 mems; Secretariat of Cen. Cttee Dr NAJIBULLAH, NUR AHMAD NUR, NIAZ MUHAMMAD MOHMAND, SULTAN ALI KESHTMAND, MIR SAHEB KARWAL, NAJMUDDIN KAWIANI, HAYDAR MASUD, MUHAMMAD DAUD RAZMYAR, ABD AL-QADER ASHNA, MUHAMMAD KHALIL SEPAHI, MUHAMMAD ANWAR ESAR, MUHAMMAD SHARIF.
National Front (NF): POB 4010, Kabul; tel. (93) 40439; telex 232; f. 1981, as National Fatherland Front, as union of PDPA representatives, nat. and tribal groups; aims to promote nat. unity, reconciliation and reconstruction; became a collective organization for all legal political activity in 1987, when it was renamed National Front; Exec. Board of 51 mems; Chair. Cen. Council ABD AR-RAHIM HATIF; First Dep. Chair. SAYED EKRAM PAYGIR; c. 800,000 mems.

In July 1987 a law permitting the formation of other political parties was introduced. In order to be officially recognized, a party must support national reconciliation, have at least 500 members and be based in Kabul.

The following organizations have been approved and registered as political parties by the Government since November 1987:

Islamic Party of the People of Afghanistan (IPPA): Kabul; Chair. Qari ABD AS-SATAR SERAT; Vice-Chair. ABD AL-GHAFUR BAHER.
Ittehad-i-Ansarollah (Union of Followers of God): Kabul; f. 1988; Islamic; Pres. Haji ZAFAR MOHAMMAD KHADEM.
Peasants' Justice Party of Afghanistan (PJPA): Kabul; Chair. ABD AL-HAKIM TAWANA.
Solidarity Movement of Afghan People: Kabul; f. 1988; Chair. SARWAR NURESTANI.
Toilers' Organization of Afghanistan (TOA): Kabul; left-wing; signed co-operation agreement with the PDPA in 1987; First Sec. HAMIDOLLAH GRAN.
Toilers' Revolutionary Organization of Afghanistan (TROA): Kabul; f. 1968; left-wing; signed co-operation agreement with the PDPA in 1987; Leaders MAHBUBOLLAH KOSHANI, MUHAMMAD BASHIR BAGHLANI, MUHAMMAD ESHAQ KAWA.

There are many insurgent groups of Mujaheddin fighting against the Government in Afghanistan. The different groups co-operate to varying degrees, but relations are often strained by rivalry and feuding. In May 1985 seven major groups (each with its headquarters in Pakistan) formed a grand alliance, called the **Ittehad-i-Islami Afghan Mujaheddin** (Islamic Unity of Afghan Mujaheddin—IUAM; POB 185, Charsadda Rd, Peshawar, Pakistan; Chair. and Spokesman October 1988–January 1989: Prof. BURHANUDDIN RABBANI; the leadership is changed every three months; c. 100,000 mems), comprising three moderate/traditionalist groups:

Harakat-i-Inqilab-i-Islami (Movement for Islamic Revolution): Leaders MAULVI MUHAMMAD NABI MUHAMMADI and NASRULLAH MANSUR.
Jebha-i-Nejat-i-Melli Afghanistan (Afghan National Liberation Front): Leader Prof. SIBGHATULLAH MOJADDEDI.
Mahaz-i-Melli-i-Islami (National Islamic Front): Leader Pir SAYED AHMAD GAILANI.

and four fundamentalist groups:

Hizb-i Islami (Islamic Party): split into two factions in 1979; Leaders GULBUDDIN HEKMATYAR and MAULVI MUHAMMAD YUNUS KHALIS.
Jamiat-i Islami (Islamic Society): f. 1970; Leader Prof. BURHANUDDIN RABBANI.
Ittehad-i-Islami (Islamic Unity): Leader Prof. ABD AR-RASUL SAYEF; Deputy Leader AHMAD SHAH.

In June 1987 eight Afghan Islamic factions (based in Teheran, Iran) formed the **Islamic Coalition Council of Afghanistan** (ICCA Spokesman: Hojatoleslam ALEMI), comprising the **Afghan Nasr Organization**, the **Guardians of Islamic Jihad of Afghanistan**, the **United Islamic Front of Afghanistan**, the **Islamic Force of Afghanistan**, the **Dawa Party of Islamic Unity of Afghanistan**, the **Harakat-e Eslami Afghanistan** (the Islamic Movement of Afghanistan; Leader: Ayatollah ASEF MOHSENI), the **Hezbollah**, and the **Islamic Struggle for Afghanistan**.

Diplomatic Representation

EMBASSIES IN AFGHANISTAN*

Austria: POB 24, Zarghouna Wat, Kabul; tel. (93) 32720; telex 218; Ambassador: (vacant).
Bangladesh: POB 510, House 19, Sarak 'H', Wazir Akbar Khan Mena, Kabul; tel. (93) 25783; Chargé d'affaires a.i.: MAHMOOD HASAN.
Bulgaria: Wazir Akbar Khan Mena, Kabul; tel. (93) 22996; Ambassador: IVAN MATEEV.
China, People's Republic: Shah Mahmud Wat, Shar-i-Nau, Kabul; tel. (93) 20446; Chargé d'affaires a.i.: ZHANG DELIANG.
Cuba: Shar Rahi Haji Yaqub, opp. Shar-i-Nau Park, Kabul; tel. (93) 30863; Ambassador: REGINO FARINAS CANTERO.
Czechoslovakia: Taimani Wat, Kala-i-Fatullah, Kabul; tel. (93) 32082; Ambassador: BOHUSLAV HANDL.
France: Shar-i-Nau, Kabul; tel. (93) 23631; Chargé d'affaires a.i.: CHRISTIAN LAMBERT.

AFGHANISTAN
Directory

German Democratic Republic: Ghazi Ayub Khan Wat, Shar-i-Nau, Kabul; tel. (93) 20782; telex 249; Ambassador: KRAFT BUMBEL.

Germany, Federal Republic: POB 83, Wazir Akbar Khan Mena, Kabul; tel. (93) 22432; telex 25; Chargé d'affaires a.i.: Dr GERD MASSMANN.

Hungary: POB 830, Sin 306–308, Wazir Akbar Khan Mena, Kabul; tel. (93) 20469; Ambassador: MIHALY GOLUB.

India: Malalai Wat, Shar-i-Nau, Kabul; tel. (93) 30557; Ambassador: INDER PAL KHOSLA.

Indonesia: POB 532, Wazir Akbar Khan Mena, District 10, House 93, Kabul; tel. (93) 23334; telex 239; Chargé d'affaires a.i.: ABDULLAH FUAD RACHMAN.

Iran: Shar-i-Nau, Kabul; tel. (93) 26255; Chargé d'affaires a.i.: AHMAD KHUDADADI.

Iraq: POB 523, Wazir Akbar Khan Mena, Kabul; tel. (93) 24797; Ambassador: BURHAN KHALIL GHAZAL.

Italy: POB 606, Khoja Abdullah Ansari Wat, Kabul; tel. (93) 24624; telex 55; Chargé d'affaires a.i.: CALAMAI.

Japan: POB 80, Wazir Akbar Khan Mena, Kabul; tel. (93) 26844; telex 216; Chargé d'affaires a.i.: KEIKI HIRAGA.

Korea, Democratic People's Republic: Wazir Akbar Khan Mena, House 28, Sarak 'H' House 103, Kabul; tel. (93) 22161; Ambassador: KANG HUI-SUN.

Libya: 103 Wazir Akbar Khan Mena, Kabul; tel. (93) 25947; Secretary: SALEM A. EL-HUNI.

Mongolia: Wazir Akbar Khan Mena, Sarak 'T' House 8714, Kabul; tel. (93) 22138; Ambassador: AGVAANDORJIYN TSOLMON.

Pakistan: Zarghouna Wat, Shar-i-Nau, Kabul; tel. (93) 21374; Chargé d'affaires a.i.: S. FIDA YUNAS.

Poland: Gozargah St, Kabul; tel. (93) 42461; Ambassador: EDWARD PORADKO.

Turkey: Shar-i-Nau, Kabul; tel. (93) 20072; Chargé d'affaires a.i.: SALIH ZEKI KARACA.

USSR: Darulaman Wat, Kabul; tel. (93) 41541; Ambassador: YULIY MIKHAILOVICH VORONTSOV.

United Kingdom: Karte Parwan, Kabul; tel. (93) 30511; Chargé d'affaires a.i.: IAN W. MACKLEY.

USA: Khwaja Abdullah Ansari Wat, Kabul; tel. (93) 24231; Chargé d'affaires a.i.: JOHN GLASSMANN.

Viet-Nam: 3 Nijat St, Wazir Akbar Khan Mena, Kabul; tel. (93) 26596; Ambassador: (vacant).

Yugoslavia: 923 Main Rd, Wazir Akbar Khan Mena, Kabul; tel. (93) 23671; Ambassador: (vacant).

* Not all of the above-mentioned countries recognize the Soviet-backed administration as the legitimate government of Afghanistan.

Judicial System

The functions and structure of the judiciary are established in Articles 107–121 of the Constitution ratified by the Loya Jirgah in November 1987.

The courts apply the provisions of the Constitution and the laws of the Republic of Afghanistan, and, in cases of ambivalence, will judge in accordance with the rules of Shari'a (Islamic religious law). Trials are held in open session except when circumstances defined by law deem the trial to be held in closed session. Trials are conducted in Pashtu and Dari or in the language of the majority of the inhabitants of the locality. The right to speak in court in one's mother tongue is guaranteed to the two sides of the lawsuit.

The judiciary comprises the Supreme Court, provincial, city, divisional, precinct and sub-district courts, the courts of the armed forces and other such special courts as are formed in accordance with the directives of the law.

The highest judicial organ is the Supreme Court, which consists of a Chief Justice, deputy Chief Justices and judges, all of whom are appointed by the President for a term of six years. It supervises the judicial activities of the courts and ensures the uniformity of law enforcement and interpretation by those courts.

Death sentences are carried out after ratification by the President.

Chief Justice of the Supreme Court: NEZAMUDDIN TAHZIB.

The Public Prosecution Department consists of the Attorney-General, provincial, divisional, district, sub-district, city and precinct attorney offices, the attorney office of the armed forces, and other such special offices as are formed in accordance with the directives of the law. The Attorney-General supervises the activities of all the attorney offices, which are independent of local organs and answerable only to the Attorney-General himself. The Attorney-General and his deputies, who are appointed by the President for a term of six years, supervise the implementation and observance of all laws.

Attorney-General: MUHAMMAD OSMAN RASEKH.

Religion

The official religion of Afghanistan is Islam. Muslims comprise 99% of the population, approximately 80% of them of the Sunni and the remainder of the Shi'ite sect. There are small minority groups of Hindus, Sikhs and Jews.

ISLAM

The High Council of Ulema and Clergy of Afghanistan: Kabul; Chair. MAWLAWI GHOLAM SARWAR MANZUR.

The Press

The newspapers and periodicals marked * were reported to be the only ones appearing regularly in 1988.

PRINCIPAL DAILIES

*Anis: (Friendship): Kabul; f. 1927; evening; independent; Dari and Pashtu; news and literary articles; organ of the NF; Chief Editor MOHAMMAH S. KHARNIKASH; circ. 25,000.

Badakhshan: Faizabad; f. 1945; Dari and Pashtu; Chief Editor HADI ROSTAQI; circ. 3,000.

Bedar: Mazar-i-Sharif; f. 1920; Dari and Pashtu; Chief Editor ROZEQ FANI; circ. 2,500.

Ettehadi-Baghlan: Baghlan; f. 1930; Dari and Pashtu; Chief Editor SHAFIQULLAH MOSHFEQ; circ. 1,200.

*Haqiqat-e Enqelab-e Saur (Truth of the April Revolution): Kabul; f. 1980; Dari; organ of the PDPA; Editor BAREQ SHAFII; circ. 50,000.

*Hewad: Kabul; f. 1959; Dari and Pashtu; State-owned; Editor-in-Chief ABDULLAH BAKHTIANAE; circ. 12,200.

*Ittifak Islam: Herat; Dari and Pashtu.

Jawzjan: Jawzjan; f. 1942; Dari and Pashtu; Chief Editor A. RAHEM HAMRO; circ. 1,500.

*Kabul New Times: POB 983, Ansari Wat, Kabul; tel. (93) 61847; f. 1962 as Kabul Times, renamed 1980; English; State-owned; Editor-in-Chief M. SEDDIQ RAHPOE; circ. 5,000.

Nangarhor: Jalalabad; f. 1919; Pashtu; Chief Editor MORAD SANGARMAL; circ. 1,500.

Sanae: Parwan; f. 1953; Dari and Pashtu; Chief Editor G. SAKHI ESHANZADA; circ. 1,700.

*Seistan: Farah; f. 1947; Dari and Pashtu; Editor-in-Chief M. ANWAR MAHAL; circ. 1,800.

Tulu-i-Afghan: Qandahar; f. 1924; Pashtu; Chief Editor TAHER SHAFEQ; circ. 1,500.

Wolanga: Paktia; f. 1943; Pashtu; Chief Editor M. ANWAR; circ. 1,500.

PERIODICALS

*Adalat (Justice): Kabul; f. 1988; monthly; organ of the Peasants' Justice Party.

*Afghanistan: Historical Society of Afghanistan, Kabul; tel. (93) 30370; f. 1948; quarterly; English and French; historical and cultural; Editor MALIHA ZAFAR.

*Afghanistan Today: POB 1013, Ansari Wat, Kabul; tel. (93) 61353; monthly; State-owned.

*Al-Eslam: Kabul; f. 1988; monthly; organ of the Islamic Party of the People of Afghanistan; Editor-in-Chief Mawlawi NASROLLAH HANIFI; circ. 5,000.

*Aryana: Historical Society of Afghanistan, Kabul; tel. (93) 30370; f. 1943; quarterly; Pashtu and Dari; cultural and historical; Editor ABD AL-HADI HAND.

*Awaz: Kabul; f. 1940; monthly; Pashtu and Dari; radio and television programmes; Editor NASIR TOHORI; circ. 20,000.

*Eqtesad (Economics): Afghan Chambers of Commerce and Industry, Mohd Jan Khan Wat, Kabul; tel. (93) 26796; telex 45; f. 1922; weekly; Dari and Pashtu; Editor FAQIR MUHAMMAD.

*Erfan: Ministry of Education, Mohd Jan Khan Wat, Kabul; f. 1923; monthly; Dari and Pashtu; Chief Editor KUBRA MAZHARI MALORAW; circ. 2,500.

AFGHANISTAN

Ershad-e-Islam (Islamic Precepts): Kabul; f. 1987; publ. by the Ministry of Islamic Affairs; Editor MUHAMMAD SALEM KHARES.

Geography: Kabul; f. 1965; monthly; Pashtu and Dari; Editor-in-Chief STANAMIR ZAHER; circ. 2,500.

*Gharjestan: Kabul; f. 1988; every two months; political and cultural; for the people of Hazara.

Gorash: Ministry of Information and Culture, Mohd Jan Khan Wat, Kabul; f. 1979; weekly; Turkmani; Chief Editor S. MISEDIQ AMINI; circ, 1,000.

*Haqiqat-e-Sarbaz: Ministry of National Defence, Kabul; f. 1980; 3 a week; Dari and Pashtu; Chief Editor MER JAMALUDDIN FAKHR; circ. 18,370.

Helmand: Bost; f. 1954; 2 a week; Pashtu; Editor-in-Chief M. OMER FARHAT BALEGH; circ. 1,700.

Herat: Ministry of Information and Culture, Mohd Jan Khan Wat, Kabul; f. 1923; monthly; Dari and Pashtu; Chief Editor JALIL SHABGER FOLADYON.

*Kabul: Academy of Sciences, Scientific Research Centre for Languages and Literature, Kabul; f. 1931; monthly; Pashtu; literature and language research; Editor N. M. SAHEEM.

*Kar: POB 756, Kabul; tel. (93) 23040; weekly; publ. by the Central Council of Afghanistan Trade Unions; circ. 26,000.

*Kunar Periodical Journal: Asadabad; f. 1987; Pashtu; news and socio-economic issues; circ. 5,000.

Mojala-e-Ariana (Light): Kabul; f. 1978; monthly; Dari and Pashtu; Editor-in-Chief RASHID ASHTI; circ. 1,000.

*Muhasel-e-Emroz (Today's Student): Kabul; f. 1986; monthly; State-owned; juvenile; circ. 5,000.

Nengarhar: Kabul; f. 1919; weekly; Pashtu; Editor-in-Chief KARIM HASHIMI; circ. 1,500.

*Pamir: Micro-Rayon, Kabul; tel. (93) 20585; f. 1952; fortnightly; Dari and Pashtu; combined organ of the Kabul Cttee and Municipality; Chief Editor ENAYET POZHOHAN GURDANI; circ. 30,000.

Payam-e-Haq: Kabul; f. 1953; monthly; Dari and Pashtu; Editor-in-Chief FARAH SHAH MOHIBI; circ. 1,000.

*Qaria (Village): Kabul; f. 1987; weekly; life and developments in the countryside.

Samangon: Aibak; f. 1978; weekly; Dari; Editor-in-Chief M. MOHSEN HASSAN; circ. 1,500.

Sawad (Literacy): Kabul; f. 1954; monthly; Dari and Pashtu; Editor-in-Chief MALEM GOL ZADRON; circ. 1,000.

*Seramiasht: POB 3066, Afghan Red Crescent Society, Puli Artal, Kabul; tel. (93) 30969; telex 318; f. 1958; 2 a month; Dari, Pashtu and English; Editor H. R. JADIR; circ. 2,000.

Sob: Kabul; tel. (93) 25240; f. 1979; weekly; Balochi; Editor-in-Chief WALIMUHAMMAD ROKHSHONI; circ. 1,000.

Talim wa Tarbia (Education): Kabul; f. 1954; monthly; publ. by Institute of Education.

Urdu (Military): Kabul; f. 1922; quarterly; Dari and Pashtu; military journal; issued by the Ministry of National Defence; Chief Editor KHALILULAH AKBARI; circ. 500.

*Voice of Peace: The Extraordinary Supreme Commission for National Reconciliation of Afghanistan, Kabul; f. 1987; fortnightly; Dari and Pashtu; peace and reconciliation.

*Yulduz (Star): Ministry of Information and Culture, Mohd Jan Khan Wat, Kabul; f. 1979; weekly; Uzbeki and Turkmani; Chief Editor EKHAN BAYONI; circ. 2,000.

*Zendagi-e Hezbi (Party Life): Kabul; f. 1987; 6 a year; Dari and Pashtu; issued by the Central Committee of the PDPA.

Zeray: Academy of Sciences, Scientific Research Centre for Languages and Literature, Kabul; f. 1938; weekly; Pashtu; Pashtu folklore, literature and language; Editor MUHAMMAD NASSER; circ. 1,000.

*Zhwandoon (Life): Kabul; tel. (93) 26849; f. 1944; weekly; Pashtu and Dari; illustrated; Editor ROHELA ROSEKH KHORAMI; circ. 1,400.

NEWS AGENCIES

Bakhtar News Agency: Ministry of Information and Culture, Mohd Jan Khan Wat, Kabul; tel. (93) 24089; f. 1939; Pres. GHOLAM SARWAR YURESH; Dir ABD AL-QUDDUS TANDER.

Foreign Bureaux

Československá tisková kancelář (ČTK) (Czechoslovakia): POB 673, Kabul; tel. (93) 23419; telex 79.

The following foreign agencies are also represented in Kabul: APN (USSR; Correspondent ALEKSANDR TRUBIN) and Tanjug (Yugoslavia).

PRESS ASSOCIATION

Union of Journalists of Afghanistan: Wazir Akbar Khan Mena, St 13, Kabul; f. 1980; Sec. MAHMUD HABIBI.

Publishers

Afghan Book: POB 206, Kabul; f. 1969; books on various subjects, translations of foreign works on Afghanistan, books in English on Afghanistan and Dari language textbooks for foreigners; Man. Dir JAMILA AHANG.

Afghanistan Today Publishers: POB 983, c/o The Kabul Times, Ansari Wat, Kabul; tel. (93) 61847; publicity materials; answers enquiries about Afghanistan.

Balhaqi Book Publishing and Importing Institute: POB 2025, Kabul; tel. (93) 26818; f. 1971 by co-operation of the Government Printing House, Bakhtar News Agency and leading newspapers; publishers and importers of books; Pres. MUHAMMAD ANWAR NUMYALAI.

Book Publishing Institute: Herat; f. 1970 by co-operation of Government Printing House and citizens of Herat; books on literature, history and religion.

Book Publishing Institute: Qandahar; f. 1970; supervised by Government Printing House; mainly books in Pashtu language.

Educational Publications: Ministry of Education, Shar Rahi Malek Asghar, Kabul; tel. (93) 21716; textbooks for primary and secondary schools in the Pashtu and Dari languages; also three monthly magazines in Pashtu and in Dari.

Franklin Book Programs Inc: POB 332, Kabul.

Historical Society of Afghanistan: Kabul; tel. (93) 30370; f. 1931; mainly historical and cultural works and two quarterly magazines: *Afghanistan* (English and French), *Aryana* (Dari and Pashtu); Pres. AHMAD ALI MOTAMEDI.

Institute of Geography: Kabul University, Kabul; geographical and related works.

Kabul University Press: Kabul; tel. (93) 42433; f. 1950; textbooks; two quarterly scientific journals in Dari and in English, etc.

Pashtu Tolana (Pashtu Academy): Shar Alikhan St, Kabul; tel. (93) 20350; f. 1937 by the Dept of Press and Information; research works on Pashtu language and literature; Pres. POHAND RSHTEENE; publs *Zeray* (weekly), *Kabul* (monthly).

Government Publishing House

Government Printing House: Kabul; tel. (93) 26851; f. 1870 under supervision of the Ministry of Information and Culture; four daily newspapers in Kabul, one in English; weekly, fortnightly and monthly magazines, one of them in English; books on Afghan history and literature, as well as textbooks for the Ministry of Education; 13 daily newspapers in 13 provincial centres and one journal and also magazines in three provincial centres; Dir MUHAMMAD AYAN AYAN.

Radio and Television

In 1986 there were an estimated 135,000 radio receivers and 12,800 television receivers in use. Television broadcasting in colour began in August 1978 with a transmission range of 50 km. In March 1985 new radio stations were commissioned in Qandahar, Herat, Jalalabad, Ghazni and Asadabad, in addition to existing main stations in the provinces of Kabul and Nangarhar. Further radio stations were to be established in the provinces of Paktia, Farah and Badakhshan.

State Committee for Radio, TV and Cinematography: Ansari Wat, Kabul; Tel. (93) 25241; Chair. (vacant).

Radio Afghanistan and TV Afghanistan: POB 544, Ansari Wat, Kabul; tel. (93) 25241; under the supervision of the Ministry of Communications; in 1988 TV Afghanistan was broadcast 10 hours daily; home service (Radio) in Dari, Pashtu, Pashai, Nuristani, Uzbeki, Turkmani and Balochi; foreign service in Urdu, Arabic, English, Russian, German, Dari and Pashtu; Pres. (Radio) SAYED YAQUB WASIQ; Pres. (Television) ABDULLAH SHADAN.

Finance

(cap. = capital; auth. = authorized; p.u. = paid up; res = reserves; m. = million; brs = branches; amounts in afghanis)

BANKING

In June 1975 all banks were nationalized. There are no foreign banks operating in Afghanistan.

AFGHANISTAN

Da Afghanistan Bank (Central Bank of Afghanistan): Ibne Sina Wat, Kabul; tel. (93) 24075; telex 223; f. 1939; main functions: banknote issue, foreign exchange regulation, credit extensions to banks and leading enterprises and companies, govt and private depository, govt fiscal agency; cap. 4,000m., res 5,299m., dep. 15,008m. (1985); Gov. MUHAMMAD HAKIM; Pres. ABD AL-BASHIR RANJBAR; 70 brs.

Agricultural Development Bank of Afghanistan: POB 414, Kabul; tel. (93) 24459; telex 274; f. 1959; makes available credits for farmers, co-operatives and agro-business; aid provided by IBRD and UNDP; cap. 666.8m., res 438.0m. (March 1986); Chair. Dr BASSIR; Pres. M. IBRAHIM DILZADA.

Banke Milli Afghan (Afghan National Bank): Ibne Sina Wat, Kabul; tel. (93) 25451; telex 31; f. 1932; cap. p.u. 1,000m.; res 100.7m.; total resources 6,954.8m. (1986); Chair. H. E. ABD AL-WAKIL; Pres. MUHAMMAD AKRAM KHALIL; 68 brs.

Export Promotion Bank of Afghanistan: 24 Mohammad Jan Khan Wat, Kabul; tel. (93) 24447; telex 02; f. 1976; provides financing for exports and export-oriented investments; cap. and res 308m.; dep. 819m. (March 1984); Pres. GHULAM MUHAMMAD YEILAQI.

Industrial Development Bank of Afghanistan: POB 14, Jade Maiwand, Kabul; tel. (93) 25641; f. 1973; provides financing for industrial development; total financial resources including cap. 1,498m.; Pres. H. AZIZI; Vice-Pres. A. YARMAND.

Mortgage and Construction Bank: Bldg No. 2, First Part Jade Maiwand, Kabul; tel. (93) 23341; f. 1955 to provide short- and long-term building loans; auth. cap. 200m.; cap. p.u. 100m. (1987); Pres. FAIZ MUHAMMAD ALOKOZI.

Pashtany Tejaraty Bank (Afghan Commercial Bank): Mohd Jan Khan Wat, Kabul; tel. (93) 25641; telex 243; f. 1954 to provide short-term credits, forwarding facilities, opening letters of credit, purchase and sale of foreign exchange; cap. p.u. 1,000m., dep. 7,085.7m., total assets 19,826.4m. (1987); Pres. and CEO ZIR GUL WARDAK; Vice-Pres A. Q. FAZLY, A. K. KAKAR; 17 brs in Afghanistan and abroad.

INSURANCE

There is one national insurance company:

Afghan National Insurance Co: POB 329, Afghan Insurance Bldg, Timore Shahi Park, Kabul; tel. (93) 26518; telex 31; f. 1964; mem. of Asian Reinsurance Corpn; marine, aviation, fire, motor and accident insurance; cap. 75m.; Pres. M. Y. DEEN; Vice-Pres. ABD AR-RAZAQUE.

No foreign insurance companies are permitted to operate in Afghanistan.

Trade and Industry

CHAMBERS OF COMMERCE AND INDUSTRY

Afghan Chamber of Commerce and Industry: Mohd Jan Khan Wat, Kabul; tel. (93) 26796; telex 45; Pres. MUHAMMAD HAKIM.

Federation of Afghan Chambers of Commerce and Industry: Darulaman Wat, Kabul; f. 1923; includes chambers of commerce and industry in Ghazni, Qandahar, Kabul (Chair. Mr KARIMZADA), Herat (Chair. Mr SIDIQI), Mazar-i-Sharif, Fariab, Jawzjan, Kunduz, Jalalabad and Andkhoy; Pres. MEHAR CHAND VERMA; Deputy Pres. MUHAMMAD HAKIM.

TRADING CORPORATIONS

Afghan Carpet Exporters' Guild: POB 3159, Darulaman Wat, Kabul; tel. (93) 41765; telex 34; f. 1968; a non-profit making asscn of carpet manufacturers and exporters; Pres. AHMAD J. RATEB; 861 mems.

Afghan Cart Company: POB 61, Zarghona-Maidan, Kabul; tel. (93) 21952; telex 57; the largest export/import company in Afghanistan.

Afghan Fruits Processing Co: POB 261, Industrial Estate, Puli Charkhi, Kabul; tel. (93) 5184; telex 61; exports raisins, other dried fruits and nuts.

Afghan Raisin and Other Dried Fruits Institute: POB 3034, Sharara Wat, Kabul; tel. (93) 30463; telex 48; exporters of dried fruits and nuts.

Afghan Wool Enterprises: Shar-i-Nau, Kabul; tel. (93) 31963.

Afghanistan Karakul Institute: POB 506, Puli Charkhi, Kabul; tel. (93) 21952; exporters of furs.

Afghanistan Plants Enterprise: POB 122, Puli Charkhi, Kabul; tel. (93) 31962; exports medicines, plants and spices.

Handicraft Promotion and Export Centre: POB 3089, Sharara Wat, Kabul; tel. (93) 32935; telex 34; Pres. MOMENA RANJBAR.

TRADE UNIONS

In January 1988 union membership stood at 300,500.

Central Council of Afghanistan Trade Unions: POB 756, Kabul; tel. (93) 23040; f. 1978 to establish and develop the trade union movement, including the setting up of councils and organizational cttees in the provinces; 285,000 mems; Pres. ABD AS-SATAR PURDELI; Vice-Pres. AHMADULLAH POYA.

Balkh Council of Trade Unions: Mazar-i-Sharif; Pres. MUHAMMAD KABIR KARGAR.

Central Council of the Union of Craftsmen: Kabul; f. 1987; 72 mems.

Central Council of the Union of Peasant Co-operatives: Kabul; 125,000 mems; Chair. KHODAYNUR BAWAR.

Kabul Council of Trade Unions: Kabul; Chair. WASEI KARGAR.

Kabul Union of Furriers: Kabul; Leader ABD AL-KHALIQ.

Nangarhar Council of Trade Unions: Jalalabad; Deputy Chair. MUQREBUDDIN KARGAR.

Traders' Union of Afghanistan: Kabul; Chair. REZWANQOL TAMANA.

Writers' Union of Afghanistan: Kabul; Chair. AKRAM OSMAN.

Transport

RAILWAYS

In 1977 the Government approved plans for the creation of a railway system. The proposed line (of 1,815 km) was to connect Kabul to Qandahar and Herat, linking with the Iranian State Railways at Islam Quala and Tarakun, and with Pakistan Railways at Chaman. By 1988, however, work had not yet begun on the proposed railway.

A combined road and rail bridge was completed across the Amu-Dar'ya (Oxus) river in 1982, linking the Afghan port of Hairatan with the Soviet port of Termez. There are plans for a 200-km railway line from Hairatan to Pul-i-Khomri, 160 km north of Kabul, but work had not begun by 1988. It has been reported that Afghan personnel are receiving training in the USSR.

ROADS

Ministry of Communications and **Ministry of Construction Affairs:** Kabul; in 1986 there were 22,000 km of roads. All-weather highways now link Kabul with Qandahar and Herat in the south and west, Jalalabad in the east and Mazar-i-Sharif and the Amu-Dar'ya river in the north.

Land Transport Company: Khoshal Mena, Kabul; tel. (93) 20345; f. 1943; commercial transport within Afghanistan.

Afghan International Transport Company: Kabul.

Afghan Container Transport Company Ltd: POB 3234, Shar-i-Nau, Kabul; tel. (93) 23088; telex 17.

Afghan Transit Company: POB 530, Ghousy Market, Mohd Jan Khan Wat, Kabul; tel. (93) 22654; telex 76.

The Milli Bus Enterprise: Ministry of Transport, Kabul; state-owned and -administered; Pres. Eng. AZIZ NAGHABAN.

INLAND WATERWAYS

There are 1,200 km of navigable inland waterways, including the Amu-Dar'ya (Oxus) river. River ports on the Amu-Dar'ya are linked by road to Kabul.

CIVIL AVIATION

There are international airports at Kabul and Qandahar. The expansion of Kabul airport was due for completion in late 1987. There were also plans to construct six airports in the north-east, with Soviet help. There are 29 local airports.

Ministry of Civil Aviation: POB 165, Ansari Wat, Kabul; tel. (93) 26541; Dir-Gen. of Air Operations ABD AL-WASEH HAIDARI.

National Airline

Bakhtar Afghan Airlines: POB 76, Afghan Air Authority Bldg, Ansari Wat, Kabul; tel. (93) 24043; f. 1967; merged with Ariana Afghan Airlines Co Ltd in October 1985; internal services between Kabul and 14 regional locations; external services to the USSR, Czechoslovakia, Saudi Arabia, Iraq, India and the UAE; Pres. NIAZ MUHAMMAD; Gen. Man. S. L. SABHARWAL; fleet of 2 Boeing 727-100, 2 Tu-154M, 2 Antonov-26, 2 Antonov-24, 2 YAK-40, 1 DHC-6 Twin Otter.

Tourism

Afghanistan's potential attractions for the foreign visitor include: Bamian, with its high statue of Buddha and thousands of painted caves; Bandi Amir, with its suspended lakes; the Blue Mosque of Mazar; Herat, with its Grand Mosque and minarets; the towns of Qandahar and Girishk; Balkh (ancient Bactria), 'Mother of Cities', in the north; Bagram, Hadda and Surkh Kotal (of interest archaeologists); and the high mountains of the Hindu Kush. There were 9,200 visitors (including 4,700 from the USSR) in 1981, and about the same number in 1982.

Afghan Tour: Ansari Wat, Shar-i-Nau, Kabul; tel. (93) 30323; official travel agency supervised by ATO.

Afghan Tourist Organization (ATO): Ansari Wat, Shar-i-Nau, Kabul; tel. (93) 30323; f. 1958; Pres. M. OMAR KARIMZADA.

Atomic Energy

Atomic Energy Commission: Faculty of Science, Kabul University, Kabul; Pres. Dr MUHAMMAD RASUL.

ALBANIA

Introductory Survey

Location, Climate, Language, Religion, Flag, Capital

The People's Socialist Republic of Albania lies in south-eastern Europe. It is bordered by Yugoslavia to the north and east, by Greece to the south and by the Adriatic and Ionian Seas (parts of the Mediterranean Sea) to the west. The climate is Mediterranean throughout most of the country. The sea plays a moderating role, although frequent cyclones in the winter months make the weather unstable. The average temperature is 14°C (57°F) in the north-east and 18°C (64°F) in the south-west. The language is Albanian, the principal dialects being Gheg (north of the Shkumbini river) and Tosk (in the south). The literary language is being formed on the basis of a strong fusion of the two dialects, with the phonetic and morphological structure of Tosk prevailing. The State recognizes no religion and supports atheist propaganda. All religious institutions have been closed. Before 1946 Islam was the predominant faith, and there were small groups of Christians (mainly Roman Catholic in the north and Eastern Orthodox in the south). The national flag (proportions 7 by 5) is red, with a two-headed black eagle, above which is a gold-edged, five-pointed red star, in the centre. The capital is Tirana (Tiranë).

Recent History

On 28 November 1912, after more than 400 years of Turkish rule, Albania declared its independence under a provisional government. The country was occupied by Italy in 1914 but its independence was re-established in 1920. A republic was proclaimed in 1925 and Ahmet Beg Zogu was elected President. He was proclaimed King Zog in 1928 and reigned until the occupation of Albania by Italy in April 1939, after which Albania was united with the Italian crown for four years. Albania was occupied by German forces in 1943, but they withdrew after a year. A provisional government was formed in October 1944.

The Communist-led National Liberation Front (NLF), established with help from Yugoslav Communists in 1941, was the most successful wartime resistance group and took power on 29 November 1944. Elections in December 1945 were based on a single list of candidates, sponsored by the Communists. The new regime was led by Enver Hoxha, head of the Albanian Communist Party since 1943. King Zog was deposed and the People's Republic of Albania was proclaimed on 11 January 1946. The Communist Party was renamed the Party of Labour of Albania (PLA) in 1948.

The NLF regime had close links with Yugoslavia, including a monetary and customs union, until the latter's expulsion from the Cominform in 1948. Albania's leaders, fearing Yugoslav expansionism, quickly turned against their former mentors. Albania became a close ally of the USSR and joined the Moscow-based Council for Mutual Economic Assistance (CMEA) in 1949. Albania's adherence to the Eastern bloc was weakened by the relaxation of Soviet policy towards Yugoslavia after the death of Marshal Stalin, the Soviet leader, in 1953.

Hoxha resigned as Head of Government in 1954 but retained effective national leadership as First Secretary of the PLA. Albania joined the Warsaw Pact in 1955 but relations with the USSR deteriorated when Soviet leaders attempted a *rapprochement* with Yugoslavia. Albania supported Beijing in the Sino-Soviet ideological dispute. The USSR denounced Albania and broke off relations in 1961. Albania turned increasingly to the People's Republic of China for support, ended participation in the CMEA in 1962 and withdrew from the Warsaw Pact in 1968. However, following the improvement of relations between China and the USA after 1972, Albania became disenchanted with its alliance with Beijing. Sino-Albanian relations deteriorated further upon the death of Mao Zedong, the Chinese leader, in 1976. A new constitution was adopted in December 1976, declaring Albania a People's Socialist Republic, and reaffirming its policy of self-reliance.

In 1974 the Minister of Defence, Gen. Beqir Balluku, was dismissed, but it was not until 1978 that the Government chose to reveal that he had been involved in a plot against it on behalf of China, and that he had been executed in 1975. In 1978 Albania announced its full support of Viet-Nam in its dispute with Beijing, and China formally terminated all economic and military co-operation with Albania. Albania recognized the Vietnamese-backed government of Kampuchea in 1983.

In September 1979 Hysni Kapo, a member of the PLA's Politburo and one of Hoxha's closest collaborators, died. A government reshuffle took place in April 1980, and Mehmet Shehu, Chairman of the Council of Ministers since 1954, was relieved of his concurrent post of Minister of Defence. In December 1981 Shehu died as a result of a shooting incident. It was officially reported that he had committed suicide, but other sources suggested his involvement in a leadership struggle with Hoxha. (A year later Hoxha claimed that Shehu had been the leader of a plot to assassinate him, and in March 1985, amidst suggestions that Shehu had in fact been executed—which were subsequently denied by the Government—allegations that Shehu had worked as a secret agent, successively for the USA, the USSR and Yugoslavia, were repeated.) Following the death of Shehu, a new government was formed under Adil Çarçani, hitherto First Deputy Chairman. Feçor Shehu, Minister of the Interior and nephew of Mehmet Shehu, was not reappointed.

In September 1982 a group of armed Albanian exiles landed on the coast, but were promptly disposed of by the authorities. The Pretender to the throne of Albania, Leka I, while not directly involved, admitted his acquaintance with the rebels' leader. In November Ramiz Alia replaced Haxhi Lleshi as President of the Presidium of the People's Assembly (Head of State), and the Council of Ministers was reshuffled. A number of former state and Party officials, including Feçor Shehu and two other former Ministers, were reportedly executed in September 1983. In February 1984 an additional Deputy Chairman of the Council of Ministers was appointed.

Enver Hoxha died in April 1985. No foreign delegations were permitted to attend the funeral, and a Soviet message of condolence was rejected. Ramiz Alia replaced Hoxha as First Secretary of the PLA, and pledged that he would uphold the independent policies of his predecessor. In mid-1985 the Chairman of the State Planning Commission and the Minister of Finance were replaced. To celebrate the 40th anniversary of the proclamation of the Republic, in January 1986 an amnesty for certain categories of prisoners was announced. In March 1986 Nexhmije Hoxha, widow of Enver Hoxha, was elected to the chair of the General Council of the Democratic Front of Albania.

The Ninth PLA Congress was held in November 1986. The new Central Committee re-elected Ramiz Alia as First Secretary, and the number of full members of the Political Bureau was increased from 10 to 13. Following the election of a new People's Assembly in February 1987, Ramiz Alia was also re-elected President of its Presidium. Adil Çarçani was reappointed Chairman of the Council of Ministers, and the number of Deputy Chairmen was increased from three to four. The Ministry of Light and Foodstuff Industry was divided into two separate Ministries, and a State Control Commission was established at ministerial level. In February 1988 Farudin Hoxha was appointed to the newly-created post of Minister to the Presidium of the Council of Ministers.

Albania has diplomatic relations with over 100 countries. Albania remains hostile to the USSR, and Soviet attempts to renew links have been repeatedly rebuffed. In November 1986 Albania reiterated its determination not to have any relations with the USSR or the USA. Since the rift with Beijing, Albania has shown an interest in emerging from its isolation and in improving relations with Western nations. Two separate border incidents during 1984, in which a Frenchman employed on the Greek island of Corfu and a Greek citizen were shot dead by Albanian frontier guards, created only temporary setbacks. In 1985 delegations from the Italian and the French Ministries of Foreign Affairs visited Tirana, and it was reported that secret talks were taking place between Albania and the United Kingdom with a view to re-establishing diplomatic relations (severed as a result of the sinking of two British warships in the Corfu channel in 1946). In October 1985 the Albanian Minister of Foreign Trade, Shane Korbeci, visited Italy and was received by the Italian Prime Minister, Bettino Craxi. Relations between the two countries were subsequently strained, however, following an incident involving six Albanian citizens who entered the Italian embassy in Tirana in December 1985 in search of political asylum. In 1987 the Albanian family remained inside the embassy. In December 1986 two Italian trawlers were seized by the Albanian authorities while allegedly fishing illegally in Albania's territorial waters in the vicinity of Vlorë. The eight fishermen concerned were brought to trial in January 1987. Six Italians received suspended prison sentences of between four and 10 months, and the one-year sentences to the two captains were also suspended upon appeal to the Supreme Court. In January 1988 a delegation from the French National Assembly was received in Tirana, and in the following month the French Secretary of State for Foreign Affairs also visited Albania. Diplomatic relations with Spain were established in September 1986, and with Canada and the Federal Republic of Germany in September 1987. In October the Federal German Minister of Foreign Affairs paid an official visit to Albania, and in September 1988 the Albanian Minister of Foreign Affairs went to Bonn.

Negotiations between Albania and Greece took place in Athens in 1984, and in December the visit to Tirana by the Greek Minister of State for Foreign Affairs resulted in the signing of several co-operation agreements. In January 1985 the Albanian/Greek border crossing at Kakavija was reopened. In August 1987 Greece formally ended the technical state of war with Albania, in existence since 1945. Relations with Greece continued to improve in 1988, following a visit to Athens in April by the Albanian Minister of Foreign Affairs. However, the question of the status of the Greek minority in Albania, estimated to number 400,000, remains a sensitive issue, as does that of the 2m. ethnic Albanians resident in Yugoslavia. Ideological differences also prevent friendly relations with Yugoslavia. Since 1981, following riots in the Yugoslav province of Kosovo by ethnic Albanians demanding better conditions, relations between Albania and Yugoslavia have been strained. During 1985, however, talks on trade and transport between the two countries were successful. In October 1986 the Albanian Minister of Foreign Affairs and the Yugoslav Federal Secretary for Foreign Affairs held discussions at the UN in New York. The meeting was reportedly the first between the two countries' Foreign Ministers since 1946. In 1987 tension was renewed, owing to the failure of the Shkodër–Titograd railway line, but in December the Yugoslav Secretary for Foreign Trade visited Tirana for talks on bilateral co-operation. Links with Turkey were strengthened in August 1988, when the Turkish Minister of Foreign Affairs paid an official visit to Albania. In the same month the Japanese Deputy Minister of Foreign Affairs had talks in Tirana.

Albania was not represented at the 1984 Stockholm Conference on Security and Co-operation in Europe, and did not attend the Athens Conference on Balkan Co-operation and the creation of a nuclear-free zone. In February 1988, however, Albania attended a meeting of Balkan Foreign Ministers, held in Yugoslavia. At the conference, the first of all six Balkan nations for more than 50 years, the Albanian Minister of Foreign Affairs displayed a positive approach and emphasized the need for realism in regional co-operation. The participants agreed that ministerial delegations should meet on a regular basis in order to discuss multilateral co-operation. A meeting of Foreign Ministry officials was to be held in Tirana in January 1989. A further modification of Albanian policy was indicated in March 1988 when, for the first time since 1954, the anniversary of Stalin's death was reportedly not commemorated in Albania.

A report released in December 1984 by the human rights organization, Amnesty International, was highly critical of Albania's detention of thousands of political and religious dissidents.

Government

Nominally the supreme organ of government is the People's Assembly, a single-chamber legislature of 250 deputies. In practice the Assembly meets for only a few days each year to ratify actions taken in its name by the Presidium of the Assembly, whose President is Head of State. Executive authority is held by the Council of Ministers, whose Chairman is Head of Government. The Council is elected by the Assembly.

Real power is held by leaders of the (Communist) Party of Labour of Albania, or Workers' Party, the only political party in the country. The Party has a political monopoly; it controls the entire functioning of government, and all the country's leaders are members. The Party Congress, convened every five years, elects the Central Committee (85 full members and 46 candidate members were elected in November 1986), which, in turn, elects the Political Bureau (Politburo) and the Secretariat.

Elections to the People's Assembly, held every four years, are based on a single list of candidates standing for the Communist-led Democratic Front of Albania.

For local government, Albania is divided into 26 districts, each under a People's Council elected every three years.

Defence

Defence in Albania is conducted under the auspices of the People's Army, which was founded in 1943. Military service lasts for two years in the Army, and three years in the Air Force, Navy and paramilitary units. In July 1987, according to Western estimates, the total strength of the armed forces was 42,000 (including 22,400 conscripts), comprising Army 31,500, Air Force 7,200 and Navy 3,300. The internal security forces number 5,000 and the frontier force 7,000. Defence expenditure in 1986 was estimated at 978m. lekë.

Economic Affairs

In material terms, Albania is the poorest country in Europe. The World Bank's estimate of GNP per caput in 1981 was only US $820. There are, however, considerable mineral resources, and Albania is self-sufficient in grain. The economy operates on the principles of public ownership of the means of production. Long-term planning began in 1951, and by 1965 the semi-feudal society had been replaced by the state-run agrarian-industrial system. In 1987, however, there were indications that some measure of economic decentralization might be permitted. The need for improvements was also acknowledged.

The fifth Five-Year Plan (1971–75) aimed to develop production through extensive capital investments and large industrial building projects. During the sixth Five-Year Plan (1976–80) the annual growth in net material product (NMP) averaged 5%. Industrial output increased by an average annual rate of 6.8%. Agricultural production rose by 21.4% over the previous five-year period. Exports increased by 33%, with processed and semi-processed goods accounting for 70% of the total. The seventh Five-Year Plan (1981–85) envisaged an increase of 35–37% in NMP, but growth of only 16% was achieved. Industrial production was expected to rise by 36–38%, but went up by only 27%. Agricultural output increased by 13%, compared with a target of 30–32%. Exports were planned to increase by 58–60% but rose by only 29%. Imports went up by 23%, compared with a target of 56–58%.

The eighth Five-Year Plan (1986–90) continued to stress the development of energy and mineral resources, particularly the petroleum industry. Compared with 1985, the 'global social product' (gross output of goods and material services) was to increase by 31–33% and NMP was to rise by 35–37%. The volume of industrial production was to grow by 29–31%. Compared with the 1981–85 period, average annual agricultural output during the 1986–90 Plan was to go up by 35–37%. The volume of foreign trade was due to expand by 34–36% during the 1986–90 period, with exports alone increasing by 44–46%. Real income per head in 1990 was to rise by 7–9% over 1985. Basic investment during the 1986–90 Plan was to be 11–13% higher than during the 1981–85 Plan, with about 25,000m. lekë to be invested in the country's socio-economic development.

In comparison with the previous year, in 1986 the social product rose by 4.5% and NMP by 7.2%. Total industrial production increased by 5.8% and agricultural production by 2.8%. The population's real income went up by 2%. In an attempt to stimulate production, a new system of bonuses and incentives for certain workers was introduced in 1987. State budget expenditure was estimated at 9,350m. lekë in 1987 and at 9,450m. lekë in 1988.

Albania's hydroelectric potential is being expanded rapidly. In 1988 only 25% of this potential was being utilized. Nevertheless, hydroelectricity accounted for over 80% of total electricity production. Output of electric energy reached an estimated 2,975m. kWh in 1985. Compared with the previous five-year period, the total output of electricity rose by 46% in 1981–85, and was to increase by 78–80% in 1986–90. The largest hydroelectric project is the Enver Hoxha station at Koman (planned eventually to be capable of producing 2,000m. kWh annually), the third phase of the River Drini system in northern Albania. The third 150-MW turbine was connected to the national grid in March 1987. A major project of the 1986–90 Five-Year Plan is the construction of a new hydroelectric power and irrigation complex on the River Devoll at Bënjë, in Gramsh District, which will generate 250m. kWh per year. The Light of the Party hydropower station in Fierza has a generating capacity of 500,000 kW.

Albania has its own reserves of petroleum, producing an estimated 3.4m. metric tons in 1985, and its own refining facilities. Geological surveys are being intensified. By 1990, compared with 1985, extraction was to increase by 33–35%. One-third of investment in industry during the 1986–90 Plan was to be devoted to the oil sector. Albania is one of the world's largest producers and exporters of chromite (chromium ore), with an estimated output of 237,000 metric tons (chromium content) in 1985. In 1984 chromite accounted for more than 17% of Albania's total exports. Production was scheduled to increase by 36% between 1986 and 1990. Todo Manço mine, at Bulqize in Dibër District, accounted for 44% of all chromium extracted in Albania in 1982. Output of coal, which is mined in central and southern Albania, rose by 48% in the 1981–85 period, and was to increase by 42–44% during the 1986–90 Plan. One of the most important coal mines is that of Memaliaj in Tepelenë District. Other important minerals include copper, nickel, bitumen and pyrite. Copper smelting and processing plants are located at Rubik, Kukës, Shkodër and Laç. Production of blister copper increased by 25% in 1981–85, and output of copper wires and cables was almost double that of the previous Five-Year Plan. Under the 1986–90 Plan, a total of 1,100m. lekë was to be invested in the chrome and copper industries. Copper output was planned to rise by 42%. An iron and steel plant opened at Elbasan in 1976, and a second blast furnace began production in 1981. The plant's output of steel rose from 10,000 tons in 1985 to 14,000 tons in 1986. By 1988 it was expected that domestic production of iron and steel would meet 70% of Albania's requirements.

Industrial production represented almost 60% of general social product by 1985. Under the 1986–90 Plan, investment in the industrial sector was to total 10,000m. lekë. Industry is based on the processing of agricultural raw materials and the production of machinery and equipment, chemicals, fertilizers, building materials and textiles, the latter accounting for 65% of total light industrial output. The chemical and fertilizer industries have expanded rapidly since the mid-1960s. In the 1981–85 period production of phosphatic fertilizers doubled, and that of sulphuric acid rose by 160%. Production of chemical fertilizers was scheduled to reach 500,000 tons by 1990, 55% more than in 1985. It was envisaged that output of the chemical industry in 1990 would be 38–40% higher than in 1985. In 1987, compared with the previous year, the chemical industry's production rose by 7%. The light and foodstuffs industries meet over 85% of domestic needs, with the 125 enterprises and combines employing some 100,000 people. In 1987 these two industries accounted for 38% of gross industrial production and for 40% of the country's total exports. The 1986–90 Plan emphasized increased output in light industry, especially the production of consumer goods. Output by the light and foodstuffs industries was to rise by 30–32%. In 1987 the food industry's production was 5% higher than in 1986. General industrial output was planned to rise by 4.9% in 1988. Major industrial projects commissioned in 1986 included the lubricant oils plant in Ballsh, extension of the existing superphosphate factory and the building of a new sulphuric acid factory at Laç, and a new urea factory (to produce 100,000 tons a year) at Fier. In 1988 work was to begin on the construction of a new ferro-chrome plant at Burrel and on the second stage of an extension of the copper wires and electric cables plant at Shkodër.

Agriculture was transformed after 1945 by land reclamation and mechanization, and complete collectivization was achieved in 1967. Albania became self-sufficient in bread grain in 1976. Besides wheat and maize, other important crops are rice, potatoes, dry beans, olives, citrus fruits and grapes. Industrial crops include tobacco, cotton, sunflowers and sugar beet. During the 1986–90 Plan tobacco production was to increase by 90–92%. In 1983 709,800 ha were under cultivation. In 1981–85 42,000 ha were brought under irrigation and 11,000 ha of existing irrigated land underwent improvements. By 1987 57% of arable land was under irrigation. With investment of 980m. lekë, this was to increase to 63% by the end of the 1986–90 Plan. When completed in 1990, the Bënjë irrigation system will provide 500m. cu m of water a year, sufficient to irrigate 100,000 ha. In 1983 the 421 co-operatives accounted for 73.6% of total agricultural production. The severe weather of early 1985 led to the loss of large numbers of livestock. Compared with 1986, agricultural output was expected to rise by 5% in 1987, but, owing to exceptionally cold weather in early 1987, this target was not achieved. An increase of 7.2% was planned for 1988. About 35% of Albania is forested. Between 1986 and 1990 the afforested areas were to be extended. About 15,000 ha of forests were to be improved and 1,300 ha renewed annually. Timber production was to increase by 13% in 1990, compared with 1985.

Albania's principal exports, other than chromite, include ferro-nickel ore, coal, copper wire, bitumen, tobacco and cigarettes, timber and furniture, textiles, canned foods, wine, fruit and vegetables, and handicrafts. In 1982 fuels made up 27.1% of total exports, minerals and metals 26.2%, and electricity 13.2%. Of total imports, fuels, minerals and metals accounted for 33.3%, machinery and equipment for 22.2%, and chemical and rubber products for 16.6%; foodstuffs accounted for only 5.2%. The export of electricity to neighbouring countries is of increasing significance. In 1987 Albania had electricity export agreements with Austria, Bulgaria, Greece, Romania and Yugoslavia. In the 1981–85 period exports totalled 4.8m. MWh. Compared with 1985, exports of electric power were to increase 20-fold in 1986–90. In 1987, however, production of electricity was badly affected by a prolonged drought, which continued in early 1988.

The Constitution forbids the acceptance of foreign credits, and the principle of self-reliance was reiterated in 1986. Economic growth has been hindered by the Government's inflexible trading policies and by the ending of all agreements with the People's Republic of China which, until 1978, accounted for about one-half of Albania's foreign trade. A *rapprochement* began in 1983, however, when a Chinese trade delegation visited Albania, resulting in trade accords worth US $5m.–7m. Commercial relations with both Western and Eastern European countries are also improving steadily. In 1984 Albania's trade with Western European countries accounted for 40% of total foreign trade. In 1985 trade with CMEA member countries was worth an estimated 261m. roubles, or 37% of the total. The exchange agreement with Greece was renewed in January 1987, and in April 1988 the two countries signed an accord to promote local trade between their border areas. Albania's main trading partners are Yugoslavia, Czechoslovakia and Italy. Trade with Yugoslavia and Italy in 1984 totalled an estimated US $88m. and $60m. respectively. The value of trade with Czechoslovakia exceeded 70m. roubles in 1986. A goods exchange agreement for 1986–90 was signed with Yugoslavia in 1985, setting the total value of their bilateral trade at $680m. Similar five-year agreements were also concluded with all CMEA member countries except the USSR and Mongolia, and with Algeria, Argentina, Austria, the People's Republic of China and Finland. A three-year agreement (1986–88) was signed with Turkey. In November 1985 the first visit to Albania by an economic delegation from the Federal Republic of Germany was made, and in 1987 trade exchanges between Albania and the Federal Republic were estimated to have reached DM 100m. In June 1988 the two countries signed a co-operation agreement. In May 1986 a French trade delegation visited Tirana. A goods exchange agreement with Egypt was signed in July 1987. In August 1988 Albania signed a trade agreement with Japan.

Social Welfare

All medical services are free of charge, and medicines are supplied free to children up to one year of age. Between 1985 and 1990 expenditure on the health service was to be increased by 17.3%. In 1983 the number of health institutions throughout the country exceeded 5,165, and there were 17,600 beds available. There were 4,957 doctors and dentists, or one for every 573 persons. Kindergartens and nursery schools receive large subsidies. Women are entitled to 180 days' maternity leave,

ALBANIA

receiving 80% of salary. There is a non-contributory state social insurance system for all workers, with 70–100% of salary being paid during sick leave, and a pension system for the old and disabled. Retirement pensions represent 70% of the average monthly salary. Men retire between the ages of 50 and 60, and women between 45 and 55. Income tax has been abolished, government expenditure being met by surpluses earned by state enterprises.

Education

Education in Albania is provided free at primary and secondary level. Students in higher education pay a fee in accordance with the family income. The state budget allocated 891m. lekë to education and culture in 1983. Children in the age group of three to six years may attend nursery school (kopshte). Children between the ages of seven and 15 years attend an 'eight-grade school' which is compulsory. In 1985 nearly 57% of pupils leaving the 'eight-grade school' went on to secondary education. Secondary schools in Albania may be divided into three main categories, namely '12-year schools' (shkollat 12-vjeçare) giving four-year courses, secondary technical-professional schools (shkollat e mesme tekniko-profesionale) which combine vocational training with a general education, and lower vocational schools (shkollat e ulte profesionale) which train workers in the fields of agriculture and industry. The school-year in secondary schools lasts six and a half months. All secondary-school graduates are required to spend a year working in factories or on collective farms.

In the 1988/89 school year a total of 760,000 pupils and students enrolled at educational institutes. The Enver Hoxha University at Tirana has eight faculties and had 12,500 full- and part-time students in 1987. Students at higher education institutes spend seven months of every year at the institute, two months in production or construction work, one month in physical culture and military training, and two months on vacation.

Public Holidays

1989: 1 January (New Year's Day), 11 January (Proclamation of the Republic), 1 May (May Day), 7 November (Victory of the October Socialist Revolution), 28 November (Proclamation of Independence), 29 November (Liberation Day 1944).

1990: 1 January (New Year's Day), 11 January (Proclamation of the Republic), 1 May (May Day), 7 November (Victory of the October Socialist Revolution), 28 November (Proclamation of Independence), 29 November (Liberation Day 1944).

Weights and Measures

The metric system is in force.

Statistical Survey

Source (unless otherwise stated): Drejtoria e Statistikës, Tirana.

Area and Population

AREA, POPULATION AND DENSITY

Area (sq km)	
Land	27,398
Inland water	1,350
Total	28,748*
Population (census result)	
January 1979	2,591,000
Population (official estimates at mid-year)	
1985	2,962,200
1986	3,022,000
1987	3,082,700†
Density (per sq km) at mid-1987	107.2

* 11,100 sq miles.
† Comprising 1,588,500 males and 1,494,200 females.

DISTRICTS (1987)

	Area (sq km)	Population (mid-year)	Density (per sq km)
Berat	1,027	171,000	166.5
Dibër	1,568	150,300	95.8
Durrës	848	237,900	280.5
Elbasan	1,481	234,500	158.3
Fier	1,175	235,200	200.2
Gramsh	695	43,100	62.0
Gjirokastër	1,137	64,800	57.0
Kolonjë	805	24,000	29.8
Korçë	2,181	212,500	97.4
Krujë	607	103,700	170.8
Kukës	1,330	99,100	74.5
Lezhë	479	58,900	123.0
Librazhd	1,013	70,800	69.9
Lushnjë	712	127,700	179.3
Mat	1,028	75,100	73.0
Mirditë	867	50,100	57.8
Përmet	929	39,600	42.6
Pogradec	725	68,500	94.5
Pukë	1,034	51,000	49.3
Sarandë	1,097	83,800	76.4
Shkodër	775	45,900	59.2
Skrapar	2,528	225,800	89.3
Tepelenë	817	50,000	61.2
Tiranë	1,238	343,500	277.5
Tropojë	1,043	44,500	42.7
Vlorë	1,609	171,400	106.5
Total	**28,748**	**3,082,700**	**107.2**

Source: *Statistical Yearbook of the PSR of Albania 1988.*

ALBANIA

PRINCIPAL TOWNS (population at mid-1987)

Tiranë (Tirana, the capital)	225,700
Durrës (Durazzo)	78,700
Elbasan	78,300
Shkodër (Scutari)	76,300
Vlorë (Vlonë or Valona)	67,600
Korçë (Koritsa)	61,500
Berat	40,500
Fier	40,300
Lushnjë	26,900
Gjirokastër	26,400
Kavajë	24,200

Source: *Statistical Yearbook of the PSR of Albania*.

BIRTHS, MARRIAGES AND DEATHS

	Registered live births		Registered marriages		Registered deaths	
	Number	Rate (per 1,000)	Number	Rate (per 1,000)	Number	Rate (per 1,000)
1983	73,762	26.0	25,607	9.0	17,416	6.1
1984	79,177	27.3	26,397	9.1	16,618	5.7
1985	77,535	26.2	25,271	8.5	17,179	5.8
1986	76,435	25.3	25,718	8.5	17,369	5.7
1987	79,696	25.9	27,370	8.9	17,119	5.6

* Provisional.

Average Life Expectation (1986/87): 71.6 years (Males 68.7 years, Females 74.3 years).

Source: *Statistical Yearbook of the PSR of Albania*.

ECONOMICALLY ACTIVE POPULATION
(ILO estimates, '000 persons at mid-1980)

	Males	Females	Total
Agriculture, etc.	338	339	677
Industry	237	74	311
Services	144	79	223
Total	**719**	**492**	**1,211**

Source: ILO, *Economically Active Population Estimates and Projections, 1950–2025*.

Mid-1986 (estimates in '000): Agriculture, etc. 740; Total 1,435 (Source: FAO, *Production Yearbook*).

EMPLOYMENT IN THE 'SOCIALIZED' SECTOR
(excluding agricultural co-operatives)

	1986	1987
Industry	272,300	287,000
Construction	78,300	77,800
Agriculture	182,100	190,300
Transport and communications	38,000	39,600
Trade	55,400	56,400
Education and culture	55,800	57,600
Health service	37,200	37,700
Others	40,300	41,800
Total	**759,400**	**788,200**

Source: *Statistical Yearbook of the PSR of Albania*.

Agriculture

PRINCIPAL CROPS ('000 metric tons)

	1984	1985*	1986*
Wheat and spelt	580*	530	540
Rice (paddy)	14*	14	14
Barley	34*	36	36
Maize	400*	400	410
Rye	10*	10	10
Oats	30*	30	30
Sorghum	35*	36	36
Potatoes	135*	136	136
Dry beans	20*	21	21
Sunflower seed	53*	54	55
Seed cotton	16*	16	16
Cotton seed	10*	10	10
Olives	25*	40	30
Vegetables	185*	186	186
Grapes	82*	83	83
Sugar beet	320	320	320
Apples	22*	15	18
Plums	20*	20	20
Oranges	14*	12	14
Tobacco (leaves)	19*	20	20
Cotton (lint)	6*	4†	4

* FAO estimates.   † Unofficial estimate.
Source: FAO, *Production Yearbook*.

LIVESTOCK

	1985	1986	1987
Horses	50,000	53,100	56,400
Mules	19,800	18,200	17,900
Asses	84,900	90,800	95,300
Cattle	590,800	618,600	671,900
Pigs	204,500	209,200	214,400
Sheep	1,318,400	1,346,500	1,432,300
Goats	864,700	918,900	979,100

Source: *Statistical Yearbook of the PSR of Albania*.
Poultry (FAO estimates, million): 5 in 1984; 5 in 1985; 5 in 1986.

LIVESTOCK PRODUCTS (FAO estimates, metric tons)

	1984	1985	1986
Beef and veal	27,000	27,000	27,000
Mutton and lamb	18,000	18,000	18,000
Goats' meat	8,000	8,000	8,000
Pig meat	9,000	9,000	9,000
Poultry meat	13,000	13,000	14,000
Cows' milk	342,000	345,000	345,000
Sheep's milk	46,000	41,000	41,000
Goats' milk	31,000	31,000	31,000
Cheese†	16,000*	12,900	13,200
Butter	3,690	3,775	3,838
Hen eggs	13,000	13,200	13,200
Wool:			
greasy	3,150	3,200	3,200
scoured (clean)	1,890	1,920	1,920
Cattle hides	3,894	3,982	3,982
Sheep and lamb skins	2,337	2,386	2,394
Goat and kid skins	664	664	664

* Unofficial estimate.
† Cheese from whole or partly skimmed milk of cows or buffaloes.
Source: FAO, *Production Yearbook*.

Forestry

ROUNDWOOD REMOVALS ('000 cubic metres)

Annual total 2,330 (Industrial wood 722, Fuel wood 1,608) in 1971 (official estimates) and in 1972–86 (FAO estimates).

ALBANIA

SAWNWOOD PRODUCTION ('000 cubic metres)
Annual total 200 (coniferous 105, broadleaved 95) in 1966–71 (official estimates) and in 1972–86 (FAO estimates).
Source: FAO, *Yearbook of Forest Products*.

Fishing

('000 metric tons, live weight)

	1985
Inland waters	3.6
Mediterranean Sea	10.1
Total catch	**13.7**

1986: Catch as in 1985 (FAO estimate).
Source: FAO, *Yearbook of Fishery Statistics*.

Mining

PRODUCTION (estimates, '000 metric tons)

	1983	1984	1985
Brown coal (incl. lignite)	1,700	1,775	1,790
Crude petroleum	3,990	3,410	3,415
Natural gas (terajoules)	16,000	17,000	17,000
Copper*†	15.0	14.1	15.0
Nickel*†	9.0	9.7	10.0
Chromium*‡	197	207	237

* Figures relate to the metal content of ores.
† Estimated by Metallgesellschaft Aktiengesellschaft (Frankfurt).
‡ Estimated by the US Bureau of Mines.
Source: UN, *Industrial Statistics Yearbook*.

Industry

SELECTED PRODUCTS (metric tons unless otherwise stated)

	1983	1984	1985
Olive oil[1]	7,000	3,000	7,000
Raw sugar[2]	38,000	40,000	33,000
Wine (hectolitres)[1]	220,000	230,000	230,000
Cigarettes (million)[3]	6,100	6,200	6,000
Nitrogenous fertilizers (a)[4]	73,000	75,000	n.a.
Phosphate fertilizers (b)[4]	25,000	18,000	n.a.
Motor spirit (Petrol)	260,000	270,000	280,000
Kerosene	85,000	90,000	95,000
Distillate fuel oils	365,000	380,000	390,000
Bitumen (Asphalt)	1,450,000	1,500	1,550
Cement[5]	840,000	840,000	848,000
Copper (unrefined)[6]	12,000	12,600	13,000
Electric energy (million kWh)	2,725	2,850	2,975

[1] Estimated by the FAO.
[2] Estimated by the International Sugar Organization (London).
[3] Estimated by the US Department of Agriculture.
[4] Figures for fertilizer production are unofficial estimates quoted by the FAO. Output is measured in terms of (a) nitrogen or (b) phosphoric acid.
[5] Estimated by the US Bureau of Mines.
[6] Estimated by Metallgesellschaft Aktiengesellschaft (Frankfurt).
Source: mainly UN, *Industrial Statistics Yearbook*.
1986: Olive oil 4,000 metric tons (FAO estimate).

Finance

CURRENCY AND EXCHANGE RATES
Monetary Units
100 qindarka (qintars) = 1 new lek.

Denominations
Coins: 5, 10, 20 and 50 qintars; 1 lek.
Notes: 1, 3, 5, 10, 25, 50 and 100 lekë.

Sterling and Dollar Equivalents (30 September 1988)
£1 sterling = 11.84 lekë;
US $1 = 7.00 lekë (non-commercial rates);
1,000 lekë = £84.48 = $142.86.

Exchange Rate
The non-commercial rate, applicable to tourism, has been fixed at US $1 = 7.000 lekë since June 1979.

STATE BUDGET (million lekë, provisional)

Revenue	1987	1988
National economy	9,009	9,140
Non-productive sector and other income from the socialist sector	341	360
Total revenue	**9,350**	**9,500**

Expenditure	1987	1988
National economy	5,076	5,820
Socio-cultural measures	2,682	2,747
Defence	1,055	1,600
Administration	148	161
Total expenditure	**9,300**	**9,450**

Source: Albanian Telegraphic Agency.

INVESTMENT
Capital investment during the 1986–90 Five-Year Plan was estimated at 24,450 million lekë, 2,800 million more than during the previous Five-Year Plan.
Source: Albanian Telegraphic Agency.

External Trade

No figures are available for the total value of trade since 1964, when imports totalled 4,906.4m. old lekë and exports 2,996.2m. old lekë. The old lek was replaced in August 1965 by the new lek (1 new lek = 10 old lekë). Prior to this change the official rate of exchange was US $1 = 50 old lekë.

TRADE WITH OECD COUNTRIES* (US $ million)

Imports†	1979	1980
Austria	4.3	6.8
Belgium/Luxembourg	1.0	—
Canada	—	0.1
Denmark	0.3	0.3
Finland	0.5	0.1
France	7.5	5.1
Germany, Federal Republic	—	20.5
Greece	13.0	28.8
Italy	20.6	23.1
Japan	4.0	2.0
Netherlands	6.0	4.2
Sweden	2.5	2.0
Switzerland	2.5	3.0
United Kingdom	1.3	3.0
USA	10.0	7.0

* Compiled from data of partner countries.
† OECD exports to Albania.

ALBANIA

Statistical Survey, Directory

Exports‡	1979	1980
Austria	9.1	7.0
Belgium/Luxembourg	0.5	2.0
Denmark	0.5	0.3
Finland	—	1.0
France	0.2	9.5
Germany, Federal Republic	—	9.1
Greece	9.0	9.0
Italy	31.4	42.0
Japan	4.0	—
Netherlands	5.6	5.6
Norway	0.8	—
Spain	4.5	4.0
Sweden	18.2	7.0
Switzerland	1.4	2.0
United Kingdom	—	0.3
USA	10.8	12.0

‡ OECD imports from Albania.

Transport

ROADS AND RAILWAYS

1987: Total road freight 76,840,000 metric tons; total railway freight: 7,666,000 metric tons.
Source: *Statistical Yearbook of the PSR of Albania.*

INTERNATIONAL SEA-BORNE SHIPPING
(estimated freight traffic, '000 metric tons)

	1983	1984	1985
Goods loaded	1,150	1,150	1,077
Goods unloaded	631	635	626

Source: UN, *Monthly Bulletin of Statistics.*

1987: Total sea-borne freight: 1,025,000 metric tons. Source: *Statistical Yearbook of the PSR of Albania.*

Communications Media

	1983	1984	1985
Book production:			
Titles*	997	1,130	939
Copies ('000)*	6,224	6,506	5,710
Daily newspapers:			
Number	n.a.	2	n.a.
Average circulation	n.a.	145,000	n.a.
Radio receivers in use	476,000	n.a.	493,000
Television receivers in use	196,000	n.a.	232,000

* Figures include pamphlets (130 titles and 419,000 copies in 1983; 158 titles and 494,000 copies in 1984; 95 titles and 300,000 copies in 1985).
Source: UNESCO, *Statistical Yearbook.*

1987: Book production: titles: 1,091; copies: 7,972,000; Daily newspapers: number: 2; average circulation: 150,000.
Source: *Statistical Yearbook of the PSR of Albania.*

Education

(1986)

	Institutions	Teachers	Pupils
Pre-primary	3,102	5,005	113,840
Primary (8-year)	1,651	27,378	541,564
Secondary:			
general	67	2,060	47,168
vocational	330	5,725	130,969
Higher	8	1,509	22,403

Source: *Directory of Statistics.*

Directory

The Constitution

A new constitution was adopted on 28 December 1976. The following is a summary of its main provisions:

THE SOCIAL ORDER

The Political Order

Articles 1-15. Albania is a People's Socialist Republic, based on the dictatorship of the proletariat. The Party of Labour of Albania (Workers' Party) is the sole leading political force of the State and society. Marxism-Leninism is the ruling ideology.

The representative bodies are the People's Assembly and the People's Councils, elected by the people through universal suffrage by equal, direct and secret ballot. Officials serve the people and render account to them. They also participate directly in production work, in order to prevent the creation of a privileged stratum.

In the construction of socialism, Albania relies primarily on its own efforts.

The Economic Order

Articles 16-31. The economy is a socialist economy, which relies on the socialist ownership of the means of production. Socialist property is inviolable and state property belongs to all the people. The State works to narrow the differences between the countryside and the cities. The personal property of the citizens is recognized and protected by the State.

Foreign trade is a state monopoly.

The granting of concessions to, and the creation of foreign or joint economic or financial institutions with, capitalist, bourgeois and revisionist monopolies and States, as well as the acceptance of credits from them, is prohibited.

Citizens pay no levies or taxes whatsoever.

Education, Science and Culture

Articles 32-37. The State carries out broad ideological and cultural activity for the communist education of the working people. Education is organized by the State and is free of charge.

The State organizes the development of science and technology.

The State recognizes no religion and supports and carries out atheist propaganda.

THE FUNDAMENTAL RIGHTS AND DUTIES OF CITIZENS

Articles 38-65. The rights and duties of citizens are founded on the reconciliation of the interests of the individual with those of the socialist society.

All citizens are equal before the law. Women enjoy the same rights as men.

Citizens reaching the age of 18 have the right to take part in voting for, and to be elected to, all organs of state power.

Citizens enjoy the right to work and to recreation. Workers are guaranteed the necessary material means for life in old age and sickness.

Marriage and the family are under the care and protection of the State and society. Marriage is contracted before the competent state organs.

Citizens enjoy freedom of speech.

The creation of all organizations of a fascist, anti-democratic, religious or anti-socialist nature is prohibited.

SUPREME BODIES OF STATE POWER

The People's Assembly

Articles 66-74. The People's Assembly is the supreme body of state power and sole law-making body. It defines the main directions of the domestic and foreign policy of the State. It elects, appoints and dismisses the Presidium of the People's Assembly, the Council of Ministers, the Supreme Court, the Attorney-General and his deputies.

The People's Assembly is composed of 250 deputies, elected for a period of four years, and meets in regular session twice a year.

The Presidium of the People's Assembly

Articles 75-79. The Presidium of the People's Assembly is the supreme body of state power, with permanent activity, and is composed of a President, three Vice-Presidents, a Secretary and 10 members. It convenes the sessions of the People's Assembly and, between sessions, supervises the implementation of the laws and decisions of the People's Assembly, and controls all state organs.

The Presidium directs and controls the activity of the People's Councils.

The Supreme Organs of State Administration

Articles 80-86. The Council of Ministers is the supreme executive and order-issuing body, and is composed of the Chairman, Vice-Chairmen and ministers. It directs activity for the realization of the domestic and foreign policies of the State. It directs and controls the activity of the ministries, other central organs of the state administration and the executive committees of the People's Councils.

The Chairman and Vice-Chairmen of the Council of Ministers constitute the Presidium of the Council of Ministers.

The Country's Defence and the Armed Forces

Articles 87-91. The State protects the victories of the people's revolution and of socialist construction, and defends the freedom, national independence and territorial integrity of the country.

The armed forces are led by the Party of Labour of Albania. The First Secretary of the Central Committee of the Party of Labour of Albania is the Supreme Commander of the armed forces and Chairman of the Defence Council. The stationing of foreign bases and military forces in Albania is not permitted.

LOCAL ORGANS OF STATE POWER AND STATE ADMINISTRATION

Articles 92-100. The People's Councils are organs of state power, which carry out the administration in the respective administrative-territorial units with the broad participation of the working masses. The People's Councils are elected for a term of three years.

A Higher People's Council may dissolve a lower People's Council. Executive committees are an executive and order-issuing organ of the People's Councils.

THE PEOPLE'S COURTS

Articles 101-103. The People's Courts are bodies which administer justice. At the head of the organs of justice stands the Supreme Court, which directs and controls the activity of the courts. The Supreme Court is elected at the first session of the People's Assembly. The other People's Courts are elected by the people.

THE ATTORNEY-GENERAL'S OFFICE

Articles 104-106. It is the duty of the Attorney-General's Office to supervise the implementation of the laws. The Attorney-General and his deputies are appointed at the first session of the People's Assembly. Attorneys are appointed by the Presidium of the Assembly.

THE EMBLEM, THE FLAG, THE CAPITAL

Articles 107-109. The emblem of the People's Socialist Republic of Albania consists of a black double-headed eagle, encircled by two sheaves of wheat with a five-pointed red star at the top and tied at the bottom by a red ribbon bearing the inscription '24th May 1944'.

The state flag has a red background with a black double-headed eagle in the middle and a red five-pointed star outlined in gold at the top.

The capital is Tirana.

FINAL PROVISIONS

Articles 110-112. The Constitution is the fundamental law of the State. Drafts for amendments may be presented by the Presidium of the People's Assembly, the Council of Ministers or two-fifths of the deputies. The approval of the Constitution and amendments to it requires a two-thirds majority of all deputies.

The Government
(October 1988)

HEAD OF STATE

President of the Presidium of the People's Assembly: RAMIZ ALIA (elected 22 November 1982, re-elected 19 February 1987).

PRESIDIUM OF THE PEOPLE'S ASSEMBLY

President: RAMIZ ALIA.
Vice-Presidents: RITA MARKO, XHAFER SPAHIU, EMINE GURI.
Secretary: SIHAT TOZAJ.
Members:
SIMON BALLABANI
FAIK ÇINAJ
PETRIT GAÇE
RAHMAN HANKU
SOTIR KOÇOLLARI
TEREZINA MARUBI
STEFAN QIRJAKO
KRISTAQ RAMA
LUMTURI REXHA
ELENI SELENICA

COUNCIL OF MINISTERS

Chairman: ADIL ÇARÇANI.
Deputy Chairman: BESNIK BEKTESHI.
Deputy Chairman and Minister of Home Affairs: HEKURAN ISAI.
Deputy Chairman: MANUSH MYFTIU.
Deputy Chairman: VANGJEL ÇERRAVA.
Minister of Foreign Affairs: REIS MALILE.
Minister of People's Defence: PROKOP MURRA.
Chairman of the State Planning Commission: NIKO GJYZARI.
Chairman of the State Control Commission: ENVER HALILI.
Minister of Finance: ANDREA NAKO.
Minister of Industry and Mining: LLAMBI GEGPRIFTI.
Minister of Energy: LAVDOSH HAMETAJ.
Minister of Light Industry: VITO KAPO.
Minister of the Foodstuff Industry: JOVAN BARDHI.
Minister of Agriculture: THEMIE THOMAI.
Minister of Construction: ISMAIL AHMETI.
Minister of Transport: LUAN BABAMETO.
Minister of Home Trade: OSMAN MURATI.
Minister of Foreign Trade: SHANE KORBECI.
Minister of Public Services: XHEMAL TAFAJ.
Minister of Education: SKËNDER GJINUSHI.
Minister of Health Service: AHMET KAMBERI.
Minister to the Presidium of the Council of Ministers: FARUDIN HOXHA.

MINISTRIES

All Ministries are in Tirana.
Ministry of Foreign Affairs: Ministria e Punëvet të Jashtme, Tirana; telex 2164.
Ministry of Foreign Trade: Ministria e Tregetisë të Jashtme, Tirana; telex 2152.

POLITBURO OF THE CENTRAL COMMITTEE OF THE PARTY OF LABOUR OF ALBANIA

Full Members:
RAMIZ ALIA
MUHO ASLLANI
BESNIK BEKTESHI
FOTO ÇAMI
ADIL ÇARÇANI
HAJREDIN ÇELIKU
LENKA ÇUKO
HEKURAN ISAI
RITA MARKO
PALI MISKA
PROKOP MURRA
MANUSH MYFTIU
SIMON STEFANI

Candidate Members:
VANGJEL ÇERRAVA
LLAMBI GEGPRIFTI
PIRRO KONDI
QIRJAKO MIHALI
KIÇO MUSTAQI

Legislature

KUVENDI POPULLOR
(People's Assembly)

President: PETRO DODE.
Vice-Presidents: Mrs VITORI CURRI, IBRAHIM HAMZA.
Secretary: SALI SHIJAKU.

ALBANIA

The Assembly has 250 members, elected (unopposed) for a four-year term. At the general election held on 1 February 1987, it was reported that 100% of the electorate voted: 1,830,652 votes were cast in favour of the 250 candidates and one vote was invalid.

Political Organizations

Partia e Punës e Shqipërisë (Party of Labour of Albania, PLA): Tirana; f. 1941; the Communist Party of Albania, which adopted its present name in 1948; also known as the Workers' Party; the country's only permitted political party; Marxist-Leninist; 128,000 members, 15,300 candidate members (Jan. 1986); First Sec. of Central Cttee RAMIZ ALIA; Secs FOTO ÇAMI, HAJREDIN ÇELIKU, LENKA ÇUKO, SIMON STEFANI.

Fronti Demokratik i Shqipërisë (Democratic Front of Albania): Tirana; tel. 79-57; f. 1942; serves as the main link between the people and the PLA and the people's state power in the struggle for the construction of socialism and in the defence of the homeland; the Front is responsible for the enlightenment and education of the working people, according to the party line, and serves as a powerful means for the active participation of the broad working masses in the solution of major social and state problems; nominates all candidates in elections; Gen. Council has 25-mem. Presidency; Chair. of Gen. Council NEXHMIJE HOXHA.

Bashkimi i Rinisë së Punës të Shqipërisë (Union of Albanian Working Youth): Tirana; tel. 78-18; f. 1941; political organization for young people, sponsored by the Party of Labour of Albania, playing an important role in the political, economic, social, educational and cultural life of the country; at the 9th Congress, held in October 1987, 15 mems and 6 candidate mems were elected to the Presidium of the Central Cttee; 175 mems were elected to the Central Cttee; First Sec. of the Central Cttee MEHMET ELEZI.

Bashkimi të Grave të Shqipërisë (Women's Union of Albania): Tirana; tel. 79-59; f. 1943 for the ideological, political and social education of women, aiming to achieve their complete emancipation, to help build a socialist society, and to consolidate the international solidarity of women; at the 9th Congress, held in June 1983, a General Council of 167 mems, a Presidium of 27 and a Secretariat of 5 were elected; Pres. of General Council LUMTURI REXHA; Sec.-Gen. LEONORA ÇARO.

Diplomatic Representation

EMBASSIES IN ALBANIA

Bulgaria: Rruga Skënderbeu 12, Tirana; tel. 26-72; Ambassador: KHRISTAKI KUNEV.

China, People's Republic: Rruga Skënderbeu 57, Tirana; tel. 26-00; telex 2148; Ambassador: FAN CHENGZUO.

Cuba: Rruga Kongresi i Përmetit, Tirana; tel. 51-77; telex 2155; Ambassador: (vacant).

Czechoslovakia: Rruga Skënderbeu 10, Tirana; telex 2162; Ambassador: ANTON SIMKOVIČ.

Egypt: Rruga Skënderbeu 43, Tirana; tel. 30-13; telex 2156; Ambassador: MANZUR AHMAD AL-DALI.

France: Rruga Skënderbeu 14, Tirana; tel. 28-04; telex 2150; Ambassador: PHILIPPE LEGRAIN.

German Democratic Republic: Rruga Asim Zeneli, Tirana; tel. 23-01; telex 2161; Ambassador: DIETER KULITZKA.

Germany, Federal Republic: Hotel Dajti, Bulevardi Dëshmorët e Kombit 6, Tirana; tel. 54-05; telex 2148; Ambassador: FRIEDRICH KRONECK.

Greece: Rruga Frederick Shiroka 3, Tirana; tel. 68-50; Ambassador: SPYRIDON A. DOKIANOS.

Hungary: Rruga Skënderbeu 16, Tirana; tel. 20-14; telex 2169; Ambassador: KÁROLY KRISTON.

Italy: Rruga Labinoti 103, Tirana; tel. 28-00; telex 2166; Ambassador: GIORGIO DE ANDREIS.

Korea, Democratic People's Republic: Rruga Skënderbeu 55, Tirana; tel. 22-58; Ambassador: PAK YONG-SI.

Poland: Rruga Kongresi i Përmetit 123, Tirana; Chargé d'affaires a.i.: WŁADYSŁAW CIASTON.

Romania: Rruga Themistokli Gërmenji 2, Tirana; tel. 22-59; Ambassador: GHEORGHE POP.

Turkey: Rruga Konferenca e Pezës 31, Tirana; tel. 24-49; Ambassador: TEOMAN SÜRENKÖK.

Viet-Nam: Rruga Lek Dukagjini, Tirana; tel. 25-56; Ambassador: LE NGOC THANH.

Yugoslavia: Rruga Kongresi i Përmetit 192–196, Tirana; tel. 30-42; telex 2167; Ambassador: NOVAK PRIBICEVIĆ.

Judicial System

Justice is administered under the Constitution by the Supreme Court, by Territorial Division Courts, by District Courts and by Village, City and City Quarter Courts. There is no Ministry of Justice. The Supreme Court is elected for a four-year term by the People's Assembly; between sessions of the Assembly, individual members of the Court are elected by the Presidium of the People's Assembly. The Territorial Division Courts are elected for a three-year term by the People's Councils of the districts in which they exercise their jurisdiction. The District Courts are elected for a three-year term by all voting citizens through a direct and secret ballot. The Village, City and City Quarter Courts are bodies of a social character, and are elected by the people for a three-year term. Military Tribunals are held at the Supreme Court and at District Courts. Courts of Justice are independent in the exercise of their functions, and are separated from the administration.

A revised Penal Code came into effect in October 1977, followed by a Code of Penal Procedure (1980), a Labour Code (1980), a Civil Code, together with a Code of Civil Procedure (1982) and a Family Code (1982). Trials are held in public. The accused is assured the right of defence, and the principle of presumption of innocence is sanctioned by the Code of Penal Procedure. First-degree cases are normally tried by District Courts or, exceptionally, by Territorial Division Courts or the Supreme Court. For first-degree cases, the tribunal comprises a professional judge and two assistant judges. Trials in the Village, City and City Quarter Courts are held before an assistant judge from the District Court and two social activists. These Courts try simple cases, and are empowered to punish a guilty person with a fine or social reprimand. Second-degree cases are held in the Territorial Division Courts or in the Supreme Court, before three judges and two assistant judges. The verdicts of the lower courts may be altered, within the law, by the higher courts, and judges may be recalled before the expiration of their term by their electors or the organ that has elected them. Both the President of the Supreme Court and the Attorney-General have the right to issue a demand for the protection of legality against the peremptory verdicts of the courts. The demand for the protection of legality is presented, within the law, before the Penal Tribunal (College), the Civil Tribunal, the Military Tribunal or the Plenary Meeting of the Supreme Court.

The Office of Investigation is a state organ that investigates criminal acts. This department is separated from the organs of internal affairs and from the other administrative organs. The Chairman of the General Department of Investigation and his deputies are appointed by the People's Assembly. The chairmen of the district's offices of investigation are appointed by the Chairman of the General Department of Investigation. Attorneys' offices are state organs that control strictly and uniformly the application of the laws from Ministries and other central and local organs, from courts, organs of investigation, enterprises, institutions and citizens' organizations. The Attorney-General and his deputies are appointed by the People's Assembly, and District Attorneys by the Presidium of the People's Assembly.

President of the Supreme Court: ARANIT ÇELA.

Attorney-General: RRAPI MINO.

Chairman of the General Department of Investigation: QEMAL LAME.

Religion

There is no formal practice of the previously predominant Muslim religion, although certain social traditions persist. All religious institutions were closed by the Government in 1967. Article 37 of the 1976 Constitution states that Albania recognizes no religion and supports and carries out atheist propaganda. All of the old mosques have now been shut down and are preserved as centres of cultural interest. Formerly the population was approximately 70% Muslim, 10% Roman Catholic (in the north) and 20% Greek Orthodox (in the south). A small number of Albanians are believed to be adherents of the Jewish faith.

CHRISTIANITY

The Roman Catholic Church

Albania formally comprises the archdioceses of Durrës (directly responsible to the Holy See) and Shkodër (Shkodër), three dioceses, one territorial abbacy and Southern Albania (previously the responsibility of an Apostolic Administrator). There are no longer any resident prelates holding office in the country.

Apostolic Administrator of Durrës and Lezhë: NICOLA TROSHANI, Titular Bishop of Cisamo.

Apostolic Administrator of Shkodrë: ERNESTO ÇOBA, Titular Bishop of Mideo.

ALBANIA   Directory

The Press

The Albanian press recognizes itself as a powerful medium of educational and organizational propaganda with a profound Marxist-Leninist ideological content. It expresses party doctrine probably more forcefully than any other European communist press. There are numerous local newspapers, generally the organs of the regional party committees. In 1985 the 23 newspapers and 77 magazines had a total circulation of 64m. copies. The most important publications are the Party of Labour daily, *Zëri i Popullit*, and *Bashkimi*, the organ of the Democratic Front. In 1984 there were 14 district newspapers, published twice a week. The Albanian Telegraphic Agency (ATA), has a monopoly of news distribution in Albania.

PRINCIPAL DAILIES

Zëri i Popullit (The Voice of the People): Bulevardi Stalin, Tirana; tel. 78-13; f. 1942; publ. by the Central Committee of the Party of Labour; Editor-in-Chief ARSHIN XHEZO; circ. 105,000.

Bashkimi (Unity): Bulevardi Stalin, Tirana; tel. 81-10; f. 1943; publ. by the Democratic Front; Editor-in-Chief HAMIT BORIÇI; circ. 30,000.

PERIODICALS
Tirana

Bibliografia Kombëtare e Librit Shqiptar (National Bibliography of Albanian Books): Tirana; quarterly; published by the National Library of Albania.

Bibliografia Kombëtare e Periodikeve Shqip (National Bibliography of Albanian periodicals): Tirana; monthly; published by the National Library of Albania.

Bujqësia Socialiste (Socialist Agriculture): Tirana; monthly; publ. by the Ministry of Agriculture; Editor FAIK LABINOTI.

Buletini i Shkencave Bujqësore (Agricultural Sciences Bulletin): Tirana; quarterly; summaries in French; publ. by the Agricultural Scientific Research Institute; Editor-in-Chief LEFTER VESHI.

Buletini i Shkencave të Natyrës (Natural Sciences Bulletin): Tirana; f. 1957; quarterly; summaries in French; publ. by the Enver Hoxha University of Tirana; Editor-in-Chief MUHARREM FRASHERI.

Buletini i Shkencave Mjekësore (Medical Sciences Bulletin): Tirana; quarterly; summaries in French; publ. by the Enver Hoxha University of Tirana; Editor-in-Chief YLVI VEHBIU.

Buletini i Shkencave Teknike (Technical Sciences Bulletin): Tirana; quarterly; summaries in French; publ. by the Enver Hoxha University of Tirana.

Buletini i Studimeve Gjeologjike (Bulletin of Geological Studies): Tirana; quarterly; publ. by Ministry of Industry and Mining.

Drejtësia Popullore (People's Law): Tirana; f. 1948; quarterly; publ. of Supreme Court and Attorney-General's Office; Chief Editor ELENI SELENICA.

Drita (The Light): Baboci 37z, Tirana; f. 1960; weekly; publ. by Union of Writers and Artists of Albania; Chief Editor ŽIJA ÇELA.

Estrada (Variety Shows): Tirana; every 2 months; publ. by the Central House of Popular Creativity.

Fatosi (The Valiant): Tirana; fortnightly; publ. by Cen. Cttee of Union of Working Youth.

Gazeta Zyrtare e RPS të Shqipërisë (Official Gazette of the PSR of Albania): Tirana; occasional government review.

Gjuha Jonë (Our Language): Tirana; 3 a year; organ of the Institute of Language and Literature at the Academy of Sciences; Editor ALI DHRIMO.

Horizonti (Horizon): Tirana; fortnightly; publ. by Cen. Cttee of Union of Working Youth.

Hosteni (The Goad): Tirana; f. 1945; fortnightly; political review of humour and satire; publ. by the Union of Journalists; Editor-in-Chief NIKO NIKOLLA.

Iliria (Illyria): Qendra e Kërkimeve Arkeologjike, Tirana; 2 a year; summaries in French; publ. by Archaeological Centre at Academy of Sciences.

Kënga Jonë (Our Song): Tirana; f. 1960; every 2 months; publ. by the Central House of Popular Creativity.

Kultura Popullore (Popular Culture): Tirana; 2 a year; annually in French; publ. by the Institute of Folk Culture at the Academy of Sciences; Editor-in-Chief ALFRED UÇI.

Laiko Vima (People's Step): Gjirokastër; f. 1945; 2 a week; monthly literary edn; in Greek; publ. by the Democratic Front for the Greek minority; Editor-in-Chief VASIL ÇAMI.

Les Lettres Albanaises: Rruga Konferenca e Pezës, Tirana; tel. 26-91; quarterly; in French; literary and artistic review; publ. by Union of Writers and Artists of Albania; Editor-in-Chief ISMAIL KADARE.

Luftëtari (The Fighter): Tirana; f. 1945; 2 a week; publ. by the Ministry of National Defence; Editor-in-Chief DEMOKRAT ANASTASI.

Mbrëmje Tematike (Evening Parties): Tirana; publ. by the Central House of Popular Creativity.

Mësuesi (The Teacher): Tirana; f. 1961; weekly; publ. by the Ministry of Education and Culture; Editor-in-Chief THOMA QENDRO.

Monumentet (Monuments): Tirana; f. 1971; 2 a year; summaries in French; publ. by the Institute of Monuments and Culture; Editor-in-Chief SOTIR KOSTA.

Ndërtuesi (The Builder): Tirana; quarterly; publ. by the Ministry of Construction.

Në shërbim të popullit (In the Service of the People): Tirana; f. 1955; Editor-in-Chief THOMA NAQE.

Në skenën e fëmijëve (On the Children's Stage): Tirana; published by the Central House of Popular Creativity.

Nëna dhe Fëmija (Mother and Child): Tirana; 3 a year; publ. by Ministry of Public Health.

Nëntori (November): Baboci 37z, Tirana; f. 1954; monthly; publ. by the Union of Writers and Artists of Albania; Chief Editor KIÇO BLUSHI.

Për Mbrojtjen e Atdheut (For the Defence of the Fatherland): Tirana; f. 1948; publ. of the Ministry of National Defence; Editor-in-Chief BEGE TENA.

Përmbledhje Studimesh (Collection of Studies): Tirana; quarterly; summaries in French; bulletin of the Ministry of Industry and Mining.

Pionieri (The Pioneer): Tirana; f. 1944; fortnightly; publ. by the Cen. Cttee of the Union of Working Youth; Editor-in-Chief SKENDER HASKO; circ. 38,000.

Political-Social Studies: Tirana; f. 1988; publ. by Institute of Marxist-Leninist Studies.

Probleme Ekonomike: Tirana; quarterly; organ of Institute for Economic Studies.

Puna (Labour): Bulevardi Dëshmorët e Kombit, Tirana; f. 1945; 2 a week; also quarterly in French; organ of the Central Council of Albanian Trade Unions; Editor-in-Chief NAMIK DOKLE.

Radio Përhapja: Tirana; fortnightly; organ of Albanian Radio and Television.

Revista Mjekësore (Medical Review): Tirana; every 2 months; publ. by Ministry of Health.

Revista Pedagogjike: Tirana; quarterly; organ of the Institute of Pedagogical Studies; Editor SOTIR TEMO.

Rruga e Partisë (The Party's Road): Tirana; f. 1954; monthly; publ. by Cen. Cttee of the Party of Labour; Editor STEFI KOTMILO; circ. 9,000.

Shëndeti (Health): Tirana; f. 1949; monthly; publ. by the Ministry of Public Health; Editor-in-Chief ROZA THEOHARI.

Shkenca dhe Jeta (Science and Life): Tirana; every 2 months; organ of the Central Committee of the Union of Working Youth; Editor-in-Chief KUDRET ISAI.

Shqipëria e Re (New Albania): Rruga Themistokli Gërmenji 6, Tirana; f. 1947; published monthly in Albanian; every 2 months in Arabic, English, French, German, Italian, Russian and Spanish; organ of the Committee for Foreign Cultural Relations; illustrated political and social magazine; Editor YMER MINXHOZI; circ. 170,000.

Shqipëria Sot (Albania Today): Tirana; every 2 months; published in English, French, German, Italian and Spanish; political, cultural and social review; Editor-in-Chief DHIMITER VERLI.

Shqiptarja e Re (The New Albanian Woman): Tirana; f. 1943; monthly; publ. by the Women's Union of Albania; political and socio-cultural review; Editor-in-Chief VALENTINA LESKAJ.

Skena dhe Ekrani (Stage and Screen): Tirana; quarterly; publ. by the Committee for Culture and Arts.

Sporti Popullor (People's Sport): Tirana; f. 1945; weekly; publ. by the Ministry of Education and Culture; Editor BESNIK DIZDARI; circ. 60,000.

Studenti (The Student): Tirana; f. 1967; weekly; publ. by the Committee of the University Working Youth Union.

Studia Albanica: Tirana; f. 1964; 2 a year; history and philology; in French; publ. by the Albanian Academy of Sciences; Editor-in-Chief LUAN OMARI.

Studime Filologjike (Philological Studies): Tirana; f. 1964; quarterly; summaries in French; publ. by the Institute of Language and Literature at the Albanian Academy of Sciences; Editor-in-Chief ANDROKLI KOSTALLARI.

ALBANIA

Studime Historike (Historical Studies): Tirana; f. 1964; quarterly; summaries in French; publ. by the Institute of History at the Albanian Academy of Sciences; historical sciences; Editor-in-Chief STEFANAQ POLLO.

Teknika (Technology): Tirana; f. 1954; quarterly; publ. by the Ministry of Industry and Mining; Editor NATASHA VARFI.

Teatri (Theatre): Tirana; f. 1960; every 2 months; publ. by the Central House of Popular Creativity.

Tirana: Tirana; f. 1987; publ. by Tirana District Party of Labour Cttee.

Tregtia e Jashtme Popullore (Albanian Foreign Trade): Rruga Konferenca e Pezës 6, Tirana; tel. 29-34; telex 2179; f. 1961; every 2 months; in English and French; organ of the Albanian Chamber of Commerce; Editor AGIM KORBI.

Tribuna e Gazetarit (The Journalist's Tribune): Tirana; every 2 months; publ. by the Union of Journalists of Albania; Editor ADRIATIK KANANI.

Vatra e Kulturës (Centre of Culture): Tirana; publ. by the Central House of Popular Creativity.

Ylli (The Star): Tirana; f. 1951; monthly; socio-political and literary review; Editor-in-Chief NEVRUZ TURHANI.

Yllkat (Little Stars): Tirana; monthly; publ. by Institute of Pedagogical Studies.

Zëri i Rinisë (The Voice of the Youth): Tirana; f. 1942; 2 a week; publ. by Cen. Cttee of the Union of Albanian Working Youth; Editor-in-Chief REMZI LANI; circ. 53,000.

10 Korriku (10 July): Tirana; f. 1947; monthly; publ. by the Ministry of People's Defence; Editor-in-Chief SELAMI VEHBIU.

Other Towns

Adriatiku (Adriatic): Durrës; f. 1967; 2 a week; publ. by Durrës District Party of Labour Cttee.

Drapër e Çekan (Hammer and Sickle): Fier; f. 1967; 2 a week.

Fitorjë (Victory): Sarandë; f. 1971; 2 a week; Editor-in-Chief BELUL KORKUTI.

Jehona e Skraparit (Echo of Skrapar): Skrapar; 2 a week.

Jeta e Re (New Life): Shkodër; f. 1967; 2 a week.

Kastrioti: Krujë; f. 1971; 2 a week; publ. by Krüje District Party of Labour Cttee.

Kukësi i Ri (New Kukës): Kukës; 2 a week.

Kushtrimi (Clarion Call): Berat; f. 1967; 2 a week.

Pararoja (Vanguard): Gjirokastër; f. 1967; 2 a week; publ. by Gjirokastër District Party of Labour Cttee.

Përpara (Forward): Korçë; f. 1967; 2 a week; publ. by Korçë District Party of Labour Cttee; Editor-in-Chief STRATI MARKO; circ. 4,000.

Shkëndija (The Spark): Lushnjë; f. 1971; 2 a week; publ. by Lushnjë District Party of Labour Cttee.

Shkumbimi: Elbasan; 2 a week; publ. by Elbasan District Party of Labour Cttee; Editor-in-Chief MEFAIL PUPULEKU.

Ushtimi i Maleve (Rumble of the Mountains): Peshkopi; 2 a week.

Zëri i Vlorës (The Voice of Vlorë): Vlorë; f. 1967; 2 a week; publ. by Vlorë District Party of Labour Cttee; Editor-in-Chief DASHO METODASHAJ.

In addition, 11 new local newspapers, published by the District Party Committees of Lezhë, Përmet, Pukë, Pogradec, Mirditë, Tepelenë, Mat, Gramsh, Kolonjë, Tropojë and Librazhd, were established in 1988.

NEWS AGENCY

Albanian Telegraphic Agency (ATA): Bulevardi Marcel Cachin 23, Tirana; tel. 44-12; telex 2142; f. 1945; domestic and foreign news; branches in provincial towns; Dir TAQO ZOTO.

Foreign Bureau

Xinhua (New China) News Agency (People's Republic of China): Rruga Skënderbeu 57, Tirana; tel. 26-00; telex 2148; Bureau Chief WANG HONGQI.

PRESS ASSOCIATION

Bashkimi i Gazetarëve të Shqipërisë (Union of Journalists of Albania): Tirana; tel. 79-77; f. 1949; Chair. MARASH HAJATI; Sec.-Gen. YMER MINXHOZI.

Publishers

In 1985 a total of 939 book titles (including 803 first editions) were published.

Drejtoria Qëndrore e Përhapjes dhe e Propagandimit të Librit (Central Administration for the Dissemination and Propagation of the Book): Tirana; tel. 78-41; directed by the Ministry of Education and Culture.

Botime të Akademisë së Shkencave të RPSSH: Tirana; publishing house of the Albanian Academy of Sciences.

Botime të Drejtorisë së Arsimit Shëndetësor dhe të Shtëpisë së Propagandës Bujqësore: Tirana; medicine, sciences and agriculture.

Botime të Institutit të Lartë Bujqësor: Tirana; publishing house of the Higher Institute of Agriculture.

Botime të Shtëpisë Botuese 8 Nëntori: Tirana; books and journals on Albania, political sciences, translations of Albanian works into foreign languages, technical and scientific books; Dir PAVLLO GJIDEDE.

Botime të Shtëpisë Botuese të Librit Shkollor: Tirana; f. 1967; educational books; Dir FEJZI KOÇI.

Botime të Shtëpisë Botuese Naim Frashëri: Tirana; tel. 79-06; novels, poetry, popular literature.

Botime të Universitetit të Tiranës Enver Hoxha: Tirana; publishing house of the Enver Hoxha University of Tirana; sciences, engineering, geography, history, literature, economics, etc.

Government Publishing House

N.I.SH. Shtypshkronjave Mihal Duri (Mihal Duri State Printing House): Tirana; government publications, politics, law, education; Dir HAJRI HOXHA.

WRITERS' UNION

Lidhja e Shkrimtarëve dhe e Artistëve të Shqipërisë (Union of Writers and Artists of Albania): Baboci 37z, Tirana; tel. 79-89; f. 1945; 1,750 mems; Chair. DRITËRO AGOLLI

Radio and Television

It was estimated that there would be about 500,000 radio receivers and 300,000 television sets in use by 1987.

Radiotelevisioni Shqiptar: Rruga Ismail Qemali, Tirana; tel. 81-34; f. 1944; Dir-Gen. SEFEDIN ÇELA.

RADIO

Radio Tirana: broadcasts more than 24 hours of internal programmes daily from Tirana; regional stations in Berat, Fier, Gjirokastër, Korçë, Kükes, Pukë, Rogozhina, Sarandë and Shkodër; wire-relay service in Tirana and in factories, mines and clubs all over the country.

External Service: broadcasts for 83 hours daily in Albanian, Arabic, Bulgarian, Chinese, Czech, English, French, German, Greek, Hungarian, Indonesian, Italian, Persian, Polish, Portuguese, Romanian, Russian, Serbo-Croat, Spanish, Swedish and Turkish; Dir AGIM PAPAPROKO.

TELEVISION

There are stations at Tirana, Berat, Elbasan, Gjirokastër, Kükes, Peshkopi and Pogradec. Programmes are broadcast in colour in Tirana only and in black and white elsewhere for 5 hours daily (8 hours on Sundays).

Finance

Banka e Shtëtit Shqiptar (Albanian State Bank): Head Office: Sheshi Skënderbeu 1, Tirana; tel. 24-35; telex 2153; f. 1945; sole credit institution; branches in 34 towns; Gen. Dir KAMBER MYFTARI.

State Agricultural Bank: Tirana; tel. 77-38; f. 1970; gives short- and long-term credits to agricultural co-operatives and enterprises; Dir S. KUCI.

Drejtoria e Përgjithshme e Kursimeve dhe Sigurimeve (Directorate of Savings and Insurance): Tirana; tel. 25-42; f. 1949; Dir SEIT BUSHATI.

In 1984 there were 115 savings offices and 3,600 agencies.

Trade and Industry

CHAMBER OF COMMERCE

Dhoma e Tregtisë e Republikës Popullore Socialiste të Shqipërisë (Chamber of Commerce of the People's Socialist Republic of

ALBANIA

Albania): Rruga Konferenca e Pezës 6, Tirana; tel. 79-97; telex 2179; f. 1958; Chair. LIGOR DHAMO; Vice-Chair. SIMON POREÇI.

Durrës Chamber of Commerce: Durrës; f. 1988; promotes trade with southern Italy.

Gjirokastër Chamber of Commerce: Gjirokastër; f. 1988; promotes trade with Greek border area; Chair. NAXHI MAMANI.

SUPERVISORY ORGANIZATION

Albkontroll: Bul. Enver Hoxha 45, Durrës; tel. 23-54; telex 2181; f. 1962; brs throughout Albania; independent control body for inspection of goods for import and export, means of transport, etc.; Dir HITO MINGA.

FOREIGN TRADE ORGANIZATIONS

Agroeksport: Rruga 4 Shkurti 6, Tirana; tel. 52-27; telex 2137; export of vegetables, fruit, canned fish, wine, tobacco, etc.; Gen. Man. LUAN SHAHU.

Albkoop: Rruga 4 Shkurti 6, Tirana; tel. 41-79; telex 2187; f. 1986; import and export of consumer goods, incl. textiles, handicrafts, stationery, jewellery; Gen. Man. JETON HAJDARAJ.

Durrësimpeks: Rruga Skënderbeu 177, Durrës; tel. 21-99; telex 2181; f. 1988; industrial and agricultural goods.

Gjirokastërimpeks: Rruga Nacionale 55, Gjirokastër; tel. 707; f. 1988; industrial and agricultural goods.

Industrialimpeks: Rruga 4 Shkurti 6, Tirana; tel. 45-40; telex 2140; export of textiles, clothing, kitchenware, paper, timber, wooden articles, cement, etc.; import of cotton, wool, paper, etc.; Gen. Man. HAZBI GJIKONDI.

Makinaimport: Rruga 4 Shkurti 6, Tirana; tel. 52-20; telex 2127; import of factory installations and machine parts; Gen. Man. THEODHOR DUMA.

Metalimport: Rruga 4 Shkurti 6, Tirana; tel. 38-48; telex 2116; imports ferrous and non-ferrous metals, electrodes, oil lubricants, minerals, etc.; Dir T. BORODNI.

Mineralimpeks: Rruga 4 Shkurti 6, Tirana; tel. 33-70; telex 2123; import and export of chromium ore, ferro-nickel ore, electricity, etc.; Gen. Dir NIQIFOR ALIKAJ.

Transshqip: Rruga 4 Shkurti 6, Tirana; tel. 30-76; telex 2131; transport of foreign trade goods by sea and road; agents in Durrës, Vlorë and Sarandë; Gen. Dir GIOLEKË ZENELI.

CO-OPERATIVE ORGANIZATIONS

Centrocoop: Sheshi Skënderbeu, Tirana; co-operative import and export organization.

Bashkimi Qëndror i Kooperativave të Artizanatit (Central Union of Handicraft Workers' Co-operatives): Tirana; Pres. KRISTO THEMELKO.

Bashkimi Qëndror i Kooperativave Tregtare (Central Union of Commercial Co-operatives): Tirana.

Bashkimi Qëndror i Kooperativave të Shit-Blerjes (Central Union of Buying and Selling Co-operatives): Tirana.

TRADE UNIONS

The principal function of Albanian trade unions is to mobilize the working class to carry out the task of socialist construction. In every work and production centre there is a trade union grass-root organization which elects the trade union committee, while in each ward and district there is a ward committee and a district council.

Këshilli Qëndror i Bashkimeve Profesionale të Shqiperisë (Central Council of Albanian Trade Unions): Bulevardi Dëshmorët e Kombit, Tirana; f. 1945; 743,894 mems; a 201-member General Council, a 21-member Presidium and four secretaries were elected at the 10th Congress, held in June 1987; Pres. of Gen. Council SOTIR KOÇOLLARI.

Transport

RAILWAYS

In 1988 there were 509 km of railway track, with lines linking Tirana–Vorë–Sukth–Durrës, Durrës–Kavajë–Rrogozhinë–Elbasan–Librazhd–Prenjas–Pogradec, Rrogozhinë–Lushnje–Fier–Ballsh, Vorë–Laç–Lezhë–Shkodër and Selenicë–Vlorë. A standard-gauge line is being built between Fier and Selenicë. A new 35-km line between Fier and Vlorë was opened in 1985. In March 1986 work began on the Milot–Rrëshen–Klos railway, to comprise 66 km of main line and 34 km of secondary lines. The Milot–Rrëshen section opened in October 1987.

In 1979 Albania and Yugoslavia agreed to construct a 50-km line between Shkodër and Titograd. Construction of the 35-km extension from Laç to Shkodër was completed in 1981, and the Shkodër–Hani i Hotit link (35.5 km) was completed in 1984. Work on the Yugoslav section was completed in late 1985. The Shkodër–Titograd line opened to international freight traffic in September 1986. In mid-1988, however, Yugoslavia suspended all traffic on the Titograd–Shkodër line, following heavy financial losses.

Drejtoria e Hekurudhave: Tirana; railways administration; Gen. Dir VIKTOR CAPRAZI.

ROADS

In 1988 the road network comprised 6,700 km of main roads and 10,000 km of other roads. All regions are linked by the road network, but many roads in mountainous districts are unsuitable for motor transport. Private cars are banned in Albania. Bicycles and mules are widely used.

SHIPPING

Albania's merchant fleet had an estimated total displacement of 56,000 grt in 1982. The chief ports are the Enver Hoxha Port of Durrës, Vlorë, Sarandë and Shëngjin. Durrës harbour has been dredged to allow for bigger ships. In 1980 construction of a new port near Vlorë began. When completed, by 1990, the port will have a cargo-handling capacity of more than 4m. tons per year. A ferry service for the transport of freight between the Enver Hoxha Port of Durrës and Trieste (Italy) was inaugurated in November 1983. An agreement to establish a ferry service between Albania and the Greek island of Corfu was confirmed in 1988.

Drejtoria e Agjensisë së Vaporave: Enver Hoxha Port of Durrës; shipping administration.

CIVIL AVIATION

Albania has air links with Athens, Belgrade, Bucharest, Budapest, East Berlin, London, Rome, Vienna (summer only) and Zürich. An agreement to establish air links between Albania and Turkey was signed in February 1984. There is a small but modern airport at Rinas, 28 km from Tirana. There is no regular internal air service.

Albtransport: Rruga Kongresi i Përmetit 202, Tirana; tel. 30-26; telex 2124; air agency.

Tourism

Only a few thousand foreign visitors, mostly from Western Europe, are permitted to enter Albania each year. The main tourist centres include Tirana, Durrës, Sarandë and Shkodër. The Roman amphitheatre at Durrës is one of the largest in Europe. The ancient towns of Apollonia and Butrint are important archaeological sites, and there are many other towns of historic interest.

Albturist: Bulevardi Dëshmorët e Kombit 6, Tirana; tel. 79-56; telex 2148; Gen. Dir RUHI SHEQI.

ALGERIA

Introductory Survey

Location, Climate, Language, Religion, Flag, Capital

The Democratic and Popular Republic of Algeria lies in north Africa, with the Mediterranean Sea to the north, Mali and Niger to the south, Tunisia and Libya to the east, and Morocco and Mauritania to the west. The climate on the Mediterranean coast is temperate, becoming more extreme in the Atlas mountains immediately to the south. Further south is part of the Sahara, a hot and arid desert. Temperatures in Algiers, on the coast, are generally between 9°C (48°F) and 29°C (84°F), while in the interior they may exceed 50°C (122°F). Arabic is the official language but French is still widely used. There is a considerable Berber-speaking minority. Islam is the state religion, and almost all Algerians are Muslims. The national flag (proportions 3 by 2) has two equal vertical stripes, of green and white, with a red crescent moon and a five-pointed red star superimposed in the centre. The capital is Algiers (el-Djezaïr).

Recent History

Algeria was conquered by French forces in the 1830s and annexed by France in 1842. For most of the colonial period, official policy was to colonize the territory with French settlers, and many French citizens became permanent residents. Unlike most of France's overseas possessions, Algeria was not formally a colony but was 'attached' to metropolitan France. However, political and economic power within Algeria was largely held by the white settler minority, as the indigenous Muslim majority did not have equal rights.

On 1 November 1954 the major Algerian nationalist movement, the Front de libération nationale (FLN), began a war for national independence, in which about 1m. Muslims were killed or wounded. Despite resistance from the Europeans in Algeria, the French Government agreed to a cease-fire in March 1962 and independence was declared on 3 July 1962. In August the Algerian provisional government transferred its functions to the Political Bureau of the FLN, and in September a National Constituent Assembly was elected (from a single list of FLN candidates) and the Republic proclaimed. A new government was formed, with Ahmed Ben Bella, founder of the FLN, as Prime Minister. As a result of the nationalist victory, about 1m. French settlers emigrated from Algeria.

A draft constitution, providing for a presidential regime with the FLN as the sole party, was adopted by the Constituent Assembly in August 1963. In September the Constitution was approved by popular referendum and Ben Bella was elected President. Under his leadership, economic reconstruction was begun and the foundation was laid for a single-party socialist state. However, the failure of the FLN to function as an active political force left real power with the bureaucracy and the army. In June 1965 the Minister of Defence, Col Houari Boumedienne, deposed Ben Bella in a bloodless coup and took control of the State as President of a Revolutionary Council of 26 members, chiefly army officers.

Boumedienne faced considerable opposition from left-wing members of the FLN, but by 1971 the Government felt strong enough to adopt a more active social policy. French petroleum interests were nationalized and an agrarian reform programme was initiated. In June 1975 Boumedienne announced a series of measures to consolidate the regime and his personal power, including the drawing up of a National Charter and a new constitution, and the holding of elections for a President and National Assembly. Following public discussion of the National Charter, which formulated the principles and plans for creating a socialist system and maintaining Islam as the state religion, a referendum was held in June 1976, at which the Charter was adopted by 98.5% of the electorate. In November a new constitution was approved by another referendum, and in December Boumedienne was elected President unopposed, winning more than 99% of the votes cast. The new formal structure of power was completed in February 1977 by the election of FLN members to the National Assembly.

In December 1978 President Boumedienne died, and the Council of the Revolution (now consisting of only eight members) took over the government. An FLN Congress in January 1979 adopted a new party structure, electing a Central Committee which was envisaged as the highest policy-making body both of the party and of the nation as a whole: this Committee was to choose a party leader who would automatically become the sole presidential candidate. Their choice of Col Ben Djedid Chadli, commander of Oran military district, was upheld by a national referendum in February, and was seen as representing a compromise between liberal and radical contenders. Unlike Boumedienne, Chadli appointed a Prime Minister, Col Muhammad Abd al-Ghani, anticipating constitutional changes which were approved by the National Assembly in June and which included the obligatory appointment of a Prime Minister. Further changes in the party structure of the FLN were made in June 1980, when the FLN authorized Chadli to form a smaller Political Bureau of seven members (increased to 10 in July 1981) with more limited responsibilities, thereby increasing the power of the President. Membership of the National Assembly was increased to 281 in the legislative elections of March 1982, when the electorate was offered a choice of three candidates per seat. Of the successful candidates, 55 were FLN party officials and 142 were government officials, so executive control of the Assembly was expected to increase.

At the fifth conference of the FLN, held in December 1983, Chadli was re-elected to the post of secretary-general of the party, and became the sole candidate for the presidential election, which was held on 12 January 1984. His candidature was endorsed by 95.4% of the electorate, and he was therefore returned to office for another five years. Immediately after his re-election, President Chadli named a new Prime Minister, Abd al-Hamid Brahimi, the former Minister of Planning. In 1985 Chadli initiated a public debate on Boumedienne's National Charter of 1976, which resulted in the adoption of a new National Charter at a special congress of the FLN in December. The revised Charter sought a balance between socialism and Islam as the state ideology, and encouraged the private sector. At a referendum in January 1986, 98.37% of the votes cast (with 95.92% of the electorate participating) favoured the adoption of the new Charter. The number of seats in the National Assembly was increased to 295, all candidates being nominated by the FLN, for a general election in February 1987, when a record 87.29% of the electorate participated. Of the votes cast, however, 15.26% were invalid. In June a new Minister of the Interior was appointed, and Chadli introduced further changes in the military hierarchy, in order to strengthen the position of the Chief of Staff of the Army and to create a more professional army. In July the National Assembly passed legislation to permit the formation of local organizations without prior government authorization. The new law, however, continued to forbid associations that were deemed to threaten Algeria's security or the policies of the Charter.

Meanwhile, the Government encountered criticism and violent protests from students, Islamic fundamentalists and the Berbers of the Kabyle region, who felt that their culture and language were being suppressed. In 1985 18 alleged supporters of Ben Bella were sentenced to terms of imprisonment, following their conviction on charges of threatening state security. In a separate trial, a total of 22 human rights and Berber cultural activists were found guilty of membership of illegal organizations, and received short prison sentences. In November 1986 four people were killed and 186 people were arrested during three days of rioting at Constantine and Sétif, which followed protests by students against government plans to reform the *baccalauréat* examination, and against poor living conditions and tuition facilities at the University of Constantine. The 186 detainees later received prison sentences for unlawful assembly, disturbing the peace and damage to property. Several human rights activists were exiled to southern Algeria, and in January 1987 security forces shot dead the leader, Mustafa Bouiali, and several other members of a clandestine Islamic fundamentalist group, who had been in hiding for 18 months, following the theft of weapons from a police barracks. In March and April the Government issued amnesties to human rights activists and to the 186 people imprisoned after the riots in Constantine, and approved the formation of a new human rights organization. In June 12 alleged supporters of Ben Bella received 'moderate' sentences of between two and 10 years' imprisonment for attacking the State, distributing subversive literature and receiving funds from abroad. At the end of a large trial in July, involving 202 defendants charged with involvement in the activities of Bouiali's Islamic fundamentalist group, four people received death sentences for plotting against the State, murder, armed attacks and robbery. Other defendants received sentences ranging from life to one year's imprisonment, while 15 people were acquitted. During an amnesty to commemorate the 25th anniversary of Algerian independence in August, the four death sentences were commuted to life imprisonment.

In response to a sharp decline in the price of petroleum in 1986 and an increase in Algeria's external debt, the Government introduced austerity measures and began to remove state controls from various economic sectors (see Economic Affairs). In November 1987 the Ministry of Planning, which had previously been responsible for the close supervision of every aspect of Algeria's economy, was abolished, in accordance with the latter policy. In the same month a new Ministry of Education and Training was created, in response to increasing demands for employment and educational opportunities for young people, manifested by a student boycott of lectures earlier that month. With the aim of accelerating the implementation of new economic measures, in December President Chadli announced a series of administrative reforms, intended to improve the efficiency of Algeria's slow-moving and complex bureaucratic procedures. In February 1988 Chadli appointed 'technocratic' ministers to deal with the economic problems of the health and agricultural sectors.

Meanwhile, Algeria's economic difficulties and the rapid increase in the country's population, along with the Government's austerity policies, had resulted in decaying infrastructure, shortages of food and other essential goods, high prices, unemployment and increasing social polarization. Since July 1988 there had been a wave of strikes, but in September President Chadli reaffirmed his commitment to economic reform and vowed to dismiss any officials attempting to obstruct the implementation of austerity measures. Rumours subsequently emerged of government plans to introduce further austerity measures, including a rise in bread prices. There were demands for a general strike, and in early October riots broke out in the working-class districts of Algiers. As violent unrest spread through the capital and to Oran and Annaba, the Government declared a state of emergency, and armed soldiers were deployed at Algiers harbour and outside important buildings. Official sources announced that 3,743 people had been arrested, and that 176 had died during clashes with government forces, although other estimates of deaths ranged from 200 to 500. After six days, the state of emergency was revoked and, during a national television broadcast, Chadli promised to introduce political reforms. It was subsequently announced that a referendum would be held on 3 November, seeking approval for a series of constitutional amendments which included proposals to make the Prime Minister accountable to the National Assembly, rather than to the FLN. Meanwhile, food and other essential goods, drawn from emergency stockpiles, were delivered to shops in Algiers, and 923 detainees, mostly minors, were released. In late October Chadli dismissed the uncompromising Muhammad Cherif Messaadia from the deputy leadership of the FLN and replaced him with the more liberal Abd al-Hamid Mehri. Chadli also announced plans to make the FLN more democratic by broadening its membership and by introducing elections for most party posts. It was also proposed that non-party members would be allowed to contest seats in popularly-elected organizations. These plans were to form the subject of a referendum in early 1989.

At the referendum on constitutional amendments, held on 3 November 1988, 92.27% of votes cast (with 83.08% of the electorate participating) favoured the adoption of the reforms proposed in October. Immediately after the referendum, Chadli appointed Kasdi Merbah, who had been the Minister of Health since February, to be Prime Minister. Merbah appointed a new 22-member Council of Ministers, which included 13 newcomers. The principal ministries were allocated to 'technocrats'

or to veteran politicians. The new Government subsequently presented the National Assembly with an emergency programme of reforms, which aimed to remove causes of discontent by addressing problems experienced by Algerian youth and by the unemployed. In November the FLN congress approved the constitutional amendments and nominated Chadli as sole candidate in the presidential election, due to be held on 22 December.

Since independence, Algeria has been one of the most prominent non-aligned states and, as such, played an important part in the release of the US hostages in Iran in January 1981. The Algerian Government has supported various liberation movements in Africa and the Middle East, providing military, financial and diplomatic aid for the Polisario Front in Western Sahara (see chapter on Morocco).

In the early 1980s there was a noticeable improvement in relations with the USA, culminating, in April 1985, in a meeting between the US and Algerian Presidents in Washington. As a result of this visit, Chadli succeeded in having Algeria removed from the list of countries that the US Government had declared 'ineligible' to purchase US military equipment. Algeria's relations with the USA were temporarily strained in April 1988, when Algeria successfully negotiated the release of hostages being held on a hijacked Kuwaiti airliner, while agreeing to provide the hijackers with a safe passage from Algiers airport to Iran or Lebanon. The Algerian authorities' decision to allow the hijackers to escape unpunished attracted severe criticism from the USA and the UK. However, any tension with the USA was defused shortly afterwards by the visit to Algeria of the US Deputy Secretary of State, John Whitehead, who used the occasion to request Algeria to assist in the release of US hostages being held in Lebanon.

The protracted struggle in Western Sahara embittered Algeria's relations with France, which supported the claims of Morocco and Mauritania. Algeria also criticized French military intervention elsewhere in Africa, while further grievances were the heavy trade surplus in France's favour, and France's determination to reduce the number of Algerians resident in France. By the early 1980s, relations had improved, and in 1982 President Chadli made the first official visit to France by an Algerian head of state since independence. In September 1986 relations were strained by the French Government's announcement of proposals to introduce visa requirements for visitors from non-EEC countries to France. In October Algeria retaliated by introducing similar requirements for French visitors. In the same month, however, the French Government expelled 13 Algerian members of the Mouvement pour la Démocratie en Algérie (MDA—founded by Ben Bella in 1984) from France and banned the MDA newspaper, Al-Badil, after Algerian security forces co-operated with France following a series of bombings in Paris. In April 1987 the Algerian Government agreed to release the assets of former French settlers, which had been 'frozen' since independence. Further agreements allowed former French property-owners to sell their land in Algeria to the Algerian State, and permitted French workers in Algeria to transfer their income to France. In return, the French Government agreed to provide financial assistance to Algeria for three years. In July the two countries concluded an agreement relating to children from mixed Algerian-French marriages, and the French authorities suppressed another MDA publication. In the following months Algeria assisted in negotiations between France and Iran over the blockading of the French embassy in Teheran and the Iranian embassy in Paris. Algeria also conducted negotiations with Islamic groups in Lebanon, in an attempt to obtain the release of French hostages. Meanwhile, in January 1988 France announced the arrests of two MDA members on charges which included illegal possession of arms. In June Algeria and France signed an agreement guaranteeing French mothers access to children living with their Algerian fathers. The two countries also agreed to establish a bilateral commission to adjudicate on contentious cases of child custody. In July the French Government banned the MDA newspaper, Al-Badil démocratique, which had been established as a replacement for the outlawed Al-Badil. In September, however, relations between France and Algeria cooled, as parents occupied the French embassy in Algiers to protest against the Algerian Government's decision that children from Algerian-French marriages should attend Arabic-speaking schools. Relations continued to deteriorate during the riots in Algiers in October (see above), as Algerian state newspapers accused the French media of exaggerating the extent of the unrest, and the Algerian Government criticized the French Minister of Co-operation for objecting to the stern measures taken against rioters. Meanwhile, the French Prime Minister maintained an embarrassed silence on the unrest, in an attempt to balance French support for human rights with the French interest in preventing the unrest from spreading across the Maghreb and into the North African community in France.

Relations with Spain improved in 1987, after deteriorating in 1986 owing to Algerian suspicion of Spain's pro-Moroccan position in the conflict in Western Sahara and the presence in Algiers of a leader of ETA, the Basque separatist movement. In December 1986 the Spanish Deputy Prime Minister visited President Chadli, and in the following month Spain announced that Algeria would be incorporated into its programme of overseas military co-operation. In August the two countries signed a pact which allowed an Algerian security official to be stationed in Spain to monitor the activities of Algerian dissidents, in exchange for closer supervision of members of ETA, exiled in Algeria. In December an MDA activist was arrested by the Spanish authorities and expelled to Algeria.

Algeria's relations with other Maghreb states (Libya, Mauritania, Morocco and Tunisia) improved considerably in the 1980s. Algeria partially opened its frontier with Morocco in February 1983, and signed the Maghreb Fraternity and Co-operation Treaty, which normalized relations with Tunisia, in March. It was hoped that this treaty would eventually form the basis of the long-discussed Great Arab Maghreb. It was therefore left open for other countries to sign; Mauritania did so in December 1983. However, the *rapprochement* with Morocco continued to be hindered by Algeria's continuing support of the Polisario Front. In May 1987 President Chadli met King Hassan of Morocco at a location on the Algeria/Morocco border, under the auspices of King Fahd of Saudi Arabia. After the meeting, the two leaders issued a communiqué announcing that consultations to resolve existing problems between the two countries would continue. Later in the month, the Algerian Government released 150 Moroccan soldiers, in exchange for 102 Algerian prisoners, held in Morocco.

Meanwhile, relations with Libya improved, following President Chadli's meetings with the Libyan Secretary for Foreign Liaison in November 1985, and with Col Muammar al-Qaddafi, the Libyan leader, in January 1986. In an attempt to consolidate its good relations with Algeria, Libya advocated a treaty of union with Algeria in March and June 1986. In June 1987 a proposal for a political union between Libya and Algeria was submitted to Chadli by Col Qaddafi's deputy, Maj. Abd as-Salam Jalloud, during his visit to Algeria. After Jalloud's visit, Algeria suggested that the Maghreb Fraternity and Co-operation Treaty of 1983 already provided a framework for a new Algerian-Libyan relationship. Later in June, Col Qaddafi arrived unexpectedly in Algeria to attempt to persuade Chadli to agree to the union proposals, but he succeeded only in gaining several minor co-operation agreements. In the following month Chadli visited Tunisia to discuss the Libyan proposals with Habib Bourguiba, the Tunisian President. The two leaders subsequently issued a joint communiqué announcing that discussions had been held on the means of developing unity within the Maghreb region. In October Algeria agreed, in principle, to a treaty of political union with Libya, but the official announcement of the treaty was postponed, following diplomatic pressure from the USA (in addition to opposition from within the Algerian Government), and Chadli again proposed that Libya should sign the Maghreb Fraternity and Co-operation Treaty.

Towards the end of 1987 and during 1988 the process of achieving Maghreb unity gained momentum. In November 1987 President Chadli received the Moroccan Minister of Foreign Affairs, and they discussed means of accelerating the establishment of the Great Arab Maghreb and of resolving the conflict in Western Sahara. In January 1988, during a meeting in Tunis, Chadli and the new Tunisian President, Zine al-Abidine ben Ali, issued directives to intensify bilateral co-operation, demanded a just resolution of the Western Sahara conflict, and pledged to work for regional stability and the early creation of the Great Arab Maghreb. Chadli then visited Col Qaddafi in an apparent attempt to persuade him to sign the Maghreb Fraternity and Co-operation Treaty in March, on the fifth anniversary of its inception. At a tripartite meeting in Tunis in February, Chadli, President Ben Ali of Tunisia and Col Qaddafi of Libya all expressed their determination to work towards the creation of the Great Arab Maghreb. Libya's failure to sign the Maghreb Fraternity and Co-operation Treaty was a major factor underlying Algeria's efforts to improve relations with Morocco. In early May the head of the secretariat (i.e. deputy leader) of the FLN, Muhammad Cherif Messaadia, visited Rabat to invite King Hassan to a 'summit' conference of the Arab League in Algiers, which Chadli had convened for June, with the aim of rallying support for the Palestinian uprising in the Israeli-occupied territories. A few days later, King Hassan dispatched two senior advisers to Algiers for further consultations, and on 16 May the two countries announced the re-establishment of diplomatic relations at ambassadorial level. The Moroccan-Algerian border was subsequently opened in early June, before the Arab League 'summit'.

The creation of the Great Arab Maghreb became a reality in June 1988, when the first meeting of the five heads of state of the Maghreb countries was held in Algiers, following the conclusion of the Arab League 'summit'. The five leaders issued a joint communiqué announcing the creation of a Maghreb commission whose responsibility was to focus on the establishment of a semi-legislative, semi-consultative council to harmonize legislation in the region, and to prepare joint economic projects. At the end of June, Algeria and Libya agreed to hold referendums on a proposed union of the two countries. Unlike the proposals issued by Col Qaddafi in 1987 (which envisaged a total merger), this revised proposal aimed merely to establish a federation between the two countries. President Chadli later announced that the Algerian referendum on the union would be held in 1989. In July 1988 Algeria signed a co-operation agreement with Morocco, and the two countries announced plans to harmonize their railway, postal and telecommunications systems. Later in the month, the Maghreb commission met in Algiers and announced the creation of five working groups to examine areas of regional integration. The working groups, each chaired by a representative of a member country, met during the following three months, in order to prepare for the second meeting of the Maghreb commission in October.

Government

Under the 1976 Constitution (with modifications adopted by the National Assembly in June 1979 and with further amendments approved by popular referendum in November 1988), Algeria is a socialist single-party state. The Head of State is the President of the Republic, who is nominated by a Congress of the FLN (the only authorized party) and is elected for a five-year term by universal adult suffrage. The President presides over a Council of Ministers and a High Security Council. The President may appoint Vice-Presidents and must appoint a Prime Minister, who initiates legislation and appoints a Council of Ministers. The Prime Minister is responsible to the unicameral National People's Assembly, which comprises 295 members, elected by universal adult suffrage for a five-year term. The President is empowered to legislate by decree, after consultations with the Prime Minister, when the Assembly is not in session. The country is divided into 48 departments (wilayat), sub-divided into communes. Each wilaya and commune has an elected assembly. All candidates for election, whether to local or national assemblies or to the Presidency of the Republic, are nominated by the FLN, but the electorate may be offered a choice of candidates.

Defence

In June 1988 the estimated strength of the armed forces was 139,000 (including 70,000 conscripts), comprising an army of 120,000, a navy of 7,000 and an air force of 12,000. The 1987 defence budget was estimated at 5,810m. dinars. The USSR provides military equipment and training. Military service is compulsory for six months, and there is a gendarmerie of 30,000, controlled by the Ministry of the Interior.

Economic Affairs

Following Algeria's long war of independence, and the consequent departure of French personnel, the economy was severely disrupted and suffered from a shortage of skilled workers. In the period following independence, the Government nationalized large agricultural estates, important manufacturing enterprises and banks. The main sector of the economy, the extraction and processing of hydrocarbons (petroleum and natural gas), was brought under state control in 1971. Assisted by the sharp rises in petroleum prices after

1973, Algeria experienced rapid economic expansion and industrialization, with a consequent decline in the importance of agriculture. In 1987 various state controls were removed from agricultural co-operatives and public enterprises, in an attempt to move away from the collectivization of the 1970s, which was being increasingly criticized for its inefficiency. In 1987, according to estimates by the World Bank, Algeria's gross national product (GNP), measured at average 1985–87 prices, was US $63,560m., equivalent to $2,760 per head. Algeria's GNP per head in that year was the second highest level among African countries. It was estimated that GNP per head increased, in real terms, at an average rate of 0.9% per year between 1980 and 1987. The average annual rate of inflation rose from an estimated 12% in 1985 and 1986 to an estimated 15% in 1987 and 1988.

Only about 10% of Algeria's land can be used for agriculture, which accounts for around 8% of gross domestic product (GDP), and employed 26.1% of the working population in 1986. In an attempt to discourage population drift away from rural areas (particularly among young people), farmers' earnings have been more closely related to those of their industrial counterparts. Land reforms led to the establishment of large co-operatives, but about one-half of the cultivated land remained under private ownership. In 1987 the Government introduced major reforms, which allowed farmers to form collectives, comprising at least three members, and to lease land in units, formed from the subdivision of existing co-operatives. The farmers were also allowed to transfer or trade their leases after five years, to control their own operations, to work directly with the banks and to make a profit. The State, as owner of the land, was to restrict its role to the provision of aid and to mediation in disputes over land division. Algeria's major agricultural products are cereals, wine and citrus fruits. However, the country produces only 35% of domestic cereal requirements, and large quantities of foodstuffs (dairy produce, vegetable oils and sugar, as well as cereals) have to be imported. In 1986 agricultural production increased by 12%, although the cereal harvest for 1986/87 declined to 2.1m. tons. The 1987/88 cereal harvest was initially expected to reach 3.5m. tons, but in early 1988 Algeria was a victim of a plague of locusts over the Sahel region. In 1987 imports of food accounted for 25% of the total import bill. The importance of the agricultural sector was stressed by the Government's Development Plan for 1985–89, which increased investment in agriculture to 14.4% of the total, compared with 11.8% of total investment allocated to the sector under the 1980–84 Plan.

Algeria is rich in minerals, notably iron ore, phosphates, petroleum and natural gas. It is a relatively small petroleum producer: annual output declined from 54m. metric tons in 1978 to 27.9m. tons in 1986. In 1987 Algeria's reserves were estimated at 8,500m. barrels. Algeria is a member of OPEC (see p. 196). Under OPEC agreements, Algeria's production quota for the second half of 1987 and for the whole of 1988 was 667,000 barrels per day. Algeria's proven recoverable reserves of natural gas, estimated at 2,950,000m. cu m, are the world's fourth largest. Production of natural gas totalled 97,400m. cu m in 1986 and 110,810m. cu m in 1987, of which 24,930m. cu m was liquefied for export. The hydrocarbons industry contributed about 22% of GDP and 97.4% of export revenues in 1987. Hydrocarbon exports totalled about $8,000m. per year in 1986 and 1987. In 1986 liquefied natural gas (LNG) represented 27%, and crude petroleum 20%, of hydrocarbon export revenue. In 1988 hydrocarbon exports were projected to rise to $9,000m.–$10,000m. In 1987 Algeria, Libya and Tunisia agreed to construct a gas pipeline to supply Libya with Algerian natural gas, and in mid-1988 the three countries formed a joint venture, the Société Arabe pour le Transport de Gaz Naturel, to conduct studies for the proposed pipeline. In September 1988 an agreement was signed with Morocco for the construction of a gas pipeline by an Algerian-Moroccan joint venture, to supply both Morocco and Spain with Algerian gas. Algeria is aiming at self-sufficiency in cement, iron and steel, plastics, chemicals and fertilizers, although in the mid-1980s many plants were still working below their full potential. In 1987 Algerian and Italian companies agreed to establish a joint venture to construct Algeria's first car assembly plant. Commerce and industry are dominated by state-controlled enterprises. Socialist management of companies by their workers was introduced in 1974. In December 1987 state-controlled enterprises were allowed to adopt their own annual plans, to determine the prices of their products and to invest their profits freely, in order to increase profitability and efficiency. The capital and shares of these enterprises were to be held by eight state holding companies, which were established in mid-1988.

After the large increases in the price of petroleum in 1973–74, the Government introduced an intensive investment programme, using increased revenue to expand the economy. Increased earnings from gas and petroleum exports led to a trade surplus of an estimated US $4,223m. in 1985. The rapid fall in oil prices, however, resulted in a sharp decline of the trade surplus to an estimated $177m. in 1986, according to IMF figures. In 1987 the price of petroleum recovered slightly and the trade surplus increased to $1,023m. In 1984 there was a current account surplus of $74m., which rose to $1,015m. in 1985. In 1986, however, the current account registered a deficit of $2,230m., but in 1987 the current account achieved a small surplus, estimated at $70m., owing to higher oil and gas prices. In mid-1988 legislation was introduced to ease state controls on external trade.

Revenues from the hydrocarbon sector led to a rapid growth in GDP during the 1970s, reaching a peak of 16.3% growth in 1980. However, the world recession, decreased petroleum production and loss of gas revenues (owing to pricing disagreements and voluntary conservation of reserves) meant that real GDP rose by only 1.2% in 1981, by 3.4% in 1982 and by an estimated 3.5% in 1983. Annual GDP growth was estimated at 6% in 1984 and 1985, but declined to 2.9% in 1986 and to 0.8% in 1987. The 1988 budget proposals projected GDP growth at 4.1% for that year, well below the annual growth rate of 6.5% projected in the 1985–89 Development Plan. Algeria's external debt reached an estimated US $21,000m. in 1987 and was estimated at $20,700m. in 1988. The cost of servicing the debt in 1988 was expected to total $5,200m.

Algeria's development has been concentrated in heavy industry along the northern coastal strip, emphasizing capital-intensive production for export. Reliance on the existing infrastructure, together with an annual population growth rate of 4.8% in the cities in the period 1977–87, has caused a general decline in urban living standards. The Government aimed to create 116,000 jobs in 1988, insufficient to offset an overall population increase of an estimated 3.1% per year. In 1987 about 17% of the work-force were unemployed. About 1m. Algerians work abroad, and in 1985 remittances from overseas workers totalled an estimated US $373.2m. In December 1987 the Government introduced measures which aimed to improve living standards by creating special funds, such as the housing fund. In October 1988, however, economic factors, particularly low urban living standards, were the main grievances underlying the most serious unrest in Algeria since independence (see Recent History).

The 1985–89 Development Plan, approved in July 1984, envisaged total investment of 550,000m. dinars, and GDP growth of 6.5% annually. Like its predecessors, the Plan continued to emphasize the agricultural sector and the importance of increasing the share of export revenue coming from non-hydrocarbons; there was also to be considerable investment in the country's infrastructure, particularly in the railway network and in housing, which was to take 16% of the total investment.

In June 1988 the World Bank approved two loans, totalling US $303m., towards railway and energy projects in Algeria. Receipts from tourism totalled $60m. in 1983. In 1986 the Government announced measures to encourage tourism as an alternative means of earning foreign exchange, following the decline in the hydrocarbon sector. A new banking and credit law was introduced in 1986 to restructure the credit system, by giving greater autonomy to the five commercial banks, and to upgrade the functions of the Central Bank. In 1987 the Conseil National du Crédit (CNC) was set up to supervise the banking reforms and determine Algeria's foreign borrowing. During the last four months of 1986, the dinar was devalued by an estimated 7%, to promote non-hydrocarbon exports.

In 1987 the Ministry of Light Industry began to prepare a Development Plan for 1990–94, which aimed to encourage industries in the high-technology sector and develop export potential. The 1988 budget proposals projected investment expenditure at 88,700m. dinars, substantially below the annual target of 110,000m. dinars set by the 1985–89 Development Plan, with an expected deficit of 10,000m. dinars. The Government introduced tax incentives to encourage the establishment of joint ventures with foreign companies, industrial maintenance operations, and the expansion of the agricultural and tourism sectors. Meanwhile, price increases were announced for petrol, diesel oil, passport duties and excise stamps, in an attempt to control the budgetary deficit.

Social Welfare

Since 1974, all Algerian citizens have had the right to free medical attention. In 1979 Algeria had 367 hospital establishments, with a total of 47,116 beds, and there were 6,881 physicians working in the country. In 1984 a new health plan was announced. In 1987 the administrative investment budget allocated 3,961m. dinars to expenditure on health and social services. Under the 1984 plan, several new health centres and clinics were to be built, an institution for training health care administrators was to be founded, and vaccinations were to be made more readily available.

Education

Education is officially compulsory for nine years between six and 15 years of age. Primary education begins at the age of six and lasts for six years. Secondary education begins at 12 years of age and lasts for up to seven years (a first cycle of four years and a second of three years). In 1985 the total enrolment at primary and secondary schools was equivalent to 73% of the school-age population (82% of boys; 63% of girls). Enrolment at primary schools in 1985 included an estimated 86% of children in the relevant age-group (95% of boys; 78% of girls). The 1985–89 Development Plan envisaged expenditure of 31,500m. dinars on new educational schemes, in addition to 33,300m. dinars on projects carried over from the previous five-year plan. More than 27% of total planned expenditure in the 1988 budget was allocated to education and training. In accordance with the National Charter, the various primary and secondary schools were unified in 1976, private education was abolished and a nine-year 'enseignement fondamental' was introduced. Priority is being given to teacher-training, to the development of technical and scientific teaching programmes, and to adult literacy and training schemes. In 1987 there were eight universities and a number of 'Centres Universitaires' and technical colleges. In 1986/87 there were about 156,700 undergraduates and post-graduates studying at university. In 1985, according to UNESCO estimates, the average rate of adult illiteracy was 50.4% (males 37%; females 63%).

Public Holidays

1989: 2 January (for New Year), 1 May (Labour Day), 7 May* (Id al-Fitr, end of Ramadan), 19 June (Ben Bella's Overthrow), 5 July (Independence), 14 July* (Id al-Adha, Feast of the Sacrifice), 4 August* (Islamic New Year), 13 August* (Ashoura), 13 October* (Mouloud, Birth of Muhammad), 1 November (Anniversary of the Revolution).

1990: 1 January (New Year), 27 April* (Id al-Fitr, end of Ramadan), 1 May (Labour Day), 19 June (Ben Bella's Overthrow), 4 July* (Id al-Adha, Feast of the Sacrifice), 5 July (Independence), 24 July* (Islamic New Year), 2 August* (Ashoura), 2 October* (Mouloud, Birth of Muhammad), 1 November (Anniversary of the Revolution).

* Religious holidays, which are dependent on the Islamic lunar calendar, may differ by one or two days from the dates given.

Weights and Measures

The metric system is in force.

ALGERIA

Statistical Survey

Source (unless otherwise stated): Office National des Statistiques, Ministère de la Planification et de l'Aménagement du Territoire, 8 rue des Moussebiline, BP 55, Algiers; tel. 64-77-90; telex 52620.

Area and Population

AREA, POPULATION AND DENSITY

Area (sq km)	2,381,741*
Population (census results)†	
12 February 1977‡	16,948,000
April 1987‡	22,971,558
Population (official estimates at mid-year)‡	
1985	21,850,000
1986	22,520,000
Density (per sq km) at April 1987	9.6

* 919,595 sq miles.
† Provisional.
‡ Excluding Algerian nationals residing abroad, numbering an estimated 828,000 at 1 January 1978.

AREA AND POPULATION BY WILAYA (ADMINISTRATIVE DISTRICT)*

	Area (sq km)	Population (estimates at 1 Jan. 1984)†
Adrar	422,498.0	161,936
el-Asnam (ech-Cheliff)	8,676.7	1,040,563
Laghouat	112,052.0	391,817
Oum el-Bouaghi (Oum el-Bouagul)	8,123.0	464,806
Batna	14,881.5	691,079
Béjaia	3,442.2	659,040
Biskra (Beskra)	109,728.0	662,778
Béchar	306,000.0	184,069
Blida (el-Boulaïda)	3,703.8	1,126,303
Bouira	4,517.1	454,805
Tamanrasset (Tamenghest)	556,000.0	62,680
Tébessa (Tbessa)	16,574.5	439,638
Tlemcen (Tilimsen)	9,283.7	678,025
Tiaret (Tihert)	23,455.6	731,542
Tizi-Ouzou	3,756.3	1,028,864
Algiers (el-Djezaïr)	785.7	2,442,303
Djelfa (el-Djelfa)	22,904.8	403,500
Jijel	3,704.5	604,319
Sétif (Stif)	10,350.4	1,776,673
Saida	106,777.4	450,594
Skikda	4,748.3	597,530
Sidi-Bel-Abbès	11,648.2	604,773
Annaba	3,489.3	650,096
Guelma	8,624.4	633,733
Constantine (Qacentina)	3,561.7	807,245
Médéa (Lemdiyya)	6,704.1	575,305
Mostaganem (Mestghanem)	7,023.6	396,765
M'Sila	19,824.6	540,013
Mascara (Mouaskar)	5,845.6	526,644
Ouargla (Wargla)	559,234.0	261,760
Oran (Ouahran)	1,820.0	889,800
Total	**2,381,741.0**	**20,841,000**

* In December 1983 an administrative reorganization created 17 new *wilayat*, bringing the total number to 48.
† Excluding Algerian nationals abroad, estimated to total 828,000 at 1 January 1978.

PRINCIPAL TOWNS
(estimated population at 1 January 1983)

Algiers (el-Djezaïr, capital)	1,721,607	Tlemcen (Tilimsen)	146,089
Oran (Ouahran)	663,504	Skikda	141,159
Constantine (Qacentina)	448,578	Béjaia	124,122
		Batna	122,788
Annaba	348,322	El-Asnam (ech-Cheliff)	118,996
Blida (el-Boulaïda)	191,314	Boufarik	112,000*
Sétif (Stif)	186,978	Tizi-Ouzou	100,749
Sidi-Bel-Abbès	146,653	Médéa (Lemdiyya)	84,292

* 1977 figure.

April 1987 (census results, not including suburbs): Algiers 1,483,000; Constantine 438,000; Oran 590,000.

BIRTHS AND DEATHS (UN estimates, annual averages)

	1970–75	1975–80	1980–85
Birth rate (per 1,000)	48.0	45.0	42.7
Death rate (per 1,000)	15.4	13.4	10.7

Source: UN, *World Population Prospects: Estimates and Projections as Assessed in 1984*.

EMPLOYMENT
(household survey, '000 persons, excluding armed forces, 1985)

	Males	Females	Total
Agriculture, hunting, forestry and fishing	987	12	999
Mining and quarrying			
Manufacturing	556	39	595
Electricity, gas and water			
Construction	661	9	670
Trade, restaurants and hotels	302	9	311
Transport, storage and communications	192	10	202
Financing, insurance, real estate and business services			
Community, social and personal services	860	247	1,107
Total	**3,558**	**326**	**3,884**

Source: ILO, *Year Book of Labour Statistics*.

ALGERIA

Statistical Survey

Agriculture

PRINCIPAL CROPS ('000 metric tons)

	1984	1985	1986
Wheat	1,200	1,478	1,445
Barley	588	1,330	1,100
Oats	64	108	80
Potatoes	521	800	850
Pulses	45	46	63
Sugar beets	110†	112	112
Onions (dry)	196	100	152
Tomatoes	266	300	275
Grapes	415	469	465†
Olives	133†	140†	140*
Oranges	183	200	220
Tangerines and mandarins	83	90	105
Dates	183	220†	190†
Water-melons	243	252†	350†
Tobacco	6	3	3

* FAO estimate. † Unofficial figure.
Source: FAO, *Production Yearbook*.

LIVESTOCK ('000 head, year ending September)

	1984	1985	1986
Sheep	14,725	15,000	14,795
Goats	3,000	3,010	3,090
Cattle	1,404	1,592†	1,557
Horses	92	120	120*
Mules	155	160	160*
Asses	403	473*	475*
Camels	125	130	130

Chickens (FAO estimates, million): 21 in 1984; 22 in 1985; 22 in 1986.

* FAO estimate. † Unofficial figure.
Source: FAO, *Production Yearbook*.

LIVESTOCK PRODUCTS (FAO estimates, '000 metric tons)

	1984	1985	1986
Beef and veal	46	49	47
Mutton and lamb	85	81*	77*
Goat's meat	14	14	14
Poultry meat	50	52	53
Other Meat	9	10	11
Cows' milk	600	536*	539*
Sheep's milk	190	195	197
Goats' milk	160	162	164
Hen eggs	64.0	90.0*	123.0*
Wool:			
greasy	35.0	42.0	40.0
clean	18.0	22.0	20.0
Cattle hides	7.3	7.5	7.2
Sheep skins	13.8	12.5	11.8
Goat skins	2.8	2.9	2.8

* Unofficial figure.
Source: FAO, *Production Yearbook*.

Forestry

ROUNDWOOD REMOVALS
(FAO estimates, '000 cu m, excluding bark)

	1984	1985	1986
Sawlogs, veneer logs and logs for sleepers*	20	20	20
Other industrial wood	203	210	216
Fuel wood	1,604	1,654	1,708
Total	1,827	1,884	1,944

* Assumed to be unchanged since 1975.
Source: FAO, *Yearbook of Forest Products*.

Fishing

(FAO estimates, '000 metric tons, live weight)

	1984	1985	1986
European sardine (pilchard)	36.4	36.6	38.9
Other marine fishes	26.2	26.4	28.0
Marine crustaceans	2.9	3.0	3.2
Total catch	65.5	66.0	70.0

Source: FAO, *Yearbook of Fishery Statistics*.

Mining

('000 metric tons, unless otherwise indicated)

	1983	1984	1985
Coal*	7	7	8
Iron ore:			
gross weight	3,680	3,660	3,370*
metal content*	1,991	1,980	1,825
Salt	150	150	182
Lead ore*†	3.0	3.6	3.6
Zinc ore†	11.4	14.6	12.0
Copper ore*†	0.1	0.1	—
Mercury‡	0.3	0.8	0.9
Phosphate rock	893	1,000	1,207
Crude petroleum	31,292	29,700	29,357
Natural gas (petajoules)	873	936	1,161

* Provisional or estimated data.
† Figures refer to the metal content of concentrates and ores.
‡ Estimates by the US Bureau of Mines.
1986: Crude petroleum 27,910,000 metric tons; Natural gas 1,341 petajoules.
1987: Crude petroleum 30,410,000 metric tons.

ALGERIA

Industry

SELECTED PRODUCTS
('000 metric tons, unless otherwise indicated)

	1983	1984	1985
Olive oil (crude)*	24	14	24
Margarine	13.4*	n.a.	n.a.
Flour	650	n.a.	n.a.
Raw sugar	5*	7*	0
Wine ('000 hectolitres)*	1,880	2,150	2,200
Cigarettes (metric tons)	1,750	1,800	1,850
Woven cotton fabrics (million sq metres)	105	105	103
Footwear—excl. rubber ('000 pairs)	16,780	n.a.	n.a.
Nitrogenous fertilizers (a)†	47.0	65.0*	101.5
Phosphate fertilizers (b)†	53.0	77.5	84.2
Naphtha	3,677	4,022	4,060
Motor spirit (petrol)	1,400	1,774	1,800
Kerosene	110	120	130
Jet fuel	520	487	500
Distillate fuel oils	6,456	7,260	7,300
Residual fuel oils	5,177	5,108	5,200
Liquefied petroleum gas	1,481	2,806	2,910*
Cement*	4,808	5,534	5,534
Pig-iron	1,113	1,100	1,100*
Crude steel	892	700*	750*
Television receivers ('000)	194	225	n.a.
Buses and coaches—assembled (number)	700	731	n.a.
Lorries—assembled (number)	6,500	7,344*	n.a.
Electric energy (million kWh)	10,216	11,182	12,274

* Provisional or estimated data.
† Production in terms of (a) nitrogen or (b) phosphoric acid. Phosphate fertilizers include ground rock phosphate.

Source: mainly UN, *Industrial Statistics Yearbook*.

Finance

CURRENCY AND EXCHANGE RATES

Monetary Units
100 centimes = 1 Algerian dinar (AD).

Denominations
Coins: 1, 2, 5, 10, 20 and 50 centimes; 1 and 5 dinars.
Notes: 5, 10 and 100 dinars.

Sterling and Dollar Equivalents (31 August 1988)
£1 sterling = 10.854 dinars;
US $1 = 6.445 dinars;
1,000 Algerian dinars = £92.14 = $155.16.

Average Exchange Rate (dinars per US $)
1985   5.0278
1986   4.7023
1987   4.8497

Statistical Survey

ADMINISTRATIVE BUDGET (estimates, million AD)

Expenditure	1985	1986	1987*
Presidency	611.8	640.0	585.0
National defence	4,793.1	5,459.0	5,805.0
Foreign affairs	583.5	619.3	583.0
Light industry	137.6	149.5	132.0
Housing and construction	359.4	460.9	439.0
Finance	1,252.4	1,446.1	1,613.0
Home affairs	n.a.	3,543.0	4,003.0
Commerce	130.6	146.8	148.0
Youth and sport	403.6	446.6	396.0
Information	350.8	384.8	373.0
Ex-servicemen	2,984.5	3,289.0	3,192.0
Culture and tourism	218.3	258.2	226.0
Agriculture and fishing	766.0	838.1	772.0
Health	2,720.6	3,518.3	3,961.0
Transport	373.7	414.0	413.0
Justice	477.4	556.4	668.0
Professional training	1,397.9	1,539.8	1,562.0
Religious affairs	363.7	403.1	473.0
Public works	690.8	784.1	697.0
Education	11,026.7	13,626.7	15,886.0
Higher education and scientific research	2,764.4	2,931.6	3,494.0
Heavy industry	94.6	108.3	107.0
Water, environment and forests	798.3	866.0	810.0
Energy and petrochemicals industries	201.5	220.9	216.0
Planning and land development	n.a.	165.9	—
Social protection	476.7	530.1	501.0
Extra expenditure	25,197.5	23,384.4	15,779.0
Total (incl. others)	**62,200.0**	**67,000.0**	**63,000.0**

* As announced in November 1985. A revised administrative budget, announced in April 1986, projected total expenditure of 59,500 million AD.

1988 (million AD): Revenue 103,000; Administrative expenditure 64,500.

INVESTMENT BUDGET (million AD)

Expenditure	1988
Hydrocarbons	700
Manufacturing industries	1,300
Mines and energy (incl. rural electrification)	1,000
Agriculture and water projects	7,450
Services	135
Economic and administrative infrastructure	8,369
Education and training	7,100
Social and cultural infrastructures	3,294
Construction	2,142
Infrastructure and training linked to the reform of state enterprises	470
Grants to new enterprises	150
Financial restructuring of State enterprises	3,400
Total (incl. others)	**47,500**

Source: *Al-Moudjahid*.

CENTRAL BANK RESERVES
(US $ million at 31 December)

	1985	1986	1987
Gold*	215	239	277
IMF special drawing rights	138	167	202
Reserve position in IMF	168	181	153
Foreign exchange	2,513	1,312	1,285
Total	**3,034**	**1,899**	**1,917**

* Valued at 35 SDRs per troy ounce.
Source: IMF, *International Financial Statistics*.

ALGERIA

MONEY SUPPLY (million AD at 31 December)

	1985	1986	1987
Currency outside banks	76,642	89,360	96,892
Demand deposits at deposit money banks	104,623	95,935	103,801
Checking deposits at post office	18,315	18,312	22,247
Private sector demand deposits at treasury	2,650	1,145	929
Total money	202,230	204,752	223,869

Source: IMF, *International Financial Statistics*.

COST OF LIVING (Consumer Price Index for Algiers; average of monthly figures; base: 1982 = 100)

	1984	1985	1986
Food	113.4	127.5	149.2
Clothing	111.1	118.3	123.9
Rent, electricity, gas and water	111.4	115.7	127.5
All items (incl. others)	114.6	126.6	142.2

Source: ILO, *Year Book of Labour Statistics*.

NATIONAL ACCOUNTS
(million AD at current prices)
Expenditure on the Gross Domestic Product

	1983	1984	1985
Government final consumption expenditure	34,700	40,800	45,800
Private final consumption expenditure	106,200	118,300	136,200
Increase in stocks	7,500	7,300	4,800
Gross fixed capital formation	80,300	87,400	92,700
Total domestic expenditure	228,700	253,800	279,500
Exports of goods and services	65,300	67,700	69,200
Less Imports of goods and services	60,300	61,600	59,500
GDP in purchasers' values	233,800	259,900	289,200

Source: IMF, *International Financial Statistics*.

BALANCE OF PAYMENTS (US $ million)

	1984	1985	1986
Merchandise exports f.o.b.	12,792	13,034	8,066
Merchandise imports f.o.b.	−9,235	−8,811	−7,889
Trade balance	3,557	4,223	177
Exports of services	778	722	1,361
Imports of services	−4,442	−4,132	−3,976
Balance on goods and services	−107	813	−2,438
Private unrequited transfers (net)	186	191	209
Government unrequited transfers (net)	−5	11	
Current balance	74	1,015	−2,230
Long-term capital (net)	−404	−36	364
Short-term capital (net)	193	−85	319
Net errors and omissions	−197	126	349
Total (net monetary movements)	−333	1,020	−1,198
Valuation changes (net)	−45	334	39
Changes in reserves	−379	1,355	1,159

Source: IMF, *International Financial Statistics*.

External Trade

PRINCIPAL COMMODITIES (million AD)

Imports c.i.f.	1982	1983	1984
Foodstuffs and tobacco	8,745	9,200	8,815
Energy and lubricants	317	881	1,053
Primary products and raw materials	1,273	1,557	3,174
Semi-finished products	15,984	16,136	15,208
Capital goods	11,983	12,854	15,130
Consumer goods	3,760	3,959	7,242
Total (incl. others)	49,384	49,782	51,257

1986 (million AD): Foodstuffs 8,709; Semi-finished products 10,858; Industrial equipment 13,272; Consumer goods 6,283; Total (incl. others) 43,415.
Source: Office National des Statistiques.
1987 (million AD): Foodstuffs 8,524; Semi-finished products 8,850; Raw materials 2,424; Industrial equipment 9,064; Consumer goods 4,374; Total (incl. others) 34,196.
Source: Direction Générale des Douanes, *Actualité Economique*.

Exports f.o.b.	1982	1983	1984
Foodstuffs and tobacco	324	178	239
Energy and lubricants	59,391	59,824	57,646
Primary products and raw materials	756	702	976
Total (incl. others)	60,478	60,722	59,106

1986 (million AD): Foodstuffs 123; Energy and lubricants 35,964; Semi-finished products 761; Total 36,848.
Source: Office Nationale des Statistiques.
1987 (million AD): Foodstuffs 145; Energy and lubricants 38,137; Semi-finished products 518; Total (incl. others) 39,156.
Source: Direction Générale des Douanes, *Actualité Economie*.

PRINCIPAL TRADING PARTNERS (million AD)*

Imports	1981	1982	1984†
Belgium-Luxembourg	1,855	1,965	2,170
Brazil	1,385	823	1,407
Canada	3,936	1,974	1,985
France	9,016	10,360	12,063
Germany, Federal Republic	6,631	6,841	5,478
Italy	6,417	3,335	4,501
Japan	2,527	3,607	n.a.
Netherlands	1,240	1,205	1,296
Romania	207	368	n.a.
Spain	3,106	3,746	2,252
Sweden	534	547	n.a.
Switzerland	794	531	n.a.
USSR	303	363	n.a.
United Kingdom	1,733	1,730	n.a.
USA	1,677	3,746	2,894
Total (incl. others)	48,780	49,384	51,257

* Imports by country of production; exports by country of consignment.
† No data are available for 1983.
Source: Ministère du Commerce, Algiers.

1985 (US $ million): Imports: France 2,688, Germany, Federal Republic 1,088, Italy 1,051, Total (incl. others) 9,169. Exports: France 2,085, Germany, Federal Republic 1,275, Italy 2,280, Japan 2,206, Netherlands 948, Spain 765, Total (incl. others) 9,169.
Source: IMF, *Direction of Trade Statistics*.

ALGERIA

Statistical Survey

Exports	1981	1982	1984†
Belgium-Luxembourg	238	665	454
Brazil	1,181	907	410
France	11,383	19,172	16,806
Germany, Federal Republic	7,578	3,205	1,777
Italy	5,952	8,588	10,715
Japan	3,251	2,038	n.a.
Netherlands	4,569	7,536	7,085
Romania	2	91	n.a.
Spain	2,569	3,332	2,034
Sweden	448	121	n.a.
USSR	541	878	n.a.
United Kingdom	782	907	852
USA	19,149	9,199	12,809
Total (incl. others)	62,837	60,478	59,106

Transport

RAILWAYS (traffic)

	1982	1983	1984
Passengers carried ('000)	24,842	34,043	35,700
Freight carried ('000 metric tons)	11,355	11,437	11,400
Passenger-km (million)	1,774	1,804	1,835
Freight ton-km (million)	2,765	2,671	2,631

1987: Passengers carried ('000) 43,000, Freight carried ('000 metric tons) 12,700.

ROAD TRAFFIC (motor vehicles in use at 31 December)

	1977	1978	1981
Passenger cars	355,125	411,894	573,573
Lorries and vans	174,801	186,169	248,258
Coaches and buses	5,484	6,401	8,417
Motorcycles	16,637	16,812	17,608

Source: Ministère de la Planification et de l'Aménagement du Territoire, Algiers; and (1981) International Road Federation. Figures for 1979 and 1980 are not available.

INTERNATIONAL SEA-BORNE SHIPPING
(estimated freight traffic, '000 metric tons)

	1983	1984	1985
Goods loaded	54,677	53,370	50,543
Goods unloaded	16,676	15,865	15,450

Source: UN, *Monthly Bulletin of Statistics*.

CIVIL AVIATION (traffic on scheduled services)

	1982	1983	1984
Kilometres flown ('000)	29,800	31,200	36,400
Passengers carried ('000)	3,150	3,411	3,781
Passenger-km (million)	2,610	2,798	3,312
Freight ton-km ('000)	15,900	28,200	14,900
Mail ton-km ('000)	1,800	1,900	1,900
Total ton-km ('000)	253,000	282,000	306,000

Source: UN, *Statistical Yearbook*.

Tourism

FOREIGN VISITORS BY COUNTRY OF ORIGIN

	1984	1985	1986
France	167,811	108,278	91,181
Germany, Federal Republic	27,562	19,720	17,347
Italy	30,844	23,318	21,937
Morocco	1,537	821	624
Tunisia	9,233	8,203	10,169
United Kingdom	9,684	7,969	6,868
USA	4,070	3,279	2,607
Total (incl. others)	250,747	171,588	150,733

Hotel Capacity (1986): 200 hotels; 32,862 beds.

Source: Ministère de la Culture et du Tourisme, Algiers.

Communications Media

	1982	1983	1984
Radio receivers ('000 in use)	4,200	4,400	n.a.
Television receivers ('000 in use)	n.a.	1,325	n.a.
Book production: titles*	504	n.a.	718
Daily newspapers:			
Number	4	n.a.	5
Average circulation ('000 copies)	445	n.a.	570
Non-daily newspapers:			
Number	15	n.a.	n.a.
Average circulation ('000 copies)	309	n.a.	n.a.
Other periodicals:			
Number	27	n.a.	n.a.
Average circulation ('000 copies)	476	n.a.	n.a.

* Including pamphlets (167 in 1984).

1985: Radio receivers ('000 in use) 4,800; Television receivers ('000 in use) 1,600.

Source: UNESCO, *Statistical Yearbook*.

Telephones: 709,000 in use (1984).

Education

(state institutions only, 1984)

	Institutions	Teachers	Pupils
Primary	11,360	125,034	3,481,288
Middle and Secondary			
General	1,250*	80,055	1,756,506
Teacher training	40†	2,458	27,364
Technical	174*	2,163	66,886
Higher (Universities, etc.)	13*	12,509‡	11,507

* 1981/82 figures.
† 1978/79 figures.
‡ 1983/84 figures.

Source: mainly UNESCO, *Statistical Yearbook*.

Directory

The Constitution

A new constitution for the Democratic and Popular Republic of Algeria, approved by popular referendum on 19 November 1976, was promulgated on 22 November 1976. The Constitution was amended by the National People's Assembly on 30 June 1979. Further amendments were approved by referendum on 3 November 1988. The main provisions of the Constitution, as amended, are summarized below:

The preamble recalls that Algeria owes its independence to a war of liberation which will go down in history as one of the epic struggles in the resurrection of the peoples of the Third World. It emphasizes that the institutions which have been established since June 1965 are intended to transform the progressive ideas of the revolution into real achievements, affecting daily life, and to develop the content of the revolution by thought and action towards a definitive commitment to socialism.

FUNDAMENTAL PRINCIPLES OF THE ORGANIZATION OF ALGERIAN SOCIETY

The Republic

The State is socialist. Islam is the state religion and Arabic is the official national language. National sovereignty resides in the people. The National Charter is the fundamental source of national policy and law. It is to be referred to on ideological questions and for the interpretation of the Constitution. The popular assemblies are the basic institution of the State.

Socialism

The irreversible option of socialism is the only path to complete national independence. The individual ownership of property for personal or family use is guaranteed. Non-exploitative private property is an integral part of the new social system. The cultural, agrarian and industrial revolutions and socialist management of enterprises are the bases for the building of socialism.

The State

The State is exclusively at the service of the people. Those holding positions of responsibility must live solely on their salaries and may not, directly or by the agency of others, engage in any remunerative activity.

Fundamental Freedoms and the Rights of Man and the Citizen

Fundamental rights and freedoms are guaranteed. All discrimination on grounds of sex, race or occupation is forbidden. Law cannot operate retrospectively and a person is presumed innocent until proved guilty. Victims of judicial error shall receive compensation from the State.

The State guarantees the inviolability of the home, of private life and of the person. The State also guarantees the secrecy of correspondence, the freedom of conscience and opinion, freedom of intellectual, artistic and scientific creation, and freedom of expression and assembly.

The State guarantees the right to join a trade union, the right to work, to protection, to security, to health, to leisure, to education, etc. It also guarantees the right to leave the national territory, within the limits set by law. The law lays down the conditions under which the fundamental rights and freedoms may be withdrawn from anyone who uses them to attack the Constitution, the essential interests of the nation, the unity of the people and of the national territory, the internal and external security of the State, and the socialist revolution.

Duties of citizens

Every citizen must protect public property and safeguard national independence. The law sanctions the duty of parents to educate and protect their children, as well as the duty of children to help and support their parents. Women must participate fully in the building of socialism and national development.

The National Popular Army

The Army safeguards national independence and sovereignty. It participates in the development of the country and the building of socialism.

Principles of foreign policy

Algeria subscribes to the objectives of the UN, the OAU and the League of Arab States. It supports Arab, Maghreb and African unity, on a basis of popular liberation. It is non-aligned and advocates peace and non-interference in the internal affairs of states. It fights against colonialism, imperialism and racial discrimination and supports the peoples of Africa, Asia and Latin America in their liberation struggles.

POWER AND ITS ORGANIZATION

Political power

The Algerian institutional system rests on the principle of the single-party state. The Front de Libération Nationale (FLN) is a vanguard force, guiding and organizing the people for the building of socialism. Party and state organs work in different frameworks and with different means to attain the same objectives. The decisive posts in the state organization are held by members of the party leadership.

The Executive

The President of the Republic is Head of State, Head of the Armed Forces and responsible for national defence. He must be of Algerian origin, a Muslim and more than 40 years old. He is nominated by the FLN Congress and elected by universal, secret, direct suffrage. His mandate is for five years, and is indefinitely renewable. The President embodies the unity of the nation. The President presides over joint meetings of the party and the executive. The President presides over meetings of the Council of Ministers. He may appoint one or more Vice-Presidents, to whom he may delegate some of his powers, and must appoint a Prime Minister, who is responsible to the National People's Assembly. The Prime Minister must appoint a Council of Ministers. He drafts, co-ordinates and implements his government's programme, which he must present to the Assembly for ratification. Should the Assembly reject the programme, the Prime Minister and the Council of Ministers resign, and the President appoints a new Prime Minister. Should the newly-appointed Prime Minister's programme be rejected by the Assembly, the President dissolves the Assembly, and a general election is held. Should the President be unable to perform his functions, owing to a long and serious illness, the President of the National People's Assembly assumes the office for a maximum period of 45 days (subject to the approval of two-thirds majorities in the FLN Central Committee and the National Assembly). If the President is still unable to perform his functions after 45 days, the Presidency is declared vacant. Should the Presidency fall vacant, the President of the National People's Assembly temporarily assumes the office (subject to the approval of two-thirds majorities in the FLN Central Committee and the National Assembly) and organizes presidential elections within 45 days. He may not himself be a candidate in the election. The President presides over a High Security Council which advises on all matters affecting national security.

The Legislature

The National People's Assembly prepares and votes the law. Its members are nominated by the party leadership and elected by universal, direct, secret suffrage for a five-year term. The deputies enjoy parliamentary immunity. The Assembly sits for two ordinary sessions per year, each of not more than three months' duration. The commissions of the Assembly are in permanent session. The Assembly may be summoned to meet for an extraordinary session on the request of the President, or of the Prime Minister, or of two-thirds of the members of the Assembly. Both the Prime Minister and the Assembly may initiate legislation. The Assembly may legislate in all areas except national defence. In the periods between sessions of the Assembly the President may legislate by decree, in accordance with the Prime Minister's recommendations, but all such legislation must be submitted to the Assembly in the following session.

The Judiciary

Judges obey only the law. They defend the socialist revolution. The right of the accused to a defence is guaranteed. The Supreme Court regulates the activities of courts and tribunals. The Higher Court of the Magistrature is presided over by the President of the Republic; the Minister of Justice is Vice-President of the Court. All magistrates are answerable to the Higher Court for the manner in which they fulfil their functions.

Constitutional revision

The Constitution can be revised on the initiative of the President of the Republic by a two-thirds majority of the National Assembly. The basic principles of the Constitution may not be revised.

ALGERIA

The Government

HEAD OF STATE

President: BEN DJEDID CHADLI (elected 7 February 1979; re-elected 12 January 1984).

COUNCIL OF MINISTERS
(December 1988)

President and Minister of Defence: BEN DJEDID CHADLI.
Prime Minister: KASDI MERBAH.
Minister of the Interior and Environment: BOUBAKER BELKAÏD.
Minister of Foreign Affairs: BOUALEM BESSAÏEH.
Minister of Agriculture: NOUREDDINE KADRA.
Minister of Public Works: AISSA ABD AL-LAOUI.
Minister of Energy, Chemicals and Petrochemical Industries: SADOK BOUSSENA.
Minister of Light Industry: MUHAMMAD TAHAR BOUZGHOUB.
Minister of Heavy Industry: MUHAMMAD GHRIB.
Minister of Finance: SID-AHMAD GHOZALI.
Minister of Construction and Regional Development: NADIR BEN MAATI.
Minister of Public Health: Prof. MESSAOUD ZITOUNI.
Minister of Higher Education: Prof. ABD AL-HAMID ABERKANE.
Minister of Education and Training: SLIMANE CHEÏK.
Minister of Commerce: MOURAD MEDELCI.
Minister of Posts and Telecommunications: YACINE FERGANI.
Minister of War Veterans: MUHAMMAD DJEGHABA.
Minister of Religious Affairs: BOUALEM BAKI.
Minister of Youth and Sport: CHERIF RAHMANI.
Minister of Transport: AL-HADI KHEDIRI.
Minister of Justice: ALI BEN FLIS.
Minister of Information and Culture: MUHAMMAD ALI-AMMAR.
Minister of Hydraulics: AHMAD BEN FREHA.
Minister of Labour and Social Affairs: MUHAMMAD NABI.

MINISTRIES

Office of the President: Présidence de la République, el-Mouradia, Algiers; tel. (2) 60-03-60; telex 53761.
Office of the Prime Minister: Palais du Gouvernement, Algiers; tel. (2) 60-23-40; telex 52073.
Ministry of Agriculture: 12 blvd Col Amirouche, Algiers; tel. (2) 63-89-50; telex 52984.
Ministry of Commerce: 44 rue Muhammad Belouizdad, Algiers; tel. (2) 63-33-66; telex 52768.
Ministry of Construction, Housing and Regional Development: route des 4 Canons, Tagarins, Algiers; tel. (2) 61-20-14; telex 53880.
Ministry of Culture and Tourism: Palais de la Culture, Algiers; tel. (2) 58-91-10; telex 52555.
Ministry of Defence: ave des Tagarins, Algiers; tel. (2) 61-15-15; telex 52627.
Ministry of Education and Training: 8 ave de Pékin, el-Mouradia, Algiers; tel. (2) 60-54-41; telex 52443.
Ministry of Energy and Petrochemical Industries: 80 rue Ahmad Ghermoul, Algiers; tel. (2) 66-33-00; telex 52790.
Ministry of Finance: Palais du Gouvernement, Algiers; tel. (2) 63-23-40; telex 52062.
Ministry of Foreign Affairs: 6 rue 16n- Batran, el-Mouradia, Algiers; tel. (2) 60-47-44; telex 52794.
Ministry of Health: 25 blvd Laala Abd ar-Rahmane, el-Madania, Algiers; tel. (2) 66-33-15; telex 51263.
Ministry of Heavy Industry: 6 rue Ahmad Bey, Immeuble le Colisée, Algiers; tel. (2) 60-11-14; telex 52707.
Ministry of Higher Education: 1 rue Bachir Attar, Palais du 1er Mai, Algiers; tel. (2) 66-33-61; telex 52720.
Ministry of Hydraulics, Forestry and Fishing: le Grand Seminaire, Kouba, Algiers; tel. (2) 58-95-00; telex 62560.
Ministry of Information: 11 chemin Doudon Mokhtar ben-Aknoun, Algiers; tel. (2) 79-23-23; telex 52469.
Ministry of the Interior: Palais du Government, Algiers; tel. (2) 63-23-40; telex 52073.
Ministry of Justice: 8 rue de Khartoum, el-Biar, Algiers; tel. (2) 78-20-90; telex 52761.
Ministry of Labour and Social Affairs: rue Farid Zouieoueche, Kouba, Algiers; tel. (2) 77-91-33; telex 53447.
Ministry of Light Industry: 3 rue Ahmad Bey, Algiers; tel. (2) 60-11-44; telex 52707.
Ministry of Posts and Telecommunications: 4 blvd Salah Bouakouir, Algiers; tel. (2) 61-12-20; telex 52020.
Ministry of Public Works: 135 rue Didouche Mourad, Algiers; tel. (2) 59-00-29; telex 52713.
Ministry of Religious Affairs: 2 ave Timgad, Hydra, Algiers; tel. (2) 60-85-55; telex 52648.
Ministry of Transport: chemin Abd al-Kader Gadouche, Hydra, Algiers; tel. (2) 60-60-33; telex 52775.
Ministry of War Veterans (Moudjahidine): 2 rue Lt Benafa, Château-Neuf, Algiers; tel. (2) 78-23-55; telex 52011.
Ministry of Youth and Sport: 3 place du 1er Mai, Algiers; tel. (2) 66-33-70; telex 52110.

Legislature

ASSEMBLÉE NATIONALE POPULAIRE

The National People's Assembly comprises 295 deputies, elected by universal suffrage for a five-year term. The most recent general election took place on 26 February 1987. A single-party list of candidates was presented by the FLN, but the electorate was offered a choice of three candidates per seat. Electoral participation was 87.29%. However, 15.26% of the votes cast were invalid.

President of the National Assembly: RABAH BITAT.

Political Organizations

Front de Libération Nationale (FLN): blvd Zirout Yousuf, Algiers; telex 53931; f. 1954; sole legal party; socialist in outlook, the party is organized into a Secretariat, a Central Committee, a Political Bureau, Federations, Kasmas and cells; according to party statutes adopted at the FLN Congress in January 1979, the Central Committee (elected by Congress and consisting of 120–160 full members and 30–40 alternate members, meeting twice annually) chooses a party Secretary-General who automatically becomes the candidate for the Presidency of the Republic. Members of the Political Bureau (between seven and 11, meeting monthly) are chosen by the Secretary-General and endorsed by the Central Committee; Sec.-Gen. Col BEN DJEDID CHADLI; Head of Secretariat ABD AL-HAMID MEHRI.

Political Bureau: BEN DJEDID CHADLI (President), RABAH BITAT, ABDALLAH BELHOUCHET, MUHAMMAD BEN AHMAD ABD AL-GHANI, ABD AL-HAMID MEHRI, AHMAD TALEB IBRAHIMI, BOUALEM BAKI, BOUALEM BEN HAMOUDA. Deputy Members: ABD AL-HAMID BRAHIMI, RACHID BEN YELLES, BACHIR ROUIS, ABDALLAH KHALEF.

Under the aegis of the FLN there exists a number of mass political organizations, including the Union Nationale de la Jeunesse Algérienne (UNJA) and the Union Nationale des Femmes Algériennes (UNFA).

There are several small opposition groups: all are officially proscribed and in exile in France or in other Arab countries. These include:

Parti de l'avant-garde socialiste: successor to the Algerian Communist Party.

Mouvement pour la Démocratie en Algérie (MDA): f. 1984 in Paris; seeks pluralist democratic system of government; Pres. AHMAD BEN BELLA.

In December 1985 AHMAD BEN BELLA and Dr HOCINE AIT AHMAD announced the formation of a united democratic front.

Diplomatic Representation

EMBASSIES IN ALGERIA

Albania: 19 bis rue Abdelkrim Lagoune, el-Mouradia, Algiers; Ambassador: DHIMITËR STAMO.
Angola: 34 chemin Abd al-Kader, el-Mouradia, Algiers; tel. (2) 56-15-24; telex 62204; Ambassador: HENRIQUE TELES CARREIRA.
Argentina: 7 rue Hamani, Algiers; tel. (2) 64-74-08; telex 67485; Ambassador: VICENTE ESPECHE-GIL.
Australia: 12 ave Emile Marquis, Djenane-el-Malik, Hydra, Algiers; tel. (2) 60-28-46; telex 66105; Ambassador: Dr J. N. SKINNER.
Austria: Les Vergers, rue 2, Villa 9, DZ-16330 Bir Khadem, Algiers; tel. (2) 56-26-99; telex 62302; Ambassador: HANS G. KNITEL.

ALGERIA

Bangladesh: 141 blvd Salah Bouakouir, Algiers; telex 52565; Ambassador: REAZ RAHMAN.

Belgium: 22 chemin Youcef Tayebi, el-Biar, Algiers; tel. (2) 78-57-12; telex 61365; Ambassador: ANDRÉ ADAM.

Benin: rue 3, Villa no. 4, Beaulieu, el-Harrach, Algiers; telex 52447; Ambassador: ANTOINE LALEYE.

Brazil: 48 blvd Muhammad V, Algiers; telex 52470; Ambassador: RONALD L. M. SMALL.

Bulgaria: 13 blvd Col Bougara, Algiers; Ambassador: GRIGOR TODOROV KRUCHMARSKI.

Burundi: 116 bis blvd des Martyrs, Algiers; telex 53501; Ambassador: ANDRÉ NADAYIRAGE.

Cameroon: 26 chemin Cheikh Bachir Ibrahimi, el-Biar, Algiers; telex 52421; Ambassador: SIMON NKO'O ETOUNGOU.

Canada: 27 bis rue Ali Massoudi, POB 225, Hydra, Algiers; tel. (2) 60-66-11; telex 66043; Ambassador: GILLES MATHIEL.

Chad: 6 rue Sylvain Fourastier, Le Golf, Algiers; telex 52642; Ambassador: MBAILAOU NAIMBAYE LOSSIMIAN.

China, People's Republic: 34 blvd des Martyrs, Algiers; telex 53233; Ambassador: JIN SEN.

Congo: 13 rue Rabah Noël, Algiers; telex 52069; Ambassador: BENJAMIN BOUNKOULOU.

Côte d'Ivoire: Immeuble 'Le Bosquet', Le Paradou, Hydra, Algiers; telex 52881; Ambassador: LAMBERT AMON TAMOH.

Cuba: 22 rue Larbi Alik, Hydra, Algiers; telex 52963; Ambassador: CLAUDIO RAMOS BORREGO.

Czechoslovakia: Villa Malika, 7 chemin Zyriab, BP 999, Algiers; tel. (2) 60-05-25; telex 66281; Ambassador: FRANTIŠEK KAN.

Denmark: 29 blvd Zirout Youcef, BP 500, DZ-16000 Alger-Gare, Algiers; tel. 63-88-71; telex 67328; Ambassador: PREBEN HANSEN.

Egypt: Chargé d'affaires: Dr HUSSAIN AHMAD AMIN.

Finland: BP 256, 16035 Hydra, Algiers; telex 66296; Ambassador: RISTO RÄNNÄLI.

France: 6 rue Larbi Alik, Hydra, Algiers; telex 52644; Ambassador: JEAN AUDIBERT.

Gabon: 136 bis blvd Salah Bouakouir au 80 rue Allili, BP 85, Algiers; tel. (2) 72-02-64; telex 52242; Ambassador: YVES ONGOLLO.

German Democratic Republic: 16 rue Payen, Hydra, Algiers; tel. (2) 60-96-28; telex 62374; Ambassador: GERHARD HAIDA.

Germany, Federal Republic: 165 chemin Sfindja, BP 664, Algiers; tel. (2) 63-48-45; telex 67343; Ambassador: Dr WILFRIED M. HOFMANN.

Ghana: 62 rue Parmentier, Hydra, Algiers; tel. (2) 56-23-32; telex 62234; Ambassador: VICTOR KWASI DEY.

Greece: 31 rue A. les Crêtes, 16035 Hydra, Algiers; tel. (2) 60-08-55; telex 66071; Ambassador: GEORGES HELMIS.

Guinea: 43 blvd Central Said Hamdine, Hydra, Algiers; telex 53451; Ambassador: FODE BERETE.

Guinea-Bissau: Cité DNC, rue Ahmad Kara, Hydra, Algiers; tel. (2) 60-01-51; Ambassador: Dr LEONEL VIEIRA (also representing Cape Verde).

Holy See: 1 rue Nourredine Mekiri, 16090 Bologhine, Algiers; tel. (2) 62-34-30; Pro-Nuncio: Mgr GIOVANNI DE ANDREA.

Hungary: 18 ave des Frères Oughlis, BP 68, el-Mouradia, Algiers; tel. (2) 60-77-09; telex 62217; Ambassador: ZOLTÁN ZSIGMOND.

India: 119 ter rue Didouche Mourad, Algiers; tel. (2) 59-46-00; telex 66138; Ambassador: V. K. NAMBIAR.

Indonesia: 6 rue Muhammad Chemlal, BP 62, 16070 el-Mouradia, Algiers; tel. (2) 60-20-51; telex 62214; Ambassador: MUHAMMAD SINGGIH HADIPRANOWO.

Iran: 60 rue Didouche Mourad, Algiers; telex 52880; Ambassador: SIAVASH ZARGARAN YAQOUBI.

Iraq: 4 rue Arezki Abri, Hydra, Algiers; telex 53067; Ambassador: IBRAHIM SHUJAA SULTAN.

Italy: 18 rue Muhammad Ouidir Amellal, el-Biar, Algiers; tel. (2) 78-33-99; telex 61357; Ambassador: MICHELANGELO JACOBUCCI.

Japan: 1 chemin Macklay, el-Biar, Algiers; tel. (2) 78-62-00; telex 61389; Ambassador: NISHIYAMA TAKEHIKO.

Jordan: 6 rue du Chenoua, Algiers; telex 52464; Ambassador: YASIN ISTANBULI.

Korea, Democratic People's Republic: 49 rue Hamlia, Bologtrine, Algiers; telex 53929; Ambassador: LI MAN-SOK.

Kuwait: 1 ter rue Didouche Mourad, Algiers; telex 52267; Ambassador: ABDEL-LATIF HAMAD AL-SALIH.

Lebanon: 9 rue Kaïd Ahmad, el-Biar, Algiers; telex 52416; Ambassador: SALHAD NASRI.

Libya: 15 chemin Cheikh Bachir Ibrahimi, Algiers; telex 52700; Ambassador: ABDEL-FATTAH NAAS.

Madagascar: 22 rue Abd al-Kader Aouis Bologhine, Algiers; tel. (2) 62-31-96; telex 61156; Ambassador: SAMUEL LAHADY.

Mali: Villa no. 15, Cité DNC/ANP, chemin du Kaddous, Algiers; telex 52631; Ambassador: BOUBACAR KASSE.

Mauritania: BP 276, el-Mouradia, Algiers; telex 53437; Ambassador: OULD MUHAMMAD MAHMOUD MUHAMMADOU.

Mexico: 8 chemin du Kaddous, BP 880, DZ-16300 Alger-Gare, Algiers; tel. (2) 59-12-13; telex 66090; Ambassador: JORGE PALACIOS.

Mongolia: 4 rue Belkacem Amani, Hydra, Algiers; Ambassador: TSEBEENGOMBYN DEMIDDAGBA.

Morocco: Algiers; Ambassador Prof. ABD AL-LATIF BERBICHE.

Netherlands: 23 chemin Cheikh Bachir Ibrahimi, BP 72, El-Biar, Algiers; tel. 78-28-29; telex 61364; Ambassador: JAN TONNY WARMENHOVEN.

Niger: 54 rue Vercors Rostamia Bouzareah, Algiers; telex 52625; Ambassador: MOUSTAPHA TAHI.

Nigeria: 27 bis rue Blaise Pascal, BP 629, Algiers; tel. (2) 60-60-50; telex 52523; Ambassador: B. A. OKI.

Oman: 126 rue Didouche Mourad, Algiers; telex 52223; Ambassador: SALEM ISMAIL SUWAID.

Pakistan: 14 ave Soudani Boudjemâa, Algiers; tel. (2) 60-57-81; telex 66277; telex 66277; Ambassador: KARAMATULLAH KHAN GHORLI.

Philippines: Algiers; Ambassador: PACIFICO CASTRO.

Poland: 37 ave Mustafa Ali Khodja, el-Biar, Algiers; telex 52562; Ambassador: STANISŁAW PICHLA.

Portugal: 67 chemin Muhammad Gacem, Algiers; tel. (2) 56-61-95; telex 62202; Ambassador: FERNANDO ANDRESEN GUIMARÃES.

Qatar: BP 118, 25 bis allée Centrale, Clairval, Algiers; tel. (2) 79-80-56; telex 52224; Ambassador: KHALIFA SULTAN AL-ASSIRY.

Romania: 24 rue Si Arezki, Hydra, Algiers; telex 52915; Ambassador: (vacant).

Saudi Arabia: 4 rue Arezki Abri, Hydra, Algiers; telex 53039; Ambassador: HASAN FAQQI.

Senegal: 1 rue Arago, Algiers; tel. (2) 60-32-85; telex 52133; Ambassador: IBRAHIMA WONE.

Somalia: 11 impasse Tarting, blvd des Martyrs, Algiers; telex 52140; Ambassador: ABD AL-HAMID ALI YOUCEF.

Spain: 10 rue Azil Ali, Algiers; telex 67330; Ambassador: GUMERSINDO RICO Y RODRÍGUEZ VILLAR.

Sweden: BP 23, place Allendé, Bir-Mourad-Rais B, Algiers; tel. (2) 59-42-90; telex 66069; Ambassador: JEAN-CHRISTOPHE ÖBERG.

Switzerland: 27 blvd Zirout Youcef, DZ-16000 Alger-Gare, Algiers; tel. (2) 63-39-02; telex 67342; Ambassador: O. UHL.

Syria: Domaine Tamzali, chemin A. Gadouche, Hydra, Algiers; telex 52572; Ambassador: AHMAD MADANIYA.

Tunisia: 11 rue du Bois de Boulogne, Hydra, Algiers; telex 52968; Ambassador: M'HEDI BACCOUCHE.

Turkey: Villa dar el Ouard, chemin de la Rochelle, blvd Col Bougara, Algiers; tel. (2) 60-12-57; telex 66244; Ambassador: ERDIL K. AKAY.

USSR: impasse Boukhandoura, el-Biar, Algiers; telex 52511; Ambassador: VASILIY TARATUTA.

United Arab Emirates: 26 rue Aouis Mokrane, POB 454, el-Mouradia, Algiers; tel. (2) 56-46-47; telex 62208; Ambassador: MUHAMMAD I. AL-JOWAIED.

United Kingdom: 7 chemin des Glycines, BP 43, DZ-16000 Alger-Gare, Algiers; tel. (2) 60-56-01; telex 66151; Ambassador: PATRICK EYERS.

USA: 4 chemin Cheikh Bachir Brahimi, Algiers; tel. (2) 60-11-86; telex 66047; Ambassador: CHRISTOPHER ROSS.

Venezuela: 38 rue Jean Jaurès, el-Mouradia, Algiers; telex 52695; Ambassador: FRANCISCO SALAZAR MARTÍNEZ.

Viet-Nam: 30 rue de Chenoua, Hydra, Algiers; telex 52147; Ambassador: VO TOAN.

Yemen Arab Republic: 74 rue Bouraba, Algiers; telex 53582; Ambassador: HAMOD MUHAMMAD BAYDER.

Yemen, People's Democratic Republic: 12 ave Chahid el-Wali Mustafa Sayed, Algiers; Ambassador: ABD AL-WAKIL ISMAIL AS-SAROURI.

Yugoslavia: 7 rue des Frères Benhafid, BP 662, Hydra, Algiers; tel. (2) 60-47-04; telex 66076; Ambassador: BORISLAV MILOŠEVIĆ.

Zaire: 12 rue A, Les Crêtes, Hydra, Algiers; telex 52749; Ambassador: IKOLO BOLELAMA W'OKONDOLA.

ALGERIA

Zimbabwe: 24 rue Arab Si Ahmad, Birkhadem, Algiers; Ambassador: SOLOMON RAKOBE NKOMO.

Judicial System

The highest court of justice is the Supreme Court (Cour suprême) in Algiers. Justice is exercised through 183 courts (tribunaux) and 31 appeal courts (cours d'appel), grouped on a regional basis. Three special Criminal Courts were set up in Oran, Constantine and Algiers in 1966 to deal with economic crimes against the State. From these there is no appeal. In April 1975 a Cour de sûreté de l'état, composed of magistrates and high-ranking army officers, was established to try all cases involving state security. The Cour des comptes was established in 1979. A new penal code was adopted in January 1982, retaining the death penalty.

President of Supreme Court: A. MEDJHOUDA.
Procurator-General: Y. BEKKOUCHE.

Religion

ISLAM

Islam is the official religion, and the whole Algerian population, with a few rare exceptions, is Muslim.

President of the Superior Islamic Council: AHMAD HAMANI; place Cheik Abd al-Hamid ibn Badis, Algiers.

CHRISTIANITY

The Europeans, and a few Arabs, are Christians, mostly Roman Catholics.

The Roman Catholic Church

Algeria comprises one archdiocese and three dioceses (including one directly responsible to the Holy See). In 1988 there were an estimated 50,000 adherents in the country.

Bishops' Conference: Conférence Episcopale Régionale du Nord de l'Afrique, 13 rue Khélifa-Boukhalfa, DZ-16000 Alger-Gare, Algiers; tel. (2) 63-42-44; f. 1985; Pres. Mgr HENRI TEISSIER, Archbishop of Algiers.

Archbishop of Algiers: Mgr HENRI TEISSIER, Archevêché, 13 rue Khélifa-Boukhalfa, DZ-16000 Alger-Gare, Algiers; tel. (2) 63-42-44.

Protestant Church

Protestant Church of Algeria: 31 rue Reda Houhou, 16000 Algiers; tel. (2) 66-22-16; telex 65172; three parishes; 1,000 mems; Pastor (Algiers) Dr HUGH G. JOHNSON; Pastor (Oran) Dr DAVID W. BUTLER; Pastor (Constantine) KAYIJ-A-MUTOMBU.

The Press

DAILIES

Ach-Cha'ab (The People): 1 place Maurice Audin, Algiers; f. 1962; national information journal in Arabic; Dir MUHAMMAD BOUARROUDJ; circ. 80,000.

Horizons 2000: Algiers; f. 1985; evening; French; circ. 100,000.

Al-Joumhouria (The Republic): 6 rue ben Cenoussi Hamida, Oran; f. 1963; Arabic language; Editor AÏSSA ADJINA; circ. 70,000.

Al-Massa: Algiers; f. 1985; evening; Arabic; circ. 100,000.

Al-Moudjahid (The Fighter): 20 rue de la Liberté, Algiers; f. 1965; FLN journal in French and Arabic; Dir MAUR ED-DINE NAIT-MAZI; circ. 392,000.

An-Nasr (The Victory): Zone Industrielle, BP 388, La Palma, Constantine; tel. (4) 93-92-16; f. 1963; Arabic language; Editor ABDALLAH GUETTAT; circ. 340,000.

WEEKLIES

Algérie Actualité: 2 rue Jacques Cartier, 16000 Algiers; tel. (2) 63-54-20; telex 66475; f. 1965; French; Dir KAMEL BELKACEM; circ. 250,000.

Bulletin Officiel des Marchés de l'Operateur Publique: Algiers; f. 1987; publ. by Entreprise Nationale d'Edition et Publicité; list of international tenders; French.

Al-Hadef (The Goal): Zone Industrielle, BP 388, La Palma, Constantine; tel. (4) 93-92-16; f. 1972; sports; French; Editor-in-Chief MUSTAFA MANCERI; circ. 110,000.

Révolution Africaine: 7 rue du Stade, Hydra, Algiers; FLN journal in French; socialist; Dir ZOUBIR ZEMZOUM; circ. 50,000.

OTHER PERIODICALS

Al-Acala: rue Timgad, Hydra, Algiers; f. 1970; published by the Ministry of Religious Affairs.

Algérie Médicale: 3 blvd Zirout Youcef, Algiers; f. 1964; publ. of Union médicale algérienne; 2 a year; circ. 3,000.

Alouan (Colours): 119 rue Didouche Mourad, Algiers; f. 1973; cultural review published by the Ministry of Culture; monthly; Arabic.

Arab Steel: BP 4, Cheriga, Algiers; telex 52553; monthly; Arabic, English and French.

Bibliographie de l'Algérie: Bibliothèque Nationale, 1 ave Docteur Fanon, Algiers 16000; tel. (2) 63-06-32; f. 1964; lists books, theses, pamphlets and periodicals published in Algeria; 2 a year; Arabic and French.

Ach-Cha'ab ath-Thakafi (Cultural People): Algiers; f. 1972; cultural monthly; Arabic.

Ach-Chabab (Youth): 2 rue Khélifa Boukhalfa; journal of the UNJA; bi-monthly; French and Arabic.

Culture et Société: 7 blvd Ché Guévara, Algiers; tel. (2) 62-10-00; telex 66380; f. 1984; summary of items issued by State news agency; Dir BELKACEM AHCENE-DJABALLAH.

Développement et Wilayate: 7 blvd Ché Guévara, Algiers; tel. (2) 62-10-00; telex 66380; f. 1984; summary of items issued by State news agency; Dir BELKACEM AHCENE-DJABALLAH.

Al-Djeza'ir Réalités (Algeria Today): BP 95–96, Bouzareah, Algiers; f. 1972; organ of the Popular Assembly of the Wilaya of Algiers; monthly; French and Arabic.

Al-Djeza'iria (Algerian Woman): Villa Joly, 24 ave Franklin Roosevelt, Algiers; f. 1970; organ of the UNFA; monthly; French and Arabic.

Al-Djeich (The Army): Office de l'Armée Nationale Populaire, 3 chemin de Gascogne, Algiers; f. 1963; monthly; Algerian army review; Arabic and French; circ. 10,000.

Economie: 7 blvd Ché Guévara, Algiers; tel. (2) 62-10-00; telex 66380; f. 1963; monthly; summary of items issued by State news agency; Dir BELKACEM AHCENE-DJABALLAH.

Journal Officiel de la République Algérienne Démocratique et Populaire: 7, 9 and 13 ave A. ben Barek; f. 1962; French and Arabic.

Al-Kitab (The Book): 3 blvd Zirout Youcef, Algiers; f. 1972; bulletin of SNED; every 2 months; French and Arabic.

Libyca: 3 blvd Zirout Youcef, Algiers; f. 1953; anthropology and ethnography; irregular; French; Dir MOULOUD MAMMERI.

Nouvelles Economiques: 6 blvd Amilcar Cabral, Algiers; f. 1969; publ. of Institut Algérien du Commerce Extérieur; monthly; French and Arabic.

Révolution et Travail: 48 rue Khellifa Boukhalfa, Algiers; journal of UGTA (central trade union) with Arabic and French editions; monthly; Editor-in-Chief ZIANE FARRAH.

Revue Algérienne du Travail: 28 rue Hassiba ben Bouali, Algiers; f. 1964; Ministry of Labour publication; quarterly; French.

Revue d'Histoire et de Civilisation du Maghreb: 3 blvd Zirout Youcef, Algiers; f. 1966; history and civilization; irregular; French and Arabic; circ. 4,000; Dir M. KADDACHE.

Sports Panorama: 7 blvd Ché Guévara, Algiers; tel. (2) 62-10-00; telex 66380; f. 1985; summary of items issued by State news agency; Dir BELKACEM AHCENE-DJABALLAH.

Ath-Thakafa (Culture): 2 place Cheikh ben Badis, BP 96, Algiers; tel. (2) 62-20-73; f. 1971; published by the Ministry of Culture and Tourism; every 2 months; cultural review; circ. 10,000; Editor-in-Chief CHEBOUB OTHMANE.

NEWS AGENCIES

Algérie Presse Service (APS): 7 blvd Ché Guévara, Algiers; tel. (2) 62-10-00; telex 66380; f. 1962; Dir-Gen. BELKACEM AHCENE-DJABALLAH.

Foreign Bureaux

Agence France-Presse (AFP): 6 rue Abd al-Karim el-Khettabi, Algiers; tel. (2) 63-62-01; telex 67427; Chief JEAN-FRANÇOIS RICHARD.

Agencia EFE (Spain): 4 ave Pasteur, Algiers; tel. (2) 61-64-16; telex 66458; Chief MANUEL OSTOS.

Agentstvo Pechati Novosti (APN) (USSR): BP 24, el-Mouradia, Algiers; Chief Officer YURI S. BAGDASAROV.

Agenzia Nazionale Stampa Associata (ANSA) (Italy): 4 ave Pasteur, Algiers; tel. (2) 63-73-14; telex 66467; Chief CESARE RIZZOLI.

Allgemeiner Deutscher Nachrichtendienst (ADN) (German Democratic Republic): 38 rue Larbi Alik, Hydra, Algiers; tel. (2) 60-07-14; telex 66167; Chief DIETER GRAU.

ALGERIA

Associated Press (AP) (USA): 4 ave Pasteur, BP 769, Algiers; tel. (2) 63-59-41; telex 67365; Representative RACHID KHINRI.

Bulgarska Telegrafna Agentsia (BTA) (Bulgaria): Zaatcha 5, el-Mouradia, Algiers; Chief GORAN GOTEV.

Prensa Latina (Cuba): Algiers; tel. (2) 61-39-49; telex 52972; Bureau Chief JULIO HERNÁNDEZ.

Reuters (UK); 4 ave Pasteur, Algiers.

Telegrafnoye Agentstvo Sovetskovo Soyuza (TASS) (USSR): 21 rue de Boulogne, Algiers; Chief KONSTANTIN DUDAREV.

Xinhua (New China) News Agency (People's Republic of China): 32 rue de Carthage, Hydra, Algiers; tel. (2) 60-76-85; telex 66204; Chief BAI GUORUI.

Wikalat al-Maghreb al-Arabi (Morocco) and the Middle East News Agency (Egypt) are also represented.

Publishers

Entreprise Nationale du Livre (ENAL): 3 blvd Zirout Youcef, BP 49, Algiers; tel. (2) 63-97-12; telex 53845; f. 1966 as Société Nationale d'Edition et de Diffusion, name changed 1983; publishes books of all types, and is sole importer, exporter and distributor of all printed material, stationery, school and office supplies; also holds State monopoly for commercial advertising; Dir-Gen. SEGHIR BENAMAR.

Office des Publications Universitaires: 1 place Centrale de Ben, Aknoun, Algiers; tel. (2) 78-87-18; telex 61396; controlled by Ministry of Higher Education; publishes university textbooks.

Radio and Television

In 1985 there were 4.8m. radio receivers and 1,557,000 television receivers in use, of which an estimated 300,000 were colour sets.

Radiodiffusion Télévision Algérienne (RTA): Immeuble RTA, 21 blvd des Martyrs, Algiers; tel. (2) 60-23-00; telex 52042; government-controlled; Dir of RTA MUHAMMAD OUZEGHDOU; Dirs of Radio M. ABD AL-KADER, HACHEMI SOUAMI; Dir of TV ABD AL-KADER BRAHIMI.

RADIO

Arabic Network: transmitters at Aïn Beïda, Algiers, Batna, Béchar, Oran, Touggourt and Souk-Ahras.

French Network: transmitters at Algiers, Constantine, Oran and Tipaza.

Kabyle Network: transmitters at Algiers and Michelet.

TELEVISION

The principal transmitters are at Algiers, Batna, Sidi-Bel-Abbès, Constantine, Souk-Ahras and Tlemcen. The national network was completed during 1970. Television is taking a major part in the national education programme.

Finance

(cap. = capital; dep. = deposits; res = reserves; brs = branches; m. = million; amounts in Algeriand dinars)

BANKING

Central Bank

Banque Centrale d'Algérie: 8 blvd Zirout Youcef, 16000 Algiers; tel. (2) 64-75-00; telex 66499; f. 1962; cap. 40m.; central bank of issue; Gov. BADER ED-DINE NOUIOUA; Gen. Man. BACHIR SAÏL.

Nationalized Banks

From November 1967 only the following nationalized banks were authorized to conduct exchange transactions and to deal with banks abroad, and by May 1972 these three banks had absorbed all foreign and private banks. It was announced in June 1982 that the banking system was to be restructured. New legislation on banking and credit, approved in August 1986, enabled the five commercial banks (Banque Extérieure d'Algérie, Banque Nationale d'Algérie, Crédit Populaire d'Algérie, Banque de l'Agriculture et du Développement Rural and Banque de Développement Local) to improve their project assessment capabilities. The Central Bank was given a greater role in managing money supply, the exchange rate and foreign exchange reserves, and was authorized to borrow internationally.

Banque Extérieure d'Algérie (BEA): 11 blvd Col Amirouche, Algiers; tel. (2) 61-12-52; telex 67072; f. 1967; cap. 1,000m., dep. 41,368.7m, res 10,459.8m. (1986); chiefly concerned with energy and maritime transport sectors; Pres. and Gen. Man. MOURAD KHELLAF; 60 brs.

Banque Nationale d'Algérie (BNA): 8 blvd Ernesto Ché Guévara, Algiers; tel. (2) 62-05-44; telex 52788; f. 1966; cap. 1,000m., res 3,774.9m. (1986); specializes in heavy industry and transport sectors; Chair. and Pres. MUHAMMAD THAMINY; Gen. Man. ABD AL-MOUMENE FAOUZI BEN MALEK; 85 brs.

Crédit Populaire d'Algérie (CPA): 2 blvd Col Amirouche, Algiers; tel. (2) 61-13-34; telex 67170; f. 1966; cap. 800m., dep. 14,413.3m. (1986); bank for building and public works, light industry, transport and tourism; Gen. Man. MAHFOUD ZEROUTA; 90 brs.

Development Banks

Banque de l'Agriculture et du Développement Rural (BADR): 1 rue Mustapha Bouhired, BP 544, Algiers; tel. (2) 64-72-64; telex 62240; f. 1982; cap. 1,000m., dep. 50,027.4m., res 1,422.7m. (1985); finance for the agricultural sector; Man. Dir MUSTAFA ACHOUR.

Banque Algérienne de Développement (BAD): 12 blvd Col Amirouche, Algiers; tel. (2) 63-81-46; telex 66092; f. 1963; cap. and res 1,200m. (1987), dep. 3,596.5m. (Dec. 1984); a public establishment with fiscal sovereignty, to contribute to Algerian economic development through long-term investment programmes; Pres. and Dir-Gen. SASSI AZIZA.

Banque de Développement Local (BDL): 5 rue Gaci Amar, Staoueli, (W. Tipaza); tel. (2) 81-58-00; telex 63171; f. 1985; regional development bank; cap. 500m., dep. 6,457m. (1986); Dir-Gen. MUHAMMAD BEN HALIMA; 83 brs.

Caisse Nationale d'Epargne et de Prévoyance (CNEP): 40–42 rue Larbi ben M'Hidi, Algiers; tel. (2) 63-25-10; telex 52037; savings and housing bank; Man. JAKHDAR BENOUATAF.

INSURANCE

Insurance is a state monopoly.

Caisse Algérienne d'Assurance et de Réassurance: 48 rue Didouche Mourad, Algiers; tel. (2) 63-11-95; telex 52894; f. 1963 as a public corporation; Dir-Gen. MAHFOUD BATTATA.

Caisse Nationale de Mutualité Agricole: 24 blvd Victor Hugo, Algiers; tel. (2) 63-72-88; telex 673333; Dir-Gen. YAHIA CHERIF BRAHIM.

Compagnie Centrale de Réassurance: 21 blvd Zirout Youcef, Algiers; tel. (2) 63-72-88; telex 67092; f. 1973; general; Chair. and Gen. Man. DJAMEL CHOUAÏB CHOUITER.

Société Algérienne d'Assurances (SAA): 5 blvd Ernesto Ché Guévara, Algiers; tel. (2) 62-29-44; telex 61216; f. 1963; state-sponsored company; Chair. MAHFOUD BATTATA; Dir-Gen. ABD AL-KRIM DJAFRI.

Trade and Industry

EXPORT INSTITUTE

Office Nationale des Foires et des Exportations (ONAFEX): Palais des Expositions, Pins Maritimes, BP 656, Alger-Gare, Algiers; tel. (2) 76-31-00; telex 64212; f. 1982; Dir-Gen. ZAHIR ABD AR-RAHIM.

DEVELOPMENT

Entreprise Nationale d'Engineering et de Développement des Industries Légères (EDIL): 50 rue Khélifa Boukhalfa, BP 1140, Algiers; tel. (2) 66-33-90; telex 52883; f. 1982; Dir-Gen. MISSOUM ABD AL-HAKIM.

Société Centrale pour l'Equipement du Territoire (SCET) International: Algiers; Dir A. GAMBRELLE.

NATIONALIZED INDUSTRIES

A large part of Algerian industry is nationalized. The following are some of the most important nationalized industries, each controlled by the appropriate Ministry.

Entreprise Nationale de Cellulose et de Papier (CELPAP): route de la Salamandre, BP 128, Mostaganem; tel. (6) 26-54-99; telex 14058; Man. Dir ENWAR TEWFIK BERBAR.

Entreprise Nationale de Commerce: 6-9 rue Belhaffat-Ghazali, Hussein Dey, Algiers; tel. (2) 77-43-20; telex 52063; monopoly of imports and distribution of materials and equipment; Dir-Gen. MUHAMMAD LAÏD BELARBIA.

Entreprise Nationale de Développement et de Coordination des Industries Alimentaires (ENIAL): 2 rue Ahmad Ait Muhammad-el-Harrach, Algiers; tel. (2) 76-51-42; telex 54-031; f. 1965; semolina, pasta, flour and couscous; Dir-Gen. MUSTAFA MOKRAOUI.

ALGERIA

Entreprise Nationale des Pêches (ENAPECHES): Quai d'Aigues Mortes, Port d'Alger; tel. (2) 62-01-00; telex 61346; f. 1979 to replace (with ECOREP which deals with fishing equipment) former Office Algérien des Pêches; production, marketing, importing and exporting fish; Man. Dir AL-OKBI BENOUAAR.

Entreprise Nationale de la Sidérurgie (SIDER): Chaiba, el-Hadjar, BP 342, Annaba; tel. (8) 83-49-99; telex 81661; f. 1964 as Société Nationale de la Sidérurgie, restructured 1983; steel, cast iron, zinc and products; Man. Dir MESSAOUD CHETTIH.

Office Régional des Produits Oléicoles du Centre (ORPO Centre): rue Bey Muhammad, Domaine Garidi, Kouba, Algiers; tel. (2) 58-41-70; telex 77098; production and marketing of olives and olive oil; Dir-Gen. MUSTAFA CHABOUR.

Pharmacie Centrale Algérienne: 2 rue Bichat, Algiers; tel. (2) 65-18-27; telex 52993; f. 1969; pharmaceutical products; Man. Dir M. MORSLI.

Secrétariat d'Etat aux Forêts et au Reboisement: Immeuble des Forêts, Bois du Petit Atlas, el-Mouradia, Algiers; tel. (2) 60-43-00; telex 52854; f. 1971; production of timber, care of forests; Man. Dir DANIEL BELBACHIR.

Société de Gestion et de Développement des Industries Alimentaires (SOGEDIA): 13 ave Claude Debussy, Algiers; tel. (2) 64-38-01; telex 52837; food industry; Dir-Gen. M. AICHOUR.

Société Nationale de l'Artisanat Traditionnel (SNAT): Algiers; tel. (2) 62-68-02; telex 53093; traditional crafts; Man. Dir SAÏD AMRANI.

Société Nationale de Constructions Mécaniques (SONACOME): Birkhadem, Algiers; tel. (2) 65-93-92; telex 52800; f. 1967; to be reorganized into 11 smaller companies, most of which will specialize in manufacture or distribution of one of SONACOME's products; Dir DAOUD AKROUF.

Société Nationale de Constructions Métalliques (SN METAL): Algiers; tel. (2) 63-29-30; telex 52889; f. 1968; production of metal goods; Chair. HACHEM MALIK; Man. Dir ABD AL-KADER MAIZA.

Société Nationale des Eaux Minérales Algériennes (SN-EMA): 21 rue Bellouchat Mouloud, Hussein Dey, Algiers; tel. (2) 77-17-91; telex 52310; mineral water; Man. Dir TAHAR KHENEL.

Société Nationale de l'Electricité et du Gaz (SONELGAZ): 2 blvd Salah Bouakouir, BP 841, Algiers; tel. (2) 64-82-60; telex 66381; monopoly of production, distribution and transportation of electricity and gas; Man. Dir MUSTAFA HARRATI.

Société Nationale de Fabrication et de Montage du Matériel Electrique (SONELEC): 4 & 6 blvd Muhammad V, Algiers; tel. (2) 63-70-82; telex 52867; electrical equipment.

Société Nationale des Industries Chimiques (SNIC): 4-6 blvd Muhammad V, BP 641, Algiers; tel. (2) 64-07-73; telex 52802; production and distribution of chemical products; Dir-Gen. RACHID BEN IDDIR.

Société Nationale des Industries des Lièges et du Bois (SNLB): 1 rue Kaddour Rahim, BP 61, Hussein Dey, Algiers; tel. (2) 77-99-99; telex 52726; f. 1973; production of cork and wooden goods; Chair. MALEK BELLANI.

Société Nationale des Industries des Peaux et Cuirs (SONIPEC): 100 rue de Tripoli, BP 113, Hussein Dey, Algiers; tel. (2) 77-66-00; telex 52832; f. 1967; hides and skins; Chair. and Man. Dir MUHAMMAD CHERIF AZI; Man. Dir HASSAN BEN YOUNES.

Société Nationale des Industries Textiles (SONITEX): 4-6 rue Patrice Lumumba, BP 41, Algiers; tel. (2) 63-41-35; telex 52929; f. 1966; split in 1982 into separate cotton, wool, industrial textiles, silk, clothing and distribution companies; 22,000 employees; Man. Dir MUHAMMAD AREZKI ISLI.

Société Nationale des Matériaux de Construction (SNMC): Algiers; tel. (2) 64-35-13; telex 52204; f. 1968; production and import monopoly of building materials; Man. Dir ABD AL-KADER MAIZI.

Société Nationale de Recherches et d'Exploitations Minières (SONAREM): 127 blvd Salah Bouakouiz, BP 860, Algiers; tel. (2) 63-15-55; telex 52910; f. 1967; mining and prospecting; Dir-Gen. OUBRAHAM FERHAT.

Société Nationale pour la Recherche, la Production, le Transport, la Transformation et la Commercialisation des Hydrocarbures (SONATRACH): 10 rue du Sahara, Hydra, Algiers; tel. (2) 56-18-56; telex 62103; f. 1963; State-owned organization for exploration, exploitation, transport and marketing of petroleum, natural gas and their products; Dir-Gen. SADOK BOUSENA.

In May 1980 it was announced that SONATRACH was to be split up and its functions divided among 12 companies (including SONATRACH itself). The other 11 were:

Entreprise Nationale de Canalisation (ENAC): ave de la Palestine, BP 514, Algiers; tel. (2) 70-35-90; telex 42939; piping; Dir-Gen. HAMID MAZRI.

Entreprise Nationale de Raffinage et de Distribution des Produits Pétroliers (ENRDP): route des Dunes, BP 73, Chéraga, Algiers; tel. (2) 81-09-69; telex 53079; f. 1980; export and internal distribution of products; Dir-Gen. ABD AL-MADJID KAZI-TANI.

Entreprise Nationale d'Engineering Pétrolier (ENEP): 2 blvd Muhammad V, Algiers; tel. (2) 63-08-92; telex 66493; engineering.

Entreprise Nationale de Forage (ENAFOR): BP 211, Hassi Messaoud, Algiers; tel. (2) 73-85-40; telex 44077; drilling; Dir-Gen. ABD AR-RACHID ROUABAH.

Entreprise Nationale de Génie Civil et Bâtiments (ENGCB): route de Corso, BP 23, Boudouaou, Algiers; tel. (2) 41-65-26; telex 53653; civil engineering; Dir-Gen. MUHAMMAD TAHAR ZEMZOUM.

Entreprise Nationale de Géophysique (ENAGEO): BP 213, Hassi Messaoud, Ouargla; tel. (9) 78-80-03; telex 44053; geophysics; Dir-Gen. ALI OUARTSI.

Entreprise Nationale des Grands Travaux Pétroliers (ENGTP): Zone Industriel, BP 09, Reghaïa, Boumerdes; tel. (2) 80-06-80; telex 68150; major industrial projects; Dir-Gen. FAROUK HOUHOU; Asst Dir-Gen. M. BEN AMEUR.

Entreprise Nationale de Pétrochimie et d'Engrais (ENPE): route des Dunes, Chéraga, Algiers; tel. (2) 81-09-69; telex 53876; petrochemicals and fertilizers.

Entreprise Nationale des Plastiques et de Caoutchouc (ENPC): rue des Frères Meslim, BP 452, Aïn Turk, Sétif; tel. (5) 90-33-40; telex 86040; production and marketing of rubber and plastics; Dir-Gen. MAHIEDDINE ECHIKH.

Enterprise Nationale de Raffinage des Produits Pétroliers (ENRP): f. 1987; refining of products.

Entreprise Nationale de Service aux Puits (ENSP): 1 blvd Anatole France, BP 53, Hassi Messaoud, Ouargla; tel. (9) 73-89-84; telex 44018; oil-well servicing; Dir-Gen. L. MOSTEFAI.

Entreprise Nationale des Travaux aux Puits (ENTP): BP 71, In-Amenas, Illizi; telex 44052; oil-well construction; Dir-Gen. ABD AL-AZIZ KRISSAT.

Société Nationale des Tabacs et Alumettes (SNTA): 40 rue Hocine-Nourredine, Algiers; tel. (2) 66-18-68; telex 52780; monopoly of manufacture and trade in tobacco, cigarettes and matches; Dir-Gen. MUHAMMAD TAHAB BOUZEGHOUB.

STATE TRADING ORGANIZATIONS

Since 1972 all international trading has been carried out by state organizations, of which the following are the most important:

Entreprise Nationale d'Approvisionnements en Produits Alimentaires (ENAPAL): 29 rue Larbi ben M'hidi, BP 659, Algiers; tel. (2) 64-02-75; telex 52991; f. 1983; monopoly of import, export and bulk trade in basic foodstuffs; brs in more than 40 towns; Chair. LAID SABRI; Man. Dir BRAHIM DOUAOURI.

Entreprise Nationale d'Approvisionnement et de Régulation en Fruits et Légumes (ENAFLA): 12 ave des 3 Frères Bouadou, BP 42, Birmandreis, Algiers; tel. (2) 56-90-83; telex 62113; f. 1983; division of the Ministry of Commerce; fruit and vegetable marketing, production and export; Man. Dir ALI BENSEGUENI.

Office Algérien Interprofessionel des Céréales (OAIC): 5 rue Ferhat-Boussaad, Algiers; tel. (2) 66-38-14; telex 52121; f. 1962; monopoly of trade in wheat, rice, maize, barley and products derived from these cereals; Man. Dir M. DOUAOURI.

Office National de la Commercialisation des Produits Viti-Vinicoles (ONCV): 112 Quai-Sud, Algiers; tel. (2) 63-09-40; telex 67074; f. 1968; monopoly of importing and exporting products of the wine industry; Man. Dir DOUAOURI BRAHIM.

TRADE FAIR

Foire Internationale d'Alger: Palais des Expositions, Pins Maritimes, BP 656, Algiers; tel. (2) 76-31-00; telex 64212.

PRINCIPAL TRADE UNIONS

Union Générale des Travailleurs Algériens (UGTA): Maison du Peuple, place du 1er mai, Algiers; tel. 66-89-47; telex 65051; f. 1956; 1,000,000 mems; Sec.-Gen. TAYEB BELAKHDAR.

There are 10 national 'professional sectors' affiliated to UGTA. These are:

Secteur Alimentation, Commerce et Tourisme (Food, Commerce and Tourist Industry Workers): Gen. Sec. ABD AL-KADER GHRIBLI.

Secteur Bois, Bâtiments et Travaux Publics (Building Trades Workers): Gen. Sec. LAIFA LATRECHE.

Secteur Education et Formation Professionnelle (Teachers): Gen. Sec. SAÏDI BEN GANA.

ALGERIA *Directory*

Secteur Energie et Pétrochimie (Energy and Petrochemical Workers): Gen. Sec. ALI BELHOUCHET.

Secteur Finances (Financial Workers): Gen. Sec. MUHAMMAD ZAAF.

Secteur Information, Formation et Culture (Information, Training and Culture).

Secteur Industries Légères (Light Industry): Gen. Sec. ABD AL-KADER MALKI.

Secteur Industries Lourdes (Heavy Industry).

Secteur Santé et Sécurité Sociale (Health and Social Security Workers): Gen. Sec. ABD AL-AZIZ DJEFFAL.

Secteur Transports et Télécommunications (Transport and Telecommunications Workers): Gen. Sec. EL-HACHEMI BEN MOUHOUB.

Union Nationale des Paysans Algériens—UNPA: f. 1973; 700,000 mems; Sec.-Gen. AÏSSA NEDJEM.

Transport

RAILWAYS

In 1982 plans were announced for the investment of US $11,000m. in constructing new railways by 1990. Studies were carried out in 1982 for an underground railway in Algiers, which was eventually to cover a 64-km network. As the economy encountered difficulties in 1985–86, the construction of the metro system and other major projects were postponed or cancelled, and emphasis was given to the rehabilitation of the existing network. In February 1988 the metro project was revived in a modified form. Work on the first 26-km line of the network, to be constructed by local companies, was to begin in late 1988. The line was to incorporate the existing rail network, with the construction of only 8 km underground, and was expected to take seven years to complete.

Société Nationale des Transports Ferroviaires (SNTF): 21–23 blvd Muhammad V, Algiers; tel. 61-15-10; telex 52455; f. 1976 to replace Société Nationale des Chemins de Fer Algériens; 3,761 km of track, of which 296 km are electrified and 1,112 km are narrow gauge; daily passenger services from Algiers to the principal provincial cities and a service to Tunis; Dir-Gen. M. MAHERZI.

ROADS

There are about 82,000 km of roads and tracks, of which 24,000 km are main roads and 19,000 km are secondary roads. The total is made up of 55,000 km in the north, including 24,000 km of good roads, and 27,000 km in the south, including 3,200 km with asphalt surface. The French administration built a good road system, partly for military purposes, which since independence has been allowed to deteriorate in parts, and only a small percentage of roads are surfaced. New roads have been built linking the Sahara oil fields with the coast, and the Trans-Sahara highway is a major project. The first 360-km stretch of the highway, from Hassi Marroket to Aïn Salah, was opened in April 1973, and the next section, ending at Tamanrasset, was opened in June 1978. In 1987 Algeria received a loan of US $120m. from the World Bank to rehabilitate 386 km of primary roads and to establish a road maintenance project.

Société Nationale des Transports Routiers (SNTR): 27 rue des 3 Frères Bouadou, Birmandreis, Algiers; tel. (2) 56-21-21; telex 52962; f. 1967; holds a monopoly of goods transport by road; Chair. HAOUSSINE EL-HADJ; Dir-Gen. BEN AOUDA BEN EL-HADJ DJELLOUL.

Société Nationale des Transports des Voyageurs (SNTV): 19 rue Rabah Midat, Algiers; tel. (2) 66-00-52; telex 52603; f. 1967; holds monopoly of long-distance passenger transport by road; Man. Dir M. DIB.

SHIPPING

Algiers is the main port, with anchorage of between 23 m and 29 m in the Bay of Algiers, and anchorage for the largest vessels in Agha Bay. The port has a total quay length of 8,380 m. There are also important ports at Annaba, Arzew, Béjaia, Djidjelli, Ghazaouet, Mostaganem, Oran and Skikda. The contract for a new port for steel at Djenden was awarded to an Italian firm in 1984. Petroleum and liquefied gas are exported through Arzew, Béjaia and Skikda. Algerian crude petroleum is also exported through the Tunisian port of La Skhirra.

Compagnie Algéro-Libyenne de Transports Maritimes (CALTRAM): 21 rue des Frères, Bouadou, Birmandreis, Algiers; tel. (2) 63-58-07; telex 62112; Chair. M. O. DAS.

Entreprise Nationale de Consignation et d'Activités Annexes aux Transports Maritimes (ENCATM): Algiers; f. 1987 as part of restructuring of SNTM-CNAN; responsible for merchant traffic.

Entreprise Nationale de Réparations Navales (ERENAV): Algiers; f. 1987; ship repairs.

Entreprise Nationale de Transport Maritime de Voyageurs—Algérie Ferries (ENTMV): Algiers; f. 1987 as part of restructuring of SNTM-CNAN; responsible for passenger transport; operates coastal car ferry services between Algiers, Annanba and Oran.

NAFTAL Direction Aviation Maritime: Aéroport Houari Boumedienne, Dar-el-Beida, BP 70, Algiers; tel. (2) 75-73-75; telex 64315; Dir Z. BEN MERABET.

Office National des Ports (ONP): quai d'Arcachon, BP 830, Algiers-Port; tel. (2) 62-57-48; telex 52738; f. 1971; responsible for management and growth of port facilities and sea pilotage; Man. Dir M. HARRATI.

Société Nationale de Manutention (SONAMA): 6 rue de Béziers, Algiers; tel. (2) 64-65-61; telex 52339; monopoly of port handling; Man. Dir AMOS BELALEM.

Société Nationale de Transports Maritimes et Compagnie Nationale Algérienne de Navigation (SNTM-CNAN): 2 quai d'Ajaccio, Nouvelle Gare Maritime, BP 280, Algiers; tel. (2) 63-74-13; telex 52980; f. 1964; state-owned company which has the monopoly of conveyance, freight, chartering and transit facilities in all Algerian ports; operates fleet of freight and passenger ships; office in Marseilles and reps. in Paris, most French ports and the principal ports in many other countries. In September 1987 the company was restructured, and two new shipping companies were formed to deal with passenger transport and merchant traffic; Chair. MUHAMMAD GUENDOUZ; Man. Dir AMMAR BOUSBAH.

Société Nationale de Transports Maritimes des Hydrocarbures et des Produits Chimiques (SNTM-HYPROC): BP 60, Arzew; tel. (6) 37-30-99; telex 12097; Dir-Gen. MOURAD BELGUEDJ.

CIVIL AVIATION

Algeria's main airport, Dar-el-Beïda, 20 km from Algiers, is a class A airport of international standing. At Constantine, Annaba, Tlemcen and Oran there are also airports which meet international requirements. There are also 65 aerodromes of which 20 are public, and a further 135 airstrips connected with the oil industry.

Air Algérie (Entreprise Nationale d'Exploitation des Services Aériens Internationaux de Transport Public) and **Inter-Air Services (Entreprise Nationale d'Exploitation des Services Aériens de Transport Intérieur et Travail Aériens):** 1 place Maurice Audin, Immeuble el-Djazair, BP 858, Algiers; tel. (2) 63-12-82; telex 52436; Air Algérie f. 1953 by merger; state-owned from 1972; divided into Inter-Air Services (internal flights) and Air Algérie (external flights) 1983; internal services and extensive services to Europe, North, Central and West Africa, the Middle East and Asia; Man. ELHADJU HAOUSSINE; fleet of 2 Airbus A310-200, 11 Boeing 727, 13 Boeing 737, 3 Boeing 737-200C, 3 Lockheed L-100-30, 14 Grumman AG-CAT, 8 Fokker F27, 11 Beechcraft, 1 Alouette 2.

Tourism

Algeria's tourist attractions include the Mediterranean coast, the Atlas mountains and the desert. In 1986 a total of 150,733 tourists visited Algeria. Receipts from tourism totalled about US $60m. in 1983. In 1986 there were 200 hotels, with a total of 32,862 beds, and in 1987 a development programme planned to provide a further 120,000 beds by 1999, through joint ventures with foreign companies. The Government identified 19 potential tourist centres and aimed to attract 900,000 tourists per year by 1999.

Office National Algérien de l'Animation de la Promotion et de l'Information Touristique (ONAT): 25–27 rue Khélifa-Boukhalfa, Algiers; tel. (2) 61-29-86; telex 66339; Dir-Gen. MAARIF RACHID.

Atomic Energy

Haut Commissariat à la Recherche (HCR): BP 100, el-Madania, Algiers; tel. (2) 66-33-25; telex 65303; f. 1986; formerly Commissariat aux Energies Nouvelles; government-funded; research and development in the field of renewable sources of energy, including atomic, solar, wind and geothermal energy.

Subsidiary organizations include:

Centre for Experimentation on Solar Energy Equipment: research and development of alternative energy sources, including solar, wind and geothermal energy.

ALGERIA

Centre for Nuclear and Solar Studies: basic and applied research, nuclear physics, gamma irradiation technology, training.

Centre for the Development of Advanced Techniques: robotics, remote sensing, laser technology, plasma physics, systems design, micro-computers, electronic instruments.

Centre for the Development of Energy Conversion: reactor physics and technology, nuclear and process instrumentation, turbo-machinery, heat-transfer technology.

Centre for the Development of Materials: ore processing, metallurgy, semi-conductors, analytical chemistry, geochemistry.

Centre for the Development of Technics in Health Physics and Nuclear Safety: regulations and standards on ionizing radiation, radioactive release, inspection and security during conversion, transport and storage of radioactive materials.

ANDORRA

Introductory Survey

Location, Climate, Language, Religion, Flag, Capital

The Valleys of Andorra form an autonomous co-principality in western Europe. The country lies in the eastern Pyrenees, bounded by France and Spain, and is situated roughly midway between Barcelona and Toulouse. The climate is alpine, with much snow in winter and a warm summer. The official language is Catalan, but French and Spanish are also widely spoken. Most of the inhabitants are Christians, mainly Roman Catholics. The flag (proportions 3 by 2) has three equal vertical stripes, of blue, yellow and red, with the state coat of arms (a quartered shield above the motto *Virtus unita fortior*) in the centre of the yellow stripe. The capital is Andorra la Vella.

Recent History

Owing to the lack of distinction between the competence of the General Council of Andorra and the co-princes who have ruled the country since 1278, the Andorrans have encountered many difficulties during recent years in their attempts to gain international status for their country and control over its essential services.

Until 1970 the franchise was granted only to third-generation Andorran males who were more than 25 years of age. Thereafter, women, persons aged between 21 and 25, and second-generation Andorrans were allowed to vote in elections to the General Council. In 1977 the franchise was extended to include all first-generation Andorrans of foreign parentage who were aged 28 and over. The electorate remained small, however, when compared with the size of the population, and Andorra's foreign residents (who comprise 70% of the total population) increased their demands for political and nationality rights. Immigration is on a quota system, being restricted to French and Spanish nationals intending to work in Andorra.

Political parties are not directly represented in the General Council, but there are loose groupings with liberal and conservative sympathies. The country's only political organization, the Partit Democràtic d'Andorra, is technically illegal, and in the 1981 elections to the General Council the party urged its supporters to cast blank votes.

During discussions on institutional reform, held in 1980, representatives of the co-princes and the General Council agreed that an executive council should be formed, and that a referendum should be held on changes in the electoral system. In January 1981 the co-princes formally requested the General Council to prepare plans for reform, in accordance with these proposals. After elections to the General Council in December 1981, the new Council elected Oscar Ribas Reig as Head of Government. He then appointed an executive of six ministers who expressed their determination to give Andorra a full constitution, to defend local industry and to encourage private investment.

Severe storm damage in November 1982, and the general effects of the world recession, led to a controversial vote by the General Council, in August 1983, in favour of the introduction of income tax, to help to alleviate Andorra's budgetary deficit of 840m. pesetas, and to provide the Government with extra revenue to pursue development projects. Subsequent government proposals for an indirect tax on bank deposits, hotel rooms and property sales encountered strong opposition from financial and tourism concerns, and prompted the resignation of the Government in April 1984. Josep Pintat Solans, a local businessman, was elected unopposed by the General Council as Head of Government in May. In August, however, the Ministers of Finance, and Industry, Commerce and Agriculture resigned from their posts over disagreements concerning the failure to implement economic reforms. Major extensions of citizenship rights were proposed in August 1985.

In December 1985 a general election was held for the General Council, which later re-elected Francesc Cerqueda i Pascuet to the post of First Syndic. The electorate was increased by about 27% as a result of the newly-introduced lower minimum voting age of 18 years. The Council also re-elected Josep Pintat Solans as President of Government in January 1986, when he won the support of 27 of its 28 members.

In September 1986 President François Mitterrand of France (the French co-prince of Andorra) and his Spanish counterpart, Dr Joan Martí Alanis (the Bishop of Urgel) met in Andorra to discuss the co-principality's status in relation to the EEC, and to discuss the question of free exchange of goods between the members of the Community and Andorra, following Spain's admission to the EEC in January 1986. Discussions also focused on this matter at a meeting held in Spain in February 1987.

In April 1987 the Consejo Sindical Interregional Pirineos-Mediterráneo (CSI), a collective comprising French and Spanish trade unions, in association with the Andorran Asociación de Residentes Andorranos (ARA) began to claim rights, including those of freedom of expression and association and the right to strike, for 20,000 of its members who were employed as immigrant workers in Andorra. A meeting of six small European nations was held in Andorra in September 1987.

A document proposing further institutional reforms was approved by the General Council in October 1987. The transfer to the Andorran Government of responsibility for such matters as public order was proposed, while the competence of the co-princes in the administration of justice was recognized. The document also envisaged the drafting of a constitution for Andorra. The implementation of the reforms, however, was dependent on the agreement of the co-princes. In 1988 a commission from the Council of Europe (see p. 128) was to investigate the question of human rights in Andorra.

In December 1987 municipal elections were held, in which 80% of the electorate voted. The number of citizens eligible to vote, however, represented only 13% of Andorra's total population. For the first time, the election campaign involved the convening of meetings and the use of the media, in addition to the traditional 'door-to-door' canvassing. Although Andorra has no political parties as such, four of the seven seats were won by candidates promoting a conservative stance.

In June 1988 the first Andorran workers' trade union was established by the French unions, CFDT and FO, and by the Spanish union, UGT. (There are about 20,000 salaried workers in Andorra, 90% of whom are of French or Spanish origin.) In the following month, however, the General Council unanimously rejected the formation of the union, as it does not recognize the right of association of workers and prohibits the existence of any union. It warned the foreign members of the union that they risked immediate expulsion from Andorra.

Government

Andorra has no proper constitution, and its peculiar autonomy is a legacy of feudal conditions; the country, although administratively independent, has no clear international status. Andorra is a co-principality, under the suzerainty of the President of France and the Spanish Bishop of Urgel. The valleys pay a nominal biannual tax, the *questia*, to France and to the Bishop of Urgel. The French President is represented in Andorra by the Veguer de França, and the Bishop by the Veguer Episcopal. Each co-ruler has set up a permanent delegation for Andorran affairs. The Permanent Delegates are, respectively, the prefect of the French department of Pyrénées-Orientales and one of the vicars general of the Urgel diocese.

The General Council of the Valleys submits motions and proposals to the permanent delegation. The 28 members of the Council (four from each of the seven parishes) are elected by Andorran citizens for a term of four years, one-half of the Council being renewed every two years until December 1981, when an election was held for the whole Council. The Council elects as its head, for a three-year term, the First Syndic (Syndic Procurador General), who until 1982 also acted as chief executive, and the Second Syndic, who cease to be members of the Council on their election. The General Council appointed an Executive Council for the first time in January 1982. This entails the separation of powers between an executive and a legislature and represents an important step towards institutional reform. Proposals for further reforms were approved by the General Council in October 1987.

ANDORRA

Introductory Survey, Statistical Survey

In a 'popular consultation' on electoral reform, held in May 1982, some 30% of voters supported the existing majority vote system, while 42% preferred a new system of proportional representation; approval of such a reform, however, still depended on the consent of the co-princes.

Economic Affairs

Andorra's products are mainly agricultural, with potatoes and tobacco being the principal crops; in 1981 production was 472 and 264 metric tons respectively. Livestock is raised and in 1982 there were approximately 9,000 sheep and 1,115 cattle. Iron, lead, alum, stone and timber are produced. Since the Second World War, Andorra has become a market for numerous European and overseas goods, owing to favourable excise conditions, and consequently the economy has expanded rapidly. However, Spain's accession to membership of the EEC on 1 January 1986, and the consequent removal of Spanish tariff barriers, threatened this lucrative trade in duty-free consumer goods. Under the terms of Spain's entry to the EEC, Andorra was granted a period of two years in which to negotiate a new customs arrangement with the EEC. The Government hoped to negotiate a trade agreement that would give the country a special status within the Community and thereby preserve the co-principality's economic livelihood. By October 1987, however, agreement had not been reached. Andorra therefore proposed to request that the EEC allow it to continue as a free-trade area, in exchange for modifications in the co-principality's fiscal and social policies. In July 1988 (following a delay of six months) negotiations took place between Andorra and the EEC, concerning Andorra's request for special status within the Community. Andorra hoped to retain the present system of exchange and to establish a customs union for industrial products from EEC countries. It also proposed to charge customs duty on products from countries outside the EEC at the EEC rate, and to purchase agricultural products at subsidized EEC rates.

Concern within Andorra over the social implications of rapid development has led to demands for a curb on economic expansion, although the authorities, as yet, have had little real control over managing this development. Tourism is an important source of revenue, both in winter and summer, and is much encouraged. In 1982 about 10m. foreign tourists entered Andorra, most of them visitors in transit. There are an estimated 250 hotels in Andorra.

French and Spanish currencies are in use. The absence of income tax or other forms of direct taxation has favoured the development of Andorra as a tax haven. The Government derives its revenue from a small levy on imports, indirect taxes on petrol and other items, stamp duty and the sale of postage stamps. The failure to balance revenue and expenditure has produced an increasing budget deficit, financed by borrowing. There is minimal company law or property registration within the principality, and land speculation has led to a rapid growth in construction. Banking is an important sector of the economy, although an informal agreement limits the number of banks operating within the country to five.

In November 1987 the Andorran Government announced its intention of acquiring two electricity companies, Forces Hidroelèctriques Andorranes SA and Electricidad Andorrana SA, for 3,500m. pesetas, of which 2,000m. pesetas were to be loaned from Andorran banks in 'block' investments until 1989. The two companies were to be merged to form Forces Elèctriques d'Andorra (FEDA). It was envisaged that Redesa (Spain) and EDF (France) would be able to satisfy the 60% of Andorra's electricity requirement which cannot be provided by FEDA.

Education

Education is provided by both French- and Spanish-language schools. Instruction in Catalan has only recently become available, at a school under the control of the local Roman Catholic Church. In 1986/87 there were a total of 8,845 pupils attending the 18 schools. The total number of teaching staff in 1982 was 305.

Public Holidays

1989: 2 January (for New Year's Day), 8 September (National Holiday), 25 December (Christmas).

1990: 1 January (New Year's Day), 8 September (National Holiday), 25 December (Christmas).

Each Parish also holds its own annual festival, which is taken as a public holiday, usually lasting for three days, in July, August or September.

Weights and Measures

The metric system is in force.

Statistical Survey

AREA AND POPULATION

Area: 467 sq km (180 sq miles).

Population: 46,976 (1986 census), comprising 12,843 Andorrans, 25,880 Spanish, 3,492 French and 4,761 others. *Capital:* Andorra la Vella, population 18,463. Source: Consellería de Turisme i Esports.

Births and Deaths (1987): Live births 527 (birth rate 11.1 per 1,000); Deaths 175 (death rate 3.7 per 1,000).

FINANCE

Currency and Exchange Rates: French and Spanish currencies are both in use. *French currency:* 100 centimes = 1 franc. *Coins:* 1, 5, 10, 20 and 50 centimes; 1, 2, 5 and 10 francs. *Notes:* 10, 20, 50, 100 and 500 francs. *Sterling and Dollar Equivalents* (30 September 1988): £1 sterling = 10.77 francs; US $1 = 6.37 francs; 1,000 French francs = £92.83 = $156.99. *Average Exchange Rate* (francs per US dollar): 8.985 in 1985; 6.926 in 1986; 6.011 in 1987. *Spanish currency:* 100 céntimos = 1 peseta. *Coins:* 50 céntimos; 1, 5, 25, 50 and 100 pesetas. *Notes:* 100, 500, 1,000 and 5,000 pesetas. *Sterling and Dollar Equivalents* (30 September 1988): £1 sterling = 209.25 pesetas; US $1 = 123.70 pesetas; 1,000 Spanish pesetas = £4.779 = $8.084. *Average Exchange Rate* (pesetas per US dollar): 170.04 in 1985; 140.05 in 1986; 123.48 in 1987.

Budget (million pesetas, 1983): Expenditure 3,683.4; Revenue 3,719.7.

EXTERNAL TRADE

Imports (1986): from France 31,525,222,000 pesetas; from Spain 20,036,199,000 pesetas; Total (incl. others) 74,312,755,085 pesetas. *Exports* (1986): to France 1,261,917 pesetas; to Spain 762,196 pesetas (estimate); Total (incl. others) 2,325,252 pesetas.

TOURISM

Tourist Arrivals (1977): via France 2,200,000; via Spain 4,500,000; Total 6,700,000. Source: data supplied by French and Spanish Customs.

COMMUNICATIONS MEDIA

Radio Receivers (1986): 8,000 in use.

Television Receivers (1986): 4,000 in use.

EDUCATION

Enrolment (1986/87): 3- to 6-year-olds 1,875; 7- to 15-year-olds 5,642; 15 and over 1,328; Total 8,845.

Directory

The Government
(November 1988)

Episcopal Co-Prince: Dr JOAN MARTÍ ALANIS, Bishop of Urgel.
French Co-Prince: FRANÇOIS MITTERRAND.
Permanent Episcopal Delegate: NEMESI MARQUES.
Permanent French Delegate: MAURICE JOUBERT.
Veguer Episcopal: FRANCESC BADIA-BATALLA.
Veguer de França: LLUÍS DEBLÉ.

EXECUTIVE COUNCIL
President of Government: JOSEP PINTAT SOLANS.
Minister of Finance: BONAVENTURA RIBERAYGUA MIQUEL.
Minister of Commerce, Industry and Agriculture: LLUÍS MOLNE ARMENGOL.
Minister of Public Services: MERCÈ SANSA REÑÉ.
Minister of Education and Culture: ROC ROSSELL DOLCET.
Minister of Tourism and Sport: JOSEP MIÑO GUITART.
Minister of Health, Labour and Welfare: MAGI MAESTRE CAMPDERROS.

Legislature

CONSELL GENERAL DE LAS VALLS D'ANDORRÀ
(General Council of the Valleys)

First Syndic: FRANCESC CERQUEDA I PASCUET.
Second Syndic: ANTONI GARRALLÀ ROSSELL.

There are 28 members (four from each of the seven parishes), directly elected for a term of four years. The most recent general election was held on 12 December 1985.

Political Organizations

Although political parties are not officially allowed in Andorra, conservative and liberal groupings exist, in addition to the following party:

Partit Democràtic d'Andorra (PDA): Andorra la Vella; f. 1979 to succeed Agrupament Democràtic d'Andorra; technically illegal; advocates representative and parliamentary democracy, while accepting Andorra's status as a co-principality.

Judicial System

In Civil Law judicial power is exercised in civil matters in the first instance by four judges (Battles), two appointed by the French Veguer and two by the Veguer Episcopal. There is a Judge of Appeal appointed alternately by France and Spain, and in the third instance (Tercera Sala) cases are heard in the Supreme Court of Andorra at Perpignan or in the court at Urgel.

Criminal Law is administered by the Tribunal des Corts, consisting of the two Veguers, the Judge of Appeal, the two Battles and two members of the General Council (Parladors).

The Press

Poble Andorra: Avinguda Meritxell 112, Andorra la Vella; tel. (078) 22500; f. 1974; weekly; Publr ANTONI CORNELLA SERRA; circ. 3,000.

Radio and Television

In 1986 there were an estimated 8,000 radio receivers and 4,000 television receivers in use. In February 1987 a private TV company, Antenna 7, began to transmit one hour of Andorran-interest programmes per day from the Spanish side of the border.

Radio Andorra: BPI, Avinguda Meritxell, Andorra la Vella; f. 1984 as an Andorran-owned commercial public broadcasting service, to replace two stations which closed in 1981, following the expiry of their contracts with French and Spanish companies; Dir GUALBERTO OSSORIO.

Finance

(cap. = capital; res = reserves; dep. = deposits; m. = million; brs = branches; amounts in Spanish pesetas)

PRINCIPAL BANKS

Banc Agricol i Comercial d'Andorra SA: Carrer Mossèn Cinto Verdaguer 6, Andorra la Vella; tel. (078) 21333; telex 201; f. 1930; cap. 1,800m., res 3,538m., dep. 62,716m. (Dec. 1987); brs at Les Escaldes, Pas de la Casa and Sant Julià de Lòria; Pres. and Man. Dir MANUEL CERQUEDA-ESCALER.

Banc Internacional: Avinguda Meritxell 32, Andorra la Vella; tel. (078) 20037; telex 206; f. 1958; affiliated to Banco de Bilbao, Spain; cap. 2,646m., res 4,344m., dep. 145,374m. (Dec. 1986); Chair. JOAN MORA FONT; Gen. Man. JORDI ARISTOT MORA; 3 brs.

Banca Cassany SA: Avinguda Meritxell 39-41, Andorra la Vella; tel. (078) 20138; f. 1958; Dir ALAIN FRECHU; Sec. J. PIERRE CANTURRI.

Banca Mora SA: Plaça Coprinceps 2, Les Escaldes; tel. (078) 20607; telex 222; f. 1952; affiliated to Banco de Bilbao; cap. 1,512m., res 2,205m., dep. 70,304m. (Dec. 1986); Chair. F. MORA FONT; CEO MANUEL ESTEVE; 6 brs.

Banca Reig: Sant Julià de Lòria; tel. (078) 41074; telex 240; Chair. J. REIG.

Crèdit Andorrà: Avinguda Princep Benlloch 19, Andorra la Vella; tel. (078) 20326; telex 200; f. 1955; cap. 5,000m., res 4,325m., dep. 135,045m. (Dec. 1987); Chair. A. PINTAT; Man. Dir P. ROQUET; 9 brs.

Transport

RAILWAYS

There are no railways in Andorra, but the nearest stations are Ax-les-Thermes, Hospitalet and La Tour de Carol, in France (with trains from Toulouse and Perpignan), and Puigcerdà, in Spain, on the line from Barcelona. There is a connecting bus service from all four stations to Andorra.

ROADS

Roads are maintained by the General Council of Andorra. A good road connects the Spanish and French frontiers, passing through Andorra la Vella. In 1986 there were 31,246 motor vehicles in use.

CIVIL AVIATION

There is an airport at Seo de Urgel in Spain, 20 km from Andorra la Vella, with three flights daily from Barcelona. A bus service connects to Andorra.

Tourism

Andorra has attractive mountain scenery. Winter sports facilities are available at five skiing centres.

Consellería de Turisme i Esports: Govern d'Andorra, Edifici Administratiu, Andorra la Vella; tel. (078) 21234; telex 469.

Sindicat d'Initiativa de las Valls d'Andorra: Carrer Dr Vilanova, Andorra la Vella; tel. (078) 20214.

ANGOLA

Introductory Survey

Location, Climate, Language, Religion, Flag, Capital

The People's Republic of Angola lies on the west coast of Africa. The Cabinda district is separated from the rest of the country by the estuary of the River Congo and Zairean territory, with the Congo lying to its north. Angola is bordered by Zaire to the north, Zambia to the east and Namibia to the south. The climate is tropical, locally tempered by altitude. There are two distinct seasons (wet and dry) but little seasonal variation in temperature. It is very hot and rainy in the coastal lowlands but temperatures fall inland. The official language is Portuguese, but African languages (mainly Ovimbundu, Kimbundu, Bakongo and Chokwe) are also in common use. Much of the population follows traditional beliefs, although there is a large minority of Christians, mainly Roman Catholics. The flag (proportions 3 by 2) has two equal horizontal stripes, of red and black; superimposed in the centre, in gold, are a five-pointed star, half a cog-wheel and a machete. The capital is Luanda.

Recent History

Formerly a Portuguese colony, Angola became an overseas province in 1951. Small nationalist groups began to form in the 1950s. There was an unsuccessful nationalist rebellion in 1961. Severe repression followed and there was a lull in nationalist activity until 1966. After a new wave of fighting, nationalist guerrilla groups were able to establish military and political control in large parts of eastern Angola and to press westward. Three major nationalist organizations were formed: the Movimento Popular de Libertação de Angola (MPLA) in 1956, the Frente Nacional de Libertação de Angola (FNLA) in 1962 and the União Nacional para a Independência Total de Angola (UNITA) in 1966. Following the April 1974 coup d'état in Portugal, Angola's right to independence was recognized, and negotiations between the Portuguese Government and the nationalist groups began in September. After the formation of a common front by these groups, it was agreed that Angola would become independent in November 1975.

In January 1975 a transitional government was established, comprising representatives of the MPLA, the FNLA, UNITA and the Portuguese Government. However, violent clashes between the MPLA and the FNLA occurred in March, as a result of the groups' political differences, and continued throughout the country. By the second half of 1975 control of Angola was effectively divided between the three major nationalist groups, each aided by foreign powers. The MPLA (which held the capital) was supported by the USSR and Cuba, the FNLA by Zaire and Western powers (including the USA), while UNITA was backed by South African forces. The FNLA and UNITA formed a united front to fight the MPLA.

The Portuguese Government proclaimed Angola independent from 11 November 1975, transferring sovereignty to 'the Angolan people' rather than to any of the liberation movements. The MPLA proclaimed the People's Republic of Angola and the establishment of a government in Luanda under the presidency of the movement's leader, Dr Agostinho Neto. The FNLA and UNITA proclaimed the People's Democratic Republic of Angola and a coalition government, based in Nova Lisboa (renamed Huambo). The involvement of South African and Cuban troops caused an international furore. By the end of February 1976, however, the MPLA, aided by Cuban technical and military expertise, had effectively gained control of the whole country. South African troops were withdrawn from Angola in March, but Cuban troops remained to assist the MPLA regime in countering guerrilla activity by the remnants of the defeated UNITA forces.

In May 1977 an abortive coup, led by Nito Alves, a former minister, resulted in the deaths of about 200 people. The task of national reconstruction was severely hampered by subsequent arrests and a purge of state and party officials. In December 1977 the MPLA was restructured as a political party, the Movimento Popular de Libertação de Angola—Partido de Trabalho (MPLA–PT), but further divisions were evident in December 1978, when President Neto abolished the post of Prime Minister and ousted several other ministers.

President Neto died in September 1979, and José Eduardo dos Santos, then Minister of Planning, was unanimously elected party leader and President by the MPLA–PT Central Committee. President dos Santos has continued to encourage strong links with the Soviet bloc, and has led campaigns to eliminate corruption and inefficiency. Elections to the National People's Assembly, which replaced the Council of the Revolution, were first held in 1980. Fresh elections, due to be held in 1983, were postponed until 1986, owing to political and military problems.

The MPLA Government's recovery programme has been continually hindered by security problems. Although the FNLA rebel movement reportedly surrendered to the Government in 1984, UNITA has, with considerable material aid from South Africa, conducted sustained and disruptive guerrilla activities, mainly in southern and central Angola. The South Africans themselves have also mounted numerous armed incursions over the Angolan border with Namibia, ostensibly in pursuit of guerrilla forces belonging to the South West Africa People's Organisation (SWAPO), who have bases within Angola. The Angolan Government formed regional military councils in the provinces affected by the fighting, and a new Defence and Security Council. Although the Government's military campaign against the rebels appeared to be increasingly successful during 1985, UNITA's position was strengthened in April 1986, when US military aid began to arrive. A visit to the European Parliament by Jonas Savimbi, the President of UNITA, in October 1986 failed to improve the international standing of the group. UNITA continued to seek international recognition in March 1987, when it offered to allow non-military traffic to operate on the Benguela railway, which had been effectively closed since 1975, owing to persistent sabotage by the rebels. In the following month Angola, Zambia and Zaire signed a declaration of intent to reopen the Benguela railway. However, UNITA continued to conduct sabotage attacks against the railway; in an ambush in June 1988, the rebels inflicted heavy damage on the Benguela line, destroying 11 diesel locomotives and killing 12 railway employees. During 1987 and early 1988 UNITA's position was consolidated, both by South African military support, and by the announcement by the US Government, in June 1987, that it was intending to continue providing covert military aid to UNITA in 1987 and 1988.

Nevertheless, UNITA was excluded from a series of major peace negotiations which commenced in May 1988 (see below). In July and August Jonas Savimbi travelled to the USA and to several European and African capitals in an attempt to gain support for UNITA's demands to be included in the negotiations. Although movement for a negotiated settlement between the MPLA Government and UNITA then gathered momentum, UNITA's position became vulnerable in August, when a cease-fire between Angola and South Africa was declared (see below) and when South African troops were reportedly withdrawn from Angola. UNITA, which openly refused to adhere to the cease-fire, continued to be active; in an offensive conducted by the Angolan Government against UNITA in September, several rebel bases were captured. Large numbers of UNITA forces were then moved to northern Angola, where they continued to receive US military support, allegedly through Zaire. In early October Savimbi offered a truce to the Cuban forces, on condition that they refrain from attacking UNITA guerrillas.

Angola, along with the other 'front-line' states, supports proposals for the attainment of independence by Namibia, following a UN-supervised cease-fire and elections. However, South Africa and the USA have insisted since 1982 that any withdrawal of South African troops from Namibia must be preceded, or at least accompanied, by the withdrawal of Cuban troops from Angola. The rejection by the Angolan Government of this stipulation prevented progress towards a settlement of the Namibia issue until December 1983, when South Africa proposed a complete withdrawal of its forces from Angola, on condition that the Angolan Government undertook to prevent SWAPO and Cuban forces from entering the areas vacated by the South African troops. Angola eventually accepted this proposal, and a cease-fire was established in the occupied area in early 1984. In February, as part of the settlement (which came to be known as the Lusaka agreement), Angola and South Africa established a Joint Monitoring Commission (JMC) to supervise the progress of the South African disengagement. Although some South African forces remained inside Angolan territory in early 1985, the cease-fire was maintained, and in September and October 1984, in talks held with US delegates, President dos Santos proposed a peace plan for Namibia involving a phased withdrawal of most of the Cuban forces in Angola. Under the plan, the Cuban withdrawal would be conditional on the withdrawal of the remaining South African forces from Angola, and would begin only after the implementation of Namibian independence was under way. The peace proposals were conveyed to South Africa by the USA in November, but differences between South Africa and Angola concerning the timetable for (and the extent of) the Cuban withdrawal prevented the conclusion of an agreement, although in April 1985 South Africa officially 'withdrew' virtually all of its remaining troops from Angola, and in May the JMC was dissolved.

From that time, however, South Africa periodically deployed military forces in Angola and mounted 'hot-pursuit' operations, ostensibly to curb continued activity by guerrillas of SWAPO and the African National Congress (ANC, a banned South African opposition movement). In June 1986 South Africa denied responsibility for a raid on the port of Namibe, in southern Angola, seriously damaging fuel storage tanks and cargo ships. In November South Africa claimed that its forces raided southern Angola in order to pre-empt a planned advance by SWAPO into Namibia. This claim was dismissed by SWAPO as a diversionary tactic to cover South African incursions into Angola. By mid-1987 it was apparent that South African security forces were becoming increasingly active inside Angola and in Namibia, along the southern border with Angola. In July units of the South African-led South West African Territory Force claimed to have launched a raid in southern Angola in which some 190 FAPLA (Angolan government forces) and SWAPO troops were killed. As the year progressed, the security situation in Angola deteriorated considerably: in October the South African Government confirmed, for the first time, that it was maintaining a 'limited presence' of troops inside Angola. At the time, the Angolan Government was conducting a major offensive against the rebel forces, which UNITA claimed to have defeated by early November. In late October units of the South African Defence Force launched a 'pre-emptive' raid on a SWAPO base in an unspecified part of southern Angola, in which some 150 SWAPO troops and 12 South African soldiers were reportedly killed. In the following month South Africa confirmed that it was providing military support to UNITA, and announced that it had engaged in direct action against Soviet and Cuban forces, in which several South African soldiers were reportedly killed. Later in November, the UN Security Council demanded the unconditional withdrawal of South African troops from Angola within two weeks. Having eventually agreed to comply with this demand, South Africa nevertheless continued to be active in Angola in the first half of 1988. In March it was reported that South African troops were conducting an offensive about 600 km within Angolan territory. When negotiations aiming to achieve a peace settlement in Angola and Namibia commenced in May, the security situation worsened, as the parties involved in the discussions attempted, through military consolidation, to strengthen their bargaining positions. Following progress in the peace negotiations (see below), a cease-fire was announced in August, and South African troops had reportedly withdrawn from Angola by the end of the month. Although an uneasy truce was maintained between Angola and South Africa at this time, it was reported in September that both Cuba and South Africa were reinforcing their troops along the border between Namibia and Angola, thereby endangering the cease-fire. During September FAPLA troops conducted an offensive against the guerrilla rebels who rejected the cease-fire; the apparent absence of South African soldiers, in support of UNITA, facilitated the success of FAPLA troops in capturing several UNITA bases. This offensive was not considered sufficiently serious to invalidate advances made in the negotiations for a peace settlement.

In September 1987 Maj. Wynand de Toit, a South African commando who had been captured in Angola in 1985, was exchanged for 133 Angolan prisoners being held by UNITA, together with Pierre Albertini, a French national being held prisoner in the South African 'Independent Homeland' of Ciskei, and Klaas de Jonge, a Dutch national who had been confined to Dutch Embassy offices in South Africa since 1985.

From the mid-1980s Angolan relations with the USA deteriorated, largely as a result of the reverse in US policy towards UNITA. In July 1985 the US Congress repealed legislation (the so-called Clark Amendment) which had prohibited US military support for UNITA since 1976. Angola subsequently suspended all contacts with the USA, although the Angolan proposals of 1984, concerning the Cuban withdrawal, remained valid. Following a visit by Jonas Savimbi to the USA in January 1986, the Reagan administration announced its decision, endorsed by the US Congress in September 1986, to grant $15m. in covert military aid to UNITA. In response, the Angolan Government requested that the UN should replace the US Government as primary mediator in negotiations concerning Namibia. As a result of Angola's deteriorating relations with the USA and with South Africa, exacerbated by Pretoria's installation of an 'interim government' in Namibia in June 1985, the prospects for a Namibian agreement became increasingly remote. In August 1986, however, the Angolan Government requested a meeting with the US Government, with a view to improving relations. However, the US administration was not receptive to this request, as was reflected by the unabated pressure on US oil companies in Angola to cease operations there.

In early 1987 there were reports that the US Government was considering the development of a disused airbase in Zaire, which had reportedly been used to convey aid to UNITA. In April Angola and the USA resumed discussions concerning a negotiated settlement over Namibia, and the Angolan Government made considerable efforts to secure diplomatic recognition from the USA, in spite of the announcement by the US administration, in June, of its intentions to continue to provide some $15m. in covert military aid to UNITA in both 1987 and 1988. In July 1987 it was reported that the discussions concerning Namibia had failed to produce agreement, but negotiations were resumed in September 1987 and January 1988. Angola's readiness to establish good relations with the USA was reflected in the change in the direction of the Government's economic policy, indicated in August 1987 by President dos Santos' announcement that Angola was applying for membership of the International Monetary Fund (IMF). In the following month the President made visits to several European capitals, including Paris and Lisbon, aimed at securing economic and, in some cases, military aid, and at obtaining support for Angola's proposed membership of the IMF. The visit to Lisbon was particularly significant, in that it was the first by an Angolan President to Portugal since Angola gained independence in 1975.

In March 1988 it appeared that, in spite of an intensification of armed hostilities, a state of military deadlock had again been reached, and a series of negotiations subsequently took place. During discussions between Angola, Cuba and the USA in March, Angola indicated a willingness to be flexible regarding the timetable for the evacuation of Cuban forces from southern Angola. The USA and the USSR played a prominent role in negotiations, and in early June they announced a target date of 29 September 1988 for reaching a peace settlement. The USA also acted as unofficial mediator in a series of major discussions which began in May 1988 between Angola, Cuba and South Africa. By mid-July the participants had agreed to a document containing 14 'essential principles' for a peaceful settlement, which provided for independence for Namibia, in accordance with the terms of the UN Security Council's Resolution 435 (see chapter on Namibia, Vol. II), and for the withdrawal of Cuban troops from Angola. In early August discussions in Geneva resulted in an agreement on a 'sequence of steps' for a peace settlement, whereby South African troops were to withdraw from Angola by 1 September, a cease-fire was to begin on 8 August, and was to be maintained, pending the achievement of an agreement by 1 September on a timetable for the total withdrawal of Cuban troops from Angola. In addition, the implementation of independence for Namibia was to commence on 1 November, with a general election, supervised by the UN, to be held in Namibia by 1 June 1989. It was reported that the South African troops were duly evacuated from Angola in late August 1988, when further discussions were held at Brazzaville, in the Congo, between Angola, Cuba and South Africa (and the USA). Although the participants in these talks failed to reach an agreement on a timetable for the Cuban withdrawal by the target date of 1 September, the cease-fire remained in force. In further negotiations in September and October, the gap was narrowed between Angolan and South African proposals for the timetable of the withdrawal of Cuban troops. On 13 December 1988 Angola, Cuba and South Africa finally signed a protocol requiring all 50,000 Cuban troops to be withdrawn from Angola by July 1991, and naming 1 April 1989 as the implementation date for a seven-month transition to Namibian independence, culminating in a general election on 1 November 1989.

In addition to these US-sponsored negotiations, peace initiatives emerged from within Africa. Efforts by President Botha of South Africa to improve the diplomatic standing of his country in the region included an official visit, in October, to Zaire, where the security situation in Angola was discussed, At the time, Zaire was one of several African states involved in efforts, supported by the USA, to pressurize the Angolan Government into negotiating an internal settlement with UNITA. Following discussions in Gabon, in late September, between the Heads of State of Angola, Gabon and the Congo, reports suggested that a 'summit' conference involving these countries and Zaire and Zambia was to be held in Zambia in early October, at which the participants were to discuss recent South African diplomatic overtures and the security situation in Angola and Namibia; these reports were, however, denied by President Kaunda of Zambia. Shortly after visiting Moscow in late October, President dos Santos conferred, in early November, with King Hassan of Morocco, an ally of the UNITA rebels; observers suggested that these talks were indicative of a readiness on the part of dos Santos to negotiate with UNITA.

The USA has hitherto made the withdrawal of Cuban forces a precondition for diplomatic recognition of the Angolan Government, which has been withheld since independence. Angola has diplomatic and economic links with most other countries, both Eastern and Western. In January 1982 Angola and the USSR signed a major co-operation agreement, whereby Soviet assistance, worth about US $2,000m., was to be given for the construction of dams and a second petroleum refinery. In 1983 diplomatic relations were established with the People's Republic of China, which had supported the MPLA's opponents in the civil war. In February 1985 Angola and Zaire signed a defence and security agreement which reportedly included an undertaking that neither country would allow its territory to be used as a base for attacks against the other. The efficacy of this agreement was brought into question in March 1986, when it appeared that a UNITA raid on the diamond-mining town of Andrada in northern Angola, in which 178 foreign workers were taken hostage, had been launched from Zaire. The two countries reaffirmed the terms of the 1985 agreement at talks held in July 1986. Zaire's tacit complicity with Jones Savimbi was, however, indicated by the spread of UNITA activity in the area that borders Zaire in late 1986 and early 1987, and by the reputed plans of the US Government to develop a disused airbase in Zaire. This resulted in renewed tension between the two Governments. Nevertheless, in April 1987 Angola, Zaire and Zambia signed a declaration of intent to restore services on the Benguela railway, which had been effectively closed since 1975. However, continued acts of sabotage by UNITA thwarted attempts to reopen the railway line. Efforts by Zaire to mediate in the armed conflict in Angola during 1988 were resisted by President dos Santos, owing to Zaire's alleged support for UNITA.

In August 1988 an Angolan fighter aircraft shot down a civilian plane travelling over Angolan territory, which was carrying President Masire of Botswana; although Masire was slightly injured, the explanation by the Angolan Government that the presidential jet had been mistaken for an enemy aircraft proved sufficient to preserve good relations between Angola and Botswana.

In July 1988 the Ministries of Domestic and Foreign Trade were merged, reportedly for administrative reasons, and the former Minister of Foreign Trade, Domingo das Chagas Simões Rangel, was appointed as the new Minister of Trade.

Government

According to the 1975 constitution (amended in October 1976 and September 1980), the Movimento Popular de Libertação de Angola—Partido do Trabalho (Workers' Party) or MPLA—PT, a Marxist-Leninist vanguard party, is responsible for the country's political, economic and social leadership. No other political parties are permitted. The MPLA—PT's supreme organ is the Congress, which normally meets every four years. In December 1985 the Congress elected the MPLA—PT's President and a 90-member Central Committee (75 full and 15 alternate members) to supervise the movement's work. The Committee elected an eight-member Secretariat to recommend policies to the Council of Ministers. In addition, the Central Committee appointed a new 13-member Political Bureau, which is the principal policy-making body of the MPLA—PT, and is effectively senior to the Central Committee Secretariat.

The supreme organ of state is the National People's Assembly, which comprises 318 members (including 29 alternate members) chosen by electoral colleges, composed of representatives elected by all 'loyal' citizens. The Assembly's term of office is normally three years, but the elections due in 1983 were postponed until 1986. The Head of State is the President of the Republic, who is also President of the MPLA—PT, Commander-in-Chief of the armed forces, Chairman of the Political Bureau of the MPLA—PT and Chairman of the Council of Ministers. The President appoints the Council of Ministers to exercise executive authority.

Defence

Military service is by compulsory conscription. In June 1988 the armed forces, FAPLA (Forças Armadas Populares de Libertação de Angola), had an estimated total strength of 100,000: 91,500 (including 10,000 guerrilla forces and 24,000 conscripts) serving in the army, 1,500 in the navy and 7,000 in the air force. The Directorate of People's Defence and Territorial Troops (formerly the People's Defence Organisation), a people's militia, has about 50,000 members. The border guard numbers 7,000. In addition, there were an estimated 50,000 Cuban troops stationed in Angola in 1988, as well as East German and Soviet advisers and technicians. The defence budget for 1986 was 32,730m. kwanza.

Economic Affairs

The Angolan economy was severely affected by the exodus in 1975 of more than 300,000 Portuguese, who had held virtually all important positions in agriculture and industry. Although Angola has ample natural resources and considerable potential, continuing civil strife and incursions by South African troops have hampered recovery. According to estimates by the UN Statistical Office, Angola's gross domestic product (GDP) increased, in real terms, at an average rate of 1.4% per year between 1975 and 1980, but declined by 2.0% in 1981. Real GDP grew by an estimated 5.4% in 1982, 1.5% in 1983, 2.5% in 1984 and 5.2% in 1985. Recent economic expansion failed, however, to keep pace with the increase in the country's population; according to UN estimates, real GDP per head declined by 0.3% per year, on average, between 1980 and 1985.

Agriculture is the largest sector of the economy, employing more than 70% of the working population, although only about 2% of Angola's arable land is cultivated. The principal subsistence crops are maize, cassava, sweet potatoes and bananas. The major commercial crops are coffee (normally the third largest export commodity), sugar cane, cotton and sisal. Livestock herds were depleted as a result of the civil war and drought in 1981, but they subsequently increased, so that in 1986 cattle numbers were estimated at 3.38m., pigs at 470,000, sheep at 255,000 and goats at 965,000. Much of Angola's territory is covered by forests, but commercial forestry has been developed only in the Cabinda and Moxico districts. The illegal export of timber by UNITA disrupts the forestry industry. Fishing was formerly an important industry but catches were drastically reduced by the withdrawal of most European-owned fleets in 1975–76. Measures to restore the industry were taken in 1981, when the Government formed a fisheries enterprise, and Angola was granted a loan of US $10m. from BADEA for the rehabilitation of fisheries facilities. In 1984 a further grant of 6.76m. ECUs ($4.9m.) was made to the sector by the EEC, and an agreement was signed with the Soviet Government for co-operation in the development of fisheries in Angola. The total catch, however, declined from 110,876 metric tons in 1983 to 58,442 tons in

1986. In February 1988 the USSR agreed to strengthen co-operation in the fisheries sector, with the possibility of the establishment of a joint fisheries venture and the construction of a fishing port in Namibe province.

The widespread disruption of transport routes, the devastation of land, and the displacement of large numbers of the population as a result of the civil war have caused a deterioration in the economy as a whole, which has been exacerbated by drought and the severe lack of skilled personnel. By 1988 it was estimated that 650,000 Angolans had been displaced from rural areas by the civil strife, and that 1m. people faced food shortages. With restrictions on the import of items that peasant producers would wish to buy, the subsequent lack of incentive to earn money and the re-emergence of a barter economy have also affected production levels adversely. Angola is now receiving financial and technical aid from several Soviet-bloc and West European countries, including Portugal.

The agricultural sector, in particular, continues to decline. Coffee is the principal cash crop and Angola was formerly the world's principal supplier of robusta coffee. Annual production of green coffee was more than 200,000 metric tons before independence, but by 1982 the coffee crop had slumped to only 17,000 tons. There was a slight improvement in production, to about 22,000 tons in 1983 and 27,000 tons in 1984, but output declined to some 25,000 tons in 1985. It was estimated that production of coffee recovered slightly, to about 35,000 tons, in 1986. In June 1983 the Government established a new state-controlled company, the Empresa de Rebenefício e Exportação do Café de Angola (CAFANGOL), to purchase and market coffee. The area of production under state control has declined in recent years, owing to labour shortages, induced by the lack of incentive to earn money. The widespread return by peasant coffee producers to subsistence farming has similarly reduced production in the private sector. The UN World Food Programme plans to spend $14.25m. on a food-for-work project to alleviate this problem, which affects the whole of the agricultural sector, and the Government is committed, in principle, to policy changes, such as the devaluation of Angola's currency, the kwanza, initially by about 40%. It was estimated that coffee provided some $55m. in export earnings (2.7% of total exports) in 1985. Coffee exports amounted to 20,000 tons in that year, and they declined in volume to 15,000 tons in 1986 and to 11,000 tons in 1987. In late 1987 it was announced that a state-run secretariat was to be established to improve the performance of the coffee sector.

Production of raw sugar was 82,000 metric tons in 1973 but only 17,000 tons in 1985. In that year Angola imported some 77,000 tons of the product. Cuban technicians are assisting with the rehabilitation of sugar estates. The staple diet of most inhabitants is cassava, and production was estimated at 1.97m. tons in 1986. Maize production was estimated at 250,000 tons in 1986. In the 1987 season total cereal production was estimated at 410,000 tons, compared with annual pre-independence levels of about 600,000 tons. Before independence, Angola was a net exporter of food, but the country now imports at least 50% of its needs. The cereal deficit for 1986/87 was estimated at 338,800 tons, and for 1987/88 at 345,000 tons. Of this amount, 187,000 tons was pledged by donors of food-aid. The Government appealed for 300,000–350,000 tons of food aid for 1988/89. At a meeting of the UN Disaster Relief Organization held in May 1988 in Geneva, Switzerland, Angola initiated an appeal for $110m. in emergency aid, of which $80m. was to cover food aid requirements; pledges of $75m. were forthcoming from donors attending the meeting.

Angola is very rich in minerals, especially petroleum, diamonds and iron ore, and there are also deposits of copper, manganese, phosphates and salt. In 1975 deposits of uranium were discovered on the border with Namibia. Petroleum is the major source of foreign exchange, accounting for nearly 50% of export earnings in 1974, rising to about 95% in 1985. Exports of crude oil accounted for some 88% of total export earnings in 1986. Petroleum officially provided 35% of GDP and 40% of state revenues in 1985. Angola's proven reserves of petroleum were estimated at about 252m. tons at the beginning of 1985. In 1987 about 65% of production came from offshore fields in Cabinda, where the Cabinda Gulf Oil Company (Cabgoc), in association with the state-controlled Sociedade Nacional de Combustíveis de Angola (SONANGOL), achieved ouput from these fields alone of 194,400 barrels per day (b/d) in 1986. Other fields, both onshore and offshore, are of increasing importance. Investment in oil operations for 1986–90 was forecast at nearly $3,000m. (of which about $1,000m. would be allocated to the Cabinda oilfields). Angola's overall petroleum production reached 231,000 b/d in 1985, about 282,000 b/d in 1986 and 358,000 b/d in 1987, as further fields came into production. With 30 new wells being drilled and 36 coming into production, total output was expected to exceed 450,000 b/d in 1988. It was forecast that by 1991 total petroleum production could reach 550,000 b/d, but, in view of the dramatic fall in prices from early 1986, this prediction may prove unrealistic. Petroleum export earnings reached $1,191m. in 1985, but fell to $1,140m. in 1986. The value of petroleum exports recovered to an estimated $2,100m. in 1987, and was projected to reach a similar level in 1988, as increased output of petroleum was expected to offset depressed prices for the commodity. Angola's sole refinery, Petrangol, at Luanda, currently processes about 1.35m. metric tons of petroleum per year. Domestic oil consumption was only 42,000 b/d in 1984, however, and most of Angola's oil output is exported in its crude form, although long-term plans to increase the refinery's capacity to 2m. tons, or to build a second refinery, are being considered. SONANGOL has trade and technical co-operation agreements with several major international oil companies, and prospects for the petroleum sector are excellent. In 1986, however, the collapse of the oil price, and increasing pressure from the US administration on US oil companies to withdraw from Angola, prompted the Angolan Government to stress the need to develop other sectors of the economy, such as agriculture. The Chevron Corporation responded to the pressure from the US administration in February 1987, when it announced its decision to sell one-fifth of its 49% interest in the Cabinda holding. This portion of its interest was sold to the Italian national oil company, AGIP.

Diamonds are the country's second largest foreign exchange earner, and between 5% and 8% of world diamond production is normally accounted for by Angola. The output of Angolan diamonds (of which a high proportion are of gem quality) was 1,960,000 carats in 1974, but fell to only 353,000 carats in 1977. Recorded output rose to 1.5m. carats in 1980, but declined thereafter, owing to UNITA attacks and to extensive diamond smuggling. Production fell to about 625,000 carats in 1985, and to around 350,000 carats in 1986, before rising to an estimated 1m. carats in 1988. Earnings from diamond sales fell from $234m. in 1980 to only $33m. in 1985, but rose to a projected $180m. in 1988. The Companhia de Diamantes de Angola (DIAMANG) was dissolved in July 1986. The state-controlled Empresa Nacional De Diamantes de Angola (ENDIAMA), which had held 77% of the shares in DIAMANG, then instigated a new national diamond policy, whereby diamond-mining was to be divided into blocks of land, to be exploited under production-sharing agreements with foreign concessionaires. In December 1987 Angola and the USSR signed a co-operation agreement, covering the mining of diamonds and quartz.

The other principal mineral is iron ore, the production of which reached 5.6m. metric tons (60% to 65% iron) in 1974. Angola is thought to have high-grade iron ore reserves of more than 1,000m. metric tons, but production was halted in August 1975, when the Cassinga mines in southern Angola were partially destroyed. Rehabilitation work was delayed by the South African raids of December 1983. The cost of rehabilitating the mines was estimated at between $25m. and $28m. The state-owned Empresa Nacional de Ferro de Angola (FERRANGOL), founded in 1981, plans to extend iron-mining to other known deposits, and development of the Cassala deposits, north of the Cuanza River, should benefit from the completion of the Kapanda dam and hydroelectricity project, to be implemented with Soviet and Brazilian assistance. This project, the largest construction scheme ever undertaken in Angola, is expected to cost about $900m. Construction work on the dam began in 1983 and is scheduled for completion in 1989–92. Although the project was to have a generating capacity of 520 MW, the dearth of capital and the security situation, combined with a severe drop in the level of energy consumption since independence, have raised doubts as to the feasibility of the project. Nevertheless, Brazil granted a credit of $100m. for the construction work in July 1988. Angola has a massive hydroelectricity potential, and there are plans to increase the capacity of the existing Cambambe dam to 650 MW by the late 1980s. In 1987 the Portuguese Government granted a credit of $140m. towards a scheme to rehabilitate the Lomaum dam on the Catumbela river. Exploratory drilling in the Cassala and Quitungo areas revealed aggregate reserves of iron and magnetite of about 200m. tons, which could eventually be mined to produce 5m.–6m. tons per year, but the development of these resources is expected to depend on trends in the market in the near future. Mining of phosphate rock started in the north in 1981, with annual production capacity of 15,000 metric tons. Research work, completed on a deposit in Cabinda province in 1984, revealed that between 400,000 and 600,000 metric tons of phosphates could be extracted annually. Important deposits of feldspar have been found in Huíla province.

As a result of the thriving petroleum industry, Angola's trade surplus increased from $196m. in 1981 to $769m. in 1982, and to $1,158m. in 1983. In 1985 a trade surplus of $747m. was recorded. In 1986, however, total exports fell to $1,280m., from $1,980m. in 1985, and, although imports were limited to $1,060m. (a reduction of 23%), the current account deficit almost doubled, to reach $447m. Until 1986, when the fall in oil prices seriously depleted earnings of foreign exchange, Angola had a good record in repayment of foreign debts. A foreign investment law of June 1979, which made arrangements for royalties, taxes and the repatriation of capital in the event of nationalization, also aimed to make the country attractive to foreign investors. The Government's ability to import vital raw materials and machinery is restricted by the need to spend about 50% of foreign exchange earnings on defence, and a further 25% on food imports. Private enterprise is permitted in some sectors of the economy, but more than 80% of industry and commerce was state-owned in 1981.

In 1983 the 1981–85 national economic plan was transformed into a General Emergency Plan, which imposed a policy of economic austerity. This continued under the 1984 annual economic plan, which emphasized defence, increased food production and restrictions on expenditure of foreign exchange, in order to limit external debt. The disbursed medium- and long-term external debt grew to only US $2,5000m. by the end of 1985, while the cost of debt servicing in that year was $324m. By December 1986 the foreign debt had reached $3,000m., and repayment arrears totalled $378m. The USSR, which was owed more than 62% of the total debt, agreed to reschedule repayments of debt principal falling due in 1987–88. The external debt was estimated at $4,000m. in late 1987. The 1986–90 plan, adopted at the second Party Congress (held in December 1985), again placed the emphasis on defence, and on the need to stimulate internal production and to restrict foreign exchange expenditure. With revenue expected to total only $2,333m., the 1987 state budget envisaged a deficit of $789m., compared with one of only $10m. in 1986. In January 1988 the Government initiated a programme for economic and financial restructuring, the Saneamento Económico e Financeiro (SEF). Under the programme state enterprises were to be restructured to allow much greater managerial and financial autonomy, the supply and distribution systems were to be improved, and more price incentives were to be introduced for state enterprises. External assistance was needed for the success of the programme, and it was hoped that membership of the International Monetary Fund (IMF), if granted (see below), would generate Western financial aid for the SEF.

In June 1987 the Minister of Finance proposed an innovative refinancing strategy, which was evolved in conjunction with a British financial consultant. Under the strategy, the repayment of debt arrears and future debt repayments were to be guaranteed by part-payments in petroleum through international oil companies, by 'restructuring' of the debt repayments with sovereign borrowers and export credit agencies, and by raising floating rate notes (FRN) on the Euromarket, to the value of some US $120m., in order to finance repayments and to raise 'modest' funds. However, the proposals received a negative response from Western countries, owing to concern over the intention to include future maturities, as well as arrears, in the strategy. In August, as a consequence of this negative response, and in accordance with a change in the Government's economic policy, President dos Santos announced Angola's intention to apply for membership of the International Monetary Fund (IMF). Angola's application was persistently opposed by the USA, but supported by many Western creditor nations who were satisfied with the early progress of the SEF in 1988. Meanwhile, the Government made new proposals for the bilateral repayment of debts, including a version of the refinancing strategy, modified to omit the element regarding the repayment of future maturities. In July 1988 Brazil agreed to reschedule arrears and debt repayments due in 1988, totalling $56m., and, in addition, to provide credit lines of $235m., of which $100m. was allocated to the Kapanda dam project.

Angola's decision to become a party to the Lomé convention (see p. 149), which it formally signed in April 1985, made the country eligible for increased aid from the EEC and for preferential trade tariffs. In 1986 the EEC granted 95m. ECUs to Angola, over a five-year period, for various development projects. In early 1988 it was announced that the African Development Bank had agreed to extend a credit of $100m., over three years, for the implementation of industrial and agricultural projects in Angola. Angola participates fully in the affairs of the Southern African Development Co-ordination Conference (SADCC, see p. 205), in which it has special responsibility for the co-ordination of energy development and conservation.

Social Welfare

Medical care is provided free of charge, but its availability is limited by a shortage of trained personnel and medicines. At independence there were 24 hospitals in Angola (eight of them in Luanda), but these were left without trained staff. In 1981 there were 460 foreign physicians in the country, mainly from Cuba, and a major training programme produces about 1,000 Angolan paramedics per year, and helps to spread basic medical knowledge to village communities. An agreement with the USSR, signed in 1984, provided for the completion and equipment of hospitals in Lubango, Luanda and Malanje. In the same year Spain approved a loan of $3m. to Angola for the construction of a medical school. The European Development Fund was expected to provide ECU 19.5m. (US $21.7m.) towards a scheme, proposed in 1988, to rehabilitate the national referral hospital Américo Boavida. War veterans are cared for by the Ministry of Defence.

Education

Education is officially compulsory for eight years, between seven and 15 years of age, but the Government's target of free universal education has not yet been reached. Primary education, beginning at seven years of age and lasting for four years, is provided free of charge. Secondary education begins at the age of 11 and lasts for up to six years, comprising a first cycle of four years and a second of two years. In 1973, under Portuguese rule, primary school pupils numbered only 300,000, but by 1985 there were 930,000. Enrolment at secondary schools (including students receiving vocational instruction and teacher-training) increased from 57,829 in 1970 to 151,759 in 1984. As a proportion of the school-age population, the total enrolment at primary and secondary schools increased from 37% in 1970 to 80% in 1980, but declined to 49% in 1984. Higher education is also being encouraged, and there were 4,493 students at the University of Angola in 1984. Much education now uses national languages rather than Portuguese. At independence the estimated adult illiteracy rate was over 85%. A national literacy campaign was launched in 1976, and the average rate of adult illiteracy in 1985 was officially estimated at 59% (males 51%).

Public Holidays

1989: 2 January (for New Year's Day), 4 February (Anniversary of the outbreak of the armed struggle against Portuguese colonialism), 27 March (Victory Day), 14 April (Youth Day)*, 1 May (Workers' Day), 1 August (Armed Forces' Day)*, 17 September (National Hero's Day, birthday of Dr Agostinho Neto), 11 November (Independence Day), 1 December (Pioneers' Day)*, 10 December (Anniversary of the Foundation of the MPLA), 25 December (Family Day).

1990: 1 January (New Year's Day), 4 February (Anniversary of the outbreak of the armed struggle against Portuguese colonialism), 27 March (Victory Day), 14 April (Youth Day)*, 1 May (Workers' Day), 1 August (Armed Forces' Day)*, 17 September (National Hero's Day, birthday of Dr Agostinho Neto), 11 November (Independence Day), 1 December (Pioneers' Day)*, 10 December (Anniversary of the Foundation of the MPLA), 25 December (Family Day).

* Although not officially recognized as public holidays, these days are popularly treated as such.

Weights and Measures

The metric system is in force.

Statistical Survey

Sources (unless otherwise stated): Direcção dos Serviços de Estatística, Luanda.

Area and Population

AREA, POPULATION AND DENSITY

Area (sq km)	1,246,700*
Population (census results)	
30 December 1960	4,480,719
15 December 1970	
Males	2,943,974
Females	2,702,192
Total	5,646,166
Population (UN estimates at mid-year)	
1984	8,540,000
1985	8,754,000
1986	8,981,000
Density (per sq km) at mid-1986	7.2

* 481,354 sq miles.

1986: Population 8,989,800 (official estimate).

DISTRIBUTION OF POPULATION BY DISTRICT
(1986 estimates)

	Area (sq km)	Population	Density (per sq km)
Cabinda	7,270	138,400	19.0
Zaire	40,130	135,700	3.4
Uíge	58,698	714,700	12.2
Luanda	2,418	1,227,100	507.5
Cuanza Norte	24,110*	343,700	14.3
Cuanza Sul	55,660*	616,900	11.1
Malanje	87,246*	805,800	9.2
Lunda-Norte	102,783	272,300	2.6
Lunda-Sul	56,985	149,600	2.6
Benguela	31,788	584,100	18.4
Huambo	34,274	1,350,400	39.4
Bié	70,314	995,200	14.2
Moxico	223,023	283,100	1.3
Cuando-Cubango	199,049	124,100	0.6
Namibe	58,137	95,700	1.6
Huíla	75,002	787,800	10.5
Bengo	31,371*	150,800	4.8
Cunene	89,342	214,400	2.4
Total	**1,246,700**	**8,989,800**	**7.2**

* Provisional estimates.

Source: Instituto Nacional de Estatística, Angola.

PRINCIPAL TOWNS (population at 1970 census)

Luanda (capital)	480,613*	Benguela	40,996
Huambo (Nova Lisboa)	61,885	Lubango (Sá de Bandeira)	31,674
Lobito	59,258	Malanje	31,559

* 1982 estimate: 1,200,000.

BIRTHS AND DEATHS (UN estimates, annual averages)

	1970–75	1975–80	1980–85
Birth rate (per 1,000)	48.0	47.5	47.3
Death rate (per 1,000)	25.4	23.6	22.2

Source: UN, *World Population Prospects: Estimates and Projections as Assessed in 1984*.

ECONOMICALLY ACTIVE POPULATION
(ILO estimates, '000 persons at mid-1980)

	Males	Females	Total
Agriculture, etc.	1,281	1,237	2,518
Industry	304	22	326
Services	442	128	569
Total	**2,027**	**1,386**	**3,414**

Source: ILO, *Economically Active Population Estimates and Projections, 1950–2025*.

Mid-1986 (estimates in '000): Agriculture, etc. 2,706; Total (incl. others) 3,789. Source: FAO, *Production Yearbook*.

Agriculture

PRINCIPAL CROPS (FAO estimates, '000 metric tons)

	1982	1983	1984
Wheat	10	10	10
Rice (paddy)	20	22	22
Maize	250	275	260
Millet and sorghum	50	50	50
Potatoes	40	40	40
Sweet potatoes	180	180	180
Cassava (Manioc)	1,950	1,950	1,950
Dry beans	40	40	40
Groundnuts (in shell)	20	20	20
Sunflower seed	10	10	10
Seed cotton	33	33	33
Cottonseed	22	22	22

1985: Harvests assumed to be unchanged since 1984, with the following exceptions (FAO estimates, '000 metric tons): Maize 250; Sugar cane 250; Coffee (green) 25; Tobacco 3*.

* Unofficial estimates.

1986: Harvests assumed to be unchanged since 1985, with the following exception: Coffee (green) 35,000 metric tons (unofficial estimate).

Source: FAO, *Production Yearbook*.

	1982	1983	1984
Cotton (lint)	11	11	11
Palm kernels	12	12	12
Palm oil	40	40	40
Vegetables	227	227	227
Citrus fruit	80	80	80
Pineapples	35	35	35
Bananas	280	280	280
Sugar cane	250	350	240
Coffee (green)	17	22*	27*
Tobacco	3	3	3
Sisal	n.a.	3	3

LIVESTOCK
(FAO estimates, '000 head, year ending September)

	1984	1985	1986
Cattle	3,350	3,360	3,380
Pigs	460	465	470
Sheep	245	250	255
Goats	955	960	965

Poultry (FAO estimates, million): 6 in 1984; 6 in 1985; 6 in 1986.
Source: FAO, *Production Yearbook*.

ANGOLA

LIVESTOCK PRODUCTS (FAO estimates, '000 metric tons)

	1984	1985	1986
Beef and veal	53	54	55
Goats' meat	3	3	3
Pig meat	15	16	16
Poultry meat	7	7	7
Other meat	7	6	6
Cows' milk	148	148	148
Butter	0.8	0.8	0.8
Cheese	2.5	2.5	2.5
Hen eggs	3.9	3.9	3.9
Cattle hides	7.7	7.9	8.1

Honey: 15,000 metric tons per year (FAO estimate).
Source: FAO, *Production Yearbook*.

Forestry

ROUNDWOOD REMOVALS
('000 cubic metres, excluding bark)

	1984	1985	1986
Sawlogs, veneer logs and logs for sleepers	116	134	108
Pulpwood*†	140	140	140
Other industrial wood*	719	737	756
Fuel wood*	3,805	3,900	4,005
Total*	4,780	4,911	5,009

* FAO estimates.
† Assumed to be unchanged since 1973.
Source: FAO, *Yearbook of Forest Products*.

SAWNWOOD PRODUCTION ('000 cubic metres)

	1984	1985	1986
Total (incl. boxboards)	2	5	5

Source: FAO, *Yearbook of Forest Products*.

Fishing

('000 metric tons, live weight)

	1984	1985	1986
Freshwater fishes*	8.0	8.0	8.0
Cunene horse mackerel	5.9	19.3	19.1
Sardinellas	12.6	28.7	21.6
Other marine fishes (incl. unspecified)	46.2	17.6	9.7
Total fish	72.7	73.6	58.4
Crustaceans and molluscs	0.0	0.9	0.1
Total catch	72.7	74.5	58.4

* Assumed to be unchanged since 1973.
Source: FAO, *Yearbook of Fishery Statistics*.

Mining

(estimates, '000 metric tons, unless otherwise indicated)

	1983	1984	1985
Crude petroleum	8,304	10,292	11,427
Natural gas (petajoules)	4	5	5
Salt (unrefined)*	55	50	10
Diamonds ('000 carats)*	1,034	902	625
Gypsum (crude)*	20	20	20

* Based on data from the US Bureau of Mines.
Source: UN, *Industrial Statistics Yearbook*.
Crude petroleum ('000 metric tons): 13,930 in 1986; 17,080 in 1987 (Source: UN, *Monthly Bulletin of Statistics*).

Industry

SELECTED PRODUCTS
(estimates, '000 metric tons, unless otherwise indicated)

	1983	1984	1985
Raw sugar*	60	50	50
Cigarettes (million)†	2,400	2,400	2,400
Jet fuels	70	65	70
Motor spirit	70	70	75
Distillate fuel oils	250	225	250
Residual fuel oils	600	575	600
Cement‡	220	350	350
Crude steel‡	10	10	10
Electric energy (million kWh)	1,740	1,790	1,790

* Estimates by the International Sugar Organization.
† Estimates by the US Department of Agriculture.
‡ Estimates by the US Bureau of Mines.
Source: UN, *Industrial Statistics Yearbook*.

Finance

CURRENCY AND EXCHANGE RATES

Monetary Units
100 lwei = 1 kwanza (K).

Denominations
Coins: 50 lwei; 1, 2, 5, 10 and 20 kwanza.
Notes: 20, 50, 100, 500 and 1,000 kwanza.

Sterling and Dollar Equivalents (30 September 1988)
£1 sterling = 50.09 kwanza;
US $1 = 29.62 kwanza;
1,000 kwanza = £19.965 = $33.761.

Exchange Rate
Since 1976 the official rate has been fixed at US $1 = 29.62 kwanza.

BUDGET (million kwanza)

Revenue	1983	1984	1985
State enterprises	10,126	9,896	12,154
Taxes	38,669	54,897	56,393
Other*	6,796	9,763	9,981
Total	55,591	74,556	78,528

* Excluding loans (million kwanza): 7,746 in 1984; 11,960 in 1985.

ANGOLA

Expenditure	1983	1984	1985
Economic development	17,907	21,961	23,465
Social services	14,838	16,754	18,780
Defence and security	23,295	31,943	34,306
Administration	9,159	8,787	9,874
Other	2,378	2,857	4,063
Total	67,577	82,302	90,488

Source: Instituto Nacional de Estatística, Angola.

NATIONAL ACCOUNTS
(estimates, million kwanza at current prices)
Composition of the Gross National Product

	1984	1985
Gross domestic product (GDP) at factor cost	129,214.2	137,209.3
Indirect taxes	21,502.1	21,668.2
Less Subsidies	9,146.1	14,130.9
GDP in purchasers' values	141,570.2	144,746.6
Net factor income from abroad	−1,716.0	−6,977.0
Gross national product	139,854.2	137,769.6

Gross Domestic Product by Economic Activity (at factor cost)

	1984	1985
Agriculture and livestock	13,470.2	11,526.9
Manufacturing and mining (excl. petroleum)	11,576.0	12,616.4
Fishing	2,604.1	2,783.7
Transport and communications	7,489.3	7,914.4
Construction	3,377.6	6,131.4
Extraction and refining of petroleum	41,417.5	44,601.1
Other energy	725.5	1,030.0
Trade and other productive sectors	14,000.0	14,656.0
Other services	34,554.0	35,949.4
Total	129,214.2	137,209.3

Source: Instituto Nacional de Estatística, Angola.

BALANCE OF PAYMENTS (million kwanza)

	1982	1983	1984
Trade balance	11,021	17,785	20,850
Services (net)	−19,007	−19,792	−23,613
Unrequited transfers	794	986	1,047
Current balance	−7,192	−1,021	−1,716
Long-term capital (net)	3,026	1,628	6,103
Short-term capital, errors and omissions	3,901	−466	−2,557
Changes in reserves	−265	141	1,830

Source: Banco Nacional de Angola.

External Trade

SELECTED COMMODITIES (million kwanza)

Imports	1983	1984	1985
Animal products	1,315	1,226	1,084
Vegetable products	2,158	3,099	2,284
Fats and oils	946	1,006	1,196
Food and beverages	2,400	1,949	1,892
Mineral products	317	130	127
Industrial chemical products	1,859	1,419	1,702
Plastic materials	431	704	454
Paper products	376	380	411
Textiles	1,612	1,816	1,451
Shoes and hats	207	265	218
Base metals	1,985	3,730	2,385
Electrical equipment	3,296	2,879	2,571
Transport equipment	2,762	2,240	3,123
Masonry products	132	137	132
Optical instruments	230	192	271
Total (incl. others)	20,197	21,370	19,694

Source: Instituto Nacional de Estatística, Angola.

Exports	1984	1985
Animal products	188	670
Vegetable products	2,363	1,624
Mineral products	55,209	62,319
Industrial chemical products	27	2
Timber	100	106
Textiles	4	5
Pearls, gemstones, precious metals	2,837	2,204
Base metals	34	5
Electrical equipment	35	28
Transport equipment	8	3
Total (incl. others)	60,823	66,968

SELECTED TRADING PARTNERS (million kwanza)

Imports	1983	1984	1985
Argentina	n.a.	780	848
Brazil	1,639	1,611	2,116
France	2,449	2,080	2,208
Germany, Federal Republic	1,023	1,347	1,519
Italy	861	1,022	725
Netherlands	1,633	1,520	1,424
Portugal	3,282	3,027	2,607
Sweden	688	511	1,090
United Kingdom	955	785	968
USA	1,462	3,300	1,406

Source: Instituto Nacional de Estatística, Angola.

Exports	1983	1984	1985
Belgium and Luxembourg	897	802	1,016
Brazil	4,899	3,539	4,194
German Democratic Republic	1,079	1,446	950
Japan	76	126	71
Netherlands	5,650	4,724	2,417
Portugal	255	700	2,144
Spain	4,432	5,234	7,873
United Kingdom	5,674	9,868	6,937
USA	26,090	23,667	29,077

Transport

GOODS TRANSPORT ('000 metric tons)

	1983	1984	1985
Road	691.5	725	996
Railway	399.2	458	522
Shipping (inshore and offshore)	401.3	444	512
Air	21.5	33	43
Total	1,513.5	1,660	2,073

PASSENGER TRANSPORT ('000 journeys)

	1983	1984	1985
Road	75,956.5	35,165	29,797
Railway	8,007.6	7,105	7,201
Air	959.3	727	927
Total	84,923.4	42,997	37,925

Sources: Instituto Nacional de Estatística, Angola; Ministry of Transport and Communications, Luanda.

INTERNATIONAL SEA-BORNE SHIPPING (estimated freight traffic, '000 metric tons)

	1983	1984	1985
Goods loaded	8,301	9,675	10,140
Goods unloaded	940	912	980

Source: UN, *Monthly Bulletin of Statistics*.

CIVIL AVIATION (traffic on scheduled services)

	1982	1983	1984
Kilometres flown (million)	11.4	15.7	15.1
Passengers carried ('000)	891	952	690
Passenger-km (million)	858	980	917
Freight ton-km (million)	20.8	46.2	25.1

Source: UN, *Statistical Yearbook*.

Communications Media

	1981	1982	1983
Radio receivers ('000 in use)	138	150	163
Television receivers ('000 in use)	31	32	33
Telephones ('000 in use)	40	n.a.	n.a.

Radio receivers: 230,000 in 1985.
Television receivers: 1,557,000 in 1985.
Book production: 57 titles (books 33, pamphlets 24) and 430,000 copies (books 239,000, pamphlets 191,000) in 1979; 47 titles in 1985.
Daily newspapers: 4 (estimated circulation 112,000) in 1984.
Source: UNESCO, *Statistical Yearbook*; UN, *Statistical Yearbook*.

Education

1981

	Teachers	Pupils
Pre-primary*	40,027	342,316
Primary		1,258,858
Secondary:		
general	3,870	134,578
teacher-training	410	2,564
vocational		2,642
Higher	374	2,666

* Initiation classes in which pupils learn Portuguese.

1984 (pupils): Pre-primary 208,459; Primary 870,410; Secondary: general 144,612, teacher-training 3,586, vocational 3,561; Higher 4,493.
Source: UNESCO, *Statistical Yearbook*.
1985 ('000 pupils): Pre-primary 217; Primary 930.
Source: Instituto Nacional de Estatística, Angola.

Directory

The Constitution

The MPLA regime adopted an independence constitution for Angola in November 1975. It was amended in October 1976 and September 1980. The main provisions of the Constitution are summarized below:

BASIC PRINCIPLES

The People's Republic of Angola shall be a sovereign, independent and democratic state. All sovereignty shall be vested in the Angolan people. The Movimento Popular de Libertação de Angola—Partido do Trabalho (MPLA–PT), their legitimate representative, shall be responsible for the political, economic and social leadership of the nation. The people shall be guaranteed broad effective participation in the exercise of political power through the development of people's power organizations.

The People's Republic of Angola shall be a unitary and indivisible State. Economic, social and cultural solidarity shall be promoted between all the Republic's regions for the common development of the entire nation and the elimination of regionalism and tribalism.

Defence
Under the leadership of the MPLA–PT and with its President as Commander-in-Chief, the People's Armed Forces for the Liberation of Angola (FAPLA) shall be institutionalized as the national army of the Republic. It shall be the responsibility of FAPLA to defend the country and to participate alongside the people in production and hence in national reconstruction. The Commander-in-Chief of FAPLA shall appoint and dismiss high-ranking officers.

Religion
The Republic shall be a secular state and there shall be complete separation of the State and religious institutions. All religions shall be respected.

The Economy
Agriculture shall be regarded as the base and industry as the decisive factor in the Republic's development. The Republic shall promote the establishment of just social relations in all sectors of production, furthering and developing the public sector and fostering co-operatives. It shall recognize, protect and guarantee private activities and property, including that of foreigners, provided that they are useful to the country's economy and in the interests of the Angolan people. The fiscal system shall be guided by the principle of graduated direct taxation.

Education
The Republic shall vigorously combat illiteracy and obscurantism and shall promote the development of education and of a true national culture.

FUNDAMENTAL RIGHTS AND DUTIES

The State shall respect and protect the human person and human dignity. All citizens shall be equal before the law. They shall be

ANGOLA

subject to the same duties, without any distinction based on colour, race, ethnic group, sex, place of birth, religion, level of education, or economic or social status.

It shall be the right and duty of every citizen to participate in the defence of the country and to defend and extend the revolution. All citizens over the age of 18 shall have the right and duty to take an active part in public life, to vote and be elected or appointed to any State organ. All elected citizens shall be accountable to the electorate, which shall at any given time have the right to revoke the mandate given.

There shall be freedom of expression, assembly and association provided that the basic objectives of the Republic are adhered to. Every citizen has the right to a defence. Individual freedoms are guaranteed. Freedom of conscience and belief shall be inviolable. Work shall be the right and duty of all citizens. The State guarantees medical and health care and the right to assistance in childhood, motherhood, disability, old age, etc. It also guarantees access to education and culture.

STATE ORGANS

President of the Republic

The President of the Republic shall be the President of the MPLA–PT. As Head of State the President shall represent the Angolan nation and shall have the following specific functions:

to swear in the government appointed by the People's Assembly on the recommendation of the MPLA–PT;

to preside over the Council of Ministers;

to declare war and make peace, following authorization by the People's Assembly;

to nominate, swear in and dismiss the Provincial Commissioners;

to sign, promulgate and publish the laws of the People's Assembly, government decrees and statutory decrees;

to direct national defence;

to decree a state of siege or state of emergency;

to pardon and commute sentences;

to indicate from among the members of the Political Bureau who shall deputize when the President is absent or temporarily prevented from exercising presidential functions;

to discharge all the other functions conferred on the President by the People's Assembly.

In the case of the death, resignation or permanent incapacity of the president, the Central Committee shall designate from among its members the person who shall provisionally exercise the duties of the president of the Republic.

People's Assembly

The People's Assembly is the supreme State body, to which the government is responsible. Members are elected by colleges composed of representatives chosen by all loyal citizens over 18 years old in their work- or living-places. Elections are held every three years. (Between sessions of the People's Assembly, affairs are conducted by its Permanent Commission. Local People's Assemblies are currently being elected at municipal and provincial level, although the security situation has hindered this process, and such bodies are also to be established at village, neighbourhood and communal level.)

Government

The Government shall comprise the President of the Republic, the ministers and the secretaries of state, and other members whom the law shall indicate, and shall have the following functions:

to guarantee the safety of persons and property;

to draw up and implement the general state budget once it is approved by the People's Assembly;

to follow guidelines laid down by the People's Assembly.

The Government may exercise by decree the legislative functions delegated to it by the People's Assembly.

Judiciary

The organization, composition and competence of the courts shall be established by law. Judges shall be independent in the discharge of their functions.

Local Administration

The People's Republic of Angola shall be administratively divided into provinces (províncias), municipalities (municipios), communes (comunas), neighbourhoods (bairros) and villages (povoações).

Local administration shall be guided by the combined principles of unity, decentralization and local initiative.

In a province, the provincial commissioner shall be the direct representative of the government. The government shall be represented in the district by the local commissioner, and in the commune by the commune commissioner, who shall be appointed on the recommendation of the MPLA–PT. The administrative bodies of the district, commune, neighbourhood and village shall be, respectively, the local commission, the commune commission, and the people's neighbourhood or village commission.

Eighteen provincial assemblies of 55–85 deputies are elected every three years by all loyal citizens over 18 years old.

The local authorities shall have legal personality and shall enjoy administrative and financial autonomy. The structure and jurisdiction of the administrative bodies and other organs of local administration shall be established by law.

FINAL PROVISIONS

An amendment to the Constitution is made by the People's Assembly. Laws and regulations may be repealed or amended if they conflict with the spirit of the present law or the Angolan revolutionary process.

The Government

HEAD OF STATE

President: José Eduardo dos Santos (assumed office 21 September 1979).

COUNCIL OF MINISTERS
(December 1988)

Chairman of the Council of Ministers: José Eduardo dos Santos.

Minister of State for Town Planning, Housing and Water: Filipe Joaquim Fragata.

Minister of State for Inspection and Control: Kundi Paihama.

Minister of State for the Productive Sphere, Minister of Energy and Petroleum: Lt-Col Pedro de Castro dos Santos Van-Dúnem (Loy).

Minister of State for the Economic and Social Sphere: (vacant).

Minister of External Relations: Afonso Van-Dúnem (Mbinda).

Minister of Planning: António Henriques da Silva.

Minister of Defence: Col Pedro Maria Tonha (Pedalé).

Minister of Justice: Fernando José França Van-Dúnem.

Minister of Health: Flávio João Fernandes.

Minister of the Interior: Manuel Alexandre Duarte Rodrigues (Kito).

Minister of Education: Augusto Lopes Teixeira (Tutu).

Minister of Finance: Augusto Teixeira de Matos.

Minister of Labour and Social Security: Diogo Jorge de Jesus.

Minister of Trade: Domingo das Chagas Simões Rangel.

Minister of Construction and Housing: João Henriques Garcia (Cabelo Branco).

Minister of Industry: Henrique de Carvalho Santos (Onambwe).

Minister of Transport and Communications: Carlos António Fernandes.

Minister of Fisheries: Francisco José Ramos da Cruz.

Minister of Agriculture: Fernando Faustino Muteka.

Minister of State Security: Kundi Paihama.

Secretary of the Council of Ministers: José Leitão da Costa e Silva.

MINISTRIES

Office of the President: Luanda; telex 3072.

Ministry of Agriculture and Forestry: Avda Norton de Matos 2, Luanda; telex 3322.

Ministry of Construction: Prédio da Mutamba, Luanda; telex 3067.

Ministry of Defence: Rua Silva Carvalho ex Quartel General, Luanda; telex 3138.

Ministry of Education and Culture: Avda Comandante Jika, Luanda.

Ministry of Energy and Petroleum: Avda 4 de Fevereiro 105, CP 1279, Luanda; tel. 372300; telex 3300.

Ministry of Finance: Avda 4 de Fevereiro, Luanda; tel. 44628; telex 3363.

Ministry of Fisheries: Ilha do Cabo Cais do Carvão, Luanda; telex 3273.

Ministry of Foreign Affairs: Avda Comandante Jika, Luanda; telex 3127.

Ministry of Health: Rua Diogo Cão, Luanda.

ANGOLA

Ministry of Industry: Prédio Gomes Irmão, Rua Cerqueira Lukoki 25, Luanda; tel. 334700; telex 3373.
Ministry of Information: CP 1240, Luanda; telex 3376.
Ministry of the Interior: Avda 4 de Fevereiro, Luanda.
Ministry of Justice: Largo do Palácio, Luanda.
Ministry of Labour and Social Security: Largo do Palácio, Luanda.
Ministry of Planning: Largo do Palácio, Luanda; telex 3082.
Ministry of Provincial Co-ordination: Luanda.
Ministry of State Security: Luanda.
Ministry of Trade: Largo Kinaxixi 14, Luanda; tel. 344525; telex 3282.
Ministry of Transport and Communications: POB 1250-C, Avda 4 de Fevereiro 42, Luanda; tel. 70061; telex 3108.

PROVINCIAL COMMISSIONERS*

Bengo: MALAMBA DEOLINDO ROSA FACHO.
Benguela: Maj. MANUEL JOÃO GONÇALVES LOURENÇO.
Bié: LUÍS PAULINO DOS SANTOS.
Cabinda: JORGE BARROS TCHIMPUATI.
Cunene: PEDRO MUTINDE.
Huambo: MARCOLINO JOSÉ CARLOS (MOCO).
Huíla: LOPO FORTUNATO FERREIRA DO NASCIMENTO.
Kuando-Kubango: MANUEL FRANCISCO TUTA (BATALHA DE ANGOLA).
Kwanza Norte: PAULO TEIXEIRA JORGE.
Kwanza-Sul: AURELIO SEGUNDA.
Luanda: CRISTOVÃO FRANCISCO DA CUNHA.
Lunda Norte: NORBERTO FERNADES DOS SANTOS.
Lunda Sul: GARCIANO MENDE.
Malanje: JOÃO ERNESTO DOS SANTOS (LIBERDADE).
Moxico: JAIME BAPTISTA NDONJE.
Namibe: DOMINGOS JOSÉ.
Uije: DOMINGOS MUTALENO.
Zaire: JOSÉ ANIBAL LOPES ROCHA.

*All Provincial Commissioners are ex-officio members of the Government.

Legislature

NATIONAL PEOPLE'S ASSEMBLY

The People's Assembly, established in November 1980, is the legislative body, and has 318 members (including 29 alternate members) who are chosen for a three-year term by electoral colleges, composed of representatives elected by all 'loyal' citizens. The elections due in 1983 were postponed until 1986.

Political Organizations

Movimento Popular de Libertação de Angola—Partido do Trabalho (MPLA—PT) (People's Movement for the Liberation of Angola—Workers' Party): Luanda; telex 3369; f. 1956; in 1961-74, as MPLA, waged guerrilla war against the Portuguese armed forces; ruling party since 1975; reorganized as MPLA—PT, a Marxist-Leninist political party, in December 1977; cen. cttee of 90 mems (75 full and 15 alt. mems); political bureau, comprising a maximum of 13 mems and two alt. mems, is overall policy-making body and is effectively senior to cen. cttee secretariat of eight depts; Chair. JOSÉ EDUARDO DOS SANTOS.

Political Bureau

Members:
JOSÉ EDUARDO DOS SANTOS (President).
AFONSO VAN-DÚNEM (MBINDA).
Col ANTÓNIO DOS SANTOS FRANÇA (NDALU).
Lt-Col FRANCISCO MAGALHÃES PAIVA (NVUNDA).
Col JULIÃO MATEUS PAULO (DINO MATROSS).
KUNDI PAIHAMA.
MANUEL ALEXANDRE DUARTE RODRIGUES (KITO).
PASCOAL LUVUALU.
Lt-Col PEDRO DE CASTRO DOS SANTOS VAN-DÚNEM (LOY).
Col PEDRO MARIA TONHA (PEDALÉ).
Maj. ROBERTO ANTÓNIO FRANCISCO VICTOR DE ALMEIDA.

Alternate Members:
ANTÓNIO JACINTO DO AMARAL MARTINS.
MARIA MAMBO CAFÉ.

Central Committee Secretariat

Secretary for Cadres and Organization: JOSÉ EDUARDO DOS SANTOS.
Secretary for Ideology: Maj. ROBERTO ANTÓNIO FRANCISCO VICTOR DE ALMEIDA.
Secretary for State and Judicial Bodies: Col JULIÃO MATEUS PAULO (DINO MATROSS).
Secretary for Youth, Mass and Social Organization: MARIA MAMBO CAFÉ.
Secretary for Economic and Social Affairs and Production: PAULO MIGUEL JÚNIOR.
Secretary for Agrarian Policy: SANTANA ANDRÉ PITRA (PETROFF).
Secretary for Foreign Relations: AFONSO VAN-DÚNEM (MBINDA).
Secretary for Administration and Finance: JACINTO VENANCIO (CHIPOPA).

The following groups are in conflict with the Government:

Frente de Libertação do Enclave de Cabinda (FLEC): f. 1963; comprises several factions seeking the secession of Cabinda province; estimated strength of 200-300; Pres. FRANCISCO XAVIER LUBOTA.

União Nacional para a Independência Total de Angola (UNITA): f. 1966 to secure independence from Portugal; later received Portuguese support to oppose the MPLA; UNITA and the Frente Nacional de Libertação de Angola (FNLA, f. 1962 but inactive since 1984) conducted military campaign against the MPLA govt with aid from some Western nations, 1975-76; openly supported by South Africa until 1984; US aid was received from 1986; operates mainly in central and southern Angola, with an estimated strength of 28,000 regular soldiers and 37,000 militia; Pres. Dr JONAS SAVIMBI; Sec.-Gen. MIGUEL N'ZAU PUNA.

Diplomatic Representation

EMBASSIES IN ANGOLA

Algeria: Luanda; Ambassador: HANAFI OUSSEDIK.
Belgium: CP 1203, Luanda; tel. 372368; telex 3356; Ambassador: GUIDO COURTOIS.
Brazil: CP 5428, Luanda; tel. 43275; telex 3365; Ambassador: PAULO DYRCEU PINHEIRO.
Bulgaria: Luanda; telex 3375; Ambassador: BOYAN MIHAYLOV.
Cape Verde: Luanda; telex 3247; Ambassador: CORSINO FORTES.
China, People's Republic: Luanda; Ambassador: HU LIPENG.
Congo: Luanda; Ambassador: ANATOLE KHONDO.
Côte d'Ivoire: Rua Karl Marx 43, Luanda; Ambassador: JEAN-MARIE KACOU GERVAIS.
Cuba: Luanda; telex 3236; Ambassador: RODOLFO PUENTE FERRO.
Czechoslovakia: Rua Amílcar Cabral 5, Luanda; Ambassador: MILOSLAV POLANSKY.
Denmark: Avda 4 de Fevereiro 42, CP 1402, Luanda; tel. 70420; telex 3233; Chargé d'affaires a.i.: MOGENS PREHN.
Egypt: Luanda; telex 3380; Ambassador: AHMED NABIL EL-SALAWY.
France: Luanda; Ambassador: JACQUES GASSEAU.
Gabon: Avda 4 de Fevereiro 95, Luanda; tel. 72614; telex 3263; Ambassador: RAPHAËL NKASSA-NZOGHO.
German Democratic Republic: Rua Agostinho Pedro Neto 3133, CP 3182, Luanda; tel. 336871; telex 3383; Ambassador: GOTTHELF SCHULZE.
Germany, Federal Republic: CP 1295, Luanda; tel. 334516; telex 3372; Ambassador: HANNSPETER DISDORN.
Ghana: Luanda; telex 3331; Ambassador: (vacant).
Guinea: Luanda; telex 3177.
Holy See: Rua Luther King 123, CP 1030, Luanda; tel. 330532; Apostolic Delegate: FORTUNATO BALDELLI.
Hungary: Rua Vereador Jaime de Amorim 22-28, Alvalade, CP 2977, Luanda; telex 3084; Ambassador: JÓZSEF NÉMETH.
India: Hotel Turismo, Rua Rainha Ginga, Luanda; tel. 393681; telex 4098; Ambassador: VAMAN SARDESAI.
Italy: Luanda; tel. 393533; telex 3265; Ambassador: FRANCESCO LANATA.
Korea, Democratic People's Republic: Luanda; Ambassador: KIM CHUNG NAM.
Netherlands: CP 3624, Luanda; telex 3051; Ambassador: CORNELIS DE SROOT.

ANGOLA

Nigeria: CP 479, Luanda; tel. 40084; telex 3014; Ambassador: VICTOR N. CHIBUNDU.
Poland: CP 1340, Luanda; telex 3222; Ambassador: JAN BOJKO.
Portugal: Rua Karl Marx 50, CP 1346, Luanda; tel. 33027; telex 3370; Ambassador: ANTÓNIO D'OLIVEIRA PINTO DA FRANÇA.
Romania: Rua 5 de Outubro 68, Luanda; tel. 36757; telex 3022; Ambassador: MARIN ILIESCU.
São Tomé and Príncipe: Luanda; Ambassador: ARIOSTO CASTELO DAVID.
Spain: CP 3061, Luanda; tel. 71952; telex 3526; Ambassador: (vacant).
Sweden: Luanda; telex 3126; Ambassador: STEN RYLANDER.
Switzerland: CP 3163, Luanda; tel. 38314; telex 3172; Chargé d'affaires: FERMO GEROSO.
Tanzania: Luanda; Ambassador: CRISPIN MBADILA.
USSR: CP 3141, Luanda; tel. 45028; Ambassador: VLADIMIR NIKOLAYEVICH KAZIMIROV.
United Kingdom: Rua Diogo Cão 4, CP 1244, Luanda; tel. 334582; telex 3130; Ambassador: M. J. C. GLAZE.
Viet-Nam: Luanda; telex 3226; Ambassador: NGUYEN HUY LOI.
Yugoslavia: Luanda; telex 3234; Ambassador: ZIVADIN JOVANOVIĆ.
Zaire: Luanda; Ambassador: ILANGWA-E-YOKA.
Zambia: CP 1496, Luanda; tel. 31145; telex 3439; Ambassador: BONIFACE ZULU.

Judicial System

There is a Supreme Court and Court of Appeal in Luanda. There are also civil, criminal, military and revolutionary people's courts.

Religion

Much of the population follows traditional beliefs.

CHRISTIANITY

Conselho Angolano de Igrejas Evangélicas (Angolan Council of Evangelical Churches): Rua Amílcar Cabral 182, 1° andar, CP 1659, Luanda; tel. 330415; telex 3255; f. 1977; 12 mem. churches; two assoc. mems; Pres. Rev. MALUNGO ANTÓNIO PEDRO (Evangelical Reformed Church of Angola); Gen. Sec. Rev. AUGUSTO CHIPESSE.

Protestant Churches

Evangelical Congregational Church in Angola (Igreja Evangélica Congregacional em Angola: CP 551, Huambo; 100,000 mems; Gen. Sec. Rev. JÚLIO FRANCISCO.
Evangelical Pentecostal Church of Angola (Missão Evangélica Pentecostal de Angola): CP 219, Porto Amboim; 13,600 mems; Sec. Rev. JOSÉ DOMINGOS CAETANO.
United Evangelical Church of Angola (Igreja Evangélica Unida de Angola): CP 122, Uíge; 11,000 mems; Gen. Sec. Rev. A. L. DOMINGOS.

Other denominations active in the country include the African Apostolic Church, the Church Full of the Word of God, the Church of Apostolic Faith in Angola, the Evangelical Baptist Church, the Evangelical Church in Angola, the Evangelical Church of the Apostles of Jerusalem, the Evangelical Reformed Church of Angola, the Kimbanguist Church in Angola and the United Methodist Church.

The Roman Catholic Church

Angola comprises three archdioceses and 11 dioceses. At 31 December 1985 there were an estimated 4.7m. adherents in the country.
Bishops' Conference: Conferência Episcopal de Angola e São Tomé, CP 87, Luanda; tel. 34640; f. 1981; Pres. Most Rev. MANUEL FRANKLIN DA COSTA, Archbishop of Lubango.
Archbishop of Huambo: Most Rev. FRANCISCO VITI, Arcebispado, CP 10, Huambo; tel. 2371.
Archbishop of Luanda: Cardinal ALEXANDRE DO NASCIMENTO, Arcebispado, CP 87, 1230C, Luanda; tel. 34640.
Archbishop of Lubango: Most Rev. MANUEL FRANKLIN DA COSTA, Arcebispado, CP 231, Lubango; tel. 20405.

The Press

The press was nationalized in 1976.

DAILIES

Diário da República: CP 1306, Luanda; official govt news sheet.
O Jornal de Angola: CP 1312, Luanda; tel. 31623; telex 3341; f. 1923; Dir-Gen. ADELINO MARQUES DE ALMEIDA; mornings and Sunday; circ. 41,000.
Newspapers are also published in several regional towns.

PERIODICALS

Angola Norte: POB 97, Malanje; weekly.
A Célula: Luanda; political journal of MPLA—PT.
Jornal de Benguela: CP 17, Benguela; 2 a week.
Lavra & Oficina: CP 2767-C, Luanda; tel. 322155; f. 1975; journal of the Union of Angolan Writers; monthly; circ. 5,000.
Noticia: Calçada G. Ferreira, Luanda; weekly.
Novembro: CP 3947, Luanda; tel. 31660; monthly; Dir ROBERTO DE ALMEIDA.
O Planalto: CP 96, Huambo; 2 a week.
A Voz do Trabalhador: CP 28, Luanda; journal of União Nacional de Trabalhadores Angolanos (National Union of Angolan Workers); monthly.

NEWS AGENCIES

ANGOP: Rua Marechal Tito 13B, CP 2181, Luanda; tel. 41438; telex 3311; Dir-Gen. and Editor-in-Chief JÚLIO AUGUSTO CARDOSO.

Foreign Bureaux

Agence France-Presse (AFP): Prédio Mutamba, CP 2357, Luanda; tel. 34939; telex 3334; Bureau Chief MANUELA TEIXEIRA.
Agentstvo Pechati Novosti (APN) (USSR): Luanda; Chief Officer VLADISLAV Z. KOMAROV.
Allgemeiner Deutscher Nachrichtendienst (ADN) (German Democratic Republic): CP 3193, Luanda; telex 3323; Correspondent GUDRUN GROSS.
Inter Press Service (IPS) (Italy): Rua Alberto Lemos 34, CP 3593, Luanda; tel. 38724; telex 3304; Correspondent JUAN PEZZUTO.
Prensa Latina (Cuba): Rua D. Miguel de Melo 92-2, Luanda; tel. 36804; telex 3253; Chief Correspondent ELOY CONCEPCIÓN.
Telegrafnoye Agentstvo Sovetskovo Soyuza (TASS) (USSR): Rua Marechal Tito 75, Luanda; telex 3244; Correspondent NIKOLAI SEMYONOV.
Xinhua (New China) News Agency (People's Republic of China): Rua Karl Marx 57-3, andar E, Bairro das Ingombotas, Zona 4, Luanda CP; tel. 32415; telex 4054; Correspondent ZHAO XIAOZHONG.

Publishers

Empresa Distribuidora Livreira (EDIL), UEE: Rua da Missão 107, CP 1245, Luanda; tel. 34034.
Neográfica, SARL: CP 6518, Luanda; publ. *Novembro*.
Nova Editorial Angolana, SARL: CP 1225, Luanda; f. 1935; general and educational; Man. Dir POMBO FERNANDES.
Offsetográfica Gráfica Industrial Lda: CP 911, Benguela; tel. 2568.

Government Publishing House

Imprensa Nacional, UEE: CP 1306, Luanda; f. 1845; Gen. Man. Dr ANTÓNIO DUARTE DE ALMEIDA E CARMO.

Radio and Television

In 1988 there were an estimated 1.2m. radio receivers and 200,000 television receivers in use.

RADIO

Rádio Nacional de Angola: Rua Comandante Jika, CP 1329, Luanda; tel. 321190; telex 3066; broadcasts in Portuguese, English, French, Spanish and vernacular languages (Chokwe, Kikongo, Kimbundu, Kwanyama, Fiote, Ngangela, Luvale, Songu, Umbundu); Dir-Gen. GUILHERME MOGAS.

TELEVISION

Televisão Popular de Angola (TPA): Rua Ho Chi Minh, CP 2604, Luanda; tel. 320025; telex 3238; f. 1975; parastatal company; Dir CARLOS GARCIA.

ANGOLA   *Directory*

Finance

(cap. = capital; dep. = deposits; res = reserves; m. = million; brs = branches; amounts in kwanza)

BANKING

All banks were nationalized in 1975.

Central Bank

Banco Nacional de Angola: Avda 4 de Fevereiro 151, CP 1298, Luanda; tel. 39141; telex 3005; f. 1976 to supersede Banco de Angola; bank of issue; cap. and res 7,657m.; dep. 111,975m. (1983); Gov. ANTÓNIO DA SILVA INÁCIO (acting); 55 brs and agencies.

Commercial Banks

Banco de Crédito Comercial e Industrial: CP 1395, Luanda.

Banco Popular de Angola: Avda 4 de Fevereiro, Luanda; tel. 36598; telex 3367; dep. 17,102m. (1983); Dir-Gen. JOÃO ABEL DAS NEVES; brs throughout Angola.

Foreign Bank

Banque Paribas: CP 1385, Rua Dr Al. Troni, Edificio BPA 18, Luanda; tel. 90877; telex 4068; Rep. ALAIN PFEIFFER.

INSURANCE

Empresa Nacional de Seguros e Resseguros de Angola (ENSA), UEE: Avda 4 de Fevereiro 93, CP 5778, Luanda; tel. 70169; telex 3087.

Trade and Industry

SUPERVISORY BODIES

National Planning Committee: Ministry of Planning, CP 1205, Luanda; tel. 39052; telex 3082; f. 1977; responsible for drafting and supervising the implementation of the National Plan and for co-ordinating economic policies and decisions; Chair. Minister of Planning.

National Supplies Commission: Luanda; f. 1977 to combat sabotage and negligence.

CHAMBER OF COMMERCE

Associação Comercial de Luanda: Edifício Palácio de Comércio, 1° andar, CP 1275, Luanda; tel. 22453.

STATE TRADING ORGANIZATIONS

Angomédica, UEE: Rua Dr Américo Boavida 85/87, CP 2698, Luanda; tel. 332945; telex 4195; f. 1981 to import pharmaceutical goods; Gen. Dir Dr A. PITRA.

Direcção dos Serviços de Comércio (Dept of Trade): Largo Diogo Cão, CP 1337, Luanda; f. 1970; brs throughout Angola.

Epmel, UEE: Rua Karl Marx 35-37, Luanda; tel. 30943; industrial agricultural machinery.

Exportang, UEE: Rua dos Enganos 1A, CP 1000, Luanda; tel. 32363; telex 3318; co-ordinates exports.

Importang, UEE: Calçada do Município 10, CP 1003, Luanda; tel. 37994; telex 3169; f. 1977; co-ordinates majority of imports; Dir-Gen. LOURENÇO M. NETO.

Maquimport, UEE: Rua Rainha Ginga 152, CP 2975, Luanda; tel. 39044; telex 4175; f. 1981 to import office equipment.

Mecanang, UEE: Rua dos Enganos, 1°-7° andar, CP 1347, Luanda; tel. 90644; telex 4021; f. 1981 to import agricultural and construction machinery, tools and spare parts.

STATE INDUSTRIAL ENTERPRISES

Companhia do Açúcar de Angola: 77 Rua Direita, Luanda; production of sugar.

Companhia Geral dos Algodões de Angola (COTONANG): Avda da Boavista, Luanda; production of cotton textiles.

Empresa Abastecimento Técnico Material (EMATEC), UEE: Largo Rainha Ginga 3, CP 2952, Luanda; tel. 38891; telex 3349; technical and material suppliers to the Ministry of Defence.

Empresa Açucareira Centro (OSUKA), UEE: Rua Estrada Principal Lobito, CP 037, Lobito; tel. 91459; telex 08268; sugar industry.

Empresa Açucareira Norte (ACUNOR), UEE: Rua Robert Shilds, CP 225, Caxito, Bengo; tel. 71720; sugar production.

Empresa Angolana de Embalagens (METANGOL), UEE: Rua Estrada do Cacuaco, CP 151, Luanda; tel. 70680; production of non-specified metal goods.

Empresa de Cimento de Angola (CIMANGOLA-UEM): Avda 4 de Fevereiro 42, Luanda; tel. 371190; telex 3142; f. 1954; 69% state-owned; cement production; exports to several African countries.

Empresa de Construção de Edificações (CONSTROI), UEE: Rua Alexandre Peres, CP 2566, Luanda; tel. 33930; telex 3165; construction.

Empresa de Pesca de Angola (PESCANGOLA), UEE: Luanda; f. 1981; state fishing enterprise, responsible to Ministry of Fisheries.

Empresa de Rebenefício e Exportação do Café de Angola (CAFANGOL), UEE: Avda 4 de Fevereiro 107, CP 342, Luanda; tel. 73452-37916; telex 3274-3011; f. 1983; national coffee-processing and trade organization.

Empresa de Tecidos de Angola (TEXTANG), UEE: Rua N'gola Kiluanji-Kazenga, CP 5404, Luanda; tel. 380723; telex 3146; production of textiles.

Empresa Nacional de Cimento (ENCIME), UEE: CP 157, Lobito; tel. 2325; cement production.

Empresa Nacional de Comercialização e Distribuição de Produtos Agrícolas (ENCODIPA): Luanda; central marketing agency for agricultural produce; numerous brs throughout Angola.

Empresa Nacional de Construções Eléctricas (ENCEL), UEE: Rua Comandante Che Guevara 0191, RC 187, Luanda; tel. 31411; electric energy.

Empresa Nacional de Diamantes de Angola (ENDIAMA), UEE: Luanda; f. 1986 to control diamond mining, following the dissolution of the Companhia de Diamantes de Angola (DIAMANG).

Empresa Nacional de Electricidade (ENE), UEE: Edifício Geominas, 6°-7° andar, CP 772, Luanda; tel. 21499; telex 3170; distribution of electricity.

Empresa Nacional de Ferro de Angola (FERRANGOL): Rua João de Barros 26, CP 2692, Luanda; tel. 73800; state-owned; iron production; Dir ARMANDO DE SOUSA (MACHADINHO).

Empresa Nacional de Manutenção (MANUTECNICA), UEE: Rua 7ª Avda do Cazenga 10L, CP 3508, Luanda; tel. 83646; assembly of machines and specialized equipment for industry.

Empresa Publica de Telecomunicacões (EPTEL), UEE: Rua I Congresso 26, CP 625, Luanda; tel. 392285; telex 3012; international telecommunications.

Empresa Texteis de Angola (ENTEX), UEE: Avda Comandante Kima Kienda, CP 5720, Luanda; tel. 36182; telex 3086; weaving and tissue finishing.

Fina Petróleos de Angola SARL: CP 1320, Luanda; telex 3246; petroleum production, refining and exploration; operates Luanda oil refinery, Petrangol, with capacity of 35,000 b/d; also operates Quinfuquena terminal; Man. Dir J. G. REBELO.

Siderurgia Nacional, UEE: CP Zona Industrial do Forel das Lagostas, Luanda; tel. 73028; telex 3178; f. 1963, nationalized 1980; steelworks and rolling mill plant.

Sociedade Nacional de Combustíveis de Angola (SONANGOL): Rua I Congresso do MPLA, CP 1318, Luanda; tel. 31690; telex 3148; f. 1976 for exploration, production and refining of crude oil, and marketing and distribution of petroleum products; sole concessionary in Angola, supervises foreign oil companies working onshore and offshore; majority shareholding in jt ventures with Cabinda Gulf Oil Co, Fina Petróleos de Angola and Texaco Petróleos de Angola; Dir-Gen. (vacant).

Cabinda Gulf Oil Company: CP 2950, Luanda; tel. 392646; telex 3167; exploration and production of petroleum in Cabinda province; subsidiary of Chevron Corpn; 51% owned by SONANGOL (see above); Man. Dir W. M. LEWIS.

Sociedade Unificada de Tabacos de Angola (SUT): Rua Deolinda Rodrigues 537, CP 1263, Luanda; tel. 360170; telex 3237; f. 1919; tobacco products; Gen. Man. A. CAMPOS.

TRADE UNION

União Nacional de Trabalhadores Angolanos (UNTA) (National Union of Angolan Workers): Avda 4 de Fevereiro 210, CP 28, Luanda; telex 3387; f. 1960; Sec.-Gen. PASCOAL LUVUALU; 600,000 mems.

Transport

In early 1988 a US $340m. emergency programme was launched to rehabilitate the transport infrastructure, which has been severely disrupted by the civil war.

RAILWAYS

The total length of track operated was 2,952 km in 1987. There are plans to extend the Namibe line beyond Menongue and to construct north-south rail links. Under the emergency transport

ANGOLA

programme launched in early 1988, $121m. was allocated to the rehabilitation of the Namibe (Moçamêdes) and Luanda railways.

Caminhos de Ferro de Angola: CP 1250c, Luanda; tel. 70061; telex 3108; national network operating four fmrly independent systems; Nat. Dir A. DE S. E. SILVA; Dep. Dir (Tech.) Eng. R. M. DA C. JUNIOR.

Amboim Railway: Porto Amboim; f. 1945; 123 km of track; Dir A. V. FERREIRA.

Benguela Railway (Companhia do Caminho de Ferro de Benguela): Rua Praça 11 Novembro 3, CP 32, Lobito; tel. 2645; telex 8253; f. 1903; owned 90% by Tank Consolidated Investments (which is wholly owned by Société Générale de Belgique), 10% by govt of Angola; passenger and freight line running from the port of Lobito across Angola, via Huambo and Luena, to the Zaire border, where it connects with the Société Nationale des Chemins de Fer Zaïrois system, which in turn links with Zambia Railways, thus providing the shortest west coast route for central African trade; 1,394 km of track; guerrilla operations by UNITA have suspended all international traffic since 1975, with only irregular services from Lobito to Huambo being maintained; a declaration of intent to reopen the cross-border lines was signed in April 1987 by Angola, Zambia and Zaire, although its implementation was placed in doubt by continued sabotage against the railway by UNITA; Vice-Pres. F. G. DE MAGALHÃES FALCÃO; Dir-Gen. CLEOFAS SILINGE.

Luanda Railway (Empresa de Caminho de Ferro de Luanda, UEE): CP 1250c, Luanda; tel. 70061; telex 3108; f. 1886; serves an iron, cotton and sisal-producing region between Luanda and Malanje; 536 km of track; Dir J. M. FERREIRA DO NASCIMENTO.

Namibe Railway: Namibe; f. 1905; main line from Namibe (Moçamêdes) to Menongue, via Lubango, with branch lines to Chibia and iron ore mines at Cassinga; 899 km of track; Dir L. DA M. G. CIPRIANO.

ROADS

In 1984 Angola had 72,300 km of roads, of which 18,600 km were main roads and 28,700 km were secondary roads. A total of 180 bridges and pontoons that were destroyed in the civil war had been rebuilt by the end of 1979. Rehabilitation of roads was to receive $142m. under the emergency transport programme launched in early 1988.

SHIPPING

The main harbours are at Lobito, Luanda and Namibe; the commercial port of Porto Amboim, in Kwanza-Sul province, has been closed for repairs since July 1984. The expansion of port facilities in Cabinda was planned. In May 1983 a regular shipping service began to operate between Luanda and Maputo (Mozambique). Under the emergency transport programme launched in early 1988, refurbishment work was to be undertaken on the ports of Luanda and Namibe (Moçamêdes).

Angonave—Linhas Marítimas de Angola: Rua Gov. Eduardo Costa 31, CP 5953, Luanda; tel. 30144; telex 3313; national shipping line; receives Cuban assistance in training crews; operates 11 vessels; Dir-Gen. FRANCISCO VENÂNCIO.

Cabotang–Cabotagem Nacional Angolana: Avda 4 de Fevereiro 83a, Luanda; tel. 73133; telex 3007; operates 2 vessels off the coasts of Angola and Mozambique; Dir-Gen. JOÃO OCTAVIO VAN-DUNEN.

Empresa Portuaria do Lobito: Rua Avda da Independencia, CP 16, Lobito; tel. 2711; telex 8233; long-distance sea transport.

Empresa Portuaria de Moçâmedes—Namibe, UEE: Rua Pedro Benje 10-A and 10-C, CP 49, Namibe; tel. 60643; long-range sea transport; Dir HUMBERTO DE ATAIDE DIAS.

Secil Marítima SARL: 82 Avda Paulo Dias de Novais, Luanda; telex 1342; operates 3 vessels.

CIVIL AVIATION

TAAG—Linhas Aéreas de Angola: Rua da Missão, Luanda; tel. 3235; telex 3442; f. 1939; internal services, and services from Luanda to Cape Verde, the Congo, Guinea-Bissau, Mozambique, Nigeria, São Tomé, Zaire, Zambia, Brazil, Cuba, France, Italy, Portugal, the German Democratic Republic, and the USSR; Dir-Gen. JOSÉ FERNANDES; fleet of 1 Boeing 707-320B, 7 Boeing 707-320C, 4 Boeing 737-200, 1 Boeing 737-200C, 2 Lockheed L100-20, 3 Antonov An-26, 1 Fokker F27-400M, 1 Fokker F27-500, 3 Fokker F27-600, 3 Yakovlev Yak-40, 2 Il-62.

Tourism

National Tourist Agency: Palácio de Vidro, CP 1240, Luanda; tel. 72750.

ANTARCTICA

Source: British Antarctic Survey, High Cross, Madingley Rd, Cambridge, CB3 0ET, England; tel. (0223) 61188; telex 817725.

The Continent of Antarctica is estimated to cover 13,900,000 sq km. There are no indigenous inhabitants, but since 1944 a number of permanent research stations have been established.

Major Stations

(The following list includes major stations south of latitude 60° occupied during 1988.)

	Latitude	Longitude
ARGENTINA		
Belgrano II	77° 52′ S	34° 37′ W
Esperanza	63° 24′ S	56° 59′ W
Jubany	62° 14′ S	58° 40′ W
Marambio	64° 14′ S	56° 38′ W
Orcadas	60° 45′ S	44° 43′ W
San Martín	68° 08′ S	67° 04′ W
AUSTRALIA		
Casey	66° 17′ S	110° 32′ E
Davis	68° 35′ E	77° 58′ E
Mawson	67° 36′ S	62° 52′ E
BRAZIL		
Comandante Ferraz	62° 05′ S	58° 23′ W
CHILE		
Arturo Prat	62° 30′ S	59° 41′ W
Bernardo O'Higgins	63° 19′ S	57° 54′ W
Rodolfo Marsh	62° 12′ S	58° 54′ W
PEOPLE'S REPUBLIC OF CHINA		
Great Wall	60° 13′ S	58° 58′ W
FRANCE		
Dumont d'Urville	66° 40′ S	140° 01′ E
FEDERAL REPUBLIC OF GERMANY		
Georg von Neumayer	70° 37′ S	8° 22′ W
INDIA		
Dakshin Gangotri	70° 05′ S	12° 00′ E
JAPAN		
Mizuho	70° 42′ S	44° 20′ E
Syowa	69° 00′ S	39° 35′ E
NEW ZEALAND		
Scott	77° 51′ S	166° 46′ E
POLAND		
Arctowski	62° 09′ S	58° 28′ W
SOUTH AFRICA		
Sanae	70° 19′ S	2° 25′ W
USSR		
Bellingshausen	62° 12′ S	58° 54′ W
Leningradskaya	69° 30′ S	159° 23′ E
Mirny	66° 33′ S	93° 01′ E
Molodezhnaya	67° 40′ S	45° 51′ E
Novolazarevskaya	70° 46′ S	11° 50′ E
Russkaya	74° 46′ S	136° 52′ W
Vostok	78° 27′ S	106° 51′ E
UNITED KINGDOM		
Faraday	65° 15′ S	64° 16′ W
Halley	75° 36′ S	26° 45′ W
Rothera	67° 34′ S	68° 08′ W
Signy	60° 43′ S	45° 36′ W
USA		
McMurdo	77° 51′ S	166° 40′ W
Palmer	64° 46′ S	64° 03′ W
Siple	75° 56′ S	84° 15′ W
South Pole	South Pole	
URUGUAY		
Artigas	62° 11′ S	58° 53′ W

Territorial Claims

Territory	Claimant State
Antártida Argentina	Argentina
Antártida Chilena	Chile
Australian Antarctic Territory	Australia
British Antarctic Territory	United Kingdom
Dronning Maud Land	Norway
Ross Dependency	New Zealand
Terre Adélie	France

These claims are not recognized by the USA or the USSR. No formal claims have been made in the sector of Antarctica between 90° W and 150° W.

See also Article 4 of the Antarctic Treaty below.

Research

Scientific Committee on Antarctic Research (SCAR) of the **International Council of Scientific Union (ICSU):** Secretariat: Scott Polar Research Institute, Lensfield Rd, Cambridge, CB2 1ER, England; tel. (0223) 62061; f. 1958 to further the co-ordination of scientific activity in Antarctica, with a view to framing a scientific programme of circumpolar scope and significance; mems 18 countries.

President: Dr C. Lorius (France).

Vice-Presidents: Prof. Dr G. Hempel (Federal Republic of Germany), Prof. E. S. Korotkevich (USSR).

Secretary: Dr A. C. Rocha Campos (Brazil).

The Antarctic Treaty

The Treaty (summarized below) was signed in Washington, DC, on 1 December 1959 by the 12 nations co-operating in the Antarctic during the International Geophysical Year, and entered into force on 23 June 1961.

Article 1. Antarctica shall be used for peaceful purposes only.

Article 2. On freedom of scientific investigation and co-operation.

Article 3. On exchange of information and personnel.

Article 4. i. Nothing contained in the present Treaty shall be interpreted as:

(a) a renunciation by any Contracting Party of previously asserted rights of or claims to territorial sovereignty in Antarctica;

(b) a renunciation or diminution by any Contracting Party of any basis of claim to territorial sovereignty in Antarctica which it may have whether as a result of its activities or those of its nationals in Antarctica, or otherwise;

(c) prejudicing the position of any Contracting Party as regards its recognition or non-recognition of any other State's right of or claim or basis of claim to territorial sovereignty in Antarctica.

ii. No acts or activities taking place while the present Treaty is in force shall constitute a basis for asserting, supporting or denying a claim to territorial sovereignty in Antarctica or create any rights of sovereignty in Antarctica. No new claim, or enlargement of an existing claim, to territorial sovereignty in Antarctica shall be asserted while the present Treaty is in force.

Article 5. Any nuclear explosions in Antarctica and the disposal there of radioactive waste material shall be prohibited.

Article 6. On geographical limits and rights on high seas.

ANTARCTICA

Article 7. On designation of observers and notification of stations and expeditions.
Article 8. On jurisdiction over observers and scientists.
Article 9. On consultative meetings.
Articles 10–14. On upholding, interpreting, amending, notifying and depositing the Treaty.

SIGNATORIES

Argentina	France	South Africa
Australia	Japan	USSR
Belgium	New Zealand	United Kingdom
Chile	Norway	USA

ACCEDING STATES

Austria, Brazil, Bulgaria, Canada, the People's Republic of China, Cuba, Czechoslovakia, Denmark, Ecuador, Finland, the German Democratic Republic, the Federal Republic of Germany, Greece, Hungary, India, Italy, the Democratic People's Republic of Korea, the Republic of Korea, the Netherlands, Papua New Guinea, Peru, Poland, Romania, Spain, Sweden, Uruguay.

Brazil, the People's Republic of China, the German Democratic Republic, the Federal Republic of Germany, India, Italy, Poland, Spain, Sweden and Uruguay have achieved consultative status under the Treaty, by virtue of their scientific activity in Antarctica.

ANTARCTIC TREATY CONSULTATIVE MEETINGS

Meetings of representatives from all the original signatory nations of the Antarctic Treaty and acceding nations accorded consultative status are held periodically to discuss scientific and political matters. The 13th meeting was held in Brussels (Belgium) in October 1985, and the 14th meeting was held in Rio de Janeiro (Brazil) in October 1987. The 15th meeting was to be held in Paris (France) in 1989. The representatives elect a Chairman and Secretary. Committees and Working Groups are established as required.

Among the numerous measures which have been agreed and implemented by the Consultative Parties are several designed to protect the Antarctic environment and wildlife. These include Agreed Measures for the Conservation of Antarctic Flora and Fauna, the designation of Specially Protected Areas and Sites of Special Scientific Interest, and a Convention for the Conservation of Antarctic Seals. A Convention on the Conservation of Antarctic Marine Living Resources, concluded at a diplomatic conference in May 1980, entered into force in April 1982. The text of a Convention on the Regulation of Antarctic Mineral Resource Activities was agreed in June 1982. The Convention was opened for signature on 25 November 1988 and nine countries immediately signed it. To enter into force, the Convention requires the ratification of 16 of the 22 Consultative Parties (including the USSR, the USA and all countries having territorial claims).

ANTIGUA AND BARBUDA

Introductory Survey

Location, Climate, Language, Religion, Flag, Capital

The country comprises three islands: Antigua (280 sq km—108 sq miles), Barbuda (161 sq km—62 sq miles) and the uninhabited rocky islet of Redonda (1.6 sq km—0.6 sq mile). They lie along the outer edge of the Leeward Islands chain in the West Indies. Barbuda is the most northerly (40 km—25 miles north of Antigua), and Redonda is 40 km south-west of Antigua. The climate is tropical, although tempered by constant sea breezes and the trade winds, and the mean annual rainfall of 1,000mm (40 inches) is slight for the region. The temperature averages 27°C (81°F) but can rise to 33°C (93°F) during the hot season between May and October. English is the official language but an English patois is commonly used. The majority of the inhabitants profess Christianity, and are mainly adherents of the Anglican Communion. The national flag consists of an inverted triangle centred on a red ground and divided horizontally into three bands, of black, blue and white, with the black stripe bearing a symbol of the rising sun in gold. The capital is St John's, on Antigua.

Recent History

Antigua was colonized by the British in the 17th century. The island of Barbuda, formerly a slave stud farm for the Codrington family, was annexed to the territory in 1860. Until December 1959 Antigua and other nearby British territories were administered, under a federal system, as the Leeward Islands. The first elections under universal adult suffrage were held in 1951. The colony participated in the West Indies Federation, which was formed in January 1958 but dissolved in May 1962.

Attempts to form a smaller East Caribbean Federation failed, and most of the eligible colonies subsequently became Associated States in an arrangement which gave them full internal self-government while the United Kingdom retained responsibility for defence and foreign affairs. Antigua attained associated status in February 1967. The Legislative Council was replaced by a House of Representatives, the Administrator became Governor and the Chief Minister was restyled Premier.

In the first general election under associated status, held in February 1971, the Progressive Labour Movement (PLM) ousted the Antigua Labour Party (ALP), which had held power since 1946, by winning 13 of the 17 seats in the House of Representatives. George Walter, leader of the PLM, replaced Vere C. Bird, Sr as Premier. However, a general election in February 1976 was won by the ALP, with 11 seats, while the seat representing Barbuda was won by an independent. Vere Bird, the ALP's leader, again became Premier, while Lester Bird, one of his sons, became Deputy Premier.

In 1975 the Associated States agreed that they would seek independence separately. In the 1976 elections the PLM campaigned for early independence while the ALP stood against it. In September 1978, however, the ALP Government declared that the economic foundation for independence had been laid, and a premature general election was held in April 1980, when the ALP won 13 of the 17 seats. There was strong opposition from Barbuda to independence as part of Antigua, and at local elections in March 1981 the Barbuda People's Movement (BPM), which continued to campaign for secession from Antigua, won all the seats on the Barbuda Council. However, the territory finally became independent, as Antigua and Barbuda, on 1 November 1981, remaining within the Commonwealth. The grievances of the Barbudans concerning control of land and devolution of power were unresolved, although the ALP Government had made concessions, yielding a certain degree of internal autonomy to the Barbuda Council. The Governor, Sir Wilfred Jacobs, became Governor-General, while the Premier, Vere Bird, became the country's first Prime Minister.

Following disagreements within the opposition PLM, George Walter, the former Premier, formed his own political party, the United People's Movement (UPM), in 1982. At the first general election since independence in April 1984, divisions within the opposition allowed the ALP to win convincingly in all of the 16 seats that it contested. The remaining seat, representing Barbuda, was retained by an unopposed independent. In March 1985 the Organization for National Reconstruction (ONR), a Barbudan party advocating co-operation with the ALP Government in Antigua, won a majority on the Barbuda Council in local elections. A new opposition party, the National Democratic Party (NDP), was formed in Antigua in 1985. In April 1986 it merged with the UPM to form the United National Democratic Party (UNDP). George Walter declined to play any significant public role in the UNDP, and Dr Ivor Heath, who had led the NDP, was elected leader of the new party.

In November 1986 a political crisis arose over a rehabilitation scheme at the international airport on Antigua. In January 1987, after a cabinet reshuffle, the Government appointed a former Chief Justice of Grenada, Sir Archibald Nedd, to conduct an official inquiry into the contract conditions and cost of the US $11.5m. project (worth no more than $0.5m. by World Bank estimates), negotiated by Vere Bird, Jr (eldest son of the Prime Minister). The report, published in August, stated that, while there was no evidence of criminal activity, Bird, Jr had acted 'in a manner unbecoming a minister of government' by awarding part of the contract to a company of which he was both the Chairman and the Legal Adviser. The controversy divided the ALP, with eight Ministers (including Lester Bird, the Deputy Prime Minister) demanding the resignation of Vere Bird, Jr, and Prime Minister Bird refusing to dismiss him. The UNDP and the Antigua Caribbean Liberation Movement (ACLM) united in the demand for resignation but, despite the expectation of an early election, failed to make an electoral pact. The rifts within the ALP and the Bird family continued into 1988. Despite the increasing bitterness, all the sitting MPs were confirmed as candidates for the next election. In August 1988 new allegations of corruption by government members were made, this time implicating Lester Bird. Also in 1988 economic concerns grew, particularly about the size of the national debt, which prompted a controversial proposal, in May, for large increases in charges for services by public utilities.

In foreign relations, the ALP Government follows a policy of non-alignment, although the country has strong links with the USA, and actively assisted in the US military intervention in Grenada in October 1983 as a member of the Organization of Eastern Caribbean States (OECS, see p. 107). Antigua and Barbuda is also a member of CARICOM (see p. 106), but in 1988 proved to be one of the main opponents of closer political federation within either organization. Since 1982, Antigua has intensified its programme of foreign relations, strengthening its links with Canada, the People's Republic of China, the Republic of Korea, and in Latin America. Relations with Trinidad and Tobago were disrupted in 1988 when Antigua allegedly reneged on an agreement that would have allowed BWIA, Trinidad's national airline, access to the profitable London Heathrow–Antigua route. The two Governments placed each other's goods under trade licence but, in March 1988, Antigua agreed to seek 'fifth freedom' rights for BWIA to land *en route* to London, and all trade barriers between the two countries were removed.

Government

Antigua and Barbuda is a constitutional monarchy. Executive power is vested in the British sovereign, as Head of State, and exercised by the Governor-General, who represents the sovereign locally and is appointed on the advice of the Antiguan Prime Minister. Legislative power is vested in Parliament, comprising the sovereign, a 17-member Senate and a 17-member House of Representatives. Members of the House are elected from single-member constituencies for up to five years by universal adult suffrage. The Senate is composed of 11 members (of whom one must be an inhabitant of Barbuda) appointed on the advice of the Prime Minister, four appointed on the advice of the Leader of the Opposition, one appointed

ANTIGUA AND BARBUDA

at the discretion of the Governor-General and one appointed on the advice of the Barbuda Council. Government is effectively by the Cabinet. The Governor-General appoints the Prime Minister and, on the latter's recommendation, selects the other Ministers. The Prime Minister must be able to command the support of a majority of the House, to which the Cabinet is responsible.

Defence

There is a small defence force of about 700 men. The US Government finances two military bases on Antigua. In 1984 the USA provided a patrol boat for the newly-formed coast-guard service.

Economic Affairs

Since the mid-1960s, economic growth has only just matched the increase in the islands' population. In 1987, according to estimates by the World Bank, Antigua and Barbuda's gross national product (GNP) per head, measured at average 1985–87 prices, was US $2,570, a real increase of 5.7% on the previous year's figure. Between 1980 and 1987 it is estimated that GNP per head increased, in real terms, at an average rate of 3.9% per year.

Tourism is the main economic activity. Antigua was one of the first Caribbean states actively to encourage tourism in the early 1960s, and by 1981 the industry accounted for approximately 25% of employment and made a direct contribution to the gross domestic product (GDP) of 12% and an estimated 40% contribution indirectly through services. After a period of stagnation during 1981 and 1982, owing to the world recession, the tourist industry began to expand again in 1983. Tourist arrivals increased by 28% in 1984, with the largest increase being derived from the USA. Stop-over arrivals increased by a more moderate 8.2% in 1985, and by 6.5% in 1986. However, cruise-ship visitor arrivals rose by 51.8% in 1985 and by 21.6% in 1986, when tourism earnings were estimated at EC $283m., accounting for around 60% of GDP. In 1987 stop-over arrivals increased by 6.6% and cruise-ship arrivals by 25.2%, to a total of 312,749 visitors. A major expansion of tourist facilities is in progress, and the Government aims to double the number of hotel rooms available to 6,000 between 1986 and 1991. In 1988 the St John's waterfront development came into use.

The Government estimated in 1987 that 60% of tourism earnings were remitted abroad. Fears of over-reliance on winter tourism have led towards a policy of diversification, encouraging manufacturing, agriculture and fishing. Agriculture, including livestock, forestry and fishing, contributed 4.3% of GDP in 1986. Local agriculture has been encouraged, and several new crops have been introduced in order to lessen the country's dependence on imported food, much of it consumed by the tourism industry. The sugar industry, which had collapsed in 1972, was revived in 1981 with the refurbishment of the sugar factory at Gunthorpes, to supply the local market, but financial problems led to its closure in 1985. In 1985 the FAO approved assistance of EC $270,000 for the country's agricultural sector. A wide variety of vegetables and the speciality 'Antigua Black' pineapple are cultivated, and in 1985 the Government embarked on a four-year livestock development programme, aimed at making the country self-sufficient in meat. As a result of increased investment and improved conditions for farmers, some increases in agricultural output were achieved in 1983, but the effects of prolonged drought contributed to a decline of 8.7% in agricultural and livestock production during 1984. Agricultural output increased sufficiently during 1985 to reduce imports of fresh vegetables by two-thirds, and by 1988 there were export hopes for cucumbers and pumpkins. In October 1988, however, strong winds across the Atlantic brought about a brief infestation by African desert locusts.

It has been estimated that up to 4,000 tons of fish per year could be yielded from the deep-sea fishing grounds, but in 1985 only about one-half of this figure was caught, despite the use of new ships, which increased catches. The Government is also hoping to increase the area currently under sea-island cotton, which was formerly Antigua's principal export crop. At the end of 1987 there were plans for a US $15m. development of the industry, supported by Japanese and Canadian interests. One of the main problems confronting all economic sectors is the lack of available water, aggravated during 1983 and 1984 by low rainfall. Emergency aid was obtained from the EEC, enabling Antigua to purchase water from neighbouring Guadeloupe and Dominica. A new desalinization plant at Crabb's Point, intended to increase Antigua's water supply by 2m. gallons per day, was completed at the end of 1987.

There are a number of light industries manufacturing rum, garments and household appliances, and assembling electronic components for export. The output of manufacturing industry has been adversely affected by the contraction of regional markets, by shortage of labour, and by the lack of an established private industrial sector within Antigua and Barbuda. To provide an additional source of revenue, the establishment of offshore banks in Antigua and Barbuda has been encouraged. Legislation which was approved in 1982 allowed the foundation of offshore institutions which would bring in up to EC $4m.

Two major sources of government revenue are the annual rental of EC $4.1m. for the two military bases on Antigua, paid by the US Government, and the 40% company tax which provided more than EC $20m. in 1986. Income tax was abolished in 1977. The combination of increased government expenditure and declining economic growth produced rising budget deficits in the early 1980s. However, the strong recovery in the tourist industry, and the introduction of fiscal adjustment measures by the Government, reduced the budget deficit to EC $16.7m. in 1984. With the aim of reducing expenditure, the Government announced that no further workers would be engaged in the public sector during 1986. For the first time in 15 years, the projected recurrent budget deficit was below EC $1m. for 1986. In 1987 increases in planned expenditure meant that the projected recurrent budget deficit was EC $6m. The actual 1987 deficit, however, was EC $27m. The projected budget deficit for 1988 rose to EC $15m. Antigua and Barbuda also has one of the highest debt-servicing commitments in the Eastern Caribbean, and in 1986 about 17% of recurrent revenue was devoted to repayments on the country's external debt, which stood at US $63m. By the end of 1987 the external debt had increased to US $240m., and repayments absorbed 20% of recurrent revenue. During 1987 the Government developed a debt-rescheduling programme, in an attempt to reduce its repayment arrears. The trade deficit increased from EC $379.1m. in 1985 to EC $472.2m. in 1986, increasing again in 1987, as a consequence of declining exports and large increases in imported goods. Antigua receives aid for development projects, capital investment and skills training from a number of governmental and international organizations. In 1984 the country began to benefit from an agricultural and educational assistance programme by the People's Republic of China.

Real growth in GDP averaged 7.5% annually between 1977 and 1979, but was only 2.5% by 1982. However, GDP was estimated to have grown by 6.4% in 1983, with the growth rate rising to 6.7% by 1985. In 1986 growth was 8.0%, and in 1987 it was 8.7%, the highest in CARICOM. The average annual rate of inflation declined steadily from 19% in 1980 to only 2.3% in 1983. The rate was 3.9% in 1984, but only 1.0% in 1985. An estimated 21% of the labour force were unemployed in 1983 and 1984.

Social Welfare

There are two state welfare schemes providing free health care, and a range of pensions, benefits, and grants. Antigua has a 220-bed general hospital and four health centres. In 1986 there were 37 physicians working in the islands.

Education

Education is compulsory for 11 years between five and 16 years of age. Primary education begins at the age of five and normally lasts for six years. Secondary education, beginning at 11 years of age, lasts for five years, comprising a first cycle of three years and a second cycle of two years. In 1984 enrolment at primary and secondary schools was equivalent to 63% of the school-age population. In 1986 there were 77 schools providing pre-primary, primary and secondary education; the majority of schools are administered by the Government. Teacher training and technical training are available at the State Island College. An extra-mural department of the University of the West Indies offers several foundation courses leading to higher study at branches elsewhere.

ANTIGUA AND BARBUDA

Public Holidays

1989: 2 January (for New Year's Day), 24 March (Good Friday), 27 March (Easter Monday), 1 May (Labour Day), 15 May (Whit Monday), 5 June (Queen's Official Birthday), 7–8 August (Carnival), 1 November (Independence Day), 25–26 December (Christmas).

1990: 1 January (New Year's Day), 13 April (Good Friday), 16 April (Easter Monday), 7 May (Labour Day), 4 June (Whit Monday), 11 June (Queen's Official Birthday), 6–7 August (Carnival), 1 November (Independence Day), 25–26 December (Christmas).

Weights and Measures

The imperial system is in use but a metrication programme is being introduced.

Statistical Survey

Source (unless otherwise stated): Ministry of Finance, Redcliffe St, St John's.

AREA AND POPULATION

Area: 441.6 sq km (170.5 sq miles).
Population: 65,525 (males 31,054, females 34,471) at census of 7 April 1970; 76,296 (estimate, mid-1986).
Density (1986): 172.8 per sq km.
Principal Town: St John's (capital), population 36,000.
Births, Marriages and Deaths (1986): Live births 1,130 (birth rate 14.8 per 1,000); Marriages 309 (marriage rate 4.1 per 1,000); Deaths 383 (death rate 5.0 per 1,000).
Economically Active Population (estimates, 1985): Employed 25,455 (males 14,257, females 11,198); Unemployed 6,799 (males 5,075, females 1,724); Total labour force 32,254.

AGRICULTURE, ETC.

Principal Crops (metric tons, 1986): Cucumbers 329.0, Aubergines 186.2, Pumpkins 176.7, Limes 188.8, Mangoes ('000) 1,001.4, Coconuts ('000) 514.
Livestock (FAO estimates, '000 head, year ending September 1986): Cattle 18, Pigs 4, Sheep 13, Goats 13 (Source: FAO, *Production Yearbook*).
Fishing (metric tons, 1985): Fish 2,290, Lobsters 117.0.

INDUSTRY

Production (estimates, 1985): Rum and alcohol 2,776.8 hectolitres; Wines and vodka 380.4 hectolitres; Electric energy 76.5m. kWh.

FINANCE

Currency and Exchange Rates: 100 cents = 1 East Caribbean dollar (EC $). *Coins:* 1, 2, 5, 10, 25 and 50 cents, 1 dollar. *Notes:* 1, 5, 10, 20 and 100 dollars. *Sterling and US Dollar equivalents* (30 September 1988): £1 sterling = EC $4.566; US $1 = EC $2.700; EC $100 = £21.90 = US $37.04. *Exchange rate:* Fixed at US $1 = EC $2.700 since July 1976.
Budget (estimates, EC $ million, 1988): Recurrent expenditure 231.8; Recurrent revenue 217.1.
International Reserves (US $ million at 31 December 1987): Foreign exchange 25.6; Total 25.6 (Source: IMF, *International Financial Statistics*).
Money Supply (EC $ million at 31 December 1987): Currency outside banks 42.24; Demand deposits at deposit money banks 68.39; Total money 110.62 (Source: IMF, *International Financial Statistics*).
Cost of Living (Consumer Price Index; base: 1980 = 100): 118.8 in 1983; 123.4 in 1984; 124.7 in 1985 (Source: IMF, *International Financial Statistics*).
Gross Domestic Product (EC $ million at current prices): 392.6 in 1984; 454.5 in 1985; 509.9 in 1986.

Balance of Payments (US $ million, 1986): Merchandise exports f.o.b. 24.7; Merchandise imports f.o.b. −181.4; *Trade balance* −156.7; Exports of services 119.2; Imports of services −56.2; *Balance on goods and services* −93.7; Unrequited transfers (net) 17.9; *Current balance* −75.8; Direct capital investment (net) 13.0; Other long-term capital (net) 61.6; Other short-term capital (net) −6.3; Net errors and omissions 4.8; *Total (net monetary movements)* −2.1; Valuation changes (net) 8.7; Exceptional financing (net) 6.4; *Changes in reserves* 13.0 (Source: IMF, *International Financial Statistics*).

EXTERNAL TRADE

Principal Commodities (EC $ million, 1984): *Imports:* Food and live animals 69.8; Beverages and tobacco 11.7; Mineral fuels, lubricants, etc. 89.1; Chemicals 22.7; Basic manufactures 44.7; Machinery and transport equipment 77.8; Miscellaneous manufactured articles 32.2; Total (incl. others) 356.1. *Exports:* Mineral fuels, lubricants, etc. 5.5; Chemicals 3.6; Basic manufactures 3.3; Machinery and transport equipment 14.3; Miscellaneous manufactured articles 18.0; Total (incl. others) 47.5.
Principal Trading Partners (EC $ million): *Imports* (1984): Canada 12.0; United Kingdom 37.6; USA 134.7; Yugoslavia 13.7; Total (incl. others) 356.1. *Exports* (1978): Saint Lucia 3.6; Trinidad and Tobago 7.0; United Kingdom 2.6; USA 11.9; Total (incl. others) 33.8.

TRANSPORT

Road Traffic (registered vehicles, 1986): Passenger motor cars 11,188; Motor cycles 834, Station wagons, vans, pick-ups, jeeps, lorries and buses 3,321.
Shipping (freight traffic, '000 metric tons, 1986): Goods loaded 15.6; Goods unloaded 346.6.

TOURISM

Foreign Tourist Arrivals (1987): 159,207 visitors by air; 153,542 cruise-ship passengers.

COMMUNICATIONS MEDIA

Radio Receivers (1986): 35,000 in use.
Television Receivers (1986): 27,000 in use.
Telephones (1986): 6,724 in use.

EDUCATION

Pre-primary (1983): 21 schools; 23 teachers; 677 pupils.
Primary (1983): 48 schools; 426 teachers; 9,933 students.
Secondary (1983): 16 schools; 331 teachers; 4,197 students.
Tertiary (1986): 2 colleges; 631 students.

Directory

The Constitution

The Constitution, which came into force at the independence of Antigua and Barbuda on 1 November 1981, states that Antigua and Barbuda is a 'unitary sovereign democratic state'. The main provisions of the Constitution are summarized below:

FUNDAMENTAL RIGHTS AND FREEDOMS

Regardless of race, place of origin, political opinion, colour, creed or sex, but subject to respect for the rights and freedoms of others and for the public interest, every person in Antigua and Barbuda is entitled to the rights of life, liberty, security of the person, the enjoyment of property and the protection of the law. Freedom of movement, of conscience, of expression (including freedom of the press), of peaceful assembly and association is guaranteed and the inviolability of family life, personal privacy, home and other property is maintained. Protection is afforded from discrimination on the grounds of race, sex, etc., and from slavery, forced labour, torture and inhuman treatment.

THE GOVERNOR-GENERAL

The Queen, as Head of State, is represented in Antigua and Barbuda by a Governor-General of local citizenship.

PARLIAMENT

Parliament consists of the Queen, a 17-member Senate and the House of Representatives composed of 17 elected members. Senators are appointed by the Governor-General: 11 on the advice of the Prime Minister (one of whom must be an inhabitant of Barbuda), four on the advice of the Leader of the Opposition, one at his own discretion and one on the advice of the Barbuda Council. The Barbuda Council is the principal organ of local government in that island, whose membership and functions are determined by Parliament. The life of Parliament is five years.

Each constituency returns one Representative to the House who is directly elected in accordance with the Constitution.

The Attorney-General, if not otherwise a member of the House, is an ex-officio member but does not have the right to vote.

Every citizen over the age of 18 is eligible to vote.

Parliament may alter any of the provisions of the Constitution.

THE EXECUTIVE

Executive authority is vested in the Queen and exercisable by the Governor-General. The Governor-General appoints as Prime Minister that member of the House who, in the Governor-General's view, is best able to command the support of the majority of the members of the House, and other Ministers on the advice of the Prime Minister. The Governor-General may remove the Prime Minister from office if a resolution of no confidence is passed by the House and the Prime Minister does not either resign or advise the Governor-General to dissolve Parliament within seven days.

The Cabinet consists of the Prime Minister and other Ministers and the Attorney-General.

The Leader of the Opposition is appointed by the Governor-General as that member of the House who, in the Governor-General's view, is best able to command the support of a majority of members of the House who do not support the Government.

CITIZENSHIP

All persons born in Antigua and Barbuda before independence who, immediately prior to independence, were citizens of the United Kingdom and Colonies automatically become citizens of Antigua and Barbuda. All persons born outside the country with a parent or grandparent possessing citizenship of Antigua and Barbuda automatically acquire citizenship as do those born in the country after independence. Provision is made for the acquisition of citizenship by those to whom it would not automatically be granted.

The Government

Head of State: HM Queen ELIZABETH II.

Governor-General: Sir WILFRED EBENEZER JACOBS (took office 1 November 1981).

CABINET
(October 1988)

Prime Minister: VERE C. BIRD, Sr.
Deputy Prime Minister and Minister of Economic Development, External Affairs, Tourism and Energy: LESTER BRYANT BIRD.
Minister of Finance: JOHN E. ST LUCE.
Attorney-General and Minister of Legal Affairs: KEITH B. FORD.
Minister of Public Utilities and Aviation: ROBIN YEARWOOD.
Minister of Agriculture, Fisheries, Housing and Lands: HILLROY HUMPHRIES.
Minister of Home Affairs: CHRISTOPHER MANASSEH O'MARD.
Minister of Education, Culture and Youth Affairs: REUBEN H. HARRIS.
Minister of Labour and Health: ADOLPHUS ELEAZER FREELAND.
Minister of Public Works and Communications: VERE C. BIRD, Jr.
Ministers without Portfolio: DONALD CHRISTIAN, DONALD SHEPHERD, HUGH MARSHALL, EUSTACE COCHRANE, HENDERSON SIMON, MOLWYN JOSEPH.

MINISTRIES

Office of the Prime Minister: Factory Rd, St John's; tel. 20773; telex 2127.
Ministry of Agriculture, Fisheries, Housing and Lands: High St, St John's; tel. 21007.
Ministry of Education, Culture and Youth Affairs: Church St, St John's; tel. 20192.
Ministry of Economic Development, External Affairs, Tourism and Energy: Queen Elizabeth Highway, St John's; tel. 20092; telex 2122.
Ministry of Finance: High St, St John's; tel. 21199.
Ministry of Labour and Health: St John's; tel. 20011.
Ministry of Legal Affairs: Hadeed Bldg, Redcliffe St, St John's; tel. 20017.
Ministry of Public Works: St John's St, St John's; tel. 20894.

Legislature

PARLIAMENT
Senate

President: BRADLEY CARROT.
There are 17 nominated members.

House of Representatives

Speaker: CASFORD MURRAY.
Ex-Officio Member: The Attorney-General.
Clerk: L. DOWE.

General Election, 17 April 1984

Party	Seats
Antigua Labour Party	16
Progressive Labour Movement	—
United People's Movement	—
Independent	1

Political Organizations

Antigua Caribbean Liberation Movement (ACLM): POB 493, St John's; f. 1979; left-wing; Chair. TIM HECTOR.

Antigua Labour Party (ALP): St Mary's St, St John's; tel. 21059; f. 1968; Leader VERE C. BIRD, Sr; Chair. LESTER BRYANT BIRD; Sec. J. E. ST LUCE.

Barbuda People's Movement (BPM): Codrington; campaigns for separate status for Barbuda.

Barbuda Independence Movement: Codrington; f. 1988; advocates self-government for Barbuda.

ANTIGUA AND BARBUDA

Organization for National Reconstruction (ONR): Codrington; f. 1983 to promote the economic development of Barbuda by co-operating with central government; Pres. ARTHUR NIBBS.

Progressive Labour Movement (PLM): St John's; f. 1970; Leader ROBERT HALL.

United National Democratic Party (UNDP): St John's; f. 1986 by merger of the United People's Movement (f. 1982) and the National Democratic Party (f. 1985); Chair. Dr IVOR HEATH.

Diplomatic Representation

EMBASSIES AND HIGH COMMISSION IN ANTIGUA AND BARBUDA

United Kingdom: British High Commissioner's Office, 38 St Mary's Street, POB 483, St John's; tel. 20008; telex 2113 (High Commissioner resident in Barbados).

USA: Queen Elizabeth Highway, St John's; tel. 23505; telex 2140 (Ambassador resident in Barbados).

Venezuela: Cross St, POB 1201, St John's; tel. 21570; Chargé d'affaires: CARLOS CRISTANCHO.

Judicial System

Justice is administered by the Eastern Caribbean Supreme Court, based in Saint Lucia, which consists of a High Court of Justice and a Court of Appeal. One of the Court's Puisne Judges is responsible for Antigua and Barbuda, and presides over the Court of Summary Jurisdiction on the islands. There are also Magistrate's Courts for lesser cases.

Religion

CHRISTIANITY

Antigua Christian Council: POB 863, St John's; tel. 20261; f. 1964; 5 mem. churches; Pres. Rev. NEVILLE BRODIE; Exec. Sec. Miss EDRIS ROBERTS.

The Anglican Communion

Anglicans in Antigua and Barbuda are adherents of the Church in the Province of the West Indies. The diocese of the North Eastern Caribbean and Aruba comprises 12 islands: Antigua, Saint Christopher (St Kitts), Nevis, Anguilla, Barbuda, Montserrat, Dominica, Saba, St Maarten, Aruba, St Bartholomew and St Eustatius; the total number of Anglicans is about 60,000. The See City is St John's.

Bishop of the North Eastern Caribbean and Aruba and Archbishop of the West Indies: Rt Rev. ORLAND LINDSAY, Bishop's Lodge, POB 23, St John's; tel. 20151.

The Roman Catholic Church

The diocese of St John's-Basseterre, suffragan to the archdiocese of Castries (Saint Lucia), includes Anguilla, Antigua and Barbuda, the British Virgin Islands, Montserrat and Saint Christopher and Nevis. At 31 December 1986 there were an estimated 14,053 adherents in the diocese. The Bishop participates in the Antilles Episcopal Conference (based in Jamaica).

Bishop of St John's-Basseterre: Rt Rev. DONALD J. REECE; Catholic Offices, POB 836, St John's; tel. 21135.

Other Christian Churches

Antigua Baptist Association: POB 277, St John's; tel. 21254; Pres. IVOR CHARLES.

Evangelical Lutheran Church: POB 968, St John's; tel. 22896; Pastors R. SEEGER, M. HENRICH.

There are also Methodist, Pentecostal, Seventh-day Adventist, Moravian, Nazarene, Salvation Army and Wesleyan Holiness places of worship.

The Press

The Herald: 2nd Floor, Redcliffe House, Cross 8, Redcliffe Street, St John's; tel. 23752; weekly; Editor EVERTON BARNES; circ. 2,500.

The Nation's Voice: Public Information Division, POB 590, Church St and Independence Ave, St John's; tel. 20090; weekly; Editor ROBIN BASCUS; circ. 1,500.

The Outlet: Cross St and Tanner St, POB 493, St John's; tel. 24425; f. 1975; weekly; publ. by the Antigua Caribbean Liberation Movement (ACLM); Editor JAMES KNIGHT; circ. 5,500.

The Worker's Voice: 46 North St, POB 1281, St John's; tel. 20090; f. 1943; 2 a week; official organ of the Antigua Labour Party and the Antigua Trades and Labour Union; Editor LESLIE JOHN; circ. 3,000.

FOREIGN NEWS AGENCY

Inter Press Service (IPS) (Italy): Old Parham Rd, St John's; tel. 23602; Correspondent LOUIS DANIEL.

Radio and Television

In 1986 there were an estimated 35,000 radio receivers and 27,000 television receivers in use.

Antigua Government Public Information Division: Office of the Prime Minister, Factory Rd, St John's; tel. 20260; comprises:

Antigua and Barbuda Broadcasting Service (Radio): POB 590, St John's; tel. 20112; f. 1956.

Antigua and Barbuda Broadcasting Service (Television): POB 1280, St John's; tel. 20821; f. 1964.

Caribbean Radio Lighthouse: Box 1057, St John's; tel. 21454; religious broadcasts; f. 1975; Dir CURTIS L. WAITE.

Radio ZDK: Grenville Radio Ltd, POB 1100, St John's; tel. 21100; f. 1970; Man. IVOR BIRD.

CTV cable television transmits 12 channels of US television 24 hours a day to subscribers.

Finance

(cap. = capital; brs = branches)

BANKING

Antigua Commercial Bank: corner of St Mary's and Thames Sts, POB 95, St John's; tel. 21217; telex 2175; f. 1955; auth. cap. $5m.; Man. JOHN BENJAMIN; 2 brs.

Antigua and Barbuda Development Bank: 27 St Mary's St, POB 1279, St John's; tel. 20838; f. 1974; Man. BERNARD S. PERCIVAL.

Bank of Antigua: POB 315, corner of High and Thames Sts, St John's; tel. 24282; telex 2180; 1 br.

Fidelity Trust Bank Ltd: High St, St John's.

Foreign Banks

Bank of Nova Scotia (Canada): High St, POB 342, St John's; tel. 21104; telex 2118; Man. L. J. NELSON.

Barclays Bank PLC (UK): High St, POB 225, St John's; tel. 20334; telex 2135; Man. I. C. LAYNE; 2 brs.

Canadian Imperial Bank of Commerce: 28 High St, POB 28, St John's; tel. 20836; telex 2150; Man. G. R. HILTS.

Royal Bank of Canada: High St and Market St, POB 252, St John's; tel. 20325; telex 2120; offers a trustee service.

Swiss American National Bank: High St, POB 1302, St John's; tel. 24460; telex 2181.

INSURANCE

Several foreign companies have offices in Antigua. Local insurance companies include the following:

Diamond Insurance Co Ltd: POB 489, Camacho's Ave, St John's; tel. 23474; telex 2173.

General Insurance Agency Co Ltd: POB 340, Redcliffe St, St John's; tel. 22346.

Sentinel Insurance Co Ltd: POB 207, Antigua Mill Hotel, St John's; tel. 20808.

State Insurance Corpn: POB 290, Redcliffe St, St John's; tel. 20110; telex 2177.

Trade and Industry

Antigua and Barbuda Manufacturers' Association: POB 1158, St John's; tel. 21912; Chair. P. HARKER; Exec. Sec. B. STUART YOUNG.

Antigua Chamber of Commerce Ltd: Cross and Redcliffe Sts, St John's; tel. 20743; telex 2105; f. 1944; 90 mems; Pres. EUSTACE FRANCIS; Exec. Dir LIONEL BOULOS.

Antigua Cotton Growers' Association: Dunbars, St John's; tel. 24962; telex 2122; Chair. FRANCIS HENRY; Sec. PETER BLANCHETTE.

Antigua Employers' Federation: 7 Redcliffe Quay, Redcliffe St, POB 298, St John's; tel. 20449; f. 1950; 94 mems; Chair. ARMALD DERRICK; Sec. HENDERSON BASS.

Antigua Fisheries Corpn: St John's; partly funded by the Antigua and Barbuda Development Bank; aims to help local fishermen.

Antigua Sugar Industry Corpn: POB 899, Gunthorpes, St George's; tel. 20653.

DEVELOPMENT AGENCIES

Barbuda Development Agency: St John's; economic development projects for Barbuda; Chair. HAKIM AKBAR.

Industrial Development Board: Newgate St, St John's; tel. 21038; f. 1984 to stimulate investment in local industries.

St John's Development Corporation: c/o Ministry of Economic Development, Queen Elizabeth Highway, St John's; tel. 23925.

TRADE UNIONS

Antigua and Barbuda Public Service Association (ABPSA): POB 747, St John's; Pres. LINDBERG DOWE; Gen. Sec. ELLOY DE FREITAS; 500 mems.

Antigua Trades and Labour Union (ATLU): 46 North St, St John's; tel. 20090; f. 1939; affiliated to the Antigua Labour Party; Pres. WILLIAM ROBINSON; Gen. Sec. NOEL THOMAS; about 10,000 mems.

Antigua Workers' Union (AWU): Freedom Hall, Newgate St, St John's; tel. 22005; f. 1967 after a split with ATLU; affiliated to the Progressive Labour Movement; Pres. MALCOLM DANIEL; Gen. Sec. KEITHLYN SMITH; 10,000 mems.

National Assembly of Workers: Cross St, St John's; affiliated to the Antigua Caribbean Liberation Movement.

Transport

ROADS

There are 384 km (239 miles) of main roads and 781 km (485 miles) of secondary dry-weather roads. In early 1986 it was announced that Antigua and Barbuda was to receive US $3.5m. from the EEC to finance the first phase of a major road rehabilitation programme.

SHIPPING

The main harbour is the St John's Deep Water Harbour. There are two tugs for the berthing of ships, and modern cargo handling equipment. The harbour can also accommodate three large cruise ships, and is used by a number of foreign shipping lines. In May 1987 a contract was signed for the dredging of St John's Harbour and the building of a deep-water pier for cruise ships, allowing passengers immediate access to central St John's. In November 1987 a new high-speed passenger and cargo ferry began operations to neighbouring islands, extending its services with a second vessel in May 1988.

Caribbean Link: St John's; f. 1987; scheduled services to 10 islands; Dirs DON MARSHALL, KEVIN BELIZAIRE; 2 vessels.

CIVIL AVIATION

Antigua's V.C. Bird (formerly Coolidge) International Airport, 7 km north-east of St John's, is modern and accommodates jet-engined aircraft. During 1986 and 1987 controversial redevelopment of the airport took place, financed by a US $11.1m. loan from a consortium of five banks (see Recent History). There is a small airstrip at Codrington on Barbuda.

LIAT (1974): POB 819, V.C. Bird International Airport, Antigua; tel. 20700; telex 2124; f. 1956 as Leeward Islands Air Transport Services; shares are held by the governments of Antigua and Barbuda, Montserrat, Grenada, Barbados, Trinidad and Tobago, Jamaica, Guyana, Dominica, Saint Lucia, Saint Vincent and the Grenadines and Saint Christopher and Nevis; scheduled passenger and cargo services to 22 islands in the West Indies and to Caracas; charter flights are also undertaken; Chair. IAN ARCHER; Man. Dir ARTHUR FOSTER; fleet of 4 HS.748, 5 Dash 8-100, 6 Twin Otter, 6 Islander, 1 Trislander; 2 BAe ATP on order.

Four Island Air Services Ltd: wholly-owned subsidiary of LIAT; runs scheduled services between Antigua, Barbuda and Saint Christopher and Nevis.

Inter Island Air Services Ltd: wholly-owned subsidiary of LIAT; runs scheduled services between Saint Vincent and the Grenadines, Grenada and Saint Lucia.

Tourism

Tourism is the main industry. Antigua and Barbuda offer a reputed 365 beaches, the annual attractions of an international sailing regatta and Carnival week, and the historic Nelson's Dockyard in English Harbour (a national park since 1985). In 1986 the Government established the St John's Development Corporation to oversee the redevelopment of the capital as a commercial duty-free centre, with extra cruise-ship facilities. In 1987 there were 159,207 stop-over visitors and 153,542 cruise-ship passengers, most of whom came from the USA, Canada, the United Kingdom and from other Caribbean countries. There were an estimated 42 hotels with a total of 4,256 beds in 1987. A modern luxury 500-room hotel with conference facilities was opened at Deep Bay at the end of 1987.

Antigua Department of Tourism: High St and Corn Alley, POB 363, St John's; tel. 20029; Man. EDIE HILL-THIBOU.

Antigua Hotels and Tourist Association (AHTA): POB 454, St John's; tel. 20374; telex 2172; Pres. JOHN HAWLEY.

ARGENTINA

Introductory Survey

Location, Climate, Language, Religion, Flag, Capital

The Argentine Republic occupies almost the whole of South America south of the Tropic of Capricorn and east of the Andes. It has a long Atlantic coastline stretching from Uruguay and the River Plate to Tierra del Fuego. To the west lie Chile and the Andes mountains, while to the north are Bolivia, Paraguay and Brazil. Argentina also claims the Falkland Islands (known in Argentina as the Islas Malvinas), South Georgia, the South Sandwich Islands and part of Antarctica. The climate varies from sub-tropical in the Chaco region of the north to sub-arctic in Patagonia, generally with moderate summer rainfall. Temperatures in Buenos Aires are generally between 5°C (41°F) and 29°C (84°F). The language is Spanish. The great majority of the population profess Christianity: more than 90% are Roman Catholics and about 2% Protestants. The national flag (proportions 2 by 1) has three equal horizontal stripes, of light blue, white and light blue. The state flag (proportions 3 by 2) has the same design with, in addition, a gold 'Sun of May' in the centre of the white stripe. The capital is Buenos Aires, but the transfer to a new capital at the twin towns of Viedma-Carmen de Patagones is expected to be completed by 1995.

Recent History

In 1916 Hipólito Yrigoyen, a member of the reformist Unión Cívica Radical (UCR), became Argentina's first President to be freely elected by direct popular vote. He remained in office until 1922, when another UCR politician became President. In 1928 Yrigoyen was elected for a second term, but in 1930 he was overthrown by an army coup, and the country's first military regime was established. Civilian rule was restored in 1932. Conservative politicians and landowners held power from then until June 1943, when another coup took place. Military rule was imposed until 1946.

A leading figure in the military regime was Col (later Lt-Gen.) Juan Domingo Perón Sosa, who became Secretary for Labour and Social Welfare in November 1943. In this post, he promoted labour reforms and encouraged unionization. Subsequently, Col Perón became also Vice-President and Minister of War, but in October 1945 he was forced to resign all his posts. This led to popular protests and demonstrations. Perón won a presidential election in February 1946, and took office in June. The new Government extended the franchise to women in 1947. President Perón founded the Peronista party in 1948, and was re-elected in November 1951. His position was greatly enhanced by the popularity, particularly among industrial workers and their families, of his second wife, Eva ('Evita') Duarte de Perón, who died, aged 33, in July 1952. As President, Gen. Perón pursued a policy of extreme nationalism and social improvement. In 1954, however, his measures of secularization and the legalization of divorce brought him into conflict with the Roman Catholic Church. In September 1955 President Perón was deposed by a revolt of the armed forces. He went into exile, eventually settling in Spain, from where he continued to direct the Peronist movement.

Following the overthrow of Gen. Perón, Argentina entered a lengthy period of political instability. The provisional government that took power after the coup was replaced in November 1955 by a military junta, with Gen. Pedro Aramburu, the Chief of the General Staff, as President. Congressional and presidential elections were held in February 1958. The presidential election was won by Dr Arturo Frondizi, a left-wing Radical, who took office in May. His party, the UCR Intransigente (UCRI), won large majorities in both chambers of Congress. In March 1962, following Peronist successes in national and provincial elections, President Frondizi was deposed by a military coup. He was replaced by Dr José María Guido, hitherto the President of the Senate, who resigned from the UCRI as a result of criticism from party members. The next presidential election, in July 1963, was won by another Radical, Dr Arturo Illía, who took office in October. However, President Illía was overthrown by a coup in June 1966. Power was assumed by a military junta, led by Lt-Gen. Juan Carlos Onganía, a former Commander-in-Chief of the Army. The legislature was closed, and political parties were banned. In May 1970 Gen. Aramburu, the former President, was abducted by members of the Montoneros, a guerrilla group of left-wing Peronists. In June he was killed by his captors. Later that month, President Onganía was deposed by his military colleagues, and a junta of the three armed forces' leaders took power. The junta appointed Brig.-Gen. Roberto Levingston, a former Minister of Defence, to be President. In March 1971, however, President Levingston was overthrown by the junta, which nominated one of its members, Lt-Gen. Alejandro Lanusse (Commander-in-Chief of the Army since October 1968), to be President. Urban guerrilla groups intensified their activities in 1971 and 1972.

Congressional and presidential elections were held in March 1973. The Frente Justicialista de Liberación, a Peronist coalition, won control of the National Congress, while the presidential election was won by the party's candidate, Dr Héctor Cámpora, who took office in May. However, President Cámpora resigned in July, to enable the holding of a fresh presidential election which Gen. Perón, who had returned to Argentina in June (after nearly 18 years in exile), would be eligible to contest. This election, in September 1973, returned the former President to power, with more than 60% of the votes. He took office in October, with his third wife, María Estela ('Isabelita') Martínez de Perón, as Vice-President.

General Perón died in July 1974 and was succeeded as President by his widow. The Government's economic austerity programme and the soaring rate of inflation caused widespread strikes and dissension among industrial workers. This increasingly chaotic situation resulted in demands for the resignation of President Perón. In March 1976 the armed forces, led by Lt-Gen. Jorge Videla (Commander of the Army), overthrew the President and installed a three-man junta: Gen. Videla was sworn in as President. The junta made substantial alterations to the Constitution, dissolved Congress, suspended all political and trade union activity and removed most government officials from their posts. Several hundred people were arrested, while Señora Perón was detained and later went into exile.

The new military regime launched a successful, although ferocious, offensive against left-wing guerrillas and opposition forces, and reintroduced the death penalty for abduction, subversion and terrorism. The imprisonment, torture and murder of many people who were suspected of left-wing political activity by the armed forces provoked protests over violations of human rights, from within Argentina and from abroad. The number of people who 'disappeared' after the coup was estimated to be between 6,000 and 15,000. Repression eased in 1978, after all armed opposition had been eliminated.

In May 1978 the junta confirmed President Videla in office until March 1981. In August 1978 he retired from the army and ceased to be part of the junta. In March 1981 Gen. Roberto Viola, a former member of the junta, succeeded President Videla and promised to extend the dialogue with the political parties as a prelude to an eventual return to democracy. After suffering a heart attack, he was replaced in December by Lt-Gen. Leopoldo Galtieri, the Commander-in-Chief of the Army, who attempted to cultivate popular support by continuing the process of political liberalization which had been begun by his predecessor.

To distract attention from the unstable domestic situation, and following unsuccessful negotiations with the United Kingdom in February over Argentina's long-standing sovereignty claim, President Galtieri ordered the invasion of the Falkland Islands (Islas Malvinas) in April 1982 (see chapter on the Falkland Islands, Vol. II). The United Kingdom recovered the islands after a short war during which about 750 Argentine lives were lost. Argentine forces surrendered in June 1982 but no formal cessation of hostilities was signed. The defeat brought about the final humiliation of the armed forces: Galtieri was forced to resign, and the rest of the junta were replaced. The army, under the control of Lt-Gen. Cristino Nicolaides, installed a retired general, Reynaldo Bignone, as President in

July 1982. The armed forces were held responsible for the disastrous economic situation, and, unable to resolve the crisis, were forced to move rapidly towards the transfer of power to a civilian government. Moreover, in 1983 a Military Commission of Inquiry into the war concluded in its report that the main responsibility for Argentina's defeat lay with members of the former junta, who were recommended for trial. Galtieri was given a prison sentence, while several other officers were put on trial for corruption, murder and insulting the honour of the armed forces. Meanwhile, in August 1983 the regime approved the Ley de Pacificación Nacional, an amnesty law which granted retrospective immunity to the police, the armed forces and others for political crimes that had been committed over the previous 10 years.

In February 1983 the Government had announced that general and presidential elections would be held on 30 October. In April the ban on 'Isabelita' Perón and 25 former government and trade union officials was lifted. Señora Perón was retained as titular head of the Peronist party, the Partido Justicialista, but remained in Spain. The other main party, the UCR, which was supported by some socialist and some conservative groups, announced its candidate, Dr Raúl Alfonsín, in July. At the elections, the UCR succeeded in attracting the votes of many former Peronist supporters. It won 317 of the 600 seats in the presidential electoral college, and 129 of the 254 seats in the Chamber of Deputies, although the Peronists won a narrow majority of provincial governorships. Dr Alfonsín took office as President on 10 December.

Shortly after taking office, President Alfonsín announced a radical reform of the armed forces, which led to the immediate retirement of more than one-half of the military high command. In addition, he repealed the Ley de Pacificación Nacional and ordered the court martial of the first three military juntas to rule Argentina after the coup of 1976, for offences including abduction, torture and murder. Public opposition to the former military regime was strengthened by the discovery and exhumation of hundreds of unmarked graves throughout the country. It was believed that between 15,000 and 30,000 people had disappeared during the so-called 'dirty war' between the former military regime and its opponents from 1976 until 1983. In December the Government announced the formation of the National Commission on the Disappearance of Persons (CONADEP) to investigate the events of the 'dirty war'. A report by CONADEP, published in September 1984, gave details of 8,960 people who had disappeared during the 'dirty war' and implicated 1,300 officers of the armed forces in the campaign of repression and violence. In October President Alfonsín announced that the court martial of the former leaders would be transferred to the civilian Federal Court of Appeal.

The trial of the former leaders began in April 1985. Several hundred prosecution witnesses gave testimonies which revealed the systematic atrocities and the campaign of terror perpetrated by the former military leaders. The verdicts on the nine accused officers were announced in December 1985. Four of the accused were acquitted, but sentences were passed on the remaining five, including sentences of life imprisonment for two former junta members, Gen. Videla and Adm. Eduardo Massera. The public response to the verdicts was generally one of dissatisfaction; many people believed that the sentences were too lenient. Furthermore, there remained for the Government the problem of its policy towards the several hundred lower-ranking officers who were also under suspicion of violations of human rights.

The court martial of the members of the junta which had held power during the Falklands war was conducted concurrently with the trial of the former military leaders. In May 1986 all three members of that junta were found guilty of negligence and received prison sentences, including a term of 12 years for Galtieri. In July 1988 an appeal by Galtieri and five other military leaders against their sentences began at the civilian Federal Court of Appeals. In late October the Court announced its decision to uphold the sentence against Galtieri.

Public approval of the Government's policies was reflected in the results of the national and local elections in November 1985. At the elections for one-half of the seats in the Chamber of Deputies, the UCR received 43.5% of the votes and increased its strength by one seat. In January 1986 President Alfonsín announced the formation of an 18-member advisory body, the Consejo para la Consolidación de la Democracia, which was to advise the Government on the proposed reform of the Constitution. In May the President announced plans to transfer the capital of Argentina from Buenos Aires to the twin towns of Viedma-Carmen de Patagones, about 750 km south of the present capital. The announcement aroused considerable controversy, principally because such a move was expected to cost in excess of US $3,000m. A further conflict broke out with the Roman Catholic Church over the administration's plans to legalize divorce, which had been overwhelmingly approved by the Chamber of Deputies in August. Following some amendment, the legislation was eventually approved in June 1987.

In late 1986 the Government sought approval for the Punto Final ('Full Stop') Law, whereby civil and military courts were to begin new judicial proceedings against members of the armed forces accused of violations of human rights within a 60-day period, ending on 22 February 1987. The legislation provoked widespread opposition but was, nevertheless, approved by the Senate in December. In early 1987 Adm. Ramón Arosa, the Navy Chief of Staff, warned the Government that more trials of military personnel would further undermine military morale. His warning was seemingly vindicated when, in April, a series of rebellions broke out at army garrisons throughout the country. The most serious insurrection occurred at the Campo Mayo base and involved more than 100 middle-ranking officers, who proclaimed their opposition to the Government's policy on the prosecution of members of the armed forces, and demanded a general amnesty and changes in the High Command. News of the mutinies caused an internal crisis which abated only following the personal intervention of President Alfonsín. Although the rebellions were resolved without incident, many observers considered that the President had made significant concessions to the rebel officers, a view supported by the Government's disclosure, in May, of new legislation governing violations of human rights, known as the Obediencia Debida ('Due Obedience') Law. Under the legislation, an amnesty was to be declared for all members of the armed forces below the rank of colonel. By June the legislation had been approved by the Senate and the Supreme Court, and had been extended to absolve all military and police officers holding the rank of Brigadier-General. Therefore, under the new law, of the 350–370 officers hitherto due to face prosecution for violations of human rights, only 30–50 senior officers were now to be tried.

The legislation provoked great controversy, and was a decisive factor in the ruling party's appeal to voters at the gubernatorial and legislative elections of 6 September 1987, when voting was held for 127 seats in the Chamber of Deputies, 22 provincial governorships, more than 700 provincial legislative seats and more than 10,000 municipal posts. The Partido Justicialista made significant gains, while the UCR suffered an unexpected and severe defeat, losing its overall majority in the lower house and five of the seven provincial governorships that it had previously held, including the key governorship of Buenos Aires province.

The UCR's defeat also attributed to its imposition, in July 1987, of an unpopular programme of strict austerity measures. Following the elections, however, further stringent measures were introduced to reverse the economic decline, which immediately led to protests by the powerful trade union, the Confederación General del Trabajo (CGT). Since 1984 the CGT had held a series of general strikes in protest at the Government's economic policy, and two further strikes were organized in early November and December, leaving the Government's plans for a 'Pacto de Garantías', a new social and economic accord with the trade unions and Peronists, in jeopardy.

In January 1988 the administration was again placed under pressure by military unrest, when Lt-Col Aldo Rico, a leading figure in the insurrection of April 1987 (see above), staged a rebellion at the garrison town of Monte Caseros. The Government acted swiftly to curb the unrest, and after three days the revolt was quashed. More than 330 rebels, nearly all members of the army, were detained. Although the Government appeared to have regained the initiative in its struggle to contain dissent within the armed forces, relations between the administration and the forces as a whole remained delicate, principally because of military resentment at low salaries and a reduction in government expenditure on defence. Moreover, the unresolved fate of the 36 senior officers, still awaiting trial under the Obediencia Debida Law for alleged violations of human rights, was a continual source of disquiet within military circles.

ARGENTINA

In July 1988 the UCR and the Partido Justicialista selected their candidates for the forthcoming presidential election. Contrary to expectations, Carlos Saúl Menem, a firm advocate of the traditional Peronist ideology and policies, defeated the party's president, Antonio Cafiero, in an internal poll for the candidature. Menem's main opponent at the election was expected to be Eduardo César Angeloz, presidential candidate of the UCR. The presidential election was scheduled for May 1989, with the transfer of power due to take place in December 1989. In view of the proximity of the electoral contest, President Alfonsín announced, in September 1988, the postponement of his proposed reform of the Constitution. This decision represented a severe disappointment for the Alfonsín administration, which had frequently sought, but ultimately failed to secure, any consensus with the other political parties on this issue. This set-back, coupled with mounting opposition to the Government's economic policy, contributed to the climate of dissatisfaction and uncertainty (exacerbated by a further army mutiny in December), which seemed likely to dominate the final phase of Alfonsín's presidency.

For many years, Argentina had a territorial dispute with Chile over three small islands in the Beagle Channel, south of Tierra del Fuego. In January 1979 the two countries agreed to accept an offer of mediation from the Pope. The Vatican proposals of December 1980, which awarded the disputed islands to Chile, were rejected in March 1981 by the Argentine Government, which continued to threaten military action in 1983. The civilian government which came to power in December 1983 was in favour of accepting the proposals, and signed a declaration of peace and friendship with Chile in January 1984, pending a more detailed settlement of the dispute. In October it was announced that the two countries had reached a broad agreement which guaranteed Argentine rights over deposits of petroleum and other minerals in the disputed waters in the South Atlantic. In November the treaty was approved by a national referendum and by the Senate. In May 1985 the treaty was formally ratified by representatives of the Argentine and Chilean Governments.

Government

Argentina comprises a Federal District, 23 provinces and the National Territory of Tierra del Fuego.

Legislative power is vested in the bicameral Congress: the Chamber of Deputies has 254 members, elected by universal adult suffrage for a term of four years (with one-half of the seats renewable every two years), while the Senate has 46 members, nominated by provincial legislatures for a term of nine years (with one-third of the seats renewable every three years). Executive power is vested in the President, elected by an electoral college for a six-year term. Each province has its own elected Governor and legislature, concerned with all matters not delegated to the Federal Government.

Defence

A period of national service is compulsory for men between the ages of 18 and 45 years. The length of service is 6–12 months in the army, 12 months in the air force and 14 months in the navy; some conscripts may serve less. The total strength of the regular armed forces in June 1988 was 95,000 (including 40,000 conscripts), of which the army had 55,000 with a further 250,000 trained reservists, the navy had 25,000 and the air force 15,000 men. There were also paramilitary forces numbering 18,000 men. Defence expenditure for 1988 was estimated to be 4,400m. australes.

Economic Affairs

Argentina has experienced economic decline in recent years. In 1987, according to estimates by the World Bank, the country's gross national product (GNP), measured at average 1985–87 prices, was US $74,490m., equivalent to $2,370 per head. Between 1980 and 1987, it was estimated, GNP declined, in real terms, at an average annual rate of 0.4%, with real GNP per head falling by 1.9% per year.

Argentina is rich in natural resources. The agricultural sector (including livestock and fishing) accounted for about 70% of export revenue and 14.6% of gross domestic product (GDP) in 1986. The principal crops are wheat, maize, oilseeds, sorghum, soybeans and sugar. The Government planned to increase the annual output of grain crops by 30% between 1984 and 1989 by introducing a programme of pesticides, new machinery, fertilizers and new crop species. Argentina is one of the world's major exporters of wheat and other cereals. In recent years, however, falling world prices and increased competition from sales of subsidized grain by other countries have caused the sector to decline. Between 1984 and 1986 Argentina lost $2,100m. in export earnings as a result of falling grain prices. In 1980 the USSR signed an agreement to import a minimum of 4.5m. metric tons of grain and 60,000 metric tons of beef annually until 1985. In 1986 the USSR agreed to the renewal of (substantially reduced) imports of Argentine wheat for five years. Flooding in late 1985 caused extensive damage to crops; the wheat crop declined from 13.2m. metric tons in 1884 to 8.7m. tons in 1985 and 8.9m. tons in 1986. Further declines were also recorded in the production of linseed, soybeans and sorghum, and gross agricultural production fell by 3.5% in 1985. Total plantings of cereals and oilseeds increased in 1987: wheat sowings amounted to more than 4.8m. ha, and linseed sowings increased to 675,000 ha. However, a period of drought during the first half of 1988 resulted in a reduction in sowings in that year. The area planted with wheat declined to an estimated 4.4m. ha, and linseed plantings fell to some 621,000 ha. In July 1987, the Government announced plans to eliminate or reduce export taxes on selected agricultural products, but this decision was not expected to provide any short-term benefits for the sector, which has continued to suffer from the mounting costs of raw materials, high interest rates and depressed prices. Argentina's low trade surplus of an estimated $2,123m., registered in 1986, was caused, mainly, by a decline of 26% in the value of agricultural exports. Severe flooding in 1987 adversely affected the harvest. However, some improvement was expected in 1988, when exports of cereals were expected to reach 23.7m. tons. In addition, the agricultural sector was expected to benefit from the increase in world prices for cereals, prompted by the drought in US farming areas. Export earnings for the sector were projected to rise from some $3,000m. in 1987 to $5,000m. in 1988 and $7,000m. in 1989.

In recent years the importance of beef to the Argentine economy has declined significantly; beef exports are now no more than 25% of their peak, recorded in the 1920s, and they contribute only 5% of export revenue. The number of cattle fell from 61m. in 1977 to 52.5m. in 1986. The decline in herds, coupled with the Argentinians' exceptionally high consumption of beef per head, have contributed to speculation that Argentina may become a net importer of beef by the 1990s. Intense competition from Brazil and Uruguay and subsidized meat produced in the EEC have been particularly damaging to the sector. Other agricultural exports include dairy produce, cotton and wool.

In 1985 the Government announced plans for increased investment in the agricultural sector over the following five years. In 1986 the World Bank agreed to lend $350m. to Argentina to facilitate the reform of the agricultural sector by reducing agricultural taxes, in order to increase exports and to reduce costs for producers. In 1988 the World Bank allocated a loan of $106.5m. to assist the development of the sector. In July 1986 Argentina signed a two-year fishing agreement with the USSR and Bulgaria, whereby the Soviet and Bulgarian fleets obtained access to Argentine territorial waters, including the disputed waters around the Falkland Islands. In October, however, the British Government announced plans unilaterally to extend its fishing limits around the Falkland Islands to 150 nautical miles (278 km) from February 1987.

Industry has been one of the sectors most severely affected by the recession. Employment in manufacturing contracted by 36.4% between 1974 and 1983, while production was affected by a shortage of raw materials and by debts, together with a sharp drop in domestic demand. Industrial output declined by an estimated 23% between 1974 and 1985. However, certain sectors, such as chemicals, textiles, pulp and paper, began to increase production in 1983, as a result of cuts in imports. The output of motor cars, which had shrunk from 218,600 in 1980 to 106,890 in 1982, continued to fluctuate; production was estimated at 166,000 in 1987. It was reported that the sector was experiencing a severe economic recession in 1987–88. The manufacturing sector began to recover during the last quarter of 1985, led by the capital goods industries. In 1986 the industrial sector as a whole grew by 12.8%. In early 1987 the Government introduced a series of measures to reduce costs, to increase investment and productivity, and to encourage the growth of small and medium-sized companies.

ARGENTINA

Introductory Survey

In 1978, for the first time, foreign oil companies were allowed to drill for petroleum in Argentina. By 1982 the state oil company, Yacimientos Petrolíferos Fiscales (YPF), had extended its operations as far south as Tierra del Fuego and to the west central provinces from Mendoza to Neuquén. The major oilfield is at Comodoro Rivadavia in the south, discovered in 1907, and providing over 30% of national output. Argentina's petroleum refining capacity in 1983 was 700,000 barrels per day (b/d), of which 430,000 b/d was under YPF's control. The major refining installations are at La Plata and Luján de Cujo. Argentina's proven reserves of petroleum amount to 2,428m. barrels. In 1985 the Government announced plans to encourage foreign investment in the sector, in order to increase production by 30%. Although foreign investors were thought to have been deterred by the decline in world petroleum prices, in August 1986 YPF agreed terms on an exploration project with a consortium of foreign companies, including Esso and Chevron. An important site for exploration is the offshore field at Tierra del Fuego; in October 1987 it was announced that Total was to undertake extensive exploration work in the region. It has been estimated that US $30,000m. must be invested in the sector from 1985 until 2000 if Argentina is to remain self-sufficient in petroleum and generate exports. In 1986 production averaged 433,425 b/d, less than 40% of national petroleum consumption, and in 1987 a further decline in production prompted Argentina to import petroleum, amounting to 1m. cu m, for the first time in 25 years. In 1987 YPF's operating losses and overseas debt amounted to an estimated $4,000m. The company's poor performance in recent years was an important factor in the Government's decision, in April 1988, to permit private-sector companies to operate in Argentine oil fields, where hitherto YPF had been the sole operator.

In 1988 the Neuba Dos gas pipeline (1,477 km in length) was inaugurated, linking fields in Neuquén, where there are proven reserves of 700,000m. cu m of natural gas, to Buenos Aires. Gas production averaged 19,000m. cu m per year in 1986. In early 1988 extensive gas and oil fields were discovered off Tierra del Fuego; the gas find was estimated to total 160,000m. cu m. Under a contract signed in 1972, Bolivia exports 5.7m. cu m of natural gas per day to Argentina. Coal output rose by 3.5% in 1982, to 515,000 metric tons, providing 40% of domestic requirements, but fell to an estimated 400,000 tons in 1985. The Alfonsín Government undertook a programme of development in the mining industry, which recorded a growth rate of only 0.4% between 1979 and 1983. In late 1987 the Government announced plans to seek overseas investors to participate in the development of recently discovered steam and lignite coal reserves. Moreover, reserves of steam coal rose to 752.3m. tons, following the discovery of new fields in Patagonia. In December 1983 work began on the Yacyretá hydroelectric project on the Paraná, jointly undertaken with Paraguay, which is expected to cost US $6,000m. Yacyretá is scheduled to have a generating capacity of 2,700 MW, and should be the second largest hydroelectric scheme in the world when it becomes fully operational in 1997. The Salto Grande project with Uruguay, 340 km north of Buenos Aires, was completed in 1982: Argentina takes 82% of production, totalling some 6,400m. kWh per year. In 1988 a hydroelectric complex with a capacity of 2,100 MW was under construction at Piedra del Aguila, on the Limay river, and was expected to contribute 9% of Argentina's energy requirements. In 1985 hydroelectric power provided 45% of Argentina's electricity requirements.

Argentina is the leading nuclear power in Latin America. There are proven reserves of 30,000 metric tons of uranium concentrates. The Atucha I nuclear power station (capacity 640 MW) came into operation in 1974, and the Embalse Río Tercero 600 MW reactor in Córdoba went 'on stream' in March 1983. Atucha II (capacity 690 MW) due to begin operating in 1993; two more 380 MW reactors were also planned, and were to begin operations in 1997 and 2000. In 1984 the Government implemented a programme of spending cuts in the nuclear power sector, which have led to delays in construction and a decline in development. Argentina aims to have a capacity of 4,500 MW in nuclear-generated power by the end of the century. Argentina has so far resisted strong international pressure, principally from the USA, to sign the Treaty on the Non-Proliferation of Nuclear Weapons and to ratify the Treaty of Tlatelolco (see p. 59).

On taking office in December 1983, the civilian Government inherited a major economic crisis from the military regime. Argentina's GDP, measured in constant prices, had fallen by 5.9% in 1981 and by 5.7% in 1982. By 1983 inflation had reached 433.7% and Argentina's total foreign debt was estimated to be US $43,600m., with outstanding interest payments of $2,700m. dating from the last quarter of 1983. The Government immediately introduced a series of price controls and made a commitment to lowering unemployment and to raising real wages. In January 1985 the Government revealed details of its five-year economic plan, which based its strategy for Argentina's economic recovery on an increase in exports. In spite of the plan's commitment to fiscal and financial reform and to a reduction in public spending (policies which formed part of the existing agreement between the IMF and Argentina), the IMF announced the suspension of its aid programme to Argentina in March. The Fund's action had been prompted by the Government's failure to control inflation and by its reluctance to use foreign reserves to reduce arrears on the foreign debt of $48,400m. In an attempt to reach a new agreement with the IMF, President Alfonsín announced further austerity measures in May, as part of the Government's 'war economy' policy. In June the Government, under pressure to reach an agreement with the IMF and alarmed at the rise in the annual rate of inflation to 1,128.9%, announced a new and much stricter austerity programme, known as the Austral Plan, which marked a radical departure from the administration's hitherto restrained approach. The programme's aims were to reduce inflation, to increase revenues and to cut public expenditure. A new unit of currency, the austral (equivalent to 1,000 pesos argentinos), was introduced, and a 90-day 'freeze' on prices and wages was imposed. In spite of opposition to the programme from the Peronists and the CGT, the Government was able to claim some measure of success: the annual rate of inflation declined from 688% in 1984 to 385% in 1985.

In February 1986 the Government announced the introduction of the second phase of the Austral Plan, which emphasized the administration's commitment to the modernization of the economy and to the attainment of economic growth. One controversial aspect of the new phase was the proposed 'privatization' of some of the 353 state-owned manufacturing companies, principally in the steel and petrochemical sectors. The Government hoped that privatization would reduce Argentina's foreign debt of more than US $50,000m. by eliminating a proportion of the $11,000m. owed by public sector companies. Further amendments to the Austral Plan were announced in April, including a 3.75% devaluation of the austral (to be followed by further small devaluations).

In February 1987 the Government launched its second Austral Plan, which was intended to correct the deficiencies of the first plan and, in particular, to curb inflation, mainly by imposing a 'freeze' on wages and prices. However, in July, only a few weeks prior to the crucial gubernatorial and legislative elections, the Government announced a further series of economic measures, specifically designed to reduce the public-sector deficit. The Government's unpopular decision to impose austerity measures proved costly for the UCR at the elections, but, despite calls for the resignation of its economic team, the Government seemed committed to its economic programme. However, a new set of wide-ranging economic measures, including a new 'freeze' on wages and prices, a limited privatization programme, the introduction of a two-tier system for the foreign exchange rate and an end to regulated bank interest rates, was introduced in October and appeared to signal the end of the Austral Plan. The new measures had been prompted, in part, by the dramatic increase in the monthly rate of inflation in October, when retail prices rose by 19.5% and wholesale prices by 30.4%. Despite the failure of the Austral Plan and continuing disagreement with the trade unions, the annual rate of GDP growth recovered from −4.5% in 1985 to 5.7% in 1986.

In January 1987 Argentina reached a preliminary agreement with the IMF on a stand-by credit of $1,350m. and funding of SDR 519m. to cover a shortfall in export earnings in 1986. In March Argentina reached agreement with its creditor banks on the rescheduling of about $30,000m. in outstanding debt and on new funds of $1,950m. In May the World Bank allocated a loan of $500m. to Argentina and disclosed plans for further lending of $2,000m. in 1987–88. Also in May, Argentina's Paris Club creditors assented to the rescheduling of $2,100m. in debts; the accord represented a significant concession to Argentina, as it provided for the rescheduling of 100% of principal and interest payments falling due between 1986 and 1988. The accord was contingent on Argentina's ability to fulfil the terms of its agreement with the IMF; by October it was apparent that the Fund's economic targets would not be achieved, and the IMF delayed disbursement of some $215m., a move which, in turn, resulted in a refusal by Argentina's commercial bank creditors to release $500m. in new funds. In November, however, following talks between the Government and the IMF, the IMF approved the Government's new economic programme.

In March 1988 the IMF resumed the disbursement of funds to Argentina. However, relations with the IMF and international creditor banks remained precarious, in the light of a relatively poor economic performance in 1987: inflation increased to 174.8%, and GDP grew by only 1.6%. In mid-1988 the Government announced plans to seek funding of US $4,700m., including $1,500m. from the IMF, to cover the fiscal deficit in 1988 and interest payments in 1988–89. In August the Government launched a new economic programme, the 'Primavera' Plan, under which the commercial rate of the austral was devalued by 11.42%, public spending was to be cut by $500m. in 1988, some 30,000 civil servants were to be offered voluntary retirement, and a 'freeze' on salary and prices was to be imposed. The new measures were favourably received by the international financial community but not by Argentina's trade unions. During a general strike in September, held in protest at the economic programme, violent clashes occurred between the police and demonstrators, and further industrial unrest was anticipated. However, in the same month, the World Bank confirmed the allocation of $1,250m. in funds for Argentina, mainly conditional on a reduction in the public sector deficit. Moreover, the Government was confident of securing further financing from other international sources.

In early 1988 Argentina and Spain reached agreement on a 'Special Co-operation' Treaty, under which Argentina was to receive US $3,000m. in aid and investment projects over a period of three years.

Argentina's balance of payments has recently been characterized by a growing trade surplus, rising from US $712m. in 1981 to $3,982m. in 1984. However, because of a large deficit on services (including interest payments), the current deficit in 1984 was $2,495m. Following a trade surplus of $4,582m. in 1985, a substantial increase in imports, to $4,714m., and a fall in exports, to $6,837m., resulted in a reduced trade surplus of $2,123m. in 1986. In 1987 the trade surplus was reported to have declined to less than $1,000m., principally as a result of low world prices for Argentina's agricultural goods. However, some improvement was forecast for 1988, and a trade surplus of $2,200m. was anticipated.

During 1988 the Government attempted to extend its privatization programme, prompted by the need to curb excessive public spending: in 1987 the public-sector deficit was estimated at US $2,210m. In 1988 the Government announced plans to privatize two television channels, 15 radio stations and the shipping company, ELMA. Two other major projects were the proposed sale of a 40% stake in Aerolíneas Argentinas to the Scandinavian airline, SAS, and that of an equivalent stake in the Empresa Nacional de Telecomunicaciones (Entel) to a Spanish concern, the Compañía Telefónica Nacional de España. The Aerolíneas Argentinas sale, in particular, aroused considerable controversy, and it seemed unlikely that legislation concerning the privatization would be approved by Congress, where it was strongly opposed by the Peronists.

In August 1986 Argentina and Brazil signed a trade pact which was expected to have significant economic and political implications for trade integration in the region. Under the terms of the agreement, economic links between the two countries were to be founded on extensive co-operation in the development of high-technology industries; energy, communications and transport links were to be improved, and trading between the countries was to be on a balanced basis, with preferential treatment for industrial and agricultural products from each country. Specific projects included the formation of a customs union, the purchase by Brazil of 1.3m. tons of Argentine wheat annually over the following five years and the construction of a jointly-financed hydroelectric plant at Garabí on the River Uruguay. In April 1988 Argentina and Brazil signed a further 22 accords to extend the process of economic integration, including a significant agreement to share information on the development of nuclear technology.

Social Welfare

Social welfare benefits fall into three categories: retirement, disability and survivors' pensions; family allowances; and health insurance. The first is administered by the Subsecretaría de Seguridad Social (part of the Ministry of Social Welfare) and funded by compulsory contributions from all workers, employed and self-employed, over 18 years of age. The second is supervised by the Subsecretaría and funded by employers. The third is administered by means of public funds and may be provided only by authorized public institutions. Work insurance is the responsibility of the employer. Expenditure by the central government on social security and welfare represented 33% of total government spending in 1985, while expenditure on health services accounted for a further 1.3%.

In 1975 there were 48,693 physicians working in Argentina, equivalent to one for every 530 inhabitants: the best doctor-patient ratio of any country in Latin America.

Education

Education from pre-school to university level is available free of charge. Education is officially compulsory for all children at primary level, between the ages of six and 14 years. Secondary education lasts for between four and six years, depending on the type of course: the normal certificate of education (bachillerato) course lasts for five years, whereas a course leading to a commercial bachillerato may last for four or five years, and one leading to a technical or agricultural bachillerato lasts for six years. Non-university higher education, usually leading to a teaching qualification, is for three or four years, while university courses last for four years or more. There are 29 state universities and 23 private universities.

According to census results, the average rate of adult illiteracy declined from 7.4% in 1970 to only 6.1% (males 5.7%, females 6.4%) in 1980. According to estimates by UNESCO, the illiteracy rate in 1985 was only 4.5%. The total enrolment at primary and secondary schools in 1985 was equivalent to 94% of the school-age population.

Public Holidays

1989: 2 January (for New Year's Day), 1 April (Good Friday), 1 May 1989: 2 January (for New Year's Day), 24 March (Good Friday), 1 May (Labour Day), 25 May (Anniversary of the 1810 Revolution), 10 June (Occupation of the Islas Malvinas), 20 June (Flag Day), 10 July (Independence Day), 17 August (Death of Gen. José de San Martín), 12 October (Discovery of America), 25 December (Christmas).

1990: 1 January (New Year's Day), 13 April (Good Friday), 1 May (Labour Day), 25 May (Anniversary of the 1810 Revolution), 10 June (Occupation of the Islas Malvinas), 20 June (Flag Day), 10 July (Independence Day), 17 August (Death of Gen. José de San Martín), 12 October (Discovery of America), 25 December (Christmas).

Weights and Measures

The metric system is in force.

ARGENTINA

Statistical Survey

Statistical Survey

Sources (unless otherwise stated): Instituto Nacional de Estadística y Censos, Hipólito Yrigoyen 250, 12°, Of. 1210, 1310 Buenos Aires; tel. (1) 33-7872; telex 21952; and Banco Central de la República Argentina, Reconquista 266, 1003 Buenos Aires; tel. (1) 394-8111; telex 1137.

Area and Population

AREA, POPULATION AND DENSITY

Area (sq km)	2,766,889*
Population (census results)†	
30 September 1970	23,362,204
22 October 1980	
Males	13,755,983
Females	14,191,463
Total	27,947,446
Population (official estimates at mid-year)	
1985	30,563,833
1986	31,029,694
1987	31,497,000
Density (per sq km) at mid-1987	11.4

* 1,068,302 sq miles. The figure excludes the Falkland Islands (Islas Malvinas) and Antarctic territory claimed by Argentina.
† Figures exclude adjustment for underenumeration, estimated to have been 1% at the 1980 census.

PROVINCES (census of 22 October 1980)

	Population	Capital
Buenos Aires—Federal District	2,922,829	
Buenos Aires—Province	10,865,408	La Plata
Catamarca	207,717	Catamarca
Córdoba	2,407,754	Córdoba
Corrientes	661,454	Corrientes
Chaco	701,392	Resistencia
Chubut	263,116	Rawson
Entre Ríos	908,313	Paraná
Formosa	295,887	Formosa
Jujuy	410,008	Jujuy
La Pampa	208,260	Santa Rosa
La Rioja	164,217	La Rioja
Mendoza	1,196,228	Mendoza
Misiones	588,977	Posadas
Neuquén	243,850	Neuquén
Río Negro	383,354	Viedma
Salta	662,870	Salta
San Juan	465,976	San Juan
San Luis	214,416	San Luis
Santa Cruz	114,941	Río Gallegos
Santa Fé	2,465,546	Santa Fé
Santiago del Estero	594,920	Santiago del Estero
Tucumán	972,655	Tucumán
Territory		
Tierra del Fuego	27,358	Ushuaia

PRINCIPAL TOWNS (population at 1980 census)

Buenos Aires (capital)	2,922,829*	Mar del Plata	414,696
Córdoba	983,969	Santa Fé	291,966
Rosario	957,301	San Juan	291,707
Mendoza	605,623	Bahía Blanca	223,818
La Plata	564,750	Resistencia	220,104
San Miguel de		Corrientes	180,612
Tucumán	498,579	Paraná	161,638

* The population of the metropolitan area was 9,967,826.

BIRTHS AND DEATHS

	Registered live births		Registered deaths	
	Number	Rate (per 1,000)	Number	Rate (per 1,000)
1980	697,461	24.7	241,125	8.5
1981	680,292	23.7	241,898	8.4
1982	663,429	22.8	233,071	8.0
1983	655,876	22.1	251,301	8.5

Marriages: 161,422 (marriage rate 5.6 per 1,000) in 1981; 177,010 (marriage rate 6.0 per 1,000) in 1983.
Source: UN, mainly *Demographic Yearbook*.

ECONOMICALLY ACTIVE POPULATION*
(persons aged 14 years and over, census of 22 October 1980)

	Males	Females	Total
Agriculture, hunting, forestry and fishing	1,123,138	77,854	1,200,992
Mining and quarrying	44,194	2,977	47,171
Manufacturing	1,566,028	429,967	1,985,995
Electricity, gas and water	94,789	8,467	103,256
Construction	981,251	21,924	1,003,175
Wholesale and retail trade, restaurants and hotels	1,221,063	481,017	1,702,080
Transport, storage and communication	424,671	35,805	460,476
Finance, insurance, real estate and business services	265,475	130,229	395,704
Community, social and personal services	1,044,416	1,354,623	2,399,039
Activities not adequately described	494,678	196,624	691,302
Total labour force	7,249,703	2,739,487	9,989,190

* Figures exclude persons seeking work for the first time, totalling 44,608 (males 28,331; females 16,277).

Source: ILO, *Year Book of Labour Statistics*.

Mid-1985 (official estimates): Total labour force 11,467,983 (males 8,375,912; females 3,092,071).

ARGENTINA

Agriculture

PRINCIPAL CROPS ('000 metric tons)

	1984	1985	1986
Wheat	13,200	8,700	8,900
Rice (paddy)	476	410	405
Barley	238	118	190*
Maize	9,500	11,530	12,400
Rye	140	105	94
Oats	610	400	560*
Millet	136	140	240
Sorghum	6,930	6,200	4,200
Potatoes	2,118	2,000†	2,100†
Sweet potatoes	325	377	149
Cassava (Manioc)†	140	140	140
Soybeans	7,000	6,500	7,100
Groundnuts (in shell)	329	229	205
Sunflower seed	2,200	3,430	4,200
Linseed	550	500	565*
Seed cotton	610	536	340†
Cotton lint	180	171	109
Tomatoes	589	751	750†
Onions (dry)	291	290†	290†
Grapes	2,746	2,279	2,750†
Sugar cane	15,468	14,300	14,000*
Tea (green)	41	47	47†
Tobacco (leaves)	75	61	66*

* Estimate. † FAO estimate.

Source: FAO, *Production Yearbook*.

LIVESTOCK ('000 head, year ending September)

	1984	1985	1986
Horses*	2,900	3,000	3,000
Cattle	54,594	54,000*	53,000*
Pigs*	3,800	3,800	4,000
Sheep*	33,800	29,441	29,243
Goats†	3,098	3,100	3,100

Chickens (million): 42 in 1984; 42† in 1985; 45† in 1986.
Ducks (million): 2 in 1984; 2† in 1985; 2† in 1986.
Turkeys (million): 3 in 1984; 3† in 1985; 3† in 1986.

* Estimate. † FAO estimate.

Source: FAO, *Production Yearbook*.

LIVESTOCK PRODUCTS ('000 metric tons)

	1984	1985	1986
Beef and veal	2,548	2,760*	2,800*
Mutton and lamb*	109	104	91
Goats' meat†	6	6	6
Pig meat	235*	240*	245†
Horse meat†	50	50	51
Poultry meat	381†	372	382
Cows' milk*	5,200	5,823	6,200
Butter	28	33	33*
Cheese	212	215	245
Hen eggs	270*	274†	279†
Wool:			
greasy*	153	140	138
scoured*	102	95	92
Cattle hides (fresh)†	369	411	414

* Estimate. † FAO estimate.

Source: FAO, *Production Yearbook*.

Forestry

ROUNDWOOD REMOVALS
('000 cubic metres, excl. bark)

	1984	1985	1986
Sawlogs, veneer logs and logs for sleepers	1,935	1,935*	1,935*
Pulpwood	3,043	3,043*	3,043*
Other industrial wood	436	436	436
Fuel wood	5,900	6,483*	7,148*
Total	11,314	11,897	12,562

* FAO estimates.

Source: FAO, *Yearbook of Forest Products*.

SAWNWOOD PRODUCTION
('000 cubic metres, incl. boxboards)

	1982	1983	1984
Coniferous (soft wood)	269	304	175
Broadleaved (hard wood)	856	866	846
Total	1,125	1,170	1,021

Railway sleepers: 96,000 cubic metres in 1984.
1985–86: Annual production as in 1984 (FAO estimates).
Source: FAO, *Yearbook of Forest Products*.

Fishing

('000 metric tons, live weight)

	1984	1985	1986
Freshwater fishes	9.3	9.6	8.5
Argentine hake	183.2	259.3	270.6
Other marine fishes	67.1	102.8	119.4
Crustaceans	23.4	10.6	7.3
Argentine shortfin squid	29.0	21.5	12.5
Other molluscs	2.8	2.6	2.0
Total catch	314.8	406.4	420.3

Source: FAO, *Yearbook of Fishery Statistics*.

Mining

('000 metric tons, unless otherwise indicated)

	1983	1984*	1985*
Hard coal	485.8	509.0	400.0
Crude petroleum ('000 cu metres)	28,474	24,637	23,634
Natural gas ('000 terajoules)*	457	478	570
Iron ore*†	390	346	367
Lead ore*†	31.7	28.5	28.6
Zinc ore*†	36.6	34.9	36.4
Tin concentrates (metric tons)*†	291	274	451
Silver ore (metric tons)*†	78	62	68
Uranium ore (metric tons)*†	179	129	170‡

* Source: UN, *Industrial Statistics Yearbook*.
† Figures refer to the metal content of ores and concentrates.
‡ Provisional figures.

ARGENTINA

Industry

SELECTED PRODUCTS
('000 metric tons, unless otherwise indicated)

	1984	1985	1986
Edible vegetable oils	1,185.2	1,435.5	1,565.1
Wheat flour	2,753.6	2,801.0	2,761.6
Sugar	1,411.6	1,099.2	1,052.3
Beer and malt ('000 litres)	407,926	382,698	551,801
Cigarettes (metric tons)	30,843	31,092*	32,112*
Paper	764	690	799
Mechanical wood pulp	121	125	129
Chemical and semi-chemical pulp	440	458	501
Quebracho extract	66	62	n.a.
Rayon and acetate continuous filaments (metric tons)	2,127	1,424	3,619
Non-cellulosic continuous filaments (metric tons)	30,159	20,106	33,644
Non-cellulosic discontinuous fibres (metric tons)	20,868	16,616	27,008
Sulphuric acid (metric tons)	253,566	235,454	250,840
Rubber tyres ('000)	7,922	5,664	7,489
Portland cement	5,096	4,693	5,558
Crude steel	2,338	2,586	n.a.
Ferro-alloys	63	59	n.a.
Diesel oil ('000 cu metres)	1,098	1,031	962
Fuel oil ('000 cu metres)	6,229	6,126	5,736
Gas oil ('000 cu metres)	7,844	8,053	7,860
Kerosene ('000 cu metres)	566	518	514
Passenger motor vehicles (number)	142,188	119,733	147,063
Commercial motor vehicles (number)	28,513	21,365	28,835
Domestic sewing machines (number)	41,496	31,778*	n.a.
Refrigerators and washing machines (number)	429,577	271,150	378,200
Television receivers (number)	430,090	599,255	800,975
Plastic footwear ('000 pairs)	1,570	n.a.	n.a.

* Provisional figures.

Finance

CURRENCY AND EXCHANGE RATES

Monetary Units:
100 centavos = 1 austral (A).

Denominations:
Coins: 1, 5, 10 and 50 centavos.
Notes: 1, 5, 10, 50 and 100 australes.

Sterling and Dollar Equivalents (30 September 1988)
£1 sterling = 20.155 australes;
US $1 = 11.960 australes;
100 australes = £49.62 = $83.61.

Average Exchange Rate (australes per US $)
1985	0.6018
1986	0.9430
1987	2.1443

Note: The austral was introduced on 15 June 1985, replacing the peso argentino at the rate of 1 austral = 1,000 pesos argentinos. The peso argentino, equal to 10,000 former pesos, had itself been introduced on 1 June 1983. Some figures in this survey are in terms of pesos argentinos or old pesos.

BUDGET (thousand australes)*

Revenue	1983	1984	1985
Taxation	92,855	705,006	7,484,492
Taxes on income, profits, etc.	4,581	24,455	405,968
Social security contributions	17,983	188,800	2,241,830
Taxes on property	3,436	21,077	403,087
Value-added tax	13,822	93,495	1,141,502
Excises	25,621	228,344	1,850,342
Other domestic taxes on goods and services	1,481	11,462	105,974
Import duties, etc.	6,726	34,313	328,598
Export duties	9,504	60,516	774,045
Foreign exchange conversion tax	935	5,194	51,734
Stamp duties	380	624	93,615
Other tax revenue	8,386	36,726	87,797
Property income	1,273	15,817	287,069
Administrative fees and charges, etc.	2,064	11,058	141,773
Other current revenue	10,072	50,350	371,655
Capital revenue	57	117	1,352
Total revenue	**106,321**	**782,348**	**8,286,341**

Expenditure†	1983	1984	1985
General public services	13,040	43,329	663,576
Defence	13,531	77,993	490,873
Education	11,369	84,213	566,307
Health	2,039	16,014	119,773
Social security and welfare	49,646	334,927	3,056,401
Housing	867	4,410	39,388
Other community and social services	702	5,778	42,695
Economic services	33,847	179,483	1,730,372
General administration, regulation and research	5,530	34,022	226,905
Agriculture, forestry and fishing	1,300	7,786	65,691
Electricity, gas, steam and water	10,286	46,479	593,112
Roads	4,686	34,743	300,131
Inland and coastal waterways	882	1,061	27,848
Other transport and communications	9,997	47,271	451,101
Other purposes	40,623	120,422	2,333,090
Interest payments	17,098	120,422	1,076,832
Sub-total	**165,664**	**866,569**	**9,042,480**
Adjustment to cash basis	−16,872	19,204	338,539
Total expenditure	**148,792**	**885,773**	**9,381,019**
Current	133,623	804,744	8,583,087
Capital	15,169	81,029	797,932

* Figures refer to the consolidated accounts of the central government, including special accounts, government agencies and the national social security system. The budgets of provincial and municipal governments are excluded.
† Excluding net lending (thousand australes): 44,524 in 1983; 163,943 in 1984; 1,829,123 in 1985.

Source: IMF, *Government Finance Statistics Yearbook*.

1986 (estimate, million australes): Revenue 11,674.7; Expenditure 14,312.9.
1987 (estimate, million australes): Expenditure 28,548.5.
1988 (estimate, million australes): Revenue 83,050.4, Expenditure 116,052.9.

CENTRAL BANK RESERVES*
(US $ million at 31 December)

	1985	1986	1987
Total	3,273	2,718	1,617

* Figures exclude reserves of gold, totalling 4,372,000 troy ounces in 1985, and 4,373,000 ounces in 1986 and 1987.

Source: IMF, *International Financial Statistics*.

ARGENTINA

Statistical Survey

MONEY SUPPLY
(million australes at 31 December)

	1984	1985	1986
Currency outside banks	313.4	2,022.3	3,989.6
Demand deposits at commercial banks	121.4	992.0	1,597.9

Source: IMF, *International Financial Statistics*.

COST OF LIVING
(Consumer Price Index for Buenos Aires. Base: 1974 = 100)

	1985	1986	1987
Food and drink	80,955,909.3	160,384,935.1	373,316,515.9
Clothing	32,802,284.5	61,744,791.7	128,392,651.7
Rent, fuel and light	73,173,644.4	123,690,853.2	283,004,584.2
Domestic goods	73,927,370.3	121,569,664.5	267,107,003.2
Medical services	107,582,667.1	241,943,992.5	560,741,029.2
Transport and communications	97,461,261.2	164,729,249.7	373,415,295.4
Education	89,597,663.3	172,298,387.5	400,644,832.3
Other goods and services	96,285,001.0	179,448,333.9	446,496,441.6
All items	78,650,895.1	149,510,305.5	345,863,651.6

NATIONAL ACCOUNTS (australes at constant 1970 prices)
Expenditure on the Gross Domestic Product

	1984	1985	1986
Final consumption expenditure	8,593	8,065	8,991
Increase in stocks	−13	−124	−58
Gross fixed capital formation	1,374	1,210	1,293
Total domestic expenditure	9,954	9,151	10,226
Exports of goods and services	1,463	1,671	1,536
Less Imports of goods and services	956	837	1,102
GDP in purchasers' values	10,461	9,986	10,660

Gross Domestic Product by Economic Activity (at factor cost)

	1984	1985	1986
Agriculture, forestry and fishing	1,444	1,407	1,379
Mining and quarrying	253	245	240
Manufacturing	2,274	2,035	2,297
Construction	336	308	309
Electricity, gas and water	412	418	449
Transport and communications	1,075	1,037	1,082
Trade, restaurants and hotels	1,223	1,128	1,370
Finance	702	693	741
Other services	1,550	1,579	1,575
Total	9,268	8,847	9,444

BALANCE OF PAYMENTS (US $ million)

	1984	1985	1986
Merchandise exports f.o.b.	8,100	8,396	6,852
Merchandise imports f.o.b.	−4,118	−3,518	−4,406
Trade balance	3,982	4,878	2,446
Exports of services	1,809	1,933	1,989
Imports of services	−8,288	−7,763	−7,296
Balance of goods and services	−2,497	−952	−2,861
Unrequited transfers (net)	2	—	2
Current balance	−2,495	−952	−2,859
Direct capital investment (net)	268	919	574
Other long-term capital (net)	−1,502	665	317
Short-term capital (net)	1,297	387	573
Net errors and omissions	−55	−532	302
Total (net monetary movements)	−2,487	487	−1,093
Valuation changes	−150	−213	−93
Exceptional financing (net)	2,459	761	210
Official financing (net)	194	−219	−8
Changes in reserves	16	817	−984

Source: IMF, *International Financial Statistics*.

External Trade

PRINCIPAL COMMODITIES (distribution by BTN, US $ '000)

Imports c.i.f.	1982	1983	1984*
Vegetable products	153,138	115,399	136,052
Coffee, tea, maté, etc.	85,577	64,971	64,282
Mineral products	815,550	585,739	613,160
Metallurgical minerals, slag and cinder	91,690	73,756	77,107
Mineral fuels and oils, bituminous substances, etc.	687,864	470,055	490,076
Chemical products	920,163	942,080	1,001,067
Inorganic chemicals, compounds of precious metals, etc.	158,907	126,276	159,154
Organic chemicals and products	402,260	439,085	436,957
Artificial resins and plastics, natural and synthetic rubber, etc.	271,367	298,567	275,339
Artificial resins and plastics, cellulose, etc.	186,342	185,356	178,735
Paper-making material, paper and manufactures	198,228	139,040	90,297
Paper and paper products	99,020	95,374	57,037
Basic metals and manufactures	538,320	486,785	514,171
Iron and steel, and manufactures	375,664	356,089	370,378
Machinery and apparatus, incl. electrical	1,478,263	1,114,594	1,061,103
Boilers, machinery and mechanical appliances	903,059	738,681	668,450
Electrical machinery	575,204	375,913	392,653
Transport equipment	329,554	289,943	349,225
Land vehicles	214,855	198,978	256,215
Sea and river vehicles	31,521	25,450	1,618
Scientific and precision instruments, audiovisual equipment, etc.	196,194	171,995	156,841
Total (incl. others)	5,336,914	4,504,156	4,584,706

* Provisional figures.

ARGENTINA

Exports f.o.b.	1982	1983	1984*
Live animals and animal products	882,186	679,572	459,992
Meat and edible offal	598,786	430,084	257,012
Vegetable products	2,611,932	3,540,295	3,474,893
Edible fruits	182,455	134,009	106,420
Cereals	1,822,180	2,894,058	2,239,846
Oilseeds and nuts	459,665	365,740	952,472
Animal and vegetable fats and oils	429,326	538,157	930,482
Prepared foodstuffs, beverages and tobacco	884,478	1,148,737	1,114,117
Meat and fish preparations	207,557	173,638	148,487
Sugar and preserves	64,434	186,304	107,508
Residues and waste from food industry; prepared animal fodder	438,617	644,337	723,701
Chemical products	348,944	297,567	270,393
Hides, skins, furs, etc.	364,055	300,057	331,000
Hides and skins	298,290	264,330	304,884
Paper-making material, paper and manufactures	46,967	38,907	42,547
Textiles and manufactures	338,439	224,452	307,328
Wool and other animal hair	233,667	188,007	216,442
Cotton	91,006	25,880	79,077
Base metals and manufactures	514,100	318,358	316,324
Iron and steel and manufactures	351,332	207,201	202,457
Machinery and apparatus, incl. electrical	295,250	180,679	210,889
Boilers, machinery and mechanical appliances	250,371	152,248	177,777
Transport equipment	215,984	92,222	168,207
Land vehicles	112,242	68,351	91,765
Total (incl. others)	7,624,936	7,836,063	8,107,413

* Provisional figures.

PRINCIPAL TRADING PARTNERS (US $ '000)

Imports c.i.f.	1984	1985	1986
Austria	26,913	29,534	14,409
Belgium	98,532	70,594	148,741
Bolivia	391,745	382,860	352,741
Brazil	831,200	611,521	691,298
Canada	66,857	35,752	49,518
Chile	118,393	84,409	148,585
Colombia	24,440	24,288	69,372
Denmark	22,133	10,812	12,682
France	204,120	207,867	236,703
Germany, Federal Republic	442,544	404,001	523,375
Italy	190,480	233,880	239,469
Japan	375,870	265,580	336,618
Mexico	78,523	59,816	100,135
Netherlands	65,805	63,151	97,093
Peru	34,985	36,500	60,120
Poland	25,476	22,639	24,884
Spain	89,762	67,869	102,846
Sweden	47,952	35,956	51,133
Switzerland	99,012	103,307	92,221
USSR	35,554	41,876	51,170
USA	837,212	685,028	824,811
Uruguay	98,129	65,957	92,967
Total (incl. others)	4,584,672	3,814,148	4,724,053

Exports f.o.b.	1984	1985	1986
Belgium	207,161	148,762	190,460
Bolivia	88,224	69,252	60,478
Brazil	478,214	496,297	698,070
Canada	49,004	58,752	53,852
Chile	149,910	111,050	136,780
China, People's Republic	74,851	311,004	252,053
Colombia	60,633	132,749	60,970
Czechoslovakia	93,665	58,013	91,832
Denmark	35,211	20,658	8,430
France	132,084	122,179	102,924
Germany, Federal Republic	297,559	289,221	352,756
India	163,724	55,442	38,484
Iran	430,210	313,936	256,318
Israel	38,436	31,064	30,675
Italy	377,164	300,646	285,330
Japan	271,153	360,890	391,074
Mexico	171,542	255,472	158,356
Netherlands	892,516	856,348	735,825
Paraguay	94,431	72,236	67,443
Peru	127,945	161,968	189,125
Poland	121,508	98,197	100,749
Portugal	59,155	73,841	96,071
Spain	222,808	213,093	170,578
USSR	1,187,797	1,212,699	208,840
USA	847,887	1,003,560	677,917
Uruguay	82,913	99,017	129,322
Venezuela	113,948	72,846	44,804
Total (incl. others)	8,107,405	8,396,017	6,852,195

Transport

RAILWAYS (traffic)

	1984	1985	1986
Passengers carried (million)	291	300	359
Freight carried ('000 tons)	19,502	34,436	15,018
Passenger-km (million)	10,469	10,544	12,459
Freight ton-km (million)	11,207	18,981	8,761

Source: Ferrocarriles Argentinos.

ROAD TRAFFIC (motor vehicles in use at 31 December)

	1984	1985	1986
Passenger cars	3,685,000	3,773,600	3,898,000
Buses and coaches	56,000	57,300	59,700
Goods vehicles	1,332,000	1,338,700	1,375,000

Source: IRF, *World Road Statistics*.

SHIPPING (vessels entering Argentine ports)

	1984	1985	1986
Displacement ('000 net reg. tons)	33,618	35,605	31,026

Source: Ministerio de Obras y Servicios Públicos.

CIVIL AVIATION (traffic)

	1984	1985	1986
Passengers carried ('000)	6,378	5,869	6,749
Freight carried (tons)	74,691	76,231	89,282
Kilometres flown ('000)	80,897	86,144	94,236

ARGENTINA

Tourism

FOREIGN VISITORS BY ORIGIN

	1982	1983	1984
North and South America	1,111,026	1,114,047	1,412,968
Europe	153,243	143,878	147,108
Asia, Africa and Oceania	31,975	55,027	48,131
Total	1,296,244	1,312,952	1,608,207

Source: Dirección Nacional de Migraciones.

Communications Media

	1982	1983	1985
Radio receivers ('000 in use)	n.a.	16,000	20,000
Television receivers ('000 in use)	n.a.	5,910	6,500
Telephones ('000 in use)*	2,385	2,518	2,580†
Book production‡:			
Titles	4,962	4,216	n.a.
Copies ('000)	14,763	13,526	n.a.
Daily newspapers	191	n.a.	188†

* Source: Empresa Nacional de Telecomunicaciones.
† Figures refer to 1984.   ‡ Including pamphlets.
Source: mainly UNESCO, *Statistical Yearbook*.

Education

(1985—provisional)

	Institutions	Students	Teachers
Pre-primary	8,015	693,259	36,287
Primary	26,275	4,811,736	254,970
Secondary	5,405	1,683,520	220,003
Universities*	462	664,200	44,038
Colleges of higher education*	912	181,945	26,661
Other	4,061	255,953	20,442

Source: Ministerio de Educación y Justicia.

Directory

Note: In June 1987 Congress approved a law to transfer the federal capital from Buenos Aires to the twin towns of Viedma-Carmen de Patagones. The transfer was expected to take place between 1987 and 1995.

The Constitution

The return to civilian rule in 1983 represented a return to the principles of the 1853 Constitution, with some changes in electoral details. The Constitution is summarized below:

DECLARATIONS, RIGHTS AND GUARANTEES

Each province has the right to exercise its own administration of justice, municipal system and primary education. The Roman Catholic religion, being the faith of the majority of the nation, shall enjoy State protection; freedom of religious belief is guaranteed to all other denominations. All the inhabitants of the country have the right to work and exercise any legal trade; to petition the authorities; to leave or enter the Argentine territory; to use or dispose of their properties; to associate for a peaceable or useful purpose; to teach and acquire education, and to express freely their opinion in the press without censorship. The State does not admit any prerogative of blood, birth, privilege or titles of nobility. Equality is the basis of all duties and public offices. No citizens may be detained, except for reasons and in the manner prescribed by the law; or sentenced other than by virtue of a law existing prior to the offence and by decision of the competent tribunal after the hearing and defence of the person concerned. Private residence, property and correspondence are inviolable. No one may enter the home of a citizen or carry out any search in it without his consent, unless by a warrant from the competent authority; no one may suffer expropriation, except in case of public necessity and provided that the appropriate compensation has been paid in accordance with the provisions of the laws. In no case may the penalty of confiscation of property be imposed.

LEGISLATIVE POWER

Legislative power is vested in the bicameral Congress, comprising the Chamber of Deputies and the Senate. The Chamber of Deputies has 254 directly-elected members, chosen for four years and eligible for re-election; one-half of the membership of the Chamber shall be renewed every two years. The Senate has 46 members, chosen by provincial legislatures for a nine-year term, with one-third of the seats being renewed every three years.

The powers of Congress include regulating foreign trade; fixing import and export duties; levying taxes for a specified time whenever the defence, common safety or general welfare of the State so require; contracting loans on the nation's credit; regulating the internal and external debt and the currency system of the country; fixing the budget and providing for whatever is conducive to the prosperity and welfare of the nation. Congress also approves or rejects treaties, authorizes the Executive to declare war or make peace, and establishes the strength of the armed forces in peace and war.

EXECUTIVE POWER

Executive power is vested in the President, who is the supreme chief of the nation and handles the general administration of the country. The President issues the instructions and rulings necessary for the execution of the laws of the country, and himself takes part in drawing up and promulgating those laws. The President appoints, with the approval of the Senate, the judges of the Supreme Court and all other competent tribunals, ambassadors, civil servants, members of the judiciary and senior officers of the armed forces and bishops. The President may also appoint and remove, without reference to another body, his cabinet ministers. The President is Commander-in-Chief of all the armed forces.

JUDICIAL POWER

Judicial power is exercised by the Supreme Court and all other competent tribunals. The Supreme Court is responsible for the internal administration of all tribunals.

PROVINCIAL GOVERNMENT

The 22 States retain all the power not delegated to the Federal Government. They are governed by their own institutions and elect their own governors, legislators and officials.

The Government

HEAD OF STATE

President of the Republic: Dr Raúl Ricardo Alfonsín Foulkes (took office 10 December 1983).
Vice-President: Dr Víctor Martínez.

ARGENTINA

MINISTERS
(December 1988)

Minister of the Interior: ENRIQUE NOSIGLIA.
Minister of Foreign Affairs and Worship: Lic. DANTE CAPUTO.
Minister of Education and Justice: JORGE SÁBATO.
Minister of National Defence: HORACIO JUAN JUANARENA.
Minister of the Economy: JUAN VITAL SOURROUILLE.
Minister of Labour and Social Security: IDELER TONELLI.
Minister of Public Health and Welfare: RICARDO BARRIOS ARRECHEA.
Minister of Public Works and Services: RODOLFO TERRAGNO.
Secretary-General to the Presidency: CARLOS BECERRA.

MINISTRIES

General Secretariat to the Presidency: Balcarce 50, 1064 Buenos Aires; tel. (1) 46-9841.
Ministry of the Economy: Hipólito Yrigoyen 250, 1310 Buenos Aires; tel. (1) 34-6411; telex 21952.
Ministry of Education and Justice: Pizzurno 935, 1020 Buenos Aires; tel. 42-4551; telex 22646.
Ministry of Foreign Affairs and Worship: Reconquista 1088, 1003 Buenos Aires; tel. (1) 311-0071; telex 21194.
Ministry of the Interior: Balcarce 24, 1064 Buenos Aires; tel. (1) 46-9841.
Ministry of Labour and Social Security: Avda Julio A. Roca 609, 1067 Buenos Aires; tel. (1) 33-7888; telex 18007.
Ministry of National Defence: Avda Paseo Colón 255, 1063 Buenos Aires; tel. (1) 30-1561; telex 22200.
Ministry of Public Health and Welfare: Defensa 120, 1345 Buenos Aires; tel. (1) 30-4322; telex 25064.
Ministry of Public Works and Services: Avda 9 de Julio 1925, 1332 Buenos Aires; tel. (1) 37-1339; telex 22577.

President and Legislature

PRESIDENT

Election, 30 October 1983*

Candidates	Votes	%	Seats in electoral college
Dr RAÚL ALFONSÍN FOULKES (Unión Cívica Radical)	7,659,530	51.8	317
Dr ITALO LUDER (Partido Justicialista—Peronists)	5,936,556	40.2	259
OSCAR ALENDE (Partido Intransigente)	344,434	2.3	2
Others	838,719	5.7	22
Total	14,779,239	100.0	600

* The election on 30 October was for a 600-member presidential electoral college, which met on 30 November to elect the President.

Note: A presidential election was due to be held on 14 May 1989. The transfer of power was scheduled for 10 December 1989.

CONGRESS

Cámara de Diputados
(Chamber of Deputies)

President: Dr JUAN CARLOS PUGLIESE.
Vice-President: ROBERTO PASCUAL SILVA.

The Chamber has 254 members, who hold office for a four-year term, with one-half of the seats renewable every two years.

General Election, 6 September 1987*

	Seats
Unión Cívica Radical	117
Partido Justicialista	105
Unión del Centro Democrático	7
Partido Intransigente	5
Pacto Autonomista-Liberal	4
Partido Demócrata Cristiano	3
Partido Demócrata Progresista	2
Movimiento Popular Neuquino	2
Renovador de Salta	2
Others	7
Total	254

* The table indicates the distribution of the total number of seats, following the election for one-half of the membership.

Senado
(Senate)

President: Dr VÍCTOR MARTÍNEZ.

The 46 members of the Senate are nominated by the legislative bodies of each province (two Senators for each), with the exception of Buenos Aires, which elects its Senators by means of a special Electoral College. The Senate's term of office is nine years, with one-third of the seats renewable every three years.

Political Organizations

Alianza Federal: Buenos Aires; f. 1983; right-wing; Pres. FRANCISCO MANRIQUE.
Frente de Izquierda Popular: Buenos Aires; left-wing; Leader JORGE ABELARDO RAMOS.
Movimiento de Integración y Desarrollo (MID): Buenos Aires; f. 1963; Pres. ROGELIO FRIGERIO; 145,000 mems.
Movimiento al Socialismo (MAS): Leaders RUBÉN VISCONTI, LUIS ZAMORA; 55,000 mems.
Partido Comunista de Argentina: Buenos Aires; f. 1918; Sec.-Gen. ATHOS FAVA; 76,000 mems.
Partido Demócrata Cristiano (PDC): Buenos Aires; f. 1954; Leader (vacant); 68,000 mems.
Partido Demócrata Progresista (PDP): Chile 1934, 1227 Buenos Aires; Leader RAFAEL MARTÍNEZ RAYMONDA; 85,000 mems.
Partido Intransigente: Buenos Aires; f. 1957; left-wing; Leaders Dr OSCAR ALENDE, LISANDRO VIALE; Sec. MARIANO LORENCES; 90,000 mems.
Partido Justicialista: Buenos Aires; Peronist party; f. 1945; 3m. mems; Pres. ANTONIO CAFIERO; three factions within party:
  Frente Renovador, Justicia, Democracia y Participación—Frejudepa: f. 1985; reformist wing; Leaders CARLOS SAÚL MENEM, ANTONIO CAFIERO, CARLOS GROSSO.
  Movimiento Nacional 17 de Octubre: Leader HERMINIO IGLESIAS.
  Oficialistas: Leaders JOSÉ MARÍA VERNET, LORENZO MIGUEL.
Partido Nacional de Centro: Buenos Aires; f. July 1980; conservative; Leader RAÚL RIVANERA CARLES.
Partido Obrero: Ayacucho 444, Buenos Aires; tel. (1) 953-8433; f. 1982; Trotskyist; Leaders JORGE ALTAMIRA, CHRISTIAN RATH; 61,000 mems.
Partido Popular Cristiano: Leader JOSÉ ANTONIO ALLENDE.
Partido Socialista Democrático: Rivadavia 2307, 1034 Buenos Aires; Leader AMÉRICO GHIOLDI; 39,000 mems.
Partido Socialista Popular: f. 1982; Leaders GUILLERMO ESTÉVEZ BOERO, EDGARDO ROSSI; 60,500 mems.
Unión del Centro Democrático (UCD): Buenos Aires; f. Aug. 1980 as coalition of eight minor political organizations to challenge the 'domestic monopoly' of the populist movements; Leader ALVARO ALSOGARAY.
Unión Cívica Radical (UCR): Buenos Aires; tel. (1) 49-0036; telex 21326; moderate; f. 1890; Leader Dr RAÚL ALFONSÍN FOULKES; First Vice-Pres. CÉSAR JAROSLAVSKY; 1,410,000 mems.
Unión para la Nueva Mayoría: Buenos Aires; f. 1986; centre-right; Leader JOSÉ ANTONIO ROMERO FERIS.

Other parties and groupings include: Alianza Socialista, Confederación Socialista Argentina, Movimiento Línea Popular, Movimiento Popular Neuquino, Pacto Autonomista-Liberal, Partido Bloquista de San Juan, Partido Conservador Popular, Partido Obrero Comunista Marxista-Leninista, Partido Socialista Auténtico, Partido Socialista Unificado and Renovador de Salta.

ARGENTINA

The following political parties and guerrilla groups are illegal:

Intransigencia y Movilización Peronista: Peronist faction; Leader NILDA GARRES.

Partido Peronista Auténtico (PPA): f. 1975; Leaders MARIO FIRMENICH, ÓSCAR BIDEGAIN, RICARDO OBREGÓN CANO (in prison).

Partido Revolucionario de Trabajadores: political wing of the Ejército Revolucionario del Pueblo (ERP); Leader LUIS MATTINI.

Triple A—Alianza Anticomunista Argentina: extreme right-wing; Leader ANÍBAL GORDON (in prison).

The dissolution of the Movimiento Peronista Montonero (MPM) was announced in December 1983. Mario Firmenich, the former leader of the MPM, was arrested in Brazil in 1983 and was transferred into the custody of the Argentine authorities in 1984.

Diplomatic Representation

EMBASSIES IN ARGENTINA

Albania: 3 Febrero 1365, 1426 Buenos Aires; tel. (1) 783-2888; telex 22658; Ambassador: PIRO ANDONI.

Algeria: Montevideo 1889, 1021 Buenos Aires; tel. (1) 22-1271; telex 22467; Ambassador: ABDELMADJID AOUCHICHE.

Australia: Avda Santa Fé 846, 8°, 1059 Buenos Aires; tel. (1) 312-6841; telex 21946; Ambassador: KEITH DOUGLAS-SCOTT.

Austria: French 3671, 1425 Buenos Aires; tel. (1) 802-7195; telex 18853; Ambassador: Dr ALBERT ROHAN.

Belgium: Defensa 113, 8°, 1065 Buenos Aires; tel. (1) 33-0066; telex 22070; Ambassador: LUC STEYAERT.

Bolivia: Corrientes 545, 2°, 1043 Buenos Aires; tel. (1) 45-0082; telex 24362; Ambassador: EUFRONIO PADILLA CAERO.

Brazil: Arroyo 1142, 1007 Buenos Aires; tel. (1) 44-0035; telex 21158; Ambassador: CARLOS F. DUARTE GONÇALVES DA ROCHA.

Bulgaria: Manuel Obarrio 2967, 1425 Buenos Aires; tel. (1) 83-7458; telex 21314; Ambassador: PURVAN NIKOLOV CHERNEV.

Canada: Edif. Brunetta 25°, Suipacha 1111, Casilla 1598, 1368 Buenos Aires; tel. (1) 312-9081; telex 21383; Ambassador: CLAYTON BULLIS.

Chile: Tagle 2762, 1425 Buenos Aires; tel. (1) 802-7020; telex 21669; Ambassador: SERGIO GAETE ROJAS.

China, People's Republic: Republiquetas 5349, 1431 Buenos Aires; tel. (1) 52-0084; telex 22871; Ambassador: SHEN YUNAO.

Colombia: Avda Santa Fé 782, 1°, 1059 Buenos Aires; tel. (1) 312-5538; telex 22254; Ambassador: VICENTE BORREGO RESTREPO.

Costa Rica: Esmeralda 135, 6°, 1035 Buenos Aires; tel. (1) 45-8427; telex 21394; Ambassador: FERNANDO SALAZAR NAVARRETE.

Cuba: Virrey del Pino 1810, 1426 Buenos Aires; tel. (1) 782-9049; telex 22433; Ambassador: Dr FERNANDO LÓPEZ MUIÑO.

Czechoslovakia: Figueroa Alcorta 3240, 1425 Buenos Aires; tel. (1) 801-3804; telex 22748; Ambassador: JAROSLAV PAVLICEK.

Denmark: Avda Leandro N. Alem 1074, 1001 Buenos Aires; tel. (1) 312-7680; telex 22173; Ambassador: KARL-FREDERIK HASLE.

Dominican Republic: Avda Santa Fé 1206, 2°, 1059 Buenos Aires; tel. (1) 41-4669; Ambassador: CIRILIO JOSÉ CASTELLANOS.

Egypt: Callao 1033, 2°, 1023 Buenos Aires; tel. (1) 41-5455; Ambassador: MUSTAFA MOHAMED TAWFIK.

El Salvador: Florida 868, 12°, 1005 Buenos Aires; tel. (1) 312-3444; Ambassador: CARLOS HUMBERTO FIGUEROA.

Finland: Avda Santa Fé 846, 5°, 1059 Buenos Aires; tel. (1) 312-0600; telex 21702; Ambassador: (vacant).

France: Cerrito 1399, 1010 Buenos Aires; tel. (1) 393-1071; telex 24300; Ambassador: ANTOINE BLANCA.

Gabon: Avda Figueroa Alcorta 3221, 1425 Buenos Aires; tel. (1) 801-9840; telex 18577; Ambassador: J.-B. EYI-NKOUMOU.

German Democratic Republic: Olazábal 2201-51, 1428 Buenos Aires; tel. (1) 781-2002; telex 21786; Ambassador: HORST NEUMANN.

Germany, Federal Republic: Villanueva 1055, 1426 Buenos Aires; tel. (1) 771-5054; telex 21668; Ambassador: HANS WERNER Graf FINCK VON FINCKENSTEIN.

Greece: Avda Roque Sáenz Peña 547, 4°, 1352 Buenos Aires; tel. (1) 34-4958; telex 22426; Ambassador: DIMITRI MANOLATOS.

Guatemala: Lavalle 1759, 6° B, 1048 Buenos Aires; tel. (1) 46-4647; Ambassador: Prof. CARLOS HUMBERTO PACAY Y PACAY.

Haiti: Esmeralda 626, 3° A, 1405 Buenos Aires; tel. (1) 392-1868; Ambassador: IVES FRANÇOIS.

Directory

Holy See: Avda Alvear 1605, 1014 Buenos Aires; tel. (1) 42-9697; telex 17406; Apostolic Nuncio: Monsignor UBALDO CALABRESI.

Honduras: Avda Roque Sáenz Peña 336, 2°, 1020 Buenos Aires; tel. (1) 40-0484; telex 18008; Ambassador: CARLOS VILLANUEVA DOBLADO.

Hungary: Coronel Díaz 1874, 1425 Buenos Aires; tel. (1) 824-5845; telex 22843; Ambassador: MARTON KLEIN.

India: Paraguay 580, 3°, 1057 Buenos Aires; tel. (1) 31-3020; telex 23413; Ambassador: (vacant).

Indonesia: M. Ramón Castilla 2901, 1425 Buenos Aires; tel. (1) 801-6622; telex 21781; Ambassador: J. B. SOEDARMANTO KADARISMAN.

Iran: Figueroa Alcorta 3229, 1425 Buenos Aires; tel. (1) 802-1470; telex 21288; Ambassador: MUHAMMAD MEHDI POURMOHAMMADI.

Iraq: Buenos Aires; tel. (1) 552-6565; telex 17134; Chargé d'affaires: ADEL AHMED ZAIDAN.

Ireland: Avda Santa Fé 1391, 4°, 1059 Buenos Aires; tel. (1) 44-9987; telex 17654 Ambassador: PATRICK A. WALSHE.

Israel: Arroyo 916, 1007 Buenos Aires; tel. (1) 392-4481; telex 17106; Ambassador: DOV B. SCHMORAK.

Italy: Avda San Martín 2100, Buenos Aires; tel. (1) 83-00-71; telex 21961; Ambassador: UBERTO BOZZINI.

Japan: Azcuénaga 1035, Casilla 4595, 1115 Buenos Aires; tel. (1) 83-1031; telex 22516; Ambassador: SENKURO SAIKI.

Korea, Republic: Coronel Díaz 2860, 1425 Buenos Aires; tel. (1) 802-2737; Ambassador: SOO WOO RYEE.

Lebanon: Avda Libertador 2354, 1425 Buenos Aires; tel. (1) 802-4493; telex 22866; Ambassador: EDMOND KHAYAT.

Libya: Posadas 1650, 3°, 1112 Buenos Aires; tel. (1) 41-1620; telex 22682; Chargé d'affaires: (vacant).

Mexico: Larrea 1230, 1117 Buenos Aires; tel. (1) 826-2161; telex 21869; Ambassador: EUGENIO ANGUIANO.

Morocco: Calle Mariscal Ramón Castilla No. 2952, CP 1425, Buenos Aires; tel. (1) 801-8154; telex 18161; Ambassador: (vacant).

Netherlands: Edif. Holanda 2°, Maipú 66, 1084 Buenos Aires; tel. (1) 33-6066; telex 21824; Ambassador: EDUARD O. VAN SUCHTELEN.

Nicaragua: Montevideo 373, 6°, 1019 Buenos Aires; tel. (1) 45-0732; telex 23481; Ambassador: ERNESTO MEJÍA SÁNCHEZ.

Nigeria: 3 de febrero 1365, 1462 Buenos Aires; tel. (1) 783-288; telex 23565; Ambassador: J. A. FAKAYODE.

Norway: Esmeralda 909, 3°, Casilla 2286, 1000 Buenos Aires; tel. (1) 312-2204; telex 22811; Ambassador: HENRIK F. HOLO.

Pakistan: Avda Alvear 1402, Buenos Aires; tel. (1) 22-0355; Ambassador: RAJA TRIDIV ROY.

Panama: Montevideo 373, 6°, 1019 Buenos Aires; tel. (1) 49-2621; Ambassador: ROBERTO PUELLO ARAÚZ.

Paraguay: Las Heras 2545, 1425 Buenos Aires; tel. (1) 802-4948; telex 21687; Ambassador: MIGUEL BESTARD.

Peru: Avda Libertador 1720, 1425 Buenos Aires; tel. (1) 802-6427; telex 17807; Ambassador: ALFONSO GRADOS BERTORINI.

Philippines: Juramento 1945, 1428 Buenos Aires; tel. (1) 781-4170; Ambassador: SIME D. HIDALGO.

Poland: Alejandro María de Aguado 2870, 1425 Buenos Aires; tel. (1) 802-9681; Ambassador: JAN JANISZEWSKI.

Portugal: Córdoba 315, 3°, 1054 Buenos Aires; tel. (1) 31-2586; telex 22736; Ambassador: (vacant).

Romania: Arroyo 962, 1007 Buenos Aires; tel. (1) 393-0883; telex 24301; Ambassador: MIHAIL MUNTEAN.

Saudi Arabia: Alejandro María de Aguado 2881, 1425 Buenos Aires; tel. (1) 802-4735; telex 23291; Ambassador: FUAD A. NAZIR.

Spain: Mariscal Ramón Castilla 2720, 1425 Buenos Aires; tel. (1) 802-6031; telex 21660; Ambassador: RAIMUNDO BASSOLS JACAS.

Sweden: Corrientes 330, 3°, 1378 Buenos Aires; tel. (1) 311-3088; telex 21340; Ambassador: ANDERS SANDSTRÖM.

Switzerland: Avda Santa Fé 846, 12°, 1059 Buenos Aires; tel. (1) 311-6491; telex 22418; Ambassador: JEAN-PIERRE KEUSCH.

Syria: Calloa 956, 1023 Buenos Aires; tel. (1) 42-2113; Ambassador: ABDEL SALAM AKIL.

Thailand: Virrey del Pino 2458, 6°, 1426 Buenos Aires; tel. (1) 785-6504; Ambassador: SIRAJAYA BUDDHI-BAEDYA.

Turkey: Avda Roque Sáenz Peña 852, 1035 Buenos Aires; tel. (1) 46-8779; telex 21135; Ambassador: GÜNDÜZ TUNÇBILEK.

USSR: Avda Rodríguez Peña 1741, 1021 Buenos Aires; tel. (1) 42-1552; telex 22147; Ambassador: OLEG KVASOV.

USA: Avda Colombia 4300, Palermo, 1425 Buenos Aires; tel. (1) 774-7611; telex 18156; Ambassador: THEODORE E. GILDRED.

Uruguay: Avda Las Heras 1907, 1127 Buenos Aires; tel. (1) 821-6032; telex 25526; Ambassador: LUIS BARRIOS TASSANO.

ARGENTINA

Venezuela: Avda Santa Fé 1461, 2°, 1060 Buenos Aires; tel. (1) 42-0033; telex 21089; Ambassador: GUIDO GROOSCORS.
Yugoslavia: Marcelo T. de Alvear 1705, 1060 Buenos Aires; tel. (1) 41-2860; telex 21479; Ambassador: FILIP MATIĆ.
Zaire: Villanueva 1356, 2°, Casilla 5589, 1426 Buenos Aires; tel. (1) 771-0075; telex 22324; Ambassador: KAMANDA NGONGO.

Judicial System

SUPREME COURT

Corte Suprema: Talcahuano 550, 4°, 1013 Buenos Aires; tel. (1) 40-1540.

All members of the Supreme Court are appointed by the Executive, with the agreement of the Senate. Members are dismissed by impeachment.

President: Dr JOSÉ SEVERO CABALLERO.
Justices: ENRIQUE SANTIAGO PETRACCHI, CARLOS SANTIAGO FAYT, AUGUSTO CÉSAR BELLUSCIO, Dr JORGE ANTONIO BACQUÉ.
Attorney-General: ANDRÉS D'ALESSIO.

OTHER COURTS

Judges of the lower, national or further lower courts are appointed by the President, with the agreement of the Senate, and are dismissed by impeachment.

The Federal Court of Appeal in Buenos Aires has three courts: civil and commercial, criminal, and administrative. There are six other courts of appeal in Buenos Aires: civil, commercial, criminal, peace, labour, and penal-economic. There are also federal appeal courts in: La Plata, Bahía Blanca, Paraná, Rosario, Córdoba, Mendoza, Tucumán and Resistencia.

The provincial courts each have their own Supreme Court and a system of subsidiary courts. They deal with cases originating within and confined to the provinces.

Religion

CHRISTIANITY

More than 90% of the population are Roman Catholics and about 2% are Protestants.

Federación Argentina de Iglesias Evangélicas (Argentine Federation of Evangelical Churches): José María Moreno 873, 1424 Buenos Aires; tel. (1) 922-5356; f. 1958; 29 mem. churches; Pres. Rev. RODOLFO ROBERTO REINICH (Evangelical Church of the River Plate); Exec. Sec. Rev. ENRIQUE LAVIGNE.

The Roman Catholic Church

Argentina comprises 13 archdioceses, 51 dioceses (including one for Catholics of the Ukrainian rite) and three territorial prelatures. The Archbishop of Buenos Aires is also the Ordinary for Catholics of Oriental rites.

Bishops' Conference: Conferencia Episcopal Argentina, Calle Suipacha 1034, 1008 Buenos Aires; tel. (1) 311-0993; f. 1959; Pres. Cardinal RAÚL FRANCISCO PRIMATESTA, Archbishop of Córdoba.

Armenian Rite

Apostolic Exarch of Latin America: VARTAN WALDIR BOGHOSSIAN (Titular Bishop of Mardin), Exarcado Apostólico Armenio, Charcas 3529, 1425 Buenos Aires; tel. (1) 824-1613.

Latin Rite

Archbishop of Bahía Blanca: JORGE MAYER, Avda Colón 164, 8000 Bahía Blanca; tel. (091) 22-070.
Archbishop of Buenos Aires: Cardinal JUAN CARLOS ARAMBURU, Arzobispado, Rivadavia 415, 1002 Buenos Aires; tel. (1) 30-3925.
Archbishop of Córdoba: Cardinal RAÚL FRANCISCO PRIMATESTA, Avda Hipólito Yrigoyen 98, 500 Córdoba; tel. (051) 38-942.
Archbishop of Corrientes: FORTUNATO ANTONIO ROSSI, 9 de Julio 1543, 3400 Corrientes; tel. (0783) 22-436.
Archbishop of La Plata: ANTONIO QUARRACINO, Calle 14, No 1009, 1900 La Plata; tel. (021) 21-8286.
Archbishop of Mendoza: CÁNDIDO GENARO RUBIOLO, Catamarca 98, 5500 Mendoza; tel. (061) 233-862.
Archbishop of Paraná: ESTANISLAO ESTEBAN KARLICH, Monte Caseros 77, 3100 Paraná; tel. (043) 211-440.
Archbishop of Resistencia: JUAN JOSÉ IRIARTE, Bartolomé Mitre 363, Casilla 35, 3500 Resistencia; tel. (0711) 26867.
Archbishop of Rosario: JORGE MANUEL LÓPEZ, Córdoba 1677, 2000 Rosario; tel. (041) 21-5175.

Directory

Archbishop of Salta: MOISÉS JULIO BLANCHOUD, España 596, 4400 Salta; tel. (087) 214-306.
Archbishop of San Juan de Cuyo: ITALO SEVERINO DI STEFANO, Bartolomé Mitre 240, Oeste, 5400 San Juan de Cuyo; tel. (064) 22-2578.
Archbishop of Santa Fé: EDGARDO GABRIEL STORNI, Avda General López 2720, 3000 Santa Fé; tel. (042) 35-791.
Archbishop of Tucumán: HORACIO ALBERTO BÓZZOLI, Avda Sarmiento 895, 4000 Tucumán; tel. (081) 22-6345.

Ukrainian Rite

Bishop of Santa María del Patrocinio en Buenos Aires: ANDRÉS SAPELAK, Ramón L. Falcón 3960, Casilla 28, 1407 Buenos Aires; tel. (2) 67-4192.

The Anglican Communion

The Iglesia Anglicana del Cono Sur de América (Anglican Church of the Southern Cone of America) was formally inaugurated in Buenos Aires in April 1983. The Church comprises five dioceses, covering six countries: Argentina, Bolivia, Chile, Paraguay, Peru and Uruguay.

Presiding Bishop: Rt Rev. DAVID LEAKE (Bishop of Northern Argentina), Casilla 187, 4400 Salta.
Bishop of Argentina: Rt Rev. RICHARD STANLEY CUTTS, 25 de Mayo 282, 1002 Buenos Aires; tel. (1) 34-4618.

Protestant Churches

Baptist Evangelical Convention: Rivadavia 3476, 1203 Buenos Aires; tel. (1) 88-8924; Pres. Rev. Dr CARLOS CARAMUTTI.
Iglesia Evangélica Congregacionalista (Evangelical Congregational Church): Perón 525, 3100 Paraná; tel. (043) 21-6172; f. 1924; 100 congregations, 8,000 mems, 24,000 adherents; Supt Rev. GERARDO ARNDT.
Iglesia Evangélica Luterana Argentina: Silveyra 1655, 1607 Villa Adelina, Buenos Aires; tel. (1) 766-7948; f. 1905; 30,000 mems; Pres. ROBERTO M. KROEGER.
Iglesia Evangélica del Río de la Plata: Mariscal Sucre 2855, 1428 Buenos Aires; tel. (1) 784-1029; f. 1899; 50,000 mems; Pres. RODOLFO R. REINICH.
Iglesia Evangélica Metodista Argentina (Methodist Church of Argentina): Rivadavia 4044, 1205 Buenos Aires; tel. (1) 982-3712; f. 1836; 6,040 mems; 9,000 adherents; seven regional superintendents; Bishop FEDERRICO J. PAGURA; Admin. HUMBERTO SHIKIYA; Exec. Sec. Gen. Board Rev. DAVID DELGADO.

JUDAISM

Delegación de Asociaciones Israelitas Argentinas—DAIA (Delegation of Argentine Jewish Associations): Pasteur 633, 5°, Buenos Aires; f. 1935; there are about 400,000 Jews, mostly in Buenos Aires; Pres. Dr DAVID GOLDBERG; Sec.-Gen. Dr HÉCTOR UMASCHI.

The Press

PRINCIPAL DAILIES

Buenos Aires

Ambito Financiero: Carabelas 241, 3°, 1009 Buenos Aires; tel. (1) 35-1621; f. 1976; morning (Mon.–Fri.); business; Dir JULIO A. RAMOS.
Buenos Aires Herald: Azopardo 455, 1107 Buenos Aires; tel. (1) 34-8477; f. 1876; English; morning; independent; Editor RONALD HANSEN; circ. 20,000.
Boletín Oficial de la República Argentina: Suipacha 767, 1008 Buenos Aires; tel. (1) 322-4164; f. 1893; morning (Mon.–Fri.); official records publication; Dir HORACIO GASTIABURO.
Clarín: Piedras 1743, 1140 Buenos Aires; tel. (1) 27-0061; f. 1945; morning; independent; Dir Sra ERNESTINA LAURA HERRERA DE NOBLE; circ. 480,000 (daily), 750,000 (Sunday).
Crónica: Garay 130, 1063 Buenos Aires; tel. (1) 361-1001; f. 1963; morning and evening; Dir MARIO ALBERTO FERNÁNDEZ (morning), RICARDO GANGEME (evening); circ. 330,000 (morning), 190,000 (evening), 450,000 (Sunday).
El Cronista Comercial: Alsina 547, 1087 Buenos Aires; tel. (1) 33-3015; f. 1908; morning; Editor DANIEL DELLA COSTA; circ. 100,000.
Diario Popular: Beguerestain 182, 1870 Avellaneda, Buenos Aires; tel. (1) 204-6056; f. 1974; morning; Dir ALBERTO ALBERTENGO; circ. 145,000.
La Gaceta: Beguerestain 182, Avellaneda, Buenos Aires; Dir RICARDO WEST OCAMPO; circ. 35,000.
El Heraldo de Buenos Aires: Azopardo 455, 1107 Buenos Aires; tel. (1) 34-8479; f. 1988; evening; independent; Editor LORENZO AMENGUAL.

ARGENTINA

La Nación: Bouchard 557, 1106 Buenos Aires; tel. (1) 313-1003; telex 18558; f. 1870; morning; independent; Dir BARTOLOMÉ MITRE; circ. 210,648.

Página 12: Buenos Aires; f. 1987; morning; left-wing.

La Prensa: Avda de Mayo 567, 1319 Buenos Aires; tel. (1) 331-1001; f. 1869 by José C. Paz; morning; independent; Dir MÁXIMO GAINZA; circ. 65,000.

La Razón: Gral Hornos 690, 1272 Buenos Aires; tel. (1) 26-9051; f. 1905; morning and evening; Exec. Dir PATRICIO PERALTA RAMOS; circ. 180,000.

The Southern Cross: Medrano 107, 1178 Buenos Aires; tel. (1) 983-1371; f. 1875; Dir P. FEDERICO RICHARDS.

Tiempo Argentino: Lafayette 1910, 1286 Buenos Aires; tel. (1) 28-1929; telex 22276; Editor Dr TOMÁS LEONA; circ. 75,000.

La Voz: Tabaré 1641, 1437 Buenos Aires; tel. (1) 922-3800; Dir VICENTE LEÓNIDAS SAADI.

PRINCIPAL PROVINCIAL DAILIES

Bahía Blanca

La Nueva Provincia: Sarmiento 54/64, 8000 Bahía Blanca, Provincia de Buenos Aires; tel. 20201; telex 81826; f. 1898; morning; independent; Dir DIANA JULIO DE MASSOT; circ. 36,000 (weekdays), 55,000 (Sunday).

Catamarca

El Sol: Esquiú 551, 4700 San Francisco del Valle de Catamarca; tel. 23844; f. 1973; morning; Dir TOMÁS NICOLÁS ALVAREZ SAAVEDRA.

Comodoro Rivadavia

Crónica: Namuncurá 122, 9000 Comodoro Rivadavia, Provincia del Chubut; tel. 26015; telex 86996; f. 1962; morning; Dir Dr DIEGO JOAQUÍN ZAMIT; circ. 10,000.

Concordia

El Heraldo: Quintana 46, 3200 Concordia; tel. (045) 215304; telex 46508; f. 1915; evening; Editor Dr CARLOS LIEBERMANN; circ. 10,000.

Córdoba

Comercio y Justicia: Mariano Moreno 378, 5000 Córdoba; tel. 33788; telex 51563; f. 1939; morning; economic and legal news; Editor JORGE RAÚL EGUÍA; circ. 12,000.

Córdoba: Santa Rosa 167, 5000 Córdoba; tel. (051) 22072; f. 1928; evening; Dir GUSTAVO ALONSO OBIETA; circ. 25,000.

La Voz del Interior: Avellaneda 1661, 5000 Córdoba; tel. (051) 72-9535; f. 1904; morning; independent; Dir LUIS EDUARDO REMONDA; circ. 87,000.

Corrientes

El Liberal: 25 de Mayo 1345, 3400 Corrientes; tel. (0783) 22069; f. 1909; evening; Dir JUAN FRANCISCO TORRENT.

El Litoral: H. Yrigoyen 990, 3400 Corrientes; tel. (0783) 22264; f. 1960; morning; Dir GABRIEL FERIS; circ. 25,000.

La Plata

El Día: Avda Ameghino Diagonal 80, No 817/21, 1900 La Plata, Provincia de Buenos Aires; tel. 21-0101; telex 31165; f. 1884; morning; independent; Dir RAÚL E. KRAISELBURD; circ. 54,868.

Mar del Plata

El Atlántico: Bolívar 2975, 7600 Mar del Plata, Provincia de Buenos Aires; tel. 3-5462; f. 1938; morning; Dir OSCAR ALBERTO GASTIARENA; circ. 20,000.

La Capital: Avda Champagnat 2551, 7600 Mar del Plata, Provincia de Buenos Aires; tel. 77-1164; telex 39884; f. 1905; Dir TOMÁS R. STEGAGNINI; circ. 32,000.

Mendoza

Los Andes: San Martín 1049, 5500 Mendoza; tel. (061) 2-44500; f. 1882; morning; independent; Dir ELCIRA V. SCHIAPPA DE AZEVEDO; circ. 60,662.

Mendoza: San Martín 947, 5500 Mendoza; tel. (061) 2-41064; f. 1969; Dir ALFREDO ORTIZ BARILI; circ. 6,670.

Paraná

El Diario: Buenos Aires y Urquiza, 3100 Paraná, Entre Ríos; tel. (043) 21-0082; telex 45108; f. 1914; morning; democratic; Dir Dr LUIS F. ETCHEVEHERE; circ. 20,000.

Quilmes, B.A.

El Sol: H. Yrigoyen 122, Quilmes 1878; tel. 253-4595; f. 1927; Dir JOSÉ MARÍA GHISANI; circ. 25,000.

Resistencia

El Territorio: Casilla 320, Carlos Pellegrini 211/231, 3500 Resistencia; f. 1919; morning; Dir RAÚL ANDRÉS AGUIRRE; circ. 15,000.

La Rioja

La Gaceta Riojana: 25 de Mayo 76, 5300 La Rioja; tel. 26443; f. 1988; Editor RAÚL NICOLÁS CHACÓN.

Río Negro

Río Negro: Gral Roca (8332), Río Negro; tel. (0941) 22021; f. 1912; morning; Editor JAMES NEILSON.

Rosario

La Capital: Sarmiento 763, 2000 Rosario, Santa Fé; tel. 392-2193; f. 1867; morning; independent; Dir CARLOS OVIDIO LAGOS; circ. 93,920.

Salta

El Tribuno: Ruta 68, Km 1592, 4400 Salta; tel. 24-0000; telex 65126; f. 1949; morning; Dir ROBERTO EDUARDO ROMERO; circ. 41,215.

San Juan

Diario de Cuyo: Mendoza 380 Sur, 5400 San Juan; tel. 29680; f. 1947; morning; independent; Dir FRANCISCO MONTES; circ. 25,000.

Tribuna de la Tarde: Mitre 85 Oeste, 5400 San Juan; tel. 40-0923; f. 1931; evening; Dir DANTE AMÉRICO MONTES.

Santa Fé

Hoy: 1° de Mayo 2820, 3000 Santa Fé; f. 1986; Dir ANDRÉS SAAVEDRA; circ. 30,000.

El Litoral: San Martín 2651-59, 3000 Santa Fé; tel. (041) 20101; f. 1918; morning; independent; Dir ENZO VITTORI; circ. 40,000.

Santiago del Estero

El Liberal: Libertad 263, 4200 Santiago del Estero; tel. (05484) 22-4400; telex 64114; f. 1898; morning; Editors Dr ALDO CLAUDIO CASTIGLIONE, Dr JULIO CÉSAR CASTIGLIONE; circ. 30,000.

Tucumán

La Gaceta: Mendoza 654, 4000 San Miguel de Tucumán; tel. 219260; telex 61208; f. 1912; morning; independent; Dir EDUARDO GARCÍA HAMILTON; circ. 80,552.

La Tarde: Mendoza 654, San Miguel de Tucumán 4000; tel. 219260; telex 61208; f. 1981; evening; Dir ENRIQUE R. GARCÍA HAMILTON.

WEEKLY NEWSPAPER

El Informador Público: Buenos Aires; right-wing; Editor JESÚS IGLESIAS ROUCO.

PERIODICALS

Aeroespacio: Casilla 37, Sucursal 12B, 1412 Buenos Aires; tel. (1) 322-2753; telex 21763; f. 1931; bi-monthly; aeronautics; Dir JOSÉ CÁNDIDO D'ODORICO; circ. 26,000.

ARS, Revista de Arte: Rodríguez Peña 339, 9°A, Buenos Aires; annually; art magazine; Dir Dr I. I. SCHLAGMAN.

Billiken: Azopardo 579, 1307 Buenos Aires; tel. (1) 30-7040; telex 21163; f. 1919; weekly; children's magazine; Dir CARLOS SILVEYRA; circ. 240,000.

Canal TV: Azopardo 579, 1307 Buenos Aires; weekly; TV guide.

Casas y Jardines (Houses and Gardens): Sarmiento 643, 1382 Buenos Aires; tel. (1) 45-1793; f. 1932; every 2 months; publ. by Editorial Contémpora SRL; Dir NORBERTO M. MUZIO.

Chacra & Campo Moderno: Editorial Atlántida SA, Azopardo 579, 1307 Buenos Aires; tel. (1) 333-4591; telex 21163; f. 1930; monthly; farm and country magazine; Dir CONSTANCIO C. VIGIL; circ. 35,000.

Claudia: Avda Leandro N. Alem 896, 1001 Buenos Aires; tel. (1) 312-6010; telex 9229; f. 1957; monthly; women's magazine; Dir MERCEDES MARQUES; circ. 17,100.

El Derecho: Tucumán 1436, 1050 Buenos Aires; tel. (1) 45-3302; law.

Desarrollo Económico-Revista de Ciencias Sociales: Güemes 3950, 1425 Buenos Aires; tel. (1) 71-3738; every 3 months; publication of Instituto de Desarrollo Económico y Social; circ. 2,500.

El Economista: Avda Córdoba 632, 1054 Buenos Aires; tel. (1) 392-3308; f. 1951; weekly; financial; Dir Dr D. RADONJIC; circ. 33,000.

Gente: Azopardo 579, 3°, 1307 Buenos Aires; tel. (1) 33-4591; telex 21163; f. 1965; weekly; general; Dir JORGE DE LUJÁN GUTIÉRREZ; circ. 133,000.

ARGENTINA

El Gráfico: Azopardo 579, 1307 Buenos Aires; tel. (1) 33-4591; telex 21163; f. 1919; weekly; sport; Dir Constancio C. Vigil; circ. 127,000.

Humor: Venezuela 842, 1095 Buenos Aires; tel. (1) 334-5400; telex 9072; f. 1978; every 2 weeks; satirical revue; Editor Andrés Cascioli; circ. 180,000.

Jurisprudencia Argentina: Talcahuano 650, 1013 Buenos Aires; tel. (1) 40-7850; f. 1918; weekly; law; Dir Ricardo Estévez Boero; circ. 10,000.

Legislación Argentina: Talcahuano 650, 1013 Buenos Aires; tel. (1) 40-0528; f. 1958; Dir Ricardo Estévez Boero; circ. 15,000.

Mercado: Perú 263, 2°, 1067 Buenos Aires; tel. (1) 34-6713; f. 1969; weekly; commerce; Dir Alberto Borrini.

Mundo Israelita: Lavalle 2615, 1°, 1052 Buenos Aires; tel. (1) 961-7999; f. 1923; weekly; Editor Dr José Kestelman; circ. 26,000.

Nuestra Arquitectura (Our Architecture): Sarmiento 643, 5°, 1382 Buenos Aires; tel. (1) 45-1793; f. 1929; every 2 months; publ. by Editorial Contémpora SRL; Dir Norberto M. Muzio.

Nueva Presencia: Castelli 330, 1032 Buenos Aires; tel. (1) 89-2727; weekly; Editor Herman Schiller.

Para Ti: Azopardo 579, 1307 Buenos Aires; tel. (1) 33-4591; f. 1922; weekly; women's interest; Dir Aníbal C. Vigil; circ. 104,000.

Pensamiento Económico: Avda Leandro N. Alem 36, 1003 Buenos Aires; tel. (1) 331-8051; telex 18542; f. 1925; every 3 months; review of Cámara Argentina de Comercio; Dir Lic. Pedro Naón Argerich.

Perfil: Sarmiento 1113, 1041 Buenos Aires; tel. (1) 35-2552; telex 18213; Editor Daniel Pliner.

El Periodista: Buenos Aires; weekly; Dir Carlos Gabetta.

Política Obrera: Avda Belgrano 2608, Buenos Aires; tel. (1) 943-2439; every 2 months; magazine of Partido Obrero; circ. 5,000.

La Prensa Médica Argentina: Junín 845, 1113 Buenos Aires; tel. (1) 961-9793; f. 1914; monthly; medical; Editor Dr P. A. López; circ. 8,000.

Prensa Obrera: Ayacucho 444, Buenos Aires; tel. (1) 953-8433; f. 1982; weekly; publication of Partido Obrero; circ. 16,000.

Review of the River Plate: Austria 1828, 1425 Buenos Aires; tel. (1) 982-4961; f. 1891; 3 a month; agricultural, financial, economic and shipping news and comment; Dir Archibald B. Norman; circ. 3,500.

Satiricon: Buenos Aires; satirical review; circ. 28,000.

La Semana: Sarmiento 1113, 1041 Buenos Aires; tel. (1) 35-2552; telex 18213; general; Editor Daniel Pliner.

La Semana Médica: Arenales 3574, 1425 Buenos Aires; tel. (1) 824-5673; f. 1894; weekly; Dir Prof. Dr Guillermo R. Jáuregui; circ. 7,000.

Siete Días: Avda Leandro N. Alem 896, 1001 Buenos Aires; tel. (1) 32-6010; f. 1967; weekly; general; Dir Ricardo Cámara.

Somos: Azopardo 579, 1307 Buenos Aires; tel. (1) 33-4591; f. 1976; weekly; general; anti-Peronist; Dir Aníbal C. Vigil; circ. 21,000.

Técnica e Industria (Technology and Industry): Rodríguez Peña 694, 5°, 1020 Buenos Aires; tel. (1) 46-3193; f. 1922; monthly; Dir E. R. Fedele; circ. 5,000.

Visión: Montevideo 496, 6°, 1019 Buenos Aires; tel. (1) 49-3652; telex 21926; f. 1950; every 2 weeks; Latin American affairs, politics; Dir Dr Mariano Grondona.

Vosotras: Avda Leandro N. Alem 896, 3°, 1001 Buenos Aires; tel. (1) 32-6010; f. 1935; women's weekly; Dir Abel Zanotto; circ. 33,000. Monthly supplements: **Labores:** circ. 130,000, **Modas:** circ. 70,000.

NEWS AGENCIES

Agencia TELAM SA: Bolívar 531, 1066 Buenos Aires; tel. (1) 34-2162; telex 21077; Editor-in-Chief Mario R. Monteverde.

Diarios y Noticias (DYN): Chacabuco 314, 6°, 1069 Buenos Aires; tel. (1) 33-3971; telex 23058; Dir Jorge Carlos Brinsek.

Noticias Argentinas SA (NA): Chacabuco 314, 8°, 1069 Buenos Aires; tel. (1) 33-8688; telex 18363; f. 1973; Dir Raúl Eduardo García.

Foreign Bureaux

Agence France-Presse (AFP): Avda Corrientes 456, 6°, Of. 61/62, 1366 Buenos Aires; tel. (1) 394-8169; telex 24349; Bureau Chief Jean-Pierre Gallois.

Agencia EFE (Spain): Guido 1770, 1016 Buenos Aires; tel. (1) 41-0666; telex 17568; Bureau Chief Manuel M. Meseguer Sánchez.

Agenzia Nazionale Stampa Associata (ANSA) (Italy): Calle San Martín 320, 6°, 1004 Buenos Aires; tel. (1) 394-7568; telex 24214; Bureau Chief Vincenzo Fiaschitello.

Associated Press (AP) (USA): Bouchard 551, 5°, Casilla 1296, 1106 Buenos Aires; tel. (1) 311-0081; telex 121053; Bureau Chief William H. Heath.

Deutsche Presse-Agentur (dpa) (Federal Republic of Germany): Avda Corrientes 456, 10°, Of. 104, 1366 Buenos Aires; tel. (1) 394-0990; Bureau Chief Gerd Reuter.

Inter Press Service (IPS) (Italy): Perú 590, 10°, Of. C, 1068 Buenos Aires; tel. (1) 34-7124; telex 24712; Correspondent Gustavo Capdevilla.

Magyar Távirati Iroda (MTI) (Hungary): Avda José Hernández 2010, 11°, Buenos Aires; Correspondent Endre Simó.

Prensa Latina (Cuba): Corrientes 456, 2°, Of. 27, Buenos Aires; tel. (1) 394-0565; telex 24410; Correspondent Elmer Rodríguez Menéndez.

Reuters (UK): Avda Eduardo Madero 940, 25°, 1106 Buenos Aires; tel. (1) 313-2021; Chief Correspondent R. Jarvie.

Telegrafnoye Agentstvo Sovetskovo Soyuza (TASS) (USSR): Avda Córdoba 652, 11°'E', 1054 Buenos Aires; tel. (1) 392-2044; Dir Isidoro Gilbert.

United Press International (UPI) (USA): Casilla 796, Correo Central 1000, Avda Belgrano 271, 1092 Buenos Aires; tel. (1) 34-5501; telex 350-1225; Dir Alberto J. Schazín.

Xinhua (New China) News Agency (People's Republic of China): Calle Tucumán 540, 14°, Apto D, 1049 Buenos Aires; tel. (1) 313-9755; telex 23643; Bureau Chief Ju Qingdong.

The following are also represented: Central News Agency (Taiwan), Interpress (Poland), Jiji Press (Japan).

PRESS ASSOCIATION

Asociación de Entidades Periodísticas Argentinas: Esmeralda 356, 1035 Buenos Aires.

Publishers

Editorial Abril, SA: Avda Belgrano 1580, 4°, 1093 Buenos Aires; tel. (1) 37-7355; telex 22630; f. 1961; fiction, non-fiction, children's books, textbooks; Dir Fernando Costanzó.

Editorial Acme SA: Santa Magdalena 632, 1277 Buenos Aires; tel. (1) 28-2014; f. 1949; general fiction, children's books, agriculture, textbooks; Man. Dir Eduardo A. Ederra.

Editorial Alfa Argentina SA: Defensa 599, 3°, 1065 Buenos Aires; tel. (1) 33-1199; f. 1971; general fiction, literature, philosophy, psychology; textbooks; Man. Dir Leonardo Milla.

Aguilar Argentina SA de Ediciones: Balcarce 363, 1064 Buenos Aires; tel. (1) 30-1197; telex 22835; f. 1946; general non-fiction; Man. Manuel Rodríguez.

Editorial Albatros, SACI: Hipólito Yrigoyen 3920, 1208 Buenos Aires; tel. (1) 981-1161; f. 1967; technical, non-fiction, social sciences, medicine and agriculture; Man. Gustavo Gabriel Canevaro.

Amorrortu Editores, SA: Paraguay 1225, 7°, 1057 Buenos Aires; tel. (1) 393-8812; f. 1967; anthropology, religion, economics, sociology, philosophy, psychology, pschoanalysis, current affairs; Man. Dir Horacio de Amorrortu.

Angel Estrada y Cía, SA: Bolívar 462, 1066 Buenos Aires; tel. (1) 331-6521; telex 17990; f. 1869; textbooks, children's books; Pres. Patricia de Estrada.

El Ateneo, Librería—Editorial: Patagones 2463, 1282 Buenos Aires; tel. (1) 942-9002; f. 1912; medicine, engineering, economics and general; Dirs Pedro García Rueda, Eustasio A. García.

Editorial Atlántida, SA: Florida 643, 1005 Buenos Aires; tel. (1) 311-2261; telex 21163; f. 1918; fiction and non-fiction, children's books; Founder Constancio C. Vigil; Man. Dir Alfredo J. Vercelli.

Ediciones La Aurora: Deán Funes 1823/25, 1244 Buenos Aires; tel. (1) 941-8940; f. 1925; general, religion, spirituality, theology, philosophy, psychology, history, semiology, linguistics; Dir Dr Hugo O. Ortega.

Editorial Bruguera: Avalos 365, 1427 Buenos Aires; tel. (1) 553-2885; Man. Dir F. J. J. Texidó.

Centro Editor de América Latina, SA: Juan D. Perón 1228, 1038 Buenos Aires; tel. (1) 35-9449; f. 1967; literature, history; Man. Dir José B. Spivacow.

Centro de Documentación e Información Educativa: Ministerio de Educación y Justicia, Paraguay 1657, 1°, 1062 Buenos Aires; tel. (1) 41-5420; education, bibliography, directories, etc.; Dir Laureano García Elorrio.

Editorial Ciordia, SRL: Defensa 613, 1065 Buenos Aires; tel. (1) 30-4497; f. 1938; general educational and fiction; Man. Dir Miguel Angel Braga.

ARGENTINA

Editorial Claretiana: Lima 1360, 1138 Buenos Aires; tel. (1) 27-9250; f. 1956; Catholic religion; Dir P. ANDRÉS BERASAIN.

Editorial Claridad, SA: San José 1627, Buenos Aires; tel. (1) 23-5573; f. 1922; literature, biographies, social science, politics; Pres. Dra ANA MARÍA CABANELLAS.

Club de Lectores: Avda de Mayo 624, 1084 Buenos Aires; tel. (1) 34-3955; f. 1938; non-fiction; Dir JUAN MANUEL FONTENLA.

Club de Poetas: Casilla 189, 1401 Buenos Aires; f. 1975; poetry and literature; Exec. Dir JUAN MANUEL FONTENLA.

Editorial Columba, SA: Sarmiento 1889, 5°, 1044 Buenos Aires; tel. (1) 45-4297; f. 1953; classics in translation, 20th century; Man. Dir CLAUDIO A. COLUMBA.

Editorial Contémpora, SRL: Sarmiento 643, 1382 Buenos Aires; tel. (1) 45-1793; architecture, town-planning, interior decoration and gardening; Dir NORBERTO M. MUZIO.

Cosmopolita, SRL: Piedras 744, 1070 Buenos Aires; tel. (1) 361-8049; f. 1940; science and technology; Man. Dir RUTH F. DE RAPP.

Ediciones Depalma SRL: Talcahuano 494, 1013 Buenos Aires; tel. (1) 46-1815; f. 1944; law, politics, sociology, philosophy, history and economics; Dir ROBERTO SUARDIAZ.

Editorial Difusión, SA: Sarandi 1065-67, Buenos Aires; tel. (1) 941-0118; f. 1937; literature, philosophy, religion, education, textbooks, children's books; Dir DOMINGO PALOMBELLA.

Emecé Editores, SA: Carlos Pellegrini 1069, 9°, 1009 Buenos Aires; tel. (1) 311-4710; telex 17736; f. 1939; fiction, non-fiction, biographies, history, art, poetry, essays; Pres. BONIFACIO DEL CARRIL; Editors JORGE NAVEIRO, BONIFACIO P. DEL CARRIL.

Espasa Calpe Argentina, SA: Tacuarí 328, 1071 Buenos Aires; tel. (1) 34-0073; f. 1937; literature, science, dictionaries; publ. *Colección Austral*; Dir RAFAEL OLARRA JIMÉNEZ.

EUDEBA—Editorial Universitaria de Buenos Aires: Rivadavia 1573, 1033 Buenos Aires; tel. (1) 37-2202; f. 1958; university text books and general interest publications; Gen. Man. GUILLERMO MINA.

Fabril Editora, SA: California 2098, 1289 Buenos Aires; tel. (1) 21-3601; f. 1958; non-fiction, science, arts, education and reference; Editorial Man. ANDRÉS ALFONSO BRAVO; Business Man. RÓMULO AYERZA.

Editorial Glem, SACIF: Avda Caseros 2056, 1264 Buenos Aires; tel. (1) 26-6641; f. 1933; psychology, technology; Pres. JOSÉ ALFREDO TUCCI.

Editorial Guadalupe: Julián Alvarez 2215, 1425 Buenos Aires; tel. (1) 84-6066; f. 1895; social sciences, religion, anthropology, children's books, and pedagogy; Man. Dir P. LUIS O. LIBERTI.

Editorial Hachette, SA: Rivadavia 739, 1002 Buenos Aires; tel. (1) 334-8481; telex 17479; f. 1931; general non-fiction; Man. Dir J. A. MUSSET.

Editorial Heliasta, SRL: Viamonte 1730, 1°, 1055 Buenos Aires; tel. (1) 45-1843; f. 1970; literature, biography, politics, social science; Pres. Dra ANA MARÍA CABANELLAS.

Editorial Hemisferio Sur, SA: Pasteur 743, 1028 Buenos Aires; tel. (1) 48-9825; telex 18522; f. 1966; agriculture, science; Man. Dirs JUAN ÁNGEL PERI, ADOLFO LUIS PEÑA.

Editorial Hispano-Americana, SA (HASA): Alsina 731, 1087 Buenos Aires; tel. (1) 331-5051; f. 1934; science and technology; Pres. Prof. HÉCTOR OSCAR ALGARRA.

Editorial Inter-Médica, SAICI: Junín 917, 1°, Casilla 4625, Buenos Aires; tel. (1) 83-3234; f. 1959; science, medicine, dentistry, psychology, odontology; Pres. JORGE MODYEIEVSKY.

Editorial Inter-Vet, SA: Avda de los Constituyentes 3141, Buenos Aires; tel. (1) 51-2382; f. 1987; veterinary; Pres. JORGE MODYEIEVSKY.

Editorial Kapelusz, SA: Moreno 372, 1091 Buenos Aires; tel. (1) 34-6451; telex 18342; f. 1905; textbooks, psychology, pedagogy, children's books; Man. Dir RICARDO PASCUAL ROBLES.

Editorial Kier, SACIFI: Avda Santa Fé 1260, 1059 Buenos Aires; tel. (1) 41-0507; f. 1907; Eastern doctrines and religions, astrology, parapsychology, tarot, Ching, occultism, natural medicine; Pres. ALFONSO F. PIBERNUS.

Editorial Labor Argentina, SA (Spain): Venezuela 613, 1095 Buenos Aires; tel. (1) 33-4135; f. 1924; technology, science, art; Man. Dir PEDRO CLOTAS CIERCO.

Editorial Víctor Lerú, SA: Don Bosco 3834, 1000 Buenos Aires; tel. (1) 981-6098; f. 1944; art and architecture, music, history, technology, school books; Man. Dir VÍCTOR NEP.

Carlos Lohlé, SA: Tacuarí 1516, Casilla 3097, 1000 Buenos Aires; tel. (1) 27-9969; f. 1953; philosophy, religion, belles-lettres; Pres. CARLOS F. P. LOHLÉ; Dir FRANCISCO M. LOHLÉ.

Editorial Losada, SA: Moreno 3362/64, 1209 Buenos Aires; tel. (1) 88-8608; f. 1938; general; Pres. GONZALO PEDRO LOSADA.

Ediciones Macchi, SA: Alsina 1535 PB, 1088 Buenos Aires; tel. (1) 46-0594; f. 1947; economic sciences; Man. Dir RAÚL LUIS MACCHI.

Editorial Médica Panamericana, SA: Junín 831, 1113 Buenos Aires; tel. (1) 961-8815; telex 17666; f. 1962; health sciences; Pres. ROBERTO BRIK.

Editorial Nova, SACI: Buenos Aires; tel. (1) 34-8698; f. 1945; arts, philosophy, religion, medicine, textbooks, science and technology; Dir HORACIO D. ROLANDO.

Ediciones Nueva Visión, SAIC: Tucumán 3748, 1189 Buenos Aires; tel. (1) 89-5050; f. 1954; psychology, art, social sciences, architecture; Man. Dir JORGE J. GRISETTI.

Editorial Paidós: Defensa 599, 1°, 1065 Buenos Aires; tel. (1) 331-2275; f. 1945; social sciences, medicine, philosophy, religion, history, literature, textbooks; Man. Dir ENRIQUE BUTELMAN.

Plaza y Janés, SA: Lambaré 893, Buenos Aires; tel. (1) 86-6769; popular fiction and non-fiction; Man. Dir JORGE PÉREZ.

Editorial Plus Ultra, SAI & C: Callao 572, 1022 Buenos Aires; tel. (1) 46-5092; f. 1964; literature, history, textbooks, law, economics, politics, sociology, pedagogy, children's books; Man. Editor CARLOS ALBERTO LOPRETE.

Schapire Editor, SRL: Uruguay 1249, 1016 Buenos Aires; tel. (1) 44-0765; f. 1941; music, art, theatre, sociology, history, fiction; Dir MIGUEL SCHAPIRE DALMAT.

Ediciones Siglo Veinte, SA: Maza 177, 1206 Buenos Aires; tel. (1) 88-2758; telex 22146; f. 1943; fiction and non-fiction; Gen. Man. GREGORIO SCHVARTZ.

Editorial Sigmar, SACI: Belgrano 1580, 1093 Buenos Aires; tel. (1) 38-2844; telex 9073; f. 1941; children's books; Man. Dir SIGFRIDO CHWAT.

Editorial Sopena Argentina, SACI e I: Moreno 957, 7°, Of. 2, Casilla 1075, 1091 Buenos Aires; tel. (1) 38-7182; f. 1918; dictionaries, classics, chess, health, politics, history, children's books; Exec. Pres. DANIEL CARLOS OLSEN.

Editorial Stella: Viamonte 1984, 1056 Buenos Aires; tel. (1) 46-0346; Prop. Asociación Educacionista Argentina; general non-fiction and textbooks.

Editorial Sudamericana, SA: Humberto 531, 1°, 1103 Buenos Aires; tel. (1) 362-2128; telex 25644; f. 1939; general fiction and non-fiction; Gen. Man. JAIME RODRIGUÉ.

Editorial Troquel, SA: Garay 1454, 1153 Buenos Aires; tel. (1) 23-0771; f. 1954; general literature, technology and textbooks; Pres. GUSTAVO ARMANDO RESSIA.

Sudamericana/Planeta, SA (Editores): Humberto 545, 1°, 1103 Buenos Aires; tel. (1) 362-1332; telex 25644; f. 1983; general fiction and non-fiction; Pres. JAIME RODRIGUÉ.

PUBLISHERS' ASSOCIATION

Cámara Argentina de Publicaciones: Reconquista 1011, 6°, 1003 Buenos Aires; tel. (1) 311-6855; f. 1970; Pres. AGUSTÍN DOS SANTOS; Man. LUIS FRANCISCO HOULIN.

Radio and Television

In 1986 there were an estimated 19.9m. radio receivers in use, and in 1987 there were an estimated 5,950,000 television receivers in use.

Secretaría de Comunicaciones: Sarmiento 151, 4°, 1000 Buenos Aires; tel. (1) 312-1283; telex 21706; co-ordinates 30 stations and the international service; Sec. Lic. JUAN MANUEL MAGLIANO.

Subsecretaría de Planificación y Gestión Tecnológica: Sarmiento 151, 4°, 1000 Buenos Aires; tel. 311-5909; telex 21706; Under-Sec. Ing. LEONARDO JOSÉ LEIBSON.

Subsecretaría de Radiodifusión: Sarmiento 151, 4°, 1000 Buenos Aires; tel. (1) 311-5909; telex 21706; Under-Sec. Dr ROBERTO HORACIO TEZÓN.

Subsecretaría de Telecomunicaciones: Sarmiento 151, 4°, 1000 Buenos Aires; tel. (1) 311-5909; telex 21706; Under-Sec. Dr GUILLERMO GUSTANO KLEIN.

Comité Federal de Radiodifusión (CFR): Suipacha 765, 1008 Buenos Aires; tel. 394-4274; f. 1972; controls various technical aspects of broadcasting and transmission of programmes; Head PEDRO RAÚL SÁNCHEZ.

RADIO

There are three privately-owned stations in Buenos Aires and 72 in the interior. There are also 37 state-controlled stations, four provincial, three municipal and three university stations. The principal ones are Radio El Mundo, Radio del Plata, Radio Nacional, Radio Rivadavia, Radio Belgrano, Radio Argentina,

ARGENTINA

Radio Continental, Radio Mitre, Radio Antartida, Radio Excelsior, Radio Ciudad de Buenos Aires and Radio Splendid, all in Buenos Aires.

Servicio Oficial de Radiodifusión (SOR): Sarmiento 151, 1000 Buenos Aires; tel. (1) 30-2121; Dir FLORENCINO RODRÍGUEZ CROSS; runs:

Cadena Argentina de Radiodifusión (CAR): Avda Entre Ríos 149, 3°, 1079 Buenos Aires; tel. (1) 45-2113; groups all national state-owned commercial stations which are operated directly by the Subsecretaría Operativa.

LRA Radio Nacional: Ayacucho 1556, 1112 Buenos Aires; tel. (1) 803-5555; telex 21250; f. 1937; Dir OSCAR MARTÍNEZ ZEMBORAÍN.

Radiodifusión Argentina al Exterior (RAE): Casilla 555, 1000 Buenos Aires; tel. (1) 803-2351; f. 1958; broadcasts in 8 languages to all areas of the world; Gen.-Dir Lic. LUIS ROMEO ROJAS.

Asociación de Radiodifusoras Privadas Argentinas (ARPA): Juan D. Perón 1561, 8°, 1037 Buenos Aires; tel. (1) 35-4412; f. 1958; Pres. EVARISTO R. A. ALONSO.

TELEVISION

There are four television channels in the federal capital of Buenos Aires, 26 in the province of Buenos Aires, 41 in the interior, and 117 relay stations. There are 26 private television channels, 16 state-supervised stations (both provincial and national) and two university channels. The national television network is controlled by the Secretariat of Culture (part of the Ministry of Education and Justice).

The following are some of the more important television stations in Argentina: Argentina Televisora Color LS82 Canal 7, LS83 Canal 9, LS84 Canal 11, LS85 Canal 13, Telenueva, Teledifusora Bahiense, Telecor, Dicor Difusión Córdoba, TV Universidad Nacional Córdoba, and TV Mar del Plata.

Asociación de Teleradiodifusoras Argentinas (ATA): Córdoba 323, 6°, 1054 Buenos Aires; tel. (1) 312-4208; telex 17253; f. 1959; association of 21 private television stations; Pres. ALEJANDRO ENRIQUE MASSOT.

ATC—Argentina Televisora Color LS82 TV Canal 7: Avda Figueroa Alcorta 2977, 1425 Buenos Aires; tel. (1) 802-6001; state-controlled channel; Dir RAMIRO CASABELLAS.

LS83 TV Canal 9: Gelly 3378, 1425 Buenos Aires; tel. (1) 801-3065; private channel; Dir ALEJANDRO RAMAY.

LS84 Canal 11: Pavón 2444, 1248 Buenos Aires; tel. (1) 941-0091; telex 22780; state-controlled channel; Dir-Gen. CARLOS M. NEGRI.

LS85 TV Canal 13: San Juan 1170, 1147 Buenos Aires; tel. (1) 27-3661; telex 21762; f. 1960; state-controlled channel; Dir EDUARDO METZGER.

Finance

(cap. = capital; p.u. = paid up; res = reserves; dep. = deposits; m. = million; amounts in pesos argentinos and australes—₳)

BANKING

In 1986 there were 25 government-owned provincial banks, five government-owned municipal banks, 38 private commercial banks in the city of Buenos Aires and 90 private commercial banks in the rest of Argentina. There were also 31 foreign-owned banks operating in Argentina. In March 1984 President Alfonsín's Government disclosed plans to reform the banking sector. Fourteen financial institutions were to be liquidated and six others were to be placed under government control. In October 1986 the Government announced a reform of banking regulations, under which reserve requirements on deposits in Argentine banks were substantially reduced.

Central Bank

Banco Central de la República Argentina: Reconquista 266, 1003 Buenos Aires; tel. (1) 394-8411; telex 1137; f. 1935 as a central reserve bank; it has the right of note issue; all capital is held by the state; cap. and res 745,018m. (Dec. 1983); Pres. JOSÉ LUIS MACHINEA; Vice-Pres. MARCELO KIGUEL.

Government-Owned Commercial Banks

Banco de la Ciudad de Buenos Aires: Florida 302, 1313 Buenos Aires; tel. (1) 45-0726; telex 22365; municipal bank; f. 1878; cap. and res ₳527.7m., dep. ₳2,875.7m. (April 1988); Pres. Dr LUIS A. REMAGGI ALBERRO; 37 brs.

Banco de Entre Ríos: Monte Caseros 128, 3100 Paraná; tel. (042) 22-3700; telex 45115; f. 1935; provincial bank; cap. and res ₳126.7m., dep. ₳444.2m. (April 1988); Pres. HUGO REINALDO DOVAL; 37 brs.

Banco de Mendoza: Gutiérrez 51, POB 19, 5500 Mendoza; tel. (061) 25-1200; telex 55204; f. 1934; provincial bank; cap. ₳230.2m., dep. ₳519.1m. (April 1988); Pres. HUGO REINALDO DOVA; 77 brs.

Banco de la Nación Argentina: Bartolomé Mitre 326, 1039 Buenos Aires; tel. (1) 30-1011; telex 21407; f. 1891; national bank; cap. and res ₳8,579.6m., dep. ₳10,123.6m. (April 1988); Pres. MARIO LUIS KENNY; Gen. Man. GUIDO OSCAR ROMERO; 577 brs.

Banco de la Provincia de Buenos Aires: Avda San Martín 137, 1004 Buenos Aires; tel. (1) 33-2561; telex 18276; f. 1822; provincial bank; cap. and res ₳2,771.5m., dep. ₳6,541.2m. (April 1988); Pres. ALDO FERRER; Gen. Man. ANTONIO CASTELLO; 322 brs.

Banco del Chaco: Güemes 102, 3500 Resistencia; tel. (0722) 21077; telex 71214; f. 1958; provincial bank; cap. and res ₳365.0m., dep. ₳209.5m. (April 1988) Pres. Dr MANUEL WALDEMAR AGUIRRE; Gen. Man. RUBÉN ABEL MARCÓN; 26 brs.

Banco de la Provincia de Córdoba: San Jerónimo 166, 5000 Córdoba; tel. 051-42001; telex 51610; f. 1873; provincial bank; cap. and res ₳528.1m., dep. ₳3,231.6m. (April 1988); Pres. Dr JOAQUÍN CENDOYA; 157 brs.

Banco de la Provincia de Corrientes: 9 de Julio y San Juan, 3400 Corrientes; tel. (0783) 66637; telex 74106; cap. and res ₳166.4m., dep. ₳379.5m. (1988); Pres. RICARDO J. G. HARVEY; 30 brs.

Banco de la Provincia de Neuquén: Argentina 41/45, Neuquén; tel. 31-459; telex 84128; cap. and res ₳203.2m., dep. ₳283.6m. (April 1988); Pres. OMAR SANTIAGO NEGRETTI; 21 brs.

Banco Provincial de Santa Fé: San Martín 715, 2000 Rosario, Santa Fé; tel. (041) 21-1370; telex 41751; f. 1874; provincial bank; cap. and res ₳273.4m., dep. ₳680.1m. (April 1988); Pres. JORGE DOMÍNGUEZ.

Private Commercial Banks

Banco Alas: Sarmiento 528/32, 1041 Buenos Aires; tel. (1) 313-3400; telex 9127; cap. and res ₳16.3m., dep. ₳57.5m. (March 1986); Government Administrator LUIS PEDERNERA; 55 brs.

Banco Comercial del Norte: Esmeralda 25, Buenos Aires; tel. (1) 394-9199; telex 23879; f. 1912; cap. and res ₳290.1m., dep. ₳972.0m. (April 1988); Pres. FEDERICO J. L. ZORRAQUÍN; Gen. Man. N. POZZOLI; 75 brs.

Banco de Crédito Argentino, SA: Rivadavia 401, Buenos Aires; tel. (1) 334-1181; telex 18077; f. 1887; cap. and res ₳322.9m., dep. ₳1,352.0m. (April 1988); merged with Banco Financiero Argentino in 1987; Pres. Dr RICARDO CAIROLI; Gen. Man. OSVALDO CORTESI; 65 brs.

Banco Español del Río de la Plata Ltdo: Juan D. Perón 402, 1003 Buenos Aires; tel. (1) 331-2951; telex 21562; f. 1886; cap. and res ₳337.1m., dep. ₳1,109.8m. (April 1988); Pres. Dr PABLO TERÁN NOGUÉS; 66 brs.

Banco Francés del Río de la Plata: Reconquista 165, 1003 Buenos Aires; tel. (1) 331-7071; telex 9119; f. 1886; cap. and res ₳241.4m., dep. ₳914.0m. (April 1988); Pres. Dr LUIS MARÍA OTERO MONSEGUR; 26 brs.

Banco de Galicia y Buenos Aires: Juan D. Perón 407, Casilla 86, 1038 Buenos Aires; tel. (1) 394-7080; telex 23805; f. 1905; cap. and res ₳471.9m., dep. ₳2,312.6m. (April 1988); Pres. ROBERTO J. BULLRICH; 129 brs.

Banco Mercantil Argentino: Avda Corrientes 629, 1324 Buenos Aires; tel. (1) 334-9999; telex 9122; f. 1923; cap. and res ₳149.1m., dep. ₳680.1m. (April 1988); Pres. NOEL WERTHEIN; 45 brs.

Banco Quilmes, SA: Juan D. Perón 564, 2°, 1038 Buenos Aires; tel. (1) 331-8110; telex 17895; f. 1907; cap. and res ₳199.7m., dep. ₳1,265.7m. (April 1988); Pres. Dr PEDRO O. FIORITO; 58 brs.

Banco Río de la Plata, SA: Bartolomé Mitre 480, 1004 Buenos Aires; tel. (1) 331-8361; telex 9215; f. 1908; cap. and res ₳1,502.0m., dep. ₳3,413.2m. (April 1988); Exec. Vice-Pres. ROQUE MACCARONE; 84 brs.

Banco Shaw, SA: Sarmiento 355, 1041 Buenos Aires; tel. (1) 311-6271; telex 21226; f. 1959; cap. and res ₳143.8m., dep. ₳821.6m. (April 1988); Pres. Dr ALEJANDRO SHAW; 30 brs.

Other National Banks

Banco Hipotecario Nacional: Defensa 192, 1065 Buenos Aires; tel. (1) 34-2001; f. 1886; mortgage bank; cap. and res ₳1,018.8m., dep. ₳1,039.7m. (April 1988); Pres. Dr LUIS ANÍBAL REYNALDO.

Banco Nacional de Desarrollo: 25 de Mayo 145, 1002 Buenos Aires; tel. (1) 33-2091; telex 9179; f. 1944; development bank; cap. and res ₳1,392.3m., dep. ₳1,513.4m. (April 1988); Pres. (vacant).

Caja Nacional de Ahorro y Seguro: Hipólito Yrigoyen 1770, 1308 Buenos Aires; tel. (1) 11-1568; telex 22642; f. 1915; savings bank and insurance institution; cap. and res ₳162.1m., dep. ₳2,377.1m. (April 1988); Pres. Dr CARLOS AUGUSTO FONTE; Gen. Man. CONSTANTINO DIZ; 61 brs.

ARGENTINA *Directory*

Foreign Banks

Banca Nazionale del Lavoro, SA—BNL (Italy): Florida 32-36, Buenos Aires; tel. (1) 331-1580; telex 24028; cap. and res ₳418.5m., dep. ₳469.0m. (April 1988); took over Banco de Italia y Río de la Plata in 1987; Gen. Man. (vacant).

Banco do Brasil, SA: Sarmiento 487, 1041 Buenos Aires; tel. (1) 394-9861; f. 1960; cap. and res ₳120.6m., dep. ₳12.7m. (April 1988); Gen. Man. ERNANI SCHMITT.

Banco Europeo para América Latina, SA: Juan D. Perón 338, 1038 Buenos Aires; tel. (1) 331-6544; telex 9152; f. 1914; cap. and res ₳176.6m., dep. ₳323.2m. (June 1988); Gen. Man. MARC LEFLOT.

Banco Holandés Unido (Netherlands): Florida 361, 1005 Buenos Aires; tel. (1) 394-1022; telex 9160; f. 1914; cap. and res ₳94.5m., dep. ₳285.8m. (April 1988); Regional Man. (Argentina, Paraguay and Uruguay) F. T. BRILL; Man. (Argentina) P. C. VAN DIJK.

Banco di Napoli (Italy): Bartolomé Mitre 699, 1036 Buenos Aires; tel. (1) 30-5555; f. 1930; cap. and res ₳128.0m., dep. ₳61.2m. (April 1988); Gen. Man. PASCUAL FILOMENO.

Banco Popular Argentino: Florida 201 esq. Juan D. Perón, Casilla 3650, 1005 Buenos Aires; tel. (1) 33-6075; telex 9220; f. 1887; cap. and res ₳185.9m., dep. ₳441.0m. (April 1988); Pres. RICARDO TEJERO MAGRO; 27 brs.

Banco de Santander, SA (Spain): Bartolomé Mitre 575, 1036 Buenos Aires; tel. (1) 33-0014; f. 1964; cap. and res ₳62.6m., dep. ₳198.1m. (April 1988); Pres. EMILIO BOTÍN, Gen. Man. A. MARIANO MARTÍNEZ PÉREZ.

Banco Sudameris: Juan D. Perón 500, 1038 Buenos Aires; tel.(1) 33-4061; telex 9186; f. 1910; cap. and res ₳107.8m., dep. ₳679.5m. (April 1988); Man. PATRICK DE VILLEMANDY.

Banco Supervielle Société Générale SA: Reconquista 330, 1003 Buenos Aires; tel. (1) 394-4051; telex 24024; f. 1887; cap. and res ₳146.2m., dep. ₳465.7m. (April 1988); Chair. FRANCISCO SÉNECA.

Banco Tornquist, SA: Bartolomé Mitre 531, 1036 Buenos Aires; tel. (1) 30-7841; telex 9193; f. 1960; cap. and res ₳242.8m., dep. ₳475.4m. (April 1988); Pres. SERGE BOUTISSOU; Vice-Pres. DANIEL CHOQUART; 33 brs.

Bank of America NT & SA (USA): Juan D. Perón 525, 1038 Buenos Aires; tel. (1) 394-3266; f. 1940; cap. and res ₳80.2m., dep. ₳421.3m. (April 1988); Senior Vice-Pres. and Country Man. J. M. FORN.

Lloyds Bank (Bank of London and South America) Ltd (UK): Reconquista 101-51, Casilla 128, 1003 Buenos Aires; tel. (1) 33-0920; telex 21558; f. 1862; part of Lloyd's Bank Group; cap. and res ₳338.0m., dep. ₳1,239.5m. (April 1988); Dir-Gen. Gen. A. G. G. MCWILLIAM; 41 brs.

Bank of Tokyo Ltd (Japan): Corrientes 420, 1043 Buenos Aires; tel. (1) 393-8097; f. 1956; cap. and res ₳98.5m., dep. ₳116.8m. (April 1988); Man. HIROYOSHI KASAI.

Banque Nationale de Paris (France): 25 de Mayo 471, 1002 Buenos Aires; tel. (1) 311-4490; telex 23285; f. 1981; cap. and res ₳315.0m., dep. ₳312.0m. (July 1988); Gen. Man. PHILIPPE DE BOISSIEU.

Barclays Bank International PLC (UK): Juan D. Perón 655, 1038 Buenos Aires; tel. (1) 49-1001; telex 22080; f. 1979; cap. and res ₳42.9m., dep. ₳5.9m. (April 1988); Chief Man. M. N. JOHNSON.

Chase Manhattan Bank, NA (USA): 25 de Mayo 140, 1002 Buenos Aires; tel. (1) 30-1135; telex 9138; f. 1904; cap. and res ₳134.1m., dep. ₳278.2m. (April 1988); Gen. Man. HARRY TETHER.

Citibank, NA (USA): Bartolomé Mitre 530, 1036 Buenos Aires; tel. (1) 33-4041; f. 1914; cap. and res ₳385.4m., dep. ₳937.6m. (April 1988); Vice-Pres. RICHARD HANDLEY; 16 brs.

Deutsche Bank AG (Federal Republic of Germany): Reconquista 134 y Bartolomé Mitre 401, 1003 Buenos Aires; tel. (1) 30-2510; telex 9115; f. 1960; cap. and res ₳188.2m., dep. ₳609.9m. (April 1988); Dirs RAÚL G. STOCKER, KARL OSTENRIEDER, JÜRGEN REBOUILLON; 14 brs.

First National Bank of Boston (USA): Florida 99, 1005 Buenos Aires; tel. (1) 34-3051; f. 1784; cap. and res ₳425.4m., dep. ₳2,183.1m. (April 1988); Vice-Pres. and Gen. Man Ing. MANUEL SACERDOTE; 22 brs.

Royal Bank of Canada: Florida 202, 1005 Buenos Aires; tel. (1) 46-9851; f. 1869; cap. and res ₳56.9m., dep. ₳104.3m. (April 1988); Gen. Man. EGON WILHELM TEGTMEYER; 2 brs.

Bankers' Associations

Asociación de Bancos Argentinos (ADEBA): San Martín 229, 10°, 1004 Buenos Aires; tel. (1) 394-1430; telex 23704; f. 1972; Pres. ROQUE MACCARONE; Exec. Dir Dr NORBERTO C. PERUZZOTTI; 26 mems.

Asociación de Bancos de la República Argentina (ABRA): Reconquista 458, 2°, 1358 Buenos Aires; tel. (1) 394-1871; telex 28165; f. 1919; Pres. Dr MANUEL R. SACERDOTE; Exec. Sec. Dr FRANCISCO RODRÍGUEZ LÓPEZ; 37 mems.

Asociación de Bancos de Provincia de la República Argentina (ABAPRA): Florida 470, 1°, 1005 Buenos Aires; tel. 392-6321; f. 1959; Pres. RENÉ SANTIAGO GIORGIS; Man. EDUARDO R. D'AMATO; 31 mems.

Asociación de Bancos del Interior de la República Argentina (ABIRA): Corrientes 538, 4°, 1043 Buenos Aires; tel. (1) 394-3439; telex 28273; f. 1956; Pres. Dr JORGE FEDERICO CHRISTENSEN; Dir IGNACIO J. C. PREMOLI; 40 mems.

Federación de Bancos Cooperativos de la República Argentina (FEBANCOOP): Maipú 374, 9°/10°, 1006 Buenos Aires; tel. (1) 394-9949; telex 23650; f. 1973; Pres. RAÚL MEILÁN SALGADO; Exec. Dir Lic. SAMUEL GLEMBOCKI; 37 mems.

STOCK EXCHANGES

Mercado de Valores de Buenos Aires, SA: 25 de Mayo 367, 9°, 1002 Buenos Aires; tel. (1) 313-4522; telex 17445; Pres. GUIDO C. M. TAVELLI.

There are also stock exchanges at Córdoba, San Juan, Rosario, Mendoza and Mar del Plata.

INSURANCE

Superintendencia de Seguros de la Nación: Avda Julio A. Roca 721, 1067 Buenos Aires; tel. (1) 30-6653; f. 1938; Superintendent Lic. DIEGO PEDRO PELUFFO.

In June 1985 it was announced that all existing companies should have a minimum capital of ₳279,090 (australes) for all classes of insurance.

In June 1983 there were nearly 260 insurance companies operating in Argentina, of which 14 were foreign. The following is a list of those offering all classes or a specialized service.

La Agrícola, SA: Corrientes 447, Buenos Aires; tel. (1) 394-5031; f. 1905; associated company La Regional; all classes; Pres. LUIS R. MARCO; First Vice-Pres. JUSTO J. DE CORRAL.

Aseguradora de Créditos y Garantías, SA: San Martín 379, 6°, 1004 Buenos Aires; tel. (1) 394-1018; telex 24334; f. 1965; Pres. ALEJANDRO E. FRERS; Man. CARLOS GUSTAVO KRIEGER.

Aseguradora de Río Negro y Neuquén: Avda Alem 503, Cipolletti, Río Negro; f. 1960; all classes; Gen. Man. ERNESTO LÓPEZ.

Aseguradores de Cauciones SA: Paraguay 580, 1057 Buenos Aires; tel. (1) 312-5321; telex 17321; f. 1969; all classes; Pres. Dr AGUSTÍN DE VEDIA.

Aseguradores Industriales SA: Juan D. Perón 650, 6°, 1038 Buenos Aires; tel. (1) 46-5425; f. 1961; all classes; Exec. Pres. Dir LUIS ESTEBAN LOFORTE.

La Austral: Juncal 1319, 1062 Buenos Aires; tel. (1) 42-9881; telex 21078; f. 1942; all classes; Pres. RODOLFO H. TAYLOR.

Colón, Cía de Seguros Generales SA: San Martín 548-550, 1004 Buenos Aires; tel. (1) 393-5069; telex 23923; f. 1962; all classes; Gen. Man. L. D. STÜCK.

Columbia, SA: Juan D. Perón 690, 1038 Buenos Aires; tel. (1) 46-1240; f. 1918; all classes; Pres. EUGENIO M. BLANCO.

El Comercio, Compañía de Seguros a Prima Fija SA: Maipú 53, 1084 Buenos Aires; tel. (1) 34-2181; f. 1889; all classes; Pres. FELIPE JOSÉ LUIS M. GAMBA; Man. PABLO DOMINGO F. LONGO.

Compañía Argentina de Seguro de Crédito a la Exportación SA: Sarmiento 440, 4°, 1347 Buenos Aires; tel. (1) 394-7979; telex 24207; f. 1967; covers credit and extraordinary and political risks for Argentine exports; Pres. LUIS ORCOYEN.

Compañía Aseguradora Argentina SA: Casilla 3398, Avda Roque S. Peña 555, 1035 Buenos Aires; tel. (1) 30-1571; telex 012-2876; f. 1918; all classes; Man. GUIDO LUTTINI; Vice-Pres. ALBERTO O. ARGENTO.

La Continental, SA: Corrientes 655, 1043 Buenos Aires; tel. (1) 393-8051; telex 121832; f. 1912; all classes; Pres. RAÚL MASCARENHAS.

La Franco-Argentina, SA: Hipólito Yrigoyen 476, 1086 Buenos Aires; tel. (1) 30-3091; telex 17291; f. 1896; all classes; Pres. Dr GUILLERMO MORENO HUEYO; Gen. Man. Dra HAYDÉE GUZIAN DE RAMÍREZ.

Hermes, SA: Edif. Hermes, Bartolomé Mitre 754/60, 1034 Buenos Aires; tel. (1) 34-8441; f. 1926; all classes; Pres. CARLOS ANÍBAL PERALTA; Gen. Man. DIONISIO KATOPODIS.

Iguazú, SA: San Martín 442, 1004 Buenos Aires; tel. (1) 394-6661; f. 1947; all classes; Pres. RAMÓN SANTAMARINA.

India, SA: Avda Roque S. Peña 730, 1035 Buenos Aires; tel. (1) 30-6001; f. 1950; all classes; Pres. CARLOS DE ALZAGA; Vice-Pres. MATILDE DÍAZ VÉLEZ.

Instituto Italo-Argentino de Seguros Generales, SA: Avda Roque S. Peña 890, 1035 Buenos Aires; tel. (1) 45-5814; f. 1920; all classes; Pres. LUIS GOTTHEIL.

ARGENTINA

La Meridonal, SA: Juan D. Perón 646, 1038 Buenos Aires; tel. (1) 33-0941; f. 1949; life and general; Pres. G. G. LASCANO.

Plus Ultra, Cía Argentina de Seguros SA: San Martín 548-50, 1004 Buenos Aires; tel. (1) 393-5069; telex 23923; f. 1956; all classes; Gen. Man. L. D. STÜCK.

La Primera, SA: Blvd Villegas y Oro, Trenque Lauquén, Prov. Buenos Aires; tel. (1) 393-8125; all classes; Pres. ENRIQUE RAÚL U. BOTTINI; Man. Dr RODOLFO RAÚL D'ONOFRIO.

La Rectora, SA: Corrientes 848, 1043 Buenos Aires; tel. (1) 394-6081; f. 1951; all classes; Pres. PEDRO PASCUAL MEGNA; Gen. Man. ANTONIO LÓPEZ BUENO.

La República, SA: San Martín 627/29, 1374 Buenos Aires; tel. (1) 393-9901; f. 1928; group life and general; Pres. ARTURO EDBROOKE; Man. RODNEY C. SMITH.

Sud América Terrestre y Marítima Cía de Seguros Generales SA: Avda Pdte R. S. Peña 530, 1035 Buenos Aires; tel. (1) 30-8570; telex 24256; f. 1919; all classes; Mans ALAIN HOMBREUX, JORGE O. SALVIDIO.

La Unión Gremial, SA: Casilla 300, Gen. Mitre 665/99, 2000 Rosario, Santa Fé; tel. 47071; f. 1908; general; Pres. Cont. VÍCTOR MANUEL CABANELLAS; Gen. Man. Cont. EDUARDO IGNACIO LLOBET.

La Universal: Juncal 1319, 1062 Buenos Aires; tel. (1) 42-9881; telex 21078; f. 1905; all classes; Pres. Dr E. MAYER.

Reinsurance

Instituto Nacional de Reaseguros: Avda Julio A. Roca 694, 1067 Buenos Aires; tel. (1) 34-0084; telex 1170; f. 1947; reinsurance in all branches except credit; Pres. and Man. FELICIANO SALVIA.

Insurance Associations

Asociación Argentina de Compañías de Seguros: 25 de Mayo 565, 1002 Buenos Aires; tel. (1) 313-6974; telex 23837; f. 1894; 132 mems; Pres. Dr RODOLFO R. D'ONOFRIO.

Asociación de Aseguradores Extranjeros en la Argentina: San Martín 201, 7°, 1004 Buenos Aires; tel. (1) 394-3881; f. 1875; association of 10 foreign insurance companies operating in Argentina; Pres. Dr PEDRO ZUPPELLI; Sec. RICHARD MACGRATH.

Trade and Industry

CHAMBERS OF COMMERCE

Cámara Argentina de Comercio: Avda Leandro N. Alem 36, 1003 Buenos Aires; tel. (1) 331-8051; telex 18542; f. 1924; Pres. CARLOS R. DE LA VEGA.

Cámara de Comercio, Industria y Producción de la República Argentina: Florida 1, 4°, 1005 Buenos Aires; tel. (1) 33-0813; telex 18693; f. 1913; Pres. JOSÉ CHEDIEK; Vice-Pres. Dr FAUSTINO S. DIÉGUEZ, Dr JORGE M. MAZALAN; 1,500 mems.

Cámara de Comercio Exterior de la Federación Gremial del Comercio e Industria: Avda Córdoba 1868, Rosario, Santa Fé; tel. 21-3896; f. 1958; deals with import-export; Pres. EDUARDO C. SALVATIERRA; Vice-Pres. HUGO ULPIANO ARROYO; 120 mems.

Cámara de Exportadores de la República Argentina: Diag. Roque Sáenz Peña 740, 1°, 1035 Buenos Aires; f. 1943 to promote exports; Pres. Ing. DANIEL BRUNELLA; Vice-Pres. Ing. ALEJANDRO ACHAVAL; 700 mems.

Similar chambers are located in most of the larger centres and there are many foreign chambers of commerce.

GOVERNMENT REGULATORY AND SUPERVISORY BODIES

Consejo Federal de Inversiones: San Martín 871, 1004 Buenos Aires; tel. (1) 313-2034; federal board to regulate domestic and foreign investment; Sec.-Gen. Ing. JUAN JOSÉ CIACERA.

Instituto de Desarrollo Económico y Social (IDES): Güemes 3950, 1425 Buenos Aires; tel. (1) 71-3738; f. 1961; 700 mems; Pres. TORCUATO S. DITELLA; Sec. Dr CATALINA WAINERMAN.

Instituto Forestal Nacional (IFONA): Avda Pueyrredón 2446, 1119 Buenos Aires; tel. (1) 803-3146; telex 21535; national forestry commission; f. 1940; Dir Ing. HUGO H. KUGLER.

Junta Nacional de Carnes: San Martín 459, 1004 Buenos Aires; tel. (1) 394-5161; telex 24210; national meat board; in 1978 was granted a new national autonomous organic structure and was charged with the promotion and control of livestock and meat sales; Pres. Dr ALFREDO BEGATTI.

Junta Nacional de Granos: Paseo Colón 359, Buenos Aires; tel. (1) 30-0641; telex 21793; national grain board; supervises commercial practices and organizes the construction of farm silos and port elevators; Pres. JORGE CORT.

DEVELOPMENT ORGANIZATIONS

Instituto Argentino del Petróleo: Maipú 645, Buenos Aires; tel. (1) 392-3244; established to promote the development of petroleum exploration and exploitation.

Secretaría de Planificación: Hipólito Yrigoyen 250, 8°, Buenos Aires; tel. (1) 331-1722; f. 1961 to formulate national long-term development plans; Sec. Dr BERNARDO GRINSPUN.

Sociedad Rural Argentina: Florida 460, 1005 Buenos Aires; tel. (1) 392-2030; telex 23414; f. 1866; private organization to promote the development of agriculture; Pres. Dr GUILLERMO E. ALCHOURÓN; 9,400 mems.

STATE ENTERPRISES

Directorio de Empresas Públicas (DEP): Buenos Aires; f. 1986; holding company for state enterprises; Pres. Lic. HORACIO A. LOSOVIZ.

Sindicatura General de Empresas Públicas: Lavalle 1429, 1048 Buenos Aires; tel. (1) 45-6081; f. 1978 to replace the Corporación de Empresas Nacionales; to exercise external control over wholly- or partly-owned public enterprises; Pres. Dr HÉCTOR CONSTANTINO RODRÍGUEZ.

Agua y Energía Eléctrica Sociedad del Estado (AyEE): Avda Leandro N. Alem 1134, 1001 Buenos Aires; tel. (1) 311-6364; telex 21889; f. 1947; state water and electricity board; Pres. Ing. HORACIO V. QUAINI.

Empresa Nacional de Correos y Telégrafos (ENCOTEL): Sarmiento 151, 1000 Buenos Aires; tel. (1) 311-5031; telex 22045; f. 1972; postal services; Gen. Administrator Adm. Ing. JORGE RAÚL DUPONT.

Empresa Nacional de Telecomunicaciones (Entel): Defensa 143, 1065 Buenos Aires; tel. (1) 49-9684; telex 18003; f. 1949; state telecommunications corporation; Gen. Administrator Dr GUILLERMO G. KLEIN.

Gas del Estado: Alsina 1169, 1088 Buenos Aires; tel. (1) 37-2091; f. 1946; state gas corporation; Pres. Ing. CARLOS M. BECHELLI.

Hidroeléctrica Norpatagónica SA (Hidronor): Avda Leandro N. Alem 1074, 1001 Buenos Aires; tel. (1) 312-6030; telex 18097; f. 1967; state hydroelectric corporation; Pres. VÍCTOR POCHAT.

Obras Sanitarias de la Nación: Marcelo T. de Alvear 1840, Buenos Aires; tel. (1) 41-1081; f. 1973; sanitation; Gen. Administrator Lic. LUCIO F. DUARTE.

Petroquímica General Mosconi SAI y C: Perú 103, 1067 Buenos Aires; tel. (1) 33-5964; telex 22850; f. 1970; state petrochemical industry; Pres. Lic. JUAN C. COLOMBETTI.

Servicios Eléctricos del Gran Buenos Aires SA (SEGBA): Balcarce 184, Buenos Aires; tel. (1) 33-1901; f. 1958; state electricity enterprise; Pres. Ing. PABLO L. CARABELLI.

Yacimientos Carboníferos Fiscales (YCF): Avda Roque S. Peña 1190, Buenos Aires; tel. (1) 1958; state coal mining enterprise; Gen. Administrator Ing. JOSÉ A. MATAR IBÁÑEZ.

Yacimientos Mineros de Agua de Dionisio: Avda Julio A. Roca 710, Buenos Aires; tel. (1) 34-8024; f. 1958; state mining enterprise; Pres. Lic. PABLO ENRIQUE CHISTIK.

Yacimientos Petrolíferos Fiscales Sociedad del Estado (YPF): Avda Roque S. Peña 777, 1364 Buenos Aires; tel. (1) 46-7270; telex 21999; f. 1922; public corporation authorized to formulate national petroleum policy and to develop, process and market hydrocarbon resources; in July 1987, as part of the deregulation of the petroleum industry, it was announced that YPF was to be separated into four operational divisions; Pres. GUSTAVO DANIEL MONTAMAT; Vice-Pres. Ing. JORGE ENRICH BALADA.

TRADE ASSOCIATIONS

Asociación de Importadores y Exportadores de la República Argentina: Sarmiento 767, 1°, 1041 Buenos Aires; tel. (1) 325-3170; telex 25761; f. 1966; Pres. Lic. FERNANDO A. RAIMONDO; Man. ESTELIA D. DE AMATI.

Asociación de Industriales Textiles Argentinos: Uruguay 291, 4°, 1015 Buenos Aires; tel. (1) 49-2256; f. 1945; textile industry; Pres. MANUEL CYWIN; 250 mems.

Asociación de Industrias Argentinas de Carnes: Avda Córdoba 991, 1° A, 1054 Buenos Aires; tel. (1) 392-0587; telex 17304; meat industry; refrigerated and canned beef and mutton; Pres. JORGE BORSELLA.

Asociación Vitivinícola Argentina: Güemes 4464, 1425 Buenos Aires; tel. (1) 774-3370; f. 1904; wine industry; Pres. LUCIANO COTUMACCIO; Man. Lic. MARIO J. GIORDANO.

Cámara de Sociedades Anónimas: Sarmiento 299, Buenos Aires; tel. (1) 312-7434; Pres. Dr JORGE ENRIQUE RIVAROLA; Man. Dr ADALBERTO ZELMAR BARBOSA.

ARGENTINA

Centro de Exportadores de Cereales: Bouchard 454, 7°, 1106 Buenos Aires; tel. (1) 311-1697; telex 18644; f. 1943; grain exporters; Pres. Pedro E. García Oliver.

Confederación de Productores y Exportadores de la República Argentina: Bartolomé Mitre 2241, 1039 Buenos Aires; tel. (1) 48-6010; Pres. Jacobo Raies.

Confederaciones Rurales Argentinas: México 682, 2°, 1097 Buenos Aires; tel. (1) 261-1501; Pres. Dr Raúl Romero Feris.

Federación Lanera Argentina: Paseo Colón 823, 5°, 1063 Buenos Aires; tel. (1) 361-4604; telex 22021; f. 1929; wool industry; Pres. Ricardo G. Gravenhorst; Sec. Jorge D. Srodek; 119 mems.

EMPLOYERS' ORGANIZATION

Unión Industrial Argentina (UIA): Avda Leandro N. Alem 1067, 11°, 1001 Buenos Aires; tel. (1) 313-2762; telex 21749; f. 1887; Argentine association of manufacturers; re-established in 1974 with the fusion of the Confederación Industrial Argentina (CINA) and the Confederación General de la Industria; following the dissolution of the CINA in 1977, the UIA was formed in 1979; Pres. Eduardo de la Fuente; Exec. Sec. Dr Jorge Prina.

TRADE UNIONS

Confederación General del Trabajo—CGT (General Confederation of Labour): Buenos Aires; f. 1984; Peronist; Sec.-Gen. Saúl Edolver Ubaldini; represents approximately 90% of Argentina's 1,100 trade unions and consists of three groups:

CGT: Buenos Aires.

Renovadores: Buenos Aires.

62 Organizaciones: Buenos Aires.

Transport

Ministerio de Obras y Servicios Públicos: Avda 9 de Julio 1925, 1332 Buenos Aires; tel. (1) 37-1339; telex 22577; controls:

Secretaría de Transportes: Avda 9 de Julio 1925, 14°, 1332 Buenos Aires; tel. (1) 38-1435; Sec. (vacant).

Subsecretaría de Transporte: Avda 9 de Julio 1925, 8°, 1332 Buenos Aires; tel. (1) 38-5838, ext. 407; Under-Sec. (vacant).

Subsecretaría de Planificación del Transporte: Avda 9 de Julio 1925, 11°, 1332 Buenos Aires; tel. (1) 37-2571, ext. 465; Under-Sec. (vacant).

Subsecretaría de Marina Mercante: Julio A. Roca 734, 1067 Buenos Aires; tel. (1) 30-2857; telex 21091; Under-Sec. (vacant).

Dirección Nacional de Transporte Aerocomercial: Avda 9 de Julio 1925, 22°, 1332 Buenos Aires; tel. (1) 37-8365; telex 22577; Dir (vacant).

RAILWAYS

Lines: General Belgrano (narrow gauge), General Roca, General Bartolomé Mitre, General San Martín, Domingo Faustino Sarmiento (all wide gauge), General Urquiza (medium gauge) and Línea Metropolitana, which controls the railways of Buenos Aires and its suburbs. There are direct rail links with the Bolivian Railways network to Santa Cruz de la Sierra and La Paz; with Chile, through the Las Cuevas-Caracoles tunnel (across the Andes) and between Salta and Antofagasta; with Brazil, across the Paso de los Libres and Uruguayana bridge; with Paraguay (between Posadas and Encarnación by ferry-boat) and with Uruguay (between Concordia and Salto). In 1987 there were 34,509 km of tracks. In the Buenos Aires commuter area 270.4 km of wide gauge track and 52 km of medium gauge track are electrified. In mid-1988 work commenced on the construction of the 'Expreso del Sud' railway, linking Buenos Aires with the Bolivian capital, La Paz.

Ferrocarriles Argentinos (FA): Avda Ramos Mejía 1302, 1302 Buenos Aires; tel. (1) 312-4713; telex 22507; f. 1948 with the nationalization of all foreign property; autonomous body but policies are established by the Ministry of Public Works and Services through the Secretaría de Transportes; Supt Julio Quevedo.

Cámara de Industriales Ferroviarios: Alsina 1607, 1°, 1088 Buenos Aires; tel.(1) 40-5571; private organization to promote the development of Argentine railway industries; Pres. Ing. Guillermo Nottage.

Buenos Aires has an underground railway system:

Subterráneos de Buenos Aires: Bartolomé Mitre 3342, 1312 Buenos Aires; tel. (1) 89-4780; telex 18979; f. 1952; became completely state-owned in 1978; controlled by the Municipalidad de la Ciudad de Buenos Aires; five underground lines totalling 36 km; Pres. José María García Arecha.

ROADS

In 1986 there were 211,369 km of roads, of which 378 km were motorways, 36,928 km were other main roads and 174,063 km were secondary roads. In 1983 the network carried about 80% of all freight tonnage and 85% of all medium- and long-distance passengers. Four branches of the Pan-American highway run from Buenos Aires to the borders of Chile, Bolivia, Paraguay and Brazil.

Dirección Nacional de Vialidad: Comodoro Py 2002, 1104 Buenos Aires; tel. (1) 312-9021; telex 17879; controlled by the Secretaría de Transportes; Gen. Man. Ing. Saúl Martínez.

Asociación Argentina Empresarios Transporte Automotor (AAETA): Bernardo de Yrigoyen 330, 6°, 1072 Buenos Aires; Pres. Luis Carral.

Federación Argentina de Entidades Empresarias de Autotransporte de Cargas (FADEAC): Avda de Mayo 1370, 3°, 1372 Buenos Aires; tel. (1) 37-3635; Pres. Rogelio Cavalieri Iribarne.

There are several international passenger and freight services including:

Autobuses Sudamericanos SA: Bernardo de Yrigoyen 1370, 1°, Casilla 40, 1401 Buenos Aires; tel. (1) 27-6591; telex 17870; f. 1928; international bus services; car and bus rentals; charter bus services; Pres. Armando Samuel Schleker; Gen. Man. María Antonia Aprea.

INLAND WATERWAYS

There is considerable traffic in coastal and river shipping, mainly carrying petroleum and its derivatives. In 1983 the total displacement of vessels entering Argentine ports for such transport was 28.2m. nrt.

Dirección Nacional de Construcciones Portuarias y Vías Navegables: Avda España 221, 4°, Buenos Aires; tel. (1) 361-5964; responsible for the maintenance and improvement of waterways and dredging operations; Dir Ing. Enrique Casals de Alba.

SHIPPING

There are more than 100 ports, of which the most important are Buenos Aires, Quequén, Rosario and Bahía Blanca. There are specialized terminals at Ensenada, Comodoro Rivadavia, San Lorenzo and Campana (petroleum); Bahía Blanca, Rosario, Santa Fé, Villa Concepción, Mar del Plata and Quequén (cereals); and San Nicolás and San Fernando/San Isidro (raw and construction materials). In May 1987 the World Bank allocated a loan of US $50m. to Argentina to help finance the rehabilitation of Bahía Blanca. Argentina's merchant fleet totalled 2,066,661 grt in 1985; it comprised 64 cargo vessels, 26 bulk carriers, 58 tankers and 41 miscellaneous vessels.

Administración General de Puertos: Avda Julio A. Roca 734/42, 1067 Buenos Aires; tel. (1) 34-5621; telex 21879; f. 1956; state enterprise for direction, administration and exploitation of all national sea and river ports; Chair. Ing. Ricardo N. Gastaldi.

Capitanía General del Puerto: Avda Julio A. Roca 734, 2°, 1067 Buenos Aires; tel. (1) 34-9784; f. 1967; co-ordination of port operations; Port Captain Capt. Pedro Taramasco.

The chief state-owned organizations are:

Empresa Líneas Marítimas Argentinas SA (ELMA): Avda Corrientes 389, 1043 Buenos Aires; tel. (1) 312-8111; telex 21807; f. 1941; state line operating 50 vessels (474,445 grt) to Northern Europe, Scandinavia, the Mediterranean, West and East Coasts of Canada and the USA, Gulf of Mexico, Caribbean ports, Brazil, Pacific ports of Central and South America, Far East, North and South Africa and the Near East; Pres. Dr Luis Suárez Herter.

Yacimientos Petrolíferos Fiscales (YPF): Avda Roque S. Peña 777, 1035 Buenos Aires; tel. (1) 46-7271; telex 21792; Pres. Gustavo Daniel Montamat; fleet of 368,701 grt of cargo, tankers and tanker craft and motor launches.

Private shipping companies operating on coastal and overseas routes include:

Astra Compañía Argentina de Petróleo, SA: Leandro N. Alem 621, 1001 Buenos Aires; tel. (1) 311-0091; telex 17478; Pres. Dr Ricardo Gruneisen; fleet of 40,163 grt of tankers and tanker craft.

Bottachi, SA de Nàvegación: Avda Madero 940, 17°, 1106 Buenos Aires; tel. (1) 361-0252; telex 17269; fleet of 79,696 grt of tankers and cargo craft.

Compañía Argentina de Transportes Marítimos, SA: Avda Corrientes 327, 3°, 1043 Buenos Aires; tel. (1) 311-6300; telex 23524; Pres. Juan L. Martín; Vice-Pres. R. E. Vásquez; fleet of 54,153 grt.

CIVIL AVIATION

Argentina has 10 international airports (Aeroparque Jorge Newbery, Córdoba, Corrientes, El Plumerillo, Ezeiza, Jujuy, Resistencia, Río Gallegos, Salta and San Carlos de Bariloche). Ezeiza, 35

ARGENTINA

km from Buenos Aires, is one of the most important air terminals in Latin America. All aviation companies, with the exception of LADE, are controlled by the Dirección Nacional de Transporte Aerocomercial.

Aerolíneas Argentinas: Paseo Colón 185, 1063 Buenos Aires; tel. (1) 30-2071; telex 22517; f. 1950; nationalized industry; services to New York, Los Angeles, Miami, Mexico, Montreal and Europe. Its South American services link Argentina with Bolivia, Chile, Colombia, Ecuador, Uruguay, Brazil, Peru, Venezuela and Paraguay. The internal network covers the whole country. Passengers, mail and freight are carried. Pres. EDUARDO GONZÁLEZ DEL SOLAR; Vice-Pres. OSCAR CARBONE; fleet comprises 6 Boeing 747-200B, 1 747SP, 2 707, 8 727-200, 10 737-200, 2 737-200C, 4 Fokker F.28-1000, 1 F.28-4000.

Austral Líneas Aéreas (ALA): Corrientes 485, 1398 Buenos Aires; tel. (1) 313-3777; telex 22098; f. 1971; taken over by the state in 1980 to prevent financial collapse; 'privatized' in Sept. 1987; domestic flights linking 27 cities in Argentina; Pres. AMADEO RIVAS; fleet comprises 8 BAC 1-11 series 500, 3 DC-9-80.

Líneas Aéreas del Estado (LADE): Perú 710, Buenos Aires; tel. (1) 361-7174; telex 22040; f. 1940; controlled by the Air Ministry and operates through the Argentine Air Force. LADE operates from El Palomar Air Base, Buenos Aires, to 31 domestic points, all south of the capital; Sub-Dir MARCELO AUGUSTO CONTE; passenger fleet comprises 1 Fokker F.28-1000C, 2 F.27-600, 2 Twin Otter.

Tourism

Argentina's superb tourist attractions include the Andes mountains, the lake district centred on Bariloche (where there is a National Park), Patagonia, the Atlantic beaches and Mar del Plata, the Iguazú falls, the Pampas and Tierra del Fuego. Visitors to Argentina numbered 1,608,207 in 1984.

Secretaría de Turismo de la Nación: Calle Suipacha 1111, 21°, 1368 Buenos Aires; tel. (1) 312-5621; telex 24882; Sec. Dr ENRIQUE J. OLIVERA.

Asociación Argentina de Agencias de Viajes y Turismo (AAAVYT): Viamonte 640, 10°, 1053 Buenos Aires; tel. (1) 322-2804; telex 25449; f. 1951; Pres. PEDRO BACHRACH; Gen. Man. HÉCTOR J. TESTONI.

Atomic Energy

Comisión Nacional de Energía Atómica (CNEA): Avda del Libertador 8250, 1429 Buenos Aires; telex 21388; f. 1950; Pres. EMMA V. PÉREZ FERREIRA.

Consejo Consultivo Nacional de Energía Atómica: Buenos Aires; f. 1987; to advise the CNEA's Pres. (see above) in the drawing-up of studies and projects concerned with the reorganization of nuclear activities.

Argentina's first nuclear reactor, with a capacity of 350 MW, at Atucha, on the River Paraná de las Palmas, began to operate in 1974. A second plant at Embalse (Córdoba), with an estimated capacity of 600 MW, came into operation in March 1983. A third plant, Atucha II, with an estimated capacity of 700 MW, was under construction in 1988, and was expected to begin operating in 1993. Argentina's first nuclear fuel production plant opened in April 1982, and a plutonium processing plant was due to begin operating in early 1987. In recent years the development of the atomic energy sector has been severely hindered by lack of funds. In 1985 nuclear power supplied 11.5% of Argentina's total energy requirements.

Research reactors: The following research reactors are in operation:

RA-1 Centro Atómico Constituyentes: maximum capacity 150 kW.
RA-2 Centro Atómico Constituyentes: maximum capacity 30 MW.
RA-3 Centro Atómico Ezeiza: maximum capacity 8 MW.

AUSTRALIA

Introductory Survey

Location, Climate, Language, Religion, Flag, Capital

The Commonwealth of Australia occupies the whole of the island continent of Australia, lying between the Indian and Pacific Oceans, and its offshore islands, principally Tasmania to the south-east. Australia's nearest neighbour is Papua New Guinea, to the north. In the summer there are tropical monsoons in the northern part of the continent (except for the Queensland coast), but the winters are dry. Both the north-west and north-east coasts are liable to experience tropical cyclones between December and April. In the southern half of the country, winter is the wet season; rainfall decreases rapidly inland. Very high temperatures, sometimes exceeding 50°C (122°F), are experienced during the summer months over the arid interior and for some distance to the south, as well as during the pre-monsoon months in the north. The official language is English. In 1966 more than 88% of the population professed Christianity. The national flag (proportions 2 by 1) is blue, with a representation of the United Kingdom flag in the upper hoist, a large seven-pointed white star in the lower hoist and five smaller white stars, in the form of the Southern Cross constellation, in the fly. The capital, Canberra, lies in one of two enclaves of federal territory known as the Australian Capital Territory (ACT).

Recent History

Since the Second World War, Australia has taken an important place in Asian affairs and has strengthened its political and economic ties with India, South-East Asia and Japan. The country co-operates more closely than formerly with the USA (see ANZUS, p. 92). As a founder-member of the Colombo Plan (p. 110), Australia has given much aid to Asian countries. Australia is also a member of the South Pacific Commission (p. 201) and of the South Pacific Bureau for Economic Co-operation (p. 203).

In January 1966 Sir Robert Menzies resigned after 16 years as Prime Minister, and was succeeded by Harold Holt, who was returned to office at elections later that year. However, Holt died in a swimming accident in December 1967. His successor, Senator John Gorton, took office in January 1968 but resigned, after losing a vote of confidence, in March 1971. William McMahon was Prime Minister from March 1971 until December 1972, when, after 23 years in office, the Liberal-Country Party coalition was defeated at a general election for the House of Representatives. The Australian Labor Party (ALP), led by Gough Whitlam, won 67 of the 125 seats in the House. Following a conflict between the Whitlam Government and the Senate, both Houses of Parliament were dissolved in April 1974, and general elections were held in May. The ALP was returned to power, although with a reduced majority in the House of Representatives. However, the Government failed to gain a majority in the Senate, and in October 1975 the Opposition in the Senate obstructed legislative approval of budget proposals. The Government was not willing to consent to a general election over the issue but in November the Governor-General, Sir John Kerr, intervened and took the unprecedented step of dismissing the Government. A caretaker ministry was installed under Malcolm Fraser, the Liberal leader, who formed a coalition government with the National Country Party. This coalition gained large majorities in both Houses of Parliament at general elections in December 1975, but the majorities were progressively reduced at general elections in December 1977 and October 1980.

Fraser's coalition government was defeated by the ALP at federal elections in March 1983. Robert Hawke, who had replaced William Hayden as Labor leader in the previous month, became the new Prime Minister and immediately organized a meeting of representatives of government, employers and trade unions to reach agreement on a prices and incomes policy that would allow economic recovery. Hawke called a general election for December 1984, 15 months earlier than necessary, and the ALP was returned to power with a reduced majority in the House of Representatives. The opposition coalition between the Liberal Party and the National Party collapsed in April 1987, when 12 National Party MPs withdrew from the agreement and formed the New National Party (led by Sir Joh Bjelke-Petersen, the right-wing Premier of Queensland), while the remaining 14 National Party MPs continued to support their leader, Ian Sinclair, who wished to remain within the alliance. Both Houses of Parliament were dissolved in June, in preparation for an early general election in July. The election campaign was dominated by economic issues. The ALP was returned to office with an increased majority, securing 86 of the 148 seats in the House of Representatives. Following his victory, Hawke announced an extensive reorganization of government departments, aimed at reducing public expenditure. The new Inner Cabinet comprised only 16 members; 14 junior ministers were also appointed. The Liberal and National Parties announced the renewal of the opposition alliance in August. Four months later, Bjelke-Petersen was forced to resign as Premier of Queensland, under pressure from National Party officials who blamed him for the sharp decline in support for the National Party in Queensland.

Several substantial defeats at by-elections held in early 1988, followed (in September) by the rejection in a referendum of four government proposals for constitutional reform, testified to the growth of general disaffection with the Hawke administration. A decline in living standards and commitment to a policy of wage restraint led to a lack of confidence in the Government. In March 1988 the ALP was decisively defeated at state elections in New South Wales, where it had held power for 12 years. In October the party retained power in the state of Victoria, but with a reduced majority. Hawke had been sharply criticized in August for nominating the former Labor leader, William Hayden, to succeed Sir Ninian Stephen as Governor-General. Hayden had, in the past, been openly critical of the office, and it was speculated that his appointment would hasten the replacement of the present constitutional monarchy by a modified system.

Owing to Australian opposition to French test explosions of nuclear weapons at Mururoa Atoll in the South Pacific Ocean, a ban on uranium sales was introduced. However, in August 1986 the Government announced its decision to resume uranium exports, claiming that the sanction had been ineffective and that the repeal of the ban—which provoked strong opposition among Labor MPs—would increase government revenue by $A66m., through the repayment of compensation that had been awarded to the mining industry. In December 1986 Australia ratified a treaty declaring the South Pacific area a nuclear-free zone. In May 1987 Australia and the United Kingdom began a joint operation to ascertain the extent of plutonium contamination resulting from British nuclear weapons testing at Maralinga between 1956 and 1967. Many Australians were highly critical of the UK's apparent disregard for the environmental consequences of the tests and of the British authorities' failure to make adequate arrangements to protect the local Aborigines, who were now campaigning for a thorough decontamination of their traditional lands.

The sensitive issue of Aboriginal land rights was addressed by the Government in August 1985, when it adopted proposals for legislation that would give Aborigines inalienable freehold title to national parks, vacant Crown land and former Aboriginal reserves, in spite of widespread opposition from state governments (which had formerly been responsible for their own land policies), from mining companies and from the Aborigines themselves, who were angered by the Government's withdrawal of its earlier support for the Aboriginal right to veto mineral exploitation. In October 1985 Ayers Rock, in the Northern Territory, was officially transferred to the Mutijulu Aboriginal community, on condition that continuing access to the rock (the main inland tourist attraction) be guaranteed. In 1986, however, the Government abandoned its pledge to impose such federal legislation on unwilling state governments, and this led to further protests from Aboriginal leaders. Legislation to facilitate the granting of exploration permits to mining companies, while preserving Aboriginal rights, was under consideration in 1987. In September the Prime Minister proposed a treaty of understanding with the Aboriginal people, to coincide with the 200th anniversary, in 1988, of European settlement in Australia. In November 1987 an official commission of inquiry into the cause of the high death rate among Aboriginal prisoners recommended immediate government action, and in July 1988 it was announced that 108 cases remained to be investigated. Amid fears that discontented Aborigines would disrupt Australia's bicentennial celebrations, Hawke advanced proposals for an enlarged Ministry for Aboriginal Affairs, but by late 1988 little had been achieved. In August a United Nations report had accused Australia of being in violation of international human rights in its treatment of the Aboriginal people. In November the Government announced an enquiry into the Aboriginal Affairs Department, following accusations, voiced by the opposition coalition, of nepotism and misuse of funds. Statements made by members of the opposition coalition, criticizing the continued influx of Asian immigrants into the country, caused further debate on the issue of race relations throughout 1988. John Howard, the leader of the Liberal Party, warned that the high rate of immigration was damaging Australia's 'social cohesion'. About 5m. people have migrated to Australia since 1945.

In its foreign policy, the Hawke Government placed greater emphasis on links with South-East Asia. Australian relations with Indonesia, which had been strained since the Indonesian annexation of the former Portuguese colony of East Timor in 1976, improved in August 1985, when Robert Hawke made a statement recognizing Indonesian sovereignty over the territory, but subsequently deteriorated, following the publication in a Sydney newspaper, in April 1986, of an article containing allegations of corruption against the Indonesian President, Gen. Suharto. Relations between the two countries improved slightly in September 1988, when agreement was reached, in principle, to develop offshore petroleum resources in the Timor Gap, an area of sea forming a boundary between the two countries. In December 1986 the Australian Government announced the imposition of further trading sanctions against South Africa, as a protest against the system of racial apartheid in that country. Imports of South African coal, iron, steel and agricultural products were banned from June 1987.

The viability of the ANZUS military pact, linking Australia, New Zealand and the USA, was disputed by the US Government after the New Zealand Government of David Lange had declared, in July 1984, that vessels believed to be powered by nuclear energy, or to be carrying nuclear weapons, would be barred from the country's ports. Hawke did not support the New Zealand initiative, and Australia continued to participate with the USA in joint military exercises from which New Zealand had been excluded. However, the Hawke Government declined directly to endorse US retaliation against New Zealand, and in 1986 stated that Australia regarded its 'obligations to New Zealand as constant and undiminishing'. In late 1988 Australia signed a 10-year agreement with the USA, extending its involvement in the management of US-staffed military bases in Australia. The pact was regarded as confirmation of Australia's continuing commitment to alliance with the West. In response to growing Soviet influence in the Pacific region, the Government announced in early 1987 that Australia's defence ties with South Pacific nations were to be given the same priority as traditional links with South-East Asian countries. In March proposals for an ambitious new defence strategy were published, following the recommendations of a government-commissioned report advocating a comprehensive restructuring of the country's military forces, on the basis of greater self-reliance. The cost of the plan, however, was estimated at $A25,000m. over 15 years.

In March 1986 the last vestiges of Australia's constitutional links with the United Kingdom were finally severed by the Australia Act, which abolished the UK Parliament's residual legislative, executive and judicial controls over Australian state law.

Government

Australia comprises six States and two Territories. Executive power is vested in the British monarch and exercised by the monarch's appointed representative, the Governor-General, who normally acts on the advice of the Federal Executive Council (the Cabinet), led by the Prime Minister. The Governor-General appoints the Prime Minister and, on the latter's recommendation, other Ministers.

Legislative power is vested in the Federal Parliament. This consists of the monarch, represented by the Governor-General, and two chambers elected by universal adult suffrage (voting is compulsory). The Senate has 76 members (12 from each State and two from each of the Territories), who are elected by a system of proportional representation for six years when representing a State, with half the seats renewable every three years, and for a term of three years when representing a Territory. The House of Representatives has 148 members, elected for three years (subject to dissolution) from single-member constituencies. The Federal Executive Council is responsible to Parliament.

Each State has a Governor, representing the monarch, and its own legislative, executive and judicial system. The State Governments are essentially autonomous, but certain powers are placed under the jurisdiction of the Federal Government. All except the Northern Territory, which acceded to self-governing status in 1978, and Queensland have an Upper House, the Legislative Council, and a Lower House, the Legislative Assembly or House of Assembly. The chief ministers of the States are known as Premiers, as distinct from the Federal Prime Minister.

Defence

Australia's defence policy is based on collective security and it is a member of the British Commonwealth Strategic Reserve and ANZUS, with New Zealand and the USA. In June 1988 Australia's armed forces numbered 70,500 (army 32,000, navy 15,800, air force 22,600). The defence budget for 1987/88 was $A7,410m. Service in the armed forces is voluntary.

Economic Affairs

Australia has a diversified economy, with a generally high level of material prosperity. In 1987, according to estimates by the World Bank, Australia's gross national product (GNP), measured at average 1985–87 prices, was US $176,301m., equivalent to $10,900 per head (comparable to the average levels in industrialized West European countries). It was estimated that Australia's GNP per head increased, in real terms, at an average rate of 1.5% per year between 1980 and 1987. The average annual real growth of overall gross domestic product (GDP) was 4.0% in 1965–80, slowing to 3.1% in 1980–86.

Greatly-accelerated development of mineral and energy resources followed net increases in foreign capital inflow during the early 1980s. Although foreign investment declined in 1983/84, following a decision in December 1983 to 'float' the Australian dollar and to abolish most foreign exchange controls, it subsequently rose sharply, reaching $A19,900m. in 1985/86 and $A25,500m. in 1986/87. Australia has vast reserves of coal, petroleum, natural gas, nickel, iron ore and bauxite, and there is a major diamond field in the Kimberley Mountains of Western Australia, which by 1986 was producing at a rate that would yield 25m. carats of mainly industrial-quality diamonds per year, equivalent to almost 40% of 1984 world output. In addition, the Government lifted the ban on uranium exports in 1977, subject to stringent nuclear safeguards, and sales abroad were worth $A360m. in 1982/83. Uranium production totalled an estimated 4,100 metric tons in 1987. Gold, silver, lead, zinc and copper are also exploited. In 1986/87 output of gold reached 81,856 kg and lead production totalled 142,000 metric tons. In 1986 exports of gold were valued at $A941m. In 1987 there were plans for the development of the Cadjebut lead and zinc deposit, in the West Kimberley region of Western Australia. Exploitable reserves were estimated at 2.5m. metric tons, and mining of 320,000 tons of ore per year was expected to begin in 1988, with an annual production rate of 44,000 tons of zinc and 13,000 tons of lead contained in concentrates. The Olympic Dam project in South Australia is expected to yield large amounts of gold, copper and uranium, although their exploitation was unlikely to begin before the late 1980s. In late 1988 a new silicon plant in Kemerton, Western Australia, announced anticipated annual production of 24,300 metric tons of metal by 1990. About 70% of Australia's petroleum requirements are now met by domestic sources, but it is estimated that, in the absence of major new discoveries, self-sufficiency will fall to 42% by 1993/94. Petroleum production declined from 26.7m. metric tons in 1985 to 23.8m. tons in 1986. However, there have been recent discoveries of offshore petroleum deposits in the Timor Sea. Coal is Australia's principal source of foreign exchange earnings, and production is being raised, both for export and to fuel the domestic aluminium smelting industry. The production of hard coal increased from 155.6m. metric tons in 1985/86 to an estimated 182.3m. tons in 1986/87, and in 1986 Australia overtook the USA as the world's leading coal exporter, with exports of coal in that year reaching a record 92m. tons, accounting for export earnings of $A5,200m. (more than 15% of total export revenue). In mid-1988 the Government advocated an extensive reorganization of the coal industry, after production had been drastically reduced by prolonged industrial action. Work on a project to produce liquefied natural gas on the North-West Shelf, costing $A14,000m., resulted in 1984 in the first deliveries of unprocessed natural gas for domestic use, and in 1985 Japanese customers contracted to buy large quantities of gas, beginning in 1989. In 1983/84 the output of natural gas from Bass Strait, and from new fields in South and Western Australia, totalled 12.1m. cu m. In 1987 the China Metallurgical Import and Export Corporation (CMIEC) of Beijing signed an agreement to form a joint venture to exploit a rich outcrop of iron ore at Mount Channar, in the Pilbara region of Western Australia. Production was scheduled to begin in 1990, initially at a rate of 5m. metric tons per year, which was expected to increase to 10m. tons per year by 1996. The CMIEC undertook to provide 40% of development costs and to purchase the new mine's entire output. In the same year an iron ore export agreement, estimated to be worth $A1,500m., was secured with Romania, whereby Australia was to supply 53m. metric tons of iron ore to Romania's steel industry over a period of 11 years, beginning in January 1988. It was hoped that these agreements would help to offset an anticipated decline in the level of iron ore exports to Japan (hitherto Australia's principal customer), where the steel industry was experiencing a depression. (Revenue from iron ore exports decreased from $A1,940m. in 1985/86 to $A1,750m. in 1986/87.) The production of iron ore reached a record 100.4m. metric tons (64% iron) in 1986/87, and the output of nickel totalled 74,654 tons. In 1986 an important platinum deposit, which was judged to have export potential, was discovered in the Northern Territory, and it was hoped that exploitation of this reserve would end Australia's dependence on South Africa for the mineral. In 1987 the discovery was announced of a new, allegedly vast, field of opals near Coober Pedy, in South Australia. South Australia supplies 80% of the world demand for opals, mostly from mines in the Coober Pedy region, which contain gems estimated to be worth more than $A24m.

In 1985/86 minerals accounted for about 39% of export revenue and contributed 5.5% of GDP, although mining employed only 1.4% of the working population. Many of Australia's minerals are being exploited as raw materials for Japan's industries. The pattern of Australia's dependence on foreign trade has thus undergone a change, with Japan overtaking Western countries as the major market, taking 28.5% of Australian exports in 1985/86, and as the major source of imports, providing 23.8% of the total in 1985/86, slightly ahead of the USA, which supplied 21.0%; ASEAN countries together accounted for 6.5% of exports and 4.6% of imports, while EEC member-states together took about 14% of exports and provided 23% of imports. Australia had a trade surplus of $A517.7m. in 1984/85, when the value of exports totalled $A30,537.7m. and that of imports $A30,020.0m. In 1986/87, however, there was a trade deficit of $A1,239.3m., with exports totalling $A35,782.6m. and imports $A37,021.9m. The trade deficit was $A3,000m. in 1987/88. Relations with the EEC have been strained since 1980, owing to the fact that the subsidized prices of certain EEC products, particularly meat and sugar, make Australian goods uncompetitive in their traditional markets, but in February 1985 Australia secured an assurance that EEC subsidies on exports of beef to the Far East would not be extended.

Manufacturing, which in 1987/88 contributed about 17% of GDP and employed about 16% of the labour force, mainly in the iron and steel and engineering sectors, has become very diversified under the protection of tariffs, which in 1986 ranged from 4% for mineral manufactures to 66% for clothing. Other important industries are food-processing, machinery, motor vehicles, chemicals, electrical goods and electronic equipment. In May 1988 the Government announced that substantial reductions in the general levels of protection would be progressively introduced over the next few years. However, commitments to maintain protection to the clothing, footwear and related industries were affirmed.

The phenomenal mineral discoveries of recent years have eroded Australia's traditional reliance on the agricultural sector, which contributed only 4.5% of GDP in 1986/87. Severe drought affected agricultural production in 1979–83, with the important wheat crop decreasing to 8.8m. tons in 1982/83. Wheat production subsequently recovered, reaching a record 17.4m. tons in 1986. The area planted to wheat, however, fell from 11.2m. ha in 1986/87 to 9.4m. ha in 1987/88, reflecting the shift of emphasis from crops to livestock. Wool, wheat, meat, sugar and dairy products are major export items; as a source of foreign exchange earnings, wool is second in importance only to coal, accounting for export earnings of $A3,400m. in 1986/87. Total agricultural exports reached a record $A11,700m. in 1986/87.

The Hawke Government sought to curtail public expenditure, and embarked on a programme of economic austerity. In 1986 and 1988 the Government signed agreements with trade-union leaders for further wage restraint. The 1986/87 budget aimed to curb the rise in interest rates and to halt the rapid depreciation of the Australian dollar, which had been 'floated' in December 1983 and had declined in value by 54% in relation to the Japanese yen, and by 25% against the US dollar, between January 1985 and July 1986. Projected revenue of $A71,300m. was to be obtained partly through increased excise and indirect taxes on fuel, alcohol and luxury goods, and was to include $A1,400m. in new taxes. The 1987/88 budget resulted in a surplus of $A2,300m., the first occasion on which a surplus had been achieved for more than 20 years. A further surplus of $A5,470m. was forecast for the 1988/89 financial year, equivalent to 1.7% of GDP. A decline in the rates of inflation and unemployment and a reduction in the current account deficit were envisaged. In 1986/87 the current account deficit had reached $A13,600m., equivalent to 5% of GDP or 37% of total annual export receipts. The equivalent figure for 1987/88 was 28%, and in 1988/89 the deficit was expected to decline to $A9,500m. In 1983/84 GDP grew, in real terms, by 4.9%; growth subsequently declined to 4.6% in 1984/85, to 3.7% in 1985/86 and to 2.0% in 1986/87, but rose to 3.6% in 1987/88. GDP was projected to increase by 3.5% in 1988/89. The annual rate of inflation declined to 4.3% in the year 1984/85, owing largely to a restraint in wage settlements, arising from the Government's tripartite agreement with employers and trade unions. However, inflation in the year to June 1988 was 7.1%, although it was forecast to fall to 4.5% by mid-1989. The seasonally-adjusted unemployment rate in Australia was 7.4% of the labour force in June 1988, and was expected to decline to 7.25% by the end of the 1988/89 financial year. Wide-ranging measures to deregulate the banking system were announced in 1984, and trading licences were granted to 16 foreign banks in February 1985. Plans to 'privatize' certain state-owned concerns were under consideration in 1988.

Social Welfare

Australia provides old-age, invalid and widows' pensions, unemployment, sickness and supporting parents' benefits, family allowances and other welfare benefits and allowances. Reciprocal welfare agreements operate between Australia and New Zealand and the United Kingdom. In 1984 Australia had 3,535 hospital establishments, including nursing homes, with a total of 166,237 beds, equivalent to one for every 66 inhabitants. In 1984 there were 35,000 physicians registered in the country. The desert interior is served by the Royal Flying Doctor Service. Of total expenditure by the Federal Government and its agencies in the financial year ending 30 June 1986, $A6,751m. (9.5%) was for health services, while a further $A19,325m. (27.3%) was for social security and welfare. Expenditure on health by all levels of government in 1985/86 was $A12,949m. (14.1% of total government spending).

In February 1984 the Government introduced a system of universal health insurance, known as Medicare, whereby every Australian is protected against the costs of medical and hospital care. Where medical expenses are incurred, Medicare covers patients for 85% of the government-approved Schedule Fee for any service provided by a doctor in private practice. For hospital care, Medicare pays the full cost of shared-ward accommodation in public hospitals when treatment is provided by doctors employed by the hospital. Out-patient treatment is also free. Private health insurance is available to cover private hospital accommodation and the choice of doctor in a public hospital. The Medicare scheme is financed in part by a 1% levy on taxable incomes above a certain level.

AUSTRALIA

Education

Education is the responsibility of each of the States and the Federal Government. It is compulsory, and available free of charge, for all children from the ages of six to 15 years. Primary education generally begins at six years of age and lasts for six years. Secondary education, beginning at the age of 12, usually lasts for five years. As a proportion of children in the relevant age-groups, the enrolment ratios in 1985 were 97% in primary schools and 86% in secondary schools. In 1987 there were 2,196,742 children enrolled in government primary and secondary schools, and 808,141 attending private schools. Special services have been developed to meet the needs of children living in the remote 'outback' areas, notably Schools of the Air, using two-way receiver sets. A system of one-teacher schools and correspondence schools also helps meet these needs. Australia has 19 universities, with a total of 175,476 students in 1985. Expenditure on education by all levels of government in the financial year 1985/86 was $A13,043m. (14.2% of total government spending).

Public Holidays

1989: 2 January (for New Year's Day), 26 January (Australia Day), 24–27 March (Easter), 25 April (Anzac Day), 12 June* (Queen's Official Birthday), 25 December (Christmas Day), 26 December (Boxing Day)†.

1990: 1 January (New Year's Day), 26 January (Australia Day), 13–16 April (Easter), 25 April (Anzac Day), 12 June* (Queen's Official Birthday), 25 December (Christmas Day), 26 December (Boxing Day)†.

* In Western Australia this holiday will be held on 25 September in 1989. No date has yet officially been announced for 1990.
† Boxing Day is not a public holiday in South Australia.

There are also numerous state holidays.

Weights and Measures

The metric system is in force.

Statistical Survey

Source (unless otherwise stated): Australian Bureau of Statistics, POB 10, Belconnen, ACT 2616; tel. (062) 526627; telex 62020.

Area and Population

AREA, POPULATION AND DENSITY

Area (sq km)	7,682,300*
Population (census results)†	
30 June 1976	14,033,100
30 June 1981	
Males	7,448,300
Females	7,475,000
Total	14,923,300
Population (official estimates at mid-year)†	
1986	15,973,900
1987	16,249,000
1988	16,531,900
Density (per sq km) at mid-1988	2.2

* 2,966,151 sq miles.
† Figures include Australian residents temporarily overseas. Census results also include an adjustment for underenumeration, estimated to have been 2.7% in 1976 and 1.9% in 1981. The enumerated totals were: 13,548,448 in 1976; 14,576,330 (males 7,267,076; females 7,309,254) in 1981.

STATES AND TERRITORIES (30 June 1986)

	Area (sq km)	Population	Density (per sq km)
New South Wales (NSW)	801,600	5,543,500	6.9
Victoria	227,600	4,164,700	18.3
Queensland	1,727,200	2,592,600	1.5
South Australia	984,000	1,373,100	1.4
Western Australia	2,525,500	1,440,600	0.6
Tasmania	67,800	446,900	6.6
Northern Territory	1,346,200	148,100	0.1
Australian Capital Territory	2,400	264,400	110.2
Total	7,682,300	15,973,900	2.1

PRINCIPAL TOWNS (estimated population at 30 June 1985)*

Canberra (national capital)	273,600†
Sydney (capital of NSW)	3,391,600
Melbourne (capital of Victoria)	2,916,600
Brisbane (capital of Queensland)	1,157,200
Perth (capital of W Australia)	1,001,000
Adelaide (capital of S Australia)	987,100
Newcastle	423,300
Wollongong	236,800
Gold Coast	208,100
Hobart (capital of Tasmania)	178,100
Geelong	147,100
Townsville	101,700
Darwin (capital of Northern Territory)	68,500

* Figures refer to metropolitan areas, each of which normally comprises a municipality and contiguous urban areas.
† Including Queanbeyan, in NSW.

BIRTHS, MARRIAGES AND DEATHS*

	Registered live births		Registered marriages		Registered deaths	
	Number	Rate (per 1,000)	Number	Rate (per 1,000)	Number	Rate (per 1,000)
1980	225,527	15.3	109,240	7.3	108,695	7.4
1981	235,842	15.8	113,905	7.6	109,003	7.3
1982	239,903	15.8	117,275	7.7	114,771	7.6
1983	242,570	15.8	114,860	7.5	110,084	7.2
1984	238,472	15.3	108,655	7.0	111,889	7.2
1985	242,910	15.4	115,493	7.3	116,833	7.4
1986	243,408	15.2	114,913	7.2	114,981	7.2
1987†	244,148	15.0	114,085	7.0	117,366	7.2

* Data are tabulated by year of registration rather than by year of occurrence.
† Provisional.

AUSTRALIA

PERMANENT AND LONG-TERM MIGRATION*

	1985	1986	1987
Arrivals			
Males	83,490	97,500	103,810
Females	79,760	88,890	100,650
Total	163,260	186,400	204,460
Departures			
Males	49,260	48,720	49,980
Females	45,990	43,750	45,340
Total	95,250	92,470	95,320
Net Increase	68,010	93,930	109,140

* Persons intending to stay for more than one year. Figures are rounded to the nearest 10.

ECONOMICALLY ACTIVE POPULATION ('000 persons aged 15 years and over, excluding armed forces, at August)

	1984	1985	1986*
Agriculture and services to agriculture	373.1	394.5	390.6
Forestry, logging, fishing and hunting	27.1	19.8	24.3
Mining	93.2	102.4	95.9
Manufacturing	1,141.4	1,109.4	1,126.7
Electricity, gas and water	147.9	137.9	137.0
Construction	423.2	468.8	491.0
Transport and storage	354.1	375.1	394.2
Wholesale and retail trade	1,271.4	1,318.8	1,383.6
Communications	131.6	148.3	148.2
Finance, property and business services	619.3	663.7	699.2
Public administration and defence	321.7	323.6	324.0
Community services	1,138.4	1,155.2	1,216.0
Recreational, personal and other services	420.0	428.5	455.0
Total employed	6,462.3	6,646.1	6,885.7
Unemployed	604.6	571.2	595.6
Total labour force	7,066.9	7,217.2	7,481.4
Males	4,393.9	4,437.1	4,527.8
Females	2,673.0	2,780.1	2,953.6

* Beginning in 1986, unpaid family workers who worked for one hour or more are included among employed persons.

1987 (estimates, '000 persons at November): Total employed 7,159.9; Unemployed 566.5; Total labour force 7,726.4.

Agriculture

PRINCIPAL CROPS
('000 metric tons)

	1984	1985	1986
Wheat	18,666	16,127	17,356
Rice (paddy)	632	864	687
Barley	5,554	4,913	3,530
Maize	238	291	228
Oats	1,367	1,339	1,580
Sorghum	1,885	1,369	1,285
Potatoes	1,020	992	933
Dry peas	137	167	246
Soybeans (Soya beans)	89	110	106
Sunflower seed	170	293	228
Rapeseed	32	88	85
Cottonseed	230	410	382
Cotton (lint)	141	249	258
Tomatoes	270	300*	295*
Cauliflower	100	100*	100*
Onions (dry)	152	125*	127*
Green peas	150*	151*	155*
Carrots	131	125*	118*
Grapes	841	890	865
Sugar cane	25,450	22,409	25,410
Apples	267	352	290
Pears	122	139	125
Oranges	445	489	519
Pineapples	125	131	135
Bananas	145	132	107

* FAO estimate.

1986/87 ('000 metric tons, year ending 31 March): Wheat 16,119; Rice (paddy) 608; Barley 3,548; Oats 1,584; Rapeseed 76; Tomatoes 266; Onions (dry) 165; Sugar cane 24,742; Apples 325; Pears 145; Oranges 504; Pineapples 142; Bananas 158.

1987/88 ('000 metric tons, year ending 31 March, provisional): Wheat 12,444; Rice (paddy) 701; Barley 3,635; Oats 1,736; Rapeseed 65; Tomatoes 301; Onions (dry) 166; Sugar cane 25,390; Oranges 467.

Source: FAO, *Production Yearbook*, and Australian Bureau of Statistics.

LIVESTOCK ('000 head at 31 March)

	1985	1986	1987
Horses	416	346	312
Cattle	22,797	21,820	21,915
Pigs	2,512	2,512	2,611
Sheep	149,747	146,776	149,157
Goats	460	366	548

Chickens (million): 50 in 1985; 53 in 1986; 58 in 1987.

1988 ('000 head, provisional): Cattle 22,188; Pigs 2,492; Sheep 153,956.

Source: FAO, *Production Yearbook*, and Australian Bureau of Statistics.

DAIRY PRODUCE (year ending 30 June)

	1983/84	1984/85	1985/86
Whole milk (intake by factories, million litres)	5,923	6,038	6,038
Factory butter ('000 metric tons)	111	114	n.a.
Factory cheese ('000 metric tons)	161	160	n.a.
Market milk sales by factories (million litres)	1,572	1,593	1,625

AUSTRALIA

OTHER LIVESTOCK PRODUCTS
('000 metric tons, year ending 30 June)

	1984/85	1985/86	1986/87
Beef and veal	1,310	1,385	1,508
Mutton	215	258	286
Lamb	301	320	297
Pig meat	260	271	282
Poultry meat	345	367	384
Hen eggs	179	n.a.	n.a.
Wool:			
greasy	814	819	833*
clean	523	527	536*

* Provisional.

Forestry

ROUNDWOOD REMOVALS
('000 cubic metres)

	1984	1985	1986
Sawlogs, veneer logs and logs for sleepers	7,281	8,241	8,144
Pulpwood	6,790	7,419	7,859
Other industrial wood	1,005	1,169	1,116
Fuel wood	2,874	2,874*	2,880*
Total	17,950	19,703*	19,999*

* FAO estimate.
Source: FAO, *Yearbook of Forest Products*.

SAWNWOOD PRODUCTION
('000 cubic metres)

	1984	1985	1986
Coniferous sawnwood	1,096	1,218	1,226
Broadleaved sawnwood	1,711	1,802	1,772
Sub-total	2,807	3,020	2,998
Railway sleepers	196	196	196
Total	3,003	3,216	3,194

Source: FAO, *Yearbook of Forest Products*.

Fishing

('000 metric tons, live weight, year ending 30 June)

	1983/84	1984/85*	1985/86*
Inland waters	2.9	2.3	2.2
Indian Ocean	107.0	103.4	101.2
Pacific Ocean	58.0	54.3	53.2
Total catch	167.9	160.0	156.6

* FAO estimates.
Source: FAO, *Yearbook of Fishery Statistics*.

Mining*

(year ending 30 June, '000 metric tons, unless otherwise indicated)

	1984/85	1985/86	1986/87
Coal (black)	145,173	155,600	182,250
Coal, brown (lignite)[1]	36,369	33,312	39,712
Coal, brown (briquettes)	802	851	828
Bauxite	32,400	31,864	33,168
Zircon (metric tons)[2]	314,544	n.a.	n.a.
Iron ore	91,340	97,790	100,370
Lead	189	206	142
Zinc	299	297	300
Copper	165	163	171
Titanium[3]	859	n.a.	n.a.
Tin (metric tons)	2,824	2,208	784
Crude petroleum (million litres)[4]	30,919	31,669	30,205
Natural gas (million megajoules)	463,473	512,409	524,330
Gold (kg)	40,501	56,928	81,856
Silver (kg)	284,963	315,337	270,608
Nickel (metric tons)	82,267	80,528	74,654

* Figures for metallic minerals represent metal contents based on chemical assay, except figures for bauxite and iron ore, which are in terms of gross quantities produced. The estimated iron content of iron ore is 64%.
[1] Excludes coal used in making briquettes.
[2] In terms of zircon (ZrO_2) contained in zircon and rutile concentrates.
[3] In terms of TiO_2 contained in bauxite and mineral sands.
[4] Including condensate.

1987/88: Natural gas 533,329m. megajoules.

Industry

SELECTED PRODUCTS (year ending 30 June, '000 metric tons, unless otherwise indicated)

	1985/86	1986/87	1987/88
Coke	3,534	3,253	n.a.
Pig-iron	5,925	5,783	5,455
Steel (ingots)	6,826	6,387	6,091
Electric motors—under 720 watts ('000)	1,918	2,061	2,279
Clay bricks (million)	1,980	1,850	1,868
Sulphuric acid	1,788	1,678	1,814
Nitric acid (metric tons)	192,514	203,484	203,300
Television receivers ('000)	238	211	177
Refrigerators ('000)	328	289	386
Cotton yarn	21	21	21
Cotton cloth ('000 sq m)	38,508	38,237	39,454
Tinplate	312	292	307
Electricity (million kWh)	124,381	130,212	139,025
Cement	6,106	5,912	6,139
Concrete—ready-mixed ('000 cu m)	14,132	13,782	n.a.
Soap (metric tons)	26,199	27,361	n.a.
Paper	1,123	1,209	n.a.
Motor vehicles ('000)	390	322	340

AUSTRALIA

Finance

CURRENCY AND EXCHANGE RATES

Monetary Units
100 cents = 1 Australian dollar ($A).

Denominations
Coins: 1, 2, 5, 10, 20 and 50 cents; 1 dollar.
Notes: 2, 5, 10, 20, 50 and 100 dollars.

Sterling and US Dollar Equivalents (30 September 1988)
£1 sterling = $A2.1465;
US $1 = $A1.2740;
$A100 = £46.59 = US $78.49.

Average Exchange Rate (US $ per Australian dollar)
1985   0.7008
1986   0.6709
1987   0.7009

GENERAL GOVERNMENT BUDGET*
($A million, year ending 30 June)

Revenue	1984/85	1985/86	1986/87
Income from public enterprises	1,456	2,624	3,413
Interest, etc.	3,724	4,474	4,493
Indirect taxes	29,380	32,372	35,710
Direct taxes (paid) on income	35,327	39,401	45,429
Other direct taxes, fees, fines, etc.	1,236	1,312	1,420
Total	71,123	80,183	90,465

Expenditure	1984/85	1985/86	1986/87
Final consumption	40,255	45,001	48,864
Subsidies	3,676	3,878	3,879
Interest, etc.	6,765	8,537	9,781
Personal benefits to residents	21,196	22,896	24,702
Current grants to non-profit institutions	2,469	2,700	2,972
Transfers overseas	950	980	947
Total	75,311	83,992	91,145

* Consolidated accounts of Commonwealth, State and local authorities, excluding public financial enterprises. Figures relate to current transactions only.

STATE GOVERNMENT FINANCES*
($A million, year ending 30 June)

	Receipts		Expenditure	
	1983/84	1984/85	1983/84	1984/85
New South Wales	11,128	13,064	11,804	13,850
Victoria	9,805	10,941	10,174	11,436
Queensland	6,033	6,599	6,164	6,764
South Australia	3,193	3,459	3,270	3,604
Western Australia	3,920	4,155	4,052	4,305
Tasmania	1,372	1,550	1,389	1,582
Northern Territory	942	1,053	976	1,094

* Includes all State Government Authorities.

OFFICIAL RESERVES (US $ million at 30 June)

	1986	1987	1988
Gold*	2,718	3,566	3,580
IMF special drawing rights	325	339	334
Reserve position in IMF	222	241	248
Foreign exchange	5,557	8,526	11,863
Total	8,823	12,673	16,024

* Valued at market-related prices.
Source: IMF, *International Financial Statistics*.

Statistical Survey

MONEY SUPPLY ($A million at 30 June)

	1986	1987	1988
Currency outside banks	8,717	9,598	10,979
Demand deposits at trading and savings banks	14,621	17,029	20,612

Source: IMF, *International Financial Statistics*.

COST OF LIVING (Consumer Price Index*. Base: 1970 = 100)

	1983	1984	1985
Food	351.3	370.4	393.6
Fuel and light	392.3	414.1	444.5
Clothing	340.0	360.6	385.1
Rent	333.9	357.9	388.0
All items	361.3	375.4	400.8

* Weighted average of six state capitals.

NATIONAL ACCOUNTS
($A million at current prices, year ending 30 June)

National Income and Product

	1984/85	1985/86	1986/87
Compensation of employees	110,904	121,899	133,130
Operating surplus	41,685	46,728	51,332
Domestic factor incomes	152,589	168,627	184,462
Consumption of fixed capital	33,622	38,694	44,074
Gross domestic product (GDP) at factor cost	186,211	207,321	228,536
Indirect taxes, *less* subsidies	25,704	28,494	31,831
GDP in purchasers' values	211,915	235,815	260,367
Net factor income from abroad	−6,274	−7,776	−9,343
Gross national product	205,641	228,039	251,024
Less Consumption of fixed capital	33,622	38,694	44,074
National income in market prices	172,019	189,345	206,950

Expenditure on the Gross Domestic Product

	1984/85	1985/86	1986/87
Government final consumption expenditure	40,255	45,001	48,864
Private final consumption expenditure	126,870	141,041	153,904
Increase in stocks	1,040	1,284	−1,410
Gross fixed capital formation	50,490	57,952	62,456
Statistical discrepancy	−1,878	−1,980	1,881
Total domestic expenditure	216,777	243,298	265,695
Exports of goods and services	34,143	37,952	42,217
Less Imports of goods and services	39,005	45,435	47,545
GDP in purchasers' values	211,915	235,815	260,367
GDP at constant 1979/80 prices	139,466	145,452	149,331

AUSTRALIA

Gross Domestic Product by Economic Activity (at factor cost)

	1984/85	1985/86	1986/87
Agriculture, hunting, forestry and fishing	9,103	9,072	10,284
Mining	8,999	10,662	10,855
Manufacturing	33,757	36,586	39,678
Electricity, gas and water	7,268	8,134	8,438
Construction	14,462	16,311	17,880
Wholesale and retail trade	25,333	28,775	31,361
Transport, storage and communications	16,881	18,841	21,157
Ownership of dwellings	16,024	18,235	20,753
Finance, property and business services	18,973	21,331	25,592
Public administration and defence	8,889	9,833	10,597
Other community, social and personal services	32,572	35,913	39,930
Sub-total	192,261	213,693	236,525
Less Imputed bank service charge	−6,050	−6,372	−7,989
Total	186,211	207,321	228,536

BALANCE OF PAYMENTS (US $ million)

	1985	1986	1987
Merchandise exports f.o.b.	22,275	22,189	26,316
Merchandise imports f.o.b.	−23,559	−24,292	−26,827
Trade balance	−1,284	−2,103	−512
Exports of services	5,192	5,707	7,247
Imports of services	−13,158	−14,086	−16,454
Balance on goods and services	−9,250	−10,482	−9,719
Private unrequited transfers (net)	686	817	1,119
Government unrequited transfers (net)	−154	−145	−76
Current balance	−8,717	−9,810	−8,676
Direct capital investment (net)	331	624	37
Other long-term capital (net)	7,053	9,586	6,810
Short-term capital (net)	−756	−695	−488
Net errors and omissions	−193	999	2,687
Total (net monetary movements)	−2,282	705	371
Valuation changes (net)	628	776	1,123
Official financing (net)	−19	−2	4
Changes in reserves	−1,674	1,479	1,497

Source: IMF, *International Financial Statistics*.

FOREIGN INVESTMENT ($A million, year ending 30 June)

Inflow	1982/83	1983/84	1984/85
EEC—United Kingdom	2,429	2,366	2,033
—Other	1,023	1,191	1,841
Switzerland	214	97	328
USA	328	925	2,052
Canada	30	91	192
Japan	3,239	1,226	3,153
ASEAN*	1,517	2,131	807
Other countries	1,174	1,290	2,183
Total	9,954	9,317	12,589

Outflow	1982/83	1983/84	1984/85
EEC—United Kingdom	133	111	66
—Other	4	14	13
New Zealand	126	150	154
USA	5	8	70
Papua New Guinea	33	77	31
ASEAN*	73	133	56
Other countries	73	67	72
Total	447	560	462

* Indonesia, Malaysia, the Philippines, Singapore and Thailand; also Brunei from 1 January 1984.

FOREIGN AID EXTENDED BY AUSTRALIA*
($A million, year ending 30 June)

	1983/84	1984/85	1985/86
Aid payments:			
Bilateral:			
Papua New Guinea	302	320	326
Other	395	438	422
Multilateral	216	235	259
Administration	19†	18†	24
Total	932	1,011	1,031

* Official only; excludes transfers by private persons and organizations to overseas recipients.
† Includes the cost of administration of overseas students by other government agencies.

Source: Statistical summary, Australian Official Development Assistance to Developing Countries.

External Trade

PRINCIPAL COMMODITIES
($A million, year ending 30 June)

Imports	1984/85	1985/86	1986/87
Food and live animals	1,246.6	1,418.1	1,612.0
Coffee, tea, cocoa and spices	344.4	418.8	404.9
Fish, crustaceans and molluscs	304.1	333.4	422.6
Beverages and tobacco	225.4	297.6	326.8
Crude materials (inedible) except fuels	932.1	1,022.7	1,083.3
Cork and wood	325.6	328.4	297.6
Mineral fuels, lubricants, etc.	2,299.0	1,927.4	1,749.2
Petroleum, petroleum products, etc.	2,291.2	1,924.0	1,742.2
Chemicals and related products	2,548.9	3,024.4	3,472.0
Organic chemicals	672.4	765.6	880.6
Basic manufactures	4,919.3	5,619.9	6,185.8
Paper, paperboard and manufactures	838.3	842.2	1,012.8
Textile yarn, fabrics, etc.	1,443.7	1,678.3	1,831.3
Machinery and transport equipment	11,900.4	15,141.5	15,422.6
Road vehicles and parts (excl. tyres, engines and electrical parts)	3,087.8	3,771.3	2,720.0
Miscellaneous manufactured articles	3,865.7	4,669.1	5,184.8
Total merchandise (incl. others)	29,049.4	n.a.	n.a.
Non-merchandise trade	970.5	n.a.	n.a.
Total	30,019.9	34,691.2	37,021.9

AUSTRALIA   Statistical Survey

Exports	1984/85	1985/86	1986/87
Food and live animals	7,526.7	8,086.1	7,993.5
Meat and meat preparations	1,373.8	1,700.6	2,249.4
Dairy products and birds' eggs	420.3	437.1	467.6
Cereals and cereal preparations	4,023.9	3,928.6	2,800.6
Sugar, sugar preparations and honey	612.1	649.5	694.0
Beverages and tobacco	71.5	84.7	151.6
Crude materials (inedible) except fuels	7,991.1	9,011.0	9,904.0
Textile fibres and waste*	2,622.8	3,207.2	3,871.5
Hides, skins and fur-skins (raw)	320.7	395.4	543.3
Metalliferous ores and metal scrap	4,577.9	4,850.7	4,853.1
Mineral fuels, lubricants, etc.†	7,484.5	7,976.6	7,309.1
Animal and vegetable oils, fats and waxes	124.4	142.3	123.3
Chemicals and related products	542.9	593.3	663.4
Basic manufactures	2,960.5	3,279.7	3,834.7
Machinery and transport equipment	1,479.8	1,611.8	2,612.2
Machinery	939.1	1,144.3	1,596.5
Transport equipment	540.7	467.5	1,015.7
Miscellaneous manufactured articles	584.9	659.4	853.7
Other commodities and transactions‡	941.8	1,350.1	2,337.1
Total merchandise	29,708.1	n.a.	n.a.
Non-merchandise trade	830.2	n.a.	n.a.
Total	30,538.3	32,795.0	35,782.6

* Excluding wool tops.
† Excluding natural and manufactured gas.
‡ Including natural and manufactured gas.

PRINCIPAL TRADING PARTNERS
($A '000, year ending 30 June)

Imports	1985/86	1986/87
Bahrain	28,336	19,479
Belgium/Luxembourg	287,112	311,927
Brazil	245,972	219,549
Canada	691,157	750,501
China, People's Republic	435,032	588,829
Denmark	172,886	176,861
Finland	208,463	262,631
France	776,124	827,302
Germany, Federal Republic	2,743,163	2,782,116
Hong Kong	676,476	800,037
India	170,527	203,352
Indonesia	209,310	310,556
Ireland	150,248	184,332
Italy	1,094,688	1,110,296
Japan	8,248,305	7,737,074
Korea, Republic	556,666	897,907
Kuwait	297,025	162,629
Malaysia	325,432	409,667
Netherlands	430,680	486,656
New Zealand	1,454,427	1,431,969
Papua New Guinea	170,946	189,747
Philippines	122,519	113,354
Saudi Arabia	470,822	437,267
Singapore	745,209	755,917
South Africa	157,831	154,717
Sweden	657,791	655,277
Switzerland	428,478	489,826
Taiwan	1,161,078	1,517,523
Thailand	200,874	284,383
United Arab Emirates	134,806	175,845
United Kingdom	2,515,632	2,705,511
USA	7,283,677	8,118,424
Other countries	1,439,505	1,750,449
Total	34,691,197	37,021,910

Exports	1985/86	1986/87
Bangladesh	27,997	41,488
Belgium/Luxembourg	266,901	297,577
Canada	460,187	637,088
China, People's Republic	1,497,376	1,590,458
Egypt	508,129	362,472
Fiji	204,587	174,202
France	707,983	908,850
Germany, Federal Republic	878,874	1,101,130
Hong Kong	727,099	1,086,099
India	428,291	425,413
Indonesia	522,211	527,585
Iran	305,249	343,798
Iraq	206,497	194,714
Italy	686,584	823,709
Japan	9,307,147	9,088,020
Korea, Republic	1,318,790	1,499,601
Kuwait	132,177	86,871
Malaysia	515,995	589,994
Netherlands	438,631	598,220
New Zealand	1,505,577	1,775,912
Papua New Guinea	561,593	651,051
Philippines	203,587	258,749
Poland	137,593	107,416
Saudi Arabia	486,447	297,951
Singapore	728,235	779,813
South Africa	137,678	154,130
Taiwan	1,060,655	1,227,646
Thailand	163,994	223,649
USSR	969,719	687,725
United Arab Emirates	178,791	222,213
United Kingdom	1,153,888	1,374,905
USA	3,242,413	4,194,630
Other countries	3,124,132	3,449,504
Total	32,795,007	35,782,583

Transport

	1982/83	1983/84	1984/85
Railways:			
Route kilometres (number)*	39,065	39,251	n.a.
Passengers ('000)	394,937	403,456	n.a.
Goods and livestock ('000 metric tons)	124,093	142,183	n.a.
Road traffic:			
Motor vehicles registered ('000)*	8,590	8,833	9,118
Overseas shipping:			
Vessels entered ('000 tons)†	223,817	263,614	310,228
Vessels cleared ('000 tons)†	230,385	267,264	309,152
Air transport, internal services:			
Kilometres flown ('000)	127,952	126,087	n.a.
Passengers carried	10,332,934	10,597,651	n.a.
Freight (metric tons)	141,853	149,879	n.a.
Mail (metric tons)	16,767	17,571	n.a.
Air transport, overseas services‡:			
Kilometres flown ('000)	64,898	65,670	71,046
Passengers carried	2,101,788	2,189,669	2,449,596
Freight (metric tons)	75,375	84,844	90,357
Mail (metric tons)	4,219	4,410	4,744

* Figures as at end of period.
† Figures are for deadweight tonnage of vessels.
‡ Refers only to services operated by Qantas Airways Ltd.

Tourism

	1982	1983†	1984†
Number of visitors (arrivals)*	954,674	943,900	1,015,100

* i.e. intending to stay for less than one year.
† Total is rounded to the nearest 100.

1986: Total number of visitors 1,429,400.
1987: Total number of visitors 1,784,900.

Communications Media

	1983	1984	1985
Telephones in use ('000 at 30 June)	8,267	8,329	8,727

Radio receivers (1982): 17,600,000 in use (estimate).
Television receivers (1982): 6,500,000 in use (estimate).
Books (1982): 2,358 titles (including 599 pamphlets) produced.
Newspapers (1979): 63 dailies (combined circulation 4,851,000); 470 non-dailies (circulation 8,930,000).

Education

(1985)

	Institutions	Teaching staff*	Students
Government schools	7,561	150,383	2,230,833
Non-government schools	2,502	46,747	775,336
Universities	19	11,751	175,476
Colleges of advanced education	45	11,039	195,231
Technical and further education	233†	52,587‡	1,316,551§

1986 (students): Government schools 2,034,539; Non-government schools 737,285; Universities 188,662; Colleges of advanced education 137,315.
1987: Government schools: Institutions 7,575; Teaching staff 148,972; Students 2,196,742. Non-government schools: Institutions 2,504; Teaching staff 49,543; Students 808,141.

* Full-time staff plus full-time equivalents of part-time staff.
† Figure refers to major institutions only.
‡ Figure comprises 17,637 full-time staff and 34,950 part-time staff.
§ Figure comprises 859,194 vocational and preparatory students and 457,357 adult education students.

Directory

The Constitution

The Federal Constitution was adopted on 9 July 1900 and came into force on 1 January 1901. Its main provisions are summarized below:

PARLIAMENT

The legislative power of the Commonwealth of Australia is vested in a Federal Parliament, consisting of HM the Queen (represented by the Governor-General), a Senate, and a House of Representatives. The Governor-General may appoint such times for holding the sessions of the Parliament as he or she thinks fit, and may also from time to time, by proclamation or otherwise, prorogue the Parliament, and may in like manner dissolve the House of Representatives. By convention, these powers are exercised on the advice of the Prime Minister. After any general election Parliament must be summoned to meet not later than 30 days after the day appointed for the return of the writs.

THE SENATE

The Senate is composed of 12 senators from each State, two senators representing the Australian Capital Territory and two representing the Northern Territory. The senators are directly chosen by the people of the State or Territory, voting in each case as one electorate, and are elected by proportional representation. Senators representing a State have a six-year term and retire by rotation, one-half from each State on 30 June of each third year. The term of a senator representing a Territory is limited to three years. In the case of a State, if a senator vacates his or her seat before the expiration of the term of service, the Houses of Parliament of the State for which the senator was chosen shall, in joint session, choose a person to hold the place until the expiration of the term or until the election of a successor. If the State Parliament is not in session, the Governor of the State, acting on the advice of the State's Executive Council, may appoint a senator to hold office until Parliament reassembles, or until a new senator is elected.

The Senate may proceed to the dispatch of business notwithstanding the failure of any State to provide for its representation in the Senate.

THE HOUSE OF REPRESENTATIVES

In accordance with the Australian Constitution, the total number of members of the House of Representatives must be as nearly as practicable double that of the Senate. The number in each State is in proportion to population, but under the Constitution must be at least five. The House of Representatives is composed of 148 members, including two members for the Australian Capital Territory and one member for the Northern Territory.

Members are elected by universal adult suffrage and voting is compulsory. Only Australian citizens are eligible to vote in Australian elections. British subjects, if they are not Australian citizens or already on the rolls, have to take out Australian citizenship before they can enrol and before they can vote.

Members are chosen by the electors of their respective electorates by the preferential voting system.

The duration of the Parliament is limited to three years.

To be nominated for election to the House of Representatives, a candidate must be 18 years of age or over, an Australian citizen, and entitled to vote at the election or qualified to become an elector.

THE EXECUTIVE GOVERNMENT

The executive power of the Federal Government is vested in the Queen, and is exercisable by the Governor-General, advised by an Executive Council of Ministers of State, known as the Federal Executive Council. These ministers are, or must become within three months, members of the Federal Parliament.

The Australian Constitution is construed as subject to the principles of responsible government and the Governor-General acts on the advice of the ministers in relation to most matters.

THE JUDICIAL POWER

See Judicial System, p. 382.

THE STATES

The Australian Constitution safeguards the Constitution of each State by providing that it shall continue as at the establishment of the Commonwealth, except as altered in accordance with its own provisions. The legislative power of the Federal Parliament is limited in the main to those matters that are listed in section 51 of the Constitution, while the States possess, as well as concurrent powers in those matters, residual legislative powers enabling them to legislate in any way for 'the peace, order and good Government' of their respective territories. When a state law is inconsistent with a law of the Commonwealth, the latter prevails, and the former is invalid to the extent of the inconsistency.

The States may not, without the consent of the Commonwealth, raise or maintain naval or military forces, or impose taxes on any property belonging to the Commonwealth of Australia, nor may the Commonwealth tax State property. The States may not coin money.

The Federal Parliament may not enact any law for establishing any religion or for prohibiting the exercise of any religion, and no religious test may be imposed as a qualification for any office under the Commonwealth.

The Commonwealth of Australia is charged with protecting every State against invasion, and, on the application of a State Executive Government, against domestic violence.

Provision is made under the Constitution for the admission of new States and for the establishment of new States within the Commonwealth of Australia.

ALTERATION OF THE CONSTITUTION

Proposed laws for the amendment of the Constitution must be passed by an absolute majority in both Houses of the Federal Parliament, and not less than two or more than six months after its passage through both Houses the proposed law must be submitted in each State to the qualified electors.

In the event of one House twice refusing to pass a proposed amendment that has already received an absolute majority in the other House, the Governor-General may, notwithstanding such refusal, submit the proposed amendment to the electors. By convention, the Governor-General acts on the advice of the Prime Minister. If in a majority of the States a majority of electors voting approve the proposed law and if a majority of all the electors voting also approve, it shall be presented to the Governor-General for Royal Assent.

No alteration diminishing the proportionate representation of any State in either House of the Federal Parliament, or the minimum number of representatives of a State in the House of Representatives, or increasing, diminishing or altering the limits of the State, or in any way affecting the provisions of the Constitution in relation thereto, shall become law unless the majority of the electors voting in that State approve the proposed law.

STATES AND TERRITORIES

New South Wales

The State's executive power is vested in the Governor, appointed by the Crown, who is assisted by a Cabinet.

The State's legislative power is vested in a bicameral Parliament, the Legislative Council and the Legislative Assembly. The Legislative Council, formerly consisting of 60 members, began, in late 1978, a process of reconstitution at the end of which it was to consist of 45 members directly elected for the duration of three parliaments, 15 members retiring every four years. The Legislative Assembly consists of 99 members and sits for four years.

Victoria

The State's legislative power is vested in a bicameral Parliament: the Upper House, or Legislative Council, of 44 members, elected for six years, and the Lower House, or Legislative Assembly, of 88 members, elected for four years. One-half of the members of the Council retires every three years.

In the exercise of the executive power the Governor is assisted by a Cabinet of responsible ministers. Not more than five members of the Council and not more than 13 members of the Assembly may occupy salaried office at any one time.

The State has 88 electoral districts, each returning one member, and 22 electoral provinces, each returning two Council members.

Queensland

The State's legislative power is vested in a unicameral Parliament composed of 82 members who are elected from 82 districts for a term of three years.

South Australia

The State's Constitution vests the legislative power in a Parliament elected by the people and consisting of a Legislative Council and a House of Assembly. The Council is composed of 22 members, one-half of whom retires every three years. Their places are filled by new members elected under a system of proportional representation, with the whole State as a single electorate. The executive has no authority to dissolve this body, except in circumstances warranting a double dissolution.

The 47 members of the House of Assembly are elected for three years from 47 electoral districts.

The executive power is vested in a Governor, appointed by the Crown, and an Executive Council consisting of 13 responsible ministers.

Western Australia

The State's administration is vested in the Governor, a Legislative Council and a Legislative Assembly.

The Legislative Council consists of 34 members, each of the 17 provinces returning two members. Election is for a term of six years, one-half of the members retiring every three years.

The Legislative Assembly consists of 57 members, elected for three years, each representing one electorate.

Tasmania

The State's executive authority is vested in a Governor, appointed by the Crown, who acts upon the advice of his premier and ministers, who are elected members of either the Legislative Council or the House of Assembly. The Council consists of 19 members who sit for six years, retiring in rotation. The House of Assembly has 35 members elected for four years.

Northern Territory

On 1 July 1978, the Northern Territory was established as a body politic with executive authority for specified functions of government. Most functions of the government were transferred to the Territory Government in 1978 and 1979, major exceptions being Aboriginal affairs and uranium mining.

The Territory Parliament consists of a single house, the Legislative Assembly, with 25 members. The first parliament stayed in office for three years, but as from the election held in August 1980 members are elected for a term of four years.

The office of Administrator continues. The Northern Territory (Self-Government) Act provides for the appointment of an Administrator by the Governor-General charged with the duty of administering the Territory. In respect of matters transferred to the Territory Government, the Administrator acts with the advice of the Territory Executive Council; in respect of matters retained by the Commonwealth, the Administrator acts on Commonwealth advice.

Australian Capital Territory

The Australian Capital Territory, within which the Federal Seat of Government is situated, is administered by the Federal Government. Under legislation passed by the Parliament the Governor-General is given power to make ordinances for the peace, order and good government of the Territory. There is established in the Territory an elected House of Assembly, consisting of 18 elected members, which may advise the Government on matters affecting the Territory.

The Government

Head of State: HM Queen ELIZABETH II.

Governor-General: WILLIAM GEORGE HAYDEN (from February 1989).

THE MINISTRY
(December 1988)

Prime Minister: ROBERT J. L. HAWKE*.

Deputy Prime Minister, Attorney-General and Minister Assisting the Prime Minister on Commonwealth–State Relations: LIONEL F. BOWEN*.

Minister for Justice: Senator MICHAEL TATE.

Minister for Consumer Affairs and Minister Assisting the Treasurer for Prices: Senator NICK BOLKUS.

Minister for Industry, Technology and Commerce: Senator JOHN N. BUTTON*.

Minister for Science, Customs and Small Business: BARRY O. JONES.

Minister for Transport and Communications: RALPH WILLIS*.

Minister for Transport and Communications Support, Minister Assisting the Prime Minister and Minister Assisting the Treasurer: GARY PUNCH.

Treasurer: PAUL J. KEATING*.

Minister for Finance: Senator PETER A. WALSH*.

Minister for Foreign Affairs and Trade: Senator GARETH J. EVANS*.

Minister for Trade Negotiations, Minister Assisting the Minister for Industry, Technology and Commerce and Minister Assisting the Minister for Primary Industries and Energy: MICHAEL J. DUFFY*.

Minister for Industrial Relations and Minister Assisting the Prime Minister for Public Service Matters: PETER F. MORRIS*.

Minister for Employment, Education and Training: JOHN S. DAWKINS*.

Minister for Employment and Education Services: PETER DUNCAN.

Minister for Aboriginal Affairs: GERARD L. HAND.

Minister for Defence: KIM C. BEAZLEY*.

Minister for Defence Science and Personnel: ROS KELLY.

Minister for Primary Industries and Energy: JOHN C. KERIN*.

Minister for Resources: PETER COOK.

Minister for Social Security: BRIAN L. HOWE*.

Minister for Administrative Services: J. STEWART WEST*.

AUSTRALIA

Minister for Community Services and Health: Dr NEAL BLEWETT*.
Minister for Housing and Aged Care: PETER STAPLES.
Minister for Veterans' Affairs: BENJAMIN C. HUMPHREYS.
Minister for the Arts, Sport, the Environment, Tourism and Territories: Senator GRAHAM RICHARDSON*.
Minister for the Arts and Territories: A. CLYDE HOLDING.
Minister for Immigration, Local Government and Ethnic Affairs and Minister Assisting the Prime Minister for Multicultural Affairs: Senator ROBERT F. RAY*.
Minister for Local Government and Minister Assisting the Prime Minister for the Status of Women: Senator MARGARET REYNOLDS.

* Denotes member of the Inner Cabinet.

DEPARTMENTS

Department of the Prime Minister and Cabinet: 3-5 National Circuit, Barton, ACT 2600; tel. (062) 715111; telex 61616.
Department of Aboriginal Affairs: MLC Tower, Woden Town Centre, Phillip, ACT 2606; tel. (062) 891222; telex 62471.
Department of Administrative Services: POB 1920, Canberra City, ACT 2601; tel. (062) 753000; telex 62482.
Department of the Arts, Sport, the Environment, Tourism and Territories: Tobruk House, 15 Moore St, Canberra City, ACT 2601; tel. (062) 689411; telex 61716.
Attorney-General's Department: Robert Garran Offices, Barton, ACT 2600; tel. (062) 719111; telex 62002.
Department of Community Services and Health: POB 9848, Canberra, ACT 2601; tel. (062) 891555; telex 62149.
Department of Defence: Russell Offices, Canberra, ACT 2600; tel. (062) 659111; telex 62053.
Department of Employment, Education and Training: POB 826, Woden, ACT 2606; tel. (062) 837777; telex 62116.
Department of Finance: Newlands St, Parkes, ACT 2600; tel. (062) 632222; telex 62639.
Department of Foreign Affairs and Trade: Bag 8, Queen Victoria Terrace, Canberra, ACT 2600; tel. (062) 619111; telex 62007.
Department of Immigration, Local Government and Ethnic Affairs: Benjamin Offices, Chan St, Belconnen, ACT 2617; tel. (062) 641111; telex 62077.
Department of Industrial Relations: POB 9879, Canberra, ACT 2601; tel. (062) 437333; telex 62944.
Department of Industry, Technology and Commerce: 51 Allara St, Canberra, ACT 2601; tel. (062) 761000; telex 62654.
Department of Primary Industries and Energy: Edmund Barton Bldg, Broughton St, Barton, ACT 2601; tel. (062) 458211; telex 62101.
Department of Social Security: Juliana House, Bowes St, Phillip, ACT 2606; tel. (062) 844844; telex 62143.
Department of Transport and Communications: cnr Northbourne Ave and Cooyong St, Canberra, ACT 2600; POB 594, Canberra, ACT 2601; tel. (062) 687111; telex 62065.
Department of the Treasury: Parkes Place, Parkes, ACT 2600; tel. (062) 632111; telex 62372.
Department of Veterans' Affairs: MLC Tower, Keltie St, Phillip, ACT 2606; tel. (062) 891111; telex 62706.

ADMINISTRATORS OF TERRITORIES

Northern Territory: Cdre E. E. JOHNSTON.
Norfolk Island: Cdre JOHN A. MATTHEW.
Cocos (Keeling) Islands: (vacant).
Christmas Island: T. F. PATERSON.

Legislature

FEDERAL PARLIAMENT

Senate

President: Senator KERRY WALTER SIBRAA (Lab.).
Chairman of Committees: Senator DAVID HAMER (Lib.).
Leader of the Government in the Senate: Senator JOHN N. BUTTON (Lab.).
Leader of the Opposition in the Senate: Senator FREDERICK MICHAEL CHANEY (Lib.).

Election, 11 July 1987

Party	Seats at election	Seats at Dec. 1988
Labor Party	32	32
Liberal Party	27	27
National Party	8	7
Australian Democrats	5	7
Independents and others	4	3
Total	76	76

House of Representatives

Speaker: JOAN CHILD (Lab.).
Chairman of Committees: LEO MCLEAY (Lab.).
Leader of the House: KIM C. BEAZLEY (Lab.).
Leader of the Opposition: JOHN HOWARD (Lib.).

Election, 11 July 1987

Party	Seats at election	Seats at Dec. 1988
Labor Party	86	85
Liberal Party	43	45
National Party	19	18
Total	148	148

State Governments

NEW SOUTH WALES

Governor: Rear-Adm. DAVID J. MARTIN.

Liberal–National Party Ministry
(December 1988)

Premier: NICK GREINER.

Legislature

Legislative Council: Pres. JOHN RICHARD JOHNSON; Chair. of Cttees CLIVE HEALEY.
Legislative Assembly: Speaker LAWRENCE BORTHWICK KELLY; Chair. of Cttees JACK RICHARD FACE.

VICTORIA

Governor: Rev. Dr JOHN DAVIS MCCAUGHEY.

Labor Ministry
(December 1988)

Premier: JOHN CAIN.

Legislature

Legislative Council: Pres. RODERICK ALEXANDER MACKENZIE; Chair. of Cttees GIOVANNI ANTONIO SGRO; Clerk of the Council ROBERT KEEGAN EVANS.
Legislative Assembly: Speaker CYRIL THOMAS EDMUNDS; Chair. of Cttees WILLIAM FRANCIS FOGARTY; Clerk of the Assembly RAYMOND KEITH BOYES.

QUEENSLAND

Governor: Sir WALTER CAMPBELL.

National Party Ministry
(December 1988)

Premier: MICHAEL JOHN AHERN.

Legislature

Legislative Assembly: Speaker L. W. POWELL; Chair. of Cttees E. C. Row; Clerk A. R. WOODWARD.

SOUTH AUSTRALIA

Governor: Lt-Gen. Sir DONALD BEAUMONT DUNSTAN.

Labor Ministry
(December 1988)

Premier: JOHN CHARLES BANNON.

Legislature

Legislative Council: Pres. and Chair. of Cttees ANNE LEVY; Clerk of the Council C. H. MERTIN.

AUSTRALIA

House of Assembly: Speaker J. P. TRAINER; Chair. of Cttees D. M. FERGUSON; Clerk of the House G. D. MITCHELL.

WESTERN AUSTRALIA
Governor: Prof. GORDON REID.

Labor Ministry
(December 1988)

Premier: PETER DOWDING.

Legislature

Legislative Council: Pres. CLIVE EDWARD GRIFFITHS; Chair. of Cttees DAVID JOHN WORDSWORTH; Clerk of the Council LAURENCE BERNHARD MARQUET.

Legislative Assembly: Speaker MICHAEL BARNETT; Chair. of Cttees GRAHAM JOHN BURKETT; Clerk of the Assembly BRUCE LEFROY OKELY.

TASMANIA
Governor: Gen. Sir PHILIP BENNETT.

Liberal Ministry
(December 1988)

Premier: ROBIN TREVOR GRAY.

Legislature

Legislative Council: Pres. ALBERT JAMES BROADBY; Chair. of Cttees R. T. HOPE; Clerk of the Council ADRIAN JACK SHAW.

House of Assembly: Speaker R. CORNISH; Chair. of Cttees JOHN BEATTIE; Clerk of the House PAUL TREVOR MCKAY.

NORTHERN TERRITORY
Administrator: Cdre E. E. JOHNSTON.

Liberal–National Party Ministry
(December 1988)

Chief Minister: M. B. PERRON.

Legislature

Legislative Assembly: Speaker ROGER W. S. VALE.

Political Organizations

Australian Democratic Labor Party: 155–159 Castlereagh St, Sydney, NSW; f. 1956 following a split in the Australian Labor Party; Pres. P. J. KEOGH; Gen. Sec. JOHN KANE.

Australian Democrats Party: 96 St Kilda Rd, St Kilda, Vic 3182; tel. (03) 537-1611; telex 39117; f. 1977; comprises the fmr Liberal Movement and the Australia Party; Leader Senator JANINE HAINES.

Australian Labor Party: John Curtin House, 22 Brisbane Ave, Barton, ACT 2600; f. 1891; advocates the democratic socialization of industry, production, distribution and exchange, with the declared aim of eliminating exploitation and other anti-social features in these fields; Fed. Parl. Leader ROBERT J. L. HAWKE; Nat. Pres. JOHN BANNON; Nat. Sec. ROBERT HOGG.

Communist Party of Australia: 635 Harris St, Ultimo, NSW 2007; tel. (02) 281-2899; telex 3188 (domestic), 121822 (international); f. 1920; independent of both Soviet and Chinese influence; Nat. Exec.: B. AARONS, R. DURBRIDGE, P. RANALD, T. BURKE, L. CONNOR, W. NEILLEY, J. GILLETT, J. STEVENS.

Communist Party of Australia (Marxist-Leninist): f. 1967 following a split in Communist Party of Australia; Maoist; Chair. E. F. HILL.

Liberal Party of Australia: Federal Secretariat, cnr Blackall and Macquarie Sts, Barton, ACT 2600; tel. (062) 732564; telex 62630; f. 1944; advocates private enterprise, social justice, individual liberty and initiative; committed to national development, prosperity and security; Fed. Pres. JOHN D. ELLIOTT; Fed. Parl. Leader JOHN HOWARD.

National Party of Australia: John McEwen House, National Circuit, Barton, ACT 2600; tel. (062) 733822; telex 62543; f. 1916 as the Country Party of Australia; adopted present name in 1982; advocates balanced national development based on free enterprise, with special emphasis on the needs of people outside the major metropolitan areas; Fed. Pres. STUART MCDONALD; Fed. Parl. Leader IAN SINCLAIR; Fed. Dir PAUL DAVEY.

New National Party of Australia: f. 1987 following split in National Party; right-wing; Leader Sir JOH BJELKE-PETERSEN.

Socialist Party of Australia: 65 Campbell St, Surry Hills, NSW 2010; tel. (02) 212-6855; telex 126784; f. 1971; advocates public ownership of the means of production, working-class political power; Pres. J. MCPHILLIPS; Gen. Sec. P. SYMON.

Other political parties include the **Farm and Town Party.**

Diplomatic Representation
EMBASSIES AND HIGH COMMISSIONS IN AUSTRALIA

Argentina: MLC Tower, Suite 102, 1st Floor, Woden, ACT 2606; POB 262, Woden, ACT 2606; tel. (062) 824855; telex 62195; Ambassador: RAFAEL GOWLAND.

Austria: 12 Talbot St, Forrest, ACT 2603; tel. (062) 951533; telex 62726; Ambassador: Dr JAMES PREUSCHEN.

Bangladesh: 11 Molineaux Place, Farrer, ACT 2607; POB 197, Mawson, ACT 2607; tel. (062) 863992; telex 61729; High Commissioner: Air Vice-Marshal Sultan MAHMUD BU (designate).

Belgium: 19 Arkana St, Yarralumla, ACT 2600; tel. (062) 732501; telex 62601; Ambassador: Dr WILFRIED DE PAUW.

Brazil: 19 Forster Crescent, Yarralumla, ACT; POB 1540, Canberra, ACT 2601; tel. (062) 732372; telex 62327; Ambassador: MARCOS HENRIQUE CAMILLO CÔRTES.

Burma: 22 Arkana St, Yarralumla, Canberra, ACT 2600; tel. (062) 733811; telex 61376; Ambassador: U MAUNG MAUNG SOE TINT.

Canada: Commonwealth Ave, Canberra, ACT 2600; tel. (062) 733844; telex 62017; High Commissioner: R. ALLEN KILPATRICK.

Chile: 10 Culgoa Circuit, O'Malley, ACT 2606; tel. (062) 862430; telex 62685; Ambassador: JAIME HERRERA CARGILL.

China, People's Republic: 14 Federal Highway, Watson, Canberra, ACT 2602; tel. (062) 412446; telex 62489; Ambassador: ZHANG ZAI.

Cyprus: 37 Endeavour St, Red Hill, ACT 2603; tel. (062) 952120; telex 62499; High Commissioner: Dr PROKOPIS VANEZIS.

Czechoslovakia: 47 Culgoa Circuit, O'Malley, ACT 2606; tel. 866755; Ambassador PETR KADLEC.

Denmark: 15 Hunter St, Yarralumla, ACT 2600; tel. (062) 732195; telex 62661; Ambassador: BIRGER ABRAHAMSON.

Egypt: 125 Monaro Crescent, Red Hill, ACT 2603; tel. (062) 950394; telex 62497; Ambassador NABIL MUHAMMAD BADR.

Fiji: 9 Beagle St, Red Hill, ACT 2600; POB E159, Queen Victoria Terrace, ACT 2600; tel. (062) 959148; telex 62345; Chargé d'affaires: AKUILA MAKUTU WARADI (acting).

Finland: 10 Darwin Ave, Yarralumla, ACT 2600; tel. (062) 733800; telex 62713; Ambassador: ULF-ERIK SLOTTE.

France: 6 Perth Ave, Yarralumla, ACT 2600; tel. (062) 905111; telex 61346; Ambassador: ROGER DUZER.

German Democratic Republic: 8 Dalman Crescent, O'Malley, ACT 2606; tel. (062) 862300; telex 62496; Ambassador: JOACHIM ELM.

Germany, Federal Republic: 119 Empire Circuit, Yarralumla, ACT 2600; tel. (062) 701911; telex 62035; Ambassador: Dr HANS SCHAUER.

Greece: 9 Turrana St, Yarralumla, ACT 2600; tel. (062) 733011; telex 62724; Ambassador: EFTHYMIOS TZAPHERIS.

Holy See: 2 Vancouver St, Red Hill, ACT 2603; tel. (062) 953876; Apostolic Pro-Nuncio: Mgr FRANCO BRAMBILLA.

Hungary: 79 Hopetoun Circuit, Yarralumla, ACT 2600; tel. (062) 823226; telex 62737; Ambassador: ZOLTÁN JUHÁR.

India: 3–5 Moonah Place, Yarralumla, ACT 2600; tel. (062) 733999; telex 62362; High Commissioner: MUHAMMAD HAMID ANSARI.

Indonesia: 8 Darwin Ave, Yarralumla, ACT 2600; tel. (062) 733222; telex 62525; Ambassador: Air Vice-Marshal ROESMAN.

Iran: 14 Torres St, Red Hill, ACT 2603; POB 219, Manuka, ACT 2603; tel. (062) 952544; telex 62490; Ambassador: MEHDI KHANDAGHABADI.

Iraq: 48 Culgoa Circuit, O'Malley, ACT 2606; tel. (062) 861333; telex 61520; Ambassador: ANWAR A. K. AL-HADITHI.

Ireland: 20 Arkana St, Yarralumla, ACT 2600; tel. (062) 733022; telex 62720; Ambassador: JAMES A. SHARKEY.

Israel: 6 Turrana St, Yarralumla, ACT 2600; tel. (062) 731309; telex 62224; Ambassador: ZVI KEDAR.

Italy: 12 Grey St, Deakin, ACT 2600; POB 360, Canberra City, ACT 2601; tel. (062) 733333; telex 62028; Ambassador: Dr ERIC DA RIN.

Japan: 112 Empire Circuit, Yarralumla, ACT 2600; tel. (062) 733244; telex 62034; Ambassador: KENICHI YANAGI.

Jordan: 20 Roebuck St, Red Hill, ACT 2603; tel. (062) 959951; telex 62551; Ambassador: Dr SULEIMAN DAJANI.

AUSTRALIA

Kenya: Amdahl House, 6th Floor, 33-35 Ainslie Ave, Canberra, ACT; POB 1990, Canberra, ACT 2601; tel. (062) 474788; telex 61929; High Commissioner: Maj.-Gen. JOSEPH MBYATI MUSOMBA.

Korea, Republic: 113 Empire Circuit, Yarralumla, ACT 2600; tel. (062) 733044; Ambassador: CHANG SOO LEE.

Laos: 1 Dalman Crescent, O'Malley, ACT 2606; tel. (062) 864595; telex 61627; Chargé d'affaires a.i.: OUAN PHOMMACHACK.

Lebanon: 27 Endeavour St, Red Hill, ACT 2603; tel. (062) 957378; telex 61762; Ambassador: LATIF ABUL-HUSN.

Malaysia: 7 Perth Ave, Yarralumla, ACT 2600; tel. (062) 731543; High Commissioner: Tan Sri Datuk ZAKARIA BIN Haji MUHAMMAD ALI.

Malta: 261 La Perouse St, Red Hill, ACT 2603; tel. (062) 951586; telex 62817; High Commissioner: VICTOR J. GAUCI.

Mauritius: 43 Hampton Circuit, Yarralumla, ACT 2600; tel. (062) 811203; telex 62863; High Commissioner: JEAN-CLAUDE BIBI.

Mexico: 14 Perth Ave, Yarralumla, ACT 2600; tel. (062) 733963; telex 62329; Ambassador: JESÚS FRANCISCO DOMENE.

Netherlands: 120 Empire Circuit, Yarralumla, ACT 2600; tel. (062) 733111; telex 62047; Ambassador: JORIS MICHAEL VOS.

New Zealand: Commonwealth Ave, Canberra, ACT 2600; tel. (062) 733611; telex 7162019; High Commissioner: GRAHAM K. ANSELL.

Nigeria: 7 Terrigal Crescent, O'Malley, ACT 2606; POB 241, Civic Square, ACT 2608; tel. (062) 861322; High Commissioner: G. J. N. ANIEMENA.

Norway: 17 Hunter St, Yarralumla, ACT 2600; tel. (062) 733444; telex 62569; Ambassador: PER THELIN HAUGESTAD.

Pakistan: 59 Franklin St, Forrest, ACT 2603; POB 198, Manuka, ACT 2603; tel. (062) 950021; Ambassador: Adm. (retd) TARIQ KAMAL KHAN.

Papua New Guinea: Forster Crescent, Yarralumla, ACT 2600; POB 572, Manuka, ACT 2603; tel. (062) 733322; telex 62592; High Commissioner: PAUL BERNARD SONGO.

Peru: Qantas House, Suite 1, 9th Floor, 197 London Circuit, Canberra City, ACT 2601; POB 971, Civic Square, ACT 2608; tel. (062) 572953; telex 61664; Ambassador: GONZALO BEDOYA DELBOY.

Philippines: 1 Moonah Place, Yarralumla, ACT 2600; POB 297, Manuka, ACT 2603; tel. (062) 732535; telex 62665; Ambassador: ROMUALDO A. ONG.

Poland: 7 Turrana St, Yarralumla, ACT 2600; tel. (062) 731208; telex 62584; Ambassador: ANTONI PIERZCHALA.

Portugal: 6 Campion St, 1st Floor, Deakin, ACT 2600; POB 92, Deakin, ACT 2600; tel. (062) 852084; telex 62649; Ambassador: Dr JOSÉ LUIS GOMES.

Saudi Arabia: 12 Culgoa Circuit, O'Malley, ACT 2606; POB 63, Garran, ACT 2605; tel. (062) 862099; telex 61454; Ambassador: A. RAHMAN N. ALOHALY.

Singapore: 17 Forster Crescent, Yarralumla, ACT 2600; tel. (062) 733944; telex 62192; High Commissioner: J. F. CONCEICAO.

South Africa: cnr State Circle and Rhodes Place, Yarralumla, ACT 2600; tel. (062) 732424; telex 62734; Ambassador: CORNELIUS A. BASTIAANSE.

Spain: 15 Arkana St, Yarralumla, ACT 2600; POB 76, Deakin, ACT 2600; tel. (062) 733555; telex 62485; Ambassador: Dr JOSÉ LUIS PARDOS.

Sri Lanka: 35 Empire Circuit, Forrest, ACT 2603; tel. (062) 953521; telex 61620; High Commissioner: Dr WICKREMA SENA WEERASOORIA.

Sweden: 5 Turrana St, Yarralumla, ACT 2600; tel. (062) 733033; telex 62303; Ambassador: HANS BJÖRK.

Switzerland: 7 Melbourne Ave, Forrest, ACT 2603; tel. (062) 733977; telex 62275; Ambassador: (vacant).

Thailand: 111 Empire Circuit, Yarralumla, ACT 2600; tel. (062) 731149; telex 62533; Ambassador: JETN SUCHARITKUL.

Turkey: 60 Mugga Way, Red Hill, ACT 2603; tel. (062) 950227; telex 62764; Ambassador: FARUK SAHİNBAS.

USSR: 78 Canberra Ave, Griffith, ACT 2603; tel. (062) 959033; telex 62239; Ambassador: YEVGENI M. SAMOTEIKIN.

United Kingdom: Commonwealth Ave, Canberra, ACT 2600; tel. (062) 706666; telex 62222; High Commissioner: JOHN COLES.

USA: Chancery, Yarralumla, ACT 2600; tel. (062) 705000; telex 62104; Ambassador: LAURENCE WILLIAM LANE, Jr.

Uruguay: Bonner House, Suite 5, Woden, ACT 2606; POB 318, Woden, ACT 2606; tel. (062) 824418; telex 61486; Chargé d'affaires a.i.: JULIO GIAMBRUNO.

Venezuela: MLC Tower, Suite 106, 1st Floor, Woden, ACT 2606; POB 37, Woden, ACT 2606; tel. (062) 824827; telex 62110; Ambassador: Dr RAMÓN DELGADO.

Viet-Nam: 6 Timbarra Crescent, O'Malley, ACT 2606; tel. (062) 866059; telex 62756; Chargé d'affaires a.i.: DO NGOC AN.

Yugoslavia: 11 Nuyts St, Red Hill, ACT 2603; POB 161, Manuka, ACT 2603; tel. (062) 951458; telex 62317; Ambassador: Dr BORIS CIZELJ.

Zambia: Amdahl Bldg, 3rd Floor, 33-35 Ainslie Ave, Canberra, ACT 2608; tel. 472088; telex 61796; High Commissioner: JASON C. MFULA.

Judicial System

The judicial power of the Commonwealth of Australia is vested in the High Court of Australia, in such other Federal Courts as the Federal Parliament creates, and in such other courts as it invests with Federal jurisdiction.

The High Court consists of a Chief Justice and six other Justices, each of whom is appointed by the Governor-General in Council, and has both original and appellate jurisdiction.

The High Court's original jurisdiction extends to all matters arising under any treaty, affecting representatives of other countries, in which the Commonwealth of Australia or its representative is a party, between States or between residents of different States or between a State and a resident of another State, and in which a writ of mandamus, or prohibition, or an injunction is sought against an officer of the Commonwealth of Australia. It also extends to matters arising under the Australian Constitution or involving its interpretation, and to many matters arising under Commonwealth laws.

The High Court's appellate jurisdiction has, since June 1984, been discretionary. Appeals from the Federal Court, the Family Court and the Supreme Courts of the States and of the Territories may now be brought only if special leave is granted, in the event of a legal question that is of general public importance being involved, or of there being differences of opinion between intermediate appellate courts as to the state of the law.

Legislation enacted by the Federal Parliament in 1976 substantially changed the exercise of Federal and Territory judicial power, and, by creating the Federal Court of Australia in February 1977, enabled the High Court of Australia to give greater attention to its primary function as interpreter of the Australian Constitution. The Federal Court of Australia has assumed, in two divisions, the jurisdiction previously exercised by the Australian Industrial Court and the Federal Court of Bankruptcy and has additionally been given jurisdiction in trade practices and in the developing field of administrative law. Jurisdiction has also been conferred on the Federal Court of Australia, subject to a number of exceptions, in matters in which a writ of mandamus, or prohibition, or an injunction is sought against an officer of the Commonwealth of Australia. The Court also hears appeals from the Court constituted by a single Judge, from the Supreme Courts of the Territories, and in certain specific matters from State Courts, other than a Full Court of the Supreme Court of a State, exercising Federal jurisdiction.

In March 1986 all remaining categories of appeal from Australian courts to the Queen's Privy Council in the UK were abolished by the Australia Act.

FEDERAL COURTS

High Court of Australia

POB E435, Queen Victoria Terrace, Canberra, ACT 2600; tel. (062) 706861; telex 61430.

Chief Justice: Sir ANTHONY FRANK MASON.

Justices:
Sir RONALD DARLING WILSON, Sir FRANCIS GERARD BRENNAN, Sir WILLIAM PATRICK DEANE, Sir DARYL MICHAEL DAWSON, JOHN LESLIE TOOHEY, MARY GENEVIEVE GAUDRON.

Federal Court of Australia

Chief Judge: Sir NIGEL HUBERT BOWEN.

There are 30 other Judges.

Family Court of Australia

Chief Judge: ALISTAIR BOTHWICK NICHOLSON.

There are more than 50 other Judges.

NEW SOUTH WALES

Supreme Court

Chief Justice: Sir LAURENCE WHISTLER STREET.

President of the Court of Appeal: MICHAEL DONALD KIRBY.

Chief Judge in Equity: MICHAEL MANIFOLD HELSHAM.

Chief Judge of Common Law: JOHN PATRICK SLATTERY.

AUSTRALIA

VICTORIA
Supreme Court
Chief Justice: Sir JOHN MCINTOSH YOUNG.

QUEENSLAND
Supreme Court
Southern District (Brisbane)
Chief Justice: D. G. ANDREWS.
Senior Puisne Judge: J. KELLY.

Central District (Rockhampton)
Puisne Judge: A. G. DEMACK.

Northern District (Townsville)
Puisne Judge: Sir GEORGE KNEIPP.

SOUTH AUSTRALIA
Supreme Court
Chief Justice: LEONARD JAMES KING.

WESTERN AUSTRALIA
Supreme Court
Chief Justice: DAVID MALCOLM.

TASMANIA
Supreme Court
Chief Justice: Sir GUY STEPHEN MONTAGUE GREEN.

AUSTRALIAN CAPITAL TERRITORY
Supreme Court
Chief Justice: JEFFREY ALLAN MILES.

NORTHERN TERRITORY
Supreme Court
Chief Justice: K. J. A. ASCENE.

Religion

CHRISTIANITY

Australian Council of Churches: 379 Kent St, POB C199, Sydney, NSW 2000; tel. (02) 29-2215; telex 17175; f. 1946; 13 mem. churches; Pres. Most Rev. Dr DAVID J. PENMAN (Anglican Archbishop of Melbourne); Gen. Sec. Rev. DAVID GILL.

The Anglican Communion

The constitution of the Church of England in Australia came into force in January 1962. The body was renamed the Anglican Church of Australia in August 1981. The Church comprises five provinces (together containing 23 dioceses) and the extra-provincial diocese of Tasmania. In 1985 there were an estimated 3,750,000 adherents.

National Office of the Anglican Church: General Synod Office, Box Q190, Queen Victoria PO, Sydney, NSW 2000; tel. (02) 265-1525; Gen. Sec. JOHN G. DENTON.

Primate of Australia, Archbishop of Brisbane and Metropolitan of Queensland: Most Rev. JOHN B. R. GRINDROD, Bishopsbourne, Box 421, GPO, Brisbane, Queensland 4001.

Archbishop of Adelaide and Metropolitan of South Australia: Most Rev. KEITH RAYNER, Bishop's Court, 45 Palmer Place, North Adelaide, South Australia 5006.

Archbishop of Melbourne and Metropolitan of Victoria: Most Rev. Dr DAVID J. PENMAN, Bishopscourt, 120 Clarendon St, Melbourne, Victoria 3002.

Archbishop of Perth and Metropolitan of Western Australia: Most Rev. PETER F. CARNLEY, Bishop's House, 90 Mounts Bay Rd, Perth, Western Australia 6000; also has jurisdiction over Christmas Island and the Cocos (Keeling) Islands.

Archbishop of Sydney and Metropolitan of New South Wales: Most Rev. DONALD W. B. ROBINSON, Box Q190, Queen Victoria PO, Sydney, NSW 2000.

The Roman Catholic Church

Australia comprises seven archdioceses (including two directly responsible to the Holy See) and 25 dioceses (including one each for Catholics of the Maronite, Melkite and Ukrainian rites). There are an estimated 4m. adherents in the country.

Australian Catholic Bishops Conference: 63 Currong St, Braddon (POB 368, Canberra), ACT 2601; tel. (062) 472011; f. 1979; Pres. Cardinal EDWARD BEDE CLANCY, Archbishop of Sydney.

Archbishop of Adelaide: Most Rev. LEONARD A. FAULKNER, Catholic Diocesan Centre, 39 Wakefield St, Adelaide, South Australia 5000; tel. (08) 210-8108.

Archbishop of Brisbane: Most Rev. FRANCIS R. RUSH, Catholic Centre, 790 Brunswick St, Brisbane, Queensland 4005; tel. (07) 224-3361.

Archbishop of Canberra and Goulburn: Most Rev. FRANCIS P. CARROLL, Archbishop's House, POB 89, Commonwealth Ave, Canberra, ACT 2601; tel. (062) 486411.

Archbishop of Hobart: (vacant), Catholic Church Office, POB 62A, Hobart, Tasmania 7001.

Archbishop of Melbourne: Most Rev. THOMAS F. LITTLE, Catholic Diocesan Centre, POB 146, 383 Albert St, East Melbourne, Victoria 3002; tel. (03) 667-0377.

Archbishop of Perth: Most Rev. WILLIAM J. FOLEY, St Mary's Cathedral, 21 Victoria Sq., Perth, Western Australia 6000; tel. (09) 325-9177.

Archbishop of Sydney: Cardinal EDWARD BEDE CLANCY, Archdiocesan Chancery, Polding House, 13th Floor, 276 Pitt St, Sydney, NSW 2000; tel. (02) 264-7211.

Orthodox Churches

Greek Orthodox Archdiocese: 242 Cleveland St, Redfern, Sydney, NSW 2016; tel. (02) 698-5066; f. 1924; 700,000 mems; offices in Melbourne, Adelaide and Perth; Leader in Australia Archbishop STYLIANOS.

The Antiochian, Coptic, Romanian, Serbian and Syrian Orthodox Churches are also represented.

Other Christian Churches

Baptist Union of Australia: POB 377, Hawthorn, Vic 3122; tel. (03) 818-0341; f. 1926; 60,024 mems; 748 churches; Nat. Pres. W. C. MCFARLANE; Nat. Sec. O. C. ABBOTT.

Churches of Christ in Australia: 7 Elm Rd, Glen Iris, Victoria 3146; tel. (03) 256085; 400,000 mems; Pres. Rev. G. POWELL; Sec. Rev. I. E. ALLSOP.

Lutheran Church of Australia: Lutheran Church House, 58 O'Connell St, North Adelaide, SA 5006; tel. (08) 267-4922; telex 87519; f. 1966; 111,040 mems; Pres. Rev. L. G. STEICKE; Sec. Rev. K. J. SCHMIDT.

Uniting Church in Australia: POB E266, St James, NSW 2000; tel. (02) 287-0900; f. 1977 with the union of Methodist, Presbyterian and Congregational Churches; 1.1m. mems; Pres. Sir RONALD WILSON; Sec. Rev. GREGOR HENDERSON.

Other active denominations include the Armenian Apostolic Church, the Assyrian Church of the East and the Society of Friends (Quakers).

JUDAISM

Great Synagogue: 166 Castlereagh St, Sydney, NSW; tel. (02) 267-2477; f. 1828; Sr Minister Rabbi RAYMOND APPLE.

The Press

The total circulation of Australia's daily newspapers is very high but in the remoter parts of the country weekly papers are even more popular. Most of Australia's newspapers are published in sparsely populated rural areas where the demand for local news is strong. The only newspapers that may fairly claim a national circulation are the dailies *The Australian* and *Australian Financial Review*, and the weeklies *The Bulletin*, the *National Times* and the *Nation Review*, the circulation of most newspapers being almost entirely confined to the State in which each is produced.

The trend in recent years towards the concentration of media ownership has led to the development of three principal groups of newspapers. Economic conditions have been conducive to the expansion of newspaper companies into magazine and book publishing, radio and television, etc. The principal groups are as follows:

Consolidated Press Holdings Ltd: 54 Park St, Sydney, NSW 2000; tel. (02) 282-8000; telex 120514; publishes *Australian Women's Weekly*, *The Bulletin*, *Australian Business*, *Cleo* and other magazines.

The John Fairfax Group: 235 Jones St, Broadway, NSW 2007; POB 506, Sydney, NSW 2001; f. 1841; controls *The Sydney Morning Herald*, *Australian Financial Review* and *Sun-Herald* (Sydney), *The Age* (Melbourne), *Illawarra Mercury* (Wollongong), *The Newcastle Herald* (Newcastle), *Business Review Weekly* (New Zealand).

The Herald and Weekly Times Ltd: 44-74 Flinders St, Melbourne, Vic 3000; tel. (03) 652-1111; telex 30104; acquired by News Ltd in 1987; Chair. and CEO JOHN J. D'ARCY; publs include *The Herald*,

AUSTRALIA

The Sun News-Pictorial, The Weekly Times, The Sporting Globe, The Bendigo Advertiser and *The Geelong Advertiser* (Melbourne), *Papua New Guinea Post-Courier, Fiji Times.*

News Ltd: 2 Holt St, Surry Hills, Sydney, NSW 2010; tel. (02) 288-3000; telex 20124; Chair. R. H. SEARBY; CEO K. RUPERT MURDOCH; controls *Adelaide News, The Australian, Daily Mirror* (Sydney), *Northern Territory News* (Darwin), *Sunday Times* (Perth), *Sunday Sun* (Brisbane), *Daily Telegraph* and *Sunday Telegraph* (Sydney), *Northern Daily Leader* (Tamworth), *Townsville Bulletin*, Progress Press (Melbourne). Assoc. publs: *New Idea* and *TV Week* (Melbourne), *The Sun, News of the World, The Times* and *The Sunday Times* (London), *Boston Herald* (Boston), *Express-News* (San Antonio, Texas).

David Syme & Co Ltd: 250 Spencer St, Melbourne, Vic 3000; tel. (03) 600-4211; telex 30449; f. 1834; wholly-owned by John Fairfax Group (see above); publishes *The Age* and other newspapers and magazines in Victoria; Man. Dir G. J. TAYLOR.

NEWSPAPERS

Australian Capital Territory

The Canberra Times: 9 Pirie St, Fyshwick 2609; tel. (062) 802122; telex 62069; f. 1926; daily and Sun.; morning; Editor-in-Chief I. R. MATHEWS; circ. 44,000.

New South Wales
Dailies

The Australian: News Ltd, 2 Holt St, Surry Hills 2010, POB 4245; tel. 288-3000; telex 20124; f. 1964; edited in Sydney, simultaneous edns in Sydney, Melbourne, Perth, Townsville and Brisbane; Propr K. RUPERT MURDOCH; Editor FRANK DEVINE; circ. 138,000.

Australian Financial Review: 235 Jones St, Broadway, POB 506, Sydney 2001; tel. (02) 282-2833; telex 24851; f. 1951; Mon.-Fri.; distributed nationally; Editor-in-Chief PETER ROBINSON; circ. 78,000.

Daily Commercial News: POB 1552, Sydney 2001; tel. (02) 211-4055; telex 121874; f. 1891; Gen. Man. C. S. WYNDHAM.

Daily Mirror: 2 Holt St, Surry Hills 2010; tel. (02) 288-3000; telex 20124; f. 1941; evening; CEO K. RUPERT MURDOCH; Editor ROY MILLER; circ. 395,000.

Daily Telegraph: 2 Holt St, Surry Hills 2010; tel. 288-3000; telex 20124; f. 1879; morning; Editor JOHN HARTIGAN; circ. 326,000.

The Manly Daily: 26 Sydney Rd, Manly 2095; tel. (02) 977-3333; f. 1906; Tues.-Sat.; Man. G. H. MCGAY; circ. 81,000.

The Newcastle Herald: 28-30 Bolton St, Newcastle 2300; tel. 263222; telex 28269; f. 1858; morning; 6 a week; Editor B. W. POMFRETT; circ. 56,000.

The Sydney Morning Herald: 235 Jones St, Broadway, POB 506, Sydney 2001; tel. (02) 282-2822; telex 20121; f. 1831; morning; Editor-in-Chief J. H. ALEXANDER; circ. 266,000 (Mon.-Fri.), 400,000 (Sat.).

Weeklies

Bankstown Canterbury Torch: 398 Marion St, Bankstown 2200; tel. 709-3433; f. 1920; Wed.; Publr J. P. ENGISCH; circ. 78,000.

Northern District Times: 116 Rowe St, Eastwood 2122; tel. 858-1766; f. 1921; Wed.; Man. R. HAYLES; Editor R. BENDALL; circ. 65,000.

The Parramatta Advertiser: 142 Macquarie St, Parramatta 2150; tel. (02) 689-5500; telex 72133; Wed.; Editor S. STICKNEY; circ. 80,531.

Parramatta and District Mercury: 38 George St, 1st Floor, Parramatta 2150; f. 1977; Tues.; circ. 102,000.

St George and Sutherland Shire Leader: 172 Forest Rd, Hurstville 2220; tel. 579-5033; f. 1960; Tues. and Thurs.; Man. IAN MUDDLE; Editor MICHAEL GARDNER; circ. 124,000.

Sun-Herald: 235 Jones St, Broadway, POB 506, Sydney 2001; tel. (02) 282-2822; telex 20121; f. 1953; Sunday; Editor DAVID HICKIE; circ. 671,000.

Sunday Telegraph: 2 Holt St, Surry Hills 2010; tel. 288-3000; telex 20124; f. 1938; Editor IAN MOORE; circ. 665,000.

Northern Territory
Daily

Northern Territory News: 3 Printers Place, POB 1300, Darwin 5794; tel. (089) 828200; telex 85574; f. 1952; Mon. to Sat.; Man. Editor J. HOGAN; circ. 19,000.

Weeklies

The Darwin Star: 31 Bishop St, POB 39330 Winnellie, Darwin 5789; f. 1976; Thurs.; Man. Editor PATRICK CUSICK; circ. 13,000.

Sunday Territorian: Printers Place, POB 1300, Darwin 5794; tel. (089) 828200; telex 85574; Sun.; Editor G. SHIPWAY; circ. 21,000.

Queensland
Dailies

Courier-Mail: Campbell St, Bowen Hills, Brisbane 4006; tel. (07) 2526011; telex 40101; f. 1933; morning; Editor G. T. CHAMBERLIN; circ. 257,000.

Daily Sun: GPO Box 222, Brisbane 4001; tel. (07) 533333; telex 40105; f. 1982; morning; Editor MIKE QUIRK; circ. 125,000.

Weeklies

The Suburban: 10 Aspinall St, Nundah; POB 10, Nundah 4012; tel. 266-6666; five suburban edns; Publr Mrs HEATHER JEFFERY; combined circ. 117,000.

Sunday Mail: Campbell St, Bowen Hills, Brisbane 4006; tel. (07) 2526011; telex 40110; f. 1923; Editor DES HOUGHTON; circ. 320,000.

Sunday Sun: cnr Brunswick and McLachlan Sts, Fortitude Valley, Brisbane 4000; tel. (07) 528050; f. 1971; Man. Editor M. QUIRK; circ. 371,000.

South Australia
Dailies

Advertiser: 121 King William St, Adelaide 5001; tel. (08) 218-9218; telex 82101; f. 1858; morning; Man. Editor J. L. SCALES; circ. 216,000.

News: 112 North Terrace, Adelaide 5000, POB 1771, GPO Adelaide 5001; tel. (08) 510351; telex 82131; f. 1923; evening; Mon.-Fri.; Man. Editor ROGER HOLDEN; circ. 167,000.

Weekly

Sunday Mail: 116-120 North Terrace, Adelaide 5000; f. 1912; Editor REX JORY; circ. 250,000.

Victoria
Dailies

The Age: 250 Spencer St (cnr Lonsdale St), Melbourne 3000; tel. (03) 600421; telex 30449; f. 1854; independent; morning; Man. Dir G. J. TAYLOR; Editor CREIGHTON BURNS; circ. 236,000.

The Herald: 44-74 Flinders St, Melbourne 3000; tel. (03) 652-1111; telex 30104; f. 1840; evening; Editor E. BEECHER; circ. 217,000.

Sun News-Pictorial: 44-74 Flinders St, Melbourne 3000; tel. (03) 652-1111; telex 30104; f. 1922; morning; Editor COLIN DUCK; circ. 570,000.

Weeklies

Regional Progress: 92 Atherton Rd, Oakleigh 3166; tel. 568-4644; f. 1960; publ. by Leader Group; Wed.; Editor CHRISTINA RATCLIFFE; circ. 67,000.

Sporting Globe: 44 Flinders St, Melbourne 3000; tel. (03) 652-1111; telex 30104; f. 1922; Mon.; Editor NEVILLE WILLMOTT.

Sunday Observer: 46-49 Porter St, Prahran 3181; tel. 520-5555; telex 30880; f. 1971; Editor JIM LAWRENCE; circ. 135,000.

Sunday Press: 61 Flinders Lane, Melbourne 3000; tel. (03) 652-1111; telex 30104; f. 1973; Editor MARTIN THOMAS; circ. 175,000.

Truth: 272 Rosslyn St, West Melbourne 3003; tel. (03) 329-0277; telex 30562; f. 1890; Mon. and Thurs.; Editor C. SMITH; circ. 210,000.

Tasmania
Dailies

Advocate: POB 63, Burnie 7320; tel. 301409; telex 59049; f. 1890; morning; Editor D. J. CHERRY; circ. 27,000.

Examiner: 71-75 Paterson St, POB 99A, Launceston 7250; tel. (003) 315111; telex 58511; f. 1842; morning; independent; Editor M. C. P. COURTNEY; circ. 39,000.

Mercury: 91-93 Macquarie St, Hobart 7000; tel. (002) 300622; telex 58104; f. 1854; morning; Editor B. J. DARGAVILLE; circ. 58,000.

Weeklies

Advocate Weekender: POB 63, Burnie 7320; tel. 301409; telex 59049; f. 1968; Saturday; Editor D. J. CHERRY; circ. 14,000.

Sunday Examiner: 71-75 Paterson St, Launceston 7250; tel. (003) 315111; telex 58511; f. 1924; Editor M. C. P. COURTNEY; circ. 39,000.

Sunday Tasmanian: 91-93 Macquarie St, Hobart 7000; tel. (002) 300622; f. 1984; morning; Editor B. J. DARGAVILLE; circ. 40,000.

The Tasmanian Mail: 130 Collins St, Hobart 7000; tel. (002) 211211; telex 57150; f. 1978; Man. Editor W. A. J. HASWELL; circ. 131,000.

AUSTRALIA

Western Australia

Dailies

Daily News: 120 Roe St, Northbridge, Perth 6000; tel. (09) 427-1400; f. 1882; evening, Mon.-Fri.; Editor JACK HARRISON; circ. 100,000.

The West Australian: 219 St George's Terrace, POB D162, GPO Perth 6001; tel. (09) 482-3111; f. 1833; morning; Editor R. E. CRONIN; circ. 281,000.

Weeklies

The Countryman: 219 St George's Terrace, POB D162, Perth 6001; tel. (09) 482-3111; telex 94999; f. 1885; Thurs.; farming; Editor R. C. RAYMOND; circ. 13,000.

Sunday Times: 34–42 Stirling St, Perth 6000; tel. (09) 326-8326; telex 92015; f. 1897; Man. Dir D. THOMPSON; Editor-in-Chief DON SMITH; circ. 280,000.

PRINCIPAL PERIODICALS

Weeklies and Fortnightlies

The Advocate: 196–200 Lygon St, Carlton, Vic 3053; tel. (03) 662-1100; f. 1868; Thurs.; Roman Catholic; Editor NEVILLE WEERERATNE; circ. 19,000.

Australasian Post: 32 Walsh St, West Melbourne, Vic 3003; tel. (03) 320-7000; f. 1946; factual, general interest, Australiana; Mon.; Editor-in-Chief TONY BERRY; circ. 225,000.

The Bulletin: 54 Park St, Sydney, NSW 2000; tel. (02) 282-8200; telex 120514; f. 1880; Wed.; Editor DAVID DALE.

The Medical Journal of Australia: 77–79 Arundel St, Glebe, NSW 2037; tel. (02) 660-6055; telex 24814; f. 1914; fortnightly; Editor Dr KATHLEEN KING; circ. 23,000.

New Idea: 32 Walsh St, Melbourne, Vic; tel. (03) 320-7000; weekly; women's; Editor-in-Chief D. BOLING.

News Weekly: POB 66A, GPO Melbourne, Vic 3001; tel. (03) 602-1133; f. 1943; publ. by National Civic Council; Wed.; political, social, educational and trade union affairs; Editor PETER WESTMORE; circ. 17,000.

People Magazine: POB 5201, Sydney, NSW 2001; tel. (02) 282-8000; telex 25027; weekly; Editor CHRIS BLACK; circ. 257,000.

Queensland Country Life: 432 Queen St, Brisbane, Qld; telex 42523; f. 1935; Thurs.; Editor-in-Chief PETER OWEN; circ. 35,000.

Scene: 61 Flinders Lane, Melbourne, Vic 3000; tel. (03) 652-1111; telex 30104; f. 1925; Wed.; Editor GARRY MANSFIELD; circ. 80,000.

The South Sea Digest: 46 Kippax St, 4th Floor, Surry Hills, NSW 2010; POB 4245, Sydney, NSW 2001; tel. (02) 288-3000; telex 20124; f. 1981; fortnightly; business and politics in South Pacific; Editor JOHN CARTER.

Stock and Land: POB 1386, Collingwood, Vic 3066; tel. (03) 418-7900; telex 35668; f. 1914; weekly; livestock, land and wool market journal; Editor P. F. DOWNE; circ. 24,000.

TV Week: 32 Walsh St, Melbourne, Vic; tel. (03) 320-7000; telex 31824; f. 1957; Mon.; colour national; Editor-in-Chief JOHN HALL; circ. 850,000.

Video Business: POB 1024, Richmond North, Vic 3121; tel. (03) 429-5599; telex 38225; f. 1984; fortnightly; circ. 3,000.

Weekly Times: Box 751F, GPO Melbourne, Vic 3001; tel. (03) 652-1111; telex 30104; f. 1869; farming, gardening, country life and sport; Wed.; Editor KEVIN BOYLE; circ. 110,000.

Woman's Day: 54 Park St, POB 5245, Sydney, NSW 2001; tel. (02) 282-8000; telex 20514; weekly; circulates throughout Australia and NZ; Editor NENE KING; circ. 720,000.

Monthlies and Others

Archaeology in Oceania: University of Sydney, NSW 2006; tel. (02) 692-2666; f. 1966; 3 a year; archaeology and physical anthropology; Editor J. PETER WHITE.

Architecture Media Australia Pty Ltd: 11 Beach St, Suite 4, Port Melbourne, Vic 3207; tel. (03) 646-4760; f. 1904; 11 a year; Editor TOM HEATH; circ. 10,000.

Australian Cricket: 200 Crown St, Darlinghurst, NSW 2010; tel. (02) 331-5655; telex 74488; f. 1968; monthly; Editor NOEL MENGEL.

Australian Electrical World: POB 1024, Richmond North, Vic 3121; tel. (03) 429-5599; telex 38225; f. 1935; monthly; Editor WENDY PARKER; circ. 7,361.

Australian Hi-Fi Magazine: POB 341, Mona Vale, NSW 2103; tel. (02) 997-1188; f. 1970; monthly; Editor GREG BORROWMAN; circ. 25,000.

Australian Historical Studies: Dept of History, University of Melbourne, Parkville, Vic 3052; tel. (03) 344-4000; telex 35185; f. 1940; 2 a year; Editor STUART MACINTYRE; circ. 1,500.

Australian Home Beautiful: 32 Walsh St, West Melbourne, Vic 3003; tel. (03) 320-7521; telex 30578; f. 1925; monthly; Editor-in-Chief TONY FAWCETT.

Australian House and Garden: 168 Castlereagh St, Sydney, NSW 2000; tel. (02) 282-8041; telex 20514; monthly; building, furnishing, decorating, handicrafts, gardening, entertaining; Editor-in-Chief DAWN SWAIN.

Australian Journal of Agricultural Research: CSIRO, 314 Albert St, POB 89, East Melbourne, Vic 3002; tel. (03) 418-7333; telex 30236; f. 1950; quarterly; Man. Editor G. A. FORSTER.

Australian Journal of Marine and Freshwater Research: CSIRO, 314 Albert St, POB 89, East Melbourne, Vic 3002; tel. (03) 418-7333; telex 30236; f. 1950; 6 a year; Man. Editor ANN GRANT.

Australian Journal of Mining: POB 1024, Richmond North, Vic 3121; tel. (03) 429-5599; telex 38225; f. 1986; monthly; Editor LIZ REID; circ. 9,032.

Australian Journal of Pharmacy: 40 Burwood Rd, Hawthorn, Vic 3122; tel. (03) 810-9800; f. 1886; monthly; journal of the associated pharmaceutical orgs; Editor S. L. DICKSON; Man. G. E. SIMONSEN; circ. 7,600.

Australian Journal of Physics: CSIRO, 314 Albert St, POB 89, East Melbourne, Vic 3002; tel. (03) 418-7333; telex 30236; f. 1953; 6 a year; Man. Editor R. P. ROBERTSON.

Australian Journal of Politics and History: University of Queensland, St Lucia, Qld 4067; tel. 377-2265; f. 1955; 3 a year; Editor J. A. MOSES; circ. 1,000.

Australian Law Journal: 44–50 Waterloo Rd, North Ryde, NSW 2113; tel. 887-0177; telex 27995; f. 1927; monthly; Gen. Editor J. G. STARKE; circ 7,000.

Australian Left Review: POB A247, South Sydney PO, NSW 2000; f. 1966; 6 a year.

Australian Photography: POB 606, Sydney, NSW 2001; tel. (02) 281-2333; telex 121887; monthly; journal of the Australian Photographic Soc.; Editor DAVID ADERMANN.

Australian Quarterly: 72 Bathurst St, Sydney, NSW 2000; tel. (02) 264-8923; f. 1929; quarterly; Editors HUGH PRICHARD, ELAINE THOMPSON; circ. 3,000.

Australian Wildlife Research: CSIRO, 314 Albert St, POB 89, East Melbourne, Vic 3002; tel. (03) 418-7333; telex 30236; f. 1974; 6 a year; Man. Editor GREGG BERRY.

Australian Women's Weekly: 54 Park St, Sydney, NSW 2000; telex 20514; f. 1933; monthly; Publr RICHARD WALSH; Editor JENNIFER ROWE; circ. 1,166,000.

The Australian Worker incorporating The Worker: 35 Regent St, 3rd Floor, Chippendale, NSW 2008; tel. (02) 698-7393; telex 73231; f. 1891; 6 a year; journal of the Australian Workers' Union; circ. 105,000.

Cleo: 54 Park St, Sydney, NSW 2000; POB 4088, Sydney, NSW 2001; tel. (02) 282-8617; telex 120514; women's monthly; Editor LISA WILKINSON.

Current Affairs Bulletin: 72 Bathurst St, Sydney, NSW 2000; tel. (02) 264-5726; f. 1947; monthly; Exec. Editor R. HOWARD; circ. 6,000.

Economic Record: Dept of Econometrics, University of Sydney, NSW 2006; tel. (02) 692-3069; f. 1925; quarterly; journal of Economic Soc. of Australia; Jt Editors Prof. A. D. WOODLAND, Prof. G. BRENNAN.

Ecos: CSIRO, POB 225, Dickson, ACT 2602; tel. (062) 484584; telex 62003; f. 1974; quarterly; reports of CSIRO environmental research findings for the non-specialist reader; Editor ROBERT LEHANE; circ. 8,000.

Electronics Australia: POB 227, Waterloo, NSW 2017; tel. (02) 693-6620; telex 74488; f. 1922; monthly; technical, radio, television, microcomputers, hi-fi and electronics; Man. Editor JAMIESON ROWE.

Fashion Business: POB 1024, Richmond North, Vic 3121; tel. (03) 429-5599; telex 38225; f. 1986; 6 a year; Editor ANGELA ANG; circ. 12,000.

Industrial and Commercial Photography: POB 606, Sydney, NSW 2001; tel. (02) 281-2333; telex 121887; every 2 months; journal of the Professional Photographers Asscn of Australia, Australian Cinematographers Soc., Australian Inst. of Medical and Biological Illustration and Photographic Industrial Marketing Asscn of Australia; Editor MICHAEL ROOKSBERRY.

Journal of Pacific History: Australian National University, POB 4, Canberra, ACT 2601; f. 1966; 3 a year; Editors NIEL GUNSON, DOROTHY SHINEBERG.

Manufacturer's Monthly: 68–72 Wentworth Ave, Darlinghurst, NSW 2010; tel. (02) 211-4055; telex 23036; f. 1961; circ. 12,000.

AUSTRALIA

Modern Boating: The Federal Publishing Co Pty Ltd, 180 Bourke Rd, Alexandria, NSW 2015; tel. (02) 693-6666; telex 74488; f. 1965; monthly; Editors BARRY TRANTER, PETER NIELSEN.

Modern Motor: 54–58 Park St, Sydney, NSW 2000; tel. (02) 282-8350; telex 120514; f. 1954; monthly; Editor BARRY LAKE; circ. 50,200.

Music Business: POB 1024, Richmond North, Vic 3121; tel. (03) 429-5599; telex 38225; f. 1985; monthly; Editor GAIL CORK; circ. 4,000.

Nation Review: POB 1024, Richmond North, Vic 3121; tel. (03) 429-5599; telex 38225; f. 1958; independent, progressive monthly; Editor-in-Chief GEOFFREY M. GOLD; circ. 46,000.

New Horizons in Education: c/o Dept of Education, University of Queensland, St Lucia, Qld 4067; f. 1938; 2 a year; Editor Dr L. MILLER.

Oceania: The University of Sydney, Sydney, NSW 2006; tel. (02) 692-2666; telex 20056; f. 1930; quarterly; social anthropology; Editors L. R. HIATT, F. MERLAN.

The Open Road: 151 Clarence St, Sydney, NSW; tel. (02) 260-9302; f. 1927; every 2 months; journal of National Roads and Motorists' Assen (NRMA); Editor C. WHEILDON; circ. 1,700,000.

Overland: POB 249, Mt Eliza, Vic 3930; tel. (03) 787-1545; f. 1954; quarterly; literary, social, political; Editor S. MURRAY-SMITH; circ. 3,000.

Pacific Islands Monthly: 64–76 Kippax St, Surry Hills, NSW 2010; POB 4245, Sydney, NSW 2001; tel. (02) 288-3000; telex 20142; f. 1930; political, economic and cultural affairs in the Pacific Islands; Editor HELEN FRASER.

Photoworld Magazine: POB 341, Mona Vale, NSW 2103; tel. (02) 997-1188; f. 1978; monthly; photographic equipment and travel; Editor NEIL SUDBURY; circ. 20,000.

Publishing and Marketing Australia: 3rd Floor, 480 St Kilda Rd, Melbourne, Vic 3004; tel. (03) 267-3611; telex 33770; f. 1904; 8 a year; Editor TOM HEATH; circ. 10,000.

Queensland Countrywoman: 89–95 Gregory Terrace, Brisbane, Qld; f. 1929; monthly; journal of the Qld Countrywomen's Assen; Editor Mrs BERYL SYMONS.

Reader's Digest: POB 4353, Sydney, NSW 2001; tel. (02) 690-6111; telex 120260; monthly; Editor HUGH VAUGHAN-WILLIAMS; circ. 460,649.

Robotic Age: POB 1024, Richmond North, Vic 3121; tel. (03) 429-5599; telex 38225; f. 1983; quarterly; Editor GEOFFREY M. GOLD; circ. 8,000.

Salon Australia: POB 1024, Richmond North, Vic 3121; tel. (03) 429-5599; telex 38225; Editor DARYL MANNELL; circ. 11,000.

Search—Science and Technology in Australia and New Zealand: POB 873, Sydney, NSW 2001; tel. (02) 556-1693; f. 1970; 6 a year; journal of Australia and NZ Assen for the Advancement of Science; Exec. Editor B. J. WALBY; circ. 5,000.

Stereo Buyer's Guide: POB 341, Mona Vale, NSW 2103; tel. (02) 997-1188; f. 1971; 5 a year; Editor DON NORRIS; circ. 18,000.

Video: POB 163, Chippendale, NSW 2008; tel. 699-3622; telex 25027; f. 1982; monthly; Editor STEWART FIST.

Video Business: POB 1024, Richmond North, Vic 3121; tel. (03) 429-5599; telex 38225; Editor SEVEGNE NEWTON; circ. 2,895.

Videoworld Magazine: POB 341, Mona Vale, NSW 2103; tel. (02) 997-1188; f. 1982; monthly; circulated with *Australian Hi-Fi Magazine* and *Photoworld Magazine*; Editor GREG BORROWMAN; combined circ. 45,000.

What's on Video and Cinema: POB 1024, Richmond North, Vic 3121; tel. (03) 429-5599; telex 38225; f. 1981; monthly; Editor PETER BARRETT; circ. 183,000.

Wildlife Australia: 8 Clifton St, Petrie Terrace, Brisbane, Qld 4000; tel. (07) 369-4586; quarterly; journal of the Wildlife Preservation Soc. of Qld; Editor DON HENRY.

World Review: c/o Australian Institute of International Affairs, POB E181, Queen Victoria Terrace, Canberra, ACT 2600; tel. (062) 822133; f. 1962; quarterly; Editor Dr GLEN ST J. BARCLAY.

Your Computer: 706 Military Rd, Mosman, NSW 2088; telex 60469; circ. 30,000.

Your Garden: 32 Walsh St, West Melbourne, Vic 3002; tel. (03) 320-7000; monthly; Editor-in-Chief SHEILA TRYK; circ. 90,000.

NEWS AGENCIES

Australian Associated Press: 364 Sussex St, Sydney, NSW 2000; POB 3888, Sydney 2001; tel. (02) 236-8800; telex 25510; f. 1935; owned by major daily newspapers of Australia; Chair. E. J. L. TURNBULL; CEO C. L. CASEY.

Foreign Bureaux

Agence France-Presse (AFP): POB K389, Haymarket, NSW 2000; tel. (02) 264-1822; telex 176518; Bureau Chief PETER MACKLER.

Agencia EFE (Spain): 5 Erldunda Circuit, Hawker, Canberra, ACT 2614; tel. (062) 543732; Correspondent ANTONIO-JOSÉ ARJONILLA.

Agenzia Nazionale Stampa Associata (ANSA) (Italy): Angus and Coote House, 8th Floor, 500 George St, Sydney, NSW 2000; tel. (02) 264-8348; telex 71770; Bureau Chief CLAUDIO MARCELLO.

Associated Press (AP) (USA): 4th Floor, 364 Sussex St, Sydney, NSW 2000; POB K378, Haymarket, NSW 2000; tel. (02) 267-2122; telex 121181; Bureau Chief PETER O'LOUGHLIN.

Deutsche Presse-Agentur (dpa) (Federal Republic of Germany): 67 Kipling Ave, Mooroolbark, Melbourne, Vic 3138; tel. (03) 726-5551; telex 33131; Bureau Chief BORIS B. BEHRSING.

Jiji Tsushin-Sha (Japan): Paxton House, 5th Floor, 90 Pitt St, Sydney, NSW 2000; tel. (02) 291229; telex 75974; Bureau Chief IKUHIRO KISHIDA.

Kyodo Tsushin (Japan): 364 Sussex St, Sydney, NSW 2000; tel. (02) 264-7390; telex 75851; Bureau Chief KOJI MURAI.

Reuters Australia Pty Ltd: POB K342, Haymarket, NSW 2000; tel. (02) 264-5083; telex 72835.

Telegrafnoye Agentstvo Sovetskovo Soyuza (TASS) (USSR): 8 Elliott St, Campbell, Canberra, ACT 2601; Correspondent SERGEI SOLOVEV.

United Press International (UPI) (USA): News House, 2 Holt St, 3rd Floor, Sydney, NSW 2010; tel. (02) 212-3899; telex 20578; Man. BRIAN DEWHURST.

Xinhua (New China) News Agency (People's Republic of China): 50 Russell St, Hackett, Canberra, ACT 2602; tel. (062) 486369; telex 61507; Correspondent JIN MINGYUAN.

The Central News Agency (Taiwan) and the New Zealand Press Association are represented in Sydney, and Antara (Indonesia) is represented in Canberra.

PRESS ASSOCIATIONS

Australian Newspapers Council: 44–74 Flinders St, Melbourne, Vic 3000; tel. (03) 652-1111; telex 30104; f. 1958; 5 mems, confined to metropolitan daily or Sunday papers; Pres. G. J. TAYLOR; Sec. A. L. GREEN.

Country Press Association of New South Wales Inc: POB C599, Clarence St, Sydney, NSW 2000; tel. (02) 294658; f. 1900; Exec. Dir D. J. SOMMERLAD; 75 mems.

Country Press Association of South Australia Incorporated: 130 Franklin St, Adelaide, SA 5000; tel. (08) 2312626; f. 1912; represents South Australian country newspapers; Pres. K. JEFFREY; Exec. Dir M. R. TOWNSEND.

Country Press Australia: POB C599, Clarence St, Sydney, NSW 2000; tel. (02) 294658; f. 1906; Exec. Dir D. J. SOMMERLAD; 250 mems.

Queensland Country Press Association: POB 103, Paddington, Qld 4064; tel. (07) 369-6088; Pres. MARK HODGSON; Sec. G. P. W. WILLCOCKS.

Regional Dailies of Australia Ltd: 247 Collins St, Melbourne, Vic 3000; tel. (03) 654-2022; f. 1936; Chair. J. M. MORWOOD; CEO R. W. SINCLAIR; 35 mems.

Tasmanian Press Association Pty Ltd: 71–75 Paterson St, Launceston, Tas; tel. (003) 315111; telex 58511; Sec. B. J. MCKENDRICK.

Victoria Country Press Association Ltd: 33 Rathdowne St, Carlton, Vic 3053; tel. (03) 662-3244; f. 1910; Pres. R. L. J. BEKS; Exec. Dir R. C. MCDIARMID; 103 mems.

Publishers

Addison-Wesley Publishing Co: Unit 1A, 6–8 Byfield St, North Ryde, NSW 2113; tel. (02) 888-2733; telex 71919; educational, scientific, technical, computer, general; Gen. Man. DEREK HALL.

Allen and Unwin: 12th Floor, NCR House, 8 Napier St, POB 764, North Sydney, NSW 2059; tel. (02) 922-6399; telex 24331; fiction, trade, educational; Chair. R. P. HYMAN; Man. Dir P. A. GALLAGHER.

Angus and Robertson Publishers: 4 Eden Park, 31 Waterloo Rd, POB 290, North Ryde, NSW 2113; tel. (02) 888-4111; telex 26452; f. 1886; fiction, non-fiction, general and children's; Gen. Man. JOHN OLDMEADOW; CEO TERRY HUGHES.

Ashton Scholastic: Railway Crescent, Lisarow, POB 579, Gosford, NSW 2250; tel. (043) 283555; telex 24881; f. 1968; educational and children's; Chair. M. SINCLAIR; Man. Dir KEN JOLLY.

AUSTRALIA

Australasian Medical Publishing Co Ltd: 71–79 Arundel St, Glebe, NSW 2037; tel. 660-6055; f. 1913; scientific, medical and educational; Man. GEOFFREY F. HILL.

The Australasian Publishing Co Pty Ltd: cnr Bridge Rd and Jersey St, Hornsby, NSW 2077; tel. 476-2000; telex 23274; f. 1937; general; Man. Dir G. A. RUTHERFORD.

Bacon Publishing Pty Ltd: 9 Kingston Town Close, POB 223, Oakleigh, Vic 3166; tel. (03) 563-1044; f. 1938; theology and Christian education, educational; Chair. Mrs M. BACON; Man. Dir A. R. TOSTEVIN.

Butterworths Pty Ltd: 271–273 Lane Cove Rd, North Ryde, NSW 2113; tel. (02) 887-3444; telex 122033; f. 1910; law, medical, tax, technical, scientific and commercial; Chair. G. R. N. CUSWORTH; Man. Dir D. J. JACKSON.

Cambridge University Press (Australia): 10 Stamford Road, Oakleigh, Melbourne, Vic 3166; tel. (03) 568-0322; scholarly and educational; Dir KIM W. HARRIS.

Century Hutchinson Australia Pty Ltd: 89–91 Albion St, Surry Hills, NSW 2010; tel. (02) 211-3233; telex 37972; general; CEO E. F. MASON.

Collins, Wm., Pty Ltd: 55 Clarence St, Sydney, NSW 2000; tel. (02) 229-2800; telex 26292; fiction, general non-fiction, children's and Australiana; Man. Dir T. J. KITSON.

Commonwealth Scientific and Industrial Research Organization (CSIRO): 314 Albert St, East Melbourne, Vic 3002; tel. (03) 418-7333; telex 30236; f. 1948; scientific journals, books and indices; Man. Editorial Services P. W. REEKIE.

Encyclopaedia Britannica (Australia) Inc: 22 Lambs Rd, Artarmon, NSW 2064; tel. (02) 438-4544; telex 23044; reference, education, art, science and commerce; Pres. H. W. DE WEESE.

Golden Press Pty Ltd: 46 Egerton St, Silverwater, NSW 2141; tel. (02) 648-5697; telex 26070; children's, general non-fiction, education; Publr MARK NEWMAN; Gen. Man. ROSS ALEXANDER.

Gordon and Gotch Ltd: 25–37 Huntingdale Rd, POB 29, Burwood, Vic 3125; tel. (03) 2851700; telex 37381; Man. Dir I. D. GOLDING.

Harcourt Brace Jovanovich Group (Australia) Pty Ltd: 30–52 Smidmore St, Marrickville, NSW 2204; tel. (02) 517-8999; telex 23394; educational, technical, scientific, medical; Man. Dir BARRY DINGLEY.

Harper and Row (Australasia) Pty Ltd: Unit 3B, Artarmon Industrial Estate, cnr Reserve Rd and Frederick St, POB 226, Artarmon, NSW 2064; tel. (02) 439-6155; telex 72598; reference, educational, medical; Man. Dir B. D. WILDER.

Hodder and Stoughton (Australia) Pty Ltd: 10–16 South St, Rydalmere, NSW 2116; tel. (02) 638-5299; telex 24858; fiction, general, educational, technical, children's; Man. Dir MICHAEL H. DUFFETT.

Horwitz Grahame Pty Ltd: 506 Miller St, POB 306, Cammeray, NSW 2062; tel. (02) 929-6144; telex 127833; fiction, reference, educational, Australiana, general; Man. Dir L. J. MOORE.

Hyland House Publishing Pty Ltd: 23 Bray St, South Yarra, Vic 3141; tel. (03) 241-6336; trade, general; Rep. AL KNIGHT.

Jacaranda Wiley Ltd: 33 Park Rd, Milton, Qld 4064; POB 859, Brisbane, Qld 4001; tel. (07) 369-9755; telex 41845; f. 1954; educational, technical and cartographic; Man. Dir JOHN COLLINS.

The Law Book Co Ltd: 44–50 Waterloo Road, North Ryde, NSW 2113; tel. (02) 887-0177; telex 27995; legal and professional; Man. Dir W. J. MACKARELL.

Longman Cheshire Pty Ltd: Kings Gardens, 95 Coventry St, South Melbourne, Vic 3205; tel. (03) 697-0666; telex 33501; f. 1957; incorporates Pitman Publishing Pty Ltd; mainly educational, legal, professional, some general; Man. Dir N. J. RYAN.

Lothian Books: 11 Munro St, Port Melbourne, Vic 3207; tel. (03) 645-1544; telex 39476; f. 1888; general, gardening, health, juvenile; Man. Dir PETER H. LOTHIAN.

McGraw-Hill Publishing Co Australia Pty Ltd: 4 Barcoo St, East Roseville, Sydney, NSW 2069; tel. (02) 406-4288; telex 120849; educational and technical; Man. Dir D. F. FOWKE.

Macmillan Company of Australia Pty Ltd: 107 Moray St, South Melbourne, Vic 3205; tel. (03) 699-8922; telex 34454; f. 1967; general and educational; Exec. Chair. BRIAN STONIER; Man. Dir JOHN ROLFE.

McPhee Gribble Publishers Pty Ltd: 66 Cecil St, Fitzroy, Vic 3065; tel. (03) 419-9855; telex 31494; f. 1975; general fiction and non-fiction, children's; Man. Dirs HILARY MCPHEE, DIANA GRIBBLE.

Majura Press: POB 25, Hackett, ACT 2602; tel. (062) 413329; f. 1984; non-fiction; Man. S. FRENCH.

Melbourne University Press: 268 Drummond St, Carlton South, Vic 3053; tel. (03) 347-3455; telex 35185; f. 1923; academic, educational, Australiana, general except fiction and children's; Chair. Prof. J. R. V. PRESCOTT; Dir (vacant).

National Library of Australia: Canberra, ACT 2600; tel. (062) 621111; telex 62100; national bibliographical publs, facsimiles of materials in the library's collections; Dir-Gen. W. M. HORTON.

Thomas Nelson Australia: 480 La Trobe St, Melbourne, Vic 3000; tel. (03) 329-5199; telex 33088; educational, vocational, professional and specialized; Man. Dir B. J. RIVERS.

New South Wales University Press Ltd: POB 1, Kensington, NSW 2033; tel. (02) 697-3403; telex 26054; f. 1961; general and educational; Man. Dir DOUGLAS HOWIE.

Octopus Publishing Group Australia Pty Ltd: 81–85 Abinger St, Richmond, Melbourne, Vic 3121; tel. (03) 429-3622; telex 35347; educational and general; Man. Dir SANDY GRANT.

Oxford University Press: POB 2784Y, Melbourne, Vic 3001; tel. (03) 646-4200; telex 35330; f. 1908; general non-fiction and educational; Man. Dir SANDRA MCCOMB.

Penguin Books Australia Ltd: 487/493 Maroondah Highway, POB 257, Ringwood, Vic 3134; tel. (03) 871-2400; telex 32458; f. 1946; general; Man. Dir P. J. FIELD; Publishing Dir ROBERT SESSIONS.

Pergamon Press (Australia) Pty Ltd: 19A Boundary St, Rushcutter's Bay, NSW 2011; tel. (02) 331-5211; telex 27458; f. 1949; educational, general, scientific; Chair. I. R. MAXWELL; Man. Dir J. MAYER.

Reader's Digest Services Pty Ltd: 26–32 Waterloo St, Surry Hills, NSW 2010; POB 4353, Sydney, NSW; tel. (02) 699-0111; general; Man. Dir M. MATON.

Reed Books Pty Ltd: 2 Aquatic Drive, French's Forest, Sydney, NSW 2086; tel. (02) 451-8122; f. 1964; Australiana, general non-fiction; Publr W. A. TEMPLEMAN; Gen. Man. D. A. MACLELLAN.

Rigby Education: 484 St Kilda Rd, Melbourne, Vic 3004; tel. (03) 269-4760; telex 36521; educational; CEO JOHN GILDER.

Rigby Publishers: POB 71, Burnside, SA 5066; tel. (08) 311344; telex 88090; f. 1859; general; Gen. Man. FRANK W. THOMPSON.

Schwartz Publishing: 45 Flinders Lane, Melbourne, Vic 3000; tel. (03) 654-2000; telex 30625; fiction, non-fiction; Dir MORRY SCHWARTZ.

Simon and Schuster Prentice-Hall of Australia Pty Ltd: 7 Grosvenor Place, POB 151, Brookvale, NSW 2100; tel. (02) 939-1333; telex 74010; educational, trade, reference and general; Gen. Man. JON ATTENBOROUGH.

Thames and Hudson (Australia) Pty Ltd: 86 Stanley St, West Melbourne, Vic 3003; tel. (03) 329-8454; art and general; Man. Dir RICHARD M. GILMOUR.

D. W. Thorpe: 20–24 Stokes St, POB 146, Port Melbourne, Vic 3207; tel. (03) 645-1511; biographies, trade, paperbacks; Man. Dir M. WEBSTER.

Time Life Books (Australia) Pty Ltd: 7th Floor, Philips Building, 15 Blue St, North Sydney, NSW 2060; tel. (02) 929-0933; telex 24027; Man. Dir BONITA L. BOEZEMAN.

Transworld Publishers (Aust.) Pty Ltd: 20 Young St, Neutral Bay, NSW 2089; tel. (02) 908-4366; telex 71471; general, fiction, juvenile, education; Man. Dir GEOFFREY S. RUMPF.

University of Queensland Press: POB 42, St Lucia, Qld 4067; tel. (07) 377-2127; telex 40315; f. 1948; scholarly and general cultural interest; Gen. Man. LAURIE MULLER.

University of Western Australia Press: Tuart House, cnr Mounts Bay Rd and Crawley Ave, Nedlands, WA 6009; tel. (09) 380-3182; f. 1954; educational, secondary and university, technical, scientific, scholarly, humanities; Man. V. S. GREAVES.

Weldon-Hardie: 372 Eastern Valley Way, Willoughby, NSW 2068; tel. (02) 406-9222; telex 121546; general non-fiction, literature, Australiana; CEO KEVIN WELDON.

Government Publishing House

Australian Government Publishing Service: POB 84, Canberra, ACT 2601; tel. (062) 954411; telex 62013; f. 1970; Dir of Publishing F. W. THOMPSON.

PUBLISHERS' ASSOCIATION

Australian Book Publishers Association: 161 Clarence St, Sydney, NSW 2000; tel. (02) 295422; f. 1949; c. 150 mems; Pres. SUE DONOVAN; Dir SUSAN BLACKWELL.

Radio and Television

The programmes for the National Broadcasting Service and National Television are provided by the non-commercial statutory corporation, the Australian Broadcasting Corporation (ABC).

The Corporation operates 131 medium-wave stations, 39 FM, 6 domestic and 10 overseas (Radio Australia) short-wave stations broadcasting in English, French, Indonesian, Japanese, Standard

AUSTRALIA

Chinese, Cantonese, Neo-Melanesian, Thai and Vietnamese. In 1983 the Government agreed to provide funds to establish a second regional radio network for the ABC, due to be completed by 1990.

There is one national television network of 11 stations with 76 transmitters and 233 translator stations.

Commercial radio and television services are provided by stations operated by companies under licences granted and renewed by the Australian Broadcasting Tribunal. They rely for their income on the broadcasting of advertisements. On 1 January 1983, there were 136 commercial radio stations in operation, and in August 1987 there were 51 commercial television stations.

In 1982 there were an estimated 17.6m. radio receivers and 6.5m. television receivers in use.

Australian Broadcasting Corporation (ABC): 150 William St, POB 9994, Sydney, NSW 2001; tel. (02) 339-0211 (radio), (02) 437-8000 (television); telex 26506 (corporate), 176464 (radio), 120432 (television); f. 1932 as Australian Broadcasting Commission; Chair. ROBERT SOMERVAILLE; Man. Dir DAVID HILL.

RADIO

Federation of Australian Radio Broadcasters: POB 294, Milson's Point, NSW 2061; tel. (02) 929-4866; telex 25161; asscn of privately-owned stations; Fed. Dir M. J. HARTCHER.

Major Commercial Broadcasting Station Licensees

5KA Broadcasters Pty Ltd: 106 Currie St, Adelaide, SA 5000; tel. (08) 2315511; operates one station.

6IX Radio Network Pty Ltd: POB 77, Tuart Hill, WA 6060; tel. (09) 344-0777; telex 94273; operates three stations; Gen. Man. GRAEME EDWIN.

AWA Ltd: 422 Lane Cove Rd, North Ryde, NSW 2113; tel. (02) 8877111; telex 121515; f. 1913; operates eight stations; Chair. P. MASON; CEO Dr P. CRAWFORD.

Associated Broadcasting Services Ltd: Walker St, Ballarat, Vic 3350; tel. (053) 313166; telex 32011; f. 1957; operates two television and two radio stations; Chair. W. H. HEINZ; CEO MICHAEL J. FAULKNER.

Australian Radio Network: 9 Rangers Rd, POB 1107, Neutral Bay, NSW 2089; tel. (02) 908-1900; telex 22797; operates eight stations; CEO B. E. BYRNE.

Broadcasting Station 2SM Pty Ltd: 186 Blues Point Rd, North Sydney, NSW 2060; tel. (02) 922-1270; telex 25350; operates five stations; CEO G. W. RUTHERFORD.

Consolidated Broadcasting System (WA) Pty Ltd: 283 Rokeby Rd, Subiaco, WA; tel. (09) 381-4488; operates four stations; CEO R. BIGUM.

Macquarie Broadcasting Holdings Ltd: 364 Sussex St, Sydney, NSW 2000; POB 4290, Sydney, NSW 2001; tel. (02) 269-0646; telex 21502; operates more than 26 stations; Man. Dir W. M. CASSIDY.

Southern Cross Communications Ltd: Lily St, POB 888, Bendigo, Vic 3550; tel. (054) 439677; telex 32885; f. 1961; operates one station; CEO GRAEME L. EDDY.

Southern State Broadcasters Pty Ltd: 121 King William St, Adelaide, SA 5000; tel. (08) 211-7666; telex 82000; operates two stations; Gen. Man. BRIAN NIELSEN.

Tamworth Radio Development Company Pty Ltd: POB 497, Tamworth, NSW 2340; tel. (067) 657055; telex 63166; operates five stations; Man. E. C. WILKINSON.

Wesgo Communications Pty Ltd: 2 Leabons Lane, Seven Hills, NSW 2147; tel. (02) 671-2411; telex 23614; operates 16 stations; CEO T. J. O'KEEFE.

TELEVISION

Federation of Australian Commercial Television Stations: 447 Kent St, Sydney, NSW 2000; tel. (02) 264-5577; telex 121542; f. 1960; represents all commercial television stations; Chair. L. A. MAUGER; Fed. Dir DAVID MORGAN.

Commercial Television Station Licensees

Amalgamated Television Services Pty Ltd: TV Centre, Epping, NSW 2121; tel. 858-7777; telex 20250; f. 1956; operates one station; Gen. Man. E. F. THOMAS.

Austarama Television Pty Ltd: POB 42, Hawthorn Rd, Nunawading, Vic 3131; tel. (03) 234-1010; telex 30628; f. 1964; operates one station at Melbourne; Man. Dir W. MCKENZIE.

Australian Capital Television Pty Ltd: POB 777, Dickson, ACT 2602; tel. (062) 411000; telex 62046; f. 1962; operates three stations; Gen. Man. P. HUNNIFORD.

Ballarat and Western Victoria Television Ltd: POB 464, Ballarat, Vic 3350; tel. (053) 313166; telex 32011; f. 1962; operates five stations; Chair. W. H. HEINZ; CEO M. J. FAULKNER.

Brisbane TV Ltd: POB 604, Brisbane, Qld 4001; tel. (07) 369-7777; telex 41653; f. 1959; operates one station; Man. Dir D. BLACK.

Broadcast Operations Ltd: Remembrance Driveway, Griffith, NSW 2680; tel. (069) 624500; telex 169991; f. 1965; operates one television station and four radio stations; Chief Exec. B. MEADLEY; Gen. Man. M. BISHOP.

Broken Hill Television Ltd: POB 472, Broken Hill, NSW 2880; tel. (080) 6013; telex 80874; f. 1968; operates one station; Chair. P. MARTIN; Man. Dir J. M. STURROCK.

Country Television Services Ltd: POB 465, Orange, NSW 2800; tel. (063) 622288; telex 163012; f. 1962; operates two television stations and one radio station; Man. Dir I. RIDLEY; Station Mans D. STURGISS (television), S. WARD (radio).

Darling Downs TV Ltd: POB 670, Toowoomba, Qld 4350; tel. (076) 322288; telex 140058; f. 1962; operates three stations; Man. Dir L. R. BURROWS; Gen. Man. B. M. FINLAY.

Far Northern Television Ltd: POB 596, Cairns, Qld 4870; tel. (070) 516322; telex 48401; f. 1966; operates one station; Chair. JACK GLEESON; Gen. Man. DAVID ASTLEY.

General Television Corporation Pty Ltd: 22–46 Bendigo St, POB 100, Richmond, Vic 3121; tel. (03) 420-3111; telex 30189; f. 1957; operates one station; Man. Dir G. RICE; Gen. Man. I. J. JOHNSON.

Geraldton Telecasters Pty Ltd: 7 Fore St, Perth, WA 6000; tel. (09) 328-9833; telex 94382; f. 1977; operates one station; Gen. Man. BRIAN HOPWOOD.

Golden West Network Ltd: POB 112, Bunbury, WA 6230; tel. (097) 214466; telex 92305; f. 1967; CEO W. G. RAYNER.

Goulburn-Murray Television Ltd: POB 666, Shepparton, Vic 3630; tel. (058) 215666; telex 30742; f. 1961; operates one station; Chair. W. H. HEINZ; Gen. Man. TONY KENISON.

HSV Channel 7 Pty Ltd: POB 215D, GPO Melbourne, Vic 3001; tel. (03) 697-7777; telex 30707; f. 1956; operates one station; Chair. C. C. SKASE; Man. Dir G. B. CARRINGTON.

Mackay Television Ltd: POB 496, PO Mackay, Qld 4740; tel. (079) 576333; telex 48152; f. 1968; operates one station; Gen. Man. RAY COX.

Mt Isa Television Pty Ltd: 110 Camooweal St, Mt Isa, Qld 4825; tel. (077) 438888; telex 49947; f. 1971; operates one station; Chair. Sir ASHER JOEL; Man. Dir A. JOEL; Gen. Man. B. HILLIER; Production and Operations Man. L. J. CONNOLLY.

NBN Ltd: Mosbri Crescent, POB 750L, Newcastle, NSW 2300; tel. (049) 20321; telex 28039; f. 1962; operates one station; CEO JOE SWEENEY.

Northern Rivers Television Ltd: Peterson Rd, POB 920, Coffs Harbour, NSW 2450; tel. (066) 522777; telex 66961; f. 1965; operates two stations; Gen. Man. RON LAWRENCE.

Northern Television (TNT9) Pty Ltd: Watchorn St, Launceston, Tas 7250; tel. (003) 440202; telex 58512; f. 1962; operates one station; Gen. Man. DAVID W. WHITE.

Queensland Television Ltd: POB 72, GPO Brisbane, Qld 4001; tel. (07) 369-9999; telex 42347; f. 1959; operates one station; Exec. Dir SAM CHISHOLM; Gen. Man. IAN R. MÜLLER.

Regional Television Australia Pty Ltd: 82–84 Sydenham Rd, Marrickville, NSW 2204; POB 285, Sydney, NSW 2001; tel. (02) 516-1233; telex 120581; CEO LLOYD D. BARWELL.

Riverina and North East Victoria TV Pty Ltd: POB 2, Kooringal via Wagga, NSW 2650; tel. (069) 211222; telex 69022; f. 1964; Man. A. COOK.

Riverland Television Pty Ltd: Murray Bridge Rd, POB 471, Loxton, SA 5333; tel. (085) 846891; telex 80313; f. 1976; operates one station; Exec. Chair. E. H. URLWIN; Gen. Man. W. L. MUDGE.

Rockhampton Television Ltd: Dean St, POB 568 Rockhampton, Qld 4700; tel. (079) 285222; telex 49008; f. 1963; Gen. Man. TONY SHIELDS.

South Australian Telecasters Ltd: 45–49 Park Terrace, Gilberton, SA 5081; tel. (08) 269-7777; telex 82084; f. 1965; operates one station; Gen. Man. D. EARL.

South East Telecasters Ltd: POB 821, Mount Gambier, SA 5290; tel. (087) 256366; telex 80013; f. 1966; operates one station; Chair. G. T. BARNFIELD; Man. Dir G. J. GILBERTSON.

Southern Cross Communications Ltd: Lily St, POB 888, Bendigo, Vic 3550; tel. (054) 439677; telex 32885; f. 1961; operates seven stations; CEO GRAEME L. EDDY.

Southern Television Corporation Ltd: 202 Tynte St, North Adelaide, SA 5006; tel. (08) 267-0111; telex 82238; f. 1958; operates one station; Gen. Man. TYRRELL TALBOT.

Spencer Gulf Telecasters Ltd: POB 305, 4 Port Pirie, SA 5540; tel. (086) 322555; telex 80320; f. 1968; operates five stations; Man. R. M. DAVIS.

AUSTRALIA

Sunraysia Television Ltd: 18 Deakin Ave, Mildura, Vic 3500; tel. (050) 230204; telex 55304; f. 1965; Chair P. M. JOHANSEN; Man. A. D. SHARPE; CEO E. G. PRESSER.

Swan Television and Radio Broadcasters Ltd: POB 99, Tuart Hill, WA 6060; tel. (09) 349-9999; telex 92142; f. 1965; operates one station; Gen. Man. KEN GANNAWAY.

Tasmanian Television Ltd: 52 New Town Rd, Hobart, Tas; tel. (002) 780666; telex 58019; f. 1959; operates one station; Gen. Man. D. ROUSE.

TCN Channel Nine Pty Ltd: 24 Artarmon Rd, POB 27, Willoughby, NSW 2068; tel. (02) 430-0444; telex 20689; f. 1956; operates one station; Exec. and Man. Dir (Bond Television) SAMUEL CHISHOLM.

Telecasters North Queensland Ltd: 12 The Strand, POB 1016, Townsville, Qld 4810; tel. (077) 213377; telex 47023; f. 1962; operates one station; Chair. J. F. GLEESON; Gen. Man. DAVID ASTLEY.

Television New England Ltd: Radio Centre, Calala, POB 317, Tamworth, NSW 2340; tel. (067) 657066; telex 63214; f. 1965; operates two stations; Chair. H. JOSEPH; Gen. Man. M. M. MORONEY.

Television Wollongong Transmissions Ltd: Fort Drummond, Mt St Thomas, POB 1800, Wollongong, NSW 2500; tel. (042) 285444; telex 29029; f. 1962; Chair. W. LEAN; Gen. Man. J. RUSHTON.

Territory Television Pty Ltd: Blake St, Gardens Hill, POB 1764, Darwin, NT 5794; tel. (089) 818888; telex 85138; f. 1971; operates one station; Gen. Man. PETER DOOLEY.

TV Broadcasters Ltd: 125 Strangways Terrace, North Adelaide, SA 5006; tel. (08) 267-0777; telex 82141; f. 1959; operates one station; Gen. Man. J. S. DOHERTY.

TVW Enterprises Ltd: POB 77, Tuart Hill, WA 6060; tel. (09) 344-0777; telex 92235; f. 1959; Chair. C. B. HUGALL; Man. Dir K. V. CAMPBELL.

United Telecasters Sydney Ltd: Epping and Pittwater Rds, North Ryde, NSW 2113; tel. (02) 887-0222; telex 21767; f. 1965; operates one station; Man. Dir GEORGE BROWN.

Universal Telecasters Qld Ltd: POB 751, GPO Brisbane, Qld 4001; tel. (07) 369-0000; telex 40354; f. 1965; operates one station; Gen. Man. R. CAMPBELL.

Wide Bay-Burnett Television Ltd: 187-189 Cambridge St, POB 30, Granville, Qld 4650; tel. (071) 222288; telex 49702; f. 1965; Man. Dir G. J. MCVEAN.

Finance

(cap. = capital; p.u. = paid up; res = reserves; dep. = deposits; m. = million; brs = branches; amounts in Australian dollars)

BANKING
Central Bank

Reserve Bank of Australia: 65 Martin Place, Sydney, NSW 2000; GPO Box 3947, Sydney, NSW 2001; tel. (02) 234-9333; telex 20106; f. 1911; bank of issue; cap. and res 4,664.6m., dep. and other accounts 6,467.8m. (June 1988); Gov. R. A. JOHNSTON; Dep. Gov. M. J. PHILLIPS.

Commonwealth Banks

Commonwealth Banking Corporation: Pitt St and Martin Place, Sydney, NSW 2000; POB 2719, Sydney, NSW 2001; tel. (02) 227-7111; telex 120345; f. 1960; controlling body for three mem. banks; res and provisions 704.2m. (1987); Chair. M. A. BESLEY; Man. Dir D. N. SANDERS.

Commonwealth Bank of Australia: Pitt St and Martin Place, Sydney, NSW 2000; POB 2719, Sydney, NSW 2001; tel. (02) 227-7111; telex 120345; f. 1912; cap. and res 1,226.9m., dep. 11,838m. (1987); Chief Gen. Mans B. A. POULTER, C. J. KER, H. L. SPENCER; more than 1,200 brs world-wide.

Commonwealth Development Bank of Australia: Prudential Bldg, 39 Martin Place, Sydney, NSW 2000; POB 2719, Sydney, NSW 2001; tel. (02) 227-7111; telex 120345; f. 1960; cap. and res 213.9m., dep. 915.6m. (1986); Gen. Man. J. W. FLETCHER.

Commonwealth Savings Bank of Australia: Pitt St and Martin Place, Sydney, NSW 2000; POB 2719, Sydney, NSW 2001; tel. (02) 227-7111; telex 120267; f. 1912; cap. and res. 934.3m., dep. 13,200.6m. (1987); Gen. Man. H. L. SPENCER.

Development Banks

Australian Resources Development Bank Ltd: 379 Collins St, POB 53, Melbourne, Vic 3000; tel. (03) 616-2800; telex 32078; f. 1967 by major Australian trading banks, with support of Reserve Bank of Australia, to marshal funds from local and overseas sources for the financing of Australian participation in projects of national importance; acquired Australian Banks' Export Re-Finance Corpn in 1980; cap. and res 21.7m., dep. 744.1m. (Sept. 1986); Chair. W. H. HODGSON; Gen. Man. A. LOCKE.

Primary Industry Bank of Australia Ltd: 115 Pitt St, Sydney, NSW 2000; POB 4577, Sydney, NSW 2001; tel. (02) 231-5655; telex 23495; f. 1978; cap. and res 11m., dep. 808.8m. (1986); Chair. WALTER C. IVES; Man. Dir JOHN C. FREARSON.

Trading Banks

Australia and New Zealand Banking Group Ltd: Collins Place, 55 Collins St, Melbourne, Vic 3000; POB 537 E, Melbourne, Vic 3001; tel. (03) 658-2955; telex 39920; f. 1836; present name adopted in 1970; cap. and res 3,138.6m., dep. 34,191.4m. (1987); over 1,690 points of representation in Australia, New Zealand and worldwide; Chair. Sir WILLIAM VINES; Deputy Chair. and CEO W. J. BAILEY.

Australian Bank Ltd: 17 O'Connell St, POB 1631, Sydney, NSW 2000; tel. (02) 264-8000; telex 72253; f. 1981; cap. p.u. 70m. (1987); CEO DICK MORATH.

Bank of Queensland Ltd: 229 Elizabeth St, POB 898, Brisbane, Qld 4001; tel. (07) 231-0421; telex 41565; f. 1874; cap. and res 63m., dep. 377.3m. (1988); Chair. HARRY BAYNES; Gen. Man. NEVILLE H. BLUNT; 57 brs.

Macquarie Bank Ltd: Level 26, 20 Bond St, Sydney, NSW 2000; tel. (02) 237-3333; telex 122246; f. 1969 as Hill Samuel Australia Ltd; present name adopted in 1985; cap. and res 115.7m., dep. 570.5m. (1988); Chair. DAVID S. CLARKE; Man. Dir ANTHONY R. BERG; 3 brs.

National Australia Bank Ltd: 500 Bourke St, Melbourne, Vic 3000; POB 84A, Melbourne, Vic 3001; tel. (03) 605-3500; telex 30241; f. 1981 by merger of Commercial Banking Co of Sydney with National Bank of Australasia; cap. and res 1,782.8m., dep. 21,631.6m. (Sept. 1986); Chair. Sir RUPERT CLARKE; Man. Dir N. R. CLARK; 1,219 brs.

Rural and Industries Bank of Western Australia: 54–58 Barrack St, POB E237, Perth, WA 6001; tel. (09) 320-6206; telex 92417; f. 1945; WA govt bank; cap. and res 303m., dep. 4,609m. (1988); Chair. Dr ROSS GARNAUT; Man. Dir DAVID P. FISCHER; Group Gen. Man. ANDREW J. GORDON; 112 brs.

State Bank of New South Wales: 52 Martin Place, POB 41, Sydney, NSW 2001; tel. (02) 226-8000; telex 74238; f. 1933; cap. 607.3m., dep. 5,826m. (1987); Chair. R. F. W. WATSON; Man. Dir J. A. O'NEILL; 275 brs in Australia.

State Bank of South Australia: 97 King William St, Adelaide, SA 5000; POB 399, Adelaide, SA 5001; tel. (08) 210-4411; telex 82082; f. 1984 by merger; cap. 1,010.4m., dep. 7,695.9m. (June 1988); Chair. L. BARRETT; Man. Dir TIM MARCUS CLARK; 177 brs.

Westpac Banking Corporation: 60 Martin Place, Sydney, NSW 2001; tel. (02) 226-3311; telex 20122; f. 1982 by merger; cap. p.u. 554.2m., dep. 42,384m. (1987); Chair. Sir JAMES FOOTS; Man. Dir STUART FOWLER.

Savings Banks

Advance Bank Australia Ltd: POB R221, Royal Exchange, Sydney, NSW 2000.

Civic Advance Bank Ltd: Northgate Bldg., 60 Marcus Clarke St, Canberra City, ACT 2601; tel. (062) 496699; telex 62093; Chair. J. G. SERVICE; CEO G. B. MEYER.

The Savings Bank of Tasmania (The Hobart Savings Bank): 39 Murray St, Hobart, Tas 7000; tel. (002) 304777; telex 58296; f. 1845; Chair. R. J. HARRIS; Gen. Man. P. W. KEMP.

State Bank of Victoria: 385 Bourke St, Melbourne, Vic 3000; POB 267D, Melbourne, Vic 3001; tel. (03) 604-7000; telex 32910; f. 1842; dep. 10,730m., total resources 12,435m. (June 1986); Chair. J. ARNOLD HANCOCK; CEO L. G. C. MOYLE; 529 brs.

Tasmania Bank: 79 St John St, POB 288, Launceston, Tas 7250; tel. (003) 329-6001; telex 58579; f. 1835; fmrly the Launceston Bank for Savings, restyled Tasmania Bank in 1988; res 26.8m., dep. 410.5m. (1986); Chair. CLIVE N. HILL; Gen. Man. MARCUS T. ATHERTON; 30 brs.

Westpac Savings Bank Ltd: 60 Martin Place, Sydney, NSW 2001; tel. (02) 226-3311; telex 20122; f. 1956; cap. p.u. 90m., dep. 7,704m. (1987); Chair. Sir JAMES FOOTS; Man. Dir S. A. FOWLER.

Foreign Banks

Bankers' Trust (Australia) Ltd (USA): POB H9, Australia Sq., Sydney, NSW 2000.

Bank of America (Australia) Ltd (USA): POB 490, Sydney, NSW 2001.

Bank of China (People's Republic of China): 65 York St, Sydney, NSW 2000.

Bank of New Zealand: POB 507, Sydney, NSW 2001; tel. (02) 290-6666; telex 123240; Chair. M. G. KING.

AUSTRALIA

Bank of Singapore (Australia) Ltd: Bank of Singapore House, 99 Queen St, Melbourne, Vic 3000; tel. (03) 602-2700; telex 152696; f. 1986; Gen. Man. and CEO J. BRUCE BRAWN; 5 brs.

Bank of Tokyo (Australia) Ltd (Japan): Level 15, State Bank Centre, 52 Martin Place, Sydney, NSW 2000; POB 4210, Sydney, NSW 2001; tel. (02) 225-9700; telex 73354; f. 1985; cap. 50.0m., res 2.7m., dep. 198.2m. (1986); Chair. and Man. Dir HIDEHIRO KIKUCHI.

Banque Nationale de Paris (France): 12 Castlereagh St, Sydney, NSW 2000; POB 269, Sydney, NSW 2001; tel. (02) 232-8733; telex 20132; Gen.-Man. ROBERT AMZALLAG; 6 brs.

Barclays Bank (Australia) Ltd (UK): POB 3357, Sydney, NSW 2001; tel. (02) 233-6622; telex 22114.

Chase AMP Bank Ltd (USA): 36th Floor, Qantas International Centre, 1 Jamison St, Sydney, NSW 2000.

Citibank Ltd (USA): POB 5343, Sydney, NSW 2001.

Deutsche Bank (Australia) Ltd (Federal Republic of Germany): 1 Collins St, Melbourne, Vic 3000; tel. (03) 654-1277; telex 15231; Man. Dir Dr KLAUS L. ALBRECHT.

Habib Finance (Australia) Ltd (Pakistan): Level 7, National Australia Bank House, 255 George St, Sydney, NSW 2000; tel. (02) 233-5233; telex 121098; f. 1987.

HongkongBank of Australia Ltd (Hong Kong): 99 William St, Melbourne, Vic 3000; POB 763G, Melbourne, Vic 3001; tel. (03) 619-0338; telex 152117; Man. Dir J. C. S. RANKIN.

IBJ Australia Bank Ltd: Chancery House, 37 St George's Terrace, Perth, WA 6000; tel. (09) 220-9777; telex 96993; f. 1985; cap. 100m.; Chair. Sir HAROLD KNIGHT.

Lloyds Bank NZA PLC (UK): 35 Pitt St, POB R220, Royal Exchange, Sydney, NSW 2000; tel. (02) 239-5555; telex 26115; f. 1985; cap. 47.7m., res 33.6m., dep. 694.2m. (1986); Chair. Sir JOHN MASON; CEO TONY DAVIES.

Mitsubishi Bank (Australia) Ltd (Japan): Level 1, 255 George St, Sydney, NSW 2000; tel. (02) 250-1800; telex 27234; f. 1985; Man. Dir SHUICHI TAKAHASHI.

NatWest Australia Bank Ltd (UK): Qantas International Centre, International Sq., Sydney, NSW 2001; tel. (02) 250-8500; telex 177326.

Standard Chartered Bank (Australia) PLC (UK): POB 2633, Adelaide, SA 5001.

STOCK EXCHANGES

Australian Stock Exchange Ltd: Level 9, Plaza Bldg, Australia Sq., Sydney, NSW 2000; tel. (02) 233-5266; telex 24628; f. 1987 by merger of the stock exchanges in the six capital cities (listed below), to replace the fmr Australian Associated Stock Exchange; Exec. Dir RONALD L. COPPEL.

Australian Stock Exchange (Adelaide) Ltd: 55 Exchange Place, Adelaide, SA; tel. (08) 212-3702; telex 82186; f. 1887; 50 mems; Chair. A. H. COUNSELL; Man. Dir A. S. CUNNINGHAM.

Australian Stock Exchange (Brisbane) Ltd: 123 Eagle St, Brisbane, Qld 4000; POB 7055, Riverside Centre, Brisbane, Qld 4000; tel. (07) 831-1499; telex 40264; f. 1884; 39 mems; Chair. L. A. DRAPER; Man. G. P. CHAPMAN.

Australian Stock Exchange (Hobart) Ltd: 86 Collins St, Hobart, Tas; tel. (002) 347333; telex 58111; f. 1891.

Australian Stock Exchange (Melbourne) Ltd: 351 Collins St, Melbourne, Vic; tel. (03) 617-8611; telex 30550; f. 1884, inc. 1970; 257 mems; Chair. L. G. COX; Gen. Man. R. B. LEE.

Australian Stock Exchange (Perth) Ltd: Exchange House, 68 St George's Terrace, Perth, WA 6001; tel. (09) 327-0000; telex 92159; f. 1889; 43 mems; Chair. P. E. MARFLEET; Man. Dir JOHN G. THOMPSON.

Australian Stock Exchange (Sydney) Ltd: Exchange Centre, 20 Bond St, Australia Sq., POB H224, Sydney, NSW 2000; tel. (02) 225-6600; telex 20630; f. 1871; 245 mems; Chair. KEVIN J. TROY; Man. Dir PETER W. MARSHMAN.

PRINCIPAL INSURANCE COMPANIES

AMP Fire & General Insurance Co Ltd: 8 Loftus St, Sydney Cove, NSW 2000; tel. (02) 850-2607; telex 177001; f. 1958; Chair. J. W. UTZ; Man. Dir J. K. STAVELEY.

Australian Guarantee Ltd: 130 Phillip St, Sydney, NSW 2000; tel. (02) 234-1122; telex 26612; f. 1938; Chair. I. MATHIESON; Man. Dir R. ROBSON.

Australian Natives' Association Insurance Co Ltd: 114-124 Albert Rd, South Melbourne, Vic 3205; f. 1948; Chair. G. D. WEARNE; Man. B. O. FENTON.

Australian Reinsurance Co Ltd: 31 Queen St, Melbourne, Vic 3000; tel. (03) 616-9200; telex 34201; f. 1962; reinsurance; Chair. S. C. G. MACINDOE; Man. Dir P. C. HEFFERNAN; Gen. Mans S. V. F. BRAIN, S. M. WESTWOOD.

Capita Financial Group Ltd: 60-66 Hunter St, Sydney, NSW 2000; tel. (02) 221-1788; telex 24086; f. 1878 as the City Mutual Life Assurance Society Ltd; present name adopted in 1986; life insurance, superannuation and financial services; Chair. GERALD WELLS; Man. Dir DAVID S. GREATOREX.

Catholic Church Insurances Ltd: 387 St Kilda Rd, Melbourne, Vic 3004; tel. (03) 267-5900; f. 1911; Chair. Mgr P. H. JONES; Gen. Man. C. R. O'MALLEY.

The Chamber of Manufactures Insurance Ltd: 368-374 St Kilda Rd, Melbourne, Vic 3004; tel. (03) 699-4211; telex 39482; f. 1914; Chair. W. D. MCPHERSON; Gen. Man. and CEO T. R. LONGES.

Colonial Mutual General Insurance Co Ltd: 330 Collins St, Melbourne, Vic 3000; tel. (03) 607-6111; telex 34059; f. 1958; Chair. P. C. TRUMBLE; Gen. Man. G. D. C. SWANTON.

The Colonial Mutual Life Assurance Society Ltd: 330 Collins St, Melbourne, Vic 3000; tel. (03) 607-6111; telex 34059; f. 1873; Chair. P. C. TRUMBLE; Man. Dir JOHN MILBURN-PYLE.

Commercial Union Assurance Co of Australia Ltd: Commercial Union Centre, 485 La Trobe St, Melbourne, Vic; tel. (03) 605-8222; telex 33100; f. 1960; fire, accident, marine; Chair. J. A. HANCOCK; Man. Dir W. S. MANSFIELD.

Copenhagen Reinsurance Co (Aust.) Ltd: 60 Margaret St, Sydney, NSW 2000; tel. (02) 277266; telex 26721; f. 1961; reinsurance; Chair. DAVID BROWN; Gen. Man. PAUL ALLISON.

FAI Insurances Ltd: FAI Insurance Group, 185 Macquarie St, Sydney, NSW 2000; tel. (02) 221-1155; telex 21755; f. 1956; Chair. J. L. ADLER; Gen. Man. Dr T. MAINPRIZE.

Farmers Grazcos Co-operative Ltd: 3 Spring St, Sydney, NSW 2000; tel. (02) 279284; f. 1980; Gen. Man. F. D. LUXFORD.

The Federation Insurance Ltd: 342-348 Flinders St, Melbourne, Vic 3000; tel. (03) 620101; telex 30847; f. 1926; Chair. R. L. M. SUMMERBELL; Gen. Man. A. J. KELL.

GRE Insurance Ltd: 604 St Kilda Rd, Melbourne, Vic 3004; tel. (03) 520-6233; telex 31259; fire, marine, accident; Man. Dir H. N. LEVICK.

Manufacturers' Mutual Insurance Ltd: 60-62 York St, Sydney, NSW 2000; tel. (02) 290-6222; telex 126666; f. 1914; workers' compensation; fire, general accident, motor and marine; Chair. C. W. LOVE; Man. Dir A. T. C. VENNING.

Mercantile & General Life Reinsurance Group of Australia Ltd: Royal Exchange Bldg, 56 Pitt St, Sydney, NSW 2000; tel. (02) 2518000; telex 120318; f. 1956; reinsurance; Chair. G. T. KRYGER; Man. Dir S. R. B. FRANCE.

Mercantile Mutual Holdings Ltd: 55 Clarence St, Sydney, NSW; tel. (02) 234-8111; telex 176577; f. 1878; Chair. Sir HAROLD KNIGHT; Man. Dir P. R. SHIRRIFF.

MLC Insurance Ltd: 44 Martin Place, Sydney, NSW 2000; tel. (02) 957-8000; telex 74679; f. 1958; Chair. R. C. GARROWAY; Gen. Man. D. A. WHIPP.

MLC Life Ltd: 105-153 Miller St, POB 200, North Sydney, NSW 2060; tel. (02) 957-8000; telex 121290; f. 1886; Chair. V. E. MARTIN; Man. Dir I. K. CROW.

National & General Insurance Co Ltd: 5 Blue St, Sydney, NSW 2060; tel. (02) 922-3822; f. 1954; fire, marine, general; Chair. Sir ARVI PARBO; Gen. Man. A. J. SCOTT.

The National Mutual Life Association of Australasia Ltd: 447 Collins St, Melbourne, Vic 3000; tel. (03) 616-3911; telex 35654; f. 1869; Chair. S. B. MYER; Man. Dir E. A. MAYER.

NRMA Insurance Ltd: 151 Clarence St, Sydney, NSW 2000; tel. (02) 260-9222; telex 22348; f. 1926; associated with National Roads and Motorists' Asscn; Gen. Man. R. J. LAMBLE.

NZI Life Ltd: 118 Mount St, North Sydney, NSW 2060; tel. (02) 925-1999; f. 1921 as South British United Life Assurance Co Ltd; present name adopted in 1985; Gen. Man. CHRISTOPHER C. MOORE.

QBE Insurance Group Ltd: 82 Pitt St, Sydney, NSW 2000; tel. (02) 235-4444; telex 26914; f. 1886; general insurance; Chair. J. D. O. BURNS; Man. Dir E. J. CLONEY.

Reinsurance Co of Australasia Ltd: 1 York St, Sydney, NSW 2000; tel. (02) 221-2144; telex 24504; f. 1961; reinsurance, fire, accident, marine; Chair. M. T. SANDOW; Man. Dir P. J. MILLER.

Southern Pacific Insurance Co Ltd: 80 Alfred St, Milson's Point, NSW 2061; f. 1935; fire, accident, marine; Chair. C. H. V. CARPENTER; Chief Gen. Man. B. A. SELF.

Sun Alliance Australia Ltd: Sun Alliance Bldg, 22-34 Bridge St, Sydney, NSW 2000; fire, accident and marine insurance; Gen. Man. J. J. MALLICK.

Wesfarmers Insurance Ltd: 184 Railway Parade, Bassendean, WA 6054; tel. (09) 279-0333; telex 96159; Man. T. I. CORNFORD.

AUSTRALIA Directory

Westpac Life Insurance Services Ltd: 60 Martin Place, Sydney, NSW 2001; tel. (02) 226-2888; f. 1986; CEO MONTY HILKOWITZ.

Insurance Associations

Australian Insurance Association: Capital Centre, 4th Floor, 54 Marcus Clarke St, POB 2013, Canberra, ACT 2601; tel. (062) 49-7666; telex 62708; f. 1968; Pres. A. T. C. VENNING; Exec. Sec. M. T. DRINKWATER.

Australian Insurance Institute: 31 Queen St, Melbourne, Vic 3000; tel. (03) 6294021; telex 139668; f. 1919; Pres. F. D. MCGHEE; CEO A. V. SMYTHE; 8,475 mems.

Insurance Council of Australia Ltd: 31 Queen St, Melbourne, Vic 3000; tel. (03) 614-1077; telex 37334; f. 1975; CEO R. G. A. SMITH.

Life Insurance Federation of Australia Inc: 31 Queen St, Melbourne, Vic 3000; tel. (03) 629-5751; f. 1979; Chair. I. F. STANWELL; Exec. Dir D. A. PURCHASE; 49 mems.

Trade and Industry

CHAMBERS OF COMMERCE

International Chamber of Commerce: POB E118, Queen Victoria Terrace, Canberra, ACT 2600; tel. (062) 951961; f. 1927; 65 mems; Chair. R. J. GRAHAM.

Australian Chamber of Commerce: Brisbane Ave, Barton, ACT 2600; tel. (062) 732381; telex 62507; f. 1901; mems include Chambers of Commerce in Sydney, Melbourne, Canberra, Brisbane, Adelaide, Perth, Hobart, Newcastle, Darwin, Gove, Tamworth, Cairns, Norfolk Island, and State Feds of Chambers of Commerce in Vic, Qld and WA; Pres. A. O. HAY; Exec. Dir Dr G. R. WEBB.

Chamber of Commerce and Industry, SA, Inc: 136 Greenhill Road, Unley, SA 5061; tel. (08) 373-1422; telex 88370; 3,100 mems; Gen. Man. L. M. THOMPSON.

Hobart Chamber of Commerce: 65 Murray St, Hobart, Tas 7000; POB 969K, Hobart, Tas 7001; tel. (002) 344325; telex 346034; f. 1851; Dir V. J. BARRON.

Launceston Chamber of Commerce: 99 George St, Launceston, Tas 7250; POB 780, Launceston, Tas 7250; tel. (003) 318988; f. 1849; Sec. A. G. HART.

State Chamber of Commerce and Industry: 93 York St, POB 4280, GPO Sydney, NSW 2001; tel. (02) 299-7888; telex 127113; f. 1826; Dir DAVID ABBA; Dep. Dir JACKIE PETERSON.

State Chamber of Commerce and Industry (Qld): 243 Edward St (cnr Adelaide St), Brisbane, Qld 4000; POB 1390, Brisbane, Qld 4001; tel. (07) 221-1766; telex 145636; f. 1868; Dir P. ROUBICEK.

State Chamber of Commerce and Industry (Victoria): Commerce House, World Trade Centre, cnr Flinders and Spencer Sts, Melbourne, Vic 3005; tel. (03) 611-2233; telex 31255; f. 1851; Exec. Dir D. C. JONES.

Western Australian Chamber of Commerce and Industry (Inc): 14 Parliament Place, West Perth, WA 6005; tel. (09) 322-2688; telex 93609; f. 1890; 4,000 mems; Dir C. BARNETT.

AGRICULTURAL AND INDUSTRIAL ORGANIZATIONS

The Australian Agricultural Council: Dept of Primary Industries and Energy, Barton, Canberra, ACT 2600; tel. (062) 725220; telex 62188; f. 1934 to provide means for consultation between individual States and the Commonwealth on agricultural production and marketing (excluding forestry and fisheries), to promote the welfare and standards of Australian agricultural industries and to foster the adoption of national policies in regard to these industries; eight mems comprising the agricultural Ministers of the six States and the Northern Territory and the Commonwealth Minister for Primary Industries and Energy; Sec. D. C. AYLIFFE.

Standing Committee on Agriculture: f. 1934; an advisory body to the Australian Agricultural Council; implements co-ordination of agricultural research and of quarantine measures relating to pests and diseases of plants and animals; comprises the State and Northern Territory Dirs of Agriculture and reps of Commonwealth Depts with an interest in agriculture; Sec. D. C. AYLIFFE.

Australian Dairy Corporation: 1601 Malvern Rd, Glen Iris, Vic 3146; tel. (03) 298-3777; telex 30503; promotes local consumption and controls the export of dairy produce; Chair. Sir NEIL CURRIE; Man. Dir JOHN L. GIBSON.

Australian Industry Development Corporation: 212 Northbourne Ave, Canberra, ACT 2601; tel. (062) 479411; telex 62307; f. 1970; a Commonwealth statutory corpn providing finance and financial services, including the arrangement of project finance and equity participations, to promote the development of Australian industries and assist Australian participation in the ownership and control of industries and resources; brs in Sydney, Melbourne, Perth, Adelaide and Brisbane; cap. p.u. $A87.5m., total assets $A1,511.5m. (1985); Chair. Sir GORDON JACKSON; CEO J. ROBERT THOMAS.

Australian Meat and Livestock Corporation: POB 4129, Sydney, NSW 2001; tel. (02) 260-3111; telex 22887; statutory federal govt authority assisting the Australian meat and livestock industries in domestic and international trade; Chair. R. AUSTEN.

Australian Trade Development Council: c/o Dept of Trade, Canberra, ACT 2600; f. 1958; advises the Minister for Trade on all aspects of the development of overseas trade; Chair. Dr B. W. SCOTT.

Australian Wheat Board: Ceres House, 528 Lonsdale St, Melbourne, Vic 3000; tel. (03) 605-1555; telex 130196; f. 1939; marketing authority for wheat on the export market; 11 mems; Chair. CLINTON CONDON.

Australian Wool Corporation: Wool House, 369 Royal Parade, Parkville, Vic 3052; tel. 341-9111; telex 30548 (general), 34128 (sales); f. 1973; responsible for wool marketing and research; board of 10 mems (chair., four wool growers, four from commerce, one govt mem.); Chair. DAVID ASIMUS.

Department of Primary Industries and Energy: Edmund Barton Bldg, Broughton St, Barton, Canberra, ACT 2600; tel. (062) 723933; telex 62188; f. 1987 to replace the fmr Depts of Primary Industry and of Resources and Energy; responsible for national resources and energy policy and for the promotion and development of primary industries; Chair. Minister for Primary Industries and Energy; Sec. GRAHAM EVANS.

Wool Council of Australia: POB E10, Queen Victoria Terrace, Canberra, ACT 2600; tel. (062) 732531; telex 62683; comprises 20 mems; levies wool tax for research and development, promotion and market support; consults with Australian Wool Corpn on reserve prices; represents wool-growers to govt and industry; Pres. K. M. SAWERS; Exec. Dir D. M. MOORE.

EMPLOYERS' ORGANIZATIONS

Confederation of Australian Industry: POB E14, Queen Victoria Terrace, Canberra, ACT 2600; tel. (062) 732311; telex 62733; f. 1977 by merger of Associated Chambers of Mfrs of Australia and the Australian Council of Employers' Feds; mems: 38 nat. asscns representing over 100,000 firms; Pres. B. E. HELSON; Chief Exec. D. S. GEORGE; Sec. R. J. GARDINI.

Dairy Farmers Co-operative Ltd: 55 Chandos St, St Leonard's, NSW 2065; tel. 430-1222; telex 21438; f. 1900; Gen. Man. D. S. KINNERSLEY.

The Master Builders' Association of New South Wales: POB 9, Broadway, NSW 2007; tel. 660-7188; telex 27308; f. 1873; Exec. Dir R. L. ROCHER; 4,500 mems.

Meat and Allied Trades Federation of Australia: 25–27 Albany St, 1st Floor, Crows Nest, NSW 2065; POB 1208, Crows Nest, NSW 2065; tel. (02) 438-5144; telex 22480; f. 1928; Pres. J. H. MEDWAY; Nat. Dir R. H. J. NOBLE.

Metal Trades Industry Association of Australia: 51 Walker St, North Sydney, NSW 2060; tel. (02) 929-5566; telex 121257; f. 1873; Nat. Pres. Dr W. W. UHLENBRUCH; Dir and CEO A. C. EVANS; 7,000 mems.

New South Wales Farmers' Association: 56 Young St, Sydney, NSW 2000; POB 1068, GPO Sydney, NSW 2001; tel. (02) 251-1700; telex 26638; f. 1978 as The Livestock and Grain Producers' Asscn of NSW.

New South Wales Flour Millers' Council: BNZ House, 333 George St, POB 2125, Sydney, NSW 2001; Sec. K. G. WILLIAMS.

Screen Production Association of Australia: 33 Albany St, Suite 4, Crows Nest, NSW 2065; tel. (02) 436-4077; Pres. ROSS DIMSEY; Exec. Dir JOHN DANIELL.

Timber Trade Industrial Association: 155 Castlereagh St, Sydney, NSW 2000; f. 1940; 530 mems; Man. H. J. MCCARTHY.

MANUFACTURERS' ORGANIZATIONS

The Australian Chamber of Manufactures (NSW): Private Bag 938, North Sydney, NSW 2059; tel. (02) 957-5792; telex 122050; f. 1885; Nat. CEO W. J. HENDERSON; Dir NSW Div. G. D. JOHN.

The Australian Chamber of Manufactures (Victoria): Industry House, 370 St Kilda Rd, POB 1469N, GPO Melbourne, Vic 3001; tel. (03) 698-4111; telex 32596; f. 1877; 8,500 mems; Nat. CEO W. J. HENDERSON; Dir, Victoria Div. K. C. CROMPTON.

Australian Manufacturers' Export Council: Industry House, POB E14, Queen Victoria Terrace, Canberra, ACT 2600; tel. (062) 732311; telex 62733; f. 1955; Exec. Officer G. J. CHALKER.

Business Council of Australia: 10 Queen's Rd, Melbourne, Vic 3004; POB 387D, Melbourne, Vic 3001; tel. (03) 267-6288; telex 36733; public policy research and advocacy; governing council

AUSTRALIA

comprises chief execs of Australia's major cos; Pres. Sir RODERICK CARNEGIE; Exec. Dir P. A. MCLAUGHLIN.

Confederation of Western Australian Industry, Inc: POB 6209, Hay St East, Perth, WA 6004; tel. (09) 325-0111; telex 94124; Exec. Dir W. J. BROWN.

Queensland Confederation of Industry: Industry House, 375 Wickham Terrace, Brisbane, Qld 4000; tel. (07) 831-1699; telex 41369; f. 1976; 2,500 mems; Gen. Man. ROGER M. BRYCE.

Tasmanian Confederation of Industries: 242 Liverpool St, Hobart, Tas 7000; tel. (002) 345933; telex 57210; f. 1898; Exec. Dir E. C. ILES.

PRINCIPAL TRADE UNIONS

Australian Council of Trade Unions (ACTU): 393-397 Swanston St, Melbourne, Vic 3000; tel. (03) 663-5266; telex 33943; f. 1927; br. in each State, generally known as a Trades and Labour Council; 158 affiliated trade unions; Pres. SIMON CREAN; Sec. WILLIAM J. KELTY.

Administrative and Clerical Officers' Association: 245 Castlereagh St, Sydney, NSW 2000; tel. (02) 267-3000; telex 26021; Nat. Sec. P. ROBSON; 54,000 mems.

Amalgamated Footwear and Textile Workers' Union of Australia: 132-138 Leicester St, Carlton, Vic 3053; tel. (03) 347-2766; f. 1919; Fed. Pres J. ROUGHLEY, W. BURKE; 30,000 mems.

Amalgamated Metal Workers' Union: 136 Chalmers St, Surry Hills, NSW 2010; tel. 690-1411; telex 23763; 155,730 mems.

Australasian Meat Industry Employees' Union: 377 Sussex St, Sydney, NSW 2000; tel. 264-2279; 38,158 mems.

Australian Building Construction Employees' and Builders Labourers' Federation: 190 Sturt St, Adelaide, SA 5000; tel. (08) 211-8977; telex 33748; Gen. Sec. N. L. GALLAGHER; 45,000 mems.

Australian Postal and Telecommunications Union: 139 Queensberry St, 1st Floor, Carlton, Vic 3053; 48,000 mems.

Australian Public Service Association: 41-43 Drummond St, Carlton, Vic 3053; POB 147, Carlton South, Vic 3053; tel. (03) 663-5933; telex 35702; f. 1912; Pres. JOY PALMER; Sec. GARY MCMORRAN; 29,000 mems.

Australian Railways Union: 377 Sussex St, 6th Floor, Sydney, NSW 2000; tel. (02) 267-6116; Nat. Sec. R. C. TAYLOR; 42,416 mems.

Australian Teachers' Federation: POB 415, Carlton South, Vic 3053; tel. (03) 348-1700; telex 152486; f. 1920; Pres. DI FOGGO; Gen. Sec. ROBERT V. BLUER; 177,000 mems.

Australian Telecommunications Employees' Association: 270 Flinders St, 11th Floor, Melbourne, Vic 3000; tel. (03) 632675; Pres. J. HALL; Sec.-Treas. C. P. COOPER; 25,200 mems.

Australian Workers' Union: 35 Regent St, 3rd Floor, Chippendale, NSW 2008; tel. (02) 690-1022; telex 73231; f. 1886; Pres. A. BEGG; Gen. Sec. G. A. BARR; 122,000 mems.

Building Workers' Industrial Union of Australia: 490 Kent St, 3rd Floor, Sydney, NSW 2000; tel. (02) 267-3929; f. 1945; Pres. N. A. CURRIE; Gen. Sec. P. M. CLANCY; 41,260 mems.

Electrical Trades Union of Australia: National Council, 302-306 Elizabeth St, Sydney, NSW 2010; tel. (02) 211-5888; telex 73372; f. 1919; Pres. R. C. LUCKMAN; Nat. Sec. T. A. JOHNSON; 88,569 mems.

Federal Clerks' Union of Australia: 53 Queen St, 2nd Floor, Melbourne, Vic 3000; 100,000 mems.

Federated Ironworkers' Association of Australia: 51-65 Bathurst St, Sydney, NSW 2000; tel. (02) 264-2877; telex 176770; f. 1911; Nat. Pres. BOB REDMOND; Nat. Sec. STEVE HARRISON; 69,000 mems.

The Federated Miscellaneous Workers Union of Australia: Federal Council, 365 Sussex St, 1st Floor, Sydney, NSW 2000; tel. (02) 267-9681; telex 75879; f. 1916; Gen. Sec. M. J. FERGUSON; 127,000 mems.

Federated Municipal and Shire Council Employees' Union of Australia: Labor Council Bldg, Suite 2, 5th Floor, 377 Sussex St, Sydney, NSW 2000; tel. (02) 264-9918; Fed. Sec. B. MCCARNEY; 49,158 mems.

Hospital Employees' Federation: 240 Macquarie Rd, Greystanes, NSW 2145; 30,579 mems.

Printing and Kindred Industries Union: 596 Crown St, Surry Hills, NSW 2010; tel. (02) 690-1000; telex 71708; f. 1916; Sec. J. P. CAHILL; 48,000 mems.

Transport Workers' Union of Australia: 17-25 Lygon St, Carlton, Vic 3053; tel. (03) 663-6399; 94,499 mems.

Vehicle Builders Employees' Federation of Australia: 1st Floor, 61-65 Drummond St, Carlton South, Vic 3053; tel. (03) 663-5866; telex 30705; Gen. Sec. WAYNE BLAIR; 33,671 mems.

Waterside Workers' Federation of Australia: 365-375 Sussex St, Sydney, NSW 2000; tel. (02) 267-9134; telex 25645; f. 1902; Gen. Sec. T. I. BULL.

Transport

Australian Transport Advisory Council: POB 594, Canberra, ACT 2601; tel. (062) 687851; telex 62018; f. 1946; Mems: Federal Minister for Transport and Communications, State and Territory Ministers of Transport, Roads and Marine and Ports; Observer: the New Zealand Minister of Transport; initiates discussion, and reports as necessary, on any matter which will tend to promote a better co-ordination of transport development, while encouraging modernization and innovation; promotes research; Sec. T. ARROWSMITH.

Urban Transit Authority of New South Wales: 11-31 York St, Sydney, NSW 2000; telex 25702; co-ordinates bus, rail and ferry services in Sydney, Newcastle and Wollongong; operates publicly-owned buses and ferries; exercises broad policy control over privately operated public vehicles in the above areas; Chair. G. A. BAYUTTI; Man. Dir J. BREW (acting).

RAILWAYS

Before July 1975 there were seven government-owned railway systems in Australia. In July 1975 Australian National was formed to incorporate the Commonwealth Railways, non-metropolitan South Australian Railways and the Tasmanian Government Railways. In 1984 there were 40,807 km of railway in Australia.

Australian National: 1 Richmond Rd, Keswick, SA 5035; tel. (08) 217-4111; telex 88445; f. 1978; a federal statutory authority operating 7,315 km of track (1987); Chair. Dr D. G. WILLIAMS; Gen. Man. R. M. KING (acting).

Queensland Railways: Railway Centre, 305 Edward St, Brisbane, Qld 4000; POB 1429, Brisbane, Qld 4001; tel. (07) 225-0211; telex 41514; operates 10,079 km of track; Commr R. T. SHEEHY; Dep. Commr and Sec. R. W. DUNNING.

State Rail Authority of New South Wales: 11-31 York St, Sydney, NSW 2000; POB 29, Sydney, NSW 2001; tel. (02) 219-8888; telex 25702; administers passenger and freight rail service in NSW over a track network of 9,909 km; Chair. R. SAYERS; CEO R. A. SCHWARZER.

State Transport Authority (South Australia): 136 North Terrace, Adelaide, SA 5000; POB 2351, GPO Adelaide, SA 5001; tel. (08) 218-2200; telex 87115; f. 1978; operates 152 km of metropolitan track, and bus and tram services; Chair. J. D. RUMP; Gen. Man. J. V. BROWN.

State Transport Authority (Victoria): 589 Collins St, Melbourne, Vic 3000; tel. (03) 619-1111; telex 33801; f. 1983; operates 5,809 km of track; Chair. J. KING; Man. Dir K. M. FITZMAURICE.

Western Australian Government Railways (Westrail): Westrail Centre, POB S1422, Perth 6001, WA; tel. (09) 326-2222; telex 92879; operates passenger and freight transport services mainly in the south of WA; 5,553 main line route-km of track; Commr W. I. MCCULLOUGH.

ROADS

At 31 December 1985 there were 852,986 km of roads, including 787 km of motorways, 38,728 km of other main roads and 91,777 km of secondary roads.

SHIPPING

Commonwealth of Australia, Australian National Line: (Australian Shipping Commission), 432 St Kilda Rd, Melbourne, Vic 3004; POB 2238T, Melbourne, Vic 3001; tel. (03) 269-5555; telex 130584; f. 1956; shipping agents; coastal trade and coastal and overseas bulk shipping; container management services; overseas container services to Europe, Hong Kong, New Zealand, Taiwan, the Philippines, Korea, Singapore, Malaysia, Thailand, Indonesia and Japan; bulk services to Japan, India, Pakistan, Malaysia, Indonesia, New Zealand; Chair. W. BOLITHO; Man. Dir M. MOORE-WILTON.

The Adelaide Steamship Co Ltd: 123 Greenhill Rd, Unley, SA 5061; tel. (08) 272-3077; telex 82133; f. 1875; Man. Dir J. G. SPALVINS.

Ampol Ltd: 84 Pacific Highway, North Sydney, NSW 2060; tel. (02) 929-6222; telex 121325; f. 1936; bulk carriage of crude oil to Brisbane and Sydney, and carriage of refined products and black oils from the Brisbane refinery to Qld out-ports; Chair. Sir TRISTAN ANTICO; Man. Dir A. J. HURLSTONE; 2 vessels.

John Burke Shipping: 14-24 Macquarie St, New Farm, POB 509, Fortitude Valley, Qld 4006; tel. (07) 852-1701; telex 40483; f. 1887;

AUSTRALIA

coastal services and trade with Papua New Guinea; Man. D. J. DALY; 5 vessels.

Burns, Philp and Co Ltd: 7 Bridge St, Sydney, NSW; POB 543, Sydney, NSW 2001; tel. (02) 259-1111; telex 120290; f. 1883; Chair. J. D. O. BURNS; CEO ANDREW TURNBULL.

Holyman and Sons Pty Ltd: Remount Rd, Mowbray, POB 70, Launceston, Tas; tel. (003) 263388; telex 58517; coastal services; Chair. K. C. HOLYMAN.

Howard Smith Industries Pty Ltd: POB N364, Grosvenor St, Sydney, NSW 2000; tel. (02) 230-1777; telex 24505; ship and tug services; Chair. W. J. TROTTER; CEO D. A. W. THOMSON.

McIlwraith McEacharn Ltd: Barclays House, 25 Bligh St, Sydney, NSW 2000; tel. (02) 232-1200; telex 178116; 114 William St, Melbourne, Vic 3000; tel. (03) 609-1011; telex 30339; f. 1875; tug and launch owners and operators; shipping agents and ship management, repair and cleaning; mfrs of hyperbaric equipment, computer software. Chair. Sir IAN POTTER; Man. Dir A. B. LAWRANCE.

Mason Shipping: Tingira St, POB 840, Portsmith, Cairns, Qld 4870; tel. (070) 516933; telex 48405; a division of Portsmith Stevedoring Co Pty Ltd; coastal services and stevedoring; Man. D. W. SIMS; 4 vessels.

TNT Shipping and Development Ltd: TNT Plaza, Tower 1, Lawson Sq., Redfern, NSW 2016; tel. (02) 698-9222; telex 27343; f. 1958; wholly owned subsidiary of Thomas Nationwide Transport Ltd; shipowner and operator; charters vessels; Man. Dir Sir PETER ABELES; Dir ROLAND J. HOY.

Western Australian Coastal Shipping Commission (Stateships): Port Beach Rd, North Fremantle, WA; POB 394, Fremantle, WA; tel. (09) 430-0200; telex 92054; Chair. and Gen. Man. D. F. WILSON.

CIVIL AVIATION

In the sparsely-populated areas of central and western Australia, air transport is extremely important, and Australia has pioneered services such as the Flying Doctor Service to overcome the problems of distance. The country is also well served by international airlines.

Air New South Wales: Kingsford Smith Airport, Mascot, Sydney, NSW 2020; tel. (02) 268-1678; telex 20143; f. 1934; a division of Ansett Transport Industries (Operations) Pty Ltd; extensive services from Sydney throughout NSW and Qld's Sunshine Coast; Chair. Sir RODEN CUTLER; Gen. Man. J. HUTCHISON; fleet includes 3 Fokker F-28-1000, 4 Fokker F-50.

Ansett Airlines of Australia: 501 Swanston St, Melbourne, Vic 3000; tel. (03) 668-1211; telex 30085; f. 1936; a division of Ansett Transport Industries (Operations) Pty Ltd; passenger and air cargo services throughout Australia and to New Zealand; Chair. and Jt Man. Dirs K. RUPERT MURDOCH, Sir PETER ABELES; Gen. Man. G. J. MCMAHON; fleet includes 5 Boeing 767, 12 Boeing 727-200, 1 Boeing 727-200F, 7 Fokker F-27, 5 Fokker F-50.

Ansett NT: 31 Smith St, Darwin, NT 5290; tel. (089) 819800; telex 85187; f. 1981; a division of Ansett Transport Industries (Operations) Pty Ltd; services link Darwin with Katherine, Tennant Creek, Alice Springs, Gove, Ayers Rock, Groote Eylandt, Cairns, Mt Isa and Hamilton Island; Gen. Man. PETER HILLAS; fleet includes 1 Fokker F-28-1000, 1 BAe 146-200.

Ansett WA: Perth Airport, Cloverdale, Perth, WA 6105; tel. (09) 478-9222; telex 92147; f. 1934; a division of Ansett Transport Industries (Operations) Pty Ltd; services from Perth to Darwin via north-west ports and throughout Western Australia; State Man. G. W. COURT; Admin. Man. R. SMITH; fleet of 4 Fokker F-28-1000, 2 Fokker F-28-4000, 1 Fokker F-28-3000, 5 BAe 146-200.

Australian Airlines: 50 Franklin St, POB 2806AA, Melbourne, Vic 3001; tel. (03) 665-1333; telex 30109; f. 1946 as Trans-Australia Airlines (TAA); present name adopted in 1986; services to all States; Chair. A. E. HARRIS; CEO JAMES A. STRONG; fleet includes 4 Airbus A300B4, 12 Boeing 737-300, 10 Boeing 727-276, 5 Douglas DC-9-30, 1 Boeing 727-77F, 3 Fokker F-27.

East-West Airlines Ltd: Level 3, 431 Glebe Point Rd, Glebe, NSW 2037; telex 176198; f. 1947; routes total 16,619 km; services to all States, the Northern Territory and Norfolk Island; Gen. Man. NEIL BERKETT; fleet includes 8 F-28, 7 F-27.

Qantas Airways Ltd: Qantas International Centre, International Sq., POB 489, Sydney, NSW 2001; tel. (02) 263-3636; telex 20113; f. 1920; govt-owned; services to 42 cities in 24 countries including destinations in the UK, Europe, the USA, Canada, Japan, South-East Asia, India, the Middle East, Africa and the South-West Pacific, including New Zealand; Chair. J. B. LESLIE; CEO J. L. MENADUE; fleet of 31 Boeing 747 and Boeing 767.

Tourism

The main attractions are swimming and surfing on the Pacific beaches, sailing from Sydney and other harbours, skin-diving along the Great Barrier Reef, winter sports in the Australian Alps, notably the Snowy Mountains, and summer sports in the Blue Mountains. The town of Alice Springs and the sandstone monolith of Ayers Rock are among the attractions of the desert interior. Much of Australia's wildlife is unique to the country. Australia received an estimated 1.8m. foreign tourist visitors in 1987.

Australian Tourist Commission: 80 William St, Woolloomooloo, Sydney, NSW 2011; tel. (02) 360-1111; telex 22322; f. 1967 for promotion of tourism; 10 offices, of which nine are overseas; Chair. JOHN HADDAD; Man. Dir JOHN S. ROWE.

Atomic Energy

Australian Institute of Nuclear Science and Engineering: PMB, Menai, NSW 2234; supports university research and training projects in all branches of nuclear science and engineering; mems comprise 19 universities, ANSTO and CSIRO; Scientific Sec. Dr R. GAMMON.

Australian Nuclear Science and Technology Organisation (ANSTO): Lucas Heights Research Laboratories, New Illawarra Rd, Lucas Heights, NSW 2234; PMB 1, Menai, NSW 2234; tel. (02) 543-3111; telex 24562; f. 1987 to replace the Australian Atomic Energy Commission (AAEC), which had been in existence since 1953; aims to bring the benefits of nuclear science and technology to industry, to medicine and to the community; Chair. Prof. R. E. COLLINS; Exec. Dir Dr DAVID J. COOK; 900 employees.

HIFAR: 10-MW thermal research reactor; critical 1958; for production of radioisotopes, studies of effects of high-intensity radiation on materials and of the use of neutrons to analyse crystal lattices, molecular structure, trace element concentrations and uranium in ores.

MOATA: 100-kW thermal research reactor; critical 1962; provides neutron radiography, fission and alpha track analyses, activation services and research in physical chemistry and materials.

Australian School of Nuclear Technology: PMB 1, Menai, NSW 2234; tel. (02) 543-3111; telex 24562; provides short-term, intensive courses for participants from Australia and overseas, covering radionuclides in medicine, radioisotope techniques and radiation protection; Dep. Prin. B. TONER.

AUSTRALIAN EXTERNAL TERRITORIES

CHRISTMAS ISLAND

Introduction

Christmas Island covers an area of about 135 sq km (52 sq miles) and lies 360 km south of Java Head in the Indian Ocean. The nearest point on the Australian coast is North West Cape, 1,408 km to the south-east.

Following annexation by Britain in 1888, Christmas Island was incorporated for administrative purposes with the Straits Settlements in 1900. Japanese forces occupied the island from March 1942 until the end of the Second World War, and in 1946 Christmas Island became a dependency of Singapore.

Administration was transferred from Singapore to the United Kingdom on 1 January 1958, pending final transfer to Australia. It became an Australian territory on 1 October 1958. Christmas Island has no indigenous population. In June 1987 the population was estimated at 2,000, comprising mainly Chinese and Malays and a small number of Indians, Europeans and Eurasians. Residents consist almost entirely of employees of the Phosphate Mining Corporation of Christmas Island and the administration and their families. Since 1981, all residents of the island have been eligible to acquire Australian citizenship.

The economy has been based on the recovery of phosphates. During the year ending 30 June 1984 about 463,000 metric tons were exported to Australia, 332,000 tons to New Zealand and 341,000 tons to other countries. Reserves were estimated to be sufficient to enable production to be maintained until 1991. In November 1987, however, the Australian Government announced the closure of the phosphate mine, owing to industrial unrest. Efforts are to be made to develop the island's considerable potential for tourism. In April 1986 initial plans were announced for a hotel and casino complex.

Directory

The Government

An Administrator, appointed by the Governor-General of Australia and responsible to the Minister for Territories, is the senior government representative on the island. There is a nine-member island council, to which elections are held annually.
Administrator: T. F. PATERSON.

Judicial System

The judicial system comprises a Supreme Court, a District Court, a Magistrate's Court and a Children's Court.

Supreme Court: c/o Government Offices, Christmas Island 6798, Indian Ocean; tel. 8501; telex 1078001; Judge: Sir WILLIAM FORSTER (non-resident); Additional Judge: JOHN F. GALLOP (non-resident).

Religion
Christianity

Within the Anglican Church of Australia, Christmas Island forms part of the archdiocese of Perth, Western Australia.

The Press

Christmas Island News: weekly; Editor DAVID WENTWORTH-PERRY; circ. 200.

Radio and Television

There were an estimated 2,500 radio receivers in use in 1985.
Christmas Island Broadcasting: Christmas Island 6798, Indian Ocean; tel. 8301; telex 78002; f. 1967; owned and operated by the Christmas Island Services Corporation; daily broadcasting service by Radio VLU-2 on 1422 KHz, in English, Malay and Mandarin; Station Man. JAY BUSCH.
Christmas Island Television: Station Man. DOUGLAS MALEY.

Industry

Phosphate Mining Corporation of Christmas Island (PMCI): Christmas Island 6798, Indian Ocean; tel. 8402; telex 78006; f. 1981 as the Phosphate Mining Co of Christmas Island, reorg. under present name as an Australian govt statutory authority in 1985; responsible for mining, treatment and sale of Christmas Island phosphates; proposed closure announced in Nov. 1987.

Transport

In 1987 railway lines, with a total length of 24 km, served the island's phosphate mines. There are good roads in the developed areas. Australian government charter aircraft operate a weekly service from Perth via the Cocos (Keeling) Islands. The Australian National Line operates ships to the Australian mainland. In 1987 the Phosphate Mining Corporation of Christmas Island operated a cargo-shipping service to Singapore and shipped phosphate to Australia and New Zealand, and to Malaysian and other Asian ports. It also operated weekly flights from Singapore to Christmas Island.

COCOS (KEELING) ISLANDS

Introduction

The Cocos (Keeling) Islands are 27 in number and lie 2,768 km north-west of Perth, in the Indian Ocean. The islands, which have an area of 14 sq km (5.4 sq miles), form two low-lying coral atolls, densely covered with coconut palms. The population at 30 June 1986 was 616, comprising 414 residents on West Island and 202 on Home Island, the only inhabited islands in the group. The Cocos Malays are descendants of the people who were brought to the islands in 1826 by Alexander Hare and of labourers who were subsequently introduced by John Clunies-Ross.

The islands were declared a British possession in 1857 and came successively under the authority of the governors of Ceylon (1878) and the Straits Settlements (1886); in the same year, the British crown granted all land on the islands above the high-water mark to John Clunies-Ross and his heirs and successors in perpetuity. In 1946, when the islands became a dependency of the Colony of Singapore, a resident administrator, responsible to the governor of Singapore, was appointed. Administration of the islands was transferred to the Commonwealth of Australia on 23 November 1955.

In June 1977 the Australian government announced new policies concerning the islands, which resulted in its purchase from John Clunies-Ross of the whole of his interests in the islands, with the exception of his residence and associated buildings. The purchase took effect on 1 September 1978. An attempt by the Australian government to acquire Clunies-Ross' remaining property was deemed by the Australian high court in October 1984 to be unconstitutional.

In July 1979 the Cocos (Keeling) Islands council was established, with a wide range of functions in the Home Island village area (which the government has transferred to the council on trust for the benefit of the Cocos Malay community) and, since September 1984, in the greater part of the rest of the territory.

On 6 April 1984 a referendum to decide the future political status of the islands was held by the Australian government, with United Nations observers present. A large majority voted in favour of integration with Australia. As a result, the islanders were to acquire the rights, privileges and obligations of all Australian citizens. The powers and functions of the islands council were to be expanded to give it greater responsibility, and the inhabitants of the territory were to have full voting rights in elections to the Australian parliament.

Although local fishing is good and domestic gardens provide vegetables, bananas and pawpaws, the islands are not self-sufficient, and other foodstuffs, fuels and consumer items are imported from mainland Australia. A Cocos postal service (including a philatelic bureau) came into operation in September 1979, and revenue from the service is used for the benefit of the community.

Coconuts, grown throughout the islands, are the sole cash crop: total output was an estimated 5,000 metric tons in 1984, and total exports in 1984/85 were 202 metric tons.

Primary education is provided at the schools on Home and West Islands. Secondary education is provided to the age of 16 years on West Island. A bursary scheme enables Cocos Malay children to continue their education on the Australian mainland.

Directory

The Government

An Administrator, appointed by the Governor-General of Australia and responsible to the Minister for Territories, is the senior government representative in the islands.

Administrator: (vacant).

Chairman of the Cocos (Keeling) Islands Council: Parson BIN YAPAT.

Judicial System

Supreme Court, Cocos (Keeling) Islands: Cocos (Keeling) Islands 6799, Indian Ocean; tel. 6660; telex 67002; Judge: Sir WILLIAM FORSTER (non-resident); Additional Judge: R. FRENCH (non-resident).

Magistrates' Court, Cocos (Keeling) Islands: Special Magistrate: HAROLD BINGHAM.

Religion
Christianity

Within the Anglican Church of Australia, the Cocos Islands form part of the archdiocese of Perth, Western Australia.

Radio

There were an estimated 250 radio receivers in use in 1985. There is no television service.

Radio VKW Cocos: POB 70, Cocos Islands 6799, Indian Ocean; tel. 6666; non-commercial; daily broadcasting service in Cocos Malay and English; Station Man. D. WILLIAMS; Programme Man. R. F. CAREY.

Industry

Cocos Islands Co-operative Society Ltd: Home Island, Cocos Islands, Indian Ocean; tel. 7598; telex 67001; f. 1979; conducts the business enterprises of the Cocos Islanders; activities include boat construction and repairs, copra and coconut production, sail-making, stevedoring; Chair. MEDOUS BIN BYNIE.

Transport

Australian government charter aircraft from Perth provide a weekly service for passengers, supplies and mail to and from the airport on West Island. Cargo vessels from Perth deliver supplies, at intervals of six to eight weeks.

NORFOLK ISLAND

Introduction

Norfolk Island lies off the eastern coast of Australia, about 1,400 km east of Brisbane. It is about 8 km long and 4.8 km wide. The island was uninhabited when discovered in 1774 by a British expedition, led by Capt. James Cook. Norfolk Island was used as a penal settlement from 1788 to 1814 and again from 1825 to 1855, when it was abandoned. In 1856 it was resettled by 194 emigrants from Pitcairn Island, which had become overpopulated. Norfolk Island was administered as a separate colony until 1897, when it became a dependency of New South Wales. In 1913 control was transferred to the Australian government. The capital of the territory is Kingston.

Under the Norfolk Island Act 1979, Norfolk Island is progressing to responsible legislative and executive government, enabling it to run its own affairs to the greatest practicable extent. Wide powers are exercised by the nine-member legislative assembly (the fourth elections for which were held on 21 May 1986) and by an executive council comprising the executive members of the legislative assembly who have ministerial-type responsibilities. The Act preserves the Australian government's responsibility for Norfolk Island as a territory under its authority, with the minister for territories and local government as the responsible minister. The Act indicated that consideration would be given within five years to an extension of the powers of the legislative assembly and the political and administrative institutions of Norfolk Island. In 1985 legislative and executive responsibility was assumed by the Norfolk Island Government for public works and services, civil defence, betting and gaming, territorial archives and matters relating to the exercise of executive authority. The further extension of powers is continuing.

About 400 ha of land are arable. The main crops are Kentia palm seed, cereals, vegetables and fruit. Some flowers and plants are grown commercially. The administration is increasing the area devoted to Norfolk Island pine and hardwoods. Seed of the Norfolk Island pine is exported. Tourism is the island's main industry.

Statistical Survey

AREA AND POPULATION

Area: 34.5 sq km (13.3 sq miles).

Population (census results): 2,175 (males 1,067; females 1,108) at 30 June 1981; 2,367 (males 1,170; females 1,197), including visitors, at 30 June 1986.

Births and Deaths (1986): Live births 25 (birth rate 10.6 per 1,000); Deaths 15 (death rate 6.3 per 1,000).

Economically Active Population (persons aged 10 years and over, 1981 census): 985 (males 583; females 402).

FINANCE

Currency: Australian currency is used.

Budget (estimates, year ending 30 June 1988): Revenue $A4,872,000; Expenditure $A4,840,128.

EXTERNAL TRADE

1985/86 (year ending 30 June): *Imports*: $A23,272,284, mainly from Australia. *Exports*: $A2,592,118.

TOURISM

Visitors (1986): 29,428.

Directory

The Government

The Administrator is appointed by the Governor-General of Australia and is responsible to the Minister for Territories. A form of responsible legislative and executive government was extended to the island in 1979, as outlined above.

Administrator: Cdre JOHN A. MATTHEW.

EXECUTIVE COUNCIL
(December 1988)

Minister for Commerce, Tourism and Health: GEOFFREY JAMES BENNETT.

Minister for Finance: EDWARD HOWARD.

Minister for Planning: WILLIAM WINTON SANDERS.

All Ministries are in Kingston.

AUSTRALIAN EXTERNAL TERRITORIES

Legislature

ASSEMBLY

President: JOHN TERENCE BROWN.

Members: GERARDUS HENDRIKUS AAFJES, GEOFFREY JAMES BENNETT, DAVID ERNEST BUFFETT, ROSEMARIE GAYE EVANS, EDWARD HOWARD, DAVID JOHN RODGERS, HELEN VICTORIA SAMPSON, WILLIAM WINTON SANDERS.

Judicial System

Supreme Court of Norfolk Island: appeals lie to the Federal Court of Australia.

Judges: R. W. FOX (Chief Judge), T. R. MORLING.

The Press

Norfolk Island Government Gazette: Kingston, Norfolk Island 2899; tel. 2001; telex 30003; weekly.

Norfolk Islander: 'Greenways Press', POB 150, Norfolk Island 2889; tel. 2159; f. 1965; weekly; Co-Editors Mr and Mrs THOMAS LLOYD; circ. 1,300.

Radio and Television

There were an estimated 1,500 radio receivers in use in 1987. In August 1987 a television service was introduced, with programmes relayed via satellite from the Australian Broadcasting Corporation in Sydney.

Norfolk Island Broadcasting Service: New Cascade Rd; tel. 2137; non-commercial; broadcasts 112 hours per week; Broadcasting Officer Mrs K. M. LECREN.

Finance

BANKING

There are branches of the Commonwealth Banking Corpn (Australia) and Westpac Banking Corporation Savings Bank Ltd (Australia).

Trade

Norfolk Island Chamber of Commerce: POB 370, Norfolk Island 2899; f. 1966; affiliated to the Australian Chamber of Commerce; 60 mems; Pres. BOB GOLDSWORTHY; Sec. PETER BEAUMONT.

Transport

ROADS

There are about 80 km of roads, including 53 km of sealed road.

SHIPPING

The Compagnie des Chargeurs Calédoniens operates cargo services from Sydney, Australia, and Auckland, New Zealand. A small tanker from Nouméa (New Caledonia) delivers petroleum products to the island and another from Australia delivers liquid propane gas. Sofrana Unilines and the South Pacific Shipping Co also operate vessels on these routes.

CIVIL AVIATION

Norfolk Island has one airport, with two runways (of 1,900 m and 1,550 m), capable of taking medium jet aircraft.

Norfolk Airlines: National Bank House, cnr Adelaide and Creek Sts, POB 905, Brisbane, Qld 4001, Australia; tel. 229-5872; telex 41421; f. 1973; operates regular flights from Brisbane and Sydney to Lord Howe Island (a dependency of New South Wales) and Norfolk Island, and charters throughout Australia and the South Pacific; Chair. JOHN BROWN; Gen. Man. MICHAEL CHILDS; fleet of 30 aircraft, including Lear Jets and Beechcraft Super King Air 200s.

Tourism

Norfolk Island Government Tourist Board: Burnt Pine, POB 211, Norfolk Island 2899; tel. (672) 2147; telex 32010; Chair. IAN W. KENNY.

Norfolk Island Government Visitors' Information Bureau: Burnt Pine, POB 211, Norfolk Island 2899; tel. (672) 2147; telex 32010; CEO BARRY J. SCHIPPLOCK.

OTHER TERRITORIES

Ashmore and Cartier Islands

The Ashmore Islands (known as West, Middle and East Islands) and Cartier Island are situated in the Timor Sea, about 850 km and 790 km west of Darwin respectively. The islands are small and uninhabited, consisting of sand and coral, surrounded by shoals and reefs. Grass is the main vegetation. Maximum elevation is about 2.5 m above sea-level. The islands abound in sea-cucumbers (*bêches-de-mer*) and, seasonally, turtles.

The United Kingdom took formal possession of the Ashmore Islands in 1878, and Cartier Island was annexed in 1909. The islands were placed under the authority of the Commonwealth of Australia in 1931. They were annexed to, and deemed to form part of, the Northern Territory of Australia in 1938. On 1 July 1978 the Australian government assumed direct responsibility for the administration of the islands, which rests with the minister for territories. Periodic visits are made to the islands by the Royal Australian Navy and aircraft of the Royal Australian Air Force, and the Civil Coastal Surveillance Service makes aerial surveys of the islands and neighbouring waters.

The area is thought to hold good prospects for petroleum exploration. In August 1983 Ashmore Reef was declared a national nature reserve.

Australian Antarctic Territory

The Australian Antarctic Territory was established by Order in Council, proclaimed in August 1936, subsequent to the Australian Antarctic Territory Acceptance Act (1933). It consists of the portion of Antarctica (divided by the French territory of Adélie Land) lying between 45°E and 136°E, and between 142°E and 160°E. The Australian National Antarctic Research Expeditions (ANARE) maintains three permanent scientific stations, Mawson, Davis and Casey, in the territory. The area of the territory is 6,120,000 sq km (2,320,000 sq miles).

Coral Sea Islands Territory

The Coral Sea Islands became a Territory of the Commonwealth of Australia under the Coral Sea Islands Act of 1969. It comprises several islands and reefs east of Queensland between the Great Barrier Reef and longitude 156° 06'E, and between latitude 12° and 24°S. The islands have been acquired by Australia by numerous acts of sovereignty since the early years of the 20th century.

Spread over a sea area of approximately 780,000 sq km (300,000 sq miles), all the islands and reefs in the Territory are very small, totalling only a few sq km of land area. They include Cato Island, Chilcott Islet in the Coringa Group, and the Willis Group. A meteorological station, operated by the Commonwealth Bureau of Meteorology and with a staff of three, has provided a service on one of the Willis Group since 1921. The other islands are uninhabited. There are six automatic weather stations distributed throughout the Territory.

The Act constituting the Territory did not establish an administration on the islands but provides means of controlling the activities of those who visit them. The Lihou Reef and Coringa-Herald National Nature Reserves were established in 1982 to provide protection for the wide variety of terrestrial and marine wildlife, which include rare species of birds and sea turtles. The increasing range and scope of international fishing enterprises made desirable an administrative framework and system of law. The Governor-General of Australia is empowered to make ordinances for the peace, order and good government of the Territory and, by ordinance, the laws of the Australian Capital Territory apply. The Supreme Court and Court of Petty Sessions of Norfolk Island have jurisdiction in relation to the Territory. The Minister for

AUSTRALIAN EXTERNAL TERRITORIES

Territories is responsible for matters affecting the Territory, and the area is visited regularly by the Royal Australian Navy.

Heard Island and McDonald Islands

These islands are situated about 4,000 km (2,500 miles) south-west of Perth, Western Australia, and have been administered by the Australian Government since 1947, when it established a scientific research station on Heard Island (which functioned until 1955). The area is 370 sq km (143 sq miles). There are no permanent inhabitants, but Australian expeditions visit the island from time to time. Heard Island is about 44 km (27 miles) long and 20 km (12 miles) wide. The McDonald Islands, with an area of about 1 sq km (0.4 sq mile), lie approximately 40 km (25 miles) west of Heard Island.

AUSTRIA

Introductory Survey

Location, Climate, Language, Religion, Flag, Capital

The Republic of Austria lies in central Europe, bordered by Switzerland and Liechtenstein to the west, by the Federal Republic of Germany and Czechoslovakia to the north, by Hungary to the east, and by Italy and Yugoslavia to the south. The climate varies sharply, owing to great differences in elevation. The mean annual temperature lies between 7° and 9°C (45° and 48°F). The population is 99% German-speaking, with small Croat and Slovene-speaking minorities. Almost all of the inhabitants profess Christianity: about 89% are Roman Catholics, while about 6% are Protestants. The national flag (proportions 3 by 2) consists of three equal horizontal stripes, of red, white and red. The state flag has, in addition, the coat of arms (a small shield, with horizontal stripes of red separated by a white stripe, superimposed on a black eagle, wearing a golden crown and holding a sickle and a hammer in its feet, with a broken chain between the legs) in the centre. The capital is Vienna (Wien).

Recent History

Austria was formerly the centre of the Austrian (later Austro-Hungarian) Empire, which comprised a large part of central Europe. The Empire, under the Habsburg dynasty, was dissolved in 1918, at the end of the First World War, and Austria proper became a republic. The first post-war Council of Ministers was a coalition led by Dr Karl Renner, who remained Chancellor until 1920, when a new constitution introduced a federal form of government. Most of Austria's inhabitants favoured union with Germany but this was forbidden by the post-war peace treaties. In March 1938, however, Austria was occupied by Nazi Germany's armed forces and incorporated into the German Reich.

After liberation by Allied forces, a provisional government, under Dr Renner, was established in April 1945. In July, following Germany's surrender, Austria was divided into four zones, occupied by forces of the USA, the USSR, the United Kingdom and France. These four approved the first post-war elections, held in November 1945, when the conservative Österreichische Volkspartei (ÖVP, Austrian People's Party) won 85, and the Sozialistische Partei Österreichs (SPÖ, Socialist Party of Austria) 76, of the 165 seats in the Nationalrat (National Council). These two parties formed a coalition government. In December Dr Renner became the first President of the second Austrian Republic, holding office until his death in December 1950. However, it was not until May 1955 that the four powers signed a State Treaty with Austria, ending the occupation and recognizing Austrian independence, effective from 27 July. Occupation forces left in October 1955.

More than 20 years of coalition government came to an end in April 1966 with the formation of a Council of Ministers by the ÖVP alone. Dr Josef Klaus, the Federal Chancellor since April 1964, remained in office. Dr Bruno Kreisky, a former Minister of Foreign Affairs, was elected leader of the SPÖ in 1967. The SPÖ achieved a relative majority in the March 1970 general elections and formed a minority government, with Kreisky as Chancellor. In April 1971 the incumbent President, Franz Jonas of the SPÖ, was re-elected, defeating the ÖVP candidate, Dr Kurt Waldheim, a former Minister of Foreign Affairs (who subsequently served two five-year terms as UN Secretary-General, beginning in January 1972). The SPÖ won an absolute majority of seats in the Nationalrat at general elections in October 1971 and October 1975. Meanwhile, President Jonas died in April 1974. A presidential election, held in June, was won by Dr Rudolf Kirchschläger, who had been Minister of Foreign Affairs since 1970. He took office for a six-year term, and was re-elected in 1980.

In November 1978 the Government was defeated in a national referendum on whether to commission Austria's first nuclear power plant, and it was widely expected that Kreisky would resign. However, the SPÖ gave him its full support and he emerged in an apparently even stronger position. The possible use of nuclear power remains a controversial issue. At the general election in May 1979 the SPÖ increased its majority in the Nationalrat. In January 1981 Kreisky announced a government reshuffle, following the resignation of the Vice-Chancellor and Minister of Finance, Hannes Androsch, who had been criticized for his personal financial practices. In January 1988 Androsch was found guilty of making false statements concerning his financial affairs, and was forced to resign from his post as director of a major bank.

The general election of April 1983 marked the end of the 13-year era of one-party government, when the SPÖ lost its absolute majority in the Nationalrat, and Kreisky, unwilling to participate in a coalition government, resigned as Chancellor. The reduction in the SPÖ's representation was partly attributed to the emergence of two environmentalist 'Green' parties, both founded in 1982. The two parties together received more than 3% of the total votes, but failed to win any seats. Kreisky's successor, Dr Fred Sinowatz (the former Vice-Chancellor and Minister of Education), took office in May, leading a coalition of the SPÖ and the small liberal Freiheitliche Partei Österreichs (FPÖ, Freedom Party of Austria). The new Government continued the social welfare policy of its predecessor, also maintaining Austria's foreign policy of 'active neutrality'.

A presidential election was held in 1986, when Dr Kirchschläger retired after two six-year terms of office as Head of State. The SPÖ candidate for the election was Dr Kurt Steyrer (the Minister of Health and Environment), while Dr Waldheim, the former UN Secretary-General, stood as an independent candidate but with the support of the ÖVP. There were also two other candidates: Freda Meissner-Blau, an environmentalist, and Otto Scrinzi, a right-wing nationalist. The campaign was dominated by allegations that Waldheim, a former officer in the army of Nazi Germany, had been implicated in atrocities committed by the Nazis in the Balkans in 1942–45, provoking a bitter controversy which divided the country and brought unexpected international attention to the election. No candidate achieved the required 50% of the vote at the first ballot on 4 May (Waldheim received 49.65% of the votes cast, while Steyrer received 43.67%); a second 'run-off' ballot between the two principal candidates was therefore held on 8 June. Waldheim then won a clear victory, with 53.89% of the votes, compared with Steyrer's 46.11%. The election of Waldheim, who took office in July, drew criticism from some foreign governments, and relations with Israel and the USA, in particular, were severely strained. Waldheim's presidency has remained controversial, both at home and abroad, and since his election he has been ostracized by large sections of the international community. In February 1988 a specially-appointed international commission of historians concluded that Waldheim must have been aware of the atrocities that had been committed, but the President refused to resign, despite a substantial decline in his popular support within the country. The issue inevitably provoked divisions within the ruling coalition, and ceremonies to mark the 50th anniversary of the occupation by Nazi Germany, held in March 1988, brought renewed attention to the question.

After the defeat of the SPÖ presidential candidate, Chancellor Sinowatz and four of his ministers resigned. Dr Franz Vranitzky, who had been Minister of Finance, became the new Chancellor, and replaced several ministers. In September the ruling coalition collapsed, when the FPÖ elected a new leader, Jörg Haider, who represented the right wing of his party. This precipitated the end of the partnership between the SPÖ and the FPÖ, and the general election for the Nationalrat, scheduled for April 1987, was brought forward to 23 November 1986. At the election no party won an absolute majority: the SPÖ won 80 seats, the ÖVP 77, the FPÖ 18 and the alliance of 'Green' parties 8. Dr Vranitzky tendered his resignation on 25 November, but was immediately requested by President Waldheim to initiate negotiations on the formation of a new coalition. The preceding Government remained in power while these negotiations took place. On 25 January 1987 the formation of a 'grand coalition' of the SPÖ and the ÖVP was announced.

AUSTRIA

Introductory Survey

The programme of the new Government focused on the reduction of the budget deficit and modernization of the economy; the improvement of the environment; electoral reform and widening the scope of direct democracy and civic rights; and Austria's standing abroad. At regional elections in Burgenland and municipal elections in Vienna in late 1987 the ÖVP suffered set-backs, while the FPÖ increased its representation in the two provincial assemblies.

Government

Austria is a federal republic, divided into nine provinces, each with its own provincial assembly and government. Legislative power is held by the bicameral Federal Assembly. The first chamber, the Nationalrat (National Council), has 183 members, elected by universal adult suffrage for four years (subject to dissolution) on the basis of proportional representation. The second chamber, the Bundesrat (Federal Council), has 63 members, elected for varying terms by the provincial assemblies. The Federal President, elected by popular vote for six years, is the Head of State, and normally acts on the advice of the Council of Ministers, led by the Federal Chancellor, which is responsible to the Nationalrat.

Defence

After the ratification of the State Treaty in 1955, Austria declared its permanent neutrality. To protect its independence, the armed forces were instituted. Military service is compulsory and consists of six months' initial training, followed by a maximum of 60 days' reservist training and 30 to 90 days' specialist training for 15 years. In June 1988 the total armed forces numbered 54,700 (including 27,300 conscripts), comprising an army of 50,000 (25,000 conscripts) and an air force of 4,700 (2,300 conscripts). Austrian air units are an integral part of the army. Total reserves are 242,000, of whom 70,000 undergo refresher training each year. The defence budget for 1988 amounted to 17,646m. Schilling.

Economic Affairs

In 1987, according to estimates by the World Bank, Austria's gross national product (GNP), measured at average 1985-87 prices, was US $90,484m., equivalent to $11,970 per head. GNP per head increased by an average of 1.7% per year between 1980 and 1987. The Austrian economy depends mainly on manufacturing, while agriculture is of declining importance. The proportion of the labour force in agriculture and forestry dropped steadily from 17.3% in 1971 to only 8.4% in 1987. The contribution of the agricultural sector to the gross domestic product (GDP) was 4.0% in 1984, falling to 3.4% by 1987. Austrian farms produce more than 90% of the country's food requirements, and surplus dairy products are exported.

Austria has iron ore and petroleum deposits, lignite, magnesite, lead and some copper. Hydroelectric power resources provide the major domestic source of energy, accounting for 71% of total electricity production in 1986, but the development of several big hydroelectric and nuclear power projects remains controversial, following protests by powerful environmentalist groups. Austria's electricity needs have grown considerably in recent years, and, as a result, the country is heavily dependent on imports of energy, mainly from the Eastern bloc.

After the Second World War, about one-quarter of Austrian industry was nationalized, including most of the heavy industry (particularly iron and steel, chemicals, non-ferrous metals, engineering and mining). The nationalized sector accounted for about 20% of industrial output in the late 1980s. During the 1980s the Government has given substantial financial support to ÖIAG, the state holding company, with subsidies to the group in 1981-85 totalling 12,500m. Schilling, but in 1987 ÖIAG announced losses of 8,000m. Schilling. The Government has implemented a major restructuring of the state sector, permitting the sale of shares in some nationalized companies to private or foreign partners, although ÖIAG is to maintain a controlling interest of at least 51%. The Government also agreed to provide further financial support to the nationalized industries, totalling 33,000m. Schilling during the period 1987-90. Most of this was destined for Voest-Alpine, the steel and engineering company, which recorded losses of 4,500m. Schilling in 1987. The labour force employed by the state sector was also to be reduced: Voest-Alpine alone planned to cut 10,000 jobs in 1987-90. The first partial privatization took place in November 1987, when 15% of ÖMV, the oil and gas group, was sold by the Government, and in June 1988 the State reduced its holding in Austrian Airlines from 99.2% to 75%. The Government is committed to continuing this programme: privatization of the state-owned electricity utility began in late 1988, and the country's two principal banks, Creditanstalt and Österreichische Länderbank, were also chosen for future flotation.

Industrial relations are good, in keeping with the traditional Austrian social consensus. Manufacturing employed 28.2% of the labour force in 1987, and provided 27.5% of GDP. Older industries, such as textiles, steel and machinery, have been declining in recent years, but new industries, such as chemicals, electronics and vehicles, have become significant. Industrial output rose by 4.5% in 1985, but by only 1% in 1986, and actually declined by 2% in 1987. Tourism is a leading source of external revenue, providing receipts of 105,000m. Schilling in 1987.

Austria's GDP grew by only 1.3% in 1987, after an increase of 1.7% in 1986. The average rate of unemployment was 5.2% in 1986 and 5.6% in 1987, and by May 1988 the rate stood at 4.7%. The Government has traditionally been committed to a policy of full employment, but the current restructuring of the state sector incorporates plans to reduce its labour force. Inflation averaged 3.2% in 1985 and 1.7% in 1986, falling to 1.4% in 1987; it was forecast to rise to 2% in 1988.

In 1986 the trade deficit increased to US $4,612m., from $4,406m. in 1985. In 1987 the deficit amounted to $4,471m.; in that year imports rose by less than 1%, while exports fell by about 1%. Energy imports generally account for around 90% of Austria's trade deficit. The current account of the balance of payments showed a deficit of 1,100m. Schilling in 1987, compared with a surplus of 2,600m. Schilling in 1986; a small deficit was forecast for 1988.

The federal budget deficit amounted to 5.1% of GDP in 1986 and 4.7% in 1987. The Government has set a target of reducing this proportion to 2.5% by 1992, and the 1988 budget included several measures to cut public spending, including a pay 'freeze' for the public sector, a reduction in pensions and cutbacks in some social services. In March 1988 the Government announced wide-ranging tax reforms, to be implemented from 1989. Provisions included reducing income tax brackets and raising taxes on tobacco and gambling.

Austria is a member of the European Free Trade Association (EFTA, see p. 152) and has a bilateral free trade agreement with the EEC, whose member states accounted for 68.0% of Austria's imports and 63.4% of exports in 1987. The Austrian Government has recognized that, after the implementation of the EEC's single European market (planned for 1992), Austrian traders may face competitive disadvantages, and in 1988 a commission was appointed in Vienna to consider the question of integration with the EEC.

Social Welfare

The social insurance system covers all wage-earners and salaried employees, agricultural and non-agricultural self-employed and dependants, regardless of nationality. The coverage is compulsory and provides earnings-related benefits in case of old age, invalidity, death, sickness, maternity and injuries at work. About 95% of the population are protected. There are separate programmes which provide unemployment insurance, family allowance, benefits for war victims, etc. In 1986 Austria had 79,083 hospital beds (one for every 96 inhabitants), and in 1987 there were 22,529 physicians working in the country. Health was allocated 12% of total central government expenditure in the 1986 budget, while social security and welfare accounted for 42%.

Education

The central controlling body is the Federal Ministry of Education, the Arts and Sport. Higher education and research are the responsibility of the Federal Ministry of Science and Research. Provincial boards (Landesschulräte) supervise school education in each of the nine federal provinces.

Education is free and compulsory between the ages of six and 15 years. All children undergo four years' primary education at a Volksschule, after which they choose between two principal forms of secondary education. This may be a Hauptschule which, after four years, may be followed by one of a variety of schools offering technical, vocational and other specialized training, some of which provide a qualification for university. Alternatively, secondary education may be obtained in an Allgemeinbildende höhere Schule, which provides an eight-year general education covering a wide range of subjects,

AUSTRIA

culminating in the Reifeprüfung or Matura. This gives access to all Austrian universities. Since 1977/78, however, all Austrian citizens over the age of 24, and with professional experience, may attend certain university courses in connection with their professional career or trade.

Opportunities for further education exist in six universities as well as 14 specialist colleges, all of which have university status, and schools of technology, art and music. Institutes of adult education (Volkshochschulen) are found in all provinces, as are other centres run by public authorities, church organizations and the Austrian Trade Union Federation.

Public Holidays

1989: 2 January (for New Year's Day), 6 January (Epiphany), 27 March (Easter Monday), 1 May (Labour Day), 4 May (Ascension Day), 15 May (Whit Monday), 25 May (Corpus Christi), 15 August (Assumption), 26 October (National Holiday), 1 November (All Saints' Day), 8 December (Immaculate Conception), 25 December (Christmas Day), 26 December (St Stephen's Day).

1990: 1 January (New Year's Day), 6 January (Epiphany), 16 April (Easter Monday), 1 May (Labour Day), 24 May (Ascension Day), 4 June (Whit Monday), 14 June (Corpus Christi), 15 August (Assumption), 26 October (National Holiday), 1 November (All Saints' Day), 8 December (Immaculate Conception), 25 December (Christmas Day), 26 December (St Stephen's Day).

Weights and Measures

The metric system is in force.

Statistical Survey

Source (unless otherwise stated): Austrian Central Statistical Office, 1033 Vienna, Hintere Zollamtsstr. 2B; tel. (01) 711-28; telex 132600.

Area and Population

AREA, POPULATION AND DENSITY

Area (sq km)	83,855*
Population (census results)	
12 May 1971	7,491,526†
12 May 1981‡	
Males	3,572,426
Females	3,982,912
Total	7,555,338
Population (official estimates at mid-year)‡	
1985	7,555,000
1986	7,565,000
1987	7,576,000
Density (per sq km) at mid-1987	90.3

* 32,377 sq miles.
† Total includes foreign workers with families abroad.
‡ Figures include all foreign workers.

PROVINCES

	Area (sq km)	Population (1987 annual average)	Density (per sq km)	Provincial Capital (with 1981 population)
Burgenland	3,965.4	266,900	67.3	Eisenstadt (10,102)
Kärnten (Carinthia)	9,533.8	541,900	56.8	Klagenfurt (87,321)
Niederösterreich (Lower Austria)	19,172.1	1,425,800	74.4	Sankt Pölten (50,419)*
Oberösterreich (Upper Austria)	11,979.6	1,294,200	108.0	Linz (199,910)
Salzburg	7,154.0	461,900	64.6	Salzburg (139,426)
Steiermark (Styria)	16,387.1	1,181,000	72.1	Graz (243,166)
Tirol (Tyrol)	12,647.1	609,800	48.2	Innsbruck (117,287)
Vorarlberg	2,601.3	314,400	120.9	Bregenz (24,561)
Wien (Vienna)*	414.9	1,479,800	3,566.6	—
Total	**83,855.3**	**7,575,700**	**90.3**	—

* Vienna, the national capital, has separate provincial status. The area and population of the city are not included in the province of Lower Austria, which is also administered from Vienna, pending the completion of provincial government buildings at Sankt Pölten, which became the provincial capital on 10 July 1986.

PRINCIPAL TOWNS (population at 1981 census)

Vienna (capital)	1,531,346	Klagenfurt	87,321
Graz	243,166	Villach	52,692
Linz	199,910	Wels	51,060
Salzburg	139,426	Sankt Pölten	50,419
Innsbruck	117,287	Steyr	38,942

BIRTHS, MARRIAGES AND DEATHS

	Registered live births		Registered marriages		Registered deaths	
	Number	Rate (per 1,000)	Number	Rate (per 1,000)	Number	Rate (per 1,000)
1980	90,872	12.1	46,435	6.2	92,442	12.3
1981	93,942	12.4	47,768	6.3	92,693	12.3
1982	94,840	12.5	47,643	6.3	91,339	12.1
1983	90,118	11.9	56,171	7.4	93,041	12.3
1984	89,234	11.8	45,823	6.1	88,466	11.7
1985	87,440	11.6	44,867	5.9	89,578	11.9
1986	86,964	11.5	45,821	6.1	87,071	11.5
1987	86,503	11.4	76,205	10.1	84,907	11.2

Expectation of life at birth: Males 71.5 years; females 78.2 years (1987).

ECONOMICALLY ACTIVE POPULATION
('000 persons, 1987 average*)

	Males	Females	Total
Agriculture, forestry, hunting and fishing	153	134	287
Mining and quarrying	14	1	15
Manufacturing	699	264	963
Construction	261	20	281
Electricity, gas, water and sanitary services	35	6	41
Commerce (incl. storage)	193	266	459
Transport and communications	181	40	222
Services	500	614	1,113
Other activities (not adequately described)	14	23	37
Total	**2,050**	**1,368**	**3,418**

* Yearly average based on the results of quarterly sample surveys.

Agriculture

PRINCIPAL CROPS ('000 metric tons)

	1985	1986	1987
Wheat	1,562.8	1,414.6	1,450
Barley	1,521.4	1,292.5	1,180
Maize	1,726.7	1,739.7	1,690
Rye	338.7	283.6	308
Oats	283.9	269.9	245
Mixed grain	117.7	108.0	85
Potatoes	1,042.2	982.4	879
Sugar beet	2,407.4	1,570.9	2,130
Apples	293.2	368.6	264
Pears	117.9	159.7	106
Plums	76.0	82.9	51
Cherries	22.8	24.7	24
Currants	28.9	26.8	15

Grapes ('000 metric tons): 170 in 1985; 320 in 1986; 311 in 1987 (unofficial estimates).

LIVESTOCK ('000 head at December)

	1985	1986	1987
Horses	44.9	43.6	45.2
Cattle	2,650.6	2,637.2	2,590.0
Pigs	3,925.9	3,800.5	3,950.0
Sheep	244.9	255.7	261.0
Goats	32.6	30.7	33.5
Chickens	14,439.8	14,197.8	14,500.0
Ducks	153.1	146.1	130.0
Geese	23.4	25.4	25.2
Turkeys	243.8	267.0	377.0

LIVESTOCK PRODUCTS ('000 metric tons)

	1985	1986	1987
Milk	3,797.0	3,776.5	3,720.0
Butter	43.5	45.5	41.0
Cheese	105	99.5	78.0
Hen eggs*	1,798	1,832.0	1,817.5
Beef	208	221.0	220.0
Veal	16.5	17.0	17.5
Pig meats	374.5	362.5	361.5
Poultry meat	79	81.5	84.0

* Millions.

Forestry

ROUNDWOOD REMOVALS
('000 cubic metres, excluding bark)

	1985	1986	1987
Sawlogs, veneer logs and logs for sleepers	6,548	6,745	6,688
Pitprops (mine timber), pulpwood, and other industrial wood	2,637	2,868	2,568
Fuel wood	2,441	2,518	2,504
Total	11,626	12,131	11,760

SAWNWOOD PRODUCTION ('000 cubic metres)

	1985	1986	1987
Coniferous sawnwood*	5,743	5,544	5,686
Broadleaved sawnwood*	222	204	199
Sub-total	5,965	5,748	5,885
Railway sleepers	37	35	24
Total	6,002	5,783	5,909

* Including boxboards.

Mining

('000 metric tons, unless otherwise indicated)

	1985	1986	1987
Brown coal (incl. lignite)	3,081	2,969	2,790
Crude petroleum	1,147	1,116	1,063
Iron ore:			
gross weight	3,270	3,120	3,050
metal content	1,019	976	949
Magnesite (crude)	1,225	1,084	947
Salt (unrefined)	734	743	703
Antimony ore (metric tons)*	550	558	399
Lead ore (metric tons)*	7,500	5,697	6,437
Tungsten (metric tons)*	1,565	n.a.	n.a.
Zinc ore (metric tons)*	24,259	17,844	16,983
Graphite (natural)	31	36	36
Gypsum (crude)	694	702	702
Kaolin	501	445	445
Talc	131	133	133
Natural gas (million cu metres)	1,164	1,112	1,167

* Figures refer to the metal content of ores.

AUSTRIA

Industry

SELECTED PRODUCTS ('000 metric tons, unless otherwise indicated)

	1985	1986	1987
Wheat flour	354	362	351
Raw sugar	431	283	359
Margarine (metric tons)	47,854	46,757	46,977
Wine ('000 hectolitres)	1,125.7	2,229.8	2,183.6
Beer ('000 hectolitres)	8,836	9,017	8,640
Cigarettes (million)	16,051	15,354	15,100
Cotton yarn—pure and mixed (metric tons)	15,056	15,298	18,362
Woven cotton fabrics—pure and mixed (metric tons)	16,363	15,625	18,078
Wool yarn—pure and mixed (metric tons)	9,122	8,834	7,367
Woven woollen fabrics—pure and mixed (metric tons)	4,426	4,289	3,652
Mechanical wood pulp	197	183	192
Chemical and semi-chemical wood pulp	1,124	1,162	728
Newsprint	241	234	246
Other printing and writing paper	850	873	989
Other paper	696	725	755
Paperboard	340	351	392
Nitrogenous fertilizers (metric tons)[1]	232,500	240,000	n.a.
Phosphate fertilizers (metric tons)[1]	99,100	75,300	n.a.
Plastics and resins	606	591	743
Liquefied petroleum gas	90	65	72
Motor spirit (petrol)[2]	2,078	2,095	2,325
Kerosene	7	6	4
Jet fuel	180	173	196
Distillate fuel oils	2,209	2,491	2,536
Residual fuel oils	2,408	2,032	1,864
Lubricating oils	86	227	—
Petroleum bitumen (asphalt)	225	235	228
Coke-oven coke	1,751	1,744	1,727
Cement	4,560	4,569	4,520
Pig-iron (excl. ferro-alloys)	3,704	3,349	3,451
Crude steel	4,660	4,292	4,301
Aluminium—unwrought (metric tons): primary	94,106	92,453	93,414
secondary[3]	79,703	81,013	62,731
Refined copper—unwrought (metric tons): primary	7,771	7,067	3,855
secondary	36,136	36,010	39,215
Refined lead—unwrought (metric tons): primary	6,415	6,064	6,809
secondary	13,281	12,743	16,032
Refined zinc—unwrought (metric tons): primary	18,973	18,369	18,282
secondary	1,523	1,084	1,467
Motorcycles, etc. ('000)	161	99	61
Construction: new dwellings completed (number)	41,143	38,838	38,494
Electric energy (million kWh)	44,534	44,653	50,518
Manufactured gas (million cu metres): from gasworks	38	36	37
from cokeries	702	722	712

[1] Estimated production during 12 months ending 30 June of the year stated. Figures for nitrogenous fertilizers are in terms of nitrogen, and those for phosphate fertilizers are in terms of phosphoric acid. Source: FAO, *Monthly Bulletin of Statistics*.
[2] Including aviation gasoline.
[3] Secondary aluminium produced from old scrap and remelted aluminium.

Finance

CURRENCY AND EXCHANGE RATES

Monetary Units
100 Groschen = 1 Schilling.

Denominations
Coins: 1, 2, 5, 10 and 50 Groschen; 1, 5, 10, 25, 50, 100, 500 and 1,000 Schilling.
Notes: 20, 50, 100, 500 and 1,000 Schilling.

Sterling and Dollar Equivalents (30 September 1988)
£1 sterling = 22.36 Schilling;
US $1 = 13.22 Schilling;
1,000 Schilling = £44.72 = $75.66.

Average Exchange Rate (Schilling per US $)
1985   20.690
1986   15.267
1987   12.643

FEDERAL BUDGET (million Schilling)

Revenue	1985	1986	1987*
Direct taxes on income and wealth	113,852	119,456	114,834
Social security contributions—unemployment insurance	18,736	19,969	20,747
Indirect taxes	131,562	137,349	143,111
Current transfers	15,320	11,854	19,324
Sales and charges	11,230	11,833	12,494
Interest, shares of profit and other income	12,325	12,278	16,636
Sales of assets	456	526	6,713
Repayments of loans granted	651	561	529
Capital transfers	1,168	1,157	733
Borrowing	89,644	125,205	113,090
Other revenue	1,584	6,071	4,866
Total	**396,528**	**446,259**	**453,077**

Expenditure	1985	1986	1987*
Current expenditure on goods and services	90,948	98,054	98,957
Interest on public debt	36,775	40,444	46,778
Current transfers to:			
Regional and local authorities	31,189	33,482	34,675
Other public bodies	52,808	56,651	63,058
Households	72,421	76,332	82,013
Other	37,369	45,079	44,163
Deficits of government enterprises	5,405	4,261	6,102
Gross capital formation	11,950	12,230	10,466
Capital transfers	16,834	18,083	13,920
Acquisition of assets	3,779	3,866	2,913
Loans granted	974	806	711
Debt redemption	31,659	33,625	35,105
Other expenditure	6,551	4,856	6,007
Total	**398,662**	**427,769**	**444,868**

* Preliminary figures.

NATIONAL BANK RESERVES
(US $ million at 31 December)

	1985	1986	1987
Gold*	2,283	2,888	3,523
IMF special drawing rights	210	186	292
Reserve position in IMF	445	442	468
Foreign exchange	4,112	5,534	6,772
Total	**7,050**	**9,050**	**11,055**

* Valued at 60,000 Schilling per kilogram.
Source: IMF, *International Financial Statistics*.

AUSTRIA

Statistical Survey

MONEY SUPPLY ('000 million Schilling at 31 December)

	1985	1986	1987
Currency outside banks	84.5	87.9	93.0
Demand deposits at deposit money banks	97.4	105.7	120.5
Total money	181.9	193.5	213.5

Source: IMF, *International Financial Statistics*.

COST OF LIVING (Consumer Price Index. Base: 1976 = 100)

	1985	1986	1987*
Food	144.4	147.9	100.7
Rent (incl. maintenance and repairs)	176.1	181.6	103.8
Fuel and light	194.3	180.3	94.7
Clothing	140.8	144.5	101.5
Total (incl. others)	152.9	155.5	101.4

* Base: 1986 = 100.

NATIONAL ACCOUNTS ('000 million Schilling at current prices)

National Income and Product

	1985	1986	1987
Compensation of employees	716.88	760.41	791.21
Operating surplus*	277.00	298.45	307.74
Domestic factor incomes	993.88	1,058.86	1,098.95
Consumption of fixed capital	167.53	176.20	183.87
Gross domestic product at factor cost	1,161.40	1,235.06	1,282.82
Indirect taxes	225.93	234.04	244.86
Less Subsidies	39.20	46.05	46.13
GDP in purchasers' values	1,348.13	1,423.05	1,481.56
Factor income received from abroad	66.49	58.45	56.94
Less Factor income paid abroad	73.56	70.41	69.52
Gross national product	1,341.06	1,411.08	1,468.98
Less Consumption of fixed capital	167.53	176.20	183.87
National income in market prices	1,173.54	1,234.89	1,285.10
Other current transfers from abroad	16.15	16.67	17.50
Less Other current transfers paid abroad	13.90	14.13	17.89
National disposable income	1,175.80	1,237.43	1,284.71

* Including a statistical discrepancy.

Expenditure on the Gross Domestic Product

	1985	1986	1987
Government final consumption expenditure	255.00	270.95	280.99
Private final consumption expenditure	775.04	803.34	830.07
Increase in stocks*	13.77	16.00	24.49
Gross fixed capital formation	301.99	319.58	334.14
Total domestic expenditure	1,345.81	1,409.88	1,469.69
Exports of goods and services	549.13	522.97	526.01
Less Imports of goods and services	546.81	509.80	514.13
GDP in purchasers' values	1,348.13	1,423.05	1,481.56
GDP at 1976 prices	878.84	890.80	904.47

* Including a statistical discrepancy.

Gross Domestic Product by Economic Activity

	1985	1986	1987
Agriculture, hunting, forestry and fishing	44.99	47.47	48.60
Mining and quarrying	5.87	5.81	6.37
Manufacturing	362.92	388.31	390.39
Electricity, gas and water	39.85	44.03	49.24
Construction	89.08	93.37	99.65
Wholesale and retail trade	169.88	174.25	178.87
Restaurants and hotels	44.96	49.76	52.04
Transport, storage and communications	78.46	81.52	86.28
Owner-occupied dwellings	86.63	96.16	101.01
Finance, insurance and real estate	117.31	126.07	134.05
Public administration and defence	185.07	197.09	206.00
Other community, social and personal services	47.02	50.82	54.64
Private non-profit services to households	9.60	10.10	10.61
Domestic services of households	0.64	0.69	0.66
Sub-total	1,282.28	1,365.45	1,418.41
Value-added tax	125.37	128.69	131.78
Import duties	9.08	9.00	9.86
Less Imputed bank service charges	68.56	75.07	80.46
Total*	1,348.13	1,423.05	1,481.56

* Including a statistical discrepancy.

BALANCE OF PAYMENTS (US $ million)

	1985	1986	1987
Merchandise exports f.o.b.	16,683	21,565	26,666
Merchandise imports f.o.b.	−21,089	−26,176	−31,137
Trade balance	−4,406	−4,612	−4,471
Exports of services	13,423	16,908	18,850
Imports of services	−9,198	−12,168	−14,576
Balance on goods and services	−181	128	−197
Private unrequited transfers (net)	−55	2	65
Government unrequited transfers (net)	−39	−44	−71
Current balance	−275	86	−203
Direct capital investment (net)	195	−39	136
Other long-term capital (net)	−291	641	1,589
Short-term capital (net)	−256	640	−1,435
Net errors and omissions	713	−600	314
Total (net monetary movements)	88	728	402
Monetization of gold	−68	−60	−84
Valuation changes (net)	500	723	1,049
Changes in reserves	520	1,392	1,367

Source: IMF, *International Financial Statistics*.

AUSTRIA

External Trade

Note: Austria's customs territory excludes Mittelberg im Kleinen Walsertal (in Vorarlberg) and Jungholz (in Tyrol). The figures also exclude trade in silver specie and monetary gold.

PRINCIPAL COMMODITIES
(distribution by SITC, million Schilling)

Imports c.i.f.	1985	1986	1987
Food and live animals	23,478.6	23,302.6	21,962.0
Vegetables and fruit	8,083.1	7,706.1	8,219.0
Coffee, tea, cocoa and spices	6,401.6	6,613.2	4,556.8
Crude materials (inedible) except fuels	27,138.4	22,280.2	21,301.4
Metalliferous ores and metal scrap	7,684.2	5,018.1	4,257.0
Mineral fuels, lubricants, etc. (incl. electric current)	64,092.2	35,355.0	29,808.6
Coal, coke and briquettes	8,647.1	6,934.6	5,614.0
Petroleum, petroleum products, etc.	41,564.6	19,451.8	18,594.2
Crude petroleum oils, etc.	26,768.0	11,340.8	10,943.7
Refined petroleum products	12,996.9	7,070.7	6,687.1
Gas (natural and manufactured)	12,992.9	7,847.3	4,825.2
Petroleum gases, etc., in the gaseous state	12,227.3	7,469.1	4,488.2
Chemicals and related products	43,034.3	41,142.7	42,428.2
Organic chemicals	7,297.5	5,586.3	5,884.1
Medicinal and pharmaceutical products	7,002.3	7,237.7	7,920.3
Artificial resins, plastic materials, etc.	12,243.7	12,277.8	12,751.3
Products of polymerization, etc.	7,975.4	7,787.6	8,095.1
Basic manufactures	78,301.6	78,389.8	78,950.0
Paper, paperboard and manufactures	7,002.1	7,310.1	7,795.6
Textile yarn, fabrics, etc.	18,707.5	18,744.0	18,870.5
Non-metallic mineral manufactures	7,084.6	7,374.9	7,914.7
Iron and steel	12,107.4	12,186.5	10,953.9
Non-ferrous metals	10,365.3	8,929.2	8,681.6
Other metal manufactures	13,738.7	14,555.2	14,850.1
Machinery and transport equipment	128,610.9	137,905.4	143,082.2
Power generating machinery and equipment	7,233.9	7,512.2	7,324.8
Machinery specialized for particular industries	14,639.1	15,040.8	16,904.4
General industrial machinery, equipment and parts	20,636.2	22,253.9	22,980.9
Office machines and automatic data processing equipment	11,415.0	12,422.0	11,606.1
Telecommunications and sound equipment	6,967.8	8,529.0	10,048.3
Other electrical machinery, apparatus, etc.	23,610.9	23,684.5	25,816.6
Road vehicles and parts*	37,551.4	41,534.4	40,477.1
Passenger motor cars (excl. buses)	23,226.2	26,458.8	23,969.9
Parts and accessories for cars, buses, lorries, etc.*	6,038.3	6,319.7	6,696.2
Miscellaneous manufactured articles	61,974.7	65,907.1	71,097.3
Furniture and parts	6,214.5	6,554.8	7,433.0
Clothing and accessories (excl. footwear)	18,265.1	19,547.9	21,579.6
Professional, scientific and controlling instruments, etc.	6,481.8	7,136.8	7,356.2
Photographic apparatus, etc., optical goods, watches and clocks	5,767.4	5,964.7	5,957.6
Total (incl. others)	430,969.3	407,954.1	411,858.8

* Excluding tyres, engines and electrical parts.

Exports f.o.b.	1985	1986	1987
Food and live animals	13,480.6	12,104.9	10,661.3
Crude materials (inedible) except fuels	19,288.5	18,093.6	18,222.0
Cork and wood	9,127.2	8,688.7	8,762.0
Simply worked wood and railway sleepers	8,097.8	7,736.1	7,888.0
Simply worked coniferous wood	7,698.6	7,370.1	7,515.2
Sawn coniferous wood	7,499.6	7,129.4	7,228.0
Chemicals and related products	32,354.5	29,637.4	30,765.3
Organic chemicals	5,883.5	4,937.2	4,984.0
Artificial resins, plastic materials, etc.	10,498.9	9,583.7	10,917.5
Products of polymerization, etc.	7,459.9	6,366.9	7,681.5
Basic manufactures	119,785.8	112,521.9	112,907.4
Paper, paperboard and manufactures	19,864.3	19,126.2	20,165.5
Paper and paperboard (not cut to size or shape)	14,195.6	13,897.7	14,822.4
Printing and writing paper in bulk (incl. newsprint)	9,981.8	9,771.1	10,659.4
Textile yarn, fabrics, etc.	19,193.8	18,665.6	18,350.3
Non-metallic mineral manufactures	11,682.2	11,633.4	11,476.4
Iron and steel	31,514.5	26,291.6	25,490.4
Universals, plates and sheets	11,014.7	10,065.1	9,917.4
Tubes, pipes and fittings	7,127.6	5,601.2	5,517.5
Non-ferrous metals	8,375.5	7,321.1	8,021.0
Aluminium and aluminium alloys	5,484.4	5,132.5	5,300.0
Other metal manufactures	17,029.7	16,785.1	16,422.1
Machinery and transport equipment	110,801.8	113,744.3	114,530.2
Power generating machinery and equipment	14,246.1	16,035.5	17,036.8
Internal combustion piston engines and parts	10,641.0	12,543.6	12,794.3
Engines for road vehicles, tractors, etc.	9,381.1	11,156.5	11,264.0
Machinery specialized for particular industries	20,338.0	20,282.2	20,302.9
General industrial machinery, equipment and parts	19,550.1	19,718.4	19,000.3
Telecommunications and sound equipment	9,301.6	11,230.9	11,325.9
Other electrical machinery, apparatus, etc.	21,972.0	22,161.0	23,944.7
Road vehicles and parts (excl. tyres, engines and electrical parts)	15,010.6	14,912.4	14,179.0
Miscellaneous manufactured articles	48,713.4	50,737.2	47,846.6
Clothing and accessories (excl. footwear)	11,802.4	12,175.2	12,075.5
Footwear	6,042.9	5,427.3	4,739.8
Total (incl. others)	353,962.4	342,478.7	342,433.4

AUSTRIA

PRINCIPAL TRADING PARTNERS* (million Schilling)

Imports c.i.f.	1985	1986	1987
Algeria	3,428.7	1,696.7	1,291.0
Belgium/Luxembourg	9,156.7	9,850.6	9,985.8
Brazil	3,724.1	2,335.0	2,007.1
Czechoslovakia	8,329.0	6,540.6	5,917.7
France	15,636.4	15,988.7	16,687.1
Germany, Federal Republic	176,384.5	179,461.9	181,950.9
Hungary	8,501.9	6,647.7	6,178.1
Italy	35,466.5	36,500.9	38,674.0
Japan	14,149.9	17,881.0	17,945.7
Libya	4,511.5	3,828.2	3,200.5
Netherlands	11,401.6	11,288.1	11,369.9
Nigeria	4,555.0	1,598.8	1,047.9
Poland	4,773.4	4,341.4	4,017.1
Saudi Arabia	2,340.4	798.4	504.7
Sweden	7,781.2	7,141.1	7,234.7
Switzerland	19,435.5	19,750.6	19,401.1
USSR	19,150.9	12,497.0	8,501.4
United Kingdom	9,816.7	9,355.5	9,886.7
USA	16,044.4	13,111.7	14,236.7
Yugoslavia	4,749.4	3,974.7	3,929.0
Total (incl. others)	430,969.3	407,954.1	411,858.8

* Imports by country of production; exports by country of consumption.

Exports f.o.b.	1985	1986	1987
Algeria	3,731.9	2,203.3	1,080.0
Belgium/Luxembourg	8,017.2	8,965.6	8,130.0
Czechoslovakia	3,888.2	3,992.9	3,935.6
Denmark	3,846.4	4,103.9	3,811.8
France	14,023.0	14,725.8	15,349.3
German Democratic Republic	4,413.9	3,786.7	5,970.4
Germany, Federal Republic	106,618.8	112,142.7	119,271.2
Hungary	9,162.2	7,804.8	6,624.0
Iran	3,602.6	1,999.0	1,733.6
Iraq	4,214.6	2,263.4	1,211.6
Italy	31,772.1	31,765.1	35,492.3
Netherlands	8,337.7	8,816.7	9,214.0
Poland	4,288.5	3,433.3	2,985.8
Saudi Arabia	3,770.6	2,642.8	1,482.9
Spain (excl. Canary Is.)	5,592.2	6,523.8	6,271.1
Sweden	6,563.3	6,786.6	6,672.5
Switzerland	23,878.7	26,832.4	25,385.6
USSR	13,409.9	10,483.1	8,503.1
United Kingdom	16,277.0	15,296.7	15,649.6
USA	16,504.2	13,796.5	12,185.2
Yugoslavia	8,249.0	3,674.0	6,780.8
Total (incl. others)	353,962.4	342,478.7	342,433.4

Transport

RAILWAYS (Federal Railways only)

	1985	1986	1987
Passenger-km (millions)	7,290	7,332	7,434
Freight (net ton-km) (millions)	11,903	11,273	11,008
Freight tons carried ('000)	58,209	58,073	54,730

ROAD TRAFFIC (motor vehicles in use at 31 December)

	1985	1986	1987
Private cars	2,530,800	2,609,390	2,684,780
Buses and coaches	9,183	9,209	9,267
Goods vehicles	206,746	212,463	221,139
Motorcycles and scooters	84,640	85,952	87,980
Mopeds	563,756	543,151	522,115

SHIPPING (freight traffic in '000 metric tons)

	1985	1986	1987
Goods loaded	2,122	1,931	1,846
Goods unloaded	4,873	5,249	5,418

CIVIL AVIATION (Austrian Airlines, '000)

	1985	1986	1987
Kilometres flown	23,022	23,656	24,656
Passenger ton-km	132,021	127,442	152,184
Cargo ton-km	18,516	18,788	19,056
Mail ton-km	4,150	4,067	3,978

Tourism

FOREIGN TOURIST ARRIVALS (by country of origin)

	1985	1986	1987
Belgium-Luxembourg	339,113	329,554	348,000
France	664,933	722,937	692,000
Germany, Federal Republic	8,145,318	8,393,619	8,450,000
Italy	543,756	641,313	695,000
Netherlands	1,247,378	1,243,350	1,301,000
Switzerland	457,955	530,175	575,000
United Kingdom	785,973	772,650	762,000
USA	987,722	509,472	672,000
Total (incl. others)	15,167,830	15,092,283	15,761,400

Communications Media

	1985	1986	1987
Telephones in use	2,729,389	2,818,437	2,907,000
Radio licences issued	2,627,297	2,639,497	2,690,871
Television licences issued	2,425,920	2,434,250	2,483,846
Book titles produced	9,339	10,281	9,786

1986: Non-daily newspapers 152; Other periodicals 2,123.
1987: Daily newspapers 32 (average circulation 2,646,814).

Education
(1987/88)

	Institutions	Staff	Students
Primary	3,394	28,652	350,907
General secondary	2,048	57,233	462,975
Compulsory vocational	1,160	21,713	331,204
Teacher training: second level	35	838	8,575
third level	26	1,894	7,050
Universities and other higher schools	18	10,517	175,510

Directory

The Constitution

The Austrian Constitution of 1920, as amended in 1929, was restored on 1 May 1945. Its main provisions are summarized below:

Austria is a democratic republic, having a president (Bundespräsident), elected directly by the people, and a two-chamber legislature, the Federal Assembly. The republic is organized on the federal system, comprising the provinces (Länder) of Burgenland, Carinthia, Lower Austria, Upper Austria, Salzburg, Styria, Tyrol, Vorarlberg and Vienna. There is universal suffrage for men and women who are more than 19 years of age.

The Nationalrat (National Council) consists of 183 members, elected by universal direct suffrage, according to a system of proportional representation. It functions for a period of four years.

The Bundesrat (Federal Council) represents the federal provinces. Vienna sends 12 members, Lower Austria 12, Upper Austria 10, Styria 10, Carinthia 4, Tyrol 5, Salzburg 4, Burgenland and Vorarlberg 3 each, making 63 in all. The seats are divided between the parties according to the number of seats they hold in the provincial assemblies and are held during the life of the provincial government which they represent. Each province in turn provides the chairman for six months.

For certain matters of special importance the two chambers meet together; this is known as a Bundesversammlung.

The President, elected by popular vote, is the Head of State and holds office for six years. The President is eligible for re-election only once in succession. Although invested with special emergency powers, the President normally acts on the authority of the Government, and it is the Government which is responsible to the National Council for governmental policy.

The Government consists of the Chancellor, the Vice-Chancellor and the other ministers, who may vary in number. The Chancellor is chosen by the President, usually from the party with the strongest representation in the newly-elected National Council, and the other ministers are then chosen by the President on the advice of the Chancellor.

If the National Council passes an explicit vote of 'no confidence' in the Federal Government or individual members thereof, the Federal Government or the Federal Minister concerned shall be removed from office.

All new acts must be read and put to the vote in both houses. A new bill goes first to the National Council, where it usually has three readings, and secondly to the Federal Council, where it can be held up, but not vetoed.

The Constitution also provides for appeals by the Government to the electorate on specific points by means of referendum. There is further provision that if 200,000 or more electors present a petition to the Government, the Government must lay it before the National Council.

The Landtag (Provincial Assembly) exercises the same functions in each province as the National Council does in the State. The members of the Landtag elect a government (Landesregierung) consisting of a provincial governor (Landeshauptmann) and his councillors (Landesräte). They are responsible to the Landtag.

The spheres of legal and administrative competence of both national and provincial governments are clearly defined. The Constitution distinguishes four groups:

1. Law-making and administration are the responsibility of the State: e.g. foreign affairs, justice and finance.

2. Law-making is the responsibility of the State, administration is the responsibility of the provinces: e.g. elections, population matters and road traffic.

3. The State lays down the rudiments of the law, the provinces make the law and administer it: e.g. charity, rights of agricultural workers, land reform.

4. Law-making and administration are the responsibility of the provinces in all matters not expressly assigned to the State: e.g. municipal affairs, building theatres and cinemas.

The Government

HEAD OF STATE

Federal President: Dr KURT WALDHEIM (sworn in 8 July 1986).

COUNCIL OF MINISTERS
(November 1988)

A coalition of the Socialist Party of Austria (SPÖ) and the Austrian People's Party (ÖVP).

Federal Chancellor: Dr FRANZ VRANITZKY (SPÖ).
Vice-Chancellor and Minister of Foreign Affairs: Dr ALOIS MOCK (ÖVP).
Minister of Economic Affairs: ROBERT GRAF (ÖVP).
Minister of the Interior: KARL BLECHA (SPÖ).
Minister of Agriculture and Forestry: Dipl.-Ing. JOSEF RIEGLER (ÖVP).
Minister of the Public Sector and Transport: Dipl.-Ing. Dr RUDOLF STREICHER (SPÖ).
Minister of Justice: Dr EGMONT FOREGGER (Independent).
Minister of Employment and Social Affairs: ALFRED DALLINGER (SPÖ).
Minister of Finance: Dkfm. FERDINAND LACINA (SPÖ).
Minister of National Defence: Dr ROBERT LICHAL (ÖVP).
Minister of Science and Research: Dr HANS TUPPY (ÖVP).
Minister of Education, the Arts and Sport: Dr HILDE HAWLICEK (SPÖ).
Minister of Environment, Youth and Family: Dr MARILIES FLEMMING (ÖVP).
Minister of the Federal Chancellery (Health and Public Service): Dr FRANZ LÖSCHNAK (SPÖ).
Secretary of State to the Federal Chancellery: JOHANNA DOHNAL (SPÖ).
Minister of the Federal Chancellery (Federalism and Administrative Reform): Dr HEINRICH NEISSER (ÖVP).
Secretary of State in the Ministry of Finance: Dr GÜNTHER STUMMVOLL (ÖVP).

MINISTRIES

Office of the Federal Chancellor: 1014 Vienna, Ballhausplatz 2; tel. (01) 53-11-50; telex 1370900.
Ministry of Agriculture and Forestry: 1010 Vienna, Stubenring 1; tel. (01) 75-0-00.
Ministry of Economic Affairs: 1010 Vienna, Stubenring 1; tel. (01) 75-0-00; telex 111780.
Ministry of Education, the Arts and Sport: 1014 Vienna, Minoritenplatz 5; tel. (01) 53-1-20.
Ministry of Employment and Social Affairs: 1010 Vienna, Stubenring 1; tel. (01) 75-0-00.
Ministry of Environment, Youth and Family: 1031 Vienna, Radetzkystr. 2; tel. (01) 71-1-58; telex 3221371.
Ministry of Finance: 1010 Vienna, Himmelpfortgasse 4-8B; tel. (01) 51-4-33; telex 111688.
Ministry of Foreign Affairs: 1014 Vienna, Ballhausplatz 2; tel. (01) 53115; telex 01371.
Ministry of the Interior: 1014 Vienna, Herrengasse 7; tel. (01) 66-2-60.
Ministry of Justice: 1074 Vienna, Museumstr. 7; tel. (01) 96-2-20.
Ministry of National Defence: 1031 Vienna, Dampfschiffstr. 2; tel. (01) 51595; telex 112145.
Ministry of the Public Sector and Transport: 1030 Vienna, Radetzkystr. 2; tel. (01) 75-76-31; telex 111800.
Ministry of Science and Research: 1014 Vienna, Minoritenplatz 5; tel. (01) 53-1-20; telex 111157.

President and Legislature

PRESIDENT

Presidential Election, First Ballot, 4 May 1986

Candidates	Votes	%
Dr KURT WALDHEIM	2,343,387	49.65
Dr KURT STEYRER (SPÖ)	2,061,162	43.67
FREDA MEISSNER-BLAU	259,471	5.49
OTTO SCRINZI	55,940	1.18

Second Ballot, 8 June 1986

Candidates	Votes	%
Dr KURT WALDHEIM	2,460,203	53.89
Dr KURT STEYRER (SPÖ)	2,105,118	46.11

AUSTRIA

NATIONALRAT
President of the Nationalrat: LEOPOLD GRATZ.

General Election, 23 November 1986

	Votes	% of Total	Seats
Socialist Party (SPÖ)	2,092,024	43.12	80
People's Party (ÖVP)	2,003,663	41.30	77
Freedom Party (FPÖ)	472,205	9.73	18
United Green Party/ Alternative List (VGÖ/ALÖ)	234,028	4.82	8

BUNDESRAT
(September 1988)

President of the Bundesrat: Dr HELMUT FRAUSCHER (Jan.–June 1989).

Provinces	Total seats	SPÖ	ÖVP	FPÖ
Burgenland	3	2	1	—
Carinthia	4	3	1	—
Lower Austria	12	5	7	—
Upper Austria	10	4	6	—
Salzburg	4	2	2	—
Styria	10	4	6	—
Tyrol	5	1	4	—
Vorarlberg	3	1	2	—
Vienna	12	8	3	1
Total	63	30	32	1

Political Organizations

Alternative Liste Österreich (ALÖ) (Austrian Alternative List): 1050 Vienna, Margarethen-Gürtel 122–124/1/K; tel. (01) 54-23-07; f. 1982; radical ecologist party, linked to the anti-nuclear Green Party in the Federal Republic of Germany; aims for an alternative energy policy; Leader DORIS EISENRIEGLER.

Freiheitliche Partei Österreichs (FPÖ) (Freedom Party of Austria): 1010 Vienna I, Kärntnerstr. 28; f. 1955; Liberal party which partially succeeds the Verband der Unabhängigen (League of Independents), dissolved in 1956, and stands for moderate social reform, for the participation of workers in management, for European co-operation and for good relations with all the countries of Free Europe; Chair. Dr JÖRG HAIDER; Leader of Parliamentary Group Abg. Dr FRIEDHELM FRISCHENSCHLAGER.

Die Grüne Alternative (Grüne) (The Green Alternative): 1060 Vienna, Millergasse 40/9; tel. (01) 59-79-181; f. 1986; campaigns for environmental protection, peace and social justice; Leaders FREDA MEISSNER-BLAU, Mag. WALTER GEYER.

Kommunistische Partei Österreichs (KPÖ) (Communist Party of Austria): 1206 Vienna, Höchstädtplatz 3; tel. (01) 33-46-11; telex 114082; f. 1918; strongest in the industrial centres and trade unions; advocates a policy of strict neutrality and friendly relations with neighbouring states and with the USSR; Chair. FRANZ MUHRI; Secs HANS KALT, Dr WALTER SILBERMAYR.

Nationale Demokratische Partei (NDP) (National Democratic Party of Austria): 1030 Vienna, Landstrassergürtel 19/3; extreme right-wing party; Chair. Dr NORBERT BURGER.

Österreichische Volkspartei (ÖVP) (Austrian People's Party): 1010 Vienna I, Kärntnerstr. 51; f. 1945; Christian-Democratic party; the 'Salzburg programme' (1972) defines it as 'progressive centre party'; 760,000 mems; Chair. Dr ALOIS MOCK; Sec.-Gen. HELMUT KUKACKA.

Sozialistische Partei Österreichs (SPÖ) (Socialist Party of Austria): 1014 Vienna I, Löwelstr. 18; tel. (01) 63-27-31; telex 114198; founded as the Social-Democratic Party in 1889; advocates democratic socialism and Austria's permanent neutrality; 700,000 mems; Chair. Dr FRANZ VRANITZKY; Secs GÜNTHER SALLABERGER, JOSEF CAP.

Vereinte Grüne Österreichs (VGÖ) (United Green Party of Austria): 4020 Linz, Göthestr. 9; tel. (0732) 66-83-91; f. 1982; ecologist party; Chair. JOSEF BUCHNER; Gen. Sec. WOLFGANG PELIKAN.

Diplomatic Representation

EMBASSIES IN AUSTRIA

Afghanistan: 1020 Vienna, Taborstr. 12; tel. (01) 24-24-12; Ambassador: (vacant).

Albania: 1030 Vienna, Jacquingasse 41; tel. (01) 78-37-95; telex 133248; Ambassador: ENGJËLL KOLONECI.

Algeria: 1010 Vienna, Rudolfinergasse 18; tel. (01) 36-88-53; telex 134163; Ambassador: HOCINE MESLOUB.

Argentina: 1010 Vienna, Goldschmiedgasse 2/1; tel. (01) 63-85-77; telex 114512; Ambassador: Dr ROBERTO ENRIQUE GUYER.

Australia: 1040 Vienna, Mattiellistr. 2–4/III; tel. (01) 512-85-80; telex 74313; Ambassador: JOHN ROBERT KELSO.

Belgium: 1040 Vienna, Operngasse 20B; tel. (01) 56-75-79; telex 113364; Ambassador: Graf FRANCIS DE LA BARRE D'ERQUELINNES.

Bolivia: 1010 Vienna, Doblhofgasse 3/8; tel. (01) 484412; telex 131556; Ambassador: ORLANDO DONOSO.

Brazil: 1010 Vienna, Lugeck 1/V/15; tel. (01) 512-06-310; telex 111925; Ambassador: JOÃO TABAJARA DE OLIVEIRA.

Bulgaria: 1040 Vienna, Schwindgasse 8; tel. (01) 65-64-44; Ambassador: CHRISTO DORTSCHEV.

Canada: 1010 Vienna, Luegerring 10/IV; tel. (01) 63-36-91; telex 75320; Ambassador: MICHAEL SHENSTONE.

Chile: 1010 Vienna, Lugeck 1/III/9; tel. (01) 512-33-70; telex 75952; Ambassador: RAFAEL ENRIQUE ORTIZ NAVARRO.

China, People's Republic: 1030 Vienna, Metternichgasse 4; tel. (01) 75-31-49; telex 135794; Ambassador: YANG CHENGXU.

Colombia: 1010 Vienna, Stadiongasse 6–8; tel. (01) 42-42-49; telex 116798; Ambassador: Dr MARIO LASERNA PINZÓN.

Côte d'Ivoire: 1090 Vienna, Alser Str. 28; tel. (01) 48-37-23; Ambassador: ADONIT MANOUAN.

Cuba: 1130 Vienna, Eitelbergergasse 24; tel. (01) 82-81-98; telex 131398; Ambassador: GUSTAVO MAZORRA HERNÁNDEZ.

Czechoslovakia: 1140 Vienna, Penzinger Str. 11–13; tel. (01) 82-26-29; telex 131702; Ambassador: MILAN RUSŇÁK.

Denmark: 1015 Vienna, Führichgasse 6; tel. (01) 512-79-04; telex 113261; Ambassador: JENS CHRISTENSEN.

Ecuador: 1010 Vienna, Goldschmiedgasse 10/II/24; tel. (01) 535-32-08; telex 134958; Ambassador: Dr JULIO CORREA PAREDES.

Egypt: 1190 Vienna, Gallmeyergasse 5; tel. (01) 36-11-34; telex 15623; Ambassador: Dr MOHAMED IBRAHIM SHAKER.

Finland: 1020 Vienna, Untere Donaustr. 13–15; tel. (01) 24-75-21; telex 135230; Ambassador: MATTI KAHILUOTO.

France: 1040 Vienna, Technikerstr. 2; tel. (01) 65-47-47; Ambassador: JEAN NOIVILLE.

German Democratic Republic: 1130 Vienna, Frimbergergasse 6–8; tel. (01) 82-36-54; telex 133591; Ambassador: KLAUS WOLF.

Germany, Federal Republic: 1030 Vienna, Metternichgasse 3; tel. (01) 71-1-54; telex 134261; Ambassador: DIETRICH Graf VON BRÜHL.

Greece: 1040 Vienna, Argentinierstr. 14; tel. (01) 65-57-91; telex 133176; Ambassador: GEORGES CLADAKIS.

Guatemala: 1010 Vienna, Opernring I/R/4/407; tel. (01) 56-91-01; Ambassador: EDUARDO CASTILLO ARRIOLA.

Holy See: 1040 Vienna, Theresianumgasse 31; tel. (01) 505-13-27; Apostolic Nuncio: Mgr MICHELE CECCHINI.

Hungary: 1010 Vienna, Bankgasse 4–6; tel. (01) 63-26-31; telex 135546; Ambassador: JÁNOS NAGY.

India: 1015 Vienna, Kärntner Ring 2; tel. (01) 65-86-66; telex 113721; Ambassador: JAGDISH RUDRAYA HIREMATH.

Indonesia: 1180 Vienna, Gustav-Tschermak-Gasse 5–7; tel. (01) 34-25-34; telex 115579; Ambassador: S. WIRYONO.

Iran: 1030 Vienna, Jaurèsgasse 3; tel. (01) 72-26-50; telex 131718; Ambassador: HUSSEIN NOQREKAR SHIRAZI.

Iraq: 1010 Vienna, Johannesgasse 26; tel. (01) 73-81-95; telex 135397; Ambassador: Dr WAHBI ABDEL RAZZAK AL-QARAGULI.

Ireland: 1030 Vienna, Hilton Centre; tel. (01) 75-42-46; telex 136887; Ambassador: JOSEPH SMALL.

Israel: 1180 Vienna, Anton Frank-Gasse 20; tel. (01) 31-15-06; telex 4005; Ambassador: (vacant).

Italy: 1030 Vienna, Rennweg 27; tel. (01) 75-51-21; telex 132620; Ambassador: GIROLAMO NISIO.

Japan: 1040 Vienna, Argentinierstr. 21; tel. (01) 501-71-0; telex 135810; Ambassador: ATSUHIKO YATABE.

Korea, Democratic People's Republic: 1140 Vienna, Beckmanngasse 10–12; tel. (01) 89-23-11; telex 131750; Ambassador: CHO GI CHOL.

AUSTRIA

Directory

Korea, Republic: 1030 Vienna, Kelsenstr. 2; tel. (01) 78-63-18; telex 131252; Ambassador: LEE SIE-YONG.
Kuwait: 1010 Vienna, Universitätsstr. 5; tel. (01) 42-56-46; telex 135898; Ambassador: ABDUL-HAMID ABDULLAH AL-AWADHI.
Lebanon: 1010 Vienna, Schwedenplatz 2/15; tel. (01) 63-88-21; telex 115273; Chargé d'affaires: CHRISTIANE GEZRAWI-BASSILE.
Libya: 1170 Vienna, Dornbacherstr. 27; tel. (01) 45-36-11; telex 116267; Secretary of People's Bureau: ENBEIA MANSUR WADI.
Luxembourg: 1190 Vienna, Hofzeile 27; tel. (01) 36-21-86; telex 115276; Ambassador: EDOUARD MOLITOR.
Malaysia: 1040 Vienna, Prinz Eugen-Str. 18; tel. (01) 505-10-42; telex 133830; Ambassador: ABDUL HALIM BIN ALI.
Mexico: 1040 Vienna, Renngasse 4; tel. (01) 535-17-76; telex 115660; Ambassador: CUEVAS CANCINO.
Morocco: 1020 Vienna, Untere Donaustr. 13–15; tel. (01) 24-25-68; Ambassador: TAOUFIK KABBAJ.
Netherlands: 1020 Vienna, Untere Donaustr. 13–15/VIII; tel. (01) 24-85-87; telex 135462; Ambassador: LODEWIJK H. J. B. VAN GORKOM.
New Zealand: 1010 Vienna, Lugeck 1; tel. (01) 52-66-36; telex 136582; Ambassador: DONALD JAMES WALKER.
Nicaragua: 1010 Vienna, Schwedenplatz 2/7/64; tel. (01) 63-81-13; Ambassador: IVÁN MEJÍA-SOLÍS.
Nigeria: 1030 Vienna, Rennweg 25; tel. (01) 72-66-85; telex 131583; Ambassador: TIMOTHY ANAELE MGBOKWERE.
Norway: 1030 Vienna, Bayerngasse 3; tel. (01) 75-66-92; telex 132768; Ambassador: KNUT HEDEMANN.
Oman: 1090 Vienna, Währingerstr. 2-4/24–25; tel. (01) 31-64-52; telex 116662; Chargé d'affaires: MUNIR A. MAKKI.
Pakistan: 1190 Vienna, Hofzeile 13; tel. (01) 36-73-81; telex 135634; Ambassador: Dr KHURSHID HYDER.
Panama: 1030 Vienna, Strohgasse 3516; tel. (01) 73-46-33; Ambassador: ERNESTO KOREF.
Peru: 1030 Vienna, Gottfried-Keller-Gasse 2; tel. (01) 73-43-77; telex 135524; Ambassador: JORGE MORELLI PANDO.
Philippines: 1190 Vienna, Nedergasse 34; tel. (01) 31-59-30; Ambassador: NELSON D. LAVIÑA.
Poland: 1130 Vienna, Hietzinger Hauptstr. 42c; tel. (01) 82-74-44; Ambassador: MARIAN KRZAK.
Portugal: 1040 Vienna, Operngasse 20B; tel. (01) 56-75-36; telex 113237; Ambassador: CARLOS ARY-DOS-SANTOS.
Qatar: 1090 Vienna, Strudlhofgasse 10; tel. (01) 31-66-39; Ambassador: ALI ABDUL-RAHMAN AL-MUFTAH.
Romania: 1040 Vienna, Prinz Eugen-Str. 60; tel. (01) 65-32-27; telex 133335; Ambassador: TRANDAFIR COCARLA.
Saudi Arabia: 1190 Vienna, Formanekgasse 38; tel. (01) 36-23-16; telex 115757; Ambassador: ESSA A. AL-NOWAISER.
South Africa: 1190 Vienna, Sandgasse 33; tel. (01) 32-64-93; telex 116671; Ambassador: NAUDÉ STEYN.
Spain: 1040 Vienna, Argentinierstr. 34; tel. (01) 65-57-80; telex 131545; Ambassador: Dr JESÚS NÚÑEZ.
Sweden: 1020 Vienna, Obere Donaustr. 49–51; tel. (01) 33-45-45; telex 114720; Ambassador: DAG E. J. MALM.
Switzerland: 1030 Vienna, Prinz Eugen-Str. 7; tel. (01) 78-45-21; telex 132960; Ambassador: JEAN-PIERRE RITTER.
Thailand: 1180 Vienna, Weimarer-Str. 68; tel. (01) 34-83-61; telex 133893; Ambassador: SAWANIT KONGSIRI.
Tunisia: 1030 Vienna, Ghegastr. 3; tel. (01) 78-65-52; telex 111748; Ambassador: DALI JAZI.
Turkey: 1040 Vienna, Prinz Eugen-Str. 40; tel. (01) 65-55-59; telex 131927; Ambassador: ERDEM ERNER.
USSR: 1030 Vienna, Reisnerstr. 45–47; tel. (01) 73-12-15; Ambassador: GENNADI SERAFIMOVICH SHIKIN.
United Arab Emirates: 1190 Vienna, Peter-Jordan-Str. 66; tel. (01) 36-14-55; telex 74106; Ambassador: ABDUL AZIZ AL-OWAIS.
United Kingdom: 1030 Vienna, Reisnerstr. 40; tel. (01) 73-15-75; telex 132810; Ambassador: ROBERT JAMES O'NEILL.
USA: 1090 Vienna, Boltzmanngasse 16; tel. (01) 31-55-11; telex 114634; Ambassador: HENRY ANATOLE GRUNWALD.
Uruguay: 1010 Vienna, Krugerstr. 3/1/4–6; tel. (01) 513-22-40; telex 112589; Ambassador: JOAQUÍN COSTANZO.
Venezuela: 1030 Vienna, Marokkanergasse 22; tel. (01) 75-32-19; telex 136219; Ambassador: Dr FRANCISCO SUCRE FIGARELLA.
Yugoslavia: 1030 Vienna, Rennweg 3; tel. (01) 713-25-95; Ambassador: MILOŠ KRSTIĆ.
Zaire: 1030 Vienna, Marokkanergasse 22/1/6; tel. (01) 73-88-75; Ambassador: BULAMBO WA MWENDA.

Judicial System

The Austrian legal system is based on the principle of a division between legislative, administrative and judicial power. There are three supreme courts (Verfassungsgerichtshof, Verwaltungsgerichtshof and Oberster Gerichtshof). The judicial courts are organized into about 200 local courts (Bezirksgerichte), 17 provincial and district courts (Landes-und Kreisgerichte), and 4 higher provincial courts (Oberlandesgerichte) in Vienna, Graz, Innsbruck and Linz.

SUPREME ADMINISTRATIVE COURTS

Verfassungsgerichtshof (Constitutional Court): Vienna I, Judenplatz 11; f. 1919; deals with matters affecting the Constitution, examines the legality of legislation and administration; Pres. Univ. Doz. Dr LUDWIG ADAMOVICH; Vice-Pres. Prof. Dr KURT RINGHOFER.
Verwaltungsgerichtshof (Administrative Court): Vienna I, Judenplatz 11; deals with matters affecting the legality of administration; Pres. Dr VIKTOR HELLER; Vice-Pres. Dr INGRID PETRIK.

SUPREME JUDICIAL COURT

Oberster Gerichtshof: Vienna I, Museumstr. 12; Pres. Dr WALTER MELNIZKYI); Vice-Pres. Prof. HERBERT HARBICH, Dr KARL PISKA.

Religion

CHRISTIANITY
The Roman Catholic Church

The vast majority of Austrians belong to the Roman Catholic Church. Austria comprises two archdioceses, seven dioceses and the territorial abbacy of Wettingen-Mehrerau (directly responsible to the Holy See). The Archbishop of Vienna is also the Ordinary for Catholics of the Byzantine rite in Austria (totalling an estimated 3,500 at 31 December 1984).

Bishops' Conference: Österreichische Bischofskonferenz, 1010 Vienna, Rotenturmstrasse 2; tel. (01) 51-5-52; f. 1979; Pres. D.Dr KARL BERG, Archbishop of Salzburg; Sec. Dr ALFRED KOSTELECKY, Titular Bishop of Aggar.
Archbishop of Salzburg: D.Dr KARL BERG, 5010 Salzburg, Kapitelplatz 2, Postfach 62; tel. (0662) 42-5-91.
Archbishop of Vienna: Cardinal HANS HERMANN GROËR, 1010 Vienna, Rotenturmstr. 2; tel. (01) 51-5-52.

Protestant Churches

Baptist Union of Austria: 1160 Vienna, Mörikeweg 16/1; tel. 94-84-465; Pres. Rev. AUGUST HIRNBÖCK.
Evangelische Kirche AB in Österreich (Protestant Church of the Augsburgian Confession): 1180 Vienna, Severin-Schreiber-Gasse 3; tel. (01) 47-15-23; 352,585 mems; Bishop D. DIETER KNALL.
Evangelische Kirche HB (Helvetischen Bekenntnisses) (Protestant Church of the Helvetic Confession): 1010 Vienna, Dorotheergasse 16; tel. (01) 512-83-93; 15,863 mems; Landessuperintendent Pfr. Mag. PETER KARNER.

Other Christian Churches

Old Catholic: 1010 Vienna, Schottenring 17; tel. (01) 34-83-94-0; approx. 25,000 mems; Bishop NIKOLAUS HUMMEL.

JUDAISM

There are about 10,000 Jews in Austria.

Israelitische Kultusgemeinde (Israelite Religious Community): 1190 Vienna, Bauernfeldgasse 4; tel. (01) 36-16-55; telex 136298; Pres. PAUL GROSZ.

The Press

Austria's *Wiener Zeitung*, founded in 1703, is the oldest daily paper published in the world, and Austria's press history dates back to 1605, when its first newspaper was published. Article 13 of the 1867 Constitution gave citizens of the Austro-Hungarian Empire the right to express opinions freely and stated that the Press could not be censored. Restrictions on this freedom of the Press are permissible only within the framework of Article 10 (2) of the European Convention of Human Rights.

By the 1922 Press Law, any person who had been subject to an incorrect statement in the Press was granted the right to publish a reply free of charge. This right of reply, which was unsatisfactory to the newspapers as well as to the person in question, was fundamentally reformed by the Media Law of 1982: the post of Verantwortlicher Redakteur (Responsible Editor—who had been

AUSTRIA

penally liable if the newspaper refused to publish a reply) was abolished and the liability was removed. Now a newspaper may refuse to accept the reply if it is untrue.

Any person who feels himself to have been maligned by a newspaper has, in addition to the right of reply, the right to sue the author of the article. Furthermore, he may demand compensation of up to 100,000 Schilling from the publisher. This right is lost, however, if the newspaper can prove that the publication was true or that 'journalistic care' was taken.

In 1961 the Austrian Press Council (Presserat) was founded. It consists of representatives of the publishers and journalists and its principal duties are to watch over the freedom of the Press and to ascertain grievances of the Press. The political parties each have at least one newspaper, and independent papers tend to follow a political line. Although there is a strong Press in some provinces, the country's Press is centred in Vienna. The three highest circulation dailies are the *Neue Kronen-Zeitung*, the *Kurier*, and the *Kleine Zeitung* (Graz).

PRINCIPAL DAILIES

Bregenz

Neue Vorarlberger Tageszeitung: 6901 Bregenz, Kornmarktstr. 18; tel. (05574) 24-6-01; telex 57730; f. 1972; morning; independent; Editor WALTER ZEINER; circ. weekdays 35,827, Saturday 36,380.

Vorarlberger Nachrichten: Bregenz, Kirchstr. 35; tel. (05574) 512-0; telex 57710; morning; Editors EUGEN A. RUSS, THOMAS ORTNER; circ. weekdays 63,387, Saturday 65,915.

Graz

Kleine Zeitung: 8011 Graz, Schönaugasse 64; tel. (0316) 70-63-0; telex 31782; f. 1904; independent; Editor Dr FRITZ CSOKLICH; circ. weekdays and Sunday 155,630, Friday 194,596.

Neue Zeit: 8054 Graz, Ankerstr. 4; tel. (0316) 28-08-0; telex 31703; f. 1945; morning; Editor JOSEF RIEDLER; circ. 78,443, Friday 84,423.

Innsbruck

Neue Tiroler Zeitung: 6021 Innsbruck, Südtiroler Platz 6; tel. (05222) 35-1-44; f. 1945; morning; Austrian People's Party.

Tiroler Tageszeitung: 6020 Innsbruck, Ing.-Etzel-Str. 30; tel. (05222) 74-20; telex 54482; morning; independent; Editor JOSEPH S. MOSER; circ. weekdays 95,178, Saturday 105,560.

Klagenfurt

Kärntner Tageszeitung: 9020 Klagenfurt, Viktringer Ring 28; tel. (04222) 55-1-66; telex 422415; f. 1946; morning except Monday; Socialist; Editor Dr HELLWIG VALENTIN; circ. weekdays 65,437, Friday 68,535.

Kleine Zeitung: 9020 Klagenfurt, Funderstr. 1A; tel. (04222) 55-6-65; telex 42413; independent; Editor HEINZ STRITZL; circ. weekdays and Sunday 96,887, Friday 117,718.

Neue Volkszeitung: 9020 Klagenfurt, Völkermarkter Ring 25; tel. (0463) 54-44-00; telex 422430; morning; Austrian People's Party; Chief Editor KURT MARKARITZER; circ. weekdays 31,207, Saturday 33,107.

Linz

Neues Volksblatt: 4020 Linz, Hafenstr. 1–3; tel. (0732) 28-19-01; telex 21235; f. 1869; Austrian People's Party; Editor PETER KLAR; circ. weekdays 28,474, Friday 34,625.

Oberösterreichische Nachrichten: 4010 Linz, Promenade 23; tel. (0732) 28050; f. 1865; morning; independent; Editor Dr HERMANN POLZ; circ. weekdays 98,127, Saturday 139,335.

Oberösterreichisches Tagblatt: 4010 Linz, Anastasius-Grün-Str. 6; tel. (0732) 55-2-11; telex 21270; Socialist Party; Editor GERALD HÖCHTLER; circ. weekdays 31,657, Friday 34,388.

Salzburg

Neues Salzburger Tagblatt: 5020 Salzburg, Auerspergstr. 42; tel. (0662) 72491; Socialist Party; Editor Dr MANFRED SCHEUCH; circ. weekdays 8,727.

Salzburger Nachrichten: 5021 Salzburg, Bergstr. 14; tel. (0662) 77-5-91; telex 633583; f. 1945; morning; independent; Editor-in-Chief Prof. Dr KARL-HEINZ RITSCHL; circ. weekdays 67,035, Saturday 107,250.

Salzburger Volkszeitung: 5020 Salzburg, Elisabethkai 58; tel. (06222) 79-49-10; telex 06/633627; Austrian People's Party; Editor WILLI SAUBERER; circ. weekdays 12,537.

Vienna

*Kurier: 1072 Vienna, Lindengasse 52; tel. (01) 96-2-10; telex 132631; f. 1954; independent; Editor Dr GÜNTHER WESSIG; circ. weekdays 402,252, Saturday 523,588, Sunday 662,759.

Directory

*Neue A-Z: 1030 Vienna, Viehmarktgasse 4; tel. (01) 79-02-0; f. 1889; morning; Socialist Party; Editor Dr MANFRED SCHEUCH; circ. weekdays 72,487, Friday 129,199, Saturday 78,328.

*Neue Kronen-Zeitung: 1190 Vienna, Muthgasse 2; tel. (01) 3601-0; telex 114327; f. 1900; independent; Editor HANS DICHAND; circ. weekdays 958,135, Sunday 1,293,946.

*Die Presse: 1010 Vienna, Parkring 12A; tel. (01) 51-4-14; telex 114110; f. 1848; morning; independent; Editor Dr THOMAS CHORHERR; circ. Mon.-Thur. 68,527, Friday 87,872, Saturday 87,283.

*Volksstimme: 1206 Vienna, Höchstädtplatz 3; tel. 33-56-01; f. 1945; morning; Communist Party; Editor MICHAEL GRABER; circ. weekdays 39,574, Sunday 72,663.

*Wiener Zeitung: 1037 Vienna, Rennweg 12A; tel. (01) 78-76-31; telex 131805; f. 1703; morning; official government paper; Editor HEINZ FAHNLER; circ. 50,000.

* National newspapers.

PRINCIPAL WEEKLIES

Agrar Post: 3430 Tulln, Königstetter Str. 132; f. 1924; independent; agriculture.

Blickpunkt: 6410 Telfs, Blickpunkt-Verlagshaus; tel. (05262) 4611; telex 534006; Editor NORBERT WALSER; circ. 42,700.

Die Furche: 1010 Vienna, Singerstr. 7; tel. (01) 52-52-61; f. 1945; Catholic; Editor HANNES SCHOPF; circ. 13,003.

Die ganze Woche: 1160 Vienna, Odoakergasse 34–36; tel. (01) 46-26-91; telex 134008; Chief Editor Dr FRANZ ENDLER; circ. 820,000.

Die Industrie: 1010 Vienna, Bösendorferstr. 2/16; tel. (01) 65-72-15; Editor HERBERT KREJCI.

Kärntner Nachrichten: 9020 Klagenfurt, Dr-Arthur-Lemisch-Platz 4; tel. (04222) 51-38-69; Austrian Liberal Party; Editor KURT KNAPPINGER.

Neue Illustrierte Wochenschau: 1070 Vienna VII, Kaiserstr. 8–10; tel. (01) 93-56-46; telex 113556; f. 1908; Editors GERHARD LEIMER, REINHOLD PILZ; circ. 132,120.

Die neue IW-Internationale Wirtschaft: 1050 Vienna, Nikolsdorfer Gasse 7–11; tel. (01) 55-55-85; economics; Editor NIKOLAUS GERSTMAYER; circ. 11,400.

NFZ—Neue Freie Zeitung: 1010 Vienna, Kärntner Str. 28; tel. (01) 512-94-52; telex 113610; Austrian Liberal Party; Editor Mag. CHRISTIAN WEHRSCHÜTZ; circ. 40,000.

Niederösterreichische Nachrichten: 3100 St Pölten, Gutenbergstr. 12; tel. (02742) 61-5-61; telex 15512; Editor HANS STRÖBITZER; circ. 124,350.

Oberösterreichische Rundschau: 4010 Linz, Hafenstr. 1–3; tel. (0732) 278-1-21; telex 02/1014; circ. 112,500.

Der Österreichische Bauernbündler: 1014 Vienna, Bankgasse 1–3; tel. (01) 533-96-76; Editor Ing. PAUL GRUBER; circ. 78,100.

Präsent: 6020 Innsbruck, Exlgasse 20; tel. (05222) 81-5-41; telex 05/33620; f. 1892; independent Catholic; Chief Editor BENEDIKT POSCH.

Samstag: 1081 Vienna, Strozzigasse 8; tel. (01) 43-59-11; f. 1951; weekly; independent; Editor DIETMAR GRIESER; circ. 101,900.

Tiroler Bauernzeitung: 6021 Innsbruck, Brixner Str. 1; tel. (05222) 35-5-21; telex 53804; published by Tiroler Bauernbund; Chief Editor NR. Dr Ing. ALOIS LEITNER; circ. 23,000.

Videňské Svobodné Listy: 1050 Vienna, Margaretenplatz 7; weekly for Czech and Slovak communities in Austria; Editor JOSEF JONÁŠ.

Vorarlberger Volksbote: 6901 Bregenz, Anton-Schneider-Str. 32; tel. (05574) 23-6-71; Editor ALFONS J. KOPF; circ. 21,467.

Die Wirtschaft: 1051 Vienna, Nikolsdorfer Gasse 7–11; tel. (01) 55-55-85; telex 111669; economics; circ. 25,500.

Wochenpost: 8011 Graz, Parkstr. 1; tel. (0316) 77-5-11; independent; illustrated; non-political; Chief Editor Dr MARGIT GRATZER; circ. 25,556.

POPULAR PERIODICALS

Austria-Ski: 6020 Innsbruck, Olympiastr. 10; tel. (05222) 59501; telex 533876; 6 a year; official journal of Austrian Skiing Assn; Editor Mag. JOSEF SCHMID.

Auto Touring: 1010 Vienna, Schubertring 3; tel. (01) 72-99-0; telex 133907; monthly; official journal of the Austrian Automobile Organizations; Editor WALTER PRSKAWETZ; circ. 759,900.

Basta: 1050 Vienna, Krongasse 6; tel. (01) 56-75-31; monthly; Chief Editor WOLFGANG FELLNER.

Bunte Österreich: 1190 Vienna, Muthgasse 2; tel. (01) 3601-0; illustrated weekly; circ. 124,621.

AUSTRIA

Frauenblatt: 1081 Vienna, Strozzigasse 8; tel. (01) 43-59-11; women's weekly; Editor TRAUDE WINKLBAUER; circ. 53,000.

Neue Frau: 1030 Vienna, Viehmarktgasse 4; tel. (01) 79-02-0; women's weekly magazine; Editor DORIS STOISSER; circ. 79,336.

Profil: 1010 Vienna, Marc-Aurel-Str. 12; tel. (01) 66-16-70; telex 136404; fortnightly; political general; independent; circ. 88,300.

RZ Illustrierte Romanzeitung: 1072 Vienna, Kaiser Str. 8–10; tel. (01) 93-56-46; f. 1936; weekly illustrated; Editor HANS ADLASSNIG; circ. 35,223.

Sport und Toto: 1080 Vienna, Piaristengasse 16; tel. (01) 43-34-63; weekly sports illustrated; Editor RALPH ZEILINGER.

Sportfunk: 1010 Vienna, Walfischgasse 14/4/15; tel. (01) 513-76.05; telex 113191; sporting weekly.

Trend: 1010 Vienna, Marc-Aurel-Str. 12; tel. (01) 53-4-70; telex 136404; monthly; economics; circ. 80,000.

Welt der Frau: 4020 Linz, Lustenauerstr. 21; tel. (0732) 27-02-91; women's monthly magazine; circ. 80,000.

Wiener: 1060 Vienna, Lehargasse 11; tel. (01) 56-76-77; telex 111853; monthly; Chief Editor ANDREAS DRESSLER.

Wochenpresse: 1070 Vienna, Lindengasse 52; tel. (01) 96-21-0; telex 135869; f. 1946; independent; weekly news magazine; Chief Editor Dr HANS MAGENSCHAB; circ. 47,744.

SPECIALIST PERIODICALS

Acta Chirurgica Austriaca: 1238 Vienna, Feldgasse 13; tel. (01) 88-56-46; 6 a year; journal of the Austrian Surgical Soc.; Editor Mag. RICHARD HOLLINEK.

Acta Mechanica: Springer Verlag, 1010 Vienna, Mölkerbastei 5; tel. (01) 533-96-14-0; f. 1965; irregular; Editors S. LEIBOVICH (Ithaca, NY), H. TROGER (Vienna), G. J. WENG (New Brunswick, NJ), F. ZIEGLER (Vienna), J. ZIEREP (Karlsruhe).

Acta Medica Austriaca: 1238 Vienna, Feldgasse 13; tel. (01) 88-56-46; 5 a year; journal of the Austrian Soc. for Internal Medicine and associated societies; Editor Mag. RICHARD HOLLINEK.

Computing: Springer Verlag, 1010 Vienna, Mölkerbastei 5; tel. (01) 533-96-14-0; f. 1966; irregular; Editors R. ALBRECHT (Innsbruck), R. L. CONSTABLE (Ithaca), W. HÄNDLER (Erlangen), W. KNÖDEL (Stuttgart), W. L. MIRANKER (Yorktown Heights), H. J. STETTER (Vienna), H. WACKER (Linz).

Forum: 1070 Vienna, Museumstr. 5; tel. (01) 93-27-33; f. 1954; every 2 months; international magazine for cultural freedom and political equality; Editor-in-Chief GERHARD OBERSCHLICK.

itm praktiker: 1040 Vienna, Phorusgasse 8; tel. (01) 57-67-65; telex 12553; technical hobbies; Chief Editor GERHARD K. BUCHBERGER; circ. 18,800.

Juristische Blätter mit Beilage 'Wirtschaftsrechtliche Blätter': Springer Verlag, 1010 Vienna, Mölkerbastei 5; tel. (01) 533-96-14-0; f. 1872; monthly; Editors F. BYDLINSKI, H. R. KLECATSKY, G. WILHELM (Beilage 'Wirtschaftsrechtliche Blätter').

Die Landwirtschaft: 1011 Vienna, Seilergasse 6–8; tel. (01) 51-5-46; telex 111349; f. 1923; monthly; agriculture and forestry; owned and published by Österreichischer Agrarverlag; Editor Ing. FRANZ GEBHART; circ. 95,000.

Literatur und Kritik: Otto Müller Verlag, 5021 Salzburg, Ernest-Thun-Str. 11; tel. (0662) 72-1-52; f. 1966; 5 a year; Austrian and East European literature and criticism; Editor KURT KLINGER.

Monatshefte für Chemie: 1010 Vienna, Mölkerbastei 5; tel. (01) 533-96-14-0; f. 1880; monthly; chemistry; Man. Editor K. SCHLÖGL.

Monatshefte für Mathematik: Springer Verlag, 1010 Vienna, Mölkerbastei 5; tel. (01) 533-96-14-0; f. 1890; irregular; Editor H. REITER.

Österreichische Ärztezeitung: 1010 Vienna, Weihburggasse 10–12; tel. (01) 52-44-86; telex 11270; f. 1945; fortnightly; organ of the Austrian Medical Board; Editor Dr MONIKA BANNERT.

Österreichische Ingenieur-und Architekten-Zeitschrift: 1010 Vienna, Mölkerbastei 5; tel. (01) 533-96-14-0; f. 1958; monthly; Editors W. KOENNE, R. MAYR-HARTING, G. WIDTMANN.

Österreichische Monatshefte: 1010 Vienna, Kärntnerstr. 51; tel. (01) 52-26-21; telex 01/1771; f. 1945; monthly; organ of Austrian People's Party; Editor Dr ALFRED GRINSCHGL.

Österreichische Musikzeitschrift: 1010 Vienna, Hegelgasse 13/22; tel. (01) 52-68-69; f. 1946; monthly; Editors E. LAFITE, Dr M. DIEDERICHS-LAFITE.

Pädiatrie und Pädologie: Springer Verlag, 1010 Vienna, Mölkerbastei 5; tel. (01) 533-96-14-0; f. 1965; irregular; Editor G. WEIPPL.

Reichsbund-Aktuell: 1010 Vienna, Ebendorferstr. 6/V; tel. (01) 42-54-06; monthly; Catholic; organ of Reichsbund, Bewegung für christliche Gesellschaftspolitik und Sport; Editor ERICH RAPHAEL MÜLLER.

Reiseland Österreich: 1110 Vienna, Leberstr. 122; tel. (01) 74-15-95; telex 13/2312; f. 1928; monthly; Editor-in-Chief GEORG KARP; circ. 35,000.

Trotzdem: 1070 Vienna, Neustiftgasse 3; tel. (01) 93-41-23; monthly; organ of the Socialist Youth of Austria; Editor ALFRED GUSENBAUER.

Welt der Arbeit: 1030 Vienna, Viehmarktgasse 4; tel. (01) 79-02-0; socialist industrial journal; Editor KURT HORAK; circ 69,516.

Wiener klinische Wochenschrift: 1010 Vienna, Mölkerbastei 5; tel. (01) 533-96-14-0; f. 1887; medical bi-weekly; Editors O. KRAUPP, E. DEUTSCH.

Wiener Medizinische Wochenschrift: 1238 Vienna, Feldgasse 13; tel. (01) 88-56-46; 2 a month; journal of graduate medical education; Editor Mag. RICHARD HOLLINEK.

Zukunft: 1014 Vienna, Loewelstr. 18; tel. (01) 53-427-306; monthly; Socialist party; Editor ALBRECHT K. KONECNY.

NEWS AGENCIES

APA (Austria Presse-Agentur): Internationales Pressezentrum (IPZ), 1199 Vienna, Gunoldstr. 14; tel. (01) 36-05-0; telex 114721; f. 1946; co-operative agency of the Austrian Newspapers and Broadcasting Co (private company); 37 mems; Man. Dir Dr WOLFGANG VYSLOZIL; Chief Editor JOSEF NOWAK.

Foreign Bureaux

Agence France-Presse (AFP): IPZ, 1199 Vienna, Gunoldstr. 14; tel. (01) 36-31-87; telex 115833; Correspondent BERNARD MEIXNER.

Agenzia Nazionale Stampa Associata (ANSA) (Italy): IPZ, 1199 Vienna, Gunoldstr. 14; tel. (01) 36-13-00; telex 114891; Bureau Chief LUCIANO COSSETTO.

Allgemeiner Deutscher Nachrichtendienst (ADN) (German Democratic Republic): 1030 Vienna, Reisnerstr. 18/4/18; Correspondent HEINZ SCHINDLER.

Associated Press (AP) (USA): IPZ, 1199 Vienna, Gunoldstr. 14; tel. 36-14-58; telex 115930; Bureau Chief ALISON SMALE.

Československá tisková kancelář (ČTK) (Czechoslovakia): 1080 Vienna, Auerspergstr. 15; tel (01) 42-03-75; telex 114215.

Deutsche Presse-Agentur (dpa) (Federal Republic of Germany): IPZ, 1199 Vienna, Gunoldstr. 14; tel. 362158; telex 114633; Correspondent ALEX WACHSMUTH.

Inter Press Service (IPS) (Italy): IPZ, 1199 Vienna, Gunoldstr. 14; tel. (01) 36-85-06; telex 136081; Dir FEDERICO NIER-FISCHER.

Kyodo Tsushin (Japan): IPZ, 1199 Vienna, Gunoldstr. 14; tel. (01) 36-15-20; telex 135736; Bureau Chief KIYOSHI HASUMI.

Magyar Távirati Iroda (MTI) (Hungary): 1010 Vienna, Teinfaltstr. 4; tel. (01) 63-31-38; telex 115025; Correspondent ANDRÁS HELTAI.

Novinska Agencija Tanjug (Tanjug) (Yugoslavia): IPZ, 1190 Vienna, Gunoldstr. 14.

Reuters (UK): 1010 Vienna 1, Börsegasse 11; tel. (01) 531-12-0; telex 114645; Chief Correspondent COLIN A. MCINTYRE.

Telegrafnoye Agentstvo Sovetskovo Soyuza (TASS) (USSR): 1040 Vienna, Grosse Neugasse 28; tel. (01) 56-11-46.

United Press International (UPI) (USA): 1199 Vienna, Gunoldstr. 14/2; tel. (01) 369-12-58; telex 111662.

Xinhua (New China) News Agency (People's Republic of China): 1030 Vienna, Reisnerstr. 21; tel. (01) 73-41-40; telex 134384; Correspondent LI CHUNGUANG.

Central News Agency (CNA) (Taiwan) is also represented.

PRESS ASSOCIATIONS

Österreichischer Zeitschriftenverband (Assen of Periodical Publishers): 1090 Vienna, Hörlgasse 18/5; tel. (01) 31-70-01; f. 1945; 164 mems; Pres. Dr RUDOLF BOHMANN.

Verband Österreichischer Zeitungsherausgeber und Zeitungsverleger (Austrian Newspaper Publishers' Asscn): 1010 Vienna, Schreyvogelgasse 3; tel. (01) 533-61-78; telex 114223; f. 1945; all daily and most weekly papers are mems; Pres. Dir JULIUS KAINZ; Sec.-Gen. Mag. FRANZ IVAN.

Publishers

Akademische Druck- und Verlagsanstalt: 8010 Graz, Neufeldweg 75, Postfach 598; tel. (0316) 41-1-53; telex 312234; f. 1949; scholarly reprints and new works, facsimile editions of Codices; Dir MANFRED KRAMER.

Bergland Verlag GmbH: 1051 Vienna, Spengergasse 39; tel. (01) 55-56-41; f. 1937; belles-lettres, art, history, fiction; Owner and Dir FRIEDRICH GEYER.

AUSTRIA

Betz, Annette, Verlag GmbH: 1091 Vienna, Alserstr. 24; tel. (01) 48-15-38; telex 114802; f. 1962; Dir Dr OTTO MANG.

Böhlau Verlag GmbH: 1011 Vienna, Dr Karl Lueger-Ring 12; tel. (01) 63-87-35; f. 1947; history, law, philology, the arts, sociology; Owner Dr PETER RAUCH.

Bohmann Druck und Verlag GmbH & Co KG: 1110 Vienna, Leberstr. 122; tel. (01) 74-15-95; telex 132312; f. 1936; trade, technical and industrial books and periodicals; Dirs Dr RUDOLF BOHMANN, HEINZ KELLER.

Christian Brandstätter, Verlag und Edition: 1080 Vienna, Wickenburggasse 26; tel. (01) 48-38-14.

Wilhelm Braumüller, GmbH: 1092 Vienna, Servitengasse 5; tel. (01) 34-81-24; f. 1783; sociology, politics, history, ethnology, linguistics, psychology and philosophy; university publrs; Dir BRIGITTE KALTSCHMID.

Franz Deuticke Verlagsgesellschaft mbH: 1011 Vienna, Helferstorferstr. 4; tel. (01) 533-43-45; f. 1878; science text books, school books; Dir Dr SCHARETZER.

Ludwig Doblinger, KG: 1010 Vienna I, Dorotheergasse 10; tel. (01) 51-50-30; telex 133008; f. 1876; music; Dir HELMUTH PANY.

Europa Verlag GmbH: 1232 Vienna, Altmannsdorfer Str. 154-156; tel. (01) 67-26-22; telex 131326.

Freytag-Berndt und Artaria KG Kartographische Anstalt: 1071 Vienna VII, Schottenfeldgasse 62; tel. (01) 93-95-01; telex 133526; f. 1879 (1770—Artaria); geography, maps and atlases; Chair. Dr WALTER PETROWITZ, HARALD HOCHENEGG.

Gerold & Co: 1011 Vienna, Graben 31; tel. (01) 533-50-14; telex 136157; f. 1867; philology, literature, Eastern Europe, sociology and philosophy; Dir HANS NEUSSER.

Globus Zeitungs-, Druck- und Verlagsanstalt GmbH: 1206 Vienna, Höchstädtplatz 3; tel. (01) 334501; telex 114629; f. 1945; newspapers, political science, popular sciences, fiction; Gen. Man. Dr H. ZASLAWSKI.

Herder & Co: 1011 Vienna, Wollzeile 33, Postfach 248; tel. (01) 512-14-13; telex 01/1046; f. 1886; religion, theology, history, juvenile; Dir ERICH M. WOLF.

Herold Druck- und Verlagsgesellschaft mbH: 1080 Vienna, Strozigasse 8; tel. (01) 43-15-51; telex 111760; f. 1947; art, history, politics, religion; Dirs FRANZ HÖRMANN, LEOPOLD KURZ.

Hölder-Pichler-Tempsky Verlag: 1096 Vienna, Frankgasse 4; tel. (01) 43-89-93; f. 1922; school text-books; Man. Dir GUSTAV GLÖCKLER.

Brüder Hollinek: 1238 Vienna, Feldgasse 13; tel. (01) 88-56-46; f. 1872; science, medicine, law and administration, dictionaries; Dir Mag. RICHARD HOLLINEK.

Jugend und Volk Verlagsgesellschaft mbH: 1153 Vienna, Anschützgasse 1; tel. (01) 87-25-15; telex 136103; f. 1921; pedagogics, art, literature, children's books; Dir Dr OTTO SCHIMPF.

Verlag Kremayr & Scheriau: 1121 Vienna, Niederhofstr. 37; tel. (01) 83-45-01; telex 1/31405; f. 1951; non-fiction, history.

Kunstverlag Wolfrum: 1010 Vienna, Augustinerstr. 10; tel. (01) 512-41-78; f. 1919; art; Dirs HUBERT WOLFRUM, MONIKA ENGEL.

Leykam Verlag: 8011 Graz, Stempfergasse 3; tel. (0316) 76-6-76-0; telex 32209; art, literature, academic, law; Dir Dr K. OKTABETZ.

Manz'sche Verlags- und Universitätsbuchhandlung: 1014 Vienna, Kohlmarkt 16; tel. (01) 533-17-81; telex 75310631; f. 1849; law, political and economic sciences; textbooks and schoolbooks; Exec. Principals Dkfm. FRANZ STEIN, Dr ANTON C. HILSCHER.

Wilhelm Maudrich: 1097 Vienna, Lazarettgasse 1; tel. (01) 42-47-12; telex 135177; f. 1909; medical; Dir GERHARD GROIS.

Otto Müller Verlag: 5021 Salzburg, Ernest-Thun-Str. 11; tel. (0662) 88-19-74; f. 1937; general; Man. ARNO KLEIBEL.

Paul Neff Verlag KG: 1140 Vienna, Hackingerstr. 52; tel. (01) 94-06-11; f. 1829; fiction, biographies, music, theatre, etc.

R. Oldenbourg KG: 1030 Vienna, Neulinggasse 26/3; tel. (01) 72-62-59; f. 1959; Dirs Dr KARL CORNIDES, Dr THOMAS CORNIDES.

Verlag Orac: 1010 Vienna, Graben 17; tel. (01) 53-4-52; telex 136365; f. 1946; Dir HELMUT HANUSCH.

Österreichischer Gewerbeverlag GmbH: 1014 Vienna, Herrengasse 10; tel. (01) 63-07-68; f. 1945; general; Man. F. SCHARETZER.

Pinguin Verlag Pawlowski KG: 6021 Innsbruck, Lindenbühelweg 2; tel. (05222) 81-1-83; illustrated books; Dirs OLAF PAWLOWSKI, HELLA PFLANZER.

Residenz Verlag GmbH: 5020 Salzburg, Gaisbergstr. 6; tel. (0662) 25-7-71; telex 6/32887; Dir Dr JOCHEN JUNG.

Anton Schroll & Co: 1051 Vienna, Spengergasse 39; tel. (01) 55-56-41; f. 1884; also in Munich; art books; Man. F. GEYER.

Springer-Verlag: 1010 Vienna, Mölkerbastei 5; tel. (01) 533-96-14; telex 114506; f. 1924; medicine, science, technology, law, sociology, economics, periodicals; Dirs K. F. SPRINGER, C. MICHALETZ, D. GÖTZE, W. JOOS, R. SIEGLE.

Leopold Stocker Verlag: 8011 Graz, Bürgergasse 11; tel. (0316) 71636; f. 1917; history, nature, hunting, fiction, poetry, textbooks; Dir Dr ILSE DVORAK-STOCKER.

Verlag Styria: 8011 Graz, Schönaugasse 64; tel. (0316) 8063-0; telex 312387; f. 1869; literature, history, theology, philosophy; Gen. Dir Dr HANNS SASSMANN.

Verlagsanstalt Tyrolia GmbH: 6020 Innsbruck, Exlgasse 20; tel. (05222) 81-5-41; f. 1907; geography, history, science, religion, fiction; Chair. Dr GEORG SCHIEMER.

Carl Ueberreuter Verlag: 1091 Vienna, Alser Str. 24; tel. (01) 48-15-38; telex 114802; non-fiction, children's; Dir Dr OTTO MANG.

Universal Edition: 1015 Vienna, Postfach 3, Bösendorfer Str. 12; tel. (01) 505-86-95; telex 11397; f. 1901; music; Dir Dr J. JURANEK.

Urban & Schwarzenberg, KG: 1096 Vienna, Frankgasse 4; tel. (01) 42-27-31; f. 1866; science, medicine; Dir MICHAEL URBAN.

Paul Zsolnay Verlag GmbH: 1041 Vienna, Prinz Eugen-Str. 30 (also in Darmstadt); tel. (01) 505-76-61; telex 132279; f. 1923; fiction, non-fiction; Dir GERHARD BECKMANN.

Government Publishing Houses

Österreichische Staatsdruckerei (Austrian State Printing Office): 1037 Vienna, Rennweg 12A; tel. (01) 78-76-310; f. 1804; law, art reproductions; Dir ARIBERT SCHWARZMANN.

Österreichischer Bundesverlag GmbH: 1015 Vienna, Schwarzenbergstr. 5; tel. (01) 512-25-61; telex 131159; f. 1772 by Empress Maria Theresia; school textbooks, education, educational periodicals, science, children's books, books about Austria and sports; foundation administered by the State; Dir Komm. Rat Dkfm. KURT BIAK.

PUBLISHERS' ASSOCIATION

Hauptverband des österreichischen Buchhandels (Association of Austrian Publishers and Booksellers): 1010 Vienna I, Grünangergasse 4; tel. (01) 512-15-35; f. 1859; Pres. OTTO HAUSA; Gen. Sec. Dkfm. Dr GERHARD PROSSER; 670 mems.

Radio and Television

In January 1988 there were 619 radio transmitters in the provinces, broadcasting two national programmes (one for 18 hours and one for 24 hours), 10 local programmes and an overseas service on shortwave. At the same time there were 913 television transmitters. In 1988 there were 2,681,390 registered radio receivers and 2,475,076 television receivers.

Österreichischer Rundfunk (ORF) (Austrian Broadcasting Company): 1136 Vienna, Würzburggasse 30; tel. (01) 82-91-0; f. 1955; controls all radio and television in Austria; Dir-Gen. THADDÄUS PODGORSKI; Dirs JOHANNES KUNZ, ERNST WOLFRAM MARBOE (Television Programmes), ERNST GRISSEMANN (Radio Programmes), HEINZ DOUCHA (Technology), Dr PETER RADEL (Finance and Administration).

Finance

(cap. = capital; p.u. = paid up; dep. = deposits; m. = million; brs = branches; amounts in Schilling)

BANKS

Banks in Austria, apart from the National Bank, belong to one of six categories. The first category comprises banks that are organized as corporations (i.e. joint stock banks), and special purpose credit institutions. In July 1987 these numbered, respectively, 50 and 64. The second category comprises private banks, which numbered five, and the third category comprises savings banks, which numbered 129. The fourth category comprises co-operative banks. These include rural credit co-operatives (Raiffeisenkassen), which numbered 879 in July 1988, and industrial credit co-operatives (Volksbanken), which numbered 105. The remaining two categories comprise the mortgage banks of the various Austrian 'Länder', which numbered nine in July 1988, and the building societies, which numbered four in July 1988. The majority of Austrian banks (with the exception of the building societies) operate on the basis of universal banking, although certain categories have specialized. Banking operations are governed by the Banking Act of 1979 (Kreditwesengesetz–KWG), as amended in 1986.

Central Bank

Oesterreichische Nationalbank (Austrian National Bank): 1090 Vienna, Otto Wagner-Platz 3; tel. 4360-0; telex 114778; f. 1922; Pres. Dr HELLMUTH KLAUHS; Gen. Man. ADOLF WALA; 7 brs.

AUSTRIA

Commercial Banks

AVA—Bank GmbH: 1015 Vienna, Operngasse 2; tel. (01) 51-5-71; telex 111173; f. 1927; cap. 200m., dep. 8,290m. (1987); Gen. Man. Dr JOHANN BURGEMEISTER; 37 brs.

Banco do Brasil AG: 1010 Vienna, Tegetthoffstr. 4; tel. (01) 52-66-63; telex 111997; cap. 50m. (1987); Chair. NIVALDO VOIGT.

Bank der Österreichischen Postsparkasse AG: 1015 Vienna, Opernring 3–5; tel. (01) 58809-0; telex 112268; cap. 160m., dep. 11,000m. (1987); Chair. and Gen. Man. Komm. Rat FREIMUT DOBRETSBERGER.

Bank für Arbeit und Wirtschaft AG: 1010 Vienna, Seitzergasse 2–4; tel. (01) 53-4-53-0; telex 115311; f. 1947; cap. 6,348m., dep. 170,713m. (1987); Chair. and Gen. Man. Komm. Rat WALTER FLÖTTL; 125 brs.

Bank für Wirtschaft und Freie Berufe AG: 1072 Vienna, Zieglergasse 5; tel. (01) 96-15-46; telex 132346; f. 1914; cap. 50m., dep. 1,217m. (Dec. 1987); Mans PETER SCHLADOFSKY, PETER WENINGER, HANNES ROTTER.

Bank Gebrüd. Gutmann Nfg AG: 1011 Vienna, Schwarzenbergplatz 16; tel. (01) 65-76-36; telex 136506; f. 1922; cap. 40m.; Gen. Man. Dr HELMUTH E. FREY.

Bank Winter & Co AG: 1011 Vienna, Singerstr. 10; tel. (01) 51-50-40; telex 112462; cap. 300m., dep. 26,200m. (1987); Chair. SIMON MOSKOVICS; Man. Dirs THOMAS MOSKOVICS, ADA HAFNER; 1 br.

Bankhaus Feichtner & Co AG: 1011 Vienna, Wipplingerstr. 1; tel. (01) 533-16-06; telex 114260; cap. 100m., dep. 4,485m. (1987); Chair. Dr WOLFGANG WIPLER.

Bankhaus Rössler AG: 1015 Vienna, Kärntner Ring 17; tel. (01) 512-96-96; telex 131815; cap. 30m. (1985); Management Board HANNS CHRISTIAN, Dr GERHARD TANEW.

Bankhaus Schelhammer & Schattera: 1011 Vienna, Goldschmiedgasse 3; tel. (01) 53-4-34; telex 13206; f. 1832; cap. 120m., dep. 2,623m. (Dec. 1987); private bank; Partners Komm. Rat Dipl.-Ing. JOSEF MELCHART, Dr ROBERT NORDEN; 1 br.

Bankhaus C. A. Steinhäusser: 1014 Vienna, Kohlmarkt 1/10; tel. (01) 533-10-10; telex 133146; cap. 50m. (1987); Man. JOSEPH BUCHEGGER.

Central Wechsel- und Creditbank AG: 1015 Vienna, Kärntner Str. 43; tel. (01) 515-66-0; telex 112387; cap. 200m. (1988); Gen. Man. Dr KÁLMÁN MÉSZÁROS.

Centro Internationale Handelsbank AG: 1015 Vienna, Tegetthoffstr. 1; tel. (01) 51-5-20-0; telex 136990; f. 1973; cap. 250m., dep. 6,112m. (Dec. 1987); Exec. Bd Dr GERHARD VOGT, JAN WOLOSZYN, CHRISTIAN SPERK.

Chase Manhattan Bank (Austria) AG: 1011 Vienna, Parkring 12A, Postfach 582; tel. (01) 51-5-89; telex 112570; cap. 20m., total resources 3,206m. (Dec. 1987); Chair. RICHARD MOUNCE; Gen. Man. ANDREAS TREICHL.

Citibank (Austria) AG: 1015 Vienna, Lothringer Str. 7; tel. (01) 71-71-70; telex 112105; cap. 100m., dep. 8,220m.; Gen. Man. STEPHAN HANDL.

Creditanstalt-Bankverein: 1010 Vienna, Schottengasse 6; tel. (01) 531-31-0; telex 133030; f. 1855; cap. 3,100m., dep. 412,635m. (Dec. 1987); Chair. Dr G. SCHMIDT-CHIARI; 345 brs.

Donau-Bank AG: 1011 Vienna, Parkring 6; tel. (01) 5-15-35; telex 116473; f. 1974; jointly owned by the State Bank of the USSR and the Bank for Foreign Economic Affairs of the USSR; cap. 270m., dep. 14,476m. (1987); Chair. ANDREJ I. AKIMOV.

Elsässische Bank AG: 1015 Vienna, Schwarzenbergplatz 1; tel. (01) 712-51-03-0; telex 133766; f. 1872; wholly-owned subsidiary of Société Générale Alsacienne de Banque (France); cap. 75m., dep. 5,828m. (1987); Pres. RENÉ GERONIMUS; Gen. Mans Dr ALBERT MÜRSCH (Strasbourg); Dr MANFRED KUNZE (Vienna).

Focobank (Austria) AG: 1011 Vienna, Rathausstr. 20, Postfach 306; tel. (01) 43-61-61; telex 114911; cap. 45m., dep. 1,361m.; Chair. and Gen. Man. Dkfm. Dr ERICH STÖGER.

Internationale Bank für Aussenhandel AG: 1011 Vienna, Neuer Markt 1; tel. (01) 51-5-56-0; telex 113564; f. 1970; cap. 75m., dep. 5,788m. (1986); Gen. Mans Dkfm. Dr WALTER BEYER, Dkfm. HUBERT WIELEBNOWSKI.

Kathrein & Co Bank AG: 1013 Vienna, Wipplingerstr. 25; tel. 53401; telex 1 14123; f. 1924; Dirs Dr FELIX ANSELMI, STEFAN BREZOVICH, HEINZ HÖDL, MANFRED WOLZT.

Länderbank-Exportbank AG: 1010 Vienna, Wallnerstr. 8; tel. (01) 53-13-40; telex 133468; Chair. HELMUT BOHUNOVSKY.

Meinl Bank AG: 1015 Vienna, Kärntner Ring 2; tel. (01) 65-47-31; telex 132256; cap. 40m., dep. 3,200m. (1987); Dirs JULIUS MEINL, WOLFGANG SAMESCH, ERNST WIMMER.

Mercurbank GmbH: 1015 Vienna, Kärntner Ring 8; tel. (01) 6 50132-0; telex 131439; cap. 90m., dep. 3,549m. (1987); Mans. MANFRED KOPRIVA, Dkfm. ROBERT SCHILDER; 31 brs.

Österreichische Länderbank AG: 1011 Vienna, Am Hof 2; tel. (01) 531-24-0; telex 115561; f. 1880; cap. 1,700m., dep. 198,883m. (Dec. 1987); Chair. and CEO Dkfm. GERHARD WAGNER; 141 brs.

Österreichische Verkehrskreditbank AG: 1081 Vienna, Auerspergstr. 17; tel. (01) 42-76-48-0; telex 115965; cap. 50m. (1987); Chair. and Gen. Man. Dr OTTO ASCHENBRENNER.

Österreichisches Credit-Institut AG: 1010 Vienna, Herrengasse 12; tel. (01) 531-30-0; telex 115260; f. 1896; cap. 350m., dep. 24,061m.; Gen. Man. Dr GEROLD PIRINGER; Man. Dr FRIEDRICH GEHART; 42 brs.

Sao Paolo Bank (Austria) AG: 1010 Vienna, Rotenturmstr. 5-9; tel. (01) 535-36-01; telex 114266; cap. 200m.; Gen. Man. PIERO ZAINO; 1 br.

Schoeller & Co Bank AG: 1011 Vienna, Renngasse 1–3; tel. (01) 53471; telex 114219; f. 1833; cap. 200m., dep. 16,808m. (1987); Chair. and Gen. Man. Dr HERBERT SCHOELLER; 12 brs.

Regional Banks

Bank für Handel und Industrie AG: 8011 Graz, Herrengasse 28; tel. (0316) 71-6-87; telex 31298; f. 1956; cap. 30m.; Pres. GOTTFRIED PENGG; Mans REINHARD FISCHER, ERHARD WRESSNIG; 3 brs.

Bank für Kärnten und Steiermark AG: 9010 Klagenfurt, Dr Arthur Lemisch-Platz 5; tel. (0463) 51-15-55; telex 422454; f. 1922; cap. 300m., dep. 17,012m. (1987); Gen. Man. MAXIMILIAN MERAN; Dir Dr HEIMO PENKER; 28 brs.

Bank für Oberösterreich und Salzburg: 4010 Linz, Hauptplatz 10-11; tel. (0732) 2802/0; telex 21802; f. 1869; cap. 500m., dep. 37,837m. (Dec. 1987); Chair. Dr HERMANN BELL; 75 brs.

Bank für Tirol und Vorarlberg AG: 6021 Innsbruck, Erlerstr. 5–9; tel. (0512) 5333-0; telex 533535; f. 1904; cap. 300m., dep. 14,375m. (1987); Gen. Man. Komm. Rat Dr GERHARD MOSER; Dirs Dr OTTO KASPAR, Dr JÜRGEN WAGENSONNER; 34 brs.

Bankhaus Daghofer & Co AG: 5010 Salzburg, Griesgasse 11; tel. (0662) 84-15-01-0; telex 633267; Chair. ARMIN HITZENBERGER; 2 brs.

Eisenstädter Bank AG: 7001 Eisenstadt, Hauptstr. 31; tel. (02682) 2501; telex 17610; cap. 35m.; Dirs MANFRED SCHNEIDER, ERNST GASSNER; 6 brs.

Salzburger Kredit- und Wechsel-Bank AG: 5024 Salzburg, Makartplatz 3; tel. (0662) 72516-0; telex 633625; f. 1921; cap. 60m.; Dirs KLAUS BÖNING, GEORG EBNER; 3 brs.

Steiermärkische Bank GmbH: 8011 Graz, Hauptplatz, Rathaus; tel. (0316) 7032; telex 311930; f. 1922; cap. 120m.; Gen. Man. Dr JAN OHMS.

Specialized Banks

Österreichische Investitionskredit AG: 1013 Vienna, Renngasse 10; tel. (01) 53135; telex 114495; cap. 465m.; Chair. and Gen. Man. Dr ANTON OSOND.

Österreichische Kommunalkredit AG: 1011 Vienna, Renngasse 10; tel. (01) 533-26-77; cap. 100m.

Österreichische Kontrollbank AG: 1010 Vienna, Am Hof 4; tel. (01) 531-27-0; telex 132747; f. 1946; export financing, stock exchange clearing, money market operations; cap. 440m. (Dec. 1987); Chair. and Gen. Man. Komm. Rat HELMUT H. HASCHEK.

Savings Banks

Girozentrale und Bank der österreichischen Sparkassen AG (GZ) (Central Bank of the Austrian Savings Banks): 1011 Vienna, Schubertring 5; tel. (01) 71-194-0; telex 132591; f. 1937; central institution of savings banks; cap. 2,725m., dep. 242,630m. (1987); Chair. and Gen. Man. Komm. Rat Dr KARL PALE.

Die Erste Österreichische Spar-Casse (First Austrian Savings Bank): 1010 Vienna, Graben 21; tel. (01) 53100; telex 114012; f. 1819; cap. and reserves 4,086.6m., dep. 114,285.4m. (Dec. 1986); Chair. and CEO Dr HANS HAUMER; 110 brs.

Österreichische Postsparkasse: 1018 Vienna, Georg-Coch Platz 2; tel. (01) 51-40-00; telex 111663; f. 1883; cap. 2,307m., dep. 149,279m. (1986); Gov. Dkfm. KURT NÖSSLINGER; Vice-Govs Dr V.WOLF, Dr. E. HAMPEL; 12 brs.

Zentralsparkasse und Kommerzialbank Wien (Z) (Savings Bank): 1030 Vienna, Vordere Zollamtsstr. 13; tel. (01) 7292-0; telex 133615; f. 1905; cap. 7,691m., dep. 185,901m. (1987); Chair. Prof. Dr HELMUT ZILK; 173 brs.

Co-operative Banks

Genossenschaftliche Zentralbank AG (GZB-Vienna): 1011 Vienna, Herrengasse 1; tel. (01) 6662-0; telex 136989; f. 1927; cap. 2,000m., dep. 107,795m. (Dec. 1987); central institute of the Austrian Raiffeisen banking group; Pres. Dr KARL GRUBER; Gen. Man. Dr KLAUS LIEBSCHER; 3 brs.

AUSTRIA *Directory*

Österreichische Volksbanken-AG: 1090 Vienna, Peregringasse 3; tel. (01) 3134-0; telex 134206; f. 1922; cap. 525m., dep. 54,575m. (1987); Chair. and CEO ROBERT MÄDL.

Bankers' Organization

Verband österreichischer Banken und Bankiers (Asscn of Austrian Banks and Bankers): 1013 Vienna, Börsegasse 11; tel. (01) 535-17-71; telex 132824; f. 1945; Pres. GUIDO SCHMIDT-CHIARI; Gen. Sec Dr FRITZ DIWOK; 52 mems.

STOCK EXCHANGE

Wiener Börsekammer (Vienna Stock Exchange): 1011 Vienna, Wipplingerstr. 34; tel. (01) 53-4-99; telex 132447; f. 1771; two sections: Stock Exchange, Commodity Exchange; Pres. Dkfm. GERHARD WAGNER; Gen. Sec. Dr KURT NEUTEUFEL.

INSURANCE COMPANIES

In 1988 there were 69 insurance organizations in Austria. A selection of companies is given below.

Anglo-Elementar Versicherungs-AG: 1015 Vienna, Kärntner Ring 12; tel. (01) 65-57-67; telex 132355; Gen. Man. ERIK SKREINER.

Austria Österreichische Versicherungs-AG: 1021 Vienna II, Untere Donaustr. 25; tel. (01) 21-1-75; telex 135308; f. 1936; Gen. Man. HERBERT SCHIMETSCHEK.

Donau Allgemeine Versicherungs-AG: 1010 Vienna, Schottenring 15; tel. (0222) 31-46-11; f. 1867; all classes; Gen. Man. Dr GERHARD PUSCHMANN.

Erste Allgemeine Versicherungs-AG: 1011 Vienna, Landskrongasse 1-3; tel. (01) 6338-0; telex 114085; f. 1882; Gen. Man. Dr DIETRICH KARNER.

Grazer Wechselseitige Versicherung: 8011 Graz, Herrengasse 18–20; tel. (0316) 7037-0; telex 31414; f. 1828; all classes; Gen. Man. Dr FRIEDRICH FALL.

Internationale Unfall- und Schadenversicherung AG: 1011 Vienna, Tegetthoffstr. 7; tel. (01) 51403-0; telex 112111; cap. 200,000m. (1985); all classes except life insurance and annuity insurance; Gen. Man. Mag. Dr JOSEF CUDLIN.

Versicherungsanstalt der österreichischen Bundesländer Versicherungs-AG: 1021 Vienna, Praterstr. 1-7; tel. (01) 2619-0; telex 134800; Gen. Man. Dr WALTER PETRAK.

Wiener Allianz Versicherungs-AG: 1131 Vienna, Hietzinger Kai 101-105; tel. (01) 94-85-11-0; telex 134222; f. 1860; all classes except life insurance; Gen. Man. Dr ERNST BAUMGARTNER.

Wiener Städtische Wechselseitige Versicherungsanstalt (Municipal Insurance Co of the City of Vienna): 1011 Vienna I, Schottenring 30; tel. (01) 531-39-0; telex 135140; f. 1898; all classes; Chair. The Mayor of Vienna; Gen. Man. Dipl. Kfm. Dr ERICH GÖTTLICHER.

Zürich Kosmos Versicherungen AG: 1015 Vienna I, Schwarzenbergplatz 15; tel. (01) 501-25-0; telex 133375; f. 1910; all classes; Gen. Man. Dr WERNER FABER.

Insurance Organization

Verband der Versicherungsunternehmungen Österreichs (Asscn of Austrian Insurance Companies): 1030 Vienna III, Schwarzenbergplatz 7; tel. (01) 711-56-0; telex 133289; f. 1945; Pres. HERBERT SCHIMETSCHEK; Gen. Sec. Dr HERBERT PFLÜGER.

Trade and Industry

CHAMBERS OF COMMERCE

All Austrian enterprises must by law be members of the Economic Chambers. The Federal Economic Chamber promotes international contacts and represents the economic interest of trade and industry on a federal level. Its Foreign Trade Organization includes about 90 offices abroad.

Bundeskammer der gewerblichen Wirtschaft (Federal Economic Chamber): 1045 Vienna, Wiedner Hauptstr. 63; tel. (01) 50105; telex 111871; f. 1946; six sections: Commerce, Industry, Smallscale Production, Banking and Insurance, Transport and Tourism; these divisions are subdivided into branch associations; Local Economic Chambers with divisions and branch associations in each of the nine Austrian provinces; Pres. Abg. z. Nationalrat RUDOLF SALLINGER; Sec.-Gen. D.Dr KARL KEHRER; 271,600 mems.

INDUSTRIAL ASSOCIATIONS

Bundeskammer der gewerblichen Wirtschaft—Bundessektion Industrie: 1045 Vienna I, Wiedner Hauptstr. 63; tel. (01) 6505; telex 11871; f. 1896 as Zentralverband der Industrie Österreichs (Central Federation of Austrian Industry), merged into present organization 1947; Chair. Dipl. Volksw. PHILIPP SCHOELLER; Deputy Chair. Pres. Dr CHRISTIAN BEURLE; Dir Dr FRIEDRICH PLACEK; comprises the following industrial federations:

Fachverband der Audiovisions- und Filmindustrie (Films): 1045 Vienna, Wiedner Hauptstr. 63; tel. (01) 6505; telex 111871; Chair. Prof. WALTHER K. STOITZNER, Dr ELMAR A. PETERLUNGER; 1,200 mems.

Fachverband der Bauindustrie (Building): 1030 Vienna, Engelsberggasse 4, Postfach 87; tel. (01) 713-65-04-0; telex 135284; Chair. Dipl.-Ing. FRIEDRICH FELLERER; Dir Dr JOHANNES SCHENK; 136 mems.

Fachverband der Bekleidungsindustrie (Clothing): 1030 Vienna III, Schwarzenbergplatz 4; tel. (01) 72-12-96; telex 134891; Chair. ALFONS SCHNEIDER; Dir Mag. CHRISTOPH HAIDINGER; 606 mems.

Fachverband der Bergwerke und Eisenerzeugenden Industrie (Mining and Iron Producing): 1015 Vienna, Goethegasse 3, Postfach 300; tel. (01) 52-46-01-0; Chair. Gen. Dir K.R. Dr Ing. FRIEDRICH SCHMOLLGRUBER; Sec. Ing. Mag. HERMANN PRINZ; 112 mems.

Fachverband der Chemischen Industrie (Chemicals): 1045 Vienna 4, Wiedner Hauptstr. 63; tel. (01) 6505; telex 111871; Chair. Gen. Dir Komm. Rat Dipl.-Ing Dr WOLFGANG UNGER; Dir Mag. Dr HARALD STRASSNITZKY; 1,071 mems.

Fachverband der Eisen- und Metallwarenindustrie Österreichs (Iron and Metal Goods): 1045 Vienna 4, Wiedner Hauptstr. 63, Postfach 335; tel. (01) 501-05; telex 113872; f. 1908; Chair. Komm. Rat HANNES FOLTER; Dir Dipl. Kfm. GOTTFRIED TAURER; 800 mems.

Fachverband der Elektro-und Elektronikindustrie (Electrical): 1010 Vienna, Rathausplatz 8; tel. (01) 42-55-97; Chair. Dipl. Ing. ALFRED MOSBECK; Dir Dr HEINZ RASCHKA; 558 mems.

Fachverband der Erdölindustrie (Oil): 1031 Vienna, Erdbergstr. 72; tel. (01) 713-23-48; telex 132138; f. 1947; Gen. Dir Dr HERBERT KAES; Gen. Sec. Dr HERBERT LANG; 21 mems.

Fachverband der Fahrzeugindustrie (Vehicles): 1045 Vienna 4, Wiedner Hauptstr. 63; tel. (01) 6505; telex 111871; Pres. Dipl.-Ing. OTTO VOISARD; Gen. Sec. Mag. ERIK BAIER; 160 mems.

Fachverband der Gas- und Wärmeversorgungsunternehmungen (Gas and Heating): 1010 Vienna, Schubertring 14; tel. (01) 513-15-88; Chair. Gen. Dir Komm. Rat Dr KARL REISINGER; Dir Dkfm. GERHARD JANACZEK; 104 mems.

Fachverband der Giessereiindustrie (Foundries): 1045 Vienna 4, Wiedner Hauptstr. 63, Postfach 339; tel. (01) 50105-3463; telex 111871; Chair. Ing. MICHAEL ZIMMERMANN; Dir Dr KURT KRENKEL; 133 mems.

Fachverband der Glasindustrie (Glass): 1045 Vienna 4, Wiedner Hauptstr. 63, Postfach 328; tel. (01) 6505; telex 111871; Chair. Dipl. Ing. RAIMUND CRAMMER; Dir Dr PETER SCHOEPF; 65 mems.

Fachverband der Holzverarbeitenden Industrie (Wood Processing): 1037 Vienna III, Schwarzenbergplatz 4, Postfach 123; tel. (01) 712-26-01; telex 134891; f. 1946; Chair. Komm. Rat HANNO WEISS; Dir Dr GEORG PENKA; 613 mems.

Fachverband der Ledererzeugenden Industrie (Leather Producing): 1045 Vienna 4, Wiedner Hauptstr. 63, Postfach 312; tel. (01) 50105; telex 111871; f. 1945; Chair. Ing. HELMUTH SCHMIDT; Dir Dr HEINRICH LEOPOLD; 14 mems.

Fachverband der Lederverarbeitenden Industrie (Leather Processing): 1045 Vienna 4, Wiedner Hauptstr. 63, Postfach 313; tel. (01) 50105; telex 111871; f. 1945; Chair. GERHARD WALLNER; Dir Dr HEINRICH LEOPOLD; 83 mems.

Fachverband der Maschinen- und Stahlbauindustrie (Machinery and Steel Construction): 1045 Vienna, Wiedner Hauptstr. 63; f. 1908; Pres. Dr JOSEF BERTSCH; Dir Mag. OTTO NEUMAYER; 1,086 mems.

Fachverband der Metallindustrie (Metals): 1045 Vienna 4, Wiedner Hauptstr. 63, Postfach 338; tel. (01) 6505; telex 111871; f. 1946; Chair. Komm. Rat Dr OTHMAR RANKL; Dir Dr GÜNTER GREIL; 69 mems.

Fachverband der Nahrungs- und Genussmittelindustrie (Provisions): Vienna III, Zaunergasse 1-3; tel. (01) 72-21-21; telex 131247; Chair. Ing. MARTIN PECHER; Dir Dr KLAUS SMOLKA; 674 mems.

Fachverband der Papier und Pappe verarbeitenden Industrie (Paper and Board Processing): 1041 Vienna, Brucknerstr. 8; tel. (01) 505-53-82-0; Chair. Komm. Rat HEINZ KONWALLIN; Dir Dkfm. Dr WERNER HOSCHKARA; 188 mems.

Fachverband der Papierindustrie (Paper): 1061 Vienna, Gumpendorferstr. 6; tel. (01) 58-886-0; telex 111734; Chair. Dr ROBERT LAUNSKY-TIEFFENTHAL; Dir Dr GEROLF OTTAWA; 63 mems.

Fachverband der Sägeindustrie (Sawmills): 1011 Vienna I, Uraniastr. 4/1; tel. (01) 75-76-25; telex 61322301; f. 1947; Chair.

Dipl. Ing HERBERT KULTERER; Dir Dr GERHARD ALTRICHTER; 2,401 mems.

Fachverband der Stein- und Keramischen Industrie (Stone and Ceramics): 1045 Vienna, Wiedner Hauptstr. 63, Postfach 329; tel (01) 6505-3531; telex 111871; f. 1946; Chair. Dr CARL HENNRICH; Pres. Ing. LEOPOLD HELBICH; 470 mems.

Fachverband der Textilindustrie (Textiles): 1013 Vienna I, Rudolfsplatz 12; tel. (01) 533-37-26-0; telex 114125; Pres. Dr THEODOR HLADIK; Dir Dr HELMUT HUBER; 400 mems.

TRADE UNIONS

The Trade Union Federation represents employees at all levels, except top managerial. By law all employees are subject to collective agreements which are negotiated annually by the Federation. About 60% of workers are members.

Österreichischer Gewerkschaftsbund (OGB) (Austrian Trade Union Federation): 1011 Vienna I, Hohenstaufengasse 10-12; tel. (01) 53-444; telex 114316; non-party union organization with voluntary membership; f. 1945; organized in 15 trade unions, affiliated with ICFTU and ETUC; Pres. FRIEDRICH VERZETNITSCH; Exec. Secs KARL DROCHTER, HERBERT TUMPEL; 1,652,839 mems (1987).

Bundesfraktion Christlicher Gewerkschafter im Österreichischen Gewerkschaftsbund (Christian Trade Unionists' Section of the Austrian Trade Union Federation): 1010 Vienna I, Hohenstaufengasse 12; tel. (01) 53-444; organized in Christian Trade Unionists' Sections of the following 15 trade unions; affiliated with WCL; Sec.-Gen. GÜNTHER ENGELMAYER.

Gewerkschaft der Bau- und Holzarbeiter (Building Workers and Woodworkers): 1082 Vienna I, Ebendorferstr. 7; tel. (01) 42-36-41; telex 114833; Chair. JOSEF HESOUN; 184,224 mems (1987).

Gewerkschaft der Chemiearbeiter (Chemical Workers): 1060 Vienna VI, Stumpergasse 60; tel. (01) 597-15-01; Chair. ERWIN HOLZERBAUER; 59,833 mems (1984).

Gewerkschaft Druck und Papier (Printing and Paper Trade Workers): 1072 Vienna, Postfach 91, Seidengasse 15-17; tel. (01) 93-82-31; f. 1842; Chair. HERBERT BRUNA; 23,160 mems (1986).

Gewerkschaft der Eisenbahner (Railwaymen): 1051 Vienna V, Margaretenstr. 166; tel. (01) 55-46-47; Chair. FRITZ PRECHTI; 117,511 mems (1984).

Gewerkschaft der Gemeindebediensteten (Municipal Employees): 1090 Vienna IX, Maria-Theresien-Str. 11; tel. (01) 34-36-00; Chair. RUDOLF PÖDER; 168,897 mems (1984).

Gewerkschaft Land-Forst-Garten (Agricultural and Forestry Workers): 1013 Vienna I, Wipplingerstr. 35; tel. (01) 53-444-480; f. 1906; Chair. ERICH DIRNGRABNER; 19,828 mems (1984).

Gewerkschaft Handel, Transport, Verkehr (Workers in Commerce and Transport): 1010 Vienna, Teinfaltstr. 7; tel. (01) 53-4-54; f. 1904; Chair. ROBERT ZEHENTHOFER; 37,385 mems (1987).

Gewerkschaft Hotel, Gastgewerbe, Persönlicher Dienst (Hotel and Restaurant Workers): 1013 Vienna I, Hohenstaufengasse 10; tel. (01) 534-44; f. 1906; Chair. ERWIN NIEMITZ; 50,867 mems (1987).

Gewerkschaft Kunst, Medien, freie Berufe (Musicians, Actors, Artists, Journalists, etc.): 1090 Vienna IX, Maria-Theresien-Str. 11; tel. (01) 34-36-00; f. 1945; Chair. Ing. STEFAN MÜLLER; Sec.-Gen. WALTER BACHER; 17,872 mems (1986).

Gewerkschaft der Lebens- und Genussmittelarbeiter (Food, Beverage and Tobacco Workers): 1080 Vienna, Albertgasse 35; tel. (01) 42-15-45; Chair. Dr JOSEF STARIBACHER; 42,881 mems (1985).

Gewerkschaft Metall-Bergbau-Energie (Metal Workers, Miners and Power Supply Workers): 1041 Vienna IV, Plösslgasse 15; tel. (01) 65-46-91; f. 1890; Chair. SEPP WILLE; 251,112 mems (1986).

Gewerkschaft Öffentlicher Dienst (Public Employees): 1010 Vienna I, Teinfaltstr. 7; tel. (01) 63-96-61; telex 114402; f. 1945; Chair. RUDOLF SOMMER; Gen. Secs ALFRED STIFTER, HANNS WAAS; 220,654 mems (1984).

Gewerkschaft der Post- und Fernmeldebediensteten (Postal and Telegraph Workers): 1010 Vienna, Biberstr. 5; tel. (01) 52-55-11; telex 112042; Chair. NORBERT TMEJ; 77,485 mems (1987).

Gewerkschaft der Privatangestellten (Commercial, Clerical and Technical Employees): 1013 Vienna, Deutschmeisterplatz 2; tel. (01) 34-35-20; telex 114114; Chair. ALFRED DALLINGER; 346,126 mems (1984).

Gewerkschaft Textil, Bekleidung, Leder (Textile, Garment and Leather Workers): 1010 Vienna I, Hohenstaufengasse 10; tel. (01) 63-37-11; f. 1945; Chair. HARALD ETTL; 50,303 mems (1984).

NATIONALIZED INDUSTRIES

After the Second World War the Nationalrat passed a law giving the State control in the sectors concerned with coal and ore mining, iron and steel, non-ferrous metals, petroleum production and processing, chemical production, electricity and engineering and shipbuilding. Nationalized industries now employ about one-fifth of industrial workers and contribute almost one-quarter of the country's industrial production. To rationalize the administration of the State's interest in these concerns and their subsidiaries, a Federal Law passed in January 1970 transferred the controlling interest to the Austrian Nationalized Industries Holding Company (ÖIAG).

Österreichische Industrieholding Aktiengesellschaft (ÖIAG) (Austrian Nationalized Industries Holding Company): 1015 Vienna, Kantgasse 1, Postfach 99; tel. (01) 71-114; telex 132047; f. 1970 to form an effective co-ordination of the nationalized enterprises on the basis of economic management and to promote research activities in the subsidiary companies; Chair. Board of Dirs Dr HUGO MICHAEL SEKYRA; Chair. Supervisory Board Dr JOSEF STARIBACHER; controls the following concerns and their subsidiaries:

Austria Metall AG: 5280 Braunau am Inn-Ranshofen; tel. (07722) 2341; telex 27745; f. 1939; aluminium production and processing, copper and copper alloy semi-finished products; Chair. Board of Dirs Dr ROBERT EHRLICH; Chair. Supervisory Board Dr HUGO MICHAEL SEKYRA; 4,600 employees.

Bleiberger Bergwerks-Union: 9010 Klagenfurt, Radetzkystr. 2, Postfach 95; tel. (04222) 55-525; telex 422434; f. 1867; lead and zinc mining and processing; Chair. Board of Dirs Dr JULIUS STAINER; Chair. Supervisory Board Dipl. Ing. ERICH STASKA; 1,568 employees.

Chemie Holding AG: 4021 Linz, St Peter-Str. 25, Postfach 296; tel. (0732) 5910; telex 21324; f. 1939; chemical products; Chair. Board of Dirs Gen. Dir Dr RICHARD KIRCHWEGER; Chair. Supervisory Board Dkfm. Dr OSKAR GRÜNWALD; 6,000 employees.

Elin Union AG: 1140 Vienna, Penzingerstr. 76; tel. (01) 82-900; telex 112763; f. 1892; electrical industry; Chair. Board of Dirs GUIDO KLESTIL; Chair. Supervisory Board Dkfm. HANS RUTKOWSKI; 6,639 employees.

ÖMV AG: 1090 Vienna, Otto-Wagner-Platz 5, Postfach 15; tel. (01) 48-900; telex 114801; partially privatized in 1987; exploration, production, import and transport of crude oil, semi-finished products and natural gas; f. 1955 as Österreichische Mineralölverwaltung; Chair. Board of Dirs, Dipl. Ing. Dr HERBERT KAES; Chair. Supervisory Board Dkfm. Dr OSKAR GRÜNWALD; 6,300 employees.

Simmering-Graz-Pauker AG: 1110 Vienna, Brehmstr. 16; tel. (01) 74-69; telex 132574; f. 1831; heavy engineering; Chair. Board of Dirs Dipl. Ing. Dr KLAUS WOLTRON; Chair. Supervisory Board Dkfm. HANS RUTKOWSKI; 3,564 employees.

Voest-Alpine AG: 4010 Linz, POB 2; tel. (0732) 585; telex 2207444; iron and steel works, steel processing, mechanical engineering, design and supply of industrial plants; Chair. Board of Dirs Dr HERBERT C. LEWINSKY; Chair. Supervisory Board Dr HUGO MICHAEL SEKYRA; 38,079 employees.

Wolfsegg-Traunthaler Kohlenwerks AG: 4010 Linz, Waltherstr. 22, Postfach 65; tel. (0732) 27-05-01; telex 26543; f. 1911; coal; Dirs Dr HANS SCHABEL, Dipl. Ing. FALKO PEBALL; Chair. Supervisory Board Dipl. Ing. ERICH STASKA; 620 employees.

TRADE FAIRS

Trade Fairs play an important part in the economic life of Austria. The largest are held during the spring and autumn at Vienna, but there are also a number of important fairs held in the provinces.

Dornbirner Messe GmbH: 6854 Dornbirn, Messestr. 4, Postfach 100; tel. (05572) 65-6-94; telex 059108; annually (July); average number of visitors 200,000.

Grazer Messe International: 8011 Graz, Postfach 63; f. 1906; twice yearly (May and October); exhibits of all categories, but special emphasis on agriculture, iron and steel, hotel and building equipment; average number of visitors 500,000; once yearly: Technova, international high-tech, innovation fair; Dir GERD NOVAK.

Innsbrucker Messe GmbH: 6020 Innsbruck, Falkstr. 2-4; tel. (05222) 585911; annually (April, May and September); mainly devoted to tourism and equipment for the tourist; average number of visitors 200,000.

Österreichische Holzmesse-Klagenfurter Messe (Austrian Timber Fair): Messedirektion, 9021 Klagenfurt, Postfach 79, Valentin-Leitgeb-Str. 11; annually (summer season); main emphasis on timber and articles made of wood; average number of visitors 300,000.

Rieder Messe: 4910 Ried im Innkreis, Postfach 61; tel. (07752) 4011; telex 027/720; holds International Agricultural Fair and Ried Spring Fair in alternate years; over 1m. visitors.

Vienna Fairs and Congress Ltd: 1071 Vienna, Messeplatz 1, Postfach 124; tel. (01) 93-15-24; telex 133491; f. 1921; three annual general fairs (February, March and September), 22-26 specialized

AUSTRIA

fairs per year at two sites; exhibits of all categories; average number of visitors 1,200,000; Pres. MANFRED MAUTNER MARKHOF; Dirs Dr REGINALD FÖLDY, GERD A. HOFFMANN.

Welser Messe: 4601 Wels, Messehaus; tel. (07242) 8-22-22; telex 25400; every 2 years; agriculture, cattle-breeding, industry, trade; average number of visitors approx. 1m.

Transport

RAILWAYS

The Austrian Federal Railways operate 90% of all the railway routes in Austria. There are approximately 5,800 km of track and all main lines are electrified.

Österreichische Bundesbahnen (ÖBB) (Austrian Federal Railways): Head Office: 1010 Vienna, Elisabethstr. 9; tel. (01) 56-50-0; telex 1377; Dir-Gen. Dr HEINRICH ÜBLEIS.

Innsbruck Divisional Management: 6020 Innsbruck, Claudiastr. 2; Pres. Dipl.-Ing. S. KIENPOINTNER.

Linz Divisional Management: 4020 Linz, Bahnhofstr. 3; tel. (0732) 56411; Pres. Dr GUSTAV HAMMERSCHMID.

Vienna Divisional Management: 1020 Vienna, Nordbahnstr. 50; Pres. Dr ERWIN SEMMELRATH.

Villach Divisional Management: 9500 Villach, 10.-Oktober-Str. 20; Pres. Dr RUDOLF REISP.

Other railway companies include: Achensee Railway, Graz–Köflach Railway, Györ–Sopron–Ebenfurt Railway, Montafon Railway, Salzburg-Lamprechtshausen, Stern and Hafferl Light Railways Co, Styrian Provincial Railways, Tirol Zugspitze Railway, Vienna Local Railways, Zillertal Railway (Jenbach–Mayrhofen).

ROADS

At 31 December 1987 Austria had 107,503 km of classified roads, of which 1,376 km were modern motorway, 10,143 km main roads, 24,987 km secondary roads and an estimated 70,000 km communal roads.

INLAND WATERWAYS

The Danube (Donau) is Austria's only navigable river. It enters Austria from Germany at Passau and flows into Czechoslovakia near Hainburg. The length of the Austrian section of the river is 351 km. Danube barges carry up to 1,800 tons, but loading depends on the water level, which varies considerably during the year. Cargoes are chiefly petroleum and derivatives, coal, coke, iron ore, iron, steel, timber and grain. A passenger service is maintained on the Upper Danube and between Vienna and the Black Sea. Passenger services are also provided on Bodensee (Lake Constance) and Wolfgangsee by Austrian Federal Railways, and on all the larger Austrian lakes.

Ministry of the Public Sector and Transport: 1030 Vienna, Radetzkystr. 2; tel. (01) 711-62-0; telex 111800; responsible for the administration of inland waterways.

Erste Donau-Dampfschiffahrts-Gesellschaft (First Danube Steamship Co): 1021 Vienna, Handelskai 265; tel. (01) 217-10-0; telex 131698; fleet consists of 11 passenger vessels, 8 pushers, 29 motor-cargoships, 107 cargo-barges and lighters, 9 motor tankships, 30 tank-barges and lighters.

CIVIL AVIATION

The main international airport is at Schwechat, near Vienna. There are also international flights from Innsbruck, Salzburg, Graz, Klagenfurt and Linz, and internal flights between these cities.

Österreichische Luftverkehrs AG (Austrian Airlines): 1107 Vienna, Fontanastr. 1; tel. (01) 68-35-11; telex 131811; f. 1957; 75% state-owned; serves 57 cities in 37 countries of Europe, North Africa and the Middle East, also New York and Tokyo, covering 57,930 km; external flights from Vienna, Graz, Linz, Klagenfurt and Salzburg to 45 European and Middle East destinations; Chair. and Dir-Gen. OTTO BINDER; Man. Dirs D.Dr A. HESCHGL, Dr H. PAPOUSEK; fleet of 2 Airbus A310, 2 MD-87, 13 MD-81, 3 DC-9-32, 4 Fokker 50; on order: 4 MD-87, 1 Airbus A 310.

Tourism

Tourism plays an important part in the Austrian economy; receipts from tourism were estimated at 105,000m. Schilling in 1987, when Austria received 15.8m. foreign visitors. The country's mountain scenery attracts visitors in both summer and winter, while Vienna and Salzburg, where internationally-renowned art festivals are held, are important cultural centres.

Österreichische Fremdenverkehrswerbung (Austrian National Tourist Office): Vienna IV, Margaretenstr. 1; tel. (01) 588-66; telex 3222306.

Atomic Energy

Construction of Austria's first nuclear power station, at Zwentendorf on the Danube, was begun in 1971. A referendum was held in November 1978, when it was decided that the plant should not be put into operation, and public opinion remains divided on the issue. In March 1985 a formal decision to dismantle the plant was taken, in view of the high maintenance costs, and it seemed likely that parts of the installation would be sold.

Österreichisches Forschungszentrum Seibersdorf GmbH–ÖFZS (Austrian Research Centre, Seibersdorf): 2444 Seibersdorf; tel. (02254) 800; telex 014353; f. 1956; a limited company of which the capital is shared by the Austrian Government (51%), State industries (25%) and private enterprises (24%). Man. Dirs Prof. Dr PETER KOSS (Science and Technology), Prof. Dr WINFRIED SCHENK (Industry and Marketing); Chair. Dipl.-Ing. Dr ERICH STASKA.

THE BAHAMAS

Introductory Survey

Location, Climate, Language, Religion, Flag, Capital

The Commonwealth of the Bahamas consists of about 700 islands and more than 2,000 cays and rocks, extending from off the Florida coast of the USA to just north of Cuba and Haiti, in the West Indies. The main islands are New Providence, Grand Bahama, Andros, Eleuthera and Great Abaco. More than 60% of the population reside on the island of New Providence. The remaining members of the group are known as the 'Family Islands'. A total of 29 of the islands are inhabited. The climate is mild and sub-tropical, with average temperatures of about 30°C (86°F) in summer and 20°C (68°F) in winter. The average annual rainfall is about 1,000 mm (39 in). The official language is English. Most of the inhabitants profess Christianity, the largest denominations being the Anglican, Baptist, Roman Catholic and Methodist churches. The national flag has three equal horizontal stripes, of blue, gold and blue, with a black triangle at the hoist, extending across one-half of the width. The capital is Nassau, on the island of New Providence.

Recent History

A former British colonial territory, the Bahamas attained internal self-government in January 1964, although the parliamentary system dates back to 1729. The first elections under universal adult suffrage were held in January 1967 for an enlarged House of Assembly. The Progressive Liberal Party (PLP), supported mainly by Bahamians of African origin and led by Lynden (later Sir Lynden) Pindling, won 18 of the 38 seats, as did the ruling United Bahamian Party (UBP), dominated by Europeans. With the support of another member, the PLP formed a government and Pindling became Premier. At the next election, in April 1968, the PLP won 29 seats and the UBP only seven.

Following a constitutional conference in September 1968, the Bahamas government was given increased responsibility for internal security, external affairs and defence in May 1969. In the elections of September 1972, which were dominated by the issue of independence, the PLP maintained its majority. Following a constitutional conference in December 1972, the Bahamas became an independent nation, within the Commonwealth, on 10 July 1973. Pindling remained Prime Minister. The PLP increased its majority in the elections of July 1977 and was again returned to power in the June 1982 elections, with 32 of the 43 seats in the House of Assembly. The remaining 11 seats were won by the Free National Movement (FNM), which had reunited for the elections after splitting into several factions over the previous five years.

Trading in illicit drugs, mainly for the US market, has become a major problem for the country, since many of the small islands and cays are being used by drug traffickers in their smuggling activities. In 1983 allegations were made of widespread corruption, and the abuse of Bahamian bank secrecy laws by drug financiers and US tax evaders. These claims were denied by Sir Lynden Pindling, who announced, in November 1983, the appointment of a Royal Commission to investigate thoroughly all aspects of the drug trade in the Bahamas. The Commission's hearings revealed the extent to which money deriving from the drug trade had permeated Bahamian social and economic affairs. By November 1985 a total of 51 suspects had been indicted, including the assistant police commissioner, Howard Smith, who was charged with bribery and dismissed from the force. In October 1984 two Cabinet ministers, implicated by the evidence presented to the Commission, resigned. The Commission also revealed that Sir Lynden had received several million dollars in gifts and loans from businessmen, although the Commission stated that there was no evidence that the payments were drug-related. After unsuccessfully demanding Sir Lynden's resignation, the Deputy Prime Minister, Arthur Hanna, resigned, and two further ministers were dismissed. The opposition FNM staged demonstrations, demanding Pindling's resignation, but the Prime Minister refused to accept any personal responsibility for corruption by public officials, and the PLP convention at the end of October unanimously endorsed Pindling as party leader.

An early general election was held on 19 June 1987. The issue of the illegal drug trade and of drugs-related corruption within the Government dominated the campaign, but the PLP was returned to power for a fifth consecutive term, obtaining 53% of the total votes and winning 31 of the 49 seats in the enlarged House of Assembly. The FNM won 16 seats, while the remaining two seats were won by independents. The opposition later claimed that the election had been fraudulent, and in December the courts agreed to examine the allegations in nearly one-half of the constituencies.

Controversy over the drugs issue continued into 1988. Statistics relating to crime in 1987 indicated unprecedented levels of violent and drug-related offences, and in February 1988 new claims of official corruption were made at the trial in Florida, USA, of a leading Colombian drugs trafficker. Pindling and the Deputy Prime Minister were alleged to have accepted bribes, but this was vehemently denied. Furthermore, new measures were announced against the drug trade and corruption, and in May 1988 the Bahamas requested US naval co-operation. Also in May, the Judicial Committee of the Privy Council, in London, finally rejected accusations by the opposition that Sir Lynden and Lady Pindling's financial affairs had not been sufficiently investigated.

The Bahamas' traditionally close relationship with the USA has been strained by the increasingly aggressive attitudes of the US Government towards the bank secrecy laws and the drug smuggling in the islands. In July 1988 the Bahamas led a protest of the CARICOM (see p. 106) nations at US attempts to impose its extraterritorial jurisdiction on small neighbours. Nevertheless, the USA and the Bahamas have collaborated in a series of operations to intercept drug smugglers; financial and institutional co-operation has increased; and in June 1987 a legal assistance treaty was signed with the USA. In mid-1988 the US Senate approved the certification of the Bahamas as 'fully co-operative' in the campaign against illicit drugs. Relations with the Bahamas' other neighbours, Haiti and Cuba, have been strained by the influx of large numbers of illegal Haitian immigrants, and the sinking of a Bahamian patrol boat by Cuba in 1980.

Government

Legislative power is vested in the bicameral Parliament. The Senate has 16 members, of whom nine are appointed by the Governor-General on the advice of the Prime Minister, four by the Leader of the Opposition and three after consultation with the Prime Minister. The House of Assembly has 49 members, elected for five years (subject to dissolution) by universal adult suffrage. Executive power is vested in the British monarch, represented by a Governor-General, who is appointed on the Prime Minister's recommendations and who acts, in almost all matters, on the advice of the Cabinet. The Governor-General appoints the Prime Minister and, on the latter's recommendation, selects the other Ministers. The Cabinet is responsible to the House.

Defence

The paramilitary Coastguard is the only security force in the Bahamas, and numbered 600 in June 1988. The defence budget in 1987 was a record US $60m., most of which was to finance the anti-drug trafficking campaign.

Economic Affairs

In 1987, according to estimates by the World Bank, the Bahamas' gross national product (GNP) per head, measured at average 1985–87 prices, was US $10,320, the highest level among Caribbean countries. It was estimated that GNP per head increased, in real terms, at an average rate of 2.8% per year between 1980 and 1987.

Tourism is the main source of income, accounting for about 54% of gross domestic product (GDP) in 1985 and employing some 43% of the working population. In response to a decline in the number of visitors in 1981 and to competition from other islands, the Government increased the budget for tourism by nearly 40% in 1982. Tourist arrivals increased by 5%, to 2.3m., in 1984, and to 2.6m. in 1985. In 1986 the number of cruise-ship passenger arrivals increased by 32% over the previous year's figure, and total arrivals reached 3.0m. Almost 90% of visitors to the Bahamas are from the USA, and this market seems to have been particularly affected by the sharp decline in stock market prices in October 1987. Therefore, despite continued substantial increases in the number of European and Canadian visitors (due to favourable exchange rates), total arrivals in 1987 rose to only 3.1m. In 1988 the tourism budget was increased by B $5m., to B $34.2m. Receipts from tourism in 1987 were estimated at US $1,170.3m. The revival of the tourist industry has encouraged foreign investment in the sector, and in 1986 the Government enhanced its Tourism Development Plan. The state-owned Bahamas Hotel Corporation planned to double the amount of tourist accommodation by 1995. In addition, improvements are being carried out at Nassau Airport and Nassau Harbour, and cruise-ship facilities are being developed in several outer islands (a B $50m. contract was awarded in May 1988).

The Government is attempting to broaden the country's economic base by developing agriculture and fishing, which together accounted for less than 5% of GDP in 1981, and industrial activity. Approximately 80% of food supplies are imported. The reduction of these imports, which are mainly required for the tourist trade, is a primary aim of the Government's 1980-90 Master Plan to promote economic growth. The plan provides for improvements to agricultural and fisheries infrastructure. The cultivation of citrus fruit for export has been encouraged in order to take advantage of the damage caused by frost and disease to citrus fruit plantations in the southern USA. More than 20,000 acres (8,000 ha) are expected to be converted to fruit farming by 1995. In January 1986 the UN Food and Agriculture Organization (FAO) announced that it was to conduct a survey of pine forests on Andros, Abaco and Grand Bahama to assess potential for developing a lumber industry.

The Government also plans to create more jobs in the primary sector. At mid-1987 it was estimated that more than 18% of the labour force were unemployed and that among the under-25-year-olds the rate of unemployment was as high as 35%. However, the rate was on the decline by 1988. It was hoped that people could be encouraged to enter the agricultural and light industry sectors. About 450,000 acres (180,000 ha) of land were reserved for farmers in 1981, and improvements were made in the treatment of smallholders.

Industrial development includes the production of salt, cement, pharmaceuticals and spirits. Also, in 1985, Heineken and two Bahamian partners began construction of a brewery in Nassau, with production capacity of 1.2m. cases of beer per year. The distillery at Nassau is the largest exporter of light rums in the Caribbean, selling more than 12m. litres per year. However, growth in the output of rum (which increased in value by B $2.5m., or 19%, in 1987) and cement (which almost doubled in 1987, by B $0.3m.) was offset by the decline in production of pharmaceuticals, salt and aragonite. In 1987, therefore, exports from the manufacturing sector fell by 4.1%, following a drop of 3% in 1986. This sector has suffered a decline since 1982 (when it accounted for about 10% of GDP), despite continuing government incentives to light manufacturing industries.

Until 1986 the industrial sector was based on petroleum refining and transhipment. However, the petroleum sector has suffered from fluctuations in the price of, and demand for, petroleum and its derivatives. Refining activity at the large petroleum refinery on Grand Bahama, which had been operating at a greatly reduced level, ceased in August 1985. There are two transhipment terminals on Grand Bahama, which are operated as joint ventures by Chevron and the Bahamas Oil Refining Company (Borco) and handle crude petroleum and petroleum products from the USA, Venezuela, Colombia, Mexico and the Far East. By 1987, as a result of renewed interest, three foreign oil companies were actively exploring for petroleum in the Bahamas and were negotiating with the Government for additional exploration rights. Since 1986 there has been particularly strong growth in the construction sector, mainly as a result of harbour developments and hotel-building.

The Bahamas established its own shipping registry in 1976. After an initial lull, many ships have registered; the addition of 10 tankers in 1983 brought the fleet's displacement to a total of 2.5m. grt (the third largest 'open-registry' fleet in the world). By 1986 the fleet had reached 4.0m. grt, and in 1988 it stood at 8.9m. grt.

The Government is committed to retaining the Bahamas' status as a tax haven, and the country has become a leading 'offshore' financial centre. In 1988, however, there was some concern in the banking community as a result of government criticism and the doubling of fees payable by banks in order to operate in the Bahamas. With almost 400 banks in the Bahamas, holding at least US $100m. in deposits at the end of 1986, banking is second only to tourism in importance.

The economy was estimated to have grown by 3.5% in 1986 and by 5% in 1987. Inflation averaged 4.3% in 1987, compared with 6.8% for the previous 12 months. The 1988 budget projected total expenditure of $592m. In December 1987 the country's total national debt stood at an estimated B $597.2m. The current account deficit rose from B $25.9m. in 1986 to B $165.2m. in 1987. Owing to the decline in export earnings, the trade deficit increased by B $162.5m. to reach B $881.6m. in 1987. The Bahamas' principal trading partner is the USA.

Social Welfare

The health service is centralized in Nassau at the government general hospital. In the Family Islands there are 15 clinics with a resident doctor or nurse. In 1980 the Bahamas had six hospital establishments, with a total of 925 beds, and there were 197 physicians working in the country. A Flying Doctor Service supplies medical attention to islands that lack resident personnel. Flying Dental Services and nursing personnel from the Community Nursing Service are also provided. In 1988 the Government announced plans for expenditure of B $4.5m., over four years, on modernizations and on hospitals in Nassau and Grand Bahama. A National Insurance Scheme, established in 1972, provides a wide range of benefits, including sickness, maternity, retirement and widows' pensions as well as social assistance payments. An Industrial Injuries Scheme has been established. Expenditure by the central Government in 1986 included B $64.8m. on health, and a further B $45.0m. on social security and welfare.

Education

Education is compulsory between the ages of five and 14 years, and is provided free of charge in government schools. There is an extensive primary and secondary school system, with 122 schools in 1985. There are several private and denominational schools. Primary education begins at five years of age and lasts for six years. Secondary education, beginning at the age of 11, also lasts for six years and is divided into two equal cycles. The University of the West Indies has an extra-mural department in Nassau, and in 1979 opened a branch in the Bahamas, offering degree courses in hotel management and tourism. Technical, teacher-training and professional qualifications can be obtained at the two campuses of the College of the Bahamas, while the Universities of Miami and St John's, New York, also run degree programmes. Government expenditure on education in 1987 was B $96.5m., or 22.1% of total government spending.

Public Holidays

1989: 2 January (for New Year's Day), 24 March (Good Friday), 27 March (Easter Monday), 15 May (Whit Monday), 3 June (Labour Day), 10 July (Independence Day), 4 August (for Emancipation Day), 12 October (Discovery Day/Columbus Day), 25-26 December (Christmas).

1990: 1 January (New Year's Day), 13 April (Good Friday), 16 April (Easter Monday), 2 June (Labour Day), 4 June (Whit Monday), 10 July (Independence Day), 6 August (for Emancipation Day), 12 October (Discovery Day/Columbus Day), 25-26 December (Christmas).

Weights and Measures

The imperial system is used.

Statistical Survey

Source (unless otherwise stated): Central Bank of the Bahamas, POB N-4868, Frederick St, Nassau; tel. 322-2193; telex 20115.

AREA AND POPULATION

Area: 13,939 sq km (5,382 sq miles).

Population: 175,192 at census of 7 April 1970; 209,505 (males 101,774, females 107,731) at census of 12 May 1980; 240,000 (official estimate for mid-1987). *By island* (1980): New Providence 135,437 (including the capital, Nassau); Grand Bahama 33,102; Andros 8,397; Eleuthera 8,326.

Density (mid-1987): 17.2 per sq km.

Principal Town: Nassau (capital), estimated population 110,000 (1980).

Births, Marriages and Deaths (1986): Registered live births 5,559 (birth rate 24.0 per 1,000); Registered marriages (1985) 1,959 (marriage rate 8.4 per 1,000); Registered deaths 1,181 (death rate 5.1 per 1,000).

Economically Active Population (1980 census): Agriculture, hunting, forestry and fishing 4,554; Mining and quarrying 346; Manufacturing 4,957; Electricity, gas and water 1,271; Construction 6,675; Trade, restaurants and hotels 24,474; Transport, storage and communications 6,176; Financing, insurance, real estate and business services 6,441; Community, social and personal services 24,094; Activities not adequately defined 1,705; Total employed 80,693; Total unemployed 6,359; Total labour force 87,052 (males 48,275; females 38,777) (Source: ILO, *Year Book of Labour Statistics*).

AGRICULTURE, ETC.

Principal Crops (FAO estimates, '000 metric tons, 1986): Sugar cane 232; Tomatoes 9; Bananas 8 (Source: FAO, *Production Yearbook*).

Livestock (FAO estimates, '000 head, year ending September 1986): Cattle 5; Pigs 20; Sheep 40; Goats 18 (Source: FAO, *Production Yearbook*).

Fishing (metric tons, live weight): Total catch 5,341 in 1984; 7,629 in 1985; 5,893 in 1986.

MINING AND INDUSTRY

Production (estimates, '000 metric tons, 1985): Unrefined salt 850; Cement (1984) 63; Motor spirit (petrol) 20; Naphthas 600; Jet fuels 400; Distillate fuel oils 600; Residual fuel oils 1,900; Liquefied petroleum gas 10; Electric energy 854m. kWh (Source: UN, *Industrial Statistics Yearbook*).

FINANCE

Currency and Exchange Rates: 100 cents = 1 Bahamian dollar (B $). *Coins:* 1, 5, 10, 15, 25 and 50 cents; 1, 2 and 5 dollars. *Notes:* 50 cents; 1, 3, 5, 10, 20, 50 and 100 dollars. *Sterling and dollar equivalents* (30 September 1988): £1 sterling = B $1.691; US $1 = B $1.000; B $100 = £59.14 = US $100.00. *Exchange rate:* Since February 1970 the official exchange rate, applicable to most transactions, has been US $1 = B $1, i.e. the Bahamian dollar has been at par with the US dollar. There is also an investment currency rate, applicable to certain transactions between residents and non-residents. The average of this exchange rate (B $ per US $) was: 1.180 in 1985; 1.175 in 1986; 1.199 in 1987.

Budget (B $ million, 1987): *Revenue:* Taxation 353.5 (Import tax 246.3); Other receipts 45.1; Total 398.7. *Expenditure:* General public services 88.4; Defence 13.1; Education 96.5; Health 74.5; Social services 14.7; Housing 3.9; Other community services 4.0; Economic services 100.3 (Transport 19.9, Tourism 33.4, Public works and water supply 36.3); Public debt interest 40.7; Total 436.0 (current 383.2; capital 52.8). *1988* (estimates, B $ million): Total revenue 515.8; Total expenditure 511.9.

International Reserves (US $ million at 31 December 1987): IMF special drawing rights 0.4; Reserve position in IMF 15.2; Foreign exchange 154.5; Total 170.1 (Source: IMF, *International Financial Statistics*).

Money Supply (B $ million at 31 December 1987): Currency outside banks 74.8; Demand deposits at deposit money banks 202.9; Total money 277.7.

Cost of Living (consumer price index for Nassau; base: 1971 = 100): 248.4 in 1984; 260.4 in 1985; 278.2 in 1986.

Gross Domestic Product (B $ million at current prices): 2,011.8 in 1984; 2,252.3 in 1985; 2,214.1 in 1986.

Balance of Payments (B $ million, 1987*): Merchandise exports f.o.b. 273.1; Merchandise imports f.o.b. −1,154.7; *Trade balance* −881.6; Exports of services 1,389.4; Imports of services −670.2; *Balance on goods and services* −162.4; Private unrequited transfers (net) −17.8; Government unrequited transfers (net) 14.2; *Current balance* −166.0; Direct capital investment (net) 10.8; Other long-term capital (net) −37.8; Short-term capital (net) 8.2; Net errors and omissions 125.2; *Total (net monetary movements)* −59.6; Valuation changes (net) −1.8; *Changes in reserves* −61.4.

* The figures for merchandise exports and imports exclude petroleum and petroleum products (export value B $460m.).

EXTERNAL TRADE

Principal Commodities (B $ million, 1985): *Imports c.i.f.:* Food and live animals 154.2; Petroleum and petroleum products 2,286.0; Chemicals 119.2; Basic manufactures 138.3; Machinery and transport equipment 199.2; Miscellaneous manufactured articles 150.5; Total (incl. others) 3,077.9. *Exports f.o.b.:* Petroleum and petroleum products 2,329.1; Chemicals 199.9; Total (incl. others) 2,630.0.

Principal Trading Partners (B $ million 1985): *Imports:* Indonesia 89.0, Mexico 237.1, Puerto Rico 72.5, Saudi Arabia 39.0, United Kingdom 131.2, USA 841; Total (incl. others) 3,077.9. *Exports:* Belgium 23.8, Canada 27.0, Puerto Rico 134.9, United Kingdom 81.2, USA 2,162.0; Total (incl. others) 2,630.0.

TRANSPORT

Road Traffic (registered vehicles, 1983): Private motor cars 59,561, Other vehicles 5,199, Total 64,760.

Shipping: *Merchant fleet* (displacement, million grt) 2.5 in 1983; 4.0 in 1986; 8.9 in 1988. *International sea-borne freight traffic* (estimates, '000 metric tons, 1985): Goods loaded 9,325; Goods unloaded 8,710 (Source: UN, *Monthly Bulletin of Statistics*).

TOURISM

Tourist Arrivals: 2,631,970 in 1985; 3,007,300 in 1986; 3,081,370 (by air 1,455,920; by sea 1,625,450) in 1987.

COMMUNICATIONS MEDIA

Radio Receivers (1985): 116,000 in use (Source: UNESCO, *Statistical Yearbook*).

Television Receivers (1985): 51,000 in use (Source: UNESCO, *Statistical Yearbook*).

Telephones (1984): 75,207 in use.

Daily Newspapers (1984): 3 titles (total circulation 38,000 copies) (Source: UNESCO, *Statistical Yearbook*).

EDUCATION

Primary (1985): 84 schools, 24,224 students.

Junior High (1985): 7 schools, 6,264 students.

Junior-Senior High (1985): 22 schools, 10,462 students.

Senior High (1985): 9 schools, 6,847 students.

All-Age Schools (1985): 95 schools, 12,665 students.

Special Schools (1985): 5 schools, 292 students.

In August 1988 there were about 2,000 students registered at the College of the Bahamas.

Directory

The Constitution

A new Constitution for the Commonwealth of the Bahamas came into force at independence on 10 July 1973. The main provisions of the Constitution are summarized below:

Parliament consists of a Governor-General (representing the British monarch), a nominated Senate and an elected House of Assembly. The Governor-General appoints the Prime Minister and, on the latter's recommendation, the remainder of the Cabinet. Apart from the Prime Minister, the Cabinet has not fewer than eight other ministers, of whom one is the Attorney-General. The Governor-General also appoints a Leader of the Opposition.

The Senate (upper house) consists of 16 members, of whom nine are appointed by the Governor-General on the advice of the Prime Minister, four on the advice of the Opposition Leader, and three on the Prime Minister's advice after consultation with the Opposition Leader. The House of Assembly (lower house) has 49 members. A Constituencies Commission reviews numbers and boundaries at intervals of not more than five years and can recommend alterations for approval of the House. The life of Parliament is limited to a maximum of five years.

The Constitution provides for a Supreme Court and a Court of Appeal.

The Government

Head of State: HM Queen ELIZABETH II.
Governor-General: Sir HENRY TAYLOR (took office 26 June 1988).

THE CABINET
(November 1988)

Prime Minister and Minister of Finance: Sir LYNDEN OSCAR PINDLING.
Deputy Prime Minister, Minister of Foreign Affairs and Tourism: CLEMENT T. MAYNARD.
Minister of Housing and National Insurance: GEORGE W. MACKEY.
Minister of Education and Attorney-General: PAUL L. ADDERLEY.
Minister of Agriculture, Trade and Industry: ERVIN KNOWLES.
Minister of Employment and Immigration: ARTHUR T. MAYCOCK.
Minister of Health: Dr NORMAN GAY.
Minister of Transport and Local Government: PHILIP M. BETHEL.
Minister of Youth, Sports and Community Affairs: PETER J. BETHEL.
Minister of Works and Utilities: DARRELL E. ROLLE.

MINISTRIES

Office of the Prime Minister: POB N-3733, Rawson Sq., Nassau; tel. 322-2805.
Ministry of Agriculture, Trade and Industry: POB N-3028, East Bay St, Nassau; tel. 323-1777.
Ministry of Education: POB N-3913, Shirley St, Nassau; tel. 322-8140.
Ministry of Employment and Immigration: Nassau.
Ministry of Finance: POB N-3017, Rawson Sq., Nassau; tel. 322-4151; telex 20255.
Ministry of Foreign Affairs: POB N-3746, East Hill St, Nassau; tel. 322-7624; telex 20264.
Ministry of Health: POB N-3730, Post Office Bldg, East Hill St, Nassau; tel. 322-7425.
Ministry of Housing and National Insurance: POB N-275, Mosko Bldg, Hawkins Hill, Nassau; tel. 323-5896.
Ministry of Tourism: POB N-3701, Bay St, Nassau; tel. 322-7500; telex 20164.
Ministry of Transport and Local Government: POB N-3008, Post Office Bldg, East Hill St, Nassau; tel. 323-7814; telex 20263.
Ministry of Works and Utilities: POB N-8156, J. F. Kennedy Drive, Nassau; tel. 322-4830.
Ministry of Youth, Sports and Community Affairs: POB N-10114, Nassau; tel. 322-3140.

Legislature

SENATE

President: EDWIN COLEBY.
There are 16 nominated members.

HOUSE OF ASSEMBLY

Speaker: Sir CLIFFORD DARLING.
The House has 49 members.

General Election, 19 June 1987

Party	Seats
Progressive Liberal Party	31
Free National Movement	16
Independents	2
Total	49

Political Organizations

Free National Movement (FNM): POB N-8181, Nassau; tel. 325-0637; telex 20238; f. 1972; Leader CECIL WALLACE-WHITFIELD; Senate Leader JOHN HENRY BOSTWICK.
Progressive Liberal Party (PLP): POB N-1107, Gambier House, Farrington Rd, Nassau; tel. 325-2900; f. 1953; centrist party; Leader Sir LYNDEN PINDLING; Chair. SEAN MCWEENEY.

Diplomatic Representation

EMBASSY AND HIGH COMMISSION IN THE BAHAMAS

United Kingdom: POB N-7516, Bitco Bldg, East St, Nassau; tel. 325-7471; telex 20112; High Commissioner: COLIN G. MAYS.
USA: POB N-8197, Queen St, Nassau; tel. 322-4733; telex 20138; Ambassador: Mrs CAROL BOYD HALLETT.

Judicial System

The Judicial Committee of Her Majesty's Privy Council (which sits in London), the Bahamas Court of Appeal, the Supreme Court and the Magistrates' Courts are the main courts of the Bahamian judicial system.

All courts have both a criminal and civil jurisdiction. The Magistrates' Courts are presided over by professionally qualified Stipendiary and Circuit Magistrates in New Providence and Grand Bahama and by Commissioners sitting as Magistrates in the other Family Islands.

Whereas all magistrates are empowered to try offences which may be tried summarily, a Stipendiary and Circuit Magistrate may, with the consent of the accused, also try certain less serious indictable offences. However, a Stipendiary and Circuit Magistrate may in no case pass a sentence of imprisonment of more than two years for any one offence and may only in certain cases impose a fine in excess of B $1,500.

All magistrates may make maintenance orders, and, in certain circumstances, orders for separation and custody of children. Where title to land is not in dispute and the value of the land is B $142.85 or less, a magistrate may hear and determine the case.

A commissioner has a jurisdiction of up to B $285.71 for matters of contract or tort. The limit for a Stipendiary and Circuit Magistrate is B $571.43.

The Supreme Court consists of the Chief Justice and not more than four and not less than two justices.

Appeals in almost all matters lie from the Supreme Court to the Court of Appeal with further appeal in certain instances to the Judicial Committee of Her Majesty's Privy Council in the United Kingdom.

Justices of the Supreme Court: Prof. PHILIP TELFORD GEORGES (Chief Justice), Sir DENIS MALONE (Senior Justice), BERTRAND O. ADAMS, NEVILLE L. SMITH, JOAQUIM GONSALVES-SABOLA.
Justices of the Court of Appeal: Sir JOSEPH LUCKHOO (President), KENNETH G. SMITH, KENNETH HENRY.

THE BAHAMAS

Directory

Stipendiary and Circuit Magistrates: Joseph B. Alfred, Cleopatra Christie, George van Sertima, Sylvia Bonaby, Sharon R. Wilson (acting).
Registrar of the Supreme Court: Joseph C. Strachan.
Deputy Registrar of the Supreme Court: Carolita D. Luckhoo.

Religion

CHRISTIANITY

In 1980 there were approximately 38,400 Anglicans, 50,000 Baptists, 40,000 Roman Catholics, 12,000 Methodists and 10,000 Seventh-day Adventists. The Assemblies of Brethren, Greek Orthodox, Lutheran and Pentecostal Churches and the Salvation Army are also represented.

Bahamas Christian Council: POB SS-5863, Shirley St Post Office, Nassau; tel. 323-2153; f. 1948; 10 mem. churches; Sec. Rev. Charles A. Sweeting.

The Roman Catholic Church

The Bahamas comprises the single diocese of Nassau, suffragan to the archdiocese of Kingston in Jamaica. In 1988 there were an estimated 44,024 adherents in the Bahamas. The Bishop participates in the Antilles Episcopal Conference (based in Kingston, Jamaica).

Bishop of Nassau: Most Rev. Lawrence A. Burke, POB N-8187, The Hermitage, Eastern Road, Nassau; tel. 322-8919.

The Anglican Communion

Anglicans in the Bahamas are adherents of the Church in the Province of the West Indies. The diocese of Nassau and the Bahamas also includes the Turks and Caicos Islands.

Bishop of Nassau and the Bahamas: Right Rev. Michael Eldon, POB N-7107, Addington House, Nassau.

The Methodist Church

General Superintendent of the Methodist Church in the Bahamas: Rev. Dr Kenneth Huggins, POB N-3702, Nassau.

The Press

NEWSPAPERS

Freeport News: POB F7, Freeport; tel. 352-8321; f. 1961; daily; Dir Dudley N. Byfield; Editor Richardson Campbell; circ. 5,000.

Nassau Daily Tribune: POB N-3207, Shirley St, Nassau; tel. 322-2766; f. 1903; Publr/Editor Eileen Dupuch Carron; circ. 12,000.

Nassau Guardian: POB N-3011, Oakes Field, Nassau; tel. 323-5654; telex 20100; f. 1844; daily; Publr/Gen. Man. Kenneth W. Francis; Editor Christopher Symonette; circ. 11,044.

PERIODICALS

The Bahamas Financial Digest: POB N-4271, Nassau; tel. 322-1149; telex 20447; f. 1973; 4 a year; business and investment; Publr/Editor Michael A. Symonette.

Bahamas Tourist News: POB N-4855, Baypari Bldg, Parliament St, Nassau; monthly; Editor Paul Bower; circ. 240,000 (annually).

Bahamian Review Magazine: POB N-494, Collins Ave, Nassau; tel. 322-8922; f. 1952; monthly; Editor William Cartwright; circ. 25,000.

Nassau: POB N-1914 Nassau; tel. 322-1149; f. 1984; literature, current affairs, reviews; 4 a year; Publr Michael A. Symonette.

Official Gazette: c/o Cabinet Office, POB N-7147, Nassau; tel. 322-2805; weekly; published by the Cabinet Office.

Publishers

Bahama Publishers Ltd: POB F-7, Cedar St, Freeport; tel. 352-8321.

Bahamas International Publishing Co Ltd: POB N-1914, Baypari Bldg, Parliament, New Providence; tel. 322-1149.

Commonwealth Publications Ltd: POB N-4826, Nassau; tel. 322-1038; telex 20275; f. 1979; publishes *Bahamas Business Guide* (a guide to doing business in the Bahamas and the Government's economic and financial policies) and *An Economic History of the Bahamas*.

Etienne Dupuch Jr Publications Ltd: POB N-7513, Oakes Field, New Providence; tel. 323-5665; publishes *Bahamas Handbook*, *What To Do* magazines, *Welcome Bahamas*, *Tadpole* (educational colouring book) series and *Dining and Entertainment Guide*; Dirs Etienne Dupuch, Jr, S. P. Dupuch.

Radio and Television

In 1985 there were approximately 116,000 radio receivers and about 51,000 television receivers in use.

Broadcasting Corporation of the Bahamas (Radio Bahamas): POB N-1347, Centreville, New Providence; tel. 322-4623; telex 20253; f. 1936; government-owned; commercial; three channels; a northern (Grand Bahama) service of Radio Bahamas was established in 1973 at Freeport; Gen. Man. Calsey Johnson.

Bahamas Television: f. 1977; owned by Broadcasting Corporation of the Bahamas; transmitting power of 50,000 watts; full colour; Gen. Man. Calsey Johnson.

Bahamas Television covers the Central Bahamas and the main capital of New Providence. Freeport, the second city, is covered by cable television. US television programmes and some satellite programmes can be received.

Finance

In recent years the Bahamas has developed into one of the world's foremost financial centres, and finance has become a significant feature of the economy. At 31 December 1987 there were 382 financial institutions in the Bahamas: 281 dealt with the general public while the remaining 101 were restricted, non-active or nominee institutions. There were 130 Bahamian-incorporated banks and/or trust companies; 95 were subsidiaries of foreign institutions and 35 were Bahamian-based.

There are no corporation, income, capital gains or withholding taxes or estate duty, but higher stamp, property, immigration and company registration fees were introduced for non-Bahamian companies in 1976. In 1988 the fees payable by banks in order to operate in the Bahamas were doubled.

BANKING

(cap. = capital; dep. = deposits; res = reserves; m. = million; brs = branches; amounts in Bahamian dollars)

Central Bank

The Central Bank of the Bahamas: POB N-4868, Frederick St, Nassau; tel. 322-2193; telex 20115; f. 1973; bank of issue; external res B $210.3m. (June 1988); Gov. James H. Smith.

Development Bank

The Bahamas Development Bank: Bay St, POB N-3034, Nassau; tel. 322-8721; telex 20297; f. 1978 to fund approved projects and channel funds into appropriate investments; Chair. Ishmael Lightbourne.

Principal Bahamian-based Banks

African-Arabian Islamic Bank Ltd: POB N-10051, Nassau; f. 1981; telex 20457.

Ahlia Banking Ltd: POB N-7768, Nassau; f. 1963.

Akida Islamic Bank International Ltd: POB N-4877, Nassau; f. 1981.

Artoc Bank and Trust Ltd: POB N-8319, Harrison Bldg, Malbourgh, Nassau; tel. 325-1183; telex 20270; f. 1977.

Bahama Bank Ltd: POB N-272, Nassau; f. 1964.

Bank of International Trade Ltd: POB N-1372, Nassau; f. 1981.

Bank of New Providence Ltd: POB N-4723, Claughton House, Shirley and Charlotte Sts, Nassau; tel. 322-3824; telex 20464; Gen. Man. Byrd Osborne.

Capital Industrial Bank Ltd: POB N-4805, Nassau; f. 1973.

Commonwealth Industrial Bank Ltd: POB SS-5541, 610 Bay St, Nassau; tel. 322-1421; f. 1960; Exec. Vice-Pres. Vernon G. R. Beares; 5 brs.

Dominion Charter Bank Ltd: POB N-3229, Nassau; tel. 322-2754; telex 20409; f. 1980.

Equator Bank Ltd: POB SS-6273, Norfolk House, Frederick St, Nassau; tel. 322-2754; telex 20409; f. 1974.

Fidenas International Bank Ltd: POB N-4816, Nassau; tel. 325-6052; telex 20278; f. 1981; cap. US $5m., dep. US $43m.; Chair./CEO Geoffrey P. Jurick.

Finance Corporation of Bahamas Ltd (FINCO): POB N-3038, Frederick St, Nassau; tel. 322-4822; f. 1953; Man. Dir Peter Thompson; 3 brs.

THE BAHAMAS   *Directory*

First Home Banking Centre Ltd: POB F-2644, The Mall, Freeport; tel. 352-6676; f. 1978; Pres. ALFRED STEWART.

First Imexco Bank Ltd: POB N-1348, Nassau; f. 1967.

Independent Bank and Trust Company Ltd: POB N-3908, 50 Frederick House, Nassau; tel. 325-0940; f. 1981.

Latin Bank and Trust Company Ltd: POB N-7788, Nassau; f. 1979.

Meridien International Bank Ltd: POB N-3209, Nassau; tel. 393-4857; telex 20386; f. 1980; Chair. A. S. SARDINAS.

Offshore Trust Banking Corporation Ltd: POB N-7525, Nassau; telex 20111; f. 1981.

People's Penny Savings Bank: POB N-1484, Market St, Nassau; tel. 322-4140; telex 20353; f. 1952; 3 brs.

Principal Foreign Banks

In 1983 there were more than 100 foreign banks with branches in the Bahamas, including 91 from the USA.

Banca della Svizzera Italiana (Overseas) Ltd (Italy): Norfolk House, Frederick St, POB N-7130, Nassau; tel. 323-8312; telex 20197.

Bank of Montreal (Bahamas and Caribbean) Ltd (Canada): POB N-7118, Harrison Bldg, Marlborough St, Nassau; tel. 322-1690; telex 20141; f. 1970; cap. B $3m., res B $2m., dep. B $139m. (Sept. 1981); Man. Dir BRAD BELLIS; 3 brs.

Bank of Nova Scotia (Canada): POB N-7518, Rawson Sq., Nassau; tel. 322-1071; telex 20187; Man. GEORGE E. MARSHALL; Deputy Man. JAMES BRAMMER; 11 brs.

Barclays Bank PLC (UK): POB N-8350, Bay St, Nassau; tel. 322-4921; telex 20149; Man. H. G. SANDS.

Canadian Imperial Bank of Commerce: POB N-7125, Shirley St, Nassau; tel. 322-8455; telex 20169; Area Man. TERRY HILTS; 9 brs.

Charterhouse Japhet Bank and Trust International Ltd (UK): POB N-3045, E. D. Sassoon Bldg, Parliament St, Nassau; tel. 322-4643; telex 20142; Bahamas incorporated 1950; cap. B $2m.; Chair. and CEO RENO J. BROWN; Dir PETER F. JAKOBSEN.

Chase Manhattan Bank NA (USA): POB N-4921, Shirley and Charlotte Sts, Nassau; tel. 322-8792; telex 20140; Gen. Man. KEN BROWN; 4 brs.

Citibank, NA (USA): POB N-8158, Thompson Blvd, Oakes Field, Nassau; tel. 322-4240; telex 20153; Gen. Man. PAUL D. MAJOR; 2 brs.

Lloyds Bank International (Bahamas) Ltd (UK): POB N-1262, King and George Sts, Nassau; tel. 322-8711; telex 20107; Gen. Man. ENRIQUE NYBORG-ANDERSEN; Asst Man. R. FUNES; 1 br.

The Royal Bank of Canada Ltd: POB N-7537, Nassau; tel. 322-8700; telex 20393; Man. Dir G. B. GREENSLAND; 16 brs.

Swiss Bank Corpn (Overseas) Ltd: 3rd Floor, Claughton House, Shirley St, POB N-7757, Nassau; tel. 322-7570; telex 20348.

Principal Bahamian Trust Companies

Bahamas International Trust Co Ltd: POB N-7768, Bitco Bldg, Bank Lane, Nassau; tel. 322-1161; telex 20143; incorporated 1957; cap. B $1m.; Chair. L. B. JOHNSON; Man. Dir JAMES M. KNOTT.

Euro-Dutch Trust Co (Bahamas) Ltd: POB N-9204, Charlotte House, Nassau; f. 1975; tel. 325-1033; telex 20303.

Leadenhall Trust Co Ltd: POB N-1965, Marlborough St, Nassau; tel. 325-5508; telex 20584; f. 1976; Man. Dir ROBERT MONTGOMERY.

NatWest International Trust Corp. (Bahamas) Ltd: POB N-7788, West Bay St, Nassau; tel. 326-0404; telex 20177; f. 1936; Chair DONALD R. KESTER; Deputy Chair. J. D. FRIZELL.

Rawson Trust Co Ltd: POB N-4465, Charlotte House, Nassau; tel. 322-7461; telex 20172; f. 1969.

Bankers' Organizations

Association of International Banks and Trust Companies in the Bahamas: POB N-7880, Nassau; tel. 326-0041.

Bahamas Institute of Bankers: POB N-3202, Bolam House, George St, Nassau; tel. 322-1456.

INSURANCE

The leading British and a number of US and Canadian companies have agents in Nassau and Freeport. Local insurance companies include the following:

Bahamas First General Insurance Co Ltd: POB N-1216, Centreville House, Second Tce, West Collins Ave, Nassau; tel. 326-5439; telex 20576.

Bahamas International Assurance Co: POB SS-6201, Palmdale Ave, Nassau; tel. 322-3196.

Bahamas Pioneer Insurance Co Ltd: POB SS-6207, East Shirley and Kemp Rd, Nassau; tel. 325-7468.

International Bahamian Insurance Co: POB N-10280, Peek Bldg, New Providence; tel. 322-2504.

Trade and Industry

Bahamas Chamber of Commerce: POB N-665, Shirley St, Nassau; tel. 322-2145; telex 20569; f. 1935 to promote, foster and protect trade, industry and commerce; Pres. WILLIAM U. WONG; Exec. Dir RUBY L. SWEETING; 900 mems.

Bahamas Agricultural and Industrial Corporation (BAIC): POB N-4940, BAIC Building, East Bay St, Nassau; tel. 322-3740; telex 20646; f. 1971 as Bahamas Development Corporation to promote investment in all sectors of the economy and to act as a clearance agency for all projects; name changed 1981; Chair. ALFRED T. MAYCOCK.

Nassau/Cable Beach/Paradise Island Promotion Board: POB N-7799, Dean's Lane, Fort Charlotte, Nassau; tel. 322-8381; f. 1970; Chair. C. RICHARD COOK; Sec. MICHAEL C. RECKLEY; 30 mems.

EMPLOYERS' ASSOCIATIONS

Bahamas Association of Architects: POB N-1207, Shirley St, Nassau; tel. 325-6115; Pres. WINSTON JONES.

Bahamas Association of Land Surveyors: POB N-7782, Nassau; tel. 322-4569; Pres. ANDREW C. LAVILLE; Vice-Pres./Sec. SHERLYN W. HALL; 30 mems.

Bahamas Association of Shipping Agents: POB N-1451, Nassau.

Bahamas Boatmen's Association: f. 1974; POB ES-5212, Nassau; Pres. and Sec. FREDERICK GOMEZ.

Bahamas Contractors' Association: POB N-8049, Nassau; Pres. BRENDON C. WATSON; Sec. EMMANUEL ALEXIOU.

Bahamas Employers' Confederation: POB N-166, Nassau; tel. 328-1757; telex 20392; f. 1963; Pres. TYRONE D'ARVILLE.

Bahamas Hotel Employers' Association: POB N-7799, Dean's Lane, Fort Charlotte, Nassau; tel. 322-2262; telex 20392; f. 1958; Pres. J. BARRIE FARRINGTON; Exec. Dir MICHAEL C. RECKLEY; 26 mems.

Bahamas Institute of Chartered Accountants: POB N-7037, Nassau; Pres. WILLIAM WALLACE.

Bahamas Institute of Professional Engineers: POB N-4312, Nassau; Pres. IVERN DAVIES.

Bahamas Motor Dealers' Association: POB N-4824, Nassau; tel. 322-1149; Pres. PERCY CAMPBELL.

Bahamas Real Estate Association: POB N-8860, Bahamas Chamber Building, Nassau; tel. 325-4942; Pres. FRANK CAREY.

Nassau Association of Shipping Agents: Nassau.

Soft Drink Bottlers' Association: POB N-272, Nassau.

TRADE UNIONS

The Commonwealth of the Bahamas Trade Union Congress (CBTUC): POB GT-2514, Nassau; affiliated to the Caribbean Congress of Labour; Pres. DAVID KNOWLES; 11,000 mems.

The main unions are as follows:

Bahamas Airport, Service and Industrial Workers' Union: POB N-3364, Workers House, Balfour Ave, Nassau; tel. 323-5030; f. 1958; Pres. HENRY DEAN; Gen. Sec. RAMON NEWBALL; 532 mems.

Bahamas Brewery, Distillers and Allied Workers' Union: POB N-299, Nassau; f. 1968; Pres. BRADICK CLEARE; Gen. Sec. DAVID KEMP; 140 mems.

Bahamas Communication and Public Officers' Union: POB N-3190, East St, Nassau; tel. 322-1537; f. 1973; Pres. KEITH E. ARCHER; Sec.-Gen. AUDLEY G. WILLIAMS; 1,611 mems.

Bahamas Doctors' Union: POB N-3911, Nassau; Pres. Dr EUGENE NEWERY; Gen. Sec. GEORGE SHERMAN.

Bahamas Electrical Workers' Union: POB GT-2535, East West Highway, Nassau; tel. 323-1838; telex 2535; Pres. SAMUEL MITCHELL; Gen. Sec. JONATHAN CAMBRIDGE.

Bahamas Hotel Catering and Allied Workers' Union: POB GT-2514, St Charles Vincent St, Nassau; tel. 323-5933; f. 1958; Pres. THOMAS BASTIAN; Gen. Sec. LEONARD WILSON; 5,500 mems.

Bahamas Housekeepers' Union: POB 898, Nassau; f. 1973; Pres. MERLENE DECOSTA; Gen. Sec. MILLICENT MUNROE.

Bahamas Maritime Port and Allied Workers' Union: POB 10517, Nassau; Pres. JAMES BLATCH; Gen. Sec. ANTHONY WILLIAMS.

Bahamas Musicians' and Entertainers' Union: POB N-880, Horseshoe Drive, Nassau; tel. 322-3734; f. 1958; Pres. LEROY DUKE' HANNA; Sec. RONALD SIMMS; 410 mems.

Bahamas Oil and Fuel Services Workers' Union: POB 10597, Nassau; f. 1956; Pres. VINCENT MUNROE.

Bahamas Public Services Union: POB N-4692, Wulff Rd, Nassau; tel. 325-0038; f. 1959; Pres. ARLINGTON MILLER; Sec.-Gen. ERIC DARVILLE; 4,247 mems.

Bahamas Taxi-Cab Union: POB N-1077, Nassau; tel. 323-5952; telex 20480; Pres. OSWALD NIXON; Gen. Sec. ROSCOE WEECH.

Bahamas Transport, Agricultural, Distributive and Allied Workers' Trade Union: POB N-7821, Wulff Rd, Nassau; tel. 323-4538; f. 1959; Pres. RANDOLF FAWKES; Gen. Sec. MAXWELL N. TAYLOR; 1,362 mems.

Bahamas Union of Teachers: POB N-3482, 104 Bethel Ave, Stapledon Gdns, Nassau; tel. 323-7085; f. 1945; Pres. DONALD SYMONETTE; Gen. Sec. LESLIE DEAN; 1,985 mems.

Bahamas Utilities Services and Allied Workers' Union: POB GT-2515, Nassau; Pres. DREXEL DEAN; Gen. Sec. HERMAN ROKER.

Bahamas Workers' Council International: POB 5337 M.S., Nassau; f. 1969; Chair. DUDLEY WILLIAMS.

Commonwealth Cement and Construction Workers' Union: POB N-8680, Nassau; Pres. AUDLEY HANNA; Gen. Sec. ERMA MUNROE.

Commonwealth Electrical Workers' Union: POB F-1983, Grand Bahama; Pres. OBED PINDER, Jr; Gen. Sec. CHRISTOPHER COOPER.

Commonwealth Transport Union: POB F-1983, Freeport; Pres. LEO DOUGLAS; Gen. Sec. KENITH CHRISTIE.

Commonwealth Union of Hotel Services and Allied Workers: POB F-1983, White House of Labour, Cedar St, Freeport; tel. 352-9361; Pres. HURIE BODIE; Gen. Sec. (vacant).

Commonwealth Wholesale, Retail and Allied Workers' Union: POB F-1983, Freeport; tel. 352-9361; Pres. MERLENE THOMAS; Gen. Sec. KIM SMITH.

Eastside Stevedores' Union: POB 1176, Nassau; f. 1972; Pres. SALATHIEL MACKEY; Gen. Sec. CURTIS TURNQUEST.

Grand Bahama Commercial, Clerical and Allied Workers' Union: POB F-839, 33A Kipling Bldg, Freeport; tel. 352-7438; Pres. NEVILLE SIMMONS; Gen. Sec. LIVINGSTONE STUART.

Grand Bahama Construction, Refinery and Maintenance Workers' Union: POB F-839, 33A Kipling Bldg, Freeport; tel. 352-7438; f. 1971; Pres. JAMES TAYLOR; Gen. Sec. EPHRAIM BLACK.

Grand Bahama Entertainers' Union: POB F-2672, Freeport; Pres. CHARLES SMITH; Gen. Sec. IRMA THOMPSON.

Grand Bahama Telephone and Communications Union: POB F-2478, Freeport; Pres. NAAMAN ELLIS; Gen. Sec. DOROTHY CLARKE.

United Brotherhood of Longshoremen's Union: POB N-7317, Wulff Rd, Nassau; f. 1959; Pres. J. MCKINNEY; Gen. Sec. W. SWANN; 157 mems.

Transport

ROADS

There are about 966 km (600 miles) of roads in New Providence and 1,368 km (850 miles) in the Family Islands, mainly on Grand Bahama, Cat Island, Eleuthera, Exuma and Long Island.

SHIPPING

The principal seaport is at Nassau. In 1988 work began on a two-year improvement and expansion programme, which will enable the harbour to accommodate the very largest cruise ships. Berthing facilities at Potters Cay (New Providence), Governor's Harbour (Eleuthera), Morgan's Bluff (North Andros) and George Town (Exuma) were also to be improved.

The Bahamas converted to free-flag status in 1976, and by 1983 possessed the world's third largest open-registry fleet. The fleet's displacement was 8.9m. grt in 1988.

The following are the chief shipping and cruise lines calling at Nassau: P & O, Pacific Steam Navigation Co, Tropical Shipping, Home Lines, Eastern Steamship Co, Norwegian-American Lines, Costa Lines, NCL Norwegian Caribbean Lines, Holland American Lines, and the Scandinavian World Cruises.

There is a weekly mail and passenger service to all the Family Islands.

Cavalier Shipping: POB N-8170, Crawford St, Oakes Field, New Providence; tel. 323-3821.

R. R. Farrington & Sons: POB N-93, Union Dock, Nassau; tel. 322-2203; telex 20123.

Grand Bahama Port Authority: POB F-2666, Freeport, Grand Bahama; tel. 352-6711.

Pioneer Shipping Ltd: POB N-3044, Union Dock Bay, Nassau; tel. 325-7889; telex 20350.

United Shipping Co Ltd: POB F-2552, Freeport, Grand Bahama; tel. 352-9315; telex 30048.

CIVIL AVIATION

Nassau International Airport and Freeport International Airport are the main terminals for international and internal services.

Bahamasair: POB N-4881, Windsor Field, Nassau; tel. 327-8451; telex 20239; f. 1973; scheduled services between Nassau, Freeport, Miami, Fort Lauderdale, Atlanta, Tampa, Newark, Orlando, Turks and Caicos Islands, West Palm Beach and 20 locations within the Family Islands; Chair. PHILIP M. BETHEL; Gen. Man. CARLTON A. CARTWRIGHT; fleet of 4 Boeing 737, 4 HS.748.

Tourism

The mild climate and beautiful beaches attract many tourists. In 1986 there were 205 hotels, with a total of 12,660 rooms. In 1987 there were 3.1m. tourist arrivals (including 1.6m. cruise-ship passengers), mostly from the USA, Canada and the United Kingdom. Receipts from tourism reached an estimated US $1,170.3m. in that year.

Ministry of Tourism: POB N-3701, Bay St, Nassau; tel. 322-7500; telex 20164; Dir-Gen. BALTRON BETHEL.

Bahamas Hotel Association: POB N-7799, West Bay St, Nassau; tel. 322-8381; telex 20392.

BAHRAIN

Introductory Survey

Location, Climate, Language, Religion, Flag, Capital

The State of Bahrain consists of a group of about 35 islands, situated midway along the Persian (Arabian) Gulf, about 24 km (15 miles) from the east coast of Saudi Arabia (to which it is linked by a causeway), and 28 km (17 miles) from the west coast of Qatar. There are six principal islands in the archipelago, and the largest of these is Bahrain itself, which is about 50 km (30 miles) long and between 13 km and 25 km (8 to 15 miles) wide. To the north-east of Bahrain island, and linked to it by a causeway and motor-road, lies Muharraq island, which is approximately 6 km (4 miles) long. Another causeway links Bahrain with Sitra island. The climate is temperate from December to the end of March, with temperatures ranging between 19°C (66°F) and 25°C (77°F), but becomes very hot and humid during the summer months. In August and September temperatures can rise to 40°C (104°F). The official language is Arabic, but English is also widely spoken. Almost all Bahraini citizens are Muslims, divided into two sects: Shi'ites (almost 60%) and Sunnis (over 40%). Non-Bahrainis, who comprise more than 30% of the total population, include Muslims, Christians and adherents of other religions. The national flag (proportions 5 by 3) is scarlet, with a vertical white stripe at the hoist, the two colours being separated by a serrated line. The capital is Manama.

Recent History

Bahrain, a traditional Arab monarchy, became a British Protected State in the 19th century. Under this arrangement, government was shared between the ruling sheikh and his British adviser. Following a series of territorial disputes in the 19th century, Persia (now Iran) made renewed claims to Bahrain in 1928. This disagreement remained unresolved until May 1970, when Iran accepted the findings of a report, commissioned by the UN, which showed that the inhabitants of Bahrain overwhelmingly favoured complete independence, rather than union with Iran.

During the reign of Sheikh Sulman bin Hamad al-Khalifa, who became ruler of Bahrain in 1942, social services and public works were considerably expanded. Sheikh Sulman died in November 1961 and was succeeded by his eldest son, Sheikh Isa bin Sulman al-Khalifa. Extensive administrative and political reforms came into effect in January 1970, when a 12-member Council of State was established. The formation of this new body, which became Bahrain's supreme executive authority, represented the first formal derogation of the ruler's powers. Sheikh Khalifa bin Sulman al-Khalifa, the ruler's eldest brother, became President of the Council.

Meanwhile, in January 1968 the United Kingdom had announced its intention to withdraw British military forces from the area by 1971. In March 1968 Bahrain joined the nearby territories of Qatar and the Trucial States (now the United Arab Emirates), which were also under British protection, in a Federation of Arab Emirates. It was intended that the Federation should become fully independent, but the interests of Bahrain and Qatar proved to be incompatible with those of the smaller sheikhdoms, and both seceded from the Federation. Bahrain thus became a separate independent state on 15 August 1971, when a new treaty of friendship was signed with the United Kingdom. Sheikh Isa took the title of Amir, while the Council of State became the Cabinet, with Sheikh Khalifa as Prime Minister. A Constituent Assembly, convened in December 1972, produced a new constitution, providing for a National Assembly which would contain Cabinet ministers and 30 elected members. On 6 December 1973 the Constitution came into force, and on the following day elections were held for the new Assembly. In the absence of political parties, candidates stood in an individual capacity. In August 1975 the Prime Minister submitted his resignation, complaining of obstruction by the National Assembly. However, Sheikh Khalifa was reappointed and, at his request, the Assembly was dissolved by Amiri decree. New elections were promised, but by late 1988 there were no signs that the National Assembly would be reconvened. Without the Assembly, the ruling family has almost absolute powers.

Although major international territorial claims were brought to an end by the 1970 agreement with Iran, the Iranian revolution of 1979 led to uncertainty about possible future claims to Bahrain. There has also been evidence of tension between Shi'ite Muslims, who form a slender majority in Bahrain, and the dominant Sunni Muslims, the sect to which the ruling family belongs. In December 1981 more than 70 people, mainly Bahrainis, were arrested when a supposedly Iranian-backed plot to overthrow the Government was thwarted. In 1984 there were renewed fears of Iranian attempts to disrupt the country's stability when a cache of weapons was discovered in a Bahraini village, and in June 1985 six men were deported from the United Kingdom, following the discovery of a planned coup against the Bahraini Government.

In March 1981 Bahrain was one of the six founder-members of the Gulf Co-operation Council (GCC) (see p. 122), which by 1983 had settled agreements aimed at co-ordinating defence strategy and at freer trading and co-operative economic protection among Gulf states. In 1983 and 1984 Bahrain participated in joint military exercises, organized by the GCC, which were held as part of a strategy to develop a rapid deployment force for the region.

In April 1986 the US Vice-President, George Bush, visited Bahrain to reaffirm the USA's readiness to preserve Gulf security in the event of an escalation of the Iran–Iraq war, which began in September 1980. In January 1987 the USA announced its intention to sell 12 F-16 fighter aircraft to Bahrain as part of a contract, valued at $400m., to provide military equipment. Bahrain would thereby become the first Gulf nation to receive any of these aircraft. Work began on the construction of an air-force base, in the south of the island, to accommodate the F-16 aircraft. Bahrain already provides an onshore 'facility' for the US forces, and there is a large US navy presence. In September the US Secretary of Defense, Caspar Weinberger, presented Sheikh Isa with a letter from President Reagan, expressing his gratitude to Bahrain for its assistance in enabling US warships to escort 'reflagged' Kuwaiti merchant vessels in Gulf waters. In December a controversial sale of 70 Stinger anti-aircraft missiles and 14 launchers, worth $7m., was agreed between Bahrain and the USA. The weapons were to be delivered as soon as possible. Conditions of sale included the stipulation that Bahrain sell back the weapons either when another US air defence system could be found for the country, or after 18 months.

In July 1987, as a result of the escalation of tension in the Gulf (exacerbated by the presence of US and Soviet naval forces), the UN Security Council adopted Resolution 598, urging an immediate cease-fire. Iraq agreed to observe a cease-fire if Iran would reciprocate, but Iran prevaricated, attaching conditions to its acceptance of the Resolution. In November 1987, at an extraordinary meeting of the League of Arab States in Amman, Jordan, representatives of the member states, including Bahrain, unanimously condemned Iran for prolonging the Gulf War, deplored its occupation of Arab (i.e. Iraqi) territory, and urged it to accept Resolution 598 without preconditions. (For more detailed coverage of the Gulf War and of the events that led to a cease-fire, in August 1988, which, if permanent, will benefit all the states of the Gulf area, see the chapters on Iran and Iraq.) In February 1988 three Bahrainis were convicted by the security court for their involvement in an Iranian-supported plot, revealed in December 1987, to sabotage Bahrain's petroleum refinery.

In recent years Bahrain has acquired focal importance in the Gulf region. Its international airport is the centre of Gulf aviation, and Bahrain was chosen as the site of a proposed Arabian Gulf University. Plans to establish a stock exchange for Gulf countries in Bahrain were approved by the Cabinet in August 1986, and it was expected that the exchange would open in early 1989. A further indication of Bahrain's growing importance within the region was the construction of a causeway linking Bahrain and Saudi Arabia, which was opened in November 1986.

In April 1986 Qatari military forces raided the island of Fasht ad-Dibal, a coral reef situated midway between Bahrain and Qatar, over which both claim sovereignty. During the raid Qatar seized 29 foreign workers (most of whom were subsequently released), who were constructing a Bahraini coastguard station on the island. Officials of the GCC met representatives from both states in an attempt to reconcile them and avoid a split within the Council. Fasht ad-Dibal became the third area of dispute between the two countries, the others being Zubara, on mainland Qatar, and Hawar island. In December 1987 Bahrain and Qatar accepted a proposal from Saudi Arabia to submit their dispute over Fasht ad-Dibal to arbitration at the International Court of Justice in The Hague.

In June 1988 Bahrain held its first official talks with the USSR, when the Amir of Bahrain met the Soviet Ambassador to Kuwait, to discuss ways of developing links between the two countries.

Government

Bahrain is ruled by an Amir through an appointed Cabinet. In August 1975 the National Assembly was dissolved.

Defence

In June 1988 the Bahrain Defence Force consisted of 2,850 men (2,300 army, 350 navy, 200 air force). The defence budget for 1988 was BD 62.0m. In 1982 the GCC states pledged defence aid of some US $1,000m. for the modernization of equipment, and in 1984 this was followed by a further grant, for the same amount, to be shared between Bahrain and Oman.

Economic Affairs

During the 19th century, Bahrain's economy was dominated by pearl-diving and trade. Fishing also played an important part, while agriculture, although restricted by the harsh environment, principally involved the cultivation of dates. However, the exploitation of petroleum, first discovered in commercial quantities in 1932, has transformed the islands. The sale of refined petroleum products has become the mainstay of Bahrain's economy. In 1986, according to estimates by the World Bank, Bahrain's gross national product (GNP) per head, measured at average 1984–86 prices, was US $8,510, considerably below the level of other petroleum-producing countries in the Gulf, but comparable with European industrial countries. Between 1973 and 1985, it was estimated, Bahrain's GNP expanded, in real terms, at an average rate of 5.2% per year. Over the same period, real GNP per head increased by only 0.8% per year. In 1986 GNP per head declined by about 3%.

Industrial pollution threatens the fishing industry: the virtual disappearance of shrimps from the Gulf forced the Bahrain Fishing Company to close in 1979. The total catch of the fishing industry declined from 5,747 metric tons in 1981 to 4,812 tons in 1983. However, a revival began in 1985, when the total catch was 7,763 tons, and in 1986 the catch increased to 8,299 tons. In 1985 the Government announced an investment of BD 20,000 (US $53,200) to revive the pearling industry. Agriculture, which contributed only about 1% of Bahrain's gross domestic product (GDP) during the early 1980s, is heavily dependent on irrigation, and has been adversely affected, both by the increasing salinity of the soil and by the attraction of other sectors of the economy. In 1986 work began on a two-stage project, expected to cost BD 12m., to expand the Tubli sewage works and to make further use of treated effluent for irrigation purposes. The first phase of this scheme, which was due to be completed in 1988, was expected to double the plant's daily production capacity to 110,000 cu m of water; and the second phase involves the connection of more towns to the network and the construction of a major reservoir at Buhayr. By 1987 it was hoped that 16% of demand for food would be met by indigenous production. A poultry farm, which opened in 1983, met 85% of total demand for eggs in that year. By 1986 poultry production had risen to meet 51% of local demand, and egg production had risen to meet 90% of total demand. A five-year agricultural plan, announced in 1984, aimed to increase output of dairy produce, and in 1985 the Bahrain National Dairy Company was established, to concentrate on the production of milk for the domestic market.

Because Bahrain was already a well-established commercial centre, its petroleum industry developed more rapidly than that of other Gulf countries. By 1936, 16 wells were producing petroleum, which was refined at a complex in Sitra. Bahrain's annual output of crude petroleum reached a peak in 1970, with production of almost 28m. barrels, equivalent to 76,639 barrels per day (b/d). Bahrain also joined the Organization of Arab Petroleum Exporting Countries (OAPEC, see p. 193) in that year. The nation's petroleum reserves, estimated to be 100m. barrels at 1 January 1988, are small in comparison with those of other petroleum-producing countries. At 1987 levels of production, Bahrain's reserves will be exhausted by 1994. In 1968 Bahrain and Saudi Arabia signed an agreement whereby output from an oilfield to which both countries had claims, Abu Safah, was to be shared equally between them. By 1983 this field accounted for more than 50% of Bahrain's revenues from petroleum. However, production at the Abu Safah field ceased in early 1987, and Saudi Arabia agreed to provide 75,000 b/d of crude petroleum in compensation.

In 1976 the Government made its first moves to take control of the petroleum industry, and by 1980 it had acquired all rights over petroleum production and exploration, and a 60% share in the Sitra refinery. Bahrain's output of crude petroleum averaged 42,000 b/d in 1983, but declined to 41,774 b/d in 1984. In 1985, however, production rose to 41,922 b/d. The capacity of the Sitra refinery had been expanded to 250,000 b/d by 1983, although a decline in petroleum production and a reduction in demand limited average throughput to 174,987 b/d in that year, compared with 197,400 b/d in 1982. Throughput in 1984 rose to an average of 209,000 b/d, but in the 12 months preceding December 1985 production fell to only 75% of capacity. In 1986 the refinery was producing 243,000 b/d. A plan to upgrade the Sitra refinery, which was expected to cost US $1,000m., was announced in July 1986. To supplement declining reserves, exploration for further sources of petroleum is under way, and a total of 20 new wells were drilled in 1986, increasing average output for that year to 42,422 b/d. In the first nine months of 1987, 13 wells were drilled, and production averaged 41,688 b/d. Total crude petroleum output in 1987 reached 15.2m. barrels. In 1986 a five-year plan for the production of petroleum and gas was initiated, in an attempt to maintain output at between 40,000 b/d and 43,000 b/d until 1991. As a result of the decline of Bahrain's petroleum sector, its contribution to GDP fell from 35.6% in 1975 to 16.3% in 1986. Bahrain has substantial deposits of natural gas, with known reserves estimated at 209,000 cu m in 1985. Most of the gas is found unassociated with petroleum, and it is used as feedstock and fuel for Bahrain's indigenous industry. Bahrain's output of natural gas fell from 6,332m. cu m in 1985 to 5,803m. cu m in 1986, before rising slightly, to 5,843m. cu m, in 1987. At 1985 rates of extraction, the country's gas reserves will be exhausted by the year 2018.

In the 1970s, in an attempt to avoid dependence upon limited resources of hydrocarbons, Bahrain embarked on a vigorous programme of industrial diversification. An aluminium smelter, operated by Aluminium Bahrain (ALBA), was inaugurated in 1971, and, despite the fall in world aluminium demand which occurred in the early 1980s, production of primary aluminium rose from 171,454 metric tons in 1982 to 180,344 tons in 1987. Expansion of the plant, scheduled for completion in 1990, was expected to increase total annual capacity to 225,000 tons. Ancillary industry includes the production of atomized aluminium powder and extruded products (such as rods, sheets, windows and doors), and an aluminium rolling mill, with an annual capacity of 40,000 tons of sheet and coil aluminium, began commercial production in January 1986. In its first full year of production the Gulf Aluminium Rolling Mill Company produced 30,000 tons of rolled aluminium, and by late 1988 the plant was using 55,000 tons of aluminium per year, a requirement that was expected to increase to 60,000 tons in 1989. Plans for an aluminium foil plant, with a capacity of 6,000 tons per year, were postponed in 1988. Plans for the development of further aluminium plants elsewhere in the Gulf may reduce ALBA's profitability in the future, despite the increase in world-wide aluminium prices in 1987-88. An iron and steel pelletization plant was opened in December 1984, but, owing to problems of litigation and lack of orders, it was forced to close in mid-1986. However, in March 1988 the Arab Iron and Steel Company (AISCO) was purchased by a newly-formed subsidiary of the Kuwait Petroleum Corporation, the Gulf Industrial Investment Company, and production at the plant was due to recommence in December 1988. A dry dock for shipbuilding and repairs opened in 1977. This enterprise had failed to become profitable by 1984, but nevertheless received renewed financial support from OAPEC in that year. In 1987 the dock's occupancy rate rose, as a result of an increase in demand (caused by attacks on shipping in the Gulf), and its revenue was $22m., compared with $11.3m. in 1986. The company was expected to achieve its first full-year profit in 1987. In 1979 a plant for the production of liquefied petroleum gas (LPG) was opened, to process 120m. cu ft (3.4m. cu m) of associated gas per day, and to produce propane, butane and naphtha. In 1988 a contract, with a projected cost of $74m., was signed for the expansion of the Bahrain National Gas Company's LPG plant, thereby increasing its capacity by 50% and creating 70 new jobs. The expansion work will increase the production of propane, butane and naphtha to 250m. cu ft (7.1m. cu m) per day and was expected to commence in January 1989, for completion at the end of the following year. A further plant had opened in 1985 and had begun producing ammonia in June, and methanol in the following month. By September 1986 this plant had produced a combined 840,000 tons of ammonia and methanol. Light industry, including the production of supplementary gas, asphalt, prefabricated buildings, plastics, soft drinks, air-conditioning equipment and paper products, also continued to develop. In 1987 the Government imposed a 20% tariff on competing imported goods for a trial period of 12 months, as part of a programme to support the expansion of light industry. In 1987 Bahrain exported its first industrial product, aluminium fly mesh, to the Far East.

A major reason for Bahrain's prosperity was the government decision, in 1975, to license 'offshore banking units' (OBUs) in Bahrain. OBUs are not involved in local banking, but serve to channel money from the petroleum-producing region back into world markets. In 1985 there were 74 OBUs, with total assets of US $56,805m., which fell to $55,680m. in 1986. In 1987 the number of operational OBUs was reduced to 68, and in September their total assets stood at $59,500m. In January 1988 the number of OBUs further declined to 65. The end of the Gulf War was expected to lead to increased confidence in the region and to a revival of Bahrain's banking system, one of the main contributors to the country's economy. It was hoped that the establishment of a stock exchange, plans for which were approved in 1986, would stimulate investment in Bahrain. The stock exchange was expected to open in early 1989.

According to census results, Bahrain's population increased by 245% between 1959 and 1981. This rapid rise, combined with an increase of over 50% in water consumption between 1979 and 1983, necessitated considerable expansion of power and desalination facilities. By the early 1980s Bahrain had major power stations in four towns, with a combined generating capacity of 992 MW, and in 1987 the Government began to study proposals for a fifth power station, with a generating capacity of 400 MW, to be constructed by 1992. In 1985 expansion work was under way on desalination units at Sitra, where it is hoped to increase capacity to 20m. gallons per day (g/d). There were also plans for a 10m. g/d reverse osmosis plant to provide water for 22% of the population. Much of the funding for development in Bahrain is supplied by its neighbours in the Gulf, on whose generosity and co-operation its relative poverty leads it to depend.

As a result of the collapse of international prices for petroleum in the first half of 1986, revenue from the petroleum sector accounted for only 53% of total government revenue in that year, compared with 70% in 1983. Owing to the shortfall in revenue, government expenditure in 1986 was reduced from BD 550m. to BD 487.1m. Government revenue declined to BD 467.6m. in 1986, and a budget deficit of BD 19.5m. was therefore recorded. The deficit was funded largely by the Government's drawing on its cash balances and by the issuing of bonds by the Treasury. In 1987 the economy became more stable, and the 1988 budget (issued for one year only, in an attempt further to stabilize the economy) envisaged expenditure of BD 490m. and revenue of BD 430m., thus resulting in a projected deficit of BD 60m. Revenue from petroleum and petroleum products was expected to provide almost 59% of total budget revenue. In 1985 a surplus of US $264.9m. on the current account of the balance of payments was recorded. In 1986, however, a deficit of $50.0m. was registered, and in 1987 the balance of payments deteriorated sharply, resulting in a current account deficit of $318.9m. The trade surplus rose from $100.3m. in 1985 to $177.4m. in 1986, but in 1987 a trade deficit of $63.3m. was recorded. Measured at constant prices, GDP declined in both 1985 and 1986. In September 1986 various measures to stimulate the economy were introduced, including a 2% reduction in interest rates and the abolition of re-export fees.

Social Welfare

The state-administered medical service provides comprehensive treatment for all residents, including expatriates. There are also physicians, dentists and opticians in private practice. In 1983 Bahrain had six hospitals, 27 health centres and 16 child welfare centres. In 1982 there were 397 physicians working in the country. In 1987 plans for the construction of a new hospital and the upgrading of the Sulmaniya Medical Centre were revived. Of total expenditure by the central Government in 1986, BD 31.8m. (6.4%) was for health services, and a further BD 10.8m. (2.2%) for social security and welfare. A Social Security Law covers pensions, industrial accidents, sickness, unemployment, maternity and family allowances.

Education

Education is not compulsory, but state education is available free of charge. Private and religious education are also available. There are five different types of schooling: primary and religious schooling (for children aged six to 11 years), intermediate (12-14 years), secondary or commercial streaming (15-17 years). The University of Bahrain, created by Amiri decree in 1986, constitutes four colleges: the College of Engineering, the College of Arts and Science, the College of Education and the College of Management and Business Administration. Construction of the Arabian Gulf University, funded by six Arab governments, was under way in the mid-1980s, with the first intake of students scheduled for mid-1988. However, owing to lack of funding, the opening of the university was postponed for an indefinite period. In 1985 an estimated 94% of children aged six to 11 years (94.6% of boys; 93.8% of girls) attended primary schools, 52.4% of those aged 12 to 14 were enrolled at intermediate schools, and 41% of those aged 15-17 were enrolled at secondary schools. In 1986 there were 85,867 students in 139 schools. In early 1988, according to the Ministry of Education, more than 65% of teachers were native Bahrainis. Expenditure on education by the central Government in 1986 was BD 53m., representing 10.7% of total spending. Plans have been formulated for the construction of 18 new schools, at a cost of BD 14.4m., by 1990. In 1987 four new schools and a technical institute, built at a cost of BD 8m., were opened. In 1981 the average rate of adult illiteracy among the indigenous Bahraini population was 31.3% (males 21.2%; females 41.4%). In 1985, according to UNESCO estimates, the illiteracy rate among all adults was 27.3% (males 20.7%; females 35.9%).

Public Holidays

1989: 1 January (New Year's Day), 5 March* (Leilat al-Meiraj, Ascension of the Prophet), 7 April* (Ramadan begins), 7 May* (Id al-Fitr, end of Ramadan), 14 July* (Id al-Adha, Feast of the Sacrifice), 4 August* (Muharram, Islamic New Year), 13 August* (Ashoura), 13 October* (Mouloud, Birth of the Prophet), 16 December (National Day).

1990: 1 January (New Year's Day), 23 February* (Leilat al-Meiraj), 28 March* (Ramadan begins), 27 April* (Id al-Fitr), 4 July* (Id al-Adha), 24 July* (Muharram), 2 August* (Ashoura), 2 October* (Mouloud), 16 December (National Day).

* These holidays are dependent on the Islamic lunar calendar and may vary by one or two days from the dates given.

Weights and Measures

The metric system is being introduced.

Statistical Survey

Source (unless otherwise stated): Central Statistics Organization, POB 5835, Manama; tel. 242353; telex 8853.

AREA AND POPULATION

Area: 691.2 sq km (266.9 sq miles).

Population: 350,798 (males 204,793, females 146,005), comprising 238,420 Bahraini citizens (males 119,924, females 118,496) and 112,378 aliens (males 84,869, females 27,509), at census of 5 April 1981; 421,040 (official estimate for mid-1988).

Principal Towns (population at 1981 census): Manama (capital) 121,986; Muharraq Town 61,853.

Births and Deaths (UN estimates, 1980–85): Average annual birth rate 32.2 per 1,000; Death rate 4.5 per 1,000; Life expectancy at birth (1981): males 65.9 years, females 68.9 years.

Labour Force (manpower survey, 1984): Agriculture 1,496; Mining, quarrying, petroleum and gas extraction 433; Manufacturing 10,228 (petroleum, chemicals and plastics 4,533, other 5,695); Construction 27,555; Trade 11,280; Communications 1,761; Transport and storage 7,804; Financing 4,107; Other non-manufacturing industries 12,308; Total 81,503. Of the total labour force, 28.2% were Bahrainis, and 71.8% non-Bahrainis.

AGRICULTURE, ETC.

Principal Crops (FAO estimates, '000 metric tons, 1986): Tomatoes 13; Other vegetables and melons 30; Dates 41 (Source: FAO, *Production Yearbook*).

Livestock (FAO estimates, '000 head, year ending September 1986): Cattle 6; Sheep 7; Goats 15 (Source: FAO, *Production Yearbook*).

Livestock Products (FAO estimates, '000 metric tons, 1986): Poultry meat 4; Cows' milk 6; Hen eggs 3.6 (Source: FAO, *Production Yearbook*).

Fishing ('000 metric tons, live weight): Total catch 5.6 in 1984; 7.8 in 1985; 8.3 in 1986. (Source: FAO, *Yearbook of Fishery Statistics*).

MINING

Production (1987): Crude petroleum 15,216,000 barrels; Natural gas 5,843 million cu metres.

INDUSTRY

Production ('000 barrels, 1987): Liquefied petroleum gas 296; Naphtha 12,785; Motor spirit (petrol) and aviation gasoline 19,418; Kerosene 2,681; Fuel oil 21,225; Diesel oil 42; Gas oil 28,029; Heavy lubricant distillate 1,161; Petroleum bitumen (asphalt) 967; Electric energy 2,996 million kWh; Aluminium (unwrought, '000 metric tons) 180.3.

FINANCE

Currency and Exchange Rates: 1,000 fils = 1 Bahrain dinar (BD). *Coins:* 1, 5, 10, 25, 50 and 100 fils. *Notes:* 500 fils; 1, 5, 10 and 20 dinars. *Sterling and Dollar Equivalents* (30 September 1988): £1 sterling = 635.8 fils; US $1 = 376.0 fils; 100 Bahrain dinars = £157.28 = $265.96. *Exchange Rate:* Fixed at US $1 = 376.0 fils (BD 1 = $2.6596) since November 1980.

Budget (estimates, BD million): 1986 and 1987: Revenue 1,110; Expenditure 1,110 (550* in 1986; 560 in 1987). 1988: Revenue 430 (Petroleum receipts 252); Expenditure 490 (Recurrent 365, Capital 125).

* Actual expenditure in 1986 was BD 487 million.

Development Plan (proposed expenditure, BD million, 1982–87*): Infrastructure 768 (Electricity 260, Water and Sewerage 192, Housing 182, Roads 72, Ports and Airport 37, Other 25); Social Services 86 (Education 37, Health 12, Other 37); Economic Services 34 (Agriculture 21, Industry 11, Other 2); Administrative Services 93 (Defence and Security 80, Other 13); Other sectors 41; Total 1,022 (Source: Statistical Bureau, Ministry of Finance and National Economy).

* In May 1983 the Five-Year Plan was extended for a further year.

International Reserves (US $ million at 31 December 1987): Gold (valued at cost of acquisition) 6.6; IMF special drawing rights 20.7; Reserve position in IMF 38.7; Foreign exchange 1,089.1; Total 1,155.1 (Source: IMF, *International Financial Statistics*).

Money Supply (BD million at 31 December 1987): Currency outside banks 84.06; Demand deposits at commercial banks 162.61; Total money 246.67 (Source: IMF, *International Financial Statistics*).

Cost of Living (Consumer Price Index; base: March 1983–February 1984 = 100): 96.2 in 1985; 94.8 in 1986; 93.3 in 1987.

Gross Domestic Product (BD million at current prices): 1,733.9 in 1984; 1,602.9 in 1985; 1,383.0 in 1986 (Source: IMF, *International Financial Statistics*).

Balance of Payments (US $ million, 1987): Merchandise exports f.o.b. 2,361.2; Merchandise imports f.o.b. −2,424.5; *Trade balance* −63.3; Exports of services 828.7; Imports of services −576.3; *Balance on goods and services* 189.1; Private unrequited transfers (net) −621.3; Government unrequited transfers (net) 113.3; *Current balance* −318.9; Long-term capital (net) −62.0; Short-term capital (net) −58.2; Net errors and omissions −9.7; *Total* (net monetary movements) −448.8; Valuation changes (net) 107.9; *Changes in reserves* −340.9 (Source: IMF, *International Financial Statistics*).

EXTERNAL TRADE

Principal Commodities (BD million, 1987): *Imports c.i.f.:* Crude petroleum 470.9; Total (incl. others) 982.3. *Exports f.o.b.:* Petroleum and petroleum products 739.5; Aluminium 61.0; Total (incl. others) 881.3 (Source: IMF, *International Financial Statistics*).

TRANSPORT

Road Traffic (registered motor vehicles, 1986): Private cars 81,872; Taxis 973; Vans and lorries 22,557; Private buses 2,394; Public buses 528; Motorcycles 1,658; Total 109,982.

Shipping (international sea-borne freight traffic, '000 dwt, 1986): *Goods loaded:* Dry cargo 1,954; Petroleum products 89,543,000 barrels. *Goods unloaded:* 1,109.

Civil Aviation (Bahrain International Airport, 1987): 20,398 aircraft arrived and departed.

COMMUNICATIONS MEDIA

Radio Receivers: 142,000 in use (1985).

Television Receivers: 170,000 in use (1985).

Telephones: 76,792 in use (1987).

Book Production: 46 titles (1983).

Daily Newspapers: 3 (1984).

EDUCATION

Government Institutions (1986): *Primary:* 1,454 classes; 50,936 students. *Intermediate:* 566 classes; 19,838 students. *Secondary* (general): 256 classes, 7,815 students; (commercial): 145 classes, 4,534 students; (technical): 95 classes, 2,630 students. *Religious education:* 9 classes, 114 students.

Directory

The Constitution

A 108-article Constitution was ratified in June 1973. It states that 'all citizens shall be equal before the law' and guarantees freedom of speech, of the Press, of conscience and religious beliefs. Other provisions include the outlawing of the compulsory repatriation of political refugees. The Constitution also states that the country's financial comptroller should be responsible to Parliament and not to the Government, and allows for national trade unions 'for legally justified causes and on peaceful lines'. Compulsory free primary education and free medical care are also laid down in the Constitution. The Constitution, which came into force on 6 December 1973, also provided for a National Assembly, composed of the members of the Cabinet and 30 members elected by popular vote, although this was dissolved in August 1975.

The Government

HEAD OF STATE

Amir: Sheikh ISA BIN SULMAN AL-KHALIFA (succeeded to the throne on 2 November 1961; took the title of Amir on 16 August 1971).

THE CABINET
(December 1988)

Prime Minister: Sheikh KHALIFA BIN SULMAN AL-KHALIFA.
Minister of Defence: Maj.-Gen. Sheikh KHALIFA BIN AHMAD AL-KHALIFA.
Minister of Finance and National Economy: IBRAHIM ABD AL-KARIM MUHAMMAD.
Minister of Foreign Affairs: Sheikh MUHAMMAD BIN MUBARAK BIN HAMAD AL-KHALIFA.
Minister of Education: Dr ALI MUHAMMAD FAKHRO.
Minister of Health: JAWAD SALIM AL-ARRAYEDH.
Minister of the Interior: Sheikh MUHAMMAD BIN KHALIFA BIN HAMAD AL-KHALIFA.
Minister of Information: TARIQ ABD AR-RAHMAN AL-MOAYED.
Minister of Justice and Islamic Affairs: Sheikh ABDULLAH BIN KHALID AL-KHALIFA.
Minister of Development and Industry and Acting Minister of State for Cabinet Affairs: YOUSUF AHMAD ASH-SHIRAWI.
Minister of Transport: IBRAHIM MUHAMMAD HUMAIDAN.
Minister of Labour and Social Affairs: Sheikh KHALIFA BIN SULMAN BIN MUHAMMAD AL-KHALIFA.
Minister of Housing: Sheikh KHALID BIN ABDULLAH BIN KHALID AL-KHALIFA.
Minister of Public Works, Power and Water: MAJID JAWAD AL-JISHI.
Minister of Commerce and Agriculture: HABIB AHMAD QASSIM.
Minister of State for Legal Affairs: Dr HUSSAIN MUHAMMAD AL-BAHARNA.

MINISTRIES

Amiri Court: POB 555, Riffa Palace, Manama; tel. 661451; telex 8666.
Office of the Prime Minister: POB 1000, Government House, Government Rd, Manama; tel. 262266; telex 9336.
Ministry of Commerce and Agriculture: POB 5479, Diplomatic Area, Manama; tel. 531531; telex 9171.
Ministry of Defence: POB 245, West Rifa'a; tel. 665599; telex 8429.
Ministry of Development and Industry: POB 1435, Manama; tel. 291511; telex 8344.
Ministry of Education: POB 43, Khalid bin al-Walid Rd, Qudhaibiya, Manama; tel. 258400; telex 9094.
Ministry of Finance and National Economy: POB 333, Government House, Government Rd, Manama; tel. 262400; telex 8933.
Ministry of Foreign Affairs: POB 547, Government House, Government Rd, Manama; tel. 258200; telex 8228.
Ministry of Health: POB 12, Sheikh Sulman Rd, Manama; tel. 250834; telex 8511.
Ministry of Housing: POB 802, Diplomatic Area, Manama; tel. 533000; telex 8599.
Ministry of Information: POB 253, Isa Town; tel. 681555; telex 8399.
Ministry of the Interior: POB 13, Police Fort Compound, Manama; tel. 254021; telex 8333.
Ministry of Justice and Islamic Affairs: POB 450, Diplomatic Area, Manama; tel. 531333.
Ministry of Labour and Social Affairs: POB 32333, Isa Town, Manama; tel. 687800; telex 9062.
Ministry of Public Works, Power and Water: POB 6000, Muharraq Causeway Rd, Manama; tel. 533133; telex 8515.
Ministry of State for Cabinet Affairs: POB 1000, Government House, Government Road, Manama; tel. 262266; telex 7424.
Ministry of State for Legal Affairs: POB 790, Government House, Government Rd, Manama; tel. 259990.
Ministry of Transport: POB 10325, Diplomatic Area, Manama; tel. 232023; telex 8989.

Legislature

NATIONAL ASSEMBLY

In accordance with the 1973 Constitution, elections to a national assembly took place in December 1973. About 30,000 electors elected 30 members for a four-year term. Since political parties are not allowed, all 114 candidates stood as independents but, in practice, the National Assembly was divided almost equally between conservative, moderate and more radical members. In addition to the 30 elected members, the National Assembly contained the members of the Cabinet. In August 1975 the Prime Minister resigned because, he complained, the National Assembly was preventing the Government from carrying out its functions. The Amir invited the Prime Minister to form a new Cabinet, and two days later the National Assembly was dissolved by Amiri decree. It has not been revived.

Diplomatic Representation

EMBASSIES IN BAHRAIN

Algeria: POB 26402, Adiliya 336, Villa 579, Rd 3622, Manama; tel. 713783; telex 2775; Ambassador: BELAID MOHAND OUSSAID.
Bangladesh: POB 23434, House 159, Rd 2004, Area 320, Hoora; tel. 293371; telex 7029; Chargé d'affaires: A. MOMEN CHOUDHURY.
Egypt: POB 818, Adiliya; tel. 712011; telex 8248; Ambassador: MUHAMMAD MAHMOUD ABU ZEID.
France: POB 11134, King Faisal Rd, Diplomatic Area, Manama; tel. 291734; telex 9281; Ambassador: PIERRE BOILLOT.
Germany, Federal Republic: POB 10306, Diplomatic Area 317, Al-Hasan Bldg, Sheikh Hamad Causeway, Manama; tel. 530210; telex 7128; Ambassador: Dr BERND WULFFEN.
India: POB 26106, Bldg 182, Rd 2608, Qudhaibiya, Area 326, Adliya, Manama; tel. 712785; telex 9047; Ambassador: M. P. MURALIDHARA MENON.
Iran: Sheikh Isa Rd 2709, Manama; tel. 712151; telex 8238; Chargé d'affaires: (vacant).
Iraq: Ar-Raqeeb Bldg, No 17, Rd 2001, Comp 320, King Faisal Rd, Manama; tel. 290999; telex 9620; Ambassador: TAHA M. ALLAWI AL-QAISI.
Japan: POB 23720, House 403, Rd 915, Salmaniya, Manama; tel. 243364; Ambassador: TOSHIRO OGUSHI.
Jordan: POB 5242, Bldg 462, Villa 1-2, Rd 3308, Manama; tel. 721520; Ambassador: AMJAD AL-MAJALI.
Korea, Republic: POB 11700, King Faisal Rd, Manama; tel. 291629; telex 8736; Ambassador: HAE YUNG CHUNG.
Kuwait: POB 786, Diplomatic Area, 76 Rd 1703, Manama; tel. 242330; telex 8830; Ambassador: AHMAD AL-MUBARAKI.
New Zealand: POB 5881, Manama Centre, Government Rd, Manama; tel. 271600; telex 8748; Ambassador: J. D. L. RICHARDS.
Oman: POB 26414, Diplomatic Area, Bldg 37, Rd 1901, Manama; tel. 293663; telex 9332; Ambassador: GHALIB BIN ABDULLAH BIN JUBRAN.

BAHRAIN

Pakistan: POB 563, House 75, Rd 3403, Area 334, Mahooz, Manama; tel. 712470; Chargé d'affaires a.i.: I. A. ANSARI.
Saudi Arabia: POB 1085, Bldg 1450, Rd 4043, Jufair, Manama; tel. 727223; Ambassador: Dr GHAZI ABD AR-RAHMAN AL-GOSAIBI.
Tunisia: POB 26911, al-Mahouz, Manama; tel. 721431; Ambassador: BORHANODDINE BEN ASHORE.
United Kingdom: POB 114, 21 Government Rd, Manama; tel. 254002; telex 8213; Ambassador: JOHN ALAN SHEPHERD.
USA: POB 26431, Off Sheikh Isa Rd, Manama; tel. 714151; telex 9398; Ambassador: Dr SAM H. ZAKHEM.

Judicial System

Since the termination of British legal jurisdiction in 1971, intensive work has been undertaken on the legislative requirements of Bahrain. The Criminal Law is at present contained in various Codes, Ordinances and Regulations. All nationalities are subject to the jurisdiction of the Bahrain courts which guarantee equality before the law irrespective of nationality or creed.

Directorate of Courts: POB 450, Government House, Government Rd, Manama; tel. 531333.

Religion

At the April 1981 census the population was 350,798, distributed as follows: Muslims 298,140; Christians 25,611; Others 27,033; No religion 14.

ISLAM

Muslims are divided between the Sunni and Shi'ite sects. The ruling family is Sunni, although the majority of the Muslim population (almost 60%) are Shi'ite.

CHRISTIANITY
The Anglican Communion

Within the Episcopal Church in Jerusalem and the Middle East, Bahrain forms part of the diocese of Cyprus and the Gulf. There are two Anglican churches in Bahrain, St Christopher's Cathedral in Manama and the Community Church in Awali, and the congregations are entirely expatriate. The Bishop in Cyprus and the Gulf is resident in Cyprus, while the Archdeacon in the Gulf is resident in the United Arab Emirates.

Provost: Very Rev. JOHN F. PARKINSON, St Christopher's Cathedral, POB 36, Al-Mutanabi Ave, Manama; tel. 253866.

The Press

DAILIES

Akhbar al-Bahrain (Bahrain News): POB 253, Manama; Arabic; publ. by the Ministry of Information.
Akhbar al-Khalij (Gulf News): POB 5300, Manama; tel. 620111; telex 8565; f. 1976; Arabic; Chair IBRAHIM AL-MOAYED; Man. Dir ANWAR M. ABD AR-RAHMAN; Editor-in-Chief AHMAD KAMAL; circ. 22,000.
BAPCO Daily News: Awali; tel. 755047; telex 8214; publ. by the Bahrain Petroleum Co BSC; English; Saturday to Wednesday inclusive; Editor SAMUEL KNIGHT; circ. 1,000.
Daily News Bulletin: POB 1062, Manama; tel. 251881.
Gulf Daily News: POB 5300, Manama; tel. 620222; telex 8565; f. 1978; English; Editor-in-Chief CLIVE JACQUES; Editor GEORGE WILLIAMS; circ. 11,500.

WEEKLIES

Al-Adhwaa' (Lights): POB 250, Manama; tel. 245251; telex 8564; f. 1965; Arabic; publ. by Arab Printing and Publishing House; Editor MAHMOUD AL-MARDI; circ. 7,000.
Akhbar BAPCO (BAPCO News): Bahrain Petroleum Co BSC, POB 25149, Awali; tel. 755055; telex 8214; f. 1981; formerly known as an-Najma al-Usbou' (The Weekly Star); Arabic; house journal; Editor KHALID F. MEHMAS; circ. 8,000.
Al-Bahrain: POB 253, Isa Town; Arabic; tel. 681555; telex 8399; publ. by the Ministry of Information; Editor SALMAN TAKI; circ. 5,000.
Al-Jaridat ar-Rasmiya (The Official Gazette): POB 253, Isa Town; f. 1957; Arabic; publ. by the Ministry of Information.
Al-Masirah: POB 5981, Manama; tel. 258882; telex 7421; f. 1977; Arabic; politics; publ. by Al-Masirah Journalism, Printing and Publishing House; Chair. and Editor-in-Chief KHALIFA HASAN QASSIM.
Al-Mawakif (Situations): POB 1083, Manama; tel. 231231; f. 1973; Arabic; general interest; Editor MANSOOR RADHI; circ. 4,000.
Sada al-Usbou' (Weekly Echo): POB 549, Bahrain; tel. 291234; telex 8880; f. 1969; Arabic; Owner and Editor-in-Chief ALI SAYYAR; circ. 25,000 (in various Gulf States).

OTHER PERIODICALS

Arab Travel: POB 224, Manama; tel. 231122; telex 8981; monthly; travel trades; publ. by Al-Hilal Publishing and Marketing Co; Editor ANN PAYLOR; circ. 11,700.
Gulf Panorama: POB 1122, Manama; tel. 277677; monthly; Editor IBRAHIM BASHMI; circ. 15,000.
Al-Hayat at-Tijariya (Commerce Review): POB 248, Manama; tel. 233913; telex 8691; monthly; English and Arabic; publ. by Bahrain Chamber of Commerce and Industry; Editor HAFEDH ASH-SHAIKH; circ. 3,500.
Link: POB 5981, Manama; tel. 258882; telex 7421; f. 1986; monthly; social and cultural magazine; publ. by Al-Masirah Journalism, Printing and Publishing House; Chair. and Editor-in-Chief KHALIFA HASAN KASIM.
Al-Mujtama' al-Jadid (The New Society): POB 590, Manama; monthly; general interest.
Al-Murshid (The Guide): POB 553, Manama; English and Arabic; monthly guide, including 'What's on in Bahrain'; publ. by Arabian Printing and Publishing House; Editor M. SOLIMAN.
Oil & Gas News: POB 224, Manama; tel. 231122; telex 8981; monthly; publ. by Al-Hilal Publishing and Marketing Co.
This is Bahrain & What's On: POB 726, Manama; tel. 250014; telex 8494; f. 1975; quarterly; English, with an Arabic section; general interest; publ. by Gulf Advertising and Marketing Co; Editor FENELLA FLANAGAN; circ. 20,000.
This Is Our Country: POB 5127, Manama; monthly; English and Arabic.

NEWS AGENCIES

Agence France-Presse (France): Direction Régionale pour le Golfe, POB 5890, Manama; tel. 259115; telex 8987; Correspondent ASSAD SABOUNJI.
Associated Press (AP) (USA): POB 26940, Al-Moosa Bldg, Manama; tel. 530101; telex 9470; Chief of Bureau ALI MAHMOUD.
Deutsche Presse-Agentur (dpa) (Federal Republic of Germany): POB 26995, Rd 3435, Bldg 1464, Apt 2, Al-Mahouz, Manama; tel. 727523; telex 9542; Correspondent NABIL MEGALLI.
Gulf News Agency: POB 301, Manama; tel. 687272; telex 9030.
Reuters (UK): Middle East Headquarters, POB 1030, Manama; tel. 255455; telex 8301.

United News of India also has an office in Bahrain.

Publishers

Arab Printing and Publishing House: POB 553, Manama.
ArabCommunicators: POB 551, Manama; tel. 254258; telex 8263; publrs of annual Bahrain Business Directory; Dirs AHMAD A. FAKHRI, HAMAD A. ABDUL.
Falcon Publishing WLL: POB 5028, Manama; tel. 253162; telex 8917; Chair and Man. Dir A. A. ASH-SHO'ALA; Group Gen. Man. RODNEY PEAKE.
Gulf Advertising and Marketing Co: POB 726, Manama; tel. 250014; telex 8494.
Al-Hilal Publishing and Marketing Co: POB 224, Manama; tel. 231122; telex 8981; specialist magazines of commercial interest; Chair. A. M. ABD AR-RAHMAN; Man. Dir R. MIDDLETON.
Al-Masirah Journalism, Printing and Publishing House: POB 5981, Manama; tel. 258882; telex 7421.

Government Publishing House

Directorate of Publications: POB 26005, Manama; tel. 689077; Dir MUHAMMAD AL-KHOZAI.

Radio and Television

In 1985 there were an estimated 142,000 radio receivers and 170,000 television receivers in use. English language programmes, broadcast from Saudi Arabia by the US Air Force in Dhahran and by the Arabian-American Oil Co (Aramco), can be received in Bahrain, as can the television service provided by the latter.

BAHRAIN

Bahrain Broadcasting Station: POB 194, Manama; tel. 712278; telex 9259; f. 1955; state-owned and -operated enterprise; two 10 kW transmitters; programmes are in Arabic and English, and include news, plays and talks; Station Mans HASSAN SALMAN KAMAL (Arabic service), AHMAD M. SULAIMAN (English service).

Radio Bahrain: POB 702, Manama; tel. 640022; telex 8311; f. 1977; commercial radio station in English language; Man. AHMAD M. SULAIMAN.

Bahrain Television: POB 1075, Manama; tel. 681811; telex 8311; commenced colour TV broadcasting in 1973; second channel in English began broadcasting in October 1981; the station takes advertising; covers Bahrain, eastern Saudi Arabia, Qatar and the UAE; Dir H. AL-UMRAN; Adviser JOHN SHAW.

Finance

(cap. = capital; p.u. = paid up; dep. = deposits; m. = millions; res = reserves; brs = branches; amounts in Bahraini dinars unless otherwise stated)

BANKING
Central Bank

Bahrain Monetary Agency (BMA): POB 27, Manama; tel. 241241; telex 9144; f. 1973, in operation from January 1975; controls issue of currency, regulates exchange control and credit policy, organization and control of banking system and bank credit; cap. p.u. 20m., dep. 105.9m., res 108.4m., total assets 324.6m. (Dec. 1986); Governor ABDULLAH HASSAN SAIF; Chair. Sheikh KHALIFA BIN SALMAN AL-KHALIFA; Deputy Chair. IBRAHIM ABD AL-KARIM MUHAMMAD.

Locally Incorporated Commercial Banks

Al-Ahli Commercial Bank BSC: POB 5941, Manama; tel. 244333; telex 9130; f. 1977; full commercial bank; total assets 155.2m. (Dec. 1987); Chair. MUHAMMAD YOUSUF JALAL; Gen. Man. GREGORY KRIKORIAN.

Arlabank International EC: POB 5070, Manama Centre, Manama; tel. 232124; telex 9345; f. 1983; wholly owned subsidiary: Arab-Latin American Bank (Banco Arabe Latinoamericano) in Peru; total assets US $1,298m. (Dec. 1987); Chair. ABDULLAH A. SAUDI; Gen. Man. CHRISTIAN RODRIGUEZ-CAMILLONI.

Bahrain Middle East Bank EC: POB 797, Manama; tel. 532345; telex 9706; f. 1982; owned by Burgan Bank (28%) and GCC nationals (72%); total assets US $503m. (Dec. 1987); Chair. ABD AR-RAHMAN SALEM AL-ATIQI; Gen. Man. and CEO K. J. A. KATCHADURIAN.

Bahraini Saudi Bank BSC (BSB): POB 1159, Government Rd, Manama; tel. 263111; telex 7010; f. 1983; commenced operations in early 1985; licensed as a full commercial bank; total assets 81.2m. (Dec. 1987); Chair. Sheikh IBRAHIM BIN HAMAD AL-KHALIFA; Gen. Man. MANSOOR AS-SAYED (acting).

Bank of Bahrain and Kuwait BSC (BBK): POB 597, Manama; tel. 253388; telex 8919; f. 1971; total assets 666.7m. (1987); Chair. RASHID ABD AR-RAHMAN AZ-ZAYANI; Gen. Man. MURAD ALI MURAD; 18 local brs, 3 brs overseas.

Gulf International Bank BSC (GIB): POB 1017, Ad-Dowali Bldg, King Faisal Rd, Manama; tel. 256245; telex 8802; f. 1975; owned by governments of Bahrain, Iraq, Kuwait, Oman, Qatar, Saudi Arabia and the UAE; cap. US $530.5, total assets US $8,963m. (Dec. 1987); Chair. ABDULLAH HASSAN SAIF; Gen. Man. GHAZI M. ABD AL-JAWAD.

National Bank of Bahrain BSC (NBB): POB 106, Government Rd, Manama; tel. 258800; telex 8242; f. 1957; commercial bank with Government of Bahrain as major shareholder; cap. p.u. 28.0m., dep. 575.1m., total assets 650.5m. (Dec. 1987); Chair. AHMAD ALI KANOO; Gen. Man. and CEO HUSSAIN ALI JUMA; 19 brs.

Foreign Commercial Banks

Algemene Bank Nederland NV (Netherlands): POB 350, Manama; tel. 255420; telex 8356; Gen. Man. and Regional Man. (Middle East and Africa) W. J. VAN DER MEI.

Arab Bank Ltd (Jordan): POB 395, Manama Centre, Manama; tel. 255988; telex 8232; Regional Man. Dr MAKRAM A. RAHAL; 4 brs.

Bank Melli Iran: POB 785, Government Rd, Manama; tel. 259910; telex 8266; Asst Man. MANOCHEHR KHEEZRI; 1 br.

Bank Saderat Iran: POB 825, Manama; tel. 255318; telex 8688; Man. Y. M. SHENOY; 2 brs.

Banque du Caire (Egypt): POB 815, Manama; tel. 254454; telex 8298; Man. MAHMOUD ABBAS ABU AL-KHAIR.

Banque Paribas FCB (France): POB 5241, Manama; tel. 253119; telex 8458; Gen. Man. M. APTHORPE.

British Bank of the Middle East (BBME) (Hong Kong): POB 57, Manama; tel. 242555; telex 8230; Area Man. ALAN D. WHYTE; 5 brs.

Chase Manhattan Bank NA (USA): POB 368, Manama; tel. 251401; telex 8286; Vice-Pres. and Man. STEVE FULLENKAMP; 1 br.

Citibank NA (USA): POB 548, Manama; tel. 257124; telex 8225; Vice-Pres. ROSS DI BACCO; 1 br.

Grindlays Bahrain Bank BSC: POB 793, Manama; tel. 250805; telex 8335; f. 1984 when Bahraini citizens took over 60% of equity held by Grindlays Bank PLC (London); total assets 40.8m.; Chair. MUHAMMAD ABDULLAH AZ-ZAMIL; Gen. Man. J. J. CANNING; 3 brs.

Habib Bank Ltd (Pakistan): POB 566, Manama Centre, Manama; tel. 271402; telex 9448; f. 1941; cap. US $287m.; dep. US $4,940m.; Sr Vice-Pres. and Gen. Man. ABD AL-HANNAN MIRZA.

Hongkong and Shanghai Banking Corpn (Hong Kong): POB 5497, BBME Bldg, Al-Khalifa Ave, Manama; tel. 255828; telex 8707; Man. ALAN D. WHYTE.

National Bank of Abu Dhabi: POB 5247, Manama; tel. 250824; telex 8483; Man. ROGER C. V. BACKETT; 1 br.

Rafidain Bank (Iraq): POB 607, Manama; tel. 255456; telex 8332; f. 1979; Man. ABBAS HADI AL-BAYATI; 1 br.

Saudi National Commercial Bank: POB 20363, Manama; tel. 231182; telex 9298; Gen. Man. SAID CHAUDHRY.

Standard Chartered Bank (UK): POB 29, Manama; tel. 255946; telex 8229; f. in Bahrain 1920; Gen. Man. ROSS HOLDEN; 5 brs.

United Bank Ltd (Pakistan): POB 546, Government Rd, Manama; tel. 254032; telex 8247; Man. YOUSUF AHMAD AL-MADINI; 2 brs.

Specialized Financial Institutions

Arab Banking Corpn: POB 5698, ABC Tower, Diplomatic Area, Manama; tel. 532235; telex 9433; f. 1980 by Amiri decree; jointly owned by Kuwait Ministry of Finance, Central Bank of Libya and Abu Dhabi Investment Authority; offers full range of commercial, merchant and investment banking services; total assets US $17,548m. (Dec. 1987); Pres. and Chief Exec. ABDULLAH A. SAUDI; Chair. ABD AL-MOHSEN YOUSUF AL-HUNAIF; 6 brs.

Bahrain Housing Bank: POB 5370, Diplomatic Area, Manama; tel. 233321; telex 8599; f. 1979; Chair. Sheikh KHALID BIN ABDULLAH BIN KHALID AL-KHALIFA; Gen. Man. ISA SULTAN ATH-THAWADI.

Bahrain Islamic Bank BSC: POB 5240, Government Rd, Manama; tel. 231402; telex 9388; f. 1979; total assets BD 63.7m. (1986); Pres. and Gen. Man. ABD AL-LATIF A. RAHIM JANAHI.

'Offshore' Banking Units

Bahrain has been encouraging the establishment of 'offshore' banking units (OBUs) since October 1975. An OBU is not allowed to provide local banking services but is allowed to accept deposits from governments and large financial organizations in the area and make medium-term loans for local and regional capital projects.

Operational OBUs

Algemene Bank Nederland NV (ABN BANK): POB 350; tel. 255420; telex 8356.

Allied Banking Corporation: POB 20493; tel. 246616; telex 9349.

ALUBAF Arab International Bank EC: POB 11529; tel. 531212; telex 9671.

American Express Bank Ltd: POB 93; tel. 531383; telex 8536.

Arab Asian Bank EC: POB 5619; tel. 233129; telex 8583.

Arab Bank Ltd: POB 395; tel. 555988; telex 8232.

Arab Banking Corporation: POB 5698; tel. 232235; telex 9432.

Arab International Bank: POB 1114; tel. 261611; telex 9489.

Arab Investment Company SAA (TAIC): POB 5559; tel. 271126; telex 8334.

Arab Malaysian Development Bank: POB 5619; tel. 257059; telex 9393.

Arab Saudi Bank: POB 10100; tel. 530011; telex 7218.

Arlabank International EC: POB 5070; tel. 232124; telex 9345.

Al-Bahrain Arab African Bank EC (Al-Baab); POB 20488; tel. 230491; telex 9380.

Bahrain International Bank EC: POB 5016; tel. 274545; telex 9832.

Banco de Vizcaya SA: POB 5307; tel. 253340; telex 9060.

Banco do Estado de São Paulo SA (BANESPA): POB 25615; tel. 232241; telex 9347.

Bank Bumiputra Malaysia Berhad: POB 20392; tel. 231073; telex 8884.

Bank Negara Indonesia 1946: POB 20715; tel. 277562; telex 8208.

Bank of America NT & SA: POB 5280; tel. 245000; telex 8616.

Bank of Bahrain and Kuwait BSC: POB 597; tel. 253388; telex 8919.

Bank of Baroda: POB 1915; tel. 253681; telex 9449.

Bank of Credit and Commerce International SA: POB 569; tel. 256501; telex 8346.

BAHRAIN

Bank of Oman Ltd: POB 20654; tel. 232882; telex 9565.
Bank of Tokyo Ltd: POB 5850; tel. 26518; telex 9066.
Bank Saderat Iran: POB 825; tel. 255318; telex 8688.
Bankers' Trust Co: POB 5905; tel. 259841; telex 9020.
Banque Arabe et Internationale d'Investissement (BAII): POB 5333; tel. 258258; telex 8542.
Banque Indosuez: POB 5410; tel. 257019; telex 8976.
Banque Nationale de Paris: POB 5253; tel. 250852; telex 8595.
Banque Paribas: POB 5993; tel. 259272; telex 9078.
Barclays Bank PLC: POB 5120; tel. 242024; telex 8747.
British Bank of the Middle East: POB 57; tel. 255933; telex 8230.
Canadian Imperial Bank of Commerce: POB 774; tel. 250551; telex 8593.
Chase Manhattan Bank NA: POB 368; tel. 251401; telex 8286.
Chemical Bank: POB 5492; tel. 252619; telex 8562.
Citibank NA: POB 548; tel. 257124; telex 8225.
Commercial Bank of Australia: POB 5467; tel. 254792; telex 8687.
Crédit Suisse: POB 5100; tel. 232123; telex 8422.
FRAB-Bank (Middle East) EC: POB 5290; tel. 259862; telex 9024.
Grindlays Bank PLC: POB 5793; tel. 233210; telex 8723.
Gulf International Bank BSC (GIB): POB 1017; tel. 256245; telex 8802.
Gulf Riyad Bank EC: POB 20220; tel. 232030; telex 9088.
Habib Bank Ltd: POB 566; tel. 271811; telex 8240.
Hanil Bank Ltd: POB 1151; tel. 243503; telex 7048.
Korea Exchange Bank: POB 5767; tel. 255418; telex 8846.
Kuwait Asia Bank EC: POB 10401; tel. 532111; telex 9611.
Manufacturers Hanover Trust Co: POB 5471; tel. 254375; telex 8556.
Massraf Faysal al-Islami of Bahrain EC: POB 20492; tel. 275040; telex 9270.
Midland Bank PLC: POB 5675; tel. 257100; telex 8719.
National Bank of Abu Dhabi: POB 5886; tel. 255776; telex 8982.
National Bank of Bahrain: POB 106; tel. 258800; telex 8242.
National Bank of Pakistan: POB 775; tel. 244191; telex 9221.
Overseas Trust Bank Ltd: POB 5628; tel. 245145; telex 9238.
Al-Saudi Banque (Paris): POB 5820; tel 257319; telex 8969.
Saudi European Bank SA: POB 26380; tel. 232884; telex 8732.
Saudi National Commercial Bank: POB 20363; tel. 231182; telex 9298.
Scandinavian Bank Group PLC: POB 5345; tel. 532244; telex 8530.
Security Pacific National Bank: POB 5589; tel. 259956; telex 9034.
Société Générale: POB 5275; tel. 242002; telex 8568.
Standard Chartered Bank PLC: POB 29; tel. 255946; telex 8229.
State Bank of India: POB 5466; tel. 253640; telex 8804.
Swiss Bank Corporation: POB 5560; tel. 257221; telex 9173.
Union de Banques Arabes et Françaises (UBAF): POB 5595; tel. 250985; telex 8840.
United Bank of Kuwait PLC: POB 5494; tel. 256774; telex 8649.
United Gulf Bank EC: POB 5964; tel. 533233; telex 9556.
Yamaichi International (Middle East) EC: POB 26894; tel. 253922; telex 9468.
Yapi Ve Kredi Bankasi: POB 1104; tel. 270089; telex 9931.

Representative Offices
In January 1988 a total of 59 banks maintained representative offices in Bahrain.

Investment Banks
Investment banks operating in Bahrain include the following: Arab Financial Services Co EC, Arab Multinational Investment Co (AMICO), Arabian Investment Banking Corpn (INVESTCORP) EC, BAII Corpn EC, Bahrain International Investment Centre (BIIC), Bahrain Investment Bank BSC, Bahrain Islamic Investment Co BSC, Bahraini Kuwaiti Investment Group (BKIG), Al-Baraka Islamic Investment Bank BSC, Citicorp Investment Bank (CIB), Elders IXL, Gulf Investments Co, EF Hutton International Inc., Islamic Investment Company of the Gulf (Bahrain) EC, Merrill Lynch Int. Inc., National Bank of Pakistan, Nikko Investment Banking (Middle East) EC, Nomura Investment Banking (Middle East) EC, Okasan Int. (Middle East) EC, Robert Fleming Holdings Ltd, Sumitomo Finance (Middle East) EC, Trans-Arabian Investment Bank EC (TAIB), United Gulf Investment Co, Yamaichi International (Middle East) EC, Az-Zayani Investments Ltd.

INSURANCE

Al-Ahlia Insurance Co BSC: POB 5282, Manama; tel. 258860; telex 8761; f. 1976.

Arab Insurance Group BSC (ARIG): POB 26992, Arig House, Diplomatic Area, Manama; tel. 531110; telex 9395; f. 1980; owned by governments of Kuwait, Libya and Abu Dhabi; cap. p.u. US $150m.; all non-life reinsurance; Chair. ABD AL-WAHAB A. AT-TAMMAR; Gen. Man. and CEO NOOR UD-DIN A. NOOR UD-DIN.

Atlas Assurance Co Ltd: POB 20449, Manama; tel. 254709; telex 8223; general insurance.

Bahrain Insurance Co BSC (BIC): POB 843, Suite 310, Sh. Mubarak Bldg, Government Ave, Manama; tel. 255641; telex 8463; f. 1969; all classes including life insurance; cap. BD 1.2m.; 66.66% Bahraini-owned; 33.33% Iraqi-owned; Gen. Man. HISHAM SHUKRI BABAN; 4 brs.

Bahrain Kuwait Insurance Co BSC: POB 10166, Diplomatic Area, Manama; tel. 532323; telex 8672; Gen. Man. PETER L. ATKINSON.

National Insurance Co BSC (NIC): POB 1818, Unitag House, Government Rd, Manama; tel. 244181; telex 8908; f. 1982; all classes of general insurance; Chair. J. A. WAFA; Pres. SAMIR AL-WAZZAN.

In July 1985, 13 foreign insurance companies were represented.

Trade and Industry

CHAMBER OF COMMERCE

Bahrain Chamber of Commerce and Industry: POB 248, Manama; tel. 233913; telex 8691; f. 1939; 3,647 mems; Pres. QASSIM AHMAD FAKHROO; Sec.-Gen. JASSIM MUHAMMAD ASH-SHATTI.

STATE ENTERPRISES

Aluminium Bahrain BSC (ALBA): POB 570, Manama; tel. 752222; telex 8253; f. 1971; operates a smelter owned by the governments of Bahrain (57.9%) and Saudi Arabia (20%), the remainder being held privately; in 1987 output at the smelter had increased to 180,344 tons; Chief Exec. GUDVIN K. TOFTE.

Bahrain Aluminium Extrusion Co BSC (BALEXCO): POB 1053, Manama; tel. 730111; telex 8634; f. 1976; generally supplies 'unfinished' systems to the construction industry; 100% owned by the Government of Bahrain; Chair. Dr ABD AL-LATIF KANOO; Gen. Man. ABD AL-MONEM SHIRAWI.

Bahrain Atomizers International: POB 5328, Manama; tel. 261158; telex 8253; f. 1973; produces atomized aluminium powder; owned by the Government of Bahrain (51%) and Breton Investments (49%); Chair. Y. SHIRAWI.

Bahrain National Gas Co BSC (BANAGAS): POB 29099, Rifa'a; tel. 756222; telex 9317; f. 1979; responsible for extraction, processing and sale of hydrocarbon liquids from associated gas derived from onshore Bahrain fields; ownership is 75% Government of Bahrain, 12.5% Caltex and 12.5% Arab Petroleum Investments Corporation (APICORP); produced 161,000 tons of LPG and 140,000 tons of natural gasoline in 1987; Chair. Sheikh IBRAHIM BIN RASHID AL-KHALIFA; Production Man. ALI A. GINDI.

Bahrain National Oil Co (BANOCO): POB 25504, Awali; tel. 754666; telex 8670; f. 1976; responsible for exploration for petroleum and other hydrocarbons and involved in their refining, transport, storage, local distribution and sales of petroleum products, international marketing of crude oil and petroleum products, supply and sales of aviation fuels; CEO MUHAMMAD SALEH SHEIKH ALI.

Bahrain Petroleum Co BSC (BAPCO): Awali; tel. 754444; telex 8214; f. 1980; a refining company owned by the Government of Bahrain (60%) and Caltex Bahrain (40%); Chair. YOUSUF AHMAD ASH-SHIRAWI (Minister of Development and Industry); Chief Exec. DON F. HEPBURN.

Bahrain-Saudi Aluminium Marketing Co (BALCO): POB 20079, Manama; tel. 234164; telex 9110; f. 1976; to market ALBA products; owned by the Government of Bahrain (74.33%) and Saudi Basic Industries Corporation (25.67%); Gen. Man. MAHMOUD M. A. AS-SOUFI.

Bahrain Telecommunications Co BSC (BATELCO): POB 14, Manama; tel. 270270; telex 8201; f. 1981; operates all telecommunications services; cap. BD 60m.; 60% owned by Bahrain, 40% by Cable and Wireless PLC (United Kingdom); Chair. IBRAHIM MUHAMMAD HASSAN HUMAIDAN; Gen. Man. BRIAN WOOD.

General Poultry Co: POB 5472, Bahrain; tel. 631001; telex 8678; fully-owned by Government of Bahrain; produces poultry feed and eggs; Chair. SIDDIQ AL-ALAWI.

Gulf Aluminium Rolling Mill Co (GARMCO): POB 20725, Manama; tel. 731000; telex 9786; f. 1980 as a joint venture between the governments of Bahrain, Saudi Arabia, Kuwait, Iraq (20% each), Oman and Qatar (10% each); initial capacity of 40,000 tons per year of aluminium sheet and coil; production in 1986, the first year of operation, reached 30,000 tons of rolled aluminium; Gen. Man. JOHN KAY.

Gulf Industrial Investment Co (GIIC): POB 50177, Hidd; tel. 673311; telex 9993; f. 1988; owned by Kuwait Petroleum Corpn (KPC); Chair. AWWAD AL-KHALDI; Gen. Man. Dr MAHMOUD MARDI.

Gulf Petrochemical Industries Co BSC (GPIC): POB 26730, Sitra; tel. 731777; telex 9897; f. 1979 as a joint venture between the governments of Bahrain, Kuwait and Saudi Arabia, each with one-third equity participation; cap. p.u. BD 60m.; a petrochemical complex at Sitra, inaugurated in 1981, began production of ammonia and methanol in 1985; Chair. Dr TAWFIQ AL-MOAYED; Gen. Man. MUSTAFA AS-SAYED.

TRADE UNIONS

There are no trade unions in Bahrain.

Transport

ROADS

Most inhabited areas of Bahrain are linked by bitumen-surfaced roads. By 1987 the number of private cars in Bahrain had risen to 115,000, compared with 20,000 in 1971. Public transport consists of taxis and privately-owned bus services. A national bus company provides public services throughout the country. A modern network of dual highways is being developed, and a 25-km causeway link with Saudi Arabia was opened in November 1986. In its first year of operation, more than 4.5m. people and more than 1.3m. vehicles used the King Fahd Causeway. A three-lane dual carriageway links the causeway to Manama. A joint Bahraini-Saudi bus company was formed in 1986, with capital of US $266,600, to operate along the causeway. A second causeway, linking Manama with Muharraq, is planned for construction between 1989 and 1992.

Directorate of Roads and Sewerage: POB 5, Exhibition Rd, Hoora, Manama; tel. 273003; responsible for road maintenance and construction; Adviser JACK K. MCDADE.

SHIPPING

Numerous shipping services link Bahrain and the Gulf with Europe, the USA, Pakistan, India, the Far East and Australia.

The deep-water harbour of Mina Sulman was opened in April 1962; it has 14 conventional berths, two container terminals and a roll-on/roll-off berth. In the vicinity are two slipways able to take vessels of up to 1,016 tons and 73 m in length, with services available for ship repairs afloat. The second container terminal, which has a 400-m quay (permitting two 180-m container ships to be handled simultaneously), was opened in April 1979. Further development of Mina Sulman, to allow handling of larger quantities of container cargo, began in 1983. The extension was expected to cost US $13m. During 1985 Mina Sulman handled approximately 2m. metric tons of cargo. An agreement to lease a floating dry dock was expected to be signed by ASRY by the end of 1988. The floating dock would take vessels of up to 70,000 dwt (from March 1989), compared with the 500,000-dwt vessels that can be accommodated in the present fixed dry dock.

Directorate of Customs and Ports: POB 15, Manama; tel. 243533; telex 8642; responsible for customs activities and acts as port authority; President of Customs and Ports Sheikh DAIJ BIN KHALIFA AL-KHALIFA; Port Director EID ABDULLAH YOUSUF; Harbour Master SALIH MUSALLAM.

Arab Shipbuilding and Repair Yard Co (ASRY): POB 50110, Hidd; tel. 671111; telex 8455; f. 1974 by OAPEC members; 500,000-ton dry dock opened 1977; cap. US $340m.; Chair. Sheikh DAIJ BIN KHALIFA AL-KHALIFA; Gen. Man. ANTONIO J. MACHADO LOPES.

CIVIL AVIATION

Bahrain International Airport has a first-class runway, capable of taking the largest aircraft in use, and expansion is still in progress. In 1986 Gulf Air carried a total of 2,589,697 passengers.

Directorate of Civil Aviation: POB 586, Bahrain International Airport, Muharraq; tel. 321332; telex 9186; Asst Under-Sec. Sheikh HAMAD BIN ABDULLAH AL-KHALIFA.

Gulf Air Co GSC (Gulf Air): POB 138, Manama; tel. (enquiries) 322200; telex 8255; f. 1950; jointly owned by the Governments of Bahrain, Oman, Qatar and Abu Dhabi; network includes Abu Dhabi, Amman, Athens, Baghdad, Bahrain, Bangkok, Bombay, Cairo, Colombo, Damascus, Dar es Salaam, Delhi, Dhahran, Dhaka, Doha, Dubai, Frankfurt, Fujairah, Hong Kong, Istanbul, Jeddah, Karachi, Khartoum, Kuwait, Larnaca, London, Manila, Muscat, Nairobi, Paris, Ras al-Khaimah, Riyadh, Salalah, San'a, Sharjah, Shiraz, Teheran and Tunis; Chair. of Board ABDULLAH BIN NASSER AS-SUWEIDI (Bahrain); Pres. and Chief Exec. ALI IBRAHIM AL-MALKI (Qatar); fleet consists of 11 TriStar, 8 Boeing 737-200, 2 Boeing 747-200.

Tourism

There are several archaeological sites of importance. Bahrain is the site of the ancient trading civilization of Dilmun. There is a wide selection of hotels and restaurants. In 1982 a total of 203,141 tourists were recorded on arrival in Bahrain, and in 1984 the number of tourists from other Gulf countries reached 154,000.

Bahrain Tourism Co (BTC): POB 5831, Manama; tel. 530530; telex 8929; total assets BD 13m. (1986).

Directorate of Tourism and Archaeology: Manama; tel. 727111; Dir Sheikh RASHID AL-KHALIFA.

BANGLADESH

Introductory Survey

Location, Climate, Language, Religion, Flag, Capital

The People's Republic of Bangladesh lies in southern Asia, surrounded by Indian territory except for a short south-eastern frontier with Burma and a southern coast fronting the Bay of Bengal. The country has a tropical monsoon climate and suffers from periodic cyclones. The average temperature is 19°C (67°F) from October to March, rising to 29°C (84°F) between May and September. The average annual rainfall in Dhaka is 188 cm (74 in), of which about three-quarters occurs between June and September. About 95% of the population speak Bengali, the state language, while the remainder mostly use tribal dialects. More than 85% of the people are Muslims, Islam being the state religion, and there are small minorities of Hindus, Buddhists and Christians. The national flag is green, with a red disc in the centre. The capital is Dhaka (Dacca).

Recent History

Present-day Bangladesh was formerly East Pakistan, one of the five provinces into which Pakistan was divided at its initial creation, when Britain's former Indian Empire was partitioned in August 1947. East Pakistan and the four western provinces were separated by about 1,000 miles (1,600 km) of Indian territory. East Pakistan was formed from the former Indian province of East Bengal and the Sylhet district of Assam. Although the East was more populous, government was based in West Pakistan. Dissatisfaction in East Pakistan at its dependence on a remote central government flared up in 1952, when Urdu was declared Pakistan's official language. Bengali, the main language of East Pakistan, was finally admitted as the joint official language in 1954, and in 1955 Pakistan was reorganized into two wings, east and west, with equal representation in the central legislative assembly. However, discontent continued in the eastern wing, particularly as the region was under-represented in the administration and armed forces, and received a disproportionately small share of Pakistan's development expenditure. The leading political party in East Pakistan was the Awami League, led by Sheikh Mujibur Rahman, who demanded autonomy for the East. General elections in December 1970 gave the Awami League an overwhelming victory in the East, and thus a majority in Pakistan's National Assembly; Sheikh Mujib should have become Prime Minister, but Pakistan's President, Gen. Yahya Khan, would not accept this, and negotiations on a possible constitutional compromise broke down. The convening of the new National Assembly was postponed indefinitely in March 1971, leading to violent protests in East Pakistan. The Awami League decided that the province should unilaterally secede from Pakistan, and on 26 March Mujib proclaimed the independence of the People's Republic of Bangladesh ('Bengal Nation').

Civil war immediately broke out. President Yahya Khan outlawed the Awami League and arrested its leaders. By April 1971 the Pakistan army dominated the eastern province. In August Sheikh Mujib was secretly put on trial in West Pakistan. Resistance continued, however, from the Liberation Army of East Bengal (the 'Mukhti Bahini'), a group of irregular fighters who launched a major offensive in November. As a result of the fighting, an estimated 9.5m. refugees crossed into India. On 4 December India declared war on Pakistan, with Indian forces intervening in support of the 'Mukhti Bahini'. Pakistan surrendered on 16 December and Bangladesh's independence became a reality. Pakistan was thus confined to its former western wing. In January 1972 Sheikh Mujib was freed by Pakistan's new President, Zulfiqar Ali Bhutto, and became Prime Minister of Bangladesh. Under a provisional constitution, Bangladesh was declared to be a secular state and a parliamentary democracy. The new nation quickly achieved international recognition, causing Pakistan to withdraw from the Commonwealth in January 1972. Bangladesh joined the Commonwealth in April. The members who had been elected from the former East Pakistan for the Pakistan National Assembly and the Provincial Assembly in December 1970 formed the Bangladesh Constituent Assembly. A new constitution was approved by this Assembly in November 1972 and came into effect in December. A general election for the country's first Jatiya Sangsad (Parliament) was held in March 1973. The Awami League received 73% of the total votes and won 292 of the 300 directly elective seats in the legislature. Bangladesh was finally recognized by Pakistan in February 1974. Stability was threatened by opposition groups which resorted to terrorism and included both political extremes. In December a state of emergency was declared and constitutional rights were suspended. In January 1975 parliamentary government was replaced by a presidential form of government. Sheikh Mujib became President, assuming absolute power, and created the Bangladesh Peasants' and Workers' Awami League. In February Bangladesh became a one-party state.

In August 1975 Sheikh Mujib and his family were assassinated in a right-wing coup, led by a group of Islamic army majors. Khandakar Mushtaq Ahmed, the former Minister of Commerce, was installed as President, declared martial law and banned political parties. A counter-coup on 3 November brought to power Brig. Khalid Musharaf, the pro-Indian commander of the Dhaka garrison, who was appointed Chief of Army Staff, but on 7 November a third coup overthrew Brig. Musharaf's four-day-old regime and power was assumed by the three service chiefs jointly, under a non-political President, Abusadet Mohammed Sayem, the Chief Justice of the Supreme Court. A neutral non-party government was formed, in which the reinstated Chief of Army Staff, Major-Gen. Ziaur Rahman (Gen. Zia), took precedence over his colleagues. Political parties were legalized again in July 1976.

An early return to representative government was promised, but in November 1976 elections were postponed indefinitely and, in a major shift of power, Gen. Zia took over the powers of Chief Martial Law Administrator from President Sayem, assuming the presidency also in April 1977. He amended the Constitution, making Islam, instead of secularism, its first basic principle. In a national referendum in May 1977, 99% of voters affirmed their confidence in President Zia's policies, and in June 1978 the country's first direct presidential election resulted in a clear victory for Zia, who formed a Council of Ministers to replace his Council of Advisers. Parliamentary elections followed in February 1979 and, in an attempt to persuade opposition parties to participate in the elections, President Zia met some of their demands by repealing 'all undemocratic provisions' of the 1974 constitutional amendment, releasing political prisoners and withdrawing press censorship. Consequently, 29 parties contested the elections, in which President Zia's Bangladesh Nationalist Party (BNP) received 49% of the total votes and won 207 of the 300 directly elective seats in the Jatiya Sangsad. In April a new Prime Minister was appointed, and martial law was repealed. The state of emergency was revoked in November.

Political instability recurred, however, when Gen. Zia was assassinated on 30 May 1981 during an attempted military coup, supposedly led by Maj.-Gen. Mohammad Abdul Manzur, an army divisional commander who was himself later killed in confused circumstances. The elderly Vice-President, Justice Abdus Sattar, took over as acting President but was faced by strikes and demonstrations in protest against the execution of several officers who had been involved in the coup, and pressure from opposition parties to have the date of the presidential election moved. As the only person acceptable to the different groups within the BNP, Sattar was nominated as the party's presidential candidate, gaining an overwhelming victory at the November election. President Sattar announced his intention of continuing the policies of the late Gen. Zia. He found it increasingly difficult, however, to retain civilian control over the country, and in January 1982 he formed a National Security Council, which included military personnel, led by the Army Chief of Staff, Lt-Gen. Hossain Mohammad Ershad. On 24 March Gen. Ershad seized power in a bloodless coup, claiming that political corruption and economic mismanagement had become intolerable. The country was placed under martial law, with Ershad as Chief Martial Law Administrator (in October his title was changed to Prime Minister), aided by a mainly military Council of Advisers; a retired judge, Justice Abul Chowdhury, was nominated as President by Ershad. Political activities were banned. Later in the year, several former ministers were tried and imprisoned on charges of corruption.

Although the Government's economic policies achieved some success and gained a measure of popular support for Ershad, there were increasing demands in 1983 for a return to democratic government. The two principal opposition groups that emerged were a 15-party alliance, headed by a faction of the Awami League under Sheikh Hasina Wajed (daughter of the late Sheikh Mujib), and a seven-party group which was led by a faction of the BNP under the former President Sattar (who died in October 1985) and Begum Khalida Zia (widow of Gen. Zia). In September 1983 the two groups formed an alliance, the Movement for the Restoration of Democracy (MRD), and jointly issued demands for an end to martial law, for the release of political prisoners and for the holding of parliamentary elections before any others. In November permission was given for the resumption of political activity, and it was announced that a series of local elections between December 1983 and March 1984 were to precede a presidential election and a parliamentary election later in the year. A new political party, the Jana Dal (People's Party), was formed in November 1983 to support Ershad as a presidential candidate. Following demonstrations demanding civilian government, the ban on political activity was reimposed at the beginning of December, only two weeks after it had been rescinded, and leading political figures (including, temporarily, Begum Zia and Sheikh Hasina) were detained. On 11 December Ershad declared himself President.

Bangladesh remained disturbed in 1984, with frequent strikes and political demonstrations. Local elections to *upazilla* (subdistrict) councils, due to take place in March, were postponed, as the opposition objected to their being held before the presidential and parliamentary elections, on the grounds that Ershad was trying to improve his power-base. The presidential and parliamentary elections, scheduled for May, were also postponed, until December, because of persistent opposition demands for the repeal of martial law and for the formation of an interim neutral government to oversee a fair election. In October Ershad agreed to repeal martial law in three stages in November and December if the opposition would participate in these elections. They responded with an appeal for a campaign of civil disobedience, which led to the announcement in October that the elections were to be indefinitely postponed.

In January 1985 it was announced that a parliamentary election would be held in April, to be preceded by a relaxation of martial law in certain respects: the Constitution was to be fully restored after the election. The announcement was followed by the formation of a new Council of Ministers, composed entirely of military officers and excluding all members of the Jana Dal, in response to demands by the opposition parties for a 'neutral' government during the pre-election period. Once more, the opposition threatened to boycott the election, as President Ershad would not relinquish power to an interim government, and in March political activity was banned again. This was immediately followed by a referendum, held in support of the presidency, in which Ershad received 94% of the total votes. Local elections for *upazilla* councils in rural areas were held in May, without the participation of the opposition, and Ershad claimed that 85% of the elected council chairmen were his supporters, although not necessarily of his party. In September a new five-party political alliance, the National Front (comprising the Jana Dal, the United People's Party, the Gonotantrik Party, the Bangladesh Muslim League and a breakaway section of the Bangladesh Nationalist Party), was established to proclaim government policies.

In January 1986 the 10-month ban on political activity was ended. The five components of the National Front formally became a single pro-Government entity, named the Jatiya Dal (National Party). Further strikes and demonstrations were organized by opposition groups, who continued to demand the repeal of martial law before the holding of any parliamentary or presidential elections. In March President Ershad announced that parliamentary elections were to be held (under martial law) at the end of April. He relaxed martial law, however, by removing all army commanders from important civil posts and by abolishing more than 150 military courts and the martial law offices. These concessions fulfilled some of the opposition's demands and, as a result, candidates from eight parties of the Awami League alliance (including Sheikh Hasina herself), the Jamit-i-Islami and other smaller opposition parties participated in the general election for a new Jatiya Sangsad on 7 May (postponed from 26 April). However, the BNP alliance, led by Begum Zia, boycotted the polls. The election was characterized by allegations of extensive fraud, violence and intimidation. The Jatiya Dal won 153 of the 300 directly elective seats. In addition, the 30 seats reserved for women in the legislature were filled by nominees of the Jatiya Dal.

In June 1986, while the Constitution remained suspended, the Awami League alliance again demanded the repeal of martial law, the resignation of Ershad and the restoration of a complete democratic system. At the beginning of July Ershad announced that martial law would be repealed only after a presidential election. Although the Awami League members had been sworn in as MPs, they refused to attend the inauguration of the Jatiya Sangsad. In late July the Jatiya Sangsad was prorogued for an indefinite period. A civilian Council of Ministers was sworn in. Mizanur Rahman Chowdhury, former general-secretary of the Jatiya Dal, became Prime Minister.

In order to be a candidate in the presidential election in October 1986, Ershad retired as Army Chief of Staff in August and appointed Maj.-Gen. M. Atiqur Rahman in his place, while remaining as Chief Martial Law Administrator and Commander-in-Chief of the Armed Forces. In early September Ershad joined the Jatiya Dal, being elected as chairman of the party and nominated as its presidential candidate. At the presidential election in mid-October, which was boycotted by both the BNP and the Awami League, Ershad won an overwhelming victory over his 11 opponents, receiving nearly 22m. votes, according to official results. Alleged malpractice was reportedly more discreet than in the May legislative elections.

In November 1986 Ershad summoned the Jatiya Sangsad, which approved indemnity legislation, legalizing the military regime's actions since March 1982. Ershad repealed martial law and restored the 1972 Constitution. The opposition alliances criticized the indemnity law, stating that they would campaign for the dissolution of the Jatiya Sangsad and the overthrow of the Ershad Government. In December 1986, in an attempt to curb increasing dissension, President Ershad formed a new Council of Ministers, including four MPs from the Awami League. The Justice Minister, Justice A. K. M. Nurul Islam, was appointed Vice-President.

In 1987 the opposition groups continued to hold anti-Government strikes and demonstrations, often with the support of the trade unions and student groups, demanding the resignation of President Ershad and his Government, the installation of an interim neutral government, and the holding of fresh elections. The Government, in turn, continued to reject these demands. In July the Jatiya Sangsad approved the Zilla Parishad (District Council) Amendment Bill, enabling army representatives to participate in the 64 district councils, along with the elected representatives. The adoption of this controversial legislation led to widespread and often violent strikes and demonstrations, organized by the opposition groups, who claimed that the bill represented an attempt by the President to secure an entrenched military involvement in the governing of the country, despite the ending of martial law in November 1986. Owing to the intensity of public opposition, President Ershad was forced to withdraw the bill in August 1987 and return it to the Jatiya Sangsad for reconsideration. A major government reshuffle followed. Political events were overshadowed in August and September, however, when the most severe floods in Bangladesh for 40 years resulted in widespread devastation. In a renewed effort to oust President Ershad, the opposition groups combined forces and organized further protests in November. Thousands of activists (including Sheikh Hasina and Begum Zia) were detained, but demonstrations, strikes and opposition rallies continued, leading to numerous clashes between police units and protesters. After 16 days of violent agitation, the Dhaka police chief imposed a 30-day ban on marches and rallies in the capital. The unrest had caused considerable economic dislocation, and the Government claimed that the country was losing US $50m. per day. As a result of this, and in an attempt to forestall another general strike being planned by opposition groups, President Ershad declared a nationwide state of emergency on 27 November, suspending political activity and civil rights, and banning all anti-Government protests, initially for 120 days. In spite of the imposition of curfews on the main towns, reports of disturbances continued, as the opposition maintained its campaign to force Ershad's resignation. In early December, when about 6,000 people were being detained in prison as a result of the unrest, opposition parties in the Jatiya Sangsad announced that their representatives would resign their seats. On 6 December, after 12 opposition members had resigned and the 73 Awami League members had agreed to do likewise, President Ershad dissolved the Jatiya Sangsad. Sheikh Hasina and Begum Zia were subsequently released, after being under house arrest for four weeks, but both women rejected President Ershad's offer of peace negotiations and pledged to continue the campaign for his resignation. In January 1988 the President announced that a general election for the Jatiya Sangsad would be held on 28 February, but leaders of the main opposition parties declared their intention to boycott the proposed poll while Ershad remained in office. As a result of the boycott campaign organized by the opposition, the general election was postponed until 3 March. In January, however, an alliance of 76 very minor political parties formed a government-approved 'Combined Opposition Group' (COG), led by the head of the left-wing Jatiya Samajtantrik Dal (R), A.S.M. Abdur Rab, to contest the general election. Local elections to the Union Parishads, which were held throughout Bangladesh in February and which were not boycotted by the opposition, were marred by serious outbreaks of violence. The general election was also characterized by widespread violence, as well as by alleged fraud and malpractice. The opposition's boycott campaign proved to be highly successful and the actual level of participation by the electorate appeared to have been considerably lower than the Government's estimate of 50%. As expected, the Jatiya Dal won a large majority of the seats.

In late March a radical reshuffle of the Council of Ministers included the appointment of a new Prime Minister, Moudud Ahmed, hitherto the Minister of Industry and a Deputy Prime Minister. Owing to an abatement in the opposition's anti-Government campaign, Ershad repealed the state of emergency in April. Despite strong condemnation by the opposition and sections of the public, legislation to amend the Constitution, establishing Islam as Bangladesh's state religion, was approved by an overall majority in the Jatiya Sangsad in June. The opposition movement suffered a serious set-back in July, when the Secretary-General of the BNP, A.K.M. Obaidur Rahman, was dismissed, together with several other senior party members, following internal disputes. He subsequently formed a rival faction, challenging the leadership of Begum Zia. By early September, however, political events had been completely overshadowed by a new wave of disastrous monsoon floods, which began in August and proved to be the most severe in the area's recorded history (see Economic Affairs). In November Bangladesh suffered further flooding as the result of a cyclone, which caused an estimated 3,000 deaths.

In foreign affairs, Bangladesh has maintained a policy of non-alignment. Relations with Pakistan improved in 1976: ambassadors were exchanged, and trade, postal and telecommunication links were resumed. Pakistan, however, refuses to accept the 300,000 Bihari Muslims (who supported Pakistan in Bangladesh's war of liberation in 1972) still remaining in refugee camps in Bangladesh, unless it does not have to bear the cost of absorbing them. Relations with India have been strained over the questions of cross-border terrorism (especially around the area of the Chittagong Hill Tracts, where Buddhist tribal rebels, the Shanti Bahini, have been waging guerrilla warfare against the Bangladeshi police and the Bengali settlers for several years) and of the Farrakka barrage, which has been constructed by India on the Ganga (Ganges) river, so depriving Bangladesh of water for irrigation and river transport during the dry season. In August 1985 Bangladesh and Burma completed work on the demarcation of their common border, in accordance with a May 1979 agreement.

Bangladesh is a member of the South Asian Association for Regional Co-operation (SAARC, see p. 220), formally constituted in December 1985, with Bhutan, India, Maldives, Nepal, Pakistan and Sri Lanka. Included in SAARC's newly-drafted charter were pledges of non-interference by members in each other's internal affairs and a joint effort to avoid 'contentious' issues whenever the association meets.

Government

With the ending of martial law, constitutional government was revived in November 1986 (having been suspended in March 1982). Bangladesh has a presidential form of government. The President is elected by universal suffrage for a five-year term and appoints his Council of Ministers from the 330-member Jatiya Sangsad (Parliament), 300 members of which are elected by universal suffrage. An additional 30 women members are appointed by the other members. The Jatiya Sangsad serves a five-year term, subject to dissolution. In 1983 a system of 493 local administrative sub-districts (*upazillas*), each containing an average of 260,000 people, was established as part of a move to decentralize government. These *upazillas* are staffed by civil servants from Dhaka but headed by local chairmen, who hold office for five years. They have increased local involvement in development schemes, and development funds are allocated yearly to each of them.

Defence

Military service is voluntary. In June 1988 the armed forces numbered 101,500: an army of 90,000, a navy of 7,500 and an air force of 4,000. The paramilitary forces totalled 55,000, and included the Bangladesh Rifles (border guard) of 30,000. Budget expenditure on defence was estimated at 6,640m. taka for 1986/87.

Economic Affairs

Apart from small city-states, Bangladesh is the most densely populated country in the world, with an estimated population of 102.6m. at mid-1987, averaging 713 inhabitants per sq km. The population is increasing at about 1.9% annually, and was expected to be more than 130m. by the year 2000. In the year ending 30 June 1986 the expansion of domestic food production exceeded the rate of population growth, but the country was still unable to halt the increase in poverty. In terms of average income, Bangladesh is among the world's poorest countries. In 1987, according to estimates by the World Bank, the gross national product (GNP), measured at average 1985–87 prices, was US $17,408m., equivalent to about $160 per head. Between 1980 and 1987, it was estimated, Bangladesh's GNP per head increased, in real terms, at an average rate of only 1.0% per year. However, the average annual increase in overall gross domestic product (GDP), measured in constant prices, was 2.4% between 1965 and 1980, rising to 3.7% between 1980 and 1986. Because of the extensive damage caused by widespread flooding in 1987, real GDP growth was only 2.5% in 1987/88, compared with the official target of 5.1%. Owing to the even more severe monsoon floods which devastated the country in 1988, some observers predicted a decline in real GDP in 1988/89.

Agriculture, which employs about 60% of the working population, contributed about 40% of GDP in 1986/87 and 1987/88. Agricultural output expanded by an estimated 4.9% in 1985/86. The land is fertile, but crops are often destroyed by floods, cyclone and drought. Production of rice, which is grown on about 75% of cultivated land, fell sharply after independence and did not regain former levels until 1974. Rice harvests continued to improve: output of milled rice reached 14.8m. long tons in 1985/86 and 15.2m. tons in 1986/87. In 1985/86 the total irrigated area in Bangladesh was 6.2m. acres (2.5m. ha), which was expected to increase to 9.2m. acres (3.7m. ha) by 1989/90. Domestic demand for fertilizer increased from 210,000 tons in 1969/70 to 1.3m. tons in 1987/88. The Chittagong Urea Fertilizer Project, upon completion in 1987, was to produce about 561,000 metric tons of fertilizer annually. Between 1980 and 1985, efforts were made to increase output of wheat, as it is more nutritious than rice and cheaper to produce. Production of wheat reached 1,440,000 tons in 1984/85, fell to 1,030,000 tons in 1985/86, but rose again to 1,070,000 tons in 1986/87. Output of food grains (including rice on a milled basis) increased from 14.37m. tons in 1981/82 to a record 16.3m. tons in 1985/86. However, despite this improvement, it was still necessary to import grain (1.5m. tons in 1985/86). There was a slight rise in the production of food grains (to 16.5m. tons) in 1986/87. Owing to the prolonged and extensive flooding which occurred in Bangladesh between July and September 1987, however, total output in 1987/88 was projected to fall to around 14m. tons. Because of this decrease in production, the Government was compelled to import 2.9m. tons of food grains (mostly wheat), compared with the planned target of 1.8m. tons, in 1987/88. The condition of the agricultural sector deteriorated further in September 1988, when the most severe floods ever recorded in Bangladesh destroyed 2.7m.–3m. tons of food grains. The Government estimated that 2m. tons of food grains would have to be imported (the state food warehouses held surplus stocks of 1.2m. tons).

Jute and tea are the main cash crops. Bangladesh supplies about 90% of world exports of raw jute. In 1986 the jute industry employed about 250,000 workers. Because of competition from synthetic substitutes for jute, general world recession and increased competition from India, Nepal and Thailand, annual output declined from 7m. bales (each of 400 lb or 181.4 kg) in 1969/70 to just over 4m. bales in 1980/81. In 1982/83 production rose marginally, to 4.8m. bales, but in 1983/84 floods destroyed an estimated 1m. bales, bringing production down to 4m. bales, although, because of a world shortage, jute sales earned double the average 1983 price per bale. Output of jute rose to 6m. bales in 1984/85, and the Government had to reduce the export price by one-third. The lower price was insufficient to cover the cost of production. International prices for raw jute declined by 45% in 1985/86, with no prospect of immediate recovery. Accordingly, despite the high output of 7.5m. bales, the jute industry incurred a total financial loss of 2,130m. taka in 1985/86. The long-term difficulty for Bangladesh is to ensure regular and reliable supplies to satisfy demand. Total jute production fell by 22% in 1986/87, to less than 6m. bales. Jute and jute products provided 46% of export revenue in 1985/86, and 35% in 1986/87. Because of the extensive flooding in August and September 1987, the Government reduced the jute production target for 1987/88 from 4.5m. bales to 4m. bales. Actual output, however, was projected to amount to only 3.8m. bales and to fall even lower in 1988/89, following the devastating monsoon floods that inundated the country in August and September 1988.

In 1979 a programme to improve the quality of locally-produced tea was introduced. Exports of tea were valued at 1,570.4m. taka (6.0% of total export receipts) in 1984/85, but declined to 997.3m. taka (3.6% of total export receipts) in 1985/86, and to 903.2m. taka (2.7% of total export receipts) in 1986/87. The considerable decrease in export receipts from tea was due to the decline in international prices for tea in 1985–87. Potatoes, sugar cane, tobacco, spices and tropical fruits are also produced, while the output of cotton is being increased to lessen the burden of imports. The Government planned to increase the area under cotton cultivation from 6,000 ha in 1980 to 129,090 ha by 1990.

Mineral resources are few. There are large reserves of natural gas, and by 1985 a total of 13 gas fields had been discovered (including one off shore). In 1986 the Government inaugurated the Second Gas Development Project, aiming to increase gas supplies from existing fields and to produce the first significant quantities of liquid hydrocarbons (kerosene and gasoline) in Bangladesh. In July 1988 a 100-MW gas-turbine power station project was inaugurated at Haripur. Low-grade coal reserves of 700m. tons have also been discovered. As part of the third Five-Year Plan (1985–90), the Government has intensified mineral exploration activities in the north of the country. After many years of exploration, reserves of petroleum, estimated at 40m. barrels, were discovered in the district of Sylhet in December 1986. The cost of petroleum imports was 9,698m. taka in 1985 and 6,434m. taka in 1986. In 1986 Bangladesh imported about 1.1m. tons of crude petroleum and 500,000 tons of refined oil products.

Industry accounted for only about 14% of GDP in 1986. Manufactured products comprised about 43% of imports in 1983/84. Between 1983 and 1987, however, the expansion of annual industrial output increased from about 6% to about 10%. About 20% of the industrial labour force are employed in jute-based industries. Other major products are cotton textiles, chemicals and sugar. Output declined in nearly all the main industries after 1971, owing to war damage, the departure of the largely non-Bengali financier and managerial class and the loss of many skilled Bengali workers. Most organized industry was nationalized, and state corporations were created for the major commodities. General Zia's Government, however, changed industrial policy, encouraging private investment and compensating foreign investors whose assets had been nationalized in 1971, on condition that the money was reinvested in Bangladesh. Many tea plantations and state-owned industrial units were returned to the private sector during 1976 and 1977, and in 1981 the private sector was permitted to establish cotton textile spinning mills. The cotton textile industry expanded rapidly during the 1980s and established itself as an important source of export earnings. Most of this expansion was achieved through private initiative, and in 1985/86 nearly 600 new companies (providing 150,000 new jobs) were formed. During 1984/85 the textile industry exported goods worth US $100m., a three-fold expansion over 1983/84. In 1986 the US Government fixed Bangladesh's annual quota of cotton textile exports to the USA at 4.2m. dozen pieces for at least the next two years. In 1987/88 cotton textiles overtook jute as Bangladesh's most important source of foreign exchange, with exports of garments valued at US $435m., compared with jute exports of $339m. The value of garment exports in 1988/89 was expected to increase by 20%, to $525m.

In mid-1980 Parliament legislated for the establishment of three export-processing zones to increase trade and foreign investment, and by 1985 the first factories were in operation. In 1982, in an attempt to stimulate private investment, about one-half of the nationalized jute and textile industries returned to the private sector. In 1986 the policy of 'privatization' continued to dominate plans for economic development, and the Industrial Policy (1986) aimed to raise the contribution of the industrial sector to GDP and to achieve industrial growth, with emphasis on private-sector participation. The proportion of the country's industrial assets under government ownership was reduced from 85% in 1972 to 45% (of a considerably larger industrial base) in 1986. In 1985 the Government decided on a phased divestment of 49% of the shares in three of the four nationalized banks.

Trade patterns were disrupted by the separation from Pakistan, to which the tea crop had largely been exported before the war. In 1976, however, direct trade links were re-established with Pakistan: shipping and banking arrangements were agreed, and a joint trade committee was established by the two countries. In 1984/85 the two-way trade between Bangladesh and Pakistan amounted to US $103.17m. Bangladesh's persistent trade deficit is partly offset by remittances sent home by Bangladeshi workers abroad. Remittances from workers abroad averaged $476m. per year over the period 1980–85. Remittances reached $696m. in 1987 and were expected to increase further in 1988. Between 1979/80 and 1981/82, owing largely to reductions in international prices for jute, there was a 35% decline in the terms of trade (export prices relative to import costs). In 1982/83 the Government imposed import restrictions and devalued the currency by 22%, and again by 20%, in relation to the US dollar. Economic policies gave priority to reducing dependence on imported food, energy and manufactures by increasing domestic production. In spite of the declines in prices for commodities such as tea and jute, the trade deficit decreased from 35,543.4m. taka in 1985/86 to 35,009.1m. taka in 1986/87.

Bangladesh is heavily dependent on large amounts of foreign aid, particularly commodity aid, to meet the requirements of budget plans and development programmes, and to offset the deficit on trade in goods and services. In 1986 foreign aid accounted for over 40% of total government resources. Foreign aid disbursements were expected to reach US $1,520m. in 1986/87, compared with about $1,400m. in the previous year. Two major suppliers of funds are the World Bank and Japan. The Japanese bilateral aid commitment for 1985/86 was $140m. The World Bank approved credits (in the form of loans, at concessionary rates, from the International Development Association) totalling $389m. in 1986/87 and $227.8m. in 1987/88. In February 1987 the IMF approved immediate assistance of SDR 88.9m., with a further SDR 135.1m. (increased to SDR 182.6m. in August) to be made available over three years under a structural adjustment facility (SAF). In November the IMF approved a loan of SDR 86.25m. for the second year of the SAF arrangement. Total pledges of aid by the main donor countries and agencies amounted to $2,056m. for 1988/89, which represented a real increase of about 13.6% over the pledges for 1987/88.

The country's first Five-Year Plan (1973–78) aimed at an annual growth of 5.5% in GDP. This target was exceeded, with an average annual rate of growth of 6.7%. After an interim two-year plan for 1978–80, the second Five-Year Plan, covering 1980–85, was formulated with a total proposed outlay of 255,950m. taka, of which 201,250m. was to go to the public sector and 54,700m. to the private sector. An average annual GDP growth rate of 8.4% was projected; however, the actual rise in GDP averaged only 3.8% per year over the Plan period. A third Five-Year Plan (1985–89), initiated in July 1985, envisaged total investment of 284,810m. taka, average annual GDP growth of 5.4%, a reduction in the annual rate of population increase, an annual growth rate in agricultural output of

4%, an annual growth rate in industrial output of 10.1%, and a food-grain production target of 20.7m. tons per year. A greater emphasis on the promotion of small-scale and cottage industries in the rural areas was included in the third Five-Year Plan. In 1986 the co-operative movement was being fully supported by the national development policy. The aims of this movement were to shun dependence on aid and to promote policies of self-help. The proposed budget expenditure for 1988/89 totalled an estimated 105,650m. taka, of which 52,500m. taka was for recurrent expenses and 53,150m. for development spending. The overall deficit was estimated at 49,960m. taka.

In August and September 1988 Bangladesh suffered extremely serious floods (the most severe in the area's recorded history). Three-quarters of Bangladesh, including two-thirds of Dhaka, were flooded, vast areas of crop-growing land were submerged, transport and communications were severely disrupted, the number of dead was unofficially estimated at more than 2,600, while more than 30m. people were left homeless. According to official figures, the floods caused damage estimated at $1,500m.–$2,000m. The Government established a national Disaster Prevention Council, appealed for immediate aid from friendly countries and donor agencies, and urged the use of regional co-operation to evolve a comprehensive solution to the problem of flooding.

Social Welfare

The principal medical objective after independence was to prevent epidemics and widespread malnutrition, and to treat and rehabilitate war victims. Basic health services remain relatively undeveloped: in the early 1980s about 25% of all live-born children died before reaching five years of age. Health programmes give particular priority to the popularization of birth control. In 1981 Bangladesh had 504 hospital establishments, with a total of only 19,727 beds, equivalent to one for every 4,545 inhabitants: one of the lowest levels of provision in the world. In 1981 there were 10,065 physicians working in the country. The Government's annual expenditure on health rose from 899m. taka in 1982/83 to 2,418m. taka in 1986/87.

In 1986 the Government adopted a policy of 'Health for All', and several programmes were incorporated in the third Five-Year Plan with the aim of achieving this objective: the number of health centres was to be increased (in 1985 a total of 355 *upazilla* health complexes were in operation), more people were to be given medical training, and the public education programme on family planning was to be expanded.

Education

Education is not compulsory but the Government provides free primary schooling for five years. Primary education begins at five years of age and lasts for five years. Secondary education, beginning at the age of 10, lasts for up to seven years, comprising a first cycle of five years and a second cycle of two further years. In 1985 an estimated 54% of children (63% of boys; 45% of girls) in the relevant age-group attended primary schools, while the comparable enrolment ratio at secondary schools was 17%. Some pilot schemes for compulsory attendance in primary schools are in progress, and there are plans to introduce universal primary education by the late 1980s. Secondary schools and colleges in the private sector vastly outnumber government institutions: in 1976 government high schools comprised only about 2% of the country's total. There are seven universities, including one for agriculture, one for Islamic studies and one for engineering. Educational reform is designed to assist in satisfying the manpower needs of the country, and most importance is given to primary, technical and vocational education. In 1986 the rate of adult illiteracy was about 74%, despite a five-year government programme that was initiated in 1980 in an attempt to eradicate illiteracy. In 1987 another mass literacy programme was initiated by the Government. The aim of this programme was to reduce the rate of adult illiteracy to 40% by the year 2000. Government expenditure on education rose from 2,337m. taka in 1982/83 to 6,879m. taka in 1986/87.

Public Holidays

1989: 1 January (New Year's Day), 21 February (National Mourning Day), 24 March (Good Friday), 26 March (Independence Day), 27 March (Easter Monday), 1 May (May Day), 7 May* (Id al-Fitr, end of Ramadan), May* (Buddha Purinama), 14 July* (Id al-Adha, Feast of the Sacrifice), July* (Jamat Wida), 4 August* (Muharram, Islamic New Year), September* (Shab-i-Bharat), September* (Durga Puja), 13 October* (Birth of the Prophet), 7 November (National Revolution Day), 16 December (National Day), 25 December (Christmas), 26 December (Boxing Day).

1990: 1 January (New Year's Day), 21 February (National Mourning Day), 26 March (Independence Day), 13 April (Good Friday), 16 April (Easter Monday), 27 April* (Id al-Fitr), 1 May (May Day), May* (Buddha Purinama), 4 July* (Id al Adha), 24 July* (Muharram, Islamic New Year), July* (Jamat Wida), September* (Shab-i-Bharat), September* (Durga Puja), 2 October* (Birth of the Prophet), 7 November (National Revolution Day), 16 December (National Day), 25 December (Christmas), 26 December (Boxing Day).

* Dates of certain religious holidays are subject to the sighting of the moon, and there are also optional holidays for different religious groups.

Weights and Measures

The imperial system of measures is in force, pending the introduction of the metric system. The following local units of weight are also used:

1 maund = 82.28 lb (37.29 kg).
1 seer = 2.057 lb (932 grams).
1 tola = 180 grains (11.66 grams).

Statistical Survey

Source (unless otherwise stated): Bangladesh Bureau of Statistics, 14/2 Topkhana Rd, Dhaka; tel. (2) 409871.

Area and Population

AREA, POPULATION AND DENSITY

Area (sq km)	143,998*
Population (census results)†	
1 March 1974	76,398,000
6 March 1981	
Males	46,295,000
Females	43,617,000
Total	89,912,000
Population (official estimates at mid-year)	
1985	98,657,000
1986	100,616,000
1987	102,563,000
Density (per sq km) at mid-1987	712.3

* 55,598 sq miles.
† Including adjustment for net underenumeration, estimated to have been 6.9% in 1974 and 3.2% in 1981. The enumerated totals were: 71,479,071 in 1974; 87,119,965 (males 44,919,191, females 42,200,774) in 1981.

POPULATION BY DIVISIONS

	1974 Census	1981 Census
Chittagong	19,914,000	23,322,000
Dhaka	22,780,000	27,091,000
Khulna	15,177,000	17,695,000
Rajshahi	18,527,000	21,804,000
Total	76,398,000	89,912,000

PRINCIPAL TOWNS (population at 1981 census)

Dhaka (capital)	3,430,312*	Barisal	172,905
Chittagong	1,391,877	Sylhet	168,371
Khulna	646,359	Rangpur	153,174
Rajshahi	253,740	Jessore	148,927
Comilla	184,132	Saidpur	126,608

* Including Narayanganj (population 270,680 in 1974).

BIRTHS AND DEATHS*

	Registered live births Rate (per 1,000)	Registered deaths Rate (per 1,000)
1982	34.8	12.2
1983	35.0	12.3
1984	34.8	12.3
1985	34.6	12.0
1986	34.4	11.9

* Registration is incomplete. According to UN estimates, the average annual rates in 1980–85 were: Births 44.8 per 1,000; Deaths 17.5 per 1,000.

ECONOMICALLY ACTIVE POPULATION*
('000 persons, 1983/84)

	Males	Females	Total
Agriculture, hunting, forestry and fishing	16,231	216	16,448
Mining and quarrying	46	—	46
Manufacturing	1,785	698	2,483
Electricity, gas and water	68	—	68
Construction	477	9	487
Trade, restaurants and hotels	3,115	140	3,255
Transport, storage and communications	1,077	11	1,088
Financing, insurance, real estate and business services	133	3	136
Community, social and personal services	2,080	214	2,294
Activities not adequately defined	534	1,137	1,671
Total employed	25,547	2,429	27,976
Unemployed	411	106	517
Total labour force	25,958	2,535	28,493

* All figures are rounded, so totals may not always be the sum of their component parts.

Source: ILO, *Year Book of Labour Statistics*.

Agriculture

PRINCIPAL CROPS (million long tons, year ending 30 June)

	1984/85	1985/86	1986/87
Rice (milled)	14.39	14.80	15.16
Wheat	1.38	1.03	1.07
Sugar cane	6.77	6.54	6.79
Potatoes	1.14	1.09	1.05
Sweet potatoes	0.67	0.60	0.54
Pulses	0.20	0.19	0.18
Oilseeds	0.27	0.26	0.25
Jute	0.91	1.55	1.21

Tobacco (production in '000 metric tons): 48 in 1984; 49 in 1985; 52 (unofficial estimate) in 1986 (Source: FAO, *Production Yearbook*).

LIVESTOCK ('000 head at 30 June)

	1984/85	1985/86	1986/87
Cattle	22,811	23,137	23,468
Buffaloes	584	605	626
Sheep	524	526	528
Goats	10,178	10,420	10,667
Chickens	58,307	60,845	63,493
Ducks	26,140	28,775	31,675

BANGLADESH

Livestock Products (year ending 30 June)

	1984/85	1985/86	1986/87
Beef and veal (metric tons)	274,580	278,499	282,530
Buffalo meat (metric tons)	4,330	4,554	4,703
Mutton and lamb (metric tons)	933	933	933
Goats' meat (metric tons)	47,480	48,638	49,795
Poultry meat (metric tons)	61,478	65,211	n.a.
Edible offals (metric tons)	7,497	7,640	7,787
Cows' and buffalo milk (metric tons)	1,218,290	1,234,341	1,251,138
Sheep's milk (metric tons)*	17,000	17,000	17,000
Goats' milk (metric tons)*	517,000	522,000	528,000
Butter (metric tons)	21,612	21,911	22,210
Cheese (metric tons)	1,530	1,530	1,568
Hen eggs ('000)	839,628	876,168	914,292
Other poultry eggs ('000)	980,250	1,079,100	1,187,775
Wool:			
greasy (metric tons)*	1,320	1,330	1,300
clean (metric tons)*	810	810	813
Cattle and buffalo hides ('000)	5,211	5,299	5,377
Sheep and goat skins ('000)	5,862	5,999	6,138

* FAO estimates for 1984–86.

Forestry

Roundwood Removals ('000 cubic metres)

	1984	1985	1986
Sawlogs, veneer logs and logs for sleepers	484	467	467*
Pulpwood	104	76	69
Other industrial wood*	295	303	311
Fuel wood*	25,600	26,298	26,993
Total	26,483	27,144	27,840

* FAO estimates.
Source: FAO, *Yearbook of Forest Products*.

Sawnwood Production
('000 cubic metres)

	1984	1985	1986
Total (incl. boxboards)	148*	93	73

* FAO estimate.
Source: FAO, *Yearbook of Forest Products*.

Fishing

('000 long tons, year ending 30 June)

	1984/85	1985/86	1986/87
Inland	588	587	594
Marine	185	207	210
Total catch	773	794	804

Source: Directorate of Fisheries.

Mining

	1985	1986	1987
Natural gas (million cu ft)	94,580	106,652	125,315

Industry

SELECTED PRODUCTS ('000 long tons, unless otherwise indicated, public sector only, year ending 30 June)

	1984/85	1985/86	1986/87
Jute textiles	520	451	540
Hessian	208	163	204
Sacking	223	217	248
Carpet backing	81	66	80
Others	8	5	8
Cotton cloth (million yards)	69	65	65
Cotton yarn (million lb)	106	95	100
Newsprint	46	48	47
Other paper	39	42	43
Cement	240	292	310
Steel ingots	101	96	82
Re-rolled steel products	13	13	34
Petroleum products	943	949	974
Urea fertilizer	741	835	846
Ammonium sulphate	10	10	9
Chemicals	19	20	25
Refined sugar	88	82	182
Wine and spirits ('000 liquid proof galls)	1,104	1,153	1,187
Tea (million lb)*	94	87	87
Edible oil and vegetable ghee	15	15	27
Cigarettes ('000 million)	14	14	15

* Including production in the private sector.

Finance

Currency and Exchange Rates

Monetary Units
100 poisha = 1 taka.

Denominations
Coins: 1, 2, 5, 10, 25 and 50 poisha.
Notes: 1, 5, 10, 50, 100 taka.

Sterling and Dollar Equivalents (30 September 1988)
£1 sterling = 54.11 taka;
US $1 = 32.00 taka;
1,000 taka = £18.48 = $31.25.

Average Exchange Rate (taka per US $)
1985   27.995
1986   30.407
1987   30.950

Note: The foregoing information refers to the official exchange rate, applicable to most transactions. There is also a secondary rate, determined by bidding for foreign exchange by importers in an auction market. At 31 August 1988 this auction market rate was US $1 = 32.91 taka.

Budget (estimates, million taka, year ending 30 June)

Revenue	1984/85	1985/86	1986/87
Customs duties	16,799	12,020	14,480
Excise duties	6,780	8,730	9,000
Sales tax	4,129	4,400	6,000
Stamps	1,313	1,250	1,300
Motor vehicle taxes	63	140	150
Income taxes	3,735	4,587	5,097
Land revenue	416	510	560
Other taxes and duties	81	108	n.a.
Interest receipts	7	2,331	1,800
Railways	1,652	1,800	n.a.
Other revenue	2,502	6,294	n.a.
Total	37,477	42,170	47,170

BANGLADESH

Statistical Survey

Expenditure	1984/85	1985/86	1986/87
General administration	7,691	9,601	10,689
Justice and police	2,570	3,508	3,532
Defence	5,068	5,970	6,603
Scientific departments	120	187	n.a.
Education	4,470	6,012	6,879
Health	1,826	1,140	2,418
Social welfare	172	156	n.a.
Agriculture	755	583	1,174
Manufacturing and construction	83	126	n.a.
Transport and communication	976	940	n.a.
Railways	2,279	2,330	n.a.
Other expenditure	2,153	2,049	n.a.
Total	28,163	32,602	39,560

Source: Ministry of Finance.

1987/88 (revised estimates, million taka): Revenue 51,460; Expenditure 47,300.
1988/89 (estimates, million taka): Revenue 55,690; Expenditure 52,500.

PUBLIC-SECTOR DEVELOPMENT EXPENDITURE
(estimates, million taka, year ending 30 June)

	1983/84	1984/85	1985/86
Agriculture	7,479	10,315	1,983
Rural development	453	743	768
Water and flood control	3,382	6,272	4,653
Industry	2,873	2,555	5,462
Power, scientific research and natural resources	7,357	8,926	12,165
Transport	3,041	4,296	3,715
Communication	767	1,151	460
Physical planning and housing	1,074	833	1,205
Education and training	1,276	1,375	1,185
Health	762	887	784
Population planning	706	756	972
Social welfare	108	153	133
Manpower and employment	206	251	74
Miscellaneous	237	281	244
Total development expenditure	29,721	38,794	33,803

Source: Ministry of Finance.

1986/87 (revised estimate): Total development expenditure 45,134m. taka.
1987/88 (revised estimate): Total development expenditure 46,506.1m. taka.
1988/89 (estimate): Total development expenditure 53,150m. taka.

INTERNATIONAL RESERVES
(US $ million at 31 December)

	1985	1986	1987
Gold*	12.9	16.8	22.8
IMF special drawing rights	13.1	10.3	53.3
Reserve position in IMF	24.6	27.4	31.8
Foreign exchange	298.8	371.4	758.1
Total	349.4	425.9	866.0

* Valued at market-related prices.
Source: IMF, *International Financial Statistics*.

MONEY SUPPLY (million taka at 31 December)

	1985	1986	1987
Currency outside banks	17,672	19,027	22,490
Demand deposits at scheduled banks	28,279	30,968	n.a.
Total money*	45,955	49,996	n.a.

* Including private-sector deposits held by monetary authorities.
Source: IMF, *International Financial Statistics*.

COST OF LIVING (Consumer Price Index for middle-class families in Dhaka; base: 1969/70 = 100)

	1984/85	1985/86	1986/87
Food	934	1,024	1,170
Fuel and lighting	1,057	1,210	1,264
Housing and household requisites	1,114	1,269	1,416
Clothing and footwear	926	968	1,034
Miscellaneous	796	818	877
All items	931	1,014	1,130

NATIONAL ACCOUNTS
(million taka at current prices, year ending 30 June)
Expenditure on the Gross Domestic Product

	1984/85	1985/86*	1986/87*
Government final consumption expenditure	29,793	35,762	42,914
Private final consumption expenditure	377,680	412,924	465,615
Increase in stocks	667	6,767	15,227
Gross fixed capital formation	51,345	47,915	42,260
Total domestic expenditure	459,485	503,368	566,016
Exports of goods and services	25,712	27,117	28,598
Less Imports of goods and services	68,235	70,575	72,975
GDP in purchasers' values	416,962	459,910	521,639

* Figures are provisional. Revised totals (in million taka) are: 462,013 in 1985/86; 539,174 in 1986/87.

Gross Domestic Product by Economic Activity

	1985/86	1986/87	1987/88*
Agriculture and hunting	179,490	210,558	230,726
Forestry and logging	20,294	23,587	24,638
Fishing	16,999	20,917	22,426
Mining and quarrying	8	6	6
Manufacturing	37,335	40,208	43,946
Electricity, gas and water	2,713	3,545	4,769
Construction	26,058	28,839	31,805
Wholesale and retail trade	39,174	46,877	52,486
Transport, storage and communications	33,328	36,640	37,948
Owner-occupied dwellings	31,771	34,817	35,622
Finance, insurance, real estate and business services	8,935	10,116	12,524
Public administration and defence	19,810	23,735	28,318
Other services	46,098	59,329	68,890
Total	462,013	539,174	594,104

* Provisional.

BANGLADESH

BALANCE OF PAYMENTS (US $ million)

	1985	1986	1987
Merchandise exports f.o.b.	999.5	880.0	1,076.9
Merchandise imports f.o.b.	−2,286.4	−2,300.7	−2,458.2
Trade balance	−1,287.0	−1,420.7	−1,381.3
Exports of services	279.5	246.7	304.3
Imports of services	−631.6	−670.2	−655.1
Balance on goods and services	−1,639.1	−1,844.2	−1,732.1
Private unrequited transfers (net)	449.4	618.1	682.3
Government unrequited transfers (net)	650.2	611.4	711.6
Current balance	−539.5	−614.7	−338.3
Long-term capital (net)	457.1	740.3	586.3
Short-term capital (net)	−31.3	−26.2	−74.7
Net errors and omissions	13.4	−3.5	−23.7
Total (net monetary movements)	−100.3	96.0	149.7
Valuation changes (net)	−21.1	−19.2	5.8
Exceptional financing (net)	2.8	1.8	0.8
Official financing (net)	−4.3	−40.0	−40.3
Changes in reserves	−122.9	38.6	115.9

Source: IMF, *International Financial Statistics*.

FOREIGN AID (US $ million, year ending 30 June)

Donor	1983/84	1984/85	1985/86
Canada	137	80	98
India	3	4	6
Japan	94	126	139
Netherlands/Belgium	49	61	43
Sweden	17	3	12
USSR	51	17	22
United Kingdom	44	45	42
USA	161	195	104
Total	556	531	466

Source: Ministry of Finance.

External Trade

PRINCIPAL COMMODITIES
(million taka, year ending 30 June)

Imports	1984/85	1985/86	1986/87
Food and live animals	15,016.8	7,717.6	11,375.4
Wheat	6,505.8	3,820.3	6,078.5
Rice	3,992.1	332.6	1,288.8
Beverages and tobacco	93.1	60.3	159.3
Crude materials (inedible) except fuels	4,094.1	3,615.6	3,825.1
Mineral fuels, lubricants, etc.	10,588.6	12,161.3	10,132.3
Animal and vegetable oils and fats	4,957.4	5,139.2	4,272.7
Chemicals	7,157.6	7,711.0	6,133.1
Basic manufactures	13,099.5	13,260.8	16,313.0
Machinery and transport equipment	11,835.3	11,449.0	14,170.9
Miscellaneous manufactured articles	1,327.4	1,639.9	1,850.9
Other commodities and transactions	93.1	175.0	263.4
Total	68,262.9	62,929.6	68,496.1

Exports	1984/85	1985/86	1986/87
Raw jute and jute cuttings	3,899.7	3,437.9	2,754.2
Jute goods	10,053.7	9,068.4	8,905.7
Tea	1,570.4	997.3	903.2
Hides, skins and leather goods	1,947.9	2,394.0	3,652.5
Fish and fish preparations	2,333.0	3,580.4	4,450.1
Newsprint and other paper	219.9	0.3	12.8
Spices	8.0	3.3	90.3
All other items	6,192.3	7,904.6	12,718.2
Total	26,224.9	27,386.2	33,487.0

PRINCIPAL TRADING PARTNERS (million taka)

Imports c.i.f.	1984/85	1985/86	1986/87
Australia	1,921.4	844.7	1,103.3
Canada	1,490.4	1,083.6	7,442.0
China, People's Republic	3,004.3	2,370.2	3,150.7
France	1,311.9	516.5	1,184.3
Germany, Federal Republic	2,342.5	2,489.0	3,398.8
Hong Kong	1,050.4	788.3	1,267.7
India	2,431.8	3,057.6	3,632.8
Japan	7,473.7	8,006.8	8,982.0
Korea, Republic	2,961.7	n.a.	n.a.
Malaysia	1,567.5	1,276.9	1,022.3
Netherlands	1,460.8	1,106.7	1,569.0
Singapore	7,944.5	9,070.8	5,582.9
USSR	1,360.3	749.7	880.2
United Kingdom	2,042.5	2,360.2	2,911.0
USA	9,340.0	3,608.9	4,780.7

Exports f.o.b.	1984/85	1985/86	1986/87
Belgium	1,834.0	1,015.2	1,234.2
India	945.0	76.8	56.1
Italy	1,220.6	1,488.3	2,897.0
Japan	1,778.4	1,946.3	2,149.6
Singapore	1,000.4	1,272.2	1,577.6
USSR	950.7	587.9	986.8
United Kingdom	1,357.6	1,568.8	1,913.9
USA	4,912.4	6,408.5	10,478.5

Transport

RAILWAYS (year ending 30 June)

	1984/85	1985/86	1986/87
Passenger-kilometres (million)	6,031.3	6,005	6,155
Freight ton-kilometres (million)	812.9	612	512

Source: Bangladesh Railway.

ROAD TRAFFIC (motor vehicles in use)

	1984	1985	1986
Private motor cars	25,020	25,675	26,388
Taxis	1,259	1,293	1,325
Buses and coaches	8,131	8,350	8,575
Trucks	15,132	15,537	15,950
Jeeps	8,370	8,596	8,828
Station wagons	4,016	4,124	4,235
Auto-rickshaws	13,574	13,941	14,316
Motor cycles	50,192	51,548	52,339
Others	4,059	4,169	4,282
Total	129,753	133,233	136,238

Source: Ministry of Communications.

BANGLADESH

INTERNATIONAL SEA-BORNE SHIPPING
(freight traffic, '000 long tons, year ending 30 June)

	1984/85	1985/86	1986/87
Chalna			
Goods loaded	555	762	730
Goods unloaded	1,821	1,561	1,557
Chittagong			
Goods loaded	341	334	402
Goods unloaded	6,829	5,902	5,836
Total goods loaded	898	1,096	1,132
Total goods unloaded	8,650	7,463	7,393

Tourism

	1985	1986	1987
Tourist arrivals	145,634	129,070	106,765

Communications Media

	1984	1985	1986
Radio receivers ('000 licensed)	548	587	551
Television receivers ('000 in use)	245	311	369
Telephones ('000 in use)	143	151	164
Book production: titles	708	720	n.a.
Daily newspapers:			
Number of titles	64	54	n.a.
Average circulation ('000)	546	554	n.a.

Education

(1985/86)

	Institutions	Students
Primary schools	43,712	10,776,000
Secondary schools	8,793	2,745,000
Technical colleges and institutes (government)*	98	26,393
Universities†	6	29,201

* In addition to government-owned and managed institutes, there are many privately-administered vocational training centres.
† An Islamic university was opened in 1986, bringing the total number of universities in Bangladesh to seven.

Directory

The Constitution

The members who were returned from East Pakistan (now Bangladesh) for the Pakistan National Assembly and the Provincial Assembly in the December 1970 elections formed the Bangladesh Constituent Assembly. A new Constitution for the People's Republic of Bangladesh was approved by this Assembly on 4 November 1972 and came into effect on 16 December 1972. The Constitution was amended in 1973, 1974, 1975, 1977, 1979, 1981 and 1988. Following the military coup of 24 March 1982, the Constitution was suspended, and the country was placed under martial law. On 10 November 1986 martial law was lifted and the suspended Constitution was revived.

SUMMARY

Fundamental Principles of State Policy

The Constitution was initially based on the fundamental principles of nationalism, socialism, democracy and secularism, but in 1977 an amendment replaced secularism with Islam. The amendment states that the country shall be guided by 'the principles of absolute trust and faith in the Almighty Allah, nationalism, democracy and socialism'. A further amendment in 1988 established Islam as the state religion. The Constitution aims to establish a society free from exploitation in which the rule of law, fundamental human rights and freedoms, justice and equality are to be secured for all citizens. A socialist economic system is to be established to ensure the attainment of a just and egalitarian society through state and co-operative ownership as well as private ownership within limits prescribed by law. A universal, free and compulsory system of education shall be established. In foreign policy the State shall endeavour to consolidate, preserve, and strengthen fraternal relations among Muslim countries based on Islamic solidarity.

Fundamental Rights

All citizens are equal before the law and have a right to its protection. Arbitrary arrest or detention, discrimination based on race, age, sex, birth, caste or religion, and forced labour are prohibited. Subject to law, public order and morality, every citizen has freedom of movement, of assembly and of association. Freedom of conscience, of speech, of the press and of religious worship are guaranteed.

GOVERNMENT

The President

The President is the constitutional Head of State and is elected for a term of five years. He is eligible for re-election. The supreme control of the armed forces is vested in the President. He appoints the Vice-President, the Prime Minister and other Ministers as well as the Chief Justice and other judges. The President is elected by universal adult suffrage.

The Executive

Executive authority shall rest in the President and shall be exercised by him either directly or through officers subordinate to him in accordance with the Constitution.

There shall be a Council of Ministers to aid and advise the President. All ministers shall hold office during the pleasure of the President.

The Legislature

Parliament (Jatiya Sangsad) is a unicameral legislature. It comprises 300 members and an additional 30 women members elected by the other members. Members of Parliament, other than the 30 women members, are directly elected on the basis of universal adult franchise from single territorial constituencies. Persons aged 18 and over are entitled to vote. The parliamentary term lasts for five years unless Parliament is dissolved sooner by the President. War can be declared only with the assent of Parliament. In the case of actual or imminent invasion, the President may take whatever action he may consider appropriate.

THE JUDICIARY

The Judiciary comprises a Supreme Court with High Court and an Appellate Division. The Supreme Court consists of a Chief Justice and such other judges as may be appointed by the President. The High Court division has such original appellate and other jurisdiction and powers as are conferred on it by the Constitution and by other law. The Appellate Division has jurisdiction to determine appeals from decisions of the High Court division. Subordinate courts, in addition to the Supreme Court, have been established by law.

ELECTIONS

An Election Commission supervises elections for the Presidency and for Parliament, delimits constituencies and prepares electoral rolls. It consists of a Chief Election Commissioner and other Commissioners as may be appointed by the President. The Election Commission is independent in the exercise of its functions. Subject to the Constitution, Parliament may make provision as to elections where necessary.

The Government

HEAD OF STATE

President: Lt-Gen. (retd) HOSSAIN MOHAMMAD ERSHAD (assumed power as Chief Martial Law Administrator 24 March 1982; took office as President 11 December 1983, confirmed by referendum 21 March 1985; re-elected 15 October 1986).

COUNCIL OF MINISTERS
(December 1988)

President of the Council of Ministers and Minister of Defence and of Establishment and Reorganization: Lt-Gen. (retd) HOSSAIN MOHAMMAD ERSHAD.

Vice-President and Minister of Islam and of Law and Justice: Justice A. K. M. NURUL ISLAM.

Prime Minister and Minister of Industry: MOUDUD AHMED.

Deputy Prime Minister and Minister of Home Affairs: Prof. M. A. MATIN.

Deputy Prime Minister, Minister of Information and Political Adviser to the President: Kazi ZAFAR AHMED.

Deputy Prime Minister and Minister of Labour and Manpower: SHAH MOAZZEM HOSSAIN.

Minister of Finance: Dr WAHIDUL HUQ.

Minister of Foreign Affairs: ANISUL ISLAM MAHMUD.

Minister of Social Welfare and Women's Affairs: MOHAMMAD REZWANUL HAQ CHOWDHURY.

Minister of Communications: ANWAR HUSSAIN MANZUR.

Minister of Energy and Mineral Resources: A. B. M. GHOLAM MUSTAFA.

Minister of Fisheries and Livestock: Sardar AMZAD HUSSAIN.

Minister of Education: Sheikh SHAHIDUL ISLAM.

Minister of Irrigation, Water Development and Flood Control: MAHBUBUR RAHMAN.

Minister of Jute: A. K. M. MOYEEDUL ISLAM.

Minister of Textiles: Lt-Col (retd) ZAFAR IMAM.

Minister of Ports, Shipping and Inland Water Transport: M. KORBAN ALI.

Minister of Planning: Air Vice-Marshal (retd) A. K. KHANDAKAR.

Minister of Health and Family Planning: Maj.-Gen. (retd) MOHAMMAD ABDUL MUNIM.

Minister of Youth and Sports: Maj. (retd) IQBAL HOSSAIN CHOWDHURY.

Minister of Agriculture: Maj.-Gen. (retd) MAHMUDUL HASAN.

Minister of Land Administration and Land Reform: SUNIL GUPTA.

Minister of Works: MOSTAFA JAMAL HAIDER.

Minister of Commerce: M. A. SATTAR.

Minister of Relief and Rehabilitation: SERAJUL HOSSAIN KHAN.

Minister of State for Civil Aviation and Tourism: ZIAUDDIN AHMED.

Minister of State for Post and Telecommunications: Kazi FEROJ RASHID.

Minister of State for Local Government, Rural Development and Co-operatives: NAZIUR RAHMAN MIAH.

Minister of State for Religious Affairs: NAZIMUDDIN KHAN AZAD.

Minister of State for Cultural Affairs: NUR MOHAMMAD KHAN.

MINISTRIES

Ministry of Agriculture: Bangladesh Secretariat, Bhaban 4, 2nd Storey, Dhaka.

Ministry of Commerce and Industry: Shilpa Bhaban, Motijheel C/A, Dhaka; telex 642201.

Ministry of Communications: Bangladesh Secretariat, Bhaban 7, 1st 9-Storey Bldg, 8th Floor, Dhaka; telex 65712.

Ministry of Cultural Affairs: Dhaka.

Ministry of Defence: Old High Court Bldg, Dhaka; tel. (2) 259082.

Ministry of Energy and Mineral Resources: Bangladesh Secretariat, Bhaban 6, New Bldg, 2nd Floor, Dhaka.

Ministry of Education: Bangladesh Secretariat, Bhaban 7, 2nd 9-Storey Bldg, 6th Floor, Dhaka.

Ministry of Finance and Planning: Bangladesh Secretariat, Bhaban 7, 1st 9-Storey Bldg, 3rd Floor, Dhaka; telex 65886.

Ministry of Foreign Affairs: Topkhana Rd, Dhaka: tel. (2) 236020; telex 642200.

Ministry of Food: Bangladesh Secretariat, Bhaban 4, 2nd 9-Storey Bldg, 3rd Floor, Dhaka; telex 65671.

Ministry of Health and Family Planning: Bangladesh Secretariat, Main Bldg, 3rd Floor, Dhaka.

Ministry of Home Affairs: School Bldg, 2nd and 3rd Floors, Bangladesh Secretariat, Dhaka.

Ministry of Information: Bangladesh Secretariat, 2nd 9-Storey Bldg, 8th Floor, Dhaka; tel. (2) 235111.

Ministry of Irrigation, Water Development and Flood Control: Dhaka.

Ministry of Jute and Textiles: Dhaka.

Ministry of Labour and Manpower: Bangladesh Secretariat, 1st 9-Storey Bldg, 4th Floor, Dhaka.

Ministry of Law and Land Reform: Bangladesh Secretariat, Bhaban 4, 2nd 9-Storey Bldg, 3rd Floor, Dhaka.

Ministry of Local Government: Bangladesh Secretariat, Bhaban 7, 1st 9-Storey Bldg, 6th Floor, Dhaka.

Ministry of Ports, Shipping and Inland Water Transport: Dhaka; tel. (2) 404345.

Ministry of Religious Affairs: Dhaka.

Ministry of Social Welfare and Women's Affairs: Bangladesh Secretariat, Bhaban 6, New Bldg, Dhaka.

Ministry of Works: Bangladesh Secretariat, Main Extension Bldg, 2nd Floor, Dhaka.

President and Legislature

PRESIDENT

A total of 12 candidates contested the presidential election held on 15 October 1986. According to official results, Lt-Gen. (retd) Hossain Mohammad Ershad won 21,795,337 votes (83.5% of the votes cast). His nearest rivals were Maulana M. H. Huzur (1,510,456 votes) and Lt-Col (retd) Said Faruq Rahman (1.17m. votes).

JATIYA SANGSAD
(Parliament)

Speaker: SHAMSUL HUDA CHOWDHURY.
Deputy Speaker: M. RIAZUDDIN AHMED.

General Election, 3 March 1988

	Seats
Jatiya Dal	252
Combined Opposition Group (COG)	18
Jatiya Samajtantrik Dal (S)	3
Freedom Party	2
Independents	25
Total	**300**

In addition to the 300 directly-elected members, a further 30 seats are reserved for women members.

Political Organizations

Since August 1975, when all political parties were banned, political activity has been prohibited intermittently. Political activity was again prohibited from November 1987. Numerous groups oppose the Government of President Ershad. The principal opposition alliances are led by the Awami League and the Bangladesh National Party, and comprised eight and seven parties respectively in 1987. A third alliance, led by Rashed Khan Menon and Hasanul Huq Inu, comprises five Marxist-Leninist parties. The following parties are among the more influential of those currently active:

Awami League: 23 Bangabandhu Ave, Dhaka; f. 1949; supports parliamentary democracy; advocates socialist economy, but with private sector, and a secular state; pro-Soviet and pro-Indian; Pres. Sheikh HASINA WAJED; Gen.-Sec. Begum SAJEDA CHOWDHURY; c. 1,025,000 mems.

Bangladesh Communist Party: Dhaka; f. 1948; pro-Soviet; allied to Awami League; Gen.-Sec. SAIFUDDIN AHMED MANIQ; c. 2,500 mems; banned November 1987.

Bangladesh Jatiya League: 500A Dhanmandi R/A, Rd 7, Dhaka; f. 1970 as Pakistan National League, renamed in 1972; supports parliamentary democracy; Leader ATAUR RAHMAN KHAN; c. 50,000 mems.

Bangladesh Jatiyatabadi Dal (Bangladesh Nationalist Party—BNP): Sattar House 19A, Rd 27 (Old) and 16 (New), Dhanmandi R/A, Dhaka; f. 1978 by merger of groups supporting Ziaur Rahman, including Jatiyatabadi Gonotantrik Dal (Jagodal—Nationalist Democratic Party); right of centre; favours democratic presidential system of govt; Chair. Begum KHALIDA ZIA; Vice-Chair. Prof. A. Q. M. BADRUDDOZA CHAUDHRY; Sec.-Gen. ABDUS SALAM TALUKDAR; in July 1988 a group of dissidents, led by a fmr Sec.-Gen., A. K. M. OBAIDUR RAHMAN, formed a rival faction.

Bangladesh Khilafat Andolon: Lalbagh, Dhaka.

Bangladesh Krishak Sramik Party (Peasants' and Workers' Party): Sonargaon Bhavan, 99 South Kamalapur, Dhaka 17; f. 1914, renamed 1953; supports parliamentary democracy, non-aligned foreign policy and socialism; Pres. A. S. M. SULAIMAN; Gen.-Sec. MUHAMMAD EMDAD HUSSAIN; c. 125,000 mems.

Bangladesh People's League: House 72, Dhanmandi R/A, Rd 7A, Dhaka; f. 1976; supports parliamentary democracy; c. 75,000 mems.

Combined Opposition Group (COG): f. 1988; a govt-approved alliance of 76 minor political parties; Leader A. S. M. ABDUR RAB.

Democratic League: 68 Jigatola, Dhaka 9; f. 1976; conservative; Leader KHANDAKAR MUSHTAQ AHMED.

Freedom Party: f. 1987; Islamic; opposed to Awami League; Co-Chair. Lt-Col (retd) SAID FARUQ RAHMAN, Lt-Col (retd) KHANDAKAR ABDUR RASHID.

Gonoazadi League: 30 Banagran Lane, Dhaka.

Islamic Democratic League: 84 Testari Bazar, Dhaka; Leader Maulana ABDUR RAHIM.

Jamit-i-Islami: 505 Elephant Rd, Bara Maghbazar, Dhaka 17; tel. (2) 401581; f. 1941; Islamic fundamentalist; Pres. ABBAS ALI KHAN (acting).

Jatiya Dal (National Party): Dhaka; f. 1983 as Jana Dal; reorg. 1986, when the National Front (f. 1985), a five-party alliance of the Jana Dal, the United People's Party, the Gonotantrik Dal, the Bangladesh Muslim League and a breakaway section of the Bangladesh Nationalist Party, formally converted itself into a single pro-govt grouping; advocates nationalism, democracy, Islamic ideals and progress; Chair. Lt-Gen. (retd) HOSSAIN MOHAMMAD ERSHAD; Sec.-Gen. SHAH MOAZZAM HOSSAIN.

Jatiya Janata Party: 6 Folder St, Wari, Dhaka 3; f. 1976; social democratic; Chair. FERDAUS AHMAD QUARISHI; Secs-Gen. A. K. MUJIBUR RAHMAN, ABDUL MATIN CHOWDHURY, YUSUF ALI; c. 25,000 mems.

Jatiya Samajtantrik Dal (R): breakaway faction of JSD; Leader A. S. M. ABDUR RAB.

Jatiya Samajtantrik Dal (JSD—(S)) (National Socialist Party): 23 DIT Ave, Malibagh Choudhury Para, Dhaka; f. 1972; left-wing; Leader SHAJAHAN SIRAJ; c. 5,000 mems.

National Awami Party—Bhashani (NAP): 226 Outer Circular Rd, Dhaka; f. 1957; Maoist; Pres. ABU NASSER KHAN BHASHANI; Gen.-Sec. ABDUS SUBHANI.

National Awami Party—Muzaffar (NAP-M): 21 Dhanmandi Hawkers' Market, 1st Floor, Dhaka 5; f. 1957, reorg. 1967; pro-Soviet; c. 500,000 mems; Leader MUZAFFAR AHMED; Gen.-Sec. PIR HABIBUR RAHMAN.

Samyabadi Dal: Dhaka; Maoist; Leader MOHAMMAD TOAHA.

Diplomatic Representation

EMBASSIES AND HIGH COMMISSIONS IN BANGLADESH

Afghanistan: House CWN(C)-2A Gulshan Ave, Gulshan Model Town, Dhaka 12; tel. (2) 603232; Chargé d'affaires a.i.: ABDUL AHAD WOLASI.

Algeria: 4 CWN(C) Gulshan Ave, Gulshan Model Town, Dhaka 12; tel. (2) 605021; Ambassador: MUHAMMAD CHADLY.

Australia: 184 Gulshan Ave, Gulshan Model Town, Dhaka 12; tel. (2) 600091; telex 642317; High Commissioner: SUSAN J. D. BOYD.

Belgium: House 40, Rd 21, Block B, Banani, Dhaka; tel. (2) 600138; telex 642304; Ambassador: Baron OLIVIER GILLES.

Bhutan: House 58, Rd 3A, Dhanmandi R/A, POB 3141, Dhaka; tel. (2) 505418; Ambassador: D. K. CHHETRI.

Brazil: House 23, Rd 5, Baridhara Model Town, Dhaka 1212; tel. (2) 605390; telex 642334; Chargé d'affaires a.i.: BERNARDINO RAIMUNDO DA SILVA.

Bulgaria: House 12, Rd 127, Gulshan Model Town, Dhaka 12; tel. (2) 602344; telex 642310; Ambassador: DIMITAR STANOEV.

Burma: 89(B), Rd 4, Banani, Dhaka; tel. (2) 601915; Ambassador: U SOE MYINT.

Canada: House 16A, Rd 48, Gulshan Model Town, POB 569, Dhaka 12; tel. (2) 607071; telex 642328; High Commissioner: EMILE GAUVREAU.

China, People's Republic: Plot NE(L)6, Rd 83, Gulshan Model Town, Dhaka 12; tel. (2) 601037; Ambassador: CHEN SONGLU.

Czechoslovakia: House 3A NE(O), Rd 90, Gulshan Model Town, Dhaka 12; tel. (2) 601673; telex 65730; Ambassador: JIŘÍ MAJSAJDR.

Denmark: House NW(H)1, Rd 51, Gulshan Model Town, POB 2056, Dhaka 12; tel. (2) 600108; telex 642320; Ambassador: JOERN KROGBECK.

Egypt: House NE(N)-9, Rd 90, Gulshan Model Town, Dhaka 12; tel. (2) 600158; Ambassador: MUHAMMAD MUSTAFA BADR.

France: POB 22, House 18, Rd 108, Gulshan Model Town, Dhaka 12; tel. (2) 607083; Ambassador: STANISLAS FILLIOL.

German Democratic Republic: 32/34, Rd 74, Gulshan Model Town, Dhaka 12; tel. (2) 600202; telex 642332; Ambassador: KLAUS MAESER.

Germany, Federal Republic: 178 Gulshan Ave, Gulshan Model Town, POB 108, Dhaka 12; tel. (2) 600166; telex 642331; Ambassador: KLAUS MAX FRANKE.

Holy See: Plot 1–2, Baridhara Model Town, POB 6003, Dhaka 1212; tel. (2) 600218; Apostolic Pro-Nuncio: Most Rev. LUIGI ACCOGLI.

Hungary: 80 Gulshan Ave, Gulshan Model Town, POB 6012, Dhaka 1212; tel. (2) 608101; telex 642314; Ambassador: JÓZSEF OLAH.

India: House 120, Rd 2, Dhanmandi R/A, Dhaka 1205; tel. (2) 503606; telex 642336; High Commissioner: INDRAJIT SINGH CHADHA.

Indonesia: 75 Gulshan Ave, Gulshan Model Town, Dhaka 12; tel. (2) 600131; telex 65639; Ambassador: MUHAMMAD ACHIRUL AEN.

Iran: CWN(A)-12 Kamal Ataturk Ave, Gulshan Model Town, Dhaka 12; tel. (2) 601432; telex 65714; Ambassador: GHOLAM REZA YOUSEFI.

Iraq: 112 Gulshan Ave, Gulshan Model Town, Dhaka 12; tel. (2) 600298; telex 642307; Ambassador: ZUHAIR MUHAMMAD ALOMAR.

Italy: House NWD(4), Rd 58/62, Gulshan Model Town, Dhaka 12; tel. (2) 603161; telex 642313; Ambassador: Dr SANDRO MARIA SIGGIA.

Japan: Plot 110, Rd 27, Block A, Banani Model Town, Dhaka 13; tel. (2) 608191; telex 65872; Ambassador: TAKEO IGUCHI.

Korea, Democratic People's Republic: House 6, Rd 7, Baridhara Model Town, Dhaka; tel. (2) 601250; Ambassador: KO YON-SIK.

Korea, Republic: House NW(E)17, Rd 55, Gulshan Model Town, Dhaka 12; tel. (2) 604921; Ambassador: MAN SOON CHANG.

Kuwait: Plot 39, Rd 23, Block J, Banani, Dhaka 13; tel. (2) 600233; telex 65600; Ambassador: AHMAD MURSHED AL-SULIMAN.

Libya: NE(D), 3A, Gulshan Ave (N), Gulshan Model Town, Dhaka 12; tel. (2) 600141; Secretary of People's Committee: MUSBAH ALI A. MAIMOON (acting).

Malaysia: House 4, Rd 118, Gulshan Model Town, Dhaka 12; tel. (2) 600291; High Commissioner: ZAINUDDIN A. RAHMAN.

Nepal: United Nations Rd 2, Baridhara Model Town, Dhaka; tel. (2) 601790; telex 65643; Ambassador: Dr MOHAN PRASAD LOHANI.

Netherlands: House 49, Rd 90, Gulshan Model Town, Dhaka 12; tel. (2) 600278; Ambassador: J. H. J. JEURISSEN.

Pakistan: House NEC-2, Rd 71, Gulshan Model Town, Dhaka 12; tel. (2) 600276; Ambassador: RIAZ H. KHOKHAR.

Philippines: House NE(L) 5, Rd 83, Gulshan Model Town, Dhaka 12; tel. (2) 605945; Ambassador: REYNALDO O. ARCHILLA.

Poland: 53 Gulshan Ave, Gulshan Model Town, Dhaka 12; tel. (2) 606098; telex 642316; Ambassador: EDWARD BARADZIEJ.

Qatar: House 23, Rd 108, Gulshan Model Town, Dhaka 12; tel. (2) 604477; Chargé d'affaires a.i.: ABDULLAH AL-MUTAWA.

Romania: House 33, Rd 74, Gulshan Model Town, Dhaka 12; tel. (2) 601467; telex 65739; Chargé d'affaires a.i.: ALEXANDRU VOINEA.

Saudi Arabia: House SW(A)-25, Rd 10, Gulshan Model Town, Dhaka 12; tel. (2) 600221; telex 642305; Ambassador: ABDUL LATIF ABDULLAH IBRAHIM AL-MAIMANEE.

Sri Lanka: House 22 (NW), Rd 56, Gulshan Model Town, Dhaka 12; tel. (2) 604009; telex 642321; High Commissioner: A. K. DAVID.

Sweden: 73 Gulshan Ave, Gulshan Model Town, POB 304, Dhaka 12; tel. (2) 607061; telex 642303; Ambassador: EVA HECKSCHER.

Thailand: 21, Block B, Rd 16, Banani Residential Area, Dhaka 13; tel. (2) 601475; Ambassador: CHAIYA CHINDAWONGSE.

BANGLADESH *Directory*

Turkey: House 7, Rd 62, Gulshan Model Town, Dhaka 12; tel. (2) 602198; Ambassador: MUAMMER TUNCER.
USSR: NE(J) 9, Rd 79, Gulshan Model Town, Dhaka 12; tel. (2) 601050; Ambassador: VITALY STEPANOVICH SMIRNOV.
United Arab Emirates: House CEN(H)41, Rd 113, Gulshan Model Town, Dhaka 12; tel. (2) 604775; telex 642301; Ambassador: IBRAHIM JAWAD AL-RIDHA.
United Kingdom: Abu Bakr House, Plot 7, Rd 84, Gulshan Model Town, POB 6079, Dhaka 12; tel. (2) 600133; telex 642470; High Commissioner: TERENCE G. STREETON.
USA: Park Rd, Baridhara Model Town, Dhaka 1212; telex 642319; Ambassador: WILLIARD AMES DE PREE.
Yugoslavia: House 10, Rd 62, Gulshan Model Town, Dhaka 12; tel. (2) 601505; Ambassador: KALMAN FEHER.

Judicial System

A judiciary, comprising a Supreme Court with High Court and Appellate Divisions, is in operation. See under Constitution.
Chief Justice: Dr F. K. M. A. MUNIM.
Attorney-General: M. NURULLAH.

Religion

Preliminary results of the 1981 census classified 86.6% of the population as Muslims, 12.1% as caste Hindus and scheduled castes, and the remainder as Buddhists, Christians and tribals.

Freedom of religious worship is guaranteed under the Constitution but, under the 1977 amendment to the Constitution, Islam was declared to be one of the nation's guiding principles and, under the 1988 amendment, Islam was established as the state religion.

BUDDHISM

World Federation of Buddhists Regional Centre: Buddhist Monastery, Kamalapur, Dhaka 14; Leader Ven. VISUDDHANANDA MAHATHERO.

CHRISTIANITY

Jatio Church Parishad (National Council of Churches): 395 New Eskaton Rd, Moghbazar, Dhaka 2; tel. (2) 402869; f. 1949 as East Pakistan Christian Council; four mem. churches; Pres. Dr SAJAL DEWAN; Gen. Sec. M. R. BISWAS.

Church of Bangladesh—United Church

After Bangladesh achieved independence, the Diocese of Dacca (Dhaka) of the Church of Pakistan (f. 1970 by the union of Anglicans, Methodists, Presbyterians and Lutherans) became the autonomous Church of Bangladesh. In 1986 the Church had an estimated 12,000 members.
Bishop of Dhaka: Rt Rev. BARNABAS DWIJEN MONDAL, St Thomas' Church, 54 Johnson Rd, Dhaka 1100; tel. (2) 234650.

The Roman Catholic Church

For ecclesiastical purposes, Bangladesh comprises one archdiocese and four dioceses. At 31 December 1986 there were an estimated 227,204 adherents in the country.
Catholic Bishops' Conference: Archbishop's House, POB 3, 1 Kakrail Rd, Dhaka 1000; tel. (2) 408879; f. 1978; Pres. Most Rev. MICHAEL ROZARIO, Archbishop of Dhaka.
Archbishop of Dhaka: Most Rev. MICHAEL ROZARIO, Archbishop's House, POB 3, 1 Kakrail Rd, Dhaka 1000; tel. (2) 408879.

Other Christian Churches

Bangladesh Baptist Sangha: Sadarghat, POB 1108, Dhaka 1; tel. (2) 234644; 26,500 mems (1985); Pres. M. S. ADHIKARY; Exec. Sec. Rev. R. N. BAROI.

Among other denominations active in Bangladesh are the Bogra Christian Church, the Evangelical Christian Church (12,350 mems in 1985), the Garo Baptist Union (16,000 mems), the Reformed Church of Bangladesh and the Sylhet Presbyterian Synod (9,500 mems).

The Press

PRINCIPAL DAILIES

Bengali

Azad: 27K Dhakeshari Rd, Ramna, Dhaka 5; tel. (2) 502043; f. 1936; morning; Editor MD JAINUL ANAM KHAN; circ. 12,000.
Azadi: 9 C.D.A. C/A, Momin Rd, Chittagong; tel. (31) 221278; f. 1960; Editor Prof. MOHAMMAD KHALED; circ. 13,000.
Banglar Bani: 1 Motijheel C/A, Dhaka 1000; tel. (2) 235341; f. 1972, relaunched 1981; publication suspended in August 1987; Editor SHEIKH FAZLUL KARIM SALIM; circ. 20,000.
Dainik Abarta: 141 Arambagh, Motijheel, POB 628, Dhaka 2; tel. (2) 254333; Editor S. M. TAUFIQUL ISLAM; circ. 4,000.
Dainik Bangla: 1 DIT Ave, Dhaka 1000; tel. (2) 235065; f. 1964; govt-owned; Editor AHMED HUMAYUN; circ. 50,000.
Dainik Barta: Natore Rd, Rajshahi; tel. (2) 2424; f. 1976; morning; govt-owned; Editor MOSLEM ALI BISWAS; circ. 6,000.
Dainik Desh: 5 Segun Bagicha, Dhaka; tel. (2) 244040; f. 1979; publ. of the Bangladesh Jatiyatabadi Dal (BNP) party; Chief Editor ANWARUL ISLAM; circ. 18,000.
Dainik Inquilab: 2/1 Ramkrishna Mission Rd, Dhaka; tel. (2) 237449; Editor M. A. BAHAUDDIN; circ. 42,000.
Dainik Ittefaq: 1 Ramkrishna Mission Rd, Dhaka 3; tel. (2) 256075; f. 1953; Editor AKTHER-UL-ALAM; circ. 195,000.
Dainik Jahan: Bicic Silpanagari, Maskanda, Mymensingh; tel. 5677; Editor MUHAMMAD HABIBUR RAHMAN SHEIKH; circ. 4,000.
Dainik Janata: 24 Aminbag, Shanti Nagar, Dhaka 1217; tel. (2) 400498; Editor SANAULLAH NOORI.
Dainik Janmobhumi: 15 Iqbal Nagar Mosque Rd, Khulna 9100; tel. (41) 21280; f. 1982; Editor HUMAYUN KABIR; circ. 5,000.
Dainik Khabar: 137 Shanti Nagar, Dhaka 17; tel. (2) 406601; f. 1985; Editor MIZANUR RAHMAN MIZAN; circ. 18,000.
Dainik Kishan: 309 Outer Circular Rd, Raja Bazar, Dhaka; tel. (2) 600360; f. 1976; Editor KAZI ABDUL QADER; circ. 4,000.
Dainik Nava Avijan: Lalkuthi, North Brook Hall Rd, Dhaka; tel. (2) 257516; Editor A. S. M. REZAUL HAQUE; circ. 15,000.
Dainik Patrika: 85 Elephant Rd, Dhaka 17; tel. (2) 415057; Editor MIA MUSA HOSSAIN.
Dainik Purbanchal: 38 Iqbal Nagar Mosque Lane, Khulna; tel. (41) 21944; f. 1974; Editor LIAQUAT ALI; circ. 3,000.
Dainik Rupashi Bangla: Natun Chowdhury Para, Bagichagaon, Comilla; tel. (2) 6689; f. 1971 (a weekly until 1979); Editor Prof. ABDUL WAHAB; circ. 4,000.
Dainik Samachar: 31/32 P.K. Ray Rd, Ispahani Bldg, Bangla Bazar, Dhaka; tel. (2) 281060; Editor SEKANDAR HAYAT MAJUMDER.
Dainik Sangram: 423 Elephant Rd, Bara Mogh Bazar, Dhaka 1217; tel. (2) 405279; Man. Dir MOHAMED SHAMSUR RAHMAN; Editor ABUL ASAD; circ. 19,000.
Dainik Shakti: 64/1 Purana Paltan, Dhaka 1000; tel. (2) 405535; Editor A. Q. M. ZAIN-UL-ABEDIN; circ. 4,000.
Dainik Sphulinga: Amin Villa, P-5 Housing Estate, Jessore 7401; tel. (8) 6433; f. 1971; Editor Begum RASHIDA SATTAR; circ. 14,000.
Dainik Uttara: Bahadur Bazar, Dinajpur Town, Dinajpur; tel. (531) 415911; f. 1974; Editor Prof. MUHAMMAD MOHSIN; circ. 4,000.
Ganakantha: 24G Tipu Sultan Rd, Dhaka; tel. (2) 606784; telex 642696; f. 1979; morning; Editor JAHANGIR KABIR CHOWDHURY; circ. 10,000.
Janabarta: 5 Babul Khan Rd, Khulna; tel. (41) 21075; f. 1974; Editor SYED SOHRAB ALI; circ. 4,000.
Karatoa: Chani Bazar, Bogra; tel. (51) 5238; f. 1976; Editor MOZAMMEL HAQUE LALU; circ. 3,000.
Naya Bangla: 101 Momin Rd, Chittagong; tel. (31) 202816; f. 1978; Editor ABDULLAH AL-SAGIR; circ. 12,000.
Probaho: 2 Raipara Cross Rd, Khulna; tel. (41) 23650; f. 1977; Editor ASHRAFUL HUQUE; circ. 3,000.
Protidin: Ganeshtola, Dinajpur; tel. (2) 4555; f. 1980; Editor ABDUS SAMAD; circ. 3,000.
Runner: Pyari Mohan Das Rd, Bejpara, Jessore; tel. (2) 6943; f. 1980; Editor R. M. SAIFUL ALAM MUKUL; circ. 2,000.
Sangbad: 263 Bangshal Rd, Dhaka 1; tel. (2) 238147; telex 642454; f. 1951; Editor AHMEDUL KABIR; circ. 57,000.
Swadhinata: 99A Zamal Khan Lane, Chittagong; tel. (31) 209644; f. 1972; Editor ABDULLAH-AL-HARUN; circ. 4,000.
Zamana: Kazir Dewry, 2nd Lane, Chittagong; tel. (31) 205424; f. 1955; morning; Editor MOYEENUL ALAM; circ. 17,000.

English

Bangladesh Observer: Observer House, 33 Toyenbee Circular Rd, Motijheel C/A, Dhaka 1000; tel. (2) 235105; f. 1949; morning; Editor Prof. K. M. A. MUNIM; circ. 43,000.
Bangladesh Times: 1 DIT Ave, Dhaka 1000; tel. (2) 258840; f. 1974; morning; Editor SHAHIDUL HUQ; circ. 20,000.
Daily Capital News: 29 Nabaray Lane, Islampur, Dhaka; tel. (2) 257985; Editor SEKANDER HAYAT MAJUMDER.

BANGLADESH

Directory

Daily Life: 27 Sadarghat Rd, Chittagong; tel. (31) 207300; f. 1977; Editor ANWARUL ISLAM BOBBY; circ. 10,000.

Daily News: 76A Segunbagicha, Dhaka 1000; tel. (2) 413027; f. 1982; supports the government; Editor MUJIBUL HAIDER CHOWDHURY; circ. 8,000.

Daily Tribune: 38 Iqbal Nagar Mosque Lane, Khulna; tel. (41) 21013; f. 1978; morning; Editor FERDOUSI ALI; circ. 6,000.

Morning Post: 280 New Eskaton Rd, Dhaka 1000; tel. (2) 413256; f. 1969; Editor HABIBUL BASHAR; circ. 20,000.

New Nation: 1 Ramkrishna Mission Rd, Dhaka 1203; tel. (2) 256071; f. 1981; Editor ENAMUL HAQ; circ. 10,000.

People's View: 129 Panchlaish R/A, Chittagong; tel. (31) 204993; f. 1969; Editor SHABBIR ISLAM; circ. 3,000.

PERIODICALS

Bengali

Aachal: 100B Malibagh Chowdhury Para, Dhaka 1219; tel. (2) 414043; weekly; Editor FERDOUSI BEGUM.

ADAB Sangbad: 1/3 Block F, Lalmatia, Dhaka 1207; tel. (2) 313318; telex 642940; f. 1974; monthly; publ. by the Assen of Devt Agencies in Bangladesh (ADAB); Editor-in-Chief S. M. AKHTARUZZAMAN; circ. 7,000.

Ad-Dawat: Rajshahi Town; f. 1976; monthly; Editor MOHAMMAD ABUL QASEM.

Ahmadi: 4 Bakshi Bazar, Dhaka; f. 1925; fortnightly; Editor A. H. M. ALI ANWAR.

Ajker Samabaya: 114 Motijheel C/A, Dhaka 1000; f. 1974; fortnightly; Editor KH. REASUL KARIM; circ. 10,000.

Amod: Comilla Sadar, Comilla; tel. (2) 6193; f. 1955; weekly; Editor SHAMSUN NEHAR RABBANI; circ. 2,000.

Ananda Bichitra: 1 DIT Ave, Dhaka; tel. (2) 241639; f. 1986; fortnightly; Editor SHAHADAT CHOWDHURY; circ. 32,000.

Ananda Chitra: 55 Inner Circular Rd, Shanti Nagar, Dhaka; Editor K. G. KARIM.

Ananda Patra: 188 Motijheel Circular Rd, Dhaka 1000; tel. (2) 406988; weekly; Editor MOSTAFA JABBAR.

Bangla Dak: 12 Avoy Das Lane, Dhaka; Editor SALEH AHMED; circ. 2,000.

Begum: 66 Loyal St, Dhaka 1; tel. (2) 233789; f. 1947; women's illustrated weekly; Editor NURJAHAN BEGUM; circ. 25,000.

Bichitra: Dainik Bangla Bhaban, 1 DIT Ave, Dhaka 1000; tel. (2) 232086; f. 1972; weekly; Editor SHAHADAT CHOWDHURY; circ. 42,000.

Biplav: 5 Shegunbagicha, Dhaka 2; f. 1982; weekly; Editor SIKDER AMINUL HUQUE.

Chakra: 2/10 Mymensingh Rd, Dhaka; tel. (2) 504278; Editor HUSNE ARA AZIZ.

Chitra Bangla: 137 Shanti Nagar, Dhaka; tel. (2) 407601; weekly; Editor FULLORA BEGUM FLORA; circ. 46,000.

Chitra Desh: 24 Ramkrishna Mission Rd, Dhaka 1203; weekly; Editor HENA AKHTAR CHOWDHURY.

Chitrakalpa: 12 Folder St, Dhaka 3; Editor ASIRUDDIN AHMED.

Chitrali: Observer House, 33 Toyenbee Circular Rd, Motijheel C/A, Dhaka 1000; tel. (2) 235105; f. 1963; film weekly; Editor AHMED ZAMAN CHOWDHURY; circ. 25,000.

Chutti: 87 Bijoy Nagar, Dhaka 1000; tel. (2) 241112; weekly; Editor JAWADUL KARIM; circ. 18,000.

Desh Bandhu: 55 Inner Circular Rd, Dhaka; Editor ALAMGIR KABIR.

Dhaka Digest: 34 Topkhana Rd, Dhaka; f. 1974; monthly; Editor RASHID CHOWDHURY; circ. 7,000.

Ekota: 240 Bangshal Rd, Dhaka; tel. (2) 242123; weekly; Editor MOTIUR RAHMAN.

Fashal: 28J Toyenbee Circular Rd, Motijheel C/A, Dhaka 1000; tel. (2) 233099; f. 1965; agricultural weekly; Chief Editor ERSHAD MAZUMDAR; circ. 8,000.

Ispat: Majampur, Kushtia; tel. (2) 3676; f. 1976; weekly; Editor WALIUR BARI CHOUDHURY; circ. 3,000.

Jahan-e-Nau: 13 Karkun Bari Lane, Dhaka; tel. (2) 252205; f. 1960; weekly; Editor MD HABIBIUR RAHMAN; circ. 9,000.

Janakatha: 130 DIT Extension Rd, Dhaka; Editor IBRAHIM RAHMAN.

Jhorna: 4/13 Block A, Lalmatia, Dhaka; tel. (2) 415239; Editor MUHAMMAD JAMIR ALI.

Jugabheri: Ambarkhana, Sylhet; tel. 7659; f. 1931; weekly; Editor AMINUR RASHID CHOWDHURY; circ. 1,000.

Kalantar: 87 Khanjahan Ali Rd, Khulna; tel. (41) 61424; f. 1971; weekly; Editor NOOR MOHAMMAD; circ. 12,000.

Kankan: Nawab Bari Rd, Bogra; tel. (51) 6424; f. 1974; weekly; Editor Mrs SUFIA KHATUN; circ. 6,000.

Kanak: 144 DIT Extension Rd, Dhaka; tel. (2) 415110; weekly; Editor AMIR HOSSAIN.

Kirajagat: National Sports Control Board, 62/63 Purana Paltan, Dhaka; f. 1977; weekly; Editor ALI MUZZAMAN CHOWDHURY; circ. 7,000.

Kishore Bangla: Observer House, Motijheel C/A, Dhaka 1000; juvenile weekly; f. 1976; Editor RAFIQUL HAQUE; circ. 5,000.

Krishi Katha: 3 Ramkrishna Mission Rd, Dhaka; f. 1957; monthly; Editor NURJAHAN KORESHI; circ. 6,000.

Laboni: 404B Chowdhury Para, Dhaka; Editor LINA KABIR.

Mallika: 51 Lalchan-Mokim Lane, Roth Khola, Dhaka; tel. (2) 251408; Editor Dr JHORNA DATTA.

Meghna: 55 Inner Circular Rd, Shanti Nagar, Dhaka 1217; tel. (2) 404983; weekly; Editor MOSTAFA AMIR FAISAL; circ. 16,000.

Moha Nagar: 4 Dilkusha C/A, Dhaka 1000; tel. (2) 255282; Editor SYED MOTIUR RAHMAN.

Moshal: 4 Dilkusha C/A, Dhaka 1000; tel. (2) 231092; Editor MUHAMMAD ABUL HASNAT; circ. 3,000

Muktibani: Toyenbee Circular Rd, Motijheel C/A, Dhaka 1000; tel. (2) 253712; telex 642474; f. 1972; weekly; Editor NIZAM UDDIN AHMED; circ. 35,000.

Natun Bangla: 44A Hatirpur, Dhaka; tel. (2) 508102; weekly; Editor MAJIBUR RAHMAN.

Natun Katha: 31E Topkhana Rd, Dhaka; weekly; Editor HAJERA SULTANA; circ. 4,000.

Nayajug: 32 Purana Paltan, Dhaka; tel. (2) 283510; f. 1976; weekly; Editor KAZI ZAFAR AHMED; circ. 9,000.

Nopun: 520 Peyarabag, Magbazar, Dhaka 11007; tel. (2) 312156; monthly; Editor SHAJAHAN CHOWDHURY.

Palli Samachar: 144 DIT Extension Rd, Dhaka; tel. (2) 404671; Editor MUHAMMAD MOZIBUR RAHMAN; circ. 7,000.

Parikrama: 65 Shanti Nagar, Dhaka; tel. (2) 415640; Editor MOMTAZ SULTANA.

Patuakhali Samachur: Patuakhali Town; f. 1970; fortnightly; Editor SHAMSUL HAQ KHAN.

Prohar: 35 Siddeswari Rd, Dhaka 1217; tel. (2) 404206; Editor MUJIBUL HUQ.

Protirodh: Dept of Answar and V.D.P. Khilgoan, Ministry of Home Affairs, School Bldg, 2nd and 3rd Floors, Bangladesh Secretariat, Dhaka; tel. (2) 405971; f. 1977; fortnightly; Editor ZAHANGIR HABIBULLAH; circ. 20,000.

Purbani: 1 Ramkrishna Mission Rd, Dhaka 1203; tel. (2) 256503; f. 1951; film weekly; Editor KHONDKER SHAHADAT HOSSAIN; circ. 22,000.

Reporter: 28J Toyenbee Circular Rd, Motijheel C/A, Dhaka; tel. (2) 257589; f. 1976; news weekly; Chief Editor ERSHAD MAZUMDAR; circ. 5,000.

Robbar: 1 Ramkrishna Mission Rd, Dhaka; tel. (2) 256071; f. 1978; weekly; publication suspended Dec. 1987; Editor ABDUL HAFIZ; circ. 20,000.

Rokshena: 13B Avoy Das Lane, Tiktuli, Dhaka; tel. (2) 255117; Editor SYEDA AFSANA.

Rupashi: 7 Segunbagicha, Dhaka; tel. (2) 239622; Editor GULSHAN AHMED.

Sachitra: 50F Inner Circular Rd, Naya Paltan, Dhaka; tel. (2) 403242; Editor KHALID MAHMOUD.

Sachitra Bangladesh: 112 Circuit House Rd, Dhaka 1000; tel. (2) 402129; f. 1979; fortnightly; Editor A. B. M. ABDUL MATIN; circ. 8,000.

Sachitra Sandhani: 68/2 Purana Paltan, Dhaka; tel. (2) 409680; f. 1978; weekly; Editor GAZI SHAHABUDDIN MAHMUD; circ. 13,000.

Sandip: 28/A/3 Toyenbee Circular Rd, Dhaka; tel. (2) 235542; weekly; Editor MOHSEN ARA RAHMAN.

Satodal: 33 Johanson Rd, Dhaka; Editor A. L. ZAHIRUL HUQ KHAN.

Shishu: Shishu Academy, Old High Court Area, Dhaka; f. 1977; children's weekly; Editor JOBAYEDA KHANAM; circ. 5,000.

Sonar Bangla: 423 Elephant Rd, Mogh Bazar, Dhaka 1217; tel. (2) 400637; f. 1961; Editor MUHAMMED QAMARUZZAMAN; circ. 25,000.

Superstar: 46A Razmoni Cinema Complex, Kakrail, Dhaka; tel. (2) 416079; f. 1986; socio-cultural newspaper; Editor KHONDAKER MOZAMMEL HUQ; circ. 50,000.

Swadesh: 19 B.B. Ave, Dhaka; tel. (2) 256946; weekly; Editor ZAKIUDDIN AHMED; circ. 8,000.

Tarokalok: 8/3 Neelkhet, Babupura, Dhaka 1205; tel. (2) 507952; weekly; Editor SAJJAD KADIR.

BANGLADESH

Tide: 56/57 Motijheel C/A, Dhaka 1000; tel. (2) 259421; Editor ENAYET KARIM.

Tilotwoma: 14 Bangla Bazar, Dhaka; Editor ABDUL MANNAN.

English

ADAB News: 1/3, Block F, Lalmatia, Dhaka 1207; tel. (2) 313318; telex 642940; f. 1974; 6 a year; publ. by the Asscn of Devt Agencies in Bangladesh (ADAB); Editor-in-Chief AZFAR HUSSAIN; circ. 4,000.

Bangladesh: 112 Circuit House Rd, Dhaka 1000; tel. (2) 402013; fortnightly; Editor A. B. M. ABDUL MATIN.

Bangladesh Gazette: Bangladesh Government Press, Tejgaon, Dhaka; f. 1947, name changed 1972; weekly; official notices; Editor M. HUDA.

Bangladesh Illustrated Weekly: 31A Rankin St, Wari, Dhaka; tel. (2) 23358; Editor ATIQUZZAMAN KHAN; circ. 3,000.

Bangladesh Today: 27 Naya Paltan, Dhaka; Editor SERAJUL ISLAM CHOWDHURY.

Cinema: 81 Motijheel C/A, Dhaka 1000; Editor SHEIKH FAZLUR RAHMAN MARUF; circ. 11,000.

Consumer-Economist: Yasmin Palace, Jubilee Rd, Chattagram; tel. (31) 204038; f. 1980; weekly; Editor MOYEENUL ALAM; circ. 16,000.

Detective: Polwell Bhaban, Naya Paltan, Dhaka 2; tel. (2) 402757; f. 1960; weekly; also publ. in Bengali; Editor SYED AMJAD HOSSAIN; circ. 3,000.

Dhaka Courier: 62/61 Purana Paltan, Dhaka; tel. (2) 238222; weekly; Editor ENAYET ULLAH KHAN; circ. 5,000.

Eastern Tribune: 62/1 Purana Paltan, Dhaka; tel. (2) 282258; f. 1969; weekly; Editor ABUL HOSSAIN MALLICK; circ. 3,500.

Friday: 17/1 Eskaton Garden Rd, Dhaka; tel. (2) 409589; Editor SHAWFIKUL GHAANI SHAPAN.

Herald: 87 Bijoy Nagar, Dhaka; tel. (2) 231533; f. 1981; weekly; Editor JAQADUL KARIM; circ. 4,000.

Holiday: 40/1 Naya Paltan, Dhaka 1000; tel. (2) 403495; f. 1965; weekly; independent; Editor FAZAL M. KAMAL; circ. 14,000.

Karnaphuli Shipping News: 88 Ghat Farhadbag, Kazem Ali Rd, Chittagong; tel. (31) 220366; f. 1977; twice a week; Editor F. KARIM; circ. 10,000.

Motherland: Khanjahan Ali Rd, Khulna; tel. (41) 61685; f. 1974; weekly; Editor M. N. KHAN.

Muslim Times: 21/4C Rankin St, Wari, Dhaka; Editor GIASUDDIN.

Saturday Post: 280 New Eskaton Rd, Dhaka 1000; tel. (2) 413256; f. 1975; weekly; Man. Editor ZAKIR HOSSAIN; Editor HABIBUL BASHAR; circ. 15,000.

Sunday Star: 149/A DIT Extension Ave, Dhaka; tel. (2) 403980; f. 1981; weekly; Editor MOHIUDDIN AHMED.

Tide: 56/57 Motijheel C/A, Dhaka; tel. (2) 259421; Editor ENAYET KARIM.

Voice From the North: Dinajpur Town, Dinajpur; tel. (2) 3256; f. 1981; weekly; Editor Prof. MUHAMMAD MOHSIN; circ. 5,000.

NEWS AGENCIES

Bangladesh Sangbad Sangstha (BSS) (Bangladesh News Agency): 68/2 Purana Paltan, Dhaka 1000; tel. (2) 235036; telex 5526; Man. Dir. and Chief Editor MAHBUBUL ALOUN.

Eastern News Agency (ENA): 3/3C Purana Paltan, Dhaka 1000; tel. (2) 234206; telex 642410; f. 1970; Man. Dir and Chief Editor GOLAM RASUL MALLICK.

Foreign Bureaux

Agence France-Presse (AFP): Shilpa Bank, 5th Floor, 8 DIT Ave, nr Dhaka Stadium, Dhaka; tel. (2) 242234; telex 5526; Correspondent GOLAM TAHABOOR.

Associated Press (AP) (USA): 8/6 Segun Bagicha, Dhaka 1000; tel. (2) 233061; telex 642967; Representative HASAN SAEED.

Inter Press Service (IPS) (Italy): c/o Bangladesh Sangbad Sangstha, 68/2 Purana Paltan, Dhaka 1000; tel. (2) 280356; Correspondent A. K. M. TABIBUL ISLAM.

Reuters Ltd (UK): POB 3993, Dhaka; tel. (2) 505061; telex 642540; Bureau Chief ATIQUL ALAM.

Xinhua (New China) News Agency (People's Republic of China): 22 New Eskaton Rd, Dhaka 1000; tel. (2) 403167; Correspondent XUAN ZENGPEI.

PRESS ASSOCIATIONS

Bangladesh Council of Newspapers and News Agencies: Dhaka; tel. (2) 413256; Chair. MOINUL HOSSAIN; Sec.-Gen. HABIBUL BASHAR.

Bangladesh Federal Union of Journalists: National Press Club Bldg, 18 Topkhana Rd, Dhaka 1000; tel. (2) 254777; f. 1973; Pres. REAZUDDIN AHMED; Sec.-Gen. SYED ZAFAR AHMED.

Bangladesh Sangbadpatra Karmachari Federation (Newspaper Employees' Fed.): 47/3 Toyenbee Circular Rd, Bikrampur House, Dhaka 1000; tel. (2) 235065; f. 1972; Pres. RAFIQUL ISLAM; Sec.-Gen. MIR MOZAMMEL HOSSAIN.

Bangladesh Sangbadpatra Press Sramik Federation (Newspaper Press Workers' Federation): 1 Ramkrishna Mission Rd, Dhaka; f. 1960; Pres. M. ABDUL KARIM; Gen.-Sec. BELAYAT HOSSAIN.

Dhaka Union of Journalists: National Press Club, Dhaka; f. 1947; Pres. ABEL KHAIR; Gen.-Sec. ABDUL KALAM AZAD.

Overseas Correspondents' Association Bangladesh (OCAB): 18 Topkhana Rd, Dhaka 1000; f. 1979; Pres. GOLAM TAHABOOR; Gen. Sec. TAHMINA SAYEED; 51 mems.

Publishers

Adeyle Brothers: 60 Patuatuly, Dhaka 1.

Ahmed Publishing House: 7 Zindabahar 1st Lane, Dhaka 1; tel. (2) 36492; f. 1942; literature, history, science, religion, children's, maps and charts; Man. Dir KAMALUDDIN AHMED; Man. MESBAHUDDIN AHMED.

Ashrafia Library: 4 Hakim Habibur Rahman Rd, Chawk Bazar, Dhaka 1000; Islamic religious books, texts, and reference works of Islamic institutions.

Asiatic Society of Bangladesh: 5 Old Secretariat Rd, Ramna, Dhaka; tel. (2) 239390; f. 1951; periodicals on science and humanities; Pres. A. K. M. ZAKARIA; Sec. Prof. SERAJUL.

Bangla Academy: Burdwan House, Dhaka 1000; tel. (2) 500131; f. 1955; higher education textbooks in Bengali, research works in language, literature and culture, popular science, drama, children's books, translations of world classics, dictionaries; Dir-Gen. ABU HENA MUSTAFA KAMAL.

Bangladesh Book Corporation: 73/74 Patuatuly, Dhaka.

Bangladesh Publishers: 45 Patuatuly, Dhaka.

Bangladesh Books International Ltd: Ittefaq Bhaban, 1 Ramkrishna Mission Rd, POB 377, Dhaka 3; tel. (2) 256071; f. 1975; reference, academic, research, literary, children's in Bengali and English; Chair. MOINUL HOSSEIN; Man. Dir ABDUL HAFIZ.

Barnamala Prakashani: 30 Bangla Bazar, Dhaka.

Boi Prakashani: 38A Bangla Bazar, Dhaka.

Boighar: 149 Government New Market, Dhaka.

Book Society: 38 Bangla Bazar, Dhaka.

Co-operative Book Society Ltd: Motijheel, Dhaka.

Didar Publishing House: 45 Johnson Rd, Dhaka.

Emdadia Library: Chawk Bazar, Dhaka.

Great Bengal Library: Islampur, Dhaka.

Habibia Library: Chawk Bazar, Dhaka.

Islamia Library: Patuatuly, Dhaka.

Islamic Foundation: Baitul Mukarram, Dhaka.

Jatiya Sahitya Prakashani: 51 Purana Paltan, POB 3416, Dhaka 1000; f. 1970; Prin. Officer MOFIDUL HOQUE.

Khan Brothers & Co: 67 Pyari Das Rd, Dhaka.

Knowledge House: Pyari Das Rd, Dhaka.

Liaquat Publications: 34 North Brook Hall Rd, Dhaka.

Model Publishing House: 34 Bangla Bazar, Dhaka.

Mofiz Book House: 37 Bangla Bazar, Dhaka.

Mowla Brothers: Bangla Bazar, Dhaka.

Muktadhara: 74 Farashganj, Dhaka; f. 1971; educational, literary and general; Bengali and English; Man. Dir C. R. SAHA; Chief Editor S. P. LAHIRY.

Mullick Brothers: 3/1 Bangla Bazar, Dhaka; educational.

Osmania Book Depot: 42/43 North Brook Hall Rd, Dhaka 1.

Paramount Book Corpn: Ashraf Chamber, 66 Bangabandhu Ave, Dhaka; literary.

Puthighar: 74 Farashganj, Dhaka; f. 1951; educational; Bengali and English; Man. Dir C. R. SAHA; Chief Editor S. P. LAHIRY.

Puthipatra: 1/6 Shirish Das Lane, Banglabazar, Dhaka 1; f. 1952.

Rahman Brothers: 5/1 Gopinath Datta, Kabiraj St, Babu Bazar, Dhaka; tel. (2) 282633; educational.

Rangpur Publications: 13/3 Haramohan St, Amligola, Dhaka.

Royal Library: Ispahani Bldg, 31/32 P. K. Roy Rd, Banglabazar, Dhaka 1; tel. (2) 250863.

Sahitya Kutir: Bogra.

BANGLADESH

Sahityika: 6 Bangla Bazar, Dhaka.
Samakal Prakashani: 36A Toyenbee Circular Rd, Dhaka 1000.
Standard Publishers Ltd: Dhaka Stadium, Dhaka 1.
Student Ways: 9 Bangla Bazar, Dhaka.
University Press Ltd: POB 2611, Red Cross Bldg, 114 Motijheel C/A, Dhaka 1000; tel. (2) 232950; f. 1975; educational, academic and general; Man. Dir. MOHIUDDIN AHMED; Editor MAHBOOB HASSAN.

Government Publishing Houses

Bangladesh Bureau of Statistics: Bldg 8, Room 12, Bangladesh Secretariat, Dhaka; tel. (2) 409571; f. 1971; statistical yearbooks and monthly bulletins; Publ. Officer MENHAJUDDIN AHMAD; Sec. ABDUS SALAM.
Bangladesh Government Press: Tejgaon, Dhaka; tel. (2) 603897; f. 1972.
Department of Films and Publications: 112 Circuit House Rd, Dhaka 1000; tel. (2) 402263.
Press Information Department: Bhaban 6, Bangladesh Secretariat, Dhaka 1000; tel. (2) 400958; telex 65619.

PUBLISHERS' ASSOCIATIONS

Bangladesh Publishers' and Booksellers' Association: 3rd Floor, 3 Liaquat Ave, Dhaka 1; f. 1972; Pres. JANAB JAHANGIR MOHAMMED ADEL; 2,500 mems.
National Book Centre of Bangladesh: 67A Purana Paltan, Dhaka 1000; f. 1963 to promote the cause of 'more, better and cheaper books'; organizes book fairs, publs a monthly journal; Dir FAZLE RABBI.

Radio and Television

In 1986 there were an estimated 551,000 licensed radio receivers and 369,000 television receivers in use.

National Broadcasting Authority: NBA House, Shahbag Ave, Dhaka; tel. (2) 503342; telex 642228; f. 1984 by merger of Radio Bangladesh and Bangladesh Television; Chair. SAIFUL BARI.

Radio Bangladesh: f. 1971; govt-controlled; regional stations at Chittagong, Dhaka, Khulna, Lalma, Rajshahi, Rangpur and Sylhet broadcast a total of 90 hours 35 minutes daily; external service broadcasts 10 programmes daily in Arabic, Bengali, English, Hindi, Nepalese and Urdu; Chair. and Dir-Gen. ENAMUL HUQ.

Bangladesh Television (BTV): POB 456, Rampura, Dhaka 1219; tel. (2) 400131; telex 65624; f. 1971; govt-controlled; colour transmissions from 1980; daily broadcasts on one channel from Dhaka station for 7 hours; transmissions also from relay stations at Chittagong, Khulna, Mymensingh, Natore, Noakhali, Rangpur, Satkhira, Sylhet, Cox's Bazar and Rangamati were opened between 1975 and 1983; Chair. SAIFUL BARI; Gen. Man. MOSTAFA KAMAL SYED.

Finance

(cap. = capital; p.u. = paid up; res = reserves; dep. = deposits; m. = million; brs = branches; amounts in taka)

BANKING

Central Bank

Bangladesh Bank: Motijheel C/A, POB 325, Dhaka 1000; tel. (2) 235000; telex 65657; f. 1971; cap. p.u. 30m., total assets 71,563m., dep. 33,782m. (Dec. 1987); Gov. and Chair. SHEGUFTA BAKHT CHAUDHURI; Dep. Govs MAHBUBUR RAHMAN KHAN, A. S. M. FAKHRUL AHSAN; 7 brs.

Nationalized Commercial Banks

Agrani Bank: 9D Dilkusha C/A, Motijheel, POB 531, Dhaka 1000; tel. (2) 250906; telex 642757; f. 1972; cap. and res 114m., dep. 23,811m. (Dec. 1987); Chair. IMAMUDDIN AHMED CHAUDHURY; Man. Dir HUMAYUN HAMID; 851 brs.
Janata Bank: 110 Motijheel C/A, Motijheel, POB 468, Dhaka 1000; tel. (2) 236216; telex 65840; f. 1972; cap. and res 154.2m., dep. 24,103m. (Dec. 1987); Chair. Brig. (retd) M. RAHMAN MAJUMDAR; Man. Dir M. AHSANUL HAQUE; 878 brs.
Rupali Bank Ltd: Rupali Bhaban, 34 Dilkusha C/A, POB 719, Dhaka 1000; tel. (2) 256021; telex 65635; f. 1972; cap. and res 334.9m., dep. 13,851.3m. (Dec. 1987); Chair. F. M. EHSANUL KABIR CHOWDHURY; Man. Dir QAZI BAHARUL ISLAM; 508 brs.
Sonali Bank: Motijheel C/A, POB 147, Dhaka 1000; tel. (2) 252990; telex 642644; f. 1972; cap. and res 317.6m., dep. 39,629.2m. (Dec. 1987); Chair. M. KERAMAT ALI; Man. Dir M. M. NURUL HAQUE; 1,262 brs.

In 1985 the Government announced a phased divestment of 49% of the shares of the Agrani, Janata and Rupali Banks. The Sonali Bank has remained under full government ownership.

Private Commercial Banks

Al Baraka Bank Bangladesh Ltd: Dhaka; f. 1987 on Islamic banking principles; 70% owned by private Saudi Arabian interests, 12% by Bangladesh investors and 5% by Bangladesh govt; cap. p.u. 150m. (1988).
Arab Bangladesh Bank Ltd: BCIC Bhaban, 30-31 Dilkusha C/A, POB 3522, Dhaka 1000; tel. (2) 281193; telex 642520; f. 1982 as first jt-venture Bangladeshi private sector commercial bank; cap. and res 136.7m., dep. 2,809.4m. (Dec. 1987); Chair. M. MORSHED KHAN; Man. Dir A. K. M. GHAFFAR; 24 brs.
City Bank Ltd: 1A Dilkusha C/A, POB 3381, Dhaka 1000; tel. (2) 235071; telex 642581; f. 1983; cap. and res 74.2m., dep. 1,780.4m. (Dec. 1987); Chair. M. A. HASHEM; Man. Dir M. ALTAFUR RAHMAN; 24 brs.
International Finance Investment and Credit Bank (IFICB): BSB Bldg, 17th-19th Floors, 8 DIT Ave, POB 2229, Dhaka 1000; tel. (2) 243020; telex 642703; f. 1983; cap. and res 177.8m., dep. 3,722.1m. (Dec. 1987); Chair. JAHURUL ISLAM; Man. Dir M. FAZLUR RAHMAN; 26 brs.
Islamic Bank of Bangladesh Ltd (IBB): 71 Dilkusha C/A, POB 233, Dhaka 1000; tel. (2) 252921; telex 642525; f. 1983 on Islamic banking principles; cap. and res 128.9m., dep. 2,419.7m. (Dec. 1987); Chair. Cdre (retd) M. ATAUR RAHMAN; Man. Dir M. AZIZUL HAQ (acting); 22 brs.
National Bank Ltd: 18 Dilkusha C/A, POB 3838, Dhaka 1000; tel. (2) 235056; telex 642791; f. 1983; cap. and res 213.5m., dep. 4,031.2m. (Dec. 1987); Chair. Dr AZIZUR RAHMAN MALLICK; Man. Dir R. A. HOWLADAR; 43 brs.
Pubali Bank Ltd: Pubali Bank Bhaban, 26 Dilkusha C/A, POB 853, Dhaka 1000; tel. (2) 251781; telex 65844; f. 1972; cap. and res 162.8m., dep. 7,141.1m. (Dec. 1987); Chair. EMADUDDIN AHMED CHOWDHURY; Man. Dir Sk. AMINUL ISLAM; 363 brs.
United Commercial Bank Ltd: 60 Motijheel C/A, POB 2653, Dhaka 1000; tel. (2) 235075; telex 642733; f. 1983; cap. and res 103.5m., dep. 2,360.6m. (Dec. 1987); Chair. S. M. SHAFIUL AZAM; Man. Dir S. A. SHAKOOR; 33 brs.
Uttara Bank: 94 Motijheel C/A, POB 818, Dhaka 1000; tel. (2) 231162; telex 642915; f. 1965; cap. and res 236.8m., dep. 6,065.5m. (Aug. 1988); Chair. Dr SYEDA FEROZA BEGUM; Man. Dir Dr A. K. M. SYEDUR RAHMAN; 185 brs.

Foreign Banks

American Express Bank Ltd (USA): ALICO Bldg, 18-20 Motijheel C/A, POB 420, Dhaka 1000; tel. (2) 238351; telex 65618; f. 1966; dep. 2,142m. (Dec. 1987); Gen. Man. DENNIS REYNARD; 5 brs.
Bank of Credit and Commerce International (Overseas) Ltd (Cayman Islands): Jiban Bima Bhaban, Dilkusha C/A, POB 896, Dhaka 1000; tel. (2) 236360; telex 65615; f. 1976; CEO M. A. RASHID; 3 brs.
Banque Indosuez (France): 47 Motijheel C/A, POB 3490, Dhaka 1000; tel. (2) 238285; telex 642438; f. 1981; dep. 1,807m. (Dec. 1987); Man. (Bangladesh) MARC DUMETZ; Jt Gen. Man. D. DAS GUPTA; 3 brs.
Grindlays Bank PLC (UK): 2 Dilkusha C/A, POB 502, Dhaka 1000; tel. (2) 230225; telex 642597; f. 1905; Gen. Man. A. J. COOPER; 9 brs.
Habib Bank Ltd (Pakistan): 53 Motijheel C/A, POB 201, Dhaka 1000; tel. (2) 235091; telex 65772; f. 1976; Vice-Pres. and Man. HABIB H. MIRZA; 1 br.
Standard Chartered Bank (UK): ALICO Bldg, 18-20 Motijheel C/A, POB 536, Dhaka 1000; tel. (2) 231046; telex 65859; f. 1966; cap. and res 71.1m., dep. 769m. (Dec. 1987); Chair. and Man. Dir RODNEY GALPIN; 2 brs.
State Bank of India: 24-25 Dilkusha C/A, POB 981, Dhaka 1000; tel. (2) 253914; telex 642431; f. 1975; cap. p.u. 8m., dep. 97m. (Dec. 1987); Man. Dir P. GANGULY; 1 br.

DEVELOPMENT FINANCE ORGANIZATIONS

Bangladesh House Building Finance Corpn (BHBFC): HBFC Bldg, 22 Purana Paltan, POB 2167, Dhaka 1000; tel. (2) 415315; f. 1952; provides low-interest credit for house-building; cap. and res 125.7m., dep. 127.1m. (Dec. 1987); 5 zonal offices and 13 regional offices; Chair. HASHIMUDDIN AHMED; Man. Dir KHAWJA ZAHURUL HAQ; 20 brs.

BANGLADESH

Bangladesh Krishi Bank: 83–85 Motijheel C/A, POB 357, Dhaka 1000; tel. (2) 240031; telex 642526; f. 1961; provides credit for agricultural and rural devt; cap. and res 953.7m., dep. 5,247.2m. (June 1988); Chair. Maj.-Gen. (retd) MAHABBAT JAN CHOWDHURY; Man. Dir Dr A. M. M. SHAWKAT ALI; 823 brs.

Bangladesh Samabaya Bank Ltd (BSBL): 'Samabaya Sadan', 9D Motijheel C/A, POB 505, Dhaka 1000; tel. (2) 231129; f. 1948; provides credit for agricultural co-operatives; cap. and res 210.6m., dep. 20.2m. (Dec. 1987); Chair. MUHAMMAD HASAN UDDIN SARKER; Man. Dir MUHAMMAD NAZRUL ISLAM.

Bangladesh Shilpa Bank (BSB) (Industrial Development Bank): Shilpa Bank Bhaban, 8 DIT Ave, POB 975, Dhaka; tel. (2) 235151; telex 642950; f. 1972; fmrly Industrial Devt Bank; provides finance for industrial devt; cap. and res 1,503.3m., dep. 893.4m. (Dec. 1987); Chair. K. M. RABBANI; Man. Dir Dr MUHIUDDIN KHAN ALAMGIR; 13 brs.

Bangladesh Shilpa Rin Sangstha (BSRS) (Industrial Loan Agency): 5th–7th Floors, BIWTA Bhaban, 141–143 Motijheel C/A, POB 473, Dhaka 1000; tel. (2) 252016; f. 1972; cap. and res 1,077.3m., dep. 14.2m. (Dec. 1987); Chair. MIR ATAUL HOQUE KHANDKER; Man. Dir M. SEKANDAR ALI; 4 brs.

Grameen Bank: Mirpur-2, Dhaka 1210; tel. (2) 381138; telex 642601; f. 1983; provides credit for the landless rural poor; cap. p.u. 72m., dep. 244m. (July 1988); Chair. Prof. IQBAL MAHMOOD; Man. Dir Dr MUHAMMAD YUNUS; 460 brs.

Investment Corpn of Bangladesh (ICB): BSB Bldg, 12th–14th Floors, 8 Rajuk Ave, POB 2058, Dhaka 1000; tel. (2) 254112; f. 1976; provides devt financing; cap. and res 345.4m. (Dec. 1987); Chair. Maj.-Gen. (retd) M. A. MATIN; Man. Dir GHIASUDDIN AHMED; 5 brs.

STOCK EXCHANGE

Dhaka Stock Exchange: Dhaka; f. 1960; 91 mems.

INSURANCE

Department of Insurance (attached to Ministry of Commerce): 74 Motijheel C/A, Dhaka 1000; state-owned; controls activities of all insurers, home and foreign; Controller of Insurance SHAMSUDDIN AHMAD.

In 1973 the two corporations below were formed, one for life insurance and the other for general insurance.

Jiban Bima Corpn: 24 Motijheel C/A, Dhaka 1000; tel. (2) 232047; state-owned; comprises 36 national life insurance cos; life insurance; Man. Dir M. A. RAHIM.

Shadharan Bima Corpn: 33 Dilkusha C/A, Dhaka 1000; tel. (2) 252026; state-owned; general insurance; Man. Dir M. SHAMSUL ALAM.

Trade and Industry

In 1972 the Government took over all cotton, jute and other major industrial enterprises and the tea estates. Management Boards were appointed by the Government. During 1976 and 1977 many tea plantations and the smaller industrial units were returned to the private sector. Further privatization, particularly in the jute and textile industries, was carried out in 1982. By 1986 the proportion of the country's industrial assets under government ownership had fallen to 45% (from 85% in 1972).

Export Promotion Bureau: 122–124 Motijheel C/A, Dhaka 1000; tel. (2) 230500; telex 642204; f. 1972; attached to Ministry of Commerce; regional offices in Chittagong, Khulna and Rajshahi; brs in Comilla, Sylhet, Bogra and Barisal; Vice-Chair. RUHUL AMIN MAJUMDER.

Planning Commission: Planning Commission Secretariat, G.O. Hostel, Sher-e-Bangla Nagar, Dhaka; f. 1972; govt agency responsible for all aspects of economic planning and development including the preparation of the five-year plans and annual development programmes (in conjunction with appropriate govt ministries), promotion of savings and investment, compilation of statistics and evaluation of development schemes and projects.

GOVERNMENT-SPONSORED ORGANIZATIONS

Bangladesh Chemical Industries Corpn: Shilpa Bhaban, 2nd Floor, Motijheel C/A, Dhaka 1000; tel. (2) 231954; telex 65847; Chair. A. K. M. MOSHARRAF HOSSAIN.

Bangladesh Export Processing Zones Authority: 222 New Eskaton Rd, Dhaka 1000; tel. (2) 405032; telex 642268; f. 1983 to operate and control export processing zones in Bangladesh; Chair. Brig. (retd) A. K. M. AZIZUL ISLAM.

Bangladesh Fisheries Development Corpn: 24/25 Dilkusha C/A, Motijheel, Dhaka 1000; tel. (2) 259190; telex 255518; f. 1964; Chair. Brig. (retd) SIRAJUL HAQUE.

Bangladesh Forest Industries Development Corpn: 186 Circular Rd, Motijheel C/A, Dhaka 1000; Chair. M. ATIKULLAH.

Bangladesh Jute Mills Corpn: Adamjee Court, 4th Floor, Motijheel C/A, Dhaka 1000; tel. (2) 238192; telex 65676; f. 1972; operates 35 jute mills with over 15,808 looms (there are also 35 mills in the private sector); Chair. SYED AHMED.

Bangladesh Mineral Exploration and Development Corpn: HBFC Bldg, 8th–9th Floors, 22 Purana Paltan, Dhaka 1000; telex 65737; Chair. M. W. ALI.

Bangladesh Oil, Gas and Mineral Corpn (Petrobangla): 122–124 Motijheel C/A, Chamber Bldg, Dhaka 1000; tel. (2) 253131; telex 725; Chair. ABDUS SATTAR (acting).

Bangladesh Small and Cottage Industries Corpn (BSCIC): 137/138 Motijheel C/A, Dhaka 1000; tel. (2) 233202; f. 1957; Chair. MUHAMMAD SIRAJUDDIN.

Bangladesh Steel and Engineering Corpn: Bangladesh Steel House, Airport Rd, Kawran Bazar, Dhaka; tel. (2) 315145; telex 642225; Chair. NEFAUR RAHMAN.

Bangladesh Sugar and Food Industries Corpn: Shilpa Bhaban, Motijheel C/A, Dhaka 1000; tel. (2) 258084; telex 642210; f. 1972; Chair. M. NEFAUR RAHMAN.

Bangladesh Textile Mills Corpn: Shadharan Bima Bhaban, 33 Dilkusha C/A, Dhaka 1000; tel. (2) 252504; telex 65703; f. 1972; Chair. M. NURUNNABI CHOWDHURY.

Trading Corpn of Bangladesh: HBFC Bldg, 22 Purana Paltan, Dhaka 1000; telex 642217; f. 1972; Chair. A. K. M. AZIZUL ISLAM.

CHAMBERS OF COMMERCE

Federation of Bangladesh Chambers of Commerce and Industry: 60 Motijheel C/A, 4th Floor, POB 2079, Dhaka 1000; tel. (2) 282880; telex 642418; f. 1973; Pres. M. A. SATTAR.

Agrabad Chamber of Commerce and Industry: Chamber Bldg, Bangabandhu Rd, POB 70, Chittagong; tel. (2) 501031; Pres. L. D. B. BRYCESON.

Barisal Chamber of Commerce and Industry: Asad Mansion, 1st Floor, Sadar Rd, Barisal; tel. (2) 3984; Pres. KAZI ISRAIL HOSSAIN.

Bogra Chamber of Commerce and Industry: Raja Bazar, Bogra; tel. (51) 6257; f. 1963; Pres. TAHER UDDIN CHOWDHURY.

Chittagong Chamber of Commerce and Industry: Chamber House, Agrabad C/A, POB 481, Chittagong; tel. (31) 502325; telex 66472; f. 1959; 3,516 mems; Pres. AMIR KHOSRU MAHMUD CHOWDHURY; Sec. M. H. CHOWDHURY.

Comilla Chamber of Commerce and Industry: Rammala Rd, Ranir Bazar, Comilla; tel. (2) 5444; Pres. AFZAL KHAN.

Dhaka Chamber of Commerce and Industry: Dhaka Chamber Bldg, 65–66 Motijheel C/A, POB 2641, Dhaka 1000; tel. (2) 234383; telex 642418; f. 1958; 5,000 mems; Pres. A. S. MAHMUD; Sr Vice-Pres. A. M. MUBASH-SHAR.

Dinajpur Chamber of Commerce and Industry: Jail Rd, Dinajpur; tel. (2) 3189; Pres. KHAIRUL ANAM.

Faridpur Chamber of Commerce and Industry: Chamber House, Niltuly, Faridpur; tel. (2) 3530; Pres. KHANDOKER MOHSIN ALI.

Khulna Chamber of Commerce and Industry: 6 Lower Jessore Rd, Khulna; tel. (41) 24135; f. 1934; Pres. S. K. ZAHOIUL ISLAM.

Khustia Chamber of Commerce and Industry: 15, NS Rd, Khustia; tel. (2) 3448; Pres. DIN MOHAMMAD.

Metropolitan Chamber of Commerce and Industry: Chamber Bldg, 4th Floor, 122–124 Motijheel C/A, Dhaka 1000; tel. (2) 257614; telex 642413; f. 1904; 238 mems; Pres. HABIBULLAH KHAN; Sec. C. K. HYDER.

Noakhali Chamber of Commerce and Industry: Noakhali Pourshara Bhaban, 2nd Floor, Maiydee Court, Noakhali; tel. (2) 5229; Pres. MOHAMMAD NAZIBUR RAHMAN.

Rajshahi Chamber of Commerce and Industry: Chamber Bldg, Station Rd, Ghoramara; tel. (2) 2215; f. 1960; 48 mems; Pres. MESBAHUDDIN AHMED.

Sylhet Chamber of Commerce and Industry: POB 97, Chamber Bldg, Jail Rd, Sylhet; Admin. ABDUL KHALEQUE KHAN.

TRADE ASSOCIATIONS

Bangladeshiyo Cha Sangsad (Tea Asscn of Bangladesh): 6 Jahan Bldg, 2nd Floor, 93 Agrabad C/A, POB 287, Chittagong; tel. (31) 501009; f. 1952; Chair. AHMADUL KABIR; Sec. M. A. H. AL-AZAD.

Bangladesh Jute Association: BJA Bldg, 137 Banga Bandhu Rd, POB 59, Narayanganj, Dhaka; tel. (2) 72193; Chair. Capt. (retd) M. S. ALI; Sec. ABUL FAZL CHOWDHURY.

Bangladesh Jute Goods Association: 3rd Floor, 150 Motijheel C/A, Dhaka 1000; tel. (2) 253640; f. 1979; 17 mems; Chair. M. A. KASHEM, Haji MOHAMMAD ALI.

Bangladesh Jute Mills Association: 8th Floor, Hadi Mansion, 2 Dilkusha C/A, Dhaka 1000; tel. (2) 253279; Chair. SYED MOHSEN ALI.

Bangladesh Jute Spinners Association: 55 Purana Paltan, 3rd Floor, Dhaka; tel. (2) 282566; telex 642413; f. 1979; 29 mems; Chair. MOHAMMAD SHAMS-UL HAQUE; Sec. AHMED JAMAL.

Bangladesh Tea Board: 111/113 Motijheel C/A, Dhaka 1000; telex 642208; Chair. QUAMRUL HUDA.

Jute Marketing and Export Corporation: 14 Topkhana Rd, Dhaka; tel. (2) 236090; Chair. MUSTAFIZUR RAHMAN.

CO-OPERATIVES

Bangladesh Co-operative Marketing Society: 9D Motijheel C/A, Dhaka 1000.

Chattagram Bahini Kalyan Shamabaya Samity Ltd: 70 Agrabad C/A, Osman Court, Chittagong; f. 1972.

TRADE UNIONS

The ban on trade union activity was lifted in January 1986. Anti-government strikes were banned in November 1987.

In 1986 only about 3% of the total labour force was unionized. There were 2,614 registered unions, organized mainly on a sectoral or occupational basis. There were about 17 national trade unions to represent workers at the national level.

Transport

RAILWAYS

Bangladesh Railway: Railway HQ, Chittagong; tel. (31) 500120; telex 66200; supervised by the Railway Division of the Ministry of Communications; divided into East and West zones, with HQ at Chittagong and Rajshahi (tel. 2576); total length of track 4,550.9 km (1985); Dir-Gen. (Railway Div.) S. HASAN AHMAD; Gen. Man. (East Zone) M. MATIUR RAHMAN; Gen. Man. (West Zone) A. K. M. ZAINUL ABEDIN; Gen. Man. (Projects) A. K. M. AMANUL ISLAM CHOWDHURY.

ROADS

Of the 6,240 km of road, about 3,840 km are metalled. More than 3,500 km of road and 250 bridges were destroyed in the disastrous monsoon floods in 1988.

Bangladesh Road Transport Corpn: Paribhaban, DIT Ave, Dhaka; f. 1961; transportation services including a truck division, transports govt foodgrain; 700 vehicles (1980).

INLAND WATERWAYS

In Bangladesh there are some 8,430 km of navigable waterways, which transport 70% of total domestic and foreign cargo traffic and on which are located the main river ports of Dhaka, Narayanganj, Chandpur, Barisal and Khulna. A river steamer service connects these ports several times a week. Vessels of up to 175-m overall length can be navigated on the Karnaphuli river.

Bangladesh Inland Water Transport Corpn: 5 Dilkusha C/A, Dhaka 1000; tel. (2) 257092; f. 1972; 273 vessels (1986).

SHIPPING

The chief ports are Chittagong, where the construction of a second dry-dock is planned, and Chalna. A modern seaport is being developed at Mangla.

Atlas Shipping Lines Ltd: Jiban Bima Bhaban, S. K. Mujib Rd, Agrabad, Chittagong 2; tel. (31) 504287; telex 66213; Man. Dir S. U. CHOWDHURY; Man. SHAHADAT HOSSAIN.

Bangladesh Shipping Corpn: Pine View, 100 Agrabad C/A, POB 641, Chittagong; tel. (31) 501855; telex 66277; f. 1972; maritime shipping; 21 vessels, 270,153 tons capacity (1987); Chair. JANAB M. KORBAN ALI; Man. Dir TARECK ANIS AHMED.

Bangladesh Steam Navigation Co Ltd: Red Cross Bldg, 87 Motijheel C/A, Dhaka 1000; coastal services; Chair. A. K. KHAN; Man. Dir A. M. Z. KHAN.

Chittagong Port Authority: POB 2013, Chittagong; tel. (31) 500101; telex 66264; provides bunkering and lighterage facilities as well as provisions and drinking water supplies.

United Shipping Corpn Ltd: 4th Floor, Parachi Bldg, 54 Dilkusha C/A, POB 755, Dhaka 2; tel. (2) 24565; telex 65749.

CIVIL AVIATION

There is an international airport at Dhaka (Zia International Airport) situated at Kurmitola and opened in 1980, with the capacity to handle 5m. passengers annually. There are also airports at all major towns.

Bangladesh Biman (Bangladesh Airlines): Biman Bhaban, Motijheel C/A, Dhaka 1000; tel. (2) 255911; telex 626649; f. 1972; 100% state-owned; internal services to all major towns; international services to Bahrain, Bhutan, Burma, Greece, India, Italy, Kuwait, Libya, Malaysia, Nepal, the Netherlands, Oman, Pakistan, Qatar, Saudi Arabia, Singapore, Thailand, the UAE and the United Kingdom; Chair. Minister of Civil Aviation and Tourism; Man. Dir MUHAMMAD FAIZUR RAZZAQUE; fleet of 3 F-27, 2 F-28, 4 Boeing 707-320C and 3 DC 10-30.

Tourism

Tourist attractions include the cities of Dhaka and Chittagong, Cox's Bazar—which has the world's longest beach (120 km)—on the Bay of Bengal, and Teknaf, at the southernmost point of Bangladesh. Tourist arrivals totalled 106,765 in 1987. The majority of visitors are from India, Japan, the United Kingdom and the USA. Earnings from tourism increased from 230m. taka in 1981 to 900m. taka in 1985.

Bangladesh Parjatan Corpn (National Tourist Organization): 233 Airport Rd, Tejgaon, Dhaka 15; tel. (2) 325155; telex 642206; there are two tourist information centres in Dhaka, and one each in Bogra, Chittagong, Cox's Bazar, Khulna, Rajshahi, Rangamati; Chair. Col (retd) SYED SHAHABUDDIN AHMED; Man. S. KUTUBUDDIN AHMED.

Atomic Energy

Bangladesh Atomic Energy Commission (BAEC): 7 Kazi Nazrul Islam Ave, POB 158, Dhaka 1000; tel. (2) 505021; f. 1965 as Atomic Energy Centre of the fmr Pakistan Atomic Energy Comm. in East Pakistan, reorg. 1973; operates an atomic energy research establishment and a nuclear reactor (inaugurated in January 1987) at Savar, an atomic energy centre at Dhaka, six nuclear medicine centres at Chittagong, Dhaka, Dinajpur, Rajshahi and Sylhet, a beach-sand exploitation centre at Cox's Bazar and a nuclear power project involving the exploitation of uranium and thorium; construction to begin by late 1988 of a 320-MW nuclear power plant at Rooppur, with tech. assistance from Fed. Repub. of Germany; Chair. (vacant); Sec. ABU NAIM AHMED.

BARBADOS

Introductory Survey

Location, Climate, Language, Religion, Flag, Capital
Barbados is the most easterly of the Caribbean islands, lying about 320 km (200 miles) north-east of Trinidad. There is a rainy season from July to November and the climate is cool during the rest of the year. The mean annual temperature is about 26°C (78°F). The language is English. Almost all of the inhabitants profess Christianity but there are small groups of Hindus, Muslims and Jews. The majority of the population are Anglicans but about 90 other Christian denominations are represented. The national flag (proportions 3 by 2) has three equal vertical stripes, of blue, gold and blue; superimposed on the centre of the gold band is the head of a black trident. The capital is Bridgetown.

Recent History
Barbados was formerly a British colony. The Barbados Labour Party (BLP) won a general election in 1951, when universal adult suffrage was introduced, and held office until 1961. Although the parliamentary system dates from 1639, ministerial government was not established until 1954, when the BLP's leader, Sir Grantley Adams, became the island's first Premier. He was subsequently Prime Minister of the West Indies Federation from January 1958 until its dissolution in May 1962.

Barbados achieved full internal self-government in October 1961. An election in December 1961 was won by the Democratic Labour Party (DLP), formed in 1955 by dissident members of the BLP. The DLP's leader, Errol Barrow, became Premier, succeeding Dr Hugh Cummins of the BLP. When Barbados achieved independence on 30 November 1966, Barrow became the island's first Prime Minister, having won another election earlier in the month.

The DLP retained power in 1971 but in the general election of September 1976 the BLP, led by J. M. G. M. ('Tom') Adams (Sir Grantley's son), ended Barrow's 15-year rule. The BLP successfully campaigned against alleged government corruption, winning a large majority over the DLP. Both parties were committed to retaining a system of free enterprise and alignment with the USA. At a general election in June 1981 the BLP was returned to office, owing mainly to its economic achievements in government, with 17 of the 27 seats in the newly enlarged House of Assembly. The remainder of the seats were won by the DLP. A Cabinet reshuffle took place in early 1983, and in September the Minister of Health, Dr Donald Blackman, left the Cabinet following allegations that he had publicly criticized a fellow Minister. There was also disagreement between the Government and the opposition concerning the amount spent on defence. Adams died suddenly in March 1985 and was succeeded as Prime Minister by his deputy, Bernard St John, a former leader of the BLP.

At a general election in May 1986 the DLP won a decisive victory, receiving 59.4% of the total votes and winning 24 of the 27 seats in the House of Assembly. Bernard St John and all but one of his Cabinet Ministers lost their seats, and Errol Barrow returned as Prime Minister after 10 years in opposition. The new Government later introduced a programme of tax reforms, which was intended to reduce spending and borrowing by the public sector. Emphasizing the Government's policy of job creation, a new Ministry of Employment was established, and a comprehensive employment survey was begun, with technical assistance from the OAS (see p. 190). In June 1986 it was announced that Barrow was to review Barbados' participation in the US-supported Regional Security System (RSS), the defence force that had been established soon after the US invasion of Grenada in October 1983. Barbados, under Adams, was one of the countries whose troops supported the invasion. In November 1986 Barrow announced a halt in recruitment to the Barbados Defence Force. In June 1987 Barrow died suddenly. He was succeeded by L. Erskine Sandiford (hitherto the Deputy Prime Minister), who pledged to continue Barrow's economic and social policies.

In September 1987, however, the Minister of Finance, Richie Haynes, resigned, accusing Sandiford of failing to consult him over financial appointments. Sandiford assumed the financial portfolio, but acrimony over government policy continued to trouble the DLP into 1988. The budget proposals for the financial year 1988/89, announced in April 1988, renewed controversy, both inside and outside the ruling party. Economic concerns had prompted reductions in planned expenditure and, reversing previous policy, an increase in taxes.

Relations with Trinidad and Tobago were strained between 1982 and 1985 by publicly-stated differences over the intervention in Grenada, and by Trinidad's imposition of import restrictions (a compromise on this was reached in August 1986). In May 1988 talks were held with Trinidad to resolve a fishing dispute. In 1988 relations with Jamaica were strained over the approach to events in Haiti, and the Barbadian pressure for closer integration within CARICOM (see p. 106). Moves towards a Caribbean internal market continued, despite political differences and trade tensions with the OECS (see p. 107) in late 1987. In June 1988 import duties were abolished for all but four CARICOM countries.

Government
Executive power is vested in the British monarch, represented by a Governor-General, who acts on the advice of the Cabinet. The Governor-General appoints the Prime Minister and, on the latter's recommendation, other members of the Cabinet. Legislative power is vested in the bicameral Parliament, comprising a Senate of 21 members, appointed by the Governor-General, and a House of Assembly with 27 members, elected by universal adult suffrage for five years (subject to dissolution) from single-member constituencies. The Cabinet is responsible to Parliament. Elected local government bodies were abolished in 1969 in favour of a division into 11 parishes, all of which are administered by the central government.

Defence
The Barbados Defence Force, established in April 1978, consists of 154 regular personnel. It is divided into regular defence units and a coastguard service with armed patrol boats; there is also a volunteer force and a reserve. Government spending on defence in the 1987/88 financial year was Bds $21.3m., representing 2.8% of total budget expenditure.

Economic Affairs
Traditionally, the economy of Barbados was based mainly on the cultivation of sugar cane and related activities, including the production of raw sugar, rum and molasses. In recent times, the island's economy has become diversified, so reducing the importance of sugar. Services, particularly tourism, are now the leading source of employment in Barbados, while exports of manufactured goods have overtaken agricultural exports in value. In 1987, according to estimates by the World Bank, the island's gross national product (GNP), measured at average 1985–87 prices, was US $1,358m., equivalent to $5,330 per head. Between 1980 and 1987, it was estimated, GNP per head increased, in real terms, at an average rate of 0.4% per year.

After independence, the island's output of cane sugar fell steadily. In the late 1970s depressed world prices and increasing costs contributed to the industry's difficulties, which were compounded in 1983 by smut disease. By 1984 the contribution of the sugar industry to gross domestic product (GDP) was only 2.8%. In 1985 raw sugar output of 100,247 tons was heavily subsidized. The 1986 harvest produced 111,149 tons. In December 1986 the US Government announced that its 1987 quota for imports of Barbadian sugar was to be 7,500 tons, 40% lower than in 1986. The area under sugar cane cultivation was reduced from 32,000 acres (12,950 ha) in 1986 to 25,000 acres (10,117 ha) in 1987. Exceptionally dry weather reduced 1987 output to 83,431 tons, more than 7% below target and the lowest annual total since 1948. Sugar export earnings of Bds $68m., however, were slightly higher than in 1986, as the export price per ton had increased. For 1988 the USA again reduced its quota, only to revise it in July to 8,205 tons, making it the first increase on the previous annual quota for some years. The EEC quota of 54,400 tons remained unchanged. Continued labour shortages and a late crop resulted in a further decline in raw sugar output in 1988, to about 80,000 tons, nearly 10% below the target level. The closure of two sugar factories was announced in July 1988. Exports of rum totalled Bds $8m. in 1985 (Bds $2m. more than in 1984, helped by a bulk shipment to the United Kingdom), then rose to Bds $8.8m. in 1986, before declining to Bds $7m. in 1987.

Owing to volatile fluctuations in the international price of sugar on the free market, the Barbados Government has encouraged a policy of agricultural diversification. A rural development project, announced in 1980, invested Bds $5m. in agro-industries, and in February 1987 the World Bank announced that it was to provide a loan of US $4m. for a project designed to improve the diversity and viability of the agricultural sector. Supplementary crops have been planted, most of them in rotation with sugar.

Sea-island cotton, the island's original export crop, has been revived, with 754 acres (305 ha) under cultivation in 1985/86 and 1,050 acres (425 ha) planted for the 1986/87 crop. Output of cotton lint increased from 128 metric tons in the 1985/86 season to 161 tons in 1986/87, but the latter total represented only about one-half of the annual target. Furthermore, the sharp decline in contractual export prices meant that export receipts were about 25% lower, at US $2.1m. Problems continued for the 1988 harvest, with the poorest yields per acre for five years and production of lint reaching only 119 tons. Later that year, however, a Canadian investor and the Governments of Barbados and the three Eastern Caribbean producers announced a large investment project with the establishment of the Caribbean Sea Island Cotton Company.

Production of maize and groundnuts has increased, although heavy rains at the beginning of 1986 devastated the 1986 groundnut crop. By the end of 1985 the island was virtually self-sufficient in tomatoes, carrots and onions. In 1986 the Government announced a three-year pilot scheme, designed to increase production of fruits such as mango, grapefruit, avocado and papaya. In October 1988, however, strong winds across the Atlantic brought about an infestation by African desert locusts that caused temporary anxiety. A fishing complex, costing Bds $5m., was opened at Oistins in June 1983, as part of an overall plan to modernize the industry and to make Barbados self-sufficient in fish. As a consequence, landings of fish increased from 3,411 metric tons in 1981 to 6,522 tons in 1983. However, adverse weather conditions in subsequent years led to a decline in fish landings, and in 1986 the total catch was only 2,956 tons.

Tourism was greatly affected by the world recession. The steady expansion of the 1960s slowed in the mid-1970s and again between 1980 and 1982. Increased charter business and cheaper flights from the USA helped the industry in 1983, when tourist arrivals rose by 8%, boosted by short-stay visitors from the USA. Although tourism continued to grow in 1984 and between January and April 1985, Barbados experienced one of its worst summer seasons for several years between May and December 1985, with tourist arrivals declining by 13%. However, during 1986 total tourist arrivals increased by 3%, to 369,770, helped by an increase of 23% in the number of visitors from the United Kingdom. Real earnings in the sector were estimated to have fallen by 3% in 1985, to a total of Bds $618m., but increased facilities and improved pricing produced a 6% increase in earnings during 1986. In the 1987 season, real earnings were estimated to have risen by 14% and tourist arrivals reached a record 421,859, as a result of strong growth during the summer season and an increase in the number of visitors from Canada and especially the UK, visitor arrivals from the latter rising by 66%.

In February 1984 the Government disclosed details of a five-year development plan, with emphasis on expansion by the private sector. Government policy is to reduce dependence on tourism and to diversify industry and agriculture, thus forming a more stable, broad-based economy. It has succeeded in attracting light manufacturing industry through tax incentives. However, these industries also suffered the effects of recession in the USA, the main market for their products. The revival of the US economy in 1983 and 1984 helped to boost manufacturing exports, but local sales of clothing and furniture were depressed by the imposition in 1982 of import restrictions by Trinidad and Tobago (the island's main trading partner in the CARICOM region), which reduced its imports by about one-half in 1985, and by the decline of the Jamaican economy. In 1987 an increase in the extra-regional consumption tax on garments helped the sector's ability to compete at home, and prompted growth (of 16%), which continued into 1988. During 1984 production of electronic components increased by 26%, but in 1985 exports fell by 20%, to Bds $301.7m., as a result of a slump in the US computer market and increased competition from Asia. By the end of 1985, four large component assembly plants had been closed, and 1,200 jobs lost. In August 1986 the largest manufacturing enterprise in Barbados, Intel, announced that it was to close, with a loss of 950 jobs and an estimated US $15m. in annual government revenue. Following Intel's closure, exports of electronic components declined by a further 23.5% during 1986, to Bds $230.8m., and by a massive 67% in 1987. This contraction distorted the level of output for the manufacturing sector as a whole, which consequently showed a decline of 9.5% in 1985 and of 6% in 1987, but nevertheless had achieved expansion of 8% during 1986. Among other sectors, growth was particularly strong in food-processing and the manufacture of beverages for the domestic market, and, since 1987, in data-processing (this and the garment sector are the two largest government-assisted industries).

Infrastructure is well-developed in Barbados, and the Government's road-building programme kept the construction industry buoyant through 1987. The completion of the northern access road (at a cost of Bds $52m.) in December 1987 caused a decline in the demand for quarry products, but increased activity in the private housing sector ensured continued growth in the industry as a whole. A cement plant, capable of producing 1,000 tons of clinker per day, which was financed jointly by the governments of Barbados and Trinidad and Tobago, was completed in 1984.

Reserves of petroleum and natural gas have been discovered. In 1983 petroleum was being exploited at the rate of approximately 1,500 barrels per day (b/d). In 1982 the Government purchased facilities for onshore petroleum drilling and production at a cost of US $12m. Output from the Woodbourne field was increased substantially in 1983 and 1984, and in 1985, although the increase in output was more moderate, total production (of 679,000 barrels) satisfied about 50% of the country's oil requirements. In 1986 output declined by 17.7%, to 558,970 barrels, and the Barbados National Oil Co Ltd (BNOCL) reduced its drilling operations by about 40% from mid-year, when a prolonged period of low international petroleum prices made it more economically viable to increase petroleum imports. However, in February 1987 it was announced that production at the Woodbourne field was to be increased by 25%, following a recovery in petroleum prices. The recovery was short-lived, and BNOCL incurred a loss of Bds $4.5m. for the financial year 1986/87, with a 62% fall in revenue from sales of crude petroleum and natural gas. Barbados uses about 1.2m. barrels per year; the Government's aim is to be self-sufficient in petroleum (requiring production of about 4,000 b/d).

After a five-year period of economic growth, real GDP declined by 2.5% in 1981, and by a further 4.4% in 1982, despite stringent economic measures, introduced in 1981, to halt the fall in government revenue and to improve the balance of payments. However, the fall in GDP had been stopped by 1983, and there was a rise of 3.6%, in real terms, in 1984. In 1985 GDP rose by only 1%, but increased government spending and budgetary tax concessions helped to stimulate growth of 5% in 1986 and 2.2% in 1987. In October 1982 the IMF agreed to provide Bds $70m. under a stand-by arrangement in support of a 20-month economic adjustment programme; compensatory financing of Bds $28m. was also approved to offset a reduction in earnings from tourism and sugar exports. After three years of growth averaging 25.5%, the value of total domestic exports declined by about 13% in 1985, by 15.3% in 1986 (to Bds $420.6m.), and to Bds $214.5m. in 1987 (owing mainly to the collapse of the electronic components industry). Retained imports fell by 9% in 1985, to Bds $1,016m., the lowest level in three years, but increased by 4% in 1986, only to fall by 11% in 1987. The trade deficit in 1986 totalled Bds $646.8m., an increase of 26% on the 1985 deficit. In 1987 the trade deficit rose to Bds $722.2m., the largest figure since the record Bds $760.0m. of 1981. Foreign debt repayments increased substantially during 1986 and were equivalent to 8.7% of the total value of exports of goods and services, compared with 3.8% in 1985. In December 1987 the national debt stood at Bds $1,500m.

(more than one-half of which was owed externally), 17% higher than in the previous year. The 1988/89 budget envisaged expenditure of Bds $981.1m.

In 1987 the Government rejected a proposal from the World Bank for a devaluation of the Barbados dollar, claiming that reduced taxation and the rationalization of state enterprises incurring heavy financial losses would improve the country's export competitiveness. At the end of March 1987 the Government suspended scheduled services of the national airline, Caribbean Airways, which, by December 1986, had accumulated liabilities of more than Bds $24m. Unemployment averaged 13.9% of the labour force in 1982, but by December 1985 had risen to 18.2%. The rate declined slightly during 1986, to an average of 17.8%, and remained stable, at an average of 17.9%, in 1987. The average rate of inflation fell from 10.3% in 1982 to 5.3% in 1983, 4.6% in 1984, 3.9% in 1985, and to only 1.3% in 1986. The rate rose to 3.3% in 1987, and reached 6.5% in the year to February 1988.

In 1985 the US Congress approved a Barbados-US Double Taxation Agreement, signed in February 1986, which has led to strong interest in 'offshore' financial facilities in Barbados. Similar agreements with the Nordic countries were under negotiation in 1988. By the end of 1986 there were some 650 companies registered in the offshore sector, including 150 international business companies and 220 foreign sales corporations, and by the end of March 1987 60 insurance firms had opened offices in Bridgetown. There was a particular interest in the establishment of exempt insurance companies, their number more than doubling in a year to 110 by the end of 1987. One new offshore bank was licensed in 1987, bringing the total of such banks to five. During the financial year 1986/87 the sector contributed Bds $5m. to GDP. The unrest in Panama in 1988 was expected to stimulate the offshore sector significantly.

Social Welfare

A social security scheme was established in 1967, and a National Drug Plan, introduced in 1980, is the first stage in a national health service, due to be completed by 1986. Old-age pensions and unemployment insurance are available. The Government has also created a building scheme of group housing for lower-income families. In 1982 Barbados had 11 hospital establishments, with a total of 2,151 beds, and there were 221 physicians working on the island. Government expenditure on health services in the 1987/88 financial year represented 14.7% of current budget spending, while social security and welfare received a further 8.9% of the total.

Education

Education is compulsory for 11 years, between five and 16 years of age. Primary education begins at the age of five and lasts for six years. Secondary education, beginning at 11 years of age, also lasts for six years, divided into two equal cycles. Enrolment of children in the primary age-group was 99% in 1982. The ratio for secondary schoolchildren was 89% in 1984. Tuition at all government schools is free, and the state provides for approximately 86% of those eligible for primary and secondary education. The adult literacy rate was believed to be 98% in 1985. In 1986 there were 126 primary and secondary schools, six senior schools, a community college, a teacher training college, a theological college, a technical institute and a polytechnic. Degree courses in arts, law, education, natural sciences and social sciences are offered at the Barbados branch of the University of the West Indies. The faculty of medicine administers the East Caribbean Medical Scheme, while an in-service training programme for graduate teachers in secondary schools is provided by the School of Education. Government expenditure on education represented 22% of current budget spending in the 1987/88 financial year. In 1986 plans were announced for improvements to the primary and secondary education system, and for expansion of the technical training programme. The project is to be funded by the Inter-American Development Bank, the World Bank and the Government.

Public Holidays

1989: 2 January (for New Year's Day), 24 March (Good Friday), 27 March (Easter Monday), 1 May (May Day), 15 May (Whit Monday), 7 August (Kadooment Day), 7 October (United Nations Day), 30 November (Independence Day), 25–26 December (Christmas).

1990: 1 January (New Year's Day), 13 April (Good Friday), 16 April (Easter Monday), 7 May (May Day), 4 June (Whit Monday), 6 August (Kadooment Day), 7 October (United Nations Day), 30 November (Independence Day), 25–26 December (Christmas).

Weights and Measures

The metric system is used.

Statistical Survey

Sources (unless otherwise stated): Barbados Statistical Service, National Insurance Bldg, Fairchild St, Bridgetown; tel. 427-7841; Central Bank of Barbados, POB 1016, Bridgetown; tel. 436-6870.

AREA AND POPULATION

Area: 430 sq km (166 sq miles).
Population: 252,029 (males 119,665, females 132,364) at census of 12 May 1980; 253,881 (males 119,975, females 133,906) at 31 December 1987 (official estimate).
Density (1987): 590 per sq km.
Principal Town: Bridgetown (capital), population 7,517 at 1980 census.
Births and Deaths (registrations, 1987): Live births 3,839 (birth rate 15.1 per 1,000); Deaths 2,049 (death rate 8.2 per 1,000).
Economically Active Population (labour force sample survey, annual average, '000 persons, excluding institutional households, 1986): Agriculture, forestry and fishing 7.8; Manufacturing 11.6; Electricity, gas and water 2.3; Construction and quarrying 7.9; Trade, restaurants and hotels 20.7; Transport, storage and communications 5.4; Financing, insurance, real estate and business services 3.3; Community, social and personal services 37.2; Total employed 96.2 (males 53.6, females 42.6); Unemployed 20.7 (males 8.0, females 12.7); Total labour force 116.9 (males 61.6, females 55.3).

AGRICULTURE, ETC.

Principal Crops (metric tons, 1985): Roots and tubers 6,000; Vegetables 8,000; Sugar cane (1987) 689,022.

Livestock (FAO estimates, '000 head, year ending September 1986): Cattle 18; Pigs 49; Sheep 55; Goats 33 (Source: FAO, *Production Yearbook*).
Livestock Products (metric tons, 1987): Beef 397; Veal 8; Chicken meat 8,123; Mutton 25; Pig meat 1,296; Cows' milk 11,735; Hen eggs 1,830.
Fishing (metric tons, live weight): Total catch 5,913 in 1984; 3,915 in 1985; 4,227 in 1986 (Source: FAO, *Yearbook of Fishery Statistics*).

MINING

Production: (1987) Natural gas 29.5 million cu m.; Crude petroleum 496,800 barrels.

INDUSTRY

Production: (1987) Raw sugar 83,431 metric tons; Rum 3,146,000 litres; Beer 7,290,000 litres; Cigarettes 163 metric tons; Batteries 14,322; Electric energy 425m. kWh.

FINANCE

Currency and Exchange Rates: 100 cents = 1 Barbados dollar (Bds $). *Coins:* 1, 5, 10 and 25 cents; 1 dollar. *Notes:* 1, 2, 5, 10, 20 and 100 dollars. *Sterling and US Dollar equivalents* (30 September

BARBADOS

Statistical Survey, Directory

1988): £1 sterling = Bds $3.401; US $1 = Bds $2.011; Bds $100 = £29.40 = US $49.72. *Exchange Rate*: Fixed at US $1 = Bds $2.0113 since August 1977.

Current Budget (Bds $ '000, year ending 31 March 1987): *Revenue*: Tax revenue 614,866 (Taxes on income and profit 135,686; Taxes on property 36,058; Taxes on goods and services 220,751; Import duties 116,039); Non-tax revenue 111,855 (Government departments 65,901); Total 726,721. *Expenditure*: General public services 114,028; Defence 21,290; Education 164,824; Health 109,812; Social security and welfare 67,008; Housing and community amenities 38,422; other community and social services 11,055; Economic services 121,991 (Agriculture 19,164; Roads and other transport 67,020); Debt charges 105,584; Total 754,014.

International Reserves (US $ million at 31 December 1987): Gold 3.89; IMF special drawing rights 0.89; Reserve position in IMF 3.08; Foreign exchange 141.24; Total 149.10 (Source: IMF, *International Financial Statistics*).

Money Supply (Bds $ million at 31 December 1987): Currency outside banks 156.64; Demand deposits at commercial banks 278.48 (Source: IMF, *International Financial Statistics*).

Cost of Living (retail price index; base: March 1980 = 100): 149.7 in 1985; 151.2 in 1986; 156.8 in 1987.

Gross Domestic Product (Bds $ million in current purchasers' values): 2,410.0 in 1985; 2,646.0 in 1986; 2,913.7 in 1987.

Balance of Payments (US $ million, 1986): Merchandise exports f.o.b. 244.4; Merchandise imports f.o.b. −522.6; *Trade balance* −278.2; Exports of services 526.6; Imports of services −265.4; *Balance on goods and services* −17.0; Unrequited transfers (net) 11.6; *Current balance* −5.4; Direct capital investment (net) 5.0; Other long-term capital (net) −1.2; Short-term capital (net) 45.8; Net errors and omissions −24.1; *Total (net monetary movements)* 20.1; Valuation changes (net) −0.2; *Changes in reserves* 19.9 (Source: IMF, *International Financial Statistics*).

EXTERNAL TRADE

Principal Commodities (Bds $ '000, 1987): *Imports:* Food and live animals 166,953; Beverages and tobacco 23,687; Crude materials (inedible) except fuels 32,170; Mineral fuels, lubricants, etc. 111,468; Animal and vegetable oils and fats 9,420; Chemicals 107,585; Basic manufactures 186,434; Machinery and transport equipment 250,498; Miscellaneous manufactured articles 122,585; Other commodities and transactions 25,374; Total 1,035,891. *Exports:* Sugar 56,876; Molasses and syrup 5,304; Rum 7,187; Semi-processed and other food products 3,574; Basic manufactures 63,040; Machinery and transport equipment 67,445; Chemicals 33,428; Mineral fuels, lubricants, etc. 58,228; Other items 18,629; Total 313,708.

Principal Trading Partners (Bds $ '000, 1987): *Imports:* Canada 81,283; CARICOM countries 143,271 (Trinidad and Tobago 94,774); Guyana 4,268; Japan 54,476; United Kingdom 120,553; USA 333,552; Total (incl. others) 1,035,891. *Exports:* Canada 13,203; CARICOM countries 74,027 (Trinidad and Tobago 18,938); Guyana 3,094; Puerto Rico 18,883; United Kingdom 55,963; USA 67,608; Total (incl. others) 313,708.

TRANSPORT

Road Traffic (motor vehicles in use, 1986): Passenger cars (incl. hired cars and taxis) 34,850; Pick-ups, vans and station wagons 2,503; Lorries, buses and tractors 2,779; Motor cycles 1,934.

International Shipping (estimated freight traffic, '000 metric tons, 1985): Goods loaded 211; Goods unloaded 460 (Source: UN, *Monthly Bulletin of Statistics*).

Civil Aviation (1987): Aircraft movements 31,600; Freight loaded 4,054.9 metric tons; Freight unloaded 7,741.4 metric tons.

TOURISM

Tourist Arrivals: 359,135 in 1985; 369,770 in 1986; 421,859 in 1987.

COMMUNICATIONS MEDIA

Radio Receivers (1986): 200,000 in use.

Television Receivers (1988): 62,000 in use.

Telephones (1987): 94,338 in use.

Book Production (1983): 87 titles (18 books, 69 pamphlets).

Daily Newspapers (1984): 2 (circulation 40,000) (Source: UNESCO, *Statistical Yearbook*).

EDUCATION

Institutions and Enrolment (1985/86):

Primary: 105 schools, 28,235 students.

Secondary: 21 schools, 21,501 students.

Senior: 6 schools, 1,050 students.

Technical: 1 institution, 1,852 students.

Teacher Training: 1 institution, 87 students.

Theological: 1 institution, 20 students.

Community College: 1 institution, 1,750 students.

University of the West Indies: 1 institution, 1,932 students.

There are also 15 government-aided independent schools and 23 non-aided independent schools, with 4,311 and 3,586 students respectively in 1985/86.

Directory

The Constitution

The Constitution came into force on 30 November 1966, when Barbados became independent. Under its terms, protection is afforded to individuals from slavery and forced labour, from inhuman treatment, deprivation of property, arbitrary search and entry, and racial discrimination; freedom of conscience, of expression, assembly, and movement are guaranteed.

Executive power is nominally vested in the British monarch, as Head of State, represented in Barbados by a Governor-General, who appoints the Prime Minister and, on the advice of the Prime Minister, appoints other Ministers and some Senators.

The Cabinet consists of the Prime Minister, appointed by the Governor-General as being the person best able to command a majority in the House of Assembly, and not fewer than five other Ministers. Provision is also made for a Privy Council, presided over by the Governor-General.

Parliament consists of two houses, the Senate and the House of Assembly. The Senate has 21 members, 12 appointed by the Governor-General on the advice of the Prime Minister, two on the advice of the Leader of the Opposition, and seven as representatives of such interests as the Governor-General considers appropriate. The House of Assembly has (since 1981) 27 members, elected by universal adult suffrage for a term of five years (subject to dissolution). The minimum voting age is 18.

The Constitution also provides for the establishment of Service Commissions for the Judicial and Legal Service, the Public Service, the Police Service and the Statutory Boards Service. These Commissions are exempt from legal investigation; they have executive powers to deal with appointments, dismissals and disciplinary control of the services for which they are responsible.

The Government

Head of State: HM Queen ELIZABETH II.

Governor-General: Sir HUGH SPRINGER (took office 24 February 1984).

THE CABINET
(November 1988)

Prime Minister and Minister of Economic Affairs and Finance: L. ERSKINE SANDIFORD.

Deputy Prime Minister and Minister of International Transport, Telecommunications and Immigration: PHILIP M. GREAVES.

Attorney-General and Minister of Legal Affairs: MAURICE A. KING.

Minister of Health: BRANDFORD M. TAITT.

Minister of Foreign Affairs: Sir JAMES TUDOR.

Minister of Trade, Industry and Commerce: E. EVELYN GREAVES.

Minister of Housing and Lands: HAROLD A. BLACKMAN.

BARBADOS — Directory

Minister of Agriculture, Food and Fisheries: WARWICK O. FRANKLYN.
Minister of Transport and Works: DONALD BLACKMAN.
Minister of Tourism and Sports: WESLEY W. HALL.
Minister of Employment, Labour Relations and Community Development: N. KEITH SIMMONS.
Minister of Education and Culture: CYRIL V. WALKER.
Minister of State, Civil Services: L. V. HARCOURT LEWIS.
Minister of State for Finance: Dr CARL CLARKE.

MINISTRIES

Office of the Prime Minister: Government Headquarters, Bay St, St Michael; tel. 436-6435.
Ministry of Agriculture, Food and Fisheries: POB 505, Graeme Hall, Christ Church; tel. 428-4150.
Ministry of Education and Culture: Jemmot's Lane, St Michael; tel. 427-3272.
Ministry of Employment, Labour Relations and Community Development: Marine House, Hastings, St Michael 29; tel. 427-5420.
Ministry of Finance: Government Headquarters, Bay St, St Michael; tel. 436-6435.
Ministry of Foreign Affairs: 1 Culloden Rd, St Michael; tel. 436-2990; telex 2222.
Ministry of Health: Jemmott's Lane, St Michael; tel. 426-5080.
Ministry of Housing and Lands: Marine House, Hastings, Christ Church; tel. 427-5420.
Ministry of Legal Affairs: Marine House, Hastings, Christ Church; tel. 427-5420.
Ministry of State, Civil Services: Government Headquarters, Bay St, St Michael; tel. 436-6435.
Ministry of Tourism and Sports: PO Building, Cheapside, Bridgetown; tel. 436-4830.
Ministry of Trade, Industry and Commerce: Reef Rd, Fontabelle, St Michael; tel. 427-5270.
Ministry of Transport and Works: POB 25, Bridgetown; tel. 429-2191; telex 2203.

Legislature

PARLIAMENT
Senate
President: FRANK WALCOTT.
There are 20 other members.

House of Assembly
Speaker: LAWSON WEEKES.
Clerk of Parliament: GEORGE BRANCKER.

General Election, 28 May 1986

Party	Votes	%	Seats
Democratic Labour Party	80,028	59.45	24
Barbados Labour Party	54,367	40.38	3
Others	227	0.17	—
Total	134,622	100.00	27

Political Organizations

Barbados Labour Party: Grantley Adams House, 111 Roebuck St, Bridgetown; tel. 426-2277; f. 1938; moderate social democrat; Leader and Chair. HENRY FORDE; Gen. Sec. PATRICIA SYMMONDS.
Democratic Labour Party: George St, Belleville, St Michael; tel. 429-3104; f. 1955; Leader L. ERSKINE SANDIFORD; Pres. BRANDFORD TAITT; Gen. Sec. CORA CUMBERBATCH.
People's Pressures Movement: Bridgetown; f. 1979; Leader ERIC SEALY.
Workers' Party of Barbados: Bridgetown; tel. 425-1620; f. 1985; small left-wing organization; Gen. Sec. Dr GEORGE BELLE.

Diplomatic Representation

EMBASSIES AND HIGH COMMISSIONS IN BARBADOS

Brazil: Sunjet House, Independence Square, Bridgetown; tel. 427-1735; telex 2434; Ambassador: AMAURY BIER.
Canada: Bishops Court Hill, St Michael; tel. 429-3550; telex 2247; High Commissioner: ART WRIGHT.
China, People's Republic: 17 Golf View Terrace, Rockley, Christ Church; tel. 436-6042; telex 2363; Ambassador: LU ZONGQING.
Colombia: Hastings Towers, Apt 3A, Hastings Main Road, Christ Church; tel. 427-8804; telex 2499; Chargé d'affaires: Mrs LUZ BEATRIZ PEDRAZA BERNAL.
Costa Rica: 'Windley', Garden Gap, Worthing No. 2, Christ Church; tel. 436-8442; Ambassador: RENÉ CASTRO HERNÁNDEZ.
Korea, Republic: 2nd Floor, Barbados Mutual Life Building, Collymore Rock, St Michael; tel. 429-9650; telex 2532; Ambassador: CHONG JONG-GYU.
Trinidad and Tobago: Cockspur House, Nile St, Bridgetown; tel. 429-9600/1; telex 2326; High Commissioner: MAURICE ST JOHN.
United Kingdom: POB 676, Lower Collymore Rock, Bridgetown; tel. 436-6694; telex 2219; High Commissioner: KEVIN F. X. BURNS.
USA: POB 302, Canadian Imperial Bank of Commerce Bldg, Broad St, Bridgetown; tel. 436-4950; telex 2259; Ambassador: (vacant).
Venezuela: El Sueno, Worthing, Christ Church; tel. 435-7619; telex 2339; Ambassador: ORESTES DI GIACOMO.

Judicial System

Justice is administered by the Supreme Court of Judicature, which consists of a High Court and a Court of Appeal. Final appeal lies with the Judicial Committee of the Privy Council, in London. There are Magistrates' Courts for lesser offences.

Chief Justice: Sir DENYS A. WILLIAMS.
Puisne Judges: C. S. HUSBANDS, J. HUSBAND, C. A. ROCHEFORD, E. F. BELGRAVE.
Registrar: MARIE MACCORMACK.
Magistrates' Courts: Appeals lie to a Divisional Court of the High Court.

Religion

More than 90 religious denominations and sects are represented in Barbados. According to the 1970 census, there were about 150,000 Anglicans, while the Methodist, Moravian and Pentecostal groups are next in importance. There are about 24,000 Roman Catholics (including adherents in Saint Vincent and the Grenadines), and other Christian groups have a combined membership of 50,000. There are also small groups of Hindus, Muslims and Jews.

CHRISTIANITY
The Anglican Communion

Anglicans in Barbados are adherents of the Church in the Province of the West Indies, comprising eight dioceses. The Archbishop of the Province is the Bishop of the North Eastern Caribbean and Aruba, resident at St John's, Antigua. In Barbados there is a Provincial Office (St George's Church, St George) and an Anglican Theological College (Codrington College, St John).

Bishop of Barbados: Rt Rev. DREXEL GOMEZ, Diocesan Office, Mandeville House, Bridgetown; tel. 426-2761.

The Roman Catholic Church

The diocese of Bridgetown-Kingstown, comprising Barbados and Saint Vincent and the Grenadines, is suffragan to the archdiocese of Port of Spain (Trinidad and Tobago). The Bishop participates in the Antilles Episcopal Conference (based in Kingston, Jamaica).

Bishop of Bridgetown-Kingstown: Rt Rev. ANTHONY H. DICKSON, POB 1223, St Patrick's Cathedral, Jemmott's Lane, Bridgetown; tel. 426-2325.

Protestant Churches

Baptist Church: Baptist Convention, President Kennedy Dr., Bridgetown; tel. 429-2697.
Caribbean Atlantic Assembly of the Church of God: St Michael's Laza, St Michael's Row, Bridgetown; tel. 427-5770.
Church of Jesus Christ of Latter-day Saints: Carleigh House, 3 Golf Club Rd, Bridgetown; tel. 435-7853; telex 2561.
Church of the Nazarene: Eagle Hall, Bridgetown; tel. 425-1067.
East Caribbean Conference of Seventh-day Adventists: Britton's Hill, St Michael; tel. 429-7234.
Methodist Church: Bethel Church Office, Bay St, Bridgetown; tel. 426-2223; Chair. Rev. LEONARD W. B. ROCK.
Moravian Church: Roebuck St, Bridgetown; tel. 426-2337; Superintendent Rev. RUDOLPH HOLDER.

BARBADOS

New Testament Church of God: River Rd, St Michael; tel. 426-1359.

Wesleyan Holiness Church: General Headquarters, Bank Hall; tel. 429-4864.

The Press

Barbados Advocate (News): POB 230, Fontabelle, Bridgetown; tel. 426-1210; telex 2613; f. 1895; daily; Man. Dir and Publr PATRICK HOYOS; Man. Editor ROBERT BEST; circ. 19,000.

The Beacon: 111 Roebuck St, Bridgetown; organ of the Barbados Labour Party; weekly; circ. 15,000.

The Nation: Fontabelle, St Michael; tel. 436-6240; telex 2310; f. 1973; daily; Dir HAROLD HOYTE; circ. 22,008 (weekday), 33,714 (weekend).

The New Bajan: Carib Publicity Co, Nation House, Fontabelle, St Michael; tel. 436-6420; f. 1953; monthly; illustrated magazine; Man. Editor TREVOR A. D. GALE; circ. over 8,000.

Official Gazette: Government Printing Office, Bay St, Bridgetown; tel. 436-6776; Mon. and Thur.

Sunday Advocate (News): POB 230, Fontabelle, Bridgetown; tel. 426-1210; telex 2613; f. 1895; Man. Dir and Publr PATRICK HOYOS; Editor ULRIC RICE; circ. 30,308.

The Sunday Sun: Fontabelle, St Michael; tel. 436-6240; telex 2310; f. 1977; Dir HAROLD HOYTE; circ. 34,830.

NEWS AGENCIES

Caribbean News Agency (CANA): Culloden View, Beckles Road, St Michael; tel. 429-2903; telex 2228; f. 1976; public and private shareholders from English-speaking Caribbean; Gen. Man. HARRY R. MAYERS.

Foreign Bureaux

Agencia EFE (Spain): 48 Gladioli Drive, Husbanos, St James; tel. 425-1542; Rep. YUSSUFF HANIFF.

Inter Press Service (IPS) (Italy): Silver Hill, Christ Church; tel. 86646; Correspondent ALBERT BRANDFORD.

Xinhua (New China) News Agency (People's Republic of China): POB 22A, 29 Newton Tce, Christ Church, Bridgetown; telex 2458; Chief Correspondent DING BAOZHONG.

Publishers

Caribbean Contact Ltd: c/o Caribbean Conference of Churches, POB 616, Bridgetown; tel. 427-2681; telex 2335; religion, social sciences, children's books.

Caribbean Publishing Co Ltd: Nation House, Fontabelle, St Michael; tel. 436-5889.

Nation Publishing Co Ltd: Nation House, Fontabelle, St Michael; tel. 436-6240; telex 2310.

Radio and Television

In 1986 there were an estimated 200,000 radio receivers and in 1988 62,000 television receivers in use.

Caribbean Broadcasting Corporation: POB 900, Bridgetown; tel. 429-2041; telex 2560; f. 1963; Chair. Prof. E. R. WALROND.

RADIO

Barbados Broadcasting Service: St George; f. 1981.

Barbados Rediffusion Service Ltd: River Rd, Bridgetown; tel. 426-0820; f. 1934; commercial wired service with island-wide coverage; Gen. Man. F. DUESBURY; Programme Dir A. PRAGNELL.

CBC Radio: POB 900, Bridgetown; tel. 429-2041; telex 2560; f. 1963; administered by the Caribbean Broadcasting Corporation; broadcasts 20 hours per day; Gen. Man. SAM TAITT.

Radio Liberty FM: POB 900, Bridgetown; f. 1984; administered by the Caribbean Broadcasting Corporation; broadcasts 13 hours Sun.–Thur., 18 hours Fri. and Sat.; Gen. Man. SAM TAITT.

Voice of Barbados: River Rd, Bridgetown; tel. 426-0820; f. 1981; commercial station covering Barbados and Eastern Caribbean; Gen. Man. F. G. DUESBURY; Programme Dir J. E. ROGERS.

YESS Ten-Four: River Rd, Bridgetown; tel. 426-0820; operated by Barbados Rediffusion Service Ltd.

TELEVISION

CBC TV: POB 900, Bridgetown; tel. 429-2041; telex 2560; f. 1964; Channel Nine operated by Caribbean Broadcasting Corporation; since 1987 two subscription channels, 14 and 18, have been available; Gen. Man. SAM TAITT.

Finance

(cap. = capital; auth. = authorized; dep. = deposits; res = reserves; brs = branches; m. = million)

BANKING

Central Bank

Central Bank of Barbados: POB 1016, Church Village, Bridgetown; tel. 436-6870; telex 2251; f. 1972; bank of issue; cap. Bds $2m., res Bds $18.5m., dep. Bds $207.6m. (Dec. 1987); Gov. Dr KURLEIGH KING; Gen. Man. (vacant).

National Development Bank

Barbados Development Bank: POB 50, Level 7, Central Bank Bldg, Church Village, Bridgetown; tel. 436-8870; telex 2295; f. 1969; auth. cap. Bds $30m.; Gen. Man. RICHARD LESLIE.

National Bank

Barbados National Bank: 11 James St, POB 1002, Bridgetown; tel. 427-5920; telex 2271; f. 1978 by the merger of the Barbados Savings Bank, Sugar Industry Agricultural Bank, Agricultural Credit Bank and The Public Officers Housing Loan Fund; cap. Bds $12.5m., dep. Bds $409.8m. (Dec. 1986); Chair. Sen. AMORY PHILLIPS; Man. Dir L. G. FRANCIS; 5 brs.

Foreign Banks

Bank of Nova Scotia (Canada): POB 202, Broad St, Bridgetown; tel. 426-0230; telex 2223; Man. A. C. ALLEN; 7 brs.

Barclays Bank PLC (UK): POB 301, Broad St, Bridgetown; tel. 429-5151; telex 2348; f. 1837; Man. K. L. LEWIS; 12 brs.

Canadian Imperial Bank of Commerce: POB 405, Broad St, Bridgetown; tel. 426-0571; telex 2230; Man. T. MULLOY; 10 brs and 2 sub-brs.

Caribbean Commercial Bank (Trinidad and Tobago): Lower Broad St, Bridgetown; tel. 426-5022; telex 2289; f. 1984; Pres. MICHAEL WRIGHT.

Chase Manhattan Bank NA (USA): Lower Broad St, Bridgetown; tel. 436-6900; telex 2269.

Royal Bank of Canada: POB 1011, Trident House, Broad St, Bridgetown; tel. 426-5200; telex 2242; f. 1911; Man. LARRY A. DAVIS; 7 brs.

United International Bank Ltd: Room 203, Kay's House, Roebuck St, Bridgetown; tel. 429-7690.

Trust Companies

Bank of Commerce Trust Company Barbados Ltd: POB 503, Bridgetown; tel. 426-2740.

Bank of Nova Scotia Trust Co (Caribbean) Ltd: POB 1003B, Bank of Nova Scotia Bldg, Broad St, Bridgetown; tel. 426-5285; telex 2223.

Royal Bank (Barbados) Financial Corporation: POB 48B, Royal Bank House, Bush Hill, Garrison, St Michael; tel. 429-5249; Man. N. L. SMITH.

STOCK EXCHANGE

Barbados Securities Exchange: 6th Floor, Central Bank Bldg, Church Village, Bridgetown; tel. 436-9871; f. 1987; Gen. Man. ANTHONY K. JOHNSON.

INSURANCE

The leading British and a number of US and Canadian companies have agents in the territory. Local insurance companies include the following:

Barbados Commercial Insurance Co Ltd: Harrison's Bldg, 1 Broad St, Bridgetown; tel. 436-6560.

Barbados Fire & General Insurance Co: POB 150, Beckwith Place, Broad St, Bridgetown; tel. 426-4291; telex 2393; f. 1880.

Barbados Mutual Life Assurance Society: Collymore Rock, St Michael; tel. 436-6750; telex 2423; f. 1840; Chair. P. McG. PATTERSON; Man. D. W. ALLAN.

C. F. Harrison & Co Ltd: POB 304, 1 Broad St, Bridgetown; tel. 426-0720; telex 2307; Man. Dir ROBERT W. GODDARD; Gen. Man. FLOYD CODRINGTON.

Insurance Corporation of Barbados: Roebuck St, Bridgetown; tel. 427-5590; telex 2317; f. 1978; cap. Bds $3m.; Chair. JOHN MAYERS; Gen. Man. DAVID DEANE.

BARBADOS

Life of Barbados Ltd: Plantations Bldg, Lower Broad St, Bridgetown; tel. 426-1060; telex 2392; f. 1971; Pres. CECIL F. DE CAIRES.

United Insurance Co Ltd: POB 1215, Cavan House, Lower Broad St, Bridgetown; tel. 436-1991; telex 2343; f. 1976; Dir G. M. CHALLENOR.

Trade and Industry

CHAMBERS OF COMMERCE

Barbados Chamber of Commerce and Industry: 1st Floor, Nemwil House, Collymore Rock, POB 189, St Michael; tel. 426-2056; f. 1825; 150 mem. firms, 260 reps; Pres. JOHN BELLAMY; Exec. Dir STANLEY L. TAYLOR.

Barbados Junior Chamber of Commerce: Bridgetown; Pres. AVRIL BREWSTER; Sec. VINCENT HAYNES.

DEVELOPMENT

Barbados Agricultural Development Corporation: Fairy Valley, Christ Church; tel. 428-0001; f. 1965; programme of diversification and land reforms; Chair. E. R. S. CUMBERBATCH; Gen. Man. G. V. J. GARVEY; Sec. FRANK B. TAYLOR.

Barbados Export Promotion Corporation: Pelican Industrial Park, St Michael; tel. 427-5758; telex 2486; co-ordinates activities of Barbadian manufactures; Chief Exec. PHILIP WILLIAMS.

Barbados Industrial Development Corporation: Pelican House, Princess Alice Highway, POB 250, Bridgetown; tel. 427-5350; telex 2295; f. 1969; operates industrial estates; encourages foreign investment; advises potential customers; promotes domestic manufacturing; Chair. CECIL WILLIAMS; Gen. Man. RAWLE G. B. CHASE.

Barbados Marketing Corporation: POB 703C, Bridgetown; tel. 427-5250; telex 2253; Chair. ROBERT MORRIS; Gen. Man. CLYDE KING.

British Development Division in the Caribbean: POB 167, Collymore Rock, St Michael; tel. 436-6694; telex 2236; Head MICHAEL G. BAWDEN.

STATE-OWNED COMPANIES

Barbados National Oil Company Ltd (BNOCL): Woodbourne, St Philip; tel. 423-0918; telex 2334; f. 1982; exploration for petroleum and natural gas.

National Petroleum Corporation (NPC): Wildey, St Michael; tel. 426-5012; f. 1951; gas distribution; Chair. of Board J. CLIVESTON KING; Gen. Man. E. HERMAN BRATHWAITE.

ASSOCIATIONS

Barbados Agricultural Society: The Grotto, Culloden and Beckles Rd, St Michael; tel. 436-6680; Pres. PATRICK BETHELL.

Barbados Association of Medical Practitioners: Noranda, Lower Collymore Rock, Bridgetown; tel. 429-7569.

Barbados Association of Professional Engineers: Noranda, Lower Collymore Rock, Bridgetown; tel. 426-9123.

Barbados Hotel Association: 4th Ave, Belleville, St Michael; tel. 426-5041; telex 2314; Pres. RALPH TAYLOR; Exec. Dir RUSSELL KELLMAN.

Barbados Manufacturers' Association: Prescod Blvd, Harbour Rd, St Michael; tel. 426-4474; f. 1964; Pres. ALFRED KNIGHT; Exec. Sec. RITA ALKINS; 112 mem. firms.

Barbados National Association of Co-operative Societies: James St, Bridgetown; tel. 436-2270.

Barbados Small Business Association: Princess Alice Highway, Bridgetown; tel. 429-7849.

Barbados Sugar Industry Ltd: POB 719C, Warrens, St Thomas; tel. 425-0010; telex 2418; Man. Dir E. A. B. DEANE; Sec. D. H. A. JOHNSON.

West Indian Sea Island Cotton Association (Inc): c/o Barbados Agricultural Development Corporation, Fairy Valley, Christ Church; tel. 428-0250; Pres. E. LEROY WARD; Sec. MICHAEL I. EDGHILL; 8 mem. associations.

EMPLOYERS' ORGANIZATION

Barbados Employers' Confederation: 1st Floor, Nemwil House, Lower Collymore Rock, St Michael; tel. 426-1574; f. 1956; Pres. CHRISTOPHER ST JOHN; Exec. Dir JAMES A. WILLIAMS; Sec.-Treas. DEBORAH GREEN; 156 mems.

TRADE UNIONS

Principal unions include:

Barbados Industrial and General Workers' Union: Bridgetown; f. 1981; Leader ROBERT CLARKE; Gen. Sec. LADEPOO SALANKEY; c. 2,000 mems.

Barbados Secondary Teachers' Union: Ryeburn House, 8th Ave, Belleville, St Michael; tel. 429-7676; f. 1948; Pres. GEORGE JACKMAN; Sec. PATRICK FROST; 350 mems.

Barbados Union of Teachers: POB 127, Bridgetown; f. 1974; tel. 436-6139; Pres. M. MARSHALL; Gen. Sec. CARLISLE BASCOMBE; 2,000 mems.

Barbados Workers' Union: Harmony Hall, St Michael; tel. 426-3492; f. 1941; Sec.-Gen. FRANK WALCOTT; 30,000 mems.

National Union of Public Workers: POB 174, Dalkeith Rd, Bridgetown; tel. 426-1764; f. 1944; Pres. NIGEL O. HARPER; Gen. Sec. JOSEPH GODDARD; 6,000 mems.

National Union of Seamen: 34 Tudor St, Bridgetown; tel. 436-6137.

Transport

ROADS

Ministry of Transport and Works: POB 25, The Pine, St Michael; tel. 429-2191; telex 2203; maintains a network of about 1,642 km (1,020 miles) of roads, of which 1,300 km (808 miles) have an asphalt surface; Chief Technical Officer C. H. ARCHER.

SHIPPING

Inter-island traffic is catered for by a fortnightly service of one vessel of the West Indies Shipping Corporation operating from Trinidad as far north as Jamaica. The CAROL container service consortium connects Bridgetown with West European ports and several foreign shipping lines call at the port. Bridgetown harbour has berths for eight ships and simultaneous bunkering facilities for five.

Barbados Shipping and Trading Co Ltd: Carlisle House, Hincks St, Bridgetown; tel. 426-1754.

Shipping Association of Barbados: Carlisle House, Hincks St, Bridgetown; tel. 427-9860.

DaCosta Ltd: POB 103, Carlisle House, Hincks St, Bridgetown; tel. 426-0850; telex 2328.

Tore Torsteinson: Fairfield House, St Philip; tel. 423-6125.

CIVIL AVIATION

The principal airport is Grantley Adams International Airport, 18 km (11 miles) from Bridgetown.

Caribbean Air Cargo Ltd (CARICARGO): Grantley Adams Intl Airport, Christ Church; tel. 428-4180; telex 2417; f. 1979 by the governments of Barbados and Trinidad and Tobago (joint shareholders); services between Miami, New York, Houston, Puerto Rico and the Eastern Caribbean; Chair. PETER LOOK HONG; Man. Dir KINGSLEY CLARKE; fleet of 2 Boeing 707-320C.

Caribbean Airways: Old Terminal Bldg, Grantley Adams Intl Airport; tel. 428-0812; telex 22265; f. 1970; ceased operating scheduled services from 1 April 1987; Chair. H. YEARWOOD; Gen. Man. W. BLACKMAN; fleet of 1 DC-10-30 (on lease).

Tourism

The natural attractions of the island consist chiefly of the healthy climate and varied scenery. In addition, there are many facilities for outdoor sports of all kinds. Bathsheba, on the east coast, is a well-known health resort. Revenue from tourism increased from Bds $13m. in 1960 to an estimated Bds $749.9m. in 1987. The number of tourist arrivals rose from 303,778 in 1980 to 421,859 in 1987.

Barbados Board of Tourism: POB 242, Harbour Rd, Bridgetown; tel. 427-2623; telex 2420; f. 1958; offices in London, New York, Montreal, Toronto, California and Frankfurt; Chair. CLEVEDON MAYERS; Dir of Tourism PATRICIA NEHAUL.

BELGIUM

Introductory Survey

Location, Climate, Language, Religion, Flag, Capital

The Kingdom of Belgium lies in north-western Europe, bounded to the north by the Netherlands, to the east by Luxembourg and the Federal Republic of Germany, to the south by France, and to the west by the North Sea. The climate is temperate. It is mild and humid on the coast, with hotter summers and colder winters inland. Temperatures in Brussels are generally between 0°C (32°F) and 23°C (73°F). Dutch, spoken in the north (Flanders), and French, spoken in the south (Wallonia), are the two main official languages. A 1963 law established four linguistic regions, the French, Dutch and German-speaking areas and Brussels, which is situated in the Flemish part but has bilingual status. Approximately 57% of the population are Dutch-speaking, 42% are French-speaking and 0.6% speak German. Almost all of the inhabitants profess Christianity, and the great majority are Roman Catholics. The national flag (proportions 15 by 13) consists of three equal vertical stripes, of black, yellow and red. The capital is Brussels.

Recent History

Since the Second World War, Belgium has become recognized as a leader of international co-operation in Europe. It is a founder member of many important international organizations, including the Council of Europe, the European Communities and the Benelux Economic Union. King Leopold III, who had reigned since 1934, abdicated in July 1951 in favour of his son, Baudouin.

In the post-war period the language dispute between French and Dutch speakers has been the country's main political problem, exacerbated by political polarization between Flanders, in the north (supporting mainly the conservative Christian Social Party and the nationalist Volksunie—VU), and francophone Wallonia, in the south (predominantly Socialist). All the major parties have both French and Flemish sections, although linguistic conflicts frequently override political considerations, as a result of the trend away from centralized administration towards greater regional control. Moderate constitutional reforms, produced in July 1971, were the first steps towards regional autonomy; in 1972 further concessions were made, with the German-speaking community being represented in the Cabinet for the first time, and in 1973 linguistic parity was assured in central government. Provisional legislation, passed in 1974, established separate Regional Councils and Ministerial Committees. One of the main disputes has concerned the status of Brussels, as 85% of the city's inhabitants are francophone but the Flemish parties have been unwilling to grant it equal status with the other two regional bodies.

In June 1977 Leo Tindemans formed a coalition between the Christian Social parties, the Socialists and two 'linguistic' parties, the Front Démocratique des Francophones (FDF) and the VU. The Cabinet, in what became known as the Egmont Pact, proposed the abolition of the virtually defunct nine-province administration, and devolution of power from the central government to create a federal Belgium, comprising three political and economic regions (Flanders, Wallonia and Brussels), and two linguistic communities. These proposals, however, were not implemented. Tindemans resigned in October 1978 and the Minister of Defence, Paul Vanden Boeynants, took over as Prime Minister in a transitional government. Elections were held in December but the results showed little change in the distribution of seats in the Chamber of Representatives. Four successive Prime Ministers-designate failed to form a new government, the main obstacle again being the future status of Brussels. The six-month crisis was finally resolved when a new coalition government was formed in April 1979 under Dr Wilfried Martens, president of the Flemish Christian Social Party (CVP).

In 1980 the linguistic conflict worsened, sometimes involving violent incidents. The Government, which was also under pressure over the proposed installation of NATO nuclear missiles in Belgium and over its plans to reduce public spending at a time of high unemployment, decided that Flanders and Wallonia would be administered by regional assemblies, with control of cultural matters, public health, roads, urban projects and 10% of the national budget, while Brussels was to retain its three-member executive.

Internal disagreement over Martens' proposals for economic recovery resulted in the formation of four coalition governments between April 1979 and October 1980. The announcement of austerity measures including a 'freeze' on wages, resulted in demonstrations and lost him the support of the Socialist parties. In April 1981 a new government was formed, led by Mark Eyskens (CVP), hitherto Minister of Finance. It was a coalition of the Christian Social parties and the Socialist parties: the Cabinet remained virtually unchanged, and expressed its intention to promote investment and industrial development while cutting public spending. Lack of parliamentary support for his policies led to Eyskens' resignation in September. In December Martens formed a new centre-right government, comprising the two Christian Social parties and the two Liberal parties. In 1982 Parliament granted special powers for the implementation of austerity measures (see Economic Affairs); these were effective until 1984, and similar powers were approved in March 1986. Opposition to reductions in public spending has been vigorous, with public-sector unions undertaking damaging strike action in November 1982, September 1983 and May 1986, when two one-day general strikes took place.

The issue of the installation of 48 US 'cruise' nuclear missiles on Belgian territory led to a two-day debate in the Chamber of Representatives in November 1983 and a deferral of the final decision until 1985. A series of bombings, directed against NATO-connected targets, was carried out during 1984, and included six explosions along an oil pipeline in December. Responsibility for the attacks was claimed by an extreme left-wing organization, the Cellules Communistes Combattantes (CCC), suspected of having close links with a French terrorist group, Action Directe. In March 1985 the Chamber finally carried a majority vote in favour of the cruise sitings, and 16 missiles were installed at Florennes. However, these missiles were removed in December 1988, under the terms of the Intermediate-range Nuclear Forces treaty concluded by the USA and the USSR in December 1987.

Following a riot in May 1985 at a football match between English and Italian clubs (in the final of the European Cup competition) at the Heysel Stadium in Brussels, which resulted in 39 deaths, calls were made for the resignation of the Interior Minister, Charles-Ferdinand Nothomb, over accusations of inefficient policing. The Deputy Prime Minister, Jean Gol, resigned over the issue in July, taking five other Liberal Cabinet members with him, and causing the collapse of the coalition. Martens offered the resignation of his Government, but this was 'suspended' by King Baudouin, and a general election was called for 13 October 1985, with the Government handling only a minimal programme until that time. A further row over education, which developed into a dispute between the two linguistic groups, led to the final dissolution of Parliament in September 1985. The general election returned the Christian Social-Liberal alliance to power, and Martens formed his sixth Cabinet in November 1985.

The incidence of terrorist attacks gathered momentum in the weeks following the election. The new Cabinet held an extraordinary session following the violent deaths of 16 people in two armed attacks on supermarkets in the Brabant region and the bombing of four banks within a week. Responsibility for the bank attacks was again claimed by the CCC. Further attacks, mainly centred on NATO targets, were carried out before a number of arrests were made. In January 1986 the Government announced new, more stringent security legislation, which placed tighter restrictions on the sale of weapons and ammunition. In October 1988 four members of the CCC were sentenced to life imprisonment, with hard labour, for their part in 21 attacks, carried out in 1984 and 1985, while two alleged members of an associated group, the Front Révolutionnaire d'Action Prolétarienne (FRAP), received five-year

BELGIUM

prison sentences, after being found guilty of a number of acts of urban violence.

In 1983 the election of a francophone mayor in the Flemish commune of Voeren (known in French as Les Fourons), which had been transferred from the French-speaking Liège province to Dutch-speaking Limburg in 1963, had caused a linguistic conflict which had split the Cabinet. A compromise solution failed to prevent the problem from re-emerging in October 1986, when the mayor in question, José Happart, was dismissed from his post for refusing to take a fluency test in Dutch. The incident provoked another bitter conflict between the two linguistic groups in the coalition, leading Nothomb, the Interior Minister, to resign from the Government, and causing Martens to tender his resignation as Prime Minister. This, however, was refused by King Baudouin. The issue continued to generate tension between the coalition parties during 1987, as Happart was repeatedly re-elected as acting mayor despite the Limburg authorities' frequent attempts to remove him from office, and finally caused the Government to collapse in October, when its resignation was accepted by King Baudouin. At a general election in December, the CVP sustained significant losses in Flanders, while the French-speaking Socialist Party (PS) gained seats in Wallonia, and the Socialists became the largest overall grouping in the Chamber of Representatives. However, no party had a clear mandate for power, and the ensuing negotiations for a new coalition lasted 146 days. During this time, Martens assumed a 'caretaker' role, pending the formation of a new government, and a series of mediators, appointed by King Baudouin, attempted to reach a compromise. In May 1988 Martens was sworn in at the head of his eighth administration, after agreement was finally reached by the French- and Dutch-speaking wings of both the Christian Social and Socialist parties and by the VU.

The five-party coalition agreement committed the new Government to a programme of further austerity measures, together with tax reforms and increased federalization. In August 1988 Parliament approved the first phase of the federalization plan, intended ultimately to lead to a constitutional amendment, whereby increased autonomy would be granted to the country's three linguistic regions in several areas of jurisdiction, including education and economic policy. Further legislation, allocating the public funds necessary to give effect to such regional autonomy, was presented to Parliament in November. Agreement was also reached by which Brussels was to have its own regional council, with an executive responsible to it, giving the city equal status with Flanders and Wallonia. In an attempt to end linguistic conflicts such as that generated by Happart, it was announced that officials in communes such as Voeren would have to demonstrate proficiency in both French and Dutch.

Government

Belgium is a constitutional and hereditary monarchy, comprising nine provinces. Legislative power is vested in the King and the bicameral Parliament (the Senate and the Chamber of Representatives). The Senate has 182 members, including 106 directly elected by universal adult suffrage, 50 elected by provincial councils, 25 co-opted by the elected members and one Senator by right, the heir to the throne. The Chamber has 212 members, all directly elected by popular vote, on the basis of proportional representation. Members of both Houses serve for up to four years. Executive power, nominally vested in the King, is exercised by the Cabinet. The King appoints the Prime Minister and, on the latter's advice, other Ministers. The Cabinet is responsible to Parliament. There are political organs representing each of the linguistic regions and the capital (see Recent History).

Defence

Belgium is a member of NATO. In June 1988 the total strength of the armed forces was 88,300 (of whom 26,500 were conscripts), comprising army 65,100, navy 4,500 and air force 18,700. The defence budget for 1987 was 129,870m. Belgian francs. Military service lasts 10 months for postings to Germany and one year for conscripts serving in Belgium.

Economic Affairs

Belgium is among the most densely populated countries in Europe, and its economy is based on diversified industrial and commercial activity. In 1987, according to estimates by the World Bank, Belgium's gross national product (GNP), measured at average 1985–87 prices, was US $112,009m., equivalent to $11,360 per head. Between 1980 and 1987, it was estimated, GNP per head increased at an average rate of 1.0% per year in real terms. The average annual growth of overall gross domestic product (GDP) was 3.9% in 1965–80, falling to 0.9% in 1980–86. GDP growth was estimated at 1.8% in 1987. Industrial activity has concentrated in recent years in the increasingly populous Flemish areas of the north, but governments have encouraged re-investment in the southern, Walloon, region. Apart from coal and, to a lesser extent, clay, sand and stone, the country has no natural resources, and it purchases essential raw materials abroad: the vital export trade is therefore dependent largely on the state of the world market. Agriculture (with forestry and fishing) employed 2.5% of the total working population in 1986, and contributed 2% of GDP.

In 1986 69% of Belgium's GDP was exported, making it one of the world's principal per caput exporters. Over 70% of Belgium's external trade was with other members of the EEC in 1986, when the country's three main trading partners (the Federal Republic of Germany, France and the Netherlands) together accounted for 56.1% of total trade (57.0% of imports; 55.2% of exports). Belgium and Luxembourg constitute the Belgo-Luxembourg Economic Union (BLEU) and form a single customs region. The dual exchange rate being operated by the BLEU is to be abolished by 1992, to comply with plans to remove all capital controls within the EEC. Belgium transferred from the European currency 'snake' to the new European Monetary System (EMS) in 1979. In February 1982 the Belgian franc was devalued by 8.5% in relation to the other currencies participating in the EMS: in March 1983 and January 1987 it was revalued by 1.5% and by 2% respectively in EMS realignments.

Unemployment, which affected an average of 6.4% of the total labour force between 1972 and 1981, rose to 14.4% in 1984, but by July 1988 it had declined to 10.3%. There are distinct regional differences in rates of unemployment, due to the concentration of declining traditional industries, such as steel and textiles, in Wallonia. Government schemes to alleviate the problem include job-creation programmes and the introduction of a shorter working week, with legal restraints on pay settlements being adopted in January 1983 and reinforced in 1986.

Industrial output declined by 5% in 1980, as recession affected Belgium's heavy industries, and there were several factory closures in the steel, motor vehicle and textile sectors. The two largest steel concerns merged in 1981, but the sector continued to incur severe financial losses. In 1983 the industry was granted a loan of BF 14,000m. by the EEC, and the Belgian Government approved a scheme to finance restructuring of the steel industry at a cost of BF 24,750m., under which output was to be reduced by 27%, and 35% of jobs in the state-owned Cockerill Sambre group, which in 1983 incurred a net loss of BF 34,000m., were to be lost. In January 1984 the Belgian and Luxembourg Governments reached a 10-year agreement on the joint restructuring of their steel industries. Cockerill Sambre and ARBED (its Luxembourg equivalent) agreed to divide steel production between them so as to avoid competing with each other's products. Following approval by the Commission of the European Communities for the Government's plans to aid the steel sector in March 1984, Cockerill Sambre received BF 51,200m., but steel production was cut from 7.1m. metric tons to 4m. tons annually. In May 1985 trade unions finally agreed a programme of early retirement and a 36-hour week, as part of the restructuring, with BF 27,000m. in state support promised. The need to reduce excess steel capacity throughout the EEC resulted in uncertainty regarding the future of the loss-making Cockerill Sambre group. However, a further programme of restructuring, including reductions in wages and the loss of 2,200 jobs, reduced the group's net loss to BF 1,800m. in 1987, compared with BF 4,500m. in the previous year, reflecting the return to profitability of some of the group's 50 subsidiaries. The coal-mining industry has also experienced serious financial difficulties. In 1985 the four mines of Kempense Steenkolenmijnen (KS) received subsidies of BF 8,000m. In 1986 KS made a loss of BF 16,000m., and a restructuring programme, announced in January 1987, aimed to reduce the work-force by 8,200, and capacity from 6.1m. tons per year to 3.2m. tons per year, by 1996. Overall industrial output began to recover in 1984, particularly in the Flanders region, and continued to improve in subsequent years. The industrial sector accounted for 33% of GDP in 1986.

In 1978 Belgium began a programme of borrowing to finance the public-sector deficit, which had been aggravated by large payments of unemployment benefits, job-creation projects, rising petroleum prices and public investment. By March 1985 the public debt had reached BF 4,639,800m. Debt servicing therefore represented a heavy burden, accounting for an estimated 22% of current expenditure in the 1986 and 1987 budgets. By 1988 the accumulated public-sector debt was equivalent to 130% of annual GNP.

Under emergency powers, the Martens Government began in 1982 to impose a series of austerity measures, including tax increases, wage restraints, and reductions in planned expenditure on health services, social security, education, defence and public works. These measures were strongly opposed by the trade unions, but they had a mitigative effect on the budget deficit, which fell from 14.9% of GDP in 1983 to about 8% in 1987. The rate of inflation fell steadily from an average of 7.7% in 1983 to 1.3% in 1986. Having risen to 1.6% in 1987, the average rate in the year to August 1988 was 0.9%.

The 1989 budget, announced in August 1988, envisaged spending cuts of BF 77,000m., one-third of which was to result from an earlier debt-rescheduling agreement made with Belgium's financial institutions, in an attempt to reduce the budget deficit from an estimated 8.5% of GNP in 1988 to 7%, or BF 403,200m., in 1989. Reductions in spending were to be made in several fields, including health care, defence and payments to provinces and communes. However, the new Martens administration demonstrated a willingness to temper its austerity measures with increases in some welfare payments and renewed assistance for the long-term unemployed. Owing to export growth and a fall in the volume of imports, Belgium recorded a current surplus on its balance of payments in 1985 (US $669m.), 1986 ($3,009m.) and 1987 ($2,920m.).

Plans to introduce a computerized dealing system to the Brussels Stock Exchange, scheduled for September 1988, were postponed in August when the Finance Minister, Philippe Maystadt, proposed the immediate establishment of a government commission to draft legislation to end antiquated trading practices, including the quasi-monopoly held by stockbroking companies, in Belgium's four stock exchanges. Fears that such practices were resulting in a loss of business to other European exchanges, together with a number of attempts by foreign investors to acquire major Belgian companies (notably Société Générale de Belgique, the country's largest holding company), exemplified the need for reform. Following an unsuccessful bid by an Italian businessman, Carlo De Benedetti, to gain control of Société Générale de Belgique, the Cabinet approved new legislation in June 1988, requiring investors to disclose the acquisition of more than 5% of shares in a listed company.

The first major tax reforms since 1962, including proposals to reduce the upper limit of personal taxation from 70% to 55% and to lower other personal taxes by 10%, were approved by Parliament in December 1988. Any consequent loss in revenue was to be offset by a reduction in tax allowances for businesses, increases in duty on a number of goods and by an intensified campaign against tax evasion.

Social Welfare

Social welfare is administered mainly by the National Office for Social Security. Contributions are paid by employers and employees towards family allowances, health insurance, unemployment benefit and pensions. Most allowances and pensions are periodically adjusted in accordance with changes to the consumer price index. Workers and employees are entitled to four weeks' holiday for every 12-month period of work. They are insured against accidents occurring on the work premises or on the way to and from work. Medical care is free to widows, pensioners, orphans and the disabled. Ordinary and supplementary family allowances are the entitlement of all families. Social welfare is also administered at a local level by Public Assistance Commissions which have been set up in every municipality. In 1982 Belgium had 531 hospital establishments, with a total of 92,686 beds (one for every 106 inhabitants), and there were 26,593 physicians working in the country. Of total expenditure by the central government in 1984, about 42,100m. francs (1.7%) was for health, and 1,018,000m. francs (41.0%) was for social security and welfare.

Education

Full-time education in Belgium is compulsory from the ages of six to 16 years. Thereafter, pupils must remain in part-time education for a further two-year period. Secular education may be provided by the State or be subsidized by provincial or municipal authorities, while denominational (usually Roman Catholic) schools are generally subsidized by private bodies. In accordance with the 1963 Language of Instruction Act, teaching is given in the language of the region: in the Brussels district teaching is in the mother language of the pupil. In June 1986 it was announced that the study of Dutch as a second language in Wallonian schools was to be introduced, and was eventually to become compulsory.

There are state-financed nursery schools for children under five years old, attended by about 90% of infants. Elementary education is for children aged six to 12 years and consists of three courses of two years each. Secondary education lasts for six years and is divided into three two-year cycles or, in a few cases, two three-year cycles. The Diploma of Secondary Education may be gained after an additional two years of higher teacher training.

The requirement for university entrance is a pass in the 'examination of maturity', taken after the completion of secondary studies. Courses are divided into 2-3 years of general preparation followed by 2-3 years of specialization. There are five universities, two of which are divided into French and Dutch-speaking sections, and several university centres or faculties. There are also non-university institutions of higher education for those who have successfully completed their secondary studies. These provide arts education, technical training or higher teacher training (i.e. for secondary school).

The National Study Fund provides grants where necessary and nearly 20% of students receive scholarships. Government expenditure on education in 1987 was equivalent to 16.2% of the total budget, compared with 15.6% in 1986.

Legislation granting increased autonomy in the formulation of education policy to Belgium's three linguistic regions, as part of the Government's federalization programme, was due to come into effect in January 1989.

Public Holidays

1989: 2 January (for New Year's Day), 27 March (Easter Monday), 1 May (Labour Day), 4 May (Ascension Day), 15 May (Whit Monday), 21 July (Independence Day), 15 August (Assumption), 1 November (All Saints' Day), 11 November (Armistice Day), 25 December (Christmas Day).

1990: 1 January (New Year's Day), 16 April (Easter Monday), 1 May (Labour Day), 24 May (Ascension Day), 4 June (Whit Monday), 21 July (Independence Day), 15 August (Assumption), 1 November (All Saints' Day), 11 November (Armistice Day), 25 December (Christmas Day).

Weights and Measures

The metric system is in force.

Statistical Survey

Source: mainly Institut National de Statistique, 44 rue de Louvain, 1000 Brussels; tel. (02) 513-96-50.

Area and Population

AREA, POPULATION AND DENSITY

Area (sq km)	30,519*
Population (census results)†	
31 December 1970	9,650,944
1 March 1981	
Males	4,810,349
Females	5,038,298
Total	9,848,647
Population (official estimates at 31 December)†	
1985	9,858,895
1986	9,867,751
1987	9,875,716
Density (per sq km) at 31 December 1987	323.6

* 11,783 sq miles.   † Population is *de jure*.

PROVINCES (population at 31 December 1987)

	Population	Capital (with population)
Antwerp	1,587,450	Antwerp (476,044*)
Brabant	2,221,818	Brussels (970,346*)
Flanders (East)	1,328,779	Ghent (232,620)
Flanders (West)	1,095,193	Bruges (117,857)
Hainaut	1,271,649	Mons (89,515)
Liège	992,068	Liège (200,312)
Limburg	736,982	Hasselt (65,798)
Luxembourg	226,452	Arlon (22,209)
Namur	415,326	Namur (103,104)

* Including suburbs.

PRINCIPAL TOWNS (population at 31 December 1987)

Bruxelles (Brussel, Brussels)	970,346*
Antwerpen (Anvers, Antwerp)	476,044†
Gent (Gand, Ghent)	232,620
Charleroi	208,938
Liège (Luik)	200,312
Brugge (Bruges)	117,857
Namur (Namen)	103,104
Mons (Bergen)	89,515
Kortrijk (Courtrai)	76,314
Mechelen (Malines)	75,718
Oostende (Ostend)	68,397
Hasselt	65,798

* Including Schaerbeek, Anderlecht and other suburbs.
† Including Deurne and other suburbs.

BIRTHS, MARRIAGES AND DEATHS

	Registered live births		Registered marriages*		Registered deaths†	
	Number	Rate (per 1,000)	Number	Rate (per 1,000)	Number	Rate (per 1,000)
1980	124,794	12.7	66,413	6.7	114,364	11.6
1981	124,827	12.7	65,011	6.6	113,308	11.5
1982	120,382	12.2	62,423	6.3	112,506	11.4
1983	117,395	11.9	59,652	6.1	114,814	11.6
1984	115,790	11.8	58,989	6.0	110,577	11.2
1985	114,283	11.6	57,630	6.0	112,691	11.4
1986	117,271	11.9	56,657	5.7	111,671	11.3
1987	117,448	11.9	56,588	5.7	105,840	10.7

* Including marriages among Belgian armed forces stationed outside the country and alien armed forces in Belgium, unless performed by local foreign authority.
† Including Belgian armed forces stationed outside the country but excluding alien armed forces stationed in Belgium.

ECONOMICALLY ACTIVE POPULATION
(ISIC Major Divisions, '000 persons at 30 June each year)

	1984	1985	1986
Agriculture, forestry and fishing	106.1	105.0	103.2
Mining and quarrying	25.5	23.7	22.6
Manufacturing	812.6	810.7	799.1
Electricity, gas and water	32.8	32.1	31.7
Construction	203.2	202.7	204.6
Trade, restaurants and hotels	696.7	702.6	712.7
Transport, storage and communications	263.4	262.5	260.5
Finance, insurance, real estate and business services	271.1	289.5	301.5
Community, social and personal services*	1,214.4	1,233.4	1,262.0
Total in home employment	3,634.7	3,662.3	3,697.9
Persons working abroad	33.9	33.9	35.8
Total in employment	3,668.6	3,696.2	3,733.7
Unemployed†	545.7	505.9	477.9
Total labour force	4,214.3	4,202.2	4,211.6
Males	2,561.2	2,531.0	2,514.0
Females	1,653.2	1,671.1	1,697.7

* Including members of the armed forces ('000): 89.4 in 1984; 89.3 in 1985; 89.3 in 1986.
† Figures from 1985 onward exclude older unemployed persons not seeking employment: 38,284 in 1985; 59,003 in 1986.

Agriculture

PRINCIPAL CROPS ('000 metric tons)

	1985	1986	1987
Wheat	1,149.6	1,256.9	1,046.5
Spelt	37.6	37.9	36.5
Barley	685.4	793.1	678.1
Maize	50.4	56.9	40.3
Rye	22.5	19.3	16.7
Oats	93.6	59.3	60.4
Potatoes	1,521.7	2,055.4	1,620.3
Linseed	8.3	6.2	6.7
Flax fibre	15	11	15
Sugar beet	5,952.2	5,886.2	5,425.2

BELGIUM

LIVESTOCK ('000 head at 1 December)

	1985	1986	1987
Horses	26.0	24.4	23.1
Cattle	2,943.5	2,967.4	2,950.2
Pigs	5,412.1	5,762.7	5,880.8
Sheep	123.5	128.0	133.1
Goats	7.0	7.7	7.8

Poultry ('000 head at 1 December): Chickens 30,937 in 1986; Ducks 62 in 1986; Turkeys 207 in 1986.

LIVESTOCK PRODUCTS ('000 metric tons)

	1985	1986	1987
Beef and veal	317	316	317
Pig meat	717	738	779
Milk	3,796	3,918	3,777
Butter	97	100	86
Cheese	51	51	56
Hen eggs	174	176	174

Fishing*

('000 metric tons)

	1985	1986	1987
Marine fishes	31.1	28.2	29.2
Crustaceans and molluscs	2.6	2.3	2.2
Total catch	33.7	30.5	31.4

* Figures refer to marketable quantities landed in Belgium, which may be less than the live weight of the catch. The total catch (in '000 metric tons) was: 35.4 in 1985; 31.3 in 1986; 32.9 in 1987.

Mining

	1985	1986	1987
Hard coal ('000 metric tons)	6,212	5,589	4,356
Natural gas* (million cu metres)	52	37	38

* From coal mines.

Industry

SELECTED PRODUCTS
('000 metric tons, unless otherwise indicated)

	1985	1986	1987
Wheat flour[1]	937.6	851.3	931.8
Raw sugar	961	988	915
Margarine	171.8	171.3	184.4
Beer ('000 hectolitres)	13,930.9	13,715.4	13,987.7
Cigarettes (million)	30,183.9	28,619.4	28,953.1
Cotton yarn—pure and mixed (metric tons)	47,796	50,660	56,969*
Woven cotton fabrics—pure and mixed (metric tons)[2]	53,250	55,139	53,945

SELECTED PRODUCTS—continued
('000 metric tons, unless otherwise indicated)

	1985	1986	1987
Flax yarn (metric tons)[3]	9,009	7,688	7,689
Jute yarn (metric tons)	13,615	11,505	10,917
Other vegetable textile yarns (metric tons)	18,338	13,021	7,867
Wool yarn—pure and mixed (metric tons)	90,632	86,202	84,846
Woven woollen fabrics—pure and mixed (metric tons)[2]	35,734	35,681	33,858
Rayon continuous filaments (metric tons)	5,180	5,145	4,491
Woven rayon and acetate fabrics—pure and mixed (metric tons)[4]	28,617	27,973	29,783
Mechanical wood pulp	111	125	168
Chemical and semi-chemical wood pulp	256	231	270
Newsprint	100.0	96.0	110.7
Other paper and paperboard	832.3	834.9	1,003.7
Ethyl alcohol—Ethanol ('000 hectolitres)	175.8	156.7	117.9
Sulphuric acid (100%)	2,106.9	1,956.6	2,069.4
Nitric acid (100%)	1,532.9	1,453.6	1,469.5
Nitrogenous fertilizers[5]	760	750	n.a.
Phosphate fertilizers[6]	364	361	n.a.
Liquefied petroleum gas	345	520	533
Naphtha	1,304	998	1,421
Motor spirit (petrol)	3,853	4,906	4,857
Aviation gasoline	207.9	155.3	139.7
Kerosene	22	73	35
White spirit	257.5	361.3	327.7
Jet fuel	1,196.1	1,265.2	1,243.1
Distillate fuel oils	7,336.0	9,482.9	9,073.3
Residual fuel oil	3,638.2	7,316.3	7,773.4
Lubricating oils	28	10	2
Petroleum bitumen (asphalt)	516.1	665.7	652.3
Coke-oven coke	5,964	5,130	5,226
Cement	5,537	5,760	5,689
Pig-iron	8,719.0	8,014.5	8,242.4
Crude steel	10,687.3	9,764.6	9,786.4
Refined copper—unwrought (metric tons)[7]	455,459	457,779	475,906
Refined lead—unwrought (metric tons)[8]	114,293	98,313	108,030
Tin: primary (metric tons)	2,298	2,712	3,904
Zinc—unwrought (metric tons)[9]	289,562	288,787	308,580
Radio receivers ('000)[10]	1,097	1,233	1,165
Television receivers ('000)[10]	833	930	917
Merchant vessels launched ('000 gross reg. tons)[11]	74	102	52
Passenger motor cars ('000)[12]	997.3	1,063.7	1,140.6
Commercial motor vehicles ('000)[12]	37.5	54.2	54.4
Electric energy (million kWh)	57,321.4	58,675.1	63,367.0
Manufactured gas (million cu metres)	2,526	2,199	2,237

* Provisional figure.
[1] Industrial production only. [2] Including blankets.
[3] Including yarn made from tow.
[4] Including fabrics of natural silk and blankets and carpets of cellulosic fibres.
[5] Estimated production in Belgium and Luxembourg during 12 months ending 30 June of the year stated. Figures are in terms of nitrogen. Source: FAO, *Monthly Bulletin of Statistics*.
[6] Estimated production in Belgium and Luxembourg during 12 months ending 30 April of the year stated. Figures are in terms of phosphoric acid. Source: FAO, *Monthly Bulletin of Statistics*.
[7] Including alloys and the processing of refined copper imported from Zaire.
[8] Primary and secondary production, including alloys and remelted lead.
[9] Including alloys and remelted zinc.
[10] Factory shipments.
[11] Source: *Lloyd's Register of Shipping*.
[12] Assembled wholly or mainly from imported parts.

BELGIUM

Finance

CURRENCY AND EXCHANGE RATES

Monetary Units
100 centimes (centiemen) = 1 franc belge (frank) or Belgian franc (BF).

Denominations
Coins: 50 centimes; 1, 5, 10, 20 and 250 francs.
Notes: 50, 100, 500, 1,000 and 5,000 francs.

Sterling and Dollar Equivalents (30 September 1988)
£1 sterling = 66.55 francs;
US $1 = 39.35 francs;
1,000 Belgian francs = £15.03 = $25.41.

Average Exchange Rate (francs per US $)
1985   59.378
1986   44.672
1987   37.334

Note: The information on the exchange rate refers to the official market rate, used for most current transactions. There is also a free exchange market rate, applicable to most capital transactions. The average of this latter rate (francs per US dollar) was: 59.74 in 1985; 45.08 in 1986; 37.57 in 1987.

BUDGET (million Belgian francs)

Revenue	1987*	1988†
Direct taxation	902,414	929,727
Customs and excise	104,970	106,078
VAT, stamp, registration and similar duties	378,795	388,621
Other current taxes	59,752	55,129
Capital revenues	3,768	11,569
Total	1,449,699	1,491,124

Expenditure	1987*	1988†
Government departments	746,650	746,013
Public debt	397,393	409,578
Pensions	181,048	194,578
Education and cultural services	283,545	285,055
Defence	104,002	103,100
Other expenditure	146,696	154,017
Total	1,859,334	1,892,341

* Provisional.   † Official estimates.

NATIONAL BANK RESERVES*
(US $ million at 31 December)

	1985	1986	1987
Gold	1,443	1,443	1,421
IMF special drawing rights	361	342	700
Reserve position in IMF	519	565	557
Foreign exchange	3,969	4,630	8,363
Total	6,292	6,980	11,041

* Figures for gold and foreign exchange refer to the monetary association between Belgium and Luxembourg. Gold is valued at $42.22 per troy ounce. Figures exclude deposits made with the European Monetary Co-operation Fund.

MONEY SUPPLY ('000 million Belgian francs at 31 December)

	1985	1986	1987
Currency outside banks	379.9	400.5	410.7
Demand deposits at commercial banks	427.9	469.5	505.4
Monetary liabilities of other monetary institutions	160.7	178.4	180.3

COST OF LIVING (Consumer Price Index. Base: 1981 = 100)

	1985	1986	1987
Food	132.1	134.5	133.66
Fuel and light	138.8	115.1	104.47
Clothing	128.0	137.7	145.23
All items (incl. others)	129.9	131.6	133.60

NATIONAL ACCOUNTS ('000 million Belgian francs at current prices)

National Income and Product

	1984	1985	1986
Compensation of employees	2,521.0	2,659.0	2,783.7
Operating surplus	1,115.5	1,234.9	1,364.0
Domestic factor incomes	3,636.5	3,893.9	4,147.7
Consumption of fixed capital	426.5	457.9	498.7
Gross domestic product (GDP) at factor cost	4,063.0	4,351.8	4,646.4
Indirect taxes	529.8	558.9	575.8
Less Subsidies	67.4	67.7	74.0
GDP in purchasers' values	4,525.4	4,843.0	5,148.2
Factor income from abroad	387.1	469.6	419.7
Less Factor income paid abroad	414.9	500.9	434.6
Gross national product (GNP)	4,497.6	4,811.7	5,133.3
Less Consumption of fixed capital	426.5	457.9	498.7
National income in market prices	4,071.1	4,353.8	4,634.6
Other current transfers from abroad	39.3	44.3	37.9
Less Other current transfers paid abroad	77.6	73.2	67.9
National disposable income	4,032.8	4,324.9	4,604.6

1987 ('000 million francs): GDP in purchasers' values 5,306; GNP 5,296 (Source: IMF, *International Financial Statistics*).

Expenditure on the Gross Domestic Product

	1984	1985	1986
Government final consumption expenditure	799.7	852.5	881.3
Private final consumption expenditure*	2,962.7	3,176.8	3,297.8
Increase in stocks†	−3.2	−21.1	−9.1
Gross fixed capital formation	709.6	743.2	806.6
Total domestic expenditure	4,468.8	4,751.4	4,976.6
Exports of goods and services	3,332.1	3,466.7	3,360.5
Less Imports of goods and services	3,275.5	3,375.1	3,188.9
GDP in purchasers' values	4,525.4	4,843.0	5,148.2
GDP at constant 1980 prices	3,609.4	3,660.5	3,748.3

* Including statistical discrepancy ('000 million francs): −25.0 in 1984; −18.8 in 1985; −36.7 in 1986.
† Including adjustment in connection with gross fixed capital ('000 million francs): −6.0 in 1984; −4.3 in 1985; −8.9 in 1986.

BELGIUM

Statistical Survey

Gross Domestic Product by Economic Activity

	1984	1985	1986
Agriculture and livestock	104.5	103.7	105.1
Forestry and logging	6.2	6.8	6.9
Fishing	1.7	2.0	2.2
Mining and quarrying	24.3	23.6	22.4
Manufacturing[1]	1,022.3	1,087.9	1,164.5
Electricity, gas and water	162.5	181.9	190.8
Construction	236.1	248.2	260.4
Wholesale and retail trade[2]	656.6	742.8	845.3
Distribution of petroleum products[2]	225.0	224.1	221.5
Transport, storage and communications	362.3	389.4	381.9
Finance and insurance	249.5	272.2	318.0
Real estate[3]	257.9	277.8	295.3
Business services	190.0	190.8	218.7
Public administration and defence	372.7	397.2	415.3
Education	272.3	286.5	292.7
Health services	120.3	129.0	137.7
Other community, social and personal services[4]	341.5	367.9	387.8
Domestic service of households	47.3	49.5	51.3
Sub-total	4,653.0	4,981.3	5,317.8
Imputed bank service charge	−72.2	−78.7	−96.3
Value-added tax deductible from capital formation	−77.6	−85.5	−96.9
Statistical discrepancy[5]	22.2	25.9	23.6
Total	4,525.4	4,843.0	5,148.2

[1] Including garages. [2] Including import duties. [3] Including imputed rent of owner-occupied dwellings. [4] Including restaurants and hotels.
[5] Including a correction to compensate for the exclusion of certain own-account capital investments ('000 million francs): 6.1 in 1984; 6.8 in 1985; 7.6 in 1986.

BALANCE OF PAYMENTS (US $ million)*

	1985	1986	1987
Merchandise exports f.o.b.	47,336	59,938	76,100
Merchandise imports f.o.b.	−47,808	−59,399	−76,256
Trade balance	−472	539	−156
Exports of services	33,467	41,259	48,218
Imports of services	−31,670	−37,797	−43,743
Balance on goods and services	1,325	4,001	4,319
Private unrequited transfers (net)	−129	−212	−116
Government unrequited transfers (net)	−527	−781	−1,283
Current balance	669	3,009	2,920
Direct capital investment (net)	755	−993	−411
Other long-term capital (net)	−5,312	−5,788	−1,709
Short-term capital (net)	4,379	3,644	1,021
Net errors and omissions	−140	247	414
Total (net monetary movements)	350	118	2,235
Monetization of gold (net)	—	—	287
Valuation changes (net)	505	711	1,665
Official financing (net)	−426	−362	161
Changes in reserves	429	467	4,348

* Including Luxembourg.
Source: IMF, *International Financial Statistics*.

External Trade of Belgium and Luxembourg

Note: Figures exclude trade in monetary gold, non-commercial military goods and silver specie.
Exports include stores and bunkers for foreign ships and aircraft.

PRINCIPAL COMMODITIES
(distribution by SITC, million Belgian francs)

Imports c.i.f.	1985	1986	1987*
Food and live animals	293,685	279,841	273,122
Dairy products and birds' eggs	40,832	38,367	40,539
Cereals and cereal preparations	60,041	49,877	50,461
Vegetables and fruit	53,478	52,966	56,064
Coffee, tea, cocoa and spices	41,446	39,029	28,863
Animal feeding-stuff (excl. cereals)	31,552	30,175	27,173
Beverages and tobacco	37,814	37,505	38,242
Crude materials (inedible) except fuels[1]	246,214	191,108	194,423
Oil seeds and oleaginous fruit	32,506	25,374	26,729
Textile fibres and waste[2]	33,979	28,700	28,782
Metalliferous ores and metal scrap[1]	89,649	59,201	59,786
Non-ferrous base metal waste and scrap	32,124	21,121	22,427
Mineral fuels, lubricants, etc. (incl. electric current)	550,962	325,310	288,192
Coal, coke and briquettes	51,366	41,500	34,618
Coal, lignite and peat	37,856	29,793	25,496
Petroleum, petroleum products, etc.	396,326	219,026	205,027
Crude petroleum oils, etc.	187,819	112,993	117,835
Refined petroleum products	200,174	100,351	82,563
Gas oils (distillate fuels)	64,956	34,256	26,056
Residual fuel oils	75,451	35,906	30,094
Gas (natural and manufactured)	95,089	58,933	43,108
Petroleum gases, etc., in the gaseous state	85,165	54,926	34,529
Animal and vegetable oils, fats and waxes	20,847	12,972	10,148
Chemicals and related products[2]	338,836	318,188	323,899
Organic chemicals[2]	116,289	99,750	99,119
Hydrocarbons and their derivatives[2]	56,076	38,535	43,167
Artificial resins, plastic materials, etc.[2]	78,776	76,014	79,050
Products of polymerization, etc.[2]	51,420	48,868	51,605
Basic manufactures[1,2]	675,929	663,873	669,387
Paper, paperboard and manufactures[2]	66,151	69,344	73,953
Paper and paperboard (not cut to size or shape)[2]	46,025	48,607	52,019
Textile yarn, fabrics, etc.	102,755	99,732	99,480
Textile yarn	45,847	42,150	40,998
Non-metallic mineral manufactures	205,171	212,147	219,060
Pearls, precious and semi-precious stones	167,608	171,459	176,910
Non-industrial diamonds (unset)	166,453	170,342	175,812
Sorted diamonds (rough or simply worked)	106,105	106,096	112,171
Cut diamonds (unmounted)	60,333	63,751	61,596
Iron and steel	94,375	89,779	90,117
Non-ferrous metals[1,2]	103,121	85,091	77,083
Copper and copper alloys[1]	46,533	37,707	31,768
Unwrought copper and alloys[1]	40,377	32,108	26,079
Aluminium and aluminium alloys	34,943	32,010	31,469
Other metal manufactures	66,020	67,818	68,344

BELGIUM

Statistical Survey

Imports c.i.f.—*continued*	1985	1986	1987*
Machinery and transport equipment	766,995	854,617	909,747
Power generating machinery and equipment	67,293	69,687	73,248
Internal combustion piston engines (incl. parts)	50,985	51,999	56,790
Machinery specialized for particular industries	56,264	64,169	70,639
General industrial machinery, equipment and parts	81,551	84,287	86,598
Office machines and automatic data processing equipment	64,653	66,463	71,849
Automatic data processing machines, etc.	38,309	40,357	44,084
Electrical machinery, apparatus, etc.	121,324	139,956	135,695
Road vehicles and parts[3]	334,694	380,796	419,391
Passenger motor cars (excl. buses)	104,707	126,222	136,786
Parts and accessories for cars, buses, lorries, etc.	199,161	213,740	236,844
Miscellaneous manufactured articles	266,663	289,126	315,348
Clothing and accessories (excl. footwear)[2]	78,966	86,343	94,331
Other commodities and transactions	119,868	92,699	76,699
Non-monetary gold (excl. gold ores and concentrates)	35,031	27,891	23,493
Unwrought or semi-manufactured gold (excl. rolled gold)	34,854	27,757	23,397
Confidential transactions	70,850	55,061	45,949
Total	3,317,812	3,065,239	3,099,209

* Provisional.
[1] Copper matte, usually classified with metal ores and concentrates (under 'crude materials'), is included in non-ferrous metals (under 'basic manufactures').
[2] Figures exclude the value of certain confidential transactions, included in the last item of the table.
[3] Excluding tyres, engines and electrical parts.

Exports f.o.b.	1985	1986	1987*
Food and live animals[1]	273,220	272,483	277,368
Meat and meat preparations	49,696	54,225	55,123
Fresh, chilled or frozen meat	36,370	39,991	40,658
Dairy products and birds' eggs	41,624	44,712	48,571
Cereals and cereal preparations	45,766	36,082	39,844
Vegetables and fruit	38,800	41,826	44,507
Beverages and tobacco	24,556	24,225	25,514
Crude materials (inedible) except fuels[1,2]	88,019	76,467	77,223
Mineral fuels, lubricants, etc. (incl. electric current)	208,617	152,578	117,056
Petroleum, petroleum products, etc.	188,964	137,815	104,007
Refined petroleum products	178,311	129,739	97,565
Motor spirit (petrol) and other light oils	54,702	38,917	27,790
Motor spirit (incl. aviation spirit)	36,388	27,480	15,157
Gas oils (distillate fuels)	40,061	26,525	17,021
Residual fuel oils	51,440	37,046	31,171
Animal and vegetable oils, fats and waxes[1]	24,983	15,395	12,541
Chemicals and related products[1]	406,701	382,931	388,315
Organic chemicals[1]	77,552	66,562	61,816
Medicinal and pharmaceutical products[1]	39,400	39,755	40,233
Artificial resins, plastic materials, etc.	143,043	137,476	147,527
Products of polymerization, etc.[1]	101,456	92,749	101,883

Exports f.o.b.—*continued*	1985	1986	1987*
Basic manufactures[1]	977,502	915,058	908,878
Paper, paperboard and manufactures	44,264	46,006	50,756
Textile yarn, fabrics, etc.[1]	178,456	174,478	174,291
Textile yarn	39,955	36,976	37,070
Floor coverings, etc.[1]	56,046	55,382	56,370
Carpets, carpeting, rugs, mats, etc.	55,425	54,908	55,584
Non-metallic mineral manufactures[1]	252,084	243,605	250,425
Pearls, precious and semi-precious stones	189,110	177,223	180,833
Non-industrial diamonds (unset)	187,977	176,214	179,922
Sorted diamonds (rough or simply worked)	91,898	92,211	93,179
Cut diamonds (unmounted)	96,074	84,003	86,696
Iron and steel[1]	265,575	236,659	224,215
Ingots and other primary forms	47,697	44,520	45,900
Bars, rods, angles, shapes, etc.	53,785	48,364	39,494
Universals, plates and sheets	111,531	100,698	102,064
Thin sheets and plates (rolled but not further worked)	47,833	44,139	42,087
Non-ferrous metals[1,2]	117,433	98,137	92,546
Copper and copper alloys[1,2]	49,108	40,348	38,854
Aluminium and aluminium alloys	33,211	30,861	31,842
Other metal manufactures	68,968	65,166	66,461
Machinery and transport equipment[1]	735,635	792,348	834,623
Power generating machinery and equipment[1]	48,501	19,523	19,474
Machinery specialized for particular industries[1]	74,254	75,460	82,291
General industrial machinery, equipment and parts[1]	54,967	54,641	53,699
Telecommunications and sound equipment	48,821	66,109	67,177
Other electrical machinery, apparatus, etc.	67,051	70,158	71,390
Road vehicles and parts[1,3]	378,012	432,960	464,669
Passenger motor cars (excl. buses)	286,936	329,207	356,444
Parts and accessories for cars, buses, lorries, etc.[3]	44,687	46,106	50,593
Miscellaneous manufactured articles[1]	229,457	239,628	251,103
Furniture and parts	33,198	33,691	35,568
Clothing and accessories (excl. footwear)	44,853	47,849	50,960
Photographic apparatus, etc., optical goods, watches and clocks[1]	47,890	47,341	46,370
Photographic and cinematographic supplies	44,588	43,064	41,882
Photographic film, plates and paper	40,832	39,306	37,624
Other commodities and transactions	199,003	199,213	200,447
Confidential transactions	175,363	184,024	184,482
Total	3,167,691	3,070,327	3,093,069

* Provisional.
[1] Figures exclude the value of certain confidential transactions, included in the last item of the table.
[2] Copper matte, usually classified with metal ores and concentrates (under 'crude materials'), is included in non-ferrous metals (under 'basic manufactures').
[3] Excluding tyres, engines and electrical parts.

BELGIUM   *Statistical Survey*

PRINCIPAL TRADING PARTNERS*
(million Belgian francs)

Imports c.i.f.	1985	1986	1987†
Austria	23,147	25,782	23,900
Brazil	29,598	15,836	17,317
Canada	18,772	16,054	21,554
France	498,946	485,655	487,456
Germany, Federal Republic	695,513	709,252	754,379
Iraq	10,973	3,373	12,100
Italy	118,169	129,985	132,177
Japan	70,275	84,798	82,477
Libya	3,548	8,091	13,661
Netherlands	614,602	547,563	532,663
Nigeria	39,107	16,541	5,685
Norway	26,803	13,409	19,334
Saudi Arabia	22,801	33,173	16,608
South Africa and Namibia	20,688	16,094	14,357
Spain (excl. Canary Is.)	37,804	34,745	37,021
Sweden	62,566	64,458	70,525
Switzerland	77,349	67,529	60,336
USSR	74,001	46,778	47,867
United Kingdom	295,654	255,848	241,700
USA	187,924	154,716	146,863
Zaire	32,605	27,832	23,925
All countries (incl. others)	3,304,322	3,058,497	3,092,428
Not distributed	13,490	6,742	6,781
Total	**3,317,812**	**3,065,239**	**3,099,209**

* Imports by country of production; exports by country of last consignment.
† Provisional.

Exports f.o.b.	1985	1986	1987†
Algeria	20,071	11,658	9,349
Austria	26,493	29,896	29,145
Canada	21,848	18,434	14,989
Denmark	34,470	37,043	32,842
France	600,637	614,836	633,088
Germany, Federal Republic	588,662	605,794	613,904
India	41,809	36,185	38,451
Israel	34,769	41,179	46,692
Italy	172,280	179,134	197,444
Japan	25,589	28,346	31,650
Netherlands	451,006	461,131	465,061
Norway	23,449	26,874	21,965
Saudi Arabia	28,160	18,402	14,953
Spain (excl. Canary Is.)	31,269	41,863	57,051
Sweden	45,871	45,411	44,441
Switzerland	76,326	72,607	70,790
USSR	37,305	22,164	18,323
United Kingdom	309,865	267,140	260,677
USA	200,790	162,608	160,922
All countries (incl. others)	3,141,180	3,045,512	3,070,875
Not distributed	26,511	24,815	22,194
Total	**3,167,691**	**3,070,327**	**3,093,069**

Transport

RAILWAYS (traffic)

	1985	1986	1987
Passenger-km (million)	6,572	6,069	6,970
Freight ton-km (million)	8,254	7,423	7,266

ROAD TRAFFIC (motor vehicles in use at 31 December)

	1985	1986	1987
Private cars	3,342,704	3,408,721	3,497,818
Buses and coaches	16,817	16,449	16,095
Goods vehicles	272,839	282,286	296,415
Tractors (non-agricultural)	29,243	30,170	31,627

SHIPPING

Fleet (at 30 June)

	1986	1987	1988
Merchant shipping:			
Steamships:			
number	2	1	1
displacement*	113.7	78.5	78.5
Motor vessels:			
number	94	91	77
displacement*	2,104.5	2,178.5	1,960.9
Inland waterways:			
Powered craft:			
number	2,327	1,914	1,828
displacement*	1,405.8	1,135.8	1,095.7
Non-powered craft:			
number	181	177	167
displacement*	323.6	346.2	334.0

* '000 gross registered tons.

Freight Traffic ('000 metric tons)

	1985	1986	1987
Sea-borne shipping:			
Goods loaded	49,804	46,170	45,485
Goods unloaded	74,127	77,028	82,407
Inland waterways:			
Goods loaded	50,414	51,794	50,843
Goods unloaded	60,922	61,013	62,692

CIVIL AVIATION (traffic)

	1985	1986	1987
Kilometres flown ('000)	53,094	53,181	57,910
Passenger-km ('000)	5,664,363	5,561,536	5,976,593
Ton-km ('000)	509,677	500,512	538,000
Mail ton-km ('000)	18,246	19,220	23,000

Figures refer to Sabena—Belgian World Air Lines.

Tourism

	1985	1986	1987
Number of tourist nights*	9,843,452	9,815,769	10,064,504

* Foreign visitors only.

BELGIUM   Statistical Survey, Directory

Communications Media

	1985	1986	1987
Telephones in use	4,346,369	4,555,955	4,719,273
Television receivers in use	2,971,596	2,984,119	3,172,636
Radio licences	4,526,291	4,515,973	4,608,450

Newspapers (1984): 26 general interest dailies (combined circulation 2,209,000).

Book titles (production, 1984): 6,527, of which 5,722 were first editions.

Source: partly UNESCO, *Statistical Yearbook*.

Education

(1982/83)

	Institutions	Students
Pre-school	4,234	395,883
Primary	4,790	768,207
Secondary	2,272	858,625
Non-academic higher education	477	114,291
Universities and equivalent	19	102,354

1985: Pre-school 19,763 teachers, 391,848 students; Primary 44,190 teachers, 730,288 students; Secondary 824,997 students; Universities and equivalent 103,598 students (Source: UNESCO, *Statistical Yearbook*).

1986/87 Students: Pre-school 381,787; Primary 755,085; Secondary 843,674; Non-academic higher education 121,478; Universities and equivalent 103,505 (Sources: Ministerie van Onderwijs and Ministère de l'Education Nationale).

Directory

The Constitution

The Belgian Constitution has been considerably modified by amendments since its origin in 1831. Belgium is a constitutional monarchy. The central legislature consists of a Chamber of Representatives and a Senate. The Chamber of Representatives consists of 212 members, who are elected for four years unless the Chamber is dissolved before that time has elapsed. Belgium entered 1971 with a rewritten Constitution, differing from its predecessor mainly in its treatment of the three cultural entities: French-speaking, Dutch-speaking and German-speaking. Each community has regional powers in cultural and economic affairs. Before this there had been juridical recognition of the separate, bilingual status of Brussels, and provision made for the creation of regional political organs for Brussels, Flanders and Wallonia.

ELECTORAL SYSTEM

Members must be 25 years of age, and they are elected by secret ballot according to a system of proportional representation. Suffrage is universal for citizens of 18 years or over, and voting is compulsory.

The Senate, or Second Chamber, is chosen in the following manner. It is composed of:

(1) Half as many members as the Chamber of Representatives, elected directly by the same electors.

(2) Members chosen by the Provincial Councillors, in the proportion of one for every 200,000 population.

(3) Members co-opted by groups (1) and (2), up to half the number of group (2).

(4) One Senator by right, the heir to the throne.

There are now 182 Senators.

All Senators must be over 40, with the exception of a small number of members of the royal family, who become Senators by right at the age of 18. Members are elected for four years.

THE CROWN

The King has the right to veto legislation, but he does not exercise it. Though he is supreme head of the executive, he in fact exercises his control through the Cabinet, which is responsible for all acts of government to the Chamber of Representatives. Though the King, according to the Constitution, appoints his own ministers, in practice, since they are responsible to the Chamber of Representatives and need its confidence, they are generally the choice of the Representatives. Similarly, the royal initiative is in the hands of the ministry.

LEGISLATION

Legislation is introduced either by the Government or the members in the two Houses, and as the party complexion of both Houses is generally almost the same, measures passed by the Chamber of Representatives are usually passed by the Senate. Each House elects its own President at the beginning of the session, who acts as an impartial Speaker, although he is a party nominee. The Houses elect their own committees, through which all legislation passes. They are so well organized that through them the Legislature has considerable power of control over the Cabinet. Nevertheless, according to the Constitution (Article 68), certain treaties must be communicated to the Chamber only as soon as the 'interest and safety of the State permit'. Further, the Government possesses an important power of dissolution which it uses; a most unusual feature is that it may be applied to either House separately or to both together (Article 71).

Revision of the Constitution is to be first settled by an ordinary majority vote of both Houses, specifying the article to be amended. The Houses are then automatically dissolved. The new Chambers then determine the amendments to be made, with the provision that in each House the presence of two-thirds of the members is necessary for a quorum, and a two-thirds majority of those voting is required.

LOCAL ADMINISTRATION

The system of local government conforms to the general European practice of being based on a combination of central officials as the executive agent and locally elected councillors as the deliberating body. The areas are the provinces and the communes, and the latter are empowered by Article 108 of the Constitution to associate for the purposes of better government.

The Government

HEAD OF STATE

King of the Belgians: HM King BAUDOUIN (BOUDEWIJN) (took the oath 17 July 1951).

THE CABINET

(November 1988)

(CVP) and (PSC) Christian Social Party; (PS) Parti Socialiste; (SP) Socialistische Partij; (VU) Volksunie.

Prime Minister: Dr WILFRIED MARTENS (CVP).

Deputy Prime Minister, Minister for the Brussels Region and of Institutional Reforms (French Sector): PHILIPPE MOUREAUX (PS).

Deputy Prime Minister, Minister of Economic Affairs and Planning and National Education (Flemish Sector): WILLY CLAES (SP).

BELGIUM

Deputy Prime Minister, Minister of Communications and Institutional Reforms (Flemish Sector): JEAN-LUC DEHAENE (CVP).
Deputy Prime Minister, Minister of Justice and the Middle Classes: MELCHIOR WATHELET (PSC).
Deputy Prime Minister, Minister of the Budget and Scientific Policy: HUGO SCHLITZ (VU).
Minister of Foreign Affairs: LEO TINDEMANS (CVP).
Minister of Finance: PHILIPPE MAYSTADT (PSC).
Minister of Foreign Trade: ROBERT URBAIN (PS).
Minister of the Civil Service: MICHEL HANSENNE (PSC).
Minister of Posts and Telecommunications: FREDDY WILLOCKX (SP).
Minister of Social Affairs: PHILIPPE BUSQUIN (PS).
Minister of National Defence: GUY COËME (PS).
Minister of Public Works: PAULA D'HONDT-VAN OPDENBOSCH (CVP).
Minister of the Interior and for the Modernization of the Civil Service and National Scientific and Cultural Institutions: LOUIS TOBBACK (SP).
Minister of National Education (French Sector): YVAN YLIEFF (SP).
Minister of Development Co-operation: ANDRÉ GEENS (VU).
Minister of Pensions: ALAIN VAN DER BIEST (PS).
Minister of Employment and Labour: LUC VAN DEN BRANDE (CVP).

There are 13 Secretaries of State.

MINISTRIES

Office of the Prime Minister: 16 rue de la Loi, 1000 Brussels; tel. (02) 513-80-20; telex 62400.
Ministry for the Brussels Region: 21-23 blvd du Régent, 1000 Brussels; tel. (02) 513-82-00; telex 25190.
Ministry of the Budget and Scientific Policy: 26 rue de la Loi, 1040 Brussels; tel. (02) 237-93-11; telex 22292.
Ministry of the Civil Service: Lynton Building, 31 rue du Commerce, 1040 Brussels; tel. (02) 513-88-40.
Ministry of Communications and Institutional Reforms (Flemish Sector): 65 rue de la Loi, 1040 Brussels; tel. (02) 237-67-11; telex 25183.
Ministry of Development Co-operation: 2 rue des Quatre Bras, 1000 Brussels; tel. (02) 516-84-11.
Ministry of Economic Affairs and Planning: 23 square de Meeûs, 1040 Brussels; tel. (02) 511-19-30; telex 21062.
Ministry of Employment and Labour: 51-53 rue Belliard, 1040 Brussels; tel. (02) 233-41-11; telex 22937.
Ministry of Finance: 12 rue de la Loi, 1000 Brussels; tel. (02) 233-81-11.
Ministry of Foreign Affairs: 2 rue des Quatre Bras, 1000 Brussels; tel. (02) 516-81-11; telex 23979.
Ministry of Foreign Trade: 2 rue des Quatre Bras, 1000 Brussels; tel. (02) 516-83-11.
Ministry of Institutional Reforms (French Sector): 21-23 blvd du Régent, 1000 Brussels; tel. (02) 513-82-00.
Ministry of the Interior and for the Modernization of Public Services and National Scientific and Cultural Institutions: 2 rue de la Loi, 1000 Brussels; tel. (02) 511-06-60; telex 21762.
Ministry of Justice: 4 place Poelaert, 1000 Brussels; tel. (02) 513-67-88; telex 62440.
Ministry of the Middle Classes: 61 rue de la Régence, 1000 Brussels; tel. (02) 511-19-48.
Ministry of National Defence: 8 rue Lambermont, 1000 Brussels; tel. (02) 512-16-10; telex 61104.
Ministry of National Education (Flemish Sector): 3 rue Ducale, 1000 Brussels; tel. (02) 513-28-90; telex 26750.
Ministry of National Education (French Sector): 68A rue du Commerce, 1040 Brussels; tel. (02) 511-72-60; telex 24619.
Ministry of Pensions: 31 rue du Commerce, 1040 Brussels; tel. (02) 513-63-70.
Ministry of Posts and Telecommunications: 56 rue de la Loi, 1040 Brussels; tel. (02) 230-13-30.
Ministry of Public Works: 9th Floor, 155 rue de la Loi, 1040 Brussels; tel. (02) 734-91-07; telex 63477.
Ministry of Social Affairs: 5th Floor, 56 rue de la Loi, 1040 Brussels; tel. (02) 230-01-70.

Legislature

CHAMBRE DES REPRÉSENTANTS/KAMER VAN VOLKSVERTEGENWOORDIGERS
(Chamber of Representatives)

General Election, 13 December 1987

	Votes	%	Seats
CVP	1,194,687	19.45	43
PS	961,429	15.66	40
SP	913,975	14.88	32
PVV	709,137	11.55	25
PRL	577,897	9.41	23
PSC	491,839	8.01	19
VU	494,229	8.05	16
Agalev	275,307	4.48	6
Ecolo	157,985	2.57	3
FDF	71,340	1.16	3
Vlaams Blok	116,410	1.90	2
PCB/KPB	51,074	0.83	0
PvdA/PTB	45,162	0.74	0
Others	80,741	1.31	0
Total	6,141,212	100.00	212

SÉNAT/SENAAT

General Election, 13 December 1987

	Votes	%	Seats
CVP	1,169,539	19.20	22
PS	958,760	15.74	20
SP	896,114	14.71	17
PRL	564,221	9.26	12
PVV	686,608	11.27	11
PSC	474,708	7.79	9
VU	494,432	8.12	8
Agalev	299,051	4.91	3
Ecolo	168,381	2.76	2
Vlaams Blok	122,925	2.02	1
FDF	77,596	1.27	1
PCB/KPB	52,322	0.86	0
PvdA/PTB	43,381	0.71	0
Others	84,522	1.39	0
Total	6,092,560	100.00	106

In addition, the Senate has 50 members elected by provincial councils, a further 25 co-opted by the elected members and one Senator by right, the heir to the throne.

Political Organizations

Anders Gaan Leven (Agalev) (Ecologist Party—Dutch-speaking): 78 Twee Kerkenstraat, 1040 Brussels; tel. (02) 230-66-66; f. 1982; Pres. LÉO COX.

Ecolo (Ecologist Party—French-speaking): 28 rue Basse-Marcelle, 5000 Namur; tel. (081) 22-78-71; Pres. PAUL LANNOYE.

Front Démocratique des Bruxellois Francophones (FDF) (French-speaking Democratic Front): 127 chaussée de Charleroi, 1060 Brussels; tel. (02) 538-83-20; f. 1964; aims at the preservation of the French character of Brussels and the establishment of a federal state; Pres. GEORGES CLERFAYT; Sec.-Gen. JEAN-PIERRE CORNELISSEN.

Front National: f. 1988; extreme right-wing nationalist party; Leader WERNER VAN STEEN.

Partei der Deutschsprachigen Belgier (PDB) (German-speaking Party): 6 Kaperberg, 4700 Eupen; f. 1971; aims at equality of rights for the German-speaking minority (65,000 approx.) as recognized in the national constitution; Pres. ALFRED KEUTGEN (Eupen).

Parti Communiste de Belgique (PCB)/Kommunistische Partij van België (KPB) (Communist Party): 18-20 ave Stalingrad, 1000 Brussels; tel. (02) 512-90-12; f. 1921; c. 7,000 mems; Pres. LOUIS VAN GEYT; Vice-Pres. (French-speaking) CLAUDE RENARD; Secs MARCEL COUTEAU, ROEL JACOBS, L. LOOSE, ROBERT DUSSART, DANIEL FEDRIGO.

Parti Féministe Unifié (PFU): 35 ave des Phalènes, BP 14, Ixelles, 1050 Brussels; tel. (02) 648-87-38; f. 1972; aims at the creation of a humanistic, self-governing, egalitarian republic where the basic rights of the individual and of society are respected; non-hierarchical structure.

BELGIUM

Parti de la Liberté du Citoyen (PLC): 46 ave de Scheut, 1070 Brussels; tel. (02) 524-39-66; Pres. LUC EYKERMAN.

Parti Réformateur Libéral (PRL) (Liberal Party—French-speaking wing): Centre International Rogier, 26e étage, BP 570, 1210 Brussels; tel. (02) 219-43-30; f. 1979; 60,000 mems; formerly the Parti des Réformes et de la Liberté en Wallonie; Pres. LOUIS MICHEL.

Parti Social Chrétien (PSC)/Christelijke Volkspartij (CVP) (Christian Social Party): 41 rue des deux Eglises, 1040 Brussels; tel. (02) 238-01-11 (PSC); (02) 230-60-70 (CVP); f. 1945; 186,000 mems; Pres. (PSC) GÉRARD DEPREZ; Pres. (CVP) FRANK SWAELEN; Secs JACQUES LEFÈVRE (PSC), LUDO WILLEMS (CVP).

Parti Socialiste (PS) (Socialist Party—French-speaking wing): Maison du PS, 13 blvd de l'Empereur, 1000 Brussels; tel. (02) 513-82-70; f. in 1885 as the Parti Ouvrier Belge; split from the Flemish wing in 1979; Pres. GUY SPITAELS; Sec. ROGER GAILLIEZ.

Parti Wallon (PW) (Walloon Party): 2 rue Maurice Lange, 1381 Quenast; f. 1985 by amalgamation of the Rassemblement Wallon (f. 1968), the Rassemblement Populaire Wallon and the Front Indépendantiste Wallon; advocates an independent Walloon state; ideologically a left-wing socialist party; Pres. JEAN-CLAUDE PICCIN.

Partij van de Arbeid van België (PvdA)/Parti du Travail de Belgique (PTB) (Belgian Labour Party): f. 1979; Marxist-Leninist; Leader LUDO MARTENS.

Partij voor Vrijheid en Vooruitgang (PVV) (Liberal Party—Dutch-speaking wing): 47–48 Regentlaan, bus 2, 1000 Brussels; tel. (02) 512-78-70; telex 65865; f. 1961; succeeded the former Liberal Party; Pres. ANNEMIE NEYTS-UYTTEBROECK.

Socialistische Partij (SP) (Socialist Party—Flemish wing): 13 blvd de l'Empereur, 1000 Brussels; tel. (02) 513-28-78; f. 1885; Pres. KAREL VAN MIERT; Sec. CARLA GALLE.

Union Démocrate pour le Respect du Travail (UDRT)/Respect voor Arbeid en Democratie (RAD) (Employers' Party): 56 blvd Lambermont, 1030 Brussels; tel. (02) 242-76-60; f. 1978; aims at fiscal reform and the defence of private property and free enterprise; Pres. ROBERT HENDRICK; Co-Pres. MICHEL DEMEY; Sec. (French-speaking) PASCAL DE ROUBAIX; Sec. (Dutch-speaking) MICHEL VAN HOUTTE.

Vlaams Blok (Flemish Nationalist Party): 17 Schipperijkaai, 1210 Brussels; tel. (02) 219-60-09; f. 1979; Chair. KAREL DILLEN.

Volksunie (VU) (People's Union): 12 Barrikadenplein, 1000 Brussels; tel. (02) 219-49-30; f. 1954; 60,000 mems; Flemish nationalist party aiming at federal structure for the country; Pres. JAAK GABRIELS; Sec. P. VAN GREMBERGEN.

Terrorist organizations include the extreme left-wing Cellules Communistes Combattantes (CCC) and the associated Front Révolutionnaire d'Action Prolétarienne (FRAP), and the extreme right-wing Westland New Post (WNP).

Diplomatic Representation

EMBASSIES IN BELGIUM

Algeria: 209 ave Molière, 1060 Brussels; tel. (02) 343-50-78; telex 64142; Ambassador: SIDAHMED GHOZALI.

Angola: 182 rue Franz Merjay, 1180 Brussels; tel. (02) 344-49-80; telex 63170; Ambassador: EMÍLIO CARVALHO GUERRA.

Argentina: 225 ave Louise, BP 6, 1050 Brussels; tel. (02) 647-78-12; Ambassador: TEODORO GABRIEL MATZKIN.

Australia: 6–8 rue Guimard, 1040 Brussels; tel. (02) 231-05-00; telex 21834; Ambassador: PETER C. J. CURTIS.

Austria: 47 rue de l'Abbaye, 1050 Brussels; tel. (02) 649-91-70; telex 22463; Ambassador: HEINZ WEINBERGER.

Bangladesh: 29–31 rue Jacques Jordaens, 1050 Brussels; tel. (02) 640-55-00; telex 63189; Chargé d'affaires a.i.: MASUM CHOWDHURY.

Barbados: 14 ave Lloyd George, 1050 Brussels; tel. (02) 648-13-58; telex 63926; Ambassador: RASHID ORLANDO MARVILLE.

Benin: 5 ave de l'Observatoire, 1180 Brussels; tel. (02) 374-91-92; telex 24568; Ambassador: TAIRON DJAOUGA-MAMADOU.

Bolivia: 176 ave Louise, BP 6, 1050 Brussels; tel. (02) 647-27-18; telex 63494; Ambassador: AUGUSTO CUADROS SÁNCHEZ.

Botswana: 169 ave de Tervueren, 1040 Brussels; tel. (02) 735-20-70; telex 22849; Ambassador: ERNEST SIPHO MPOFU.

Brazil: 350 ave Louise, BP 5, 1050 Brussels; tel. (02) 640-20-15; telex 26758; Ambassador: DAVID SILVEIRA DA MOTA, Jr.

Bulgaria: 58 ave Hamoir, 1180 Brussels; tel. (02) 374-59-63; telex 22473; Ambassador: YORDAN KIROV.

Burkina Faso: 16 place Guy d'Arezzo, 1060 Brussels; tel. (02) 345-99-12; Ambassador: AMADÉ OUEDRAOGO.

Burundi: 46 square Marie-Louise, 1040 Brussels; tel. (02) 230-45-35; telex 23572; Ambassador: ASTÈRE NZISABIRA.

Cameroon: 131 ave Brugmann, 1060 Brussels; tel. (02) 345-18-70; telex 24117; Ambassador: ISABELLE BASSONG.

Canada: 2 ave de Tervueren, 1040 Brussels; tel. (02) 513-79-40; telex 21613; Ambassador: JACQUES J. A. ASSELIN.

Central African Republic: 416 blvd Lambermont, 1030 Brussels; tel. (02) 242-28-80; telex 22493; Chargé d'affaires a.i.: GRÉGOIRE WILLYBIRO-NGOUTOU.

Chad: 52 blvd Lambermont, 1030 Brussels; tel. (02) 215-19-75; Ambassador: ABDOULAYE LAMANA.

Chile: 17 rue Montoyer, 1040 Brussels; tel. (02) 512-67-00; telex 61955; Chargé d'affaires a.i.: JOSÉ MANUEL OVALLE BRAVO.

China, People's Republic: 443–445 ave de Tervueren, 1150 Brussels; tel. (02) 771-58-57; Ambassador: LIU SHAN.

Colombia: 44 rue Van Eyck, BP 5-6, 1050 Brussels; tel. (02) 649-56-79; telex 25254; Ambassador: RAFAEL RIVAS FOSADA.

Comoros: c/o Senegal Embassy, Brussels (see below); Ambassador: ALI MLAHAI LI (resident in Paris).

Congo: 16-18 ave F. D. Roosevelt, 1050 Brussels; tel. (02) 648-38-56; telex 23677; Ambassador: AMBROISE GAMBOUELE.

Costa Rica: 437 ave Louise, 1050 Brussels; tel. (02) 640-55-41; telex 23548; Ambassador: DANIEL RATTON THIERY.

Côte d'Ivoire: 234 ave F. D. Roosevelt, 1050 Brussels; tel. (02) 672-23-57; telex 21993; Ambassador: CHARLES VALY TUHO.

Cuba: 77 rue Roberts-Jones, 1180 Brussels; tel. (02) 343-00-20; telex 21945; Ambassador: TERESITA AVERHOFF PURÓN.

Cyprus: 83 rue de la Loi (4e étage), 1040 Brussels; tel. (02) 230-12-95; telex 25172; Ambassador: ANGELOS ANGELIDES.

Czechoslovakia: 152 ave Adolphe Buyl, 1050 Brussels; tel. (02) 647-68-09; telex 21455; Ambassador: KAREL LUKAS.

Denmark: 221 ave Louise, BP 7, 1050 Brussels; tel. (02) 648-25-25; telex 22591; Ambassador: GEORG F. K. HARHOFF.

Dominica: 12 rue des Bollandistes, 1040 Brussels; tel. (02) 733-43-28; Ambassador: CHARLES SAVARIN.

Ecuador: 70 chaussée de Charleroi, 1060 Brussels; tel. (02) 537-91-30; telex 63292; Ambassador: DIEGO PAREDES PEÑA.

Egypt: 44 ave Léo Errera, 1180 Brussels; tel. (02) 648-18-01; telex 64809; Ambassador: FAWZI MOHAMED EL IBRASHI.

Ethiopia: 32 blvd St Michel, 1040 Brussels; tel. (02) 733-49-29; telex 62285; Chargé d'affaires a.i.: ALEMAYEHU RAMETO.

Fiji: 66–68 ave de Cortenberg (7e étage), BP 7, 1040 Brussels; tel. (02) 736-90-51; telex 26934; Chargé d'affaires: IAN PERKS.

Finland: 489 ave Louise, 1050 Brussels; tel. (02) 648-84-84; telex 23099; Ambassador: PENTTI TALVITIE.

France: 65 rue Ducale, 1000 Brussels; tel. (02) 512-17-15; telex 21478; Ambassador: Comte XAVIER DE CAUZE DE NAZELLE.

Gabon: 112 ave W. Churchill, 1180 Brussels; tel. (02) 343-00-55; telex 23383; Ambassador: MARCEL ODONGUI-BONNARD.

Gambia: 126 ave F. D. Roosevelt, 1050 Brussels; tel. (02) 640-10-49; telex 24344; Ambassador: MAMADU KALIFO BOJANG.

German Democratic Republic: 80 blvd St Michel, 1040 Brussels; tel. (02) 743-91-00; telex 21585; Ambassador: ERNST WALKOWSKI.

Germany, Federal Republic: 190 ave de Tervueren, 1150 Brussels; tel. (02) 770-58-30; telex 21382; Ambassador: Frau RENATE FINKE-OSIANDER.

Ghana: 44 rue Gachard, 1050 Brussels; tel. (02) 649-01-63; telex 22572; Ambassador: JOSEPH AHWA LARYEA.

Greece: 430 ave Louise (3e étage), 1050 Brussels; tel. (02) 648-33-02; telex 25521; Ambassador: GEORGES VANDALIS.

Grenada: 24 ave des Arts (7e étage), BP 2, 1040 Brussels; tel. (02) 230-62-65; telex 64015; Chargé d'affaires a.i.: SAMUEL ORGIAS.

Guatemala: 53 blvd Général Wahis, 1030 Brussels; tel. (02) 736-03-40; telex 25130; Ambassador: J. ALEXEI DE SYNEGUB.

Guinea: 75 ave Roger Vandendriessche, 1150 Brussels; tel. (02) 771-01-90; telex 64731; Ambassador: IBRAHIMA SYLLA.

Guinea-Bissau: 70 ave F. D. Roosevelt, 1050 Brussels; tel. (02) 230-41-21; telex 63631; Ambassador: BUBACAR TURÉ.

Guyana: 21–22 ave des Arts, 1040 Brussels; tel. (02) 230-60-65; telex 26180; Ambassador: JAMES MATHESON.

Haiti: 160A ave Louise, BP 21, 1050 Brussels; tel. (02) 649-73-81; Chargé d'affaires a.i.: MARYSE PENETTE.

Holy See: 5–9 ave des Franciscains, 1150 Brussels; tel. (02) 762-20-05; Apostolic Nuncio: Archbishop ANGELO PEDRONI.

Honduras: 3 ave des Gaulois (5e étage), 1040 Brussels; tel. (02) 734-00-00; telex 63175; Ambassador: MANUEL LÓPEZ LUNA.

BELGIUM

Hungary: 41 rue Edmond Picard, 1180 Brussels; tel. (02) 343-67-90; telex 21428; Ambassador: Dr József Németh.
Iceland: 5 rue Archimède (8e étage), 1040 Brussels; tel. (02) 231-03-95; telex 29459; Ambassador: Einar Benediktsson.
India: 217 chaussée de Vleurgat, 1050 Brussels; tel. (02) 640-91-40; telex 22510; Ambassador: Dr N. P. Jain.
Indonesia: 294 ave de Tervueren, 1150 Brussels; tel. (02) 771-20-14; telex 21200; Ambassador: Atmono Suryo.
Iran: 415 ave de Tervueren, 1150 Brussels; tel. (02) 762-37-45; telex 24083; Chargé d'affaires a.i.: Abolghassem Ardakani.
Iraq: 131 ave de la Floride, 1180 Brussels; tel. (02) 374-59-92; telex 26414; Ambassador: Zaid Hwaishan Haidar.
Ireland: 19 rue du Luxembourg (3e étage), 1040 Brussels; tel. (02) 513-66-33; telex 24598; Ambassador: Dr Edward J. Brennan.
Israel: 40 ave de l'Observatoire, 1180 Brussels; tel. (02) 374-90-80; telex 24290; Ambassador: Avraham Primor.
Italy: 28 rue Emile Claus, 1050 Brussels; tel. (02) 649-97-00; telex 23950; Ambassador: Giovanni Saragat.
Jamaica: 83–85 rue de la Loi (5e étage), 1040 Brussels; tel. (02) 230-11-70; telex 26644; Ambassador: Leslie Wilson.
Japan: 58 ave des Arts (7e étage), 1040 Brussels; tel. (02) 513-92-00; telex 22174; Ambassador: Yoshiva Kato.
Jordan: 104 ave F. D. Roosevelt, 1050 Brussels; tel. (02) 640-77-55; telex 62513; Ambassador: Hasan Abu Nimah.
Kenya: 1–5 ave de la Joyeuse Entrée, 1040 Brussels; tel. (02) 230-30-65; telex 62568; Ambassador: Francis Kirimi Muthaura.
Korea, Republic: 3 ave Hamoir, 1180 Brussels; tel. (02) 375-39-80; telex 26256; Ambassador: Yoo Chong Ha.
Kuwait: 43 ave F. D. Roosevelt, 1050 Brussels; Ambassador: Ali Husain Saleh al-Sammak.
Lebanon: 2 rue Guillaume Stocq, 1050 Brussels; tel. (02) 649-94-60; telex 22547; Ambassador: Dr Saïd al-Assaad.
Lesotho: 66 ave de Cortenbergh, BP 5, 1040 Brussels; tel. (02) 736-39-76; telex 25852; Chargé d'affaires a.i.: Ntebaleng Mothepu.
Liberia: 55 ave F. D. Roosevelt, 1050 Brussels; tel. (02) 648-13-49; telex 61384; Chargé d'affaires a.i.: Roosevelt Anderson.
Libya: 28 ave Victoria, 1050 Brussels; tel. (02) 649-21-12; Sec. of People's Bureau: Dr Mohamed Saraf Edin Alfaituri.
Luxembourg: 75 ave de Cortenbergh, 1040 Brussels; tel. (02) 733-99-77; Ambassador: Guy de Muyser.
Madagascar: 276 ave de Tervueren, 1150 Brussels; tel. (02) 770-17-26; telex 61197; Ambassador: Christian Rémi Richard.
Malawi: 15 rue de la Loi, 1040 Brussels; tel. (02) 231-09-80; telex 24128; Ambassador: Lawrence P. Anthony.
Malaysia: 414A ave de Tervueren, 1150 Brussels; tel. (02) 762-67-67; telex 26396; Ambassador: Dato Noor Adlan bin Yahyauddin.
Mali: 487 ave Molière, 1060 Brussels; tel. (02) 345-74-32; telex 22508; Ambassador: Lamine Keïta.
Malta: 44 rue Jules Lejeune, 1060 Brussels; tel. (02) 343-01-95; telex 26616; Ambassador: Joseph Licari.
Mauritania: 1 rue Paul Lauters, BP 11, 1050 Brussels; tel. (02) 660-49-38; Ambassador: Ely Ould Allaf.
Mauritius: 68 rue des Bollandistes, 1040 Brussels; tel. (02) 733-99-88; telex 23114; Ambassador: Raymond Chasle.
Mexico: 6 rue Paul Emile Janson, 1050 Brussels; tel. (02) 648-26-71; telex 22355; Ambassador: Alfredo del Mazo González.
Monaco: 17 place Guy d'Arezzo, BP 7, 1060 Brussels; tel. (02) 347-49-87; Ambassador: François Giraudon.
Morocco: 29 blvd St Michel, 1040 Brussels; tel. (02) 647-34-52; telex 21233; Ambassador: Abdelmalek Cherkaoui.
Mozambique: 97 blvd Saint-Michel, 1040 Brussels; tel. (02) 736-25-64; Ambassador: Frances Vitoria Velho Rodrigues.
Netherlands: 35 rue de la Science, 1040 Brussels; tel. (02) 230-30-20; telex 21311; Ambassador: Hein Theo Schaapveld.
New Zealand: 47–48 blvd du Régent, 1000 Brussels; tel. (02) 512-10-40; telex 22025; Ambassador: Gerard Francis Thompson.
Nicaragua: 255 chaussée de Vleurgat, 1050 Brussels; tel. (02) 345-19-25; telex 63553; Ambassador: Giovanni Delgado Campos.
Niger: 78 ave F. D. Roosevelt, 1050 Brussels; tel. (02) 648-61-40; telex 22857; Ambassador: Yacouba Sandi.
Nigeria: 288 ave de Tervueren, 1150 Brussels; tel. (02) 762-98-31; telex 22435; Ambassador: Joshua O. B. Iroha.
Norway: Europe Centre, 17 rue Archimède (4e et 5e étage), 1040 Brussels; tel. (02) 230-78-65; telex 21071; Ambassador: Knut Sverre.

Pakistan: 57 ave Delleur, 1170 Brussels; tel. (02) 673-80-07; telex 61816; Ambassador: Munir Akram.
Panama: 8 blvd Brand Whitlock, 1050 Brussels; tel. (02) 733-90-89; telex 25169; Chargé d'affaires a.i.: Novidad Morón Zanet.
Papua New Guinea: 17–19 rue Montoyer, 1040 Brussels; tel. (02) 640-34-95; telex 62249; Chargé d'affaires a.i.: Joseph Gabut.
Paraguay: 42 ave de Saturne, 1180 Brussels; tel. (02) 374-87-48; telex 26535; Ambassador: Dido Florentín-Bogado.
Peru: 179 ave de Tervueren, 1150 Brussels; tel. (02) 733-33-19; telex 24577; Ambassador: Julio Ego-Aguirre Alvarez.
Philippines: 299 ave Molière, 1060 Brussels; tel. (02) 343-64-00; telex 23631; Chargé d'affaires a.i.: Norberto Basilio.
Poland: 29 ave des Gaulois, 1040 Brussels; tel. (02) 733-77-48; telex 21562; Ambassador: Stanisław Matosek.
Portugal: 115 rue Defacqz (5e étage), 1050 Brussels; tel. (02) 539-38-50; telex 24570; Ambassador: António Augusto de Medeiros Patricio.
Qatar: 37 ave F. D. Roosevelt, 1050 Brussels; tel. (02) 640-29-00; telex 63754; Ambassador: Abdulrahman Abdalla al-Wohaibi.
Romania: 105 rue Gabrielle, 1180 Brussels; tel. (02) 345-26-80; telex 21859; Ambassador: George Ciucu.
Rwanda: 1 ave des Fleurs, 1150 Brussels; tel. (02) 763-07-02; telex 26653; Ambassador: Ildéphonse Munyeshyaka.
San Marino: 44 ave Brugman, BP 6, 1060 Brussels; tel. (02) 344-60-67; Ambassador: Adalmiro Bartolini.
São Tomé and Príncipe: 42 ave Brugman, 1060 Brussels; tel. (02) 347-53-75; telex 65313; Ambassador: Maria Manuela Margarido.
Saudi Arabia: 45 ave F. D. Roosevelt, 1050 Brussels; tel. (02) 649-57-25; telex 64626; Ambassador: Ibrahim Saleh Bakr.
Senegal: 196 ave F. D. Roosevelt, 1050 Brussels; tel. (02) 672-90-51; telex 63951; Ambassador: Falilou Kane.
Sierra Leone: 410 ave de Tervueren, 1150 Brussels; tel. (02) 771-00-53; telex 63624; Ambassador: Marian Judith Tanner Kamara.
Singapore: 198 ave F. D. Roosevelt, 1050 Brussels; tel. (02) 660-30-98; telex 26731; Ambassador: Francis Yeo Teng Yang.
Somalia: 66 ave F. D. Roosevelt, 1050 Brussels; tel. (02) 640-16-69; telex 24807; Ambassador: Saïd Hagi Mohamoud Farah.
South Africa: 26 rue de la Loi, BP 7 & 8, 1040 Brussels; tel. (02) 230-68-45; telex 23495; Ambassador: Douwe Gerbrand Grobler.
Spain: 19 rue de la Science, 1040 Brussels; tel. (02) 230-03-40; telex 22092; Ambassador: Mariano Berdejo Rivera.
Sri Lanka: 21–22 ave des Arts, 1040 Brussels; tel. (02) 230-48-90; telex 26927; Ambassador: Anthony N. Wiratunga.
Sudan: 124 ave F. D. Roosevelt, 1050 Brussels; tel. (02) 647-51-59; telex 24370; Ambassador: Farouk A. Rahman A. Eisa.
Suriname: 379 ave Louise, BP 20, 1050 Brussels; tel. (02) 640-11-72; telex 62680; Ambassador: Franklin Juliaan Leefland.
Swaziland: 71 rue Joseph II (5e étage), 1040 Brussels; tel. (02) 230-00-44; Chargé d'affaires a.i.: Harry Mabuza.
Sweden: 148 ave Louise, 1050 Brussels; tel. (02) 649-21-58; telex 21148; Ambassador: Kaj Sundberg.
Switzerland: 26 rue de la Loi, BP 9, 1040 Brussels; tel. (02) 230-61-45; telex 63711; Ambassador: Gaspard Bodmer.
Syria: 3 ave F. D. Roosevelt, 1050 Brussels; tel. (02) 648-01-35; telex 26669; Ambassador: Siba Nasser.
Tanzania: 363 ave Louise (7e étage), 1050 Brussels; tel. (02) 640-65-00; telex 63616; Ambassador: Prof. Simon M. Mbilinyi.
Thailand: 2 square du Val de la Cambre, 1050 Brussels; tel. (02) 640-68-10; telex 63510; Ambassador: Danai Tulalamba.
Togo: 264 ave de Tervueren, 1150 Brussels; tel. (02) 770-55-63; telex 25093; Ambassador: Affionjbon Ekoue.
Trinidad and Tobago: ave de la Faisanderie, 1150 Brussels; tel. (02) 762-94-15; telex 23539; Ambassador: Terence Baden-Semper.
Tunisia: 278 ave de Tervueren, 1150 Brussels; tel. (02) 771-73-95; telex 22078; Ambassador: Rachid Sfar.
Turkey: 4 rue Montoyer, 1040 Brussels; tel. (02) 344-22-16; telex 24677; Ambassador: Ecmel Barutou.
Uganda: 317 ave de Tervueren, 1150 Brussels; tel. (02) 762-58-25; telex 62814; Ambassador: Charles Katungi.
USSR: 66 ave de Fré, 1180 Brussels; tel. (02) 374-34-06; telex 65272; Ambassador: Feliks Petrovich Bogdanov.
United Arab Emirates: 73 ave F. D. Roosevelt, 1050 Brussels; tel. (02) 640-60-00; telex 26559; Chargé d'affaires a.i.: Salem Rached Salem al-Agroobi.
United Kingdom: 28 rue Joseph II, 1040 Brussels; tel. (02) 217-90-00; telex 22703; Ambassador: Sir Peter Charles Petrie.

BELGIUM

USA: 27 blvd du Régent, 1000 Brussels; tel. (02) 513-38-30; telex 21336; Ambassador: MAYNARD GLITMAN.

Uruguay: 437 ave Louise, 1050 Brussels; tel. (02) 640-11-69; telex 24663; Ambassador: MIGUEL J. BERTHET.

Venezuela: 23 ave des Phalènes, 1050 Brussels; tel. (02) 649-44-16; telex 63787; Ambassador: ANDRÉS EDUARDO BRITO MARTÍNEZ.

Western Samoa: 95 ave F. D. Roosevelt, 1050 Brussels; tel. (02) 660-84-54; Ambassador: FEESAGO SIAOSI FEPULEA'I.

Yugoslavia: 11 ave Emile de Mot, 1050 Brussels; tel. (02) 647-26-52; telex 26156; Ambassador: KUZMAN DIMCEVSKI.

Zaire: 30 rue Marie de Bourgogne, 1040 Brussels; tel. (02) 513-66-10; telex 21983; Ambassador: KABALA KISEKE SEKA.

Zambia: 469 ave Molière, BP 2, 1060 Brussels; tel. (02) 343-56-49; Ambassador: KAPEMBE N'SINGO.

Zimbabwe: 21–22 ave des Arts, BP 5/6, 1040 Brussels; tel. (02) 230-85-35; telex 24133; Chargé d'affaires a.i.: CHRISPEN MAVODZA.

Judicial System

The independence of the judiciary is based on the constitutional division of power between the legislative, executive and judicial bodies, each of which acts independently. Judges are appointed by the crown for life, and cannot be removed except by judicial sentence. The law of 1967, in force since 1970, unified civil procedure in the district courts, and reorganized the courts' areas of competence. Each of Belgium's nine provinces is divided into judicial districts, and these, in turn, into judicial cantons. The judiciary is organized on four levels, from the judicial canton to the district, regional and national courts. The lowest courts are those of the Justices of the Peace, of which there are 222, and the 20 Police Tribunals; each type of district court numbers 26, one in each district, including the Tribunals of the First Instance, Tribunals of Commerce, and Labour Tribunals. There are five regional Courts of Appeal, five regional Labour Courts, and one Court of Assizes in each province. The highest courts are the five civil and criminal Courts of Appeal, the five Labour Courts and the supreme Court of Cassation. The Military Court of Appeal is in Brussels.

COUR DE CASSATION/HOF VAN CASSATIE (SUPREME COURT OF JUSTICE)

First President: M. CHATEL.

President: R. SCREVENS.

Counsellors: R. JANSSENS, R. SOETAERT, O. STRANARD, H. BOSLY, J. SACE, E. BOON, C. CAENEPEEL, J. VERVLOET, J. RAUWS, J. MATTHIJS, J. D'HAENENS, J. POUPART, P. MARCHAL, J. DE PEUTER, D. HOLSTERS, P. GHISLAIN, Y. RAPPE, M. LAHOUSSE, Y. BELLE-JEANMART, M. CHARLIER, H. D. BAETE-SWINNEN, G. DE BAETS, L. WILLEMS.

General Prosecutor: J. KRINGS.

First Attorney-General: L. F. DUCHATELET.

Attorneys-General: H. LENAERTS, J. VELU, A. TILLEKAERTS, R. DECLERCQ, E. LIEKENDAEL, B. JANSSENS DE BISTHOVEN, G. D'HOORE, J. M. PIRET, J. DU JARDIN.

COURS D'APPEL/HOVEN VAN BEROEP (CIVIL AND CRIMINAL HIGH COURTS)

Antwerp: First Pres. A DE MAN; Gen. Prosecutor (vacant).

Brussels: First Pres. L. SLACHMUYLDER; Gen. Prosecutor V. VAN HONSTÉ.

Ghent: First Pres. G. NUYTINCK; Gen. Prosecutor G. VERHEGGE.

Liège: First Pres. R. LAURENT; Gen. Prosecutor L. GIET.

Mons: First Pres. P. GUERITTE; Gen. Prosecutor G. DEMANET.

Religion

CHRISTIANITY

The Roman Catholic Church

Belgium comprises one archdiocese and seven dioceses. At 31 December 1985 there were an estimated 8,720,000 adherents (about 88% of the total population).

Bishops' Conference: Bisschoppenconferentie van België/Conférence Episcopale de Belgique, 15 Wollemarkt, 2800 Mechelen; tel. (015) 21-65-01; f. 1981; Pres. Cardinal GODFRIED DANNEELS, Archbishop of Mechelen-Brussels.

Archbishop of Mechelen-Brussels: Cardinal GODFRIED DANNEELS, Aartsbisdom, 15 Wollemarkt, 2800 Mechelen; tel. (015) 21-65-01.

Protestant Churches

Belgian Evangelical Lutheran Church: 26 rue du Major René Dubreucq, 1050 Brussels; tel. (02) 511-92-47; f. 1950; 425 mems; Pres C. J. HOBUS.

Church of England: 29 rue Capitaine Crespel, 1050 Brussels; tel. (02) 511-71-83; Ven. JOHN LEWIS, Archdeacon of North-West Europe (Diocese of Gibraltar in Europe) and Chancellor of the Pro-Cathedral of the Holy Trinity, Brussels.

Eglise Protestante Unie de Belgique: 5 rue du Champ de Mars, 1050 Brussels; tel. (02) 511-44-71; 35,000 mems; Pres. Rev. M. J. BEUKENHORST; Sec. Mme R. FRAISSE-LHEUREUX.

Mission Evangélique Belge: 7 rue du Moniteur, 1000 Brussels; tel. (02) 217-23-83; f. 1918; about 2,000 mems.

Union of Baptists in Belgium (UBB): 35 rue Laplace, 4100 Seraing; tel. (041) 37-31-15; f. 1922 as Union of Evangelical Baptist Churches; Pres. HENRY BENS; Sec. GASTON WATHIEU.

JUDAISM

There are about 35,000 Jews in Belgium.

Consistoire Central Israélite de Belgique (Central Council of the Jewish Communities of Belgium): 2 rue Joseph Dupont, Brussels; tel. (02) 512-21-90; f. 1808; Chair. M. GEORGES SCHNEK.

The Press

Article 18 of the Belgian constitution states: 'The Press is free; no form of censorship may ever be instituted; no cautionary deposit may be demanded from writers, publishers or printers. When the author is known and is resident in Belgium, the publisher, printer or distributor may not be prosecuted.'

There are 34 general information dailies, 16 of which are autonomous, the remainder depending largely or totally on the former (some are only, under a different title, regional editions of a larger paper). In 1986 the combined circulation of all daily newspapers averaged 2,161,720 copies per issue.

There is a trend towards concentration. The 'Le Soir' group consists of five dailies. The only other significant group consists of three Catholic newspapers, linked with *De Standaard*.

There are few official political organs, but nearly all the Belgian dailies have political or trade union leanings. It is not, however, possible to establish a parallel between the supporters of the parties and the readership of the dailies.

There is no easy division of the daily newspapers into popular and serious press, but most newspapers strive to give a serious news coverage. The most widely-circulating dailies in French in 1987 were: *Le Soir* (208,833), *La Meuse/La Lanterne* (132,844), *La Libre Belgique* (80,813) and *La Dernière Heure* (92,577); and in Dutch: *Het Laatste Nieuws/De Nieuwe Gazet* (301,306), *De Standaard/Nieuwsblad/De Gentenaar* (378,697), *Het Volk/De Nieuwe Gids* (189,513) and *Gazet van Antwerpen/Gazet van Mechelen* (189,971). The major weeklies include *Flair* (350,645), *Humo* (213,161), *TV Ekspres* (220,000) and *Le Soir Illustré* (118,460), the latter associated with the daily *Le Soir*; and the cultural periodicals *Pourquoi Pas?* (70,086) and *Knack* (120,000). The popular women's periodical *Femmes d'Aujourd'hui* (352,083) has considerable sales in France. Some periodicals are printed in French and in Dutch.

PRINCIPAL DAILIES

Antwerp

De Financieel Ekonomische Tijd: 5 Brouwersvliet, bus 3, 2000 Antwerp; tel. (03) 231-57-56; telex 32614; f. 1968; Dutch economic and financial paper; Gen. Man. J. LAMERS; Chief Editor JERRY VAN WATERSCHOOT; circ. 24,830.

Gazet van Antwerpen: 2 Katwilgweg, 2050 Antwerp; tel. (03) 210-02-10; telex 31385; f. 1891; Christian Democrat; Dir-Gen. R. VAN TONGERLOO; Editor L. DE CLERCK; circ. 189,971 (with *Gazet van Mechelen*).

Lloyd Anversois-De Lloyd: 23 Eiermarkt, 2000 Antwerp; tel. (03) 234-05-50; telex 31446; f. 1858; shipping transport, commerce, industry, finance; Dir ROGER JAUMOTTE; circ. 10,000.

De Nieuwe Gazet: 10 Leopoldstraat, 2000 Antwerp; tel. (03) 231-96-80; telex 71382; f. 1897; Liberal; Editor FRANS STRIELEMAN; circ. 301,306 (with *Het Laatste Nieuws*).

Arlon

L'Avenir du Luxembourg: 38 rue des Déportés, 6700 Arlon; tel. (063) 22-03-49; telex 41503; f. 1897; Catholic; Editor JO MOTTET; circ. 34,252.

Brussels

La Côte Libre: 131 rue de Birmingham, 1070 Brussels; tel. (02) 526-56-06; telex 22648; f. 1868; financial; Editor O. DE BEAUFORT; circ. 7,000.

BELGIUM

Courrier de la Bourse: 131 rue de Birmingham, 1070 Brussels; tel. (02) 526-56-06; telex 22648; f. 1896; financial, economic, industrial and political; Admin. Dir O. DE BEAUFORT; circ. 8,500.

La Dernière Heure/Les Sports: 127 blvd Emile Jacqmain, 1000 Brussels; tel. (02) 211-28-88; telex 21448; f. 1906; independent Liberal; Dir P. LE HODEY; Chief Editor DANIEL VAN WYLICK; circ. 95,000.

Le Drapeau Rouge: 33 rue de la Caserne, 1000 Brussels; tel. (02) 512-87-00; f. 1921; Communist; Editor PIERRE BEAUVOIS; Man. JACQUES MOINS; circ. 15,000.

L'Echo de la Bourse: 131 rue de Birmingham, 1070 Brussels; tel. (02) 526-55-11; telex 23396; f. 1881; economic and financial; Dir R. WATSON; Editor F. MELAET; circ. 30,000.

Het Laatste Nieuws: 105 Emile Jacqmainlaan, 1000 Brussels; tel. (02) 219-32-90; telex 21495; f. 1888; Dutch; independent; Dir F. VINK; Editor L. SIAENS; circ. 301,306 (with *De Nieuwe Gazet*).

La Lanterne: 134 rue Royale, 1000 Brussels; tel. (02) 217-77-50; telex 22751; f. 1944; independent; Gen. Man. C. MATRIGE; Chief Editor W. MEURENS; circ. 132,844 (with *La Meuse*).

La Libre Belgique: 127 blvd Emile Jacqmain, 1000 Brussels; tel. (02) 211-27-77; telex 21550; f. 1884; Catholic; independent; Dir P. LE HODEY; Chief Editor J. FRANCK; circ. 80,813.

De Nieuwe Gids: 105 Koningsstraat, 1000 Brussels; tel. (02) 218-56-05; f. 1944; Dutch; Dir-Gen. ANTOON VAN MELKEBEEK; circ. 189,513 (with *Het Volk*).

Le Soir: 21 place de Louvain, 1000 Brussels; tel. (02) 217-77-50; telex 21485; f. 1887; independent; Dir-Gen. ANDRÉ DE BETHUNE; Chief Editor M. Y. TOUSSAINT; circ. 208,833.

Krantengroep De Standaard (Group combining **De Standaard, Het Nieuwsblad, De Gentenaar**): published by Vlaamse Uitgeversmaatschappij NV, 28-30 Gossetlaan, 1720 Groot-Bijgaarden; tel. (02) 467-22-11; telex 63435; Christian Socialist; Dir G. VERDEYEN; Editorial Dirs M. RUYS, L. BOSTOEN; circ. 378,697.

Charleroi

Le Journal & Independance/Le Peuple: 9 quai de Flandre, 6000 Charleroi; tel. (071) 31-01-90; telex 51277; f. 1837; Gen. Man. C RENARD; Editor JEAN GUY; circ. 20,249.

La Nouvelle Gazette (Charleroi, Namur, La Louvière, Philippeville); **La Province** (Mons): 2 quai de Flandre, 6000 Charleroi; tel. (071) 32-00-35; telex 51218; f. 1878; Man. Dir MICHEL FROMONT; Editor J.-P. VANDERMEUSE; circ. 87,581.

Eupen

Grenz-Echo: 8 Marktplatz, 4700 Eupen; tel. (087) 55-47-05; f. 1927; German; independent Catholic; Dir A. KÜCHENBERG; Editor HEINZ WARNY; circ. 13,000.

Ghent

De Gentenaar: 53 Vlaanderenstraat, 9000 Ghent; tel. (091) 25-76-86; telex 11244; f. 1879; Catholic; Man. G. VERDEYEN.

De Morgen/Vooruit: 84 Moutstraat, 9000 Ghent; tel. (091) 21-80-91; telex 11264; f. 1978; independent; Editor PAUL GOOSSENS; circ. 51,947.

Het Volk: 22 Forelstraat, 9000 Ghent; tel. (091) 25-57-01; telex 11228; f. 1891; Catholic; Dir A. VAN MELKEBEEK; Editor P. DE BAERE; circ. 189,513 (with *De Nieuwe Gids*).

Hasselt

Het Belang van Limburg: 10 Herckenrodesingel, 3500 Hasselt; tel. (011) 29-42-11; telex 39034; f. 1879; Christian Social; Dir PETER BAERT; Editor LUC VAN LOON; circ. 99,027.

Liège

La Libre Belgique/Gazette du Liège: 26–28 blvd d'Avnoy, 4000 Liège; tel. (041) 23-19-33; telex 41297; f. 1846; Dir LILY PORTUGAELS; circ. 80,813.

La Meuse: 8-12 blvd de la Sauvenière, 4000 Liège; tel. (041) 20-08-11; telex 41521; f. 1855; independent; Man. Dir C. MATRIGE; Gen. Man. M. FROMONT; Editor W. MEURENS; circ. 132,844 (with *La Lanterne*).

La Wallonie: 55 rue de la Régence, 4000 Liège; tel. (041) 20-18-11; telex 41143; f. 1919; progressive; Dir ROBERT GILLON; Editor P. GRUSELIN; circ. 48,000.

Mechelen

Gazet van Mechelen: 13 Befferstraat, 2800 Mechelen; tel. (015) 20-83-83; telex 31385; f. 1896; Christian Democrat; Gen. Man. R. VAN TONGERLOO; Editor L. DE CLERCK; circ. 189,971 (with *Gazet van Antwerpen*).

Namur

Vers l'Avenir: 12 blvd Ernest Mélot, 5000 Namur; tel. (081) 24-88-11; telex 59121; f. 1918; Christian Democrat; Editor JEAN-CLAUDE BAFFREY; circ. 64,327.

Tournai

Le Courrier de l'Escaut: 24 rue du Curé Notre-Dame, 7500 Tournai; tel. (069) 22-81-43; telex 57147; f. 1829; Christian Social; Dir MARC LESTIENNE; circ. 25,000.

Verviers

Le Jour/Le Courrier: 14 rue du Brou, 4800 Verviers; tel. (087) 31-33-61; f. 1894; independent; Dir J. DE THYSEBAERT; Chief Editor R. MONAMI; circ. 13,565.

WEEKLIES

Antwerpse Post: 2 Katwilgweg, 2050 Antwerp; news magazine; circ. 32,590.

BS (Bonne Soirée): 46 De Jonckerstraat, 1060 Brussels; tel. (02) 537-08-00; telex 23291; f. 1922; women's magazine in French; Chief Editor MARIE-HÉLÈNE ADLER; circ. 56,124.

La Cité: 26 rue St Laurent, 1000 Brussels; tel. (02) 217-23-90; telex 22998; f. 1950 as daily, weekly 1988; Christian Democrat; Editor JOS SCHOONBROODT; circ. 20,000.

De Boer en de Tuinder: 8 Minderbroedersstraat, 3000 Louvain; telex 24166; f. 1891; agriculture and horticulture; circ. 52,000.

De Bond: 170 Langestraat, 1150 Brussels; tel. (02) 782-00-00; general interest; circ. 316,823.

Brugsch Handelsblad: 4 Eekhoutstraat, 8000 Bruges; tel. (050) 33-06-61; telex 81222; f. 1906; local, national and international news; Dirs J. HERREBOUDT and P. OP DE BEECK; Editor J. HERREBOUDT; circ. 40,000.

Dag Allemaal: Luchthavenlei 7, 2100 Antwerp; tel. (03) 218-76-40; telex 33451; f. 1984; general interest; circ. 101,190.

Femmes d'Aujourd'hui: 9 ave Frans van Kalken, 1070 Brussels; tel. (02) 523-20-60; telex 25104; f. 1933; women's magazine; Dir L. HIERGENS; Chief Editor L. LUCAS; circ. 164,512 (French), 187,571 (Dutch).

Flair: 7 Jan Blockxstraat, 2018 Antwerp; tel. (03) 247-45-11; telex 32979; Dutch and French; women's magazine; Dir K. HUYSMANS; circ. (in Belgium) 350,645.

Humo: 46 De Jonckerstraat, 1060 Brussels; tel. (02) 537-08-00; telex 23291; general weekly and TV and radio guide in Dutch; Chief Editor G. MORTIER; circ. 213,161.

Joepie: Luchthavenlei 7, 2100 Antwerp; tel. (03) 218-76-40; telex 33451; f. 1973; teenagers' interest; circ. 144,422.

Kerk en Leven: 92 Halewijnlaan, 2050 Antwerp; tel. (03) 219-38-00; religious; circ. 800,000.

Knack: 97 Louis Schmidtlaan, 1040 Brussels; telex 25425; independent news magazine; Dir FRANS VERLEYEN; Chief Editors HUBERT VAN HUMBEECK, FRANK DEMOOR; circ. 120,000.

Kwik: 105-107 Emile Jacqmainlaan, 1000 Brussels; tel. (02) 219-32-90; telex 21495; f. 1962; Dir FRANS VINK; Editor K. VANDER MIJNSBRUGGE; circ. 78,927.

Landbouwleven: 92 ave Léon Grosjean, 1140 Brussels; agriculture; circ. 45,489.

Libelle: 7 Jan Blockxstraat, 2018 Antwerp; tel. (03) 237-01-20; telex 32979; f. 1945; Dutch and French; women's magazine; Dir K. HUYSMANS; Chief Editor M. DE BORGER; circ. 274,683.

Panorama/Ons Land: 7 Jan Blockxstraat, 2018 Antwerp; tel. (03) 247-45-11; telex 32979; f. 1956; Dutch; general interest; Dir K. HUYSMANS; Chief Editor K. ANTHIERENS; circ. 85,000.

De Post: 105 Emile Jacqmainlaan, 1000 Brussels; tel. (02) 219-32-90; f. 1949; general illustrated; Dir K. VANDER MIJNSBRUGGE; circ. 77,322.

Pourquoi Pas?: 95 blvd Emile Jacqmain, 1000 Brussels; tel. (02) 211-08-11; telex 21180; f. 1910; news; Editor A. LEMOINE; circ. 70,086.

Het Rijk der Vrouw: 9 Frans van Kalkenlaan, 1070 Brussels; tel. (02) 523-20-60; telex 25104; f. 1932; women's interest; Dir L. HIERGENS; Chief Editor L. LUCAS; circ. 200,000.

Le Sillon Belge: 92 ave Léon Grosjean, 1140 Brussels; agriculture; circ. 44,636.

Le Soir Illustré: 21 place de Louvain, 1000 Brussels; tel. (02) 217-77-50; f. 1928; independent illustrated; Dir A. DECLERQ; circ. 118,460.

Spirou/Robbedoes: 637 chemin de Waterloo, 1060 Brussels; tel. (02) 344-13-60; children's interest; circ. 63,000.

Sport '90: 153 ave de Tervueren, 1040 Brussels; sport; circ. 100,000.

Story: 7 Jan Blockxstraat, 2018 Antwerp; tel. (03) 237-01-20; telex 32979; f. 1975; Dutch; women's interest; Dir K. HUYSMANS; circ. 179,557.

TeVe-Blad: 18 Kammenstraat, 2000 Antwerp; tel. (03) 231-47-90; f. 1981; illustrated; Chief Editor ROB JANS; circ. 250,000.

BELGIUM

Télémoustique: 46 De Jonckerstraat, 1060 Brussels; tel. (02) 537-08-00; telex 23291; f. 1924; radio and TV; Dir LOUIS CROONEN; Editor ALAIN DE KUYSEHE; circ. 204,000.

TV Ekspres en TV Strip: 18 Kammenstraat, 2000 Antwerp; tel. (03) 231-47-90; telex 33134; Chief Editor ROB JANS; circ. 220,000.

Le Vif/L'Express: 33 place Jamblinne de Meux, 1040 Brussels; tel. (02) 736-79-00; telex 63186; Dir GÉRALD JACOBY; Chief Editor JEAN-PIERRE STROOBANTS; circ. 80,000.

Het Wekelijks Nieuws: 5 Nijverheidslaan, 8970 Poperinge; tel. (057) 33-67-21; Christian news magazine; Dirs H. and L. SANSEN; Editor H. SANSEN; circ. 56,000.

ZIE-Magazine: 18 Kammenstraat, 2000 Antwerp; tel. (03) 231-47-90; f. 1930; illustrated; Chief Editor ROB JANS; circ. 80,000.

Zondag Nieuws: 105 E. Jacqmainlaan, 1000 Brussels; tel. (02) 219-32-90; telex 21495; f. 1958; general interest; Editor R. SCHOLLIERS; circ. 115,250.

Zondagsblad: 22 Forelstraat, 9000 Ghent; tel. (091) 25-57-01; f. 1949; Catholic; Dir A. VAN MELKEBEEK; Editor J. NIJS; circ. 85,000.

SELECTED OTHER PERIODICALS

Belgian Business Magazine: 42 ave du Houx, 1170 Brussels; tel. (02) 673-81-70; telex 23830; monthly; management; circ. 65,700.

Het Beste uit Reader's Digest: 12A Grote Markt, 1000 Brussels; monthly; general; circ. 100,000.

International Equipment News: 216 Groenstraat, 1030 Brussels; tel. (02) 242-29-92; business; Dir H. BRIELS.

Jet Limburg: 21 Bedryfstraat, 3500 Hasselt; fortnightly; general interest; circ. 240,614.

Marie Claire: 68 ave Winston Churchill, 1180 Brussels; tel. (02) 345-99-20; telex 64104; monthly; women's interest; circ. 80,000.

Le Moniteur de l'Automobile: 181 chaussée de la Hulpe, BP 2, 1170 Brussels; tel. (02) 660-19-20; telex 26379; fortnightly; motoring; Editor ÉTIENNE VISART; circ. 85,000.

The Office: 81 ave Franklin Roosevelt, 1050 Brussels; tel. (02) 640-69-80; telex 64028; f. 1935; English; monthly; Editor WILLIAM R. SCHULHOF; circ. 160,000.

Rock This Town/Fabiola: 41 ave de Sumatra, 1180 Brussels; tel. (02) 374-99-04; f. 1982; monthly; popular music; Chief Editor PIERRE ARNOULD; circ. 60,000.

Santé: 51 rue A. Danse, 1180 Brussels; monthly; popular medicine; circ. 100,000.

Sphere: 140B blvd Lambermont, 1030 Brussels; 6 a year; travel; circ. 77,000.

Temps Nouveaux: 41 rue des Deux Églises, 1040 Brussels; tel. (02) 238-01-11; monthly; current affairs; circ. 90,000.

Vie Féminine: 26 rue Saint-Laurent, 1000 Brussels; monthly; women's interest; circ. 88,654.

Vrouw & Wereld: 170 Langestraat, 1150 Brussels; tel. (02) 782-00-00; monthly; women's interest; circ. 319,400.

NEWS AGENCIES

Agence Belga (Agence Télégraphique Belge de Presse SA)—Agentschap Belga (Belgisch Pers-telegraafagentschap NV): 1 blvd Charlemagne, BP 51, 1041 Brussels; tel. (02) 230-50-55; telex 21408; f. 1920; largely owned by daily papers; Chair. G. VERDEYEN; Gen. Man. R. DE CEUSTER.

Agence Europe: 10 blvd St Lazare, 1210 Brussels; tel. (02) 219-02-56; telex 21108; f. 1952; daily bulletin on EEC activities.

Centre d'Information de Presse (CIP): 1 chemin de Maecht, 1030 Brussels; f. 1946; Chair LOUIS MEERTS.

Foreign Bureaux

Agence France-Presse (AFP): 1 blvd Charlemagne, BP 3, 1041 Brussels; tel. (02) 230-83-94; telex 24889; Dir CHARLES SCHIFFMANN.

Agencia EFE (Spain): 1 blvd Charlemagne, BP 20, 1041 Brussels; tel. (02) 230-45-68; telex 23185; Dir RAMÓN CASTILLO MESEGUER.

Agentstvo Pechati Novosti (APN) (USSR): 22 rue Général Lotz, 1180 Brussels; tel. (02) 343-26-58; telex 23798; Dir IGOR ROUJENSTEV.

Agenzia Nazionale Stampa Associata (ANSA) (Italy): 1 blvd Charlemagne, BP 7, 1040 Brussels; tel. (02) 230-81-92; telex 63717; Dir GIAMPIERO GRAMAGLIA.

Algemeen Nederlands Persbureau (ANP) (Netherlands): 1 blvd Charlemagne, 1041 Brussels; tel. (02) 230-85-27; Correspondents MARTINUS VAN DIJK, RIK WINKEL.

Allgemeiner Deutscher Nachrichtendienst (ADN) (German Democratic Republic): 8 rue J. E. Raymond, BP 3, 1160 Brussels; Dir RALF KLINGSIECK.

Associated Press (AP) (USA): 1 blvd Charlemagne, BP 49, 1041 Brussels; tel. (02) 230-52-49; telex 21741; Dir ROBERT WIELAARD.

Československá tisková kancelář (ČTK) (Czechoslovakia): 2 rue des Egyptiens, BP 6, 1050 Brussels; tel. (02) 648-01-33; telex 23092; Correspondent J. PRUSEK.

Deutsche Presse-Agentur (dpa) (Federal Republic of Germany): 1 blvd Charlemagne, BP 17, 1041 Brussels; tel. (02) 230-36-91; telex 22356; Dir HARTWIG NATHE.

Inter Press Service (IPS) (Italy): (French-speaking) 35 rue du Framboisier, 1180 Brussels; tel. (02) 374-77-18; Correspondent JACQUES ELIAS; (Dutch-speaking) 21 Inquisitiestraat, 1040 Brussels; tel. (02) 736-18-31; Dir DIRK PEETERS.

Jiji Press (Japan): 1 blvd Charlemagne, BP 26, 1041 Brussels; tel. (02) 736-80-15; telex 25029; Dir MAHITO TSUCHIYAMA.

Kyodo Tsushin (Japan): 1 blvd Charlemagne, BP 37, 1041 Brussels; tel. (02) 238-09-10; Dir AKIHIRO ONODA.

Magyar Távirati Iroda (MTI) (Hungary): 41 rue Jean Chapelie, 1060 Brussels; tel. (02) 343-75-35; telex 24455; Dir FERENC FÁBIÁN.

Reuters (UK): 61 rue de Trèves, 1040 Brussels; tel. (02) 230-92-15; telex 21633; Editor G. RATZIN.

United Press International (UPI) (USA): 17 rue Philippe le Bon, 1040 Brussels; tel. (02) 230-43-30; telex 26997; Correspondents STEPHAN KETELE, HERMAN SAEN.

Xinhua (New China) News Agency (People's Republic of China): 32 square Ambiorix, Résidence le Pavois, BP 4, 1040 Brussels; tel. (02) 230-32-54; telex 26555; Chief Correspondent LE ZUDE.

Novinska Agencija Tanjug (Yugoslavia) and **TASS** (USSR) also have bureaux in Brussels.

PRESS ASSOCIATIONS

Association générale des Journalistes professionnels de Belgique/Algemene Vereniging van de Beroeps-journalisten in België: 1 blvd Charlemagne, BP 54, 1041 Brussels; tel. (02) 238-09-44; f. 1979 on merger of Association Générale de la Presse Belge (f. 1885) and Union Professionnelle de la Presse Belge (f. 1914); 1,375 mems (1981); affiliated to IFJ (International Federation of Journalists); Pres. MARCEL BAUWENS; Sec.-Gen. J. VANDEN HOECK.

Association belge des Editeurs de Journaux/Belgische Vereniging van de Dagbladuitgevers: 20 rue Belliard, 1040 Brussels; tel. (02) 512-17-32; telex 26854; f. 1964; 23 mems; Pres ANDRÉ DE BÉTHUNE; Sec.-Gen. JEAN HOET.

Fédération de la Presse Périodique de Belgique/Federatie van de periodieke pers van België (FPPB): 54 rue Charles Martel, 1040 Brussels; tel. (02) 230-09-99; f. 1891; Sec.-Gen. JEAN-LOUIS DUCHÊNE.

Principal Publishers

Acco, CV: 134-136 Tiensestraat, 3000 Louvain; tel. (016) 23-35-20; telex 62547; f. 1960; general reference, school-books, periodicals; Dir HUBERT VAN SLAMBROUCK.

Altiora NV (Publishing Dept): 1 Abdijstraat, BP 54, 3281 Averbode; tel. (013) 77-17-51; telex 39104; f. 1934; general, fiction, juvenile and religious (Roman Catholic); weekly children's periodicals; Dir T. G. SECUIANU.

Editions Atlen: 55 ave Huart-Hamoir, 1030 Brussels; tel. (02) 242-39-00; telex 63698; f. 1978; reference; Dir J. THURMAN.

De Boeck-Wesmael, SA: 203 ave Louise, BP 1, 1050 Brussels; tel. (02) 640-72-72; telex 65701; f. 1795; school, technical and university textbooks, youth, nature and documentaries; Dirs CHR. DE BOECK, G. HOYOS.

Brepols IGP, NV: 8 Baron F. du Fourstraat, 2300 Turnhout; tel. (014) 41-54-51; telex 34182; f. 1975; religion, history; Man. Dir MICHEL ROLIN.

Casterman, SA: 28 rue des Soeurs Noires, 7500 Tournai; tel. (069) 25-42-11; telex 57328; f. 1780; fiction, encyclopaedias, education, periodicals and children's books; Man. Dir R. VANGENEBERG.

Didier-Hatier, SA: 18 rue Antoine Labarre, 1050 Brussels; tel. (02) 649-99-45; f. 1979; school books, general literature; Dir M. MARCHAL.

Die Keure, NV: 108 Oude Gentweg, 8000 Bruges; tel. (050) 33-12-35; telex 81411; f. 1948; textbooks, law, political and social sciences; Dir J. P. STEEVENS.

Editions et Imprimerie J. Duculot SA: rue de la Posterie, Parc Industriel, 5800 Gembloux; tel. (081) 61-00-61; telex 59309; f. 1919; literature, art, religion, juveniles, linguistics, general science, school and university textbooks, guides, regional literature; Gen. Man. JEAN VEROUGSTRAETE.

BELGIUM
Directory

Editions Dupuis SA: 7 blvd Tirou, 6000 Charleroi; tel. (071) 32-44-47; telex 51370; f. 1898; children's fiction, periodicals for children and adults; Dir JEAN DENEUMOSTIER.

Elsevier Librico NV: 325 Leuvensesteenweg, 1940 Sint-Stevens-Woluwe; tel. (02) 720-90-90; telex 21831; f. 1960; biography, history, literature, reference, juveniles, art, practical guides, nature, documentaries, children's books, travel; Dir-Gen. ÉLIE BERWAERTS.

Etablissements Emile Bruylant: 67 rue de la Régence, 1000 Brussels; tel. (02) 512-98-45; f. 1838; law; Chief Man. Dir J. VANDEVELD; Gen. Man. Mme A. VAN SPRENGEL.

Halewijn NV: 92 Halewijnlaan, 2050 Antwerp; tel. (03) 219-38-00; f. 1953; general, periodicals; Dir-Gen. J. CORNILLE.

Heideland, NV: 1 Grote Markt, 3500 Hasselt; tel. (011) 22-45-05; telex 39831; f. 1945; general, paperbacks and periodicals; Dir L. NAGELS.

Editions Hemma SA: 106 rue de Chevron, BP 32, 4081 Stoumont-Chevron; tel. (086) 43-36-36; telex 41507; f. 1956; juveniles, educational books and materials; Dir ALBERT HEMMERLIN.

Kluwer Algemene Uitgeverijen België (KAUB): 21-23 Santvoortbeeklaan, 2100 Deurne; tel. (03) 360-02-11; telex 33649; f. 1986; fiction and popular non-fiction, general reference books; Dir C. VAN BAELEN.

Editions Labor-Nathan: 156-158 chaussée de Haecht, 1030 Brussels; tel. (02) 216-81-50; telex 25532; f. 1925; general; *L'Ecole 2000* (periodical); Gen. Man. JACQUES FAUCONNIER.

Maison Ferdinand Larcier, SA: 39 rue des Minimes, 1000 Brussels; tel. (02) 512-47-12; f. 1839; legal publications; Dir J. M. RYCKMANS.

Editions du Lombard SA: 1-11 ave Paul-Henri Spaak, 1070 Brussels; tel. (02) 522-56-00; telex 23097; f. 1946; juveniles, games, education, geography, history, religion; Man. Dir LUCIEN LOTTEFIER.

Imprimerie Robert Louis Editions: 35-43 rue Borrens, 1050 Brussels; tel. (02) 640-10-40; f. 1952; science and technical; Mans PIERRE LOUIS, ALBAN LOUIS.

Mercatorfonds: 85 Meir, 2000 Antwerp; tel. (03) 231-38-40; telex 71876; f. 1965; art, ethnography, literature, music, geography and history; Dirs JAN MARTENS, R. DE VOCHT.

De Nederlandsche Boekhandel, NV: 222 Kapelsestraat, 2080 Kapellen; tel. (03) 664-53-20; telex 32242; f. 1893; school books, scientific; Dirs J. and R. PELCKMANS.

Nouvelles Editions Marabout SA: 30 ave de l'Energie, 4430 Alleur; tel. (041) 61-18-63; telex 42072; f. 1977; paperbacks; Man. Dir SERGE MARTIANO; Dir JEAN-PAUL MICHAUD.

Reader's Digest SA: 12A Grand'Place, 1000 Brussels; tel. (02) 423-25-11; telex 21876; f. 1967; education, sport, games, geography, history, travel; Dir-Gen. R. MORLEY.

Roularta NV: 33 Meiboomlaan, 8800 Roeselare; tel. (051) 23-23-11; telex 81642; f. 1954; Man. Dir IWAN BEKAERT.

De Sikkel: 8 Nijverheidsstraat, 2150 Malle; tel. (03) 312-47-61; telex 34641; f. 1919; education, literature, art, history of art, technical, sciences, sports, school magazines, trade papers and journals; Dir K. DE BOCK.

Snoeck-Ducaju en Zoon NV: 464 Begijnhoflaan, 9000 Ghent; tel. (091) 23-48-97; telex 12765; f. 1948; art books, holiday guides; Pres. SERGE SNOECK.

Société Belgo-Française de Presse et de Promotion (SBPP) SA: 68 ave Winston Churchill, 1180 Brussels; tel. (02) 345-99-20; telex 64104; periodicals; Dir CLAUDE CUVELIER.

J. B. Wolters Leuven, NV: 50 Blijde-Inkomststraat, 3000 Louvain; tel. (016) 23-34-88; telex 24525; f. 1959; education; Dir JACQUES GERMONPREZ.

Zuidnederlandse Uitgeverij, NV: 8 Cleydaellaan, 2630 Aartselaar; tel. (03) 887-83-00; telex 31739; f. 1956; general fiction and non-fiction, children's books; Dir J. VANDE VELDEN.

PUBLISHERS' ASSOCIATIONS

Association des Editeurs Belges (ADEB): 140 blvd Lambermont, 1030 Brussels; tel. (02) 241-65-80; f. 1922; asscn of French-language book publishers; Dir BERNARD GÉRARD.

Cercle Belge de la Librairie: 35 rue de la Chasse Royale, 1160 Brussels; tel. (02) 640-52-41; f. 1883; asscn of Belgian booksellers and publishers; 205 mems; Pres. M. DESTREBECQ.

Vereniging van Uitgevers van Nederlandstalige Boeken: 93 Frankrijklei, 2000 Antwerp; tel. (03) 232-46-84; asscn of Dutch-language book publishers; Sec. (vacant).

Radio and Television

In 1987 there were an estimated 3,172,636 television sets in use and 4,608,450 radio licences.

FRENCH

Radio-Télévision Belge de la Communauté Culturelle Française: 52 blvd Auguste Reyers, 1040 Brussels; tel. (02) 737-21-11; telex 21437; Chair. M. VAN CAMPENHOUDT; Admin-Gen. ROBERT STEPHANE; Dir of Radio Programmes PHILIPPE DASNOY; Dir of Television Programmes GEORGES KONEN; Dir of Information Service (Radio and Television) PIERRE DEVOS.

DUTCH

Belgische Radio en Televisie: Instituut der Nederlandse Uitzendingen, 52 August Reyerslaan, 1040 Brussels; tel. (02) 737-31-11; telex 22486; Chair. ELS WITTE; Admin.-Gen. CASIMIR GOOSSENS; Dir of Radio Programmes PIET VAN ROE; Dir of Television Programmes BERT HERMANS; Dir of News Department KAREL HEMMERECHTS; Dir Educational Broadcasting LEA MARTEL; Dir Technical Department MICHEL GEWILLIG.

Finance

(cap. = capital; m. = million; res = reserves;
dep. = deposits; brs = branches; frs = Belgian francs)

BANKING

Commission Bancaire: 99 ave Louise, 1050 Brussels; telex 62107; f. 1935 to supervise the application of the law relating to the legal status of banks and bankers and to the public issue of securities; also the application of the legal status of common trust funds (1957), of certain non-banking financial enterprises (1964), of holding companies (1967) and of the private savings banks (1976); Pres. W. VAN GERVEN; Man. Dirs H. BIRON, P. DUBOIS, G. GELDERS, J. VERTENEUIL.

Central Bank

Banque Nationale de Belgique: 5 blvd de Berlaimont, 1000 Brussels; tel. (02) 219-46-00; telex 21355; f. 1850; bank of issue; cap. 400m. frs, res 22,291m. frs, dep. 11,346m. frs (Dec. 1987); Gov. J. GODEAUX; Vice Gov. A. VERPLAETSE; Exec. Dirs G. JANSON, W. FRAEYS, F. JUNIUS, J.-P. PAUWELS, G. QUADEN; 2 brs.

Development Banks

Gewestelijke Investeringsmaatschappij voor Vlaanderen: 37 Karel Oomstraat, 2018 Antwerp; tel. (03) 233-83-83; telex 34167; f. 1980; promotes creation, restructuring and extension of private enterprises, stimulation of public initiatives, implementation of the industrial policy of state and regions; cap. 2,674m. frs; Pres. R. VAN OUTRYVE D'YDEWALLE; CEO G. VAN ACKER.

Institut de Réescompte et de Garantie (IRG)/Herdiscontering-en Waarborginstituut (HWI): 78 rue du Commerce, 1040 Brussels; tel. (02) 511-73-30; f. 1935; deals with banks, public credit institutions, private savings banks and other financial intermediaries (money-market dealer and administrator of a deposit protection scheme); cap. and res 2,415.7m. frs; Chair. MARCEL D'HAEZE; Gen. Man. WILLY VAN HOECK.

Nationale Investeringsmaatschappij (NIM)/Société Nationale d'Investissement (SNI): 63-67 rue Montoyer, 1040 Brussels; tel. (02) 237-06-11; telex 25744; f. 1962; reconstituted in 1976 as a 100% state-owned holding company; cap. 14,000m. Belgian francs; wide cash-raising powers to muster equity capital; private sector representation on governing body and investment committee; Pres. P. WILMES.

Société Régional d'Investissement de Wallonie: 19 place Joséphine-Charlotte, 5100 Jambes; tel. (081) 30-64-11; telex 59415; f. 1979; shareholding company; promotion of creation, restructuring and extension of private enterprises; stimulation of the industrial policy of state and provinces; cap. 3,920m. frs; Pres. BERNARD MARCHAND.

Major State-owned Banks

Caisse Nationale de Crédit Professionnel/Nationale Kas voor Beroepskrediet: 16 blvd de Waterloo, 1000 Brussels; tel. (02) 513-64-80; telex 22026; f. 1929; res 2,158m. frs; Gen. Man. D. PONLOT.

Crédit Communal de Belgique/Gemeentekrediet van België: 44 blvd Pachéco, 1000 Brussels; tel. (02) 214-41-11; telex 25068; f. 1860; cap. 3,500m. frs, res 19,531m. frs, dep. 1,401,919m. frs (Dec. 1987); Chair. F. SWAELEN; Man. Dir FRANÇOIS NARMON; 1,357 brs.

Institut National de Crédit Agricole/Nationaal Instituut voor Landbouwkrediet: 56 rue Joseph II, 1040 Brussels; tel. (02) 234-12-11; telex 26863; f. 1937; agricultural credits; credits granted to agricultural associations; financing of agricultural products and foodstuffs; Pres. J. DETRY.

Société Nationale de Crédit à l'Industrie (SNCI)/Nationale Maatschappij voor Krediet aan de Nijverheid (NMKN): 14 ave

BELGIUM

de l'Astronomie, 1030 Brussels; tel. (02) 214-12-11; telex 25996; f. 1919; semi-public credit institution; extends long-, medium- and short-term credits to industrial and commercial enterprises; cap. 410m. frs, res 8,978m. frs, dep. 478,184m. frs (Dec. 1986); Chair. K. DIERCKX; Gen. Man. ALFRED RAMPEN; 16 brs.

Major Commercial Banks

Algemene Bank Nederland (België) NV: 53 Regentlaan, 1000 Brussels; tel. (02) 518-02-11; telex 26194; f. 1960 as Internationale Handels- en Diamantbank NV, name changed 1984; cap. 900m. frs, res 769m. frs, dep. 65,350m. frs (Dec. 1986); Chair. P. J. PISTOR; Man. Dirs W. J. KOLFF, M. EENHOORN, H. GOOSSENS.

Antwerpse Diamantbank NV/Banque Diamantaire Anversoise SA: 54 Pelikanstraat, 2018 Antwerp; tel. (03) 233-90-80; telex 31673; f. 1934; cap. 1,385m. frs, dep. 2,383m. frs (March 1988); Chair. HENRI FAYT; Man. Dir PAUL M. DE GROOTE.

Antwerpse Hypotheekkas/Caisse Hypothécaire Anversoise: 214 Grote Steenweg, 2600 Antwerp; tel. (03) 218-21-11; telex 33100; f. 1881; savings bank; cap. 2,000m. frs, res 4,270m. frs, dep. 132,328m. frs (Dec. 1985); Chair. Baron JEAN VAN DE PUT; Gen. Man. JOZEF VAN RIET; 67 brs.

BACOB SC: 25 Trierstraat, 1040 Brussels; tel. (02) 237-82-11; telex 62199; f. 1924; savings bank; cap. 13,427m. frs, dep. 296m. frs (Dec. 1987); Chair. H. DETREMMERIE; 536 brs.

Bank of Yokohama (Europe) SA: 287 ave Louise, BP 1, 1050 Brussels; tel. (02) 648-82-85; telex 21709; f. 1983; cap. 500m. frs, res 241m. frs, dep. 52,154m. frs (March 1987); Man. Dir MASAHIRO TAKANO.

Bank van Roeselare en West-Vlaanderen NV: 38 Noordstraat, 8800 Roeselare; tel. (051) 23-52-11; telex 81734; f. 1924, name changed 1935 and 1955; commercial and savings bank; cap. 700m. frs, res 1,858m. frs, dep. 48,669m. frs (Dec. 1987); Chair. J. SERCU; 73 brs.

Banque Belgo-Zaïroise (Belgolaise) SA: 1 Cantersteen, 1000 Brussels; tel. (02) 518-72-11; telex 21375; f. 1960, name changed 1972; cap. 1,000m. frs, res 2,102m. frs, dep. 26,572m. frs (Dec. 1987); Pres. JACQUES VERDICKT; Man. Dir MICHEL ISRALSON.

Banque Bruxelles Lambert SA: 24 ave Marnix, 1050 Brussels; tel. (02) 517-21-11; telex 21421; f. 1975 by merger; cap. 15,004m. frs, res 14,897m. frs, dep. 1,616,132m. frs (Sept. 1987); Pres. JACQUES THIERRY; 985 brs.

Banque Européenne pour l'Amérique Latine SA: 59 rue de l'Association, 1000 Brussels; tel. (02) 219-00-15; telex 22431; f. 1974; cap. 1,575m. frs, res 1,391m. frs, dep. 38,756m. frs (Dec. 1987); Chair. XAVIER MALOU; Man. Dir NESTOR RIGA.

Banque Indosuez Belgique SA: 9–13 Grote Markt, 2000 Antwerp; tel. (03) 225-07-80; telex 31730; f. 1954, present name from Oct. 1986; cap. 700m. frs, res 515m. frs, dep. 64,407m. frs (March 1986); capital increased to 1,000m. frs in June 1986; Chair. of Board of Dirs JO HOLVOET; 5 brs.

Banque Ippa SA: 45 Brusselstraat, 2018 Antwerp; tel. (03) 247-72-11; telex 35664; f. 1969; cap. and res 2,933m. frs, dep. 39,521m. frs; Chair. of Management Board A. VAN HOUTTE; Gen. Man. D. DE VEUSSER; 30 brs.

Banque Nagelmackers SA: 18 place de la Cathédrale, 4000 Liège; tel. (041) 20-02-11; telex 41271; f. 1747; cap. 930m. frs, res 860m. frs, dep. 30,400m. frs (Sept. 1987); Exec. Cttee GÉRARD FIEVET, BAUDOUIN NAGELMACKERS, L.-J. BORSU, ANDRÉ PAQUOT; 44 brs.

Banque Paribas Belgique SA/Paribas Bank België NV: 162 blvd E. Jacqmain, BP 2, 1210 Brussels; tel. (02) 219-30-10; telex 21349; f. 1968; cap. 3,000m. frs, res 3,245m. frs, dep. 215,243m. frs (Dec. 1986); Chair. F. ROBERT VANES; 58 brs.

Caisse Générale d'Epargne et de Retraite (CGER)/Algemene Spaar-en Lijfrentekas (ASLK): BP 1436, 1000 Brussels; tel. (02) 213-61-11; telex 26860; f. 1865; res 22,444m. frs, dep 1,150,382m. frs (Dec. 1987); Pres. LUC AERTS; 1,160 brs.

CERA Spaarbank: 52 Parijsstraat, 3000 Leuven; tel. (016) 24-49-99; telex 24166; f. 1935 as Centrale Raiffeisenkas CV/Centrale des Caisses Rurales; central organization of co-operative banks; cap. 10,122m. frs, res 15,200m. frs, dep. 379,475m. frs (Dec. 1987); Chair. of Board of Dirs R. EECKLOO; Chair. of Exec. Cttee. W. DANCKAERT.

Chase Banque de Commerce SA/Chase Handelsbank NV: 9 Lange Gasthuisstraat, 2000 Antwerp; tel. (03) 223-71-11; telex 31232; f. 1893, name changed 1985; cap. 330m. frs, res 739m. frs, dep. 29,772m. frs (Dec. 1987); took over retail activities of Manufacturers Hanover Bank Belgium SA in September 1986; Chair. RICHARD LOWRY; Gen. Man. ALFRED BOUCKAERT; 20 brs.

Continental Bank SA: 227 rue de la Loi, 1040 Brussels; tel. (02) 230-61-06; telex 21219; f. 1914; present name from 1970; cap. 650m. frs, res 3,240m. frs, dep. 47,600m. frs (Dec. 1986); Chair. EDWARD S. BOTTUM; Man. Dir TIMOTHY WOOD.

Crédit du Nord Belge SA: 32 rue du Fossé-aux-Loups, 1000 Brussels; tel. (02) 211-32-11; telex 21670; f. 1896, name changed 1919; cap. 750m. frs, res 161m. frs, dep. 20,321m. frs (Dec. 1987); Man. Dir and Chair. Exec. Cttee BERNARD HUE; 22 brs.

Crédit Général SA de Banque: 5 Grand'Place, 1000 Brussels; tel. (02) 516-12-11; telex 64540; f. 1958; cap. 2,000m. frs, res 919m. frs, dep. 80,527m. frs (Dec. 1986); Chair. V. WELTJENS.

Generale Bank NV/Générale de Banque SA: 3 Montagne du Parc, 1000 Brussels; tel. (02) 518-21-11; telex 21283; f. 1965 as Société Générale de Banque/Generale Bankmaatschappij, name changed 1985; cap. and res 47,550m. frs, dep. 2,005,905m. frs (Dec. 1987); Chair. of Board of Man. Dirs PAUL-EMMANUEL JANSSEN (designate); Chair. of Board of Dirs JACQUES GROOTHAERT; 1,157 brs.

Générale de Banque Belge pour l'Etranger: 3 Montagne du Parc, 1000 Brussels; tel. (02) 511-26-31; f. 1935, present name from Nov. 1985; cap. 1,100m. frs, res 126m. frs, dep. 31,283m. frs (Dec. 1985); Chair. HENRI FAYT.

Kredietbank NV: 7 Arenbergstraat, 1000 Brussels; tel. (02) 517-41-11; telex 21207; f. 1935; cap. and res 28,583m. frs (March 1987); Pres. JAN HUYGHEBAERT; Chair. A. VLERICK.

The Long-Term Credit Bank of Japan (Europe) SA: 40 blvd du Régent, BP 4, 1000 Brussels; tel. (02) 513-90-20; telex 61393; f. 1976 as Nippon European Bank SA; cap. 800m. frs, res 471m. frs (Mar. 1988); Chair. KOICHI INAMURA; Man. Dir HIROMI YOKOYAMA.

Royal Bank of Canada (Belgium) SA: 1 rue de Ligne, 1000 Brussels; tel. (02) 217-40-40; telex 21780; f. 1934, name changed 1983; cap. 540m. frs, res 552m. frs, dep. 30,801m. frs (Sept. 1987); Chair. W. C. C. MACKAY; Man. Dir D. LEPAGE.

Saitama Bank (Europe) SA: 27 ave des Arts, BP 4, 1040 Brussels; tel. (02) 230-81-00; telex 24368; f. 1980; cap. 560m. frs, res 401m. frs, dep. 27,237m. frs (Dec. 1987); Chair. SCHOICHI KAMIO; Gen. Man. SHIGENOBU GOTO.

Takugin International Bank (Europe) SA: 17 ave Marnix, 1050 Brussels; tel. (02) 512-67-53; telex 23568; f. 1981; cap. 585m. frs, res 447m. frs (March 1988); Chair. HIROJI NAKAMURA; Man. Dir MASARU TAKANO.

Banking Associations

Association Belge des Banques/Belgische Vereniging der Banken: 36 rue Ravenstein, BP 5, 1000 Brussels; tel. (02) 512-58-68; telex 25575; f. 1936; represents only privately-owned banks; 83 mems; affiliated to Fédération des Entreprises de Belgique; Pres. LÉO GOLDSCHMIDT; Dir-Gen. MICHEL DE SMET.

Groupement Belge des Banques d'Epargne (GBE) (Savings Banks): 34-35 place Jamblinne de Meux, 1040 Brussels; tel. (02) 736-99-20; affiliated to Fédération des Entreprises de Belgique; Pres. RAYMOND BAVAY; Sec.-Gen. C. DE NOOSE.

STOCK EXCHANGE

La Bourse de Fonds Publics de Bruxelles et la Commission de la Bourse (Stock Exchange): Palais de la Bourse, Place de la Bourse, Brussels; tel. (02) 509-12-11; telex 21374; Pres. JEAN PETERBROECK; Sec. JACQUES LELEUX.

There are also stock exchanges in Antwerp, Ghent and Liège.

INSURANCE COMPANIES

Abeille-Paix, Société Anonyme Belge d'Assurances: 80 rue de la Loi, 1040 Brussels; telex 21819; fire, accident, general; Chair. M. J. ARVIS; Gen. Man. M. P. MEYERSON.

Abeille-Paix Vie, Société Anonyme Belge d'Assurances: 80 rue de la Loi, 1040 Brussels; telex 21819; life; Chair. M. M. GARNIER; Gen. Man. M. P. MEYERSON.

Assubel-Vie: Brussels; Pres. PIERRE SCOHIER.

Aviabel, Compagnie Belge d'Assurances Aviation, SA: 10 ave Brugmann, 1060 Brussels; tel. (02) 349-12-11; telex 21928; f. 1935; aviation, insurance, reinsurance; Chair. G. CAMBRON; Gen. Man. J. VERWILGHEN.

AG de 1824—Compagnie Belge d'Assurances Générales 'Vie': 53 blvd Emile Jacqmain, 1000 Brussels; tel. (02) 214-81-11; telex 22766; f. 1969; life, pensions, loans; Chair. and Man. Dir M. LIPPENS; Gen. Man. V. CROES.

AG 1830—Compagnie Belge d'Assurances Générales: 53 blvd Emile Jacqmain, 1000 Brussels; tel. (02) 214-81-11; telex 22766; f. 1830; all forms of insurance; Chair. and Man. Dir M. LIPPENS; Gen. Man. V. CROES.

Belgamar, Compagnie Belge d'Assurances Maritimes SA: 54 St-Katelijnevest, Bus 39/40, 2000 Antwerp; tel. (03) 231-56-62; telex 33411; f. 1945; marine reinsurance; Chair. P. VAN DER MEERSCH; Dir-Man. A. THIÉRY.

BELGIUM
Directory

La Belgique, Compagnie d'Assurances SA: 61 rue de la Régence, 1000 Brussels; tel. (02) 511-38-40; telex 63869; f. 1855; cap. 400m. frs; Chair. HERVÉ NAGELMACKERS; Gen. Man. P. ROUSSELLE.

Compagnie d'Assurance de l'Escaut: 10 rue de la Bourse, Antwerp; f. 1821; fire, accident, life, burglary, reinsurance; Man E. DIERCXSENS.

Compagnie Belge d'Assurance-Crédit SA (COBAC): 15 rue Montoyer, 1040 Brussels; tel. (02) 513-89-30; telex 22337; f. 1929; Chair. R. LAMY; Man. Dir A. STAS DE RICHELLE.

Compagnie Financière et de Réassurance du Groupe AG: 53 blvd Emile Jacqmain, 1000 Brussels; f. 1824; all forms of reinsurance world-wide; Chair. and Man. Dir M. LIPPENS; Gen. Man. V. CROES.

Generali Belgium SA: 149 ave Louise, 1050 Brussels; tel. (02) 536-72-11; telex 21772; fire, accident, marine, life, reinsurance; Pres. Baron LAMBERT; Dir-Gen. C. DENDAL.

Groupe Eagle-Star-Compagnie de Bruxelles 1821 SA d'Assurances: 62 rue de la Loi, 1040 Brussels; tel. (02) 237-12-11; telex 24443; f. 1821; fire, life, general; Pres. G. H. LOCKWOOD; Gen. Man. JEAN BUISSERET.

Groupe Josi Compagnie Centrale d'Assurances 1909 SA: 11 rue des Colonies, 1000 Brussels; tel. (02) 515-12-11; telex 21463; f. 1909; accident, fire, marine, general; Pres. and Dir-Gen. J. P. LAURENT JOSI.

Les Patrons Réunis SA: 60 Chaussée de Charleroi, 1060 Brussels; tel. (02) 537-30-50; telex 64654; f. 1887; fire, life, accident; Chair. H. LIEKENS; Gen. Man. R. NICOLAS.

Royale Belge: 25 blvd Souverain, 1170 Brussels; tel. (02) 661-61-11; telex 23000; f. 1853; life, accident, fire, theft, reinsurance, and all other risks; Pres. PIERRE VAN DER MEERSCH; Vice-Pres. JEAN DROMER, ALBERT FRÈRE; Man. Dirs PIERRE GARNY, PIERRE LABADIE, JEAN-MARIE DE MUNTER.

Société Mutuelle des Administrations Publiques: 24 rue des Croisiers, 4000 Liège; tel. (041) 20-31-11; telex 41216; institutions, civil service employees, public administration and enterprises.

Urbaine UAP Compagnie Belge d'Assurances et de Réassurances SA: 32 rue Belliard, 1040 Brussels; tel. (02) 230-10-01; telex 62060; f. 1900; all risks; Chair. J. P. DE LAUNOIT; Man. Dir R. CORNEMILLOT.

Utrecht Risques Divers: 13 rue de la Loi, 1000 Brussels; tel. (02) 512-00-58; telex 61069; f. 1948; Dirs R. WEBER, M. LACROIX.

Insurance Associations

Fédération des Producteurs d'Assurances de Belgique: 40 ave Albert Elisabeth, 1200 Brussels; tel (02) 733-35-22; f. 1934; 900 mems; Pres. JAN HENDRICKX; Dir JEAN SCHOUTERDEN.

Union Professionnelle des Entreprises d'Assurances Belges et Etrangères Opérant en Belgique—Beroepsvereniging der Belgische en Buitenlandse Verzekeringsondernemingen: 29 square de Meeûs, 1040 Brussels; tel. (02) 513-68-45; telex 63652; f. 1921; 181 mems; affiliated to Fédération des Entreprises de Belgique; Pres. JOHN VAN WATERSCHOOT; Dir-Gen. RENÉ VAN GOMPEL.

Trade and Industry

PRINCIPAL CHAMBERS OF COMMERCE

There are chambers of commerce and industry in all major towns and industrial areas.

Kamer van Koophandel en Nijverheid van Antwerpen: 12 Markgravestraat, 2000 Antwerp; tel. (03) 232-22-19; telex 71536; f. 1969; Gen. Man. M. VERBOVEN.

Chambre de Commerce de Bruxelles: 500 ave Louise, 1050 Brussels; tel. (02) 648-50-02; telex 22082; f. 1875.

TRADE AND INDUSTRIAL ASSOCIATIONS

Fédération des Entreprises de Belgique (Belgian Business Federation): 4 rue Ravenstein, 1000 Brussels; tel. (02) 515-08-11; telex 26576; f. 1895; federates all the main industrial and non-industrial associations; Pres. PHILIPPE BODSON; Man. Dir RAYMOND PULINCKX.

Association Belge des Entreprises d'Alimentation à Succursales (ABEAS) (Food Chain Stores): 60 rue St Bernard, 1060 Brussels; tel. (02) 537-30-60; f. 1941; Pres. GUY BECKERS; Dir-Gen. ALPHONSE DE VADDER.

Association des Centrales Electriques Industrielles de Belgique (Industrial Electricity): 36 rue Joseph II, 1040 Brussels; f. 1922; Pres. PAUL RENDERS; Admin. MARCEL DE LEENER; Man. MAURICE DE BECKER.

Association des Entreprises Exportatrices de l'Industrie Alimentaire Belge/Vereniging van de uitvoerende Bedrijven van de Belgische Voedingsindustrie—VITABEL (Exporting Food Manufacturers): 172 ave de Cortenbergh, BP 7, 1040 Brussels; tel. (02) 735-81-70; telex 26246; f. 1984; Pres. E. VAN BELLE.

Association des Exploitants de Carrières de Porphyre (Porphyry): 64 rue de Belle-Vue, 1050 Brussels; tel. (02) 648-68-60; f. 1967; Pres. PHILIPPE NOTTÉ; Dir GEORGES HANSEN.

Association des Fabricants de Pâtes, Papiers et Cartons de Belgique (COBELPA) (Paper): 39–41 rue d'Arlon, 1040 Brussels; tel. (02) 230-70-20; telex 22713; f. 1940; co-operative asscn; Pres. BERNARD ANCION; Dir ALFRED ROSE.

Association des Groupements et Entreprises de Distribution de Belgique (AGED) (Distribution): 3 rue de la Science, 1040 Brussels; tel. (02) 537-30-60; f. 1946; Pres. MICHEL BUISSERET; Dir-Gen. ALFONS DE VEDDER.

Association des Industries des Carrières (AIC) (Federation of Quarrying Industries): 64 rue de Belle-Vue, 1050 Brussels; tel. (02) 648-68-60; f. 1975; Pres. PHILIPPE NOTTÉ; Dir GEORGES HANSEN.

Confédération des Brasseries de Belgique (Breweries): Maison des Brasseurs, 10 Grand' Place, 1000 Brussels; tel. (02) 511-49-87; f. 1971; Pres. ROGER VAN DER SCHUEREN; Dir MICHEL BRICHET.

Confédération Nationale de la Construction (CNC) (Civil Engineering, Road and Building Contractors and Auxiliary Trades): 34–42 rue du Lombard, 1000 Brussels; tel. (02) 510-46-11; telex 64956; f. 1946; 15,000 mems; Pres. ROLAND MAES; Admin. Dir FREDDY FEYS, Man. Dir EDWIN JACOBS.

Confédération Professionnelle du Sucre et de ses Dérivés (Sugar): 182 ave de Tervueren, 1150 Brussels; tel. (02) 771-01-30; f. 1938; mems 10 groups, 66 firms; Pres. ANDRÉ FOUYN; Dir-Gen. ALAIN JOLLY.

Fédération Belge de l'Industrie de la Chaussure (FEBIC) (Footwear): 53 rue François Bossaerts, 1030 Brussels; tel. (02) 735-27-01; telex 65625; f. 1968; Pres. ROELAND SMETS.

Fédération Belge des Dragueurs de Gravier et de Sable (BELBAG-DRAGBEL) (Dredging): 12 ave Hippocrate, BP 19, 1940 Woluwé-Saint-Etienne; tel. (02) 736-02-15; f. 1967; Pres. DANIEL DE GROOTE.

Fédération Belge des Entreprises de Distribution (FEDIS): 60 rue St-Bernard, 1060 Brussels; tel. (02) 537-30-60; telex 63201; Pres. JACQUES DOPCHIE; Man. Dir ROBERT VAN ASSCHE.

Fédération Belge des Entreprises de la Transformation du Bois (FEBELBOIS) (Wood): Maison du Bois, 109–111 rue Royale, 1000 Brussels; tel. (02) 217-63-65; telex 64143; Gen. Pres. GUSTAAF NEYT; Man. Dir HUBERT FONDERIE.

Fédération Belge des Industries Graphiques (FEBELGRA) (Graphic Industries): 20 rue Belliard, BP 16, 1040 Brussels; tel. (02) 512-36-38; telex 26854; f. 1978; 1,000 mems; Pres. POL VERWAEST; Sec.-Gen. JOS ROSSIE.

Fédération Belge des Industries de l'Habillement (Clothing and Outfitting): 24 rue Montoyer, BP 11, 1040 Brussels; tel. (02) 230-88-90; telex 61055; f. 1946; Pres. ANDRÉ DELFOSSE; Dir JOSÉ DÉCAT.

Fédération Belge du Commerce Alimentaire (FEBECA) (Foodstuffs Trade): 60 rue St-Bernard, 1060 Brussels; tel. (02) 537-30-60; telex 63201; f. 1941; Pres. GEORGES DE MEYERE; Dir-Gen. J. DEGRAVE.

Fédération Belgo-Luxembourgeoise des Industries du Tabac (FEDETAB) (Tobacco): 270–272 ave de Tervueren, boîte 20, 1150 Brussels; tel. (02) 762-57-20; telex 64888; f. 1947; Pres. EMMANUEL VAN OUTRYVE D'YDEWALLE; Chief Exec. GUY DEMOULIN; Sec.-Gen. D. VUIJLSTEKE.

Fédération Charbonnière de Belgique (Coal): 21 ave des Arts, 1040 Brussels; tel. (02) 230-37-40; f. 1909; Pres. PIERRE VANDERGOTEN; Dir GUY VAN BRUYSTEGEM.

Fédération de l'Industrie Cimentière (Cement): 46 rue César Franck, 1050 Brussels; tel. (02) 649-98-50; telex 21431; f. 1949; Pres. RENÉ CELIS; Dir-Gen. JEAN-PIERRE LATTEUR.

Fédération de l'Industrie du Béton (FeBe) (Precast Concrete): 207–209 blvd August Reyers, 1040 Brussels; tel. (02) 735-80-15; f. 1936; Pres. RAF BULCKE; Dir WILLY SIMONS.

Fédération de l'Industrie du Gaz (FIGAZ) (Gas): 4 ave Palmerston, 1040 Brussels; tel. (02) 230-43-85; Pres. ROBERT-GEORGES HAVAUX; Sec.-Gen. LIEVEN BLOM.

Fédération de l'Industrie du Verre (Glass): 47 rue Montoyer, 1040 Brussels; tel. (02) 509-15-20; telex 21287; f. 1947; Pres. GÉRY LIVREMONT; Dir PIERRE VAN DE PUTTE.

Fédération de l'Industrie Textile Belge (FEBELTEX) (Textiles): 24 rue Montoyer, 1040 Brussels; tel. (02) 230-93-30; telex 20183; f. 1945; 1,800 mems; Pres. LUC SANTENS; Dir-Gen. PIERRE JANSSENS.

BELGIUM

Fédération des Carrières de Grès (Sandstone): 73 rue Franz Merjay, 1060 Brussels; f. 1947; Pres. PIERRE-ETIENNE DAPSENS; Sec. ÉLAINE MEERT.

Fédération des Carrières de Petit Granit (Granite): BP 3, 7400 Soignies; tel. (067) 33-41-21; telex 57444; f. 1948; Pres. JEAN-FRANZ ABRAHAM.

Fédération des Entreprises de l'Industrie des Fabrications Métalliques, Mécaniques, Electriques, Electroniques et de la Transformation des Matières Plastiques (FABRIMETAL) (Metalwork, Engineering, Electrics, Electronics and Plastic Processing): 21 rue des Drapiers, 1050 Brussels; tel. (02) 510-23-11; telex 21078; f. 1946; Pres. EUGÈNE A. VAN DYCK; Man. Dir PHILIPPE DE BUCK VAN OVERSTRAETEN.

Fédération des Entreprises de Métaux non Ferreux (Nonferrous Metals): 47 rue Montoyer, 1040 Brussels; tel. (02) 513-86-34; telex 22077; f. 1918; 40 mems; Pres. LEANDRO ALIMENTI; Admin. Dir CHRISTIAN PIRLOT DE CORBION.

Fédération des Industries Agricoles et Alimentaires/Verbond der Landbouw en Voedingsnijverheid (Food and Agricultural Industries): 172 Kortenberglaan, bus 7, 1040 Brussels; tel. (02) 735-81-70; telex 26246; f. 1937; Pres. PIERRE GODFROID; Dir-Gen. PAUL VERHAEGHE.

Fédération des Industries Céramiques de Belgique et du Luxembourg (FEDICER) (Ceramics): 4 ave Gouverneur Cornez, 7000 Mons; tel. (065) 34-80-00; telex 57865; f. 1919; Pres. C. Y. DUMOLIN; Dir P. DE BRUYCKER.

Fédération des Industries Chimiques de Belgique (Chemical Industries): 49 square Marie-Louise, 1040 Brussels; tel. (02) 230-40-90; telex 23167; f. 1919; Pres. ETIENNE DE WOLF; Man. Dir PAUL-F. SMETS.

Fédération des Industries Transformatrices de Papier et Carton (FETRA) (Paper and Cardboard): 715 chaussée de Waterloo, BP 25, 1180 Brussels; tel. (02) 344-19-62; telex 23442; f. 1947; 300 mems; Pres. PHILIPPE DE SOMER; Dir PHILIPPE DELLA FAILLE DE LEVERGHEM.

Fédération Nationale Belge de la Fourrure et de la Peau en Poil (Furs and Skins): 4 rue de l'Autonomie, BP 4, 1070 Brussels; tel. (02) 521-79-35; f. 1947; Pres. J. ASCAREZ; Sec.-Gen. C. KOHNER.

Fédération Patronale des Ports Belges (Port Employers): 33 Brouwersvliet, bus 7, 2000 Antwerp; tel. (03) 232-19-27; f. 1937; Pres. KAREL NOENINCKX; Sec. FRANS GIELEN.

Fédération Pétrolière Belge (Petroleum): 4 rue de la Science, 1040 Brussels; tel. (02) 512-30-03; telex 26930; f. 1926; Pres. GEORGES DE GRAEVE.

Groupement National de l'Industrie de la Terre Cuite (Terracotta): 13 rue des Poissonniers, BP 22, 1000 Brussels; tel. (02) 511-25-81; f. 1947; Pres. LUC JANSEN; Dir GIOVANNI PEIRS.

Groupement Patronal des Bureaux Commerciaux et Maritimes (Employers' Association of Trade and Shipping Offices): 33 Brouwersvliet, bus 7, 2000 Antwerp; tel. (03) 232-19-27; f. 1937; Pres. KAREL NOENINCKX; Sec. FRANS GIELEN.

Groupement de la Sidérurgie (Iron and Steel): 47 rue Montoyer, 1040 Brussels; tel. (02) 509-14-11; telex 21287; f. 1982; Pres. and Dir-Gen. CHRISTIAN OURY.

Groupement des Sablières (Sand and Gravel): 49 Quellinstraat, 2018 Antwerp; tel. (03) 223-66-83; f. 1937; Pres. ALFRED PAULUS; Sec. PAUL DE NIE.

Industrie des Huiles Minérales de Belgique (IHMB) (Mineral Oils): 49 square Marie-Louise, 1040 Brussels; tel. (02) 230-40-90; telex 23167; f. 1921; 90 mems; Pres. R. VANDATTE; Sec. M. DONCKERWOLCKE.

Union de la Tannerie et de la Mégisserie Belges (UNITAN) (Tanning and Tawing): 161 rue Th. de Cuyper, BP 32, 1200 Brussels; tel. (02) 771-32-06; f. 1962; 13 mems; Pres. GUY VANDERHAEGEN; Sec. MARC VANWELDEN.

Union des Armateurs Belges (Shipowners): 9 Lijnwaadmarkt, 2000 Antwerp; tel. (03) 232-72-31; Chair. JACQUES SAVERYS; Man. R. VAN HERCK.

Union des Carrières et Scieries de Marbres de Belgique (UCSMB) (Marble): 40 rue Bosquet, 1060 Brussels; tel. (02) 538-46-61; telex 24235; Pres. J. VAN DEN WILDENBERG; Vice-Pres. P. STONE.

Union des Exploitations Electriques en Belgique (UEEB) (Electricity): 4 galerie Ravenstein, BP 6, 1000 Brussels; tel. (02) 511-19-70; telex 62409; f. 1911; Pres. PHILIPPE COLS; Dir-Gen. E. R. MARICQ.

Union des Producteurs Belges de Chaux, Calcaires, Dolomies et Produits Connexes (UCCD) (Lime, limestone, dolomite and related products): 61 rue du Trône, 1050 Brussels; tel. (02) 511-61-73; f. 1942; co-operative society; Co-Pres. GUY CUVELIER, CHARLES MOREAU DE MELEN; Dir EMILE WOUTERS.

Union Professionnelle des Producteurs de Fibres-Ciment (Asbestos-Cement): World Trade Centre, 162 blvd Emile Jacqmain, BP 37, 1210 Brussels; tel. (02) 211-04-11; telex 21696; f. 1941; Pres. ETIENNE VAN DER REST; Sec. PAUL VAN REETH.

TRADE UNIONS AND PROFESSIONAL ORGANIZATIONS

Fédération Générale du Travail de Belgique (FGTB)/Algemeen Belgisch Vakverbond: 42 rue Haute, 1000 Brussels; tel. (02) 511-80-67; telex 24620; f. 1899; affiliated to ICFTU; Pres. ANDRÉ VANDEN BROUCKE; has 11 affiliated unions with an estimated total membership of 1,036,028 (1986). Affiliated unions:

De Algemene Centrale/La Centrale Générale (Central Union): 26–28 rue Haute, 1000 Brussels; tel. (02) 513-06-25; telex 62559; Pres. JUAN FERNANDEZ; Sec.-Gen. HENRI LORENT; Nat. Secs EDDY SCHELSTRAETE, MICHEL NOLLET, ALFONS VAN NOOTEN, HANS RAES, MAURICE CORBISIER; 239,239 mems (1986).

Algemene Diamantbewerkersbond van België (Diamond Workers): 57 Lange Kievitstraat, bus 1, 2018 Antwerp; tel. (03) 232-48-60; f. 1896; Pres. C. DENISSE; 3,672 mems (1986).

Belgische Transportarbeidersbond (Belgian Transport Workers): 66 Paardenmarkt, 2000 Antwerp; tel. (03) 231-18-40; telex 73080; f. 1913; Pres. REMI VAN CANT; 24,433 mems (1986).

Centrale de l'Industrie du Livre et du Papier (Graphical and Paper Workers): galerie du Centre, bloc 2, 17 rue des Fripiers, 1000 Brussels; tel. (02) 511-09-66; f. 1945; Secs ROGER DEMEYER, ROBERT LELOUP, ROGER SAGON; 11,918 mems (1987).

Centrale der Kleding en aanverwante vakken van België (Clothing Workers): 32 Ommeganckstraat, 2018 Antwerp; tel. (03) 233-56-72; f. 1898; Pres. JEAN SCHOUPPE; Gen. Sec. FIRMIN VAN DE CALSEYDE; 27,040 mems (1986).

Centrale des Métallurgistes de Belgique (Metal Workers): 17 rue Jacques Jordaens, 1050 Brussels; tel. (02) 647-83-14; f. 1887; Sec.-Gen. GERMAIN DUHIN; 196,795 mems (1986).

Centrale des Travailleurs de l'Alimentation et de l'Hôtellerie (Catering and Hotel Workers): 18 rue des Alexiens, 1000 Brussels; tel. (02) 512-97-00; f. 1912; Pres. ARTHUR LADRILLE; Nat. Sec. EDUARD PEPERMANS; 57,380 mems.

Centrale Générale des Services Publics (Public Service Workers): Maison des Huit Heures, 9–11 place Fontainas, 1000 Brussels; tel. (02) 539-39-60; telex 22563; f. 1945; Pres. R. PITON; Gen. Secs G. LONNOY, R. FERNANDEZ, G. SERET, P. STEENHAUT; 227,448 mems (1986).

Nationale Centrale der Mijnwerkers van België (Miners): 8 J. Stevensstraat, bus 4, 1000 Brussels; tel. (02) 511-96-45; f. 1889; Pres. J. OLYSLAEGERS; 19,142 mems (1987).

Syndicat des Employés, Techniciens et Cadres de Belgique (Employees, Technicians and Administrative Workers): 42 rue Haute, 1000 Brussels; tel. (02) 513-18-91; f. 1891; Pres. FRANÇOIS JANSSENS; Gen. Sec. GILBERT CLAJOT; 174,528 mems (1986).

Textielarbeiderscentrale van België (Textile Workers): 143 Opvoedingsstraat, 9000 Ghent; tel. (091) 21-75-11; f. 1898; Nat. Pres. DONALD WITTEVRONGEL; Nat. Sec. XAVIER VERBOVEN; 38,389 mems (1986).

Confédération des Syndicats Chrétiens (CSC): 121 rue de la Loi, 1040 Brussels; tel. (02) 233-34-11; telex 61770; Pres. WILLY PEIRENS; has 18 affiliated unions with an estimated total membership of 1,336,000 (1987). Affiliated unions:

Centrale Chrétienne de l'Alimentation et des Services (Food and Service Industries): 27 rue de l'Association, 1000 Brussels; tel. (02) 218-21-71; f. 1919; Pres. W. VIJVERMAN; Sec.-Gen. F. BOCKLANDT; 111,049 mems (1982).

Centrale Chrétienne des Industries Graphiques et du Papier (Paper Workers): 26 ave d'Auderghem, 1040 Brussels; tel. (02) 231-00-90; Sec.-Gen. MARCEL NEIRYNCK; 21,712 mems (1976).

Centrale Chrétienne des Métallurgistes de Belgique (Metal Workers): 127 rue de Heembeek, 1120 Brussels; tel. (02) 215-88-40; Pres. T. JANSSEN; 232,000 mems.

Centrale Chrétienne des Ouvriers des Industries des Mines, de l'Energie, de la Chimie, du Cuir et Diverses (Mines, Power, Chemical, Leather, etc., Workers): 26–32 ave d'Auderghem, 1040 Brussels; tel. 021-231-00-90; f. 1912; Pres. A. VAN GENECHTEN; Nat. Sec. A. CUYVERS; Gen. Sec. M. SOMMEREYNS; 77,651 mems (1987).

Centrale Chrétienne des Ouvriers du Textile et du Vêtement de Belgique (Textile and Clothing Workers): 27 Koning Albertlaan, 9000 Ghent; tel. (091) 22-57-01; f. 1886; Pres. L. FRURU; Gen. Sec. A. DUQUET; 100,000 mems (1987).

Centrale Chrétienne des Ouvriers du Transport et des Ouvriers Diamantaires (Transport and Diamond Workers): 12–14 Entrepotplaats, 2000 Antwerp; tel. (03) 231-47-85; Pres. JOHN JANSSENS.

BELGIUM   *Directory*

Centrale Chrétienne des Services Publics—Christelijke Centrale van de Openbare Diensten (Public Service Workers): 26 ave d'Auderghem, 1040 Brussels; tel. (02) 231-00-90; f. 1921; Pres. Filip Wieers; Sec.-Gen. Guy Rasneur; 93,000 mems (1976).

Centrale Chrétienne des Travailleurs du Bois et du Bâtiment (Wood and Building Workers): 31 rue de Trèves, 1040 Brussels; tel. (02) 230-85-70; Pres. A. Desloovere; Sec.-Gen. Bernard Baert; 188,300 mems (1987).

Centrale Chrétienne des Travailleurs de la Pierre, du Ciment, de la Céramique et du Verre (Stone, Cement, Ceramic and Glass Workers): 26–32 ave d'Auderghem, 1040 Brussels; tel. (02) 231-00-90; Pres. August de Decker; Secs Léo Dusoleil, Raymond Groetembril; 26,000 mems (1981).

Centrale Chrétienne du Personnel de l'Enseignement Moyen et Normal Libre (Lay Teachers in Secondary and Teacher-Training Institutions): 26–32 ave d'Auderghem, 1040 Brussels; tel. (02) 231-00-90; f. 1924; f. 1950; Pres. Roger Denis; 18,000 mems (1987).

Centrale Chrétienne du Personnel de l'Enseignement Technique (Teachers in Technical Education): 26 ave d'Auderghem, 1040 Brussels; tel. (02) 231-00-90; f. 1924; Pres. Jean-Pierre van den Berghe; Sec.-Gen. Wilfried Kiekens; 33,000 mems (1982).

Centrale des Francs Mineurs (Miners' Union): 26 ave d'Auderghem, 1040 Brussels; Pres. André Daemen; Sec. Frans Vanderlinden; 31,725 mems (1976).

Centrale Nationale des Employés/Landelijke Bedienden Centrale (Employees): (Northern Region) 1 Beggaardenstraat, 2000 Antwerp; tel. (03) 234-15-00; (Southern Region) 33–35 ave d'Auderghem, 1040 Brussels; tel. (02) 230-65-73; f. 1912; Secs-Gen. L. Stragier (Northern), José Roisin (Southern); 240,000 mems (1979).

Fédération des Instituteurs Chrétiens de Belgique/Christen Onderwijzersverbond van België (School Teachers): 203 Koningsstraat, 1210 Brussels; tel. (02) 217-40-50; f. 1893; Pres. Régis Dohogne; Sec.-Gen. L. van Beneden; 50,876 mems (1988).

Service Syndical Sports (Sport): 7 Poel, 9000 Ghent; tel. (091) 24-00-42; Pres. E. Laenen; Sec. M. Lippens.

Syndicat Chrétien des Communications et de la Culture (Christian Trade Unions of Railway, Post and Telecommunications, Shipping, Civil Aviation, Radio, TV and Cultural Workers): 26 ave d'Auderghem, 1040 Brussels; tel. (02) 231-00-90; f. 1919; Pres. M. Bovy; Secs P. Bertin, E. Jans, R. Frippiat, J. Hinnekens, P. van den Dooren, E. van Elsacker; 60,000 mems (1987).

Union Chrétienne des Membres du Personnel de l'Enseignement Officiel: 26 ave d' Auderghem, 1040 Brussels; tel. (02) 231-00-90; Pres. A. Pollet; Secs E. Bodson, J. Luyten.

Centrale Générale des Syndicats Libéraux de Belgique (CGSLB) (General Federation of Liberal Trade Unions of Belgium): 2 rue Brederode, 1000 Brussels; tel. (02) 511-15-95; f. 1889; National Pres. Armand Colle; 250,000 mems.

Syndicat Libre de la Fonction Publique (Public Services' Union): 25 rue de Spa, 1000 Brussels; Pres. Frans Mievis; Gen. Sec. Guy de Witte.

Fédération Nationale des Unions Professionnelles Agricoles de Belgique: 94–96 rue Antoine Dansaert, 1000 Brussels; tel. (02) 511-07-37; f. 1919; Pres. L. Ernoux; Sec.-Gen. J. P. Champagne.

Nationale Unie der Openbare Diensten (NUOD)/Union Nationale des Services Publics (UNSP): 54 Paviljoenstraat, 1210 Brussels; tel. (02) 215-66-70; Pres. Gerald van Acker; Sec.-Gen. Freddy Malfrooid.

TRADE FAIRS

Foire Internationale de Bruxelles (Brussels International Trade Fair): Parc des Expositions, 1020 Brussels; tel. (02) 478-48-60; telex 23643; f. 1919; holds more than 25 fairs and trade shows each year, as well as 60 congresses and technical exhibitions; Gen. Man. J. Isaac Castiau.

International Fair of Flanders: Congrescentrum (5th floor), 9000 Ghent; tel. (091) 22-40-22; telex 12666; f. 1946; holds several fairs annually.

Transport

RAILWAYS

The Belgian railway network is one of the densest in the world. The main lines are operated by the SNCB under lease from the State Transport Administration and the system is complemented by the SNCV bus and light railway network for local traffic. Six regional companies run trams, rapid transit systems and metros.

Société Nationale des Chemins de Fer Belges (SNCB)/Nationale Maatschappij der Belgische Spoorwegen (NMBS): 85 rue de France, 1070 Brussels; tel. (02) 525-21-11; f. 1926; 142.2m. passengers were carried in 1987; directed by a board of 16 members; 3,568 km of lines, of which 2,200 km are electrified; Gen. Man. M. E. Schouppe.

ROADS

At 31 December 1987 there were 1,567 km of motorways, 12,902 km of other main or national roads and 13,850 km of secondary or regional roads. In addition, there are about 100,000 km of minor roads.

Société Nationale des Chemins de Fer Vicinaux (SNCV) (Light railways, buses and trams): 14 rue de la Science, 1040 Brussels; f. 1884; operates all public bus and tram services; Pres. R. Denison; Dir-Gen. Hugo Vanwesemael.

INLAND WATERWAYS

There are over 1,500 km of inland waterways in Belgium, of which 657 km are navigable rivers and 860 km are canals. In 1982 an estimated 91,222,000 metric tons of cargo were carried on the inland waterways. Under the Investment Plan started in 1957 canals and rivers have been modified to accommodate more traffic.

Ministerie van Openbare Werken: Hoofdbestuur der Waterwegen, Residence Palace, Wetstraat 155, 1040 Brussels; tel. (02) 733-96-70; telex 63477; Dir-Gen. Ir. J. Demoen.

SHIPPING

The modernized port of Antwerp is the second biggest in Europe and handles 80% of Belgian foreign trade by sea and inland waterways. It is also the largest railway port and has one of the largest petroleum refining complexes in Europe. It has 98 km of quayside and 17 dry docks, and is currently accessible to vessels of up to 75,000 tons: extensions are being carried out which will increase this limit to 125,000 tons. The port receives some 19,000 vessels and handled 90 million tons of cargo in 1986. Other ports include Zeebrugge, Ostend, Ghent, Liège and Brussels.

Régie Belge des Transports Maritimes (Belgian Maritime Transport Authority): 30 rue Belliard, 1040 Brussels; tel. (02) 230-01-80; telex 23851; Gen. Man. P. Muyldermans; Ostend–Dover lines; 1 passenger vessel, 2 jetfoils and 6 multi-purpose vessels.

De Keyser Thornton: 38 Huidevettersstraat, 2000 Antwerp; tel. (03) 233-01-05; telex 72511; liner and ship agents, forwarders and warehousemen; f. 1853; Man. Dir M. P. Ingham.

Ahlers Lines NV: 139 Noorderlaan, 2030 Antwerp; tel. (03) 543-72-11; telex 72154; services to Finland, Poland, USSR, Morocco; Dirs H. Coppieters, J. Gelens, H. Knoche.

Belfranline NV: 24–29 Meir, 2000 Antwerp; tel. (03) 234-84-11; telex 34115; f. 1957; liner services to Venezuela, Dominican Republic, Haiti, Netherlands Antilles, Trinidad and Tobago, Barbados and Jamaica; also to Central America (East Coast); Pres. J. E. Sasse; Man. Dir E. J. Sasse.

CMB SA/NV: (Reg. Office) 61 St Katelijnevest, 2000 Antwerp; (Commercial Office) 1 Meir, 2000 Antwerp; tel. (03) 223-21-11; telex 72304; f. 1895, formerly known as Compagnie Maritime Belge (Lloyd Royal) SA, merged with Methania SA/NV in 1985; European service and lines to North and South America, Africa, Middle East and Indian sub-continent; Chair. and Man. Dir P. Pluys; Dir/Gen. Man. J. Saverys; 17 vessels for freight (conventional, container, bulk) and passengers.

ESSO Belgium SA/NV: 101 Frankrijklei, 2000 Antwerp; tel. (03) 231-96-00; telex 31144; tanker service, refining/marketing; Pres. R. Dahan; Vice-Pres. D. A. Schram.

North Sea Ferries (Belgium) NV: Leopold II Dam, 13, 8380 Zeebrugge; tel. (050) 54-34-11; telex 81469; operated in conjunction with North Sea Ferries Ltd, UK; roll-on/roll-off ferry services between Hull and Zeebrugge; Dirs R. E. Speld, M. L. van Leeuwen, M. Storme.

Northern Shipping Service NV: 54 St Katelijnevest, 2000 Antwerp; tel. (03) 233-99-85; telex 32315; forwarding, customs clearance, liner and tramp agencies, chartering, Rhine and inland barging, multi-purpose bulk/bags fertilizer terminal; Pres. L. M. Heintz.

Petrofina SA: 52 rue de l'Industrie, 1040 Brussels; tel. (02) 233-91-11; telex 21556; integrated oil company active in exploration and production, transportation and oil refining, petrochemicals, marketing of petroleum products and research; Pres. and Man. Dir Jean-Pierre Amory.

BELGIUM
Directory

Société Belge de Navigation Maritime/Navibel SA: 54 St Katelijnevest, 2000 Antwerp; tel. (03) 233-99-85; telex 32315; tramp, European, Mediterranean and North West African cargo services; Pres. R. DE VLAMINCK.

Ubem NV/SA: 150 Mechelsesteenweg, 2018 Antwerp; tel. (03) 237-29-50; telex 32515; bulk carriers and car ferry services; Man. Dir E. DE LAET.

CIVIL AVIATION

The main international airport is at Brussels, with a direct train service from the air terminal. There are also international airports at Antwerp, Liège, Charleroi and Ostend.

SABENA (Société anonyme belge d'exploitation de la navigation aérienne) (Belgian World Air Lines): Air Terminal, 35 rue Cardinal Mercier, 1000 Brussels; tel. (02) 511-90-60; telex 21322; f. 1923; 54% state-owned; services to most parts of the world; Chair. CARLOS VAN RAFELGHEM; Vice-Chair. ANDRÉ PAHAUT; fleet of 3 Boeing 747, 16 Boeing 737, 3 Airbus A310, 5 DC-10-30 CF, 2 Cessna, 8 SF-260, 5 EMB 121 Xingu.

Delta Air Transport (DAT) NV: Deurne Airport, BP 4, 2100 Antwerp; tel. (03) 239-58-35; telex 32602; f. 1966; Antwerp and Brussels to Amsterdam, Frankfurt, Stuttgart, Düsseldorf, London (Heathrow), Munich, Zurich, Copenhagen and Dublin; charter service in Europe; Pres. C. VAN RAFELGHEM; Gen. Man. TONY VANGRIEKEN; fleet of 3 FH227B, 2 F.28, 5 EMB 120.

Sobelair (Société Belge de Transports par Air) NV: 131 ave Frans Courtens, 1030 Brussels; tel. (02) 216-21-75; telex 22095; f. 1946; subsidiary of Sabena, operating charter and inclusive-tour flights; Man. Dir P. JONNART; Dir R. MINET; Man. J. EDOM; fleet of 3 Boeing 737-200, 1 Boeing 737-300, 2 Boeing 707-320C.

Trans European Airways (TEA): Bldg 117, Melsbroek Airport, 1910 Melsbroek; telex 21886; f. 1970; charter and inclusive-tour flights; Man. Dir G. P. GUTELMAN; fleet of 1 Airbus A300B2, 5 Boeing 737-200, 3 Boeing 737-300.

Tourism

Belgium has several towns of rich historic and cultural interest, such as Bruges, Ghent and Antwerp. Ostend and other seaside towns attract many visitors. The forest-covered Ardennes region is excellent hill-walking country.

Office de Promotion du Tourisme de la Communauté Française: 61 rue Marché-aux-Herbes, 1000 Brussels; tel. (02) 513-90-90; telex 63245; f. 1981; promotion of tourism in French-speaking Belgium; Dir JOSÉ CLOSSEN.

Tourist Information Brussels (TIB): Hôtel de Ville, Grand-Place, 1000 Brussels; tel. (02) 513-89-40; telex 65206; Pres. VIVIANE BARO (acting); Dir GEORGES RENDERS.

Tourist Office for Flanders: 61 Grasmarkt, 1000 Brussels; tel. (02) 513-90-90; telex 63245; f. 1985; official promotion and policy body for tourism in Flemish part of Belgium; Gen. Commissioner URBAIN CLAEYS.

Atomic Energy

In 1986 an estimated 67.2% of Belgium's electricity was produced by nuclear power. There were seven reactors in all, with a total capacity of 5,486 MW.

Commissariat à l'Energie Atomique (Atomic Energy Commission): Administration de l'Energie, Ministère des Affaires Economiques, 30 rue de Mot, 1040 Brussels; tel. (02) 233-61-11; telex 23509; f. 1950; deals with nuclear matters falling within the competence of the Ministry of Economic Affairs.

Centre d'Etude de l'Energie Nucléaire (CEN)/Studiecentrum voor Kernenergie (SCK): 1 rue Ch. Lemaire, 1160 Brussels; tel. (02) 661-08-11; telex 22718; laboratories: 200 Boeretang, 2400 Mol; tel. (014) 31-18-01; telex 31922; f. 1952; currently engaged in basic research, contract and service activities in a number of sectors; staff of 1,200 including 300 senior scientists; Pres. I. VAN VAERENBERGH; Gen. Sec. R. DE CORT.

Institut Interuniversitaire des Sciences Nucléaires/Interuniversitair Instituut voor Kernwetenschappen: 5 rue d'Egmont, 1050 Brussels; f. 1947 to promote research in nuclear science and solid state physics in advanced teaching and research establishments, including departments in the universities and centres at the State University (formerly Polytechnic Institute) of Mons and the Royal Military School at Brussels; 170 scientific researchers; Pres. S. LOCCUFIER; Sec.-Gen. P. LEVAUX, DR.SC.

Organisme National de Déchets Radioactifs et des Matières fissiles (ONDRAF/NIRAS): 1 place Madou, 1000 Brussels; tel. (02) 212-10-11; telex 65784; f. 1981; management of radioactive waste; Gen. Man. E. DETILLEUX.

BELIZE

Introductory Survey

Location, Climate, Language, Religion, Flag, Capital

Belize lies on the Caribbean coast of Central America, with Mexico to the north-west and Guatemala to the south-west. The climate is sub-tropical, tempered by trade winds. The temperature averages 24°C (75°F) from November to January, and 27°C (81°F) from May to September. Annual rainfall ranges from 51 inches (1,290 mm) in the north to 175 inches (4,450 mm) in the south. The average annual rainfall in Belize City is 65 inches (1,650 mm). English is the official language but Spanish is the mother tongue of about one-half of the population, and there are small communities of Garifuna (Carib) and Maya speakers in the south. An English 'creole' is almost universally understood. Most of the population profess Christianity, dividing approximately into 60% Roman Catholics and 40% Protestants. The national flag is dark blue, with narrow horizontal red stripes at the upper and lower edges; at the centre is a white disc containing the state coat of arms, bordered by an olive wreath. The capital is Belmopan.

Recent History

Belize, known as British Honduras until June 1973, was first colonized by British settlers in the 17th century, but was not recognized as a British colony until 1862. In 1954 a new constitution granted universal adult suffrage and provided for the creation of a Legislative Assembly. The territory's first general election, in April 1954, was won by the only party then organized, the People's United Party (PUP), led by George Price. The PUP won all subsequent elections until 1984. In 1961 Price was appointed First Minister under a new ministerial system of government. The colony was granted internal self-government in 1964, with the United Kingdom retaining responsibility for defence, external affairs and internal security. Following an election in 1965, Price became Premier and a bicameral legislature was introduced. In 1970 the capital of the territory was moved from Belize City to the newly built town of Belmopan.

Much of the recent history of Belize has been dominated by the territorial dispute with Guatemala, particularly in the years prior to Belize's independence (see below). This was achieved on 21 September 1981, within the Commonwealth, and with George Price becoming Prime Minister. However, the failure of the 1981 draft treaty with Guatemala, and the clash of opposing wings within the ruling party, undermined the dominance of the PUP. Internal disputes within the PUP intensified during 1983, although Price succeeded in keeping the factions together. However, at the general election, held in December 1984, the PUP's 30 years of rule ended when the United Democratic Party (UDP) received 53% of the total votes and won 21 of the 28 seats in the enlarged House of Representatives. The remaining seven seats were won by the PUP, with 44% of the votes, but Price and several of his ministers lost their seats. The UDP's leader, Manuel Esquivel, became Prime Minister. The new Government pledged itself to reviving Belize's economy through increased foreign investment. In January 1985 Louis Sylvestre, the leading right-wing member of the PUP, resigned from the party and subsequently formed his own party, the Belize Popular Party (BPP).

By 1988, however, the UDP was suffering from internal dissension, after municipal elections in March, when the opposition had won control of four out of seven Town Boards. The PUP had been able to take advantage of the controversy surrounding the Government's creation of a Security and Intelligence Service (SIS, a body intended to operate secretly against the illegal drugs trade, but also responsible for scrutinizing appointments to the civil service), and the alleged attempts by the Government to stifle any expression of opposition. The PUP campaigned vigorously against the adoption of the legislation to establish the SIS, but it was enacted in January 1988. At the same time, there was an arson attack on the home of the Deputy Prime Minister, who was also the minister responsible for the SIS. The Government retaliated strongly against the PUP, alleging its involvement in the incident, although this claim was rejected in court. This was in addition to a series of court actions against the PUP's newspaper, *The Belize Times*, a controversy over the limiting of opposition broadcasts, and the dismissals of some senior public officials. Despite this acrimony, there was a bipartisan consensus on negotiations with Guatemala in 1988.

The frontier with Guatemala was agreed by a convention in 1859 but this was declared invalid by Guatemala in 1940. Guatemalan claims to sovereignty of Belize date back to the middle of the 19th century and were written into Guatemala's constitution in 1945. In November 1975 and July 1977 British troops and aircraft were sent to protect Belize from the threat of Guatemalan invasion, and a battalion of troops and a detachment of fighter aircraft remained in the territory. Negotiations between the United Kingdom and Guatemala began in 1977. In 1980 Britain warned that it might unilaterally grant independence to Belize if no settlement with Guatemala were forthcoming, and later that year the British Government finally excluded the possibility of any cession of land to Guatemala, although offering economic and financial concessions. In November the UN General Assembly overwhelmingly approved a resolution urging that Belize be granted independence (similar resolutions having been adopted in 1978 and 1979), and the United Kingdom decided to proceed with a schedule for independence. A tripartite conference in March 1981 appeared to produce a sound basis for a final settlement, with Guatemala accepting Belizean independence in exchange for access to the Caribbean Sea through Belize and the use of certain offshore cays and their surrounding waters. A state of emergency was declared for three weeks in April, following strikes and serious rioting, apparently organized by the opposition in protest at the preliminary 'Heads of Agreement' which had been reached in the previous month. A constitutional conference nevertheless went ahead in April. However, further tripartite talks in May and July collapsed as a result of renewed claims by Guatemala to Belizean land. With Belizean independence imminent, Guatemala made an unsuccessful appeal to the UN Security Council to intervene, breaking off diplomatic relations with the United Kingdom and sealing its border with Belize on 7 September. However, on 21 September, as scheduled, Belize achieved independence. Guatemala alone refused to recognize Belize's new status, and during 1982 requested the reopening of negotiations with the United Kingdom, alleging that Belize was not legally independent. Tripartite talks in January 1983 collapsed after Belize rejected Guatemala's proposal that Belize should cede the southern part of the country. This claim was subsequently suspended. Belize is a member of CARICOM (see p. 106), whose summit conferences in 1982, 1983 and again in 1988 expressed support for Belize's territorial integrity against claims by Guatemala.

At independence the United Kingdom had agreed to leave troops as protection and for training of Belizean defence forces 'for an appropriate time'. In 1984 Prime Minister Esquivel was given renewed assurances from the British Government over its commitment to keep British troops in Belize until the resolution of the territorial dispute with Guatemala. Discussions with Guatemala resumed in February 1985, with greater optimism shown by all three parties. In July the new draft Guatemalan Constitution omitted the previous unconditional claim to Belize, while Esquivel had previously acknowledged Guatemala's right of access to the Caribbean Sea, but no settlement was forthcoming. In January 1986 Dr Marco Vinicio Cerezo was inaugurated as the elected President of Guatemala, representing a change from a military to a civilian government. In August the United Kingdom and Guatemala renewed diplomatic relations at a consular level, and in December the restoration of full diplomatic relations was announced. Meanwhile, a six-member select committee of the Belize House of Representatives was established in June 1986, to examine information on Guatemala's claim to Belize. In March 1987 and July 1988 Guatemalan trade delegations visited Belize. In April 1987 fresh talks were held between Guatemala, the United Kingdom and Belize (although Belize was still regarded by Guatemala as being only an observer). Tripartite negotiations continued, and in May 1988 the formation of a permanent Joint Commission (which, in effect, entailed a recognition of the Belizean state by Guatemala) was announced. This body was to attempt to draft a treaty that would be validated by referendums in both Guatemala and Belize. The agreement was sanctioned by Florencio Marin, parliamentary Leader of the Opposition, despite the tension between the PUP and the ruling UDP over other matters. In November 1988, however, there was a minor incident in the disputed waters of the Gulf of Honduras, when an unarmed British naval vessel was fired upon by a Guatemalan gunboat.

Government

Belize is a constitutional monarchy, with the British sovereign as Head of State. Executive authority is vested in the sovereign and is exercisable by the Governor-General, who is appointed on the advice of the Prime Minister, must be of Belizean nationality, and acts in almost all matters on the advice of the Cabinet. The Governor-General is also advised by an appointed Belize Advisory Council. Legislative power is vested in the bicameral National Assembly, comprising a Senate (eight members appointed by the Governor-General) and a House of Representatives (28 members elected by universal adult suffrage for five years, subject to dissolution). The Governor-General appoints the Prime Minister and, on the latter's recommendation, other Ministers. The Cabinet is responsible to the House.

Defence

The Belize Defence Force was formed in 1978 and was based on a combination of the existing Police Special Force and the Belize Volunteer Guard. The Force is of battalion size, made up of regular, volunteer and reserve elements, and includes small maritime and air wings. Provision has been made for the establishment of National Service if necessary to supplement normal recruitment. The Belize Government assumed the recurrent charges of about BZ $4m. per annum from 1981. Military service is voluntary. In June 1988 the regular armed forces totalled 700, and there were approximately 1,500 British troops in Belize. The estimated defence budget for 1988 was BZ $17.9m.

Economic Affairs

The economy of Belize is primarily agricultural, based mainly on the production of sugar, bananas and citrus fruits. In 1987, according to estimates by the World Bank, the country's gross national product (GNP), measured at average 1985–87 prices, was US $219m., equivalent to $1,250 per head. Between 1980 and 1987, it was estimated, GNP per head declined, in real terms, at an average annual rate of 0.5%. Over this period, Belize's population increased by 2.6% per year, but real GNP rose by only 2.1% per year. In 1987, however, GNP per head increased by 2.0% in real terms.

Although 40% of the country is considered suitable for agriculture, only 15% of this area was under cultivation in 1986. Nevertheless, agriculture, forestry and fishing employed 37% of the working population in 1980 and contributed 19.4% of gross domestic product (GDP) in 1985. Belize's crops are susceptible to adverse weather conditions such as hurricanes, or heavy rains which, for example, halved the 1988 crop of red kidney beans.

Following the introduction of smut-resistant varieties of sugar cane, production of raw sugar rose to 114,300 long tons in 1983. Production fell to 101,500 long tons in 1984, but sugar exports still accounted for about 46% of the total value of domestic exports, earning BZ $65.1m. Production rose slightly in 1985, to 102,000 long tons, but export earnings fell to BZ $45.9m., before rising to BZ $62.9m. in 1986, despite a decline in production to 93,353 long tons. The cane harvest in 1986 had been 854,000 long tons, but in 1987 it was 789,000 long tons, despite a milling requirement of some 850,000 long tons. Output of raw sugar was also lower, at 82,300 long tons, but export earnings were maintained at BZ $62.6m. The 1988 cane harvest was only 756,559 long tons, compared with a target of 800,025 long tons, while production of raw sugar was 81,747 long tons. Belize was protected from the most severe effects of the decline in free-market international sugar prices by quota agreements, at preferential prices, with the USA and the European Economic Community, which accept more than two-thirds of Belize's sugar exports. Between 1985 and 1987, however, the USA's annual quota for imports of Belizean sugar was reduced from 24,500 long tons to 9,000 tons. After revision, the 1988 US quota was increased slightly, to 9,862 long tons. The drastic quota reductions and lower prices had contributed, however, to the reluctance of farmers to cultivate sugar cane, hence the failure to achieve production targets.

In March 1986 the Belizean Government announced that the national petroleum company of Jamaica (Petrojam) was to invest US $12.5m. in the Libertad sugar mill (closed in 1985), which was to be reopened for the production of wet alcohol, to be shipped to Jamaica for conversion into ethyl alcohol (ethanol) and then exported to the USA. Production was expected to begin in April 1988, achieving full capacity of 7.6m. gallons per year by 1989, but various delays and the shortfall in cane production resulted in postponement of the starting date until the end of 1989. In a parallel agreement, Petrojam was to supply the Belizean Government with petroleum for a five-year period beginning in 1988.

Production of bananas was 10,545 metric tons in 1984. In 1985, when the banana plantations were privatized, 10,298 tons were harvested from 1,300 acres (526 ha), but in 1986, despite an increase in the area to 4,000 acres (1,619 ha), output rose only slightly, to 11,325 metric tons. The entire crop was sold to the United Kingdom, under provisions of the Lomé Convention (see p. 149), and earned BZ $9.1m. in export revenue. The 1987 crop of more than 22,000 metric tons earned BZ $14.3m. The Government plans to make bananas the country's principal export crop by 1991. The citrus crop totalled 59,586 metric tons in 1985, providing export earnings of BZ $24.2m. In 1986 the crop reached 74,886 metric tons. Major expansion of the citrus industry was planned by a consortium headed by the US company, Coca-Cola Foods, which bought 686,186 acres (277,690 ha) of virgin forest land in north-western Belize in 1985. The project was finally abandoned, however, in 1987, mainly for economic reasons, and after pressure from environmentalists and the Florida citrus industry. Coca-Cola Foods itself donated 32,000 acres (12,950 ha) of its total 190,000 acres (76,890 ha) for a nature reserve, although it intended to retain some 50,000 acres (20,000 ha) for a possible smaller project. Nevertheless, by 1987 the annual citrus crop totalled a record 99,838 metric tons, and provided export earnings of BZ $31.0m. The 1988 crop was about 83,500 metric tons.

Rice, red kidney beans and maize are the principal domestic food crops, and the development of other crops, such as cocoa, coconuts and soya beans, is being encouraged. Dairy-farming, livestock and bee-keeping are also being developed. A dairy plant in the Cayo district, with a capacity of processing 400 gallons of milk per day, began operations in July 1986. Fishing provided export earnings of BZ $15m. in 1985, of which nearly 90% were accounted for by lobster sales. In 1987, however, export earnings from fish products declined to BZ $11m. Belize has considerable timber reserves, particularly of tropical hardwoods, and there were government plans to revitalize the forestry sector.

A Five-Year Plan for 1985–89 aimed to promote private investment, through tax incentives, to increase and diversify production, and to reduce dependence on imported goods. An improvement of infrastructure and a development of the international telecommunications network were also planned, and contracts were awarded in 1987 and 1988. Manufacturing, especially of clothing, accounted for 15% of GDP in 1985. In June 1984 the unemployment rate was 13.6% (of a total labour force of 46,500), and in 1988 the rate remained high. Immigration from neighbouring Central American countries, especially El Salvador, is offset by emigration to the USA, while remittances from Belizean workers abroad provide an important source of income.

GDP, in real terms, increased by only 0.7% in 1983 and by 1.3% in 1984, followed by rises of 2.6% in 1985, 3.9% in 1986 and 4.5% in 1987. The trade deficit rose from BZ $69.8m. in 1984 to BZ $77.4m. in 1985, but in 1986 it declined to BZ $58.7m., before rising to BZ $87.2m. in 1987. In November 1984 the Government was forced to seek assistance from the IMF for balance-of-payments support and help in reducing the growing budget deficit. The IMF support programme was ended in March 1987, but, with other policies, it had improved financial performance. The budget deficit for the financial year 1986/87 was estimated at BZ $46m. The 1987/88 budget envisaged expenditure of BZ $226.4m. At the end of 1987 the public external debt totalled BZ $240m., while reserves of foreign exchange rose from US $24.6m. at the end of 1986 to US $54.6m. by mid-1988. The rate of inflation remained low,

BELIZE

Introductory Survey, Statistical Survey

averaging 1.0% in 1986 and 2.3% in 1987. Development assistance from the United Kingdom, Canada and various international organizations is used to improve infrastructure and public utilities.

In an attempt to diversify the economy, exploration for petroleum has been encouraged. Tourism is being promoted, but has suffered from unfavourable publicity over the Guatemalan dispute and the problems resulting from drug trafficking in various parts of the country. The cultivation of hemp (marijuana), and the trafficking in illicit drugs, has proved to be an increasing problem for the Government. In January 1988, following various other initiatives, the Government established a Security and Intelligence Service (SIS) to lead the efforts to contain the drug problem. Although Mexico, with financial assistance from the USA, has helped in spraying the drug plantations with herbicides, enough of the crop survives to provide an estimated annual income of US $55m., equal to one-third of Belize's GDP.

Social Welfare

There were 10 urban and 20 rural health centres in 1980; pre-natal and child welfare clinics are sponsored by the Ministry of Health. In 1987 there were 583 hospital beds and 77 registered physicians. The infant mortality rate declined from 51 per 1,000 live births in 1970 to 20 per 1,000 in 1987. Of total budgetary expenditure by the central Government (including the Social Security Board) in the financial year 1985/86, BZ $10.2m. (9.0%) was for health, and a further BZ $8.9m. (7.8%) for social security and welfare.

Education

Education is compulsory for all children between the ages of six and 14 years. Primary education, beginning at six years of age and lasting for eight years, is provided free of charge, principally through subsidized denominational schools under government control. Secondary education, beginning at the age of 14, lasts for four or five years. In 1984 the total enrolment at primary and secondary schools was equivalent to 84% of the school-age population. In 1985 there were also four technical colleges, four vocational schools and a teacher-training college. The Government contributed up to 60% of the operational costs for 17 of the 22 secondary schools in 1982, while the remaining five were government-controlled. The Belize College of Arts, Science and Technology (BELCAST), founded in 1980, was planned as the first stage in a new University of Belize. In March 1986, however, the Government announced that it planned to divide BELCAST, with the result that it would continue as a vocational training school, with a greatly reduced budget. The Belize Teachers' College and the Bliss School of Nursing were to be re-established as independent institutions. There is an extra-mural branch of the University of the West Indies in Belize. Budgetary expenditure on education in the financial year 1985/86 was BZ $17.6m., representing 15.5% of total spending by the central Government. The estimated adult literacy rate is over 93%.

Public Holidays

1989: 2 January (for New Year's Day), 6 March (Baron Bliss Day/Commonwealth Day), 24–27 March (Easter), 1 May (Labour Day), 12 June (Queen's Official Birthday), 11 September (for St George's Cay Day), 21 September (Independence Day), 12 October (Columbus Day, anniversary of the discovery of America), 20 November (for Garifuna Settlement Day), 25–26 December (Christmas).

1990: 1 January (New Year's Day), 5 March (Baron Bliss Day/Commonwealth Day), 13–16 April (Easter), 7 May (for Labour Day), 11 June (Queen's Official Birthday), 10 September (St George's Cay Day), 21 September (Independence Day), 12 October (Columbus Day, anniversary of the discovery of America), 19 November (Garifuna Settlement Day), 25–26 December (Christmas).

Weights and Measures

Imperial weights and measures are used, but petrol and paraffin are measured in terms of the US gallon (3.785 litres).

Statistical Survey

Source (unless otherwise stated): Statistical Office of the Ministry of Economic Development, Belmopan; tel. 8-22207.

AREA AND POPULATION

Area: 22,965 sq km (8,867 sq miles).

Population: 144,857 (males 73,213, females 71,644) at census of 12 May 1980; 175,600 (official estimate, 1987).

Density (1987): 7.6 per sq km.

Principal Towns (estimated population at mid-1985): Belmopan (capital) 4,500; Belize City (former capital) 47,000; Corozal 10,000; Orange Walk 9,600; Dangriga (formerly Stann Creek) 7,700.

Births, Marriages and Deaths (1986): Registered live births 6,178 (birth rate 36.1 per 1,000); Registered marriages 1,025 (marriage rate 6.0 per 1,000); Registered deaths 716 (death rate 4.2 per 1,000) (Source: UN, *Demographic Yearbook* and *Population and Vital Statistics Report*).

Economically Active Population (1980 census): Agriculture, hunting, forestry and fishing 14,745; Mining and quarrying 32; Manufacturing 4,142; Electricity, gas and water 604; Construction 1,772; Trade, restaurants and hotels 5,646; Transport, storage and communications 1,725; Financing, insurance, real estate and business services 360; Community, social and personal services 8,956; Activities not adequately defined 1,791; Total employed 39,773 (males 31,749, females 8,024); Unemployed 7,554 (males 4,836, females 2,718); Total labour force 47,327 (males 36,585, females 10,742) (Source: ILO, *Year Book of Labour Statistics*).

AGRICULTURE, ETC.

Principal Crops (1987): Sugar cane 789,000 long tons; Bananas 1,184,000 boxes (each of 42 lb or 19 kg); Oranges 1,672,000 boxes (each of 90 lb or 40.7 kg); Grapefruit 883,000 boxes (each of 80 lb or 36 kg); Rice (paddy) 11.1 million lb; Maize 59.5 million lb; Red kidney beans 5.6 million lb.

Livestock (FAO estimates, '000 head, year ending September 1986): Horses 5; Mules 4; Cattle 49; Pigs 25; Sheep 4; Goats 1 (Source: FAO, *Production Yearbook*).

Livestock Products (FAO estimates, '000 metric tons, 1986): Meat 6; Cows' milk 4 (Source: FAO, *Production Yearbook*); (official estimates, 1987): Beef 2.5 million lb; Honey 620,000 lb.

Forestry (FAO estimates, '000 cu m, 1986): Roundwood removals: Industrial wood 29; Fuel wood 126; Total 155 (Source: FAO, *Yearbook of Forest Products*).

Fishing (metric tons, live weight): Total catch 1,301 in 1984; 1,389 in 1985; 1,434 in 1986 (Source: FAO, *Yearbook of Fishery Statistics*).

INDUSTRY

Production (1987): Raw sugar 82,300 long tons; Molasses 24,300 long tons; Cigarettes 98.8 million; Beer 568,000 gallons; Batteries 6,600; Flour 8,036 long tons; Fertilizers 7,896 long tons; Garments 2,592,000; Citrus concentrate 1,919,000 gallons; Soft drinks 817,000 cases.

FINANCE

Currency and Exchange Rates: 100 cents = 1 Belizean dollar (BZ $). *Coins:* 1, 5, 10, 25 and 50 cents. *Notes:* 1, 5, 10, 20 and 100 dollars. *Sterling and US Dollar equivalents:* (30 September 1988): £1 sterling = BZ $3.382; US $1 = BZ $2.000; BZ $100 = £29.57 = US $50.00. *Exchange rate:* Fixed at US $1 = BZ $2.000 since May 1976.

Budget (BZ $ '000, year ending 31 March 1986): *Revenue:* Taxation 88,649 (Import duties 45,538); Other current revenue 13,064; Capital revenue 157; Total 101,870 (excl. grants 1,400); *Expenditure:* General public services 18,274; Defence 6,465; Education 17,576; Health 10,227; Social security and welfare 8,903; Housing and community amenities 4,185; Economic services 29,286; Other purposes 18,789; Total 113,705 (current 99,891, capital 13,814). Figures refer to the consolidated accounts of the central Government, including the operations of the Social Security Board. (Source: IMF, *Government Finance Statistics Yearbook*).

International Reserves (US $ million at 31 December 1987): Reserve position in the IMF 2.71; Foreign exchange 33.62; IMF special drawing rights 0.09; Total 36.41 (Source: IMF, *International Financial Statistics*).

Money Supply (BZ $ million at 31 December 1987): Currency outside banks 29.56; Demand deposits at commercial banks 36.80 (Source: IMF, *International Financial Statistics*).

Cost of Living (retail price index; base: February 1980 = 100): 134.1 in 1985; 135.4 in 1986; 138.6 in 1987 (Source: IMF, *International Financial Statistics*).

Gross Domestic Product (BZ $ million at current purchasers' values): 387.9 in 1984; 396.6 in 1985; 431.3 in 1986 (Source: IMF, *International Financial Statistics*).

Balance of Payments (US $ million, 1987): Merchandise exports f.o.b. 86.7; Merchandise imports f.o.b. −116.2; *Trade balance* −29.5; Exports of services 65.2 Imports of services −39.5; *Balance on goods and services* −3.8; Private unrequited transfers (net) 17.9; Government unrequited transfers (net) 12.3; *Current balance* 26.3; Direct capital investment (net) 1.9; Other long-term capital (net) 1.1; Short-term capital (net) −3.1; Net errors and omissions −14.3; *Total* (net monetary movements) 11.9; Valuation changes (net) −2.1; *Changes in reserves* 9.8 (Source: IMF, *International Financial Statistics*).

EXTERNAL TRADE

Principal Commodities (BZ $ million, 1987): *Imports:* Total 285.9. *Exports:* Sugar 62.6; Molasses 1.1; Bananas 14.3; Citrus products 31.0; Fish products 11.0; Timber 4.8; Garments 31.3; Total 156.1 (excl. re-exports 31.8).

Principal Trading Partners (US $ million, 1985): *Imports:* Guatemala 4.2; Japan 5.6; Mexico 7.3; Netherlands 7.4; Netherlands Antilles 5.7; United Kingdom 10.1; USA 63.6; Total (incl. others) 128.1; *Exports:* Mexico 20.4; United Kingdom 18.1; USA 41.8; Total (incl. others) 90.1. (Source: UN, *International Trade Statistics Yearbook*).

TRANSPORT

Road Traffic (motor vehicles licensed, 1987): 12,752.

International Shipping (sea-borne freight traffic, '000 metric tons, 1985): Goods loaded 136; Goods unloaded 144 (Source: UN, *Monthly Bulletin of Statistics*).

Civil Aviation (1987): Passenger movements 372,800.

TOURISM

Tourist arrivals (1985): 93,440.

COMMUNICATIONS MEDIA

Radio Receivers (1986): 88,000 in use.

Telephones (1983): 8,600 in use.

Newspapers (1986): There are no daily newspapers but seven non-dailies are published.

EDUCATION

Primary (1987): 226 schools, 1,575 teachers, 40,000 students.
Secondary (1987): 24 schools, 522 teachers, 7,155 students.
Higher (1987): 8 institutions, 69 teachers, 932 students.

Directory

The Constitution

The Constitution came into effect at the independence of Belize on 21 September 1981. Its main provisions are summarized below:

FUNDAMENTAL RIGHTS AND FREEDOMS

Regardless of race, place of origin, political opinions, colour, creed or sex, but subject to respect for the rights and freedoms of others and for the public interest, every person in Belize is entitled to the rights of life, liberty, security of the person, and the protection of the law. Freedom of movement, of conscience, of expression, of assembly and association and the right to work are guaranteed and the inviolability of family life, personal privacy, home and other property and of human dignity is upheld. Protection is afforded from discrimination on the grounds of race, sex, etc, and from slavery, forced labour and inhuman treatment.

CITIZENSHIP

All persons born in Belize before independence who, immediately prior to independence, were citizens of the United Kingdom and Colonies automatically become citizens of Belize. All persons born outside the country having a husband, parent or grandparent in possession of Belizean citizenship automatically acquire citizenship, as do those born in the country after independence. Provision is made which permits persons who do not automatically become citizens of Belize to be registered as such. (Belizean citizenship is also offered, under the Belize Loans Act 1986, in exchange for interest-free loans of US $25,000 with a 10-year maturity.)

THE GOVERNOR-GENERAL

The British monarch, as Head of State, is represented in Belize by a Governor-General, a Belizean national.

Belize Advisory Council

The Council consists of not less than six people 'of integrity and high national standing', appointed by the Governor-General for up to 10 years upon the advice of the Prime Minister. The Leader of the Opposition must concur with the appointment of two members and be consulted about the remainder. The Council exists to advise the Governor-General, particularly in the exercise of the prerogative of mercy, and to convene as a tribunal to consider the removal from office of certain senior public servants and judges.

THE EXECUTIVE

Executive authority is vested in the British monarch and exercised by the Governor-General. The Governor-General appoints as Prime Minister that member of the House of Representatives who, in the Governor-General's view, is best able to command the support of the majority of the members of the House, and appoints a Deputy Prime Minister and other Ministers on the advice of the Prime Minister. The Governor-General may remove the Prime Minister from office if a resolution of 'no confidence' is passed by the House and the Prime Minister does not, within seven days, either resign or advise the Governor-General to dissolve the National Assembly. The Cabinet consists of the Prime Minister and other Ministers.

The Leader of the Opposition is appointed by the Governor-General as that member of the House who, in the Governor-General's view, is best able to command the support of a majority of the members of the House who do not support the Government.

THE LEGISLATURE

The Legislature consists of a National Assembly comprising two chambers: the Senate, with eight nominated members; and the House of Representatives, with (since 1984) 28 elected members. The Assembly's normal term is five years. Senators are appointed by the Governor-General: five on the advice of the Prime Minister; two on the advice of the Leader of the Opposition or on the advice of persons selected by the Governor-General; and one after consultation with the Belize Advisory Council. If any person who is not a Senator is elected to be President of the Senate, he or she shall be an *ex-officio* Senator in addition to the eight nominees.

Each constituency returns one Representative to the House, who is directly elected in accordance with the Constitution.

If a person who is not a member of the House is elected to be Speaker of the House, he or she shall be an *ex-officio* member in addition to the 28 members directly elected. Every citizen older than 18 years is eligible to vote. The National Assembly may alter any of the provisions of the Constitution.

The Government

Head of State: HM Queen ELIZABETH II.

Governor-General: Dame ELMIRA MINITA GORDON (assumed office 21 September 1981).

BELIZE

THE CABINET
(December 1988)

Prime Minister, Minister of Finance and of Defence: Manuel Esquivel.
Deputy Prime Minister and Minister of Home Affairs and of Local Government: Curl Thompson.
Attorney-General and Minister of Foreign Affairs and of Economic Development: Dean Barrow.
Minister of Commerce, Industry and Tourism: Edwardo Juan.
Minister of Natural Resources: Charles Wagner.
Minister of Agriculture: Dean Lindo.
Minister of Labour and Social Services: Philip Goldson.
Minister of Education, Youth and Sport: Elodio Aragón.
Minister of Health: Israel Alpuche.
Minister of Housing and Public Works: Hubert Elrington.
Minister of Transport, Energy and Communications: Derek Aikman.

MINISTRIES

Office of the Prime Minister: Belmopan; tel. 8-2346; telex 102.
Ministry of Foreign Affairs: Belmopan; telex 102.
All other Ministries are also situated in Belmopan.

Legislature

NATIONAL ASSEMBLY
The Senate
President: Doris Garcia.
There are eight nominated members.

House of Representatives
Speaker: Carlos Castillo.
Clerk: A. E. Johnson.

General Election, 14 December 1984

	Seats
United Democratic Party	21
People's United Party	7*
Total	28

* Reduced to 6 seats in January 1985, prior to the formation of the Belize Popular Party.

Political Organizations

Belize Popular Party (BPP): Belize City; f. 1985 by dissident mems of PUP; Leader Louis Sylvestre; Chair. Mark Cuellar.
People's United Party (PUP): Belize City; f. 1950; based on organized labour; merged with Christian Democratic Party in 1988; Leader George Price; Chair. Said Musa; Leader in the House of Representatives Florencio Marin.
United Democratic Party (UDP): 21 King St, Belize City; f. 1974 by merger of People's Development Movement, Liberal Party and National Independence Party; conservative; Leader Manuel Esquivel; Chair. Derek Aikman.

Diplomatic Representation

EMBASSIES AND HIGH COMMISSION IN BELIZE

Colombia: Belmopan; tel. 8-22547; Chargé d'affaires: Dr Edilberto Ramírez de la Pava.
France: POB 230, 5574 Princess Margaret Drive, Belize City; tel. 2-44556; telex 291; Ambassador: Jean Claude Fortuit.
Honduras: POB 285, 91 North Front St, Belize City; tel. 2-45889; telex 103; Chargé d'affaires: Marco A. Caballero.
Mexico: 20 North Park St, Belize City; tel. 2-44301; telex 277; Ambassador: Lic. Marco A. Alcázar.
Panama: 3 Orchid Gardens, Belmopan; tel. 8-22504; Chargé d'affaires: José Paredes.

United Kingdom: POB 91, Embassy Sq., Belmopan; tel. 8-22146; telex 284; High Commissioner: Peter Alexander Bremner Thomson.
USA: 29 Gabourel Lane, Belize City; tel. 2-77161; telex 213; Ambassador: Robert G. Rich, Jr.

Judicial System

Summary Jurisdiction Courts (criminal jurisdiction) and District Courts (civil jurisdiction), presided over by magistrates, are established in each of the six judicial districts. Summary Jurisdiction Courts have a wide jurisdiction in summary offences and a limited jurisdiction in indictable matters. The maximum civil claim in which District Courts may exercise jurisdiction was increased in 1985 from BZ $500 to BZ $5,000. Appeals lie to the Supreme Court, which has jurisdiction corresponding to the English High Court of Justice and where a jury system is in operation. From the Supreme Court further appeals lie to a Court of Appeal, established in 1968, which holds an average of four sessions per year. Final appeals are made to the Judicial Committee of the Privy Council in the United Kingdom.

Court of Appeal: James Smith (President), Sir Joseph Luckhoo, Justice K. Saint L. Henry.
Chief Justice: Taufik S. Cotran.
Puisne Judges: George Brown, Satchi Ponnambalam.
Registrar of the Supreme Court: K. L. Munnings.
Magistrates: Traodio Gonzalez (Chief Magistrate), Lee F. J. Longsworth, Merlene Matute, Griffith Mitchell, Ramon Ramirez, Marie Anderson, Frederick B. Lyle.

Religion

At mid-1985 an estimated 102,650 of the population were adherents of the Roman Catholic Church, while 63,668 were Anglican, Methodist or members of various Protestant sects, including a community of Mennonites.

CHRISTIANITY

Belize Christian Council: POB 508, 149 Allenby St, Belize City; tel. 2-77077; f. 1957 as Church World Service Committee, reorg. 1961 and 1978; seven mem. churches, four assoc. bodies; Pres. Rev. Harold A. Gill (Methodist Church); Gen. Sec. Sadie Vernon.

The Roman Catholic Church
Belize comprises the single diocese of Belize City—Belmopan, suffragan to the archdiocese of Kingston in Jamaica. The Bishop participates in the Antilles Episcopal Conference (based in Jamaica).
Bishop of Belize City—Belmopan: Osmond Peter Martin, POB 616, Bishop's House, 144 North Front St, Belize City; tel. 2-72122.

The Anglican Communion
Anglicans in Belize are of the Church in the Province of the West Indies, comprising eight dioceses. The Archbishop of the Province is the Bishop of the North Eastern Caribbean and Aruba, resident at St John's, Antigua.
Bishop of Belize: (vacant) POB 535, Bishopthorpe, Southern Foreshore, Belize City; tel. 2-73380.

The Methodist Church
Chairman and General Superintendent, Belize/Honduras District: Rev. Harold A. Gill, POB 212, Belize City; 2,017 mems.

Other Churches
Denominations active in the country include the Church of God in Christ, the Presbyterian Church, the Salvation Army and the Seventh-day Adventist Church.

OTHER RELIGIONS
There are also small communities of Hindus, Muslims and Bahá'ís.

The Press

Amandala: Amandala Press, POB 15, 3304 Partridge St, Belize City; tel. 2-77276; f. 1969; weekly; independent; Editor Evan X. Hyde; circ. 8,000.
The Beacon: 7 Church St, Belize City; weekly; supports UDP; Publr and Editor Michael Finnigan; circ. 4,200.

BELIZE

Directory

The Belize Times: POB 506, 3 Queen St, Belize City; tel. 2-45757; f. 1956; weekly; party political paper of People's United Party; Editor AMALIA MAI; circ. 5,000.

Belize Today: Government Information Service, Belmopan; tel. 8-22159; telex 138; monthly; official; circ. 12,000.

Government Gazette: Government Printery, Belmopan; official; weekly.

People's Pulse: c/o 21 King St, Belize City; f. 1988; weekly; organ of the United Democratic Party.

The Reporter: POB 707, 63 Cemetry Rd, Belize City; tel. 2-72503; f. 1968; weekly; Editor HARRY LAWRENCE; circ. 6,500.

NEWS AGENCY

Agencia EFE (Spain): Belmopan; tel. 8-22159; Correspondent M. A. ROMERO.

PRESS ASSOCIATION

Belize Newspaper Association: POB 707, Belize City.

Radio and Television

In 1986 there were about 88,000 radio receivers in use. In August 1986 the Belize Broadcasting Authority issued licences to eight television operators for 14 channels, which mainly retransmit US satellite programmes, thus placing television in Belize on a fully legal basis for the first time. In June 1988 zoning regulations were issued for Belize City also.

RADIO

Belize Broadcasting Network: POB 89, Albert Cattouse Bldg, Belize City; tel. 2-77246; f. 1937; government-operated semi-commercial service; transmissions for some 133 hours per week on AM and 112 hours per week on FM; broadcasts in English (75%) and Spanish; Dir RENÉ R. VILLANUEVA.

TELEVISION

Tropical Vision Channel 7: Belize City; tel. 2-72825; Man. NESTOR VASQUEZ.

CTV-Channel 9: Belize City; tel. 2-44400; Man. MARIE HOARE.

Finance

(cap. = capital; brs = branches)

BANKING
Central Bank

Central Bank of Belize: POB 852, Treasury Lane, Belize City; tel. 2-77216; telex 225; f. 1982; cap. BZ $10m.; Gov. ALAN SLUSHER.

Development Bank

Development Finance Corporation: Bliss Parade, Belmopan; tel. 8-22350; issued cap. BZ $10m.; Chair. MICHAEL C. E. YOUNG; Man. SANDRA BEDRAN.

Other Banks

Atlantic Bank Ltd: POB 481, 6 Albert St, Belize City; tel. 2-77301; telex 216; f. 1971; Gen. Man. ROBERTO C. STANLEY; 1 br.

Bank of Nova Scotia: POB 708, Albert St, Belize City; tel. 2-77028; telex 218; Man. JOSÉ R. ROSADO; 4 brs.

Barclays Bank PLC: POB 363, 21 Albert St, Belize City; tel. 2-77211; telex 217; Man. JORGE M. AUIL; 2 brs and 1 sub-br.

Belize Bank: POB 364, 60 Market Sq., Belize City; tel. 2-77132; telex 229; Man. JOHN MILLER.

There is also a Government Savings Bank.

INSURANCE

General insurance is carried on by local companies, and British, American and Jamaican companies are also represented.

Trade and Industry

Belize Export and Investment Promotion Unit: joint government and private-sector institution to encourage export and investment; Dir DENTON BELISLE.

Ministry of Economic Development: Belmopan; administration of public and private sector investment; statistics agency; Head SHARMAN YVONNE HYDE.

STATUTORY BODIES

Banana Control Board: management of banana industry.

Belize Beef Corporation: f. 1978; semi-governmental organization to aid development of cattle-rearing industry.

Citrus Control Board: f. 1966; determines basic quota for each producer, fixes annual price of citrus; Chair. C. SOSA.

Marketing Board: POB 479, Belize City; tel. 2-77402; f. 1948 to encourage the growing of staple food crops; purchases crops at guaranteed prices, supervises processing, storing and marketing; Chair. SANTIAGO PERDOMO.

Belize Sugar Board: 2nd St South, Corozal Town; tel. 4-22005; f. 1960 to control the sugar industry and cane production; includes representatives of the Government, sugar manufacturers, cane farmers and the public sector; Exec. Sec. I. E. CRUZ.

CHAMBER OF COMMERCE

Belize Chamber of Commerce: POB 291, 7 Cork St, Belize City; telex 121; f. 1918; Pres. ADDY CASTILLO; Sec. DAVID USHER; 540 mems.

DEVELOPMENT ORGANIZATION

Belize Reconstruction and Development Corporation: POB 92, Belize City; 2-77424; Chair. HART TILLETT; Gen. Man. A. BRYAN CARD.

EMPLOYERS' ASSOCIATIONS

Cane Farmers' Association: San Antonio Rd, Orange Walk; tel. 3-22005; f. 1959 to assist cane farmers and negotiate with the Sugar Board and manufacturers on their behalf; 14 district brs; Chair. SANTIAGO ROSADO.

Citrus Growers' Association: POB 7, Dangriga; tel. 5-22145; f. 1966; citrus crop farmers' association; Chair. ROY DIAZ; Sec. GASPAR MARTIN.

Livestock Producers' Association: POB 1052, 24 Craig St, Belize City; tel. 2-44748; Pres. JOHN CARR.

TRADE UNIONS

National Trades Union Congress of Belize (NTUCB): Pres. EDBERT HIGINIO,

Principal Unions

United General Workers' Union: 1259 Lakeland City, Dangriga; tel. 5-22105; f. 1979 by amalgamation of the Belize General Development Workers' Union and the Southern Christian Union; three branch unions affiliated to the central body; affiliated to ICFTU; Pres. ANTONIO GONZÁLEZ; Gen. Sec. PABLO LAMBEY.

Belize National Teachers' Union: POB 382, Belize City; tel. 2-72857; Pres. JOHN PINNELO; Sec. MIGUEL WONG; 600 mems.

Christian Workers' Union: 23 George St, Belize City; tel. 2-72150; f. 1962; general; Pres. DESMOND VAUGHN; 2,000 mems.

Democratic Independent Union: POB 695, Belize City; Pres. CYRIL DAVIS; 1,250 mems.

Public Service Union of Belize: 3 Kut Avenue, Belize City; tel. 2-72318; f. 1922; public workers; Pres. GODWIN SUTHERLAND; Sec.-Gen. CARL SMITH; 1,150 mems.

CO-OPERATIVES

In 1981 there were 38 Credit Unions, 52 Agricultural, Producer and Marketing Co-operatives, nine Fishing Co-operatives, seven Bee-Keepers' Co-operatives, two Housing Co-operatives, six Transport Co-operatives and one Supplies Co-operative.

There were also three co-operative groups: Belize Credit Union League (22 mems), Fishing Co-operative Association (five mems), Honey Producers Federation (five mems).

Transport

There are no railways.

ROADS

There are about 1,600 km (1,000 miles) of all-weather main and feeder roads and about 400 km (250 miles) of cart roads and bush trails. A number of logging and forest tracks are usable by heavy-duty vehicles in the dry season.

SHIPPING

A new deep-water port at Belize City was opened to traffic in 1980. There is a second port at Dangriga (formerly Stann Creek), to the south of Belize City, and in 1988 preliminary work began

BELIZE

in the development of Big Creek as a banana port, to be in use by 1990. Seven major shipping lines call at Belize City, including the Carol Line (consisting of Harrison, Hapag-Lloyd, Nedlloyd and CGM).

CIVIL AVIATION

Philip S. W. Goldson International Airport, 14 km (9 miles) from Belize City, can accommodate medium-sized jet-engined aircraft, and there are plans for the construction of a new terminal. There are airstrips for light aircraft on internal flights near the major towns and offshore islands.

Maya Airways Ltd: POB 458, 6 Fort St, Belize City; tel. 2-77215; telex 280; f. 1961; internal services; Dir GORDON A. ROE; fleet of 4 BN-2A Islander, 2 Cessna U206.

Tourism

The main tourist attractions are the beaches and the barrier reef, hunting and fishing, and remains of the Mayan civilization. There are plans to establish wildlife reserves. There were 163 hotels in Belize in 1987. In 1985 there were 93,440 tourist arrivals, and income from tourism was estimated at between BZ $9m. and BZ $13m.

Belize Tourist Bureau: POB 325, 53 Regent St, Belize City; tel. 2-77213; f. 1964; 13 mems; Chair. Minister of Tourism; Sec. FRANK TILLETT (acting).

BENIN

Introductory Survey

Location, Climate, Language, Religion, Flag, Capital

The People's Republic of Benin is a narrow stretch of territory in West Africa. The country has an Atlantic coastline of about 100 km (60 miles), flanked by Nigeria to the east and Togo to the west; its northern borders are with Burkina Faso and Niger. The climate is tropical in the north, with one rainy season and a maximum temperature of 46°C (115°F), and equatorial in the south, with average temperatures of 20°–34°C (68°–93°F) and two rainy seasons. French is the official language but each of the indigenous ethnic groups has its own language. Bariba and Fulani are the major languages in the north, while Fon and Yoruba are widely spoken in the south. The majority of the people follow traditional beliefs and customs. About 15% of the inhabitants are Christians, mainly Roman Catholics, and about 13% are Muslims. The national flag (proportions 3 by 2) is green, with a five-pointed red star in the upper hoist. The capital is Porto-Novo, but most government offices and other state bodies are in Cotonou.

Recent History

Benin, called Dahomey until 1975, was formerly part of French West Africa. It became a self-governing republic within the French Community in December 1958, and an independent state on 1 August 1960. The country's history from independence until 1972 was marked by chronic political instability, with five successful coups involving the army.

Elections in December 1960 were won by the Parti Dahoméen de l'Unité, whose leader, Hubert Maga, a northerner, became the country's first President. In October 1963, following riots by workers and students, President Maga was deposed by a military coup, led by Col (later Gen.) Christophe Soglo, Chief of Staff of the Army. Soglo served as interim Head of State until the election in January 1964 of a government headed by Sourou-Migan Apithy, a southerner who had been Vice-President under Maga. Another southerner, Justin Ahomadegbé, became Prime Minister. This regime was resented in the north, where rioting occurred. In November 1965, following a series of political crises, Gen. Soglo forced Apithy and Ahomadegbé to resign. A provisional government was formed but the army intervened again in December, when Gen. Soglo assumed power at the head of a military regime. In December 1967 industrial unrest, following a ban on trade union activity, led to another coup, this time by younger officers, led by Maj. (later Lt-Col) Maurice Kouandété. An interim regime was established, with Lt-Col Alphonse Alley, formerly Chief of Staff, as Head of State and Kouandété as Prime Minister.

A return to civilian rule was attempted in 1968. A referendum in March approved a new constitution, based on a strong presidency, and a presidential election was held in May. However, leading politicians, including all former Presidents, were banned from participation in the presidential poll and called on their supporters to boycott the election. As a result, only about 26% of the electorate voted, with the abstention rate reaching 99% in the north. The election was declared void, and in June the military regime nominated Dr Emile-Derlin Zinsou, formerly Minister for Foreign Affairs, as President. In July 1968 President Zinsou was sworn in, and confirmed in office by a referendum, but in December 1969 he was deposed by Lt-Col Kouandété, then Commander-in-Chief of the Army. A Military Directorate, led by Lt-Col Paul-Emile de Souza, assumed power.

In March 1970 a presidential election was held amid violent incidents and widespread claims of irregularities. The poll was abandoned when counting revealed roughly equal support for the three main candidates, Ahomadegbé, Apithy and Maga. In May, however, the Directorate handed over power to a Presidential Council comprising these three veteran politicians. It was agreed that each member of the triumvirate would act as Head of State, in rotation, for a two-year period. As a concession to the north, Maga became the first to hold this office, being succeeded in May 1972 by Ahomadegbé.

On 26 October 1972, however, the collective civilian leadership was deposed by Maj. (later Brig.-Gen.) Mathieu Kerekou, Deputy Chief of Staff of the armed forces, who established a military regime. Kerekou promised that the new regime would be based on equal representation between northern, central and southern regions. He proclaimed a resolutely progressive policy, and in September 1973 the National Council of the Revolution (CNR) was established to carry it out.

In November 1974 Kerekou announced that the country would follow the path of 'scientific socialism', based on Marxist-Leninist principles. The vital sectors of the economy, including the banks and the distribution of petroleum products, were taken over by the State. In February 1975 the country's co-operation agreements with France were renegotiated. Between 1974 and 1978 a decentralized local administration was set up, the education system taken over and the legal system put under review. The army and the gendarmerie were merged to form a National Defence Force. In November 1975 the Parti de la Révolution Populaire du Bénin (PRPB) was established as the 'highest expression of the political will of the people of Benin', and in December the country's name was changed from Dahomey to the People's Republic of Benin.

In August 1977 the CNR adopted a Loi Fondamentale which decreed new structures in government. Under its terms, a National Revolutionary Assembly was instituted as the supreme authority of the state, following an election, held in November 1979, for the 336 members of the Assembly: a single list of candidates was presented and approved by 97.5% of the voters. The CNR was disbanded and a National Executive Committee was established. At the first Ordinary Congress of the PRPB, held in December, it was decided that Kerekou would be the sole candidate for President of the Republic; the Assembly unanimously elected him to this office in February 1980. In April 1981 it was announced that the three members of the former Presidential Council, who had been imprisoned following their overthrow in the coup of 1972, had been released from house arrest. A gradual moderation in Benin's domestic policies followed, and ministerial reshuffles in April and December 1982 reflected the Government's campaign against corruption and inefficiency, and indicated the importance of rural development in its economic policies. The changes also removed members of an extreme left-wing faction ('Les Ligueurs') from power, and resulted, for the first time, in a minority of army officers in the Government.

In February 1984, at an extraordinary session of the National Revolutionary Assembly, the Loi Fondamentale was amended to increase the mandates of Assembly members (People's Commissioners) and of the President from three years to five years. Moreover, the number of People's Commissioners was reduced from 336 to 196. At legislative elections held in June, 97.9% of voters approved the single list of candidates for the Assembly, which then, in July, re-elected Kerekou, the sole candidate, as President. In a subsequent government reshuffle the membership of the National Executive Council was reduced from 22 ministers to 15. Upon his re-election, Kerekou announced an amnesty for several political prisoners, including Alphonse Alley, the former Head of State.

Following a boycott of classes by students in April 1985, riots broke out in May at the University of Benin and in schools, which led to the closure by the Government of all educational establishments until the beginning of June. Several students were detained following the riots, and, in an ensuing government reshuffle, both the Minister of Secondary and Higher Education and the Minister of Culture, Youth and Sports were replaced. In November some 100 people, including teachers, engineers and high-ranking officials, were arrested on suspicion of belonging to the banned Parti communiste dahoméen (PCD). Although Kerekou ordered the release of 50 of those implicated in the 1985 student riots in September 1986, it was subsequently claimed by Amnesty International that at least 88 detainees were still being held, in unhealthy conditions, while no specific charges had been brought against them. Further student unrest occurred in 1987 and 1988.

BENIN

Introductory Survey

In late 1986 the steadily deteriorating domestic economic situation caused Kerekou to make a series of visits to Western European donor nations, where he negotiated several important new aid agreements. In January 1987 Benin joined the World Bank-affiliated International Finance Corporation, a move which was perceived as indicative of a shift towards a more liberal economic management policy. In the same month Kerekou resigned from the army to become a civilian Head of State, and in February a ministerial reshuffle was carried out in which both the Minister of Foreign Affairs and the Minister of Finance and Economy were replaced.

Growing concern among army officers at widespread corruption within Kerekou's civilian Government, together with opposition to the proposed establishment of a Court of State Security, culminated in a coup attempt in March 1988. Almost 150 officers, including members of the presidential guard, were reported to have been arrested following the incident. Kerekou's failure to acknowledge publicly the attempted coup was believed to be linked to the presence in Cotonou at that time of an IMF delegation to discuss the country's economic programme. Unofficial reports later indicated that a further attempt to overthrow the Government had taken place in June, while President Kerekou had been attending the ECOWAS summit in Togo. In July five ministers were dismissed, accused of economic incompetence, and the Ministry of Finance and Economy was replaced by two new ministries, with responsibility for finance and for industry and energy.

In August 1988 Amnesty International reported that many of those who had been arrested in the aftermath of the two incidents were being detained without charge. The organization also claimed that a large number of Benin's detainees could be classified as prisoners of conscience, and revealed that political prisoners were being tortured. In the same year, it was alleged that Benin had agreed to accept shipments of toxic waste from several Western countries.

On several occasions Benin has accused foreign powers of conspiring with internal opposition to destabilize the regime. Its international standing has improved, however, with the relaxation of Kerekou's regime during the 1980s. Relations with France, Benin's main trading partner and supplier of aid, deteriorated sharply in 1977 following an airborne mercenary attack on Cotonou, in which French involvement was alleged. Dialogue between the two countries resumed in full in 1978, however, and relations continued to improve, with a visit to Benin by President Mitterrand in January 1983 being the first undertaken by a French president since Benin's independence. Later that year Benin and the USA exchanged ambassadors.

In 1988, however, relations with the USA deteriorated when that country accused Benin of allowing Libyan agents to use its territory as a base for terrorist activities. Kerekou responded by ordering the head of the Libyan diplomatic mission in Cotonou, who had allegedly been involved in the transfer of explosives, to leave the country, and by closing the offices of a Libyan-supported import-export agency that was implicated in the affair. New restrictions on the entry of Libyan nationals into the country and the rejection of a Libyan offer of economic aid were perceived to be further indications of Benin's wish to restrict its relations with the Qaddafi regime.

Benin's relations with Nigeria improved following a meeting of representatives of the two countries in 1988 to discuss trans-border co-operation. It was agreed that precise frontier markings would make smuggling and illegal immigration easier to control, and the establishment of a special force to police the border was discussed.

Government

In accordance with the Loi Fondamentale, adopted in August 1977 and amended in February 1984, a National Revolutionary Assembly, a body of 196 People's Commissioners representing socio-professional classes, is elected by universal suffrage every five years. The Assembly, in turn, elects the President of the Republic, also for a five-year term of office. Government is in the hands of the National Executive Council (NEC), under the President of the Republic, which includes heads of departments and heads of provinces, meeting monthly, and, more important, the Permanent Committee of the NEC, which comprises only ministers, meeting weekly. The 45-member Central Committee of the Parti de la Révolution Populaire du Bénin, the only legal political party, plays a leading role in government. The Central Committee elects from its members a political bureau to direct policy.

Local administration is based on six provinces, divided into 84 districts. Each province is governed by a Prefect and a Secretary-General, assisted by a Provincial Revolutionary Council, a Regional Planning and Development Committee and a Conference of Heads of Regional Departments. There is a considerable degree of decentralization and financial autonomy.

Defence

Citizens of both sexes are liable for military service between the ages of 18 and 51. The army strength in June 1988 was 3,800, the air force 350 and the navy 200. In addition, there were paramilitary forces numbering at least 3,500 men. France provides technical assistance and equipment. In 1977 a central organization, the Headquarters People's Armed Forces of Benin, was established to unify the police, customs service, armed forces and gendarmerie. It comprises three units: national defence, public security and people's militia. In 1988 the estimated defence budget was 11,420m. francs CFA.

Economic Affairs

Benin's economy is based mainly on agriculture. The agricultural sector (including forestry and fishing) engaged an estimated 63% of the labour force in 1986, compared with 70% in 1980, and provided about 49% of gross domestic product (GDP) in 1986. Despite the official policy of Marxism-Leninism, several sectors of the economy have reverted to private control. However, Benin is one of the world's less developed countries, with a low level of industrialization and literacy. In 1987, according to estimates by the World Bank, gross national product (GNP), measured at average 1985–87 prices, was US $1,315m., equivalent to $300 per head. Between 1980 and 1987, it was estimated, GNP per head decreased, in real terms, at an average rate of 0.6% per year. The average annual growth of overall GDP, measured in constant prices, was 2.3% in 1965–80, rising to 3.6% in 1980–86. Real GNP per head fell by an estimated 5.7% in 1987.

In 1975 the agricultural sector was reformed, with the introduction of a co-operative system. The land is under-utilized, however: in 1982 there were 1,200,000 ha under cultivation, representing only about 10% of potential farming area. In 1985 it was announced that the OAU was to provide $750,000 for research into agricultural production in semi-arid zones. Regional production efforts are the responsibility of the Centres d'Action Régionale pour le Développement Rural (CARDERs), through which operate regional development projects.

Benin's principal food crops are cassava (manioc), yams, maize and sorghum. The major cash crops are the oil palm and cotton. Production of palm oil and palm kernel oil declined following the 1976–77 drought, which caused extensive damage to oil palm trees. Output recovered somewhat during the early 1980s, totalling around 35,000 metric tons annually in 1982–85: however, production remains well below oil-processing capacity, which was estimated at 215,000 tons in 1986. Increased investment in the cotton sector resulted in a strong growth during the 1980s, with output of seed (unginned) cotton totalling 89,325 metric tons in 1985/86, and 142,800 tons in 1986/87. In 1985 the French Central Fund for Economic Co-operation (CCCE) granted 75m. French francs for the construction of two cotton-ginning mills, each with an annual capacity of 20,000 tons, and in January 1988 the Société Internationale Financière pour les Investissements et le Développement en Afrique (SIFIDA) agreed to pre-finance one-fifth of 1987/88 production. However, the 1988/89 crop was threatened by heavy rains in Borgou province, which normally produces about one-half of the total annual crop. There are large unrecorded exports of food to Nigeria, where prices are higher and where farmers do not have to contend with the bureaucratic problems of state marketing agencies. Benin normally covers its demand for staple foods. Livestock and fisheries are both small but increasingly significant sectors. The major livestock project under way is a 37,000-ha ranch at Okpara. The national fishing company is jointly owned by Benin and Libya.

The industrial sector, based on small-scale processing of primary production, employed only 7% of the labour force in 1980 and contributed 13% of GDP in 1986. The 1981–90 Development Plan had envisaged an increase to 15.3% of GDP by 1985. Although some sectors of industry and commerce have been nationalized since December 1974, this has mainly affected Benin's external trade, and in 1978 about 60% of internal trade was conducted privately. Reserves of gold, phosphates (5m. tons) and marble have been discovered, although by 1987 the only mineral to be exploited, apart from petroleum (see below), was limestone, supplying the cement factory at Onigbolo. This factory, operational since 1982, was jointly financed by Nigeria and has a total annual capacity of 500,000 metric tons. However, it was thought to be producing only 85,000 tons per year in 1985. Similarly, the sugar factory at Savé, also co-financed by Nigeria with an annual capacity of 45,000 tons, has operated only intermittently since its inauguration in 1983. Owing to unfavourable economic circumstances, Nigeria has been unable to honour an agreement to accept 60% of output from the two concerns. A new textiles complex, built by the People's Republic of China, was inaugurated at Lokossa in May 1987.

Petroleum has been discovered off shore, and there are estimated recoverable reserves of about 22m. barrels. Production at the Sémé field began in 1982, and in 1984 output averaged 6,900 barrels per day (b/d), almost double Benin's petroleum needs. The Norwegian Government provided 90% of the $100m. needed to finance the project. A second phase of exploitation began in 1984, and in August 1985 oil exploration rights were unexpectedly sold to a Swiss-based company, Panoco, in a US $2,000m. joint-venture agreement. By September 1986 output was estimated at only 9,000 b/d, compared with the 25,000 b/d projected upon Panoco's take-over of the Sémé field. The agreement was cancelled in September, with the Beninois Government assuming temporary control of production. However, by the end of 1987 production had declined to about 6,000 b/d, emphasizing the need to find a new contractor. Some reserves of natural gas have been discovered in the oil fields.

Other projects include a major water-supply programme for Cotonou and Porto-Novo, initiated in late 1986, and a transport infrastructure rehabilitation programme aiming to upgrade the highway network and improve facilities at Cotonou port, initiated in May 1987. The construction of a 65-MW hydro-electric installation at Nangbeto, on the Mono river, jointly with Togo, was completed in 1988. The dam will help to irrigate 42,000 ha of land in Benin, and, with a maximum production capacity of 150m. kWh per year, will substantially reduce the country's reliance on imported energy. The project, which cost an estimated US $140m., was co-financed by the OPEC Fund for International Development and the Islamic Development Bank (IDB).

In December 1986 the World Bank gave support of US $15m. towards a $31.5m. programme of rehabilitation for the public services sector, under which a number of wholly or partly state-owned companies were likely to be restructured or liquidated.

Current budget spending rose steadily to reach 60,600m. francs CFA in 1983. As a result of the Kerekou regime's austerity programme, expenditure was reduced, to 51,200m. francs CFA, in 1986 and declined sharply, to an estimated 47,800m. francs CFA, in 1987. Spending was projected to increase to an estimated 53,737m. francs CFA in 1988. Benin's chronic balance-of-payments deficit decreased from an estimated US $76.3m. in 1983 to $54.7m. in 1984, largely owing to reduced imports. The trade deficit, which declined from an estimated 60,600m. francs CFA in 1986 to 49,700m. francs CFA in the following year, is partly offset by unrecorded exports to Nigeria, by remittances from workers abroad, and by foreign aid. (The principal donor of foreign aid is France, which in 1983–85 provided assistance worth 32,250m. francs CFA, with the aid given in 1985 including a budget subsidy of 2,000m. francs CFA.) In December 1986 the total external debt was estimated at about US $889.6m. Debt-servicing obligations rose from $8.8m. in 1980 to $60m. in 1985, and to $120.8m. in 1986, of which less than one-half was paid. The Government attributed the escalation of the external debt to the contracting of loans for the industrial projects at Onigbolo, Savé and Sémé (see above).

Beginning in 1986, Beninois representatives held a series of discussions with both the IMF and the World Bank, as it became increasingly evident that only by the conclusion of an agreement with these institutions, leading to the implementation of a structural adjustment programme, would Benin begin to solve its acute budgetary and balance-of-payments problems, and thus facilitate a rescheduling of the country's debts and the granting of new credits. In 1988, in anticipation of such an agreement, the Government introduced further austerity measures, affecting, in particular, the public sector, with the intention of reducing the budget deficit in that year to about 1,808m. francs CFA, compared with a deficit of 5,877m. francs CFA in 1987.

Benin is a member of the Economic Community of West African States (ECOWAS, see p. 132), of the West African Monetary Union (UMOA, p. 154), which shares a common currency (linked to the French franc), and of the West African Economic Community (CEAO, p. 119).

Social Welfare

In 1980 Benin had 204 physicians (one for every 17,000 inhabitants). In 1982 there were six hospitals, 31 health centres, 186 dispensaries and 65 maternity clinics. Two further hospitals were opened at Abomey and Natitingou in 1985 and 1986 respectively. There is a minimum hourly wage for workers.

Education

Following legislation in 1975, the State took control of all education, which is public, secular and provided free of charge. Education is officially compulsory for six years, to be completed by children between the ages of five and 12 years. Primary education begins at five or six years of age and lasts for six years. Secondary education, beginning at 11 or 12 years of age, lasts for up to seven years, comprising a first cycle of four years and a second of three years. In 1986 enrolment at primary schools was equivalent to 59% of children in the relevant age-group (74% of boys; 42% of girls). In 1984 the comparable ratio for secondary enrolment was only 20% (boys 29%; girls 12%). In 1985, according to UNESCO estimates, the average rate of adult illiteracy was 74.1% (males 63.3%; females 84.3%).

The University of Benin was founded at Cotonou in 1970, and teacher-training colleges were opened at Lokossa, Natitingou and Parakou in September 1987. A major education project, launched in 1986 with funding from UNESCO, aimed to construct 67 new primary schools in the northern provinces of Atacora and Borgou and in the southern province of Mono.

Public Holidays

1989: 2 January (for New Year's Day), 16 January (Anniversary of Mercenary Attack on Cotonou), 1 May (Labour Day), 7 May* (Id al-Fitr, end of Ramadan), 14 July* (Id al-Adha, Feast of the Sacrifice), 26 October (Armed Forces Day), 30 November (National Day), 25 December (Christmas Day), 31 December (Harvest Day).

1990: 1 January (New Year's Day), 16 January (Anniversary of Mercenary Attack on Cotonou), 27 April* (Id al-Fitr, end of Ramadan), 1 May (Labour Day), 4 July* (Id al-Adha, Feast of the Sacrifice), 26 October (Armed Forces Day), 30 November (National Day), 25 December (Christmas Day), 31 December (Harvest Day).

* These holidays are dependent on the Islamic lunar calendar and may vary by one or two days from the dates given.

Weights and Measures

The metric system is in force.

Statistical Survey

Source (unless otherwise stated): Institut National de la Statistique et de l'Analyse Economique, BP 323, Cotonou; tel. 31-40-81.

Area and Population

AREA, POPULATION AND DENSITY

Area (sq km)	112,622*
Population (census of 20–30 March 1979)	
Males	1,596,939
Females	1,734,271
Total	3,331,210
Population (official estimates at mid-year)	
1985	4,040,000
1986	4,169,000
1987	4,304,000
Density (per sq km) at mid-1987	38.2

* 43,484 sq miles.

ETHNIC GROUPS

1959 estimates: Fon 47.0%; Adja 12.2%; Bariba 9.7%; Yoruba and Mali 8.8%; Aizo 5.1%; Somba 5.0%; Fulani 3.8%; Coto-Coli 2.5%; Dendi 1.7%; others 4.4%.

POPULATION BY PROVINCE (1979 census)

Atacora	479,604
Atlantique	686,258
Borgou	490,669
Mono	477,378
Ouémé	626,868
Zou	570,433
Total	**3,331,210**

PRINCIPAL TOWNS

(estimated population at 1 July 1981)
Cotonou 383,250; Porto-Novo (capital) 144,000.

BIRTHS AND DEATHS (UN estimates, annual averages)

	1970–75	1975–80	1980–85
Birth rate (per 1,000)	49.8	51.1	50.7
Death rate (per 1,000)	26.6	24.6	21.2

Souce: UN, *World Population Prospects: Estimates and Projections as Assessed in 1984.*

ECONOMICALLY ACTIVE POPULATION

(ILO estimates, '000 persons at mid-1980)

	Males	Females	Total
Agriculture, etc.	598	648	1,246
Industry	91	28	118
Services	218	193	410
Total	**906**	**869**	**1,775**

Source: ILO, *Economically Active Population Estimates and Projections, 1950–2025.*

Mid-1986 (estimates in '000): Agriculture, etc. 1,305; Total 2,008 (Source: FAO, *Production Yearbook*).

Agriculture

PRINCIPAL CROPS ('000 metric tons)

	1984	1985	1986
Rice (paddy)	8	6	9
Maize	379	425	384
Millet	11	12	18
Sorghum	3	79	90
Sweet potatoes	5	40	34
Cassava (Manioc)	685	708	726
Yams	819	778	858
Taro (Coco yam)	1	1	2
Dry beans	43	39	44
Groundnuts (in shell)	58	69	67
Cottonseed*	58	57	92
Cotton (lint)*	28	27	44
Coconuts*	20	20	20
Palm kernels	18.2	24.7	18†
Tomatoes	32	48	73
Chillies and peppers (green)*	20	20	21
Oranges*	13	12	12
Mangoes*	13	12	12
Bananas*	13	13	13
Pineapples*	3	3	3
Coffee (green)	3†	4*	4*

* FAO estimates.   † Unofficial estimate.
Source: FAO, *Production Yearbook.*

LIVESTOCK ('000 head, year ending September)

	1984	1985	1986*
Horses*	6	6	6
Asses*	1	1	1
Cattle	892	912	930
Pigs	541	570	600
Sheep	1,085	1,122	1,160
Goats	1,035	1,071	1,100

Poultry (million): 18 in 1984; 21 in 1985; 22* in 1986.
* FAO estimates.
Source: FAO, *Production Yearbook.*

LIVESTOCK PRODUCTS (FAO estimates, '000 metric tons)

	1984	1985	1986
Beef and veal	13	13	13
Mutton and lamb	3	3	3
Goats' meat	3	3	3
Pig meat	6	6	7
Poultry meat	21	24	25
Other meat	6	7	7
Cows' milk	15	14	15
Goats' milk	5	6	6
Hen eggs	13.0	15.1	16.0

Source: FAO, *Production Yearbook.*

BENIN — Statistical Survey

Forestry

ROUNDWOOD REMOVALS
('000 cubic metres, excluding bark)

	1984	1985	1986*
Sawlogs, veneer logs and logs for sleepers	23	20	20
Other industrial wood*	196	202	209
Fuel wood*	4,056	4,178	4,309
Total	4,275	4,400	4,538

* FAO estimates.
Source: FAO, *Yearbook of Forest Products*.

Fishing

(FAO estimates, '000 metric tons, live weight)

	1984	1985	1986
Inland waters	16.4	16.5	16.0
Atlantic Ocean	3.9	3.8	7.5
Total catch	20.3	20.3	23.5

Source: FAO, *Yearbook of Fishery Statistics*.

Mining

('000 metric tons)

	1983	1984	1985
Crude petroleum	1	1*	1*

* Provisional or estimated figures.
Source: UN, *Industrial Statistics Yearbook*.

Industry

SELECTED PRODUCTS ('000 metric tons, unless otherwise indicated)*

	1983	1984	1985
Palm oil and palm kernel oil	33	34	37
Salted, dried or smoked fish	2.0	2.0	2.0
Cement	300	300	300
Electric energy (million kWh)	5	5	5

* Provisional or estimated figures.
Source: UN, *Industrial Statistics Yearbook*.

Finance

CURRENCY AND EXCHANGE RATES

Monetary Units
100 centimes = 1 franc de la Communauté financière africaine (CFA).

Denominations
Coins: 1, 2, 5, 10, 25, 50 and 100 francs CFA.
Notes: 50, 100, 500, 1,000 and 5,000 francs CFA.

French Franc, Sterling and Dollar Equivalents (30 September 1988)
1 French franc = 50 francs CFA;
£1 sterling = 538.6 francs CFA;
US $1 = 318.5 francs CFA;
1,000 francs CFA = £1.857 = $3.140.

Average Exchange Rate (francs CFA per US $)
1985   449.26
1986   346.30
1987   300.54

BUDGET ESTIMATES (current budget, million francs CFA)

Revenue	1985	1986
Direct taxes	14,500	18,120
Indirect taxes	29,950	34,090
Registration and stamp duty	610	540
Income from property, operations and services	5,260	3,580
Contributions from local communities and public companies	100	250
Receipts from previous years	350	450
Total	50,770	57,030

Expenditure	1985	1986
Public debt	80	80
Personnel	37,070	42,340
Equipment	4,800	5,370
Subsidies, grants and aid	8,820	3,410
Other	—	5,830
Total	50,770	57,030

1987 (million francs CFA): Budget balanced at 47,800.
Source: *La Zone Franc—Rapport 1986*.
1988 (estimates, million francs CFA): Revenue 51,929; Expenditure 53,737.

Investment Budget (estimates, million francs CFA): 40,588 in 1985; 49,800 in 1986; 50,800 in 1987; 54,100 in 1988.

DEVELOPMENT PLAN, 1981–90
(planned public investment, '000 million francs CFA)

Agriculture	55.6
Industry/Mining	44.5
Infrastructure	297.2
Railways	188.3
Ports	30.1
Water/Dams	42.7
Roads	14.2
Total (identified)	397.3
Total (planned)	958.8

Source: *Bulletin de l'Afrique Noire*, December 1981.

BENIN

Statistical Survey

CENTRAL BANK RESERVES (US $ million at 31 December)

	1985	1986	1987
Gold*	3.6	4.5	5.2
IMF special drawing rights	—	—	0.1
Reserve position in IMF	2.2	2.5	2.9
Foreign exchange	1.9	1.4	0.6
Total	7.7	8.4	8.8

* Valued at market-related prices.
Source: IMF, *International Financial Statistics*.

MONEY SUPPLY (million francs CFA at 31 December)

	1985	1986	1987
Currency outside banks	20.26	26.17	19.61
Demand deposit at deposit money banks*	63.63	49.86	38.90
Checking deposits at post office	2.90	2.74	3.00
Total money*	87.09	78.93	61.84

* Beginning in 1986, figures for demand deposits are not strictly comparable with those for 1985.
Source: IMF, *International Financial Statistics*.

NATIONAL ACCOUNTS (million francs CFA at current prices)

National Income and Product

	1982	1983	1984
Compensation of employees	92,849	91,966	98,961
Operating surplus	250,196	274,910	296,500
Domestic factor incomes	343,045	366,876	395,461
Consumption of fixed capital	34,964	45,336	48,565
Gross domestic product (GDP) at factor cost	378,009	412,212	444,026
Indirect taxes, *less* subsidies	33,872	27,173	22,175
GDP in purchasers' values	411,881	439,385	466,201
Net factor income from abroad	−2,305	−15,762	−38,727
Gross national product	409,576	423,623	427,474
Less Consumption of fixed capital	34,964	45,336	48,665
National income in market prices	374,612	378,287	378,809
Other current transfers from abroad (net)	39,576	44,924	48,010
National disposable income	414,188	423,211	426,819

Expenditure on the Gross Domestic Product

	1984	1985	1986
Government final consumption expenditure	41,824	42,168	43,585
Private final consumption expenditure	385,069	404,322	435,262
Increase in stocks	5,200	−1,604	13,600
Gross fixed capital formation	60,472	77,462	82,820
Total domestic expenditure	492,565	522,348	575,267
Exports of goods and services	91,945	106,700	−72,601
Less Imports of goods and services	118,309	129,200	
GDP in purchasers' values	466,201	499,848	502,666
GDP at constant 1978 prices	265,400	271,900	263,210

Gross Domestic Product by Economic Activity

	1984	1985	1986
Agriculture, hunting, forestry and fishing	177,798	179,571	200,183
Mining and quarrying	42,403	46,599	28,335
Manufacturing			
Electricity, gas and water	3,584	3,556	4,282
Construction	17,045	23,432	24,564
Trade, restaurants and hotels	86,632	96,618	96,637
Transport, storage and communications	43,280	46,014	48,100
Finance, insurance, real estate, etc.*	34,813	38,293	34,476
Public administration and defence	38,471	38,814	39,321
GDP at factor cost	444,026	472,897	475,898
Indirect taxes, *less* subsidies	22,175	26,951	26,768
GDP in purchasers' values	466,201	499,848	502,666

* Including community, social and personal services (other than government services).

BALANCE OF PAYMENTS (million francs CFA)

	1985*	1986†	1987†
Merchandise exports f.o.b.	79,100	53,200	48,600
Merchandise imports f.o.b.	−97,800	−113,800	−98,300
Trade balance	−18,700	−60,600	−49,700
Services (net)	−27,800	−20,300	−13,900
Balance on goods and services	−46,500	−80,900	−63,600
Private unrequited transfers (net)	22,600	22,800	22,800
Government unrequited transfers (net)	18,400	16,800	16,800
Current balance	−5,500	−41,300	−24,000
Long-term capital (net)	4,400	18,100	13,500
Short-term capital (net)	n.a.	25,500	−15,200
Net errors and omissions	−5,200	−1,100	1,200
Total (net monetary movements)	−6,300	1,200	−24,500

* Provisional figures.   † Estimated figures.
Sources: Banque Centrale des Etats de l'Afrique de l'Ouest.

External Trade

Source: Banque Centrale des Etats de l'Afrique de l'Ouest.

PRINCIPAL COMMODITIES (million francs CFA)

Imports c.i.f.	1981	1982	1983
Cereals	4,574	6,727	8,510
Beverages and tobacco	22,281	20,858	16,320
Refined petroleum products	7,376	5,930	1,484
Non-electrical machinery	13,179	13,263	8,955
Electrical machinery	8,128	11,920	8,238
Road transport equipment	8,539	9,352	7,544
Chemicals	6,596	9,378	7,891
Miscellaneous manufactured articles	62,986	60,178	35,432
Cotton yarn and fabrics	20,213	24,060	14,113
Total (incl. others)	147,499	152,553	112,032

BENIN

Statistical Survey

Exports f.o.b.	1981	1982	1983
Coffee	320	932	661
Cocoa beans	n.a.	282	1,740
Palm products	2,329	1,886	2,701
Fuels	2	551	13,584
Cottonseed	123	49	176
Raw cotton	2,548	1,465	4,938
Shea-nuts (Karité nuts)	n.a.	14	n.a.
Machinery and transport equipment	378	518	90
Chemicals	255	71	1
Miscellaneous manufactured articles	1,155	479	101
Lime, cement and clinker	443	76	66
Cotton yarn and fabrics	425	132	16
Total (incl. others)	9,141	7,837	25,351

PRINCIPAL TRADING PARTNERS (million francs CFA)

Imports	1981	1982	1983
Algeria	2,844	1,145	0.3
Austria	881	1,629	1,213
Belgium and Luxembourg	8,583	6,714	1,819
China, People's Republic	8,369	9,385	6,951
Côte d'Ivoire	2,259	1,444	1,153
France	29,308	37,530	29,977
Germany, Federal Republic	7,889	8,567	5,389
Ghana	1,059	1,546	2,936
India	13,381	6,762	2,462
Italy	4,316	5,619	5,029
Japan	8,341	8,540	4,760
Netherlands	11,852	11,704	7,189
Nigeria	3,238	3,832	1,711
Senegal	1,203	1,887	1,208
Spain	1,318	1,400	2,053
Taiwan	2,239	2,023	1,536
United Kingdom	14,878	18,758	13,705
USA	9,692	8,030	4,889
Total (incl. others)	147,499	152,553	112,032

Exports	1981	1982	1983
China, People's Republic	703	n.a.	n.a.
Côte d'Ivoire	24	98	n.a.
France	1,858	1,131	1,645
Germany, Federal Republic	724	604	322
Ghana	124	1	n.a.
Italy	103	46	128
Japan	600	969	2,507
Malaysia	640	n.a.	n.a.
Netherlands	951	1,723	5,727
Niger	682	798	944
Nigeria	536	868	421
Sweden	183	n.a.	n.a.
Togo	250	147	305
United Kingdom	256	546	482
USA	44	n.a.	10,636
Total (incl. others)	9,141	7,837	25,351

Transport

RAILWAYS (traffic)

	1979	1980	1981
Passengers carried ('000)	1,665	1,800	1,934
Passenger-km (million)	143	163	187.6
Freight carried ('000 tons)	352	344	419
Freight ton-km (million)	140.4	143	176.5

1983 (million): Passenger-km 157; Freight ton-km 145 (Source: UN Economic Commission for Africa, *African Statistical Yearbook*).

ROAD TRAFFIC (motor vehicles in use at 31 December)

	1977	1978	1979
Private cars	9,536	9,549	9,592
Buses and coaches	7,439	7,271	6,927
Goods vehicles			

Sources: *World Road Statistics* (International Road Federation, Geneva); UN, *Statistical Yearbook*.

INTERNATIONAL SEA-BORNE SHIPPING (freight traffic at Cotonou, '000 metric tons)

	1985	1986	1987
Goods loaded	107.5	137.1	172.7
Goods unloaded	1,059.1	1,030.1	1,094.7

Source: Port Autonome de Cotonou.

CIVIL AVIATION (traffic on scheduled services)*

	1982	1983	1984
Kilometres flown (million)	1.8	2.0	1.9
Passengers carried ('000)	81	80	80
Passenger-km (million)	212	211	211
Freight ton-km (million)	21.2	18.7	17.4

* Including an apportionment of the traffic of Air Afrique.
Source: UN, *Statistical Yearbook*.

Tourism

	1981	1982	1983
Estimated tourist arrivals ('000)	46	48	48

Source: UN, *Statistical Yearbook*.

Communications Media

	1981	1982	1983
Radio receivers ('000 in use)	250	270	290
Television receivers ('000 in use)	7	10	13

Radio receivers (1985): estimated 300,000 in use.
Television receivers (1985): estimated 15,000 in use.
Telephones (1978): 16,000 in use.
Books (1978): 13 titles (18,000 copies) produced.
Daily newspapers (1984): 1 (estimated average circulation 1,000).
Source: mainly UNESCO, *Statistical Yearbook*.

Education

(1987/88)

	Schools	Teachers	Pupils Males	Females	Total
Pre-primary	334	722	7,513	5,937	13,450
Primary	2,850	15,319	312,650	158,366	471,016
Secondary:					
general	151	2,711	64,863	25,321	90,184
vocational	33	687	4,196	2,683	6,879
Higher	13	1,110	8,519	1,593	10,112

Source: Ministère des Enseignements Moyers et Supérieur, Cotonou.

Directory

The Constitution

On 23 May 1977 legislation (a Loi Fondamentale) was announced by the Parti de la révolution populaire du Bénin (PRPB) as preparation for the 'people's democratic revolution'. In August the Loi Fondamentale was approved by the National Revolutionary Council. In its place, a National Revolutionary Assembly was established in November 1979, comprising directly elected People's Commissioners. They, in turn, elect the President, who is Head of State. The People's Commissioners represent socio-professional classes, not geographical constituencies. At local levels, state powers are exercised by elected provincial district town and village councils. The judiciary is responsible to the National Revolutionary Assembly and the Armed Forces are under the control of the PRPB.

The Government

HEAD OF STATE

President: MATHIEU KEREKOU (assumed office 27 October 1972; elected President 5 February 1980; re-elected 31 July 1984).

NATIONAL EXECUTIVE COUNCIL
(November 1988)

Head of Military Revolutionary Government and Minister of Defence: MATHIEU KEREKOU.

Minister Delegate to the Presidency in charge of Interior, Security and Territorial Administration: Maj. EDOUARD ZODEHOUGAN.

Minister Delegate to the Presidency in charge of Planning and Statistics: SIMON IFEDE OGOUMA.

Minister of Rural Development and Co-operative Action: GANDOUNO KODJA.

Minister of Equipment and Transport: MARTIN DOHOU AZONHIHO.

Minister of Finance and Economy: DIDIER DASSI.

Minister of Trade, Crafts and Tourism: GIRIGISSOU GADO.

Minister of Primary Education: Capt. PHILIPPE AKPO.

Minister of Secondary and Higher Education: VINCENT GUEDZODJE.

Minister of Culture, Youth and Sports: ALI HOUDOU.

Minister of Labour and Social Affairs: IRENÉE ZINSOU.

Minister of Public Health: SOULÉ DANKORO.

Minister of Information and Communications: OUSMANE BATOKO.

Minister of Foreign Affairs and Co-operation: GUY LANDRY HAZOUMÉ.

Minister of Justice and Inspection of Parastatal Enterprises: SALIOU ABOUDOU.

Minister of Industry and Energy: JUSTIN GNIDEHOU.

The Prefects of the six provinces also have ministerial status.

MINISTRIES

Office of the President and Ministry of Defence: BP 2028, Cotonou; tel. 30-00-90; telex 5222.

Ministry of Culture, Youth and Sports: BP 65, Porto-Novo; tel. 21-24-30.

Ministry of Equipment and Transport: Cotonou; tel. 31-46-64.

Ministry of Finance and Economy: BP 302, Cotonou; tel. 31-40-53; telex 5009.

Ministry of Foreign Affairs and Co-operation: BP 318, Cotonou; tel. 30-04-00; telex 5200.

Ministry of Industry and Energy: Cotonou.

Ministry of Information and Communications: BP 180, Cotonou; tel. 31-43-34; telex 5208.

Ministry of Inspection of Parastatal Enterprises: Cotonou; tel. 31-33-49.

Ministry of Interior, Security and Territorial Administration: Cotonou; tel. 30-11-06.

Ministry of Justice: BP 967, Cotonou; tel. 31-31-46.

Ministry of Labour and Social Affairs: BP 907, Cotonou; tel. 31-31-12.

Ministry of Planning and Statistics: BP 342, Cotonou; tel. 30-05-41; telex 5252.

Ministry of Primary Education: Porto-Novo; tel. 21-26-51.

Ministry of Public Health: BP 882, Cotonou; tel. 31-26-70.

Ministry of Rural Development and Co-operative Action: BP 34, Porto-Novo; tel. 21-30-53.

Ministry of Secondary and Higher Education: Cotonou; tel. 30-06-81.

Ministry of Trade, Crafts and Tourism: BP 2037, Cotonou; tel. 31-52-58.

Legislature

ASSEMBLÉE NATIONALE RÉVOLUTIONNAIRE

In August 1977 the Loi Fondamentale provided for the disbanding of the National Revolutionary Council, which was to be replaced by a National Revolutionary Assembly. The Assembly was elected by direct universal suffrage in November 1979, then consisting of 336 People's Commissioners (reduced to 196 at elections in June 1984) who, in turn, elect the President. The People's Commissioners represent socio-professional groups, not geographical constituencies. In June 1984 the tenure of the National Assembly and the President of the Republic was extended from three years to five.

President of Permanent Committee: ROMAIN VILON GUEZO.

Political Organization

Parti de la révolution populaire du Bénin (PRPB): Cotonou; f. 1975; Marxist-Leninist ruling party; cen. cttee of 45 mems, from which an 11-mem. political bureau is elected; Chair. Cen. Cttee MATHIEU KEREKOU.

Diplomatic Representation

EMBASSIES IN BENIN

Algeria: BP 1809, Cotonou; telex 5030; Ambassador: ABDELAZIZ YADI.

Bulgaria: Cotonou; Chargé d'affaires a.i.: DIMITER PERLIDANSKI.

China, People's Republic: BP 196, Cotonou; Ambassador: ZHU XIANSONG.

Cuba: BP 948, Cotonou; telex 5277; Ambassador: CARLOS CALANAS.

Egypt: BP 1215, Cotonou; telex 5274; Ambassador: ABDEL AZIZ KHALIL.

France: route de l'Aviation, BP 966, Cotonou; tel. 31-22-24; telex 5209; Ambassador: FRANÇOIS-XAVIER GENDREAU.

German Democratic Republic: Cotonou; Ambassador: GERHARD HAIDA.

Germany, Federal Republic: 7 route Inter-Etats, BP 504, Cotonou; tel. 31-29-67; telex 5224; Ambassador: FRITZ HERMANN FLIMM.

Ghana: BP 488, Cotonou; tel. 30-07-46; Ambassador: C. T. K. QUARSHIE.

Korea, Democratic People's Republic: BP 317, Cotonou; Ambassador: AN KI-POK.

Libya: 'Les Cocotiers', Cotonou; telex 5254; People's Bureau Representative: (vacant).

Niger: BP 352, Cotonou; tel. 31-40-30; telex 5005; Ambassador: SALOU YARO.

Nigeria: Lot 21, Patte d'Oie, Cotonou; telex 5247; Ambassador: Ms J. J. AYORINDE.

USSR: BP 2013, Cotonou; Ambassador: VALENTIN PAVLOV.

USA: rue Caporal Anani Bernard, BP 2012, Cotonou; tel. 30-17-92; Ambassador: WALTER E. STADLER.

Zaire: BP 130, Cotonou; tel. 30-19-83; Ambassador: BINDO N'KETA KIBIBI.

Judicial System

The Central People's Court controls the judicial operations of all the People's Courts at various levels. It is responsible to the National Revolutionary Assembly and to the National Executive Council.

At the lowest level, each commune, village and city ward has its own court, which does not, however, have executive powers. There is a court in each district, which has the power to try cases. There is also a court in each province which acts as an appeals court and an assizes court. The Central Court is composed of a chairman, three divisional chairmen who are professional judges, six judges and 12 lay people's judges who have the same powers as the professional judges and magistrates in judicial decision-making. The professional judges are appointed by the National Executive Council. The lay people's judges are elected for three years by the National Revolutionary Assembly on the advice of the Central Committee of the PRPB.

In April 1988 the National Revolutionary Assembly adopted a law establishing a Court of State Security, with special jurisdiction over all affairs relating to the internal and external security of the country.

Cour populaire centrale (Central People's Court): Cotonou; Chair. LÉANDRE AMLON.

Cour criminelle d'exception (Court of State Security): Cotonou; Chair. HENRI AMOUSSOU KAPKA.

Religion

According to the 1961 census, 65% of the population held animist beliefs, 15% were Christians (Roman Catholic 12%, Protestant 3%) and 13% Muslims. Since 1975, religious and spiritual cults have been discouraged.

CHRISTIANITY

There are 257 Protestant mission centres with a personnel of about 120. At 31 December 1985 there were an estimated 670,650 Roman Catholics (over one-sixth of the population), mainly in the south of the country.

The Roman Catholic Church

Benin comprises one archdiocese and five dioceses.

Bishops' Conference: Conférence Episcopale du Bénin, Archevêché, BP 491, Cotonou; tel. 31-31-45; Pres. Mgr CHRISTOPHE ADIMOU, Archbishop of Cotonou.

Archbishop of Cotonou: Mgr CHRISTOPHE ADIMOU, Archevêché, BP 491, Cotonou; tel. 30-01-45.

Protestant Church

Eglise protestante méthodiste en République populaire du Bénin: Carré 206, BP 34, 54 ave Sékou Touré, Cotonou; tel. 31-25-20; f. 1843; 62,000 mems (1985); Pres. Rev. HARRY Y. HENRY; Sec. Rev. SAMUEL J. DOSSOU.

The Press

L'Aube Nouvelle: Cotonou; daily.

Bénin-Magazine: BP 1210, Cotonou; monthly; social and economic affairs; circ. 5,000.

Bénin-Presse Information: BP 120, Cotonou; tel. 31-26-55; publ. by the Agence Bénin-Presse; weekly.

Bulletin de l'Agence Bénin-Presse: BP 120, Cotonou; tel. 31-26-55; daily.

La Croix du Bénin: BP 105, Cotonou; tel. 32-11-19; f. 1946; Roman Catholic; fortnightly; Dir BARTHÉLEMY CAKPO ASSOGBA.

Ehuzu: BP 1210, Cotonou; tel. 30-08-75; govt-owned; daily; Dir MAURICE CHABI; circ. 10,000.

La Gazette du Golfe: Cotonou; f. 1988; privately-owned; six a year.

Journal Officiel de la République Populaire du Bénin: Porto-Novo; official govt bulletin; fortnightly.

NEWS AGENCIES

Agence Bénin-Presse (ABP): BP 72, Cotonou; tel. 31-26-55; telex 5221; f. 1961; national news agency; section of the Ministry of Information and Communications; Dir EVARISTE DEGLA.

Foreign Bureaux

Agentstvo Pechati Novosti (APN) (USSR): 'Les Cocotiers', Lot F-12, BP 968, Cotonou; tel. 30-10-23; telex 5204; Dir V. MIKHAILOV.

Telegrafnoye Agentstvo Sovetskovo Soyuza (TASS) (USSR): Lot 186, Patte d'Oie, BP 928, Cotonou 6; tel. 30-01-33; telex 5204; Correspondent ALEKSANDR PROSVETOV.

Publisher

Government Publishing House

Office National d'Edition, de Presse et d'Imprimerie (ONEPI): BP 1210, Cotonou; tel. 30-08-75; f. 1975; Dir-Gen. BONI ZIMÉ MAKO.

Radio and Television

According to UNESCO, there were an estimated 300,000 radio sets and 15,000 television receivers in use in 1985.

Office de Radiodiffusion et de Télévision du Bénin: BP 366, Cotonou; tel. 31-20-41; telex 5132; state-owned; radio broadcasts in French, English and 18 local languages; TV transmissions 12 hours weekly; Dir of Radio SYLVESTRE ZOMAHOUN; Dir of TV MICHÈLE BADAROU.

Finance

(cap. = capital; dep. = deposits; res = reserves; m. = million; brs = branches; amounts in francs CFA)

BANKING

Central Bank

Banque Centrale des Etats de l'Afrique de l'Ouest (BCEAO): route de Lomé, BP 325, Cotonou; tel. 31-24-66; telex 5211; br. in Parakou; headquarters in Dakar, Senegal; f. 1955; bank of issue for the seven states of the Union monétaire ouest-africaine (UMOA), comprising Benin, Burkina Faso, Côte d'Ivoire, Mali, Niger, Senegal and Togo; cap. and res 171,495m. (Dec. 1987); Gov. ALASSANE OUATTARA; Dir in Benin GILBERT MEDJE; br. at Parakou.

State Banks

Banque Béninoise pour le Développement (BBD): 2 rue des Cheminots, BP 300, Cotonou; tel. 31-34-76; telex 5238; f. 1962; cap. 1,500m. (Sept. 1987); Pres. PROSPER VIGBE; Man. Dir JUSTIN K. AGBODJINOU; 3 brs.

Banque Commerciale du Bénin (BCB): rue du Révérend Père Colineau, BP 85, Cotonou; tel. 31-37-13; telex 5216; f. 1962; cap. 1,500m. (Sept. 1987); conducts all govt business; Pres. SYLVAIN LADIKPO; Dir-Gen. RAMANOU AMOUSSA; 22 brs.

Caisse Nationale de Crédit Agricole (CNCA): BP 999, Cotonou; tel. 31-53-86; telex 5018; f. 1975; 91% state-owned; cap. 300m., dep. 7,089m.; Pres. ISIDORE AMOUSSOU; Dir-Gen. ASSOUMA YAKOUBOU; activities currently suspended.

INSURANCE

Société Béninoise d'Assurance: angle ave Steinmetz et rue du roi Dokodonou, Cotonou; f. 1974; cap. 40m.; Pres. VALENTIN HODONOU.

Société Nationale d'Assurance et de Réassurance (SONAR): BP 2030, Cotonou; tel. 31-16-49; telex 5231; f. 1974; cap. 300m.; state-owned; Pres. ANTOINE URSULE CAKPO; Dir-Gen. MATHIEU-AIMÉ LAWSON; 8 brs.

Trade and Industry

DEVELOPMENT ORGANIZATIONS

Caisse Centrale de Coopération Economique (CCCE): blvd de France, BP 38, Cotonou; tel. 31-35-80; telex 5082; Dir JACQUES BENIER.

Mission de Coopération et d'Action Culturelle (Mission Française d'Aide et de Coopération): BP 476, Cotonou; tel. 30-08-24; telex 5209; centre for administering bilateral aid from France according to the co-operation agreement signed in February 1975; Dir BERNARD HADJADJ.

MARKETING BOARDS

Office National du Bois (ONAB): BP 1238, Cotonou; tel. 33-19-56; telex 5160; f. 1983; forest development and marketing of wood products; cap. 300m. francs CFA; Man. Dir D. GABRIEL LOKOUN.

Société Béninoise des Matériaux de Construction (SOBEMAC): BP 1209, Cotonou; tel. 31-25-93; telex 5262; f. 1975; cap. 100m. francs CFA; state-owned; monopoly of cement marketing; Pres. MAMOUD MOUSTAPHA SOULE; Man. Dir RENÉ DOSSA MEGNIHO.

BENIN — *Directory*

Société Nationale de Commercialisation et d'Exportation du Bénin (SONACEB): BP 933, Cotonou; tel. 31-28-22; telex 5248; f. 1972; monopoly of internal marketing of all agricultural produce except palm products, cotton and tobacco; monopoly of cement exports; Pres. ARMAND ALAPINI; Man. Dir POLYCARPE AGOSSA.

Société Nationale de Commercialisation des Produits Pétroliers (SONACOP): ave d'Ornano, BP 245, Cotonou; tel. 31-22-90; telex 5245; f. 1974; cap. 1,500m. francs CFA; state-owned; importer and distributor of petroleum products; Pres. RICHARD ADJAHO; Man. Dir EDMOND-PIERRE AMOUSSOU.

Société Nationale pour le Développement des Fruits et Légumes (SONAFEL): BP 2040, Cotonou; tel. 31-52-34; telex 5031; headquarters at Bohicon; f. 1975; cap. 50m. francs CFA; state-owned; development of fruit and vegetable production; monopoly of export of fruit and vegetable produce; Man. Dir JOACHIM PHILIPPE D'ALMEIDA.

Société Nationale pour la Promotion Agricole (SONAPRA): BP 933, Cotonou; tel. 33-08-20; telex 5248; f. 1983; cap. 500m. francs CFA; state-owned; marketing of agricultural products; Pres. VALENTIN AGBO; Dir-Gen. ROBERT TETEVI VINYOR.

Société Nationale d'Equipement (SONAE): BP 2042, Cotonou; tel. 31-31-26; telex 5201; f. 1975; cap. 300m. francs CFA; state-owned; import and distribution of capital goods; Man. Dir NICOLAS ADAGBE.

CHAMBER OF COMMERCE

Chambre de Commerce, d'Agriculture et d'Industrie de la République Populaire du Bénin (CCIB): ave du Général de Gaulle, BP 31, Cotonou; tel. 31-32-99; Pres. RAFFET LOKO; Vice-Pres. J.-V. ADJOVI, M. T. LALEYE; Sec.-Gen. N. A. VIADENOU.

EMPLOYERS' ORGANIZATIONS

Association des Syndicats du Bénin (ASYNBA): Cotonou; Pres. PIERRE FOURN.

Groupement Interprofessionnel des Entreprises du Bénin (GIBA): BP 6, Cotonou; Pres. A. JEUKENS.

Syndicat des Commerçants Importateurs et Exportateurs du Bénin: BP 6, Cotonou; Pres. M. BENCHIMOL.

Syndicat Interprofessionnel des Entreprises Industrielles du Bénin: Cotonou; Pres. M. DOUCET.

Syndicat National des Commerçants et Industriels Africains du Bénin (SYNACIB): BP 367, Cotonou; Pres. URBAIN DA SILVA.

Syndicat des Transporteurs Routiers du Bénin: Cotonou; Pres. PASCAL ZENON.

STATE ENTERPRISES

In 1987, under a programme to rationalize the public sector, studies began on the future of 11 state-owned enterprises, including ONPB, AGB, La Béninoise and a number of transport organizations, with a view to their rehabilitation or liquidation.

Société Agro-Animale Bénino-Arabe-Libyenne (SABLI): BP 03-1200, Cotonou; tel. 31-19-50; telex 5353; f. 1979; cap. 1,112m. francs CFA; 51% state-owned, 49% Libya; poultry and poultry products; Man. Dir SALÉ IMOROU.

Société d'Alimentation Générale du Bénin (AGB): 21 route de Porto-Novo, BP 53, Cotonou; tel. 33-07-28; telex 5062; f. 1978; cap. 300m. francs CFA; 100% state-owned; monopoly importer and distributor of basic foodstuffs, drink and tobacco; chain of 23 supermarkets and 3 wholesale stores; Man. Dir CHRISTOPHE YEBE SEMAKO.

Société Bénino-Arabe-Libyenne de Pêche Maritime (BELI-PECHE): BP 1516, Cotonou; tel. 31-51-36; f. 1977; cap. US $5m.; 51% state-owned, 49% Libya; fish and fish products; Pres. LAURENT FAGBOHOUN; Dir SALEH AREIBI.

Société Bénino-Arabe-Libyenne des Mines (BELIMINES): BP 1913, Cotonou; tel. 31-59-24; telex 5128; f. 1979; cap. US $2m.; 51% state-owned, 49% Libya; mining and commercialization of marble; Pres. ANDRÉ YORO; Man. Dir HASSAN A. RAGHI.

Société Béninoise d'Electricité et d'Eau (SBEE): BP 123, Cotonou; tel. 31-24-10; telex 5207; f. 1973; production and distribution of electricity and water; Man. Dir EMILE LOUIS PARAISO.

Société Béninoise de Palmier à Huile (SOBEPALH): ave Victor Regis, BP 12, Porto-Novo; tel. 21-29-03; f. 1961, nationalized 1975; cap. 425m. francs CFA; 100% state-owned; production of palm oil and cotton seed oil; refineries at Mono, Hinvy and Agonvy; Pres. PHILIPPE AKPO; Man. Dir MARIUS KOKOU QUENUM.

Société des Ciments d'Onigbolo (SCO): Onigbolo; f. 1975; cap. 6,000m. francs CFA; 51% state-owned, 43% Nigeria; production and marketing of cement; Pres. JUSTIN GNIDEHOU; Man. Dir R. J. K. FRYMANN.

Société de Fabrication des Portes Isolantes (SFPI): route Inter-Etats, quartier Agbocodji, Godomey, BP 52, Cotonou; f. 1984; cap. 125m. francs CFA; 51% state-owned; Pres. RODOLPHE DAIZO.

Société Nationale de Boissons (La Béninoise): route de Porto-Novo, BP 135, Cotonou; tel. 33-10-61; telex 5275; f. 1957, nationalized 1975; cap. 3,200m. francs CFA; production of beer, soft drinks and ice; Pres. BARNABÉ MIDOUZO; Dir-Gen. DENIS YABI.

Société Nationale de Construction et de Travaux Publics (SONACOTRAP): BP 286, Cotonou; tel. 30-15-35; f. 1976; cap. 200m. francs CFA; Dir-Gen. THÉODORE AHOUSSOU.

Société Nationale d'Irrigation et d'Aménagement Hydro-Agricole (SONIAH): BP 312, Porto-Novo; tel. 21-34-20; f. 1972; cap. 350m. francs CFA; development of irrigation and rice-growing projects; Dir-Gen. YENAKPONDJI CAPOCHICHI; Sec.-Gen. TOSSA JÉRÔME TONI.

Société Nationale pour l'Industrie des Corps Gras (SONICOG): BP 312, Cotonou; tel. 31-33-71; telex 5205; f. 1962; cap. 600m. francs CFA; production of palm oil, palm kernel and groundnut oils and cakes, sheanut butter and soaps; factories at Porto-Novo, Bohicon and Cotonou; Dir-Gen. ZULKIFL SALAMI.

TRADE UNION

Union Nationale des Syndicats des Travailleurs du Bénin (UNSTB): BP 69, Cotonou; tel. 31-56-13; telex 5200; f. 1974, when it absorbed all pre-existing trade union organizations; Sec.-Gen. ROMAIN VILON GUEZO; 300,000 mems in 16 sectoral federations.

Transport

RAILWAYS

A 650-km extension north from Parakou to Gaya, and on through Niger to Niamey, was under construction in 1988. In 1987 the network handled 444,000 metric tons of goods.

Organisation Commune Bénin-Niger des Chemins de Fer et des Transports (OCBN): BP 16, Cotonou; tel. 31-33-80; telex 5210; f. 1959; Benin has a 63% share, Niger 37%. The main line runs for 438 km from Cotonou to Parakou in the interior; a branch runs westward via Ouidah to Segboroué (34 km). There is also a line of 107 km from Cotonou via Porto-Novo to Pobé near the Nigerian border. Total length of railways: 579 km; Gen. Man. R. M. DE SOUZA.

ROADS

The system is well developed. In 1985 there were 7,445 km of classified roads (including 3,359 km of main roads) and a further 1,200 km of tracks that are suitable for motor traffic in the dry season. The roads along the coast and those from Cotonou to Bohicon and from Parakou to Malanville, a total of 700 km, are bitumen-surfaced. A major highways rehabilitation project was announced in May 1987 as part of a wider transport infrastructure programme.

Société de Transit et de Consignation du Bénin (SOTRACOB): BP 253, Cotonou; tel. 31-25-65; telex 5219; f. 1975; cap. 100m. francs CFA; 51% state-owned; Man. Dir CYRIAQUE GANDJI.

Société des Transports Routiers du Bénin (TRANS-BENIN): BP 703, Cotonou; tel. 31-32-28; f. 1977; cap. 300m. francs CFA; 49% state-owned; passenger and goods transport; Man. Dir PROSPER DJIDJOHO.

SHIPPING

The main port is at Cotonou. In 1987 the port handled 1,267,400 metric tons of goods, of which 296,500 tons were from Niger, 18,300 tons from Mali and 5,500 tons from Burkina Faso.

Capacity was 2m. metric tons in 1986. Further improvements were to be carried out under the transport infrastructure rehabilitation project announced in May 1987, with finance from France and multilateral agencies and with a loan from the Islamic Development Bank, announced in March 1988.

Association des Professionnels Agréés en Douanes du Bénin (APRAD): BP 2141, Cotonou; tel. 31-55-05; telex 5355; Chair. GATIEN HOUNGBEDJI.

Cie Béninoise de Navigation Maritime (COBENAM): BP 2032, Cotonou; tel. 31-47-87; telex 5225; f. 1974; cap. 500m. francs CFA; 51% state-owned, 49% Algerian; agents for shipping companies from France, Japan, UK, China; Man. Dir NOUHOUM ASSOUMAN.

Delmas–Bénin: ave Pierre Dehorme, BP 7, Cotonou; tel. 30-07-69; telex 5308; f. 1986; cap. 50m. francs CFA; Dir ALEXIS AHOUANSOU.

Office Béninois des Manutentions Portuaires (OBEMAP): BP 35, Cotonou; tel. 31-39-83; telex 5135; cap. 50m. francs CFA; state-owned; Man. Dir PAUL AWANOU.

Port Autonome de Cotonou: BP 927, Cotonou; tel. 31-28-90; telex 5004; f. 1965; cap. 16,577m. francs CFA; state-owned; Man. Dir ODON BRICE HOUNCANRIN.

CIVIL AVIATION

The international airport at Cotonou has a 2.4-km runway, and there are secondary airports at Parakou, Natitingou, Kandi and Abomey. There were 81,000 passengers at Cotonou in 1982. In 1981 9,763 metric tons of freight were handled.

Air Afrique: ave du Gouverneur Ballot, BP 200, Cotonou; tel. 31-21-07; Benin has a 7% share in Air Afrique (see under Côte d'Ivoire); Dir (Benin) DOKLO KONE.

Transports Aériens du Bénin (TAB): BP 824, Cotonou; tel. 30-07-97; telex 5297; f. 1978; state-owned; domestic passenger and cargo services to Savé, Parakou, Natitingou, Djougou and Kandi; regional services to Lagos, Lomé, Ouagadougou and Niamey; Man. Dir MANASSE AYAYI; fleet of 1 Fokker 28-4000, 2 Twin Otter 300, 4 DC-3.

Tourism

In 1985, some 72,000 tourists visited Benin.

Office National du Tourisme et de l'Hôtellerie (ONATHO): BP 89, Cotonou; tel. 31-26-87; telex 5032; f. 1974; state tourist agency; Dir HILAIRE SAPONDU.

BHUTAN

Introductory Survey

Location, Climate, Language, Religion, Flag, Capital

The Kingdom of Bhutan lies in the Himalaya range of mountains, with the People's Republic of China to the north and India to the south. Average monthly temperature ranges from 4.4°C (40°F) in January to 17°C (62°F) in July. Rainfall is heavy, ranging from 150 cm (60 inches) to 300 cm (120 inches) per year. The official language is Dzongkha, spoken mainly in western Bhutan. Written Dzongkha is based on the Tibetan script. The state religion is Mahayana Buddhism, mainly the Drukpa school of the Kagyupa sect. The national flag (proportions 5 by 4) is divided diagonally from the lower hoist to the upper fly, so forming two triangles, one orange and the other maroon, with a white dragon superimposed in the centre. The capital is Thimphu.

Recent History

The first hereditary King of Bhutan was installed on 17 December 1907. An Anglo-Bhutanese Treaty, signed in 1910, placed Bhutan's foreign relations under the supervision of the Government of British India. After India became independent, that treaty was replaced in August 1949 by the Indo-Bhutan Treaty of Friendship, whereby Bhutan agrees to seek the advice of the Government of India with regard to its foreign relations, but remains free to decide whether or not to accept such advice. King Jigme Dorji Wangchuk, installed in 1952, established the National Assembly (Tshogdu) in 1953 and a Royal Advisory Council in 1965. He formed the country's first Cabinet in May 1968. He died in July 1972 and was succeeded by the Western-educated 16-year-old Crown Prince, Jigme Singye Wangchuk. The new King stated his wish to maintain the Indo-Bhutan Treaty and further to strengthen friendship with India. In 1979, however, during the Non-Aligned Conference and later at the UN General Assembly, Bhutan voted in opposition to India, in favour of Chinese policy. In December 1983 India and Bhutan made a new trade agreement concerning overland trade with Bangladesh and Nepal. India raised no objection to Bhutan's decision to negotiate directly with the People's Republic of China over the Bhutan-China border, and discussions were begun in April 1984. At the fifth round of negotiations, held in Beijing in May 1988, further progress was made when the two sides agreed on the 'guiding principles' towards the demarcation of the border.

When Chinese authority was established in Tibet (Xizang) in 1959, Bhutan granted asylum to about 4,000 Tibetan refugees. As a result of the discovery that many refugees were engaged in spying and subversive activities, the Bhutan Government decided in 1976 to disperse them in small groups, introducing a number of Bhutanese families into each settlement. In early 1978 discussions with the Dalai Lama, the spiritual leader of Tibet, collapsed after four years. In June 1979 the National Assembly approved a directive establishing the end of the year as a time-limit for the refugees to decide whether to acquire Bhutanese citizenship or accept repatriation to Tibet. In October India announced that it would not be able to accept refugees who refused Bhutanese nationality as there were still about 10,000 Tibetans in India who were awaiting rehabilitation. By July 1980, however, most of the Tibetans had chosen Bhutanese citizenship, and the remainder were to be accepted by India.

Bhutan has asserted itself as a fully sovereign, independent state, becoming a member of the UN in 1971 and of the Non-Aligned Movement in 1973. By 1987 Bhutan had established diplomatic relations with 13 countries, and maintained diplomatic missions at the UN in New York, in New Delhi, Dhaka and Kathmandu.

In 1983 Bhutan was an enthusiastic founder-member of the South Asian Regional Co-operation (SARC) organization, with Bangladesh, India, Maldives, Nepal, Pakistan and Sri Lanka. In May 1985 Bhutan was host to the first meeting of ministers of foreign affairs from SARC member countries, which agreed to give their grouping the formal title of South Asian Association for Regional Co-operation (SAARC, see p. 220).

Government

Bhutan is an absolute monarchy, without a written constitution. The system of government is unusual in that power is shared by the monarchy (assisted by the Royal Advisory Council), the Council of Ministers, the National Assembly (Tshogdu) and the Head Abbot (Je Khempo) of Bhutan's 3,000–4,000 Buddhist monks. The National Assembly, which serves a three-year term, has 151 members, including 106 directly elected by adult suffrage. Ten seats in the Assembly are reserved for religious bodies, while the remainder are occupied by officials, ministers and members of the Royal Advisory Council.

Defence

The strength of the Royal Bhutanese Army, which is under the direct command of the King, is classified information. Army training facilities are provided by an Indian military training team. Although India is not directly responsible for the country's defence, the Indian Government has indicated that any act of aggression against Bhutan would be regarded as an act of aggression against India.

Economic Affairs

In terms of average income, Bhutan is one of the poorest countries in the world. In 1987, according to estimates by the World Bank, the kingdom's gross national product (GNP), measured at average 1985–87 prices, was US $201m., equivalent to about $150 per head. It was, however, estimated that GNP per head increased, in real terms, by 10.6% in 1987, one of the highest growth rates in the world.

The economy is predominantly agrarian. An estimated 95% of the economically active population were employed in agriculture, forestry and fishing in 1985, although only about 9% of the land was under cultivation. In 1983 lack of rain caused a serious decline in the production of food grains, and, as a result, food prices increased sharply. The total annual production of cereals was expected to rise from 166,000 metric tons in 1982 to more than 200,000 tons in 1986/87. Forests cover about 70% of the country's area, and further afforestation is envisaged. Roundwood removals (mainly for fuel) totalled an estimated 3.2m. cu m in 1986. The first phase of a forest-based industrial complex at Gedu has begun, and a plant for the production of particle board was being constructed in 1983. Timber and fruit, including apples, are exported.

Bhutan has some small-scale industry (contributing only about 4% to total annual gross domestic product—GDP), producing, for example, textiles, soap, matches, candles and carpets. Centres for the production of traditional handicrafts, such as bamboo-work, lacquer woodwork and woven carpets, have been established. Several minerals of economic importance have been discovered, and small mineral-based units have been formed, such as a graphite beneficiation plant at Paro. The Government is encouraging private entrepreneurs to establish small units, and a number of small industrial estates have been created, producing a variety of consumer goods and industrial raw materials. In 1981 a cement plant was established at Penden, and now has a daily capacity of 400 tons. In 1983 cement exports were worth US $3.5m. A second cement plant, at Nanglam, with a potential output of 1,500–2,500 tons per day, is scheduled for completion by 1991. Commercial production at a new calcium carbide plant at Pasakha, near Phuntsholing, was expected to commence by the end of 1987. There are also plans to establish a gypsum-mining plant at Kothakpa. As an under-populated country, Bhutan is dependent on foreign labour, particularly from Nepal; to reduce this dependence, many construction activities are to be mechanized. In the Sixth Plan (1987–92) considerable emphasis was placed on the formulation of a strategy for the rapid expansion of export-oriented industries. The production of low-cost electricity by the Chukha hydroelectric project (see below) was expected to help to stimulate growth in the industrial sector.

A series of Economic Plans began in 1961, the first two being financed entirely by India. More than 30% of the total outlay of the Fifth Plan (1981–87) was financed by India. The Sixth Plan (1987–92) envisaged expenditure of Nu 9,485m. (more than double the total expenditure of the previous Plan), of which about 29% was to be allocated to trade, industry and power, and about 28% to social services. Nine major policy objectives were declared in the Sixth Plan: the strengthening of government administration (including the continued campaign against corruption and nepotism), the preservation and promotion of national identity (particularly through the strengthening of the newly-formed Special Commission for Cultural Affairs and of traditional institutions), the mobilization of internal resources, the enhancement of rural incomes, the improvement of rural housing and resettlement, the consolidation and improvement of services, the development of human resources, the promotion of popular participation in the formulation and execution of development plans and strategies, and the promotion of national self reliance. Grants from the Government of India in the 1987/88 Annual Plan provided 29% of total expenditure, compared with 55% in 1978/79, and direct grants from international agencies amounted to nearly 9%, compared with 10% in 1978/79. Both Indian development grants (budgetary and project) and international assistance, however, have been increasing in absolute terms since the late 1970s. Each Plan since 1982 has been administered through local government institutions, in order to encourage investment at local levels. Considerable improvements have been achieved in roads, animal husbandry, irrigation, forestry and electricity generation. Six hydroelectricity stations have been established, and exports of electric energy to India began in 1988, with the inauguration of the Chukha hydroelectric project. India was to receive 85% of the total electricity generated by this project. The Indian Government is financing the establishment of an Indo-Bhutanese microwave link to provide Bhutan with instant communication internally and abroad. In 1987 the link provided 60 channels out of a total capacity of 300, and Thimphu subscribers could communicate directly, through operator trunk dialling, with Calcutta and New Delhi and thence to third countries. Bhutan joined the Asian Development Bank (ADB, see p. 98) in 1982, and received its first US $5m. multi-project loan in September 1983, to finance agricultural equipment, construction of roads and bridges, development of solar power, and improvement of water supplies and sewerage. A second multi-project loan of $7.4m. was approved in 1984, and in 1985 the ADB provided a loan of $3.48m. for the Chirang Hill Irrigation Project (scheduled for completion in 1991), in addition to approving support for five technical assistance projects, totalling $1.5m. In September 1986 the ADB approved a loan of $4.5m. towards a $8.2m. roadworks mechanization project.

Since the 1960 ban on trade with Tibet, Bhutan's main trading partner has been India, although timber, liquor and cardamom are also exported to the Middle East and Western Europe. After the inauguration of the postal system in 1972, Bhutan's postage stamps became the main source of foreign exchange, but in 1976 this category was overtaken by tourism, which provided an estimated US $2.4m. in 1987. In the year ending March 1988 there was an estimated deficit of Nu 802.5m. on merchandise trade.

The average annual increase of GDP, in real terms, was estimated at 6.4% during the Fifth Plan period (1981–86). Fiscal reforms, introduced in 1982/83, led to an increase in government revenue, and were expected to result in a reduction in the budget deficit, until then equivalent to about 20% of GDP annually. Total borrowing amounted to Nu 948.6m. in 1987/88, compared with Nu 259.3m. in 1986/87, while internal revenue rose from Nu 331.4m. in 1986/87 to Nu 503.3m. in 1987/88. Debt-service repayments increased from $120,000 in 1985/86 to $736,000 in 1987/88, and were expected to rise rapidly, to an estimated $2.5m. per year by 1991/92. The budget proposals for 1987/88 envisaged total revenue of Nu 1,698m. and total expenditure of Nu 2,020m., leaving an estimated deficit of Nu 322m.

Social Welfare

At the end of 1986 there were 27 hospitals (including five leprosy hospitals). Because of a shortage of medical personnel and a lack of funds, local dispensaries are being converted into basic health units (of which there were 70 in 1986), providing basic medical services. Malaria and tuberculosis are still widespread. The budget for the financial year 1987/88 allocated Nu 77.8m. (3.8% of total projected expenditure) to health.

Education

Education is not compulsory. Primary education begins at six years of age and lasts for six years. Secondary education, beginning at the age of 12, lasts for a further five years, comprising a first cycle of three years and a second cycle of two years. Free education is available, but there are insufficient facilities to accommodate all school-age children. In 1985 the total enrolment at primary schools was equivalent to an estimated 25% of children in the relevant age-group (32% of boys, 18% of girls), while the comparable ratio for secondary schools was only 4% (boys 6%, girls 1%). All schools are co-educational and follow a British syllabus. English is the language of instruction. Bhutan has no mission or private schools, and all schools are subsidized by the Government. Many Indian teachers are employed. In 1987 the total number of enrolled students was 57,262 and the total number of teachers was 2,365. In 1987 there were more than 200 educational institutions under the supervision of the Department of Education, including 148 primary schools, 21 junior high schools, nine high schools, one junior college, one degree college, six technical schools, 22 schools for Buddhist studies and monastic schools, two teacher-training schools and four schools for Tibetan refugees. A number of Bhutanese students were receiving higher education abroad. The 1987/88 budget allocated Nu 183.8m. (9.1% of total projected expenditure) to education. In 1988 the rate of adult illiteracy in Bhutan was about 85%.

Public Holidays

1989 and 1990: The usual Buddhist holidays are observed, as well as the Birthday of HM Jigme Singye Wangchuk (11 November) and the National Day of Bhutan (17 December).

Weights and Measures

The metric system is in operation.

Statistical Survey

Source (unless otherwise stated): Royal Government of Bhutan, Thimphu.

Area and Population

AREA, POPULATION AND DENSITY

Area (sq km)	46,500*
Population (1980 census)	1,165,000
Population (official estimates at mid-year)	
1985	1,286,275
1986	1,312,700
Density (per sq km) at mid-1986	28.2

* 17,954 sq miles.
Capital: Thimphu (estimated population 15,000 at 1 July 1987).

POPULATION OF DISTRICTS*
(mid-1985 estimates, based on 1980 census)

Bumthang	23,842
Chirang	108,807
Dagana	28,352
Gasa†	16,907
Gaylegphug	111,283
Haa	16,715
Lhuntshi	39,635
Mongar	73,239
Paro	46,615
Pema Gatshel	37,141
Punakha†	16,700
Samchi	172,109
Samdrup Jongkhar	73,044
Shemgang	44,516
Tashigang	177,718
Thimphu	58,660
Tongsa	26,017
Wangdiphodrang	47,152
Total rural population	1,119,452
Total urban population	167,823
Total	1,286,275

* The above figures are approximate, and predate the creation of a new district, Chukha, in August 1987. Chukha has an estimated total population of about 13,372 (based on the figure of 3,343 households, with an estimated average of four persons per household), who were formerly included in Samchi, Paro or Thimphu districts. A new and more extensive census is scheduled to take place in 1990.
† Gasa and Punakha were merged into a single district in August 1987.

BIRTHS AND DEATHS (UN estimates, annual averages)

	1970-75	1975-80	1980-85
Birth rate (per 1,000)	41.8	40.0	38.4
Death rate (per 1,000)	21.3	19.8	18.1

Source: UN, *World Population Prospects: Estimates and Projections as Assessed in 1984.*
Official estimates (Demographic Sample Survey, 1984): Birth rate 39.1 per 1,000; Death rate 19.3 per 1,000.

LIFE EXPECTANCY
45.6 years (1985 estimate).

ECONOMICALLY ACTIVE POPULATION
(estimates, '000 persons, 1981/82)

Agriculture, etc.	613
Industry	6
Trade	9
Public services	22
Total	650

Agriculture

PRINCIPAL CROPS (estimates, '000 metric tons)

	1984	1985	1986
Rice (paddy)	61	62	63
Wheat	10	11	11
Barley	5	5	5
Maize	85	86	88
Millet	7	7	8
Other cereals	7	8	7
Potatoes	27	27	28
Other roots and tubers	17	18	18
Pulses	3	3	3
Tobacco	1	1	1
Jute	4	4	4
Vegetables	10	11	11
Citrus fruit	26	26	27
Other fruits	22	24	24

Source: FAO, *Production Yearbook.*

LIVESTOCK ('000 head)

	1984	1985	1986
Cattle	316	347	339
Pigs	58	60	89
Sheep	38	39	44
Goats	40	52	32
Buffaloes	n.a.	n.a.	5
Asses	23	n.a.	24
Poultry	176	179	211
Yaks	30	31	36

Livestocks Products ('000 metric tons, 1984): Milk 30.2, butter 1.7, cheese 2.4, pork 0.9, beef 4.7, eggs (total number) 4,989,915.
Source: Central Statistical Organization, Royal Government of Bhutan.

BHUTAN   Statistical Survey

Forestry

ROUNDWOOD REMOVALS
(FAO estimates, '000 cubic metres, excl. bark)

	1979	1980	1981
Sawlogs, veneer logs and logs for sleepers	240*	240	240
Other industrial wood	38*	38	38
Fuel wood	2,814	2,884	2,946
Total	3,092	3,162	3,224

* Unofficial figure.

1982-86: Annual output as in 1981 (FAO estimates).
Sawnwood production: 5,000 cubic metres per year (FAO estimates, 1982-86).
Source: FAO, *Yearbook of Forest Products*.
Logging ('000 cu m): 122,200 in 1982/83; 126,957 in 1983/84; 121,395 in 1984/85.
Source: Department of Forestry, Ministry of Agriculture.

Fishing

Total catch 1,000 metric tons of freshwater fishes per year (FAO estimate).

Mining

	1984	1985	1986
Gypsum (metric tons)	13,532	12,000	24,837
Coal* ('000 metric tons)	8.6	30	30
Limestone ('000 metric tons)	126	144	172
Slate ('000 sq ft)	503.3	540.8	614.2
Dolomite (metric tons)	111,535	162,014	217,371

* The coal industry was nationalized in 1984.
Source: Department of Industries and Mines, Royal Government of Bhutan.

Industry

SELECTED PRODUCTS (year ending 31 March)

	1981/82	1982/83	1983/84
Minerals (metric tons)	136,010	33,188	37,988
Cement (metric tons)	99,008	88,688	169,624
Electric energy (million kWh)	22	24	26

Source: Department of Industries and Mines, Royal Government of Bhutan.

Finance

CURRENCY AND EXCHANGE RATES
Monetary Units
100 chetrum (Ch) = 1 ngultrum (Nu).

Denominations
Coins: 5, 10, 25 and 50 chetrum; 1 ngultrum.
Notes: 1, 2, 5, 10, 20, 50 and 100 ngultrum.

Sterling and Dollar Equivalents (30 September 1988)
£1 sterling = 24.55 ngultrum;
US $1 = 14.52 ngultrum;
1,000 ngultrum = £40.73 = $68.88.

Average Exchange Rate (ngultrum per US $)
1985 12.369
1986 12.611
1987 12.962

Note: The ngultrum is at par with the Indian rupee.

BUDGET (estimates, '000 ngultrum, year ending 31 March)

Revenue	1986/87*	1987/88
Internal revenue	345,142	411,369
Grants from Government of India	611,621	836,744
Grants from UN and other international agencies	223,936	340,000
Internal borrowing	10,200	100,000
External borrowing	249,083	n.a.
Private equity participation in industrial sector	9,600	10,000
Total	1,449,582	1,698,113

* Revised budget.

Expenditure	1986/87*	1987/88
Public works department (incl. urban development)	163,046	281,485
Power (excl. Chukha hydroelectric project)	205,218	272,872
Agriculture and irrigation (incl. Food Corpn of Bhutan)	108,079	123,360
Education (incl. Royal Institute of Management)	86,436	183,788
Ministry of Finance	175,555	108,834
Health	45,910	77,779
Industry and mining	188,164	328,185
Trade and commerce	1,155	5,009
Forestry	40,426	57,543
District administration	106,666	61,339
Post and telecommunications	21,923	81,423
Animal husbandry	15,414	65,547
Foreign affairs	27,184	44,838
Police	18,599	25,130
Planning commission (incl. statistics)	8,707	15,478
Home affairs (excl. police and dzongkhag administration)	16,141	20,747
Administration of justice	5,718	9,838
Civil aviation	1,717	24,641
Information and broadcasting	70,570	34,888
Communications and tourism policy unit	906	1,580
Special Commission	7,491	13,641
Central monastic affairs	13,350	21,712
Other departments	147,810	159,910
Total	1,496,005	2,019,567

* Revised budget.
Source: Budget Bureau, Royal Government of Bhutan.

BHUTAN

Statistical Survey

SIXTH DEVELOPMENT PLAN (1987–92)
(sectoral allocation of proposed expenditure, million ngultrum)

	Total	% of total
Agriculture and irrigation	708.2	7.5
Food Corpn of Bhutan	86.2	0.9
Animal husbandry	348.4	3.7
Forestry	311.4	3.3
Industry and mining	1,553.6	16.4
Geological Survey of Bhutan	36.0	0.4
Trade and commerce	24.1	0.3
Public works	1,122.7	11.8
Power	1,135.1	11.9
Bhutan Government Transport Service	5.0	0.1
Civil aviation	48.8	0.5
Telephones	256.6	2.7
Postal, telegraph and radio services	73.0	0.8
Information and broadcasting	99.7	1.1
Education (incl. Royal Institute of Management)	1,112.8	11.7
Health	400.6	4.2
Urban Development Corpn	337.0	3.5
General development	1,826.3	19.3
Total	**9,485.3**	**100.0**

Source: Planning Commission, Royal Government of Bhutan.

BANK OF BHUTAN RESERVES (year ending 31 March)

	1984/85	1985/86	1986/87
Indian rupee reserves (million Indian rupees)	369.3	362.9	436.2
Convertible currency reserves (US $ million)	6.3	0.8	1.1

Source: Royal Monetary Authority of Bhutan.

MONEY SUPPLY (million ngultrum at 31 December)

	1984	1985	1986
Currency outside banks*	126.2	146.4	163.7
Demand deposits	111.2	132.5	140.9
Total money	**237.4**	**278.9**	**304.6**

* Including an estimate for Indian rupees (million): 80 in 1984; 76 in 1985; 73 in 1986.

Source: Royal Monetary Authority of Bhutan.

COST OF LIVING
(Consumer Price Index at 31 December; base: 1979 = 100)

	1984	1985	1986
All items	160.9	165.6	182.0

NATIONAL ACCOUNTS (million ngultrum at current prices)
Gross Domestic Product by Economic Activity

	1984	1985	1986
Agriculture and livestock	884.3	989.4	1,109.7
Forestry and logging	131.9	170.7	264.1
Mining	6.7	10.9	14.8
Manufacturing	79.1	94.9	96.0
Electricity	3.2	3.6	96.0
Construction	268.5	242.3	234.4
Trade, restaurants and hotels	230.7	259.1	290.1
Transport	50.3	60.0	68.8
Financing, insurance and real estate	175.5	191.2	192.6
Public administration	221.1	322.8	355.1
Sub-total	**2,051.3**	**2,344.9**	**2,721.6**
Less Imputed bank service charges	38.5	44.6	43.3
GDP in purchasers' values	**2,012.8**	**2,300.3**	**2,678.3**
GDP at constant 1983 prices	**1,850.2**	**1,911.0**	**2,086.6**

BALANCE OF PAYMENTS
(estimates, million ngultrum, year ending 31 March)

	1984/85	1985/86	1986/87
Merchandise exports f.o.b.	206.4	272.0	323.0
Merchandise imports c.i.f.	−825.2	−926.9	−1,125.5
Trade balance	**−618.9**	**−654.9**	**−802.5**
Exports of services	204.2	216.9	256.6
Imports of services	−511.2	−525.1	−665.7
Balance on goods and services	**−925.9**	**−963.1**	**−1,211.6**
Foreign aid	990.8	1,024.1	1,381.8
Net errors and omissions	68.8	6.3	15.3
Total (net monetary movements)	**133.7**	**67.3**	**185.6**

Source: Royal Monetary Authority of Bhutan.

External Trade

SELECTED COMMODITIES (US $'000)

Imports c.i.f.	1982	1983
Aircraft	—	4,219
Diesel fuel	4,041	4,039
Rice	1,743	1,344
Motor cars	1,151	1,100
Metal containers	n.a.	959
Soya-fortified bulgar	n.a.	792

Exports f.o.b.	1982	1983
Cement	3,809	3,516
Talc powder	459	1,428
Fruit products	980	1,095
Rosin	808	870
Cardamom	1,274	798
Sawn timber, coniferous	703	575
Potatoes	943	508

PRINCIPAL TRADING PARTNERS (US $'000)

Imports c.i.f.	1985	1986
India	66,667	71,940
Other countries	7,794	11,590

BHUTAN

Exports f.o.b.	1985	1986
India	22,500	25,580
Other countries	148	240

Source: Trade Information Bureau, Royal Government of Bhutan.

Transport

ROAD TRAFFIC

In 1986 there were 3,660 registered vehicles, of which 716 were private cars, 781 were four-wheel-drive vehicles, 1,157 were scooters, 90 were taxis, 780 were trucks, and 136 were buses.

CIVIL AVIATION (traffic, year ending 30 June)

Passengers flown: 4,745 in 1984/85; 6,296 in 1985/86 (year ending 31 March); 7,253 in 1986/87.

Tourism

Arrivals: 1,896 in 1985; 2,486 in 1986; 2,524 in 1987.
Receipts (US $ million): 1.8 in 1985; 2.2 in 1986; 2.4 in 1987.
Source: Bhutan Tourism Corpn.

Communications Media

In 1985 there were 1,800 telephones in use, 8,121 registered radio receivers and 200 television receivers. There are no television transmission stations in Bhutan, but broadcasts from Bangladesh can be received in Phuntsholing.

Education

(at 30 April 1987)

Primary schools	148
Junior high schools	21
High schools	9
Teachers' training institutes	2
Schools for Buddhist studies and monastic schools	22
Junior college	1
Degree college*	1
Technical schools	6
Schools for Tibetan refugees	4
Total pupils	57,262
Total teachers	2,365

* Affiliated to the University of Delhi.
Source: Department of Education, Royal Government of Bhutan.

Directory

The Constitution

The Kingdom of Bhutan has no formal constitution. However, the state system is a modified form of constitutional monarchy. Written rules, which are changed periodically, govern procedures for the election of members of the Royal Advisory Council and the Legislature, and define the duties and powers of those bodies.

The Government

Head of State: HM Druk Gyalpo ('Dragon King') JIGME SINGYE WANGCHUCK (succeeded to the throne in July 1972).

LODOI TSOKDE
(Royal Advisory Council)
(December 1988)

The Royal Advisory Council (Lodoi Tsokde), established in 1965, comprises 10 members: one nominee of the King, two monks representing the state religion, six people's representatives and a Chairman (Kalyon), also nominated by the King. The people's representatives have their names endorsed at village assemblies, forwarded by district Dzongdas (local administrative officials) and voted on by all members of the Tshogdu (National Assembly). The Council's principal task is to advise the King, as head of government, and to supervise all aspects of administration. The Council is in permanent session, virtually as a government department, and acts as the *de facto* Standing Committee of the Tshogdu. Members serve for five years and may be re-elected.

Chairman: Dasho KUNZANG TANGBI.
Councillors: Dasho KIPCHU DORJI (HM Government), LOPEN YONTEN GYALTSHEN (Central Monastic Body), GELONG SAMDRUP (District Monastic Bodies), TEKNATH RIZAL (South Bhutan-West), B. B. BHANDARI (South Bhutan-East), Dasho RINZIN DORJI (West Bhutan), Dasho KESANG (East Bhutan), JAMJANG GAYLEG (Central Bhutan), JAZIG (Thimphu/Paro/Ha).

LHENGYE SHUNGTSOG
(Council of Ministers)
(December 1988)

Chairman: HM Druk Gyalpo JIGME SINGYE WANGCHUCK.
Representative of His Majesty in the Ministry of Finance: HRH Ashi (Princess) SONAM CHHODEN WANGCHUCK.
Representative of His Majesty in the Ministry of Agriculture: HRH Ashi (Princess) DECHEN WANGMO WANGCHUCK.
Minister of Trade, Industries and Power: (vacant).
Minister of Home Affairs: HRH NAMGYEL WANGCHUCK.
Minister of Foreign Affairs and Secretary of the Council of Ministers: Lyonpo DAWA TSERING.
Minister of Social Services and of Communications and Tourism: Lyonpo Dr T. TOBGYAL.
Minister of Agriculture: (vacant).

MINISTRIES

All Ministries are in Thimphu.

Ministry of Finance: Thimphu; telex 890201.
Ministry of Foreign Affairs: Tashichhodzong, Thimphu; telex 890214.
Ministry of Social Services: Thimphu; telex 890203.
Ministry of Trade, Industries and Power: Thimphu; telex 890215.

Legislature

TSHOGDU

A National Assembly (Tshogdu) was established in 1953. The Assembly has a three-year term and meets twice yearly, in spring (May–June) and autumn (October–November). The size of the membership is based, in part, on the population of the districts, and is subject to periodic revision. In 1987 the Assembly had 151 members, of whom 106 were directly elected by the public. Ten seats were reserved for religious bodies, one was assigned to a representative of industry (elected by the Bhutan Chamber of Commerce and Industry), and the remainder were occupied by officials nominated by the Government (including the 18 Dzongdas). The Assembly elects its own Speaker from among its members. It enacts laws, advises on constitutional and political matters and debates all important issues. Both the Royal Advisory Council and the Council of Ministers are responsible to the Assembly.

LOCAL ADMINISTRATION

There are 18 districts (dzongkhags), each headed by a Dzongda (in charge of administration and law and order) and a Thrimpon (in

BHUTAN

Directory

charge of judicial matters). Dzongdas were previously appointed by the King, but are now appointed by the Royal Civil Service Commission, established in 1982. The Dzongdas are responsible to the Royal Civil Service Commission and the Ministry of Home Affairs, while the Thrimpons are responsible to the High Court. The principal officers under the Dzongda are the Dzongda Wongma and the Dzongrab, responsible for locally administered development projects and fiscal matters respectively. Seven of the districts are further sub-divided into sub-districts (dungkhags), and the lowest administrative unit in all districts is the bloc (gewog) of several villages.

Under provisions of the 1981–87 Plan, with the introduction of decentralization, Punakha and Thimphu were merged as one district for a few years in the early 1980s. However, this did not prove successful, and by 1985 they were once more administered separately. In August 1987 Gasa and Punakha were amalgamated into a single district, and a new district, named Chukha, was created from portions of three existing districts in western Bhutan. There are two municipal corporations (in Thimphu and Phuntsholing), each of which is headed by a Thrompon (mayor) and is composed of government officials.

Political Organizations

There are no political parties in Bhutan.

Diplomatic Representation

EMBASSIES IN BHUTAN

Bangladesh: POB 178, Thorilam, Thimphu; tel. 2539; Ambassador: MAHMOOD ATIS.

India: India House Estate, Lungtenzampa, Thimphu; tel. 2162; telex 890211; Ambassador: NARESHWAR DAYAL.

Judicial System

Bhutan has Civil and Criminal Codes, which are based on those laid down by the Shabdrung Ngawang Namgyal in the 17th century. Law was mostly administered at the district level until 1968. Existing laws were consolidated in 1982.

Appeal Court: The Supreme Court of Appeal is the King.

High Court (Thrimkhang Gongma): Established 1968 to review appeals from Lower Courts, although some cases are heard at the first instance; eight Judges (six nominated by the King and two elected by the Tshogdu, who serve for a five-year period), headed by the Chief Justice. Three judges form a quorum. The judges are assisted by seven senior Ramjams (judges in training).

Chief Justice: Lyonpo SANGYE PENJOR.

Magistrates' Courts (Dzongkhag Thrimkhang): Each district has a court, headed by the Thrimpon (magistrate) and aided by a junior Ramjam, which tries most cases. Appeals are made to the High Court, and less serious civil disputes may be settled by a Gup or Mandal (village headman) through written undertakings.

All citizens have the right to make informal appeal for redress of grievances directly to the King, through the office of the Gyalpoi Zimpon (court chamberlain).

Religion

The state religion is Mahayana Buddhism, but the southern Bhutanese are predominantly followers of Hinduism. Buddhism was introduced into Bhutan in the eighth century AD by the Indian saint Padmasambhava, known in Bhutan as Guru Rimpoche. In the 13th century Phajo Drugom Shigpo made the Drukpa school of Kagyupa Buddhism pre-eminent in Bhutan, and this sect is still supported by the dominant ethnic group, the Drukpas. The main monastic group, the Central Monastic Body (comprising 1,160 monks), is led by an elected Head Abbot (Je Khempo), is directly supported by the state and spends six months of the year at Tashichhodzong and at Punakha respectively. A further 2,120 monks, who are members of the District Monastic Bodies, are sustained by the lay population. The Central Monastic Secretariat, established in 1985, oversees all religious bodies. Monasteries (Gompas) and shrines (Lhakhangs) are numerous.

Central Monastic Secretariat (Dratshang Lhentshog): established in 1985, replacing the Central Board for Monastic Studies, to oversee all Buddhist meditational centres and schools of Buddhist studies, as well as the Central and District Monastic Bodies; Chair. The Je Khempo, His Holiness LOPON KUENLEY; Sec. Dasho RIGZIN DORJI.

The Press

Kuensel: Dept of Information and Broadcasting, POB 204, Thimphu; telex 890212; f. 1965 as a news bulletin; reorg. as a national weekly newspaper in 1986; in English, Dzongkha and Nepali; Editor-in-Chief RINZIN DORJI; Asst Editors G. S. UPADHYA (Nepali), KINLEY DORJI (English), GOEMPO DORJI (Dzongkha); circ. 2,000 (Nepali), 6,000 (English), 2,500 (Dzongkha).

Radio

There are 36 radio stations for administrative communications. Of these, 34 are for internal communications (to which the public has access), and two are external stations serving the Bhutanese diplomatic missions in India and Bangladesh. A further eight stations are for hydrological and meteorological purposes. In 1985 there were an estimated 15,000 radio receivers in use, of which 8,121 were registered.

Bhutan Broadcasting Service (BBS): Dept of Information and Broadcasting, POB 1, Thimphu; tel. 2533; f. 1973 as Radio National Youth Association of Bhutan (NYAB); present name adopted 1986; short-wave radio station broadcasting 30 hours per week in Dzongkha, Sharchopkha, Nepali and English; a daily FM programme (for Thimphu only) began in 1987; Sec. LOUISE DORJI; Programme Officer TASHI DORJI.

Finance

(cap. = capital; auth. = authorized; p.u. = paid up;
res = reserves; dep. = deposits; m. = million; brs = branches;
amounts in ngultrum)

BANKING

Central Bank

Royal Monetary Authority (RMA): POB 154, Thimphu; tel. 2540; telex 890206; f. 1982; bank of issue; frames and implements official monetary policy, co-ordinates the activities of financial institutions and holds foreign-exchange deposits on behalf of the govt; cap. 1.5m.; Chair. HRH Ashi SONAM CHHODEN WANGCHUCK; Man. Dir BAP KESANG.

Commercial Bank

Bank of Bhutan: POB 75, Phuntsholing; tel. 225; telex 890304; f. 1968; 26%-owned by the State Bank of India; cap. and res 161.9m., dep. 830m. (Dec. 1987); Dirs nominated by the Bhutan Govt: Chair. Dasho Dr DORJI TSHERING; Dirs Dasho PEMA WANGCHUCK, Dasho CHENKYAB DORJI, YESHEY ZIMBA, BAP KESANG; Dirs nominated by the State Bank of India: P. K. HAJRA, B. MISRA; Man. Dir RAM NATH; 2 brs.

Development Bank

Bhutan Development Finance Corporation (BDFC): c/o Royal Monetary Authority, POB 154, Thimphu; tel. 2540; telex 890206; f. 1988; provides long-term development loans and shorter-term agricultural credit; cap. p.u. 12.5m.; CEO PEMA TENZIN.

Savings Institution

Unit Trust of Bhutan: POB 77, Phuntsholing; tel. 434; offers various forms of investment in unit trusts (mutual funds) guaranteed by the govt; Gen. Man. SANGAY DORJI.

INSURANCE

Royal Insurance Corporation of Bhutan: POB 77, Phuntsholing; tel. 309; telex 890305; f. 1975; cap. 12m., total investments 218.3m. (1986); Chair. HRH Ashi SONAM CHHODEN WANGCHUCK; Man. Dir Dasho U. DORJI.

Trade and Industry

CHAMBER OF COMMERCE

Bhutan Chamber of Commerce and Industries: POB 147, Thimphu; tel. 2506; telex 89011; f. 1980; reorg. 1987, with membership restricted to 25–30 mems; Pres. Dasho U. DORJI; Gen. Sec. THINLEY PENJORE.

BHUTAN

GOVERNMENT ORGANIZATIONS

Export Development Corporation: Industrial Estate, Phuntsholing; tel. 353; telex 890312; operated by State Trading Corpn of Bhutan; manages export trade on behalf of govt.

Food Corporation of Bhutan (FCB): Phuntsholing; tel. 241; f. 1974; activities include retailing, marketing, storage, import and export of agricultural products and establishment of regulated market yards and horticultural processing units in the country; operates a rural finance scheme, receiving loans from the Bank of Bhutan and the Royal Insurance Corpn, to assist farmers; Man. Dir (vacant).

National Commission for Trade and Industry: Thimphu; tel. 403; fmrly Industrial Development Corpn; regulates the type, quality and quantity of proposed industrial projects; Chair. HM Druk Gyalpo JIGME SINGYE WANGCHUCK.

State Trading Corpn of Bhutan (STCB): POB 76, Phuntsholing; tel. 286; telex 890301; manages imports and exports (see above) on behalf of the Govt; Man. Dir L. B. GURUNG; brs in Thimphu, Gomtu and in Calcutta, India.

TRADE UNIONS

Trade union activity is illegal in Bhutan.

Transport

ROADS AND TRACKS

In 1987 there were 2,165 km of roads (1,703 km of which were surfaced). In addition, surfaced roads link the important border towns of Phuntsholing, Gaylegphug, Sarbhang and Samdrup Jongkhar in southern Bhutan to towns in West Bengal and Assam in India. Under the Sixth Development Plan (1987–92), the Government proposes to construct and upgrade about 1,000 km of roads to provide vital links to the national road network. In 1986 the Asian Development Bank approved a loan of US $4.5m. towards a $8.2m. roadworks mechanization project. In 1985 there were 840 licensed drivers (387 for light vehicles, 453 for heavy vehicles) in Bhutan. There is a shortage of road transport. Yaks, ponies and mules are still the chief means of transport on the rough mountain tracks. The Government operates a bus company (see below) and there are several privately-owned bus companies, which operate services between major towns.

Bhutan Government Transport Service (BGTS): Phuntsholing; tel. Thimphu 2345; f. 1962; operates a fleet of 111 buses (1985); services include a twice-daily minibus service between Thimphu and Phuntsholing; Man. Dir LHENDUP DORJI; brs in most towns.

Transport Corpn of Bhutan: POB 7, Phuntsholing; tel. 476; telex 890305; f. 1982; subsidiary of Royal Insurance Corpn of Bhutan; operates direct coach service between Phuntsholing and Calcutta.

Lorries for transporting goods are operated by the private sector.

CIVIL AVIATION

There is an international airport at Paro, and a domestic airport at Yangphulla which serves the east of the country. There are numerous helicopter landing pads.

Druk-Air Corpn (Royal Bhutan Airlines): POB 209, Tashidekhang, Main Market, Thimphu; tel. 2215; telex 890219; national airline; f. 1981; became fully operational in February 1983; daily service between Paro and Calcutta and a weekly service between Paro and Dhaka; charter services also undertaken; operates a minibus service between Paro and Thimphu; Chair. HRH Ashi SONAM CHHODEN WANGCHUCK; Man. Dir UGYEN NAMGYAL; fleet of 1 BAe 146-100 and 2 18-seat Dornier 228200 aircraft.

Tourism

Bhutan was opened to tourism in 1974, and the tourist seasons are from March to June and September to December. From 1974 to 1982 all tourists arrived by road via India. In 1983 Druk-Air began regular flights between Calcutta and Paro. In 1986 Druk-Air began daily flights between Calcutta and Paro. By 1988 there was also a weekly service between Dhaka and Paro. In 1987 the total number of foreign visitors was 2,524. Tourists travel in organized 'package' or trekking tours, or individually accompanied by government-appointed guides. Hotels have been constructed by the Department of Tourism and Communications at Phuntsholing, Paro and Thimphu, with lodges at Tongsa, Bumthang and Manas. Government-operated guest-houses are maintained in the principal towns. There are also many small privately-operated hotels and guest-houses. The first mountaineering expedition took place in 1983, to Mt Jichudrake. In early 1987 Mt Gangar Phunsum, one of the world's highest unclimbed mountains, was forbidden to climbers, to respect the wishes of the local people. Central Bhutan was opened for trekkers and coach tours in 1982, and tours to eastern Bhutan commenced in 1988. The Government exercises close control over the development of tourism. In July 1987 the National Assembly resolved that all monasteries, mountains and other holy places should be inaccessible to tourists from 1988.

Bhutan Tourism Corpn (BTC): POB 159, Thimphu; tel. 2647; telex 890217; state organization; operates two hotels for tourists; Dir JIGME TSHULTIM; Sales and Promotion Man. DAGO BEDA.

BOLIVIA

Introductory Survey

Location, Climate, Language, Religion, Flag, Capital

The Republic of Bolivia is a land-locked state in South America, bordered by Chile and Peru to the west, by Brazil to the north and east, and by Paraguay and Argentina to the south. The climate varies, according to altitude, from humid tropical conditions in the northern and eastern lowlands, which are less than 500 m (1,640 ft) above sea-level, to the cool and cold zones at altitudes of more than 3,500 m (about 11,500 ft) in the Andes mountains. The official languages are Spanish, Quechua and Aymará. Almost all of the inhabitants profess Christianity, and the great majority are adherents of the Roman Catholic Church. The national flag (proportions 3 by 2) has three equal horizontal stripes, of red, yellow and green. The state flag has, in addition, the national emblem (an oval cartouche enclosing a mountain, an alpaca, a breadfruit tree and a sheaf of grain, all surmounted by a condor and superimposed on crossed cannons, rifles and national banners) in the centre of the yellow stripe. The legal capital is Sucre. The administrative capital and seat of government is La Paz.

Recent History

The Incas of Bolivia were conquered by Spain in 1538 and, although there were many revolts against Spanish rule, independence was not achieved until 1825. Bolivian history has been characterized by recurrent internal strife, resulting in a succession of presidents, and frequent territorial disputes with its neighbours, including the 1879–83 War of the Pacific between Bolivia, Peru and Chile, and the Chaco Wars of 1928–30 and 1933–35 against Paraguay.

At a presidential election in May 1951 the largest share of the vote was won by Dr Víctor Paz Estenssoro, the candidate of the Movimiento Nacionalista Revolucionario (MNR), who had been living in Argentina since 1946. He was denied permission to return to Bolivia and contested the election *in absentia*. However, he failed to gain an absolute majority, and the incumbent President transferred power to a junta of army officers. This regime was itself overthrown in April 1952, when a popular uprising, supported by the MNR and a section of the armed forces, enabled Dr Paz Estenssoro to return from exile and assume the presidency. His government, a coalition of the MNR and the Labour Party, committed itself to profound social revolution. It nationalized the tin mines and introduced universal suffrage (the franchise had previously been limited to literate adults) and land reform. Dr Hernán Siles Zuazo, a leading figure in the 1952 revolution, was elected President for the 1956–60 term, and Dr Paz Estenssoro was again elected President in 1960. However, the powerful trade unions came into conflict with the Government, and in November 1964, following widespread strikes and disorder, President Paz Estenssoro was overthrown by the Vice-President, Gen. René Barrientos Ortuño, supported by the army. After serving with Gen. Alfredo Ovando Candía as Co-President under a military junta, Gen. Barrientos resigned in January 1966 to campaign for the presidency. He was elected in July 1966.

President Barrientos met strong opposition from left-wing groups, including mineworkers' unions. There was also a guerrilla uprising in south-eastern Bolivia, led by Dr Ernesto ('Che') Guevara, the Argentine-born revolutionary who played a leading role in the Castro regime in Cuba. However, the insurgency was suppressed by government troops, with the help of US advisers, and guerrilla warfare ended in October 1967, when Guevara was captured and killed. In April 1969 President Barrientos was killed in an air crash and Dr Luis Adolfo Siles Salinas, the Vice-President, succeeded to the presidency. In September 1969, however, President Siles Salinas was deposed by the armed forces, who installed Gen. Ovando in power again. He was forced to resign in October 1970, when, after a power struggle between right-wing and left-wing army officers, Gen. Juan José Torres González, who had support from leftists, emerged as President, pledging support for agrarian reform and worker participation in management. A 'People's Assembly', formed by Marxist politicians, radical students and leaders of trade unions, was allowed to meet and called for extreme socialist measures, causing disquiet in right-wing circles. President Torres was deposed in August 1971 by Col (later Gen.) Hugo Bánzer Suárez, who drew support from the right-wing Falange Socialista Boliviana and a section of the MNR, as well as from the army. In June 1973 President Bánzer announced an imminent return to constitutional government but elections were later postponed to June 1974. The MNR withdrew its support and entered into active opposition.

Following an attempted military coup in June 1974, the Cabinet was replaced by an all-military one. After an attempt to overthrow him in November 1974, President Bánzer declared that elections had been postponed indefinitely and that his military regime would retain power until at least 1980. All political and union activity was banned. Political and industrial unrest in 1976 led President Bánzer to announce that elections would be held in July 1978. Allegations of fraud rendered the elections void but Gen. Juan Pereda Asbún, the armed forces candidate in the elections, staged a successful military coup. In November 1978 his right-wing government was overthrown in another coup, led by Gen. David Padilla Aranciba, Commander-in-Chief of the Army, with the support of national left-wing elements.

Elections were held in July 1979 for a President and a bicameral Congress. The presidential poll resulted in almost equal support for two ex-Presidents, Dr Siles Zuazo (with 36.0% of the vote) and Dr Paz Estenssoro (with 35.9%), who were now leading rival factions of the MNR. Congress, convened in August to resolve the issue, failed to give a majority to any candidate. An interim government was formed under Walter Guevara Arce, President of the Senate, but this administration was overthrown on 1 November by a right-wing army officer, Col Alberto Natusch Busch. He withdrew 15 days later after failing to gain the support of Congress, which elected Dra Lidia Gueiler Tejada, President of the Chamber of Deputies, as interim Head of State pending presidential and legislative elections scheduled for June 1980.

The 1980 presidential election also yielded no clear winner and in July, before Congress could meet to decide between the two main contenders (again Dr Siles Zuazo and Dr Paz Estenssoro), a military junta led by the army commander, Gen. Luis García Meza, staged a coup—the 189th in Bolivia's 154 years of independence. In August 1981 a military uprising forced Gen. García to resign. In September the junta transferred power to the army commander, Gen. Celso Torrelio Villa, who declared his intention to fight official corruption and to return the country to democracy within three years. Labour unrest, provoked by Bolivia's severe economic crisis, was appeased by restitution of trade union and political rights, and a mainly civilian Cabinet was appointed in April 1982. Elections were scheduled for April 1983. The political liberalization disturbed the armed forces, who attempted to create a climate of violence, and President Torrelio resigned in July 1982, amid rumours of an impending coup. The junta installed the less moderate Gen. Guido Vildoso Calderón, the Army Chief of Staff, as President. Unable to resolve the worsening economic crisis or to control a general strike, the military regime announced in September 1982 that power would be handed over in October to the Congress which had originally been elected in 1980. Dr Siles Zuazo, who had obtained most votes in both 1979 and 1980, was duly elected President by Congress, and was sworn in for a four-year term in October 1982.

President Siles Zuazo appointed a coalition Cabinet consisting of members of his own party, the Movimiento Nacionalista Revolucionario de Izquierda (MNRI), the Movimiento de la Izquierda Revolucionaria (MIR) and the Partido Comunista de Bolivia (PCB). Economic aid from the USA and Europe was resumed but the Government found itself unable to fulfil the expectations that had been created by the return to democratic rule. The entire Cabinet resigned in August 1983, and the President appointed a Cabinet in which the number of portfolios that were held by the right-wing of the MNRI, the

Partido Demócrata Cristiano and independents was increased. The MIR joined forces with the MNR and business interests in rejecting the Government's policy of complying with IMF conditions for assistance, which involved harsh economic measures. The Government lost its majority in Congress and faced strikes and mass labour demonstrations. In November the opposition-dominated Senate approved an increase of 100% in the minimum wage, in defiance of the Government's austerity measures. Following a 48-hour general strike, the whole Cabinet resigned once again on 14 December, in anticipation of an opposition motion of censure; the ministers accused the Senate of planning a 'constitutional coup' and called for the formation of a government of national unity. In January 1984 President Siles Zuazo appointed a new coalition Cabinet, including 13 members of the previous Government.

The new Cabinet's main priority was to tackle Bolivia's grave economic decline. However, constant industrial agitation by the trade union confederation, the Central Obrera Boliviana (COB), coupled with rumours of an imminent coup, seriously undermined public confidence in the President. The subsequent introduction of austerity measures resulted in widespread protests. The Government therefore agreed to a series of economic concessions, including a moratorium on Bolivia's foreign debt to commercial banks. In June, however, the country was again thrown into turmoil by the temporary abduction of President Siles Zuazo. Two former Cabinet ministers and some 100 right-wing army officers were arrested in connection with the kidnapping, which was believed to have been supported by leading drug dealers.

In September 1984 the Government faced another crisis, following the discovery of a plot by extreme right-wing groups to overthrow the President. Following the disclosure that Congress had ordered an enquiry into suspected links between the Government and cocaine dealers, President Siles Zuazo undertook a five-day hunger strike in a bid to secure national unity and stability. In November another general strike was held, and the President announced that he would leave office a year early, in August 1985, after a general election, to be held in June. In January 1985 a new Cabinet was formed, comprising only members of the MNRI and independents. In the same month it was announced that an attempted coup by former military officers had been thwarted.

Following the Government's decision to introduce a new series of austerity measures, in March 1985 the COB called a general strike, which lasted for 16 days. The Government's offer to form a 'co-administrative' joint government with the trade unions was rejected by the COB, whose leaders advocated a revolution as the only solution to the crisis. The strike was eventually halted when a majority of union leaders accepted the Government's offer of a pay increase of more than 300%.

The principal consequence of the general strike was the Government's decision to postpone the general election until July 1985. At the election, amid reports of electoral malpractice and poor organization, the right-wing Acción Democrática Nacionalista (ADN), whose presidential candidate was Gen. Hugo Bánzer Suárez (the former dictator), received 28.6% of the votes cast, and the MNR obtained 26.4%, while the MIR was the leading left-wing party. At a further round of voting in Congress in August, an alliance between the MNR and the leading left-wing groups, including the MIR, enabled Dr Víctor Paz Estenssoro of the MNR to secure the presidency (which he had previously held in 1952–56 and 1960–64). The armed forces pledged their support for the new Government.

On taking office in August, the new Government immediately introduced a very strict economic programme, designed to reduce inflation, which was estimated to have reached 14,173% in the year to August. The COB rejected the programme and called an indefinite general strike in September. The Government responded by declaring the strike illegal and by ordering a 90-day state of siege throughout Bolivia. Leading trade unionists were detained or banished, and thousands of strikers were arrested. The strike was called off in October, when union leaders agreed to hold talks with the Government. The conclusion of the strike was regarded as a considerable success for the new administration which, in spite of having achieved office with the assistance of left-wing parties, had subsequently found a greater ally in the right-wing ADN. The alliance between the two parties was consolidated by the signing of a 'pacto por la democracia' in October. The collapse of the world tin market in late 1985 had a catastrophic impact on the Bolivian economy. In January 1986 the Cabinet resigned to enable the President to modify government policies, but Paz Estenssoro remained fully committed to the economic programme.

In July the Government was strongly criticized by opposition groups and trade unions when 160 US soldiers arrived in Bolivia to participate in a joint campaign with the Bolivian armed forces to eradicate illegal coca plantations. The Government was accused of having contravened the Constitution and of compromising national sovereignty. The allocation of US aid, however, was to be conditional upon the elimination of Bolivia's illegal cocaine trade. In October the US administration agreed to provide more than US $100m. in aid to continue the drug eradication campaign, and US troops were withdrawn, so that the Bolivian authorities could assume responsibility for the campaign. However, within a few months of the troops' withdrawal, cocaine production was once again flourishing; the price of coca leaves recovered, and workshops for the conversion of coca paste into cocaine had resumed operations.

Throughout 1986, demonstrations and strikes were held by the COB in protest at the Government's austerity measures. Following a 48-hour general strike in August, the Government imposed a state of siege for 90 days. Opposition politicians and trade unionists were detained, while a strike by miners, protesting at reductions in tin production, continued until union leaders were released in exchange for a promise to return to work. However, social unrest persisted in 1987, and President Paz Estenssoro threatened to reimpose the state of siege. Several ministers were replaced in a Cabinet reshuffle in February 1987.

Discontent with the Government's austerity policies was demonstrated by the results of the municipal elections of December 1987. The ADN and MIR emerged as the two major parties. Nevertheless, the 'pacto por la democracia' between the MNR and the ADN remained in force, as the ADN had lost a considerable amount of its support to the MIR. After the election, the Government entered into negotiations with the COB, in an attempt to avert further social unrest. In February 1988 discussions were halted, after the price of petrol was raised again. Widescale unrest followed, culminating in April with a national hunger strike, called by the COB, to protest against the Government's plans for the decentralization of the health and education services and against the continuing austerity measures. These problems led to the resignation of the Cabinet, after the MNR party congress in August, although all but four ministers were reappointed. Presidential and legislative elections were to be held in May 1989. In September 1988 Gonzalo Sánchez de Losada, hitherto Minister of Planning, was confirmed as the MNR's presidential candidate. The ADN candidate was to be Gen. Hugo Bánzer Suárez, as in 1985.

Further measures to reduce the production of coca were taken during 1988. An anti-narcotics department was established in April. The drug control troops, UMOPAR, were provided with greater resources and were further supported by a coca limitation law (adopted by the Bolivian Congress in July), restricting to 12,000 ha the land allowed for coca production (the leaves to be used for 'traditional' purposes only). In the same month, Roberto Suárez, Bolivia's leading cocaine-trafficker, was arrested and imprisoned for trading in illicit drugs. Suárez's arrest led to the exposure of drug-trading involving leading members of the ADN, and was linked to a bomb attack on US Secretary of State George Shultz's motorcade in La Paz in August, during a visit to show support for the campaign against coca production.

The long-standing issue of possible Bolivian access to the Pacific Ocean through Chilean territory, tension over which caused a break in diplomatic relations between the two countries in 1978, has yet to be resolved. The Government of Paz Estenssoro affirmed its intention to reopen negotiations on the issue. In September 1986 the Bolivian and Chilean Governments signed an agreement to promote improved political, social and economic ties between both countries. In November 1987, after repeated Chilean intransigence, the OAS voted in favour of giving Bolivia access to the sea. Only Chile voted against the proposal. The Chilean Ministry of Foreign Affairs rejected a proposal of papal mediation as a solution to the dispute.

BOLIVIA

Government

Legislative power is held by the bicameral Congress, comprising a Senate (27 members) and a Chamber of Deputies (130 members). Both houses are elected for a four-year term by universal adult suffrage. Executive power is vested in the President and the Cabinet, which the President appoints. The President is also directly elected for four years. If no candidate gains a majority of votes, the President is chosen by Congress. The country is divided, for administrative purposes, into nine departments, each of which is governed by a prefect, appointed by the President.

Defence

Military service, for one year, is selective. In June 1988 the armed forces numbered 27,600 men, of whom the army had 20,000 (including 15,000 conscripts), the air force 4,000, and the navy 3,600. The defence budget for 1986 was the equivalent of 180.49m. bolivianos.

Economic Affairs

Although well endowed with natural resources, Bolivia is a relatively poor country in terms of average income. The main sector of the economy is agriculture, which contributed 24% of gross domestic product (GDP) in 1987, and is largely traditional and labour-intensive, with low levels of productivity. Between 1980 and 1987, according to estimates by the World Bank, the average annual growth in Bolivia's population was 2.9%, while, over the same period, real gross national product (GNP) per head declined by an average rate of 5.4% per year. In 1987, according to World Bank data, GNP (measured at average 1985–87 prices) was US $4,150m., equivalent to $570 per head. The average annual growth of GDP, measured in constant prices, was 4.5% in 1965–80, but in 1980–86 GDP declined by an average annual rate of 3.0%.

Bolivia possesses large reserves of petroleum, natural gas and metalliferous ores, as well as potential for large-scale agricultural development, but lack of investment has left most of these resources unexploited. Agriculture employs almost one-half of the working population. Although subsistence farming predominates in the central highlands, agricultural production is more effective in the tropical lowlands. Potatoes, maize, rice and wheat are the principal agricultural products for domestic consumption, while cane sugar, cotton, coffee and, increasingly, timber are the principal agricultural exports. In the mid-1980s severe drought and floods resulted in a decline in agricultural production, and caused severe hardship. Sugar and cotton crops were particularly affected. The output of paddy rice was 173,200 metric tons in 1985, but declined to 137,000 tons in 1986, and to 130,000 tons in 1987. In 1986 the Government announced that a proportion of a US $55m. loan from the World Bank would be allocated to the agricultural sector.

Between 1976 and 1980 there was rapid expansion in the cultivation of coca, a shrub whose leaves are the source of the stimulant drug cocaine, which is traded illicitly. By 1984 it was calculated that 75% of all cultivated land was used for coca production. It was reported that Bolivia's annual exports of semi-pure cocaine base were in excess of 12,000 metric tons, with a value of between $1,000m. and $2,000m. The principal coca-growing area is El Chaparé. Although a joint Bolivian-US campaign to eradicate illegal coca plantations, launched in mid-1986, was moderately successful, one negative consequence of the campaign was expected to be a substantial increase in the rate of unemployment, caused by the elimination of the only source of income for many of the rural population. In 1987 the US Government announced a reduction in aid to Bolivia of $8.7m. because the Bolivian Government's efforts to eradicate the coca crop had not been sufficiently effective. In September 1988 Bolivia launched an international appeal in an attempt to raise $380m. in order to finance the coca eradication programme.

For many years, Bolivia has been a leading producer of tin, antimony and tungsten (wolfram), but, as a high-cost producer, the country has been vulnerable to changes in market demand. By 1984 Bolivia's mining sector was operating at only 50% of total capacity, and contributed only 8% of GDP. Low world prices (below the costs of production and transport) since 1980 have led to a serious decline in tin production. In 1987 output fell to 8,128 metric tons, a fall of 50% from 1985. COMIBOL, the state mining corporation, incurred a financial loss of US $258.5m. in 1985. The suspension of tin trading on the London Metal Exchange in October 1985 proved to be disastrous for the Bolivian mining industry. Foreign exchange earnings from tin exports fell from $247.7m. in 1984 to only $68.5m. in 1987. In August 1986 the Government announced plans to rationalize COMIBOL's operations, whereby control of 24 mines passed to the Government, leaving COMIBOL to manage 13 mines as subsidiaries. Two further mines were to be closed, and nine mines were to be made available for leasing. In the year to mid-1987 the COMIBOL labour force declined from 27,500 to 7,000. Other mineral deposits include lead, gold, silver, zinc and copper. Output of these metals has also fallen since 1980 but, with the exception of copper, there was some recovery in 1987. In March 1984 COMIBOL was granted rights to control the export of all minerals and to exploit Bolivia's gold deposits. Gold exports rose from 610 kg in 1986 to 1,587 kg in 1987. Export earnings from lead increased from $537,000 in 1985 to $20.8m. in 1986, but fell to $3.9m. in 1987. Earnings from silver increased from $10.2m. in 1985 to $31.7m. in 1987. In August 1985 the Government announced plans to exploit the reserves of lithium and potassium at Uyuni, which are estimated to be the largest of their kind in the world.

By August 1984 production of crude petroleum had fallen to 22,000 barrels per day (b/d), while domestic consumption had reached 21,000 b/d. In 1984 the Government announced emergency measures to stimulate an increase in production, which included the use of a loan of $134m. from the Inter-American Development Bank (IDB, see p. 156) for further exploration and the development of oilfields in Santa Cruz and Camiri. In 1987 production averaged 24,753 b/d, all of which was consumed domestically. Petroleum reserves were estimated at 151m. barrels in mid-1986. In spite of a significant discovery north of La Paz in 1985, Bolivia was expected to begin importing petroleum to meet domestic demand. The Government has expressed its eagerness to attract foreign investors to the sector, and in August 1988 Occidental Petroleum signed an agreement for oil prospecting in Madre de Dios and Lapachos, while part of a $115m. loan from the IDB, made in March, went towards an oil development project. Between 1983 and 1986 natural gas was Bolivia's main legal export, providing $328.6m. in export earnings in 1986. In 1987, however, revenue from gas exports fell to $148.6m., owing to a decline in international prices. In 1984 reserves of gas were estimated at 142,000m. cu m. Production of natural gas totalled 161,200m. cu ft (nearly 4,565m. cu m) in 1987. Bolivia is under contract to supply 21m. cu m per day to Argentina until 1992. In 1988 Brazil agreed to buy 3m. cu m per day for 25 years from 1992. A 660-km pipeline was to be built for the purpose. The Bolivia Power Company was nationalized in 1982.

The embryonic industrial sector has received some impetus from Andean Group agreements (see p. 90). Production expanded rapidly in the 1960s and 1970s. In August 1979 the Instituto Nacional de Inversiones approved 18 new industrial projects, including schemes involving the processing of mineral and agricultural products and the establishment of textile and engineering plants. Industrial production has, however, suffered from social unrest and political instability; it declined by an average annual rate of 7.5% in 1980–86, with manufacturing output falling by 9.0% per year. The manufacturing sector contributed 13% of GDP in 1986.

After achieving an economic growth rate averaging 6.3% annually between 1973 and 1977, Bolivia's GDP increased by only 0.8% in 1980, and there were falls in GDP in all subsequent years to 1986, largely as a result of declining production of petroleum, gas and metallic minerals, and falling agricultural output. The level of gross domestic investment decreased by an average rate of 17.3% annually in 1980–86. On taking office in August 1985, President Víctor Paz Estenssoro affirmed his commitment to renegotiating Bolivia's foreign debt, estimated at $4,900m., and to encouraging foreign investment in the petroleum and metal-mining sectors. However, the Government's main priority was to reduce inflation, estimated at 14,173% in the year to August. The Government's economic programme was based on a series of drastic anti-inflation measures, including: a 95% devaluation of the peso, a 10-fold increase in petroleum prices, the elimination of all price subsidies, a four-month 'freeze' on wages in the public sector and the lifting of currency controls. By 1986 the budget deficit had fallen to 4% of GDP, compared with 28% of GDP in 1984. A new unit of currency, the boliviano (equivalent to 1m. pesos), was introduced in January 1987. Although the Government's policies won the immediate support of the business community and international agencies, protests and strikes by workers continued. The Government, however, remained committed to its original programme of austerity measures. Although Bolivia failed to meet all the economic targets that had been established as conditions for financial aid from the IMF and international lending agencies, inflation was successfully reduced, from an average annual rate of 11,973% in 1985, to below 100% in 1986. In July 1987 the annual rate of inflation stood at only 10.5%, although by July 1988 it had risen to 15.3%. The economy as a whole, however, remained fragile. Unemployment affected 20% of the economically active population in 1986, compared with 18% in 1985. In mid-1987 the COB claimed that 28% of workers were without full-time employment, whereas the Government claimed that the proportion was 18%. After several years of decline, real GDP increased by 2.2% in 1987.

In September 1986 the Government announced plans to invest US $2,100m., over the following three years, in a series of schemes to promote Bolivia's economic recovery, concentrating, in particular, on the promotion of exports of timber, coffee, soya and vegetable oil. A new programme to revitalize the economy was announced in July 1987. To be financed mainly by external aid, the plan envisaged expenditure of more than $1,500m., of which $480m. was to be provided in 1987–89 by the IDB and $322m. by bilateral agencies. A total of $1,079m. was to be allocated to the public sector, and included investment in hydrocarbons, transport, agricultural and mining projects. These projects helped to increase industrial output by 7.2% in 1987. This increase, coupled with the reduction in inflation, drew praise from the World Bank and ensured further lending. In June 1988, in addition to the $27m. agreed in March for the support of the Bolivian Government's social programme, the World Bank approved a credit of $70m. to improve the balance of trade, while loans were granted from the IDB, Italy and Japan to stimulate industrial production and improve communications.

A sharp decline in tin prices in 1985, followed by a dispute with Argentina over payment for gas sales, had contributed to an increase in the current deficit on the balance of payments in 1986 and early 1987. However, this situation was eased, firstly by the IMF's endorsement of a proposal for three years' extended credit of $173.3m. in mid-1987, and subsequently when a settlement was reached with Argentina which, it was hoped, would result in annual revenue of $300m. from the sale of gas. The IMF also administered a trust fund, to which donations had been made by supportive governments. This enabled Bolivia, in March 1988, to buy back 47% of its private bank debt for $33.5m., which was 11% of its original value. In July the IMF announced a loan arrangement of $236m. (to be disbursed over three years), to offset the decline in Bolivia's export earnings and the rise in imports. In November the 'Paris Club' of creditor governments agreed to defer Bolivia's debt repayments until 1995. In mid-1988 the Government introduced a series of emergency price controls to neutralize the effect of the rise in the price of petrol on inflation. Two investment programmes, to be implemented over three years (1988–90), were also announced: a total of $1,710m. was to be invested in various projects. Another scheme to assist Bolivia in meeting some of its foreign debt obligations is in the form of 'debt-for-nature' exchanges. In 1987 a US environmental group agreed to purchase some $650,000 of Bolivia's external debt in return for the country's commitment to a conservation programme in the Amazon river basin. At mid-1988 Bolivia's total foreign debt stood at $4,209m. The Central Bank's gross and net reserves stood at $300m. and $200m. respectively in September 1988.

Bolivia's principal trading partners in 1987 were Argentina, which supplied 14% of imports and took 46% of exports, the USA, which supplied 19% of imports and took 17% of exports, and Brazil. Bolivia participates in the trade agreements negotiated by the Latin American Integration Association (see p. 170). In July 1988 a joint commission was established with Brazil to correct the imbalance in trade between the two countries by removing duties on Bolivian products and permitting the entry of more goods into Brazil.

Social Welfare

There are benefits for unemployment, accident, sickness, old age and death. In 1978 the Government established a social security and health scheme covering 1.66m. rural workers. In 1978 there were 1,158 hospitals, clinics and medical posts, with 3,410 physicians. Of total expenditure by the central Government in 1984, about 102,200m. pesos (1.5%) was for health, and a further 359,300m. pesos (5.2%) for social security and welfare.

Education

Primary education, beginning at six years of age and lasting for eight years, is officially compulsory and is available free of charge. Secondary education, which is not compulsory, begins at 14 years of age and lasts for up to four years. In 1984 the total enrolment at primary and secondary schools was equivalent to 75% of the school-age population (80% of boys; 70% of girls). In 1984 an estimated 81% of children in the relevant age-group (86% of boys; 77% of girls) attended primary schools, while the comparable ratio for secondary enrolment was only 25% (27% of boys; 23% of girls). There are eight state universities and two private universities. In 1976 the average rate of adult illiteracy was 36.8% (males 24.2%; females 48.6%), but by 1985, according to UNESCO estimates, the rate had declined to 25.8% (males 16.2%; females 34.9%). Expenditure on education by the central Government in 1984 was about 843,100m. pesos, representing 12.2% of total spending.

Public Holidays

1989: 2 January (for New Year), 22 February (Oruro only), 24 March (Good Friday), 15 April (Tarija only), 2 May (for Labour Day), 25 May (Sucre only), 2 June (Corpus Christi), 16 July (La Paz only), 6 August (Independence), 14 September (Cochabamba only), 24 September (Santa Cruz and Cobija only), 1 November (All Saints' Day), 10 November (Potosí only), 18 November (Beni only), 25 December (Christmas).

1990: 1 January (New Year), 22 February (Oruro only), 13 April (Good Friday), 15 April (Tarija only), 1 May (Labour Day), 25 May (Sucre only), 14 June (Corpus Christi), 17 July (La Paz only), 6 August (Independence), 14 September (Cochabamba only), 25 September (Santa Cruz and Cobija only), 1 November (All Saints' Day), 10 November (Potosí only), 18 November (Beni only), 25 December (Christmas).

Weights and Measures

The metric system is officially in force, but various old Spanish measures are also used.

Statistical Survey

Sources (unless otherwise indicated): Instituto Nacional de Estadística, Plaza Mario Guzmán Aspiazu No. 1, Casilla 6129, La Paz; tel. (02) 367443; Banco Central de Bolivia, Ayacucho esq. Mercado, Casilla 3118, La Paz; tel. (02) 350726; telex 2286.

Area and Population

AREA, POPULATION AND DENSITY

Area (sq km)	
Land	1,084,391
Inland water	14,190
Total	1,098,581*
Population (census results)†	
5 September 1950	2,704,165
29 September 1976	
Males	2,276,029
Females	2,337,457
Total	4,613,486
Population (official estimates at mid-year)	
1985	6,380,580
1986	6,557,959
1987	6,740,417
Density (per sq km) at mid-1987	6.1

* 424,164 sq miles.
† Figures exclude adjustment for underenumeration. This was estimated at 8.4% in 1950 and 6.99% in 1976. The adjusted total for 1950 is 3,019,031, including an estimate of 87,000 for the tribal Indian population.

DEPARTMENTS (estimated population at mid-1987)

	Population	Capital
Beni	273,285	Trinidad
Chuquisaca	485,979	Sucre
Cochabamba	1,043,616	Cochabamba
La Paz	2,081,733	La Paz
Oruro	427,797	Oruro
Pando	53,644	Cobija
Potosí	829,805	Potosí
Santa Cruz	1,260,711	Santa Cruz de la Sierra
Tarija	283,847	Tarija

PRINCIPAL TOWNS (estimated population at mid-1987)

La Paz (administrative capital)	1,013,688
Santa Cruz de la Sierra	577,803
Cochabamba	360,446
Oruro	189,278
Potosí	111,215
Sucre (legal capital)	92,917
Tarija	65,657

BIRTHS AND DEATHS

	Average birth rate (per 1,000)		Average death rate (per 1,000)	
	Rural	Urban	Rural	Urban
1984	41.8	44.5	12.4	18.2
1985	41.6	44.3	12.1	17.9

ECONOMICALLY ACTIVE POPULATION (1976 census)*

	Males	Females	Total
Agriculture, hunting, forestry and fishing	604,078	88,971	693,049
Mining and quarrying	57,194	3,405	60,599
Manufacturing	88,978	56,426	145,404
Electricity, gas and water	1,987	156	2,143
Construction	81,918	529	82,447
Trade, restaurants and hotels	49,650	57,212	106,862
Transport, storage and communications	54,250	1,722	55,972
Financing, insurance, real estate and business services	10,627	2,314	12,941
Community, social and personal services	165,688	116,223	281,911
Activities not adequately described	44,963	8,637	53,600
Total labour force	1,159,333	335,595	1,494,928

* Excluding persons seeking work for the first time, numbering 6,463 (males 5,286; females 1,177).

1986: Total labour force 1,661,426 (males 1,230,951; females 430,475).

1987: Total labour force 1,673,820.

Agriculture

PRINCIPAL CROPS ('000 metric tons)

	1985	1986	1987
Wheat	74.3	81.2	84.5
Rice (paddy)	173.2	137	130
Barley	75	78	67
Maize	554	457.2	497
Sorghum	68.3	59.3	63.2
Potatoes	768.2	697	610
Cassava (Manioc)	376.2	420	425
Other roots and tubers	80.1	88.7	94.8
Soya beans	83.3	80.9	112
Groundnuts (in shell)	15.2	15	15
Cottonseed	6.9	n.a.	6.4
Cotton (lint)	4.7	4.7	5.5
Sugar cane	3,157.0	2,870.0	2,730.0
Oranges	38.2	40	69
Bananas and plantains	366.5	396	450
Coffee (green)	23.4	23.7	25.2
Natural rubber*	5‡	5‡	n.a.

* Source: FAO, *Production Yearbook*.
† Unofficial estimate.   ‡ FAO estimate.

Source: Departamento de Estadísticas, Ministerio de Asuntos Campesinos y Agropecuarios (MACA).

BOLIVIA

LIVESTOCK ('000 head, year ending September)

	1985*	1986	1987
Horses	311	385†	388‡
Mules	80†	n.a.	n.a.
Asses	600†	n.a.	n.a.
Cattle	5,851	5,300	5,380
Pigs	1,136	1,650	1,690
Sheep	9,287	8,115	8,440
Goats	3,200†	2,360	2,290

* Source: FAO, *Production Yearbook*.
†FAO estimates.   ‡ Unofficial estimates.
Poultry (million): 6.6 in 1984; 7.8 in 1985; 8.1 in 1986.
Source: Departamento de Estadísticas, Ministerio de Asuntos Campesinos y Agropecuarios.

LIVESTOCK PRODUCTS (FAO estimates, '000 metric tons)

	1984	1985	1986
Beef and veal	120	122	115
Mutton and lamb	22	22	22
Goats' meat	3	3	3
Pig meat	35	35	35
Poultry meat	9	10	10
Cows' milk	90	95	95
Sheep's milk	29	30	30
Goats' milk	11	11	11
Cheese	6.9	6.9	7.7
Hens eggs	26.0*	26.0	26.4
Wool:			
greasy	9.3	9.4	9.5
scoured	4.9	5.0	5.1
Cattle hides (fresh)	15.4	15.6	14.4
Sheep skins (fresh)	5.9	6.0	6.0

* Unofficial estimate.
Source: FAO, *Production Yearbook*.

Forestry

ROUNDWOOD REMOVALS
(FAO estimates, '000 cubic metres, excluding bark)

	1984	1985	1986
Sawlogs, veneer logs and logs for sleepers*	136	136	136
Other industrial wood†	13	13	13
Fuel wood	1,133	1,168	1,199
Total	1,282	1,317	1,348

* Assumed to be unchanged since 1983.
† Assumed to be unchanged since 1982.
Source: FAO, *Yearbook of Forest Products*.

SAWNWOOD PRODUCTION ('000 cubic metres)

	1981	1982	1983
Broadleaved sawnwood	168	113	93
Railway sleepers*	4	4	4
Total	172	117	97

* FAO estimates.
1984–86: Annual production as in 1983 (FAO estimates).
Source: FAO, *Yearbook of Forest Products*.

Fishing

('000 metric tons, live weight)

	1984	1985	1986
Total catch	4.4	4.7	4.8*

* FAO estimate.
Source: FAO, *Yearbook of Fishery Statistics*.

Mining

(metric tons, unless otherwise indicated)

	1985	1986	1987
Tin	16,136	10,462	8,128
Lead	6,242	2,568	9,043
Zinc	38,110	33,295	39,122
Copper	1,665	331	9
Tungsten (Wolfram)	2,072	1,360	803
Antimony	8,925	10,240	10,635
Silver	111.0	87	140
Gold	0.6	0.7	2.7
Petroleum (million barrels)	7.2	6.4	6.9
Natural gas ('000 million cu ft)	164.1	160.8	161.2

Sources: Ministerio de Minería y Metalurgia; Yacimientos Petrolíferos Fiscales Bolivianos.

Industry

SELECTED PRODUCTS (metric tons, unless otherwise indicated)

	1985	1986	1987*
Flour	193,750	199,200	100,719
Cement	760,577	863,532	1,352,079
Refined sugar	189,846	173,501	160,649
Coffee	19,732	20,324	22,881
Alcohol ('000 litres)	22,379	20,329	19,193

* Estimates.
Electric Energy (million kWh): 1,668 in 1983; 1,695 in 1984; 1,725 in 1985 (Source: UN, *Industrial Statistics Yearbook*).

Finance

CURRENCY AND EXCHANGE RATES
Monetary Units
  100 centavos = 1 boliviano (B).

Denominations
  Coins: 2, 5, 10, 20 and 50 centavos; 1 boliviano.
  Notes: 2, 5, 10, 20, 50, 100 and 200 bolivianos.

Sterling and Dollar Equivalents (30 September 1988)
  £1 sterling = 4.058 bolivianos;
  US $1 = 2.400 bolivianos;
  100 bolivianos = £24.64 = $41.67.

Average Exchange Rate (bolivianos per US $)
  1985   0.440
  1986   1.922
  1987   2.055

Note: In January 1987 the Bolivian peso was replaced by a new currency, the boliviano, with a value equivalent to 1,000,000 former pesos. Some figures in this Survey are still expressed in terms of pesos.

BOLIVIA

BUDGET ('000 million pesos bolivianos)*

Revenue†	1982	1983	1984
Taxation	17.2	54.4	572.5
Taxes on income, profits and capital gains	3.4	8.4	45.6
Taxes on property	0.4	2.1	6.1
Sales taxes	1.1	3.7	30.7
Excises	6.6	10.2	88.7
Other domestic taxes on goods and services	0.2	19.2	169.7
Import duties	4.4	6.9	146.5
Export duties	0.1	0.2	0.1
Exchange taxes and profits	0.3	2.3	72.4
Taxes on international transport	0.1	0.5	4.3
Stamp taxes	0.5	0.7	9.4
Interest on taxes	0.0	0.2	1.8
Adjustment to tax revenue	0.1	0.0	−2.8
Property income	1.8	5.4	166.9
Administrative fees, charges, etc.	0.0	0.8	4.6
Fines and forfeits	0.0	0.1	0.4
Other current revenue	0.2	1.3	0.3
Total revenue	19.2	62.1	744.7

* Figures refer to the transactions of central government units covered by the General Budget. From 1983, the data also include the activities of other units (government agencies and 32 social security institutions) with their own budgets.
† Excluding grants received ('000 million pesos): 1.4 in 1983; 47.2 in 1984.

Expenditure‡	1982	1983	1984
General public services	10.4	33.0	n.a.
Defence	6.5	17.1	372.1
Education	11.8	42.7	843.1
Health	1.7	4.9	102.2
Social security and welfare	0.3	27.9	359.3
Housing and community amenities	0.5	0.7	13.8
Other community and social services	0.2	0.3	7.2
Economic services	5.4	20.6	364.5
Agriculture, forestry and fishing	0.7	2.1	36.3
Mining, manufacturing and construction	0.2	0.6	10.2
Roads	1.4	4.1	110.6
Other transport	2.5	6.8	142.2
Communications	0.2		15.3
Other purposes	n.a.	11.7	n.a.
Total expenditure	n.a.	158.9	6,891.2
Current§	n.a.	148.2	6,761.1
Capital	1.4	10.7	130.1

‡ Excluding net lending ('000 million pesos): 0.1 in 1982; 0.5 in 1983; 16.0 in 1984.
§ Including interest payments ('000 million pesos): 9.3 in 1983; 150.0 in 1984.
Source: IMF, *Government Finance Statistics Yearbook*.

INTERNATIONAL RESERVES
(US $ million at 31 December)

	1984	1985	1986
Gold*	37.9	37.8	37.8
IMF special drawing rights	—	—	2.0
Foreign exchange	251.6	200.0	161.2
Total	289.5	237.8	201.0

* National valuation.
Source: IMF, *International Financial Statistics*.

MONEY SUPPLY (million bolivianos at 31 December)

	1985	1986	1987
Currency outside banks	174	294	397
Private sector deposits at Central Bank	0	6	6
Demand deposits at commercial banks	24	69	105
Total money	198	369	508

Source: IMF, *International Financial Statistics*.

COST OF LIVING (Consumer Price Index; Base: 1966 = 100)

	1985	1986	1987
Food	15,976,045.04	60,176,942.26	66,345,504.17
Housing	6,579,300.47	22,717,098.15	26,308,337.64
Clothes	9,878,271.51	32,644,777.06	40,628,938.28
Various	9,860,448.76	43,223,610.43	55,669,564.37
All items	12,686,008.01	47,742,001.03	54,702,174.85

NATIONAL ACCOUNTS (million pesos at 1980 prices)
Gross Domestic Product by Economic Activity

	1985*	1986*	1987
Agriculture	26,789	25,534	25,489
Mining (incl. petroleum exploration)	14,284	12,062	11,013
Manufacturing	10,815	11,038	11,037
Electricity	948	987	981
Construction	3,168	2,918	3,080
Transport and fuel	7,337	7,557	8,008
Commerce and finance	27,212	27,867	28,984
Services and rent	3,322	3,356	3,313
Public administration	15,643	14,646	15,056
Sub-total	109,518	105,965	107,761
Taxes on international trade	927	1,246	1,763
Total	110,445	107,211	109,524

* Estimates.

BALANCE OF PAYMENTS (US $ million)

	1985	1986	1987
Merchandise exports f.o.b.	623.4	545.5	470.0
Merchandise imports f.o.b.	−462.8	−596.5	−658.0
Trade balance	160.6	−51.0	−188.0
Exports of services	114.0	138.7	143.0
Imports of services	−636.5	−571.9	−572.0
Balance on goods and services	−361.9	−484.2	−617.0
Private unrequited transfers (net)	19.7	18.5	20.2
Government unrequited transfers (net)	59.8	81.5	109.0
Current balance	−282.4	−384.2	−487.8
Direct capital investment (net)	10.0	10.0	22.0
Other long-term capital (net)	−244.8	−172.4	−90.8
Short-term capital (net)	−2.2	107.5	7.8
Net errors and omissions	190.0	136.2	9.4
Total (net monetary movements)	−329.4	−302.9	−539.4
Monetization of gold (net)	−0.1	—	—
Valuation changes (net)	3.8	−7.2	−23.8
Exceptional financing (net)	352.6	468.4	441.8
Official financing (net)	−62.7	−59.2	40.9
Changes in reserves	−35.8	99.1	−80.5

Source: IMF, *International Financial Statistics*.

BOLIVIA

External Trade

PRINCIPAL COMMODITIES (US $ million)

Imports	1985	1986	1987
Consumer goods	132.5	174.3	124.8
Non-durable	26.6	42.6	52.0
Durable	69.9	70.6	72.8
Raw materials	182.1	248.8	314.1
Materials for agriculture	14.6	21.6	21.8
Materials for industry	184.6	200.2	245.3
Capital goods	231.8	283	322.5
Construction	21.0	34	43.7
Agriculture	21.8	44.7	37.6
Industry	109.2	172.7	180.2
Transport equipment	71.1	112.9	104.7
Total (incl. others)	551.9	711.5	776.0

Exports	1985	1986	1987
Minerals	263.7	196.8	202.2
Natural gas	372.5	328.6	148.6
Coffee	13.9	13.2	11.5
Sugar	1.7	4.8	8.6
Wood	5.8	23.3	n.a.
Rubber	5.3	3.7	1.8
Chestnuts	1.4	3.5	6.6
Hides	1.6	6.4	8.1
Cattle	1.1	13.4	6.7
Total (incl. others)	672.7	637.5	569.6

Source: Ministerio de Industria, Comercio y Turismo.

EXPORTS OF MINING PRODUCTS (US $ '000)

	1985	1986	1987
Tin	186,647	104,100	68,480
Tungsten	10,292	6,649	5,050
Antimony	15,928	14,499	22,860
Lead	537	20,810	3,940
Zinc	29,485	28,010	32,521
Copper	1,709	777	12*
Silver	10,192	27,293	31,740

* Source: Instituto Nacional de Estadística; Departamento Comercio Exterior.
Source: Ministerio de Minería y Metalurgia.

PRINCIPAL TRADING PARTNERS (US $ '000)

Imports	1985*	1986	1987
Argentina	82,800	75,610	45,689
Belgium	4,400	16,416	4,863
Brazil	115,900	124,405	73,990
Canada	4,900	4,697	3,974
Chile	27,600	34,301	23,252
France	9,900	6,239	2,269
Germany, Federal Republic	39,700	45,873	20,428
Italy	4,400	5,497	2,482
Japan	38,600	65,333	30,598
Netherlands	9,400	5,783	2,752
Peru	27,600	14,890	5,716
Sweden	3,900	8,719	4,309
Switzerland	5,000	4,826	3,519
United Kingdom	11,000	31,009	2,652
USA	121,400	150,052	63,476
Total (incl. others)	551,900	674,033	327,165

* Estimates.

Exports	1985*	1986	1987
Argentina	375,741	340,744	259,886
Belgium	13,962	10,933	17,725
Brazil	4,470	26,037	19,479
Chile	10,659	19,913	16,640
Colombia	3,872	1,873	4,071
France	7,773	5,629	5,232
Germany, Federal Republic	33,542	37,902	33,416
Netherlands	21,730	674	192
Peru	12,716	22,263	24,036
Switzerland	10,554	7,502	6,956
United Kingdom	59,631	50,863	61,004
USA	90,858	97,072	96,077
Total (incl. others)	672,536	640,338	569,793

* Preliminary.

Transport

RAILWAYS (traffic)

	1985	1986
Passengers carried	2,214,000	2,395,000
Passenger-kilometres	748,000	790,386
Freight carried (metric tons)	993,000	1,089,000
Freight ton-kilometres	494,000	531,754

Source: Dirección General de Ferrocarriles.

ROAD TRAFFIC (motor vehicles in use)

	1986	1987
Cars	69,836	78,160
Buses	11,271	11,911
Trucks	38,329	41,677
Lorries	36,639	40,169
Vans	26,639	29,978
Jeeps	17,918	19,241
Motor cycles	47,379	47,814

CIVIL AVIATION (traffic on scheduled services)

	1982	1983	1984
Kilometres flown (million)	10.5	9.7	11.0
Passengers carried ('000)	1,160	1,299	1,359
Passenger-km (million)	780	787	877
Freight ton-km (million)	27.6	17.2	38.0

Source: United Nations, *Statistical Yearbook*.

Tourism

	1982	1983	1984
Arrivals at hotels	150,142	175,903	163,183

Education

(1986)

	Institutions*	Teachers†	Students
Primary and elementary	9,093	51,038	1,355,338
Pre-basic	1,065	1,954	137,018
Basic	6,633	40,104	947,291
Intermediate	1,395	8,980	271,029
Middle	909	7,970	206,405
Other	—	2,405	18,551
Total	10,002	62,413	1,580,294

* 1984 figures. † 1985 figures.

Directory

The Constitution

Bolivia became an independent republic in 1825 and received its first constitution in November 1826. Since that date a number of new constitutions have been promulgated. Following the *coup d'état* of November 1964, the Constitution of 1947 was revived. Under its provisions, executive power is vested in the President. According to the revised Constitution, the President is elected by direct suffrage for a four-year term and is not eligible for immediate re-election. In the event of the President's death or failure to assume office, the Vice-President or, failing the Vice-President, the President of the Senate becomes interim Head of State.

The President has power to appoint members of the Cabinet, diplomatic representatives, and archbishops and bishops from a panel proposed by the Senate. The President is responsible for the conduct of foreign affairs and is also empowered to issue decrees, and initiate legislation by special messages to Congress.

Congress consists of a Senate (27 members) and a Chamber of Deputies (130 members). Congress meets annually and its ordinary sessions last only 90 working days, which may be extended to 120. Each of the nine departments (La Paz, Chuquisaca, Oruro, Beni, Santa Cruz, Potosí, Tarija, Cochabamba and Pando), into which the country is divided for administrative purposes, elects three senators. Members of both houses are elected for four years.

The supreme administrative, political and military authority in each department is vested in a prefect appointed by the President. The sub-divisions of each department, known as provinces, are administered by sub-prefects. The provinces are further divided into cantons. There are 94 provinces and some 1,000 cantons. The capital of each department has its autonomous municipal council and controls its own revenue and expenditure.

Public order, education and roads are under national control.

A decree issued in July 1952 conferred the franchise on all persons who had reached the age of 21 years, whether literate or illiterate. Previously the franchise had been restricted to literate persons. (The voting age for married persons was to be lowered to 18 years at the 1989 elections.)

The death penalty was restored in October 1971 for terrorism, kidnapping and crimes against government and security personnel. In 1981 its scope was extended to drug trafficking.

The Government

HEAD OF STATE

President: Dr VÍCTOR PAZ ESTENSSORO (took office 6 August 1985).

Vice-President: JULIO GARRET AYLLÓN.

THE CABINET
(December 1988)

Minister of Foreign Affairs, Economic Integration and Religion: GUILLERMO BEDREGAL GUTIÉRREZ.
Minister of Finance: RAMIRO CABEZAS.
Minister of Planning and Co-ordination: ORLANDO ROMERO.
Minister of Education and Culture: Prof. ENRIQUE IPIÑA MELGAR.
Minister of Labour: ALFONSO RUEDA PEÑA.
Minister of Urban Development and Housing: FRANKLIN ANAYA.
Minister of the Interior and Justice: JUAN CARLOS DURÁN SAUCEDO.
Minister of National Defence: ALFONSO WALTER REVOLLO THENIER.
Minister of Industry, Commerce and Tourism: LUIS PALENQUE.
Minister of Transport and Communications: ANDRÉS PETRICEVIC.
Minister of Public Health and Social Security: JOAQUÍN ARCE.
Minister of Mining and Metallurgy: JAIME VILLALOBOS.
Minister of Rural and Farming Affairs: JOSÉ JUSTINIANO PASTOR.
Minister of Energy and Hydrocarbons: FERNANDO ILLANES.
Minister of Aviation: Gen. JAIME ZEGADA HURTADO.
Minister of Information: HERNÁN ANTELO.
Secretary-General of the Presidency: WALTER ZULETA RONCAL.

MINISTRIES

Office of the President: Palacio de Gobierno, Plaza Murillo, La Paz; tel. (02) 371317; telex 5242.
Ministry of Aviation: Avda Arce 2579, Casilla 6176, La Paz; tel. (02) 374142; telex 3413.
Ministry of Economic Planning: Avda Arce 2147, La Paz; tel. (02) 372060; telex 5321.
Ministry of Education and Culture: Avda Arce, La Paz; tel. (02) 373260; telex 5242.
Ministry of Energy and Hydrocarbons: Avda Mariscal Santa Cruz 1322, La Paz; tel. (02) 374050; telex 5366.
Ministry of Finance: Calle Bolívar, La Paz; tel. (02) 379240; telex 2617.
Ministry of Foreign Affairs, Economic Integration and Religion: Edif. BCB, 6° piso, La Paz; tel. (02) 371152; telex 5242.
Ministry of Industry, Commerce and Tourism: Avda Camacho esq. Bueno, Casilla 1372, La Paz; tel. (02) 372044; telex 3259.
Ministry of the Interior and Justice: Avda Arce, La Paz; tel. (02) 370460; telex 5437.
Ministry of Labour: Calle Yanacocha esq. Calle Mercado, La Paz; tel. (02) 374351; telex 5242.
Ministry of Mining and Metallurgy: Avda 16 de Julio 1769, La Paz; tel. (02) 379310; telex 5564.
Ministry of National Defence: Plaza Abaroa esq. 20 de Octubre, La Paz; tel. (02) 377130; telex 5242.
Ministry of Public Health and Social Security: Plaza del Estudiante, La Paz; tel. (02) 375460; telex 5242.
Ministry of Rural and Farming Affairs: Avda Camacho 1407, La Paz; tel. (02) 374260; telex 5242.
Ministry of Transport and Communications: Edif. La Urbana, Avda Camacho, La Paz; tel. (02) 377220; telex 2648.
Ministry of Urban Development and Housing: Avda 20 de Octubre esq. F. Guachalla, Casilla 5926, La Paz; tel. (02) 372240; telex 5242.

Legislature

NATIONAL CONGRESS

Election, 14 July 1985
(names of the presidential candidates are given in parentheses)

Party	Seats
Movimiento Nacionalista Revolucionario (Histórico) (Dr VÍCTOR PAZ ESTENSSORO)	59
Acción Democrática Nacionalista (Gen. HUGO BÁNZER SUÁREZ)	51
Movimiento de la Izquierda Revolucionaria (JAIME PAZ ZAMORA)	16
Movimiento Nacionalista Revolucionario de Izquierda (ROBERTO JORDÁN PANDO)	8
Movimiento Nacionalista Revolucionario—Vanguardia Revolucionaria 9 de Abril (CARLOS SERRATE REICHE)	6
Partido Socialista-Uno—Marcelo Quiroga (JOSÉ MARÍA PALACIOS)	5
Frente del Pueblo Unido (ANTONIO ARANÍBAR QUIROGA)	4
Falange Socialista Boliviana (DAVID AÑEZ)	3
Partido Demócrata Cristiano (Dr LUIS OSSIO SANJINES)	3
Movimiento Revolucionario Tupac Katarí (GENARO FLORES SANTOS)	2
Total	**157***

* Comprising 27 Senators and 130 members of the Chamber of Deputies.

President of the Senate: CIRO HUMBOLT BARRERO (MNR).

President of the Chamber of Deputies: WALTER SORIANO (ADN).

Note: As no candidate in the presidential election obtained a clear majority of direct votes, a choice between the three leading contenders was made by the new National Congress on 4–5 August 1985. After two ballots, Dr VÍCTOR PAZ ESTENSSORO (MNR) was

BOLIVIA

declared to have won with 94 votes. Gen. HUGO BÁNZER SUÁREZ (ADN) obtained 51 votes.

The next presidential and legislative elections were to be held on 7 May 1989.

Political Organizations

Acción Democrática Nacionalista (ADN): La Paz; f. 1979; right-wing; Leader and 1989 Presidential Candidate Gen. HUGO BÁNZER SUÁREZ; Sec.-Gen. GUILLERMO FORTÚN.

Alianza Patriótica (AP): La Paz; left-wing; absorbed MIR—Masas (breakaway faction of MIR, f. 1985); Leader WALTER DELGADILLO.

Centro Nacionalista (CEN): Héroes del Arce 1746, Of. La Voz del Pueblo, La Paz; right-wing; Leader Dr ROBERTO ZAPATA DE LA BARRA.

Falange Socialista Boliviano (FSB): La Paz; f. 1937; right-wing; Leaders DAVID AÑEZ, REMY SOLARES; divided into two factions:

  Gutiérrez: Sánchez Lima 2278, La Paz; f. 1937; Leader Dr MARIO GUTIÉRREZ.

  Moreira: Canoniga Ayllón esq. Boquerón 597, Casilla 4937, La Paz; Leader GASTÓN MOREIRA OSTRÍA; Sec.-Gen. Dr AUGUSTO MENDIZÁBAL; 100,000 mems.

Falange Socialista Boliviana de la Izquierda (FSBI): Casilla 1649, La Paz; f. 1970; Leader Dr ENRIQUE RIVEROS ALIAGA; 150,000 mems.

Frente del Pueblo Unido (FPU): left-wing; comprising dissident members of the PRIN, the MIR and the PCB (see below).

Frente Revolucionario de Izquierda (FRI): Mercado 996, 2°, Of. 2, La Paz; left-wing; Leader Dr MANUEL MORALES DÁVILA.

Mandato de Acción y Unidad Nacional (MAN): Comercio 1057, 3°, Casilla 2169, La Paz; f. 1972; Leader Dr GONZALO ROMERO ALVAREZ GARCÍA; Sec. Dr FERNANDO OBLITAS MENDOZA; 2,000 mems.

Movimiento Agrario Revolucionario del Campesinado Boliviano (MARC): Yanacocha 448, Of. 17, La Paz; f. 1978; nationalist movement; Pres. Gen. (retd) RENÉ BERNAL ESCALANTE; Exec. Sec. Dr JOSÉ ZEGARRA CERRUTO.

Movimiento Bolivia Libre (MBL): Calle Potosí No 1315, Casilla 10382, La Paz; tel. 340257; f. 1985; left-wing; breakaway faction of MIR; allied to FPU (see above); Leader ANTONIO ARANÍBAR QUIROGA.

Movimiento de la Izquierda Nacional (MIN): La Paz; left-wing; Leader Dr LUIS SANDOVAL MORÓN.

Movimiento de la Izquierda Revolucionaria (MIR): Avda América 119, 2°, La Paz; telex 3210; f. 1971; split into several factions in 1985; left-wing; Leader JAIME PAZ ZAMORA; Sec.-Gen. OSCAR EID FRANCO.

Movimiento Nacionalista Revolucionario (Histórico)—MNR: Genaro Sanjines 541, Pasaje Kuljis, La Paz; formerly part of the Movimiento Nacionalista Revolucionario (MNR, f. 1942); centre-right; Leader Dr VÍCTOR PAZ ESTENSSORO; Sec.-Gen. JOSÉ LUIS HARB; 1989 Presidential Candidate GONZALO SÁNCHEZ DE LOSADA; 700,000 mems.

Movimiento Nacionalista Revolucionario de Izquierda (MNRI): La Paz; f. 1979; formerly part of the Movimiento Nacionalista Revolucionario (MNR, f. 1942); left of centre; Leader Dr HERNÁN SILES ZUAZO; Sec.-Gen. FEDERICO ALVAREZ PLATA.

Movimiento Nacionalista Revolucionario (MNR)—Julio: Claudio Pinilla 1648, La Paz; formerly part of the Movimiento Nacionalista Revolucionario (MNR, f. 1942); Leader RUBÉN JULIO CASTRO.

Movimiento Nacionalista Revolucionario del Pueblo (MNRP): Casilla 3030, La Paz; f. 1965; nationalist movement; Leader JAIME ARELLANO CASTEÑADA; 50,000 mems.

Movimiento Revolucionario Tupac Katarí (MRTK): Linares esq. Sagáruaga 901, Casilla 3636, La Paz; f. 1978; peasant party; Pres. JUAN CONDORI URUCHI; Leader GENARO FLORES SANTOS; 80,000 mems.

Ofensiva de la Izquierda Democrática (OID): Edif. Herrmann 11°, Plaza Venezuela 1440, La Paz; f. 1979; Leader LUIS ADOLFO SILES SALINAS.

Organización de Unidad Revolucionaria (OUR): Comercio 979, 1°, Of. 14, La Paz; f. 1977; Sec.-Gen. Dr MARIO LANZA SUÁREZ; 5,000 mems.

Partido Comunista de Bolivia (PCB): La Paz; f. 1950; follows Moscow line; First Sec. SIMÓN REYES RIVERA.

Partido Comunista Marxista Leninista de Bolivia: c/o Palacio Legislativo, Palacio Murillo, La Paz; f. 1965; formerly part of the PCB; First Sec. OSCAR ZAMORA MEDINACELLI.

Partido Demócrata Cristiano: Casilla 4345, La Paz; f. 1954; Pres. Dr JORGE AGREDA VALDERRAMA; Sec. ANTONIO CANELAS-GALATOIRE; 50,000 mems.

Partido Indio: La Paz.

Partido Obrero Revolucionario (POR): Correo Central, La Paz; f. 1935; Trotskyist; Leader GUILLERMO LORA.

Partido de la Revolución Nacional (PRN): Saavedra 1026, Casilla 8466, La Paz; f. 1966; left-wing; Leader RUBÉN ARIAS ALVIS; Sec.-Gen. LUIS JIMÉNEZ ESPINOZA; 50,000 mems.

Partido Revolucionario Auténtico (PRA): Yanacocha 448, Of. 2, La Paz; f. 1960; formerly part of the Movimiento Nacionalista Revolucionario (MNR, f. 1942); Leader Dr WALTER GUEVARA ARCE.

Partido Revolucionario de la Izquierda Nacional Gueiler (PRING): Mercado 996, 2°, La Paz; Leader Dra LIDIA GUEILER TEJADA.

Partido Revolucionario de la Izquierda Nacionalista (PRIN): Colón 693, La Paz; f. 1964; left-wing; Leader JUAN LECHÍN OQUENDO.

Partido Social Demócrata (PSD): Edif. Barrosquira 6°, La Paz; f. 1945; Leader Dr ANTONIO CHIQIE DIPP.

Partido Socialista-Uno (PS-1): La Paz; Leader RAMIRO VELASCO.

Partido Socialista-Uno—Marcelo Quiroga: La Paz; Leader JOSÉ MARÍA PALACIOS.

Partido Unión Boliviana (PUB): Pichincha 729 esq. Indaburo, La Paz; Leader WALTER GONZALES VALDA.

Partido de la Unión Socialista Republicana (PURS): Casilla 3724, La Paz; f. 1945; left-wing; Leader Dr CONSTANTINO CARRIÓN V.; Sec.-Gen. PEDRO MONTAÑO; 30,000 mems.

Partido de Vanguardia Obrera: Plaza Venezuela 1452, La Paz; Leader FILEMÓN ESCOBAR.

Vanguardia Revolucionaria 9 de Abril: Casilla 5810, La Paz; tel. 320311; telex 2613; Leader Dr CARLOS SERRATE REICH.

In September 1988 the formation of **Izquierda Unida (IU)**, an electoral alliance of eight left-wing parties, was announced. Members included the MBL, PCB, AP and PS-1 (1989 Presidential Candidate: ANTONIO ARANÍBAR QUIROGA).

Diplomatic Representation

EMBASSIES IN BOLIVIA

Argentina: Calle Aspiazu 497, La Paz; tel. (02) 322172; telex 3300; Ambassador: EDUARDO HÉCTOR IGLESIAS.

Belgium: Sánchez Lima 2400, Casilla 2433, La Paz; tel. (02) 328942; telex 3274; Ambassador: RAYMOND VAN ROY.

Brazil: Fernando Guachalla 494, Casilla 429, La Paz; tel. (02) 350718; telex 2494; Ambassador: JOÃO TABAJARA DE OLIVEIRA.

China, People's Republic: La Paz; telex 5558; Ambassador: CHEN DONGSHENG.

Colombia: Calle Montevideo 115, Casilla 1418, La Paz; tel. (02) 351383; telex 3661; Ambassador: ROBERTO LIEVANO PERDOMO.

Costa Rica: Avda Vera 6870, Casilla 2780, La Paz; Ambassador: GUILLERMO GAGO PÉREZ.

Cuba: Avda Arequipa 8037, Calacoto, La Paz; tel. (02) 792616; telex 2447; Ambassador: (vacant).

Czechoslovakia: Urb. Las Colinas, Calle 24, No 6, Calacoto, Casilla 2780, La Paz; telex 2530; Ambassador: STANISLAV NOVOTNÝ.

Ecuador: Edif. Herrman 14°, Plaza Venezuela, Casilla 406, La Paz; tel. (02) 321208; telex 3388; Ambassador: OLMEDO MONTEVERDE PAZ.

Egypt: Avda Ballivián 599, Casilla 2956, La Paz; tel. (02) 786511; telex 2612; Ambassador: Dr GABER SABRA.

France: Avda Hernando Silés 5390, esq. calle 8, Obrajes, Casilla 824, La Paz; tel. (02) 786114; telex 2484; Ambassador: PIERRE MUTTER.

Germany, Federal Republic: Avda Arce 2395, Casilla 5265, La Paz; tel. (02) 352389; telex 3303; Ambassador: Dr HERMANN SAÜMWEBER.

Holy See: Avda Arce 2990, Casilla 136, La Paz; tel. (02) 375007; telex 2393; Apostolic Nuncio: Mgr SANTOS ABRIL Y CASTELLO.

Israel: Edif. Esperanza 10°, Avda Mariscal Santa Cruz, Casilla 1309, La Paz; tel. (02) 325463; telex 3297; Ambassador: BERL ZERUBAVEL.

Italy: Avda 6 de Agosto 2575, Casilla 626, La Paz; tel. (02) 327329; telex 2654; Ambassador: Dr GIOVANNI MINGAZZINI.

Japan: Calle Rosendo Gutiérrez 497, Casilla 2725, La Paz; tel. (02) 373152; telex 2548; Ambassador: (vacant).

BOLIVIA   *Directory*

Korea, Democratic People's Republic: La Paz; Ambassador: Kim Chan Sik.
Korea, Republic: Avda 6 de Agosto 2592, Casilla 1559, La Paz; tel. (02) 364485; telex 3262; Ambassador: Cho Kab-Dong.
Mexico: Avda 6 de Agosto 2652, POB 430, La Paz; tel. (02) 329505; telex 3316; Ambassador: Ricardo Galán.
Panama: Calle Potosí 1270, Casilla 678, La Paz; tel. (02) 371277; telex 2314; Ambassador: Lic. Jaime Ramírez Morales.
Paraguay: Edif. Venus, Avda Arce esq. Montevideo, Casilla 882, La Paz; tel. (02) 322018; Ambassador: Gen. Ramón Duarte Vera.
Peru: Calle Rosendo Gutiérrez 113 esq. Capitán Ravelo, Casilla 668, La Paz; tel. (02) 353550; telex 2475; Ambassador: Jaime Cacho Sousa.
Romania: Calle Capitán Ravelo (Pasaje Isaac G. Eduardo) 2173, Casilla 20879, La Paz; tel. (02) 378632; telex 3260; Ambassador: Ion Flores.
South Africa: Calle 22, Calacoto No. 7810, Casilla 6018, La Paz; tel. (02) 792101; telex 3279; Ambassador: (vacant).
Spain: Avda 6 de Agosto 2860, Casilla 382, La Paz; tel. (02) 323245; telex 3304; Ambassador: Fausto Navarro.
Switzerland: Edif. Petrolero, Avda 16 de Julio 1616, Casilla 657, La Paz; tel. (02) 353091; telex 2325; Ambassador: (vacant).
USSR: Avda Arequipa 8128, Casilla 5494, La Paz; tel. (02) 792048; telex 2480; Ambassador: Takhir Byashimovich Durdiyev.
United Kingdom: Avda Arce 2732-2754, Casilla 694, La Paz; tel. (02) 351400; telex 2341; Ambassador: Colum John Sharkey.
USA: Edif. Banco Popular del Perú, Calle Colón 290, Casilla 425, La Paz; tel. (02) 350120; telex 3268; Ambassador: Robert Sidney Gelbard.
Uruguay: Avda Arce 2985, Casilla 441, La Paz; tel. (02) 353857; telex 2378; Ambassador: José M. Alvarez.
Venezuela: Calle Méndez Arcos 117, Casilla 960, La Paz; tel. (02) 320872; telex 2383; Ambassador: Eduardo Morreo Bustamante.
Yugoslavia: Benito Juárez 315, La Florida, Casilla 1717, La Paz; tel. (02) 792148; Ambassador: Miodrag Radović.

Judicial System

SUPREME COURT

Corte Suprema: Calle Yanacocha 417, La Paz; tel. (02) 377032; telex 2320.

Judicial power is vested in the Supreme Court. There are 12 members, appointed by Congress for a term of 10 years. The court is divided into four chambers of three justices each. Two chambers deal with civil cases, the third deals with criminal cases and the fourth deals with administrative, social and mining cases. The President of the Supreme Court presides over joint sessions of the courts and attends the joint sessions for cassation cases.

President of the Supreme Court: (vacant).

DISTRICT COURTS

There is a District Court sitting in each Department, and additional provincial and local courts to try minor cases.

ATTORNEY-GENERAL

In addition to the Attorney-General at Sucre (appointed by the President on the proposal of the Senate), there is a District Attorney in each Department as well as circuit judges.

Attorney-General: Dr José Hugo Vilar Tufino.

Religion

The majority of the population are Roman Catholics; there were an estimated 5,121,019 adherents in 1982. Religious freedom is guaranteed. There is a small Jewish community, as well as various Protestant denominations, in Bolivia.

CHRISTIANITY
The Roman Catholic Church

Bolivia comprises four archdioceses, four dioceses, two Territorial Prelatures and six Apostolic Vicariates.

Bishops' Conference: Conferencia Episcopal de Bolivia, Casilla 2309, La Paz; tel. (02) 321254; f. 1972; Pres. Mgr Julio Terrazas Sandoval, Bishop of Oruro.
Archbishop of Cochabamba: Gennaro María Prata Vuolo, Calle Baptista 6036, Casilla 129, Cochabamba; tel. 22984.
Archbishop of La Paz: Luis Sáinz Hinojosa, Calle Ballivián 1277, Casilla 259, La Paz; tel. (02) 341920.
Archbishop of Santa Cruz de la Sierra: Luis Rodríguez Pardo, Casilla 25, Ingavi 49, Santa Cruz de la Sierra; tel. 24286.
Archbishop of Sucre: Cardinal René Fernández Apaza, Calle Bolívar 702, Casilla 205, Sucre; tel. (064) 21703.

The Anglican Communion

Within the Iglesia Anglicana del Cono Sur de América (Anglican Church of the Southern Cone of America), Bolivia forms part of the diocese of Peru. The Bishop is resident in Lima, Peru.

Protestant Churches

Baptist Convention of Bolivia: Casilla 3147, Santa Cruz; tel. 4-0717; f. 1947; Pres. Zacarías Flores.
Baptist Union of Bolivia: Casilla 1408, La Paz; Pres. Rev. Augusto Chuijo.
Iglesia Evangélica Metodista en Bolivia (Evangelical Methodist Church in Bolivia): Casilla 356, La Paz; tel. (02) 342702; autonomous since 1969; 5,000 mems; Bishop Rt Rev. Rolando Villena Villegas.

BAHÁ'Í FAITH

National Spiritual Assembly of the Bahá'ís of Bolivia: Casilla 1613, La Paz; tel. (02) 785058; mems resident in 5,601 localities.

The Press

DAILY NEWSPAPERS
Cochabamba

Los Tiempos: Santivañez 2110, Casilla 525, Cochabamba; tel. 28586; f. 1943; morning; independent; right-wing; Dir Carlos Canelas; circ. 18,000.

La Paz

El Diario: Loayza 118, Casilla 5, La Paz; tel. (02) 356835; telex 5530; f. 1904; morning; conservative; Dir Jorge Carrasco Villalobos; circ. 45,000.
Hoy: Avda 6 de Agosto 2170, Casilla 477, La Paz; tel. (02) 326683; telex 2613; f. 1968; morning and midday editions; independent; Dir Dr Carlos Serrate Reich; circ. 25,000.
Jornada: Junín 608, Casilla 1628, La Paz; tel. (02) 353844; f. 1964; evening; independent; Dir Jaime Ríos Chacón; circ. 11,500.
Presencia: Avda Mariscal Santa Cruz, Casilla 1451, La Paz; tel. (02) 372344; telex 2659; f. 1952; morning and evening; Catholic; Dir Lic. Armando Mariaca V.; Man. Lic. Felicísimo Tarilonte P.; circ. 90,000.
Ultima Hora: Avda Camacho 309, Casilla 5920, La Paz; tel. (02) 370416; f. 1939; evening; independent; Dir Jorge Siles Salinas; Editor Jorge Canelas; circ. 35,000.

Oruro

El Expreso: Potosí 319 esq. Oblitas, Oruro; f. 1973; morning; independent; right-wing; Dir Genaro Frontanilla Vistas; circ. 1,000.
La Patria: Avda Camacho 1892, Casilla 48, Oruro; tel. (052) 50761; f. 1919; morning; independent; Dir Enrique Miralles; circ. 5,000.

Potosí

El Siglo: Calle Linares 99, Casilla 389, Potosí; f. 1975; morning; Dir Wilson Mendieta Pacheco; circ. 1,500.

Santa Cruz

El Deber: Suárez Arana 264, Casilla 2144, Santa Cruz; tel. 23588; f. 1965; morning; independent; Dir Pedro Rivero Mercado; circ. 8,000.
El Mundo: Calle Beni 169, Santa Cruz; tel. 34770; f. 1979; morning; owned by Santa Cruz Industrialists' Association; Dir Sixto Nelson Fleig; circ. 20,000.

Tarija

La Verdad: Tarija; Dir José Lanza; circ. 3,000.

Trinidad

La Razón: Trinidad; Dir Carlos Vélez.

PERIODICALS

Actualidad Boliviana Confidencial: Fernando Guachalla 969, Casilla 648, La Paz; f. 1966; weekly; Dir Hugo González Rioja; circ. 6,000.

BOLIVIA — *Directory*

Aquí: Casilla 20441, La Paz; tel. (02) 343524; f. 1979; weekly; circ. 10,000.

Bolivia Libre: Edif. Esperanza 5°, Avda Mariscal Santa Cruz 2150, Casilla 6500, La Paz; fortnightly; published by the Ministry of Information.

Carta Cruceña de Integración: Casilla 2735, Santa Cruz de la Sierra; weekly; Dirs HERNÁN LLANOVARCED A., JOHNNY LAZARTE J.

Comentarios Económicos de Actualidad (CEA): Casilla 12097, La Paz; tel. (02) 354520; fortnightly; articles and economic analyses.

Extra: Oruro; weekly; Dir JORGE LAZO.

Información Política y Económica (IPE): Calle Comercio, Casilla 2484, La Paz; weekly; Dir GONZALO LÓPEZ MUÑOZ.

Notas: Casilla 5782, La Paz; tel. 373773; telex 3236; weekly; political and economic analysis; Editor JOSÉ GRAMUNT DE MORAGAS.

El Noticiero: Sucre; weekly; Dir DAVID CABEZAS; circ. 1,500.

Servicio de Información Confidencial (SIC): Elías Sagárnaga 274, Casilla 5035, La Paz; weekly; publ. by Asociación Nacional de Prensa; Dir JOSÉ CARRANZA.

Unión: Sucre; weekly; Dir JAIME MERILES.

PRESS ASSOCIATIONS

Asociación Nacional de Periodistas: Avda 6 de Agosto 2170, Casilla 477, La Paz; Pres. ALBERTO ZUAZO NATHES.

Asociación Nacional de Prensa: Comercio 1048, Casilla 3089, La Paz; Pres. Dr CARLOS SERRATE REICH.

Asociación de Periodistas de La Paz: Comercio 1048, Casilla 3089, La Paz; tel. 369916; Pres. ANA MARÍA DE CAMPERO.

NEWS AGENCIES

Agencia de Noticias Fides (ANF): Edif. Mariscal de Ayacucho, 6°, Of. 601, Calle Loayza, Casilla 5782, La Paz; tel. (02) 365152; telex 3236; owned by Catholic Church; Dir JOSÉ GRAMUNT DE MORAGAS.

Foreign Bureaux

Agencia EFE (Spain): Edif. Esperanza, Avda Mariscal Santa Cruz 2150, Casilla 7403, La Paz; tel. (02) 367205; telex 2535; Bureau Chief FERNANDO RUIZ.

Agentstvo Pechati Novosti (APN) (USSR): Edif. Mariscal Ballivián, Of. 401, Calle Mercado, La Paz; tel. (02) 373857; telex 3285; Correspondent VLADIMIR RAMÍREZ.

Agenzia Nazionale Stampa Associata (ANSA) (Italy): Edif. Credinform 4°, Of. 404, Calle Ayacucho 378, esq. Calle Potosí, Casilla 7768, La Paz; tel. (5912) 365530; telex 3410; Bureau Chief MABEL AZCUI.

Associated Press (AP) (USA): Edif. Mariscal de Ayacucho, Of. 1209, Calle Loayza, Casilla 4364, La Paz; tel. (02) 370128; telex 3283; Correspondent PETER J. MCFARREN.

Deutsche Presse-Agentur (dpa) (Fed. Republic of Germany): Plaza Venezuela 1456, 1°, Of. F, Casilla 135, La Paz; tel. (02) 352684; telex 2601; Correspondent ANA MARÍA CAMPERO.

Inter Press Service (IPS) (Italy): Edif. Esperanza 6°, Of. 6, Avda Mariscal Santa Cruz, Casilla 11130, La Paz; tel. (02) 361227; Correspondent OSCAR PEÑA FRANCO.

Prensa Latina (Cuba): Edif. Aries, Apto 15, Calle 10 de Obrajes esq. Hernando Siles, La Paz; tel. (02) 785357; telex 2525; Correspondent JORGE LUNA MENDOZA.

Reuters (UK): Calle Loayza, 11°, Of. 1112-3, Casilla 4057, La Paz; tel. (02) 351106; telex 2573; Correspondent JUAN JAVIER ZEBALLOS.

Telegrafnoye Agentstvo Sovetskovo Soyuza (TASS) (USSR): Casilla 6839, San Miguel, Bloque 0-33, Casa 958, La Paz; tel. (02) 792108; Correspondent ELDAR ABDULLAEV.

United Press International (UPI) (USA): Plaza Venezuela 1456, 1°, Of. B, Casilla 1219, La Paz; tel. (02) 371278; telex 2453; Correspondent ALBERTO ZUAZO NATHES.

Agence France-Presse and Telam (Argentina) are also represented.

Publishers

Editorial los Amigos del Libro: Avda Heroínas E-0311, Casilla 450, Cochabamba; tel. 22920; f. 1945; general; Man. Dir WERNER GUTTENTAG.

Editorial Bruño: Casilla 4809, Calles Loayza esq. Juan de la Riva, La Paz; tel. (02) 320198; f. 1964; Dir IGNACIO LOMAS.

Editorial Difusión: Avda 16 de Julio 1601, Casilla 1510, La Paz; tel. (02) 328126; f. 1960; literature, history, politics, social studies; Man. Dir JORGE F. CATALANO.

Librería Dismo Ltda: Comercio 806, Casilla 988, La Paz; tel. (02) 353119; Dir TERESA GONZÁLEZ DE ALVAREZ.

Editorial Don Bosco: Avda 16 de Julio 1899, Casilla 4458, La Paz; tel. (02) 371149; social sciences, literature and the cinema; Dir JULIAN BELLOMO MUSCI.

Gisbert y Cía, SA: Comercio 1270, Casilla 195, La Paz; tel. (02) 356806; f. 1907; textbooks, history, law and general; Pres. JAVIER GISBERT; Dirs CARMEN G. DE SCHULCZEWSKI, ARMANDO PAGANO.

Icthus Editorial: Avda 16 de Julio 1800, Casilla 8353, La Paz; tel. (02) 354007; f. 1967; general and textbooks; Man. Dir SALVADOR DE LA SERNA.

Ivar American: Calle Potosí 1375, Casilla 6016, La Paz; tel. (02) 361519; Man. Dir HÉCTOR IBÁÑEZ.

Editorial y Librería Juventud: Plaza Murillo 519, Casilla 1489, La Paz; tel. (02) 341694; f. 1946; textbooks and general; Man. Dir RAFAEL URQUIZO.

Editora Khana Cruz SRL: Avda Camacho 1372, Casilla 5920, La Paz; tel. (02) 370263; Dir JORGE SILES.

Librería La Paz: Colón 618, Casilla 539, La Paz; tel. (02) 353323; f. 1900; Dir CARLOS BURGOS.

Librería La Universal: Calle Genaro Sanjines 538, Casilla 2888, La Paz; tel. (02) 342961; f. 1958; Man. Dir ROLANDO CONDORI.

Editora Lux: Edif. Esperanza, Avda Mariscal Santa Cruz, Casilla 1566, La Paz; tel. (02) 329102; f. 1952; Dir MARCOS JENARO MERCADO R.

Editorial Popular: Plaza Pérez Velasco 787, Casilla 4171, La Paz; tel. (02) 324258; f. 1935; textbooks, postcards, tourist guides, etc; Man. Dir GERMÁN VILLAMOR.

Editorial Puerta del Sol: Calle Juan de la Riva 1448, La Paz; tel. (02) 360746; f. 1965; Man. Dir OSCAR CRESPO.

Librería San Pablo: Calle Colón 627, Casilla 3152, La Paz; tel. (02) 326084; f. 1967; Man. Dirs The Daughters of San Pablo.

PUBLISHERS' ASSOCIATION

Cámara Boliviana del Libro: Edif. Las Palmas, Avda 20 de Octubre 2005, Casilla 682, La Paz; tel. (02) 327039; Pres. JAVIER GISBERT C.

Radio and Television

In 1986 there were an estimated 3m. radio receivers and 390,000 television receivers in use.

Dirección General de Telecomunicaciones: Edif. Guerrero, Mercado 1115, Casilla 4475, La Paz; tel. (02) 368788; telex 2595; government-controlled broadcasting authority; Dir-Gen. Ing. FREDDY CANAVIRE PARDO.

RADIO

There were 158 radio stations in 1985, the majority of which were commercial. Broadcasts are in Spanish, Aymará and Quechua.

Asociación Boliviana de Radiodifusoras (ASBORA): Potosí 920, Casilla 7958, La Paz; tel. (02) 328513; broadcasting authority; Pres. MIGUEL A. DUERI; Vice-Pres. ENRIQUE COSTAS.

TELEVISION

Empresa Nacional de Televisión: Ayacucho 467, Casilla 900, La Paz; tel. (02) 323292; telex 2312; f. 1969; government network operating stations in La Paz, Oruro, Cochabamba, Potosí, Beni, Tarija and Santa Cruz; Dir-Gen. J. BARRAGÁN; Gen. Man. JUAN RECACOCHEA.

Televisión Universitaria (University Service): División de Infrastructura, Universidad Boliviana, Casilla 2255, La Paz; tel. (02) 359297; telex 3252; educational programmes; stations in Oruro, Cochabamba, Potosí, Sucre, Tarija, Beni and Santa Cruz; Dir ALFONSO VILLEGAS.

Finance

(cap. = capital; p.u. = paid up; res = reserves; dep. = deposits; m. = million; brs = branches; amounts are in Bolivian pesos unless otherwise stated)

BANKING

Supervisory Authority

Superintendencia de Bancos: Edif. Banco Central de Bolivia 16°, Ayacucho esq. Mercado 200, Casilla 3118, La Paz; tel. (02) 362679; f. 1928; Man. Lic. LUIS DEL RÍO CHÁVEZ.

BOLIVIA

State Banks

Banco Central de Bolivia: Ayacucho esq. Mercado, Casilla 3118, La Paz; tel. (02) 355535; telex 2286; f. 1928; bank of issue; cap. and res 671.7m. (Dec. 1981); Pres. JACQUES TRIGO; Gen. Man. MILTON PAZ CARDOZO.

Banco del Estado: Calle Colón esq. Mercado, Casilla 1401, La Paz; tel. (02) 352868; telex 3267; f. 1970; state bank incorporating banking department of Banco Central de Bolivia; cap. and res 27,589m., dep. 785,523m. (Dec. 1984); Pres. Lic. ALFREDO BUCHÓN; Gen. Man. JAVIER PANTOJA ROMERO; 55 brs.

Banco Agrícola de Bolivia: Avda Mariscal Santa Cruz esq. Almirante Grau, Casilla 1179, La Paz; tel. (02) 365876; telex 3278; f. 1942; cap. 179m. (Dec. 1976); Pres. Ing. ARTURO SORNCO V.; Gen. Man. Ing. VÍCTOR G. RIVERA.

Banco Minero de Bolivia: Calle Comercio 1290, Casilla 1410, La Paz; tel. (02) 352168; telex 2568; f. 1936; finances private mining industry; cap. p.u. and res 770m. (1981); Gen. Man. RIGOBERTO PÉREZ.

Banco de la Vivienda: Avda Camacho 1336, Casilla 8155, La Paz; tel. (02) 343510; telex 2295; f. 1964; to encourage and finance housing developments; 51% state participation; initial cap. 100m.; Pres. (vacant); Gen. Man. Lic. JOSÉ RAMÍREZ MONTALVA.

Commercial Banks

Banco Boliviano Americano: Calle Loayza esq. Camacho, Casilla 478, La Paz; tel. (02) 350861; telex 2553; f. 1957; cap. and res 7,625.8m., dep. 136,507.5m. (Dec. 1984); Pres. LUIS EDUARDO SILES; Exec. Vice-Pres. JOSÉ A. ARIAS; 13 brs.

Banco de Cochabamba, SA: Avda Camacho esq. Colón, Casilla 4314, La Paz; tel. (02) 358123; telex 5468; cap. p.u. 159.2m., res 545m., dep. 1,326m. (Aug. 1983); Exec. Pres. GUIDO QUIROGA Q.; Vice-Pres. FERNANDO SÁNCHEZ DE LOZADA; 5 brs.

Banco de Financiamiento Industrial, SA: Washington 1402, Casilla 51, Oruro; tel. 356876; telex 2234; f. 1974 to encourage and finance industrial development; cap. p.u. 105m., res 76m. (Aug. 1983); Pres. Lic. HUGO CAMPOS; Man. FRANCISCO BERMÚDEZ.

Banco Hipotecario Nacional: Avda 16 de Julio 1630, Casilla 4824, La Paz; tel. (02) 359351; telex 2290; f. 1890; cap. 491.9m. (Dec. 1985); Pres. FERNANDO ROCHERO; Gen. Man. DAVID BLANCO ZABALA.

Banco Industrial, SA: Avda 16 de Julio 1628, La Paz; tel. (02) 359471; telex 2584; f. 1963; industrial credit bank; cap. p.u. US $500m. (June 1985); Chair. of Board of Dirs JULIO LEÓN PRADO; Gen. Man. ALFREDO MOSCOSO VELARDE; 1 br.

Banco Industrial y Ganadero del Beni, SA: Calle Mercado esq. Socabaya, Edif. Guerrero, Casilla 8717, La Paz; tel. (02) 369342; telex 2381; cap. 5,943m., res 71.5m., dep. 35,994m. (Dec. 1986); Pres. JAIME MUSTAFÁ; Gen. Man. JORGE JORDAN FERRUFINO; 11 brs.

Banco de Inversión Boliviano, SA: Edif. Herrmann 15°, Plaza Venezuela, Casilla 8639, La Paz; tel. (02) 354233; telex 2465; f. 1977; cap. p.u. 77.3m., res 32m., dep. 938m.; Pres. JAIME GUTIÉRREZ MOSCOSO; Vice-Pres. MAURICIO URQUIDI U.

Banco de La Paz: Avda 16 de Julio 1473, Casilla 6826, La Paz; tel. (02) 358344; telex 2423; cap. 3,014,996m.; dep. 80,756.5m. (Dec. 1985); Pres. Lic. GUIDO E. HINOJOSA; Vice-Pres. Dr JORGE RENGEL SILLERICO; 11 brs.

Banco Mercantil SA: Ayacucho esq. Mercado, Casilla 423, La Paz; tel. (02) 356902; telex 2270; f. 1905; cap. and res US $6,389m., dep. $26,176m.; Pres. JAVIER ZUAZO CHÁVEZ; Gen. Man. EMILIO UNZUETA; 6 brs.

Banco Nacional de Bolivia: Avda Camacho esq. Colón, Casilla 360, La Paz; tel. (02) 354616; telex 2310; f. 1872; cap. and res 11.5m., dep. 98.9m. (June 1987); Pres. Dr FERNANDO BEDOYA BALLIVIÁN; Gen. Man. Dr FERNANDO CALVO U; 10 brs.

Banco de Santa Cruz de la Sierra, SA: Junín 154, Casilla 865, Santa Cruz; tel. 39911; telex 4230; f. 1966; cap. and res 31,420,389m., dep. 253,353,351m. (June 1988); Pres. Ing. LYDERS PAREJA EGUEZ; Gen. Man. Ing. LUIS FERNANDO SAAVEDRA BRUNO; 18 brs.

Banco de la Unión SA: Calle René Moreno esq. Republiquetas, No 418, Casilla 4057, La Paz; tel. (33) 46869; telex 4285; f. 1982; cap. and res US $7m., dep. $36m. (June 1988); Pres. Arq. CRISTÓBAL RODA DAZA; Vice-Pres. JORGE CÓRDOVA SERRUDO; 3 brs.

Caja Central de Ahorro y Préstamo para la Vivienda: Avda Mariscal Santa Cruz 1364, 20°, Casilla 4808, La Paz; telex 5611; f. 1967; assets US $28m. (1983); Pres. ERNESTO WENDE.

Foreign Banks

Banco do Brasil SA: Avda Camacho 1448, Casilla 1650, La Paz; tel. (02) 343007; telex 2316; f. 1960; Man. BELMIRO CANDIDO NAZARIO; 3 brs.

Banco de la Nación Argentina: Avda 16 de Julio 1486, Casilla 2745, La Paz; tel. (02) 359211; telex 2282; Man. ROBERTO VAGLIODORO MEDICI; 3 brs.

Banco Popular del Perú: Mercado esq. Colón, Casilla 907, La Paz; tel. (02) 360025; telex 2344; f. 1942; Central Man. MANUEL BARRETO; 6 brs.

Citibank N.A. (USA): Casilla 260, La Paz; tel. (02) 321742; telex 2546; Vice-Pres. RICARDO LINALE.

Deutsch-Südamerikanische Bank AG (Banco Germánico de la América del Sud) and Dresdner Bank AG (Fed. Repub. of Germany): Joint representation: Avda Mariscal Santa Cruz, esq. Yanacocha, Edif. Hansa 4°, Casilla 1077, La Paz; tel. (02) 374450; telex 2311; Rep. CARLOS A. MARTINS.

Banking Association

Asociación de Bancos e Instituciones Financieras de Bolivia: Edif. Cámara Nacional de Comercio, 15°, Avda Mariscal Santa Cruz esq. Colombia, Casilla 5822, La Paz; tel. (02) 321379; telex 2439; f. 1957; Pres. Dr FERNANDO BEDOYA BALLIVIÁN; Exec. Sec. Dr FERNANDO ROLLANO MORALES; 22 mems.

INSURANCE

Supervisory Authority

Superintendencia Nacional de Seguros y Reaseguros: Calle Batallón Colorados 162, 4°, Casilla 6118, La Paz; tel. (02) 374137; f. 1975; Superintendent Dr CARLOS CASTAÑÓN BARRIENTOS; Man. Lic. WÁLTER SÁNCHEZ SANDOVAL.

National Companies

(p.i. = premium income; amounts in Bolivian pesos, $bs)

Argos, Cía de Seguros, SA: Calle Potosí 1320, Casilla 277, La Paz; tel. (02) 340029; telex 2297; f. 1962; all classes except life; p.i. $bs38,317,794 (1982); Pres. JOSÉ T. KAWAI; Gen. Man. JORGE LUIS GUMUCIO.

Bolívar SA de Seguros: Avda Mariscal Santa Cruz 1287, Casilla 1459, La Paz; tel. (02) 351441; telex 2392; f. 1952; all classes; p.i. $bs1,800m. (1982); Pres. Lic. ALFREDO OPORTO CRESPO; Gen. Man. FREDDY OPORTO M.

Cía Americana de Seguros y Reaseguros, SA: Edif. Sáenz 3°, Avda Camacho 1377, Casilla 6180, La Paz; tel. (02) 329374; telex 2589; f. 1970; all classes; p.i. $bs27,134,698.8 (1982); Pres. MARIO PATIÑO MILÁN; Gen. Man. JULIO BUTRÓN MENDOZA.

Cía Andina de Seguros y Reaseguros, SA: Edif. Alborada 2°, Mercado esq. Loayza, Casilla 4723, La Paz; tel. (02) 374371; telex 4723; f. 1974; all classes; p.i. $bs396.7m. (1982); Pres. Lic. LUIS ADOLFO DE UGARTE; Dir RAMÓN ESCÓBAR AGUILAR.

Cía Boliviana de Seguros, SA: Colón 282, 1°, Casilla 628, La Paz; tel. (02) 351643; telex 2562; f. 1946; all classes; cap. and res US $5,273m. (1987); Pres. GONZALO BEDOYA H.; Gen. Man. ALFONSO IBÁÑEZ.

Cía de Seguros y Reaseguros Santa Cruz, SA: Edif. CIACRUZ, Calle Pari No 28, Santa Cruz; tel. (033) 3-6410; f. 1980; all classes; p.i. US $620m. (1981); Pres. JUAN MANUEL PARADA PERDRIEL; Gen. Man. ANTONIO OLEA BAUDOIN.

La Continental de Seguros y Reaseguros, SA: Edif. Herrmann 1°, Avda 16 de Julio, Casilla 5959, La Paz; tel. (02) 356926; telex 2336; f. 1975; all classes; p.i. US $3m. (1988); Pres. GONZALO BEDOYA; Mans F. GÓMEZ, J.L. CONTRERAS.

Credinform International SA de Seguros: Edif. Credinform, Potosí esq. Ayacucho, Casilla 1724, La Paz; tel. (02) 356931; telex 2304; f. 1954; all classes; p.i. $bs4,709m.; Pres. Dr ROBÍN BARRAGÁN PELAEZ; Gen. Man. MIGUEL ANGEL BARRAGÁN IBARGUEN.

Delta Insurance Co, SA: 25 de Mayo, Casilla 920, Cochabamba; tel. 26006; f. 1965; all classes except life; Pres. JUAN JOSÉ GALINDO B.; Gen. Man. CARLOS CHRISTIE J.

Fénix Boliviana SA de Seguros y Reaseguros: Edif. Naira, Of. 5, Potosí esq. Loayza, Casilla 4409, La Paz; tel. (02) 370271; telex 3470; f. 1978; all classes; $bs40m. (1982); Pres. Lic. WALTER SÁNCHEZ; Gen. Man. Lic. ORLANDO NOGALES.

La Mercantil de Seguros y Reaseguros, SA: Mercado 1121, Casilla 2727, La Paz; tel. (02) 355893; telex 3313; f. 1957; all classes; p.i. $bs50m. (1982); Pres. Dr HUGO ECHEVERRÍA; Gen. Man. LUIS SAUCEDO PAZ.

Real Bolivia de Seguros, SA: Edif. Litoral, Colón 150, Casilla 1847, La Paz; tel. (02) 328823; telex 2431; f. 1980; all classes; p.i. $bs30.7m.; Pres. SEBASTIAO BERNARDES RENGEL; Gen. Man. FRANCISCO FREITAS.

Reaseguradora Boliviana, SA: Edif. El Condor 15° y 16°, Calle Batallón Colorados, Casilla 6227, La Paz; tel. (02) 322991; telex 2315; f. 1977; p.i. US $350m.; Pres. FERNANDO ARCE GRANDCHAND; Gen. Man. DAVID ALCOREZA MARCHETTI.

BOLIVIA

Seguros Illimani, SA: Edif. Mariscal de Ayacucho 10°, Calle Loayza, Casilla 133, La Paz; tel. (02) 371090; telex 3261; f. 1979; all classes; p.i. $bs66.8m.; Pres. GASTÓN IBÁÑEZ; Gen. Man. FERNANDO ARCE G.

Union Insurance Company, SA (Cía Union de Seguros): Landaeta 221, Casilla 2922, La Paz; tel. 323408; telex 2347; all classes; Exec. Pres. LUIS SAENZ PACHECO; Gen. Man. CARMEN SEEGHERS DE ZWAHLEN.

There are also three foreign-owned insurance companies operating in Bolivia: American Life Insurance Co, American Home Assurance Co and United States Fire Insurance Co, and one company with mixed capital: Cooperativa de Seguros Cruceña Ltda.

Insurance Association

Asociación Boliviana de Aseguradores: Edif. Castilla 5°, Of. 506, Loayza 250, Casilla 4804, La Paz; tel. (02) 328804; f. 1962; Pres. DAVID ALCOREZA MARCHETTI; Exec. Sec. BLANCA M. DE OTERMÍN.

Trade and Industry

CHAMBERS OF COMMERCE

Cámara Nacional de Comercio: Edif. Cámara Nacional de Comercio, Avda Mariscal Santa Cruz 1392, Casilla 7, La Paz; tel. (02) 354255; telex 2305; f. 1890; 30 brs and special brs; Pres. DANIEL PAZ PACHECO; Gen. Man. RENÉ CANDÍA NAVARRO.

Cámara Departamental de Industria y Comercio de Santa Cruz: Avda Suárez de Figueroa 127, 3° y 4°, Casilla 180, Santa Cruz; tel. 34555; telex 4298; f. 1915; Pres. JOSÉ LUIS CAMACHO; Dir-Gen. Ing. JUSTO YÉPEZ KAKUDA.

Cámara Departamental de Comercio de Cochabamba: Calle Sucre E-0336, Casilla 493, Cochabamba; tel. 22905; telex 6380; f. 1922; Pres. Dr VÍCTOR HUGO ESCOBAR HERBAS; Dir-Gen. Dr FRANZ E. RIVERO V.

Cámara Departamental de Comercio de Oruro: Pasaje Guachalla, Casilla 148, Oruro; tel. 50606; telex 2230; f. 1895; Pres. JOSÉ FERNÁNDEZ FUENTES; Gen. Man. LUIS CAMACHO VARGAS.

Cámara Departamental de Comercio de Potosí: Casilla 159, Potosí; tel. 22641; telex 2266; Pres. ARMANDO GUERRA VIDAURRE; Gen. Man. WALTER ZABALA AYLLON.

Cámara Departamental de Comercio de Sucre: Casilla 33, Sucre; tel. 21320; telex 2694; Pres. JORGE LANDIVAR; Gen. Man. ANTONIO LANDIVAR.

Cámara Nacional de Exportadores: Avda 20 de Octubre No 2427 (Plaza Avaroa), Casilla 20744, La Paz; tel. (02) 341220; telex 2565; f. 1970; Pres. JAVIER CASTELLANOS HOCHKOFLER; Gen. Man. FRANZ ONDARZA LINARES.

STATE INSTITUTES AND DEVELOPMENT ORGANIZATIONS

Cámara Agropecuaria del Oriente: Bolívar 559, Casilla 116, Santa Cruz; tel. 23164; telex 4438; f. 1964; agriculture and livestock association for eastern Bolivia; Pres. Ing. OSMAN LANDIVAR.

Cámara Agropecuaria de La Paz: Calle Santa Cruz 266, Casilla 1620, La Paz; tel. 321496; Pres. FERNANDO PALACIOS; Gen. Man. HÉCTOR ELÍAS AYOROA.

Cámara Nacional Forestal: Calle Manuel Ignacio Salvatierra 1055, Casilla 346, Santa Cruz; tel. 23996; telex 4330; f. 1971; represents the interests of the Bolivian timber industry; Pres. EDGAR LANDÍVAR LANDÍVAR; Man. Lic. ARTURO BOWLES O.

Cámara Nacional de Industria: Edif. Cámara Nacional de Comercio 14°, Avda Mariscal Santa Cruz 1392, Casilla 611, La Paz; tel. (02) 374478; telex 3533; f. 1931; Pres. JAVIER LUPO GAMARRA; Gen. Man. Dr ALFREDO ARANA RUCK.

Cámara Nacional de Minería: Pasaje Bernardo Trigo 429, Casilla 2022, La Paz; tel. (02) 350623; f. 1953; mining institute; Pres. Dr JORGE GUTIÉRREZ DEL RÍO; Sec.-Gen. ADOLFO CASTRO.

Comité Boliviano de Productores de Antimonio: Pasaje Bernardo Trigo 429, Casilla 2022, La Paz; tel. 350623; f. 1978; controls the marketing, pricing and promotion policies of the antimony industry; Pres. MARIO MERCADO VACA GUZMÁN.

Comité Boliviano del Café (COBOLCA): Avda Villazón 1970, Casilla 21173, La Paz; tel. (02) 341553; controls the export, marketing and growing policies of the coffee industry; Gen. Man. Lic. GONZALO MARTÍNEZ BARRABINO.

Consejo Nacional de Planificación (CONEPLAN): Edif. Banco Central de Bolivia 26°, La Paz; tel. (02) 377115; f. 1985; under the direction of the Ministry of Planning and Co-ordination.

Corporación de las Fuerzas Armadas para el Desarrollo Nacional (Cofadena): Avda 6 de Agosto 2649, Casilla 1015, La Paz; tel. (02) 377305; telex 3286; f. 1972; industrial, agricultural and mining holding company and development organization owned by the Bolivian armed forces; Gen. Man. CRISÓLOGO ROJAS ZAPATA.

Corporación Minera de Bolivia (COMIBOL): Avda Mariscal Santa Cruz 1092, Casilla 349, La Paz; tel. (02) 357979; telex 2420; f. 1952; state mining corporation; taken over by FSTMB (miners' union) in April 1983; owns both mines and processing plants; Gen. Man. Ing. GONZALO BARRIENTOS CARREAGA.

Corporación Regional de Desarrollo de La Paz (Cordepaz): Edif. Santa Isabel, 2°, Bloque A, Avda Arce esq. Pinilla, Casilla 6102, La Paz; tel. (02) 342352; telex 3256; f. 1972; decentralized government institution to foster the development of the La Paz area; Pres. OSCAR CORNEJO CLAVIJO; Gen. Man. Dr ALBERTO MUÑOZ DE LA BARRA.

Empresa Minera Estatal del Oriente (EMEDO): Calle Tarija 55, Casilla 3079, Santa Cruz; tel. 27037; telex 4353; Pres. Ing. MARCELO CLAURE; Gen. Man. Ing. ROLANDO IBÁÑEZ.

Empresa Nacional de Electricidad, SA (ENDE): Colombia No 655, esq. Falsuri, Casilla 565, Cochabamba; tel. 46322; telex 6251; f. 1962; state electricity company; Pres. Minister of Energy and Hydrocarbons; Gen. Man. CLAUDE BESSE ARCE.

Empresa Metalúrgica Vinto (EMV): Casilla 612, Oruro; tel. 52857; telex 2255; state company for the smelting of non-ferrous minerals and special alloys; Gen. Man. Ing. EDUARDO FUENTES U.

Empresa Nacional de Telecomunicaciones (ENTEL): Edif. ENTEL, Calle Ayacucho No 267, Casilla 4450, La Paz; tel. (02) 367474; telex 2227; Gen. Man. Ing. ALBERTO ALARCÓN CLAVIJO.

Instituto Nacional de Inversiones (INI): Edif. Cristal 10°, Calle Yanacocha, Casilla 4393, La Paz; tel. (02) 375730; f. 1971; state institution for the promotion of new investments and the application of the Investment Law; Exec. Dir Lic. GASTÓN MURILLO.

Yacimientos Petrolíferos Fiscales Bolivianos (YPFB): Calle Bueno 185, Casilla 2376, La Paz; tel. (02) 356540; telex 2369; f. 1936; state petroleum enterprise; Pres. Minister of Energy and Hydrocarbons; Vice-Pres. for Operations Ing. JORGE FLORES LÓPEZ; Vice-Pres. for Administration and Finance Dr MAURICIO GONZALES.

EMPLOYERS' ASSOCIATIONS

Asociación Nacional de Mineros Medianos: Edif. Petrolero 5°, Avda 16 de Julio 1616, Of. 4, Casilla 6094, La Paz; tel. (02) 371112; telex 3377; f. 1939; association of the 27 private medium-sized mining companies; Pres. Dr OSCAR BONIFAZ; Sec.-Gen. ROLANDO JORDÁN POZO.

Confederación de Empresarios Privados de Bolivia (CEPB): Edif. Cámara Nacional de Comercio, 7°, Avda Mariscal Santa Cruz 1392, Casilla 20439, La Paz; tel. (02) 356831; telex 2305; largest national employers' organization; Pres. Lic. CARLOS ITURRALDE BALLIVIÁN; Exec. Sec. Dr JAVIER MURILLO DE LA ROCHA.

There are also employers' federations in Santa Cruz, Cochabamba, Oruro, Potosí, Beni and Tarija.

TRADE UNIONS

Central Obrera Boliviana (COB): Edif. Confederación de Ferroviarios, Calle Ayacucho 286, Casilla 6552, La Paz; tel. (02) 352426; f. 1952; main union confederation; 500,000 mems; Exec. Sec. SIMÓN REYES RIVERA; Sec.-Gen. EDIBERTO MAMANI.

Affiliated unions:

Central Obrera Departamental de La Paz: Estación Central 284, La Paz; tel. (02) 352898; Sec.-Gen. PABLO TICONA.

Confederación Sindical Unica de los Trabajadores Campesinos de Bolivia (CSUTCB): Calle Sucre esq. Manacocha; tel. 369433; f. 1979; peasant farmers' union; Exec. Sec. JUAN DE LA CRUZ VILLCA.

Federación de Empleados de Industria Fabril: Edif. Fabril, Plaza de San Francisco 5°, La Paz; tel. (02) 372759; Exec. Sec. DANIEL SANTALLA.

Federación Sindical de Trabajadores Mineros Bolivianos (FSTMB): Plaza Venezuela 1470, La Paz; tel. (02) 359656; mineworkers' union; Exec. Sec. VÍCTOR LÓPEZ; 27,000 mems.

Federación Sindical de Trabajadores Petroleros de Bolivia: Calle México 1504, La Paz; tel. (02) 351748; Exec. Sec. PEDRO GARCÍA.

Confederación General de Trabajadores de Bolivia (CGTB): f. 1985; Leader FRANCISCO CHAMBI MANGULA.

Transport

RAILWAYS

Empresa Nacional de Ferrocarriles (ENFE): Estación Central de Ferrocarriles, Plaza Zalles, Casilla 428, La Paz; tel. (02) 327401;

BOLIVIA

Avda Manco Kapac, La Paz; tel. (02) 355694; telex 2405; f. 1964; administers most of the railways in Bolivia. Total networks: 3,733 km (1987); Western Network: Total 2,307 km; Eastern Network: Total 1,426 km; Gen. Man. Ing. CARLOS BELMONTE ICHAZO.

A former private railway, Machacamarca–Uncia, owned by Corporación Minera de Bolivia (105 km), merged with the Western network of ENFE in February 1987. There are plans to construct a railway line with Brazilian assistance, to link Cochabamba and Santa Cruz.

ROADS

In 1984 Bolivia had 40,987 km of roads, of which 1,538 km were paved and 9,268 km were all-weather roads. Almost the entire road network is concentrated in the *altiplano* region and the Andes valleys. A 560-km highway runs from Santa Cruz to Cochabamba, serving a colonization scheme on virgin lands around Santa Cruz. The Pan-American highway, linking Argentina and Peru, crosses Bolivia from south to north-west.

INLAND WATERWAYS

By agreement with Paraguay in 1938 (confirmed in 1939) Bolivia has an outlet on the River Paraguay. This arrangement, together with navigation rights on the Paraná, gives Bolivia access to the River Plate and the sea. The River Paraguay is navigable for vessels of 12-ft draught for 288 km beyond Asunción in Paraguay and for smaller boats another 960 km to Corumbá in Brazil.

In 1974 Bolivia was granted free duty access to the Brazilian coastal ports of Belém and Santos and the inland ports of Corumbá and Port Velho. In 1976 Argentina granted Bolivia free port facilities at Rosario on the River Paraná. Most of Bolivia's foreign trade is handled through the ports of Matarani (Peru), Antofagasta and Arica (Chile), Rosario and Buenos Aires (Argentina) and Santos (Brazil).

Bolivia has over 14,000 km of navigable rivers which connect most of Bolivia with the Amazon basin.

Bolivian River Navigation Company: f. 1958; services from Puerto Suárez to Buenos Aires (Argentina).

OCEAN SHIPPING

Líneas Navieras Bolivianas (LINABOL): Edif. Hansa 16°, Avda Mariscal Santa Cruz, Apdo 8695, La Paz; tel. 369512; telex 5475; Pres. J. DEL CARPIO BRAVO; Vice-Pres. W. STAHLKE.

CIVIL AVIATION

Bolivia has 30 airports including the two international airports at La Paz (El Alto) and Santa Cruz (Viru-Viru). In 1979 air transport accounted for 4% of cargo carried compared with 25% by rail.

Lloyd Aéreo Boliviano, SAM (LAB): Casilla 132, Aeropuerto 'Jorge Wilstermann', Cochabamba; tel. (02) 25900; telex 6290; f. 1925; partly state-owned since 1941; operates internal services linking the main localities in Bolivia, and joint services with other national lines to Argentina, Brazil, Chile, Paraguay, Panama, Peru, the USA, Uruguay and Venezuela; Pres. Gen. JAIME NIÑO DE GUZMAN; Gen. Man. Lic. FERNANDO VARGAS; fleet: 2 Boeing 727-100, 3 Boeing 727-200, 1 Fokker F.27-600, 1 F.27-200, 2 Boeing 707-323C (passenger), 1 Boeing 727-100C.

Transportes Aéreos Militares: Avda Panamericana Alto, La Paz; tel. (02) 389433; internal passenger and cargo services; Dir-Gen. Col J. M. COQUIS; fleet: 1 DC-54, 4 CV-440, 20 C-47, 1 C-46, 6 IAI Arava.

Tourism

Lake Titicaca, at 3,810 m (12,500 ft) above sea-level, offers excellent fishing and the 'reed' island of Suriqui, while on its shore stands the famous Roman Catholic sanctuary of Copacabana. There are pre-Incan ruins at Tiwanaku. The Andes peaks include Chacaltaya, which has the highest ski-run in the world. In 1984 about 163,000 foreign visitors arrived at Bolivian hotels and similar establishments. In 1985 receipts from tourism totalled US $30m. Tourists come mainly from the USA, Europe and South American countries.

Instituto Boliviano de Turismo: Edif. Herrmann 4°, Plaza Venezuela, Casilla 1868, La Paz; tel. (02) 367463; telex 2534; f. 1973; Exec. Dir MARÍA TERESA CHÁVEZ VIDOVIC.

Asociación Boliviana de Agencias de Viajes y Turismo: Edif. Litoral, Mariscal Santa Cruz 1351, POB 3967, La Paz; f. 1984; Pres. EUGENIO MONROY VÉLEZ.

Atomic Energy

Instituto Boliviano de Ciencia y Tecnología Nuclear (IBTEN): Avda 6 de Agosto 2905, Casilla 4821, La Paz; tel. (02) 356877; telex 2220; f. 1983; main activities include: nuclear engineering, agricultural and industrial application of radio-isotopes, radiochemical analysis, neutron generating, nuclear physics and dosimetry; Exec. Dir Ing. JUAN CARLOS MÉNDEZ FERRY (acting).

BOTSWANA

Introductory Survey

Location, Climate, Language, Religion, Flag, Capital

The Republic of Botswana is a land-locked country in southern Africa, with South Africa to the south and east, Zimbabwe to the north-east and Namibia (South West Africa) to the west and north. A short section of the northern frontier adjoins Zambia. The climate is generally sub-tropical, with hot summers. Annual rainfall averages about 457 mm (18 in), varying from 635 mm (25 in) in the north to 228 mm (9 in) or less in the western Kalahari desert. The country is largely near-desert, and most of its inhabitants live along the eastern border, close to the main railway line. English is the official language, and Setswana the national language. Most of the population follow African religions, but several Christian churches are also represented. The national flag (proportions 3 by 2) consists of a central horizontal stripe of black, edged with white, between two blue stripes. The capital is Gaborone.

Recent History

Botswana was formerly the Bechuanaland Protectorate, under British rule. Bechuanaland became a British protectorate, at the request of the local rulers, in 1885. It was administered as one of the High Commission Territories in southern Africa, the others being the colony of Basutoland (now Lesotho) and the protectorate of Swaziland. The British Act of Parliament that established the Union of South Africa in 1910 also allowed for the inclusion in South Africa of the three High Commission Territories, on condition that the local inhabitants were consulted. Until 1960, successive South African governments asked for the transfer of the three territories, but the native chiefs always objected to such a scheme.

Within Bechuanaland, gradual progress was made towards self-government, mainly through nominated advisory bodies. A new constitution was introduced in December 1960, and a Legislative Council (partly elected, partly appointed) first met in June 1961. Bechuanaland was made independent of High Commission rule in September 1963, and the office of High Commissioner was abolished in August 1964. The seat of government was transferred from Mafeking (now Mafikeng), in South Africa, to Gaberones (now Gaborone) in February 1965. On 1 March 1965 internal self-government was achieved, and the territory's first direct election, for a Legislative Assembly, was held on the basis of universal adult suffrage. Of the Assembly's 31 seats, 28 were won by the Bechuanaland Democratic Party (BDP or Domkrag), founded in 1962. The leader of the BDP, Seretse Khama, was sworn in as the territory's first Prime Minister. Bechuanaland became the independent Republic of Botswana, within the Commonwealth, on 30 September 1966, with Sir Seretse Khama (as he had just become) taking office as the country's first President. The BDP, restyled the Botswana Democratic Party at independence, won elections to the National Assembly, with little opposition, in 1969, 1974 and 1979. Sir Seretse, a liberal conservative, consolidated his leadership of the country while pursuing a national programme of democracy, development, self-reliance and unity.

Sir Seretse Khama died in July 1980. His successor to the presidency was Dr Quett Masire, previously Vice-President and Minister of Finance. Dr Masire's presidency was renewed in September 1984, when, in a general election to the National Assembly, the ruling BDP again achieved a decisive victory. Although the BDP's success in the general election consolidated its position, some discontent among the population at the country's high level of unemployment was reflected in the outcome of the simultaneous elections to local government offices, in which the BDP lost control of all the town councils except that of Selebi-Phikwe. The elections to the leadership of the BDP, held in July 1985, resulted in a number of changes in the membership of the party's Central Committee, although the principal officers of the party retained their posts.

During 1987 there was growing tension between the BDP and the main opposition party, the Botswana National Front (BNF). In March an unprecedented outbreak of rioting was attributed by observers to popular dissatisfaction with the Government as a result of increasing unemployment. The BNF was subsequently accused of provoking the unrest. Several members of the BDP suggested that BNF youths were being trained by Libya and the USSR in order to overthrow the Government. In a letter to President Masire, Dr Kenneth Koma, the leader of the BNF, protested against the allegations and urged the President not to ban the BNF. At five parliamentary by-elections held in August 1987, four seats were held by the BDP, while the BNF retained the fifth. In September 1987 a referendum was held on constitutional amendments concerning the electoral system; a large majority reportedly voted in favour of endorsing the reforms, although the BNF boycotted the referendum. A general election to the National Assembly was scheduled to be held in 1989; Dr Koma announced in February 1988 that the BNF was to present candidates in all parliamentary constituencies.

In southern African politics, Botswana occupies a delicate position which is reflected in a foreign policy of moderation and non-alignment. Although Botswana does not have diplomatic links with South Africa, and is openly critical of apartheid, it depends heavily on its neighbour for trade and communications. In April 1980 Sir Seretse chaired the Lusaka summit meeting which established the Southern African Development Co-ordination Conference (SADCC), an economic union of nine southern African states committed to reducing their dependence on South Africa. In July 1981 the SADCC decided to establish a permanent secretariat in Gaborone (see p. 205).

In May 1984 President Masire accused South Africa of exerting pressure on Botswana to sign a non-aggression pact, aimed at preventing the use of Botswana's territory by guerrilla forces of the African National Congress (ANC), a black nationalist movement that is officially outlawed in South Africa. Relations deteriorated sharply in June 1985, when South African forces launched a raid, in which 12 people were killed, on alleged ANC bases in Gaborone. In November a car-bomb, planted outside a hospital in Mochudi, killed four people. Relations improved in February 1986, when Botswana reiterated its pledge to prohibit the use of its territory as a base for terrorist attacks. In March the Botswana Government expelled ANC representatives. However, relations deteriorated in May, when, in conjunction with attacks on Zambia and Zimbabwe, South African forces launched attacks on buildings at Mogaditsane, causing one death. South Africa again claimed that the action had been directed against ANC bases, but the attacks were internationally condemned. At a meeting of the SADCC in August, when sanctions against South Africa were 'commended' (but not agreed upon), Botswana did not commit itself to applying sanctions.

In early 1987, with the approach of the South African whites-only general election in May, tension mounted as South Africa warned that it would launch attacks against Botswana in order to pre-empt disruption of the election by the ANC. In April four people were killed in a bomb explosion in Gaborone; South African involvement was strongly suspected. In August Steven Burnett, a former member of the British Army, was sentenced to five years' imprisonment for the attempted murder of Ronald Watson, a prominent South African businessman, rugby player and anti-apartheid activist; Burnett had gained access to Watson's Gaborone hotel room by masquerading as a British agent, and it was alleged that he had attempted to force Watson to disclose the names and addresses of members of the ANC in Gaborone.

During 1988 there was speculation that South Africa was again attempting to coerce the Botswana Government into signing a security accord. In March South Africa openly admitted responsibility for a commando raid on a house in Gaborone, in which four alleged members of the ANC were killed. In June President Masire reported the arrest of two members of a South African defence force unit which had allegedly opened fire on Botswana security forces near Gaborone while attempting to conduct a commando raid. South Africa claimed that the unit had been on a mission only to gather information, and that the members of the unit had been fired on by the

Botswanans before opening fire themselves. South Africa was also thought to have been responsible for a car-bomb attack in Gaborone shortly afterwards, although no link was established between the two incidents. An abortive attempt to rescue the two South African gunmen from gaol in September led to the arrests of the defence lawyer in the case and a South African soldier. In addition, two South African civilians faced charges, in October, of helping a third South African to conceal information concerning the June raid. Five alleged members of the ANC were killed by South African police near the South African border with Botswana in early August; later in the month the South African army announced plans to erect an electrified fence along a section of the border between Botswana and South Africa, in order to halt the reputed threat of guerrilla infiltration into South Africa via Botswana. In late September South Africa issued warnings to Botswana that it would take action to prevent attacks by ANC guerrillas via Botswanan territory, which were allegedly planned to disrupt South African municipal elections held in late October.

The transfer of control of the railways in Botswana, from National Railways of Zimbabwe to Botswana Railways, was delayed in early 1987, amid growing tension between the authorities of the South African 'Homeland' of Bophuthatswana and the Botswana Government, which was being pressurized to recognize the 'Homeland' as independent. In late 1986 Bophuthatswana announced that all Botswana train crews would be required to obtain visas to travel through its territory. Major disruption to the rail service was, however, avoided by the introduction of South African train crews to operate the section of rail lines crossing Bophuthatswana, and less harm was inflicted on Botswana than on the 'Homeland' and traders from Mafikeng in South Africa. In February 1987 Botswana began construction of a railway line to bypass Bophuthatswana boundaries, and the dispute ended in April, when the 'Homeland' offered to abandon the new visa requirements.

As one of the five 'front-line' states, Botswana played an important role in the attempts to encourage a peaceful solution to the constitutional problems of Zimbabwe, and continues to do so for Namibia. The Botswana Defence Force was formed in 1977, mainly to control security problems extending from Botswana's neighbours. Relations with Zimbabwe became strained in early 1983, when it was alleged that armed Zimbabwean dissidents were being sheltered among the 3,000 Zimbabwean refugees encamped in Botswana. The first meeting of the Botswana-Zimbabwe joint commission for co-operation was held in October 1984. A new influx of refugees, following the Zimbabwe general election in July 1985, threatened to disrupt relations. In May 1988, however, President Masire expressed confidence that the remaining Zimbabwean refugees would return to their country as a result of an apparent improvement in the political climate in Zimbabwe, following the signing of a unity agreement between the country's two main political parties in December 1987. A border post at Mpandamatenga, between northern Botswana and Zimbabwe, was reopened in September 1988, after 10 years of closure; the reopening was aimed, in part, at assisting tourism in the area. Improved relations between Botswana and Zimbabwe were consolidated in September 1988, when the two countries signed an amended customs agreement.

In August 1987 Botswana and Mozambique agreed to establish a permanent joint commission to develop and strengthen political, economic and cultural links.

While travelling to a 'summit' conference of African countries in Luanda, Angola, in August 1988, President Masire suffered minor injuries when his presidential aircraft was shot down over Angolan territory by an Angolan fighter aircraft. Angola issued an apology, claiming that the presidential aircraft had been mistaken for an enemy aircraft, and the incident was not expected to impair relations between Botswana and Angola.

Government

Legislative power is vested in the National Assembly, with 36 members holding office for five years, including 30 elected by universal adult suffrage and four appointed by the President. Executive power is vested in the President, elected by the Assembly for its duration. He appoints and leads a Cabinet, which is responsible to the Assembly. The President has powers to delay implementation of legislation for six months, and certain matters also have to be referred to the 15-member House of Chiefs for approval, although this body has no power of veto. Local government is effected through nine district councils and four town councils.

Defence

Botswana established a permanent Defence Force in 1977. In June 1988 its total strength was 3,250, including 150 in an air arm. In addition there was a paramilitary police force of 1,000. The defence budget for 1987/88 was 45.3m. pula.

Economic Affairs

With a semi-arid climate, and periodically subject to drought, Botswana is not well suited to agriculture. Nevertheless, the country's economy was traditionally based on the nomadic herding of livestock and on the cultivation of subsistence crops. Since the 1970s, however, the exploitation of mineral deposits has become a major activity in terms of Botswana's exports and gross national product (GNP), although the mining sector provides employment for only about 4% of the labour force. The recent development of mining has made an important contribution to the country's rapid economic growth. In 1987, according to estimates by the World Bank, Botswana's GNP (at average 1985–87 prices) was US $1,175m., equivalent to $1,030 per head. Between 1980 and 1987, it was estimated, GNP per head increased, in real terms, at an average rate of 9.0% per year, the second highest growth rate among all the countries of the world for which data are available over this period. Measured in purchasers' values, Botswana's gross domestic product (GDP) increased, in real terms, at an annual average of 14.3% between 1965 and 1980. The average real growth rate in GDP was 11.9% per year between 1980 and 1986.

More than 80% of the country's working population are engaged in agriculture. Until the early 1970s, this sector was the source of almost all of Botswana's exports. From the early 1980s, however, agriculture was adversely affected by successive years of drought, and in 1986 the contribution of the agricultural sector (including forestry and fishing) to total GDP was only 4%. In normal years the cattle industry is a significant source of foreign exchange earnings, and livestock accounts for about 80% of the total agricultural output. Under the provisions of the Lomé Convention (see p. 149), Botswana exports beef to the countries of the EEC on favourable terms. The national herd is very unevenly distributed among the rural population, of whom almost 50% have no direct access to cattle. It is estimated that one-half of the total herd is owned by 5% of households, with about 20% of the total held by the country's 360 large-scale commercial farms. The Botswana Meat Commission (BMC) slaughtered a record 239,000 head of cattle in 1984, when beef sales earned some P119.9m. However, the BMC's throughput declined to 193,843 head in 1986, despite slightly better rains during the year. Although the carcass weight of beef exports declined, fluctuations in the exchange rate resulted in an increase in the value of beef exports from some P95m. in 1984 to P125.4m. in 1986, when beef exports accounted for 7% of Botswana's foreign earnings. The drought reduced the national herd to some 2.4m. head by mid-1987, about 600,000 fewer than pre-drought levels, and the number of cattle slaughtered in 1987 declined by 25%, to some 146,000 head. However, an annual growth rate of 5% was forecast in the beef industry up to 1991, in view of planned expansion and development projects, such as the construction of a new abattoir in Francistown, due to be completed in 1989.

Arable farming is largely undeveloped and extremely vulnerable to adverse weather conditions. The total production of the four major crops (maize, sorghum, millet and beans) declined to some 7,300 metric tons in 1984, owing to drought. Production rose to some 19,000 tons in 1985. In spite of improved rainfall in 1986, locust swarms limited output in that year to only 20,000 tons. However, government incentives led to an increase of 25% in the planted area in 1987, to 306,000 ha, so that overall output of grain rose from 21,000 metric tons in 1986 to 25,000 tons in the following year. The outlook for 1988 was uncertain. Crop production satisfies only about 10% of national requirements, which were 190,000 tons in 1985, and were projected to exceed 200,000 tons per year by 1991. In early 1987 it was estimated that almost 80% of the population required supplementary food aid. In 1984 a National Food Strategy was introduced, whereby new measures to co-ordinate food distribution were to be undertaken. In the following year the Government introduced a Labour-based Relief Programme, whereby local inhabitants were to be paid to develop the rural infrastructure. In the 1987/88 budget proposals, more than P5m. was allocated for drought relief, to supplement external assistance. There are also projects to bring extensive new areas of land under irrigation in the Chobe and Okavango regions.

Mining is now the major source of exports and government revenues, accounting for 46.1% of Botswana's total GDP in 1985/86. In addition to the established extraction of diamonds, copper-nickel and coal, there are also deposits of asbestos, chromite, copper, fluorspar, iron, manganese, silver, talc and uranium. There have been large-scale discoveries of salt and natural sodium carbonate (soda ash) in the north-east, and indications of the presence of platinum, gold, petroleum and natural gas in southern Botswana.

Diamond production began in 1971, and in 1987 diamonds accounted for 85% of total export earnings. All current diamond production is by the De Beers Botswana Mining Company (Debswana), which is owned equally by the Botswana Government and the South African company De Beers, although Botswana takes about 70% of the profits. In July 1987 Debswana and De Beers signed an agreement whereby the South African company bought Botswana's diamond stockpile in return for some US $500m. and a 5.27% shareholding in De Beers. This entitled Debswana to two seats on the board of directors of De Beers and on the board of its international trading arm, the Diamond Trading Company. The value of Botswana's diamond exports has risen significantly in recent years, reaching P1,066m. in 1985, P1,226m. in 1986, and a record P2,253m. in 1987. The surge in earnings in 1987 was largely attributable to the sale by Debswana of its stockpile. Output rose to 12.9m. carats in 1984, making Botswana the third largest diamond producer in the world. Output fell slightly, to 12.6m. carats, in 1985, but rose to 13.1m. carats in 1986, and a record 13.2m. in 1987. In 1984 it was estimated that production at the two chief mines would continue for at least 25–30 years. Output was expected to increase further in 1990, with the planned opening of a plant, at Jwaneng mine, to sift ore tailings for stones.

The Selebi-Phikwe copper and nickel operation, in which the Government has a 15% share, began production in 1974. More than 40m. metric tons of ore were located, and production of copper-nickel matte reached an estimated 58,000 tons in 1985. However, the decline in world metal prices and markets after 1981 reduced earnings and caused considerable financial problems for the operating company, whose accumulated losses were estimated to have reached P1,189m. by 1986. The position of the company improved in 1987, when accumulated losses fell to P1,165m. Operating profits increased from P18.2m. in 1986 to P20.4m. in 1987, reflecting an increase in the volume and value of sales. The upward trend was expected to continue in 1988, as production levels were projected to rise considerably and as metal prices remained buoyant. In July 1988 the company announced plans to develop a new copper-nickel mine near Selebi-Phikwe; the mine was projected to reach full capacity of 1,500 tons of ore per day by mid-1990. There are further high-grade copper deposits in the Ghanzi area, but development of these will be partly subject to a sustained improvement in world copper prices.

Coal-mining in Botswana began in 1972, and 499,400 metric tons were produced in 1986. It is believed that there may be reserves of 17,000m. tons in the east of the country. Development of Botswana's coal resources would require the development of rail links, either through South Africa or by a trans-Kalahari railway passing through Namibia to the port of Walvis Bay, and their profitability would depend on a recovery in world coal prices. The prospects for world prices in 1987 suggested that any development would be unlikely until after 1990. With the inauguration of a new power station at the Morupule coalfield in May 1987, Botswana was expected to reduce dependence on South African electricity supplies.

The sole major minerals project to be scheduled under the Sixth National Development Plan is the exploitation of the soda ash deposits at Sua-Pan, where there are estimated reserves of 1,000m. tons of salt and 200m. tons of soda ash. Agreement on the exploitation of soda ash deposits was reached between the Governments of Botswana and South Africa in October 1987. Arrangements for financing the scheme, projected to cost US $456m. at 1988 prices, were finalized in November 1988.

In 1987 a joint venture, Shashe Mines, was formed by the Government, a Canadian company and a US company, to conduct exploration work on gold deposits at Map Nova, near Francistown; exploitation of the mineral, with a projected annual value of P8m., was due to begin in 1988/89.

Botswana, with Lesotho and Swaziland, is linked to South Africa in a customs union. However, Botswana left the Rand Monetary Area and established its own currency and central bank in 1976. The dramatic rise in diamond output and earnings caused a revival in the economy from 1982/83, when GDP, at 1979/80 prices, grew by 24%, until 1984/85, when the growth rate of GDP was estimated at some 8%. GDP grew by about 14% in 1985/86, and by 14.7% in 1986/87, owing to unexpected increases in diamond production and price levels. Growth in 1987/88 was expected to reach about 8.7%. Botswana had a persistent trade deficit, which was partly offset by remittances sent home by migrant workers, for more than 20 years until 1983. A surplus of P502m. was recorded in 1986, owing largely to the rise in diamond exports. According to preliminary estimates, the surplus for 1987 was P1,146m., reflecting the effect of the sale of Debswana's diamond stockpile to De Beers in July. The balance-of-payments surplus rose from P566m. in 1986 to a record P950m. in 1987. There was also a considerable rise in foreign exchange reserves, which stood at more than P2,500m. in early 1988, sufficient to cover imports for about 30 months. A budget surplus of P377m. was recorded in 1987/88. The 1988/89 budget envisaged a surplus of P280m. Inflation reached an annual rate of about 10% in 1985 and 1986, and was reduced to 8% in 1987, with another reduction projected for 1988.

The Sixth National Development Plan (1985–91) involves total projected investment of P1,220m., and emphasizes employment-creation, rural and infrastructural development, and education. The Botswana Development Corporation (BDC), established in 1970, aims to promote investment and assists various companies, particularly in the fields of industry and agriculture. The BDC planned a five-year programme of investment, covering 1985/86–1989/90. In an attempt to encourage general investment in the economy, the Government announced a liberalization of exchange controls in early 1988.

Social Welfare

Health services are being developed, and in 1980 there were 13 general hospitals, one mental hospital, 103 clinics (32 with maternity wards), 215 health posts and 341 mobile health stops. There were 111 registered physicians, 10 dentists and 1,071 nurses. The construction at Francistown of a new hospital, the largest in the country, was due to be completed in 1987. Medical treatment for children under 11 years of age is provided free of charge. Of development expenditure in the 1988/89 budget, P26.1m. was allocated to health.

Education

Adult illiteracy averaged 59% (males 63%; females 56%) in 1971, but, according to estimates by UNESCO, the rate had declined to 29.2% (males 27.4%; females 30.5%) by 1985. A National Literacy Programme was initiated in 1980, and about 40,000 adults were enrolled under the programme in 1986. Free primary education from the age of six years was also introduced in 1980. The Government aimed to provide universal primary education by 1990, and at least two years of intermediate schooling for all soon after that date. It also aimed to make available, by 1991, secondary education for 70% of children who complete primary education. Fees for secondary education were to be abolished in 1988. Under the Sixth National Development Plan, P198m. is to be spent on education, including the construction of primary and secondary schools, and the expansion of technical education and of the training of teachers. Education was allocated P79.7m. of development expenditure in the 1988/89 budget.

Education is not compulsory. Primary education begins at seven years of age and lasts for up to six years. Secondary education, beginning at the age of 13, lasts for a further five years, comprising a first cycle of three years and a second of two years. As a proportion of the school-age population, the total enrolment at primary and secondary schools increased from 52% (boys 48%; girls 56%) in 1975 to 73% (boys 69%; girls 77%) in 1985. Enrolment at primary schools in 1985 included 88% of children in the relevant age-group (83% of boys; 93% of girls), while the comparable ratio for secondary enrolment was only 22% (boys 20%; girls 25%). In 1986 there were 235,941 pupils in primary schools, mostly financed by district councils, assisted by government grants in aid. In that year, there were also 35,966 secondary students, 652 technical

BOTSWANA

students, and 1,700 students at the University of Botswana. In addition, there were 932 students at brigades, which are small, semi-autonomous units providing craft and practical training. There were also 1,633 students enrolled at teacher-training colleges. In 1985 a teacher-training college for the secondary level was opened.

Public Holidays
1989: 1–2 January (New Year), 24–27 March (Easter), 4 May (Ascension Day), 15–16 July (for President's Day), 30 September–1 October (for Botswana Day), 25–26 December (Christmas).

1990: 1–2 January (New Year), 13–16 April (Easter), 24 May (Ascension Day), 15–16 July (for President's Day), 30 September–1 October (for Botswana Day), 25–26 December (Christmas).

Weights and Measures
The metric system is in use.

Statistical Survey

Source (unless otherwise stated): Central Statistics Office, Private Bag 0024, Gaborone; tel. 52521.

Area and Population

AREA, POPULATION AND DENSITY

Area (sq km)	582,000*
Population (census results)	
31 August 1971	574,094†
12–26 August 1981‡	
Males	443,104
Females	497,923
Total	941,027
Population (official estimates at mid-year)	
1985	1,088,000
1986	1,128,000
1987	1,169,000
Density (per sq km) at mid-1987	2.0

* 224,711 sq miles.
† Excluding 10,550 nomads and 10,861 non-citizens.
‡ Excluding 42,069 citizens absent from the country during enumeration.

POPULATION BY CENSUS DISTRICT
(1981 census results)

Barolong	15,471	Kweneng	117,127	
Central	323,328	Lobatse	19,034	
Chobe	7,934	Ngamiland	68,063	
Francistown	31,065	Ngwaketse	104,182	
Gaborone	59,657	North-East	36,636	
Ghanzi	19,096	Orapa	5,229	
Jwaneng	5,567	Selebi-Phikwe	29,469	
Kgalagadi	24,059	South-East	30,649	
Kgatleng	44,461			

PRINCIPAL TOWNS (population at 1981 census)

Gaborone (capital)	59,657	Kanye	20,215
Francistown	31,065	Lobatse	19,034
Selebi-Phikwe	29,469	Mochudi	18,386
Serowe	23,661	Maun	14,925
Mahalapye	20,712	Ramotswa	13,009
Molepolole	20,565		

BIRTHS AND DEATHS
1981: Birth rate 47.2 per 1,000; death rate 12.9 per 1,000 (census estimates).

ECONOMICALLY ACTIVE POPULATION
(persons aged 12 years and over, 1981 census)

	Males	Females	Total
Agriculture, hunting, forestry and fishing	86,436	67,135	153,571
Mining and quarrying	10,550	654	11,204
Manufacturing	3,473	1,007	4,480
Electricity, gas and water	2,238	166	2,404
Construction	16,298	787	17,085
Trade, restaurants and hotels	5,837	6,292	12,129
Transport, storage and communications	2,832	290	3,122
Financing, insurance, real estate and business services	816	661	1,477
Community, social and personal services	40,551	30,607	71,158
Activities not adequately defined	5,273	2,359	7,632
Total employed	174,304	109,958	284,262
Unemployed	14,766	17,460	32,226
Total labour force	189,070	127,418	316,488

1984/85 (survey results): Total labour force 367,949 (males 172,763; females 195,186).

Mid-1986 (estimates in '000): Agriculture, etc. 259; Total labour force 393. Source: FAO, *Production Yearbook*.

EMPLOYMENT (formal sector only; August each year)

	1983	1984	1985*
Agriculture	4,500	5,400	4,000
Mining and quarrying	7,200	7,500	7,300
Manufacturing	9,800	9,500	10,100
Electricity and water	1,900	2,000	1,900
Construction	9,600	11,100	11,600
Trade, restaurants and hotels	15,300	18,100	18,300
Transport and communications	3,900	5,500	5,700
Finance and business services	6,000	6,200	6,800
Community, social and personal services	42,400	44,700	51,400
Total	100,600	110,000	117,100

* September 1985.

The number of Batswana employed in South African mines was 18,849 in 1983, 18,894 in 1984, and 16,397 in 1985.

BOTSWANA   Statistical Survey

Agriculture

PRINCIPAL CROPS ('000 metric tons)

	1984	1985	1986
Maize	1	1	0
Millet	1	2	1*
Sorghum	6	15	8*
Roots and tubers*	7	7	7
Pulses*	13	14	14
Groundnuts (in shell)	1	1*	1*
Sunflower seed	0	0	1*
Cottonseed*	2	2	2
Cotton (lint)*	1	1	1
Vegetables*	16	16	16
Fruit*	11	11	11

* FAO estimates.
Source: FAO, *Production Yearbook*.

LIVESTOCK ('000 head, year ending September)

	1984	1985	1986
Cattle	2,685	2,459	2,720*
Horses*	23	24	24
Donkeys	138	143	143*
Sheep	167	200	210
Goats	889	1,138	1,000*
Pigs*	8	8*	8*

* FAO estimates.
Source: FAO, *Production Yearbook*.

LIVESTOCK PRODUCTS (FAO estimates, '000 metric tons)

	1984	1985	1986
Beef and veal	41	42	43
Goats' meat	3	3	3
Other meat	8	8	8
Cows' milk	94	96	98
Goats' milk	3	3	3
Cheese	1.1	1.1	1.2
Butter and ghee	1.3	1.3	1.4
Hen eggs	0.7	0.7	0.7
Cattle hides	5.5	5.6	5.8

Source: FAO, *Production Yearbook*.

Forestry

ROUNDWOOD REMOVALS
(FAO estimates, '000 cubic metres)

	1984	1985	1986
Industrial wood	70	73	76
Fuel wood	1,066	1,107	1,149
Total	1,136	1,180	1,225

Source: FAO, *Yearbook of Forest Products*.

Fishing

	1984	1985	1986
Total catch (metric tons)	1,500	1,700	1,900

Source: FAO, *Yearbook of Fishery Statistics*.

Mining

(metric tons, unless otherwise indicated)

	1984	1985	1986
Coal	392,854	437,088	499,400
Copper ore*	21,517	21,703	21,337
Nickel ore*	18,562	19,560	18,972
Cobalt ore*	259	222	162
Diamonds ('000 carats)	12,904	12,608	13,100

* Figures refer to the metal content of ores.

Industry

SELECTED PRODUCTS

	1982	1983	1984
Beer ('000 litres)	58,600	63,600	63,800
Electric energy (million kWh)	604	622	661

1985: Electric energy 701 million kWh.
1986: Electric energy 725 million kWh.

Finance

CURRENCY AND EXCHANGE RATES
Monetary Units
100 thebe = 1 pula (P).

Denominations
Coins: 1, 2, 5, 10, 25 and 50 thebe; 1 pula.
Notes: 1, 2, 5, 10 and 20 pula.

Sterling and Dollar Equivalents (30 September 1988)
£1 sterling = 3.377 pula;
US $1 = 1.997 pula;
100 pula = £29.62 = $50.08.

Average Exchange Rate (US $ per pula)
1985   0.5296
1986   0.5354
1987   0.5960

BUDGET ('000 pula, year ending 31 March)

Revenue*	1984/85	1985/86†	1986/87‡
Taxation	628,760	794,300	995,310
Mineral revenues	376,480	560,260	685,750
Customs pool revenues	155,790	145,360	193,500
Non-mineral income tax	87,180	82,190	109,410
Other current revenue	131,400	189,280	156,300
Interest	25,500	16,340	20,490
Other property income	79,470	150,330	75,470
Fees, charges, etc.	26,430	22,610	60,340
Sales of fixed assets and land	3,240	2,150	1,860
Total	763,400	985,730	1,153,470

* Excluding grants received ('000 pula): 39,520 in 1984/85; 29,440 in 1985/86; 41,210 in 1986/87. All figures are rounded to the nearest 10,000 pula.
† Estimates.   ‡ Budget forecasts.

BOTSWANA

Expenditure*	1984/85	1985/86†	1986/87‡
Office of the President	42,510	51,014	59,658
Finance and development planning	24,613	18,353	19,514
Labour and home affairs	9,179	11,093	13,109
Agriculture	28,810	34,872	45,092
Education	67,261	82,482	98,123
Commerce and industry	3,956	5,398	7,365
Local government and lands	50,792	64,744	72,582
Works and communications	52,550	66,253	81,586
Mineral resources and water affairs	13,435	18,424	25,068
Health	22,344	26,227	32,850
External affairs	3,097	5,662	10,300
Appropriations from revenue	244,385	282,329	598,232
Public debt interest	44,046	61,849	51,102
Total (incl. others)	622,377	748,831	1,144,467

* Figures refer to operations of the Consolidated Fund only.
† Estimates. ‡ Budget forecasts.

Source: *Financial Statements, Tables and Estimates of Consolidated and Development Fund Revenues 1986/87.*

NATIONAL DEVELOPMENT PLAN, 1985–91
(projected expenditure in million pula)

Office of the President	72.5
Finance and development planning	19.8
Home affairs	15.3
Agriculture	52.8
Education	198.0
Commerce and industry	19.3
Local government and lands	133.4
Works and communications	322.9
Mineral resources and water affairs	93.8
Health	69.8
Non-allocated expenditures	240.0
Total	1,222.3

Source: Ministry of Finance and Development Planning, Gaborone.

INTERNATIONAL RESERVES
(US $ million at 31 December)

	1985	1986	1987
IMF special drawing rights	10.65	17.14	21.82
Reserve position in IMF	14.20	19.06	22.32
Foreign exchange	758.35	1,161.48	2,012.95
Total	783.21	1,197.67	2,057.08

Source: IMF, *International Financial Statistics.*

MONEY SUPPLY (million pula at 31 December)

	1985	1986	1987
Currency outside banks	43.4	58.5	68.6
Demand deposits at commercial banks	144.9	184.9	243.6
Total money	188.2	243.5	312.1

Source: IMF, *International Financial Statistics.*

COST OF LIVING
(Consumer Price Index; base: 1980 = 100)

	1984	1985	1986
Food, beverages and tobacco	165.6	181.5	198.8
Clothing and footwear	137.4	145.0	156.9
All items (incl. others)	152.7	165.0	181.6

NATIONAL ACCOUNTS
(million pula at current prices, year ending 30 June)
Expenditure on the Gross Domestic Product

	1983/84	1984/85	1985/86
Government final consumption expenditure	362.8	443.1	526.7
Private final consumption expenditure	629.3	746.3	817.0
Increase in stocks	−19.8	15.2	−6.0
Gross fixed capital formation	337.6	484.0	511.9
Total domestic expenditure	1,309.9	1,688.6	1,849.6
Exports*	772.3	970.3	1,472.0
Less Imports†	780.1	998.2	1,128.1
GDP in purchasers' values	1,302.1	1,660.7	2,193.5
GDP at constant 1979/80 prices	1,122.2	1,211.5	1,380.6

* Exports of goods only.
† Imports of goods plus net imports of services.

1986/87 (million pula): GDP 2,747.4 at current prices; 1,583.9 at 1979/80 prices.

Source: IMF, *International Financial Statistics.*

Cost-Structure of the Gross Domestic Product*

	1982/83	1983/84	1984/85
Compensation of employees	409.8	476.4	534.1
Operating surplus	358.2	485.9	652.2
Domestic factor incomes	768.0	962.3	1,186.3
Consumption of fixed capital	129.1	151.2	172.6
GDP at factor cost	897.1	1,113.5	1,358.9
Indirect taxes, *less* subsidies	131.9	165.4	164.6
GDP in purchasers' values	1,029.0	1,278.9	1,523.5

* Figures are preliminary. Revised totals of GDP in purchasers' values (in million pula) are: 1,049.7 in 1982/83; 1,302.1 in 1983/84; 1,660.7 in 1984/85.

Source: Bank of Botswana, Gaborone.

Gross Domestic Product by Economic Activity*

	1983/84	1984/85	1985/86
Agriculture, hunting, forestry and fishing	76.1	78.5	84.0
Mining and quarrying	405.3	553.1	1,005.3
Manufacturing	82.0	92.9	129.4
Electricity, gas and water	32.3	32.5	40.0
Construction	70.5	59.2	61.3
Trade, restaurants and hotels	276.9	312.6	377.0
Transport, storage and communication	32.7	38.7	42.5
Finance, insurance, real estate and business services	86.5	95.8	109.5
Government services	202.0	247.4	284.8
Other services	43.5	46.0	49.1
Sub-total	1,307.8	1,556.7	2,182.9
Less Imputed bank service charge	28.9	33.2	38.0
Total	1,278.9	1,523.5	2,144.9

* Figures are preliminary. Revised totals (in million pula) are: 1,302.1 in 1983/84; 1,660.7 in 1984/85; 2,193.5 in 1985/86.

BOTSWANA

Statistical Survey

BALANCE OF PAYMENTS (US $ million)

	1985	1986	1987
Merchandise exports f.o.b.	727.8	852.5	1,582.2
Merchandise imports f.o.b.	−494.1	−608.7	−852.3
Trade balance	233.6	243.8	729.9
Exports of services	161.2	216.6	284.1
Imports of services	−381.0	−432.3	−553.9
Balance on goods and services	13.8	28.1	460.1
Private unrequited transfers (net)	−3.2	−2.6	−1.8
Government unrequited transfers (net)	76.9	115.5	138.9
Current balance	87.6	140.0	597.2
Direct capital investment (net)	52.1	90.5	125.1
Other long-term capital (net)	61.5	51.6	
Short-term capital (net)	27.5	−14.3	−1.2
Net errors and omissions	25.5	33.8	−145.5
Total (net monetary movements)	254.3	301.6	575.6
Valuation changes (net)	54.7	112.8	283.8
Changes in reserves	308.9	414.5	859.4

Source: IMF, *International Financial Statistics*.

External Trade

PRINCIPAL COMMODITIES ('000 UA*)

Imports	1984	1985	1986†
Food, beverages and tobacco	186,459	231,743	269,607
Fuel	104,201	130,049	147,664
Chemicals and rubber	85,795	100,852	154,505
Wood and paper	33,752	37,402	57,677
Textiles and footwear	92,357	104,649	123,227
Metal and metal products	92,360	102,389	153,828
Machinery and electrical goods	166,657	221,730	280,058
Vehicles and transport equipment	130,096	175,633	242,274
Other commodities	124,735	169,958	188,677
Total	1,016,412	1,274,405	1,617,517

* Figures are in terms of the Unit of Account (UA) used by the Customs Union of Southern Africa. This is equivalent to the South African rand. Its average value was: 1.455 pula in 1984; 1.166 pula in 1985; 1.216 pula in 1986.
† Estimates.

Exports	1984	1985	1986†
Meat and meat products	70,224	113,696	146,688
Diamonds	697,095	1,237,227	1,455,606
Copper-nickel matte	77,041	140,604	147,117
Textiles	45,551	37,730	50,923
Hides and skins	12,718	21,852	11,801
Other commodities	66,498	80,091	150,872
Total	969,127	1,631,200	1,963,007

PRINCIPAL TRADING PARTNERS ('000 UA)

Imports	1984	1985	1986†
CUSA*	793,357	966,229	1,256,682
Other Africa	89,156	100,962	118,593
United Kingdom	31,656	58,955	45,335
Other Europe	67,468	96,095	98,975
USA	8,678	35,146	59,115
Others	10,451	17,018	38,817
Total	1,016,412	1,274,405	1,617,517

* Customs Union of Southern Africa, of which Botswana is a member; also including Lesotho, Namibia, South Africa and Swaziland.
† Estimates.

Exports	1984	1985	1986†
CUSA*	65,277	95,021	109,779
Other Africa	37,913	59,746	117,895
United Kingdom	20,032	83,550	89,855
Other Europe	734,384	1,269,153	1,631,557
USA	79,061	115,856	3,302
Others	32,460	7,854	10,600
Total	969,127	1,631,180	1,962,988

Transport

RAILWAYS (year ending 30 June)

	1982/83	1983/84	1984/85
Passenger journeys*	529,984	487,298	542,692
Freight (net ton-km)	1,378,732	1,336,650	1,296,735

* Internal traffic only.

ROAD TRAFFIC

	1983	1984	1985
Vehicles registered*	38,108	41,197	45,748

* Excluding government vehicles (4,371 in 1983).

CIVIL AVIATION (traffic)

	1983	1984*	1985
Passenger journeys ('000)	127	112	136
Freight (metric tons)	278	338	n.a.
Mail (metric tons)	93	104	n.a.

* Preliminary figures.

Tourism

	1981	1982	1983
Tourist arrivals ('000)	227	305	306
Tourist receipts (US $ million)	22	36	47

Source: UN, *Statistical Yearbook*.

Communications Media

	1981	1982	1983
Radio receivers ('000 in use)	80	100	120

Radio receivers ('000 in use, 1985): 140.
Book production (first editions only, 1980): 97 titles (books 70; pamphlets 27).
Daily newspapers (1984): 1 title (estimated circulation 18,000 copies).
Sources: UNESCO, *Statistical Yearbook*; Central Statistics Office, Gaborone.
Telephones in use: 17,409 in 1983; 17,912 in 1984; 19,109 in 1985.

Education

(1986)

	Institutions	Teachers	Students
Primary	537	7,324	235,941
Secondary	73	1,619	35,966
Brigades	15	125	932
Teacher training	5	106	1,633
Technical education	2	86	652
University	1	249	1,700

1984: There were 218 Batswana studying abroad.
Source: *Education Statistics*, 1986 (Central Statistics Office, Gaborone).

Directory

The Constitution

The Constitution of the Republic of Botswana came into operation at independence on 30 September 1966.

EXECUTIVE

President
Executive power lies with the President of Botswana, who is also Commander-in-Chief of the armed forces. Election for the office of President is linked with the election of members of the National Assembly. Presidential candidates must be over 30 years of age and receive at least 1,000 nominations. If there is more than one candidate for the Presidency, each candidate for office in the Assembly must declare support for a presidential candidate. The candidate for President who commands the votes of more than half the elected members of the Assembly will be declared President. If the Presidency falls vacant the members of the National Assembly will themselves elect a new President. The President will hold office for the duration of Parliament. After the 1974 elections the President became an ex officio member of the Assembly. The President chooses four members of the National Assembly.

Cabinet
There is also a Vice-President, whose office is Ministerial. The Vice-President is appointed by the President and deputizes in the absence of the President. The Cabinet consists of the President, the Vice-President and 10 other Ministers appointed by the President. The Cabinet is responsible to the National Assembly.

LEGISLATURE

The legislative power is vested in Parliament, consisting of the President and the National Assembly, acting after consultation in certain cases with the House of Chiefs. The President may withhold assent to a Bill passed by the National Assembly. If the same Bill is again presented after six months, the President is required to assent to it or to dissolve Parliament within 21 days.

House of Chiefs
The House of Chiefs has the Chiefs of the eight principal tribes of Botswana as ex-officio members, four members elected by sub-chiefs from their own number, and three members elected by the other 12 members of the House. Bills and motions relating to chieftaincy matters and alterations of the Constitution must be referred to the House, which may also deliberate and make representations on any matter.

National Assembly
The National Assembly consists of the Speaker, the Attorney-General, who does not have a vote, 30 elected members and four specially elected members chosen by the President. There is universal adult suffrage. The life of the Assembly is five years.

The Constitution contains a code of human rights, enforceable by the High Court.

The Government

HEAD OF STATE

President: Dr QUETT KETUMILE JONI MASIRE (took office 18 July 1980; re-elected for a five-year term 10 September 1984).

CABINET
(December 1988)

President: Dr QUETT KETUMILE JONI MASIRE.

Vice-President and Minister of Finance and Development Planning: PETER MMUSI.

Minister of External Affairs: Dr GAOSITWE K. T. CHIEPE.

Minister of Mineral Resources and Water Affairs: ARCHIE M. MOGWE.

Minister of Presidential Affairs and Public Administration: PONATSHENGO H. K. KEDIKILWE.

Minister of Agriculture: DANIEL KWELAGOBE.

Minister of Works and Communications: CHAPSON BUTALE.

Minister of Commerce and Industry: MOATLAGOLA P. K. NWAKO.

Minister of Health: JAMESON LESEDI T. MOTHIBAMELE.

Minister of Education: KEBATHLAMANG PITSEYOSI MORAKE.

Minister of Home Affairs: ENGLISHMAN M. K. KGABO.

Minister of Local Government and Lands: PATRICK BALOPI.

Assistant Minister of Agriculture: GEOFFREY OTENG.

Assistant Minister of Finance and Development Planning: OBED CHILUME.

Assistant Ministers of Local Government and Lands: MICHAEL R. TSHIPINARE, RONALD SEBEGO.

MINISTRIES

Office of the President: Private Bag 001, Gaborone; tel. 355434; telex 2414.

Ministry of Agriculture: Private Bag 003, Gaborone; tel. 351171.

Ministry of Commerce and Industry: Private Bag 004, Gaborone; tel. 353881; telex 2674.

Ministry of Education: Private Bag 005, Gaborone; tel. 355294; telex 2944.

Ministry of Finance and Development Planning: Private Bag 008, Gaborone; tel. 355272; telex 2401.

Ministry of Health: Private Bag 0038, Gaborone; tel. 355557.

Ministry of Home Affairs: Private Bag 002, Gaborone; tel. 355212.

Ministry of Local Government and Lands: Private Bag 006, Gaborone; tel. 352091.

Ministry of Mineral Resources and Water Affairs: Private Bag 0018, Gaborone; tel. 352454; telex 2503.

Ministry of Works, Transport and Communications: Private Bag 007, Gaborone; tel. 355303; telex 2743.

Legislature

NATIONAL ASSEMBLY

Speaker: JAMES G. HASKINS.

BOTSWANA

General Election, 8 September 1984

Party	Votes	%	Seats
Botswana Democratic Party	154,863	68.0	29*†
Botswana National Front	46,550	20.4	4†
Botswana People's Party	14,961	6.6	1
Botswana Independence Party	7,288	3.2	—
Botswana Progressive Union	3,036	1.3	—
Independent	1,058	0.5	—
Total	227,756	100.0	34

* Of the 29 members of the BDP in the National Assembly, four were specially elected by the President.

† A by-election held in December 1984 (following a disputed result) increased the total number of seats held by the BNF to 5 and reduced the BDP total to 28. Five by-elections held in August 1987 did not alter the distribution of seats in the National Assembly.

There are two additional members of the Assembly: the Speaker and the Attorney-General. The President is an ex-officio member.

HOUSE OF CHIEFS

The House has a total of 15 members.

Chairman: Chief SEEPAPITSO.

Political Organizations

Botswana Democratic Party (BDP): POB 28, Gaborone; f. 1962; Pres. Dr QUETT MASIRE; Chair. P. S. MMUSI; Sec.-Gen. DANIEL KWELAGOBE.

Botswana Independence Party (BIP): POB 3, Maun; f. 1962; Pres. MOTSAMAI K. MPHO; Sec.-Gen. EMMANUEL R. MOKOBI.

Botswana Liberal Party (BLP): POB 258, Francistown; f. 1983; Pres. MARTIN CHAKALISA.

Botswana National Front (BNF): POB 42, Mahalapye; f. 1967; Pres. Dr KENNETH KOMA; Parl. Leader ex-Chief BATHOEN II GASEITSIWE; Sec.-Gen. MARELEDI GIDDIE.

Botswana People's Party (BPP): POB 159, Francistown; f. 1960; Pres. Dr KNIGHT MARIPE; Chair. KENNETH MKHWA; Sec.-Gen. JOHN MOSOJANE.

Botswana Progressive Union (BPU): POB 10229, Francistown; f. 1982; Pres. D. K. KWELE; Chair. G. G. BAGWASI; Sec.-Gen. R. K. MONYATSIWA.

United Front for the Unemployed: PO Gaborone; f. 1984; Pres. M. T. MOOKETSANE.

Diplomatic Representation

EMBASSIES AND HIGH COMMISSIONS IN BOTSWANA

China, People's Republic: POB 1031, Gaborone; telex 2428; Ambassador: LU DEFENG.

France: Gaborone; telex 2374; Ambassador: JEAN PIERRE GUYOT.

Germany, Federal Republic: POB 315, Gaborone; tel. 353143; telex 2225; Ambassador: EGON KATZKI.

India: Tirelo House, The Mall, Private Bag 249, Gaborone; tel. 372676; telex 2622; High Commissioner: HARSH KUMAR BHASIN.

Libya: POB 180, Gaborone; telex 2501; Secretary of People's Bureau: S. A. EL FALLAH.

Mozambique: Gaborone; Ambassador: RAFAEL MAGUNI.

Nigeria: POB 274, Gaborone; telex 2415; High Commissioner: R. O. OMOTOYE.

Romania: Gaborone; Ambassador: GHEORGHE BADRUS.

Sweden: Private Bag 0017, Gaborone; telex 2421; Ambassador: KARL-GÖRAN ENGSTRÖM.

USSR: POB 81, Gaborone; telex 2595; Ambassador: MIKHAIL NIKOLAYEVICH PETROV.

United Kingdom: Private Bag 0023, Gaborone; tel. 352841; telex 2370; High Commissioner: PETER A. RAFTERY.

USA: POB 90, Gaborone; tel. 353982; telex 2554; Ambassador: JOHN KORDEK.

Zambia: POB 362, Gaborone; telex 2416; High Commissioner: N. N. K. KALALA.

Zimbabwe: POB 1232, Gaborone; tel. 314495; telex 2701; High Commissioner: A. M. CHIDODA.

Judicial System

There is a High Court at Lobatse and a branch at Francistown, and Magistrates' Courts in each district. Appeals lie to the Court of Appeal of Botswana.

Chief Justice: EBEN LIVESEYLUKE.

Puisne Judges: N. O. G. MURRAY, J. C. BARRINGTON-JONES.

President of the Court of Appeal: I. A. MAISELS.

Justices of Appeal: L. BARON, T. A. AGUDA, S. KENTRIDGE, A. N. E. AMISSAH, L. VAN WINSEN.

Registrar and Master of the High Court: FAQIR MUHAMMAD.

Chief Magistrates: R. F. HUNT, A. D. AMSTELL, G. M. OKELLO.

Senior Magistrates: K. OBENG, G. RWELENGERA, Y. D. PETKAR, S. HOOPER, M. WANNIAPPA, F. B. SWANNIKER.

Attorney-General: M. D. MOKAMA.

Religion

The majority of the population are animists; an estimated 30% are thought to be Christians. There are Islamic mosques in Gaborone and Lobatse. The Bahá'ís are also represented.

CHRISTIANITY

Lekgotla la Sekeresete la Botswana (Botswana Christian Council): POB 355, Gaborone; tel. 315191; f. 1966; comprises 20 churches and seven other organizations; Chair. Rev. JACOB T. LIPHOKO; Gen. Sec. NATHANIEL T. K. MMONO.

The Anglican Communion

Anglicans are adherents of the Church of the Province of Central Africa, comprising 10 dioceses and covering Botswana, Malawi, Zambia and Zimbabwe. The Province was inaugurated in 1955, and the diocese of Botswana was formed in 1972.

Archbishop of the Province of Central Africa and Bishop of Botswana: Most Rev. WALTER PAUL KHOTSO MAKHULU, POB 769, Gaborone.

Protestant Churches

African Methodist Episcopal Church: POB 141, Lobatse; Rev. L. M. MBULAWA.

Evangelical Lutheran Church in Botswana: POB 1976, Gaborone; tel. 352227; telex 2882; Bishop Rev. PHILIP ROBINSON; 15,553 mems.

Evangelical Lutheran Church in Southern Africa (ELCSA): POB 5394, Johannesburg 2000, South Africa; tel. 3377113; telex 86519; Gen. Sec. Rev. MERVYN D. ASSUR; six dioceses (one in Botswana).

   Botswana Diocese: Bishop Rev. M. NTUPING, POB 400, Gaborone; tel. 353976.

Methodist Church in Botswana: POB 260, Gaborone; Dist. Supt Rev. Z. S. M. MOSAI.

United Congregational Church of Southern Africa: POB 1263, Gaborone; tel. 352491; autonomous since 1980; Chair. (elect) Rev. S. R. PHETO; Sec. Rev. K. F. MOKOBI; 14,000 mems.

Other denominations active in Botswana include the Church of God in Christ, the Dutch Reformed Church and the United Methodist Church.

The Roman Catholic Church

Botswana comprises a single diocese. The metropolitan see is Bloemfontein, South Africa. The church was established in Botswana in 1928, and had an estimated 44,000 adherents in the country at 31 December 1986. The Bishop participates in the Southern African Catholic Bishops' Conference, based in Pretoria, South Africa.

Bishop of Gaborone: Mgr BONIFACE TSHOSA SETLALEKGOSI, Bishop's House, POB 218, Gaborone; tel. 312958.

The Press

DAILY NEWSPAPER

Dikgang Tsa Gompieno (Botswana Daily News): Private Bag 0060, Gaborone; tel. 352261; telex 2409; f. 1964; publ. by Dept of Information and Broadcasting; Setswana and English; Mon.–Fri.; circ. 30,000.

PERIODICALS

Agrinews: Private Bag 003, Gaborone; f. 1971; monthly; technical journal on agriculture and rural development; circ. 6,000.

Botswana Advertiser: POB 130, Gaborone; tel. 2844; telex 2351; weekly.

BOTSWANA   *Directory*

Botswana Guardian: POB 1641, Gaborone; tel. 314937; telex 2692; weekly; Editor (vacant); circ. 13,408.

The Gazette: POB 1605, Gaborone; tel. 312833; telex 2631; weekly; circ. 9,500.

Government Gazette: Private Bag 0081, Gaborone; tel. 314441; telex 2414.

Kutlwano: Private Bag 0060, Gaborone; telex 2409; monthly; Setswana and English; publ. by Dept of Information and Broadcasting; circ. 7,000.

Mmegi Wa Dikgang: POB 20906, Gaborone; tel. 374784; telex 2753; weekly; Setswana and English; publ. by Mmegi Publishing Trust.

Northern Advertiser: POB 402, Francistown; f.1985; weekly; advertisements, local interest, sport; publ. by Premier Investments (Pty) Ltd.

The Zebra's Voice: Private Bag 00114, Gaborone; f. 1982; quarterly; cultural magazine; publ. by the National Museum, Monuments and Art Gallery; circ. 4,000.

NEWS AGENCIES

Botswana Press Agency (BOPA): Private Bag 060, Gaborone; tel. 313601; telex 2284; f. 1981.

Foreign Bureaux

Inter Press Service (IPS) (Italy): POB 1605, Gaborone; tel. 312833; telex 2631.

Xinhua (New China) News Agency (People's Republic of China): Plot 5379, President's Drive, POB 1031, Gaborone; tel. 353434; telex 2428; Correspondent CHEN GUOWEI.

Publishers

A.C. Braby (Botswana) (Pty) Ltd: POB 1549, Gaborone; telex 2371; telephone directories.

Department of Information and Broadcasting: Private Bag 0060, Gaborone; tel. 352541; telex 2409; publs include *Dikgang Tsa Gompieno*, *Daily News* and material on Botswana.

Longman Botswana (Pty) Ltd: POB 1083, Gaborone; tel. 313969.

Printing and Publishing Co (Botswana) (Pty) Ltd: 5647 Nakedi Rd, POB 130, Broadhurst, Gaborone; tel. 312844; telex 2351; publs *Botswana Advertiser*.

Government Publishing House

Department of Government Printing and Publishing Services: Private Bag 0081, Gaborone; tel. 314441; telex 2414.

Radio and Television

RADIO

There were an estimated 150,000 radio receivers in use in 1988. The introduction of a commercial radio network is under consideration.

Radio Botswana: Private Bag 0060, Gaborone; tel. 352541; telex 2633; broadcasts in Setswana and English; f. 1965; Dir Mrs M. NASHA.

TELEVISION

TV Association of Botswana: Gaborone; two transmitters relaying SABC-TV programmes from South Africa, and BOP-TV programmes from Bophuthatswana; plans for a national TV service are under consideration.

Finance

(cap. = capital; dep. = deposits; res = reserves;
m. = million; brs = branches; amounts in pula)

BANKING

Bank of Botswana: POB 712, Gaborone; tel. 351911; telex 2405; f. 1975; bank of issue; cap. and res 381.5m., dep. 1,518.4m., (Dec. 1986); Gov. H. C. L. HERMANS; Dir of Operations A. SABINE.

Bank of Credit and Commerce (Botswana) Ltd: Lobatse House, Industrial Sites, POB 871, Gaborone; tel. 352867; telex 2556; f. 1982; cap. and res 5.0m., dep. 49.6m. (Dec. 1987); Chair. E. A. GARDA; Man. Y. H. PATEL; 4 brs.

Barclays Bank of Botswana Ltd: Commerce House, The Mall, POB 478, Gaborone; tel. 352041; telex 2417; f. 1975; cap. and res 31.9m., dep. 306.7m. (Dec. 1987); Chair. LOUIS G. NCHINDO; Man. Dir ROBERT A. BIRD; 18 brs.

Botswana Co-operative Bank Ltd: Co-operative Bank House, Broadhurst Mall, POB 40106, Gaborone; tel. 371398; telex 2298; f. 1974; cap. and res 2.2m., loans 5.9m. (1985); central source of credit for registered co-operative societies; Pres. M. L. SETLHARE; Gen. Man. L. LINDKVIST.

National Development Bank: Development House, The Mall, POB 225, Gaborone; tel. 352801; telex 2553; f. 1964; cap. and res 7.7m., dep. 50.1m. (March 1986); priority given to agricultural credit for Botswana farmers, and co-operative credit and loans for local business ventures; Chair. C. G. MOGAMI; Gen. Man. B. I. GASENNELWE; 6 brs.

Standard Chartered Bank Botswana Ltd: Standard House, The Mall, POB 496, Gaborone; tel. 353111; telex 2258; f. 1975; cap. and res 14.5m., dep. 147.2m. (Dec. 1986); Chair. J. G. HASKINS; Man. Dir A. O'DWYER; 13 brs.

INSURANCE

Associated Insurance Brokers of Botswana (Pty) Ltd: Standard House, POB 624, Gaborone; tel. 351481; telex 2539; f. 1982 by merger of Insurance Brokers Botswana (Pty) Ltd and Minet Botswana (Pty) Ltd; Man. Dir C. P. M. COWPER.

Botswana Eagle Insurance Co Ltd: 501 Botsalano House, POB 1221, Gaborone; telex 2259.

Botswana Insurance Co (Pty) Ltd: BIC House, POB 336, Gaborone; tel. 351791; telex 2359; Gen. Man. P. B. SUMMER.

ECB Insurance Brokers (Botswana) (Pty) Ltd: Botsalano House, POB 1195, Gaborone.

IGI Botswana (Pty) Ltd: IGI House, POB 715, Gaborone; tel. 351521; telex 2430; Gen. Man. J. M. WALKIN.

Trade and Industry

PUBLIC CORPORATIONS

Botswana Housing Corporation: POB 412, Gaborone; tel. 353341; telex 2729; cap. P1.3m. (March 1983); provides housing for government and local authorities, assists with housing schemes and provision of housing for other persons; Chair. P. O. MOLOSI, the Perm. Sec., Ministry of Local Govt and Lands; Gen. Man. J. D. RICHARDSON; 557 employees.

Botswana Meat Commission (BMC): Private Bag 4, Lobatse; tel. 330321; telex 2420; f. 1966; cap. and res P40m. (Sept. 1986); slaughter of livestock, exports of hides and skins, carcasses, frozen and chilled boneless beef, offal tannery and cannery producing wet blue leather, canned tongue, pet foods and corned beef; Exec. Chair. D. W. FINLAY; Gen. Man. F. BOAKGOMO; 1,600 employees.

Botswana Power Corporation: Motlakase House, POB 48, Gaborone; tel. 352211; telex 2431; irredeemable cap. P19.4m.; Chair. the Dep. Perm. Sec., Ministry of Mineral Resources and Water Affairs; CEO E. D. BELL.

Botswana Telecommunications Corporation: POB 700, Gaborone; tel. 353611; telex 2252; f. 1980; cap. 17.3m. (March 1985); CEO M. T. CURRY.

Water Utilities Corporation: Private Bag 00276, Gaborone; tel. 352521; telex 2545; f. 1970; public water supply undertaking for principal townships; assets P154m.; revenue P27m.; Chair. the Perm. Sec., Ministry of Mineral Resources and Water Affairs; CEO T. WATERS.

CHAMBER OF COMMERCE

Botswana National Chamber of Commerce and Industry: POB 20344, Gaborone; tel. 52677.

MARKETING BOARD

Botswana Agricultural Marketing Board: Private Bag 0053, Gaborone; tel. 351341; telex 2530; cap. P4.2m.; Chair. the Perm. Sec., Ministry of Agriculture; Gen. Man. P. R. J. MULLIGAN.

DEVELOPMENT ORGANIZATIONS

Botswana Development Corporation Ltd: Madirelo House, Mmanaka Rd, POB 438, Gaborone; tel. 351811; telex 2251; f. 1985/86; cap. p.u. P19.0m. (June 1987); Chair. the Perm. Sec., Ministry of Finance and Development Planning, BALDEZI GAOLATHE; Gen. Man. M. O. MOLEFANE.

Botswana Enterprise Development Unit (BEDU): Plot No. 1269, Lobatse Rd, PB 0014, Gaborone; f. 1974 to promote industrialization and rural development; Dir J. LINDFORS.

Botswana Livestock Development Corporation (Pty) Ltd: POB 455, Gaborone; tel. 351949; telex 2543; f.1977; cap. P3.8m. (1987); Chair. M. L. MOKONE; Gen. Man. S. M. R. BURNETT.

Financial Services Company of Botswana (Pty) Ltd: POB 1129, Gaborone; tel. 351363; telex 2207; f. 1974; cap. and res P1.9m.; provides hire purchase, mortgage and industrial leasing facilities; Chair. J. E. ANDERSON; Gen. Man. G. H. WILSON.

Trade and Investment Promotion Agency (TIPA), Ministry of Commerce and Industry: Private Bag 004, Gaborone; tel. 353881; telex 2674; promotes diversification of the industrial sector by encouraging investment, provides consultancy services and monitors projects, participates in trade missions and international trade fairs; Dir J. R. MONAMETSI.

EMPLOYERS' ASSOCIATION

Botswana Confederation of Commerce, Industry and Manpower: Botsalano House, POB 432, Gaborone; f. 1971; Chair. R. MANNATHOKO; Sec.-Gen. MODIRE J. MBAAKANYI; 600 affiliated mems.

TRADE UNIONS

Botswana Federation of Trade Unions: POB 440, Gaborone; tel. 352534; f. 1977; Gen. Sec. RONALD DUST BAIPIDI.

Affiliated Unions

Air Botswana Employees' Union: POB 92, Gaborone; Gen. Sec. JOYCE MOTHUPI.

Botswana Bank Employees' Union: POB 111, Gaborone; Gen. Sec. KEOLOPILE GABORONE.

Botswana Commercial and General Workers' Union: POB 62, Gaborone; Gen. Sec. ALFRED J. KEBAWETSE.

Botswana Commercial Banks Supervisory and Managerial Staff Union: c/o Standard Chartered Bank Botswana Ltd, Standard House, The Mall, POB 496, Gaborone; Gen. Sec. CYNTHIA MOGAMI.

Botswana Construction Workers' Union: POB 1508, Gaborone; Gen. Sec. J. MOLAPISI.

Botswana Co-operative Managers' Union: POB 70, Gaborone; Gen. Sec. A. P. RAMOSAKO.

Botswana Diamond Sorters-Valuators' Union: POB 1186, Gaborone; Gen. Sec. FELIX T. LESETEDI.

Botswana Housing Corporation Staff Union: POB 412, Gaborone; Gen. Sec. M. G. K. MOTOWANE.

Botswana Local Government Workers' Union: POB 20048, Francistown; Gen. Sec. ALLISON MANGENA.

Botswana Meat Industry Workers' Union: POB 181, Lobatse; Gen. Sec. RUSSIA SESINYE.

Botswana Mining Workers' Union: POB 14, Selebi-Phikwe; Gen. Sec. BALEKAMANG GABASIANE.

Botswana Railway Staff and Artisan Employees' Union: POB 1486, Gaborone; Gen. Sec. P. MAGOWE.

Botswana Railway Workers' Union: POB 181, Gaborone; Gen. Sec. E. T. G. MOHUTSIWA.

Botswana Telecommunication Employees' Union: POB 2032, Gaborone; Gen. Sec. LOFTUS S. MOTLOKWA.

Central Bank Union: POB 712, Gaborone; Gen. Sec. G. S. SHAGWA.

Insurance Employees' Union of Botswana: POB 1863, Gaborone; Gen. Sec. G. T. MMATLI.

National Union of Government, Parastatal and Statutory Bodies' Manual Workers: POB 374, Gaborone; Gen. Sec. ALLISON T. MANGENA.

Orapa and Letlhakane Mines Staff Union: POB 220, Orapa; Gen. Sec. C. M. TANGANE.

CO-OPERATIVES

Department of Co-operative Development: POB 86, Gaborone; f. 1964; by 1976 there were 116 co-operatives, of which 57 were marketing and supply co-operatives, 20 consumers' co-operatives, 29 thrift and loan societies, four credit societies, two dairy co-operatives, a horticultural co-operative, a fisheries co-operative, a co-operative union and a co-operative bank.

Botswana Co-operative Union: Gaborone; telex 2298.

Transport

RAILWAYS

The main railway line from Mafikeng, South Africa, to Bulawayo, Zimbabwe, a distance of 960 km, passes through the country. There are 705 km of 1,067mm-gauge track within Botswana, including two spurs serving the Selebi-Phikwe mining complex (59 km) and the Morupule colliery (14 km). The entire main railway line in Botswana is to be rehabilitated under an SADCC project, estimated to cost US $114m. Feasibility studies were undertaken in 1984 for the construction of a trans-Kalahari rail link, about 875 km in length, which would provide Botswana with an outlet to the Atlantic Ocean on the coast of Namibia, but this project is unlikely to proceed in the near future.

Botswana Railways: Private Bag 00125, Gaborone; telex 2980; the railway has been owned and operated by National Railways of Zimbabwe (NRZ), but Botswana Railways has been effecting a gradual take-over. The section of railway from Ramatlabama to Mahalapye came under the control of Botswana Railways in April 1984, and it was planned that the entire length of track within Botswana should be completely controlled by Botswana Railways by January 1987. These plans were delayed in January 1987, owing to a dispute with the authorities of Bophuthatswana, the South African 'independent Homeland', who declared that all Botswana train crews would require visas to travel through the 'Homeland'. South African train crews agreed to operate the section of railway running through Bophuthatswana, and the construction of a new line to bypass Bophuthatswana was begun in February 1987. In April 1987 the 'Homeland' offered to abandon the new visa requirements, thereby ending the dispute. Progress towards a formal hand-over of the railway was made in July 1988, when it was reported that agreement had been reached on the amount that Botswana was to pay NRZ in compensation for its local assets.

ROADS

In 1986 there were about 13,500 km of roads, of which 2,040 km were main roads and 1,023 km were secondary roads. There is a tarred road from Gaborone, via Francistown, to Kazungula, where the borders of Botswana, Namibia, Zambia and Zimbabwe meet. The Government plans the construction of a road between Orapa and Serowe, and the Palapye to Serowe road was completed in 1983. Under the Sixth National Development Plan, there are plans to construct several main roads and to extend the networks of both feeder and rural roads serving the remoter areas. In 1988 bids for contracts for the construction of a 300-km road between Nata and Maun were being considered. It is possible to cross the Zambezi river into Zambia by ferry. Plans to build a bridge at the crossing are being considered.

CIVIL AVIATION

The centre of Botswana's air network is Seretse Khama Airport, the international airport at Gaborone, which opened in 1984. There are three regional airports, and airfields at all population centres and tourist areas. Air Botswana is investigating the possibility of operating a scheduled service to the village of Kasane in the Chobe area of northern Botswana. The service is projected to begin after the completion of the new Kasane Airport, which is scheduled to be fully operational by early 1991. The present scheduled services of Air Botswana are supplemented by an active charter and business sector which carries 40% of the total passengers. British Airways operates a service between London and Gaborone, via Zambia, instigated in March 1987 to counter the effect of a possible ban on flights to South Africa. In January 1987 Air Tanzania began a weekly service to Gaborone. In April 1988 it was announced that Botswana was planning to assume control of its airspace from South Africa.

Air Botswana (Pty) Ltd: POB 92, Gaborone; tel. 352812; telex 2413; f. 1972; owned by the Botswana Development Corpn; domestic services between Gaborone, Maun, Francistown and Selebi-Phikwe, connecting with regional services to Kenya, Lesotho, Mozambique, South Africa, Swaziland, Zambia and Zimbabwe; also operates world-wide cargo charters; Chair. M. O. MOLEFANE; Gen. Man. KEITH PETCH; fleet of 1 Fokker F-27-200, 1 Fokker F-27-400, Dornier 228; 3 ATR-42 to replace the Fokker F-27s in 1988.

Tourism

There are six game reserves, including Chobe, only a short drive from Victoria Falls (on the Zambia-Zimbabwe border) by first-class roads. Some 60,000 tourists visited Botswana in 1986, compared with 82,000 visitors in 1983, when earnings from tourism were about P40m. Efforts to expand the tourist industry include plans for the construction of new hotels and the rehabilitation of existing ones. The Botswana Development Corporation was to begin construction of a luxury hotel near Gaborone in early 1988, for completion by 1990.

Department of Wildlife and National Parks: POB 131, Gaborone; tel. 351461; Dir. K. T. NGWAMOTSOKO.

Tourism Development Unit, Ministry of Commerce and Industry: Private Bag 0047, Gaborone; tel. 353024; telex 2414; f. 1973; promotion of tourism in Botswana; Dir CHAWA BOGOSI.

BRAZIL

Introductory Survey

Location, Climate, Language, Religion, Flag, Capital

The Federative Republic of Brazil, the fifth largest country in the world, lies in central and north-eastern South America. To the north are Venezuela, Colombia, Guyana, Suriname and French Guiana, to the west Peru and Bolivia, and to the south Paraguay, Argentina and Uruguay. Brazil has a very long coastline on the Atlantic Ocean. Climatic conditions vary from hot and wet in the tropical rain forest of the Amazon basin to temperate in the savannah grasslands of the central and southern uplands, which have warm summers and mild winters. In Rio de Janeiro temperatures are generally between 17°C (63°F) and 29°C (85°F). The language is Portuguese. Almost all of the inhabitants profess Christianity, and about 90% are adherents of the Roman Catholic Church. The national flag (proportions 10 by 7) is green, bearing, at the centre, a yellow diamond containing a blue celestial globe with 23 white five-pointed stars (one for each state), arranged in the pattern of the southern firmament, and an equatorial scroll with the motto 'Ordem e Progresso' ('Order and Progress'). The capital is Brasília, although some administrative offices still remain in Rio de Janeiro, which was the capital of Brazil until 1960.

Recent History

Formerly a Portuguese possession, Brazil became an independent monarchy in 1822, and a republic in 1889. A federal constitution for the United States of Brazil was adopted in 1891. Following social unrest in the 1920s, the economic crisis of 1930 resulted in a major revolt, led by Dr Getúlio Vargas, who was installed as President. He governed the country as a benevolent dictator until forced to resign by the armed forces in December 1945. During Vargas's populist rule, Brazil enjoyed internal stability and steady economic progress. He established a strongly authoritarian corporate state, similar to fascist regimes in Europe, but in 1942 Brazil entered the Second World War on the side of the Allies. Brazil was the first South American country to dispatch fighting troops to Europe, sending an expeditionary force to Italy in 1944.

In 1946 Gen. Eurico Dutra was elected President and a new constitution was adopted. Vargas was re-elected President in 1950, but failed to create the necessary stability and committed suicide in August 1954. The next President was Dr Juscelino Kubitschek, who took office in 1956. Brazil's capital was moved in 1960 from Rio de Janeiro to the newly-constructed city of Brasília, sited on a previously uninhabited jungle plateau about 1,000 km (600 miles) inland. President Kubitschek was succeeded by Dr Jânio Quadros, who was elected in October 1960 and took office in January 1961. President Quadros resigned after only seven months in office, and in September 1961 the Vice-President, João Goulart, was sworn in as President.

Military leaders suspected Goulart, the leader of the Partido Trabalhista Brasileiro (PTB), of Communist sympathies, and they were reluctant to let him succeed to the presidency. As a compromise, the Constitution was amended to restrict the powers of the President and to provide for a Prime Minister. Upon taking office, President Goulart appointed Dr Tancredo de Almeida Neves, a member of the Partido Social Democrático (PSD) and a former Minister of Justice, to be Prime Minister. However, Dr Neves and most of his Cabinet resigned in June 1962. He was succeeded by Dr Francisco Brochada da Rocha, also of the PSD, who was Prime Minister from July to September 1962. His successor was Dr Hermes Lima of the PTB, hitherto Minister of Labour, but a referendum in January 1963 approved a return to the presidential system of government, whereupon President Goulart formed his own Cabinet.

Following a period of rapid inflation and allegations of official corruption, the left-wing regime of President Goulart was overthrown by a bloodless army revolution on 31 March-1 April 1964. The leader of this right-wing military coup was Gen. (later Marshal) Humberto Castelo Branco, the Army Chief of Staff, who was elected President by Congress. In October 1965 President Castelo Branco assumed dictatorial powers, and all of Brazil's 13 existing political parties were banned. In December, however, two artificially-created parties, the pro-Government Aliança Renovadora Nacional (ARENA) and the opposition Movimento Democrático Brasileiro (MDB), were granted official recognition. President Castelo Branco nominated as his successor the Minister of War, Marshal Artur da Costa e Silva, who was elected President in October 1966 and took office in March 1967. At the same time, a new constitution, changing the country's name to the Federative Republic of Brazil, was introduced. The ailing President da Costa e Silva was forced to resign in September 1969, being replaced by a triumvirate of military leaders.

During its early years the military regime promulgated a series of Institutional Acts which granted the President wide-ranging powers to rule by decree. On 20 October 1969 the ruling junta introduced a revised constitution, vesting executive authority in an indirectly-elected President. Congress, suspended since December 1968, was recalled and elected Gen. Emílio Garrastazú Médici, who took office as President on 30 October 1969. Urban guerrilla activity was widespread during 1970 but was largely eliminated by stern security measures. The next President was Gen. Ernesto Geisel, chosen by an electoral college, who took office in March 1974. Despite President Geisel's more liberal outlook, the MDB made sweeping gains in the congressional elections of November 1974, and calls were made for an end to military government.

In January 1978 President Geisel's choice of Gen. João Baptista de Figueiredo as his successor was endorsed by the national convention of the ARENA. General Figueiredo was duly elected President by an electoral college in October 1978 and took office in March 1979, promising to continue the *abertura*, or opening to democratization, begun by President Geisel. In the face of growing political agitation, Congress approved various reforms that had been proposed by President Geisel. In November 1979 Congress approved legislation to end the controlled two-party system. The new parties that were subsequently formed included the first independent labour party, the Partido dos Trabalhadores (PT).

President Figueiredo suffered a heart attack in September 1981 and was temporarily replaced by Vice-President Antônio Aureliano Chaves de Mendonça, the first civilian to hold presidential office since 1964. Congressional, state and municipal elections were held in November 1982. The government-sponsored Partido Democrático Social (PDS) gained a majority of seats in the Senate, but failed to win an absolute majority in the Chamber of Deputies, and was also defeated in elections for the governorships of 10 states and in municipal elections in more than 75% of the main towns. The pre-election legislative measures ensured, however, that the PDS would have a majority in the presidential electoral college, due to choose a successor to Gen. Figueiredo in 1985.

In February 1983, to limit the strength of the opposition, the President issued a decree which reduced the authority of the state governors before they had even taken office, and the regime introduced other measures which concentrated political power in Brasília. Lacking a working majority in the Chamber of Deputies, the President ruled by decree laws until May 1983, when he was able to form an alliance of the PDS with the small Partido Trabalhista Brasileiro (PTB, unrelated to the former PTB, banned in 1965), thereby obtaining 248 out of 479 seats. In August 1983 the PTB withdrew from its pact with the PDS, and in October a 60-day state of emergency was declared in Brasília. In December 1983, responding to opposition demands for direct voting in the presidential election, President Figueiredo confirmed that the system of indirect election, through an electoral college, would be retained.

Throughout 1984 Brazil's political life was dominated by the issue of succession. In February the four opposition parties announced the formation of the Free Elections Movement and proposed a constitutional amendment to provide for an immediate return to direct presidential elections. In an attempt to regain the political initiative, President Figueiredo presented his own draft amendment, which proposed the return of Brazil to full democracy (including the holding of direct presidential elections) by 1988, a reduction in the presidential term of office from six to four years and the curtailment of the President's exceptional powers. In April Congress voted on the opposition's amendment; in spite of considerable backing from members of the PDS, the opposition narrowly failed to obtain the two-thirds majority that was required.

In July 1984 Vice-President Chaves de Mendonça and the influential Marco de Oliveira Maciel, a former Governor of Pernambuco State, announced the formation of an alliance of liberal PDS members with members of the Partido do Movimento Democrático Brasileiro (PMDB). This offered the opposition a genuine opportunity to defeat the PDS in the electoral college. In August Senator Tancredo Neves, the Governor of Minas Gerais State (who had been Prime Minister in 1961-62), was named presidential candidate for the liberal alliance, while the former president of the PDS, José Sarney, was declared vice-presidential candidate. In December the liberal alliance formed an official political party, the Partido Frente Liberal (PFL). At the presidential election, held in January 1985, Neves was elected as Brazil's first civilian President for 21 years, winning 480 of the 686 votes in the electoral college. Prior to the inauguration ceremony in March 1985, however, Neves was taken ill, and in April, following a series of operations, he died. José Sarney, who had assumed the role of Acting President in Neves' absence, took office as President in April. President Sarney made no alterations to the Cabinet selected by Neves, and he affirmed his commitment to fulfilling the objectives of the late President-designate. In May Congress approved a constitutional amendment restoring direct elections by universal suffrage. The right to vote was also extended to illiterate adults. The first direct elections took place in November, when municipal elections were held in 31 cities.

The introduction in February 1986 of an anti-inflation programme, the Cruzado Plan (see Economic Affairs), proved, initially, to be a considerable success for the Government and boosted the personal popularity of President Sarney. The Government hoped to capitalize on its popularity at elections for the National Congress, to act as the Constitutional Assembly, in November 1986, when an electorate of some 69m. Brazilians was eligible to vote for 49 senators and 487 federal deputies. Gubernatorial elections were held concurrently with the congressional elections. At the elections the PMDB emerged as the leading party within the ruling coalition: its representatives secured a majority in the Constitutional Assembly and more than 20 state governorships. The Constitutional Assembly was to draft a new constitution and determine the length of the presidential term of office.

In addition to the problems posed by the constitutional issue, President Sarney's first months in office were further complicated by his Government's controversial proposals for agrarian reform, announced in May 1985, which exacerbated the already tense relations between landowners and peasants. The National Agrarian Reform Programme was launched in October. Under the programme, the Government planned to distribute 40.2m. ha of land to 1.4m. landless families by 1989. However, violent clashes between landowners and peasants, especially in the east Amazonian region, continued throughout 1986, resulting in the deaths of 125 people between January and June. The Roman Catholic Church strongly condemned the Government's apparent lack of commitment to agrarian reform, and supported the illegal occupation of land by peasant groups. Moreover, public dissatisfaction with the Government's economic policies resulted, in November, in the first anti-Government protests since the end of military rule.

The Constitutional Assembly was installed in February 1987, and it was soon apparent that the constitutional debate was to be dominated by the issue of the length of the presidential mandate. The issue caused serious divisions within not only the Assembly but also the PMDB. In May President Sarney attempted to take the initiative in the debate by offering to reduce his term of office from six to five years, and to step down in March 1990. The President's difficulties with the Assembly and the decline in his popularity were compounded by the failure of the Cruzado Plan in early 1987. In February Brazil declared a unilateral moratorium on the repayment of $68,000m. of debt to commercial banks; this decision had serious repercussions for Brazil's overall debt-restructuring programme, but the Government was unable to devote its attention to the problem of the country's foreign debt until the question of the new Constitution had been resolved.

At an extraordinary convention of the PMDB, in July 1987, a majority of the PMDB's members refused to endorse Sarney's offer to relinquish office in 1990, asserting that the Constitutional Assembly was the only appropriate forum to resolve such an issue. In November the Systematization Committee of the Constitutional Assembly voted to reduce the presidential mandate to four years and to introduce a parliamentary form of government. The Committee's vote represented a humiliating blow for the President, who subsequently announced that he would not contest the Assembly's decision, and that he would act as an 'independent arbitrator' at the forthcoming presidential election.

In March 1988, however, President Sarney's administration was bolstered by the Constitutional Assembly's vote in favour of maintaining a presidential system of government. President Sarney was reported to have threatened to resign if the Assembly voted for the introduction of a parliamentary form of government, and his stance on the issue was reported to have caused a serious division within the PMDB. In June the Constitutional Assembly reversed the earlier decision by the Systematization Committee, and approved a presidential mandate of five years. The first round of voting for the presidential election was provisionally set for 15 November 1989, thereby enabling Sarney to remain in office until March 1990. This *de facto* victory for the President precipitated a series of resignations from the PMDB by some of its leading members, who subsequently formed a new centre-left party, the Partido da Social Democracia Brasileira. In July the Assembly began the process of drawing up the definitive version of the new Constitution. President Sarney made a concerted attempt to persuade the Assembly to delete or amend more than 20 articles, on the grounds that they would render Brazil ungovernable. Moreover, he expressed concern at the potential cost of many of the new social programmes envisaged by the Constitution, and by the nationalist slant of some articles. The President's views brought him into direct conflict with the President of the Assembly, Ulysses Guimarães, and led to the resignation of three Ministers opposed to the President's interference in the matter. In spite of last-minute disagreements, the Constitution was approved by the National Congress on 2 September 1988, and was promulgated on 5 October. Among its 245 articles were provisions transferring many hitherto presidential powers to the National Congress. In addition, censorship was abolished; the voting age was lowered to 16 years; and the principle of habeas corpus was introduced. However, the Constitution offered no guarantees of land reform, and was thought by many to be nationalistic and protectionist.

In addition to the new Constitution, the other main issue confronting the administration throughout 1988 was that of economic policy. Following the appointment of three new Ministers of Finance within only nine months, the Government eventually revealed its commitment to drastic cuts in public-sector expenditure, primarily based on a 'freeze' on salary increases for state employees. The adoption of such an unpopular policy led to widespread strikes in the state sector, and in June 1988 both the Head of the General Staff of the Armed Forces and the president of the state petroleum company, PETROBRÁS, left office, following public criticism by them of the Government's economic programme. Despite the announcement, in November, of the formation of a tripartite social pact (composed of the Government and representatives of trade unions and the business sector), protests occurred throughout Brazil, following violent clashes at a state-run steel mill at Volta Redonda, near Rio de Janeiro, in the course of which government troops shot dead at least three protesters. The combination of industrial unrest and social tension was thought to have been a decisive factor in the generally poor results obtained by the PMDB at municipal elections held on 15 November, when the left-wing Partido Democrático Trabalhista and Partido dos Trabalhadores made important gains at the expense of the ruling party. Hence, the final year of the Sarney administration was expected to be dominated by continuing social and economic difficulties and by fierce competition between presidential candidates.

Following the tensions created by the war in 1982 between Argentina and the United Kingdom, after the invasion of the Falkland Islands by Argentine forces, Brazil's relations with the USA improved in 1983, and Brazil gave support to US foreign policy in return for economic aid. In recent years Brazil's relations with the USA have deteriorated as a result of trade disputes. Brazilian troops were mobilized on the frontiers with Venezuela, Guyana and Suriname. Close relations were established with Suriname, and military and economic assistance was provided, in an attempt to weaken Suriname's links with Cuba. In 1988 the Uruguayan Government announced its intention to seek talks with Brazil on some 22,000 ha of Brazilian land claimed by Uruguay, and the sovereignty of a Brazilian island in the Quarai river.

Government

Brazil had a military-backed government from 1964 to 1985. Under the 1969 Constitution, amended by presidential decree in 1977 and 1978, the country is a federal republic comprising 23 States, three Territories and a Federal District (Brasília). Legislative power is exercised by the bicameral National Congress, comprising the Chamber of Deputies (members elected for four years) and the Federal Senate (members elected in rotation for eight years). The number of deputies is based on the size of the population. Election is by universal adult suffrage (the franchise was extended to illiterate adults in 1985) and voting is compulsory. One-third of the Senators are elected indirectly. Executive power is exercised by the President, elected for six years. At the presidential election in January 1985, the President was chosen by an electoral college. A subsequent constitutional amendment provides that future Presidents will be elected by direct balloting. The President appoints and leads the Cabinet. Each State has a directly elected Governor and an elected legislature. A Constitutional Assembly, which was installed in February 1987, drew up a new constitution, which was ratified by the National Congress in September 1988 and promulgated in October.

Defence

Military service, lasting 12 months, is compulsory for men between 18 and 45 years of age. In June 1988 the armed forces comprised 319,200 men: army 218,000, navy 50,500 and air force 50,700. Public security forces number about 243,000 men. Defence expenditure for 1988 was estimated at 275,000m. cruzados.

Economic Affairs

Brazil occupies about 48% of the South American continent. It is the world's fifth largest country, in terms of area, and the sixth most populous. Much of Brazil's interior is covered by tropical forests, on land drained by the world's largest river system, the Amazon and its many tributaries. In terms of aggregate gross national product (GNP), Brazil is among the world's 10 leading countries. Since 1945 the country has experienced rapid industrialization and a generally high rate of economic growth, notably in the period 1967-74, when GNP expanded at an average rate of 11% per year in real terms. In terms of employment, the major sector of the economy is still agriculture, which (along with forestry and fishing) engaged 28.5% of the working population in 1985. Manufacturing employed 14.7% of the working population in 1985. The contribution of the manufacturing sector to gross domestic product (GDP) in 1986 was 28%, compared with 11% from the agricultural sector. In 1987, according to estimates by the World Bank, Brazil's GNP (at average 1985-87 prices) was US $314,642m., equivalent to $2,020 per head. Although annual population growth is more than 2%, it was estimated that GNP per head increased at an average rate of 1.0% per year, measured in constant prices, between 1980 and 1987. The average annual increase in overall GDP, in real terms, was 9.0% in 1965-80, slowing to 2.7% in 1980-86. In 1985 and 1986, however, rates of growth of 8.3% and 8.0% were achieved. In 1987 GDP growth was estimated at only 2.9%.

Agriculture, forestry and fishing provided 11.1% of Brazil's GDP in 1985. In 1977 Brazil became the world's second-largest exporter of agricultural products. The principal agricultural exports are coffee, sugar, soya beans (soybeans), orange juice, beef, poultry and cocoa, and other crops include sisal, tobacco, maize and cotton. Agricultural production expanded by 5% and 8.8% in 1984 and 1985 respectively. Soya beans are Brazil's most important crop, and Brazil is the world's second leading producer. The soya bean crop increased from 16m. metric tons in 1984 to 18m. tons in 1985, but fell to 13m. tons in 1986. However, production recovered to 17m. tons in 1987. The area planted with soya beans increased from 9.2m. ha in 1986/87 to more than 10.3m. ha in 1987/88; consequently, the 1988 crop was expected to reach 19m. tons. Brazil is normally the world's leading producer of coffee, which accounted for more than 8% of export revenue in 1987. Between May and October 1985 Brazil experienced its most severe drought for 40 years: the south and south-east of the country were the regions most seriously affected. As a consequence, agricultural output declined by 7% in 1986, with an estimated decline of 11.4% in the crops sector. The coffee crop fell from 33m. bags (each of 60 kg) in 1985 to 14m. bags in 1986, of which only 9.9m. bags were suitable for export. In order to satisfy the domestic demand for coffee, Brazil imported 1.5m. bags in 1986, and Colombia displaced Brazil as the world's leading exporter of coffee. The 1987 crop recovered to a record level of 35.8m. bags, but, in view of unfavourable weather conditions, the 1988 crop was expected to reach only 25m. bags. In spite of high international prices (principally in early 1986), Brazil's export earnings from coffee declined from US $2,632m. in 1985 to $2,347m. in 1986. Export revenue fell to $2,185m. in 1987. Early estimates for 1989 indicated a crop of between 30m. and 40m. bags. In October 1987 a major reform of Brazil's coffee export system was announced.

Brazil is also the world's leading producer of sugar cane; production increased from 239m. metric tons in 1986 to 269m. tons in 1987. Drought in the north-east region of Brazil was reported to have damaged more than 13% of the 1988 harvest. Output of raw sugar (in which Brazil also leads the world) rose from an estimated 8.3m. metric tons in 1985 to an estimated 8.5m. tons in 1986. Wheat production increased from 4.3m. metric tons in 1985 to 5.7m. tons in 1986 and to 6.1m. tons in 1987. Favourable climatic conditions in 1987 contributed to a record grain harvest of 66m. metric tons in 1988, and agricultural exports were expected to reach $12,000m. in that year. Brazil was reported to be planning to increase its grain production in 1989 to 75m. tons, in order to take advantage of the severe drought afflicting the grain-producing areas of the USA in 1988. Severe frost in the USA in late 1983 led to a significant increase in Brazil's overseas sales in 1984, making orange juice Brazil's fourth most important source of foreign exchange and resulting in export earnings of $1,470m. Following the recovery of the US orange juice industry, export earnings fell to $725m. in 1985. As a consequence, Brazil began to seek new markets in Europe, and EEC countries were collectively the largest consumer of Brazilian orange juice for the June-July 1987 harvest. Brazil is the world's largest exporter of orange juice concentrate, accounting for 60% of the total world market. Brazil supplies 23% of world demand for cocoa. However, production of cocoa has suffered from lack of investment, although exports of cocoa beans earned $273m. in 1986 and $266m. in 1987. In late 1987 Bahia, the main cocoa-producing region, was severely affected by drought, and this development, coupled with low world prices, was expected to result in serious difficulties for the industry in 1988, when the cocoa harvest was estimated at between 2.9m. and 3.5m. bags (each of 60 kg).

Total production of poultry meat was 1.5m. metric tons in 1985 and 1.6m. tons in 1986. The 1986-89 Development Plan, announced in August 1985 by the Sarney administration, stressed the importance of developing the agricultural sector to meet the domestic demand for food. The Government intended to increase the output of food crops by 4.5% annually from 1986 respectively. In 1986 the Government announced a three-year agricultural programme which envisaged investment of CZ $71,000m. in the sector. The plan's objectives included a 10% increase in annual grain production and the establishment of a National Agricultural Fund. In June 1986 the World Bank approved a loan of US $149m. to Brazil for irrigation projects in the north-east region. In June 1988 the Government announced a $600m. investment programme for agro-industrial projects. Funding was to be supplied by the World Bank ($300m.) and by farmers and commercial banks. The agricultural and livestock sector expanded by an estimated 14% in 1987.

Throughout 1988 international attention was drawn increasingly to the effects of the extensive burning of the tropical rain forests in the state of Amazonas. Large-scale burning of trees began in the 1970s, following the construction of new roads which provided access to hitherto impenetrable areas for cattle ranchers, squatter farmers and lumber companies. Cattle ranchers, in particular, have been responsible for almost 80% of the destruction in the region; in 1987 an estimated 200,000 sq km of forest was burned down, including at least 75,000 sq km of virgin forest. In addition to the extensive destruction of animal and plant life, the emission of carbon dioxide from the fires has caused incalculable damage to the earth's ozone layer. In October 1988 the Brazilian Government, under pressure from international organizations, announced a series of measures designed to protect the rain forests, including a total ban on the export of logs and the imposition of rigorous environmental controls on all agricultural and industrial projects in the region.

Industrial production, which accounted for 39% of GDP in 1986, is concentrated on machinery, electrical goods, construction materials, rubber, sugar and wood processing, chemicals and vehicle production. Traditional industries (textiles, clothing, food and beverages) still account for 50% of total industrial production. Industrial production grew by 6.7% in 1984 and by 9% and 11% in 1985 and 1986 respectively. However, in 1987 the sector was reported to have grown by only 0.2%. In 1986 Brazil's total production of crude steel was 21.2m. metric tons and exports totalled 6.5m. tons. Output in 1987 increased to 22.2m. tons. The Tubarão steel mill, with an annual capacity of 3.2m. tons, was inaugurated in November 1983, but future expansion of the industry has been hindered by resistance from overseas markets, and in particular from the USA, which in 1984 imposed surcharges of up to 100% on all imports of Brazilian sheet steel. The Açominas integrated steel works in Minas Gerais, inaugurated in February 1985, were expected to come into operation in 1987–88, and were to produce 2m. tons of steel annually. The Albras aluminium refinery, with an annual capacity of 320,000 tons, was inaugurated in 1986. The construction of its associated alumina smelter, Alunorte, with an annual capacity of 1.3m. tons, has been delayed, and was not expected to resume before 1987. A new processing plant at São Luís de Maranhão, opened in 1984, will be able to produce annually 100,000 tons of aluminium and 500,000 tons of alumina. Brazil is the world's sixth largest producer of motor vehicles; exports represented 20% of total production and 12.5% of Brazil's total exports in 1985. Production was expected to increase from 683,000 cars in 1987 to 759,000 in 1988, and to an estimated 970,000 in 1993. Brazil is also the world's ninth largest exporter of armaments; in 1987 exports of military materials earned an estimated $369m. (at 1985 prices). The country is also a major producer of naval vessels (in 1986 Brazil constructed 429,855 gross tons of ships) and has a diversified and successful aerospace industry.

In September 1988 the Government announced plans to modernize the industrial sector, principally by alleviating the protectionist conditions in which the sector had hitherto been operating. Under the new policy, export-processing zones were to be established in the north and north-east regions, and would receive fiscal incentives from the Government; some US $9,700m. was to be invested in the textiles industry; and import privileges were to be allocated to companies participating in a benefit scheme for exports.

Brazil possesses vast mineral reserves, particularly in Minas Gerais and the Amazon area, and in 1981 the Grand Carajás project (in Amazonia) was opened. Reserves of iron ore at Carajás are estimated to be 18,000m. metric tons. Production began in January 1986, and planned output was 35m. tons of iron ore per year by 1987. Investment in the project was expected to be about US $125,000m., and the value of the Carajás minerals was assessed at $543,000m. The leading mineral export is iron ore, and Brazil is the world's largest exporter. In 1986 Brazil exported 100m. tons of iron ore, out of total production of 168m. tons. New mineral discoveries, including phosphates, uranium, manganese, titanium, copper, tin and coal, are constantly being made. Brazil is the fourth largest producer of bauxite, and extensive reserves have been located in Minas Gerais and the Amazon region, where known reserves amount to 4,600m. tons. Lack of demand, however, has 'frozen' future investment. Gold deposits at Serra Pelada, found in 1980, raised Brazil's annual gold production from 14 metric tons in 1980 to 32 tons in 1985. Output was 24 tons in 1986. Reserves were estimated at 341 tons in 1984. Following foreign investment of $600m. in 1986–88, the sector was expected to expand, and production in 1987 was reported to be 84 tons, although more than 50% of total output was undeclared, having been disposed of by smugglers. In 1989 a major new mine, at Igarape Bahía (with reserves of 65 tons), was scheduled to commence operations. Coal reserves are estimated at 15,000m. metric tons. Tin production increased from 13,100 metric tons in 1983 to more than 26,500 tons in 1985. Production was expected to increase from 29,000 tons in 1987 to a record level of 34,000 tons in 1988. Brazil is the world's most rapidly expanding producer of tin. In addition, Brazil is the world's sixth largest tin consumer and has a smelting capacity of 13,000 tons. The world's largest tin mine, Pitinga, is located in the Amazon region, supplies 12% of global production and has reserves of 575,000 tons. Recent discoveries of platinum could contain one-half of the world's known reserves of the mineral. Brazil has reserves of the largest variety of gems in the world, and supplies 65% of world demand for precious stones.

Reserves of crude petroleum were estimated at 2,300m. barrels in 1988, and were expected to increase by 300%, following the discovery of the enormous 'Marlim' field in the Baia de Campos, which was thought to contain recoverable reserves of more than 2,000m. barrels. Dependence on imported petroleum was reduced from 82.5% in 1979 to 58% in 1983, when domestic output averaged 340,000 barrels per day (b/d). Production averaged more than 600,000 b/d in 1986 and 1987, and was projected to reach 780,000 b/d by 1989. To reduce the cost of oil imports, an alternative energy plan, PROALCOOL, was devised in 1976, aiming to replace 40% of petrol consumption by combustible alcohol (ethanol), derived from sugar and cassava, by 1985. By 1986 more than 50% of fuel oil consumption was of ethanol, and between 1979 and September 1987 Brazil produced some 3.5m. cars to operate on ethanol. By 1988 an estimated 90% of all new cars were designed to operate on ethanol. However, in view of the decline in world petroleum prices and the subsequent fall in Brazil's petroleum import bill, the Government banned the construction of new plants for the programme until 1989, in an attempt to reduce costs. In 1988 the Government announced a reduction in the subsidy to ethanol users which had previously maintained the cost of ethanol at only 35% of petroleum prices. The Government planned to invest $11,600m., mainly in petroleum exploration and production projects, between 1986 and 1989. Intensive offshore exploration has revealed proven reserves of 81,600m. cu m of natural gas. A new field, 'Albacora', may contain reserves of 150,000m. cu. m. Production reached 16.5m. cu m per day in late 1987. Under Brazil's new Constitution, approved by the National Congress in September 1988, foreign mining companies were banned from holding majority shareholdings in any exploration, extraction or refining operations on Brazilian territory. In addition, new risk contracts for oil companies were prohibited. The new laws were expected to have radical and possibly prejudicial consequences for the mining and petroleum sectors.

In the mid-1980s some 95% of Brazil's total electricity consumption was hydro-generated. The Itaipú hydroelectric power station, on the Paraná river, has a generating capacity of 12,600 MW and is the largest in the world. This project, undertaken with Paraguay and inaugurated in 1984, was to increase Brazil's installed capacity to 77,500 MW by 1990. The Tucuruí plant, on the Tocantins river, came into operation in November 1984. The estimated total hydroelectric generating potential is 213,000 MW. Brazil plans to construct two dams, at Santa Isabel and São Félix, to supply 4,000 MW to the northern region, beginning in 1992. However, the Sarney Government's austerity programme resulted in the cancellation in July 1985 of 10 planned hydroelectric projects and development of the Tucuruí plant. It was estimated that the nuclear programme would be producing 2.5% of the nation's power requirements by the late 1980s. In 1977, following the discovery of two large uranium deposits, Brazil signed an agreement with the Federal Republic of Germany to build eight nuclear power stations by the year 2000. The programme has been delayed: in 1985 one of the stations, Angra I (656 MW), commenced operations; work on Angra II was expected to be completed in 1995, but work on Angra III has been suspended until 1995. Plans for two other stations were also suspended. In 1988 the Government announced an extensive reorganization of the nuclear sector, in order to improve efficiency and reduce costs. By 1983 Brazil was able to produce plutonium. In 1987 a plant for enriching uranium was under construction at Iperó.

Between 1967 and 1974 Brazil's GDP grew, in real terms, by an average of 11.3% per year. The 'economic miracle' ended in 1974 at a time of worldwide recession, but real growth averaged 6.5% annually in 1975–80. During the early 1980s GDP continued to fluctuate, but between 1984 and 1986 the economy experienced a period of growth, expanding by 4.5% in 1984, 8.3% in 1985 and 8.0% in 1986. Unemployment has continued to increase and, including underemployment, may affect 60% of the labour force. Inflation has also continued to rise, reaching 224% in 1984 and 248.5% in 1985. Following the introduction of the Cruzado Plan (see below) in early 1986, inflation fell to 63.5% in 1986. Large-scale foreign borrowing for huge, unproductive 'prestige' projects, combined with the world recession and resultant low prices for primary exports, have led Brazil to incur a massive foreign debt, the largest of any country in the world, estimated at US $105,126m. in 1985 and $111,045m. in 1986. In January 1985 Brazil reached a preliminary agreement with its commercial bank creditors on the rescheduling of $45,300m. in debts falling due between 1985 and 1991. In February, however, negotiations were halted, following the IMF's decision to suspend its economic agreement with Brazil (dating from 1983). Attempts to reach a new agreement on economic targets with the IMF were hampered by a dispute within the Cabinet between the Minister of Finance, who favoured the IMF's policy, and the Minister of Planning. Contrary to the IMF's proposals for lower inflation and austerity, President Sarney rejected economic recession as a means of enabling Brazil to meet its debt commitments. Instead, the Government's 1986-89 Development Plan emphasized the need for economic growth and social spending. In addition, the Government planned to allocate $2,500m. to combat unemployment and poverty.

Throughout 1986 the Government maintained its opposition to the IMF's involvement in the formulation of economic policy. However, Brazil's commercial bank creditors were reluctant to agree to any rescheduling plan in the absence of an IMF-approved economic programme. In February 1986 the Government, prompted by an increase of 16.2% in the monthly rate of inflation for January, announced an economic stabilization programme, the Cruzado Plan, under which a new currency, the cruzado, was introduced; prices were to be 'frozen' for one year; and salaries were to be readjusted in accordance with the rate of inflation. One unforeseen consequence of the anti-inflation programme, however, was a dramatic rise in consumer spending, which the Government intended to curb by introducing a further programme of economic adjustment. Under this programme, the Government was to honour its commitment to the redistribution of wealth in favour of the poor by allocating increased funds to health, education, housing and food. Two supplementary programmes of austerity measures, Cruzado II and III, were introduced in July and November 1986, and included increases of up to 100% on taxes on luxury goods and an extensive revision of the consumer price index. A trade surplus of US $8,300m. was recorded in 1986 (following surpluses of $13,086m. in 1984 and $12,466m. in 1985).

By early 1987, however, it was apparent that the optimism surrounding the Cruzado Plan had been misplaced. Inflation began to rise at the end of 1986, reaching a monthly rate of 23.2% in May 1987. In June the Government introduced a new 'Macroeconomic Control Plan', which included a devaluation of the cruzado by 8.5%, a 50% reduction in the target for GDP growth in 1987 (to 3.5%), and the implementation of a programme of price readjustment. The new measures appeared to show some signs of success: the monthly rate of inflation declined to 6.4% and 5.7% in August and September respectively. However, the plan's long-term success was jeopardized by the Government's decision to make concessions on wage rises and public expenditure. In late 1987 plans for new tax reforms, including the introduction of capital gains tax, and the proposed abolition of several state enterprises in a bid to reduce government spending, were announced. A trade surplus of $11,173m. was recorded in 1987, although GDP growth declined to only 2.9%. Moreover, despite the new economic measures, the annual rate of inflation rose to 366%.

In February 1987 Brazil declared a unilateral moratorium on $68,000m. of medium- and long-term debt to commercial banks. In November, however, the Government, anxious to avoid the downgrading of Brazil's debts, agreed to an interim debt accord, whereby it was to resume interest payments in exchange for a short-term bridging loan of $3,000m. In 1987 Brazil's foreign debt was estimated at $116,900m. Moreover, in February 1988 the Brazilian Government publicly acknowledged that the debt moratorium had been an error, and that during its enforcement Brazil had lost funds amounting to $710m. Following the resumption of negotiations with its commercial bank creditors, Brazil announced that a preliminary accord had been agreed, in February–March 1988, on the rescheduling of $62,000m. of medium- and long-term debt and on the provision of new funding of $5,200m. The accord was contingent on the successful submission by Brazil of an economic programme to the IMF. In August the Fund approved the new programme (see below) and agreed to allocate a stand-by facility of SDR 1,096m. to Brazil. The debt accord was finally signed in November, when Brazil also repaid $3,760m. in interest on its commercial bank debt, thereby erasing all interest arrears due to the banks dating from February 1987. Despite the new agreement, Brazil remained the leading debtor country in the world, with a foreign debt of $120,300m. in April 1988.

Throughout 1988 one of the major economic problems for the Sarney administration was the public-sector deficit, which equalled 5.4% of GDP in 1987. In particular, the Government planned to reduce federal expenditure on salaries, which had increased from 37% of total expenditure in 1982 to 60% in 1987. In April the Government announced a series of measures designed to reduce the deficit, including the imposition of a 'freeze' on increases in salaries for civil servants and members of the armed forces. This decision proved highly unpopular, and led to widespread industrial action by civil servants. In May the Government revealed a new economic programme, aimed at the modernization of the Brazilian economy through liberalizing trade and reducing the state's role in the industrial sector. The programme envisaged the privatization of the majority of state companies; a reduction in import taxes by 90%; and the repeal of some export controls. A trade surplus of $10,500m. was anticipated for 1988.

By November 1988 it was apparent that the Government had been unable to reverse the trend towards hyperinflation; the monthly rate of inflation increased from 22% in June to 24% in September, and to a record level of 27% in October. Inflation in the 12 months to October was 714%, and the annual rate for 1988 was expected to reach 900%. Despite the announcement, in November, of the formation of a tripartite social pact (between the Government, the trade unions and the business sector), in an attempt to reverse inflation and check salary increases, reports of large-scale transfers of Brazilian capital to other countries, coupled with an intensification of protests and strikes in the public sector, indicated that Brazil's economic situation remained critical.

In August 1985 Brazil and Argentina signed a trade accord (see chapter on Argentina p. 351).

Social Welfare

The social security system, in existence since 1923, was rationalized in 1960, and the Instituto Nacional de Previdência Social (INPS) was formed in 1966. All social welfare programmes were consolidated in 1977 under the National System of Social Insurance and Assistance (SINPAS). The INPS administers benefits to urban and rural employees and their dependants. Employers and employees contribute 53.19%, the Federal Union 8.23% and other sources 36.37%. SINPAS revenue for 1983 was estimated at CR$6,636,898m. equal to 5.48% of GNP. Benefits include sickness benefit, invalidity, old age, length of service and widows' pensions, maternity and family allowances and grants. There are three government agencies: the Instituto de Administração Financeira da Previdência e Assistência Social collects contributions and revenue and supplies funds, the Instituto Nacional de Assistência Médica da Previdência Social is responsible for medical care, and CEME (Central Medicines) supplies medicines at a low price.

In 1982 there were 171,585 physicians in Brazil's hospitals; in 1984 the country had 12,175 hospital establishments, with a total of 538,721 beds. The private medical sector controls 90% of Brazil's hospitals. In response to a highly critical report on the health services, made in 1981, the Government introduced a health and welfare programme, Prevsaúde. This has been replaced by the Plan for the Reorientation of Health Aid, which proposes to adapt available resources to the requirements of the public. The plan has been co-ordinated by the Ministries of Social Welfare, Education and Health and by the State and Municipal Secretaries for Health. Expenditure by the central Government in 1985 included CZ $22,547m. on health services and CZ $82,108m. on social security and welfare. Under the 1986-89 Development Plan, announced in August 1985, US $4,000m. will be invested in social development schemes. In early 1988, however, the World Bank strongly criticized the misallocation of funds in the health sector, of which only 15% were assigned to preventative health care, for example immunization programmes and child health.

BRAZIL

The welfare of the dwindling population of indigenous American Indians is the responsibility of the Fundação Nacional do Indio (FUNAI), which was formed to assign homelands to the Indians, most of whom are landless and threatened by the exploitation of the Amazon forest, and lack political rights.

Education

Education is free in official pre-primary schools and is compulsory between the ages of seven and 14 years. Primary education begins at seven years of age and lasts for eight years. Secondary education, beginning at 15 years of age, lasts for four years and is also free in official schools. In 1984 an estimated 79.5% of children aged seven to 14 attended primary schools, while only 14.4% of those aged 15 to 17 were enrolled at secondary schools. The Federal Government is responsible for higher education, and in 1985 there were 68 universities, of which 47 were state-administered. There are a large number of private institutions in all levels of education.

Despite an anti-illiteracy drive, launched in 1971, the adult illiteracy rate in 1985 averaged 22.2% (males 20.9%; females 23.4%).

Public Holidays

1989: 2 January (for New Year's Day), 21 April (Tiradentes Day), 1 May (Labour Day), 4 May (Ascension Day), 25 May (Corpus Christi), 7 September (Independence Day), 12 October (Our Lady Aparecida, patroness of Brazil), 2 November (All Souls' Day), 15 November (Proclamation of the Republic), 25 December (Christmas Day).

1990: 1 January (New Year's Day), 21 April (Tiradentes Day), 1 May (Labour Day), 24 May (Ascension Day), 14 June (Corpus Christi), 7 September (Independence Day), 12 October (Our Lady Aparecida, patroness of Brazil), 2 November (All Souls' Day), 15 November (Proclamation of the Republic), 25 December (Christmas Day).

Other local holidays include 20 January (Foundation of Rio de Janeiro) and 25 January (Foundation of São Paulo).

Weights and Measures

The metric system is in force.

Statistical Survey

Sources (unless otherwise stated): Banco Central do Brasil, Brasília, DF; tel. (061) 224-1453; telex (61) 1702; Fundação Instituto Brasileiro de Geografia e Estatística (FIBGE), Av. Franklin Roosevelt 166, 20.021 Rio de Janeiro, RJ; tel. (021) 252-3501; telex (21) 30939.

Area and Population

AREA, POPULATION AND DENSITY

Area (sq km)	8,511,965*
Population (census results)†	
1 September 1970	93,139,037
1 September 1980	
Males	60,298,897
Females	60,849,685
Total	121,148,582
Population (official estimates at mid-year)†	
1985	135,564,000
1986	138,493,000
1987	141,452,000
Density (per sq km) at mid-1987	16.6

* 3,286,488 sq miles.
† Excluding Indian jungle population, numbering 45,429 in 1950. Census results also exclude an adjustment for underenumeration.

ADMINISTRATIVE DIVISIONS (mid-1987, official estimates)

State	Population ('000)	Capital
Acre (AC)	386	Rio Branco
Alagoas (AL)	2,303	Maceió
Amazonas (AM)	1,843	Manaus
Bahia (BA)	11,087	Salvador
Ceará (CE)	6,122	Fortaleza
Espírito Santo (ES)	2,382	Vitória
Goiás (GO)	4,632	Goiânia
Maranhão (MA)	4,865	São Luís
Mato Grosso (MT)	1,581	Cuiabá
Mato Grosso do Sul (MS)	1,674	Campo Grande
Minas Gerais (MG)	15,100	Belo Horizonte
Pará (PA)	4,587	Belém
Paraíba (PB)	3,104	João Pessoa
Paraná (PR)	8,530	Curitiba
Pernambuco (PE)	6,990	Recife
Piauí (PI)	2,518	Teresina
Rio de Janeiro (RJ)	13,267	Rio de Janeiro
Rio Grande do Norte (RN)	2,194	Natal
Rio Grande do Sul (RS)	8,749	Porto Alegre
Rondônia (RO)	982	Porto Velho
Santa Catarina (SC)	4,236	Florianópolis
São Paulo (SP)	30,943	São Paulo
Sergipe (SE)	1,345	Aracajú
Distrito Federal (DF)	1,684	Brasília
Federal Territory:		
Amapá (AP)	232	Macapá
Roraima (RR)	110	Boa Vista

BRAZIL

PRINCIPAL TOWNS (estimated population at mid-1987)

Brasília (capital)	1,567,709	Natal	510,106
São Paulo	10,063,110	Maceió	482,195
Rio de Janeiro	5,603,388	Teresina	473,901
Belo Horizonte	2,114,429	Santos	460,100
Salvador	1,804,438	São João de	
Fortaleza	1,582,414	Meriti	457,753
Nova Iguaçu	1,319,491	Niterói	441,684
Recife	1,287,623	Jaboatão	409,528
Curitiba	1,279,205	João Pessoa	396,197
Porto Alegre	1,272,121	Campo Grande	384,398
Belém	1,116,578	Contagem	383,904
Goiânia	923,333	Ribeirão Preto	383,125
Campinas	841,016	São José dos	
Manaus	809,914	Campos	372,578
São Gonçalo	728,469	Campos	366,716
Guarulhos	713,582	Aracaju	360,013
Duque de Caxias	664,105	Feira de Santana	355,201
Santo André	635,129	Juíz de Fora	349,720
Osasco	591,568	Londrina	346,676
São Bernardo do		Olinda	334,686
Campo	562,485	Sorocaba	327,468
São Luís	561,859		

BIRTHS AND DEATHS:
Average annual birth rate 33 per 1,000 in 1970–80; death rate 8.2 per 1,000 in 1970–80.

ECONOMICALLY ACTIVE POPULATION (persons aged 10 years and over, household survey, September 1985*)

	Males	Females	Total
Agriculture, hunting, forestry and fishing	11,913,894	3,276,499	15,190,393
Manufacturing	5,779,898	2,067,419	7,847,317
Construction	3,041,620	55,766	3,097,386
Other industrial activities	753,598	85,677	839,275
Wholesale and retail trade	3,959,635	1,855,025	5,814,660
Transport and communications	1,766,730	149,279	1,916,009
Services (incl. restaurants and hotels)	3,142,549	5,711,610	8,854,159
Social services	1,118,558	3,032,370	4,150,928
Public administration	1,754,379	592,357	2,346,736
Other activities (not adequately described)	2,232,071	948,002	3,180,073
Persons seeking employment	1,162,439	699,119	1,861,558
Total economically active	36,625,371	18,473,123	55,098,494

* Figures exclude the rural population of the northern region.

Agriculture

PRINCIPAL CROPS ('000 metric tons)

	1985	1986	1987
Coffee*	3,821	2,083	4,220
Seed cotton	2,857	2,314	1,672
Maize	22,018	20,531	26,787
Dry beans	2,549	2,209	2,006
Rice (paddy)	9,025	10,374	10,425
Cassava (Manioc)	23,125	25,621	23,500
Wheat	4,320	5,690	6,099
Potatoes	1,947	1,836	2,343
Soybeans	18,279	13,330	16,979
Sugar cane	247,199	239,178	268,585
Cocoa beans	431	459	329
Oranges	14,214†	13,327†	14,787†
Tobacco (leaves)	410	387	398
Bananas	4,815†	5,042†	5,225†
Groundnuts (in shell)	339	217	195
Natural rubber	40.4	32.6	26.6

* Figures are in terms of dry cherries. The proportion of coffee beans is estimated at 50%.
† Source: FAO, *Quarterly Bulletin of Statistics*.

LIVESTOCK ('000 head)

	1984	1985*	1986*
Cattle	127,655	126,391	128,918
Horses	5,442	5,500†	5,500†
Asses	1,246	1,250†	1,250†
Mules	1,946	1,980†	2,000†
Pigs	32,327	32,327	33,000
Sheep	18,447	18,356‡	18,473‡
Goats	9,675	9,500‡	9,800‡

* Chickens (million): 463 in 1984; 479‡ in 1985; 500† in 1986.
* Ducks (million): 6 in 1984; 6† in 1985; 6† in 1986.
* Turkeys (million): 3 in 1984; 3† in 1985; 3† in 1986.
* Source: FAO, *Production Yearbook*.   †FAO estimate.
‡ Estimate.

LIVESTOCK PRODUCTS ('000 metric tons)

	1984	1985	1986
Beef and veal	2,548	2,760*	2,800*
Mutton and lamb†	29	29	29
Goats' meat†	23	23	23
Pig meat†	780	770	1,100
Horse meat	24	21	24
Poultry meat	1,416	1,549	1,629
Cows' milk	12,303	12,580†	11,860†
Goats' milk†	90	90	90
Butter*	70	70†	65
Cheese†	59	59	59
Dried milk*	170	150	150
Hen eggs	964	1,000†	1,050†
Wool:			
greasy	30	30†	31†
scoured†	19	19	19
Cattle hides (fresh)*	310*	320†	315†

* Unofficial estimates.   † FAO estimates.
Source: FAO, *Production Yearbook*.

Forestry

ROUNDWOOD REMOVALS
(FAO estimates, '000 cubic metres, excluding bark)

	1984	1985	1986
Sawlogs, veneer logs and logs for sleepers	39,924	39,924	39,983
Pulpwood*	20,900	20,900	20,900
Other industrial wood	5,026	5,137	5,245
Fuel wood	164,507	168,124	171,646
Total	230,357	234,085	237,774

* Assumed to be unchanged since 1980.
Source: FAO, *Yearbook of Forest Products*.

SAWNWOOD PRODUCTION
(FAO estimates, '000 cubic metres)

	1984	1985	1986
Coniferous (softwood)	8,384	8,384	8,384
Broadleaved (hardwood)	9,397	9,397	9,679
Total	17,781	17,781	18,063

Source: FAO, *Yearbook of Forest Products*.

BRAZIL
Statistical Survey

Fishing

(metric tons)

	1984	1985	1986
Total catch	958,908	971,537	847,889*

* FAO estimate (Source: FAO, *Yearbook of Fishery Statistics*).

Mining

	1984	1985	1986
Bauxite ('000 metric tons)	10,355	9,963	11,153
Coal ('000 metric tons)	22,776	24,414	22,574
Iron ore ('000 metric tons)*	143,842	167,232	168,200
Manganese ore ('000 metric tons)*	3,494	3,516	3,600
Lead ('000 metric tons)*	366	418	255
Dolomite ('000 metric tons)	1,917	2,208	2,816
Sea salt ('000 metric tons)	3,578	1,734	1,600
Gold (kilograms)	37,218	31,583	24,124
Silver (kilograms)	25,195	49,523	63,616
Crude petroleum ('000 cu metres)	26,838	31,709	34,394
Natural gas (million cu metres)	4,902	5,468	5,686

* Figures refer to the gross weight of ores. The metal content (in '000 metric tons) was: Iron 111,311 in 1984, 127,730 in 1985, 129,405 in 1986, 134,100 in 1987; Manganese 2,457 in 1984, 2,320 in 1985, 2,499 in 1986, 2,870 in 1987; Lead 16.7 in 1984, 17.0 in 1985, 13.6 in 1986.

1987: Crude petroleum 34,208,000 cu metres; Natural gas 5,786 million cu metres.

Source: *Anuário Mineral Brasileiro*, Ministério das Minas e Energia.

Other ores (metal content, metric tons): Copper 35,212 in 1984, 40,999 in 1985, 40,183 in 1986; Nickel 23,532 in 1984, 20,300 in 1985, 21,423 in 1986; Zinc 72,000* in 1984, 72,000* in 1985; Tin 19,957 in 1984, 26,514 in 1985, 27,663 in 1986; Chromium 129,000 in 1984, 131,000 in 1985, 131,000 in 1986; Tungsten 1,892 in 1984, 2,050 in 1985; Uranium 117 in 1984, 110† in 1985.

* Estimate (Source: US Bureau of Mines).
† Estimate (Source: UN, *Industrial Statistics Yearbook*).

Industry

SELECTED PRODUCTS
('000 metric tons, unless otherwise indicated)

	1985	1986	1987
Asphalt	986	1,375	1,263
Electric power (million kWh)	187,111	201,774	209,026
Coke	6,204	6,449	n.a.
Pig iron	18,961	20,353	21,335
Crude steel	20,450	21,240	22,228
Cement*	20,635	25,252	25,470
Tyres ('000 units)	24,928	27,046	25,341
Synthetic rubber (metric tons)	265,940	270,817	251,547
Passenger cars (units)	758,958	814,445	683,308
Commercial vehicles (units)	207,814	240,921	236,678
Tractors (units)	48,850	61,077	53,904
Sugar	7,995	7,537	7,003
Newsprint	208	n.a.	n.a.
Other paper and board	3,814	n.a.	n.a.

* Portland cement only.

Finance

CURRENCY AND EXCHANGE RATES

Monetary Units
100 centavos = 1 cruzado (CZ $).

Denominations
Coins: 1, 5, 10 and 50 centavos; 1 cruzado.
Notes: 100, 200, 500, 1,000, 5,000, 10,000, 50,000 and 100,000 cruzeiros. (Notes are stamped in cruzados.)

Sterling and Dollar Equivalents (30 September 1988)
£1 sterling = 610.74 cruzados;
US $1 = 361.17 cruzados;
1,000 cruzados = £1.637 = $2.769.

Average Exchange Rates (cruzados per US $)
1985   6.200
1986 13.656
1987 39.229

Note: In March 1986 the cruzeiro (CR $) was replaced by a new currency unit, the cruzado, equivalent to 1,000 cruzeiros. Notes and coins issued in cruzeiros were to circulate concurrently with the cruzado, and were to remain as legal tender until the issue of cruzado coins and notes. Some figures in this Survey continue to be in terms of cruzeiros.

BUDGET (estimates, CZ $ million)

Revenue	1986	1987	1988
Taxes	213,606,400	306,600,000	2,471,000,000
Patrimonial revenue	1,205,540	1,811,700	12,000,000
Industrial revenue	24,710	69,200	395,200
Currency transfers	214,814	460,900	1,500,000
Miscellaneous	221,404,537	245,358,200	2,044,499,908
Other revenue	2,160,499	2,353,000	15,767,700
National Treasury total	438,616,500	556,653,000	4,545,162,808
Other resources	20,671,770	35,192,000	122,801,000
General total	459,288,270	591,845,000	4,667,963,808

Source: Secretaria de Planejamento da Presidência da República and Secretaria de Orçamento e Finanças.

Expenditure	1986	1987	1988
Legislative and auxiliary	2,774,729	4,450,609	22,602,000
Judiciary	2,645,383	6,166,924	30,422,400
Executive	453,868,158	581,227,467	4,614,939,408
Presidency (including Planning Secretariat)	3,743,621	14,888,785	85,453,157
Air	14,537,450	23,853,027	118,759,295
Agriculture	6,728,342	11,949,691	66,582,500
Communications	1,220,083	7,906,516	6,991,626
Education and culture	27,936,551	39,732,623	215,795,782
Army	8,283,398	14,910,993	74,692,054
Finance	4,144,447	7,249,700	34,846,286
Industry and commerce	2,464,678	17,251,708	103,191,968
Interior	2,936,768	14,339,588	52,129,100
Justice	1,378,783	2,609,429	12,982,000
Marine	9,160,221	15,386,412	81,546,378
Mines and power	1,566,333	2,237,780	73,287,769
Foreign affairs	2,559,264	3,357,416	16,388,554
Health	8,640,627	14,505,614	75,769,793
Work and social welfare	8,755,019	9,619,219	7,798,937
Transport	47,240,708	60,768,380	224,481,888
Unspecified items	302,571,868	320,660,586	3,364,242,321
Total	459,288,270	591,845,000	4,667,963,808

BRAZIL

Statistical Survey

CENTRAL BANK RESERVES (US $ million at 31 December)

	1985	1986	1987
Gold	1,004	958	1,159
IMF special drawing rights	1	—	—
Foreign exchange	10,604	5,803*	6,299*
Total	11,609	6,761*	7,458*

* Excluding holdings of foreign exchange by the Bank of Brazil.
Source: IMF, *International Financial Statistics*.

MONEY SUPPLY (CZ $ million at 31 December)

	1985	1986	1987
Currency outside banks	23,846	n.a.	n.a.
Demand deposits at commercial banks	70,800	279,300	567,700

Source: IMF, *International Financial Statistics*.

COST OF LIVING (Consumer Price Index, Rio de Janeiro; annual averages; base: March 1986 = 100)

	1985	1986	1987
Foodstuffs	41.3	102.5	322.9
Clothing	42.8	105.0	311.2
Housing	42.2	93.0	283.3
Household articles	45.1	101.1	300.0
Medicines and hygiene products	43.8	102.4	398.3
Personal services	38.6	101.2	364.7
Utilities and urban transport	47.9	100.9	400.8
All items	41.8	102.0	338.2

Source: Fundação Getúlio Vargas.

NATIONAL ACCOUNTS (CZ $ million at current prices)
Composition of the Gross National Product

	1983	1984	1985*
Gross domestic product (GDP) at factor cost	106,277	353,857	1,281,835
Indirect taxes	15,024	40,257	146,167
Less Subsidies	3,106	6,147	21,925
GDP in purchasers' values	118,195	387,968	1,406,077
Factor income received from abroad	661	3,080	12,700
Less Factor income paid abroad	7,501	25,021	86,361
Gross national product	111,355	366,027	1,332,416

* Figures are provisional. For revised total of GDP in purchasers' values, see the table below.
Source: UN, *National Accounts Statistics*.

Expenditure on the Gross Domestic Product

	1985	1986	1987
Government final consumption expenditure	136,591	390,867	1,562,798
Private final consumption expenditure	973,740	2,629,852	8,326,409
Increase in stocks			
Gross fixed capital formation	236,521	709,201	2,514,763
Total domestic expenditure	1,346,852	3,729,920	12,403,970
Exports of goods and services	169,331	324,852	1,089,369
Less Imports of goods and services	98,094	228,504	704,761
GDP in purchasers' values	1,418,089	3,826,268	12,788,578
GDP at constant 1980 prices	13,758	14,865	15,298

Source: IMF, *International Financial Statistics*.

Gross Domestic Product by Economic Activity (at factor cost)

	1982	1983	1984
Agriculture, hunting, forestry and fishing	3,695	11,775	40,541
Mining and quarrying	351	1,196	5,418
Manufacturing	13,062	30,288	102,270
Electricity, gas and water	1,020	2,350	8,386
Construction	2,997	6,363	20,351
Trade, restaurants and hotels	6,572	16,033	52,585
Transport, storage and communications	2,504	5,737	18,761
Finance, insurance, real estate and business services	8,861	24,186	78,576
Government services	3,224	7,752	21,832
Other community, social and personal services	5,704	14,350	48,068
Sub-total	47,990	120,030	396,789
Less Imputed bank service charge	4,942	13,755	42,932
Total	43,047	106,276	353,857

Source: UN, *National Accounts Statistics*.

BALANCE OF PAYMENTS (US $ million)

	1984	1985	1986
Merchandise exports f.o.b.	27,002	25,634	22,392
Merchandise imports f.o.b.	−13,916	−13,168	−14,044
Trade balance	13,086	12,466	8,348
Exports of services	3,203	3,675	2,910
Imports of services	−16,418	−16,569	−15,821
Balance on goods and services	−129	−428	−4,563
Private unrequited transfers (net)	161	139	95
Government unrequited transfers (net)	10	16	−9
Current balance	42	−273	−4,477
Direct capital investment (net)	1,556	1,267	331
Other long-term capital (net)	−4,358	−7,944	−9,645
Short-term capital (net)	−3,195	−1,614	498
Net errors and omissions	398	−530	−530
Total (net monetary movements)	−5,557	−9,094	−13,823
Monetization of gold	336	257	135
Valuation changes (net)	229	−672	−846
Exceptional financing (net)	10,434	8,968	10,195
Official financing (net)	491	−385	396
Changes in reserves	5,933	−926	−3,942

Source: IMF, *International Financial Statistics*.

OVERSEAS INVESTMENT IN BRAZIL, 1987 (US $ '000)

Countries of origin	Investments	Reinvestments	Total
Belgium	251,716	205,800	457,516
Canada	1,013,373	421,397	1,434,770
France	635,080	754,272	1,389,352
Germany, Federal Republic	3,533,935	1,817,262	5,351,197
Japan	2,396,480	564,531	2,961,011
Luxembourg	413,595	138,907	552,502
Netherlands	551,992	398,135	950,127
Netherlands Dependencies	225,477	21,405	246,882
Panama	919,855	434,398	1,354,253
Sweden	335,649	176,741	512,390
Switzerland	1,406,185	1,398,291	2,804,476
United Kingdom	963,254	934,833	1,898,087
USA	5,556,490	2,784,207	8,340,697
Others	2,762,336	442,440	3,204,776
Total	20,965,417	10,492,619	31,458,036

BRAZIL

External Trade

PRINCIPAL COMMODITIES (US $ '000)

Imports f.o.b.	1985	1986	1987
Vegetable products	958,117	1,195,248	722,246
Mineral products	6,454,820	3,873,910	5,077,298
Products of the chemical and allied industries	1,478,920	2,126,747	2,212,983
Plastic materials, resins and rubber	331,128	417,171	475,517
Paper-making materials, paper	119,206	192,470	269,101
Base metals and articles of base metal	417,918	636,653	706,026
Machinery and mechanical appliances, electrical equipment	1,971,451	2,714,276	3,011,282
Transport equipment	508,455	749,644	946,736
Optical, photographic and measuring instruments, clocks and watches	371,498	586,949	520,950
Total (incl. others)	13,153,491	14,044,304	15,051,864

Exports f.o.b.	1985	1986	1987
Live animals and animal products	751,584	603,438	677,234
Vegetable products	3,489,341	2,594,040	2,901,827
Coffee	2,632,471	2,347,400	2,185,270
Animal and vegetable oils and fats	848,116	267,096	446,727
Food, beverages, vinegar and tobacco	4,479,294	4,337,018	4,500,650
Cocoa beans	360,614	273,322	265,587
Sugar	368,682	381,397	324,612
Tobacco leaf	437,427	394,520	405,497
Mineral products	3,548,775	2,540,715	2,777,843
Haematite	1,658,143	1,615,310	1,615,395
Products of chemical and allied industries	1,124,071	964,656	1,165,642
Hides and skins	262,387	247,166	265,373
Wood, charcoal and cork	303,306	311,111	400,113
Textiles and textile articles	1,000,607	890,099	1,202,007
Cotton (raw)	76,754	16,756	160,179
Machinery and mechanical appliances, electrical equipment	2,170,903	2,239,973	2,519,628
Transport equipment	1,694,158	1,568,887	2,774,916
Total (incl. others)	25,639,011	22,348,603	26,225,115

PRINCIPAL TRADING PARTNERS (US $ '000 f.o.b.)

Imports	1985	1986	1987
Argentina	468,865	736,988	580,063
Belgium-Luxembourg	75,174	102,515	128,235
Canada	397,942	433,559	409,233
Chile	216,282	278,393	353,098
France	301,955	568,934	601,036
Germany, Federal Republic	863,551	1,285,123	1,448,937
Italy	187,583	348,641	333,409
Japan	549,879	881,584	843,377
Netherlands	163,716	253,013	287,152
Poland	137,179	180,949	155,052
Saudi Arabia	945,394	879,818	861,485
Sweden	92,112	136,453	161,184
Switzerland	224,867	350,430	345,839
USSR	63,718	44,811	70,197
United Kingdom	251,131	346,153	378,987
USA	2,575,321	3,186,733	3,142,781
Venezuela	257,777	95,583	157,058
Total (incl. others)	13,153,491	14,044,304	15,051,864

Imports (US $ million): Iraq 2,018 in 1984, 1,800 in 1985; Kuwait 227 in 1984.

Exports	1985	1986	1987
Argentina	547,793	678,336	831,782
Belgium-Luxembourg	569,761	484,486	611,388
Canada	414,332	436,057	561,551
Chile	238,756	246,074	354,824
Denmark	112,321	108,505	94,367
France	779,674	717,635	678,153
Germany, Federal Republic	1,274,415	1,099,200	1,228,522
Italy	1,124,878	910,439	1,269,706
Japan	1,394,103	1,513,585	1,676,476
Mexico	220,157	155,981	171,342
Netherlands	1,551,944	1,298,558	1,607,786
Nigeria	841,710	247,106	216,672
Norway	84,498	89,782	76,978
Peru	92,058	156,442	215,752
Poland	161,604	223,910	292,680
Saudi Arabia	168,029	211,752	481,181
Spain	523,128	447,035	444,428
Sweden	181,016	193,348	138,311
Switzerland	165,397	185,480	230,998
USSR	450,199	265,721	379,062
United Kingdom	663,339	646,217	755,740
USA	6,689,294	6,174,415	7,191,844
Venezuela	302,810	348,383	374,074
Total (incl. others)	25,639,011	22,348,603	26,225,115

Transport

RAILWAYS

	1983	1984	1985
Passengers ('000)	499,484	587,500	624,199
Passenger-km (million)	13,797	15,578	16,036
Passenger revenue (million cruzeiros)	37,893	97,207	351,311
Freight ('000 metric tons)	172,266	205,707	217,213
Freight ton-km (million)	74,966	92,440	100,226
Freight revenue (million cruzeiros)	428,322	1,537,275	5,554,891

Source: Empresa Brasileira de Planejamento de Transportes (GEIPOT).

ROAD TRAFFIC (motor vehicles in use at 31 December)

	1983	1984	1985
Passenger cars	8,761,457	9,198,447	9,527,296
Lorries	929,712	959,714	979,096
Buses	126,501	129,947	130,179
Commercial vehicles	812,861	861,372	905,200

Source: GEIPOT.

SHIPPING

	1983	1984	1985
Brazilian fleet (vessels)	1,890	2,135	2,193
Capacity ('000 dwt)	2,344	10,001	10,462
Freight (million metric tons):			
Total shipping	155.0	n.a.	n.a.
Brazilian share (percentage)	44.5	n.a.	n.a.

Source: Sunamam.

BRAZIL

CIVIL AVIATION (embarked passengers, mail and cargo)

	1984	1985	1986
Number of passengers ('000)	12,136	13,182	16,285
Freight (metric tons)	287,264	1,038,826	1,225,885
Mail (metric tons)	20,360	22,161	20,167

Source: Departamento de Aviação Civil (DAC).

Tourism

	1984	1985	1986*
Arrivals	1,595,726	1,735,982	1,934,091

* Provisional estimate.
Source: Empresa Brasileira de Turismo.

Education

(1985)

	Institutions	Teachers	Students
Pre-primary*	37,337	109,514	2,481,848
First grade	187,274	1,040,566	24,769,736
Second grade	9,260	206,111	3,016,138
Higher	859	122,486	1,367,609

* Figures refer to 1984.
Source: Serviço de Estatística da Educação e Cultura.

Directory

The Constitution

A revised constitution was introduced on 20 October 1969; the following is a summary of the main provisions (major subsequent amendments are listed below on p. 542):

Brazil is a Federative Republic consisting of 23 States, one Federal District and three Territories indissolubly united under a representative form of government to constitute the Union. The Federal District is the capital of the Union.

The Union's competence includes maintaining relations with foreign states and making treaties with them, and taking part in international organizations; declaring war and making peace; decreeing a state of siege; organizing the armed forces, planning and guaranteeing national security, issuing currency; supervising credits, etc.; establishing national services, including communications, development and education services; legislating on the execution of the Constitution and federal services and on civil, commercial, penal, procedural, electoral, agrarian, maritime and labour law. The Union, States, Federal District and Municipalities are forbidden to make any distinction between Brazilians, establish any religious cults or churches against the public interest, and to deny public documents.

The Union may intervene in state affairs only in matters of extreme urgency, such as national security, and then only by Presidential decree. The States are responsible for electing their Governors by universal suffrage by direct secret ballot. The state law will decree the establishment of Municipalities, after due consultation with the local population; it will also decree the division of the States into districts; municipal organization may vary from state to state.

LEGISLATIVE POWER

The legislative power is exercised by the National Congress, which is composed of the Chamber of Deputies and the Federal Senate. Elections for deputies and senators take place simultaneously throughout the country; candidates for Congress must be Brazilian by birth and have full exercise of their political rights. They must be at least 21 years of age in the case of deputies and at least 35 years of age in the case of senators. Congress meets twice a year in ordinary sessions, and extraordinary sessions may be convened on demand of a third of the members of either House or the President. Each Chamber arranges its own internal procedure.

The Chamber of Deputies is made up of representatives of the people, elected by direct secret ballot by men and women over 18 years of age, for a period of four years. The number of inhabitants determines the number of deputies per state. Each Territory will have one deputy.

The Federal Senate is composed of representatives of the States, elected by direct secret ballot. Each State will elect three senators with a mandate for eight years, with elections after four years of one-third of the members and after another four years of the remaining two-thirds. Each Senator is elected with his substitute. The Senate approves, by secret ballot, the choice of Magistrates, when required by the Constitution; of the Attorney-General of the Republic, of the Ministers of the Accounts Tribunal, of the Governor of the Federal District, of the Territorial Governors and of the permanent heads of diplomatic missions.

The National Congress is responsible for legislating on all matters within the competence of the Union; national and regional plans and programmes, the strength of the armed forces in times of peace and territorial limits. Both houses vote on the budget in joint session. It is also responsible for making definitive resolutions on Presidential treaties, authorizing the President to leave the country, declaring war and approving boundary changes in the States or Territories. The Executive power must send any bills proposed by the President to the National Congress within 15 days of signing. Constitutional amendments must be proposed by at least one-third of the total number of members of both houses or by the President. Amendments are ratified by a simple majority. No changes may be made to the Constitution during a state of siege. Any Presidential bill must be considered by Congress within 45 days if so requested by the President. The President is exclusively responsible for legislation concerning finance, creating new public offices, etc., and matters concerning the administration of the Federal District and the Territories.

EXECUTIVE POWER

Executive power is exercised by the President of the Republic, aided by the Ministers of State. Candidates for the Presidency and Vice-Presidency must be Brazilian-born, be in full exercise of their political rights and be over 35 years of age. The President and Vice-President will be elected by a simple majority in open session of an electoral college composed of all members of the National Congress and delegates appointed by the State Legislatures on the basis of three for each state and one more for each 500,000 voters registered in the state. The President holds office for a term of five years and is not eligible for re-election. If the President violates any of his responsibilities he may be impeached by a two-thirds majority of the Deputies and judged by the Supreme Tribunal or the Senate according to the nature of his crime.

The Ministers of State are chosen by the President and their duties include carrying out the President's decrees, expediting instructions for the enactment of laws, decrees and regulations, and presentation to the President of an annual report of their activities.

National security is the responsibility of every citizen. There is a National Security Council, composed of the President and the Vice-President of the Republic, all the Ministers of State and the Chiefs of Staff of the armed services.

JUDICIAL POWER

Judicial power in the Union is exercised by the Supreme Federal Tribunal; the Federal Appeal Tribunals and federal judges; Military Tribunals and judges; Electoral Tribunals and judges; Labour Tribunals and judges; and State Tribunals and judges. Judges are appointed for life; they may not undertake any other employment, receive any benefits from cases tried by them or engage in any

BRAZIL

party political activity. The Tribunals elect their own presidents and organize their own internal structure.

The Supreme Federal Tribunal, situated in the Union capital, has jurisdiction over the whole national territory and is composed of 11 Ministers. The Ministers are nominated by the President after approval by the Senate, from Brazilian-born citizens, over the age of 35, of proved judicial knowledge and experience.

POLITICAL AND PERSONAL RIGHTS

Registration and voting are compulsory for all Brazilian citizens who are more than 18 years of age, except those who are illiterate or unable to express themselves in the national language or are temporarily or definitively deprived of political rights.* The organization of political parties is regulated by federal law, with the guarantee of the fundamental human rights. Congressional representation is achieved when 5% of the total electorate votes for one party, with a minimum of 7% in each of seven states.

All citizens are equal in the eyes of the law, regardless of sex, race, employment, religion or political convictions; any racialism will be prosecuted; there is no death penalty (except under military legislation in case of external war), no life imprisonment, banishment or confiscation of property. Rights concerning citizens' life, liberty, security and property are inviolable.

The President may declare a state of siege in cases of serious breaches of order or the likelihood of their occurring; or war. Except in cases of war, the state of siege may not last longer than 60 days, with the possibility of extension with the approval of Congress. During a state of siege Congress may suspend constitutional guarantees, and also the immunity of federal deputies and senators.

The Constitution also lays down principles of economic and social order, concerning freedom of enterprise, dignity of human labour, social function of ownership, harmony and solidarity in production, economic development and repression of abuse of economic power. Strikes are not permitted in public services and essential activities, as defined by law. The Constitution lays down certain rights for workers, including limited hours of work, paid holidays and social welfare benefits; voting in trade union elections is compulsory.

The law protects family life; education is the right of all, with equal opportunity. Education will be organized by the States and the Federal District and the Union will give technical and financial assistance to develop education.

AMENDMENTS

In April 1977 the following constitutional amendments were promulgated by presidential decree:

1. The presidential term of office was increased from five to six years as from the expiry of the then incumbent's term, 15 March 1979, and the date for the presidential elections was brought forward from January 1979 to October 1978.

2. Henceforth, constitutional amendments must be approved by Congress by a simple majority, not the two-thirds majority as at present.

3. From 1978 state governors and one-third of the seats in the Senate were to be elected indirectly by electoral colleges comprising members of the state assemblies and municipal councils. Those elected (including mayors) in November 1976 were to hold office until 1982 instead of 1980. The Government restored direct elections in 1980.

4. Federal deputies to be allocated on the basis of population and not on the number of registered voters as before. Each state elects not fewer than six and not more than 55 representatives.

5. Non-budgetary tax measures will no longer require congressional approval.

6. No election candidates to be allowed to appear on radio or television to discuss campaign issues.

In December 1977 the Senate approved rules for allowing marriages to be dissolved. Brazilian citizens will be able to apply for one divorce only during their lifetime. In the case of a marriage partner becoming mentally ill, divorce proceedings cannot begin until five years after the illness has been proved.

In September further amendments were promulgated which came into force in January 1979:

1. The repeal of Institutional Act 5 which gave the President the power to close Congress, suspend a citizen's political rights for 10 years and remove members of the federal, state or municipal legislatures.

2. The repeal of Article 185 of the Constitution which imposed political ineligibility for life on those citizens penalized under Institutional Act 5.

---

* By virtue of this clause, American Indians are classed as minors and do not, therefore, have any political rights.

3. The promulgation of a new National Security Law under which the death penalty, perpetual imprisonment and banishment were abrogated and under which the right of *habeas corpus* was restored for political detainees.

4. The creation of a constitutional council with the President as Chairman and comprising the Vice-President, the President of the Senate and representatives of the armed forces, to approve Presidential decrees with regard to measures designed to safeguard national security:

(a) emergency measures where public order is gravely disturbed in specific regions;

(b) state of emergency for 90 days, renewable, where public security is threatened;

(c) state of siege for 180 days, includes powers of detention, censorship, etc.

5. The creation of a new law on the formation of political parties under which a new party must have 10% of the votes in Congress or the support of 5% of the electorate.

In May 1985 the National Congress approved the following constitutional amendments:

1. The President is to be elected by direct balloting with universal suffrage.

2. Illiterate citizens are permitted to vote.

Note: Following congressional elections in November 1986, a Constitutional Assembly was installed in February 1987 to draft a new constitution and determine the length of the current presidency. The new Constitution, composed of 245 articles, was ratified by the National Congress on 2 September 1988, and was promulgated on 5 October. Under the Constitution, the presidential term of office is five years. The legislature is empowered to sanction the President, to amend the national budget and to determine international treaties. Other provisions include the abolition of censorship; the lowering of the minimum voting age to 16 years; the introduction of the principle of habeas corpus; the granting of the right to strike, and payment in the event of dismissal, to workers; and the establishment of a 44-hour working week.

The Government

HEAD OF STATE

President: José Sarney (took office as acting President on 15 March 1985, and as President on 22 April 1985, following the death of President-elect Tancredo Neves).

CABINET
(December 1988)

The Cabinet is composed of members of an alliance, the Aliança Democrática, formed in 1984 by the Partido Frente Liberal (PFL) and the Partido do Movimento Democrático Brasileiro (PMDB).

Minister, Head of the Secretariat for Planning: João Batista de Abreu (PMDB).

Minister of Justice: Paulo Brossard de Souza Pinto (PMDB).

Minister of the Navy: Adm. Henrique Saboia.

Minister of the Army: Gen. Leônidas Pires Gonçalves.

Minister of the Air Force: Brig. Octávio Júlio Moreira Lima.

Minister of Foreign Affairs: Roberto Costa de Abreu Sodré (PFL).

Minister of Finance: Mailson Ferreira da Nobrega.

Minister of Transport: José Reinaldo Carneiro Tavares (PFL).

Minister of Agriculture: Iris Rezende Machado (PMDB).

Minister of Education: Hugo Napoleão do Rego Neto (PMDB).

Minister of Labour: Almir Pazzianotto Pinto Urban (PMDB).

Minister of Health: Luiz Carlos Borges da Silveira (PMDB).

Minister of Industry and Commerce: Roberto Cardoso Alves (PMDB).

Minister of Mines and Energy: Iris Rezende Machado (PMDB) (acting).

Minister of the Interior: João Alves (PDS).

Minister of Communications: Antônio Carlos Peixoto de Magalhães (PFL).

Minister of Social Welfare: Jáder Fontenelle Barbalho (PMDB).

Head of the President's Military Household: Gen. Rubens Bayma Denys.

Minister of the Presidency and Head of the President's Civilian Household: Ronaldo Costa Couto.

BRAZIL

Head of the National Information Service (SNI): Gen. IVAN DE SOUZA MENDES.

Head of the General Staff of the Armed Forces (EMFA): Adm. VALBERT LISIEUX MEDEIROS DE FIGUEIREDO.

Minister of Land Reform and Development: LEOPOLDO BESSONE (PMDB).

Minister of Culture: JOSÉ APARECIDO DE OLIVEIRA (PMDB).

Minister of Administration: ALUÍZIO ALVES (PMDB).

Minister of Science and Technology: RALPH BIASI (PMDB).

Minister of Urban Development and Environment: LUIZ PRISCO VIANNA (PMDB).

Minister of Irrigation: VICENTE FIALHO (PMDB).

MINISTRIES

Office of the President: Palácio do Planalto, Praça dos Três Poderes, 70.150 Brasília, DF; tel. (061) 223-2714; telex (61) 1451.

Ministry of Administration: Esplanada dos Ministérios, Bloco C, 70.046 Brasília, DF; tel. (061) 224-1149; telex (61) 1086.

Ministry of the Air Force: Esplanada dos Ministérios, Bloco M, 8°, 70.045 Brasília, DF; tel. (061) 224-7548; telex (61) 1152.

Ministry of Agriculture: Esplanada dos Ministérios, Bloco D, 8°, 70.043 Brasília, DF; tel. (061) 218-2800; telex (61) 1138.

Ministry of the Army: Esplanada dos Ministérios, Bloco 4, 70.042 Brasília, DF; tel. (061) 224-6797; telex (61) 1094.

Ministry of Communications: Esplanada dos Ministérios, Bloco R, 70.044 Brasília, DF; tel. (061) 223-4992; telex (61) 1994.

Ministry of Culture: SBN, Quadra 2, Bloco F, Edif. Central, 70.040 Brasília, DF; tel. (061) 223-5614; telex (61) 1068.

Ministry of Education: Esplanada dos Ministérios, Bloco L, 70.047 Brasília, DF; tel. (061) 223-7306; telex (61) 9105.

Ministry of Finance: Esplanada dos Ministérios, Bloco P, 5°, 70.048 Brasília, DF: tel. (061) 223-2729; telex (61) 1142.

Ministry of Foreign Affairs: Palácio do Itamaraty, Esplanada dos Ministérios, 70.040 Brasília, DF; tel. (061) 226-1762; telex (61) 1319.

Ministry of Health: Esplanada dos Ministérios, Bloco 11, 70.058 Brasília, DF; tel. (061) 223-8158; telex (61) 1752.

Ministry of Industry and Commerce: Esplanada dos Ministérios, Bloco 6, 70.053 Brasília, DF; tel. (061) 223-7784; telex (61) 1066.

Ministry of the Interior: Esplanada dos Ministérios, Bloco 23, 70.054 Brasília, DF; tel. (061) 226-2820; telex (61) 1015.

Ministry of Justice: Esplanada dos Ministérios, Bloco T, 70.064 Brasília, DF; tel. (061) 224-2964; telex (61) 1088.

Ministry of Labour: Esplanada dos Ministérios, Bloco F, 10°, 70.059 Brasília, DF; tel. (061) 224-6864; telex (61) 1158.

Ministry of Land Reform and Development: SBN, Edif. Palácio do Desenvolvimento, 18°, 70.057 Brasília, DF; tel. (061) 223-3503; telex (61) 1476.

Ministry of Mines and Energy: Esplanada dos Ministérios, Bloco 3, 70.056 Brasília, DF; tel. (061) 223-3489; telex (61) 1140.

Ministry of the Navy: Esplanada dos Ministérios, Bloco 3, 70.055 Brasília, DF; tel. (061) 224-3489; telex (61) 1392.

Ministry of Science and Technology: SAS, Quadra 5, Lote 6, Bloco H, 9°, 70.070 Brasília, DF; tel. (061) 226-6211; telex (61) 2481.

Ministry of Social Security and Welfare: Esplanada dos Ministérios, Bloco U, 70.065 Brasília, DF; tel. (061) 224-3445; telex (61) 1694.

Ministry of Transport: Esplanada dos Ministérios, Bloco 9, 70.062 Brasília, DF; tel. (061) 226-5225; telex (61) 1096.

Ministry of Urban Development and Environment: SEPN, Q 505, Bloco B, 70.730 Brasília, DF; tel. (061) 272-8413; telex (61) 4220.

Legislature

CONGRESSO NACIONAL
(National Congress)

President of the Federal Senate: Senator HUMBERTO LUCENA.

President of the Chamber of Deputies: ULYSSES GUIMARÃES.

General Election, 15 November 1986

Party	Federal Senate*	Chamber of Deputies
Partido do Movimento Democrático Brasileiro (PMDB)	44	259
Partido da Frente Liberal (PFL)	16	115
Partido Democrático Social (PDS)	5	36
Partido Democrático Trabalhista (PDT)	2	24
Partido dos Trabalhadores (PT)	—	19
Partido Trabalhista Brasileiro (PDB)	1	19
Partido Liberal (PL)	1	7
Partido Democrata Cristão (PDC)	1	3
Partido Comunista Brasileiro (PCB)	—	2
Partido Comunista do Brasil (PC do B)	—	2
Partido Socialista Brasileiro (PSB)	2	1
Total	**72**	**487**

* Elections for 49 Senate seats were held on 15 November 1986.

Note: The new National Congress was also to act as the Constitutional Assembly. The Assembly was installed in February 1987. The President of the Constitutional Assembly is ULYSSES GUIMARÃES.

Governors

STATES

Acre: FLAVIANO BAPTISTA DE MELO (PMDB).
Alagoas: FERNANDO COLLOR DE MELLO (PMDB).
Amazonas: AMAZONINO ARMANDO MENDES (PMDB).
Bahia: FRANCISCO WALDIR PIRES DE SOUZA (PMDB).
Ceará: TASSO RIBEIRO JEREISSATI (PMDB).
Espírito Santo: MAX FREITAS MAURO (PMDB).
Goias: HENRIQUE SANTILLO (PMDB).
Maranhão: EPITÁCIO CAFETEIRA AFONSO PEREIRA (PMDB).
Mato Grosso: CARLOS GOMES BEZERRA (PMDB).
Mato Grosso do Sul: MARCELO MIRANDA SOARES (PMDB).
Minas Gerais: NEWTON CARDOSO (PMDB).
Pará: HÉLIO MOTA GUEIROS (PMDB).
Paraíba: TARCÍSIO DE MIRANDA BURITY (PMDB).
Paraná: ALVARO FERNANDES DIAS (PMDB).
Pernambuco: MIGUEL ARRAES DE ALENCAR (PMDB).
Piauí: ALBERTO TAVARES SILVA (PMDB).
Rio de Janeiro: WELLINGTON MOREIRA FRANCO (PMDB).
Rio Grande do Norte: GERALDO FERREIRA DE MELO (PMDB).
Rio Grande do Sul: PEDRO JORGE SIMON (PMDB).
Rondônia: JERÔNIMO GARCIA DE SANTANA (PMDB).
Santa Catarina: PEDRO IVO FIGUEIREDO DE CAMPOS (PMDB).
São Paulo: ORESTES QUÉRCIA (PMDB).
Sergipe: ANTÔNIO CARLOS VALDARES (PFL).

FEDERAL TERRITORIES

Amapá: JORGE NOVA DA COSTA.
Roraima: ROBERTO PINHEIRO KLEIN (acting).

FEDERAL DISTRICT

Brasília: JOAQUIM RORIZ.

Note: The Governors of the Federal Territories and Brasília are Federal Government nominees.

Political Organizations

In May 1985 the National Congress approved a constitutional amendment providing for the free formation of political parties. The following parties are represented in Congress:

Aliança Democrática (AD): f. 1984; electoral alliance formed to support the candidacy of the late Tancredo Neves in the presidential election of January 1985; comprises:

  Partido da Frente Liberal (PFL): f. 1984 by moderate members of the PDS and PMDB; Pres. MARCOS MACIEL; Gen. Sec. SAULO QUEIROZ.

BRAZIL — *Directory*

Partido do Movimento Democrático Brasileiro (PMDB): f. 1980; moderate elements of former MDB; merged with Partido Popular February 1982; Pres. ULYSSES GUIMARÃES; Gen.-Sec. MILTON REIS; factions include:

Históricos: f. 1988.

Movimento da Unidade Progressiva (MUP).

Partido Comunista Brasileiro (PCB): f. 1922; pro-Moscow; Sec.-Gen. SALOMÃO MALINA.

Partido Comunista do Brasil (PC do B): f. 1962; pro-Albanian; Sec.-Gen. JOÃO AMAZONAS; 5,000 mems.

Partido Democrata Cristão (PDC): Leader SIQUEIRA CAMPOS.

Partido Democrático Social (PDS): Senado Federal Anexo II, Presidência do PDS, 70.000 Brasília, DF; telex (61) 2402; f. 1980 as pro-Government party in succession to ARENA (see above); (in 1984 some liberal members of the PDS united with members of the PMDB (see above) to contest the presidential election of January 1985); Pres. JARBAS PASSARINHO; Sec.-Gen. AMARAL NETO.

Partido Democrático Trabalhista (PDT): Rua 7 de Setembro 141, 4°, 20.050 Rio de Janeiro, RJ; f. 1980; formerly the PTB (Partido Trabalhista Brasileiro) renamed 1980 when the name was awarded to a dissident group after controversial judicial proceedings; Pres. LEONEL BRIZOLA; Gen. Sec. Dra CARMEN CYNIRA.

Partido Liberal (PL): Pres. ÁLVARO VALLE.

Partido da Social Democracia Brasileira (PSDB): Brasília, DF; f. 1988; centre-left; formed by dissident members of the PMDB (incl. Históricos), PFL, PDS, PDT, and the PSB and PTB (see below); Pres. MÁRIO COVAS.

Partido Socialista Brasileiro (PSB): Pres. JAMIL HADAD.

Partido dos Trabalhadores (PT): Congresso Nacional, 70.160, Brasília, DF; tel. (061) 224-1699; f. 1980; first independent labour party; associated with the *autêntico* branch of the trade union movement; 350,000 mems; Pres. LUÍS IGNÁCIO (LULA) DA SILVA; Vice-Pres. JACÓ BITTAR; Sec.-Gen. OLÍVIO DUTRA.

Partido Trabalhista Brasileiro (PTB): f. 1980; Pres. LUIZ GONZAGA DE PAIVA MUNIZ; Gen. Sec. JOSÉ CORREIA PEDROSO, Jr.

Other political parties include:

Partido Verde: Brasília, DF; Green party; Pres. FERNANDO GABEIRA.

Diplomatic Representation

EMBASSIES IN BRAZIL

Algeria: SHIS, Q1 09, Conj. 13, Casa 01, Lago Sul, 71.600 Brasília, DF; tel. (061) 248-4039; telex (61) 1278; Ambassador: ABDELOUAHAB KERAMANE.

Angola: Brasília, DF; Ambassador: FRANCISCO ROMÃO DE OLIVEIRA E SILVA.

Argentina: SEPN, Av. W-3 Quadra 513, Bloco D, Edif. Imperador, 4° andar, 70.442 Brasília, DF; tel. (061) 273-3737; telex (61) 1013; Ambassador: HÉCTOR ALBERTO SUBIZA.

Australia: SHIS, QI 09 Conj. 16, Casa 01, Lago Sul, 70.469 Brasília, DF; tel. (061) 248-5569; telex (61) 1025; Ambassador: WARWICK EDUARD WEEMAES.

Austria: SES, Av. das Nações, Lote 40, CP 07-1215, Brasília, DF; tel. (061) 243-3111; telex (61) 1215; Ambassador: Dr NIKOLAUS HORN.

Bangladesh: SHIS, QL 10, Conj. 01, Casa 17, 70.468 Brasília, DF; tel. (061) 248-4609; Ambassador: MUJIB-UR RAHMAN.

Belgium: Av. das Nações, Lote 32, 70.422 Brasília, DF; tel. (061) 243-1354; telex (61) 1261; Chargé d'affaires a.i. CLAUDE MISSON.

Bolivia: SCS, Edif. Camargo Correia, 10°, 70.302 Brasília, DF; tel. (061) 223-2688; telex (61) 1946; Ambassador: JAIME BALCAZAR.

Bulgaria: SEN, Av. das Nações, Lote 8, 70.432 Brasília, DF; tel. (061) 223-5193; telex (61) 1305; Ambassador: GEORGI JEKOV GEUROV.

Cameroon: QI 3, Conj. 5, Casa 2, Lago Sul, 71.600 Brasília, DF; tel. (061) 248-4433; telex (61) 2235; Ambassador: MARTIN NGUELE MBARGA.

Canada: SES, Av. das Nações, Lote 16, CP 07-0961, 70.410 Brasília, DF; tel. (061) 223-7615; telex (61) 611296; Ambassador: JOHN PETER BELL.

Chile: SES, Av. das Nações, Lote 11, 70.407 Brasília, DF; tel. (061) 226-5545; telex (61) 1075; Ambassador: RAÚL SCHMIDT DUSSAILLANT.

China, People's Republic: SES, Av. das Nações, Lote 51, 70.443 Brasília, DF; tel. (061) 244-8695; telex (61) 1300; Ambassador: TAO DAZHAO.

Colombia: SES, Av. das Nações, Lote 10, 70.444 Brasília, DF; tel. (061) 226-8902; telex (61) 1458; Ambassador: GERMÁN RODRÍGUEZ FONNEGRO.

Costa Rica: SCS, Edif. Ceará 501/502, 70.303 Brasília, DF; tel. (061) 226-7212; Ambassador: MIGUEL ANGEL CAMPOS.

Côte d'Ivoire: SEN, Av. das Nações, Lote 09, 70.473 Brasília, DF; tel. (061) 321-4656; telex (61) 1095; Ambassador: Gen. BERTIN ZEZE BAROAN.

Cuba: QI 05, Conj. 18, Casa 01, Lago Sul, 71.600 Brasília, DF; tel. (061) 248-2018; Ambassador: RENÉ RODRÍGUEZ.

Czechoslovakia: SES, Av. das Nações, Lote 21, 70.414 Brasília, DF; tel. (061) 243-1263; telex (61) 1073; Ambassador VLADIMIR GULLA.

Denmark: SES, Av. das Nações, Lote 26, CP 07-0484, 70.416 Brasília, DF; tel. (061) 242-8188; telex (61) 1494; Ambassador: ERIK LYRTOFT-PETERSEN.

Dominican Republic: QI 19, Conj. 09, Casa 01, Lago Sul, 70.000 Brasília, DF; tel. (061) 248-1405; Ambassador: OSCAR HAZIM SUBERO.

Ecuador: QI 11, Conj. 09, Casa 24, 71.600 Brasília, DF; tel. (061) 248-5560; telex (61) 1290; Ambassador: LUIS PONCE ENRÍQUEZ.

Egypt: SEN, Av. das Nações, Lote 12, 70.435 Brasília, DF; tel. (061) 225-8517; telex (61) 1387; Ambassador: MEDHAT IBRAHIM TEWFIK.

El Salvador: QI 07, Conj. 12, Casa 01, Lago Sul, 71.600 Brasília, DF; tel. (061) 248-6409; telex (61) 2763; Chargé d'affaires: RAFAEL ANTONIO BOLAÑOS.

Finland: SES, Av. das Nações, Lote 27, 70.417 Brasília, DF; tel. (061) 242-8555; telex (61) 1155; Ambassador: RISTO KAUPPI.

France: SES, Av. das Nações, Lote 4, 70.404 Brasília, DF; tel. (061) 321-5354; telex (61) 1078; Ambassador: PHILIPPE CUVILLIER.

German Democratic Republic: CP 13-1971, SHI-Sul, QL 6, Conj. 8, Casa 17, 71.600 Brasília, DF; tel. (061) 248-1008; telex (61) 1417; Ambassador: Dr WERNER HÄNOLD.

Germany, Federal Republic: CP 07-0752, SES, Av. das Nações, Lote 25, 70.415 Brasília, DF; tel. (061) 243-7466; telex (61) 1198; Ambassador: HEINZ DITTMANN.

Ghana: SHIS QL 10, Conj. 08, Casa 02, 71.600 Brasília, DF; tel. (061) 248-6047; Ambassador: KOFI N. AWOONOR.

Greece: SHIS, QL 04, Conj. 1, Casa 18, 70.461 Brasília, DF; tel. (061) 248-1756; telex (61) 1843; Ambassador: ALEXIS D. ZAKYTHINOS.

Guatemala: SHIS, QL 08, Conj. 05, Casa 11, 70.460 Brasília, DF; tel. (061) 248-3318; Ambassador: CARLOS ALBERTO PRERA.

Guyana: Edif. Venâncio III, salas 410–414, 70.438 Brasília, DF; tel. (061) 224-9229; Ambassador: HUBERT O. JACK.

Haiti: SHIS, QI 7, Conj. 16, Casa 13, Lago Sul, 70.465 Brasília, DF; tel. (061) 248-6860; Ambassador: RAYMOND MATHIEU.

Holy See: SES, Av. das Nações, Lote 1, 70.401 Brasília, DF; tel. (061) 223-0794; telex (61) 2125; Apostolic Nuncio: Mgr CARLO FURNO.

Honduras: SBN, Edif. Eng. Paulo Mauricio Sampaio, 12°, sala 1209, CEP 70.040, Brasília, DF; tel. (061) 223-2773; telex (61) 3736; Ambassador: ROBERTO ARITA QUINÓÑEZ.

Hungary: SES, Av. das Nações, Lote 19, 70.413 Brasília, DF; tel. (061) 243-0822; telex (61) 1285; Ambassador: GABOR SUTO.

India: SDS, Edif. Venâncio VI, 5°, CP 11-1097, Brasília, DF; tel. (061) 226-1585; telex (61) 1245; Ambassador: DILBAGH SINGH.

Indonesia: SES, Av. das Nações, Lote 20, 70.200 Brasília, DF; tel. (061) 243-0102; Ambassador: (vacant).

Iran: SES, Av. das Nações, Lote 31, 70.421 Brasília, DF; tel. (061) 242-5733; telex (61) 1347; Ambassador: MAHMOUD MOVAHEDI.

Iraq: SES, Av. das Nações, Lote 64, Brasília, DF; tel. (061) 243-1804; telex (61) 1331; Ambassador: OAIS TAWFIG ALMUKHFAR.

Israel: SES, Av. das Nações, Lote 38, 70.424 Brasília, DF; tel. (061) 244-7675; telex (61) 1093; Ambassador: ITZHAK SARFATY.

Italy: SES, Av. das Nações, Lote 30, 70.420 Brasília, DF; tel. (061) 244-0044; telex (61) 1488; Ambassador: ANTONIO CIARRAPICO.

Japan: SES, Av. das Nações, Lote 39, 70.425, Brasília, DF; tel. (061) 242-6866; telex (61) 1376; Ambassador: KOICHI KOMURA.

Korea, Republic: SEN Av. das Nações, Lote 14, 70.436, Brasília, DF; tel. (061) 223-3466; telex (61) 1085; Ambassador: TAE WOONG KWON.

Kuwait: SHI-Sul, QI 5, Ch. 30, 70.467 Brasília, DF; tel. (061) 248-1634; telex (61) 1367; Ambassador: SAISAL AL-GHAIS.

Lebanon: SES, Av. das Nações, Q.805, Lote 17, 70.411 Brasília, DF; tel. (061) 242-4801; telex (61) 1295; Ambassador: SAMIR HOBEICA.

BRAZIL
Directory

Libya: SHIS, QI 1S, Chácara 26, CP 3505, 71.600 Brasília, DF; tel. (061) 248-6710; telex (61) 1099; Ambassador: ALI SULEIMAN AL-AUJALI.

Malaysia: SHIS, QI 05, Chácara 62, Lago Sul, 70.477 Brasília, DF; tel. (061) 248-5008; telex (61) 3666; Ambassador: Dato AJIT SINGH.

Mexico: SES, Av. das Nações, Lote 18, 70.412 Brasília, DF; tel. (061) 244-1011; telex (61) 1101; Ambassador: ANTONIO GONZÁLEZ DE LEÓN.

Morocco: SHIS, QI 11, Conj. 05, Casa 13, Lago Sul, 71.600 Brasília, DF; Ambassador: MOHAMED LARBI MESSARI.

Netherlands: SEN Av. das Nações, Lote 05, 70.405, Brasília, DF; POB 07-0098, 70.000; tel. (061) 223-20-25; telex (61) 1492; Ambassador: Jonkheer HUBERT VAN NISPEN.

Nicaragua: SCS, Edif. Venâncio da Silva 1301/1310, 70.302 Brasília, DF; tel. (061) 225-0283; telex (61) 2495; Ambassador: JORGE JAVIER JENKINS MOLIERI.

Nigeria: SHIS QL 6, Conj. 5, Casa 1, 70.459 Brasília, DF; tel. (061) 248-6768; telex (61) 1315; Ambassador: PATRICK COLE.

Norway: SES, Av. das Nações, Lote 28, 70.418, CP 07-0670, 70.418 Brasília, DF; tel. (061) 243-8720; telex (61) 1265; Ambassador: SIGURD ENDRESEN.

Pakistan: SCS, Edif. Central, 5°, 70.458 Brasília, DF; tel. (061) 224-2922; telex (61) 2252; Ambassador: TARIQ KHAN AFRIDS.

Panama: SCS, Edif. JK, 13° andar, 132/133, 70.449 Brasília, DF; tel. (061) 225-0859; Ambassador: GUSTAVO GARCÍA DE PAREDES.

Paraguay: SES, Av. das Nações, Lote 42, CP 14-2314, 70.427 Brasília, DF; tel. (061) 242-3723; telex (61) 1845; Ambassador: SALVADOR PEREDES SORIA.

Peru: SES, Av. das Nações, Lote 43, 70.428 Brasília, DF; tel. (061) 242-9435; telex (61) 1108; Ambassador: HUGO PALMA VALDERRAMA.

Philippines: SEN, Av. das Nações, Lote 1, 70.431 Brasília, DF; tel. (061) 223-5143; telex (61) 1420; Ambassador: LAURO L. BAJA, Jr.

Poland: SES, Av. das Nações, Lote 33, 70.423 Brasília, DF; tel. (061) 243-3438; telex (61) 1165; Ambassador: STANISŁAW PAWLISZEWSKI.

Portugal: SES, Av. das Nações, Lote 2, 70.042 Brasília, DF; tel. (061) 223-1090; telex (61) 1033; Ambassador: ADRIANO DE CARVALHO.

Romania: SEN, Av. das Nações, Lote 6, 70.456 Brasília, DF; tel. (061) 226-0746; Ambassador: GEORGHE APOSTOL.

Saudi Arabia: SHI-Sul, QL 10, Conj. 9, Casa 20, 70.471 Brasília, DF; tel. (061) 248-3523; telex (61) 1656; Ambassador: ABDULLAH SALEH HABABI.

Senegal: SEN, Av. das Nações, Lote 18, 70.437 Brasília, DF; tel. (061) 226-4405; telex (61) 1377; Ambassador: DEMBA NIANG (acting).

South Africa: Av. das Nações, Lote 6, CP 11-1170, 70.406 Brasília, DF; tel. (061) 223-4873; telex (61) 1683; Ambassador: ALEXANDRE VAN ZYL.

Spain: SES, Av. das Nações, Lote 44, 70.429 Brasília, DF; tel. (061) 242-1074; telex (61) 1313; Ambassador: JOSÉ LUIS CRESPO DE VEGA.

Suriname: SCS, Edif. OK, 2° andar, 70.000 Brasília, DF; tel. (061) 248-1780; telex (61) 1414; Ambassador: HARVEY HAROLD NAARENDORP.

Sweden: SES, Av. das Nações, Lote 29, 70.419 Brasília, DF; tel. (061) 243-1444; telex (61) 1225; Ambassador: KRISTER KUMLIN.

Switzerland: SES, Av. das Nações, Lote 41, 70.448 Brasília, DF; tel. (061) 244-5500; telex (61) 1135; Ambassador: CHARLES HENRY BRUGGMANN.

Syria: SEN, Av. das Nações, Lote 11, 70.434 Brasília, DF; tel. (061) 226-0970; telex (61) 1721; Ambassador: GHASSOUB RIFAI.

Thailand: SEN, Av. das Nações Norte, Lote 10, 70.433 Brasília, DF; tel. (061) 224-6943; telex (61) 3763; Ambassador: PRADEEP SOCHIRATNA.

Togo: SHIS QI 11, Conj. 9, Casa 10, CP 13-1998, 71.600 Brasília, DF; tel. (061) 248-4752; telex (61) 1837; Ambassador: LAMBANA TCHAOU.

Trinidad and Tobago: SHIS, QL 8, Conj. 4, Casa 5, 71.600 Brasília, DF; tel. (061) 248-1922; telex (61) 1844; Ambassador: SURUJRATTAN RAMBACHAN.

Turkey: SES Av. das Nações, Lote 23, 70.452 Brasília, DF; tel. (061) 242-1850; telex (61) 1663; Ambassador: METIN KUSTALOGLU.

USSR: SES, Av. das Nações, Lote A, 70.476 Brasília, DF; tel. (061) 223-3094; telex (61) 1273; Ambassador: LEONID FILIPPOVICH KUZMIN.

United Kingdom: SES, Quadra 801, Conj. K, CP 07-0586, 70.408 Brasília, DF; tel. (061) 225-2710; telex (61) 1360; Ambassador: MICHAEL J. NEWINGTON.

USA: SES, Av. das Nações, Lote 3, 70.403 Brasília, DF; tel. (061) 321-7272; telex (61) 41167; Ambassador: HARRY W. SHLAUDEMAN.

Uruguay: SES, Av. das Nações, Lote 14, 70.450 Brasília, DF; tel. (061) 224-2415; telex (61) 1173; Ambassador: Dr ROBERTO VIVO BONOMI.

Venezuela: SES, Av. das Nações, Lote 13, Q-803, 70.451 Brasília, DF; tel. (061) 223-9325; telex (61) 1325; Ambassador: FERNANDO GERBASI.

Yemen Arab Republic: Brasília, DF; Ambassador: (vacant).

Yugoslavia: SES, Quadra 803, Lote 15, 70.409 Brasília, DF; tel. (061) 223-7272; Ambassador: BRANKO TRPENOVSKI.

Zaire: SHIS, QI 9, Conj. 8, Casa 20, Lago Sul, CP 07-0041, 71.600 Brasília, DF; tel. (061) 248-3348; telex (61) 1435; Ambassador: LUALABA EMELEME ALEKIA.

Judicial System

The judiciary powers of the State are held by the following tribunals: the Supreme Federal Tribunal, the Federal Tribunal of Appeal, the State Tribunals of Justice, the Superior Military, the Electoral, and the Labour Tribunals; and by judges of other courts.

The Supreme Federal Court comprises 11 ministers, nominated by the President and approved by the Senate. It judges offences committed by persons exempt from appearing before the normal courts, such as the President, Ministers of State, its own members, judges of other courts, and chiefs of permanent diplomatic missions. It also litigates in disputes between the Union and the states, between the states, or between foreign nations and the Union or the states; disputes as to jurisdiction between justices and/or tribunals of the different states, including those of the federal district and of the territories; in cases involving the extradition of criminals, in certain special cases involving the principle of *habeas corpus*, and in other cases.

The Federal Tribunal of Appeal judges the cases in which the Federal Union has interest.

The State Tribunals of Justice, apart from their normal function as a court of appeal, can sit in judgment on their own members. The number of judges varies according to the judiciary organization of each state.

The organs of the Electoral Tribunal (the Superior Tribunal, the Regional Tribunals, and the electoral judges) register the names of political parties, fix the date of elections, supervise the listing of voters, and deal with all infractions of the electoral laws. The seven judges of the Superior Electoral Tribunal are chosen: three from the Supreme Federal Tribunal, two from the Federal Tribunal of Appeal and two by the President of the Republic.

The functions of the Military Court are no more than the name implies. The Labour Tribunal deals with labour disputes.

Civil offenders usually come before the courts of the separate states and of the Federal District. Each state organizes its own judiciary system on the principles established in the Constitution, and appoints its own judges from those who have passed the State examination in law.

THE SUPREME FEDERAL TRIBUNAL

Supreme Federal Tribunal: Praça dos Três Poderes, 70.175 Brasília, DF; tel. (061) 224-7179; telex (61) 1473.

President: LUIZ RAFAEL MAYER.

Vice-President: JOSÉ NÉRI DA SILVEIRA.

Justices: JOSÉ FRANCISCO REZEK, DJACI ALVES FALCÃO, CÉLIO DE OLIVEIRA BORJA, LUIZ OCTÁVIO PIRES E ALBUQUERQUE GALLOTTI, CARLOS ALBERTO MADEIRA, JOSÉ CARLOS MOREIRA ALVES, SYDNEY SANCHES, OSCAR DIAS CORRÊA, ALDIR GUIMARÃES PASSARINHO.

Procurator-General: JOSÉ PAULO SEPÚLVEDA PERTENCE.

Director-General (Secretariat): SEBASTIÃO DUARTE XAVIER.

Religion

CHRISTIANITY

Conselho Nacional de Igrejas Cristãs do Brasil—CONIC (National Council of Christian Churches in Brazil): Rua Senhor dos Passos 202, CP 2876, 90.020 Porto Alegre, RS; tel. (0512) 245010; telex (51) 2332; f. 1982; six mem. churches; Pres. Pastor Dr GOTTFRIED BRAKEMEIER (Pres. of Igreja Evangélica de Confissão Luterana no Brasil); Exec. Sec. Rev. GODOFREDO G. BOLL.

The Roman Catholic Church

Brazil comprises 36 archdioceses, 188 dioceses (including one each for Catholics of the Maronite, Melkite and Ukrainian Rites), 16

BRAZIL

territorial prelatures and two territorial abbacies. The Archbishop of São Sebastião do Rio de Janeiro is also the Ordinary for Catholics of other Oriental Rites in Brazil (estimated at 8,500 in 1978). The great majority of Brazil's population are adherents of the Roman Catholic Church.

Bishops' Conference: Conferência Nacional dos Bispos do Brasil, SES, Quadra 801, Conj. B, CP 13-2067, 70.401 Brasília, DF; tel. (061) 225-2955; telex (61) 1104; f. 1980 (statutes approved 1986); Pres. Mgr LUCIANO P. MENDES DE ALMEIDA, Archbishop of Mariana, MG.

Latin Rite

Archbishop of São Salvador da Bahia, BA: Cardinal LUCAS MOREIRA NEVES, Primate of Brazil, Palácio da Sé, Praça da Sé 1, 40.000 Salvador; tel. (071) 243-5411.

Archbishop of Aparecida do Norte, SP: GERALDO MARIA DE MORAIS PENIDO.

Archbishop of Aracajú, SE: LUCIANO JOSÉ CABRAL DUARTE.

Archbishop of Belém do Pará, PA: ALBERTO GAUDÊNCIO RAMOS.

Archbishop of Belo Horizonte, MG: SERAFIM FERNANDES DE ARAÚJO.

Archbishop of Botucatú, SP: VICENTE MARCHETTI ZIONI.

Archbishop of Brasília, DF: Cardinal JOSÉ FREIRE FALCÃO.

Archbishop of Campinas, SP: GILBERTO PEREIRA LOPES.

Archbishop of Campo Grande: VITÓRIO PAVANELLO.

Archbishop of Cascavel, PR: ARMANDO CIRIO.

Archbishop of Cuiabá, MT: BONIFÁCIO PICCININI.

Archbishop of Curitiba, PR: PEDRO ANTÔNIO MARCHETTI FEDALTO.

Archbishop of Diamantina, MG: GERALDO MAJELA REIS.

Archbishop of Florianópolis, SC: AFONSO NIEHUES.

Archbishop of Fortaleza, CE: Cardinal ALOISIO LORSCHEIDER.

Archbishop of Goiânia, GO: ANTÔNIO RIBEIRO DE OLIVEIRA.

Archbishop of Juiz de Fora, MG: JUVENAL RORIZ.

Archbishop of Londrina, PR: GERALDO MAJELA AGNELO.

Archbishop of Maceió, AL: EDVALDO GONÇALVES AMARAL.

Archbishop of Manaus, AM: CLÓVIS FRAINER.

Archbishop of Mariana, MG: LUCIANO P. MENDES DE ALMEIDA.

Archbishop of Maringá, PR: JAIME LUÍZ COELHO.

Archbishop of Natal, RN: ALAIR VILAR FERNANDES DE MELO.

Archbishop of Niterói, RJ: JOSÉ GONÇALVES DA COSTA.

Archbishop of Olinda e Recife, PM: JOSÉ CARDOSO SOBRINHO.

Archbishop of Paraíba, PB: JOSÉ MARIA PIRES.

Archbishop of Porto Alegre, RS: JOÃO CLÁUDIO COLLING.

Archbishop of Porto Velho, RO: JOSÉ MARTINS DA SILVA.

Archbishop of Pouso Alegre, MG: JOSÉ D'ANGELO NETO.

Archbishop of Ribeirão Prêto, SP: (vacant).

Archbishop of São Luís do Maranhão, MA: PAULO EDUARDO DE ANDRADE PONTE.

Archbishop of São Paulo, SP: Cardinal PAULO EVARISTO ARNS.

Archbishop of São Sebastião do Rio de Janeiro, RJ: Cardinal EUGÊNIO DE ARAÚJO SALES.

Archbishop of Teresina, PI: MIGUEL FENELON CÂMARA.

Archbishop of Uberaba, MG: BENEDITO DE ULHÔA VIEIRA.

Archbishop of Vitória, ES: SILVESTRE LUÍS SCANDIÁN.

Maronite Rite

Bishop of Nossa Senhora do Libano em São Paulo, SP: JEAN CHEDID.

Melkite Rite

Bishop of Nossa Senhora do Paraíso em São Paulo, SP: SPIRIDON MATTAR.

Ukrainian Rite

Bishop of São João Batista em Curitiba, PR: EFREM BASILIO KREVEY.

The Anglican Communion

Anglicans form the Episcopal Church of Brazil (Igreja Episcopal do Brasil), comprising seven dioceses.

Igreja Episcopal do Brasil: POB 11.510, 90.641 Porto Alegre, RS; tel. (0512) 360651; f. 1890; 65,000 mems (1987); Primate: Rt Rev. OLAVO VENTURA LUIZ, Bishop of Southwestern Brazil.

Protestant Churches

Igreja Cristã Reformada do Brasil: CP 2808, 01.000 São Paulo, SP; Pres. Rev. JANOS APOSTOL.

Igreja Evangélica de Confissão Luterana no Brasil (IECLB): Rua Senhor dos Passos 202, 2° andar, CP 2876, 90.020 Porto Alegre, RS; tel. (051) 213433; telex (51) 2332; f. 1949; 870,000 mems; Pres. Pastor Dr GOTTFRIED BRAKEMEIER.

Igreja Evangélica Congregacional do Brasil: CP 414, 98.700 Ijuí, RS; tel. (055) 332-4656; f. 1942; 41,000 mems, 310 congregations; Pres. Rev. H. HARTMUT W. HACHTMANN.

Igreja Evangélica Luterana do Brasil: Rua Cel. Lucas de Oliveira 894, CP 1076, 90.001 Porto Alegre, RS; tel. (0512) 32-2111; telex (51) 515741; 186,544 mems; Pres. JOHANNES H. GEDRAT.

Igreja Metodista do Brasil: General Communication Secretariat, Rua Artur Azevedo 1192, Apdo 81, Pinheiros, 05.404 São Paulo, SP; Exec. Sec. Dr ONÉSIMO DE OLIVEIRA CARDOSO.

Igreja Presbiteriana Unida do Brasil (IPU): CP 2368, 29.001 Vitória, ES.

BAHÁ'Í FAITH

National Spiritual Assembly: Rua Eng. Gama Lobo 267, Vila Isabel, 20.551 Rio de Janeiro, RJ; tel. (021) 288-9846; mems resident in 1,250 localities.

BUDDHISM

Federação das Seitas Budistas do Brasil: Av. Paulo Ferreira 1133, Piqueri, São Paulo, SP.

Sociedade Budista do Brasil (Rio Buddhist Vihara): Dom Joaquim Mamede 45, Santa Tereza, 20.241 Rio de Janeiro, RJ; tel. (021) 220-7486; f. 1972; Pres. JOÃO REIS MARQUES.

The Press

The most striking feature of the Brazilian press is the relatively small circulation of newspapers in comparison with the size of the population. The newspapers with the largest circulations are *O Día* (207,000), *O Globo* (350,000), *Fôlha de São Paulo* (212,000), and *O Estado de São Paulo* (230,000). The low circulation is mainly due to high costs resulting from distribution difficulties. In consequence there are no national newspapers. In 1988 a total of 288 newspaper titles were published in Brazil. The last remaining censorship on books and newspapers was abolished in July 1985.

DAILY NEWSPAPERS

Belém, PA

O Liberal: Rua Gaspar Viana 253, 66.000 Belém, PA; tel. (091) 222-3000; telex (91) 1026; f. 1946; Pres. LUCIDEA MAIORANA; circ. 20,000.

Belo Horizonte, MG

Diário da Tarde: Rua Goiás 36, 30.000 Belo Horizonte, MG; tel. (031) 226-2322; telex (31) 1253; f. 1930; evening; Dir PEDRO AGUINALDO FULGÊNCIO; circ. 35,000.

Diário de Minas: Praça Raul Soares 339, 30.180 Belo Horizonte, MG; tel. (031) 212-7107; telex (31) 5113; f. 1949; Pres. FREDERICO O. ZANAM PEREIRA; circ. 50,000.

Estado de Minas: Rua Goiás 36, 30.000 Belo Horizonte, MG; tel. (031) 272-2322; telex (31) 1166; f. 1928; morning; independent; Dir PEDRO AGNALDO FULGÊNCIO; circ. 65,000.

Blumenau, SC

Jornal de Santa Catarina: Rua São Paulo 1120, 89.010 Blumenau, SC; tel. (0473) 22-6400; telex (473) 120; f. 1971; Pres. NILTON J. REIS; circ. 25,000.

Brasília, DF

Correio Braziliense: SIG, Q2, Lote 340, 70.610 Brasília, DF; tel. (061) 321-1314; telex (61) 1727; f. 1960; Dir-Gen. PAULO C. DE ARAÚJO; circ. 30,000.

Jornal de Brasília: SIG Trecho 1, Lotes 585/645, 70.610 Brasília, DF; tel. (61) 225-2515; telex (61) 1208; f. 1972; Dir JORGE DE MORÃES JARDIM, Filho; circ. 25,000.

Campinas, SP

Correio Popular: Rua Conceição 124, 13.015 Campinas, SP; tel (019) 32-8588; telex (19) 1021; f. 1927; Pres. SYLVINO DE GODOY NETO; circ. 15,000.

Curitiba, PR

O Estado do Paraná: Rua João Tachannerl 800, 80.520 Curitiba, PR; tel. (041) 233-8811; telex (41) 5388; f. 1951; Pres. PAULO CRUZ PIMENTEL; circ. 15,000.

Gazeta do Povo: Praça Carlos Gomes 04, 80.010 Curitiba, PR; tel. (041) 224-0522; telex (41) 6520; f. 1919; Pres. FRANCISCO CUNHA PEREIRA, Filho; circ. 40,000.

BRAZIL

A Tribuna do Paraná: CP 869, Jardim Mercês, Cidade da Comunicaçãos, 80.520 Curitiba PR; tel. (041) 233-8811; telex (41) 5388; f. 1956; Pres. PAULO CRUZ PIMENTEL; circ. 15,000.

Florianópolis, SC

O Estado: Rodovia SC-401, Km 3, 88.030 Florianópolis, SC; tel. (0482) 33-5555; telex (482) 179; f. 1915; Pres. JOSÉ MATUSALÉM COMELLI; circ. 20,000.

Fortaleza, CE

O Povo: Av. Aguanambi 282, 60.055 Fortaleza, CE; tel. (085) 211-9666; telex (85) 1107; f. 1928; evening; Pres. DEMÓCRITO ROCHA DUMMAR; circ. 20,000.

Tribuna do Ceará: Av. Desemb. Moreira 2900, 60.000 Fortaleza, CE; tel. (085) 247-3066; telex (85) 1207; Pres. JOSÉ A. SANCHO; circ. 12,000.

Goiânia, GO

Diário da Manhã: Av. 24 de Outubro 1240, 74.000 Goiânia, GO; tel. (062) 233-5013; telex (62) 1055; f. 1980; Pres. JULIO NASSER CUSTÓDIO DOS SANTOS; circ. 16,000.

O Popular: Rua Thomaz Edson Q7, Sector Serrinha, 74.610 Goiânia, GO; tel. (062) 241-5533; telex (62) 1110; f. 1938; Pres. JAIME CÂMARA, Jr; circ. 20,000.

Londrina, PR

Fôlha de Londrina: Rua Piauí 241, 86.010 Londrina PR; tel. (0432) 22-3636; telex (432) 123; f. 1948; Pres. JOÃO MILANEZ; circ. 35,000.

Manaus, AM

A Critica: Rua Lobo D'Álmeida 278, 69.007 Manaus; tel. (092) 232-1400; telex (92) 2103; f. 1949; Dir UMBERTO CALDERARO, Filho; circ. 19,000.

Niterói, RJ

O Fluminense: Rua Visconde de Iboraí 184, 24.035 Niterói, RJ; tel. (021) 719-3311; telex (21) 32054; f. 1878; Dir ALBERTO FRANCISCO TORRES; circ. 80,000.

A Tribuna: Rua Barão do Amazonas 31, 24.030 Niterói, RJ; tel. (021) 719-1886; f. 1926; Dir-Gen. MARIA MADALENA A. TANURE; circ. 18,000.

Porto Alegre, RS

Zero Hora: Av. Erico Veríssimo s/n, 90,000 Porto Alegre, RS; tel. (0512) 223-1110; telex (51) 3157; f. 1964; Pres. MAURÍCIO SIROTSKY; circ. 110,000 (Mon.), 115,000 weekdays, 250,000 Sunday.

Recife, PE

Diário de Pernambuco: Praça da Independência 12, 2° andar, 50.018 Recife, PE; tel. (081) 231-6222; telex (81) 1057; f. 1925; morning; independent; Pres. GLADSTONE VIERA BELO; circ. 31,000.

Ribeirão Preto, SP

Diário da Manhã: Rua Duque de Caxias 179, 14.100 Ribeirão Preto, SP; tel. (016) 634-0909; f. 1898; Dir PAULO M. SANT'ANNA; circ. 17,000.

Rio de Janeiro, RJ

Brazil Herald: Rua do Rezende 65, 20.231 Rio de Janeiro, RJ; tel. (021) 221-2772; f. 1946; daily, except Mondays; morning; only English language daily in Brazil; Dir MAURO SALLES; circ. 18,000.

O Dia: Rua Riachuelo 359, 20.235 Rio de Janeiro, RJ; tel. (021) 292-2020; telex (21) 22385; f. 1951; morning; popular labour; Pres. ANTÔNIO ARY DE CARVALHO; circ. 207,000 weekdays, 400,000 Sundays.

O Globo: POB 1090, Rua Irineu Marinho 35, 20.233 Rio de Janeiro, RJ; tel. (021) 272-2000; telex (21) 22595; f. 1925; morning; Dir ROBERTO MARINHO; circ. 350,000 weekdays, 520,000 Sundays.

Jornal do Brasil: Av. Brasil 500, São Cristovão, 20.940 Rio de Janeiro, RJ; tel. (021) 585-4422; telex (21) 23690; f. 1891; morning; Catholic, conservative; Pres. J. ANTÔNIO DO NASCIMENTO BRITO; circ. 200,000 weekdays, 325,000 Sundays.

Jornal do Comércio: Rua do Livramento 189, 20.221 Rio de Janeiro, RJ; tel. (021) 253-6675; telex (21) 22165; f. 1927; morning; Pres. AUSTREGÉSILO DE ATHAYDE; circ. 31,000 weekdays.

Jornal dos Sports: Rua Tenente Possolo 15/25, Cruz Vermelha, 20.230 Rio de Janeiro, RJ; tel. (021) 232-8010; telex (21) 23093; f. 1931; morning; sporting daily; Dir VENÂNCIO P. VELLOSO, Filho; circ. 38,000.

Ultima Hora: Rua Equador 702, 20.220 Rio de Janeiro, RJ; tel. (021) 223-2444; telex (21) 22385; f. 1951; evening; Dir-Gen. JOSÉ NUNES, Filho; circ. 56,000.

Salvador, BA

A Tarde: Av. Magalhães Neto s/n, 40.000 Salvador, BA; tel. (071) 231-0077; telex (71) 1299; f. 1912; evening; Pres. REGINA SIMÕES DE MELLO LEITÃO; circ. 54,000.

Correio da Bahia: Av. Luiz Viana Filho s/n, 40.000 Salvador, BA; tel. (71) 231-2811; telex (71) 1594; f. 1978; Pres. ARMANDO GONÇALVES.

Jornal da Bahia: Rua Djalma Dutra 121, 40.000 Salvador, BA; tel. (071) 233-7446; telex (71) 1296; f. 1958; Pres. CARLOS EDUARDO V. BARRAL; circ. 20,000.

Santo André, SP

Diário do Grande ABC: Rua Catequese 562, 09.090 Santo André SP; tel. (011) 449-5533; telex (11) 44034; f. 1958; Pres. EDSON DANILLO DOTTO; circ. 85,000.

Santos, SP

A Tribuna: Rua General Câmara 90/94, 11.010 Santos, SP; tel. (013) 232-7711; telex (13) 1058; f. 1984; Pres. GIUSFREDO SANTINI; circ. 35,000.

São Paulo, SP

Diário Comércio e Indústria: Rua Alvaro de Carvalho 354, 01.050 São Paulo, SP; tel. (011) 256-5011; telex (11) 21436; f. 1924; morning; Pres. WALDEMAR DOS SANTOS; circ. 50,000.

Diário Popular: Rua Major Quedinho 28, 1°-6°, 01.050 São Paulo, SP; tel. (011) 258-2133; telex (11) 21213; f. 1884; evening; independent; Pres. RODRIGO L. SOARES; circ. 90,000.

O Estado de São Paulo: Av. Eng. Caetano Álvares 55, 02.550 São Paulo, SP; tel. (011) 856-2122; telex (11) 23511; f. 1875; morning; independent; Pres. ANTÔNIO O. SCATOLIN; circ. 230,000 weekdays, 460,000 Sundays.

Fôlha de São Paulo: Alameda Barão de Limeira 425, Campos Elísios, 01.202 São Paulo, SP; tel. (011) 874-2222; telex (11) 22930; f. 1921; morning; Editorial Dir OCTÁVIO FRIAS O., Filho; circ. 211,900 weekdays, 314,830 Sundays.

Gazeta Mercantil: Rua Major Quedinho 90, 8°, 01.050 São Paulo, SP; tel. (011) 256-3133; telex (11) 23748; f. 1920; business paper; Pres. LUIZ FERREIRA LEVY; circ. 80,000.

Jornal da Tarde: Av. Eng. Caetano Álvares 55, 02.550 São Paulo, SP; tel. (011) 856-2122; telex (11) 23511; f. 1966; evening; independent; Pres. JOSÉ V. C. MESQUITA; circ. 120,000, 180,000 Mondays.

Notícias Populares: Alameda Barão de Limeira 425, 01.202 São Paulo, SP; tel. (011) 874-2222; telex (11) 22930; f. 1963; Dirs: see *Fôlha de São Paulo*, above; circ. 150,000.

Vitória, ES

A Gazeta: Rua Chafic Murad 902, 29.050 Vitória, ES; tel. (027) 222-8338; telex (27) 2273; f. 1928; Pres. EUGÊNIO PACHECO QUEIROZ; circ. 19,000.

PERIODICALS
Rio de Janeiro, RJ

Amiga: Rua do Russell 766/804, 22.210 Rio de Janeiro, RJ; tel. (021) 265-2012; telex (21) 21525; weekly; women's interest; Pres. ADOLPHO BLOCH; circ. 88,000.

Antenna-Eletrônica Popular: Av. Marechal Floriano 143, CP 1131, 20.060 Rio de Janeiro, RJ; tel. (021) 223-2442; f. 1926; monthly; telecommunications and electronics, radio, TV, hi-fi, amateur and CB radio; Dir GILBERTO AFFONSO PENNA; circ. 25,000.

Carinho: Rua do Russell 766/804, 22.214 Rio de Janeiro, RJ; tel. (021) 265-2012; telex (21) 21525; monthly; women's interest; Pres. ADOLPHO BLOCH; circ. 100,000.

Casa e Jardim: Rua Felizbelo Freire 671, 20.071 Rio de Janeiro, RJ; tel. (021) 270-6262; f. 1953; monthly; homes and gardens, illustrated; Editor MILTON MADEIRA; circ. 80,000.

Conjuntura Econômica: Praia de Botafogo 188, 22.253 Rio de Janeiro, RJ; tel. (021) 551-0246; f. 1947; monthly; economics and finance; published by Fundação Getúlio Vargas; Editor Dr PAULO RABELLO DE CASTRO; circ. 22,000.

Criativa: Rua Itapiri 1209, 21.251 Rio de Janeiro, RJ; tel. (021) 273-5522; telex (21) 23365; monthly; women's interest; Pres. OSCAR D. NEVES; circ. 121,000.

Desfile: Rua do Russell 766/804, 22.214 Rio de Janeiro, RJ; tel. (021) 265-2012; telex (21) 21525; f. 1969; monthly; women's interest; Dir ADOLPHO BLOCH; circ. 140,000.

Ele Ela: Rua do Russell 766/804, 22.210 Rio de Janeiro RJ; tel. (021) 265-2012; telex (21) 21525; f. 1969; monthly; men's interest; Dir ADOLPHO BLOCH; circ. 210,000.

Fatos e Fotos: Rua do Russell 766/804, 20.210 Rio de Janeiro, RJ; tel. (021) 285-0033; telex (21) 21525; illustrated weekly; general interest; Pres. ADOLPHO BLOCH; circ. 110,000.

BRAZIL   *Directory*

Manchete: Rua do Russell 766/804, 20.210 Rio de Janeiro, RJ; tel. (021) 265-2012; telex (21) 22751; f. 1952; weekly; general; Dir ADOLPHO BLOCH; circ. 160,000.

São Paulo, SP

Capricho: Rua Geraldo Flausino Gomes 61, 04.575 São Paulo, SP; tel. (011) 545-8122; telex (11) 24134; monthly; women's interest; Dir VICTOR CIVITA; circ. 167,000.

Claudia: Rua Geraldo Flausino Gomes 61, 04.575 São Paulo, SP, CP 2372; tel. (011) 545-8122; telex (11) 24134; f. 1962; monthly; women's magazine; Dir VICTOR CIVITA; circ. 254,000.

Digesto Econômico: Associação Comercial de São Paulo, Rua Boa Vista 51, 01.014 São Paulo, SP; tel. (011) 234-3382; telex (11) 23355; every 2 months; Pres. ROMEU TRUSSARDI, Filho.

Dirigente Rural: Rua Afonso Celso 243, 04.119 São Paulo, SP; tel. (011) 549-4344; telex (11) 23552; monthly; agriculture; Dir HENRY MAKSOUD; Editor ISAAC JORDANOVSKI; circ. 64,577.

Exame: Rua Geraldo F. Gomes 61, 04.574 São Paulo, SP; tel. (011) 545-8122; telex (11) 24134; fortnightly; business; Dir VICTOR CIVITA; circ. 85,000.

Iris: Rua Jacucaim 67, Brooklin, 04.563 São Paulo, SP; tel. (011) 531-1299; f. 1947; monthly; photography, video; Dirs BEATRIZ AZEVEDO MARQUES, SUSANNE AZEVEDO MARQUES; circ. 75,000.

Manequim: Rua Geraldo Flausino Gomes 61, 04.575 São Paulo, SP; tel. (011) 545-8122; telex (11) 24134; monthly; fashion; Dir VICTOR CIVITA; circ. 300,000.

Máquinas e Metais: Rua Dona Elisa 167, 01.155 São Paulo, SP; tel. (011) 826-4511; f. 1964; monthly; machine and metal industries; Editor JOSÉ ROBERTO GONÇALVES; circ. 20,000.

Mickey: Rua Bela Cintra 299, 01.415 São Paulo, SP; tel. (011) 257-0999; telex (11) 70522; every 2 weeks; children's magazine; Dir VICTOR CIVITA; circ. 150,000.

Micromundo-Computerworld do Brasil: Rua Caçapava 79, 01.408 São Paulo, SP; tel. (011) 881-6844; telex (11) 32017; monthly; computers; Gen. Dir ERIC HIPPEAU; circ. 38,000.

Mundo Elétrico: Rua Consórcio 59, 04.535 São Paulo, SP; tel. (011) 853-7185; telex (11) 30410; f. 1959; monthly; electricity; Pres. MANFREDO GRUENWALD.

Nova: Rua Geraldo Flausino Gomes 61, 04.575 São Paulo, SP; tel. (011) 545-8122; telex (11) 24134; f. 1973; monthly; women's interest; Dir VICTOR CIVITA; circ. 156,000.

Pato Donald: Rua Bela Cintra 299, 01.415 São Paulo, SP; tel. (011) 257-0999; telex (11) 70522; every 2 weeks; children's magazine; Dir VICTOR CIVITA; circ. 186,600.

Placar: Rua Geraldo Flausino Gomes 61, 04.575 São Paulo, SP; tel. (011) 545-8122; telex (11) 24134; f. 1970; weekly; sports magazine; Dir VICTOR CIVITA; circ. 119,000.

Quatro Rodas: Rua Geraldo Flausino Gomes 61, Brooklin, 04.575 São Paulo, SP; tel. (011) 545-8122; telex (11) 24134; f. 1960; monthly; motoring; Pres. VICTOR CIVITA; circ. 167,000.

Revista O Carreteiro: Rua Palacete das Águias 284, 04.635 São Paulo, SP; tel. (011) 533-5237; monthly; transport; Dir JOSÉ A. DE CASTRO; circ. 160,000.

Saúde: Av. Marquês de São Vicente 1771, 01.139 São Paulo, SP; tel. (011) 826-6777; telex (11) 26070; monthly; health; Dir ANGELO ROSSI; circ. 180,000.

Veja: Av. Otaviano Alves de Lima 4400, 02.901 São Paulo, SP; tel. (011) 856-1322; telex (11) 22115; f. 1968; news weekly; Dir VICTOR CIVITA; circ. 523,000.

Video Business: Rua Jacucaim 102/112, Brooklin, 01.457 São Paulo, SP; tel. (011) 211-8499; f. 1987; monthly; video; Dirs BEATRIZ A. MARQUES, SILVIA H. A. MARQUES PILZ; circ. 80,000.

Visão: Rua Afonso Celso 243, 01.419 São Paulo, SP; tel. (011) 549-4344; telex (11) 23552; f. 1952; weekly; news magazine; Editor HENRY MAKSOUD; circ. 148,822.

NEWS AGENCIES

Editora Abril SA: Av. Otaviano Alves de Lima 4400, CP 2372, 02.909 São Paulo, SP; tel. (011) 266-0056; telex (11) 2215; Mans EDGARD S. FARIA, AUTA ROJAS BARRETO.

Agência ANDA: Edif. Correio Braziliense, Setor das Indústrias Gráficas 300/350, Brasília, DF; Dir EDILSON VARELA.

Agência o Estado de São Paulo: Av. Eng. Caetano Alvares 55, 02.550 São Paulo, SP; tel. (011) 856-2122; telex (11) 22700; Rep. SAMUEL DIRCEU F. BUENO.

Agência Fôlha de São Paulo: Alameda Barão de Limeira 425, Campos Elísios, 01.290 São Paulo; tel. (011) 243-6428; Dir TARSIO NITRINI.

Agência Globo: Rua Irineu Marinho 35, 2° andar, Centro, 20.030 Rio de Janeiro, RJ; tel. (021) 292-2000; Dir LUCIANO DE MORAIS.

Agência Jornal do Brasil: Av. Brasil 500, 6° andar, São Cristovão, 20.940 Rio de Janeiro, RJ; tel. (021) 264-4422; Rep. JAIR SOARES.

Foreign Bureaux

Agence France-Presse (AFP) (France): CP 2575-ZC-00, Rua México 21, 7° andar, 20.031 Rio de Janeiro, RJ; tel. (021) 240-6634; telex (21) 22494; Bureau Chief JACQUES THOMET; Rua Sete de Abril 230, 11° andar, Bloco B, 01.044 São Paulo, SP; tel. (011) 255-2566; telex (11) 21454; Bureau Chief RICARDO UZTARROZ; SDS, Edif. Venâncio IV, sala 307, Brasília, DF; tel. (061) 224-3576; telex (61) 1291; Bureau Chief MICHEL GALAN.

Agencia EFE (Spain): Av. Rio Branco 25, 13° andar, 20.090 Rio de Janeiro, RJ; tel. (021) 253-4465; telex (21) 30073; Bureau Chief ZOILO G. MARTÍNEZ DE LA VEGA; SHIS, QI 3, Conj. 8, Casa 13, Lago Sul, 71.600 Brasília, DF; tel. (061) 248-1375; Bureau Chief RICARDO PALMÁS.

Agenzia Nazionale Stampa Associata (ANSA) (Italy): Av. Pres. Antônio Carlos 40, Cobertura, CP 16095, Rio de Janeiro, RJ; tel. (021) 220-5528; telex (21) 22296; Bureau Chief MANUEL HORACIO PALLAVIDINI; Av. São Luís 258, 13° andar, Of. 1302, São Paulo, SP; tel. (011) 256-5835; telex (11) 21421; Bureau Chief RICCARDO CARUCCI; c/o Correio Brasiliense, 70.610 Brasília, DF; tel. (061) 226-1755; telex (61) 2211; Bureau Chief HUMBERTO ANTONIO GIANNINI; Rua Barão do Rio Branco 556, Curitiba, PA; tel. (041) 24-5000; Bureau Chief ELOIR DANTÉ ALBERTI.

Allgemeiner Deutscher Nachrichtendienst (ADN) (German Democratic Republic): SHI-SUL, QL 14, Conj. 10, Casa 13, CP 7079, 71.600 Brasília, DF; tel. (061) 248-6499; telex (61) 3856; Correspondent WOLFGANG WAGNER.

Associated Press (AP) (USA): Av. Brasil 500, sala 847, CP 72-ZC-00, 20.001 Rio de Janeiro, RJ; tel. (021) 580-4422; telex (21) 21888; Bureau Chief BRUCE HANDLER; Rua Major Quedinho 28, 6° andar, CP 3815, 01.050 São Paulo, SP; tel. (011) 256-0520; telex (11) 21595; Correspondent STAN LEHMAN; a/c Sucursal Folha de São Paulo, CLS 104 Bloco C Loja 41, CP 14-2260, 70.343 Brasília, DF; tel. (061) 223-9492; telex (61) 1454; Correspondent JORGE MEDEROS.

Deutsche Presse-Agentur (dpa) (Federal Republic of Germany): Av. Brasil 500, 6° andar, 20.940 Rio de Janeiro, RJ; tel. (021) 248-9156; telex (21) 22550; Bureau Chief SIEGFRIED NIEBUHR.

Inter Press Service (IPS) (Italy): Rua do Russell 450/602, 22.210 Rio de Janeiro; tel. (021) 285-7982; telex (21) 34845; Correspondent MARIO CHIZUO OSAVA.

Jiji Tsushin-Sha (Japan): Rua Tenente Otavio Gomes 37, Aclimação, 01.526 São Paulo, SP; tel. (011) 278-5790; telex (11) 24594; Chief Correspondent YUKIO YOSHINAGA.

Kyodo Tsushin (Japan): Praia do Flamengo 168-701, Flamengo, 22.210 Rio de Janeiro, RJ; tel. (021) 285-2412; telex (21) 33653; Bureau Chief HIROAKI IDAKA.

Prensa Latina (Cuba): Marechal Mascarenhas de Moraes 121, Apto 203, Copacabana, 22.030 Rio de Janeiro, RJ; tel. (021) 256-7259; telex (21) 36510; Correspondent SERGIO PINEDA.

Reuters (UK): SCS, Edif. Gilberto Salamão, salas 807–810, 70.300 Brasília, DF; tel. (061) 223-5918; telex (61) 11982; Rua Líbero Badaró 377, 21°, 01.009 São Paulo, SP; tel. (011) 35-1046; telex (11) 23796; Av. Rio Branco 25, 12°, Conj. C/D, CP 266, 20.090 Rio de Janeiro, RJ; tel. (021) 233-5430; telex (21) 23222; Chief Correspondent RICHARD JARVIE.

Telegrafnoye Agentstvo Sovetskovo Soyuza (TASS) (USSR): Rua General Barbosa 34, Apto 802, Rio de Janeiro, RJ; Correspondent ALEKSANDR MAKSIMOV; Av. das Naçoes, Lote A, 70.000 Brasília, DF; Correspondent YURIY BESPALCO.

United Press International (UPI) (USA): Rua Uruguaina 94, 18°, Centro, 20.050 Rio de Janeiro, RJ; tel. (021) 224-4194; telex (21) 22680; Chief Correspondent BRIAN LEONARD NICHOLSON; Rua Sete de Abril 230, Bloco B, 6°, 01.044 São Paulo, SP; tel. (011) 257-5262; telex (11) 22235; Correspondent CHRISTIAN BOFILL; Edif. Gilberto Salamão, Sala 813, 70.300 Brasília, DF; tel. (061) 24-6413; telex (61) 1507; Correspondent WALTER SOTOMAYOR.

Xinhua (New China) News Agency (People's Republic of China): SHI/S QI 15, Conj. 16, Casa 14, CP 7089; 71.600 Brasília, DF; tel. (061) 248-5489; telex (61) 2788; Chief Correspondent WANG ZHIGEN.

Central News Agency (Taiwan) and Novosti (USSR) are also represented in Brazil.

PRESS ASSOCIATIONS

Associação Brasileira de Imprensa: Rua Araújo Pôrto Alegre 71, Castelo, 20.030 Rio de Janeiro, RJ; f. 1908; 4,000 mems; Pres. BARBOSA LIMA SOBRINHO; Sec. JOSUÉ ALMEIDA.

Federação Nacional dos Jornalistas Profissionais—FENAJ: SCRS 502, Bloco A, 1°-2°, 70.330, Brasília, DF; tel. (061) 223-7002; telex (61) 1792; f. 1946; represents 26 regional unions; Pres. ARMANDO SOBRAL ROLLEMBERG.

Publishers

There are nearly 500 publishers in Brazil. The following is a list of the most important by virtue of volume of production.

Rio de Janeiro, RJ

Bloch Editores, SA: Rua do Russell 766/804, Glória, 22.210 Rio de Janeiro, RJ; tel. (021) 265-2012; telex (21) 21525; f. 1953; general; Pres. ADOLPHO BLOCH.

Distribuidora Record de Serviços de Imprensa, SA: Rua Argentina 171, São Cristóvão, CP 884, 20.921 Rio de Janeiro, RJ; tel. (021) 580-3668; telex (21) 30501; f. 1941; general fiction and non-fiction, education, textbooks, fine arts; Pres. ALFREDO C. MACHADO.

Ebid-Editora Páginas Amarelas Ltda: Av. Pres. Wilson 165, 3° andar, 20.080 Rio de Janeiro, RJ; tel. (021) 292-6116; telex (21) 21678; commercial directories.

Editora Artenova, SA: Rua Pref. Olímpio de Mello 1774, Benfica, 20.030 Rio de Janeiro, RJ; tel. (021) 264-9198; f. 1971; sociology, psychology, occultism, cinema, literature, politics and history; Man. Dir ALVARO PACHECO.

Editora Brasil-América (EBAL) SA: Rua Gen. Almérico de Moura 302/320, São Cristóvão, 20.921 Rio de Janeiro, RJ; tel. (021) 580-0303; telex (21) 21293; f. 1945; children's books; Dir ADOLFO AIZEN.

Editora Delta SA: Av. Almirante Barroso 63, 26° andar, CP 2226, 20.031 Rio de Janeiro, RJ; tel. (021) 240-0072; f. 1958; reference books.

Editora Globo SA: Rua Itapiru 1209, Rio Comprido, 20.251 Rio de Janeiro, RJ; tel. (021) 273-5522; telex (21) 23365; f. 1957; general.

Editora e Gráfica Miguel Couto SA: Rua da Passagem 78, Loja A, Botafogo, 22.290 Rio de Janeiro, RJ; tel. (021) 541-5145; f. 1969; engineering; Dir PAULO KOBLER PINTO LOPES SAMPAIO.

Editora Monterrey Ltda: Rio de Janeiro, RJ; f.1963; fiction; Dir J. GUEIROS.

Editora Nova Fronteira, SA: Rua Bambina 25, Botafogo, 22.251 Rio de Janeiro, RJ; tel. (021) 286-7822; telex (21) 34695; f. 1965; fiction, psychology, history, politics, science fiction, poetry, leisure, reference; Pres. SÉRGIO C. A. LACERDA.

Editora Tecnoprint, SA: Rua da Proclamação 109, 21.040 Rio de Janeiro, RJ; tel. (021) 260-6122; f. 1939; general.

Editora Vecchi, SA: Rua do Rezende 144, Esplanada do Senado, 20.234 Rio de Janeiro, RJ; tel. (021) 221-0822; telex (21) 32756; f. 1913; general literature, juvenile, reference, cookery, magazines; Dir DELMAN BONATTO.

Editora Vozes, Ltda: Rua Frei Luís 100, 25.600 Petrópolis, RJ; tel. (021) 43-5112; f. 1901; Catholic publishers; management, theology, anthropology, fine arts, history, linguistics, science, fiction, education, data processing, etc.; Dir Dr MIGUEL GOMES MOURÃO DE CASTRO.

Exped—Espansão Editorial Ltda: Estrada dos Bandeirantes 1700, Bloco H, Jacarepeguá, 22.700 Rio de Janeiro, RJ; tel. (021) 342-0669; telex (21) 33280; f. 1967; textbooks, literature, reference; Gen. Man. FERDINANDO BASTOS DE SOUZA.

Fundação de Assistência ao Estudante (FAE): Rua Miguel Ângelo 96, Maria da Graça, 20.781 Rio de Janeiro, RJ; tel. (021) 261-7750; f. 1967; education; Dir EGBERTO DA COSTA GAIA.

Gráfica Editora Primor, Ltda: Rodv. Pres. Dutra 2611, 21.530 Rio de Janeiro, RJ; tel. (021) 371-6622; telex (21) 22150; f. 1968.

Livraria Francisco Alves Editora, SA: Rua 7 de Setembro 177, 20.050 Rio de Janeiro, RJ; tel. (021) 221-3198; f. 1854; textbooks, fiction, non-fiction; Dir Supt LEO MAGARINOS DE SOUZA LEÃO.

Livraria José Olympio Editora, SA: Rua Marquês de Olinda 12, CP 9018, Botafogo, 22.252 Rio de Janeiro, RJ; tel. (021) 551-0642; telex (21) 21327; f. 1931; juvenile, science, history, philosophy, psychology, sociology, fiction; Dir LUIZ OCTÁVIO DO ESPÍRITO SANTO.

Ao Livro Técnico SA Indústria e Comércio: Rua Sá Freire 40, São Cristóvão, 20.930 Rio de Janeiro, RJ; tel. (021) 580-1168; telex (21) 30472; f. 1946; technical, scientific, children's, languages, textbooks; Man. Dir REYNALDO MAX PAUL BLUHM.

Otto Pierre Editores Ltda: Rua Dr Nunes 1225, Olaria, 21.021 Rio de Janeiro, RJ.

Tesla Publicações Ltda: Rua da Quitanda 49, 1° andar, salas 110/12, 20.011 Rio de Janeiro, RJ; tel. (021) 242-0135; f. 1960; children's books.

São Paulo, SP

Atual Editora Ltda: Rua José Antônio Coelho 785, Vila Mariana, 04.011 São Paulo, SP; tel. (011) 575-1544; f. 1973; school books; Dirs GELSON IEZZI, OSVALDO DOLCE.

Cedibra Editora Brasileiro Ltda: Rua Particular 300, km 102 Via Anhauguera, Campinas, 13.100 São Paulo, SP; tel. (0192) 419911; literature and children's books; Man. Dir JAN RAIS.

Cia Editora Nacional: Rua Joli 294, Brás, 03.016 São Paulo, SP; tel. (011) 291-2355; f. 1925; textbooks, history, science, social sciences, philosophy, fiction, juvenile; Dirs JORGE YUNES, PAULO C. MARTI.

Cia Melhoramentos de São Paulo, Indústrias de Papel: Rua Tito 479, 05.051 São Paulo, SP; tel. (011) 262-6866; telex (11) 23151; f. 1890; history, science, juvenile education, history; Gen. Man. RAINER OELLERS.

Editora Abril SA: Av. Octaviano Alves de Lima 4400, CP 02909, São Paulo, SP; tel. (011) 856-1322; telex (11) 22115; f. 1950; Dir VICTOR CIVITA.

Editora Atica, SA: Rua Barão de Iguape 110, 01.507 São Paulo, SP; tel. (011) 278-9322; telex (11) 32969; f. 1965; education, economics, literature, accountancy; Pres. ANDERSON FERNANDES DIAS.

Editora Atlas SA: Rua Conselheiro Nébias 1384, Campos Elíseos, CP 7186, 01.803 São Paulo, SP; tel. 221-9144; f. 1944; business administration, data-processing, economics, accounting, law, education, social sciences; Pres. LUIZ HERRMANN.

Editora Brasiliense: Rua Gal. Jardim 160, 01.223 São Paulo, SP; tel. (011) 231-1422; f. 1943; education, sociology, history, administration, psychology, literature, children's books; Mans CAIO GRACO DA SILVA PRADO, THEOPHILO ISIDORE DE ALMEIDA, Filho.

Editora do Brasil SA: Rua Conselheiro Nébias 887, Campos Elíseos, 01.263 São Paulo, SP; tel. (011) 222-0211; f. 1943; commerce, education, history, psychology and sociology.

Editora Caminho Suave Ltda: Rua Fagundes 157, Liberdade, 01.508 São Paulo, SP; tel. (011) 278-5840; f. 1965; textbooks.

Editora e Encadernadora Formar Ltda: Rua dos Trilhos 1126, Mooca, CP 13250, 03.168 São Paulo, SP; tel. (011) 93-5133; f. 1962; general.

Editora F.T.D. SA: Rua Pereira Nunes 323, 20.511 Rio de Janeiro, RJ; tel. (021) 288-5846; f. 1965; textbooks; Pres. JOÃO TISSI.

Editora Moderna Ltda: Rua Afonso Brás 431, Ibirapuera, 04.511 São Paulo, SP; tel. (011) 531-5099; f. 1969; education and children's books.

Editora Nova Cultural Ltda: Av. Brigadeiro Faria Lima 2000, Torre Norte, 3°/4°/5° andares, 01.452 São Paulo, SP; tel. (011) 815-8055; telex (11) 83765; f. 1965; general encyclopaedias, pocket books, children's activities manuals, elementary educational books; Man. Dir FLAVIO BARROS PINTO.

Editora Revista dos Tribunais Ltda: Rua Conde do Pinhal 78, 01.501 São Paulo, SP; tel. (011) 37-2433; f. 1955; law and jurisprudence, administration, economics and social sciences; Dir ALVARO MALHEIROS.

Editora Rideel Ltda: Alameda Afonso Schmidt 877, Santa Terezinha, 02.450 São Paulo, SP; tel. (011) 267-8344; f. 1971; general; Dir ITALO AMADIO.

Editora Rio Gráfica Ltda: Rua do Curtume 665, Bl. D 705 Bl. E, São Paulo, SP; tel. (011) 262-3100; telex (11) 54071.

Encyclopaedia Britannica do Brasil Publicações Ltda: Rua Rego Freitas 192, Vila Buarque, CP 31027, 01.220 São Paulo, SP; tel. (011) 221-7122; telex (11) 21460; f. 1951; reference books.

Ênio Matheus Guazzelli & Cia Ltda (Livraria Pioneira Editora): Praça Dirceu de Lima 313, Casa Verde, 02.515 São Paulo, SP; tel. (011) 858-3199; f. 1964; architecture, political and social sciences, business studies, languages, children's books; Dir ÊNIO MATHEUS GUAZZELLI.

Gráfica-Editora Michalany SA: Rua Biobedas 321, Saúde, CP 12933, 04.302 São Paulo, SP; tel. (011) 275-9716; f. 1965; biographies, economics, textbooks, geography, history, religion, maps; Dir DOUGLAS MICHALANY.

Instituto Brasileiro de Edições Pedagógicas Ltda: Rua Joli 294, Brás, CP 5321, 03.016 São Paulo, SP; tel. (011) 291-2355; f. 1972; textbooks, foreign languages, reference books and chemistry.

Lex Editora SA: Rua Machado de Assis 47/57, Vila Mariana, CP 12888, 04.106 São Paulo, SP; tel. (011) 549-0122; f. 1937; legislation and jurisprudence; Dir AFFONSO VITALE SOBRINHO.

Editora Luzeiro Ltda: Rua Almirante Barroso 730, Brás, 03.025 São Paulo, SP; tel. (011) 292-3188; f. 1973; folklore and literature.

Saraiva SA Livreiros Editores: Av. Marquês de São Vicente 1697, CP 2362, 01.139 São Paulo, SP; tel. (011) 826-8422; f. 1914; education, textbooks, law, economics; Pres. PAULINO SARAIVA.

Editora Scipione Ltda: Praça Carlos Gomes 46, 01.501 São Paulo, SP; tel. (011) 37-4151; f. 1983; textbooks, mathematics; Dir MAURÍCIO FERNANDES DIAS.

BRAZIL — *Directory*

Belo Horizonte, MG

Editora Lê SA: Av. D. Pedro II, 4550 Jardin Montanhês, CP 2585, 30.730 Belo Horizonte, MG; tel. (031) 462-6262; telex (31) 3340; f. 1967; textbooks.

Editora Lemi SA: Av. Nossa Senhora de Fátima 1945, CP 1890, 30.000 Belo Horizonte, MG; tel. (031) 201-8044; f. 1967; administration, accounting, law, ecology, economics, textbooks, children's books and reference books.

Editora Vigília Ltda: Rua Felipe dos Santos 508, Bairro de Lourdes, CP 2468, 30.180 Belo Horizonte, MG; tel. (031) 337-2744; f. 1960; general.

Curitiba, PR

Editora Educacional Brasileira SA: Rua XV de Novembro 178, salas 101/04, CP 7498, 80.000 Curitiba, PR; tel. (041) 223-5012; f. 1963; biology, textbooks and reference books.

PUBLISHERS' ASSOCIATIONS

Associação Brasileira do Livro: Av. 13 de Maio 23, 16°, 20.031 Rio de Janeiro, RJ; tel. (021) 232-7173; Dir ALBERJANO TORRES.

Câmara Brasileira do Livro: Av. Ipiranga 1267, 10°, 01.039 São Paulo, SP; tel. (011) 229-7855; telex (11) 23151; f. 1946; Pres. ALFREDO WEISZFLOG.

Sindicato Nacional dos Editores de Livros: Av. Rio Branco 37, 15°, 20.097 Rio de Janeiro, RJ; tel. (021) 233-5484; telex (21) 37063; 190 mems; Pres. ALFREDO C. MACHADO; Exec. Sec. MARIA CRISTINA RAMALHO.

There are also regional publishers' associations.

Radio and Television

In 1986 there were an estimated 75m. radio receivers and 34m. television receivers in use. In 1988, as part of the Government's privatization scheme, plans were announced to privatize 14 radio stations and one television station.

Departamento Nacional de Telecomunicações (Dentel) (National Telecommunications Council): Via N2, Anexo do Ministério das Comunicações, Esplanada dos Ministérios, Bloco R, 70.066 Brasília, DF; tel. (061) 223-3229; telex (61) 1175; Dir-Gen. ROBERTO BLOIS MONTES DE SOUZA.

Empresa Brasileira de Comunicação, SA (Radiobrás) (Brazilian Communications Company): SCRN 702/3, Bloco B, no. 18, 70.710 Brasília, DF; tel. (061) 224-3949; telex (61) 1682; f. 1988 following merger of Empresa Brasileira de Radiodifusão and Empresa Brasileira de Notícias; Chair. ANTÔNIO MARTINS DE VASCONCELOS.

RADIO

In 1988 there were 2,529 radio stations in Brazil, including 19 in Brasília, 38 in Rio de Janeiro, 32 in São Paulo, 24 in Curitiba, 24 in Porto Alegre and 23 in Belo Horizonte.

The main broadcasting stations in Rio de Janeiro are: Rádio Nacional, Rádio Globo, Rádio Eldorado, Rádio Jornal do Brasil, Rádio Tupi and Rádio Mundial. In São Paulo the main stations are Rádio Bandeirantes, Rádio Mulher, Rádio Eldorado, Rádio Gazeta and Rádio Excelsior; and in Brasília: Rádio Nacional, Rádio Alvorada, Rádio Planalto and Rádio Capital.

TELEVISION

In 1988 there were 216 television stations in Brazil, of which 106 were in the state capitals and six in Brasília. PAL-M colour television was adopted in 1972 and the Brazilian system is connected with the rest of the world by satellite.

The main television networks are:

TV Bandeirantes—Canal 13: Rádio e Televisão Bandeirantes, SA, Rua Radiantes 13, Morumbí, CP 372, 05.699 São Paulo, SP; tel. (011) 842-3011; telex (11) 37878; 23 television networks throughout Brazil; Pres. JOÃO JORGE SAAD.

RBS TV—Canal 12: Rua TV Gaúcha 189, 90.659 Porto Alegre, RS; tel. (0512) 235-5000; telex (51) 4118; Dir JAIME SIROTSKY.

TV Globo—Canal 4: Rua Lopes Quintas 303, 22.463 Rio de Janeiro, RJ; tel. (021) 294-7732; telex (21) 22795; f. 1965; 12 stations; national network; Pres. ROBERTO MARINHO.

TV Manchete-Canal 6: Rua do Russel 804, 22.210 Rio de Janeiro, RJ; tel. (021) 265-2012; telex (21) 35998; Pres. ADOLPHO BLOCH.

TV Record—Canal 7: Av. Miruna 713, Aeroporto, 04.085 São Paulo, SP; tel. (011) 542-9000; telex (11) 22245; Dir-Pres. PAULO MACHADO DE CARVALHO, Filho.

TVS—Canal 4 de São Paulo, SA: Rua Dona Santa Veloso 575, Vila Guilherme, 02.050 São Paulo, SP; tel. (011) 292-9044; telex (11) 22126; Vice-Pres. GUILHERME STOLIAR.

BROADCASTING ASSOCIATIONS

Associação Brasileira de Emissoras de Rádio e Televisão (ABERT): Mezanino do Hotel Nacional, salas 5 a 8, 70.322 Brasília, DF; tel. (061) 224-4600; telex (61) 2001; f. 1962; mems: 32 shortwave, 643 FM, 1,294 medium-wave and 84 tropical-wave radio stations and 177 television stations (mid-1986); Pres. JOAQUIM MENDONÇA; Exec. Dir ANTÔNIO ABELIN.

There are regional associations for Bahia, Ceará, Goiás, Minas Gerais, Paraná, Pernambuco, Rio de Janeiro and Espírito Santo (combined), Rio Grande do Sul, Santa Catarina, São Paulo, Amazonas, Distrito Federal, Mato Grosso and Mato Grosso do Sul (combined) and Sergipe.

Finance

(cap. = capital; p.u. = paid up; dep. = deposits; res = reserves; m. = million; brs = branches; amounts in cruzados, unless otherwise stated)

BANKING

In September 1988 the Conselho Monétario Nacional approved legislation to allow foreign banks to hold up to 33% of the voting stock and 50% of the total capital of local financial institutions.

Conselho Monétario Nacional: SBS, Edif. Banco do Brasil, 6° andar, Brasília, DF; f. 1964 to formulate monetary policy and to supervise the banking system; Pres. Minister of Finance.

Central Bank

Banco Central do Brasil: Av. Pres. Vargas 84, 70.074 Brasília, DF; tel. (061) 214-2000; telex (61) 2098; f. 1965 to execute the decisions of the Conselho Monetário Nacional; bank of issue; total assets 8,976,293.8m. (June 1987); Pres. ELMO DE ARAÚJO CAMÕES.

State Commercial Banks

Banco do Brasil, SA: Sector Bancário Sul, Lote 32, Quadra 4, CP 562, Brasília, DF; tel. (061) 212-2211; telex (61) 2107; f. 1808; cap. and res 244,653.7m., dep. 1,336,715.5 (June 1987); Pres. MÁRIO BERARD; 3,314 brs.

Banco do Estado de Minas Gerais, SA: Rua Rio de Janeiro 471, CP 300, 30.160 Belo Horizonte, MG; tel. (031) 239-1111; telex (31) 2134; f. 1967; cap. and res 2,017.7m., dep. 18,553.1 (June 1987); Pres. JOSÉ LUIZ ROCHA; 260 brs.

Banco do Estado do Paraná, SA: Rua Máximo João Kopp 274, CP 3331, 80.000 Curitiba, PR; tel. (041) 251-8250; telex (41) 6515; f. 1928; cap. and res 2,975.8m., dep. 26,870.7m. (May 1987); Pres. SERGIO MIGUEL DE SOUZA; 309 brs.

Banco do Estado do Rio Grande do Sul, SA: Rua Capitão Montanha 177, CP 505, 90.010 Porto Alegre, RS; tel. (051) 21-5023; telex (51) 512474; f. 1928; cap. 1,072.7m., res 8,613.3m., dep. 25,045.7m. (Dec. 1987); Pres. ODACIR KLEIN; 295 brs.

Banco do Estado do Rio de Janeiro, SA (BANERJ): Av. Nilo Peçanha 175, 17° andar, CP 21090, 20.020 Rio de Janeiro, RJ; tel. (021) 533-2272; telex (21) 23290; f. 1945; cap. and res 730.2m., dep. 8,072.9m. (Dec. 1985); Pres. JORGE HILÁRIO GOUVEIA VIEIRA; 2 brs; taken over by Banco Central do Brasil in March 1987.

Banco do Estado de São Paulo, SA: Praça Antônio Prado 6, CP 30-565, 01.010 São Paulo, SP; tel. (011) 32-8565; telex (11) 22052; f. 1926; cap. and res 15,478.7m., dep. 70,731.2m. (May 1987); Pres. JOÃO DE OLIVEIRA; 837 brs.

Banco do Nordeste do Brasil, SA: Praça Murillo Borges 1, 60.000 Fortaleza, CE; tel. (085) 231-0688; telex (85) 1132; f. 1954; cap. and res 10,419.5m., dep. 8,751.9m. (June 1987); Pres. JOSÉ PEREIRA E SILVA; 163 brs.

Private Banks

Banco América do Sul, SA: Av. Brig. Luís Antônio 2020, CP 8075, 01.318 São Paulo, SP; tel. (011) 288-4933; telex (11) 21354; f. 1940; cap. and res 4,000.0m., dep. 8,913.4m. (June 1987); Pres. YOSUKE YOSHIDA; 103 brs.

Banco Bamerindus do Brasil, SA: Rua Comendador Araújo 551, 80.420 Curitiba, PR; tel. (041) 223-8407; telex (41) 5303; f. 1952; cap. and res 11,731.0m., dep. 19,950.8m. (June 1987); Pres. JOSÉ EDUARDO DE ANDRADE VIEIRA; Dir OTTORINO MARINI; 990 brs.

Banco Bandeirantes, SA: Rua Boa Vista 162, 7°, CP 8260, 01.014 São Paulo, SP; tel. (011) 239-5622; telex (11) 412353; f. 1944; cap. and res 611.3m., dep. 941.6m. (June 1987); Pres. Dr GILBERTO DE ANDRADE FARIA; 165 brs.

Banco Boavista, SA: Praça Pio X 118, CP 1560-ZC-00, 20.092 Rio de Janeiro, RJ; tel. (021) 291-6633; telex (21) 30053; f. 1924; cap. and res 1,160.3m., dep. 9,726.7m. (May 1987); Pres. LINNEO DE PAULA MACHADO; 64 brs.

BRAZIL
Directory

Banco Bozano Simonsen SA: Av. Rio Branco 138, 20.057 Rio de Janeiro, RJ; tel. (021) 271-8000; telex (21) 22963; f. 1972; cap. and res 558.3m., dep. 1,108.7m. (June 1987); Pres. JÚLIO RAFAEL DE ARAGÃO BOZANO; 17 brs.

Banco Brasileiro de Descontos, SA (BRADESCO): Cidade de Deus CX, CP 8250, 06.000 Osasco, SP; tel. (011) 704-3311; telex (11) 74001; f. 1943; cap. and res 60,708.5m., dep. 180,615.9m. (June 1987); Pres. AMADOR AGUIAR; 1,735 brs.

Banco Chase Manhattan, SA: Rua do Ouvidor 98, CP 221, 20.040 Rio de Janeiro, RJ; tel. (021) 216-6112; telex (21) 21837; fmrly Banco Lar Brasileiro, SA; cap. and res 1,476.9m., dep. 30,240.8m. (April 1987); Pres. ALFREDO SALAZAR, Filho; Exec. Vice-Pres. MILTON TESSEROLLI; 44 brs.

Banco Cidade: Praça Dom José Gaspar 106, CP 30735, 01.047 São Paulo, SP; tel. (011) 258-8233; telex (11) 22198; f. 1965; cap. and res 1,235.2m., dep. 9,355.6m. (June 1987); Pres. EDMUNDO SAFDIE; 25 brs.

Banco de Crédito Nacional, SA (BCN): Rua Boa Vista 228, CP 30-243, 01.014 São Paulo, SP; tel. (011) 229-4011; telex (11) 21284; f. 1924; cap. and res 7,263.4m., dep. 9,448.5m. (June 1987); Pres. Dr ANTÔNIO GRISI; 181 brs.

Banco de Crédito Real de Minas Gerais, SA: Rua Espírito Santo 495, POB 90, 30.000 Belo Horizonte, MG; tel. (031) 212-2100; telex (31) 1351; f. 1889; cap. 216.6m., res −171.5m., dep. 2,443.0m. (Dec. 1985); Pres. Dr DERMEVAL JOSÉ PIMENTA; 204 brs.

Banco Econômico, SA: Rua Miguel Calmon 285, 40.000 Salvador, BA; tel. (071) 254-1834; telex (71) 1197; f. 1834; cap. and res 8,314.1m., dep. 16,835.1m. (May 1987); Pres. ÂNGELO CALMON DE SÁ; 541 brs.

Banco Europeu para a América Latina (BEAL), SA: Rua Bela Cintra 952, 01.415 São Paulo, SP; tel. (011) 257-0422; telex (11) 23985; f. 1911; formerly Banco Ítalo-Belga; cap. and res 894.4m., dep. 4,447.5m. (June 1987); Gen. Man. M. BARDINI; 6 brs.

Banco Francês e Brasileiro, SA: Av. Paulista 1318, 01.310 São Paulo, SP; tel. (011) 251-4522; telex (11) 23340; f. 1948; affiliated with Crédit Lyonnais; cap. and res 7,918.7m., dep. 32,723.1m. (June 1987); Dir PIERRE JEAN DOSSA; 52 brs.

Banco Hispano Americano: Alameda Santos 960, 01.418 São Paulo, SP; tel. (011) 284-9355; telex (11) 35596; f. 1981; cap. and res 266.9m., dep. 603.1m. (June 1987); Dir RAMÓN JARABA TELLO.

Banco Holandês Unido SA: Rua do Ouvidor 107, 20.040 Rio de Janeiro, RJ; tel. (021) 297-2055; telex (21) 23663; f. 1917; cap. and res 537.5m., dep. 1,240.4m. (May 1987); Gen. Man. DURK VISSERMAN (acting); 5 brs.

Banco Itaú, SA: Rua Boa Vista 176, CP 30341, 01.092 São Paulo, SP; tel. (011) 239-8000; telex (11) 22131; f. 1944; cap. and res 34,694.7m., dep. 122,949.8m. (June 1987); Pres. JOSÉ CARLOS DE MORÃES ABREU; 130 brs.

Banco Mercantil de São Paulo, SA: Av. Paulista 1450, CP 4077, 01.310 São Paulo, SP; tel. (011) 252-2121; telex (11) 37701; f. 1938; cap. and res 1,476.9m., dep. 30,240.8m. (April 1987); Pres. GASTÃO AUGUSTO DE BUENO VIDIGAL; 333 brs.

Banco Mercantil do Brasil, SA: Rua Rio de Janeiro 680, CP 836, 30.000 Belo Horizonte, MG; tel. (031) 201-6122; telex (31) 1762; f. 1941; cap. and res 3,568.6m., dep. 11,357m. (May 1987); Pres. OSWALDO DE ARAÚJO; 224 brs.

Banco Meridional do Brasil, SA: Rua 7 de Setembro 1028, CP 26, 90.010 Porto Alegre, RS; tel. (051) 225-9954; telex (51) 3250; f. 1985, formerly Banco Sulbrasileiro, SA; Pres. CARLOS TADEU AGRIFOGLIO VIANNA; 361 brs; taken over by the Government in Feb. 1985.

Banco Mitsubishi Brasileiro: Rua Líbero Badaró 641, CP 30179, 01.009 São Paulo, SP; tel. (011) 239-5244; telex (11) 21854; f. 1933; cap. and res 850.0m., dep. 2,852.5m. (April 1987); Pres. MOTOCHIKA KOBORI; 19 brs.

Banco Nacional, SA: Av. Rio Branco 123, 2° andar, 20.040 Rio de Janeiro, RJ; tel. (021) 296-7722; telex (21) 21265; f. 1944; cap. and res 6,254.3m., dep. 23,369m. (April 1987); Pres. MARCOS DE MAGALHÃES PINTO; 567 brs.

Banco Noroeste SA: Rua Alvares Penteado 216, CP 8119, 01.012 São Paulo, SP; tel. (011) 239-0844; telex (11) 36810; f. 1923; cap. and res 3,481.2m., dep 32,407.6m. (June 1987); Pres. JORGE WALLACE SIMONSEN; 151 brs.

Banco Real, SA: Av. Paulista 1374, POB 5766, 01.310 São Paulo, SP; tel. (011) 286-4988; telex (11) 23520; f. 1925; cap. and res 13,913.5m., dep. 27,870.3m. (June 1987); Pres. Dr ALOYSIO DE ANDRADE FARIA; 610 brs.

Banco Royal do Canada, SA: Rua XV de Novembro 240, 01.013 São Paulo, SP; tel. (011) 239-4533; telex (11) 23351; f. 1984; fmrly Banco Internacional SA; cap. and res 514.2m., dep. 716.4m. (June 1987); Pres. M. A. BRENNAN; 4 brs.

Banco Safra, SA: Av. Paulista 2100, 16°, 01.310 São Paulo, SP; tel. (011) 234-6755; telex (11) 21396; cap. 2,000.0m., res 21,667.1m., dep. 70,264.2m. (Dec. 1987); Pres. CARLOS ALBERTO VIEIRA; 73 brs.

Banco Sudameris Brasil, SA: Av. Paulista 1000, 01.310 São Paulo, SP; tel. (011) 283-9633; telex (11) 30397; f. 1910; cap. and res 4,245.6m., dep. 14,941.3m. (June 1987); Dir GIOVANNI LENTI; 74 brs.

Banco Sumitomo Brasileiro: Av. Paulista 949, CP 7961, São Paulo, SP; cap. and res 1,095.6m., dep. 4,146.8m. (June 1987); Pres. ATSUSHI SAKAI; 5 brs.

Banco de Tokyo SA: Av. Paulista 1274, 01.310 São Paulo, SP; tel. (011) 285-6011; telex (11) 21192; f. 1972; cap. 411.8m., res 2,089.8m., dep. 16,856.2m. (Dec. 1987); Pres. TOSHIRO KOBAYASHI; 7 brs.

Unibanco—União de Bancos Brasileiros, SA: Praça do Patriarca 30, POB 8185, 01.000 São Paulo, SP; tel. (011) 817-4322; telex (11) 34074; f. 1924; cap. and res 14,811.1m., dep. 83,137.3m. (June 1987); Pres. WALTHER MOREIRA SALLES; 896 brs.

Development Banks

Banco de Desenvolvimento de Minas Gerais—BDMG: Rua da Bahia 1600, Belo Horizonte, MG; tel. (031) 212-3822; telex (31) 1343; cap. and res 5,236.2m., dep. 22,936.6m. (June 1987); Pres. CARLOS TEIXEIRA DE OLIVEIRA.

Banco de Desenvolvimento do Espírito Santo, SA: Av. Princesa Isabel 54, CP 1168, 29.000 Vitoria, ES; tel. (027) 223-8333; telex (27) 2131; cap. 2.3m. (1984); Pres. ANTÔNIO DE CALDAS BRITO.

Banco do Desenvolvimento do Estado da Bahia, SA: Av. Magalhães Neto, S/N°, 40.000 Salvador, BA; tel. (071) 231-2322; telex (71) 1665; f. 1937; cap. and res 1,476.8m., dep. 1,973m. (March 1987); Pres. ARNALDO MURILO NOGUEIRA LEITE.

Banco de Desenvolvimento do Estado de São Paulo, SA (BADESP): Av. Paulista 1776, 01.310 São Paulo, SP; tel. (011) 289-2233; Pres. JOSÉ TIACCI KIRSTEN.

Banco de Desenvolvimento do Estado do Rio Grande do Sul, SA (BADESUL): Rua 7 de Setembro 666, 90.000 Porto Alegre, RS; tel. (051) 21-6655; telex (51) 1159; f. 1975; cap. and res 661.6m., dep. 2,481.0m. (June 1987); Pres. JAMES GIACOMONI.

Banco de Desenvolvimento do Paraná, SA: Av. Vicente Machado 445, CP 6042, 80.420 Curitiba, PR; tel. (041) 224-9711; telex (41) 5083; f. 1962; cap. 838.2m. (1987); Pres. CELSO DA COSTA SABÓIA.

Banco Nacional de Crédito Cooperativo, SA: SBN, Q.01-BL.C-2° e s/n Edif. Palácio do Desenvolvimento-Asa Norte 70.057 Brasília, DF; tel. 224-5515; telex (61) 2292; established in association with the Ministry of Agriculture and guaranteed by the Federal Government to provide co-operative credit; cap. and res 22.1m., dep. 3,832.0m. (May 1987); Pres. DEJANDIR DALPASQUALE; 39 brs.

Banco Nacional do Desenvolvimento Econômico e Social (BNDES): Av. República do Chile 100, 20.031 Rio de Janeiro, RJ; tel. (021) 277-7447; telex (21) 22466; f. 1952 to act as main instrument for financing of development schemes sponsored by the Government and to support programmes for the development of the national economy; cap. and res 57,209.3m., dep. 263,503.1m. (Dec. 1986); disbursements 48,774.5m. (1986); Pres. ANDRÉ FRANCO MONTORO, Filho.

Banco Regional de Desenvolvimento do Extremo Sul (BRDE): Rua Uruguai 155, POB 139, 90.010 Porto Alegre, RS; tel. (051) 221-9200; telex (51) 1229; f. 1961; cap. and res 1,998m., dep. 8,434m. (1986); development bank for the states of Paraná, Rio Grande do Sul and Santa Catarina; acts as agent for numerous federal financing agencies and co-operates with IBRD and Eximbank; finances small- and medium-sized enterprises; Dir-Pres. WALDEMAR ALLEGRETTI; 3 brs.

Investment Banks

Banco Bozano, Simonsen de Investimento, SA: Av. Rio Branco 138, 20.057 Rio de Janeiro, RJ; tel. (021) 271-8000; telex (21) 22963; f. 1967; investment bank catering for medium- and long-term capital requirements, mergers, acquisitions; cap. and res 3,263.8m., dep. 5,814.1m. (June 1987); Pres. JÚLIO RAFAEL DE ARAGÃO BOZANO; 6 brs.

Banco Finasa de Investimento, SA: Av. Paulista 1450, 01.310 São Paulo, SP; tel. (011) 252-2121; telex (11) 37701; f. 1965; medium- and long-term financing for industrial and commercial activities; underwriting shares and debentures; investment advisers; cap. and res 3,013.8m., dep. 3,074.6m. (June 1987); Pres. GASTÃO AUGUSTO DE BUENO VIDIGAL; 7 brs.

Banco de Montreal Investimento SA (Montrealbank): Travessa Ouvidor 4, 20.149 Rio de Janeiro, RJ; tel. (021) 291-1122; telex (21) 21956; cap. and res 1,185.1m., dep. 4,961.7m. (May 1987); Pres. PEDRO LEITÃO DA CUNHA; 6 brs.

BRAZIL
Directory

Foreign Banks

Banca Commerciale Italiana: Av. Paulista 407, CP 30461, 01.311 São Paulo, SP; tel. (011) 289-4666; telex (11) 23679; cap. and res 489.2m., dep. 1,317.8m. (June 1987); Man. ANTÔNIO RAMPONE; 2 brs.

Banco de la Nación Argentina: Av. Rio Branco 134-A, 20.040 Rio de Janeiro, RJ; tel. (021) 252-2029; telex (21) 23673; f. 1892; cap. and res 247.6m., dep. 305.2m. (June 1987); Man. FERNANDO LUIS ALVES; 2 brs.

Banco Unión (Venezuela): Av. Paulista 1708, 01.310 São Paulo, SP; tel. (011) 283-3722; telex (11) 30476; f.1892; cap. and res 529.7m., dep. 1,459.6m. (June 1987); Dir-Gen. DONALDISON MARQUES DA SILVA.

Citibank NA (USA): Av. Paulista 1111, 01.311 São Paulo, SP; telex (11) 310980; f. 1812; cap. and res 3,928.1m., dep. 17,519.0m. (April 1987); Dir ARNOLDO SOUZA DE OLIVEIRA; 13 brs.

Deutsche Bank AG (Federal Republic of Germany): Rua 15 de Novembro 137, CP 30427, 01.013 São Paulo, SP; tel. (011) 229-0422; telex (11) 22692; f. 1969; cap. and res 625.5m., dep. 3,754.6m. (June 1987); Man. CHRISTIAN RECKMANN.

The First National Bank of Boston (USA): Rua Líbero Badaró 487, 01.009 São Paulo, SP; tel. (011) 234-5622; telex (11) 22285; cap. and res 2,259.4m., dep. 7,604.7m. (June 1987); Pres. HENRIQUE DE CAMPOS MEIRELLES; 8 brs.

Lloyds Bank PLC (UK): Av. Brig. Faria Lima 2020, 01.452 São Paulo, SP; tel. (011) 814-1488; telex (11) 24061; cap. and res 3,901.2m., dep. 12,299.4m. (June 1987); Gen. Man. FREDERICK H. CIBBS; 14 brs.

Unión de Bancos del Uruguay: Rua 7 de Setembro 64, 20.050 Rio de Janeiro, RJ; tel. (021) 252-8070; telex (21) 31571; cap. 42.0m., res 45.4m., dep. 14.4m. (June 1987); Man. NELSON VAZ MOREIRA.

Banking Associations

Federação Nacional dos Bancos: Rua Líbero Badaró 425, 17° andar, 01.009 São Paulo, SP; tel. (011) 239-3000; telex (11) 24710; f. 1966; Pres. ANTÔNIO DE PÁDUA ROCHA DINIZ; Vice-Pres PEDRO CONDE, THEÓPHILO AZEREDO SANTOS.

Sindicato dos Bancos dos Estados do Rio de Janeiro e Espírito Santo: Av. Rio Branco 81, 19°, Rio de Janeiro, RJ; Pres. THEÓPHILO DE AZEREDO SANTOS; Vice-Pres. Dr MUFAREJ.

Sindicato dos Bancos dos Estados de São Paulo, Paraná, Mato Grosso e Mato Grosso do Sul: Rua Líbero Badaró 293, 13° andar, 01.905 São Paulo, SP; f. 1924; Pres. PAULO DE QUEIROZ.

There are eight other banking associations in Maceió, Salvador, Fortaleza, Belo Horizonte, João Pessoa, Recife, Rio de Janeiro and Porto Alegre.

STOCK EXCHANGES

Comissão de Valores Mobiliários CVM: Rua 7 de Setembro 111, 20.050 Rio de Janeiro, RJ; tel. (021) 292-5117; telex (21) 21549; f. 1977 to supervise the operations of the stock exchanges and develop the Brazilian securities market; Chair. ARNOLDO WALD.

Bolsa de Valores do Rio de Janeiro: Praça 15 de Novembro 20, 20.010 Rio de Janeiro, RJ; tel. (021) 291-5354; telex (21) 35100; f. 1843; 700 stocks quoted; Pres. Dr SÉRGIO BARCELLOS; Vice-Pres. PEDRO SALGADO.

Bolsa de Valores de São Paulo: Rua Líbero Badaró 471, 3°, São Paulo, SP; tel. (011) 258-7222; 500 stocks quoted; Pres. Dr EDUARDO ROCHA DE AZEVEDO.

There are commodity exchanges at Porto Alegre, Vitória, Recife, Santos and São Paulo.

INSURANCE

Supervisory Authorities

Superintendência de Seguros Privados (SUSEP): Rio de Janeiro, RJ; tel. (021) 231-3092; f. 1966; within Ministry of Finance; Superintendent JOÃO RÉGIS RICARDO DOS SANTOS.

Conselho Nacional de Seguros Privados (CNSP): Rio de Janeiro, RJ; tel. (021) 222-1423; f. 1966; Pres. Minister of Finance; Sec. VANICE DA SILVEIRA ARAÚJO LIMA.

Instituto de Resseguros do Brasil (IRB): Av. Marechal Câmara 171, 20.023 Rio de Janeiro, RJ; tel. (021) 297-1212; telex (21) 21237; f. 1939; reinsurance; Pres. RONALDO DO VALLE SIMÕES.

Principal National Companies

(p.i. = premium income; o.l. = operational limit; cap. = capital; m. = million; amounts in cruzados, unless otherwise stated)

The following is a list of the 23 principal national insurance companies, selected on the basis of premium income.

Rio de Janeiro, RJ

Bradesco Seguros, SA: Rua Barão de Itapagipe 225, 20.261 Rio de Janeiro, RJ; tel. (021) 264-0101; telex (21) 22055; f. 1935; o.l. 21.9m., cap. 100.0m. (1985); general; Pres. ARARINO SALLUM DE OLIVEIRA.

Cia Internacional de Seguros: Rua Ibituruna 81, Maracanã, CP 1137, 20.271 Rio de Janeiro, RJ; tel. (021) 284-1222; f. 1920; p.i. US $40m., net assets $40m. (1985); property, life and risk; Pres. Dr MAURICE ALBERT BERCOFF.

Generali do Brasil, Cia Nacional de Seguros: Av. Rio Branco 128, 7° andar, Rio de Janeiro, RJ; tel. (021) 292-0144; telex (21) 22846; f. 1945; p.i. 1.9m., cap. 958.5m. (1987); general; Pres. CLÁUDIO BIETOLINI.

Nacional, Cia de Seguros: Av. Pres. Vargas 850, 20.091 Rio de Janeiro, RJ; tel. (021) 296-2112; telex (21) 30881; f. 1946; o.l. 5.0m., cap. 60.0m. (1985); life and risk; Pres. VICTOR ARTHUR RENAULT.

Sasse, Cia Nacional de Seguros Gerais: Av. Rio Branco 125, 4°-5°, 20.031, Rio de Janeiro, RJ; tel. (021) 275-4022; f. 1967; o.l. 4.0m., cap. 101.7m. (1985); general; Pres. OYAMA PEREIRA.

Sul América, Cia Nacional de Seguros: Rua da Quitanda 86, 20.091 Rio de Janeiro, RJ; tel. (021) 291-2020; telex (21) 30407; f. 1895; o.l. 12.3m., cap. 139.2m. (1985); life and risk; Pres. RONY CASTRO DE OLIVEIRA LYRIO; offices in São Paulo, Porto Alegre, Belo Horizonte and Recife.

Sul América Terrestres, Marítimos e Acidentes Cia de Seguros: Rua da Quitanda 86, 20.091 Rio de Janeiro, RJ; tel. (021) 291-2020; telex (21) 30677; f. 1914; general; o.l. 13.6m., cap. 455.8m. (1985); Pres. RONY CASTRO DE OLIVEIRA LYRIO.

Yorkshire-Corcovado Cia de Seguros: Av. Almirante Barroso 52, 24° andar, 20.031 Rio de Janeiro, RJ; tel. (021) 292-1125; telex (21) 22343; f. 1943; p.i. 1.1m., cap. 50m. (1985); life and risk; Pres. MANOEL PIO CORRÊA, Filho.

São Paulo, SP

Brasil, Cia de Seguros Gerais: Rua Luiz Coelho 26, 01.309 São Paulo, SP; tel. (011) 285-1533; telex (11) 21401; f. 1904; o.l. 3.2m., cap. 60.0m. (1985); general; Pres. JEAN-MARIE MONTEIL.

Cia Paulista de Seguros: Rua Líbero Badaró 158, CP 709, 01.008 São Paulo, SP; tel. (011) 229-0811; telex (11) 37787; f. 1906; o.l. 2.2m., cap. 39.0m. (1985); general; Pres. ROBERTO PEREIRA DE ALMEIDA, Filho.

Cia Real Brasileira de Seguros: Av. Paulista 1374, 6° andar, 01.310 São Paulo, SP; tel. (011) 285-0255; telex (11) 24744; f. 1965; o.l. 1.1m., cap. 23.7m. (1985); Pres. ALOYSIO DE ANDRADE FARIA.

Cia de Seguros do Estado de São Paulo: Rua Pamplona 227, 01.405 São Paulo, SP; tel. (011) 284-4888; telex (11) 21999; f. 1967; cap. 350,000m. (1987); life and risk; Pres. HERBERT JÚLIO NOGUEIRA.

Iochpe Seguradora SA: Rua Dr Miguel Couto 58, 5° andar 01.008 São Paulo, SP; tel. (011) 239-1822; telex (11) 37776; f. 1964; p.i. 274.0m., cap. 290.0m. (1987); life and risk; Dir-Pres. PEDRO PEREIRA DE FREITAS.

Itaú Seguros SA: POB 1798, Rua das Guajuviras 100, Bloco A, 04.390 São Paulo, SP; tel. (011) 582-3322; telex (11) 32125; f. 1921; p.i. US $169.9m., cap. $30.7m. (1985); all classes; Pres. EUDORO LIBANIO VILLELA.

Porto Seguro Cia de Seguros Gerais: Av. Rio Branco 1489, 01.311 São Paulo, SP; tel. (011) 223-0022; telex (11) 32613; f. 1945; o.l. 1.7m., cap. 39.3m. (1985); life and risk; Pres. ROSA GARFINKEL.

Skandia-BRADESCO Cia Brasileira de Seguros: Av. Paulista 1415, 01.311 São Paulo, SP; tel. (011) 287-4710; f. 1914; p.i. 30m., cap. 12m. (1986); Man. Dir SVEN SCHÉLE.

Sul América Bandeirante Seguros, SA: Rua Anchieta 35, 01.016 São Paulo, SP; tel. (011) 259-3555; telex (11) 24021; f. 1944; o.l. 4.0m., cap. 65.0m. (1985); life and risk; Pres. RONY CASTRO DE OLIVEIRA LYRIO.

Sul América Unibanco Seguradora SA: Rua Líbero Badaró 293, 32°andar, 01.009 São Paulo, SP; tel. (011) 235-5000; telex (11) 34826; f. 1866; o.l. 8.8m. (1983), cap. 60.0m. (1985); Pres. RONY CASTRO DE OLIVEIRA LYRIO.

Vera Cruz Seguradora SA: Av. Maria Coelho Aguiar 215, Bloco D, 2° andar, 05.804 São Paulo, SP; tel. (011) 545-4944; f. 1955; o.l. 6.9m., (1983), cap. 41.8m. (1985); general; Pres. HORÁCIO IVES FREYRE.

Provincial Companies

The following is a list of the principal provincial insurance companies, selected on the basis of premium income.

Bamerindus Cia de Seguros: Rua Marechal Floriano Peixoto 5500, Curitiba, PR; tel. (041) 221-2121; telex (41) 5672; f. 1938; cap. 129.1m. (1985); all classes; Pres. HAMILCAR PIZZATTO.

BRAZIL

Directory

Cia de Seguros Aliança da Bahia: Rua Pinto Martins 11, 9° andar, 40.000 Salvador, BA; tel. 242-1065; f. 1870; o.l. 9.1m., cap. 153.6m. (1985); general; Pres. PAULO S. FREIRE DE CARVALHO.

Cia de Seguros Minas-Brasil: Rua dos Caetés 745, 30.120 Belo Horizonte, MG; tel. (031) 201-5799; telex (31) 1506; f. 1938; p.i. 15.5m., cap. 130,000 (March 1986); life and risk; Pres. JOSÉ CARNEIRO DE ARAÚJO.

Cia União de Seguros Gerais: Av. Borges de Medeiros 261, 90.020 Porto Alegre, RS; tel. (051) 26-7933; telex (51) 2530; f. 1891; cap. 100.4m. (1986); Pres. ATTILA SÁ D'OLIVEIRA.

Trade and Industry

GOVERNMENT ADVISORY BODIES

Carteira de Comércio Exterior (CACEX): Av. Pres. Vargas 328, 11° andar, 20.091, Rio de Janeiro, RJ; tel. (021) 271-7504; telex (21) 23753; f. 1954; state foreign trade agency; dept of Banco Central do Brasil; Dir NAMIR SALEK.

Comissão de Fusão e Incorporação de Empresa (COFIE): Ministério da Fazenda, Esplanada dos Ministérios, Edif. Sede, Ala B, 1° andar, Brasília, DF; tel. (061) 225-3405; telex (61) 1539; mergers commission; Pres. SEBASTIÃO MARCOS VITAL; Exec. Sec. EDGAR BEZERRA LEITE, Filho.

Conselho de Desenvolvimento Comercial (CDC): Ministério da Indústria e do Comércio, SCS, Q02, Edif. Pres. Dutra, 2° andar, Bloco C, Sala 227, Esplanada dos Ministérios, 70.300 Brasília, DF; tel. (061) 223-0308; telex (61) 2537; commercial development council; Exec. Sec. Dr RUY COUTINHO DO NASCIMENTO.

Conselho de Desenvolvimento Econômico (CDE): Esplanada dos Ministérios, Bloco K, 7° andar, 70.063 Brasília, DF; tel. (061) 215-4100; f. 1974; economic development council; Gen. Sec. JOÃO BATISTA DE ABREU.

Conselho de Desenvolvimento Industrial (CDI): Ministério da Indústria e do Comércio, Lotes 2/5-2/8, Bloco G, 8°, 70.070 Brasília, DF; tel. (061) 225-0822; telex (61) 2225; f. 1969; industrial development council; offers fiscal incentives for selected industries and for producers of manufactured goods under the Special Export Programme; Exec. Sec. Dr ERNESTO CARRARA.

Conselho de Desenvolvimento Social (CDS): Esplanada dos Ministérios, Bloco K, 3° andar, 382, 70.063 Brasília, DF; tel. (061) 215-4477; social development council; Exec. Sec. JOÃO A. TELES.

Conselho Federal de Desestacização: f. 1988; responsible for proposed privatization of some 70 state companies; Sec. PAULO GALLETA.

Conselho Interministerial de Preços (CIP): Av. Pres. Antônio Carlos 375, 10° andar, 20.020 Rio de Janeiro, RJ; tel. (021) 240-2281; telex (21) 33314; prices commission; Exec. Sec. WENCESLAU D'AVILA FERNANDES MAGALHÃES.

Conselho Nacional do Comércio Exterior (CONCEX): Fazenda, 5° andar, Gabinete do Ministro, Esplanada dos Ministérios, Bloco 6, 70.048 Brasília, DF; tel. (061) 223-4856; telex (61) 1142; f. 1966; responsible for foreign exchange and trade policies and for the control of export activities; Exec. Sec. NAMIR SALEK.

Conselho Nacional de Desenvolvimento Científico e Tecnológico (CNPq): Av. W-3 Norte, Quadra 507, Bloco B, 70.740 Brasília, DF; tel. (061) 274-1155; telex (61) 1089; f. 1951; scientific and technological development council; Pres. Dr CRODOVALDO PAVAN.

Conselho Nacional de Desenvolvimento Pecuário (CONDEPE): to promote livestock development.

Conselho de Não-Ferrosos e de Siderurgia (CONSIDER): Ministério da Indústria e do Comércio, Esplanada dos Ministérios, Bloco 6, 5° andar, 70.053 Brasília, DF; tel. (061) 224-6039; telex (61) 1012; f. 1973; exercises a supervisory role over development policy in the non-ferrous and iron and steel industries; Exec. Sec. WILLIAM ROCHA CANTAL.

Conselho Nacional do Petróleo (CNP): SGA Norte, Quadra 603, Módulos H, I, J, 70.830 Brasília, DF; tel. (061) 226-0403; telex (61) 1673; f. 1938; directs national policy on petroleum; Pres. Gen. ROBERTO FRANCO DOMINGUES.

Fundação Instituto Brasileiro de Geografia e Estatística (IBGE): Av. Franklin Roosevelt 166, Castelo, 20.021 Rio de Janeiro, RJ; tel. (021) 220-6671; telex (21) 30939; f. 1936; produces and analyses statistical, geographical, cartographic, geodetic, demographic and socio-economic information; Pres. CHARLES CURT MUELLER; Dir-Gen. DAVID WU TAI.

Instituto Nacional de Metrologia, Normalização e Qualidade Industrial (INMETRO): SCS, Edif. Chams, 2° andar, 70.300 Brasília, DF; tel. (061) 224-2315; telex (61) 1834; in 1981 INMETRO absorbed the Instituto Nacional de Pesos e Medidas (INPM), the weights and measures institute; Pres. Dr MASAO ITO.

Instituto de Planejamento Econômico e Social (IPEA): SBS, Edif. BNDE, 6° andar, 70.076 Brasília, DF; tel. (061) 225-4350; telex (61) 01979; planning institute; Pres. RICARDO SANTIAGO.

Superintendência do Desenvolvimento da Pesca (SUDEPE): Edif. da Pesca, Av. W-3 Norte, Quadra 506, Bloco C, 70.040 Brasília, DF; tel. (061) 272-3229; telex (61) 1179; attached to the Ministry of Agriculture; assists development of fishing industry; Superintendent AÉCIO MOURA DA SILVA.

REGIONAL DEVELOPMENT ORGANIZATIONS

Companhia de Desenvolvimento do Vale do São Francisco (CODEVASF): SGAN, Q 601, Lote 1, Edif. Sede, 70.830 Brasília, DF; tel. (061) 223-8913; telex (61) 1157; f. 1974; Pres. ELISEU ROBERTO DE ANDRADE ALVES.

Superintendência do Desenvolvimento da Amazônia (SUDAM): Av. Almirante Barroso 426, Bairro do Marco, 66.000 Belém, PA; tel. (091) 226-0044; telex (91) 1117; f. 1966 to develop the Amazon regions of Brazil; attached to the Ministry of the Interior; supervises industrial, cattle breeding and basic services projects; Superintendent Eng. HENRY CHECRALLA KAYATH.

Superintendência do Desenvolvimento do Nordeste (SUDENE): Praça Supt João Gonçalves de Souza, Cidade Universitária, 50.000 Recife, PE; tel. (081) 271-1044; telex (81) 1245; f. 1959; attached to the Ministry of the Interior; assists development of north-east Brazil; Superintendent PAULO GANEM SOUTO.

Superintendência do Desenvolvimento da Região Centro Oeste (SUDECO): SAS, Quadra 1, Bloco A, lotes 9/10, 70.070 Brasília, DF; tel. (061) 225-6111; telex (61) 1616; f. 1967 to co-ordinate development projects in the States of Goiás, Mato Grosso, Mato Grosso do Sul, Rondônia and Distrito Federal; Superintendent RAMEZ TEBET.

Superintendência do Desenvolvimento da Região Sul (SUDESUL): Rua Caldas Júnior 120, 20°, 90.018 Porto Alegre, RS; tel. (0512) 286-400; telex (51) 1005; f. 1967 to co-ordinate development in the states of Rio Grande do Sul, Santa Catarina and Paraná; attached to the Ministry of the Interior; Superintendent NAPOLEÃO DE OLIVEIRA.

Superintendência da Zona Franca de Manaus (SUFRAMA): Rua Ministro João Gonçalves de Souza, Cidade Universitária, Distrito Industrial, 69.000 Manaus, AM; tel. (092) 237-3288; telex (92) 2146; to assist in the development of the Manaus Free Zone; Superintendent JADYR CARVALHEDO MAGALHÃES.

Other regional development organizations include Poloamazônia (agricultural and agro-mineral nuclei in the Amazon Region), Polocentro (woodland savannah in Central Brazil), Poloeste (agricultural and agro-mineral nuclei in the Centre-West), Polonordeste (integrated areas in the North-East), Procacau (expansion of cocoa industry), Prodoeste (development of the Centre-South), Proterra (land distribution and promotion of agricultural industries in the North and North-East), Provale (development of the São Francisco basin).

COMMERCIAL, AGRICULTURAL AND INDUSTRIAL ORGANIZATIONS

ABRASSUCOS: São Paulo, SP; association of orange juice industry; Pres. MÁRIO BRANCO PERES.

Associação do Comércio Exterior do Brasil: Av. General Justo 335, Rio de Janeiro, RJ; tel. (021) 240-5048; exporters' association; Pres. NORBERTO INGO ZABROZNY.

Companhia Vale do Rio Doce, SA (CVRD): Av. Graça Aranha 26, Bairro Castelo, 20.005 Rio de Janeiro, RJ; tel. (021) 272-4477; telex (21) 23162; f. 1942; state-owned mining company; owns and operates the Vitória–Minas railway, the port of Tubarão and the Carajás iron ore project; also involved in forestry and pulp production; Pres. AGRIPINO ABRANCHES VIANA.

Confederação das Associações Comerciais do Brasil: Brasília, DF; confederation of chambers of commerce in each state; Pres. AMAURY TENPORAL.

Confederação Nacional da Agricultura (CNA): Brasília, DF; tel. (061) 225-3150; national agricultural confederation; Pres. CORREA LEITE.

Confederação Nacional do Comércio (CNC): SCS, Edif. Presidente Dutra, 4° andar, Quadra 11, 70.327 Brasília, DF; tel. (061) 223-0578; national confederation comprising 35 affiliated federations of commerce; Pres. ANTÔNIO JOSÉ DOMINGUES DE OLIVEIRA SANTOS.

Confederação Nacional da Indústria (CNI): SBN, Edif. Roberto Simonsen, 16° andar, 70.040 Brasília, DF; tel. (061) 224-1328; f. 1938; national confederation of industry comprising the 21 state industrial federations; Pres. Dr ALBANO DO PRADO FRANCO; Vice-Pres. EDGAR ARP.

Confederação Nacional dos Transportes Terrestres (CNTT): Edif. Sofia, 2° andar, Setor Comercial Sul, Brasília, DF; tel. (061)

BRAZIL

223-2300; confederation of land transport federations; Pres. Camilo Cola.

Departamento Nacional da Produção Mineral (DNPM): SAN, Quadra 1, Bloco B, 3° andar, 70.040 Brasília, DF; tel. (061) 224-2670; telex (61) 1116; f. 1934; attached to the Ministry of Mines and Energy; responsible for geological studies and control of exploration of mineral resources; Dir-Gen. José Belfort dos Santos Bastos.

Federação das Indústrias do Estado de São Paulo (FIESP): Av. Paulista 1313, 01.311 São Paulo, SP; tel. (011) 251-3522; telex (11) 22130; regional manufacturers' association; Pres. Mário Amato; Vice-Pres. Carlos Eduardo Moreira Ferreira.

Instituto do Açúcar e do Álcool (IAA): Largo do Paço 42, Edif. Taquara, 20.010 Rio de Janeiro, RJ; tel. (021) 224-6463; telex (21) 50201; f. 1933; government agency for the promotion and development of the sugar industry; sole exporter of raw sugar; Pres. Dr Marcelo Piancastelli de Siqueira.

Instituto Brasileiro do Café (IBC): Av. Rodrigues Alves 129, 10°, Praça Mauá, 20.081 Rio de Janeiro, RJ; tel. (021) 263-5121; telex (21) 23119; f. 1952; controls and promotes production of and commerce in coffee and gives technical advice to producers; government agency; Pres. Dr Jório Dauster Magalhães.

Instituto Brasileiro do Desenvolvimento Florestal (IBDF): Setor de Áreas Isoladas, L4 Norte, 70.080 Brasília, DF; tel. (061) 223-5966; telex (61) 1711; f. 1967; independent organization affiliated to the Ministry of Agriculture; responsible for the annual formulation of national and regional forest plans; merged with SEMA (National Environmental Agency) in 1988; Pres. Antônio Costa de Freitas Guimaraes.

Instituto Nacional da Propriedade Industrial (INPI): Praça Mauá 7, 11° andar, 20.081 Rio de Janeiro, RJ; tel. (021) 223-4182; telex (21) 22992; f. 1970; Pres. Mauro Fernando Maria Arruda.

Instituto Nacional de Tecnologia (INT): Av. Venezuela 82, 8°, 20.081 Rio de Janeiro, RJ; tel. (021) 223-1320; telex (21) 30056; f. 1921; co-operates in national industrial development; Dir Paulo Roberto Krahe.

União Democrática Ruralista (UDR): f. 1986; landowners' organization; Pres. Ronaldo Caiado.

PRINCIPAL STATE ENTERPRISES

In November 1986 the Government announced the closure or merger of 15 state enterprises. A further 32 organizations were to be closed or merged over the following months. Moreover, in 1988 the Government announced plans to sell the majority of Brazil's state enterprises to the private sector.

Centrais Elétricas Brasileiras, SA (ELETROBRÁS): Av. Pres. Vargas 642, 20.071 Rio de Janeiro, RJ; tel. (021) 291-1222; telex (21) 22395; f. 1962; government holding company (6 subsidiary and 23 associated electricity companies) responsible for planning, financing and managing Brazil's electrical energy programme; Pres. Mario Penna Bhering.

Companhia Siderúrgica Nacional, SA (CSN): Av. 13 de Maio 13, 8° andar, Centro 20.031 Rio de Janeiro, RJ; tel. (021) 297-7177; telex (21) 23025; f. 1941; iron and steel; Pres. Juvenal Osório Gomes.

Empresa Brasileira de Aeronáutica, SA (EMBRAER): Av. Brigadeiro Faria Lima 2170, CP 343, 01.220 São José dos Campos, SP; tel. (123) 25-1000; telex (123) 3589; f. 1969; aeronautics industry; Chief Executive Officer Ozílio Carlos da Silva.

Empresa Brasileira de Assistência Técnica e Extensão Rural (EMBRATER): SAIN, Parque Rural, Edif. Sede EMBRATER, CP 070530, 70.770 Brasília, DF; tel. (061) 274-4650; telex (61) 1916; Pres. Romeu Padilha de Figueiredo.

Empresa Brasileira de Correios e Telégrafos (ECT): Ed. Sede, 19° andar, SBN, Conj. 3, Bloco A, 70.002 Brasília, DF; tel. (061) 224-9262; telex (61) 1119; posts and telegraph; Pres. Joel Marciano Rauber.

Empresa Brasileira de Pesquisa Agropecuária (EMBRAPA): SCS, Supercenter Venâncio 2000, Q.08, Bloco B, No 50, 9° andar, 70.333 Brasília, DF; tel. (061) 216-5110; telex (61) 1620; f. 1973; attached to the Ministry of Agriculture; agricultural research; Pres. Ormuz Freitas Rivaldo.

Empresa Brasileira de Telecomunicações, SA (EMBRATEL): Av. Pres. Vargas 1012, CP 2586, 20.071 Rio de Janeiro, RJ; tel. (021) 253-1744; telex (21) 21185; f. 1965; operates national and international telecommunications system; Pres. José Eugênio Guisard Ferraz.

Petróleo Brasileiro, SA (PETROBRÁS): Av. República do Chile 65, 20.035 Rio de Janeiro, RJ; tel. (021) 212-4477, ext. 3442/3; telex (21) 23335; f. 1953; has monopoly on development and production of petroleum and petroleum products; 1985 budget US $1,743m.; 50,304 employees; Pres. Armando Guedes Coelho.

Directory

Petrobrás Comércio Internacional, SA (INTERBRÁS): Rua do Rosário 90, Rio de Janeiro, RJ; tel. (021) 296-2033; telex (21) 21709; Pres. Carlos Sant'Anna; Vice-Pres. Hamilton Sérgio Albertazzi.

Petrobrás Distribuidora, SA: Praça 22 de Abril 36, 8° andar, Castelo, 20.021 Rio de Janeiro, RF; tel. (021) 217-8066; telex (21) 21222; f. 1971; marketing of all petroleum by-products; Pres. Albérico Barroso Alves; Vice-Pres. Marcus Túlio Roberto Sampaio de Melo.

Petrobrás Fertilizantes, SA (PETROFÉRTIL): Praça Mahatma Gandhi 14, 9°/13° andares, 20.031 Rio de Janeiro, RJ; tel. (021) 217-5335; telex (21) 23880; f. 1976; Pres. Maximiano da Silva Fonseca; Vice-Pres. Aurílio Fernandes Lima.

Petrobrás Internacional, SA (BRASPETRO): Praça Pio X 119, 20.040 Rio de Janeiro, RJ; tel. (021) 297-0102; telex (21) 21889; f. 1972; international division with operations in Algeria, Angola, People's Republic of China, Colombia, the Congo, Ghana, Guatemala, Libya, Norway, South Yemen, Trinidad and Tobago and Uruguay; Pres. Wagner Freire; Vice-Pres. Antônio Seabra Moggi.

Petrobrás Mineraçao, SA (Petromisa): Av. Pres. Vargas 583, 20.076 Rio de Janeiro, RJ; tel. (021) 224-7805; telex (21) 32509; potassium exploration and non-petroleum mining; Pres. José Edilson de Melo Távora; Exec. Vice-Pres. Ruben Lahyr Schneider.

Petrobrás Química, SA (PETROQUISA): Rua Buenos Aires 40, 20.070 Rio de Janeiro, RJ; tel. (021) 297-6677; telex (21) 21496; f. 1968; petrochemicals industry; controls 27 affiliated companies and 4 subsidiaries; Pres. Paulo Vieira Belotti; Vice-Pres. Tarcisio de Vasconcelos Maia.

Siderurgia Brasileira, SA (SIDERBRÁS): SAS, Quadra 2, Bloco E, Edif. Siderbrás, 9° andar, 70.070 Brasília, DF; tel. (061) 223-9104; telex (61) 1542; f. 1974; steel industry; Pres. Manoel Moacélio de Aquiar Mendes.

Other state enterprises include Aços Finos Piratini, SA, Companhia Coque e Álcool de Madeira (COALBRA), Companhia Ferro e Aço de Vitória, Companhia Nacional de Álcalis, SA, Companhia Siderúrgica de Mogi das Cruzes, Companhia Siderúrgica Paulista, SA, Usinas Siderúrgicas da Bahia and Usinas Siderúrgicas de Minas Gerais.

TRADE UNIONS

Following the return to civilian government in March 1985, the ban on trade union associations, which had been in force under military rule, was repealed.

Central Unica dos Trabalhadores (CUT): Rua Ouvidor Peleja, 112 Bosque da Saúde, 04.123 São Paulo, SP; tel. (011) 577-4833; telex (11) 54282; f. 1983; central union confederation; left-wing; Pres. Jair Meneguelli; Gen. Sec. Avelino Ganzer.

Confederação General dos Trabalhadores (CGT): São Paulo, SP; f. 1986; fmrly Coordenação Nacional das Classes Trabalhadoras; represents 1,258 labour organizations linked to PMDB; Pres. Joaquim dos Santos Andrade.

Confederação Nacional dos Metalúrgicos (Metal Workers): f. 1985; Pres. Joaquim dos Santos Andrade.

Confederação Nacional das Profissões Liberais (CNPL) (Liberal Professions): SCS, Edif. Gilberto Salomão, Gr. 1.306/1.312, 70.305 Brasília, DF; tel. (061) 223-1683; telex (61) 3883; f. 1953; confederation of liberal professions; Pres. Dr José Augusto de Carvalho.

Confederação Nacional dos Trabalhadores na Indústria (CNTI) (Industrial Workers): Av. W 3 Norte, Quadra 505, Lote 01, 70.730 Brasília, DF; tel. (061) 274-4150; telex (61) 4230; f. 1946; Pres. José Calixto Ramos.

Confederação Nacional dos Trabalhadores no Comércio (CNTC) (Commercial Workers): Av. W/5 Sul, Quadra 902, Bloco C, 70.390 Brasília, DF; tel. (061) 224-3511; f. 1946; Pres. Antônio de Oliveira Santos.

Confederação Nacional dos Trabalhadores em Transportes Marítimos, Fluviais e Aéreos (CONTTMAF) (Maritime, River and Air Transport Workers): Av. Pres. Vargas 446, gr. 2205, 20.071 Rio de Janeiro, RJ; tel. (021) 233-8329; f. 1957; Pres. Aloysio Ribeiro.

Confederação Nacional dos Trabalhadores em Transportes Terrestres (CNTTT) (Land Transport Workers): SBS Edif. Seguradoras, 11° andar, 70.072 Brasília, DF; tel. (061) 224-5011; telex (61) 1593; f. 1952; 300,000 mems; Pres. Orlando Coutinho.

Confederação Nacional dos Trabalhadores em Comunicações e Publicidade (CONTCOP) (Communications and Advertising Workers): Edif. Serra Dourada, 7° andar, Gr. 705/708, Quadra 11, SCS, 70.365 Brasília, DF; tel. (061) 224-7926; f. 1964; Pres. José Alceu Portocarrero.

BRAZIL — Directory

Confederação Nacional dos Trabalhadores nas Empresas de Crédito (CONTEC) (Workers in Credit Institutions): Av. W4, SEP-SUL EQ 707/907 Lote E, 70.351 Brasília, DF; tel. (061) 224-5833; f. 1958; 730,052 mems (1987); Pres. LOURENÇO FERREIRA DO PRADO.

Confederação Nacional dos Trabalhadores em Estabelecimentos de Educação e Cultura (CNTEEC) (Workers in Education and Culture): SAS, Quadra 4, Bloco B, 70.302 Brasília, DF; tel. (061) 226-2988; f. 1967; Pres. MIGUEL ABRAHÃO.

Confederação Nacional dos Trabalhadores na Agricultura (CONTAG) (Agricultural Workers): MSPW, Conjunto 502, Lote 2, Núcleo Bandeirante, 70.750 Brasília, DF; tel. (061) 552-0259; f. 1964; Pres. JOSÉ FRANCISCO DA SILVA.

Transport

Conselho Nacional de Transportes: Ministério dos Transportes, Esplanada dos Ministérios, Bloco 9, 7°, 70.062 Brasília, DF; tel. (061) 224-5622; telex (61) 1096; f. 1961 to study, co-ordinate and execute government transport policy and reorganize railway, road and ports and waterways councils; Pres. JOSÉ REINALDO CARNEIRO TAVARES; Exec. Sec. LAURY PEREIRA BARCELLOS.

Empresa Brasileira de Planejamento de Transportes (GEIPOT): SAN, Quadra 3, Blocos N/O, Edif. Núcleo dos Transportes, 70.040 Brasília, DF; tel. (061) 226-7335; telex (61) 1316; f. 1973; agency for the promotion of an integrated modern transport system; advises the Minister of Transport on transport policy; Pres. STANLEY FORTES BAPTISTA.

Empresa Brasileira de Transportes Urbanos (EBTU): SAN, Quadra 3, Lote A, 3°, 70.040 Brasília, DF; tel. (061) 226-7335; telex (61) 1604; f. 1975 to administer resources for national urban transportation programmes costing 88,438.7m. cruzeiros between 1976 and 1982; Pres. TELMO BORBA MAGADAN.

RAILWAYS

In 1985 the Government announced plans to invest US $422m. in a project to modernize and expand the railway network. Out of a total network of 29,901 km, 2,094 km of track has been electrified. In 1987 the Government announced controversial plans to construct a 1,600-km north–south railway, at an estimated cost of US $2,600m., to link the city of Açailândia, in the state of Marahão, with Brasília. Work was scheduled to start in 1987, and the railway was to be completed by early 1990.

Rêde Ferroviária Federal, SA (RFFSA) (Federal Railway Corporation): Praça Procópio Ferreira 86, 20.221 Rio de Janeiro, RJ; tel. (021) 291-2185; telex (21) 21372; f. 1957 as a holding company for 18 railways grouped into 7 regional networks, with a total of 22,184 km in 1987; a mixed company in which the government holds the majority of the shares; Pres. PAULO MUNHOZ DA ROCHA; Vice-Pres. FERNANDO JORGE FAGUNDES NETTO.

There are also railways owned by State Governments and several privately-owned railways:

Carajás Railway: Retorno Itaqui-Pedrinhas, Km 7, BR 135, 65.000 São Luís, MA; tel. (0982) 222-8844; telex (982) 164/205; state-owned; transportation of iron ore, wood and rice; 902 km inaugurated in February 1985; Dir ROMILDO COELHO VELLO.

Companhia Vale de Rio Doce (Vitória–Minas Railway): Av. Graça Aranha 26, Castelo, 20.005 Rio de Janeiro, RJ; tel. (021) 272-4477; telex (21) 23162; f. 1942; state-owned; transportation of iron ore, general cargo, passengers; Estrada de Ferro Carajás (890 km) and Estrado de Ferro Vitória Minas (720 km); Pres. AGRIPINO ABRANCHES VIANA.

Estrada de Ferro do Amapá: Praia de Botafogo 300, 11-A, 22.259 Rio de Janeiro, RJ; tel. (021) 552-4422; telex (21) 23774; opened 1957; 194 km open in 1985; operated by Indústria e Comércio de Minérios, SA; Pres. OSWALDO LUIZ SENRA PESSOA.

FEPASA—Ferrovia Paulista, SA: Praça Julio Prestes 148, 01.218 São Paulo, SP; tel. (011) 223-7211; telex (11) 22724; formed by merger of five railways operated by São Paulo State; 5,036 km open in 1985; Pres. ANTÔNIO CARLOS RIOS CORRAL.

Other privately-owned mineral lines are: Estrada de Ferro Campos do Jordão (47 km open in 1985), Estrada de Ferro Perus–Pirapora (33 km open in 1985), Estrada de Ferro Votorantim (15 km open in 1985) and Estrada de Ferro Mineração Rio do Norte (f. 1984; 35 km open in 1985). In 1988 a private company, Companhia Ferroviária Paraná-Oeste (Ferroeste), was set up to build a 420-km railway to serve the grain production regions in Paraná and Mato Grosso do Sul.

ROADS

In 1987 there were 1,675,040 km of roads in Brazil, of which 8% were paved. Brasília has been a focal point for inter-regional development, and paved roads link the capital with every region of Brazil. The building of completely new roads has taken place predominantly in the north. Roads are the principal mode of transport, accounting for 70% of freight and 97% of passenger traffic, including long-distance bus services, in 1979. Major projects include the 5,000-km Trans-Amazonian Highway, running from Recife and Cabedelo to the Peruvian border, the 4,138-km Cuibá–Santarém highway, which will run in a north–south direction, and the 3,555-km Trans-Brasiliana project which will link Marabá, on the Trans-Amazonian highway, with Aceguá on the Uruguayan frontier.

Departamento Nacional de Estradas de Rodagem (DNER) (National Roads Development): Av. Pres. Vargas 522/534, 20.071 Rio de Janeiro, RJ; tel. (021) 233-2493; telex (21) 23535; f. 1945 to plan and execute federal road policy and to supervise state and municipal roads with the aim of integrating them into the national network; Dir ANTÔNIO ALBERTO CANABRAVA.

INLAND WATERWAYS

River transport plays only a minor part in the movement of goods, although total freight carried increased from 4.7m. tons in 1980 to 6.9m. tons in 1985. There are three major river systems, the Amazon, Paraná and the São Francisco. The Amazon is navigable for 3,680 km, as far as Iquitos in Peru, and ocean-going ships can reach Manaus, 1,600 km upstream. Plans have been drawn up to improve the inland waterway system and one plan is to link the Amazon and Upper Paraná to provide a navigable waterway across the centre of the country.

Companhia Docas do Pará: Av. Pres. Vargas 41, 2° andar, 66.000 Belém, PA; tel. (091) 223-2055; telex (91) 2320; f. 1967; administers the port of Belém; Dir-Pres. AFFONSO LOPES FREIRE.

Empresa de Navegação da Amazônia, SA (ENASA): Av. Pres. Vargas 41, CP 1068, 66.000 Belém, PA; tel. (091) 223-3011; telex (91) 1311; f. 1967; cargo and passenger services on the Amazon river and its principal tributaries, connecting the port of Belém with Marajó, Santarém, Parintins, Manaus and other river ports; Pres. VICENTE DE PAULA QUEIROZ; fleet of 10 vessels amounting to 8,564 grt.

SHIPPING

There are 36 deep-water ports in Brazil, five of which, including the port of Santos which handles 30% of all cargo, are privately owned. The largest ports are Santos, Rio de Janeiro, Paranaguá, Recife and Vitória. Tubarão, an iron ore port, and Santana (Amapá) on the Amazon, from where manganese is exported, are among the ports already equipped with automated facilities. Both ports are being expanded, as are Recife and Maceió, the sugar ports, and Ilheus, the cocoa port, on the eastern seaboard. The two main oil terminals, at São Sebastião (São Paulo) and Madre de Jesus (Bahia), are being expanded. Port expansion plans also include the building of terminals at Areia Branca, Paranaguá and Rio Grande. A new iron ore terminal is under construction at Sepetiba, and a sugar terminal is to be built in São Paulo State. All ports will be deepened to accommodate vessels of over 40,000 tons. In 1988 the World Bank allocated a loan of US $20m. to Brazil for a project to increase the efficiency of the country's ports. Brazil's merchant fleet is the largest in Latin America. In 1984 it comprised 1,636 vessels (10m. tons), of which 150 were oil tankers and 1,486 were cargo vessels. In 1984 Brazil reached agreement with Bolivia on the construction of a port on the Caceres lagoon and the dredging of the Tamengo channel.

Superintendência Nacional da Marinha Mercante (SUNAMAM): Av. Rio Branco 115, 14°, 20.040 Rio de Janeiro, RJ; tel. (021) 221-4015; telex (21) 21652; f. 1941; supervisory board of the merchant marine; Superintendent MURILLO R. H. DE MAIA.

Empresa dos Portos do Brasil (Portobrás): SAS, Quadra 1, Blocos 1, E/F, Brasília, DF; tel. (061) 224-1700; telex (61) 1112; f. 1975 to supervise, control and develop policies for the ports and navigable waterways; Pres. CARLOS THEOFILO DE S. MELLO.

Companhia Brasileira de Transporte de Granéis, Ltda: Rua da Assembléia 100, 21°, 20.011 Rio de Janeiro, RJ; tel. (021) 224-9232; telex (21) 30603; f. 1976 for the carriage of liquid and solid bulk cargoes; Pres. JOSÉ CELSO MACEDO SOARES; Exec. Dir MARCIO SALLES; 8 vessels amounting to 255,863 grt.

Companhia de Navegação Lloyd Brasileiro: Rua do Rosario 1, CP 1501, 20.041 Rio de Janeiro, RJ; tel. (021) 233-6957; telex (21) 23364; f. 1890; partly government-owned; operates between Brazil, the USA, Northern Europe, Scandinavia, the Mediterranean, East and West Africa, the Far East, the Arabian Gulf, Japan, Australia and New Zealand, and around the South American coast through the associated company **Lloyd-Libra**. Operates with pelletized, containerized and frozen cargoes, as well as with general and bulk cargoes; Pres. ELMO SEREJO FARIAS; 47 vessels.

BRAZIL
Directory

Companhia de Navegação Marítima (NETUMAR): Rua Monsenhor Coutinho 340, Centro Manaus, AM; Av. Presidente Vargas 482, 22°, 20.000 Rio de Janeiro, RJ; tel. (021) 223-1660; telex (21) 23069; f. 1959; coastal traffic including Amazon region, foreign trade to USA and Canada, east coast and Great Lakes ports, Argentina and Uruguay; Dir José Carlos Leal; 14 vessels, 229,309 dwt.

Companhia de Navegação do Norte (CONAN): Av. Rio Branco 45, 23° e 25° andares, Rio de Janeiro, RJ; tel. (021) 223-4155; telex (21) 22713; f. 1965; services to Brazil, Argentina, Uruguay and inland waterways; Chair. J. R. Ribeiro Salomão; 10 vessels amounting to 121,900 grt.

Empresa de Navegação Aliança, SA: Av. Pasteur 110, Botafogo, 22.290 Rio de Janeiro, RJ; tel. (021) 546-1122; telex (21) 23778; f. 1950; cargo services to Argentina, Europe, Baltic, Atlantic and North Sea ports; Pres. Carlos G. E. Fischer; 14 vessels.

Frota Amazônica, SA: Av. Presidente Vargas 112, CP 1367, Belém, PA; tel. (091) 224-0477; telex (91) 1041; cargo services between the Amazon region and the US Gulf ports, the east coast of the USA and Canada and Northern Europe; Pres. José Carlos Fragoso Pires; 6 vessels of 35,150 grt.

Frota Oceânica Brasileira, SA: Av. Venezuela 110, CP 21-020, 20.081 Rio de Janeiro, RJ; tel. (021) 291-5153; telex (21) 22224; f. 1947; Pres. José Carlos Fragoso Pires; Vice-Pres. Luiz Joaquim Campos Alhanati; 14 vessels amounting to 365,731 grt.

Linhas Brasileiras de Navegação SA (LIBRA): Av. Rio Branco 25, 15° andar, 20.090 Rio de Janeiro, RJ; tel. (021) 223-2102; telex (21) 21382; Exec. Dir Sylvio Silva Gonçalves; 13 cargo vessels amounting to 176,573 grt.

Petróleo Brasileiro SA (Petrobrás) (Frota Nacional de Petroleiros—Fronape): Rua Carlos Seidl, 188 Caju, CP 51015, 20.931 Rio de Janeiro, RJ; tel. (021) 580-4581; telex (21) 22286; Supt Telmo B. Schneider; tanker fleet of 4,980,805 dwt.

Vale do Rio Doce Navegação, SA (DOCENAVE): Rua Voluntários da Pátria 143, Botafogo, 20.000 Rio de Janeiro, RJ; tel. (021) 286-8002; telex (21) 22142; bulk carrier to Japan, Persian Gulf, Europe, North America and Argentina; Dir Carlos Auto de Andrade; 20 bulk and 3 ore/oil carriers amounting to 1,153,826 grt (bulk) and 538,823 grt (ore/oil).

CIVIL AVIATION

There are about 1,500 airports and airstrips. Of the 48 principal airports 21 are international, although most international traffic is handled by the two airports at Rio de Janeiro and two at São Paulo. A new international airport was opened at Guarulhos, near São Paulo, in January 1985.

Serviços Aéreos Cruzeiro do Sul, SA: Av. Sílvio de Noronha 361 gr. 311, CP 190, 200.21 Rio de Janeiro, RJ; telex (21) 21765; f. 1927; in 1975 VARIG purchased an 86% participation in the company; network routes: Brazil, Argentina, Barbados, Bolivia, Colombia, French Guiana, Suriname, Trinidad and Tobago, Uruguay; Pres. Dr Aguinaldo de Melo Junqueira; 1986 fleet: 6 Boeing 767-100, 6 Boeing 737-200, 2 Airbus A-300 B-4.

Transbrasil SA Linhas Aéreas: Rua Santa Luzia 651, 18°, Rio de Janeiro, RJ; tel. (021) 220-6066; telex (21) 22744; f. 1955 as Sadia, renamed 1972; scheduled passenger and cargo services to major Brazilian cities and Orlando; cargo charter flights to the USA; Pres. Dr Omar Fontana; 1986 fleet: 9 Boeing 707-320C, 3 Boeing 767-200, 2 Boeing 737-300, 8 Boeing 727-100, 2 Boeing 727-100C.

VARIG, SA (Viação Aérea Rio Grandense): Edif. Varig., Av. Almte Sílvio Noronha 365, 20.021 Rio de Janeiro, RJ; tel. (021) 297-5141; telex (21) 22363; f. 1927; international services; Argentina, Chile, Colombia, Costa Rica, Ecuador, Panama, Paraguay, Peru, Uruguay, Venezuela, Mexico, Canada, the USA, Angola, Côte d'Ivoire, Japan, Nigeria, Mozambique, South Africa and Western Europe; domestic services to major cities of the country; cargo services; Pres. Hélio Smidt; Vice-Pres. Rubel Thomas; 1987 fleet: 7 Boeing 707-320-C, 10 Boeing 727-100, 12 Boeing 737-200, 4 Boeing 747-200B, 2 Boeing 747-300, 2 Boeing 767-200, 2 Airbus A-300, 12 Douglas DC-10-30, 14 Lockheed 188-A.

Viação Aérea São Paulo, SA (VASP): 04695 Edif. VASP, Aeroporto Congonhas, São Paulo, SP; tel. (011) 533-7011; telex (11) 37913; f. 1933; controlled by São Paulo State Government; domestic services covering all Brazil; Pres. Sidnei Franco da Rocha; 1987 fleet: 2 Boeing 727-200, 22 Boeing 737-200 Super Advanced, 6 Boeing 737-300, 3 Airbus A-300 B2K.

In addition to the airlines listed above, there are a number of others operating regional services.

Tourism

In 1986 about 1.9m. tourists visited Brazil. Rio de Janeiro, with its famous beaches, is the centre of the tourist trade. Like Salvador, Recife and other towns, it has excellent examples of Portuguese colonial and modern architecture. The modern capital, Brasília, incorporates a new concept of city planning and is the nation's show-piece. Other attractions are the Iguaçu Falls, the seventh largest (by volume) in the world, and the tropical forests of the Amazon basin.

Centro Brasileiro de Informação Turística (CEBITUR): Rua Mariz e Barros 13, 6° andar, Praça da Bandeira, 20.270 Rio de Janeiro, RJ; tel. (021) 293-1313; telex (21) 21066.

Conselho Nacional de Turismo (CNTUR) (National Tourism Office): Ministério da Indústria e do Comércio, Rua Mariz e Barros 13, 5°, 20.270 Rio de Janeiro, RJ; tel. (021) 273-0691; f. 1966; Exec. Sec. José Roberto Novais Bueno.

Coordenadoria de Promoção Comercial Conselho de Desenvolvimento Comercial: SCS, Q02, Bloco C, No 227, Ministério da Indústria e do Comércio, Edif. Pres. Dutra, 2° andar, 70.300 Brasília, DF; tel. (061) 223-0129; telex (61) 2537; f. 1967; organizes fairs and exhibitions; Co-ordinator Sebastião Gomes de Medeiros; Sec.-Gen. Ruy Coutinho do Nascimento.

Divisão de Feiras e Turismo/Departamento de Promoção Comercial: Ministério das Relações Exteriores, Esplanada dos Ministérios, 2°, 70.170 Brasília, DF; tel. (061) 211-6644; f. 1977; organizes Brazil's participation in trade fairs and commercial exhibitions abroad; Dir Sergio Barcellos Telles.

Empresa Brasileira de Turismo—EMBRATUR: Rua Mariz e Barros 13, 7° andar, 20.270 Rio de Janeiro, RJ; tel. (021) 273-2212; telex (21) 21066; f. 1966; studies tourist development projects; Pres. João Dória Júnior.

Atomic Energy

Brazil's first nuclear power station, at Angra dos Reis, RJ, commenced commercial operation (power of 657 MW) in early 1985, after design deficiencies had caused delays. Following an agreement between Brazil and the Federal Republic of Germany, two other plants, of 1,300 MW (Angra II and III), were to be constructed at the same site, with Brazilian participation, and were originally expected to become operational in 1992 and 1995 respectively. Work on two further planned plants was postponed in 1983 owing to lack of available finance. In September 1985 construction of the Angra III plant and of two further plants, Iguape I and II, was postponed indefinitely. The construction of the Angra II plant was to be completed by 1995. Development within the sector has been severely hampered by government spending cuts in recent years. In 1987 the Angra I plant was closed for several months because of generating difficulties. A plant for enriching uranium was under construction at Iperó.

In 1988 the Government announced an extensive reorganization of the nuclear power sector, including the creation of the Conselho Superior de Política Nuclear and the dissolution of Nucleares Brasileiras (NUCLEBRÁS). In addition, the management and development of nuclear power plants was transferred to the electricity sector, principally to ELETROBRÁS.

Research reactors: The following research reactors are in operation:

(CDTN-RI) CDTN-NUCLEBRÁS, Belo Horizonte, MG; thermal power 250 kW.

(IPEN-RI) IPEN, São Paulo, SP; thermal power 5 MW.

(IEN-RI) IEN-CNEN, Rio de Janeiro, RJ; thermal power 10 kW.

(URANIE) CDTN-NUCLEBRÁS, Belo Horizonte, MG (subcritical).

(RESUCO) DEN-UFPe, Recife, Pe (subcritical).

(NC-9000) CTA, São José dos Campos, SP (subcritical).

(CAPITU) CDTN-NUCLEBRÁS, Belo Horizonte, MG (subcritical).

(SUBLIME) IME, Rio de Janeiro, RJ (planned).

Conselho Superior de Política Nuclear (CSPN): f. 1988; to determine and supervise the implementation of Brazil's nuclear power programme.

Comissão Nacional de Energia Nuclear (CNEN): Rua General Severiano 90, Botafogo, 20.040 Rio de Janeiro, RJ; tel. (021) 295-9596; telex (21) 21280; f. 1956; controlling organization for: Centro de Desenvolvimento da Tecnologia Nuclear—CDTN (nuclear research); Instituto de Engenharia Nuclear—IEN (nuclear engineering); Instituto de Radioproteção e Dosimetria—IRD (radiation protection and dosimetry) and Instituto de Pesquisas Energéticas e Nucleares—IPEN (energetics and nuclear research); in 1988 assumed responsibility for management of nuclear power programme; 1988 budget estimate: CZ $10,000m.; Pres. Rex Nazaré Alves.

Indústrias Nucleares do Brasil: f. 1988 to replace NUCLEBRÁS; responsible for construction and financing of nuclear power plants; Pres. JOHN FOREMAN.

Urânio do Brasil: f. 1988 to replace NUCLEBRÁS; responsible for fuel-cycle (from extraction of uranium to processing stage).

As a result of the Brazil-Federal Republic of Germany nuclear agreement signed in July 1975, four joint-ventures between NUCLEBRÁS and Federal German firms were established: NUCLAM (mining), NUCLEI (enrichment by the nozzle method), NUCLEN (engineering) and NUCLEP (heavy equipment) and NUSTEP (in the Federal Republic of Germany). In accordance with the Government's reorganization of the sector, announced in 1988, NUCLAM and NUSTEP were closed down; NUCLEI's activities were transferred to Urânio do Brasil; NUCLEN became a subsidiary of ELETROBRÁS; and NUCLEP was to be privatized.

BRUNEI

Introductory Survey

Location, Climate, Language, Religion, Flag, Capital

The Sultanate of Brunei (Negara Brunei Darussalam) lies in South-East Asia, on the north-west coast of the island of Kalimantan (Borneo, most of which is Indonesian territory). It is surrounded and bisected on the landward side by Sarawak, one of the two eastern states of Malaysia. The country has a tropical climate, characterized by consistent temperature and humidity. Average annual rainfall ranges from about 2,400 mm (95 in) in lowland areas to about 4,000 mm (158 in) in the interior. Temperatures are high, with the annual extreme range being 23°C (73°F) to 35.8°C (96.4°F). The principal language is Malay, although Chinese is also spoken and English is widely used. The Malay population (nearly 65% of the total) are mainly Sunni Muslims, Islam being the official religion. Most of the Chinese in Brunei are Buddhists, Confucians or Daoists. Europeans and Eurasians are predominantly Christians. The flag (proportions 2 by 1) is yellow, with two diagonal stripes, of white and black, running from the upper hoist to the lower fly; superimposed in the centre is the state emblem (in red, with yellow Arabic inscriptions). The capital is Bandar Seri Begawan (formerly called Brunei Town).

Recent History

Brunei, a traditional Islamic monarchy, formerly included most of the coastal regions of North Borneo (now Sabah) and Sarawak, which later became states of Malaysia. During the 19th century the rulers of Brunei ceded large parts of their territory to the United Kingdom, reducing the sultanate to its present size. In 1888, when North Borneo became a British protectorate, Brunei became a British Protected State. In accordance with an agreement made in 1906, a British Resident was appointed to the court of the ruling Sultan as an adviser on administration. Under this arrangement, a form of government that included an advisory State Council emerged.

Brunei was invaded by Japanese forces in December 1941, but reverted to its former status in 1945, when the Second World War ended. The British-appointed Governor of Sarawak was High Commissioner for Brunei from 1948 until the territory's first written constitution was promulgated in September 1959, when a further agreement was made between the Sultan and the British Government. The United Kingdom continued to be responsible for Brunei's defence and external affairs until the attainment of independence in 1984.

In December 1962 a large-scale revolt broke out in Brunei and in parts of Sarawak and North Borneo. The rebellion was carried out by the 'North Borneo Liberation Army', an organization linked with the Parti Ra'ayat Brunei (Brunei People's Party), led by A. M. Azahari, which was strongly opposed to the planned entry of Brunei into the Federation of Malaysia. The rebels proclaimed the 'revolutionary State of North Kalimantan', but the revolt was suppressed, after 10 days' fighting, with the aid of British forces from Singapore. A state of emergency was declared, the People's Party was banned, and Azahari was given asylum in Malaya. In the event, the Sultan decided in 1963 against joining the Federation. From 1962 he ruled by decree, and the state of emergency remained in force. Sir Omar Ali Saifuddin, who had been Sultan since 1950, abdicated in October 1967 in favour of his son, Hassanal Bolkiah, who was then 21 years of age. Under an agreement signed in November 1971, Brunei was granted full internal self-government.

In December 1975 the UN General Assembly passed a resolution which called for British withdrawal from Brunei, for the return of political exiles and for the holding of a general election. Negotiations in 1978, following assurances by Malaysia and Indonesia that they would respect Brunei's sovereignty, resulted in an agreement (signed in January 1979) that Brunei would become fully independent within five years. Independence was duly proclaimed on 1 January 1984, and the Sultan took office as Prime Minister and Minister of Finance and of Home Affairs, presiding over a Cabinet of six other ministers (including two of the Sultan's brothers and his father, the former Sultan).

The future of the Chinese population, who controlled much of Brunei's private commercial sector but had become stateless since independence, appeared threatened in 1985, when the Sultan indicated that Brunei would become an Islamic state in which the indigenous, mainly Malay, inhabitants, known as *bumiputras* ('sons of the soil'), would receive preferential treatment. Several Hong Kong and Taiwan Chinese, who were not permanent Brunei residents, were repatriated.

In May 1985 a new political party, the Brunei National Democratic Party (BNDP), was formed. The new party, which comprised businessmen loyal to the Sultan, based its policies on Islam and a form of liberal nationalism. However, the Sultan forbade employees of the Government (about 40% of the country's working population) to join the party. Persons belonging to the Chinese community were also excluded from membership. Divisions within the new party led to the formation of a second group, the Brunei National United Party, in February 1986. This party, which also received the Sultan's official approval, placed greater emphasis on co-operation with the Government, and was open to both Muslim and non-Muslim ethnic groups.

Although the Sultan was not expected to allow any relaxation of restrictions on radical political activities, it became clear during 1985 and 1986 that a more progressive style of government was being adopted. The death of Sir Muda Omar Ali Saifuddin, the Sultan's father, in September 1986 was expected to hasten modernization. In October the Cabinet was enlarged to 11 members when the Sultan carried out a government reshuffle, in which commoners and aristocrats were assigned portfolios that had previously been given to members of the royal family. In February 1988, however, the BNDP was dissolved by the authorities after it had demanded the resignation of the Sultan as Head of Government (although not as Head of State), an end to the 26-year state of emergency and the holding of democratic elections. The official reason for the dissolution of the party was its connections with a foreign organization, the Pacific Democratic Union. The leaders of the BNDP, Abdul Latif Hamid and Abdul Latif Chuchu, were arrested, under provisions of the Internal Security Act, and remained in detention in December 1988.

Relations with the United Kingdom had become strained during 1983, following the Brunei Government's decision, in August, to transfer the management of its investment portfolio from the British Crown Agents to the newly-created Brunei Investment Agency. However, normal relations were restored in September, when the British Government agreed that a battalion of Gurkha troops, stationed in Brunei since 1971, should remain in Brunei after independence, at the Sultanate's expense, specifically to guard the oil and gas fields. This arrangement could, however, be under threat, owing to British uncertainty concerning the future of Gurkha forces after 1997, when Hong Kong (the site of the main Gurkha base) reverts to Chinese rule. The level of co-operation between Brunei and the United Kingdom was demonstrated in the extensive joint military exercise which took place in August 1988.

Brunei has developed close relations with the members of ASEAN (see p. 101), in particular Singapore, and became a full member of the organization immediately after independence. Royal visits were made to Thailand and Indonesia in 1984, and diplomatic relations with Japan were established in the same year. Brunei also joined the UN, the Commonwealth and the Organization of the Islamic Conference in 1984.

In 1986 and 1987 Brunei appeared anxious to promote good relations with the USA, the United Kingdom, Indonesia and Malaysia. In early 1987 the Government was highly embarrassed by the disclosure that the Sultan had arranged a contribution of US $10m. in 'humanitarian' aid to Nicaraguan 'Contra' rebels, and that this donation (made in response to a request by US officials at a time when all aid to the Contras from the USA had been prohibited by the US Congress) had been mistakenly deposited in a Swiss businessman's bank account.

BRUNEI

In March 1987 Brunei showed interest in joining the Five-Power Defence Agreement, linking the United Kingdom, Malaysia, Singapore, Australia and New Zealand. Brunei's relations with Malaysia improved considerably in early 1987, when Malaysia offered to help Brunei with the establishment of an army reserve force, and in March, when the Malaysian Prime Minister, Datuk Seri Dr Mahathir Mohamad, visited Brunei for discussions. In September the two countries announced possible future co-operation in the production of defence equipment.

Following the death of the Sultan's father in September 1986, relations with Indonesia also improved, and in September 1987 the Sultan offered Indonesia a $100m. interest-free loan for industrial and transport projects, repayable over 25 years with a seven-year grace period. In August 1988 the President of the Philippines, Corazon Aquino, made a state visit to Brunei. The Sultan offered, in principle, to participate in an international group to finance Philippine economic development plans.

Government

The 1959 Constitution confers supreme executive authority on the Sultan. He is assisted and advised by four Constitutional Councils: the Religious Council, the Privy Council, the Council of Cabinet Ministers and the Council of Succession. Since the rebellion of 1962, certain provisions of the Constitution have been suspended, and the Sultan has ruled by decree.

Defence

The Royal Brunei Malay Regiment numbered 4,000 (including 250 women) in June 1988, all services forming part of the army. Military service is voluntary. Paramilitary forces comprised 1,900 Royal Brunei Police. The defence budget for 1986 was B $505m. A Gurkha battalion of the British army has been stationed in Brunei since 1971.

Economic Affairs

Brunei's economy depends almost entirely on its petroleum and natural gas resources. By world standards, Brunei is not a major producer of oil and gas, but the country has a relatively small population and the development of the hydrocarbons sector has provided the inhabitants with a very high level of material prosperity. Brunei's gross domestic product (GDP), measured in current prices, reached a peak of US $4,848m. ($25,500 per head) in 1980, but falls in petroleum production and prices led to reduced GDP in subsequent years. Between 1975 and 1984, GDP expanded, in real terms, at an average rate of 3.9% annually, compared with a target growth rate of 6%. After expanding by an average of 12.2% per year during 1975–79, GDP contracted by 1.4% annually between 1980 and 1986. Nevertheless, in terms of average income, Brunei remains one of the world's richest countries. In 1986, according to estimates by the World Bank, Brunei's GDP, measured at average 1984–86 prices, was US $3,571m., equivalent to US $15,390 per head. Between 1980 and 1986, it was estimated, real GDP per head declined at an average rate of 5.1% per year.

In 1988 six offshore and two onshore fields were producing crude petroleum. Output reached a peak of about 260,000 barrels per day (b/d) in 1979, but in subsequent years production steadily decreased. Falls in international prices for crude petroleum and a reduced world demand in the 1980s accelerated a policy to conserve resources, such that by 1988 production had decreased to 150,000 b/d. Export earnings from crude petroleum, which were B $762m. in 1973, rose to B $4,778m. in 1981 but had fallen to B $1,619.9m. by 1986, reflecting reductions in both production and prices. Average output of natural gas has remained roughly constant, at about 900m. cu ft per day since 1983. Earnings from natural gas, B $46.5m. in 1973, increased to B $3,397m. in 1981, but declined to B $2,110.7m. in 1986. Sales of oil and natural gas, which in 1986 accounted for 97.2% of total exports, are almost entirely responsible for Brunei's favourable trade balance. Brunei's principal customer is Japan, which takes 46% of petroleum and about 97% of the total gas output; Brunei exports more than 5m. metric tons of liquefied natural gas (LNG) per year to Japan on a long-term contract. The USA and ASEAN countries are the next largest importers of Bruneian petroleum. The trade surplus fell from B $5,629m. in 1983 to B $2,539.7m. in 1986, owing to a decline in international petroleum prices, which caused a reduction in export earnings, and to an increase in imports of manufactured goods. However, Brunei's official international reserves continue to rise, and in 1988 they were estimated at US $25,000m. These reserves are managed largely by the government-controlled Brunei Investment Agency, established in August 1983 to invest reserves abroad. In 1988 there was no external public debt.

Development projects are hampered by lack of skilled labour and by the small size of the population; foreign workers, principally from the Philippines and Malaysia, have helped to ease the labour shortage and comprised about one-third of the total labour force of 85,300 in 1985. Among the major projects which have already been completed are an international airport, a deep-water port at Muara, a petroleum refinery, with a capacity of 10,000 b/d, a natural gas liquefaction plant, the largest in the world, at Lumut, and a co-generation power plant, completed in 1987 at a cost of B $327m. Brunei's GDP more than doubled in the five years before 1979, when it reached an estimated B $5,795m. In 1984 GDP in current purchasers' values rose to B $8,210.3m., but in 1985 it fell to B $7,529.3m., 71% of which was derived from production of oil and gas. In 1986 GDP declined further, to an estimated B $5,773.3m. Manufacturing and mining accounted for 76% of GDP in 1983, and for 69.3% in 1984.

In 1975 highly favourable tax concessions were introduced, with the aim of encouraging investment in new industries. The areas most suitable for industrial development are timber, paper, fertilizers, petro-chemicals and glass. Government policy is to encourage local (especially indigenous or *bumiputra*) enterprises with greater participation by Bruneians. The 1980–84 Development Plan was designed to achieve a high level of employment, to diversify the economy through the development of agriculture, forestry and fisheries, and aimed at a minimum annual growth rate of 6%. The plan involved total expenditure of B $2,000m.

The average annual rate of inflation was 6.4% in 1982 and only 1.2% in 1983, kept down by state-controlled prices for some basic commodities, including rice. The rate increased to 3.1% in 1984, but declined to 1.4% in the year to March 1986. Government revenue, largely financed by taxes from the petroleum companies, increased significantly from 1979, and in 1985 there was an estimated surplus of B $4,985m. Expenditure in the 1985 budget totalled B $2,071m., or B $580m. less than the total allocation in 1984, although defence expenditure was increased. In 1986, however, revenue totalled B $3,331.5m. and expenditure B $2,720.4m., leaving a surplus of only B $611.1m. The decline in revenue was attributed to a reduction in both production and international prices of petroleum. Government figures for 1987 showed revenue, excluding investment income (unofficially estimated at between US $1,500m. and US $2,500m.), of B $2,700m. and expenditure of B $2,400m., resulting in a surplus of B $300m. Government estimates for expenditure in 1988 included a 24% allocation to the armed forces, 15% to education and 7% to health.

In 1986, after a year of readjustment, the Government introduced a fifth Development Plan (1986–90), which aimed to reduce dependence on income from petroleum and natural gas (reserves of which were expected to be exhausted after about another 25 years), to achieve self-sufficiency in food production, and to promote import substitution. The largest projects were new port developments and improvements to water supplies, sewerage and telecommunications. The plan also included a review of the 1975–84 period, drawing attention to the failure of the two preceding plans to diversify the economy and to achieve significant expansion in agriculture, forestry and fishing.

The 1986–90 Plan envisaged total expenditure of B $6,200m. Of the B $3,730m. allocated to development, industry and commerce were to receive 10% of projected expenditure, while social services were to continue to receive the largest proportion (29%). Manufacturing, timber production and agriculture were also emphasized. In 1985 Brunei imported 80% of its total food requirements, in spite of the objectives of previous plans to achieve self-sufficiency in home-grown crops and to develop potential areas of agricultural land. The only reported success has been in egg production where Brunei reached 90% self-sufficiency in 1987. In 1986 it was announced that a 20-year master plan for Brunei was under consideration, of which the 1986–90 Plan was to form a part. The Government's recognition of the need to diversify the economy was reflected in the new emphasis that it placed on the development of the private sector, aided by: the conversion of Brunei into a centre for banking and finance, and for trade and maintenance services; the establishment of a development bank to replace the Economic Development Board; and national pension and training schemes. The Government also proposed that Brunei's vast reserves of high-grade silica should be used to develop the manufacture of microchips and components for optical instruments. In November 1986 the Government closed down the National Bank of Brunei, following allegations of irregularities. It was announced in December 1988 that creditors were to be paid in full, following civil claims against the financier involved.

Social Welfare

Free medical services are provided by the Government. In 1982 there were 107 physicians working in the country. The main 550-bed central referral hospital is in Bandar Seri Begawan, but there are three other hospitals (in Kuala Belait, Tutong and Temburong), as well as private facilities provided by Brunei Shell. For medical care not available in Brunei, citizens are sent abroad at the Government's expense. There is a 'flying doctor' service, as well as various clinics, travelling dispensaries and dental clinics. A non-contributory state pensions scheme for the old and disabled came into operation in 1955. The state also provides financial assistance to the poor, the destitute and widows. Under the 1986-90 Development Plan, B $756.9m. was allocated to health and social services. National pension schemes were to be introduced by the Government under the 1986-90 Plan.

Education

Education is free, and Islamic studies form an integral part of the school curriculum. Pupils who are Brunei citizens and live more than 8 km (5 miles) from their schools are entitled to free accommodation in hostels, free transport or a subsistence allowance. Schools are classified according to the language of instruction, i.e. Malay, English or Chinese (Mandarin). In 1986 the total enrolment in the 146 primary schools was 36,983, while in the 29 general secondary schools and sixth-form centres the enrolment was 18,714. In 1987 there were two teacher-training colleges and two colleges for vocational and technical education. The University of Brunei Darussalam was formally established in 1985, but many students continue to be sent to universities abroad, at government expense. In 1987 515 students were enrolled at the four faculties. A new campus is scheduled to be completed in 1992, and intake is to be expanded to 2,000 students. Adult illiteracy fell from 36% in 1971 to an estimated 29% in 1981. The 1985 budget allocated B $231m. to education.

Public Holidays

1989: 1 January (New Year's Day), February* (Chinese New Year), 23 February (National Day), 5 March† (Meraj, Ascension of the Prophet), 7 April† (First Day of Ramadan), 23 April† (Anniversary of the Revelation of the Koran), 7 May† (end of Ramadan), May/June (Anniversary of the Royal Brunei Malay Regiment), 14 July† (Hari Raya Haji, Feast of the Sacrifice), 15 July (Sultan's Birthday), 4 August† (Islamic New Year), 13 October† (Mouloud, Birth of the Prophet), 25 December (Christmas).

1990: 1 January (New Year's Day), February* (Chinese New Year), 23 February (National Day), 23 February† (Meraj, Ascension of the Prophet), 28 March† (First Day of Ramadan), 13 April† (Anniversary of the Revelation of the Koran), 27 April† (end of Ramadan), May/June (Anniversary of the Royal Brunei Malay Regiment), 4 July† (Hari Raya Haji, Feast of the Sacrifice), 15 July (Sultan's Birthday), 24 July† (Islamic New Year), 2 October† (Mouloud, Birth of the Prophet), 25 December (Christmas).

* From the first to the third day of the first moon of the lunar calendar.

† These holidays are dependent on the Islamic lunar calendar and may vary by one or two days from the dates given.

Weights and Measures

The imperial system is in operation but local measures of weight and capacity are used. These include the gantang (1 gallon), the tahil (1⅓ oz) and the kati (1⅓ lb).

Statistical Survey

Source (unless otherwise stated): Economic Planning Unit, Ministry of Finance, Bandar Seri Begawan; tel. (02) 41991; telex 2676.

AREA, POPULATION AND DENSITY

Area: 5,765 sq km (2,226 sq miles); *by district:* Brunei/Muara 570 sq km (220 sq miles), Seria/Belait 2,725 sq km (1,052 sq miles), Tutong 1,165 sq km (450 sq miles), Temburong 1,305 sq km (504 sq miles).

Population (excluding transients afloat): 192,832 (males 102,942, females 89,890) at census of 25 August 1981; 226,300 (males 116,800, females 109,500) at mid-1986 (official estimates). *Capital:* Bandar Seri Begawan, population 50,500 (1986 estimate).

Density (per sq km): 39.0 (1986).

Ethnic Groups (1986): Malay 155,600, Chinese 41,400, Other indigenous 11,400, Others 17,900, Total 226,300.

Births and Deaths (1986): Live births 6,928 (birth rate 30.6 per 1,000); Deaths 726 (death rate 3.2 per 1,000).

Economically Active Population (1981 census): Agriculture, hunting, forestry and fishing 3,435; Mining and quarrying 3,863; Manufacturing 2,783; Electricity, gas and water 1,961; Construction 12,644; Trade, restaurants and hotels 7,363; Transport, storage and communications 4,529; Financing, insurance, real estate and business services 2,010; Community, social and personal services 29,282; Activities not adequately defined 258; Total employed 68,128 (males 52,737; females 15,391); Unemployed 2,562 (males 1,122; females 1,440); Total labour force 70,690 (males 53,859; females 16,831). *1986 estimate:* Total labour force 81,000.

AGRICULTURE, ETC.
(Source: FAO)

Principal Crops (FAO estimates, '000 metric tons, 1986): Rice (paddy) 3, Cassava (Manioc) 1, Bananas 1, Pineapples 1, Vegetables (incl. melons) 9.

Livestock (FAO estimates, '000 head, year ending September 1986): Cattle 4, Buffaloes 12, Pigs 14, Goats 1.

Livestock Products (FAO estimates, metric tons, 1986): Poultry meat 4,000; Hen eggs 1,900; Cattle and buffalo hides (fresh) 224.

Forestry (FAO estimates, '000 cu m, 1984): *Roundwood removals:* Sawlogs, veneer logs and logs for sleepers 206; Other industrial wood 8; Fuel wood 79; Total 293. *Sawnwood production:* Total (incl. boxboards) 90. **1985-86:** Annual output as in 1984 (FAO estimates).

Fishing (metric tons, live weight, 1986): Inland waters 129 (Freshwater fishes 90, Giant river prawn 39); Pacific Ocean 2,629 (Marine fishes 2,131, Crustaceans and molluscs 498); Total catch 2,758.

MINING

Production (1985): Crude petroleum 54,373,117 barrels; Natural gasoline 414,301 barrels; Natural gas 317,048m. cu ft.

INDUSTRY

Production ('000 metric tons, 1986): Motor spirit (petrol) 117.3; Distillate fuel oils 83.9; Kerosene 28.6; Naphthas 6.8 (1985).

FINANCE

Currency and Exchange Rates: 100 sen (cents) = 1 Brunei dollar (B $). *Coins:* 1, 5, 10, and 50 cents. *Notes:* 1, 5, 10, 50, 100, 500 and 1,000 dollars. *Sterling and US Dollar Equivalents* (30 September 1988): £1 sterling = B $3.440; US $1 = B $2.040; B $100 = £29.07 = US $49.02. *Average Exchange Rate* (Brunei dollars per US $): 2.2002 in 1985; 2.1774 in 1986; 2.1060 in 1987. Note: The Brunei dollar is at par with the Singapore dollar.

Budget (estimates, B $ million, 1984): *Revenue:* Total 6,500; *Expenditure:* Royal Brunei Malay Regiment 340.2, Public works 231.3, Education 216.2, Transfer to Development Fund 950, Total (incl. others) 2,651.

BRUNEI
Statistical Survey, Directory

Cost of Living (Consumer Price Index; base: 1977 = 100): 143.1 in 1984; 146.4 in 1985; 149.0 in 1986.

Gross Domestic Product (B $ million in current purchasers' values): 8,210.3 in 1984; 7,529.3 in 1985; 5,773.3 in 1986 (provisional).

EXTERNAL TRADE

Principal Commodities (B $ million, 1986): *Imports:* Food and live animals 209.1, Beverages and tobacco 84.9, Crude materials (inedible) except fuels 17.4, Mineral fuels, lubricants, etc. 14.6, Animal and vegetable oils and fats 5.5, Chemicals 101.5, Basic manufactures 305.7, Machinery and transport equipment 550.8, Miscellaneous manufactured articles 160.0, Total (incl. others) 1,450.4. *Exports:* Crude petroleum 1,619.9, Petroleum products 146.7, Natural gas 2,110.7, Total (incl. others) 3,990.1.

Principal Trading Partners (B $ million, 1985): *Imports:* Australia 37.2, China, People's Republic 27.4, Germany, Federal Republic 87.7, Japan 256.5, Malaysia (Peninsular) 75.5, Netherlands 48.4, Singapore 373.6, Taiwan 34.2, Thailand 45.2, United Kingdom 114.7, USA 177.2. *Exports:* Australia 33.3, Japan 2,667.9, Korea, Republic 293.6, Malaysia (Sarawak) 40.5, Singapore 266.7, Taiwan 67.1, Thailand 323.9, USA 243.2.

TRANSPORT

Road Traffic (registered vehicles, 1986): Private cars 84,410, Taxis 117, Motor-cycles and scooters 3,582, Goods vehicles 10,629, Buses 422, Other vehicles 1,849, Total 101,009.

International Sea-borne Shipping (1986): *Vessels* ('000 net registered tons): Entered 11,458.9, Cleared 9,271.9. *Goods* ('000 metric tons): Loaded 18,627.0, Unloaded 671.7.

Civil Aviation (1986): Aircraft landings 4,812, aircraft take-offs 4,811; passenger arrivals 178,259, passenger departures 175,643; freight loaded 5,409,131 kg, freight unloaded 580,753 kg.

TOURISM

Tourist Arrivals (1986): 6,578.

COMMUNICATIONS MEDIA

Radio receivers (1986): 78,000 in use.
Television receivers (1986): 49,500 in use.
Telephones (1986): 35,636 in use.
Book Production (1982): 72 titles (50 books, 22 pamphlets); 360,000 copies (341,000 books, 19,000 pamphlets).
Newspapers (1984): 1 (average circulation 46,000 copies per issue).
Other Periodicals (1984): 19 (combined circulation 128,000 copies per issue).

EDUCATION

1986:
Pre-primary: 145 schools; 392 teachers; 7,958 pupils.
Primary: 146 schools; 2,225 teachers; 36,983 pupils.
General Secondary: 29 schools; 1,636 teachers; 18,714 pupils.
Teacher Training: 2 colleges; 95 teachers; 519 pupils.
Vocational: 6 colleges; 319 teachers; 1,169 pupils.
Higher Education: 1 institute; 33 teachers; 176 pupils.

Directory

The Constitution

Note: Certain sections of the Constitution have been in abeyance since 1962.

A new constitution was promulgated on 29 September 1959. Under its provisions, sovereign authority is vested in the Sultan and Yang Di-Pertuan, who is assisted and advised by four Councils:

THE RELIGIOUS COUNCIL

In his capacity as head of the Islamic faith in Brunei, the Sultan and Yang Di-Pertuan is advised on all Islamic matters by the Religious Council, whose members are appointed by the Sultan and Yang Di-Pertuan.

THE PRIVY COUNCIL

This Council, presided over by the Sultan and Yang Di-Pertuan, is to advise the Sultan on matters concerning the Royal prerogative of mercy, the amendment of the Constitution and the conferment of ranks, titles and honours.

THE COUNCIL OF CABINET MINISTERS

Presided over by the Sultan and Yang Di-Pertuan, the Council of Cabinet Ministers considers all executive matters.

THE COUNCIL OF SUCCESSION

Subject to the Constitution, this Council is to determine the succession to the throne, should the need arise.

The State is divided into four administrative districts, in each of which is a District Officer (Malay) responsible to the Prime Minister and Minister of Home Affairs.

The Government

HEAD OF STATE

Sultan and Yang Di-Pertuan: HM Sir MUDA HASSANAL BOLKIAH MU'IZZADDIN WADDAULAH (succeeded 4 October 1967; crowned 1 August 1968).

COUNCIL OF CABINET MINISTERS
(December 1988)

Prime Minister and Minister of Defence: The Sultan and Yang Di-Pertuan, HM Sir MUDA HASSANAL BOLKIAH MU'IZZADDIN WADDAULAH.

Minister of Home Affairs and Special Adviser to the Prime Minister: Pehin Dato Haji ISA.
Minister of Foreign Affairs: Pengiran Perdana Wazir Pengiran MUDA MOHAMAD BOLKIAH.
Minister of Finance: Pengiran Di-Gadong Pengiran MUDA JEFRI BOLKIAH.
Minister of Industry and Primary Resources: Pehin Dato ABDUL RAHMAN BIN TAIB.
Minister of Law: Pengiran BAHRIN BIN Pengiran Haji ABAS.
Minister of Education: Pehin Dato Haji ABDUL RAHMAN.
Minister of Development: Pengiran Dr ISMAIL.
Minister of Communications: AWANG ZAKARIA BIN Haji SULEIMAN.
Minister of Religious Affairs: Pehin Dato Haji MOHD ZAIN.
Minister of Culture, Youth and Sports: Pehin Dato Haji HUSSEIN.
Minister of Health: Dato Dr Haji JOHAR.

MINISTRIES

Office of the Prime Minister: Istana Nurul Iman, Bandar Seri Begawan; tel. (02) 29988; telex 2727.
Ministry of Communications: Batu 2½, Jalan Gadong, Bandar Seri Begawan; tel. (02) 23845.
Ministry of Culture, Youth and Sports: Jalan McArthur, Bandar Seri Begawan; tel. (02) 40585.
Ministry of Defence: Bolkiah Garrison, Bandar Seri Begawan 1110; tel. (02) 32092; telex 2220.
Ministry of Development: Lapangan Terbang Lama Berakas; tel. (02) 41911; telex 2722.
Ministry of Education and Health: Lapangan Terbang Lama Berakas, Bandar Seri Begawan 1170; tel. (02) 44233; telex 2577.
Ministry of Finance: Bandar Seri Begawan; tel. (02) 42405; telex 2674.
Ministry of Foreign Affairs: Jalan Subok, Bandar Seri Begawan; tel. (02) 41177; telex 2292.
Ministry of Home Affairs: Bandar Seri Begawan; tel. (02) 23225.
Ministry of Law: Bandar Seri Begawan; tel. (02) 44872.

Political Organizations

Partai Perpaduan Kebang-Saan Brunei—PPKB (Brunei National United Party—BNUP): Bandar Seri Begawan; f. 1986 after split in BNDP (see below); pro-govt party; Sec.-Gen. AWANG HATTA Haji ZAINAL ABIDDIN.

There were formerly four other political organizations: **Parti Ra'ayat Brunei** (PRB, Brunei People's Party), which is banned and whose members are all in exile; **Barisan Kemerdeka'an Rakyat** (BAKER, People's Independence Front), f. 1966 but no longer active; **Parti Perpaduan Kebang-Saan Ra'ayat Brunei** (PERKARA, Brunei People's National United Party), f. 1968 but no longer active, and **Parti Kebang-Saan Demokratik Brunei—PKDB** (BNDP, Brunei National Democratic Party), f. 1985 and dissolved by government order in 1988.

Diplomatic Representation
EMBASSIES AND HIGH COMMISSIONS IN BRUNEI

Australia: 4th Floor, Teck Guan Plaza, cnr Jalan Sultan and Jalan McArthur, Bandar Seri Begawan; tel. (02) 29435; telex 2582; High Commissioner: JOHN MACARTNEY STAREY.

Bangladesh: 5 Olympic Garden, Kampong Anggerek Desa, Bandar Seri Begawan; High Commissioner: (vacant).

France: POB 3027, Bandar Seri Begawan; Ambassador: PATRICK AMIOT.

Germany, Federal Republic: 49–50 Jalan Sultan, POB 3050, Bandar Seri Begawan; tel. (02) 25547; telex 2742; Ambassador: GREGOR KOEBEL.

Indonesia: LB 711, Jalan Kumbang Pasang, Bandar Seri Begawan; tel. (02) 21852; Ambassador: ZUWIR DJAMAL.

Japan: LB 16464 Kampong Mabohai, Jalan Kebangsaan, POB 3001; tel. (02) 29265; telex 2564; Chargé d'affaires: YUTAKA SHIMOMOTO.

Korea, Republic: Kampong Sungai Tilong, Batu 7, Jalan Muara; tel. (02) 30383; telex 2615; Ambassador: KANG SUNG-KU.

Malaysia: 6th Floor, Darussalam Bldg, Jalan Sultan, Bandar Seri Begawan; tel. (02) 28410; telex 2401; High Commissioner: ZAINAL ABIDIN BIN MOKHTAR.

Pakistan: LB 277, Kampong Telanai, Mile 3, Jalan Tutong; tel. (02) 51623; Ambassador: MIR ABAD HUSSAIN.

Philippines: 4th–5th Floors, Badi-ah Bldg, Mile 1, Jalan Tutong, Bandar Seri Begawan 1930; tel. (02) 28241; telex 2673; Ambassador: EUSEBIO A. ABAQUIN.

Singapore: 5th Floor, RBA Plaza, Jalan Sultan, Bandar Seri Begawan; tel. (02) 27583; telex 2385; High Commissioner: EDWARD LEE KWONG FOO.

Thailand: LB 241, Jalan Elia Fatimah, Kampong Kiarong, POB 2989, Bandar Seri Begawan 1929; tel. (02) 29653; telex 2607; Ambassador: SOMCHIT INSINGHA.

United Kingdom: 3rd Floor, Hongkong and Shanghai Bank Chambers, Jalan Pemancha, POB 2197, Bandar Seri Begawan; tel. (02) 22231; telex 2211; High Commissioner: ROGER WESTBROOK.

USA: 3rd Floor, Teck Guan Plaza, cnr Jalan Sultan and Jalan McArthur, Bandar Seri Begawan; tel. (02) 29670; telex 2609; Ambassador: THOMAS C. FERGUSON.

Judicial System
SUPREME COURT

The Supreme Court consists of the Court of Appeal and the High Court.

Chief Registrar, Supreme Court: E. T. S. WOOLLEY.

The Court of Appeal: composed of the President and two Commissioners appointed by the Sultan. The Court of Appeal considers criminal and civil appeals against the decisions of the High Court. **President:** Sir TI-LIANG YANG.

The High Court: composed of the Chief Justice and such Commissioners as the Sultan may appoint. In its appellate jurisdiction, the High Court considers appeals in criminal and civil matters against the decisions of the Subordinate Courts. The High Court has unlimited original jurisdiction in criminal and civil matters. **Chief Justice:** Dato Sir DENYS ROBERTS.

OTHER COURTS

The Subordinate Courts: presided over by the Chief Magistrate and magistrates, with limited original jurisdiction in civil and criminal matters.

The Courts of Kathis: deal solely with questions concerning Islamic religion, marriage and divorce. Appeals lie from these courts to the Sultan in the Religious Council. **Chief Kathi:** Pehin Haji ABDUL HAMID BIN BAKAL.

Religion

The official religion of Brunei is Islam, and the Sultan is head of the Islamic population. The majority of the Malay population (about 130,000) are Muslims of the Sunni sect. The Chinese population is either Buddhist, Confucianist, Daoist or Christian. Large numbers of the indigenous ethnic groups are animists of various types. The remainder of the population are mostly Christians, generally Roman Catholics, Anglicans or members of the American Methodist Church of Southern Asia.

CHRISTIANITY
The Anglican Communion

Brunei is within the jurisdiction of the Anglican diocese of Kuching (Malaysia).

The Roman Catholic Church

Brunei is within the jurisdiction of the Roman Catholic archdiocese of Kuching (Malaysia).

The Press
NEWSPAPERS

Borneo Bulletin: 74 Jalan Sungei, POB 69, Kuala Belait; tel. (03) 34344; telex 3336; f. 1953; weekly (Sat.); English; independent; Gen. Man. I. M. MACGREGOR; Editor HAN J. LING; circ. 35,000.

Brunei Darussalam Newsletter: Information Section, Broadcasting and Information Dept, Ministry of Culture, Youth and Sports, Jalan McArthur, Bandar Seri Begawan; monthly; English; circ. 14,000.

Pelita Brunei: Information Section, Broadcasting and Information Dept, Ministry of Culture, Youth and Sports, Jalan McArthur, Bandar Seri Begawan; f. 1956; weekly (Wed.); Malay; govt newspaper; distributed free; circ. 45,000.

Salam: c/o Brunei Shell Petroleum Co Sdn Bhd, Seria; tel. (037) 2106; f. 1953; monthly; Malay and English; distributed free to employees of the Brunei Shell Petroleum Co Sdn Bhd; circ. 9,000.

Publishers

Borneo Printers & Trading Sdn Bhd: POB 2211, Bandar Seri Begawan 1922; tel. (02) 24856.

The Brunei Press: POB 69, Kuala Belait; tel. (03) 34344; telex 3336; f. 1959; Gen. Man. I. M. MACGREGOR.

Capital Trading & Printing Pte Ltd: POB 1089; tel. (02) 44541.

Eastern Printers & Trading Co Ltd: POB 2304; tel. (02) 20434.

Leong Bros: 52 Jalan Bunga Kuning, POB 164, Seria; tel. (03) 22381.

Offset Printing House: POB 1111; tel. (02) 24477.

Government Publishing House

Government Printer: Government Printing Office, Lapangan Terbang Lama, Berakas; tel. (02) 44541.

Radio and Television

In 1988 there were an estimated 82,000 radio receivers and 54,000 television receivers in use.

Radio Television Brunei: Dept of Broadcasting and Information, Bandar Seri Begawan 2042; tel. (02) 43111; telex 2311; f. 1957; two radio networks, one broadcasting in Malay and local dialects, the other in English, Chinese (Mandarin) and Gurkha; a colour television service transmits programmes in Malay and English; Dir Pengiran BADARUDIN Pengiran GHANI.

Finance
BANKING

The Treasury Department performs most of the functions of a central bank.

Commercial Bank

International Bank of Brunei: Bangunan IBB, Lot 155, Jalan Roberts, POB 2725, Bandar Seri Begawan; tel. (02) 20686; telex 2320; f. 1981 as Island Development Bank; Man. Dir AZIZ BIN ABDUL RAHMAN; 25 brs.

BRUNEI
Directory

Foreign Banks

Bank of America NT and SA (USA): Ground Floor, Suri Bldg, Jalan Tutong, POB 2280, Bandar Seri Begawan; tel. (02) 24911; telex 2235; f. 1972; Vice-Pres. and Country Man. BRUNO CORNELIO; 2 brs.

Citibank NA (USA): 147 Jalan Pemancha, Bandar Seri Begawan 2085; tel. (02) 43983; telex 2224; Country Corporate Officer DAVID CONNER; 2 brs.

The Hongkong and Shanghai Banking Corpn (Hong Kong): cnr Jalan Sultan and Jalan Pemancha, POB 59, Bandar Seri Begawan; tel. (02) 42305; telex 2273; f. 1947; acquired assets of National Bank of Brunei in 1986; Man. I. C. A. KING-HOLFORD; 9 brs.

Malayan Banking Bhd (Malaysia): 148 Jalan Pemancha, POB 167, Bandar Seri Begawan; tel. (02) 42494; telex 2316; f. 1960; Man. WAN MOHD DEN WAN MOHD ZIN; 3 brs.

Overseas Union Bank Ltd (Singapore): Unit G5, RBA Plaza, Jalan Sultan, Bandar Seri Begawan 2085; tel. (02) 25477; telex 2256; f. 1973; Man. LAU KUIN SAM; 2 brs.

Standard Chartered Bank (UK): 51–55 Jalan Sultan, POB 186, Bandar Seri Begawan 1901; tel. (02) 42386; telex 2223; f. 1958; Man. M. G. PALIN; 11 brs.

United Malayan Banking Corpn Bhd (Malaysia): 141 Jalan Pemancha, POB 435, Bandar Seri Begawan; tel. (02) 22516; telex 2207; f. 1963; Man. LIOW CHEE HWA; 1 br.

INSURANCE

There are several locally-incorporated insurance companies and a number of international insurance companies.

Trade and Industry

Trade in Brunei is largely conducted by European and Chinese agency houses and by Chinese merchants.

CHAMBERS OF COMMERCE

Brunei State Chamber of Commerce: POB 2246, Bandar Seri Begawan 1922; tel. (02) 28533; telex 2203; Chair. KIYOSHI SAWAMURA; Sec. ALASTAIR SEYB; 89 mems.

Chinese Chamber of Commerce: POB 281, 9 Jalan Pretty, Bandar Seri Begawan; tel. (02) 34374; Chair. LIM ENG MING.

Indian Chamber of Commerce: POB 974, Bandar Seri Begawan; tel. (02) 23886; Pres. BIKRAMJIT BHALLA.

Malay Chamber of Commerce: POB 156, Room 411, Malay Teachers' Bldg, Jalan Kianggeh, Bandar Seri Begawan; f. 1964; Chair. A. A. HAPIZ LAKSAMANA; 120 mems.

TRADE UNIONS

Total membership of the four trade unions was c. 4,000 in 1983.

Brunei Government Junior Officers' Union: Bandar Seri Begawan; Pres. Haji ALI BIN Haji NASAR; Gen. Sec. Haji OMARALI BIN Haji MOHIDDIN.

Brunei Government Medical and Health Workers' Union: POB 459, Bandar Seri Begawan; Pres. Pengiran Haji MOHIDDIN BIN Pengiran TAJUDDIN; Gen. Sec. HANAFI BIN ANAI.

Brunei Oilfield Workers' Union: POB 175, Seria; f. 1961; 505 mems; Pres. SEMITH BIN SABLI; Vice-Pres. MOHD ALI Haji YUSOF; Sec.-Gen. ABDUL WAHAB JUNAIDI.

Royal Brunei Custom Department Staff Union: Custom Dept, Kuala Belait; f. 1972; Pres. HASSAN BIN BAKAR; Gen. Sec. ABDUL ADIS BIN TARIP.

Transport

RAILWAYS

There are no public railways in Brunei. The Brunei Shell Petroleum Co Sdn Bhd maintains a 19.3-km section of light railway between Seria and Badas.

ROADS

In 1988 there were about 1,450 km of roads in Brunei. The main highway connects Bandar Seri Begawan, Tutong and Kuala Belait. A 59-km coastal road links Muara and Tutong. Bus services operate between Brunei/Muara, Tutong and Belait districts.

Land Transport Department: Ministry of Communications, Batu 2½, Jalan Gadong, Bandar Seri Begawan; tel. (02) 24775; Controller Haji MOHD KASSIM BIN Haji JOHAN.

SHIPPING

Most sea traffic is handled by a deep-water port at Muara, 27 km from the capital. The original, smaller port at Bandar Seri Begawan itself is mainly used for local river-going vessels. There is a port at Kuala Belait which takes shallow-draught vessels and serves mainly the Shell oil field and Seria. Owing to Brunei's shallow waters at Seria, tankers are unable to come up to the shore to load and crude oil from the oil terminal is pumped through an underwater loading line to a single buoy mooring, to which the tankers are moored. At Lumut there is a 4.5-km jetty for liquefied natural gas (LNG) carriers.

Rivers are the principal means of communication in the interior and boats or water taxis the main form of transport for most residents of the water villages. Larger water taxis operate daily to Temburong district.

Bee Seng Shipping Co: 1½ Miles Jalan Tutong, POB 92, Bandar Seri Begawan; telex 2219.

Brunei Shell Tankers Sendirian Berhad: Seria, Berhad; tel. (02) 373999; telex 3313; operated by Shell Tankers BV; 7 vessels.

CIVIL AVIATION

There is an international airport at Bandar Seri Begawan. Substantial upgrading work was completed in 1987. The Brunei Shell Petroleum Co Sdn Bhd operates a private airfield at Anduki for helicopter services.

Directorate of Civil Aviation: Brunei International Airport; tel. (02) 30142; telex 2267; Dir JOB LIM.

Royal Brunei Airlines Ltd: RBA Plaza, POB 737, Bandar Seri Begawan; tel. (02) 40500; telex 2737; f. 1974; operates services to Bangkok, Dubai, Darwin, Hong Kong, Jakarta, Kota Kinabalu, Kuala Lumpur, Kuching, Manila, Singapore and Taiwan; Chair. Prince JEFRI BOLKIAH; Man. Dir Pengiran TENGAH METASSIM; fleet of 1 B737-200, 1 B737-200 QC and 2 B757-@200.

Tourism

Tourism is relatively underdeveloped: in 1986 only 6,578 tourists visited Brunei.

Information Bureau: Information Section, Broadcasting and Information Dept, Prime Minister's Office, Bandar Seri Begawan 2041; tel. (02) 4040007; telex 2614.

BULGARIA

Introductory Survey

Location, Climate, Language, Religion, Flag, Capital

The People's Republic of Bulgaria lies in the eastern Balkans, in south-eastern Europe. It is bounded by Romania to the north, by Turkey and Greece to the south and by Yugoslavia to the west. The country has an eastern coastline on the Black Sea. The climate is one of fairly sharp contrasts between winter and summer. Temperatures in Sofia are generally between $-5°C$ (23°F) and 28°C (82°F). The official language is Bulgarian, a member of the Slavonic group, written in the Cyrillic alphabet. Minority languages include Turkish and Macedonian. Most Christians adhere to the Bulgarian Orthodox Church, while there is a substantial minority of Muslims. The national flag (proportions 3 by 2) has three equal horizontal stripes, of white, green and red, with the state emblem (a lion, flanked by sheaves of grain and surmounted by a five-pointed red star) in the upper hoist. The capital is Sofia.

Recent History

Formerly a monarchy, Bulgaria allied with Nazi Germany in the Second World War and joined in the occupation of Yugoslavia in 1941. King Boris died in 1943 and was succeeded by his young son, Simeon II. In September 1944 the Fatherland Front, a left-wing alliance formed in 1942, seized power, with help from the USSR, and installed a government led by Kimon Georgiyev. In September 1946 the monarchy was abolished by popular referendum, and a republic was proclaimed. The first post-war election was held in October, when the Fatherland Front received 70.8% of the votes and won 364 seats, of which 277 were held by the Bulgarian Communist Party (BCP), in the 465-member National Assembly. In November Georgi Dimitrov, the First Secretary of the BCP and a veteran international revolutionary, became Chairman of the Council of Ministers (Prime Minister) in a government formed from members of the Fatherland Front. All opposition parties were abolished, and a new constitution, based on the Soviet model, was adopted in December 1947. Dimitrov was replaced as Chairman of the Council of Ministers by Vasil Kolarov in March 1949, but remained leader of the BCP until his death in July. His successor as Party leader, Vulko Chervenkov, also became Chairman of the Council of Ministers in February 1950. Political trials and executions became less frequent after the death in 1953 of Iosif Stalin, the Soviet leader, and the rehabilitation of those who had been disgraced began in 1956.

Todor Zhivkov succeeded Chervenkov as leader of the BCP in March 1954, although the latter remained Chairman of the Council of Ministers until April 1956, when he was replaced by Anton Yugov. Following an ideological struggle within the BCP, Zhivkov also became Chairman of the Council of Ministers in November 1962. In April 1965 an attempted coup against the Government was discovered. In May 1971 a new constitution was adopted, and in July Zhivkov relinquished his position as Chairman of the Council of Ministers to become the first President of the newly-formed State Council. He was re-elected in 1976, in 1981 and in 1986. In September 1978 a purge of BCP membership commenced. At the twelfth BCP Congress, held in March and April 1981, the party's leader was restyled General Secretary. In June, following elections to the National Assembly, a new government was formed, headed by Grisha Filipov, a member of the BCP's Political Bureau, in succession to Stanko Todorov, who had been Chairman of the Council of Ministers since 1971. A broad reshuffle, affecting senior posts in the BCP and the Government, was announced in January 1984; it included the merging of four ministries into two in the sphere of trade and industry, and was widely believed to have economic, rather than political, ends. In 1985 the BCP leadership initiated a campaign against corruption and inefficiency, resulting in the dismissal and replacement of a number of ministers and senior officials. In 1986 the Council of Ministers underwent extensive reorganization. Several ministries and state committees were restructured. In March Georgi Atanasov, a former Vice-President of the State Council, replaced Filipov as Chairman of the Council of Ministers.

At the thirteenth BCP Congress, held in April 1986, Zhivkov advocated the elimination of excessive bureaucracy, an improvement in the integration of self-governing organizations with centralized state management and an increase in the scope for initiative among such organizations. He also placed great emphasis on the importance to the national economy of an acceleration of scientific and technological progress. Following elections to the National Assembly in June, Zhivkov was unanimously re-elected President of the State Council.

In August 1987 the National Assembly approved further structural reforms and personnel changes in the Council of Ministers. The number of Deputy Chairmen was reduced from nine to one. Other changes included the abolition of four councils (the Council for Agriculture and Forestry, the Council for Economic Affairs, the Council for Social Affairs and the Council for Intellectual Development, which were founded only in 1986). Three ministries and several state committees were also abolished, including the Ministry of Trade (which was itself established only in 1986 to replace three ministries), and four new ministries were created in their place. The National Assembly also approved extensive administrative reform, aimed at increased efficiency and the promotion of the principles of self-government. The reforms included the creation of nine administrative regions to replace the existing 28 districts and involved the relocation of nearly 100,000 government employees. Amendments to the Constitution were also under consideration.

Proposals to restrict the tenure of office by high-ranking officials of the BCP to two five-year terms were approved, in principle, at a BCP conference in January 1988. This was followed in March by local elections, for which the authorities permitted, for the first time, the nomination of candidates other than those endorsed by the BCP, and in which candidates who had been presented by independent public organizations and workers' collectives obtained about one-quarter of the total votes cast. However, much of the Soviet-style programme of reform (*perestroistvo*), advocated at the 1987 session of the National Assembly, was not implemented in 1988. At a plenum of the BCP, held in July 1988, several prominent proponents of reform, including one member of the party's Political Bureau, were dismissed from office. The leading campaigners of an environmental pressure group, which had been established earlier in the year without official sanction, were expelled from the BCP at the same plenum.

In January 1985 reports were received in the West that Bulgaria had begun a campaign to force the country's Turkish minority to adopt Slavic names in advance of the next census, planned for the end of that year, and loss of life was claimed to have occurred where the campaign had met resistance. It was suggested that such action might have been taken in order to disguise the fact that the ethnic Turkish population, which constitutes nearly 10% of Bulgaria's total population, has a much higher rate of natural increase than the Slav population. The Bulgarian Government denied that coercion was being used in a programme in which the ethnic Turks were claimed to be participating voluntarily. Attempts have been made in the West, without proof, to link this issue with a series of bomb attacks by unidentified terrorists in Bulgaria in 1984, in which several people were killed. Following the population census (held in December 1985), Bulgaria was condemned by the Turkish Government for 'seeking to eliminate all statistical evidence of its ethnic Turks'. The census questionnaires were criticized for allowing no scope for members of national minorities to register themselves as anything other than Bulgarian. In 1986 the Bulgarian Government continued to refute allegations, made by Amnesty International, that more than 250 ethnic Turks had been arrested or imprisoned for refusing to accept new identity cards, and that many more had been forced to resettle away from their homes, in other regions of the country. In December 1986 Naim Süleymanoglu (formerly Naum Shalamanov), a 19-year old Bulgarian world champion weight-lifter of Turkish ancestry, defected to the West during a tournament in Australia. Süleymanoglu repeated earlier Turkish claims, and asserted that Turks were being tortured by the Bulgarian authorities. In September 1987 Bulgaria's decision to declare 3 March a public holiday, to commemorate the establishment of the first Bulgarian state after 500 years of Turkish occupation, was criticized by the Turkish Government as further evidence of Bulgarian determination forcibly to assimilate its ethnic Turkish population. Bulgaria responded by condemning what it regarded as the pan-Turkish tendencies of the Turkish Government, denouncing them as a threat to peace between the two countries.

In foreign affairs, Bulgaria has close links with other Eastern European countries through its membership of the Warsaw Pact (see p. 207) and of the CMEA (see p. 124). Relations with Western states have steadily improved, and co-operation in economic and technical fields is increasing. However, relations between Bulgaria and Italy became strained in November 1982 after Mehmet Ağca, a Turkish citizen, had claimed Bulgarian involvement in his attempt to assassinate Pope John Paul II in 1981. In spite of the related arrest and detention of Sergei Antonov, a Bulgarian airline official in Rome, Ağca's claim remained unsubstantiated, and in April 1986 Antonov returned to Bulgaria, having been acquitted in the previous month, on the grounds that there was insufficient evidence to convict him. In February 1988 the Ministers of Foreign Affairs of the six Balkan nations met, in the first conference at such a senior level, to discuss plans for increased regional co-operation. On the eve of the conference, Bulgaria and Turkey signed a pledge to further bilateral economic and social relations, an agreement which was expected to lead to discussions on the situation of the ethnic Turkish community in Bulgaria.

Government

Under the 1971 constitution, the supreme organ of state power is the unicameral National Assembly, with 400 members elected for five years by universal adult suffrage in single-member constituencies. The Assembly elects the State Council (27 members were elected in June 1986) to be its permanent organ. There is no constitutional provision for a Head of State, but some of the equivalent functions are exercised by the President of the State Council. The Council of Ministers, the highest organ of state administration, is elected by (and responsible to) the Assembly. Political power is held by the Bulgarian Communist Party (BCP), which dominates the Fatherland Front. The Front presents an approved list of candidates for elections to all representative bodies (members of the National Assembly were elected unopposed in June 1986). The BCP's highest authority is the Party Congress, convened every five years. The Congress elects a Central Committee (195 members were elected in April 1986) to supervise Party work. To direct its policy, the Committee elects a Political Bureau (Politburo), with nine full members and six candidate members in late 1988. For local administration, Bulgaria comprises nine regions (divided into a total of 273 municipalities), each with a Regional People's Council. Each region comprises a number of municipalities and has its own administrative centre.

Defence

Bulgaria is a member of the Warsaw Pact. Military service is for two years in the army and air force, and for three years in the navy. According to Western estimates, the total strength of the armed forces in June 1988 was 157,800 (including 94,000 conscripts), comprising an army of 115,000, an air force of 34,000 and a navy of 8,800. Paramilitary forces include 15,000 border troops and 7,500 security police. There is a voluntary People's Militia of 150,000. Defence expenditure for 1988 was estimated at 1,405m. leva.

Economic Affairs

Bulgaria is a very fertile country. After 1945, agriculture was organized on a large-scale co-operative and mechanized basis, centred on huge state-controlled agro-industrial complexes. These became self-financing in 1987, when there were 295 complexes in all, encompassing about 83% of the total land area under cultivation. Between 1965 and 1975 the labour force in agriculture and forestry declined from 1,891,000 (44.4% of the total working population) to 1,049,000 (23.6%). The principal crops are wheat, maize, barley, sugar beet, grapes and tobacco, and in 1985 agriculture (excluding forestry) accounted for 13.5% of net material product (NMP). Tobacco is an increasingly important crop. Although it occupies scarcely 2.5% of land under cultivation, it accounts for 20% of all agricultural production and 40% of the revenue of the National Agro-Industrial Union. In 1985 about 27% of Bulgaria's total agricultural output came from private plots, which occupied nearly 14% of the total area under cultivation, and accounted for almost 40% of total meat production. There is a large exportable surplus of processed agricultural products. Owing to adverse weather conditions prevalent in 1987, agricultural output declined by 4.3% compared with 1986. Industry (mining, manufacturing and utilities) provided 60% of NMP in 1987.

Between 1965 and 1975 the labour force in manufacturing increased from 991,000 (23.3% of the total) to 1,438,000 (32.3%). Food, beverages and tobacco form the largest manufacturing sector, accounting for about 24% of total output in 1987. The engineering and electronics sectors, in particular, have been greatly developed, with production increasing by 11% in 1987, as have the chemical fertilizer and metallurgical industries.

The 1976–80 Five-Year Plan achieved a 35% increase in industrial production, and a 20% increase in agricultural output, with three-quarters of the Plan's budget spent on further modernization and reconstruction of industry. Foreign trade increased by 80%. The Five-Year Plan for 1981–85 projected a continuation of the slowdown in economic growth, and NMP rose by 20%. Priority was given to the development of heavy industry. Encouragement was also given to the fusion of state and co-operative ownership. In 1982 a 'new economic mechanism' was introduced to increase efficiency and to ensure the elimination of the weakest enterprises: subsidies to individual companies were reduced, while wages were linked to output. Bulgaria was compelled to import grain from the West in 1985, when the harvest declined to only about 5m. metric tons. However, output increased to more than 8m. tons in 1986, and exceeded 7m. tons in 1987. Foreign trade turnover for the 1981–85 period increased at an average annual rate of 6.6%, with a little more than 50% of export earnings derived from products of the mechanical engineering and electronic industries. In the first six months of 1988 trade increased by 6.2% compared with the equivalent period in 1987, with import and export transactions both rising (by 5.6% and 6.8% respectively). In 1985 Bulgaria imported 13.4m. metric tons of petroleum, and, in common with other CMEA countries, was unfavourably affected by the fall in the international price of oil, paying more than the average world market price for its imports from the USSR and earning little convertible currency from its re-exports.

Bulgaria has one of the lowest debts to the West of all CMEA countries. The gross external debt rose from US $4,100m. in 1986 to nearly $6,000m. by mid-1988. In 1985 the Government borrowed a total of $470m. in three major loans from Western banks, both to help to develop its electronic and high-technology industries and to offset some of the economic consequences of the adverse weather conditions. The drought affected not only crop production and water supplies but also electric power generation, and caused the Government to introduce wide-ranging price increases and to enforce the rationing of electricity.

The draft Five-Year Plan for 1986–90 envisaged an acceleration of the development of science and technology and, accordingly, an increase in the production of machine tools and technical equipment. It also provided for a restructuring of foreign-trade activities and for reforms in the structure and policies of domestic economic management, with a limited amount of decentralization of decision-making and a higher degree of independence for self-governing enterprises, more than 1,500 of which were to be established during the five-year period. A new law on public enterprises was scheduled to be introduced in January 1989, providing for a comprehensive 'privatization' of all state-controlled industries. It was believed that shares in the newly-formed companies would be available to foreign, as well as Bulgarian, investors. A major reorganization of the banking system began in June 1987. As a result of a rise in the country's foreign debt in convertible currencies, the Government established eight new commercial banks to function as self-financing, joint-stock companies. The role of the new banks was to work in close co-operation with industrial enterprises in an advisory capacity, and they were to have the additional power both to liquidate companies that experienced serious financial difficulties and to enforce mergers. However, the new banks were not to be entirely independent, as they were required to deposit one-half of their capital with the Bulgarian National Bank prior to registration. Furthermore, the National Bank retained the right to dissolve any banks incurring a financial loss. Tax reductions and other financial incentives for increased agricultural production in the private sector were also to be introduced. In 1986 it was estimated that NMP would increase by 30% over the 1986-90 period, foreign trade by 32-37% and industrial production by 27%. By 1990 production of the electronic and mechanical engineering industries would rise by 70-75% and account for 70% of total exports. Compared with the previous year, NMP rose by 5.1% in 1987 and was expected to increase by 6.1% in 1988. In 1987 industrial production increased by 4.3% (and was expected to grow by 5% in 1988) and agricultural output fell by 3.8%, although it was predicted to increase by 5.5% in 1988. Production in the engineering sector rose by 9.3%.

Bulgaria produces less than one-third of its energy needs, and priority is being given to the full development of indigenous energy resources. Bulgaria's first nuclear power station, constructed by Soviet engineers, opened in 1974, and nuclear power, which was providing 29% of electric energy in 1985, was expected to provide 40% by 1990 and 60% by 2000. Loading of the fifth reactor at the nuclear power station at Kozlodui was completed in January 1988. Construction of a sixth reactor was under way. When completed, this would enable the station to produce 43% of the national electricity supply. A second nuclear power station was being built at Belene, on the Danube. Bulgaria's first wind power station, at the Frangen plateau, north of Varna, was due to begin operating in the mid-1980s. Production of electricity increased by 6.6% in 1987. In the first six months of 1988 electricity supplied 35% of total energy consumption. Coal, iron ore, copper, lead and zinc are mined, while petroleum is extracted on the Black Sea coast. Compared with the previous year, total coal output rose by 4.4% in 1987, to reach 36.8m. metric tons. Bulgaria became self-sufficient in pig-iron in 1980 and produced 1.7m. tons in 1987.

In June 1986 the construction of a 1,635-km gas pipeline, linking Bulgaria to the USSR, was completed. In the mid-1980s the USSR supplied Bulgaria with 5,500m. cu m of gas per year, and the gas being conveyed through the new pipeline is expected to meet one-fifth of Bulgaria's demand for hydrocarbon products.

Foreign trade is a state monopoly, and in 1987 81.5% was with the other members of the CMEA, and 59.3% with the USSR alone. Since 1980, in an attempt to increase trade and co-operation with the West, foreign companies have been encouraged to establish joint enterprises in Bulgaria. Long-term reciprocal trade agreements with Czechoslovakia and the People's Republic of China were signed in December 1985, and in January 1986 a 10-year agreement on economic, scientific and technical co-operation was signed with France. In 1987, according to provisional estimates, import expenditure totalled 14,067m. leva, with revenue from exports amounting to 13,802m. leva. Considerable tourist development has played an important part in alleviating Bulgaria's shortage of foreign exchange.

Budget proposals for 1988 envisaged total expenditure of 22,952m. leva, of which 10,842m. leva was to be allocated to the national economy, 4,304m. leva to education, culture and health, and 3,914m. leva to social security. Projected revenue was to balance at 22,952m. leva.

Social Welfare

State social insurance is directed by the Department of Public Insurance and the Pensions Directorate. In 1987 3,726.9m. leva (18% of the state budget) were allotted to social security. Workers are paid compensation during sick leave. Women are entitled to full paid leave before and after childbirth. All pensions are non-contributory. Retirement pensions consist of a basic sum plus up to 12% allowance for additional service, over the minimum requirement. The basic pension is related to the average monthly pay in three of the last 15 years of service. Retirement age varies from 45 to 60 years, depending on the job. Women retire five years earlier than men.

Since 1951 all medical services and treatment have been provided free for the whole population. In 1988 there were 88,000 hospital beds and 22,000 beds in sanatoriums and health spas. In 1983 there were 24,000 physicians. All medical treatment establishments and medical schools, training colleges and research institutes are controlled by the Ministry of Public Health and Social Welfare. Departments of Public Health in the regional People's Councils supervise medical work, together with the Bulgarian Red Cross.

Education

Education in Bulgaria is compulsory, and provided free of charge, between the ages of six and 16 years. It is administered by the Bulgarian Ministry of National Education, although direct organization of kindergartens and schools is exercised by specialized organs of local People's Councils. In 1986 kindergartens were attended by 83.2% of all children between the ages of three and six, but in 1988 plans were being discussed to make attendance at kindergartens compulsory from the age of five. The unified secondary polytechnical school was first introduced in the 1981/82 school year to provide primary and secondary education in three stages, in accordance with plans to restructure the Bulgarian system of education. The first stage covers schooling from the first to the 10th grade, while in the second stage, which lasts one and a half school years, students obtain general vocational qualifications, and at the third stage, which lasts six months, they acquire vocational qualifications in a narrow speciality, as well as specific job-training in an industrial environment. In addition, vocational-technical schools provide primary education and workers' professional qualifications, secondary vocational-technical schools provide secondary education and workers' professional qualifications, and technical colleges (tekhnikums) offer secondary training for specialists in industry, construction, agriculture, transport, trade and public health. After completing secondary education, students are entitled to continue their training in semi-higher institutes or in higher educational institutions. In the 1986/87 school year 349,131 pupils attended kindergartens, 1,261,544 attended primary and secondary schools, and 117,138 students took courses at semi-higher and higher educational institutions.

Public Holidays

1989: 2 January (for New Year), 3 March (Liberation Day), 1-2 May (Labour Days), 24 May (Education Day), 9-10 September (National Days), 7 November (Anniversary of Russia's October Revolution).

1990: 1 January (New Year), 3 March (Liberation Day), 1-2 May (Labour Days), 24 May (Education Day), 9-10 September (National Days), 7 November (Anniversary of Russia's October Revolution).

Weights and Measures

The metric system is in force.

Statistical Survey

Source (unless otherwise stated): Central Statistical Office at the Council of Ministers, Sofia, Panayot Volov St 2; tel. 46-01; telex 22001.

Area and Population

AREA, POPULATION AND DENSITY

Area (sq km)*	110,912†
Population (census results)	
2 December 1975	8,727,771
4 December 1985	
Males	4,430,061
Females	4,518,327
Total	8,948,388
Population (official estimates at 31 December)	
1985	8,949,900
1986	8,966,500
1987	8,973,596
Density (per sq km) at 31 December 1987	80.9

* Including territorial waters of frontier rivers (267.8 sq km).
† 42,823 sq miles.

PRINCIPAL TOWNS
(population at 1985 census)

Sofia (capital)	1,114,759	Stara Zagora	150,803
Plovdiv	342,131	Pleven	129,766
Varna	302,211	Tolbukhin	109,066
Ruse (Roussé)	183,746	Sliven	102,423
Burgas (Bourgas)	182,549	Shumen	100,116

1987 (estimates at 31 December): Sofia 1,128,707; Plovdiv 349,000; Varna 303,000; Ruse 186,000; Burgas 186,000; Stara Zagora 153,000.

BIRTHS, MARRIAGES AND DEATHS

	Registered live births		Registered marriages*		Registered deaths	
	Number	Rate (per 1,000)	Number	Rate (per 1,000)	Number	Rate (per 1,000)
1980	128,190	14.5	69,726	7.9	97,950	11.1
1981	124,372	14.0	66,539	7.5	95,441	10.7
1982	124,166	13.9	67,154	7.5	100,293	11.2
1983	122,993	13.8	67,032	7.5	102,182	11.4
1984	122,303	13.6	65,361	7.3	101,419	11.3
1985	118,955	13.3	66,682	7.4	107,485	12.0
1986†	120,414	13.4	65,153	7.3	101,836	11.4
1987†	115,586	12.9	n.a.	n.a.	107,909	12.0

* Including marriages of Bulgarian nationals outside the country but excluding those of aliens in Bulgaria.
† Provisional.

Expectation of Life (years at birth, 1978–80): Males 68.35; Females 73.55.

ECONOMICALLY ACTIVE POPULATION (1975 census)

	Males	Females	Total
Agriculture, hunting, forestry and fishing	498,545	550,594	1,049,139
Mining and quarrying	62,534	22,310	84,844
Manufacturing	761,321	676,921	1,438,242
Electricity, gas and water	21,368	6,615	28,253
Construction	288,429	61,927	350,356
Trade, restaurants and hotels	127,031	228,721	355,752
Transport, storage and communication	231,007	67,575	298,582
Financing, insurance, real estate and business services	8,273	23,528	31,801
Community, social and personal services	366,604	443,325	809,929
Activities not adequately described	326	560	886
Total labour force	**2,365,708**	**2,082,076**	**4,447,784**

1985 census: Total labour force 4,802,005 (males 2,515,894; females 2,286,111) aged 16 years and over.

EMPLOYEES IN THE 'SOCIALIZED' SECTOR*
(annual averages, '000)

	1985	1986	1987
Agriculture*	878.8	848.1	821.5
Forestry	16.3	24.3	25.5
Industry†	1,411.1	1,403.0	1,422.3
Construction	360.6	359.2	359.1
Commerce	355.2	360.7	361.4
Transport and storage	257.0	263.2	259.5
Communications	42.5	43.1	43.8
Finance and insurance services	22.2	22.4	23.0
Education and culture	311.7	317.2	317.6
Public health, welfare and sports	201.0	201.8	207.7
Administration	54.1	54.3	57.2
Science and scientific institutes	82.1	83.0	85.8
Housing and community services‡	54.4	56.7	58.7
Total (incl. others)	**4,094.7**	**4,076.5**	**4,083.6**

* Excluding agricultural co-operatives (employing more than 280,000 people in 1975) but including state farms and machine-tractor stations.
† Mining, manufacturing and electricity.
‡ Including water supply.

BULGARIA

Agriculture

PRINCIPAL CROPS ('000 metric tons)

	1984	1985	1986
Wheat	4,836	3,068	4,327
Rice (paddy)	61	55	69†
Barley	1,279	800	1,144
Maize	2,994	1,350	2,848
Rye	37	49	35†
Oats	25	41	25†
Potatoes	418	439	491
Dry beans	46	43	46
Dry peas	20	17	18*
Soybeans	72	37	54
Sunflower seed	462	365	489
Seed cotton	15	14	18
Cabbages	143	102	150*
Tomatoes	905	781	760
Cauliflowers	4	2	4*
Pumpkins, squash and gourds	59	48	57*
Cucumbers and gherkins	169	150	150*
Green chillies and peppers	247	222	250*
Dry onions	62	77	90*
Green beans	18	16	20*
Green peas	17	11	12*
Water-melons	274	260	321*
Grapes	1,120	905	924
Apples	526	336	543
Pears	92	84	82
Plums	123	148	115
Peaches and nectarines	82	73	55
Apricots	24	57	26
Strawberries	20	11	15
Sugar beets	1,133	832	870
Tobacco leaves	141	126	107
Flax fibre and tow	2	2	2*
Hemp fibre and tow	4	2	4*

* FAO estimate.
† Unofficial figure.

1987 ('000 metric tons): Wheat 4,127; Barley 1,096; Maize 1,968; Soybeans 34; Dry beans 30; Potatoes 318; Sunflower seed 400; Seed cotton 17; Tomatoes 835; Grapes 916; Apples 323; Strawberries 13; Sugar beets 772; Tobacco leaves 105.

Source: FAO, mainly *Production Yearbook*.

LIVESTOCK ('000 head at 1 January each year)

	1986	1987	1988
Horses	120	121	123
Asses	345	n.a.	n.a.
Cattle	1,706	1,678	1,649
Pigs	3,912	4,050	4,034
Sheep	9,724	9,563	8,886
Goats	460	441	n.a.
Buffaloes	29	26	24
Poultry	39,227	39,735	41,424

LIVESTOCK PRODUCTS (metric tons)

	1984	1985	1986
Beef and veal	128,000	131,000	130,000
Buffalo meat	2,000	2,000	2,000
Mutton and lamb	79,000	77,000	83,000
Goats' meat	5,000	5,000	7,000
Pigmeat	335,000	334,000	361,000
Poultry meat	166,000	158,000	157,000
Edible offals	46,000*	45,000*	47,000*
Cow milk	2,162,000	2,118,000	2,176,000
Buffalo milk	25,000	23,000	22,000
Sheep milk	324,000	319,000	328,000
Goat milk	79,000	77,000	79,000
Butter	24,657	24,633	24,345
Cheese (all kinds)	185,857	179,235	191,000
Hen eggs	150,052	153,543	155,918
Other poultry eggs	2,313	2,767	2,015
Honey	10,030	9,731	10,760
Raw silk	205	206	180*
Wool:			
greasy	36,158	33,751	32,365
scoured	18,300	17,300	16,600
Cattle and buffalo hides	20,550*	20,550*	21,050*
Sheep skins	31,000*	31,000*	32,100*

* FAO estimate.

1987 (metric tons): Butter 26,000; Wool (greasy) 31,000; Honey 11,011.

Source: FAO, mainly *Production Yearbook*.

Forestry

ROUNDWOOD REMOVALS
('000 cubic metres, state forests only)

	1984	1985	1986
Sawlogs, veneer logs and logs for sleepers	1,287	1,218	1,090
Pulpwood	1,173	1,219	1,080
Other industrial wood	604	604	586
Fuel wood	1,727	1,769	1,769
Total	4,791	4,810	4,525

Source: FAO, *Yearbook of Forest Products*.

SAWNWOOD PRODUCTION ('000 cubic metres, incl. boxboards)

	1984	1985	1986
Coniferous (soft wood)	1,052	1,082	974
Broadleaved (hard wood)	407	413	341
Total	1,459	1,495	1,315

Railway sleepers ('000 cubic metres): 24 in 1984; 20 in 1985; 21 in 1986.

Source: FAO, *Yearbook of Forest Products*.

BULGARIA

Fishing

('000 metric tons, live weight)

	1984	1985	1986
Common carp	11.0	9.9	10.4
Southern blue whiting	2.6	4.8	10.7
Hakes	6.0	0.5	0.4
Atlantic redfishes	3.0	5.8	11.4
Chilean jack mackerel	14.7	2.3	—
Cape horse mackerel	50.5	42.8	48.5
European sprat	13.9	15.9	11.7
Other fishes (incl. unspecified)	6.1	9.9	8.6
Crustaceans	—	0.3	0.0
Molluscs	5.1	7.8	7.5
Total catch	112.9	100.2	109.2
of which:			
Inland waters	13.0	11.9	14.1
Mediterranean and Black Seas	15.4	17.0	12.9
Atlantic Ocean	69.8	68.9	82.2
Pacific Ocean	14.7	2.3	—

Source: FAO, *Yearbook of Fishery Statistics*.

Mining

('000 metric tons, unless otherwise indicated)

	1983	1984	1985
Anthracite	83 }	223	223
Other hard coal	160 }		
Lignite	26,805 }	32,136	30,657
Other brown coal	5,342 }		
Iron ore*	554	622	607
Copper ore*†	68	73	78
Lead ore*†	95	95	97
Zinc ore*†	68	65	68
Manganese ore*	13.1	13.0	11.3
Salt (refined)	87	89	89
Crude petroleum‡	300	300	300
Natural gas ('000 terajoules)	6	6	5

* Figures relate to the metal content of ores.
† Source: Metallgesellschaft Aktiengesellschaft (Frankfurt am Main).
‡ UN estimates.

1986 ('000 metric tons): Hard and brown coal 35,222; Iron ore (metal content) 661; Manganese ore (gross weight) 37.
1987 ('000 metric tons): Hard and brown coal 36,780; Iron ore (metal content) 567; Manganese ore (gross weight) 38.

Sources: UN, *Industrial Statistics Yearbook*; Committee for Social Information at the Council of Ministers, Sofia.

Industry

SELECTED PRODUCTS
('000 metric tons, unless otherwise indicated)

	1985	1986	1987
Refined sugar	457	n.a.	n.a.
Wine ('000 hectolitres)	3,859	n.a.	n.a.
Beer ('000 hectolitres)	5,838	6,025	6,209
Cigarettes and cigars (metric tons)	93,975	90,000	90,300
Cotton yarn (metric tons)[1]	82,700	85,100	83,900
Woven cotton fabrics ('000 metres)[2]	351,300	349,500	351,900
Flax and hemp yarn (metric tons)	9,500	8,500	8,200
Wool yarn (metric tons)[1]	35,100	35,200	32,200
Woven woollen fabrics ('000 metres)[2]	41,900	42,022	40,803
Woven fabrics of man-made fibres ('000 metres)[3]	36,400	37,200	37,800
Leather footwear ('000 pairs)	22,800	n.a.	n.a.
Rubber footwear ('000 pairs)	8,217	n.a.	n.a.
Chemical wood pulp	174.3	162.0	141.6
Paper	370.4	377.2	366.6
Rubber tyres ('000)[4]	1,659	1,668	1,851
Sulphuric acid (100%)	810.1	806.6	688.5
Caustic soda (96%)	157.1	143.6	108.6
Soda ash (98%)	1,036.6	1,054.2	1,070.2
Nitrogenous fertilizers (metric tons)[5]	837,736	817,900	801,400
Phosphate fertilizers (metric tons)[5]	171,705	132,400	130,800
Soap (metric tons)	25,800	n.a.	n.a.
Coke (gas and coke-oven)	1,087	1,156	1,314
Unworked glass—rectangles ('000 sq metres)	23,459	19,500	20,300
Clay building bricks (million)	1,122	1,145	1,077
Cement	5,296	5,640	5,589
Pig-iron and ferro-alloys	1,754	1,651	1,706
Crude steel	2,944	2,965	3,044
Tractors—10 h.p. and over (number)	5,350	5,094	4,751
Metal-working lathes (number)	5,477	5,912	4,888
Cranes (number)	1,457	n.a.	n.a.
Fork-lift trucks (number)	85,432	84,852	85,160
Refrigerators—household (number)	122,100	118,000	110,500
Washing machines—household (number)	155,900	159,200	171,700
Radio receivers (number)	41,500	38,000	56,100
Television receivers (number)	110,600	153,700	198,500
Electric energy (million kWh)	41,629	41,817	43,464

[1] Pure and mixed yarn. Figures for wool include yarn of man-made staple.
[2] Pure and mixed fabrics, after undergoing finishing processes.
[3] Finished fabrics, including fabrics of natural silk.
[4] Tyres for road motor vehicles (passenger cars and commercial vehicles).
[5] Figures for nitrogenous fertilizers are in terms of nitrogen, and for phosphate fertilizers in terms of phosphoric acid. Data for nitrogenous fertilizers include urea.

Finance

CURRENCY AND EXCHANGE RATES

Monetary Units
100 stotinki (singular: stotinka) = 1 lev (plural: leva).

Denominations
Coins: 1, 2, 5, 10, 20 and 50 stotinki; 1, 2 and 5 leva.
Notes: 1, 2, 5, 10 and 20 leva.

Sterling and Dollar Equivalents (31 July 1988)
£1 sterling = 2.241 leva;
US $1 = 1.310 leva;
100 leva = £44.63 = $76.34.

BULGARIA

STATE BUDGET (million leva)

Revenue	1986	1987*	1988*
National economy	20,384.8	19,011.8	21,109.0
Other receipts	1,622.7	1,661.0	1,843.0
Total	22,007.5	20,672.8	22,952.0

Expenditure	1986	1987*	1988*
National economy	11,377.6	9,590.1	10,842.0
Education, health, science, art and culture	3,736.8	3,884.1	4,304.0
Social security†	3,631.7	3,726.9	3,914.0
Administration	3,163.6	336.9	355.0
Other expenditure		3,124.8	3,537.0
Total	21,909.7	20,662.8	22,952.0

* Approved budget proposals.
† Including the pension fund for agricultural co-operatives.

COST OF LIVING
(Consumer Price Index; base: 1980 = 100)

	1984	1985	1986
All items	102.9	104.6	108.4

Source: ILO, *Year Book of Labour Statistics*.

NATIONAL ACCOUNTS
Net Material Product* (million leva at current market prices)

Activities of the Material Sphere	1984	1985	1986
Agriculture and livestock	4,511.8	3,425.1	4,062.1
Forestry	87.2	87.1	
Industry†	14,090.7	15,169.9	16,676.8
Construction	2,366.8	2,489.6	2,564.3
Trade, restaurants, etc.‡	1,328.0	1,801.0	1,227.0
Transport and storage	1,644.5	1,516.2	1,752.2
Communications	267.2	291.2	
Others	610.8	670.4	569.0
Total	24,907.0	25,450.5	26,851.4

* Defined as the total net value of goods and 'productive' services, including turnover taxes, produced by the economy. This excludes economic activities not contributing directly to material production, such as public administration, defence and personal and professional services.
† Principally manufacturing, mining, electricity, gas and water supply. The figures also include the value of hunting, fishing and logging when these activities are organized.
‡ Includes material and technical supply.

1987 (million leva): Agriculture and forestry 3,645; Industry 16,690; Construction 2,663; Total (incl. others) 28,213.

External Trade

PRINCIPAL COMMODITIES (million leva)

Imports f.o.b.	1982	1983	1984
Machinery and equipment	3,717.5	4,097.3	4,373.5
Power and electro-technical machinery	286.4	346.2	568.7
Mining, metallurgical and oil-drilling equipment	254.3	221.5	253.9
Tractors and agricultural machinery	261.6	288.1	287.7
Transport rolling stock	1,488.7	1,733.1	1,801.6
Fuels, mineral raw materials and metals	5,077.4	5,538.5	6,026.4
Solid fuels	452.1	483.2	495.8
Ferrous metals	864.6	938.2	946.3
Chemicals, fertilizers and rubber	605.4	620.6	682.5
Chemicals	245.2	259.2	312.3
Agricultural crop and livestock crude materials (except foods)	501.3	588.3	640.7
Timber, cellulose and paper products	216.7	229.1	236.3
Textile raw materials and semi-manufactures	129.9	180.0	172.4
Raw materials for food production	280.3	310.8	321.5
Other industrial goods for consumption	529.2	514.9	526.2
Commodities for cultural purposes	246.0	220.8	209.3
Total (incl. others)	10,975.9	11,966.0	12,842.3

1985 (million leva): Machinery and equipment 4,673.6; Fuels, mineral raw materials and metals 6,600.5; Chemicals, fertilizers and rubber 670.0; Agricultural crop and livestock crude materials (except foods) 664.9; Raw materials for food production 569.8; Other industrial goods for consumption 528.3; Total (incl. others) 14,066.5.

1986 (million leva): Machinery and equipment 5,371; Fuels, mineral raw materials and metals 6,307; Chemicals, fertilizers and rubber 647; Agricultural crop and livestock crude materials (except foods) 635; Raw materials for food production 472; Other industrial goods for consumption 580; Total (incl. others) 14,353.3.

1987 (million leva, provisional): Machinery and equipment 5,565; Fuels, mineral raw materials and metals 5,682; Chemicals, fertilizers and rubber 692; Agricultural crop and livestock crude materials (except foods) 632; Raw materials for food production 416; Other industrial goods for consumption 642; Total (incl. others) 13,966.

BULGARIA

Statistical Survey

Exports f.o.b.*	1984	1985	1986
Machinery and equipment	6,197.2	7,342.9	7,719.8
Power and electro-technical machinery	392.5	563.7	620.2
Hoisting and hauling equipment	1,252.6	1,370.2	1,361.3
Agricultural machinery	247.6	268.4	273.0
Transport rolling stock	1,055.1	n.a.	n.a.
Fuels, mineral raw materials and metals	1,399.9	1,377.6	1,071.3
Ferrous metals	422.1	399.5	353.6
Chemicals, fertilizers and rubber	588.7	545.0	443.8
Chemicals	387.4	344.9	278.7
Building materials and components	255.1	253.1	271.0
Agricultural crop and livestock crude materials (except foods)	216.1	203.9	181.9
Raw materials for food production (incl. tobacco)	407.2	432.6	334.0
Foodstuffs, beverages and tobacco products	2,268.3	1,897.5	1,759.7
Meat and dairy products, animal fats and eggs	272.2	244.7	249.0
Fruit and vegetables	501.0	n.a.	n.a.
Wine, brandy and spirits	459.4	454.8	306.3
Cigarettes	679.6	691.1	670.8
Other industrial goods for consumption	1,315.3	1,332.3	1,434.7
Clothing and underwear	304.3	304.8	313.3
Medical, sanitary and cosmetic products	611.1	n.a.	n.a.
Total (incl. others)	12,987.3	13,739.4	13,350.5

* Figures include foreign aid and loans, and exports of ships' stores and bunkers for foreign vessels.

1987 (million leva, provisional): Total 13,816, of which: Machinery and equipment 8,359.0; Fuels, mineral raw materials and metals 977.0; Chemicals, fertilizers and rubber 420.0; Raw materials for food production 359.0; Foodstuffs, beverages and tobacco products 1,671.0; Other industrial goods for consumption 1,459.

PRINCIPAL TRADING PARTNERS* (million leva)

Imports f.o.b.	1985	1986	1987†
Cuba	234.7	194.2	252.3
Czechoslovakia	583.5	652.8	697.1
German Democratic Republic	712.0	746.2	804.2
Germany, Federal Republic	547.5	699.3	694.9
Italy	163.0	160.0	164.6
Japan	86.6	104.7	145.1
Libya	400.9	509.1	135.7
Poland	640.2	593.7	669.9
Switzerland	189.5	201.5	192.7
USSR	7,898.1	8,098.0	8,056.1
USA	152.4	130.9	91.8
Total (incl. others)	14,066.5	14,353.3	14,067.3

* Imports by country of purchase; exports by country of sale.
† Figures are provisional.

Exports f.o.b.	1985	1986	1987†
Cuba	232.0	235.2	199.1
Czechoslovakia	626.5	609.8	673.4
German Democratic Republic	700.8	742.0	756.9
Germany, Federal Republic	198.8	145.2	159.7
Greece	202.1	127.9	n.a.
Hungary	264.6	263.6	254.0
Iran	121.1	83.0	81.7
Iraq	421.3	303.9	394.8
Italy	68.2	109.8	82.5
Libya	594.8	376.3	469.1
Poland	476.3	540.8	598.1
Romania	292.7	318.4	287.5
Switzerland	141.3	131.3	131.8
Turkey	151.4	n.a.	n.a.
USSR	7,775.8	8,154.5	8,437.3
United Kingdom	228.4	74.0	n.a.
Yugoslavia	118.1	113.2	n.a.
Total (incl. others)	13,739.4	13,350.5	13,802.0

Transport

RAILWAY TRAFFIC (million)

	1985	1986	1987
Passenger-kilometres	7,785	8,004	8,075
Freight ton-kilometres	18,172	18,327	17,842

INLAND WATERWAYS (million)

	1985	1986	1987
Passenger-kilometres	18	14	17
Freight ton-kilometres	2,039	2,425	1,971

SEA-BORNE SHIPPING
(international and coastal traffic, million)

	1985	1986	1987
Passengers	0.6	0.5	0.5
Freight (metric tons)	23	25	26

CIVIL AVIATION (million)

	1985	1986	1987
Passenger-kilometres	3,231	2,961	3,578
Freight ton-kilometres	44	43	42

Tourism

	1985	1986	1987
Foreign visitor arrivals	7,295,244	7,567,062	7,593,637

BULGARIA

VISITORS TO BULGARIA BY COUNTRY OF ORIGIN

	1985	1986	1987
Austria	46,239	48,253	53,828
Belgium	12,226	12,981	14,047
Czechoslovakia	444,638	383,682	398,053
France	39,546	27,252	32,872
German Democratic Republic	268,214	260,231	283,329
Germany, Federal Republic	188,593	225,958	267,891
Greece	98,657	76,305	149,888
Hungary	252,107	213,432	243,163
Iran*	32,687	36,255	42,887
Iraq*	3,268	3,192	3,889
Italy	17,655	18,396	23,624
Jordan*	5,854	4,515	4,866
Netherlands	16,516	11,834	18,135
Poland	477,653	527,715	746,644
Romania	207,653	181,512	193,034
Sweden	15,472	16,969	28,185
Switzerland	9,430	9,852	9,747
USSR	363,516	303,613	384,054
United Kingdom	73,350	45,996	74,897
USA	17,626	9,702	13,320
Yugoslavia	1,435,112	1,916,036	1,436,384
Unspecified (mainly Turkey)*	3,269,232	3,233,381	3,170,900
Total	7,295,244	7,567,062	7,593,637

* Mainly visitors in transit.

Communications Media

	1983	1984	1985
Telephone subscribers	1,655,000	1,810,500	1,946,300
Radio licences	2,055,139	2,043,500	2,017,400
Television licences	1,691,115	1,697,200	1,696,500
Daily newspapers (titles)	14	12	n.a.
Book production:			
Titles*	4,924	5,367	5,171
Copies ('000)*	59,840	60,933	63,106

* Figures include pamphlets (816 titles and 9,312,000 copies in 1983; 927 titles and 6,510,000 copies in 1984; 849 titles and 8,263,000 copies in 1985).

1986: Telephone subscribers 2,079,000; Radio licences 1,997,400; Television licences 1,692,700.
1987: Telephone subscribers 2,229,000; Radio licences 1,982,900; Television licences 1,692,400.

Education

(1986/87)

	Institutions	Teachers	Students
Kindergarten	4,977	27,276	349,131
Unified secondary polytechnical	3,501	71,825	1,261,544
Special	128	2,369	17,272
Vocational technical	4	47	1,292
Secondary vocational technical	260	7,657	110,615
Technical colleges and schools of arts	237	10,014	104,953
Semi-higher institutes (teacher training)	19	856	10,428
Higher educational	31	16,453	106,710

Source: Ministry of Culture, Science and Education, Sofia.

Directory

The Constitution

Bulgaria was formerly a monarchy but on 15 September 1946 King Simeon was deposed and Bulgaria was declared a Republic. The Constitution of 1947 was replaced by a new Constitution, which was adopted by a referendum held on 16 May 1971, and proclaimed by the Fifth National Assembly on 18 May. The following are its main provisions:

The People's Republic of Bulgaria is a socialist state of the working people of towns and villages, headed by the working class. The Bulgarian Communist Party is the leading force in society and in the State. It guides the construction of a developed socialist society in the country in close fraternal co-operation with the Bulgarian Agrarian Union.

The State serves the people. It defends their interests and socialist acquisitions; directs the country's socio-economic development according to a plan; creates conditions for the constant improvement of the welfare, education and health services of the people, as well as for the all-round development of science and culture; ensures the free development of man, guarantees his rights and protects his dignity; organizes the defence of national independence, state sovereignty and the country's territorial integrity; develops and consolidates the friendship, co-operation and mutual assistance with the Union of Soviet Socialist Republics and the other socialist countries; conducts a policy of peace and understanding with all countries and peoples.

In the People's Republic of Bulgaria all power comes from the people and belongs to the people. It is realized by the people through the freely elected representative organs—the National Assembly and the People's Councils—or directly. The representative organs are elected on the basis of a general, equal and direct right to vote by secret ballot.

All the citizens of the People's Republic of Bulgaria who are 18 years of age, irrespective of sex, nationality, race, religion, education, profession, official, public or property status, excluding those under restraint, are eligible to vote and to be elected.

The People's Republic of Bulgaria is governed strictly in accordance with the Constitution and the country's laws. It belongs to the world socialist community, which is one of the main conditions for its independence and all-round development.

SOCIAL-ECONOMIC ORGANIZATION

The economic system of the People's Republic of Bulgaria is socialist. It is based on public ownership of the means of production.

The forms of ownership are: state (all people's) ownership, co-operative ownership, ownership of public organizations, and personal ownership.

Plants and factories, banks, underground resources, the natural sources of power, nuclear energy, forests, pasture land, roads, railway, water and air transport, posts, telegraphs, telephones, the radio and television are state (all people's) property.

Co-operative property belongs to collective bodies of working people who have united of their own free will for the joint carrying out of economic activity, to co-operative unions and inter-co-operative organizations. The State fosters and aids the activity of co-operatives and of co-operative farms.

The property of public organizations serves for achieving their goals, including the realization of the activities entrusted to them by state organs, and for meeting public interests.

The citizens of the People's Republic of Bulgaria have the right of personal ownership on real and movable property to meet personal needs and those of the family. The State protects the personal property, including savings, acquired by work or in some other lawful manner. Citizens cannot exercise their rights of personal ownership and their other property rights to the detriment of the public interest. The right to inherit is recognized and guaranteed.

The State directs the national economy and the other spheres of public life on the basis of unified plans for social-economic development.

Foreign trade is the exclusive right of the State.

Labour is a fundamental social-economic factor. The socialist principle 'From everyone according to his abilities, to everyone according to his work' is applied in the People's Republic of Bulgaria. The protection of labour is dealt with by the law.

THE NATIONAL ASSEMBLY

The National Assembly is the supreme representative organ which expresses the will of the people and their sovereignty. As a supreme organ of state power it combines the legislative and executive activities of the State and exercises supreme control. The term of its mandate is five years. It is composed of 400 people's representatives who are elected in constituencies with an equal number of inhabitants. The people's representatives are responsible and account to their electorate. They may be recalled before the expiry of the term for which they have been elected. Their recall is effected by decision of the electorate in a manner laid down by law. The Assembly is convened to sessions by the State Council at least three times a year.

The National Assembly is the only legislative organ of the People's Republic of Bulgaria and the supreme organizer of the planned management of social development. It realizes the supreme leadership of the home and foreign policy of the State; approves and amends the Constitution; determines which questions should be decided by referendum, and in what manner; passes, amends and revokes laws; passes the unified plans for the social-economic development of the country and the reports on their fulfilment and the State budget and the report of the Government on its realization the preceding year; establishes taxes and fixes their rate; grants amnesty; decides the questions of declaring war and concluding peace; appoints and relieves of his duties the Commander-in-Chief of the Armed Forces; may set up state-public organs with the status of ministries; elects and relieves of their duties the State Council, the Council of Ministers, the Supreme Court and the Chief Prosecutor of the People's Republic; passes laws, decisions, declarations and appeals.

Legislative initiative belongs to the State Council, the Council of Ministers, the permanent commissions of the National Assembly, the people's representatives, the Supreme Court and the Chief Prosecutor. The right of legislative initiative belongs also to public organizations in the person of the National Council of the Fatherland Front, the Central Council of Bulgarian Trade Unions, the Central Committee of the Dimitrov Young Communist League and the Executive Council of the Central Co-operative Council on questions referring to their activity.

THE STATE COUNCIL

The State Council of the People's Republic of Bulgaria is a supreme permanent organ of state power which unites the taking of decisions with their realization. Being a supreme organ of the National Assembly, the State Council ensures the blending of legislative with executive activities. It is responsible for all its activities and reports on them to the National Assembly. At its first session the National Assembly elects a State Council from among the people's representatives by a majority of more than one-half of the total number of deputies.

The powers of the State Council are in force until the newly elected National Assembly elects a State Council.

The State Council realizes the general leadership of the home and foreign policy of the State. It represents the People's Republic of Bulgaria in her international relations. The President of the State Council receives the credentials and letters of recall of foreign diplomatic representatives in the country.

The State Council appoints elections for a National Assembly and for people's councils; determines the date for holding a referendum when a decision has been passed by the National Assembly that a referendum should take place on a certain question and in a certain manner; convenes the National Assembly at sessions; issues decrees and other juridical acts on the basic questions arising from the laws and the decisions of the National Assembly; issues decrees also on questions of principle; in urgent cases by decree amends or amplifies individual provisions of the laws; carries out the general guidance of the country's defence and security; appoints and relieves of their duties the members of the State Defence Committee and of the supreme commanding staff of the Armed Forces; controls the activities of the Council of Ministers and of the heads of the Ministries and of the other Departments; at the proposal of the Chairman of the Council of Ministers relieves of their duties and appoints individual members of the Council of Ministers—it is the duty of the State Council to submit this decision to be approved at the next session of the National Assembly; issues decrees and passes decisions, appeals and declarations.

THE COUNCIL OF MINISTERS

The Council of Ministers (the Government) is a supreme executive and administrative organ of the State Power. The Council effects its activities under the leadership and control of the National Assembly, and—when the latter is not in session—under the leadership and control of the State Council.

The Council of Ministers is responsible for the conducting of the internal and external policy of the State. It exercises the right of legislative initiative and secures conditions for carrying through the rights and freedoms of citizens. It also ensures public order and the country's security. It is responsible for the general leadership of the Armed Forces and concludes international agreements. It directly guides, co-ordinates and controls the activities of the ministries and other departments. The Council organizes both the implementation of the acts of the National Assembly, and of the State Council. It guides and controls the activities of the executive committees of the people's councils. It adopts decrees, instructions and decisions.

LOCAL GOVERNMENT

The territory of the Republic is divided for administrative purposes into nine regions (each comprising several municipalities), which are governed by Regional People's Councils, elected by the local population. Their function is to implement all economic, social and cultural undertakings of local significance in conformity with the laws of the country. They prepare local economic plans and budgets within the framework of the State Economic Plan and the State Budget, and direct its execution. They are responsible for the correct administration of state property and economic enterprises in their areas, and for the maintenance of law and order. These councils report at least once a year to their electors on their activities.

JUSTICE

The judicial authorities apply the law. Justice is independent and subject only to the law. Lay judges (Assessors) also take part in the dispensation of justice. Judges of all ranks and assessors are elected except in special cases fixed by law. Supreme judicial control over every kind of court is exercised by the Supreme Court of the People's Republic, which is elected by the National Assembly for a term of five years.

Citizens whose rights have been violated by government organs may appeal against such violations before higher-ranking organs and courts, in accordance with the Law of Administrative Procedure, 1970.

The Chief Prosecutor, who is also elected by the National Assembly for five years, and is answerable to it alone, has supreme supervision over the correct observance of the law by Government organs, officials, and all citizens. It is his particular duty to attend to the prosecution and punishment of crimes that are detrimental to the national and economic interests of the Republic or affect its independence.

THE RIGHTS AND DUTIES OF CITIZENS

All citizens are equal before the law. No privileges or restrictions in rights based on nationality, origin, religion, sex, race, education or property are recognized. All preaching of racial, national or religious hatred is punishable by law.

Women have equal rights with men in all spheres, including equal pay for equal work. The State pays special attention to the needs of mothers and children. Marriage and the family are under State protection, although only civil marriage is legally valid. Children born out of wedlock have equal rights with legitimate offspring.

All citizens have the right to free medical treatment in hospitals.

Labour is recognized as the basic factor of public and economic life. All citizens have the right to work, and it is their duty to engage in socially useful labour, according to their abilities. Holidays, limited working hours, pensions and medical treatment are guaranteed.

All citizens have the right to free education, which is secular and democratic. Elementary education is compulsory. National minorities have the right to be educated in their own tongue, and to develop their national culture, although the study of Bulgarian is compulsory.

The Church is separate from the State. Citizens have freedom of religion and conscience. However, misuse of the Church and religion for political ends and the formation of religious organizations with a political basis is prohibited.

BULGARIA

Citizens are guaranteed freedom of speech and of the Press, secrecy of correspondence, inviolability of persons and dwellings, and the right of meetings and rallies.

Military service is compulsory for all male citizens.

The Government
(December 1988)

HEAD OF STATE

President of the State Council: Todor Zhivkov (elected 7 July 1971; re-elected 17 June 1981 and 17 June 1986).

STATE COUNCIL

President: Todor Zhivkov.
First Vice-President: Petur Tanchev.
Vice-Presidents: Georgi Dzhagarov, Yaroslav Radev.
Secretary: Nikola Manolov.
Members: Chudomir Aleksandrov, Mrs Asya Angelova Emilova, Milko Balev, Acad. Angel Balevsky, Vladimir Bonev, Andrei Bundzhulov, Angel Dimitrov, Petur Dyulgerov, Kostadin Dzhatev, Grisha Filipov, Ginyo Ganev, Pencho Kubadinsky, Mrs Elena Lagadinova, Yanko Markov, Mrs Emilya Mircheva Kostova, Boril Orlinov Kosev, Ivan Panev, Dimitur Yordanov Dimitrov, Yordan Yotov, Acad. Pantelei Zarev, Nikolai Zhishev, Zhivko Zhivkov.

COUNCIL OF MINISTERS

Chairman: Georgi Atanasov.
Deputy Chairman: Grigor Stoichkov.
Minister of Economics and Planning: Stoyan Kostov Ovcharov.
Minister of Foreign Economic Relations: Andrei Lukanov.
Minister of the Interior: Georgi Tanev.
Minister of National Defence: Gen. Dobri Dzhurov.
Minister of Foreign Affairs: Petur Mladenov.
Minister of Agriculture and Forestry: Georgi Menov.
Minister of Culture, Science and Education: Georgi Yordanov.
Minister of Transport: Trifon Pashov.
Minister of Public Health and Social Welfare: Mincho Peychev.
Minister of Justice: Mrs Svetla Daskalova.
Minister, the Ambassador Extraordinary and Plenipotentiary to the USSR: Georgi Pankov.
President of the Bulgarian National Bank: Vasil Kolarov.
Chairman of the Committee for State and People's Control: Georgi Georgiyev.
First Deputy Minister of Foreign Economic Relations: Khristo Khristov (with the rank of Minister).

MINISTRIES

Council of Ministers: 1000 Sofia, Blvd Dondukov 1; tel. 86-91.
Ministry of Agriculture and Forestry: Sofia, 55 Blvd Botev.
Ministry of Culture, Science and Education: 1000 Sofia, Blvd A. Stamboliisky 18; tel. 84-81; telex 22384.
Ministry of Economics and Planning: 1000 Sofia, Blvd Dondukov 21.
Ministry of Foreign Affairs: 1000 Sofia, 2 Al. Zhendov St; telex 22530.
Ministry of Foreign Economic Relations: 1000 Sofia, Sofiiska Komuna St 12.
Ministry of the Interior: Sofia, ul. Shesti Septemvri.
Ministry of Justice: Sofia; telex 22933.
Ministry of National Defence: Sofia, Levsky St.
Ministry of Public Health and Social Welfare: 1000 Sofia, pl. Lenina 5; tel. 86-31; telex 22430.
Ministry of Transport: 1000 Sofia, Levsky St 9-11; tel. 87-10-81.

POLITICAL BUREAU OF THE CENTRAL COMMITTEE OF THE COMMUNIST PARTY

Members: Georgi Atanasov, Milko Balev, Gen. Dobri Dzhurov, Grisha Filipov, Pencho Kubadinsky, Petur Mladenov, Ivan Panev, Lt-Gen. Dimitur Stoyanov, Yordan Yotov, Todor Zhivkov (General Secretary).

Candidate Members: Petko Danchev, Petur Dyulgerov, Andrei Lukanov, Stoyan Kostov Ovcharov, Grigor Stoichkov, Georgi Yordanov.

Legislature

NARODNO SOBRANIYE
(National Assembly)

The Ninth National Assembly, elected for a five-year term on 8 June 1986, has 400 members (276 are members of the Bulgarian Communist Party, 99 of the Bulgarian Agrarian Union and 25 are non-party members), who were all elected unopposed.

Chairman: Stanko Todorov.
Deputy Chairmen: Atanas Dimitrov, Milena Stamboliiska, Drazha Vulcheva.

Political Organizations

Fatherland Front: Sofia, Blvd Vitosha 18; a mass organization unifying both political parties and social organizations; it has elected local councils throughout the country, controlled by the National Council in Sofia; the supreme body is the Congress, which is elected every five years; 4,388,000 mems.; Chair. Pencho Kubadinsky.

Bulgarian Agrarian People's Union (Bulgarsky Zemedelsky Naroden Soyuz—BZNS): Sofia, Yanko Zabunov St 1; tel. 88-19-51; telex 23302; f. 1899; peasant political organization participating in the Fatherland Front Government; 120,000 mems; Sec. Petur Tanchev.

Bulgarian Communist Party (Bulgarska Komunisticheska Partiya—BKP): Sofia; f. 1891 as the Bulgarian Social Democratic Party (BSDP); re-established as the BKP in 1919; absorbed the remaining BSDP in 1947; the dominant party in the Fatherland Front; 932,055 mems (1986); Gen. Sec. of Central Committee Todor Zhivkov; Secs Milko Balev, Grisha Filipov, Emil Khristov, Dimitur Stanishev, Lt-Gen. Dimitur Stoyanov, Vasil Tsanov, Yordan Yotov; Chair. of Central Control and Auditing Commission Nacho Papazov.

Committee of the Movement of Bulgarian Women: Sofia, Blvd Patriyarkh Evtimii 82; f. 1948; 171 mems; Pres. Mrs Elena Lagadinova; First Vice-Pres. Yordanka Tropolova.

Dimitrov Pioneer-Children's Organization Septemvriiche: Sofia, Blvd A. Stamboliisky 11; tel. 86-81; telex 22552; f. 1944; a mass social and political organization of children; Pres. of Central Council Magdalena Yankova.

Dimitrov Young Communist League: Sofia, Blvd A. Stamboliisky 11; f. 1947; a mass social and political organization of youth, controlled by a Central Committee; First Sec. Andrei Bundzhulov.

Diplomatic Representation

EMBASSIES IN BULGARIA

Afghanistan: Sofia, L. Karavelov St 34; tel. 88-23-98; Ambassador: Mehrabuddin Paktiawal.

Albania: Sofia, Khan Asparuh St 8; tel. 52-24-14; Ambassador: Bashkim Rama.

Algeria: Sofia, Slavyanska St 16; tel. 87-56-83; telex 22519; Ambassador: Zine el-Abidine Hachichi.

Argentina: Sofia, Blvd Klement Gottwald 42; tel. 44-38-21; Ambassador: Raúl Medina Muñoz.

Austria: 1000 Sofia, Ruski St 13; tel. 52-28-07; telex 22566; Ambassador: Dr Manfred Kiepach.

Belgium: Sofia, ul. Frédéric Joliot-Curie 19; tel. 72-35-27; telex 22455; Ambassador: Michael Dooms.

Brazil: Sofia, Blvd Rusky 27; tel. 44-36-55; telex 22099; Chargé d'affaires a.i.: Sonja Maria de Castro.

China, People's Republic: Sofia, Blvd Rusky 18; tel. 87-87-24; telex 22545; Ambassador: Teng Shaozhi.

Colombia: Sofia, Vasil Aprilov 17; tel. 44-61-77; telex 23393; Ambassador: Evelio Ramírez Martínez.

Congo: Sofia, Blvd Klement Gottwald 54; tel. 44-65-18; Ambassador: Henri Djombo.

Cuba: Sofia, Mladezhka St 1; tel. 72-09-96; telex 22428; Ambassador: Manuel Pérez Hernández.

BULGARIA

Czechoslovakia: Sofia, Blvd Vladimir Zaimov 9; tel. 44-62-81; Ambassador: VÁCLAV JANOUŠEK.
Denmark: 1000 Sofia, Blvd Rusky 10, POB 1393; tel. 88-04-55; telex 22099; Chargé d'affaires a.i.: MOGENS MUNCK.
Egypt: Sofia, Ovcha Koupel, Boriana St 61; tel. 56-71-21; telex 22270; Ambassador: MUHAMMAD AL-ATRIBI.
Ethiopia: Sofia, Vasil Kolarov St 28; tel. 88-39-24; Chargé d'affaires a.i.: AYELLE MAKONEN.
Finland: Sofia, Volokamsko St 57; tel. 68-33-26; telex 22776; Ambassador: KLAUS KRISTIAN SNELLMAN.
France: Sofia, Oborishte St 29; tel. 44-11-71; telex 22336; Ambassador: BERTRAND GUILHEM DE LATAILLADE.
German Democratic Republic: Sofia, ul. Frédéric Joliot-Curie 25; tel. 68-13-61; telex 22449; Ambassador: EGON ROMMEL.
Germany, Federal Republic: Sofia, Henri Barbusse St 7; tel. 72-21-27; telex 22590; Ambassador: KARL WALTER LEWALTER.
Ghana: 1113 Sofia, Pierre Degeyter St 9, Apt 37-38; tel. 70-65-09; Ambassador: COFFI AKUWA-HARRISON.
Greece: Sofia, Blvd Klement Gottwald 68; tel. 44-37-70; telex 22458; Ambassador: GEORGIOS CHRISTOYANNIS.
Hungary: Sofia, ul. Shesti Septemvri 57; tel. 66-20-21; telex 22459; Ambassador: SÁNDOR SIMICS.
India: Sofia, Blvd Patriyarkh Evtimii 31; tel. 87-39-44; telex 22954; Chargé d'affaires: DIVYABH MANCHANDA.
Indonesia: Sofia, G. Gheorghiu-Dej St 32; tel. 44-23-49; telex 22358; Ambassador: ABDEL KOBIR SASRADIPOERA.
Iran: Sofia, Blvd Klement Gottwald 70; tel. 44-10-13; telex 22303; Ambassador: ALI MUHAMMAD FARMANBAR.
Iraq: Sofia, Anton Chekhov St 21; tel. 87-00-13; telex 22307; Ambassador: FAWSI DAKIR AL-ANI.
Italy: Sofia, Shipka St 2; tel. 88-17-05; telex 22173; Ambassador: PAOLO TARONI.
Japan: Sofia, Lyulyakova Gradina St 14; tel. 72-39-84; telex 22397; Ambassador: MASAMI TANIDA.
Kampuchea: Sofia, Mladost 1, Blvd S. Aliende Res. 2; tel. 75-51-35; Chargé d'affaires a.i.: SIM SUONG.
Korea, Democratic People's Republic: Sofia, Mladost 1, Blvd S. Aliende Res. 4; tel. 77-53-48; Ambassador: KIM PYONG-IL.
Kuwait: Sofia, Blvd Klement Gottwald 47; tel. 44-19-92; telex 23586; Ambassador: TALIB JALAL AD-DIN AL-NAQIB.
Laos: Sofia, Ovcha Kupel, Buket St 80; tel. 56-55-08; Ambassador: THALEUNE WARRINTRASAK.
Lebanon: Sofia, ul. Frédéric Joliot-Curie 19; tel. 72-04-31; telex 23140; Ambassador: HUSSEIN MOUSSAWI.
Libya: Sofia, Oborishte St 10; tel. 44-19-21; telex 22180; Secretary of People's Bureau: OMAR MUFTAH DALLAL.
Mexico: Sofia, Todor Strashimirov St 1; tel. 44-32-82; telex 22087; Ambassador: JAIME FERNÁNDEZ-MACGREGOR.
Mongolia: Sofia, ul. Frédéric Joliot-Curie 52; tel. 70-02-62; telex 22274; Ambassador: MANGALJAVIN DASH.
Morocco: Sofia, Blvd Klement Gottwald 44; tel. 44-27-94; Ambassador: ABDELHAMID BENNANI.
Mozambique: Sofia; Ambassador: GONÇALVES RAFAEL SENGO.
Netherlands: Sofia, Denkoglu St 19a; tel. 87-41-86; telex 22686; Ambassador: VIVIAN H. MEERTINS.
Nicaragua: Sofia, Mladost 1, Blvd Aliende, Res. 1; tel. 75-41-57; Ambassador: ROGER VÁSQUEZ BARRIOS.
Peru: Sofia, ul. Frédéric Joliot-Curie 19, Apt. 20; tel. 70-32-63; telex 23182; Chargé d'affaires: JULIO VEGA ERAUSQUÍN.
Poland: Sofia, Khan Krum St 46; tel. 88-51-66; telex 22595; Ambassador: WIESŁAW BEK.
Portugal: Sofia, Ivats Voivoda St 6; tel. 44-35-48; telex 22082; Chargé d'affaires a.i.: LUIZ GONZAGA FERREIRA.
Romania: Sofia, Sitnyakovo St 4; tel. 70-70-47; telex 22321; Ambassador: VASILE PUNGAN.
Spain: Sofia, Oborishte St 47; tel. 43-00-17; telex 22308; Ambassador: JOAQUÍN PÉREZ GÓMEZ.
Sweden: Sofia, pl. Veltchova Zavera 1; tel. 65-10-02; telex 22373; Ambassador: AKE BERG.
Switzerland: 1000 Sofia, Shipka St 33; tel. 44-31-98; telex 22792; Ambassador: MICHAEL VON SCHENCK.
Syria: Sofia, Hristo Georguiev 10; tel. 44-15-85; telex 23464; Ambassador: TAHA KHAYRAT.
Turkey: Sofia, Blvd Tolbukhin 23; tel. 87-23-06; telex 22199; Ambassador: ÖMER ENGIN LÜTEM.
USSR: Sofia, Blvd Bulgaro-savetska druzhba 28; tel. 66-88-19; Ambassador: VIKTOR VASILEVICH SHARAPOV.
United Kingdom: Sofia, Blvd Tolbukhin 65-67; tel. 88-53-61; telex 22363; Ambassador: JOHN HAROLD FAWCETT.
USA: Sofia, Blvd A. Stamboliisky 1; tel. 88-48-01; telex 22690; Ambassador: SOL POLANSKY.
Uruguay: Sofia, Tsar Ivan Asen II St 91, POB 213; tel. 44-19-57; telex 23087; Ambassador: ALEXANDRO LORENZO Y LOSADA.
Venezuela: Sofia, ul. Frédéric Joliot-Curie 17; tel. 72-39-77; telex 23495; Ambassador: JOSÉ GREGORIO GONZÁLEZ RODRÍGUEZ.
Viet-Nam: Sofia, Ilya Petrov St 1; tel. 72-08-79; telex 22717; Ambassador: NGUYEN TIEN THONG.
Yemen, People's Democratic Republic: Sofia, Blvd S. Aliende, Res. 3; tel. 75-61-63; Ambassador: ALI MUNASSAR MUHAMMAD.
Yugoslavia: Sofia, G. Gheorghiu-Dej St 3; tel. 44-32-37; telex 23537; Ambassador: MILENKO STEFANOVIĆ.

Judicial System

Justice in the People's Republic of Bulgaria is administered by the district, regional and military courts and by the Supreme Court. All labour disputes are considered by the conciliation committees of the enterprises and by the regional courts. Civil law disputes among state enterprises, offices and co-operative and public organizations are heard by the State Court of Arbitration, and disputes connected with international trade by the Foreign Trade Court of Arbitration at the Bulgarian Chamber of Commerce and Industry.

The district court judges and assessors are elected by the district people's councils for a term of five years. Judges and assessors of the Supreme Court are elected for a term of five years by the National Assembly. Judicial control over the activities of all courts is exercised by the Supreme Court. Control for the correct observance of the law by Governmental local government authorities and officials, and by the citizens, is exercised by the Chief Prosecutor of the Republic, who is elected by the National Assembly for a term of five years. All other prosecutors of courts are appointed and discharged by the Chief Prosecutor. All courts and prisons are under the Ministry of Justice. All lawyers are organized in consultation offices and citizens have the right to choose their own legal representatives from among the members of any such group. State enterprises may employ their own legal adviser.

President of the Supreme Court: IVAN VELINOV.
Chief Prosecutor: VASIL ZHELYAZKOV MRUCHKOV.

Religion

Committee for Affairs of the Bulgarian Orthodox Church and the Religious Denominations: Sofia, Al. Zhendov St 2; deals with relations between religious organizations and the Government; Chair. LYUBOMIR POPOV.

CHRISTIANITY
The Orthodox Churches

Armenian-Apostolic-Orthodox Church: Sofia, Naicho Tzanov St 31; tel. 88-02-08; 20,000 adherents (1985); administered by Bishop DIRAYR MARDIKIYAN (resident in Bucharest); Chair. of the Diocesan Council in Bulgaria GARO DERMESROBIYAN.

Bulgarian Orthodox Church: 1000 Sofia, Synod Palace, 4 Oborishte St; tel. 87-56-11; f. 865; administered by the Bulgarian Patriarchy; there are 11 dioceses in Bulgaria and three foreign dioceses, each under a Metropolitan; adherents in Bulgaria comprise 80% of the church-going population; Patriarch MAXIM.

The Roman Catholic Church

Bulgarian Catholics may be adherents of either the Latin or the Bulgarian (Byzantine-Slav) Rite. The country comprises two dioceses, both directly responsible to the Holy See.

Latin Rite

Bishop of Nikopol: SAMUIL SERAFIMOV DZHUNDRIN, 7000 Ruse, Rost. Blaskov St 14; tel. 2-81-88; 20,000 adherents (1968).

Diocese of Sofia and Plovdiv: GEORGI IVANOV YOVCHEV (Apostolic Administrator) 4000 Plovdiv, Lilyana Dimitrova St 3; tel. 22-84-30; 45,000 adherents (1980).

Bulgarian Rite

Apostolic Exarch of Sofia: METODI IVANOV STRATIYEV (Titular Bishop of Diocletianopolis in Thrace), Sofia, ul. Pashovi 10/B; tel. 52-02-97; 10,000 adherents (1985).

The Protestant Churches

Supreme Episcopal Council of the Bulgarian Evangelical Methodist Church: Sofia, Rakovsky St 86; tel. 87-33-58; Head Pastor IVAN NOZHAROV.

BULGARIA

Union of the Churches of the Seventh-day Adventists: Sofia, Vasil Kolarov St 10; tel. 88-12-18; Head Pastor NIKOLA TANEV.

Union of the Evangelical Baptist Churches: Varna, Georgi Dimitrov St 100; tel. 45-64-22; Head Pastor GEORGI TODOROV.

Union of the Evangelical Congregational Churches: Sofia, Vasil Kolarov St 49; tel. 88-05-93; Head Pastor PAVEL IVANOV.

Union of the Evangelical Pentecostal Churches: 1557 Sofia, Bacho Kiro St 21; tel. 83-22-33; f. 1928; Head Pastor DINKO JELEV.

ISLAM

Supreme Muslim Theological Council: Sofia, Bratya Miladinovi St 27; tel. 87-73-20; adherents estimated at 14% of the actively religious population, with an estimated 500 acting regional imams; Chief Mufti of the Turkish Muslims in Bulgaria NEDYO GEDZHEV; Mufti of the Bulgarian Muslims CHAVDAR ILIYEV, Smolyan.

JUDAISM

Central Jewish Theological Council: 1000 Sofia, Eksarkh Yosif St 16; tel. 83-12-73; 5,000 adherents; Head YOSSIF LEVI.

The Press

As in most Communist countries, the press in Bulgaria is considered a powerful instrument of the Party and part of the educational system, and for that reason it is subject to strict control by the Government. It is largely dominated by the Communist Party and by organizations attached to the Fatherland Front, and much of its news originates from TASS, the Soviet news agency. Censorship is not usually necessary, since editors are Party members and aware of their responsibility to the Government.

There are 14 daily newspapers in Bulgaria, eight of which are published in Sofia, and their total daily circulation was about 2m. copies in 1980. Until late 1988 the most important was *Rabotnichesko Delo*, the organ of the Communist Party. However, in government proposals expected to be implemented in early 1989, *Otechestven Front*, the Fatherland Front daily, was to be the sole newspaper expressing the official views of the Government, while *Rabotnichesko Delo* was to concentrate on more general issues. Another important newspaper is *Narodna Mladezh*, the youth newspaper.

PRINCIPAL DAILIES

Chernomorsky Front (Black Sea Front): Burgas, Milin Kamak 9; f. 1950; organ of the district committees of the Communist Party, the Fatherland Front and the District People's Council; Editor-in-Chief STOICHO GOTSEV; circ. 100,000.

Dunavska Pravda (Danubian Truth): Russe; f.1944; organ of the district committees of the Communist Party, the Fatherland Front and the District People's Council; Editor-in-Chief TSVYATKO TSVETKOV; circ. 27,500.

Kooperativno Selo (For Co-operative Farming): Sofia, 11 August St 18; tel. 83-50-33; telex 23174; f. 1951; organ of the Ministry of Agriculture; Editor-in-Chief GEORGI AVRAMOV; circ. 193,000.

Narodna Armiya (People's Army): Sofia, Ivan Vasov St 12; f. 1944; organ of the Ministry of National Defence; Editor-in-Chief Col RANGEL ZLATKOV; circ. 55,000.

Narodna Mladezh (People's Youth): Sofia, Blvd Lenin 47; f. 1944; organ of the Central Committee of the Dimitrov Communist Youth Union; Editor-in-Chief GEORGI TULIISKY; circ. 250,000.

Narodno Delo (People's Cause): 9000 Varna, Khristo Botev St 3; organ of the district committees of the Communist Party and the Fatherland Front and of the district People's Council; f. 1950; midday; Editor-in-Chief YORDAN DONCHEV; circ. 100,000.

Otechestven Front (Fatherland Front): Sofia, Blvd Lenin 47; f. 1942; organ of the National Council of the Fatherland Front; morning and evening editions; Editor-in-Chief GENCHO BUCHVAROV; total circ. 280,000.

Otechestven Glas (The Voice of the Fatherland): 4000 Plovdiv, Krakra St 9; telex 44506; f. 1943; organ of the district committees of the Communist Party, the Fatherland Front and the District People's Council; Editor-in-Chief MIKHAIL MILCHEV; circ. 104,000.

Pirinsko Delo (Pirin's Cause): Blagoevrad, Assen Khristov St 19; organ of the district people's council, the district committees of the Communist Party and the Fatherland Front; Editor-in-Chief ILYA SARIN; circ. 33,000.

Rabotnichesko Delo (Workers' Cause): Sofia, Blvd Lenin 47; f. 1927; organ of the Communist Party; Editor-in-Chief RADOSLAV RADEV; circ. 850,000.

Trud (Labour): Sofia, Blvd Dondukov 82; tel. 87-25-01; telex 22427; f. 1923; organ of the Central Council of Trade Unions; Editor-in-Chief LYUBEN GENOV; circ. 300,000.

Vecherny Novini (Evening News): Sofia, Blvd Lenin 47; f. 1951; a popular advertising paper; Editor-in-Chief DELCHO KRUSTEV; circ. 125,000.

Zemedelsko Zname (Agrarian Banner): Sofia, Yanko Zabunov St 23; f. 1899; organ of the Agrarian People's Party; Editor-in-Chief Prof. DIMITUR DIMITROV; circ. 165,000.

PRINCIPAL PERIODICALS

Anteni (Antennae): Sofia, Khan Krum St 12; weekly on politics and culture; Editor-in-Chief VESELIN YOSIFOV; circ. 150,000.

Bulgaria: Sofia, Levsky St 1; monthly; Russian, German and Spanish; illustrated magazine; Editor-in-Chief (vacant); circ. 157,000.

Bulgaria Today: Sofia, Levsky St 1; monthly; French, English and Italian; Editor-in-Chief NIKOLA ZAKHARIYEV; total circ. 25,000.

Bulgarian Films: 1000 Sofia, Rakovsky St 96; tel. 87-66-11; telex 22447; f. 1960; 8 a year; magazine in English, French and Russian; cinema; Editor-in-Chief IVAN STOYANOVICH; circ. 21,000.

Bulgarian Foreign Trade: Sofia, Parchvich 42; tel. 8-51-51; telex 23318; f. 1952; fortnightly; French, German, English and Russian; organ of the Bulgarian Chamber of Commerce and Industry; Editor-in-Chief VENTSESLAV DIMITROV; circ. 13,000.

Bulgaro-Suvetska Druzhba: Sofia, Blvd Klement Gottwald 4; organ of the All-National Committee for Bulgarian-Soviet Friendship; Editor-in-Chief BORIS PETKOV; circ. 68,000.

Bulgarsky Voin (Bulgarian Soldier): Sofia, 11 August St 6; monthly organ of the Chief Political Department of the People's Army; literature and arts; Editor-in-Chief ORLIN ORLINOV; circ. 23,000.

Chitalishte (Reading Room): Sofia, Sofiiska Komuna St 4; monthly; organ of the Committee for Art and Culture; Editor-in-Chief BOYAN BALABANOV; circ. 5,000.

Computer for You: 1000 Sofia, Blvd Tolbukhin 51A; tel. 87-78-04; f. 1985; monthly; hardware and software; circ. 20,000.

Darzhaven Vestnik (State Newspaper): 1123 Sofia; 2 a week; publishes the laws, decrees, etc., of the National Assembly; Editor-in-Chief EMIL MITEV; circ. 63,587.

Discover Bulgaria: 1000 Sofia, Rakovsky St 127; tel. 88-37-39; f. 1958; every 2 months; French, English, German and Russian; Editor-in-Chief LILIYA GERASIMOVA; circ. 47,000.

Do It Yourself: 1000 Sofia, Blvd Tolbukhin 51A; tel. 87-50-45; f. 1981; monthly; circ. 180,000.

Economic News of Bulgaria: Sofia, Blvd A. Stamboliisky 11A; monthly; English, French, German, Spanish and Russian; published by the Bulgarian Chamber of Commerce and Industry; Editor-in-Chief LYUBEN MIKHAILOV; circ. 15,000.

Fakel (The Torch): 1000 Sofia, Angel Kanchev St 5; tel. 88-00-31; f. 1981; every 2 months; translations of Soviet literature; published by the Committee for Culture, the Bulgarian Writers' Union and the Union of Translators; Editor-in-Chief BOZHIDAR BOZHILOV; circ. 20,000.

Ikonomicheska Misal (Thoughts on Economics): Sofia, Aksakov 3; 10 a year; organ of the Institute of Economics of the Bulgarian Academy of Sciences; Editor-in-Chief KLEMANSO GROZDANOV; circ. 7,000.

Ikonomika (Economics): Sofia, Blvd Dondukov 21; f. 1946 as *Planovo Stopanstvo* (Planning of the Economy); present name adopted in 1985; monthly; organ of the State Planning Commission, Ministry of Finance, Bulgarian National Bank and Central Statistical Office; Editor-in-Chief ZVETAN MARINOV; circ. 5,000.

Izkustvo (Art): 1504 Sofia, ul. Shipka 18; 1404 Sofia, POB 139; tel. 43-01-92; f. 1951; 10 a year; organ of the Committee for Art and Culture, and of the Union of Bulgarian Artists; Editor-in-Chief Prof. IVAN MARAZOV; circ. 5,000.

Kinoizkustvo (Cinematic Art): Sofia, pl. Slaveikov 11; f. 1946; monthly; cinema; Editor-in-Chief EMIL PETROV; circ. 9,000.

LIK: Sofia, Blvd Lenin 49; weekly publication of the Bulgarian Telegraph Agency; literature, art and culture; Editor-in-Chief SIRMA VELEVA; circ. 17,600.

Literaturen Front (Literary Front): Sofia, Angel Kanchev St 5; f. 1944; organ of the Bulgarian Writers' Union; Editor-in-Chief LILYANA STEFANOVA; circ. 40,000.

Lov i Ribolov (Hunting and Fishing): 1000 Sofia, Blvd Vitosha 31–33; tel. 88-42-20; f. 1895; monthly organ of the Hunting and Angling Union; Editor-in-Charge KHRISTO RUSKOV; circ. 60,000.

Mladezh (Youth): Sofia, Blvd Khristo Botev 48; f. 1945; monthly organ of the Central Committee of the Dimitrov Communist Youth Union; Editor-in-Chief LYUBOMIR STOIKOV; circ. 70,000.

Naroden Sport (People's Sport): Sofia, ul. Rakitin 2; tel. 44-44-29; telex 22504; f. 1944; 3 a week; organ of the Bulgarian Union for Physical Culture and Sports; Editor-in-Chief CHAVDAR KALEV; circ. 270,000.

BULGARIA

Narodna Kultura (National Culture): 1040 Sofia, Sofiiska Komuna St 4; tel. 88-33-22; organ of the Committee for Culture; Editor-in-Chief STEFAN PRODEV; circ. 50,000.

Narodna Prosveta (National Education): Sofia, Blvd Lenin 125; monthly organ of Ministry of Education and the Union of Bulgarian Teachers; Editor DIMITUR TSVETKOV; circ. 12,125.

Nasha Rodina (Our Country): Sofia, Blvd Lenin 47; monthly; socio-political and literary; illustrated; Editor-in-Chief DIMITUR METODIYEV; circ. 35,500.

Novo Vreme (New Time): Sofia, Blvd Lenin 47; f. 1897; monthly theoretical organ of the Central Committee of the Communist Party of Bulgaria; Editor-in-Charge NIKOLAI IRIBADZHAKOV; circ. 32,000.

Orbita: 1000 Sofia, 8 Tsar Kaloyan St; tel. 88-51-68; f. 1969; weekly publication of the Central Committee of the Dimitrov Young Communist League; science and technology; Editor-in-Chief Dr DIMITUR PEEV; circ. 110,000.

Otechestvo (Fatherland): Sofia, Blvd Vitosha 18; fortnightly illustrated publication of the National Council of the Fatherland Front; Editor-in-Chief SERAFIM SEVERNYAK; circ. 100,000.

Paralleli: Sofia, Blvd Lenin 49; weekly illustrated publication of the Bulgarian Telegraph Agency; Editor-in-Chief VENELIN MITEV; circ. 135,000.

Plamak (Flame): Sofia, Angel Kanchev 5; f. 1924; every 2 weeks; literature, art and publishing; organ of the Union of Bulgarian Writers; Editor-in-Chief GEORGI KONSTANTINOV; circ. 11,000.

Pogled: Sofia, 11 August St 6; organ of the Union of Bulgarian Journalists; Editor-in-Chief EVGENI STANCHEV; circ. 310,000.

Science and Technology: Sofia, Blvd Lenin 49; tel. 84-61; f. 1964; weekly of the Bulgarian Telegraph Agency; Editor-in-Chief VESELIN SEIKOV; circ. 18,000.

Septemvri (September): Sofia, pl. Slaveikov 2a; monthly; organ of the Union of Bulgarian Writers; literary; Editor-in-Chief VLADIMIR GOLEV; circ. 15,000.

Septemvriiche (Septembrist): Sofia, Blvd Lenin 47; 2 a week; organ of the Central Committee of the Dimitrov Union of People's Youth; Editor-in-Chief NIKOLAI ZIDAROV; circ. 300,000.

Slavyani (Slavs): Sofia, Tsar Kaloyan St 1; monthly organ of the Slav committee in Bulgaria; Editor-in-Chief KATYA GEORGIYEVA; circ. 20,000.

Sofiiska Pravda (Sofia Truth): Sofia, Tsar Kaloyan St 3; f. 1955; 3 a week; organ of the District People's Council and the district committees of the Communist Party and the Fatherland Front; Editor-in-Chief VASIL MILUSHEV; circ. 13,000.

Sturshel (Hornet): 1504 Sofia, Blvd Lenin 47; f. 1946; weekly; humour and satire; Editor-in-Chief KHRISTO PELITEV; circ. 375,000.

Teater (Theatre): Sofia, Blvd Dondukov 82; monthly organ of the Committee of Culture and Art, Bulgarian Writers' Union and Union of Actors; Editor-in-Chief Prof. YULIYAN VUCHKOV; circ. 4,500.

Televiziya i Radio: Sofia, ul. Shishman 30; organ of the Committee for Television and Radio; Editor-in-Chief KHRISTO CHAVDAROV; circ. 100,000.

Turist: Sofia, Blvd D. Blagoev 24; tel. 51-16-41; f. 1902; monthly organ of the Bulgarian Tourist Union; Editor-in-Chief KHRISTO GEORGIYEV; circ. 25,000.

Vanshna Targoviya (Foreign Trade): Sofia, Tsar Kaloyan 8; monthly publication of the Ministry for Foreign Trade; Editor-in-Chief ALEXANDUR CHICHOVSKY; circ. 3,000.

The World Over: 1000 Sofia, Blvd Lenin 39; telex 22821; f. 1964; weekly publication of the Bulgarian Telegraph Agency; international politics; Editor-in-Chief YOSSIF DAVIDOV.

Zdrave (Health): Sofia, Byalo More St 8; published by Bulgarian Red Cross; Editor-in-Chief MARIYA NIKOLOVA; circ. 200,000.

Zhenata Dnes: Sofia, pl. Narodno Sabranie 12; monthly organ of the Committee of the Movement of Bulgarian Women; also in Russian; Editor-in-Chief Mrs ELEONORA TURLAKOVA; circ. 580,000.

NEWS AGENCIES

Bulgarska Telegrafna Agentsia (BTA): (Bulgarian Telegraph Agency): 1040 Sofia, Blvd Lenin 49; tel. 84-61; telex 22821; f. 1898; the official news agency, having agreements with the leading foreign agencies and correspondents in all major capitals; publishes weekly surveys of science and technology, international affairs, literature and art; Dir-Gen. BOYAN TRAIKOV.

Sofia-Press Agency: Sofia 2, Levsky St 1; telex 22622; f. 1967 by the Union of Bulgarian Writers, the Union of Bulgarian Journalists, the Union of Bulgarian Artists and the Union of Bulgarian Composers; publishes socio-political and scientific literature, fiction, children's and tourist literature, publications on the arts, a newspaper, magazines and bulletins in foreign languages; Dir-Gen. STEFAN PETROV.

Foreign Bureaux

Agence France-Presse (AFP): 1000 Sofia, Blvd Tolbukhin 16; tel. 88-33-94; telex 22572; Correspondent VESSELA SERGEVA-PETROVA.

Agentstvo Pechati Novosti (APN) (USSR): Sofia, 11 Avgust St 1, Apt 3; Bureau Man. YURI KOVALENKO.

Allgemeiner Deutscher Nachrichtendienst (ADN) (German Democratic Republic): 1000 Sofia, Moskovska 27A; Correspondent HEIDEMARIE DREISNER.

Československá tisková kancelář (ČTK) (Czechoslovakia): 1113 Sofia, ul. Gagarin, blok 154, Apt 19; tel. 87-21-69; telex 22537; Correspondent VĚRA IVANOVICHOVÁ.

Magyar Távirati Iroda (MTI) (Hungary): Sofia, ul. Frédéric Joliot-Curie 15, blok 156/3, Apt 28; Correspondent KÁROLY NAGY.

Prensa Latina (Cuba): 1113 Sofia, ul. Yuri Gagarin 22, blok 154B, Apt 2; tel. 71-91-90; Correspondent SUSANA UGARTE SOLER.

Telegrafnoye Agentstvo Sovetskovo Soyuza (TASS) (USSR): 1000 Sofia, ul. A. Gendov 1, Apt 29; Correspondent ALEKSANDR STEPANENKO.

Xinhua (New China) News Agency (People's Republic of China): Sofia, pl. Narodno Sobraniye 3, 2nd Floor; tel. 88-49-41; telex 22539; Correspondent LI FUPIN.

The following agencies are also represented: PAP (Poland), Reuters (UK) and Tanjug (Yugoslavia).

PRESS ASSOCIATION

Union of Bulgarian Journalists: Sofia, Graf Ignatiyev St 4; tel. 87-27-73; telex 22635; f. 1955; Pres. BOYAN TRAIKOV; First Vice-Pres. STOINE KRASTEV; 4,500 mems.

Publishers

Darzhavno Izdatelstvo 'Khristo G. Danov': Plovdiv, ul. Petko Karavelov 17; tel. 22-52-32; f. 1855; fiction, poetry, literary criticism; Dir PETUR ANASTASSOV.

Darzhavno Izdatelstvo Meditsina i Fizkultura: 1080 Sofia, pl. Slaveikov 11; tel. 87-13-08; medicine, physical culture and tourism; Dir PETUR GOGOV.

Darzhavno Izdatelstvo 'Narodna Kultura': Sofia, ul. Gavril Genov 4; tel. 87-80-63; f. 1944; foreign fiction and poetry in translation; Dir VERA GANCHEVA.

Darzhavno Izdatelstvo 'Narodna Prosveta': Sofia, ul. Vasil Drumev 37; educational publishing house; Dir SVYATKO GAGOV.

Darzhavno Izdatelstvo 'Nauka i Izkustvo': Sofia, Blvd Rusky 6; tel. 87-57-01; f. 1948; general publishers; Dir GANKA SLAVCHEVA.

Darzhavno Izdatelstvo 'Tekhnika': 1000 Sofia, Blvd Rusky 6; tel. 87-57-01; f. 1958; textbooks for technical and higher education and technical literature; Dir PETRANA WURGOVA.

Darzhavno Izdatelstvo 'Zemizdat': 1504 Sofia, Blvd Lenin 47; tel. 46-31; f. 1949; specializes in works on agriculture, shooting, fishing, forestry, livestock-breeding, veterinary medicine and popular scientific literature and textbooks; Dir PETUR ANGELOV.

Darzhavno Voyenno Izdatelstvo: Sofia, ul. Ivan Vazov 12; military publishing house; Head Col GEORGI GEORGIYEV.

Izdatelstvo na Bulgarskata Akademiya na Naukite (Publishing House of the Bulgarian Academy of Sciences): 1113 Sofia, Acad. Georgi Bonchev St, blok 6; tel. 72-09-22; telex 23132; f. 1869; scientific works and periodicals of the Academy of Sciences; Dir Prof. Dr IVAN GARBUCHEV.

Izdatelstvo 'Bulgarsky Khudozhnik': 1000 Sofia, Slaveikov 6; tel. 88-47-49; art books, children's books; Dir STEFAN KURTEV.

Izdatelstvo 'Bulgarsky Pisatel': Sofia, ul. Shesti Septemvri 35; publishing house of the Union of Bulgarian Writers; Bulgarian fiction and poetry, criticism; Dir SIMEON SULTANOV.

Izdatelstvo na CC na DKMS 'Narodna Mladezh' (People's Youth Publishing House): Sofia, ul. Kaloyan 10; politics, history, original and translated fiction, and original and translated poetry for children; Dir ROSEN BOSEV.

Izdatelstvo na Natsionalniya Savet na Otechestveniya Front (Publishing House of the National Council of the Fatherland Front): Sofia, Blvd Dondukov 32; Dir SLAV KHRISTOV KARASLAVOV.

Izdatelstvo 'Profizdat' (Publishing House of the Central Council of Bulgarian Trade Unions): Sofia, Blvd Dondukov 82; specialized literature and fiction; Dir STOYAN POPOV.

Knigoizdatelstvo 'Georgi Bakalov' Varna: Varna, pl. Deveti septemvri 6; popular science, science fiction, economics, *belles-lettres*; Dir PANKO ANCHEV.

BULGARIA

Partizdat—Izdatelstvo na Bulgarskata Komunisticheska Partiya (Publishing House of the Bulgarian Communist Party): 1000 Sofia, Blvd Lenin 47; tel. 43-431; f. 1944; Dir PENJO ASTARDJIEV.

Sinodalno Izdatelstvo: Sofia; religious publishing house; Dir KIRIL BOINOV.

STATE ORGANIZATION

Jusautor: 1463 Sofia, Ernst Thälmann Ave 17; tel. 80-51-59; telex 23042; Bulgarian copyright agency; represents Bulgarian authors of literary, scientific, dramatic and musical works, and deals with all formalities connected with the grant of options, authorization for translations, drawing up of contracts for the use of their works by foreign publishers and producers; negotiates for the use of foreign works in Bulgaria; controls the application of copyright legislation; Dir-Gen. YANA MARKOVA.

WRITERS' UNION

Union of Bulgarian Writers: Sofia, Angel Kanchev 5; f. 1913; 370 mems; Pres. LYUBOMIR LEVCHEV.

Radio and Television

Radio and television are supervised by the Committee for Television and Radio of the Committee for Culture of the Council of Ministers.

There were an estimated 2,100,000 radio receivers in use in 1985. There were about 2,100,000 television receivers in 1987. Colour television was introduced in 1977.

Bulgarian Committee for Television and Radio: 1504 Sofia, San Stefano St 29; tel. 46-81; telex 22581; Chair. LYUBOMIR PAVLOV.

RADIO

Bulgarsko Radio: 1421 Sofia, Blvd Dragan Tsankov 4; tel. 85-41; telex 22557; there are four Home Service programmes and local stations at Blagoevgrad, Plovdiv, Shumen, Stara Zagora and Varna. The Foreign Service broadcasts in Bulgarian, Turkish, Greek, Serbo-Croat, French, Italian, German, English, Portuguese, Spanish, Albanian and Arabic.

TELEVISION

Bulgarska Televiziya: 1504 Sofia, ul. San Stefano 29; tel. 46-31; telex 22581; programmes are transmitted daily.

Finance

(cap. = capital; dep. = deposits; res = reserves; m. = million; amounts in leva)

BANKING

A major restructuring of the banking system began in 1987, when eight new commercial banks were established as self-managing shareholders' societies. The new trading banks will give credit only to organizations that are profitable and will be legally responsible for their financial dealings. The National Bank of Bulgaria will remain the only issuing bank.

National Bank

Bulgarska Narodna Banka (National Bank of Bulgaria): 1000 Sofia, Sofiiska Komuna St 2; tel. 85-51; telex 22392; f. c. 1879; issuing bank; Pres. VASIL KOLAROV; Deputy Dir VESSELIN RANKOV.

Other Banks

Avtotekhnika (Motor and Engineering Bank): f. 1987.

Bank for Economic Projects (Mineralbank): 1000 Sofia, Legué St 17, POB 589; tel. 80-17-37; telex 23390; f. 1980, reorganized 1987; cap. 120m., dep. 839m., res 75m. (Dec. 1986); Pres. RUMEN GEORGIYEV.

Biokhim (Commercial Bank): 1040 Sofia, 1 Ivan Vazov St; tel. 54-13-66; telex 23862; f. 1987; cap. 60m., dep. 463m. (1987); Chair. BORIS MITEV.

Bulgarian Foreign Trade Bank: 1000 Sofia, Sofiiska Komuna St 2; tel. 85-51; telex 22031; f. 1964; shares held by National Bank of Bulgaria and other state institutions; incorporating the Maritime Commercial Bank Ltd; co-ordinates foreign trade activities of the other commercial banks; cap. 120m.; res 340.4m. (Dec. 1985); Pres. IVAN DRAGNEVSKY.

Elektronika (Electronics Bank): 1574 Sofia, 55 Chapaev St; tel. 70-74-47; telex 23745; f. 1987.

State Savings Bank: Sofia, Moskovska 19; f. 1951; provides general individual banking services; dep. 16,000m. (1986).

Stopanska banka (Commercial Bank): Sofia; f. 1987; Chair. ZVETAN PETKOV.

Stroybank Ltd: 1202, Sofia 46 Dunav Str., POB 112; tel. 8-38-41; telex 23887; f. 1987; cap. 30m., dep. 661m. (June 1988); Pres. CHRISTOMIR YORDANOV.

Transportna (Transport Bank): 9000 Varna, 5 Shipka St; tel. 22-30-73; telex 77303; f. 1987; Chair. TODOR DUKOV.

Zemedelska i kooperativna (Agricultural and Co-operative Bank): 4018 Plovdiv, G. Dimitrov Blvd 37; tel. 23-18-76; telex 44324; f. 1987; supplies credit for reconstruction and modernization, technology transfer and quality improvement; Chair. YANKO MUSURLIEV.

INSURANCE

State Insurance Institute: Sofia, Rakovsky St 102; all insurance firms were nationalized during 1947, and were reorganized into one single State insurance company; Chair. TOMA TOMOV.

Bulstrad (Bulgarian Foreign Insurance and Reinsurance Co, Ltd): 1000 Sofia, Dunav St 5; POB 627; tel. 8-51-91; telex 22564; f. 1961; deals with all foreign insurance and reinsurance; Chair. S. DARVINGOV.

Trade and Industry

CHAMBER OF COMMERCE

Bulgarian Chamber of Commerce and Industry: 1040 Sofia, Blvd A. Stamboliisky 11A; tel. 87-26-31; telex 22374; promotes economic relations and business contacts between Bulgarian and foreign companies and organizations; organizes official participation in international fairs and exhibitions and manages the international fairs in Plovdiv; publishes economic publications in Bulgarian and foreign languages; patents inventions and registers trade marks and industrial designs; organizes foreign trade advertising and publicity; provides legal consultations etc.; Pres. PETUR RUSEV.

FOREIGN TRADE ORGANIZATIONS

Foreign trade is a state monopoly, and is conducted through foreign trade organizations and various state enterprises and corporations. Principal organizations include:

Agrocommerce: 1000 Sofia, Blvd Dondukov 86; tel. 80-33-12; telex 23223; exports the produce of the member organizations of the National Agro-Industrial Union; import and maintenance of industrial equipment; import of consumer products and utilization of waste products; Dir-Gen. VLADIMIR DAMIYANOV.

Agromachinaimpex: 1040 Sofia, Stoyan Lepoyev St 1; tel. 20-03-91; telex 22563; export and import, maintenance and repair of agricultural equipment; Dir-Gen. TODOR PASHALIYEV.

Balkancarimpex: 1040 Sofia, Kliment Okhridsky Blvd 18; tel. 7-53-01; telex 23431; export of trucks, lorries and other vehicles; construction of vehicle parts.

Banimpex: 1113 Sofia, G. Bonchev St 107, POB 98; tel. 71-31; telex 23688; import of scientific equipment and chemicals; export of software products and chemicals.

Bulgarcoop: 1000 Sofia, Rakovsky St 99; tel. 84-41; telex 23429; export of live snails, live game and game meat; honey and bee products; nuts, pulses, medicinal plants, rose hips and rose-hip shells, fruit and vegetables (fresh and processed), essential oil seeds, etc.; onions and mushrooms; natural mineral water; consumer goods; Gen. Man. NENKO LECHEV.

Bulgariafilm: 1000 Sofia, Rakovsky St 96; tel. 87-66-11; telex 22447; export and import of films; participation in international film events; publication of film magazines; Dir ALEKSANDER ILIYEV.

Bulgarplodexport: 1040 Sofia, Blvd A. Stamboliisky 7; tel. 88-59-51; telex 23297; f. 1947; production, import and export of fresh and preserved fruit and vegetables; Dir-Gen. TSVETAN KARAMOCHEV.

Bulgartabac: 1000 Sofia, Blvd A. Stamboliisky 14; POB 96; tel. 87-52-11; telex 23288; covers manufacture, import and export of raw and manufactured tobacco; Dir-Gen. DIMITER YADKOV.

Chimimport: 1000 Sofia, Sofiiska Komuna St 1; tel. 88-38-11; telex 22521; import and export of chemicals, fertilizer, plant protection preparations, tyres, synthetic rubber and rubber wares, photographic paper, aniline dyes, crude petroleum and oil products, paraffins, petrochemicals, plastic and plastic products, fuels, etc.; Dir-Gen. BELO BELOV.

Electroimpex: 1000 Sofia, George Washington St 17; tel. 8-61-81; telex 22075; covers the export and import of electrical and power

BULGARIA

equipment and components for the electrical engineering industry; Gen. Man. KIRIL TSOCHEV.

Electronimpex: 1309 Sofia, Kiril Pchelinksy St 1; tel. 21-90-61; telex 23455; foreign trade in the fields of radio-location, radio-navigation and communications.

Energoimpex: 1463 Sofia, Ernst Thaelmann Blvd 17A; tel. 51-88-67; telex 22669; import and export of coal, electric power; delivery of machines and power equipment.

Hemus: 1000 Sofia, Levsky St 7; tel. 80-30-00; telex 22267; import and export of books, periodicals, numismatic items, antique objects, philatelic items, art products, musical instruments, gramophone records, cinematographic equipment and souvenirs; Gen. Man. IVAN ABADZHIYEV.

Hranexport: 1080 Sofia, Alabin St 56; tel. 88-22-51; telex 22525; import and export of grain, cocoa, sugar, oils, feed, pulses, vegetable oils, mixtures, etc.; Gen. Man. YOVCHO RUSEV.

Industrialimport: 1040 Sofia, Pozitano St 3; tel. 87-30-21; telex 22092; import and export of cotton, woollen and silk ready-made garments, knitwear, cotton, woollen and silk textiles, leather goods, china and glassware, sports equipment; Gen. Man. ANGEL ANGELOV.

Inflot: 1504 Sofia, Blvd Vl. Zaimov 88; 1000 Sofia, POB 634; tel. 87-25-34; telex 22376; agency for foreign and Bulgarian shipping, inland and maritime; Dir-Gen. DIMITUR BOTZEV.

Information Systems and System-Engineering Services: 1618 Sofia, 9 Septemvri Blvd 140; tel. 56-30-74; telex 23109; import and export of information systems, software products and system-engineering services; Dir-Gen. OGNYAN BOZAROV.

Intercommerce: 1040 Sofia, pl. Lenina 16; POB 676; tel. 87-93-64; telex 22067; all kinds of multilateral, compensation and barter deals, import and export, participation in foreign firms; Dir-Gen. KONSTANTIN GLAVANAKOV.

Interpred: 1057 Sofia, Blvd Bulgarosavetska Droujba 16; tel. 46-46-46; telex 23284; agency for the representation of foreign firms in Bulgaria; Chair. PETER VALCHEV.

Isotimpex: 1113 Sofia, Chapayev St 51; tel. 70-72-41; telex 22731; import and export of computing and organizational equipment, semi-conductors, radio parts, office equipment, materials for computing equipment; maintenance and service of computer systems; Dir-Gen. LYUBOMIR VITANOV.

Kintex: 1407 Sofia, Blvd Anton Ivanov 66; tel. 66-23-11; telex 22471; import and export of sports and hunting goods and explosives for industrial and mining purposes; Dir-Gen. IVAN DAMIYANOV.

Koraboimpex: 9000 Varna, D. Blagoev Blvd 128; tel. 88-18-25; telex 77550; imports and exports ships, marine and port equipment; Dir-Gen. KIRIL KOSTOV.

Lessoimpex: 1303 Sofia, Antim I St 17; tel. 8-61-71; telex 23407; import and export of timber, furniture and wooden products; Dir-Gen. STEFAN STEFANOV.

Machinoexport: 1000 Sofia, Aksakov St 5; tel. 88-53-21; telex 23425; export of metal-cutting and wood-working machines, industrial robots, hydraulic and pneumatic products and other equipment, tools and spare parts; Gen. Man. NENO MITEV.

Maimex: 1431 Sofia, D. Nestorov Blvd 15; tel. 5-81-01; telex 22712; import and export of specialized medical equipment and pharmaceutical products; Dir TSONCHO TSONCHEV.

Matchim: 1303 Sofia, Aprilsky Quarter 11; tel. 26-73-87; telex 23807; import and export of technology, equipment and materials.

Metalokeramikaimpex: 1113 Sofia, Chapaev St 49; tel. 70-00-43; telex 23622; import and export of products for the cement, machine-building and electrical engineering industries.

Metal Technology: 1574 Sofia, Chapaev St 53; tel. 7-14-21; telex 22903; export and import of machinery and industrial equipment.

Mineralimpex: 1156 Sofia, Kliment Okhridsky Blvd 44, Bl. 1A; tel. 77-95-06; telex 22973; export of mineral raw materials, drilling tools and products; import of machinery, minerals and diamond tools; Dir-Gen. STOIKO NIKOLOV.

Pharmachim: 1220 Sofia, Iliyensko chaussée 16; tel. 38-55-31; telex 22097; import and export of drugs, pharmaceutical, microbiological and veterinary products, essential oils, cosmetics and dental materials; Dir-Gen. IVAN ANDONOV.

Pirin: 1000 Sofia, Levsky St 19; tel. 88-14-43; telex 22761; f. 1965; production, export and import of leather goods; Dir-Gen. T. MANOLOV.

Prodexim: 1000 Sofia, Alabin St 56; tel. 88-06-42; telex 22212; import and export of machines and equipment for the light and food industries, textile products and household equipment.

Raznoiznos: 1040 Sofia, Tsar Assen St 1; tel. 88-02-11; telex 23244; export and import of industrial and craftsmen's products, timber products, paper products, glassware, kitchen utensils, furniture, carpets, toys, sports equipment, musical instruments, etc.; Dir-Gen. BOTZHO BOTEV.

Ribno Stopanstvo: 1000 Sofia, Parchevich St 42; tel. 80-10-01; telex 22796; import and export of fish and fish products; Dir KHRISTO YANEV.

Rodopaimpex: 1000 Sofia, Gavril Genov St 2; tel. 88-26-61; telex 22541; export of cattle, sheep, breeding animals, meat, meat products; dairy products, poultry, eggs; import of meat, breeding animals, tallow, artificial casing and equipment for the meat industry; Dir-Gen. SVETOSLAV ALEKSIYEV.

Rudmetal: 1000 Sofia, Dobrudzha St 1; tel. 88-12-71; telex 22027; f. 1952; export and import of metal and metal products, lead, zinc, copper, pure lead, ores, coal, etc.; Dir-Gen. YOSIF YOSIFOV.

Stroyimpex: 1000 Sofia, Triyaditsa St 5; tel. 80-30-47; telex 22385; export of cement, lime, cement slabs, floor tiles, prefabricated wooden houses; etc.; import of building materials, machines and equipment; Dir-Gen. ATANAS VLAKHOV.

Technoexportstroy: 1303 Sofia, Antim I St 11; tel. 87-85-11; telex 22128; design and construction abroad of all types of public, utility, industrial and infrastructural projects; supply of machines and technical assistance; Gen. Man. MARIN DZHERMANOV.

Technoimpex: 1000 Sofia, Tsar Kaloyan St 8, POB 932; tel. 88-15-71; telex 23783; scientific and technological assistance abroad in the fields of industry, architecture, construction, transport and communications and education; Dir-Gen. TSOKO KRIVIRADEV.

Techno-import-export: 1113 Sofia, ul. Frédéric Joliot-Curie 20, POB 541; tel. 73-81; telex 22193; import and export of machines and complete plants in the fields of power generation, metallurgy, mining and construction; Dir-Gen. VELIMIR DIMITROV.

Technoprogress: 1233 Sofia, Vranya St 20; tel. 31-20-26; telex 23141; research and development, design and marketing in construction industry.

Telecom: 1309 Sofia, Kiril Pchelinsky St 2; tel. 2-13-01; telex 22077; export and import of radioelectronic equipment and technology for the communications industry; Dir-Gen. NIKOLA MONOV.

Transimpex: 1606 Sofia, Skobelev Blvd 65; tel. 52-23-21; telex 22123; import and export of railway equipment, wagons, locomotives, boats and shipping parts.

Vinimpex: 1080 Sofia, Lavele St 19; tel. 88-39-21; telex 22467; import and export of wine and spirits and equipment and spares for the wine industry; Dir-Gen. GEORGI TOROMANOV.

TRADE UNIONS AND CO-OPERATIVES

Central Council of Bulgarian Trade Unions: Sofia, pl. D. Blagoev 1; tel. 86-61; telex 22446; f. 1904; the central Trade Union organization, to which are affiliated 17 individual federations and trade unions; Chair. PETUR DYULGEROV; Sec. ANDON TRAYKOV; total mems 4,000,000.

Trade Unions

Federation of Trade Union Organizations of Agricultural and Food Industry Workers: Sofia, ul. Dimo Hadzhidimov 29; Pres. MILADIN SHATEROV; 1,150,000 mems.

Federation of Trade Union Organizations of Biotechnical and Chemical Industry Workers: Sofia, ul. Alabin 3; Pres. IVAN SIMOV; 101,855 mems.

Federation of Trade Union Organizations of Communications Workers: Sofia, ul. Shesti Septemvri 4; Chair. VIOLETA STOYANOVA; 45,000 mems.

Federation of Trade Union Organizations of Construction and Building Industry Workers: Sofia, pl. Lenina 4; Chair. IVAN TODOROV; 274,500 mems.

Federation of Trade Union Organizations of Workers in Electronics: Sofia, pl. Lenina 4; Chair. NEDYALKO NEDYALKOV; 160,000 mems.

Federation of Trade Union Organizations of Forestry and Timber Industry Workers: 1606 Sofia, ul. Dimo Hadzhidimov 29; Pres. NIKOLA ABADJIEV; 111,000 mems.

Federation of Trade Union Organizations of Light Industry Workers: Sofia, ul. Shesti Septemvri 4; Chair. PETUR PETROV; 215,000 mems.

Federation of Trade Union Organizations of Machine-Building Workers: Sofia, pl. Lenina 4; Chair. DOYCHO DINEV; 420,000 mems.

Federation of Trade Union Organizations of Miners, Geologists, Metallurgic and Power Industry Workers: Sofia, pl. Lenina 4; Chair. STEFAN MILENKOV; 178,000 mems.

Federation of Trade Union Organizations of Transport Workers: Sofia, Blvd Georgi Dimitrov 106; f. 1911; Chair. ATANAS STANEV; 330,000 mems.

BULGARIA

Trade Union of Workers in Administration and Social Organization: Sofia, ul. Alabin 52; Chair. STOYAN CHOBANOV; 147,000 mems.

Trade Union of Health Service Workers: Sofia, pl. Lenina 4; Chair. Dr IVAN SECHANOV; 157,000 mems.

Trade Union of Workers in the Polygraphic Industry and Cultural Institutions: Sofia, Zdanov St 7; Pres. BOICHO PAVLOV; 49,300 mems.

Trade Union of Trade Workers: Sofia, ul. Shesti Septemvri 4; Chair. PETUR TSEKOV; 520,000 mems.

Union of Bulgarian Actors: 1000 Sofia, ul. Pope Andrei 1; tel. 87-71-96; f. 1919; Chair. VANCHA DOYCHEVA; 4,000 mems.

Union of Bulgarian Cinematographers: Chair. LYUDMIL STAYKOV.

Union of Bulgarian Teachers: Sofia, pl. Lenina 4; tel. 88-10-07; f. 1905; Chair. PANKA BABUKOVA; 238,000 mems.

Union of Musicians in Bulgaria: Sofia, ul. Alabin 52; Chair. Prof. GEORGI ROBEV; 6,000 mems.

Co-operatives

Central Co-operative Union: 1000 Sofia, Rakovsky 99, POB 55; tel. 84-41; telex 23229; f. 1947; the central body of all the co-operative organizations in the country. There are 384 consumers' co-operatives, 326 agrarian industrial complexes and 167 producers' co-operatives; more than 2,202,000 mems are affiliated to the Central Union; Pres. IVAN PEHLIVANOV.

TRADE FAIR

Plovdiv International Fair: Plovdiv, Blvd G. Dimitrov 37; tel. 55-31-91; telex 44432; f. 1933; in 1988: International Fair of consumer goods and foodstuffs (9–15 May), (in 1989: 8–14 May, in 1990: 7–13 May), International Technical Fair (26 September–2 October), (in 1989: 25 September–1 October, in 1990: 24–30 September); organized by Bulgarian Chamber of Commerce and Industry; Dir-Gen. KIRIL ASPARUKHOV.

Transport

Ministry of Transport: 1080 Sofia, ul. Levsky 9; tel. 31-71-21; directs the state rail, road, water and air transport organizations.

Despred: 1000 Sofia, Slavyanska St 2; tel. 87-60-16; telex 23306; state forwarding enterprise; Dir-Gen. TRAIKO VARGOV.

RAILWAYS

There were 4,586 km of track in Bulgaria in 1987, of which more than 2,050 km were electrified. In June 1986 the new Sofia–Gorna Oryakhovitsa–Varna main-line railway was opened. Construction of an underground railway in Sofia began in 1979, and was still in progress in 1988. The system was to have a total length of 100 km.

Bulgarian State Railways (BDZ): 1080 Sofia, Ivan Vazov St 3; tel. 87-30-45; telex 22423; owns and controls all railway transport; Chair. VESELIN PAVLOV.

ROADS

There were 36,908 km of roads in Bulgaria at the beginning of 1988, including 242 km of motorways, 2,955 km of main roads and 3,812 km of secondary roads. A major motorway runs from Sofia to the coast.

Autotransport: Sofia, Gurko St 5; tel. 87-62-32; telex 22332; f. 1965; Dir-Gen. T. PEYUVSKY.

SHIPPING AND INLAND WATERWAYS

The Danube river is the main waterway. External services link Black sea ports to the USSR, the Mediterranean and Western Europe.

Bulgarian River Lines: 7000 Ruse, pl. Otets Paisi 2; tel. 3-43-62; telex 62403; Dir YORDAN RADOYEV.

Navigation Maritime Bulgare: 9000 Varna, Blvd Chervenoarmeiska 1; tel. 22-24-74; telex 77351; f. 1892; sole enterprise in Bulgaria employed in sea transport; owns tankers, bulk carriers and container, ferry and passenger vessels with a displacement of more than 1,800,000 dwt; Dir-Gen. Capt. ATANAS YONKOV.

Shipping Corporation: Varna, Panagyurishte St 17; tel. 22-63-16; telex 077524; organization of sea and river transport; carriage of goods and passengers on waterways; controls all aspects of shipping and shipbuilding, also engages in research, design and personnel training; Dir-Gen. NIKOLAI YOVCHEV.

CIVIL AVIATION

Balkan Bulgarian Airlines: 1540 Sofia, Sofia Airport; pl. Narodno Sobraniye 12 (Head Office); tel. 7-12-01; telex 22342; f. 1947; state economic internal passenger and cargo services to Varna, Burgas, Ruse, Plovdiv, Kurdzhali, Targovishte, Silistra, Vidin and Gorna Oriakhovitsa; external services to Abu Dhabi, Algiers, Amsterdam, Ankara, Athens, Baghdad, Barcelona, Beirut, Belgrade, Berlin, Bratislava, Brussels, Bucharest, Budapest, Cairo, Casablanca, Copenhagen, Damascus, Dresden, Frankfurt am Main, Geneva, Harare, Helsinki, Istanbul, Khartoum, Kiev, Kuwait, Lagos, Leipzig, Leningrad, London, Luanda, Luxembourg, Madrid, Milan, Moscow, Nicosia, Paris, Prague, Rome, Stockholm, Tripoli, Tunis, Valletta, Vienna, Warsaw, Zürich; also agricultural aviation services; carried about 2.8m. passengers in 1987; fleet of 16 TU-134, 20 TU-154, 8 AN-24, 7 Il-18, 12 Yak-40, 6 Mil Mi-8 and 3 AN-12; Dir-Gen. VELICHKO VELICHKOV.

Tourism

Bulgaria's tourist attractions include the resorts on the Black Sea coast and the mountain scenery. There were 7,593,637 foreign visitor arrivals in 1987, mainly from other Eastern European countries.

Balkantourist: 1040 Sofia, Blvd Vitosha 1; tel. 4-33-31; telex 22583; f. 1948; the state tourist enterprise; Dir-Gen. IVAN MILKOV.

Atomic Energy

A heterogeneous swimming-pool reactor, with a thermal capacity of 2,000 kW, came into operation near Sofia in 1961. The reactor, supplied under a bilateral agreement by the USSR, is used for the production of radioactive isotopes as well as for experimental work.

Bulgaria's first nuclear power station at Kozlodui, which opened in 1974 with an initial generating capacity of 440 MW, was expanded to provide a capacity of 2,585 MW by 1988. A second nuclear power station, rated at 6,000 MW, was due to begin production at Belene in 1990. In 1988 the Kozlodui station was producing 40% of the country's electricity.

Institute for Nuclear Research and Nuclear Energy of the Bulgarian Academy of Sciences: 1784 Sofia, Blvd Lenin 72; tel. 75-80-32; telex 23561; f. 1973; Dir Acad. KHR. KHRISTOV.

BURKINA FASO

Introductory Survey

Location, Climate, Language, Religion, Flag, Capital

Burkina Faso (formerly the Republic of Upper Volta) is a landlocked state in West Africa, bordered by Mali to the west and north, by Niger to the east, and by Benin, Togo, Ghana and Côte d'Ivoire to the south. The climate is hot and mainly dry, with an average annual temperature of 28°C (82°F). Humidity reaches 80% in the south during the rainy season, which occurs between June and October but is often very short. The official language is French, and there are numerous indigenous languages (principally Mossi), with many dialects. The majority of the population follow animist beliefs, about 30% are Muslims and fewer than 10% Christians, mainly Roman Catholics. The national flag (proportions 3 by 2) has two equal horizontal stripes, of red and green, with a five-pointed gold star in the centre. The capital is Ouagadougou.

Recent History

Burkina Faso (known as Upper Volta until August 1984) was formerly a province of French West Africa. It became a self-governing republic within the French Community in December 1958 and achieved full independence on 5 August 1960, with Maurice Yaméogo as President. In January 1966 President Yaméogo was deposed in a military coup, led by Lt-Col (later Gen.) Sangoulé Lamizana, the Army Chief of Staff, who took office as President and Prime Minister. The military regime dissolved the National Assembly, suspended the Constitution and established a Supreme Council of the Armed Forces. Political activities were suspended in September 1966 but the restriction was lifted in November 1969. A new constitution, approved by popular referendum in June 1970, provided for a return to civilian rule after a four-year transitional regime of joint military and civilian administration. Elections for a National Assembly were held in December, and the Union démocratique voltaïque (UDV) won 37 of the 57 seats. In January 1971 the President appointed the UDV leader, Gérard Ouedraogo, as Prime Minister. He took office in February at the head of a mixed civilian and military Council of Ministers.

In late 1973 conflicts between the Government and the National Assembly led to deadlock, and in February 1974 the President, Gen. Lamizana, announced that the army had assumed power again. He dismissed the Prime Minister and dissolved the National Assembly. The Constitution and political activity were suspended, and the President assumed the functions of the premiership. In May the new military regime banned political parties. The Assembly was replaced by a National Consultative Council for Renewal, formed in July 1974, with 65 members nominated by the President.

Political parties were allowed to resume their activities from October 1977. A referendum in November approved a draft constitution which provided for a return to civilian democratic rule. Seven parties registered to contest elections for a new National Assembly, held in April 1978. The UDV won 28 of the 57 seats, while the newly-formed Union nationale pour la défense de la démocratie (UNDD) won 13. Gen. Lamizana was elected President in May, and the seven parties grouped themselves into three alliances in the Assembly, as required by the Constitution. The main opposition front was formed by the UNDD and the Union progressiste voltaïque (UPV). In July the Assembly elected the President's nominee, Dr Joseph Conombo (a leading member of the UDV), to be Prime Minister. The new Government's attempts to accommodate the various groups and to improve the economy were made difficult by the tacit hostility of the army and trade unions, and by the divisions in the National Assembly.

Largely as a result of the deteriorating economic situation, the country suffered a series of strikes during 1979 and 1980. After prolonged industrial unrest, President Lamizana was overthrown in November 1980 in a bloodless coup, led by Col Saye Zerbo, the military commander of the capital region, who had been Minister of Foreign Affairs during the previous period of military rule. A Comité militaire de redressement pour le progrès national (CMRPN), with 31 members (all soldiers), was established, and in December the new regime formed a Government of National Recovery, comprising both army officers and civilians. The Constitution was suspended, and the National Assembly was dissolved. Political parties and activities were banned, and a curfew was imposed. During 1981 Col Zerbo faced increasing opposition from the trade unions, a conflict which culminated in the suspension of one of the union associations and the revocation of the right to strike between November 1981 and February 1982. In November 1982, however, Col Zerbo was ousted in another military coup, led by non-commissioned army officers, in which five people were killed. Major Jean-Baptiste Ouedraogo emerged as leader of the new military regime, setting up the Conseil de salut du peuple (CSP). The CMRPN was dissolved, and a predominantly civilian government was formed. In February 1983 several soldiers and opposition figures were arrested, following the discovery of an alleged plot to reinstate the Zerbo regime. A power struggle within the CSP became apparent with the arrest, in May 1983, of radical left-wing elements within the Government, including the recently-appointed Prime Minister, Capt. Thomas Sankara. Maj. Ouedraogo announced the withdrawal of the armed forces from political life and disbanded the CSP. Sankara and his supporters were released after two weeks' detention, following a rebellion by pro-Sankara commandos at Pô, near the Ghana border, under the leadership of Capt. Blaise Compaoré.

In August 1983 Capt. Sankara seized power in a coup, in which an estimated 15 people were killed. Opposition politicians were placed under house arrest, a strict curfew was imposed and a Conseil national révolutionnaire (CNR) set up. Capt. Compaoré, as Minister of State to the presidency, became the regime's second-in-command. Citizens were encouraged to join local administrative committees, Comités pour la défense de la révolution (CDRs), in an attempt to mobilize popular support for the regime. In September ex-President Zerbo was formally arrested, after his supporters attempted to overthrow the new Government. Administrative, judicial and military reforms were announced, and Tribunaux populaires révolutionnaires (TPRs) were inaugurated to consider cases of alleged corruption. Several former politicians, including Zerbo, appeared before these tribunals and were subsequently imprisoned.

In March 1984 a prominent teachers' union staged a 48-hour strike in protest at the arrest of three of its leaders. In June seven people were executed, convicted of plotting to overthrow the Government. Sankara accused an outlawed political group, the Front Progressiste Voltaïque (which comprised members of the former UPV and other left-wing groups), of complicity in the plot, alleging that it had been supported by France and other foreign powers: the French Government vigorously denied any involvement, and relations between the two countries underwent some strain. In August 1984, on the first anniversary of the coup that had brought him to power, Sankara announced that Upper Volta would henceforth be known as Burkina Faso ('Land of the Incorruptible Men'), and a new national flag and anthem were introduced. Later that month, following signs of growing factionalism within the CNR, Sankara dissolved and re-formed the Government, reducing the influence of the Ligue patriotique pour le développement (LIPAD), a Marxist faction which had begun to oppose Sankara's populist rhetoric.

During 1985 the Sankara regime again encountered opposition from trade unions. The secretary-general of the LIPAD-affiliated Confédération syndicale burkinabê, Soumane Touré, was arrested in January, after having accused members of the CNR of embezzling public funds, and in February a total of 20 union leaders were detained, following a brief 'leaflet war', organized in protest against the introduction of austerity measures. In rural districts, however, it had begun to appear that the extended role of the CDRs in imposing government policy and organizing local affairs had consolidated both the revolution and Sankara's position as leader. In August the Government repealed the curfew that had been in force since August 1983.

The intensification, during 1986, of measures aimed at furthering the development of the rural economy increased tension between the Government and the trade unions, despite the granting of an amnesty for all political prisoners, announced in October. In early 1987 it was announced that austerity measures were to be introduced and that the public sector and the tax system were to undergo reform: a major tax-recovery operation was carried out in May and June, which reportedly led to the closure of many small businesses. In late May several influential trade-union activists, including Soumane Touré (who had been released under the October 1986 amnesty), were detained on charges of 'counter-revolutionary activities'. In August, during a speech commemorating the fourth anniversary of the coup that had brought him to power, Sankara appealed for unity among the country's political factions.

Growing disharmony within the CNR itself was evidenced when, as a result of a 're-formation' of the Government, several members of a leading left-wing faction, the Union de lutte communiste reconstruite (ULCR), lost their ministerial posts. On 15 October 1987 a 'Popular Front', under the leadership of Capt. Blaise Compaoré (Sankara's second-in-command), took power in a violent coup in which Sankara was killed, along with 13 of his close associates. The CNR was dissolved, and a curfew was imposed, while Burkina's land and air borders remained closed for two weeks. The former President was denounced, firstly as an 'autocrat' and subsequently as a 'revolutionary gone astray'. The new regime pledged a continuation of the revolutionary process begun in August 1983, but stated that only by the instigation of a 'rectification process' would popular confidence in the revolution be restored. The new 27-member Council of Ministers, announced on 31 October 1987, included only seven members of the previous Government and four military representatives. Compaoré became Head of State, assuming the title of Chairman of the Popular Front rather than that of President. A brief rebellion at the Koudougou garrison, led by Capt. Boukary Kaboré, was rapidly quelled, and Kaboré was reported to have fled the country. However, Sankara's death continued to be mourned widely, and in November a clandestine movement of resistance to the new regime, the Rassemblement démocratique et populaire–Thomas Sankara, was formed in Ouagadougou. The curfew was repealed in early January 1988.

Many of Sankara's close associates, including former ministers and members of his family, were arrested and detained without trial in the months following the coup. In January 1988 the Popular Front denied allegations, made by Amnesty International, that some detainees had been tortured. Soumane Touré was released from detention shortly after the coup, but LIPAD declined an invitation to participate in the Popular Front.

In March 1988 it was announced that the CDRs were to be disarmed and replaced by Comités révolutionnaires (CRs), under Capt. Arsène Yè Bognessan; the powers of the TPRs were also to be curtailed. In August a reshuffle of the Council of Ministers consolidated Compaoré's position at the head of the new regime, with the appointment of a number of civilian ministers to oversee the implementation of the Popular Front's economic programme (see Economic Affairs). In the same month Compaoré announced a campaign against 'laziness and amateurism' among state employees.

In December 1985 a long-standing border dispute with Mali erupted into a six-day war which left some 50 people dead. The conflict centred on an area known as the Agacher strip, reputed to contain significant deposits of minerals. Political tension between the two governments had been rising since mid-1985, when the Malian secretary-general of the Communauté économique de l'Afrique de l'Ouest (CEAO, see p. 119) was expelled from Burkina for criticizing austerity measures that had been imposed on the CEAO by Sankara. Following the cease-fire, which was arranged by the CEAO's defence grouping ANAD (Accord de non-agression et d'assistance en matière de défense), and as a result of the interim decision on the dispute that the International Court of Justice (ICJ) delivered in January 1986, troops were withdrawn from the Agacher area. Ambassadors were exchanged in June, and the ICJ's ruling, made in December, that the territory be divided equally between the two countries (with Burkina Faso gaining sovereignty over the eastern district of Beli) was formally accepted by both countries.

Under the Sankara regime, Burkina Faso established close links with neighbouring Ghana: a series of co-operation and security agreements were consolidated in 1984, and preliminary proposals for the eventual political and economic integration of the two countries were announced in August 1986. Summit meetings of leaders from Burkina Faso and Ghana, together with Benin and Libya, were held regularly to demonstrate 'revolutionary solidarity'. In September 1986 both Burkina Faso and Ghana were implicated by the Togolese Government in an alleged coup attempt in Lomé, and relations with Togo remained strained for several months.

The October 1987 coup had a generally favourable effect on Burkina Faso's external relations. In the months following his accession to power, Compaoré and other members of the Popular Front visited neighbouring countries, in an attempt to rally support for the new regime. Among the first West African states to support Compaoré were Togo and Côte d'Ivoire, although suggestions that the latter country had assisted in the overthrow of Sankara were denied. The Libyan leader, Col Qaddafi, also expressed a desire to maintain close links with the Popular Front. Those countries that had enjoyed particularly cordial contacts with Sankara, notably Ghana, Gabon and the Congo, condemned the coup, although relations with Ghana improved following meetings between the leaders of the two nations in early 1988. France, Burkina Faso's major trading partner, reacted with caution to the Compaoré regime, but the two countries' long-term relations seemed unlikely to be adversely affected.

Government

The National Assembly was dissolved in November 1980. All legislative and executive power rests with the Popular Front, whose Chairman is Head of State. For administrative purposes, the country is divided into 30 provinces, which, in turn, are divided into 250 departments, districts and villages. Local government is carried out by Comités révolutionnaires (CRs).

Defence

National service is voluntary, and lasts for two years on a part-time basis. In June 1988 the armed forces numbered 8,700, including a small air force, and there were 1,750 men in paramilitary forces. Defence expenditure was 15,338m. francs CFA in 1987.

Economic Affairs

The economy is predominantly agricultural. More than 80% of the working population are farmers or livestock-raising nomads. The agricultural sector contributed about 45% of gross domestic product (GDP) in 1986. The principal crops are sorghum, sugar cane, millet, beans and maize, most of which are consumed domestically. The major export crop is cotton, followed by shea-nuts (karité nuts). Production of seed (unginned) cotton increased from 58,000 metric tons in 1981/82 to 169,593 tons in 1986/87, and to an estimated 180,000 tons in 1987/88, largely reflecting an increase in the area cultivated and the introduction of government incentives. Livestock and livestock products provided about one-eighth of the country's export earnings in the mid-1980s.

Recovery in the agricultural sector, following the devastating droughts that affected the whole Sahel region from 1968 to 1974, was hampered by erratic rainfall patterns in the late 1970s and early 1980s, with the result that by May 1985 it was estimated that nearly 1.5m. Burkinabê were suffering from the effects of famine. Output of cereals was particularly affected, and in 1984 the overall cereal deficit reached 170,000 tons. However, following the return of normal rainfall, output of cereals totalled 1.6m. tons in 1985/86, increasing to an estimated 1.8m. tons in 1986/87. Several regional development projects that had been initiated by the Sankara regime, including a programme to irrigate 55,700 ha of land in the Sourou valley (for the cultivation of rice, sorghum and maize), were to be continued under the new Government, and several new projects, including a programme of agricultural research (to be funded by the International Development Association), were due to commence in 1988.

The People's Development Plan, introduced in May 1984 by the Sankara regime, aimed to achieve self-sufficiency in basic foods and essential capital goods, through economic decentralization and small-scale agricultural projects. The 1986-90 development programme, involving estimated total investment of 630,000m. francs CFA (of which 133,000m. francs CFA were to be provided from domestic resources), was to allocate a large proportion of resources to the manufacturing sector. It was hoped to achieve an average annual growth rate of 3.1% over the five-year period. In August 1984 the traditional land-ownership system was abolished, and all land and mineral rights were nationalized. The development of the agricultural sector was to remain a major economic priority for the Compaoré regime, with particular emphasis being placed on increased mechanization. The state-farm system was, however, to be progressively eliminated under the Popular Front.

Construction of a 15-MW hydroelectric dam at Kompienga, near the Togo border, which was expected to provide irrigation for 7,000 ha of land, began in June 1985, with completion scheduled for the end of 1988. Further hydroelectric projects are in progress at Bagre, on the Nankabe (White Volta), and at Noumbiel, on the Mouhoun (Black Volta), where a 60-MW installation is to be constructed.

In 1988 the Compaoré Government announced its intention of exploiting the country's mining potential. Development of mineral reserves has been hindered by poor communications and uncertainty concerning international markets. The Tambao manganese deposits are estimated to contain over 12m. tons of high-grade ore, and plans to extend the existing railway from Ouagadougou, to facilitate the exploitation of the deposits, were to be revived, following their suspension in mid-1986. The Poura gold mine, which closed in 1966, was reopened in 1984, and it was hoped to achieve annual production of 3.4 tons by 1990. Initial exploration of zinc and silver deposits at Perkoa, near Koudougou, began in 1984, financed by the World Bank: potential reserves are estimated at 10m. tons. A project to extract 450,000 tons of zinc ore per year from this region was to be implemented in 1988. Manufacturing contributed about 14% of GDP in the mid-1980s: the major concerns are food-processing, tobacco and textiles. A plan for the extension of existing cotton-ginning facilities at Bobo-Dioulasso was announced in 1987.

The country remains exceptionally poor, even by the standards of the developing countries. In 1987, according to estimates by the World Bank, Burkina Faso's gross national product (GNP), measured at average 1985–87 prices, was US $1,426m., equivalent to $170 per head, the latter figure representing an average annual decrease of 0.6% since 1980. The estimated average increase in overall GDP, in real terms, was 3.5% per year in 1965–80, falling to 2.5% per year in 1980–86. In recent years the growth of GDP has failed to keep pace with the rate of population increase. The country's critical financial situation has been aggravated by a chronic trade deficit, which in 1982 totalled 95,902m. francs CFA (more than five times the total value of exports), and in 1987 totalled almost 70,000m. francs CFA. France remains the major trading partner, providing 29.5% of imports and taking 26.4% of exports in 1986. Burkina's foreign debt totalled US $665m. at the end of 1986, according to the World Bank. A budget deficit of 5,990m. francs CFA was forecast for 1988, compared with an estimated 12,600m. francs CFA in 1987, with external debt-service payments projected to fall to 15,000m. francs CFA in 1988, from some 18,000m. francs CFA in the previous year. The Government depends on foreign sources for up to three-quarters of its national budget, with France alone providing some 30,000m. francs CFA in aid in 1987. Population density is high for a country with such limited resources. Traditionally, there has been substantial emigration to the coastal countries of the region, in particular to Côte d'Ivoire, which is estimated to accommodate some 1m. Burkinabê. Remittances that are sent home by emigrant workers contribute significantly to Burkina's balance of payments.

In 1988, in view of the country's persistent economic problems, the Government sought the assistance of the IMF and the World Bank in formulating a medium-term structural adjustment programme. (Such recourse had been strongly resisted by the Sankara regime.) The programme was likely to reflect Compaoré's advocacy of a system of 'state capitalism', by encouraging the development of private enterprise, to the detriment of the generally unprofitable state sector.

Social Welfare

The Government provides hospitals and rural medical services. A special medical service for schools is in operation. In 1980 there were five main hospitals, with a total of 2,042 beds. There were also 254 dispensaries, 11 medical centres and 65 regional clinics. A new hospital, built with aid from the People's Republic of China, was inaugurated at Koudougou in 1988. In 1981 only 127 physicians were employed in official medical services (one per 55,858 inhabitants). By 1987, however, every village had its own elected health committee and a primary health centre, and there was one physician per 40,000 inhabitants. In addition, a major vaccination programme, involving 2.5m. Burkinabé children, had been implemented. An old-age and veterans' pension system was introduced in 1960, and extended workers' insurance schemes have been in operation since 1967. Of total expenditure by the central Government in 1985, 3,911m. francs CFA (6.3%) was for health, and a further 5,191m. francs CFA (8.3%) was for social security and welfare.

Education

Education is provided free of charge. Primary education, which is officially compulsory, begins at seven years of age and lasts for up to six years. Secondary education, beginning at the age of 13, lasts for a further seven years, comprising a first cycle of four years and a second of three years. It was estimated that in 1985 about 27% of children in the relevant age-group attended primary schools (35% of boys; 20% of girls), while the comparable ratio for secondary school enrolment was only about 4% (boys 5%; girls 3%). The number of students in higher education increased, however, from 1,067 in 1975 to 3,869 in 1986. There is a university in Ouagadougou, and government grants are available for higher education in European and African universities. A rural radio service has been established to further general and technical education in rural areas. Adult 'functional literacy' programmes in national languages were introduced in 1983. In 1985, according to UNESCO estimates, adult illiteracy averaged 86.8% (males 79.3%; females 93.9%). Budget expenditure on education in 1987 was estimated at 16,826m. francs CFA, representing almost 19% of total government spending.

Public Holidays

1989: 2 January (for New Year), 3 January (Anniversary of the 1966 Revolution), 27 March (Easter Monday), 1 May (May Day), 4 May (Ascension Day), 7 May* (Id al-Fitr, end of Ramadan), 15 May (Whit Monday), 14 July* (Id al-Adha, Feast of the Sacrifice), 4 August (National Day), 15 August (Assumption), 13 October* (Mouloud, Birth of the Prophet), 1 November (All Saints' Day), 25 December (Christmas).

1990: 1 January (New Year), 3 January (Anniversary of the 1966 Revolution), 16 April (Easter Monday), 27 April* (Id al-Fitr, end of Ramadan), 1 May (May Day), 24 May (Ascension Day), 4 June (Whit Monday), 4 July* (Id al-Adha, Feast of the Sacrifice), 4 August (National Day), 15 August (Assumption), 2 October* (Mouloud, Birth of the Prophet), 1 November (All Saints' Day), 25 December (Christmas).

* These holidays are dependent on the Islamic lunar calendar and may vary by one or two days from the dates given.

Weights and Measures

The metric system is in force.

BURKINA FASO

Statistical Survey

Source (except where otherwise stated): Institut National de la Statistique et de la Démographie, BP 374, Ouagadougou; tel. 33-55-37.

Area and Population

AREA, POPULATION AND DENSITY

Area (sq km)	274,200*
Population (census results)	
1–7 December 1975	5,638,203
10–20 December 1985	
Males	3,833,237
Females	4,131,468
Total	7,964,705
Population (estimates at mid-year)	
1986	8,080,000
1987 (UN estimate)	8,305,000
Density (per sq km) at mid-1987	30.3

* 105,870 sq miles.

PRINCIPAL TOWNS (population at 1985 census)

Ouagadougou (capital)	441,514	Ouahigouya	38,902
Bobo-Dioulasso	228,668	Banfora	35,319
Koudougou	51,926	Kaya	25,814

BIRTHS AND DEATHS (UN estimates, annual averages)

	1970–75	1975–80	1980–85
Birth rate (per 1,000)	49.3	48.1	47.8
Death rate (per 1,000)	26.1	24.0	20.1

Source: UN, *World Population Prospects: Estimates and Projections as assured in 1984.*

ECONOMICALLY ACTIVE POPULATION
(ILO estimates, '000 persons at mid-1980)

	Males	Females	Total
Agriculture, etc.	1,550	1,414	2,964
Industry	89	57	146
Services	145	165	310
Total	1,784	1,637	3,421

Source: ILO, *Economically Active Population Estimates and Projections, 1950–2025.*

1985 census (provisional): Total labour force 4,051,409 (males 2,060,410; females 1,990,999).

Agriculture

PRINCIPAL CROPS ('000 metric tons)

	1984	1985	1986
Maize	74	142*	155
Millet	417.2	587*	679
Sorghum	594	798*	1,011
Rice (paddy)	41	50*	38
Sweet potatoes*	33	25†	16
Cassava (Manioc)*	31	32†	33†
Yams*	32†	33†	33†
Vegetables*	107	119†	123†
Fruit*	63	66	68†
Pulses*	460†	475†	475†
Groundnuts (in shell)	72	110†	158
Cottonseed	79	88	115
Cotton (lint)	30	34	46
Sesame seed	5	6	5
Tobacco (leaves)*	1†	1†	1†
Sugar cane*	320	340	345†

* Source: FAO, *Production Yearbook.*
† FAO estimates.

LIVESTOCK ('000 head)

	1985	1986	1987
Cattle	3,045	3,051	3,057
Sheep	2,148	2,158	2,169
Goats	3,236	3,252	3,268
Pigs	206	206	206
Horses	70	70	70
Asses	200	200	200
Camels*	6	6†	n.a.

Poultry (million)*: 20 in 1984; 20 in 1985; 21 in 1986.
* Source: FAO, *Production Yearbook.*
† FAO estimates.

LIVESTOCK PRODUCTS (FAO estimates, '000 metric tons)

	1984	1985	1986
Beef and veal	27	28	28
Mutton and lamb	4	4	4
Goats' meat	7	8	8
Pigs' meat	4	4	4
Horse meat	1	1	1
Poultry meat	18	18	19
Cows' milk	87	88	89
Goats' milk	9	10	10
Butter	0.7	0.7	0.7
Hen eggs	14.0	14.3	14.7
Cattle hides	4.6	4.7	4.8
Sheep skins	1.0	1.0	1.1
Goat skins	2.2	2.3	2.4

Source: FAO, *Production Yearbook.*

BURKINA FASO

Forestry

ROUNDWOOD REMOVALS
('000 cubic metres, excluding bark)

	1984	1985	1986*
Sawlogs, veneer logs and logs for sleepers	2	1	1
Other industrial wood*	297	304	312
Fuel wood*	6,294	6,443	6,618
Total	6,593	6,748	6,931

* FAO estimates.
Source: FAO, *Yearbook of Forest Products*.

Fishing

('000 metric tons, live weight)

	1980	1981	1982
Total catch	6.5	7.5	7.0

1983–86: Catch as in 1982 (FAO estimate).
Source: FAO, *Yearbook of Fishery Statistics*.

Industry

SELECTED PRODUCTS (metric tons, unless otherwise indicated)

	1984	1985	1986
Flour	17,677	25,682	25,518
Raw sugar	26,773	27,939	n.a.
Soap	11,971	13,456	n.a.
Cottonseed oil (refined)	4,116	5,945	n.a.
Beer (hectolitres)	623,160	n.a.	389,269
Soft drinks (hectolitres)	122,611	n.a.	128,644
Cigarettes ('000 packets)	33,569	33,569	25,492
Footwear ('000 pairs)	911	1,318	890
Cotton yarn	393	392	238
Bicycles, motor cycles and scooters ('000)	26.5	32.3	52.8
Bicycle and motor cycle tyres ('000)	714.4	994.6	526.1
Electric power ('000 kWh)	123,191	123,306	130,567

Finance

CURRENCY AND EXCHANGE RATES

Monetary Units
100 centimes = 1 franc de la Communauté financière africaine (CFA).

Denominations
Coins: 1, 2, 5, 10, 25, 50 and 100 francs CFA.
Notes: 100, 500, 1,000, 5,000 and 10,000 francs CFA.

French Franc, Sterling and Dollar Equivalents (30 September 1988)
1 French franc = 50 francs CFA;
£1 sterling = 538.6 francs CFA;
US $1 = 318.5 francs CFA;
1,000 francs CFA = £1.857 = $3.140.

Average Exchange Rate (francs CFA per US $)
1985 449.26
1986 346.30
1987 300.54

BUDGET (million francs CFA)*

Revenue†	1984	1985	1987
Taxation	49,260	55,109	74,231
Taxes on income, profits, etc.	10,812	9,004	17,115
Individual taxes	6,567	6,413	7,312
Social security contributions	5,293	5,539	n.a.
Domestic taxes on goods and services	10,091	10,047	18,832
Turnover tax	4,618	3,567	5,900
Excises	3,088	4,106	7,975
Taxes on international trade	18,674	24,609	32,661
Import duties	16,362	21,267	29,060
Other current revenue	6,267	18,989	8,721
Property income	2,866	3,240	3,617
Sub-total	55,527	74,098	82,952
Adjustment to cash basis	6,734	−1,490	—
Total current revenue	62,261	72,608	82,952
Capital revenue	17	99	64
Total revenue	62,278	72,707	83,016

* Figures represent a consolidation of the operations of the General Budget, covering the major units of the central government, and (except for 1987) the National Social Security Fund. Data for 1985 also include four extrabudgetary accounts. No figures are available for 1986.
† Excluding grants received (million francs CFA): 810 in 1984; 801 in 1985.

Expenditure‡	1984	1985	1987
General public services	6,935	7,200	11,000
Defence	11,784	12,178	15,338
Education	10,851	11,242	16,826
Health	3,576	3,911	5,128
Social security and welfare	4,349	5,191	1,698
Housing and community amenities	82	84	1,332
Other community and social services	964	989	1,360
Economic services	7,664	8,835	9,575
General administration, regulation and research	1,660	3,246	n.a.
Agriculture, forestry and fishing	2,784	2,688	2,512
Mining, manufacturing and construction	209	73	111
Transport and communications	507	438	1,289
Other economic services	2,504	2,295	2,688
Other purposes	7,810	5,129	13,617
Sub-total	57,750	62,353	88,562
Adjustment to cash basis	6,941	1,092	—
Total expenditure	64,691	63,445	88,562
Current§	60,854	57,903	75,874
Capital	3,837	5,542	12,688

‡ Excluding net lending (million francs CFA): 1,747 in 1984; 2,358 in 1985; −907 in 1987.
§ Including interest payments (million francs CFA): 3,698 in 1984; 6,455 in 1985; 8,538 in 1987.
Note: All figures for 1987 are provisional.
Source: IMF, *Government Finance Statistics Yearbook*.

1988 (budget proposals, million francs CFA): Revenue 90,295; Expenditure 96,285.

CENTRAL BANK RESERVES (US $ million at 31 December)

	1985	1986	1987
Gold*	3.6	4.5	5.2
IMF special drawing rights	6.2	6.9	8.0
Reserve position in IMF	8.3	9.2	10.7
Foreign exchange	125.1	217.4	303.9
Total	143.1	238.0	327.8

* Valued at market-related prices.
Source: IMF, *International Financial Statistics*.

BURKINA FASO

Statistical Survey

MONEY SUPPLY ('000 million francs CFA at 31 December)

	1985	1986	1987
Currency outside banks	30.97	43.43	43.71
Demand deposits at deposit money banks*	36.36	39.75	44.09
Checking deposits at post office	1.98	2.14	2.79

* Excluding the deposits of public establishments of an administrative or social nature.

Source: IMF, *International Financial Statistics*.

COST OF LIVING (Consumer Price Index for Africans in Ouagadougou; base: 1980 = 100)

	1985	1986	1987
All items	146.3	142.5	138.5

Source: IMF, *International Financial Statistics*.

NATIONAL ACCOUNTS (million francs CFA at current prices)
National Income and Product

	1982	1983	1984
Compensation of employees	82,516	86,595	92,066
Operating surplus	202,212	214,964	221,951
Domestic factor incomes	284,728	301,559	314,017
Consumption of fixed capital	21,248	20,405	22,872
Gross domestic product (GDP) at factor cost	305,976	321,964	336,889
Indirect taxes	30,168	28,195	27,263
Less Subsidies	1,080	331	350
GDP in purchasers' values	335,064	349,827	363,801
Factor income received from abroad	4,525	4,600	4,600
Less Factor income paid abroad	5,527	5,300	5,400
Gross national product	334,062	349,127	363,001
Less Consumption of fixed capital	21,248	20,405	22,872
National income in market prices	312,814	328,722	340,129
Other current transfers received from abroad	105,119	107,300	111,700
Less Other current transfers paid abroad	13,983	14,600	15,700
National disposable income	403,950	421,422	436,129

Expenditure on the Gross Domestic Product

	1982	1983	1984
Government final consumption expenditure	55,481	56,719	57,689
Private final consumption expenditure	321,352	327,822	325,386
Increase in stocks	5,338	1,580	942
Gross fixed capital formation	72,701	73,906	76,183
Total domestic expenditure	454,872	460,027	460,201
Exports of goods and services	56,185	63,800	75,000
Less imports of goods and services	175,993	174,000	171,400
GDP in purchasers' values	335,064	349,827	363,801
GDP at constant 1975 prices	161,671	153,922	150,650

Gross Domestic Product by Economic Activity
(million francs CFA)

	1982	1983	1984
Agriculture and hunting	127,688	135,880	146,197
Forestry and logging	9,584	9,765	9,948
Fishing	1,441	1,549	1,699
Mining and quarrying	181	77	304
Manufacturing	39,453	46,415	50,861
Electricity, gas and water	3,250	4,055	4,246
Construction	6,935	7,749	4,934
Trade, restaurants and hotels	47,544	46,343	42,186
Transport, storage and communications	21,074	18,816	23,554
Finance, insurance, real estate and business services	14,287	15,344	15,956
Government services	46,818	49,300	52,050
Other community, social and personal services	639	515	350
Private non-profit services to households / Domestic services of households	2,444	2,606	2,769
Sub-total	321,338	338,415	355,055
Import duties	20,482	18,131	16,219
Less Imputed bank service charge	6,755	6,720	7,472
GDP in purchasers' values	335,064	349,827	363,801

Source: UN, *National Accounts Statistics*.

BALANCE OF PAYMENTS (million francs CFA)

	1985*	1986*	1987†
Merchandise exports f.o.b.	55,900	61,900	72,000
Merchandise imports f.o.b.	−142,000	−145,000	−152,500
Trade balance	−86,100	−83,100	−80,500
Services (net)	−52,500	−53,000	−56,000
Balance on goods and services	−138,600	−136,100	−136,500
Private unrequited transfers (net)	47,300	52,000	53,000
Government unrequited transfers (net)	58,000	66,000	68,000
Current balance	−33,300	−18,100	−15,500
Long-term capital (net)	29,200	37,700	21,000
Short-term capital (net) / Net errors and omissions	2,500	3,000	2,000
Total (net monetary movements)	−1,600	22,600	7,500

* Provisional figures. † Estimated figures.

Source: Banque Centrale des Etats de l'Afrique de l'Ouest.

BURKINA FASO

Statistical Survey

External Trade

Source: Banque Centrale des Etats de l'Afrique de l'Ouest.

PRINCIPAL COMMODITIES (million francs CFA)

Imports c.i.f.	1984	1985	1986
Dairy products	4,629	5,122	5,331
Cereals	17,401	23,076	7,753
Beverages and tobacco	2,857	3,309	3,522
Refined petroleum products	16,372	18,643	15,413
Other raw materials	3,648	4,263	3,823
Fats and oils	3,233	6,782	3,295
Non-electrical machinery	6,906	9,035	15,121
Electrical machinery	3,153	5,327	5,265
Road transport equipment	8,945	13,327	17,703
Chemicals	11,990	14,825	15,749
Miscellaneous manufactured articles	20,663	25,725	33,564
Hydraulic cement	3,353	3,340	4,052
Total (incl. others)	111,264	146,243	139,640

Exports f.o.b.	1984	1985	1986
Livestock and livestock products	3,839	3,491	2,725
Vegetables	712	685	595
Sesame seeds	781	1,348	422
Shea-nuts (Karité nuts)	4,006	2,190	737
Hides and skins	1,422	1,891	1,408
Cotton (ginned)	19,179	11,660	10,633
Fats and oils	977	410	168
Machinery and transport equipment	889	763	1,684
Miscellaneous manufactured articles	2,155	7,649	9,214
Rubber manufactures	934	808	15
Total (incl. others)	34,872	31,157	28,665

PRINCIPAL TRADING PARTNERS (million francs CFA)

Imports	1984	1985	1986
Algeria	1,213	2,701	17
Belgium/Luxembourg	1,312	1,595	1,760
Canada	1,916	1,117	2,305
China, People's Republic	3,530	3,618	1,603
Côte d'Ivoire	24,959	33,269	29,971
France	28,941	34,568	41,124
Germany, Federal Republic	2,799	6,963	5,108
Ghana	1,111	2,563	n.a.
Italy	1,812	3,139	6,893
Japan	4,199	4,309	6,067
Netherlands	5,137	5,978	6,922
Nigeria	799	1,549	1,080
Senegal	1,304	1,144	1,733
Spain	825	1,162	2,001
Thailand	151	2,148	1,314
Togo	1,831	1,844	3,553
United Kingdom	3,210	2,921	2,468
USA	11,159	21,941	12,553
Total (incl. others)	111,264	146,243	139,640

Exports	1984	1985	1986
Belgium/Luxembourg	865	520	151
Canada	356	271	110
China, People's Republic	1,648	1,374	165
Côte d'Ivoire	5,149	4,681	4,337
Denmark	464	578	404
France	3,669	9,046	7,572
Germany, Federal Republic	2,792	439	606
Ghana	242	372	134
Italy	1,252	1,410	881
Japan	2,502	635	281
Mali	176	389	368
Morocco	138	929	0
Niger	270	213	436
Spain	870	338	905
Sweden	246	418	488
Switzerland	340	2,205	2,192
Taiwan	8,792	5,279	7,166
Togo	352	343	253
Tunisia	503	n.a.	n.a.
United Kingdom	3,075	694	694
Total (incl. others)	34,872	31,157	28,665

Transport

RAILWAYS (traffic)

	1980	1981	1982
Passenger journeys ('000)	3,646	3,277	2,867
Passenger-km (million)	1,250	988	856
Freight ton-km (million)	600	634	668

Passengers carried: 2.4 million in 1985; 1.5 million in 1986.
Freight: 233,009 metric tons in 1985; 227,870 metric tons in 1986.

ROAD TRAFFIC (motor vehicles in use at 31 December)

	1982	1983
Cars	19,196	21,182
Buses and coaches	543	583
Goods vehicles	4,658	5,146
Tractors and trailers	1,710	1,885
Motor cycles and mopeds	7,159	13,411

Source: International Road Federation, *World Road Statistics*.

CIVIL AVIATION (traffic on scheduled services)*

	1982	1983	1984
Kilometres flown (million)	2.1	2.3	2.2
Passengers carried ('000)	81	93	93
Passenger-km (million)	215	222	222
Freight ton-km (million)	21.2	18.8	17.4
Mail ton-km (million)	0.8	0.8	0.8
Total ton-km (million)	41	40	38

* Including an apportionment of the traffic of Air Afrique.
Source: UN, *Statistical Yearbook*.

Tourism

	1984	1985	1986
Number of tourist arrivals	40,249	44,375	60,704

Receipts from tourism (million francs CFA): 1,788 in 1984; 2,193 in 1985; 2,212 in 1986.

Source: Division du Tourisme et de l'Hôtellerie, Ouagadougou.

BURKINA FASO

Communications Media

	1981	1982	1983
Radio receivers ('000 in use)	118	120	123
Television receivers ('000 in use)	11	19	35

Telephones (1984): 14,000 in use.
Book production (1985): 4 titles.
Daily newspapers (1984): 1 (average circulation 2,000 copies).
Source: mainly UNESCO, *Statistical Yearbook*.

Education

(1986)

	Insti-tutions	Teachers	Pupils		
			Male	Female	Total
Primary	1,758	6,091	221,969	129,838	351,807
Secondary:					
General	107	1,519	33,208	15,667	48,875
Vocational	18	421	2,601	2,207	4,808
Teacher training	1	n.a.	231	116	347
Higher	1	325	2,955	914	3,869

Source: Ministère de l'Education nationale, Ouagadougou.

Directory

The Constitution

The 1977 Constitution was suspended following the military coup of 25 November 1980.

The Government

HEAD OF STATE

Chairman of the Popular Front: Capt. BLAISE COMPAORÉ (assumed power 15 October 1987).

COUNCIL OF MINISTERS
(November 1988)

Chairman of the Popular Front and Head of Government: Capt. BLAISE COMPAORÉ.
Minister of Popular Defence and Security: Maj. JEAN-BAPTISTE BOUKARY LINGANI.
Minister of Economic Promotion: Capt. HENRI ZONGO.
Minister of External Relations: JEAN-MARC PALM.
Minister of Health and Social Action: ALAIN ZOUGBA.
Minister of Secondary and Higher Education and Scientific Research: OUMAROU CLÉMENT OUEDRAOGO.
Minister of Planning and Co-operation: YOUSSOUF OUEDRAOGO.
Minister of Primary Education and Mass Literacy: ALICE TIENDRÉBÉOGO.
Minister of Peasant Affairs: Capt. LAURENT SEDEGO.
Minister of Information and Culture: SERGE THÉOPHILE BALIMA.
Minister of the Environment and Tourism: BÉATRICE DAMIBA.
Minister of Trade and Popular Supply: FRÉDÉRIC KORSAGA.
Minister of Transport and Communications: ISSA KONATÉ.
Minister of Territorial Administration: JEAN-LÉONARD COMPAORÉ.
Minister of Justice and Keeper of the Seals: SALIF SAMPEBOGO.
Minister of Equipment: Capt. DAPROU KAMBOU.
Minister of Sports: Lt KILIMITÉ HIEN.
Minister of Labour, Social Security and the Public Service: KANIDOUA NABOHO.
Minister of Finance: BINTOU SANOGO.
Minister of Agriculture and Livestock: ALBERT DJIDMA.
Minister of Water Resources: ALFRED NOMBRE.
Secretary of State for Housing and Urban Affairs: MOÏSE TRAORÉ.
Secretary of State for the Budget: CÉLESTIN TIENDRÉBÉOGO.
Secretary of State for Culture: ALIMATA SALEMBÉRÉ.
Secretary of State for Mines: JEAN YADO TOÉ.
Secretary of State for Social Action: ELIE SARÉ.
Secretary of State for Livestock: AMADOU GUIAO.
Secretary of State for Secondary Education: OUEMIDOUN BOLEHO.
Secretary-General of the Government and of the Council of Ministers: PROSPER VOKOUMA.

Secretary-General of the Revolutionary Committees: Capt. ARSÈNE YÈ BOGNESSAN.

MINISTRIES

Chairman's Office: Ouagadougou.
Ministry of Agriculture and Livestock: BP 7005, Ouagadougou.
Ministry of Economic Promotion: Ouagadougou.
Ministry of the Environment and Tourism: BP 7044, Ouagadougou; tel. 33-41-65; telex 5555.
Ministry of Equipment: BP 7011, Ouagadougou.
Ministry of External Relations: BP 7038, Ouagadougou; telex 5222.
Ministry of Finance: BP 7008, Ouagadougou; tel. 33-40-74; telex 5256.
Ministry of Health and Social Action: BP 7009, Ouagadougou.
Ministry of Information and Culture: BP 7045, Ouagadougou; tel. 33-44-67; telex 5285.
Ministry of Justice: BP 526, Ouagadougou.
Ministry of Labour, Social Security and the Public Service: BP 7006, Ouagadougou.
Ministry of Peasant Affairs: Ouagadougou.
Ministry of Planning and Co-operation: BP 7050, Ouagadougou; telex 5319.
Ministry of Popular Defence and Security: BP 496, Ouagadougou; telex 5297.
Ministry of Primary Education and Mass Literary: BP 7032, Ouagadougou; telex 5555.
Ministry of Secondary and Higher Education and Scientific Research: BP 7130, Ouagadougou.
Ministry of Sports: BP 7035, Ouagadougou.
Ministry of Territorial Administration: BP 7034, Ouagadougou.
Ministry of Trade and Popular Supply: BP 365, Ouagadougou.
Ministry of Transport and Communications: BP 7701, Ouagadougou.
Ministry of Water Resources: Ouagadougou.
Office of the Secretary-General: BP 7030, Ouagadougou.

Legislature

ASSEMBLÉE NATIONALE

The National Assembly was dissolved following the coup of November 1980.

Political Organizations

The following groups were in existence in 1988:

Front progressiste voltaïque (FPV): fusion of the fmr Union progressiste voltaïque and other left-wing parties; officially banned; Sec.-Gen. Prof. JOSEPH KI-ZERBO (in exile).
Groupe communiste burkinabé (GCB): Ouagadougou; Marxist-Leninist splinter group.
Ligue patriotique pour le développement (LIPAD): Ouagadougou; f. 1973; Marxist and pro-Soviet; Pres. HAMIDOU COULIBALY.

BURKINA FASO

Rassemblement démocratique et populaire—Thomas Sankara: Ouagadougou; f. Nov. 1987; clandestine resistance movement; Leader VINCENT OUEDRAOGO.

Union communiste burkinabê (UCB): Ouagadougou; f. 1985; Leader WATAMOU LAMIEN.

Union démocratique voltaïque (UDV): Burkina Faso section of the fmr Rassemblement démocratique africain, f. 1946; officially banned; Leader MALO TRAORÉ.

Union de Lutte communiste (ULC): Ouagadougou; f. 1978.

Union de Lutte communiste reconstruite (ULCR): Ouagadougou; f. 1984; Maoist; Leaders VALÈRE SOMÉ, BASILE GUISSOU.

Diplomatic Representation

EMBASSIES IN BURKINA FASO

Algeria: BP 3893, Ouagadougou; telex 5359.

China, People's Republic: quartier Rotonde, BP 538, Ouagadougou; Ambassador: JIANG XIANG.

Cuba: BP 3422, Ouagadougou; telex 5360; Ambassador: REME REMIGIO RUIZ.

Egypt: BP 668, Ouagadougou; telex 5289; Ambassador: Dr MOHAMAD ALEY EL-KORDY.

France: 902 ave de l'Indépendance, BP 504, Ouagadougou; tel. 33-38-92; telex 5211; Ambassador: ALAIN DESCHAMPS.

Germany, Federal Republic: BP 600, Ouagadougou; tel. 33-60-94; telex 5217; Ambassador: MICHEL GEIER.

Ghana: BP 212, Ouagadougou; tel. 33-28-75; Ambassador: (vacant).

Korea, Democratic People's Republic: BP 370, Ouagadougou; Ambassador: YI TAE-KYUN.

Korea, Republic: BP 618, Ouagadougou; telex 5307; Ambassador: CHOI KEUN-BAE.

Libya: BP 1601, Ouagadougou; telex 5311; Secretary of People's Bureau: (vacant).

Netherlands: BP 1302, Ouagadougou; telex 5303; Ambassador: P. R. BROUWER.

Nigeria: BP 132, Ouagadougou; tel. 33-42-41; telex 5236; Chargé d'affaires a.i.: A. K. ALLI ASSAYOUTI.

USSR: BP 7041, Ouagadougou; Ambassador: YEVGENI NIKOLAYEVICH KORENDYASOV.

USA: BP 35, Ouagadougou; tel. 30-67-23; telex 5290; Ambassador: DAVID SHINN.

Judicial System

Following the August 1983 coup, Tribunaux populaires révolutionnaires (TPRs) were established, to operate under the jurisdiction of the Appeal Courts at Ouagadougou and Bobo-Dioulasso. Tribunals consist of three magistrates from the judiciary, three military personnel and representatives of local Comités révolutionnaires.

Religion

An estimated 57% of the population follow animist beliefs.

ISLAM

At 31 December 1986 there were an estimated 2,514,261 Muslims in Burkina Faso.

CHRISTIANITY

Protestant Churches

At 31 December 1986 there were an estimated 106,467 adherents.

The Roman Catholic Church

Burkina Faso comprises one archdiocese and eight dioceses. At 31 December 1986 there were an estimated 868,116 adherents.

Bishops' Conference: Conférence Épiscopale du Burkina Faso et du Niger, BP 1195, Ouagadougou; tel. 30-60-26; f. 1966, legally recognized 1978; Pres. Rt Rev. ANSELME TITIANMA SANON, Bishop of Bobo-Dioulasso.

Archbishop of Ouagadougou: Cardinal PAUL ZOUNGRANA, BP 1472, Ouagadougou; tel. 39-67-04.

The Press

Direction de la presse écrite: Ouagadougou; official govt body responsible for media direction.

DAILIES

Bulletin Quotidien d'Information: BP 507, Ouagadougou; tel. 30-61-14; f. 1959; publ. by the Direction de la presse écrite; simultaneous edn publ. in Bobo-Dioulasso; Dir-Gen. HUBERT BAZIÉ; Editor PIERRE-CLAVIER TASSEMBEDO; circ. 1,500.

Dunia: Ouagadougou.

Jamaa (Voice of the Masses): Ouagadougou; f. 1988; organ of the Popular Front.

Lolowulein (Red Star): Ouagadougou; f. 1985; state-owned.

Notre Combat: BP 507, Ouagadougou.

Sidwaya (Truth): Ouagadougou; f. 1984; govt-owned; Dir BABOU PAULIN BAMOUNI; circ. 5,000.

PERIODICALS

Armée du Peuple: Ouagadougou; f. 1982; monthly; armed forces and defence information; Editor-in-Chief Lt SEYDOU NIANG.

Bulletin Economique et Fiscal: BP 502, Ouagadougou; tel. 33-61-48; telex 5268; f. 1971; monthly; legislative and statutory notices; distributed by the Chambre de Commerce, d'Industrie et d'Artisanat du Burkina; circ. 350.

Bulletin Mensuel de Statistique: BP 374, Ouagadougou; tel. 33-55-37; monthly; economic and demographic statistics; publ. by National Statistics Office.

Carrefour Africain: BP 368, Ouagadougou; f. 1960; weekly; state-owned; Dir-Gen. BABOU PAULIN BAMOUNI; circ. 6,000.

Courrier Consulaire du Burkina: BP 502, Ouagadougou; tel. 30-61-14; telex 5268; f. 1960; monthly; legislative and statutory notices; publ. by the Chambre de Commerce, d'Industrie et d'Artisanat du Burkina; circ. 350.

L'Intrus: Ouagadougou; f. 1986; weekly; satirical humour.

Journal Officiel du Burkina: BP 568, Ouagadougou; weekly.

Manegda: Mooré; weekly.

NEWS AGENCIES

Agence Burkinabê de Presse: BP 2507, Ouagadougou; tel. 33-28-20; telex 5327; f. 1963; state-controlled.

Foreign Bureaux

Agence France-Presse (AFP): BP 391, Ouagadougou; tel. 33-56-56; telex 5204; Bureau Chief KIDA TAPSOBA.

TASS (USSR) also has a bureau in Ouagadougou.

Publishers

Presses Africaines SA: BP 1471, Ouagadougou; tel. 33-43-07; telex 5344; general fiction, religion, primary and secondary textbooks; Man. Dir A. WININGA.

Société Nationale d'Edition et de Presse (SONEPRESS): BP 810, Ouagadougou; f. 1972; general, periodicals; Pres. MARTIAL OUEDRAOGO.

Government Publishing House

Imprimerie Nationale du Burkina Faso (INBF): route de l'Hôpital Yalgado, BP 7040, Ouagadougou; tel. 33-52-92; f. 1963; Dir LATY SOULEYMANE TRAORÉ.

Radio and Television

There were an estimated 123,000 radio receivers and 35,000 television receivers in use in 1983.

RADIO

Radiodiffusion-Télévision Burkina: BP 7029, Ouagadougou; tel. 33-68-05; telex 5132; f. 1959; services in French and 13 vernacular languages; Tech. Dir JOSEPH GUISSOU. There is a second station at Bobo-Dioulasso.

REP: Ouagadougou; f. 1987; private commercial station; Dir JEAN-HUBERT BAZIE.

TELEVISION

Télévision Nationale du Burkina (Voltavision): BP 7029, Ouagadougou; tel. 33-68-01; telex 5231; f. 1963; daily transmissions; currently received only in Ouagadougou and Bobo-Dioulasso; public viewing centres are being set up; Dir S. BALIMA.

BURKINA FASO
Directory

Finance

(cap. = capital; res = reserves; dep. = deposits; m. = million; brs = branches; amounts in francs CFA)

BANKING

Central Bank

Banque Centrale des Etats de l'Afrique de l'Ouest (BCEAO): ave Gamal-Abdel-Nasser, BP 356, Ouagadougou; tel. 33-67-15; telex 5205; headquarters in Dakar, Senegal; f. 1955; bank of issue for the seven states of the Union monétaire ouest-africaine (UMOA), comprising Benin, Burkina Faso, Côte d'Ivoire, Mali, Niger, Senegal and Togo; cap. and res 171,495m. (Dec. 1987); Gov. ALASSANE OUATTARA; Dir in Burkina Faso MOUSSA KONÉ; br. in Bobo-Dioulasso.

State Banks

Banque Burkinabê-Libyenne pour le Commerce et le Développement (BALIB): Ouagadougou; f. 1987; cap. 800m.; 50% state-owned, 50% Libyan-owned.

Banque pour le Financement du Commerce et des Investissements du Burkina (BFCI-B): 4 rue du Marché, BP 585, Ouagadougou; tel. 30-60-35; telex 5269; f. 1973; cap. and res 14,201m. (Sept. 1987); Pres. M. N'GOLO KONÉ; Dir-Gen. JEAN-BAPTISTE CONFÉ.

Banque Internationale du Burkina SA (BIB): rue Patrice Lumumba, BP 362, Ouagadougou; tel. 33-33-75; telex 5210; f. 1974; cap. 1,638m. (Sept. 1986); 53% state-owned, 40% owned by BIAO (France); Pres. YACOUBA SANOU; Gen. Man. ROC KABORÉ; 13 brs.

Banque Internationale pour le Commerce, l'Industrie et l'Agriculture du Burkina SA (BICIA-BF): ave Dr Nkwamé N'Kruma, BP 8, Ouagadougou; tel. 33-21-63; telex 5203; f. 1973; cap. 1,250m. (Sept. 1986); 51% state-owned; Pres. SOW DIÉ MARTIN; Man. Dir D. AUGUSTIN DER SOMDA; 11 brs.

Banque Nationale de Développement du Burkina Faso (BND): BP 148, Ouagadougou; tel. 33-29-96; telex 5225; f. 1962; cap. 2,500m. (Sept. 1986); 92% state-owned; Pres. GUY SOMÉ; Man. Dir BOUKARY OUEDRAOGO; 6 brs.

Caisse Nationale de Crédit Agricole du Burkina Faso (CNCA-BF): BP 1644, Ouagadougou; tel. 33-23-60; telex 5443; f. 1979; cap. 1,300m. (Sept. 1986); 54% state-owned; Pres. AMBROISE BATIENON; Dir-Gen. NOËL KABORÉ.

Caisse Nationale des Dépôts et des Investissements (CNDI): 4 rue du Marché, BP 585, Ouagadougou; tel. 33-41-72; telex 5269; f. 1973; cap. 2,857m.; 100% state-owned; Pres. of Admin. Council N'GOLO KONÉ; Dir-Gen. FRÉDÉRIC ASSOMPTION KORSAGA.

Union Révolutionnaire des Banques (UREBA): 2 ave Nelson Mandela, BP 4414, Ouagadougou; tel. 33-22-05; telex 5458; f. 1984; cap. 1,529m. (Sept. 1987); 51% owned by govt and provinces; Pres. MARCELLIN ZONGO; Man. Dir KOUKA VICTOR NIKIEMA.

INSURANCE

Société Nationale d'Assurance et de Réassurance (SONAR): BP 406, Ouagadougou; tel. 33-63-43; telex 5294; f. 1973; cap. 120m.; 51% state-owned; Man. Dir BABLO FÉLIX HEMA.

Trade and Industry

ADVISORY BODY

Conseil Révolutionnaire Economique et Social: Ouagadougou; f. 1985; 38 mems; Pres. KADER CISSÉ.

GOVERNMENT REGULATORY BODIES

Autorité des Aménagements des Vallées des Voltas (AVV): BP 524, Ouagadougou; tel. 30-61-10; telex 5401; f. 1974; integrated rural development, including economic and social planning; Man. Dir EMMANUEL NIKIEMA.

Bureau des Mines de la Géologie du Burkina (BUMIGEB): BP 601, Ouagadougou; tel. 30-02-27; telex 5340; f. 1978; cap. 818m. francs CFA; research into geological and mineral resources; Man. Dir KOUDOUBI FRÉDÉRIC KOALA.

Caisse de Stabilisation des Prix des Produits Agricoles (CSPPA): BP 1453, Ouagadougou; tel. 30-62-13; telex 5202; f. 1964; cap. 25m.; responsible for stabilization of agricultural prices; supervises trade and export; Dir EMMANUEL ANDRÉ YAMÉOGO; br. at Bobo-Dioulasso.

Office National des Céréales (OFNACER): BP 53, Ouagadougou; tel. 30-26-05; telex 5317; responsible for stabilization of the supply and price of cereals; Dir GOAMA HENRI KABORÉ.

Office National du Commerce Exterieur (ONAC): BP 389, Ouagadougou; tel. 30-62-23; telex 5258; f. 1974; supervises external trade; Man. Dir BENOÎT ZABREMBA.

Office National de l'Eau et de l'Assainissement (ONEA): BP 170, Ouagadougou; tel. 30-60-73; telex 5226; f. 1977; cap. 3,086m. francs CFA; storage, purification and distribution of water; Dir VICTOR WANDÉ OUEDRAOGO.

Office National de l'Exploitation des Ressources Animales: BP 7058, Ouagadougou; tel. 30-66-95; telex 5312; Dir-Gen. ROGER MOUSSA TALL.

CHAMBER OF COMMERCE

Chambre de Commerce, d'Industrie et d'Artisanat du Burkina: BP 502, Ouagadougou; tel. 30-61-14; telex 5268; Pres. PAUL BALKOUMA; Sec.-Gen. SYLVIE KABORE; br. in Bobo-Dioulasso.

DEVELOPMENT AGENCIES

Caisse Centrale de Coopération Economique (CCCE): ave Binger, BP 529, Ouagadougou; tel. 33-60-76; telex 5271; Dir FRANÇOIS PEYREDIEU DU CHARLAT.

Mission Française de Coopération: BP 510, Ouagadougou; tel. 30-67-71; telex 5211; centre for administering bilateral aid from France under co-operation agreements signed in 1961; Dir FRANÇOIS MIMIN.

EMPLOYERS' ORGANIZATIONS

Association Professionnelle des Banques et Établissements Financiers (APBEF): Ouagadougou; Pres. JEAN-BAPTISTE CONFÉ.

Conseil National du Patronat Burkinabé: Ouagadougou.

Groupement Professionnel des Industriels: BP 810, Ouagadougou; tel. 33-28-81; f. 1974; Pres. MARTIAL OUEDRAOGO.

Syndicat des Commerçants Importateurs et Exportateurs (SCIMPEX): BP 552, Ouagadougou; Pres. PIERRE LINAS.

Syndicat des Entrepreneurs et Industriels: Ouagadougou.

CO-OPERATIVES

Groupement Coopératif de Ventes Internationales des Produits du Burkina (Cooproduits): BP 91, Ouagadougou; telex 5224; agricultural co-operative; exports seeds, nuts and gum arabic; Chair. and Man. Dir KÉOULÉ NACOULIMA.

Société de Commercialisation du Burkina 'Faso Yaar': BP 531, Ouagadougou; tel. 30-61-28; telex 5274; BP 375, Bobo-Dioulasso; tel. 98-18-31; f. 1967; 97% state-owned marketing organization with 30 retail outlets; Pres. Minister of Trade and Popular Supply; Man. Dir MAMADOU KARAMBIRI.

Union des Coopératives Agricoles et Maraîchères du Burkina (UCOBAM): BP 277, Ouagadougou; tel. 30-65-27; telex 5287; f. 1968; cap. 128m. francs CFA; comprises 8 regional co-operative unions (20,000 mems); production and marketing of fruit and vegetables; Dir-Gen. ISSAKA DERME; Commercial Dir ANDRÉ BICABA.

TRADE UNIONS

There are over 20 autonomous trade unions. The five trade union syndicates are:

Confédération Générale du Travail Burkinabé (CGTB): Ouagadougou; f. 1988; confederation of several autonomous trade unions.

Confédération Nationale des Travailleurs (CNT): BP 445, Ouagadougou; f. 1972; Pres. EMANUEL OUEDRAOGO.

Confédération Syndicale Burkinabé (CSB): BP 299, Ouagadougou; f. 1974; affiliated to Ligue patriotique pour le développement (LIPAD); mainly public service unions; Sec.-Gen. YACINTHE OUEDRAOGO.

Organisation Nationale des Syndicats Libres (ONSL): BP 99, Ouagadougou; f. 1960; Sec.-Gen. BONIFACE KABORÉ; 6,000 mems (1983).

Union Syndicale des Travailleurs Burkinabé (USTB): BP 381, Ouagadougou; f. 1958; Sec.-Gen. BONIFACE SOMDAH; 35,000 mems in 45 affiliated orgs.

Transport

RAILWAY

In mid-1988 there were around 550 km of track in Burkina Faso, comprising 517-km of the 1,175-km RAN line linking Ouagadougou to Abidjan (see below) and a 33-km extension of that line from Ouagadougou to Donsin, constructed by voluntary labour. Work on a further, 77-km, extension from Donsin to Kaya began in March 1987, while plans to construct a 210-km extension to the manganese deposits at Tambao, a project which was postponed in 1986 (owing to a lack of external funding), were revived in 1988.

La Régie du Chemin de Fer Abidjan–Niger (RAN): BP 192, Ouagadougou; tel. 33-46-97; telex 5433; Head Office: BP 1394,

BURKINA FASO

Abidjan, Côte d'Ivoire; f. 1904; 1,173 km of track linking Ouagadougou via Bobo-Dioulasso with the coast at Abidjan (Côte d'Ivoire); 517 km of this railway are in Burkina Faso; the co was to be reorganized as two independent railways by 1989.

ROADS

At 31 December 1986 there were 11,231 km of roads, including 4,576 km of main roads and 4,108 km of secondary roads. The Ghana-Burkina Faso Road Transport Commission, based in Accra, was set up to implement the 1968 agreement on improving communications between the two countries.

An internationally-aided programme of rehabilitation aiming to improve more than 6,000 km of roads, particularly in the north-east, and providing for the maintenance of 1,640 km, at a cost of US $73m., was begun in 1981. In 1986 plans were announced for a 133-km tarred road, to connect Bobo-Dioulasso to the Mali border via Orodara.

Régie X9: Ouagadougou; tel. 30-42-96; telex 5313; Dir NEBAMA KERE.

CIVIL AVIATION

There are international airports at Ouagadougou and Bobo-Dioulasso, 49 small airfields and 13 private airstrips. The renovation and expansion of the airport at Ouagadougou, including the extension of the runway from 2,500 m to 3,000 m, was due for completion in early 1989. Plans to extend the runway at Bobo-Dioulasso, from 2,050 m to 2,500 m, were announced in 1987.

Air Afrique: Burkina Faso has a 7% share; see under Côte d'Ivoire.
Air Burkina: BP 1459, Ouagadougou; tel. 30-61-43; telex 203; f. 1967; 66% state-owned airline with a monopoly of domestic services; also operates flights to and from Bamako (Mali), Lomé (Togo), Cotonou (Benin), Niamey (Niger), Accra (Ghana), Bouaké and Abidjan (Côte d'Ivoire); Man. Dir (vacant); fleet of 1 DHG6 Twin Otter, 1 EMB 110 P2 Bandeirante, 1 Fokker F28.

Tourism

The principal tourist attraction is big game hunting in the east and south-west, and along the banks of the Mouhoun (Black Volta) river. There is a wide variety of wild animals in the game reserves. In 1987 there were 68,308 tourist arrivals at hotels, and receipts from tourism totalled 2,300m. francs CFA.

Direction Générale du Tourisme et de l'Hôtellerie: BP 624, Ouagadougou; tel. 30-63-96; telex 5555; Dir-Gen. ABDOULAYE SANKARA.

Faso Tours: BP 1318, Ouagadougou; tel. 30-66-71; telex 5377.

BURMA

Introductory Survey

Location, Climate, Language, Religion, Flag, Capital

The Union of Burma lies in the north-west region of South-East Asia, between the Tibetan plateau and the Malay peninsula. The country is bordered by Bangladesh and India to the north-west, by the People's Republic of China and Laos to the north-east and by Thailand to the south-east. The climate is tropical, with an average temperature of 27°C (80°F) and monsoon rains from May to October. Temperatures in Rangoon are generally between 18°C (65°F) and 36°C (97°F). The official language is Burmese, and there are also a number of tribal languages. About 85% of the population are Buddhists. There are animist, Muslim, Hindu and Christian minorities, and there is a Chinese community of some 350,000. The national flag is red, with a blue canton, in the upper hoist, bearing two ears of rice within a cogwheel and a ring of 14 five-pointed stars (one for each state), all in white. The capital is Rangoon.

Recent History

Burma was annexed to British India during the 19th century, and became a separate British dependency, with a limited measure of self-government, in 1937. Japanese forces invaded and occupied the country in February 1942, and Japan granted nominal independence under a government of anti-British nationalists. The Burmese nationalists later turned against Japan and aided Allied forces to reoccupy the country in May 1945. They formed a resistance movement, the Anti-Fascist People's Freedom League (AFPFL), led by Gen. Aung San, which became the main political force after the defeat of Japan. Aung San was assassinated in July 1947 and was succeeded by U Nu. On 4 January 1948 the Union of Burma became independent, outside the Commonwealth, with U Nu as the first Prime Minister.

During the first decade of independence Burma was a parliamentary democracy, and the Government successfully resisted revolts by communists and other insurgent groups. In 1958 the ruling AFPFL split, and U Nu invited the Army Chief of Staff, Gen. Ne Win, to head a caretaker government. Elections in February 1960 gave an overwhelming majority to U Nu, leading the Union Party, and he resumed office in April. Despite its popularity, however, the U Nu administration proved ineffective, and in March 1962 Gen. Ne Win intervened again, staging a coup to depose U Nu. The new Revolutionary Council suspended the Constitution and instituted authoritarian control through the government-sponsored Burma Socialist Programme Party (BSPP). All other political parties were outlawed in March 1964.

The next decade saw the creation of a more centralized system of government, attempting to win popular support and nationalizing important sectors of the economy. A new constitution, aiming to transform Burma into a democratic socialist state, was approved in a national referendum in December 1973. New governmental organizations were created, the BSPP became the sole authorized political party, and the country's name was changed to the Socialist Republic of the Union of Burma. In March 1974 the Revolutionary Council was dissolved, and U Ne Win (who, together with other senior army officers, became a civilian in 1972) was elected President by the State Council. Burma's economic problems increased, however, and in 1974 there were riots over food shortages and social injustices, and student demonstrations followed in 1976, as social problems increased. Following an attempted coup by members of the armed forces in July 1976, the BSPP reviewed its economic policies, and in 1977 a new plan was adopted to quell unrest.

An election in January 1978 gave U Ne Win a mandate to rule for a further four years, and in March he was re-elected Chairman of the State Council. In May 1980 a general amnesty was declared for political prisoners and political exiles and rebels, including the former Prime Minister, U Nu, who returned from exile in July. More than 2,000 exiles surrendered, but few senior members of the rebel forces did so. Gen. San Yu, formerly the Army Chief of Staff, was elected Chairman of the State Council in November 1981; U Ne Win, however, remained Chairman of the BSPP. The Citizenship Law of 1982 provided for three categories of citizen, and precluded members of non-indigenous races from holding important positions. In November 1983 sentences of life imprisonment were imposed on Brig. Tin Oo, formerly a member of the State Council and Joint General Secretary of the BSPP, and Col Bo Ni, formerly Minister of Home and Religious Affairs, for corruption and misuse of state funds. At the fifth congress of the BSPP, in August 1985, U Ne Win was re-elected for a further four-year term as Chairman. U San Yu, the Chairman of the State Council, was elected to the new post of Vice-Chairman of the party. The congress also approved the enlargement of the party's Central Executive Committee, from 15 to 17 members, and of the Central Committee, from 260 to 280 members. Elections for a new People's Assembly were held in November. U Aye Ko, the General Secretary of the BSPP, was elected by the Assembly to the new position of Vice-President.

In August 1987, owing to the country's increasing economic problems, an unprecedented extraordinary meeting, comprising the BSPP Central Committee, the organs of the State Council and other state organs, was convened. U Ne Win proposed a review of the policies of the past 25 years, and acknowledged the need to correct any shortcomings. In September the announcement of the withdrawal from circulation of high-denomination banknotes, coupled with rice shortages following a poor harvest, provoked student riots, the first public display of civil unrest since 1974. Owing to continued economic deprivation, further student unrest in Rangoon in March 1988 culminated in serious riots which were violently suppressed by the *lon htein* (riot police), under the direct command of U Sein Lwin, the BSPP Joint General Secretary. Fresh demonstrations, to demand the release of persons who had been detained in March, started in June. The Government's response was again extremely brutal, and many demonstrators were killed. In July vain attempts were made to counter the growing unpopularity of the Government, including the removal from office of Maj.-Gen. Min Gaung, the Minister of Home and Religious Affairs, and U Thien Aung, the head of the People's Police Force in Rangoon, for their alleged responsibility for events during March and June. (The Prime Minister, also, was subsequently dismissed.) Finally, at an extraordinary meeting of the BSPP congress in July, U Ne Win resigned as party Chairman and asked the congress to approve the holding of a national referendum on the issue of a multi-party system. The congress rejected the referendum proposal and the resignation of four other senior members of the BSPP, including that of U Sein Lwin, but accepted the resignation of U San Yu, the BSPP Vice-Chairman.

The subsequent election of U Sein Lwin to the chairmanship of the BSPP by the party's Central Executive Committee, and his appointment as Chairman of the State Council and as state President, increased popular discontent and provoked further student-led riots. Martial law was imposed on Rangoon, and thousands of unarmed demonstrators were reportedly massacred by the armed forces throughout the country, in an attempt to regain control. In August students called a general strike, and U Sein Lwin was forced to resign after only 17 days in office. He was replaced by the more moderate Dr Maung Maung, hitherto the Attorney-General, whose response to the continued rioting was conciliatory. Martial law was revoked; Brig.-Gen. Aung Gyi (a former close colleague of U Ne Win but subsequently an outspoken critic of the regime), who had been detained under U Sein Lwin, was released; and permission was given for the formation of the All Burma Students' Union. Demonstrations continued, however, and by September students and Buddhist monks had assumed control of the municipal government of many towns. In early September U Nu, the former Prime Minister, requested foreign support for his formation of an alternative government. The emerging opposition leaders, Brig.-Gen. Aung Gyi, Aung San Suu Kyi (daughter of Gen. Aung San) and Gen. Tin U (a former Chief of Staff and Minister of Defence), then formed the

BURMA

National United Front for Democracy, which was subsequently renamed the League for Democracy and later the National League for Democracy (NLD).

At an emergency meeting of the BSPP congress in September, it was decided that free elections would be held within three months and that members of the armed forces, police and civil service could no longer be affiliated to a political party. Now distanced from the BSPP, the armed forces, led by Gen. Saw Maung, seized power on 18 September, ostensibly to maintain order until multi-party elections could be arranged. The State Law and Order Restoration Council (SLORC) was formed, all state organs (including the People's Assembly, the State Council and the Council of Ministers) were abolished, demonstrations were banned and a nationwide dusk-to-dawn curfew was imposed. Despite this, opposition movements demonstrated in favour of an interim civilian government, and it was estimated that more than 1,000 demonstrators were killed in the first few days following the coup. The SLORC announced the formation of a nine-member government, with Gen. Saw Maung as Minister of Defence and of Foreign Affairs and subsequently also Prime Minister. It was widely believed, however, that U Ne Win, although ostensibly in retirement, probably retained a controlling influence over the new leaders, all of whom, including Gen. Saw Maung, were known to be his supporters. The new Government changed the official name of the country to the Union of Burma (as it had been before 1973).

The law maintaining the BSPP as the sole party was abrogated, and new parties were encouraged to register for the forthcoming elections. The BSPP registered under a new name, the National Unity Party, with U Tha Kyaw, the former Minister of Transport, as Chairman. By mid-December, a total of 167 parties had registered. Although the NLD registered, it was uncertain whether it would contest elections, which, it asserted, could not be held fairly under military rule. In December, owing to disagreements with Aung San Suu Kyi, Brig.-Gen. Aung Gyi was expelled from the NLD, after he had founded the Union National Democracy Party.

The largest of the various insurgent groups, which have been fighting government forces since independence in 1948, is the Burmese Communist Party (BCP), which has gained control of areas in northern Burma and is well organized militarily. Secret peace talks with the Government in 1981 failed to reach any agreement, and government forces have continued to resist the guerrillas. The BCP formerly received support and aid from the Chinese Communist Party, but this funding gradually diminished, as relations between the Burmese Government and the People's Republic of China began to improve.

In early 1984 the Government launched one of its heaviest offensives in 35 years against the Karen National Liberation Army (KNLA), which then had an estimated 4,000 armed members. The KNLA is the military wing of the Karen National Union (KNU), founded in 1948, which has led a protracted campaign for the establishment of an independent state for the Karen ethnic group. By 1986 serious fighting near the Thai border, with reportedly heavy casualties on both sides, had forced more than 17,000 civilian refugees to flee into Thailand. The KNU is a member of the anti-communist National Democratic Front (NDF), an organization of 10 ethnic minority groups, formed in 1975 (by five groups, originally) with the aim of making Burma a federal union and opposing both the Government and, initially, the BCP. In September 1983 the NDF was joined by the Kachin Independence Army (KIA), an insurgent group which, by 1985, numbered about 5,000 armed members. As well as Karen and Kachin, the NDF also comprises Karenni, Mon, Shan, Pa-O, Palaung, Wa, Arakanese and Lahu parties. By May 1986 the various minority groups in the NDF had agreed to relinquish their individual demands for autonomy, in favour of a unified demand for a federal system of government. At the same time, the BCP withdrew its demand for a 'one-party' government in Burma, and entered into an alliance with the NDF. In spite of opposition from the KNU, the NDF maintained its alliance with the BCP during 1987. At the second NDF congress in June 1987, Maj.-Gen. Bo Mya, the President of the KNU and Chief of Staff of the KNLA, was replaced as NDF President by Saw Maw Reh, a former Chairman of the Karenni National Progressive Party, and further leadership changes removed all KNU representatives from senior NDF positions. The new NDF leaders advocated the establishment, mainly through political means, of autonomous, ethnic-based states within a Burmese union. At the congress it was emphasized that the alliance with the BCP was of a military, rather than ideological, nature.

In November 1986 the BCP, aided militarily by some NDF groups, launched a surprise attack on government forces in the north-east of the country. In a series of counter-attacks, government troops recaptured much territory, and in January 1987 Burmese army units captured the border town of Panghsai, which had been controlled by the BCP since 1970. In February the Government launched further offensives against Karen and Shan insurgents in eastern areas, near the border with Thailand; by May, government forces had captured the headquarters of the KIA at Momauk, and had also regained control of 60 km of border areas. Fierce fighting continued along the Thai border in subsequent months, and there were reports of heavy casualties.

Part of the Government's campaign against the insurgent groups has been an attempt to intercept the smuggling routes on the border with Thailand, from which the insurgents have earned large levies from the sale of 'black market' goods. This has caused the guerrillas to deal increasingly in illicit drugs, notably opium and its derivatives (including heroin). In 1986, however, the Government launched a five-year programme, aided by the UN, to suppress drug-trafficking, and in February 1987 government forces launched a campaign in Shan state against Khun Sa, the 'opium warlord' and leader of the 15,000-strong rebel Shan United Army, who controlled much of the drug trade in the 'Golden Triangle' (the world's major opium-producing area, where the borders of Burma, Laos and Thailand meet).

The insurgent groups were sympathetic to the anti-Government movements in Rangoon and other major cities. Continued attacks throughout 1988 engaged the government forces in the border areas, leaving fewer of them to impose order in the towns. In late September the Karens announced plans to co-operate with protesting students and Buddhist monks to work towards the achievement of democracy. After the armed forces seized power, insurgents intensified operations, aided by at least 3,000 students whom the Karen rebels agreed to train and arm. In mid-October the Karens and their new recruits captured Mae Ta Waw, on the Thai border, their most significant victory for a decade. In November 22 anti-Government groups, led by members of the NDF, formed an alternative government, called the Democratic Alliance of Burma. The KNU leader, Maj.-Gen. Bo Mya, was elected President, while Brang Seng (Chairman of the Kachin Independence Organization) and Nai Shwe Kyin (a Mon) were elected Vice-Presidents.

Government

Under the Constitution which entered into force in January 1974, the highest organ of state is the 489-member People's Assembly (Pyithu Hluttaw), a legislative body elected by the people. From among its members the Assembly elects a State Council of 29 members. The Council is the chief decision-making organ of government and co-ordinates the work of central and local governmental organs. The Assembly also elects the Council of Ministers (which is responsible for the public administration of the State), the Council of People's Justices, the Council of People's Attorneys and the Council of People's Inspectors. Burma, formerly a federation, is now unitary, and is divided into States or Divisions. These, in turn, are divided into townships, and townships into wards or village-tracts. People's Councils exist for every sub-division at each of these levels. Following the military coup of September 1988, all state organs, including the People's Assembly, the State Council and the Council of Ministers, were abolished by the State Law and Order Restoration Council.

Defence

Burma maintains a policy of neutrality and has no external defence treaties. Military service is voluntary. The armed forces are largely engaged in internal security duties. In June 1988 the armed services totalled 186,000 men, of whom 170,000 were in the army, 7,000 in the navy and 9,000 in the air force. Paramilitary forces comprise a People's Police Force of 38,000 men and a People's Militia of 35,000 men. Defence expenditure allocated for 1987/88 was an estimated 1,900m. kyats.

BURMA

Economic Affairs

Burma is potentially rich in agricultural, fishery, timber, mineral and water resources, of which large parts remain unexploited. In terms of average income, Burma is one of the poorest countries in Asia; in 1986, according to estimates by the World Bank, Burma's gross national product (GNP), measured at average 1984–86 prices, was US $200 per head. Between 1965 and 1986, it was estimated, GNP per head increased, in real terms, at an average rate of 2.3% per year. The average annual increase in overall gross domestic product (GDP), measured in constant prices, was 3.9% in 1965–80, rising to 4.9% in 1980–86.

The agricultural sector continues to use mainly traditional methods, and remains mostly in private ownership. In 1986 agriculture, including livestock and fishing, produced 48% of GDP. In 1987 this sector employed 62.8% of the labour force. The output of the agricultural sector expanded, in real terms, by 4.7% per year in 1982–86. Rice, timber and other agricultural products have traditionally been the principal export items; agricultural commodities provided 52% of total export earnings in 1985. The introduction of high-yield agricultural programmes, concentrating initially on rice, allowed the output of paddy rice to rise by more than 50% between 1975/76 and 1984/85, when the rice harvest reached a record 14.4m. metric tons. In 1984/85 Burma exported 803,000 tons of milled rice, but in 1985/86 rice exports totalled 646,000 tons, although paddy production had increased slightly (to 14.5m. tons). Rice contributed 37% of total exports in 1984, but only 25% in 1985. Production of milled rice remained relatively stable, rising from 7.78m. tons in 1986/87 to 8.02m. tons in 1987/88. Exports, however, declined from 600,000 tons in 1986/87 to only 150,000 tons in 1987/88. This reduction was largely due to the relaxation of restrictions on domestic trade in September 1987, permitting individuals to engage in private enterprise, which created difficulties for the Government in rice procurement, as official prices were uncompetitive with those obtainable on the 'black market'. Burma has the potential to increase its rice output significantly by introducing double-cropping. In 1985/86 about 2.55m. ha of paddy, or 52% of total rice-growing land, was sown with high-yielding varieties. The Government has also encouraged diversification into other crops, including jute, maize, tobacco and pulses, although in 1987 rice was grown on 90% of cultivated land. Burma has the world's largest stands of broadleaved (hardwood) trees. In 1984/85 the total output of broadleaved roundwood was 1.47m. cu tons (each of 50 cu ft or 1.416 cu m), including 400,000 cu tons of teak, and export earnings from timber reached 1,003m. kyats, compared with 281m. kyats in 1975/76. In 1986 roundwood removals totalled 19.1m. cu m, and in 1986/87 teak became Burma's principal source of foreign exchange: providing US $138m., compared with $73m. from rice exports. More than 63% of forestry production was in the private sector in 1985/86.

Burma has significant deposits of petroleum, tin, copper and coal. However, insurgent activity and an inefficient and expensive system of internal transport have prevented Burma from attaining many previous production levels. Since 1980 Burma has not been self-sufficient in crude petroleum, and annual output declined from a peak of 11m. barrels in 1979/80 to 6.3m. barrels in 1987. Output in 1986 averaged 24,000 barrels per day (b/d) according to official reports, compared with the 30,000 b/d necessary for self-sufficiency. By 1988, it was estimated that production had declined to 15,000 b/d, and, for the first time in its history, Burma imported crude petroleum from Australia, financed by the Asian Development Bank (ADB, see p. 98). In January 1988 the ADB approved a technical assistance grant of US $220m. for a three-year programme to develop petroleum and gas resources. Three commercially viable oilfields were discovered in 1981, with estimated total recoverable reserves of 1,717m. barrels of crude petroleum, but more recent explorations have not been successful. Burma's output of natural gas has increased significantly, however, from 8.8m. cu ft in 1977/78 to 32.6m. cu ft in 1985/86. In 1982 offshore natural gas deposits were discovered in the Gulf of Martaban, but in 1986 the Government decided to abandon a development project for the area, owing mainly to lack of funds. In 1986 proven onshore reserves of natural gas totalled 2,000,000m. cu ft (57,000m. cu m), and there were also large undeveloped deposits in the region of the Irrawaddy delta. In 1987 the International Development Association (IDA) provided US $63m. for an onshore gas development project, whereby 12 new wells would be drilled at Payagon, to increase gas production to 1m. cu m (35m. cu ft) per day. Since the 1970s, Burma has made increasing use of hydroelectric power as the main source of domestic energy, accounting for 55% of all electricity generated in 1985/86, while natural gas power stations accounted for 38%. Other minerals known to exist in Burma include tungsten, zinc and lead.

The manufacturing sector in Burma is small, accounting for 10.7% of the country's GDP in 1987, and for 8.7% of the labour force; output in manufacturing failed to reach its target growth rate during the third Four-Year Plan (1978–82), increasing by 6.6% annually instead of the projected 12%. The sector grew by 10.5% (according to official estimates) in 1984/85, but by only 6% in 1985/86. The principal industrial activities are related to agriculture: food processing and the manufacture of tobacco products. In 1984/85 1,001.1m. kyats of public-sector investment was for agro-based industries. Petroleum refining and textiles are also important. In January 1988 refineries were working at 30% of capacity, owing to a shortage of crude petroleum. In 1985/86 factories were estimated to be operating at 20%–50% of their full capacity. Of the 41,721 factories and enterprises in operation in 1985/86, 39,239 were controlled by private interests.

Industry, transport, internal and external trade, communications and finance have been nationalized since the 1962 revolution. In 1973 Burma joined the ADB, which, together with the World Bank (see p. 60), provides most of Burma's multilateral support. In February 1986 the ADB granted a US $35m. loan towards an edible-oil project, and in May the IDA approved a $30m. credit for a grain storage and processing project. In 1986 the United Nations Development Programme (UNDP) provided aid for more than 50 projects, and in 1987 it provided US $675,000 for a new edible-oil project, which was to establish 10 expeller oil mills and to convert one existing mill into a solvent-extraction plant. In November 1985 the Japanese Government agreed to provide 49,050m. yen for eight projects, including the construction of an integrated plant to produce liquefied petroleum gas. Japan is the principal unilateral aid donor, providing the Burmese Government with 231m. kyats (60% of total foreign aid) for 1987/88 under four 'memoranda of understanding', signed in Rangoon in July 1987. In December 1987, owing to a decline in export revenue and a sharp rise in debt-servicing costs, the UN granted Burma the status of a 'least developed country'. The Federal Republic of Germany (Burma's second largest aid-donor) accordingly converted loans worth US $31.6m. into grants, and pledged to provide all future aid in this form. Japan announced that it would reimburse Burma with grants equal to scheduled debt repayments. However, owing to disapproval of political developments, Japan, the USA, the Federal Republic of Germany and other Western donors suspended aid to Burma in August–September 1988, pending the introduction of political and economic reforms.

A total of 7,500m. kyats was invested in the state sector in 1987/88. Burma's external debt increased from $300m. in 1975 to approximately $3,300m. at 31 March 1984, of which slightly less than one-half was undisbursed. In April 1988 the Burmese Government announced foreign debts of US $4,000m., and the debt-service ratio, which had been estimated at 48% in 1987, was unofficially estimated to have reached 80% of the country's earnings of foreign exchange. Burma's official reserves of foreign exchange declined from $253.7m. at the end of 1980 to only $27.1m. at the end of 1987. The annual trade deficit, which increased sharply in 1982/83 to US $422.4m., improved considerably in 1983/84, narrowing to $221.6m. In 1986/87 the trade deficit declined to $196.7m., but in 1987/88 it rose to $324.6m., according to government statistics. Continuing trade deficits have led to large balance-of-payments deficits; in 1986/87 the overall balance-of-payments deficit was 44.2m. kyats. Owing to political turmoil, there were no exports between July and December 1988. Burma defaulted on foreign debt payments (totalling US $292.1m. for the whole of 1988), and foreign exchange reserves fell to less than $20m.

The 1982–86 Four-Year Plan emphasized the development of agriculture, rather than an increase in industrial capacity, and envisaged average annual growth of 6.2%. In 1986 the Government announced that an average annual GDP growth of 5.5% had been achieved during the Plan period. The annual rate of inflation was officially 4.4% in 1984/85 and 5% in 1985/86.

The Four-Year Plan for 1986–90 aimed to improve economic self-sufficiency, to encourage new investment projects, to diversify exports and to reduce the public-sector deficit and reliance on foreign aid and loans. In March 1986 the Plan's target for average GDP growth was revised from 6.1% to 4.5%. During the first year of the 1986–90 Plan, GDP grew by 3.7%, compared with a target rate of 3.6%.

The budget proposals for 1987/88 envisaged expenditure of 42,400m. kyats and revenue of 38,600m. kyats. The resulting deficit of 3,800m. kyats, equivalent to 6.2% of projected GDP, was to be financed by borrowing from the state-owned banking system, as in previous years. A total of 7,500m. kyats was to be provided for public-sector investment, of which 35% would be funded by foreign aid and loans. The 1987/88 budget aimed to generate real GDP growth of 5%; however, GDP totalled $1,420m., a growth of only 2.2%. The government forecast for GDP growth in 1988/89 was 2.3%, with output in agriculture expanding by 2.8%. Exports generated 1,452.7m. kyats in 1987/88, compared with a target of 3,322.7m. kyats. During 1986/87 the annual rate of inflation rose from 7% to 26%, but in 1988 it was unofficially estimated at 400%.

The economy continues to suffer from extensive trading of goods in the 'black market'; in 1985 about two-thirds of such goods were smuggled in from Thailand, and total illegal trade was thought to have a turnover of up to 50% of official trading. In November 1985, in an effort to counter this, the Government withdrew certain large-denomination banknotes from circulation, with only limited success. In September 1987 a second demonetization took place, when the three higher-denomination banknotes were withdrawn from circulation. There was, however, no attempt to reduce the difference between the official exchange rate (about 7 kyats = US $1) and the 'black market' rate (about 40 kyats = US $1), which is a major factor ensuring the continuation of 'black market' trade. In December 1988 a law was promulgated to allow foreign investment. Teak, petroleum, natural gas and gems remain under government monopoly, but private enterprise was to be encouraged in all other sectors. To create favourable conditions for investment, the Government announced a three-year exemption from tax liability for foreign investors, and guarantees against nationalization.

Burma's principal trading partner is Japan, which supplied 33.7% of the value of imports and took 6.7% of exports in 1983/84, while the European Community provided 25.8% of imports and took 12.3% of exports. India was the largest market for Burma's exports, accounting for 12.8% of total export earnings. In 1987 Japanese exports to Burma totalled US $175m., while Japan's imports from Burma were valued at only $34m.

Social Welfare

Burma has fairly well-developed health facilities but they are not comprehensive. In 1986/87 the country had 10,579 physicians and 7,895 nurses. There were 636 hospitals, with a total of 25,839 beds. Health treatment is available free of charge. In 1986/87 government expenditure on public health was 616m. kyats. About 550,000 workers are covered by social security insurance, and all workers are entitled to state pensions.

Education

Education is provided free of charge, where available, but is not compulsory. In 1980, according to UNESCO estimates, adult illiteracy averaged 34% (males 24%, females 44%), a relatively small proportion for a low-income country. Primary education begins at five years of age and lasts for five years. Secondary education, beginning at 10 years of age, lasts for a further six years, comprising a first cycle of four years and a second of two years. In 1983 the total enrolment at primary and secondary schools was equivalent to 61% of the school-age population. In 1986/87 the total enrolment of students was 6.8m., of whom 5.1m. were at primary school level, 1,125,632 in secondary education, 238,498 in high schools, 27,723 in technical, vocational and teacher training colleges, and 211,493 in universities and colleges. There were 227,622 teachers in the 36,156 schools and colleges and the three universities in 1986/87. Emphasis is placed on vocational and technical training. In 1986/87 expenditure on education was estimated at 1,200m. kyats.

Public Holidays

1989: 4 January (Independence Day), 12 February (Union Day), 2 March (Peasants' Day, anniversary of the 1962 coup), March* (Full Moon of Tabaung), 27 March (Armed Forces Day), April* (Maha Thingyan—Water Festival), 17 April (Burmese New Year), 1 May (Workers' Day), May* (Full Moon of Kason), 14 July† (Id al-Adha—Feast of the Sacrifice), 19 July (Martyrs' Day), August* (Full Moon of Waso), October* (Full Moon of Thadingyut), October* (Devali), November* (Tazaungdaing Festival), 3 December (National Day), 25 December (Christmas Day).

1990: 4 January (Independence Day), 12 February (Union Day), 2 March (Peasants' Day, anniversary of the 1962 coup), March* (Full Moon of Tabaung), 27 March (Armed Forces Day), April* (Maha Thingyan—Water Festival), 17 April (Burmese New Year), 1 May (Workers' Day), May* (Full Moon of Kason), 4 July† (Id al-Adha—Feast of the Sacrifice), 19 July (Martyrs' Day), August* (Full Moon of Waso), October* (Full Moon of Thadingyut), October* (Devali), November* (Tazaungdaing Festival), 3 December (National Day), 25 December (Christmas Day).

* A number of Burmese holidays depend on lunar sightings.
† These holidays are regulated by the Islamic calendar and may vary by one or two days from the dates given.

Weights and Measures

The imperial system is in force.

Statistical Survey

Sources (unless otherwise stated): *Report to the Pyithu Hluttaw on the Financial, Economic and Social Conditions of the Socialist Republic of the Union of Burma* (annual), Ministry of Planning and Finance, Ministers' Office, Rangoon; tel. (01) 76066.

Area and Population

AREA, POPULATION AND DENSITY

Area (sq km)	676,552*
Population (census results)	
31 March 1973	28,885,867
31 March 1983†	
Males	17,507,837
Females	17,798,352
Total	35,306,189
Population (official estimates at mid-year)	
1983	36,747,000
1984	37,614,000
1986‡	39,411,000
Density (per sq km) at mid-1986	58.3

* 261,218 sq miles.
† Figures exclude adjustment for underenumeration. Also excluded are 7,716 Burmese citizens (5,704 males; 2,012 females) abroad.
‡ Official estimate for 1985 is not available.

PRINCIPAL TOWNS (census of 31 March 1983)

Rangoon	2,458,712		Taunggyi	107,907
Mandalay	532,895		Sittwe	107,607
Moulmein	219,991		Manywa	106,873
Pegu	150,447			
Bassein	144,092			

BIRTHS AND DEATHS

Crude birth rate 28.4 per 1,000 in 1984; crude death rate 8.7 per 1,000 in 1984 (estimates).

EMPLOYMENT
(official estimates, '000 persons, year ending 31 March 1985)

	State sector	Co-operative and private sector	Total
Agriculture	80	9,312	9,392
Livestock and fishing	16	182	198
Forestry	93	89	182
Mining and quarrying	72	13	85
Manufacturing	178	1,056	1,234
Electricity, gas and water	16	—	16
Construction	162	78	240
Transport and communications	114	374	488
Social services	231	84	315
Administration	541	29	570
Trade	68	1,376	1,444
Activities not adequately defined	—	628	628
Total	**1,571**	**13,221**	**14,792**

Agriculture

PRINCIPAL CROPS ('000 metric tons)

	1984	1985	1986
Wheat	214	206	246
Rice (paddy)	14,255	15,219	15,000*
Maize	303	323	350*
Millet	165	191	200*
Potatoes	156	184	164
Sugar cane	3,663	3,767	3,786
Pulses	571	580	671
Groundnuts (in shell)	532	667	651
Cottonseed	69	83	80*
Cotton (lint)	35	42	40*
Sesame seed	207	253	269
Tobacco (leaves)	64	69	65†
Jute and substitutes	55	52	50
Natural rubber	16	16	16
Vegetables (incl. melons)	2,052	2,068	2,103*
Fruit (excl. melons)*	1,008	1,020	1,023*

* FAO estimate.   † Unofficial estimate.
Source: FAO, *Production Yearbook*.

LIVESTOCK ('000 head, year ending September)

	1984	1985	1986*
Horses*	115	117	119
Cattle	9,502	9,718	9,981
Buffaloes	2,079	2,143	2,196
Pigs	2,706	2,955	3,116
Sheep	316	322	347
Goats	1,119	1,195	1,280

Chickens (million): 33 in 1984; 33 in 1985; 35* in 1986.
Ducks (million): 6 in 1984; 6 in 1985; 7* in 1986.

* FAO estimates.
Source: FAO, *Production Yearbook*.

LIVESTOCK PRODUCTS ('000 metric tons)

	1984	1985	1986
Beef and veal*	79	79	80
Buffalo meat*	20	20	21
Mutton and lamb*	2	2	2
Goats' meat*	6	6	6
Pig meat*	82	83	85
Poultry meat	103	104	108*
Cows' milk	560†	560*	601*
Buffaloes' milk*	65	68	70
Goats' milk*	6	6	6
Butter and ghee*	12.3	12.3	13.2
Cheese*	35.1	35.1	37.7
Hen eggs	43.6*	48.0	51.0*
Other poultry eggs	10.1	7.2†	8.2†
Cattle and buffalo hides*	25.0	25.2	25.5

* FAO estimates.   † Unofficial estimates.
Source: FAO, *Production Yearbook*.

Forestry

ROUNDWOOD REMOVALS
('000 cu m, excl. bark)

	1984	1985	1986
Sawlogs, veneer logs and logs for sleepers	1,720	1,717	1,805
Other industrial wood*	1,093	1,114	1,135
Fuel wood*	15,548	15,853	16,156
Total	18,361	18,684	19,096

* FAO estimates.
Source: FAO, *Yearbook of Forest Products*.

SAWNWOOD PRODUCTION ('000 cu m)

	1984	1985	1986
Sawnwood (incl. boxboards)	494	513	472
Railway sleepers	11	11	11
Total	505	524	483

Source: FAO, *Yearbook of Forest Products*.

Fishing

('000 metric tons, live weight)

	1983	1984	1985
Inland waters	142.9	144.0	146.8
Indian Ocean	444.7	465.7	497.0
Total catch	587.6	609.7	643.8

1986: Catch as in 1985 (FAO estimates).
Source: FAO, *Yearbook of Fishery Statistics*.

Mining

(long tons, unless otherwise indicated, year ending 31 March)

	1982/83	1983/84*	1984/85*
Coal	28,660	35,401	42,500
Crude petroleum ('000 barrels)	9,789	10,168	11,761
Natural gas (million cu ft)	17,400	18,190	24,796
Refined lead	8,001	7,505	7,500
Antimonal lead	273	308	250
Zinc concentrates	7,650	7,775	9,000
Tin concentrates	1,354	1,349	1,644
Tungsten concentrates	592	875	997
Copper concentrates	—	—	36,000
Iron ore (metric tons)	9,045	7,764	—
Refined silver ('000 troy oz)	576	576	576

* Provisional.
Note: Figures for metallic minerals refer to the metal content of ores mined.

Industry

SELECTED PRODUCTS (year ending 31 March)

	1982/83	1983/84*	1984/85*
Salt ('000 long tons)	265	276	296
Sugar ('000 long tons)	39	56	62
Cigarettes (million)	3,189	2,882	2,760
Cotton yarn ('000 long tons)	18.0	15.1	14.1
Soap ('000 metric tons)	49.9	34.6	48.2
Cement ('000 metric tons)	335	324	328
Motor spirit (petrol) ('000 gallons)	720	704	907
Kerosene ('000 gallons)	60	52	100
Diesel oil ('000 gallons)	992	939	1,178

* Provisional.

Finance

CURRENCY AND EXCHANGE RATES

Monetary Units
100 pyas = 1 kyat.

Denominations
Coins: 1, 5, 10, 25 and 50 pyas; 1 kyat.
Notes: 1, 5, 10, 15, 45 and 90 kyats.

Sterling and Dollar Equivalents (30 September 1988)
£1 sterling = 11.260 kyats;
US $1 = 6.659 kyats;
1,000 kyats = £88.81 = $150.17.

Average Exchange Rate (kyats per US $)
1985 8.4749
1986 7.3304
1987 6.6535

Note: Since January 1975 the value of the kyat has been linked to the IMF's special drawing right (SDR). Since May 1977 the exchange rate has been fixed at a mid-point of SDR 1 = 8.5085 kyats.

CENTRAL GOVERNMENT BUDGET
(million kyats, year ending 31 March)

Revenue*	1983/84	1984/85	1985/86
Taxes on income and profits	266	313	369
Taxes on goods and services	3,111	3,135	3,043
Import duties	1,225	1,153	1,210
Property income	2,062	2,071	1,936
Fees, charges and sales	974	1,067	1,059
Sale of fixed assets	2	2	3
Total	7,640	7,741	7,620

* Excluding grants from abroad (million kyats): 405 in 1983/84; 404 in 1984/85; 587 in 1985/86.

Expenditure*	1983/84	1984/85	1985/86
General public services	1,147	1,131	1,249
Defence	1,540	1,576	1,698
Education	1,017	998	1,058
Health	545	625	695
Social security and welfare	448	516	475
Housing and community amenities	258	278	282
Economic services	2,590	2,999	3,163
Agriculture, forestry and fishing	1,771	2,162	2,213
Roads	478	505	581
Total (incl. others)	7,936	8,509	9,015
Current	5,706	6,341	6,558
Capital	2,230	2,168	2,457

* Excluding net lending (million kyats): −198 in 1983/84; −271 in 1984/85; −365 in 1985/86.

Source: IMF, *Government Finance Statistics Yearbook*.

BURMA

Statistical Survey

INTERNATIONAL RESERVES
(US $ million at 31 December)

	1985	1986	1987
Gold*	9.7	10.8	12.5
IMF special drawing rights	—	—	0.1
Foreign exchange	33.9	33.1	27.1
Total	43.6	43.9	39.7

* Valued at SDR 35 per troy ounce.
Source: IMF, *International Financial Statistics*.

MONEY SUPPLY
(million kyats at 31 December)

	1984	1985	1986
Currency outside banks	11,768	10,504	15,218

Source: IMF, *International Financial Statistics*.

COST OF LIVING
(Consumer Price Index for Rangoon. Base: 1978 = 100)

	1981/82	1982/83	1983/84
Food and beverages	105.4	111.5	120.7
Tobacco	103.4	105.6	109.1
Fuel and light	136.4	136.2	139.0
Clothing	99.6	111.2	113.0
Rent and repairs	103.6	114.8	111.8
Miscellaneous goods and services	110.1	112.1	113.4
All items	107.8	113.4	119.8

Source: Central Statistical Organization.

NATIONAL ACCOUNTS
(million kyats at current prices, year ending 31 March)
National Income and Product

	1983/84	1984/85*	1985/86*
Compensation of employees	18,998	20,637	22,014
Operating surplus	22,005	24,328	26,134
Domestic factor incomes	41,003	44,965	48,148
Consumption of fixed capital	4,484	4,871	5,271
Gross domestic product (GDP) at factor cost	45,487	49,836	53,419
Indirect taxes, *less* subsidies	4,336	4,288	4,314
GDP in purchasers' values	49,823	54,124	57,733
Net factor income from abroad	−510	−517	−585
Gross national product	49,313	53,607	57,148
Less Consumption of fixed capital	−4,484	−4,871	−5,271
National income in market prices	44,829	48,736	51,877

* Provisional.
Source: UN, *Monthly Bulletin of Statistics*.

Expenditure on the Gross Domestic Product

	1984/85	1985/86	1986/87
Final consumption expenditure	47,396	49,863	51,013
Increase in stocks	−367	−189	−894
Gross fixed capital formation	8,476	8,643	9,921
Total domestic expenditure	55,505	58,317	60,040
Exports of goods and services	3,133	2,566	2,925
Less Imports of goods and services	5,041	4,802	4,513
GDP in purchasers' values	53,597	56,081	58,452

Source: IMF, *International Financial Statistics*.

Gross Domestic Product by Economic Activity

	1983/84	1984/85*	1985/86*
Agriculture, hunting, forestry and fishing	23,711	26,054	27,594
Mining and quarrying	504	595	661
Manufacturing	4,775	5,235	5,735
Electricity	227	247	317
Construction	872	946	968
Wholesale and retail trade	12,272	13,141	14,009
Transport, storage and communications	1,985	2,070	2,191
Other services (incl. gas and water)	5,476	5,836	6,258
GDP in purchasers' values	49,823	54,124	57,733

* Figures are provisional. Revised totals (in million kyats) are: 53,597 in 1984/85; 56,081 in 1985/86.
Source: UN, *Monthly Bulletin of Statistics*.

BALANCE OF PAYMENTS (US $ million)

	1983	1984	1985
Merchandise exports f.o.b.	375.2	364.1	310.8
Merchandise imports f.o.b.	−728.2	−564.5	−512.9
Trade balance	−353.0	−200.4	−202.1
Exports of services	68.1	66.4	69.0
Imports of services	−141.3	−151.7	−152.9
Balance on goods and services	−426.2	−285.7	−286.0
Unrequited transfers (net)	82.2	67.9	80.5
Current balance	−344.1	−217.8	−205.5
Long-term capital (net)	213.4	193.5	132.5
Short-term capital (net)	32.2	0.2	16.4
Net errors and omissions	72.4	9.3	38.7
Total (net monetary movements)	−26.1	−14.7	−18.1
Valuation changes (net)	1.6	−1.0	−4.6
Changes in reserves	−24.5	−15.7	−22.6

Source: IMF, *International Financial Statistics*.

BURMA

External Trade

PRINCIPAL COMMODITIES
(million kyats, year ending 31 March)

Imports c.i.f.	1981/82	1982/83*	1983/84*
Milk and milk products	84.4	67.5	44.8
Animal and vegetable oils, fats and waxes	88.5	43.3	6.8
Pharmaceuticals	130.7	129.1	53.4
Chemicals	133.0	144.9	118.7
Fertilizers	368.6	164.1	107.6
Cotton yarn	60.4	75.7	50.1
Refined petroleum products	68.2	70.1	7.6
Scientific instruments	180.1	84.3	38.2
Base metals and base metal manufactures	699.1	593.6	454.8
Machinery (non-electric)	2,063.7	2,978.2	720.8
Transport equipment	852.3	588.6	376.0
Electric machinery	228.9	425.4	204.9
Paper and paper products	115.2	102.4	77.0
Rubber manufactures	77.2	50.1	69.6
Total (incl. others)	5,611.3	6,313.6	5,197.3

* Provisional.
Source: Central Statistical Organization.

Exports f.o.b.	1981/82	1982/83*	1983/84*
Rice and rice products	1,509.4	1,143.5	1,395.6
Matpe	134.7	111.3	138.9
Prawns	77.6	87.8	44.9
Teak	707.3	730.8	839.7
Hardwood	65.1	73.1	44.1
Base metals and ores	264.7	208.2	301.4
Silver	38.2	42.9	53.5
Oilcakes	41.0	51.6	55.9
Raw jute	28.3	4.7	—
Raw rubber	81.3	60.3	62.6
Cement	37.8	21.6	33.9
Total (incl. others)	3,452.8	3,036.3	3,419.5

PRINCIPAL TRADING PARTNERS
(million kyats, year ending 31 March)

Imports	1981/82	1982/83	1983/84*
African countries	96.0	3.6	99.8
Australia, New Zealand and Pacific	80.5	86.0	99.9
Bangladesh	45.0	48.6	31.0
China, People's Repub.	180.4	250.5	237.1
Eastern Europe	490.4	322.6	843.8
EEC	1,415.8	1,809.9	1,340.1
India	35.1	46.7	15.6
Japan	2,107.7	2,366.7	1,752.4
North America	284.7	514.3	207.8
South-East Asian countries	381.5	426.7	251.4
Total (incl. others)	5,611.3	6,313.6	5,197.3

* Provisional.
1984/85: Total imports 5,650.0m. kyats; Total exports 3,653.8m. kyats (provisional).

Exports	1981/82	1982/83	1983/84*
African countries	844.3	211.1	271.3
Bangladesh	92.9	129.1	67.9
China, People's Repub.	29.2	8.4	30.5
Eastern Europe	153.4	29.4	1.0
EEC	302.4	528.1	419.3
India	57.8	121.3	437.8
Japan	329.4	246.1	227.5
Middle East	82.2	97.3	181.9
North America	13.6	6.7	13.5
Pakistan	43.1	30.2	21.7
Sri Lanka	183.3	349.4	167.2
Total (incl. others)	3,452.8	3,036.3	3,419.5

Transport

RAILWAYS (BURMA RAILWAYS CORPN) ('000)

	1982/83	1983/84*	1984/85*
Passengers	62,111	61,198	63,428
Passenger-miles	2,341,642	2,283,283	2,403,936
Freight tons	2,257	2,208	2,208
Freight-ton-miles	353,235	350,308	333,320

* Provisional.

ROAD TRAFFIC (ROAD TRANSPORT CORPN) ('000)

	1982/83	1983/84*	1984/85*
Passengers	154,943	111,420	118,529
Passenger-miles	789,060	648,402	754,984
Freight tons	1,248	1,217	1,238
Freight-ton-miles	157,062	147,602	150,072

* Provisional.

INLAND WATER TRANSPORT CORPN ('000)

	1982/83	1983/84*	1984/85*
Passengers	19,134	18,618	19,715
Passenger-miles	352,828	377,026	415,647
Freight tons	1,870	2,128	2,028
Freight-ton-miles	236,553	263,026	279,841

* Provisional.

INTERNATIONAL SEA-BORNE SHIPPING
(freight traffic, '000 metric tons, year ending 31 March)

	1981/82	1982/83	1983/84
Goods loaded	1,229	1,078	1,124
Goods unloaded	692	759	475

CIVIL AVIATION (BURMA AIRWAYS CORPN)
('000, internal and external flights)

	1982/83	1983/84*	1984/85*
Passengers	552	501	422
Passenger-miles	138,795	134,462	118,402
Freight tons	5.0	5.1	3.5
Freight-ton-miles	1,528	1,411	1,604

* Provisional.

Tourism

	1982	1983	1984*
Number of visitors	29,910	29,668	28,575
Tourist revenue (million kyats)	75.4	82.9	80.1

* Provisional.

Communications Media

	1982/83	1983/84*	1984/85*
Telephones in use . . .	50,312	51,304	52,604

* Provisional.

Radio receivers (1985): 3m. in use.
Television receivers (1985): 20,000 in use.
Daily newspapers (1984): 7 titles (combined circulation 511,000 copies per issue).

Education

(1984/85, provisional)

	Institutions	Teachers	Students
Primary schools	27,499	104,754	4,855,963
Middle schools	1,562	28,024	993,585
High schools	676	13,644	257,897
Teacher training colleges . .	18	438	3,834
Agricultural, technical and vocational schools and institutes	56	598	10,736
Universities and colleges . .	35	5,524	174,279

Directory

The Constitution

The Constitution came into force on 3 January 1974, following a national referendum held in December 1973. It is the basic law of the State. A summary of the main provisions follows:

GENERAL PRINCIPLES

The Socialist Republic of the Union of Burma is a sovereign, independent, socialist state. There shall be only one political party, the Burma Socialist Programme Party. Sovereign power rests with the people as represented by the People's Assembly. The State is the ultimate owner of all natural resources and shall exploit them in the interests of the people. The means of production shall be nationalized. National groups shall have the right to practise their religion and culture freely within the law and the national interest. The State shall follow an independent and peaceful foreign policy.

STATE ORGANS*

The structure of the State is based on a system of local autonomy under central leadership. Government operates at four levels of administration: wards or village tracts, townships, states or divisions and at national level.

People's Assembly (Pyithu Hluttaw)

The People's Assembly is a unicameral legislature, and the highest organ of state power. It exercises sovereign power on behalf of the people. It is elected directly by secret ballot for a term of four years. Regular sessions take place twice a year, the intervening period being no more than eight months. The People's Assembly may be dissolved if three-quarters of its members agree to it. It may delegate executive and judicial power to central and local state organs. It has the power to enact economic legislation, declare war and peace and the right to call referenda. It may constitute committees and commissions and invest them with powers and duties. Under certain circumstances the People's Assembly may dissolve the People's Councils.

State Council

The State Council is composed of 29 members including one representative from each of the 14 states and divisions, and the Prime Minister, elected by the People's Assembly from its members. The State Council elects from its members a Chairman who becomes President of the Union and represents the State. The term of office of the Council and the President is the same as that of the People's Assembly. The State Council is vested with executive power to carry out the provisions of the Constitution. It has the power to convene the People's Assembly in consultation with the panel of Chairmen of the Assembly. It interprets and promulgates legislation and makes decisions concerning diplomatic relations, international treaties and agreements. It is responsible for the appointment of the heads of the public services. The State Council has the power to grant pardons and amnesties. It may make orders with the force of law between sessions of the People's Assembly, and may order military action in defence of the State. It may also declare a state of emergency and martial law, subject to the approval of the People's Assembly.

Council of Ministers

The Council of Ministers is the highest organ of public administration, elected by the People's Assembly from a list of candidates submitted by the State Council. Its term of office is the same as that of the People's Assembly. The Prime Minister is elected by the Council of Ministers from its members. It is responsible for the management of public administration, and for drafting economic measures and submitting them to the People's Assembly for enactment.

Council of People's Justices

This is the highest judicial organ, elected by the People's Assembly from a list of members submitted by the State Council. Its term of office is the same as that of the People's Assembly.

Council of People's Attorneys

The Council of People's Attorneys is elected by the People's Assembly from a list of members submitted by the State Council. Its term of office is the same as that of the People's Assembly. It is responsible to the People's Assembly for directing state, divisional and township law officers, protecting the rights of the people and supervising the central and local organs of state power.

Council of People's Inspectors

This is elected by the People's Assembly from a list of candidates submitted by the State Council. Its term of office is the same as that of the People's Assembly. It is responsible to the People's Assembly for the inspection of the activities of the local organs of state power, ministries and public bodies. There are also local inspectorates at each administrative level, responsible to the People's Council concerned.

People's Councils

The term of office of the People's Councils is the same as that of the People's Assembly. The People's Councils are elected at different levels according to law. They are responsible for local economic and social affairs and public administration, the administration of local justice, local security, defence and the maintenance of law and order. Each of the People's Councils elects an executive committee to implement its decisions. The Executive Committees each elect a Chairman and a Secretary, who also act as the Chairman and Secretary of that particular People's Council.

* On 18 September 1988 all state organs were abolished by the State Law and Order Restoration Council.

FUNDAMENTAL RIGHTS AND DUTIES OF CITIZENS

All citizens are equal before the law, irrespective of race, religion, sex or other distinction. Every citizen has the right to enjoy the benefits derived from labour, to inherit, to settle anywhere in the State according to law, to receive medical treatment, education and rest and recreation. Freedom of thought, conscience and expression are upheld subject to the law and the interests of state security. All citizens are bound to abstain from undermining the sovereignty and security of the State and the socialist system.

ELECTORAL SYSTEM

All citizens over 18 years are entitled to vote. Those whose parents are both citizens may stand for election to office having attained the age of 20 years (Village and Township Councils), 24 years (State and Divisional Councils), and 28 years (People's Assembly). Members of religious orders and others disqualified by law are prohibited from voting or standing for election.

BURMA
Directory

The Government

HEAD OF STATE

Chairman of the State Law and Order Restoration Council: Gen. SAW MAUNG (took office 18 September 1988).

STATE LAW AND ORDER RESTORATION COUNCIL
(December 1988)

Gen. SAW MAUNG (Chairman)
Brig.-Gen. KHIN NYUNT (First Secretary)
Col TIN U (Second Secretary)
Lt-Gen. THAN SHWE
Rear-Adm. MAUNG MAUNG KHIN
Maj.-Gen. TIN TUN
Brig-Gen. AUNG YE KYAW
Maj.-Gen. PHONE MYINT
Maj.-Gen. SEIN AUNG
Maj.-Gen. CHIT SWE
Brig.-Gen. KYAW BA
Col MAUNG THINT
Brig.-Gen. MAUNG AYE
Brig.-Gen. NYAN LIN
Brig.-Gen. MYINT AUNG
Brig.-Gen. MYA THINN
Brig.-Gen. TUN KYI
Brig.-Gen. AYE THAUNG
Brig.-Gen. MYO NYUNT

MINISTERS
(December 1988)

Prime Minister, Minister of Defence and of Foreign Affairs: Gen. SAW MAUNG.
Minister of Planning and Finance, of Energy and of Mines: Rear-Adm. MAUNG MAUNG KHIN.
Minister of Transport and Communications and of Construction: Maj.-Gen. TIN TUN.
Minister of Home and Religious Affairs and of Information and Culture: Maj.-Gen. PHONE MYINT.
Minister of Education and of Labour and Social Welfare: Brig.-Gen. AUNG YE KYAW.
Minister of Industry (No. I) and of Industry (No. II): Maj.-Gen. SEIN AUNG.
Minister of Co-operatives, of Fisheries and Livestock Breeding and of Agriculture and Forests: Maj.-Gen. CHIT SWE.
Minister of Trade: Col ABEL.
Minister of Health: Dr PE THEIN.

MINISTRIES

President's Office: Ady Rd, Rangoon; tel. (01) 60776.
Prime Minister's Office: Ministers' Office, Rangoon; tel. (01) 83742.
Office of the State Council: 15-16 Windermere Park, Rangoon; tel. (01) 32318.
Ministry of Agriculture and Forests: Ministers' Office, Rangoon; tel. (01) 75080.
Ministry of Construction: Ministers' Office, Rangoon; tel. (01) 76773.
Ministry of Co-operatives: 259-263 Bogyoke Aung San St, Rangoon; tel. (01) 77096.
Ministry of Culture: 26-42 Pansodan St, Rangoon; tel. (01) 81321.
Ministry of Defence: Signal Pagoda Rd, Rangoon; tel. (01) 71611; telex 21316.
Ministry of Education: Ministers' Office, Rangoon; tel. (01) 78597.
Ministry of Energy: 74-80 St John's Rd, Rangoon; telex 21307.
Ministry of Foreign Affairs: Prome Court, Prome Rd, Rangoon; tel. (01) 83333; telex 21313.
Ministry of Health: Ministers' Office, Rangoon; tel. (01) 72075.
Ministry of Home and Religious Affairs: Ministers' Office, Rangoon; tel. (01) 71952.
Ministry of Industry (No. I): 192 Kaba Aye Pagoda Rd, Rangoon; tel. (01) 50701; telex 21513.
Ministry of Industry (No. II): Ministers' Office, Rangoon; tel. (01) 78142; telex 21500.
Ministry of Information: Ministers' Office, Rangoon; tel. (01) 71409.
Ministry of Labour and Social Welfare: Ministers' Office, Rangoon; tel. (01) 78350.
Ministry of Livestock Breeding and Fisheries: Ministers' Office, Rangoon; tel. (01) 80398.
Ministry of Mines: Ministers' Office, Rangoon; tel. (01) 73996.
Ministry of Planning and Finance: Ministers' Office, Rangoon; tel. (01) 76066.
Ministry of Trade: 228-240 Strand Rd, Rangoon; tel. (01) 73613; telex 21338.
Ministry of Transport and Communications: Ministers' Office, Rangoon; tel. (01) 78438.

Legislature

PYITHU HLUTTAW
(People's Assembly)

Following national elections early in 1974, the inaugural session of the Pyithu Hluttaw was convened on 2 March 1974. New elections were held in November 1985. All the candidates were members of the Burma Socialist Programme Party. There were 489 seats. Following the military coup of 18 September 1988, the Pyithu Hluttaw, together with all other state organs, was abolished.

Political Organizations

Following the military coup of 18 September 1988, the Government announced that political organizations other than the ruling party would be permitted to function, on condition that such groups obtained official registration. By mid-December 1988, a total of 167 political parties had registered, although many had no serious political ambitions (being encouraged by financial incentives) and others were believed to be controlled by the NUP, in an attempt to split support for the opposition parties and to discredit student and ethnic minority groups.

Anti-Fascist People's Freedom League: f. 1988; assumed name of wartime resistance movement which became Burma's major political force after independence; formed by those who separated from U Nu in 1958; Chair. BO KYAW NYUNT.

Democracy Party: f. 1988; comprises supporters of fmr Prime Minister U NU; Chair. U THU WAI; Vice-Chair. U KHUN YE NAUNG.

National League for Democracy (NLD): 54-56 University Avenue, Rangoon; f. 1988; initially known as the National United Front for Democracy, and subsequently as the League for Democracy; present name adopted in Sept. 1988; comprises two broadly-based opposition groups demanding the replacement of the mil. govt with an interim admin. to prepare for multi-party elections and the full restoration of democracy; exec. cttee of 12 mems; Chair. Gen. TIN U; Gen. Sec. AUNG SAN SUU KYI.

National Unity Party (NUP): 93c Windermere Rd, Kamayut, Rangoon; tel. 78180; f. 1962 as the Burma Socialist Programme Party (Lanzin Party); sole legal political party until Sept. 1988, when present name was adopted; 15-mem. cen. exec. cttee and 280-mem. cen. cttee; Chair. U THA KYAW; Jt Gen. Secs U TUN YI, U THAN TIN.

People's Democratic Party: 150 Lewis St, Kyauktada Township, Rangoon; f. 1988; initially known as the National Democratic Party; Chair. Thakin LWIN; Gen. Sec. U TIN SHWE.

Union National Democracy Party (UNDP): 2-4 Shinsawpu Rd, Sanchaung Township, Rangoon; f. 1988 by Brig.-Gen. AUNG GYI (fmr chair. of the National League for Democracy).

The following groups are in armed conflict with the Government:

Communist Party of Burma (CPB): f. 1939, reorg. 1946; has operated clandestinely since 1948; receives limited support from the People's Repub. of China; est. strength 10,000 troops; has participated since 1986 in jt mil. operations with sections of the National Democratic Front; Chair. of Cen. Cttee Thakin BA THEIN TIN; Army Chief of Staff TIN YEE.

National Democratic Front (NDF): f. 1975; aims to establish a federal union based on national self-determination; Pres. SAW MAW REH (KNPP); Vice-Pres. NOR MONG ONN (SSPP); Gen. Sec. TU JA (KIO); in 1988 comprised 10 organizations (each representing an ethnic minority group); three regional commands:

Northern Command:

Kachin Independence Organization (KIO): Chair. BRANG SENG/**Kachin Independence Army (KIA):** f. 1961; c. 8,000 troops; Chief of Staff Maj.-Gen. ZAU MAI.

Palaung State Liberation Organization (PSLO): Vice-Chair. KHRUS SANGAI (acting)/**Palaung State Liberation Army (PSLA):** c. 500 troops; Chief of Staff Maj. AI MONG.

Shan State Progress Party (SSPP): f. 1971; Gen. Sec. Col SAI LAK/**Shan State Army (SSA):** c. 2,500 troops; Chief of Staff Lt-Col GAW LIN DA.

Central Command:

Karenni National Progressive Party (KNPP): Chair. BYA REH/**Karenni Revolutionary Army (KRA):** c. 400 troops; Chief of Staff Brig.-Gen. BEE HTOO.

BURMA

Pa-O National Organization (PNO): Chair. AUNG KHAM HTI/**Pa-O National Army (PNA):** c. 300–400 troops; Chief of Staff Col HTOON YI.

Wa National Organization (WNO)/Wa National Army (WNA): c. 600–700 troops; Chair. and Chief of Staff AI CHAU HSEU.

Southern Command:

Arakan Liberation Party (ALP)/Arakan Liberation Army (ALA): f. 1974; Chair. and Chief of Staff Maj. KHAING YE KHAING.

Karen National Union (KNU): f. 1948; opposed to alliance with BCP/**Karen National Liberation Army (KNLA):** c. 3,500–3,700 troops; Pres. and Chief of Staff Maj.-Gen. BO MYA.

Lahu National Army (LNA): accepted as member of NDF in June 1988.

New Mon State Party (NMSP)/Mon National Liberation Army (MNLA): c. 300 troops; Pres. and Chief of Staff NAI NOL LAR.

Diplomatic Representation

EMBASSIES IN BURMA

Australia: 88 Strand Rd, Rangoon; tel. (01) 80711; telex 21301; Ambassador: CHRISTOPHER L. LAMB.

Bangladesh: 340 Prome Rd, Rangoon; tel. (01) 32900; telex 21320; Ambassador: A. Z. M. ENAYETULLAH KHAN.

China, People's Republic: 1 Pyidaungsu Yeiktha Rd, Rangoon; tel. (01) 72087; telex 21346; Ambassador: CHENG RUISHENG.

Czechoslovakia: 326 Prome Rd, Rangoon; tel. (01) 30515; telex 21337; Ambassador: JAROSLAV RICHTER.

Egypt: 81 Pyidaungsu Yeiktha Rd, Rangoon; tel. (01) 81011; telex 21315; Ambassador: MAHMUD ISMAIL SAYID ISSA.

France: 102 Pyidaungsu Yeiktha Rd, POB 858, Rangoon; tel. (01) 82122; telex 21314; Ambassador: GEORGES SIDRE.

German Democratic Republic: 18E Inya Rd, Rangoon; tel. (01) 30933; telex 21501; Ambassador: Dr WOLFGANG SEYFARTH.

Germany, Federal Republic: 32 Natmauk Rd, POB 12, Rangoon; tel. (01) 50477; telex 21401; Ambassador: Dr Baron WALTHER VON MARSCHALL.

India: 545-547 Merchant St, Rangoon; tel. (01) 82933; telex 21201; Ambassador: Dr I. P. SINGH.

Indonesia: 100 Pyidaungsu Yeiktha Rd, Rangoon; tel. (01) 81714; Ambassador: SOEHARTO PONTOATNADJO.

Israel: 49 Prome Rd, Rangoon; tel. (01) 84188; telex 21319; Ambassador: MENASHE ZIPORI.

Italy: 3 Lowis Rd, Golden Valley, Rangoon; tel. (01) 30966; telex 21317; Ambassador: Dr PIERFRANCO SIGNORINI.

Japan: 100 Natmauk Rd, Rangoon; tel. (01) 52288; telex 21400; Ambassador: HIROSHI OHTAKA.

Korea, Republic: 97 University Ave, Rangoon; tel. (01) 30655; telex 21324; Ambassador: KWON PYONG-HYON.

Laos: A1 Diplomatic Quarters, Fraser Rd, Rangoon; tel. (01) 85837; telex 21519; Ambassador: SALY KHAMSY.

Malaysia: 65 Windsor Rd, Rangoon; tel. (01) 20251; telex 21321; Ambassador: SALLEHUDDIN ABDULLAH.

Nepal: 16 Natmauk Yeiktha Rd, Rangoon; tel. (01) 50633; telex 21402; Ambassador: Dr DIBYA DEO BHATT.

Pakistan: 18 Windsor Rd, Rangoon; tel. (01) 84788; Chargé d'affaires: SALAHUDDIN CHOUDHRY.

Philippines: 56 Prome Rd, 6½ Mile, Rangoon; tel. (01) 32080; Ambassador: ALFREDO L. ALMENDRALA.

Romania: 71 Mission Rd, Rangoon; tel. (01) 75891; telex 21323; Chargé d'affaires: CONSTANTIN POPESCU.

Singapore: 287 Prome Rd, Rangoon; tel. (01) 33200; telex 21356; Chargé d'affaires: LAM PECK HENG.

Sri Lanka: 34 Fraser Rd, Rangoon; tel. (01) 22812; telex 21352; Ambassador: W. K. M. DE SILVA.

Thailand: 91 Prome Rd, Rangoon; tel. (01) 82471; telex 21341; Ambassador: THONGCHAN CHOTIKASATHIEN.

USSR: 38 Newlyn Rd, Rangoon; tel. (01) 72427; telex 21331; Ambassador: SERGEI PAVLOVICH PAVLOV.

United Kingdom: 80 Strand Rd, POB 638, Rangoon; tel. (01) 81700; telex 21216; Ambassador: MARTIN R. MORLAND.

USA: 581 Merchant St, Rangoon; tel. (01) 82055; Ambassador: BURTON LEVIN.

Viet-Nam: 40 Komin Kochin Rd, Rangoon; tel. (01) 50361; Ambassador: NGUYEN HOA.

Yugoslavia: 39 Windsor Rd, POB 943, Rangoon; tel. (01) 20238; telex 21325; Ambassador: BRANKO VULETIĆ.

Judicial System

A new judicial structure was established in March 1974. Its highest organ, composed of members of the People's Assembly, was the Council of People's Justices, which functioned as the central Court of Justice. Below this Council were the state, divisional, township, ward and village tract courts formed with members of local People's Councils. These arrangements ceased to operate following the imposition of military rule in September 1988, when it was announced that a Supreme Court was being appointed. In November 1988 it was announced that all courts would be closed until April 1989.

Religion

Freedom of religious belief and practice is guaranteed. About 85% of the population are Buddhists; the remainder are animists (5%), Muslims (4%), Hindus (1.5%) and Christians (4.5%).

CHRISTIANITY

Myanma Naingan Chrityan Athin-daw-mya Kaung-si (Burma Council of Churches): Central YMCA Bldg, 263 Maha Bandoola St, POB 1400, Rangoon; tel. (01) 73290; f. 1974 to succeed the Burma Christian Council; 12 mem. churches; Pres. Most Rev. ANDREW MYA HAN, Anglican Archbishop of Burma; Gen. Sec. Prof. WILLIAM PAW.

The Roman Catholic Church

Burma comprises two archdioceses, six dioceses and one Apostolic Prefecture. At 31 December 1986 there were an estimated 432,000 adherents in the country, representing 1.1% of the total population.

Burma Catholic Bishops' Conference: 292 Prome Rd, Sanchaung PO, Rangoon; f. 1982; Pres. Rt Rev. PAUL ZINGHTUNG GRAWNG, Bishop of Myitkyina.

Archbishop of Mandalay: Most Rev. ALPHONSE U THAN AUNG, Archbishop's House, 82nd and 25th St, Mandalay; tel. (02) 21997.

Archbishop of Rangoon: Most Rev. GABRIEL THOHEY MAHN GABY, Archbishop's House, 289 Theinbyu St, Rangoon; tel. (01) 72752.

The Anglican Communion

Anglicans are adherents of the Church of the Province of Burma, comprising four dioceses. The Province was formed in February 1970, and contained an estimated 45,000 adherents in 1985.

Archbishop of Burma and Bishop of Rangoon: Most Rev. ANDREW MYA HAN, Bishopscourt, 140 Pyidaungsu Yeiktha Rd, Dagon PO, Rangoon; tel. (01) 72668.

Protestant Churches

Burma Baptist Convention: 143 St John's Rd, POB 506, Rangoon; tel. (01) 21465; f. 1865 as Burma Baptist Missionary Convention; present name adopted 1954; 398,000 mems (1985); Pres. Rev. U AYE MYAT KYAW; Gen. Sec. Rev. M. ZAU YAW.

Burma Methodist Church: Methodist Headquarters, 22 Signal Pagoda Rd, Rangoon; Bishop C. F. CHU.

Lutheran Bethlehem Church: 181-183 Theinbyu St, Kandawgalay PO 11221, POB 773, Rangoon; tel. (01) 78148; Rev. J. J. ANDREWS.

Presbyterian Church of Burma: Synod Office, Falam, Chin State; 22,000 mems; Rev. SUN KANGLO.

Other denominations active in Burma include the Lisu Christian Church and the Salvation Army.

BAHÁ'Í FAITH

National Spiritual Assembly: 355 Bowlane, Tamwe PO 11211, Rangoon; tel. (01) 51271; mems resident in 487 localities.

The Press

DAILIES

Botahtaung Daily (Vanguard Daily): 22-30 Strand Rd, Botahtaung PO, POB 539, Rangoon; tel. (01) 74310; f. 1958; state-owned; morning; Chief Editor U THEIN; circ. 140,000.

Guardian: 392-396 Merchant St, Botahtaung PO, POB 1522, Rangoon; tel. (01) 70150; f. 1956; state-owned; morning; English; Chief Editor U SOE MYINT; circ. 19,000.

BURMA

Directory

Kyemon Daily (Mirror Daily): 77 52nd St, Dazundaung PO, POB 819, Rangoon; tel. (01) 82777; f. 1951; state-owned; morning; Chief Editor U Tin Soe; circ. 140,000.

Loktha Phyithu Nezin (Working People's Daily): 212 Theinbyu Rd, Botahtaung PO, POB 40, Rangoon; tel. (01) 73182; f. 1963; morning; Chief Editor Sao Kai Hpa; circ. 160,000.

Myanma Alin (New Light of Burma): 58 Komin Kochin Rd, Bahan PO, POB 21, Rangoon; tel. (01) 50777; f. 1914; nationalized 1969; morning; Chief Editor (vacant); circ. 50,000.

Working People's Daily: 212 Theinbyu Rd, Botahtaung PO, POB 43, Rangoon; tel. (01) 73206; f. 1963; morning; English; Chief Editor U Ko Ko Lay; circ. 24,000.

PERIODICALS

Aurora (Moethaukpan): Myawaddy Press, 184 32nd St, Rangoon; monthly; Burmese and English; circ. 50,000.

Do Kyaung Tha: Myawaddy Press, 184 32nd St, Rangoon; monthly; circ. 100,000.

Gita Padetha: Rangoon; journal of Burma Music Council; circ. 10,000.

Guardian Magazine: 392/396 Merchant St, Botahtaung PO, POB 1522, Rangoon; tel. (01) 70150; f. 1953; nationalized 1964; monthly; English; literary; circ. 50,000.

Myawaddy Magazine: 184 32nd St, Rangoon; tel. (01) 74655; f. 1952; monthly; literary magazine; circ. 20,000.

Pyinnya Lawka Journal: 529 Merchant St, Rangoon; publ. by Sarpay Beikman Management Board; quarterly; circ. 18,000.

Shetho (Forward): 22/24 Pansodan St, Rangoon; monthly; Burmese and English; govt. publ.; circ. 36,000.

Shu Ma Wa Magazine: 146 Western Wing, Bogyoke Market, Rangoon; monthly; literary.

Shwe Thwe: 529 Merchant St, Rangoon; weekly; bilingual children's journal; publ. by Sarpay Beikman Management Board; circ. 100,000.

Teza: Myawaddy Press, 184 32nd St, Rangoon; monthly; English and Burmese; circ. 60,100.

Thwe/Thauk Magazine: 185 48th St, Rangoon; f. 1946; monthly; literary.

NEWS AGENCIES

News Agency of Burma (NAB): 212 Theinbyu Rd, Rangoon; tel. (01) 70893; f. 1963; govt-controlled; Chief Editors U Ye Tint (domestic section), U Kyaw Min (external section).

Foreign Bureaux

Agence France-Presse (AFP) (France): 58A Golden Valley, Rangoon; tel. (01) 32360; Correspondent U Khin Maung Thwin.

Agenzia Nazionale Stampa Associata (ANSA) (Italy): POB 270, Rangoon; tel. 50916; telex 21201; Rep. U Myo Thant.

Associated Press (AP) (USA): 283 U Wisara Rd, Sanchaung PO, Rangoon; tel. (01) 30176; telex 21327; Rep. U Sein Win.

Deutsche Presse-Agentur (dpa) (Federal Republic of Germany): 55 Kalagar St, Kemmendine PO, Rangoon; Correspondent U Chit Tun.

Reuters: 162 Phayre St, Rangoon; tel. (01) 71419; telex 21202; Correspondent U Hla Kyi.

Telegrafnoye Agentstvo Sovetskovo Soyuza (TASS) (USSR): 41-3 Lowis Rd, Golden Valley, Rangoon; tel. (01) 31513; Correspondent Yevgeniy Shevelev.

Xinhua (New China) News Agency (People's Republic of China): 67A Prome Rd, Rangoon; tel. (01) 75714; telex 21351; Rep. Lui Jimin.

Publishers

Hanthawaddy Press: 157 Bo Aung Gyaw St, Rangoon; f. 1889; books and journals; Man. Editor U Zaw Win.

Knowledge Publishing House: 130 Bo Gyoke Aung San St, Yegyaw, Rangoon; travel, fiction, religion, politics and directories.

Kyipwaye Press: 84th St, Letsaigan, Mandalay; arts, travel, religion, fiction and children's.

Myawaddy Press: 184 32nd St, Rangoon; tel. (01) 74655; journals and magazines; Chief Editor (vacant).

Sarpay Beikman Management Board: 529 Merchant St, Rangoon; tel. (01) 83611; f. 1947; Burmese encyclopaedia, literature, fine arts and general; also magazines and translations; Chair. U Taik Soe; Vice-Chair. U Maung Maung Khin.

Shumawa Press: 146 West Wing, Bogyoke Market, Rangoon; non-fiction.

Thu Dhama Wadi Press: 55-56 Maung Khine St, POB 419, Rangoon; f. 1903; religious; Propr U Tin Htoo; Man. U Pan Maung.

Government Publishing House

Printing and Publishing Corpn: 228 Theinbyu St, Rangoon; tel. (01) 81033; Man. Dir Col Maung Maung Khin.

PUBLISHERS' ASSOCIATION

Burmese Publishers' Union: 146 Bogyoke Market, Rangoon.

Radio and Television

There were an estimated 1m. radio receivers and 40,000 television receivers in use in 1986.

Burma Broadcasting Service (BBS): GPO Box 1432, Yangon Taing, Rangoon; tel. (01) 31355; telex 21360; f. 1946; broadcasts in Burmese, Arakanese, Mon, Shan, Karen, Chin, Kachin, Kayah and English; colour television transmissions began in 1980; Dir-Gen. U Kyaw Minn; Dir of Broadcasting U Aung Kyi; Dir of Television U Ko Ko Gyi (acting).

Finance

(cap. = capital; p.u. = paid up; res = reserves; dep. = deposits; m. = million; amounts in kyats)

BANKING

All banks in Burma were nationalized and amalgamated in 1963 to form the People's Bank of the Union of Burma. In 1972 this was renamed the Union of Burma Bank, and in 1976 it was reconstituted as the central bank. There are also three state-owned banks with specialist functions.

Central Bank

Union of Burma Bank: 24-26 Sule Pagoda Rd, Rangoon; tel. (01) 85300; telex 21213; f. 1976; bank of issue; cap. p.u. 200m.; dep. 948m.; Chair. U Maung Maung Hla.

State Banks

Myanma Agricultural Bank: 1-7 Latha St, Rangoon; tel. (01) 73018; provides agricultural credit for farmers; cap. 40m.; Man. Dir U Sein Bann.

Myanma Economic Bank: 564 Merchant St, Rangoon; tel. (01) 81819; telex 21213; provides savings and credit facilities and extends loans to state economic organizations, municipal bodies and co-operatives; Man. Dir U Maung Maung Than.

Myanma Foreign Trade Bank: 80-86 Maha Bandoola Garden St, POB 203, Rangoon; tel. (01) 84911; telex 21300; f. 1976; cap. and res 69m., dep. 252m. (March 1987); handles all foreign exchange and international banking transactions; Man. Dir U Maung Maung Than; Dep. Gen. Mans U Mya U, U Khin Maung Kyi.

INSURANCE

Myanma Insurance Corpn: 163-167 Pansodan St, Rangoon; tel. (01) 84466; telex 21203; f. 1975; Man. Dir U Ko Ko Gyi.

Trade and Industry

Socialist Economic Planning Committee: Rangoon; f. 1967; 10 mems.

GOVERNMENT CORPORATIONS

Agricultural and Farm Produce Trade Corpn: 70 Pansodan Rd, Rangoon; tel. (01) 84044; telex 21305; Man. Dir U Ohn Kin.

Agriculture Corpn: 72-74 Shwedagon Pagoda Rd, Rangoon; tel. (01) 83480; telex 21311; Man. Dir U Tin Hlaing.

Construction Corpn: 60 Shwedagon Pagoda Rd, Rangoon; tel. (01) 80955; telex 21336; Man. Dir U Khin Maung Yin.

Electric Power Corpn: 197-199 Lower Kemmendine Rd, Rangoon; tel. (01) 85366; telex 21306; Man. Dir U Khin Maung Thein.

Fisheries Corpn: 654 Merchant St, Rangoon; tel. (01) 78022; telex 21310; f. 1972; Man. Dir U Kan Nyunt.

Foodstuff Industries Corpn: 523 Merchant St, Rangoon; tel. (01) 84494; telex 21500; Man. Dir Col Soe Lwin.

General Industries Corpn: 192 Kaba Aye Pagoda Rd, Rangoon; tel. (01) 56055; telex 21500; Man. Dir Saw Myint.

BURMA

Heavy Industries Corpn: 23A Kaba Aye Pagoda Rd, POB 370, GPO Rangoon; tel. (01) 62863; telex 21503; Man. Dir Lt-Col THAN SHWE.

Hotel and Tourist Corpn (Tourist Burma): 77–91 Sule Pagoda Rd, POB 1398, Rangoon; tel. (01) 77571; telex 21330; govt-controlled; manages all hotels, tourist offices, diplomatic stores and duty-free shops; Man. Dir U THAW DA SEIN; Gen. Man. Col TANKA DHOJ; Dep. Gen. Man. (Hotels) U TIN YEE; Dep. Gen. Man. (Tourism and Diplomatic Stores) U MYO LWIN.

Industrial Planning Department: 192 Kaba Aye Pagoda Rd, POB 11201, Bahan PO, Rangoon; tel. (01) 50744; f. 1952; Dir-Gen. Lt-Col AYE KYIN.

Inspection and Agency Corpn: Rangoon; works on behalf of state-owned enterprises to promote business with foreign companies; Man. Dir U WIN KYI.

Livestock Breeding Corpn: Veterinary Institute Estate, Insein, POB 1457, Rangoon; tel. (01) 40726; telex 21310; Man. Dir U KHIN LATT.

Metal Industries Corpn: 354 Prome Rd, Rangoon; tel. (01) 31518; telex 21500; Man. Dir U MYO THANT.

Myanma Export-Import Corpn: 577 Merchant St, Rangoon; tel. (01) 80260; telex 21305; Man. Dir U AUNG KYI.

Myanma Gems Corpn: 66 Kaba Aye Pagoda Rd, POB 1397, Rangoon; tel. (01) 61901; telex 21506; govt-controlled; Man. Dir U HLA THEIN.

Myanma Oil Corpn: 74–80 St. John's Rd, Rangoon; tel. (01) 82266; telex 21307; fmrly Burma Oil Co; nationalized 1963; govt-controlled; Man. Dir TINT LWIN.

No. 1 Mining Corpn: 226 Maha Bandoola St, Rangoon; tel. (01) 74711; telex 21307; fmrly Myanma Bawdwin Corpn; govt-controlled; development and mining of non-ferrous metals; Man. Dir U MYO NYUNT.

No. 2 Mining Corpn: Kanbe, Yankin, Rangoon; tel. (01) 50166; telex 21511; fmrly Myanma Tin Tungsten Development Corpn; govt-controlled; development and mining of tin, tungsten and antimony; Man. Dir U NYAN LIN.

No. 3 Mining Corpn: Kanabe, Yankin PO, Rangoon; tel. (01) 57444; telex 21511; govt-controlled; production of pig iron, carbon steel, steel grinding balls, coal, barytes, gypsum, limestone and various clays, etc.; Man. Dir U HLA THEIN.

Petrochemical Industries Corpn: 23 Prome Rd, Rangoon; tel. (01) 22822; telex 21329; f. 1975; govt-controlled; Man. Dir U HLAING MYINT SAN.

Petroleum Products Supply Corpn: 74–80 St. John's Rd, Rangoon; tel. (01) 82011; telex 21307; govt-controlled; Man. Dir Col MYINT SOE.

Pharmaceuticals Industries Corpn: 192 Kaba Aye Pagoda Rd, Rangoon; tel. (01) 56740; telex 21500; Man. Dir U BA NYUNT.

Posts and Telecommunications Corpn: 43 Bo Aung Gyaw St, Rangoon; tel. (01) 85499; telex 21222; Man. Dir U TIN.

Textiles Industries Corpn: 192 Kaba Aye Pagoda Rd, Rangoon; tel. (01) 56333; telex 21500; Man. Dir U MYA SOE NYEIN.

Timber Corpn: POB 206, Ahlone, Rangoon; tel. (01) 83933; telex 21312; f. 1948; extraction, processing, and main exporter of Burma teak and other timber, veneers, plywood and other forest products; Man. Dir U KHIN MAUNG GYI.

CO-OPERATIVES

There were 21,250 co-operative societies in 1984/85.

Central Co-operative Society (CCS) Council: 334/336 Strand Rd, Rangoon; tel. (01) 74550; Chair. U THAN HLANG; Sec. U TIN LATT.

WORKERS' AND PEASANTS' COUNCILS

Conditions of work are stipulated in the Workers' Rights and Responsibilities Law, enacted in 1964. Regional workers' councils ensure that government directives are complied with, and that targets are met on a regional basis. In January 1985 there were 293 workers' councils in towns, with more than 1.8m. members. They are co-ordinated by a central workers' asiayone in Rangoon, formed in 1968 to replace trades union organizations which had been abolished in 1964.

Peasants' Asiayone (Organization): Rangoon; tel. (01) 82819; f. 1977; peasants representative org.; Chair. Brig.-Gen. U THAN NYUNT; Sec. U SAN TUN.

Workers' Asiayone: Central Body Headquarters, Strand Rd, Rangoon; f. 1968; workers representative org.; Chair. U OHN KYAW; Sec. UNYUNT THEIN.

Transport

All railways, domestic air services, passenger and freight road transport services and inland water facilities are owned and operated by state-controlled enterprises.

RAILWAYS

The railway network comprised 3,156 km of track in 1984/85.

Burma Railways Corpn: Bogyoke Aung San St, POB 118, Rangoon; tel. (01) 84455; telex 21361; f. 1972; govt-operated; Man. Dir Col WIN SEIN; Gen. Man. U SAW CLYDE.

ROADS

In 1984/85 the total length of roads in Burma was 23,067 km of which 3,946 km were highways and 19,121 km were main roads.

Road Transport Corpn: 375 Bogyoke Aung San St, Rangoon; tel. (01) 82252; f. 1963 to carry out phased nationalization of passenger and freight road transport; in 1984/85 operated 2,695 haulage trucks and 1,335 passenger buses; Man. Dir (vacant).

INLAND WATERWAYS

The principal artery of traffic is the River Irrawaddy, which is navigable as far as Bhamo, about 1,450 km inland, while parts of the Salween and Chindwin rivers are also navigable.

Inland Water Transport Corpn: 50 Pansodan St, Rangoon; tel. (01) 83244; govt-owned; operates cargo and passenger services throughout Burma; 19.7m. passengers and 2m. tons of freight were carried in 1984/85; Man. Dir U KHIN MAUNG THEIN.

SHIPPING

Rangoon is the chief port. Vessels with a displacement of up to 15,000 tons can be accommodated. In 1985 a modernization plan for Rangoon port was announced in anticipation of increased foreign trade by 1990. A large container yard was under construction in 1988 and due to be completed in 1990. There are also plans for the construction of a new international port at Thilawa, 13 km from Rangoon, which would also deal with the increased trade.

Burma Ports Corpn: 10 Pansodan St, POB 1, Rangoon; tel. (01) 83122; telex 21208; f. 1880; general port and harbour duties; Man. Dir U TIN MAUNG SOE; Gen. Man. U TIN OO; fleet of 11 vessels totalling 817,051 grt and 36 smaller craft.

Burma Five Star Shipping Corpn: 132–136 Theinbyu Rd, POB 1221, Rangoon; tel. (01) 80022; telex 21210; f. 1959; cargo services to the Far East, South-East Asia and Europe; Man. Dir U SHWE THAN; Gen. Man. U THAN TUT; fleet of 22 coastal and ocean-going vessels.

CIVIL AVIATION

Mingaladon Airport, near Rangoon, is equipped to international standards. In 1987 work began on a five-year airport expansion project, at a possible cost of up to US $250m.

Burma Airways Corpn (BAC): 104 Strand Rd, Rangoon; tel. (01) 72911; telex 21204; f. 1948; govt-controlled; internal network operates services to 25 airports; external services to Bangkok, Calcutta, Dhaka, Kathmandu and Singapore; Man. Dir Col KYAW THEIN; Flight Operations Man. U KYAWT MYAING; fleet of 2 F-28-4000, 5 F-27, 1 F28-1000, 1 F27-400, 1 F27-200, 3 helicopters.

Tourism

Tourism is undeveloped. Rangoon, Mandalay and Pagan possess outstanding palaces, Buddhist temples and shrines. In 1985 Burma received 32,948 foreign visitors. In August 1988, owing to political turbulence, Burma closed its borders to tourists, but they were reopened in December.

Tourist Burma: 77/91 Sule Pagoda Rd, Rangoon; tel. (01) 78376; telex 21330; sole tour operator and travel agent; handles all travel arrangments for groups and individuals.

Atomic Energy

Union of Burma Atomic Energy Department: Central Research Organization, 6 Kaba Aye Pagoda Rd, Rangoon; f. 1955; Chair. Dr MAUNG MAUNG GALE.

BURUNDI

Introductory Survey

Location, Climate, Language, Religion, Flag, Capital

The Republic of Burundi is a land-locked country lying on the eastern shore of Lake Tanganyika, in central Africa, a little south of the Equator. It is bordered by Rwanda to the north, by Tanzania to the south and east, and by Zaire to the west. The climate is tropical (hot and humid) in the lowlands, and cool in the highlands, with an irregular rainfall. The official languages are French and Kirundi, while Swahili is used, in addition to French, in commercial circles. More than 60% of the inhabitants profess Christianity, with the great majority of the Christians being Roman Catholics. A large minority still adhere to traditional animist beliefs. The national flag (proportions 3 by 2) consists of a white diagonal cross on a background of red (above and below) and green (left and right), with a white circle, containing three green-edged red stars, in the centre. The capital is Bujumbura.

Recent History

Burundi (formerly Urundi) became part of German East Africa in 1899. In 1916, during the First World War, the territory was occupied by Belgian forces from the Congo (now Zaire). Subsequently, as part of Ruanda-Urundi, it was administered by Belgium under a League of Nations mandate and later as a UN Trust Territory. Elections in September 1961, held under UN supervision, were won by the Union for National Progress party (UPRONA), which had been formed in 1958 by Ganwa (Prince) Louis Rwagasore, son of the reigning Mwami (King), Mwambutsa IV. Prince Rwagasore became Prime Minister, but was assassinated after only two weeks in office. He was succeeded by his brother-in-law, André Muhirwa. Internal self-government was granted in January 1962 and full independence on 1 July 1962, when the two parts of the Trust Territory became separate states. Burundi continued to be linked to Rwanda in a customs and monetary union, until the agreements were terminated in January 1964. In July 1966 the Mwami was deposed, after a reign of over 50 years, by his son Charles, with the help of a group of army officers, and the constitution was suspended. In November 1966 Charles, now Mwami Ntare V, was himself deposed by his Prime Minister, Capt. (later Lt-Gen.) Michel Micombero, who declared Burundi a republic.

Micombero's rule confirmed the long-established dominance of the Tutsi tribe over the Hutu tribe, who form the majority of the population. Several alleged plots against the Government in 1969 and 1971 were followed in 1972 by an abortive coup during which Ntare V was killed. The Hutus were held responsible for the attempted coup and this served as a pretext for the Tutsis to conduct a series of large-scale massacres of the rival tribe, with the final death toll being estimated at around 100,000. Many Hutus fled to neighbouring countries, and repression of the tribe continued.

In 1972 Micombero began a prolonged restructuring of the executive, which resulted in 1973 in an appointed seven-man Presidential Bureau, with Micombero holding the dual office of President and Prime Minister. In July 1974 the Government introduced a new republican constitution which vested sovereignty in UPRONA, the sole legal political party in Burundi. The President was elected Secretary-General of the party and re-elected for a seven-year presidential term.

On 1 November 1976 an army coup deposed Micombero, who died in exile in July 1983. The leader of the coup, Lt-Col (later Col) Jean-Baptiste Bagaza, was appointed President by the Supreme Revolutionary Council (composed of army officers), and a new Council of Ministers was formed. The Prime Minister, Lt-Col Edouard (Ndugu) Nzambimana, announced in mid-1977 the military regime's intention to hand over power to a civilian government in 1981.

The 1978–82 five-year plan elaborated on the Government's general policy as defined in the Declaration of Fundamental Aims of 20 November 1976, with the main objectives being social justice and unity throughout the country, based on the elimination of corruption in the administration.

In October 1978 President Bagaza announced a ministerial reshuffle in which he abolished the post of Prime Minister. The first national congress of UPRONA was held in December 1979, and a party Central Committee, headed by President Bagaza, was elected to take over the functions of the Supreme Revolutionary Council in January 1980. A new constitution, adopted by national referendum in November 1981, provided for the establishment of a National Assembly, to be elected by universal adult suffrage. The first elections were held in October 1982. Having been re-elected president of UPRONA at the party's second national congress in July 1984, Bagaza was elected President of Burundi by direct suffrage for the first time in August, winning 99.63% of the votes cast; he was the only candidate for either election.

In 1985 relations between the Government and religious authorities in Burundi were affected by the arrest of several priests and the Roman Catholic Archbishop of Gitega, as well as by the expulsion of many foreign missionaries. The dispute was investigated by Amnesty International, which alleged that 20 priests were being detained without trial. An official government statement acknowledged that arrests had been made, but declared that those priests who had 'admitted their mistakes' had subsequently been released. In late 1986 the Government assumed responsibility for the organization and administration of all lower- and intermediate-level Roman Catholic seminaries, a measure that was regarded as one of retaliation against the Roman Catholic Church, which was alleged by the Government to have been 'disseminating tendentious information abroad'. Relations between the Government and church authorities deteriorated further, in 1987, when Catholic lay catechists were forbidden to administer the Eucharist, and morning prayer meetings were banned. However, in June, in a conciliatory gesture to the Church, the Government announced that all Catholic priests in custody were to be released.

On 3 September 1987 a military coup deposed President Bagaza while he was attending a conference in Canada. The coup was led by Maj. Pierre Buyoya, who accused Bagaza of corruption and immediately formed a Military Committee for National Salvation to administer the country, pending the appointment of a new President. The Constitution was suspended, and the National Assembly was dissolved. On 2 October Buyoya was sworn in as President of the Third Republic. He promptly announced the release of several hundred political prisoners. Many of the restrictions earlier imposed on the Church were also lifted, fuelling speculation that discontent at Bagaza's treatment of Catholic priests had been a major factor in the coup. The new Council of Ministers comprised civilians, but retained no minister from the previous regime. However, it was generally thought unlikely that conditions would improve for the Hutu people, as political power had, in effect, merely been transferred from one Tutsi clan to another. Tutsi domination of the army, where tribal members comprise 99.7% of soldiers, and of the administration, where Tutsis comprise 94% of party cadres and 95% of magistrates, was expected to continue.

In August 1988 tribal tensions flared in the north of the country when groups of Hutus, claiming Tutsi provocation, slaughtered hundreds of Tutsis in the towns of Ntega and Marangara. The Tutsi-dominated army was immediately dispatched to the region to restore order, and in the subsequent week large-scale tribal massacres, similar to those of 1972, occurred. More than 60,000 refugees fled to neighbouring Rwanda, as the death toll rose to an estimated 20,000. In the aftermath of the killings, a group of Hutu intellectuals were arrested for writing a letter of protest at the army's actions and for demanding the establishment of an independent commission of inquiry into the massacres. In October, however, Buyoya announced changes to the Council of Ministers, including the appointment of a Hutu to the newly-restored post of Prime Minister. The Council included, for the first time, a majority of Hutu representatives.

The violent unrest of 1988 threatened to have an economic, as well as social and political, effect on the country. Burundi is the largest recipient per caput of low-interest loans from the World Bank, and, under Buyoya, the country satisfied several criteria imposed by the Bank, namely the devaluation of its currency, the elimination of import restrictions and the abolition of passbook laws, which prevented Hutus from moving to different areas of the country. However, it was feared that the repressive military measures that the Buyoya Government adopted would discourage future aid programmes.

Government
The 1981 Constitution, which provided for the election by universal adult suffrage of a President for a five-year term, and of 52 representatives to a National Assembly for a similar period (a further 13 representatives being appointed by the President), was suspended in September 1987. Executive and legislative powers were assumed by a 31-member Military Committee for National Salvation (CMSN). The CMSN elected its Chairman as President of the Republic. A civilian Council of Ministers was appointed. The organs of UPRONA, the only authorized political party, were suspended following the coup, but were to be restored at a later date. For the purposes of local government, Burundi comprises 15 provinces, administered by civilian governors, each of which is divided into districts and further subdivided into communes.

Defence
The army was merged with the police force in 1967. The total strength of the armed forces in June 1988 was 7,200, comprising an army of 5,500, a navy of 50, an air force of 150, and a paramilitary force of 1,500 gendarmes. Defence expenditure in 1986 totalled an estimated 4,780m. Burundi francs.

Economic Affairs
In terms of average income, Burundi is one of the 20 poorest countries in the world. In 1987, according to World Bank estimates, gross national product (GNP) was US $1,205m., equivalent to $240 per head (at average 1985–87 prices), the latter figure having decreased at an average rate of 0.4% annually, in real terms, since 1980. The average increase in overall gross domestic product (GDP), measured in constant prices, was 3.6% in 1965–80, slowing to 2.3% in 1980–86. Real GDP rose by 3.3% in 1986, to total $1,090m. (at current prices). The annual rate of inflation averaged 12.0% in 1981, 5.8% in 1982, 8.4% in 1983 and 14.4% in 1984. According to official figures, consumer prices increased by 3.6% in 1985, and by only 1.9% in 1986, but inflation rose to 7.3% in 1987.

The economy is based largely on agriculture, which (with forestry and fishing) engaged about 92% of the labour force and contributed 60.6% of GDP in 1986. The main subsistence crops are cassava and sweet potatoes, while the principal cash crops are coffee, tea and cotton. The annual harvest of seed (unginned) cotton increased from 7,155 metric tons in 1985/86 to 7,894 tons in 1986/87. Burundi's annual output of made tea increased from 867 metric tons in 1975 to 4,145 tons in 1985, but declined to about 3,600 tons in 1986. Estimated production of tea in 1987 was 4,000 tons. Coffee is Burundi's principal export. In 1984 coffee output fell slightly, to an estimated 32,000 tons, but the value of coffee exports rose by 52%, with coffee sales providing 84% of total export earnings. The value of coffee exports increased by a further 12.5% in 1985, when coffee sales again accounted for 84% of total export earnings, and provided 25% of government revenue and 10% of GDP. The coffee harvest fell from 40,502 metric tons in 1985/86 to 37,839 tons in 1986/87. In 1987 exports of coffee accounted for 80% of total export earnings. Such heavy dependence on a single commodity has caused Burundi's balance of trade to react sharply to fluctuations in international prices for coffee and has prevented reliable economic planning. With proposed expenditure of 159,000m. Burundi francs, the 1988–92 five-year plan sought to expand and develop the private sector, to promote trade and to strengthen the banking and financial sectors in order to ensure stability for the economy. The EEC countries, in particular Belgium, France and the Federal Republic of Germany, are among Burundi's main trading partners, accounting for 51.3% of import costs and 60.8% of export revenue in 1987. Revenue from coffee exports rose by more than 63% in 1979 but the trade deficit continued to increase. In subsequent years the value of imports increased, while coffee earnings remained below their 1979 level. Revenue from coffee exports rose from 11,511m. Burundi francs in 1985 to a record 17,057m. francs in 1986 (when the visible trade deficit was 3,888m. francs), but fell to 7,175m. francs in 1987. The trade deficit rose to 15,007m. francs in 1987.

The mining sector was based on the exploitation of small amounts of gold, bastnaesite, cassiterite, tungsten and tantalum, although no significant production of bastnaesite has been noted since 1978, nor of cassiterite since 1979. Burundi has the world's richest deposits of vanadium, and important deposits of nickel, estimated at 5% of world reserves, and uranium are being surveyed. Petroleum has been detected beneath Lake Tanganyika and in the Ruzizi valley, and test drilling began in 1986. In December 1986 the Amoco Burundi Petroleum Company signed a contract with the Government to drill two wells under Lake Tanganyika in 1987. Manufacturing, however, is still on a small scale, accounting for 5.2% of GDP in 1986. It consists largely of the processing of agricultural products, a sector that the 1983–87 plan was to develop, with a view not only to preparing produce for export but also to establishing various import substitution industries. A native textile industry has been developed, and produced 8.5m. metres of cloth in 1986. Plantations of sugar cane have been established on the Moso plain, near Bujumbura, in association with a refinery which was due to be completed in 1987, and which was projected to meet 90% of the country's demand for sugar by 1990. Two factories at Bujumbura and Gitega, completed in 1983, are to process Burundi's entire coffee crop. Construction of a brewery, a joint venture with a Dutch company, was completed at Gitega in 1985. In 1974 trade agreements were made with the EEC, and in 1976 Burundi established, with Zaire and Rwanda, the Economic Community of the Great Lakes Countries (CEPGL, see p. 226). In 1985 Burundi became a full member of the Preferential Trade Area for Eastern and Southern African States (see p. 220). Burundi is also a member of the International Coffee Organization (see p. 223).

Most of the foreign aid to Burundi comes from Belgium, France and the Federal Republic of Germany and through the EEC's European Development Fund and the World Bank. In February 1984 the total amount of foreign aid required for the 1983–87 five-year plan was stated to be US $1,556m., which was to represent about 60% of the total planned investment. In August 1986 Burundi became the first member of the IMF to benefit from the Fund's Structural Adjustment Facility (SAF), established in the previous March. Under the new facility, the IMF approved a loan of SDR 27.1m., to be made over a period of three years, in support of the Burundi Government's programme of economic recovery, which aimed to reduce the country's dependence on coffee exports for earnings of foreign exchange, to restore real annual GDP growth to about 4%, to restrict the deficit on the current account of the balance of payments to no more than 6.5% of GDP in 1987, and to reverse the trend of escalating debt-servicing costs. (The current-account deficit increased from 3% of GDP at the beginning of the 1980s to 8.5% of GDP in 1984, while debt-servicing costs increased from 6% of export earnings in 1981 to about 20% in 1984.) The loan was approved in addition to an 18-month stand-by credit facility of SDR 21m. that had been agreed earlier in the month, and to a US $50m. structural adjustment credit, negotiated in the previous May. The first tranche, of SDR 8.54m., was made available in August 1986, and the second tranche, of SDR 12.8m., in May 1988. This had been delayed as a result of the September 1987 coup and the sharp decline in world prices for coffee. Other measures taken in 1986, as part of the Government's programme of economic reform, included the raising of official prices payable to coffee producers by 28%, and, in July, the devaluation of the Burundi franc by 13% in relation to the IMF's SDR. At the end of 1986 Burundi's external public debt totalled 66,858.4m. francs. The franc was further devalued in February 1988, by 9% against the IMF's SDR, in line with World Bank programmes designed to bring inflation down to a yearly rate of 4.5%. World Bank credits totalling US $153.5m. were approved in 1987/88.

Unemployment has always been an enormous problem but, as 90% of the population reside in rural areas, it is virtually impossible for unemployment in the countryside to decrease in absolute terms. The National Recovery Programme, initiated in 1978, aimed to mitigate this problem by continuing efforts to alleviate the food scarcity. In 1977 a stocking and trading centre was established to co-ordinate the buying and selling of foodstuffs over the whole country. The Recovery Programme also aimed to promote intensive livestock farming and new crops, such as soya beans, oil palms and sugar cane, and to create a farmers' co-operative.

Budget proposals for 1988 envisaged recurrent expenditure of 25,240m. Burundi francs and revenue of 21,861m. francs. Proposed spending represented a 23% increase on the budget for 1987, with allocations to the education sector rising by 17%, to the public health sector by 17% and to the transport sector by 23%.

Two dams are being built, and a large hydroelectric scheme on the Rwanda-Zaire border (the Ruzizi-II project) is being developed jointly with those two countries, for completion in the late 1980s, Burundi's electricity supply hitherto having been obtained almost entirely from the hydroelectric station at Bukavu in Zaire. In September 1986 a hydroelectric power station was opened in Rwegura, Cibitoke province. The station cost 5,500m. francs and was to have a generating capacity of 18 MW of electricity, one-third of the country's total. In 1987 Burundi signed a co-operation agreement with the Federal Republic of Germany, providing for the construction of two additional turbines at the Bururi hydroelectric station. The exploitation of Burundi's peat bogs provided 10,000 metric tons of peat, for use as an additional source of energy, in 1982.

In 1986 the OPEC Fund for International Development agreed to provide a loan of US $3m. for the completion of the Makamba-Butembera road, which was to receive additional funding from the Saudi Fund for Development and the Burundi Government. The construction of the new road was planned with the aim of both facilitating transport in an area with good potential for agricultural development and improving road links with Tanzania.

In February 1987 the African Development Fund agreed to lend 217,630m. francs CFA towards the construction of a shipyard in Bujumbura. Later in the year, the International Development Agency (IDA) signed a contract to provide a loan of US $4.8m. to assist in financing expansion in the telecommunications system, with a further loan of US $7.5m. to finance plans to improve economic and public enterprise management. In October 1987 the French Central Fund for Technical Co-operation signed an agreement to lend 43.5m. French francs to Burundi for a tea project in Buhoro. Plans to construct a railway linking Uganda and Tanzania were announced in 1987. The railway will run through Burundi and Rwanda and will be an estimated 961 km (597 miles) in length.

Social Welfare

Wage-earners are protected by insurance against accidents and occupational diseases and can draw on a pension fund. Medical facilities are, however, limited. In 1978 there were 22 hospitals, nine maternity units and 100 dispensaries. In 1981 Burundi had one hospital bed for every 286 inhabitants. In 1986 Burundi and the People's Republic of China signed a protocol whereby the latter undertook to provide Burundi with medical aid in the form of drugs and equipment, and by sending a team of 12 specialists to Burundi for two years.

Education

Education is provided free of charge. Kirundi is the language of instruction in primary schools, while French is used in secondary schools. Primary education, which is officially compulsory, begins at seven years of age and lasts for six years. Secondary education, which is not compulsory, begins at the age of 13 and lasts for up to seven years, comprising a first cycle of four years and a second of three years. In 1985 the total enrolment at primary and secondary schools was equivalent to 29% of the school-age population (males 35%; females 24%), whereas in 1980 the proportion had been only 16%. Enrolment at primary schools increased from 175,856 in 1980 to 343,027 in 1984. The latter total included an estimated 39% of children in the relevant age-group (45% of boys; 32% of girls). Enrolment at secondary schools, including pupils receiving vocational instruction and teacher training, rose from 19,013 in 1980 to 23,984 in 1984. However, the latter total was equivalent to only 4% of the population in the secondary age-group. There is one university, in Bujumbura, with 1,900 students in 1981. According to official estimates, the average rate of illiteracy among the population aged 10 years and over was 66.2% (males 57.2%; females 74.3%) in 1982.

Public Holidays

1989: 2 January (for New Year's Day), 27 March (Easter Monday), 1 May (Labour Day), 4 May (Ascension Day), 1 July (Independence Day), 15 August (Assumption), 18 September (Victory of UPRONA Party), 1 November (All Saints' Day), 25 December (Christmas).

1990: 1 January (New Year's Day), 16 April (Easter Monday), 1 May (Labour Day), 24 May (Ascension Day), 1 July (Independence Day), 15 August (Assumption), 18 September (Victory of UPRONA Party), 1 November (All Saints' Day), 25 December (Christmas).

Weights and Measures

The metric system is in force.

Statistical Survey

Area and Population

AREA, POPULATION AND DENSITY

Area (sq km)	27,834*
Population (census of 15–16 August 1979)	4,028,420
Population (official estimates at mid-year)	
1985	4,717,703
1986	4,857,347
1987	5,001,000
Density (per sq km) at mid-1987	179.7

* 10,747 sq miles.

PRINCIPAL TOWNS

Bujumbura (capital), population 172,201 (census of August 1979); Gitega 15,943 (1978).

Source: Banque de la République du Burundi.

BIRTHS AND DEATHS (UN estimates, annual averages)

	1970–75	1975–80	1980–85
Birth rate (per 1,000)	46.2	48.2	47.2
Death rate (per 1,000)	23.7	20.5	19.0

Source: UN, *World Population Prospects: Estimates and Projections as Assessed in 1984.*

BURUNDI

ECONOMICALLY ACTIVE POPULATION
(1983 estimates)

Traditional agriculture	2,319,595
Fishing	5,481
Traditional trades	22,820
Private sector (modern)	37,884
Public sector	95,061
Total labour force	**2,480,841**

1979 census: Total labour force 2,413,169 (males 1,133,477; females 1,279,692).

Sources: *Revue des statistiques du travail* and Centre de recherche et de formation en population.

1986 estimate: Total labour force 2,653,951 (males 1,254,041; females 1,399,910). Source: ILO, *Year Book of Labour Statistics.*

Agriculture

PRINCIPAL CROPS ('000 metric tons)

	1984	1985	1986
Wheat	8	7†	14†
Maize	139	150*	160*
Finger millet*	30	44	50
Sorghum*	160	210	220
Rice	18	12†	20†
Potatoes	37	38*	40*
Sweet potatoes	517	520*	550*
Cassava (Manioc)	511	520*	520*
Yams	6	7*	7*
Taro (Coco yam)	103	105*	105*
Dry beans	241	290*	300*
Dry peas	20	32*	32*
Palm kernels*	2.3	2.3	2.4
Groundnuts (in shell)*	80	80	80
Cottonseed	4†	4	4*
Cotton (lint)	2	2†	2*
Sugar cane	6	6*	7*
Coffee (green)	26	33†	30†
Tea (made)	3	3†	3*
Tobacco (leaves)	4	4*	4*
Bananas and plantains	1,250	1,250*	1,260*

* FAO estimates.   † Unofficial estimates.

Source: FAO, *Production Yearbook.*

1987 (FAO estimates, '000 metric tons): Millet 50, Sorghum 220, Dry beans 300, Dry peas 32.

LIVESTOCK ('000 head, year ending September)

	1984	1985	1986*
Cattle	409	415	415
Sheep	361	369	370
Goats	779	798	820
Pigs	76	78*	80

* FAO estimates.

Poultry (FAO estimates, million): 3 in 1984; 4 in 1985; 4 in 1986.

Source: FAO, *Production Yearbook.*

LIVESTOCK PRODUCTS (FAO estimates, '000 metric tons)

	1984	1985	1986
Beef and veal	6	7	7
Mutton and lamb	1	1	1
Goats' meat	2	2	2
Pig meat	5	5	5
Cows' milk	24	24	25
Goats' milk	6	7	7
Hen eggs	2.7	2.8	2.9

Source: FAO, *Production Yearbook.*

Forestry

ROUNDWOOD REMOVALS ('000 cubic metres)

	1984	1985	1986
Sawlogs, veneer logs and logs for sleepers	8	6	6
Other industrial wood*	37	38	39
Fuel wood*	3,492	3,590	3,697
Total	**3,537**	**3,634**	**3,742**

* FAO estimates.

Source: FAO, *Yearbook of Forest Products.*

Fishing

('000 metric tons, live weight)

	1984*	1985*	1986
Dagaas	7.4	7.0	5.5
Freshwater perches	4.3	4.0	1.2
Others	—	—	0.1
Total catch	**11.7**	**11.0**	**6.8**

* FAO estimates.

Source: FAO, *Yearbook of Fishery Statistics.*

Industry

SELECTED PRODUCTS

	1985	1986	1987
Beer ('000 hectolitres)	810	890	939
Soft drinks ('000 hectolitres)	127	135	130
Cigarettes (million)	293	288	271
Blankets ('000)	364	402	342
Footwear ('000 pairs)	373	368	398

Source: Banque de la République du Burundi.

Finance

CURRENCY AND EXCHANGE RATES

Monetary Units
  100 centimes = 1 Burundi franc.

Denominations
  Coins: 1, 5 and 10 francs.
  Notes: 10, 20, 50, 100, 500, 1,000 and 5,000 francs.

Sterling and Dollar Equivalents (30 September 1988)
  £1 sterling = 263.40 francs;
  US $1 = 155.77 francs;
  1,000 Burundi francs = £3.796 = $6.420.

Average Exchange Rate (Burundi francs per US dollar)
  1985   120.69
  1986   114.17
  1987   123.56

Note: Between May 1976 and November 1983 the rate was fixed at US $1 = 90.0 Burundi francs. Since November 1983 the Burundi franc has been linked to the IMF's special drawing right (SDR), with the mid-point exchange rate initially fixed at SDR 1 = 122.7 francs. This remained in force until July 1986, since when the rate has been frequently adjusted. A rate of SDR 1 = 201.0 francs was established in August 1988.

BURUNDI

Statistical Survey

BUDGET (million Burundi francs)

Revenue	1985	1986	1987
Income tax	4,020.9	4,420.0	4,159.8
Property tax	99.3	104.2	107.0
Customs duties	6,551.2	8,087.9	3,976.1
Excise duties	2,477.9	2,395.8	2,480.1
Other indirect taxes	4,264.8	4,800.5	5,098.7
Administrative receipts	839.5	2,173.5	2,007.4
Total revenue	**18,253.6**	**21,981.9**	**17,829.1**

Expenditure	1985	1986	1987
Goods and services	10,854.6	12,062.0	11,684.3
Subsidies and transfers	3,800.8	4,309.3	4,890.1
Net loans	508.8	50.9	161.5
Other	5,141.1	4,572.2	3,571.8
Total expenditure	**20,305.3**	**20,994.4**	**20,307.7**

1988 (estimates, million Burundi francs): Expenditure 25,239.8; Revenue 21,860.5.

Sources: Ministry of Finance; Banque de la République du Burundi.

CENTRAL BANK RESERVES (US $ million at 31 December)

	1985	1986	1987
Gold	5.62	6.93	8.53
IMF special drawing rights	0.12	0.65	0.06
Reserve position in IMF	10.06	11.20	12.99
Foreign exchange	19.29	57.22	47.68
Total	**35.09**	**76.00**	**69.26**

Source: Banque de la République du Burundi.

MONEY SUPPLY (million Burundi francs at 31 December)

	1985	1986	1987
Currency outside banks	7,254	8,008	8,734
Official entities' deposits at Central Bank	1,966	2,210	1,416
Demand deposits at commercial banks	7,914	8,478	8,303
Demand deposits at other monetary institutions	1,049	962	999
Total money	**18,182**	**19,658**	**19,453**

Source: Banque de la République du Burundi.

COST OF LIVING (Consumer Price Index for Bujumbura; base: January 1980 = 100)

	1985	1986	1987
Food	153.7	142.7	141.6
Clothing	125.3	140.8	166.1
Rent, fuel and light	149.0	144.0	149.3
All items (incl. others)	**153.9**	**156.8**	**167.9**

Source: Banque de la République du Burundi.

NATIONAL ACCOUNTS (million Burundi francs at current prices)
Expenditure on the Gross Domestic Product

	1985	1986	1987
Government final consumption expenditure	22,793	24,252	26,306
Private final consumption expenditure	109,478	104,340	105,451
Increase in stocks	73	3,247	649
Gross fixed capital formation	20,113	18,860	23,740
Total domestic expenditure	**152,457**	**150,699**	**156,146**
Exports of goods and services	13,937	15,625	13,088
Less Imports of goods and services	25,047	25,482	28,754
GDP in purchasers' values	**141,347**	**140,842**	**140,480**
GDP at constant 1980 prices	**108,762**	**112,916**	**117,539**

Source: Banque de la République du Burundi.

Gross Domestic Product by Economic Activity*

	1985	1986	1987
Agriculture, hunting, forestry and fishing	77,656	72,057	71,490
Mining and quarrying	639	906	989
Electricity, gas and water			
Manufacturing	5,607	6,140	7,048
Construction	5,599	4,942	5,691
Trade, restaurants and hotels	10,750	11,072	11,039
Transport, storage and communications	2,994	3,540	3,878
Other commercial services	1,781	1,851	1,925
Government services	16,605	17,856	19,532
Non-profit services to households		500	
GDP at factor cost	**121,632**	**118,864**	**121,592**
Indirect taxes, *less* subsidies	15,152	17,725	14,030
GDP in purchasers' values	**136,784**	**136,589**	**135,622**

* Excluding GDP of the artisan branch (million francs): 4,562 in 1985; 4,253 in 1986; 4,858 in 1987.

Source: Banque de la République du Burundi.

External Trade

PRINCIPAL COMMODITIES (million Burundi francs)

Imports c.i.f.	1985	1986	1987
Intermediate goods	9,295.9	9,092.6	9,495.7
Capital goods	7,604.7	7,203.5	9,053.4
Consumer goods	5,853.7	6,898.4	6,916.2
Total	**22,754.3**	**23,194.5**	**25,465.3**

Sources: Département des Etudes et Statistiques; Banque de la République du Burundi.

Exports f.o.b.	1985	1986	1987
Coffee	11,511.0	17,057.4	7,174.6
Cotton	42.4	20.2	502.3
Hides and skins	124.5	150.6	181.8
Tea	617.6	514.6	614.3
Minerals	11.5	4.9	1.5
Other products	509.6	477.4	395.7
Total	**12,816.6**	**18,225.1**	**8,870.2**

BURUNDI

PRINCIPAL TRADING PARTNERS (million Burundi francs)

Imports	1985	1986	1987
Belgium-Luxembourg	3,550.7	4,441.4	4,823.0
France	2,806.0	2,281.0	2,112.6
Germany, Federal Republic	2,665.5	2,729.7	3,324.0
Italy	1,144.7	1,157.7	909.9
Japan	1,464.3	1,557.1	2,080.7
Kenya	606.5	647.1	658.6
Netherlands	338.7	989.5	1,382.4
Tanzania	253.0	215.6	115.9
United Kingdom	414.9	509.8	521.8
USA	1,329.5	583.7	468.2
Zaire	251.8	421.0	119.4
Others	7,928.7	7,660.9	8,948.8
Total	22,754.3	23,194.5	25,465.3

Sources: Département des Etudes et Statistiques; Banque de la République du Burundi.

Exports	1985	1986	1987
Belgium-Luxembourg	1,371.5	2,112.4	995.8
France	139.2	338.4	674.8
Germany, Federal Republic	7,270.3	10,535.8	3,037.6
Italy	227.1	454.5	245.6
Netherlands	662.0	1,387.6	688.9
United Kingdom	603.0	555.4	716.2
USA	814.4	1,313.2	719.9
Others	2,354.5	2,608.9	3,379.1
Total	13,442.0	19,306.2	10,457.9

Transport

ROAD TRAFFIC (motor vehicles in use)

	1985	1986	1987
Passenger cars	8,219	8,977	9,892
Vans	2,604	2,821	3,077
Lorries	1,453	1,607	2,324
All other vehicles	2,655	2,914	3,284
Total	14,931	16,319	17,577

Sources: Département des Impôts; Banque de la République du Burundi.

LAKE TRAFFIC (Bujumbura—'000 metric tons)

	1985	1986	1987
Goods:			
Arrivals	179.9	181.8	157.2
Departures	36.5	39.2	30.8

Source: Banque de la République du Burundi.

CIVIL AVIATION (Bujumbura Airport)

	1985	1986	1987
Passengers:			
Arrivals	20,202	22,032	23,711
Departures	20,379	22,374	24,947
Freight (metric tons):			
Arrivals	5,404	5,473	4,228
Departures	3,643	3,336	2,168

Sources: Ministry of Transport and Aviation; Banque de la République du Burundi.

Tourism

	1981	1982	1983
Tourist arrivals ('000)	37	38	38*

* Estimated figure.
Source: UN, *Statistical Yearbook*.

Communications Media

	1981	1982	1983
Radio receivers ('000 in use)	152	165	178

Source: UNESCO, *Statistical Yearbook*.
Telephones (1983): 6,000 in use.

Education

(1984)

	Teachers	Pupils
Pre-primary	25	1,446
Primary	6,192	337,329
Secondary:		
General	595	9,765
Teacher training	465	7,782
Vocational	507	4,514

Source: Ministère de l'Education Nationale, *Statistiques scolaires*.

Directory

The Constitution

Following the coup of September 1987, the Constitution of November 1981 was suspended. Its main provisions were as follows:

UPRONA (Union pour le progrès national) is the sole legal political party. It determines national political orientation and state policy, and supervises the action of the Government. The Head of State and the National Assembly, which holds legislative power and meets twice a year, are elected for a term of five years by direct universal adult suffrage. The sole candidate for Head of State is the President of UPRONA.

The Government

HEAD OF STATE

President: Maj. PIERRE BUYOYA (proclaimed 2 October 1987).

MILITARY COMMITTEE FOR NATIONAL SALVATION

The CMSN comprises 31 members.

Executive Committee:
Maj. PIERRE BUYOYA (Chairman)
Lt-Col EDMOND NDAKAZI
Lt-Col GERVAIS NDIKUMAGENGE
Lt-Col GEDEON FYIROKO
Lt-Col JEAN-CLAUDE NDIYO
Lt-Col JEAN-BAPTISTE MBONYINGINGO
Lt-Col ALOYS KADOYI
Maj. GERARD CISHAHAYO
Maj. SIMON RUSUKU
Maj. ETIENNE SINDIHEBURA

COUNCIL OF MINISTERS
(December 1988)

President and Minister of National Defence: Maj. PIERRE BUYOYA.
Prime Minister and Minister of Planning: ADRIEN SIBOMANA.
Minister of Justice: EVARISTE NIYONKURU.
Minister of Internal Affairs: ALOYS KADOYI.
Minister of External Relations and Co-operation: CYPRIEN MBONIMPA.
Minister of Finance: GÉRARD NIYIBIGIRA.
Minister of Rural Development and Handicrafts: GABRIEL TOYI.
Minister of Agriculture and Animal Husbandry: JUMAINE HUSSEIN.
Minister of Industry and Trade: BONAVENTURE KIDWINGIRA.
Minister of Transport, Posts and Telecommunications: Maj. SIMON RUSUKU.
Minister of Public Works and Urban Development: EVARISTE SIMBARAKIYE.
Minister of Energy and Mines: GILBERT MIDENDE.
Minister of Public Health: Dr NORBERT NGENDABANYIKWA.
Minister for Family and Women's Development Affairs: PIA NDAYIRAGIJE.
Minister for Social Affairs: JULIE NGIRIYE.
Minister of Labour and Professional Training: CHARLES KARIKURUBU.
Minister of Youth, Sport and Culture: ADOLPHE NAHAYO.
Minister of Information: FRÉDÉRIC NGENZEBUHORO.
Minister of the Public Service: DIDACE RUDARAGI.
Minister of Development, Tourism and the Environment: BASILE SINDAHARAYE.
Minister of Higher Education and Scientific Research: NICOLAS MAYUGI.
Minister of Primary and Secondary Education: GAMALIEL NDARUZANIYE.
Secretary of State in charge of Government Planning: SALVATOR SAHINGUVU.
Secretary of State in charge of International Co-operation: FRIDOLIN HATUNGIMANA.

MINISTRIES

Office of the President and Minister of National Defence: Bujumbura; tel. 6063; telex 5049.
Ministry of Agriculture and Animal Husbandry: Bujumbura; tel. 2087.
Ministry of Energy and Mines: Bujumbura.
Ministry of External Relations and Co-operation: Bujumbura; tel. 2150; telex 5065.
Ministry of Family and Women's Development Affairs: Bujumbura; tel. 5561.
Ministry of Finance: BP 1830, Bujumbura; tel. 23988; telex 5135.
Ministry of Industry and Trade: Bujumbura; tel. 5330.
Ministry of Information: BP 4080, Bujumbura; tel. 4666; telex 56.
Ministry of Internal Affairs: Bujumbura; tel. 4242.
Ministry of Justice: Bujumbura; tel. 2148.
Ministry of Labour and Professional Training: BP 2830, Bujumbura; tel. 25058.
Ministry of Public Health: Bujumbura; tel. 6020.
Ministry of the Public Service: Bujumbura; tel. 3514.
Ministry of Public Works and Urban Development: Bujumbura; tel. 6841; telex 5048.
Ministry of Rural Development and Handicrafts: Bujumbura; tel. 5267.
Ministry of Social Affairs: Bujumbura; tel. 5039.
Ministry of Transport, Posts and Telecommunications: Bujumbura; tel. 2923; telex 5103.
Ministry of Youth, Sport and Culture: Bujumbura; tel. 6822.

Legislature

ASSEMBLÉE NATIONALE

The 65-member National Assembly was dissolved following the coup of September 1987. The new Government envisaged the restoration of the National Assembly within two years.

Political Organization

Union pour le progrès national (UPRONA): BP 1810, Bujumbura; tel. 25028; telex 5057; f. 1958; following the 1961 elections, the many small parties which had been defeated subsequently merged with UPRONA, which became the sole legal political party in November 1966; organized into local cttees, the higher cttees being those of the zone or quarter, commune, province and finally the cen. cttee, with 70 mems, and a political bureau of eight mems at mid-1987; the supreme organ is the party congress; c. 1m. mems in 1980; three affiliated movements: the Union de la Jeunesse révolutionnaire burundaise (UJRB), the Union des Femmes burundaises (UFB) and the Union des Travailleurs du Burundi (UTB).

Diplomatic Representation

EMBASSIES IN BURUNDI

Belgium: 9 ave de l'Industrie, BP 1920, Bujumbura; tel. 3676; telex 5033; Ambassador: DENIS BANNEEL.
China, People's Republic: BP 2550, Bujumbura; tel. 24252; Ambassador: WANG JIANBANG.
Cuba: 14 ave Ngozi, BP 2288, Bujumbura; tel. 26476; telex 5140; Ambassador: DIOSDADO FERNÁNDEZ GONZÁLEZ.
Egypt: 31 ave de la Liberté, BP 1520, Bujumbura; tel. 3161; telex 5040; Ambassador: MUHAMMAD MOUSA.
France: 60 ave de l'UPRONA, BP 1740, Bujumbura; tel. 26464; telex 5044; Ambassador: ROBERT RIGOUZZO.
Germany, Federal Republic: 22 rue 18 septembre, BP 480, Bujumbura; tel. 26412; telex 5068; Ambassador: KARL FLITTNER.
Holy See: 46 chaussée Prince Louis-Rwagasore, BP 1068, Bujumbura; tel. 2326; Apostolic Pro-Nuncio: Mgr PIETRO SAMBI.
Korea, Democratic People's Republic: BP 1620, Bujumbura; tel. 22881; Ambassador: SIN BYEUNG TCHEUL.
Libya: ave de l'UPRONA, BP 4619, Bujumbura; telex 5088.

BURUNDI

Romania: rue Pierre Ngendandumwe, BP 2770, Bujumbura; tel. 24135; Chargé d'affaires a.i.: ALEXANDRA ANDREI.
Rwanda: 24 avenue du Zaïre, BP 400, Bujumbura; tel. 3140; telex 5032; Ambassador: EMMANUEL RUZINDANA.
Tanzania: BP 1653, Bujumbura; Ambassador: NICHOLAS J. MARO.
USSR: 9 ave de l'UPRONA, BP 1034, Bujumbura; tel. 26098, 22984; Ambassador: VSEVOLOD SOFINSKY.
USA: chaussée Prince Rwagasore, BP 1720, Bujumbura; tel. 3454; Ambassador: JAMES D. PHILLIPS.
Zaire: 5 ave Olsen, BP 872, Bujumbura; tel. 3492; Ambassador: IKOLO MBOLOKO.

Judicial System

The Constitution prescribes a judicial system wherein the judges are subject to the decisions of UPRONA made in the light of the revolutionary concept of the law. No appeal is provided for in the case of decisions of the Supreme Court. A programme of legal reform was announced in December 1986, under which provincial courts were to be replaced by a dual system of courts of civil and criminal jurisdiction. A network of mediation and conciliation courts was to be established to arbitrate in minor disputes arising among the rural population.

Supreme Court: Bujumbura; tel. 5442. Four chambers: ordinary, cassation, constitutional and administrative.
Courts of Appeal: Bujumbura, Gitega and Ngozi.
Tribunals of First Instance: There are 15 provincial tribunals and 122 smaller resident tribunals in other areas.
Tribunal of Trade: Bujumbura.
Tribunals of Labour: Bujumbura and Gitega.
Administrative Courts: Bujumbura and Gitega.

Religion

More than 60% of the population are Christians, mostly Roman Catholics. Anglicans number about 60,000. There are about 200,000 Protestants, of whom some 160,000 are Pentecostalists. Fewer than 40% of the population are followers of traditional belief, which is mainly in a God 'Imana'. About 1% of the population are Muslims. The Bahá'í Faith is also active in Burundi.

CHRISTIANITY

Alliance des Eglises protestantes du Burundi: BP 17, Bujumbura; tel. 24216; f. 1970; five mem. churches; Pres. Bishop JEAN-ALFRED NDORICIMPA; Gen. Sec. Rev. NOÉ NZEYIMANA.

The Anglican Communion

Anglicans in Burundi form part of the Church of the Province of Burundi, Rwanda and Zaire, inaugurated in May 1980. The Church comprises nine dioceses, including three in Burundi, where it incorporates the Eglise épiscopale du Burundi. Since 1982 the Archbishop of the Province has been the Bishop of Butare (in Rwanda).

Bishop of Bujumbura: Rt Rev. SAMUEL SINDAMUKA, BP 1300, Bujumbura; tel. 22641.
Bishop of Buye: Rt Rev. SAMUEL NDAYISENGA, BP 58, Ngozi.
Bishop of Gitega: Rt Rev. JEAN NDUWAYO, BP 23, Gitega.

The Roman Catholic Church

Burundi comprises one archdiocese and six dioceses. At 31 December 1986 there were an estimated 2,773,691 adherents.

Bishops' Conference: Conférence des Evêques catholiques du Burundi, BP 1390, Bujumbura; tel. 23263; f. 1980; Pres. Rt Rev. EVARISTE NGOYAGOYE, Bishop of Bubanza.
Archbishop of Gitega: Most Rev. JOACHIM RUHUNA, Archevêché, BP 118, Gitega; tel. 2160.

Other Christian Churches

Union of Baptist Churches of Burundi: Rubura, DS 117, Bujumbura 1; Pres. PAUL BARUHENAMWO; Exec. Sec. OSIAS HABINGABWA.

Other denominations active in the country include the Evangelical Christian Brotherhood of Burundi, the Free Methodist Church of Burundi and the United Methodist Church of Burundi.

BAHÁ'Í FAITH

National Spiritual Assembly: BP 1578, Bujumbura.

The Press

All publications are strictly controlled by the Government.

NEWSPAPERS

Burundi chrétien: BP 232, Bujumbura; Roman Catholic weekly; French.
Le Renouveau du Burundi: BP 2870, Bujumbura; f. 1978; publ. by UPRONA; daily; French; circ. 20,000.
Ubumwe: BP 1400, Bujumbura; tel. 3929; f. 1971; weekly; Kirundi; circ. 20,000.

PERIODICALS

Bulletin économique et financier: BP 482, Bujumbura; bi-monthly.
Bulletin officiel du Burundi: Bujumbura; monthly.
Le Burundi en Images: BP 1400, Bujumbura; f. 1979; monthly.
Culture et Sociétés: BP 1400, Bujumbura; f. 1978; quarterly.

NEWS AGENCY

Agence burundaise de Presse (ABP): 6 ave de la Poste, BP 2870, Bujumbura; tel. 5417; telex 5056; publ. daily bulletin.

Publishers

Imprimerie du Parti: BP 1810, Bujumbura.
Les Presses Lavigerie: 5 blvd de l'UPRONA, BP 1640, Bujumbura.

Government Publishing House

Imprimerie nationale du Burundi (INABU): BP 991, Bujumbura; tel. 4046; telex 80.

Radio and Television

In 1985 there were an estimated 180,000 radio receivers, and in 1987 about 4,500 television receivers, in use. The installation of a colour television network was completed in 1985.

Voix de la Révolution/La Radiodiffusion et Télévision Nationale du Burundi (RTNB): BP 1900, Bujumbura; tel. 23742; telex 5119; f. 1960; govt-controlled; daily radio programmes in Kirundi, Swahili, French and English; Dir-Gen. ALEXIS NTAVYO; Dir 1st Programme CHRISTINE NTAHE; Dir 2nd Programme ANTOINE NTAMIKEVYO; Dir (Television) J. NZOBONIMPA.

Finance

(cap. = capital; res = reserves; dep. = deposits;
m. = million; amounts in Burundi francs)

BANKING

Central Bank

Banque de la République du Burundi (BRB): BP 705, Bujumbura; tel. 25142; telex 5071; f. 1964; cap. and res 2,222m. (Sept. 1987); Gov. ISAAC BUDABUDA; Vice-Gov. EVARISTE NIBASUMBA; Dir PASCAL NTAMASHIMIKIRO.

Commercial Banks

Banque Commerciale du Burundi (BANCOBU): chaussée Prince Louis-Rwagasore, BP 990, Bujumbura; tel. 22317; telex 5051; f. 1960; reorg. 1988, following merger with Banque Belgo-Africaine du Burundi; 51% state-owned; cap. and res 406m., dep. 4,624m. (Sept. 1987); Chair. JEAN BERCHMANS NSABIYUMVA; Man. Dir JACQUES VAN EETVELDE.
Banque de Crédit de Bujumbura (BCB): ave Patrice Emmery Lumumba, BP 300, Bujumbura; tel. 22091; telex 5063; f. 1964; cap. and res 515m., dep. 7,714m. (Sept. 1987); Chair. ASTÈRE NDORERE; Man. Dir RÉGINALD THIBAUT DE MAISIÈRES.
Caisse d'Epargne du Burundi (CADEBU): BP 615, Bujumbura; tel. 22348; telex 71; f. 1964; wholly state-owned; cap. 90m.; Chair. PASTEUR BUDEYI; Man. Dir BONIFACE BAGORIKUNDA.

Development Banks

Banque Nationale pour le Développement Economique du Burundi (BNDE): BP 1620, Bujumbura; tel. 22888; telex 5091; f. 1967; cap. 740m. (Sept. 1987); Chair. BONUS KAMWENUBUSA; Man. Dir FRANÇOIS BARWENDERE.

BURUNDI

Caisse Centrale de Mobilisation et de Financement (CAMOFI): 4 ave de l'UJRB, BP 8, Bujumbura; tel. 25642; telex 5082; f. 1977; finances public-sector development projects and businesses; cap. 100m. (Sept. 1987); Chair. Minister of Finance; Man. Dir LÉONARD NTIBAGIRIRWA.

Holding Arabe Libyen Burundais (HALB): BP 1892, Bujumbura; tel. 26635; telex 5090; f. 1975; cap. 1,036.1m. (Sept. 1987); Chair. JEAN BERCHMANS NSABIYUMVA.

Meridien Bank Burundi: Bujumbura; f. 1988; 25% owned by Meridien International Bank.

Société Burundaise de Financement (SBF): BP 270, 14-18 rue de l'Amitié, Bujumbura; tel. 22126; telex 5080; f. 1982; cap. 630m. (Sept. 1987); Chair. MATHIAS SINAMENYE.

INSURANCE

Société d'Assurances du Burundi (SOCABU): BP 2440, 14-18 rue de l'Amitié, Bujumbura; tel. 26803; telex 5113; f. 1977; partly state-owned; cap. 120m.; Man. ATHANASE GAHUNGU.

Union Commerciale d'Assurances et de Réassurance (UCAR): BP 3012, Bujumbura; tel. 23638; telex 5162; f. 1986; cap. 60m. (Sept. 1987); Chair. Lt-Col EDOUARD NZAMBIMANA; Man. Dir HENRY TARMO.

Trade and Industry

STATE TRADE ORGANIZATION

Office National du Commerce (ONC): Bujumbura; f. 1973; supervises international commercial operations between the govt of Burundi and other states or private organizations; also ensures the import of essential materials; brs in each province.

DEVELOPMENT ORGANIZATIONS

Comité de Gérance de la Reserve Cotonnière (COGERCO): Bujumbura; develops the cotton industry.

Fonds de Promotion Economique: PB 270, Bujumbura; tel. 5562; telex 80; f. 1981 to finance and promote industrial, agricultural and commercial activities; Man. Dir BONAVENTURE KIDWINGIRA.

Institut des Sciences Agronomiques du Burundi (ISABU): BP 795, Bujumbura; tel. 3384; f. 1962 for the scientific development of agriculture and livestock.

Office de la Tourbe du Burundi (ONATOUR): BP 2360, Bujumbura; tel. 6480; telex 48; f. 1977 to promote the exploitation of peat bogs.

Office des Cultures Industrielles du Burundi (OCIBU): BP 450, Bujumbura; tel. 2631; supervises coffee plantations and coffee exports.

Office du Thé du Burundi (OTB): Bujumbura; telex 5069; f. 1979; develops the tea industry.

Office National du Bois (ONB): BP 1492, Bujumbura; tel. 4416; f. 1980; exploits local timber resources and imports foreign timber; Dir LAZARE RUNESA.

Office National du Logement (ONL): BP 2480, Bujumbura; tel. 6074; telex 48; f. 1974; deals with housing construction.

Société d'Economie Mixte pour l'Exploitation du Quinquina au Burundi (SOKINABU): BP 1783, Bujumbura; tel. 23469; telex 81; f. 1975 to develop and exploit cinchona trees, the source of quinine; Man. RAPHËL REMEZO.

Société de Stockage et de Commercialisation des Produits Vivriers (SOBECOV): Bujumbura; f. 1977 to stock and sell agricultural products in Burundi.

Société Mixte, Minière et Industrielle Roumano-Burundaise (SOMIBUROM): Bujumbura; f. 1977; exploitation and marketing of mineral and industrial products.

Société Sucrière du Moso (SOSUMO): BP 835, Bujumbura; tel. 6576; telex 35; f. 1982; develops and manages sugar cane plantations.

CHAMBER OF COMMERCE

Chambre de Commerce et de l'Industrie du Burundi: BP 313, Bujumbura; tel. 2280; f. 1923; Pres. M. R. LECLERE; Hon. Sec. M. T. POJER; 130 mems.

TRADE UNION

Union des Travailleurs du Burundi (UTB): BP 1340, Bujumbura; tel. 3884; telex 57; f. 1967 by merger of all previous unions; closely allied with UPRONA; sole authorized trade union, with 18 affiliated nat. professional feds; Sec.-Gen. MARIUS RURAHENYE.

Transport

RAILWAYS

There are no railways in Burundi, but in 1987 plans were finalized for the construction of a line passing through Uganda, Rwanda and Burundi, to connect with the Kigoma-Dar es Salaam line in Tanzania, which would improve Burundi's isolated trade position.

ROADS

The road network is very dense and in 1981 there was a total of 5,144 km of roads, of which 1,710 km were national highways and 1,274 km secondary roads. In 1985 a contract was awarded to construct a 133-km road linking Rugombo and Kayanza, a town on the Rwandan border. In 1986 finance was obtained from international sources for the completion of the Makamba-Butembera road, providing improved access to agricultural areas bordering Tanzania.

INLAND WATERWAYS

Bujumbura is the principal port for both passenger and freight traffic on Lake Tanganyika, and the greater part of Burundi's external trade is dependent on the shipping services between Bujumbura and Tanzania, Zambia and Zaire.

CIVIL AVIATION

There is an international airport at Bujumbura, equipped to take large jet-engined aircraft.

Air Burundi: BP 2460, 40 ave du Commerce, Bujumbura; telex 80; f. 1971 as Société des Transports Aériens du Burundi, adopted present name in 1975; operates services to Kigali (Rwanda), Kalémié, Bukavu and Goma (Zaire), and internally from Bujumbura to Kirundo; Man. Dir ISAAC GAFURERO; fleet of 1 Caravelle, 2 Twin Otter, 2 Piper Super Cub.

Tourism

Tourism is relatively undeveloped. Tourist arrivals totalled an estimated 38,000 in 1983.

Office National du Tourisme: BP 902, Bujumbura; tel. 22202; telex 5030; f. 1972; Dir ANDRÉ NDAYIRAGIJE.

CAMEROON

Introductory Survey

Location, Climate, Language, Religion, Flag, Capital

The Republic of Cameroon lies on the west coast of Africa, with Nigeria to the west, Chad and the Central African Republic to the east, and the Congo, Equatorial Guinea and Gabon to the south. The climate is hot and humid in the south and west, with average temperatures of 26°C (80°F). The north is drier, with more extreme temperatures. The official languages are French and English, and many local languages are also spoken. Approximately 39% of Cameroonians follow traditional religious beliefs. About 40% are Christians, and about 21%, mostly in the north, are Muslims. The national flag (proportions 3 by 2) has three equal vertical stripes, of green, red and yellow, with a five-pointed gold star in the centre of the red stripe. The capital is Yaoundé.

Recent History

In 1884 a German protectorate was established in Cameroon (Kamerun). In 1916, during the First World War, the German administration was overthrown by invading British and French forces. Under an agreement made between the occupying powers in 1919, Cameroon was divided into two zones: a French-ruled area, in the east and south, and a smaller British-administered area in the west. In 1922 both zones became subject to mandates of the League of Nations, with France and the United Kingdom as the administering powers. In 1946 the zones were transformed into UN Trust Territories, with British and French rule continuing in their respective areas.

French Cameroons became an autonomous state, within the French Community, in 1957. Under the leadership of Ahmadou Ahidjo, a northerner who became Prime Minister in 1958, the territory became independent, as the Republic of Cameroon, on 1 January 1960. The first election for the country's National Assembly, held in April 1960, was won by Ahidjo's party, the Union camerounaise. In May the new Assembly elected Ahidjo to be the country's first President.

British Cameroons, comprising a northern and a southern region, was attached to neighbouring Nigeria, for administrative purposes, prior to Nigeria's independence in October 1960. Plebiscites were held, under UN auspices, in the two regions of British Cameroons in February 1961. The northern area voted to merge with Nigeria (becoming the province of Sardauna), while the south voted for union with the Republic of Cameroon, which took place on 1 October 1961.

The enlarged country was named the Federal Republic of Cameroon, with French and English as joint official languages. It comprised two states: the former French zone became East Cameroon, while the ex-British portion became West Cameroon. John Foncha, Prime Minister of West Cameroon and leader of the Kamerun National Democratic Party, became Vice-President of the Federal Republic. Under the continuing leadership of Ahidjo, who was re-elected President in May 1965, the two states became increasingly integrated, despite Cameroon's ethnic and cultural diversity. In September 1966 a one-party regime was established when the two governing parties and several opposition groups combined to form a single party, the Union nationale camerounaise (UNC). The party expanded to embrace almost all the country's political, cultural, professional and social organizations. The only significant opposition party, the extreme left-wing Union des populations camerounaises (UPC), was finally crushed in 1971, although the leaders continued activities in exile in Paris. Meanwhile, President Ahidjo was re-elected in March 1970, when Solomon Muna (who had replaced Foncha as Prime Minister of West Cameroon in 1968) became Vice-President.

In June 1972, after approval by referendum of a new constitution, the federal system was ended and the country became the United Republic of Cameroon. The office of Vice-President was abolished. A fully centralized political and administrative system was quickly introduced, and in May 1973 a new National Assembly was elected for a five-year term. After the re-election of Ahidjo as President in April 1975, the Constitution was revised, and a Prime Minister, Paul Biya (a bilingual Christian southerner), was appointed in June. Despite opposition from anglophone intellectuals who desired a return to the federal system of government, Ahidjo was unanimously re-elected for a fifth five-year term of office in April 1980.

President Ahidjo announced his resignation in November 1982 and named Paul Biya, the Prime Minister, as his successor. No official reasons for the resignation were given. Bello Bouba Maigari, a northerner, was appointed Prime Minister. Ahidjo retained the presidency of the UNC and his political influence continued. In cabinet reshuffles in April and June 1983, Biya introduced more technocrats into the Government and gradually removed supporters of the former President. On 22 August 1983 Biya announced the discovery of a plot to overthrow his Government, and simultaneously dismissed the Prime Minister and the Minister of the Armed Forces, both northern Muslims. On 27 August former President Ahidjo resigned as President of the UNC and strongly criticized the regime of President Biya. In September Biya was elected President of the ruling party, and in January 1984 he was re-elected as President of the Republic, reportedly gaining 99.98% of the votes cast. In a subsequent cabinet reshuffle, the post of Prime Minister was abolished, and it was announced that the country's name was to revert from the United Republic of Cameroon to the Republic of Cameroon.

In February 1984 Ahidjo (by then in exile in France) and two of his close military advisers were tried for their alleged complicity in the coup plot of August 1983. All three men received death sentences which were, however, commuted to life imprisonment two weeks later. On 6 April 1984 rebel elements in the presidential guard, led by Col Saleh Ibrahim, a northerner, attempted to seize power and overthrow the Biya government. After three days of heavy fighting, in which hundreds were reported to have been killed, the rebellion was crushed by forces loyal to the President. Trials of those implicated in the coup were held in May and November 1984, with a total of 51 defendants receiving death sentences. It was reported, following the May trials, that 46 executions had been carried out within hours of the announcement of the verdict. Following extensive changes within the military hierarchy, the UNC central committee and the leadership of state-controlled companies, in which supporters of the former President were dismissed, Biya reshuffled his government in July and introduced more stringent press censorship.

At the party congress in March 1985, the UNC was renamed the Rassemblement démocratique du peuple camerounais (RDPC). In August 10 ministers were replaced in a cabinet reshuffle, which also brought the Ministry of Defence, the Ministry in charge of Missions and the Ministry of Computer Services and Public Contracts into the Presidency. In January 1986 allegations of repression were made against the Biya regime by members of the exiled UPC movement, who claimed (at a press conference held in Paris) that between 200 and 300 people, mainly anglophones or members of clandestine opposition movements, had been arrested in the preceding months, and that some of the detainees were being subjected to torture. The Government subsequently released a number of detainees.

Comprehensive changes in the internal structure of the RDPC occurred as a result of elections held between January and March 1986, with more than half of the party's 49 section presidents being replaced. Many of the posts were contested by more than one candidate. In November 1986, following a reorganization of the President's office, Biya again carried out a reshuffle of the Cabinet, appointing a total of four new ministers.

In January 1987 the Minister of Foreign Affairs, William Eteki Mboumoua, was abruptly dismissed from his post after having signed an agreement to restore diplomatic relations with Hungary, supposedly without the President's knowledge. Several journalists, including the two principal officials of the government-owned daily newspaper, were detained during early 1987 for the alleged publication of secret or politically sensitive material. The composition of the staff at the state-owned publishing concerns subsequently underwent extensive changes. In July the National Assembly approved a new electoral code providing for multiple candidacy in public elections, and in October voters in more than 40% of communes had a choice of more than one candidate in elections for seats on the 196 municipal councils. All candidates were approved by the RDPC.

Popular opposition to the austerity measures that the Government introduced in June 1987 (see Economic Affairs) became evident in December, when about 300 students were arrested, following a riot at the University of Yaoundé in protest at delays in the payment of grants. Unconfirmed sources also reported that a coup attempt, led by the Commander-in-Chief of the Air Force, Gen. Nganso, had taken place in the same month.

Ostensibly for reasons of economy, the presidential election, originally scheduled for January 1989, was brought forward to coincide with elections to the National Assembly, in April 1988. (Constitutional amendments, enabling the Head of State to call a presidential election before the end of his term of office, as well as increasing the number of seats in the National Assembly from 150 to 180, had been approved by the legislature in March.) President Biya was re-elected unopposed, securing 98.75% of the votes cast. Reflecting the fact that the electorate had, for the first time in a legislative election, been presented with a choice of RDPC-approved candidates, 153 of those elected to the National Assembly were new members. In May Biya announced a cabinet reshuffle and a streamlining of administrative structures. Several ministries were merged or abolished, and the posts of Secretary-General of the Government and Director of the Presidential Cabinet were replaced by a single Secretary-General at the Presidency. A campaign against corruption led to the arrest of more than 100 ministerial officials and executives of the country's state-owned industries, in connection with the misappropriation of public funds.

In July 1973 President Ahidjo announced his country's impending withdrawal from the Organisation commune africaine, malgache et mauricienne (OCAM), a grouping of mainly French-speaking African states, then based in Yaoundé. Cameroon also negotiated a revision of its co-operation agreements with France in 1974. The independent foreign policy that was pursued under President Ahidjo has been continued by his successor. In August 1986 Cameroon was forced to appeal for international emergency aid when an explosion of underwater volcanic gases at Lake Nyos, in the north-west of the country, led to an estimated 1,700 deaths and caused widespread suffering. The disaster coincided with a much-publicized visit to Cameroon by Shimon Peres, the Prime Minister of Israel, during which the two countries renewed diplomatic links, following a 13-year suspension of relations as a result of the Arab-Israeli war in 1973. Relations with France have generally remained close, although Cameroon has sought to resist overdependence: France currently accounts for more than one-third of the country's foreign trade transactions. The close relationship between the two countries was confirmed in 1988, when President Biya made a state visit to France in order to discuss economic co-operation. In recent years, however, Cameroon has become increasingly anxious to attract investment from other countries, notably the Federal Republic of Germany, whose Chancellor, Dr Helmut Kohl, visited the country in 1987. Relations with Nigeria, which had come under some strain as a result of a series of border disputes, showed signs of improvement following a state visit by President Babangida of that country, when it was announced that joint border controls were to be established.

Government

Under the amended 1972 Constitution, executive power is vested in the President, as Head of State, while legislative power is held by the unicameral National Assembly. Both the President and the Assembly are elected for five years by universal adult suffrage. In 1988 the number of deputies to the National Assembly was increased, from 150 to 180, to take account of the increase in population. The Cabinet is appointed by the President. In May 1988 the Secretariat-General of the Government and Cabinet of the President were merged to form a single Secretariat-General at the Presidency. Local administration is based on 10 provinces, each with a Governor who is appointed by the President.

Defence

In June 1988 Cameroon had an army of 6,600 and there were 4,000 men in paramilitary forces. The navy numbered 700 and the air force had 300 men. France has a bilateral defence agreement with Cameroon. The defence budget for 1988/89 was 45,500m. francs CFA.

Economic Affairs

In recent years, owing to the rapid development of its petroleum industry and the steady performance of its agricultural sector, Cameroon has enjoyed one of the highest levels of income per head in tropical Africa. In 1987, according to estimates by the World Bank, Cameroon's gross national product (GNP), measured at average 1985–87 prices, was US $10,441m., equivalent to $960 per head. Between 1980 and 1987, it was estimated, GNP per head increased, in real terms, at an average rate of 4.2% per year. The average annual increase in overall gross domestic product (GDP), measured in constant prices, was 5.1% in 1965–80, rising to 8.2% (one of the world's highest national growth rates) in 1980–86.

Agriculture is well-diversified, and the main commercial products are cocoa (of which Cameroon is one of the world's largest producers), coffee, bananas, cotton, palm oil, natural rubber and cane sugar. Agricultural production expanded at an average rate of 4.2% annually in 1965–80, and during that period accounted for between 70% and 75% of total export trade. As the petroleum industry increased in importance, the expansion of agricultural output slowed, to an average of 2.0% in 1980–86. In 1986 the agricultural sector, including forestry and fishing, contributed 22% of GDP and employed an estimated 65% of the working population.

Output in virtually all agricultural sectors declined in 1981/82 and 1982/83, owing to persistent drought. Therefore, the attainment of self-sufficiency in agriculture was given priority under the 1986–91 Plan. Production of cereals, which was particularly affected by the drought, recovered by the mid-1980s, with maize output totalling more than 1m. tons in 1983/84, and paddy rice 103,000 tons in 1986/87, compared with just 15,000 tons in 1979/80. Owing to favourable climatic conditions, production of cocoa beans reached a record level of 128,876 metric tons in 1987/88, compared with 108,900 tons in 1983/84. In February 1988 the World Bank approved a loan of US $103m. towards a cocoa rehabilitation project. Cameroon's production of coffee totalled only 64,000 tons in 1983/84, but recovered to 114,519 tons in 1984/85, following an extensive replanting campaign. The late delivery of fertilizers was blamed for a sharp reduction in output, to 86,000 tons, in 1987/88. Output of cotton increased during the early 1980s, owing to expansion of the area under cultivation, to 100,000 ha: production of seed (unginned) cotton totalled 102,000 tons in 1983 but declined to 67,000 tons in 1984, recovering to 123,000 tons in 1986. Production of sawlogs fell to 1,298,000 cu m in 1983, as a result of the drought, but recovered to 2,093,000 cu m in 1985. Further development of Cameroon's forests, which are estimated to cover 40% of the total land area, depends on the creation of an adequate transport infrastructure.

The diversity of agricultural products has given rise to agro-industries, including a maize complex, sugar-processing plants, a rubber-processing factory, tobacco factories, and cotton-spinning and -weaving mills. Hydroelectricity provides around 95% of the country's power generation: the capacity of the Song-Loulou plant is to be extended from 288 MW to 384 MW by 1990, and there are also plants at Edéa and Lagdo. Further installations are planned for Nachtigal and Warak.

Petroleum, discovered off Rio del Rey in 1973, is the only major mineral resource currently exploited in Cameroon. Output of crude petroleum increased steadily, from 800,000 metric tons in 1978 (when the country's first oil exports were shipped) to an estimated 9.2m. tons in 1985. However, in response to the depletion of reserves and the decline in international oil prices, annual output had fallen to 8.6m. tons by 1987. Further oilfields, at Moudi and Lokelé, are now in production, but exploration ceased in February 1986. Cameroon's known reserves of petroleum are expected to be exhausted by the mid-1990s. The capacity of the petroleum refinery, opened at Limbe (formerly Victoria) in 1980, has been expanded to 2m. tons per year. Since 1982 the state oil corporation, Société Nationale des Hydrocarbures, has held a 20% interest in all the petroleum-producing companies operating in Cameroon. The decrease in international oil prices reduced export earnings from petroleum from 478,864m. francs CFA in 1984 to

CAMEROON

192,709m. francs CFA in 1986. The exploitation of bauxite deposits at Minim-Martap and Ngaoundal has been delayed, pending a recovery in the world market for this commodity. Deposits of iron ore, estimated at 120m. tons, near Kribi, as well as some 190,000 tons of rutile at Akonolinga, are likely to be developed in the near future.

Owing to an expansion in export earnings from petroleum, the current deficit on the balance of payments declined to US $179.7m. in 1984. However, since 1985, falling world prices for Cameroon's major export commodities, together with a depreciation in the value of the US dollar, have resulted in a further increase in the deficit, which reached $549.0m. in 1986.

External debt was 1,035,000m. francs CFA in 1987. The debt-service ratio, formerly one of the lowest among black African countries, was equivalent to 30% of declared export earnings in that year (compared with about 14% in 1985), as a result of declining export revenue. The sixth Five-Year Plan (1986–91) involved total projected expenditure of 7,830,000m. francs CFA, of which 26% was to be devoted to agricultural development, and aimed to achieve average GDP growth of 6.7% annually over the five-year period. Real GDP growth in 1986/87 was estimated at 4.3%. GDP was estimated to have fallen by 9% in 1987/88, and a further decline of between 5% and 6%, was expected in 1988/89. Public expenditure in 1986/87 totalled an estimated 800,000m. francs CFA, 13% less, in nominal terms, than in 1985/86, while the 1987/88 budget envisaged a further reduction in nominal expenditure, which was projected at 648,400m. francs CFA. Owing to the decline in petroleum revenues, in 1986 the Government embarked upon an austerity programme. In May plans were announced for the progressive reduction of long-term public investment in industry, envisaging the 'privatization' of some 62 wholly or partly state-owned concerns. Public expenditure was to be reduced further by means of the introduction of strict austerity measures, announced in June 1987: these were to include the regulation of salaries of public-sector employees and the closure of 'inefficient' state enterprises and overseas diplomatic missions. In the proposals for the 1988/89 budget, expenditure was to be further reduced, to 600,000m. francs CFA, while additional revenue was to be generated by increases in both direct and indirect taxation.

In spite of its deteriorating economic situation, Cameroon has, in recent years, resisted pressure from its major trading partners, such as France and the Federal Republic of Germany, to accept intervention by the IMF and the World Bank. In 1988, however, negotiations between the Government and these two bodies culminated in the announcement of a medium-term stabilization programme for Cameroon, supported by an IMF credit of US $150m. The programme envisaged further reductions in public expenditure, especially in the fields of public investment and the country's unprofitable state-owned enterprises.

Social Welfare

The Government and Christian missions maintain hospitals and medical centres. In 1979 Cameroon had 22,800 hospital beds in 126 hospitals and health centres and 900 dispensaries. There were 603 physicians working in the country (one per 13,681 inhabitants). The 1988/89 budget allocated 24,000m. francs CFA to health expenditure. A campaign aiming at 'Health for all by the year 2000' is being carried out, with the emphasis on the development of preventive medicine. The 1986–91 Plan envisaged the development of a system of social security suitable to the country's needs.

Education

Since independence, Cameroon has achieved one of the highest rates of school attendance in Africa, but provision of educational facilities varies according to region. Education is provided by the Government, missionary societies and private concerns. Education in state schools is available free of charge, and the Government provides financial assistance for other schools. Bilingual teaching was introduced for the first time in primary schools in 1972, and school curricula were standardized in 1977.

Primary education begins at six years of age. It lasts for six years in Eastern Cameroon (where it is officially compulsory), and for seven years in Western Cameroon. Secondary education, beginning at the age of 12 or 13, lasts for a further seven years. In 1984 the total enrolment at primary and secondary schools was equivalent to 67% of the school-age population (75% of boys; 59% of girls): attendance at schools in the northern region, which had been as low as 32% in 1981, was estimated at 55% in 1986. In 1976 the average rate of adult illiteracy was 59.5% (males 45.4%; females 75.5%): by 1985, according to estimates by UNESCO, the rate had declined to 43.8% (males 31.6%; females 55.3%). The State University at Yaoundé, founded in 1962, has been decentralized, and consists of five regional campuses, each being devoted to a different field of study. Budgets in recent years have given high priority to education, with an allocation of 60,000m. francs CFA in 1988/89.

Public Holidays

1989: 2 January (for New Year), 11 February (Youth Day), 24 March (Good Friday), 27 March (Easter Monday), 1 May (Labour Day), 4 May (Ascension Day), 7 May* (Djoulde Soumae, end of Ramadan), 20 May (National Day), 14 July* (Festival of Sheep), 10 December (Reunification Day), 25 December (Christmas).

1990: 1 January (New Year), 11 February (Youth Day), 13 April (Good Friday), 16 April (Easter Monday), 27 April* (Djoulde Soumae, end of Ramadan), 1 May (Labour Day), 20 May (National Day), 24 May (Ascension Day), 4 July* (Festival of Sheep), 10 December (Reunification Day), 25 December (Christmas).

* These holidays are dependent on the Islamic lunar calendar and may vary by one or two days from the dates given.

Weights and Measures

The metric system is in force.

Statistical Survey

Source (unless otherwise stated): Direction de la Statistique et de la Comptabilité Nationale, BP 25, Yaoundé; tel. 22-07-88; telex 8203.

Area and Population

AREA, POPULATION AND DENSITY

Area (sq km)	475,442*
Population (census of 9 April 1976)†	
Males	3,754,991
Females	3,908,255
Total	7,663,246
Population (official estimates at mid-year)	
1985	10,170,000
1986	10,460,000
1987	10,822,000
Density (per sq km) at mid-1987	22.8

* 183,569 sq miles.
† Including an adjustment for underenumeration, estimated at 7.4%. The enumerated total was 7,090,115 (males 3,472,786; females 3,617,329).

PROVINCES (population at 1976 census)

	Urban	Rural	Total
Centre-South	498,290	993,655	1,491,945
Littoral	702,578	232,588	935,166
West	232,315	803,282	1,035,597
South-West	200,322	420,193	620,515
North-West	146,327	834,204	980,531
North	328,925	1,904,332	2,233,257
East	75,458	290,750	366,235
Total	2,184,242	5,479,004	7,663,246

Note: In August 1983 the number of provinces was increased to 10. Centre-South province became two separate provinces, Centre and South. The northern province was split into three: Far North, North and Adamoua.

PRINCIPAL TOWNS

1976 (population at census): Douala 458,426, Yaoundé (capital) 313,706, Nkongsamba 71,298, Maroua 67,187, Garoua 63,900, Bafoussam 62,239, Bamenda 48,111, Kumba 44,175, Limbe (formerly Victoria) 27,016.
Mid-1986 (estimated population): Douala 1,029,731, Yaoundé 653,670.

BIRTHS AND DEATHS (UN estimates, annual averages)

	1970–75	1975–80	1980–85
Birth rate (per 1,000)	42.3	43.1	42.9
Death rate (per 1,000)	18.9	17.4	15.8

Source: UN, *World Population Prospects: Estimates and Projections as Assessed in 1984*.

ECONOMICALLY ACTIVE POPULATION
(1976 census, resident population)*

	Males	Females	Total
Agriculture, hunting, forestry and fishing	1,073,264	961,710	2,034,974
Mining and quarrying	1,188	70	1,258
Manufacturing	96,577	25,834	122,411
Electricity, gas and water	2,366	105	2,471
Construction	46,065	714	46,779
Trade, restaurants and hotels	80,862	27,180	108,042
Transport, storage and communication	35,541	718	36,259
Financing, insurance, real estate and business services	5,224	815	6,039
Community, social and personal services	178,937	26,550	205,487
Activities not adequately described	48,093	23,041	71,134
Total	1,568,117	1,066,737	2,634,854

* Excluding persons seeking work for the first time, totalling 123,045 (males 88,050, females 34,995).

1983/84 (official estimate): Total labour force 3,695,000.
1984/85 (official estimate): Total labour force 3,876,588.
Mid-1986 (estimates in '000): Agriculture 2,611; total labour force 4,036 (Source: FAO, *Production Yearbook*).

Agriculture

PRINCIPAL CROPS ('000 metric tons)

	1984	1985	1986
Rice (paddy)	111	105*	113*
Maize	409	337	350*
Millet and sorghum	207	443	400*
Potatoes*	160	180	200
Sweet potatoes*	130	140	150
Cassava (Manioc)	650	670*	690*
Yams	375	380*	400*
Other roots and tubers	800	810*	820*
Dry beans*	107	110	113
Groundnuts (in shell)	110	140	140*
Sesame seed*	10	10	10
Cottonseed*	60	60	63
Cotton lint†	38	40	38
Palm kernels*	44	46	52
Sugar cane*	1,150	1,200	1,250
Vegetables*	418	420	429
Avocados*	28	29	30
Pineapples*	32	32	33
Bananas	66	67*	67*
Plantains*	970	980	986
Coffee (green)	130	96	122
Cocoa beans	121	115†	120†
Tobacco (leaves)†	2	3	5
Natural rubber	18	18	19*

* FAO estimates.   † Unofficial estimates.
Source: FAO, *Production Yearbook*.

CAMEROON

LIVESTOCK ('000 head)

	1985/86	1986/87
Cattle	3,535	4,351
Sheep	1,651	2,565
Goats	2,097	3,167
Pigs	701	710
Poultry	11,000	12,000

LIVESTOCK PRODUCTS (FAO estimates, '000 metric tons)

	1984	1985	1986
Beef and veal	48	54	56
Mutton and lamb	7	7	7
Goats' meat	7	7	7
Pigmeat	17	17	17
Poultry meat	8	9	9
Other meat	4	4	4
Cows' milk	46	47	48
Hen eggs	9.6	10.0	10.4
Cattle hides	9.7	10.9	11.2
Sheepskins	1.4	1.5	1.5
Goatskins	1.4	1.4	1.4

Source: FAO, *Production Yearbook*.

Forestry

ROUNDWOOD REMOVALS ('000 cubic metres)

	1984	1985	1986*
Sawlogs, veneer logs and logs for sleepers	1,923	2,093	2,093
Other industrial wood*	647	665	684
Fuel wood*	8,885	9,129	9,389
Total	11,455	11,887	12,166

* FAO estimates.
Source: FAO, *Yearbook of Forest Products*.

SAWNWOOD PRODUCTION ('000 cubic metres)

	1984	1985	1986
Total (incl. boxboards)	552	565	565*

* FAO estimate.
Railway sleepers (FAO estimates, '000 cubic metres): 85 in 1984; 85 in 1985; 85 in 1986.
Source: FAO, *Yearbook of Forest Products*.

Fishing

('000 metric tons, live weight)

	1984	1985	1986
Freshwater fishes	20.0	20.0	20.0
Bigeye grunt	4.5	3.6	2.7
Croakers and drums	5.8	5.2	4.8
Threadfins and tasselfishes	3.3	4.0	3.5
Sardinellas	18.1	18.0	18.0
Bonga shad	18.0	18.0	18.0
Other marine fishes (incl. unspecified)	4.7	4.4	4.1
Total fish	74.4	73.3	71.1
Crustaceans and molluscs	12.9	12.7	12.9
Total catch	87.3	86.0	84.0

Source: FAO, *Yearbook of Fishery Statistics*.

Mining

('000 metric tons, unless otherwise indicated)

	1983	1984	1985
Crude petroleum	5,689	7,400	9,170
Tin (metric tons)*	24	24	24
Limestone flux and calcareous stone	51	n.a.	79

* Estimated metal content of ore (Source: International Tin Council).
Source: UN, *Industrial Statistics Yearbook* and *Monthly Bulletin of Statistics*.
Crude petroleum ('000 metric tons): 8,980 in 1986; 8,600 in 1987 (Source: UN, *Monthly Bulletin of Statistics*).

Industry

SELECTED PRODUCTS
('000 metric tons, unless otherwise indicated)

	1983	1984	1985
Palm oil	39	n.a.	n.a.
Raw sugar	58	54	70*
Cocoa butter (exports)	5.5	3.3	3.5
Beer ('000 hectolitres)	3,354	3,976	4,904
Soft drinks ('000 hectolitres)	1,033	1,244	1,397
Cigarettes (million)	1,954	2,319	2,128
Soap	25.1	30.7	26.1
Jet fuels	137	150	155
Motor spirit (petrol)	430	650	655
Kerosene	470	520	525
Distillate fuel oils	610	650	655
Residual fuel oils	975	995	997
Lubricating oils	220	210	215
Cement	598	694	785
Aluminium (unwrought)†	53.6	125.4	81.8
Radio receivers ('000)	12	36	16
Footwear ('000 pairs)	6,108	3,572	3,964
Electric energy (million kWh)	1,804	2,230	2,237

* Estimated production.   † Using alumina imported from Guinea.
Source: UN, *Industrial Statistics Yearbook*.

Finance

CURRENCY AND EXCHANGE RATES

Monetary Units
100 centimes = 1 franc de la Coopération financière en Afrique central (CFA).

Denominations
Coins: 1, 2, 5, 10, 25, 50, 100 and 500 francs CFA.
Notes: 100, 500, 1,000, 5,000 and 10,000 francs CFA.

French Franc, Sterling and Dollar Equivalents (30 September 1988)
1 French franc = 50 francs CFA;
£1 sterling = 538.6 francs CFA;
US $1 = 318.5 francs CFA;
1,000 francs CFA = £1.857 = $3.140.

Average Exchange Rate (francs CFA per US $)
1985 449.26
1986 346.30
1987 300.54

CAMEROON   Statistical Survey

BUDGET ESTIMATES
(million francs CFA, year ending 30 June)

Revenue	1986/87	1987/88
Taxation	461,700	365,000
Indirect taxes	254,800	185,000
Registration and stamp duty	24,800	20,000
Customs and miscellaneous duties	182,100	160,000
Non-tax revenue	186,700	235,000
Property income	1,800	3,000
Miscellaneous products and services	34,900	82,000
Petroleum royalties	150,000	150,000
Total revenue	**648,400**	**600,000**

Expenditure	1986/87	1987/88
Current budget	476,100	400,000
Internal debt	3,100	12,000
Public authorities	380,700	320,000
Territorial administration	31,400	19,000
State intervention	60,900	49,000
Investment budget	327,200	250,000
Public debt servicing	100,000	150,000
Infrastructure	227,200	100,000
Total expenditure	**803,300**	**650,000**

Source: *La Zone Franc—Rapport 1987*.

1988/89: Budget balanced at 600,000m. francs CFA (current expenditure 375,000m.; investment expenditure 225,000m.).

CENTRAL BANK RESERVES
(US $ million at 31 December)

	1985	1986	1987
Gold*	9.70	11.74	14.45
IMF special drawing rights	4.62	3.45	0.26
Reserve position in IMF	0.22	0.24	0.28
Foreign exchange	127.62	55.32	63.22
Total	**142.16**	**70.76**	**78.21**

* Valued at market-related prices.

Source: IMF, *International Financial Statistics*.

MONEY SUPPLY ('000 million francs CFA at 31 December)

	1985	1986	1987
Currency outside banks	148.30	167.66	171.11
Demand deposits at deposit money banks	277.28	279.21	214.80
Checking deposits at post office	1.10	1.10	1.10
Total money	**426.68**	**447.97**	**387.01**

Source: IMF, *International Financial Statistics*.

COST OF LIVING
(Consumer Price Index for Africans in Yaoundé. Base: 1980 = 100)

	1983	1984	1985
Food	154.4	161.5	160.4
Clothing	143.1	189.6	257.1
All items (incl. others)	**145.8**	**162.4**	**180.5**

Source: ILO, *Year Book of Labour Statistics*.

NATIONAL ACCOUNTS
('000 million francs CFA at current prices, year ending 30 June)

National Income and Product

	1982/83	1983/84	1984/85
Compensation of employees	747.4	875.5	989.5
Operating surplus	1,363.7	1,737.5	2,181.7
Domestic factor incomes	**2,111.1**	**2,613.0**	**3,171.2**
Consumption of fixed capital	158.1	165.2	194.7
Gross domestic product (GDP) at factor cost	**2,269.2**	**2,778.3**	**3,365.9**
Indirect taxes	355.0	434.1	485.4
Less Subsidies	6.1	17.4	12.4
GDP in purchasers' values	**2,618.0**	**3,195.0**	**3,838.9**
Factor income received from abroad	11.7	14.1	−98.2
Less Factor income paid abroad	71.5	76.2	
Gross national product	**2,558.3**	**3,132.9**	**3,740.7**
Less Consumption of fixed capital	158.1	165.2	194.7
National income in market prices	**2,400.2**	**2,967.7**	**3,546.1**
Other current transfers received from abroad	17.4	18.3	0.9
Less Other current transfers paid abroad	22.5	23.8	
National disposable income	**2,395.1**	**2,962.2**	**3,547.0**

Expenditure on the Gross Domestic Product

	1982/83	1983/84	1984/85
Government final consumption expenditure	248.7	306.4	345.3
Private final consumption expenditure	1,716.5	2,008.0	2,466.3
Increase in stocks	25.6	19.4	16.3
Gross fixed capital formation	654.5	809.5	939.0
Total domestic expenditure	**2,645.3**	**3,143.3**	**3,766.9**
Exports of goods and services	547.5	646.5	799.9
Less Imports of goods and services	574.7	594.7	727.9
GDP in purchasers' values	**2,618.0**	**3,195.0**	**3,838.9**

Gross Domestic Product by Economic Activity

	1982/83	1983/84	1984/85
Agriculture and hunting	551.2	632.1	700.6
Forestry and logging	48.5	62.9	84.8
Fishing	7.5	7.0	5.0
Mining and quarrying	400.5	520.5	629.7
Manufacturing	290.9	358.5	422.4
Electricity, gas and water	30.1	35.2	37.7
Construction	145.8	192.6	227.6
Wholesale and retail trade	297.8	401.9	564.6
Restaurants and hotels	12.9	13.0	
Transport, storage and communications	128.8	147.3	230.7
Finance, insurance, real estate and business services	355.2	396.8	455.3
Government services	171.8	212.8	248.8
Other community, social and personal services	34.5	39.3	46.3
Private non-profit services to households	11.0	13.6	15.4
Domestic services of households	22.3	26.6	27.9
Sub-total	**2,508.7**	**3,060.0**	**3,696.9**
Import duties	146.8	173.0	174.4
Less imputed bank service charges	37.5	38.1	32.4
GDP in purchasers' values	**2,618.0**	**3,195.0**	**3,838.9**

CAMEROON

BALANCE OF PAYMENTS (US $ million)

	1984	1985	1986
Merchandise exports f.o.b.	1,567.8	1,679.3	2,077.0
Merchandise imports f.o.b.	−1,058.8	−1,163.9	−1,634.5
Trade balance	509.0	515.5	442.5
Exports of services	452.5	550.4	518.5
Imports of services	−1,121.0	−1,633.8	−1,419.3
Balance on goods and services	−159.5	−568.0	−458.3
Private unrequited transfers (net)	−77.8	−102.1	−122.8
Government unrequited transfers (net)	57.6	86.6	32.1
Current balance	−179.7	−583.5	−549.0
Direct capital investment (net)	17.0	317.5	3.3
Other long-term capital (net)	366.1	153.5	87.1
Short-term capital (net)	−169.9	57.1	400.7
Net errors and omissions	−126.8	106.6	−33.6
Total (net monetary movements)	−93.4	51.3	−91.5
Valuation changes (net)	−13.0	0.7	18.2
Exceptional financing (net)	—	—	0.1
Official financing (net)	0.5	0.6	—
Changes in reserves	−105.9	52.5	−73.2

Source: IMF, *International Financial Statistics*.

External Trade

PRINCIPAL COMMODITIES (million francs CFA)

Imports c.i.f.	1984	1985	1986
Tyres	6,373	7,856	5,181
Textiles	21,067	18,031	20,827
Malt	8,895	6,380	15,029
Cement	6,630	9,667	5,575
Alumina	15,373	14,804	9,593
Lubricants	3,614	3,438	3,917
Medicine	4,583	22,404	24,460
Books and newspapers	4,363	9,369	10,733
Iron and steel pipes	7,781	4,011	1,470
Paper and allied products	8,894	8,436	16,612
Drilling equipment	12,372	4,180	7,472
Footwear	3,549	4,300	5,143
Iron and steel	48,077	38,217	35,210
Cutting machinery	5,205	8,204	7,404
Generating machinery	5,004	8,919	6,971
Road transport equipment	57,995	65,566	66,940
Air transport equipment	1,397	6,758	10,797
Maritime transport equipment	10,077	1,636	1,996
Electrical, telegraphic, telephone appliances and machinery	30,709	46,108	56,112
Fertilizers	7,395	10,452	8,223
Total (incl. others)	484,646	513,898	590,439

Exports f.o.b.	1984	1985	1986
Cocoa	100,397	85,473	87,223
Coffee (arabica)	32,706	26,038	28,330
Coffee (robusta)	61,049	87,206	88,281
Bananas	6,663	6,764	5,670
Rubber	6,843	5,991	4,319
Tobacco	3,702	5,256	4,429
Cotton fibre	10,272	5,360	12,326
Cotton fabrics	9,403	5,923	3,984
Palm nuts and kernels	1,284	511	161
Palm oil	591	336	1,567
Cocoa pulp	6,437	8,717	5,533
Cocoa butter	7,857	7,844	8,661
Logs	14,324	27,971	18,488
Sawnwood and sleepers	4,018	5,690	2,712
Aluminium	29,794	22,083	16,914
Aluminium products	5,637	6,975	5,184
Crude petroleum	478,864	445,680	192,709
Total (incl. others)	822,041	816,912	541,728

PRINCIPAL TRADING PARTNERS (million francs CFA)

Imports c.i.f.	1984	1985	1986
Belgium/Luxembourg	14,342	14,999	20,432
France	207,536	219,709	248,932
Germany, Federal Republic	32,245	36,378	53,800
Italy	22,086	25,279	27,939
Japan	34,449	37,606	45,041
Netherlands	8,470	11,221	15,691
Spain	12,192	13,101	14,663
UDEAC*	9,809	5,172	2,181
UMOA†	8,495	n.a.	n.a.
United Kingdom	16,828	20,296	21,710
USA	49,619	37,241	29,116
Total (incl. others)	484,646	513,898	590,439

Exports f.o.b.	1984	1985	1986
Belgium/Luxembourg	36,225	23,600	12,213
France	179,889	288,229	111,857
Germany, Federal Republic	34,713	49,095	39,647
Italy	50,739	52,105	29,658
Japan	3,882	n.a.	n.a.
Netherlands	138,212	120,728	148,924
Nigeria	8,264	9,870	14,533
Spain	8,559	49,785	27,669
UDEAC*	29,808	33,568	28,221
UMOA†	2,715	n.a.	n.a.
USSR	7,000	16,166	9,313
United Kingdom	3,498	n.a.	n.a.
USA	266,917	110,543	88,772
Total (incl. others)	822,041	816,912	541,728

* Union douanière et économique de l'Afrique centrale (Customs and Economic Union of Central Africa), comprising Cameroon, the Central African Republic, Chad (since December 1984), the Congo, Equatorial Guinea (since January 1985) and Gabon.

† Union monétaire ouest-africaine (West African Monetary Union), comprising Benin, Burkina Faso, Côte d'Ivoire, Mali (since February 1984), Niger, Senegal and Togo.

Source: Chambre de Commerce, d'Industrie et des Mines, Douala.

CAMEROON

Transport

RAILWAYS (traffic, year ending 30 June)

	1983/84	1984/85	1985/86
Passengers carried ('000)	2,218	2,481	2,079
Passenger-km (million)	444	438	412
Freight carried ('000 tons)	1,849	1,982	1,844
Freight ton-km (million)	838	971	871

ROAD TRAFFIC (motor vehicles in use at 31 December)

	1984	1985	1986
Passenger cars	72,449	77,105	80,757
Commercial vehicles	41,301	43,510	44,875
Tractors and trailers	2,045	2,473	2,709
Motorcycles and scooters	41,579	41,807	40,961

INTERNATIONAL SEA-BORNE SHIPPING (Douala)

	1984	1985	1986
Vessels entered	1,176	1,242	1,963
Freight loaded ('000 metric tons)	999	1,010	1,040
Freight unloaded ('000 metric tons)	2,999	3,428	3,188

Source: Office National des Ports, Douala.

CIVIL AVIATION (traffic on scheduled services)

	1982	1983	1984
Kilometres flown (million)	6.2	6.1	6.0
Passengers carried ('000)	634	631	677
Passenger-km (million)	581	568	540
Freight ton-km (million)	45.7	43.5	55.5

Source: UN, *Statistical Yearbook*.

Tourism

FOREIGN VISITORS

Foreigners staying at least two nights: 124,102 in 1985; 112,889 in 1986; 115,203 in 1987.

HOTELS

In January 1988 there were 150 classified hotels, with a total of 8,000 rooms and 12,000 beds.

Source: mainly Secrétariat d'Etat au Tourisme, Yaoundé.

Communications Media

	1983	1984	1985
Radio receivers ('000 in use)	830	n.a.	940

Telephones (1983): 47,000 in use.
Book production (first editions only, 1979): 22 titles (94,000 copies), excluding pamphlets.
Daily newspapers (1984): 1 (average circulation 35,000 copies).
Non-daily newspapers (1984): 3 (average circulation 35,000 copies).
Source: mainly UNESCO, *Statistical Yearbook*.

Education

(1986/87)

	Institutions	Pupils	Teachers
Pre-primary	626	83,963	2,952
Primary	5,941	1,795,254	35,728
Post-primary	122	9,111	927
Secondary	388	291,842	9,017
Technical	183	90,666	3,714
Teacher training	33	4,259	411
Higher*	5	19,586	975

* 1985/86 figures.
Source: Ministère de l'Education Nationale, Yaoundé.

Directory

The Constitution

The Constitution of the United Republic of Cameroon was promulgated on 2 June 1972, after approval by a referendum on 21 May 1972. It was revised on 9 May 1975.

In January 1984 the National Assembly approved a constitutional amendment, restoring the country's original name, the Republic of Cameroon. At the same time, the Assembly adopted further constitutional reforms, abolishing the post of Prime Minister and providing that the President of the Republic would be succeeded, in the event of death or incapacity, by the President of the National Assembly. Further constitutional amendments, agreed in March 1988, made provision for the holding of a presidential election before the expiry of the incumbent President's mandate, and increased the number of members in the Assembly from 150 to 180, effective from the general election of April 1988.

The main provisions of the 1972 Constitution, as amended, are summarized below:

The Constitution declares that the human being, without distinction as to race, religion, sex or belief, possesses inalienable and sacred rights. It affirms its attachment to the fundamental freedoms embodied in the Universal Declaration of Human Rights and the UN Charter. The State guarantees to all citizens of either sex the rights and freedoms set out in the preamble of the Constitution.

SOVEREIGNTY

1. The Republic of Cameroon shall be one and indivisible, democratic, secular and dedicated to social service. It shall ensure the equality before the law of all its citizens. Provisions that the official languages be French and English, for the motto, flag, national anthem and seal, that the capital be Yaoundé.

2-3. Sovereignty shall be vested in the people who shall exercise it either through the President of the Republic and the members returned by it to the National Assembly or by means of referendum. Elections are by universal suffrage, direct or indirect, by every citizen aged 21 or over in a secret ballot. Political parties or groups may take part in elections subject to the law and the principles of democracy and of national sovereignty and unity.

4. State authority shall be exercised by the President of the Republic and the National Assembly.

THE PRESIDENT OF THE REPUBLIC

5. The President of the Republic, as Head of State and Head of the Government, shall be responsible for the conduct of the affairs of the Republic. He shall define national policy and may charge the members of the government with the implementation of this policy in certain spheres.

6-7. Candidates for the office of President must hold civic and political rights and be at least 35 years old, and may not hold any other elective office or professional activity. The President is elected for five years, by a majority of votes cast by the people, and may be re-elected. A presidential election may take place before the expiry of the five-year term, if the incumbent President so decides. Provisions are made for the continuity of office in the case of the President's resignation.

CAMEROON

8–9. The Ministers and Vice-Ministers are appointed by the President to whom they are responsible, and they may hold no other appointment. The President is also head of the armed forces, he negotiates and ratifies treaties, may exercise clemency after consultation with the Higher Judicial Council, promulgates and is responsible for the enforcement of laws, is responsible for internal and external security, makes civil and military appointments, provides for necessary administrative services.

10. The President, by reference to the Supreme Court, ensures that all laws passed are constitutional.

11. Provisions whereby the President may declare a State of Emergency or State of Siege.

THE NATIONAL ASSEMBLY

12. The National Assembly shall be renewed every five years, though it may at the instance of the President of the Republic legislate to extend or shorten its term of office. It shall be composed of 180 members elected by universal suffrage.

13–14. Laws shall normally be passed by a simple majority of those present, but if a bill is read a second time at the request of the President of the Republic a majority of the National Assembly as a whole is required.

15–16. The National Assembly shall meet twice a year, each session to last not more than 30 days; in one session it shall approve the budget. It may be recalled to an extraordinary session of not more than 15 days.

17–18. Elections and suitability of candidates and sitting members shall be governed by law.

RELATIONS BETWEEN THE EXECUTIVE AND THE LEGISLATURE

19. Bills may be introduced either by the President of the Republic or by any member of the National Assembly.

20. Reserved to the legislature are: the fundamental rights and duties of the citizen; the law of persons and property; the political, administrative and judicial system in respect of elections to the National Assembly, general regulation of national defence, authorization of penalties and criminal and civil procedure etc., and the organization of the local authorities; currency, the budget, dues and taxes, legislation on public property; economic and social policy; the education system.

21. The National Assembly may empower the President of the Republic to legislate by way of Ordinance for a limited period and for given purposes.

22–26. Other matters of procedure, including the right of the President of the Republic to address the Assembly and of the Ministers and Vice-Ministers to take part in debates.

27–29. The composition and conduct of the Assembly's programme of business. Provisions whereby the Assembly may inquire into governmental activity. The obligation of the President of the Republic to promulgate laws, which shall be published in both languages of the Republic.

30. Provisions whereby the President of the Republic, after consultation with the National Assembly, may submit to referendum certain reform bills liable to have profound repercussions on the future of the Nation and National Institutions.

THE JUDICIARY

31. Justice is administered in the name of the people. The President of the Republic shall ensure the independence of the judiciary and shall make appointments with the assistance of the Higher Judicial Council.

THE SUPREME COURT

32–33. The Supreme Court has powers to uphold the Constitution in such cases as the death or incapacity of the President and the admissibility of laws, to give final judgments on appeals on the Judgment of the Court of Appeal and to decide complaints against administrative acts. It may be assisted by experts appointed by the President of the Republic.

IMPEACHMENT

34. There shall be a Court of Impeachment with jurisdiction to try the President of the Republic for high treason and the Ministers and Vice-Ministers for conspiracy against the security of the State.

THE ECONOMIC AND SOCIAL COUNCIL

35. There shall be an Economic and Social Council, regulated by the law.

AMENDMENT OF THE CONSTITUTION

36–37. Bills to amend the Constitution may be introduced either by the President of the Republic or the National Assembly. The President may decide to submit any amendment to the people by way of a referendum. No procedure to amend the Constitution may be accepted if it tends to impair the republican character, unity or territorial integrity of the State, or the democratic principles by which the Republic is governed.

The Government

HEAD OF STATE

President: Paul Biya (took office 6 November 1982, following the resignation of Ahmadou Ahidjo; elected 14 January 1984 for a five-year term; re-elected 24 April 1988).

CABINET
(December 1988)

Secretary-General at the Presidency: Paul Tessa.

Minister Delegate at the Presidency in charge of Defence: Michel Meva'a M'Eboutou.

Minister for the Presidency: Ogork Ebot Ntui.

Minister Special Adviser to the President: Titus Edzoa.

Minister of Justice and Keeper of the Seals: Benjamin Itoe.

Minister of External Relations: Jacques-Roger Booh-Booh.

Minister of Youth and Sports: Dr Joseph Fofe.

Minister of Territorial Administration: Ibrahim Mbombo Njoya.

Minister of Finance: Sadou Hayatou.

Minister of National Education: Prof. Georges Ngango.

Minister of Labour and Social Welfare: Jean Baptiste Bokam.

Minister of Public Health: Prof. Joseph Mbede.

Minister of Agriculture: John Niba Ngu.

Minister of Planning and Territorial Development: Elizabeth Tankeu.

Minister of Industrial and Commercial Development: Joseph Tsanga Abanda.

Minister of Social Affairs and Women's Affairs: Aissatou Yaou.

Minister of Posts and Telecommunications: Oumarou Sanda.

Minister of Mines, Water and Energy: Francis Wainchom Nkwain.

Minister of Housing and Town Planning: Ferdinand-Léopold Oyono.

Minister of Public Works and Transport: Claude Tchepannou.

Minister of Information and Culture: Henri Bandolo.

Minister of the Public Service and State Control: Prof. Joseph Owona.

Minister of Higher Education, Scientific Research and Computer Sciences: Abdoulaye Babale.

Minister of Livestock, Fisheries and Animal Husbandry: Hamadjoda Adjoudji.

Secretaries of State:

Agriculture: Tikela Kemonne.

Planning and Territorial Development: Ndanga Ndinga Badel.

Industrial and Commercial Development: Louis Abogo Nkono.

Finance: Ephraim Inoni.

Education: Paul Enyi Atogo.

Tourism: Dr Abdoulaye Souaibou.

Defence: Amadou Ali.

MINISTRIES

Ministries do not usually have Post Office Box numbers. Correspondence should generally be addressed to ministries c/o the Central Post Office, Yaoundé.

Office of the President: Yaoundé; tel. 23-40-25; telex 8207.

Ministry of Agriculture: Yaoundé; tel. 23-40-85; telex 8325.

Ministry of Defence: Yaoundé; tel. 23-40-55; telex 8261.

Ministry of External Relations: Yaoundé; tel. 22-01-33; telex 8252.

Ministry of Finance: BP 18, Yaoundé; tel. 23-40-00; telex 8260.

Ministry of Higher Education, Scientific Research and Computer Sciences: Yaoundé; telex 8418.

Ministry of Housing and Town Planning: Yaoundé; tel. 23-22-82; telex 8560.

Ministry of Industrial and Commercial Development: Yaoundé.

Ministry of Information and Culture: BP 1588, Yaoundé; tel. 22-31-55; telex 8215.

CAMEROON

Ministry of Justice: Yaoundé; tel. 22-01-97; telex 8566.
Ministry of Labour and Social Welfare: Yaoundé; tel. 22-01-86.
Ministry of Livestock, Fisheries and Animal Husbandry: Yaoundé; tel. 22-33-11.
Ministry of Mines, Water and Energy: Yaoundé; tel. 23-34-04; telex 8504.
Ministry of National Education: Yaoundé; tel. 23-40-50; telex 8551.
Ministry of Planning and Territorial Development: Yaoundé; telex 8268.
Ministry of Posts and Telecommunications: Yaoundé; tel. 23-40-16; telex 8582.
Ministry of Public Health: Yaoundé; tel. 22-29-01; telex 8565.
Ministry of the Public Service and State Control: Yaoundé; telex 8597.
Ministry of Public Works and Transport: Yaoundé; tel. 22-16-22; telex 8653.
Ministry of Social Affairs and Women's Affairs: Yaoundé; tel. 22-41-48.
Ministry of Territorial Administration: Yaoundé; tel. 23-40-90; telex 8503.
Ministry of Youth and Sports: Yaoundé; tel. 23-32-57; telex 8568.

Legislature

ASSEMBLÉE NATIONALE

The number of seats in the Assemblée Nationale was increased from 150 to 180, following a constitutional amendment agreed in March 1988. Elections to the enlarged Assembly were held on 24 April 1988. A total of 324 candidates, all approved by the RDPC, contested the 180 seats.

President: LAWRENCE SHANG FONKA.
Secretary-General: El Hadj AHMADOU HAYATOU.

Political Organizations

Rassemblement démocratique du peuple camerounais (RDPC): BP 867, Yaoundé; f. 1966 as Union nationale camerounaise (UNC) by merger of the Union camerounaise, the Kamerun National Democratic Party and four opposition parties; renamed in March 1985; comprises a congress which meets every five years, a 12-mem. political bureau and a cen. cttee of 65 mems and 20 alt. mems; Pres. PAUL BIYA; Political Sec. FRANÇOIS SANGAT KUOH; there are two ancillary organs: Organisation des femmes du RDPC and Jeunesse du RDPC.

In November 1987 a number of banned opposition movements in exile, including several factions of the Union des populations camerounaises (UPC), merged to form the Cameroon Democratic Front (CDF), led by Ndeh Ntumaza.

Diplomatic Representation

EMBASSIES IN CAMEROON

Algeria: BP 1619, Yaoundé; tel. 23-06-65; telex 8517; Ambassador: MISSOUM SBIH.
Belgium: BP 816, Yaoundé; tel. 22-27-88; telex 8314; Ambassador: FERNAND VAN BRUSSELEN.
Brazil: BP 348, Yaoundé; tel. 23-19-57; telex 8587; Ambassador: P. G. VILSA-BÔAS CASTRO.
Canada: Immeuble Stamatiades, BP 572, Yaoundé; tel. 23-02-03; telex 8209; Ambassador: ANDRÉ S. SIMARD.
Central African Republic: BP 396, Yaoundé; tel. 22-51-55; Ambassador: BASILE AKELELO.
Chad: BP 506, Yaoundé; tel. 22-06-24; telex 8352; Chargé d'affaires: ALI OUTMAN.
China, People's Republic: BP 1307, Yaoundé; tel. 23-00-83; Ambassador: SHEN LIANRUI.
Congo: BP 1422, Yaoundé; tel. 23-24-58; telex 8379; Ambassador: BERNADETTE BAYONNE.
Côte d'Ivoire: Immeuble Ndende, quartier Bastos, BP 203, Yaoundé; tel. 22-09-69; telex 8388; Ambassador: ANTOINE KONAN KOFFI.
Egypt: BP 809, Yaoundé; tel. 22-39-22; telex 8360; Ambassador: MOHAMED AL-KHAZINDAR.
Equatorial Guinea: BP 277, Yaoundé; tel. 22-41-49; Ambassador: POLICARPO MONSUY MBA.
France: Plateau Atémengué, BP 1631, Yaoundé; tel. 22-02-33; telex 8233; Ambassador: YVON OMNÈS.
Gabon: BP 4130, Yaoundé; tel. 22-29-66; telex 8265; Ambassador: AUGUSTIN CHANGO.
German Democratic Republic: BP 1139, Yaoundé; tel. 22-38-41; telex 8412; Ambassador: MANFRED VOSS.
Germany, Federal Republic: BP 1160, Yaoundé; tel. 23-05-66; telex 8238; Ambassador: Dr FRIEDERICH REICHE.
Greece: BP 82, Yaoundé; tel. 22-39-36; telex 8364; Chargé d'affaires a.i. ANASTASSIOS GAUALIAS.
Holy See: BP 210, Yaoundé; tel. 22-04-75; telex 8382; Apostolic Pro-Nuncio: Mgr DONATO SQUICCIARINI.
Israel: BP 5934, Yaoundé; tel. 22-16-44; telex 8632; Ambassador: JAACOV KEINAN.
Italy: Quartier Bastos, BP 827, Yaoundé; tel. 22-33-76; telex 8305; Ambassador: FRANCESCO LABBRUZZO.
Korea, Republic: BP 301, Yaoundé; tel. 23-32-23; telex 8241; Ambassador: KIM DONG-HO.
Liberia: BP 1185, Yaoundé; tel. 23-26-31; telex 8227; Ambassador: CARLTON ALEXWYN KRONYANH KARPEH.
Libya: BP 1980, Yaoundé; telex 8272; Head of People's Bureau: FANNOUSH HAMDI.
Morocco: BP 1629, Yaoundé; tel. 22-50-92; telex 8347; Ambassador: (vacant).
Netherlands: BP 310, Yaoundé; tel. 22-05-44; telex 8237; Ambassador: GEORGES WEHRY.
Nigeria: BP 448, Yaoundé; tel. 22-34-55; telex 8267; Ambassador: MOHAMMED H. SAIDU.
Saudi Arabia: BP 1602, Yaoundé; tel. 22-39-22; telex 8336; Ambassador: HAMAD AL-TOAIMI.
Senegal: Plateau 'Bastos', BP 1716, Yaoundé; tel. 22-03-08; telex 8303; Ambassador: SALOUM KANDE.
Spain: BP 877, Yaoundé; tel. 22-41-89; telex 8287; Ambassador: MANUEL PIÑEIRO-SOUTO.
Switzerland: BP 1169, Yaoundé; tel. 23-28-96; telex 8316; Ambassador: JURG STREULI.
Tunisia: rue de Rotary, BP 6074, Yaoundé; tel. 22-33-68; telex 8370; Ambassador: HÉDI DRISSI.
USSR: BP 488, Yaoundé; tel. 22-17-14; Ambassador: VLADIMIR PEDEROV.
United Kingdom: ave Winston Churchill, BP 547, Yaoundé; tel. 22-05-45; telex 8200; Ambassador: MARTIN REITH.
USA: BP 817, Yaoundé; tel. 23-40-14; telex 8223; Ambassador: MARK EDELMAN.
Zaire: BP 632, Yaoundé; tel. 22-51-03; telex 8317; Ambassador: MWEME NGABWE DEDE KABIKA.

Judicial System

Supreme Court: Yaoundé; consists of a President, nine titular and substitute judges, a Procureur Général, an Avocat Général, deputies to the Procureur Général, a Registrar and clerks.

President of the Supreme Court: MARCEL NGUINI.

High Court of Justice: Yaoundé; consists of 9 titular judges and 6 substitute judges, all elected by the National Assembly.

Religion

It is estimated that 39% of the population follow traditional animist beliefs, 21% are Muslims and 40% Christians, mainly Roman Catholics.

CHRISTIANITY

Protestant Churches

Fédération des Eglises et missions évangéliques du Cameroun (FEMEC): BP 491, Yaoundé; tel. 22-30-78; f. 1968; 10 mem. churches; Pres. Rev. Dr JEAN KOTTO (Evangelical Church of Cameroon); Admin. Sec. Rev. Dr GRÉGOIRE AMBADIANG DE MENDENG (Presbyterian Church of Cameroon).

There are about 1m. Protestants in Cameroon, with about 3,000 church and mission workers, and four theological schools.

Eglise évangélique du Cameroun (Evangelical Church of Cameroon): BP 89, Douala; tel. 42-36-11; independent since 1957; 500,000 mems (1985); Sec. Rev. CHARLES E. NJIKE.

CAMEROON

Eglise presbytérienne camerounaise (Presbyterian Church of Cameroon): BP 519, Yaoundé; tel. 32-42-36; independent since 1957; comprises four synods and 16 presbyteries; 200,000 mems (1985); Gen. Sec. Rev. GRÉGOIRE AMBADIANG DE MENDENG.

Eglise protestante africaine (African Protestant Church): BP 26, Lolodorf; active among the Ngumba people; 8,400 mems (1985); Dir-Gen. Rev. ANTOINE NTER.

Presbyterian Church in Cameroon: BP 19, Buéa; tel. 32-23-36; telex 5613; 184,257 mems (1987); 224 ministers; Moderator Rev. HENRY ANYE AWASOM.

Union des Eglises baptistes au Cameroun (Union of Baptist Churches of Cameroon): BP 6007, New Bell, Douala; tel. 42-41-06; autonomous since 1957; 37,000 mems (1985); Gen. Sec. Rev. EMMANUEL MBENDA.

Among other denominations active in the country are the Cameroon Baptist Church, the Cameroon Baptist Convention, the Church of the Lutheran Brethren of Cameroon, the Evangelical Lutheran Church of Cameroon, the Presbyterian Church in West Cameroon and the Union of Evangelical Churches of North Cameroon.

The Roman Catholic Church

Cameroon comprises four archdioceses and 12 dioceses. At 31 December 1985 there were an estimated 2,741,000 adherents (about 27% of the total population). There are several active missionary orders, and four major seminaries for African priests.

Bishops' Conference: Conférence Episcopale Nationale du Cameroun, BP 272, Garoua; tel. 27-13-53; f. 1981; Pres. Cardinal CHRISTIAN WIYGHAN TUMI, Archbishop of Garoua.

Archbishop of Bamenda: Mgr PAUL VERDZEKOV, Archbishop's House, BP 82, Bamenda; tel. 36-12-41.

Archbishop of Douala: Mgr SIMON TONYÈ, Archevêché, BP 179, Douala; tel. 42-37-14.

Archbishop of Garoua: Cardinal CHRISTIAN WIYGHAN TUMI, Archevêché, BP 272, Garoua; tel. 27-13-53.

Archbishop of Yaoundé: Mgr JEAN ZOA, Archevêché, BP 207, Yaoundé; tel. 23-04-83; telex 8681.

BAHÁ'Í FAITH

National Spiritual Assembly: BP 145, Limbe; tel. 33-21-46; mems in 1,305 localities.

The Press

The press in Cameroon has suffered from the problems of low circulations, small advertising income, high printing costs and expensive paper. Censorship has added to its difficulties. The Cameroon Press Law of December 1966 was modified in June 1981 to stipulate conditions of authorization or prohibition of newspapers, periodicals and magazines.

DAILY

Cameroon Tribune: BP 1218, Yaoundé; tel. 22-27-00; telex 8311; f. 1974; govt-controlled; French; also weekly edn in English; Dir NDEMBY YEMBE; Editor-in-Chief ABUI MAMA ELOUNDOU; circ. 66,000 (daily), 25,000 (weekly).

PERIODICALS

Afrique en Dossiers: BP 1715; Yaoundé.

Le Bamiléké: BP 329, Nkongsamba; monthly.

Bulletin de la Chambre de Commerce, d'Industrie et des Mines du Cameroun: BP 4011, Douala; tel. 42-28-88; telex 5616; monthly.

Bulletin Mensuel de la Statistique: BP 660, Yaoundé; monthly.

Cameroon Information: Ministry of Information and Culture, BP 1588, Yaoundé; telex 8215; fortnightly; French and English; circ. 5,000.

Cameroon—Magazine: 6 a year; independent; Editor-in-Chief FRANCIS EMILE MBOUNJA.

Cameroon Outlook: BP 124, Limbe; f. 1969; 3 a week; independent; English; Editor JEROME F. GWELLEM; circ. 20,000.

Cameroon Panorama: BP 46, Buéa; tel. 32-22-40; f. 1962; monthly; English; Roman Catholic; Editor Sister MERCY HORGAN; circ. 4,000.

Cameroon Post: Yaoundé; weekly; independent; English; Editor A. Y. NGALIM; circ. 20,000.

Cameroon Times: BP 200, Limbe; f. 1960; 3 a week; English; Editor-in-Chief JEROME F. GWELLEM; circ. 12,000.

Le Combattant: Yaoundé; weekly; independent; Editor BENYIMBE JOSEPH; circ. 21,000.

Courrier Sportif du Bénin: BP 17, Douala; weekly; Dir HENRI JONG.

Essor des Jeunes: BP 363, Nkongsamba; monthly; Roman Catholic; Editor Abbé JEAN-BOCO TCHAPE; circ. 3,000.

La Gazette: BP 5485, Douala; 2 a week; Editor ABODEL KARIMOU; circ. 35,000.

The Gazette: BP 408, Limbe; tel. 33-25-67; weekly; English edn of *La Gazette*; Editor JEROME F. GWELLEM; circ. 70,000.

Journal Officiel de la République du Cameroun: BP 1603, Yaoundé; tel. 23-12-77; telex 8403; fortnightly; official govt notices; circ. 1,500.

Le Libéral: Yaoundé; fortnightly.

Le Messager: Bafoussam; fortnightly; independent; Editor PUIS NJAWE; circ. 19,000.

Nleb Bekristen: Imprimerie Saint-Paul, BP 763, Yaoundé; f. 1935; fortnightly; Ewondo; Dir PASCAL BAYLON MVOE; circ. 6,000.

Les Nouvelles du Mungo: BP 1, Nkongsamba; monthly; circ. 3,000.

Le Patriote: Yaoundé.

Presbyterian Newsletter: BP 19, Buéa; telex 5613; quarterly.

Recherches et Études Camerounaises: BP 193, Yaoundé; monthly; publ. by Office National de Recherches Scientifiques du Cameroun.

Le Républicain: Yaoundé.

Revue d'Informations et d'Etudes Economiques et Financières: BP 1630, Yaoundé; quarterly.

Le Serviteur: BP 1405, Yaoundé; monthly; Protestant; Dir Pastor DANIEL AKO'O; circ. 3,000.

Le Travailleur/The Worker: BP 1610, Yaoundé; f. 1972; monthly; French and English; journal of Organisation des Sociétés de Travailleurs Camerounais; circ. 15,000.

L'Unité: BP 867, Yaoundé; weekly; French and English.

NEWS AGENCIES

CAMNEWS: c/o SOPECAM, BP 1218, Yaoundé; Dir JEAN NGANDJEU.

Foreign Bureaux

Agence France-Presse (AFP): Villa Kamdem-Kamga, BP 229, Elig-Essono, Yaoundé; telex 8218; Correspondent RENÉ-JACQUES LIGUE.

Xinhua (New China) News Agency (People's Republic of China): ave Joseph Omgba, BP 1583, Yaoundé; tel. 22-25-72; telex 8294; Chief Correspondent LIANG GUIHE.

Reuters (UK) and TASS (USSR) are also represented in Cameroon.

Publishers

Centre d'Edition et de Production pour l'Enseignement et la Recherche (CEPER): BP 808, Yaoundé; tel. 22-13-23; telex 8338; f. 1967; general non-fiction, history, Africana, paperbacks, science and technology, social science, university and secondary textbooks; Man. Dir WILFRED W. BANMBUH.

Editions Buma Kor: BP 727, Yaoundé; tel. 23-29-03; telex 8438; f. 1977; general, children's, educational and Christian; English and French; Man. Dir B. D. BUMA KOR.

Editions Clé: BP 1501, Yaoundé; tel. 22-35-54; telex 8438; f. 1963; African literature and studies; secondary and university textbooks, theology and religion; Man. Dir LAURENTIN SOMÉ.

Editions Le Flambeau: BP 113, Yaoundé; tel. 22-36-72; f. 1977; general; Man. Dir JOSEPH NDZIE.

Editions Semences Africaines: BP 5329, Yaoundé-Nlongkak; f. 1974; fiction, history, religion, textbooks; Man. Dir PHILIPPE-LOUIS OMBEDE.

Gwellem Publications: Presbook Compound (Down Beach), BP 408, Limbe; tel. 33-25-67; f. 1983; periodicals, books and pamphlets; Dir and Editor-in-Chief JEROME F. GWELLEM.

Imprimerie Saint-Paul: ave Monseigneur Vogt, BP 763, Yaoundé; education, medicine, philosophy, politics, religion and fiction.

Société Camerounaise de Publications (SCP): BP 23, Yaoundé; tel. 22-27-00; f. 1974; Man. Dir ENGELBERT NGOH-HOB.

Société Kenkoson d'Etudes Africaines: BP 4064, Yaoundé; f. 1975; law, academic; CEO M. SALOMÉ.

Government Publishing Houses

Imprimerie Nationale: BP 1603, Yaoundé; tel. 23-12-77; telex 8403; Dir AMADOU VAMOULKE.

CAMEROON

Société de Presse et d'Editions du Cameroun (SOPECAM): BP 1218, Yaoundé; tel. 23-40-12; telex 8311; f. 1978; under the supervision of the Ministry of Information and Culture; publr of the *Cameroon Tribune;* Editorial Dir PAUL CELESTIN NDEMBIYEMBE BAKOUME.

Radio and Television

In 1983 there were an estimated 820,000 radio receivers in use. In March 1985 a national television network, Cameroon Television (CTV), was inaugurated. In 1987 the two broadcasting companies, Radiodiffusion Nationale du Cameroun and CTV, were replaced by Cameroon Radio Television (CRTV). In early 1988 22 of the proposed 32 transmitters were in service, with the remainder scheduled to become fully operational by the end of the same year.

Cameroon Radio Television (CRTV): BP 281, Yaoundé; tel. 22-14-00; telex 8215; f. 1987 as a result of the merger of CTV and Radiodiffusion Nationale du Cameroun; broadcasts in French and English; Chair. IBRAHIM MBOMBO NJOYA; Gen. Man. GERVAIS MENDO ZE.

Radio Buéa: PMB, Buéa; tel. 32-25-25; programmes in English, French and 28 other local languages; Man. PETERSON CHIA YUH.

Radio Douala: BP 986, Douala; tel. 42-60-60; programmes in French, English, Douala, Bassa, Ewondo, Bakoko and Bamiléké; Dir BRUNO DJEM.

Radio Garoua: BP 103, Garoua; tel. 27-11-67; programmes in French, Hausa, English, Foulfouldé, Arabic and Choa; Dir BELLO MALGANA.

There are also provincial stations at Bertoua, Bafoussam, Maroua, Ebolowa, Ngaoundéré and Bamenda, and there is a local radio station serving Yaoundé.

Finance

(cap. = capital; res = reserves; dep. = deposits; m. = million; brs = branches; amounts in francs CFA)

BANKING

Central Bank

Banque des Etats de l'Afrique Centrale (BEAC): blvd du 20 mai, BP 1917, Yaoundé; tel. 22-25-05; telex 8343; f. 1973 as the central bank of issue for mem. states of the Customs and Economic Union of Central Africa (UDEAC), comprising Cameroon, the Central African Republic, Chad, the Congo, Equatorial Guinea and Gabon; 6 brs in Cameroon; cap. 24,000m., res 148,480m. (Dec. 1986); Gov. CASIMIR OYÉ MBA; Dir in Cameroon SIMON BASSILEKIN.

Commercial Banks

Bank of Credit and Commerce Cameroon SA (BCCC): Kennedy Bldg, ave John F. Kennedy, BP 1188, Yaoundé; tel. 22-29-86; telex 8558; f. 1981; 20% state-owned, 65% by BCCI Holdings (Luxembourg) SA; cap. 1,250m., dep. 75,494m. (1986); Pres. JEAN KANGA ZAMB; Man. Dir ENOW TANJONG; 4 brs.

Banque Internationale pour le Commerce et l'Industrie du Cameroun (BICIC—Cameroon): ave du Général de Gaulle, BP 4070, Douala; tel. 42-84-31; telex 5225; f. 1962; 39% state-owned, 13% by Barclays Bank UK, 11.5% by Banque Nationale de Paris; cap. 4,000m., res 3,044m., dep. 334,654m. (June 1985); Chair. RAYMOND MALOUMA; Gen. Man. EDOUARD AKAME MFOUMOU; 34 brs.

Banque Paribas Cameroun: 88 blvd de la Liberté, BP 1589, Douala; tel. 42-23-42; telex 5286; f. 1980; 40% owned by Paribas International; cap. 3,500m. (June 1987); br. in Yaoundé; Pres. MICHEL MEVA'A M'EBOUTOU; Dir-Gen. CHARLES TCHOMTCHOUA DJADJO.

Banque Unie de Crédit (BUC): Place Elig Essono, BP 122, Yaoundé; tel. 23-33-85; f. 1976; cap. 400m.; Pres. and Man. Dir GUSTAVE LELE.

BIAO—Cameroun: ave du Général de Gaulle, BP 4001, Douala; tel. 42-80-11; telex 5218; f. 1974; cap. 3,500m. (June 1987); 25% state-owned, 65% by Banque Internationale pour l'Afrique Occidentale (France); Pres. ABDOULAYE SOUAIBOU; Gen. Man. FRANÇOIS MPONDO MBONGUE; 42 brs.

Cameroon Bank SA: BP 1613, Yaoundé; tel. 22-25-84; telex 8342; f. 1974; cap. 705m. (June 1986); 43% owned by Caisse Nationale des Hydrocarbures, 28% by Société Nationale d'Investissement; Chair. THÉODORE EYEFFA; Gen. Man. (vacant); 11 brs.

International Bank of Africa Cameroon SA: blvd de la Liberté, BP 3300, Douala; tel. 42-84-22; telex 5734; f. 1982; 35% state-owned; cap. 3,000m.; took over activities of Bank of America Cameroon SA; Pres. THOMAS EBONGALAME; Gen. Man. PAUL J. ROELS.

Meridien Bank Cameroon SA: 83 blvd de la Liberté, BP 1132, Douala; tel. 42-98-05; telex 5580; f. 1988; cap. 1,000m.; 25% state-owned, 65% owned by Meridien International Bank (Zambia); took over activities of Chase Manhattan Overseas Banking Corpn; Pres. DAVID T. ATOGHO; Gen. Man. EMMANUEL EDING; br. in Yaoundé.

Société Camerounaise de Banque (SCB): rue Monseigneur Vogt, BP 145, Yaoundé; tel. 23-40-05; telex 8213; f. 1961; 49.4% state-owned, 25% Crédit Lyonnais (France), 16% Banque Camerounaise de Développement (BCD); cap. 5,000m. (June 1986); Pres. AHMADOU HAYATOU; Gen. Man. DANIEL POTOUONJOU TAPONJIE; 43 brs.

Société Générale de Banques au Cameroun (SGBC): 7 rue Joss, BP 4042, Douala; tel. 42-70-10; telex 5579; f. 1963; cap. 3,000m., res 5,414m., dep. 164,942m. (June 1984); 30% state-owned, 15% by BCD, 37.8% by Société Générale (France); Pres. AMADOU MOULIOM NJIFENJOU; Gen. Man. GASTON NGUENTI; 29 brs.

Standard Chartered Bank Cameroon SA: 57 blvd de la Liberté, BP 1784, Douala; tel. 42-36-12; telex 5858; f. 1981; br. in Yaoundé; cap. 1,000m. (June 1987); 66% owned by Standard Chartered Bank; Chair. HERMAN MISSE; Gen. Man. JOHN B. DOWLING.

Development Banks

Banque Camerounaise de Développement: rue du Mfoundi, BP 55, Yaoundé; tel. 22-09-11; telex 8225; f. 1960; 82% state-owned, 10% by Caisse centrale de coopération économique (see below), 8% by BEAC; provides financial and technical assistance to development projects; cap. 6,000m. (June 1985); Chair. OUSMANE MEY; Man. Dir VALÈRE ABANDA METOGO.

Crédit Agricole du Cameroun: Yaoundé; f. 1987; cap. 4,000m. francs CFA; agricultural development bank.

Crédit Foncier du Cameroun (CFC): BP 1531, Yaoundé; tel. 22-03-73; telex 8368; f. 1977; 70% state-owned; cap. 6,000m. (June 1986); provides financial assistance for social welfare and environment; Chair. EDOUARD AKAME MFOUMOU; Man. Dir JEAN PIERRE MONCEAU.

Crédit Industriel et Commercial: Yaoundé; f. 1987; industrial development bank.

Société Nationale d'Investissement du Cameroun (SNI): Place de la Poste, BP 423, Yaoundé; tel. 22-44-22; telex 8205; f. 1964; state-owned; cap. 7,000m. (June 1986); Chair. VICTOR AYISSI MVODO; Man. Dir SIMON NGANN YONN.

INSURANCE

Assurances Mutuelles Agricoles du Cameroun (AMACAM): BP 962, Yaoundé; tel. 22-49-66; telex 8300; f. 1965; cap. 100m.; Pres. JÉRÉMIE OBAM MFOU'OU; Man. Dir RAYMOND EKOUMOU.

Caisse Nationale de Réassurances SA (CNR): ave Foch, BP 4180, Yaoundé; tel. 22-37-99; telex 8262; f. 1965; cap. 1,000m.; Man. Dir (vacant); Asst Man. Dir JOACHIM FOUNGTCHO.

Compagnie Camerounaise d'Assurances et de Réassurances (CCAR): rue Franqueville, BP 4068, Douala; tel. 42-62-71; telex 5341; f. 1974; cap. 499.5m.; Pres. YVETTE CHASSAGNE; Dir FABIEN ATANGANA.

Compagnie Nationale d'Assurances (CNA): BP 12125, Douala; tel. 42-44-46; telex 5100; f. 1986; cap. 600m.; Chair. THÉODORE EBOBO; Man. Dir. PROTAIS AYANGMA AMANG.

Guardian Royal Exchange Assurance (Cameroun) Ltd (GREACAM): 56 blvd de la Liberté, BP 426, Douala; tel. 43-53-65; telex 5690; cap. 300m.; Pres. A. V. CADDICK; Man. Dir M. E. FARRAR-HOCKLEY.

Société Camerounaise d'Assurances (SOCAR): 86 blvd de la Liberté, BP 280, Douala; tel. 42-08-38; telex 5504; f. 1973; cap. 800m.; Chair. JEAN NKUETE; Man. Dir PAUL TSALA.

Société Nouvelle d'Assurances du Cameroun (SNAC): rue Manga Bell, BP 105, Douala; tel. 42-92-03; telex 5745; f. 1974; all forms of insurance; cap. 700m.; Man. Dir JEAN-CHARLES SUZEAU.

Trade and Industry

ADVISORY BODY

Economic and Social Council: BP 1058, Yaoundé; tel. 22-25-97; telex 8275; state body which advises the govt on economic and social problems; comprises 85 mems, who meet several times a year, a permanent secretariat and a president; mems are nominated for a five-year term, while the secretariat is elected annually; Pres. LUC AYANG; Sec.-Gen. Dr JOSEPH SIMON EPALE.

PRINCIPAL DEVELOPMENT ORGANIZATIONS

Caisse Centrale de Coopération Economique (CCCE) (France): BP 46, Yaoundé; tel. 22-23-24; telex 8301; Dir JACQUES CHARPENTIER.

CAMEROON

Cameroon Development Corporation (CAMDEV): Bota, Limbe; tel. 33-22-51; telex 5242; f. 1947, reorg. 1982; cap. 12,242m. francs CFA; 91.7% state-owned; a statutory agricultural enterprise established to acquire and develop plantations of tropical crops, fmrly in German ownership; operates in four of 10 provinces, and is the second largest employer of labour; planted area 40,000 ha out of 98,000 ha on lease from govt; operates two oil mills, three banana packing stations, three tea and four rubber factories; a smallholders' programme is in hand; Chair. SAMUEL MOKA LIFAFA ENDELEY; Gen. Man. PETER MAFANY MUSONGE.

Centre National d'Assistance aux Petites et Moyennes Entreprises (CAPME): BP 1377, Douala; tel. 42-58-58; telex 5590; f. 1970 by Cameroon govt and UNDP; development centre for small and medium-sized businesses; advises on industrial techniques and training and undertakes market research; Dir M. BOUBA ARDO.

Centre National du Commerce Extérieur (CNCE): 1er étage, Immeuble ONCPB, BP 2461, Douala; tel. 42-16-79; telex 5585; research into new and existing markets, commercial and economic information, and training programmes for the export market; Dir LOUIS WANSEK.

Hévéa-Cameroun (HEVECAM): BP 1298, Douala and BP 174, Kribi; tel. 42-75-64; telex 5880; f. 1975; cap. 16,518m. francs CFA; state-owned; development of 15,000 ha rubber plantation; 2,900 employees; Pres. LUC LOE; Man. Dir JEAN REMY.

Mission d'Aménagement et d'Equipement des Terrains Urbains et Ruraux (MAETUR): BP 1248, Yaoundé; tel. 22-31-13; telex 5725; f. 1977; Pres. F. OYONO; Dir JEAN-PIERRE SAVARY.

Mission de Développement des Cultures Vivrières (MIDEVIV): BP 1682, Yaoundé; tel. 22-38-29; f. 1973; development and improvement of seeds and planting materials; production and distribution of foodstuffs for urban centres; Pres. MAXIALE MAHI; Dir JEAN-BERNARD ABONG.

Mission Française de Coopération: BP 1616, Yaoundé; tel. 22-44-43; telex 8392; administers bilateral aid from France; Dir GEORGES MARTRES.

Mission de Développement de la Province du Nord-Ouest (MIDENO): BP 442, Bamenda.

Office Céréalier dans la Province du Nord: BP 298, Garoua; tel. 27-14-38; f. 1975; combating effects of drought in northern Cameroon and stabilization of cereal prices; Pres. FON FOSSI YAKUM TAW; Dir-Gen. Dr RUBEN MBON.

Office National de Commercialisation des Produits de Base (ONCPB): BP 378, Douala; tel. 42-67-76; telex 5260; f. 1978 to replace the Caisse de stabilisation des prix and the Cocoa Marketing Board; has monopoly of marketing cocoa, coffee, cotton, groundnuts and palm kernels; is responsible for the internal prices for the planters, the quality of the produce and development of production; holds 22% share in CAMDEV; Pres. LUC AYANG; Man. Dir ROGER MELINGUI.

Société de Développement de la Culture et la Transformation du Blé (SODEBLE): BP 41, Ngaoundéré; tel. 25-10-05; telex 7642; f. 1975; cap. 4,500m. francs CFA; development of wheat-growing and flour-milling in the Adamaoua region; Man. Dir MARTIN KOUEBO.

Société de Développement du Cacao (SODECAO): BP 1651, Yaoundé; tel. 22-09-91; telex 8574; f. 1974, reorganized 1980; cap. 425m. francs CFA; development of cocoa, coffee and food crop production in the Centre-Sud province; Dir-Gen. FÉLIX TONYE MBOG.

Société de Développement de l'Elevage (SODEVA): BP 50, Kousseri; cap. 50m. francs CFA; Dir Alhadji OUMAROU BAKARY.

Société de Développement et d'Exploitation des Productions Animales (SODEPA): BP 1410, Yaoundé; tel. 22-24-28; f. 1974; cap. 375m. francs CFA; development of livestock and livestock products; Man. Dir ETIENNE ENGUELEGUELE.

Société de Développement de la Haute-Vallée du Noun (UNVDA): BP 25, N'Dop and BP 43, Bamenda; f. 1978; cap. 895m. francs CFA; rice cultivation; Dir-Gen. G. A. NIBA.

Société de Développement du Nkam (SODENKAM): BP 02, Nkondjock, Yambassi-Bafang; f. 1970; cap. 136m. francs CFA; development of northern area by improving infrastructure and increasing production; marketing of agricultural products; Man. Dir ROBERT NKA MBOCK.

Société de Développement de la Riziculture dans la Plaine des Mbo (SODERIM): BP 146, Melong; f. 1977; cap. 1,535m. francs CFA; expansion of rice-growing and processing; Pres. S. ETAME; Man. Dir JOSEPH-JACQUES NGA.

Société d'Expansion et de Modernisation de la Riziculture de Yagoua (SEMRY): BP 46, Yagoua; tel. 29-62-03; telex 7655; f. 1971; cap. 4,580m. francs CFA; expansion of rice-growing in areas where irrigation is possible and commercialization of rice products; Pres. ALBERT EKONO NNA; Dir-Gen. TORI LIMANGANA.

Société Immobilière du Cameroun (SIC): BP 387, Yaoundé; tel. 23-34-11; telex 8577; f. 1952; cap. 1,000m. francs CFA; housing construction and development; Pres. GABRIEL LOUIS DJEUDJANG; Man. Dir JEAN-PAUL DSAURET.

CHAMBERS OF COMMERCE

Chambre d'Agriculture, d'Elevage et des Forêts du Cameroun: Parc Repiquet, BP 287, Yaoundé; tel. 22-38-85; telex 8243; BP 400, Douala; other delegations at Yaoundé, Bafoussam, Bamenda and Garoua; 44 mems; Pres. RENÉ GOBE; Sec.-Gen. ABEL MOUEN MAKOUA.

Chambre de Commerce, d'Industrie et des Mines du Cameroun: BP 4011, Douala; tel. 42-28-88; telex 5616; f. 1963; branches: BP 12206, Douala; BP 36, Yaoundé; BP 211, Limbe; BP 59, Garoua; BP 944, Bafoussam; BP 551, Bamenda; 138 mems; Pres. PIERRE TCHANQUÉ; Sec.-Gen. SAMUEL BATEKI.

EMPLOYERS' ASSOCIATIONS

Groupement des Femmes d'Affaires du Cameroun (GFAC): BP 1940, Douala; tel. 42-4-64; telex 6100; Pres. FRANÇOISE FONING.

Groupement Interprofessionnel pour l'Etude et la Co-ordination des Intérêts Economiques au Cameroun (GICAM): ave Konrad Adenauer, BP 1134, Yaoundé; tel. 22-27-22; also at BP 829, Douala; tel. 42-31-41; f. 1957; Acting Pres. PAUL SOPPO-PRISO.

Syndicat Professionnel des Entreprises du Bâtiment, des Travaux Publics et des Activités Annexes: BP 1134, Yaoundé; br. at BP 660, Douala; telex 8286; Pres. PAUL SOPPO-PRISO.

Syndicat des Commerçants Importateurs-Exportateurs du Cameroun (SCIEC): 16 rue Quillien, BP 562, Douala; tel. 42-60-04; Sec.-Gen. G. TOSCANO.

Syndicat des Industriels du Cameroun (SYNINDUSTRICAM): BP 673, Douala; tel. 42-30-58; telex 5342; f. 1953; Pres. SAMUEL KONDO EBELLE; Sec.-Gen. Mme NSOMO.

Syndicat des Producteurs et Exportateurs de Bois du Cameroun: BP 570, Yaoundé; tel. 22-27-22; telex 8286; Pres. SAMUEL DUCLAIR FANDJO.

Syndicat des Transporteurs Routiers du Cameroun: BP 834, Douala; tel. 42-55-21.

Syndicats Professionnels Forestiers et Activités connexes du Cameroun: BP 100, Douala.

Union des Syndicats Professionnels du Cameroun (USPC): BP 829, Douala; Pres. MOUKOKO KINGUE.

West Cameroon Employers' Association (WCEA): BP 97, Tiko.

PRINCIPAL CO-OPERATIVE ORGANIZATIONS

Bakweri Co-operative Union of Farmers Ltd: Dibanda, Tiko; produce marketing co-operative for bananas, cocoa and coffee; 14 societies, 2,000 mems; Pres. Dr E. M. L. ENDELEY.

Cameroon Co-operative Exporters Ltd: BP 19, Kumba; f. 1953; mems: 8 socs; central agency for marketing of mems' coffee, cocoa and palm kernels; Man. A. B. ENYONG; Sec. M. M. EYOH (acting).

Centre National de Développement des Entreprises Coopératives (CENADEC): BP 120, Yaoundé; f. 1970; promotes and organizes the co-operative movement; bureaux at BP 43, Kumba and BP 26, Bamenda; Dir XAVIER ONAMBELE ETOUNDI.

North-West Co-operative Association Ltd (NWCA): BP 41, Bamenda; tel. 36-12-12; telex 5842; Pres. MARTIN CHI AKUMA; Gen. Man. POLYCARP NDIBOTI NGWAYI.

Union Centrale des Coopératives Agricoles de l'Ouest (UCCAO): ave Samuel Wonko, BP 1002, Bafoussam; tel. 44-14-39; telex 7005; f. 1959; 85,000 mems; Pres. ETIENNE POUPONG; Man. Dir HENRI FANKAM.

West Cameroon Co-operative Association Ltd: BP 135, Kumba; founded as central financing body of the co-operative movement; provides short-term credits and agricultural services to mem. socs; policy-making body for the co-operative movement in West Cameroon; 142 mem. unions and socs with total membership of c. 45,000; Pres. Chief T. E. NJEA; Sec. M. M. QUAN.

There are 83 co-operatives for the harvesting and sale of bananas and coffee and for providing mutual credit.

TRADE UNIONS

National Union of Private Journalists (NUPJ): Yaoundé; f. 1984; Pres. DOMINIQUE SIMI FOUDA; Vice-Pres. PADDY TAMBE JOHN, DAVID ACHIDI NDIFANG.

Organisation des Syndicats des Travailleurs Camerounais/Organization of Cameroon Workers' Unions (OSTC): BP 1610, Yaoundé; tel. 23-00-47; f. 1985; formerly the Union National des Travailleurs du Cameroun (UNTC); Pres. DOMINIQUE FOUDA IMAH.

Transport

RAILWAYS

There are some 1,370 km of track, the West Line running from Douala to Nkongsamba (172 km) with a branch line leading southwest from Mbanga to Kumba (29 km), and the Transcameroon railway which runs from Douala to Ngaoundéré (930 km), with a branch line from Ngoumou to Mbalmayo (30 km). The section from Yaoundé to Ngaoundéré (622 km) was opened in 1974. An extension of its western branch is projected from Mbalmayo to Bangui, in the Central African Republic. Improvements to the line between Douala and Yaoundé were begun in 1974; those on the section between Yaoundé and Maloumé were completed in April 1978, and those between Douala and Edéa in 1981. Improvements to the section between Edéa and Eseka, which cut the 90 km line to 82 km, were completed in 1982. The final section, between Eseka and Maloumé, was inaugurated in May 1987.

Régie Nationale des Chemins de Fer du Cameroun (REGIFERCAM): BP 304, Douala; tel. 42-60-45; telex 5607; f. 1947; Chair. SAMUEL EBOUA; Man. Dir SAMUEL MINKO.

Office du Chemin de Fer Transcamerounais: BP 625, Yaoundé; tel. 22-44-33; telex 8293; supervises the laying of new railway lines and improvements to existing lines, and undertakes relevant research; Gen. Man. LUC TOWA FOTSO.

ROADS

At 30 June 1987 there were 52,214 km of roads, including 7,548 km of main roads and 13,666 km of secondary roads. A fast metalled road between Douala and Yaoundé was opened in August 1985. The 1986-91 Plan envisaged the construction of a further 3,000 km of tarred roads. However, improvements to Cameroon's road network, including the rehabilitation of the roads from Edéa to Kribi and from Mbalmayo to Ebolowa, as well as the construction of the Bamenda 'ring road', were likely to be delayed, following the announcement, in 1988, of a reduction in planned public expenditure.

SHIPPING

There are two sea ports at Kribi and Limbe/Tiko, a river port at Garoua, and an estuary port at Douala-Bonabéri, the largest port and main outlet. It has 2,510 m of quays and a minimum depth of 5.8 m in the channels, 8.5 m at the quays. In 1986 the port of Douala handled 4,348,906 metric tons of international goods. Extensions and modernizations to the port were completed in January 1980, and a storage zone for the use of land-locked central African countries has been constructed. Handling capacity increased to 7m. metric tons per year. Plans are under way to increase the annual capacity of the container terminal from 1.5m. tons to 2m. tons. Facilities for ship-repair have also been provided, and there is a logistic area for oil research facilities.

Office National des Ports/National Ports Authority: 5 blvd Leclerc, BP 4020, Douala; tel. 42-01-33; telex 5270; cap. 12,040m. francs CFA; Chair. ANDRÉ-BOSCO CHEUOUA; Gen. Man. SIEGFRIED DIBONG.

CAMATRANS (Delmas-Vieljeux Cameroun): rue Kitchener, BP 263, Douala; tel. 42-10-36; telex 5222; f. 1977; cap. 1,000m. francs CFA; Pres. PATRICE VIELJEUX; Dir (vacant).

Cameroon Shipping Lines SA (CAMSHIPLINES): BP 4054, Douala; tel. 42-00-38; telex 5615; f. 1975; cap. 4,365m. francs CFA; 67% state-owned; 6 vessels trading with western Europe, USA, Far East and Africa; Chair. FRANÇOIS SENGAT KUO; Man. Dir RENÉ MBAYEN.

Conseil National des Chargeurs du Cameroun (CNCC): BP 1588, Douala; tel. 42-32-06; telex 5669; f. 1986; cap. 800m. francs CFA; promotion of the maritime sector; Gen. Man. GUSTAVE TCHETGEN.

Fako Transport Shipping Lines (FTSC): Douala; f. 1985; joint-venture with USA.

Société Africaine de Transit et d'Affrètement (SATA): Vallée Tokoto, BP 546, Douala; tel. 42-82-09; telex 5239; f. 1950; cap. 625m. francs CFA; Man. Dir RAYMOND PARIZOT.

Société Agence Maritime de l'Ouest Africain Cameroun (SAMOA): place du Gouvernement, BP 1127, Douala; tel. 42-16-80; telex 5256; f. 1953; agents for Lloyd Triestino, Armada Shipping, Black Star Line, Gold Star Line, Nigerian Star Line, OT Africa Line, Spliethoff, Jeco Shipping, Van Uden; Dir PAUL STEFANI.

Société Camerounaise de Manutention et d'Acconage (SOCAMAC): BP 284, Douala; tel. 42-40-51; telex 5537; f. 1976; freight handling; Pres. MOHAMADOU TALBA; Dir-Gen. KLAUS HAYOBAUMANN.

Société Camerounaise de Transport et d'Affrètement (SCTA): BP 974, Douala; tel. 42-17-24; telex 6181; f. 1951; cap. 100m. francs CFA; Pres. JACQUES VIAULT; Dir-Gen. GONTRAN FRAUCIEL.

Société Ouest-Africaine d'Enterprises Maritimes Cameroun—SOAEM: blvd de la Liberté, BP 320, Douala; tel. 42-02-88; f. 1959; cap. 708m. francs CFA; Pres. RÉNÉ KOLOWSKI; Man. Dir JEAN-LOUIS GRECIET.

SOCOPAO (Cameroun): BP 215, Douala; tel. 42-64-64; telex 5252; f. 1951; cap. 1,440m. francs CFA; agents for Palm/Elder/Hoegh Lines, Bank Line, CNAN, CNN, Comanav, Comasersa, Dafra Line, Grand Pale, Marasia SA, Maritima del Norte, Navcoma, Nigerian Shipping Line, Niven Line, Splosna Plovba, Rossis Maritime, SSSIM, Veb Deutsche Seereederei, Polish Ocean Lines, Westwind Africa Line, Nautilus Keller Line, Estonian Shipping Co, AGTI Paris, K-Line Tokyo; Man. Dir MARC LANCREY.

Transcap Cameroun: BP 4059, Douala; tel. 42-72-14; telex 5247; f. 1960; cap. 342m. francs CFA; Pres. RÉNÉ DUPRAZ; Man. Dir MICHEL BARDOU.

CIVIL AVIATION

There are international airports at Douala and Garoua. Construction of a further international airport, at Yaoundé, began in 1988. An international airport at Bafoussam is also under construction. There are 39 smaller airports and aerodromes.

Cameroon Airlines (Cam-Air): 3 ave du Général de Gaulle, BP 4092, Douala; tel. 42-25-25; telex 5345; f. 1971; 75% govt-owned and 25% by Air France; services to Benin, Burundi, CAR, Congo, Côte d'Ivoire, Equatorial Guinea, France, Gabon, the Federal Republic of Germany, Italy, Kenya, Nigeria, Rwanda, Switzerland, the United Kingdom and Zaire and domestic flights; fleet of 3 Boeing 737, 1 Boeing 707-Combi, 1 Boeing 747-200-B and 2 Hawker Siddeley 748; Chair. ANDRÉ-BOSCO CHEUOUA; Gen. Man. YOUSSOUFA DAOUDA.

Tourism

Tourists are attracted by the cultural diversity of local customs, and by the national parks, game reserves and sandy beaches. The tourist trade is being expanded, and in 1985 there were 115,203 foreign visitors. The 1986/87 budget allotted 1,544m. francs CFA to tourism.

Secrétariat d'Etat au Tourisme: Yaoundé; tel. 22-44-11; telex 8318; f. 1960; provincial offices in Douala, Buéa, Bamenda, Ngaoundéré, Maroua, Garoua, Bafoussam, Kribi, Bertoua; Sec. of State Dr ABDOULAYE SOUAIBOU.

Société Camerounaise de Tourisme (SOCATOUR): BP 7138, Yaoundé; tel. 23-32-19; telex 8766; f. 1985; cap. 550m. francs CFA; state-owned; brs at Douala and Maroua; Pres. Bd of Admin. Dr ABDOULAYE SOUAIBOU; Gen. Man. MARC CHO NKWENTI.

CANADA

Introductory Survey

Location, Climate, Language, Religion, Flag, Capital
Canada occupies the northern part of North America (excluding Alaska and Greenland) and is the second largest country in the world, after the USSR. It extends from the Atlantic Ocean to the Pacific. Except for the boundary with Alaska in the north-west, Canada's frontier with the USA follows the upper St Lawrence Seaway and the Great Lakes, continuing west along latitude 49°N. The climate is an extreme one, particularly inland. Winter temperatures drop well below freezing but summers are generally hot. Rainfall varies from moderate to light and there are heavy falls of snow. The two official languages are English and French, the mother tongues of 62.7% and 25.4%, respectively, at the general census in 1986. More than 98% of Canadians can speak English or French. About 45% of the population are Roman Catholics. The main Protestant churches are the United Church of Canada and the Anglican Church of Canada. Numerous other religious denominations are represented. The national flag (proportions 2 by 1) consists of a red maple leaf on a white field, flanked by red panels. The capital is Ottawa.

Recent History
The Liberals, led by Pierre Trudeau, were returned to office at general elections in 1968, 1972, 1974, and again in 1980 after a short-lived minority Progressive Conservative (PC) administration. Foreign relations altered significantly under the Liberals, with less emphasis on traditional links with Western Europe and the USA, and a fostering of relations with the Far East, Africa and Latin America.

In 1975 Canada began to experience the effects of international economic recession. This led to a steady erosion of the Government's popularity, which finally resulted in the Liberals' defeat at general elections held in May 1979, although the PC administration, led by Joe Clark, lacked an overall majority. In November, Trudeau announced that he was resigning as Liberal leader, but in the following month the Government was defeated on its budget proposals. Trudeau postponed his retirement, and at general elections in February 1980 the Liberals were returned with a strong majority. Popular support for the new Government, however, fell rapidly with the persistence of adverse economic conditions, while the PC party gained substantially in popularity under the leadership of Brian Mulroney, a Québec labour lawyer and businessman with no previous political experience, who replaced Clark in June 1983.

With the Liberals' popular standing at a post-war low, Trudeau, who had earlier indicated that he would vacate the party leadership before the general elections due in 1985, resigned in June 1984 and was succeeded as Liberal leader and Prime Minister by John Turner, a former Minister of Finance. Nine days after taking office, Turner called general elections for September. The Liberals entered the pre-election period with revived popular support, but criticism of Turner's exercise of political patronage and of his general conduct of the election campaign saw the Liberals' following recede. Mulroney, an able bilingual public speaker, led the PC party to the largest electoral majority in Canadian history.

During 1986, however, the resignations in discordant circumstances of five cabinet ministers, together with the persistence of high rates of unemployment, particularly in Québec and the Atlantic Maritime Provinces, led to a diminution in the Government's popular support. Further cabinet changes were carried out in 1987 in an effort to retrieve the Government's waning popularity, which continued, none the less, to decline amid further ministerial resignations, a controversial incident concerning the operations of the Canadian Security Intelligence Service, and criticism by the Liberals and the New Democratic Party (NDP) of the Government's approach to relations with the USA, as evidenced in the terms of a new US-Canadian trade treaty (see Economic Affairs), which the Liberals and the NDP viewed as overly advantageous to US business interests and potentially damaging to Canada's national identity. Increased public discontent with Mulroney's conduct of government and with his exercise of political patronage was reflected in the loss of two seats to the NDP at federal by-elections held in July, and in decisive Liberal victories at provincial general elections in Ontario and New Brunswick.

Controversy over the proposed US-Canadian trade agreement gained momentum during the early months of 1988, amid further cabinet resignations and a sharp decline in the popularity of the PC administration. The prospect of an early general election, centring on the free trade issue, was raised in May when the Liberals and the NDP declared that, while not opposed in principle to trade liberalization, they would abandon the Mulroney accord if either party were to form a government following federal elections. In July the Federal Senate, an appointive body with a Liberal majority, indicated that it would postpone voting on the ratification of the trade agreement until after the next general election. The legislation was, however, approved in the following month by the House of Commons. In September Mulroney carried out an extensive reconstruction of the Cabinet, and in October, following indications that the PC proposals were gaining public support in the free trade debate, he called a general election for November. The PC party was re-elected, although with a reduced majority, and Senate approval of the trade agreement followed in December. Many Canadians, however, continued to express disquiet at the longer-term implications of the treaty for Canada's continued political and cultural autonomy.

Since first taking office, Prime Minister Mulroney has sought to re-establish Canada's traditional 'special relationship' with the USA, which had operated until the Trudeau period. During 1985 Canadian foreign policy moved broadly into line with that of President Reagan's administration in the USA, with the Mulroney government reinforcing its commitment to NATO defence and agreeing to the modernization of the US military radar network in northern Canada. However, Mulroney has criticized the controversial US programme of space-based defence research, the Strategic Defense Initiative (SDI).

Little progress has been made in realizing Canada's wish to secure effective US government control of the emission of gases from industrial plants, which move northwards into Canada to produce environmentally destructive 'acid rain'. In April 1985 President Reagan agreed to the formation of a joint governmental commission to examine this problem. In 1986 the commission recommended the implementation of a US $5,000m. anti-pollution programme, to be financed jointly by the US Government and the relevant industries, although no specific arrangements were set out for funding. This matter was further pursued by Mulroney at a meeting held with the US President in April 1988. The Canadian Government, meanwhile, has committed itself to the reduction by 50% of acid-pollution emissions from domestic sources by 1990.

Relations between the USA and Canada came under strain in August and September 1985, when a US coastguard ice-breaker traversed the Northwest Passage without seeking prior permission from Canada, in assertion of long-standing US claims that the channels within this 1.6m. sq km tract of ice-bound islands are international waters. The Canadian Government declared sovereignty of this area as from 1 January 1986, and in January 1988 the USA recognized Canadian jurisdiction over the Arctic islands (but not over their waters) and undertook to notify the Canadian Government in advance of all Arctic passages by US surface vessels. Canada has also pursued a disagreement with France concerning the boundary of disputed waters near the French-controlled islands of St Pierre and Miquelon, off the coast of Newfoundland.

In Québec, where four-fifths of the population speak French as a first language and which maintains its own cultural identity, the question of provincial autonomy has long been a sensitive issue. At provincial elections in 1976 the separatist Parti Québécois (PQ), led by René Lévesque, came to power, and in 1977 made French the official language of education, business and government in Québec. Certain sections of this legislation were subsequently invalidated by the Supreme

CANADA

Court of Canada. During 1977 the PQ Government reiterated its aim of sovereignty for Québec; however in 1978 Lévesque denied that unilateral separation was contemplated and stated that a 'sovereignty-association', with a monetary and customs union, would be sought. At a Québec provincial referendum held in May 1980, these proposals were rejected by an electoral margin of 59.5% to 40.5%. The PQ was re-elected at provincial general elections held in April 1981, but lost seats in all subsequent by-elections. Lévesque resigned in October 1985, and at provincial general elections held in December the PQ was replaced as the governing party by the Liberals.

Constitutional reform has been an important issue in recent years. Between 1978 and 1980, a series of proposals was made by federal and provincial governments and various advisory bodies for the patriation of the Constitution, whereby the UK Parliament would transfer to Canada authority over all matters contained in British statutes relating to Canada, opening the way for the reform of central institutions and the redistribution of legislative powers between Parliament and the Provincial Legislatures.

Trudeau and the Provincial Premiers were unable to agree on reform proposals, mainly because of the wish of several of the provinces to retain full control of their natural resources. In October 1980 the Federal Government announced that it would proceed unilaterally with a constitutional reform plan incorporating patriation and a charter of rights which would be binding on all provinces. Eight of the 10 provinces challenged the plan in the Supreme Court of Canada, which ruled in September 1981 that, while the Federal Government was acting within its powers, further efforts should be made to obtain the provinces' agreement. Renewed talks between Trudeau and the provincial leaders finally resulted in all the provinces except Québec accepting compromise proposals which included a revised charter of rights and a new formula for constitutional amendments made after patriation, whereby such amendments would require the support of at least seven provinces representing more than 50% of the population. In December the plan was overwhelmingly approved by the Federal Parliament. It was adopted by the UK Parliament in March 1982 and formally took effect in April as the Constitution Act 1982. Québec, however, maintained its opposition to the reform and its legislature claimed the right to veto constitutional provisions.

Following the return to power in 1985 of the Liberals in Québec, the Federal PC Government adopted new initiatives to bring Québec into the constitutional accord. In April 1987 Mulroney and the Provincial Premiers met at Meech Lake, Québec, to negotiate a constitutional accommodation for Québec. The resultant agreement, the Meech Lake Accord, was finalized in June. It recognized Québec as a 'distinct society' within the Canadian federation, and granted each of the provinces important new powers in the areas of federal parliamentary reform, judicial appointments and the creation of new provinces. The Accord was endorsed by the Québec provincial legislature, and is subject to ratification within three years by the Federal Parliament and all provincial legislatures. By December 1988 the Federal Parliament and eight of the 10 provincial legislatures had approved the Accord. However, opposition to certain provisions of the Accord has been expressed by the PQ, by non-Québec francophone groups and by representatives of the Inuits of the Northwest Territories (NWT) and the Yukon.

The NWT, which form one-third of Canada's land mass but contain a population of only 52,000 (of which Inuit and Indians comprise about one-half), may eventually secure a new constitutional status. In November 1982 the Federal Government agreed in principle to implement the decision of a territorial referendum held in April, in which 56% of the voters approved a division of the NWT into two parts. In April 1985 the Federal Government stated that, subject to the eventual agreement of the Provincial Premiers and of Indian and Inuit organizations, it would incorporate into the Constitution the right to self-government of Canada's 500,000 indigenous peoples. Arrangements to divide the NWT into two self-governing units, Nunavut (to the east of a proposed boundary running northwards from the Saskatchewan-Manitoba border) and Denendeh (to the west), were approved by the NWT legislature in January 1987, subject to their eventual endorsement by a plebiscite among NWT residents, and approval by the Federal Government. In September 1988, following 13 years of negotiations, the Federal Government formally transferred to indigenous ownership an area covering 673,000 sq km in the NWT. Arrangements to transfer a further 352,000 sq km tract, which includes most of Canada's Arctic islands, were expected to proceed in 1989.

Government

Canada is a federal parliamentary state. Under the Constitution Act 1982, executive power is vested in the British monarch, as Head of State, and exercisable by her representative, the Governor-General, whom she appoints on the advice of the Canadian Prime Minister. The Federal Parliament comprises the Head of State, a nominated Senate (104 members, appointed on a regional basis) and a House of Commons (295 members elected by universal adult suffrage for single-member constituencies). A Parliament may last no longer than five years. The Governor-General appoints the Prime Minister and, on the latter's recommendation, other ministers to form the Cabinet. The Prime Minister should have the confidence of the House of Commons, to which the Cabinet is responsible. Canada comprises 10 provinces (each with a Lieutenant-Governor and a Legislature, which may last no longer than five years, from which a Premier is chosen), and two territories constituted by Act of Parliament.

Defence

Canada co-operates with the USA in the defence of North America and is a member of NATO. Military service is voluntary. In June 1988 the armed forces numbered 84,600: army 22,500, navy 10,000, air force 23,100 and 29,000 not identified by service. Defence expenditure for 1988/89 was estimated at C $11,090m. In 1987 the Government announced plans to modernize and expand the defence forces. Emphasis was to be placed on naval power, with the proposed acquisition, at an estimated cost of C $8,000m., of 10–12 nuclear submarines between 1996 and 2010.

Economic Affairs

In 1987, according to estimates by the World Bank, Canada's gross national product (GNP), measured at average 1985–87 prices, was US $390,052m., equivalent to US $15,080 per head. Between 1980 and 1987, it was estimated, GNP per head increased, in real terms, at an average rate of 1.9% per year. Canada is one of the world's leading trading nations. In 1987 it was the seventh largest exporter, with export trade valued at US $98,121m. and accounting for 4.2% of the US dollar value of world exports. It was also the world's seventh largest importer, accounting for 3.8% of global imports. The Canadian economy is closely linked with that of the USA, which accounted for 75.7% of total exports and 68.1% of total imports in 1987. Prior to a free trade agreement which came into force in January 1989, about 73% of Canadian exports entering the USA were duty-free, as were approximately 72.8% of US exports to Canada. Under the new arrangements, which had been under negotiation since 1985 and were ratified by both Governments in 1988, virtually all trade tariffs between the two countries are to be progressively eliminated over a 10-year period. Since the Trudeau period, successful efforts have been made to develop alternative markets, notably in Japan, the People's Republic of China and the EEC, and in 1987 about 30% of Canada's GNP was linked with foreign trade.

Many sectors of Canadian industry rely heavily on foreign investment. Foreign control of Canadian corporations reached its peak in the early 1970s; since then, mainly as a result of government and private-sector acquisitions, such control has steadily declined. In 1985 the share of total assets held by foreign-controlled corporations in the non-financial (mainly petroleum) industries declined by 0.8%, to 23.4%. Corporations classified as US-controlled accounted for 71.5% of these assets in 1988. This proportion is expected to increase with the implementation of the US-Canada trade agreement.

Since the early 1980s, however, Canadian external investment has also increased; whereas until the mid-1970s Canada was a net capital importer, since that time it has become a net exporter, largely as a result of massive outflows of investment capital to the USA. Over the period 1983–87, Canadian-owned investments in the USA increased by 70% to a total of C $43,300m. During the same period, US investment in Canada rose by 35% to C $75,200m.

Canada, one of the world's leading industrial countries, is also a major world exporter of agricultural products and, in terms of value, the world's leading fish and seafood exporter.

CANADA

Introductory Survey

The main exports in 1987 were motor vehicles and parts, newsprint paper, wheat, crude petroleum, lumber, natural gas, wood pulp and petroleum and coal products. Canada is the world's largest producer of zinc, and the second largest of asbestos, nickel, potash, uranium, gypsum, elemental sulphur, and titanium concentrates. The country is also rich in many other minerals, including gold, silver, iron, copper, cobalt and lead. There are considerable petroleum and natural gas resources in Alberta, off the Atlantic coast and in the Canadian Arctic islands. Although the development and profitability of this industry declined after the slump in world oil prices in 1981/82, development incentives (introduced by the Federal Government in 1985), combined with a subsequent recovery in oil prices, led to a revival in investment and production. In July 1980 construction was authorized of the initial section of the Alaska Highway Gas Pipeline, which will transport US gas from Alaska to join existing pipelines in British Columbia and Alberta for distribution in the USA and, at a later date, in Canada. The advancement of this project, which was originally due for completion in the late 1980s, has been inhibited by the recent weakness in the US market for natural gas, although Canada has remained a principal source of US energy supplies, accounting in 1987 for 6% of US natural gas requirements and 5% of its petroleum imports.

In 1975 Canada began to be affected by the international slump, and inflationary pressures contributed to its economic problems. Inflation reached 12.5% in 1981 before easing to 10.8% in 1982 and responding finally to anti-inflation measures, including high interest rates, by falling to 5.8% in 1983, to 4.4% in 1984 and to 4.0% in 1985. It has since risen marginally, to 4.2% in 1986 and 4.4% in 1987. A reduction to 3.8% was forecast for 1988.

Since the first quarter of 1983, when it began to emerge from the global recession, the Canadian economy has advanced strongly. For the period 1982–87, real output in Canada expanded more rapidly on a cumulative basis than in any other major OECD country. The unemployment rate, after reaching a 'high' of 11.9% in 1983, fell to 11.3% in 1984, 10.5% in 1985, 9.6% in 1986 and 8.9% in 1987. A further fall, to under 8.0%, was forecast for 1988. The overall budget deficit for 1987/88 was C $30,083m. In February 1988 the Government projected a 1988/89 deficit of C $28,945m.

Despite the imposition of tight monetary controls and high interest rates, the Canadian dollar exchange rate has depreciated steadily since January 1976, when it last stood at par with the US dollar. In March 1988, however, assisted by the favourable level of Canadian interest rates compared with those in the USA, the exchange rate moved sharply in favour of the Canadian dollar, which rose to a four-year 'high' in relation to the US dollar, although not against the Japanese yen and the major European currencies. Following further upward movements in the Canadian-US currencies' exchange rate in April and June, the Canadian dollar retained a generally buoyant tone for the remainder of 1988.

Canada's gross domestic product (GDP) grew by an average of 4.3% per year (at constant prices) between 1983 and 1987. In 1988, however, the effects on agricultural production of a severe drought were expected to restrict GDP growth to about 4.2%. A forecast fall in the rate of Canada's economic expansion was expected to limit the advance in GDP for 1989 to under 3.0%.

Social Welfare

Almost 45% of the 1988/89 federal budget was allocated to health and social welfare. The Federal Government administers family allowances, unemployment insurance and pensions. Other services are provided by the provinces. A federal medical care insurance programme covers all Canadians against medical expenses, and a federal-provincial hospital insurance programme covers over 99% of the insurable population.

Education

Education policy is a provincial responsibility, and the period of compulsory school attendance varies. French-speaking students are entitled by law, in some provinces, to instruction in French. Primary education is from the age of five or six years to 13–14, followed by three to five years at secondary or high school. In 1984 an estimated 97% of children aged six to 11 attended primary schools, while 92% of those aged 12 to 17 were enrolled at secondary schools. There are 66 universities and 197 other institutions of higher education.

Public Holidays

1989: 2 January (for New Year), 24 March (Good Friday), 27 March (Easter Monday), 22 May (Victoria Day), 1 July (Canada Day), 4 September (Labour Day), 9 October (Thanksgiving), 11 November (Remembrance Day), 25 December (Christmas Day), 26 December (Boxing Day).

1990: 1 January (New Year), 13 April (Good Friday), 16 April (Easter Monday), 21 May (Victoria Day), 2 July (Canada Day), 3 September (Labour Day), 8 October (Thanksgiving), 11 November (Remembrance Day), 25 December (Christmas Day), 26 December (Boxing Day).

Weights and Measures

The metric system is in general use, although the imperial system, with the exception of the 2,000 lb American ton, is still occasionally used in parallel.

CANADA

Statistical Survey

Source (unless otherwise stated): Statistics Canada, Ottawa K1A 0T6; tel. (613) 990-8116; telex 053-3585.

Area and Population

AREA, POPULATION AND DENSITY

Area (sq km)	
Land	9,215,430
Inland water	755,180
Total	9,970,610*
Population (census results)	
3 June 1981	24,343,180
3 June 1986†	
Males	12,485,650
Females	12,823,680
Total	25,309,330
Population (official estimates at 1 June)	
1985	25,165,400
1986	25,353,000
1987	25,625,100
Density (per sq km) at 1 June 1987	2.6

* 3,849,674 sq miles.
† Excluding census data for one or more incompletely enumerated Indian reserves or Indian settlements.

PROVINCES AND TERRITORIES
(census results, 3 June 1986)

	Land area (sq km)	Population*	Capital
Provinces:			
Alberta	644,390	2,365,825	Edmonton
British Columbia	929,730	2,883,367	Victoria
Manitoba	548,360	1,063,016	Winnipeg
New Brunswick	72,090	709,442	Fredericton
Newfoundland	371,690	568,349	St John's
Nova Scotia	52,840	873,176	Halifax
Ontario	891,190	9,101,694	Toronto
Prince Edward Island	5,660	126,646	Charlottetown
Québec	1,356,790	6,532,461	Québec
Saskatchewan	570,700	1,009,613	Regina
Territories:			
Northwest Territories	3,293,020	52,238	Yellowknife
Yukon Territory	478,970	23,504	Whitehorse
Total	9,215,430	25,309,331	—

* Excluding census data for one or more incompletely enumerated Indian reserves or Indian settlements.

PRINCIPAL TOWNS
(census results, 3 June 1986)*

Ottawa (capital)	819,263†	St Catharine's-Niagara	343,258
Toronto	3,427,168	London	342,302
Montréal	2,921,357	Kitchener	311,195
Vancouver	1,380,729	Halifax	295,990
Edmonton	785,465	Victoria	255,547
Calgary	671,326	Windsor	253,988
Winnipeg	625,304	Oshawa	203,543
Québec	603,267	Saskatoon	200,665
Hamilton	557,029		

* Including Canadian residents temporarily in the USA, but excluding US residents temporarily in Canada.
† Including Hull.

BIRTHS, MARRIAGES AND DEATHS

	Registered live births*		Registered marriages		Registered deaths*	
	Number	Rate (per 1,000)	Number	Rate (per 1,000)	Number	Rate (per 1,000)
1979	365,475	15.2	187,711	7.9	168,183	7.1
1980	369,709	15.5	191,069	8.0	171,473	7.2
1981	371,346	15.3	190,082	7.8	171,029	7.0
1982	373,082	15.1	188,360	7.6	174,413	7.1
1983	373,689	15.0	184,675	7.4	174,484	7.0
1984	377,031	15.0	185,597	7.4	175,727	7.0
1985	375,730	14.8	184,110	7.3	181,330	7.2
1986	372,913	14.7	175,518	6.9	184,224	7.3

* Including Canadian residents temporarily in the USA but excluding US residents temporarily in Canada.

IMMIGRATION

Country of Origin	1985	1986	1987*
United Kingdom	4,719	5,088	8,547
USA	6,669	7,275	7,967
Other	72,914	86,849	134,594
Total	84,302	99,212	152,098

* Estimates.

ECONOMICALLY ACTIVE POPULATION*
('000 persons aged 15 years and over)

	1985	1986	1987
Agriculture	488	484	475
Forestry, fishing and trapping	112	106	108
Mines, quarries and oil wells	191	185	182
Manufacturing	1,981	2,015	2,044
Construction	587	627	680
Electricity, gas and water	124	121	120
Transport and communications	760	777	785
Trade	2,001	2,082	2,116
Finance, insurance and real estate	629	654	695
Public administration	802	800	814
Other services	3,648	3,783	3,934
Total employed	11,311	11,634†	11,955‡
Unemployed	1,328	1,236	1,167
Total labour force	12,639	12,870	13,121

* Figures exclude military personnel, inmates of institutions, residents of the Yukon and Northwest Territories, and Indian reserves.
† Comprising (in '000): Males 6,657; Females 4,977.
‡ Comprising (in '000): Males 6,793; Females 5,161.

CANADA   *Statistical Survey*

Agriculture

PRINCIPAL CROPS ('000 metric tons)

	1985	1986	1987
Wheat	24,252.3	31,377.9	26,342.1
Oats	2,997.1	3,251.1	2,995.2
Barley	12,443.3	14,633.6	14,382.1
Rye	598.0	609.0	492.6
Maize (Corn)	7,472.4	5,911.5	7,007.5
Buckwheat	24.7	38.6	44.1
Soybeans	1,048.0	960.0	1,266.5
Linseed	901.9	1,026.3	787.6
Rapeseed (Canola)	3,507.8	3,786.5	3,851.5
Potatoes	3,027.2	2,761.3	2,972.9
Beans	58.5	41.8	115.7
Tame hay	23,787.8	30,204.3	30,840.0

LIVESTOCK ('000 head at 1 July)

	1986	1987	1988
Milch cows	1,444	1,423	1,437
Other cattle	10,333	10,327	10,624
Sheep	694	701	679
Pigs	9,885	10,493	10,847

DAIRY PRODUCE

	1985	1986	1987
Milk (kilolitres)*	7,262,761	7,305,085	7,364,952
Creamery butter (metric tons)	94,882	98,693	95,595
Cheddar cheese (metric tons)	109,532	111,597	115,561
Ice-cream mix (kilolitres)	159,901	166,249	164,370
Eggs ('000 dozen)	472,152	472,262	475,468

* Farm sales of milk and cream.

Forestry

LUMBER PRODUCTION, 1985 (cubic metres)

	Softwoods	Hardwoods	Total
Newfoundland	34,931	12,332	47,263
Prince Edward Island	11,070	—	11,070
Nova Scotia	337,780	48,566	426,346
New Brunswick	1,243,950	59,557	1,303,507
Québec	9,482,289	37,642	9,919,931
Ontario	4,501,590	444,770	4,946,360
Manitoba	163,310	4,085	167,395
Saskatchewan	481,537	—	481,537
Alberta	2,686,676	—	2,686,676
British Columbia	32,115,846	3,356	32,119,202
Total	51,098,979	1,010,308	52,109,287

Fur Industry

NUMBER OF PELTS PRODUCED*

	1984/85	1985/86	1986/87
Newfoundland	34,982	37,840	42,022†
Prince Edward Island	36,174	41,319	42,745
Nova Scotia	306,154	323,106	345,689†
New Brunswick	79,911	85,441	85,877
Québec	722,362	774,919	687,739
Ontario	1,431,659	1,443,028	1,555,869
Manitoba	356,047	289,938	409,789
Saskatchewan	310,217	331,798	412,283
Alberta	390,395	393,321	544,377
British Columbia	329,744	286,565	330,945
Northwest Territories‡	163,176	137,008	178,071
Yukon	27,018	20,910	26,265
Total	4,170,370	4,165,193§	4,661,945§

* Including ranch-raised.
† Lynx are excluded for Nova Scotia but included in Newfoundland total in 1986/87.
‡ Seals are excluded for the Northwest Territories but included in the Canada total.
§ Hair seal are not included in the totals for 1985/86 and 1986/87.

Sea Fisheries

LANDINGS (metric tons, live weight)

	1985	1986*	1987*
Atlantic total	1,188,496	1,245,280	1,265,913
Cod	480,465	474,720	458,051
Crab	44,246	42,830	28,798
Small flatfishes	99,113	89,300	90,629
Haddock	37,095	44,720	28,071
Halibut	3,926	3,700	2,417
Pollock	44,832	49,680	50,223
Redfish	71,388	79,670	79,016
Herring	193,401	186,730	248,744
Salmon	957	1,320	1,541
Lobsters	32,639	38,030	39,431
Scallops	47,208	57,000	73,813
Tuna	129	90	222
Pacific total	209,634	220,260	262,690
Halibut	4,703	5,389	5,000
Herring	25,955	16,341	37,360
Salmon	104,014	100,241	66,060
Canada total†	1,442,130	1,508,740	1,571,603

* Preliminary.   † All sea fish.

CANADA

Mining

('000 metric tons, unless otherwise indicated)

	1985	1986	1987*
Metallic			
Bismuth (metric tons)	201	153	178
Cadmium (metric tons)	1,717	1,484	2,294
Cobalt (metric tons)	2,067	2,297	2,877
Copper (metric tons)	738,637	698,527	767,299
Gold (kilograms)	87,562	102,899	117,834
Iron ore	39,502	36,167	37,553
Lead (metric tons)	268,292	334,342	390,503
Molybdenum (metric tons)	7,852	11,251	11,581
Nickel (metric tons)	169,971	163,639	187,805
Platinum group (kilograms)	10,534	12,190	13,489
Selenium (metric tons)	361	354	496
Silver (metric tons)	1,197	1,088	1,250
Uranium oxide—U_3O_8 (metric tons)	10,441	11,502	13,202
Zinc (metric tons)	1,049,275	988,173	1,329,408
Non-metallic			
Asbestos	750	662	665
Gypsum	8,447	8,803	8,811
Nepheline syenite	467	467	499
Potash (K_2O)	6,661	6,752	7,465
Salt	10,085	10,332	10,294
Sulphur, in smelter gas	822	758	803
Sulphur, elemental	8,102	6,966	6,888
Fuels			
Coal	60,436	57,811	59,790
Natural gas (million cubic metres)†	84,344	71,896	71,962
Natural gas by-products ('000 cubic metres)‡	19,682	19,127	20,879
Petroleum, crude ('000 cubic metres)	85,564	85,468	87,108
Structural materials			
Cement	10,192	10,611	12,205
Sand and gravel	256,183	257,971	260,265
Stone	86,632	97,602	105,675

* Preliminary.
† Net withdrawals less processing and reprocessing shrinkage.
‡ Excludes sulphur.

Industry

VALUE OF SHIPMENTS (C $ '000)

	1985	1986*	1987†
Food industries	32,792,936	35,038,737	36,758,027
Beverage industries	4,863,699	5,435,295	5,806,055
Tobacco products industries	1,640,899	1,593,608	1,813,599
Rubber products industries	2,554,186	2,450,332	2,386,907
Plastic products industries	3,860,926	4,160,666	4,787,579
Leather and allied products industries	1,308,180	1,371,127	1,353,376
Primary textile industries	2,669,666	2,755,041	3,073,484
Textiles products industries	2,650,075	2,823,678	3,100,754
Clothing industries	5,543,162	5,980,887	6,336,186
Wood industries	11,121,614	12,278,396	14,882,144
Furniture and fixture industries	3,398,624	3,648,131	3,988,552
Paper and allied products industries	18,074,629	20,157,759	23,305,353
Printing, publishing and allied industries	9,534,830	10,308,765	11,238,512
Primary metal industries	16,970,955	16,994,559	18,884,197
Fabricated metal products industries	13,971,012	14,507,830	16,332,627
Machinery industries	7,450,790	7,973,070	8,972,159
Transportation equipment industries	43,116,945	44,561,068	41,644,183
Electrical and electronic products industries	13,257,862	14,381,149	15,775,235
Non-metallic mineral products industries	5,879,140	6,459,550	7,511,466

VALUE OF SHIPMENTS (C $ '000)—continued

	1985	1986*	1987†
Refined petroleum and coal products industries	24,420,831	16,930,755	16,277,220
Chemical and chemical products industries	18,268,582	18,822,346	20,156,952
Other manufacturing industries	5,065,378	5,277,927	5,481,256

Electric Energy (net production, million kWh): 447,182 in 1985; 457,007 in 1986.

* Preliminary.
† Estimates.

Finance

CURRENCY AND EXCHANGE RATES

Monetary Units
100 cents = 1 Canadian dollar (C $).

Denominations
Coins: 1, 5, 10, 25 and 50 cents; 1 dollar.
Notes: 1, 2, 5, 10, 20, 50, 100 and 1,000 dollars.

Sterling and US Dollar Equivalents (30 September 1988)
£1 sterling = C $2.058;
US $1 = C $1.217;
C $100 = £48.59 = US $82.17.

Average Exchange Rate (C $ per US $)
1985 1.3655
1986 1.3895
1987 1.3260

FEDERAL BUDGET (C $ million, year ending 31 March)

Revenue	1987/88*	1988/89†
Personal income tax	45,125	45,410
Corporate income tax	10,878	12,000
Unemployment insurance contributions	10,426	10,600
Non-resident tax	1,162	1,270
Sales tax	12,934	16,750
Customs import duties	4,384	4,160
Energy taxes	2,603	2,600
Other excise taxes and duties	3,026	3,345
Other tax revenue	206	175
Non-tax revenue: return on investments	4,548	5,060
Other non-tax revenue	2,167	1,935
Total budgetary revenue	95,459	103,305

Expenditure	1987/88*	1988/89†
Economic and regional development	14,289	13,341
Social development	56,642	59,359
Services to government	4,186	3,857
Parliament	231	237
Defence	10,772	11,090
External affairs and aid	3,439	3,541
Fiscal arrangements	7,007	7,000
Reserves net of estimated lapse	—	1,770
Programme expenditures	96,566	100,195
Public debt charges	28,976	32,055
Total expenditure	125,542	132,250

1989/90: Estimated Revenue C $106,310 million; Estimated Expenditure C $134,900 million.

* Based on preliminary financial statements for the fiscal year ending 31 March 1988.
† Figures relate to Federal Budget announced in February 1988.

CANADA

GOLD RESERVES AND CURRENCY IN CIRCULATION
(C $ million at 31 December)

	1985	1986	1987
Gold holdings*	773.0	844.5	919.5
US dollar holdings*	1,523.9	2,274.1	6,163.3
Notes in circulation	16,672.0	17,911.0	19,447.0

* US $ million.

COST OF LIVING (Consumer Price Index. Base: 1981 = 100)

	1985	1986	1987
Food	120.8	126.8	132.4
Housing	129.0	132.9	138.3
Clothing	115.6	118.8	123.8
Transport	130.8	135.0	139.9
Health and personal care	127.2	132.6	139.2
Recreation, education and reading	124.5	130.3	137.3
Tobacco and alcohol	154.0	172.3	183.9
All items	127.2	132.4	138.2

NATIONAL ACCOUNTS (C $ million at current prices)
National Income and Product

	1985	1986	1987
Compensation of employees	257,344	274,607	295,665
Operating surplus	117,832	118,481	132,684
Domestic factor incomes	375,176	393,088	428,349
Consumption of fixed capital	55,760	59,438	63,302
Gross domestic product at factor cost	430,936	452,526	491,651
Indirect taxes, *less* subsidies	47,176	53,825	58,011
Statistical discrepancy	653	132	30
GDP at market prices	478,765	506,483	549,692
Factor income from abroad*	7,574	7,207	6,987
Less Factor income paid abroad*	21,893	23,761	23,594
Gross national product	464,446	489,929	533,085
Less Consumption of fixed capital	55,760	59,438	63,302
Statistical discrepancy	−653	−132	−30
National income at market prices	408,033	430,359	469,753
Other current transfers from abroad†	1,750	2,449	2,058
Less Other current transfers paid abroad†	2,355	2,554	2,965
National disposable income	407,428	430,254	468,846

* Remitted profits, dividends and interest only.
† Transfers to and from persons and governments.

Expenditure on the Gross Domestic Product

	1985	1986	1987
Government final consumption expenditure	95,700	100,468	106,490
Private final consumption expenditure	274,946	297,304	322,970
Increase in stocks	2,981	2,936	1,954
Gross fixed capital formation	94,216	101,326	114,378
Exports of goods and services	134,979	137,459	144,213
Less Imports of goods and services	123,404	132,879	140,284
Statistical discrepancy	−653	−131	−29
GDP at market prices	478,765	506,483	549,692
GDP at constant 1981 prices	395,217	407,736	424,136

BALANCE OF PAYMENTS (US $ million)

	1985	1986	1987
Merchandise exports f.o.b.	89,654	88,719	97,871
Merchandise imports f.o.b.	−77,074	−81,137	−89,111
Trade balance	12,580	7,582	8,759
Exports of services	14,720	15,415	16,201
Imports of services	−29,317	−31,603	−34,518
Balance on goods and services	−2,017	−8,606	−9,558
Private unrequited transfers (net)	816	932	2,044
Government unrequited transfers (net)	−225	131	−461
Current balance	−1,426	−7,543	−7,975
Direct capital investment (net)	−5,942	−1,880	−963
Other long-term capital (net)	5,966	13,405	9,872
Short-term capital (net)	1,802	−2,601	4,664
Net errors and omissions	−3,680	−1,956	−2,820
Total (net monetary movements)	−3,280	−576	2,778
Valuation changes (net)	75	112	149
Exceptional financing (net)	3,207	1,055	564
Changes in reserves	1	591	3,491

Source: IMF, *International Financial Statistics*.

External Trade

PRINCIPAL COMMODITIES (C $ million)

Imports	1986	1987
Live animals	158.7	162.1
Food, feed, beverages and tobacco	6,541.2	6,630.3
Meat, fresh, chilled or frozen	412.9	493.5
Fish and marine animals	612.7	691.4
Fruit and vegetables	2,373.5	2,502.1
Raw sugar	217.2	163.0
Coffee	648.7	461.9
Distilled alcoholic beverages	173.6	157.9
Other beverages	310.1	339.0
Crude materials (inedible)	7,267.8	7,392.4
Fur skins (undressed)	185.7	231.3
Rubber and allied gums	107.9	125.6
Iron ores and concentrates	294.5	257.9
Aluminium ores, concentrates and scrap	519.1	550.2
Other metal ores, concentrates and scrap	1,077.0	760.0
Coal	744.4	732.1
Crude petroleum	2,884.6	3,159.0
Fabricated materials (inedible)	19,979.4	20,853.3
Wood and paper	1,742.9	1,978.6
Textiles	2,104.5	2,261.7
Chemicals	5,838.6	6,232.5
Iron and steel	1,840.2	2,078.7
Non-ferrous metals	3,074.0	2,484.2
End products (inedible)	76,984.0	79,368.0
General purpose machinery	3,400.5	3,482.0
Special industrial machinery	5,782.6	6,155.3
Agricultural machinery and tractors	1,727.5	1,659.6
Passenger automobiles and chassis	12,061.7	12,345.6
Trucks, truck tractors and chassis	2,947.2	3,293.1
Motor vehicle parts (excl. engines)	14,729.0	14,036.0
Televisions, radios and phonographs	915.8	878.2
Other telecommunication and related equipment	2,497.5	2,349.3
Miscellaneous electrical lighting distribution equipment	438.8	427.0
Miscellaneous measuring and laboratory equipment	893.3	912.8
Furniture and fixtures	543.7	630.2
Hand tools and cutlery	506.9	530.2
Electronic computers	4,193.1	5,009.4
Miscellaneous office machines and equipment	253.1	262.4
Miscellaneous equipment and tools	1,569.3	1,675.9
Special transactions, trade	1,746.9	2,018.3
Total	112,678.0	116,424.5

CANADA

Exports	1986	1987
Live animals	348.6	366.0
Food, feed, beverages and tobacco	9,510.6	10,266.3
Meat, fresh, chilled or frozen	939.3	1,003.2
Fish, fresh or frozen	749.3	906.3
Fish, fresh or frozen, whole	501.5	465.4
Barley	568.4	448.2
Wheat	2,835.8	3,219.2
Vegetables	384.9	424.7
Whisky	322.0	344.3
Crude materials (inedible)	15,328.2	16,797.3
Rapeseed	422.3	490.6
Iron ores and concentrates	1,107.8	968.4
Copper ores, concentrates and scrap	594.0	720.1
Nickel ores, concentrates and scrap	476.4	510.5
Crude petroleum	3,774.0	4,905.6
Natural gas	2,482.9	2,486.9
Coal and other bituminous substances	1,851.0	1,670.0
Asbestos (unmanufactured)	398.8	363.8
Fabricated materials (inedible)	38,392.3	41,742.0
Lumber, softwood	4,862.3	5,735.0
Wood pulp and similar pulp	4,072.0	5,445.1
Newsprint paper	5,667.0	6,020.7
Organic chemicals	1,143.3	1,358.1
Fertilizers and fertilizer material	1,161.5	1,269.7
Petroleum and coal products	2,097.4	2,197.8
Aluminium and alloys	2,338.9	2,751.5
Copper and alloys	729.7	809.1
Nickel and alloys	558.6	664.5
Precious metals and alloys	3,122.5	1,516.5
Electricity	1,079.7	1,211.8
End products (inedible)	52,690.8	51,953.6
Industrial machinery	3,427.3	3,453.7
Agricultural machinery and tractors	464.1	550.7
Passenger automobiles and chassis	17,677.1	14,167.5
Trucks, truck tractors and chassis	5,085.7	6,008.3
Motor vehicle engines and parts	1,795.4	1,923.5
Motor vehicle parts (excl. engines)	9,276.7	9,610.1
Office machines and equipment	1,456.6	2,030.7
Special transactions, trade	317.1	328.3
Total	**116,561.7**	**121,413.5**

PRINCIPAL TRADING PARTNERS (C $ million)

Imports	1985	1986	1987
Australia	386.6	505.4	564.1
Austria	182.2	212.9	247.5
Belgium/Luxembourg	530.1	608.5	619.0
Brazil	809.3	821.5	850.5
China, People's Repub.	403.5	566.1	770.9
Denmark	228.9	233.6	249.0
Finland	200.1	254.0	287.8
France	1,372.8	1,586.1	1,488.7
Germany, Fed. Repub.	2,715.7	3,453.4	3,534.5
Hong Kong	886.8	1,041.5	1,137.6
Ireland	217.9	244.8	199.7
Italy	1,331.1	1,671.4	1,702.8
Japan	6,114.8	7,632.2	7,750.7
Korea, Repub.	1,607.0	1,749.4	1,844.0
Malaysia	146.4	150.2	187.3
Mexico	1,330.9	1,176.5	1,169.6
Netherlands	622.9	694.8	750.2
New Zealand	160.3	174.8	199.7
Nigeria	229.8	368.2	251.5
Norway	187.9	168.0	256.8
Puerto Rico	199.2	195.1	226.9
Singapore	210.5	210.0	261.9
Spain	366.5	441.4	485.2
Sweden	682.8	788.3	883.7
Switzerland	488.8	591.5	586.8
Taiwan	1,286.2	1,744.8	2,023.0
Thailand	108.7	150.3	200.8
United Kingdom	3,280.8	3,735.7	4,339.2
USA	73,816.4	77,123.0	79,069.3
Venezuela	1,092.1	523.9	551.2
Total (incl. others)	**104,355.2**	**112,511.4**	**116,238.6**

Exports	1985	1986	1987
Algeria	330.8	193.5	200.7
Australia	626.6	624.1	689.1
Belgium/Luxembourg	702.7	823.1	1,137.2
Brazil	666.5	656.0	636.8
China, People's Repub.	1,278.3	1,119.0	1,432.1
Colombia	147.1	160.7	224.3
Cuba	328.5	364.5	272.9
France	712.7	965.1	1,037.4
Germany, Fed. Repub.	1,194.5	1,255.1	1,515.2
Hong Kong	334.0	319.1	480.1
India	492.7	352.4	271.0
Indonesia	257.6	252.0	305.1
Italy	528.7	694.6	842.8
Japan	5,707.2	5,942.0	7,036.2
Korea, Repub.	780.0	968.0	1,167.4
Mexico	391.4	397.4	522.0
Morocco	169.3	154.6	203.6
Netherlands	930.0	978.1	1,021.0
Norway	374.4	310.4	310.1
Puerto Rico	210.8	202.4	233.6
Saudi Arabia	231.0	212.0	267.9
Spain	107.7	133.4	212.5
Sweden	179.0	212.3	248.5
Switzerland	290.2	335.1	402.5
Taiwan	430.0	611.4	757.0
Turkey	220.0	201.8	266.1
USSR	1,607.9	1,215.6	800.6
United Kingdom	2,408.8	2,565.6	2,849.9
USA	90,417.5	90,319.2	91,756.4
Venezuela	307.1	323.2	336.7
Total (incl. others)	**116,145.1**	**116,733.4**	**121,462.3**

Transport

RAILWAYS (revenue traffic)*

	1985	1986	1987
Passenger-km (million)	2,228	2,090	1,917
Freight ton-km (million)	232,035	235,527	261,807

* Seven major rail carriers only.

ROAD TRAFFIC ('000 vehicles registered at 31 December)

	1984	1985	1986
Passenger cars (incl. taxis and for car hire)	10,781	11,118	11,477
Truck and truck tractors (commercial and non-commercial)	3,047	3,095	3,156
Buses (school and other)	52	54	56
Motorcycles	470	453	430
Other (ambulances, fire trucks, etc.)	20	64	72

INLAND WATER TRAFFIC
(St Lawrence Seaway, '000 metric tons)

	1985	1986	1987
Montréal—Lake Ontario	37,322	37,582	39,969
Welland Canal	41,952	41,613	42,725

Source: St Lawrence Seaway Authority.

CANADA

INTERNATIONAL SEA-BORNE SHIPPING

	1985	1986	1987
Goods ('000 metric tons)			
Loaded	143,421	144,561	158,938
Unloaded	60,669	62,012	68,106
Vessels (number)			
Arrived	26,555	28,086	29,404
Departed	26,438	28,061	29,666

CIVIL AVIATION (Canadian Carriers—Revenue Traffic, '000)

	1984	1985	1986
Passengers	23,561	24,565	26,099
Km flown	383,158	423,413	465,269
Passenger-km	34,641,763	36,604,702	40,034,760
Goods ton-km*	1,120,786	1,171,811	1,202,882

* Includes freight, express, mail and excess baggage.

Tourism

	1985	1986	1987
Travellers from the United States:			
Number ('000)	34,117	38,200	36,953
Expenditure (C $ million)	3,674	4,506	4,151
Travellers from other countries:			
Number ('000)	1,808	2,260	2,649
Expenditure (C $ million)	1,332	1,827	2,138

Communications Media

('000)

	1985	1986	1987
Total households	7,079	9,331	9,556
Homes with radio	8,961	9,244	9,444
Homes with television	8,930	9,204	9,410
Homes with telephone	8,915	9,156	9,409

Daily newspapers in French and English only (1986): 111; total circulation 5,700,000.

Education

(1987/88)

	Institutions	Teachers	Pupils*
Primary and secondary	15,768	271,053	4,935,316
Post secondary non-university	198	23,660†	319,950†
Universities and colleges‡	68	35,670	487,250§

* Full-time only.
† Estimate.
‡ Degree-granting institutions, full-time teachers and full-time students.
§ Regular winter session only.

Directory

The Constitution

Constitutional development has been based mainly upon five important acts of the British Parliament: the Quebec Act of 1774, the Constitutional Act of 1791, the Act of Union of 1840, the British North America Act of 1867, and the Canada Act of 1982. The British North America Act 1867 provided that the Constitution of Canada should be 'similar in principle to that of the United Kingdom'; that the executive authority be vested in the Sovereign, and carried on in her name by a Governor-General and Privy Council; and that legislative power be exercised by a Parliament of two Houses, the Senate and the House of Commons. The enactment of the Canada Act of 1982 was the final act of the United Kingdom Parliament in Canadian constitutional development. The Act gave to Canada the power to amend the Constitution according to procedures determined by the Constitution Act 1982, which was proclaimed in force by the Queen on 17 April 1982. The Constitution Act 1982 added to the Canadian Constitution a Charter of Rights and Freedoms, and provisions which recognize the nation's multicultural heritage, affirm the existing rights of native peoples, confirm the principle of equalization of benefits among the provinces and strengthen provincial ownership of natural resources.

THE GOVERNMENT

The national government works itself out through three main agencies. There is Parliament (consisting of the Sovereign as represented by the Governor-General, the Senate and the House of Commons) which makes the laws; the Executive (the Cabinet or Ministry) which applies the laws; and the Judiciary which interprets the laws.

Particular features similar to the British system of government are the close relation which exists between the Executive and Legislative branches, and the doctrine of cabinet responsibility which has become crystallized in the course of time. The Prime Minister is appointed by the Governor-General and is habitually the leader of the political party commanding the confidence of the House of Commons. He chooses the members of his Cabinet from members of his party in Parliament, principally from those in the House of Commons. Each Minister or member of the Cabinet is usually responsible for the administration of a department, although there may be Ministers without portfolio whose experience and counsel are drawn upon to strengthen the Cabinet, but who are not at the head of departments. Each Minister of a department is responsible to Parliament for that department, and the Cabinet is collectively responsible before Parliament for government policy and administration generally.

Meetings of the Cabinet are presided over by the Prime Minister. From the Cabinet signed orders and recommendations go to the Governor-General for his or her approval, and the Crown acts only on the advice of its responsible Ministers. The Cabinet takes the responsibility for its advice being in accordance with the support of Parliament and is held strictly accountable.

THE FEDERAL PARLIAMENT

Parliament must meet at least once a year, so that twelve months do not elapse between the last meeting in one session and the first meeting in the next. The duration of Parliament may not be longer than five years from the date of election of a House of Commons. Senators (a maximum of 104 in number) are appointed until age 75 by the Governor-General in Council. They must be at least 30 years of age, residents of the province they represent and in possession of C $4,000 of real property over and above their liabilities. Members of the House of Commons are elected by universal adult suffrage for the duration of a Parliament.

Under the Constitution, the Federal Parliament has exclusive legislative authority in all matters relating to public debt and property; regulation of trade and commerce; raising of money by any mode of taxation; borrowing of money on the public credit; postal service, census and statistics; militia, military and naval service and defence; fixing and providing for salaries and allowances of the officers of the government; beacons, buoys and lighthouses; navigation and shipping; quarantine and the establishment

CANADA

and maintenance of marine hospitals; sea-coast and inland fisheries; ferries on an international or interprovincial frontier; currency and coinage; banking, incorporation of banks, and issue of paper money; savings banks; weights and measures; bills of exchange and promissory notes; interest; legal tender; bankruptcy and insolvency; patents of invention and discovery; copyrights; Indians and lands reserved for Indians; naturalization and aliens; marriage and divorce; the criminal law, except the constitution of courts of criminal jurisdiction but including the procedure in criminal matters; the establishment, maintenance and management of penitentiaries; such classes of subjects as are expressly excepted in the enumeration of the classes of subjects exclusively assigned to the Legislatures of the provinces by the Act. Judicial interpretation and later amendment have, in certain cases, modified or clearly defined the respective powers of the Federal and Provincial Governments.

Both the Parliament of Canada and the legislatures of the provinces may legislate with respect to agriculture and immigration, but provincial legislation shall have effect in and for the provinces as long and as far only as it is not repugnant to any Act of Parliament. Both Parliament and the provincial legislatures may legislate with respect to old age pensions and supplementary benefits, but no federal law shall affect the operation of any present or future law of a province in relation to these matters.

PROVINCIAL AND MUNICIPAL GOVERNMENT

In each of the ten provinces the Sovereign is represented by a Lieutenant-Governor, appointed by the Governor-General in Council, and acting on the advice of the Ministry or Executive Council, which is responsible to the Legislature and resigns office when it ceases to enjoy the confidence of that body. The Legislatures are unicameral, consisting of an elected Legislative Assembly and the Lieutenant-Governor. The duration of a Legislature may not exceed five years from the date of the election of its members.

The Legislature in each province may exclusively make laws in relation to: amendment of the constitution of the province, except as regards the Lieutenant-Governor; direct taxation within the province; borrowing of money on the credit of the province; establishment and tenure of provincial offices and appointment and payment of provincial officers; the management and sale of public lands belonging to the province and of the timber and wood thereon; the establishment, maintenance and management of public and reformatory prisons in and for the province; the establishment, maintenance and management of hospitals, asylums, charities and charitable institutions in and for the province other than marine hospitals; municipal institutions in the province; shop, saloon, tavern, auctioneer and other licences issued for the raising of provincial or municipal revenue; local works and undertakings other than interprovincial or international lines of ships, railways, canals, telegraphs, etc., or works which, though wholly situtated within the province are declared by the Federal Parliament to be for the general advantage either of Canada or two or more provinces; the incorporation of companies with provincial objects; the solemnization of marriage in the province; property and civil rights in the province; the administration of justice in the province, including the constitution, maintenance and organization of provincial courts both in civil and criminal jurisdiction, and including procedure in civil matters in these courts; the imposition of punishment by fine, penalty or imprisonment for enforcing any law of the province relating to any of the aforesaid subjects; generally all matters of a merely local or private nature in the province. Further, provincial Legislatures may exclusively make laws in relation to education, subject to the protection of religious minorities; and to non-renewable natural resources, forestry resources and electrical energy, including their export from one province to another, and to the right to impose any mode or system of taxation thereon, subject in both cases to such laws not being discriminatory.

Under the Constitution Act, the municipalities are the creations of the provincial governments. Their bases of organization and the extent of their authority vary in different provinces, but almost everywhere they have very considerable powers of local self-government.

The Government

Head of State: HM Queen ELIZABETH II.
Governor-General: JEANNE SAUVÉ (took office 14 May 1984).

FEDERAL MINISTRY
(January 1989)*

Prime Minister: (MARTIN) BRIAN MULRONEY.
Secretary of State for External Affairs, Acting Minister of Justice and Attorney-General: (CHARLES) JOSEPH CLARK.
Minister for International Trade: JOHN CARNELL CROSBIE.
Deputy Prime Minister, President of the Queen's Privy Council for Canada and Minister of Agriculture: DONALD FRANK MAZANKOWSKI.
Minister of National Revenue: ELMER MACINTOSH MACKAY.
Minister of National Health and Welfare: ARTHUR JACOB EPP.
Minister of Regional Industrial Expansion and Minister of State for Science and Technology: ROBERT R. DE COTRET.
Minister of National Defence and Acting Solicitor-General: HENRY PERRIN BEATTY.
Minister of Finance: MICHAEL HOLCOMBE WILSON.
Minister of Consumer and Corporate Affairs: HARVIE ANDRE.
Minister of Supply and Services and Acting Minister of Public Works: OTTO JOHN JELINEK.
Minister of Fisheries and Oceans: THOMAS EDWARD SIDDON.
Minister of State (Grains and Oilseeds): CHARLES JAMES MAYER.
Minister of Indian Affairs and Northern Development and Minister of Western Economic Diversification: WILLIAM HUNTER MCKNIGHT.
Minister of Transport: BENOÎT BOUCHARD.
Minister of Energy, Mines and Resources: MARCEL MASSE.
Minister of Employment and Immigration: BARBARA JEAN MCDOUGALL.
Minister of Veterans' Affairs and Minister for the purposes of Atlantic Canada Opportunities Agency Act: GERALD STAIRS MERRITHEW.
Minister of State (Employment and Immigration) and Minister of State (Senior Citizens): MONIQUE VÉZINA.
Minister of State (Science and Technology) and Acting Minister of State (Forestry): FRANK OBERLE.
Leader of the Government in the Senate, Minister of State (Federal-Provincial Relations) and Acting Minister of Communications: LOWELL MURRAY.
Associate Minister of National Defence: PAUL WYATT DICK.
Minister of Labour: PIERRE H. CADIEUX.
Minister of State (Youth) and Minister of State (Fitness and Amateur Sport): JEAN J. CHAREST.
Minister of State (Finance): THOMAS HOCKIN.
Minister for External Relations: MONIQUE LANDRY.
Minister of State (Small Businesses and Tourism) and Minister of State (Indian Affairs and Northern Development): BERNARD VALCOURT.
Minister of State (Multiculturalism and Citizenship): GERRY WEINER.
Minister of State and Minister of State (Treasury Board) and Acting President of the Treasury Board: DOUGLAS GRINSLADE LEWIS.
Minister of State (Agriculture): PIERRE BLAIS.
Secretary of State for Canada and Acting Minister of the Environment: LUCIEN BOUCHARD.
Minister of State (International Trade) and Minister of State (Housing): JOHN HORTON MCDERMID.
Minister of State (Transport): SHIRLEY MARTIN.

* See Late Information.

MINISTRIES

Office of the Prime Minister: Ottawa K1A OA2; tel. (613) 992-4211; telex 053-3208.
Department of Agriculture: Sir John Carling Bldg, 930 Carling Ave, Ottawa K1A OC5; tel. (613) 995-5222; telex 053-3283.
Department of Communications: Journal North Tower, 300 Slater St, Ottawa K1A OC8; tel. (613) 990-4900; telex 053-3342.
Department of Consumer and Corporate Affairs: Ottawa K1A OC9; tel. (613) 997-2938; telex 053-3694.
Department of Employment and Immigration: Ottawa K1A OJ9; tel. (613) 992-4883; telex 053-3511.
Department of Energy, Mines and Resources: 580 Booth St, Ottawa K1A OE4; tel. (613) 995-3065; telex 053-3117.
Environment Canada: Terrasses de la Chaudière, Ottawa K1A OH3; tel. (819) 997-2800; telex 053-3608.
Department of External Affairs: Lester B. Pearson Bldg, 125 Sussex Drive, Ottawa K1A OG2; tel. (613) 995-1851; telex 053-3745.
Department of Finance: Place Bell Canada, 160 Elgin St, Ottawa K1A OG5; tel. (613) 992-1573; telex 053-3336.

CANADA

Department of Fisheries and Oceans: 200 Kent St, Ottawa K1A OE6; tel. (613) 993-0600; telex 053-4228.

Department of Indian and Northern Affairs: Terrasses de la Chaudière, 10 Wellington St, Ottawa K1A OH4; tel. (613) 995-5586; telex 053-3711.

Department of Justice: Justice Bldg, Kent and Wellington Sts, Ottawa K1A OH8; tel. (613) 957-4222; telex 053-3603.

Department of Labour: Labour Canada, Ottawa K1A OJ2; tel. (613) 997-2617; telex 053-3640.

Department of National Defence: 101 Colonel By Drive, Ottawa K1A OK2; tel. (613) 996-4450; telex 053-4218.

Department of National Health and Welfare: Brooke Claxton Bldg, Tunney's Pasture, Ottawa K1A OK9; tel. (613) 957-2991; telex 053-3270.

Department of Public Works: Sir Charles Tupper Bldg, Confederation Heights, Riverside Drive, Ottawa K1A OM2; tel. (613) 998-7724; telex 053-4235.

Department of Regional Industrial Expansion: 235 Queen St, Ottawa K1A OH5; tel. (613) 995-9001; telex 053-4124.

Revenue Canada (Customs and Excise): Connaught Bldg, 2nd Floor, Mackenzie Ave, Ottawa K1A OL5; tel. (613) 957-9192; telex 053-3330.

Revenue Canada (Taxation): Headquarters Bldg, 875 Heron Rd, Ottawa K1A OL8; tel. (613) 995-2960; telex 053-4974.

Department of Science and Technology: C. D. Howe Bldg, 235 Queen St, Ottawa K1A 1A1; tel. (613) 996-0326; telex 053-4396.

Secretary of State of Canada: Ottawa K1A OM5; tel. (613) 997-0055.

Solicitor-General: Sir Wilfrid Laurier Bldg, 340 Laurier Ave West, Ottawa K1A OP8; tel. (613) 991-2857; telex 053-3768.

Department of Supply and Services: Canadian Government Publishing Centre, Ottawa K1A OS9; tel. (613) 990-2309; telex 053-3580.

Department of Transport: Place de Ville, Transport Canada Bldg, 330 Sparks St, Ottawa K1A ON5; tel. (613) 996-7501; telex 053-3580.

Treasury Board: Ottawa K1A OR5; tel. (613) 996-2690; telex 053-3336.

Department of Veterans' Affairs: POB 7700, Charlottetown, PEI C1A 8M9; tel. (902) 566-8888; telex 014-44228.

Federal Legislature

THE SENATE

Speaker: GUY CHARBONNEAU.

Seats at October 1988

Liberal	59
Progressive Conservative	31
Independent	5
Independent Progressive Conservative	1
Vacant	8
Total	**104**
Ontario	24*
Québec	24†
New Brunswick	10*
Nova Scotia	10*
Alberta	6*
British Columbia	6
Manitoba	6
Newfoundland	6
Saskatchewan	6
Prince Edward Island	4
Northwest Territories	1
Yukon Territory	1
Total	**104**

* One vacancy.
† Four vacancies.

HOUSE OF COMMONS

Speaker: JOHN A. FRASER.

General Election, 21 November 1988

	Seats at election
Progressive Conservative	170
Liberal	82
New Democratic Party	43
Total	**295**

Provincial Legislatures

ALBERTA

Lieutenant-Governor: HELEN HUNLEY.
Premier: DONALD GETTY.

Election, May 1986

	Seats at election	Seats at Oct. 1988
Progressive Conservative	61	61
New Democratic Party	16	16
Liberal	4	4
Representative Party*	2	2
Total	**83**	**83**

* Elected as Independents.

BRITISH COLUMBIA

Lieutenant-Governor: DAVID LAM.
Premier: WILLIAM VANDER ZALM.

Election, October 1986

	Seats at election	Seats at Nov. 1988
Social Credit	47	45
New Democratic Party	22	23
Independent	—	1
Total	**69**	**69**

MANITOBA

Lieutenant-Governor: Dr GEORGE JOHNSON.
Premier: GARY FILMON.

Election, April 1988

	Seats at election	Seats at Oct. 1988
Progressive Conservative*	25	25
Liberal	20	20
New Democratic Party	12	12
Total	**57**	**57**

* Formed a minority government following the April 1988 election.

NEW BRUNSWICK

Lieutenant-Governor: GILBERT FINN.
Premier: FRANK McKENNA.

Election, October 1987

	Seats at election	Seats at Oct. 1988
Liberal	58	58
Progressive Conservative	—	—
New Democratic Party	—	—
Total	**58**	**58**

NEWFOUNDLAND AND LABRADOR*

Lieutenant-Governor: JAMES McGRATH.
Premier: A. BRIAN PECKFORD.

CANADA

Election, April 1985

	Seats at election	Seats at Oct. 1988
Progressive Conservative	36	35
Liberal	15	15
New Democratic Party	1	2
Total	52	52

* See Late Information.

NOVA SCOTIA
Lieutenant-Governor: ALAN R. ABRAHAM.
Premier: JOHN M. BUCHANAN.

Election, September 1988

	Seats at election
Progressive Conservative	28
Liberal	21
New Democratic Party	2
Independent	1
Total	52

ONTARIO
Lieutenant-Governor: LINCOLN M. ALEXANDER.
Premier: DAVID R. PETERSON.

Election, September 1987

	Seats at election	Seats at Nov. 1988
Liberal	95	94
New Democratic Party	16	19
Progressive Conservative	19	17
Total	130	130

PRINCE EDWARD ISLAND
Lieutenant-Governor: LLOYD G. MACPHAIL.
Premier: JOSEPH A. GHIZ.

Election, April 1986

	Seats at election	Seats at Oct. 1988
Liberal	21	22
Progressive Conservative	11	10
Total	32	32

QUÉBEC
Lieutenant-Governor: GILLES DE LAMONTAGNE.
Premier: ROBERT BOURASSA.

Election, December 1985

	Seats at election	Seats at Oct. 1988
Liberal	99	100
Parti Québécois	23	20
Independent	—	1
Vacant	—	1
Total	122	122

SASKATCHEWAN
Lieutenant-Governor: SYLVIA FEDORUK.
Premier: GRANT DEVINE.

Election, October 1986

	Seats at election	Seats at Nov. 1988
Progressive Conservative	38	37
New Democratic Party	25	27
Liberal	1	—
Total	64	64

Territorial Legislatures

NORTHWEST TERRITORIES
Commissioner: JOHN HAVELOCK PARKER.
Leader of the Legislative Assembly: NICK G. SIBBESTON.

The Legislative Assembly, elected in October 1987, consists of 24 independent members without formal party affiliation.

YUKON TERRITORY
Commissioner: DOUGLAS LESLIE DEWEY BELL.
Leader of the Territorial Council: TONY PENIKETT.

Election, May 1985

	Seats at election	Seats at Oct. 1988
New Democratic Party	8	9
Progressive Conservative	6	6
Liberal	2	1
Total	16	16

Political Organizations

British Columbia Social Credit Party: 10711 Cambie Rd, Suite 236, Richmond, BC V6X 3G5; tel. (604) 270-4040; conservative; governing party of British Columbia 1952–72 and since 1975; Leader WILLIAM VANDER ZALM.

Communist Party of Canada: 24 Cecil St, Toronto, Ont M5T 1N2; tel. (416) 979-2109; f. 1921; Chair. WILLIAM KASHTAN; Gen. Sec. GEORGE HEWISON.

Green Party of Canada: c/o Dr Seymour Trieger, RR2, Yellow Point Rd, Ladysmith, BC V0R 2E0; f. 1983; environmentalist.

Liberal Party of Canada: 200 Laurier Ave West, Suite 200, Ottawa K1P 6M8; tel. (613) 237-0740; supports Canadian autonomy, comprehensive social security, freer trade within the North Atlantic Community; Leader JOHN NAPIER TURNER; Pres. MICHEL ROBERT; Sec.-Gen. ANDRÉE BASTIEN.

Libertarian Party of Canada: POB 190, Adelaide St Postal Station, Toronto, Ont M5C 2J1; tel. (416) 323-0020; f. 1973; Leader DENNIS CORRIGAN; Pres. CHRIS BLATCHLY.

New Democratic Party: 200 Albert St, Suite 600, Ottawa K2P 1R9; tel. (613) 236-3613; f. 1961; social democratic; Leader J. EDWARD BROADBENT; Pres. JOHANNA DEN HERTOG; Sec. DENNIS YOUNG; 120,000 individual mems, 265,000 affiliated mems. (1988).

Parti Indépendantiste: 6992 rue St-Hubert, Montréal, Qué H2S 2M9; tel. (514) 272-4654; f. 1984 by breakaway faction of Parti Québécois; seeks full independence for Québec; Pres. PIERRE DE BELLEFEUILLE; Leader GILLES RHEAUME.

Parti Québécois: 7370 rue St-Hubert, Montréal, Qué H2R 2N3; tel. (514) 270-5400; f. 1968; social democratic; seeks political sovereignty for Québec in an economic association with Canada; governing party of Québec 1976–85; Pres. JACQUES PARIZEAU; Chair. Nat. Exec. NADIA ASSIMOPOULOS; c. 75,000 mems (1988).

Progressive Conservative Party: 161 Laurier Ave West, Suite 200, Ottawa K1P 5J2; tel. (613) 238-6111; f. 1854; advocates individualism and free enterprise and continued Canadian participation in NATO; Leader (MARTIN) BRIAN MULRONEY; Pres. BILL JARVIS; Nat. Dir JEAN-CAROL PELLETIER.

Rassemblement Démocratique pour l'Indépendance: 234 ouest, blvd St-Joseph, Montréal, Qué H2T 2P8; tel. (514) 271-0690; f. 1985 by breakaway faction of Parti Québécois; seeks full independence for Québec; Leader Dr CAMILLE LAURIN.

Diplomatic Representation

EMBASSIES AND HIGH COMMISSIONS IN CANADA

Algeria: 435 Daly Ave, Ottawa K1N 6H3; tel. (613) 232-9453; telex 053-3625; Ambassador: ABDELOUAHAD ABADA.

Antigua and Barbuda, Dominica, Saint Christopher and Nevis, Saint Lucia and Saint Vincent and the Grenadines: Place de Ville, Tower B, 112 Kent St, Suite 1701, Ottawa K1P 5P2; tel. (613) 236-8952; High Commissioner: Dr ASYLL M. WARNER.

Argentina: 90 Sparks St, Suite 620, Ottawa K1P 5B4; tel. (613) 236-2351; telex 053-4293; Ambassador: FRANCISCO JOSÉ PULIT.

Australia: 130 Slater St, 13th Floor, Ottawa K1P 6E2; tel. (613) 236-0841; telex 053-3391; High Commissioner: ROBERT STEPHEN LAURIE.

CANADA

Austria: 445 Wilbrod St, Ottawa K1N 6M7; tel. (613) 563-1444; telex 053-3290; Ambassador: Dr HEDWIG WOLFRAM.

Bahamas: 360 Albert St, Suite 625, Ottawa K1R 7X7; tel. (613) 232-1724; telex 053-3793; High Commissioner: IDRIS REID.

Bangladesh: 85 Range Rd, Suite 402, Ottawa K1N 8J6; tel. (613) 236-0138; telex 053-4283; High Commissioner: Maj.-Gen. K. M. SAFIULLAH.

Barbados: 151 Slater St, Suite 210, Ottawa K1P 5H3; tel. (613) 236-9517; telex 053-3375; High Commissioner: PETER G. MORGAN.

Belgium: 85 Range Rd, Suites 601–604, Ottawa K1N 8J6; tel. (613) 236-7267; telex 053-3568; Ambassador: JEAN-FRANÇOIS DE LIEDEKERKE.

Benin: 58 Glebe Ave, Ottawa K1S 2C3; tel. (613) 233-4429; telex 053-3630; Ambassador: JOSEPH LOUIS HOUNTON.

Bolivia: 77 Metcalfe St, Suite 608, Ottawa K1P 5L6; tel. (613) 236-8237; Chargé d'affaires: MARÍA RENÉE A. DE APARICIO.

Brazil: 255 Albert St, Suite 900, Ottawa K1P 6A9; tel. (613) 237-1090; telex 053-4222; Ambassador: MARCOS ANTÔNIO DE SALVO COIMBRA.

Bulgaria: 325 Stewart St, Ottawa K1N 6K5; tel. (613) 232-3215; telex 053-4386; Ambassador: VLADIMIR VELCHEV.

Burkina Faso: 48 Range Rd, Ottawa K1N 8J4; tel. (613) 238-4796; telex 053-4413; Chargé d'affaires a.i.: NORAOGO VINCENT OUÉDRAOGO.

Burma: 85 Range Rd, Suite 902, Ottawa K1N 8J6; tel. (613) 232-6434; telex 053-3334; Ambassador: THEIN AUNG.

Burundi: 151 Slater St, Suite 800, Ottawa K1P 5H3; tel. (613) 236-8483; Chargé d'affaires a.i.: DIDACE SUNZU.

Cameroon: 170 Clemow Ave, Ottawa K1S 2B4; tel. (613) 236-1522; telex 053-3736; Ambassador: PHILEMON YANG YUNJI.

Chile: 56 Sparks St, Suite 801, Ottawa K1P 5A9; tel. (613) 235-4402; telex 053-3774; Ambassador: ALBERTO BESA ALLAN.

China, People's Republic: 511–515 St Patrick St, Ottawa K1N 5H3; tel. (613) 234-2706; telex 053-3770; Ambassador: ZHANG WENPU.

Colombia: 150 Kent St, Suite 404, Ottawa K1P 5P4; tel. (613) 230-3760; telex 053-3786; Ambassador: Dr JAIME PINZÓN LÓPEZ.

Costa Rica: 150 Argyle St, Suite 115, Ottawa K2P 1B7; tel. (613) 234-5762; telex 053-4398; Ambassador: MARIO PACHECO.

Côte d'Ivoire: 9 Marlborough Ave, Ottawa K1N 8E6; tel. (613) 236-9919; Ambassador: Gen. ISSOUF KONÉ.

Cuba: 388 Main St, Ottawa K1S 1E3; tel. (613) 563-0141; telex 053-3135; Ambassador: (vacant).

Czechoslovakia: 50 Rideau Terrace, Ottawa K1M 2A1; tel. (613) 749-4442; telex 053-4224; Ambassador: JÁN JANOVIC.

Denmark: 85 Range Rd, Suite 702, Ottawa K1N 8J6; tel. (613) 234-0704; telex 053-3114; Ambassador: PER FERGO.

Egypt: 454 Laurier Ave East, Ottawa K1N 6R3; tel. (613) 234-4931; telex 053-3340; Ambassador: MAHMOUD KASSEM.

Finland: 55 Metcalfe St, Suite 850, Ottawa K1P 6L5; tel. (613) 236-2389; telex 053-4462; Ambassador: ERKKI MÄENTAKANEN.

France: 42 Sussex Drive, Ottawa K1M 2C9; tel. (613) 232-1795; Ambassador: JEAN-PIERRE CABOUAT.

Germany, Federal Republic: 1 Waverley St, Ottawa K2P 0T8; tel. (613) 232-1101; telex 053-4226; Ambassador: WOLFGANG BEHRENDS.

Ghana: 85 Range Rd, Suite 810, Ottawa K1N 8J6; tel. (613) 236-0871; telex 053-4276; High Commissioner: DANIEL O. AGYEKUM.

Greece: 80 MacLaren St, Ottawa K2P 0K6; tel. (613) 238-6271; telex 053-3852; Ambassador: LEONIDAS MAVROMICHALIS.

Guatemala: 294 Albert St, Suite 500, Ottawa K1P 6E6; tel. (613) 237-3941; telex 053-3065; Ambassador: FEDERICO URRUELA-PRADO.

Guinea: Place de Ville, Tower B, 112 Kent St, Suite 208, Ottawa K1P 5P2; tel. (613) 232-1133; telex 053-4361; Ambassador: THOMAS SEKOU.

Guyana: 151 Slater St, Suite 309, Ottawa K1P 5H3; tel. (613) 235-7249; telex 053-3684; High Commissioner: GAVIN B. KENNARD.

Haiti: Place de Ville, Tower B, 112 Kent St, Suite 1308, Ottawa K1P 5P2; tel. (613) 238-1628; telex 053-3688; Chargé d'affaires a.i.: JEAN-FRANÇOIS LIVINGSTON.

Holy See: Apostolic Nunciature, 724 Manor Ave, Rockcliffe Park, Ottawa K1M 0E3; tel. (613) 746-4914; telex 053-3380; Pro-Nuncio: Most Rev. ANGELO PALMAS.

Honduras: 151 Slater St, Suite 300A, Ottawa K1P 5H3; tel. (613) 233-8900; telex 053-4528; Ambassador: ALEJANDRO FLORES MENDOZA.

Hungary: 7 Delaware Ave, Ottawa K2P 0Z2; tel. (613) 232-1711; telex 053-3251; Ambassador: REZSOE BANYASZ.

India: 10 Springfield Rd, Ottawa K1M 1C9; tel. (613) 744-3751; telex 053-4172; High Commissioner: SURBIR JIT SINGH CHHATWAL.

Indonesia: 287 MacLaren St, Ottawa K2P 0L9; tel. (613) 236-7403; telex 053-3119; Ambassador: ADIWOSO ABUBAKAR.

Iran: 411 Roosevelt Ave, 4th Floor, Ottawa K2A 3X9; tel. (613) 729-0902; telex 053-4229; Chargé d'affaires a.i.: SEYED ABBAS KHADEM HAGHIGHAT.

Iraq: 215 McLeod St, Ottawa K2P 0Z8; tel. (613) 236-9177; telex 053-4310; Ambassador: HISHAM AL-SHAWI.

Ireland: 170 Metcalfe St, Ottawa K2P 1P3; tel. (613) 233-6281; telex 053-4240; Ambassador: SEAN GAYNOR.

Israel: 410 Laurier Ave West, Suite 601, Ottawa K1R 7T3; tel. (613) 237-6450; telex 053-4858; Ambassador: ELIASHIV BEN-HORIN.

Italy: 275 Slater St, 11th Floor, Ottawa K1P 5H9; tel. (613) 232-2401; telex 053-3278; Ambassador: VALERIO BRIGANTE COLONNA ANGELINI.

Jamaica: 275 Slater St, Suite 402, Ottawa K1P 5H9; tel. (613) 233-9311; telex 053-3287; High Commissioner: H. DALE ANDERSON.

Japan: 255 Sussex Drive, Ottawa K1N 9E6; tel. (613) 236-8541; telex 053-4220; Ambassador: YOSHIO OKAWA.

Jordan: 100 Bronson Ave, Suite 701, Ottawa K1R 6G8; tel. (613) 238-8090; telex 053-4538; Ambassador: HANI KHALIFEH.

Kenya: 415 Laurier Ave East, Ottawa K1P 5H3; tel. (613) 563-1773; telex 053-4873; High Commissioner: Lt-Gen. JOHN E. SAWE.

Korea, Republic: 85 Albert St, 10th Floor, Ottawa K1P 6A4; tel. (613) 232-1715; Ambassador: ROH JAE-WON.

Lebanon: 640 Lyon St, Ottawa K1S 3Z5; tel. (613) 236-5825; telex 053-3571; Ambassador: MAKRAM ABDEL HALIM OUAIDAT.

Lesotho: 202 Clemow Ave, Ottawa K1S 2B4; tel. (613) 236-9449; telex 053-4563; High Commissioner: BERENG AUGUSTINUS SEKHONYANA.

Malawi: 7 Clemow Ave, Ottawa K1S 2A9; tel. (613) 236-8931; telex 053-3365; High Commissioner: M. W. MACHINJILI.

Malaysia: 60 Boteler St, Ottawa K1N 8Y7; tel. (613) 237-5182; telex 053-3064; High Commissioner: Tan Sri Datuk THOMAS JAYASURIA.

Mali: 50 Goulburn Ave, Ottawa K1N 8C8; tel. (613) 232-1501; telex 053-3361; Ambassador: SADIBOU KONÉ.

Mexico: 130 Albert St, Suite 206, Ottawa K1P 5G4; tel. (613) 233-8988; telex 053-4520; Ambassador: EMILIO CARRILLO GAMBOA.

Morocco: 38 Range Rd, Ottawa K1N 8J4; tel. (613) 236-7391; telex 053-3683; Ambassador: MAATI JORIO.

Netherlands: 275 Slater St, 3rd Floor, Ottawa K1P 5H9; tel. (613) 237-5030; telex 053-3109; Ambassador: J. F. E. BREMAN.

New Zealand: Metropolitan House, 99 Bank St, Suite 801, Ottawa K1P 6G3; tel. (613) 238-5991; telex 053-4282; High Commissioner: JOHN WYBROW.

Nicaragua: 170 Laurier Ave West, Suite 908, Ottawa, K1P 5V5; tel. (613) 234-9461; telex 053-4338; Ambassador: SERGIO LACAYO.

Niger: 38 Blackburn Ave, Ottawa K1N 8A2; tel. (613) 232-4291; telex 053-3757; Ambassador: LAMBERT MESSAN.

Nigeria: 295 Metcalfe St, Ottawa K2P 1R9; tel. (613) 236-0521; telex 053-3285; High Commissioner: A. I. ATTA.

Norway: Royal Bank Centre, 90 Sparks St, Suite 932, Ottawa K1P 5B4; tel. (613) 238-6571; telex 053-4239; Ambassador: PER MARTIN ØLBERG.

Pakistan: 151 Slater St, Suite 608, Ottawa K1P 5H3; tel. (613) 238-7881; telex 053-4428; Chargé d'affaires a.i.: ANWAR KEMAL.

Peru: 170 Laurier Ave West, Suite 1007, Ottawa K1P 5V5; tel. (613) 238-1777; telex 053-3754; Ambassador: Dr OSCAR MAURTUA.

Philippines: 130 Albert St, Suite 606, Ottawa K1P 5G4; tel. (613) 233-1121; telex 053-4537; Chargé d'affaires a.i.: ELOY R. BELLO, III.

Poland: 443 Daly Ave, Ottawa K1N 6H3; tel. (613) 236-0468; telex 053-3133; Ambassador: ALOJZY BARTOSZEK.

Portugal: 645 Island Park Drive, Ottawa K1Y 0B8; tel. (613) 729-0883; telex 053-3756; Ambassador: JOÃO UVA DE MATOS PROENÇA.

Romania: 655 Rideau St, Ottawa K1N 6A3; tel. (613) 232-5345; telex 053-3101; Ambassador: EMILIAN RODEAN.

Rwanda: 121 Sherwood Drive, Ottawa K1Y 3V1; tel. (613) 722-5835; telex 053-4522; Ambassador: JOSEPH NSENGIYUMVA.

Saudi Arabia: 99 Bank St, Suite 901, Ottawa K1P 6B9; tel. (613) 237-4100; telex 053-4285; Ambassador: ZIAD SHAWWAF.

Senegal: 57 Marlborough Ave, Ottawa K1N 8E8; tel. (613) 238-6392; telex 053-4531; Ambassador: ABDELKADER FALL.

Somalia: 130 Slater St, Suite 1000, Ottawa K1P 5P2; tel. (613) 563-4541; telex 053-4739; Ambassador: MOHAMED SHEIKH HASSAN.

South Africa: 15 Sussex Drive, Ottawa K1M 1M8; tel. (613) 744-0330; telex 053-4185; Ambassador: HENDRIK DE KLERK.

CANADA   Directory

Spain: 350 Sparks St, Suite 802, Ottawa K1R 7S8; tel. (613) 237-2193; telex 053-4510; Ambassador: (vacant).
Sri Lanka: 85 Range Rd, Suites 102–104, Ottawa K1N 8J6; tel. (613) 233-8449; telex 053-3668; High Commissioner: Brig.-Gen. TISSA WEERATUNGA.
Sudan: 457 Laurier Ave East, Ottawa K1N 6R4; tel. (613) 235-4000; Ambassador: NURI KHALIL SIDDIQ.
Sweden: 441 MacLaren St, 4th Floor, Ottawa K2P 2H3; tel. (613) 236-8553; telex 053-3331; Ambassador: OLA ULLSTEN.
Switzerland: 5 Marlborough Ave, Ottawa K1N 8E6; tel. (613) 235-1837; telex 053-3648; Ambassador: ERIK LANG.
Tanzania: 50 Range Rd, Ottawa K1N 8J4; tel. (613) 232-1509; telex 053-3569; High Commissioner: FERDINAND RUHINDA.
Thailand: 85 Range Rd, Suite 704, Ottawa K1N 8J6; tel. (613) 237-1517; telex 053-3975; Ambassador: MANASPAS XUTO.
Togo: 12 Range Rd, Ottawa K1N 8J3; tel. (613) 238-5916; telex 053-4564; telex 053-4564; Ambassador: KOSSIVI OSSEYI.
Trinidad and Tobago: 75 Albert St, Suite 508, Ottawa K1P 5E7; tel. (613) 232-2418; telex 053-4343; High Commissioner: G. YET-MING.
Tunisia: 515 O'Connor St, Ottawa K1S 3P8; tel. (613) 237-0330; telex 053-4161; Ambassador: ANOUAR BERRALES.
Turkey: 197 Wurtemburg St, Ottawa K1N 8L9; tel. (613) 232-1577; telex 053-4716; Ambassador: KAYA G. TOPERI.
Uganda: 231 Cobourg St, Ottawa K1N 8J2; tel. (613) 233-7797; telex 053-4469; High Commissioner: JOSEPH TOMUSANGE.
USSR: 285 Charlotte St, Ottawa K1N 8L5; tel. (613) 235-4341; telex 053-3332; Ambassador: ALEKSEI RODIONOV.
United Kingdom: 80 Elgin St, Ottawa K1P 5K7; tel. (613) 237-1530; telex 053-3318; High Commissioner: Sir ALAN URWICK.
USA: 100 Wellington St, Ottawa K1P 5T1; tel. (613) 238-5335; telex 053-3582; Ambassador: THOMAS M. T. NILES.
Uruguay: 130 Albert St, Suite 1905, Ottawa K1P 5G4; tel. (613) 234-2727; Chargé d'affaires a.i.: ZULMA GUELMÁN.
Venezuela: 294 Albert St, Suite 602, Ottawa K1P 6E6; tel. (613) 235-5151; telex 053-4729; Ambassador: JOSÉ MACHIN.
Yugoslavia: 17 Blackburn Ave, Ottawa K1N 8A2; tel. (613) 233-6289; telex 053-4203; Ambassador: VLADIMIR PAVICEVIĆ.
Zaire: 18 Range Rd, Ottawa K1N 8J3; tel. (613) 236-7103; telex 053-4314; Ambassador: IKOLO BOLELAMA W'OKONDOLA.
Zambia: 130 Albert St, Suite 1610, Ottawa K1P 5G4; tel. (613) 563-0712; telex 053-4418; High Commissioner: Lt-Gen. BENJAMIN N. MIBENGE.
Zimbabwe: Place de Ville, Tower B, 112 Kent St, Suite 1315, Ottawa K1P 5P2; tel. (613) 237-4388; telex 053-4221; High Commissioner: STANISLAUS G. CHIGWEDERE.

Judicial System

FEDERAL COURTS

The Supreme Court of Canada: Supreme Court of Canada Bldg, Wellington St, Ottawa K1A 0J1; tel. (613) 995-4330; ultimate court of appeal in both civil and criminal cases throughout Canada. The judgment of the Court is final and conclusive. The Supreme Court is also required to advise on questions referred to it by the Governor in Council. Important questions concerning the interpretation of the Constitution Act, the constitutionality or interpretation of any federal or provincial law, the powers of Parliament or of the provincial legislatures or of both levels of government, among other matters, may be referred by the government to the Supreme Court for consideration.

In civil cases, appeals may be brought from any final judgment of the highest court of last resort in a province. The Supreme Court will grant permission to appeal if it is of the opinion that a question of public importance is involved, one that transcends the immediate concerns of the parties to the litigation. In criminal cases, the Court will hear appeals as of right concerning indictable offences where an acquittal has been set aside or where there has been a dissenting judgment on a point of law in a provincial court of appeal. The Supreme Court may, in addition, hear appeals on questions of law concerning both summary conviction and all other indictable offences if permission to appeal is first granted by the Court.

Chief Justice of Canada: R. G. Brian Dickson.
Puisne Judges: JEAN BEETZ, W. R. MCINTYRE, ANTONIO LAMER, BERTHA WILSON, GERALD LE DAIN, GÉRARD LA FOREST, CLAIRE L'HEUREUX-DUBÉ, JOHN SOPINKA.

The Federal Court of Canada: Supreme Court of Canada Bldg, Wellington St, Ottawa K1A 0H9; tel. (613) 992-4238; the Trial Division of the Federal Court has jurisdiction in claims against the Crown, claims by the Crown, miscellaneous cases involving the Crown, claims against or concerning crown officers and servants, relief against Federal Boards, Commissions, and other tribunals, interprovincial and federal-provincial disputes, industrial or industrial property matters, admiralty, income tax and estate tax appeals, citizenship appeals, aeronautics, interprovincial works and undertakings, residuary jurisdiction for relief if there is no other Canadian court that has such jurisdiction, jurisdiction in specific matters conferred by federal statutes.

The Federal Court of Appeal: Supreme Court of Canada Bldg, Wellington St, Ottawa K1A 0H9; tel. (613) 996-6795; has jurisdiction on appeals from the Trial Division, appeals from Federal Tribunals, review of decisions of Federal Boards and Commissions, appeals from Tribunals and Reviews under Section 28 of the Federal Court Act, and references by Federal Boards and Commissions. The Court has one central registry and consists of the principal office in Ottawa and local offices in major centres throughout Canada.

Chief Justice: FRANK IACOBUCCI.
Associate Chief Justice: JAMES A. JEROME.
Court of Appeal Judges: LOUIS PRATTE, DARREL V. HEALD, JOHN J. URIE, PATRICK M. MAHONEY, LOUIS MARCEAU, JAMES K. HUGESSEN, ARTHUR J. STONE, MARK R. MACGUIGAN, BERTRAND LACOMBE, ALICE DESJARDINS.
Trial Division Judges: GEORGE A. ADDY, J.-E. DUBÉ, PAUL U. C. ROULEAU, FRANCIS C. MULDOON, BARRY L. STRAYER, JOHN C. MCNAIR, BARBARA J. REED, PIERRE DENAULT, YVON PINARD, L. MARCEL JOYAL, BUD CULLEN, LEONARD A. MARTIN, MAX M. TEITELBAUM, WILLIAM ANDREW MACKAY.

PROVINCIAL COURTS

Alberta
Court of Appeal
Chief Justice of Alberta: J. H. LAYCRAFT.

Court of Queen's Bench
Chief Justice: W. K. MOORE.
Associate Chief Justice: T. H. MILLER.

British Columbia
Court of Appeal
Chief Justice of British Columbia: A. MCEACHERN.

Supreme Court
Chief Justice: B. MCLACHLIN.

Manitoba
Court of Appeal
Chief Justice of Manitoba: A. M. MONNIN.

Court of Queen's Bench
Chief Justice: B. HEWAK.
Associate Chief Justices: R. J. SCOTT, A. C. HAMILTON.

New Brunswick
Court of Appeal
Chief Justice of New Brunswick: S. G. STRATTON.

Court of Queen's Bench
Chief Justice: G. A. RICHARD.

Newfoundland
Supreme Court—Court of Appeal
Chief Justice: NOEL H. A. GOODRIDGE.

Trial Division
Chief Justice: T. A. HICKMAN.

Nova Scotia
Supreme Court—Appeal Division
Chief Justice of Nova Scotia: L. O. CLARKE.

Trial Division
Chief Justice: C. R. GLUBE.

Ontario
Supreme Court—Court of Appeal
Chief Justice of Ontario: W. G. C. HOWLAND.
Associate Chief Justice of Ontario: C. L. DUBIN.

CANADA

High Court of Justice
Chief Justice: W. D. PARKER.
Associate Chief Justice: F. W. CALLAGHAN.

Prince Edward Island
Supreme Court—Appeal Division
Chief Justice: N. H. CARRUTHERS.

Supreme Court—Trial Division
Chief Justice: K. R. MCDONALD.

Québec
Court of Appeal
Chief Justice of Québec: C. BISSON.

Superior Court
Chief Justice: ALAN B. GOLD.
Senior Associate Chief Justice: PIERRE CÔTÉ.
Associate Chief Justice: L. A. POITRAS.

Saskatchewan
Court of Appeal
Chief Justice of Saskatchewan: E. D. BAYDA.

Court of Queen's Bench
Chief Justice: MARY J. BATTEN.

Northwest Territories
Supreme Court
Judges of the Supreme Court: M. M. DE WEERDT, T. D. MARSHALL.

Court of Appeal
Chief Justice: J. H. LAYCRAFT (Alberta).

Yukon Territory
Supreme Court
Judge of the Supreme Court: H. C. B. MADDISON.

Court of Appeal
Chief Justice: A. MCEACHERN (British Columbia).

Religion

CHRISTIANITY

About 75% of the population belong to the three main Christian churches: Roman Catholic, United and Anglican. Numerous other religious denominations are represented.

Canadian Council of Churches/Conseil canadien des Eglises: 40 St Clair Ave East, Toronto, Ont M4T 1M9; tel. (416) 921-4152; telex 065-24128; f. 1944; 15 mem. churches, one assoc. mem.; Gen. Sec. Dr STUART E. BROWN.

The Anglican Communion

The Anglican Church of Canada (Eglise épiscopale du Canada) comprises four ecclesiastical provinces (each with a Metropolitan archbishop), containing a total of 30 dioceses. The Church had 912,518 members in 1982.

General Synod of the Anglican Church of Canada: Church House, 600 Jarvis St, Toronto, Ont M4Y 2J6; tel. (416) 924-9192; telex 065-24128; Gen. Sec. Archdeacon DAVID WOELLER.

Primate of the Anglican Church of Canada: MICHAEL GEOFFREY PEERS.

Archbishop of British Columbia: DOUGLAS WALTER HAMBIDGE, Bishop of New Westminster.

Archbishop of Canada: HAROLD LEE NUTTER, Bishop of Fredericton.

Archbishop of Ontario: JOHN CHARLES BOTHWELL, Bishop of Niagara.

Archbishop of Rupert's Land: WALTER HEATH JONES, Bishop of Rupert's Land.

The Orthodox Churches

Greek Orthodox Church: 40 Donlands Ave, Toronto, Ont M4J 3N6; tel. (416) 462-0833; 316,610 mems (1971 census); Bishop of Toronto His Grace SOTIRIOS.

Ukrainian Greek Orthodox Church: 9 St John's Ave, Winnipeg, Man R2W 1G8; tel. (204) 586-3093; f. 1918; 280 parishes; 150,000 mems; Metropolitan of Winnipeg and of all Canada Most Rev. WASYLY (FEDAK).

The Romanian, Syrian, Coptic and Byelorussian Churches are also represented in Canada.

The Roman Catholic Church

For Catholics of the Latin rite, Canada comprises 17 archdioceses (including one directly responsible to the Holy See), 47 dioceses and one territorial abbacy. There are also one archdiocese and four dioceses of the Ukrainian rite. In addition, the Maronite, Melkite and Slovak rites are each represented by one diocese (all directly responsible to the Holy See). In 1986 the Roman Catholic Church had 11,210,385 adherents in Canada.

Canadian Conference of Catholic Bishops/Conférence des évêques catholiques du Canada: 90 Parent Ave, Ottawa K1N 7B1; tel. (613) 236-9461; telex 053-3311; Pres. Most Rev. JAMES M. HAYES, Archbishop of Halifax; Vice-Pres. Mgr ROBERT LEBEL, Bishop of Valleyfield, Qué.

Latin Rite

Archbishop of Edmonton: JOSEPH N. MACNEIL.
Archbishop of Grouard-McLennan: HENRI LÉGARÉ.
Archbishop of Halifax: JAMES M. HAYES.
Archbishop of Keewatin-Le Pas: PETER ALFRED SUTTON.
Archbishop of Kingston: FRANCIS SPENCE.
Archbishop of Moncton: DONAT CHIASSON.
Archbishop of Montréal: Cardinal PAUL GRÉGOIRE.
Archbishop of Ottawa: JOSEPH-AURÈLE PLOURDE.
Archbishop of Québec: Cardinal LOUIS-ALBERT VACHON.
Archbishop of Regina: CHARLES A. HALPIN.
Archbishop of Rimouski: GILLES OUELLET.
Archbishop of St Boniface: MAURICE ANTOINE HACAULT.
Archbishop of St John's, Nfld: ALPHONSUS L. PENNEY.
Archbishop of Sherbrooke: JEAN-MARIE FORTIER.
Archbishop of Toronto: Cardinal G. EMMETT CARTER.
Archbishop of Vancouver: JAMES FRANCIS CARNEY.
Archbishop of Winnipeg: ADAM EXNER.

Ukrainian Rite

Ukrainian Catholic Church in Canada: 235 Scotia St, Winnipeg, Man R2V 1V7; tel. (204) 334-6363; 190,585 mems (1981 census); Archeparch-Metropolitan of Winnipeg Most Rev. MAXIM HERMANIUK.

The United Church of Canada

The United Church of Canada (Eglise unie du Canada) was founded in 1925 with the union of Methodist, Congregational and Presbyterian churches in Canada.
Other free churches have since joined. In 1988 there were 2,420 pastoral charges, 4,175 congregations, 3,897 ministers and 863,910 mems.

Moderator: Rt Rev. SANG CHUL LEE.
General Secretary: Rev. HOWARD M. MILLS, The United Church House, 85 St Clair Ave East, Toronto, Ont M4T 1M8; tel. (416) 925-5931; telex 065-28224.

Other Christian Churches

Canadian Baptist Federation: 7185 Millcreek Drive, Mississauga, Ont L5N 5R4; tel. (416) 826-0191; 1,200 churches; 131,472 mems (1986); Pres. ROBERT MACQUADE; Gen. Sec. Dr RICHARD C. COFFIN.

Christian Reformed Church in North America: 3475 Mainway, POB 5070, Burlington, Ont L7R 3Y8; tel. (416) 336-2920; f. 1857.

Church of Jesus Christ of Latter-day Saints (Mormon): 6940 Fisher Rd SE, Calgary, Alta; tel. (403) 252-1141; missions and institutes in nine major cities; 74,900 mems; Pres R. S. SPAFFORD.

Lutheran Church Canada: Winnipeg, Man; f. 1988; 325 congregations fmrly associated with the Lutheran Church Missouri Synod (USA); Pres. Rev. EDWIN LEHMAN.

Lutheran Council in Canada: 25 Old York Mills Rd, Willowdale, Toronto, Ont M2P 1B5; f. 1967; tel. (416) 488-9430; co-ordinating agency for Evangelical Lutheran Church in Canada and Lutheran Church Canada; 1,149 ministers; 1,008 congregations; 303,322 mems (1988); Exec. Dir LAWRENCE R. LIKNESS.

Mennonite Central Committee Canada: 134 Plaza Drive, Winnipeg, Man R3T 5K9; tel. (204) 261-6381; telex 075-7525; f. 1963; 95,000 mems in 560 congregations; Exec. Dir DANIEL ZEHR.

Pentecostal Assemblies of Canada: 10 Overlea Blvd, Toronto, Ont M4H 1A5; tel. (416) 425-1010; 185,257 mems; Gen. Supt Rev. J. M. MACKNIGHT; Gen. Sec. Rev. CHARLES YATES.

Presbyterian Church in Canada: 50 Wynford Drive, Don Mills, Ont M3C 1J7; tel. (416) 441-1111; f. 1875; 1,102 ministers, 1,028

CANADA

congregations; 159,179 mems (1986); Moderator Rev. TONY PLOMP; Prin. Clerk Dr E. F. ROBERTS.

Religious Society of Friends: 60 Lowther Ave, Toronto, Ont M5R 1C7; tel. (416) 922-2632; Clerk of Canadian Yearly Meeting DONALD LAITIN.

Seventh-day Adventists: 1148 King St East, Oshawa, Ont L1H 1H8; tel. (416) 433-0011; org. 1901; Pres. J. W. WILSON; Sec. D. D. DEVNICH.

BAHÁ'Í FAITH

Bahá'í Community of Canada: 7200 Leslie St, Thornhill, Ont L3T 6L8; tel. (416) 889-8168; f. 1902; 21,000 mems; Sec. Dr H. B. DANESH.

BUDDHISM

Buddhist Churches of Canada: 918 Bathurst St, Toronto, Ont M5R 3G5; tel. (416) 534-4302; Jodo Shinshu of Mahayana Buddhism; Bishop Rev. TOSHIO MURAKAMI.

ISLAM

There are an estimated 350,000 Muslims in Canada.

Council of Muslim Communities of Canada: 1521 Trinity Drive, Unit 16, Mississauga, Ont L5T 1P6; tel. (416) 672-1566; co-ordinating agency; Pres. Dr MIR IQBAL ALI.

JUDAISM

The Jews of Canada number 305,000.

Canadian Jewish Congress: 1590 ave Dr Penfield, Montréal, Qué H3G 1C5; tel. (514) 931-7531; f. 1919; Exec. Vice-Pres. ALAN ROSE.

Jewish Community Council: 151 Chapel St, Ottawa K1N 7Y2; tel. (613) 232-7306; Pres. STEPHEN VICTOR; Exec. Dir GERRY KOFFMAN.

The Press

The daily press in Canada is essentially local in coverage, influence and distribution. Through the use of satellite transmission, a national edition of the Toronto *Globe and Mail*, established in 1981, is available coast to coast, and in 1988 the *Financial Post* began publication of a national edition, also using satellite transmission.

Independently-owned daily newspapers account for 19% of the circulation of Canadian dailies. Chain ownership is predominant: over 47% of daily newspaper circulation is represented by two major groups: Thomson Newspapers Ltd (20.5% of daily newspaper circulation) and Southam Inc (27.0%). In 1987 the Québécor Group accounted for 8.7% of the total circulation, while the Sun Publishing Group also had 8.7%, and the Sterling Group had 0.8%. There are several smaller groups.

In September 1980 the Liberal government appointed a royal commission to investigate the effects of concentration of ownership in the newspaper industry. In August 1981 the commission reported that the existing concentration constituted a threat to press freedom, and recommended that some groups should be compelled to sell some of their newspaper interests in areas where there was extreme ownership concentration. While government action on the report has still to be finalized, it is expected that the Progressive Conservative government will continue to restrict cross-media ownership of newspapers, radio and television, and to prohibit non-media companies from owning daily newspapers.

In March 1988 there were 111 daily newspapers with a combined circulation of over 5.7m., representing 62% of the country's households.

In 1988 about 1,100 weekly and twice-weekly community newspapers reached an estimated 5.2m. people, mainly in the more remote areas of the country. A significant feature of the Canadian press is the number of newspapers catering for ethnic groups: there are over 80 of these daily and weekly publications appearing in over 20 languages.

There are numerous periodicals for business, trade, professional, recreational and special interest readership, although periodical publishing, particularly, suffers from substantial competition from publications originating in the USA. Among periodicals, the only one which can be regarded as national in its readership and coverage is *Maclean's Canada's Weekly Newsmagazine*.

The following are among the principal newspaper publishing groups:

Southam Newspaper Group: 150 Bloor St West, Suite 910, Toronto, Ont M5S 2Y9; tel. (416) 927-1877; Pres. PADDY SHERMAN.

Sterling Newspapers Ltd: 1827 West Fifth Ave, Second Floor, Vancouver, BC V6J 1P5; tel. (604) 732-4443; Pres. F. DAVID RADLER; Vice-Pres. and Gen. Man. STEEN O. JORGENSEN.

Directory

Thomson Newspapers Ltd: 65 Queen St West, Toronto, Ont M5H 2M8; tel. (416) 864-1710; Chair., Pres. and CEO KENNETH R. THOMSON.

DAILY NEWSPAPERS

(D = all day; E = evening; M = morning; S = Sunday; Publr = Publisher)

Alberta

Calgary Herald: POB 2400, Station M, Calgary T2P 0W8; tel. (403) 235-7100; telex 038-22793; f. 1883; Publr J. P. O'CALLAGHAN; Man. Editor GILLIAN STEWARD; circ. 138,000 (M); 124,000 (S).

Calgary Sun: 2615 12th St NE, Calgary T2E 7W9; tel. (403) 250-4200; telex 038-22734; f. 1980; Publr KENNETH M. KING; Editor-in-Chief ROBERT POOLE; circ. 73,000 (M), 98,000 (S).

Daily Herald-Tribune: 10604 100th St, Grande Prairie T8V 2M5; tel. (403) 532-1110; f. 1964; Publr B. WAYNE JOBB; Man. Editor BILL SCOTT; circ. 8,000 (E).

Edmonton Journal: 10006 101st St, Edmonton T5J 2S6; tel. (403) 429-5100; telex 037-3492; f. 1903; Publr WILLIAM NEWBIGGING; Editor LINDA HUGHES; circ. 169,000 (M); 149,000 (S).

Edmonton Sun: 9405 50th St, Edmonton T6B 2T4; tel. (403) 468-0100; telex 037-42665; f. 1978; Publr PATRICK A. HARDEN; Editor-in-Chief DAVID BAILEY; circ. 87,000 (M), 125,000 (S).

Lethbridge Herald: POB 670, Lethbridge T1J 3Z7; tel. (403) 328-4411; telex 038-49220; f. 1907; Publr and Gen. Man. DONALD R. DORAM; Man. Editor JIM HASKETT; circ. 26,000 (E).

Medicine Hat News: POB 10, Medicine Hat T1A 7E6; tel. (403) 527-1101; telex 038-48191; f. 1910; Publr GEORGE WILLCOCKS; Editor PETER MOSSEY; circ. 14,000 (E).

Red Deer Advocate: POB 5200, Red Deer T4N 5G3; tel. (403) 343-2400; f. 1901; Publr HOWARD D. JANZEN; Man. Editor JOE MCLAUGHLIN; circ. 23,000 (E).

British Columbia

Daily Courier: 550 Doyle Ave, Kelowna V1Y 7V1; tel. (604) 762-4445; f. 1904; Publr D. F. DOUCETTE; Man. Editor DAVE HENSHAW; circ. 17,000 (E).

Daily News: POB 580, Prince Rupert V8J 3R9; tel. (604) 624-6781; f. 1910; Publr IRIS CHRISTISON; circ. 4,000 (E).

Kamloops Daily News: 106-63 West Victoria St, Kamloops V2C 6J6; tel. (604) 372-2331; f. 1982; Publr BRYSON W. STONE; Editor MEL ROTHENBURGER; circ. 21,000 (E).

Nanaimo Daily Free Press: 223 Commercial St, POB 69, Nanaimo V9R 5K5; tel. (604) 753-3451; f. 1874; Publr CLYDE T. WICKS; Man. Editor FRANK PHILLIPS; circ. 10,000 (E).

Nelson Daily News: 266 Baker St, Nelson V1L 4H3; tel. (604) 352-3552; f. 1902; Publr ROBERT FIRTH; Man. Editor RYON GUEDES; circ. 5,000 (M).

Penticton Herald: 186 Nanaimo Ave West, Penticton V2A 1N4; tel. (604) 492-4002; Publr JOHN J. KOBYLNIK; Editor MIKE INGRAHAM; circ. 8,000 (E).

Prince George Citizen: POB 5700, Prince George V2L 5K9; tel. (604) 562-2441; f. 1957; Publr ALASTAIR MCNAIR; Editor ROY K. NAGEL; circ. 22,000 (E).

The Province: 2250 Granville St, Vancouver V6H 3G2; tel. (604) 732-2222; f. 1898; Publr G. HASLAM; Editor ROBERT D. MCMURRAY; circ. 188,000 (M), 220,000 (S).

The Vancouver Sun: 2250 Granville St, Vancouver V6H 3G2; tel. (604) 732-2111; telex 045-5695; f. 1886; Publr G. HASLAM; Editor BRUCE LARSEN; circ. 227,000 (E).

Times-Colonist: POB 300, Victoria V8W 2N4; tel. (604) 380-5211; telex 049-7288; f. 1858; Publr COLIN MCCULLOUGH; Man. Editor GORDON R. BELL; circ. 81,000 (M), 78,000 (S).

Manitoba

Brandon Sun: POB 460, Brandon R7A 5Z6; tel. (204) 727-2451; f. 1882; Publr ROB FORBES; Man. Editor JACK GIBSON; circ. 18,000 (E).

Daily Graphic: POB 130, Portage La Prairie R1N 3B4; tel. (204) 857-3427; Publr HUGH A. MCTAGGART; circ. 5,000 (E).

Flin Flon Reminder: 38 Main St, POB 727, Flin Flon R8A 1N5; tel. (204) 687-3454; f. 1946; Publr T. W. DOBSON; Man. Editor RON DOBSON; circ. 4,000 (E).

Winnipeg Free Press: 300 Carlton St, Winnipeg R3C 3C1; tel. (204) 943-9331; f. 1874; Publr ARTHUR E. WOOD; Man. Editor MURRAY BURT; circ. 179,000 (E), 146,000 (S).

Winnipeg Sun: 1700 Church Ave, Winnipeg R2X 2W9; tel. (204) 632-2766; f. 1980; Publr AL DAVIES; circ. 54,000 (M), 60,000 (S).

CANADA

New Brunswick

L'Acadie Nouvelle: 217 blvd St-Pierre O., Caraquet E0B 1K0; tel. (506) 727-4444; f. 1984; Gen. Man. CAMILLE MCLAUGHLIN; circ. 9,000 (M).

Daily Gleaner: POB 3370, Fredericton E3B 5A2; tel. (506) 452-6671; f. 1880; Publr TOM CROWTHER; Editor-in-Chief HAL P. WOOD; circ. 29,000 (E).

Telegraph-Journal and **Evening Times-Globe:** POB 2350, Saint John E2L 3V8; tel. (506) 632-8888; Pres. and Publr R. PAUL WILLCOCKS; Editor-in-Chief FRED HAZEL; circ. 63,000 (D).

The Times-Transcript: POB 1001, Moncton E1C 8P3; tel. (506) 853-9321; Publr JAMES D. NICHOL; Man. Editor MIKE BEMBRIDGE; circ. 44,000 (E).

Newfoundland

Telegram: POB 5970, St John's A1C 5X7; tel. (709) 364-6300; f. 1879; Publr S. R. HERDER; Editor W. R. CALLAHAN; circ. 39,000 (E), 55,000 (Saturday).

Western Star: POB 460, West St, Corner Brook A2H 6E7; tel. (709) 634-4348; f. 1900; Publr LEITH ORR; Editor-in-Chief C. HALLOWAY; circ. 11,000 (E).

Nova Scotia

Amherst Daily News: POB 280, Amherst B4H 3Z2; tel. (902) 667-5102; f. 1893; Publr EARL J. GOUCHIE; Editor JOHN CONRAD; circ. 4,000 (M).

Cape Breton Post: 255 George St, POB 1500, Sydney B1P 6K6; tel. (902) 564-5451; f. 1900; Publr JAMES P. MILNE; Man. Editor ANGUS MACDONALD; circ. 32,000 (E).

Chronicle-Herald and **Mail-Star:** 1650 Argyle St, POB 610, Halifax B3J 2T2; tel. (902) 426-2811; telex 019-21874; Pres. FRED G. MOUNCE; Man. Editor KEN FORAN; circ. 87,000 (M), 60,000 (E).

Daily News: POB 8330, Station A, Halifax; tel. (902) 465-1222; f. 1974; Editor-in-Chief DOUG MACKAY; circ. 22,000 (E).

Evening News: 352 East River Rd, New Glasgow B2H 5E2; tel. (902) 752-3000; f. 1910; Publr and Gen. Man. KEN SIMS; Man. Editor DOUG MACNEILL; circ. 11,000 (E).

Truro Daily News: POB 220, Truro B2N 5C3; tel. (902) 893-9405; f. 1891; Publr TERRENCE W. HONEY; Man. Editor ROBERT PAXTON; circ. 9,000 (E).

Ontario

Barrie Examiner: 16 Bayfield St, Barrie L4M 4T6; tel. (416) 726-6537; f. 1864; Publr P. J. KAPYRKA; Man. Editor MARK FURLONG; circ. 15,000 (E).

Beacon Herald: POB 430, Stratford N5A 6T6; tel. (519) 271-2220; f. 1854; Co-Publr and Gen. Man. CHARLES W. DINGMAN; Co-Publr and Editor STANFORD H. DINGMAN; circ. 13,000 (E).

Brampton Times: 33 Queen St West, Brampton L6Y 1M1; tel. (416) 451-2020; f. 1885; Publr VICTOR MLODECKI; Man. Editor STEVE RHODES; circ. 10,000 (E).

Cambridge Daily Reporter: 26 Ainslie St South, Cambridge N1R 3K1; tel. (519) 621-3810; f. 1846; Publr GARNET COWSILL; Man. Editor DON MOORE; circ. 14,000 (E).

Chatham Daily News: 45 Fourth St, POB 2007, Chatham N7M 2G4; tel. (519) 354-2000; f. 1862; Publr F. IAN RUTHERFORD; Man. Editor STEVE ZAK; circ. 16,000 (E).

Cobourg Daily Star: POB 400, Cobourg K9A 4L1; tel. (416) 372-0131; Publr BILL POIRIER; Man. Editor JUDY HEROD; circ. 6,000.

Daily Mercury: 8–14 Macdonnell St, Guelph N1H 6P7; tel. (519) 822-4310; f. 1854; Publr. J. PETER KOHL; Editor-in-Chief BOB BOXALL; circ. 19,000 (E).

Daily Packet and Times: 31 Colborne St East, Orillia L3V 1T4; tel. (416) 325-1355; f. 1953; Gen. Man. J. C. MARSHALL; Man. Editor JEFF DAY; circ. 10,000 (E).

Daily Press: 187 Cedar St South, POB 560, Timmins P4N 2G9; tel. (705) 268-5050; f. 1933; Publr J. C. BUTLER; Editor J. HORNYAK; circ. 14,000 (E).

Daily Sentinel-Review: POB 1000, Woodstock N4S 8A5; tel. (519) 537-2341; f. 1886; Publr PAUL J. TAYLOR; Man. Editor GARY MANNING; circ. 10,000 (E).

Le Droit: 375 Rideau St, Ottawa K1N 5Y7; tel. (613) 560-2500; f. 1913; French; Publr GILBERT LACASSE; Editor-in-Chief PIERRE ALLARD; circ. 39,000 (E).

Evening Guide: POB 296, Port Hope L1A 3W4; tel. (416) 885-2471; Publr WILLIAM POIRIER; Editor DAVID COBAIN; circ. 3,000 (E).

Expositor: POB 965, Brantford N3T 5S8; tel. (519) 756-2020; f. 1852; Publr J. HOWARD GAUL; Editor K. J. STRACHAN; circ. 34,000 (E).

Financial Post: 777 Bay St, Toronto M5G 2E4; tel. (416) 596-5649; telex 062-19547; f. 1988; Publr NEVILLE J. NANKIVELL; Editor JOHN F. GODFREY; Tues.-to-Fri.; (M).

The Globe and Mail: 444 Front St West, Toronto M5V 2S9; tel. (416) 585-5000; telex 062-19721; f. 1844; Publr A. ROY MEGARRY; Editor-in-Chief NORMAN WEBSTER; circ. 326,000 (M).

Hamilton Spectator: POB 300, Hamilton L8N 3G3; tel. (416) 526-3333; f. 1846; Publr GORDON BULLOCK; Editor ALEX M. BEER; circ. 144,000 (E).

Intelligencer: POB 5600, Belleville K8N 5C7; tel. (613) 962-9171; f. 1870; Publr and Gen. Man. H. MYLES MORTON; Man. Editor LEE BALLANTYNE; circ. 19,000 (E).

Kitchener-Waterloo Record: 225 Fairway Rd, Kitchener N2G 4E5; tel. (519) 894-2231; f. 1878; Publr K. A. BAIRD; Man. Editor WAYNE MACDONALD; circ. 79,000 (E).

Lindsay Daily Post: 15 William St North, Lindsay K9V 3Z8; tel. (705) 324-2114; Pres. J. A. MCQUARRIE; circ. 5,000 (E).

London Free Press: POB 2280, London N6A 4G1; tel. (519) 679-1111; f. 1849; Pres. J. E. ARMITAGE; Editor PHILIP R. MCLEOD; circ. 131,000 (M).

Niagara Falls Review: POB 270, Niagara Falls L2E 6T6; tel. (416) 358-5711; f. 1879; Publr GORDON A. MURRAY; Man. Editor DONALD W. MULLAN; circ. 22,000 (M).

Northern Daily News: 8 Duncan Ave, Kirkland Lake P2N 3L4; tel. (705) 567-5321; f. 1922; Publr WILLIAM MACKIE; Editor AL HOGAN; circ. 6,000 (E).

The Nugget: POB 570, North Bay P1B 8J6; tel. (705) 472-3200; f. 1909; Publr JACK R. OWENS; Editor COLIN P. VEZINA; circ. 25,000 (E).

Observer: 186 Alexander St, Pembroke K8A 4L9; tel. (613) 732-3691; f. 1855; Publr and Man. Editor W. H. HIGGINSON; circ. 7,000 (E).

Ottawa Citizen: POB 5020, Ottawa K2C 3M4; tel. (613) 829-9100; telex 053-4779; f. 1843; Publr RUSSELL A. MILLS; Editor KEITH SPICER; circ. 192,000 (D), 249,000 (Sat.).

Peterborough Examiner: POB 389, Peterborough K9J 6Z4; tel. (705) 745-4641; f. 1884; Publr and Gen. Man. BRUCE L. RUDD; Man. Editor ED ARNOLD; circ. 27,000 (E).

Recorder and Times: 23 King St West, Brockville K6V 5T8; tel. (613) 342-4441; f. 1821; Co-Publr H. S. GRANT; Co-Publr and Editor-in-Chief Mrs PERRY S. BEVERLEY; circ. 16,000 (E).

St Thomas Times-Journal: 16 Hincks St, St Thomas N5P 3W6; tel. (519) 631-2790; f. 1882; Publr and Gen. Man. L. J. BEAVIS; Man. Editor T. SHAW; circ. 9,000 (E).

Sarnia Observer: POB 3009, Sarnia N7T 7M8; tel. (519) 344-3641; f. 1917; Publr and Gen. Man. TERENCE J. HOGAN; Man. Editor COLIN BRUCE; circ. 24,000 (E).

Sault Star: POB 460, Sault Ste Marie P6A 5M5; tel. (705) 759-3030; f. 1912; Publr CLIFFORD C. SHARP; Man. Editor DOUG MILLROY; circ. 27,000 (E).

Simcoe Reformer: POB 370, Simcoe N3Y 4L2; tel. (519) 426-5710; f. 1858; Publr JOHN COWLARD; Man. Editor RON KOWALSKY; circ. 10,000 (E).

Standard: 17 Queen St, St Catharine's L2R 5G5; tel. (416) 684-7251; f. 1891; Pres. and Publr HENRY B. BURGOYNE; Man. Editor MURRAY O. G. THOMSON; circ. 44,000 (E).

Standard-Freeholder: 44 Pitt St, Cornwall K6J 3P3; tel. (613) 933-3160; Publr DON TOMCHICK; Man. Editor CRAIG ELSON; circ. 18,000 (E).

Sudbury Daily Star: 33 Mackenzie St, Sudbury P3C 4Y1; tel. (705) 674-5271; f. 1909; Publr MAURICE H. SWITZER; Man. Editor JOHN A. FARRINGTON; circ. 30,000 (E).

Sun Times: POB 200, Owen Sound N4K 5P2; tel. (519) 376-2250; f. 1853; Publr J. G. DOHERTY; Editor ROBERT HULL; circ. 24,000 (E).

The Times: 44 Richmond St West, Oshawa L1G 1C8; tel. (416) 723-3474; f. 1871; Publr A. S. TOPP; Man. Editor D. JAMES PALMATEER; circ. 22,000 (E).

Times-News and **Chronicle-Journal:** 75 Cumberland St South, Thunder Bay P7B 1A3; tel. (807) 344-3535; Publr F. M. DUNDAS; Man. Editor MICHAEL GRIEVE; circ. 40,000 (D).

Toronto Star: One Yonge St, Toronto M5E 1E6; tel. (416) 367-2000; telex 065-24387; f. 1892; Publr BELAND H. HONDERICH; Exec. Editor RAY TIMSON; circ. 519,000 (D), 806,000 (Sat.), 533,000 (S).

Toronto Sun: 333 King St East, Toronto M5A 3X5; tel. (416) 947-2222; telex 062-17688; f. 1971; Pres. and CEO J. DOUGLAS CREIGHTON; Editor JOHN DOWNING; Man. Editor PETER BREWSTER; circ. 290,000 (M), 461,000 (S).

Welland-Port Colborne Evening Tribune: POB 278, Welland L3B 5P5; tel. (416) 732-2411; f. 1863; Publr JOHN W. VANKOOTEN; Editor JAMES R. MIDDLETON; circ. 17,000 (E).

Whig-Standard: 306 King St East, Kingston K7L 4Z7; tel. (613) 544-5000; f. 1834; Publr MICHAEL L. DAVIES; Editor NEIL REYNOLDS; circ. 37,000 (E).

Windsor Star: 167 Ferry St, Windsor N9A 4M5; tel. (519) 255-5711; telex 064-77709; f. 1918; Publr J. S. THOMSON; Editor CARL MORGAN; circ. 88,000 (E).

Prince Edward Island

Guardian and Patriot: POB 760, Charlottetown C1A 4R7; tel. (902) 894-8506; f. 1887; Publr STEWART VICKERSON; Man. Editor WALTER MACINTYRE; circ. 24,000 (D).

Journal-Pioneer: POB 2480, Summerside C1N 4K5; tel. (902) 436-2121; f. 1957; Publr RALPH HECKBERT; Editor RON ENGLAND; circ. 12,000 (E).

Québec

Le Devoir: 211 rue du St-Sacrement, Montréal H2Y 1X1; tel. (514) 844-3361; f. 1910; Dir BENOÎT LAUZIÈRE; Editor-in-Chief PAUL-ANDRÉ COMEAU; circ. 29,000 (M).

The Gazette: 250 ouest, rue St-Antoine, Montréal H2Y 3R7; tel. (514) 282-2222; telex 055-61767; f. 1778; Publr CLARK DAVEY; Editor MARK HARRISON; circ. 192,000 (M), 272,000 (Sat.).

Le Journal de Montréal: 4545 Frontenac, Montréal H2H 2R7; tel. (514) 521-4545; f. 1964; Publr JOCELYNE PELCHAT; Editor NORMAND GIRARD; circ. 328,000 (M), 355,000 (Sat.), 348,000 (S).

Le Journal de Québec: 450 rue Béchard, Ville de Vanier G1M 2E9; tel. (613) 683-1573; f. 1967; Gen. Man. JEAN-CLAUDE L'ABBÉE; Chief Editor SERGE CÔTÉ; circ. 109,000 (M), 110,000 (Sat.), 98,000 (S).

Montréal Daily News: 980 ouest, rue St-Antoine, Montréal H3C 1A8; tel. (514) 877-6397; f. 1988; Publr GEORGE MACLAREN;

Le Nouvelliste: 500 rue St-Georges, Trois Rivières G9A 2K8; tel. (819) 376-2501; f. 1920; Publr CLAUDETTE TOUGAS; Man. Editor BERNARD CHAMPOUX; circ. 57,000 (M).

La Presse: 7 rue St-Jacques, Montréal H2Y 1K9; tel. (514) 285-7272; telex 052-4110; f. 1884; Publr ROGER D. LANDRY; circ. 207,000 (M), 327,000 (Sat.), 184,000 (S).

Le Quotidien du Saguenay, Lac St Jean: 1051 blvd Talbot, Chicoutimi G7H 5C1; tel. (418) 545-4474; f. 1973; Pres. GASTON VACHON; Newsroom Dir BERTRAND GENEST; circ. 35,000 (M).

The Record: 2850 rue Delorme, Sherbrooke J1K 1A1; tel. (819) 569-9525; f. 1897; Publr GEORGE R. MACLAREN; Editor CHARLES BURY; circ. 6,000 (M).

Le Soleil: 390 est, rue St Vallier, Québec G1K 7J6; tel. (418) 647-3233; telex 051-3755; f. 1896; Pres. and Gen. Man. ROBERT NORMAND; Editor-in-Chief CLAUDE GRAVEL; circ. 115,000 (M), 145,000 (Sat.), 94,000 (S).

La Tribune: 1950 rue Roy, Sherbrooke J1K 2X8; tel. (819) 564-5450; f. 1910; Publr YVON DUBÉ; Editor JEAN VIGNEAULT; circ. 42,000 (M).

La Voix de L'Est: 136 rue Principale, Granby J2G 2V4; tel. (514) 375-4555; f. 1945; Publr and Gen. Man. JEAN-GUY DUBUC; Man. Editor RÉAL MARCHESSEAULT; circ. 16,000 (M).

Saskatchewan

Leader-Post: POB 2020, Regina S4P 3G4; tel. (306) 565-8211; telex 071-3131; f. 1883; Pres. MICHAEL G. SIFTON; Editor W. IVOR WILLIAMS; circ. 72,000 (E).

Moose Jaw Times-Herald: 44 Fairford St West, Moose Jaw S6H 1V1; tel. (306) 692-6441; f. 1889; Publr PETER E. LEICHNITZ; Editor DAVE MCGEE; circ. 9,000 (E).

Prince Albert Herald: 30 10th St East, Prince Albert S6V 5R9; tel. (306) 764-4276; f. 1917; Publr and Gen. Man. R. W. GIBB; Man. Editor W. ROZNOWSKY; circ. 9,000 (M).

Star-Phoenix: 204 5th Ave North, Saskatoon S7K 2P1; tel. (306) 652-9200; telex 074-2428; f. 1902; Pres. MICHAEL C. SIFTON; Exec. Editor BILL PETERSON; circ. 66,000 (E).

Yukon Territory

Whitehorse Star: 2149-2nd Ave, Whitehorse, Yukon Y1A 1C5; tel. (403) 668-2063; f. 1985; Publr ROBERT ERLAM; Editor MASSEY PADGHAM; circ. 3,000.

SELECTED PERIODICALS

(W = weekly; F = fortnightly; M = monthly; Q = quarterly)

Alberta

Alberta Business: 340–39th Ave SE, Calgary T2G 1X6; tel. (403) 271-7508; f. 1984; Editor JOHN DODD; circ. 8,000.

Alberta Farmagazine: 4000–19th St, NE, Calgary T2E 6P8; tel. (403) 250-6633; f. 1983; Editor PETER BROUWER; circ. 92,000 (M).

Alberta Report: 17327-106th Ave, Edmonton T5S 1M7; tel. (403) 484-8884; f. 1979; news magazine; Editor STEPHEN HOPKINS; circ. 54,000 (W).

Ukrainski Visti (Ukrainian News): 10967-97th St, Edmonton T5H 2M8; tel. (403) 429-2363; f. 1929; Ukrainian and English; Editor K. SHERMAN; circ. 5,000 (W).

Western Catholic Reporter: 10562–109th St, Edmonton T5H 3B2; tel. (403) 420-1330; Editor FRANK DOLPHIN; circ. 37,000 (W).

British Columbia

BC Business: 550 Burrard St, 2nd Floor, Vancouver, V6C 2J6; tel. (604) 669-1721; telex 043-57513; f. 1973; Editor BONNIE IRVING; circ. 22,000 (M).

BC Outdoors: 1132 Hamilton St, Suite 202, Vancouver V6B 2S2; tel. (604) 687-1581; telex 045-3454; f. 1945; Editor GEORGE WILL; circ. 37,000; 7 a year.

Easy Living: 13281 Comber Way, Surrey V3W 5V8; tel. (604) 591-5101; f. 1979; Editor VIVIAN SINCLAIR; circ. 355,000 (M).

Pacific Yachting: 1132 Hamilton St, Suite 202, Vancouver V6B 2S2; tel. (604) 687-1581; f. 1968; Publr PAUL BURKHART; circ. 17,000 (M).

Vancouver Magazine: 1205 Richards St, Vancouver V6B 3G3; tel. (604) 685-5374; f. 1957; Editor BOB MERCER; circ. 82,000 (M).

Western Living: 504 Davie St, Vancouver V6B 2G4; tel. (604) 669-7525; telex 045-1484; f. 1971; Editor MALCOLM PARRY; circ. 239,000 (M).

WestWorld Magazine: 4180 Lougheed Hwy, Suite 401, Burnaby, V5C 6A7; tel. (604) 299-7311; Publr PETER LEGGE; Editor CAROL POPE; circ. 731,000 (Q).

Manitoba

The Beaver: Exploring Canada's History: 450 Portage Ave, Winnipeg R3C 0E7; tel. (204) 786-7048; f. 1920; Canadian social history; Editor CHRISTOPHER DAFOE; circ. 30,000; 6 a year.

Cattlemen: 1760 Ellice Ave, Winnipeg R3H 0B6; tel. (204) 774-1861; f. 1938; animal husbandry; Editor GREN WINSLOW; circ. 37,000 (M).

Country Guide: 1760 Ellice Ave, Winnipeg R3H 0B6; tel. (204) 774-1861; f. 1882; agriculture; Editor DAVID WREFORD; circ. 213,000 (M).

Kanada Kurier: 955 Alexander Ave, Winnipeg R3C 0A5; tel. (204) 774-1883; f. 1889; German; Editor E. PRIEBE; circ. 20,000 (W).

The Manitoba Co-operator: 220 Portage Ave, 4th Floor, Winnipeg R3C 0A5; tel. (204) 934-0401; f. 1925; agricultural; Editor and Publr W. E. MORRIS; circ. 29,000 (W).

Motor in Canada: 1077 St James St, POB 6900, Winnipeg R3C 3B1; tel. (204) 775-0201; f. 1915; Editor DAN PROUDLEY; circ. 12,000 (M).

Trade and Commerce: 1077 St James St, POB 6900, Winnipeg R3C 3B1; tel. (204) 775-0201; f. 1905; Editor GEORGE MITCHELL; circ. 13,000 (M).

New Brunswick

Atlantic Advocate: POB 3370, Fredericton E3B 5A2; tel. (506) 452-6671; f. 1956; Editor H. P. WOOD; circ. 27,000 (M).

Newfoundland

Newfoundland Lifestyle: 197 Water St, POB 2356, St John's A1C 6E7; tel. (709) 726-9300; Man. Editor EDWINA HUTTON; circ. 30,000; 6 a year.

Northwest Territories

L'Aquillon: POB 1325, Yellowknife X1A 2N9; tel. (819) 920-2919; circ. 2,000 (W).

The Drum: POB 2719, Inuvik X0E 0T0; tel. (819) 979-4545; f. 1966; English; Editor DAN HOLMAN; circ. 2,000 (W).

The Hub: POB 1250, Hay River X0E 0R0; tel. (819) 874-6577; circ. 2,000 (W).

News/North: POB 2820, Yellowknife X1A 2R1; tel. (819) 873-2661; f. 1945; circ. 9,000 (W).

Nunatsiaq News: POB 8, Iqaluit X0A 0H0; tel. (819) 979-5357; circ. 4,000 (W).

Slave River Journal: POB 990, Fort Smith X0E 0P0; tel. (819) 872-2784; circ. 2,000 (W).

Weekender: POB 2820, Yellowknife X1A 2R1; tel. (819) 873-4031.

Yellowknife: POB 2820, Yellowknife X1A 2R1; tel. (819) 873-4031; circ. 6,000 (W).

Nova Scotia

Atlantic Fisherman: 11 George St, POB 1000, Pictou B0K 1H0; tel. (902) 485-8014; f. 1984; Editor HEATHER RICHARDS; circ. 9,000 (F).

CANADA

Atlantic Insight: 1668 Barrington St, Halifax B3J 2A2; tel. (902) 421-1214; Editor SHARON FRASER; circ. 39,000 (M).

The Dalhousie Review: Dalhousie University Press, Sir James Dunn Science Bldg, Halifax B3H 3J5; tel. (902) 424-2541; f. 1921; literary and general; Editor Dr ALAN ANDREWS; (Q).

Ontario

Canada Gazette: Canadian Government Publishing Centre, Supply and Services Canada, Ottawa K1A 0S9; tel. (819) 997-1988; f. 1867; official bulletin of the Govt of Canada; Chief BEATE ALAOUI; (W).

Canada Reports: External Information Services Division, Dept of External Affairs, Ottawa K1A 0G2; telex 053-3745; English and French edns; Editor CAROLE STELMACK; (F).

Canada & the World: POB 7004, Oakville L6J 6L5; tel. (416) 338-3394; f. 1937; Editor RUPERT J. TAYLOR; circ. 24,000; 9 a year.

Canadian Aeronautics and Space Journal: 222 Somerset St West, Suite 601, Ottawa K2P 2G3; tel. (613) 234-0191; f. 1954; Chair. of Editorial Board Dr G. F. MARSTERS; circ. 3,000 (M).

Canadian Architect: 1450 Don Mills Rd, Don Mills M3B 2X7; tel. (416) 445-6641; telex 069-66612; f. 1955; Publr and Man. Editor ROBERT GRETTON; circ. 10,000 (M).

Canadian Bar Review: Canadian Bar Foundation, 50 O'Connor St, Suite 902, Ottawa K1P 6L2; tel. (613) 237-2925; telex 053-3063; f. 1923; Editor A. J. MCCLEAN; circ. 34,000 (Q).

Canadian Boating: 5200 Dixie Rd, Suite 204, Mississauga L4W 1E4; tel. (416) 625-5277; telex 069-86841; f. 1925; Editor GARY ARTHURS; circ. 17,000; 9 a year.

Canadian Chemical News: 1785 Alta Vista Drive, Ottawa K1G 3Y6; tel. (613) 526-4652; f. 1949; Editor MARGARET NEARING; circ. 10,000; 10 a year.

Canadian Construction Record: 1450 Don Mills Road, Don Mills M3B 2X7; tel. (416) 445-6641; telex 069-66612; f. 1888; Editor TED THALER; circ. 22,000 (M).

Canadian Dental Association Journal: 1815 Alta Vista Drive, Ottawa K1G 3Y6; tel. (613) 523-1770; f. 1935; Editor Dr RALPH CRAWFORD; Scientific Editors Dr ROBERT TURNBULL, Dr PIERRE DESAUTELS; (M).

Canadian Doctor: 5873 Highway 7, Markham L3P 1A3; tel. (416) 471-1490; f. 1935; Editor SHEREE L. BOND; circ. 30,000 (M).

Canadian Forest Industries: 1450 Don Mills Rd, Don Mills M3B 2X7; tel. (416) 445-6641; telex 069-66612; f. 1880; Editor TIM TOLTON; circ. 21,000 (M).

Canadian Geographic: 39 McArthur Ave, Vanier K1L 8L7; tel. (613) 745-4629; f. 1930; publ. by the Royal Canadian Geographical Soc.; Editor ROSS W. SMITH; circ. 200,000; 6 a year.

Canadian Labour: 2841 Riverside Drive, Ottawa K1V 8X7; tel. (613) 521-3400; telex 053-4750; f. 1956; trade union; Editors D. HODGSON, M. WALSH; quarterly.

Canadian Medical Association Journal: 1867 Alta Vista Drive, Ottawa K1G 3Y6; tel. (613) 731-9331; telex 053-3152; f. 1911; Scientific Editor Dr BRUCE P. SQUIRES; circ. 50,000 (F).

Canadian Nurse—L' infirmière canadienne: 50 The Driveway, Ottawa K2P 1E2; tel. (613) 237-2133; f. 1908; journal of the Canadian Nurses' Asscn; Editor JUDITH A. BANNING; circ. 101,000 (M).

Canadian Pharmaceutical Journal: 1785 Alta Vista Drive, Ottawa K1G 3Y6; tel. (613) 523-7877; f. 1869; Editor JANE DEWAR; circ. 12,000 (M).

Canadian Sportsman: 25 Townline Rd, POB 603, Tillsonburg N4G 4J1; tel. (519) 842-4824; f. 1870; Editor GARY FOERSTER; W (May–October), F (October–May).

Canadian Workshop: 130 Spy Court, Markham L3R 5H6; tel. (416) 475-8440; f. 1977; do-it-yourself; Editor CINDY LISTER; circ. 108,000 (M).

Electronics & Technology Today: 1300 Don Mills Rd, Don Mills M3B 3M8; tel. (416) 445-5600; f. 1977; Editor BILL MARKWICK; circ. 15,000 (M).

Holstein Journal: 335 Lesmill Rd, Don Mills M3B 2V1; tel. (416) 441-3030; f. 1938; Editor BONNIE E. COOPER; circ. 19,000 (M).

Legion Magazine: 359 Kent St, Suite 504, Ottawa K2P 0R6; tel. (613) 235-8741; f. 1926; Editor MALCOLM JOHNSTON; circ. 506,000; 10 a year.

Modern Medicine of Canada: 1450 Don Mills Rd, Don Mills M3B 2X7; tel. (416) 445-6641; telex 069-66612; f. 1946; Editor Dr J. A. KELLEN; English and French; circ. 35,000 (M).

Ontario Milk Producer: 6780 Campobello Rd, Mississauga L5N 2L8; tel. (416) 821-8970; f. 1925; Publr KEN SMITH; circ. 15,000.

Oral Health: 1450 Don Mills Rd, Don Mills M3B 2X7; tel. (416) 445-6641; telex 069-66612; f. 1911; dentistry; Man. Editor JANET BONELLIE; circ. 15,000 (M).

Style: 85 Scarsdale Rd, Suite 300, Don Mills M3B 2R2; tel. (416) 444-8407; telex 069-86351; f. 1888; Editor MARILYN BOLTON; circ. 8,000; 16 a year.

Teviskes Ziburiai (Lights of Homeland): 2185 Stavebank Rd, Mississauga L5C 1T3; tel. (416) 275-4672; f. 1949; Lithuanian; Editor Rev. Dr PR. GAIDA; circ. 6,000 (W).

Toronto

Anglican Journal Episcopal: 600 Jarvis St, Toronto M4Y 2J6; tel. (416) 924-9192; telex 065-24128; f. 1871; official publ. of the Anglican Church of Canada; Editor JERROLD HAMES; circ. 272,000 (M).

Arab News of Toronto (Akhbar El-Arab Toronto): 370 Queen St East, Toronto M5A 1T1; tel. (416) 362-0304; telex 065-2629; f. 1978; Arabic and English; Editor SALAH ALLAM; circ. 6,000 (F).

Books in Canada: 366 Adelaide St East, 4th Floor, Toronto M5A 3X9; tel. (416) 363-5426; f. 1971; Editor DORIS COWAN; circ. 20,000; 9 a year.

CA magazine: The Canadian Institute of Chartered Accountants, 150 Bloor St West, Toronto M5S 2Y2; tel. (416) 962-1242; telex 062-22835; f. 1911; Editor NELSON LUSCOMBE; circ. 57,000 (M).

The Campus Network: Youthstream Canada Ltd, 1541 Avenue Rd, Suite 203, Toronto M5M 3X4; tel. (416) 787-4911; 30 campus edns; Pres. CAMERON KILLORAN; circ. 257,000.

Canadian Author & Bookman: 121 Avenue Rd, Suite 104, Toronto M5R 2G3; tel. (416) 926-8084; f. 1919; publ. by the Canadian Authors Asscn; Editor DIANE KERNER; circ. 5,000 (Q).

Canadian Business: 70 The Esplanade, 2nd Floor, Toronto M5E 1R2; tel. (416) 364-4266; f. 1927; Publr ROY MACLAREN; Editor JOANN WEBB; circ. 86,000 (M).

Canadian Defence Quarterly: 310 Dupont St, Toronto M5R 1V9; tel. (416) 968-7252; telex 065-28085; Editor JOHN MARTEINSON; circ. 10,000 (Q).

Canadian Forum: 70 The Esplanade, 3rd Floor, Toronto M5E 1R2; tel. (416) 364-2431; f. 1920; political, literary and economic; Editor JOHN HUTCHESON; circ. 10,000; 10 a year.

Canadian Journal of Economics: c/o University of Toronto Press, Front Campus, Toronto M5S 1A6; tel. (416) 978-6739; f. 1968; Editor ROBIN BOADWAY; circ. 3,000 (Q).

Canadian Living: 50 Holly St, Toronto M4S 3B3; tel. (416) 482-8600; f. 1975; Editor-in-Chief JUDY BRANDOW; circ. 539,000 (M).

Canadian Musician: 20 Holly St, Suite 101, Toronto M4S 2E6; tel. (416) 485-8284; f. 1979; Editor TED BURLEY; circ. 26,000; 6 a year.

Canadian Travel Press Weekly: 310 Dupont St, Toronto M5R 1V9; tel. (416) 968-7252; telex 065-28085; Editor EDITH BAXTER; circ. 19,000.

El Popular: POB 1108, Adelaide St Station, Toronto M5C 2K5; tel. (416) 531-2495; f. 1970; Spanish; Editor MIGUEL RAKIEWICZ; circ. 14,000.

Engineering Digest: 111 Peter St, Suite 411, Toronto M5V 2W2; tel. (416) 596-1624; f. 1954; Editor H. W. MEYFARTH; circ. 66,000; 6 a year.

Farm and Country: 950 Yonge St, 7th Floor, Toronto M4W 2J4; tel. (416) 924-6209; f. 1936; Publr and Editor-in-Chief JOHN PHILLIPS; circ. 63,000; 18 a year.

Financial Times of Canada: 1231 Yonge St, Suite 300, Toronto M4T 2Z1; tel. (416) 922-1133; f. 1912; Publr DAVID TAFLER; circ. 110,000 (W).

Hockey News: 85 Scarsdale Rd, Toronto M3B 2R2; tel. (416) 445-5702; f. 1947; Editor-in-Chief BOB MCKENZIE; circ. 105,000 (W).

Magyar Élet (Hungarian Life): 6 Alcina Ave, Toronto M6G 2E8; tel. (416) 654-2551; f. 1948; Hungarian; Publr ANDREW LASZLO; circ. 8,000 (W).

New Equipment News: 111 Peter St, Suite 411, Toronto M5V 2W2; tel. (416) 596-1624; telex 062-18852; f. 1940; Editor D. B. LEHMAN; circ. 32,000 (M).

Northern Miner: 7 Labatt Ave, Toronto M5A 3P2; tel. (416) 368-3483; f. 1915; Editor J. S. BORLAND; circ. 18,000.

Ontario Medical Review: 250 Bloor St East, Suite 600, Toronto M4W 3P8; tel. (416) 963-9383; f. 1922; Editor R. DAVID FLETCHER; circ. 18,000 (M).

Quill and Quire: 56 The Esplanade, Suite 213, Toronto M5E 1A7; tel. (416) 364-3333; f. 1935; book-publishing industry; Assoc. Editor DIANA SHEPHERD; circ. 8,000 (M).

Saturday Night: 36 Toronto St, Suite 1160, Toronto M5C 2R5; tel. (416) 368-7237; f. 1887; Editor JOHN FRASER; circ. 115,000 (M).

Time (Canada edn): 620 University Ave, Suite 1120, Toronto M5G 2C5; tel. (416) 595-1229; telex 062-3245; f. 1943; Man. Dir F. P. LINTOTT; circ. 356,000 (W).

CANADA

Toronto Life Magazine: 59 Front St East, 3rd Floor, Toronto M5E 1B3; tel. (416) 364-3333; f. 1966; Editor MARQ DE VILLIERS; circ. 98,000 (M).

TV Guide: 50 Holly St, Toronto M4S 3B3; tel. (416) 482-8600; telex 065-24030; f. 1976; Editor JOHN KEYES; circ. 816,000 (W).

The following are all published by Maclean Hunter Ltd, 777 Bay St, Toronto M5W 1A7; tel. (416) 596-5000; telex 062-19547.

Canadian Aviation: tel. (416) 596-5789; telex 062-19547; f. 1928; Editor HUGH WHITTINGTON; circ. 20,000 (M).

Canadian Building: tel. (416) 596-5760; telex 062-19547; f. 1951; Editor JOHN FENNELL; circ. 18,000 (M).

Canadian Electronics Engineering: tel. (416) 596-5731; telex 062-19547; f. 1957; Editor PETER J. THORNE; circ. 19,000 (M).

Canadian Grocer: tel. (416) 596-5772; telex 062-19547; f. 1886; Editor GEORGE H. CONDON; circ. 17,000 (M).

Canadian Hotel & Restaurant: tel. (416) 596-5813; telex 062-19547; f. 1923; Editor RON STANAITIS; circ. 31,000 (M).

CAR (Canadian Auto Review): tel. (416) 596-5784; f. 1984; Editor RICHARD JACOBS; circ. 6,000 (M).

Chatelaine: tel. (416) 596-5422; telex 062-19547; f. 1928; women's journal; Editor MILDRED ISTONA; circ. 1,000,000 (M).

Civic Public Works: tel. (416) 596-5953; telex 062-19547; f. 1949; Editor CLIFF ALLUM; circ. 13,000 (M).

Design Engineering: tel. (416) 596-5833; telex 062-19547; f. 1955; Editor JAMES BARNES; circ. 18,000 (M).

Flare: tel. (416) 596-5462; telex 062-19547; f. 1984; Editor BONNIE HUROWITZ; circ. 225,000 (M).

Floor Covering News: tel. (416) 596-5940; telex 062-19547; f. 1976; Editor HELEN BAHEN; circ. 7,000; 10 a year.

Heavy Construction News: tel. (416) 596-5844; telex 062-19547; f. 1956; Editor RUSSELL B. NOBLE; circ. 26,000 (F).

Maclean's Canada's Weekly Newsmazagine: tel. (416) 596-5311; telex 065-24196; f. 1905; Editor KEVIN DOYLE; circ. 619,000 (W).

Marketing: tel. (416) 596-5835; telex 062-19547; f. 1906; Editor COLIN MUNCIE; circ. 11,000 (W).

Medical Post: tel. (416) 596-5770; telex 062-19547; f. 1965; Editor DEREK CASSELS; circ. 36,000 (F).

Office Equipment and Methods: tel. (416) 596-5920; telex 062-19547; f. 1954; Editor TOM KELLY; circ. 60,000 (M).

Prince Edward Island

Prince Edward Island Profiles: POB 36, Charlottetown C1A 7K2; tel. (902) 566-5529; f. 1988; Editor NORMA REVELER; circ. 500; 6 a year.

Québec

L'Actualité: 1001 ouest, blvd de Maisonneuve, Montréal, H3A 3E1; tel. (514) 845-2543; f. 1976; general interest; Editor JEAN PARÉ; circ. 264,000 (M).

A – Le magazine Affaires: 465 rue St-Jean, 9e étage, Montréal H2Y 3S4; tel. (514) 842-6491; telex 055-61971; f. 1978; Publr CLAUDE BEAUCHAMP; circ. 94,000; 10 a year.

Le Bulletin des Agriculteurs: 110 ouest, blvd Crémazie, Bureau 422, Montréal H2P 1B9; tel. (514) 382-4350; f. 1918; circ. 78,000 (M).

Châtelaine: 1001 ouest, blvd de Maisonneuve, Montréal H3A 3E1; tel. (514) 843-2503; f. 1960; Editor MARTINE DEMANGE; circ. 272,000 (M).

CIM Bulletin: 3400 ouest, blvd de Maisonneuve, Bureau 1210, Montréal H3Z 3B8; tel. (514) 842-3461; publ. by the Canadian Inst. of Mining and Metallurgy; Editor PIERRE MICHAUD; circ. 11,000 (M).

Cinema Canada: CP 398, Outremont, H2V 9Z9; tel. (514) 272-5354; Editor CONNIE TADROS; circ. 10,000.

Il Cittadino Canadese: 6274 est, Jean Talon, Montréal H1S 1M8; tel. (514) 253-2332; f. 1941; Italian; Editor BASILIO GIORDANO; circ. 55,000 (W).

Clin d'Oeil: 7 chemin Bates, Outremont H2V 1A6; tel. (514) 270-1100; Editor-in-Chief MARIE-JOSÉE DESMARAIS; circ. 77,000 (M).

Coup de Pouce: 2001 rue Université, Bureau 900, Montréal H3A 2A6; tel. (514) 527-9601; f. 1984; circ. 128,000 (M).

Echos Vedettes: 801 est, rue Sherbrooke, Montréal H2L 4X9; tel. (514) 525-6400; f. 1963; Editor MARC CHATELLE; circ. 168,000 (W).

Femme Plus: 404 blvd Décarie, 2e étage, Ville St-Laurent H4L 5G1; tel. (514) 748-5050; Publr SYLVIE BERGERON; circ. 60,000 (M).

Le Journal Industriel du Québec: 9500 ouest, Henri Bourassa, Ville St-Laurent H4S 1N8; tel. (514) 335-2055; f. 1985; Editor YVAN GAUTHIER; circ. 35,000; 10 a year.

Directory

Le Lundi: 404 blvd Décarie, 2e étage, Ville St-Laurent H4L 5G1; tel. (514) 748-5050; f. 1976; Editor MICHEL CHOINIÈRE; circ. 105,000 (W).

Montréal Life: 1310 ave Greene, Bureau 920, Westmount H3Z 2B5; tel. (514) 933-2555; f. 1971; Publr BOB HARRIS; circ. 54,000; 11 a year.

Photo Sélection: 910 ave Ducharme, Ville de Vanier G1M 2H6; tel. (418) 687-3550; f. 1980; Chief Editor YOLANDE RACINE; circ. 18,000; 8 a year.

Le Producteur de Lait Québécois: 555 blvd Roland-Thérrien, Longueuil J4H 3Y9; tel. (514) 679-0530; f. 1980; dairy farming; Dir HUGUES BELZILE; circ. 18,000 (M).

Progrès-Dimanche: 1051 blvd Talbot, Chicoutimi G7H 5C1; tel. (418) 545-4474; Pres. GASTON VACHON; circ. 51,000 (W).

Le Québec Industriel: 1001 ouest, blvd de Maisonneuve, Bureau 1000, Montréal H3A 3E1; tel. (514) 845-5141; f. 1946; Editor BERTRAND DIONNE; circ. 16,000 (M).

Québec Science: 2875 blvd Laurier, Ste-Foy G1V 2M3; tel. (418) 657-3551; telex 051-31623; f. 1969; Editor JACKI DALLAIRE; circ. 20,000 (M).

Reader's Digest: 215 ave Redfern, Westmount H3Z 2V9; tel. (514) 934-0751; f. 1943; French and English edns; Editor ALEXANDER FARRELL; circ. 1,706,000 (M).

Relations: 8100 blvd St-Laurence, Montréal H2P 2L9; tel. (514) 387-2541; f. 1941; Roman Catholic review; Editor-in-Chief GISÈLE TURCOT; circ. 5,000 (M).

Rénovation Bricolage: 7 chemin Bates, Outremont H2V 1A6; tel. (514) 270-1100; f. 1976; Editor-in-Chief CLAUDE LECLERC; circ. 38,000 (M).

Revue Commerce: 465 rue St-Jean, Suite 908, Montréal H2Y 2R6; tel. (514) 844-1511; telex 055-61971; f. 1898; Publr MICHEL LORD; circ. 38,000 (M).

La Terre de Chez Nous: 555 blvd Roland-Thérrien, Longueuil J4H 3Y9; tel. (514) 679-0530; f. 1929; agriculture and forestry; French; Editor-in-Chief ANDRÉ CHARBONNEAU; circ. 46,000 (W).

TV Hebdo/TV Plus: 2001 rue Université, Bureau 900, Montréal H3A 2A6; tel. (514) 499-0651; f. 1960; Publr JACQUES LINA; circ. 289,000 (W).

Saskatchewan

The Commonwealth: 1122 Saskatchewan Drive, Regina S4P 0C4; tel. (306) 525-8321; f. 1938; Editor MERRIL DEAN; circ. 9,000; 24 a year.

Farm Light & Power: 2352 Smith St, Regina S4P 2P6; tel. (306) 525-3305; f. 1959; Man. Editor DON BLACK; circ. 182,000; 10 a year.

Western Producer: POB 2500, Saskatoon S7K 2C4; tel. (306) 665-3500; f. 1923; world and agricultural news; Editor KEITH DRYDEN; circ. 131,000 (W).

Western Sportsman: POB 737, Regina S4P 3A8; tel. (306) 352-2773; f. 1968; Editor RICK BATES; circ. 31,000; 6 a year.

Yukon Territory

L'Aurore Boréal: POB 5025, Whitehorse Y1A 4Z1; tel. (403) 873-4031; circ. 1,000 (M).

Dan Sha News: 22 Nisutlin Drive, Whitehorse Y1A 3S5; tel. (403) 667-6923; f. 1973; Editor ERIC HUGGARD; circ. 3,000 (M).

Yukon News: 211 Wood St, Whitehorse Y1A 2E4; tel. (403) 667-6285; f. 1960; Editor PATRICIA LIVING; circ. 8,000; 2 a week.

NEWS AGENCIES

The Canadian Press: 36 King St East, Toronto, Ont M5C 2L9; tel. (416) 364-0321; f. 1917; 104 daily newspaper mems; national news co-operative; Chair. A. E. WOOD; Pres. KEITH KINCAID.

Foreign Bureaux

Agence France-Presse (AFP): National Press Bldg, 150 Wellington St, Ottawa K1P 5A4; tel. (613) 232-2943; also office in Montréal.

Agencia EFE (Spain): 165 Sparks St, Suite 502, Ottawa K1P 5B9; tel. (613) 230-2282.

Agenzia Nazionale Stampa Associata (ANSA) (Italy): 150 Wellington St, Press Gallery, Room 703, Ottawa K1P 5A4; tel. (613) 235-4248; telex 053-4392; Representative PIERO LACQUA.

Deutsche Presse-Agentur (dpa) (Federal Republic of Germany): 702 National Press Bldg, 150 Wellington St, Ottawa K1P 5A4; tel. (613) 234-6024; telex 0253-4812; Correspondent BARBARA HALSIG.

Inter Press Service (IPS) (Italy): 1470 rue Peel, Bureau 216, Montréal, Que H3A 1T1; tel. (514) 843-6459; Rep. ANTOINE CHAR.

Jiji Tsushin-Sha (Japan): 366 Adelaide St East, Toronto, Ont M5A 3X9; tel.(416) 368-8037; Chief MIKIO KOYAMA.

CANADA

Prensa Latina (Cuba): 221 rue du St-Sacrement, Bureau 40, Montréal, Qué H2Y 1X1; tel. (514) 844-2975; Correspondent R. RAMOS.

Reuters (UK): POB 403, Commerce Court Postal Station, Toronto, Ont M5L 1J1; tel. (416) 869-3600; telex 062-3637; Man. JOHN ADAMS; also offices in Ottawa, Montréal and Vancouver.

Telegrafnoye Agentstvo Sovetskovo Soyuza (TASS) (USSR): 200 Rideau Terrace, Suite 1305, Ottawa; tel. (613) 745-4310; telex 053-4504; Correspondent ARTEM MELIKIAN.

United Press International (UPI) (USA): 45 Richmond St West, Toronto, Ont M5H 1Z2; tel. (416) 865-1502; Man. for Canada KEN WHITEHURST; also offices in Ottawa, Montréal and Vancouver.

Xinhua (New China) News Agency: (People's Republic of China: 406 Daly Ave, Ottawa KIN 6H2; tel. (613) 234-8424; telex 053-4362; Chief Corresp. CAI SHUQI.

Associated Press (USA) and Central News Agency (Taiwan) are also represented.

PRESS ASSOCIATIONS

Canadian Business Press: 100 University Ave, Suite 508, Toronto, Ont M5J 1V6; tel. (416) 593-5497; Chair. GWEN PAGE; Admin. Man. E. SELLWOOD; three constituent asscns.

Canadian Community Newspapers' Association: 88 University Ave, Suite 705, Toronto, Ont M5J 1T6; tel. (416) 598-4277; f. 1919; Pres. KEN SOPKOW; Exec. Dir ROSS MAVIS; 650 mems.

Canadian Daily Newspaper Publishers Association: 890 Yonge St, Suite 1100, Toronto, Ont M4W 3P4; tel. (416) 923-3567; f. 1919; Chair. K. A. BAIRD; Pres. JOHN E. FOY; 83 mems.

Canadian Periodical Publishers' Association: 2 Stewart St, Toronto, Ont M5V 1H6; tel. (416) 362-2546; f. 1973; Exec. Dir CATHERINE KEACHIE.

Magazines Canada (The Magazine Asscn of Canada): 777 Bay St, 7th Floor, Toronto, Ont M5W 1A7; tel. (416) 596-2644; Chair. JAMES WARRILLOW; Vice-Chair. RON PAYNE.

Publishers

Addison-Wesley Publishers Ltd: 26 Prince Andrew Place, POB 580, Don Mills, Ont M3C 2T8; tel. (416) 447-5101; telex 069-86743; f. 1966; mathematics, science, language, business and social sciences textbooks, trade, juvenile; CEO ANTHONY J. VANDER WOUDE.

Thomas Allen and Son Ltd: 390 Steelcase Rd East, Markham, Ont L3R 1G2; tel. (416) 475-9126; telex 069-66716; f. 1916; Pres. JOHN D. ALLEN.

Annick Press Ltd: 15 Patricia Ave, Willowdale, Ont M2M 1H9; tel. (416) 221-4802; telex 069-86766; f. 1976; children's; Co-Dirs RICK WILKS, ANNE W. MILLYARD.

Arsenal Pulp Press: 1150 Homer St, Vancouver, BC V6B 2X8; tel. (604) 687-4233; f. 1972; literary, native, educational.

Avon Books of Canada: 2061 McCowan Rd, Suite 201, Scarborough, Ont M1S 3Y6; tel. (416) 293-9404; Pres. PETER AUSTIN.

Black Rose Books Ltd: 3981 blvd St-Laurent, 4e étage, Montréal, Qué H2W 1Y5; tel. (514) 844-4076; f. 1970; social studies; Pres. JACQUES ROUX.

Le Boréal Express Ltée: 5450 chemin de la Côte-des-Neiges, Bureau 212, Montréal, Qué H3T 1Y6; tel. (514) 735-6267; f. 1963; history, biography, fiction, politics, economics, educational; Pres. ANTOINE DEL BUSSO.

Borealis Press Ltd: 9 Ashburn Drive, Ottawa K2E 6N4; tel. (613) 224-6837; f. 1972; Canadian fiction and non-fiction, drama, juveniles.

Breakwater Books Ltd: 277 Duckworth St, POB 2188, St John's, Nfld A1C 6E6; tel. (709) 722-6680; f. 1973; fiction, general, children's, educational, folklore.

Butterworths: 2265 Midland Ave, Scarborough, Ont M1P 4S1; tel. (416) 292-1421; f. 1912; a division of Reed Inc; legal, professional, academic; Pres. ANDREW MARTIN.

Canada Law Book Inc: 240 Edward St, Aurora, Ont L4G 3S9; tel. (416) 773-6300; f. 1855; law reports, law journals, legal textbooks, etc.; Pres. S. G. CORBETT.

Centre Educatif et Culturel: 8101 blvd Métropolitain, Anjou, Montréal, Qué H1J 1J9; tel. (514) 351-6010; telex 055-62172; f. 1956; textbooks; Pres. and Dir-Gen. ANDRÉ ROUSSEAU.

The Coach House Press: 401 (rear) Huron St, Toronto, Ont M5S 2G5; tel. (416) 979-2217; telex 069-59372; f. 1965; fiction, poetry; Owner STAN BEVINGTON.

Collier Macmillan Canada Inc: 1200 Eglinton Ave East, Suite 200, Don Mills, Ont M3C 3N1; tel. (416) 449-6030; telex 069-59372; f. 1958; trade, textbooks, reference; Pres. RAY LEE.

Wm Collins, Sons and Co (Canada) Ltd: 100 Lesmill Rd, Don Mills, Ont M3B 2T5; tel. (416) 445-8221; f. 1932; trade, reference, bibles, dictionaries, juvenile, paperbacks; Pres. DAVID KENT.

Copp Clark Pitman: 495 Wellington St West, Toronto, Ont M5V 1E9; tel. (416) 593-9911; f. 1841; textbooks and reference material; Pres. STEPHEN MILLS.

Dominie Press Ltd: 1361 Huntingwood Drive, Unit 7, Agincourt, Ont M1S 3J1; tel. (416) 291-5857; Pres. RAYMOND YUEN.

Doubleday Canada Ltd: 105 Bond St, Toronto, Ont M5B 1Y3; tel. (416) 977-7891; f. 1944; general, trade, textbooks, mass market; Pres. ANNA PORTER.

Douglas and McIntyre Ltd: 1615 Venables St, Vancouver, BC V5L 2H1; tel. (604) 254-7191; f. 1964; general non-fiction, juvenile; Pres. SCOTT MCINTYRE.

Eden Press Inc: 31 ave Westminster, Montréal, Qué H4X 1Y8; tel. (514) 488-2066; f. 1977; scholarly, medical, scientific, general non-fiction; Pres. SHERRI CLARKSON.

Editions Bellarmin: 8100 blvd St-Laurent, Montréal, Qué H2P 2L9; tel. (514) 387-2541; f. 1891; religious, educational, politics, sociology, ethnography, history, sport, leisure; Pres. and Gen. Man. ANDRÉ BEAUCHAMP.

Editions L'Etincelle (SCE): 4920 ouest, blvd de Housonneuve, Bureau 206, Westmount, Qué H3Z 1W1; tel. (514) 488-9531; f. 1972; art, social and political sciences, geography, history, juvenile; Pres. ROBERT DAVIES.

Les Editions Fides: 5710 ave Decelles, Montréal, Qué H3S 2C5; tel. (514) 735-6406; f. 1937; juvenile, history, theology, textbooks and literature; Dir-Gen. MICHELINE TREMBLAY.

Les Editions Françaises Inc: 1411 rue Ampère, CP 395, Boucherville, Qué J4B 5W2; tel. (514) 641-0514; telex 052-5107; f. 1951; textbooks; Pres. PIERRE LESPÉRANCE.

Editions France-Québec Inc: 955 rue Amherst, Montréal, Qué H2L 3K4; tel. (514) 323-1182; telex 052-4667; f. 1965; Editor BERNARD PRÉVOST.

Editions Héritage: 300 ave Arran, St-Lambert, Qué J4R 1K5; tel. (514) 672-6710; telex 052-5134; f. 1968; history, biography, sport, juveniles; Pres. JACQUES PAYETTE.

Editions de l'Hexagone: 900 est, rue Ontario, Montréal, Qué H2L 1P4; tel (514) 525-2811; f. 1953; literature; Dir-Gen. ALAIN HORIC.

Editions Hurtubise HMH: 7360 blvd Newman, Ville LaSalle, Qué H8N 1X2; tel. (514) 364-0323; telex 055-67167; f. 1960; general academic; Pres. and Dir-Gen. HERVÉ FOULON.

Editions Libre Expression: 244 ouest, rue St-Jacques, Montréal, Qué H2Y 1L9; tel. (514) 849-5259; f. 1976; religion, social and political sciences, general fiction and non-fiction, juvenile; Pres. ANDRÉ BASTIEN.

Editions du Pélican/Le Septentrion: 1300 ave Maguire, Silliery, Qué G1T 1Z3; tel. (418) 688-3556; f. 1956; history, essays, general; Man. DENIS VAUGEOIS.

Les Editions la Presse: 44 ouest, rue St-Antoine, Montréal, Qué H2Y 1J5; tel. (514) 285-6981; telex 052-4110; f. 1971; general literature; Pres. GILLES DAOUET.

Editions du Renouveau Pédagogique Inc: 8925 blvd St-Laurent, Montréal, Qué H2N 1M5; tel. (514) 384-2690; telex 058-26756; f. 1965; textbooks; Pres. ANDRÉ DUSSAULT.

Editions du Richelieu: CP 142, Saint-Jean, Qué G3B 5W3; f. 1935; general fiction and non-fiction, Roman Catholic school religious texts; Pres. FELICIEN MESSIER.

Encyclopaedia Britannica Publications Ltd: 175 Holiday Drive, POB 2249, Cambridge, Ont N3C 3N4; tel. (519) 658-4621; telex 069-59499; f. 1937; Pres. DAVID DURNAN.

Fitzhenry & Whiteside: 195 Allstate Pkwy, Markham, Ont L3R 4T8; tel. (416) 477-0030; f. 1966; textbooks, trade, educational; Pres. ROBERT I. FITZHENRY.

Gage Educational Publishing Co: 164 Commander Blvd, Agincourt, Ont M1S 3C7; tel. (416) 293-8141; telex 065-25374; f. 1844; Pres. and CEO ROBERT M. MCELMAN.

General Publishing Co Ltd: 30 Lesmill Rd, Don Mills, Ont M3B 2T6; tel. (416) 445-3333; telex 069-86664; f. 1934; fiction, history, biography, children's, general, textbooks; Pres. JACK E. STODDART.

Ginn and Co: 3771 Victoria Park Ave, Scarborough, Ont M1W 2P9; tel. (416) 497-4600; f. 1929; textbooks; Pres. RICHARD H. LEE.

GLC Publishers Ltd: 115 Nugget Ave, Agincourt, Ont M1S 3B1; tel. (416) 291-2926; Pres. NELSON PRISKE.

Grolier Ltd: 16 Overlea Blvd, Toronto, Ont M4H 1A6; tel. (416) 425-1924; f. 1912; reference; Vice-Pres. (Publishing) KEN H. PEARSON.

Harcourt Brace Jovanovich Canada Inc: 55 Barber Greene Rd, Don Mills, Ont M3C 2A1; tel. (416) 444-7331; f. 1922; general, medical, educational, scholarly; Pres. ANTHONY W. CRAVEN.

Harlequin Books: 225 Duncan Mill Rd, Don Mills, Ont M3B 3K9; tel. (416) 445-5860; f. 1949; fiction, paperbacks; Pres. BRIAN E. HICKEY.

CANADA

Harvest House Ltd: 1200 ave Atwater, Bureau 1, Montréal, Qué H3Z 1X4; tel. (514) 932-0666; f. 1960; history, biography, environment, natural and social sciences; Dir MAYNARD GERTLER.

D. C. Heath Canada Ltd: 100 Adelaide St West, Suite 1600, Toronto, Ont M5H 1S9; tel. (416) 362-6483; Pres. ROBERT H. ROSS.

Holt, Rinehart and Winston of Canada Ltd: 55 Horner Ave, Toronto, Ont M8Z 4X6; tel. (416) 255-4491; f. 1904; educational, college, reference; Pres. ANTHONY CRAVEN.

Houghton Mifflin Canada Ltd: 150 Steelcase Rd West, Markham, Ont L3R 1B2; tel. (416) 475-1755; educational; Pres. JOHN E. CHAMP.

House of Anansi Press Ltd: 35 Britain St, Toronto, Ont M5A 1R7; tel. (416) 363-5444; f. 1967; non-fiction, contemporary social issues, belles-lettres, fiction, Canadian poetry; Publr ANN WALL.

Hurtig Publishers: 10560 105th St, Edmonton, Alta T5H 2W7; tel. (403) 426-2359; f. 1961; non-fiction, politics, Canadiana; Pres. MEL HURTIG.

Institut de Recherches Psychologiques, Inc/Institute of Psychological Research Inc: 34 ouest, rue Fleury, Montréal, Qué H3L 1S9; tel. (514) 382-3000; f. 1964; educational and psychological texts; Pres. Dr JEAN-MARC CHEVRIER.

IPI Publishing Ltd: 44 Charles St West, Suite 2704, Toronto, Ont M4Y 1R7; tel. (416) 964-6662; Pres. Dr DANIEL BAUM.

Irwin Publishing Inc: 1300 Steeles Ave West, Concord, Ont L4K 2B3; tel. (416) 660-0611; f. 1945; educational; Pres. BRIAN O'DONNELL.

Key Porter Books: 70 The Esplanade, 3rd Floor, Toronto, Ont M5E 1R2; tel. (416) 862-7777; telex 062-18092; f. 1980; general trade; Pres. ANNA PORTER.

Lancelot Press Ltd: POB 425, Hantsport, NS B0P 1P0; tel. (902) 684-9129; f. 1966; non-fiction, regional.

Leméac Editeur: 3575 blvd St-Laurent, Bureau 902, Montréal, Qué H2X 2T7; tel. (514) 848-1096; f. 1957; literary, academic, general; Pres. JULES BRILLANT; Dir-Gen. LISE P. BERGEVIN.

Lester & Orpen Dennys Ltd: 78 Sullivan St, Toronto, Ont M5T 1C1; tel. (416) 593-9602; f. 1973; fiction, non-fiction, history, young adult, politics, social issues; Pres. MALCOLM LESTER.

Libraire Beauchemin Ltée: 381 rue St-Jacques, Bureau 400, Montréal, Qué H2Y 3S2; tel. (514) 842-1427; f. 1842; textbooks and general; Pres. GUY FRENETTE.

Lidec Inc: CP 5000, succursale C, Montréal, Qué H2X 3M1; tel. (514) 843-5991; f. 1965; educational, textbooks; Pres. and Dir-Gen. MARC-AIMÉ GUÉRIN.

James Lorimer & Co Ltd: 35 Britain St, Toronto, Ont M5A 1R7; tel. (416) 362-4762; f. 1971; urban and labour studies, children's, general non-fiction.

McClelland and Stewart: 481 University Ave, Suite 900, Toronto, Ont M5G 2E9; tel. (416) 598-1114; telex 062-18603; f. 1906; trade, illustrated and educational; Pres. (vacant).

McGill-Queen's University Press: 855 ouest, rue Sherbrooke, Montréal, Qué H3A 2T7; tel. (514) 398-3750; f. 1960; scholarly and general interest; Dir PHILIP J. CERCONE.

McGraw-Hill Ryerson Ltd: 330 Progress Ave, Scarborough, Ont M1P 2Z5; tel. (416) 293-1911; telex 065-25169; f. 1944; general; Pres. ROBERT M. FREEMAN.

Merrill Publishing: 230 Barmac Drive, Weston, Ont M9L 2X5; tel. (416) 746-2200; Gen. Man. LINDA MILNE.

Methuen Publications: 150 Laird Drive, Toronto, Ont M4G 3V7; tel. (416) 425-9200; f. 1965; trade, textbooks, professional; Gen. Man. FRED D. WARDLE.

Mosaic Press: 1252 Speers Rd, Unit 2, POB 1032, Oakville, Ont L6J 5E9; tel. (416) 825-2130; f. 1974; literary, scholarly and cultural; Dir of Operations HOWARD ASTER.

Nelson Canada: 1120 Birchmount Rd, Scarborough, Ont M1K 5G4; tel. (416) 752-9100; telex 069-63813; f. 1914; school and university textbooks; Pres. A. G. COBHAM.

Oberon Press: 350 Sparks St, Suite 401A, Ottawa K1R 7S8; tel. (613) 238-3275; f. 1966; poetry, children's, fiction and general non-fiction.

OISE Press–Guidance Centre: Ontario Institute for Studies in Education, 252 Bloor St West, Toronto, Ont M5S 1V6; tel. (416) 923-6641, ext. 2531; telex 062-17720; f. 1965; educational texts, guidance and test materials and scholarly publications.

Oxford University Press: 70 Wynford Drive, Don Mills, Ont M3C 1J9; tel. (416) 441-2941; telex 069-66518; f. 1904; general, education, religious, juvenile, Canadiana; Man. Dir MICHAEL A. MORROW.

PaperJacks Ltd: 330 Steelcase Rd East, Markham, Ont L3R 2M1; tel. (416) 475-1261; f. 1971; general paperbacks; Pres. SUSAN STODDART.

Penguin Books Canada Ltd: 2801 John St, Markham, Ont L3R 1B4; tel. (416) 475-1571; telex 069-86803; f. 1974; Pres. MORTON MINT.

Pontifical Institute of Mediaeval Studies: 59 Queen's Park Crescent East, Toronto, Ont M5S 2C4; tel. (416) 926-7144; f. 1939; scholarly pubs concerning the middle ages; Dir of Publs RON B. THOMSON.

Prentice Hall Canada Inc: 1870 Birchmount Rd, Scarborough, Ont M1P 2J7; tel. (416) 293-3621; telex 065-25184; f. 1960; trade, textbooks; Pres. ROSS M. INKPEN.

Les Presses de l'Université Laval: CP 2447, Québec, Qué G1K 7R4; tel. (418) 656-3001; f. 1950; scholarly books and periodicals; Dir CLAUDE FRÉMONT.

Les Presses de l'Université de Montréal: CP 6128, succursale A, Montréal, Qué H3C 3J7; tel. (514) 343-6168; f. 1962; scholarly and general; Dir MARIE-CLAIRE BORGO.

Les Presses de l'Université du Québec: CP 250, Sillery, Qué G1T 2R1; tel. (418) 657-3551; telex 051-31623; f. 1969; scholarly and general; Dir-Gen. JACKI DALLAIRE.

Random House of Canada Ltd: 1265 Aerowood Drive, Mississauga, Ont L4W 1B9; tel. (416) 624-0672; f. 1944; Pres. GORDON BAIN.

The Reader's Digest Association (Canada) Ltd: 215 ave Redfern, Montréal, Qué H3Z 2V9; tel. (514) 934-0751; telex 052-5800; Pres. and CEO RALPH HANCOX.

W. B. Saunders Co Canada Ltd: 1 Goldthorne Ave, Toronto, Ont M8Z 5T9; tel. (416) 251-3787; telex 069-67890; Vice-Pres. PAUL S. WOLFORD.

Scholastic—TAB Publications: 123 Newkirk Rd, Richmond Hill, Ont L4C 3G5; tel. (416) 883-5300; Pres. F. LARRY MULLER.

Simon & Pierre Publishing Co Ltd: POB 280, Adelaide St Postal Station, Toronto, Ont M5C 2J4; tel. (416) 363-6767; f. 1972; drama and performing arts, fiction and non-fiction; Pres. and Editor-in-Chief MARIAN M. WILSON.

Stoddart Publishing Co Ltd: 34 Lesmill Rd, Don Mills, Ont M3B 2T6; tel. (416) 445-3333; telex 069-86664; f. 1894; a division of General Publishing Co Ltd; general; Pres. and CEO JACK E. STODDART.

Talon Books Ltd: 201–1019 East Cordova St, Vancouver, BC V6A 1M8; tel. (604) 253-5261; f. 1967; fiction and non-fiction, poetry, drama.

Turnstone Press Ltd: 100 Arthur St, Suite 607, Winnipeg, Man R3B 1H3; tel. (204) 947-1555; f. 1976; literary, regional; Man. Editor MARILYN MORTON.

University of Alberta Press: 141 Athabasca Hall, Edmonton, Alta T6G 2E8; tel. (403) 432-3662; telex 037-2979; f. 1969; scholarly, general non-fiction.

University of British Columbia Press: 6344 Memorial Rd, Vancouver, BC V6T 1W5; tel. (604) 228-3259; f. 1971; humanities, science, social science and scholarly journals; Exec. Dir JAMES J. ANDERSON.

University of Manitoba Press: 106 Curry Place, Suite 244, University of Manitoba, Winnipeg, Man R3T 2N2; tel. (204) 474-9495; scholarly; Dir PATRICIA A. DOWDALL.

University of Ottawa Press/Les Presses de l'Université d'Ottawa: 603 ave Cumberland, Ottawa K1N 6N5; tel. (613) 564-2270; f. 1936; university texts, scholarly works in English and French; general; Dir TOIVO ROHT.

University of Toronto Press: Front Campus, University of Toronto, Toronto, Ont M5S 1A6; tel. (416) 978-2239; f. 1901; academic and general university texts and journals; Dir HARALD BOHNE.

Western Legal Publications: 1 Alexander St, Suite 301, Vancouver, BC V6A 1B2; tel. (604) 687-5671; f. 1972; legal decisions, digests, manuals, texts and summaries; Gen. Man. PHILLIP W. GEORGE.

Western Producer Prairie Books: POB 2500, Saskatoon, Sask S7K 2C4; tel. (306) 665-3548; f. 1954; history, biography, photography, natural history, young adult, regional interest; Publishing Dir ELIZABETH MUNROE.

John Wiley and Sons Canada Ltd: 22 Worcester Rd, Rexdale, Ont M9W 1L1; tel. (416) 675-3580; telex 069-89189; Pres. JOHN DILL.

Government Publishing House

Canadian Government Publishing Centre: Ottawa K1A 0S9; tel. (819) 997-2560; telex 053-4296; f. 1876; books and periodicals on numerous subjects, incl. agriculture, economics, environment, geology, history and sociology; Dir PATRICIA HORNER.

CANADA *Directory*

ORGANIZATIONS AND ASSOCIATIONS

Association of Canadian Publishers: 260 King St East, Toronto, Ont M5A 1K3; tel. (416) 361-1408; f. 1976; 136 mems; trade assen of Canadian-owned English-language book publrs; represents Canadian publishing internationally; Pres. CLYDE ROSE; Exec. Dir HAMISH CAMERON.

Canadian Book Publishers' Council: 45 Charles St East, 7th Floor, Toronto, Ont M4Y 1S2; tel. (416) 964-7231; f. 1910; 50 mems; trade assen of Canadian-owned publrs and Canadian-incorporated subsidiaries of UK and USA publrs; Pres. F. C. LARRY MULLER; Exec. Dir JACQUELINE HUSHION.

La Société de Développement du Livre et du Périodique: 1151 Alexandre-De Seve, Montréal, Qué H2L 2T7; tel. (514) 524-7528; f. 1961; Pres. GUY SAINT-JEAN; Dir-Gen. LOUISE ROCHON; six constituent assens.

Radio and Television

The 1968 Broadcasting Act set out the broadcasting policy of Canada, established the Canadian Broadcasting Corporation (CBC) as the national, publicly owned, broadcasting service and created the Canadian Radio-Television and Telecommunications Commission (CRTC) as the agency regulating radio, television and cable television. The CBC is financed mainly by public funds supplemented by revenue from television advertising. Programming policy is to use predominantly Canadian creative and other resources. Services are operated in both English and French.

Radio and television service is available to over 99% of the population: 78% of Canadian homes subscribe to cable television and existing wiring makes this service, which is provided by 1,721 cable television systems, immediately available to 88% of Canadian homes. Most television programming is in colour and 93% of homes have colour TV sets.

Many privately-owned television and radio stations have affiliation agreements with the CBC and help to distribute the national services. The major private television networks which also have affiliates are CTV, TVA (which serves the province of Ontario) and Quatre Saisons (which also serves the province of Québec) and Global (serving the province of Ontario), as well as the educational networks.

Canadian Broadcasting Corporation (CBC): 1500 Bronson Ave, POB 8478, Ottawa K1G 3J5; tel. (613) 724-1200; telex 053-4260; f. 1936; financed mainly by public funds, with supplementary revenue from commercial advertising on CBC television; Pres. PIERRE JUNEAU; Exec. Vice-Pres. W. T. ARMSTRONG.

Canadian Radio-Television and Telecommunications Commission (CRTC): Ottawa K1A 0N2; tel. (819) 997-0313 (Information); telex 053-4253; f. 1968; regional offices in Montréal, Halifax, Winnipeg and Vancouver; Chair. ANDRÉ BUREAU; Vice-Chair. LOUIS R. SHERMAN (Telecommunications), MONIQUE COUPAL (Broadcasting).

RADIO

The CBC operates two AM and two FM networks, one each in English and French. The CBC's Northern Service provides both national network programming in English and French, and special local and short-wave programmes, some of which are broadcast in the languages of the Indian and Inuit peoples. In March 1987 there were 786 outlets for CBC radio (96 CBC-owned stations, 629 CBC-owned relay transmitters, 61 private affiliates and rebroadcasters). CBC radio service, which is virtually free of commercial advertising, is within reach of 99.5% of the population. Radio Canada International, the CBC's overseas short-wave service, broadcasts daily in 11 languages and distributes recorded programmes free for use world-wide.

TELEVISION

The CBC operates two television networks, one in English and one in French. CBC's Northern Service, created in 1958, now provides both radio and television service to 98% of the 90,000 inhabitants of northern Québec, the Northwest Territories and the Yukon. Almost 41% of these inhabitants are native Canadians, and programming is provided in Dene and Inuktitut languages as well as English and French. Broadcast time is also made available to native groups who produce their own programmes. As of March 1988, CBC television was carried on 868 outlets (28 CBC-owned stations, 615 CBC-owned rebroadcasters, 37 private affiliates and 188 private rebroadcasters). CBC television is available to over 98% of the population.

Canada was the first country to establish a domestic communications satellite system with the launching of Anik A-1 in November 1972, of Anik A-2 in April 1973, of Anik A-3 in May 1975 and, finally, of Anik-B in December 1978. In August 1982 Anik D-1 was put in orbit, followed by Anik C-3 in November 1982, and Anik C-2 in June 1983. These were joined by Anik D-2 in November 1984 and Anik C-1 in April 1985. Canada's commercial communications satellites are owned and operated by Telesat Canada.

Canadian Satellite Communication Inc (Cancom) of Toronto, Ontario, was licensed in April 1981 by the CRTC to carry on a multi-channel television and radio broadcasting operation via Anik satellite for the distribution of CTV, TVA and independent television and radio programmes (one AM and nine FM radio stations) to serve remote and under-served communities. In 1983 Cancom was authorized to distribute the programme output of four US television networks, via Anik satellite.

There are five educational services; TV-Ontario in Ontario and Radio-Québec in Québec operate their own television stations and networks; the Access network in Alberta purchases time for educational cultural programming on the private TV stations of the province; Knowledge Network is involved in the distribution, development and co-ordination of educational television programming to British Columbia communities via Anik C satellites and cable; and Saskmedia is involved in the production, acquisition and distribution of educationally-orientated media programming.

Canadian pay television has been in operation since 1983. All of the services initially licensed have now been reorganized in one form or another. By August 1985, Canadians had access to three general interest pay television services (one French service in eastern Canada, Premier Choix/TVEC, and two regional English services: First Choice serving eastern Canada, and Allarcom serving western Canada). New speciality discretionary services, such as MuchMusic, The Sports Network, Latinovision and Chinavision became available in 1984, and other speciality services are under consideration. In 1987 the total number of subscribers to such discretionary services represented 17.9% of potential households.

Canadian Satellite Communications Inc: 275 Slater St, Suite 1501, Ottawa K1P 5H9; tel. (613) 232-4814; Chair. J. R. PETERS; Pres. and CEO P. L. MORRISSETTE.

CTV Television Network: 42 Charles St East, Toronto, Ont M4Y 1T5; tel. (416) 928-6000; telex 062-2080; 28 privately-owned affiliated stations from coast to coast, with 243 rebroadcasters; covers 99% of Canadian TV households; Pres. and Man. Dir M. CHERCOVER; Exec. Vice-Pres. J. RUTTLE.

Global Television Network: 81 Barber Greene Rd, Don Mills, Ont M3C 2A2; tel. (416) 446-5311; telex 069-66767; one station and nine rebroadcasters serving southern Ontario; Pres. DAVID MINTZ.

Telesat Canada: 333 River Rd, Ottawa, Ont K1L 8B9; tel. (613) 746-5920; telex 053-4184; f. 1969; Chair. D. A. GOLDEN; Pres. and CEO ELDON D. THOMPSON.

TVA: 1600 est, blvd de Maisonneuve, CP 368, succursale C, Montréal, Qué H2L 4P2; tel. (514) 526-0476; telex 055-60626; f. 1971; French-language network, with 10 stations in Québec and 20 rebroadcasters serving 98% of the province and francophone communities in Ontario and New Brunswick; Pres. and Gen. Man. MICHEL HÉROUX.

ASSOCIATION

Canadian Association of Broadcasters: 350 Sparks St, POB 627, Station B, Ottawa K1P 5S2; tel. (613) 233-4035; telex 053-3127; Pres. DAVID BOND; Sr Vice-Pres. (Television) W. ROBERTS, Sr Vice-Pres. (Radio) P. NADEAU.

Finance

(cap. = capital; auth. = authorized; p.u. = paid up; res = reserves; dep. = deposits; m. = million; brs = branches; amounts in Canadian dollars)

BANKING

The first Canadian commercial bank was founded in 1817. A further 34 banks were established over the next 50 years, and following Confederation in 1867 the Bank Act of 1871 gave the Federal Government regulatory powers over banking operations throughout Canada.

The Bank Act of 1980 reorganized the banking structure by creating two categories of banking institution: 'Schedule A' banks, comprising the existing chartered banks; and 'Schedule B' banks, which are either subsidiaries of foreign banks (whose total Canadian assets cannot exceed 16% of those of the banking system in total), or Canadian-owned banks under private or semi-private ownership. The Act, which is subject to review at 10-year intervals to allow for changes in government policy and economic conditions, strictly limits the range of permitted operations outside the banking sphere, in order to curtail competition betweeen banks and commercial enterprises. In September 1988 there were seven

CANADA

'Schedule A' banks (of which no individual shareholder may control more than 10%) and 59 'Schedule B' banks.

The Bank of Canada, established as the central bank in 1934 and controlled by the Federal Government, implements government monetary and credit policies through the commercial banks. It controls the banks' clearing system and also holds the banks' primary and secondary reserves. Direct regulatory inspections of the commercial banks are carried out by the Superintendent of Financial Institutions, who reports to the Minister of Finance, and a federal agency insures individual deposits up to a limit of C $60,000 per person per institution.

At the end of 1987, there were 7,151 commercial bank branches holding deposits totalling C $216,889m. The banks' combined assets totalled C $485,997m., of which 39.4% were represented by foreign currency assets, reflecting the importance of international business in Canadian banking.

Trust and loan companies, which were originally formed to provide mortgage finance and private customer loans, now occupy an important place in the financial system, offering current account facilities and providing access to money transfer services.

Central Bank

Bank of Canada: 234 Wellington St, Ottawa K1A 0G9; tel. (613) 782-8111; telex 053-4241; f. 1934; cap. and res 30m., dep. 2,895m. (Dec. 1986); Gov. JOHN W. CROW; Sr Dep. Gov. GORDON G. THIESSEN.

Principal Commercial Banks
Schedule 'A' Banks

Bank of Montréal: 129 ouest, rue St-Jacques, Montréal, Qué H2Y 1L6; tel. (514) 877-7110; telex 052-67661; f. 1817; cap. and res 3,624m., dep. 65,054m. (July 1988); Chair. and CEO WILLIAM D. MULHOLLAND; Pres. and Chief Operating Officer MATTHEW BARRETT.

Bank of Nova Scotia (Scotiabank): 44 King St West, Toronto, Ont M5H 1H1; tel. (416) 866-6161; telex 062-2106; f. 1832; cap. and res 3,094.1m., dep. 57,597.9m. (July 1988); Chair. and CEO C. E. RITCHIE; Dep. Chair., Pres. and Chief Operating Officer J. A. G. BELL.

Canadian Imperial Bank of Commerce: Commerce Court, Toronto, Ont M5L 1A2; tel. (416) 980-2211; telex 065-24116; f. 1961; cap. and res 4,443m., dep. 72,620m. (July 1988); Chair. and CEO R. DONALD FULLERTON.

Canadian Western Bank: 10040–104 St, Edmonton, Alta T5J 3X6; tel. (403) 423-8888; telex 037-43148; f. 1987 by merger of the Bank of Alberta and the Western and Pacific Bank of Canada; cap. and res 37.7m., dep. 238.1m. (July 1988); Chair. and CEO DAVID L. EMERSON.

National Bank of Canada: 600 ouest, rue de la Gauchetière, Montréal, Qué H3B 4L2; tel. (514) 394-4000; telex 052-5181; f. 1979; cap. and res 1,486m., dep. 24,850m. (July 1988); Chair. and CEO MICHEL BÉLANGER (CEO until 30 Sept. 1989); Pres. and Chief Operating Officer ANDRÉ BEDARD (CEO from 30 Sept. 1989).

Royal Bank of Canada: 1 place Ville Marie, CP 6001, Montréal, Qué H3C 3A9; tel. (514) 874-2110; telex 055-61086; f. 1869; cap. and res 4,921m., dep. 87,882.4m (July 1988); Chair. and CEO ALLAN TAYLOR; Pres. JOHN E. CLEGHORN.

Toronto-Dominion Bank: POB 1, Toronto Dominion Centre, 55 King St West and Bay St, Toronto, Ont M5K 1A2; tel. (416) 982-8222; telex 065-24267; f. 1855; cap. and res 3,623m., dep. 47,889m. (July 1988); Chair. and CEO RICHARD M. THOMSON; Pres. ROBERT W. KORTHALS; 949 brs in Canada.

Schedule 'B' Banks

Banque Nationale de Paris (Canada): BNP Tower, 1981 ave Collège McGill, Montréal, Qué H3A 2W8; tel. (514) 285-6000; cap. p.u. and res 79.5m., total assets 1,450.6m. (April 1988); Pres. and CEO F. JONATHAN.

Barclays Bank of Canada: Commerce Court West, Suite 3500, POB 377, Toronto, Ont M5L 1G2; tel. (416) 862-0594; cap. p.u. and res 115.5m., total assets 2,186.2m. (April 1988); Pres. and CEO G. D. FARRAR.

Citibank Canada: University Place, 123 Front St West, Suite 1900, Toronto, Ont M5J 2M3; tel. (416) 947-5500; cap. p.u. and res 313.6m., total assets 4,256.4m. (April 1988); Pres. and CEO FREDERICK COPELAND, Jr.

Hongkong Bank of Canada: 885 West Georgia St, Suite 300, Vancouver, BC V6C 3E9; tel. (604) 685-1000; telex 045-07750; f. 1981; cap. p.u. and res 264.4m., total assets 3,739.5m. (April 1988); Chair. JOHN R. BOND; Pres. and CEO JAMES H. CLEAVE; 52 brs.

Lloyds Bank Canada: 130 Adelaide St West, Toronto, Ont M5H 3R2; tel. (416) 868-8000; cap. p.u. and res 291.1m., total assets 5,293.6m. (April 1988); CEO D. DRAKE.

Swiss Bank Corporation (Canada): 207 Queen's Quay West, Suite 780, POB 103, Toronto, Ont M5J 1A7; tel. (416) 865-0190; cap. p.u. and res 83.7m., total assets 1,564m. (April 1988); Pres. K. FREI.

Development Bank

Federal Business Development Bank: 800 place Victoria, Tour de la Bourse, CP 335, Montréal, Qué H4Z 1L4; tel. (514) 283-5904; f. 1975; auth. cap. 512.6m. (1988); Pres. G. A. LAVIGUEUR.

Principal Trust and Loan Companies

Canada Permanent Mortgage Corporation and Canada Permanent Trust Co: 320 Bay St, Toronto, Ont M5H 2P6; tel. (416) 361-8000; telex 062-17799; f. 1855; combined assets 6,938m. (1982); Chair., Pres. and CEO J. A. C. HILLIKER.

Canada Trustco Mortgage Co (The Canada Trust Co): POB 5703, Terminal A, London, Ont N6A 4S4; tel. (519) 663-1400; telex 064-7575; total assets 26,106m. (March 1988); Pres. PETER C. MAURICE; Chair. and CEO MERV L. LAHN.

Central Trust Co: 1801 Hollis St, POB 2343, Halifax, NS B3J 3C8; tel. (902) 425-7390; telex 019-22578; f. 1980; total assets 3,680m. (1986); Pres. and CEO DAVID A. RATTEE.

Crédit Foncier: 612 rue St-Jacques, Montréal, Qué H3C 1E1; tel. (514) 392-1880; telex 052-68622; f. 1880; total assets 2,700m. (July 1985); Chair. CLAUDE CASTONGUAY; Pres. and CEO MICHEL M. LESSARD.

Guaranty Trust Co of Canada: 366 Bay St, Toronto, Ont M5H 2W5; tel. (416) 975-4500; telex 065-24107; f. 1925; total assets 3,603.2m. (1985); Pres. and CEO ALAN R. MARCHMENT.

Montréal Trust: 1 place Ville Marie, Montréal, Qué H3B 3L6; tel. (514) 397-7000; telex 055-61286; f. 1889; total assets 1,861.1m. (1983); Chair. and Pres. ROBERT GRATTON.

National Trust Co Ltd: 18 King St East, Toronto, Ont M5C 1C4; tel. (416) 364-9141; telex 062-2028; f. 1898; total assets 2,787m. (1982); Chair. and CEO J. L. A. COLHOUN.

The National Victoria and Grey Trust Co: 1 Ontario St, Stratford, Ont N5A 6S9; f. 1844; total assets 7,800m. (1984); Pres. J. C. C. WANSBROUGH; Chair. and CEO WILLIAM H. SOMERVILLE.

Royal Trustco Ltd: Royal Trust Tower, Toronto, Ont M5W 1P9; tel. (416) 864-7000; telex 065-24237; f. 1892; total assets 71,849m. (1986); Chair. HARTLAND M. MACDOUGALL; Pres. and CEO MICHAEL A. CORNELISSEN.

Trust Général du Canada: 1100 rue Université, Montréal, Qué H3B 2G7; tel. (514) 871-7180; telex 055-61407; f. 1928; cap. and res 94m., total assets 3,038m. (1985); Pres. and CEO MAURICE JODOIN.

Savings Institutions with Provincial Charters

Province of Alberta Treasury Branches: 9925-109 St, POB 1440, Edmonton, Alta T5J 2N6; tel. (403) 493-7307; telex 037-43122; f. 1938; assets 6,153m., dep. 6,198m. (March 1988); Supt A. O. BRAY; 132 brs.

Province of Ontario Savings Office: 33 King St West, 6th Floor, Oshawa, Ont L1H 8H5; tel. (416) 433-5785; f. 1921; Exec. Dir J. S. PURDON; Dir J. L. ALLEN; 21 brs.

Bankers' Organizations

The Canadian Bankers' Association: 2 First Canadian Place, POB 348, Toronto, Ont M5X 1E1; tel. (416) 362-6092; telex 062-3402; f. 1891; Chair. A. W. MOYSEY; Pres. ROBERT M. MACINTOSH; 66 mems.

Trust Companies Association of Canada Inc: Herbert House, 335 Bay St, 7th Floor, Toronto, Ont M5H 2R3; tel. (416) 364-1207; Pres. and CEO JOHN L. EVANS; Dir of Admin. and Sec. J. SAYERS.

STOCK EXCHANGES

Alberta Stock Exchange: 300 Fifth Ave SW, 6th Floor, Calgary, Alta T2P 3C4; tel. (403) 262-7791; telex 038-21793; f. 1914; 46 mems; Pres. T. A. CUMMING.

The Montréal Exchange: Tour de la Bourse, 800 place Victoria, CP 61, Montréal, Qué H4Z 1A9; tel. (514) 871-2424; telex 055-60586; f. 1874; 76 mems; Pres. and CEO BRUNO RIVERIN.

Toronto Stock Exchange: The Exchange Tower, 2 First Canadian Place, Toronto, Ont M5X 1J2; tel. (416) 947-4700; telex 062-17759; f. 1852; 73 mems; Pres. J. P. BUNTING.

Vancouver Stock Exchange: Stock Exchange Tower, 609 Granville St, POB 10333, Vancouver, BC V7Y 1H1; tel. (604) 689-3334; telex 045-5480; f. 1907; 49 mems; Chair. J. L. MATHERS; Pres. DONALD J. HUDSON.

Winnipeg Stock Exchange: 955-167 Lombard Ave, Winnipeg, Man R3B 0V3; tel. (204) 942-8431; 19 mems; Pres. R. H. VANDEWATER.

INSURANCE
Principal Companies

Abbey Life Insurance Co of Canada: 3027 Harvester Rd, Burlington, Ont L7N 3G9; Pres. W. D. MILLAR.

CANADA   Directory

Blue Cross Life Insurance Co: POB 220, Moncton, NB E1C 8L3; tel. (506) 853-1811; telex 014-2233; Sec. D. R. Lennox.

Canada Life Assurance Co: 330 University Ave, Toronto, Ont M5G 1R8; f. 1847; Pres. E. H. Crawford.

Canada Security Assurance Co: 60 Yonge St, Toronto, Ont M5E 1H5; tel. (416) 362-2961; telex 062-19667; f. 1913; Pres. R. H. Stevens.

Canadian General Insurance Co: POB 4030, Terminal A, Toronto, Ont M5W 1K4; f. 1907; Pres. R. E. Bethell.

Canadian Home Assurance Co: 465 ouest, blvd René Lévesque, Montréal, Qué H2Z 1A8; tel. (514) 866-6531; telex 052-5169; f. 1928; Pres. J. P. Lussier.

Canadian Indemnity Co: 165 University Ave, Toronto, Ont M5H 3B9; tel. (416) 362-7231; telex 062-19747; f. 1912; Pres. D. A. Waugh.

The Canadian Surety Co: Canada Sq., 2180 Yonge St, Toronto, Ont M4S 2C2; tel. (416) 487-7195; telex 065-24212; Pres. and Gen. Man. J. Robertson.

Century Insurance Co of Canada: 1155 West Pender St, Vancouver, BC V6E 2P4; tel. (604) 683-0255; f. 1890; Pres. J. B. Murch.

Confederation Life Insurance Co: 321 Bloor St East, Toronto, Ont M4W 1H1; f. 1871; Pres. P. D. Burns.

Groupe Coopérants, inc, et Les Coopérants, société mutuelle d'assurance-vie: Maison des Coopérants, 600 ouest, blvd de Maisonneuve, Montréal, Qué H3A 3J9; tel. (514) 287-6600; f. 1876; Pres. of Board Paul Dolan; CEO Pierre Shooner.

Crown Life Insurance Co: 120 Bloor St East, Toronto, Ont M4W 1B8; tel. (416) 928-4500; telex 062-22651; f. 1900; Chair. H. M. Burns; Pres. and CEO R. F. Richardson.

Dominion Insurance Corpn: POB 4024, Terminal A, Toronto, Ont M5W 1K1; f. 1904; Pres. and Gen. Man. W. W. Ward.

Dominion of Canada General Insurance Co: 165 University Ave, Toronto, Ont M5H 3B9; tel. (416) 362-7231; telex 062-19747; f. 1887; Pres. D. A. Waugh.

Eaton Life Assurance Co: 595 Bay St, Toronto, Ont M5G 2C6; f. 1920; Chair. R. Breton; Pres. R. E. Brown.

Excelsior Life Insurance Co: 145 King St West, Toronto, Ont M5H 3T7; f. 1889; Chair. G. N. Farquhar.

Federation Insurance Co of Canada: 1080 Beaver Hall Hill, 20th Floor, Montréal, Qué H2Z 1S8; tel. (514) 875-5790; telex 055-61701; f. 1947; Pres. W. J. Green.

General Accident Assurance Co of Canada: The Exchange Tower, Suite 2600, 2 First Canadian Place, POB 410, Toronto, Ont M5X 1J1; tel. (416) 368-4733; telex 065-24272; f. 1906; Pres. Leonard G. Latham.

Gerling Global General Insurance Co: 480 University Ave, Toronto, Ont M5G 1V6; tel. (416) 598-4651; telex 065-24108; f. 1955; Pres. Dr R. R. Kern.

Gore Mutual Insurance Co: 252 Dundas St, Cambridge, Ont N1R 5T3; tel. (519) 623-1910; telex 069-59304; f. 1839; Sec. J. M. Gray.

The Great-West Life Assurance Co: 100 Osborne St North, Winnipeg, Man R3C 3A5; tel. (204) 946-1190; telex 075-7519; f. 1891; Pres. and CEO K. P. Kavanagh.

Le Groupe Commerce, compagnie d'assurances: 2450 ouest, blvd Girouard, St-Hyacinthe, Qué J2S 3B3; f. 1907; Pres. and CEO Guy St-Germain.

Guardian Insurance Co of Canada: POB 4096, Station A, Toronto, Ont M5N 1N1; f. 1911; Chair. George Alexander; Pres. N. Curtis.

Halifax Insurance Co: 75 Eglinton Ave East, Toronto, Ont M4P 3A3; tel. (416) 440-1000; f. 1809; Pres. and CEO J. N. McCarthy.

Halifax Life Insurance Co: 75 Eglinton Ave East, Toronto, Ont M4P 3A3; tel. (416) 489-5433; f. 1911; Pres. M. J. Hafeman.

Imperial Life Assurance Co of Canada: 95 St Clair Ave West, Toronto, Ont M4V 1N7; tel. (416) 926-2600; f. 1896; Chair., Pres. and CEO Claude Bruneau.

Kings Mutual Insurance Co: Berwick, NS B0P 1E0; f. 1904; Pres. M. Vissers; Man. D. C. Cook.

Laurentian General Insurance Co Inc: 1100 ouest, blvd René Lévesque, Montréal, Qué H3B 4P4; tel. (514) 392-6174; telex 055-62067; Pres. Jean Bouchard.

Le Groupe La Laurentienne: 500 est, Grande-Allée, Québec, Qué G1R 2J7; comprises 18 operating companies; Chair. and CEO Claude Castonguay.

London Life Insurance Co: 255 Dufferin Ave, London, Ont N6A 4K1; tel. (519) 432-5281; f. 1874; Pres. and CEO Earl H. Orser; Chair. A. T. Lambert.

Manufacturers Life Insurance Co: 200 Bloor St East, Toronto, Ont M4W 1E5; tel. (416) 926-0100; f. 1887; Pres. and CEO Thomas A. DiGiacomo; Chair. E. S. Jackson.

Mercantile and General Reinsurance Co of Canada: University Place, 123 Front St West, Toronto, Ont M5J 2M7; f. 1951; Pres. D. M. Batten.

Montréal Life Insurance Co: 630 ouest, rue Sherbrooke, Montréal, Qué H3A 1E4; f. 1908; Pres. N. Bauer.

Mutual Life of Canada: 227 King St South, Waterloo, Ont N2J 4C5; tel. (519) 888-2290; f. 1870; Chair. J. H. Panabaker; Pres. and CEO Jack V. Masterman.

The National Life Assurance Co of Canada: 522 University Ave, Toronto, Ont M5G 1Y7; tel. (416) 598-2122; f. 1897; Pres. and CEO S. Ross Johnson.

North American Life Assurance Co: 333 Broadway Ave, Winnipeg, Man R3C 0S9; tel. (204) 949-1660; f. 1881; Chair. D. G. Payne; Pres. Harold Thompson.

Northern Life Assurance Co of Canada: 606 4th St SW, Calgary, Alta T2P 1S9; f. 1894; Pres. and CEO G. L. Bowie; Chair. R. C. Brown.

Portage La Prairie Mutual Insurance Co: Portage La Prairie, Man R1N 3B8; tel. (204) 857-3415; f. 1884; Pres. and Gen. Man. H. G. Owens.

Québec Assurance Co: 10 Wellington St East, Toronto, Ont M5E 1L5; tel. (416) 366-7511; telex 065-24124; f. 1818; Pres. R. A. Elms.

Saskatchewan Government Insurance: 2260 11th Ave, Regina, Sask S4P 0J9; tel. (306) 565-1200; telex 071-2417; f. 1945; Pres. Alex G. Wilde.

La Sauvegarde Compagnie d'assurance sur la vie: 1 complexe Desjardins, Montréal, Qué H5B 1E2; f. 1901; Pres. Henri Leblond; Dir-Gen. Serge Beaudoin.

Seaboard Life Insurance Co: 2165 West Broadway, Vancouver, BC V6K 4N5; tel. (604) 734-1667; f. 1953; Pres. J. S. M. Cunningham.

Société Nationale d'Assurances: 425 ouest, blvd de Maisonneuve, Bureau 1500, Montréal, Qué H3A 3G5; tel. (514) 288-8711; telex 055-61190; f. 1940; Pres. Henri Joli-Coeur; Dir-Gen. Pierre Renaud.

Sovereign Life Assurance Co: 606–4th St, SW Calgary, Alta T2P 1S9; tel. (403) 298-5576; telex 038-25817; f. 1894; Pres. J. Royer.

The Stanstead and Sherbrooke Insurance Co: Toronto Dominion Centre, POB 441, Toronto, Ont M5K 1L9; f. 1835; Pres. Harold B. Greer.

Sun Life Assurance Co of Canada: POB 4150, Station A, Toronto, Ont M5W 2C9; tel. (416) 979-9966; telex 065-24389; f. 1865; Chair. and CEO John D. McNeil; Pres. John R. Gardner.

Toronto Mutual Life Insurance Co: 112 St Clair Ave West, Toronto, Ont M4V 2Y3; tel. (416) 960-3463; Pres. John T. English; Chair. Walter B. Thompson.

Travelers Canada: Travelers Tower, 400 University Ave, Toronto, Ont M5G 1S7; tel. (416) 586-3000; Pres. and CEO Daniel Damov.

United Canadian Shares Ltd: 1601 Church Ave, Winnipeg, Man R2X 1G9; tel. (204) 633-7042; telex 075-87636; f. 1951; Chair. R. H. Jones; Pres. C. S. Riley, Jr.

Victoria Insurance Co of Canada: 150 Eglinton Ave East, Toronto, Ont M4P 2Z3; tel. (416) 488-4666; telex 062-2237; Chair. and CEO R. W. Broughton.

Waterloo Insurance Co: 14 Erb St West, POB 1604, Waterloo, Ont N2J 4C8; f. 1863; Gen. Man. K. I. Tyers.

Wawanesa Mutual Insurance Co: 191 Broadway, Winnipeg, Man R3C 3P1; tel. (204) 985-3811; telex 075-7564; f. 1896; Pres. I. M. Montgomery.

Western Assurance Co: 10 Wellington St East, Toronto, Ont M5E 1L5; tel. (416) 366-7511; f. 1851; Pres. R. A. Elms.

York Fire and Casualty Insurance Co: 7501 Keele St, Suite 300, Concord, Ont L4K 1Y2; tel. (416) 738-1707; telex 069-64754; Pres. Alexander A. Thain.

Zurich Life Insurance Co of Canada: 188 University Ave, Toronto, Ont M5H 3C4; tel. (416) 593-4444; Pres. and CEO P. D. McGarry.

Insurance Organizations

Canadian Life and Health Insurance Association: 20 Queen St West, Suite 2500, Toronto, Ont M5H 3S2; tel. (416) 977-2221; f. 1894; Pres. G. M. Devlin; 110 mem. cos.

Insurance Brokers Association of Canada: 141 Adelaide St West, Suite 801, Toronto, Ont M5H 3L5; tel. (416) 367-1831; f. 1920; Gen. Man. Basil M. Steggles.

Insurance Bureau of Canada: 181 University Ave, 13th Floor, Toronto, Ont M5H 3M7; tel. (416) 362-2031; telex 062-23502; Pres. and CEO J. L. Lyndon; 180 corporate mems.

Insurance Institute of Canada: 481 University Ave, 6th Floor, Toronto, Ont M5G 2E9; tel. (416) 591-1572; f. 1952; Chair. J. Phelan; Pres. J. C. Rhind; 27,000 mems.

CANADA	Directory

Insurers' Advisory Organization Inc: 180 Dundas St West, Toronto, Ont M5G 1Z9; tel. (416) 597-1200; f. 1855; Pres. and CEO G. A. CHELLEW; 65 mems.

Life Insurance Institute of Canada: 20 Queen St, Suite 2500, Toronto, Ont M5H 3S2; tel. (416) 977-2221; Sec.-Treas. DEBBIE COLE-GAUER.

Life Underwriters' Association of Canada: 41 Lesmill Rd, Don Mills, Ont M3B 2T3; tel. (416) 444-5251; f. 1906; Exec. Vice-Pres. and Chief Operating Officer GORD WATT; 21,000 mems.

Trade and Industry

CHAMBER OF COMMERCE

The Canadian Chamber of Commerce: 55 Metcalfe St, Suite 1160, Ottawa K1P 6N4; tel. (613) 238-4000; telex 053-3360; f. 1925; mems: 500 community chambers of commerce and boards of trade, 80 nat. trade asscns and 4,000 business corpns; affiliated with all provincial chambers of commerce and with International Chamber and other bilateral orgs; Chair. JOHN D. HERRICK; Pres. R. B. HAMEL.

INDUSTRIAL ASSOCIATIONS

There are about 2,000 trades associations in Canada.

The Canadian Manufacturers' Association: One Yonge St, Toronto, Ont M5E 1J9; tel. (416) 363-7261; telex 065-24693; f. 1871; the nat. organization of mfrs of Canada; 8,000 mems; Pres and Exec. Dir J. L. THIBAULT.

Agriculture and Horticulture

Agricultural Institute of Canada: 151 Slater St, Suite 907, Ottawa K1P 5H4; tel. (613) 232-9459; f. 1920; 36 brs; 9 provincial sections; 8 affiliated societies; Gen. Man. Y. JACQUES.

Alberta Wheat Pool: 505-2nd St SW, POB 2700, Calgary, Alta T2P 2P5; tel. (403) 290-4910; telex 038-21643; Pres. D. E. LIVINGSTONE.

Canada Grains Council: 760-360 Main St, Winnipeg, Man R3C 3Z3; tel. (204) 942-2254; f. 1969; Pres. Dr DONALD A. DEVER.

Canadian Federation of Agriculture: 75 Albert St, Suite 1101, Ottawa; K1P 5E7; tel. (613) 236-3633; f. 1935; 17 mems (9 provincial feds); Pres. D. A. KNOERR; Exec. Sec. PETER MARTEN.

Canadian Horticultural Council: 3 Amberwood Crescent, Nepean, Ont K2E 7L1; tel. (613) 226-4187; telex 053-3690; f. 1922; Exec. Vice-Pres. D. DEMPSTER.

Canadian Nursery Trades Association: 1293 Matheson Blvd, Mississauga, Ont L4W 1R1; tel. (416) 629-1367; Exec. Dir CHRIS D. ANDREWS.

Canadian Seed Growers' Association: POB 8455, Ottawa K1G 3T1; tel. (613) 236-0497; f. 1904; Exec. Dir W. K. ROBERTSON; 5,000 mems.

Canadian Society of Agricultural Engineering: 151 Slater St, Suite 907, Ottawa K1P 5H4; tel. (613) 232-9459.

Dairy Farmers of Canada: 75 Albert St, Suite 1101, Ottawa K1P 5E7; tel. (613) 236-9997; f. 1934; Exec. Dir RICHARD DOYLE; 19 mem. asscns.

National Dairy Council of Canada: 141 Laurier Ave West, Suite 704, Ottawa K1P 5J3; tel. (613) 238-4116; Pres. KEMPTON L. MATTE; 250 mems.

National Farmers Union: 250c 2nd Ave South, Saskatoon, Sask S7K 2M1; tel. (306) 652-9465; 6 regional offices; Exec. Sec. STUART THIESSON.

L'Union des Producteurs agricoles: 555 blvd Roland-Therrien, Longueuil, Qué J4H 3Y9; tel. (514) 679-0530; f. 1924; Sec.-Gen. JEAN-CLAUDE BLANCHETTE; 47,000 mems.

Building and Construction

Canadian Construction Association: 85 Albert St, Ottawa K1P 6A4; tel. (613) 236-9455; f. 1918; Chair. PETER LYSAK; Pres. ROBERT E. NUTH; over 20,000 mems.

Canadian Institute of Steel Construction: 201 Consumers Rd, Suite 300, Willowdale, Ont M2J 4G8; tel. (416) 491-4552; telex 069-86547; Pres. H. A. KRENTZ; 50 mems.

Canadian Paint and Coatings Association: 9900 blvd Cavendish, Bureau 103, St-Laurent, Qué H4M 2V2; tel. (514) 745-2611; f. 1913; Pres. R. W. MURRY; 105 mems.

Construction Specifications Canada: 1 St Clair Ave West, Suite 1206, Toronto, Ont M4V 1K6; tel. (416) 922-3159; f. 1954; Exec. Vice-Pres. RENÉ GAULIN; 1,450 mems.

National Concrete Producers' Association: 1013 Wilson Ave, Suite 101, Downsview, Ont M3K 1G1; tel. (416) 635-7179; Pres. B. CLARK; Exec. Dir MARK PATAMIA.

Ontario Painting Contractors Association: 211 Consumers Rd, Suite 305, Willowdale, Ont M2J 4G8; tel. (416) 498-1897; Exec. Dir MAUREEN MARQUARDT.

Clothing and Textiles

Apparel Manufacturers' Association of Ontario: 1179 King St West, Suite 117, Toronto, Ont M6K 3C5; tel. (416) 531-5707; f. 1970; Exec. Dir F. J. BRYAN; 79 mems.

Canadian Allied Textile Trades Association: 49 Front St East, Toronto, Ont M5E 1B3; tel. (416) 363-4266.

Canadian Carpet Institute: 130 Slater St, Suite 325, Ottawa K1P 6E2; tel. (613) 232-7183; f. 1961; Pres. D. S. EDWARDS.

Canadian Textiles Institute: 280 Albert St, Suite 502, Ottawa K1P 5G8; tel. (613) 232-7195; telex 053-4290; Pres. E. L. BARRY; 4 affiliated asscns.

The Shoe Manufacturers' Association of Canada: 1010 ouest, rue Ste-Catherine, Bureau 710, Montréal, Qué H3B 3R4; tel. (514) 878-9337; f. 1918; Pres. NATHAN FINKELSTEIN; Exec. Sec. DIANE CAPPELLA; 137 mems.

Tanners Association of Canada: 50 River St, Toronto, Ont M5A 3N9; tel. (416) 364-2134; Exec. Vice-Pres. IAN C. KENNEDY.

Electrical and Electronics

Canadian Electrical Association: 1 place Westmount, Bureau 500, Montréal, Qué H3Z 2P9; tel. (514) 937-6181; telex 052-67401; f. 1891; Pres. WALLACE S. READ.

Electrical and Electronic Manufacturers Association of Canada: 10 Carlson Court, Suite 500, Rexdale, Ont M9W 6L2; tel. (416) 674-7410; telex 069-89110; Pres. N. ASPIN; Chair. of Board D. A. NOBLE; 230 mems.

Electrical Bureau of Canada: 10 Carlson Court, Suite 500, Rexdale, Ont M9W 6L2; tel. (416) 674-7410.

Fisheries

Canadian Association of Fish Exporters: 77 Metcalfe St, Suite 509, Ottawa K1P 5L6; tel. (613) 232-6325; telex 053-4556; f. 1978; Pres. B. C. DUNBAR.

Fisheries Council of British Columbia: 100 West Pender St, Suite 400, Vancouver, BC V6B 1R8; tel. (604) 684-6454; telex 045-08441; Chair. B. L. TYRER; Pres. M. HUNTER.

Fisheries Council of Canada: 77 Metcalfe St, Suite 505, Ottawa K1P 5L6; tel. (613) 238-775; telex 053-4556; Pres. R. W. BULMER; 6 mem. asscns, 192 mem. cos, 90 assoc. mem. cos.

Food and Beverages

Bakery Council of Canada: 1185 Eglinton Ave East, Suite 101, Don Mills, Ont M3C 3C6; tel. (416) 423-0262; Pres. LINDA J. NAGEL.

Brewers Association of Canada: 155 Queen St, Suite 1200, Ottawa K1P 6L1; tel. (613) 232-9601; f. 1943; Pres. R. A. MORRISON; Sec. Mrs F. T. BAMFORD.

Canadian Council of Grocery Distributors: 750 blvd Laurentien, Bureau 475, St-Laurent, Qué H4M 2M4; tel. (514) 747-6566; f. 1919; Pres. JACQUES G. AUGER; Exec. Vice-Pres. CLAUDE PIGEON; 60 mems.

Canadian Food Brokers Association: 50 River St, Toronto, Ont M5A 3N9; tel. (416) 368-5921; Pres. IAN C. KENNEDY.

Canadian Meat Council: 5233 Dundas St West, Islington, Ont M9B 1A6; tel. (416) 239-8411; f. 1919; Gen. Man. D. M. ADAMS; 83 mems.

Canadian National Millers' Association: 155 Queen St, Suite 1101, Ottawa K1P 6L1; tel. (613) 238-2293; telex 053-3964; f. 1920; Chair. ALLAN H. JAMES; Sec. STEPHEN P. MARKEY; 19 mems.

Canadian Pork Council: 75 Albert St, Suite 1101, Ottawa K1P 5E7; tel. (613) 236-9239; Pres. W. VAAGS; Exec. Sec. MARTIN RICE; 10 mem. asscns.

Chilled and Frozen Food Association of Canada: 1306 Wellington St, Suite 303, Ottawa K1Y 3B2; tel. (613) 728-6306; Exec. Dir CHRISTOPHER J. KYTE.

Confectionery Manufacturers Association of Canada: 1185 Eglinton Ave East, Don Mills, Ont M3C 3C6; tel. (416) 429-1046; f. 1919; Pres. CAROL HOCHU; mems: 23 active, 57 associate.

Grocery Products Manufacturers of Canada: 56 Sparks St, Suite 800, Ottawa K1P 5A9; tel. (613) 236-0583; Pres. GEORGE FLEISCHMANN.

Forestry, Lumber and Allied Industries

Canadian Forestry Association: 185 Somerset St West, Ottawa K2P 0J2; tel. (613) 232-1815; f. 1900; Pres. W. K. FULLERTON; Exec. Dir GLEN BLOUIN.

Canadian Lumber Standards: 1475–1055 West Hastings St, Vancouver, BC V6E 2E9; tel. (604) 687-2171.

CANADA

Canadian Lumbermen's Association: 27 Goulburn Ave, Ottawa K1N 8C7; tel. (613) 233-6205; telex 053-4519; f. 1908; Exec. Dir J. F. McCracken; 400 mems.

Canadian Pulp and Paper Association: Sun Life Bldg, 19e étage, 1155 rue Metcalfe, Montréal, Qué H3B 4T6; tel. (514) 866-6621; telex 055-60690; f. 1913; Pres. Howard Hart; Exec. Vice-Pres. and Sec. Elinor Blanchard; 62 mems.

Ontario Forest Industries Association: 130 Adelaide St West, Suite 1700, Toronto, Ont M5H 3P5; tel. (416) 368-6188; telex 065-24407; f. 1943; Pres. I. D. Bird; Exec. Asst R. M. Rauter; 24 mems.

Québec Forest Industries Association Ltd: 1200 ave Germain-des-Près, Bureau 102, Ste-Foy, Qué G1V 3M7; tel. (418) 651-9352; f. 1924; Pres. and Dir-Gen. André Duchesne; 29 mems.

Hotels and Catering

Canadian Restaurant and Foodservices Association: Nu-West Center, 80 Bloor St West, Suite 1201, Toronto, Ont M5S 2V1; tel. (416) 923-8416; f. 1944; Exec. Vice-Pres. D. Needham.

Hotel Association of Canada Inc: 34 Ross St, Toronto, Ont M5T 1Z9; tel. (416) 596-7676; Pres. Adam Borovich.

Mining

Canadian Gas Association: 55 Scarsdale Rd, Don Mills, Ont M3B 2R3; tel. (416) 447-6465; telex 069-66824; Pres. Ian C. MacNabb.

Canadian Petroleum Association: 150 Sixth Ave SW, Suite 3800, Calgary, Alta T2P 3Y7; tel. (403) 269-6721; Pres. Ian R. Smyth.

Mining Association of Canada: 350 Sparks St, Suite 809, Ottawa K1R 7S8; tel. (613) 233-9391; Pres. C. George Miller.

Northwest Territories Chamber of Mines: POB 2818, Yellowknife, NWT X1A 2R1; tel. (403) 873-5281; f. 1967.

Ontario Mining Association: 111 Richmond St West, Suite 1114, Toronto, Ont M5H 2G4; tel. (416) 364-9301; f. 1920; Pres. J. M. Gordon; Exec. Dir T. P. Reid; 35 mems.

Yukon Chamber of Mines: POB 4427, Whitehorse, Yukon Y1A 3T5; tel. (403) 667-2090.

Pharmaceutical

Canadian Cosmetic, Toiletry and Fragrance Association: 24 Merton St, Toronto, Ont M4S 1A1; tel. (416) 487-8111; f. 1928; Pres. Kenneth W. Baker; Vice-Pres. Sharron Wissler; 290 corporate mems.

Canadian Drug Manufacturers Association: 1120 Finch Ave West, Suite 604, Toronto, Ont M3J 3H7; tel. (416) 663-2362; Chair. Jack Kay; Exec. Dir Nicholas G. Leluk.

Pharmaceutical Manufacturers Association of Canada: 1111 Prince of Wales Drive, Ottawa, K2C 3T2; tel. (613) 236-9993; f. 1914; Pres. Guy Beauchemin; 65 mems.

Retailing

Retail Council of Canada: 210 Dundas St West, Suite 600, Toronto, Ont M5G 2E8; tel. (416) 598-4684; f. 1963; Chair. M. H. Ayre; Pres. A. J. McKichan; mems represent 70% of total retail store volume.

Retail Merchants' Association of Canada Inc: 1780 Birchmount Rd, Scarborough, Ont M1P 2H8; tel. (416) 291-7903; f. 1896; Pres. and CEO John Gillespie; nat. asscn of provincial groups.

Transport

Air Transport Association of Canada: see Transport—Civil Aviation.

Canadian Institute of Traffic and Transportation: 573 King St East, Toronto, Ont M5A 1M5; tel. 363-5696.

The Canadian Shippers' Council: see Transport—Shipping.

Canadian Trucking Association: Varette Bldg, 130 Albert St, Suite 300, Ottawa K1P 5G4; tel. (613) 236-9426; f. 1937; Gen. Man. L. P. Tardif.

Motor Vehicle Manufacturers' Association: 25 Adelaide St East, Suite 1602, Toronto, Ont M5C 1Y7; tel. (416) 364-9333; Pres. N. A. Clark; 9 mems.

The Railway Association of Canada: see Transport—Railways.

The Shipping Federation of Canada: see Transport—Shipping.

Wholesale Trade

Canadian Exporters' Association: 99 Bank St, Suite 250, Ottawa K1P 6B9; tel. (613) 238-8888; telex 053-4888; f. 1943; Pres. L. James Taylor; 600 mems.

Canadian Importers' Association, Inc: World Trade Centre, 60 Harbour St, Toronto, Ont M5J 1B7; tel. (416) 862-0002; telex 065-24115; f. 1932; Pres. Peter J. Dawes; over 850 mems.

Canadian Warehousing Association: 517 Wellington St West, Suite 209, Toronto, Ont M5V 2X5; tel. (416) 596-7489; f. 1917; Pres. David I. Kentish; 55 mems.

Miscellaneous

Canadian Maritime Industries Association: POB 1429, Station B, Ottawa K1P 5R4; tel. (613) 232-7127; telex 053-4848; f. 1944; Pres. J. Y. Clarke; 20 shipyards and ship repairing firms, 83 allied industries.

Canadian Tobacco Manufacturers Council: 1808 ouest, rue Sherbrooke, Montréal, Qué H3H 1E5; tel. (514) 937-7428; Pres. William H. Neville.

Council of Printing Industries of Canada: 620 University Ave, 11th Floor, Toronto, Ont M5G 2C1; tel. (416) 591-1509; Gen. Man. Franklyn R. Smith.

TRADE UNIONS

At the beginning of 1988 there were 3,841,000 union members in Canada, representing 29.6% of the civilian labour force. Of these, 33.0% belonged to unions with headquarters in the USA.

In 1988 unions affiliated to the Canadian Labour Congress represented 58.1% of total union membership.

Canadian Labour Congress: 2841 Riverside Drive, Ottawa K1V 8X7; tel. (613) 521-3400; telex 053-4750; f. 1956 by merger of the Canadian Congress of Labour and the Trades and Labour Congress of Canada; 2,231,697 mems (1988); Pres. Shirley G. E. Carr; Sec.-Treas. Richard Mercier.

Affiliated unions with over 15,000 members:

Amalgamated Clothing and Textile Workers Union: 601-15 Gervais Drive, Don Mills, Ont M3C 1Y8; tel. (416) 441-1806; Canadian Dir John Alleruzzo; 30,000 mems (1988).

American Federation of Musicians of the United States and Canada: 75 The Donway West, Suite 1010, Don Mills, Ont M3C 2E9; tel. (416) 391-5161; Vice-Pres. from Canada J. Alan Wood; 27,000 mems (1988).

Bakery, Confectionery and Tobacco Workers International Union: 3329 est, rue Ontario, Montréal, Qué H1W 1P8; tel. (514) 527-9371; Int. Vice-Pres. Alphonse de Césaré; 16,000 mems (1988).

Canadian Brotherhood of Railway, Transport and General Workers: 2300 Carling Ave, Ottawa K2B 7G1; tel. (613) 829-8764; f. 1908; Pres. J. D. Hunter; 39,900 mems (1988).

Canadian Paperworkers Union: 255 rue St-Jacques, Montréal, Qué H2Y 1M6; tel. (514) 842-8931; Pres. James M. Buchanan; 69,000 mems (1988).

Canadian Union of Postal Workers: 280 Metcalfe St, Ottawa K2P 1R7; tel. (613) 236-7238; Pres. Jean-Claude Parrot; 24,000 mems (1988).

Canadian Union of Public Employees: 21 Florence St, Ottawa K2P 0W6; tel. (613) 237-1590; telex 053-4878; Nat. Pres. Jeff Rose; 342,000 mems (1988).

Communications and Electrical Workers of Canada: 141 Laurier Ave West, Suite 906, Ottawa K1P 5J3; tel. (613) 236-6083; Pres. Fred W. Pomeroy; 40,000 mems (1988).

Energy and Chemical Workers' Union: 9940-106 St, Suite 202, Edmonton, Alta T5K 2N2; tel. (403) 422-7932; Pres. Reginald C. Basken; 37,000 mems (1988).

Fraternité nationale des charpentiers-menuisiers, forestiers et travailleurs d'usine: 3750 est, blvd Crémazie, Bureau 310, Montréal, Qué H2A 1B6; tel. (514) 374-0952; Pres. Louis-Marie Cloutier; 16,000 mems (1988).

Graphic Communications International Union: 1110 Finch Ave West, Suite 600, Downsview, Ont M3J 2T2; tel. (416) 661-9761; Int. Vice-Pres. Léonard R. Paquette; 21,679 mems (1988).

Hospital Employees Union, Local 180: 2286 West 12th Ave, Vancouver, BC V6K 2N5; Prov. Pres. Bill MacDonald; 27,000 mems (1988).

Hotel Employees and Restaurant Employees International Union: 1410 rue Stanley, Bureau 500, Montréal, Qué H3A 1P8; tel. (514) 849-7511; Int. Vice-Pres James Stamos (Montréal), Ron Bonar (Vancouver); 30,000 mems (1988).

International Association of Machinists and Aerospace Workers: 100 Metcalfe St, Suite 300, Ottawa K1P 5M1; tel. (613) 236-9761; Gen. Vice-Pres. Valérie E. Bourgeois; 58,558 mems (1988).

International Woodworkers Association of Canada (IWA–Canada): 1285 Pender St, Suite 500, Vancouver, BC V6E 4B2; tel. (604) 683-1117; f. 1937; Pres. J. J. Munro; 45,000 mems (1988).

CANADA — *Directory*

Letter Carriers' Union of Canada: 45 Auriga Drive, Ottawa K2E 7V3; tel. (613) 723-8133; Nat. Pres. BOB MCGARRY; 23,000 mems (1988).

National Automobile, Aerospace and Agricultural Implement Workers Union of Canada (CAW-Canada): 205 Placer Court, North York, Willowdale, Ont M2H 3H9; tel. (416) 497-4110; telex 069-86509; Pres. ROBERT WHITE; 143,000 mems (1988).

National Union of Provincial Government Employees: 2841 Riverside Drive, Suite 204, Ottawa K1V 8N4; tel. (613) 526-1663; Pres. JOHN L. FRYER; 292,300 mems (1988).

Office and Professional Employees' International Union: 1290 rue St-Denis, 5e étage, Montréal, Qué H6X 3J7; tel. (514) 288-6511; Canadian Dir MICHEL ROUSSEAU; 26,000 mems (1988).

Public Service Alliance of Canada: 233 Gilmour St, Ottawa K2P 0P1; tel. (613) 560-4200; telex 053-3724; f. 1966; Pres. DARYL T. BEAN; 175,759 mems (1988).

Retail, Wholesale and Department Store Union: 15 Gervais Drive, Suite 310, Don Mills, Ont M3C 1Y8; tel. (416) 441-1414; Vice-Pres. and Dir in Canada DONALD G. COLLINS; 23,615 mems (1988).

Service Employees International Union: 1 Credit Union Drive, Toronto, Ont M4A 2S6; tel. (416) 752-4073; Vice-Pres S. E. ROSCOE, AIMÉ GOHIER; 70,000 mems (1988).

Transportation Communications International Union: 130 Albert St, Suite 1700, Ottawa K1P 5G4; tel. (613) 234-5811; Nat. Pres. FRANK MAZUR; 18,000 mems (1987).

United Food and Commercial Workers International Union: 61 International Blvd, Suite 300, Rexdale, Ont M9W 6K4; tel. (416) 675-1104; f. 1979; Vice-Pres and Canadian Dirs CLIFFORD EVANS, W. E. HANLEY; 170,000 mems (1988).

United Steelworkers of America: 234 Eglinton Ave East, 7th Floor, Toronto, Ont M4P 1K7; tel. (416) 487-1571; Nat. Dir in Canada GÉRARD DOCQUIER; 160,000 mems (1988).

Other Central Congresses

Canadian Federation of Labour: 107 Sparks St, Suite 300, Ottawa K1P 5B5; tel. (613) 234-4141; f. 1982; Pres. JAMES A. MCCAMBLY; 14 affiliated unions representing over 207,736 mems (1988).

Affiliated unions with over 15,000 members:

International Brotherhood of Electrical Workers: 45 Sheppard Ave East, Suite 401, Willowdale, Ont M2N 5Y1; tel. (416) 226-5155; Int.Vice-Pres. KEN J. WOODS; 64,480 mems (1988).

International Brotherhood of Painters and Allied Trades: 9 Aspen Ave, Toronto, Ont M4B 2Z1; tel. (416) 759-6561; Gen. Vice-Pres. DAVID CAIRNS; 16,250 mems (1988).

International Union of Operating Engineers: 17704 – 103 Ave, Edmonton, Alta T5S 1J9; tel. (403) 483-0421; Canadian Dir N. BUDD COUTTS; 36,000 mems (1988).

United Association of Journeymen and Apprentices of the Plumbing and Pipe Fitting Industry of the United States and Canada: 310 Broadway Ave, Suite 702, Winnipeg, Man R3C 0S6; tel. (204) 942-0836; Vice-Pres. and Canadian Dir J. RUSS ST ELOI; 40,000 mems (1988).

Centrale de l'enseignement du Québec: 1415 est, rue Jarry, Montréal, Qué H2E 1A7; tel. (514) 374-6660; Pres. LORRAINE PAGÉ; Dir-Gen. MICHEL AGNAÏEFF; 110,000 mems (1988).

Affiliated union with over 15,000 members:

Fédération des enseignantes et des enseignants de commissions scolaires: 2336 Ste-Foy, CP 5800, Québec, Qué G1V 4E5; tel. (418) 658-5711; Pres. LUC SAVARD; 75,000 mems (1988).

Centrale des syndicats démocratiques: 1259 rue Berri, Bureau 600, Montréal, Qué H2L 4C7; tel. (514) 842-3801; f. 1972; Pres. JEAN-PAUL HÉTU; 3 federated and 262 non-federated unions representing 50,379 mems (1988).

Confederation of Canadian Unions: 1331½A St Clair Ave West, Toronto, Ont M6E 1C3; f. 1969; Pres. JESS SUCCAMORE; 20 affiliated unions representing 31,407 mems (1988).

Confédération des syndicats nationaux: 1601 ave de Lorimier, Montréal, Qué H2K 4M5; f. 1921; Pres. GÉRALD LAROSE; 2,024 affiliated locals representing 231,396 mems (1988).

Affiliated federations with over 15,000 members:

Fédération des employées et employés de services publics inc: 1601 ave de Lorimier, Montréal, Qué H2K 4M5; tel. (514) 598-2231; Pres. GINETTE GUÉRIN; 27,455 mems (1988).

Fédération des affaires sociales inc: 1601 ave de Lorimier, Montréal, Qué H2K 4M5; tel. (514) 598-2210; Pres. CATHERINE LOUMÈDE; 96,585 mems (1988).

Fédération du commerce inc: 1601 ave de Lorimier, Bureau 122, Montréal, Qué H2K 4M5; tel. (514) 598-2181; Pres. LISE POULIN; 24,500 mems (1988).

Fédération de la métallurgie: 1601 ave de Lorimier, Montréal, Qué H2K 4M5; tel. (514) 598-2136; Pres. PIERRE DUPONT; 20,000 mems (1988).

Fédération des travailleurs du papier et de la forêt: 155 est, blvd Charest, Québec, Qué G1K 3G6; tel. (418) 647-5775; Pres. CLAUDE PLAMONDON; 15,000 mems (1988).

The American Federation of Labor and Congress of Industrial Organizations (AFL-CIO), with headquarters in Washington, DC, USA, represented 224,305 members, or 5.8% of the total union membership in Canada, at the beginning of 1988. Affiliated unions with over 15,000 members:

International Association of Bridge, Structural and Ornamental Iron Workers: 284 King St West, Suite 501, Toronto, Ont M5V 1J1; tel. (416) 593-7155; Gen. Vice-Pres. DONALD W. O'REILLY; 19,940 mems (1988).

International Brotherhood of Teamsters, Chauffeurs, Warehousemen and Helpers of America: 9393 rue Edison, Bureau 200, Ville d'Anjou, Qué H1J 1T4; International Dir LOUIS LACROIX; 91,500 mems (1988).

Laborers' International Union of North America: 1177 Belanger Ave, Suite 101, Ottawa K1H 8N7; tel. (613) 738-3184; Dir DOUGLAS FORGIE; 46,715 mems (1988).

United Brotherhood of Carpenters and Joiners of America: 5799 Yonge St, Suite 807, Willowdale, Ont M2M 3V3; tel. (416) 225-8885; Officials in Canada JOHN CARRUTHERS, RONALD J. DANCER; 66,000 mems (1988).

Principal Unaffiliated Unions

Alberta Teachers' Association: 11010-142 St, Edmonton, Alta T5N 2R1; tel. (403) 453-2411; Exec. Sec. J. S. BUSKI; 38,986 mems (1988).

British Columbia Nurses' Union: 100-4259 Canada Way, Burnaby, BC V5G 1H1; tel. (604) 433-2268; Pres. COLLEEN BONNER; 19,252 mems (1988).

British Columbia Teachers' Federation: 2235 Burrard St, Vancouver, BC V6J 3H9; tel. (604) 731-8121; Pres. ELSIE MCMURPHY; 30,200 mems (1988).

Canadian Telephone Employees' Association: place du Canada, Bureau 360; Montréal, Qué H3B 2N2; tel. (514) 861-9963; Pres. ELISABETH H. ROUSSEAU; 18,000 mems (1988).

Fédération des infirmières et d'infirmiers du Québec: 1425 ouest, blvd René Lévesque, 5e étage, Montréal, Qué H3G 1T7; tel. (514) 861-9015; Pres. DIANE LAVALLE; 37,000 mems (1988).

Fédération des syndicats professionnels d'infirmières et d'infirmiers du Québec: 175 rue St-Jean, 4e étage, Québec, Qué G1R 1N4; tel. (418) 647-1102; Pres. HÉLÈNE PELLETIER; 18,000 mems (1988).

Federation of Women Teachers' Associations of Ontario: 1260 Bay St, Toronto, Ont M5R 2B8; tel. (416) 964-1232; Pres. HELEN PENFIELD; 34,000 mems (1988).

Fishermen, Food and Allied Workers' Union: Bond Bldg, 53 Bond St, POB 10, St John's, Nfld A1C 5H5; Pres. RICHARD CASHIN; 23,000 mems (1988).

Ontario English Catholic Teachers' Association: 65 St Clair Ave East, Suite 400, Toronto, Ont M4T 2Y8; tel. (416) 925-2493; Pres. JIM COONEY; 24,000 mems (1988).

Ontario Nurses' Association: 85 Grenville St, Suite 600, Toronto, Ont M5B 2E7; tel. (416) 964-8833; Pres. MONICA LESLIE; 46,680 mems (1988).

Ontario Public School Teachers' Federation: 1260 Bay St, Toronto, Ont M5R 2B7; tel. (416) 928-1128; Pres. DAVID KENDALL; 19,000 mems (1988).

Ontario Secondary School Teachers Federation: 60 Mobile Drive, Toronto, Ont M4A 2P3; tel. (416) 751-8300; Pres. JIM HEAD; 35,722 mems (1988).

Professional Institute of the Public Service of Canada: 786 Bronson Ave, Ottawa K1S 4G4; tel. (613) 237-6310; Pres. IRIS CRAIG; 20,500 mems (1988).

Syndicat des fonctionnaires provinciaux du Québec: 214 ave St-Sacrement, Bureau 200, Québec, Qué G1N 4N9; tel (418) 687-3343; Pres. JEAN-LOUIS HARGUINDEGUY; 40,000 mems (1988).

Transport

Owing to the size of the country, Canada's economy is particularly dependent upon an efficient system of transport. The St Lawrence Seaway allows ocean-going ships to reach the Great Lakes. There are almost 194,000 km (120,000 miles) of railway track, and the country's rail and canal system is being increasingly augmented by roads, air services and petroleum pipelines. The Trans-Canada

CANADA

Directory

Highway is one of the main features of a network of 392,000 km (243,600 miles) of roads and highways. In 1977 the Canadian Government extended its coastal jurisdiction to 370 km (200 nautical miles).

RAILWAYS

The Canadian Pacific and Canadian National Railways provide 88% of all rail transportation in Canada.

Algoma Central Railway: POB 7000, Sault Ste Marie, Ont P6A 5P6; tel. (705) 949-2113; telex 067-77146; f. 1899; diversified transportation co moving cargo by rail, water and road; also has interests in commercial property development; Chair. HENRY N. R. JACKMAN; Pres. L. N. SAVOIE.

BC Rail: POB 8770, Vancouver, BC V6B 4X6; tel. (604) 986-2012; telex 043-52752; f. 1912; 2,608 km; Pres. and CEO M. C. NORRIS.

Canadian National Railways: 935 ouest, rue de la Gauchetière, CP 8100, Montréal, Qué H3C 3N4; tel. (514) 399-5430; telex 055-60519; f. 1923; 45,000 km; Chair. B. O'N. GALLERY (acting); Pres. and CEO R. E. LAWLESS.

Canadian Pacific Ltd: CP 6042, succursale Windsor, Montréal, Qué H3C 3E4; tel. (514) 395-5151; f. 1881; 24,649 km of main line track; also active in road haulage and marine transport; interests in hotels, property, manufacturing and other activities; Chair. R. W. CAMPBELL; Pres. and CEO W. W. STINSON.

Ontario Northland Transportation Commission: 195 Regina St, North Bay, Ont P1B 8L3; tel. (705) 472-4500; telex 067-76103; an agency of the Govt of Ontario; operates rail services over 919.1 km of track; Chair. J. W. SPOONER; Gen. Man. P. A. DYMENT.

VIA Rail Canada Inc: 2 place Ville-Marie, 4e étage, Montréal, Qué H3B 2G6; tel. (514) 871-6000; telex 052-68530; f. 1977; operates passenger services over existing rail routes throughout Canada; Chair. L. HANIGAN; Pres. and CEO DENIS DE BELLEVAL.

Association

The Railway Association of Canada: 1117 ouest, rue Ste-Catherine, Bureau 721, Montréal, Qué H3B 1H9; tel. (514) 849-4274; telex 055-61142; f. 1917; Pres. R. H. BALLANTYNE; 13 full mems and 7 associates.

ROADS

Provincial governments are responsible for roads within their boundaries. The federal government is responsible for major roads in the Yukon and Northwest Territories and in National Parks. In 1982 there were 391,792 km of roads (excluding municipal roads), of which 41.9% were paved.

The Trans-Canada Highway extends from St John's, Newfoundland, to Victoria, British Columbia.

INLAND WATERWAYS

The St Lawrence River and the Great Lakes provide Canada and the USA with a system of inland waterways extending from the Atlantic Ocean to the western end of Lake Superior, a distance of 3,769 km (2,342 miles). There is a 10.7-m (35-foot) navigation channel from Montréal to the sea and an 8.25-m (27-foot) channel from Montréal to Lake Erie. The St Lawrence Seaway, which was opened in 1959, was initiated partly to provide a deep waterway and partly to satisfy the increasing demand for electric power. Power development has been undertaken by the Provinces of Québec and Ontario, and by New York State. In 1987 cargo traffic through the Seaway totalled 50.7m. metric tons. The navigation facilities and conditions are within the jurisdiction of the federal governments of the USA and Canada.

St Lawrence River and Great Lakes Shipping

St Lawrence Seaway Authority: 360 Albert St, Ottawa K1R 7X7; tel. (613) 598-4600; telex 053-3322; opened 1959 to allow ocean-going vessels to enter the Great Lakes of North America; operated jtly with the USA; Pres. W. A. O'NEIL.

Canada Steamship Lines Inc: 759 Victoria Sq., Montréal, Qué H2Y 2K3; tel. (514) 288-0231; telex 052-5380; f. 1913; Chair. PAUL E. MARTIN; Pres. RAYMOND LEMAY; 34 vessels; 750,000 grt.

Halco Inc: 1303 ave Greene, Westmount, Qué H3Z 2A7; tel. (514) 932-2147; telex 052-67630; Vice-Pres. GREG J. O'BRIEN.

Paterson, N. M., and Sons Ltd: POB 664, Thunder Bay, Ont P7C 4W6; tel. (807) 577-8421; telex 073-4566; bulk carriers; Vice-Pres. and Dir ROBERT J. PATERSON; 12 vessels; 95,536 grt.

Misener Shipping: 63 Church St, POB 100, St Catharine's, Ont L2R 6S1; tel. (416) 688-3500; telex 061-5155; bulk cargo; Pres. DAVID K. GARDNER; 11 vessels; 200,000 grt.

ULS International Inc: 49 Jackes Ave, Toronto, Ont M4T 1E2; tel. (416) 920-7610; telex 065-24157; Chair and Dir J. D. LEITCH; Pres. and CEO D. MAXWELL; bulk carriers; 20 vessels; 417,604 grt.

SHIPPING

British Columbia Ferry Corporation: 1112 Fort St, Victoria, BC V8W 4V2; tel. (604) 381-1401; telex 049-7483; passenger and car ferries; Gen. Man. ROD MORRISON; 39 ferries.

Esso Petroleum Canada: External Supply and Transportation Division, 55 St Clair Ave West, Toronto, Ont M5W 2J8; tel. (416) 968-5309; telex 065-28049; coastal, Great Lakes and St Lawrence River, South American, Caribbean and Gulf ports to Canadian east and US Atlantic ports; Pres. G. H. THOMSON; Man. (Marine Div.) H. M. WESTLAKE; 11 vessels; 41,836 grt.

Fednav Ltd: 600 ouest, rue de la Gauchetière, Bureau 2600, Montréal, Qué H3B 4M3; tel. (514) 878-6500; telex 055-60637; f. 1944; shipowners, operators, contractors, terminal operators; Pres. L. G. PATHY; owned and chartered fleet of c. 50 vessels.

Marine Atlantic Inc: 100 Cameron St, Moncton, NB E1C 5Y6; tel. (506) 858-3600; telex 014-2833; Pres. and CEO R. J. TINGLEY; serves Atlantic coast of Canada; 15 vessels, incl. passenger, roll-on/roll-off and freight ferries.

Papachristidis (Canada) Inc: 1350 ouest, rue Sherbrooke, Penthouse, Montréal, Qué H3G 1J1; tel. (514) 844-8404; telex 052-68780; Pres. NIKY PAPACHRISTIDIS; world-wide services; 4 vessels owned and managed; 52,309 grt.

Seaboard Shipping Co Ltd: Oceanic Plaza, 1066 West Hastings St, POB 12501, Vancouver, BC V6E 3W9; UK-Continent, Australia, New Zealand, South Africa, Mediterranean, West Indies, US Atlantic Coast; Pres. C. D. G. ROBERTS.

Soconav Inc: 1801 ave Collège McGill, Bureau 830A, Montréal, Qué H3A 2N4; tel. (514) 284-9535; telex 052-67671; Great Lakes, St Lawrence River and Gulf, Atlantic Coast, Arctic and NWT; Chair. MICHEL GAUCHER; Pres. LOUIS ROCHETTE; Vice-Pres. (Operations) GUY BAZINET; 13 tankers, 76,476 grt.

Associations

The Canadian Shippers' Council: c/o Canadian Exporters' Association, 99 Bank St, Suite 250, Ottawa K1P 6B9; tel. (613) 238-8888; telex 053-4888; Sec. J. D. MOORE.

The Shipping Federation of Canada: 300 St-Sacrement, Bureau 326, Montréal, Qué H2Y 1X4; tel. (514) 849-2325; f. 1903; Pres. J. A. CRICHTON; 69 mems.

CIVIL AVIATION

Principal Scheduled Companies

Air Canada: place Air Canada, Montréal, Qué H2Z 1X5; tel. (514) 879-7000; telex 062-17537; f. 1937; operates under jurisdiction of Ministry of Transport; 55% govt-owned; Chair. CLAUDE I. TAYLOR; Pres. and CEO PIERRE J. JEANNIOT; operates services throughout Canada and to the USA; also to the UK, Paris, Zürich, Geneva, Frankfurt, Düsseldorf, Munich, Vienna, Bombay, Singapore, Antigua, Bermuda, Barbados, Bahamas, Trinidad, Guadeloupe, Martinique, Cuba, Jamaica, Saint Lucia, the Dominican Republic and Haiti; fleet of 33 Boeing 727, 6 Boeing 747, 18 Boeing 767, 36 DC-9, 2 DC-8-63F, 6 DC-8-73F, 12 L-1011.

Canadian Airlines International: 700 Second St SW, Suite 2800, Calgary, Alta T2P 2W2; tel. (403) 294-2000; telex 043-55610; f. 1988 by merger of Canadian Pacific Airlines and Pacific Western Airlines; Chair. RHYS EYTON; Pres. MURRAY SIGLER; passenger and cargo charters and scheduled services to 68 destinations in Canada and 89 points overseas; fleet of 66 Boeing 737-200, 12 DC-10-30.

Nationair: Montréal International Airport, Administration Bldg, CP 300, Mirabel, Qué J7N 1A3; telex 052-67513; f. 1984; scheduled and charter services to Europe and South America; Pres. R. OBADIA; fleet of 3 DC-8-61, 2 DC-8-62, 2 DC-8-63, 1 DC-8-50F.

Québecair: Montréal International Airport, CP 490, Dorval 300, Qué H4Y 1B5; tel. (514) 631-9802; telex 058-22584; f. 1946; regional carrier and charter services; Chair. MARC RACICOT; Pres. and CEO MICHEL LEBLANC; fleet of 8 Convair CV-580, 2 Fokker 28-1000.

Wardair Canada: 325 Manulife Place, 10180–101st St, Edmonton, Alta T5J 3S4; tel. (403) 037-2057; f. 1946; Chair. and CEO MAXWELL W. WARD; Pres. GEORGE D. CURLEY; scheduled domestic services and international services to the UK, Puerto Rico and the Dominican Republic; fleet of 3 Boeing 747-100, 3 DC-10-30, 2 A-300-B4, 4 A-310-300.

Association

Air Transport Association of Canada: 747–99 Bank St, Ottawa K1P 6B9; tel. (613) 233-7727; f. 1934; Pres. G. M. SINCLAIR; Vice-Pres. and Sec. S. T. GRANT; 165 mems.

CANADA   Directory

Tourism

Most tourist visitors (totalling 37.0m. in 1987) are from the USA. Tourist spending in 1987 amounted to C $6,289m.

Tourism Canada: Federal Dept of Industry, Science and Technology, 235 Queen St, 4th Floor East, Ottawa K1A 0H6; tel. (613) 954-3851; telex 053-4123.

Tourism Industry Association of Canada: 130 Albert St, Suite 1016, Ottawa K1P 5G4; tel. (613) 238-3883; f. 1931; private-sector assen; encourages travel to and within Canada; promotes development of travel services and facilities; Exec. Dir JOHN LAWSON.

Atomic Energy

Atomic Energy of Canada Ltd: 344 Slater St, Ottawa K1A 0S4; tel. (613) 237-3270; telex 053-3126; f. 1952; federal govt agency for nuclear research and development, production of radioactive isotopes and design, development and marketing of power reactors; four operational research reactors at Chalk River, Ont, and one under construction at Whiteshell Nuclear Research Establishment, Pinawa, Man; prototype reactor under construction at Chalk River (isotope production); nuclear designer for CANDU (Canadian deuterium uranium) reactors; 17 commercial units now in service at four stations, providing a total capacity of 12,051 MW, representing 15.1% of Canada's total electricity generation; four others under construction in Canada; two units each in service in India, Pakistan, the Republic of Korea and Argentina, and three units under construction in Romania; Pres. and CEO JAMES DONNELLY.

Atomic Energy Control Board: POB 1046, Ottawa K1P 5S9; tel. (613) 992-9206; telex 053-3771; f. 1946; responsible for all nuclear regulatory matters; Pres. R. J. A. LÉVESQUE; Sec. P. E. HAMEL.

CAPE VERDE

Introductory Survey

Location, Climate, Language, Religion, Flag, Capital

The Republic of Cape Verde is an archipelago of 10 islands and five islets in the North Atlantic Ocean, about 500 km (300 miles) west of Dakar, Senegal. The country lies in a semi-arid belt, with little rain and an average annual temperature of 24°C (76°F). The official language is Portuguese, of which the locally spoken form is Creole (Crioulo). Virtually all of the inhabitants profess Christianity, and 98% are Roman Catholics. The national flag (proportions 3 by 2) comprises a vertical red stripe, at the hoist, and two equal horizontal stripes, of yellow and green. The red stripe bears, in the upper hoist, a five-pointed black star and a clamshell enclosed by a wreath of palms. The capital is Cidade de Praia.

Recent History

The Cape Verde Islands were colonized by the Portuguese in the 15th century. From the 1950s, liberation movements in Portugal's African colonies were campaigning for independence, and, in this context, the archipelago was linked with the mainland territory of Portuguese Guinea (now Guinea-Bissau) under one nationalist movement, the Partido Africano da Independência do Guiné e Cabo Verde (PAIGC). The independence of Guinea-Bissau was recognized by Portugal in September 1974, but the PAIGC leadership in the Cape Verde Islands decided to pursue separate independence rather than enter into an immediate federation with Guinea-Bissau. In December 1974 a transitional government, comprising representatives of the Portuguese Government and the PAIGC, was formed; members of other political parties were excluded. On 30 June 1975 elections for a National People's Assembly were held, in which only PAIGC candidates were allowed to participate. Independence was granted on 5 July, with Aristides Pereira, Secretary-General of the PAIGC, becoming Cape Verde's first President. The country's first constitution was approved in September 1980.

Although Cape Verde and Guinea-Bissau remained constitutionally separate, the PAIGC supervised the activities of both states, but progress towards the ultimate goal of unification was slow. Moreover, the Cape Verde Government disapproved of the November 1980 coup in Guinea-Bissau, and in January 1981 the Cape Verde wing of the PAIGC was renamed the Partido Africano da Independência de Cabo Verde (PAICV). In February Pereira was re-elected as President by the National Assembly, and all articles concerning ultimate union with Guinea-Bissau were removed from the Constitution. Discussions concerning reconciliation were held in June 1982, however, after the release of Luis Cabral, formerly the Head of State in Guinea-Bissau, and diplomatic relations between the two countries were subsequently normalized.

A new National Assembly was elected in December 1985. The 83 candidates on the PAICV-approved list, of whom some were not members of the PAICV, obtained 94.5% of the votes cast. In January 1986 President Pereira was re-elected for a further five-year term by the National Assembly. In the new Government several ministerial functions were redistributed: in particular, all aspects of economic management were centralized in the office of the Prime Minister, Gen. Pedro Pires. In July 1987 tension developed after the National Assembly approved legislation decriminalizing abortion, as part of a policy to promote birth control during the course of the second Development Plan for 1986–90; 16 people were arrested, following demonstrations over the dismissal of a journalist from the opposition Catholic newspaper, *Terra Nova*, and one detainee was sentenced to three months' imprisonment. Further demonstrations against abortion and for greater political freedom were held in January 1988, but Pereira dismissed them as insignificant and not indicative of any general discontent. In March the Ministry of Trade, Transport and Tourism was restructured, as a result of which a separate Ministry of Trade was established, with responsibility for civil aviation, tourism and communications. In September José Araújo, the Minister of Justice, resigned, owing to ill health, and the Prime Minister assumed control of the justice portfolio. In October the state-controlled newspaper, *Voz do Povo*, published a manifesto, signed by 24 jurists, accusing the Government of failing to respect human rights. Later in October, *Voz do Povo* published a refutation of the jurists' manifesto, signed by 29 judges. At the PAICV congress in November, Pereira and Pires were re-elected Secretary-General and Deputy Secretary-General, respectively, of the party.

Cape Verde professes a non-aligned stance in foreign affairs and maintains relations with virtually all the power blocs. Cape Verde's reputation for political independence led to its selection as the venue for several important international conferences. In July 1988 the military commanders of Angola, Cuba and South Africa met in Cape Verde to pursue peace negotiations, under the auspices of the USA. In the following month, the South African Deputy Minister of Foreign Affairs conferred with the Cape Verdean Minister of Foreign Affairs in Praia. Cape Verde also takes an active part in co-operation between the lusophone African states. In 1987 Cape Verde banned Saint Lucia Airways from the Amílcar Cabral international airport, following indications that the airline was using Cape Verde as a staging point in the transport of military equipment for the anti-Government rebels of UNITA in Angola. Cape Verde's relations with Guinea-Bissau showed further signs of improvement in 1988, when the two countries signed a co-operation agreement. In the same year Mozambique and Cape Verde pledged solidarity with each other, during a visit to the islands by the Mozambican Prime Minister, Mário Machungo.

In 1985 Cape Verde agreed to accommodate up to eight members of the Basque separatist movement, ETA, who were being deported from Spain for terrorist activities. Following negotiations in June 1986 with the Spanish Minister of the Interior, Cape Verde agreed to accept more members of ETA. In July 1987, however, an enquiry was initiated when three of the four ETA members being accommodated on Cape Verde escaped from São Vicente Island.

In 1988 Cape Verde signed a two-year co-operation agreement with Portugal, covering the rescheduling of debts owed to Portugal, education and military training. Co-operation agreements were also signed with the USSR, Ghana and Nigeria.

Government

Under the 1980 constitution, legislative power is vested in the National People's Assembly, with 83 deputies, elected by universal adult suffrage for five years. Executive power is held by the President, elected for five years by the Assembly. The President is the Head of State and governs with the assistance of an appointed Council of Ministers, led by the Prime Minister. The PAICV is the only political party permitted to operate.

Defence

The Popular Revolutionary Armed Forces were formed from ex-combatants in the liberation wars, and numbered less than 1,300 (army 1,000, navy 200, air force less than 100) in June 1988. There is also a police force and paramilitary People's Militia. National service is by selective conscription. Estimated defence expenditure in 1981 was US $3.5m. In 1988 Portugal agreed to provide military training and to allow Cape Verde to purchase light military equipment.

Economic Affairs

Little was done under Portuguese rule to develop the natural resources of the islands, such as the fishing grounds and the large reserves of underground water, or to alleviate the effects of the recurrent droughts and severe soil erosion. The World Bank has estimated that Cape Verde's gross national product (GNP) per head increased, in real terms, at an average rate of only 1.2% per year between 1980 and 1987. In 1987, however, compared with the previous year GNP per head rose by 3.5%. In that year, according to World Bank estimates, the country's

GNP (at average 1985–87 prices) was US $170m., equivalent to $500 per head.

Since the late 1960s, the agricultural subsistence economy of the islands, which normally employs about three-quarters of the working population (mainly on smallholdings), has been severely affected by an almost continuous drought. Torrential rain in September 1984, however, was so heavy that it destroyed about one-half of the country's small dams, but by 1986 these had been rebuilt, along with thousands of additional dams. The staple crops are maize (production of which totalled 12,000 metric tons in 1985/86 and was expected to reach a record 20,000 tons in 1986/87, owing to above-average rainfall), beans and sweet potatoes. Other crops normally grown include sugar cane, cassava, castor beans, bananas, coffee and groundnuts. However, about 90% of the country's total food requirements has to be imported. Since independence, most of Cape Verde's food deficit has been met by foreign aid. Food imports of 70,000 tons were envisaged for 1986, but in 1987 food import requirements declined to an estimated 56,000 tons, owing to a good harvest. External food aid for 1988 was projected at 20,000 tons. In 1987 the state-owned company, Empresa Pública de Abastecimentos (EMPA), bought 107 ha of fertile agricultural land in Paraguay for maize-growing, forestry and livestock-raising. The land cost US $1.1m., and was to be used to produce food for Cape Verde. There is extensive rural unemployment, partly remedied by government employment schemes in soil and water conservation and reafforestation projects. In 1987 Cape Verde received $10.8m. in aid from the Netherlands, to finance a major land and water conservation project on São Tiago and on Santo Antão, and a $6.7m. loan from the African Development Fund (ADF) to finance an agricultural rehabilitation programme. In the same year, the US Agency for International Development provided $1m. for a three-year agricultural research programme. In 1988 the USA provided millet worth $2m., as part of a four-year programme of food aid. Proceeds from sales of the millet were to be used to finance the employment of 4,000 people on soil-conservation and tree-planting projects. The USA also provided $1.7m. to finance the extension of the water-conservation project and, after the Cape Verdean authorities reported that swarms of locusts had been seen on the islands, a further $275,000 to train technicians. In October Cape Verde issued an urgent appeal to the international community for aid to combat locusts.

Fishing forms a large part of the islands' development potential, and sales of fish and fish products provided an estimated 83% of export earnings in 1985. The most important fish exports are usually lobster and tuna. The total annual fish catch reached 14,730 metric tons in 1981, but declined in subsequent years, to 10,180 tons in 1985. In 1981 a cold-storage plant was opened at Mindelo, with a refrigeration capacity of 6,000 tons. In 1987 BADEA (see p. 93) approved a US $4m. loan to part-finance a $10m. industrial fisheries project, which aimed to increase the annual catch of tuna from 1,700–2,500 tons to 5,000–6,000 tons. In 1988 the Government initiated a $14.4m. artisanal fisheries project, which aimed to increase the total annual fish catch to 13,500 tons, to improve the marketing of fish and to increase export earnings from the sector. The project included plans to build fishing boats locally, and to construct six techno-social centres and a central refrigeration plant on São Tiago. The project was to be financed by loans of $5.7m. from the International Fund for Agricultural Development (IFAD), $5.7m. from the ADF, $1.1m. from the UN Development Programme (UNDP) and $1.9m. from the Government.

There is little manufacturing activity except for a few small fish-processing and canning plants and clothing factories, which together employ about 1,700 people and contribute only 5% of the country's GDP. The Government is encouraging investment in this sector, and several major projects have been undertaken: in 1987 the Federal Republic of Germany agreed to finance the expansion of a plant producing butane gas. In 1988, however, a project to build a cement plant on the island of Maio, which had been approved in 1984, was cancelled, owing to a decline in domestic demand and reductions in international prices. In the same year, Cape Verde rejected offers of contracts worth US $65m. per year to process foreign industrial and domestic waste, as the islands' fishing industry would be threatened if toxic waste were illegally dumped off shore. The Government hopes to exploit the islands' resources of pozzolana, cement and salt, and to develop construction and packaging materials, soft drinks, pasta and tobacco industries.

About 95% of all goods consumed in Cape Verde are imported, with Portugal remaining the principal supplier, providing about 23% of imports in 1984. Consequently, Cape Verde suffers from a persistent trade deficit, which stood at US $78.8m. in 1984 and an estimated $57m. in 1985, while the outstanding foreign debt at the end of 1985 reached $91m., according to World Bank estimates. Between 1980 and 1984, Cape Verde's currency depreciated, in nominal terms, by 54% in relation to the US dollar. Cape Verde's annual rate of inflation averaged 16% between 1980 and 1985.

Cape Verde's first four-year Development Plan was announced in 1982. It envisaged investment of US $405m., all from external sources, the main aims being to progress towards self-sufficiency in food and to continue to combat desertification. The second four-year Development Plan, adopted by the National Assembly in December 1986, projected an annual increase of 4.5% in GDP. It envisaged investment of 33,375m. escudos, of which 31.6% was to be provided by external aid, and the remainder by remittances from Cape Verdean emigrants and by revenue from the Amílcar Cabral international airport on Sal. Annual growth was projected of 3.5% in the agricultural sector, 5% in the fishing sector, 4.8% in the tourist sector and 11.7% in industry. The Plan also aimed to reduce unemployment to 25% of the labour force, by creating 10,500 new jobs, of which 3,500 would be permanent. The Government intended to introduce reforms in agriculture, education and the civil service during the course of the Plan. In 1987 prospects to restructure the educational system were introduced, with the long-term aim of increasing the productivity of the work-force. In September 1988 the Government announced an 11% reduction in the price of petrol and diesel fuel.

There are about 600,000 Cape Verdeans living outside the country, principally in the USA, the Netherlands, Portugal and Italy. Remittances from emigrants provide about 30% of Cape Verde's GNP, and the Government has attempted to attract emigrants' capital into the light industry and fishing sectors in Cape Verde by offering favourable tax conditions to investors. In 1985 Cape Verde and the USA signed an agreement aiming to promote this new policy. In 1987 an organization was established to assess emigrants' financial and technical potential. However, the rate of emigration is expected to decline, as other countries introduce more stringent restrictions on immigration.

Foreign aid has been indispensable to Cape Verde, and in recent years the country has received assistance from European and Arab countries, Japan, the USA, the UN and the ADF. In December 1986 Cape Verde issued a proposal to its aid donors, which would fix the conditions of the intervention of each aid-donor. The proposal defined two categories of intervention, of which one was aid linked to projects, and the second covered other forms of intervention, such as aid to the balance of payments.

Development aid and bilateral co-operation agreements are being directed partly to the expansion of Cape Verde's network of transport and communications. In 1988 a US $5.1m. project to upgrade the transport and energy sectors was initiated. The project was supported by a loan of $4.7m. from the International Development Associaton (IDA), an affiliate of the World Bank. During the project, proceeds from receipts of foreign exchange were to be made available for state-owned and private transport companies to purchase buses, other vehicles, and spare parts. Reforms were to be introduced to eliminate subsidies and price controls, and to deregulate the transport sector. The Amílcar Cabral international airport, on the island of Sal, is a strategic refuelling point for long-distance flights, and, with Italian and EEC aid, the facilities were undergoing expansion in 1987. In the same year, Cape Verde opened a new air link with Boston, USA, using an aircraft leased from Mozambique. However, Cape Verde suffered a reduction of about $6m. in revenue in 1987, when South African flights to Sal, which had previously comprised 90% of air traffic, declined from 38 to seven per week (flying to European destinations). South African Airways had used Cape Verde as a stop-over for flights to the USA, but these flights were curtailed as a result of US sanctions. In November 1988 South African flights to Sal were reduced to one per week. Meanwhile, Cape Verde attempted to attract other airlines to Sal: in early 1988 discussions were held with Italian, Zambian and Botswana airlines concerning the introduction of stop-over flights to the USA, and a Belgian company agreed to establish a catering service and two restaurants at the Amílcar Cabral airport, in an attempt to encourage more custom and a growth in tourism. The main seaport is at Mindelo, on the island of São Vicente, where a ship-building and repairing yard was opened in 1983. In 1987 the ADF provided a $681,000 loan to finance feasibility studies on upgrading the Mindelo shipyard. The ports of Praia and Porto Grande were being enlarged, and in 1982 work started on a port at Palmeira, on Sal. In 1988 the USSR agreed to construct a new port at Sal-Rei, on the island of Boa Vista, and to provide technical assistance for the port undergoing construction at Palmeira and financial assistance for the construction of a new port at Tarrafal, on the island of São Nicolau. Work started in 1983 on a new telecommunications network, consisting of three automatic exchanges which would provide international telephone and telex links. In 1985 France provided 1.5m. francs for a telecommunications station.

Social Welfare
Medical facilities are limited and there is a severe shortage of staff and buildings, although plans for a national health service are being implemented. In 1980 Cape Verde had 21 hospital establishments, with a total of 632 beds, and there were 51 physicians working in government service. In 1987 Nigeria signed an agreement to construct a 200-bed hospital, as part of a technical aid programme. Development plans include the construction of more than 300 small local health units.

Education
Compulsory education is divided into Instrução Primária (for children aged seven to 12) and Escola Preparatória (for children aged 12 to 14). From the age of 14, children may attend one of the four liceus, which provide a three-year general course or a two-year pre-university course. In 1986/87 there was also one industrial and commercial school and three teacher training units. In 1987 Nigeria agreed to construct a polytechnic, as part of a technical aid programme. In 1986/87 about 49,703 pupils attended 347 primary schools and 10,304 pupils were enrolled in 16 second-stage primary schools.

A project to upgrade primary education was initiated in 1987, with the aims of reducing the high drop-out rate and of improving basic skills. The project proposed to replace the current two-cycle primary education system with a single six-year cycle, to improve teacher training and to provide better equipment. The project was to cost US $5.3m., of which $4.2m. was to be provided by a loan from the IDA. In the same year Cape Verde received a Swiss loan to finance a four-year adult literacy programme. According to official estimates, the average rate of adult illiteracy in 1985 was 52.6% (males 38.6%; females 61.4%).

Public Holidays
1989: 2 January (for New Year), 20 January (National Heroes' Day), 8 March (Women's Day), 1 May (Labour Day), 1 June (Children's Day), 5 July (Independence Day), 12 September (Day of the Nation), 25 December (Christmas Day).
1990: 1 January (New Year), 20 January (National Heroes' Day), 8 March (Women's Day), 1 May (Labour Day), 1 June (Children's Day), 5 July (Independence Day), 12 September (Day of the Nation), 25 December (Christmas Day).

Weights and Measures
The metric system is in force.

Statistical Survey

Source (unless otherwise stated): Statistical Service, Banco de Cabo Verde, Av. Amílcar Cabral, São Tiago; tel. 341; telex 99350.

AREA AND POPULATION
Area: 4,033 sq km (1,557 sq miles).
Population: 272,571 (census of 15 December 1970); 296,093 (census of 2 June 1980); 334,000 (official estimate, mid-1985). *By island:* Boa Vista 3,397, Brava 6,984, Fogo 31,115, Maio 4,103, Sal 6,006, Santo Antão 43,198, São Nicolau 13,575, São Tiago 145,923, São Vicente 41,792 (census of 2 June 1980).
Principal Town: Cidade de Praia (capital), population 57,748 at 1980 census.
Births and Deaths (1985): Registered live births 11,282 (birth rate 34.6 per 1,000); Registered deaths 2,735 (death rate 8.4 per 1,000).
Economically Active Population (ILO estimates, '000 persons at mid-1980): Agriculture 53; Industry 23; Services 26; Total 102 (males 74, females 28). Source: ILO, *Economically Active Population Estimates and Projections, 1950–2025*.

AGRICULTURE, ETC.
Principal Crops ('000 metric tons, 1986): Maize 12, Potatoes 3, Cassava 4, Sweet potatoes 7, Coconuts 10 (FAO estimate), Dates 2 (FAO estimate), Sugar cane 10 (FAO estimate), Bananas 4. Source: FAO, *Production Yearbook*.
Livestock (FAO estimates, '000 head, year ending September 1986): Cattle 13, Pigs 54, Goats 66, Asses 6. Source: FAO, *Production Yearbook*.
Fishing ('000 metric tons, live weight): Total catch 11.9 in 1983; 10.7 in 1984; 10.2 in 1985. Source: FAO, *Yearbook of Fishery Statistics*.

MINING
Production (metric tons, 1985): Salt (unrefined) 6,000; Pozzolan 10,000 (estimate by US Bureau of Mines). Source: UN, *Industrial Statistics Yearbook*.

INDUSTRY
Production (metric tons, unless otherwise indicated, 1985): Biscuits 400, Bread 2,000, Canned fish 300, Frozen fish 1,000, Manufactured tobacco 74, Alcoholic beverages 200,000 litres, Soft drinks 200,000 litres, Electric energy 26m. kWh. Source: UN, *Industrial Statistics Yearbook*.

FINANCE
Currency and Exchange Rates: 100 centavos = 1 Cape Verde escudo; 1,000 escudos are known as a conto. *Coins:* 20 and 50 centavos; 1, 2½, 10, 20 and 50 escudos. *Notes:* 100, 500 and 1,000 escudos. *Sterling and Dollar Equivalents* (30 September 1988): £1 sterling = 130.773 escudos; US $1 = 77.335 escudos; 1,000 Cape Verde escudos = £7.647 = $12.931. *Average Exchange Rate* (escudos per US dollar): 58.29 in 1982; 71.69 in 1983; 84.88 in 1984.
Budget (estimates, million escudos, 1984): Revenue 1,630; Expenditure 2,134.5.
Source: *Marchés Tropicaux et Méditerranéens*.
Currency in Circulation ('000 escudos, 1976): Notes 465,609, Coins 8,415.
Cost of Living (Consumer Price Index for Praia, excluding rent; base: 1983 = 100): 112 in 1984; 117 in 1985; 130 in 1986. Source: ILO, *Year Book of Labour Statistics*.
Gross Domestic Product by Economic Activity (estimates, million escudos at current prices, 1983): Agriculture, forestry and fishing 1,150; Mining and quarrying 38; Manufacturing 284; Electricity, gas and water 158; Construction 884; Trade, restaurants and hotels 1,337; Transport, storage and communications 712; Finance, insurance, real estate and business services 204; Public administration and defence 545; Other services 58; *GDP at factor cost* 5,370; Indirect taxes, *less* subsidies 248; *GDP in purchasers' values* 5,618. Source: UN Economic Commission for Africa, *African Statistical Yearbook*.
Balance of Payments (million escudos, 1981): Merchandise trade (net) –3,880; Net services 15, *Balance on Goods and Services* –3,865; Private transfers 1,760; Other income 25; *Current Balance* –2,080; Public transfers 1,940; Net errors and omissions 170; Total (net monetary movements) 30. Source: Centro de Estudos Economia e Sociedade, Lisbon.

EXTERNAL TRADE
Principal Commodities: *Imports* ('000 escudos, 1981): Animals and animal products 120,498, Vegetable products 475,231, Fats and

CAPE VERDE

oils 141,136, Foodstuffs and beverages 475,369, Mineral products 635,240, Chemical products 201,475, Textiles and textile products 157,187, Base metals 199,678, Machinery and electrical equipment 365,056, Transport equipment 230,763; Total (incl. others) 3,451,649. Source: Direcção Geral de Estatística, Praia. *Exports* (US $'000, 1984): Food and live animals 2,197, Crude materials (inedible) except fuels 265, Mineral fuels, lubricants, etc 42,756, Basic manufactures 642, Machinery and transport equipment 3,614, Total (incl. others) 49,657. Source: UN, *International Trade Statistics Yearbook*.

Principal Trading Partners (US $ million, 1984): *Imports*: Portugal 19.7, Netherlands 18.5, France 8.5, Spain 7.2, Belgium 4.7, Germany, Federal Republic 4.3, Brazil 3.5, Argentina 2.9, Italy 2.0, UK 1.7; Total (incl. others) 85.8. Source: IMF, *Direction of Trade Statistics Yearbook 1985*.

TRANSPORT

Road Traffic (motor vehicles in use, 1984): Passenger cars 3,000, Commercial vehicles 700.

Shipping (international freight traffic, estimates, 1985): Goods loaded 108,000 metric tons; goods unloaded 286,000 metric tons; (Source: UN, *Monthly Bulletin of Statistics*); (1981): Vessels entered 2,544; passengers embarked 97,746; passengers disembarked 97,746. Source: mainly Direcção Geral de Estatística, Praia, São Tiago.

Civil Aviation (Amílcar Cabral airport, 1982): Freight loaded 104.7 metric tons; freight unloaded 615.3 metric tons; passengers embarked 23,106; passengers disembarked 21,200. Source: Direcção Geral de Estatística, Praia, São Tiago.

COMMUNICATIONS MEDIA

Radio receivers (1985): 50,000 in use.
Television receivers (1985): 500 in use.
Telephones (1984): 2,000 in use.

EDUCATION

Primary (1986/87): 347 schools, 49,703 pupils, 1,464 teachers.
Preparatory (1986/87): 16 schools, 10,304 pupils, 321 teachers.
Secondary (1986/87): 4 schools, 5,026 pupils, 170 teachers.
Teacher training (1986/87): 3 units, 211 pupils, 53 teachers.
Industrial school (1986/87): 1 school, 531 pupils, 52 teachers.

Source: Ministério da Educação e Cultura, CP 111, Praia, São Tiago.

Directory

The Constitution

The Constitution of the Republic of Cape Verde, the first since the country's independence in 1975, was approved on 7 September 1980. It defines Cape Verde as 'a sovereign, democratic, unitary, anti-colonialist and anti-imperialist republic'. The Head of State is the President of the Republic, who is elected by the National Assembly and has a mandate of five years, as do the Assembly deputies, elected by universal adult suffrage. The Prime Minister is nominated by the same Assembly, to which he is responsible. The President of the National Assembly may act as interim Head of State if necessary. He is not a member of the government.

The Constitution abolishes both the death sentence and life imprisonment. Citizens have equality of rights and duties, without sexual, social, intellectual, religious or philosophical distinction. This extends to all Cape Verde emigrants throughout the world. Citizens also have freedom of thought, expression, association, demonstration, religion, rights and duties and the right to health care, culture and education.

On 12 February 1981 all articles concerning plans for eventual union with Guinea-Bissau were revoked, and an amendment was inserted to provide for the creation of the Partido Africano da Indepêndencia de Cabo Verde (PAICV) to replace the Cape Verde section of the PAIGC (defined in the Constitution as 'the leading force of society').

The Government

HEAD OF STATE

President: ARISTIDES MARIA PEREIRA (took office 5 July 1975; re-elected February 1981 and January 1986).

COUNCIL OF MINISTERS
(December 1988)

Prime Minister, with responsibility for Finance, Planning, Co-operation and Justice: Gen. PEDRO VERONA RODRIGUES PIRES.
Minister of the Armed Forces and Security: Col JÚLIO CÉSAR DE CARVALHO.
Minister of Trade, with responsibility for Civil Aviation, Tourism and Communications: Commdt OSVALDO LOPES DA SILVA.
Minister of Education: ANDRÉ CORSINO TOLENTINO.
Minister of Health, Labour and Social Affairs: Dr IRENEU GOMES.
Minister of Agriculture: Commdt JOÃO PEREIRA SILVA.
Minister of Local Administration and Town Planning: TITO LIVIO SANTOS DE OLIVEIRA RAMOS.
Minister of Foreign Affairs, Rural Development and Fisheries: Cmmdt SILVINO MANUEL DA LUZ.
Minister of Industry and Energy: ADÃO SILVA ROCHA.
Minister of Public Works: ADRIANO DE OLIVEIRA LIMA.
Minister of Information, Culture and Sport: Dr DAVID HOPFER ALMADA.
Deputy Minister to the Prime Minister: Cmmdt HERCULANO ADELAIDE VIEIRA.
Deputy Minister of Planning and Co-operation: JOSÉ BRITO.
Deputy Minister of Finance: Dr ARNALDO VASCONCELLOS FRANCA.
Secretary of State to the Prime Minister: JOÃO DE DEUS MAXIMIANO.
Secretary of State for Foreign Affairs: AGUINALDO LISBOA RAMOS.
Secretary of State for the Merchant Navy: Dr VIRGILIO BURGO FERNANDES.
Secretary of State for Fishing: MIGUEL LIMA.
Secretary of State for Public Administration: Dr RENATO DE SILAS CARDOSO.

MINISTRIES

Office of the President: Presidência da República, Praia, São Tiago; tel. 61-26-69; telex 6051.
Office of the Prime Minister: Praça 12 de Setembro, CP 16, Praia, São Tiago; tel. 61-33-22; telex 6052.
Ministry of Education and Culture: Avda Amílcar Cabral, CP 111, Praia, São Tiago; tel. 345; telex 6057.
Ministry of Finance: 107 Avda Amílcar Cabral, CP 30, Praia, São Tiago; tel. 61-41-42; telex 6038.
Ministry of Foreign Affairs: Praça 10 de Mayo, CP 60, Praia, São Tiago; tel. 310; telex 6070.
Ministry of Health and Social Affairs: Praça 12 de Setembro, CP 47, Praia, São Tiago; tel. 422; telex 6059.
Ministry of Information: CP 26, Praia; tel. 564; telex 99352.
Ministry of the Interior: Rua Guerra Mendes, Praia, São Tiago; tel. 255; telex 6062.
Ministry of Justice: Praça 12 de Setembro, Praia, São Tiago; tel. 336; telex 6025.
Ministry of National Defence: Avda Unidade Guiné, Praia, São Tiago; tel. 448; telex 6077.
Ministry of Rural Development: Rua António Pussich, Praia, São Tiago; tel. 335; telex 6072.
Ministry of Transport and Telecommunications: Rua Guerra Mendes, CP 15, Praia, São Tiago; tel. 601; telex 6060.

CAPE VERDE — *Directory*

Legislature

ASSEMBLÉIA NACIONAL POPULAR

The National People's Assembly consists of 83 deputies, elected for a term of five years by universal adult suffrage. The most recent general election was held on 7 December 1985, when 94.5% of the votes endorsed the single list of candidates presented by the PAICV.

President: ABÍLIO AUGUSTO MONTEIRO DUARTE.

Political Organizations

Partido Africano da Independência de Cabo Verde (PAICV): (African Party for the Independence of Cape Verde): CP 22, São Tiago; telex 6022; f. 1956 as the Partido Africano da Independência do Guiné e Cabo Verde (PAIGC); name changed in 1981, following the November 1980 coup in Guinea-Bissau, which the Cape Verde govt had opposed, having previously favoured eventual unification with Guinea-Bissau; sole legal political party; Sec.-Gen. ARISTIDES MARIA PEREIRA; Dep. Sec.-Gen. PEDRO VERONA RODRIGUES PIRES.

The **Independent Democratic Union of Cape Verde (UCID)** is an opposition movement based in Lisbon, Portugal, formed by emigrants opposed to the PAICV regime.

Diplomatic Representation

EMBASSIES IN CAPE VERDE

Brazil: Rua Guerra Menoes, CP 93, Praia, São Tiago; tel. 385; telex 6075; Ambassador: FERNANDO BUARQUE FRANCO NETTE.
China, People's Republic: Praia, São Tiago; Ambassador: LIANG TAOSHENG.
Cuba: Público CV, Praia, São Tiago; tel. 465; telex 6087; Ambassador: GILBERTO GARCÍA ALONSO.
France: CP 192, Praia, São Tiago; tel. 290; telex 6064; Ambassador: CLAUDE THULLIER.
Portugal: Achada de Santo António, CP 160, Praia, São Tiago; tel. 408; telex 6055; Ambassador: Dr ANTÓNIO BAPTISTA MARTINS.
Senegal: Praia, São Tiago; Ambassador: OMAR BEN KHATAB SOKHNA.
USSR: Praia, São Tiago; Ambassador: PAVEL MIKHAILOVICH SHMELKOV.
USA: Rua Hoji Ya Yenna 81, CP 201, Praia, São Tiago; tel. 61-43-63; telex 6068; Ambassador: VERNON DU BOIS PENNER, Jr.

Judicial System

Supremo Tribunal de Justiça: Praça 12 de Setembro, CP 117, Praia, São Tiago; tel. 61-23-69; established 1975; the highest court.

There is a network of tribunais populares at the local level.

Religion

CHRISTIANITY

At 31 December 1986 there were an estimated 309,922 adherents of the Roman Catholic Church, representing 98.4% of the total population. Protestant churches, among which the Nazarenes are prominent, represent almost 2% of the population.

The Roman Catholic Church

Cape Verde comprises the single diocese of Santiago de Cabo Verde, directly responsible to the Holy See.

Bishop of Santiago de Cabo Verde: Mgr PAULINO DO LIVRAMENTO EVORA, CP 46, Praia, São Tiago; tel. 61-11-19.

The Anglican Communion

Within the Church of the Province of West Africa, Cape Verde forms part of the diocese of The Gambia. The Bishop is resident in Banjul, The Gambia.

The Press

Boletim Informativo: CP 126, Praia, São Tiago; f. 1976; weekly; publ. by the Ministry of Foreign Affairs; circ. 1,500.

Boletim Oficial da República de Cabo Verde: Imprensa Nacional, CP 113, Praia, São Tiago; weekly; official.
Raízes: CP 98, Praia, São Tiago; tel. 319; f. 1977; quarterly; cultural review; Editor ARNALDO FRANÇA; circ. 1,500.
Terra Nova: Ilha do Fogo; weekly; Roman Catholic.
Unidade e Luta: Praia, São Tiago; organ of the PAICV.
Voz do Povo: CP 118, Praia, São Tiago; weekly; publ. by govt information service.

NEWS AGENCIES

Agence France-Presse (AFP): CP 26/118 Praia, São Tiago; tel. 61-38-89; telex 52; Rep. Mme FATIMA AZEVADO.
Inter Press Service (IPS) (Italy): CP 14, Mindelo, São Vicente; tel. 31-45-50; Rep. JUAN A. COLOMA.

Publisher

Government Publishing House

Imprensa Nacional: CP 113, Praia, São Tiago.

Radio and Television

There were an estimated 50,000 radio receivers in use in 1985, and 5,000 television receivers in use in 1987. In March 1988 France agreed to provide aid for Cape Verdean radio and television, and in October a French company agreed to install a powerful short-wave relay station on Cape Verde, which would broadcast to Latin America and Africa.

RADIO

Rádio Nacional de Cabo Verde: Praça 12 de Setembro, CP 26, Praia, São Tiago; tel. 61-38-89; govt-controlled; five transmitters and five solar relay transmitters; FM transmission only; broadcasts in Portuguese and Creole for 18 hours per day.

Voz de São Vicente: CP 29, Mindelo, São Vicente; f. 1974; govt-controlled; Dir FRANCISCO TOMAR.

TELEVISION

Televisão Experimental de Cabo Verde (TEVEC): Achada de Santo António, CP 2, Praia, São Tiago; tel. 61-40-80; one transmitter and seven relay transmitters; broadcasts in Portuguese and Creole for three hours per day.

Finance

(cap. = capital; dep. = deposits; res = reserves; m. = million; amounts in Cape Verde escudos)

BANKING

Banco de Cabo Verde: 117 Avda Amílcar Cabral, CP 101, Praia, São Tiago; tel. 61-31-53; telex 99350; f. 1976; central bank; cap. 400m., res 1,396.2m., dep. 3,790.4m. (1984); Gov. AMARO ALEXANDRE DA LUZ; 8 brs.

The **Fundo de Solidariedade Nacional** is the main savings institution; the **Fundo de Desenvolvimento Nacional** channels public investment resources; and the **Instituto Caboverdiano** administers international aid.

Trade and Industry

STATE INDUSTRIAL ENTERPRISES

Empresa Caboverdeana de Pescas (PESCAVE): CP 59, Mindelo, São Vicente; tel. 2434; telex 3084; f. 1987; co-ordinates and equips the fishing industry; manages the harbour, incl. cold-storage facilities (capacity 9,000 metric tons); operates ice supply and shipping agency.

Empresa de Comercialização de Produtos do Mar—INTERBASE, EP: CP 59, Mindelo, São Vicente; tel. 31-23-49; telex 3084; supervises marketing of fish; shipping agency and ship chandler.

Empresa Nacional de Avicultura, EP (ENAVI): CP 135, Praia, São Tiago; tel. 61-18-59; telex 6072; f. 1979; state enterprise for poultry farming.

Empresa Nacional de Combustíveis, EP: CP 1, Mindelo, São Vicente; f. 1979; state enterprise supervising import and distribution of petroleum; Dir RUI S. LOPES DOS SANTOS.

CAPE VERDE

Empresa Nacional de Produtos Farmacêuticos (EMPROFAC): CP 59, Praia, São Tiago; tel. 61-14-94; telex 6024; f. 1979; state pharmaceuticals enterprise holding monopoly of local production and medical imports.

Empresa Pública de Abastecimentos (EMPA): CP 107, Praia, São Tiago; tel. 61-11-54; telex 6054; f. 1975; state provisioning enterprise, supervising imports, exports and domestic distribution; Dir-Gen. ORLANDO JOSÉ MASCARENHAS.

Instituto Nacional de Cooperativas: Praia, São Tiago; central co-operative organization.

Secretaria de Estado das Pescas (SEP): CP 30, Praia, São Tiago; tel. 61-10-91; telex 6058; f. 1983; oversees the development of the fishing industry; Dir-Gen. VICENTE ANDRADE GOMES.

Sociedade de Comercialização e Apoio à Pesca Artesanal (SCAPA): Praia, São Tiago; state-run; co-ordinates small-scale fishing enterprises and promotes modern techniques.

CHAMBER OF COMMERCE

Associação Comercial Barlavento: CP 62, Mindelo, São Vicente; tel. 31-32-81.

TRADE UNION

União Nacional dos Trabalhadores de Cabo Verde—Central Sindical (UNTC–CS): Praia, São Tiago; f. 1978; Chair. ADOLINO MANUEL SILVA.

Transport

ROADS

In 1981 there were about 2,250 km of roads, of which 660 km were paved. In 1986 a loan of US $7.5m. from the People's Republic of China was used partly to finance new road-building projects.

SHIPPING

Cargo-passenger ships call regularly at Mindelo, on São Vicente, and Praia, on São Tiago. Praia and Porto Grande ports are being considerably enlarged, with the help of a US $7.2m. grant from the International Development Association, and a shipyard has been built at Mindelo. Work started in 1982 on a port at Palmeira, on Sal. New ports are also being constructed at Sal-Rei, on Boa Vista, and at Tarrafal, on São Nicolau, with financial and technical assistance from the USSR.

Comissão de Gestão dos Transportes Marítimos de Cabo Verde: CP 153, São Vicente; tel. 2652; telex 3031; 3,199 grt.

Companhia Nacional de Navegação Arca Verde: 5 de Julho, CP 41, Praia, São Tiago; tel. 61-10-60; telex 6067; f. 1975; 4,851 grt.

Companhia de Navegação Estrella Negra: Avda 5 de Julho 17, CP 91, São Vicente; tel. 31-54-23; telex 3030; 2,098 grt.

Companhia Nacional de Navegação Portuguesa: Agent in São Tiago: João Benoliel de Carvalho, Lda, CP 56, Praia, São Tiago.

Companhia Portuguesa de Transportes Marítimos: Agent in São Tiago: João Benoliel de Carvalho, Lda, CP 56, Praia, São Tiago.

Transportes Marítimos de Cabo Verde: Avda Kwame Nkrumah, CP 153, Mindelo, São Vicente; serves Portugal, Cádiz, Antwerp, Rotterdam, Hamburg, Ipswich, Felixstowe, Udvalla, Abidjan and Tema.

CIVIL AVIATION

The Amílcar Cabral international airport is at Espargos, on Sal Island, with capacity for aircraft of up to 50 tons. It can handle 1m. passengers per year. In 1987 work on the expansion of the airport's facilities began, with Italian and EEC aid, and in 1988 a Belgian company agreed to establish a catering service and two restaurants. There is also a small airport on each of the other main islands, except Brava.

Transportes Aéreos de Cabo Verde (TACV): 11–13 Rua Guerra Mendes, CP 1, Praia, São Tiago; telex 99365; f. 1955; connects São Vicente, Praia, Ilha do Sal, São Nicolau, Boavista, Fogo, Santo Antão and Maio; also operates weekly services to Portugal and the USA; Gen. Man. VALDEMAR FORTES DE SOUSA LOBO; fleet: 2 HS-748 Avro, 1 DC-10 and 2 DH Twin Otter.

Tourism

The islands of São Tiago, Santo Antão, Fogo and Brava offer a combination of mountain scenery and vast beaches. In 1980 the Government initiated a tourist development scheme, and by 1987 there were two international hotels on Sal Island and a tourist complex in Praia. About 2,000 tourists, mostly French and Italian, visit Cape Verde each year.

Secretaria de Estado de Comércio e Turismo: CP 105, Praia, São Tiago; tel. 573; telex 6058.

THE CENTRAL AFRICAN REPUBLIC

Introductory Survey

Location, Climate, Language, Religion, Flag, Capital

The Central African Republic is a land-locked country in the heart of equatorial Africa. It is bounded by Chad to the north, by Sudan to the east, by the Congo and Zaire to the south and by Cameroon to the west. The climate is tropical, with an average annual temperature of 26°C (79°F) and heavy rains in the south-western forest areas. The national language is Sango, but French is the official language. Many of the population hold animist beliefs, but about one-third are Christians. The national flag (proportions 5 by 3) has four horizontal stripes, of blue, white, green and yellow, divided vertically by a central red stripe, with a five-pointed yellow star and crescent in the upper hoist. The capital is Bangui.

Recent History

The former territory of Ubangi-Shari (Oubangui-Chari), within French Equatorial Africa, became the Central African Republic (CAR) on achieving self-government in December 1958. Full independence was attained on 13 August 1960. The leading figure in the campaign for self-government was Barthélemy Boganda, founder of the Mouvement d'évolution sociale de l'Afrique noire (MESAN). Boganda became the country's first Prime Minister, but he was killed in an air crash in March 1959. He was succeeded by his nephew, David Dacko, who led the country to independence and in 1962 established a one-party state, with MESAN as the sole authorized party. President Dacko was overthrown on 31 December 1965 by a military coup which brought to power his cousin, Col (later Marshal) Jean-Bédel Bokassa, Commander-in-Chief of the armed forces.

In January 1966 Col Bokassa formed a new government, rescinded the Constitution and dissolved the National Assembly. Bokassa, who became Life President in March 1972 and Marshal of the Republic in May 1974, forestalled several alleged coup attempts and used stern measures to suppress opposition. On two occasions, close associates of the President were implicated in plots to overthrow the regime. In April 1969 Lt-Col Alexandre Banza, the Minister of Public Health, was arrested and executed after being convicted of attempting to organize a coup against Bokassa. In a government reshuffle in April 1973, Auguste M'Bongo, the Minister of State for Housing and Transport, lost his post. He was subsequently accused of attempting to instigate another coup, and of having been a supporter of the 1969 plot. A government reorganization in January 1975 included the appointment of Elisabeth Domitien, the vice-president of MESAN, to the newly-created post of Prime Minister. She thus became the first woman to hold this position in any African country, but she was dismissed in April 1976, when President Bokassa assumed the premiership.

In September 1976 the Council of Ministers was replaced by the Council for the Central African Revolution, and ex-President Dacko was named personal adviser to the President. In December the Republic was renamed the Central African Empire (CAE), and a new constitution was instituted. Bokassa was proclaimed the first Emperor, and Dacko became his Personal Counsellor. The Imperial Constitution provided for the establishment of a National Assembly but no elections were held.

The elaborate preparations for Bokassa's coronation in December 1977 were estimated to have consumed about one-quarter of the country's income. In May 1978 Bokassa reshuffled the army leadership and strengthened its powers. In July he dismissed the Council of Ministers and appointed a new Council, headed by Henri Maidou, previously a Deputy Prime Minister. In January 1979 violent protests, led by students, were suppressed, reportedly with the help of Zairean troops. Following a protest by schoolchildren against compulsory school uniforms (made by a company that was owned by the Bokassa family), many children were arrested in April. About 100 of them were killed in prison, and Bokassa himself allegedly participated in the massacre. In May the Emperor's ambassador in Paris, Gen. Sylvestre Bangui, resigned in protest, and in September he became the leader of a newly-formed government-in-exile, comprising four opposition groups. On 20 September 1979, while Bokassa was in Libya, David Dacko deposed him in a bloodless coup, strongly backed by France, and resumed power as President. The country thus became a republic again, and Henri Maidou was appointed Vice-President.

The prime concern of President Dacko was to establish order and economic stability in the CAR, but his Government was not accepted without some opposition, particularly from students who objected to the continuation in office of CAE Ministers. In August 1980 Dacko accepted demands for the dismissal of both Henri Maidou and the unpopular Prime Minister, Bernard Christian Ayandho. The new Council of Ministers was led by Jean-Pierre Lebouder, formerly Minister of Planning. Bokassa, at that time in exile in Côte d'Ivoire (and subsequently in Paris), was sentenced to death *in absentia* in December 1980.

In February 1981 a new constitution, providing for a multi-party system, was approved by referendum and promulgated by President Dacko. He won a presidential election in March and was sworn in for a six-year term in April. Following accusations by his opponents of electoral malpractice, rioting broke out and a state of siege was declared in Bangui. Political tension increased after a bomb attack on a Bangui cinema in July, in which three people died. The Mouvement centrafricaine de libération nationale claimed responsibility and was subsequently banned. A state of siege was again declared, and the Government summoned assistance from army units to maintain order. The Chief of Staff of the armed forces, Gen. André Kolingba, deposed President Dacko in a bloodless coup on 1 September, citing 'gross violations of democracy' as reasons for the military take-over, and suspending all political activity. Power was assumed by a 23-member Comité militaire pour le redressement national (CMRN), and an all-military government was formed.

In March 1982 the exiled leader of the banned Mouvement pour la libération du peuple centrafricain (MLPC), Ange Patasse, returned to Bangui and was implicated in an unsuccessful coup attempt. Patasse, who had been the Prime Minister under Bokassa in 1976-78 and was runner-up in the presidential election of March 1981, sought asylum in the French embassy in Bangui, from where he was transported to exile in Togo. French support for Patasse strained the military regime's relations with France, but a visit by President Mitterrand to the CAR in October 1982 normalized relations. Some former government ministers were also implicated in the coup attempt, and in August 1984 two of the accused ex-ministers, Gaston Ouédane and Jérôme Allan, were sentenced to 10 years' imprisonment.

Opposition to Gen. Kolingba's regime continued, despite the suspension of all political activity in September 1981. In August 1983 a clandestine opposition movement was formed, uniting the three main opposition parties. In September 1984 Gen. Kolingba announced an amnesty for the leaders of banned political parties, who had been under house arrest since January, and reduced the sentences of the ex-ministers who had been imprisoned for involvement in the 1982 coup attempt. Shortly afterwards, in December 1984, President Mitterrand of France paid a state visit to the country. A total of 89 political prisoners were released in December 1985. Several students were arrested during anti-French demonstrations in Bangui in March 1986, following the death of 35 civilians, including many schoolchildren, as a result of the crash of a French military aircraft. Shortly afterwards, a bomb exploded on the road leading to Bangui-Mpoko airport. Two Libyan diplomats were expelled from the CAR, suspected of complicity in the bomb attack. The students were released in September, along with a further, unspecified number of political prisoners (including Gaston Ouédane and Jérôme Allan).

The appointment of several civilians as high commissioners (attached to the Council of Ministers, with responsibilities for various departments) in a government reshuffle in January 1984 was followed in September 1985 by the dissolution of the CMRN and the introduction of civilians into the Council of

Ministers itself, for the first time since Gen. Kolingba's assumption of power. In early 1986 a specially-convened commission drafted a new constitution providing for the creation of a sole legal political party, the Rassemblement démocratique centrafricain (RDC), and conferring strong executive powers on the President, with a legislature in a largely advisory role. The draft constitution was approved by 91.17% of the electorate in a referendum held in November 1986, in which Kolingba was also elected to serve a further six-year term as President. The Council of Ministers was reshuffled in December to include a majority of civilians, while Kolingba assumed the defence portfolio.

The RDC was officially established in February 1987, with Kolingba as founding president, and elections to the new National Assembly took place in July, with a total of 142 candidates, all nominated by the RDC, contesting the 52 seats. It was estimated that only 50% of the electorate participated in the legislative elections. The new National Assembly held its first sitting in October. In December, following reports of student unrest, the Ministers of National Education and of Higher Education and Scientific Research were dismissed, and the two portfolios were merged to form a single ministry, as part of a government reshuffle. Further reallocations of ministerial posts took place in July 1988 and in January 1989.

In October 1986 Bokassa unexpectedly returned to the CAR, and was immediately arrested. His new trial, on a total of 14 charges, opened in November, and continued until June 1987, when the former Emperor was convicted on charges of murder, conspiracy to murder, the illegal detention of prisoners and embezzlement, and was sentenced to death. An appeal for a retrial was rejected by the Supreme Court in November. In February 1988, however, President Kolingba commuted the sentence to one of life imprisonment with hard labour. (In practice, hard labour is not exacted of prisoners in the CAR.) It was widely believed that this act of clemency resulted not only from Kolingba's desire to be regarded as a moderate and humane leader, but also from a fear of unrest among Bokassa's supporters in the event of the former Emperor's execution.

Following his accession to power, Kolingba was anxious to secure international support for his regime, notably from France, which remains the country's principal source of budgetary and bilateral development aid. French military forces stationed in the CAR were used in support operations for the Government of Chad during that country's conflict with Libya. Kolingba visited France and the Federal Republic of Germany in 1988. In the same year it was announced that diplomatic relations with the USSR, which had been suspended in 1980, were to be resumed, and that the CAR and Angola were to exchange ambassadors for the first time.

Government

Under the November 1986 Constitution, executive power is vested in the President of the Republic, and legislative power in the bicameral Congress. This consists of a 52-seat National Assembly, whose sessions are held at the summons of the President, and an Economic and Regional Council, one-half of the members of which are elected by the Assembly and one-half appointed by the President. Both the President and the Assembly are elected by direct universal suffrage, the former for a six-year term and the latter for a five-year term. The Rassemblement démocratique centrafricain (RDC), officially founded in February 1987, is the sole legal political party, and its president is the President of the Republic. All 142 candidates in the July 1987 elections to the National Assembly were members of the RDC. Members of the Council of Ministers are appointed by the President. For administrative purposes, the country is divided into 16 prefectures and 52 sub-prefectures. At community level there are 18 communes de plein exercice, 39 communes de moyen exercice and 113 communes rurales.

Defence

In June 1988 the armed forces numbered about 3,800 men (army 3,500; air force 300), with a further 2,700 men in paramilitary forces. Military service is selective and lasts for two years. France maintains a force of 1,200 troops in the CAR. Estimated defence expenditure in 1987 was 5,610m. francs CFA.

Economic Affairs

Since independence, the CAR's economic growth has failed to keep pace with the increase in the country's population. In 1987, according to estimates by the World Bank, the gross national product (GNP), measured at average 1985-87 prices was US $912m., equivalent to $330 per head. Between 1980 and 1987, GNP per head decreased at an average rate of 0.5% per year, in real terms. The average annual growth of overall gross domestic product (GDP), measured in constant prices, was 2.6% between 1965 and 1980, slowing to 1.1% in 1980-86. During the early 1980s the Kolingba regime achieved a degree of economic stability through the implementation of a series of recovery programmes, with the result that real GDP expanded by an estimated 2.5% in 1985. However, growth was estimated to have slowed in 1986 and 1987.

In 1986 almost 67% of the working population were engaged in agriculture, which accounted for 41% of GDP. The most important cash crops are cotton and coffee, but subsistence farming predominates. The main subsistence crops are millet, sorghum and cassava. Since independence, both the production and export of food crops have declined. In 1986 a major livestock development programme was initiated, at a total cost of US $37.3m., of which $11.9m. was provided by a loan from the International Development Association (IDA), an affiliate of the World Bank. Manufacturing is mainly small-scale and accounted for only 4% of GDP in 1986, the main activities being in timber, tanning, textiles and brewing.

Production of cotton declined, following a record harvest of 60,000 tons (unginned) in 1971, to only 17,242 tons in 1981. Output increased to 45,500 tons in 1984/85, but was estimated to have fallen to an annual average of 34,000 tons in 1985/86 and 1986/87, as a result of a decline in international cotton prices and adverse weather conditions. The value of cotton exports declined from 8,988m. francs CFA in 1984 to 2,635m. francs CFA in 1987. Under a rationalization programme announced in early 1987, the cotton-processing and -marketing functions of the national agricultural development corporation (SOCADA) were to pass into private control, and three of the CAR's seven cotton-ginning plants were to close. Coffee production was 18,000 tons in 1982/83, but was affected by widespread drought in 1983/84, when the harvest declined to 10,000 tons. Output was estimated to have increased to 16,000 tons in 1985/86, and to 20,000 tons in 1986/87.

Forests, containing more than 60 species of valuable trees, cover 5.5% of the CAR's land area, and total exploitable potential is estimated to be 87.3m. cu m per year. Timber exports in 1984 were 337,000 cu m. In 1987 exports of wood were worth 5,976m. francs CFA. Problems of transport and organization have hampered removals, but efficiency should be increased by improvements to river navigation and by the construction of a proposed railway linking Bangui to Yaoundé, the capital of neighbouring Cameroon, and thence to the Atlantic coast.

Diamonds are found in alluvial deposits, mainly in the west of the country. Their contribution to total export earnings declined from 53% in 1968 to 17% in 1976. Following the adoption by the Government of measures to promote investment in the industry, revenue increased steadily, to reach 50% of exports in 1979. Thereafter, revenue from exports of diamonds fluctuated, accounting for about 25% of total export earnings in 1986, when declared production was 357,379 carats, compared with a peak of 609,000 carats in 1968. Earnings from official diamond exports rose from 12,273m. francs CFA in 1986 to 15,056m. francs CFA in 1987. However, there is widespread evasion of export duties, with up to 60% of total diamond production being smuggled out of the country. There is some gold mining, with official output totalling 212 kg in 1986. Reserves of uranium, estimated at some 15,000 tons, at Bakouma are unlikely to be exploited in the near future. Other known mineral deposits include limestone, iron ore, copper and manganese. Exploratory drilling for petroleum deposits on the border with Chad has begun. In 1987 it was announced that the CAR was to receive power from the Mobaye hydroelectric plant, currently under construction on the Oubangui river, in Zaire, following the signing of a co-operation agreement between the two countries, regarding the operation of hydroelectric installations on a joint basis. A further, 8.5-MW, plant is planned for Mbali, to serve the capital, while a rehabilitation project for the 10-MW station at Boali was under way in 1988.

Annual inflation averaged 10.1% in 1985. The current budget deficit was estimated at 14,750m. francs CFA in 1988. The trade deficit totalled 41,710m. francs CFA in 1986, with a 23% decline in the value of exports (due mainly to the slump in international commodity prices) being partly offset by a

THE CENTRAL AFRICAN REPUBLIC

Introductory Survey, Statistical Survey

contraction in imports in that year. The CAR relies heavily on foreign aid, especially from France, which provided 75% of gross official development aid to the country between 1981 and 1985. The current deficit on the balance of payments increased from US $33.5m. in 1984 to $48.6m. in 1985 and $86.6m. in 1986. Accumulated arrears of debt-service obligations led to the rescheduling of payments in 1982, 1983 and 1985 on the part of Western governments. Outstanding foreign debt at the end of 1987 amounted to $590m. Debt-servicing costs in the previous year totalled $17.9m.

The 1980/81 emergency plan for social and economic rehabilitation envisaged expenditure of 45,000m. francs CFA; however, political uncertainties prevented the realization of around 75% of project investment. The 1983–85 recovery programme focused on the implementation of development projects involving total investment of 31,300m. francs CFA, and succeeded in achieving a positive GDP growth rate. Both programmes concentrated on the development of agriculture and of transport infrastructure. A five-year (1986–90) development plan was formulated, but was later superseded by a series of short-term structural adjustment programmes, implemented with support from the IMF and the World Bank. The 1986/87 programme, supported by a US $30m. structural adjustment loan from the World Bank and a stand-by credit of SDR 6.08m. from the IMF, aimed to achieve annual GDP growth of 4% by continuing to give priority to the potentially rich agricultural sector, by rationalizing certain public-sector operations and by encouraging greater participation by the private sector in the economy. The 1988/89 structural adjustment programme, to be supported by credits of $40m. from the World Bank and SDR 9.12m. from the IMF, continued these policies, but aimed to achieve a more realistic target of 4% annual growth by the early 1990s.

Social Welfare

An Employment Code guarantees a minimum wage for 60,000 employees and provides for the payment of benefits to compensate for accidents at work. In 1984 there were 7,023 hospital beds in the CAR (one per 371 inhabitants), but only 112 physicians were working in the country.

Education

Education is officially compulsory for eight years between six and 14 years of age. Primary education begins at the age of six and lasts for six years. Secondary education begins at the age of 12 and lasts for up to seven years, comprising a first cycle of four years and a second of three years. In 1982 an estimated 60% of children in the relevant age-group (79% of boys; 42% of girls) attended primary schools, while secondary enrolment was equivalent to only 16% (boys 24%; girls 8%). According to estimates by UNESCO, the adult illiteracy rate in 1985 averaged 59.8% (males 46.7%; females 71.4%). In January 1986 a three-year project, aimed at improving educational facilities in rural areas, was initiated, with the African Development Fund providing US $7.6m. in finance. In 1987 the Government announced a six-year project aiming to improve the quality of primary education and the management of educational resources. The project also envisaged a scholarship system for higher education and a development plan for the University of Bangui. The International Development Association (IDA) was to assist the $20.7m. plan with a credit of $18m.

Public Holidays

1989: 2 January (for New Year), 27 March (Easter Monday), 29 March (Anniversary of death of Barthélemy Boganda), 1 May (May Day), 4 May (Ascension Day), 15 May (Whit Monday), 30 June (National Day of Prayer), 13 August (Independence Day), 15 August (Assumption), 1 November (All Saints' Day), 1 December (National Day), 25 December (Christmas).

1990: 1 January (New Year), 29 March (Anniversary of death of Barthélemy Boganda), 16 April (Easter Monday), 1 May (May Day), 24 May (Ascension Day), 4 June (Whit Monday), 30 June (National Day of Prayer), 13 August (Independence Day), 15 August (Assumption), 1 November (All Saints' Day), 1 December (National Day), 25 December (Christmas).

Weights and Measures

The metric system is officially in force.

Statistical Survey

Source (unless otherwise stated): Direction de la Statistique Générale et des Etudes Economiques, BP 696, Bangui; tel. 61-45-74.

Area and Population

AREA, POPULATION AND DENSITY

Area (sq km)	622,984*
Population (census of 8–22 December 1975)	
Males	985,224
Females	1,069,386
Total	2,054,610
Population (official estimates)	
1982 (31 December)	2,442,000
1984 (31 December)	2,607,626
1986 (mid-year)	2,740,000
Density (per sq km) at mid-1986	4.4

* 240,535 sq miles.

PRINCIPAL TOWNS

Bangui (capital), population 473,817 (Dec. 1984 estimate); Berbérati 100,000, Bouar 55,000 (1982 estimates).

BIRTHS AND DEATHS (UN estimates, annual averages)

	1970–75	1975–80	1980–85
Birth rate (per 1,000)	43.6	44.9	44.6
Death rate (per 1,000)	25.0	23.5	21.8

Source: UN, *World Population Prospects: Estimates and Projections as Assessed in 1984.*

ECONOMICALLY ACTIVE POPULATION
(ILO estimates, '000 persons at mid-1980)

	Males	Females	Total
Agriculture, etc.	436	432	868
Industry	56	20	76
Services	131	124	255
Total	**623**	**576**	**1,200**

Source: ILO, *Economically Active Population Estimates and Projections, 1950–2025.*

Mid-1986 (estimates in '000): Agriculture, etc. 868; Total 1,302 (Source: FAO, *Production Yearbook*).

THE CENTRAL AFRICAN REPUBLIC

Agriculture

PRINCIPAL CROPS ('000 metric tons)

	1984	1985	1986
Rice (paddy)	11	12	16
Maize	33	42	53
Millet and sorghum*	40	50	40
Cassava (Manioc)*	675	722	708
Yams*	197	198	198
Taro (Coco yam)*	57	58	59
Groundnuts (in shell)*	130	140	142
Sesame seed*	12	7	12
Cottonseed	46	35	42
Oranges, lemons and limes*	14	14	15
Mangoes*	6	6	6
Bananas*	82	82	83
Plantains*	65	65	65
Coffee (green)†	15	18	18
Tobacco (leaves)	1	1	1
Cotton (lint)	17	13	13†

* FAO estimates.   † Unofficial estimates.
Source: FAO, *Production Yearbook*.

LIVESTOCK ('000 head, year ending September)

	1984	1985	1986
Cattle	2,038	2,073	2,135
Goats	1,049	1,057	1,100
Sheep	97	108	112
Pigs	338	334	360

Chickens (estimates, million): 2 in 1984; 2 in 1985; 2 in 1986.
Source: FAO, *Production Yearbook*.

LIVESTOCK PRODUCTS (FAO estimates, metric tons)

	1984	1985	1986
Beef and veal	34,000	34,000	35,000
Mutton and lamb	1,000	1,000	1,000
Goats' meat	2,000	2,000	2,000
Pig meat	12,000	12,000	13,000
Poultry meat	2,000	2,000	2,000
Other meat	6,000	7,000	7,000
Cows' milk	4,000	5,000	5,000
Cattle hides (fresh)	4,930	5,016	5,166
Hen eggs	981	981	985
Honey	6,900	7,000	7,100

Source: FAO, *Production Yearbook*.

Forestry

ROUNDWOOD REMOVALS
('000 cubic metres, excluding bark)

	1984	1985	1986
Sawlogs, veneer logs and logs for sleepers	260	269	198
Other industrial wood*	218	223	229
Fuel wood	2,860	2,925	2,990*
Total	3,338	3,417	3,417

*FAO estimates.
Source: FAO, *Yearbook of Forest Products*.

SAWNWOOD PRODUCTION ('000 cubic metres)

	1984	1985	1986
Total (incl. boxboards)	58	56	54

Source: FAO, *Yearbook of Forest Products*.

Fishing

('000 metric tons, live weight)

	1984	1985	1986
Total catch (freshwater fish)	13	13	13

Source: FAO, *Yearbook of Fishery Statistics*.

Mining

	1983	1984	1985
Gold (kg)	95	236	249
Gem diamonds ('000 carats)	230	236	247
Industrial diamonds ('000 carats)	66	102	106

Source: Direction Générale des Mines et de la Géologie.

Industry

SELECTED PRODUCTS

	1983	1984	1985
Beer (hectolitres)	210,715	217,771	275,560
Soft drinks (hectolitres)	56,691	46,204	49,758
Cigarettes and cigars (million)	436	447	572
Woven cotton fabrics ('000 sq metres)*	4,000	4,000	n.a.
Footwear ('000 pairs)	266	582	611
Motor cycles (number)	5,610	4,020	4,515
Bicycles (number)	2,939	3,045	3,103
Electric energy (million kWh)	69	74	78

* UN estimates.

Finance

CURRENCY AND EXCHANGE RATES

Monetary Units
100 centimes = 1 franc de la Coopération financière en Afrique centrale (CFA).

Denominations
Coins: 1, 2, 5, 10, 25, 50 and 100 francs CFA.
Notes: 100, 500, 1,000, 5,000 and 10,000 francs CFA.

French Franc, Sterling and Dollar Equivalents
(30 September 1988)
1 French franc = 50 francs CFA;
£1 sterling = 538.6 francs CFA;
US $1 = 318.5 francs CFA;
1,000 francs CFA = £1.857 = $3.140.

Average Exchange Rate (francs CFA per US $)
1985   449.26
1986   346.30
1987   300.54

BUDGET (million francs CFA)

Revenue	1986	1987
Fiscal receipts	37,100	33,500
Other recurrent receipts	2,000	2,400
Non-recurrent receipts	1,000	2,200
Total	40,100	38,100

THE CENTRAL AFRICAN REPUBLIC

Expenditure	1986	1987
Administrative budget	40,200	42,300
Capital expenditure	38,200	36,200
Extra-budgetary expenditure	1,000	1,500
Net loans	4,000	4,800
Total	83,400	84,800

Source: *La Zone Franc—Rapport 1987*.

1988 (current budget forecasts, million francs CFA): Revenue 43,400; Expenditure 58,150.

CENTRAL BANK RESERVES (US $ million at 31 December)

	1985	1986	1987
Gold*	3.60	4.36	5.37
IMF special drawing rights	1.69	0.53	6.99
Reserve position in IMF	0.12	0.13	0.16
Foreign exchange	47.81	64.69	89.58
Total	53.22	69.71	102.10

* Valued at market-related prices.
Source: IMF, *International Financial Statistics*.

MONEY SUPPLY ('000 million francs CFA at 31 December)

	1985	1986	1987
Currency outside banks	37.15	40.61	41.46
Demand deposits at commercial and development banks	14.07	11.27	11.78
Checking deposits at post office	0.32	0.31	0.31
Total money	51.54	52.19	53.55

Source: IMF, *International Financial Statistics*.

NATIONAL ACCOUNTS (million francs CFA at current prices)
Gross Domestic Product by Economic Activity

	1983	1984	1985
Agriculture, hunting, forestry and fishing	99,372	109,275	130,927
Mining and quarrying	6,155	7,622	7,822
Manufacturing	19,065	21,691	23,149
Electricity, gas and water	1,285	2,399	2,557
Construction	5,074	7,297	7,946
Trade, restaurants and hotels	51,581	58,291	68,015
Transport, storage and communications	10,230	11,497	12,982
Finance, insurance, real estate and business services	8,962	9,756	10,806
Government services	30,289	28,443	30,372
Other community, social and personal services	11,337	12,454	13,973
Sub-total	243,350	268,725	308,549
Import duties	13,220	15,842	16,710
Less Imputed bank service charge	5,515	5,840	6,582
GDP in purchasers' values	251,055	278,727	318,677
GDP at constant 1982 prices	230,969	247,657	256,074

Source: UN, *National Accounts Statistics*.

BALANCE OF PAYMENTS (US $ million)

	1984	1985	1986
Merchandise exports f.o.b.	114.4	131.0	129.5
Merchandise imports f.o.b.	−140.1	−167.7	−201.0
Trade balance	−25.6	−36.7	−71.5
Exports of services	37.5	53.4	58.8
Imports of services	−98.8	−122.1	−156.8
Balance on goods and services	−86.9	−105.4	−169.5
Private unrequited transfers (net)	−11.2	−11.8	−19.5
Government unrequited transfers (net)	64.6	68.5	102.4
Current balance	−33.5	−48.6	−86.6
Direct capital investment (net)	4.9	2.4	6.9
Other long-term capital (net)	24.1	43.1	75.2
Short-term capital (net)	−1.7	−14.0	−9.3
Net errors and omissions	5.6	−9.6	7.5
Total (net monetary movements)	−0.6	−26.6	−6.3
Valuation changes (net)	2.5	11.8	8.0
Exceptional financing (net)	7.9	6.7	9.8
Official financing (net)	−1.0	—	−0.3
Changes in reserves	8.9	−8.2	11.2

Source: IMF, *International Financial Statistics*.

External Trade

Note: The data exclude trade with other countries in the Customs and Economic Union of Central Africa (UDEAC): Cameroon, Chad (since December 1984), the Congo, Equatorial Guinea (since January 1985) and Gabon.

PRINCIPAL COMMODITIES
(distribution by SITC, US $'000)

Imports c.i.f.	1978	1979	1980
Food and live animals	5,346	8,148	11,244
Cereals and cereal preparations	1,755	4,166	5,400
Wheat flour	803	2,653	3,603
Beverages and tobacco	3,734	2,591	5,135
Beverages	3,213	2,192	4,396
Alcoholic beverages	3,056	2,039	4,109
Chemicals and related products	5,070	9,393	9,490
Medicinal and pharmaceutical products	1,884	3,200	4,588
Medicaments	1,710	3,040	4,364
Pesticides, disinfectants, etc.	405	3,331	1,497
Basic manufactures	11,802	11,448	15,393
Non-metallic mineral manufactures	2,233	2,375	3,418
Machinery and transport equipment	21,609	27,407	27,243
Power generating machinery and equipment	1,326	4,954	1,873
Internal combustion piston engines and parts	911	4,184	1,245
Machinery specialized for particular industries	1,604	3,167	2,957
General industrial machinery, equipment and parts	3,483	5,341	3,970
Electrical machinery, apparatus, etc.	3,187	2,974	4,707

THE CENTRAL AFRICAN REPUBLIC

PRINCIPAL COMMODITIES
(distribution by SITC, US $'000)—continued

Road vehicles and parts (excl. tyres, engines and electrical parts)	11,182	9,745	13,120
Motor vehicles for goods transport and special purposes	5,022	4,417	4,409
Goods vehicles (lorries and trucks)	4,983	4,128	3,989
Miscellaneous manufactured articles	6,601	4,938	8,008
Total (incl. others)	56,662	66,530	80,461

Source: UN, *International Trade Statistics Yearbook*.

Total imports (million francs CFA): 25,646 in 1981; 41,306 in 1982; 25,951 in 1983; 38,193 in 1984; 50,686 in 1985; 87,190 in 1986 (Source: IMF, *International Financial Statistics*).

Exports f.o.b.	1978	1979	1980
Food and live animals	20,957	20,447	31,766
Coffee, tea, cocoa and spices	20,956	20,358	31,759
Coffee (green and roasted)	20,830	20,265	31,611
Crude materials (inedible) except fuels	21,441	20,893	47,678
Cork and wood	11,687	9,787	33,212
Sawlogs and veneer logs	6,547	6,777	27,407
Sawn lumber	5,140	3,010	5,805
Textile fibres and waste	4,426	5,364	8,645
Cotton	4,426	5,364	8,644
Bones, ivory, horns, etc.	3,856	4,594	4,277
Basic manufactures	26,924	35,296	28,945
Non-metallic mineral manufactures	26,860	35,019	28,908
Diamonds (non-industrial)	26,860	35,019	28,898
Gold (non-monetary)	—	—	4,163
Total (incl. others)	71,717	79,547	115,400

Source: UN, *International Trade Statistics Yearbook*.

1981 (million francs CFA): Coffee 7,263; Wood 9,642; Cotton 5,294; Diamonds 9,035; Total (incl. others) 21,323.
1982 (million francs CFA): Coffee 9,927; Wood 7,833; Cotton 2,738; Diamonds 9,046; Total (incl. others) 35,461.
1983 (million francs CFA): Coffee 14,674; Wood 8,414; Cotton 5,628; Diamonds 8,114; Total (incl. others) 28,405.
1984 (million francs CFA): Coffee 10,553; Wood 9,053; Cotton 8,988; Diamonds 13,524; Total (incl. others) 37,022.
1985 (million francs CFA): Coffee 18,469; Wood 9,025; Cotton 6,789; Diamonds 14,173; Total (incl. others) 41,217.
1986 (million francs CFA): Coffee 10,285; Wood 8,064; Cotton 4,391; Diamonds 12,273; Total (incl. others) 45,480.
1987 (million francs CFA): Coffee 5,180; Wood 5,976; Cotton 2,635; Diamonds 15,056.

Source: IMF, *International Financial Statistics*.

PRINCIPAL TRADING PARTNERS (US $'000)

Imports c.i.f.	1979	1980	1982*
Belgium/Luxembourg	1,100	1,298	1,290
Chad	226	260	1,160
Côte d'Ivoire	1,359	541	480
France	42,209	48,851	65,750
Germany, Federal Republic	2,261	2,441	3,410
Guinea-Bissau	402	1,015	n.a.
Italy	720	1,314	1,970
Japan	2,897	5,815	5,840
Netherlands	1,659	2,895	3,330
Nigeria	236	1,157	1,250
Spain	1,819	1,831	1,640
United Kingdom	2,176	2,221	1,670
USA	3,070	2,779	5,290
Zaire	952	2,145	11,130
Total (incl. others)	66,523	80,461	123,380

* **1981** (US $'000): Total imports 95,000.

Exports f.o.b.	1979	1980	1982†
Belgium/Luxembourg	16,993	16,550	24,720
Chad	527	466	1,780
Denmark	876	1,741	1,100
France	36,285	59,434	47,320
Germany, Federal Republic	154	470	2,040
Israel	9,113	8,990	9,600
Italy	1,359	2,827	970
Netherlands	1,530	1,051	260
Portugal	42	159	2,370
Romania	1,221	738	n.a.
Spain	678	3,046	690
Sudan	175	377	2,240
Switzerland	596	1,103	3,660
United Kingdom	1,669	2,873	2,300
USA	6,512	4,745	5,280
Yugoslavia	263	4,728	1,670
Total (incl. others)	79,547	111,237	107,320

† **1981** (US $'000): Total exports 79,000.
Source: UN, *International Trade Statistics Yearbook*.

Transport

ROAD TRAFFIC (motor vehicles in use at 31 December)

	1981	1982	1983
Passenger cars	23,750	38,930	41,321
Buses and coaches	79	103	118
Goods vehicles	3,060	3,190	3,720
Motorcycles and scooters	170	278	397
Mopeds	62,518	71,421	79,952

Source: IRF, *World Road Statistics*.

INLAND WATERWAYS TRAFFIC—INTERNATIONAL SHIPPING (metric tons)

	1983	1984	1985
Freight unloaded at Bangui	105,900	89,000	115,500
Freight loaded at Bangui	38,100	49,200	44,300
Total	144,000	138,200	159,800

CIVIL AVIATION (traffic on scheduled services)*

	1982	1983	1984
Kilometres flown (million)	2.3	2.4	2.4
Passengers carried ('000)	115	114	118
Passenger-km (million)	220	219	220
Freight ton-km (million)	21.3	18.8	17.5

*Including an apportionment of the traffic of Air Afrique.
Source: UN, *Statistical Yearbook*.

Tourism

	1981	1982	1983
Foreign tourist arrivals	7,000	7,000	7,000

Communications Media

	1981	1982	1983
Radio receivers	130,000	135,000	140,000
Television receivers	1,000	1,200	1,400

1985: 150,000 radio receivers in use.

Source: UNESCO, *Statistical Yearbook*.

Telephones: 11,000 in use in 1982 (Source: UN Economic Commission for Africa, *African Statistical Yearbook*).

Education

(1985)

	Institutions	Teachers	Students
Pre-primary	159	369	10,445
Primary	986	4,502	294,312
Secondary:			
General	41	914	45,166
Technical	4	127	2,233
Higher*	n.a.	105	2,133

* 1983/84 figures.

Source: Ministère de l'Education Nationale, Bangui.

Directory

The Constitution

The Constitution that had been promulgated on 6 February 1981 was suspended following the coup of 1 September 1981. All legislative and executive powers were assumed by the Military Committee for National Recovery (Comité militaire pour le redressement national—CMRN). The CMRN was dissolved on 21 September 1985, and a 22-member Council of Ministers was appointed. The present Constitution of the Central African Republic was adopted following its approval by referendum on 21 November 1986.

PREAMBLE

Affirms the adoption by the Central African people of the principles of liberty and equality before the law of all citizens, regardless of sex, race and culture; of freedom of education and equality of access to the organs of justice; of freedom of expression, movement and assembly, and of the inalienable status of the individual.

SOVEREIGNTY

The Central African Republic is one and indivisible. It is a sovereign and democratic state. The national language is Sango, and the official language is French. National sovereignty belongs to the people, who exercise it through their representative or through referenda. Suffrage is universal, equal and secret. The Rassemblement Démocratique Centrafricain is the sole political party.

THE PRESIDENCY

The President of the Republic is Head of State and Commander-in-Chief of the national armed forces. He conducts the nation's policies, negotiates and ratifies treaties, promulgates laws, has power to make regulations and is responsible for civilian and military appointments. The President is elected for a six-year term by direct universal suffrage. He is elected by an absolute majority of votes cast. If such is not obtained at the first ballot, a second ballot is to take place within two weeks of the first, contested by the two candidates gaining the largest number of votes in the first ballot. The election of the new President is to take place not less than 20 days and not more than 40 days before the expiration of the mandate of the President in office. However, the President may choose to hold a referendum to determine whether or not his mandate is to be renewed. Should the electorate reject the proposal, the President is to resign and a new presidential election is to be held two weeks after the publication of the results of the referendum. The Presidency is to become vacant only in the event of the President's death, resignation, condemnation by the High Court of Justice (see below) or permanent physical incapacitation, as certified by a Special Committee comprising the presidents of the National Assembly, the Economic and Regional Council and the Supreme Court (see below). The election of a new President must take place not less than 20 days and not more than 40 days following the occurrence of a vacancy, during which time the president of the National Assembly is to act as interim President, with limited powers.

The President appoints and dismisses ministers, who are permitted to hold no other office, and presides over the Council of Ministers. He promulgates laws adopted by the National Assembly or by the Congress, and may call referenda on proposed legislation. Laws are promulgated within two weeks of their adoption by Parliament or by referendum. The President has the power to dissolve the National Assembly, in which event legislative elections must take place not less than 20 and not more than 40 days following its dissolution. Provisions are made for the short-term implementation of decrees adopted by the Council of Ministers and for the introduction of emergency measures in the event of a serious threat to national unity.

PARLIAMENT

This is composed of the National Assembly and the Economic and Regional Council, which, when sitting together, are to be known as the Congress. The primary function of the Congress is to pass organic laws in implementation of the Constitution, whenever these are not submitted to a referendum.

The National Assembly

The National Assembly is composed of deputies elected by direct universal suffrage for a five-year term. Its formation and functioning are determined by an organic law. Its president is designated by, and from within, its bureau. Legislation may be introduced either by the President of the Republic or by a consensus of one-third of the members of the Assembly. Provisions are made for the rendering inadmissible of any law providing for the execution of projects carrying a financial cost to the State which exceeds their potential value. The National Assembly holds two ordinary sessions per year of 60 days each, at the summons of the President of the Republic, who may also summon it to hold extraordinary sessions with a pre-determined agenda. Sessions of the National Assembly are opened and closed by presidential decree.

The Economic and Regional Council

The Economic and Regional Council is composed of representatives from the principal sectors of economic and social activity. One-half of its members are appointed by the President, and the remaining half are elected by the National Assembly on the nomination of that body's president. Its formation and functioning are determined by an organic law. It acts as an advisory body in matters referred to it by the President, as well as in all legislative proposals of an economic and social nature.

The Congress

The Congress has the same president and bureau as the National Assembly. An absolute majority of its members is needed to pass organic laws, as well as laws pertaining to the amendment of the Constitution which have not been submitted to a referendum. It defines development priorities and may meet, at the summons of the President, to ratify treaties or to determine the existence of a state of war.

THE JUDICIARY

The Supreme Court

Members are appointed by the President and may hold no other office. The organization and functioning of the Supreme Court, as well as its areas of responsibility, are determined by an organic law.

THE CENTRAL AFRICAN REPUBLIC

The High Court of Justice

The High Court of Justice is composed of nine judges, of whom one-third are appointed by the President of the Republic, one-third by the president of the Congress and one-third by the president of the Supreme Court. Its president is appointed by the President of the Republic and has the casting vote. The High Court of Justice has the power to try ministers, members of the Congress and all persons guilty of breaching state security. Its organization and functioning are determined by an organic law. The President of the Republic may be judged by the High Court of Justice only if he is indicted on a charge of high treason by a three-quarters majority of members of the Congress.

Additional clauses deal with the administration of the CAR's *'collectivités territoriales'* and with the procedure for constitutional amendments.

The Government

HEAD OF STATE

President: Gen. ANDRÉ KOLINGBA (assumed power 1 September 1981; elected 21 November 1986 for a six-year term).

COUNCIL OF MINISTERS
(January 1989)

Prime Minister and Minister of Defence and War Veterans: Gen. ANDRÉ KOLINGBA.

Minister of Foreign Affairs: MICHEL GBEZERA-BRIA.

Minister of the Interior and Territorial Administration: Lt-Col CHRISTOPHE GRELOMBE.

Minister of Justice and Keeper of the Seals: THOMAS MATOUKA.

Minister of Economy and Finance, Planning and International Co-operation: DIEUDONNÉ WAZOUA.

Minister of National and Higher Education: JEAN-LOUIS PSIMHIS.

Minister of Transport and Civil Aviation: PIERRE GONIFEI-NGAIBONANOU.

Minister of the Civil Service, Labour, Social Security and Professional Training: DANIEL SEHOULIA.

Minister of Communications, Arts and Culture: JEAN BENGUE.

Minister of Public Health: JEAN WILLYBIRO-SACKO.

Minister of Rural Development: THÉODORE BAGA-YAMBO.

Minister of Energy, Mines, Geology and Water Resources: MICHEL SALLE.

Minister of Water, Forests, Wildlife, Fisheries and Tourism: RAYMOND MBITIKON.

Minister of Trade, Industry and Small- and Medium-scale Enterprises: TIMOTHÉE MARBOUA.

Minister of Posts and Telecommunications: HUGUES DOBOZENDI.

Minister of Public Works and Territorial Development: JACQUES KITTE.

Minister in charge of the Cabinet Secretariat and of Relations with the National Assembly: EDOUARD FRANCK.

Secretary of State for Economy and Finance in charge of Budget and Debt Management: JUDE ALEX KETTE.

Secretary of State for the Interior and Territorial Administration: EL-ROOSALEM HETMAN.

Secretary of State for Planning, Statistics and International Co-operation: THIERRY BINGABA.

Secretary of State for Rural Development: GEORGES ASSAS MDILAULT.

Secretary of State for Social Affairs: GENEVIÈVE LOMBILO.

MINISTRIES

Office of the President: Palais de la Renaissance, Bangui; tel. 61-03-23; telex 5253.

Ministry of the Civil Service, Labour, Social Security and Professional Training: Bangui; tel. 61-01-44.

Ministry of Communications, Arts and Culture: BP 1290, Bangui; telex 5301.

Ministry of Defence and War Veterans: Bangui; tel. 61-46-11; telex 5298.

Ministry of Economy and Finance, Planning and International Co-operation: Bangui; tel. 61-08-11; telex 5280.

Ministry of Energy, Mines, Geology and Water Resources: Bangui; telex 5243.

Ministry of Foreign Affairs: Bangui; tel. 61-15-74; telex 5213.

Ministry of the Interior and Territorial Administration: tel. 61-44-77.

Ministry of Justice: Bangui; tel. 61-16-44.

Ministry of National and Higher Education: BP 791, Bangui; telex 5333.

Ministry of Posts and Telecommunications: Bangui; tel. 61-29-46; telex 5304.

Ministry of Public Health: Bangui; tel. 61-29-01.

Ministry of Public Works and Territorial Development: Bangui; tel. 61-28-00.

Ministry of Rural Development: Bangui; tel. 61-28-00.

Ministry of Trade, Industry and Small- and Medium-scale Enterprises: Bangui; tel. 61-44-88; telex 5215.

Ministry of Transport and Civil Aviation: Bangui; tel. 61-06-36; telex 5335.

Ministry of Water, Forests, Wildlife, Fisheries and Tourism: Bangui.

Legislature

According to the November 1986 Constitution, legislative power is vested in a bicameral Congress, comprising a National Assembly and an Economic and Regional Council.

ASSEMBLÉE NATIONALE

In accordance with the provisions of the November 1986 Constitution, a 52-seat National Assembly was elected for a five-year term by direct universal suffrage on 31 July 1987. All 142 candidates were members of the Rassemblement démocratique centrafricain (RDC).

President: MAURICE METHOT.

Secretary-General: ÉMILE NICAISE MBARI.

CONSEIL ÉCONOMIQUE ET RÉGIONAL

The November 1986 Constitution provides for the establishment of an Economic and Regional Council, an advisory body.

Political Organizations

All political activity was banned between September 1981 and May 1986.

Rassemblement démocratique centrafricain (RDC): Bangui; f. Feb. 1987 as sole legal political party; to comprise a congress which will meet every three years, a political bureau and a 7-mem. exec. council; a 44-mem. provisional council was appointed to oversee activities until above bodies were elected; Pres. Gen. ANDRÉ KOLINGBA; Exec. Sec. JEAN-PAUL NGOUPANDE.

In 1983, the main active opposition groups formed the **Parti révolutionnaire centrafricain (PRC)**, comprising:

Front patriotique oubanguien-Parti du Travail (FPO-PT): f. 1979 as FPO; Leader ABEL GOUMBA.

Mouvement centrafricain pour la libération nationale (MCLN): Leader Dr IDDI LALA.

Mouvement pour la libération du peuple centrafricain (MLPC): f. 1979; Leader ANGE PATASSE.

In December 1984 several opposition leaders formed a Provisional Government for National Salvation (in exile), under the aegis of the provisional executive council of the MLPC. The President of the Provisional Government is (former Brig.-Gen.) ALPHONSE MBAIKOUA. In July 1986 the MLPC and the FPO-PT announced the formation of the **Front Uni (FU)**, which is committed to the restoration of the 1981 Constitution and the re-establishment of a multi-party system of government.

Diplomatic Representation

EMBASSIES IN THE CENTRAL AFRICAN REPUBLIC

Cameroon: BP 935, Bangui; telex 5249; Ambassador: CHRISTOPHER NSAHLAI.

Chad: BP 461, Bangui; telex 5220; Ambassador: El Hadj MOULI SEID.

China, People's Republic: BP 1430, Bangui; Ambassador: ZHOU XIANJUE.

Congo: BP 1414, Bangui; telex 5292; Chargé d'affaires: ANTOINE DELICA.

THE CENTRAL AFRICAN REPUBLIC

Directory

Côte d'Ivoire: BP 930, Bangui; telex 5279; Ambassador: JEAN-MARIE AGNINI BILE MALAN.

Egypt: BP 1422, Bangui; telex 5284; Ambassador: SAMEH SAMY DARWICHE.

France: blvd du Général de Gaulle, BP 884, Bangui; tel. 61-30-00; telex 5218; Ambassador: ALBERT PAVEC.

Gabon: BP 1570, Bangui; tel. 61-29-97; telex 5234; Ambassador: FRANÇOIS DE PAULE MOULENGUI.

Germany, Federal Republic: ave G. A. Nasser, BP 901, Bangui; tel. 61-07-46; telex 5219; Ambassador: HARRO ADT.

Holy See: ave Boganda, BP 1447, Bangui; tel. 61-26-54; Apostolic Pro-Nuncio: Most Rev. BENIAMINO STELLA, Titular Archbishop of Midila.

Iraq: BP 369, Bangui; telex 5287; Chargé d'affaires: ABDUL KARIM ASWAD.

Japan: BP 1367, Bangui; tel. 61-06-68; telex 5204; Chargé d'affaires: KIYOJI YAMAKAWA.

Korea, Democratic People's Republic: BP 1816, Bangui; Ambassador: O KYONG-HWAN.

Korea, Republic: BP 841, Bangui; tel. 61-28-88; telex 5259; Ambassador: JOUNG-SOO LEE.

Libya: BP 1732, Bangui; telex 5317; Head of Mission: EL-SENUSE ABDALLAH.

Nigeria: BP 1010, Bangui; tel. 61-39-00; telex 5269; Chargé d'affaires: T. A. O. ODEGBILE.

Romania: BP 1435, Bangui; Chargé d'affaires a.i.: MIHAI GAFTONIUC.

Sudan: BP 1351, Bangui; telex 5296; Ambassador: FAROUK ABDEL-RAHMAN.

USA: blvd David Dacko, BP 924, Bangui; tel. 61-02-00; Ambassador: DAVID C. FIELDS.

Yugoslavia: BP 1049, Bangui; Chargé d'affaires: SPIRIDON PETROVIĆ; temporarily closed February 1988.

Zaire: BP 989, Bangui; telex 5232; Ambassador: EMBE ISEA MBAMBE.

Judicial System

Supreme Court: BP 926, Bangui; tel. 61-41-33; highest judicial organ; acts as a Court of Cassation in civil and penal cases and as Court of Appeal in administrative cases; made up of four chambers: constitutional, judicial, administrative and financial.

President of the Supreme Court: ANTOINE GROTHE.

There is also a Court of Appeal, a Criminal Court, 16 tribunaux de grande instance, 37 tribunaux d'instance, six labour tribunals and a permanent military tribunal. A High Court of Justice was established following the adoption of the November 1986 Constitution, and is competent to try all cases of crimes against state security, including high treason by the President of the Republic.

Religion

An estimated 60% of the population hold animist beliefs, 5% are Muslims and 35% Christians; Roman Catholics comprise about 17% of the total population.

CHRISTIANITY

The Roman Catholic Church

The Central African Republic comprises one archdiocese and five dioceses. There were an estimated 450,000 adherents at 31 December 1986.

Bishops' Conference: Conférence Episcopale Centrafricaine, BP 1518, Bangui; tel. 61-31-48; f. 1982; Pres. Mgr JOACHIM N'DAYEN, Archbishop of Bangui.

Archbishop of Bangui: Mgr JOACHIM N'DAYEN, Archevêché, BP 798, Bangui; tel. 61-08-98.

Protestant Church

Eglise Protestante de Bangui: Bangui.

The Press

DAILY

E Le Songo: Bangui; Sango; circ. 200.

PERIODICALS

Bangui Match: Bangui; monthly.

Le Courrier Rural: BP 850, Bangui; publ. by Chambre d'Agriculture.

Journal Officiel de la République Centrafricaine: BP 739, Bangui; f. 1974; fortnightly; economic information; Dir-Gen. GABRIEL AGBA.

Renouveau Centrafricain: Bangui; weekly.

Ta Tene (The Truth): BP 1290, Bangui; monthly.

Terre Africaine: Bangui; weekly.

NEWS AGENCIES

Agence Centrafricaine de Presse (ACAP): BP 40, Bangui; tel. 61-10-88; telex 5299; f. 1974 following nationalization of the Bangui branch of Agence France-Presse; Gen. Man. VICTOR DETO TETEYA.

TASS (USSR) is the only foreign press agency represented in the CAR.

Publisher

Government Publishing House

Imprimerie Centrafricain: BP 329, Bangui; tel. 61-00-33; f. 1974; Dir-Gen. PIERRE SALAMATE-KOILET.

Radio and Television

There were an estimated 150,000 radio receivers in use in 1985. A 100-kW transmitter came into service at Bimbo in 1970, and two 50-kW transmitters were introduced in 1984. Television broadcasting began in December 1983. There were an estimated 1,400 television receivers in use in 1983.

Radiodiffusion-Télévision Centrafrique: BP 940, Bangui; telex 2355; f. 1958 as Radiodiffusion Nationale Centrafricaine; govt-controlled; radio programmes in French and Sango; Dir F. P. ZEMONIAKO.

Finance

(cap. = capital; res = reserves; dep. = deposits; m. = million; amounts in francs CFA)

BANKING

Central Bank

Banque des Etats de l'Afrique Centrale (BEAC): BP 851, Bangui; tel. 61-24-00; telex 5236; headquarters in Yaoundé, Cameroon; f. 1973 as the central bank of issue for mem. states of the Customs and Economic Union of Central Africa (UDEAC), comprising Cameroon, the Central African Republic, Chad, the Congo, Equatorial Guinea and Gabon; cap. 24,000m., res 148,480m. (Dec. 1986); Gov. CASIMIR OYE-MBA; Dir in CAR ALPHONSE KOYAMBA.

Commercial Banks

Banque de Crédit Agricole et de Développement (BCAD): place de la République, BP 801, Bangui; tel. 61-32-00; telex 5207; f. 1984; cap. 600m. (Dec. 1986); 50% owned by Banque de participation et de placement (Switzerland), 33% state-owned; Pres. MICHEL CHAUTARD; Dir-Gen. RENÉ JAULIN.

BIAO-Centrafrique: place de la République, BP 910, Bangui; tel. 61-46-33; telex 5233; f. 1980; cap. 700m. (Dec. 1986); 20% state-owned, 75% by Banque Internationale pour l'Afrique Occidentale (France); Pres. RICHARD MORIN; Dir-Gen. in Bangui FRANÇOIS EPAYE.

Union Bancaire en Afrique Centrale: rue de Brazza, BP 59, Bangui; tel. 61-29-90; telex 5225; f. 1962; cap. 1,000m. (Dec. 1986); 60% state-owned; Pres. JULES-MARC LAGUEREMA-YADINGUIN; Gen. Man. JOSEPH KOYAGBELE.

Investment Bank

Banque Centrafricaine d'Investissement (BCI): BP 933, Bangui; tel. 61-00-64; telex 5317; f. 1976; cap. 1,000m.; 34.8% state-owned; Pres. ALPHONSE KONGOLO; Man. Dir GÉRARD SAMBO.

Development Agencies

Caisse Centrale de Coopération Economique: BP 817, Bangui; tel. 61-36-34; telex 5291; Dir NILS ROBIN.

Mission Française de Coopération: BP 784, Bangui; tel. 61-30-00; telex 5218; administers bilateral aid from France; Dir MICHEL LANDRY.

THE CENTRAL AFRICAN REPUBLIC

INSURANCE

Agence Centrafricaine d'Assurances (ACA): BP 512, Bangui; tel. 61-06-23; f. 1956; cap. 3.8m.; Dir Mme R. CERBELLAUD.

Assureurs Conseils Centrafricains Faugère et Jutheau: rue de la Kouanga, BP 743, Bangui; tel. 61-19-33; f. 1968; cap. 1m.; Dir JEAN-YVES DEBOUDÉ.

Entreprise d'Etat d'Assurances et de Réassurances (SIRIRI): ave du Président Mobutu, BP 852, Bangui; tel. 61-36-55; telex 5306; f. 1972; general; cap. 100m.; Pres. EMMANUEL DOKOUNA; Dir-Gen. JEAN-MARIE YOLLOT.

Legendre, A. & Cie: rue de la Victoire, BP 896, Bangui; cap. 1m.; Pres. and Dir-Gen. ANDRÉ LEGENDRE.

Trade and Industry

CHAMBERS OF COMMERCE

Chambre d'Agriculture, d'Elevage, des Eaux, Forêts, Chasses, Pêches et Tourisme: BP 850, Bangui; Pres. MAURICE METHOT; Sec.-Gen. ANATOLE POSSITI.

Chambre de Commerce, d'Industrie, des Mines et de l'Artisanat (CCIMA): BP 813, Bangui; tel. 61-42-55; telex 5261; Pres. BERNARD-CHRISTIAN AYANDHO; Sec.-Gen. FRANÇOIS FARRA-FROND.

PRINCIPAL DEVELOPMENT ORGANIZATIONS

Agence de Développement Caféière (ADECAF): BP 1935, Bangui; tel. 61-47-30; coffee producers' association; assists coffee marketing co-operatives; Dir.-Gen. J. J. NIMIZIAMBI.

Caisse de Stabilisation et de Péréquation des Produits Agricoles (CAISTAB): BP 76, Bangui; tel. 61-08-00; telex 5278; supervises pricing and marketing of agricultural products; Dir.-Gen. M. BOUNANDELE-KOUMBA.

Comptoir National du Diamant (CND): Bangui; f. 1966; Dir-Gen. M. VASSOS.

Office National des Forêts (ONF): BP 915, Bangui; tel. 61-38-27; f. 1969; reafforestation, development of forest resources; Dir-Gen. C. D. SONGUET.

Société Centrafricaine de Développement Agricole (SOCADA): ave David Dacko, BP 997, Bangui; tel. 61-30-33; telex 5212; f. 1964; restructured 1980; cap. 1,000m. francs CFA; 75% state-owned, 25% Compagnie française pour le développement des fibres textiles (France); cotton ginning at 20 plants, production of cotton oil (at two refineries) and groundnut oil; Pres. MAURICE METHOT; Man. Dir PATRICE ENDJINGBOMA.

Société Centrafricaine de Palmiers à Huile (CENTRAPALM): BP 1355, Bangui; tel. 61-49-40; telex 5271; f. 1975; cap. 2,125m. francs CFA; state-owned; development of palm products; operates the Bossongo agro-industrial complex (inaugurated 1986); Pres. JEAN-PRIRAT MBAYE; Gen. Man. GABRIEL RAMADHANE-SAÏD.

TRADE UNION

All trade union activities were suspended in September 1981.

Transport

RAILWAYS

There are no railways at present but there is a long-term project to connect Bangui to the Transcameroon railway. A railway is also due to be constructed from Sudan's Darfur region into the CAR's Vakaga province.

ROADS

At 31 December 1987 there were about 20,278 km of roads, including 5,044 km of main roads and 3,934 km of secondary roads. Only about 2.2% of the total network is paved. Eight main routes leave Bangui, and those that are surfaced have been toll roads since 1971. Both the total road length and the condition of the roads are currently inadequate for the traffic that uses the road system. However, the Government has initiated a major project of road rehabilitation and construction. The CAR section of the Transafrican Lagos–Mombasa highway was completed in 1984, providing a link with Cameroon.

Compagnie Nationale des Transports Routiers (CNTR): BP 330, Bangui; tel. 61-46-44; cap. 35.5m. francs CFA; state-owned; Dir-Gen. GEORGES YABADA.

Compagnie de Transports Routiers de l'Oubangui Degrain & Cie (CTRO): BP 119, Bangui; f. 1940; cap. 100m. francs CFA; Man. Mme NICOLE DEGRAIN.

INLAND WATERWAYS

There are two navigable waterways. The first is open all the year, except in the dry season, and is formed by the Congo and Oubangui rivers; convoys of barges (of up to 800 tons load) ply between Bangui, Brazzaville and Pointe-Noire. The second is the river Sangha, a tributary of the Oubangui, on which traffic is seasonal. There are two ports, at Bangui and Salo, on the rivers Oubangui and Sangha respectively. Efforts are being made to develop the stretch of river upstream from Salo to increase the transportation of timber from this area, and to develop Nola as a timber port.

Agence Centrafricaine des Communications Fluviales (ACCF): BP 822, Bangui; tel. 61-02-11; telex 5256; f. 1969; state-owned; development of inland waterways transport system; Man. Dir JUSTIN NDJAPOU.

Société Centrafricaine de Transports Fluviaux (SOCATRAF): BP 1445, Bangui; telex 5256; f. 1980; cap. 400m. francs CFA; 51% owned by ACCF; Man. Dir FRANÇOIS TOUSSAINT.

CIVIL AVIATION

There is an international airport at Bangui-Mpoko, which is currently being rehabilitated at a total cost of around US $13.6m. There are also 37 small airports for internal services.

Air Afrique: BP 875, Bangui; tel. 61-46-60; telex 5281; the CAR govt has a 7% share; see under Côte d'Ivoire; Dir in Bangui ALBERT BAGNERES.

Inter-RCA: BP 1413, Bangui; telex 5239; f. 1980 to replace Air Centrafrique; 52% state-owned, 24% by Air Afrique; extensive internal services; Man. Dir JULES BERNARD OUANDE; fleet of 1 Caravelle and 1 DC-4.

Tourism

The main tourist attractions are the waterfalls, the forests and many varieties of wild animals. There are excellent hunting and fishing opportunities. There were an estimated 7,000 tourist arrivals in 1983, when tourist receipts were about US $4m.

Office National Centrafricain du Tourisme (OCATOUR): BP 655, Bangui; tel. 61-45-66.

CHAD

Introductory Survey

Location, Climate, Language, Religion, Flag, Capital

The Republic of Chad is a land-locked country in north central Africa, bordered to the north by Libya, to the south by the Central African Republic, to the west by Niger and Cameroon and to the east by Sudan. The climate is hot and arid in the northern desert regions of the Sahara but very wet (annual rainfall 500 cm) in the south. The official languages are French and Arabic, and various African languages are also widely spoken. Almost one-half of the population are Muslims, living in the north, while most of the remainder follow animistic beliefs. About 6% are Christians. The national flag (proportions 3 by 2) has three equal vertical stripes, of blue, yellow and red. The capital is N'Djamena (formerly called Fort-Lamy).

Recent History

Formerly a province of French Equatorial Africa, Chad became an autonomous state within the French Community in November 1958. François (later Ngarta) Tombalbaye, a southerner and leader of the Parti progressiste tchadien (PPT), became Prime Minister in March 1959. Chad achieved independence on 11 August 1960, with Tombalbaye as President. In 1962 President Tombalbaye banned all opposition parties and Chad became a single-party state. Civil disturbances began in 1963, with riots in the capital, and a full-scale rebellion broke out in 1965, concentrated mainly in the north, which had until that year remained under French military control. The Muslims of northern Chad have traditionally been in conflict with their black southern compatriots, who are generally animists or Christians. The banned Front de libération nationale du Tchad (FROLINAT, founded in Sudan in 1966) assumed leadership of the revolt, which was quelled in 1968 with French military intervention. In 1973 several leading figures of the regime, including the Army Chief of Staff, Gen. Félix Malloum, were imprisoned on conspiracy charges. The PPT was replaced by a new political party, the Mouvement national pour la révolution culturelle et sociale (MNRCS).

In April 1975 Tombalbaye was killed in an army coup, led by the acting Chief of Staff. Gen. Malloum was released and became President at the head of a Supreme Military Council. The provisional Government dissolved the MNRCS and launched appeals for national reconciliation. Some rebel leaders rallied to the regime, but FROLINAT maintained its opposition, receiving clandestine support from Libya, which since 1973 had occupied the 'Aozou strip' of northern Chad, covering about 114,000 sq km (44,000 sq miles) and believed to contain significant deposits of uranium. The Libyan claim to sovereignty over the Aozou region was based upon an unratified treaty signed between Vichy France and Italy in 1943.

In early 1978 FROLINAT unified its command under a Revolutionary Council, led by Goukouni Oueddei, and gained large areas of territory from government forces before its advance was halted following the arrival of French reinforcements. In August a former leader of FROLINAT, Hissène Habré, was appointed Prime Minister. Disagreements between Habré and Malloum soon arose, and by December central authority had completely broken down. Fighting between government forces and troops loyal to Habré broke out in February 1979. Habré's Forces armées du nord (FAN) took control of most of the capital, forcing Malloum to resign in March and to flee the country, leaving responsibility with the commander of the gendarmerie, Lt-Col (later Col) Wadal Abdelkader Kamougue. French troops were sent to Chad, and a cease-fire was agreed.

In April 1979, following the failure of reconciliation conferences held in Kano, Nigeria, a provisional government was formed, comprising members of FROLINAT, FAN, the MPLT (Mouvement populaire pour la libération du Tchad, also known as the 'Troisième armée') and the government armed forces (Forces armées tchadiennes—FAT). Lol Mahamat Shawwa of the MPLT was appointed President, while Goukouni Oueddei became Minister of the Interior and Habré Minister of Defence. This regime, which excluded the extreme factions of the south (now led by Kamougue) was denounced both by dissatisfied Chadian factions and by several neighbouring countries.

Sporadic fighting continued, and there was dissension within the Government between Goukouni and Habré. In August 1979, at a conference held in Lagos, an agreement was reached between 11 Chadian factions for the formation of a Gouvernement d'union nationale de transition (GUNT) under the presidency of Goukouni, with Lt-Col Kamougue of the southern extremists as Vice-President. A Council of Ministers, representing the various factions, was appointed in November.

Goukouni's authority was undermined by continual disagreements with Habré's forces, and in March 1980 the fragile truce was broken and fighting began once again in the capital. Despite numerous attempts at mediation and cease-fire agreements, the conflict remained unresolved; in May all French troops withdrew from Chad, and in June a treaty of friendship was signed between Col Muammar al-Qaddafi of Libya and a representative of President Goukouni, without the prior consent of the GUNT. During October 1980 Libyan forces intervened directly in the hostilities, resulting in the defeat of Habré and the retreat of the FAN from N'Djamena. A Libyan force of 15,000 men was established in the country.

In January 1981 proposals were made for a gradual merger of Chad and Libya, but the Libyan presence in Chad was unpopular, and guerrilla warfare continued. Habré and other FAN leaders were sentenced to death *in absentia* in June. By September President Goukouni had finally renounced the proposed merger, and in November Libyan troops were withdrawn at Goukouni's request. An inter-African peace-keeping force was installed under the auspices of the OAU, which drafted proposals for a cease-fire and the holding of elections.

In early 1982, however, these proposals were abandoned, as President Goukouni refused to negotiate with Habré. In an attempt to strengthen the GUNT, weakened by internal conflicts, Goukouni formed a Conseil d'Etat, appointed a Prime Minister and reshuffled the Council of Ministers in May. Fighting continued to intensify, however, and N'Djamena fell to Habré's forces on 7 June. The formation of a new Conseil d'Etat, with Habré as head of state, was announced on 19 June. By the end of that month the OAU force had withdrawn fully from Chad. A provisional constitution, the *acte fondamental*, was promulgated in September, and in October Habré took the oath as President and formed a new government. Goukouni, who had fled to Cameroon and thence to Algeria, continued to contest Habré's leadership. With Libyan support, his troops regained control over parts of northern Chad, and in October a rival 'government of national salvation' was formed by GUNT supporters in Bardai. Habré's regime succeeded in obtaining international recognition, having gained the support of the majority of African states by mid-1983.

In January 1983 some members of Kamougue's FAT joined the ranks of the FAN to form a new national army (FANT). In June Goukouni's rebel forces, with Libyan support, captured the northern administrative centre of Faya-Largeau. Following appeals for international assistance, Habré obtained US $10m. of military aid from the USA, as well as a contingent of Zairean paratroopers and increased logistical aid from France. Government troops counter-attacked and repossessed Faya-Largeau at the end of July, but, after prolonged bombing by Libyan aircraft, the town again fell to the rebel forces in August. In response to Habré's renewed appeals, France intervened with 'Operation Manta', sending 3,000 troops to Chad. President Mitterrand's proposal for the establishment of a federation, as a solution to the dispute, was rejected by a spokesman for Goukouni Oueddei. An 'interdiction line' separating the warring factions was set up by France along latitude 15°N, and in mid-September it was announced that fighting had ceased.

In January 1984 a meeting of representatives from all factions was held in Addis Ababa under the aegis of the OAU. The talks collapsed, however, following a disagreement over protocol and representation. Renewed fighting in January led to the shooting-down of a French aircraft and the death of its pilot, following which France decided to extend the limit of the defensive zone 100 km northwards, to latitude 16°N. In an attempt to consolidate his political power, Habré dissolved his FROLINAT-FAN faction in June 1984 and created a new official political party, the Union nationale pour l'indépendance et la révolution (UNIR). A government reshuffle followed in July. Major dissension among anti-Habré forces became increasingly evident during 1984 with the formation, by GUNT factions, of new 'splinter groups' and an anti-Goukouni movement.

Following a proposal in May 1984 by the Libyan leader, Col Qaddafi, for a simultaneous withdrawal of Libyan 'support elements' and French troops, a Franco-Libyan agreement was reached in September over joint evacuation of both countries' military forces. In mid-November it was announced that both countries' troops had been evacuated. US and Chadian intelligence reports, however, maintained that 3,000 Libyan troops were still in the country, in contravention of the agreement. At the Franco-African summit in December 1984, President Mitterrand declared that France would not use force to drive Libyans from northern Chad, but would intervene if Libyan forces moved south of the 16th parallel.

The civil war in southern Chad between Habré's forces and various guerrilla commandos ('codos') escalated in October and November 1984, with the Government reportedly carrying out summary executions in an attempt to reassert its authority in the area. To escape the increasing violence, more than 50,000 Chadians were estimated to have fled to Sudan, the Central African Republic and Cameroon. In an attempt to ease unrest in the south, Habré made several tours of the area in early 1985: calm finally returned at the end of the year, when 1,200 'codos' responded to financial inducements and rallied to the government side.

At a summit meeting held in Benin in August 1985, factions loyal to Goukouni formed a Conseil suprême de la révolution (CSR), which comprised members of seven leading anti-Government groupings. Subsequent to the realignment of the 'codos', a number of former opposition factions also declared support for the Habré regime, including the Front démocratique du Tchad (FDT), a grouping of four factions hostile to both Habré and Goukouni established in March 1985 under the leadership of Gen. Djibril Négué Djogo, and the Comité d'action et de concertation (CAC-CDR), which had split from the pro-Goukouni Conseil Démocratique Révolutionnaire (CDR) early in 1985. In response, Habré announced the release of 122 political prisoners in January 1986.

In February 1986 hostilities resumed with attacks by Libyan-backed GUNT forces on government positions to the south of the French interdiction line. Habré appealed to France for increased military aid, and a few days later French military aircraft, operating from the Central African Republic, bombed a Libyan-built airstrip at Ouadi Doum, north-east of Faya-Largeau. A retaliatory strike on N'Djamena airport caused minor damage, and France established a defensive air-strike force in the capital, an intervention which was codenamed 'Opération Epervier'. Further rebel incursions across the 'red line' in March were, however, contained by government forces alone. The USA provided US $10m. in supplementary military aid to the Habré regime during the period of hostilities, which ceased temporarily following the destruction in mid-March, by government forces, of a rebel base at Chicha, north of latitude 16°N. OAU-convened reconciliation talks, scheduled to take place in Loubomo (Congo) at the end of March, failed to materialize when Goukouni refused to attend. In the same month Habré reshuffled his Government, bringing several former opponents into the Council of Ministers.

Goukouni's failure to attend the Loubomo talks prompted the resignation, in June 1986, of GUNT vice-president Col Wadal Abdelkader Kamougue, who rallied to Habré in February 1987, joining the Government in August of that year. In August 1986 Acheikh Ibn Oumar's CDR withdrew its support from Goukouni. In October, following the onset of armed clashes in the Tibesti region between the CDR (with Libyan backing) and his own Forces armées populaires (FAP), Goukouni declared himself willing to seek a reconciliation with Habré. In November he was replaced as president of a reconstituted GUNT (comprising seven of the original 11 factions, and also known as the néo-GUNT) by Acheikh Ibn Oumar at a Libyan-supported meeting in Cotonou (Benin).

In December 1986 clashes began in the Tibesti region between Libyan troops and the now pro-Habré FAP. FANT forces moved into northern Chad, and both France and the USA increased their logistical support, with French aircraft crossing the 16th parallel to parachute arms and supplies to besieged government troops. By the end of January 1987, Habré's forces had recaptured a number of strategic targets in the north of the country, while France had responded to a Libyan military incursion in southern Chad by launching a second retaliatory air attack on Ouadi Doum. In early February France announced that it had 'redeployed' a number of troops to positions just south of the 16th parallel, and in March, following intense fighting, the Ouadi Doum airbase fell to Habré's troops. Faya-Largeau was subsequently evacuated by the retreating Libyan army, and in May it was announced that Libya was transferring control of its remaining positions south of the Aozou strip to the FAP. France subsequently extended its logistical and humanitarian aid to cover most of northern Chad, while maintaining a reduced defensive force in the south of the country.

During June and July 1987 Habré made official visits to both the USA and France. Both countries pledged further military and financial assistance, and Chad subsequently received deliveries of anti-tank missiles and anti-tank weapons from the USA. However, France advised caution regarding the resolution of the conflict with Libya over the Aozou region by military means, urging that the issue be submitted to international arbitration. In early August Habré's forces attacked and occupied the town of Aozou, the administrative centre of the disputed region. Twenty days later, following a series of Libyan air raids on Chadian targets, Col Qaddafi's forces recaptured the town, and the FANT withdrew to positions in the Tibesti. The attempt to gain control of Aozou was followed, in early September, by an incursion by Habré's forces into southern Libya, where they attacked the airbase of Maaten-es-Sarra, claimed to be an important operating point for Libyan raids into Chad. A Libyan military aircraft was subsequently shot down over N'Djamena by the French defensive force, and French positions at Abéché were bombed. In protest at this offensive, the French Government suspended supplies of arms to Chad until December, when President Mitterrand renewed his support for the Habré regime.

Efforts at mediation by the OAU intensified as the conflict escalated, and on 11 September 1987 a cease-fire took effect. In November, however, Chad claimed that FANT forces had clashed with members of Qaddafi's Islamic Legion near the Sudanese border. (The presence of Islamic Legion troops in the Darfur region of Sudan led to a deterioration of relations between that country and Chad in 1987 and 1988.) It was also claimed that Libyan aircraft were repeatedly violating Chadian airspace. Further engagements took place in November, near Goz Beïda, and to the east of Ennedi in March 1988.

In November 1987 the UN General Assembly refused to debate the question of the sovereignty of the Aozou region, concluding that the resolution of the dispute was the responsibility of the OAU. A meeting between the heads of state of the two countries, proposed by the OAU *ad hoc* committee on the dispute, was scheduled for 24 May 1988, after having been postponed several times. On the eve of the summit, it was announced that Col Qaddafi would not be attending, in protest at Chad's treatment of Libyan prisoners of war. On 25 May, however, in a speech delivered in Tripoli to commemorate the 25th anniversary of the foundation of the OAU, the Libyan leader announced his willingness to recognize the Habré regime. Qaddafi also invited Habré and Goukouni Oueddei to hold reconciliation talks in Libya, and offered to provide financial aid for the reconstruction of bombed towns in northern Chad. Habré reacted with caution to these proposals, but announced that Chad was prepared to restore diplomatic relations with Libya, which had been severed in 1982. Negotiations between the ministers of foreign affairs of the two countries, held in Gabon in July 1988, were largely inconclusive: although agreement was reached, in principle, regarding the re-establishment of diplomatic relations, the questions of the sovereignty of the Aozou region, the fate of Libyan prisoners of war in Chad and the future security of common borders remained unresolved. In October it was announced that diplomatic relations, at ambassadorial level, were to be resumed. The two countries also undertook to seek a peaceful solution to the territorial dispute, and to co-operate with the OAU committee appointed for that purpose. However, despite this apparent improvement in relations between the two countries, Chad continued to accuse Libya of violating the cease-fire agreement, and in December it was announced that a military engagement had taken place between Chadian and pro-Libyan forces near the border with Sudan.

In July 1987 reconciliation talks between UNIR and Goukouni Oueddei, who in April had appealed for the universal recognition of Habré as Chad's legitimate head of state, were reported to have failed. The cohesion of the GUNT was further undermined in 1988 by a dispute between Goukouni and Acheikh Ibn Oumar regarding the leadership of the movement. Several former opposition parties announced their support for the Habré regime, while the GUNT was reconstituted under Goukouni. In November, following the conclusion of a peace agreement with UNIR, Acheikh Ibn Oumar and his supporters returned to Chad. Meanwhile, in July a presidential decree established a committee to draft a new constitution.

Chad's relations with France underwent some strain in October 1988, when that country's Minister of Defence, Jean-Pierre Chevènement, questioned the future of the French military presence in Chad. In December President Mitterrand of France implied that the role of the 'Opération Epervier' force was likely to be reduced in 1989, putting into doubt the future of a project, announced in May 1988, to construct an airport at Faya-Largeau, with French financial assistance, which would be capable of accommodating military, as well as civilian, aircraft.

Government

The Government, which came to power through civil war, comprises a President and a Council of Ministers, appointed and led by the President. Executive and legislative power is exercised by the Council, and for administrative purposes the country is divided into 14 prefectures. In October 1982 a Conseil national consultatif was formed, consisting of two representatives of each prefecture and two representatives of the city of N'Djamena.

Defence

In January 1983 the various armed groups in Chad which rallied to Hissène Habré's Forces armées du nord (FAN) were merged to form a new national army, the Forces armées nationales tchadiennes (FANT). The total strength of the armed forces in June 1988 was estimated to be 17,200 (army 17,000, air force 200). In addition, there are paramilitary forces of approximately 5,700 men. Under defence agreements with France, the army receives technical and other aid: France had an estimated 1,900 troops in Chad in mid-1988. The USA is also a major provider of military aid. The gendarmerie, once part of the army, has been dissolved and replaced by a military police unit. Military service of three years is compulsory for men and women. Defence expenditure (excluding French and US subventions) in 1987 was an estimated 10,307m. francs CFA.

Economic Affairs

In recent years, economic difficulties in Chad, caused by unfavourable climatic conditions, an inadequate infrastructure and a paucity of known natural resources, have been exacerbated by continual civil strife. In 1987, according to estimates by the World Bank, Chad's gross national product (GNP), measured at average 1985-87 prices, was US $805m., equivalent to $150 per head (one of the lowest per caput levels in the world). It was estimated that GNP per head increased at an average rate of 2.5% annually, in real terms, between 1980 and 1987. In 1988 a report published by the Ministry of Planning and Co-operation predicted a significant recovery for the country's economy, with gross domestic product (GDP) increasing by an estimated 4.9% in that year.

Chad's economy is essentially one of subsistence, based on agriculture, stock-breeding and fishing, which together occupied an estimated 83% of the working population in 1980. The major cash crop is cotton, which has traditionally provided the basis for Chad's principal industry and around 80% of all export earnings. The country's annual output of seed (unginned) cotton declined from a peak of 174,062 metric tons in 1975/76 to 71,391 tons in 1981/82, when fighting in the southern cotton-growing area affected production severely. In 1983/84 output reached 158,491 tons, largely as a result of a 31% increase in the area under cultivation; it collapsed, however, to 98,417 tons in the drought year 1984/85. A recovery to around 105,000 tons in 1985/86 failed to offset the effects of the sudden fall in world cotton prices which occurred during that season (exacerbated by the fall in the value of the US dollar in early 1986) and which led the Habré Government, in June 1986, to introduce an emergency programme which was to be financed largely through external aid sources, such as the African Development Bank (ADB), in an attempt to avert the possible collapse of Chad's most important industry. The first phase of the programme, the total cost of which was put at US $47.4m., was to concentrate on the radical restructuring of the state-owned monopoly, Société Cotonnière du Tchad (COTONTCHAD). Under the second phase, beginning in mid-1988, price controls were introduced. As a result of this rationalization of the cotton sector, output recovered in 1987/88, to 127,000 tons, with a further increase forecast for 1988/89. The value of cotton exports was expected to rise from 13,000m. francs CFA in 1987 to 20,000m. in 1988.

Sugar cane is cultivated at a 6,000-ha agro-industrial complex at Banda, and is processed at a refinery operated by the Société nationale sucrière du Tchad. Annual domestic capacity is 30,000 tons of raw sugar, but production fell from an estimated 22,000 metric tons in 1984 to 15,000 tons in 1985.

Despite government efforts to protect agriculture by irrigation and reafforestation, crops have frequently been threatened by recurring drought. N'Djamena registered only 260mm of rain in 1984, compared with its normal annual average of 500–600mm, and the area of Lake Chad was reduced to one-third of its normal size. An estimated 2,000 Chadians died of starvation between August and October 1984, as famine spread to the normally fertile southern regions. Cereal production in 1987/88 amounted to 539,000 tons, while production was forecast at 550,000 tons in 1988/89, owing to exceptionally high rainfall levels in mid-1988. However, the cereal crop was threatened in that year by an infestation of locusts in north-west Africa. Lake Chad and the Logone-Chari basin are well stocked with fish and normally produce more than 100,000 tons annually. Livestock usually accounts for about one-fifth of Chad's GDP, and is the most important export after cotton. An estimated 80% of meat exports, however, are smuggled out of the country, depriving the Government of substantial tax revenue. The drought in 1984 severely depleted cattle stocks, with an estimated 200,000 head being lost. In mid-1988 the International Development Association (IDA), an affiliate of the World Bank, approved a credit of US $18.6m. in support of a five-year national livestock project, costing $37.2m., which aims to achieve sustained increases in livestock production, producer income and tax revenue for the Government. Export procedures were also to be reviewed under the terms of the project. Earnings from cattle exports were expected to increase from 12,700m. francs CFA in 1987 to 13,500m. in 1988.

Industry is almost entirely based on agriculture, with manufacturing accounting for only 7% of GDP in 1983. Textile production is the most important sector, followed by food and tobacco. There are proven reserves of petroleum in the Kanem region, north of Lake Chad, but development has been slow, owing to the war. In 1988 an agreement was signed with a US company, Hunt International Petroleum Company, regarding the future exploration and exploitation of petroleum reserves to the west of Lake Chad. There are also believed to be substantial deposits of uranium and manganese in the disputed northern territory.

The Habré Government's draft budget for 1988 forecast total expenditure of 25,600m. francs CFA, with revenue at 17,900m. francs CFA. The 1986 budget deficit was equivalent to 19.2% of GDP in that year, compared with a ratio of 9.9% in 1985. Chad's external public debt rose from an estimated US $150m. in 1985 to an estimated $172m. (equivalent to 21.2% of GNP) in 1986. The debt-service ratio, however, was only 2.2% of export earnings in 1986. With exports and imports predicted to total 41,900m. and 89,400m. francs CFA respectively in 1988, the trade deficit was expected to reach 47,500m. francs CFA, compared with 45,000m. in 1987.

In recent years, Chad has relied heavily on foreign aid, including emergency food aid, supplied by the UN's World Food Programme and international donors. Multilateral assistance has also been given to agricultural and communications development projects. In 1986 the African Development Fund (ADF) granted a loan of US $12.4m. towards an irrigation project in the Mamdi region, where it is hoped to cultivate maize and wheat. The total cost of the project, due to be completed in 1991, has been estimated at $25.3m. France is the main trading partner and the principal supplier of non-military aid, providing a total of 18,000m. francs CFA in budgetary aid in 1987. The USA has also become a major donor, contributing US $25m. in emergency military aid alone between December 1986 and April 1987. In July 1988 a medium-term financial rehabilitation programme was announced, to supersede the structural adjustment programme agreed with the IMF in 1987. The new programme, to be supported by a credit of US $16.2m. from the IDA and $27.9m. from the IDA's special facility for sub-Saharan Africa, envisaged significant structural changes to the country's economy, including a three-year investment programme for the agriculture, transport infrastructure, industry and energy sectors, together with tax reforms and improvements in the efficiency of budgetary procedures.

Social Welfare

An Employment Code guarantees a minimum wage and other rights for employees. There are four hospitals, 28 medical centres and several hundred dispensaries. In 1978 there were 3,373 beds in government-administered hospital establishments (one per 1,278 inhabitants), while only 90 physicians were employed in official medical services. A development programme was launched in 1986 by UNICEF, at an estimated cost of US $30m.

Education

Education is officially compulsory for six years between eight and 14 years of age. Primary education begins at the age of six and lasts for six years. Secondary education, from the age of 12, lasts for seven years, comprising a first cycle of four years and a second of three years. In 1984 enrolment at primary schools was equivalent to 38% of children in the primary age-group (55% of boys; 21% of girls), while the comparable ratio for secondary enrolment was only 6% (11% of boys; 2% of girls). The Université du Tchad was opened at N'Djamena in 1971, and there are several technical colleges. In 1985, according to estimates by UNESCO, the average rate of adult illiteracy was 74.7% (males 59.5%; females 89.1%). In 1988 the International Development Association (IDA) gave US $22m., in support of a programme to reconstruct schools in areas affected by the conflict with Libya, and to provide improved teacher-training facilities.

Public Holidays

1989: 2 January (for New Year), 27 March (Easter Monday), 1 May (Labour Day), 7 May* (Id al-Fitr, end of Ramadan), 15 May (Whit Monday), 25 May ('Liberation of Africa', anniversary of the OAU's foundation), 14 July* (Id al-Adha, Feast of the Sacrifice), 11 August (Independence Day), 15 August (Assumption), 13 October* (Maloud, Birth of the Prophet), 1 November (All Saints' Day), 28 November (Proclamation of the Republic), 25 December (Christmas).

1990: 1 January (New Year), 16 April (Easter Monday), 27 April* (Id al-Fitr, end of Ramadan), 1 May (Labour Day), 25 May ('Liberation of Africa', anniversary of the OAU's foundation), 4 June (Whit Monday), 4 July* (Id al-Adha, Feast of the Sacrifice), 11 August (Independence Day), 15 August (Assumption), 2 October* (Maloud, Birth of the Prophet), 1 November (All Saints' Day), 28 November (Proclamation of the Republic), 25 December (Christmas).

* These holidays are dependent on the Islamic lunar calendar and may vary by one or two days from the dates given.

Weights and Measures

The metric system is officially in force.

Statistical Survey

Source (unless otherwise stated): Direction de la Statistique, des Etudes Economiques et Démographiques, BP 453, N'Djamena.

Area and Population

AREA, POPULATION AND DENSITY

Area (sq km)	
Land	1,259,200
Inland waters	24,800
Total	1,284,000*
Population (sample survey)	
December 1963–August 1964	3,254,000†
Population (mid-year estimates)	
1983	4,830,000
1984	4,944,000
1985	5,061,000
Density (per sq km) at mid-1985	3.9

* 495,800 sq miles.
† Including areas not covered by the survey.

PREFECTURES

	Area (sq km)	Population (1984)	Density (per sq km)
Batha	88,800	410,000	4.6
Biltine	46,850	200,000	4.3
Borkou-Ennedi-Tibesti (BET)	600,350	103,000	0.2
Chari-Baguirmi	82,910	719,000	8.7
Guéra	58,950	234,000	4.0
Kanem	114,520	234,000	2.0
Lac	22,320	158,000	7.1
Logone Occidental	8,695	324,000	37.3
Logone Oriental	28,035	350,000	12.5
Mayo-Kebbi	30,105	757,000	25.1
Moyen-Chari	45,180	582,000	12.9
Ouadaï	76,240	411,000	5.4
Salamat	63,000	121,000	1.9
Tandjilé	18,045	341,000	18.9
Total	**1,284,000**	**4,944,000**	**3.9**

PRINCIPAL TOWNS (estimated population in 1979)

N'Djamena (capital)*	402,000	Bongor	69,000
Sarh*	124,000	Doba	64,000
Moundou	87,000	Laï	58,000
		Abéché	47,000

* Fort-Lamy was renamed N'Djamena in November 1973, and Fort-Archambault was renamed Sarh in July 1972.

CHAD

Statistical Survey

BIRTHS AND DEATHS (UN estimates, annual averages)

	1970–75	1975–80	1980–85
Birth rate (per 1,000)	44.6	44.1	44.2
Death rate (per 1,000)	24.9	23.1	21.4

Source: UN, *World Population Prospects: Estimates and Projections as Assessed in 1984.*

ECONOMICALLY ACTIVE POPULATION
(ILO estimates, '000 persons at mid-1980)

	Males	Females	Total
Agriculture, etc.	1,043	318	1,361
Industry	72	4	76
Services	154	44	197
Total	1,269	366	1,635

Source: ILO, *Economically Active Population Estimates and Projections, 1950–2025.*

Mid-1986 (estimates in '000): Agriculture 1,430; Total 1,825 (Source: FAO, *Production Yearbook*).

Agriculture

PRINCIPAL CROPS ('000 metric tons)

	1984	1985	1986
Wheat	1	5†	2*
Rice (paddy)	2	22†	25†
Maize	22	39†	53†
Millet and sorghum	254	526†	624†
Other cereals	36	113†	48†
Potatoes*	13	14	14
Sweet potatoes*	38	40	41
Cassava (Manioc)*	280	290	306
Yams*	200	210	219
Taro (Coco yam)*	8	9	9
Dry beans*	40	42	42
Other pulses*	17	18	18
Groundnuts (in shell)*	90	90	90
Sesame seed*	11	11	11
Cottonseed	60†	60*	40*
Cotton (lint)†	36	40	27
Dry onions*	13	14	14
Other vegetables*	55	60	63
Dates*	30	32	33
Mangoes*	30	32	32
Other fruit*	45	50	52
Sugar cane*	270	250	290

* FAO estimates. † Unofficial figures.

Source: FAO, *Production Yearbook.*

LIVESTOCK
('000 head, year ending September)

	1984	1985	1986
Cattle	4,784	4,899	5,017†
Goats	2,480*	2,545†	2,620†
Sheep	2,480*	2,545	2,620†
Pigs	11	11	12
Horses*	150	150	150
Asses*	255	255	255
Camels	492	539	572

Poultry *(million): 3 in 1984; 3 in 1985; 4 in 1986.

* FAO estimates.   † Unofficial figures.

Source: FAO, *Production Yearbook.*

LIVESTOCK PRODUCTS (FAO estimates, '000 metric tons)

	1984	1985	1986
Total meat	58	63	68
Beef and veal	32	36	40
Mutton and lamb	10	11	11
Goats' meat	9	9	9
Poultry meat	3	3	3
Cows' milk	105	108	110
Sheep's milk	9	10	10
Goats' milk	15	15	16
Butter	0.3	0.3	0.3
Hen eggs	3.0	3.1	3.1
Cattle hides	6.2	6.6	7.3
Sheep skins	2.1	2.1	2.1
Goat skins	1.7	1.7	1.7

Source: FAO, *Production Yearbook.*

Forestry

ROUNDWOOD REMOVALS
(FAO estimates, '000 cubic metres, excluding bark)

	1984	1985	1986
Sawlogs, etc.	2	2	2
Other industrial wood	491	502	515
Fuel wood	2,989	3,062	3,137
Total	3,482	3,566	3,654

Source: FAO, *Yearbook of Forest Products.*

Fishing

('000 metric tons, live weight)

	1984	1985	1986
Total catch (freshwater fishes)	110	115	110

Source: FAO, *Yearbook of Fishery Statistics.*

Industry

SELECTED PRODUCTS
('000 metric tons, unless otherwise indicated)

	1983	1984	1985
Salted, dried or smoked fish*	20	19	19
Wheat flour*	1	1	1
Raw sugar*	22	22	15
Electric energy (million kWh)	65	65	65

* Provisional or estimated figures.

Source: UN, *Industrial Statistics Yearbook.*

CHAD

Finance

CURRENCY AND EXCHANGE RATES

Monetary Units
100 centimes = 1 franc de la Coopération financière en Afrique centrale (CFA).

Denominations
Coins: 1, 5, 10, 25, 50, 100 and 500 francs CFA.
Notes: 500, 1,000, 5,000 and 10,000 francs CFA.

French Franc, Sterling and Dollar Equivalents
(30 September 1988)
 1 French franc = 50 francs CFA;
 £1 sterling = 538.6 francs CFA;
 US $1 = 318.5 francs CFA;
 1,000 francs CFA = £1.857 = $3.140.

Average Exchange Rate (francs CFA per US $)
 1985   449.26
 1986   346.30
 1987   300.54

GENERAL BUDGETS (million francs CFA)

Revenue	1983
Direct taxation	1,808
Poll tax	1,160
Company taxation	415
Indirect taxation	6,098
Customs receipts	5,003
Production and consumption taxes	880
Other revenue	383
Administration	260
Land	92
Extraordinary revenue	41
Total	**8,330**

Expenditure	1983	1984
Public debt interest	10	10
Services	31,946	32,844
Defence	15,000	17,496
Education	5,327	4,106
Interior	2,629	2,205
Public health	1,734	1,431
Community projects	3,440	3,427
State intervention	1,354	1,354
Total	**36,750**	**37,635**

1984 Budget: Revenue 11,200 million francs CFA.
1985 Budget: Revenue 12,434 million francs CFA; Expenditure 21,222 million francs CFA.
1986 Budget: Proposed revenue 18,700 million francs CFA; Proposed expenditure 22,700 million francs CFA.
1987 Budget: Proposed revenue 17,800 million francs CFA; Proposed expenditure 25,400 million francs CFA.
1988 Budget: Proposed revenue 17,900 million francs CFA; Proposed expenditure 25,600 million francs CFA.

CENTRAL BANK RESERVES (US $ million at 31 December)

	1985	1986	1987
Gold*	3.60	4.36	5.37
IMF special drawing rights	3.87	2.07	9.01
Reserve position in IMF	0.29	0.32	0.37
Foreign exchange	29.31	13.52	42.73
Total	**37.06**	**20.27**	**57.48**

* Valued at market-related prices.

Source: IMF, *International Financial Statistics*.

MONEY SUPPLY ('000 million francs CFA at 31 December)

	1985	1986	1987
Currency outside banks	47.35	46.67	46.70
Demand deposits at commercial and development banks	20.79	22.34	23.68
Checking deposits at post office	0.20	0.13	0.22
Total money	**68.34**	**69.14**	**70.60**

NATIONAL ACCOUNTS
(estimates, million francs CFA at current prices)
Gross Domestic Product by Economic Activity

	1981	1982	1983
Agriculture, hunting, forestry and fishing	92,940	110,610	121,630
Mining and quarrying	1,300	1,230	1,220
Manufacturing	16,450	16,440	16,820
Electricity, gas and water	1,070	1,070	1,070
Construction	3,390	3,080	2,950
Trade, restaurants and hotels	56,570	51,770	53,010
Transport, storage and communications	4,820	4,410	4,330
Finance, insurance, real estate and business services	1,580	1,440	1,460
Public administration and defence	28,360	27,580	30,430
Other services	2,780	2,550	2,540
GDP at factor cost	**209,260**	**220,180**	**235,460**
Indirect taxes, *less* subsidies	6,080	6,020	7,160
GDP in purchasers' values	**215,340**	**226,200**	**242,620**

Source: UN Economic Commission for Africa, *African Statistical Yearbook*.

BALANCE OF PAYMENTS (US $ million)

	1985	1986	1987
Merchandise exports f.o.b.	61.8	98.6	111.4
Merchandise imports f.o.b.	−166.3	−212.1	−260.9
Trade balance	**−104.5**	**−113.5**	**−149.5**
Exports of services	37.6	48.0	57.0
Imports of services	−161.2	−178.1	−219.2
Balance on goods and services	**−228.0**	**−243.6**	**−311.7**
Private unrequited transfers (net)	6.8	−5.4	−11.9
Government unrequited transfers (net)	133.9	189.5	240.4
Current balance	**−87.2**	**−59.4**	**−83.3**
Direct capital investment (net)	53.4	27.8	4.0
Other long-term capital (net)	14.1	21.5	80.6
Short-term capital (net)	2.1	−16.4	10.4
Net errors and omissions	−6.6	8.5	7.9
Total (net monetary movements)	**−24.2**	**−18.0**	**19.7**
Valuation changes (net)	7.2	−0.9	4.6
Exceptional financing (net)	2.4	2.9	1.9
Official financing (net)	−0.4	−1.5	—
Changes in reserves	**−15.0**	**−17.4**	**26.1**

Source: IMF, *International Financial Statistics*.

External Trade

PRINCIPAL COMMODITIES (million francs CFA)

Imports	1983
Beverages	71.7
Cereal products	2,272.1
Sugar, confectionery, chocolate	292.7
Petroleum products	2,280.5
Textiles, clothing, etc.	392.1
Pharmaceuticals, chemicals	1,561.9
Minerals and metals	311.2
Machinery	843.2
Transport equipment	987.6
Electrical equipment	773.3
Total (incl. others)	13,539.6

Total imports (million francs CFA): 29,349 in 1981; 35,701 in 1982; 74,802 in 1984 (Source: IMF, *International Financial Statistics*).

Exports	1983
Live cattle	49.5
Meat	23.5
Fish	2.0
Oil-cake	8.1
Natron	8.1
Gums and resins	0.4
Hides and skins	16.6
Raw cotton	3,753.7
Total (incl. others)	4,120.0

Total exports (million francs CFA): 22,665 in 1981; 18,968 in 1982; 48,563 in 1984 (Source: IMF, *International Financial Statistics*).

PRINCIPAL TRADING PARTNERS (million francs CFA)

Imports	1973	1974	1975
Belgium/Luxembourg	592.9	762.6	208.8
Cameroon	725.7	932.8	1,364.2
Central African Republic	232.6	285.1	245.4
China, People's Republic	254.8	218.7	289.1
Congo	774.5	474.9	392.4
France	7,728.8	7,642.6	10,597.2
Gabon	489.4	229.4	392.4
Germany, Fed. Republic	410.9	651.0	714.9
Italy	224.7	386.0	1,107.8
Netherlands	232.9	827.9	2,116.3
Nigeria	2,194.3	2,562.4	2,805.1
Senegal	616.0	669.0	594.0
Taiwan	418.7	281.6	412.8
United Kingdom	255.4	373.4	1,542.0
USA	720.8	2,025.1	1,786.7
Total (incl. others)	18,213.5	20,858.3	28,325.2

Source: *Bulletin de Statistique*, Sous-Direction de la Statistique, N'Djamena.

Exports	1973	1974	1975
Cameroon	197.1	128.2	251.7
Central African Republic	208.4	180.4	174.1
Congo	397.9	316.9	492.1
Denmark	44.2	10.9	n.a.
France	215.0	297.6	683.8
Gabon	75.3	64.8	54.6
Germany, Fed. Republic	92.1	10.9	6.2
Libya	129.3	70.5	11.7
Nigeria	538.9	387.8	1,976.1
Spain	54.6	68.2	37.6
United Kingdom	15.3	18.0	3.9
Zaire	121.9	496.5	152.9
Total (incl. others)	8,483.2	9,052.7	10,103.3

1983 exports (million francs CFA): Cameroon 106.3; Central African Republic 35.8; Congo 9.9; France 3,806.9; Nigeria 104.6; Total (incl. others) 4,120.0.

Transport

ROAD TRAFFIC (motor vehicles in use)

	1985
Private cars	2,741
Buses, lorries and coaches	4,000
Tractors	711
Scooters and motorcycles	3,442
Trailers	977
Total	11,871

Source: Ministère des Transports et de l'Aviation Civile.

CIVIL AVIATION (traffic on scheduled services*)

	1982	1983	1984
Kilometres flown ('000)	2,400	2,400	2,400
Passenger-km ('000)	229,000	219,000	220,000
Freight ton-km ('000)	21,600	18,800	17,500
Mail ton-km ('000)	900	900	900

* Including an apportionment of the traffic of Air Afrique.
Source: UN, *Statistical Yearbook*.

Education

(1987)

	Institutions	Teachers	Pupils
Primary	1,139	4,288	300,110
Secondary:			
General	48	1,204	42,066
Teacher training	18	94	2,896
Vocational	7	55	1,080
Higher	4	26	2,038

Source: Ministère de l'Education Nationale.

Directory

The Constitution

A provisional constitution, the *acte fondamental*, was promulgated on 29 September 1982. Work began on the drafting of a new constitution in July 1988.

The Government

HEAD OF STATE

President: HISSÈNE HABRÉ (took office 19 June 1982).

COUNCIL OF MINISTERS
(December 1988)

Minister of National Defence, Veterans and War Victims: HISSÈNE HABRÉ.
Minister of State without Portfolio: DJIDINGAR DONO NGARDOUM.
Minister of Agriculture: Col WADAL ABDELKADER KAMOUGUE.
Minister of the Civil Service: OUDALBAYE NAHAM.
Minister of Culture, Youth and Sports: DJIBRINE HISSEINE GRIENKY.
Minister of the Environment and Tourism: MBAILAO NAIMBAYE LOZIMIAN.
Minister of Finance and Data Processing: MBAILAMDANA NGARNAYAL.
Minister of Food Security and Disaster-stricken Groups: SEID BAUCHE.
Minister of Foreign Affairs: GOUARA LASSOU.
Minister of Information and Civic Orientation: ADOUM MOUSSA SEIF.
Minister of the Interior and Territorial Administration: IBRAHIM MAHAMAT ITNO.
Minister of Justice and Keeper of the Seals: KASSIRE DELWA KOUMAKOYE.
Minister of Labour, Employment and Vocational Training: ROUTOUANG YOMA GOLOM.
Minister of Livestock and Rural Hydraulics: IBN OUMAR MAHAMAT SALET.
Minister of Mines and Energy: MAHAMAT SENOUSSI KHATIR.
Minister of National Education: MAHAMAT NOUR MALLAYE.
Minister of Planning and Co-operation: SOUMAILA MAHAMAT.
Minister of Posts and Telecommunications: ASSILECK HALATA.
Minister of Public Health: Col KOTIGA GUERINA.
Minister of Public Works, Housing and Town Planning: ABDOULAYE DOUTO.
Minister of Social Affairs and Women's Promotion: Mrs RUTH YANEKO ROMBA.
Minister of Trade and Industry: BILAL SOUBIANE.
Minister of Transport and Civil Aviation: Gen. DJIBRIL NÉGUÉ DJOGO.
Minister-adviser to the President: OUANGMOTCHING HOMSALA.
Minister-delegate to the President in charge of General Inspection and State Control: AHMED KOROM.

There are 11 Secretaries of State.

MINISTRIES

Office of the President: N'Djamena; tel. 51-44-37; telex 5201.
Ministry of Agriculture: N'Djamena; tel. 51-37-52.
Ministry of the Civil Service: N'Djamena; tel. 51-56-56.
Ministry of Culture, Youth and Sports: N'Djamena; tel. 51-44-76.
Ministry of the Environment and Tourism: N'Djamena; tel. 51-56-56.
Ministry of Finance and Data Processing: N'Djamena; tel. 51-55-53; telex 5257.
Ministry of Food Security and Disaster-stricken Groups: N'Djamena; tel. 51-36-38.
Ministry of Foreign Affairs: N'Djamena; tel. 51-50-82; telex 5238.
Ministry of Information and Civic Orientation: BP 748, N'Djamena; tel. 51-56-56; telex 5240.
Ministry of the Interior and Territorial Administration: N'Djamena; tel. 51-46-59.
Ministry of Justice: N'Djamena; tel. 51-56-56.
Ministry of Labour, Employment and Vocational Training: N'Djamena; tel. 51-45-26.
Ministry of Livestock and Rural Hydraulics: N'Djamena; tel. 51-59-07.
Ministry of Mines and Energy: N'Djamena; tel. 51-20-96.
Ministry of National Defence, Veterans and War Victims: N'Djamena; tel. 51-58-89.
Ministry of National Education: BP 731, N'Djamena; tel. 51-44-76.
Ministry of Planning and Co-operation: N'Djamena; tel. 51-58-98.
Ministry of Posts and Telecommunications: N'Djamena; tel. 51-42-64; telex 5254.
Ministry of Public Health: N'Djamena; tel. 51-39-60.
Ministry of Public Works, Housing and Town Planning: N'Djamena; tel. 51-20-96.
Ministry of Social Affairs and Women's Promotion: N'Djamena; tel. 51-56-56.
Ministry of Trade and Industry: BP 453, N'Djamena; tel. 51-56-56.
Ministry of Transport and Civil Aviation: N'Djamena; tel. 51-56-56.
Office of the Minister-adviser to the President: N'Djamena; tel. 51-44-37.
Office of the Minister-delegate to the President in charge of General Inspection and State Control: N'Djamena; tel. 51-56-56.

Legislature

The National Assembly and the Economic and Social Council were both dissolved after the coup of 13 April 1975. In October 1982, following the promulgation of the *acte fondamental* (provisional constitution), a National Consultative Council (CNC) was formed, consisting of two representatives from each of Chad's 14 prefectures and two representatives from the capital, N'Djamena, all of whom are appointed by the Head of State.

Political Organizations

Union Nationale pour l'Indépendance et la Révolution (UNIR): N'Djamena; f. 1984 to succeed the cen. cttee of the Forces armées du nord (FAN), a faction of the Front de libération nationale du Tchad (FROLINAT); in control of govt since 1982; cen. cttee of 80 mems; Chair. HISSÈNE HABRÉ; Exec. Sec. GOUARA LASSOU; ancillary organ: Organisation des femmes de l'UNIR; various factions which have professed allegiance to UNIR include:

Comité d'Action et de Concertation du Conseil Démocratique Révolutionnaire (CAC-CDR): f. 1984; fmr intellectual wing of opposition CDR, declared support for Habré Nov. 1985; Pres. MAHAMAT SENOUSSI KHATIR.

Commandos Rouges (Codos): military groups representing southern interests, most of which declared support for Habré in Nov. 1985; Leader Col KOTIGA GUERINA.

Conseil Démocratique Révolutionnaire (CDR): f. 1979, split 1985; declared support for Habré Nov. 1988; Leader ACHEIKH IBN OUMAR; Head of military wing RAKHIS MANNANY.

Forces Armées Occidentales (FAO): splinter group from MPLT; fmr mem. of CSR; declared support for Habré Feb. 1988; Leader TCHARI MAINA AFONO.

Forces Armées Populaires (FAP): co-signatory to formation of CSR in 1985; c. 3,000 mems; declared support for Habré Oct. 1986; Leader HAMID MAUSSAÏ.

Forces Populaires Révolutionnaires (FPR): declared support for Habré Feb. 1988; Leader MADJO ABDELKERIM.

FROLINAT 'fondamental': fmr mem. of CSR; declared support for Habré Dec. 1987; Leader HADJERO SENOUSSI.

FROLINAT 'originel': fmr mem. of CSR; declared support for Habré Sept. 1986; Leader ABDELKADER YACINE.

Front Démocratique du Tchad (FDT): f. 1985 in Paris from four anti-Goukouni opposition groups; declared support for Habré Dec. 1985; Leader Gen. DJIBRIL NÉGUÉ DJOGO.

Rassemblement National Démocratique et Populaire (RNDP): declared support for Habré Jan. 1986; Leader KASSIRE KOUMAKOY.

Rassemblement pour l'Unité et la Démocratie Tchadienne (RUDT): declared support for Habré Jan. 1986; Leader DJIDINGAR DONO NGARDOUM.

Union Nationale Démocratique (UND): declared support for Habré Nov. 1988; Leader FACHO BALAAM.

Union Populaire Tchadienne (UPT): declared support for Habré July 1988; Leader YACOUB MAHAMAT OURADA.

Gouvernement d'Union Nationale de Transition (GUNT): coalition of opposition movements; in control of national govt 1979–82; led by GOUKOUNI OUEDDEI until Nov. 1986 (when the movement was reconstituted under the presidency of ACHEIKH IBN OUMAR) and from March 1988; in December 1988 the movement included the following factions, all of which had been signatories to the establishment of a joint council, the Conseil Suprême de la Révolution (CSR), at Bardai in 1985:

Mouvement Révolutionnaire du Peuple (MRP): mem. of CSR; Leader (vacant); Sec.-Gen. BIRE TITIMAN.

Première Armée: f. 1984; mem. of CSR; Leader MAHAMAT ABBA SAID.

Rassemblement des Forces Patriotiques (RFP): f. 1984; mem. of CSR.

The following opposition groups were also active at December 1988:

Mouvement Populaire pour la Libération du Tchad (Troisième Armée) (MPLT): breakaway group from FAP; left CSR in January 1986; Leader ABOUBAKAR ABEL RAHMANE.

Mouvement pour la Démocratie et le Socialisme au Tchad (MDST): f. 1988; based in Nigeria; Leader MAHAMAT SALEH AHMAT.

Rassemblement Nationaliste Tchadien (RNT): f. 1988; based in Belgium; Leader ISSAKA RAMAT ALHAMDOU.

Union Socialiste Tchadienne (UST): f. 1986; party aiming to negotiate with Habré regime; Leader ABDERAMAN KOULAMALLAH.

Diplomatic Representation

EMBASSIES IN CHAD

Algeria: N'Djamena; tel. 51-38-15; telex 5216; Ambassador: MAMI ABDERRAHMANE.

Central African Republic: BP 115, N'Djamena; tel. 51-32-06; Ambassador: MARTIN KOYOU-KOUMBELE.

China, People's Republic: ave Podes Blanchart, BP 1153, N'Djamena; tel. 51-37-72; telex 5235; Ambassador: YANG YONGRUI.

Egypt: BP 1094, N'Djamena; tel. 51-36-60; telex 5216; Ambassador: AZIZ M. NOUR EL-DIN.

France: BP 431, N'Djamena; tel. 51-25-75; telex 5202; Ambassador: CHRISTIAN DUTHEIL DE LA ROCHÈRE.

Germany, Federal Republic: ave Félix Eboué, BP 893, N'Djamena; tel. 51-30-90; telex 5246; Ambassador: Dr AXEL WEISHAUPT.

Iraq: N'Djamena; tel. 51-22-57; telex 5339; Chargé d'affaires: ALI MAHMOUD HASHIM.

Libya: N'Djamena; Ambassador: GAITH SALEM AN-NASSER.

Nigeria: 35 ave Charles de Gaulle, BP 752, N'Djamena; tel. 51-24-98; telex 5242; Chargé d'affaires: A. M. ALIYU BIU.

Sudan: BP 45, N'Djamena; tel. 51-34-97; telex 5235; Ambassador: TAHA MAKKAWI.

USA: ave Félix Eboué, BP 413, N'Djamena; tel. 51-28-62; telex 5203; Ambassador: ROBERT L. PUGH.

Zaire: ave du 20 août, BP 910, N'Djamena; tel. 51-59-35; telex 5322; Ambassador: Gen. MALU-MALU DHANDA.

Judicial System

The Supreme Court was abolished after the coup of April 1975. There is a Court of Appeal at N'Djamena. Criminal courts sit at N'Djamena, Sarh, Moundou and Abéché, and elsewhere as necessary, and each of these four major towns has a magistrates' court. There are 43 justices of the peace. In October 1976 a permanent court of State Security was established, comprising eight civilian military members.

Religion

It is estimated that 45% of the population are Muslims and 6% Christians, mainly Roman Catholics. Most of the remainder follow animistic beliefs.

ISLAM

Comité Islamique du Tchad: N'Djamena; tel. 51-51-80.

Head of the Islamic Community: Imam MOUSSA IBRAHIM.

CHRISTIANITY

The Roman Catholic Church

Chad comprises one archdiocese and three dioceses. There were an estimated 400,000 adherents at 31 December 1987.

Bishops' Conference: Conférence Episcopale du Tchad, BP 456, N'Djamena; tel. 51-44-43; telex 5360; Pres. Mgr CHARLES VANDAME, Archbishop of N'Djamena.

Archbishop of N'Djamena: Mgr CHARLES VANDAME, Archevêché, BP 456, N'Djamena; tel. 51-44-43; telex 5360.

Protestant Church

Eglise évangélique du Tchad: BP 127, N'Djamena; tel. 51-48-18; a fellowship of churches and missions working in Chad; includes Eglise évangélique au Tchad, Assemblées Chrétiennes, Eglise fraternelle Luthérienne and Eglise évangélique des frères.

BAHÁ'Í FAITH

National Spiritual Assembly: BP 181, N'Djamena; tel. 51-47-05; mems in 1,125 localities.

The Press

Al-Watan: N'Djamena; tel. 51-57-96; govt-owned; weekly.

Bulletin Mensuel de Statistiques du Tchad: BP 453, N'Djamena; monthly.

Comnat: BP 731, N'Djamena; tel. 29-68; publ. by UNESCO National Commission.

Info-Tchad: BP 670, N'Djamena; daily news bulletin issued by Agence Tchadienne de Presse; French.

Informations Economiques: BP 458, N'Djamena; publ. by the Chambre de Commerce, d'Agriculture et d'Industrie; weekly.

Journal Officiel de la République du Tchad: N'Djamena.

NEWS AGENCIES

Agence Tchadienne de Presse (ATP): BP 670, N'Djamena; tel. 51-58-67; telex 5240.

Foreign Bureaux

Agence France-Presse (AFP): BP 83, N'Djamena; tel. 51-54-71; telex 5248; Correspondent ALDOM NADJI TITO.

Reuters (United Kingdom): N'Djamena; tel. 51-56-57; Correspondent ABAKAR ASSIDIC.

Publisher

Government Publishing House: BP 453, N'Djamena.

Radio

There were an estimated 1.1m. radio receivers in use in 1985.

Radiodiffusion Nationale Tchadienne: BP 892, N'Djamena; govt station; programmes in French, Arabic and eight vernacular languages; there are four transmitters; Dir DJEDE KHOURTOU GAMMAR.

Radio Moundou: BP 122, Moundou; daily programmes in French, Sara and Arabic; Dir DJMANANGAR DJAÏNTA.

An anti-Government radio station, Radio Bardai, is operated by GUNT supporters at Bardai, northern Chad.

Finance

(cap. = capital; res = reserves; br. = branch; m. = million; amounts in francs CFA)

BANKING

Central Bank

Banque des Etats de l'Afrique Centrale (BEAC): BP 50, N'Djamena; Headquarters in Yaoundé, Cameroon; tel. 51-41-76; telex

5220; f. 1973 as central bank of issue for mem. states of the Customs and Economic Union of Central Africa (UDEAC), comprising Cameroon, the Central African Republic, Chad, the Congo, Equatorial Guinea and Gabon; cap. 24,000m., res 148,480m. (Dec. 1986); Gov. Casimir Oye-Mba; Dir in Chad Adam Madji; 2 brs.

Other Banks

Banque de Développement du Tchad (BDT): rue Capitaine Ohrel, BP 19, N'Djamena; tel. 51-28-29; f. 1962; cap. 520m.; 58.4% state-owned; Man. Dir Mouta Ali Zezerti.

BIAT: BP 87, N'Djamena; tel. 51-43-14; telex 5228; f. 1980; cap. 450m. (Dec. 1986); 35% state-owned, 65% by Banque Internationale pour l'Afrique Occidentale (France); Pres. Alain Lavelle; Dir-Gen. Philippe Blancard.

Banque Internationale pour le Commerce et l'Industrie du Tchad (BICIT): 15 ave Charles de Gaulle, BP 38, N'Djamena; telex 5233; 40% state-owned, 30.6% by Société Financière pour les Pays d'Outre-Mer, 29.4% by Banque Nationale de Paris; Man. Dir Hisseine Lamine; activities temporarily suspended.

Banque Tchadienne de Crédit et de Dépôts (BTCD): 6 rue Robert-Lévy, BP 461, N'Djamena; tel. 51-41-90; telex 5212; f. 1963; cap. 440m. (Dec. 1986); 40% state-owned, 34% owned by Crédit Lyonnais; Pres. Madengar Beremadji; Man. Dir Mahamat Farris; br. at Moundou.

Bankers' Organizations

Association Professionnelle des Banques au Tchad: N'Djamena.

Conseil National de Crédit: N'Djamena; f. 1965 to formulate a national credit policy and to organize the banking profession.

INSURANCE

Assureurs Conseils Tchadiens Faugère et Jutheau et Cie: N'Djamena; Dir Pierre Hubert.

Société de Représentation d'Assurances et de Réassurances Africaines (SORARAF): N'Djamena; Dir Mme Fournier.

Société Tchadienne d'Assurances et de Réassurances (STAR): BP 914, N'Djamena; tel. 51-56-77; telex 5268; Dir Philippe Sabit.

Trade and Industry

CHAMBER OF COMMERCE

Chambre Consulaire: BP 458, N'Djamena; tel. 51-52-64; f. 1938; Pres. Elie Romba; Sec.-Gen. Saleh Mahamat Rahma; brs at Sarh, Moundou, Bol and Abéché.

DEVELOPMENT ORGANIZATIONS

Caisse Centrale de Coopération Économique: BP 478, N'Djamena; tel. 51-40-71; Dir François Vincent.

Mission Française de Coopération et d'Action Culturelle: BP 898, N'Djamena; tel. 51-42-87; telex 5340; administers bilateral aid from France; Dir Jacques Compagnon.

Office National de Développement Rural (ONDR): BP 896, N'Djamena; tel. 51-48-64; f. 1968; Dir Mickael Djibrael.

Société pour le Développement de la Région du Lac (SODELAC): BP 782, N'Djamena; tel. 51-35-03; telex 5248; f. 1967; cap. 180m. francs CFA; Pres. Cherif Abdelwahab; Dir-Gen. Mahamat Moctar Ali.

TRADE

Office National des Céréales (ONC): BP 21, N'Djamena; tel. 51-37-31; f. 1978; production and marketing of cereals; Dir Ybrahim Mahamat Tidei; 11 regional offices.

Société Nationale de Commercialisation du Tchad (SONACOT): N'Djamena; telex 5227; f. 1965; cap. 150m. francs CFA; 76% state-owned; national marketing, distribution and import-export company; has monopoly of purchase and sale of gum arabic in Chad; Man. Dir Marbrouck Natroud.

TRADE UNION

Union Nationale des Syndicats du Tchad (UNST): N'Djamena; f. 1988, following a merger of the Confédération Syndicale du Tchad (CST) and the Union Nationale des Travailleurs du Tchad (UNATRAT).

Transport

RAILWAYS

In 1962 Chad signed an agreement with Cameroon to extend the Transcameroon railway from N'Gaoundéré to Sarh, a distance of 500 km. Although the Transcameroon reached N'Gaoundéré in 1974, the proposed extension into Chad has been indefinitely postponed. Other possibilities of extending Sudanese and Nigerian lines into Chad are being explored.

ROADS

In 1976 there were 30,725 km of roads, of which 4,628 km were national roads and 3,512 km were secondary roads. There are also some 20,000 km of tracks suitable for motor traffic during the October–July dry season. In July 1986 the World Bank provided a loan of US $21m. towards a major programme to rehabilitate 2,000 km of roads, with the aim of improving the movement of goods within the country. In 1988 the International Development Association (IDA) granted $47m. to support the final stage of the programme: the rehabilitation of the 30-km N'Djamena–Djermaya road and the 146-km N'Djamena–Guelengdeng road. The EEC is helping to fund the construction of a highway leading from N'Djamena to Sarh and Lere, on the Cameroon border; meanwhile, a footbridge over the Logone river was opened in February 1985, thus providing the first all-weather road link with Cameroon.

Coopérative des Transportateurs Tchadiens (CTT): BP 336, N'Djamena; tel. 51-43-55; telex 5225; road haulage; Pres. Saleh Khalifa; brs at Sarh, Moundou, Bangui (CAR), Douala and N'Gaoundéré (Cameroon).

INLAND WATERWAYS

There is a certain amount of traffic on the Chari and Logone rivers which meet just south of N'Djamena. Both routes, from Sarh to N'Djamena on the Chari and from Bongor and Moundou to N'Djamena on the Logone, are open only during the wet season, August–December, and provide a convenient alternative when roads become impassable.

CIVIL AVIATION

The international airport at N'Djamena has been in use since 1967: proposals were announced in May 1986 for a US $3.8m. improvement programme. The renewal of the runway at Abéché, with French aid, has begun, and plans were announced in 1988 to build an airport at Faya Largeau, also with French aid, capable of accommodating both civil and military aircraft. There are over 40 smaller airfields.

Air Afrique: BP 466, N'Djamena; tel. 51-40-20; Chad holds a 7% share; see under Côte d'Ivoire.

Air Tchad: 27 ave du Président Tombalbaye, BP 168, N'Djamena; tel. 51-45-64; telex 5345; f. 1966; govt majority holding with 2% UTA interest; regular passenger, freight and charter services within Chad and international charters; Dir-Gen. Mahamat Nouri; fleet of 1 Fokker F. 27-500, 2 Twin Otter, 1 Cessna 310.

Tourism

Chad's potential attractions for tourists include a variety of scenery from the dense forests of the south to the deserts of the north. Wild animals abound, especially in the two national parks and five game reserves.

Direction du Tourisme, des Parcs Nationaux et Réserves de Faune: BP 86, N'Djamena; tel. 51-45-26; also Délégation Régionale au Tourisme at BP 88, Sarh; tel. 274; f. 1962; Dir Daboulaye Ban-Ymary.

Société Hôtelière et Touristique: BP 478, N'Djamena; Dir Antoine Abtour.

CHILE

Introductory Survey

Location, Climate, Language, Religion, Flag, Capital

The Republic of Chile is a long, narrow country lying along the Pacific coast of South America, extending from Peru and Bolivia in the north to Cape Horn in the far south. Isla de Pascua (Easter Island), about 3,780 km (2,350 miles) off shore, and several other small islands form part of Chile. To the east, Chile is separated from Argentina by the high Andes mountains. Both the mountains and the cold Humboldt Current influence the climate; between Arica in the north and Punta Arenas in the extreme south, a distance of about 4,000 km (2,500 miles), the average maximum temperature varies by no more than 13°C. Rainfall varies widely between the arid desert in the north and the rainy south. The language is Spanish. There is no state religion but the great majority of the inhabitants profess Christianity, and more than 85% are adherents of the Roman Catholic Church. The national flag (proportions 3 by 2) is divided horizontally: the lower half is red, while the upper half has a five-pointed white star on a blue square, at the hoist, with the remainder white. The capital is Santiago.

Recent History

Chile was ruled by Spain from the 16th century until its independence in 1818. For most of the 19th century it was governed by a small oligarchy of land-owners. Chile won the War of the Pacific (1879–83) against Peru and Bolivia. Most of the present century has been marked by the struggle for power between right- and left-wing forces.

In September 1970 Dr Salvador Allende Gossens, the Marxist candidate of Unidad Popular (a coalition of five left-wing parties, including the Communist Party), was elected to succeed Eduardo Frei Montalva, a Christian Democrat who was President between 1964 and 1970. Allende promised to transform Chilean society by constitutional means, and imposed an extensive nationalization programme. The Government failed to obtain a congressional majority in the elections of March 1973 and was confronted with a deteriorating economic situation as well as an intensification of violent opposition to its policies. Accelerated inflation led to food shortages and there were repeated clashes between pro- and anti-Government activists. The armed forces finally intervened in September 1973, claiming that a military take-over was necessary because of the increasingly anarchic situation and economic breakdown. President Allende died during the coup.

Congress was dissolved, all political activity banned and strict censorship introduced. The military junta dedicated itself to the eradication of Marxism and the reconstruction of Chile, and its leader, Gen. Augusto Pinochet Ugarte, became Supreme Chief of State in June and President in December 1974. The junta has been widely criticized abroad for its repressive policies and violations of human rights. Critics of the regime were tortured and imprisoned, and several thousand disappeared. Some of those who had been imprisoned were released, as a result of international pressure, and sent into exile.

In September 1976 three constitutional acts were promulgated with the aim of creating an 'authoritarian democracy'. All political parties were banned in March 1977, when the state of siege was extended. Following a UN General Assembly resolution in December 1977, condemning the Government for violating human rights, Gen. Pinochet called a referendum in January 1978 to endorse the regime's policies. As more than 75% of the voters supported the President in his defence of Chile 'in the face of international aggression', the state of siege (in force since 1973) was lifted and was replaced by a state of emergency.

A plebiscite in September 1980 showed a 67% vote in favour of a new Constitution which had been drawn up by the Government, although dubious electoral practices were allegedly employed. The new Constitution was described as providing a 'transition to democracy' but, although Gen. Pinochet ceased to be head of the armed forces, additional clauses allowed him to maintain his firm hold on power until 1989. Political parties, which were still officially outlawed, began to re-emerge, and in July 1983 five moderate parties formed a coalition, the 'Alianza Democrática', demanding a return to democratic rule within 18 months. A left-wing coalition was also created.

An anti-Government campaign of bombings, begun in late 1983 and directed principally against electricity installations, continued throughout 1984. In response, in January 1984 the Government announced new anti-terrorist legislation and extensive security measures. The first May Day rally in Santiago since 1973 was attended by 150,000 people, and public protests were held throughout the country. Relations between the Roman Catholic Church and the State began to deteriorate after anti-Government demonstrations at Punta Arenas in February, for which the Government blamed the Church. Two days of violent clashes between police and demonstrators in September resulted in nine deaths, including that of a French priest. Following the demonstrations, the opposition called a further general strike in October. During the two days of protests accompanying the strike, a further nine people were killed.

Despite the Government's strenuous attempts to eradicate internal opposition, the campaign of bombings and public protests continued throughout 1985. In September 10 people were killed and several hundred were arrested during two days of anti-Government demonstrations. Opposition leaders and trade unionists were also detained and sent into internal exile. During an anti-Government protest in November, four people were killed and hundreds were arrested by the security forces. In the same month Gen. Pinochet appointed a new army representative to the junta, in what was widely regarded as a move to consolidate support for his presidency within the ruling body.

Throughout 1986 Gen. Pinochet's regime came under increasing attack from opposition groups, the Roman Catholic Church, guerrilla organizations (principally the Frente Patriótico Manuel Rodríguez—FPMR) and international critics including the US administration, which had previously refrained from condemning the regime's notorious record of violations of human rights. A bombing campaign by the FPMR continued intermittently: 267 acts of terrorism were recorded in the first half of 1986. In April leading trade union, professional and community groups, many of whom had previously been passive critics of the Government, formed the Asamblea de la Civilidad, an organization whose aim was to seek a peaceful transition to democracy. However, during a two-day general strike called by the Asamblea in July, eight people were killed and several hundred were detained. The death of an American resident, who was reported to have been deliberately set alight by a group of soldiers, provoked international condemnation and brought renewed criticism from the USA.

In September 1986 the FPMR made an unsuccessful attempt to assassinate Gen. Pinochet. The regime's immediate response was to impose a state of siege throughout Chile, under which leading members of the opposition were detained and strict censorship was introduced. One consequence of the state of siege was the reappearance of right-wing death squads, who were implicated in a series of murders which followed the assassination attempt.

In February 1984 the Council of State, a government-appointed consultative body, began drafting a law to legalize political parties and to prepare for elections in 1989. In March 1984 Gen. Pinochet confirmed that a plebiscite would be held at an unspecified time to decide on a timetable for the elections. In September, however, Gen. Pinochet firmly rejected any possibility of a return to civilian rule before 1989. In August 1985 the Roman Catholic Church sponsored talks between 11 opposition groups, which resulted in the drafting of an Acuerdo Nacional para la Transición a la Plena Democracia (National Accord for the Transition to Full Democracy). President Pinochet rejected the opposition's proposals.

In 1986 reports that Gen. Pinochet intended to extend his term of office until the late 1990s, by seeking the presidential candidacy for the plebiscite due to be held in either 1988 or

1989, caused considerable dismay among opposition groups, and gave rise to speculation that the junta and the Government were divided over the issue of a return to full democracy after 1989. In February 1987 the registration of voters opened for the presidential plebiscite. In March the Government promulgated a law under which non-Marxist political parties were to be permitted to register officially. The opposition parties, however, were divided over the question of registration, with several left-wing groups refusing to register. By mid-1987 President Pinochet had clearly indicated his intention to remain in office beyond 1989 by securing the presidential candidacy; a cabinet reshuffle in July enabled him to appoint confirmed supporters of his policies, and led to the return to the Government of the right-wing Sergio Fernández as Minister of the Interior.

Following anti-Government protests during the visit to Chile in April of Pope John Paul II, further demonstrations against the regime (resulting in the deaths of two people) occurred in October, during a general strike which was called by the trade union organization, Comando Nacional de Trabajadores (CNT). In November some 150,000–200,000 people participated in a demonstration in Santiago, organized by the Asamblea de la Cividiad and the CNT, in support of demands for the ending of military rule and for the holding of free elections. The opposition's cause was boosted, in December, by the US Congress's vote to donate US $1m. to its campaign for open elections. However, Congress's decision precipitated a further deterioration in relations between the two countries, as the Chilean Government protested strongly at US 'interference' in Chile's internal affairs.

In January 1988 the Government confirmed that the plebiscite would be held between 11 September and 12 December 1988. In February 13 political parties and opposition groups, including the Izquierda Cristiana and leading factions of the Partido Radical, Partido Socialista and the Movimiento de Acción Popular Unitario (but excluding the Partido Comunista de Chile), signed a pact to form a united front to oppose the government candidate. By May a further three organizations had joined the front, which assumed the title of El Comando por el No. The front's principal function was to co-ordinate the campaign for the anti-Government vote at the forthcoming referendum.

In July the junta announced that the selection of the government candidate would take place on 30 August. Mounting public interest in the plebiscite was demonstrated by the number of people registering to vote, which greatly exceeded both the Government's and the opposition's expectations. When the registration closed, at the end of August, some 7.4m. people, out of a potential electorate of approximately 8m., had registered. The opposition campaign was vastly overshadowed by official propaganda for the plebiscite, but in August the junta agreed to give opposition parties access to television broadcasts for the first time since 1973. Moreover, on 24 August the Government announced the lifting of the states of exception, comprising the state of emergency and the state of threat to domestic order, which had been in force almost continuously since 1973. As a result of the Government's decision, the opposition was able to hold public rallies, and it was hoped that tension surrounding the forthcoming plebiscite would be dispelled.

On 30 August Gen. Pinochet was named by the junta as the single candidate at the plebiscite scheduled for 5 October. The junta's decision provoked widespread protests by the opposition, and led to disturbances in Santiago, resulting in three deaths. In September the Government announced that all Chileans in political exile, who were believed to number 430, were henceforth permitted to return to Chile (although the cases of 177 exiles would be subject to review by the courts). Although the announcement was regarded by some as an election ploy on the part of the Government, the opposition's campaign was boosted by the return from exile of Hortensia Bussi de Allende (President Allende's widow) and her daughter, Isabel Allende. Some 200,000 people attended the first opposition rally to be held in Santiago for 15 years, and there were increasing signs that the Comando por el No was waging a successful campaign against President Pinochet. The opposition's campaign concluded in early October with a mass rally in Santiago, attended by almost 1m. people.

Prior to the plebiscite on 5 October 1988, Gen. Pinochet gave public assurances that the result would be respected by his administration. Despite some reports of electoral malpractice, the plebiscite took place without major incident. The official result gave the anti-Pinochet campaign 54.7% of the votes cast and President Pinochet 43.1%. The opposition's victory precipitated widespread public celebrations and, subsequently, clashes between government forces and opposition supporters, during which two people were killed. The cabinet members tendered their resignations, but these were initially refused by President Pinochet.

Following the plebiscite, the opposition made repeated calls for changes to the Constitution, in order to accelerate the democratic process, and sought to initiate talks with the armed forces. However, President Pinochet rejected the opposition's proposals, and affirmed his intention to remain in office until March 1990. Moreover, pro-Government supporters attempted to construe the result of the referendum as a testimony to Gen. Pinochet's personal popularity, and it was suggested that the President would stand as a candidate at the presidential election due to be held on 14 December 1989.

In late October President Pinochet announced a cabinet reshuffle, and in November he authorized the retirement of 13 generals, in the most radical revision of the army High Command since 1973. Moreover, in the same month Gen. Santiago Sinclair Oyaneder, a firm supporter of President Pinochet, was appointed the army's representative in the junta. Despite uncertainty over Gen. Pinochet's intentions concerning the forthcoming elections and his own candidacy, the democratic process had been clearly re-established in Chile, and 1989 was expected to be dominated by the election issue.

In 1985 the Chilean Government was strongly criticized by opposition groups and the inhabitants of Isla de Pascua (Easter Island) for its decision to extend and improve the island's Mataveri airstrip for use by the US National Aeronautics and Space Administration (NASA). The improved airstrip was opened in August 1987.

Chile has had border disputes: to the north with Bolivia and to the south with Argentina. In 1978 Bolivia broke off diplomatic relations with Chile on the grounds that it had not shown sufficient flexibility over the question of Bolivia's access to the Pacific Ocean. In 1987 the dispute was revived, following Chile's refusal to consider a new attempt by Bolivia to obtain a sovereign seaport. Chile's dispute with Argentina concerned three small islands in the Beagle Channel, south of Tierra del Fuego. The issue of sovereignty over these islands has, on occasions, brought the two countries to the verge of war. In December 1978 the case was referred to papal mediation and the resultant proposals were presented to the two Governments in December 1980. In October 1984 it was announced that total agreement had been reached. Under the terms of the settlement, Chile was awarded 12 islands and islets to the south of the Beagle Channel, including Lennox, Picton and Nueva. The agreement was formally approved by the ruling junta in April 1985, and was ratified in May by representatives of the Argentine and Chilean Governments.

Government

Chile is a republic, divided into 12 regions and a metropolitan area. Since the coup in September 1973 the country has been ruled by a military junta. In 1975 a Council of State was established to draft a new constitution, which was promulgated in March 1981 and will take full effect from 1989 (see Constitution). Meanwhile, executive and legislative power is vested in the President and the junta, assisted by a Cabinet. The clause stating that all Chilean nationals must obey the national authorities was effective from October 1980.

Defence

Military service lasts two years and is compulsory for men at 19 years of age. In June 1988 the army had a strength of 57,000, the air force 15,000 and the navy 29,000. Paramilitary security forces number about 27,000 carabineros. Defence expenditure for 1987 was estimated at 118,110m. pesos.

Economic Affairs

In 1973 the junta inherited an economy with inflation between 500% and 1,000%, low monetary reserves and a declining gross domestic product (GDP). The Allende Government had introduced wide-ranging state control, but the Pinochet Government attempted to establish a market-oriented economy by encouraging foreign investment, by denationalizing most of the enterprises that the Allende Government had nationalized, and by drastically reducing import tariffs. During the period

1973–87 GDP grew by an annual average rate of 1.9%. In particular, GDP expanded considerably between 1977 and 1980, growing by an average of 8.6% per year. However, the collapse of world copper prices in 1981–82 resulted in a dramatic decline in GDP, which fell by 14.5% in 1982. In 1987, according to estimates by the World Bank, Chile's gross national product (GNP), measured at average 1985–87 prices, was US $16,468m., equivalent to $1,310 per head. Between 1980 and 1987, it was estimated, GNP declined, in real terms, at an average annual rate of 0.1%, with real GNP per head falling by 1.8% per year.

In 1986 about 21% of the working population were engaged in agriculture, forestry and fishing, but the sector contributes between 6.5% and 7.5% of the GDP. Although the country has great agricultural potential, land use is inefficient, and domestic production has suffered from the Government's reluctance to take action against cheap imports, particularly of wheat, barley and oil-seeds. Consequently, by 1983 the area sown with wheat, oats, barley, maize and rye was 35% less than in 1975, and dependence on imports increased. Wheat production fell from 650,000 metric tons in 1982 to 586,000 tons in 1983, the decline being aggravated by severe drought. In 1982 imports of wheat accounted for 60% of the total consumed. In the same period imports of oil-seeds rose from 50% to 90% of the total consumed. In 1984 production of major crops improved. Wheat production rose to 988,300 tons and maize output increased from 512,000 tons in 1983 to 721,000 tons in 1984. Wheat production subsequently recovered to 1.2m. tons, 1.6m. tons and 1.7m. tons in 1985, 1986 and 1987 respectively. The annual harvest of sugar beet rose from 1.6m. metric tons in 1983 to 2.6m. tons in 1986, and to 2.5m. tons in 1987. The agricultural sector expanded by an estimated 7.1% in 1984, by 5.6% in 1985, and by 8.7% in 1986, before declining to 4% in 1987. Such growth was attributed to a boom in exports of wood products and fruit. In the year to June 1987 fruit exports accounted for 12.2% of total export earnings; some 70% of exports are taken by the US market. Chile also possesses a flourishing wine industry. Investment in the sector has fluctuated considerably in recent years, declining from 38,270m. pesos in 1983 to only 629m. pesos in 1986. However, investment increased to 3,946m. pesos in 1987, and to an estimated 2,334m. pesos in 1988.

After the coup in 1973, the military regime reversed the agricultural reforms which had been introduced by President Allende: about 30% of the agricultural land that had been redistributed was returned to its original owners, while a further 20% was auctioned. State assistance to small farmers ended.

Wood and wood products account for an increasing proportion of export earnings: in 1987 forestry products generated US $587m. in foreign revenue and accounted for more than 8% of foreign earnings. Export earnings were expected to exceed $700m. in 1988. In recent years an average of 62,000 ha of land have been reafforested annually. Fishing also has great development potential, with the total catch reaching 4,814,300 metric tons in 1987. In spite of a decline in large-scale fishing, the sector was estimated to have grown by 11.5% in 1984, by 5.6% in 1985, by 10.0% in 1986, and by 10.7% in 1987. In 1985 exports of fish accounted for 12% of foreign exchange earnings. Investment in the fishing sector increased from 932m. pesos in 1987 to an estimated 1,700m. pesos in 1988.

Chile became the world's leading producer of copper in 1982, when it accounted for 15% of global mine production of the metal. In 1987 Chile accounted for 17.2% of world output. Chile's reserves of copper ore are estimated to represent 23% of the world's proven resources and are concentrated in the Chuquicamata (output of 520,000 metric tons per year) and El Teniente (output of 370,000 tons per year) mines. Another important site is La Escondida, with estimated reserves of copper and small quantities of gold, silver and molybdenum amounting to 662m. tons. La Escondida is the site of some 20% of the non-Communist world's reserves of copper ore, and when operational, in 1991, it will become the third largest copper producer in the world, with an annual output of 320,000 tons. Exports of copper, in a processed or unprocessed form, have, until recent years, provided more than 50% of Chile's total earnings of foreign exchange, and the industry accounts for 8%–10% of GDP. Chile's production of copper rose to a record 1.3m. tons in 1984, compared with 1.1m. tons in 1981. Copper production averaged 1.4m. tons per year in 1986 and 1987, and there were plans to increase annual output to 1.7m. tons by 1990. However, copper's share of total exports by value declined from 83% in 1973 to 44% in 1981, partly as a result of fluctuations in world demand. By 1982 the world price of copper, in real terms, had fallen to its lowest level for 50 years. Prices continued to decline, and a loss in earnings of US $244m. was recorded in 1984. Although earnings increased by $141m. in 1985, copper accounted for only about 46% of total export earnings in that year. Export earnings from copper in 1987 improved by 27%, as a result of high world prices for the commodity. The Government has maintained its intention to expand the sector through investment, and in 1987 it was announced that $8,200m. was to be invested in 16 new projects for the industry. Expansion of the sector would be facilitated by the quality of Chile's high-grade ores and by the low cost of production. Investment in the mining sector increased from 40,323m. pesos in 1986 to 363,933m. pesos in 1987 and to an estimated 1,247,082m. pesos in 1988. Despite increased investment, growth in the sector has stagnated, declining from 4.4% in 1984, to 2.2% in 1985, and to 1.5% in 1986. No growth was recorded in 1987. The output of gold increased by 29% in 1982, principally as a result of the opening of the El Indio mine in 1980. Production reached 17.9 tons in 1986 and 17.0 tons in 1987. Gold metal and concentrates account for 5% of export revenues. Silver production was 500.1 metric tons in 1986 and 499.8 tons in 1987. Chile has the largest known reserves of lithium.

Other minerals of economic importance are iron ore (for domestic consumption and export, mainly to Japan), molybdenum (representing 21% of known world reserves), manganese, lead, zinc, mercury, limestone, marble, coal, nitrates and iodine. Petroleum and natural gas are found in the south. Chile imports 60,000 barrels per day (b/d) of petroleum from Ecuador and Venezuela to meet domestic requirements but, with the discovery of large new deposits in the Magellan Straits, it is hoped to satisfy domestic oil consumption by 2003. Production averaged 34,000 b/d in 1985. In addition, Chile is eager to attract foreign investment to the sector, and in 1987 ENAP, the state petroleum company, announced plans to invest some $80m. in exploration activities, mainly in the Magellan Straits, Tierra del Fuego and the Atacama desert. However, in late 1988 it was reported that the Government was considering the privatization of the petroleum industry, in the light of a decline in output. In 1986 work began on the construction of a methanol plant at Cabo Negro at a cost of more than $300m. The plant was to come into operation in 1988–89 with an annual output of 750,000 metric tons. Other domestic resources of energy, such as coal and hydroelectricity, are also being developed rapidly. Chile's potential hydroelectric generating capacity is estimated to be 18.7m. kW. The Antuco plant has a capacity of 300,000 kW and the Colbún-Machicura project, which came 'on stream' in September 1985, has an installed capacity of 490,000 kW. In 1985 the IDB allocated two loans amounting to US $230m. for the construction of a 160,000-kW plant at Alfalfal and a 130,000-kW plant at Canutillar, and in 1987 the World Bank allocated a loan of $95m. for the construction of the Pehuenche plant (capacity 500 MW), which was to be completed by the early 1990s. In mid-1988 Argentina agreed to supply Chile with a minimum of 500,000 cu m of natural gas per day for an indefinite length of time.

Manufacturing, which accounted for 20.4% of GDP in 1985 and employed an estimated 13.6% of the working population in 1986, has encountered very strong foreign competition since the Government's drastic reduction of import duties. Following the onset of the economic recession in mid-1981, demand slumped and high interest rates forced many businesses into liquidation. Industrial production fell by 21% in 1982, and by January 1983 about 61,000 small businesses had been declared insolvent. Industrial production grew by an estimated 9.8% in 1984, but fell to only 1.2% in 1985, although the construction sector grew by 16.1%. The sector was estimated to have grown by 8% in 1986, and by 5.6% in 1987, when the construction sector also grew by 10.6%. Investment in the industrial sector declined from 322,923m. pesos in 1985 to 53,045m. pesos in 1987, and to an estimated 49,357m. pesos in 1988.

Chile's economic decline, which began in 1981, was the most spectacular in Latin America. Between 1977 and 1980 gross fixed investment represented 15.2% of GNP, one of the lowest ratios in the region. Foreign loans, which had been used for importing consumer goods and for speculation on the lucrative financial market, were no longer forthcoming by mid-1981. The collapse of the domestic economy and the numerous bankruptcies of private companies led to pressure on the private banks, which were unable to service their foreign debts. A decline in world prices for copper, molybdenum and timber led to a merchandise trade deficit of $2,677m. in 1981 and only a modest surplus of $63m. in 1982. In January 1983 Chile's foreign debt, which was $3,500m. in 1973, reached $17,454m. (representing the highest level of debt per inhabitant in the world), of which 64% had been accumulated by the private sector. An agreement on a loan of $900m. from the IMF was signed in January 1983, on the condition that strict monetarist policies would be imposed. GDP declined by 0.7% in 1983.

In 1984 the economy showed signs of a modest recovery, and real GDP grew by 6.3%. Debt servicing was rendered more difficult by the continuing decline in world copper prices. However, by the end of 1984 Chile's foreign exchange reserves had risen to US $2,291m. In September the peso was devalued from 93 to 115 per US dollar. Import duties were increased to 35% to compensate for rising dollar interest rates and falling copper prices.

In May 1985 Chile reached agreement with its creditor banks on a new loan of US $1,085m. (including a loan of $300m. from the World Bank) and on the rescheduling of debts amounting to $4,450m. In addition, Chile secured further funds of $850m. from the IMF in September. In May the Government implemented a new programme of budgetary control: the currency was devalued to 168.9 pesos per US dollar, and some import tariffs were reduced to 20%. The principal obstacle to a genuine improvement in Chile's economic performance continued to be depressed market prices for leading mineral exports. Nevertheless, real GDP grew by 2.4% in 1985, and a trade surplus of $759m. was recorded. GDP growth of 5.7% was recorded in 1986, and the trade surplus increased to an estimated $1,066m.

In April 1986 Chile signed an agreement with its creditor banks on the rescheduling of US $2,600m. in principal falling due in 1985-87. In February 1987 Chile reached agreement with its foreign creditor banks on the rescheduling of $10,600m. in debts due for repayment between 1988 and 1991. By October the Government claimed that it had completed and formalized negotiations with the 'Paris Club' of creditor governments on rescheduling debts from the period 1983-87, and that Chile's entire medium- and long-term debt to its creditor banks had also been rescheduled.

In 1985, in an attempt to reduce the foreign debt of US $19,320m., the Government implemented a debt conversion programme, under which Chile's foreign creditors were able to exchange government-guaranteed loans for peso-denominated bonds. By late 1987 some $660m. of debt had been converted into equity, and, under another debt conversion scheme, a further $1,500m. of debt had been exchanged for local currency at monthly auctions held by the Central Bank. Moreover, by September 1987 Chile's foreign debt had declined to $19,250m.

The annual rate of inflation averaged 27.3% in 1983, but declined to 19.9% in 1984. An increase to 30.7% was recorded in 1985, but inflation fell to 17.4% in 1986, before increasing to 21.5% in 1987. However, in the year ending October 1987 it was estimated that workers' salaries depreciated by 2.1% in real terms. Unemployment was officially estimated at 7.9% in late 1987, but the real level was thought to exceed 30%. In addition, 13% of the labour force were engaged in a system of minimum employment. However, GDP growth of 5.4%, a trade surplus of US $1,229m. in 1987 and foreign investment of $500m. indicated favourable prospects for the Chilean economy.

In January 1988 the Government announced the devaluation of the peso by 3.9%, to 243.97 pesos per US dollar, and a reduction in customs duties to 15%. The measures had been prompted by the US administration's decision, in December 1987, to exclude Chile from the US Generalized System of Preferences for one year.

In April 1988 the Government's concerted efforts to regain the confidence of the international financial community were rewarded when Chile's foreign creditor banks agreed to reduce the interest rate levied on repayments of Chile's medium- and long-term debt of US $10,500m. In addition, the banks approved Chile's innovative proposal to repurchase a proportion of its foreign debt at discounted prices available on the secondary market. The debt accord was signed in August, and in November the Government repurchased $299m. of foreign debt for the sum of $168.4m. In December the Government announced that it expected to resume payments of principal in 1991, and to complete the payments by 2002. In August the IMF agreed, exceptionally, to extend Chile's three-year credit facility to four years, thereby increasing the funds available to Chile from SDR 750m. to SDR 825m. In August Chile's foreign debt was estimated to be $17,858m., its lowest level since 1984.

In addition to Chile's successful debt negotiations in 1988, GDP grew by an estimated 6.8% in that year, and high world prices for copper were expected to contribute to a trade surplus of more than US $2,000m. Moreover, the annual rate of inflation to October 1988 declined to an estimated 11%, although unemployment was officially reported to have increased to 8.7% by September 1988. A further indication of Chile's economic buoyancy was the dramatic increase in foreign investment authorized by the Government from January to August 1988, which amounted to $1,600m., an increase of 276% on the same period in 1987. Hence, despite political tensions and uncertainty, the Chilean economy has continued to improve, although unemployment and low wages remain serious obstacles to a full recovery.

Social Welfare

Employees, including agricultural workers, may receive benefits for sickness, unemployment, accidents at work, maternity and retirement, and there are dependants' allowances, including family allowances. In May 1981 the management of social security was transferred to the private sector, and operated by the Administradoras de Fondo de Pensiones. A National Health Service was established in 1952. There were 5,671 physicians working in official medical services in 1979. Chile had 300 hospital establishments, with a total of 37,971 beds, in 1980. Of total expenditure by the central Government in 1985, about 48,920m. pesos (6.1%) was for health services, and a further 314,070m. pesos (39.0%) for social security and welfare.

Education

Pre-primary education is widely available for all children up to the age of six years. Primary education is free and compulsory for eight years, beginning at six or seven years of age. It is divided into two cycles: the first lasts for four years and provides a general education; the second cycle offers more specialized schooling. Secondary education, beginning at the age of 13 or 14, is divided into the humanities-science programme (lasting for four years), with the emphasis on general education and possible entrance to university, and the technical-professional programme (lasting for between four and six years), designed to meet the requirements of specialist training. Higher education is provided by three kinds of institutions: universities, professional institutes and centres of technical formation. An intensive national literacy campaign, launched in 1980, reduced the rate of adult illiteracy from 11% in 1970 to an estimated 5.6% in 1983. The university law of January 1981 banned all political activity in universities, reduced the number of degree courses from 33 to 12, halved future government funding and encouraged the establishment of private specialized universities. In recent years the Government has initiated new programmes specifically designed for adult education.

Public Holidays

1989: 2 January (for New Year's Day), 24-25 March (Good Friday and Easter Saturday), 1 May (Labour Day), 21 May (Battle of Iquique), 15 August (Assumption), 18 September (Independence Day), 12 October (Day of the Race), 1 November (All Saints' Day), 8 December (Immaculate Conception), 25 December (Christmas Day), 31 December (New Year's Eve).

1990: 1 January (New Year's Day), 13-14 April (Good Friday and Easter Saturday), 1 May (Labour Day), 21 May (Battle of Iquique), 15 August (Assumption), 18 September (Independence Day), 12 October (Day of the Race), 1 November (All Saints' Day), 8 December (Immaculate Conception), 25 December (Christmas Day), 31 December (New Year's Eve).

Weights and Measures

The metric system is officially in force.

Statistical Survey

Source (unless otherwise stated): Instituto Nacional de Estadísticas, Avda Bulnes 418, Casilla 498-3, Correo 3, Santiago; tel. 6991441.

Area and Population

AREA, POPULATION AND DENSITY*

Area (sq km)	756,626†
Population (census results)‡	
22 April 1970	8,884,786
21 April 1982	
Males	5,553,409
Females	5,776,327
Total	11,329,736
Population (official estimates at mid-year)	
1986	12,327,029
1987	12,536,374
1988	12,748,498
Density (per sq km) at mid-1988	16.8

* Excluding Chilean Antarctic Territory. † 292,132 sq miles.
‡ Excluding adjustment for underenumeration, estimated at 5.12% in 1970.

REGIONS*

		Area (sq km)	Population (30 June 1988)	Capital
I	De Tarapacá	58,698	335,362	Iquique
II	De Antofagasta	126,444	375,945	Antofagasta
III	De Atacama	75,573	196,466	Copiapó
IV	De Coquimbo	40,656	468,205	La Serena
V	De Valparaíso	16,396	1,352,887	Valparaíso
VI	Del Libertador Gen. Bernardo O'Higgins	16,365	633,959	Rancagua
VII	Del Maule	30,302	816,099	Talca
VIII	Del Bío-Bío	36,929	1,641,115	Concepción
IX	De la Araucanía	31,858	768,308	Temuco
X	De Los Lagos	66,997	908,699	Puerto Montt
XI	Aisén del Gen. Carlos Ibáñez del Campo	109,025	76,430	Coihaique
XII	De Magallanes y Antártida Chilena	132,034	150,277	Punta Arenas
	Metropolitan Region (Santiago)	15,399	5,024,446	—

* Before 1975 the country was divided into 25 provinces. With the new administrative system, the 13 regions are sub-divided into 50 new provinces and the metropolitan area of Santiago.

PRINCIPAL TOWNS (population at 30 June 1985)

Gran Santiago (capital)	4,318,305*	Temuco	171,831	
Viña del Mar	315,947	Rancagua	152,132	
Valparaíso	267,025	Talca	144,656	
Talcahuano	220,910	Chillán	128,920	
Concepción	217,756	Arica	127,925	
Antofagasta	175,486	Iquique	120,732	
		Valdivia	119,977	

* Including suburbs.

BIRTHS, MARRIAGES AND DEATHS

	Registered live births*		Registered marriages		Registered deaths	
	Number	Rate (per 1,000)	Number	Rate (per 1,000)	Number	Rate (per 1,000)
1980	247,013	22.2	86,001	7.7	74,109	6.7
1981	264,809	23.4	90,564	8.0	69,971	6.2
1982	274,335	23.9	80,115	7.0	69,887	6.1
1983	260,655	22.2	82,483	7.1	74,296	6.4
1984	265,016	22.2	87,261	7.3	74,669	6.3
1985	261,978	21.6	91,099	7.5	73,534	6.1
1986	272,997	22.1	93,995	7.6	72,209	5.9

* Figures include adjustment for underenumeration, estimated at 5% for 1978–81, 6.5% for 1982–83 and 5% for 1984–85.

ECONOMICALLY ACTIVE POPULATION*
('000 persons aged 15 years and over)

	1984†	1985†	1986‡
Agriculture, forestry, hunting and fishing	536.2	585.9	801.4
Mining and quarrying	66.6	80.6	84.1
Manufacturing	463.4	487.0	530.9
Construction	120.3	126.5	184.1
Electricity, gas, water and sanitary services	26.0	27.6	24.3
Commerce	624.1	652.4	650.1
Transport, storage and communication	206.9	209.4	230.2
Financial services	111.8	148.3	155.9
Others	1,194.1	1,219.7	1,234.7
Total	**3,349.4**	**3,537.4**	**3,895.7**

* Excluding unemployed persons seeking work for the first time.
† Sample survey covering 27,500 households.
‡ Sample survey covering 36,000 households.

Agriculture

PRINCIPAL CROPS ('000 metric tons)

	1985	1986	1987
Wheat	1,165	1,626	1,734
Rice (paddy)	157	127	162
Barley	85	88	82
Oats	170	124	157
Rye	11	9	4
Maize	772	721	661
Dry beans	101	89	100
Lentils	25	29	20
Potatoes	909	791	928
Sunflower seed	33	54	49
Sugar beet	2,124	2,638	2,487
Rapeseed	32	97	123
Tomatoes	162*	308‡	414
Pumpkins, etc.	140†	140‡	120
Onions (dry)	130*	313‡	250
Water melons	172*	72‡	86
Melons	152*	51‡	78
Grapes*	1,050	1,100	1,100
Apples	400	518	580
Peaches	158	184	147
Dry peas	2	3	5
Chick-peas	9	9	8

* FAO estimates. † Source: FAO, *Production Yearbook*.
‡ ODEPA estimate.

LIVESTOCK ('000 head)

	1985	1986	1987
Horses	346	343	336
Cattle	3,217	3,222	3,371
Pigs	973	1,100	1,061
Sheep	5,806	4,955	4,836
Goats	462	462	462

LIVESTOCK PRODUCTS ('000 metric tons)

	1985	1986	1987
Beef and veal	175	177	175
Mutton and lamb	13	13	14
Pig meat	66	75	88
Horse meat	12	9	9
Poultry meat	73	78	100
Cows' milk	1,012	1,093	1,100
Butter	5.0	6.0	4.9
Cheese	13.7	17.8	16.3
Hen eggs	70.5	75.7	83.4
Wool:			
greasy	21.0	21.3	22.0
clean	10.2*	10.5*	11.7

* Unofficial figures (Source: FAO, *Production Yearbook*).

Forestry

ROUNDWOOD REMOVALS
('000 cubic metres, excluding bark)

	1984	1985	1986
Sawlogs, veneer logs and logs for sleepers	4,537	5,160	5,751
Pulpwood	3,889	3,889*	3,889*
Other industrial wood*	553	553	553
Fuel wood*	5,980	6,076	6,171
Total	14,959	15,678	16,364

* FAO estimates.
Source: FAO, *Yearbook of Forest Products*.

SAWNWOOD PRODUCTION
('000 cubic metres, incl. boxboards)

	1985*	1986	1987
Coniferous (soft wood)	1,871	1,747	2,309
Broadleaved (hard wood)	320	279	368
Total	2,191	2,026	2,677

* Unofficial estimates (Source: FAO, *Yearbook of Forest Products*).
Railway sleepers ('000 cubic metres): 3 per year (1981-85). Source: FAO, *Yearbook of Forest Products*.
Source: CORFO.

Fishing*

('000 metric tons, live weight)

	1985	1986	1987
Chilean hake	28.7	29.7	30.9
Patagonian hake	31.7	38.5	56.6
Chilean jack mackerel	1,456.9	1,184.3	1,710.0
Chilean sprat	26.9	22.9	31.8
Chilean pilchard (sardine)	2,886.6	2,585.2	2,234.3
Anchoveta (Peruvian anchovy)	142.5	1,463.4	335.9
Chub mackerel	11.3	1.6	32.8
Other marine fishes (incl. unspecified)	75.4	89.3	154.8
Total fish	4,660.0	5,414.9	4,647.1
Crustaceans	20.8	26.5	30.5
Clams	32.3	37.2	35.0
Other molluscs	56.8	63.2	72.9
Other aquatic animals	34.5	29.9	28.8
Total catch	4,804.4	5,571.7	4,814.3

* Including quantities landed by foreign fishing craft in Chilean ports.

Mining

('000 metric tons, unless otherwise indicated)

	1985	1986	1987
Copper (metal content)	1,359.8	1,399.4	1,412.9
Coal	1,384	1,453.7	1,749.9
Iron ore*	6,510	7,009	6,690
Calcium carbonate	2,470.1	2,757.1	2,428.8
Sodium sulphate—hydrous (metric tons)	815	4,616	12,406
Molybdenum—metal content (metric tons)	18,389	16,581	16,941
Manganese (metric tons)†	35,635	31,631	31,803
Gold (kilograms)	17,240	17,947	17,035
Silver (kilograms)	517,333	500,077	499,761
Petroleum (cubic metres)	2,074,350	1,940,328	1,736,398
Natural gas ('000 cubic metres)	4,638,176	4,357,477	4,352,554

* Gross weight. The estimated iron content is 61%.
† Gross weight. The estimated metal content is 32%.

CHILE

Industry

SELECTED PRODUCTS ('000 metric tons, unless otherwise indicated)

	1985	1986	1987
Sugar	285	384	348
Cement	1,429	1,441	1,500
Beer (million litres)	189	205	255
Gasoline*	960	907	n.a.
Kerosene and jet fuels*	253	302	n.a.
Distillate fuel oils*	1,193	1,313	n.a.
Residual fuel oil*	958	1,085	n.a.
Tyres ('000)	858	862	1,221
Cigarettes (million)†	8,053	n.a.	n.a.
Glass sheets ('000 sq metres)	2,977	3,134	2,310

* Source: UN, *Monthly Bulletin of Statistics*.
† Source: UN, *Industrial Statistics Yearbook*.

Finance

CURRENCY AND EXCHANGE RATES

Monetary Units
100 centavos = 1 Chilean peso.

Denominations
Coins: 1, 5, 10, 50 and 100 pesos.
Notes: 500, 1,000 and 5,000 pesos.

Sterling and Dollar Equivalents (30 September 1988)
£1 sterling = 416.63 pesos;
US $1 = 246.38 pesos;
1,000 Chilean pesos = £2.400 = $4.059.

Average Exchange Rate (pesos per US $)
1985   161.08
1986   193.02
1987   219.54

BUDGET (million pesos)

Revenue	1984	1985	1986
Income from taxes	392,506	540,745	671,077
Non-tax revenue	269,595	426,666	1,263,498
Total current revenue	662,101	967,411	1,934,575

Expenditure	1984	1985	1986
Current expenditure	630,987	917,791	1,468,602
Operational expenditure	243,700	391,865	349,963
Remunerations	139,217	168,820	161,077
Purchase of goods and services	62,477	77,977	77,721
Interest on the public debt	42,006	145,068	111,165
Transfers	311,950	405,094	753,013
Capital expenditure	75,337	117,832	182,813
Real investment	49,868	79,112	90,058
Transfers	6,794	4,195	28,509
Amortizations	18,675	34,525	64,246
Total	706,324	1,032,623	1,651,415

CENTRAL BANK RESERVES
(US $ million at 31 December)

	1985	1986	1987
Gold*	540.1	n.a.	n.a.
IMF special drawing rights	0.3	0.2	40.8
Foreign exchange	2,449.6	2,351.1	2,463.0
Total	2,990.0	2,351.3†	2,503.8†

* Valued at market-related prices.
† Excluding gold.
Source: IMF, *International Financial Statistics*.

MONEY SUPPLY (million pesos at 31 December)

	1984	1985	1986
Currency outside banks	64,101	79,512	108,560
Demand deposits at commercial banks	51,435	49,028	73,164
Total money	115,536	128,549	181,724

COST OF LIVING (Consumer Price Index, annual averages. Base: December 1978 = 100)

	1985	1986	1987
Food	377.06	467.17	579.77
Housing	445.00	501.13	579.05
Clothing	355.13	430.22	531.03
Miscellaneous	490.45	582.59	681.90
All items	423.03	505.43	605.91

NATIONAL ACCOUNTS (million pesos at current prices)
National Income and Product

	1981	1982*	1983*
Compensation of employees	515,513	514,262	n.a.
Operating surplus	456,097	423,878	n.a.
Domestic factor incomes	971,610	938,140	n.a.
Consumption of fixed capital	120,054	132,812	174,692
Gross domestic product (GDP) at factor cost	1,091,664	1,070,952	n.a.
Indirect taxes	201,488	184,867	n.a.
Less Subsidies	20,029	16,698	n.a.
GDP in purchasers' values	1,273,123	1,239,122	1,557,709
Factor income received from abroad	23,622	25,452	15,813
Less Factor income paid abroad	80,699	120,993	149,993
Gross national product (GNP)	1,216,047	1,143,581	1,423,529
Less Consumption of fixed capital	120,054	132,812	174,692
National income in market prices	1,095,993	1,010,768	1,248,837
Other current transfers received from abroad	7,527	9,250	12,346
Less Other current transfers paid abroad	3,315	3,829	5,098
National disposable income	1,100,205	1,016,189	1,256,085

* Provisional.
1984 (million pesos): GDP 1,893,394; GNP 1,700,895.
1985 (million pesos): GDP 2,576,638; GNP 2,270,844.

Expenditure on the Gross Domestic Product

	1985*	1986*	1987*
Government final consumption expenditure	367,095	410,698	475,087
Private final consumption expenditure	1,785,245	2,237,323	2,811,039
Increase in stocks	−13,213	1,387	36,335
Gross fixed capital formation	366,428	472,741	666,763
Total domestic expenditure	2,505,555	3,122,149	3,989,224
Exports of goods and services	749,205	994,168	1,394,265
Less Imports of goods and services	678,122	870,211	1,223,727
GDP in purchasers' values	2,576,638	3,246,106	4,159,762
GDP at constant 1977 prices	356,447	376,627	398,230

* Provisional.

CHILE

Gross Domestic Product by Economic Activity

	1981	1982*	1983*
Agriculture, forestry and fishing	80,710	69,371	88,800
Mining and quarrying	71,403	95,212	157,672
Manufacturing	284,241	233,969	320,807
Electricity, gas and water	28,948	40,137	52,163
Construction	81,836	69,670	73,571
Wholesale and retail trade	191,045	193,093	233,793
Transport, storage and communications	61,865	57,502	70,609
Other services	473,075	480,668	560,294
GDP in purchasers' values	1,273,123	1,239,122	1,557,709

* Provisional.

BALANCE OF PAYMENTS (US $ million)

	1985	1986	1987
Merchandise exports f.o.b.	3,804	4,199	5,224
Merchandise imports f.o.b.	−2,954	−3,099	−3,994
Trade balance	850	1,100	1,230
Exports of services	865	1,150	1,264
Imports of services	−3,104	−3,471	−3,421
Balance on goods and services	−1,389	−1,221	−927
Government unrequited transfers (net)	47	40	56
Private unrequited transfers (net)	14	44	60
Current balance	−1,328	−1,137	−811
Direct capital investment (net)	62	57	97
Other long-term capital (net)	−1,714	−2,126	−1,013
Short-term capital (net)	374	311	−158
Net errors and omissions	−3	88	−47
Total (net monetary movements)	−2,609	−2,807	−1,932
Monetization of gold	2	9	7
Valuation changes (net)	−73	−284	−116
Exceptional financing (net)	2,511	2,580	1,990
Official financing (net)	−4	−25	77
Changes in reserves	−173	−527	26

Source: IMF, *International Financial Statistics*.

External Trade

PRINCIPAL COMMODITIES (US $'000)

Imports c.i.f.	1983	1984	1985
Livestock and animal products	34,472	36,805	15,518
Vegetable products	292,491	231,969	120,860
Animal and vegetable fats	72,678	82,895	61,708
Manufactured foodstuffs, beverages and tobacco	105,747	91,413	31,135
Mineral products	607,421	619,079	553,975
Chemicals	325,144	241,405	356,064
Synthetic plastic rubber	152,795	179,304	151,366
Skins and leather goods	6,320	10,830	8,101
Paper and paper-making materials	69,847	73,767	63,235
Textiles	167,747	221,282	162,050
Plaster, cement, ceramics and glass	30,235	35,503	31,467
Metals and metal goods	132,656	204,631	165,248
Technical and electrical equipment	445,018	664,579	652,389
Transport equipment	137,644	165,376	187,005
Optical and precision instruments	71,460	80,608	70,550
Total (incl. others)	2,753,976	3,190,600	2,742,516

Total imports (US $'000): 3,156,900 in 1986; 4,023,300 in 1987.

Exports f.o.b.	1983	1984	1985
Fruit and vegetables	249,732	332,781	n.a.
Meat and fish meal fodder	307,067	275,471	275,276
Chemical wood pulp	156,426	195,942	129,672
Natural sodium nitrate	28,095	28,236	32,890
Iron ore and concentrates	112,007	109,730	90,829
Copper ores, refined and unrefined copper metal	1,864,316	1,620,051	1,760,907
Chemicals	48,417	47,635	63,972
Total (incl. others)	3,835,528	3,657,248	3,822,900

Total exports (US $'000): 4,222,400 in 1986; 5,101,900 in 1987.

PRINCIPAL TRADING PARTNERS (US $ million)

Imports	1985	1986	1987
Argentina	105.9	122.5	159.0
Brazil	248.9	247.6	380.0
Canada	59.2	54.3	66.4
Ecuador	48.1	58.8	37.2
France	78.6	94.1	129.3
Germany, Federal Republic	209.0	250.1	335.1
Italy	50.3	64.0	95.8
Japan	188.5	296.4	387.2
Korea, Republic	24.2	48.0	82.2
Nigeria	50.5	49.5	75.0
Peru	41.1	56.3	27.9
Spain	105.5	82.2	116.6
Switzerland	41.1	47.6	55.5
United Kingdom	84.3	88.5	128.3
USA	654.6	641.5	773.1
Venezuela	267.7	148.2	143.7
Total (incl. others)	2,742.5	2,914.0	4,023.3

CHILE

Exports	1985	1986	1987
Argentina	84.5	160.6	174.9
Belgium	91.0	77.9	58.6
Brazil	209.7	292.9	348.2
Canada	75.8	58.4	71.1
China, People's Republic	124.9	100.2	78.7
Colombia	44.8	40.5	51.0
France	144.6	153.1	178.6
Germany, Federal Republic	370.6	441.2	483.4
Italy	197.2	215.8	273.8
Japan	392.5	420.1	561.3
Korea, Republic	89.3	91.8	109.0
Netherlands	142.4	153.6	164.2
Peru	45.7	65.9	85.8
Spain	74.4	122.2	146.8
Taiwan	38.5	61.4	129.6
United Kingdom	256.2	219.8	317.8
USA	870.7	915.2	1,140.5
Venezuela	33.7	40.6	71.2
Total (incl. others)	3,822.9	4,222.4	5,101.9

Transport

PRINCIPAL RAILWAYS* ('000)

	1984	1985	1986†
Passengers (number)	8,672	8,914	6,243
Passenger/km	1,424,076	1,521,588	1,274,457
Freight (tons)	15,148	21,809	23,844

* Includes all international cargo of Ferrocarril Transandino.
† Provisional.

ROAD TRAFFIC (motor vehicles in use)

	1984	1985	1986
Cars	630,418	624,884	590,719
Buses and coaches	20,520	21,491	21,559
Lorries	214,831	236,371	220,492
Motor cycles	31,732	33,917	22,661

INTERNATIONAL SEA-BORNE SHIPPING
(freight traffic, '000 metric tons)

	1984	1985	1986*
Goods loaded	11,826	12,632	13,448
Goods unloaded	5,265	4,480	5,001

* Provisional.

CIVIL AVIATION

	1984	1985	1986*
Kilometres flown ('000)†	23,761	24,436	27,522
Passengers (number)	777,343	826,89	998,656
Freight ('000 ton-km)	270,256	276,27	316,304

* Provisional.
† Includes airline taxis.

Tourism

	1985	1986	1987
Arrivals	418,050	581,117	560,549

Source: Servicio Nacional de Turismo.

Communications Media

	1983	1984	1985
Radio receivers ('000 in use)	3,550	n.a.	4,000
Television receivers ('000 in use)	1,350	n.a.	1,750
Telephones ('000 in use)	629	n.a.	n.a.
Book production: titles	1,326	1,653	1,638
Daily newspapers	38	38	40

Source: mainly UNESCO, *Statistical Yearbook*.

Education

(Number of pupils)

	1985	1986	1987
Kindergarten	202,252	265,479	286,491
Basic	2,099,413	2,112,874	2,065,400
Middle	731,911	744,431	752,989
Higher (incl. universities)	197,437	214,374	224,338

Source: Ministerio de Educación.

Directory

The Constitution

Note: Since 1973 Government has been based on the three Constitutional Acts (see below). In accordance with the new Constitution approved by a plebiscite in 1980, the previous 1925 Constitution was abolished and the new Fundamental Law came into effect in March 1981. Provisions concerning the National Congress will be fully effective from 1989.

The three Constitutional Acts of 1976 provide for a 'new democratic structure' for Chilean society based on the family and rejecting class struggle. The following rights are guaranteed: the right to life and personal integrity, to a defence, to personal liberty and individual security; the right to reside in, cross or leave the country; the right of assembly, petition, association and free expression and the right to work. Men and women are accorded equal rights; no-one shall be obliged to join any association; any group considered to be contrary to morality, public order or state security shall be prohibited; the courts shall be able to prohibit any publication or broadcast considered to be contrary to public morality, order, national security or individual privacy.

The 1981 Constitution, described as a 'transition to democracy', separates the presidency from the junta and provides for presidential elections every eight years, with no re-election. The President may dissolve the legislature once during his term of office and may declare a state of emergency for up to 20 days. The bicameral legislature will consist of an upper chamber of 26 elected and nine appointed senators, who are to serve an eight-year term, and a lower chamber of 120 deputies elected for a four-year term. All former presidents are to be senators for life. There is a National Security Council consisting of the President, the Junta (comprising the heads of the armed forces and the police) and the presidents of the Supreme Court and the Senate.

All Marxist and 'totalitarian' groups are banned, limited political activity will be permitted only at the end of the 'transitional period', and there is no amnesty for terrorists. There is limited freedom of assembly and of expression: workers in public or vital sectors may not strike and other employees may strike for no more than 60 days; it is illegal to disseminate doctrines of a 'totalitarian' concept or ones which undermine public morals. The economy is based on the free market system. Abortion is prohibited.

Appended are 29 Transitory Clauses which had immediate effect in March 1981. The holding of elections is postponed until 1989, when the Junta will nominate the president and the 'no re-election' clause will be suspended. The nomination will be submitted to a referendum.

Note: Following the presidential referendum of 5 October 1988, presidential and congressional elections were due to be held on 14 December 1989. The transfer of power was scheduled to take place on 11 March 1990.

The Government

HEAD OF STATE

President: Gen. AUGUSTO PINOCHET UGARTE (assumed power as President of the Military Junta 11 September 1973; sworn in as Supreme Chief of State 27 June 1974; proclaimed President of the Republic 17 December 1974; inaugurated as President 11 March 1981).

JUNTA MILITAR DE GOBIERNO

Adm. JOSÉ TORIBIO MERINO CASTRO (Navy).
Gen. RODOLFO STANGE OELCKERS (Police).
Gen. FERNANDO MATTHEI AUBEL (Air Force).
Gen. SANTIAGO SINCLAIR OYANEDER (Army).

THE CABINET
(January 1989)

Minister of the Interior: CARLOS CÁCERES CONTRERAS.
Minister of Foreign Affairs: HERNÁN FELIPE ERRÁZURIZ CORREA.
Minister of Labour and Social Security: GUILLERMO ARTHUR ERRÁZURIZ.
Minister of Finance: HERNÁN BÜCHI BUC.
Minister of Economy, Development and Reconstruction: Brig. MANUEL CONCHA MARTÍNEZ.
Minister of Public Education: JUAN ANTONIO GUZMÁN MOLINARE.
Minister of Justice: HUGO ROSENDE SUBIABRE.
Minister of National Defence: Vice-Adm. PATRICIO CARVAJAL PRADO.
Minister of Public Works: Brig.-Gen. BRUNO SIEBERT HELD.
Minister of Transport and Telecommunications: CARLOS SILVA ECHIBURU.
Minister of Agriculture: JAIME DE LA SOTA BENAVENTE.
Minister of National Property: ARMANDO ALVAREZ MARÍN.
Minister of National Planning: SERGIO MELNICK.
Minister of Mines: PABLO BARAHONA URZÚA.
Minister of Energy: Lt-Gen. HERMÁN BRADY ROCHE.
Minister of Public Health: Dr JUAN GIACONI GANDOLFI.
Minister of Housing and Urban Development: GUSTAVO MONTERO SAAVEDRA.
Minister of Production Development (Vice-President of CORFO): Brig.-Gen. FERNANDO HORMAZÁBAL GAJARDO.
Minister Secretary-General of Government: MIGUEL ANGEL PODUJE SAPIAÍN.
Secretary-General of the Presidency: Gen. SERGIO VALENZUELA.

MINISTRIES

Ministry of Agriculture: Teatinos 40, Santiago; tel. 717436; telex 240745.
Ministry of Economy, Development and Reconstruction: Teatinos 120, Santiago; tel. 725522; telex 240558.
Ministry of Energy: Teatinos 120, 7°, Casilla 14, Correo 21, Santiago; tel. 6981757; telex 240948.
Ministry of Finance: Teatinos 120, 12°, Santiago; tel. 6982051; telex 241334.
Ministry of Foreign Affairs: Palacio de la Moneda, Santiago; tel. 6982501; telex 40595.
Ministry of Housing and Town Planning: Serrano 15, 4°, Santiago; tel. 331624; telex 240124.
Ministry of the Interior: Palacio de la Moneda, Santiago; tel. 714103; telex 241379.
Ministry of Justice: Compañía 1111, Santiago; tel. 6968151; telex 241316.
Ministry of Labour and Social Security: Huérfanos 1273, 6°, Santiago; tel. 7151333; telex 40559.
Ministry of Mines: Teatinos 120, 9°, Santiago; tel. 6965872; telex 240948.
Ministry of National Defence: Plaza Bulnes s/n, 4°, Santiago; tel. 6965271; telex 40537.
Ministry of National Planning: Ahumada 48, Casilla 9140, Santiago; tel. 722033; telex 341400.
Ministry of National Property: Avda Libertador B. O'Higgins 280, Santiago; tel. 2224669.
Ministry of Production Development (CORFO): Moneda 921, Casilla 3886, Santiago; tel. 380521; telex 240421.
Ministry of Public Education: Avda Libertador B. O'Higgins 1371, Santiago; tel. 6983351; telex 240716.
Ministry of Public Health: Enrique McIver 541, 1°, Santiago; tel. 394001; telex 240136.
Ministry of Public Works: Dirección de Vialidad, Morandé 59, 2°, Santiago; tel. 6964839; telex 240777.
Ministry of Transport and Telecommunications: Amunátegui 139, Santiago; tel. 726503; telex 240200.
Office of the Comptroller of the Republic: Teatinos 56, 9°, Santiago; tel. 724212; telex 40281.
Office of the Minister Secretary-General of Government: Palacio de la Moneda, Santiago; tel. 711680; telex 40073.

Legislature

CONGRESO NACIONAL

The bicameral National Congress (a Senate and a Chamber of Deputies) was dissolved by the armed forces on 13 September

1973. Until 1989 legislative functions will be exercised by the Junta, assisted by four legislative commissions.

Political Organizations

All 'Marxist' political parties were declared unlawful on 14 September 1973, and the activities of all political parties were suspended on 27 September 1973. All political parties and political activity were banned on 12 March 1977. In March 1987 a law to legalize political parties, with the exception of Marxist organizations, was promulgated.

The most prominent political organizations (some working from abroad) are:

Avanzada Nacional: Avda Bernardo O'Higgins 2489, Santiago; tel. 6983588; right-wing; Pres. SERGIO MIRANDA CARRINGTON.

Bloque Socialista: Santiago; tel. 395747; f. 1983; socialist alliance; members include Partido Socialista de Chile and Movimiento de Acción Popular Unitaria (see below); Co-ordinator RICARDO NÚÑEZ MUÑOZ.

Intransigencia Democrática: Santiago; tel. 724164; f. 1985; centre-left alliance; Pres. MANUEL SANHUEZA CRUZ.

Izquierda Cristiana: Christian left; Sec.-Gen. LUIS MAIRA.

Movimiento de Acción Popular Unitaria—MAPU: Marxist; Leader OSCAR GARRETÓN (in exile); Sec.-Gen. VÍCTOR BARRUETO.

Movimiento de Izquierda Revolucionaria—MIR: revolutionary left; Leader ANDRÉS PASCAL ALLENDE (in exile).

Movimiento Social Cristiano: Santiago; tel. 6961961; f. 1984; right-wing party; Pres. JUAN DE DIOS CARMONA; Sec.-Gen. MANUEL RODRÍGUEZ.

Partido Comunista de Chile (PCCh): Santiago; tel. 724164; Secs-Gen. LUIS CORVALÁN LEPE, JOSÉ SANFUENTES.

Partido Democracia Radical: Santiago; f. 1987; Pres. JAIME TORMO.

Partido Democracia Social: San Antonio 220, Of. 604, Santiago; tel. 394244; democratic socialist party; Pres. LUIS ANGEL SANTIBÁÑEZ; Sec.-Gen. JAIME CARMONA DONOSO.

Partido Demócrata de Chile (PADECHI): Santiago; registered as a political party in 1988; Leader APOLÓNIDES PARRA.

Partido Demócrata Cristiano (PDC): Carmen 8, 6°, Santiago; tel. 330251; telex 242397; f. 1957; Pres. PATRICIO AYLWIN AZÓCAR; Sec.-Gen. GUTENBERG MARTÍNEZ.

Partido Humanista: Las Urbinas 145, Depto 20, Santiago; tel. 2319089; f. 1987; humanist party; Pres. JOSÉ TOMÁS SÁENZ.

Partido Nacional: Compañía 1357, 1°, Santiago; tel. 6992793; f. 1965; traditional centre-right party; Sec.-Gen. PEDRO CORREA; divided into two factions in 1988:

  Phillips: pro-Pinochet; Leader PATRICIO PHILLIPS.

  Riesco: anti-Pinochet; Leader GERMÁN RIESCO.

Partido Radical: Avda Santa María 281, Santiago; tel. 779903; f. 1863; social democratic; mem. of Socialist International; Pres. ENRIQUE SILVA CIMMA; Sec.-Gen. RICARDO NAVARRETE.

Partido de Renovación Nacional—PARENA: Santiago; f. 1987; right-wing; Pres. SERGIO ONOFRE JARPA; 61,170 mems; comprises:

  Frente Nacional del Trabajo: Dr Barros Borgoño 21, Santiago; tel. 41923; Sec.-Gen. ANGEL FANTUZZI.

  Unión Demócrata Independiente (UDI): Suecia 286, Santiago; tel. 2322686; right-wing; Leader JAIME GUZMÁN ERRÁZURIZ (expelled from PARENA in April 1988).

  Unión Nacional: Ricardo Matte Pérez 0140, Santiago; tel. 7449915; centre-right party; Pres. ANDRÉS ALLAMAND ZAVALA.

Partido Socialdemocracia: París 815, Casilla 50.220, Correo Central, Santiago; tel. 399064; f. 1973; Pres. ARTURO VENEGAS GUTIÉRREZ; Sec.-Gen. LEVIÁN MUÑOZ PELLICER.

Partido Socialista de Chile—PS de C: Santiago; left-wing; split into factions:

  Almeyda: Santiago; Sec.-Gen. Dr CLODOMIRO ALMEYDA MEDINA.

  Mandujano: Santiago; tel. 498031; Sec.-Gen. MANUEL MANDUJANO.

  Núñez: Agustinas 853, Of. 1015, Santiago; tel. 338490; Sec.-Gen. RICARDO NÚÑEZ MUÑOZ.

Partido Socialista Auténtica: Casilla 3696, Correo Central, Santiago; tel. 92301; Sec. Gen. JUAN CARLOS MORAGA.

Partido Socialista Histórico: Nataniel 31, Of. 76, Santiago; tel. 6964704; Sec.-Gen. JUAN GUTIÉRREZ.

Unión Liberal Republicana (ULR): Santiago; f. 1987; Pres. RICARDO LAGOS; fmrly Partido por la Democracia; comprises:

Partido Liberal: San Antonio 418, Of. 803, Santiago; tel. 480738; liberal party; Pres. GUILLERMO TORO ALBORNOZ; Vice-Pres. OLGA REYES.

Partido Republicano: Sótero del Río 492, 3°, Santiago; tel. 6984167; f. 1983; centre-right party; Pres. (vacant); Sec.-Gen. GABRIEL LEÓN ECHAIZ.

Unión Socialista Popular: Teatinos 251, Of. 809, Santiago; tel. 6984269; left-wing party; Sec.-Gen. RAMÓN SILVA ULLOA.

Los Verdes: Santiago; f. 1987; environmentalist party; Pres. ANDRÉS R. KORYZMA.

In early 1988 16 political parties and opposition groups, including the Izquierda Cristiana, the Partido Humanista, Partido Demócrata Cristiana, the Unión Liberal Republicano and factions of the Partido Radical, Partido Socialista de Chile and the Movimiento de Acción Popular Unitario, united to form the **Comando por el No**, an opposition front to campaign against the government candidate in the plebiscite of 5 October 1988. Following the plebiscite, it was reported that the Comando por el No had assumed the title of **Concertación de Partidos Políticos de la Campaña**, and that the grouping intended to present a single candidate to contest the presidential election scheduled for 14 December 1989.

However, other political alliances reported to have formed since the plebiscite include:

Partido Amplio de Izquierda Socialista (PAIS): Santiago; f. 1988; Marxist; Pres. LUIS MAIRA; Sec.-Gen. RICARDO SOLARI; comprises:

  Almeyda faction of PS de C (see above).

  Izquierda Cristiana (see above).

  Partido Comunista de Chile (see above).

  Partido Radical Socialista Democrático.

Guerrilla groups:

Acción Chilena Anticomunista (ACHA): right-wing; Pres. JUAN SERRANO.

Frente Patriótico Manuel Rodríguez (FPMR): f. 1983; Communist; Leader Commdr DANIEL HUERTA.

Frente Revolucionario Nacionalista—FREN: left-wing.

Diplomatic Representation

EMBASSIES IN CHILE

Argentina: Miraflores 285, Santiago; tel. 331076; telex 240280; Ambassador: JOSÉ MARÍA ALVAREZ DE TOLEDO.

Australia: Gertrudis Echeñique 420, Casilla 33, Correo 10, Las Condes, Santiago; tel. 2285065; telex 240855; Ambassador: MALCOLM J. DAN.

Austria: Barrios Errázuriz 1968, 3°, Casilla 16196, Santiago; tel. 2234774; telex 240528; Ambassador: HARALD KREID.

Belgium: Avda Providencia 2653, 11°, Of. 1104, Santiago; tel. 2321070; telex 440088; Chargé d'affaires: MICHEL GODFRIND.

Brazil: Alonso Ovalle 1665, Santiago; tel. 6982486; telex 340350; Ambassador: RONALDO COSTA.

Canada: Ahumada 11, 10°, Casilla 427, Santiago; tel. 6962256; Ambassador: MICHEL DE GOUMOIS.

China, People's Republic: Pedro de Valdivia 550, Santiago; tel. 250755; telex 240863; Ambassador: HUANG SHIKANG.

Colombia: Darío Urzúa 2080, Santiago; tel. 747570; telex 340401; Ambassador: JORGE E. RODRÍGUEZ.

Costa Rica: Barcelona 2070, Santiago; tel. 2318915; Ambassador: FABIO CRUZ BRICEÑO.

Denmark: Avda Santa María 0182, Casilla 13430, Santiago; tel. 376056; telex 440032; Chargé d'affaires a.i.: JØRGEN ILFELDT.

Dominican Republic: Mariscal Petain 125, Santiago; tel. 2288083; Ambassador: RAFAEL VÁLDEZ HICARIO.

Ecuador: Avda Providencia 1979, 5°, Santiago; tel. 235742; telex 240717; Ambassador: CÉSAR VALDIVIESO CHIRIBOGA.

Egypt: Roberto del Río 1871, Santiago; tel. 748881; telex 440156; Ambassador: ABDEL-AZIZ FAHMY OMAR.

El Salvador: Calle Noruega 6595, Las Condes, Santiago; tel. 251096; Ambassador: Dr JOSÉ HORACIO TRUJILLO.

France: Avda Condell 65, Casilla 38-D, Santiago; tel. 2251030; telex 240535; Ambassador: FRANÇOIS MOUTON.

Germany, Federal Republic: Agustinas 785, 7° y 8°, Santiago; tel. 335031; telex 240583; Ambassador: HORST KULLAK-UBLICK.

Guatemala: Avda Américo Vespucio Norte 958, Corres 10, Casilla 36, Santiago; telex 340485; Ambassador: JULIO GÁNDARA VALENZUELA.

Haiti: Avda 11 de Septiembre 2155, Of. 801, Torre B, Santiago; tel. 2318233; Ambassador: MAX JADOTTE.

CHILE

Directory

Holy See: Calle Nuncio Sotero Sanz 200, Casilla 507, Santiago (Apostolic Nunciature); tel. 2312020; telex 241035; Nuncio: Excmo Rev. Mgr ANGELO SODANO.

Honduras: Avda 11 de Septiembre 2155, Of. 1005, Santiago; tel. 2314161; telex 440456; Ambassador: FRANCISCO LÓPEZ REYES.

India: Triana 871, Casilla 10433, Santiago; tel. 2231548; telex 340046; Ambassador: SARV KUMAR KATHPALIA.

Israel: San Sebastián 2812, 5°, Casilla 1224, Santiago; tel. 2461570; telex 240627; Ambassador: DAVID EPHRATI.

Italy: Clemente Fabres 1050, Santiago; tel. 2259029; telex 440321; Chargé d'affaires: ARMANDO SANGUINI.

Japan: Avda Providencia 2653, 19°, Casilla 2877, Santiago; tel. 2321807; telex 440132; Ambassador: SHUICHI NOMIYAMA.

Jordan: Avda Providencia 545, Apto 55, Casilla 10431, Santiago; tel. 2231177; telex 346196; Chargé d'affaires a.i.: ADIL M. ADAILEL.

Korea, Republic: Alcántara 74, Casilla 1301, Santiago; tel. 2284214; telex 340380; Ambassador: SUH KYUNG-SUK.

Lebanon: Isidoro Goyenechea 3607, Casilla 3667, Santiago; tel. 2325027; telex 440118; Ambassador: IBRAHIM KRAIDY.

Netherlands: Las Violetas 2368, Casilla 56-D, Santiago; tel. 2236825; telex 340381; Ambassador: PATRICK S. J. RUTGERS.

New Zealand: Avda Isidora Goyenechea 3516, Casilla 112, Las Condes, Santiago; tel. 2314204; telex 3440066; Ambassador: PAUL J. A. TIPPING.

Norway: Américo Vespucio Norte 548, Casilla 2431, Santiago; tel. 2281024; telex 440150; Ambassador: HELGE VINDENES.

Panama: Bustos 2199, Correo 9892, Santiago; tel. 2250147; Ambassador: RICARDO MORENO VILLALAZ.

Paraguay: Huérfanos 886, 5°, Ofs 514-515, Santiago; tel. 394640; telex 645357; Ambassador: Dr FABIO RIVAS ARAUJO.

Peru: Avda Andrés Bello 1751, Providencia, Santiago 9, Casilla 16277, Santiago; tel. 2238883; telex 440095; Ambassador: LUIS MARCHAND STENS.

Philippines: San Crecente 551, esq. Presidente Errázuriz, Las Condes, Santiago; tel. 2286135; Ambassador: RODOLFO A. ARIZALA.

Romania: Benjamín 2955, Casilla 290, Santiago; tel. 2311893; telex 440378; Chargé d'affaires a.i.: GHEORGHE PETRE.

South Africa: Carlos Antunez 1959, Casilla 16189, Santiago; tel. 2250415; telex 340484; Ambassador: Lt-Gen. ANTONIE MICHAL MULLER.

Spain: Avda Andrés Bello 1895, Casilla 16456, Santiago; tel. 742021; telex 340253; Ambassador: (vacant).

Sweden: Santiago; tel. 495052; telex 440153; Chargé d'affaires a.i.: HÅKAN WILKENS.

Switzerland: Avda Providencia 2653, Of. 1602, Casilla 3875, Santiago; telex 340870; Ambassador: SVEN MEILI.

Syria: Carmencita 111, Casilla 12, Correo 10, Santiago; tel. 2327471; telex 240095; Ambassador: HISHAM HALLAJ.

Turkey: N. Sótero Sanz 136, Casilla 16182-9, Providencia, Santiago; tel. 2318952; telex 340278; Ambassador: NURETTIN KARAKÖYLÜ.

United Kingdom: La Concepción 177, Casilla 72 D, Santiago; tel. 2239166; telex 340483; Ambassador: ALAN WHITE.

USA: Agustinas 1343, 5°, Santiago; tel. 710133; telex 240062; Ambassador: CHARLES GILLESPIE.

Uruguay: Avda Pedro de Valdivia 711, Casilla 2636, Santiago; tel. 743569; telex 340371; Ambassador: ALFREDO BIANCHI PALAZZO.

Venezuela: Mar del Plata 2055, Casilla 16577, Santiago; tel. 2250021; telex 440170; Ambassador: HÉCTOR VARGAS ACOSTA.

Judicial System

The following are the main tribunals:

The Supreme Court, consisting of 16 members, appointed for life by the President of the Republic from a list of five names submitted by the Supreme Court when vacancies arise. The President of the Supreme Court is elected by the 16 members of the Court.

There are 17 Courts of Appeal (in the cities or departments of Arica, Iquique, Antofagasta, Copiapó, La Serena, Valparaíso, Santiago, Presidente Aguirre Cerda, Rancagua, Talca, Chillán, Concepción, Temuco, Valdivia, Puerto Montt, Coyhaique and Punta Arenas) whose members are appointed for life from a list submitted to the President by the Supreme Court. The number of members of each court varies. Judges of the lower courts are appointed in a similar manner from lists submitted by the Court of Appeal of the district in which the vacancy arises.

Corte Suprema: Plaza Montt Varas, Santiago; tel. 6980561.

President of the Supreme Court: LUIS MALDONADO BOGGIANO.

Ministers of the Supreme Court:
JOSÉ M. EYZAGUIRRE ECHEVERRÍA
ISRAEL BÓRQUEZ MONTERO
RAFAEL RETAMAL LÓPEZ
OCTAVIO RAMÍREZ MIRANDA
VÍCTOR MANUEL RIVAS DEL CANTO
ENRIQUE CORREA LABRA
OSVALDO ERBETTA VACCARO
EMILIO ULLOA MUÑOZ
MARCOS ABURTO OCHOA
ESTANISLAO ZÚÑIGA COLLAO
ABRAHAM MEERSOHN SCHIJMAN
CARLOS LETELIER BOBADILLA
HERNÁN CERECEDA BRAVO
SERVANDO JORDÁN LÓPEZ
ENRIQUE ZURITA CAMPS

Attorney-General: RENÉ PICA URRUTIA.

Secretary of the President: CÉSAR DERAMOND RUBIO.

Secretary of the Court: SERGIO MERY BRAVO.

Religion

CHRISTIANITY

The Roman Catholic Church

Chile comprises five archdioceses, 16 dioceses, two territorial prelatures and two Apostolic Prefectures.

Bishops' Conference: Conferencia Episcopal de Chile, Cienfuegos 47, Casilla 517-V, Correo 21, Santiago; tel. 6981416; telex 343066; f. 1982; Pres. BERNARDINO PIÑERA CARVALLO, Archbishop of La Serena.

Archbishop of Antofagasta: CARLOS OVIEDO CAVADA, Casilla E, San Martín 2628, Antofagasta; tel. 221164.

Archbishop of Concepción: (vacant), Calle Barros Araña 544, Casilla 65-C, Concepción; tel. 25258.

Archbishop of La Serena: BERNARDINO PIÑERA CARVALLO, Los Carrera 450, Casilla 613, La Serena; tel. 212325.

Archbishop of Puerto Montt: BERNARDO CAZZARO BERTOLLO, Calle Benavente 385, Casilla 17, Puerto Montt; tel. 252215.

Archbishop of Santiago de Chile: Cardinal JUAN FRANCISCO FRESNO LARRAÍN, Erasmo Escala 1822, Casilla 30-D, Santiago; tel. 6981200.

The Anglican Communion

Anglicans in Chile are adherents of the Anglican Church of the Southern Cone of America, covering Argentina, Bolivia, Chile, Paraguay, Peru and Uruguay.

Bishop of Chile: Right Rev. COLIN FREDERICK BAZLEY, Iglesia Anglicana, Casilla 50675, Santiago; tel. 383009.

Other Christian Churches

Baptist Evangelical Convention: Casilla 1055-22, Santiago; tel. 2224085; Gen. Sec. FAUSTINO AGUILERA C.; Pres. ESTEBAN JOFRE C.

Evangelical Lutheran Church: Avda Ricardo Lyón 1483, Casilla 15167, Santiago; tel. 2255816; f. 1937 as German Evangelical Church in Chile; present name adopted in 1959; Pres. Rev. WILLIAM E. GORSKI; 2,500 mems.

Methodist Church: Sargento Aldea 1041, Casilla 67, Santiago; tel. 566074; autonomous since 1969; 6,000 mems; Bishop ISAIAS GUTIÉRREZ V.

Pentecostal Church: Calle Pena 1103, Casilla de Correo 2, Curicó; tel. 1035; f. 1945; 90,000 mems; Bishop ENRIQUE CHÁVEZ CAMPOS.

Pentecostal Mission Church: Avda Pedro Montt 1473, Casilla 5391, Santiago 3; tel. 568657; f. 1952; Sec. Rev. ARTURO PALMA CHER; Pres. Rev. NARCISO SEPÚLVEDA BARRA; 12,000 mems.

BAHÁ'Í FAITH

National Spiritual Assembly: Casilla 3731, Darío Urzúa 1588, Providencia, Santiago; tel. 2255326; telex 340436.

The Press

Most newspapers of nationwide circulation in Chile are published in Santiago. Following the assumption of power by the military government in 1973, various forms of censorship were imposed. A decree introduced in 1981 made it illegal for the press to 'emphasize or highlight news related to terrorist or extremist acts which have occurred within the country'. In 1984 more stringent regulations concerning censorship were imposed. In September 1986, following

CHILE

the imposition of a state of siege, several opposition publications were banned by the Government. In 1987 a regulatory law was introduced in order to facilitate the enforcement of legislation governing censorship. Following the curtailment of the states of exception in August 1988, opposition movements were allowed access to the media, including the press, to campaign for the October plebiscite. According to official sources, there are 128 newspapers which appear more than twice a week, with a combined circulation of more than 900,000 copies per issue.

DAILIES

Santiago

Circulation figures listed below are supplied mainly by the Asociación Nacional de la Prensa. Other sources give much lower figures.

Diario Oficial de la República de Chile: Agustinas 1269, Santiago; tel. 6983969; Dir ENRIQUE MENCHACA SALGADO; circ. 15,000.

La Época: Olivares 1229, 5°, 6° y 9°, Santiago; tel. 6990067; telex 240990; f. 1987; morning; centre; independent; Gen. Editor ASCANIO CAVALLO; circ. 50,000.

Fortín Diario: Agustinas 1849, Santiago; tel. 6990376; f. 1984; opposition; independent; Dir EDUARDO TRABUCCO PONCE.

El Mercurio: Avda Santa María 5542, Casilla 13-D, Santiago; tel. 2288147; f. 1827; morning; conservative; Man. Dir AGUSTÍN EDWARDS; circ. 120,000 (weekdays), 250,000 (Sundays).

La Nación: Agustinas 1269, Santiago; tel. 6982222; f. 1980 to replace government-subsidized *El Cronista*; morning; financial; Propr Sociedad Periodística La Nación; Dir Editor ANDRÉS SÁNCHEZ ARRIAGADA; circ. 20,000.

La Segunda: Avda Santa María 5542, Santiago; tel. 2287048; f. 1931; evening; Dir CRISTIÁN ZEGERS ARIZTÍA.; circ. 30,000.

La Tercera de la Hora: Vicuña Mackenna 1870, Santiago; tel. 517067; f. 1950; morning; Dir ARTURO ROMÁN HERRERA; circ. 170,000.

Las Ultimas Noticias: Avda Santa María 5542, Santiago; tel. 2287048; f. 1902; morning; Man. Dir HÉCTOR OLAVE VALLEJOS; owned by the Proprs of *El Mercurio*; circ. 150,000 (except Saturdays and Sundays).

Antofagasta

La Estrella del Norte: Calle Matta 2112, Antofagasta; tel. 222847; f. 1966; evening; Dir ROBERTO RETAMAL PACHECO; circ. 10,000.

El Mercurio: Manuel Antonio Matta 2112, Antofagasta; tel. 223406; f. 1906; morning; conservative independent; Proprs Soc. Chilena de Publicaciones; Dir DARÍO CANUT DE BON URRUTIA; circ. 20,000.

Arica

La Estrella de Arica: San Marcos 580, Arica; tel. 31834; telex 221051; f. 1976; Dir DARÍO CANUT DE BON URRUTIA; circ. 11,600.

Calama

La Estrella del Loa: Abaroa 1929, Calama; tel. 212535; f. 1969; Propr Soc. Chilena de Publicaciones; Dir ROBERTO RETAMAL PACHECO; circ. 4,000 (weekdays), 7,000 (Sundays).

El Mercurio: Abaroa 1929, Calama; tel. 211604; f. 1968; Propr Soc. Chilena de Publicaciones; Dir DARÍO CANUT DE BON; circ. 4,500 (weekdays), 7,000 (Sundays).

Chillán

La Discusión de Chillán: Casilla 14-D, Calle 18 de Septiembre 721, Chillán; tel. 222651; f. 1870; morning; independent; Propr Universidad de Concepción; Dir TITO CASTILLO PERALTA; circ. 8,500.

Concepción

El Sur: Casilla 8-C, Calle Freire 799, Concepción; tel. 235825; f. 1882; morning; independent; Editor HERNÁN ALVEZ C. TIRADA; circ. 38,000.

Copiapó

Atacama: Manuel Rodríguez 740, Copiapó; tel. 2255; morning; independent; Dir SAMUEL SALGADO; circ. 6,500.

Curicó

La Prensa: Casilla 6-D, Merced 373, Curicó; tel. 310453; f. 1898; morning; right-wing; Man. Dir MANUEL MASSA MAUTINO; circ. 4,000.

Iquique

La Estrella de Iquique: Luis Uribe 452, Iquique; tel. 22401; telex 223134; f. 1966; evening; Dir ARCADIO CASTILLO ORTIZ; circ. 8,500.

La Serena

El Día: Casilla 13-D, Brasil 395, La Serena; tel. 211284; f. 1944; morning; Dir ANTONIO PUGA RODRÍGUEZ; circ. 10,800.

Los Angeles

La Tribuna: Casilla 15-D, Calle Colo Colo 464, Los Angeles; tel. 321928; independent; Dir CIRILO GUZMÁN DE LA FUENTE; circ. 10,000.

Osorno

El Diario Austral: Plazuela Yungay 581, Osorno; tel. 5191; telex 373014; Dir ENRIQUE JORQUERA MÁRQUEZ; circ. 6,350.

Diario 24 Horas: Osorno; tel. 2300; Dir ROBERTO SILVA BAJIT.

Puerto Montt

El Llanquihue: Antonio Varas 167, Puerto Montt; tel. 2578; f. 1885; morning; independent; Dir MIGUEL ESTEBAN VEYL BETANZO; circ. 6,000.

Punta Arenas

La Prensa Austral: Waldo Seguel 636, Casilla 9-D, Punta Arenas; tel. 21976; telex 380029; f. 1941; morning; independent; Dir PABLO CRUZ NOCETI; circ. 10,000, Sunday (*El Magallanes*; f. 1894) 12,000.

Rancagua

El Rancagüino: O'Carroll 518, Rancagua; tel. 21729; f. 1915; independent; Dir HÉCTOR GONZÁLEZ; circ. 10,000.

Talca

La Mañana de Talca: 1 Norte 911, Talca; tel. 32520; Dir JUAN C. BRAVO; circ. 5,000.

Temuco

El Diario Austral: Bulnes 699, Casilla 1-D, Temuco; tel. 232233; f. 1916; morning; commercial, industrial and agricultural interests; Dir MARCO ANTONIO PINTO ZEPEDA; Propr Soc. Periodística Araucanía, SA; circ. 26,000.

Tocopilla

La Prensa: Matta 2112, Antofagasta, Casilla 2099, Tocopilla; tel. 222847; f. 1924; morning; independent; Dir ROBERTO RETAMAL; circ. 8,000.

Valdivia

El Correo de Valdivia: Valdivia; f. 1895; morning; non-party; Dir PATRICIO GÓMEZ COUCHOT; circ. 12,000.

El Diario Austral: Independencia 499, Valdivia; tel. 3353; telex 371011; f. 1982; Editor GUSTAVO SERRANO COTAPOS; circ. 3,500.

Valparaíso

La Estrella: Esmeralda 1002, Casilla 57-V, Valparaíso; tel. 258011; telex 230531; f. 1921; evening; independent; Dir ALFONSO CASTAGNETO; owned by the Proprs of *El Mercurio*; circ. 25,000, 30,000 (Saturdays).

El Mercurio: Esmeralda 1002, Casilla 57-V, Valparaíso; tel. 258011; telex 330445; f. 1827; morning; Dir GERMÁN CARMONA MAGER; owned by the Proprs of *El Mercurio* in Santiago; circ. 60,000.

Victoria

Las Noticias: Casilla 92, Confederación Suiza 895, Victoria; f. 1910; morning; independent; Dir TRÁNSITO BUSTAMENTE MOLINA; circ. 8,000.

El Pehuén de Curacautín: Casilla 92, Avda Central 895, Victoria; morning; independent; Dir GINO BUSTAMENTE BARRÍA; circ. 3,000.

PERIODICALS

Santiago

Análisis: Manuel Montt 425, Santiago; tel. 2234386; f. 1977; weekly; political, economic and social affairs; published by Emisión Ltda; Dir JUAN PABLO CÁRDENAS; circ. 30,000.

Apsi: Gen. Alberto Reyes 032, Providencia, Casilla 9896, Santiago; tel. 775450; f. 1976; fortnightly; Dir MARCELO CONTRERAS NIETO; circ. 30,000.

La Bicicleta: José Fagnano 614, Santiago; tel. 2223969; satirical; Dir ANTONIO DE LA FUENTE.

CA Revista Oficial del Colegio de Arquitectos de Chile AG: Manuel Montt 515, Santiago; tel. 44734; f. 1964; 4 a year; architects' magazine; Editor Arq. JAIME MÁRQUEZ ROJAS; circ. 3,000.

El Campesino: Tenderini 187, Casilla 40-D, Santiago; tel. 396710; telex 240760; f. 1838; monthly; farming; Dir PATRICIO MONTT; circ. 5,000.

Carola: San Francisco 116, Casilla 1858, Santiago; tel. 336433; telex 240656; fortnightly; women's magazine; published by Editorial Antártica, SA; Dir ISABEL MARGARITA AGUIRRE DE MAIN.

CHILE

Cauce: Monjitas 454, Of. 607, Santiago; tel. 392159; weekly; political, economic and social affairs; Dir GONZALO FIGUEROA YÁÑEZ; circ. 20,000.

Chile Agrícola: Casilla 2, Correo 13, Teresa Vial 1170; tel. 5516039; f. 1976; monthly; farming; Dir Ing. Agr. RAÚL GONZÁLEZ VALENZUELA; circ. 10,000.

Chile Filatélico: Almirante Simpson 75, Casilla 13245, Santiago; tel. 2228036; f. 1929; quarterly; Editor RICARDO BOIZARD G.

Chile Forestal: Avda Bulnes 259, Of. 706, Santiago; tel. 6966724; telex 240001; f. 1974; monthly; technical information and features on forestry sector; Dir Ing. MARÍA TERESA ARANA SILVA; circ. 5,600.

Cosas: Almirante Pastene 329, Providencia, Santiago; tel. 2258630; telex 340905; f. 1976; fortnightly; international affairs; Editor MÓNICA COMANDARI KAISER; circ. 25,000.

Creces: Manuel Montt 1922, Santiago; tel. 2234337; monthly; science and technology; Dir SERGIO PRENAFETA; circ. 12,000.

Deporte Total: Luis Thayer Ojeda 1626, Casilla 3092, Providencia, Santiago; tel. 749421; telex 341194; f. 1981; weekly; sport, illustrated; Dir DARÍO ROJAS MORALES; circ. 25,000.

Economía y Sociedad: MacIver 125, 10°, Santiago; tel. 331034; telex 340656; Dir JOSÉ PIÑERA; circ. 10,000.

Ercilla: Las Hortensias 2340, Casilla 63-D, Santiago; tel. 2255055; f. 1936; weekly; general interest; Dir MANFREDO MAYOL DURÁN; circ. 146,000.

Estanquero 11: Obispo Donoso 6, Of. A, Providencia, Santiago; tel. 2233065; f. 1985; monthly; politics; published by Sociedad Periodística Estanquero Once Ltda; Dir GASTÓN ACUÑA MACLEAN; circ. 6,000.

Estrategia: Rafael Cañas 114, Casilla 16845, Correo 9, Santiago; tel. 2746452; telex 440001; f. 1978; weekly; financial affairs; Dir VÍCTOR MANUEL OJEDA MÉNDEZ; circ. 35,000.

Gestión: Rafael Cañas 114, Santiago; tel. 2745494; telex 440001; f. 1975; monthly; business matters; Dir VÍCTOR MANUEL OJEDA MÉNDEZ; circ. 15,000.

Guía Turística: Ferrocarriles del Estado, Casilla 134-D, Santiago; tel. 796211; telex 242290; yearly tourist guides with maps, hotel, and general information; railway services; Dir AMINODOW FELLER NICKELSBERG.

Hoy: Mons. Miller 74, Clasificador 654, Correo Central, Santiago; tel. 2236102; f. 1977; weekly; general interest; Dir ABRAHAM SANTIBAÑEZ; circ. 30,000.

Jurídica del Trabajo: Avda Bulnes 180, Of. 80, Casilla 9447, Santiago; tel. 6967474; Editor MARIO SOTO VENEGAS.

Mensaje: Almirante Barroso 24, Casilla 10445, Santiago; tel. 6960653; f. 1951; monthly; national, church and international affairs; Dir RENATO HEVIA; circ. 8,000.

Microbyte: Huelén 164-B, 2°, Providencia, Santiago; tel. 2231530; telex 244259; f. 1984; monthly; computer science; Dir JOSÉ KAFFMAN; circ. 10,000.

Paula: Triana 851, Santiago; tel. 2253447; fortnightly; women's magazine; Dir ANDREA ELUCHANS; circ. 20,000.

¿Qué Pasa?: Darío Urzua 2109, Casilla 13279, Santiago; tel. 2516352; telex 341029; f. 1971; weekly; general interest; Dir ROBERTO PULIDO ESPINOSA; circ. 30,000.

Revista Médica de Chile: Avda Pdte Riesco 6007, Clasificador 1, Correo 27, Santiago; tel. 2205812; f. 1872; monthly; official organ of the Sociedad Médica de Santiago; Editor ALEJANDRO GOIĆ; circ. 2,000.

Super Rock: Luis Thayer Ojeda 1626, Casilla 3092, Providencia, Santiago; tel. 748231; telex 341194; f. 1985; weekly; Latin and European rock music, illustrated; Dir DARÍO ROJAS MORALES; circ. 40,000.

Vea: Luis Thayer Ojeda 1626, Casilla 3092, Providencia, Santiago; tel. 749421; telex 341194; f. 1939; weekly; general interest, illustrated; Dir DARÍO ROJAS MORALES; circ. 150,000.

PRESS ASSOCIATION

Asociación Nacional de la Prensa: Bandera 84, Of. 411, Santiago; tel. 6966431; Pres. CARLOS PAÚL LAMAS; Sec. JAIME MARTÍNEZ WILLIAMS.

NEWS AGENCIES

Orbe Servicios Informativos, SA: Phillips 56, 6°, Of. 66, Santiago; tel. 394774; Dir ALFREDO STEINMEYER FARIÑA.

Foreign Bureaux

Agence France-Presse (France): Avda O'Higgins 1316, 9°, Apt. 92, Santiago; tel. 6960559; telex 440074; Correspondent HUMBERTO ZUMARÁN ARAYA.

Agencia EFE (Spain): Coronel Santiago Bueras 188, Santiago; tel. 380179; Bureau Chief RAMIRO GAVILANES GRANJA.

Agenzia Nazionale Stampa Associata (ANSA) (Italy): Moneda 1040, Of. 702, Santiago; tel. 6985811; telex 344260; f. 1945; Bureau Chief GIORGIO BAGONI BETTOLLINI.

Associated Press (AP) (USA): Tenderini 85, 10°, Of. 100, Casilla 2653, Santiago; tel. 335015; telex 645493; Bureau Chief KEVIN NOBLET.

Deutsche Presse-Agentur (dpa) (Federal Republic of Germany): San Antonio 427, Of. 306, Santiago; tel. 393633; Correspondent CARLOS DORAT.

Inter Press Service (IPS) (Italy): Phillips 40, Of. 66, Santiago; tel. 397091; Dir OSCAR KNUST ROSALES; Correspondent GUSTAVO GONZÁLEZ ROSALES.

Reuters (UK): Huérfanos 1117, Of. 414, Casilla 4248, Santiago; tel. 722539; telex 240584; Correspondent RICHARD WADDINGTON.

United Press International (UPI) (USA): Nataniel 47, 9°, Casilla 71-D, Santiago; tel. 6960162; telex 240570; Bureau Chief TOM HARVEY.

Xinhua (New China) News Agency (People's Republic of China): Biarritz 1981, Providencia, Santiago; tel. 255033; telex 94293; Correspondent SUN KUOGUOWEIN.

Publishers

Ediciones Paulinas: Vicuña MacKenna 10777, Casilla 3746, Santiago; tel. 6989145; Catholic texts.

Ediciones Universitarias de Valparaíso: Universidad Católica de Valparaíso, Montt Saavedra 44, Casilla 1415, Valparaíso; tel. 252900; also Moneda 673, 8°, Santiago; tel. 332230; telex 230389; f. 1970; general literature, social sciences, engineering, education, music, arts, textbooks; Gen. Man. KARLHEINZ LAAGE H.

Editora Nacional Gabriel Mistral Ltda: Santiago; tel. 779522; literature, history, philosophy, religion, art, education; government-owned; Man. Dir JOSÉ HARRISON DE LA BARRA.

Editorial Andrés Bello/Jurídica de Chile: Avda Ricardo Lyon 946, Casilla 4256, Santiago; tel. 40436; telex 240901; f. 1947; history, arts, literature, philosophy, politics, economics, agriculture, textbooks, law and social science; Gen. Man. WILLIAM THAYER.

Editorial El Sembrador: Sargento Aldea 1041, Casilla 2037, Santiago; tel. 5569454; Dir ISAÍAS GUTIÉRREZ.

Editorial Nascimento, SA: Chiloé 1433, Casilla 2298, Santiago; tel. 5569405; f. 1898; general; Man. Dir CARLOS GEORGE NASCIMENTO MÁRQUEZ.

Editorial Universitaria, SA: María Luisa Santander 0447, Casilla 10220, Santiago; tel. 2234555; f. 1947; general literature, social science, technical, textbooks; Man. Dir GABRIELA MATTE ALESSANDRI.

Empresa Editora Zig-Zag SA: Amapolas 2075, Casilla 84-D, Santiago; tel. 2235766; telex 340455; general publishers of literary works, reference books and magazines; Pres. SERGIO MÚJICA L.; Gen. Man. RODRIGO CASTRO C.

ASSOCIATION

Cámara Chilena del Libro AG: Ahumada 312, Of. 806, Casilla 13526, Santiago; tel. 6989519; Pres. RODRIGO CASTRO CUEVAS; Exec. Sec. CARLOS FRANZ THORUD.

Radio and Television

In 1988 there were an estimated 30,000,000 radio receivers and 3,500,000 television receivers in use. There were 6 short-wave, 155 medium-wave and 215 FM stations.

RADIO

Asociación de Radiodifusores de Chile (ARCHI): Pasaje Matte 956, Of. 801, Casilla 10476, Santiago; tel. 398755; f. 1936; 340 broadcasting stations; Pres. OSCAR PIZARRO ROMERO; Vice-Pres. TOMÁS SCARPA MARTINICH; Sec.-Gen. NELSON ENCINA GÓMEZ.

Radio Nacional de Chile: San Antonio 220, 2°, Casilla 244-V, Correo 21, Santiago; tel. 339071; government station; domestic service; Dir ROBERTO MARDONES SÁEZ.

TELEVISION

In November 1988 the Government announced that Televisión Nacional de Chile—Canal 7 was to become a *Sociedad Anónima*, prior to its eventual privatization. Canal 4, Canal 11 and Canal 14 (see below) were also included in the Government's long-term proposals for privatization.

CHILE *Directory*

Televisión Nacional de Chile—Canal 7: Bellavista 0990, Casilla 16104, Santiago; tel. 774552; telex 241375; government network; 114 stations; Dir-Gen. Col ALEJANDRO BRIONES LEA-PLAZA.

Corporación de Televisión de la Universidad Católica de Chile—Canal 13: Inés Matte Urrejola 0848, Casilla 14600, Santiago; tel. 2514000; telex 440182; f. 1959; non-commercial; Exec. Dir ELEODORO RODRÍGUEZ MATTE.

Corporación de Televisión de la Universidad Católica de Valparaíso—Canal 4: Agua Santa 2455, Viña del Mar; Casilla 4059, Valparaíso; tel. 251024; f. 1957; Dir CAMILO LOBOS LEIVA.

Universidad de Chile—Canal 11: Inés Matte Urrejola 0825, Casilla 16457, Correo 9, Providencia, Santiago; tel. 776273; telex 340492; f. 1960; educational; Vice-Pres. JUAN PABLO O'RYAN GUERRERO.

Universidad del Norte—Red Telenorte de Televisión: Carrera 1625, Casilla 1045, Antofagasta; tel. 226725; telex 325142; f. 1981; operates Canal 11-Arica, Canal 12-Iquique and Canal 3-Antofagasta; Dir JOSÉ MANUEL FERNÁNDEZ SOLAR.

Empresa Nacional de Telecomunicaciones, SA—ENTEL CHILE, SA: Santa Lucía 360, Casilla 4254, Santiago; tel. 6902121; telex 240683; f. 1964; operates the Chilean land satellite stations of Longovilo, Punta Arenas and Coihaique, linked to INTELSAT system; Gen. Man. Lt-Col IVÁN VAN DE WYNGARD MELLADO.

Finance

(cap. = capital; p.u. = paid up; dep. = deposits; res = reserves; m. = million; amounts in pesos unless otherwise specified)

BANKING

In 1980 the law referring to banks was amended to eliminate the categories of commercial and provincial banks. New banking legislation, designed to limit new loans by banks to 5% of their capital, was introduced in November 1986. In December 1988 President Pinochet presented new legislation under which the Banco Central would become an autonomous body.

Supervisory Authority

Superintendencia de Bancos e Instituciones Financieras: Moneda 1123, 6°, Santiago; tel. 6990072; f. 1925; run by Ministry of Finance; Superintendent GUILLERMO RAMÍREZ VILARDELL.

Central Bank

Banco Central de Chile: Agustinas 1180, Santiago; tel. 6962281; telex 240658; f. 1926; under Ministry of Finance; bank of issue; cap. and res 233,753.7m., dep. 865,173.4m. (Dec. 1986); Pres. ENRIQUE SEGUEL MOREL; Vice-Pres. ALFONSO SERRANO SPOERER; Gen. Man. JORGE AUGUSTO CORREA GATICA; 7 brs.

State Bank

Banco del Estado de Chile: Avda B. O'Higgins 1111, Casilla 24, Santiago; tel. 716001; telex 240536; f. 1953; state bank; cap. 4,000.0m., res 48,836.6m., dep. 872,973.2m. (Dec. 1985); Pres. HERNÁN ARZE DE SOUZA FERREIRA; Gen. Man. OSVALDO PALACIOS MERY; 181 brs.

National Banks
Santiago

Banco de A. Edwards: Huérfanos 740, Santiago; tel. 394870; telex 340428; f. 1851; cap. and res US $37.5m.; Chair. AGUSTÍN EDWARDS DEL RÍO; Gen. Man. JULIO JARAQUEMADA LEDOUX; 24 brs.

Banco de Chile: Ahumada 251, Casilla 151-D, Santiago; tel. 383044; telex 440176; f. 1894; cap. and res 68,353.8m. (July 1988); Pres. ADOLFO ROJAS GANDULFO; Gen. Man. SEGISMUNDO SCHULIN-ZEUTHEN SERRANO; 101 brs.

Banco Concepción: Huérfanos 1072, Casilla 80-D, Santiago; tel. 6982741; telex 340268; f. 1871; cap. and res 10,457.1m. (July 1988); Pres. MANUEL FELIÚ; Gen. Man. JORGE DÍAZ; 35 brs.

Banco Continental: Huérfanos 1219, Casilla 10492, Santiago; tel. 6968201; telex 645347; f. 1958; cap. and res 5,077.7m. (July 1988); bought by Crédit Lyonnais in Sept. 1987; Pres. NICOLÁS YARUR LOLAS; Gen. Man. PIERRE JEAN EYMERY; 1 br.

Banco de Crédito e Inversiones: Huérfanos 1134, Casilla 136-D, Santiago; tel. 6966633; telex 340373; f. 1937; cap. and res 13,009.6m. (July 1988), dep. 236,727.7m. (Dec. 1985); Pres. JORGE YARUR BANNA; Gen. Man. LUIS ENRIQUE YARUR REY; 89 brs.

Banco del Desarrollo: Avda B. O'Higgins 949, 3°, Casilla 320-V, Correo 21, Santiago; tel. 6982901; telex 340654; f. 1983; cap. 2,747.9m. (July 1988), dep. 24,801.4 (Dec. 1985); Pres. DOMINGO SANTA MARÍA SANTA CRUZ; Gen. Man. VICENTE CARUZ MIDDLETON.

Banco Español-Chile: Agustinas 920, Casilla 76-D, Santiago; tel. 381501; telex 441102; f. 1926; cap. and res 18,671.9m. (July 1988), dep. 140.9m. (Dec. 1986); subsidiary of Banco de Santander, Spain; Pres. EMILIO BOTÍN SANZ DE SAUTUOLA Y GARCÍA DE LOS RÍOS; Gen. Man. JOSÉ ANTONIO CAMBA FERNÁNDEZ; 42 brs.

Banco Exterior SA: MacIver 225, Santiago; tel. 6962182; telex 340462; cap. and res 4,881.5m. (July 1988); Pres. CALIXTO RÍOS PÉREZ; Gen. Man. PERE CAMPISTOL SIRERA.

Banco Hipotecario de Fomento Nacional: Huérfanos 1234, Santiago; tel. 6981842; telex 340269; f. 1883; cap. and res 7,874.2m. (Dec. 1988); Pres. IGNACIO COUSIÑO ARAGÓN; Gen. Man. RICARDO BACARREZA RODRÍGUEZ; 13 brs.

Banco Industrial y de Comercio Exterior (BICE): Teatinos 220, Santiago; tel. 6982931; telex 645197; f. 1979; cap. and res US $24m., dep. US $125m. (Dec 1987); Pres. ELIODORO MATTE LARRAÍN; Gen. Man. GONZALO VALDÉS BUDGE; 2 brs.

Banco Internacional: San Antonio 76, Casilla 135-D, Santiago; tel. 723623; telex 341066; f. 1944; cap. and res 3,431.5m. (July 1988), dep. 15,438.4m. (April 1987); placed under state control Jan. 1983; Pres BORIS SUBELMAN BORTNIC; Gen. Man. CÉSAR BESIO ROLLERO; 10 brs.

Banco Nacional: Bandera 287, Casilla 131-D, Santiago; tel. 6982091; telex 340830; f. 1906; cap. and res 6,398.6m. (July 1988); Pres. FRANCISCO ERRÁZURIZ TALAVERA; Gen. Man. ALFREDO NEUT BLANCO; 31 brs.

Banco O'Higgins: Bandera 201, Casilla 51-D, Santiago; tel. 6963153; telex 341186; f. 1956; cap. and res 7,749.0m. (July 1988), dep. 117,078.5m. (Dec. 1985); Pres. ANDRÓNICO LUKSIC CRAIG; Gen. Man. GONZALO MENÉNDEZ DUQUE; 14 brs.

Banco Osorno y La Unión: Bandera 66, Casilla 57-D, Santiago; tel. 718164; telex 441215; f. 1908; cap. and res 10,967.7m. (Aug. 1988); Pres. CARLOS ABUMOHOR TOUMA; Gen. Man. ALVARO SAIEH BENDECK; 34 brs.

Banco del Pacífico: Moneda 1096, Santiago; tel. 6981873; telex 340466; cap. and res 2,131m. (July 1988); Pres. ROBERTO GUERRERO; Gen. Man. ALFREDO COMANDARI; 8 brs.

Banco de Santiago: Bandera 172, Casilla 14437, Santiago; tel. 728072; telex 240172; f. 1977; cap. and res 37,312.0 (July 1988), dep. 20,754m. (July 1983); merged with Banco Colocadora Nacional de Valores in 1986; Pres. JULIO BARRIGA SILVA; Chair. and Gen. Man. HÉCTOR VALDÉS RUÍZ; 32 brs.

Banco Security Pacific: Agustinas 621, Santiago; tel. 381620; telex 440430; f. 1981; fmrly Banco Urquijo de Chile; cap. and res US $27.4m., dep. US $93.6m. (June 1988); Pres. FRANCISCO SILVA S.; Gen. Man. RENATO PEÑAFIEL M.

Banco Sud Americano: Morandé 226, Casilla 90-D, Santiago; tel. 6982391; telex 240436; f. 1944; cap. and res 11,490.7m. (July 1988), dep. 191,481.6m. (Dec. 1985); Pres. JOSÉ BORDA AREXTABALA; Gen. Man. JUAN LUIS KOSTNER MANRÍQUEZ; 22 brs.

Banco del Trabajo: Bandera 102, Casilla 9594, Santiago; tel. 714133; telex 340370; f. 1955; cap. 7,429.4m. (July 1988), dep. 127,273.1m. (Dec. 1985); Pres. ROBERTO KELLY; Gen. Man. EMILIANO FIGUEROA SANDOVAL; 26 brs.

Morgan Bank Chile: Moneda 970, 13°, Casilla 500-D, Santiago; tel. 721037; telex 341244; cap. and res. 1,813.3m. (July 1988), dep. 5,523m. (Dec. 1986); Pres. GONZALO DE LAS HERAS MILLA; Gen. Man. DAVID W. HANSON; 1 br.

Foreign Banks

Foreign banks that have opened branches in Chile include the following:

American Express International Banking Corporation (USA), Banco do Brasil, Banco de Colombia, Banco do Estado de São Paulo (Brazil), Banco de la Nación Argentina, Banco Real (Brazil), Banco Sudameris (France), Bank of America NT & SA (USA), Bank of Tokyo (Japan), Centrobanco, Chase Manhattan Bank (USA), Chicago Continental Bank (USA), Citibank NA (USA), Hongkong and Shanghai Banking Corporation (Hong Kong), First National Bank of Boston (USA), Manufacturers Hanover Bank, Republic National Bank of New York (USA).

Association

Asociación de Bancos e Instituciones Financieras de Chile AG: Agustinas 1476, 10°, Santiago; tel. 717149; telex 340958; f. 1946; Pres. JORGE YARUR BANNA; Gen. Man. CRISTÓBAL VALDÉS SÁENZ.

STOCK EXCHANGES

Bolsa de Comercio y Valores de Santiago: La Bolsa 64, Casilla 123-D, Santiago; tel. 6982001; telex 340531; f. 1893; 32 mems; Pres. EUGENIO BLANCO RUIZ; Man. ENRIQUE GOLDFARB SKLAR.

Bolsa de Corredores y Valores de Valparaíso: Prat 798, Casilla 218-V, Valparaíso; tel. 250677; f. 1905; Pres. CARLOS F. MARRÍN ORREGO; Man. CARLOS CASTRO SANDOVAL.

CHILE   *Directory*

INSURANCE

In December 1987 there were 23 general insurance, 16 life insurance and three reinsurance companies operating in Chile.

Supervisory Authority

Superintendencia de Valores y Seguros: Teatinos 120, 6°, Casilla 2167, Santiago; tel. 6962194; telex 340260; under Ministry of Finance; Supt Fernando Alvarado Elissetche.

Principal Companies
(Selected by virtue of premium income)
(p.i. = premium income; m. = million; amounts in pesos)

Cía de Seguros La Chilena Consolidada: Bandera 131, Santiago; tel. 721525; telex 240474; f. 1905; general; p.i. 4,897m., total assets 4,263m. (Dec. 1987); Pres. Agustín Edwards Eastman.

Cía de Seguros Generales Aetna Chile, SA: Coyancura 2270, 11°, Santiago; tel. 2314566; telex 241295; f. 1900; general; p.i. 4,531m., total assets 3,369m. (Dec. 1987); Pres. Sergio Baeza Valdés.

Cía de Seguros Generales Consorcio Nacional de Seguros, SA: Bandera 236, 6°, Santiago; tel. 718232; telex 240466; f. 1920; general; p.i. 4,919m., total assets 4,348m. (Dec. 1987); Pres. Carlos Eugenio Lavín García-Huidobro.

Cía de Seguros Generales Cruz del Sur, SA: Ahumada 370, 4°, Santiago; tel. 718181; telex 340030; f. 1974; general; p.i. 6,195m., total assets 7,787m. (Dec. 1987); Pres. José Tomás Guzmán Dumas.

Cía de Seguros de Vida Aetna Chile, SA: Coyancura 2270, 10°, Of. 1020, Santiago; tel. 2314566; telex 242304; f. 1981; life; p.i. 11,166m., total assets 43,702m. (Dec. 1987); Pres. Sergio Baeza Valdés.

Cía de Seguros de Vida Consorcio Nacional, SA: Bandera 236, 8°, Santiago; tel. 721511; telex 240947; f. 1916; life; p.i. 9,957m., total assets 50,732m. (Dec. 1987); Pres. Carlos Larraín Peña.

Cía de Seguros de Vida La Construcción, SA: Avda Providencia 1933, Santiago; tel. 2326679; f. 1985; life; p.i. 4,660m., total assets 7,903m. (Dec. 1987); Pres. Sergio Orellana Salcedo.

Instituto de Seguros del Estado (ISE): Moneda 1025, 7°, Santiago; tel. 6964271; telex 240204; f. 1953; general; p.i. 6,361m., total assets 3,429m. (Dec. 1987); Pres. Gustavo Dupuis Pinillos.

Reinsurance

Caja Reaseguradora de Chile, SA: Bandera 84, 6°, Santiago; tel. 6982941; telex 340276; f. 1927; general; total assets 22,725m. (Dec. 1987); Pres. Gustavo Dupuis Pinillos.

Caja Reaseguradora de Chile, SA: Bandera 84, 6°, Santiago; tel. 6982941; telex 340276; f. 1980; life; total assets 2,637m. (Dec. 1987); Pres. Gustavo Dupuis Pinillos.

Cía Reaseguradora Bernardo O'Higgins: Huérfanos 1189, 5°, Santiago; tel. 6967929; telex 242155; f. 1981; general; total assets 1,335m. (Dec. 1987); Pres. Mahmoud Abdallah.

Insurance Association

Asociación de Aseguradores de Chile: Moneda 920, 10°, Casilla 2630, Santiago; tel. 721172; telex 340260; f. 1931; Pres. José Gandarillas Chadwick; Gen. Man. Jorge Cañas Suárez.

Trade and Industry

CHAMBER OF COMMERCE

Cámara de Comercio de Santiago de Chile, AG: Santa Lucía 302, 3°, Casilla 1297, Santiago; tel. 330962; telex 240868; f. 1919; 1,100 mems; Pres. Luis Correa Prieto; Exec. Sec. Oscar Salas Elgart.

There are Chambers of Commerce in all major towns.

STATE ECONOMIC AND DEVELOPMENT ORGANIZATIONS

In 1980 the Government began a policy of denationalization, comprising three stages, and by early 1981 over 500 state companies had been sold. Only those concerns considered to be of strategic importance continue in the state sector and each must show an annual profit of 10% of its capital. In 1985 the Government launched the third stage of the privatization programme, under which 26 state concerns were to be partially or completely sold to private interests.

Comisión Nacional de Energía: Teatinos 120, 7°, Casilla 14, Correo 21, Santiago; tel. 6981757; telex 240948; f. 1978 to determine Chile's energy policy and approve investments in energy-related projects; Pres. Min. of Energy; Exec. Sec. Sebastián Bernstein Letelier.

Corporación de Fomento de la Producción—CORFO: Moneda 921, Casilla 3886, Santiago; tel. 380521; telex 240421; f. 1939; holding group of principal state enterprises; under Ministry of Economic Affairs; grants loans and guarantees to private sector; responsible for sale of non-strategic state enterprises; Vice-Pres. Brig.-Gen. Fernando Hormazábal Gajardo; Gen. Man. Col Guillermo Letelier S.; controls:

Cía Chilena de Electricidad—CHILECTRA: Santo Domingo 789, 2°, Casilla 1557, Santiago; tel. 391096; telex 40645; f. 1921; generation, transmission and distribution of electric energy; Exec. Vice-Pres. Rubén Díaz Niera.

Cía de Acero del Pacífico SA: Casilla 167-D, Santiago; telex 240288; f. 1946; cap. US $427.1m.; iron and steel production; Gen. Man. Roberto de Andraca Barbas; 6,767 employees.

Cía de Teléfonos de Chile SA—CTC: San Martín 50, Santiago; tel. 6986616; telex 240955; f. 1930; 50.2% owned by private sector; Man. Col Gerson Echavarría Mendoza.

Complejo Forestal y Maderero Panguipulli Ltda: Agustinas 785, Of. 560, Santiago; tel. 397054; telex 346093; Gen. Man. Manuel F. Izquierdo Fernández.

Empresa Minera de Aysén Ltda: Calle 21, De Mayo 466, 3°, Coyhaique; zinc and lead mining; Gen. Man. Sergio Araneda Valdivieso.

Empresa Nacional del Carbón—ENACAR: Moneda 1025, 6°, Casilla 2056, Santiago; tel. 717201; telex 240522; in charge of coal production; Gen. Man. Col Eudoro Quiñones Silva.

Empresa Nacional de Computación e Informática SA—ECOM: José Pedro Alessandri 1495, Casilla 14796, Santiago; tel. 740076; Pres. Joaquín Prieto Pomareda.

Empresa Nacional de Electricidad, SA—ENDESA: Santa Rosa 76, Casilla 1392, Santiago; tel. 2229080; telex 240491; f. 1944; cap. p.u. 302,276m.; installed capacity 1,937 MW; Chair. Fernando Hormazábal Guajardo; Gen. Man. Mario Zenteno Carvallo.

Empresa Nacional de Explosivos, SA—ENAEX: Agustinas 1350, 3°, Casilla 255-V, Santiago; tel. 6982148; telex 440069; Gen. Man. Oscar Jadue Salvador.

Industria Azucarera Nacional—IANSA: Avda Bustamente 26, Casilla 6099, Correo 22, Santiago; tel. 2258077; telex 240670; f. 1953; cap. US $82.04m.; 1987 production 410,000 metric tons sugar, 100,000 metric tons beet pulp pellets; factories in Curicó, Linares, Rapaco, Los Angeles and Nuble; 75% owned by private sector; Gen. Man. M. Verónica González Gil.

Sociedad Química y Minera de Chile—SOQUIMICH: Moneda 970, 15°, Santiago; tel. 711121; telex 240762; nitrate mining and exploration; Exec. Gen. Man. Eduardo Bobenrieth Giglio.

Corporación Nacional del Cobre de Chile (CODELCO—Chile): Huérfanos 1270; POB 150-D, Santiago; tel. 6988801; telex 240672; f. 1976 as a state-owned enterprise with four copper-producing operational divisions at Chuquicamata, Salvador, Andina and El Teniente; attached to Ministry of Mines; Exec. Pres. Patricio Contesse.

Corporación Nacional Forestal—CONAF: Avda Bulnes 285, Of. 501, Santiago; tel. 722724; telex 440138; f. 1972 to centralize forestry activities, to enforce forestry law, to promote afforestation, to administer subsidies for afforestation projects and to increase and preserve forest resources; manages 13.3m. ha designated as National Parks, Natural Monuments and National Reserves; under Ministry of Agriculture; Exec. Dir Iván Castro Poblete.

Empresa Nacional de Minería—ENAMI: MacIver 459, 2°, Casilla 100-D, Santiago; tel. 382122; telex 240574; promotes the development of the small- and medium-sized mines; attached to Ministry of Mines; Exec. Vice-Pres. Sergio Pérez Hormazábal.

Empresa Nacional de Petróleo—ENAP: Ahumada 341, 3°, Santiago; tel. 381845; telex 240447; f. 1950; development, exploitation and refining of Chilean petroleum resources; attached to Ministry of Mines; CEO Alejandro Marty.

Oficina de Planificación Nacional—ODEPLAN: Ahumada 48, 7°, Casilla 9140, Santiago; tel. 722033; telex 341400; f. 1967 to assist the President of the Republic in all matters relating to social and economic planning; 1982–89 projected expenditure of $10,100m. on c. 15,000 projects; Dir Minister of Planning.

PROCHILE: Dirección General de Relaciones Económicas Internacionales, POB 16587, Correo 9, Santiago; tel. 2317108; telex 240836; f. 1974; bureau of international economic affairs; Dir Guillermo Lunecke Brauning.

Servicio Agrícola y Ganadero—SAG: Avda Bulnes 140, 8°, Santiago; tel. 6982244; under Ministry of Agriculture; Exec. Dir Alejandro Marchant Baeza.

CHILE

Sociedad Agrícola y Servicios Isla de Pascua: Diego de Velásquez 2094, Providencia, Santiago; tel. 2327497; administers agriculture and public services on Easter Island; Gen. Man. FERNANDO MAIRA PALMA.

Subsecretarío de Pesca: Bellavista 168, 18°, Valparaíso; tel. 212187; telex 240318; controls and promotes fishing industry; part of the Ministry of Economic Affairs; Sub-Sec. ROBERTO CABEZAS BELLO.

EMPLOYERS' ORGANIZATIONS

Confederación de la Producción y del Comercio: Estado 337, Of. 507, Casilla 9984, Santiago; tel. 333690; f. 1936; Pres. MANUEL FELIÚ J.; Gen. Man. JOSÉ FRANCISCO AGUIRRE O.

Affiliated organizations:

Asociación de Bancos e Instituciones Financieras de Chile (q.v.).

Cámara Chilena de la Construcción: Huérfanos 1052, 9°, Casilla Clasificador 679, Santiago; tel. 6960450; f. 1951; Pres. JORGE BRONFMAN HOROVITZ; Gen. Man. JAIME REYES GUTIÉRREZ; 1,300 mems.

Cámara Nacional de Comercio de Chile: Santa Lucía 302, 4°, Casilla 1015, Santiago; tel. 397694; telex 340110; f. 1858; Pres. DARÍO VIAL HERRERA; Man. HUMBERTO PRIETO CONCHA; 120 mems.

Sociedad de Fomento Fabril—SOFOFA: Agustinas 1357, 11°-12°, Casilla 44-D, Santiago; tel. 6982646; telex 34035; f. 1883; largest employers' organization; Pres. FERNANDO AGUERO GARCÉS; 2,000 mems.

Sociedad Nacional de Agricultura—SNA: Tenderini 187, 2°, Casilla 40-D, Santiago; tel. 396710; telex 240760; f. 1838; landowners' association; controls Radio Stations CB 57 and XQB8 (FM) in Santiago, CB-97 in Valparaíso, CD-120 in Los Angeles; Pres. JOSÉ MORENO AGUIRRE; Gen. Sec. RAÚL GARCÍA ASTABURUAGA.

Sociedad Nacional de Minería—SONAMI: Teatinos 20, 3°, Of. 33, Casilla 1807, Santiago; tel. 81696; f. 1883; Pres. MANUEL FELIÚ J.; Man. ALFREDO ARAYA MUÑOZ.

Confederación de Asociaciones Gremiales y Federaciones de Agricultores de Chile: Lautaro 218, Los Angeles; registered with Ministry of Economic Affairs 1981; Pres. DOMINGO DURÁN NEUMANN.

Confederación del Comercio Detallista de Chile: Merced 380, 8°, Santiago; tel. 380338; f. 1938; retail trade; registered with Ministry of Economic Affairs 1980; Pres. ELÍAS BRUGÉRE L.; Vice-Pres. IVONNE BETBEDER A.

Confederación Gremial Nacional Unida de la Mediana y Pequeña Industria, Servicios y Artesanado—CONUPIA: Santiago; registered with Ministry of Economic Affairs 1980; small- and medium-sized industries and crafts; Pres. ROBERTO PARRAQUE BONET.

There are many federations of private industrialists, organized by industry and region.

TRADE UNIONS

In September 1973 the Central Única de Trabajadores de Chile (CUT) was outlawed as it was deemed to be a political organ of the Communist Party. Trade union activities have been severely curtailed under the Pinochet regime and in 1978 seven trade union federations, representing 529 trade unions and some 400,000 workers were banned, as they were deemed to be Marxist, and their property was confiscated. However, the CUT was re-launched in August 1988.

New labour legislation introduced in 1979 and embodied in the 1981 constitution included: the right of association; that unions are to be organized only on a company basis; that the Government's right to control union budgets is to be abolished; that union representatives must not engage in any political activity; that strikes involving stoppages to essential public services or which endanger national security are to be prohibited and that strikes may last no longer than 60 days.

There are over 20 national labour federations and unions. The confederations include:

Confederación de la Construcción: Serrano 444, Santiago; tel. 397472; trade union for workers in construction industry; Pres. SERGIO TRONCOSO; Sec.-Gen. CLAUDINA GARCÍA.

Confederación de Empleados Particulares de Chile—CEPCH: Teatinos 727, 3°, Santiago; tel. 722093; trade union for workers in private sector; Pres. EDMUNDO LILLO; Sec.-Gen. FEDERICO MUJICA.

Confederación General de Trabajadores (CGT): Santiago; pro-Govt; Pres. MANUEL CONTRERAS.

Directory

Confederación Marítima de Chile—COMACH: Eleuterio Ramírez 476, 8°, Valparaíso; tel. 257656; f. 1985; Leader EDUARDO RÍOS; Sec.-Gen. SERGIO CORREA; 5,000 mems.

Confederación de Trabajadores del Cobre—CTC: MacIver 283, 5°, Santiago; tel. 380835; Pres. CARLOS OGALDE; Sec.-Gen. ROBERTO CARVAJAL.

Frente Nacional de Trabajadores Demócratas Cristianas —FNT-DC: Carmen 8, 8°, Santiago; Christian Democratic trade union organization; Pres. LUIS SEPÚLVEDA GUTIÉRREZ; Sec.-Gen. MARIO PEREDA SANDOVAL.

Grupo de los Diez: Christian Democratic trade union organization.

Unión Democrática de Trabajadores—UDT: f. 1981; 49 affiliated organizations; set up under auspices of Grupo de los Diez; Leader HERNOL FLORES; c. 780,000 mems.

The trade unions include:

Central Democrática de Trabajadores—CDT: Erasmo Escala 2170, Santiago; tel. 715338; 27 affiliated organizations; Pres. EDUARDO RÍOS ARIAS.

Central Única de Trabajadores de Chile (CUT): Santiago; f. 1988; centre-left organization; Pres. MANUEL BUSTOS; Sec.-Gen. ARTURO MARTÍNEZ M.; c. 300,000 mems; includes:

Comando Nacional de Trabajadores—CNT: Santa Mónica 2015, Santiago; tel. 6989770; f. 1983; 16 affiliated organizations.

Coordinadora Nacional Sindical—CNS: Abdón Cifuentes 67, Santiago; tel. 6985586; national co-ordinating body; 13 affiliated organizations; Pres. (vacant); Sec.-Gen. MOISES LABRAÑA; c. 700,000 mems.

Frente Nacional de Organizaciones Autónomas—FRENAO: Santa Lucía 162, Santiago; tel. 382354; Pres. MANUEL CONTRERAS LOYOLA.

Frente Unitario de Trabajadores—FUT: Compañía 3127, Santiago; tel. 96114; five affiliated organizations; Pres. CARLOS ROJAS; Sec.-Gen. HUMBERTO SOTO.

Transport

Ministerio de Transportes y Telecomunicaciones: Amunátegui 139, Santiago; tel. 726503; telex 240200.

RAILWAYS

The total length of the railway system in 1986 was 8,185 km, of which almost 90% is state-owned. The privately-owned lines are in the north. There are also five international railways, two to Bolivia, two to Argentina and one to Peru.

In 1983 management of the State Railways system was decentralized and divided into three autonomous operating regions, consisting of Northern, Southern and the Arica–La Paz railways. Further decentralization, in 1987, included the Metro Regional de Valparaíso. Future expansion of the Santiago underground transport system is to be carried out by private enterprise.

State Railways

Empresa de los Ferrocarriles del Estado: Avda Bernardo O'Higgins 3322, 3°, Casilla 134-D, Santiago; tel. 796211; telex 242290; f. 1851; 7,241 km of track (1986). The State Railways are divided between the Ferrocarril Regional de Arica (formerly Ferrocarril Arica–La Paz), Ferrocarril Regional del Norte de Chile (formerly Northern Railway), Metro Regional de Valparaíso (passenger service only) and the Ferrocarril del Sur (Southern Railway); Gen. Man. Eng. ROBERTO DARRIGRANDI CHADWICK.

Private Railways

Antofagasta (Chili) & Bolivia Railway PLC: Bolívar 255, Casilla S-T, Antofagasta; tel. 221020; telex 8954284; f. 1888; British-owned; Chair. ANDRÓNICO LUKSIC ABAROA; Gen. Man. FRANCISCO J. COURBIS GREZ. Operates an international railway to Bolivia and Argentina; cargo forwarding services; total track length 728 km.

Ferrocarril Codelco-Chile: Huérfanos 1189, 5°, Santiago; Gen. Man. M. ACEVEDO V.

Diego de Almagro a Potrerillos: 99 km; transport of forest products, minerals and manufactures.

Ferrocarril Rancagua-Teniente: 68 km; transport of forest products, livestock, minerals and manufactures.

Ferrocarril Tocopilla-Toco: Calle Olivares 1229, Santiago; telex 240762; owned by Sociedad Química y Minera de Chile, SA; 116 km; Gen. Man. E. BOBENRIETH.

In 1975 an underground railway in Santiago was begun:

Metro de Santiago: Red de Transporte Colectivo Independiente, Dirección General del Metro, Avda Libertador B. O'Higgins 1426, Santiago; tel. 6988218; telex 240777; started operations Sept. 1975;

27.25 km open in Sept. 1987; 2 lines; Gen. Man. LUDOLF LAUSEN KUHLMANN.

ROADS

Ministerio de Obras Públicas: Dirección de Vialidad, Morandé 59, 2°, Santiago; tel. 6964839; telex 240777; the authority responsible for roads; the total length of roads in Chile in 1988 was 79,222 km, of which 10,320 km were paved. The road system includes the Pan American Highway extending 3,455 km from north to south, almost completely paved. Important projects include the resurfacing of sections of the Pan American Highway and the construction of the Southern Highway Network; a four-year rehabilitation, maintenance and upgrading programme was launched in 1986, at a cost of US $280m.; investment of US $176m. annually; Dir Ing. REMBERTO URREA MUSTER.

SHIPPING

As a consequence of Chile's difficult topography, maritime transport is of particular importance. The principal ports are Valparaíso, Talcahuano, Antofagasta, San Antonio and Punta Arenas.

Chile's merchant fleet had a total capacity of 1,166,465 dwt in 1983.

Supervisory Authorities

Asociación Nacional de Armadores: Blanco 869, Valparaíso; tel. 21257; also Teatinos 20, Of. 91, 9°, Santiago; tel. 710126; shipowners' association; Pres. BELTRÁN URENDA ZEGERS; Man. SERGIO NÚÑEZ RAMÍREZ.

Cámara Marítima de Chile: Blanco 869, Valparaíso; tel. 253443; telex 230491; Pres. RONALD POLLMANN; Man. RODOLFO GARCÍA.

Dirección General de Territorio Marítimo y Marina Mercante: Errázuriz 537, 4°, Valparaíso; telex 230662; Dir Rear Adm. FERNANDO LAZCANO .

Empresa Portuaria de Chile—EMPORCHI: Blanco 839, Valparaíso; tel. 257167; telex 230313; also Huérfanos 1055, Of. 804, Santiago; tel. 6982232; telex 240624; Dir Vice-Adm. (retd) JORGE BAEZA CONCHA.

Santiago

Cía Marítima Isla de Pascua, SA (COMAIPA): MacIver 225, Of. 2001, 20°, Santiago; tel. 383036; telex 240646; Pres. FEDERICO BARRAZA; Gen. Man. ALEJANDRO BARRAZA BARRY.

Marítima Antares, SA: MacIver 225, Of. 2001, 2°, Santiago; tel. 383036; telex 340464; Pres. ALFONSO GARCÍA-MIÑAUR G.; Gen. Man. LUIS BEDRIÑANA RODRÍGUEZ.

Valparaíso

A. J. Broom y Cía, SAC: Blanco 951, POB 910, Valparaíso and Agustinas 853, 6°, POB 448, Santiago; f. 1920; Pres. Capt. JENS SORENSEN; Gen. Man. MARCELO VARGAS MUÑOZ.

Cía Chilena de Navegación Interoceánica SA: Avda Libertador B. O'Higgins 949, 2°, Casilla 4246; Santiago; tel. 6968147; telex 240486; also Plaza de la Justicia 59, Casilla 1410, Valparaíso; tel. 259001; telex 230386; f. 1930; regular sailings to Brazil, River Plate, Japan, Republic of Korea, Taiwan, Hong Kong, USA and Europe; bulk and dry cargo services; Pres. BELTRÁN URENDA Z.; Gen. Man. ANTONIO JABAT ALONSO.

Cía Sud-Americana de Vapores: Blanco 895, Casilla 49-V, Valparaíso; tel. 259061; telex 230001; also Moneda 970, 10°, 11°, Santiago; tel. 6964181; telex 240480; f. 1872; 14 cargo vessels; regular service between Chile and US/Canadian East Coast ports, US Gulf ports, North European, Mediterranean, Scandinavian and Far East ports; bulk carriers, tramp and reefer services; Pres. RICARDO CLARO VALDÉS; Man. PATRICIO FALCONE SCHIAVETTI.

Empresa Marítima del Estado (Empremar): Almirante Gómez Carreño 49, POB 105-V, Valparaíso; tel. 258061; telex 230382; f. 1953; state-owned; 14 vessels; international and coastal services; Dir RODOLFO CALDERÓN ALDUNATE; Vice-Pres. ALVARO LARENAS LETELIER.

Naviera Chilena del Pacífico, SA: Errázuriz 556, Casilla 370, Valparaíso; tel. 250551; telex 230357; also Serrano 14, Of. 502, Santiago; tel. 333063; telex 240457; cargo; 3 vessels; Pres. ARTURO FERNÁNDEZ; Gen. Man. PABLO SIMIAN.

Naviera Interoceangas, SA: Agustinas 1357, 3°, POB 2829, Santiago; tel. 6963211; telex 341234; Man. PEDRO LECAROS MENÉNDEZ.

Pacific Steam Navigation Co: Blanco 625, 6°, Casilla 24-V, Valparaíso; tel. 213191; telex 230384; also Moneda 970, 9°, Casilla 4087, Santiago; brs in Antofagasta and San Antonio; Man. DAVID KIMBER SMITH.

Sociedad Anónima de Navegación Petrolera (SONAP): Errázuriz 471, 3°, Casilla 1870, Valparaíso; tel. 259476; telex 230392; f. 1953; tanker services; 4 vessels; Deputy Man. EDUARDO RUIZ C.

Transmares Naviera Chilena Ltda: Moneda 970, 19°, Casilla 193-D, Santiago; tel. 722686; telex 240440; also Cochrane 813, 8°, Valparaíso; tel. 259051; telex 230383; f. 1969; dry cargo service Chile-Uruguay-Brazil; Gen. Man. ERICH STRELOW.

Several foreign shipping companies operate services to Valparaíso.

Ancúd

Sociedad Transporte Marítimo Chiloé-Aysén Ltda: Casilla 387, Ancúd; tel. 317; Deputy Man. PEDRO HERNÁNDEZ LEHMAN.

Puerto Montt

Naviera Magallanes SA (NAVIMAG): Avda Suiza 248, Cerrillos, POB 2829, Santiago; tel. 5572650; telex 340885; f. 1979; Gen. Man. PATRICIO LATORRE SEPÚLVEDA; Man. FRANCISCO SAHLI CRUZ.

Punta Arenas

Cía Marítima de Punta Arenas, SA: Casilla 337, Punta Arenas; telex 280009; also Casilla 2829, Santiago; tel. 6963211; telex 380041; f. 1949; shipping agents and owners operating in the Magellan Straits; Dir ROBERTO IZQUIERDO MENÉNDEZ.

San Antonio

Naviera Aysén Ltda: San Antonio; tel. 32578; telex 238603; also Huérfanos 1147, Of. 542, Santiago; tel. 6988680; telex 240982; Man. RAÚL QUINTANA A.

Naviera Paschold Ltda: Centenario 9, San Antonio; tel. 31654; telex 238603; also Huérfanos 1147, Santiago; tel. 6988680; telex 240982; Gen. Man. FERNANDO MARTÍNEZ M.

CIVIL AVIATION

There are 325 airfields in the country, of which eight have long runways. Arturo Merino Benítez, 20 km north-east of Santiago, and Chacalluta, 14 km north-east of Arica, are the principal international airports.

Línea Aérea Nacional de Chile (LAN-Chile): Huérfanos 757, Santiago; tel. 394411; telex 441061; government airline; f. 1929; operates scheduled internal passenger and cargo services, also Santiago-Easter Island; international services to Argentina, Bolivia, Brazil, Canada, French Polynesia, Peru, Spain, the USA, Uruguay and Venezuela; under the Govt's privatization programme, a 51% stake in LAN-Chile was to be sold to private interests in 1989; Gen. Man. JORGE PATRICIO SEPÚLVEDA CERÓN; fleet: 1 Boeing 747, 4 Boeing 737, 4 Boeing 707, 2 Boeing 767.

Línea Aérea del Cobre SA (LADECO): Victoria Subercaseaux 381, POB 13740, Santiago; tel. 395053; telex 240116; f. 1958; internal passenger and cargo services; international passenger and cargo services to Argentina, Brazil, Colombia, Ecuador, Paraguay and the USA; Chair. JOSÉ-LUIS IBÁÑEZ; CEO ERNESTO SILVA BAFALLUY; fleet of 7 Boeing 727-100, 1 Boeing 707-320C, 2 Fokker F27-500.

Tourism

Chile has a wide variety of attractions for the tourist, including fine beaches, ski resorts in the Andes, lakes and rivers. There are many opportunities for hunting and fishing in the southern archipelago, where there are plans to make an integrated tourist area with Argentina, requiring investment of US $120m. Isla de Pascua (Easter Island) may also be visited by tourists.

Servicio Nacional de Turismo—SERNATUR: Calle Catedral 1165, 3° y 4°, Casilla 14082, Santiago; tel. 6967141; telex 240137; f. 1975; Dir MARGARITA DUCCI BUDGE.

Asociación Chilena de Empresas de Turismo—ACHET: Moneda 973, Of. 674, Casilla 3402, Santiago; tel. 6985385; f. 1946; 205 mems; Pres. CLEMENTE GUARDA AURAS.

Atomic Energy

Comisión Chilena de Energía Nuclear: Amunátegui 95, Casilla 188-D, Santiago; tel. 6990070; telex 340468; f. 1965; government body to develop peaceful uses of atomic energy; autonomous organization that concentrates, regulates and controls all matters related to nuclear energy; Pres. Lt-Gen. HERMAN BRADY ROCHE; Exec. Dir Ing. VÍCTOR AGUILERA ACEVEDO.

In 1980 the Government decided to postpone the building of a nuclear power station until the end of the century on grounds of commercial viability.

THE PEOPLE'S REPUBLIC OF CHINA

Note: The Pinyin system of transliteration has replaced the Wade-Giles system.

Introductory Survey

Location, Climate, Language, Religion, Flag, Capital

The People's Republic of China covers a vast area of eastern Asia, with Mongolia to the north, the USSR to the north and west, Afghanistan and Pakistan to the west, and India, Nepal, Bhutan, Burma, Laos and Viet-Nam to the south. The country borders the Democratic People's Republic of Korea in the north-east, and has a long coastline on the Pacific Ocean. The climate ranges from sub-tropical in the far south to an annual average temperature of below 10°C (50°F) in the north, and from the monsoon climate of eastern China to the aridity of the north-west. The principal language is Northern Chinese (Mandarin); in the south and south-east local dialects are spoken. The Xizangzu (Tibetans), Wei Wuer (Uighurs), Menggus (Mongols) and other groups have their own languages. The traditional religions and philosophies of life are Confucianism, Buddhism and Daoism. There are also small Muslim and Christian minorities. The national flag (proportions 3 by 2) is plain red, with one large five-pointed gold star and four similar but smaller stars, arranged in an arc, in the upper hoist. The capital is Beijing (Peking).

Recent History

The People's Republic of China was proclaimed on 1 October 1949, following the victory of Communist forces over the Kuomintang government, which fled to the island province of Taiwan. The new Communist regime received widespread international recognition, but it was not until 1971 that the People's Republic was admitted to the United Nations, in place of the Kuomintang regime, as the representative of China. Most other countries now recognize the People's Republic.

With the establishment of the People's Republic, the leading figure in China's political affairs was Mao Zedong, who was Chairman of the Chinese Communist Party (CCP) from 1935 until his death in 1976. Chairman Mao, as he was known, also became Head of State in October 1949, but he relinquished this post in December 1958. His successor was Liu Shaoqi, First Vice-Chairman of the CCP, who was elected Head of State in April 1959. Liu was dismissed in October 1968, during the Cultural Revolution (see below), and died in prison in 1969. The post of Head of State was left vacant, and was formally abolished in January 1975, when a new constitution was adopted. The first Premier (Head of Government) of the People's Republic was Zhou Enlai, who held this office from October 1949 until his death in 1976. Zhou was also Minister of Foreign Affairs from 1949 to 1958, and subsequently remained largely responsible for China's international relations.

In the early years of the People's Republic, China was dependent on the USSR for economic and military aid, and Chinese planning was based on the Soviet model, with highly centralized control. From 1955 onwards, however, Mao Zedong set out to develop a distinctively Chinese form of socialism. As a result of increasingly strained relations between Chinese and Soviet leaders, caused partly by ideological differences, the USSR withdrew all technical aid to China in August 1960. Chinese hostility to the USSR increased, and was aggravated by territorial disputes between the two countries.

Sino-Soviet friction was accompanied by an improvement in China's relations with Japan and the West during the 1970s. Almost all Western countries had recognized the Government of the People's Republic as the sole legitimate government of China, and had consequently withdrawn recognition from the 'Republic of China', which had been confined to Taiwan since 1949. The People's Republic claimed Taiwan as an integral part of its territory, although the island remained to be 'liberated'. For many years, however, the USA refused to recognize the People's Republic but, instead, regarded the Taiwan regime as the legitimate Chinese government. In February 1972 President Richard Nixon of the USA visited the People's Republic and acknowledged that 'Taiwan is a part of China'. In January 1979 the USA recognized the People's Republic and severed diplomatic relations with Taiwan.

The economic progress which was achieved during the early years of Communist rule enabled China to withstand the effects of the industrialization programmes of the late 1950s (called the 'Great Leap Forward'), the drought of 1960–62 and the withdrawal of Soviet aid in 1960. To prevent the establishment of a ruling class, Chairman Mao launched the Great Proletarian Cultural Revolution in 1966. The ensuing excesses of the Red Guards caused the army to intervene; Liu Shaoqi, Head of State, and Deng Xiaoping, General Secretary of the CCP, were disgraced. In 1971 an attempted coup by the Defence Minister, Marshal Lin Biao, was unsuccessful, and by 1973 it was apparent that Chairman Mao and Premier Zhou Enlai had retained power. In 1975 Deng Xiaoping re-emerged as first Vice-Premier and Chief of the General Staff. Zhou Enlai died in January 1976. Hua Guofeng, hitherto Minister of Public Security, was appointed Premier, and Deng was dismissed. Mao died in September 1976. His widow, Jiang Qing, tried unsuccessfully to seize power, with the help of three radical members of the CCP's Politburo. The 'gang of four' and six associates of Lin Biao were tried in November 1980. All were found guilty. The 10th anniversary of Mao's death was marked in September 1986 by an official reassessment of his life; while his accomplishments were praised, it was now acknowledged that he had made mistakes, although most of the criticism was directed at the 'gang of four'.

In October 1976 Hua Guofeng succeeded Mao as Chairman of the CCP and Commander-in-Chief of the People's Liberation Army. The 11th Congress of the CCP, held in August 1977, restored Deng Xiaoping to his former posts. In September 1980 Hua Guofeng resigned as Premier but retained his chairmanship of the CCP. The appointment of Zhao Ziyang, a Deputy Premier since April 1980, to succeed Hua as Premier, confirmed the dominance of the moderate faction of Deng Xiaoping. In June 1981 Hua Guofeng was replaced as Chairman of the CCP by Hu Yaobang, former Secretary-General of the Politburo, and as Chairman of the Military Affairs Commission by Deng Xiaoping. A sustained campaign by Deng to purge the Politburo of leftist elements led to Hua's demotion to a Vice-Chairman of the CCP and, in September 1982, to his exclusion from the Politburo.

In September 1982 the CCP was reorganized and the post of Party Chairman abolished. Hu Yaobang became, instead, General Secretary of the CCP. A year later a 'rectification' (purge) of the CCP was launched, aimed at expelling 'Maoists', who had risen to power during the Cultural Revolution, and those opposed to the pragmatic policies of Deng. China's new Constitution, adopted in December 1982, restored the office of Head of State, and in June 1983 Li Xiannian, a former Minister of Finance, became President of China.

In 1983–84 several moves were made to consolidate the authority of the Government: following the announcement of a major anti-crime drive in late 1983, thousands of people were reported to have been executed, while at the same time a campaign was launched against 'spiritual pollution'; stricter censorship was introduced to limit the effects of Western cultural influences. The reorganization of the CCP continued, and several senior cadres were dismissed or discredited. During 1984–85 a programme of modernization for the armed forces was undertaken, during which several senior officers were replaced, in accordance with the policy of rejuvenation in all areas of China's leadership. In July and October 1984 five members of the State Council (Cabinet) were replaced by considerably younger politicians, and during 1985 several more ministers were replaced. In September 1985 a special CCP conference was held (for only the second time since 1949), to approve a major reshuffle of senior CCP leaders. In a move intended to give 'new vigour' to the leadership, 10 veteran Politburo members (including, most notably, Marshal Ye Jianying, one of China's most influential military leaders) resigned to make way for six new, younger members, while five new appointments were also made to the CCP secretariat. The rejuvenated Politburo was regarded as strongly pro-Deng, while the influence of the military was perceptibly reduced, and the changes were seen as an attempt to ensure the continuation of Deng's reforms until the end of the century. In September 1986 the sixth plenary session of the CCP Central Committee adopted a detailed resolution on the 'guiding principles for building a socialist society', which redefined the general ideology of the CCP, to provide a theoretical basis for the programme of modernization and the 'open door' policy.

In January 1986 a high-level 'anti-corruption' campaign was launched, to investigate reports that many officials had exploited the programme of economic reform for their own gain. In the field of culture and the arts, however, there was a significant liberalization in 1986, with a revival of the 'Hundred Flowers' movement of 1956–57, which had encouraged the development of intellectual debate. However, a wave of student demonstrations in major cities in late 1986 was regarded by China's leaders as an indication of excessive 'bourgeois liberalization', and in the ensuing government clamp-down, in January 1987, Hu Yaobang unexpectedly resigned as CCP General Secretary, being accused of 'mistakes on major issues of political principles'. Zhao Ziyang became acting General Secretary. In 1988 two leading intellectuals, Fang Lizhi and Liu Binyan, were partially politically rehabilitated, following their expulsion from the CCP in 1987. Further protests by students demanding reforms took place in Beijing in June 1988.

The campaign against 'bourgeois liberalization' was widely regarded as part of a broader, ideological struggle between those Chinese leaders who sought to extend Deng's reforms and those, generally elderly, 'conservative' leaders who opposed the reforms and the 'open door' policy. At the 13th National Congress of the CCP, which opened in October 1987, it became clear that the 'reformist' faction within the Chinese leadership had prevailed. The 'work report', delivered to the Congress by Zhao Ziyang, emphasized the need for further reform and the extension of the 'open door' policy. The composition of the new Central Committee of 285 members, appointed by the Congress, was also regarded as a victory for the 'reformist' faction, which had sought to rejuvenate the Chinese leadership. Of the 209 members of the outgoing Central Committee, only 90 were re-elected, and many of those who retired were elderly opponents of Deng's reforms. Deng Xiaoping himself retired from the Central Committee, but amendments to the Constitution of the CCP permitted him to retain the influential position of Chairman of the Central Military Commission. He was thus believed to have achieved his principal aim of resigning from some posts within the CCP, while retaining overall control of Chinese affairs.

The new Politburo, appointed by the Central Committee in November 1987, represented the fulfilment of another of Deng's goals: the promotion of his supporters within the CCP. The majority of its 18 members were relatively young officials, including the mayors, or party secretaries, of China's major industrial cities, which had been at the forefront of the urban reform programme. The membership of the new Politburo also indicated the further decline of military influence in Chinese politics. The newly-appointed Standing Committee of the Politburo consisted of Zhao Ziyang (who was also confirmed as General Secretary of the CCP and appointed Deputy Chairman of the Central Military Commission), Hu Qili, Qiao Shi, Yao Yilin and Li Peng. The new Standing Committee was regarded, on balance, as being 'pro-reform'. A further amendment to the Constitution of the CCP placed the Central Committee under the control of the Politburo, providing for its members to be nominated by the Standing Committee and responsible to it. In late November Li Peng was appointed Acting Premier of the State Council, in place of Zhao Ziyang.

At the seventh NPC, held over the period 25 March–13 April 1988, Li Peng was confirmed as Premier, and Yang Shangkun (a member of the CCP Politburo) was elected President. The trend towards reform was continued with the replacement of Peng Zhen, by Wan Li, as Chairman of the NPC Standing Committee. At a party plenum in September 1988, a programme for price reform was approved, although the poor condition of the domestic economy subsequently led to the deferment of further price reform.

Tibet (now Xizang), a semi-independent region of western China, was occupied in 1950 by Chinese Communist forces. In March 1959 there was an unsuccessful armed uprising by Tibetans opposed to Chinese rule. As a result, the Dalai Lama, the head of Tibet's Buddhist clergy and thus the region's spiritual leader, fled to India, and has since remained in exile. The Chinese ended the former dominance of the lamas (Buddhist monks) and destroyed many monasteries. Tibet became an 'Autonomous Region' of China in September 1965, but the majority of Tibetans have continued to regard the Dalai Lama as their 'god-king', and to resent the Chinese presence. In October 1987, shortly before the 37th anniversary of China's occupation of Tibet, violent clashes occurred in Lhasa (the regional capital) between the Chinese authorities and Tibetans seeking independence. Further demonstrations during a religious festival in March 1988 resulted in a riot and several deaths, and a number of Tibetan separatists were arrested and detained without trial. In December an offer from the Dalai Lama to meet Chinese representatives in Geneva was rejected, and later that month two more demonstrators were killed by security forces during a march to commemorate the 40th anniversary of the UN's adoption of the Universal Declaration of Human Rights.

China condemned Viet-Nam's invasion of Kampuchea in December 1978, and launched a punitive attack into northern Viet-Nam in February 1979. Armed clashes across the border continued, and negotiations between the two countries failed to resolve the dispute. China has given sustained financial and military support to Kampuchean resistance organizations, notably the communist Khmer Rouge, but Viet-Nam's resolution to withdraw its troops by 1990 has prompted China to reduce arms supplies to the Khmer Rouge. In November 1988 China advocated the formation of a government comprising the four active political factions in Kampuchea. Taiwan has repeatedly rejected China's proposals for reunification, whereby Taiwan would become a 'special administrative region', although trade and reciprocal visits greatly increased in 1988, as relations improved. China has, however, confirmed its intention to re-establish sovereignty over Hong Kong when the existing lease on most of the territory expires in 1997; in September 1984, following protracted negotiations, China reached agreement with the British Government over the terms of Chinese administration of the territory after that date. In June 1986 China and Portugal opened formal negotiations for the return of the Portuguese overseas territory of Macau to full Chinese sovereignty. In January 1987 the Portuguese Council of State agreed that withdrawal from Macau should take place in 1999. The agreement is based upon the 'one country, two systems' principle, which formed the basis of China's negotiated settlement regarding the return of Hong Kong.

High-level negotiations between Chinese and Soviet officials in August 1987 resulted in partial agreement concerning the demarcation of the disputed Sino-Soviet border at the Amur river. Further points of contention between China and the USSR have included Soviet support for the presence of Vietnamese troops in Kampuchea and the continued Soviet military involvement in Afghanistan. However, the phased withdrawal of all Soviet troops from Afghanistan, begun in May 1988, in addition to an undertaking, expressed by the Vietnamese Government, to remove 50,000 of its troops from Kampuchea, by the end of 1988, contributed to a significant improvement in Sino-Soviet relations throughout the year. In December 1988 the Chinese Minister of Foreign Affairs visited Moscow and it was thought likely that a 'summit' meeting between the two countries would take place in early 1989, the first since 1959. Moves to normalize Sino-Soviet relations were also facilitated by closer US-Soviet relations in 1988, and by the USSR's pledges to reduce the strength of its forces in Mongolia. The Soviet President, Mikhail Gorbachev, has, in addition, proposed the creation of joint economic zones on the Sino-Soviet border.

China's relations with the USA have also improved: Premier Zhao Ziyang visited Washington in January 1984, and President Ronald Reagan visited Beijing in April, when a bilateral agreement on industrial and technological co-operation was signed. The main obstacle to Sino-US relations remains the question of Taiwan, and, in particular, the continued sale of US armaments to Taiwan. A *rapprochement* with India was increasingly probable, following the visit by the Indian Prime Minister, Rajiv Gandhi, in December 1988. Relations between the two countries have been strained since 1962, owing to a dispute over their common border.

China's relations with Japan, its leading trading partner, began to deteriorate in 1982, after China complained that passages in Japanese school textbooks sought to justify the Japanese invasion of China in 1937. Since 1985 China has

THE PEOPLE'S REPUBLIC OF CHINA

expressed dissatisfaction at the level of its trade deficit with Japan, and at the low inflow of Japanese investment into China. Chinese leaders have also criticized the rising level of Japan's defence spending and its close commercial relations with Taiwan.

Government

China is a unitary state. Directly under the Central Government there are 22 provinces, five autonomous regions, including Xizang (Tibet), and three municipalities (Beijing, Shanghai and Tianjin). The highest organ of state power is the National People's Congress (NPC). In March 1988 the NPC had 2,970 deputies, indirectly elected for five years by the people's congresses of the provinces, autonomous regions, municipalities directly under the Central Government, and the People's Liberation Army. The NPC elects a Standing Committee to be its permanent organ. The current Constitution, adopted by the NPC in December 1982, was China's fourth since 1949. It restored the office of Head of State (President of the Republic). Executive power is exercised by the State Council (Cabinet), comprising the Premier, Vice-Premiers and other Ministers heading ministries and commissions. The State Council is appointed by, and accountable to, the NPC.

Political power is held by the Chinese Communist Party (CCP). The CCP's highest authority is the Party Congress, convened every five years. In October 1987 the CCP's Thirteenth National Congress elected a Central Committee of 175 full members and 110 alternate members. To direct policy, the Central Committee elected an 18-member Politburo.

Local people's congresses are the local organs of state power. Local revolutionary committees, created during the Cultural Revolution, were abolished in January 1980 and replaced by local people's governments.

Defence

China is divided into seven major military units. All armed services are grouped in the People's Liberation Army (PLA). In June 1988, according to Western estimates, the regular forces totalled 3,160,000: the army numbered 2,300,000, the navy 300,000 (including a naval air force of 30,000), the air force 470,000, and strategic rocket units 90,000. There is also a public security force and a civilian militia. Military service is by selective conscription, and lasts for three years in the army and naval infantry, four years in the air force and five years in the navy. Defence expenditure for 1988 was budgeted at 21,530m. yuan.

Economic Affairs

In 1987, according to estimates by the World Bank, China's gross national product (GNP), measured at average 1985-87 prices, was US $319,780m., equivalent to $300 per head. Between 1980 and 1987, it was estimated, GNP per head increased, in real terms, at an average rate of 9.1% per year, the highest growth rate in the world. In 1986 the agricultural sector employed 61% of China's labour force and contributed 35% of net material product (NMP). China, with 21% of the world's population in 1986, accounted for 19% of the world's production of cereals and 40% of the world's pig numbers in that year. China is the world's largest producer of rice, accounting for 36% of the world harvest in 1986. The gross value of China's farm output increased by about 50% in the decade up to 1978. Agricultural output increased by 4.7% in 1987, compared with an increase of 10.8% in 1986. The 1983 harvest of grain (cereals, pulses, soybeans and tubers in 'grain equivalent') exceeded all expectations, reaching 387.3m. metric tons, following the successful implementation of a system of 'rural responsibility' which provided more incentives for agricultural workers. In 1985 production of grain totalled 379.1m. tons, compared with the record 1984 harvest of 407.3m. tons. The grain harvest increased to 391.5m. tons in 1986 and to 401m. tons in 1987. A total output of 400m. tons was anticipated in 1988, and in late 1988 a severe drought was threatening the 1989 harvest. The responsibility system was taken a step further in January 1985, with the abolition of the mandatory purchase of staple crops by the State, thus permitting private grain sales by producers for the first time.

China has large mineral deposits, such as coal and iron ore, which serve the iron and steel works at Anshan, Shanghai, Baotou, Wuhan and smaller plants elsewhere. In September 1985 the first stage of the Baoshan iron and steel complex began operations. Baoshan is China's largest steel plant, with an annual production capacity of 6.5m. tons. Total production of crude steel reached 52m. tons in 1986, 56m. tons in 1987, and was forecast to reach 59m. tons in 1988. Production of hard and brown coal increased by 5.5% in 1987 to total about 950m. metric tons. Other important minerals include tungsten, molybdenum, antimony, tin, lead, mercury, bauxite, phosphate rock and manganese. The gross value of China's industrial output doubled in the decade to 1978. In 1979 emphasis shifted from heavy to light industry, but in 1982 this policy was reversed, and measures were adopted to accelerate the growth of heavy industry. In 1987 heavy industry and light industry made approximately equal contributions to the value of total industrial output, which increased by 14.6%, substantially above the planned rate of growth. For the first nine months of 1988 output rose by 17.5% over the equivalent period in 1987 and totalled 883,300m. yuan. The development of China's chemical industry is being promoted, while the electronics sector is of growing importance and has moved into areas of high technology, such as microelectronics, satellite communications and computer technology. The energy sector is being given priority in development, and the petroleum industry is expanding steadily, although around 79% of the country's fuel and power needs are still met by coal. Output of power reached 449,536m. kWh in 1986, 496,000m. kWh in 1987, and increased by around 6%, to reach 526,000m. kWh, in 1988. Since 1973 China has been self-sufficient in petroleum and its derivatives, and in 1987 the country produced 134m. tons of crude petroleum. By the end of 1984, Chinese and foreign oil companies had spent US $1,600m. on the exploration of China's offshore petroleum reserves, one of the principal areas for joint-venture contracts, and it was reported in 1985 that foreign oil companies would henceforth be permitted to explore for petroleum reserves in parts of mainland China as well. The oil trade accounted for 18% of the country's total foreign exchange earnings in 1987. China is developing its own petrochemical industries, including fibres and plastics, and is a major producer and consumer of nitrogenous fertilizers. Petrochemical products accounted for 25% of China's total export volume in 1985.

The development of the economy since 1953 has been within the framework of five-year plans, but recessions occurred in the wake of the Great Leap Forward (1958-60) and during the Cultural Revolution (1966-76). In 1980 it was decided to replace the unrealistic 1976-85 Plan by a Ten-Year Plan (1981-90) and a Five-Year Plan (1981-85), and to slow down the 'four modernizations' (agriculture, industry, defence, and science and technology). During the Sixth Five-Year Plan (1981-85) gross national product (GNP) increased at an average annual rate of 10%; industrial output increased by 12% and agricultural output by 8.1% per year. The Seventh Five-Year Plan (1986-90) aimed to continue the modernization of the economy, with priority given to reform and the expansion of the 'open door' policy. The state management of enterprises was to change gradually from direct control to indirect control, to establish 'a new socialist macroeconomic management system'. Major reforms were envisaged in the sectors of banking, pricing policy, labour law and agriculture. Target growth rates were lower than during the previous Plan: GNP was planned to increase by an annual average of 7.5%, while industrial and agricultural output was targeted to increase by 6.7%. It was acknowledged that the reforms of 1984 produced excessive growth in some areas: industrial output, for example, rose by 23.1% in the first half of 1985 (compared with the same period in 1984), well above the planned increase of 8% for the whole year, and requiring a series of measures to slow the growth rate. Since 1985 the Chinese economy has also experienced severe problems of economic control, especially control of investment. The balance of payments has become a serious problem, foreign borrowing has accelerated and foreign investment has been much lower than desired. During 1986 the economy was the object of sustained efforts to bring investment under control and to balance external payments. Excluding rural industry, the value of industrial output rose by 9.2%, while the combined output of industry and agriculture increased by 9.3%, compared with 12.3% in 1985. This moderation of growth was regarded as a positive development, although it contributed to a budget deficit of 7,080m. yuan. In 1987 GNP increased by 9.4%, to reach a value of 1,104,900m. yuan. State revenues amounted to 234,663m. yuan, with expenditure totalling 242,692m. yuan, leaving a deficit of 8,029m. yuan. GNP totalled 1,360,000m. yuan in 1988.

China's banking sector is being restructured to meet the needs of the country's rapid economic modernization, and in June 1985 the first foreign joint-venture bank was established in Shenzhen. Two more joint-venture banks were expected to be inaugurated in 1989. The services sector, in general, is of growing importance: in 1984 the output value of China's tertiary industry reached 150,200m. yuan, up 14.6% over 1983 and accounting for 22.1% of total output. In 1986 NMP reached 779,000m. yuan, an increase of 11.2% over the 1985 total. NMP rose to 915,300m. yuan in 1987, and was expected to reach 1,110,000m. yuan in 1988. An ambitious development programme is under way, calling for output from agriculture and industry to quadruple between 1980 and 2000.

In 1985, in an attempt to restrict a sizeable trade deficit, strict controls were introduced on government purchases of foreign goods, and certain import duties were increased. During 1986 there was some improvement in China's trade and balance-of-payments position, reflecting the implementation of more stringent controls on imports. The value of exports, at US $30,942.1m., increased by 13.1%, while that of imports rose by only 1.6%, to $42,904.5m. This resulted in the reduction of the visible trade deficit to $11,963m. This was further reduced in 1987, to $3,700m. During the first 11 months of 1988, the value of China's exports rose to US $41,100m., an increase of 21% compared with the corresponding period of 1987. At the same time, the value of China's imports, at US $46,500m., increased by 27% compared with the corresponding period of 1987. China's trade deficit for the first 11 months of 1988 therefore totalled US $5,400m. In 1986 a current account deficit of US $7,030m. was recorded, although this was overturned in 1987, when a surplus of $300m. was achieved. In 1988 a deficit of $2,000m. was predicted.

As part of the drive for modernization, China has pursued a much more liberal economic policy. Joint ventures and the acceptance of foreign loans are now permitted, and commercial links have been diversified. Measures to encourage the establishment of joint ventures include the adoption, in October 1986, of a new foreign investment code, which improved credit facilities for foreign investors, and the creation of four 'Special Economic Zones' ('SEZ'), with increased autonomy and flexibility; 14 coastal cities have also been opened for investment. In April 1988 it was announced that Hainan Island would be developed into China's largest 'SEZ', with the status of a separate province. In 1986 the number of joint ventures totalled 891, and during the first half of 1987 a further 725 were initiated. Around 80% of foreign investment allocated by 1986 was from Hong Kong, mainly in the fields of light industry, textiles and hotels. Outside the special zones, the commune system is being downgraded, and a degree of free enterprise is now encouraged as a means of raising living standards (the per caput annual income of peasants rose by 14.7% between 1982 and 1983). Further liberal reforms include measures to introduce capitalist-style market forces and to reduce central government control, with increased incentives for workers and a new system of taxes. China's first stock market opened in Shanghai in September 1986, and is expected to play an increasingly important role in the country's financial system. It is hoped that the successes of the reforms in China's agriculture can thus be transferred to industry. The private sector of the economy has been allowed to develop, particularly in the fields of private transport and construction companies, and the sector's output increased by 88% in 1985. In 1983 official figures for China's foreign debt were published for the first time; total debts at the end of September stood at US $3,000m., mainly to the IMF, the World Bank and Japan. In the year to June 1988 the World Bank provided China with loans totalling $1,053.7m., and IDA credits totalled $639.9m.

The external debt was estimated by Western observers to have reached $24,000m. by December 1987.

By mid-1988, however, sharp rises in the rate of inflation, which had begun in 1987, presented a major threat to the programme of reforms. In the first quarter of 1988 annual inflation rose to 13%, and in May the Politburo endorsed proposals to extend the process of price reform. However, inflation continued to rise, and following year-on-year rises in consumer prices of 24% in July and 28% in September, it was announced that further price reform would be deferred until 1990. The high rate of inflation was exacerbated by a rapid growth in industrial output, which in August 1988 was 18.3% higher than in the previous year. Industrial growth was to be slowed by a re-centralization of decision-making from local governments to the central ministries.

Social Welfare

Western and traditional Chinese medical attention is available in the cities and, to a lesser degree, in rural areas. A fee is charged. In 1984 there were 1.4m. doctors and 198,000 health establishments (including 67,000 hospitals). About 1.3m. 'barefoot doctors', semi-professional peasant physicians, assist with simple cures, treatment and the distribution of contraceptives. There were 2,165,519 hospital beds in 1984. Large factories and other enterprises provide social services for their employees. Industrial wage-earners qualify for pensions. It was announced in 1986 that China was to introduce a social security system to meet the needs of retired people and unemployed contract workers, as part of the planned reform in the labour system.

Education

The education system expanded rapidly after 1949. Fees are charged at all levels. Much importance is attached to kindergartens. Primary education begins for most children at seven years of age and lasts for five years. Secondary education usually begins at 12 years of age and lasts for a further five years, comprising a first cycle of three years and a second cycle of two years. Free higher education was abolished in 1985; instead, college students have to compete for scholarships, which are awarded according to academic ability. Since 1979 education has been included as one of the main priorities for modernization. The whole educational system is to be reformed, with the aim of introducing nine-year compulsory education in 75% of the country by 1995. As a proportion of the total school-age population, enrolment at primary and secondary schools declined from 95% in 1978 to 73% in 1982, but rose to 77% (boys 85%; girls 69%) in 1985. The average rate of adult illiteracy in 1982 was 34.5% (males 20.8%; females 48.9%). In 1986 there were about 131.8m. pupils enrolled at primary schools, while 53.7m. were at secondary schools and 1,880,000 received higher education (1,960,000 in 1987).

Public Holidays

1989: 5–7 February* (Lunar New Year), 8 March (International Women's Day), 1 May (Labour Day), 1 August (Army Day), 1–2 October (National Days).

1990: 26–28 February* (Lunar New Year), 8 March (International Women's Day), 1 May (Labour Day), 1 August (Army Day), 1–2 October (National Days).

* From the first to the third day of the first moon of the lunar calendar.

Weights and Measures

The metric system is officially in force, but some traditional Chinese units are still used.

THE PEOPLE'S REPUBLIC OF CHINA   *Statistical Survey*

Statistical Survey

Source (unless otherwise stated): State Statistical Bureau, San Li He, Beijing; tel. 868521.

Note: Wherever possible, figures in this Survey exclude Taiwan province. In the case of unofficial estimates for China, it is not always clear if Taiwan is included or excluded. Where a Taiwan component is known, either it has been deducted from the all-China figure or its inclusion is noted.

Area and Population

AREA, POPULATION AND DENSITY

Area (sq km)	9,571,300*
Population (census results)	
1 July 1964	694,580,000
1 July 1982	
Males	519,421,198
Females	488,759,540
Total	1,008,180,738
Population (official estimates at 31 December)	
1984	1,034,750,000
1985	1,045,320,000
1986	1,057,210,000
Density (per sq km) at 31 December 1986	110.5

Population (at 1 July 1988): 1,072,330,000.

* 3,695,500 sq miles.

BIRTHS AND DEATHS (sample surveys)

	1985	1986	1987
Birth rate (per 1,000)	17.80	20.77	21.04
Death rate (per 1,000)	6.57	6.69	6.65

LIFE EXPECTANCY (years at birth)

Males 61.8 in 1970–75, 66.0 in 1975–80; Females 64.6 in 1970–75, 68.6 in 1975–80 (UN estimates, including Taiwan).

1981 (official estimates): 67.88 (Males 66.43; Females 69.35).

ADMINISTRATIVE DIVISIONS (Previous spelling given in brackets)

	Area ('000 sq km)	Population (official estimates at 31 Dec. 1986)* Total ('000)	Density (per sq km)	Capital of province or region	Estimated population ('000), at 31 Dec. 1986†
Provinces					
Sichuan (Szechwan)	567	103,200	182	Chengdu (Chengtu)	2,640
Shandong (Shantung)	153	77,760	507	Jinan (Tsinan)	1,460
Henan (Honan)	167	78,080	468	Zhengzhou (Chengchow)	1,610
Jiangsu (Kiangsu)	103	62,700	611	Nanjing (Nanking)	2,290
Hebei (Hopei)	188	56,170	299	Shijiazhuang (Shihkiachwang)	1,190
Guangdong (Kwangtung)‡	212	63,460	299	Guangzhou (Canton)	3,360
Hunan (Hunan)	210	56,960	271	Changsha (Changsha)	1,190
Anhui (Anhwei)	139	52,170	374	Hefei (Hofei)	900
Hubei (Hupeh)	186	49,890	266	Wuhan (Wuhan)	3,490
Zhejiang (Chekiang)	102	40,700	400	Hangzhou (Hangchow)	1,270
Liaoning (Liaoning)	146	37,260	256	Shenyang (Shenyang)	4,290
Yunnan (Yunnan)	394	34,560	88	Kunming (Kunming)	1,520
Jiangxi (Kiangsi)	169	35,090	211	Nanchang (Nanchang)	1,190
Shaanxi (Shensi)	206	30,430	148	Xian (Sian)	2,390
Heilongjiang (Heilungkiang)	469	33,320	71	Harbin (Harbin)	2,670
Shanxi (Shansi)	156	26,550	170	Taiyuan (Taiyuan)	1,930
Guizhou (Kweichow)	176	30,080	171	Guiyang (Kweiyang)	1,400
Fujian (Fukien)	121	27,490§	227	Fuzhou (Foochow)	1,210
Jilin (Kirin)	187	23,150	124	Changchun (Changchun)	1,910
Gansu (Kansu)	454	20,710	46	Lanzhou (Lanchow)	1,390
Qinghai (Tsinghai)	721	4,120	6	Xining (Hsining)	610
Autonomous regions					
Guangxi Zhuang (Kwangsi Chuang)	236	39,460	167	Nanning (Nanning)	960
Nei Monggol (Inner Mongolia)	1,183	20,290	17	Hohhot (Huhehot)	810
Xinjiang Uygur (Sinkiang Uighur)	1,600	13,840	9	Urumqi (Urumchi)	1,040
Ningxia Hui (Ninghsia Hui)	66	4,240	64	Yinchuan (Yinchuen)	576‖
Xizang (Tibet)	1,228	2,030	2	Lhasa (Lhasa)	105‖
Municipalities					
Beijing (Peking)	17	9,750	580	—	5,970
Shanghai (Shanghai)	6	12,320	1,987	—	7,100
Tianjin (Tientsin)	11	8,190	725	—	5,460
Total	9,571	1,053,970	110		

* Excluding armed forces, totalling 3,240,000.
† Excluding population in counties under cities' administration.
‡ Including Hainan Island, which became a separate province in 1988.
§ Excluding islands administered by Taiwan, mainly Jinmen (Quemoy) and Mazu (Matsu), with 57,847 inhabitants at 31 May 1982.
‖ 1982 figures.

THE PEOPLE'S REPUBLIC OF CHINA

PRINCIPAL TOWNS
(Wade-Giles or other spellings in brackets)
Population at 31 December 1986 (official estimates in '000)*

Town	Population
Shanghai (Shang-hai)	7,180
Beijing (Pei-ching or Peking, the capital)	5,970
Tianjin (T'ien-chin or Tientsin)	5,460
Shenyang (Shen-yang or Mukden)	4,290
Wuhan (Wu-han or Hankow)	3,490
Guangzhou (Kuang-chou or Canton)	3,360
Chongqing (Ch'ung-ch'ing or Chungking)	2,830
Harbin (Ha-erh-pin)	2,670
Chengdu (Ch'eng-tu)	2,640
Xian (Hsi-an or Sian)	2,390
Zibo (Tzu-po or Tzepo)	2,330
Nanjing (Nan-ching or Nanking)	2,290
Taiyuan (T'ai-yüan)	1,930
Changchun (Ch'ang-ch'un)	1,910
Dalian (Ta-lien or Dairen)	1,680
Zhengzhou (Cheng-chou or Chengchow)	1,610
Kunming (K'un-ming)	1,520
Jinan (Chi-nan or Tsinan)	1,460
Tangshan (T'ang-shan)	1,410
Guiyang (Kuei-yang or Kweiyang)	1,400
Lanzhou (Lan-chou or Lanchow)	1,390
Fushun (F'u-shun)	1,300
Qiqihar (Ch'i-ch'i-ha-erh or Tsitsihar)	1,300
Anshan (An-shan)	1,270
Hangzhou (Hang-chou or Hangchow)	1,270
Qingdao (Ch'ing-tao or Tsingtao)	1,270
Fuzhou (Fu-chou or Foochow)	1,210
Changsha (Chang-sha)	1,190
Nanchang (Nan-ch'ang)	1,190
Shijiazhuang (Shih-chia-chuang or Shihkiachwang)	1,190
Jilin (Chi-lin or Kirin)	1,170
Baotau (Pao-t'ou or Paotow)	1,120
Huainan (Huai-nan or Hwainan)	1,090
Luoyang (Lo-yang)	1,060
Urumqi (Urumchi)	1,040
Ningbo (Ning-po)	1,030
Datong (Ta-t'ung or Tatung)	1,020
Handan (Han-tan)	1,010

* Data refer to municipalities, which may include large rural areas as well as an urban centre. The listed towns comprise those with a total population of more than 1,000,000 and a non-agricultural population of more than 500,000.

CIVILIAN EMPLOYMENT
(official estimates, '000 persons at 31 December)

	1984	1985†	1986†
Industry*	63,380	83,484	89,804
Construction and resources prospecting	18,580	21,756	23,760
Agriculture, forestry, water conservancy and meteorology	325,380	311,876	313,106
Transport, posts and telecommunications	10,800	12,221	13,050
Commerce, catering trade, service trade and supply and marketing of materials	23,540	23,631	24,844
Scientific research, culture, education, public health and social welfare	17,790	18,835	19,584
Government agencies and people's organizations	7,430	7,990	8,736
Others	9,070	18,934	19,938
Total	**475,970**	**498,727**	**512,822**

* Mining, manufacturing, electricity, gas and water.
† Figures are not strictly comparable with those for 1984.

Agriculture

PRINCIPAL CROPS
(FAO estimates, unless otherwise indicated, '000 metric tons)

	1984	1985	1986
Wheat†	87,815	85,805	90,040
Rice (paddy)†	178,255	168,569	172,224
Barley	3,300	2,700	2,700
Maize†	73,410	63,826	70,856
Rye	1,400	1,000	1,000
Oats	500	490	500
Millet†	7,025	5,977	4,540
Sorghum†	7,715	5,609	5,384
Other cereals	3,400	2,800	2,700
Potatoes	48,000	45,500	45,000
Sweet potatoes	94,400	90,000	88,500
Cassava (Manioc)	3,800	3,600	3,500
Taro (Coco yam)*	1,462	1,265	1,368
Dry beans	1,800	1,600	1,500
Dry broad beans	2,425	2,300	2,300
Dry peas	2,100	1,900	1,800
Soybeans (Soyabeans)†	9,695	10,500	11,614
Groundnuts (in shell)†	4,815	6,664	5,882
Castor beans	164‡	175‡	200
Sunflower seed†	1,704	1,732	1,544
Rapeseed†	4,205	5,607	5,881
Sesame seed†	476	691	618
Linseed	95‡	98	105
Flax fibre	68	71	72
Cottonseed	12,516	8,294	7,080
Cotton (lint)†	6,258	4,147	3,540
Vegetables and melons*	93,213	99,501	104,771
Fruit (excl. melons)*	11,152	12,853	13,623
Tree nuts*	500	502	557
Sugar cane†	39,519	51,549	50,219
Sugar beet†	8,284	8,919	8,306
Tea (made)†	414.2	432.3	460.5
Tobacco (leaves)†	1,789	2,425	1,707
Jute and jute substitutes†	1,492	4,119	1,420
Natural rubber†	188.8	187.9	209.7

* Including Taiwan. † Official estimates.
‡ Unofficial estimates.
Source: mainly FAO, *Production Yearbook*.

1987 (official estimates, '000 metric tons): Rapeseed 6,730; Cotton (lint) 4,190; Sugar cane 46,850; Sugar beet 7,970; Tea (made) 497; Jute and jute substitutes 960.

LIVESTOCK ('000 head at 31 December)

	1984	1985	1986
Horses	10,978	11,081	10,988
Mules	4,790	4,972	5,113
Asses	9,962	10,415	10,689
Cattle and buffaloes	82,128	86,820	91,667
Camels	531	530	504
Pigs	306,792	331,396	337,191
Sheep	95,193	94,210	99,009
Goats	63,207	61,674	67,220

Poultry (FAO estimates, million, year ending September): 1,200 in 1984; 1,300 in 1985; 1,400 in 1986.

1987 ('000 head at 31 December): Pigs 326,400; Sheep and goats 178,350.

THE PEOPLE'S REPUBLIC OF CHINA

LIVESTOCK PRODUCTS
(FAO estimates, unless otherwise indicated, '000 metric tons)

	1984	1985	1986
Beef and veal*	268‡	340‡	403
Buffalo meat*	113‡	135	155
Mutton and lamb*	300‡	300	325
Goats' meat*	287‡	294‡	301‡
Pig meat*	15,179	17,337	18,810‡
Horse meat*	41	43	46
Poultry meat*	1,757	1,935	2,078
Other meat*	473	497	519
Edible offals*	773	841	905
Lard*	637	685	735
Tallow*	28	31	32
Cows' milk†	2,186	2,499	2,899
Buffaloes' milk	1,560	1,620	1,700
Sheep's milk	525	531	540
Goats' milk	152	160	168
Butter*	47.9	48.9	53.1
Cheese*	206.8	211.2	215.2
Hen eggs	3,800	4,090	4,360
Other poultry eggs*	27.6	26.3	28.0
Honey*	150.7	153.4‡	156.6
Raw silk (incl. waste)†	37.6	38.9	39.1
Wool:			
greasy†	182.8	178.0	185.2
clean	114.0	107.0	110.0
Cattle and buffalo hides*	106.5	129.2	144.0
Sheep skins*	78.4	78.4	85.1
Goat skins*	62.2	63.5	66.2

* Including Taiwan.   † Official estimates.
‡ Unofficial estimates.

Source: mainly FAO, *Production Yearbook*.

Other official estimates ('000 metric tons): Beef, buffalo meat, mutton, goats' meat and pig meat 15,406 (beef and buffalo meat 373, mutton and goats' meat 586, pig meat 14,447) in 1984, 17,607 (beef and buffalo meat 467, mutton and goats' meat 593, pig meat 16,547) in 1985, 19,171 (beef and buffalo meat 589, mutton and goats' meat 622, pig meat 17,960) in 1986, 19,210 (beef, buffalo meat, mutton and goats' meat 1,410, pig meat 17,800) in 1987; Cows' milk 3,190 in 1987; Wool (greasy) 208 in 1987.

Forestry

ROUNDWOOD REMOVALS
(FAO estimates, '000 cubic metres, including Taiwan)

	1984	1985	1986
Sawlogs, veneer logs and logs for sleepers	52,872	53,885	54,592
Pulpwood	5,614	5,614	5,614
Other industrial wood	32,445	34,050	34,050
Fuel wood	167,375	170,715	174,129
Total	258,306	264,264	268,385

Source: FAO, *Yearbook of Forest Products*.

Timber production (official estimates, '000 cubic metres): 52,320 in 1983; 63,850 in 1984; 63,234 in 1985; 65,024 in 1986; 68,430 in 1987.

SAWNWOOD PRODUCTION
(FAO estimates, '000 cubic metres, including Taiwan)

	1984	1985	1986
Coniferous sawnwood	16,708	17,568	17,117
Broadleaved sawnwood	8,987	9,453	9,208
Total	25,695	27,021	26,325

Railway sleepers (FAO estimates, '000 cubic metres): 66 per year in 1980–86.
Source: FAO, *Yearbook of Forest Products*.

Fishing

('000 metric tons, live weight)

	1984	1985	1986
Fishes	4,736.2	5,467.0	6,397.9
Crustaceans	580.0	629.4	691.7
Molluscs	590.7	661.1	884.0
Jellyfishes	19.8*	21.3*	26.5*
Total catch	5,926.8	6,778.8	8,000.1
of which:			
Inland waters	2,249.7	2,943.7	3,363.5
Pacific Ocean	3,677.1	3,835.1	4,636.6

* FAO estimate.

Aquatic plants ('000 metric tons): 1,663.8 in 1984; 1,714.2 in 1985; 1,346.5 in 1986.
Source: FAO, *Yearbook of Fishery Statistics*.
Aquatic products (official estimates, '000 metric tons): 6,193.4 (marine 3,943.7, freshwater 2,249.7) in 1984; 7,051.5 (marine 4,197.5, freshwater 2,854.1) in 1985; 8,235.6 (marine 4,753.7, freshwater 3,481.9) in 1986; 9,400 in 1987.

Mining

('000 metric tons, unless otherwise indicated; unofficial estimates)

	1983	1984	1985
Hard coal	687,630*	759,120*	810,000
Brown coal (incl. lignite)	26,900*	30,110*	35,000
Crude petroleum*	106,068	114,613	124,895
Iron ore*†	56,695	63,350	69,095
Bauxite	1,600	1,600	1,650
Copper ore†	175	180	185
Lead ore†	160	160	160
Magnesite	2,000	2,000	2,000
Manganese ore†	480	480	480
Zinc ore†	160	160	190
Salt (unrefined)*	16,127	16,419	14,789
Phosphate rock	12,500	14,210	12,000
Potash‡	29	40	40
Sulphur (native)	200	200	200
Iron pyrites (unroasted)	5,200	4,700	n.a.
Natural graphite	185	185	185
Antimony ore (metric tons)†	15,000	15,000	15,000
Mercury (metric tons)	700	700	700
Molybdenum ore (metric tons)†	2,000	2,000	2,000
Silver (metric tons)†	78	78	78
Tin concentrates (metric tons)†	17,000	17,500	18,000
Tungsten concentrates (metric tons)†	12,530	13,500	15,000
Gold (kg)†	57,541	59,097	59,097
Natural gas (million cu m)*	12,212	12,425	12,927

* Official estimates.
† Figures refer to the metal content of ores and concentrates.
‡ Potassium oxide (K_2O) content of potash salts mined.

Sources for unofficial estimates: For tin, Metallgesellschaft Aktiengesellschaft (Frankfurt am Main, Federal Republic of Germany); for all other minerals, US Bureau of Mines.

Official estimates ('000 metric tons): Coal (incl. brown coal) 872,284 in 1985, 894,039 in 1986, 920,000 in 1987; Crude petroleum 130,688 in 1986, 134,000 in 1987, 140,000 in 1988; Salt 17,612 in 1986; Natural gas (million cubic metres) 13,764 in 1986.

THE PEOPLE'S REPUBLIC OF CHINA

Industry

SELECTED PRODUCTS
Unofficial Estimates
('000 metric tons, unless otherwise indicated)

	1983	1984	1985
Soyabean oil (crude)[1]	450	n.a.	n.a.
Palm oil (crude)[2]	200	184	192
Tung oil[2]	59	68	70
Rayon continuous filaments[3]	85.0	87.0	87.0
Rayon discontinuous fibres[3]	112.0	115.0	112.0
Non-cellulosic continuous filaments[3]	66.0	103.1	125.0
Non-cellulosic discontinuous fibres[3]	325.0	586.0	632.0
Plywood ('000 cu m)[2,4]	1,738	1,773	1,773
Mechanical wood pulp[2,4]	354	378	417
Chemical wood pulp[2,4]	991	1,057	1,163
Other fibre pulp[2,4]	3,918	4,386	5,467
Newsprint[2,4]	400	400	425
Other paper and paperboard[2,4]	5,696	6,510	7,673
Synthetic rubber[3]	168.9	174.1	181.1
Sulphur[6,7] (a)	350	350	350
(b)	2,300	2,300	2,300
Motor spirit (petrol)[6]	12,277	13,502	14,382
Kerosene[5]	4,102	4,080	4,075
Distillate fuel oils[6]	19,035	19,465	19,892
Residual fuel oil[6]	28,967	28,570	29,505
Aluminium (unwrought)[6]	400	400	410
Refined copper (unwrought)[6]	310	310	400
Lead (unwrought)[6]	195	195	195
Tin (unwrought)[8]	17.0	17.5	18.0
Zinc (unwrought)[6]	175	185	190

[1] Source: US Department of Agriculture. [2] Source: FAO.
[3] Source: Textile Economics Bureau Inc., New York, USA.
[4] Including Taiwan.
[5] Source: UN, *Industrial Statistics Yearbook*.
[6] Source: US Bureau of Mines.
[7] Figures refer to (a) sulphur recovered as a by-product in the purification of coal-gas, in petroleum refineries, gas plants and from copper, lead and zinc sulphide ores; and (b) the sulphur content of iron and copper pyrites, including pyrite concentrates obtained from copper, lead and zinc ores.
[8] Source: Metallgesellschaft Aktiengesellschaft, Frankfurt am Main, Federal Republic of Germany.

1986 (FAO estimates, '000 metric tons): Palm oil 222; Tung oil 75.

Official Estimates ('000 metric tons, unless otherwise indicated)

	1985	1986	1987
Raw sugar	4,513.3	5,246.4	5,110
Beer	3,104.4	4,130.1	n.a.
Cotton yarn (pure and mixed)	3,534.8	3,977.9	4,320
Woven cotton fabrics—pure and mixed (million metres)	14,668	16,473	16,700
Woollen fabrics ('000 metres)	218,160	251,870	260,000
Silk fabrics (million metres)	1,449.0	n.a.	n.a.
Chemical fibres	947.8	1,017.3	n.a.
Paper and paperboard	9,111.5	9,986.3	10,080
Rubber tyres ('000)	19,262.5	19,243.2	n.a.
Ethylene (Ethene)	652.1	695.2	n.a.
Sulphuric acid	6,763.7	7,631.1	9,620
Caustic soda (Sodium hydroxide)	2,353.1	2,518.0	n.a.
Soda ash (Sodium carbonate)	2,011.1	2,146.3	2,370
Insecticides	210.8	203.3	260
Nitrogenous fertilizers (a)*	11,438	11,592	n.a.
Phosphate fertilizers (b)*	1,760	2,340	n.a.
Potash fertilizers (c)*	24	25	n.a.
Plastics	1,234.3	1,320.8	n.a.
Coke-oven coke	38,360	40,927	n.a.
Cement	145,948	166,062	180,000
Pig-iron	43,838	50,638	n.a.

Official Estimates ('000 metric tons, unless otherwise indicated)—*continued*

	1985	1986	1987
Crude steel	46,795	52,197	56,020
Internal combustion engines ('000 horse-power)†	55,465.9	36,079.5	n.a.
Tractors—over 20 horse-power (number)	44,962	28,641	40,000
Sewing machines ('000)	9,912.0	9,894.1	n.a.
Railway locomotives—diesel (number)	746	818	909
Railway freight wagons (number)	19,325	20,592	n.a.
Road motor vehicles ('000)	437.2	369.8	472
Bicycles ('000)	32,276.7	35,682.6	40,910
Watches ('000)	54,470.7	73,319.9	n.a.
Radio receivers ('000)‡	16,003.2	15,895.2	n.a.
Television receivers ('000)	16,676.6	14,594.0	19,380
Cameras ('000)	1,789.7	2,025.4	2,390
Electric energy (million kWh)	410,690	449,536	496,000

* Production in terms of (a) nitrogen; (b) phosphoric acid; or (c) potassium oxide.
† Sales.   ‡ Portable battery sets only.

1988: Crude steel 59m. metric tons; Electric energy 526,000m. kWh.

Finance

CURRENCY AND EXCHANGE RATES
Monetary Units
100 fen (cents) = 1 jiao (chiao) = 1 renminbiao (People's Bank Dollar), usually called a yuan.

Denominations
Coins: 1, 2 and 5 fen.
Notes: 10, 20 and 50 fen; 1, 2, 5 and 10 yuan.

Sterling and Dollar Equivalents (30 September 1988)
£1 sterling = 6.294 yuan;
US $1 = 3.722 yuan;
100 yuan = £15.89 = $26.87.

Average Exchange Rate (yuan per US $)
1985   2.9367
1986   3.4528
1987   3.7221

STATE BUDGET (million yuan)

Revenue	1985	1986	1987*
Tax receipts	204,079	206,450	219,398
Funds for projects	14,679	16,000	17,700
State treasury bonds	6,061	6,200	6,000
Receipts from enterprises	4,375	3,571	16,203
Other domestic receipts	5,224	14,185	
Sub-total	234,418	246,406	259,301
Less Subsidies	50,702	32,246	35,972
Total domestic receipts	183,716	214,160	223,329
Foreign loans	2,924	7,870	14,600
Total	186,640	222,030	237,929

THE PEOPLE'S REPUBLIC OF CHINA

Expenditure	1985	1986	1987*
Capital construction	58,380	65,570	65,593
Subsidies to enterprises	10,342	12,620	10,788
Agriculture and rural communes	10,104	12,032	12,445
Education, science and health services	31,670	38,000	38,778
National defence	19,153	20,126	20,376
Administrative expenses	13,058	16,585	15,608
Total (incl. others)	184,478	229,110	245,946

* Planned figures. Actual totals (in million yuan) were: Revenue 234,663; Expenditure 242,692.

1988 (draft budget, million yuan): Revenue 255,450; Expenditure 263,450 (Capital construction 63,260; National defence 21,526).

SEVENTH FIVE-YEAR PLAN, 1986–90
(proposed investment in fixed assets, '000m. yuan)

State enterprises and institutions	896
Capital construction	500
by central departments	375
by local authorities	112.5
Special Economic Zones	12.5
Technological transformation and equipment renewal	276
Other projects	120
Collective enterprises	160
Private enterprises in towns and counties	240
Total	1,296

INTERNATIONAL RESERVES (US $ million at 31 December)

	1985	1986	1987
Gold*	486	541	629
IMF special drawing rights	483	569	640
Reserve position in IMF	332	370	429
Foreign exchange	11,913	10,514	15,236
Total	13,214	11,994	16,934

* Valued at 35 SDR per troy ounce.
Source: IMF, *International Financial Statistics*.

MONEY SUPPLY (million yuan at 31 December)

	1985	1986	1987
Currency outside banks	98,780	121,840	145,450
Deposits at People's Bank of China	33,260	39,940	45,310
Demand deposits at specialized banks	153,680	204,500	244,690
Demand deposits at rural credit co-operatives	16,010	19,620	21,950
Total money	301,730	385,900	457,400

Source: IMF, *International Financial Statistics*.

COST OF LIVING
(General Retail Price Index. Base: 1950 = 100)

	1984	1985	1986
All items	160.0	174.1	184.5

NATIONAL ACCOUNTS
Net Material Product* (million yuan at current prices)

	1984	1985	1986
Agriculture	225,100	249,200	272,000
Industry	251,600	315,200	355,100
Construction	30,300	39,600	48,900
Transport	20,300	25,000	28,200
Commerce	37,700	71,700	74,800
Total	565,000	700,700	779,000

1987: Total 915,300m. yuan.

* Defined as the total net value of goods and 'productive' services, including turnover taxes, produced by the economy. This excludes economic activities not contributing directly to material production, such as public administration, defence and personal and professional services.

BALANCE OF PAYMENTS (US $ million)

	1985	1986	1987
Merchandise exports f.o.b.	25,108	25,756	34,734
Merchandise imports f.o.b.	−38,231	−34,896	−36,395
Trade balance	−13,123	−9,140	−1,661
Exports of services	4,533	4,927	5,413
Imports of services	−3,070	−3,200	−3,676
Balance on goods and services	−11,660	−7,413	76
Private unrequited transfers	171	255	249
Government unrequited transfers	72	124	−25
Current balance	−11,417	−7,034	300
Long-term capital (net)	4,439	7,547	5,813
Short-term capital (net)	2,270	−2,295	212
Net errors and omissions	34	−263	−1,481
Total (net monetary movements)	−4,674	−2,045	4,844
Valuation changes (net)	36	39	−108
Changes in reserves	−4,638	−2,006	4,735

Source: IMF, *International Financial Statistics*.

External Trade

COMMODITY GROUPS (US $ million)

Imports c.i.f.	1984	1985	1986
Food and live animals	2,331	1,553	1,625
Beverages and tobacco	116	206	172
Crude materials (inedible) except fuels	2,542	3,236	3,143
Mineral fuels, lubricants, etc.	139	172	504
Animal and vegetable oils, fats and waxes	80	122	205
Chemicals and related products	4,237	4,469	3,771
Basic manufactures	7,318	11,898	11,192
Machinery and transport equipment	7,245	16,239	16,781
Miscellaneous manufactured articles	1,182	1,902	1,877
Other commodities and transactions	2,220	2,455	3,634
Total	27,410	42,252	42,904

1987 (provisional, US $ million): Total imports 43,392; Total exports 39,542.

THE PEOPLE'S REPUBLIC OF CHINA

Exports f.o.b.	1984	1985	1986
Food and live animals	3,232	3,803	4,448
Beverages and tobacco	110	105	119
Crude materials (inedible) except fuels	2,421	2,653	2,908
Mineral fuels, lubricants, etc.	6,027	7,132	3,683
Animal and vegetable oils, fats and waxes	144	135	114
Chemicals and related products	1,364	1,358	1,733
Basic manufactures	5,054	4,493	5,886
Machinery and transport equipment	1,493	772	1,094
Miscellaneous manufactured articles	4,697	3,486	4,948
Other commodities and transactions	1,597	3,413	6,009
Total	26,139	27,350	30,942

PRINCIPAL TRADING PARTNERS (US $ million)

Imports c.i.f.	1984	1985	1986
Argentina	93.8	333.1	347.9
Australia	950.1	1,133.9	1,403.1
Belgium	221.8	273.6	339.9
Brazil	438.9	983.5	709.2
Canada	1,126.6	1,159.2	1,010.6
France	378.2	713.2	732.2
Germany, Federal Republic	1,330.9	2,406.7	3,555.6
Hong Kong	2,952.1	4,797.0	5,609.8
Indonesia	230.0	332.0	324.0
Italy	463.8	909.0	1,138.3
Japan	8,503.7	15,035.3	12,438.5
Poland	149.5	234.2	539.8
Romania	455.3	579.8	544.5
Singapore	160.0	242.5	553.0
Spain	219.0	551.1	388.1
Switzerland	182.5	269.9	525.9
USSR	711.0	982.3	1,440.0
United Kingdom	532.7	745.7	1,011.3
USA	4,037.4	5,090.2	4,716.7
Total (including others)	27,409.6	42,252.6	42,904.5

Exports f.o.b.	1984	1985	1986
Brazil	400.1	427.6	255.7
Canada	269.6	234.5	306.5
France	243.7	224.2	321.4
Germany, Federal Republic	811.2	734.3	1,003.7
Hong Kong	6,911.7	7,204.3	9,784.6
Italy	320.3	293.7	363.1
Japan	5,417.9	6,109.0	4,779.5
Jordan	1,300.9	985.4	1,030.9
Macau	319.9	249.4	315.6
Netherlands	333.3	326.2	463.9
Philippines	245.5	315.9	156.9
Poland	128.7	256.2	441.9
Romania	312.3	275.4	260.6
Singapore	1,286.7	2,080.4	1,206.3
Syria	361.8	65.6	319.1
USSR	615.9	995.8	1,199.8
United Kingdom	348.6	353.9	1,433.4
USA	2,432.6	2,339.5	2,631.8
Total (including others)	26,139.0	27,349.8	30,942.1

Transport

	1985	1986	1987
Freight (million ton-km):			
Railways	812,600	876,500	947,100
Roads	177,000	195,800	240,900
Inland waterways	758,400	843,700	939,700
Air	415	480	660
Passenger-km (million):			
Railways	241,600	258,700	284,300
Roads	157,300	168,600	212,900
Inland waterways	17,400	17,100	19,200
Air	11,700	14,600	18,600

SEA-BORNE SHIPPING (freight traffic, '000 metric tons)

	1984	1985	1986
Goods loaded and unloaded	275,490	311,540	377,980

1987 (provisional): 397 million metric tons.

Communications Media

(million copies)

	1985	1986	1987
Newspapers	19,980	19,390	20,600
Magazines	2,560	2,400	2,640
Books	6,670	5,200	6,250

Radio receivers: 15m. in use in 1984.
Television receivers: 9.9m. in use in 1984.

Education

(1986)

	Institutions	Full-time Teachers ('000)	Students ('000)
Kindergartens	173,376	605	16,290
Primary schools	820,846	5,414	131,825
General secondary schools	92,967	2,758	48,899
Secondary technical schools	2,741	143	1,146
Teacher training schools	1,041	50	611
Agricultural and vocational schools	8,187	164	2,560
Special schools	387	7	41
Higher education	1,054	372	1,880

1987: Higher education: Institutions 1,063; Students 1.96m.

Directory

The Constitution

A new constitution was adopted on 4 December 1982 by the Fifth Session of the Fifth National People's Congress. Its principal provisions are set out below. The Preamble, which is not included here, states that 'Taiwan is part of the sacred territory of the People's Republic of China'.

GENERAL PRINCIPLES

Article 1: The People's Republic of China is a socialist state under the people's democratic dictatorship led by the working class and based on the alliance of workers and peasants.

The socialist system is the basic system of the People's Republic of China. Sabotage of the socialist system by any organization or individual is prohibited.

Article 2: All power in the People's Republic of China belongs to the people.

The organs through which the people exercise state power are the National People's Congress and the local people's congresses at different levels.

The people administer state affairs and manage economic, cultural and social affairs through various channels and in various ways in accordance with the law.

Article 3: The state organs of the People's Republic of China apply the principle of democratic centralism.

The National People's Congress and the local people's congresses at different levels are instituted through democratic election. They are responsible to the people and subject to their supervision.

All administrative, judicial and procuratorial organs of the State are created by the people's congresses to which they are responsible and under whose supervision they operate.

The division of functions and powers between the central and local state organs is guided by the principle of giving full play to the initiative and enthusiasm of the local authorities under the unified leadership of the central authorities.

Article 4: All nationalities in the People's Republic of China are equal. The State protects the lawful rights and interests of the minority nationalities and upholds and develops the relationship of equality, unity and mutual assistance among all of China's nationalities. Discrimination against and oppression of any nationality are prohibited; any acts that undermine the unity of the nationalities or instigate their secession are prohibited.

The State helps the areas inhabited by minority nationalities speed up their economic and cultural development in accordance with the peculiarities and needs of the different minority nationalities.

Regional autonomy is practised in areas where people of minority nationalities live in compact communities; in these areas organs of self-government are established for the exercise of the right of autonomy. All the national autonomous areas are inalienable parts of the People's Republic of China.

The people of all nationalities have the freedom to use and develop their own spoken and written languages, and to preserve or reform their own ways and customs.

Article 5: The State upholds the uniformity and dignity of the socialist legal system.

No law or administrative or local rules and regulations shall contravene the Constitution.

All state organs, the armed forces, all political parties and public organizations and all enterprises and undertakings must abide by the Constitution and the law. All acts in violation of the Constitution and the law must be looked into.

No organization or individual may enjoy the privilege of being above the Constitution and the law.

Article 6: The basis of the socialist economic system of the People's Republic of China is socialist public ownership of the means of production, namely, ownership by the whole people and collective ownership by the working people.

The system of socialist public ownership supersedes the system of exploitation of man by man; it applies the principle of 'from each according to his ability, to each according to his work.'

Article 7: The state economy is the sector of socialist economy under ownership by the whole people; it is the leading force in the national economy. The State ensures the consolidation and growth of the state economy.

Article 8: Rural people's communes, agricultural producers' co-operatives, and other forms of co-operative economy such as producers', supply and marketing, credit and consumers' co-operatives, belong to the sector of socialist economy under collective ownership by the working people. Working people who are members of rural economic collectives have the right, within the limits prescribed by law, to farm private plots of cropland and hilly land, engage in household sideline production and raise privately-owned livestock.

The various forms of co-operative economy in the cities and towns, such as those in the handicraft, industrial, building, transport, commercial and service trades, all belong to the sector of socialist economy under collective ownership by the working people.

The State protects the lawful rights and interests of the urban and rural economic collectives and encourages, guides and helps the growth of the collective economy.

Article 9: Mineral resources, waters, forests, mountains, grassland, unreclaimed land, beaches and other natural resources are owned by the State, that is, by the whole people, with the exception of the forests, mountains, grassland, unreclaimed land and beaches that are owned by collectives in accordance with the law.

The State ensures the rational use of natural resources and protects rare animals and plants. The appropriation or damage of natural resources by any organization or individual by whatever means is prohibited.

Article 10: Land in the cities is owned by the State.

Land in the rural and suburban areas is owned by collectives except for those portions which belong to the state in accordance with the law; house sites and private plots of cropland and hilly land are also owned by collectives.

The State may in the public interest take over land for its use in accordance with the law.

No organization or individual may appropriate, buy, sell or lease land, or unlawfully transfer land in other ways.

All organizations and individuals who use land must make rational use of the land.

Article 11: The individual economy of urban and rural working people, operated within the limits prescribed by law, is a complement to the socialist public economy. The State protects the lawful rights and interests of the individual economy.

The State guides, helps and supervises the individual economy by exercising administrative control.

Article 12: Socialist public property is sacred and inviolable.

The State protects socialist public property. Appropriation or damage of state or collective property by any organization or individual by whatever means is prohibited.

Article 13: The State protects the right of citizens to own lawfully earned income, savings, houses and other lawful property.

The State protects by law the right of citizens to inherit private property.

Article 14: The State continuously raises labour productivity, improves economic results and develops the productive forces by enhancing the enthusiasm of the working people, raising the level of their technical skill, disseminating advanced science and technology, improving the systems of economic administration and enterprise operation and management, instituting the socialist system of responsibility in various forms and improving organization of work.

The State practises strict economy and combats waste.

The State properly apportions accumulation and consumption, pays attention to the interests of the collective and the individual as well as of the State and, on the basis of expanded production, gradually improves the material and cultural life of the people.

Article 15: The State practises economic planning on the basis of socialist public ownership. It ensures the proportionate and co-ordinated growth of the national economy through overall balancing by economic planning and the supplementary role of regulation by the market.

Disturbance of the orderly functioning of the social economy or disruption of the state economic plan by any organization or individual is prohibited.

Article 16: State enterprises have decision-making power in operation and management within the limits prescribed by law, on condition that they submit to unified leadership by the State and fulfil all their obligations under the state plan.

State enterprises practise democratic management through congresses of workers and staff and in other ways in accordance with the law.

Article 17: Collective economic organizations have decision-making power in conducting independent economic activities, on condition that they accept the guidance of the state plan and abide by the relevant laws.

Collective economic organizations practise democratic management in accordance with the law, with the entire body of their workers electing or removing their managerial personnel and deciding on major issues concerning operation and management.

Article 18: The People's Republic of China permits foreign enterprises, other foreign economic organizations and individual foreigners to invest in China and to enter into various forms of economic co-operation with Chinese enterprises and other economic organizations in accordance with the law of the People's Republic of China.

All foreign enterprises and other foreign economic organizations in China, as well as joint ventures with Chinese and foreign investment located in China, shall abide by the law of the People's Republic of China. Their lawful rights and interests are protected by the law of the People's Republic of China.

Article 19: The State develops socialist educational undertakings and works to raise the scientific and cultural level of the whole nation.

The State runs schools of various types, makes primary education compulsory and universal, develops secondary, vocational and higher education and promotes pre-school education.

The State develops educational facilities of various types in order to wipe out illiteracy and provide political, cultural, scientific, technical and professional education for workers, peasants, state functionaries and other working people. It encourages people to become educated through self-study.

The State encourages the collective economic organizations, state enterprises and undertakings and other social forces to set up educational institutions of various types in accordance with the law.

The State promotes the nationwide use of Putonghua (common speech based on Beijing pronunciation).

Article 20: The State promotes the development of the natural and social sciences, disseminates scientific and technical knowledge, and commends and rewards achievements in scientific research as well as technological discoveries and inventions.

Article 21: The State develops medical and health services, promotes modern medicine and traditional Chinese medicine, encourages and supports the setting up of various medical and health facilities by the rural economic collectives, state enterprises and undertakings and neighbourhood organizations, and promotes sanitation activities of a mass character, all to protect the people's health.

The State develops physical culture and promotes mass sports activities to build up the people's physique.

Article 22: The State promotes the development of literature and art, the press, broadcasting and television undertakings, publishing and distribution services, libraries, museums, cultural centres and other cultural undertakings, that serve the people and socialism, and sponsors mass cultural activities.

The State protects places of scenic and historical interest, valuable cultural monuments and relics and other important items of China's historical and cultural heritage.

Article 23: The State trains specialized personnel in all fields who serve socialism, increases the number of intellectuals and creates conditions to give full scope to their role in socialist modernization.

Article 24: The State strengthens the building of socialist spiritual civilization through spreading education in high ideals and morality, general education and education in discipline and the legal system, and through promoting the formulation and observance of rules of conduct and common pledges by different sections of the people in urban and rural areas.

The State advocates the civic virtues of love for the motherland, for the people, for labour, for science and for socialism; it educates the people in patriotism, collectivism, internationalism and communism and in dialectical and historical materialism; it combats capitalist, feudalist and other decadent ideas.

Article 25: The State promotes family planning so that population growth may fit the plans for economic and social development.

Article 26: The State protects and improves the living environment and the ecological environment, and prevents and remedies pollution and other public hazards.

The State organizes and encourages afforestation and the protection of forests.

Article 27: All state organs carry out the principle of simple and efficient administration, the system of responsibility for work and the system of training functionaries and appraising their work in order constantly to improve quality of work and efficiency and combat bureaucratism.

All state organs and functionaries must rely on the support of the people, keep in close touch with them, heed their opinions and suggestions, accept their supervision and work hard to serve them.

Article 28: The State maintains public order and suppresses treasonable and other counter-revolutionary activities; it penalizes actions that endanger public security and disrupt the socialist economy and other criminal activities, and punishes and reforms criminals.

Article 29: The armed forces of the People's Republic of China belong to the people. Their tasks are to strengthen national defence, resist aggression, defend the motherland, safeguard the people's peaceful labour, participate in national reconstruction, and work hard to serve the people.

The State strengthens the revolutionization, modernization and regularization of the armed forces in order to increase the national defence capability.

Article 30: The administrative division of the People's Republic of China is as follows:

(1) The country is divided into provinces, autonomous regions and municipalities directly under the central government;

(2) Provinces and autonomous regions are divided into autonomous prefectures, counties, autonomous counties and cities;

(3) Counties and autonomous counties are divided into townships, nationality townships and towns.

Municipalities directly under the central government and other large cities are divided into districts and counties. Autonomous prefectures are divided into counties, autonomous counties, and cities.

All autonomous regions, autonomous prefectures and autonomous counties are national autonomous areas.

Article 31: The State may establish special administrative regions when necessary. The systems to be instituted in special administrative regions shall be prescribed by law enacted by the National People's Congress in the light of the specific conditions.

Article 32: The People's Republic of China protects the lawful rights and interests of foreigners within Chinese territory, and while on Chinese territory foreigners must abide by the law of the People's Republic of China.

The People's Republic of China may grant asylum to foreigners who request it for political reasons.

FUNDAMENTAL RIGHTS AND DUTIES OF CITIZENS

Article 33: All persons holding the nationality of the People's Republic of China are citizens of the People's Republic of China.

All citizens of the People's Republic of China are equal before the law.

Every citizen enjoys the rights and at the same time must perform the duties prescribed by the Constitution and the law.

Article 34: All citizens of the People's Republic of China who have reached the age of 18 have the right to vote and stand for election, regardless of nationality, race, sex, occupation, family background, religious belief, education, property status, or length of residence, except persons deprived of political rights according to law.

Article 35: Citizens of the People's Republic of China enjoy freedom of speech, of the press, of assembly, of association, of procession and of demonstration.

Article 36: Citizens of the People's Republic of China enjoy freedom of religious belief.

No state organ, public organization or individual may compel citizens to believe in, or not to believe in, any religion; nor may they discriminate against citizens who believe in, or do not believe in, any religion.

The State protects normal religious activities. No one may make use of religion to engage in activities that disrupt public order, impair the health of citizens or interfere with the educational system of the state.

Religious bodies and religious affairs are not subject to any foreign domination.

Article 37: The freedom of person of citizens of the People's Republic of China is inviolable.

No citizen may be arrested except with the approval or by decision of a people's procuratorate or by decision of a people's court, and arrests must be made by a public security organ.

Unlawful deprivation or restriction of citizens' freedom of person by detention or other means is prohibited; and unlawful search of the person of citizens is prohibited.

Article 38: The personal dignity of citizens of the People's Republic of China is inviolable. Insult, libel, false charge or frame-up directed against citizens by any means is prohibited.

Article 39: The home of citizens of the People's Republic of China is inviolable. Unlawful search of, or intrusion into, a citizen's home is prohibited.

Article 40: The freedom and privacy of correspondence of citizens of the People's Republic of China are protected by law. No organization or individual may, on any ground, infringe upon the freedom and privacy of citizens' correspondence except in cases where, to meet the needs of state security or of investigation into criminal offences, public security or procuratorial organs are permitted to censor correspondence in accordance with procedures prescribed by law.

Article 41: Citizens of the People's Republic of China have the right to criticize and make suggestions to any state organ or functionary. Citizens have the right to make to relevant state organs complaints and charges against, or exposures of, violation of the law or dereliction of duty by any state organ or functionary; but fabrication or distortion of facts with the intention of libel or frame-up is prohibited.

In case of complaints, charges or exposures made by citizens, the state organ concerned must deal with them in a responsible manner after ascertaining the facts. No one may suppress such complaints, charges and exposures, or retaliate against the citizen making them.

Citizens who have suffered losses through infringement of their civic rights by any state organ or functionary have the right to compensation in accordance with the law.

Article 42: Citizens of the People's Republic of China have the right as well as the duty to work.

Using various channels, the State creates conditions for employment, strengthens labour protection, improves working conditions and, on the basis of expanded production, increases remuneration for work and social benefits.

Work is the glorious duty of every able-bodied citizen. All working people in state enterprises and in urban and rural economic collectives should perform their tasks with an attitude consonant with their status as masters of the country. The State promotes socialist labour emulation, and commends and rewards model and advanced workers. The State encourages citizens to take part in voluntary labour.

The State provides necessary vocational training to citizens before they are employed.

Article 43: Working people in the People's Republic of China have the right to rest.

The State expands facilities for rest and recuperation of working people, and prescribes working hours and vacations for workers and staff.

Article 44: The State prescribes by law the system of retirement for workers and staff in enterprises and undertakings and for functionaries of organs of state. The livelihood of retired personnel is ensured by the State and society.

Article 45: Citizens of the People's Republic of China have the right to material assistance from the State and society when they are old, ill or disabled. The State develops the social insurance, social relief and medical and health services that are required to enable citizens to enjoy this right.

The State and society ensure the livelihood of disabled members of the armed forces, provide pensions to the families of martyrs and give preferential treatment to the families of military personnel.

The State and society help make arrangements for the work, livelihood and education of the blind, deaf-mute and other handicapped citizens.

Article 46: Citizens of the People's Republic of China have the duty as well as the right to receive education.

The State promotes the all-round moral, intellectual and physical development of children and young people.

Article 47: Citizens of the People's Republic of China have the freedom to engage in scientific research, literary and artistic creation and other cultural pursuits. The State encourages and assists creative endeavours conducive to the interests of the people that are made by citizens engaged in education, science, technology, literature, art and other cultural work.

Article 48: Women in the People's Republic of China enjoy equal rights with men in all spheres of life, political, economic, cultural and social, including family life.

The State protects the rights and interests of women, applies the principle of equal pay for equal work for men and women alike and trains and selects cadres from among women.

Article 49: Marriage, the family and mother and child are protected by the State.

Both husband and wife have the duty to practise family planning.

Parents have the duty to rear and educate their minor children, and children who have come of age have the duty to support and assist their parents.

Violation of the freedom of marriage is prohibited. Maltreatment of old people, women and children is prohibited.

Article 50: The People's Republic of China protects the legitimate rights and interests of Chinese nationals residing abroad and protects the lawful rights and interests of returned overseas Chinese and of the family members of Chinese nationals residing abroad.

Article 51: The exercise by citizens of the People's Republic of China of their freedoms and rights may not infringe upon the interests of the State, of society and of the collective, or upon the lawful freedoms and rights of other citizens.

Article 52: It is the duty of citizens of the People's Republic of China to safeguard the unity of the country and the unity of all its nationalities.

Article 53: Citizens of the People's Republic of China must abide by the Constitution and the law, keep state secrets, protect public property and observe labour discipline and public order and respect social ethics.

Article 54: It is the duty of citizens of the People's Republic of China to safeguard the security, honour and interests of the motherland; they must not commit acts detrimental to the security, honour and interests of the motherland.

Article 55: It is the sacred obligation of every citizen of the People's Republic of China to defend the motherland and resist aggression.

It is the honourable duty of citizens of the People's Republic of China to perform military service and join the militia in accordance with the law.

Article 56: It is the duty of citizens of the People's Republic of China to pay taxes in accordance with the law.

STRUCTURE OF THE STATE
The National People's Congress

Article 57: The National People's Congress of the People's Republic of China is the highest organ of state power. Its permanent body is the Standing Committee of the National People's Congress.

Article 58: The National People's Congress and its Standing Committee exercise the legislative power of the state.

Article 59: The National People's Congress is composed of deputies elected by the provinces, autonomous regions and municipalities directly under the Central Government, and by the armed forces. All the minority nationalities are entitled to appropriate representation.

Election of deputies to the National People's Congress is conducted by the Standing Committee of the National People's Congress.

The number of deputies to the National People's Congress and the manner of their election are prescribed by law.

Article 60: The National People's Congress is elected for a term of five years.

Two months before the expiration of the term of office of a National People's Congress, its Standing Committee must ensure that the election of deputies to the succeeding National People's Congress is completed. Should exceptional circumstances prevent such an election, it may be postponed by decision of a majority vote of more than two-thirds of all those on the Standing Committee of the incumbent National People's Congress, and the term of office of the incumbent National People's Congress may be extended. The election of deputies to the succeeding National People's Congress must be completed within one year after the termination of such exceptional circumstances.

Article 61: The National People's Congress meets in session once a year and is convened by its Standing Committee. A session of the National People's Congress may be convened at any time the Standing Committee deems this necessary, or when more than one-fifth of the deputies to the National People's Congress so propose.

When the National People's Congress meets, it elects a presidium to conduct its session.

Article 62: The National People's Congress exercises the following functions and powers:

(1) to amend the Constitution;

(2) to supervise the enforcement of the Constitution;

(3) to enact and amend basic statutes concerning criminal offences, civil affairs, the state organs and other matters;

(4) to elect the President and the Vice-President of the People's Republic of China;

(5) to decide on the choice of the Premier of the State Council upon nomination by the President of the People's Republic of China, and to decide on the choice of the Vice-Premiers, State Councillors, Ministers in charge of Ministries or Commissions and the Auditor-General and the Secretary-General of the State Council upon nomination by the Premier;

(6) to elect the Chairman of the Central Military Commission and, upon his nomination, to decide on the choice of all the others on the Central Military Commission;

(7) to elect the President of the Supreme People's Court;

(8) to elect the Procurator-General of the Supreme People's Procuratorate;

(9) to examine and approve the plan for national economic and social development and the reports on its implementation;

(10) to examine and approve the state budget and the report on its implementation;

(11) to alter or annul inappropriate decisions of the Standing Committee of the National People's Congress;

(12) to approve the establishment of provinces, autonomous regions, and municipalities directly under the Central Government;

(13) to decide on the establishment of special administrative regions and the systems to be instituted there;

(14) to decide on questions of war and peace; and

(15) to exercise such other functions and powers as the highest organ of state power should exercise.

Article 63: The National People's Congress has the power to recall or remove from office the following persons:

(1) the President and the Vice-President of the People's Republic of China;

(2) the Premier, Vice-Premiers, State Councillors, Ministers in charge of Ministries or Commissions and the Auditor-General and the Secretary-General of the State Council;

(3) the Chairman of the Central Military Commission and others on the Commission;

(4) the President of the Supreme People's Court; and

(5) the Procurator-General of the Supreme People's Procuratorate.

Article 64: Amendments to the Constitution are to be proposed by the Standing Committee of the National People's Congress or by more than one-fifth of the deputies to the National People's Congress and adopted by a majority vote of more than two-thirds of all the deputies to the Congress.

Statutes and resolutions are adopted by a majority vote of more than one half of all the deputies to the National People's Congress.

Article 65: The Standing Committee of the National People's Congress is composed of the following:

the Chairman;

the Vice-Chairmen;

the Secretary-General; and

members.

Minority nationalities are entitled to appropriate representation on the Standing Committee of the National People's Congress.

The National People's Congress elects, and has the power to recall, all those on its Standing Committee.

No one on the Standing Committee of the National People's Congress shall hold any post in any of the administrative, judicial or procuratorial organs of the state.

Article 66: The Standing Committee of the National People's Congress is elected for the same term as the National People's Congress; it exercises its functions and powers until a new Standing Committee is elected by the succeeding National People's Congress.

The Chairman and Vice-Chairmen of the Standing Committee shall serve no more than two consecutive terms.

Article 67: The Standing Committee of the National People's Congress exercises the following functions and powers:

(1) to interpret the Constitution and supervise its enforcement;

(2) to enact and amend statutes with the exception of those which should be enacted by the National People's Congress;

(3) to enact, when the National People's Congress is not in session, partial supplements and amendments to statutes enacted by the National People's Congress provided that they do not contravene the basic principles of these statutes;

(4) to interpret statutes;

(5) to examine and approve, when the National People's Congress is not in session, partial adjustments to the plan for national economic and social development and to the state budget that prove necessary in the course of their implementation;

(6) to supervise the work of the State Council, the Central Military Commission, the Supreme People's Court and the Supreme People's Procuratorate;

(7) to annul those administrative rules and regulations, decisions or orders of the State Council that contravene the Constitution or the statutes;

(8) to annul those local regulations or decisions of the organs of state power of provinces, autonomous regions and municipalities directly under the Central Government that contravene the Constitution, the statutes or the administrative rules and regulations;

(9) to decide, when the National People's Congress is not in session, on the choice of Ministers in charge of Ministries or Commissions or the Auditor-General and the Secretary-General of the State Council upon nomination by the Premier of the State Council;

(10) to decide, upon nomination by the Chairman of the Central Military Commission, on the choice of others on the Commission, when the National People's Congress is not in session;

(11) to appoint and remove the Vice-Presidents and judges of the Supreme People's Court, members of its Judicial Committee and the President of the Military Court at the suggestion of the President of the Supreme People's Court;

(12) to appoint and remove the Deputy Procurators-General and Procurators of the Supreme People's Procuratorate, members of its Procuratorial Committee and the Chief Procurator of the Military Procuratorate at the request of the Procurator-General of the Supreme People's Procuratorate, and to approve the appointment and removal of the Chief Procurators of the People's Procuratorates of provinces, autonomous regions and municipalities directly under the Central Government;

(13) to decide on the appointment and recall of plenipotentiary representatives abroad;

(14) to decide on the ratification and abrogation of treaties and important agreements concluded with foreign states;

(15) to institute systems of titles and ranks for military and diplomatic personnel and of other specific titles and ranks;

(16) to institute state medals and titles of honour and decide on their conferment;

(17) to decide on the granting of special pardons;

(18) to decide, when the National People's Congress is not in session, on the proclamation of a state of war in the event of an armed attack on the country or in fulfilment of international treaty obligations concerning common defence against aggression;

(19) to decide on general mobilization or partial mobilization;

(20) to decide on the enforcement of martial law throughout the country or in particular provinces, autonomous regions or municipalities directly under the Central Government; and

(21) to exercise such other functions and powers as the National People's Congress may assign to it.

Article 68: The Chairman of the Standing Committee of the National People's Congress presides over the work of the Standing Committee and convenes its meetings. The Vice-Chairmen and the Secretary-General assist the Chairman in his work.

Chairmanship meetings with the participation of the Chairman, Vice-Chairmen and Secretary-General handle the important day-to-day work of the Standing Committee of the National People's Congress.

Article 69: The Standing Committee of the National People's Congress is responsible to the National People's Congress and reports on its work to the Congress.

Article 70: The National People's Congress establishes a Nationalities Committee, a Law Committee, a Finance and Economic Committee, an Education, Science, Culture and Public Health Committee, a Foreign Affairs Committee, an Overseas Chinese Committee and such other special committees as are necessary. These special committees work under the direction of the Standing Committee of the National People's Congress when the Congress is not in session.

The special committees examine, discuss and draw up relevant bills and draft resolutions under the direction of the National People's Congress and its Standing Committee.

Article 71: The National People's Congress and its Standing Committee may, when they deem it necessary, appoint committees of inquiry into specific questions and adopt relevant resolutions in the light of their reports.

All organs of state, public organizations and citizens concerned are obliged to supply the necessary information to those committees of inquiry when they conduct investigations.

Article 72: Deputies to the National People's Congress and all those on its Standing Committee have the right, in accordance with procedures prescribed by law, to submit bills and proposals within the scope of the respective functions and powers of the National People's Congress and its Standing Committee.

Article 73: Deputies to the National People's Congress during its sessions, and all those on its Standing Committee during its meetings, have the right to address questions, in accordance with procedures prescribed by law, to the State Council or the Ministries and Commissions under the State Council, which must answer the questions in a responsible manner.

Article 74: No deputy to the National People's Congress may be arrested or placed on criminal trial without the consent of the presidium of the current session of the National People's Congress or, when the National People's Congress is not in session, without the consent of its Standing Committee.

Article 75: Deputies to the National People's Congress may not be called to legal account for their speeches or votes at its meetings.

Article 76: Deputies to the National People's Congress must play an exemplary role in abiding by the Constitution and the law and keeping state secrets and, in production and other work and their public activities, assist in the enforcement of the Constitution and the law.

Deputies to the National People's Congress should maintain close contact with the units which elected them and with the people, listen to and convey the opinions and demands of the people and work hard to serve them.

Article 77: Deputies to the National People's Congress are subject to the supervision of the units which elected them. The electoral units have the power, through procedures prescribed by law, to recall the deputies whom they elected.

Article 78: The organization and working procedures of the National People's Congress and its Standing Committee are prescribed by law.

The President of the People's Republic of China

Article 79: The President and Vice-President of the People's Republic of China are elected by the National People's Congress.

Citizens of the People's Republic of China who have the right to vote and to stand for election and who have reached the age of 45 are eligible for election as President or Vice-President of the People's Republic of China.

The term of office of the President and Vice-President of the People's Republic of China is the same as that of the National People's Congress, and they shall serve no more than two consecutive terms.

Article 80: The President of the People's Republic of China, in pursuance of decisions of the National People's Congress and its Standing Committee, promulgates statutes; appoints and removes the Premier, Vice-Premiers, State Councillors, Ministers in charge of Ministries or Commissions, and the Auditor-General and the Secretary-General of the State Council; confers state medals and titles of honour; issues orders of special pardons; proclaims martial law; proclaims a state of war; and issues mobilization orders.

Article 81: The President of the People's Republic of China receives foreign diplomatic representatives on behalf of the People's Republic of China and, in pursuance of decisions of the Standing Committee of the National People's Congress, appoints and recalls plenipotentiary representatives abroad, and ratifies and abrogates treaties and important agreements concluded with foreign states.

Article 82: The Vice-President of the People's Republic of China assists the President in his work.

The Vice-President of the People's Republic of China may exercise such parts of the functions and powers of the President as the President may entrust to him.

Article 83: The President and Vice-President of the People's Republic of China exercise their functions and powers until the new President and Vice-President elected by the succeeding National People's Congress assume office.

Article 84: In case the office of the President of the People's Republic of China falls vacant, the Vice-President succeeds to the office of President.

In case the office of the Vice-President of the People's Republic of China falls vacant, the National People's Congress shall elect a new Vice-President to fill the vacancy.

In the event that the offices of both the President and the Vice-President of the People's Republic of China fall vacant, the National People's Congress shall elect a new President and a new Vice-President. Prior to such election, the Chairman of the Standing Committee of the National People's Congress shall temporarily act as the President of the People's Republic of China.

The State Council

Article 85: The State Council, that is, the Central People's Government, of the People's Republic of China is the executive body of the highest organ of state power; it is the highest organ of state administration.

Article 86: The State Council is composed of the following: the Premier; the Vice-Premiers; the State Councillors; the Ministers in charge of ministries; the Ministers in charge of commissions; the Auditor-General; and the Secretary-General.

The Premier has overall responsibility for the State Council. The Ministers have overall responsibility for the respective ministries or commissions under their charge.

The organization of the State Council is prescribed by law.

Article 87: The term of office of the State Council is the same as that of the National People's Congress.

The Premier, Vice-Premiers and State Councillors shall serve no more than two consecutive terms.

Article 88: The Premier directs the work of the State Council. The Vice-Premiers and State Councillors assist the Premier in his work.

Executive meetings of the State Council are composed of the Premier, the Vice-Premiers, the State Councillors and the Secretary-General of the State Council.

The Premier convenes and presides over the executive meetings and plenary meetings of the State Council.

Article 89: The State Council exercises the following functions and powers:

(1) to adopt administrative measures, enact administrative rules and regulations and issue decisions and orders in accordance with the Constitution and the statutès;

(2) to submit proposals to the National People's Congress or its Standing Committee;

(3) to lay down the tasks and responsibilities of the ministries and commissions of the State Council, to exercise unified leadership over the work of the ministries and commissions and to direct all other administrative work of a national character that does not fall within the jurisdiction of the ministries and commissions;

(4) to exercise unified leadership over the work of local organs of state administration at different levels throughout the country, and to lay down the detailed division of functions and powers between the Central Government and the organs of state administration of provinces, autonomous regions and municipalities directly under the Central Government;

(5) to draw up and implement the plan for national economic and social development and the state budget;

(6) to direct and administer economic work and urban and rural development;

(7) to direct and administer the work concerning education, science, culture, public health, physical culture and family planning;

(8) to direct and administer the work concerning civil affairs, public security, judicial administration, supervision and other related matters;

(9) to conduct foreign affairs and conclude treaties and agreements with foreign states;

(10) to direct and administer the building of national defence;

(11) to direct and administer affairs concerning the nationalities, and to safeguard the equal rights of minority nationalities and the right of autonomy of the national autonomous areas;

(12) to protect the legitimate rights and interests of Chinese nationals residing abroad and protect the lawful rights and interests of returned overseas Chinese and of the family members of Chinese nationals residing abroad;

(13) to alter or annul inappropriate orders, directives and regulations issued by the ministries or commissions;

(14) to alter or annul inappropriate decisions and orders issued by local organs of state administration at different levels;

(15) to approve the geographic division of provinces, autonomous regions and municipalities directly under the Central Government, and to approve the establishment and geographic division of autonomous prefectures, counties, autonomous counties and cities;

(16) to decide on the enforcement of martial law in parts of provinces, autonomous regions and municipalities directly under the Central Government;

(17) to examine and decide on the size of administrative organs and, in accordance with the law, to appoint, remove and train administrative officers, appraise their work and reward or punish them; and

(18) to exercise such other functions and powers as the National People's Congress or its Standing Committee may assign it.

Article 90: The Ministers in charge of ministries or commissions of the State Council are responsible for the work of their respective departments and convene and preside over their ministerial meetings or commission meetings that discuss and decide on major issues in the work of their respective departments.

The ministries and commissions issue orders, directives and regulations within the jurisdiction of their respective departments and in accordance with the statutes and the administrative rules and regulations, decisions and orders issued by the State Council.

Article 91: The State Council establishes an auditing body to supervise through auditing the revenue and expenditure of all departments under the State Council and of the local government at different levels, and those of the state financial and monetary organizations and of enterprises and undertakings.

Under the direction of the Premier of the State Council, the auditing body independently exercises its power to supervise

THE PEOPLE'S REPUBLIC OF CHINA

through auditing in accordance with the law, subject to no interference by any other administrative organ or any public organization or individual.

Article 92: The State Council is responsible, and reports on its work, to the National People's Congress or, when the National People's Congress is not in session, to its Standing Committee.

The Central Military Commission

Article 93: The Central Military Commission of the People's Republic of China directs the armed forces of the country.

The Central Military Commission is composed of the following: the Chairman; the Vice-Chairmen; and members.

The Chairman of the Central Military Commission has overall responsibility for the Commission.

The term of office of the Central Military Commission is the same as that of the National People's Congress.

Article 94: The Chairman of the Central Military Commission is responsible to the National People's Congress and its Standing Committee.

(Two further sections, not included here, deal with the Local People's Congresses and Government and with the Organs of Self-Government of National Autonomous Areas respectively.)

The People's Courts and the People's Procuratorates

Article 123: The people's courts in the People's Republic of China are the judicial organs of the state.

Article 124: The People's Republic of China establishes the Supreme People's Court and the local people's courts at different levels, military courts and other special people's courts.

The term of office of the President of the Supreme People's Court is the same as that of the National People's Congress; he shall serve no more than two consecutive terms.

The organization of people's courts is prescribed by law.

Article 125: All cases handled by the people's courts, except for those involving special circumstances as specified by law, shall be heard in public. The accused has the right of defence.

Article 126: The people's courts shall, in accordance with the law, exercise judicial power independently and are not subject to interference by administrative organs, public organizations or individuals.

Article 127: The Supreme People's Court is the highest judicial organ.

The Supreme People's Court supervises the administration of justice by the local people's courts at different levels and by the special people's courts; people's courts at higher levels supervise the administration of justice by those at lower levels.

Article 128: The Supreme People's Court is responsible to the National People's Congress and its Standing Committee. Local people's courts at different levels are responsible to the organs of state power which created them.

Article 129: The people's procuratorates of the People's Republic of China are state organs for legal supervision.

Article 130: The People's Republic of China establishes the Supreme People's Procuratorate and the local people's procuratorates at different levels, military procuratorates and other special people's procuratorates.

The term of office of the Procurator-General of the Supreme People's Procuratorate is the same as that of the National People's Congress; he shall serve no more than two consecutive terms.

The organization of people's procuratorates is prescribed by law.

Article 131: People's procuratorates shall, in accordance with the law, exercise procuratorial power independently and are not subject to interference by administrative organs, public organizations or individuals.

Article 132: The Supreme People's Procuratorate is the highest procuratorial organ.

The Supreme People's Procuratorate directs the work of the local people's procuratorates at different levels and of the special people's procuratorates; people's procuratorates at higher levels direct the work of those at lower levels.

Article 133: The Supreme People's Procuratorate is responsible to the National People's Congress and its Standing Committee. Local people's procuratorates at different levels are responsible to the organs of state power at the corresponding levels which created them and to the people's procuratorates at the higher level.

Article 134: Citizens of all nationalities have the right to use the spoken and written languages of their own nationalities in court proceedings. The people's courts and people's procuratorates should provide translation for any party to the court proceedings who is not familiar with the spoken or written languages in common use in the locality.

In an area where people of a minority nationality live in a compact community or where a number of nationalities live together, hearings should be conducted in the language or languages in common use in the locality; indictments, judgements, notices and other documents should be written, according to actual needs, in the language or languages in common use in the locality.

Article 135: The people's courts, people's procuratorates and public security organs shall, in handling criminal cases, divide their functions, each taking responsibility for its own work, and they shall co-ordinate their efforts and check each other to ensure correct and effective enforcement of law.

THE NATIONAL FLAG, THE NATIONAL EMBLEM AND THE CAPITAL

Article 136: The national flag of the People's Republic of China is a red flag with five stars.

Article 137: The national emblem of the People's Republic of China is Tian'anmen in the centre illuminated by five stars and encircled by ears of grain and a cogwheel.

Article 138: The capital of the People's Republic of China is Beijing.

The Government

HEAD OF STATE

President: YANG SHANGKUN (elected by the Seventh National People's Congress on 8 April 1988).

Vice-President: WANG ZHEN.

STATE COUNCIL
(January 1989)

Premier: LI PENG.

Vice-Premiers: YAO YILIN, TIAN JIYUN, WU XUEQIAN.

State Councillors:

CHEN XITONG
LI GUIXIAN
LI TIEYING
WANG BINGQIAN
WANG FANG
QIN JIWEI
SONG JIAN
ZOU JIAHUA
CHEN JUNSHENG

Secretary-General: LUO GAN.

Minister of Foreign Affairs: QIAN QICHEN.

Minister of National Defence: QIN JIWEI.

Minister in Charge of the State Planning Commission: YAO YILIN.

Minister in Charge of the State Commission for Restructuring the Economy: LI PENG.

Minister in Charge of the State Education Commission: LI TIEYING.

Minister in Charge of the State Scientific and Technological Commission: SONG JIAN.

Minister in Charge of the Commission of Science, Technology and Industry for National Defence: DING HENGGAO.

Minister in Charge of the State Nationalities Affairs Commission: ISMAIL AMAT.

Minister of Machine-Building and Electronics Industry: ZOU JIAHUA.

Minister of Public Security: WANG FANG.

Minister of State Security: JIA CHUNWANG.

Minister of Civil Affairs: CUI NAIFU.

Minister of Justice: CAI CHENG.

Minister of Supervision: WEI JIANXING.

Minister of Finance: WANG BINGQIAN.

Auditor-General: LU PEIJIAN.

Governor of the People's Bank of China: LI GUIXIAN.

Minister of Commerce: HU PING.

Minister of Foreign Economic Relations and Trade: ZHENG TUOBIN.

Minister of Agriculture: HE KANG.

Minister of Forestry: GAO DEZHAN.

Minister of Energy Resources: HUANG YICHENG.

Minister of Water Resources: YANG ZHENHUAI.

Minister of Construction: LIN HANXIONG.

Minister of Geology and Mineral Resources: ZHU XUN.

Minister of Metallurgical Industry: QI YUANJING.

President of the State Nuclear Industry Corporation: JIANG XINXIONG.

THE PEOPLE'S REPUBLIC OF CHINA

Minister of Aeronautics and Astronautics Industry: LIN ZONGTANG.
President of the State Coal Corporation: YU HONGEN.
President of the State Petroleum and Natural Gas Corporation: WANG TAO.
Minister of Chemical Industry: QIN ZHONGDA.
Minister of Textile Industry: Ms WU WENYING.
Minister of Light Industry: ZENG XIANLIN.
Minister of Materials: LIU SUINIAN.
Minister of Railways: LI SENMAO.
Minister of Communications: QIAN YONGCHANG.
Minister of Posts and Telecommunications: YANG TAIFANG.
Minister of Personnel: ZHAO DONGWAN.
Minister of Labour: (vacant).
Minister of Culture: WANG MENG.
Minister of Radio, Film and Television: AI ZHISHENG.
Minister of Public Health: CHEN MINZHANG.
Minister in Charge of the State Physical Culture and Sports Commission: WU SHAOZU.
Minister in Charge of the State Family Planning Commission: Ms PENG PEIYUN.

MINISTRIES

Ministry of Aeronautics and Astronautics Industry: Beijing.
Ministry of Agriculture: Hepingli, Dongcheng District, Beijing; tel. 463061.
Ministry of Chemical Industry: Liupukang, Deshengmenwai, Beijing; tel. 446561.
Ministry of Civil Affairs: 147 Donganmen, Beijing; tel. 551731.
Ministry of Commerce: 45 Fuxingmenwai St, Beijing; tel. 668581.
Ministry of Communications: 10 Fuxing Rd, Beijing; tel. 8642371; telex 22462.
Ministry of Construction: Baiwanzhuang St, Beijing; tel. 8992833; telex 222302.
Ministry of Culture: Donganmen North St, Beijing; tel. 442131.
Ministry of Energy: Beijing.
Ministry of Finance: South Sanlihe St, Fuxingmenwai, Beijing; tel. 868731; telex 222308.
Ministry of Foreign Affairs: 225 Chaoyangmennei St, Dongsi, Beijing; tel. 553831.
Ministry of Foreign Economic Relations and Trade: 2 Changan East St, Beijing; tel. 553031; telex 22168.
Ministry of Forestry: Hepingli, Dongchang District, Beijing; tel. 463061; telex 22237.
Ministry of Geology and Mineral Resources: Xisi Yangshi St, Beijing; tel. 668741; telex 22531.
Ministry of Justice: 2 Nan Shun Cheng Jie, Xi Zhi Men, Beijing; tel. 668971.
Ministry of Labour: Beijing.
Ministry of Light Industry: Fuchengmenwai St, Beijing; tel. 890751.
Ministry of Machine-Building Industry: Beijing.
Ministry of Materials: Beijing.
Ministry of Metallurgical Industry: 46 West Dongsi St, Beijing; tel. 557431.
Ministry of National Defence: Beijing; tel. 667343.
Ministry of Personnel: Beijing.
Ministry of Posts and Telecommunications: 13 West Changan St, Beijing 100804; tel. 660540; telex 222187.
Ministry of Public Health: 44 Houhaibeiyan, Beijing; tel. 440531; telex 22193.
Ministry of Public Security: East Changan St, Beijing; tel. 553871.
Ministry of Radio, Film and Television: Outside Fu Xing Men St 2, POB 4501, Beijing; tel. 862753; telex 22236.
Ministry of Railways: 10 Fuxing Rd, Beijing; tel. 864061.
Ministry of State Security: Dongchangan St, Beijing; tel. 553871.
Ministry of Supervision: Beijing.
Ministry of Textile Industry: 12 East Changan St, Beijing; tel. 5129542; telex 22661.
Ministry of Water Resources: 1 Lane, Baiguang St, Guanganmen, Beijing; tel. 365563; telex 22466; Chief Officer LI CHENGSHI.

STATE COMMISSIONS AND CORPORATIONS

State Coal Corporation: Beijing.
State Education Commission: 37 Damucang Hutong, Xicheng District, Beijing; tel. 658731.
State Family Planning Commission: Xizhimen South Shuncheng St, Beijing; tel. 668971.
State Nationalities Affairs Commission: 252 Taipingqiao St, Beijing; tel. 666931.
State Nuclear Industry Corporation: Beijing.
State Petroleum and Natural Gas Corporation: Beijing.
State Physical Culture and Sports Commission: Chongwai Stadium Rd, Beijing; tel. 757231.
State Commission for Restructuring the Economy: Beijing.
State Scientific and Technological Commission: 52 Sanlihe, Fuxingmenwai, Beijing; tel. 868361; telex 22349.
State Commission of Science, Technology and Industry for National Defence: Beijing.

Legislature

QUANGUO RENMIN DIABIAO DAHUI
(National People's Congress)

The National People's Congress (NPC) is the highest organ of state power, and is indirectly elected for a five-year term. The First Session of the Seventh NPC opened in Beijing in March 1988. The NPC had 2,970 members. The First Session of the Seventh National Committee of the Chinese People's Political Consultative Conference (CPPCC), a revolutionary united front organization led by the Communist Party, took place simultaneously. The CPPCC holds democratic discussions and consultations on the important affairs in the nation's political life. Members of the CPPCC National Committee or of its Standing Committee may be invited to attend the NPC or its Standing Committee as observers.

Standing Committee

In March 1988, 135 members were elected to the Standing Committee.

Chairman: WAN LI.
Vice-Chairmen:

XI ZHONGXUN	RONG YIREN
PENG CHONG	YE FEI
Gen. WEI GUOQING	LIAO HANSHENG
ZHU XUEFAN	NI ZHIFU
NGAPOI NGAWANG JIGME	CHEN MUHUA
BAINQEN ERDINI QOIGYI GYAINCAIN (Panchen Lama)	FEI XIAOTONG
	SUN QIMENG
Gen. SEYPIDIN AZE	LEI JIEQIONG
ZHOU GUCHENG	WANG HANBIN
YAN JICI	

Secretary-General: PENG CHONG.

Local People's Congresses

Province	Chairman of People's Congress
Anhui	WANG GUANGYU
Fujian	CHENG XU
Gansu	XU FEIQING
Guangdong	LUO TIAN
Guizhou	ZHANG YUHUAN
Hainan Island	XU SHIJIE
Hebei	GUO ZHI
Heilongjiang	SUN WEIBEN
Henan	(vacant)
Hubei	HUANG ZHIZHEN
Hunan	LIU FUSHENG
Jiangsu	HAN PEIXIN
Jiangxi	XU QIN
Jilin	HUO MINGGUANG
Liaoning	WANG GUANGZHONG
Qinghai	HUANJUE CAILANG
Shaanxi	LI XIPU
Shandong	LI ZHEN
Shanxi	WANG TINGDONG
Sichuan	HE HAOJU
Yunnan	Miss LI GUIYING
Zhejiang	CHEN ANYU

THE PEOPLE'S REPUBLIC OF CHINA   Directory

Special Municipalities	
Beijing	Zhao Pengfei
Shanghai	Ye Gongqi
Tianjin	Wu Zhen

Autonomous Regions	
Guangxi Zhuang	Gan Ku
Nei Monggol	Batu Bagen
Ningxia Hui	Ma Sizhong
Xinjiang Uygur	Amudun Niyaz
Xizang	Ngapoi Ngawang Jigme

People's Governments

Revolutionary Committees, established during the 'Cultural Revolution' to administer each of the provinces, special municipalities and autonomous regions, were replaced by People's Governments in January 1980.

Province	Governor
Anhui	Lu Rongjing (acting)
Fujian	Wang Zhaoguo (acting)
Gansu	Jia Zhijie
Guangdong	Ye Xuanping
Guizhou	Wang Chaowen
Hainan Island	Liang Xiang (acting)
Hebei	Yue Qifeng
Heilongjiang	Hou Jie
Henan	Cheng Weigao (acting)
Hubei	Guo Zhenqian
Hunan	Xiong Qingquan
Jiangsu	Miss Gu Xiulian
Jiangxi	Wu Guanzheng
Jilin	He Zhukang (acting)
Liaoning	Li Changchun
Qinghai	Song Ruixiang
Shaanxi	Hou Zongbin (acting)
Shandong	Jiang Chunyun
Shanxi	Wang Senhao
Sichuan	Zhang Haoruo
Yunnan	He Zhiqiang
Zhejiang	Shen Zulun

Special Municipalities	Mayor
Beijing	Chen Xitong
Shanghai	Zhu Rongji
Tianjin	Li Ruihuan

Autonomous Regions	Chairman
Guangxi Zhuang	Wei Chunshu
Nei Monggol	Bu He
Ningxia Hui	Bai Lichen
Xinjiang Uygur	Tomur Dawamat
Xizang	Doje Cering

Political Organizations

COMMUNIST PARTY

Zhongguo Gongchan Dang (Chinese Communist Party—CCP): Beijing; f. 1921; more than 40m. mems in 1987. At the 13th Nat. Congress of the CCP, in October 1987, a new Cen. Cttee of 175 full mems and 110 alt. mems was elected. At its first plenary session in November, the 13th Cen. Cttee appointed a new Politburo of 17 full mems and one alt. mem.

Thirteenth Central Committee
General Secretary: Zhao Ziyang.

Politburo
Members of the Standing Committee:

Zhao Ziyang	Qiao Shi
Li Peng	Yao Yilin
Hu Qili	

Other Full Members:

Wan Li	Yang Rudai
Tian Jiyun	Yang Shangkun
Jiang Zemin	Wu Xueqian
Li Tieying	Song Ping
Li Ruihuan	Hu Yaobang
Li Ximing	Qin Jiwei

Alternate Member: Ding Guangen.

Secretariat
Full Members:

Hu Qili	Qiao Shi
Rui Xingwen	Yan Mingfu

Alternate Member: Wen Jiabao.
Chairman of Central Advisory Committee: Chen Yun.
Vice-Chairmen: Bo Yibo, Song Renqiong.

OTHER POLITICAL ORGANIZATIONS

China Association for Promoting Democracy: Beijing; tel. 447128; f. 1945; mems drawn mainly from literary, cultural and educational circles; Chair. Lei Jieqiong.

China Democratic League: 1 Beixing Dongchang Hutong, Beijing; tel. 550495; f. 1941; formed from reorganization of League of Democratic Parties and Organizations of China; mems mainly intellectuals active in education, science and culture; Chair. Fei Xiaotong.

China National Democratic Construction Association: 93 Beiheyan Dajie, Beijing; tel. 554231; telex 22044; f. 1945; mems mainly industrialists and businessmen; Chair. Sun Qimeng.

China Zhi Gong Dang: Beijing; f. 1925; reorg. 1947; mems are mainly returned overseas Chinese; Chair. Dong Yinchu.

Chinese Peasants' and Workers' Democratic Party: f. 1947; fmrly the Provisional Action Cttee of the Kuomintang; 35,000 mems, active mainly in public health and medicine; Chair. Lu Jiaxi.

Communist Youth League: f. 1922; 48.5m. mems; First Sec. of Cen. Cttee Song Defu.

Guomindang (Kuomintang) Revolutionary Committee: tel. 550388; f. 1948; mainly fmr Kuomintang mems, and those in cultural, educational, health and financial fields; Chair. Zhu Xuefan; Sec.-Gen. Peng Qingyuan.

Jiu San (3 September) Society: f. 1946; fmrly Democratic and Science Soc.; mems mainly scientists and technologists; Chair. Zhou Peiyuan.

Taiwan Democratic Self-Government League: f. 1947; recruits Taiwanese living on the mainland; Chair. Cai Zimin.

Diplomatic Representation

EMBASSIES IN THE PEOPLE'S REPUBLIC OF CHINA

Afghanistan: 8 Dong Zhi Men Wai, Da Jie Chao Yang Qu, Beijing; tel. 521582; Ambassador: (vacant).

Albania: 28 Guang Hua Lu, Beijing; tel. 521120; Ambassador: Justin Niko Papajorgji.

Algeria: Dong Zhi Men Wai Da Jie, 7 San Li Tun, Beijing; tel. 521231; telex 22437; Ambassador: Cheriet Lazhari.

Argentina: Bldg 11, 5 East Rd, San Li Tun, Beijing; tel. 522090; telex 22269; Ambassador: Arturo Enrique Ossorio Arana.

Australia: 15 Dong Zhi Men Wai Da Jie, Beijing; tel. 5322331; telex 22263; Ambassador: David Sadleir.

Austria: 5 Xiu Shui Nan Jie, Jian Guo Men Wai, Beijing; tel. 5322061; telex 22258; Ambassador: Paul Ullmann.

Bangladesh: 42 Guang Hua Lu, Beijing; tel. 521819; telex 22143; Ambassador: Farooq Sobhan.

Belgium: 6 San Li Tun Lu, Beijing; tel. 5321736; telex 22260; Ambassador: Frans Baekelandt.

Benin: 38 Guang Hua Lu, Beijing; tel. 522741; telex 22599; Ambassador: Deguenon Ahannon Cosme.

Bolivia: Beijing; Ambassador: Jorge Lema-Patino.

Brazil: 27 Guang Hua Lu, Beijing; tel. 522881; telex 22117; Ambassador: Paulo da Costa Franco.

Bulgaria: 4 Xiu Shui Bei Jie, Jian Guo Men Wai, Beijing; tel. 522231; Ambassador: Doncho Georgiev Donchev.

Burkina Faso: 52 Dong Liu Jie, San Li Tun, Beijing; telex 22666; Ambassador: Hama Arba Diallo.

Burma: 6 Dong Zhi Men Wai Da Jie, Chao Yang Qu, Beijing; tel. 5321584; telex 10416; Ambassador: U Tin Maung Myint.

Burundi: 25 Guang Hua Lu, Beijing; tel. 522328; telex 22271; Ambassador: Basile Gateretse.

Cameroon: 7 San Li Tun, Dong Wu Jie, Beijing; telex 22256; Ambassador: Eleih Elle Etian.

Canada: 10 San Li Tun Lu, Chao Yang District, Beijing; tel. 5323536; telex 22717; Ambassador: Earl G. Drake.

Central African Republic: 1 Dong San Jie, San Li Tun, Beijing; tel. 522867; telex 22142; Ambassador: Ferdinand Pierre Pounzi.

THE PEOPLE'S REPUBLIC OF CHINA

Chad: 21 Guang Hua Lu, Jianguo Men Wai, Beijing; telex 22287; Ambassador: ISSA ABBAS ALI.
Chile: 1 San Li Tun, Dong Si Jie, Beijing; tel. 5321641; telex 22252; Ambassador: PATRICIO MARTÍNEZ MOENA.
Colombia: 34 Guang Hua Lu, Beijing; tel. 523166; telex 22460; Ambassador: LUIS EDUARDO VILLAR BORDA.
Congo: 7 San Li Tun, Dong Si Jie, Beijing; tel. 521644; telex 20428; Ambassador: GABRIEL EMOUENGUE.
Côte d'Ivoire: Beijing; tel. 521482; telex 22723; Ambassador: AMOAKON EJAMPAN THIEMELE.
Cuba: 1 Xiu Shui Nan Jie, Jian Guo Men Wai, Beijing; tel. 521714; telex 22249; Ambassador: JOSÉ ARMANDO GUERRA MENCHERO.
Czechoslovakia: Ri Tan Lu, Jian Guo Men, Wai, Beijing; tel. 521531; Ambassador: ZDENKO CHEBEN.
Denmark: 1 Dong Wu Jie, San Li Tun, Beijing; tel. 5322431; telex 22255; Ambassador: ARNE BELLING.
Ecuador: 2-41 San Li Tun, Beijing; telex 22710; Ambassador: JUAN MANUEL AGUIRRE.
Egypt: 2 Ri Tan Dong Lu, Beijing; tel. 522541; telex 22134; Ambassador: AHMED A. SELIM.
Equatorial Guinea: 2 Dong Si Jie, San Li Tun, Beijing; Ambassador: EULOGIO OYO RIQUESA.
Ethiopia: 3 Xiu Shui Nan Jie, Jian Guo Men Wai, Beijing; telex 22306; Ambassador: PHILIPPOS WOLDE-MARIAM.
Finland: Tayuan Diplomatic Office Bldg, 1-10-1, Beijing; tel. 5321806; telex 22129; Ambassador: RISTO HYVÄRINEN.
France: 3 Dong San Jie, San Li Tun, Beijing; tel. 521331; telex 22183; Ambassador: MICHEL COMBAL.
Gabon: 36 Guang Hua Lu, Beijing; tel. 522810; telex 22110; Ambassador: HUBERT OKOUMA.
German Democratic Republic: 3 Dong Si Jie, San Li Tun, Beijing; tel. 521631; telex 22384; Ambassador: ROLF BERTHOLD.
Germany, Federal Republic: 5 Dong Zhi Men Wai Da Jie, Beijing; tel. 522161; telex 22259; Ambassador: HANNSPETER HELLBECK.
Ghana: 8 San Li Tun, Lu, Beijing; tel. 522288; Ambassador: OSEI BONSU AMANKWA.
Greece: 19 Guang Hua Lu, Beijing; tel. 5321317; telex 22267; Ambassador: EMMANUEL E. MEGALOKONOMOS.
Guinea: 7 Dong San Jie, San Li Tun, Beijing; tel. 523649; telex 22706; Ambassador: ADPOURAHEMANE SOW.
Guyana: 1 Xiu Shui Dong Jie, Jian Guo Men Wai, Beijing; tel. 521337; telex 22295; Ambassador: ASHIK ALTAF MOHAMED.
Hungary: 10 Dong Zhi Men Wai Da Jie, Beijing; tel. 521683; telex 22679; Ambassador: IVAN NÉMETH.
Iceland: Beijing; Ambassador BENEDIKT GRÖNDAL.
India: 1 Ri Tan Dong Lu, Beijing; tel. 5321927; telex 22126; Ambassador: CHETPUT VENKATASUBBAN RANGANATHAN.
Iran: Dong Liu Ji, San Li Tun, Beijing; tel. 5322040; telex 22253; Ambassador: ALA ED-DIN BORUJERDI.
Iraq: 3 Ri Tan Dong Lu, Chae Yang District, Beijing; tel. 521950; telex 22288; Ambassador: MOHAMED AMIN AHMED AL-JAF.
Ireland: 3 Ri Tan Dong Lu, Beijing; tel. 5322691; telex 22425; Ambassador: GEAROID O'BROIN.
Italy: 2 Dong Er Jie, San Li Tun, Beijing; tel. 5322131; telex 22414; Ambassador: ALBERTO SOLERA.
Japan: 7 Ri Tan Lu, Jian Guo Men Wai, Beijing; tel. 522361; telex 22275; Ambassador: TOSHIJIRO NAKAJIMA.
Jordan: 54 Dong Liu Jie, San Li Tun, Beijing; tel. 523906; telex 22651; Ambassador: WALID AL-SADD AL-BATAYNEH.
Kenya: 4 Xi Liu Jie, San Li Tun, Beijing; tel. 523381; telex 22311; Ambassador: JELANI HABIB.
Korea, Democratic People's Republic: Ri Tan Bei Lu, Jian Guo Men Wai, Beijing; telex 20448; Ambassador: CHU CHANG JUN.
Kuwait: 23 Guang Hua Lu, Beijing; tel. 522216; telex 22127; Ambassador: HASAN ALI AL-DABBAGH.
Laos: 11 East San Li Tun, Chao Yang District, Beijing; tel. 521244; telex 22144; Ambassador: PHONGSAVAT BOUPHA.
Lebanon: 51 Dong Liu Jie, San Li Tun, Beijing; tel. 522770; telex 22113; Ambassador: FARID SAMAHA.
Lesotho: Ta Yuan Diplomatic Bldg, San Li Tun, Beijing; tel. 5322065; telex 210278; Ambassador: BERNARD THABO MOEKETSI.
Liberia: 1 Northern Alley, San Li Tun, Beijing; tel. 5323549; telex 22165; Ambassador: JOHN CHRISTOPHER RICKS.
Libya: 55 Dong Liu Jie, San Li Tun, Beijing; telex 22310; Secretary of the People's Bureau: ABD AL-HAMID AL-ZINTANI.
Luxembourg: 21 Nei Wu Bu Jie, Beijing; tel. 556175; telex 22638; Ambassador: PAUL SCHULLER.
Madagascar: 3 Dong Jie, San Li Tun, Beijing; tel. 521353; telex 22140; Ambassador: JEAN-JACQUES MAURICE.
Malaysia: 13 Dong Zhi Men Wai Da Jie, San Li Tun, Beijing; tel. 522531; telex 22122; Ambassador: Dato ISMAIL BIN MOHAMED.
Mali: 8 Dong Si Jie, San Li Tun, Beijing; tel. 521704; telex 22257; Ambassador: NAKOUNTE DIAKITÉ.
Malta: 2-2-71 Jian Guo Men Wai, Beijing; tel. 5323114; telex 22670; Ambassador: RICHARD LAPIRA.
Mauritania: 9 Dong San Jie, San Li Tun, Beijing; tel. 521346; telex 22514; Ambassador: TAKI OULD SIDE.
Mexico: 5 Dong Wu Jie, San Li Tun, Beijing; tel. 522122; telex 22262; Ambassador: FAUSTO ZAPATA LOREDO.
Mongolia: 2 Xiu Shui Bei Jie, Jian Guo Men Wai, Beijing; tel. 521203; Ambassador: N. LUVSANCHULTEM.
Morocco: 16 San Li Tun Lu, Beijing; tel. 521489; telex 22268; Ambassador: ABDERRAHIM HARKETT.
Nepal: 1 San Li Tun Xiliujie, Beijing; tel. 521795; telex 210408; Ambassador: NAYAN BAHADUR KHATRI.
Netherlands: 1-15-2 Ta Yuan Diplomatic Missions Bldg, 14 Liang Ma He Nan Lu, Beijing; tel. 521131; telex 22277; Ambassador: Dr ROLAND VAN DEN BERG.
New Zealand: 1 Ri Tan, Dong Er Jie, Chaoyang District, Beijing; tel. 5322731; telex 22124; Ambassador: LINDSAY J. WATT.
Nicaragua: Beijing; Ambassador: ALFREDO ALANIZ DOWNING.
Niger: 50 Dong Liu Jie, San Li Tun, Beijing; tel. 521616; telex 22133; Ambassador: PIERRE AUSSEIL.
Nigeria: 2 Dong Wu Jie, San Li Tun, Beijing; telex 22274; Ambassador: ADEUGA ADEKOYE.
Norway: 1 San Li Tun, Dong Yi Jie, Beijing; tel. 5322261; telex 22266; Ambassador: JAN TORE HOLVIK.
Oman: 6 Liang Ma He Nan Lu, San Li Tun, Beijing; tel. 5323956; telex 22192; Ambassador: MUSHTAQ BIN ABDULLAH BIN JAFFER AL-SALEH.
Pakistan: 1 Dong Zhi Men Wai Da Jie, Beijing; tel. 522504; Ambassador: AKRAM ZAKI.
Peru: 2-82 San Li Tun, Beijing; tel. 5322005; telex 22278; Ambassador: ROBERTO VILLARAN KOECHLIN.
Philippines: 23 Xiu Shui Bei Jie, Jian Guo Men Wai, Beijing; tel. 523420; telex 22132; Ambassador: (vacant).
Poland: 1 Ri Tan Lu, Jian Guo Men Wai, Beijing; tel. 521235; Ambassador: MARIAN WOZNIAK.
Portugal: 2-72 San Li Tun, Beijing; tel. 5323220; telex 22326; Ambassador: OCTAVIO NETO VALERIO.
Qatar: Beijing.
Romania: Jian Guo Men Wai, Xiushui, Beijing; tel. 523255; telex 22250; Ambassador: ANGELO MICULESCU.
Rwanda: 30 Xiu Shui Bei Jie, Beijing; tel. 522193; telex 22104; Ambassador: DENIS MAGIRA BIGIRIMANA.
Senegal: 1 Ri Tan Dong Yi Jie, Jian Guo Men Wai, Beijing; tel. 522576; telex 22100; Ambassador: AHMED TIDIANE KANE.
Sierra Leone: 7 Dong Zhi Men Wai Da Jie, Beijing; tel. 521222; telex 22166; Ambassador: SHEKU BADARA BASTRU DUMBUYA.
Somalia: 2 San Li Tun Lu, Beijing; tel. 521752; telex 22121; Ambassador: YUSSUF HASSAN IBRAHIM.
Spain: 9 San Li Tun Lu, Beijing; tel. 5323742; telex 22108; Ambassador: EUGENIO BREGOLAT Y OBIOLS.
Sri Lanka: 3 Jian Hua Lu, Jian Guo Men Wai, Beijing; tel. 5321861; telex 22136; Ambassador: NANAYAKKARA PATHIRAGE SENA LAXMAN PERERA.
Sudan: 1 Dong Er Jie, San Li Tun, Beijing; telex 22116; Ambassador: MUHAMMAD HAMAD MUHAMMAD MATTAR.
Sweden: 3 Dong Zhi Men Wai Da Jie, Beijing; tel. 5323331; telex 22261; Ambassador: LARS BERGQUIST.
Switzerland: 3 Dong Wu Jie, San Li Tun, Beijing; tel. 5322736; telex 22251; Ambassador: ERWIN SCHURTENBERGER.
Syria: 6 Dong Si Jie, San Li Tun, Beijing; telex 22138; Ambassador: ZAKARIA SHURAIKI.
Tanzania: 53 Dong Liu Jie, San Li Tun, Beijing; tel. 5321408; telex 22749; Ambassador: CLEMENT GEORGE KAHAMA.
Thailand: 40 Guang Hua Lu, Beijing; tel. 5321903; telex 22145; Ambassador: TEJ BUNNAG.
Togo: 11 Dong Zhi Men Wai Da Jie, Beijing; tel. 5322202; telex 22130; Ambassador: YAO BLOUA AGBO.
Tunisia: 1 Dong Jie, San Li Tun, Beijing; tel. 5322435; telex 22103; Ambassador: TAOUFIK SMIDA.
Turkey: 9 Dong Wu Jie, San Li Tun, Beijing; tel. 5322650; telex 210168; Ambassador: BILAL SIMSIR.

Uganda: 5 Dong Jie, San Li Tun, Beijing; tel. 522370; telex 22272; Ambassador: WILLIAM WYCLIFFE RWETSIBA.
USSR: 4 Dong Zhi Men Wai Zhong Jie, Beijing; telex 22247; Ambassador: OLEG ALEKSANDROVICH TROYANOVSKY.
United Kingdom: 11 Guang Hua Lu, Jian Guo Men Wai, Beijing; tel. 5321961; telex 22191; Ambassador: Sir ALAN EWEN DONALD.
USA: 3 Xiu Shui Bei Jie, Beijing; tel. 523831; telex 22701; Ambassador: WINSTON LORD.
Venezuela: 14 San Li Tun Lu, Beijing; tel. 521295; telex 22137; Ambassador: LEONARDO DÍAZ GONZALES.
Viet-Nam: 32 Guang Hua Lu, Jian Guo Men Wai, Beijing; Ambassador: NGUYEN MINH PHUONG.
Yemen Arab Republic: 4 Dongzhi Men Wai Dajie, Beijing; tel. 523346; Ambassador: HUSSEIN ABDULKHALEK AL-GALAL.
Yemen, People's Democratic Republic: 5 Dong San Jie, San Li Tun, Beijing; telex 22279; Ambassador: IBRAHIM ABDULLA SAIDI.
Yugoslavia: 56 Dong Liu Jie, San Li Tun, Beijing; tel. 421562; telex 22403; Ambassador: ZVONE DRAGAN.
Zaire: 6 Dong Wu Jie, San Li Tun, Beijing; tel. 421966; telex 22273; Ambassador: LOMBO LO MANGAMANGA.
Zambia: 5 Dong Si Jie, San Li Tun, Beijing; tel. 521554; telex 22388; Ambassador: MATHIAS MAINZA CHONA.
Zimbabwe: 7 Dong San Jie, Beijing; tel. 521652; telex 22671; Ambassador: NICHOLAS TASUNUNGURWA GOCHE.

Judicial System

The general principles of the Chinese judicial system are laid down in Articles 123-135 of the December 1982 constitution (q.v.).

PEOPLE'S COURTS

Supreme People's Court: Dongjiaomin Xiang, Beijing; tel. 550131; f. 1949; the highest judicial organ of the state; directs and supervises work of lower courts; Pres. REN JIANXIN (five-year term of office coincides with that of National People's Congress, by which the President is elected).
Special People's Courts.
Local People's Courts.

PEOPLE'S PROCURATORATES

Supreme People's Procuratorate: Donganmen Beiheyan, Beijing; tel. 550831; acts for the National People's Congress in examining govt depts, civil servants and citizens, to ensure observance of the law; prosecutes in criminal cases. Procurator-Gen. LIU FUZHI (elected by the National People's Congress for five years).
Local People's Procuratorates: undertake the same duties at the local level. Ensure that the judicial activities of the people's courts, the execution of sentences in criminal cases, and the activities of departments in charge of reform through labour, conform to the law; institute, or intervene in, important civil cases which affect the interest of the state and the people.

Religion

During the 'Cultural Revolution' places of worship were closed. After 1977 the Government adopted a policy of religious tolerance, and the 1982 Constitution states that citizens enjoy freedom of religious belief, and that legitimate religious activities are protected. Many temples, churches and mosques are reopening.
Bureau of Religious Affairs: Beijing; Dir REN WUZHI.

ANCESTOR WORSHIP

Ancestor worship is believed to have originated with the deification and worship of all important natural phenomena. The divine and human were not clearly defined; all the dead became gods and were worshipped by their descendants. The practice has no code or dogma and the ritual is limited to sacrifices made during festivals and on birth and death anniversaries.

BUDDHISM

Buddhism was introduced into China from India in AD 67, and flourished during the Sui and Tang dynasties (6th-8th century) when eight sects were established. The Chan and Pure Land sects are the most popular.
Buddhist Association of China: f. 1953; Pres. ZHAO PUCHU.
Tibetan Institute of Lamaism: Pres. BUMI JANGBALUOCHU; Vice-Pres. CEMOLIN DANZENGCHILIE.

CHRISTIANITY

During the 19th century and the first half of the 20th century, large numbers of foreign Christian missionaries worked in China. There were c. 7m. registered Christians in China in 1988.
Three-Self Patriotic Movement Committee of Protestant Churches of China: Chair. DING GUANGXUN; Sec.-Gen. SHEN DERONG.
China Christian Council: 169 Yuan Ming Yuan Rd, Shanghai; tel. 213396; telex 34136; f. 1980; comprises provincial Christian councils; Pres. Bishop DING GUANGXUN; Gen. Sec. Bishop ZHENG JIANYE.
Anglican Church: 169 Yuan Ming Yuan Rd, Shanghai; tel. 210806; Chair. of Council Bishop DING GUANGXUN.
The Roman Catholic Church: Catholic Mission, Si-She-Ku, Beijing; Bishop of Beijing (vacant).
Chinese Catholic Patriotic Association: Chair. Mgr ZONG HUAIDE; c. 3m. mems (1988).

CONFUCIANISM

Confucianism is a philosophy and a system of ethics, without ritual or priesthood. The respects accorded Confucius are not paid to a prophet or god, but to a great sage whose teachings promote peace and good order in society and whose philosophy encourages moral living.

DAOISM

Daoism was founded by Zhang Daoling during the Eastern Han dynasty (AD 125-144). Lao Zi, a philosopher of the Zhov dynasty (born 604 BC), is its principal inspiration, and is honoured as Lord the Most High by Daoists.
China Daoist Association: Temple of the White Cloud, Beijing; tel. 367179; f. 1957; Chair. LI YUKANG.

ISLAM

According to Muslim history, Islam was introduced into China in AD 651. It had 16m. adherents in China in 1988, chiefly among the Wei Wuer and Hui people.
Beijing Islamic Association: Dongsi Mosque, Beijing; f. 1979; Chair. Imam Al-Hadji SALAH AN SHIWEI.
China Islamic Association: Beijing; f. 1953; Pres. Al-Hodji ILYAS SHEN XIAXI.

The Press

In 1986 China had 2,191 newspapers. Each province publishes its own daily. Only the major newspapers and periodicals are listed below, and only a restricted number are allowed abroad.

PRINCIPAL NEWSPAPERS

Beijing Ribao (Beijing Daily): 34 Xi Biaobei Hutong, Dongdan, Beijing; tel. 553431; f. 1952; organ of the Beijing municipal cttee of the CCP; Dir-Gen. XU WEN; Editor-in-Chief MAN YUNLAI; circ. 1m.
Beijing Wanbao (Beijing Evening News): 34 Xi Biaobei Hutong, Dongdan, Beijing; tel. 553431; telex 283642; f. 1958; Editor GU XING; circ. 500,000.
Can Kao Xiao Xi (Reference News): Beijing; reprints from foreign newspapers; publ. by Xinhua (New China) News Agency; circ. 3.6m.
China Daily: 2 Jintai Xilu, 100025 Beijing; tel. 581958; telex 22022; f. 1981; English; coverage: China's political, economic and cultural developments; world, financial and sports news; Editor-in-Chief CHEN LI; circ. 150,000.
Dazhong Ribao (Masses Daily): 99 Lishan Rd, Jinan, Shandong Province; tel. 47951; telex 9993; f. 1939; circ. 600,000; Editor-in-Chief LIU HONGXI.
Fujian Ribao (Fujian Daily): Hualin Lu, Fuzhou, Fujian; tel. 57756; daily; Editor-in-Chief LIN ZHENXIA.
Gongren Ribao (Workers' Daily): Liupukeng, Andingmen Wai, Beijing; tel. 4211561; f. 1949; trade union activities and workers' lives; also major home and overseas news; Editor-in-Chief LI JI; circ. 2.5m.
Guangming Ribao (Guangming Daily): 106 Yongan Lu, Beijing; tel. 338561; telex 20021; f. 1949; literature, art, science, education, history, economics, philosophy; Editor-in-Chief ZHAO XIHUA; circ. 1.5m.
Guangzhou Ribao (Canton Daily): 10 Dongle Lu, Renmin Zhonglu, Guangzhou, Guangdong; tel. 85812; f. 1952; daily; economic and current affairs.

Guizhou Ribao (Guizhou Daily): Guiying, Guizhou Province; circ. 300,000; Editor-in-Chief LIU XUEZHU.

Hebei Ribao (Hebei Daily): Yuhua Lu, Shijiazhuang, Hebei Province; tel. 48901; f. 1949; Editor-in-Chief YE ZHEN.

Hubei Ribao (Hubei Daily): Wuluo Lu, Wuchang, Hubei; tel. 73305; f. 1949; Dir FAN KUN.

Jiangxi Ribao (Jiangxi Daily): Nanchang, Jiangxi Province; f. 1949; Editor-in-Chief JIANG HUINENG.

Jiefang Ribao (Liberation Daily): 274 Han Kou Rd, Shanghai; tel. 221300; telex 6078; f. 1949; Chief Editor CHEN NIANYUN; circ. 1m.

Jiefangjun Bao (Liberation Army Daily): Beijing; f. 1956; official organ of the Central Military Comm.; circ. 800,000.

Jingji Ribao (Economic Daily): 9 Xi Huangchengen Nanjie, Beijing; tel. 652018; f. 1983; financial affairs, domestic and foreign trade; Editor-in-Chief FAN JINGYI; circ. 1.59m.

Nanfang Ribao (Nanfang Daily): Dongfeng Donglu, Guangzhou, Guangdong Province; tel. 77022; f. 1949; Dir DING XILING; Editor-in-Chief ZHANG CONG; circ. 1m.

Nongmin Ribao (Peasants' Daily): Shilipu Beili, Chao Yang Men Wai, Beijing; tel. 583431; telex 6592; f. 1980; 6 a week; circulates in rural areas nation-wide; Editor-in-Chief ZHANG GUANGYOU; circ. 1m.

Qingdao Ribao (Qingdao Daily): 33 Taiping Lu, Qingdao, Shandong; tel. 86237; f. 1949; daily; circ. 2.6m.

Renmin Ribao (People's Daily): 2 Jin Tai Xi Lu, Beijing; tel. 596231; telex 22320; f. 1948; organ of the CCP; also publishes overseas edn; Dir QIAN LIREN; Editor-in-Chief TAN WENRUI; circ. 5m.

Shanxi Ribao (Shanxi Daily): Shuangtasi, Taiyuan, Shanxi Province; tel. 24835; Dir WANG XIYI; Editor-in-Chief CHEN MOZHANG.

Shenzhen Tequ Bao (Shenzhen Special Zone Daily): 1 Shennan Zhonglu, Shenzhen; tel. 22840; f. 1982; reports on special economic zones, as well as Hong Kong and Macau.

Sichuan Ribao (Sichuan Daily): 70 Hongxing Zhonglu, Chengdu, Sichuan; tel. 22911; f. 1952; circ. 1.35m.; Editor-in-Chief YAO ZHINENG.

Tianjin Ribao (Tianjin Daily): 66 An Shan Rd, Heping District, Tianjin; tel. 25803; f. 1949; Editor-in-Chief LU SI; circ. 600,000.

Wenhui Bao: 149 Yuanmingyuan Lu, Shanghai; tel. 211410; telex 33080; f. 1938; Editor-in-Chief MA DA; circ. 1.7m.

World Economic Herald: Shanghai; tel. 270011; telex 33360; f. 1980; weekly; economics and current affairs; Editor-in-Chief QIN BENLI; circ. 300,000.

Xin Hua Ribao (New China Daily): 55 Zhongshan Lu, Nanjing, Jiangsu; tel. 42638; circ. 900,000.

Xin Min Wan Bao (Xin Min Evening News): Jiujianlu 41, Shanghai; tel. 217307; f. 1946; circ. 1,365,768.

Yangcheng Wanbao (Yangcheng Evening Post): 733 Dongfeng Donglu, Guangzhou, Guangdong; tel. 776211; f. 1957; circ. 1.66m.

Zhongguo Qingnian Bao (China Youth News): 2 Haiyuncang, Dongzhimen Nei, Beijing; tel. 446581; f. 1951; 4 a week; aimed at 14–25 age-group; Dir LI ZHILUN; Editor-in-Chief XU ZHUQING; circ. 3m.

SELECTED PERIODICALS

Ban Yue Tan (Fortnightly Review): Beijing; tel. 668521; f. 1980; in Chinese and Wei Wuer (Uygur); Editor-in-Chief MIN FANLU; circ. 5.3m.

Beijing Review: 24 Baiwanzhuang Rd, Beijing 100037; tel. 8314318; telex 222374; weekly; edns in English, French, Spanish, Japanese and German; Editor-in-Chief WANG YOUFEN.

Chinese Literature Press: 24 Baiwanzhuang Rd, Beijing 37; f. 1951; quarterly; in English and French; literary; includes art reproductions; Editor-in-Chief WANG MENG.

Chinese Science Abstracts: Science Press, 137 Chaoyang Men Nei St, Beijing; tel. 4411; telex 210247; f. 1982; monthly in English; science and technology; Chief Editor YAN MINGWEN.

Dianying Xinzuo (New Films): 796 Huaihai Zhonglu, Shanghai; tel. 379710; f. 1979; bi-monthly; introduces new films.

Dianzi yu Diannao (Electronics and Computers): Beijing; f. 1985; popularized information on computers and microcomputers.

Feitian (Fly Skywards): 50 Donggan Xilu, Lanzhou, Gansu; tel. 25803; f. 1961; monthly.

Guoji Xin Jishu (New International Technology): Zhanwang Publishing House, Beijing; f. 1984; also publ. in Hong Kong; international technology, scientific and technical information.

Guowai Keji Dongtai (Scientific and Technical Trends Abroad): China Institute of Scientific and Technical Information, 15 Fuxing Rd, Beijing; tel. 8015544; telex 20079; f. 1969; scientific journal.

Hai Xia (The Strait): 27 De Gui Lane, Fuzhou, Fujian Province; tel. 33656; f. 1981; quarterly; literary journal; Prin. Officers YANG YU, JWO JONG LIN.

Huasheng Bao (Voice of Overseas Chinese): 12 Bai Wan Zhuang Nan Jie, Beijing 100037; tel. 8315039; f. 1983; 2 a week; intended mainly for overseas Chinese and Chinese nationals resident abroad; Pres. and Editor-in-Chief ZHOU TI.

Jianzhu (Construction): Baiwanzhuang, Beijing; tel. 8992849; f. 1956; monthly; Editor FANG YUEGUANG; circ. 500,000.

Liaowang (Outlook): 57 Xuanwumen Xijie, Beijing; tel. 668521; f. 1981; weekly; current affairs; Gen. Man. FENG LI; Editor DABIN CHEN; circ. 500,000.

Luxingjia (Traveller): 23A Dong Jiaomin Xiang, Beijing; tel. 552631; f. 1955; monthly; Chinese scenery, customs, culture.

Meishu Zhi You (Friends of Art): 32 Beizongbu Hutong, East City Region, Beijing; tel. 5122583; telex 5019; f. 1982; every 2 months; art review journal, also providing information on fine arts pubis in China and abroad; Editors PENG SHEN, BAOLUN WU.

Nianqingren (Young People): 169 Mayuanlin, Changsha, Hunan; tel. 23610; f. 1981; monthly; general interest for young people.

Nongye Zhishi (Agricultural Knowledge): 7 Shimuyuan Dongjie, Jinan, Shandong; tel. 42238; f. 1950; fortnightly; popular agricultural science; Dir YIANG XIANFEN; circ. 400,000.

Qiushi (Seeking Truth): Beijing; f. 1988 to succeed *Hong Qi* (Red Flag); theoretical journal of the CCP; Dep. Chief Editor SU XING.

Renmin Huabao (China Pictorial): Huayuancun, West Suburbs, Beijing 28; tel. 890381; f. 1950; monthly; edns: 2 in Chinese, 4 in minority languages and 15 in foreign languages; Editor-in-Chief QIAN HAO.

Renmin Wujing Bao (People's Armed Police Newspaper): Beijing; f. 1983; journal of the CCP Cttee of the Armed Police HQ.

Shichang Zhoubao (Market Weekly): 2 Duan, Sanhao Jie, Heping District, Shenyang, Liaoning; tel. 482983; f. 1979; weekly in Chinese; trade, commodities and financial and economic affairs; circ. 1m.

Shufa (Calligraphy): 83 Kangping Lu, Shanghai; tel. 377711; f. 1978; journal on ancient and modern calligraphy.

Tiyu Kexue (Sports Science): 8 Tiyuguan Rd, Beijing; tel. 757161; f. 1981; sponsored by the China Sports Science Soc.; quarterly; in Chinese; circ. 20,000.

Wenxue Qingnian (Youth Literature Journal): Mu Tse Fang 27, Wenzhou, Zhejiang Province; tel. 3578; f. 1981; monthly; Editor-in-Chief CHEN YUSHEN; circ. 80,000.

Xian Dai Faxue (Modern Law Science): Chongqing, Sichuan; tel. 661671; f. 1979; bi-monthly; theoretical law journal, with summaries in English; Dirs LI GUOZHI, XU JINGCUN.

Yinyue Aihaozhe (Music Lovers): 74 Shaoxing Lu, 200020 Shanghai; tel. 372608; telex 33384; f. 1979; every 2 months; popular music knowledge; Editor-in-Chief SHEN TINGKANG.

Zhongguo Duiwai Maoyi (China's Foreign Trade): 1 Fu Xing Men Wai St, Beijing; tel. 863790; telex 22315; f. 1956; monthly; edns in Chinese, English, French and Spanish; carries information about Chinese imports and exports and explains foreign trade and economic policies; Editor-in-Chief LIU DEYU.

Zhongguo Ertong (Chinese Children): 21, Lane 12, Dongsi, Beijing; tel. 444761; telex 4357; f. 1980; monthly; illustrated journal for elementary school pupils.

Zhongguo Funu (Women of China): 24A Shijia Hutong, Beijing; tel. 551765; f. 1956; monthly; women's rights and status, marriage and family, education, family planning, arts, cookery, etc.

Zhongguo Guanggao Bao (China's Advertising): Editorial Dept, Beijing Exhibition Hall, Xizhimen Wai, Beijing; tel. 890661; f. 1984; weekly; all aspects of advertising and marketing; offers advertising services for domestic and foreign commodities.

Zhongguo Guangbo Dianshi (China Radio and Television): 12 Fucheng Lu, Beijing; tel. 896217; f. 1982; monthly; sponsored by Ministry of Radio, Film and Television; reports and comments.

Zhongguo Jianshe (China Reconstructs): Baiwanzhuang Lu, Beijing 37; tel. 892007; f. 1952; monthly; edns in English, Spanish, French, Arabic, Portuguese, Chinese and German; economic, social and cultural affairs; illustrated; Editor-in-Chief ISRAEL EPSTEIN.

Zhongguo Sheying (Chinese Photography): 61 Hongxing Hutong, Dongdan, Beijing; tel. 552277; f. 1957; every 2 months; reviews and comments about photography; Editor YUAN YIPING.

Zhongguo Xinwen (China News): 12 Baiwanzhuang Nanjie, Beijing; tel. 8315012; f. 1952; daily; current affairs.

Zhongguo Zhenjiu (Chinese Acupuncture and Moxibustion): Dongzhimen, Beijing 100700; tel. 446661; f. 1981; 2 a month; publ. by Chinese Soc. of Acupuncture and Moxibustion; partly in English; Editor-in-Chief Prof. WANG BENXIAN.

THE PEOPLE'S REPUBLIC OF CHINA
Directory

NEWS AGENCIES

Xinhua (New China) News Agency: 57 Xuanwumen Xidajie, Beijing; tel. 668521; telex 22316; f. 1931; offices in all Chinese provincial capitals, and about 95 overseas bureaux; news service in Chinese, English, French, Spanish, Arabic and Russian, feature and photographic services; Pres. MU QING; Editor-in-Chief NAN ZHENZHONG.

Zhongguo Xinwen She (China News Agency): POB 1114, Beijing; f. 1952; office in Hong Kong; supplies news features, special articles and photographs for newspapers and magazines in Chinese printed overseas; services in Chinese; Dir WANG SHIGU.

Foreign Bureaux

Agence France-Presse (AFP) (France): 10–83 Qi Jia Yuan, Beijing; tel. 521992; Bureau Chief BERNARD DEGDANNI.

Agencia EFE (Spain): 2-2-132 Jian Guo Men Wai, Beijing; tel. 523449; telex 22167; Rep. RAMÓN SANTAULARIA.

Agenzia Nazionale Stampa Associata (ANSA) (Italy): 2-81 Ban Gong Lou, 2-81 San Li Tun, Beijing; tel. 523651; telex 22290; Agent GIULIO PECORA.

Allgemeiner Deutscher Nachrichtendienst (ADN) (German Democratic Republic): Jian Guo Men Wai, Qi Jia Yuan Gong Yu 7-2-61, Beijing; telex 22109.

Associated Press (AP) (USA): 7-2-52 Qi Jia Yuan, Diplomatic Quarters, Beijing; tel. 523419; telex 22196; Bureau Chief JAMES ABRAMS.

Bulgarska Telegrafna Agentsia (BTA) (Bulgaria): 1-4-13 Jian Guo Men Wai, Beijing; Bureau Chief DIMITRE IVANOV MASLAROV.

Československá tisková kancelář (ČTK) (Czechoslovakia): 7-43 Qi Jia Yuan, Beijing; tel. 521 831.

Deutsche Presse-Agentur (dpa) (Federal Republic of Germany): Ban Gong Lou, San Li Tun, Apt 1-31, Beijing; tel. 5321473; telex 22297; Bureau Chief EDGAR BAUER.

Jiji Tsushin-Sha (Japan): 9-1-13 Jian Guo Men Wai, Beijing; tel. 522924; telex 22381; Correspondent YOSHIKAZU SAITO.

Kyodo Tsushin (Japan): 3-91 Jian Guo Men Wai, Beijing; tel. 522680; telex 8522324; Bureau Chief SHIGEYOSHI FUSE.

Magyar Távirati Iroda (MTI) (Hungary): 1-42 Ban Gong Lou, San Li Tun, Beijing; Correspondent FERENC KOVÁCS.

Prensa Latina (Cuba): 6 Wai Jiao Da Lou, Beijing; tel. 521831; telex 22495; Correspondent JOSÉ LUIS ROBAINA.

Reuters (UK): 1-11 Ban Gong Lou, San Li Tun, Beijing; tel. 5321921; telex 22702; Chief Representative G. V. BERGER.

Telegrafnoye Agentstvo Sovetskovo Soyuza (TASS) (USSR): Jian Guo Men Wai, Qi Jia Yuan Gong Yu, Beijing; telex 22115; Correspondent GRIGORIY ARSLANOV.

United Press International (UPI) (USA): 7-1-11 Qi Jia Yuan, Beijing; tel. 523456; telex 22197; Correspondents JANE MACARTNEY, JAMES MILES.

The following are also represented: Agerpres (Romania), Korean Central News Agency (Democratic People's Republic of Korea), Tanjug (Yugoslavia) and VNA (Viet-Nam).

PRESS ASSOCIATION

All China Journalists' Association: Xijiaominxiang, Beijing; tel. 657170; Exec. Chair. WU LENGXI.

Publishers

In 1984 there were nearly 300 publishing houses in China, including a regional 'People's Publishing House' for each province.

The Press and Publication Administration of The People's Republic of China: Beijing; administers publishing, printing and distribution under the Ministry of Culture; Dir DU DAOZHENG.

Beijing Chubanshe (Beijing Publishing House): 6 Bei Sanhuan Zhong Lu, Beijing; tel. 2012339; f. 1956; political theory, history, philosophy, economics, geography, etc.

Beijing Daxue Chubanshe (Beijing University Press): Beijing University, Haidian District, Beijing; tel. 283827; f. 1980; academic.

Dolphin Books: 24 Baiwanzhuang Rd, Beijing; tel. 890951; telex 22496; f. 1986; children's books in foreign languages.

Falü Chubanshe (Law Publishing House): POB 111, 100036 Beijing; tel. 815325; f. 1980; current laws and decrees, legal textbooks, translations of important foreign legal works.

Gaodeng Jiaoyu Chubanshe (Higher Education Press): 55 Shatan Houjie, Beijing; tel. 446891; f. 1954; academic; Pres. and Editor-in-Chief ZU ZHENQUAN.

Gongren Chubanshe (Workers' Press): Liupukeng, Andingmen Wai, Beijing; tel. 421551; f. 1949; labour movement, trade unions, science and technology related to industrial production.

Guangdong Keji Chubanshe (Guangdong Scientific and Technical Press): 25 Xinji Lu, POB 49, Guangzhou, Guangdong 510130; tel. 862931; f. 1978; natural sciences, technology, medicine; Acting Dir OU YANGLIAN.

Guoji Shudian (China International Book Trading Corporation): POB 399, Chegongzhuang Xilu 21, Beijing; tel. 8022023; telex 22496; f. 1949; foreign trade org. specializing in publs, including books, periodicals, art and crafts, microfilms, etc.; import and export distributors; Gen. Man. WANG QINGYUN.

Heilongjiang Kexue Jishu Chubanshe (Heilongjiang Scientific and Technical Publishing House): 28 Fenbu Jie, Nangang District, Harbin, Heilongjiang; tel. 35613; f. 1979; industrial and agricultural technology, natural sciences.

Huashan Wenyi Chubanshe (Huashan Literature and Art Publishing House): 45 Bei Malu, Shijiazhuang, Hebei; tel. 22501; f. 1982; novels, poetry, drama, etc.

Kexue Chubanshe (Science Press): 137 Chaoyangmen Nei Dajie, Beijing; tel. 444036; f. 1954; science and technology.

Lingnan Meishu Chubanshe (Lingnan Art Publishing House): 25 Xinji Lu, Xiti, Guangzhou, Guangdong; tel. 861251; f. 1981; works on classical and modern painting, picture albums, photographic, painting techniques; Editor-in-Chief LIN KANGSHENG.

Minzu Chubanshe (Nationalities Publishing House): Hepingli Beijie 14, 100013 Beijing; tel. 4211261; f. 1953; books and periodicals in minority languages, e.g. Mongolian, Tibetan, Kazakh, Korean, Uigur, etc.; Editor-in-Chief ZHU YINGWU.

Qunzhong Chubanshe (Masses Publishing House): 14 Dongchangan St, Beijing 100741; tel. 5121672; telex 2831; f. 1956; politics, law, judicial affairs, criminology, public security, etc.

Renmin Jiaoyu Chubanshe (People's Educational Publishing House): 55 Shatan Houjie, Beijing; tel. 442931; f. 1950; educational, scientific.

Renmin Meishu Chubanshe (People's Fine Arts Publishing House): 32 Beizongbu Hutong, Beijing; tel. 550290; f. 1951; works by Chinese and foreign painters, picture albums, photographic, painting techniques; Dir TIAN YUWEN; Editor-in-Chief LIU YUSHAN.

Renmin Weisheng Chubanshe (People's Medical Publishing House): 10 Tiantan Xi Li, Beijing 100050; tel. 755431; f. 1953; medicine (Western and traditional Chinese), pharmacology, dentistry, public health; Pres. DONG MIANGUO.

Renmin Wenxue Chubanshe (People's Literature Publishing House): 166 Chaoyangmen Nei Dajie, Beijing; tel. 553177; f. 1951; largest publr of literary works and translations into Chinese; Dir MENG WEIZAI; Editor-in-Chief TU AU.

Shanghai Guji Chubanshe (Shanghai Classics Publishing House): 272 Ruijin Erlu, Shanghai; tel. 370013; f. 1978; classical Chinese literature.

Shanghai Jiaoyu Chubanshe (Shanghai Educational Publishing House): 123 Yongfu Lu, Shanghai; tel. 377165; telex 3413; f. 1958; academic.

Shanghai Yiwen Chubanshe (Shanghai Translation Publishing House): 14 Lane 955, Yanan Zhonglu, Shanghai 200040; tel. 311890; f. 1978; translations of foreign classic and modern literature; philosophy, social sciences, dictionaries.

Shangwu Yinshuguan (Commercial Press): 36 Wangfujing Dajie, Beijing; tel. 552026; f. 1897; dictionaries and reference books in Chinese and foreign languages, translations of foreign works on social sciences; Gen. Man. LIN ERWEI.

Shaonian Ertong Chubanshe (Juvenile and Children's Publishing House): 1538 Yanan Xi Lu, Shanghai; tel. 522519; telex 5801; f. 1952; Editor-in-Chief CHEN XIANGMING; children's educational and literary works, teaching aids and periodicals.

Tianze Chubanshe (Tianze Publishing House): Beijing; f. 1988; natural sciences; Dir ZHOU YAO.

Waiwen Chubanshe (Foreign Language Press): 24 Baiwanzhuang Rd, Beijing 100037; tel. 8317390; telex 222475; f. 1952; books in foreign languages reflecting political, economic and cultural progress in People's Republic of China; Dir SHEN XIFEI; Editor-in-Chief LUO LIANG.

Wenwu Chubanshe (Cultural Relics Publishing House): 29 Wusi Dajie, Beijing; tel. 441761; f. 1956; books and catalogues of Chinese relics in museums and those recently discovered; Dir WANG DAIWEN.

Wuhan Daxue Chubanshe (Wuhan University Press): Wuhan University, Wuchang, Hubei; tel. 75941; f. 1952; academic.

Xiandai Chubanshe (Modern Press): 504 Anhua Li, Andingmenwai, Beijing; tel. 4216251; telex 210215; f. 1981; directories, reference books, etc.

Xuelin Chubanshe (Scholar Books Publishers): 710-37 Dingxi Rd, Shanghai; tel. 511802; f. 1981; academic, including personal academic works at authors' own expense; Dir LEI QUNMING; Editor-in-Chief LIU ZHAORUI.

Zhongguo Caizheng Jingji Chubanshe (China Financial and Economic Publishing House): 8 Dafosi Dongjie, Dongcheng District, Beijing; tel. 441982; f. 1961; finance, economics, commerce and accounting.

Zhongguo Dabaike Quanshu Chubanshe (Encyclopaedia of China Publishing House): 17 Fuchengmen Bei Da Jie, Beijing 100037; tel. 8315610; f. 1978; specializes in encyclopaedias; Dir MEI YI.

Zhongguo Ditu Chubanshe (China Cartographic Publishing House): 3 Baizhifang Xijie, Beijing; tel. 330808; f. 1954; cartographic publr; Dir ZHANG XUELIANG.

Zhongguo Funü Chubanshe (China Women's Publishing House): 24A Shijia Hutong, Beijing; tel. 557002; f. 1981; women's movement, marriage and family, child-care, etc.; Dir LI ZHONGXIU.

Zhongguo Qingnian Chubanshe (China Youth Publishing House): 21 Dongsi Shiertiao Hutong, Beijing 100708; tel. 444761; telex 4357; f. 1950; literature, ethics, social and natural sciences, youth work, autobiography; also periodicals; Dir CAI YUN.

Zhongguo Shehui Kexue Chubanshe (China Social Sciences Publishing House): 158A Gulou Xidajie, Beijing; tel. 441531; f. 1978; Dir ZHANG DING.

Zhongguo Xiju Chubanshe (China Theatrical Publishing House): 52 Dongsi Batiao Hutong, Beijing; tel. 4015815; telex 0489; f. 1957; traditional and modern Chinese drama.

Zhonghua Shuju (Chung Hwa Book Co): 36 Wangfujing, Dajie, Beijing; tel. 554504; f. 1912; general; Gen. Man. WANG CHUNG.

PUBLISHERS' ASSOCIATION

Publishers' Association of China: Beijing; f. 1979; arranges academic exchanges with foreign publrs; Chair. WANG ZIYE; Sec.-Gen. SONG MUWEN.

Radio and Television

In 1987 there were 215 radio broadcasting stations and in 1984 575 transmitting and relay stations. In 1978, 63% of households in the countryside had loudspeakers connected to the radio rediffusion system. There were an estimated 241.8m. radio receivers in use at 31 December 1985.

There were 204 television stations and 507 transmitting and relay stations equipped with transmitters of 1,000 Watts or more. In 1987 there were an estimated 92m. television receivers in use.

Ministry of Radio, Film and Television: Outside Fu Xing Men St 2, POB 4501, Beijing; tel. 862753; telex 22236; controls the Central People's Broadcasting Station, the Central TV Station, Radio Beijing, China Record Co., Beijing Broadcasting Institute, Broadcasting Research Institute, the China Broadcasting Art Troupe, etc.; Minister of Radio, Film and Television AI ZHISHENG.

RADIO

Central People's Broadcasting Station: Outside Fu Xing Men St 2, Beijing; domestic service in Chinese, Guanghua (Cantonese), Zang Wen (Tibetan), Chaozhou, Min Nan Hua (Amoy), Ke Jia (Hakka), Fuzhou Hua (Foochow dialect), Hasaka (Kazakh), Wei Wuer (Uygur), Menggu Hua (Mongolian) and Chaoxian (Korean); Dir YANG ZHAOLIN.

Radio Beijing: 2 Fuxing Men Wai St, Beijing; tel. 862691; telex 222271; f. 1947; foreign service in 38 languages incl. Arabic, Burmese, Czech, English, Esperanto, French, German, Indonesian, Italian, Japanese, Lao, Polish, Portuguese, Russian, Spanish, Turkish and Vietnamese; Dir CUI YULIN.

TELEVISION

Central People's Television Broadcasting Section: Bureau of Broadcasting Affairs of the State Council, Beijing; f. 1958; operates three channels.

Finance

BANKING

(cap. = capital; auth. = authorized; p.u. = paid up; res = reserves; dep. = deposits; m. = million; amounts in yuan)

Central Bank

People's Bank of China: San Li He, West City, Beijing; tel. 863907; telex 22612; f. 1948; bank of issue; Gov. LI GUIXIAN.

Other Banks

Agricultural Bank of China: 25 Fuxing Rd, Beijing; tel. 810709; telex 22017; f. 1963; functions directly under the State Council and handles state agricultural investments; dep. 6,200m. (Aug. 1979); Pres. MA YONGWEI.

Bank of China: Bank of China Bldg, 410 Fuchengmen Nei Dajie, Beijing; tel. 118311; telex 22254; f. 1912; handles foreign exchange and international settlements; cap. p.u. 5,000m., dep. 215,945m. (1986); Chair. and Pres. WANG DEYAN; 369 brs, 46 abroad.

Bank of Communications: 200 Jiang Xi Rd, Shanghai; tel. 213400; telex 33438; f. 1908; functions under the People's Bank of China; handles state investments in the joint state-private enterprises; cap. and res 645m. (1984); Pres. LI XIANGRUI.

China and South Sea Bank Ltd: 17 Xi Jiao Min Xiang, Beijing; f. 1921; cap. and res 652m. (1986); Chair. CUI PING.

China International Trust and Investment Corporation (CITIC): 19 Jianguomenwai St, Beijing; tel. 5002633; telex 22305; f. 1979; responsible to the State Council; arranges foreign investment in China and engages in jt investment ventures in China and abroad; auth. cap. 600m.; Pres. XU ZHAOLONG; Chair. RONG YIREN.

China Investment Bank: Wanshou Rd, Beijing; tel. 8011113; telex 22537; f. 1981; specializes in raising foreign funds for domestic investment and credit; Chair. ZHOU DAOJIONG.

China State Bank Ltd: 17 Xi Jiao Min Xiang, Beijing; cap. and res 525m. (1986); Gen. Man. LI PINZHOU.

Guangdong Provincial Bank: 17 Xi Jiao Min Xiang, Beijing; cap. and res 466m. (1983); Gen. Man. CHENG KEDONG.

Industrial and Commercial Bank of China: Sanlihe, Beijing; tel. 868901; f. 1984; handles industrial and commercial credits; Pres. ZHANG XIAO.

Kincheng Banking Corporation: 17 Xi Jiao Min Xiang, Beijing; telex 73405; f. 1917; cap. and res 847m. (1986); Gen. Man. XIANG KEFANG.

National Commercial Bank Ltd: 17 Xi Jiao Min Xiang, Beijing; f. 1907; cap. and res 645m. (1986); Gen. Man. WANG WEICAI.

People's Construction Bank of China: Wanshou Rd, Beijing; tel. 8011166; f. 1954 to make payments for capital construction according to plan and budget approval by the state; issues long- and medium-term loans to enterprises and short-term loans to contractors; Pres. ZHOU DAOJIONG.

Sin Hua Trust, Savings and Commercial Bank Ltd: 17 Xi Jiao Min Xiang, Beijing; cap. and res 824m. (1986); Gen. Man. CUI YANXU.

Yien Yieh Commercial Bank Ltd: 17 Xi Jiao Min Xiang, Beijing; cap. and res 805m. (1986); Gen. Man. PAN JAW LING.

Foreign Banks

Barclays Bank (UK): West 2, 23 Qianmen Ave East, Beijing; tel. 552417; telex 22589; Rep. W. H. SPEIRS.

First National Bank of Chicago (USA): CITIC Bldg, Room 1604, Jian Guo Men Wai, Beijing; tel. 5003281; telex 22433; Chief Rep. L. C. FRANKLIN.

Hongkong and Shanghai Banking Corporation (Hong Kong): 185 Yuan Ming Yuan Lu, POB 151, Shanghai; tel. 218383; telex 33058; f. 1865; Man. D. K. S. CHEUNG.

Midland Bank Group (UK): CITIC Bldg, Room 1103, Jian Guo Men Wai, Beijing; tel. 5004410; telex 22594; Group Rep. LANCE BROWNE.

Oversea-Chinese Banking Corporation Ltd (Singapore): f. 1932; brs in Xiamen (Amoy) and Shanghai; Chair. Tan Sri TAN CHIN TUAN.

Standard Chartered Bank (UK): Union Bldg, 9th Floor, 100 Yanan Dong Lu, Shanghai; tel. 218253; telex 33067; f. 1853; Rep. TIM HOOPER.

The following foreign banks also have offices in Beijing: Banca Commerciale Italiana, Bank of Brazil, Bank of Nova Scotia, Bank of Tokyo, Banque Nationale de Paris, Banque de l'Union Européenne, Banque Indosuez, Banque Paribas, Chase Manhattan, Commerzbank, Crédit Lyonnais, Deutsche Bank, Dresdner Bank, National Bank of Pakistan, National Commercial Banking Corporation of Australia, Royal Bank of Canada, Société Générale de Banque.

INSURANCE

China Insurance Co Ltd: 22 Xi Jiao Min Xiang, POB 20, Beijing; tel. 654231; telex 22102; f. 1931; cargo, hull, freight, fire, life, personal accident, industrial injury, motor insurance, reinsurance, etc.; Man. SONG GUO HUA.

THE PEOPLE'S REPUBLIC OF CHINA

The People's Insurance Co of China (PICC): 410 Fuchengmen Nei Dajie, Beijing; tel. 653150; telex 22102; f. 1949; hull, marine cargo, aviation, motor, life, fire, accident, liability and reinsurance, etc.; Pres. QIN DAOFU; Vice-Chair. LI PINZHOU, SONG GUOHUA.

Tai Ping Insurance Co Ltd: 22 Xi Jiao Min Xiang, Beijing; tel. 654231; telex 42001; marine freight, hull, cargo, fire, life, personal accident, industrial injury, motor insurance, reinsurance, etc.; Man. LIN ZHEN FENG.

Trade and Industry

EXTERNAL TRADE

All-China Federation of Industry and Commerce: 93 Beiheyan Dajie, Beijing; tel. 554231; telex 22044; f. 1953; promotes overseas trade relations; Chair. RONG YIREN.

China Council for the Promotion of International Trade: 1 Fu Xing Men Wai St, POB 4509, Beijing; tel. 8013344; telex 22315; f. 1952; encourages foreign trade and economic co-operation; sponsors and arranges Chinese exhbns abroad and foreign exhbns in China; helps foreigners to apply for patent rights and trade-mark registration in China; promotes foreign investment and organizes tech. exchanges with other countries; provides legal services; publishes trade periodicals; Chair. JIA SHI; Sec. Gen. CUI YUSHAN.

China Industry and Commerce Development Corporation (INCOMIC): 93 Bei He Yan Dajie, Beijing; tel. 554231; telex 22044; f. 1985; provides consultancy and promotion of exports and imports, both in China and internationally; Chair. HU ZIANG; Pres. ZOU SIYU.

Ministry of Foreign Economic Relations and Trade: (see under Ministries).

Export and Import Corporations

Beijing Foreign Trade Corporation: Bldg 12, Yong An Dong Li, Jian Guo Men Wai, Beijing; tel. 5001843; telex 210064; controls import-export trade, foreign trade transportation, export commodity packaging and advertising for Beijing; Dir YU XIAOSONG.

China International Book Trading Corporation: (see under Guoji Shudian in Publishers Section).

China International Water and Electric Corporation: Liupukang, Beijing; tel. 4015511; telex 22485; f. 1956 as China Water and Electric International Corpn, name changed 1983; exports equipment for projects in the field of water and electrical engineering, and undertakes such projects; Pres. ZHU JINGDE.

China Metallurgical Import and Export Corporation (CMIEC): 46 Dongsi Xidajie, Beijing; tel. 555714; telex 22461; f. 1980; imports ores, spare parts, automation and control systems, etc.; exports metallurgical products, technology and equipment; establishes joint ventures and trade with foreign companies; Pres. BAI BAOHUA.

China National Aerotechnology Import-Export Corporation: 67 Jiaonan St, Beijing; tel. 442444; telex 22318; exports signal flares, electric detonators, tachometers, parachutes, general purpose aircraft, etc.; Pres. SUN ZHAOQING.

China National Animal Breeding Stock Import and Export Corporation: Hepingli, Beijing; tel. 464344; telex 22233; sole agency for import and export of stud animals including cattle, sheep, goats, swine, horses, donkeys, camels, rabbits, poultry, etc., as well as pasture seeds and feed additives; Pres. YANG QING.

China National Arts and Crafts Import and Export Corporation: 82 Donganmen St, Beijing; tel. 552187; telex 22155; deals in jewellery, ceramics, handicrafts, pottery, wicker, bamboo, etc.; Pres. YU ZHITING.

China National Cereals, Oils and Foodstuffs Import and Export Corporation: 82 Donganmen St, Beijing; tel. 557316; telex 22281; imports and exports cereals, sugar, vegetable oils, meat, eggs, fruit, dairy produce, vegetables, wines and spirits, canned foods and aquatic products, etc.; Pres. CHEN FAXIAN.

China National Chartering Corporation (SINOCHART): Import Bldg, Erligou, Xijiao, Beijing; tel. 8314012; telex 22488; f. 1950; functions under Ministry of Foreign Economic Relations and Trade; agents for SINOTRANS (see below); arranges chartering of ships, reservation of space, managing and operating chartered vessels; Pres. PING JIAN.

China National Chemicals Import and Export Corporation: Erligou, Xijiao, Beijing; tel. 8314563; telex 22243; deals in rubber, petroleum, paints, fertilizers, inks, dyestuffs, chemicals and drugs; Pres. ZHENG DUNXUN.

China National Coal Import and Export Corporation (CNCIEC): 3A Dong Huang Si Da Jie, An Ding Men Wai, Beijing; tel. 4216061; telex 22494; imports and exports coal and tech. equipment for coal industry, joint coal development and compensation trade; Chair. WEI GUOFU.

Directory

China National Electronics Import and Export Corporation: 49 Fuxing Rd, Beijing; tel. 810910; telex 22475; Pres. LI DEGUANG.

China National Foreign Trade Transportation Corporation (SINOTRANS): Import Bldg, Erligou, Xijiao, Beijing; tel. 893566; telex 22153; f. 1950; functions under Ministry of Foreign Economic Relations and Trade; agents for Ministry's import and export corpns; arranges customs clearance, deliveries, forwarding and insurance for sea, land and air transportation; Pres. PING JIAN.

China National Import and Export Commodities Inspection Company: 12 Jianguomenwai St, Beijing; tel. 5002387; telex 210076; inspects, tests and surveys import and export commodities for overseas trade, transport, insurance and manufacturing firms; Vice-Pres. MENG QINGFA.

China National Instruments Import and Export Corporation: Erligou, Xijiao, Beijing; tel. 891179; telex 22304; imports and exports computers and technology in fields of telecommunications, electronics, navigation, chemicals, optics, nuclear physics, etc.; Pres. ZHANG BAOHE.

China National Light Industrial Products Import and Export Corporation: 82 Donganmen St, Beijing; tel. 556749; telex 22282; imports household electrical appliances, radio and TV receivers, photographic equipment, films, paper goods, building materials, etc.; exports bicycles, sewing machines, enamelware, glassware, stainless steel goods, footwear, leather goods, watches and clocks, cosmetics, stationery, electrical appliances, etc.; Pres. LI WENZHI.

China National Machine Tool Corporation: 19 Fang Jia Alley, An Nei, Beijing; tel. 4015657; telex 210088; f. 1979; imports and exports machine tools and tool products, components and equipment; supplies apparatus for machine building industry; Pres. QUAN YI LU.

China National Machinery and Equipment Import and Export Corporation: 12 Fuxing Menwai, Beijing; tel. 362561; telex 22186; f. 1978; imports and exports machine tools, all kinds of machinery, automobiles, hoisting and transport equipment, electric motors, photographic equipment, etc.; Pres. YAO MINGWEI.

China National Machinery Import and Export Corporation: Erligou, Xijiao, Beijing; tel. 891974; telex 22242; imports and exports machine tools, diesel engines and boilers and all kinds of machinery; Pres. LI GUANGYUAN (acting).

China National Medicines and Health Products Import and Export Corporation: Bldg 12, Jianguomenwai St, Beijing; tel. 5003344; telex 210103; Pres. YAN RUDAI.

China National Metals and Minerals Import and Export Corporation: Erligou, Xijiao, Beijing; tel. 8317733; telex 22241; f. 1950; principal imports and exports include steel, antimony, tungsten concentrates and ferrotungsten, zinc ingots, tin, mercury, pig iron, cement, etc.; Pres. WANG YAN.

China National Native Produce and Animal By-Products Import and Export Corporation (TUHSU): 82 Donganmen St, Beijing; tel. 554124; telex 22283; imports and exports tea, coffee, cocoa, fibres, etc.; 5 subsidiary enterprises; 73 domestic brs; Gen. Man. WANG ZHIXIN.

China National Non-ferrous Metals Import and Export Corporation: 9 Xizhang Lane, Beijing; tel. 657031; telex 22086; Pres. ZHENG RUGUI.

China National Offshore Oil Corporation (CNOOC): Nansidaokou Rd, Dazhongsi, Beijing; tel. 2014653; telex 22611; Pres. ZHONG YIMING.

China National Packaging Import and Export Corporation: 28 Donghouxiang, Andingmenwai, Beijing; tel. 4211747; telex 22490; handles import and export of packaging materials, containers, machines and tools; contracts for the processing and converting of packaging machines and materials using raw materials supplied by foreign customers; Pres. XU JIANGUO.

China National Petro-Chemical Corporation (SINOPEC): 24 Xiaoguan St, Andingmenwai, Beijing; tel. 4216731; telex 22655; f. 1983; under direct control of the State Council; petroleum refining, petrochemicals, synthetic fibres, etc.; 61 subordinate enterprises; approx. 500,000 employees; Pres. CHEN JINHUA.

China National Petroleum Corporation: Liupukang, Beijing; tel. 444313; telex 22312; Pres. WANG TAO.

China National Publications Import and Export Corporation: Chaoyangmennei St, Beijing; tel. 440731; telex 22131; imports principally foreign books, newspapers and periodicals, records, etc., exports principally Chinese scientific and technical journals published in foreign languages; Pres. CHEN WEIJIANG.

China National Publishing Industry Trading Corporation: POB 782, 504 An Hua Li, Outside An Ding Men, Beijing; tel. 4216251; telex 210215; imports and exports books, journals, paintings, woodcuts, watercolour prints and rubbings; holds book fairs abroad; undertakes joint publication; Pres. LOU MING.

China National Seed Corporation: 11 Nong Zhan Guan Nan Li, Beijing; tel. 593619; telex 22233; imports and exports crop seeds, including cereals, cotton, oil-bearing crops and vegetables; seed production for foreign seed companies etc.; Pres. LIU CHUN.

China National Technical Import Corporation: Erligou, Xijiao, Beijing; tel. 890931; telex 22244; f. 1952; imports all kinds of complete plant and equipment, acquires modern technology and expertise from abroad, undertakes co-production and jt-ventures, and technical consultation and updating of existing enterprises; Pres. XU DEEN.

China National Textiles Import and Export Corporation: 82 Donganmen St, Beijing; tel. 553793; telex 22280; imports synthetic fibres, raw cotton, wool, etc.; exports cotton yarn, cotton fabric, knitwear, woven garments, etc.; Pres. ZHONG QUANSHENG (acting).

China North Industries Corporation (NORINCO): 7A Yuetan Nan Jie, Beijing; tel. 862254; telex 22339; exports mechanical products, light industrial products, chemical products, opto-electronic products, military products, etc.; Pres. XU XIANGGUO.

China Nuclear Energy Industry Corporation (CNEIC): Sanlihe Rd, Beijing; tel. 867717; telex 22240; exports air filters, vacuum valves, dosimeters, radioactive detection elements and optical instruments; Pres. ZHANG XINDUO.

China Road and Bridge Engineering Co: 3 Waiguan Jie, An Ding Men Wai, Beijing; tel. 4213378; telex 22336; overseas building of highways, urban roads, bridges, tunnels, industrial and residential buildings, airport runways and parking areas; contracts to do all surveying, designing, pipe-laying, water supply and sewerage, building, etc., and/or to provide technical or labour services; Gen. Man. LU QIU.

Shanghai Foreign Trade Corporation: 27 Zhongshan Dong Yi Lu, Shanghai; tel. 217350; telex 33034; handles import-export trade, foreign trade transportation, chartering, export commodity packaging, storage and advertising for Shanghai municipality.

Shanghai International Trust and Service Corporation: 521 Henan Rd, POB 3066, Shanghai; tel. 226650; telex 33627; f. 1979; handles mail order and foreign trade, drafts contracts, arranges export, customs and deliveries for overseas Chinese, etc.

INTERNAL TRADE

State Administration for Industry and Commerce: 8 San Li He Dong Lu, Xichengqu, Beijing; tel. 8013300; telex 222431; functions under the direct supervision of the State Council; Dir REN ZHONGLIN.

TRADE UNIONS

All-China Federation of Trade Unions: 10 Fuxingmenwai St, Beijing 100865; tel. 8012200; telex 222290; f. 1925; organized on an industrial basis; 15 affiliated national industrial unions, 30 affiliated local trade union councils; membership is voluntary; trade unionists enjoy extensive benefits; in late 1988 there were about 100m. members; Pres. NI ZHIFU.

Principal affiliated unions:

All-China Federation of Railway Workers' Union: Chair. WU CHU.

Architectural Workers' Trade Union: Sec. SONG ANRU.

China Self-Employed Workers' Association: Pres. REN ZHONGLIN.

Light Industrial Workers' Trade Union: Chair. LI SHUYING.

Machinery Metallurgical Workers' Union: Chair. ZHANG CUNEN.

Postal and Telecommunications Workers' Trade Union of China: Chair. LUO SHUZHEN.

Seamen's Trade Union of China: Chair. QIU JIN.

TRADE FAIR

Chinese Export Commodities Fair (CECF): Guangzhou Foreign Trade Centre, 117 Lui Hua Rd, Guangzhou; tel. 677000; telex 44465; f. 1957; organized by the Ministry of Foreign Economic Relations and Trade; 2 trade fairs a year: 15 April–5 May; 15 October–5 November.

Transport

RAILWAYS

Ministry of Railways: 10 Fuxing Rd, Beijing; tel. 363875; controls all railways through regional divisions. The railway network has been extended to all provinces and regions except Xizang, where construction is in progress. Total length measured 52,500 km in 1986, of which around 4,400 km was electrified. The major routes include Beijing-Guangzhou, Tianjin-Shanghai, Manzhouli-Vladivostok, Jiaozuo-Zhicheng and Lanzhou-Badou. In addition, special railways serve factories and mines. There is an extensive development programme to improve the rail network.

There is an underground system serving Beijing. Its total length was 23 km in 1984, and further lines are under construction. In 1984 Tianjin city opened an underground line.

ROADS

In 1986 China had 962,800 km of highways. Four major highways link Lhasa with Sichuan, Xinjiang, Qinghai Hu and Kathmandu (Nepal). There are plans to build 11 motorways by 1990, with a total length of 2,000 km.

WATER TRANSPORT

Bureau of Water Transportation: Controls rivers and coastal traffic. In 1986 there were 109,400 km of navigable inland waterways in China. The main rivers are the Huanghe, Changjiang and Zhu. The Changjiang is navigable by vessels of 10,000 tons as far as Wuhan, over 1,000 km from the coast. Vessels of 1,000 tons can continue to Chongqing upstream. Over one-third of internal freight traffic is carried by water.

SHIPPING

The greater part of China's shipping is handled in nine major ports: Dalian, Qinhuangdao, Xingang, Qingdao, Lianyungang, Shanghai, Huangpu (Whampoa), Guangzhou and Zhanjiang. Three-quarters of the handling facilities are mechanical, and harbour improvement schemes are constantly in progress. In 1985 China's merchant fleet ranked ninth in the world in terms of tonnage: including chartered ships, the merchant navy had a total capacity of 14.4m. dwt.

China Ocean Shipping Co (COSCO): 6 Dongchangan St, Beijing; tel. 5121188; telex 22264; br. offices: Shanghai, Guangzhou, Tianjin, Qingdao, Dalian; merchant fleet of 614 vessels of various types with a dwt of 13m. tons; serves China/Japan, China/SE Asia, China/Australia, China/Gulf, China/Europe and China/N. America; Pres. LIU SONGJIN.

China Ocean Shipping Agency: 6 Dongchangan St, Beijing; tel. 5121924; telex 22264; f. 1953; br. offices at Chinese foreign trade ports; the sole agency which undertakes business for ocean-going vessels calling at Chinese ports; arranges sea passage, booking space, transhipment of cargoes; attends to chartering, purchase or sale of ships etc; Pres. CHEN ZHONGBIAO.

Minsheng Shipping Co: 35 Shan Xi Rd, Chongging; tel. 47152; telex 62241; f. 1984; 48 barges, 9 tugs, totalling 29,800 dwt; Gen. Man. LU GUOJI.

CIVIL AVIATION

New international airports were opened at Beijing in 1980 and Xiamen in 1983. The construction of international airports at other major centres is planned, while other airports (e.g. at Shanghai and Chengdu) are being expanded.

General Administration of Civil Aviation of China (CAAC): 115 Dong-si (West) Street, Beijing; telex 22101; f. 1949 to supersede the Civil Aviation Administration of China; controls all civil aviation activities, including a domestic network of 269 routes, with a total length of over 332,500 km and with services to all provinces and autonomous regions except Taiwan; in 1988 CAAC was restructured as a purely supervisory agency, and its operational functions were transferred to new airlines (Air China, China Eastern Airways, China Southern Airways, China Southwestern Airways and China Capital Helicopter Service); proposals to establish a sixth airline, China United Airlines (offering 11 domestic and foreign destinations), were announced in 1987; external services operate from Beijing to Addis Ababa, Baghdad, Bangkok, Belgrade, Berlin, Bucharest, Frankfurt, Fukuoka, Istanbul, Karachi, Kuwait, London, Los Angeles, Manila, Melbourne, Moscow, Nagasaki, New York, Osaka, Paris, Pyongyang, Rangoon, Rome, San Francisco, Sharjah, Singapore, Sydney, Tokyo, Vancouver and Zürich; there is a weekly charter service between Chengdu and Hong Kong; Dir-Gen. HU YIZHOU; fleet of 4 Boeing 747SP, 3 747-200B Combi, 4 767-200, 10 707-320B, C, 15 737-200, 8 737-300, 3 A310, 5 MD-82, 11 Tu-154, 7 SD-360, 7 BAe-146, 18 Y-7, Trident, Ilyushin, Antonov, and a number of smaller aircraft and helicopters.

Tourism

China has enormous potential for tourism, and the sector is developing rapidly. Attractions include dramatic scenery and places of

THE PEOPLE'S REPUBLIC OF CHINA

historical interest such as the Great Wall, the Ming Tombs, the Temple of Heaven and the Forbidden City in Beijing, and the terracotta warriors at Xian, Xizang (Tibet), with its monasteries and temples, has also been opened to tourists. Tours of China are organized for groups of visitors, and Western-style hotels have been built in many areas: by the end of 1985 there were more than 700 tourist hotels, with 242,000 beds. A total of 23.2m. tourists visited China in the first nine months of 1988 (an increase of 19.2% on the corresponding period in 1987), including many from Hong Kong and Macau. The tourist industry generated revenue of US $1,840m. in foreign exchange in 1987, and was expected to earn more than US $2,000m. in 1988.

China International Travel Service (CITS): 6 East Changan Ave, Beijing; tel. 5121122; telex 22350; makes travel arrangements for foreign parties; Gen. Man. WANG ERKANG; general agency in Hong Kong, business offices in London, Paris, New York, Los Angeles, Frankfurt, Sydney and Tokyo.

Chinese People's Association for Friendship with Foreign Countries: 1 Tai Ji Chang St, Beijing; tel. 541010; telex 210368; Pres. ZHANG WENJIN.

National Tourism Administration: 6 East Chang An Ave, Beijing; tel. 5121122; telex 22350; Dir LIU YI.

Atomic Energy

By the end of 1983 China had built 317 nuclear reactors, with a total capacity of 190m. kW. China's first 300,000-kW nuclear power station at Qinshan in Zhejiang Province, and a second plant, with two 900,000-kW units, at Daya Bay in Shenzhen Special Economic Zone, Guangdong Province (1.8m. kW), were under construction in 1986. A third station is proposed for Sunan, in Jiangsu Province. China expects to have nuclear power plants with a combined generating power of 10,000 MW by the end of the century. In October 1983 China was admitted to the International Atomic Energy Agency (IAEA).

Institute of Atomic Energy: POB 275, Beijing; tel. 868221; telex 222373; f. 1958; research and development in the field of nuclear physics, nuclear chemistry and nuclear chemical engineering, reactor engineering, preparation of isotopes, environmental and radiation protection, radiometrology, etc.; promotion of a non-nuclear application and development for the national economy; Dir SUN ZUXUN.

Atomic Research Centre: Tarim Pendi, Xingjiang; f. 1953; Dir WANG GANZHANG.

Military Scientific Council: Beijing; Dir Dr JIAN XUESAN.

CHINA (TAIWAN)

Introductory Survey

Location, Climate, Language, Religion, Flag, Capital

The Republic of China has, since 1949, been confined mainly to the province of Taiwan (comprising one large island and several much smaller ones), which lies off the south-east coast of the Chinese mainland. The territory under the Republic's effective jurisdiction consists of the island of Taiwan (also known as Formosa) and nearby islands, including the P'enghu (Pescadores) group, together with a few other islands which lie just off the mainland and form part of the province of Fujian (Fukien), west of Taiwan. The largest of these is Chinmen (Jinmen), also known as Quemoy, which (with three smaller islands) is about 10 km from the port of Xiamen (Amoy), while five other islands under Taiwan's control, mainly Matsu (Mazu), lie further north, near Fuzhou. Taiwan itself is separated from the mainland by the Taiwan (Formosa) Strait, which is about 145 km (90 miles) wide at its narrowest point. The island's climate is one of rainy summers and mild winters. Average temperatures are about 15°C (59°F) in the winter and 26°C (79°F) in the summer. The average annual rainfall is 2,565 mm (101 in). The official language is Northern Chinese (Mandarin). The predominant religion is Buddhism but there are also Muslims, Daoists and Christians (Roman Catholics and Protestants). The philosophy of Confucianism has a large following. The national flag (proportions 3 by 2) is red, with a dark blue rectangular canton, containing a white sun, in the upper hoist. The capital of Taiwan is Taipei.

Recent History

China ceded Taiwan to Japan in 1895. The island remained under Japanese rule until 1945, when the Second World War ended. As a result of Japan's defeat in the war, Taiwan was returned to Chinese control, becoming a province of the Republic of China, then ruled by the Kuomintang (KMT, Nationalist Party). The leader of the KMT was Gen. Chiang Kai-shek, President of the Republic since 1928.

The KMT Government's forces were defeated in 1949 by the Communist revolution in China. President Chiang and many of his supporters withdrew from the Chinese mainland and established themselves on Taiwan, where they set up a KMT regime in succession to their previous all-China administration. This regime continued to assert that it was the rightful Chinese Government, in opposition to the People's Republic of China, which had been proclaimed by the victorious Communists in 1949. Since establishing their base in Taiwan, the Nationalists have successfully resisted attacks by their Communist rivals and have, in turn, declared that they intend to recover control of mainland China from the Communists.

Although its effective control was limited to Taiwan, the KMT regime continued to be dominated by politicians who had formerly been in power on the mainland. In support of the regime's claim to be the legitimate government of all China, Taiwan's legislative bodies were filled mainly by surviving mainland members, and the representatives of the island's native Taiwanese majority occupied only a minority of seats. Unable to replenish their mainland representation, the National Assembly (last elected fully in 1947) and other organs extended their terms of office indefinitely, although fewer than half of the original members were alive on Taiwan in the 1980s. While it has promised eventually to reconquer the mainland, the KMT regime has been largely preoccupied with ensuring its own survival, and promoting economic development, on Taiwan. The political domination of the island by immigrants from the mainland has caused some resentment among Taiwanese, and has led to demands for increased democratization and for the recognition of Taiwan as a state independent of China. The KMT has, however, consistently rejected demands for independence, constantly restating the party's long-standing policy of seeking political reunification, although under KMT terms, with the mainland.

In 1954 the USA, which had refused to recognize the People's Republic of China, signed a mutual security treaty with the KMT Government, pledging to protect Taiwan and the Pescadores. In 1955 the islands of Quemoy and Matsu, lying just offshore from the mainland, were included in the protected area.

In spite of being confined to Taiwan, the KMT regime continued to represent China at the United Nations (and as a permanent member of the UN Security Council) until 1971, when it was replaced by the People's Republic. Nationalist China was subsequently expelled from several other international organizations and in 1988 the Taiwan regime was recognized by only about 20 countries.

In 1973 the Taiwan Government rejected an offer from the People's Republic to hold secret discussions on the reunification of China, and this policy has since been strongly reaffirmed. In October 1981 Taiwan rejected China's suggested terms for reunification, whereby Taiwan would become a 'special administrative region' and would have a substantial degree of autonomy, including the retention of its own armed forces and its relatively high standard of living. In 1983 China renewed its offer of autonomy for Taiwan, including a guarantee to maintain the status quo in Taiwan for 100 years if the province agreed to reunification. In 1984, following the agreement between the People's Republic of China and the United Kingdom that China would regain sovereignty over the British colony of Hong Kong in 1997, Chinese leaders urged Taiwan to accept similar proposals for reunification on the basis of 'one country—two systems'. The Taipei Government insisted that Taiwan would never negotiate with Beijing until the mainland regime renounced communism. In May 1986, however, the Government was forced to make direct contact with the Beijing Government for the first time, over the issue of a Taiwanese pilot who had defected to the mainland with his aircraft, and whose fellow crew-members wished to return. In March 1987 Taiwan declared the agreement that had been concluded between the People's Republic of China and Portugal, regarding the return of the Portuguese Overseas Territory of Macau to Chinese sovereignty in 1999, to be null and void. In October the Government announced the repeal of the 38-year ban on visits to the mainland by Taiwanese citizens, with the exception of civil servants and military personnel, but insisted that visits were permitted solely for 'humanitarian reasons', to allow Taiwanese of mainland descent to visit relatives 'by blood or marriage'. In late 1988 permission was extended to include visits to Taiwan by mainland Chinese, also for humanitarian purposes.

Legislative elections were held in December 1972, for the first time in 24 years, to fill 53 seats in the National Assembly. The new members, elected for a fixed term of six years, joined 1,376 surviving 'life-term' members of Assembly. President Chiang Kai-shek remained in office until his death in April 1975. He was succeeded as leader of the ruling KMT by his son, Gen. Chiang Ching-kuo, who had been Prime Minister since May 1972. The new President was Dr Yen Chia-kan, Vice-President since 1966. In May 1978 President Yen retired and was succeeded by Gen. Chiang, who appointed Sun Yun-suan, hitherto Minister of Economic Affairs, to be Prime Minister. At elections for 71 seats in the Legislative Yuan in December 1983, the KMT won an overwhelming victory, confirming its dominance over the independent 'Tangwai' (non-party) candidates. In March 1984 President Chiang was re-elected for a second six-year term, and Lee Teng-hui, a former Mayor of Taipei and a native Taiwanese, became Vice-President. In May a major government reshuffle took place, and Yu Kuo-hwa, formerly the Governor of the Central Bank, replaced Sun Yun-suan as Prime Minister. President Chiang died in January 1988 and was succeeded by Lee Teng-hui who, under the Constitution, was legally entitled to serve the remainder of President Chiang's term of office.

In September 1986 135 leading opposition politicians formed the Democratic Progress Party (DPP), in defiance of the KMT's ban on the formation of new political parties. In response, the KMT announced that it would henceforth allow the establishment of new parties (although subject to approval of their policies), and that martial law (in force since 1949) would be replaced by a new national security law. During 1987 and 1988 four new political parties were formed. Elections for 84 seats in the National Assembly and 73 seats in the Legislative Yuan were held in December 1986. The KMT achieved a decisive victory, winning 68 seats in the National Assembly and 59 in the Legislative Yuan, but the DPP received about one-quarter of the total votes, and won 11 seats in the Assembly and 12 in the Legislative Yuan, thus more than doubling the non-KMT representation. In February 1987 the KMT began to implement a programme of political reform. The most significant change was the replacement of martial law by the new National Security Law in July. Under the terms of the new legislation, political parties other than the KMT were permitted, and civilians were removed from the jurisdiction of military courts. However, the DPP remained opposed to the conditions with which opposition groups had to comply in order to gain legal recognition. The KMT also attempted to rejuvenate Taiwan's ageing leadership. Younger members of the party, who supported the reform programme, were promoted to positions of influence, and in April they secured seven major posts in a reshuffle of the Executive Yuan.

In February 1988 a plan to restructure the legislative bodies was approved by the Central Standing Committee of the KMT. Under the provisions of the plan, voluntary resignations were to be sought from 'life-term' members of the Legislative Yuan and National Assembly. In addition, seats were no longer to be reserved for representatives of mainland constituencies. In December it was announced that, subject to approval by the Legislative Yuan, members who accepted voluntary retirement would receive around NT $3.7m. in severance pay.

The 13th national Congress of the KMT was held in July 1988. In an attempt to accelerate the process of reform, the Congress decided that, for the first time, free elections would be held for two-thirds of the members of the KMT's Central Committee. In the ensuing ballot, numerous new members were elected, and the proportion of native Taiwanese increased sharply. The Central Standing Committee was similarly affected, with several of its members being replaced by younger, liberal members of the KMT. A reshuffle of the Executive Yuan, later in the month, resulted in a government comprising younger members, who were expected to hasten the programme of reform.

In November 1987 the second annual Congress of the DPP approved a resolution declaring that Taiwanese citizens had the right to advocate independence for Taiwan. In January 1988, however, two opposition activists were imprisoned, on charges of sedition, for voicing such demands. At the third annual Congress of the DPP, held in October 1988, Huang Hsin-chieh replaced Yao Chia-wen as Chairman of the party, and it was thought likely that he would be a less vigorous proponent of Taiwanese independence.

In January 1979 Taiwan suffered a serious set-back when the USA established full diplomatic relations with the People's Republic and severed relations with Taiwan. The USA also terminated the mutual security treaty with Taiwan. Commercial links are still maintained, however, under the terms of the USA's Taiwan Relations Act of March 1979. Taiwan's purchase of armaments from the USA has remained a controversial issue and has caused increased tension with mainland China. In August 1982 Taiwan's morale was further damaged when a joint Sino-US communiqué was published, in which the USA pledged to reduce gradually its sale of armaments to Taiwan. Despite this, substantial sales of weapons have continued. In April 1984 the US President, Ronald Reagan, gave an assurance that he would continue to support Taiwan, despite the improved relations between the USA and the People's Republic, which had provoked uncertainty in Taiwan.

Government

Under the provisions of the 1947 Constitution, the Head of State is the President, who is elected for a term of six years by the National Assembly. There are five Yuans (governing bodies), the highest legislative organ being the Legislative Yuan, to which the Executive Yuan (the Council of Ministers) is responsible. In July 1988 the Legislative Yuan comprised 304 members, many of whom were life members. Elections for supplementary seats are held every three years. There are also Control, Judicial and Examination Yuans. Their respective functions are: to investigate the work of the executive; to interpret the Constitution and national laws; and to supervise examinations for entry into public offices. The Legislative Yuan submits proposals to the National Assembly. Elections to the Assembly are by universal adult suffrage every six years, but in 1988 many of the Assembly seats were held by life members who formerly represented mainland constituencies. In October 1988 the Assembly had 965 members. Martial law was declared in 1949, and remained in force until July 1987, when it was replaced by a new National Security Law.

Defence

In June 1988 the armed forces totalled 405,500: army 270,000, air force 70,000, navy 35,500, with a marine corps of 30,000. Military service lasts for two years. Defence expenditure for 1988/89 was projected at NT $191,400m.

Economic Affairs

Despite the strain of maintaining large armed forces, Taiwan's economy has developed rapidly since 1950, owing mainly to the considerable expansion of foreign trade. By the 1980s, Taiwan was among the world's 20 leading exporting countries (ranking 13th in terms of total foreign trade turnover in 1988). Agriculture's role in the economy has declined significantly since the 1950s; in 1952 it provided more than 90% of total exports and contributed 56.1% of Taiwan's gross domestic product (GDP), while employing 56% of the labour force. The principal crops were rice, sugar cane and sweet potatoes. By 1983, however, agricultural products and processed food provided less than 7% of total exports. In 1987 the agricultural sector (including forestry and fishing) contributed only 5.2% of GDP (at current prices), and employed 15.3% of the working population.

Between 1970 and 1980, Taiwan's GDP expanded, in real terms, at an average rate of 9.5% per year, with the economy progressing towards self-sufficiency as the island's industrial infrastructure developed. Textiles were the main source of income, providing 32% of export earnings in 1970, but this proportion declined in the 1980s, as rising labour costs encouraged the development of more capital- and technology-intensive industries, such as the manufacture of electronic equipment and plastic products. In 1985 textiles accounted for about one-fifth of Taiwan's total exports, and were the third largest earner of foreign exchange (after exports of machinery and electronics). Other major exports include metals, plywood and furniture, and petrochemicals. Taiwan has a 65% share of the world market in shipbreaking, centred on the port of Kaohsiung. Despite Taiwan's diplomatic isolation, trade and economic links with the rest of the world have thrived. Exports continue to be dominated by the US market, which accounts for more than one-third of Taiwan's foreign trade (39% in 1988), followed by Japan and Hong Kong. However, Taiwan has come under increasing pressure from Washington to reduce its trade surplus with the USA, which totalled US $16,009m. (exports $ 23,637m., imports $7,628m.) in 1987 but declined to $10,400m. in 1988. The deficit was forecast to decline to $8,000m. in 1989 and to $1,000m. in 1992. In July 1986 Taiwan signed an agreement to allow its textile exports to the USA to expand by no more than 0.5% per year from 1986 to 1988, and a similar agreement with the EEC restricted the increase in Taiwanese textile exports to 2.3% per year for the period 1987–91. In response to such protectionist measures in its traditional markets, efforts are being made to expand and diversify export markets in Europe, Africa and South-East Asia. Taiwan has also agreed to allow access to its domestic market for US goods, and has begun by reducing tariffs on a range of products. As a result of continued trade surpluses, Taiwan's reserves of foreign exchange increased from US $2,205m. at the end of 1980 to US $74,000m. by the end of 1988, leading to pressure from abroad to revalue the New Taiwan dollar (NT $). Contrary to expectations, however, the appreciation in the currency exchange rate did not initially reduce Taiwan's trade surplus with the USA. In August 1987 the Ministry of Economic Affairs announced its opposition to any further rise in the value of the NT dollar, which had appreciated by 25% in relation to the US dollar since August 1986. In 1985 the People's Republic of China assured Taiwan that the latter's lucrative trade links with Hong Kong would not be jeopardized by China's resumption of sovereignty over Hong Kong in 1997. Indirect trade between Taiwan and the People's Republic totalled around US $2,300m. in 1988.

Mineral resources include coal, marble, gold, petroleum and natural gas, but in 1987 the mining sector contributed only 0.5% of GDP. Manufacturing employed 35% of the working population, and provided 42.8% of GDP, in 1987. Taiwan's petrochemical industry is the third largest in Asia. Energy supplies have always been a problem, and Taiwan is heavily dependent on imported petroleum, the cost of which totalled NT $80,527.5m. in 1987. There are three nuclear power plants in operation, providing 48.5% of Taiwan's total power generation in 1987.

Following the recession in world markets, Taiwan's GDP grew by only 2.8% in 1982, compared with rises of 6.1% in 1981 and 7.3% in 1980. In 1983, however, following an export-led recovery, GDP grew by 7.7%, and this economic expansion continued in 1984, with GDP rising by 9.5% in real terms. In 1985 GDP grew by 4.1% in real terms, following a virtual stagnation in exports, while the value of imports decreased by around 8%. During 1986, however, the economy was revitalized by the favourable terms of foreign trade, as a fall in petroleum prices caused the cost of Taiwan's petroleum imports to decline by 41.8%, while exports increased significantly, helped by a favourable exchange rate in relation to the Japanese yen: exports in 1986 were 23% higher than in 1985. A record trade surplus of US $19,032m. was recorded in 1987, when exports totalled $53,538.2m. and imports $34,506.5m. In 1988 the value of exports increased to about US $60,590m., while import expenditure also increased, to reach $49,650m. The trade surplus therefore declined to $10,940m. Total trade for 1989 was forecast to amount to nearly $120,000m. GDP grew by 10.6% in 1986. The 1988/89 budget envisaged record expenditure of NT $568,340m., an increase of 18% on the NT $479,673m. approved for 1987/88. The annual inflation rate, which was negligible in 1987, rose to 2.6% in the fourth quarter of 1988, and was predicted to be within a range of 4%–7% in 1989.

The unemployment rate was around 2.7% in 1983, falling to 2.45% in 1984. In 1985 the rate rose to 2.9%, but by the end of 1987 it had fallen to 1.9%. Taiwan's average gross national product (GNP) per head was US $6,045 in current prices in 1988. Overall GNP increased by 11% in 1987, but growth slowed to 7.1% in 1988. In 1989 GNP was predicted to expand by 5%–6.5%. The 1982–85 Four-Year Plan, which envisaged an average annual growth rate of 8%, aimed to increase investment, to stimulate trade and to develop industry. There are plans to develop Taiwan's role as an 'offshore' banking centre, with increased financial services, while three special export-processing zones have been established to attract further foreign investment. A science-based industrial park has been established at Hsinchu, offering special incentives for foreign investors. In 1987 the park generated sales of around US $700m., and exports worth almost US $500m. In 1984 foreign investment in Taiwan reached US $558m., representing a growth of 50% over the 1983 figure. In 1985 new foreign investment (including investment by overseas Chinese) totalled US $720m.; the highest proportion of investments went to the chemical industry, with 30.5% of the total, while the electronics and electrical appliances sector accounted for 19.8%. Enterprises which were funded by foreign investment provided 23% of total exports in 1984. New foreign and overseas Chinese investment totalled US $770m. in 1986, and reached US $1,420m. in 1988. The first offshore banking licences were granted in May 1984, as the initial move towards an eventual liberalization of Taiwan's controls on the availability of foreign exchange. In July 1987, prompted by international appeals for financial liberalization and by fears that pressure on the domestic money supply might cause inflation to rise, the Central Bank of China ended the stringent controls that it had maintained since 1949 on foreign exchange transactions. Taiwanese nationals and companies were permitted to hold and use foreign currencies, and to remit up to US $5m. abroad each year.

In 1984 a major new development plan was announced: some US $20,000m. was allocated for 14 infrastructure projects, including expansion of the China Steel Corporation, construction of the Taipei underground railway system, modernization of telecommunications facilities, exploitation of petroleum and water resources and expansion of railways and highways, among many other projects. It was announced in October 1985 that US $2,500m. was to be invested in the field of chemicals over the next 10 years, and also that the majority of state enterprises were to be 'privatized'. In late 1988 the Government announced its decision partially to privatize the China Steel Corporation, offering for sale 10% of its shares to the public. A plan to sell 49% of shares in three commercial banks was also approved. Taiwan's hopes of maintaining a high rate of export growth rely on the continued development of products employing advanced technology, and in July 1986 the Government announced a programme of investment in technology research projects (including digital communications equipment, electronics and electro-optical technology, and research on automation schemes), totalling NT $3,200m. The services sector is also regarded as an important area in Taiwan's development, with a predicted annual growth rate of 7.5% in 1986–89, and an increasing contribution to GNP.

Social Welfare

In June 1988 the Labour Insurance programme covered around 5,575,000 workers, providing benefits for injury, disability, birth, death and old age. At the same time, about 819,000 government employees and their dependants were covered by a separate scheme. In 1978 a system of supplementary benefits for those with low incomes was introduced. In 1986 Taiwan had 85 public hospitals, with a total of 29,792 beds, and 750 private hospitals, with 41,381 beds. There were 17,965 physicians (including 2,057 Chinese herb doctors) and 3,750 dentists working in the country. The number of physicians increased to 19,404 in 1987. Of total government expenditure in 1986, NT $3,748m. (1.1%) was for health, and a further NT $64,311m. (18.3%) for social security and welfare.

Education

Education at primary schools and junior high schools is free and compulsory between the ages of six and 15 years. Secondary schools consist of junior and senior middle schools, normal schools for teacher-training and vocational schools. There are also a number of private schools. Higher education is provided in universities, colleges, junior colleges and graduate schools. Government expenditure on education in 1986 totalled NT $44,474m. (12.7% of total spending). In 1987/88 there were more than 2.4m. pupils enrolled in state primary schools and more than 1.7m. in secondary schools. There are 16 universities and 11 independent colleges.

Public Holidays

1989: 1 January (Founding of the Republic), 5–7 February (Chinese New Year), 29 March (Youth Day), 5 April (Ching Ming), 8 June (Dragon Boat Festival), 14 September (Mid-Autumn Moon Festival), 28 September (Teachers' Day—Birthday of Confucius), 10 October (Double Tenth Day, anniversary of 1911 revolution), 25 October (Retrocession Day, anniversary of end of Japanese occupation), 31 October (Birthday of Chiang Kai-shek), 12 November (Birthday of Sun Yat-sen), 25 December (Constitution Day).

1990: 1 January (Founding of the Republic), 26–28 February (Chinese New Year), 29 March (Youth Day), 5 April (Ching Ming), 28 May (Dragon Boat Festival), 28 September (Teachers' Day—Birthday of Confucius), 3 October (Mid-Autumn Moon Festival), 10 October (Double Tenth Day, anniversary of 1911 revolution), 25 October (Retrocession Day, anniversary of end of Japanese occupation), 31 October (Birthday of Chiang Kai-shek), 12 November (Birthday of Sun Yat-sen), 25 December (Constitution Day).

Weights and Measures

The metric system is officially in force, but some traditional Chinese units are still used.

Statistical Survey

Source (unless otherwise stated): Directorate-General of Budget, Accounting and Statistics, Executive Yuan, 1 Chung Hsiao East Rd, Sec. 1, Taipei; tel. 3915231.

Area and Population

AREA, POPULATION AND DENSITY

Area (sq km)	36,000*
Population (census results)	
16 December 1975	16,191,609
28 December 1980	
Males	9,362,026
Females	8,587,082
Total	17,949,108
Population (official estimates at 31 December)	
1985	19,258,053
1986	19,454,610
1987	19,672,612
Density (per sq km) at 31 December 1987	546.5

Population (official estimate at 30 September 1988): 19,828,624.

* 13,900 sq miles.

PRINCIPAL TOWNS
(estimated population at 31 December 1987)

Taipei (capital)	2,637,100	Fengshan	276,259
Kaohsiung	1,342,797	Chiayi	254,875
Taichung	715,107	Chungli	247,639
Tainan	656,927	Hsinchuang	243,706*
Panchiao	506,220	Yungho	242,252
Shanchung	362,171	Taoyuan	220,255
Keelung	348,541	Changhwa	206,603
Chungho	334,663*	Hsintien	205,094
Hsinchu	309,899	Pingtun	204,990

* At 31 December 1986.

BIRTHS, MARRIAGES AND DEATHS

	Live births		Marriages		Deaths	
	Number	Rate (per '000)	Number	Rate (per '000)	Number	Rate (per '000)
1983	382,153	20.55	158,296	8.51	90,555	4.87
1984	369,725	19.59	155,052	8.22	89,576	4.75
1985	345,053	18.03	153,565	8.03	92,011	4.81
1986	308,187	15.92	145,592	7.52	94,712	4.89
1987	313,062	16.00	146,076	7.47	96,033	4.91

ECONOMICALLY ACTIVE POPULATION
(annual averages in '000)

	1985	1986	1987
Agriculture, forestry and fishing	1,297	1,317	1,226
Mining and quarrying	35	33	31
Manufacturing	2,488	2,614	2,810
Construction	521	525	554
Electricity, gas and water	34	34	35
Commerce	1,336	1,382	1,435
Transport, storage and communications	388	407	429
Finance and insurance	190	212	229
Other services	1,141	1,208	1,275
Total in employment	7,428	7,733	8,022
Unemployed	222	212	161
Total labour force	7,651	7,945	8,183

Agriculture

PRINCIPAL CROPS ('000 metric tons)

	1985	1986	1987
Rice*	2,173.5	1,973.8	1,900.5
Sweet potatoes	369.5	324.0	344.8
Asparagus	62.1	41.8	40.1
Soybeans	12.2	14.9	18.0
Maize	226.0	271.7	306.9
Tea	23.2	23.9	25.6
Tobacco	25.4	24.3	24.0
Groundnuts	89.1	77.2	111.7
Cassava (Manioc)	58.2	44.7	39.4
Sugar cane	6,823.1	6,001.5	5,162.9
Bananas	198.6	150.7	204.5
Pineapples	149.7	157.9	193.3
Citrus fruit	418.9	386.8	522.9
Vegetables	3,286.3	3,169.0	3,330.3
Mushrooms	59.9	55.2	50.3

* Figures are in terms of brown rice. The equivalent in paddy rice is approximately 30% greater.

LIVESTOCK ('000 head at 31 December)

	1985	1986	1987
Cattle	104.8	116.6	134.4
Buffaloes	38.4	36.7	35.5
Pigs	6,674.0	7,057.1	7,129.0
Sheep and goats	231.2	237.3	255.8
Chickens	59,313.0	66,101.0	69,179.0
Ducks	10,211.0	11,179.0	12,916.0
Geese	1,546.0	1,701.0	1,957.0
Turkeys	558.0	563.0	527.0

LIVESTOCK PRODUCTS

	1985	1986	1987
Beef (metric tons)	4,351	3,883	4,171
Pig meat (metric tons)	1,008,413	1,053,801	1,137,918
Goat meat (metric tons)	678	644	677
Chickens* ('000 head)	154,686	155,917	174,400
Ducks* ('000 head)	31,894	34,347	39,745
Geese* ('000 head)	3,186	3,266	3,923
Turkeys* ('000 head)	1,163	1,383	1,111
Milk (metric tons)	87,879	109,723	144,390
Duck eggs ('000)	453,247	429,246	450,752
Hen eggs ('000)	3,344,729	3,339,487	3,546,186

* Figures refer to numbers slaughtered.

Forestry

ROUNDWOOD REMOVALS ('000 cu m)

	1985	1986	1987
Industrial wood	474.6	498.7	422.6
Fuel wood	62.4	63.7	67.6
Total	537.0	562.4	490.2

CHINA (TAIWAN)

Fishing

('000 metric tons, live weight)

	1985	1986	1987
Total catch	1,037.7	1,094.6	1,236.2

Mining

(metric tons, unless otherwise indicated)

	1985	1986	1987
Coal	1,857,858	1,725,024	1,499,240
Gold (kg)	952.8	910.4	536.0
Silver (kg)	11,386.2	12,613.0	9,855.7
Electrolytic copper	46,734	50,439	46,961
Crude petroleum ('000 litres)	118,100	105,390	148,406
Natural gas ('000 cu m)	1,125,050	1,022,539	1,056,916
Salt	173,898	136,078	99,943
Gypsum	2,199	2,247	1,378
Sulphur	42,949	62,980	89,082
Marble	10,259,341	10,603,943	11,061,913
Talc	17,560	21,552	22,102
Asbestos	625	n.a.	n.a.
Dolomite	231,457	258,366	339,880

Industry

SELECTED PRODUCTS
('000 metric tons, unless otherwise indicated)

	1985	1986	1987
Wheat flour	520.0	571.6	619.2
Refined sugar	645.6	535.0	538.5
Alcoholic beverages—excl. beer ('000 hectolitres)	2,083.7	2,159.4	2,248.2
Cigarettes (million)	30,827	31,802	2,803.8
Cotton yarn	191.8	223.9	264.4
Paper	530.2	635.1	716.8
Sulphuric acid	733.0	814.6	741.8
Spun synthetic yarn	176.2	193.6	188.3
Motor spirit—petrol (million litres)	2,958.5	2,839.5	3,544.5
Diesel oil (million litres)	3,197.4	3,096.8	4,066.8
Cement	14,417.7	14,806.1	15,663.4
Pig iron	225.7	197.5	87.2
Steel ingots	1,641.9	1,813.7	1,851.3
Radio receivers ('000 units)	8,781.6	11,184.8	12,589.4
Television receivers ('000 units)	3,641.3	5,748.4	5,941.6
Ships ('000 dwt)*	516.7	552.3	564.3
Electric energy (million kWh)	52,553	59,028	65,514
Liquefied petroleum gas	426.2	517.4	554.2

* Excluding motor yachts.

Finance

CURRENCY AND EXCHANGE RATES

Monetary Units
100 cents = 1 New Taiwan dollar (NT $).

Denominations
Coins: 50 cents; 1, 5 and 10 dollars.
Notes: 10, 50, 100, 500 and 1,000 dollars.

Sterling and US Dollar Equivalents (30 September 1988)
£1 sterling = NT $48.92;
US $1 = NT $28.93;
NT $1,000 = £20.44 = US $34.57.

Average Exchange Rate (NT $ per US $)
1985   39.849
1986   37.838
1987   31.845

BUDGET (estimates, NT $ million, year ending 30 June)

Revenue	1985/86	1986/87	1987/88
Taxes	206,669	240,565	234,095
Monopoly profits	29,136	29,969	29,427
Non-tax revenue from other sources	169,916	179,720	204,092
Total	405,721	450,254	467,614

Expenditure	1985/86	1986/87	1987/88
General administration	22,266	23,743	26,591
National defence and foreign affairs	160,176	155,374	171,946
Education, science and culture	49,880	53,337	60,951
Economic construction and communications	76,361	84,010	76,336
Social welfare	68,060	72,339	85,074
Obligations	12,283	17,160	23,879
Subsidies to provincial and municipal governments	15,019	11,337	17,145
Other expenditure	1,676	32,954	5,692
Total	405,721	450,254	467,614

1988/89: (provisional estimates, NT $ million): Total revenue and expenditure to balance at 568,340.

INTERNATIONAL RESERVES
(US $ million at 31 December)

	1985	1986	1987
Gold*	964	1,313	2,698
Foreign exchange	22,556	46,310	76,748
Total	23,520	47,623	79,446

* National valuation.

MONEY SUPPLY (NT $ million at 31 December)

	1985	1986	1987
Currency outside banks	182,808	231,046	284,964
Demand deposits at deposit money banks	568,661	906,817	1,283,261
Total	751,469	1,137,863	1,568,225

CHINA (TAIWAN)

COST OF LIVING
(Consumer Price Index for urban areas. Base: 1986 = 100)

	1984	1985	1987
Food	99.35	97.83	100.45
Clothing	107.28	105.56	96.79
Housing	98.62	99.50	100.30
Transport and communications	102.56	103.52	98.41
Medicines and medical care	98.03	101.00	100.34
Education and entertainment	91.72	96.36	101.47
All items (incl. others)	98.96	99.32	99.95

NATIONAL ACCOUNTS (NT $ million in current prices)
National Income and Product

	1985	1986	1987
Compensation of employees	1,184,946	1,326,063	1,472,161
Operating surplus	702,741	872,562	971,455
Domestic factor incomes	1,887,687	2,198,625	2,443,616
Consumption of fixed capital	210,836	231,395	256,974
Gross domestic product (GDP) at factor cost	2,098,523	2,430,020	2,700,590
Indirect taxes	268,254	281,335	320,557
Less Subsidies	9,671	9,582	9,278
GDP in purchasers' values	2,357,106	2,701,773	3,013,869
Factor income from abroad	88,111	111,818	122,339
Less Factor income paid abroad	46,848	41,226	45,416
Gross national product (GNP)	2,398,369	2,772,365	3,090,792
Less Consumption of fixed capital	210,836	231,395	256,974
National income in market prices	2,187,533	2,540,970	2,833,818
Other current transfers from abroad	5,262	8,244	10,879
Less Other current transfers paid abroad	15,175	19,472	26,278
National disposable income	2,177,620	2,529,742	2,818,419

Expenditure on the Gross Domestic Product

	1985	1986	1987
Government final consumption expenditure	389,334	412,059	438,806
Private final consumption expenditure	1,205,267	1,288,575	1,404,460
Increase in stocks	−28,012	−62,568	−4,779
Gross fixed capital formation	449,149	500,802	596,610
Total domestic expenditure	2,015,738	2,138,868	2,435,097
Exports of goods and services	1,323,302	1,638,214	1,829,865
Less Imports of goods and services	981,934	1,075,309	1,251,093
GDP in purchasers' values	2,357,106	2,701,773	3,013,869
GDP at constant 1981 prices	2,212,650	2,446,775	2,718,454

Gross Domestic Product by Economic Activity

	1985	1986	1987
Agriculture and livestock	102,081	112,079	114,634
Forestry and logging	3,462	3,850	4,081
Fishing	33,485	36,341	40,099
Mining and quarrying	14,089	14,392	15,229
Manufacturing	964,629	1,160,141	1,310,506
Construction	101,717	109,465	125,449
Electricity, gas and water	100,127	104,227	115,772
Transport, storage and communications	144,308	162,584	180,851
Trade, restaurants and hotels	327,411	380,383	429,063
Finance, insurance and real estate	83,723	84,859	88,003
Housing services*	140,545	152,692	166,908
Government services	236,347	250,965	268,662
Other services	162,892	183,408	203,463
Sub-total	2,414,816	2,755,386	3,064,720
Less Imputed bank service charge	57,710	53,613	50,851
GDP in purchasers' values	2,357,106	2,701,773	3,013,869

*Including imputed rents of owner-occupied dwellings.

BALANCE OF PAYMENTS (US $ million)

	1985	1986	1987
Merchandise exports f.o.b.	30,466	39,492	53,224
Merchandise imports f.o.b.	−19,296	−22,635	−33,012
Trade balance	11,170	16,857	20,212
Exports of services	4,955	6,744	8,179
Imports of services	−6,681	−7,087	−9,770
Balance on goods and services	9,444	16,514	18,621
Private unrequited transfers (net)	−244	−304	−704
Government unrequited transfers (net)	−5	7	8
Current balance	9,195	16,217	17,925
Direct capital investment (net)	260	260	11
Other long-term capital (net)	−1,280	−1,843	−2,596
Short-term capital (net)	−2,143	8,521	12,982
Net errors and omissions	494	168	−231
Total (net monetary movements)	6,526	23,323	28,091
Monetization of gold (net)	156	223	992
Valuation changes (net)	358	558	2,739
Changes in reserves	7,040	24,104	31,822

External Trade

SELECTED COMMODITIES (NT $ million)

Imports c.i.f.	1985	1986	1987
Wheat (unmilled)	5,309.5	4,765.6	3,854.7
Maize (unmilled)	16,843.0	13,442.7	11,259.5
Soybeans	15,587.8	15,118.1	13,690.8
Logs	10,482.2	10,803.8	12,884.8
Natural rubber	2,724.1	3,362.2	3,272.7
Crude petroleum	133,149.5	77,450.5	80,527.5
Raw cotton	14,355.3	13,005.3	16,804.7
Yarn from synthetic fibres	1,613.2	3,604.8	3,039.7
Distillate fuels	4,085.4	5,511.5	4,742.4
Polyacids and derivatives	7,917.2	11,644.4	12,423.5
Thin iron and steel sheets	3,817.6	5,444.2	6,832.8
Thermoplastic resins	6,741.6	10,839.0	15,465.0
Iron and steel scrap	5,696.1	7,838.3	6,058.5
Spinning, extruding machines	6,340.9	7,933.5	13,466.1
Electrical switchgear	9,240.3	13,713.2	16,621.1
Television receivers	517.2	550.5	1,410.3
Internal combustion engines other than for aircraft	3,814.9	5,321.7	7,087.9
Ships for breaking	14,461.2	14,285.0	11,170.7
Total (incl. others)	801,847.4	916,421.5	1,099,494.7

CHINA (TAIWAN)

Exports f.o.b.	1985	1986	1987
Fresh bananas	1,706.5	1,327.4	1,716.9
Canned mushrooms	2,000.7	1,794.7	1,896.6
Canned asparagus	1,414.8	2,446.3	861.8
Raw sugar	917.7	791.7	195.3
Cotton fabrics	4,363.5	3,939.1	3,855.5
Yarn from synthetic fibres	13,988.2	14,491.6	16,108.6
Synthetic fabrics	24,409.5	29,777.1	33,048.3
Plywood	9,815.8	9,052.4	9,711.4
Clothing (incl. knitted and crocheted fabrics)	69,382.2	89,973.8	93,925.5
Thermionic articles, valves, tubes, photocells, transistors etc.	34,436.9	41,767.3	50,097.5
Calculating machines	54,655.1	83,551.9	125,320.1
Television receivers	16,007.0	22,045.7	21,455.8
Radio receivers	14,459.5	17,797.7	20,846.9
Plastic articles	105,436.7	133,349.4	148,090.8
Dolls and toys	23,675.4	27,376.3	29,028.8
Total (incl. others)	1,222,904.2	1,504,348.8	1,703,168.4

PRINCIPAL TRADING PARTNERS (US $ '000)

Imports c.i.f.	1985	1986	1987
Australia	800,647	883,494	999,059
Canada	368,974	485,637	651,046
Germany, Federal Republic	846,171	1,137,272	1,633,468
Hong Kong	319,679	378,647	706,645
Indonesia	413,795	357,325	567,239
Italy	234,490	272,898	442,160
Japan	5,548,848	8,254,716	11,822,623
Korea, Republic	186,617	328,695	531,415
Kuwait	670,769	443,043	730,154
Malaysia	481,467	500,795	729,043
Philippines	104,203	152,669	194,435
Saudi Arabia	1,361,002	909,997	1,075,312
Singapore	275,884	339,854	522,094
Thailand	146,920	162,893	200,388
United Kingdom	262,434	356,812	773,991
USA	4,746,274	5,415,788	7,628,346
Total (incl. others)	20,102,049	24,164,595	34,506,497

Exports f.o.b.	1985	1986	1987
Australia	747,332	869,790	1,100,845
Canada	944,870	1,271,457	1,558,866
Germany, Federal Republic	805,414	1,273,822	1,986,840
Hong Kong	2,539,573	2,915,387	4,112,662
Indonesia	280,900	391,656	444,451
Italy	246,076	382,342	655,065
Japan	3,460,811	4,544,841	6,962,076
Korea, Republic	253,816	349,809	637,211
Kuwait	117,163	142,490	150,263
Malaysia	194,856	205,696	271,853
Philippines	239,155	328,526	458,173
Saudi Arabia	590,013	626,323	703,471
Singapore	885,168	930,648	1,348,840
Thailand	236,208	278,383	424,114
United Kingdom	650,044	560,495	1,536,395
USA	14,772,990	18,994,694	23,637,083
Total (incl. others)	30,722,789	39,789,198	53,538,217

Transport

RAILWAYS

	1985	1986	1987
Passengers ('000)	131,268	131,782	134,367
Passenger-km ('000)	8,309,289	8,316,324	8,458,514
Freight ('000 metric tons)	29,732	28,647	31,211
Freight ton-km ('000)	2,299,840	2,365,460	2,490,214

ROAD TRAFFIC (motor vehicles in use at 31 December)

	1985	1986	1987
Passenger cars	915,598	1,046,660	1,254,955
Buses and coaches	20,845	21,698	21,608
Goods vehicles	408,526	418,212	451,100
Motorcycles and scooters	6,588,854	7,194,202	5,958,754

INTERNATIONAL SEA-BORNE SHIPPING
(freight traffic, '000 metric tons)

	1985	1986	1987
Goods loaded	16,090	16,300	18,086
Goods unloaded	60,496	70,781	83,014

CIVIL AVIATION (traffic on scheduled services)

	1985	1986	1987
Passengers carried ('000)	10,377.7	10,129.7	12,361.3
Passenger-km (million)	11,246.4	12,271.0	14,498.2
Freight carried ('000 metric tons)	328.0	424.5	510.7
Freight ton-km (million)	1,839.0	2,537.5	2,944.6

Communications Media

	1985	1986	1987
Telephones	5,653,113	6,077,889	6,458,733

Education

(1987/88)

	Schools	Full-time teachers	Pupils/Students
Pre-school	2,518	12,994	250,179
Primary	2,472	76,226	2,400,614
Secondary (incl. Vocational)	1,059	78,747	1,707,270
Higher	107	22,924	464,664
Special	10	617	2,948
Supplementary	462	4,307	298,067
Total (incl. others)	6,628	195,817	5,123,742

Directory

The Constitution

On 1 January 1947 a new constitution was promulgated for the Republic of China (confined to Taiwan since 1949). The form of government that was incorporated in the Constitution is based on a five-power system and has the major features of both cabinet and presidential government. The following are the principal organs of government:

NATIONAL ASSEMBLY

The Assembly, composed of elected delegates, meets to elect or recall the President and Vice-President, to amend the Constitution, or to vote on proposed constitutional amendments that have been submitted by the Legislative Yuan. Since the removal of the Republic of China from the mainland to Taiwan, full National Assembly elections have not been held. Many of the seats are held by 'life-term' members, originally elected to represent mainland constituencies.

PRESIDENT

Elected by the National Assembly for a term of six years, and may be re-elected for a second term (the two-term restriction is at present suspended). Represents country at all state functions, including foreign relations; commands land, sea and air forces, promulgates laws, issues mandates, concludes treaties, declares war, makes peace, declares martial law, grants amnesties, appoints and removes civil and military officers, and confers honours and decorations. He also convenes the National Assembly, and subject to certain limitations, may issue emergency orders to deal with national calamities and ensure national security.

EXECUTIVE YUAN

Is the highest administrative organ of the nation and is responsible to the Legislative Yuan; has three categories of subordinate organization:
 Executive Yuan Council (policy-making organization)
 Ministries and Commissions (executive organization)
 Subordinate organization (19 bodies, including the Secretariat, Government Information Office, Directorate-General of Budget, Accounting and Statistics, Council for Economic Planning and Development, and Environmental Protection Administration).

LEGISLATIVE YUAN

Is the highest legislative organ of the state, composed of elected members; holds two sessions a year; is empowered to hear administrative reports of the Executive Yuan, and to change government policy. Like the National Assembly, some of its seats are held by 'life-term' members.

JUDICIAL YUAN

Is the highest judicial organ of state and has charge of civil, criminal and administrative cases, and of cases concerning disciplinary measures against public functionaries (see Judicial System).

EXAMINATION YUAN

Supervises examinations for entry into public offices, and deals with personal questions of the civil service.

CONTROL YUAN

Is a body elected by local councils to impeach or investigate the work of the Executive Yuan and the Ministries and Executives; meets once a month, and has a subordinate body, the Ministry of Audit.

The Government

HEAD OF STATE

President: LEE TENG-HUI (took office 13 January 1988).
Vice-President: (vacant).
Secretary-General: SHEN CHANG-HUAN.

THE EXECUTIVE YUAN
(January 1989)

Premier: YU KUO-HWA.
Vice-Premier: SHIH CHI-YANG.
Secretary-General: ROBERT CHIEN-CHUN.
Minister of the Interior: HSU SHUI-TEH.
Minister of Foreign Affairs: LIEN CHAN.
Minister of National Defence: Gen. CHENG WEI-YUAN.
Minister of Finance: SHIRLEY W. Y. KUO.
Minister of Education: MAO KAO-WEN.
Minister of Justice: HSIAO TIEN-TSANG.
Minister of Economic Affairs: CHEN LI-AN
Minister of Communications: KUO NAN-HUNG.
Ministers of State: WANG YOU-TSAO, HUANG KUN-HUI, SHEN CHUN-SHAN, FREDRICK F. CHIEN, HENRY YU-SHU KAO, CHANG FENG-HSU, CHOW HONG-TAO.
Director-General of Council for Economic Planning and Development: FREDERICK F. CHIEN.
Chairman of the Overseas Chinese Affairs Commission: TSENG KWANG-SHUN.
Chairman of the Mongolian and Tibetan Affairs Commission: WU HUA-PENG.
Director-General of the Government Information Office: SHAW YU MING.
Director-General of Directorate-General of Budget, Accounting and Statistics: YU CHIEN-MIN.
Director-General of Central Personnel Administration: PU TA-HAI.
Director-General of Department of Health: SHIH CHUN-JEN.
Director-General of Environmental Protection Administration: EUGENE Y. H. CHIEN.
Chairman of National Council of Science: HSIA HAN-MIN.
Chairman of Council of Agriculture: YU YU-HSIEN.
Chairman of Council of Cultural Planning and Development: KUO WEI-FAN.
Chairman of Research, Development and Evaluation Commission: MA YING-JEOU.

MINISTRIES AND COMMISSIONS

Ministry of Communications: 2 Changsha St, Sec. 1, Taipei; tel. 3112661.
Ministry of Economic Affairs: 15 Foochow St, Taipei; tel. 3517271.
Ministry of Education: 5 Chungshan South Rd, Taipei 10040; tel. 3513111; telex 10894.
Ministry of Finance: 2 Aikuo West Rd, Taipei; tel. 3511611; telex 11840.
Ministry of Foreign Affairs: 2 Chiehshou Rd, Taipei 10016; tel. 3119292; telex 11299.
Ministry of the Interior: 107 Roosevelt Rd, Sec. 4, Taipei; tel. 3415241.
Ministry of Justice: 130 Chungking South Rd, Sec. 1, Taipei 10036; tel. 3146871.
Ministry of National Defence: Chiehshou Hall, Chungking South Rd, Taipei 10016; tel. 3117001.
Office of the Director-General of Budget, Accounting and Statistics: 1 Chung Hsiao East Rd, Sec. 1, Taipei; tel. 3915231.
Mongolian and Tibetan Affairs Commission: 109 Roosevelt Rd, Sec. 4, Taipei; tel. 3513131.
Overseas Chinese Affairs Commission: 30 Kungyuan Rd, Taipei; tel. 3810039.

Legislature

KUO-MIN TA-HUI
(National Assembly)

In 1988 many of the seats in the Assembly were held by members who were originally elected to represent constituencies on the Chinese mainland. Since the removal of the Republic from the mainland to Taiwan in 1949, these members hold office for an indefinite period, as full elections have not been possible. The most recent election for additional members was held on 6 December 1986, when 84 new members (68 KMT, 11 DPP, four independents and one CDSP) were elected. In October 1988 the National Assembly had 965 members. Delegates meet to elect or recall the

CHINA (TAIWAN)   *Directory*

President and Vice-President, to amend the Constitution or to vote on proposed constitutional amendments submitted by the Legislative Yuan.

LI-FA YUAN
(Legislative Yuan)

The Legislative Yuan is the highest legislative organ of state. As in the National Assembly, some of the seats are held by life members, originally elected on the Chinese mainland. The chamber also includes members appointed by the President, representing overseas Chinese communities. Other members are elected by universal suffrage for a term of three years and are eligible for re-election. Elections were held on 6 December 1986 for 73 seats, of which 59 were won by the KMT, 12 by the DPP and two by independents. In July 1988 there were 304 members, comprising 269 KMT members, 24 independents, seven members of the Young China Party and four members of the China Democratic Socialist Party.

President: LIU KUO-TSAI.

Vice-President: (vacant).

CONTROL YUAN

The 66-member Control Yuan exercises powers of investigation, impeachment and censure, and powers of consent in the appointment of the President, Vice-President and the grand justices of the Judicial Yuan, and the president, vice-president and the members of the Examination Yuan, and power of audit over central and local government finances (see the Constitution).

President: HUANG TZUEN-CHIOU.

Vice-President: MA KUNG-CHUN.

Political Organizations

China Democratic Socialist Party (CDSP): 6 Lane 357, Hoping East Rd, Sec. 2, Taipei; f. 1932 by merger of National Socialists and Democratic Constitutionalists; aims to promote democracy, to protect fundamental freedoms, and to improve public welfare and social security; 30,000 mems; Chair. YANG YU-TSE; Sec.-Gen. LIU YI-PING.

Chinese Freedom Party (CFP): Taipei; f. 1987; advocates the holding of free elections, liberalization of relations with mainland China and improved measures to combat corruption.

Chinese Republican Party (CRP): Taipei; f. 1988; advocates peaceful struggle for the salvation of China and the promotion of world peace; 1,746 mems; Chair. WANG YING-CHUN.

Democratic Liberal Party (DLP): Taipei; f. 1987; aims to promote political democracy and economic liberty for the people of Taiwan.

Democratic Progress Party (DPP): Taipei; f. 1986; aimed for the end of martial law; advocates the introduction of direct trade, tourism and postal links with mainland China, and 'self-determination' for the people of Taiwan; 1,500 mems; Chair. HUANG HSIN-CHIEH.

Kungtang (KT) (Labour Party): Taipei; f. 1987; aims to become the main political movement of Taiwan's industrial work-force; Chair. WANG YI-HSIUNG; Sec.-Gen. SU CHIN-LI.

Kuomintang (KMT) (Nationalist Party of China): 11 Chung Shan South Rd, Taipei; f. 1894; ruling party; aims to supplant communist rule in mainland China; advocates constitutional government and the unification of China under the 'Three Principles of the People'; aims to promote market economy and equitable distribution of wealth; c. 2.4m. mems; Chair. LEE TENG-HUI; Sec.-Gen. LEE HUAN; Dep. Secs-Gen. JAMES C. Y. SOONG, KAO MING-HUEY.

Young China Party: 256 King Hwa St, Taipei; f. 1923; aims to recover sovereignty over mainland China, to safeguard the Constitution and democracy, and to foster understanding between Taiwan and the non-communist world; Chair. LI HUANG.

Diplomatic Representation

EMBASSIES IN THE REPUBLIC OF CHINA

Costa Rica: Tulip Bldg, 1st Floor, 108 Chung Cheng Rd, Sec. 2, Taipei; tel. 8712422; Ambassador: SALOMAN AIZENMAN.

Dominican Republic: 110 Chung Cheng Rd, 1st Floor, Sec. 2, Tien Mou, Taipei; tel. 8717938; Ambassador: JOSÉ MANUEL LÓPEZ BALAGUER.

El Salvador: 15 Lane 34, Ku Kung Rd, Shih Lin 11102, Taipei; tel. 8819887; Ambassador: FRANCISCO RICARDO SANTANA BERRIOS.

Guatemala: 6 Lane 88, Chien Kuo North Rd, Sec. 1, Taipei; tel. 5077043; Ambassador: CARLOS ORIOL JIMÉNEZ QUIROA.

Haiti: 246 Chungshan North Rd, 3rd Floor, Sec. 6, Taipei; tel. 8317086; Ambassador: RAYMOND PERODIN.

Holy See: 87 Ai Kuo East Rd, Taipei 10605; tel. 3216847; Chargé d'affaires a.i.: Mgr PIERO BIGGIO.

Honduras: 142 Chung Hsiao East Rd, Room 701, Sec. 4, Taipei; tel. 7518737; Ambassador: AGRIPINO FLORES AGUILAR.

Korea, Republic: 345 Chung Hsiao East Rd, Sec. 4, Taipei; tel. 7619363; Ambassador: HAN CHUL-SOO.

Panama: 13 Te Huei St, 5th Floor, Taipei; tel. 5968563; Ambassador: AURELIO CHU YI.

Paraguay: 20 Lane 38 Tien Yee St, 2nd Floor, Tien Mou, Taipei; tel. 8728932; telex 13744; Ambassador: ANGEL JUAN SOUTO HERNÁNDEZ.

Saudi Arabia: 550 Chung Hsiao East Rd, 11th Floor, Sec. 4, Taipei; tel. 7035855; Ambassador: Gen. ASAAD ABDUL AZIZ AL-ZUHAIR.

South Africa: Bank Tower, 13th Floor, 205 Tun Hua North Rd, Taipei; tel. 7153251; telex 21954; Ambassador: CHRISTOFFEL PRINS.

Judicial System

The interpretative powers of the Judicial Yuan are exercised by the Council of Grand Justices nominated and appointed for nine years by the President of the Republic of China with the consent of the Control Yuan. The President of the Judicial Yuan also presides over the Council of Grand Justices.

The Judicial Yuan has jurisdiction over the high courts and district courts. The Ministry of Justice is under the jurisdiction of the Executive Yuan.

Judicial Yuan: Pres. LIN YANG-KANG; Vice-Pres. WANG TAO-YUAN; Sec.-Gen. WANG CHIA-YI; the highest judicial organ, and the interpreter of the constitution and national laws and ordinances. Other judicial powers are exercised by:

Supreme Court: Court of third and final instance for civil and criminal cases; President CHU CHIEN-HUNG.

High Courts: Courts of second instance for appeals of civil and criminal cases.

District Courts: Courts of first instance in civil, criminal and non-contentious cases.

Administrative Court: Court of final resort in cases brought against govt agencies; President WANG JUI-LIN.

Committee on the Discipline of Public Functionaries: sentences persons impeached by the Control Yuan; Chair. FAN KUEI-SHU.

Religion

BUDDHISM

Buddhists belong to the Mahayana and Theravada schools. Leader PAN SHENG. The Buddhist Association of Taiwan has 1,462 group members and more than 3.5m. adherents.

CHRISTIANITY

The Roman Catholic Church

Taiwan comprises one archdiocese, six dioceses and two apostolic administrative areas. In 1987 there were approximately 300,000 adherents, of whom 69,258 resided in the archdiocese of Taipei.

Bishops' Conference: Regional Episcopal Conference of China, POB 36603, 34 Lane 32, Kuangfu South Rd, Taipei 10552; tel. 7711295; f. 1978; Pres. Rt Rev. PAUL SHAN KUO-HSI, Bishop of Hualien.

Archbishop of Taipei: Most Rev. MATTHEW KIA YEN-WEN, Archbishop's House, 94 Loli Rd, Taipei 10668; tel. 7371311.

The Anglican Communion

Anglicans in Taiwan are adherents of the Protestant Episcopal Church. In 1988 the Church had about 2,000 members.

Bishop of Taiwan: Rt Rev. JOHN CHIH-TSUNG CHIEN, 7 Lane 105, Hangchow South Rd, Sec. 1, Taipei 10044; tel. 341-1265.

Presbyterian Church

Tai-oan Ki-tok Tiu-Lo Kau-Hoe (Presbyterian Church in Taiwan): 3 Lane 269, Roosevelt Rd, Sec. 3, Taipei; tel. 3935282; telex 20588; f. 1865; Gen. Sec. Dr C. M. KAO; 207,000 mems (1987).

DAOISM (TAOISM)

There are about 2m. adherents.

CHINA (TAIWAN)

ISLAM

Leader Dawud Fu Hsu; 55,310 adherents.

The Press

DAILIES

Taipei

Central Daily News: 260 Pa Teh Rd, Sec. 2; tel. 7213710; telex 24884; f. 1928; morning; official Kuomintang organ; Publr Shih Yung-kuei.

China News: 277 Hsinyi Rd, Sec. 2; tel. 3210882; f. 1949; afternoon; English; Publr Simone Wei; Dir Ting Wei-tung; Editor Chu Liang-jen; circ. 25,000.

China Post: 8 Fu Shun St; tel. 5969971; telex 24059; f. 1952; morning; English; Publr Nancy Yu-huang; Editor Huang Chih-hsiang.

China Times: 132 Da Li St; tel. 3087111; telex 26464; f. 1950; morning; Chinese; Chair. Yu Chi-chung; Publr Yu Chien-hsin; Editor Hu Li-tai; circ. 1.2m.

Chung Cheng Pao: 70 Li-hsing Rd, Shing-den; f. 1948; morning; armed forces; Publr Ma Chia-chen; Editor Liu Chih-hsiu.

Commercial Times: 132 Da Li St; tel. 3087111; telex 26464; f. 1978; Publr Yu Fan-ying; Editor-in-Chief Cheng Chia-chung.

Economic Daily News: 555 Chung Hsiao East Rd, Sec. 4; tel. 7681234; telex 27710; f. 1967; morning; Publr Wang Pi-ly; Editor Wang Yen-perng.

Independent Evening Post: 15 Chinan Rd, Sec. 2; tel. 3519621; f. 1947; afternoon; Chinese; Publr Wu San-lien; Editor Chang Sheu-ben.

Mandarin Daily News: 10 Fuchow St; tel. 3213479; f. 1948; morning; Publr Hsia Cheng-ying; Editor Yang Ru Der.

Min Sheng Pao: 555 Chung Hsiao East Rd, Sec. 4; tel. 7681234; telex 27710; f. 1978; Publr Wang Shaw-lan; Editor Shih Pin.

Ta Hua (Great China) Evening News: 1, Lane 61, Chiuchuan St; tel. 5919133; f. 1950; afternoon; Publr Keng Hsiu-yeh; Editor Pan Lin.

Taiwan Hsin Sheng Pao: 127 Yenping South Rd; tel. 3119634; f. 1945; morning; Chinese; Publr Shen Yueh; Editor Hsu Chang.

United Daily News: 555 Chung Hsiao East Rd, Sec. 4; tel. 7689068; telex 27710; f. 1951; morning; Publr Wang Pi-cheng; Editor Chang Tso-chin.

Youth Daily News: 3 Hsinyi Rd, Sec. 1; tel. 3212788; f. 1984; morning; Chinese; armed forces; Publr Miao Lun; Editor Nien Chen-yu.

Provincial

Chien Kuo Daily News: 36 Min Sheng Rd, Makung, Chen, Penghu; tel. 272675; f. 1949; morning; Publr Chen Tai-i; Editor Wang Lien-cherng; circ. 15,000.

China Daily News (Southern Edn): 57 Hsi Hwa St, Tainan; tel. 2202691; f. 1946; morning; Publr Chan Tien-hsing; Editor Cheng Chi-ling; circ. 260,000.

China Evening News: 243 Hsinleh St, Kaohsiung; tel. 3332203; f. 1955; afternoon; Publr Liu Hen-hsiu; Editor Yang Nien-tsu; circ. 70,000.

Daily Free Press: 57 Chung Hwa Rd, Hsin Chuang Shih; tel. 9932828; f. 1978; morning; Publr Wu A-ming; Editor Wu Ah-ming; circ. 20,000.

Keng-Sheng Daily News: 36 Wuchuan St, Hualien; tel. 23784; f. 1947; morning; Publr Hsieh Ying-yi; Editor Chen Hsing; circ. 5,000.

Kinmen Daily News: Chin Hu Village, Kinmen; tel. 2374; f. 1965; morning; Publr Chang Ming-hung; Editor Min Chyang; circ. 5,000.

Matsu Daily News: Matsu; tel. 2276; f. 1957; morning; Publr Wu Tung-lung; Editor Liao Keng-hsing.

Min Chung Daily News: 410 Chung Shan 2 Rd, Kaohsiung; tel. 3353131; f. 1950; morning; Publr Lee Jui-piao; Editor Hwang Yeh; circ. 148,000.

Shin Wen Evening News: 249 Chungcheng 4 Rd, Kaohsiung; tel. (07) 2212858; f. 1985; afternoon; Publr Yeh Chien-li; Dir Yeh Chien-li; Editor Liu Tii-chang; circ. 12,000.

Taiwan Daily News: 24 Chung Shan Rd, Taichung; tel. (04) 2815091; f. 1964; morning; Chair. Hsu Heng; Publr Chen Mao-pang; Editor Chang Chia-hsiang; circ. 250,000.

Taiwan Shin Wen Daily News: 249 Chung Cheng 4 Rd, Kaohsiung; tel. 2212154; f. 1949; morning; Publr Yeh Chien-li; Editor Yeh Yun-i.

Taiwan Times: 110 Chungshan 1 Rd, Kaohsiung; tel. 2725781; f. 1971; Publr Yu Tsang-chow; Editor Tsai Hsin-chang; circ. 148,000.

SELECTED PERIODICALS

Agri-week: 14 Wenchow St, Taipei; tel. 3938148; f. 1975; weekly; Editor Ned Liang; Publr Dr Yu Yu-hsien.

Artist Magazine: 147 Chung Ching South Rd, 6th Floor, Sec. 1, Taipei; tel. 3719692; f. 1975; monthly; Publr Ho Cheng Kwang; circ. 28,000.

Biographical Literature: 230 Hsinyi Rd, 4th Floor, Sec. 2, Taipei; tel. 3410213; Publr Liu Tsung-hsiang.

China Times Weekly: 132 Da Li St, Taipei; tel. 3087111; f. 1978; weekly; Chinese; Editor Lee Kuang-huai; Publr Chien Chih-hsin.

Continent Magazine: 11-6 Foochow St, Taipei; tel 3518310; f. 1950; fortnightly; archaeology, history and literature; Publr Wan Shao-chang.

Crown: 50 Lane 120, Tun Hwa North Rd, Taipei; tel. 7168888; monthly; Publr Ping Sin Tao.

Free China Review: 3 Chung Hsiao East Rd, Sec. 1, Taipei 10023; tel. 3313817; telex 11636; f. 1951; monthly; English; illustrated; Publr Yu-ming Shaw; Managing Editor Betty Wang.

Free China Journal: 3 Chung Hsiao East Rd, Sec. 1, Taipei 10023; tel. 3713201; telex 11636; f. 1984 (fmrly Free China Weekly); English; news review; Publr Yu-ming Shaw; Editor Yu Kuo-sheng.

The Gleaner: Kaohsiung Refinery, 2 Hung-i Rd, Nantz, Kaohsiung; tel. 3621367; Publr Chin Kai-yin.

Harvest Farm Magazine: 14 Wenchow St, Taipei; tel. 3938148; f. 1975; weekly; Publr Dr Yu Yu-hsien; Editor Ned Liang.

Information and Computer: 116 Nanking E. Rd, Sec. 2, Taipei; tel. 5422540; monthly; Chinese; Publr Fang Hsien-chi; Editor Lee Ming-feng.

Issues and Studies: Institute of International Relations, 64 Wan Shou Rd, Mucha, Taipei 11625; tel. 9394921; f. 1975; monthly; English; Chinese studies and international affairs; Publr Chang King-yuh; Editor Chou Sheu.

Jen Chien (People's World): 1st Floor, 8 Lane 737, Tunhwa S. Rd, Taipei; tel. 7091920; f. 1985; current affairs; Editor Chen Ying-chen; circ. 8,000.

Music and Audiophile: 271 Hsinyi Rd, 6th Floor, Sec. 2, Taipei; tel. 3937201; f. 1973; Publr Adam Chang.

National Palace Museum Bulletin: Wai Shuang Hsi, Shih Lin, Taipei; tel. 8812021; f. 1966; every 2 months; art history research in Chinese with summaries in English; Publr Chin Hsiao-yi; Editor-in-Chief Wu Ping; Editor Su Tu-jen; circ. 1,000.

National Palace Museum Monthly of Chinese Art: Wai Shuang Hsi, Shih Lin, Taipei; tel. 8812021; f. 1983; monthly in Chinese; Publr Chin Hsiao-yi; Editor-in-Chief Sung Lung-fei; circ. 13,000.

Ours: 4th Floor, 277 Hsinyi Rd, Sec. 2, Taipei; tel. 3921612; f. 1985; monthly; Chinese; Publr Chen Ming-hui; Editor Lisa Kuan.

Reader's Digest (Chinese Edn): 872 Min Sheng East Rd, 3rd Floor, Taipei; tel. 7637206; telex 20954; monthly; Editor-in-Chief Lin Tai-yi.

Sinorama: 16th Floor, 17 Hsu Chang St, Taipei 10015; tel. 3123342; telex 11636; f. 1976; monthly; cultural; bilingual magazine with edns in Chinese with Japanese, Spanish and English; Publr Yu-ming Shaw; Editor-in-Chief Yu Yuh-chao.

Sinwen Tienti (Newsdom): 207 Fuh Hsing North Rd, 10th Floor, Taipei; tel. 3711027; f. 1945; weekly; Chinese; Dir Pu Shao-fu; Editor Li Chi-liu.

Taiwan Pictorial: 20 Chungking South Rd, Sec. 2, Taipei 10741; tel. 3115586; f. 1954; monthly; Chinese; general illustrated; Publr Lo Sen-tung; Editor Lin Kuo-chin.

Tien Sia (Commonwealth Monthly): 87 Song Chiang Rd, 4th Floor, Taipei; tel. 5518627; monthly; business; Pres. Charles H. C. Kao; Publr and Editor Diane Ying.

Times Newsweekly: 132 Da Li St, Taipei; tel. 3087111; f. 1986; weekly; Chinese; Publr Albert C. Yu; circ. 30,000.

Unitas: 561 Chung Hsiao East Rd, Sec. 4, Taipei; tel. 7666759; monthly; Chinese; literary journal; Publr Chang Pao-ching; Editor Ma Sun.

NEWS AGENCIES

Central News Agency Inc. (CNA): 209 Sungkiang Rd, Taipei; tel 5611181; telex 11548; f. 1924; Pres. Hwang Tien-tsai; Editor-in-Chief Conrad K. Y. Lu.

Chiao Kwang News Agency: 4th Floor, 28 Tsinan Rd, Sec. 2, Taipei; tel. 3214803; Publr Hu Jenn-hua; Dir Huang Ho.

CHINA (TAIWAN)

China Youth News Agency: 131 Tun Hua North Rd, Taipei; tel. 7711542; f. 1955; Dir Peng Chao-hsiung; Editor Hu Kuei.

Foreign Bureaux

Agence France-Presse (AFP): 209 Sungkiang Rd, 6th Floor, Taipei; tel. 5011881; Correspondent Yang Hsin-hsin.

Associated Press (AP) (USA): 209 Sungkiang Rd, 6th Floor, Taipei; tel. 5036651; telex 21835; Correspondents Pan Yueh-kan, Annie Huang, Yang Chi-hsien, Shirley Lai.

Reuters (UK): 209 Sungkiang Rd, 6th Floor, Taipei; tel. 5033034; telex 22360; Correspondents K. B. Tam, Andrew Browne, C. K. Chen, Andrew Quinn.

United Press International (UPI) (USA): 209 Sungkiang Rd, 6th Floor, Taipei; tel. 5052549; Bureau Mans Shullen Shaw, Helen Berg.

PRESS ASSOCIATION

Taipei Journalists Association: 555 Chung Hsiao East Rd, Sec. 4, Taipei; tel. 7681234; c. 3,080 mems representing editorial and business executives of newspapers and broadcasting stations.

Publishers

Art Book Co: 18 Lane 283, 4th Floor, Roosevelt Rd, Sec. 3, Taipei; Publr Ho Kung Shang.

Buffalo Publishing Co: 135 Chin Shan South Rd, 2nd Floor, Sec. 1, Taipei; Publr Peng Chung Hang.

Business Publications Ltd: Hui Feng Bldg, 6th Floor, 18 Lane 14, Chi Lin Rd, Taipei 10424; tel. 5216457; telex 12393; f. 1978; international business textbooks; fine arts; Man. Dir Michelle Yang.

Cheng Chung Book Co: 20 Hengyang Rd, Taipei; humanities, social sciences, medicine, fine arts; Publr Huang Chao-heng.

Cheng Wen Publishing Co: POB 22605, Taipei; tel. 7415432; telex 13542; Publr Huang Cheng Chu.

Chinese Culture University Press: Hua Kang, Yangmingshan, Taipei; tel. 8611862; Publr Lee Fu-chen.

Chung Hwa Book Co Ltd: 94 Chungking South Rd, Sec. 1, Taipei; tel. 3117365; humanities, social sciences, medicine, fine arts, school books; Gen. Man. Hsiung Dun Seng.

The Eastern Publishing Co Ltd: 121 Chungking South Rd, Sec. 1, Taipei; tel. 3114514; Publr Cheng Li-tsu.

Far East Book Co: 66-1 Chungking South Rd, 10th Floor, Sec. 1, Taipei; tel. 3118740; art, education, history, physics, mathematics, law, literature, dictionaries; Publr George C. L. Pu.

Ho Chi Book Co: 249 Wuhsing St, Taipei; Publr Wu Fu Chang.

Hua Hsin Culture and Publications Center: 133 Kuang Fu North Rd, 2nd Floor, Taipei; tel. 7658848; f. 1960; Publr Wei Teh-mao.

International Cultural Enterprises: 25 Po Ai Rd, 6th Floor, Taipei; tel. 3318080; Publr Hu Tze-dan.

Kwang Hwa Publishing Company: 3-1 Chung Hsiao East Rd, Sec. 1, Taipei 10023; tel. 3319551; telex 11636; Publr Shaw Yu-ming.

Li-Ming Cultural Enterprise Co: 3 Hsin Yi Rd, 10th Floor, Sec. 1, Taipei; tel. 3952500; telex 27377; Publr Liu Yen-sheng; Gen. Man. Chang Ming Hong.

San Min Book Co: 61 Chungking South Rd, Sec. 1, Taipei 10036; tel. 3318484; f. 1953; literature, history, philosophy, social sciences; Publr Liu Chen-chiang.

Taiwan Kaiming Book Co: 77 Chung Shan North Rd, Sec. 1, Taipei; tel. 5415369; Publr Chao Liu Ching-ti.

The World Book Co: 99 Chungking South Rd, Sec. 1, Taipei; tel. 3311616; f. 1921; literature, textbooks; Chair. Chen Sheh Woo; Publr Yen Feng-chang.

Youth Cultural Enterprise Co Ltd: 66-1 Chungking South Rd, 3rd Floor, Sec. 1, Taipei; Publr Hu Kwei; Gen. Man. Cheng Sung-nien.

Yuan Liou Publishing Co Ltd: 7F-5, 782 Ding Chou Rd, Taipei; tel. 3923707; Publr Wang Jung-wen.

Radio and Television

In 1987 there were an estimated 18.5m. radio receivers, and 5.6m. television sets. Broadcasting stations are mostly privately owned, but the Ministry of Communications determines power and frequencies, and the Government Information Office supervises the operation of all stations, whether private or governmental.

RADIO

In 1987 there were 33 radio broadcasting corporations (with 188 stations and 379 transmitters), of which the following are the most important:

Broadcasting Corpn of China (BCC): 53 Jen Ai Rd, Sec. 3, Taipei 106; tel. (02) 7710150; telex 27498; f. 1928; domestic (7 networks) and external services in 15 languages and dialects; 45 stations, 113 transmitters; Pres. P. P. Tang; Chair. Kuo Che.

Cheng Sheng Broadcasting Corpn Ltd: 6th–8th Floors, 66-1 Chungking South Rd, Sec. 1, Taipei; tel. (02) 3617231; f. 1950; 9 stations, 9 relay stations; Chair. Joseph Ching; Pres. Yun-han Kao.

Fu Hsing Broadcasting Corpn: 5, Lane 280, Sec. 5, Chung Shan N. Rd, Taipei; 27 stations; Dir Tsay Yun-cheng.

TELEVISION

Taiwan Television Enterprise: 10 Pa Teh Rd, Sec. 3, Taipei; tel. 7711515; telex 25714; f. 1962; Chair. Hsu Chin-teh; Pres. Wang Chia-hua.

China Television Co: 120 Chung Yang Rd, Nan Kang District, Taipei; tel. 7838308; telex 25080; f. 1969; Pres. H. P. Chung; Chair. Mah Soo-lay.

Chinese Television System: 100 Kuang Fu South Rd, Taipei; tel. 751-0321; telex 24195; f. 1971; cultural and educational; Chair. Yee Chien-chiu; Pres. Wu Shih-sung.

Finance

(cap. = capital; p.u. = paid up; dep. = deposits; m. = million; brs = branches; amounts in New Taiwan dollars)

BANKING

Central Bank

Central Bank of China: 2 Roosevelt Rd, Sec. 1, Taipei; tel. 3936161; telex 21532; f. 1928; bank of issue; cap. 22,000m., dep. 2,135,908m. (June 1988); Gov. Chang Chi-cheng; Dep. Govs Chen S. Yu, Paul C. H. Chiu.

Domestic Banks

Bank of Communications: 91 Heng Yang Rd, Taipei 10003; tel. 3613000; telex 11341; f. 1907; cap. 10,000m., dep. 168,785m. (Aug. 1988); Chair. S. C. Shieh; Pres. C. Y. Lee; 13 brs.

Bank of Taiwan: 120 Chungking South Rd, Sec. 1, Taipei 10036; tel. 3147377; telex 11201; f. 1946; cap. 8,000m., dep. 574,347m. (July 1988); Chair. Dr I-Shuan Sun; Pres. Pu Chen-ming; 65 brs.

Co-operative Bank of Taiwan: 77 Kuan Chien Rd, Taipei; tel. 3118811; telex 23749; f. 1946; acts as central bank for co-operatives, and as major agricultural credit institution; dep. 547,137m. (June 1988); Chair. Hubert M. F. Hsu; Pres. H. P. Liao; 89 brs.

Export-Import Bank: 3 Nan Hai Rd, 8th Floor, Taipei; tel. 3210511; telex 26044; f. 1979; cap. 9,000m., dep. 3,593m. (June 1987); Chair. P. Y. Pai; Pres. C. S. Lo; 1 br.

Farmers Bank of China: 85 Nanking East Rd, Sec. 2, Taipei 10408; tel. 5517141; telex 21610; f. 1933; cap. 4,435m., dep. 113,921m. (June 1988); Chair. Wilson C. P. Yen; Pres. Richard M. C. Tsai; 33 brs.

International Commercial Bank of China: 100 Chi Lin Rd, Taipei 10424; tel. 5633156; telex 11300; f. 1912; cap. 5,660m., dep. 126,646m. (June 1988); Chair. C. D. Wang; Pres. Theodore S. S. Cheng; 32 brs.

Land Bank of Taiwan: 46 Kuan Chien Rd, Taipei 10038; tel. 3613020; telex 14564; f. 1946; cap. 4,000m., dep. 301,489m. (June 1987); Chair. Y. D. Sheu; Pres. T. L. Lin; 58 brs.

Commercial Banks

Bank of Kaohsiung: 21 Wu Fu 3rd Rd, Kaohsiung; tel. 2413051; telex 73266; f. 1982; cap. 650m., dep. 21,959m. (July 1988); Chair. K. C. Cheng; Pres. Chun Chung-huang; 7 brs.

Central Trust of China: 49 Wu Chang St, Sec. 1, Taipei 10006; tel. 3111511; telex 11377; f. 1935; cap. 2,850m., dep. 21,591m. (July 1987); Chair. W. S. King; Pres. T. Y. Chu; 4 brs.

Chang Hwa Commercial Bank Ltd: 38 Tsuyu Rd, Sec. 2, Taichung; tel. 2222001; telex 51248; f. 1905; 51% govt-owned; cap. 3,000m., dep. 309,728m. (July 1988); Chair. Liang Kuo-shu; Pres. K. H. Yeh; 107 brs.

City Bank of Taipei: 50, Sec. 2, Chungshan North Rd, Taipei 100; tel. 5425656; f. 1969; cap. 6,000m., dep. 171,495m. (July 1988); Chair. W. K. Wu; Pres. Shao-king Wang; 28 brs.

First Commercial Bank: 30 Chungking South Rd, Sec. 1, Taipei; tel. 3111111; telex 11310; f. 1899; 51% govt-owned; cap. 3,264m., dep. 312,478m. (July 1988); Chair. H. A. CHEN; Pres. KENNETH B. K. TSAN; 108 brs.

Hua Nan Commercial Bank Ltd: 38 Chungking South Rd, Sec. 1, Taipei; tel. 3713111; telex 11307; f. 1919; 51% govt-owned; cap. 3,024m., dep. 289,522m. (Dec. 1987); Chair. KENNETH K. H. LO; Pres. CHI TANG-LO; 94 brs.

Overseas Chinese Commercial Banking Corpn: 8 Hsiang Yang Rd, Taipei; tel. 3715181; telex 21571; f. 1961; general banking and foreign exchange; cap. p.u. 1,668m., dep. 29,437m. (July 1988); Chair. CHUA SIAO HUA; Pres. L. S. LIN; 14 brs.

Shanghai Commercial and Savings Bank Ltd: 16 Jen Ai Rd, Sec. 2, Taipei 10019; tel. 3933111; telex 22507; f. 1915; cap. p.u. 700m., dep. 15,903m. (July 1988); Chair. JU-TANG CHU; Pres. RICHARD J. R. YEN; 7 brs.

United World Chinese Commercial Bank: 65 Kuan Chien Rd, Taipei 10038; tel. 3125555; telex 21378; f. 1975; cap. 1,930m., dep. 94,912m. (Sept. 1988); Chair. SNIT VIRAVAN; Pres. T. M. YEE; 8 brs.

There are also a number of Medium Business Banks throughout the country.

Foreign Banks

American Express Bank Ltd (USA): 2nd-3rd Floor, 214 Tung Hua North Rd, Taipei; tel. 7151581; telex 11349; Vice-Pres. JAMES D. VAUGHN.

Bangkok Bank Ltd (Thailand): 121 Sung Chiang Rd, 1st-3rd Floors, POB 22419, Taipei; tel. 5073275; telex 11289; Vice-Pres. and Man. PRASONG UTHAISANGCHAI.

Bank of America NT and SA (USA): 205 Tun Hua North Rd, Taipei; tel. 7154111; telex 11610; Vice-Pres. and Man. W. LYNN ROWSELL.

Chase Manhattan Bank NA (USA): 72 Nanking East Rd, Sec. 2, POB 3996, Taipei; tel. 5378100; telex 26824; Vice-Pres. and Gen. Man. G. ROBERT HESS.

Chemical Bank (USA): Worldwide House, 7th Floor, 683-5 Ming Sheng East Rd, POB 48-11, Taipei; tel. 7121181; telex 22411; Vice-Pres. and Gen. Man. GEORGE W. MASEK.

Citibank NA (USA): 742 Min Sheng East Rd, POB 3343, Taipei; tel. 7155931; telex 23547; Vice-Pres. THOMAS M. McKEON.

Dai-Ichi Kangyo Bank Ltd (Japan): 137 Nanking East Rd, Sec. 2, Taipei; tel. 5064371; telex 11220; Pres. TOMOYUKI INOUE.

First Interstate Bank of California (USA): 221 Nanking East Rd, Sec. 3, Taipei; tel. 7153572; telex 11830; Vice-Pres. and Gen. Man. TOM L. DOBYNS.

Hongkong and Shanghai Banking Corpn (Hong Kong): 13-14th Floor, Keelung Rd, Sec.1, Taipei; tel. 7380088; telex 10934; Branch Man. IAN CAMERON MANZIES.

International Bank of Singapore: 178 Nanking East Rd, 2nd Floor, Sec. 2, Taipei; tel. 5060531; telex 25530; Branch Man. NA WU-BENG.

Irving Trust Co (USA): 4th Floor, 437 Tun Hua South Rd, Taipei; tel. 7716612; telex 21710; Vice-Pres. EDWARD J. MORIARTY.

Metropolitan Bank and Trust Co (Philippines): 107 Chung Hsiao East Rd, Sec. 4, Taipei 10646; tel. 7766355; telex 21688; Vice-Pres. and Gen. Man. HENRY SO UY.

Société Générale (France): 683 Ming Shen East Rd, Taipei 10446; tel. 7155050; telex 23904; Gen. Man. GUY PASTURAUD.

Standard Chartered Bank (UK): 337 Fu Hsing North Rd, Taipei 10483; tel. 7166261; telex 12133; Man. J. J. C. BRINSDEN.

Toronto Dominion Bank (Canada): 337 Fushing North Rd, 2nd Floor, Taipei; tel. 7162162; telex 22503; Man. BYRON JOSEPH FORDYCE.

The following foreign banks also have branches in Taiwan: Amsterdam-Rotterdam Bank (Netherlands), American Express Bank (USA), Bankers Trust Co (USA), Banque Indosuez (France), Banque Nationale de Paris (France), Banque Paribas (France), Citibank NA (USA), Crédit Lyonnais SA (France), Deutsche Bank (Federal Republic of Germany), Development Bank of Singapore, First National Bank of Boston (USA), Grindlays Bank (UK), Hollandsche Bank-Unie NV (Netherlands), Lloyds Bank PLC (UK), Manufacturers' Hanover Trust Co (USA), Rainier National Bank (USA), Royal Bank of Canada, Security Pacific National Bank (USA), Westpac Banking Corpn (Australia).

DEVELOPMENT CORPORATION

China Development Corpn: CDC Tower, 125 Nanking East Rd, Sec. 5, Taipei 10572; tel. 7638800; telex 23147; f. 1959 as privately-owned development finance co to assist in creation, modernization and expansion of private industrial enterprises in Taiwan; encourages participation of private capital in such enterprises; cap. 1,000m. (1986); Chair. YUNG-LIANG LIN; Pres. W. L. KIANG.

STOCK EXCHANGE

Taiwan Stock Exchange Corpn: City Bldg, 9th Floor, 85 Yen-Ping South Rd, Taipei 10034; tel. 3969271; telex 22914; f. 1962; Chair. YAO KU-HUAI.

INSURANCE

Cathay Insurance Co Ltd: 237 Chien Kuo South Rd, Taipei; tel. 7087890; telex 11143; f. 1961; Chair. TSAI WAN-TSAI; Gen. Man. SHIH-YEN LIAO.

Cathay Life Insurance Co Ltd: 296 Zen Ai Rd, Sec. 4, Taipei; tel. 7551399; telex 24994; f. 1962; Chair. TSAI WAN-LIN; Gen. Man. F. J. TU.

Central Insurance Co Ltd: 6 Chung Hsiao East Rd, Sec. 1, Taipei; tel. 3819910; telex 22871; f. 1962; Chair. T. C. SU; Gen. Man. THOMAS T. L. LIN.

Central Reinsurance Corpn: 53 Nan King East Rd, Sec. 2, Taipei; tel. 5115211; telex 11471; f. 1968; Chair. C. C. YANG; Gen. Man. C. F. HSU.

Central Trust of China, Life Insurance Dept: 76 Poai Rd, 5th-7th Floors, Taipei; tel. 3144327; telex 21154; f. 1941; life insurance; Pres. WEI-SHIN KING; Man. SHIH-PING WANG.

China Mariners' Assurance Corpn Ltd: 62 Hsin Sheng South Rd, Sec. 1, Taipei; tel. 3913201; telex 21748; f. 1948; Chair VICTOR D. F. FAN; Gen. Man. K. T. FAN.

Chung Kuo Insurance Co Ltd: ICBC Bldg, 10th-12th Floors, 100 Chilin Rd, Taipei; tel. 5513345; telex 21573; f. 1931; fmrly China Insurance Co Ltd; Chair. GEORGE L. T. CHIEN; Pres. C. K. LIU.

CITC Life Insurance Co Ltd: 6th Floor, 122 Tun Hua North Rd, Taipei; tel. 7134511; f. 1963; Chair. L. S. KU; Gen. Man. C. Y. KU.

The First Insurance Co Ltd: 54 Chung Hsiao East Rd, Sec. 1, Taipei; tel. 3913271; telex 28971; f. 1962; Chair. Z. T. LEE; Gen. Man. C. H. LEE.

The First Life Insurance Co Ltd: 550 Chung Hsiao East Rd, Sec. 4, Taipei; tel. 7002727; f. 1962; Chair. C. C. CHUNG.

Kuo Hua Insurance Co Ltd: 166 Chang An East Rd, Sec. 2, Taipei; tel. 7514225; telex 22554; f. 1962; Chair. J. B. WANG; Gen. Man. C. H. CHAN.

Kuo Hua Life Insurance Co Ltd: 4-6th Floor, 61 Chung Shan North Rd, Sec. 2, Taipei; tel. 5621101; telex 22486; f. 1963; Chair. JASON CHANG; Gen. Man. DANIEL I. M. OUNG.

Mingtai Fire and Marine Insurance Co Ltd: 156-1 Sung Chiang Rd, Taipei; tel. 5711231; telex 22792; f. 1961; Chair. P. C. LIN; Gen. Man. H. T. CHEN.

Nan Shan Life Insurance Co Ltd: 302 Ming Chung East Rd, Taipei; tel. 5013333; telex 11868; f. 1963; Chair. K. K. TSE; Gen. Man. W. T. KOAY.

Shin Kong Fire and Marine Insurance Co Ltd: 9-12th Floor, 13 Chien Kuo North Rd, Taipei; tel. 5415335; telex 11393; f. 1963; Chair. ANTHONY T. S. WU; Gen. Man. Y. H. CHANG.

Shin Kong Life Insurance Co Ltd: 123 Nan King East Rd, Sec. 2, Taipei; tel. 5515161; telex 21471; f. 1963; Chair. EUGENE T. C. WU; Gen. Man. WU CHIA-LU.

South China Insurance Co Ltd: 5th Floor, 560 Chung Hsiao East Rd, Sec. 4, Taipei; tel. 7038418; telex 21977; f. 1963; Chair. C. F. LIAO; Gen. Man. C. C. CHUNG.

Tai Ping Insurance Co Ltd: 550 Chung Hsiao East Rd, 3rd-5th Floors, Sec. 4, Taipei; tel. 7002700; telex 21641; f. 1929; Chair. GEORGE Y. L. WU; Gen. Man. C. C. HSU.

Taiwan Fire and Marine Insurance Co Ltd: 49 Kuan Chien Rd, Taipei; tel. 3317261; telex 21694; f. 1946; Chair. J. C. WANG; Gen. Man. K. Y. LU.

Taiwan Insurance Co Ltd: 59 Kuan Tsien Rd, Taipei; tel. 3819678; telex 21735; f. 1961; Chair. KUN-CHUNG LIN; Gen. Man. CHEN LANG-HWA.

Taiwan Life Insurance Co Ltd: 45 Kuan Chien Rd, Taipei; tel. 3116411; f. 1947; Chair. YUEH-AY WU; Gen. Man. L. C. HUNG.

Union Insurance Co Ltd: 2nd Floor, 219 Chung Hsiao East Rd, Sec. 4, Taipei; tel. 7765587; telex 27616; f. 1963; Chair. Y. T. WANG; Gen. Man. FRANK S. WANG.

Trade and Industry

CHAMBER OF COMMERCE

General Chamber of Commerce of the Republic of China: 390 Fu Hsing South Rd, 6th Floor, Sec. 1, Taipei; tel. 7012671; telex 11396; Chair. WANG YOU-THENG; Sec.-Gen. CHIANG CHI-LIN.

CHINA (TAIWAN)

TRADE AND INDUSTRIAL ORGANIZATIONS

China External Trade Development Council: 333 Keelung Rd, 4th–7th Floors, Sec. 1, Taipei 10548; tel. 7382345; telex 21676; trade promotion body; Sec.-Gen. CHIANG PIN-KUNG.

China Productivity Centre: 340 Tun Hua North Rd, 2nd Floor, Taipei; tel. 7137731; telex 22954; f. 1955; industrial management and technical consultants; Gen. Man. CASPER T. Y. SHIH.

Chinese National Association of Industry and Commerce: 390 Fu Hsing South Rd, 13th Floor, Sec. 1, Taipei; tel. 7070111; telex 10774; Chair. KOO CHEN-FU; Sec.-Gen. WU TSU-PING.

Chinese National Federation of Industries: 390 Fu Hsing South Rd, 12th Floor, Sec. 1, Taipei; tel. 7033500; telex 14565; f. 1948; 134 mem. asscns; Chair. HSUI SHENG-FA; Sec.-Gen. HO CHUN-YIH.

Taiwan Handicraft Promotion Centre: 1 Hsu Chow Rd, Taipei; tel. 3217233; telex 28944; f. 1956; Chair. PHILLIP P. C. LIU; Sec.-Gen. Y. C. WANG.

Trading Department of Central Trust of China: 49 Wuchang St, Sec. 1, Taipei; tel. 3111511; telex 26254; f. 1935; export and import agent for private and govt-owned enterprises.

CO-OPERATIVES

In December 1987 there were 4,426 co-operatives, with a total membership of 4,115,999 people and total capital of NT $10,357.7m. Of the specialized co-operatives the most important was the consumers' co-operative (3,616 co-ops; 2,589,872 mems; cap. NT $192.9m.).

The centre of co-operative financing is the Co-operative Bank of Taiwan (see Finance section), owned jointly by the Taiwan government and 605 co-operative units. The Co-operative Institute (f. 1918) and the Co-operative League (f. 1940), which has 424 institutional and 4,533 individual members, exist to further the co-operative movement's national and international interests; departments of co-operative business have been set up on three university campuses.

RURAL RECONSTRUCTION

Council of Agriculture (COA): 37 Nanhai Rd, Taipei 10728; tel. 3317541; f. 1984 to replace the Council for Agricultural Planning and Development (CAPD), and the Bureau of Agriculture (BOA); govt agency directly under the Executive Yuan, with ministerial status; administration of all affairs related to food, crops, forestry, fisheries and the animal industry; promotes technology and provides external assistance; Chair. Y. H. YU; Vice-Chair. C. C. KOH, M. Y. TJIU; Sec.-Gen. H. Y. CHEN.

TRADE UNIONS

Chinese Federation of Labour: 201-18 Tun Hua North Rd, 11th Floor, Taipei; tel. 7135111; f. 1948; mems: c. 2,758 unions representing 2,074,734 workers; Pres. HSIEH SHEN-SAN; Gen. Sec. CHIU CHING-HWUI.

National Federations

Chinese Federation of Postal Workers: 45 Chungking South Rd, 9th Floor, Sec. 2, Taipei 107; tel. 3921380; f. 1930; 23,278 mems; Pres. KO YU-CHIN.

Chinese National Federation of Railway Workers: 107 Chengchou Rd, Taipei; tel. 5119090; f. 1947; 21,527 mems; Chair. WANG TJU-WEI.

National Chinese Seamen's Union: 115 Hang-Chow South Rd, 2nd Floor, Sec. 1, Taipei; tel. 3941321; f. 1913; 27,940 mems; Pres. KING TI-HSIEN.

Regional Federations

Taiwan Federation of Textile and Dyeing Industry Workers' Unions (TFTDWU): 2 Lane 64, Chung Hsiao East Rd, Sec. 2, Taipei; tel. 3415627; f. 1957; 33,409 mems; Chair. LI HSIN-NAN.

Taiwan Provincial Federation of Labour: 4 Roosevelt Rd, 11th Floor, Sec. 2, Taipei; tel. 3916241; f. 1948; 59 mem. unions and 1.2m. mems; Pres. PENG KUANG-CHENG; Sec.-Gen. HUANG YAO-TUNG.

Transport

RAILWAYS

Taiwan Railway Administration (TRA): 2 Yen Ping North Rd, Sec. 1, Taipei; tel. 5511131; telex 21837; f. 1891; a public utility under the provincial govt of Taiwan; operates both the west line and east line systems, with a route length of 1,074.9 km; the west line is the main trunk line from Keelung, in the north, to Kaohsiung, in the south, with several branches; electrification of the main trunk line was completed in 1979; the east line runs along the east coast, linking Hualien with Taitung; the north link line, with a length of 82.3 km from New Suao to Tienpu, connecting Suao and Hualien, was opened in 1980; Man. Dir CHANG SHOU-TSEN.

There are also 1,601 km of private narrow-gauge track, operated by the Taiwan Sugar Corpn, the Forestry Administration and other organizations. These railroads are mostly used for freight but they also provide public passenger and freight services which connect with those of the TRA.

ROADS

There were 19,946 km of highways in 1987, most of them asphalt-paved. The North–South Freeway was completed in 1978. Construction of the Northern Taiwan Second Freeway began in July 1987 and was scheduled to be completed by the end of 1991.

Taiwan Highway Bureau: 70 Chung Hsiao West Rd, Sec. 1, Taipei; tel. 3110929; f. 1946; Dir-Gen. CHI-CHANG YEN.

Taiwan Motor Transport Co Ltd: 17 Hsu Chang St, 5th Floor, Taipei; tel. 3715364; f. 1980; operates national bus service; Chair. HSU JING-YUAN; Gen. Man. SHU LUNG-TAN.

SHIPPING

Taiwan has four international ports: Kaohsiung, Keelung, Taichung and Hualien. In 1987 the merchant fleet had a total displacement of 4,625,000 grt.

Evergreen Marine Corpn: 330 Minsheng East Rd, Taipei; tel. 5057766; telex 11476; f. 1968; 56 container vessels, 1 training ship; world-wide container liner services from the Far East to the USA, the Caribbean, the Mediterranean, Europe and South-East Asia; Chair. CHANG YUNG-FA; Pres. FRANK J. R. HSA.

Far Eastern Navigation Corpn Ltd: 348 Ming-Sheng East Rd, 5th Floor, Taipei; 1 bulk carrier; Chair. W. H. E. HSU.

First Steamship Co Ltd: 15 Chi Nan Rd, 7th Floor, Sec. 1, Taipei; tel. 3949412; telex 11288; 3 cargo vessels; world-wide services; Chair. S. H. HSU; Pres. S. C. CHU.

Great Pacific Navigation Co Ltd: 79 Chung Shan North Rd, 2nd Floor, Sec. 2, Taipei; tel. 5713211; telex 21983; 1 reefer vessel; fruit and refrigeration cargo services world-wide; Chair. CHEN CHA-MOU.

Taiwan Navigation Co Ltd: 7th Floor, 17 Hsuchang St, Taipei; tel. 3113882; telex 11233; 4 bulk carriers, 4 tankers, 2 barges, 3 general cargo, 2 container vessels, 2 pushers, 1 refrigerator, 1 passenger vessel; Chair. T. H. CHEN; Pres. L. S. CHEN.

Uniglory Marine Corpn: 3rd Floor, 336 Minsheng East Rd, Taipei; tel. 5019001; telex 24720; 12 container vessels; Chair. LOH YAO-FOA; Pres. LEE MAN-CHI.

Waywiser Navigation Corpn Ltd: 200 Sunkiang Rd, 7th Floor, Taipei; tel. 5221311; telex 23948; 3 bulk carriers; Chair. HSU AH-CHEN.

Yangming Marine Transport Corpn: Hwai Ning Bldg, 4th Floor, 53 Hwai Ning St, Taipei; tel. 3812911; telex 11572; 20 container vessels, 4 multi-purpose vessels, 2 ore carriers, 3 bulk carriers, 3 tankers, 1 reefer; Chair. MENG-BING CHIH; Pres. HUNG-WEI KUO.

CIVIL AVIATION

There are two international airports, Chiang Kai-shek (Taoyuan) near Taipei, which opened in 1979, and Kaohsiung. The former international airport at Sungshan is now used for domestic flights.

China Air Lines Ltd (CAL): 131 Nanking East Rd, Sec. 3, Taipei; tel. 7152626; telex 11346; f 1959; domestic services and international services to Hong Kong, Indonesia, Japan, Malaysia, the Philippines, Saudi Arabia, Singapore, Thailand, the Republic of Korea, the Netherlands, UAE and the USA; Chair. YEUH WU; Pres. Gen. CHI JUNG-CHUN; fleet of 2 Boeing 767, 4 737, 10 747, 6 Airbus-300. Taiwan has also placed an order for 3 A300-600R passenger jets, which are due to be delivered in late 1989.

Far Eastern Air Transport Corpn: 5, Alley 123, Lane 405, Tun Hua North Rd, Taipei; telex 11639; f. 1957; domestic services and chartered flights; Chair. LINDA HWOO; Pres. T. C. HWOO; fleet of 8 Boeing 737.

Tourism

The principal tourist attractions are the festivals, the ancient art treasures and the island scenery. In 1987 there were 1,760,948 foreign visitors (including overseas Chinese) to Taiwan.

Tourism Bureau, Ministry of Communications: 280 Chung Hsiao East Rd, 9th Floor, Sec. 4, Taipei; tel. 7218541; telex 26408; f. 1966; Dir-Gen. HUNTER FU.

CHINA (TAIWAN)

Taiwan Visitors' Association: 111 Minchuan East Rd, 5th Floor, Taipei; tel. 5943261; telex 20335; f. 1956; promotes domestic and international tourism; Chair. RICHARD C. C. CHAO.

Atomic Energy

Three nuclear power plants were operational in 1987. Nuclear power generation provided about 48.5% of Taiwan's total power generation in 1987.

Atomic Energy Council (AEC): 67 Lane 144, Keelung Rd, Sec. 4, 10772 Taipei; tel. 3924180; telex 26554; f. 1955; promotes the advancement of nuclear science and technology, enforces safety requirements; Chair. YEN CHEN-HSING; Sec.-Gen. LIU KUANG-CHI.

Institute of Nuclear Energy Research (INER): POB 3, Lung Tan 32500; tel. 3145384; telex 34154; f. 1968; national nuclear research centre; Dir JEN-CHANG CHOU.

COLOMBIA

Introductory Survey

Location, Climate, Language, Religion, Flag, Capital

The Republic of Colombia lies in the north-west of South America, with the Caribbean Sea to the north and the Pacific Ocean to the west. Its continental neighbours are Venezuela and Brazil to the east, and Peru and Ecuador to the south, while Panama connects it with Central America. The coastal areas have a tropical rain forest climate, the plateaux are temperate, and in the Andes mountains there are areas of permanent snow. The language is Spanish. Almost all of the inhabitants profess Christianity, and about 95% are Roman Catholics. There are small Protestant and Jewish minorities. The national flag (proportions 3 by 2) has three horizontal stripes, of yellow (one-half of the depth), dark blue and red. The capital is Bogotá.

Recent History

Colombia was under Spanish rule from the 16th century until 1819, when it achieved independence as part of Gran Colombia, which included Ecuador, Panama and Venezuela. Ecuador and Venezuela seceded in 1830, when Colombia (then including Panama) became a separate republic. In 1903 the province of Panama successfully rebelled and became an independent country. For more than a century, Colombia has been dominated by two political parties, the Conservatives (Partido Conservador) and the Liberals (Partido Liberal), whose rivalry has often led to violence. Liberal governments held power in 1860–84 and 1930–46, with Conservative governments in 1884–1930 and 1946–53. From 1922 to 1953, with one exception, every President of Colombia completed his four-year term of office. The assassination in April 1948 of Bogotá's left-wing Liberal mayor, Jorge Eliécer Gaitán, led to intense political violence, amounting to civil war, between Conservative and Liberal factions. According to official estimates, lawlessness between 1949 and 1958, known as 'La Violencia', caused the deaths of about 280,000 people.

President Laureano Gómez, who had been elected 'unopposed' in November 1949, ruled as a dictator until his overthrow by a coup in June 1953, when power was seized by Gen. Gustavo Rojas Pinilla. President Rojas established a right-wing dictatorship but, following widespread rioting, he was deposed in May 1957, when a five-man military junta took power.

In an attempt to restore peace and stability, the Conservative and Liberal Parties agreed to co-operate in a National Front. Under this arrangement, the presidency was to be held by Liberals and Conservatives in rotation, while Cabinet portfolios would be divided equally between the two parties and both would have an equal number of seats in each house of the bicameral Congress. In December 1957, in Colombia's first vote on the basis of universal adult suffrage, this agreement was overwhelmingly approved by a referendum. It was subsequently incorporated in Colombia's Constitution.

In May 1958 the first presidential election under the amended Constitution was won by the National Front candidate, Dr Alberto Lleras Camargo, a Liberal who had been President in 1945–46. He took office in August 1958, when the junta relinquished power. During the rule of President Lleras Camargo, who was in power until 1962, left-wing guerrilla groups were established in Colombia. As provided by the 1957 agreement, he was succeeded by a Conservative, Dr Guillermo León Valencia, who held office until 1966, when another Liberal, Dr Carlos Lleras Restrepo, was elected. Despite continuing political violence, President Lleras Restrepo was able to bring about some recovery in Colombia's economy.

At the presidential election of 19 April 1970, the National Front candidate, Dr Misael Pastrana Borrero of the Conservative Party, narrowly defeated Gen. Rojas, the former dictator, who campaigned as leader of the Alianza Nacional Popular (ANAPO), with policies that had considerable appeal for the poorer sections of the population. At elections to Congress, held simultaneously, the National Front lost its majority in each of the two houses, while ANAPO became the main opposition group in each. The result of the presidential election was challenged by supporters of ANAPO, who demonstrated against alleged electoral fraud. However, the result was officially upheld, after four recounts, and in August 1970 Dr Pastrana took office as President. In June 1971 ANAPO was officially constituted as a political party, advocating a populist programme of 'Colombian socialism'. However, some ANAPO supporters, in reaction to the disputed 1970 election results, formed an armed wing, the Movimiento 19 de Abril (M-19), which began guerrilla activity against the Government. They were joined by dissident members of a pro-Soviet guerrilla group, the Fuerzas Armadas Revolucionarias de Colombia (FARC), which had been established in 1966.

The bipartisan form of government ended formally with the presidential and legislative elections of April 1974, although the 1974–78 Cabinet remained subject to the parity agreement. The Conservative and Liberal Parties together won an overwhelming majority of seats in Congress, and the vote for ANAPO was greatly reduced. The presidential election was won by the Liberal Party candidate, Dr Alfonso López Michelsen, who received 56% of the total votes. President López took office in August 1974, promising wide-ranging reforms and a more equitable distribution of income. His failure to achieve these aims led to strikes, rioting and increased guerrilla violence. Meanwhile, Gen. Rojas died in January 1975 and was succeeded as leader of ANAPO by his daughter, María Eugenia Rojas de Moreno Díaz, who had been the party's presidential candidate in the 1974 election.

At elections to Congress in February 1978, the Liberal Party won a clear majority in both houses, and in June the Liberal Party candidate, Dr Julio César Turbay Ayala, won the presidential election. President Turbay kept to the National Front agreement, and attempted to tackle the problems of urban terrorism and drug trafficking, but had little success. In October 1981 a Peace Commission was set up under ex-President Lleras Restrepo. In early 1982 the guerrillas suffered heavy losses after successful counter-insurgency operations, combined with the activities of a new anti-guerrilla group which was associated with drug-smuggling enterprises, the Muerte a Secuestradores (MAS, Death to Kidnappers), whose targets later became trade union leaders, academics and human rights activists.

At congressional elections in March 1982, the Liberal Party maintained its majority in both the House of Representatives and the Senate. In the presidential election in May, the Conservative candidate, Dr Belisario Betancur Cuartas, received the most votes, benefiting from a division within the Liberal Party. President Betancur, who took office in August 1982, declared a broad amnesty for guerrillas in November, reconvened the Peace Commission and ordered an investigation into the MAS. Several hundred political prisoners were released. He embarked on a programme of radical reforms. However, the internal pacification campaign, which was begun in November 1982, met with only moderate success. An estimated 2,000 guerrillas accepted the Government's offer of amnesty.

In February 1984 President Betancur announced the resumption of talks between the Peace Commission and the principal guerrilla organizations. In late March the Peace Commission and the FARC agreed conditions for a cease-fire, which was to take effect for one year from May. Under the terms of the accord, the Government agreed to the demilitarization of rural areas. The FARC was to be allowed to assume an active political role. In July, following protracted negotiations, the M-19 group (now operating as a left-wing guerrilla movement) and the Ejército Popular de Liberación (EPL) agreed to a cease-fire but refused to relinquish their weapons. In spite of the murder of the M-19's founder, Carlos Toledo Plata, and subsequent reprisals by those guerrillas still active, the peace accord was signed in August. Factions of the FARC, EPL and the M-19 group which were opposed to the truce continued to conduct guerrilla warfare against the Government.

A major set-back to the Government's campaign for internal peace occurred in May 1984, when the Minister of Justice, Rodrigo Lara Bonilla, was assassinated. His murder was regarded as a consequence of his energetic attempts to eradicate the flourishing drugs industry, and Colombia's leading drugs dealers were implicated in the killing. The Government immediately declared a nation-wide state of siege and announced its intention to enforce its hitherto unobserved extradition treaty with the USA. The state of siege was partially lifted in October 1984.

Although members of the M-19 had begun to conduct a lawful political campaign in Colombia's main cities, reports of skirmishes between the guerrillas and the armed forces increased in early 1985. Relations between the M-19 and the armed forces continued to deteriorate, and in June the M-19 formally withdrew from the cease-fire agreement, accusing the armed forces of attempting to sabotage the truce. In November a dramatic siege by the M-19 at the Palace of Justice in Bogotá, during which more than 90 people (including 41 guerrillas and 11 judges) were killed, resulted in severe public criticism of the Government and the armed forces for their handling of events. Negotiations with the M-19 were suspended indefinitely. After three years, therefore, the only successful aspects of the Government's internal pacification programme had been the FARC's adherence to the cease-fire agreement and its foundation of a political party, the Unión Patriótica (UP), in May 1985. In response to the siege and the subsequent natural disaster caused by the eruption of the Nevado del Ruiz volcano (also in November 1985), the Government declared a state of economic and social emergency.

At congressional elections in March 1986, the traditional wing of the Partido Liberal secured a clear victory over the Partido Conservador and obtained 49% of the votes cast. The Nuevo Liberalismo wing of the Partido Liberal received only 7% of the votes and subsequently withdrew from the forthcoming presidential election. The UP won seats in both houses of Congress. At the presidential election in May, Dr Virgilio Barco Vargas, candidate of the Partido Liberal, was elected president with 58% of the votes cast. The large majority that the Partido Liberal secured at both elections obliged the Partido Conservador to form the first formal opposition to a government for 30 years. The Partido Liberal's dominant position was consolidated by the Conservatives' refusal to participate as the minority party in a coalition government with the Liberals.

On taking office in August 1986, President Barco Vargas affirmed that his Government's principal task was to solve the problem of political violence and that the new administration was committed to the peace process that had been established by former President Betancur. It was hoped that the administration's plans would benefit from the FARC's decision, in March 1986, to sign an indefinite cease-fire agreement. Further priorities for the Government were to be a campaign against poverty and the maintenance of Colombia's programme to combat the cultivation and trafficking of illicit drugs.

Despite initial optimism that the truce between the Government and the FARC would prevail and that the UP would be able to participate fully in the political process, it became apparent during 1987 that such optimism was unfounded. The deterioration in relations between the Government and the guerrillas had been largely precipitated by the Government's decision to disband the independent commissions responsible for monitoring and mediating in disputes between the authorities and guerrillas. Moreover, there was considerable hostility towards the Government because of its apparent reluctance to act against the campaign of paramilitary 'death squads' to assassinate members of the UP: between 1985 and October 1987 it was estimated that more than 450 members of the UP had been killed by such groups. In October the murder of Dr Jaime Pardo Leal, the President of the UP, heightened social tensions and led to widespread protests—many, specifically, against the Government's inadequate response to the mounting political violence. The crisis was compounded, later in the month, by the decision of six guerrilla groups, including the FARC, ELN and M-19, to form a joint front, the Coordinadora Guerrillera Simón Bolívar (CGSB). Despite the resumption of talks between representatives of the Government and the guerrillas in late October, political violence and unrest continued.

Although the Barco Government had affirmed its commitment to eradicate Colombia's role in international drugs smuggling, it was unable to make any significant progress in 1987. In December 1986 leading drugs dealers were held responsible for the murder of a prominent newspaper director in Bogotá, and in January 1987 drugs traffickers were implicated in an attempt to assassinate the Colombian ambassador to Hungary (a former Minister of Justice). Although the Government authorized an extension of police powers against drugs dealers, its campaign was severely hampered by the Colombian Supreme Court's rulings, in December 1986 and June 1987, that Colombia's extradition treaty with the USA was unconstitutional. The inadequacy of the Government's efforts was underlined, in December, when Colombian authorities first declined to extradite, and subsequently released from custody, Jorge Luis Ochoa, a leading international cocaine trafficker. In January 1988 the internal crisis worsened, following the assassination of the Attorney-General, apparently on the orders of leading drugs dealers.

The Government responded to the assassination by issuing a new anti-terrorism decree, under which the armed forces were to be increased and rewards were to be offered to informants. In addition, the Government proposed to hold a plebiscite on the question of changes to the Constitution to counter guerrilla warfare. (The plebiscite was initially scheduled to be held concurrently with mayoral elections in March 1988, but was subsequently postponed to October. However, the Government eventually withdrew its proposal, after it was deemed to be unconstitutional by the Council of State.) The first direct elections for 1,009 mayoralties were held on 13 March. Poor results for the Partido Liberal, which won in 427 municipalities, were attributed to divisions within the party. The Partido Social Conservador won in 415 municipalities, including Bogotá and Medellín. The electoral campaigns of all parties were disrupted by violence, and more than 30 candidates were killed.

In late May 1988 Colombia's internal crisis worsened, following the abduction by the M-19 group of Dr Alvaro Gómez Hurtado, a former presidential candidate of the Partido Social Conservador. Widespread protests were held in support of his release, and in June the Cabinet resigned, under public pressure. Gómez Hurtado was eventually freed by the M-19 in July, and his release appeared to give renewed impetus to the peace process; a Day of National Dialogue was held in late July, attended by representatives of political parties, trade unions and the Roman Catholic Church, although not by the Government or guerrilla groups. A Comisión de Convivencia Democrática (Commission of Democratic Cohabitation) was subsequently established, with the aim of holding further meetings between all sides in the conflict.

Moreover, at the beginning of September 1988 President Barco announced a new peace initiative, composed of three phases: pacification; transition; and definitive reintegration into the democratic system. Under the plan, the Government was committed to entering into a dialogue with those guerrilla groups that renounced violence and intended to resume civilian life. However, the Government refused to recognize territories controlled by the guerrillas, and the armed forces were to be given full powers to 'confront and punish' participants in acts of violence, terrorism or subversion. The plan encountered a favourable public response, and the CGSB was reported to have approved the President's proposals, while maintaining its demands for the suspension of the state of siege, the eradication of paramilitary groups and the repeal of the anti-terrorism decree.

In October 1988, despite reports of the guerrillas' willingness to resume the peace process, a major new offensive was launched by the leading guerrilla groups. Moreover, in November the President's effort to secure a cease-fire was placed in jeopardy by an appeal by the Minister of Defence for an 'all-out offensive' against the guerrillas. President Barco responded by dismissing the Minister and making new appointments to the military high command. However, within a few weeks of assuming his post, an unsuccessful attempt was made to assassinate the new Minister, Gen. Manuel Guerrero Paz. This development, coupled with the massacre of 43 people by a right-wing 'death squad' in the town of Segovia in November, prompted the Government to enact new measures to combat terrorism. In December it was estimated that some 18,000 murders had occurred in Colombia in 1988, of which at least 3,600 were attributed to political motives or related to drugs trafficking. However, in January 1989 it was reported that an agreement had been reached between the Government and the M-19, under which a direct dialogue was to be initiated between all political parties in Congress and the CGSB, to seek a political solution to the unrest.

COLOMBIA

During 1988 no significant progress was made by the Government in its attempt to eradicate the illegal drugs trade. Despite the decision of a US Court to sentence Carlos Lehder Rivas, a leading member of the Medellín cartel of drugs smugglers, to life imprisonment in July, other leading drugs traffickers remained at liberty within Colombia, benefiting from the continuing dispute over the country's extradition policy.

Colombia has a long-standing border dispute with Venezuela. In May 1987 Venezuela rejected Colombia's proposal for a negotiated settlement of the dispute. In August the disagreement flared again, when Venezuela claimed that a Colombian naval vessel and Colombian aircraft had violated its territorial waters and airspace. In late October 1988 14 Colombian fishermen were shot dead by Venezuelan soldiers at El Amparo, on the river border. The incident revived the controversy over military activities along the border, and it was suggested that the massacre may have been related to the large-scale smuggling of subsidized Venezuelan goods or to drugs trafficking. In 1980 Nicaragua laid claim to the Colombian-controlled islands of Providencia and San Andrés. Colombia has a territorial dispute with Honduras over cays in the San Andrés and Providencia archipelago. In October 1986 the Colombian Senate approved a delimitation treaty of marine and submarine waters in the Caribbean Sea, which had been signed by the Governments of Colombia and Honduras in August. Former President Betancur's efforts to reverse Colombian foreign policy led to improved relations with Nicaragua and Cuba, and an attempt to revive the Andean Pact. As a member of the Contadora group, Colombia sought a new peace initiative for Central America and supported the withdrawal of US forces from El Salvador and Honduras.

Government

Executive power is exercised by the President (assisted by a Cabinet), who is elected for a four-year term by universal adult suffrage. Legislative power is vested in the bicameral Congress, consisting of the Senate (112 members elected for four years) and the House of Representatives (199 members elected for four years). The country is divided into 24 Departments, three Intendencies and six Commissaries.

Defence

At 18 years of age, every male (with the exception of students) must present himself as a candidate for military service of between one and two years. In June 1988 the strength of the army was 69,000, the navy 10,600 (including 5,000 marines) and the air force 6,700. The paramilitary police force numbers about 55,000 men. Under the 1987 budget, defence expenditure was estimated at 100,445m. pesos.

Economic Affairs

Despite Colombia's internal problems in recent years, the economy has remained buoyant. In 1987, according to estimates by the World Bank, the country's gross national product (GNP), measured at average 1985–87 prices, was US $36,027m., equivalent to $1,220 per head. Between 1980 and 1987, it was estimated, GNP grew, in real terms, at an average annual rate of 2.4%, with real GNP per head increasing by 0.6% per year.

The economy depends principally on coffee, of which Colombia is the world's second largest producer, with a 16% share of the world market. Sales of coffee accounted for an estimated 62% of Colombia's legal export earnings in 1986, but the proportion declined to an estimated 43% in 1987. Production rose from 8m. bags (each of 60 kg) in 1974/75 to 13.3m. bags in 1980/81, and has subsequently averaged 11m.–12m. bags per year. However, output was expected to decline from an estimated 13.4m. bags in 1987/88 to 10m. in 1988/89. Exports declined to 9m. bags in 1981/82, as a result of a reduction in demand, but increased to 9.7m. bags in 1984/85 and to 11.5m. bags in 1985/86. In 1986/87 the sector benefited from a poor coffee harvest in Brazil and high international prices for coffee, achieving exports of more than 12m. bags and generating an estimated US $2,982m. in export earnings; Colombia became the world's leading exporter of coffee. However, declines in world prices in late 1986 and 1987 resulted in a fall in exports to 9.4m. bags in 1987/88, with a decline in earnings to $1,675m. Other major problems hampering the industry were overproduction and the occurrence of coffee rust fungus in Colombia.

Other important cash crops are cotton, bananas, sugar cane, tobacco, cocoa and cut flowers. The principal food crops are rice, sorghum, maize, wheat and barley. Agricultural output accounted for about 17% of Colombia's gross domestic product (GDP) in 1987. The output of the agricultural sector was estimated to have expanded by 4.5% in 1987 and by 4% in 1988. In recent years the fruit industry, timber production and shrimp farming have recorded dramatic growth. Bananas contribute more than 5% of export revenue, but in 1987 and 1988 production was severely disrupted by violence and strikes in Urabá, one of the main banana-producing areas. In May 1986 the World Bank allocated three loans amounting to US $250m. to Colombia for the agricultural sector. The Barco Government has announced plans to attract more private investment to the agricultural and agro-business sectors. In early 1987 the Government announced plans to spend 1,650,000m. pesos in 1987–91 on schemes to benefit the underprivileged and underdeveloped regions, including the redistribution of 470,000 ha of land. In recent years there has been renewed interest in the issue of land reform, as 68% of cultivable land is owned by only 4% of the population, and 50% of the rural population have no access to land. Moreover, an estimated 45% of Colombians live in a state of poverty, including 42.6% of rural inhabitants. The illegal trade in Colombian hemp (marijuana) and cocaine has increased dramatically in recent years, and it is believed that contraband exports of these drugs probably exceed the value of legal exports. Colombia is reported to supply an estimated 75% of all cocaine available in the USA. In addition, some 1.7m. Colombians are believed to be involved in the illegal drugs trade, representing an estimated 15% of the economically active population.

Manufacturing accounts for more than 20% of the GDP, and prominent industries are food processing, textiles, chemicals, metal products and transport equipment. By 1981, when production fell by 1% after an increase of 2.6% in 1980, the sector was suffering from loss of competitiveness abroad, and industrialists were seeking the imposition of import tariffs. In 1983 the Betancur Government introduced controls on imports and the availability of foreign exchange, and in September a ban on the import of motor cars was imposed. Import controls were eased in September 1985 and again in September 1986. The output of the manufacturing sector increased by more than 6% in 1986 and by 8.8% during the first quarter of 1987. Further growth of 6.5% was estimated in 1988. Under the 1983–86 development plan, US $21,400m. was invested in 100 projects, including the development of electric energy, mining, transport and industry. Foreign investment in the sector between January and September 1987 amounted to $1,180m. The rapidly-developing construction industry, which accounts for almost 4% of GDP and grew by 35% in 1987, received an allocation of $2,900m. to provide 400,000 additional housing units and to generate 300,000 more jobs.

In March 1982 the World Bank made a loan of US $359m. (the largest ever in Latin America) for the Guavio hydroelectric project (capacity 1,600 MW), to be completed in the late 1980s. In February 1988 the IDB allocated a loan of $360m. for completion of the project. A further loan of $70m. from the IDB has been used to construct the San Carlos hydroelectric plant (capacity 620,000 kW), near Medellín, the second stage of which came into operation in 1987. There are plans to construct five small hydro plants with an initial installed capacity of 16,100 kW. The country's estimated total installed capacity is 93,000 MW. Hydroelectricity provided 73% of energy needs in 1983, compared with 17% in 1960. Between 1987 and 1990 the Government planned to reform the sector, at a projected cost of $3,200m. Funding was to be provided by various sources, including the World Bank, which in December 1987 allocated $300m. to the project.

Production of crude petroleum averaged 219,043 barrels per day (b/d) in 1970, but fell to 123,836 b/d in 1979. Output averaged 176,459 b/d in 1985, 302,140 b/d in 1986 and 359,481 b/d in 1987. Following significant discoveries at Caño Limón in Arauca, northern Colombia, and at Vichada, proven reserves were estimated to be 1,300m. barrels. Joint projects with foreign companies enabled Colombia to produce sufficient petroleum for both domestic consumption and export in 1986. In 1987 foreign earnings from sales of petroleum were estimated at $900m. In February 1987 the state petroleum company, ECOPETROL, revealed an ambitious five-year plan, with a projected cost of $3,500m., to guarantee Colombia's self-sufficiency in petroleum beyond 1993. Under the plan, new reserves of hydrocarbons were to be sought, and $1,000m. were to be invested in two new refineries. Although the sector's production capacity is 550,000 b/d, output is restricted to 415,000 b/d because of a shortage of refineries and pipelines. In recent years the main pipeline (784 km) linking Caño Limón to Coveñas has been the frequent target of bombings by the ELN guerrilla group. Such activities were reported to have reduced production to only 315,000 b/d during the first half of 1988, when output was originally scheduled to reach 420,000 b/d. In May 1985 the Government initiated a programme to produce fuel alcohol from sugar cane. Production of natural gas exceeds local needs. Known gas reserves total 4,716,000m. cu ft (133,500m. cu m). The Guajira field came into production in 1977. The gas will supply power for the proposed Palomino petro-chemical complex.

Colombia possesses the largest proven reserves of coal in Latin America. Total proven reserves are 21,000m. metric tons, and Colombia aims to supply 10% of the world market by 1999. The richest coalfield is at El Cerrejón (with estimated reserves of 16,000m. tons), for which Exxon undertook a US $3,200m. development contract in 1980. Production began in 1984 and was hoped to yield 15m. tons per year by 1989. Colombia began exporting coal in 1983, and exports were expected to increase from 3m. tons in 1985 to 27m. tons per year after 1990. Further developments are taking place at La Loma and La Jagua. In 1987, however, low world prices for coal resulted in the decision by the state coal company (CARBOCOL) to sell 49% of its interest in the El Cerrejón project, as it was unable to repay its outstanding debt on the project's capital cost. The Cerro Matoso nickel plant, costing $400m., was inaugurated in June 1982 and was expected to produce 22,600 metric tons for export annually. Proven reserves are 25m. tons, while total reserves are estimated to be 70m. tons. Colombia produces 95% of the world's emeralds. The principal emerald-mining areas are at Muzo, Coscuez and Chivor. Silver, platinum, lead, zinc, copper, mercury, limestone and phosphates are also mined, and there are substantial reserves of uranium. Considerable optimism surrounds the future of the gold-mining industry, following the discovery of extensive reserves, mainly in the Guainía region. Production increased from 14 metric tons in 1983 to 42 tons in 1986, and may reach 100 tons per year by 1990. The total output of the mining sector expanded at an average rate of 20% per year in 1980–87, and increased by an estimated 15% in 1988.

In the late 1960s and early 1970s, Colombia's economic development was more promising than in most Latin American countries, with the annual GDP growth rate averaging 6.2% between 1966 and 1976. By 1981 the growth rate had fallen to 2.1% (from 5.4% in 1979), and by 1983 it had fallen to 1.0%. The Government continued to borrow from abroad in order to maintain economic growth, and this contributed towards high interest rates and an inflation rate of 16.8% at the end of 1983, although Colombia continued to have a low rate of indebtedness, compared with the rest of Latin America, and remained the only Latin American country that was capable of raising syndicated loans on the international markets without difficulty. Colombia received authorization from the World Bank to borrow a further $9,600m. between 1983 and 1986, at a rate of $2,000m. per year. Although export earnings began to decline in 1981, the long-term outlook was encouraging because of developments in the mining industry, which over-took coffee in terms of foreign revenue in 1987.

In 1984 Colombia's economy was severely affected by the decline in domestic demand and the recession among its neighbours. The sharp drop in exports in 1982–83, coupled with the considerable flight of capital, resulted in a significant decline in reserves of foreign exchange, which fell from $3,489m. in December 1982 to $774m. in September 1984, before improving to $1,364m. at the end of the year. Unemployment rose from 8.9% of the labour force in 1982 to 13.4% in 1984. In addition, the banking sector was severely affected by the financial difficulties of several major private concerns and by its involvement with Colombia's 'parallel' economy, centred on the flourishing trade in illicit drugs. However, in 1984 GDP grew by 3.2%, in real terms, while the annual rate of inflation averaged 16.1%.

In May 1985 the Government reached agreement with the IMF on a programme of economic adjustment. Under the terms of the agreement, Colombia received no economic aid from the IMF but the Government was able to request new funds from other creditors. In June the Government and its commercial bank creditors agreed terms for a loan of $1,000m., to cover debt-servicing commitments in 1985–86. In June 1987 Colombia's commercial bank creditors approved its request for a new loan of $1,060m., to be used to finance projects in the electricity and coal sectors and for other public investment. The loan was subsequently reduced to $1,000m. and was to be disbursed in three tranches during 1988. In December 1988 Colombia reached a preliminary agreement with its creditor banks on the provision of new funds totalling $1,700m. Colombia had initially sought $1,850m. in funding, and the banks' reluctance to assist Colombia with new financing was considered to be an important factor in the country's decision, in December, to defer, for the first time ever, repayments of debt principal until March 1989. However, Colombia remains, with Paraguay, the only Latin American country not to have rescheduled its foreign debt since the onset of the debt crisis in 1982. By late 1988 the total foreign debt was estimated to be $16,500m., of which $11,500m. had been incurred by the public sector.

Following a succession of trade deficits on the balance of payments between 1980 and 1983, Colombia recorded a surplus of $246m. in 1984. Despite another deficit of $23m. in 1985, high world prices for coffee in 1985–86 enabled Colombia to record a trade surplus of $1,922m. in 1986 and contributed to GDP growth of 5.1% in that year. A surplus of $1,826m. was achieved in 1987. On taking office in August 1986, Colombia's new Liberal Government announced that the priorities of its economic policy would be to reduce unemployment (estimated at 13.4% of the labour force in March 1987); to implement agrarian reform; to eliminate the budget deficit (equivalent to 3.9% of GDP in 1985) and to stimulate export trade. Following the decision of the Andean Pact countries, in mid-1987, to provide each member country with the legal apparatus to pursue its own interpretation of the Pact's rules governing foreign investment, the Government planned to introduce new measures to enable foreign companies to participate in nearly all sectors of the Colombian economy. Economic growth of 5.6% was recorded in 1987, and reserves of foreign exchange have continued to increase, from US $2,556m. in December 1986 to $2,796m. in August 1987, and to $3,260m. in August 1988.

The unemployment rate had fallen to 10% by early 1988, although it was reported to have increased to 12% in April. The annual rate of inflation increased from 24.8% in 1987 to 28.1% in 1988. GDP growth of 4.5% was anticipated in 1988, when foreign investment in Colombia also increased substantially. Despite some industrial unrest (a general strike was held in October 1988) and internal violence, the prospects for continuing economic growth remained favourable.

Colombia is a member of ALADI (see p. 170) and the Andean Pact (p. 90).

Social Welfare

There is compulsory social security, paid for by the Government, employers and employees, and administered by the Institute of Social Security. It provides benefits for disability, old age, death, sickness, maternity, industrial accidents and unemployment. Large enterprises are required to provide life insurance schemes for their employees, and there is a comprehensive system of pensions. In 1977 there were 12,720 physicians working in Colombia, and in 1980 the country had 849 hospital establishments, with a total of 44,495 beds. Of total expenditure by the central Government in 1987, 68,498m. pesos (7.2%) was for health. In 1984 central government expenditure on social security and welfare amounted to 114,810m. pesos. The benefits of the health service do not reach all inhabitants, and in 1981 a report by the Family Welfare Institute estimated the level of infant mortality at 64 per 1,000 live births, one of the highest rates in the world.

Education

Primary education is free and compulsory for five years, to be undertaken by children between six and 12 years of age. No child may be admitted to secondary school unless these five years have been successfully completed. Secondary education, beginning at the age of 11, lasts for up to six years. Following completion of a first cycle of four years, pupils may pursue a further two years of vocational study, leading to the Bachiller examination. In 1985 the total enrolment at primary and secondary schools was equivalent to 82% of the school-age population. Primary enrolment included 75% of children in the relevant age-group. In 1986 there were 232 institutions of higher education. There are plans to construct an Open University to satisfy the increasing demand for higher education.

COLOMBIA   Introductory Survey, Statistical Survey

Expenditure on education by the central Government in 1987 was 215,106m. pesos, representing 22.5% of total spending. In 1988 the World Bank allocated a loan of US $100m. to finance the expansion and improvement of primary education, particularly in rural areas. The rate of adult illiteracy averaged 19.2% in 1973, but, according to estimates by UNESCO, declined to 11.9% (males 10.9%; females 12.9%) in 1985.

Public Holidays

1989: 2 January (for New Year's Day), 6 January (Epiphany), 19 March (St Joseph's Day), 23 March (Maundy Thursday), 24 March (Good Friday), 1 May (Labour Day), 4 May (Ascension Day), 25 May (Corpus Christi), 9 June (Thanksgiving), 29 June (SS. Peter and Paul), 20 July (Independence), 7 August (Battle of Boyacá), 15 August (Assumption), 12 October (Discovery of America), 1 November (All Saints' Day), 11 November (Independence of Cartagena), 8 December (Immaculate Conception), 25 December (Christmas Day).

1990: 1 January (New Year's Day), 6 January (Epiphany), 19 March (St Joseph's Day), 12 April (Maundy Thursday), 13 April (Good Friday), 1 May (Labour Day), 24 May (Ascension Day), 9 June (Thanksgiving), 14 June (Corpus Christi), 29 June (SS. Peter and Paul), 20 July (Independence), 7 August (Battle of Boyacá), 15 August (Assumption), 12 October (Discovery of America), 1 November (All Saints' Day), 11 November (Independence of Cartagena), 8 December (Immaculate Conception), 25 December (Christmas Day).

Weights and Measures

The metric system is in force.

Statistical Survey

Sources (unless otherwise stated): Departamento Administrativo Nacional de Estadística (DANE), Centro Administrativo Nacional (CAN), Avda Eldorado, Apdo Aéreo 80043, Bogotá; tel. 2691100; telex 044573; Banco de la República, Carrera 7, No 14-78, Apdo Aéreo 3531, Bogotá; tel. 2831111; telex 044560.

Area and Population

AREA, POPULATION AND DENSITY

Area (sq km)	
Total	1,141,748*
Population (census results)	
24 October 1973	22,915,229
15 October 1985	
Males	13,794,327
Females	14,072,999
Total	27,867,326
Density (per sq km) at October 1985	24.4

* 440,831 sq miles.

DEPARTMENTS (population at 15 October 1985)

Department	Population	Capital
Antioquia	3,888,067	Medellín
Atlántico	1,428,601	Barranquilla
Bogotá, DE	3,982,941	Bogotá*
Bolívar	1,197,623	Cartagena
Boyacá	1,097,618	Tunja
Caldas	838,094	Manizales
Caquetá	214,473	Florencia
Cauca	795,838	Popayán
César	584,631	Valledupar
Chocó	242,768	Quibdo
Córdoba	913,636	Montería
Cundinamarca	1,382,360	Bogotá*
La Guajira	255,310	Riohacha
Huila	647,756	Neiva
Magdalena	769,141	Santa Marta
Meta	412,312	Villaricencio
Nariño	1,019,098	Pasto
Norte de Santander	883,884	Cúcuta
Quindío	377,860	Armenia
Risaralda	625,451	Pereira
Santander del Sur	1,438,226	Bucaramanga
Sucre	529,059	Sincelejo
Tolima	1,051,852	Ibagué
Valle del Cauca	2,847,087	Cali
Intendencies		
Arauca	70,085	Arauca
Casanare	110,253	Yopal
San Andrés y Providencia Islands	35,936	San Andrés

Department—continued	Population	Capital
Commissaries		
Amazonas	30,327	Leticia
Guainía	9,214	Obando
Guaviare†	35,305	San José de Guaviare
Putumayo	119,815	Mocoa
Vaupés	18,935	Mitú
Vichada‡	13,770	Puerto Carreño
Total§	27,867,326	

* The capital city, Bogotá, is the capital of two departments: Bogotá, DE, and Cundinamarca. The city's population is included only in Bogotá, DE.
† Not exact.
‡ Area not covered by the census.
§ Excludes population of Armero.

PRINCIPAL TOWNS
(population at 15 October 1985)

Bogotá, DE (capital)	3,982,941	Cúcuta	379,478
Medellín	1,468,089	Bucaramanga	352,326
Cali	1,350,565	Manizales	299,352
Barranquilla	899,781	Ibagué	292,965
Cartagena	531,426	Pereira	287,999

BIRTHS, MARRIAGES AND DEATHS*

	Registered live births	Registered deaths
1982	837,932	137,678
1983	828,348	140,298
1984	825,842	137,189
1985	835,922	153,947

1986: Registered deaths 146,346.

Registered marriages: 102,448 in 1980; 95,845 in 1981.

* Data are tabulated by year of registration rather than by year of occurrence, although registration is incomplete. According to UN estimates, the average annual rates in 1980–85 were: births 31.0 per 1,000; deaths 7.7 per 1,000.

COLOMBIA

ECONOMICALLY ACTIVE POPULATION
(household survey, 1980)

Agriculture, hunting, forestry and fishing	2,412,413
Mining and quarrying	49,740
Manufacturing	1,136,735
Electricity, gas and water	44,233
Construction	242,191
Trade, restaurants and hotels	1,261,633
Transport, storage and communications	352,623
Financing, insurance, real estate and business services	278,210
Community, social and personal services	1,998,460
Activities not adequately described	690,762
Total Labour Force	**8,467,000***

* Males 6,247,000; females 2,220,000.

Agriculture

PRINCIPAL CROPS ('000 metric tons)

	1986	1987	1988*
Wheat	81.7	74.2	81.0
Rice (paddy)	1,631.8	1,864.6	1,866.8
Barley	73.2	91.6	99.9
Maize	788.1	859.6	999.5
Sorghum	599.9	703.8	796.9
Potatoes	2,091.1	2,242.6	2,461.6
Cassava (Manioc)	1,334.9	1,285.3	1,321.5
Soybeans	167.0	128.2	153.2
Seed cotton	337.7	320.5	410.0
Cane sugar (raw)	1,296.9	1,320.6*	1,315.0
Bananas	1,036.7	1,105.1*	1,140.0
Plantains	2,301.6	2,478.4*	2,560.4
Coffee (green)	642.7	778.4	393.9†
Cocoa beans	46.7	51.0	55.4
Tobacco (blond and black)	28.6	35.3	37.0

Fruit ('000 metric tons): 697.6 in 1986; 760.4* in 1987; 806.0* in 1988.

Vegetables ('000 metric tons): 1,480.3 in 1986; 1,419* in 1987; 1,541.9 in 1988.

* Preliminary.
† Figure refers to period January–June.

Source: Ministerio de Agricultura, *Boletín Estadístico Agropecuario*.

LIVESTOCK ('000 head, year ending September)

	1984	1985	1986
Horses	1,815*	1,906*	1,950†
Mules†	600	600	600
Asses†	650	650	650
Cattle	22,441*	23,270	23,590
Pigs	2,312	2,381	2,440
Sheep	2,689*	2,714*	2,750†
Goats	797*	856*	860†
Chickens†	35,000	35,000	35,000

* Unofficial figures. † FAO estimates.
Source: FAO, *Production Yearbook*.

LIVESTOCK PRODUCTS ('000 metric tons)

	1984	1985	1986
Beef and veal	599	609	664
Pig meat	114	118	123
Cows' milk*	2,858	2,906	3,017
Cheese*	48.0	49.5	50
Butter and ghee*	13.8	14.0	14.0
Hen eggs	163	171	177
Cattle hides*	80.0	82.8	91.6

* FAO estimates.
Source: FAO, *Production Yearbook*.

Statistical Survey

Forestry

ROUNDWOOD REMOVALS (FAO estimates, '000 cu metres)

	1984	1985	1986
Sawlogs, veneer logs and logs for sleepers*	1,960	1,960	1,960
Pulpwood*	305	305	305
Other industrial wood*	408	408	408
Fuel wood	14,243	14,551	14,849
Total	**16,916**	**17,224**	**17,522**

* Assumed to be unchanged from 1982 official estimates.
Source: FAO, *Yearbook of Forest Products*.

SAWNWOOD PRODUCTION ('000 cu metres)

	1980	1981	1982
Coniferous sawnwood	30*	30*	1
Broadleaved sawnwood	900	936	680
Railway sleepers	40	40	40*
Total	**970**	**1,006**	**721**

* FAO estimates.
1983–86: Annual production as in 1982 (FAO estimates).
Source: FAO, *Yearbook of Forest Products*.

Fishing

('000 metric tons, live weight)

	1984	1985	1986
Inland waters	53.4	47.4	54.9
Atlantic Ocean	7.5	9.9	10.4
Pacific Ocean	17.7	12.4	15.2
Total catch	**78.5**	**69.7**	**80.4**

Source: FAO, *Yearbook of Fishery Statistics*.

Mining and Industry

SELECTED PRODUCTS
('000 metric tons, unless otherwise indicated)

	1985	1986	1987
Gold ('000 troy oz)	1,142.3	1,279.2	853.5
Silver ('000 troy oz)	168.8	186.8	n.a.
Salt (unrefined)	730.3	728.5	821.0
Iron ore	438.7	508.1	606.8
Crude petroleum ('000 barrels)	64,352	110,714	140,594
Diesel oil ('000 barrels)	11,150	11,152	14,054
Fuel oil ('000 barrels)	19,825	21,017	23,638
Motor fuel ('000 barrels)	21,432	24,589	28,606
Sugar	1,367.4	1,272.2	1,293.5
Cement	5,308.0	5,915.5	5,898.1
Carbonates	114.1	112.9	116.9
Caustic soda	20.2	19.1	19.5
Steel ingots	274.4	337.8	335.9

Sources: Banco de la República, Laboratorios de Fundición y Ensaye, Concesión Salinas and Empresa Colombiana de Petróleos.

COLOMBIA

Finance

CURRENCY AND EXCHANGE RATES

Monetary Units
100 centavos = 1 Colombian peso.

Denominations
Coins: 50 centavos; 1, 2, 5, 10, 20 and 50 pesos.
Notes: 50, 100, 200, 500, 1,000, 2,000 and 5,000 pesos.

Sterling and Dollar Equivalents (30 September 1988)
£1 sterling = 537.67 pesos;
US $1 = 317.96 pesos;
1,000 Colombian pesos = £1.860 = $3.145.

Average Exchange Rate (pesos per US $)
1985   142.31
1986   194.26
1987   242.61

BUDGET (million pesos)

Revenue	1985	1986	1987
Direct taxation	129,342	186,234	222,554
Indirect taxation	292,553	418,063	591,214
Rates and fines	14,756	17,883	19,351
Revenue under contracts	14,081	50,032	121,749
Credit resources	206,128	268,229	247,307
Special funds	n.a.	18,223	n.a.
Total	**656,860***	**958,664**	**1,202,175***

*Excludes special funds.

Expenditure*	1985	1986	1987
Congress and comptrollership	13,442	16,308	19,996
General administration	18,250	28,454	40,706
Government and foreign affairs	6,300	10,927	11,428
Finance and public credit	100,802	132,209	137,377
Public works and transportation	42,158	51,892	85,145
Defence	58,206	79,058	100,445
Police	44,191	53,118	74,731
Agriculture†	45,551	31,491	50,520
Health	34,896	48,384	68,498
Education	133,107	172,529	215,106
Development, labour, mines and communications	62,947	76,071	99,542
Justice and legal affairs	32,313	40,453	51,257
Total	**592,217**	**740,894**	**954,781**

*Excluding public debt.   † Investment only.
1989 (million pesos): Revenue 1,745,000m.; Expenditure 2,247,000m.

INTERNATIONAL RESERVES
(US $ million at 31 December)

	1985	1986	1987
Gold*	597	698	290
IMF special drawing rights	—	140	162
Foreign exchange	1,595	2,556	2,924
Total	**2,192**	**3,394**	**3,376**

* Valued at market-related prices.
Source: IMF, *International Financial Statistics*.

MONEY SUPPLY (million pesos at 31 December)

	1983	1984	1985
Currency outside banks	167,650	211,710	186,730
Demand deposits at commercial banks	220,890	267,300	341,180

Source: IMF, *International Financial Statistics*.

COST OF LIVING (Consumer price index for low-income families in Bogotá; base: 1980 = 100)

	1984	1985	1986
Food	216.4	287.5	343.1
Clothing	199.5	235.4	278.1
Rent	208.1	225.7	245.4
All items (incl. others)	222.8	279.1	329.6

1987: Food 430.9; All items 403.7.
Source: ILO, mainly *Year Book of Labour Statistics*.

NATIONAL ACCOUNTS (million pesos at current prices)
Composition of the Gross National Product

	1984	1985	1986
Compensation of employees	1,672,852	2,017,258	2,557,635
Operating surplus	1,823,022	2,431,847	3,346,462
Consumption of fixed capital			
Gross domestic product (GDP) at factor cost	**3,495,874**	**4,449,105**	**5,904,097**
Indirect taxes	394,501	551,948	833,864
Less Subsidies	33,791	35,170	36,536
GDP in purchasers' values	**3,856,584**	**4,965,883**	**6,701,425**
Net factor income from abroad	−99,094	−141,745	−152,548
Gross national product (GNP)	**3,757,490**	**4,824,138**	**6,548,877**

1987: GDP in purchasers' values (million pesos at current prices) 8,779,424.

Expenditure on the Gross Domestic Product

	1985	1986	1987*
Government final consumption expenditure	531,264	667,365	846,429
Private final consumption expenditure	3,445,593	4,379,396	5,672,144
Increase in stocks	75,083	19,276	24,350
Gross fixed capital formation	870,466	1,183,749	1,647,839
Total domestic expenditure	**4,922,406**	**6,249,786**	**8,190,762**
Exports of goods and services	717,413	1,259,710	1,674,709
Less Imports of goods and services	673,936	808,071	1,086,047
GDP in purchasers' values	**4,965,883**	**6,701,425**	**8,779,424**
GDP at constant 1975 prices	**587,516**	**617,527**	**650,568**

* Estimates.

Gross Domestic Product by Economic Activity

	1985	1986	1987*
Agriculture, hunting, forestry and fishing	843,738	1,162,141	1,500,045
Mining and quarrying	189,335	296,401	413,850
Manufacturing	1,079,784	1,559,868	2,069,831
Electricity, gas and water	106,839	152,665	205,764
Construction	342,422	423,255	566,108
Wholesale and retail trade	698,236	909,221	1,180,423
Transport, storage and communications	404,730	521,979	709,787
Other services	1,300,799	1,675,895	2,133,616
Total	**4,965,883**	**6,701,425**	**8,779,424**

* Estimates.

COLOMBIA

BALANCE OF PAYMENTS (US $ million)

	1985	1986	1987
Merchandise exports f.o.b.	3,650	5,331	5,700
Merchandise imports f.o.b.	−3,673	−3,409	−3,874
Trade balance	−23	1,922	1,826
Exports of services	966	1,283	1,404
Imports of services	−3,213	−3,607	−3,976
Balance on goods and services	−2,270	−402	−746
Private unrequited transfers (net)	455	793	1,001
Government unrequited transfers (net)	6	−8	—
Current balance	−1,809	383	255
Direct capital investment (net)	1,016	642	349
Other long-term capital (net)	1,334	1,825	−99
Short-term capital (net)	−113	−1,305	−182
Net errors and omissions	−273	−249	92
Total (net monetary movements)	155	1,296	415
Monetization of gold	170	64	−514
Valuation changes (net)	−39	−2	6
Official financing (net)	−1	−4	−13
Changes in reserves	285	1,354	−106

Source: IMF, *International Financial Statistics*.

External Trade

PRINCIPAL COMMODITIES (US $ '000)

Imports	1985*	1986*	1987*
Vegetables and vegetable products	243,157	225,031	260,184
Food and drink	95,964	130,254	141,714
Mineral products	464,650	238,919	171,406
Chemical products	908,761	823,534	1,016,848
Plastic and rubber products	277,014	256,586	334,762
Paper and paper products	168,416	184,811	206,602
Textiles and textile products	111,972	125,586	137,393
Metals	585,159	431,790	562,511
Mechanical and electrical equipment	971,661	1,440,345	1,543,398
Transport equipment	499,153	595,560	729,400
Total (incl. others)	4,688,876	4,874,297	5,466,245

Exports	1985*	1986*	1987*
Meat	7,045	19,315	31,277
Bananas	193,698	196,231	222,529
Raw coffee	1,769,962	2,981,506	1,674,637
Raw sugar	38,215	34,839	17,716
Fuel oil†	408,802	206,856	331,000
Cotton, raw and manufactured	105,996	91,323	111,702
Precious stones	24,800	34,264	60,039
Total (incl. others)	3,310,985	4,785,619	3,877,660

* Registrations and licences approved by INCOMEX. Export registrations do not include petroleum derivatives.
† Information according to customs declarations.

PRINCIPAL TRADING PARTNERS (US $ '000)

	1985 Imports c.i.f.	1985 Exports f.o.b.	1986 Imports c.i.f.	1986 Exports f.o.b.	1987* Imports c.i.f.	1987* Exports f.o.b.
Total ALADI	882,198	288,283	653,603	400,400	652,200	573,800
Andean Group	433,446	217,975	248,733	281,338	227,800	404,900
Bolivia	5,091	708	4,143	1,276	3,400	1,400
Ecuador	81,439	56,330	46,977	58,942	37,800	65,200
Peru	108,439	31,920	79,054	70,922	66,100	118,100
Venezuela	238,477	129,017	118,559	150,198	120,500	220,200
Other ALADI members	448,752	70,308	404,870	119,100	424,400	168,900
Argentina	106,199	36,650	85,241	67,253	58,200	41,800
Brazil	129,201	5,988	139,182	8,100	150,500	18,500
Chile	52,668	20,934	51,500	32,304	55,700	99,600
Mexico	149,274	6,351	118,370	10,945	148,600	8,200
Paraguay	1,720	60	533	51	900	200
Uruguay	9,680	325	10,044	446	10,500	600
Central American Common Market (CACM)	5,278	32,616	6,876	26,295	5,500	39,200
Rest of Latin America	95,699	63,070	88,700	87,415	133,800	151,300
Caribbean Community and Common Market (CARICOM)	1,369	5,687	658	9,893	600	15,200
USA†	1,456,624	1,165,311	1,389,385	1,529,600	1,514,700	1,997,300
Canada	158,998	39,952	116,260	73,090	174,500	67,500
Rest of North America	41,121	114,326	35,629	50,500	24,500	91,900
Eastern Europe	42,005	84,365	60,670	176,785	49,800	106,800
European Economic Community	810,600	1,233,200	894,500	2,028,000	940,000	1,358,000
European Free Trade Association	151,242	218,109	169,772	379,300	211,900	200,300
Rest of Western Europe	8,400	1,300	11,000	19,700	12,900	14,100
China, People's Republic	936	30	3,366	2,125	5,000	2,500
Asia (excluding Middle East and People's Republic of China)	453,042	181,450	374,357	264,042	420,100	221,500
Middle East	12,558	11,465	19,085	9,526	40,100	12,800
Africa (excluding Middle East)	2,524	66,092	2,228	10,659	3,800	23,000
Australasia and the Pacific	2,023	2,008	10,747	2,893	9,100	2,800
Unspecified	6,009	44,559	15,100	37,700	29,500	146,400
Total	4,130,686	3,551,886	3,852,085	5,107,900	4,228,000	5,024,400

* Preliminary figures.
† Including Puerto Rico.

COLOMBIA   Statistical Survey, Directory

Transport

RAILWAYS (traffic)

	1985	1986	1987
Passengers carried ('000)	2,369	1,420	1,429
Passenger-kilometres ('000)	228,580	177,821	171,121
Freight ('000 metric tons)	1,278	1,186	1,055
Freight ton-km ('000)	776,688	691,061	562,548

Source: Ferrocarriles Nacionales de Colombia.

ROAD TRAFFIC (motor vehicles in use)

	1984	1985	1986
Passenger cars	545,347	579,253	611,978
Buses	50,084	51,090	52,136
Goods vehicles	266,711	274,500	282,386
Heavy-duty vehicles	222,462	226,235	230,034
Total (incl. others)	1,148,944	1,196,403	1,242,650

DOMESTIC SEA-BORNE SHIPPING
(freight traffic, '000 metric tons)

	1983	1984	1985
Goods loaded and unloaded	1,254.0	1,084.8	1,488.2

INTERNATIONAL SEA-BORNE SHIPPING
(freight traffic, '000 metric tons)

	1985	1986	1987
Goods loaded	7,410	11,190	17,543
Goods unloaded	6,908	5,631	6,101

CIVIL AVIATION (traffic)

	1985	1986	1987
Domestic			
Passengers carried	5,051,319	5,448,366	5,523,842
Freight carried ('000 metric tons)	84,826	84,338	95,226
International			
Passengers:			
arrivals	519,464	516,554	525,987
departures	560,516	556,919	541,530
Freight ('000 metric tons):			
loaded	67,213	55,586	54,412
unloaded	72,314	69,594	60,698

Tourism

(visitors)

Country of Origin	1985	1986	1987
Argentina	7,483	7,919	6,624
Canada	5,248	14,426	21,684
Costa Rica	5,534	11,540	8,538
Ecuador	210,081	129,492	94,826
France	9,388	8,314	7,694
Germany, Federal Republic	9,706	10,538	11,146
Italy	6,919	7,329	7,603
Netherlands	8,723	8,239	7,300
Panama	7,620	7,941	8,549
Peru	9,473	10,026	9,611
Spain	8,319	9,125	8,457
United Kingdom	6,647	7,019	7,590
USA	68,482	66,300	70,000
Venezuela	369,477	382,582	220,677
Total (incl. others)	784,028	732,200	541,268

Source: DAS-Corporación Nacional de Turismo.

Education

(1986)

	Institutions	Teachers	Pupils
Nursery	6,640	11,518	292,741
Primary	34,520	123,006	3,740,379
Secondary (general)	5,181	83,113	1,684,731
Higher (incl. universities)*	232	44,269	417,786

* Corresponds to first academic term of 1987.

Directory

The Constitution

The Constitution which is now in force was promulgated in 1886 and has been amended from time to time. In 1957 it was amended to provide for the alternation of the presidency between the two major parties. All citizens over 18 years of age are eligible to vote. Civil rights and social guarantees include freedom of education, the right to strike (except in the public sector), public aid to those unable to support themselves, freedom of assembly, of the press, and the right to petition. All male citizens are required to present themselves for possible military service at the age of 18.

THE PRESIDENT

Executive power is vested in the President of the Republic, who is elected by popular suffrage for a four-year term of office. The President cannot hold office for two consecutive terms but may be re-elected at a later date.

The President appoints a Cabinet, which assists in the government of the country. A substitute (primer designado) is elected by Congress, subject to biannual reappointment, to act in the event of a Presidential vacancy. The President appoints the governors of the 24 Departments, the three Intendencies and the six Commissaries.

CONGRESS

Legislative power is exercised by Congress, which is composed of the Senate and the House of Representatives. Members of both chambers are elected by direct suffrage for a period of four years. The President in each House is elected for six months.

JUDICIARY

The administration of justice is in the hands of the Supreme Court, superior district tribunals, and lower courts. The magistrates of the Supreme Court of Justice are elected by serving members of the Court. The term of office is five years and the magistrates may be re-elected indefinitely.

NATIONAL ECONOMIC COUNCIL

Direction of the nation's finances is in the hands of the Consejo Nacional de Política Económica—CONPES (National Council for Economic Policy). CONPES is composed of five ministers and also representatives of banking, industrial and agricultural interests and has functioned since 1935.

LOCAL GOVERNMENT

For administrative purposes the country is divided into 24 Departments, three Intendencies and six Commissaries. The Departments are further divided into Municipalities. Governors for the Departments are appointed by the President, but regional legislatures are elected by the local inhabitants and enjoy considerable autonomy, including the management of local finances. Popular elections for mayors were held for the first time in all municipalities in 1988.

AMENDMENTS

Various constitutional reforms were promulgated in December 1968, including the following amendments: to increase the membership of the Senate from 106 to 112, and the maximum membership of the House of Representatives from 204 to 214; to increase from two to four years the term of office of representatives; to eliminate the two-thirds majority required for matters of importance; to enable the Government to legislate by decree for a maximum period of 90 days in any one year in the event of an economic crisis, though such decrees must relate only to the matters which caused the crisis; from 1970, proportional representation to be allowed in departmental and municipal elections; the same principle to apply to congressional elections after 1974. An amendment was also promulgated whereby the 'minority' party must have 'adequate' representation in government positions. Further amendments were under consideration in 1988.

Note: A state of siege has been in force intermittently since 1948.

The Government

HEAD OF STATE

President: Dr VIRGILIO BARCO VARGAS (took office 7 August 1986).
Primer Designado: Dr VÍCTOR MOSQUERA CHAUX.

CABINET
(January 1989)

Minister of Government (Interior): Dr CÉSAR GAVIRIA TRUJILLO.
Minister of Foreign Affairs: Col (retd) JULIO LONDOÑO PAREDES.
Minister of Justice: Dr GUILLERMO PLAZAS ALCID.
Minister of Finance and Public Credit: Dr LUIS FERNANDO ALARCÓN MANTILLA.
Minister of National Defence: Gen. MANUEL JAIME GUERRERO PAZ.
Minister of Agriculture: GABRIEL ROSAS VEGA.
Minister of Labour and Social Security: Dr JUAN MARTÍN CAICEDO FERRER.
Minister of Public Health: Dr LUIS H. ARRAUT ESQUIVEL.
Minister of Economic Development: Dr CARLOS ARTURO MARULANDA RAMÍREZ.
Minister of Mines and Energy: Dr OSCAR MEJÍA VALLEJO.
Minister of Education: MANUEL FRANCISCO BECERRA.
Minister of Communications: PEDRO MARTÍN LEYES HERNÁNDEZ.
Minister of Public Works and Transportation: Dr LUIS FERNANDO JARAMILLO-CORREA.

MINISTRIES

Ministry of Agriculture: Carrera 10, No 20-39, Bogotá; tel. 2419005; telex 44470.
Ministry of Communications: Edif. Murillo Toro, Carreras 7 y 8, Calle 12 y 13, Bogotá; tel. 2825465; telex 41249.
Ministry of Economic Development: Carrera 13, No 27-00, 10°, Bogotá; tel. 2419030; telex 44508.
Ministry of Education: Centro Administrativo Nacional (CAN), Of. 501, Avda Eldorado, Bogotá; tel. 2695886.
Ministry of Finance and Public Credit: 7A, No 6-45, Of. 308, Bogotá; tel. 2863676; telex 44473.
Ministry of Foreign Affairs: Palacio San Carlos, Calle 10, No 5-51, Bogotá; tel. 2421516; telex 45209.
Ministry of Government (Interior): Calle 13, No 8-38, Of. 315, Bogotá; tel. 2862324; telex 45406.
Ministry of Justice: Calle 12, No 4-65, 2°, Bogotá; tel. 2839493.
Ministry of Labour and Social Security: Calle 54, No 10-39, Bogotá; tel. 2823032; telex 45445.
Ministry of Mines and Energy: Centro Administrativo Nacional (CAN), Avda Eldorado, Bogotá; tel. 4444520; telex 45898.
Ministry of National Defence: Centro Administrativo Nacional (CAN), 2°, Avda Eldorado, Bogotá; tel. 2884184.
Ministry of Public Health: Calle 16, No 7-39, Of. 701, Bogotá; tel. 2820002.
Ministry of Public Works and Transportation: Centro Administrativo Nacional (CAN), Of. 409, Avda Eldorado, Bogotá; tel. 2223782; telex 45656.

President and Legislature

PRESIDENT

Election, 25 May 1986

Candidate	Votes Cast
Dr VIRGILIO BARCO VARGAS (Partido Liberal)	4,198,687
Dr ALVARO GÓMEZ HURTADO (Partido Conservador*)	2,578,667
JAIME PARDO LEAL (Unión Patriótica)	327,955
REGINA BETANCOURT DE LISKA (Movimiento Unitario Metapolítico)	46,772

Note: Figures exclude votes cast by Colombians resident abroad.

CONGRESO

General Election, 9 March 1986

Party	Seats Senate	House of Representatives
Partido Liberal	58	98
Partido Conservador*	43	80
Nuevo Liberalismo	6	7
Unión Patriótica	3	6
Others	4	8
Total	114	199

* In 1987 the Partido Conservador changed its name to the Partido Social Conservador Colombiano.

President of the Senate: ANCISAR LÓPEZ.
President of the House of Representatives: FRANCISCO JOSÉ JATTÍN.

Political Organizations

Alianza Nacional Popular (ANAPO): Bogotá; f. 1971 by supporters of Gen. Gustavo Rojas Pinilla; populist party; Leader MARÍA EUGENIA ROJAS DE MORENO DÍAZ.

Democracia Cristiana: Avda 42, 18-08, Apdo 25867, Bogotá; tel. 2856639; telex 45572; f. 1964; Christian Democrat party; 10,000 mems; Pres. JUAN A. POLO FIGUEROA; Sec.-Gen. DIEGO ARANGO OSORIO.

Frente por la Unidad del Pueblo (FUP): Bogotá; extreme left-wing front comprising socialists and Maoists.

Movimiento Obrero Independiente Revolucionario (MOIR): Bogotá; left-wing workers' movement; Maoist; Leader MARCELO TORRES.

Movimiento Unitario Metapolítico: Bogotá; f. 1985; populistoccultist party; Leader REGINA BETANCOURT DE LISKA.

Partido Liberal: Avda Jiménez 8-56, Bogotá; f. 1815; divided into two factions, the official group (HERNANDO DURÁN LUSSÁN, MIGUEL PINEDO) and the independent group: Nuevo Liberalismo (New Liberalism, led by Dr LUIS CARLOS GALÁN SARMIENTO, Dr ALBERTO SANTOFIMIO BOTERO, ERNESTO SAMPER, EDUARDO MESTRE).

COLOMBIA

Partido Social Conservador Colombiano: Avda 22, No 37-09, Bogotá; tel. 2680006; f. 1849; fmrly Partido Conservador; 2.9m. mems; Leader Dr MISAEL PASTRANA BORRERO; Sec.-Gen. Dr HERNANDO BARJUCH MARTÍNEZ.

Unidad Democrática de la Izquierda (Democratic Unity of the Left): Bogotá; f. 1982; Leader Dr GERARDO MOLINA; left-wing coalition incorporating the following parties:

Firmes: Bogotá; democratic party.

Partido Comunista de Colombia (PCC): Bogotá; f. 1930; Marxist-Leninist party; Leader Dr GILBERTO VIEIRA; Sec. FRANCISCO CARABALLO.

Partido Socialista de los Trabajadores (PST): Bogotá; workers' socialist party; Leader MARÍA SOCORRO RAMÍREZ.

Unión Patriótica (UP): f. 1985; Marxist party formed by FARC (see below); obtained legal status in 1986; Pres. BERNARDO JARAMILLO OSSA; Exec. Sec. OVIDIO SALINAS.

The following guerrilla groups and illegal organizations are active:

Comando Ricardo Franco-Frente Sur: f. 1984; common front formed by dissident factions from the FARC and M-19 (see below); Leader JAVIER DELGADO.

Ejército de Liberación Nacional (ELN—Unión Camilista): Castroite guerrilla movement; f. 1965; 930 mems; Leaders FABIO VÁSQUEZ CASTAÑO, MANUEL PÉREZ; factions include:

Frente Simón Bolívar: (ceased hostilities in December 1985).

Frente Antonio Nariño: (ceased hostilities in December 1985).

Ejército Popular de Liberación (EPL): left-wing guerrilla movement; splinter group from Communist Party; Leader FRANCISCO CARABALLO.

Fuerzas Armadas Revolucionarias de Colombia (FARC): fmrly military wing of the pro-Soviet Communist Party; composed of 39 armed fronts; 4,400 armed supporters in 1987; Leader MANUEL MARULANDA VELEZ (alias TIROFIJO); Gen. Sec. JACOBO ARENAS.

Movimiento de Autodefensa Obrera (MAO): workers' self-defence movement; Trotskyite; Leader ADELAIDA ABADIA REY; (reported to have joined the Unión Patriótica, July 1985).

Movimiento 19 de Abril (M-19): f. 1970 by followers of Gen. Gustavo Rojas Pinilla and dissident factions from the FARC; left-wing urban guerrilla group; 430 mems; Leader CARLOS PIZARRO LEÓN GÓMEZ (alias CABALLO LOCO); factions include:

Nuevo Frente Revolucionario del Pueblo: f. 1986; active in Cundinamarca region.

Muerte a Secuestradores (MAS) (Death to Kidnappers): right-wing paramilitary organization; funded by drug-dealers.

Patria Libre: f. 1985; left-wing guerrilla movement.

In 1984 the Government reached agreement on a cease-fire with the M-19, the FARC and the EPL. In June 1985, however, the M-19 formally withdrew from the agreement and resumed hostilities against the armed forces. In November 1985 the EPL withdrew from the agreement. The FARC maintained their commitment to the cease-fire. In late 1985 the M-19, the Comando Ricardo Franco-Frente Sur and the Comando Quintín Lame (an indigenous organization active in the department of Cauca) announced the formation of a united front, the Coordinadora Guerrillera Nacional (CGN). In 1986 the CGN participated in joint campaigns with the Movimiento Revolucionario Tupac Amarú (Peru) and the Alfaro Vive ¡Carajo! (Ecuador). The alliance operated under the name of **Batallón América**. In October 1987 six guerrilla groups, including the ELN, the FARC and the M-19, formed a joint front, to be known as the **Coordinadora Guerrillera Simón Bolívar (CGSB)**.

Diplomatic Representation

EMBASSIES IN COLOMBIA

Argentina: Avda 40A, 13-09, 16°, Bogotá; tel. 2880900; telex 44576; Ambassador: DANIEL OLMOS.

Austria: Carrera 11, No 75-29, Bogotá; tel. 2356628; telex 41489; Ambassador: Dr MANFRED ORTNER.

Belgium: Calle 26, No 4A, 45, Bogotá; tel. 2828881; telex 41203; Ambassador: WILLY J. STEVENS.

Bolivia: Calle 78, No 9-57, Bogotá; tel. 2558788; telex 45583; Ambassador: GUILLERMO RIVEROS TEJADA.

Brazil: Calle 93, No 14-20, 8°, Bogotá; Ambassador: CARLOS ALBERTO LEITE BARBOSA.

Bulgaria: Calle 81, No 7-71, Bogotá; tel. 2128028; telex 41217; Ambassador: DIMITUR PETKOV POPOV.

Canada: Calle 76, No 11-52, Apdo Aéreo 53531, Bogotá 2; tel. 217-5555; telex 44568; Ambassador: J. E. G. GIBSON.

Chile: Calle 100, No 11B-44, Bogotá; tel. 2147926; telex 44404; Ambassador: CARLOS MORALES RETAMAL.

China, People's Republic: Calle 71, No 2A-41, Bogotá; telex 45387; Ambassador: WANG YUSHENG.

Costa Rica: Carrera 15, No 80-87, Of. 401, Bogotá; tel. 2361098; Ambassador: JULIÁN ZAMORA DOBLES.

Czechoslovakia: Avda 13, No 104A-30, Bogotá; tel. 2142240; telex 44590; Ambassador: RENE HANOUSEK.

Denmark: Calle 37, No 7-43, 9°, Apdo Aéreo 52965, Bogotá; tel. 2326753; telex 44599; Ambassador: KLAUS OTTO KAPPEL.

Dominican Republic: Carrera 16, No 82-9, Bogotá 2; Ambassador: RAFAEL VALERA BENÍTEZ.

Ecuador: Calle 89, No 13-07, Bogotá; tel. 2570066; telex 45776; Ambassador: Dr RODRIGO VÁLDEZ BAQUERO.

Egypt: Carrera 18, No 88-17, Bogotá; tel. 2364803; Ambassador: MAHMOUD HAFEZ EL-KAMBASHWY.

El Salvador: Carrera 16, No 79-55, Apdo 089394, Bogotá; tel. 2361178; telex 42072; Ambassador: ANDINO SALAZAR.

Finland: Calle 72, No 8-56, Bogotá; tel. 2126111; telex 44304; Ambassador: LASSE OKA.

France: Avda 39, No 7-84, Bogotá; tel. 2854311; telex 44558; Ambassador: PAUL DIJOUD.

German Democratic Republic: Carrera 7, No 81-57, Bogotá; tel. 2490252; telex 44412; Ambassador: HEINZ LÖHN.

Germany, Federal Republic: Carrera 4, No 72-35, Apdo Aéreo 91808, Bogotá 8; tel. 2120511; telex 44765; Ambassador: GEORG JOACHIM SCHLAICH.

Guatemala: Carrera 15, No 83-43, apt 301, Bogotá; Ambassador: MARIO MARROQUÍN NÁJERA.

Haiti: Carrera 72, No 00-86, Apdo Aéreo 52224, Bogotá; tel. 2125942; Ambassador: ALIX BALMIR.

Holy See: Carrera 15, No 36-33, Apdo Aéreo 3740, Bogotá; tel. 2454260; telex 42455; Nuncio: Mgr ANGELO ACERBI.

Honduras: Carrera 13, No 63-51, Bogotá; tel. 2353158; telex 45540; Ambassador: JORGE ELÍAS FLEFIL LARACH.

Hungary: Carrera 6A, No 77-46, Bogotá; tel. 2488489; telex 43244; Ambassador: VINCE KOCZIAN.

India: Calle 93B, No 13-44, Bogotá; tel. 2369821; telex 41380; Ambassador: M. K. KHISHA.

Iran: Transversal 23, No 104-75, Bogotá; tel. 2142975; telex 42252; Ambassador: ALI ASGHAR MUSAVI.

Israel: Calle 35, No 7-25, 14°, Bogotá; tel. 2456603; telex 44755; Ambassador: YAACOV GOTEL.

Italy: Calle 70, No 10-25, Bogotá; tel. 2354300; telex 45588; Ambassador: EGONE RATZENBERGER.

Japan: Carrera 7, No 74-21, 8°–9°, Apdo Aéreo 7407, Bogotá; tel. 255-0300; telex 43327; Ambassador: RIKIWO SHIKAMA.

Korea, Republic: Calle 94, No 9-39, Bogotá; tel. 2361616; telex 41468; Ambassador: YONG HOON LEE.

Lebanon: Calle 74, No 12-44, Bogotá; tel. 2128360; telex 44333; Ambassador: SALIM NAFFAH.

Mexico: Calle 99, No 12-08, Bogotá; tel. 2566347; telex 41264; Ambassador: JOSÉ ANTONIO ALVAREZ LIMA.

Netherlands: Carrera 9, No 74-08, Bogotá; tel. 2119600; telex 44629; Ambassador: REIJNIER FLAES.

Nicaragua: Avda 19, No 133-47, Bogotá; tel. 2583356; telex 45388; Ambassador: FRANCISCO QUIÑÓNEZ REYES.

Norway: Bogotá; Ambassador: ANTON SMITH-MEYER.

Panama: Calle 87, No 11A-64, Bogotá; tel. 2367531; Ambassador: JORGE EDUARDO RITTER.

Paraguay: Calle 57, No 7-11, Of. 702, Apdo Aéreo 20085, Bogotá; tel. 2554160; Ambassador: RUBÉN RUIZ GÓMEZ.

Peru: Calle 81, No 9-73, Bogotá; tel. 2573753; telex 44453; Ambassador: JUAN JOSÉ CALLE Y CALLE.

Poland: Calle 104A, No 23-48, Bogotá; telex 44591; Ambassador: MIECZYSŁAW BIERNACKI.

Portugal: Calle 92, No 15-48, 4°, Bogotá; tel. 2563028; Ambassador: AMANDIO C. R. PINTO.

Romania: Carrera 7, No 92-58, Bogotá; tel. 2566438; telex 41238; Ambassador GEORGHE DROBA.

Spain: Calle 92, No 12-68, Bogotá; tel. 2362154; telex 44779; Ambassador: SALVADOR BERMÚDEZ DE CASTRO Y BERNALES.

Sweden: Calle 72, 5-83, Bogotá; tel. 2553777; telex 44626; Ambassador: KARL WÄRNBERG.

Switzerland: Carrera 9, No 74-08/1101, Bogotá; tel. 2553945; telex 41230; Ambassador: DANIEL DAYER.

COLOMBIA   *Directory*

USSR: Carrera 4, No 75-00, Bogotá; tel. 2357960; telex 44503; Ambassador: (vacant).
United Kingdom: Torre Propaganda Sancho, Calle 98, No 9-03, 4°, Apdo 4508, Bogotá; tel. 2185111; telex 44503; Ambassador: RICHARD A. NEILSON.
USA: Calle 37, No 8-61, Bogotá; tel. 2851300; telex 44843; Ambassador: THOMAS MCNAMARA.
Uruguay: Carrera 100, No 14-26, Bogotá; telex 43377; Ambassador: Col (retd) ARIOSTO A. FERNÁNDEZ.
Venezuela: Calle 33, No 6-94, Bogotá; tel. 2852286; telex 44504; Ambassador: LUIS LA CORTE.
Yugoslavia: Calle 93A, No 9A-22, Apdo 91074, Bogotá; tel. 2570290; telex 45155; Ambassador: UROŠ MARKIČ.

Judicial System

The Supreme Court of Justice is divided into four subsidiary divisions of Civil Cassation, Criminal Cassation, Labour Cassation and Constitutional Procedure. The 24 judges of the Supreme Court hold office until the age of 65 years, although they may be removed from office if considered to be unfit by reason of conduct or age. Vacancies are filled from within the Court by election by the members. For matters of great importance and government business, the three courts of the Supreme Court sit together as a Plenary Court.

The country is divided into judicial districts, each of which has a superior court of three or more judges. There are also other Courts of Justice for each judicial district, and judges for each province and municipality.

SUPREME COURT OF JUSTICE

Carrera 7a, No 27-18, Edif. Banco de Crédito, 15°-24°, Bogotá.
President: Dr JOSÉ ALEJANDRO BONIVENTO FERNÁNDEZ.
Vice-President: Dr RODOLFO MANTILLA JÁCOME.

Division of Civil Cassation: Carrera 7a, No 27-18, 22°, Bogotá.
President: Dr ALBERTO OSPINA BOTERO.

Division of Criminal Cassation: Carrera 7a, No 27-18, 21°, Bogotá.
President: Dr GUILLERMO DUQUE RUIZ.

Division of Labour Cassation: Carrera 7a, No 27-18, 20°, Bogotá.
President: Dr JACOBO PÉREZ ESCOBAR.

Division of Constitutional Procedure: Carrera 7a, No 27-18, 23°, Bogotá.
President: Dr JAIRO DUQUE PÉREZ.
Attorney-General: HORACIO SERPA URIBE.

Religion

Roman Catholicism is the religion of 95% of the population.

CHRISTIANITY
The Roman Catholic Church

Colombia comprises 12 archdioceses, 38 dioceses, two territorial prelatures, eight Apostolic Vicariates and six Apostolic Prefectures.
Bishops' Conference: Conferencia Episcopal de Colombia, Apdo 7448, Calle 26, No 27-48, 4°, Bogotá; tel. 2328540; f. 1978; Pres. Cardinal ALFONSO LÓPEZ TRUJILLO, Archbishop of Medellín.
Archbishop of Barranquilla: FÉLIX MARÍA TORRES PARRA, Carrera 42 F, No 75B-220, Apdo Aéreo 1160, Barranquilla 4; tel. 354108.
Archbishop of Bogotá: Cardinal MARIO REVOLLO BRAVO, Carrera 7a, No 10-20, Bogotá, DE; tel. 2437700.
Archbishop of Bucaramanga: HÉCTOR RUEDA HERNÁNDEZ, Calle 33, No 21-18, Bucaramanga; tel. 25132.
Archbishop of Cali: PEDRO RUBIANO SÁENZ, Carrera 5A, No 11-42, 2°, Cali; tel. 812066.
Archbishop of Cartagena: CARLOS JOSÉ RUISECO VIEIRA, Apdo Aéreo 400, Cartagena; tel. 45903.
Archbishop of Ibagué: JOSÉ JOAQUÍN FLÓREZ HERNÁNDEZ, Calle 10, No 2-58, Ibagué, Tolima; tel. 32680.
Archbishop of Manizales: JOSÉ DE JESÚS PIMIENTO RODRÍGUEZ, Carrera 23, No 19-22, Manizales; tel. 31179.
Archbishop of Medellín: Cardinal ALFONSO LÓPEZ TRUJILLO, Calle 57, No 49-44, Medellín; tel. 2517700.

Archbishop of Nueva Pamplona: RAFAEL SARMIENTO PERALTA, Calle 5, No 4-109, Nueva Pamplona; tel. 2816.
Archbishop of Popayán: SAMUEL SILVERIO BUITRAGO TRUJILLO, Calle 5, No 6-71, Popayán; tel. 21711.
Archbishop of Santa Fe de Antioquia: ELADIO ACOSTA ARTEAGA, Santa Fe.
Archbishop of Tunja: AUGUSTO TRUJILLO ARANGO, Calle 17, No 9-85, Tunja, Boyacá; tel. 2095.

The Episcopal Church

Bishop of Colombia: Rt Rev. BERNARDO MERINO BOTERO, Carrera 6, No 49-85, Apdo Aéreo 52964, Bogotá; tel. 2883167; there are 2,780 baptized mems, 1,320 communicant mems, 29 parishes, missions and preaching stations; 5 schools and 1 orphanage; 16 clergy.

Other Christian Churches

The Baptist Convention: Apdo Aéreo 51988, Medellín; tel. 389623; Pres. RAMÓN MEDINA IBÁÑEZ; Exec. Sec. Rev. RAMIRO PÉREZ HOYOS.
Iglesia Evangélica Luterana de Colombia: Calle 75, No 20-54, Apdo Aéreo 51538, Bogotá 2; tel. 2125735; 2,000 mems; Pres. VIESTURS PAVASARS.

BAHÁ'Í FAITH

National Spiritual Assembly: Apdo 51387, Bogotá 12; tel. 2174586; adherents in 1,013 localities.

JUDAISM

There is a community of about 25,000 with 66 synagogues.

The Press

DAILIES
Bogotá, DE

El Espacio: Carrera 61, No 45-35, Bogotá, DE; tel. 2636666; telex 44501; f. 1965; evening; Dir JAIME ARDILA CASAMITJANA; circ. 92,000.
El Espectador: Carrera 68, No 22-71, Apdo Aéreo 3441, Bogotá, DE; tel. 2606044; telex 44718, 44881; f. 1887; morning; Dir JUAN G. OSPINA; Editor LUIS GABRIEL CANO; circ. 215,000.
La República: Calle 16, No 4-96, Apdo Aéreo 6806, Bogotá, DE; tel. 2821055; f. 1953; morning; economics; Dir RODRIGO OSPINA HERNÁNDEZ; circ. 20,000.
El Siglo: Avda El Dorado No 96-50, Apdo Aéreo 5452, Bogotá, DE; tel. 2345080; telex 044458; f. 1925; Conservative; Dir ALVARO GÓMEZ HURTADO; circ. 65,000.
El Tiempo: Avda El Dorado No 59-70, Apdo Aéreo 3633, Bogotá, DE; tel. 2635555; telex 44812; f. 1911; morning; Liberal; Dir HERNANDO SANTOS CASTILLO; circ. 200,000 (weekdays), 350,000 (Sundays).

Barranquilla, Atlántico

Diario del Caribe: Calle 42, No 50B-32, Barranquilla, Atlántico; tel. 415200; telex 033473; f. 1956; daily; Liberal; Dir EDUARDO POSADA CARBÓ; circ. 30,000.
El Heraldo: Calle 53B, No 46-25, Barranquilla, Atlántico; tel. 416066; telex 033348; f. 1933; morning; Liberal; Dir JUAN B. FERNÁNDEZ; circ. 65,000.
La Libertad: Carrera 53, No 55-166, Barranquilla, Atlántico; tel. 311517; Liberal; Dir ROBERTO ESPER REBAJE; circ. 25,000.

Bucaramanga, Santander del Sur

Diario del Oriente: Bucaramanga, Santander del Sur; tel. 24759; Dir JOSÉ M. JAIMES; circ. 10,000.
El Frente: Calle 35, No 12-40, Apdo Aéreo 665, Bucaramanga, Santander del Sur; tel. 24949; telex 077777; f. 1942; morning; Conservative; Dir Dr RAFAEL ORTIZ GONZÁLEZ; circ. 13,000.
Vanguardia Liberal: Calle 34, No 13-42, Bucaramanga, Santander del Sur; tel. 27134; telex 77762; f. 1919; morning; Liberal; Sunday illustrated literary supplement and women's supplement; Dir and Man. ALEJANDRO GALVIS RAMÍREZ; circ. 42,000.

Cali, Valle del Cauca

Occidente: Calle 12, No 5-22, Cali, Valle del Cauca; tel. 851110; telex 55509; f. 1961; morning; Conservative; Dir ALVARO H. CAICEDO GONZÁLEZ; circ. 50,000.
El País: Carrera 2A, No 24-46, Apdo Aéreo 1608, Cali, Valle del Cauca; tel. 893011; telex 55527; f. 1950; Conservative; Dir ALVARO

COLOMBIA

JOSÉ LLOREDA C.; circ. 65,071 (weekdays), 72,938 (Saturdays), 108,304 (Sundays).

El Pueblo: Avda 3A, Norte 35-N-10, Cali, Valle del Cauca; tel. 688110; telex 055669; morning; Liberal; Dir LUIS FERNANDO LONDOÑO CAPURRO; circ. 50,000.

Cartagena, Bolívar

El Universal: Calle 31, No 3-81, Cartagena, Bolívar; tel. 40028; telex 37731; daily; Liberal; Dir GONZALO ZÚÑIGA; Man. GERARDO ARAÚJO; circ. 28,000.

Cúcuta, Santander del Norte

Diario de la Frontera: Calle 14, No 3-44, Cúcuta, Santander del Norte; tel. 28494; f. 1950; morning; Conservative; Dir TEODOSIO CABEZA QUIÑONES; circ. 10,000.

La Opinión: Avda 4, No 16-12, Cúcuta, Santander del Norte; tel. 21580; telex 76697; f. 1960; morning; Liberal; Dir Dr EUSTORGIO COLMENARES; circ. 18,000 (Mondays), 14,500 (Mondays–Saturdays).

Manizales, Caldas

La Patria: Carrera 20, No 21-51, Apdo Aéreo 70, Manizales, Caldas; tel. 23060; telex 042583; f. 1921; morning; Conservative; Dir Dr LUIS JOSÉ RESTREPO RESTREPO; circ. 25,000.

Medellín, Antioquia

El Colombiano: Calle 54, No 51-22, Apdo Aéreo 5236, Medellín, Antioquia; tel. 510444; telex 44727; f. 1912; morning; Conservative; Dir JUAN GÓMEZ MARTÍNEZ; circ. 123,707.

El Mundo: Calle 53, No 73-146, Apdo Aéreo 53874, Medellín, Antioquia; tel. 2642800; telex 65058; f. 1979; Dir DARÍO ARIZMENDI POSADA; circ. 60,000.

Neiva

Diario del Huila: Calle 8A, No 6-30, Neiva; tel. 22619; Dir MARÍA M. RENGIFO DE D.; circ. 10,000.

Pasto, Nariño

El Derecho: Calle 20, No 26-20, Pasto, Nariño; tel. 2170; telex 53740; f. 1928; Conservative; Pres. Dr JOSÉ ELÍAS DEL HIERRO; Dir EDUARDO F. MAZUERA; circ. 12,000.

Pereira, Risaralda

Diario del Otún: Carrera 8A, No 22-69, Apdo Aéreo 2533, Pereira, Risaralda; tel. 51313; telex 8754; f. 1982; Financial Dir JAVIER IGNACIO RAMÍREZ MÚNERA; circ. 30,000.

El Imparcial: Apdo Aéreo 57, Pereira, Risaralda; f. 1948; morning; Editor ZAHUR ZAPATA CARDONA; circ. 15,000.

La Tarde: Carrera 9A, No 20-54, Pereira, Risaralda; tel. 43013; telex 08832; f. 1975; Dir ALCIDES ARÉVALO; circ. 15,000.

Popayán, Cauca

El Liberal: Carrera 3, No 2-60, Apdo Aéreo 538, Popayán; tel. 33555; f. 1938; Dir AURA ISABEL OCANO DE MUÑOZ; circ. 10,000.

Santa Marta, Magdalena

El Informador: Santa Marta, Magdalena; f. 1921; Liberal; Dir JOSÉ B. VIVES; circ. 9,000.

Tunja, Boyacá

Diario de Boyacá: Tunja, Boyacá; Dir-Gen. Dr CARLOS H. MOJICA; circ. 3,000.

El Oriente: Tunja, Boyacá; Dir-Gen. LUIS LÓPEZ RODRÍGUEZ.

Villavicencio, Meta

Clarín del Llano: Villavicencio, Meta; tel. 23207; Conservative; Dir ELÍAS MATUS TORRES; circ. 5,000.

PERIODICALS
Bogotá, DE

Antena: Bogotá, DE; television, cinema and show business; circ. 10,000.

Arco: Carrera 5, No 35-39, Apdo Aéreo 8624, Bogotá, DE; tel. 2851500; telex 45153; f. 1959; monthly; history, philosophy, literature and humanities; Dir ALVARO VALENCIA TOVAR; circ. 10,000.

Arte en Colombia: Apdo Aéreo 90193, Bogotá, DE; tel. 2622200; telex 044611; f. 1976; quarterly; art, architecture, films and photography; English version; Dir CELIA SREDNI DE BIRBRAGHER; circ. 10,000.

El Campesino: Carrera 39A, No 15-11, Bogotá, DE; f. 1958; weekly; cultural; Dir JOAQUÍN GUTIÉRREZ MACÍAS; circ. 70,000.

Consigna: Diagonal 34, No 5-11, Bogotá, DE; tel. 2871157; fortnightly; Turbayista; Dir (vacant); circ. 10,000.

Costa Libre: Bogotá, DE; monthly; Dir MARCO ANTONIO CONTRERAS.

Coyuntura Económica: Calle 78, No 9-91, Apdo Aéreo 75074, Bogotá, DE; tel. 2116714; quarterly; economics; published by Fundación para Educación Superior y el Desarrollo (FEDESARROLLO).

Cromos Magazine: Calle 70A, No 7-81, Apdo Aéreo 59317, Bogotá, DE; f. 1916; weekly; illustrated; general news; Dir JULIO ANDRÉS CAMACHO; circ. 68,000.

As Deportes: Calle 20, No 4-55, Bogotá, DE; f. 1978; sports; circ. 25,000.

Documentos Políticos: Bogotá, DE; monthly; organ of the pro-Moscow Communist Party.

Economía Colombiana: Edif. de los Ministerios, Of. 126A, No 6-40, Bogotá, DE; f. 1984; published by Contraloría General de la República; monthly; economics.

Escala: Calle 30, No 17-70, Bogotá, DE; tel. 2878200; f. 1962; monthly; architecture; Dir DAVID SERNA CÁRDENAS; circ. 16,000.

Estrategia: Bogotá, DE; monthly; economics; Dir RODRIGO OTERO.

Guión: Carrera 16, No 36-89, Bogotá, DE; tel. 2322669; f. 1977; weekly; general; Conservative; Dir JUAN CARLOS PASTRANA; circ. 35,000.

Hit: Calle 20, No 4-55, Bogotá, DE; cinema and show business; circ. 20,000.

El Informador Andino: Bogotá, DE; economic affairs.

MD en Español: Bogotá; medicine.

Menorah: Apdo Aéreo 9081, Bogotá, DE; tel. 2433609; f. 1950; independent monthly review for the Jewish community; Dir ELIÉCER CELNIK; circ. 10,000.

Nueva Frontera: Carrera 7A, No 17-01, 5°, Bogotá, DE; tel. 2343763; f. 1974; weekly; political; Liberal; Dir CARLOS LLERAS RESTREPO; circ. 20,000.

Pluma: Apdo Aéreo 12190, Bogotá, DE; monthly; art and literature; Dir (vacant); circ. 70,000.

Que Hubo: Bogotá, DE; weekly; general; Editor CONSUELO MONTEJO; circ. 15,000.

Revista Diners: Carrera 10, No 64-65, 3°, Bogotá, DE; tel. 2122873; telex 45304; f. 1963; Dir CONSUELO MENDOZA DE RIAÑO; circ. 110,000.

Semana: Calle 85, No 10-46, Bogotá, DE; tel. 2575400; general; Dir FELIPE LÓPEZ CABALLERO.

Síntesis Económica: Bogotá, DE; tel. 2325434; weekly; economics; Dir DANIEL MAZUERA GÓMEZ.

Sucesos: Bogotá, DE; weekly; Dir NÉSTOR ESPINOZA; circ. 15,000.

Teorema: Bogotá, DE; art and literature; Dir ALBERTO RODRÍGUEZ; circ. 5,000.

Tribuna Médica: Calle 8A, No 68A-41, Bogotá, DE; tel. 2628200; telex 43195; f. 1961; fortnightly; medical and scientific; Editor SALOMÓN LERNER; circ. 55,000.

Tribuna Roja: Apdo Aéreo 19042, Bogotá, DE; tel. 2430371; f. 1971; quarterly; organ of the MOIR (pro-Maoist Communist party); Dir CARLOS NARANJO; circ. 300,000.

Vea: Calle 20, No 4-55, Bogotá, DE; weekly; popular; circ. 90,000.

Voz Proletaria: Carrera 34, No 9-28, Bogotá; tel. 2472346; telex 45152; f. 1957; weekly; left-wing; Dir MANUEL CEPEDA VARGAS; circ. 45,000.

NEWS AGENCIES

Ciep—El País: Carrera 16, No 36-55, Bogotá; tel. 2326816; Dir JORGE TÉLLEZ.

Colprensa: Diagonal 34, No 5-63, Apdo Aéreo 20333, Bogotá; tel. 2872200; telex 45153; f. 1980; Dir ALBERTO SALDARRIAGA.

Foreign Bureaux

Agence France-Presse (AFP): Carrera 5, No 16-14, Of. 807, Apdo Aéreo 4654, Bogotá 1; tel. 2818613; telex 44726; Dir DANIEL PRIOLLET.

Agencia EFE (Spain): Carrera 16, No 39A-69, Apdo 16038, Bogotá; tel. 2851576; telex 44577; Bureau Chief MANUEL RODRÍGUEZ MORA.

Agenzia Nazionale Stampa Associata (ANSA) (Italy): Carrera 4, No 67-30, Apdo Aéreo 16077, Bogotá; tel. 2125409; telex 42266; Bureau Chief ALBERTO ROJAS MORALES.

Associated Press (AP) (USA): Calle 80, No 8-14, Of. 102, Apdo 093643, Bogotá; tel. 2122040; telex 44641; Bureau Chief THOMAS G. WELLS.

Central News Agency Inc. (Taiwan): Carrera 13A, No 98-34, Bogotá; tel. 256342; Correspondent CHRISTINA CHOW.

COLOMBIA

Deutsche Presse-Agentur (dpa) (Federal Republic of Germany): Carrera 7A, No 17-01, Of. 914, Apdo Aéreo 044245, Bogotá; tel. 2818065; Correspondent CARLOS ALBERTO RUEDA.

Inter Press Service (IPS) (Italy): Calle 20, No 7-17, Of. 608, Apdo 7739, Bogotá; tel. 2418841; Correspondent MARÍA ISABEL GARCÍA NAVARRETE.

Prensa Latina (Cuba): Calle 57, No 35A-41, Apdo Aéreo 30372, Bogotá; tel. 2115266; Correspondent TOMÁS DÍAZ ACOSTA.

Reuters (UK): Carrera 6A, No 14-98, Of. 13-05, Apdo Aéreo 29848, Bogotá; tel. 2438819; telex 44537; Correspondent CHARLES LAMBELIN.

Telegrafnoye Agentstvo Sovetskovo Soyuza (TASS) (USSR): Calle 20, No 7-17, Of. 901, Bogotá; tel. 2436720; telex 43329; Correspondent GENNADY KOCHUK.

United Press International (UPI) (USA): Calle 61, No 13-23, Edif. Banco de Colombia, Of. 205, Apdo Aéreo 57570, Bogotá; tel. 2119106; telex 44892; Correspondent CLAUDIA BUSTAMANTE.

Xinhua (New China) News Agency (People's Republic of China): Calle 74, No 4-26, Apdo 501, Bogotá; tel 2115347; telex 45620; Dir HOU YAOQI.

PRESS ASSOCIATIONS

Asociación Colombiana de Periodistas: Avda Jiménez, No 8-74, Of. 510, Bogotá.

Asociación de Diarios Colombianos (ANDIARIOS): Calle 61, No 5-20, Apdo Aéreo 13663, Bogotá; tel. 2114181; f. 1962; 30 affiliated newspapers; Pres. Dr CARLOS PINILLA BARRIOS; Exec. Dir LUIS GUILLERMO ANGEL CORREA.

Círculo de Periodistas de Bogotá: Calle 26, No 13A-23, P-23, Bogotá; tel. 2824217; Pres. MARÍA TERESA HERRÁN.

Publishers

Bogotá

Comunicadores Técnicos Ltda: Calle 40A, No 13-30, Apdo Aéreo 28797, Bogotá; technical; Dir PEDRO P. MORCILLO.

Ediciones Cultural Colombiana Ltd: Calle 72, No 16-15 y 16-21, Apdo Aéreo 6307, Bogotá; tel. 2355494; f. 1951; textbooks; Dir JOSÉ PORTO VÁSQUEZ.

Ediciones Lerner Ltda: Calle 8A, No 68A-41, Apdo Aéreo 8304, Bogotá; tel. 2624224; telex 43195; f. 1959; medical science; Man. Dir JACK A. GRIMBERG.

Ediciones Paulinas: Carrera 23, No 169-98, Apdo 100383, Bogotá; tel. 2345036; f. 1956; religion, culture; Dir LUIS ERNESTO TIGREROS.

Ediciones Tercer Mundo, Ltda: Calle 69, No 6-46, Apdo Aéreo 4817, Bogotá; tel. 2484720; f. 1961; social science; Man. Dir SANTIAGO POMBO.

Editora Cinco, SA: Calle 61, No 13-23, 7°, Apdo Aéreo 15188, Bogotá; tel. 2856200; telex 15188; recreation, culture, textbooks, general; Man. PEDRO VARGAS G.

Editorial El Globo, SA: Calle 16, No 4-96, Apdo Aéreo 6806, Bogotá.

Editorial Interamericana, SA: Carrera 17, No 33-71, Apdo Aéreo 6131, Bogotá; tel. 2454786; university textbooks; Gen. Man. VÍCTOR CORTES.

Editorial Pluma Ltda: Carrera 20, No 39B-50, Apdo Aéreo 345, Bogotá; tel. 2457606; telex 45422; politics, psychology, philosophy; Man. Dir ERNESTO GAMBOA.

Editorial Presencia, Ltda: Calle 23, No 24-20, Apdo Aéreo 006642, Bogotá; tel. 2681817; textbooks, tradebooks; Gen. Man. MARÍA UMAÑA DE TANCO.

Editorial Temis SA: Calle 13, No 6-45, Apdo Aéreo 5941, Bogotá; tel. 2690713; f. 1951; law, sociology, politics; Man. Dir JORGE GUERRERO.

Editorial Voluntad, SA: Carrera 7A, No 24-89, 24°, Apdo Aéreo 29834, Bogotá; tel. 2860666; telex 42481; f. 1930; school books; Pres. GASTÓN DE BEDOUT.

Fundación Centro de Investigación y Educación Popular (CINEP): Carrera 5A, No 33A-08, Apdo Aéreo 25916, Bogotá; tel. 2324440; f. 1972; education and social sciences; Man. FRANCISCO DE ROUX, S.J.

Instituto Caro y Cuervo: Carrera 11, No 64-37, Apdo Aéreo 51502, Bogotá; tel. 2558289; f. 1942; philology, general linguistics and reference; Man. Dir IGNACIO CHAVES CUEVAS; Gen. Sec. FRANCISCO SÁNCHEZ ARÉVALO.

Inversiones Cromos SA: Calle 70A, No 7-81, Apdo Aéreo 59317; Bogotá; tel. 2171754; telex 41384; f. 1977; Pres Dr RAFAEL SANABRIA VÁSQUEZ, JULIO ANDRÉS CAMACHO C.

Legis Editores, SA: Avda Eldorado No 81-10, Apdo Aéreo 98888, Bogotá; tel. 2634100; telex 43300; f. 1952; economics, law, general; Man. VERGARA WIESNER.

Publicar SA: Calle 15, No 8-68, 6°, Apdo Aéreo 8010, Bogotá; tel. 2345600; telex 44588; f. 1954; directories; Man. Dr FABIO CABAL P.

Siglo XXI Editores de Colombia Ltda: Avda 3A, No 17-73, Apdo Aéreo 19434, Bogotá; tel. 2813906; f. 1976; arts, politics, anthropology, history, fiction, etc.; Man. Dir SANTIAGO POMBO VEJARANO.

Cali

Editorial Norma SA: 29N, No 6A-40, Apdo Aéreo 55555, Cali; tel. 675011; f. 1964; children's, textbooks, education; Gen. Man. FERNANDO GÓMEZ C.

Medellín

Aguirre Editor: Calle 53, No 49-123, Apdo Aéreo 1395, Medellín; tel. 2394801; fiction; Dir ALBERTO AGUIRRE.

Editorial Bedout, SA: Calle 61, No 51-04, Apdo Aéreo 760, Medellín; tel. 316900; f. 1889; social science, literature and textbooks; Man. HÉCTOR QUINTERO ARREDONDO.

ASSOCIATION

Cámara Colombiana de la Industria Editorial: Carrera 17A, No 37-27, Apdo Aéreo 8998, Bogotá; tel. 2880023; f. 1951; Pres. JORGE VALENCIA JARAMILLO; Exec. Dir MIGUEL LAVERDE ESPEJO; 120 mems.

Radio and Television

In 1988 there were an estimated 30,000,000 radio receivers and an estimated 7,800,000 television receivers in use.

Ministerio de Comunicaciones, División de Telecomunicaciones: Edif. Murillo Toro, Apdo Aéreo 14515, Bogotá; broadcasting authority; Dir Minister of Communications.

Instituto Nacional de Radio y Televisión—INRAVISION: Centro Administrativo Nacional (CAN), Vía del Aeropuerto Eldorado, Bogotá; tel. 2220700; telex 43311; f. 1954; government-run TV and radio broadcasting network; educational and commercial broadcasting; Dir FELIPE ZULETA.

RADIO

In 1988 there were 516 radio stations officially registered with the Ministry of Communications. Most radio stations belong to ASOMEDIOS. The principal radio networks are as follows:

Cadena Líder de Colombia: Calle 61, No 3B-05, Bogotá; tel. 2831323; Pres. EFRAÍN PÁEZ ESPÍTIA.

CARACOL (Primera Cadena Radial Colombiana, SA): Calle 19, No 8-48, Apdo Aéreo 9291, Bogotá; tel. 2822088; telex 044880; f. 1948; 126 stations; Gen. Man. RICARDO ALARCÓN GAVIRÍA.

Circuito Todelar de Colombia: Calle 57, No 18-13, Bogotá; tel. 2175687; telex 45732; f. 1953; 74 stations; Pres. GERMÁN TOBÓN MARTÍNEZ.

RCN (Radio Cadena Nacional, SA): Calle 13, No 37-32, Bogotá; 64 stations; official network; Gen. Man. RICARDO LONDOÑO LONDOÑO.

Radiodifusora Nacional: CAN, Vía Eldorado, Bogotá; tel. 2690350; Dir HJALMAR DE GREIFF BERNAL.

Super Radio: Calle 39, No 18-12, Apdo Aéreo 23316, Bogotá; 27 stations; Man. ALVARO PAVA CAMELO.

TELEVISION

Television services began in 1954 and are operated by the state monopoly, INRAVISION, which controls two commercial and one educational national stations. There are also three regional stations. Broadcasting time is distributed among competing programmers through a public tender and most of the commercial broadcast time is dominated by 28 programmers. The first channel broadcasts daily for about 17 hours, the second channel for about 15 hours. The educational station broadcasts for 5½ hours per day. The NTSC colour television system was adopted in 1979.

ASSOCIATIONS

Asociación Nacional de Medios de Comunicación (ASOMEDIOS): Carrera 22, No 85-72, Bogotá; tel. 6111300; f. 1978 and merged with ANRADIO (Asociación Nacional de Radio, Televisión y Cine de Colombia) in 1980; Pres. Dr JORGE VALENCIA JARAMILLO.

Federación Nacional de Radio (FEDERADIO): Bogotá; Dir LIBARDO TABORDA BOLÍVAR.

COLOMBIA   *Directory*

Finance

(cap. = capital; p.u. = paid up; res = reserves; dep. = deposits; m. = million; amounts in pesos, unless otherwise indicated)

Contraloría General de la República: Calle 17, No 9-82, P4, Bogotá; tel. 2823549; Controller-General Dr RODOLFO GONZÁLEZ GARCÍA.

BANKING

In early 1988 the Government announced plans to return to private ownership all financial institutions nationalized after the financial crisis of 1982.

Superintendencia Bancaria: Carrera 7, No 4-49, 5°, Apdo Aéreo 3460, Bogotá; tel. 2800187; telex 41443; Banking Superintendent NÉSTOR HUMBERTO MARTÍNEZ NEIRA.

Junta Monetaria (Monetary Board): Carrera 7, 14-78, Bogotá; regulates banking operations and monetary policy; Pres. Minister of Finance and Public Credit.

Central Bank

Banco de la República: Carrera 7, No 14-78, Apdo Aéreo 3531, Bogotá; tel. 2831111; telex 044560; f. 1923; sole bank of issue; cap. 153.9m., res 19,629.8m., dep. 553,580.1m. (Dec. 1986); Gov. Dr FRANCISCO J. ORTEGA ACOSTA; 29 brs.

The Banco de la República also administers the following financial funds that channel resources to priority sectors:

Fondo Agropecuario de Guarantías: guarantee fund for agriculture.

Fondo de Capitalización Empresarial: company capitalization fund.

Fondo de Inversiones Privadas: f. 1963; private investment fund for industrial development.

Fondo Financiero Agrario: agriculture and livestock finance fund.

Fondo Financiero Forestal: forest finance fund.

Fondo Financiero Industrial: industrial finance fund. fund.

Fondo de Desarrollo Eléctrico: electric development finance fund.

Commercial Banks

Bogotá

Banco Anglo-Colombiano (fmrly Bank of London and South America Ltd): Carrera 8A, No 15-46, Apdo Aéreo 3532, Bogotá; tel. 2868088; telex 044884; f. 1976; cap. and res 966.9m., dep. 16,069.1m. (Dec. 1985); Pres. JOSÉ JOAQUÍN CASAS FAJARDO; Regional Man. M. P. MULHOLLAND; 40 brs.

Banco de Bogotá: Calle 36, No 7-47, 15°, Apdo Aéreo 3436, Bogotá; tel. 2881188; telex 44730; f. 1870; cap. and res 10,796.8m., dep. 127,614.5m. (Dec. 1984); taken over by Government in Jan. 1986; Pres. Dr ALEJANDRO FIGUEROA JARAMILLO; 251 brs.

Banco Cafetero: Calle 28, No 13-53, POB 240332, Bogotá; tel. 2846800; telex 43422; f. 1953; cap. US $57.9m., res $7.0m., dep. $743.2m. (June 1987); government-owned; acts both as a commercial lending institution and development bank for rural coffee regions; Pres. JORGE HUMBERTO BOTERO ANGULO; 294 brs.

Banco Central Hipotecario: Carrera 6a, No 15-32, Bogotá; tel. 2813840; telex 45720; f. 1932; cap. 11,043.4m., dep. 155,059.7m. (Dec. 1986); provides urban housing development credit; Gen. Man. Dr MARIO CALDERÓN RIVERA; 131 brs.

Banco de Colombia: Calle 30A, No 6-38, Apdo Aéreo 6836, Bogotá; tel. 2850300; telex 44744; f. 1874; cap. 15,000m., res 4,395.9m., dep. 263,345.6m. (Dec. 1986); nationalized in January 1986; Pres. GUILLERMO VILLAVECES MEDINA; 270 brs.

Banco Colombo-Americano (fmrly Bank of America): Carrera 7A, No 24-89, 46°, Apdo Aéreo 12327, Bogotá; tel. 2816700; telex 44511; cap. 332.1m. (June 1984), dep. 1,175.8m. (June 1983); Pres. RODOLFO ALBORELI; 12 brs.

Banco Colpatria: Carrera 7A, No 24-89, 10°, Apdo Aéreo 7762, Bogotá; tel. 2340600; telex 44637; f. 1955; cap. and res 864.7m. (June 1984), dep. 24,608.4m. (June 1983); Pres. MARIO PACHECO CORTÉS; 26 brs.

Banco del Comercio: Calle 13, No 8-52, Apdo Aéreo 4749, Bogotá; tel. 2826400; telex 044450; f. 1949; cap. and res 2,181.9m. (June 1984), dep. 14,411.5m. (June 1983); taken over by Government in August 1987; Pres. HUGO GUILLERMO DÍAZ BÁEZ; 123 brs.

Banco de Crédito: Calle 27, No 6-48, 4°, Bogotá; tel. 2868400; telex 44789; f. 1963; cap. and res 1,586m., dep. 13,276m. (Dec. 1987); Pres. LUIS FERNANDO MESA PRIETO; 14 brs.

Banco de Crédito y Comercio (fmrly Banco Mercantil): Carrera 7A, No 14-23, Apdo Aéreo 6826, Bogotá; tel. 2848800; telex 44709; f. 1954; cap. 2,062.4m., res 1,324.9m., dep. 43,435.4m. (Dec. 1986); Exec. Pres. FEROZE SAYEEDUD DEANE; 25 brs.

Banco del Estado: Carrera 10, No 18-15, 9°, POB 11392, Bogotá; tel. 2338100; telex 44719; f. 1884; cap. 5,174.2m., res 11,127.7m., dep. 54,360.8m. (Dec. 1986); nationalized in 1986; Pres. Dr HERNÁN RINCÓN GÓMEZ; 61 brs.

Banco Exterior de Los Andes y de España de Colombia—EXTEBANDES de Colombia: Calle 74, No 6-65, Apdo Aéreo 241247, Bogotá; tel. 2127200; telex 45374; f. 1982; cap. and res 500m., dep. 4,792m. (Dec. 1984); Gen. Man. LUIS ANTONIO EFRAÍN ACEVEDO PÉREZ.

Banco Ganadero: Carrera 9A, No 72-21, 11°, Bogotá; tel. 2170100; telex 45448; f. 1956; government-owned; provides financing for cattle development; cap. 1,349.3m., res 5,504.5m., dep. 183,116.7m. (Dec. 1986); Pres. JESÚS ENRIQUE VILLAMIZAR ANGULO; 123 brs.

Banco Internacional de Colombia: Avda Jiménez, No 8-89, Bogotá; tel. 2835888; telex 44721; cap. and res 2,117.6m., dep. 26,984.9m. (Dec. 1986); Pres. AVINASH CHOPRA; 23 brs.

Banco Popular: Calle 17, No 7-43, 7°, Apdo Aéreo 6796, Bogotá; tel. 2430530; telex 45840; f. 1951; government-owned; cap. 2,400m., res 8,179m., dep. 159,925.9m. (Dec. 1986); Pres. FLORÁNGELA GÓMEZ ORDÓÑEZ; 190 brs.

Banco Real de Colombia (fmrly Banco Real SA): Carrera 7A, No 33-80, Apdo Aéreo 034262, Bogotá; tel. 2879300; telex 44688; f. 1976; cap. 274.9m., res 217.1m., dep. 4,281.8m. (Dec. 1985); Pres. Dr LUSIVANDER FURLANI LEITE; 9 brs.

Banco Santander: Carrera 10, No 28-49, 8°-13°, Edif. Bavaria Torre A, Apdo Aéreo 4740, Bogotá; tel. 2843100; telex 45417; f. 1961; cap. and res 1,202.5m., dep. 24,984.1m. (Dec. 1987); Pres. JORGE J. TRUJILLO AGUDELO; 42 brs.

Banco Sudameris Colombia (fmrly Banco Francés e Italiano): Carrera 8A, No 15-40, Apdo Aéreo 3440, Bogotá; tel. 2838700; telex 044725; cap. 419.8m., res 1,573.8m., dep. 25,830.5m. (Dec. 1987); Pres. LUCIANO DALLA BONA; 6 brs.

Banco Tequendama: Diagonal 27, No 6-70, Bogotá; tel. 2875711; telex 33475; f. 1976; cap. and res 725.8m. (June 1984); Pres. ANDRÉS ALVARO CAMACHO MARTÍNEZ; 11 brs.

Banco de los Trabajadores: Diagonal 27, No 6-27, Apdo Aéreo 17645, Bogotá; tel. 2338200; telex 41430; f. 1974; cap. and res 2,000m., dep. 4,151.3m. (Aug. 1987); Pres. Dr CARLOS ENRIQUE PINEDA DURÁN; 19 brs.

Banco Unión Colombiano (fmrly Banco Royal Colombiano): Calle 72, No 8-56, 2°-3°, POB 3438, Bogotá; tel. 2820077; telex 44609; f. 1925; cap. and res 1,074.5m., dep. 9,401.2m. (Dec. 1986); Pres. PHILLIP BRUCE ARTHUR WILLIAMS; 17 brs.

Caja de Crédito Agrario, Industrial y Minero: Carrera 8A, No 15-43, 13°, Apdo Aéreo 3534, Bogotá; tel. 2844600; telex 44738; f. 1931; cap. and res 17,519m., dep. 121,783m. (June 1986); government-owned development bank; Gen. Man. CARLOS VILLAMIL CHAUX; 878 brs.

Caja Social de Ahorros: Calle 59, No 10-60, 16°, Apdo Aéreo 53889, Bogotá; tel. 2112930; telex 45685; f. 1911; savings bank; cap. and res US $7m., dep. US $137.7m. (June 1988); Gen. Man. AUGUSTO JOSÉ ACOSTA TORRES; 110 brs.

Cali

Banco de Occidente: Carrera 5A, No 12-42, Apdo Aéreo 4400, Cali; tel. 823042; telex 55655; cap. and res 46,249m., dep. 360,170m. (June 1987); Pres. FRANCISCO CASTRO ZAWADSKY; 97 brs.

Manizales

Banco de Caldas: Carrera 22, Calle 21 esq., Apdo Aéreo 617, Manizales; tel. 841900; telex 83512; f. 1965; cap. and res 480.3m. (June 1984), dep. 1,888.7m. (June 1983); Pres. ALBERTO MEJÍA JARAMILLO; 13 brs.

Medellín

Banco Comercial Antioqueño: Edif. Vicente Uribe Rendón 14°, Carrera 46, No 52-36, Medellín; tel. 2515200; telex 65339; f. 1912; cap. and res 9,950m., dep. 74,405m., (Dec. 1987); Pres. FERNANDO CASTRO PLAZA; 143 brs.

Banco Industrial Colombiano: Calle 50, No 51-66, Apdo Aéreo 45635, Medellín; tel. 2516658; telex 06743; f. 1945; cap. 698.8m., res 5,651.7m., dep. 71,383.2m. (Dec. 1986); Pres. FRANCISCO JAVIER GÓMEZ RESTREPO; 3 brs.

Banking Association

Asociación Bancaria de Colombia: Carrera 7A, No 17-01, 3°, Apdo Aéreo 13994, Bogotá; f. 1936; 56 mem. banks; Pres. CARLOS CABALLERO ARGÁEZ; Vice-Pres. GERARDO A. MONCADA VEGA.

COLOMBIA

STOCK EXCHANGES

Comisión Nacional de Valores: Carrera 7A, No 31-10, 4°, Apdo Aéreo 39600, Bogotá; tel. 2873300; telex 44326; f. 1979 to regulate the securities market; Pres. Dr Luis Fernando Uribe Restrepo.

Bolsa de Bogotá: Carrera 8A, No 13-82, 8°, Apdo Aéreo 3584, Bogotá; tel. 2436501; telex 044807; f. 1928; Pres. Carlos del Castillo Restrepo; Vice-Pres Carlos Buraglia Gómez; Sec.-Gen. Sergio Michelsen.

Bolsa de Medellín: Carrera 50, No 50-48, 2°, Apdo Aéreo 3535, Medellín; tel. 2411814; telex 066788; Pres. Francisco Piedrahita Echeverri; Vice-Pres. Libia Barreneche Gómez.

Bolsa de Occidente SA: Calle 8A, No 3-14, 17°, Cali; tel. 817022; telex 51217; Pres. William Aguirre Peláez; Vice-Pres Jorge Ernesto Holguín B. and José Luís Munera.

INSURANCE

Principal National Companies

(selected on the basis of premium income)

(n.p.i. = net premiums issued; amounts in pesos)

Aseguradora Colseguros SA: Calle 17, No 9-82, Apdo Aéreo 3537, Bogotá DE; tel. 2839100; telex 044710; f. 1874; n.p.i. 16,141m. (1987); Pres. Dr Bernardo Botero Morales.

Aseguradora Grancolombiana SA: Calle 31, No 6-41, 4°, Apdo Aéreo 10454, Bogotá; tel. 2856520; telex 41328; n.p.i. 3,225.7m. (1983); Pres. Dr Julian Efrén Ossa Gómez.

Cía Agrícola de Seguros SA: Calle 67, No 7-94, 15°-22°, Apdo Aéreo 7212, Bogotá; tel. 2121100; telex 45501; f. 1952; n.p.i. 4,729m. (1987); Pres. Dr Ariel Jaramillo Abad.

Cía Central de Seguros: Carrera 13, No 27-47, 12°, Apdo Aéreo 5764, Bogotá; tel. 2886207; telex 45664; f. 1957; n.p.i. 3,369m. (1987); Man. Dir Julian Efrén Ossa Gómez.

Cía de Seguros Bolívar, SA: Carrera 10A, No 16-39, Apdo Aéreo 4421, Bogotá; tel. 2830100; telex 044873; f. 1939; n.p.i. 11,293m. (1987); Pres. Dr José Alejandro Cortés O.

Cía Suramericana de Seguros, SA: Centro Suramericana, Carrera 64B, No 49-30, Apdo Aéreo 780, Medellín; tel. 942302100; telex 66639; f. 1944; n.p.i. 18,158m. (1987); Pres. Dr Nicanor Restrepo Santamaría.

La Interamericana Cía de Seguros Generales, SA: Calle 78, No 9-57, 5°, Bogotá; tel. 2559700; telex 44631; n.p.i. 3,342m. (1987); Pres. Glenn A. Lawson.

La Nacional Cía de Seguros Generales, SA: Calle 42, No 56-01, Apdo 81077, Bogotá; tel. 2215800; telex 44567; f. 1952; n.p.i. 8,732m. (1987); Pres. Dr Jaime Botero Cadavid.

Seguros Caribe, SA: Carrera 7A, No 74-36, 5°-6°, Apdo 28525, Bogotá; tel. 2114183; telex 42122; n.p.i. 2,985m. (1987); Pres. Dr Fernando Escallón Morales.

Seguros del Comercio, SA: Calle 71A, No 6-30, 2°, Apdo 57227, Bogotá; tel. 2120510; telex 044582; f. 1954; n.p.i. 5,147m. (1987); Pres. Dr Maristella Sanín de Aldana.

Seguros Médicos Voluntarios, SA: Calle 72, No 6-44, 9°, Apdo 11777, Bogotá; tel. 2127611; telex 43354; n.p.i. 3,843m. (1987); Gen. Man. Dr Francisco di Domenico Asti.

Skandia Seguros de Colombia, SA: Avda 19, No 113-30, Apdo 100327, Bogotá; tel. 2141200; telex 043398; n.p.i. 8,391m. (1987); Pres. Terje Olsen.

Numerous foreign companies are also represented.

Insurance Association

Unión de Aseguradores Colombianos—FASECOLDA: Carrera 7a, No 26-20, 11° y 12°, Apdo Aéreo 5233, Bogotá; tel. 2876611; telex 41426; f. 1976; 64 mems; Pres. Dr William R. Fadul.

Trade and Industry

CHAMBERS OF COMMERCE

Confederación Colombiana de Cámaras de Comercio—CONFECAMARAS: Carrera 13, No 27-47, Of. 502, Apdo Aéreo 29750, Bogotá; tel. 2881200; telex 44416; f. 1969; 48 mem. organizations; Exec.-Pres. Nicolás del Castillo Mathieu.

Cámara de Comercio de Bogotá: Carrera 9A, No 16-21, Apdo Aéreo 29824, Bogotá; tel. 2819900; telex 45574; f. 1878; 2,500 mem. organizations; Dir Dr Mario Suárez Melo; Pres. Alvaro Hernán Mejía Pabón.

There are also local Chambers of Commerce in the capital towns of all the Departments and in many of the other trading centres.

STATE INDUSTRIAL AND TRADE ORGANIZATIONS

Carbones de Colombia—CARBOCOL: Carrera 7, No 31-10, 13°, Apdo Aéreo 29740, Bogotá; tel. 2873100; telex 45779; f. 1976; initial cap. 350m. pesos; state enterprise for the exploration, mining, processing and marketing of coal; Pres. Sergio Sokoloff; Vice-Pres. (Commerce) Roberto Iregui.

Colombiana de Minería—COLMINAS: Bogotá; state mining concern; Man. Alfonso Rodríguez Kilber.

Corporación de la Industria Aeronáutica Colombiana SA—CIAC SA: Aeropuerto Internacional Eldorado Entrada 1 Interior 2, Bogotá; tel. 2684642; telex 45254; Man. Gen. Horacio García Rodríguez.

Departamento Nacional de Planeación: Calle 26, No 13-19, Bogotá; tel. 2824055; telex 45634; supervises and administers development projects; approves foreign investments; Dir María Mercedes Cuellar de Martínez.

Empresa Colombiana de Minas—ECOMINAS: Calle 32, No 13-07, Apdo Aéreo 17878, Bogotá; tel. 2875099; administers state resources of emerald, copper, gold, sulphur, gypsum, phosphate rock and other minerals except coal, petroleum and uranium; Gen. Man. Vicente Giordanelli Durán.

Empresa Colombia de Niquel—ECONIQUEL: Carrera 7, No 26-20, Bogotá; tel. 2323839; telex 43262; administers state nickel resources; Dir Javier Restrepo Toro.

Empresa Colombiana de Petróleos—ECOPETROL: Carrera 13, No 36-24, Apdo Aéreo 5938, Bogotá; tel. 2856400; f. 1951; responsible for exploration, production and refining of petroleum; Pres. Andrés Restrepo Londoño.

ECOPETROL Internacional: Bogotá; f. 1988; conducts exploration activities in Peru and other countries in the region.

Instituto Colombiano de Petróleo: f. 1985; research into all aspects of the hydrocarbon industry; Dir Dr Jorge Bendeck Olivella.

Empresa Colombiana de Uranio—COLURANIO: Centro Administrativo Nacional (CAN), 4°, Ministerio de Minas y Energía, Bogotá; tel. 2445440; telex 45898; f. 1977 to further the exploration, processing and marketing of radio-active minerals; initial cap. US $750,000; Dir Jaime García.

Empresa de Comercialización de Productos Perecederos—EMCOPER: Bogotá; tel. 2442421; attached to Ministry of Agriculture; Dir Luis Fernando Londoño Ruiz.

Empresa Nacional de Telecomunicaciones—TELECOM: Calle 23, No 13-49, Bogotá; tel. 2694077; national telecommunications enterprise; Pres. Emilio Saravia Bravo.

Fondo de Promoción de Exportaciones—PROEXPO: Calle 28, No 13A-15, 35°-42°, Apdo Aéreo 240092, Bogotá; tel. 2825151; telex 44452; f. 1967; aims to diversify exports, strengthen the balance of payments and augment the volume of trade, by granting financial aid for export operations and acting as consultant to export firms, also undertaking market studies; Dir Federico Clarkson.

Fondo Nacional de Proyectos de Desarrollo—FONADE: Calle 26, No 13-19, 18°, 19° y 21°, Apdo Aéreo 24110, Bogotá; tel. 2829400; telex 45634; f. 1968; responsible for channelling loans towards economic development projects; administered by a committee under the head of the Departamento Administrativo de Planeación; FONADE works in close association with other official planning organizations; Dir Diana Cristina Molina Ramírez.

Fundación para el Desarrollo Integral del Valle del Cauca—FDI: Calle 8, No 3-14, 17°, Apdo Aéreo 7482, Cali; tel. 806660; telex 7482; f. 1969; industrial development organization; Pres. Gunnar Lindahl Hellberg; Exec. Pres. Fabio Rodríguez González.

Industria Militar—INUMIL: Diagonal 40, No 47-75, Apdo Aéreo 7272, Bogotá; tel. 2699911; telex 45816; attached to Ministry of Defence; Man. Maj. Gen. Hernán Hurtado Vallejo.

Instituto Colombiano Agropecuario—ICA: Calle 37, No 8-43, 4°-5°, Apdo Aéreo 7984, Bogotá; tel. 2855520; telex 44586; f. 1962; institute for promotion, co-ordination and implementation of research into and teaching and development of agriculture and animal husbandry; Dir Gabriel Montes Llamas.

Instituto Colombiano de Comercio Exterior—INCOMEX: Calle 28, No 13A-15, Apdo Aéreo 240193, Bogotá, DE; tel. 2833284; telex 44860; government agency; sets and executes foreign trade policy; Dir Arturo Saravia Better.

Instituto Colombiano de Energía Eléctrica—ICEL: Carrera 13, No 27-00, 3°, Apdo Aéreo 16243, Bogotá; tel. 2420181; telex 43319; formulates policy for the development of electrical energy; constructs systems for the generation, transmission and distribution of electrical energy; Man. Diego Otero Prada; Sec.-Gen. Germán Rueda E.

Instituto Colombiano de Hidrología, Meteorología y Adecuación de Tierras—HIMAT: Carrera 5A, No 15-80, 20°, Apdo Aéreo 20032, Bogotá; tel. 2836927; telex 44345; f. 1976; responsible for irrigation, flood control, drainage, hydrology and meteorology; Dir ENRIQUE SANDOVAL GARCÍA.

Instituto Colombiano de la Reforma Agraria—INCORA: Apdo Aéreo 151046, Bogotá; tel. 2447520; f. 1962; a public institution which, on behalf of the Government, administers public lands and those it acquires; reclaims land by irrigation and drainage facilities, roads, etc. to increase productivity in agriculture and stock-breeding; provides technical assistance and loans; supervises the redistribution of land throughout the country; Dir CARLOS OSSA ESCOBAR.

Instituto de Crédito Territorial—ICT: Carrera 13, No 18-51, Apdo Aéreo 4037, Bogotá; tel. 2343560; telex 44826; Man. (vacant).

Instituto de Fomento Industrial—IFI: Calle 16, No 6-66, Apdo Aéreo 4222, Bogotá; tel. 2822055; telex 044642; f. 1940; state finance corporation for the promotion of manufacturing activities; cap. 13,977m. pesos, res 441.4m. pesos (1986); Man. SERGIO RESTREPO LONDOÑO.

Instituto de Mercadeo Agropecuario—IDEMA: Carrera 10, No 16-82, Apdo Aéreo 4534, Bogotá; tel. 2829911; telex 43315; state enterprise for the marketing of agricultural products; Man. HELMUT BICKENBACH PLATA.

Instituto Nacional de Fomento Municipal—INSFOPAL: Centro Administrativo Nacional (CAN), Apdo Aéreo 8638, Bogotá; tel. 2690177; telex 45328; Gen. Man. JAIME M. SALAZAR VELÁSQUEZ.

Instituto Nacional de Investigaciones Geológico-Mineras—INGEOMINAS: Diagonal 53, No 34-53, Apdo Aéreo 4865, Bogotá; tel. 2211400; telex 32363500; f. 1968; responsible for mineral research, geological mapping and research including hydrogeology, remote sensing, geochemistry and geophysics; Dir Dr LUIS EDUARDO JARAMILLO.

Instituto Nacional de los Recursos Naturales Renovables y del Ambiente—INDERENA: Diagonal 34, No 5-18, 3°, Apdo Aéreo 13458, Bogotá; tel. 2854417; telex 44428; f. 1968; agency regulating the development of natural resources; Dir Dr GERMÁN GARCÍA DURÁN.

Sociedad de Gas Natural: Bogotá; f. 1988; state gas corporation; Pres. (vacant).

Sociedad Minera del Guainía (SMG): Bogotá; f. 1987; state enterprise for exploration, mining and marketing of gold; Pres. Dr JORGE BENDECK OLIVELLA.

Superintendencia de Industria y Comercio—SUPERINDUSTRIA: Carrera 13, No 27-00, 5°, Bogotá; tel. 2342035; supervises chambers of commerce; controls standards and prices; Man. Dr DIEGO NARANJO MEZA; Supt ROBERTO NAVARRO DE LA OSSA.

Superintendencia de Sociedades—SUPERSOCIEDADES: Calle 14, No 7-19, 5° al 16°, Apdo Aéreo 4188, Bogotá; tel. 2830562; oversees activities of local and foreign corporations; Supt LUIS FERNANDO SANMIGUEL CLAVIJO.

There are several other agricultural and regional development organizations.

TRADE FAIR

Corporación de Ferias y Exposiciones, SA: Carrera 40, No 22C-67, Apdo Aéreo 6843, Bogotá; tel. 2440141; telex 44553; f. 1954; holds the biannual Bogotá International Fair and the biannual International Agricultural Fair (AGROEXPO); Man. OSCAR PÉREZ GUTIÉRREZ.

EMPLOYERS' AND PRODUCERS' ORGANIZATIONS

Asociación Colombiana Popular de Industriales (ACOPI): Carrera 23, No 41-94, Apdo Aéreo 16451, Bogotá, DE; tel. 2442741; f. 1951; association of small industrialists; Pres. JUAN A. PINTO SAAVEDRA; Man. RAMIRO SERNA JARAMILLO.

Asociación de Cultivadores de Caña de Azúcar de Colombia (ASOCAÑA): Calle 58N, No 3N-15, Apdo Aéreo 4448, Cali; tel. 647902; telex 051136; f. 1959; sugar planters' association; Pres. Dr RICARDO VILLAVECES PARDO.

Asociación Nacional de Exportadores (ANALDEX): Carrera 7A, No 26-20, 27°, Apdo Aéreo 4448, Bogotá; tel. 2859303; telex 43326; exporters' association; Pres. FERNANDO BALBERI GÓMEZ.

Asociación Nacional de Exportadores de Café de Colombia: Carrera 7, No 32-33, Of. 25-04, Bogotá; tel. 2830669, 2830698; telex 44802; f. 1938; private association of coffee exporters; Pres. GILBERTO ARANGO LONDOÑO.

Asociación Nacional de Industriales (ANDI) (National Association of Manufacturers): Calle 52, No 47-48, Apdo 997, Medellín; tel. 2514444; telex 06631; f. 1944; Pres. FABIO ECHEVERRI CORREA; 7 brs; 722 mems.

Expocafé: Carrera 7A, No 74-36, Of. 302, Edif. Seguros Caribe, Apdo Aéreo 41244, Bogotá; tel. 2178900; telex 42379; f. 1985; coffee exporting organization; comprises 53 coffee co-operatives.

Federación Colombiana de Ganaderos (FEDEGAN): Carrera 14, No 36-65, Apdo Aéreo 9709, Bogotá; tel. 2453041; f. 1975; cattle raisers' association; about 350,000 affiliates; Pres. JOSÉ RAIMUNDO SOJO ZAMBRANO.

Federación Nacional de Algodoneros: Carrera 8A, No 15-73, 5°, Apdo Aéreo 8632, Bogotá; tel. 2343221; telex 44864; f. 1953; federation of cotton growers; Gen. Man. ANTONIO ABELLO ROCA; 14,000 mems.

Federación Nacional de Cacaoteros: Carrera 17, No 30-39, Apdo Aéreo 17736, Bogotá; tel. 2320806; federation of cocoa growers; Gen. Man. Dr IVÁN GARCÍA CUARTAS.

Federación Nacional de Cafeteros de Colombia (National Federation of Coffee Growers): Calle 73, No 8-13, Apdo Aéreo 3938, Bogotá; tel. 2170600; telex 44723; f. 1927; totally responsible for fostering and regulating the coffee economy; Gen. Man. JORGE CÁRDENAS GUTIÉRREZ; 203,000 mems.

Federación Nacional de Cultivadores de Cereales (FENALCE): Carrera 14, No 97-62, Apdo Aéreo 8694, Bogotá; tel. 2184160; f. 1960; federation of grain growers; Gen. Man. ADRIANO QUINTANA SILVA; 7,500 mems.

Federación Nacional de Comerciantes (FENALCO): Bogotá; federation of businessmen; Pres. ENRIQUE LUQUE CARULLO.

Sociedad de Agricultores de Colombia (SAC) (Colombian Farmers' Society): Carrera 7A, No 24-89, 44°, Apdo Aéreo 3638, Bogotá; tel. 2821989; f. 1871; Pres. ELISEO RESTREPO.

There are several other organizations, including those for rice growers, engineers and financiers.

TRADE UNIONS

According to official figures, an estimated 900 of Colombia's 2,000 trade unions are independent.

Central Unitaria de Trabajadores—CUT: Carrera 19, No 32-09, Apdo Aéreo 221, Bogotá; tel. 2457009; f. 1986; comprises 50 federations and 80% of all trade union members; Pres. JORGE CARILLO ROJAS; Sec.-Gen. ANGELINO GARZÓN.

Frente Sindical Democrática (FSD): f. 1984; centre-right trade union alliance; comprises:

Unión de Trabajadores de Colombia—UTC (National Union of Colombian Workers): Carrera 10, No 7-33, Bogotá; tel. 2333148; f. 1946; incorporates 22 regional federations, 5 industry federations and 18 national unions; affiliated to the ICFTU and ORIT; Pres. VÍCTOR M. ACOSTA VALDEBLÁNQUEZ; Gen. Sec. ALFONSO VARGAS TOVAR; 1.2m. mems.

Confederación de Trabajadores de Colombia—CTC (Colombian Confederation of Workers): Calle 16, No 14-13, 5°, Apdo Aéreo 4780, Bogotá; tel. 2430040; f. 1934; mainly Liberal; 600 affiliates, including 6 national organizations and 20 regional federations; admitted to ICFTU; Pres. ALVIS FERNÁNDEZ; 400,000 mems.

Confederación General del Trabajo—CGT: Calle 19, No 13A-12, 6° y 7°, Apdo Aéreo 5415, Bogotá; tel. 2835817; Christian Democrat; Pres. JULIO ROBERTO GÓMEZ ESGUERRA.

Transport

Land transport in Colombia is rendered difficult by high mountains, so the principal means of long-distance transport is by air. As a result of the development of the El Cerrejón coal field, Colombia's first deep-water port has been constructed at Bahia de Portete, and a 150-km rail link between El Cerrejón and the port became operational in 1986.

Instituto Nacional del Transporte (INTRA): Edif. Minobras (CAN), 6°, Apdo Aéreo 24990, Bogotá; tel. 2449100; government body; Dir Dr GUILLERMO ANZOLA LIZARAZO.

RAILWAYS

Ferrocarriles Nacionales de Colombia (National Railways of Colombia): Calle 13, No 18-24, Bogotá; tel. 2423043; telex 45468; f. 1954; Pres. Dr LUIS FERNANDO JARAMILLO CORREA; Man. Dr SERGIO HUGO AMAYA CÓRDOBA.

The Administrative Council for the National Railways operated 2,620 km of track in 1988. The system is divided into five divisions, each with its own management: Central, Pacific, Antioquia, Santander and Magdalena.

The Medellín urban transport project, which will provide a 29-km underground system with 24 stations, was scheduled to be operational by 1989. A similar transit project has been proposed for Bogotá, and in 1988 it was announced that Italy had been

COLOMBIA

selected by the Colombian Government to construct the 44-km underground system, which was due to come into operation in 1992.

ROADS

Fondo Vial Nacional: Bogotá; f. 1966; administered by the Ministerio de Obras Públicas; to execute development programmes in road transport.

In 1986 there were 106,218 km of roads. The country's main highways are the Caribbean Trunk Highway, the Eastern and Western Trunk Highways, the Central Trunk Highway and there are also roads into the interior. There are plans to construct a Jungle Edge highway to give access to the interior, a link road between Turbo, Bahía Solano and Medellín, a highway between Bogotá and Villavicencio and to complete the short section of the Pan-American highway between Panama and Colombia. In 1987 the World Bank granted a loan of US $180.3m. to Colombia for the rehabilitation and improvement of some 7,200 km of roads.

There are a number of national bus companies and road haulage companies.

INLAND WATERWAYS

Dirección de Navegación y Puertos: Edif. Minobras (CAN), Of. 562, Bogotá; tel. 2221248; telex 45656; responsible for river works and transport; the waterways system is divided into four sectors: Magdalena, Atrato, Orinoquia, and Amazonia; Dir ALBERTO RODRÍGUEZ ROJAS.

The Magdalena–Cauca river system is the centre of river traffic and is navigable for 1,500 km, while the Atrato is navigable for 687 km. The Orinoco system has more than five navigable rivers, which total more than 4,000 km of potential navigation (mainly through Venezuela); the Amazonas system has four main rivers, which total 3,000 navigable km (mainly through Brazil). There are plans to connect the Arauca with the Meta, and the Putamayo with the Amazon, and also to construct an Atrato–Truandó interoceanic canal.

SHIPPING

The four most important ocean terminals are Buenaventura on the Pacific coast and Santa Marta, Barranquilla and Cartagena on the Atlantic coast. The port of Tumaco on the Pacific coast is gaining in importance and there are plans for construction of a deep-water port at Bahía Solano. In 1986 the World Bank allocated a loan of US $43m. to Colombia for the rehabilitation of port facilities at Buenaventura, Cartagena and Santa Marta.

Empresa Puertos de Colombia—COLPUERTOS (Colombian Port Authority): Carrera 10A, No 15-22, 10°, Apdo Aéreo 13037, Bogotá; tel. 2343574; f. 1959; Man. Vice-Adm. (retd) BENJAMÍN ALZATE REYES.

Flota Mercante Grancolombiana, SA: Carrera 13, No 27-75, Apdo Aéreo 4482, Bogotá; tel. 2860200; telex 44853; owned by the Colombian Coffee Growers' Federation (80%) and Ecuador Development Bank (20%); f. 1946; one of Latin America's leading cargo carriers serving 45 countries worldwide; Pres. Dr ENRIQUE VARGAS R.; Sec.-Gen. Dr HUMBERTO VELÁSQUEZ; 16 vessels.

Colombiana Internacional de Vapores, Ltda (Colvapores): Avda Caracas, No 35-02, Apdo 17227, Bogotá; cargo services mainly to the USA.

Líneas Agromar, Ltda: Carrera 30 y Calle 4, Apdo Aéreo 3259, Barranquilla; tel. 328896; telex 33462; Pres. M. DEL DAGO F.

Several foreign shipping lines call at Colombian ports.

Directory

CIVIL AVIATION

Colombia has more than 100 airports, including 11 international airports: Bogotá (Eldorado Airport), Medellín, Cali, Barranquilla, Bucaramanga, Cartagena, Cúcuta, Leticia, Pereira, San Andrés and Santa Marta. Aerocivil operates 520 airports and the Fondo Aeronáutico Nacional operates 74 airports.

Airports Authority

Departamento Administrativo de Aeronáutica Civil (Aerocivil): Aeropuerto Internacional Eldorado, Bogotá; tel. 2669200; telex 44620; Dir YESID CASTAÑO GONZÁLEZ.

National Airlines

AVIANCA (Aerovías Nacionales de Colombia): Avda Eldorado 93-30, 4°, Bloque 1, Bogotá; telex 44427; f. 1919; operates domestic services to all cities in Colombia and international services to Argentina, Brazil, Chile, Ecuador, Mexico, Panama, Peru, Uruguay, Venezuela, the Dominican Republic, Haiti, the Netherlands Antilles, Puerto Rico, the USA, France, the Federal Republic of Germany and Spain; Pres. EDGARD LENIS; fleet: 2 Boeing 747, 10 Boeing 727-100, 7 Boeing 727-200, 4 Boeing 707.

Sociedad Aeronáutica de Medellín Consolidada, SA (SAM): Edif. SAM, Calle 52, No 52-11, Apdo Aéreo 1085, Medellín; Avda Jiménez, No 5-14, Bogotá; telex 06774; f. 1945; subsidiary of Avianca; internal services; and international cargo services to Costa Rica, El Salvador, Guatemala, Nicaragua, Panama and the USA; Gen. Man. JAVIER ZAPATA; fleet: 3 Boeing 727-100, 2 Boeing 727-100C.

Servicio Aéreo a Territorios Nacionales (Satena): Aeropuerto Internacional Eldorado, Entrada No 1, Interior No 11, Carrera 10, Bogotá; tel. 2679578; telex 44561; f. 1962; commercial enterprise attached to the Ministry of National Defence; internal services; Man. Brig. ALBERTO GUZMAN MOLINA; fleet: 1 Fokker F-28, 2 HS-748, 6 Pilatus Porter PC 6, 5 Casa 212-200.

In addition the following airlines operate scheduled domestic passenger and cargo services: Aerolíneas Centrales de Colombia, SA (ACES), Aerovías de Pesca y Colonización del Suroeste Colombiano (Aeropesca) and Aerovías Colombianas (ARCA).

Tourism

The principal tourist attractions are the Caribbean coast (including the island of San Andrés), the 16th-century walled city of Cartagena, the Amazonian town of Leticia, the Andes mountains rising to 5,700 m above sea-level, the extensive forests and jungles, pre-Columbian relics and monuments of colonial art. Since 1978 tourism has been Colombia's second most important source of foreign exchange. Most of the 541,268 visitors in 1987 came from Venezuela, Ecuador, Europe and the USA.

Corporación Nacional de Turismo: Calle 28, No 13A-15, 16°, Apdo Aéreo 8400, Bogotá; tel. 2839466; telex 441350; f. 1968; Gen. Man. ANA CECILIA GUERRERO DE URIBE; 8 brs throughout Colombia and brs in Europe, the USA and Venezuela.

Asociación Colombiana de Agencias de Viajes y Turismo—ANATO: Carrera 21, No 83-63/71, Apdo Aéreo 7088, Bogotá; tel. 2562290; f. 1949; Pres. Dr OSCAR RUEDA GARCÍA.

Atomic Energy

Instituto de Asuntos Nucleares—IAN: Avda Eldorado, Carrera 50, Apdo Aéreo 8595, Bogotá 1, DE; tel. 2220600; telex 42416; f. 1959; experimental facilities; Dir Dr ERNESTO VILLARRAL SILVA.

THE COMOROS*

Introductory Survey

Location, Climate, Language, Religion, Flag, Capital

The Federal Islamic Republic of the Comoros is an archipelago in the Mozambique Channel, between the island of Madagascar and the east coast of the African mainland. The group comprises four main islands (Njazidja, Nzwani and Mwali, formerly Grande-Comore, Anjouan and Mohéli respectively, and Mayotte) and numerous islets and coral reefs. The climate is tropical, with considerable variations in rainfall and temperature from island to island. The official languages are Arabic and French but the majority of the population speak Comoran, a blend of Swahili and Arabic. Islam is the state religion. The flag is green, with a white crescent moon and four five-pointed white stars in the centre. The capital is Moroni, on Njazidja.

Recent History

Formerly attached to Madagascar, the Comoros became a separate French Overseas Territory in 1947. The islands achieved internal self-government in December 1961, with a Chamber of Deputies and a Government Council to control local administration.

Elections in December 1972 produced a large majority for parties advocating independence, and Ahmed Abdallah became President of the Government Council. In June 1973 he was restyled President of the Government. A referendum in December 1974 resulted in a 96% vote in favour of independence, despite the opposition of the Mayotte Party, seeking the status of a French Department for the island of Mayotte.

On 6 July 1975, after France decided that any constitutional settlement must be ratified by all the islands voting separately, the Chamber of Deputies voted for immediate independence. The Chamber elected Abdallah to be first President of the Comoros and constituted itself as the National Assembly. France made no attempt to intervene but maintained control of Mayotte. President Abdallah was deposed in August, and the Assembly was abolished. A National Executive Council was established, with Prince Saïd Mohammed Jaffar, leader of the opposition Front National Uni, as its head, and Ali Soilih, leader of the coup, among its members. In November the Comoros was admitted to the UN, as a unified state comprising the whole archipelago, but France continued to support Mayotte, although recognizing the independence of the three remaining islands in December. In February 1976 Mayotte voted overwhelmingly to retain its links with France.

As relations with France deteriorated, all development aid and technical assistance were withdrawn. Ali Soilih was elected Head of State in January 1976, and a new constitution gave him extended powers. Many citizens reported political repression. In May 1978 Soilih was shot dead, following a coup by a group of about 50 European mercenaries, led by a Frenchman, Bob Denard, on behalf of the exiled former President, Ahmed Abdallah. A Federal Islamic Republic was proclaimed. In July the Comoros was expelled from the Organization of African Unity (OAU) because of the continued presence of the mercenaries.

In October 1978 a new constitution was approved in a referendum, on the three islands excluding Mayotte, by 99.31% of the votes cast. Abdallah was elected President in the same month, and in December elections were held to form a Federal Assembly. In January 1979 the Assembly approved the formation of a one-party state. Unofficial opposition groups, however, continued to exist, and 150 people were arrested in February 1981, following reports (officially denied) of an attempted coup. Ali Mroudjae, former Minister of Foreign Affairs and Co-operation, was appointed Prime Minister in February 1982, and legislative elections were held in March. Constitutional amendments, adopted in October, strengthened the President's power by reducing that of each island's Governor. In May 1983 President Abdallah announced an amnesty for all political prisoners who were serving sentences of less than 10 years. In December a plot to overthrow the Government was discovered. A group of British mercenaries was to have staged a coup on behalf of a former Comoran diplomat, Saïd Ali Kemal, but the plot was foiled by the arrest of the mercenary leaders in Australia. Abdallah was the sole candidate at a presidential election in September 1984. Despite calls by the opposition for voters to boycott the election, there was a turn-out of 98%. Abdallah's candidacy was endorsed by 99.44% of voters, and he was therefore returned to office for a further six years. In January 1985 the Constitution was amended to abolish the position of Prime Minister, and President Abdallah assumed the office of Head of Government.

In March 1985 an attempt by presidential guardsmen to overthrow Abdallah, while he was absent on a private visit to France, was foiled, and in November 17 people, including Mustapha Saïd Cheikh, secretary-general of the banned opposition movement, Front démocratique (FD), were sentenced to forced labour for life, while 50 others were also imprisoned for their part in the coup attempt. However, in December President Abdallah granted an amnesty to about 30 political prisoners, many of whom were FD members, and in May 1986 a further 15 detainees, convicted after the attempted coup, were also given amnesty. In January 1987 President Abdallah announced a further amnesty for political prisoners. In the following month Abdallah announced that elections for the Federal Assembly would be held on 22 March, and indicated that the elections would be open to individual candidates opposing the Government. However, candidates other than those selected by the Government were allowed only to contest 20 seats on Njazidja, where they received 35% of the total votes, and pro-Government candidates retained full control of the 42-seat Federal Assembly. About 65% of the electorate participated. There were allegations of widespread fraud and intimidation of opposition candidates, and, according to Comoran dissidents in Réunion, about 400 people were arrested, 200–300 of whom were later imprisoned. In June three French-based opposition movements agreed to merge, during a rally in Marseille, attended by nearly 1,000 Comorans.

In July 1987, to mark the 12th anniversary of independence, Abdallah reinstated all civil servants who had been dismissed or suspended following the coup attempt in March 1985. In mid-1987 it was reported that President Abdallah was seeking to secure a third term of office, upon the expiry of his mandate in 1990, and that the Constitution, which limited the President's tenure to two six-year terms, was to be revised accordingly. In August the Government nationalized SOCOVIA, a food-retailing company, in an apparent attempt to limit the power of the European mercenaries, with whom the director of the company was associated. In November 1987, shortly after President Abdallah's departure for a conference in France, another coup attempt by a left-wing group of 14 former members of the presidential guard and members of the Comoran armed forces was foiled by the authorities with, it was believed, assistance from French mercenaries and South African military advisers. Three rebels were killed during the attack on the main barracks, and a number of civilians also died. In March 1988 anti-Government leaflets were distributed on Mwali by the Echo Mohélien, a dissident group based on Mayotte and founded by islanders who had fled from Mwali. The group aimed to attract the attention of human rights organizations to the situation on Mwali, claiming that several people had been arrested, public funds had been diverted and civil servants had not been paid for nine months. In April President Abdallah's son, Nassuf Abdallah, founded the Union Régionale pour la Défense de la Politique du Président Ahmed Abdallah, a pro-Government party based on the island of Nzwani.

Diplomatic relations with France were resumed in July 1978, and in November the two countries signed agreements on military and economic co-operation, apparently deferring any

---

* Some of the information contained in this chapter refers to the whole Comoros archipelago, which the independent Comoran state claims as its national territory. However, the island of Mayotte (Mahoré) is, in fact, administered by France. Separate information on Mayotte may be found in the chapter on French Overseas Possessions.

THE COMOROS

decision on the future of Mayotte. In February 1979 the OAU readmitted the Comoros. At the UN General Assembly in November 1987, 128 countries voted in favour of a motion asserting the Comoran claim to Mayotte, with 22 countries abstaining and France casting the only vote against the motion. During a 10-day private visit to France in August 1988, President Abdallah conferred with the French Minister of Foreign Affairs and with the presidential adviser on African affairs.

In January 1985 the Comoros was admitted as the fourth member state of the Indian Ocean Commission (IOC), an organization founded by Madagascar, Mauritius and Seychelles to promote regional co-operation and economic development. The fourth ministerial meeting of the IOC was held in Moroni in February 1988. In June the Comoros agreed to establish diplomatic relations, and to exchange ambassadors, with Seychelles.

Government

According to the Constitution of October 1978 (q.v.), the Comoros is ruled by a President, elected for six years by universal adult suffrage. He is assisted by an appointed Council of Ministers. Legislative power lies with the Federal Assembly, with 42 members directly elected for five years, while each island has a degree of autonomy under a Governor and Council. Constitutional amendments in October 1982 gave the President the power to appoint each Governor, while the Federal Government became responsible for each island's resources.

Defence

The national army, the Forces Armées Comoriennes, has 700–800 men, and there are about 20 French officers. Current government expenditure on defence in 1986 was 872m. Comoros francs.

Economic Affairs

The economy of the Comoros is severely underdeveloped, and suffers from over-population, high unemployment, poor harvests, landlessness, lack of natural resources, poor communications and the emigration of trained personnel. In 1987, according to estimates by the World Bank, the gross national product (GNP) of the Comoros (excluding Mayotte), measured at average 1985–87 prices, was US $160m., equivalent to $380 per head. It was estimated that GNP per head increased, in real terms, at an average rate of only 0.1% per year between 1980 and 1987. In current prices, the gross domestic product (GDP) totalled 55,379m. Comoros francs in 1987, a rise of 7.6%, in real terms, over the previous year.

There is a very small industrial sector, which concentrates on the distillation of essences, vanilla processing, soft drinks and woodwork, while about 81% of the working population are engaged in agriculture and fishing, mostly using primitive techniques. The soil, however, is over-exploited, ill-suited to arable or pasture and, in places, severely eroded. Cassava, sweet potatoes, bananas and rice are the main food crops, but more than one-half of the islands' food is imported. Rice imports totalled 5,651m. Comoros francs in 1985 (following the virtual destruction of the domestic crop by a hurricane in 1984), falling to 1,821m. Comoros francs in 1986 and reaching 929m. Comoros francs in the first half of 1987. However, the Government is aiming for self-sufficiency in basic foodstuffs, and major projects involving maize, coconuts, poultry and cattle-breeding have been established.

The dominant agricultural sector, that of the colonial plantations, is devoted exclusively to the cultivation of vanilla, cloves, ylang-ylang and copra for export to a world market in recession, and earnings are quite inadequate to cover the cost of imports. In 1987 earnings from exports of vanilla and of cloves, the principal export commodities, totalled 25.5m. French francs and 31m. French francs respectively. The cost of total imports in the same year reached 311.2m. French francs. Although the Comoros is the world's leading producer of ylang-ylang, distillation costs have increased in recent years, and exports have suffered competition from Indonesian exports of canaga (a cheaper, but inferior, substitute). In 1987 production of ylang-ylang declined by 13%, as a result of adverse climatic conditions. In the same year, exports of copra were halted, owing to a sharp decline in international prices for coconut oil.

Fishing is practised on a small scale, with a total catch of about 5,000 metric tons per year. Production has gradually expanded since the early 1980s, as the number of people involved in the sector has increased and fishing boats are being motorized. Nevertheless, the catch still fails to satisfy domestic demand. According to recent studies, the Comoros has a potential annual catch of 25,000–30,000 tons of tuna, which could provide the basis for a processing industry. In July 1988 the Comoros and the EEC signed a three-year agreement which permitted 40 tuna-fishing vessels from Spain and France to operate in Comoran waters in return for financial support and assistance for a research programme on the conservation of fish stocks around the Comoros.

The Comoros has a developing tourist industry, but fewer than 2,000 tourists per year stay in the islands' four hotels. In 1986 South African developers initiated plans to build three new hotels and to refurbish existing hotels, with the aim of attracting South African and European tourists to the islands. The construction of a tourist complex at N'Galawa started in 1987. In 1988 a South African hotel company, Sun International, signed an agreement with the Comoran Government to manage two hotels on the island of Njazidja. In the same year, however, the UN Development Programme (UNDP) recommended a new emphasis on the construction of small, Comoran-owned and -managed hotels and a shift away from the encouragement of mass tourism. The UNDP proposed the implementation of a three-year programme, costing US $360,000, to provide infrastructure and service facilities, including the establishment of a hotel school on Njazidja.

A sharp decline in international prices for vanilla and a reduction in demand for ylang-ylang resulted in a substantial increase in the trade deficit in the early 1980s. There was a deficit of 9,433m. Comoros francs in 1985, falling to 5,786m. Comoros francs in 1986, owing to a reduction in import costs. In the first half of 1987, export earnings fell by 47%, in comparison with the equivalent period in 1986, as a result of the sharp decline in world prices for cloves and coconut oil, and reduced output of vanilla. Meanwhile, more capital goods were imported, resulting in a 10% increase in import costs. The current deficit on the Comoros' balance of payments also increased rapidly in the early 1980s, before falling to US $14.3m. in 1985. However, the balance-of-payments deficit increased to $15.7m. in 1986 and to $23.3m. in 1987.

Until 1975 French aid underpinned the Comoros' economy, and no effort to develop a basis for an independent economy was made. When France suspended all aid in July 1975, the islands were left virtually bankrupt until the resumption of aid, after diplomatic relations were restored in July 1978. In 1987 French aid totalled 119.5m. French francs. Saudi Arabia, Kuwait, the United Arab Emirates and the EEC also contribute to development projects. The country's first international aid donors' conference, held in July 1984, was attended by 17 countries and 24 aid agencies. The conference considered projects outlined in the 1983–90 Development Plan, and raised US $114.6m. in project finance. In 1985 the EEC agreed to allocate 7,065m. Comoros francs to finance the agricultural sector from 1986 to 1990. In 1987 the EEC provided loans for the fishing sector and to help to finance investment for small and medium-sized enterprises. In the same year, the Comoros received a $1m. loan from OPEC to rehabilitate and expand storage and handling facilities for petroleum products, and a French loan of 10m. French francs to extend and modernize the telecommunications network. France also granted a loan of 6m. French francs for the 1987–91 phase of a rice-growing project on the island of Mwali. In 1988 the EEC provided loans for the development of Moroni port and for a general import programme.

The Comoran external debt reached 1,460m. French francs in December 1987. The 1988 budget projected total expenditure of 11,700m. Comoros francs, with a planned deficit of 2,200m. Comoros francs. However, in 1988 the Comoros faced severe budgetary problems, as revenue was lower than expected, owing to fluctuations in the exchange rate, in addition to the slump in commodity sales and the problems of corruption and non-payment of customs duties. Meanwhile, the number of civil servants had doubled between 1984 and 1988 to reach 8,500, resulting in increased budgetary expenditure on salaries: by mid-1988 the payment of salaries to government employees was about three months in arrears. In early 1988 France provided a loan of 11m. French francs for the repayment of part of the external debt. French budgetary aid for 1988 was initially 29.5m. French francs, but was later increased by 3m. French francs to alleviate the Comoros' acute budgetary problems.

THE COMOROS

In November 1987 a World Bank preparatory mission visited the Comoros to draft a structural adjustment programme (SAP) for the islands. Proposed measures included the reform of state-owned companies, a reduction in numbers of state employees and the removal of subsidies on rice. In accordance with the mission's proposals, the Comoran Government announced an increase in the price of rice in the same month. Further discussions on the SAP were held in July 1988 between the Government and the World Bank, the IMF and the African Development Bank.

Social Welfare

In 1978 the Government administered six hospital establishments, with a total of 698 beds, and there were 20 physicians working in the country. In 1983 the Government was granted a loan of $2.8m. by the International Development Association (IDA), an affiliate of the World Bank, for a programme to curb population growth and to improve health facilities on the islands. Two new maternity clinics were planned, and existing health centres were to be renovated. Current expenditure on health services by the central Government in 1986 was 652m. Comoros francs (6.3% of total current spending).

Education

Education is officially compulsory for eight years between seven and 15 years of age. Primary education begins at the age of six and lasts for six years. Secondary education, beginning at 12 years of age, lasts for seven years, comprising a first cycle of four years and a second of three years. Total enrolment at primary and secondary schools, as a proportion of all school-age children, increased from 19% in 1970 to 60% (boys 72%; girls 48%) in 1980. Enrolment at primary schools in 1982 included an estimated 69% of children in the relevant age-group. Secondary education ceased after the withdrawal of all French teaching staff in late 1975, but some schools were reopened in 1976, with the aid of teachers from other French-speaking countries. Children may also receive a basic education through traditional Koranic schools, which are staffed by Comoran teachers. In 1982 there were 61,469 pupils attending primary schools, and in 1980 13,798 pupils studied at secondary schools. In 1987 the Government initiated a project to improve the education system and to make it more relevant to the country's development needs. The project was partly funded by an IDA loan of US $7.9m. About 2,000 primary-school teachers and 350 lower-secondary teachers were to receive training, while a National Centre for Technical Education and Vocational Training and a business school were to be established to provide industrial and office training. Current expenditure by the central Government on education, culture, youth and sports in 1986 was 2,477m. Comoros francs, representing 23.9% of total current spending. In 1988 the sector was allocated 28% of total planned current expenditure.

Public Holidays

1989: 5 March* (Leilat al-Meiraj, Ascension of the Prophet), 7 April* (Ramadan begins), 7 May* (Id al-Fitr, end of Ramadan), 6 July (Independence Day), 14 July* (Id al-Adha, Feast of the Sacrifice), 4 August* (Muharram, Islamic New Year), 13 August* (Ashoura), 13 October* (Mouloud, Birth of the Prophet).

1990: 23 February* (Leilat al-Meiraj, Ascension of the Prophet), 28 March* (Ramadan begins), 27 April* (Id al-Fitr, end of Ramadan), 4 July* (Id al-Adha, Feast of the Sacrifice), 6 July (Independence Day), 24 July* (Muharram, Islamic New Year), 2 August* (Ashoura), 2 October* (Mouloud, Birth of the Prophet).

* Religious holidays, which are dependent on the Islamic lunar calendar, may differ by one or two days from the dates given.

Weights and Measures

The metric system is in force.

Statistical Survey

Source (unless otherwise stated): Ministère de l'Economie et des Finances, BP 324, Moroni; tel. 2767; telex 219.
Note: Unless otherwise indicated, figures in this Statistical Survey exclude data for Mayotte.

AREA AND POPULATION

Area: 1,862 sq km (719 sq miles) *By island:* Njazidja (Grande-Comore) 1,146 sq km, Nzwani (Anjouan) 424 sq km, Mwali (Mohéli) 290 sq km.

Population: 335,150 (males 167,089; females 168,061), excluding Mayotte (estimated population 50,740), at census of 15 September 1980; 484,000 (official estimate, including Mayotte, 31 December 1986).

Principal Towns (population at 1980 census): Moroni (capital) 17,267; Mutsamudu 13,000; Fomboni 5,400.

Births and Deaths (including figures for Mayotte): 8,700 registered live births (birth rate 30.7 per 1,000) in 1973; 5,284 registered deaths (death rate 19.5 per 1,000) in 1970. Average annual birth rate 46.8 per 1,000 in 1970–75, 46.6 per 1,000 in 1975–80, 46.4 per 1,000 in 1980–85; average annual death rate 18.3 per 1,000 in 1970–75, 17.2 per 1,000 in 1975–80, 15.9 per 1,000 in 1980–85 (UN estimates).

Economically Active Population (ILO estimates, '000 persons at mid-1980, including figures for Mayotte): Agriculture, forestry and fishing 150; Industry 10; Services 20; Total 181 (males 104, females 77. Source: ILO, *Economically Active Population Estimates and Projections, 1950–2025*.

AGRICULTURE, ETC.

Principal Crops (FAO estimates, '000 metric tons, 1986): Rice (paddy) 16, Maize 6, Cassava (Manioc) 93, Sweet potatoes 18, Pulses 2, Coconuts 47, Bananas 36. Source: FAO, *Production Yearbook*.

Livestock (FAO estimates '000 head, year ending September 1986): Asses 4, Cattle 86, Sheep 9, Goats 95. Source: FAO, *Production Yearbook*.

Fishing (FAO estimates, '000 metric tons, live weight): Total catch 5.0 in 1984; 5.2 in 1985; 5.3 in 1986. Source: FAO, *Yearbook of Fishery Statistics*.

INDUSTRY

Electric energy (production by public utilities): 10 million kWh in 1985. Source: UN, *Industrial Statistics Yearbook*.

FINANCE

Currency and Exchange Rates: 100 centimes = 1 Comoros franc. *Coins:* 1, 2, 5, 10 and 20 francs. *Notes:* 50, 100, 500, 1,000 and 5,000 francs. *Sterling and Dollar Equivalents* (30 September 1988): £1 sterling = 538.6 Comoros francs; US $1 = 318.5 Comoros francs; 1,000 Comoros francs = £1.857 = $3.140. *Average Exchange Rate* (Comoros francs per US $): 449.26 in 1985; 346.30 in 1986; 300.54 in 1987. Note: The Comoros franc has a fixed link to French currency, with an exchange rate of 1 French franc = 50 Comoros francs.

Budget (estimates, million Comoros francs, 1986): *Current revenue:* Indirect taxes 5,816. *Current expenditure:* Public debt 2,840, Federal Assembly 284, President of the Republic 575, National defence 872, Foreign affairs and co-operation 395, National education, culture, youth and sports 2,477, Home affairs, information and press 221, Finance and budget 238, Equipment, planning and environment 204, Production and agriculture 136, Health and population 652, Immigration 16, Telecommunications 8, Transport and tourism 93, Justice and civil service 143, Other expenditure 1,226; Total 10,380. *Capital budget:* Revenue 17,372, Expenditure 17,372.

International Reserves (US $ million at 31 December 1986): Gold 0.24; IMF special drawing rights 0.22; Foreign exchange 17.33; Total 17.79 (Source: IMF, *International Financial Statistics*).

THE COMOROS

Statistical Survey, Directory

Money Supply (million Comoros francs at 31 December 1986): Currency outside deposit money banks 3,118; Demand deposits at deposit money banks 2,904 (Source: IMF, *International Financial Statistics*).

Gross Domestic Product by Kind of Economic Activity (estimates, million Comoros francs at current factor cost, 1983): Agriculture, hunting, forestry and fishing 14,250; Manufacturing 1,840; Electricity, gas and water 210; Construction 3,910; Trade, restaurants and hotels 4,940; Transport, storage and communications 570; Finance, insurance, real estate and business services 890; Public administration and defence 5,570; Other services 300; GDP at factor cost 32,480; Indirect taxes (net of subsidies) 4,380; GDP in purchasers' values 36,860. Source: UN Economic Commission for Africa, *African Statistical Yearbook*.

Balance of Payments (US $ million, 1987): Merchandise exports f.o.b. 11.60; Merchandise imports f.o.b. −46.15; *Trade balance* −34.55; Exports of services 16.24; Imports of services −44.62; *Balance on goods and services* −62.93; Private unrequited transfers 0.93; Government unrequited transfers 38.74; *Current balance* −23.26; Long-term capital (net) 22.45; Short-term capital (net) 7.07; Net errors and omissions 2.54; *Total* (net monetary movements) 8.79; Valuation changes (net) 0.03; *Changes in reserves* 8.82 (Source: IMF, *International Financial Statistics*).

EXTERNAL TRADE

Principal Commodities (estimates, million French francs, 1987): *Imports:* Fuels 50.3, Vehicles 32.7, Rice 19.8, Iron and Steel 18.9, Cement 10.8; Total (incl. others) 311.2. *Exports:* Cloves 31.0, Vanilla 25.5, Ylang-ylang 11.8; Total (incl. others) 69.7. Source: Banque Centrale des Comores, quoted by La Zone Franc, *Rapport 1987*.

Principal Trading Partners (million French francs, 1977): *Imports:* People's Republic of China 4.0, France 33.6, Kenya and Tanzania 7.6, Madagascar 16.1, Pakistan 6.8; Total (incl. others) 81.1. *Exports:* France 28.8, Federal Republic of Germany 1.5, Madagascar 2.2, USA 9.4; Total (incl. others) 44.0.

TRANSPORT

Road Traffic (1977): 3,600 motor vehicles in use.

International Shipping (estimated sea-borne freight traffic, '000 metric tons, 1985): Goods loaded 10; Goods unloaded 95. Source: UN, *Monthly Bulletin of Statistics*.

Civil Aviation (1973): 15,227 passenger arrivals, 15,674 passenger departures, 909 tons of freight handled.

COMMUNICATIONS MEDIA

Radio receivers (1985): 50,000 in use.

EDUCATION

Pre-Primary (1980): 600 teachers; 17,778 pupils.

Primary (1982): 1,617 teachers; 61,469 pupils.

Secondary (1980): 449 teachers (general education 432; teacher training 8; vocational 9); 13,798 pupils (general education 13,528; teacher training 119; vocational 151).

Directory

The Constitution

The Constitution of the Federal Islamic Republic of the Comoros was approved by popular referendum on 1 October 1978. Several amendments were made in October 1982 and in January 1985. It is not in effect on the island of Mayotte (q.v.), which it envisages as eventually 'rejoining the Comoran community'.

GENERAL PRINCIPLES

The preamble affirms the will of the Comoran people to derive from the state religion, Islam, inspiration for the regulation of government, to adhere to the principles laid down by the Charters of the UN and the OAU, and to guarantee the rights of citizens in accordance with the UN Declaration of Human Rights. Sovereignty resides in the people, through their elected representatives. All citizens are equal before the law.

ISLAND AND FEDERAL INSTITUTIONS

The Comoros archipelago constitutes a Federal Islamic Republic. Each island has autonomy in matters not assigned by the Constitution to the federal institutions, which comprise the Presidency and Council of Government, the Federal Assembly, and the Supreme Court. There is universal secret suffrage for all citizens over 18 in full possession of their civil and political rights. The number of political parties may be regulated by federal law.

The President of the Republic is Head of State and Head of Government and is elected for six years by direct suffrage, and may not serve for more than two terms. He nominates ministers to form the Council of Government. The Governor of each island is nominated by the President of the Republic for five years, and appoints not more than four Commissioners to whom administration is delegated. Should the Presidency fall vacant, the President of the Supreme Court temporarily assumes the office until a presidential election takes place.

The Federal Assembly is directly elected for five years. Each electoral ward elects one deputy. The Assembly meets for not more than 45 days at a time, in April and October and if necessary in extraordinary sessions. Matters covered by federal legislation include defence, posts and telecommunications, external and inter-island transport, civil, penal and industrial law, external trade, federal taxation, long-term economic planning, education and health.

The Council of each island is directly elected for four years. Each electoral ward elects one councillor. Each Council meets for not more than 15 days at a time, in March and December and if necessary in extraordinary sessions. The Councils are responsible for non-federal legislation.

THE JUDICIARY

The judiciary is independent of the legislative and executive powers. The Supreme Court acts as a Constitutional Council in resolving constitutional questions and supervising presidential elections, and as High Court of Justice it arbitrates in any case where the government is accused of malpractice.

The Government

HEAD OF STATE

President and Head of Government: AHMED ABDALLAH ABDEREMANE (elected 22 October 1978; re-elected 30 September 1984).

COUNCIL OF MINISTERS
(December 1988)

Minister of Foreign Affairs, Foreign Trade and Co-operation: SAÏD KAFE.

Minister of the Interior, Information and Broadcasting: OMAR TAMOU.

Minister of Finance, Budget, Economy, Trade, Management of State Companies and Commercial and Industrial Public Organizations: SAÏD AHMED SAÏD ALI.

Minister of Planning, Construction, Environment, Urban Development and Housing: MIKIDACHE ABDEL-RAHIM.

Minister of National Education, Culture, Youth and Sports: SALIM IDAROUSSE.

Minister of Production, Rural Development, Industry and Crafts: MOHAMMED ALI.

Minister of Justice, Public Administration, Employment and Professional Training: Dr BEN ALI BACAR.

Minister of Public Health and Population: ALI HASSAN ALI.

Secretary of State for the Interior: ABDEL-AZIZ HAMADI.

Secretary of State for Transport and Tourism: ATHOUMANE ABDOU.

Secretary of State for Posts and Telecommunications: AHMED BEN DAOUD.

MINISTRIES

Office of the Head of Government: BP 421, Moroni; tel. 2413; telex 233.

THE COMOROS   *Directory*

Ministry of Agricultural Production and Small Manufacturing: BP 41, Moroni; tel. 2292; telex 240.
Ministry of the Civil Service, Labour and Employment: BP 109, Moroni; tel. 2098; telex 219.
Ministry of Defence: BP 246, Moroni; tel. 2646; telex 233.
Ministry of Finance and Economy: BP 324, Moroni; tel. 2767; telex 219.
Ministry of Foreign Affairs and Foreign Trade: BP 428, Moroni; tel. 2306; telex 219.
Ministry of Information: BP 421, Moroni; telex 219.
Ministry of Justice: BP 520, Moroni; tel. 2411; telex 219.
Ministry of National Education, Culture, Youth and Sports: BP 446, Moroni; tel. 2420; telex 229.
Ministry of Posts and Telecommunications: Moroni; tel. 2343.
Ministry of Public Health: BP 42, Moroni; tel. 2277; telex 219.
Ministry of Transport and Tourism: Moroni; tel. 2098; telex 244.

Legislature

ASSEMBLÉE FÉDÉRALE

Elections for a Federal Assembly of 42 members were held on 22 March 1987. These elections were the first in which opposition candidates were officially permitted to stand since 1978. The Union comorienne pour le progrès (Udzima) retained control of all constituencies, although the opposition parties obtained 35.5% of the votes cast in 20 contested constituencies. In one district a second run-off poll between government and opposition candidates was held on 29 March.

President: MOHAMED TAKI ABDULKARIM.

Political Organizations

The 1978 Constitution provided for the free activity of political parties, but in January 1979 the Federal Assembly voted for the establishment of a one-party system for the following 12 years. The **Union comorienne pour le progrès (Udzima)** became the sole legal party in February 1982. In April 1988 a regional pro-government party, the **Union régionale pour la défense de la politique du Président Ahmed Abdallah**, led by NASSUF ABDALLAH, was founded on the island of Nzwani.

Various unofficial opposition groups continue to exist, mostly based in France. These include the **CHUMA** (Islands' Friendship and Unity Party), led by SAÏD ALI KEMAL, and the **Union pour une République Démocratique des Comores (URDC)**, led by MOUZAOIR ABDALLAH. In June 1987, at a meeting in France, the **FNUK-UNIKOM** (f. from the merger of the Front national uni des Komores and the Union des komoriens), led by ABUBAKAR AHMED NURDIN, the **Association des stagiares et des étudiants comoriens** and the **Mouvement pour la libération des Comores** agreed to merge into a single party. In 1988 it was reported that a group of exiles from the island of Mwali had formed the **Echo Mohélien**, based in Mayotte. A banned opposition group, the **Front démocratique (FD)**, led by MUSTAPHA SAÏD CHEIKH until his imprisonment for life in 1985, is active within the Comoros.

Diplomatic Representation

EMBASSIES IN THE COMOROS

China, People's Republic: Moroni; tel. 2721; Ambassador: LIU QINGYOU.
France: blvd de Strasbourg, BP 465, Moroni; tel. 73-07-53; telex 220; Ambassador: ROBERT SCHERRER.
Mauritius: Moroni.

Judicial System

The Supreme Court consists of two members chosen by the President of the Republic, two elected by the Federal Assembly, one by the Council of each island, and former Presidents of the Republic; Pres. HARIBOU CHEBANI.

Religion

The majority of the population are Muslims. There are an estimated 1,300 adherents of the Roman Catholic Church.

CHRISTIANITY
The Roman Catholic Church

Office of Apostolic Administrator of the Comoros: Mission Catholique, BP 46, Moroni; tel. 73-05-70.

The Press

Al Watwany: M'tsangani, BP 984, Moroni; tel. 73-08-61; f. 1985; weekly; state-owned; general; Dir ALLAOUI SAÏD OMAR; circ. 1,500.
L'Archipel: Moroni; f. 1988; weekly; independent; Publrs ABOUBACAR MCHANGAMA, SAINDOU KAMAL.

NEWS AGENCIES

Agence Comores Presse (ACP): Moroni.

Foreign Bureau

Agence France-Presse (AFP): c/o Radio-Comoros, BP 250, Moroni; tel. 2260; telex 241; Rep. ALI SOILIH.

Radio and Television

In 1985 there were an estimated 50,000 radio receivers in use. In 1986 France announced that it would be funding the construction of a television station.

Radio-Comoros: BP 250, Moroni; tel. 73-05-31; telex 241; govt-controlled since 1975; home service in Comoran and French; international services in Arabic and French; Tech. Dir KOMBO SOULAIMANA.

Finance

BANKING

(cap. = capital; dep. = deposits; res = reserves; m. = million; brs = branches; amounts in Comoros francs)

Central Bank

Banque Centrale des Comores: BP 405, Moroni; tel. 73-10-02; telex 213; f. 1981; bank of issue; cap. 500m.; Pres. AHMED DAHALANI; Dir-Gen. MOHAMED HALIFA.

Other Banks

Banque de Développement des Comores: place de France, BP 298, Moroni; tel. 73-08-18; telex 246; f. 1982; provides loans, guarantees and equity participation for small and medium-scale projects; Banque Centrale des Comores and Comoran govt hold two-thirds of shares, European Investment Bank and Caisse Centrale de Coopération Economique (France) each own one-sixth; cap. 300m. (Dec. 1986); Pres. DAROUECHE ABDALLAH; Dir-Gen. CAABI ELYACHROUTU.
Banque Internationale des Comores (BIC): place de France, BP 175, Moroni; tel. 73-02-43; telex 242; f. 1982; subsidiary of Banque Internationale pour l'Afrique Occidentale; cap. 300m., res 220.2m., dep. 8,142m. (1987); Gen. Man. EMILE EMERY; 6 brs.
BIC Afribank: Moroni; telex 274.

Trade and Industry

CEFADER: a rural design, co-ordination and support centre, with brs on each island.
Chambre de Commerce, d'Industrie et d'Agriculture: BP 763, Moroni.
Mission Permanente de Coopération: Moroni; centre for administering bilateral aid from France; Dir GABRIEL COURCELLE.
Office National du Commerce: Moroni, Njazidja; state-operated agency for the promotion and development of domestic and external trade; Chair. SAÏD MOHAMED DJOHAR.
Société de développement de la pêche artisanale des Comores (SODEPAC): state-operated agency overseeing fisheries development programme.

Other state-owned enterprises include **BAMBAO** and the **Société Comorienne des Viandes (SOCOVIA)**, a company specializing in the sale of meat and other food products, which was nationalized in 1987.

TRADE UNION

Union des Travailleurs des Comores: BP 405, Moroni.

Transport

ROADS

There are approximately 750 km of roads serviceable throughout the year, of which 398 km are paved. A major road-improvement scheme was launched in 1979, with foreign assistance, and in 1984 a French company won the contract to resurface 170 km of roads on Njazidja and Nzwani islands.

SHIPPING

Large vessels anchor off Moroni, Mutsamudu and Fomboni, and the port of Mutsamudu can now accommodate vessels of up to 11 m draught. In 1988 the EEC provided financial aid to develop Moroni port. Work on the project was expected to begin in late 1988. Goods from Europe come via Madagascar, and coasters serve the Comoros from the east coast of Africa.

Société Comorienne de Navigation: Moroni; services to Madagascar.

CIVIL AVIATION

The international airport is at Moroni-Hahaya on Njazidja and each of the three other islands has a small airfield. In 1986 the Comoros received French aid to upgrade the Moroni-Hahaya Airport.

Air Comores (Société Nationale des Transports Aériens): BP 544, Moroni; telex 218; f. 1975; state-owned; services to Nzwani, Mwali and Dzaoudzi; Gen. Man. DJAMALEDDINE AHMED; fleet of 1 Fokker F27.

Tourism

Fewer than 2,000 tourists per year visit the Comoros, whose chief attractions are the beaches, underwater fishing and mountain trips.

Société Comorienne de Tourisme et d'Hôtellerie (COMOTEL): Itsandra Hotel, Njazidja; tel. 2365; national tourist agency.

THE CONGO

Introductory Survey

Location, Climate, Language, Religion, Flag, Capital

The People's Republic of the Congo is an equatorial country on the west coast of Africa. It has a coastline of about 170 km on the Atlantic Ocean, from which the country extends northward to Cameroon and the Central African Republic. It is bordered by Gabon in the west, with Zaire to the east, while in the south there is a short frontier with the Cabinda exclave of Angola. The climate is tropical, with temperatures averaging 21°–27°C (70°–80°F) throughout the year. The average annual rainfall is about 1,200 mm (47 in). The official language is French, and many African languages are also used. More than 50% of the population follow traditional beliefs, although over 30% are Roman Catholics. There are small Protestant and Muslim minorities. The national flag is red, with the state emblem (two green palms enclosing a crossed hammer and hoe, surmounted by a gold star) in the upper hoist. The capital is Brazzaville.

Recent History

Formerly part of French Equatorial Africa, Middle Congo became the autonomous Republic of the Congo, within the French Community, in November 1958. The Congo became fully independent on 15 August 1960. The leading figure in this period was the Abbé Fulbert Youlou, a former Roman Catholic priest who, in contravention of ecclesiastical orders, became involved in politics and was suspended from priestly office. In November 1958 Youlou became Prime Minister, and in November 1959 he was elected President of the Republic by the National Assembly. After independence, the Assembly approved a new constitution for the Congo in March 1961. Under its provisions, Youlou was re-elected President (unopposed) by popular vote. Proposals to establish a one-party state were announced by President Youlou in August 1962 and overwhelmingly approved by the National Assembly in April 1963.

However, on 15 August 1963 (the third anniversary of independence and the date scheduled for the introduction of one-party rule) Youlou was forced to resign, following anti-Government demonstrations and strikes by trade unionists. On the following day, a provisional government was formed, with the support of military and trade union leaders. Alphonse Massamba-Débat, a former Minister of Planning, became Prime Minister. In December a national referendum approved a new constitution, and a general election was held for a new National Assembly. Later in the month, Massamba-Débat was elected President for a five-year term. The new regime adopted a policy of 'scientific socialism', and in July 1964 the Mouvement national de la révolution (MNR) was established as the sole political party. In June 1965 ex-President Youlou was sentenced to death *in absentia*.

Tension between the armed forces and the MNR culminated in a military coup in August 1968. The leader of the coup was Capt. (later Maj.) Marien Ngouabi, a paratroop officer, who became Chief of the General Staff. The National Assembly was replaced by the National Council of the Revolution, led by Ngouabi. The President was briefly restored to office, with reduced powers, but was dismissed again in September, when Capt. (later Maj.) Alfred Raoul, the new Prime Minister, also became Head of State, a position that he relinquished in January 1969 to Maj. Ngouabi, while remaining Prime Minister until the end of that year.

Ngouabi set up a regime which proclaimed itself Marxist but maintained close economic ties with France. The People's Republic of the Congo, as it became in January 1970, was governed by a single political party, the Parti congolais du travail (PCT). The regime was threatened by left-wing protests and attempted coups, and there were serious ethnic jealousies between the rival tribes. In 1973 Ngouabi introduced a new constitution and a National Assembly with delegates elected from a single party list. However, Ngouabi felt increasingly insecure, and in 1976 he dismissed the Political Bureau of the PCT, replacing it by a Special Revolutionary General Staff.

In March 1977 Ngouabi was assassinated. Ex-President Massamba-Débat was charged with organizing the attempted coup and later executed. The Government was taken over by an 11-member Military Committee of the PCT, and in April 1977 Col (later Brig.-Gen.) Joachim Yhombi-Opango, the Chief of Staff and, like Ngouabi, a member of the Kouyou tribe, was named as the new Head of State.

The worsening economic crisis and the inherited regional and ethnic imbalances, however, made Yhombi-Opango's regime vulnerable to both left and right. In April 1977 he abrogated the Constitution and suspended the National Assembly. In August 1978 a plot to overthrow the Government was reported. In February 1979 Yhombi-Opango and the Military Committee handed over their powers to the Central Committee of the PCT. Following an election in March, Col Denis Sassou-Nguesso (a member of the Mboshi ethnic group) became President of the Republic, having assumed power in the interim month as head of a Provisional Committee. In July a National People's Assembly and regional councils were also elected, and the new socialist Constitution was overwhelmingly approved in a referendum. At the third PCT Congress, in July 1984, Sassou-Nguesso was unanimously re-elected Chairman of the PCT Central Committee and President of the Republic for a second five-year term. Under the provisions of a constitutional amendment, he also became Head of Government. As a result of an extensive government reshuffle in August, Ange-Edouard Poungui, a former Vice-President, became Prime Minister in succession to Col Louis Sylvain Goma, who had held the post since December 1975. Sassou-Nguesso assumed control of the Ministry of Defence and Security. Legislative elections were held in September, and ex-President Yhombi-Opango, who had been detained since March 1979, was placed under house arrest in November in the northern village of Owando.

Economic decline continued, and in November 1985 the introduction of austerity measures into the system of awarding grants to students resulted in violent demonstrations in Brazzaville, during which three people were reported to have been killed. Several students were arrested. In August 1986 Claude-Ernest Ndalla, a former Minister of Education, was sentenced to death, following the trial of 10 people by the Revolutionary Court of Justice in Brazzaville. All had been accused of complicity in causing bomb attacks in the capital in 1982, in which nine people died.

In December 1985, following a reorganization of the secretariat of the PCT Central Committee, the Government was reshuffled and its membership reduced. In November 1986 the membership of the Politburo was decreased from 13 to 10, and in the following month the number of ministerial portfolios was again reduced by means of a government reshuffle.

Persistent ethnic rivalries, together with disillusionment with the Government's response to the country's worsening economic situation, resulted in an increase in opposition to the Sassou-Nguesso regime. In July 1987 some 20 army officers, most of whom were members of the Kouyou tribe, were arrested for alleged complicity in a coup plot. Shortly afterwards, fighting broke out, in the northern Cuvette region, between government forces and troops led by Pierre Anga, a former captain who had served on the Military Committee which held power under Yhombi-Opango. In early September government troops made an assault on Owando, and, with French military assistance, the rebellion was suppressed. Yhombi-Opango was taken under arrest to Brazzaville, where he was imprisoned. However, Anga fled from the attack, and evaded arrest until July 1988, when it was reported that he had been killed by the Congolese security forces.

Changes in the PCT hierarchy in July 1987 were followed by a government reshuffle in August, in which the financial and economic functions were consolidated under a Minister of Planning and Finance, and a Ministry at the Presidency in charge of Defence and Security was created. A further reallocation of portfolios took place in July 1988, following the dismissal of the Ministers of the Environment and Scientific Research and of Information: their dismissal was reported to be linked to the discovery of an agreement with a Liechtenstein-based company, regarding the import of toxic waste into the Congo.

In August 1988 an amnesty was announced for all political prisoners sentenced before July 1987, as well as for 463 common law offenders, to commemorate the 25th anniversary of the overthrow of the Youlou regime. In November the PCT approved Sassou-Nguesso as the sole candidate in the 1989 presidential election. In the same month, however, a faction of the party published a document accusing the Government of having lost its revolutionary momentum, and criticizing its recourse to the IMF and its alleged links with the South African Government.

In foreign policy, the Congo has moved away from being within the Soviet sphere of influence, as was apparent in the mid-1970s, and has fostered links with neighbouring francophone countries, and also with France, the USA and the People's Republic of China. There was an improvement in relations with France following the victory of the French left in the 1981 elections, and President Mitterrand paid an official visit to the Congo in October 1982. Western nations, particularly France, remain the chief source of development aid (French aid to the Congo represents more than one-half of total assistance to that country), but some Eastern bloc aid is received in the form of military and security assistance. The Congo is committed to the survival of the OAU (see p. 186), and is a member of the Customs and Economic Union of Central Africa (UDEAC, see p. 154). In 1986/87, during his tenure of the OAU chairmanship, President Sassou-Nguesso toured a number of Western European countries, with discussions centring on the African debt crisis and the Chad/Libya conflict. In 1988 the Congo hosted negotiations between Angola, Cuba, South Africa and the USA regarding the withdrawal of Cuban troops from Angola and the question of Namibian independence.

Government

There is only one political party, the Parti congolais du travail (PCT), which professes Marxist-Leninist principles. The Chairman of the Central Committee of the PCT is the President of the Republic, Head of State and Head of Government, elected for a five-year term by the Congress of the PCT, which also elects the 75-member Central Committee. To direct its policy, the Central Committee elects a Politburo, which comprised 10 members in December 1986. The senior executive body of the PCT is the Secretariat of the Central Committee, with eight members in December 1986. Supreme executive power rests with the Council of Ministers, under the chairmanship of the President of the Republic. The main legislative body is the National People's Assembly, which was re-established in 1979. The 153 members are elected by universal adult suffrage from a list proposed by the PCT. The Assembly is responsible to the Prime Minister, himself responsible to the PCT.

Responsibility for local administration is vested in nine People's Regional Councils, each with an Executive Committee elected by universal franchise. They act under the direction of 10 Commissars designated by the PCT Central Committee.

Defence

In June 1988 the army numbered 8,000, the navy 300 and the air force 500. There were 6,100 men in paramilitary forces, and 500 Cuban troops were stationed in the country, as were 100 Soviet troops. National service is voluntary for men and women, and lasts for two years. The defence budget for 1985 was 25,000m. francs CFA.

Economic Affairs

Prior to the development of the petroleum industry, the Congo's most important economic activity was forestry. Forests cover approximately 55% of the country's area, and more than one-half is exploitable. Reserves of timber are estimated to be between 90m. and 120m. cu m, with a production capacity of 850,000 cu m per year. Species exploited include okoumé, limba and sapele. Between 1978 and 1986 major eucalyptus plantations were installed, to supply a proposed paper-pulp factory. However, owing to weaknesses in the world paper-pulp market, the construction of the factory was cancelled, and in 1987 the timber was sold to foreign interests. Plans have been announced for the construction, by private US interests, of a telegraph- and power-transmission-pole factory near Pointe-Noire. As a result of increased public investment, both in reafforestation and in research, and of improved transport facilities, production of sawlogs rose from 572,000 cu m in 1985 to 715,000 cu m in 1986. Earnings from wood exports totalled 12,363m. francs CFA in 1985.

As a result of the rapid rise in earnings from petroleum, the agricultural sector's share of gross domestic product (GDP) declined during the early 1980s. Agriculture, forestry and fishing contributed 19% of total GDP in 1965, but only 10% in 1986. Less than 1% of the country's area is devoted to agricultural production, with the result that the Congo remains heavily dependent on food imports, which in 1984 accounted for 11% of total import expenditure. The staple crops are cassava and plantains, while maize, groundnuts and rice are also cultivated. The major cash crops are sugar cane, oil palm, cocoa and coffee. Sugar development has been taken over by a Franco-Dutch concern, and the annual output of raw sugar totalled 46,000 metric tons in 1985, compared with a low of 5,700 tons in 1979. By 1985, annual production of palm oil had declined to some 1,000 tons (compared with 2,460 tons in 1982), but output was expected to improve as a result of the implementation of development projects in the Ouesso region, which commenced in 1986. Cocoa is cultivated on 8,000 ha in the north-west Sangha region, and production of cocoa beans in 1986 was estimated at 2,000 tons. Coffee production totalled an estimated 2,000 tons in 1986. Cultivation of tobacco, once a major cash crop, has dwindled as a result of the drift of producers into more profitable crops. The Government is undertaking extensive development and plantation projects to revive production of palm oil, coffee and cocoa. In late 1986, in accordance with an IMF-sponsored structural adjustment programme, the state monopoly on food-crop marketing was abolished.

Since 1960, when the Congo's first oilfield, at Pointe-Indienne, went into production, the petroleum industry has dominated the country's economy, contributing between 60% and 70% of revenue to the national budget during the early 1980s and providing more than 90% of export earnings. The sector experienced a particularly rapid growth over this period, due to a high level of investment and increasing exports. By 1984, with seven oilfields in operation, annual production of crude petroleum had risen to 6m. tons, compared with only 2.6m. tons in 1979. However, reserves in almost all the major fields were by then declining, and further exploration was carried out on and off shore. Annual output slackened to 5.8m. tons in 1985, a level that was maintained in 1986 and 1987. Production began at the Tchibouela field, which has estimated reserves of 12m. tons, in December 1987, and at the Zatchi field, at an initial level of 6,100 barrels per day (b/d), in October 1988. In January 1987 total proven reserves of petroleum were assessed at 720m. barrels. However, revenue from this commodity has been increasingly offset by the high cost of exploitation. There are reserves of 600m. tons in the largest field, Emeraude: their heavy viscous nature would, however, necessitate expensive methods of extraction, which so far have not seemed to be viable. The operative oil companies are mainly French and Italian, and interest has been shown by US oil corporations. The Congo is not a member of OPEC. A petroleum refinery at Pointe-Noire, with an annual distillation capacity of 1m. tons, began operations in 1982 but produced only 513,013 tons in 1984. Deposits of natural gas at Pointe-Indienne and near Pointe-Noire currently yield some 760,000 cu m annually, nearly all of which is flared. Copper, gold, lead and zinc are all mined in small quantities, and iron-ore reserves are being developed with aid from the USSR.

In 1985 total output of electric energy reached 237m. kWh, mainly from the Bouenza and Djoué hydroelectric plants. In 1988 it was announced that, with assistance from the People's Republic of China, the Bouenza station was to be rehabilitated. Construction work on a new 100-MW plant at Imboulou was also in progress. Manufacturing activity, which in 1985 contributed just 6% of GDP (compared with the 47% provided by the mining sector), is concentrated mainly on the processing of agricultural and forestry products. Revenue from exports of agro-industrial products declined from 44,800m. francs CFA in 1986 to 39,600m. francs CFA in 1987. Several state-owned companies were designated for closure or sale to private interests under the 1987/88 interim investment programme.

In the mid-1980s fluctuations in the price of petroleum (and, in particular, the collapse of world oil prices in early 1986, as a result of continuing high OPEC production levels), together with weaknesses in the value of the US dollar, exemplified the need for the diversification of the Congo's economic activities away from dependence on the petroleum sector, and obliged the Government to adopt a flexible approach to planned spending. The 1982–86 Development Plan concentrated on using petroleum receipts to improve the transport infrastructure and to increase food production. An intensive programme of structural adjustment measures was commenced in 1985, and interim development programmes were implemented in 1986/87 and 1987/88. The latter programme, which aimed to reduce state participation in the economy and to increase the productive role of the private sector, was supported by structural adjustment loans from the World Bank, France and the African Development Bank (ADB). Revenue from petroleum exports was projected to total 35,200m. francs CFA in 1988, a slight increase on an estimated 34,000m. francs CFA in the previous year. Crisis budgets were announced in 1985–89. The 1989 budget was to balance at 235,800m. francs CFA, compared with 196,800m. francs CFA in 1987 (the 1988 budget, which was projected to balance at 283,976 francs CFA, was reduced in mid-1988, owing to the increasing effects of the economic crisis).

Since independence, economic growth has been closely linked with the performance of the petroleum sector. Between 1965 and 1980 the expansion of real GDP averaged 5.9% annually. Between 1980 and 1986 the average declined slightly, to 5.1%, as petroleum production was affected by the fall in international prices for that commodity.

In 1987, according to World Bank estimates, the Congo's gross national product (GNP), measured at average 1985–87 prices, was US $1,761m., equivalent to $880 per head. Owing to this high level of GNP, the Congo is classed as a lower middle-income country, despite its severe external debt crisis. It was estimated that the average annual increase in GNP per head was only 0.3%, in real terms, between 1980 and 1987. Real GNP per head declined by an estimated 8.6% in 1987.

In order to ease the burden of debt service, which in recent years has accounted for around 40% of the Congo's foreign earnings, US $500m. of the public external debt was rescheduled at a July 1986 meeting of the 'Paris Club' of Western creditor governments, following the conclusion of a SDR 22.4m. stand-by agreement with the IMF. In February 1988 the 'London Club' of commercial creditors agreed to reschedule a further 85,000m. francs CFA of the country's foreign debt, and granted some 17,000m. francs CFA in new credits. By the end of 1988, however, the Congo's foreign debt was estimated at $4,400m., compared with $1,396m. at the end of 1984.

Social Welfare

There is a state pension scheme and a system of family allowances and other welfare services. The health system consists of three general hospitals, 31 medical centres, 419 dispensaries, 98 infirmaries and seven centres for contagious diseases, giving a total of 7,048 hospital beds. Plans were announced in 1986 for the construction of a new hospital at Loubomo, in the Niari region. In 1981 there were 266 physicians and 849 qualified nurses working in the Congo.

Education

Education is officially compulsory for 10 years between six and 16 years of age. Primary education begins at the age of six and lasts for six years. Secondary education, from 12 years of age, lasts for seven years, comprising a first cycle of four years and a second of three years. In 1985, according to estimates by UNESCO, the average rate of adult illiteracy was 37.1% (males 28.6%, females 44.6%), one of the lowest in Africa. In 1965 all private schools were taken over by the Government. A number of students go to France for technical instruction. The Marien Ngouabi University, at Brazzaville, was founded in 1971.

Public Holidays

1989: 2 January (for New Year's Day), 24 March (Good Friday), 27 March (Easter Monday), 1 May (Labour Day), 15 August (Independence Day), 25 December (Christmas).

1990: 1 January (New Year's Day), 13 April (Good Friday), 16 April (Easter Monday), 1 May (Labour Day), 15 August (Independence Day), 25 December (Christmas).

Weights and Measures

The metric system is in force.

Statistical Survey

Source (unless otherwise stated): Centre National de la Statistique et des Etudes Economiques, Ministère du Plan, BP 2031, Brazzaville; tel. 81-36-94; telex 5210.

Area and Population

AREA, POPULATION AND DENSITY

Area (sq km)	342,000*
Population (census results)	
7 February 1974	1,319,790
1 January 1985	1,912,429
Density (per sq km) at 1 January 1985	5.6

* 132,047 sq miles.

REGIONS (estimated population at 1 January 1983)*

Brazzaville	456,383		Kouilou	78,738
Pool	219,329		Lékoumou	67,568
Pointe-Noire	214,466		Sangha	42,106
Bouenza	135,999		Nkayi	40,419
Cuvette	127,558		Likouala	34,302
Niari	114,229		Loubomo	33,591
Plateaux	110,379		**Total**	1,675,067

* Figures have not been revised to take account of the 1985 census results.

PRINCIPAL TOWNS (population at 1985 census)

Brazzaville (capital)	596,200
Pointe-Noire	298,014

BIRTHS AND DEATHS (UN estimates, annual averages)

	1970–75	1975–80	1980–85
Birth rate (per 1,000)	45.4	44.7	44.5
Death rate (per 1,000)	21.7	20.1	18.6

Source: UN, *World Population Prospects: Estimates and Projections as Assessed in 1984*.

THE CONGO

ECONOMICALLY ACTIVE POPULATION
(ILO estimates, '000 persons at mid-1980)

	Males	Females	Total
Agriculture, etc.	181	224	405
Industry	73	4	77
Services	136	30	166
Total	390	258	649

Source: ILO, *Economically Active Population Estimates and Projections, 1950–2025*.

Mid-1986 (FAO estimates, '000 persons): Agriculture, etc. 439; Total 724 (Source: FAO, *Production Yearbook*).

Agriculture

PRINCIPAL CROPS (FAO estimates, '000 metric tons)

	1984	1985	1986
Maize	7	7	8
Rice (paddy)	2	2	3
Sugar cane	360	510	510
Potatoes	2	2	2
Sweet potatoes	13	14	14
Cassava (Manioc)	600	610	620
Yams	14	14	14
Other roots and tubers	22	21	23
Dry beans	4	4	4
Dry peas	3	3	3
Tomatoes	9	9	9
Other vegetables	27	28	29
Avocados	20	20	21
Pineapples	105	107	110
Bananas	32	33	34
Plantains	62	63	64
Palm kernels	0.5	0.5	0.5
Groundnuts (in shell)	15	15	16
Coffee (green)*	2	3	2
Cocoa beans*	2	2	2
Natural rubber	2	2	2

* Unofficial figures.
Source: FAO, *Production Yearbook*.

LIVESTOCK
(FAO estimates, '000 head, year ending September)

	1984	1985	1986
Cattle	68	70	71
Pigs	42	43	44
Sheep	61	62	63
Goats	182	183	184

Poultry (FAO estimates, million): 1 in 1984; 1 in 1985; 1 in 1986.
Source: FAO, *Production Yearbook*.

LIVESTOCK PRODUCTS (FAO estimates, '000 metric tons)

	1984	1985	1986
Beef and veal	3	3	3
Pig meat	2	2	2
Poultry meat	5	5	5
Other meat	5	5	6
Cows' milk	3	3	3
Hen eggs	1.0	1.0	1.1

Source: FAO, *Production Yearbook*.

Forestry

ROUNDWOOD REMOVALS
('000 cubic metres, excluding bark)

	1984	1985	1986
Sawlogs, veneer logs and logs for sleepers	587	572	715
Other industrial wood*	218	224	231
Fuel wood	1,543	1,584	1,628
Total	2,348	2,380	2,574

* FAO estimates.
Source: FAO, *Yearbook of Forest Products*.

SAWNWOOD PRODUCTION ('000 cubic metres)

	1984	1985	1986
Total (incl. boxboards)	60	50	77

Fishing

('000 metric tons, live weight)

	1984	1985	1986
Freshwater fishes	12.0	13.5	12.0
Common sole	0.4	0.4	0.5
Sea catfishes	0.5	0.5	0.5
Boe drum	0.8	0.6	0.7
West African croakers	1.8	0.7	0.9
Sardinellas	12.8	9.3	11.6
Bonga shad	0.6	0.8	1.0
Other marine fishes (incl. unspecified), crustaceans and molluscs	2.8	2.0	2.8
Total catch	31.7	27.8	30.0

* FAO estimate.
Source: FAO, *Yearbook of Fishery Statistics*.

Mining

('000 metric tons, unless otherwise indicated)

	1983	1984	1985
Crude petroleum	5,365	6,007	5,830†
Copper ore*	3.9	2.5	2.9
Gold (kg)	8	3†	5†
Lead ore*	1.4	0.9	1.0
Zinc ore*	2.8	1.8	2.1

* Figures refer to the metal content of ores.
† Provisional figures.
Source: UN, *Industrial Statistics Yearbook*.

Crude petroleum ('000 metric tons): 5,860 in 1986; 5,800 in 1987 (Source: UN, *Monthly Bulletin of Statistics*).

THE CONGO

Industry

SELECTED PRODUCTS
('000 metric tons, unless otherwise indicated)

	1983	1984	1985
Palm oil	2	1	1
Wheat flour	8	3	0
Raw sugar	21	39	46
Beer ('000 hectolitres)	788	906	882
Soft drinks ('000 hectolitres)	278	279	299
Cigarettes (metric tons)	895	903	1,027
Veneer sheets ('000 cu metres)	74	63	67
Soap (metric tons)	5,100	5,500	1,900
Cement	29	n.a.	62
Electric energy (million kWh)	233	235	237
Footwear ('000 pairs)	928	995	1,128

Finance

CURRENCY AND EXCHANGE RATES

Monetary Units
100 centimes = 1 franc de la Coopération financière en Afrique centrale (CFA).

Denominations
Coins: 1, 2, 5, 10, 25, 50 and 100 francs CFA.
Notes: 100, 500, 1,000, 5,000 and 10,000 francs CFA.

French Franc, Sterling and Dollar Equivalents
(30 September 1988)
1 French franc = 50 francs CFA;
£1 sterling = 538.6 francs CFA;
US $1 = 318.5 francs CFA;
1,000 francs CFA = £1.857 = $3.140.

Average Exchange Rate (francs CFA per US $)
1985 449.26
1986 346.30
1987 300.54

ADMINISTRATIVE BUDGET (million francs CFA)

Revenue	1986	1987
Income tax and domestic taxes	64,800	56,900
Customs duties	56,900	45,500
Petroleum receipts	163,800	34,000
Various receipts	2,800	6,900
Capital resources and other mobilizable resources	43,000	15,000
Total	**331,300**	**158,300**

Expenditure	1986	1987
Public debt	159,100	46,000
Personnel	75,700	78,300
Equipment	12,800	2,200
Common services	9,000	1,400
Transfers	48,200	30,400
Capital budget	26,500	—
Total	**331,300**	**158,300**

CAPITAL BUDGET (million francs CFA)

Revenue	1986	1987
Transfer from administrative budget	26,500	—
Capital bonds	1,700	1,300
BEAC advances	4,000	—
Extraordinary receipts (incl. grants)	1,700	2,200
Various	6,300	1,600
Government borrowing	72,400	33,400
Total	**112,600**	**38,500**

Expenditure	1986	1987
Infrastructure	48,900	10,100
Economic development	34,700	14,900
Cultural and social capital	9,900	6,500
Administrative capital	8,700	7,000
Various	10,400	
Total	**112,600**	**38,500**

1988 (original budget estimates, million francs CFA): Receipts 124,800; Current expenditure 252,200; Investment expenditure 31,800.*

Source: *La Zone Franc—Rapport 1987.*

1989 (estimate): Budget to balance at 235,800 million francs CFA.

* In August 1988 the budget was reduced by an unspecified amount.

CENTRAL BANK RESERVES (US $ million at 31 December)

	1985	1986	1987
Gold*	3.60	4.36	5.37
IMF special drawing rights	1.66	4.65	2.71
Reserve position in IMF	0.53	0.59	0.68
Foreign exchange	1.78	1.58	0.01
Total	**7.56**	**11.18**	**7.77**

* Valued at market-related prices.

Source: IMF, *International Financial Statistics.*

MONEY SUPPLY ('000 million francs CFA at 31 December)

	1985	1986	1987
Currency outside banks	48.14	49.39	55.26
Demand deposits at commercial and development banks	58.31	42.66	41.82
Checking deposits at post office	5.43	5.46	5.26
Total money	**111.87**	**97.51**	**102.34**

Source: IMF, *International Financial Statistics.*

THE CONGO

NATIONAL ACCOUNTS (million francs CFA at current prices)
National Income and Product

	1982	1983	1984
Compensation of employees	206,055	225,935	257,713
Operating surplus	309,183	327,690	370,086
Domestic factor incomes	515,238	553,625	627,799
Consumption of fixed capital	89,555	120,722	176,986
Gross domestic product (GDP) at factor cost	604,793	673,347	804,785
Indirect taxes	114,759	134,493	162,290
Less Subsidies	8,038	9,454	8,566
GDP in purchasers' values	711,514	799,386	958,509
Factor income from abroad	6,452	5,258	5,077
Less Factor income paid abroad	66,037	68,147	72,723
Gross national product	651,929	736,497	890,863
Less Consumption of fixed capital	89,555	120,722	176,986
National income in market prices	562,374	615,775	713,877
Other current transfers from abroad	4,438	12,993	15,061
Less Other current transfers paid abroad	18,174	41,346	43,645
National disposable income	548,638	587,422	685,293

Source: UN, *National Accounts Statistics*.

Expenditure on the Gross Domestic Product

	1982	1983	1984
Government final consumption expenditure	95,759	120,021	141,696
Private final consumption expenditure	284,994	317,026	372,192
Increase in stocks	20,699	4,268	13,974
Gross fixed capital formation	404,695	280,185	277,265
Total domestic expenditure	806,147	721,500	805,127
Exports of goods and services	383,500	454,221	590,696
Less Imports of goods and services	478,133	376,335	437,314
GDP in purchasers' values	711,514	799,386	958,509

Gross Domestic Product by Economic Activity

	1982	1983	1984
Agriculture, hunting, forestry and fishing	60,707	65,010	71,159
Mining and quarrying	274,797	324,227	413,699
Manufacturing	30,912	40,441	41,638
Electricity, gas and water	5,642	9,351	10,119
Construction	58,374	55,866	72,112
Trade, restaurants and hotels	93,769	95,787	104,487
Transport, storage and communication	55,460	57,701	68,529
Finance, insurance, real estate, business, community, social and personal services	53,473	60,666	63,122
Government services	62,319	75,376	89,105
Other services	1,230	620	1,200
Sub-total	696,683	785,045	935,170
Import duties	30,332	29,052	37,069
Less Imputed bank service charge	15,501	14,711	13,730
GDP in purchasers' values	711,514	799,386	958,509

Source: UN, *National Accounts Statistics*.

BALANCE OF PAYMENTS (US $ million)

	1984	1985	1986
Merchandise exports f.o.b.	1,268.4	1,144.8	672.6
Merchandise imports f.o.b.	−617.6	−630.1	−512.4
Trade balance	650.8	514.7	160.2
Exports of services	86.8	83.8	111.2
Imports of services	−524.8	−762.7	−891.0
Balance on goods and services	212.8	164.2	−619.6
Private unrequited transfers (net)	−45.0	−37.5	−41.0
Government unrequited transfers (net)	42.3	40.4	59.9
Current balance	210.2	−161.3	−600.7
Direct capital investment (net)	34.9	12.7	22.4
Other long-term capital (net)	−90.4	11.8	−82.2
Short-term capital (net)	−236.7	11.0	210.7
Net errors and omissions	19.3	43.1	49.2
Total (net monetary movements)	−62.6	−82.7	−400.5
Valuation changes (net)	4.6	1.6	0.8
Exceptional financing (net)	54.2	81.2	391.1
Official financing (net)	0.6	−0.3	−0.1
Changes in reserves	−3.2	−0.2	−8.8

Source: IMF, *International Financial Statistics*.

External Trade

Note: Figures exclude trade with other states of the Customs and Economic Union of Central Africa (UDEAC).

PRINCIPAL COMMODITIES (million francs CFA)

Imports c.i.f.	1983	1984	1985
Machinery	68,257.4	54,452.5	62,481.4
Transport equipment	29,783.5	32,598.5	28,225.9
Petroleum products	5,672.6	9,766.1	8,290.2
Chemicals and related products	14,501.5	21,084.2	20,545.5
Textile materials and manufactures	6,724.0	10,495.1	8,648.9
Iron and steel	29,884.5	29,911.0	36,053.3
Food, beverages and tobacco	38,005.1	49,370.0	47,318.9
Plastic and rubber goods	7,548.8	7,923.8	7,046.5
Precision instruments, watches, etc.	5,606.7	6,143.3	6,307.1
Total (incl. others)	239,969.9	259,820.0	306,198.4

Source: Direction Générale des Douanes et des Droits Indirects.

Exports f.o.b.	1983	1984	1985
Petroleum and petroleum products	213,682.9	474,146.3	455,554.0
Wood	8,888.8	19,919.5	12,363.0
Diamonds	13,697.8	6,090.8	5,010.2
Coffee	1,103.8	2,548.8	952.4
Iron and steel	1,750.6	5,221.4	6,054.6
Total (incl. others)	243,719.7	516,700.0	488,365.7

Source: Direction Générale des Douanes et des Droits Indirects.

THE CONGO

PRINCIPAL TRADING PARTNERS (million francs CFA)

Imports c.i.f.	1983	1984	1985
Belgium/Luxembourg	5,133	4,782	6,214
China, People's Republic	3,063	5,505	4,279
France	143,637	136,793	118,797
Germany, Fed. Republic	10,853	15,412	12,176
Italy	9,353	7,778	21,567
Japan	8,001	9,480	8,917
Netherlands	6,186	5,827	7,010
Spain	4,456	8,639	11,495
USA	19,106	14,819	17,267
Total (incl. others)	239,970	259,820	306,198

Exports f.o.b.	1983	1984	1985
Belgium/Luxembourg	12,195	12,265	5,140
France	2,808	5,919	53,262
Germany, Fed. Republic	1,659	2,523	1,322
Italy	31,197	8,409	8,955
Netherlands	2,848	11,011	29,562
Spain	8,084	9,526	67,762
USA	176,032	400,780	293,112
Total (incl. others)	243,720	516,700	488,366

Transport

RAILWAYS (traffic)

	1982	1983	1984
Passenger-km (million)	390	381	408
Freight ton-km (million)	815	437	480

Source: UN, *Statistical Yearbook*.

ROAD TRAFFIC ('000 motor vehicles in use)

	1980	1981	1982
Passenger cars	45.4	49.0	30.5
Commercial vehicles	38.6	60.0	78.6

Source: Régie Nationale des Transports et des Travaux Publics.

INLAND WATERWAYS (freight traffic, '000 metric tons)

Port of Brazzaville	1981	1982	1983
Goods loaded	76.0	88.5	86.6
Goods unloaded	485.9	432.4	457.2

INTERNATIONAL SEA-BORNE SHIPPING (freight traffic, '000 metric tons)

	1983	1984	1985
Goods loaded	7,656	8,487	8,369
Goods unloaded	534	629	660

Source: UN, *Monthly Bulletin of Statistics*.

CIVIL AVIATION (traffic on scheduled services)*

	1982	1983	1984
Kilometres flown (million)	3.0	3.4	3.3
Passengers carried ('000)	161	217	228
Passenger-km (million)	247	268	274
Freight ton-km (million)	21.7	20.2	19.0

* Including an apportionment of the traffic of Air Afrique.
Source: UN, *Statistical Yearbook*.

Communications Media

	1981	1982	1983
Radio receivers ('000 in use)	98	102	100
Television receivers ('000 in use)	3.7	4.0	4.5
Telephones ('000 in use)	17	n.a.	18
Daily newspapers	n.a.	1	n.a.
Non-daily newspapers	n.a.	2	n.a.

1984: Daily newspapers 1 (average circulation 8,000 copies); Non-daily newspapers 2 (average circulation 15,000 copies).
Sources: UNESCO, *Statistical Yearbook*; UN, *Statistical Yearbook*.

Education

(1985)

	Institutions	Teachers	Pupils
Pre-primary	51	537	5,595
Primary	1,558	7,745	475,805
Secondary:			
General	n.a.	4,773	197,491
Teacher-training	n.a.	191	1,800
Vocational	n.a.	1,358	23,342
University*	1	565	9,385

* 1984 figures.
Source: UNESCO, *Statistical Yearbook*.

Directory

The Constitution

A new constitution was approved by national referendum on 8 July 1979. The Constitution was amended in July 1984. The following is a summary of its provisions:

FUNDAMENTAL PRINCIPLES

The People's Republic of the Congo is a sovereign independent state, in which all power springs from the people and belongs to the people. Treason against the people is the greatest crime. All nationals are guaranteed freedom of conscience and religion, and religious communities are free to practise their faith, but political organizations based on religion are banned. The land is the property of the people, and as necessary the state shall regulate its use. The state directs the economic life and development of the country according to the general plan. The right to own and inherit private property is guaranteed, and expropriation is governed by law.

HEAD OF STATE

The Chairman of the Central Committee of the Parti congolais du travail (PCT) is the President of the Republic, Head of State and Head of Government. He is elected for a five-year term by the Congress of the PCT.

THE EXECUTIVE

Executive power is vested in the Council of Ministers, under the Chairmanship of the President of the Republic. It directs and orientates the action of the Government; Ministers are appointed by the Prime Minister, who is responsible to the party.

THE LEGISLATURE

Most legislative powers are vested in the National People's Assembly. It has 153 members, elected for a five-year term by all adults over 18 years of age, with representatives from the PCT, mass organizations (including women and students), and workers, peasants and craftsmen. It is responsible to the Prime Minister and undertakes tasks entrusted to him by the party. The President of the National Assembly is second in rank only to the President of the Republic.

THE PARTY

The sole political party is the Parti congolais du travail (PCT). Its Political Bureau of 10 members takes part in government. Its Central Committee consists of 75 members, including the Political Bureau, most of the Ministers and the Chief of Staff of the army, chaired by the President of the Republic and Head of State. The Central Committee's powers include the initiation of revisions to the constitution, which become final when approved by the National Assembly, and the appointment of judges to the Revolutionary Court of Justice.

Note: In August 1984 a Constitutional Council was established by Presidential statute, assuming powers hitherto exercised by the Constitutional Chamber of the Supreme Court.

The Government

HEAD OF STATE

President: Col DENIS SASSOU-NGUESSO (appointed President of the Provisional Committee of the PCT 8 February 1979; elected President of the Republic 31 March 1979; re-elected July 1984).

COUNCIL OF MINISTERS
(January 1989)

Minister of Defence and Security: Col DENIS SASSOU-NGUESSO.
Prime Minister: ANGE-EDOUARD POUNGUI.
Minister of Rural Development: JUSTIN LEKOUNDZOU ITHI-OSSETOUMBA.
Minister of Administration and Local Government: Lt-Col BENOÎT MOUNDELE NGOLO.
Minister of Foreign Affairs and Co-operation: ANTOINE NDINGA OBA.
Minister of Transport and Civil Aviation: Col RAYMOND DAMAS-NGOLLO.
Minister of Planning and Finance: PIERRE MOUSSA.
Minister of Public Works, Construction, Housing and Urban Affairs: Lt-Col FLORENT TSIBA.
Minister of Health and Social Affairs: BERNARD COMBO MATSIONA.
Minister of Mines and Energy, with responsibility for Posts and Telecommunications: AIMÉ-EMMANUEL YOKA.
Minister of Industry, Fisheries and Crafts: HILAIRE MOUNTHAULT.
Minister of Trade and Small and Medium Enterprises: ALPHONSE POATI.
Minister of Basic Education and Literacy: PIERRE-DAMIEN BASSOUKOU-BOUMBA.
Minister of Forestry: AMBROISE NOUMAZALAYE.
Minister of Scientific Research and Environment: OSSEBI DOUNIAM.
Minister of Tourism, Culture and Arts: JEAN-BAPTISTE TATI-LOUTARD.
Minister of Labour, Social Security and Justice: DIEUDONNÉ KIMBEMBE.
Minister of Information: PAUL NGATSE.
Minister of Secondary and Higher Education: RODOLPHE ADADA.
Minister of Physical Culture and Sports: JEAN-CLAUDE GANGA.
Minister at the President's Office in charge of Defence and Security: (vacant).

MINISTRIES

All Ministries are in Brazzaville.
Office of the President: Palais du Peuple, Brazzaville; telex 5210.
Ministry of Education: BP 169, Brazzaville; tel. 81-24-60; telex 5210.
Ministry of Finance: Centre Administratif, quartier Plateau, BP 2093, Brazzaville; tel. 83-06-20; telex 5210.
Ministry of Foreign Affairs and Co-operation: BP 2070, Brazzaville; tel. 83-20-28; telex 5210.
Ministry of Health and Social Affairs: Palais du Peuple, Brazzaville; tel. 83-29-35; telex 5210.
Ministry of Industry, Fisheries and Crafts: Palais du Peuple, Brazzaville; tel. 83-51-30; telex 5210.
Ministry of Information: BP 2241, Brazzaville; tel. 81-03-83; telex 5291.
Ministry of Planning: BP 2031, Brazzaville; tel. 83-43-24; telex 5210.
Ministry of Trade and Small and Medium Enterprises: Brazzaville; tel. 83-18-27; telex 5210.

Legislature

ASSEMBLÉE NATIONALE POPULAIRE

The National People's Assembly is elected for a five-year term and comprises 153 members. Following the most recent elections, held on 23 September 1984, all seats were filled by PCT candidates.
President: JEAN GANGA-ZANZOU.

Political Organizations

Parti congolais du travail (PCT): Brazzaville; telex 5335; f. 1969 to replace the Mouvement national de la révolution; Marxist-Leninist party committed to 'scientific socialism'; the national party congress, the highest authority of the PCT, meets every five years; most recent meeting July 1984; a 75-mem. cen. cttee, which meets three times a year, directs party policy; an eight-mem. secretariat is the senior exec. body; a 10-mem. politburo exercises the powers of the cen. cttee between its sessions; there is also a 13-mem. mil. cttee and three specialized organs: Confédération syndicale congolaise (CSC), Union révolutionnaire des femmes congolaises (URFC) and Union de la jeunesse socialiste congolaise (UJSC). Pres. of Cen. Cttee Col DENIS SASSOU-NGUESSO; Gen. Sec. ANDRÉ OBAMI ITOU.

Mouvement patriotique du Congo (MPC): opposition movement, based in Paris; advocates pluralism and withdrawal of Cuban troops from the Congo.

THE CONGO

Diplomatic Representation

EMBASSIES IN THE CONGO

Algeria: BP 2100, Brazzaville; tel. 83-39-15; telex 5303; Ambassador: MOHAMED NACER ADJALI.
Angola: BP 388, Brazzaville; tel. 81-14-71; telex 5321; Ambassador: JOSÉ AGOSTINHO NETO.
Belgium: BP 225, Brazzaville; tel. 83-29-63; telex 5216; Ambassador: MARC FRANCK.
Bulgaria: BP 2460, Brazzaville; tel. 83-27-33; Ambassador: GEORGI VLADIKOV.
Cameroon: BP 2136, Brazzaville; tel. 83-34-04; telex 5242; Ambassador: JEAN-HILAIRE MBEA MBEA.
Central African Republic: BP 10, Brazzaville; tel. 83-40-14; Ambassador: CHARLES GUEREBANGBI.
Chad: BP 386, Brazzaville; tel. 81-22-22; Chargé d'affaires: NEATOBEI BIDI.
China, People's Republic: BP 213, Brazzaville; tel. 83-11-20; Ambassador: (vacant).
Cuba: BP 80, Brazzaville; tel. 81-20-91; telex 5308; Ambassador: DIEGO ERNESTO GONZÁLEZ PÉREZ.
Czechoslovakia: BP 292, Brazzaville; tel. 82-08-37; Ambassador: LUBOMÍR HALUSKA.
Egypt: BP 917, Brazzaville; tel. 83-44-28; telex 5248; Ambassador: MOHAMED ABDEL RAHMAN DIAB.
France: rue Alfassa, BP 2089, Brazzaville; tel. 83-14-23; telex 5239; Ambassador: ROBERT DELOS SANTOS.
Gabon: ave Fourneau, BP 2033, Brazzaville; tel. 81-05-90; telex 5225; Ambassador: CONSTANT TSOUMOU.
German Democratic Republic: rue de la Musique Tambourinée, BP 2244, Brazzaville; tel. 83-44-54; telex 5246; Ambassador: RONALD WEIDEMANN.
Germany, Federal Republic: BP 2022, Brazzaville; tel. 83-29-90; telex 5235; Ambassador: BERNHARD KALSCHEUER.
Guinea: BP 2477, Brazzaville; tel. 81-24-66; Ambassador: BONATA DIENG.
Holy See: rue Colonel Brisset, BP 1168, Brazzaville; tel. 83-15-46; Apostolic Pro-Nuncio: Most Rev. BENIAMINO STELLA, Titular Archbishop of Midila.
Italy: 2-3 blvd Lyautey, BP 2484, Brazzaville; tel. 83-40-47; telex 5251; Ambassador: TIBOR HOOR TEMPIS LIVI.
Korea, Democratic People's Republic: BP 2032, Brazzaville; tel. 83-41-98; Ambassador: PAK CHANG-SOK.
Libya: BP 920, Brazzaville; Secretary of People's Bureau: SAAD ABDESSALEM BAAIU.
Nigeria: BP 790, Brazzaville; tel. 83-13-16; telex 5263; Ambassador: LAWRENCE OLADEJO OLUFOLAHAN OYELAKIN.
Romania: BP 2413, Brazzaville; tel. 81-32-79; telex 5259; Chargé d'affaires a.i.: DIACONESCO MILCEA.
United Kingdom: ave du Général de Gaulle, Plateau, BP 1038, Brazzaville; tel. 83-49-44; telex 5385; Ambassador: ALFRED IAN GLASBY.
USSR: BP 2132, Brazzaville; tel. 83-44-39; telex 5455; Ambassador: VLADIMIR KONSTANTINOVICH LOBACHEV.
USA: BP 1015, Brazzaville; tel. 83-20-70; Ambassador: LEONARD G. SHURTLEFF.
Viet-Nam: BP 988, Brazzaville; tel. 83-26-21; Chargé d'affaires a.i.: NGUYEN DUY THI.
Yugoslavia: BP 2062, Brazzaville; tel. 83-42-46; telex 5316; Chargé d'affaires a.i.: IBRAHIM DJIKIĆ; temporarily closed Feb. 1988.
Zaire: 130 ave de l'Indépendance, BP 2450, Brazzaville; tel. 83-29-38; Ambassador: YENDE BUKU.

Judicial System

In August 1978, after the discovery of a plot to overthrow the Government, a state security court was established by decree to try 'current and future crimes against the Congolese revolution'. There is a court of appeal, labour courts, and tribunaux coutumiers (courts of common law), the latter to be replaced by tribunaux d'instance.
Supreme Court: Brazzaville; telex 5298; acts as a Cour de Cassation; Pres. CHARLES ASSEMEKANG.
Revolutionary Court of Justice: Brazzaville; f. 1969; has jurisdiction in cases involving the security of the state; comprises nine judges selected by cen. cttee of PCT; Pres. (vacant).

Directory

Religion

It is estimated that about one-half of the population follow traditional animist beliefs. The remainder are mostly Christians. In February 1978 the Government banned all religions and sects, except the Roman Catholic Church, the Congo Evangelical Church, the Salvation Army, Islam and the followers of Simon Kimbangu Prophète, Lassy Zephirin Prophète and Terynkyo.

CHRISTIANITY

The Roman Catholic Church

The Congo comprises one archdiocese and five dioceses. There were an estimated 707,200 adherents at 31 December 1985.
Bishops' Conference: Conférence Episcopale du Congo, BP 200, Brazzaville; tel. 83-06-29; f. 1966; Pres. Mgr BARTHÉLÉMY BATANTU, Archbishop of Brazzaville.
Archbishop of Brazzaville: Mgr BARTHÉLÉMY BATANTU, Archevêché, BP 2301, Brazzaville; tel. 83-17-93.

Other Christian Churches

Eglise Evangélique du Congo: BP 3205, Bacongo-Brazzaville; tel. 83-43-64; f. 1909; autonomous since 1961; 110,461 mems (1985); Pres. Rev. JEAN MBOUNGOU.
Protestant Churches: In all four equatorial states (the Congo, the CAR, Chad and Gabon) there are nearly 1,000 mission centres with a total personnel of about 2,000.

ISLAM

There are an estimated 25,000 Muslims in the Congo.
Conseil Islamique: Brazzaville; Head of Islamic community ABOUBAKAR GOLOUOLI.

The Press

Censorship has been in operation since 1972.

DAILIES

ACI: BP 2144, Brazzaville; tel. 83-05-91; telex 5285; daily news bulletin publ. by Agence Congolaise d'Information; circ. 1,000.
L'Eveil de Pointe-Noire: BP 66, Pointe-Noire.
Mweti: BP 991, Brazzaville; tel. 81-10-87; national news; Dir EMMANUEL KIALA-MATUMBA; Chief Editor JONATHAN NZOUSSI-SOUNDA; circ. 8,000.

PERIODICALS

Bakento Ya Congo: BP 309, Brazzaville; tel. 83-27-44; quarterly; Dir MARIE LOUISE MAGANGA; Chief Editor CHARLOTTE BOUSSE; circ. 3,000.
Bulletin de Statistique: Centre Nationale de la Statistique et des Etudes Economiques, BP 2031, Brazzaville; tel. 83-36-94; f. 1977; quarterly; Dir-Gen. MARCEL MOUELLE.
Bulletin Mensuel de la Chambre de Commerce de Brazzaville: BP 92, Brazzaville; monthly.
Combattant Rouge: Brazzaville; tel. 83-02-53; monthly; Dir SYLVIO GEORGES ONKA; Chief Editor GILLES OMER BOUSSI.
Congo-Magazine: BP 114, Brazzaville; tel. 83-43-81; monthly; Dir GASPARD MPAN; Chief Editor THEODORE KIAMOSSI; circ. 3,000.
Effort: BP 64, Brazzaville; monthly.
Jeunesse et Révolution: BP 885, Brazzaville; tel. 83-44-13; weekly; Dir JEAN-ENOCH GOMA-KENGUE; Chief Editor PIERRE MAKITA.
La Semaine Africaine: BP 2080, Brazzaville; tel. 83-03-28; f. 1952; weekly; Roman Catholic; circulates in the Congo, Gabon, Chad and the CAR; Dir Fr FRANÇOIS DE PAUL MOUNDANGA; Chief Editor BERNARD MACKIZA; circ. 8,000.
Le Stade: BP 114, Brazzaville; tel. 81-47-18; telex 5285; weekly; sports; Dir ROCIL PIERRE BEMBA; Chief Editor LOUIS NGAMI; circ. 10,000.
Voix de la Classe Ouvrière (Voco): BP 2311, Brazzaville; tel. 83-36-66; six a year; Dir MICHEL JOSEPH MAYOUNGOU; Chief Editor MARIE-JOSEPH TSENGOU; circ. 4,500.

NEWS AGENCIES

Agence Congolaise d'Information (ACI): ave Patrice Lumumba, BP 2141, Brazzaville; tel. 83-05-91; telex 5210; f. 1961; Dir AUGUSTIN MATONGO-AVELEY.

Foreign Bureaux

Agence France-Presse (AFP): BP 2144, Brazzaville; telex 5354; Correspondent BOY BUTA LOUMBWELE.

THE CONGO

Agentstvo Pechati Novosti (APN) (USSR): BP 170, Brazzaville; tel. 83-43-44; telex 5227; Bureau Chief DMITRI AMVROSIEV.

Telegrafnoye Agentstvo Sovetskovo Soyuza (TASS) (USSR): BP 379, Brazzaville; tel. 83-44-33; telex 5203; Correspondent BORIS PHILIPOV.

Xinhua (New China) News Agency (People's Republic of China): 40 ave Maréchal Lyauté, BP 373, Brazzaville; tel. 83-44-01; telex 5230; Chief Correspondent XU ZHENQIANG.

Reuters (UK) and Inter Press Service (Italy) are also represented in the Congo.

Publishers

Imprimerie Centrale d'Afrique (ICA): BP 162, Pointe-Noire; f. 1949; Man. Dir M. SCHNEIDER.

Société Congolaise Hachette: BP 919, Brazzaville; telex 5291; general fiction, literature, education, juvenile, textbooks.

Government Publishing House

Imprimerie Nationale: BP 58, Brazzaville.

Radio and Television

A television service began in 1963 and now operates for 46 hours per week, with most programmes in French but some in Lingala and Kikongo. Colour transmissions began in 1983. In 1983 there were an estimated 100,000 radio sets and 4,500 television receivers in use. In early 1988 the Congo and the USSR signed a co-operation agreement establishing training courses in the USSR for Congolese television personnel.

Radiodiffusion-Télévision Congolaise: BP 2241, Brazzaville; tel. 83-16-76; telex 5299; Dir FIRMIN AYESSA.

  Télévision Nationale Congolaise: BP 2241, Brazzaville; tel. 81-51-52; Dir VALENTIN MAFOUTA.

  La Voix de la Révolution Congolaise: BP 2241, Brazzaville; tel. 83-03-83; national broadcasting station; radio programmes in French, Lingala, Kikongo, Subia, English and Portuguese; transmitters at Brazzaville and Pointe-Noire; foreign service to Namibia in English and vernacular languages; Dir JEAN-PASCAL MONGO-SLYM.

Finance

(cap. = capital; res = reserves; dep. = deposits; br. = branch; m. = million; amounts in francs CFA unless otherwise stated)

BANKING
Central Bank

Banque des Etats de l'Afrique Centrale (BEAC): BP 126, Brazzaville; tel. 83-28-14; telex 5200; Headquarters in Yaoundé, Cameroon; f. 1973 as the central bank of issue for mem. states of the Customs and Economic Union of Central Africa (UDEAC), comprising Cameroon, the Central African Republic, Chad, the Congo, Equatorial Guinea and Gabon; cap. 24,000m., res 148,480m. (Dec. 1986). Gov. CASIMIR OYE MBA; Dir in the Congo GABRIEL BOKILO; br. at Pointe-Noire.

Commercial Banks

Banque Commerciale Congolaise (BCC): ave Patrice Lumumba, BP 79, Brazzaville; tel. 83-08-80; telex 5237; f. 1962; cap. 3,500m., dep. 18,200m. (Dec. 1985); 57.8% state-owned, 25% by Crédit Lyonnais (France); Chair. AMBROISE NOUMAZALAY; Gen. Man. CLÉMENT MOUAMBA; 12 brs.

Banque Internationale du Congo (BIDC): ave Patrice Lumumba, BP 33, Brazzaville; tel. 83-14-11; telex 5339; f. 1983; cap. 1,000m. (Dec. 1986); 57% state-owned, 21% by Banque Internationale pour l'Afrique Occidentale (France); Pres. LEKOUNDZOU ITIHI OSSETOUMBA; Gen. Man. MATHIAS DZON.

Union Congolaise de Banques SA (UCB): ave Amílcar Cabral, BP 147, Brazzaville; tel. 83-10-66; telex 5206; f. 1974 by the merger of Société Générale de Banques au Congo and Banque Internationale pour le Commerce et l'Industrie; cap. 3,000m., (June 1986); 51% state-owned; Chair. OSSEBI DOUANIAM; Man. Dir MATHIEU AKONGO; 12 brs.

Development Bank

Banque Nationale de Développement du Congo (BNDC): ave Foch, BP 2085, Brazzaville; tel. 83-30-13; telex 5312; f. 1961; cap. 1,087m. (Dec. 1985); 79% state-owned; provides financial and technical help for development projects; Pres. LEKOUNDZOU ITIHI OSSETOUMBA; Man. Dir ANDRÉ BATANGA; br. at Pointe-Noire.

Financial Institution

Caisse Congolaise d'Amortissement: 410 allée du Chaillu, BP 2090, Brazzaville; tel. 83-28-79; telex 5294; Man. Dir E. MABONZO.

INSURANCE

Assurances et Réassurances du Congo (ARC): ave Amílcar Cabral, BP 977, Brazzaville; tel. 83-01-71; telex 5236; f. 1973 to acquire the businesses of all insurance companies operating in the Congo; cap. 500m.; 50% govt-owned; Dir-Gen. RAYMOND IBATA; brs at Pointe-Noire, Loubomo and Ouesso.

Trade and Industry

DEVELOPMENT AGENCIES

Caisse Centrale de Coopération Economique (CCCE): BP 96, Brazzaville; tel. 83-15-95; telex 5202; French fund for economic co-operation; Dir JACQUES BENIER.

Mission Française de Coopération: BP 2175, Brazzaville; tel. 83-15-03; f. 1959; administers bilateral aid from France according to the January 1974 co-operation agreement; Dir GÉRARD LA COGNATA.

Office des Cultures Vivrières (OCV): Brazzaville; state-owned; food-crop development.

STATE MARKETING BOARDS

Office Congolais des Bois (OCB): BP 1229, Pointe-Noire; tel. 94-22-38; telex 8248; f. 1974; cap. 1,486m. francs CFA; monopoly of purchase and marketing of all timber products; Man. Dir ALEXANDRE DENGUET-ATTIKI.

Office du Café et du Cacao (OCC): BP 2488, Brazzaville; tel. 81-19-03; telex 5273; f. 1978; cap. 1,500m. francs CFA; marketing and export of coffee and cocoa; Man. Dir PAUL YORA.

Office National de Commercialisation des Produits Agricoles (ONCPA): BP 144, Brazzaville; tel. 81-24-01; telex 5273; f. 1964; marketing of all agricultural products except sugar; promotion of rural co-operatives; Dir JEAN-PAUL BOCKONDAS.

Office National du Commerce (OFNACOM): BP 2305, Brazzaville; tel. 83-43-99; telex 5309; f. 1964; proposals for privatization announced in early 1987; cap. 2,158m. francs CFA; importer and distributor of general merchandise; monopoly importer of salted and dried fish, cooking salt, rice, tomato purée, buckets, enamelled goods and blankets; Dir-Gen. VALENTIN ENOUSSA NCONGO.

Office National d'Importation et de Vente de Viande en Gros (ONIVEG): BP 2130, Brazzaville; tel. 82-30-33; telex 5240; f. 1975; cap. 177m. francs CFA; monopoly importer and distributor of wholesale meats; Man. Dir ROBERT PAUL MANGOUTA.

CHAMBERS OF COMMERCE

Chambre de Commerce, d'Agriculture et d'Industrie de Brazzaville: BP 92, Brazzaville; tel. 83-21-15; Pres. MAURICE OGNAOY; Sec.-Gen. FRANÇOIS DILOU-YOULOU.

Chambre de Commerce, d'Agriculture et d'Industrie de Loubomo: BP 78, Loubomo.

Chambre de Commerce, d'Industrie et d'Agriculture du Kouilou: 3 ave Charles de Gaulle, BP 665, Pointe-Noire; tel. 94-12-80; f. 1948; Chair. FRANÇOIS-LUC MACOSSO; Sec.-Gen. GEORGES MBOMA.

PROFESSIONAL ORGANIZATION

Union Patronale et Interprofessionnelle du Congo (UNICONGO): BP 42, Brazzaville; tel. 83-05-51; telex 5289; employers' union; Pres. JACQUES-GUY HUGUET; Sec.-Gen. MICHEL GIRARD.

NATIONALIZED INDUSTRIES

Minoterie, Aliments de Bétail, Boulangerie (MAB): BP 789, Pointe-Noire; tel. 94-19-09; telex 8283; f. 1978; cap. 2,650m. francs CFA; monopoly importer of cereals; production of flour and animal feed; Man. Dir DENIS TEMPERE.

Régie Nationale des Palmeraies du Congo (RNPC): BP 8, Brazzaville; tel. 83-08-25; f. 1966; cap. 908m. francs CFA; production of palm oil; Man. Dir RENE MAKOSSO.

Société Nationale de Construction (SONACO): BP 1126, Brazzaville; tel. 83-06-54; f. 1979; cap. 479m. francs CFA; building works; Man. Dir DENIS M'BOMO.

Société Nationale de Distribution d'Eau (SNDE): ave Sergent Malamine, BP 229 and 365, Brazzaville; tel. 83-41-69; telex 5272; f.

THE CONGO

1967; water supply and sewerage; holds monopoly over wells and import of mineral water; Chair. and Man. Dir F. S. SITA.

Société Nationale d'Elevage (SONEL): BP 81, Loutété, Massangui; f. 1964; cap. 80m. francs CFA; development of semi-intensive stock-rearing; exploitation of by-products in co-operation with SIA-CONGO; Man. Dir THÉOPHILE BIKAWA.

Société Nationale d'Exploitation des Bois (SNEB): BP 1198, Pointe-Noire; tel. 94-02-09; f. 1970; cap. 1,779m. francs CFA; production of timber; merged with wood-processing firm SONATRAB 1983; Pres. RIGOBERT NGOULOU; Man. Dir ROBERT ZINGA KANZA.

Société Nationale de Recherche et d'Exploitation Pétrolières (HYDRO-CONGO): ave Amílcar Cabral, BP 2008, Brazzaville; tel. 83-34-59; telex 5215; f. 1973; cap. 710m. francs CFA; research into and production of petroleum resources; has monopoly of distribution of petroleum products in the Congo; refinery at Pointe-Noire; Chair. RODOLPHE ADADA; Man. Dir SATURNIN OKABE.

Société des Verreries du Congo (SOVERCO): BP 1241, Pointe-Noire; tel. 94-19-19; telex 8288; f. 1977; cap. 500m. francs CFA; mfrs of glassware; Chair. A. E. NOUMAZALAYE; Man. Dir NGOYOT IBARRA.

Sucrerie du Congo (SUCO): BP 71, Nkayi; tel. 92-11-00; telex 8246; f. 1978; cap. 500m. francs CFA; sugar production; Dir Col A. RAOUL.

Unité d'Afforestation Industrielle du Congo (UAIC): BP 1120, Pointe-Noire; tel. 94-04-17; telex 8308; f. 1978; eucalyptus plantations to provide wood-pulp for export; Dir YVES LAPLACE.

TRADE UNION

Confédération Syndicale Congolaise (CSC): BP 2311, Brazzaville; tel. 83-19-23; telex 5304; f. 1964; Sec.-Gen. JEAN-MICHEL BOUKAMBA-YANGOUMA.

Transport

Agence Transcongolaise des Communications (ATC): BP 711, Pointe-Noire; tel. 94-15-32; telex 8345; f. 1969 to control nationalization of transport; is the largest state enterprise with a capital of 23,888m. francs CFA; has three sections: Congo-Océan Railway, inland waterways and general transport facilities, and the port of Pointe-Noire; Man. Dir FRANÇOIS BITA.

RAILWAYS

There are 510 km of track from Brazzaville to Pointe-Noire. A 286-km section of privately-owned line links the manganese mines at Moanda (in Gabon), via a cableway to the Congo border at M'Binda, with the main line to Pointe-Noire; a realignment of 91 km of track, from Loubomo to Bilinga, was completed in July 1985.

Chemin de Fer Congo-Océan (CFCO): BP 651, Pointe-Noire; tel. 94-25-63; telex 8231; Dir NOËL BOUANGA.

INLAND WATERWAYS

The Congo and Oubangui rivers form two axes of a highly developed inland waterway system. The Congo river and seven tributaries in the Congo basin provide 2,300 km of navigable river and the Oubangui river, developed in co-operation with the Central African Republic, 2,085 km.

ATC—Direction des Voies Navigables, Ports et Transports Fluviaux: BP 2048, Brazzaville; tel. 83-06-27; waterways authority; Dir MÉDARD OKOUMOU.

Compagnie Congolaise de Transports: BP 37, Loubomo; f. 1960; cap. 36m. francs CFA; Pres. and Dir-Gen. ROBERT BARBIER.

Société Congolaise de Transports (SOCOTRANS): BP 617, Pointe-Noire; tel. 94-23-31; f. 1977; cap. 17m. francs CFA; Mans YVES CRIQUET, HENRI BENATOUIL.

Transcap-Congo: BP 1154, Pointe-Noire; tel. 94-01-46; telex 8218; f. 1962; cap. 100m. francs CFA; Chair. J. DROUAULT.

SHIPPING

A major expansion programme for Brazzaville port was scheduled for completion in the late 1980s. The project, which was to cost an estimated 1,900m. francs CFA, was part-financed by the European Investment Bank (EIB) and aimed at making the port into a container traffic centre for several central African countries, such as Chad, the CAR and the western part of Cameroon.

ATC—Direction du Port de Brazzaville: BP 2048, Brazzaville; tel. 83-00-42; port authority; Brazzaville, on the River Congo, is an inland port; nationalized in 1977; Dir JEAN-PAUL BOCKONDAS.

ATC—Direction du Port de Pointe-Noire: BP 711, Pointe-Noire; tel. 94-00-52; telex 8318; nationalized in 1977; port authority; Pointe-Noire is the main port of the Congo; Dir ALPHONSE M'BAMA.

La Congolaise de Transport Maritime (COTRAM): f. 1984; national shipping company; state-owned; scheduled to become fully operational by 1986 and handle 40% of the Congo's traffic.

ROADS

In 1980 there were 8,246 km of roads usable throughout the year, of which 849 km were bituminized. The network consists of 4,519 km of main roads and 3,727 km of secondary roads, with the principal routes linking Brazzaville to Pointe-Noire, in the south, and to Ouesso, in the north.

Régie Nationale des Transports et des Travaux Publics: BP 2073, Brazzaville; tel. 83-35-58; f. 1965; civil engineering, upkeep of roads and public works; Man. Dir HECTOR BIENVENU OUAMBA.

CIVIL AVIATION

There are international airports at Brazzaville (Maya-Maya) and Pointe-Noire. There are also 37 smaller airfields. An aeronautical development programme covering 1982–86 included the construction of airports at six regional capitals.

Afri-Congo: Brazzaville; f. 1986; private airline operating flights to Rwanda and Burundi; fleet of one Hercules C-130.

Agence Nationale de l'Aviation Civile (ANAC): BP 128, Brazzaville; tel. 81-09-94; telex 5388; f. 1970; Gen. Man. GILBERT M'FOUO-OTSIALLY.

Air Afrique: BP 1126, Pointe-Noire; tel. 94-17-00; telex 8342; the Congo govt holds a 7% share; see under Côte d'Ivoire; Dir at Pointe-Noire JEAN-CLAUDE NDIAYE; Dir at Brazzaville I. CISSÉ DEMBA.

Lina Congo (Lignes Nationales Aériennes Congolaises): ave Amílcar Cabral, BP 2203, Brazzaville; tel. 83-30-66; telex 5243; f. 1965; state-owned; operates an extensive internal network, plus services to CAR and Gabon; Man. Dir JEAN-JACQUES ONTSA-ONTSA; fleet of 1 Boeing 737-200QC, 1 Fokker F.28-1000, 1 F.27-600, 2 Twin Otter 300.

Tourism

Brazzaville has three international hotels, but there is a shortage of accommodation in Pointe-Noire, where the oil and business sectors have increased demand. A regional hotel chain is to be established to cater for travellers in the provinces. There are plans to convert Mbamou Island into a tourist attraction.

Direction Générale du Tourisme: BP 456, Brazzaville; tel. 83-09-53; telex 5325; Dir-Gen. J. F. TABA-GOMA.

COSTA RICA

Introductory Survey

Location, Climate, Language, Religion, Flag, Capital

The Republic of Costa Rica lies in the Central American isthmus, with Nicaragua to the north, Panama to the south, the Caribbean Sea to the east and the Pacific Ocean to the west. The climate is warm and damp in the lowlands (average temperature 27°C (81°F)) and cooler on the Central Plateau (average temperature 22°C (72°F)), where two-thirds of the population live. The language is Spanish. Almost all of the inhabitants profess Christianity, and the overwhelming majority adhere to the Roman Catholic Church, the state religion. The national flag (proportions 3 by 2) has five horizontal stripes, of blue, white, red, white and blue, the red stripe being twice the width of the others. The state flag, in addition, has on the red stripe (to the left of centre) a white oval enclosing the national coat of arms, showing three volcanic peaks between the Caribbean and the Pacific. The capital is San José.

Recent History

Costa Rica was ruled by Spain from the 16th century until 1821, when independence was declared. The only significant interruption in the country's constitutional government since 1920 occurred in February 1948, when the result of the presidential election was disputed. The legislature annulled the election in March but a civil war ensued. The anti-Government forces, led by José Figueres Ferrer, were successful, and a revolutionary junta took power in April. Costa Rica's army was abolished in December 1948. After the preparation of a new constitution, the victorious candidate of the 1948 election took office in January 1949.

Figueres, who founded the socialist Partido de Liberación Nacional (PLN), dominated national politics for decades, holding presidential office in 1953–58 and 1970–74. Under his leadership, Costa Rica became one of the most democratic countries in Latin America. Since the 1948 revolution, there have been frequent changes of power, all achieved by constitutional means. Figueres' first government nationalized the banks and instituted a comprehensive social security system. The presidential election of 1958 was won by a conservative, Mario Echandi Jiménez, who reversed many PLN policies. His successor, Francisco Orlich Bolmarich (President from 1962 to 1966), was supported by the PLN but continued the encouragement of private enterprise. Another conservative, José Joaquín Trejos Fernández, held power in 1966–70. In 1974 the PLN candidate, Daniel Oduber Quirós, was elected President. He continued the policies of extending the welfare state and of establishing friendly relations with communist states. Communist and other left-wing parties were legalized in 1975. In 1978 Rodrigo Carazo Odio of the conservative Partido Unidad Opositora (PUO) coalition (subsequently the Coalición Unidad) was elected President. During Carazo's term of office the worsening instability in Central America led to diplomatic tension, and in 1981 the President was criticized for his alleged involvement in illegal arms trafficking between Cuba and El Salvador.

At presidential and legislative elections in February 1982, Luis Alberto Monge Alvarez of the PLN gained a comfortable majority when his party won 33 of the 57 seats in the Legislative Assembly. Following his inauguration in May, President Monge announced a series of emergency economic measures, in an attempt to rescue the country from near-bankruptcy. A policy of neutrality towards the left-wing Sandinista Government of Nicaragua was continued. However, after a number of cross-border raids, a national alert was declared in May. The rebel Nicaraguan leader, Edén Pastora Gómez, was expelled so as to reduce Costa Rican involvement in the Nicaraguan conflict. Relations with Nicaragua worsened as guerrilla activity spread to San José.

Throughout 1983, President Monge came under increasing pressure, from liberal members of the Cabinet and PLN supporters, to adopt a more neutral stance in foreign policy. Three leading members of the anti-Sandinista (Contra) movement were expelled from Costa Rica in May, and 80 of Pastora's supporters were arrested in September. In addition, some 82 guerrilla camps were dismantled by the Civil Guard. In November 1983 President Monge declared Costa Rica's neutrality in an attempt to elicit foreign support for his country. This declaration was opposed by the USA and led to the resignation of the Minister of Foreign Affairs.

In May 1984 there were reports of an air raid by the Nicaraguan Air Force on a border village in Costa Rica and of an increasing number of incursions by the Sandinista forces. Public opposition to any renunciation of neutrality was emphasized by a demonstration in support of peace and neutrality, held in San José and attended by over 20,000 people. An attempt was made to defuse the tense situation with the establishment of a commission, supported by the Contadora group (Colombia, Mexico, Panama and Venezuela), to monitor events in the border area. In late May, however, the attempt to assassinate Edén Pastora Gómez near the Costa Rican border exacerbated the rift within the Cabinet concerning government policy towards Nicaragua.

Relations with Nicaragua continued to deteriorate in December 1984, following an incident involving a Nicaraguan refugee at the Costa Rican embassy in Managua. Subsequently, diplomatic relations were reduced to a minimal level. Reports of clashes between Costa Rican Civil Guardsmen and Sandinista forces along the joint border became increasingly frequent. In 1985 the Government's commitment to neutrality was disputed when it decided to establish an anti-guerrilla battalion, trained by US military advisers.

During 1983 there were signs of increasing urban unrest in response to the Government's austerity measures and to the agrarian crisis, which had produced high levels of unemployment, principally among workers on banana plantations. By August 1984 the Government's position was regarded as unstable. The division within the Cabinet over policy towards Nicaragua, coupled with the effects of the unpopular austerity programme and a protracted strike by banana plantation workers, which had resulted in two deaths, led to fears of a coup. At President Monge's request, the Cabinet resigned, and in the subsequent reshuffle four Ministers were replaced.

At presidential and legislative elections in February 1986, Oscar Arias Sánchez, the candidate of the PLN, was elected President, with 52% of the votes cast. The PLN also obtained a clear majority in the Legislative Assembly. The new Government was committed to the development of a 'welfare state', whereby 25,000 new jobs and 20,000 new dwellings were to be created each year. In addition, the Government planned to renegotiate the country's external debt and to reach agreement on a social pact with the trade unions. Furthermore, President Arias Sánchez was resolved to maintain and reinforce Costa Rica's policy of neutrality, a decision which was expected to antagonize relations with the US administration.

In February 1986 diplomatic relations with Nicaragua were fully restored, and it was decided to establish a permanent inspection and vigilance commission at the common border. In accordance with the Government's pledge to protect neutrality, Costa Rica objected to the allocation of US $100m. in US aid to the Contra forces in mid-1986. In addition, the Government embarked on a series of arrests and expulsions of Contras resident in Costa Rica. In October, however, an aeroplane crash in Nicaraguan territory, involving four US citizens, caused considerable embarrassment to the Costa Rican Government and encouraged scepticism about Costa Rica's participation in the anti-Sandinista campaign.

Throughout 1986 and 1987 President Arias became increasingly involved in the quest for peace in Central America. In February 1987 President Arias' first peace proposal was discussed at a meeting of Central American Presidents, but was not endorsed. In May President Arias began a tour of Western Europe, in an attempt to secure international support and in the hope of overcoming US reservations concerning certain aspects of the peace plan. In August, at a summit meeting in Esquipulas, Guatemala, President Arias presented a modified plan which was accepted and signed by the Presidents of El Salvador, Nicaragua, Guatemala, Honduras and Costa Rica. The plan incorporated a 90-day timetable for the implementation of various measures aimed at promoting the establishment of peace in the region. The crucial provisions of the proposals were simultaneous cease-fires in Nicaragua and El Salvador, a halt to foreign assistance to rebel groups, democratic reform in Nicaragua, and a ban on the use of foreign territory as a base for attack. National reconciliation commissions were also to be formed in each of the Central American nations, including Costa Rica, to monitor the progress of the plan. This peace proposal was regarded as the most promising yet to be formulated and as a personal triumph for President Arias, who was awarded the Nobel Peace Prize in October 1987.

Despite the efforts of President Arias, the 90-day timetable for implementation of the proposals made at Esquipulas had to be extended until January 1988 before the second phase of verification and monitoring of progress could begin. In January President Arias brought Nicaraguan government officials and Contra leaders together in San José for their first discussions concerning the implementation of a cease-fire. Prior to this meeting, President Arias ordered three Contra leaders to leave Costa Rica or cease their military activities; subsequently, Alfredo César and Pedro Joaquín Chamorro agreed to leave, while Alfonso Robelo remained and agreed to modify his campaign. President Arias maintained his independent position by supporting discussions between the Contras and Sandinistas, held in Nicaragua in March, and by condemning any continuation of aid to the Contras. In November a border agreement was signed with Nicaragua in order to promote greater co-operation.

In 1988 there were renewed indications of internal unrest as a result of the Government's economic policies. In March there were two one-day stoppages by public employees, to protest against concessions made to the IMF and the World Bank. In June UNSA, the co-ordinating organization for agricultural unions, proposed a week-long protest against the Government's agricultural policies. In August there were strikes by farmers who were aggrieved at the Government's 'Agriculture for Change' policy of promoting the cultivation of cash crops, and thereby sacrificing the interests of many smallholders, to appease the IMF. The Government established a commission to consider the farmers' complaints. President Arias reshuffled the Cabinet in September 1988.

In September 1987 the Central American Vice-Presidents agreed on the future creation of a unified Parliament, in which each country was to hold 20 seats.

Government

Under the Constitution of 1949, executive power is vested in the President, assisted by two Vice-Presidents (or, in exceptional circumstances, one Vice-President) and an appointed Cabinet. The President is elected for a four-year term by compulsory adult suffrage, and a successful candidate must receive at least 40% of the votes. The legislative organ is the unicameral Legislative Assembly, with 57 members who are similarly elected for four years.

Defence

There have been no armed forces since 1948. In June 1988, rural and Civil Guards totalled 9,500 men. In 1985 an antiterrorist battalion was formed, composed of 750 Civil Guards. Spending on the security forces was estimated to be US $30.9m. in 1986. Military aid from the USA amounted to an estimated $3.7m. in 1986.

Economic Affairs

In 1987, according to estimates by the World Bank, Costa Rica's gross national product (GNP), measured at average 1985–87 prices, was US $4,299m., equivalent to $1,590 per head. Between 1980 and 1987, it was estimated, GNP per head decreased, in real terms, at an average rate of 0.9% per year. Costa Rica's economy is based mainly on the export of coffee, bananas, meat, sugar and cocoa. Staples such as maize, rice, beans and potatoes are also grown. In 1987 the agricultural sector (including forestry and fishing) employed 27.5% of the labour force. Agriculture accounted for 21% of the country's gross domestic product (GDP) in 1986. The sector typically contributes about 60% of Costa Rica's exports. In 1987 coffee and bananas accounted for 29.8% and 21.5% of export earnings respectively. Bananas were formerly Costa Rica's main export commodity, earning an average of between $240m. and $250m. per year. However, a strike by plantation workers in 1984 and the closure of the United Brands' subsidiary, Compañia Bananera de Costa Rica, severely affected the industry. Land was bought from United Brands by the Government, and converted to cocoa cultivation. Exports of bananas declined by some 25% in 1985, resulting in losses in revenue amounting to almost $40m. and precipitating a crisis in the industry. By mid-1987, however, about $30m. had been invested in development projects. A further set-back was suffered in late 1987, when an estimated 80% of the cocoa crop was ruined by disease. Coffee is Costa Rica's main export commodity, with production totalling 128,000 metric tons in 1986. The increase in the world coffee price in 1985/86 raised export earnings to $392m. in 1986. In 1987, however, the value of the coffee exports fell to an estimated $330m. In January 1988 Costa Rica's coffee export quota was reduced by the International Coffee Organization, owing to a decline in prices. In 1985 output of raw sugar was 234,000 metric tons. Costa Rica's earnings from sugar exports rose from $11m. in 1986 to an estimated $17m. in 1987. In 1987 the total output of the agricultural sector decreased by an estimated 2.5%. In October 1988 a state of emergency was declared as Hurricane Joan moved towards Costa Rica. Coffee production was particularly threatened by the hurricane, as many plantations are located on the coast.

The Government is to develop the estimated 150m. tons of bauxite which has been discovered in the Boruca region. Construction of an aluminium smelter (with a projected annual output of 280,000 metric tons) and an associated hydroelectric scheme was due to be completed by the late 1980s.

The principal branches of the manufacturing sector are food processing, textiles, chemicals and plastics. Industrial output was estimated to have increased by 5.5% in 1987. Investment is concentrated on the energy sector. Hydroelectric capacity totalled 460 MW in 1983 and was scheduled to rise to about 1,000 MW by 1988, with the opening of four new stations. Costa Rica's entire electricity requirements are expected to be fulfilled when the Arenal hydroelectricity project (opened in 1979) reaches its full capacity of 1,974 MW. In 1986 the Government announced plans to construct a 55-MW geothermal power station at Miravalle. Hydroelectric power provides 20% of commercial energy consumption, while petroleum provides 78%. Domestic petroleum production began on a small scale in June 1984. The petroleum refinery at Puerto Limón, which is supplied with crude petroleum from Mexico and Venezuela, has a capacity of 15,000 barrels per day. In 1986 imports of oil and fuel accounted for about 10% of total import costs.

According to World Bank estimates, GDP expanded at an average annual rate of 1.3% between 1980 and 1986. The average annual rate of inflation reached a peak of 90.1% in 1982, but then gradually declined, to stand at 10.9% in 1985, rising to 16.4% in 1987. Inflation was forecast to reach 18% per year by the end of 1988. Unemployment declined from 9.4% of the labour force in 1982 to 5.5% in 1987, the lowest level since 1980.

In March 1985 the IMF approved a short-term credit of SDR 54m. for Costa Rica, allowing an agreement to be made by the Government with its creditor banks on the rescheduling of $150m. in debts and on a further loan of $75m. In addition, a structural adjustment loan of $80m. was secured from the World Bank. As a result of Costa Rica's failure to attain economic targets for 1985–86, however, the IMF did not disburse the final tranche of the SDR 54m. credit. Furthermore, the World Bank and the US Agency for International Development (USAID) delayed the disbursement of loans amounting to US $80m. In May 1986, in an attempt to encourage non-traditional exports (the value of which increased by 16% in 1986) and to reduce the trade deficit, the gradual elimination of tariffs on imports of finished goods was introduced. In October 1987 the Government announced a programme of austerity measures, including a 15% increase in the price of electricity and petroleum and some reductions in planned public expenditure. Consequently, USAID decided to disburse $140m. in aid. In January 1988 the Government announced new tax reforms, and in April the IMF released the first part of a SDR 50m. stand-by loan to consolidate Costa Rica's financial position. These reforms were intended to reduce the consumption of luxury items and to yield 4,000m. colones per year through increased taxation on a wide range of goods and services. The implementation of these reforms resulted in approval by Japan, Taiwan and the Inter-American Development Bank of loans totalling US $365m., and the World Bank authorized a $100m. structural adjustment loan.

The budget deficit was reduced from 5.4% of GDP in 1986 to 3.2% in 1987. The 1989 draft budget envisaged expenditure of 66,209m. colones, compared with an estimated 54,010m. in 1988. Export earnings increased by 8.5% in 1987, including a 12% rise in non-traditional exports such as flowers. However, a 15% growth in imports resulted in a trade deficit of $227m. In August 1988 the colón was devalued for the 20th time in the year. Trade with other countries in the Central American Common Market was valued at $110m. in 1987, and should continue to develop as a result of increasing co-operation. The tourism sector is a significant source of foreign exchange, with revenue totalling $133m. in 1986. The number of tourists visiting Costa Rica increased sharply in 1988, owing partly to the unrest in neighbouring Panama.

One of Costa Rica's principal problems in the early 1980s was the high cost of servicing its external debt, which was equivalent to about 50% of the country's total export earnings. In May 1986, as a result of an acute shortage of foreign exchange, the Government announced the temporary suspension of interest payments on the foreign debt. Arrears on debt-servicing were estimated at $110m. In October 1987 the Government was still attempting to negotiate a debt-rescheduling arrangement on $1,500m. owed to foreign commercial banks. The problem remained unresolved by May 1988, when the Minister of Finance declared that the country could afford to pay only 2% of its GDP towards redeeming its foreign debt (estimated to total in excess of $4,500m.), instead of the 8% that it had been contracted to pay.

Social Welfare

Costa Rica possesses one of the world's most advanced social welfare systems, which provides a complete programme of care and assistance for all wage-earners and their dependants.

All social services are co-ordinated by the National Development Plan, administered by the Ministry of Planning, and are organized by state institutions. Approximately 7% of the GDP and 12% of public spending are allocated to the social services. The Social Security Fund provides health services and general social insurance, the National Insurance Institute provides professional insurance and the Ministry of Health operates a preventive health programme through a network of health units throughout the country. Benefits include disability and retirement pensions, workers' compensation and family assistance. In 1979 there were 1,506 registered physicians, not all resident and working in Costa Rica. In 1982 there were 28 hospitals and 76 health centres, with a total of 7,706 beds.

Education

All education is free, and elementary education is compulsory between six and 13 years of age. Official secondary education is free and consists of a three-year basic course, followed by a more highly specialized course of two years. Attendance figures are very high: in 1982 an estimated 89% of children aged six to 11 were enrolled at primary schools, while 37% of those aged 12 to 16 received secondary education. There are four universities, one of which is an 'open' university. In 1985, according to estimates by UNESCO, the average rate of adult illiteracy was only 6.4% (males 6.0%; females 6.8%). Costa Rica has the highest adult literacy rate in Central America. The education system received 8,086.2m. colones of budget expenditure in 1985.

Public Holidays

1989: 2 January (for New Year's Day), 20 March (for Feast of St Joseph), 23 March (Maundy Thursday), 24 March (Good Friday), 11 April (Anniversary of the Battle of Rivas), 1 May (Labour Day), 25 May (Corpus Christi), 29 June (St Peter and St Paul), 25 July (Anniversary of the Annexation of Guanacaste Province), 2 August (Our Lady of the Angels), 15 August (Assumption), 15 September (Independence Day), 12 October (Columbus Day), 1 December (Abolition of the Armed Forces Day), 8 December (Immaculate Conception), 25 December (Christmas Day), 28–31 December (San José only).

1990: 1 January (New Year's Day), 19 March (Feast of St Joseph), 11 April (Anniversary of the Battle of Rivas), 12 April (Maundy Thursday), 13 April (Good Friday), 1 May (Labour Day), 14 June (Corpus Christi), 29 June (St Peter and St Paul), 25 July (Anniversary of the Annexation of Guanacaste Province), 2 August (Our Lady of the Angels), 15 August (Assumption), 15 September (Independence Day), 12 October (Columbus Day), 1 December (Abolition of the Armed Forces Day), 8 December (Immaculate Conception), 25 December (Christmas Day), 28–31 December (San José only).

Weights and Measures

The metric system is in force.

Statistical Survey

Source (unless otherwise stated): Dirección General de Estadística y Censos, Ministerio de Economía y Comercio, Avda 2 y Central, Calle 10, Apdo 10.216, San José; tel. 221016; telex 2414.

Area and Population

AREA, POPULATION AND DENSITY

Area (sq km)	
Land	51,060
Inland water	40
Total	51,100*
Population (census results)†	
14 May 1973	1,871,780
11 June 1984	
Males	1,208,216
Females	1,208,593
Total	2,416,809
Population (official estimates at mid-year)	
1987	2,781,000
Density (per sq km) at mid-1987	54.4

* 19,730 sq miles.
† Excluding adjustment for underenumeration.

PROVINCES (estimated population, 1 January 1988)

	Population	Capital (with population)
Alajuela	499,623	Alajuela (147,396)
Cartago	316,379	Cartago (101,350)
Guanacaste	227,325	Liberia (33,412)
Heredia	227,950	Heredia (62,896)
Limón	200,638	Limón (62,597)
Puntarenas	313,541	Puntarenas (86,439)
San José	1,031,102	San José (278,561)
Total	**2,816,558**	—

BIRTHS, MARRIAGES AND DEATHS (rates per 1,000)

Births 31.0 in 1981, 30.7 in 1982, 29.6 in 1983, 32.3 in 1984; Marriages 7.3 in 1981, 7.7 in 1982, 7.5 in 1983, 8.5 in 1984; Deaths 3.9 in 1981, 3.9 in 1982, 3.8 in 1983, 4.1 in 1984.

COSTA RICA

ECONOMICALLY ACTIVE POPULATION
(persons aged 12 years and over, household survey, July 1987)

	Males	Females	Total
Agriculture, hunting, forestry and fishing	252,195	16,458	268,653
Mining, quarrying and manufacturing	110,394	59,843	170,237
Construction	58,009	656	58,665
Electricity, gas, water, transport, storage and communications	46,899	4,367	51,266
Commerce	119,768	62,243	182,011
Community, social and personal services	107,543	118,686	226,229
Activities not adequately described	6,703	2,184	8,887
Unemployed persons not previously employed	6,387	5,512	11,899
Total	**707,898**	**269,949**	**977,847**

Agriculture

PRINCIPAL CROPS ('000 metric tons)

	1984	1985	1986
Rice (paddy)	223	229	186
Maize	103	125	104†
Beans (dry)	23	26	31
Palm kernels*	11.8	11.8	11.8
Palm oil*	40	40	40
Sugar cane	2,936	2,950	2,650*
Bananas	1,169	1,008	1,000*
Coffee (green)	137	155	128
Cocoa beans	4	4	5

* FAO estimates.   † Unofficial figure.
Source: FAO, *Production Yearbook*.

LIVESTOCK ('000 head, year ending September)

	1984	1985	1986
Horses*	113	113	114
Cattle†	2,429	2,509	2,415
Pigs†	223	220	222

Poultry (million): 6* in 1984; 4* in 1985; 4* in 1986.
* FAO estimates.   † Unofficial figures.
Source: FAO, *Production Yearbook*.

LIVESTOCK PRODUCTS ('000 metric tons)

	1984	1985	1986
Beef and veal	77	94	109
Pig meat	11	12	11
Poultry meat	6	6	5*
Cows' milk	347	376	414
Cheese†	5.9	4.8	4.8
Butter and ghee†	3.5	2.8	2.8
Hen eggs*	9.8	9.8	11.7
Cattle hides (fresh)	8.7*	11.5†	10.8†

* Unofficial figures.   † FAO estimates.
Source: FAO, *Production Yearbook*.

Forestry

ROUNDWOOD REMOVALS
('000 cubic metres, excluding bark)

	1984	1985	1986
Sawlogs, veneer logs and logs for sleepers	415	314	314
Pulpwood*	10	10	10
Other industrial wood*	176	180	185
Fuel wood*	2,489	2,551	2,618
Total	**3,090**	**3,055**	**3,127**

* FAO estimates.
Source: FAO, *Yearbook of Forest Products*.

SAWNWOOD PRODUCTION ('000 cubic metres)

	1982	1983*	1984
Coniferous (soft wood)*	12	12	12
Broadleaved (hard wood)	366	294	400
Total	**378**	**306**	**412**

* FAO estimates.
1985–86: Annual production as in 1984 (FAO estimates).
Source: FAO, *Yearbook of Forest Products*.

Fishing

('000 metric tons, live weight)

	1984	1985	1986
Inland waters	0.2	0.3	0.3
Atlantic Ocean	0.6	0.4	0.3
Pacific Ocean	13.7	18.3	20.3
Total catch	**14.4**	**19.0**	**20.9**

Source: FAO, *Yearbook of Fishery Statistics*.

Industry

SELECTED PRODUCTS
('000 metric tons, unless otherwise indicated)

	1983	1984	1985
Cement	386	350	350
Salt (unrefined)	109*	109*	109*
Fish (tinned)	0.9*	2.3*	2.2
Palm oil	40*	40*	40*
Raw sugar	193	241	234*
Cocoa powder (metric tons)	569	400	691*
Cocoa butter (metric tons)	414	682*	985*
Cigarettes (million)	2,200	2,200	2,200
Nitrogenous fertilizers†	36*	41	n.a.
Motor spirit (petrol)	69	73	69
Kerosene	10	12	15
Distillate fuel oils	75	104	88
Residual fuel oils	144	183	202
Bitumen	12	12	12
Electric energy (million kWh)	2,918	3,069	2,826

* Estimates.
† Production in terms of nitrogen.
Source: UN, *Industrial Statistics Yearbook*.

COSTA RICA

Finance

CURRENCY AND EXCHANGE RATES
Monetary Units
  100 céntimos = 1 Costa Rican colón.

Denominations:
  Coins: 5, 10, 25 and 50 céntimos; 1, 2, 5, 10 and 20 colones.
  Notes: 5, 10, 20, 50, 100, 500 and 1,000 colones.

Sterling and Dollar Equivalents (30 September 1988)
  £1 sterling = 131.83 colones;
  US $1 = 77.96 colones;
  1,000 Costa Rican colones = £7.586 = $12.827.

Average Exchange Rate (colones per US $)
  1985 50.453
  1986 55.986
  1987 62.776

BUDGET (million colones)

Revenue	1985	1986	1987*
Taxation	28,445	35,247	42,505
Income tax	5,022	5,696	6,311
Tax on internal transactions	12,075	14,737	20,506
Import taxes and duties	5,360	7,102	9,404
Export taxes and duties	4,176	5,959	4,941
Other current revenue	1,812	1,753	1,343
Capital revenue			
Transfers	1,252	4,592	1,944
Total	29,697	39,839	44,449

Expenditure	1985	1986	1987*
Current expenditure	29,595	43,589	44,180
Consumption expenditure	12,738	16,071	17,040
Current transfers	11,783	21,298	20,575
Internal debt servicing	2,111	2,962	4,357
External debt servicing	2,963	3,258	2,208
Capital expenditure	5,480	9,083	7,727
Real investment	3,167	2,860	2,663
Capital transfers	2,313	6,223	5,064
Total	35,075	52,672	51,907

* Preliminary.
Source: Ministerio de Hacienda.

CENTRAL BANK RESERVES (US $ million at 31 December)

	1985	1986	1987
Gold	19.05	26.10	n.a.
IMF special drawing rights	0.02	0.01	0.01
Foreign exchange	506.35	523.36	488.85
Total	525.42	549.47	n.a.

Source: IMF, *International Financial Statistics*.

MONEY SUPPLY (million colones at 31 December)

	1985	1986	1987
Currency outside banks	9,938	13,241	14,777
Demand deposits at commercial banks	22,367	29,016	27,624

Source: IMF, *International Financial Statistics*.

COST OF LIVING (Consumer Price Index for San José metropolitan area; base: 1980 = 100)

	1984	1985	1986
Food	420.0	471.5	527.3
Rent	154.7	217.0	274.9
Clothing	335.4	362.2	385.6
Fuel and lighting	357.9	393.2	414.9
All items (incl. others)	386.9	442.8	497.8

1987: Food 605.1; All items 581.7.
Source: ILO, mainly *Year Book of Labour Statistics*.

NATIONAL ACCOUNTS (million colones at current prices)
Expenditure on the Gross Domestic Product

	1985	1986*	1987*
Government final consumption expenditure	31,175.0	37,950.8	43,263.9
Private final consumption expenditure	119,336.8	148,775.5	181,059.8
Increase in stocks	7,535.5	12,497.6	10,838.0
Gross fixed capital formation	37,307.6	46,148.3	56,716.3
Total domestic expenditure	195,354.9	245,372.2	291,878.0
Exports of goods and services	60,617.8	77,532.8	90,115.2
Less Imports of goods and services	63,548.0	75,153.0	99,187.2
GDP in purchasers' values	192,424.7	247,752.0	282,806.0
GDP at constant 1966 prices	9,807.8	10,317.5	10,719.0

* Preliminary.

BALANCE OF PAYMENTS (US $ million)

	1985	1986	1987
Merchandise exports f.o.b.	939.1	1,084.8	1,113.6
Merchandise imports f.o.b.	−1,004.9	−1,049.3	−1,248.5
Trade balance	−65.8	35.5	−134.9
Exports of services	331.1	355.4	375.9
Imports of services	−613.9	−626.9	−683.7
Balance on goods and services	−348.6	−236.0	−442.7
Private unrequited transfers (net)	42.6	37.4	36.5
Government unrequited transfers (net)	11.0	33.9	40.5
Current balance	−295.0	−164.7	−365.7
Direct capital investment (net)	65.2	57.4	75.0
Other long-term capital (net)	−197.0	−309.6	−505.1
Short-term capital (net)	−100.7	−51.0	−42.2
Net errors and omissions	162.8	87.8	158.9
Total (net monetary movements)	−364.7	−380.1	−679.1
Monetization of gold (net)	11.3	4.0	−3.8
Valuation changes (net)	−20.3	−20.2	−22.1
Exceptional financing (net)	495.0	459.2	723.0
Official financing (net)	−54.4	1.6	−5.5
Changes in reserves	66.9	64.4	12.5

Source: IMF, *International Financial Statistics*.

COSTA RICA

External Trade

PRINCIPAL COMMODITIES (US $ million)

Imports	1984	1985	1986
Consumer durables	72.6	78.2	64.8
Consumer non-durables	171.2	166.3	168.0
Oil and fuel	162.9	176.7	116.8
Primary commodities	432.0	395.1	468.0
Building material	36.1	42.0	36.5
Machinery and equipment	138.5	157.7	279.8
Others	80.4	82.2	13.6
Total	1,093.7	1,098.2	1,147.5

Exports	1985	1986	1987*
Coffee	310.1	391.9	330.0
Bananas	212.2	216.8	237.7
Sugar	10.5	11.1	16.9
Cattle and meat	55.7	69.8	57.2
Total (incl. others)	930.4	1,084.1	1,106.0

* Preliminary.

PRINCIPAL TRADING PARTNERS (US $ million)

Imports	1982	1983	1984
El Salvador	22.6	29.7	30.8
Germany, Federal Republic	35.1	46.7	56.2
Guatemala	56.2	59.4	59.4
Japan	37.1	52.8	82.4
Netherlands	40.6	6.1	10.5
United Kingdom	23.8	12.6	14.2
USA	316.8	372.9	394.5
Total (incl. others)	893.1	987.8	1,093.7

Exports	1982	1983	1984
El Salvador	33.1	41.6	44.5
Germany, Federal Republic	122.2	110.6	131.5
Guatemala	64.3	88.5	75.9
Japan	6.1	4.8	4.5
Netherlands	24.9	21.0	22.1
United Kingdom	26.1	12.2	16.8
USA	261.2	274.5	711.1
Total (incl. others)	870.4	872.6	1,006.4

Transport

RAILWAYS

	1982	1983	1984
Passenger journeys	2,397,147	2,508,959	2,000,933

ROAD TRAFFIC (motor vehicles in use at 31 December)

	1982	1983	1984
Cars and jeeps	91,350	101,251	106,233
Lorries	62,309	62,363	63,350
Buses	3,640	3,310	3,315
Industrial vehicles	10,322	10,812	11,109
Motor cycles	33,979	32,308	33,317
Total	201,600	210,044	217,324

1985: Cars and jeeps 109,802; Lorries 65,974; Buses 3,573.

INTERNATIONAL SEA-BORNE SHIPPING
(freight traffic, '000 metric tons)

	1983	1984*	1985*
Goods loaded	1,064	1,600	1,500
Goods unloaded	1,031	1,532	1,653

* Source: UN, *Monthly Bulletin of Statistics*.

CIVIL AVIATION

	1981	1982	1983
Passengers:			
Domestic	119,249	123,892	70,943
International	464,061	517,658	529,947
Freight (metric tons):			
Domestic	454,400	383,700	175,900
International	19,107,400	17,746,600	19,602,500

Source (all transport statistics): Ministry of Public Works and Transport, San José.

Tourism

	1984	1985	1986
Visitors	273,901	n.a.	260,840
Revenue (US $ '000)	117,139	n.a.	132,700

Source: Instituto Costarricense de Turismo.

Education

(1986)

	Institutions	Teachers	Pupils
Primary	3,107	13,529	380,384
Secondary	241	8,926	141,691

Directory

The Constitution

The present Constitution of Costa Rica was promulgated in November 1949. Its main provisions are summarized below:

GOVERNMENT

The government is unitary: provincial and local bodies derive their authority from the national Government. The country is divided into seven Provinces, each administered by a Governor who is appointed by the President. The Provinces are divided into Cantons, and each Canton into Districts. There is an elected Municipal Council in the chief city of each Canton, the number of its members being related to the population of the Canton. The Municipal Council supervises the affairs of the Canton. Municipal government is closely regulated by national law, particularly in matters of finance.

LEGISLATURE

The government consists of three branches: legislative, executive and judicial. Legislative power is vested in a single chamber, the Legislative Assembly, which meets in regular session twice a year—from 1 May to 31 July, and from 1 September to 30 November. Special sessions may be convoked by the President to consider specified business. The Assembly is composed of 57 deputies elected for four years. The chief powers of the Assembly are to enact laws, levy taxes, authorize declarations of war and, by a two-thirds vote, suspend, in cases of civil disorder, certain civil liberties guaranteed in the Constitution.

Bills may be initiated by the Assembly or by the Executive and must have three readings, in at least two different legislative periods, before they become law. The Assembly may override the presidential vote by a two-thirds vote.

EXECUTIVE

The executive branch is headed by the President, who is assisted by the Cabinet. If the President should resign or be incapacitated, the executive power is entrusted to the First Vice-President; next in line to succeed to executive power are the Second Vice-President and the President of the Legislative Assembly.

The President sees that the laws and the provisions of the Constitution are carried out, and maintains order; has power to appoint and remove Cabinet ministers and diplomatic representatives, and to negotiate treaties with foreign nations (which are, however, subject to ratification by the Legislative Assembly). The President is assisted in these duties by a Cabinet, each member of which is head of an executive department.

ELECTORATE

Suffrage is universal, compulsory and secret for persons over the age of 18 years.

DEFENCE

A novel feature of the Costa Rican Constitution is the clause outlawing a national army. Only by a continental convention or for the purpose of national defence may a military force be organized.

The Government

HEAD OF STATE

President: Lic. OSCAR RAFAEL ARIAS SÁNCHEZ (took office 8 May 1986).
Vice-Presidents: VICTORIA GARRÓN DE DORYAN, JORGE MANUEL DENGO.

THE CABINET
(November 1988)

Minister of the Presidency: Lic. RODRIGO ARIAS SÁNCHEZ.
Minister of Foreign Affairs: RODRIGO MADRIGAL NIETO.
Minister of the Interior and Police: ANTONIO ALVAREZ DESANTI.
Minister of Finance: Dr FERNANDO NARANJO VILLALOBOS.
Minister of Labour and Social Welfare: Lic. EDWIN LEÓN VILLALOBOS.
Minister of Science and Technology: Dr RODRIGO ZELEDÓN A.
Minister of Health: Dr EDGAR MOHS VILLALTA.
Minister of Public Works and Transport: Ing. GUILLERMO CONSTENLA UMAÑA.
Minister of Public Security: HERNÁN GARRÓN SALAZAR.
Minister of Agriculture and Livestock: JOSÉ MARÍA FIGUERES OLSEN.
Minister of Public Education: Dr FRANCISCO ANTONIO PACHECO.
Minister of Economy and Trade: ANTONIO BURGUES.
Minister of Industry, Energy and Mines: Dr ALVARO UMAÑA QUESADA.
Minister of Culture, Youth and Sport: Lic. CARLOS FRANCISCO ECHEVERRÍA SALGADO.
Minister of National Planning and Economic Policy: JORGE MONGE.
Minister of Housing and Human Settlement: Dr FERNANDO ZUMBADO JIMÉNEZ.
Minister of Foreign Trade: Lic. LUIS DIEGO ESCALANTE VARGAS.
Minister of Development: DANILO JIMÉNEZ VEIGA.
Minister of Justice: Dr LUIS PAULINO MORA M.
Minister of Information: GUIDO FERNÁNDEZ SABORÉ.

MINISTRIES

Ministry of Agriculture and Livestock: Apdo 10.094, 1000 San José; tel. 329420; telex 3558.
Ministry of Culture, Youth and Sport: Apdo 10.227, 1000 San José; tel. 227581.
Ministry of Economy and Trade: Apdo 10.216, 1000 San José; tel. 221016; telex 2414.
Ministry of Finance: Apdo 5.016, San José; tel. 229122; telex 2277.
Ministry of Foreign Affairs: Apdo 10.027, 1000 San José; tel. 237555; telex 2107.
Ministry of Foreign Trade: La Llacuna 12°, Avda Central, Calle 5, San José; tel. 225855; telex 2936.
Ministry of Health: Apdo 10.123, 1000 San José; tel. 230333.
Ministry of Housing and Human Settlement: Paseo Estudiantes, Apdo 222, 1002 San José; tel. 332579.
Ministry of the Interior and Police: Apdo 10.006, 1000 San José; tel. 214406; telex 3434.
Ministry of Justice: Apdo 5.685, 1000 San José; tel. 239739.
Ministry of Labour and Social Welfare: Apdo 10.133, 1000 San José; tel. 210038.
Ministry of National Planning and Economic Policy: Avda 3 y 5, Calle 4, San José; tel. 219524; telex 2962.
Ministry of Natural Resources, Energy and Mines: Avda 8–10, Calle 25, Apdo 10.104, 1000 San José; tel. 334533; telex 2363.
Ministry of the Presidency: Apdo 520, 2010 Zapote, San José; tel. 246155; telex 2106.
Ministry of Public Education: Apdo 10.087, 1000 San José; tel. 220229.
Ministry of Public Security: Apdo 4.768, 1000 San José; tel. 333208; telex 3308.
Ministry of Public Works and Transport: Apdo 10.176, San José; tel. 267311; telex 2478.
Ministry of Science and Technology: Apdo 10.318, 1000 San José; tel. 244172; telex 3338.

President and Legislature

PRESIDENT

Presidential Election, 2 February 1986

Candidates	Percentage of Votes Cast
OSCAR RAFAEL ARIAS SÁNCHEZ (PLN)	52.3
RAFAEL ANGEL CALDERÓN FOURNIER (PUSC)	45.8
ALVARO MONTERO (PU)	
ALEJANDRO MADRIGAL (ANC)	
EUGENIO JIMÉNEZ SANCHO (PI)	1.9
RODRIGO GUTIÉRREZ SÁENZ (AP)	

COSTA RICA

ASAMBLEA LEGISLATIVA
President: Dra Rosemary Kasspinsky de Murillo.

General Election, 2 February 1986

Party	Seats
Partido Liberación Nacional (PLN)	29
Partido Unidad Social Cristiana (PUSC)	25
Coalición Pueblo Unido (PU)	1
Alianza Popular (AP)*	1
Acción Agrícola Cartaginesa	1
Total	**57**

* A left-wing coalition, formed to contest the elections by the Partido del Pueblo Costarricense and several other parties.

Political Organizations

Acción del Pueblo (AP): San José; Pres. Angel Ruiz Zúñiga; Sec. Henry Mora Jiménez.

Acción Agrícola Cartaginesa: Cartago; provincial party; Pres. Juan Brenes Castillo; Sec. Rodrigo Fallas Bonilla.

Acción Democrática Alajuelense: Alajuela; provincial party; Pres. Francisco Alfaro Fernández; Sec. Juan Bautista Chacón Soto.

Alianza Nacional Cristiana (ANC): Pres. Víctor Hugo González Montero; Sec. Juan Rodríguez Venegas.

Coalición Pueblo Unido (PU): Calle 4, Avda 7 y 9, San José; tel. 230032; Sec. Alberto Salom Echeverría; left-wing coalition comprising:

    Partido del Pueblo Costarricense: Apdo 6.613, 1000 San José; tel. 225517; f. 1931; Communist; Sec.-Gen. Lenin Chacón Vargas.

    Partido Socialista Costarricense: San José; socialist; Pres. Alvaro Montero Mejía; Sec. Alberto Salom Echeverría.

    Partido de los Trabajadores: San José; Maoist; Pres. Johnny Francisco Araya Monge; Sec. Ilse Acosta Polonio.

Movimiento Nacional (MN): San José; Pres. Mario Echandi Jiménez; Sec. Rodrigo Sancho Robles.

Partido Alajuelita Nueva: Alajuelita Centro, 100W Escuela Abraham Lincoln, San José; tel. 279527; telex 3076; f. 1981; Pres. Carlos Retana Retana; Sec. William Castro Badilla.

Partido Auténtico Limonense: Limón; provincial party; Pres. Marvin Wright Lindo; Sec. Guillermo Joseph Wignall.

Partido Concordia Costarricense: Calle 2 y 4, Avda 10, San José; tel. 232497; Pres. Emilio Piedra Jiménez; Sec. Roberto Francisco Salazar Madriz.

Partido Independiente (PI): San José; Pres. Eugenio Jiménez Sancho; Sec. Gonzalo Jiménez Chaves.

Partido de Liberación Nacional (PLN): Sabana Oeste, San José; tel. 314022; f. 1948; social democratic party; affiliated to the Socialist International; 367,000 mems; Pres. Lic. Daniel Oduber Quirós; Sec.-Gen. Walter Coto Molina.

Partido Nacional Democrático: San José; Pres. Rodolfo Cerdas Cruz; Sec. Eladio Jara Jiménez.

Partido Radical Demócrata: San José; Pres. Juan José Echeverría Brealey; Sec. Rodrigo Esquivel Rodríguez.

Partido Republicano Nacional: San José; Pres. Rolando Rodríguez Varela; Sec. Fernando Peña Herrera.

Partido Unidad Social Cristiana (PUSC): San José; Pres. Rafael Angel Calderón Fournier; Sec. Roberto Tovar Faja.

Partido Unión Generaleña: Pérez Zeledón, Apdo 440-8.000, San José; tel. 710524; f. 1981; Pres. Dr Carlos A. Fernández Vega; Sec. Hugo Sáenz Marín.

Partido Unión Nacional: San José; Pres. Olga Marta Ulate Rojas; Sec. Rodrigo González Saborío.

The following party is in suspension:

Acción Socialista: San José; Pres. Marcial Aguiluz Orellana; Sec. Arnoldo Ferreto Segura.

The following guerrilla groups are active:

Ejército del Pueblo Costarricense (EPC): f. 1984; right-wing.

Patria y Libertad: f. 1985.

Diplomatic Representation

EMBASSIES IN COSTA RICA

Argentina: Calle 27, Avda Central, Apdo 1.963, San José; tel. 213438; telex 2117; Ambassador: Rubén Antonio Vela.

Belgium: 4A, entrada de Los Yoses, Apdo 3.725, 1000 San José; tel. 256255; telex 2909; Ambassador: Baron Pangaert d'Opdorp.

Brazil: Edif. Plaza de la Artillería 7°, Calle 4, Avda Central y 1, Apdo 10.132, San José; tel. 234325; telex 2270; Ambassador: R. B. Denys.

Bulgaria: Edif. Delcoré 3°, 100 m Sur Hotel Balmoral, Apdo 4.752, San José; Ambassador: Kiril Zlatkov Nikolov.

Canada: Edif. Cronos 6°, Avda Central, Calle 3, Apdo 10.303, San José; tel. 230446; telex 2179; Ambassador: Stanley E. Gooch.

Chile: De la Pulpería La Luz 125 metros Norte, Casa 19, Apdo 10.102, San José; tel. 244243; telex 2207; Ambassador: Pedro Palacios Camerón.

China (Taiwan): Edif. Mendiola 3°, Avda Central 917, Apdo 907, San José; tel. 213752; telex 2174; Ambassador: H. K. Shao.

Colombia: Apdo 3.154, 1000 San José; tel. 210725; telex 2918; Ambassador: Jaime Pinzón López.

Czechoslovakia: 200 metros sur del Rótulo de la Plaza del Sol, Residencial El Prado, Carretera a Curridabat, Apdo 3.910, 1000 San José; telex 2323; Chargé d'affaires: Ing. Václav Malý.

Dominican Republic: Frente costado al norte de la Nunciatura Apostólica, Barrio Rohrmoser, Apdo 4.746, San José; telex 3210; Ambassador: José Marcos Iglesias Iñigo.

Ecuador: Edif. Jiménez 3°, Avda 5 y Calle 1, Apdo 1.374, San José; tel. 236281; telex 2601; Ambassador: Raúl Sorrozo Encalda.

El Salvador: Edif. Trianón 3°, Avda Central y Calle 5A, Apdo 1.378, San José; tel. 225536; telex 2641; Ambassador: Carlos Matamoros Guirola.

France: Carretera a Curridabat Del Indoor Club, 200 al Sur y 25 al Oeste, Apdo 10.177, San José; tel. 250733; telex 2191; Ambassador: Pierre Sazarin.

Germany, Federal Republic: Calle 36, Avda 3A, San José; tel. 215811; telex 2183; Ambassador: Franz Elles.

Guatemala: Avda Primera detrás Más y Menos del Paseo Colón, Avda 2, San José; tel. 228991; Ambassador: Dr Carlos Urrutia-Aparicio.

Holy See: Urbanización Rohrmoser, Sabana Oeste, Apdo 992, Centro Colón, San José; tel. 322128; Apostolic Nuncio: Mgr Pier Giacomo de Nicolò.

Honduras: Edif. Jiménez de la Guardia 2°, Calle 1, Avda 5, Apdo 2.239, San José; tel. 222145; telex 2784; Ambassador: Edgardo Sevilla Idiaquez.

Israel: Calle 2, Avdas 2 y 4, Apdo 5.147, San José; tel. 216444; telex 2258; Ambassador: Shimon Moratt.

Italy: 5° entrada del Barrio Los Yoses, Apdo 1.729, San José; tel. 246574; telex 2769; Ambassador: Dr Rosario Guido Nicosia.

Japan: De la 1a entrada del Barrio Rohrmoser (Sabana Oeste) 500 metros y 100 Norte, Apdos 501 y 10.145, San José; tel. 321255; telex 2205; Ambassador: Hiroyuki Kimoto.

Korea, Republic: Calle 28, Avda 2, Barrio San Bosco, Apdo 3.150, San José; tel. 212398; telex 2512; Ambassador: Jae Hoon Kim.

Mexico: Avda 7, No 1371, Apdo 10.107, San José; tel. 225485; telex 2218; Ambassador: Jesús Cabrera Muñoz Ledo.

Netherlands: 2a entrada de Los Yoses, 100m al sur, Avda 8, Calle 37, Apdo 10.285, San José; tel. 253516; telex 2187; Ambassador: Jan-Willem Bertens.

Nicaragua: Edif. Trianón, Calle 25 y 27, Avda Central, San José; tel. 224749; telex 2316; Ambassador: Claudia Chamorro Barrios.

Panama: 200m al sur, 25m al este de Higueron, La Granja, San Pedro de Montes de Oco, San José; tel. 253401; Ambassador: (vacant).

Peru: Edif. Plaza Artillería 7°, Calle 4 y Avda Central, Apdo 4.248, San José; tel. 225644; telex 2512; Ambassador: Alfonso Espinosa Palacios.

Poland: San José; Ambassador: (vacant).

Romania: Avda 1A, Calles 29–33, Barrio Escalante 2981, San José; tel. 225479; telex 2337; Ambassador: (vacant).

Spain: c/32, Paseo Colón, Avda 2, Apdo 10.150, 1000 San José; tel. 2211933; telex 2438; Ambassador: (vacant).

Switzerland: Paseo Colón, Centro Colón, Apdo 895, San José; tel. 214829; telex 2512; Ambassador: Dr Johann Bucher.

USSR: Apdo 6.340, San José; tel. 255780; telex 2299; Ambassador: Yuri Pavlov.

United Kingdom: Edif. Centro Colón 11°, Apdo 815, 1007 San José; tel. 215566; telex 2169; Ambassador: Michael Daly.

USA: Calle 1, Avda 3, Apdo 10.054, San José; tel. 331155; Ambassador: Dean Hinton.

Uruguay: Calle 2, Avda 1, San José; tel. 232512; Ambassador: Jorge Justo Boero-Brian.

COSTA RICA
Directory

Venezuela: Avda Central 5A entrada Los Yoses, Apdo 10.230, San José; tel. 255813; telex 2413; Ambassador: MANUEL PEÑALVER.

Yugoslavia: Calles 30 y 32, Paseo Colón, San José; tel. 220619; Ambassador: (vacant).

Judicial System

Ultimate judicial power is vested in the Supreme Court, the 17 justices of which are elected by the Assembly for a term of eight years, and are automatically re-elected for an equal period, unless the Assembly decides to the contrary by a two-thirds vote. Judges of the lower courts are appointed by the Supreme Court in plenary session.

The Supreme Court may also meet as the Corte Plena, with power to declare laws and decrees unconstitutional. There are also four appellate courts, criminal courts, civil courts and special courts. The jury system is not used.

La Corte Suprema: Apdo 01, San José 1000; tel. 230666; telex 1548.

President of the Supreme Court: MIGUEL BLANCO QUIRÓS.

Religion

Under the Constitution, all forms of worship are tolerated. Roman Catholicism is the official religion of the country. Various Protestant Churches are represented. There are an estimated 7,000 members of the Methodist Church.

CHRISTIANITY

The Roman Catholic Church

Costa Rica comprises one archdiocese, three dioceses and one Apostolic Vicariate. At 31 December 1985 there were an estimated 2,325,000 adherents in the country, representing about 90% of the total population.

Bishops' Conference: Conferencia Episcopal de Costa Rica, Arzobispado, Apdo 3187, San José; tel. 210947; f. 1977; Pres. ROMÁN ARRIETA VILLALOBOS, Archbishop of San José de Costa Rica.

Archbishop of San José de Costa Rica: ROMÁN ARRIETA VILLALOBOS, Arzobispado, Apdo 497, 1000 San José; tel. 217692.

The Episcopal Church

Bishop of Costa Rica: Rt Rev. CORNELIUS JOSHUA WILSON, Apdo 2773, 1000 San José; tel. (506) 250209.

Other Churches

Baptist Convention of Costa Rica: Apdo 454, 2400 Desamparados, San José; tel. 594347; Pres. ALBERTO REYES; Sec. JULIETA CHINCHILLA DE BADILLA.

Iglesia Evangélica Metodista de Costa Rica (Evangelical Methodist Church of Costa Rica): Apdo 5.481, 1000 San José; tel. 362171; autonomous since 1973; 6,000 mems; Pres. Bishop ROBERTO DÍAZ C.

BAHÁ'Í FAITH

National Spiritual Assembly: Apdo 3.751-1000, San José; tel. 315243; telex 1050; resident in 238 localities.

The Press

General Directorate of Information and the Press: Presidential House, Apdo 520, Zapote, San José; tel. 256205; telex 2376; Dir Lic. LIDIETTE BRENES DE CHARPENTIER.

DAILIES

Boletín Judicial: La Uruca, Apdo 5.024, San José; tel. 315222; f. 1878; journal of the judiciary; Dir ISAÍAS CASTRO VARGAS; circ. 2,500.

Diario Extra: Calle 4, Avda 4, Apdo 177-1.009, San José; tel. 239505; f. 1978; morning; independent; Dir WILLIAM GÓMEZ; circ. 100,000.

La Gaceta: La Uruca, Apdo 5.024, San José; tel. 315222; f. 1878; official gazette; Dir ISAÍAS CASTRO VARGAS; circ. 5,300.

La Nación: Llorente de Tibás, Apdo 10.138, San José; tel. 351211; telex 2358; f. 1946; morning; independent; Dir EDUARDO ULIBARRI; circ. 90,000.

La Prensa Libre: Calle 4, Avda 4, Apdo 10.121, San José; tel. 236666; f. 1889; evening; independent; Dir ANDRÉS BORRASÉ SANOU; circ. 50,000.

La República: Barrio Tournón, Goicoechea, Apdo 2.130, San José; tel. 230266; f. 1950, reorganized 1967; morning; independent; Dir Lic. JOAQUÍN VARGAS GENE; circ. 60,000.

PERIODICALS

Abanico: Calle 4, esq. Avda 4, Apdo 10.121, San José; tel. 236666; weekly supplement of *La Prensa Libre*; women's interests; Editor GLADIS MIRANDA; circ. 50,000.

Acta Médica: Sabana Sur, Apdo 548, San José; tel. 323433; f. 1954; organ of the Colegio de Médicos; every 3 months; Editor Dr CLAUDIO CORDERO CABEZAS; circ. 1,000.

Contrapunto: La Uruca, Apdo 7-1.980, San José; tel. 313333; f. 1978; fortnightly; publication of Sistema Nacional de Radio y Televisión; Dir FABIO MUÑOZ CAMPOS; circ. 10,000.

Eco Católico: Avda 10, Calles 5 y 7, Apdo 1.064, San José; tel. 225903; f. 1931; Catholic weekly; Dir ARMANDO ALFARO; circ. 15,000.

Libertad: Apdo 6.613, 1000 San José; tel. 239394; f. 1962; weekly; organ of the Partido del Pueblo Costarricense; Dir RODOLFO ULLOA B.; Editor JOSÉ A. ZÚÑIGA; circ. 10,000.

Mujer y Hogar: Avda 15, Casa 1916, Apdo 89, Barrio Aránjuez, San José; tel. 223525; f. 1943; weekly; women's journal; Editor and Gen. Man. CARMEN CORNEJO MÉNDEZ; circ. 15,000.

Noticiero del Café: Calle 1, Avdas 18 y 20, Apdo 37, San José; tel. 226411; telex 2279; f. 1964; monthly; coffee journal; owned by the Instituto del Café; Dir ROCÍO BOGANTES MADRIGAL; circ. 5,500.

Perfil: Llorente de Tibás, Apdo 10.138, San José; tel. 351211; telex 2358; fortnightly; women's interest; Dir GRETTEL ALFARO.

Polémica: Icadis, Apdo 1.006, Paseo de los Estudiantes, San José; tel. 333964; f. 1981; every 4 months; left-wing; Dir GABRIEL AGUILERA PERALTA.

Rumbo: Llorente de Tibás, Apdo 10.138, 1000 San José; tel. 351211; telex 2358; f. 1984; weekly; general; Dir MARCELA ANGULO GRILLO; circ. 15,000.

San José News: Apdo 7-2.730, San José; 2 a week; Dir CHRISTIAN RODRÍGUEZ.

Semanario Universidad: Ciudad Universitaria Rodrigo Facio, San Pedro Montes de Oca, San José; tel. 246661; telex 2544; f. 1970; weekly; general; Dir Lic. CARLOS MORALES CASTRO; circ. 15,000.

The Tico Times: Calle 6, diagonal a la Corte Suprema de Justicia, Apdo 4.632, San José; tel. 220040; weekly; in English; Dir RICHARD DYER; circ. 12,000.

PRESS ASSOCIATIONS

Colegio de Periodistas de Costa Rica: Sabana Este, Calle 42, Avda 4, Apdo 5.416, San José; tel. 335850; f. 1969; 450 mems; Admin. Dir WILLIAM MONGE; Sec. Lic. JOSEFINA GUTIÉRREZ AGUERO.

Sindicato Nacional de Periodistas: Sabana Este, Calle 42, Avda 4, Apdo 5.416, San José; tel. 227589; f. 1970; 105 mems; Sec.-Gen. BERNI QUIRÓS HERRERA.

FOREIGN NEWS BUREAUX

ACAN-EFE (Central America): Costado Sur, Casa Matute Gómez, Casa 1912, Apdo 84.930, San José; tel. 226785; telex 3197; Correspondent WILFREDO CHACÓN SERRANO.

Agence France-Presse (France): Calle 13, entre Avdas 11 y 11 bis, Apdo 5.276, 1000 San José; tel. 330757; telex 2403; Correspondent DOMINIQUE PETTIT.

Agencia EFE (Spain): Avda 10, Calles 19 y 21, No 1912, Apdo 84.930, San José; tel. 226785; telex 3197.

Agentstvo Pechati Novosti (APN) (USSR): De la Casa Italiana 100 Este, 50 Norte, Apdo 1.011, San José; tel. 241560; telex 2711.

Agenzia Nazionale Stampa Associata (ANSA) (Italy): c/o Diario la República, Barrio Tournón, Guadalupe, Apdo 2.130, San José; tel. 230840; telex 2538; Correspondent YEHUDI MONESTEL ARCE.

Associated Press (AP) (USA): Apdo 769, 1250 Escazu; tel. 216146; Correspondent REID MILLER.

Deutsche Presse-Agentur (dpa) (Federal Republic of Germany): Edif. Trifami, Of. 606, Calle 2, Avda 1, Apdo 7.156, San José; tel. 330604; Correspondent DANILO ARIAS MADRIGAL.

Inter Press Service (IPS) (Italy): Calle 11 entre Avda 1 y 3, No 152, Apdo 70.1002, San José; tel. 338583; telex 3239; Dir MARICEL SEQUEIRA.

Prensa Latina (Cuba): 150 Sur Edif. Ana Lorena (IDA), Barrio Betania, San José; tel. 342606; telex 3223; Correspondent LUIS BÁEZ.

COSTA RICA

Telegrafnoye Agentstvo Sovetskovo Soyuza (TASS) (USSR): De la Casa Italia 1000 Este, 50 Norte, Casa 675, Apdo 1.011, San José; tel. 241560; telex 2711; Correspondent ENRIQUE MORA.

United Press International (UPI) (USA): Calle 15, Avda 2, Radio Reloj, Apdo 4.334, San José; tel. 222644; Correspondent WILLIAM CESPEDES CHAVARRÍA.

Xinhua (New China) News Agency (People's Republic of China): Apdo 4.774, San José; tel. 313497; telex 3066; Correspondent XU BIHUA.

Publishers

Alfalit Internacional: Apdo 292, 4050 Alajuela; f. 1961; educational; Dirs GILBERTO BERNAL, OSMUNDO PONCE.

Antonio Lehmann Librería, Imprenta y Litografía, Ltda: Calles 1 y 3, Avda Central, Apdo 10.011, San José; tel. 231212; telex 2540; f. 1896; general fiction, educational, textbooks; Man. Dir ANTONIO LEHMANN STRUVE.

Editorial Caribe: Apdo 1.307, San José; tel. 227244; f. 1949; religious textbooks; Dir JOHN STROWEL.

Editorial Costa Rica: Calle 1A, Avda 18, Apdo 10.010, San José; tel. 234875; f. 1959; government-owned; cultural; Gen. Man. GERMÁN HERNÁNDEZ.

Editorial Fernández Arce: Apdo 6.523, 1000 San José; tel. 216321; f. 1967; textbooks for primary, secondary and university education; Dir Dr MARIO FERNÁNDEZ LOBO.

Editorial Texto Ltda: Calle 26, Avdas 5 y 7, Apdo 2.988-1.000, San José; tel. 227661; f. 1963; Dir FRANK THOMAS GALLARDO; Asst Man. FRANK THOMAS ECHEVERRÍA.

Editorial de la Universidad Autónoma de Centroamérica (UACA): Apdo 7.637, 1000, San José; tel. 235822; f. 1981; Dir RODOLFO PIZA.

Editorial de la Universidad Estatal a Distancia (EUNED): Plaza González Víquez, Apdo 2, San José; tel. 235430; telex 3003; f. 1979; Dir CARLOS ALBERTO ARCE.

Editorial Universitaria Centroamericana (EDUCA): Apdo 64, Ciudad Universitaria Rodrigo Facio, 2060 San José; tel. 258740; telex 3011; f. 1969; organ of the CSUCA; science, art, philosophy; Editorial Dir CARMEN NARANJO.

Mesen Editores: Apdo 146-2.400, Desamparados, San José; tel. 592455; f. 1978; general; Dir DENNIS MESÉN SEGURA.

Trejos Hermanos Sucs, SA: Curridabat, Apdo 10.096, San José; tel. 242411; telex 2875; f. 1912; general and reference; Man. ALVARO TREJOS.

ASSOCIATION

Cámara Costarricense del Libro: San José; Pres. LUIS FERNANDO CALVO FALLAS.

Radio and Television

In 1984 there were an estimated 420,000 radio receivers and 470,000 television receivers in use.

Control Nacional de Radio: Dirección Nacional de Comunicaciones, Ministerio de Gobernación y Policia, Apdo 8.000, 1000 San José; tel. 257364; f. 1954; governmental supervisory department; Dir WARREN MURILLO MARTÍNEZ.

Cámara Nacional de Medios de Comunicación Colectiva (CANAMECC): Calle 3 Bis, Avda 7 y 9, Apdo 6.574, San José; tel. 224820; f. 1954; Pres. RODOLFO BAZO ODOR.

Cámara Nacional de Radio (CANARA): Calle 3 Bis, Avda 7 y 9, Edif. Teresa, Apdo 6.574, San José; tel. 224820; f. 1947; Pres. ARMANDO ALFARO PANIAGUA.

Asociación Costarricense para Información y Cultura (ACIC): San José; f. 1983; independent body; controls private radio stations; Pres. EUGENIO PIGNATARO PACHECO.

RADIO
Non-Commercial

Faro del Caribe: Apdo 2.710, 1000 San José; tel. 262618; f. 1948; call letters TIFC; religious and cultural programmes in Spanish and English; Man. JUAN JACINTO OCHOA F.

Radio Costa Rica: Apdo 365, 1009 San José; tel. 336628; f. 1985; broadcasts Voice of America news bulletins (in Spanish) and locally-produced educational and entertainment programmes; Pres. Lic. GONZALO MONGE.

Radio Fides: Avda 4, Curia Metropolitana, Apdo 5.079, 1000 San José; tel. 221252; f. 1952; Catholic station; Dir P. JORGE LUIS CAMPOS.

Radio Santa Clara: Santa Clara, San Carlos, Ciudad Quesada, Alajuela; tel. 471264; f. 1986; Roman Catholic station; Dir P. MARCO A. SOLÍS V.

Radio Universidad de Costa Rica: Ciudad Universitaria Rodrigo Facio, San José; tel. 253936; f. 1949; classical music; Dir JOSÉ TASIES SOLÍS.

Commercial

There are about 40 commercial radio stations including:

Cadena de Emisoras Columbia: Apdo 708, San José; tel. 340354; operates Radio Columbia, Radio Uno, Radio Sabrosa, Radio Puntarenas; Dir ARNOLDO ALFARO CHAVARRÍA.

Cadena Musical: 13 Moravia, Apdo 854, San José; tel. 362026; f. 1954; operates Radio Musical, Radio Cucu and Radio Sonora; Dir RIGOBERTO URBINA PINTO.

Circuito Radial Titania: Apdo 10.279, San José; tel. 226033; operates Radio Titania and Radio Sensación; Dir MARIO SOTELA.

Grupo Centro: Apdo 6.133, San José; tel. 354509; operates Radio Centro, Radio Turrialba, Radio W Liberia, Radio W San Isidro, Canal 28 de Televisión; Dir ROBERTO HERNÁNDEZ RAMÍREZ.

Radio Chorotega: Santa Cruz de Guanacaste, Apdo 92; tel. 680447; f. 1983; Catholic station; Dir P. ROHANY VALLEJO.

Radio Emasus: San Visto de Coto Brus; tel. 773101; f. 1962; Roman Catholic station; Dir P. ALVARO COTO.

Radio Fundación: Apdo 4.057, 1000 San José; tel. 591213; operated by the Fundación 'Ciudadelas de Libertad' to promote educational and cultural development; Man. VÍCTOR BERMÚDEZ MORA.

Radio Monumental/Radio Linda: Apdo 800, San José; tel. 220000; f. 1929; all news station; Dir NORA RUIZ DE ANGULO.

Radio Sinai/Radio Eraus: Apdo 262, San Isidro del General, Pérez Zeledón; tel. 710367; f. 1957; Dir P. ALVARO COTO OROZCO.

Sistema Radiofónico: Apdo 341, San José; tel. 224344; operates Radio Reloj and Radio Sonido 1120; Dir RÓGER BARAHONA GÓMEZ.

TELEVISION
Government-Owned

Sistema Nacional de Radio y Televisión Cultural (SINART): Apdo 7-1.980, San José; tel. 310839; telex 2374; cultural; Dir-Gen. NELSON BRENES LÓPEZ.

Commercial

Corporación Costarricense de Televisión: Apdo 1.860, San José; tel. 312222; telex 2443; Gen. Man. MARIO SOTELA BLEN.

Multivisión de Costa Rica: Apdo 4.666, San José; tel. 334444; telex 3043; operates Radio Sistema Universal A.M. (f. 1956), Channel 9 (f. 1962) and Channel 4 (f. 1964) and FM (f. 1980); Gen. Man. ARNOLD VARGAS V.

Telenac—Canal 2: Apdo 2.860, San José; tel. 312222; Pres. MARIO SOTELA BLEN.

Televisora de Costa Rica, SA (Teletica): Apdo 3.876, San José; tel. 322222; telex 2220; f. 1960; operates Channel 7; Pres. OLGA DE PICADO; Gen. Man. RENÉ PICADO COZZA.

Canal 6: Apdo 2.860, San José; tel. 329255; f. 1965; Pres. MARIO SOTELA BLEN.

Canal 11: Apdo 5.542, San José; tel. 331011; Pres. FRANZ ULRICH.

Finance

(cap. = capital; p.u. = paid up; res = reserves; dep. = deposits; m. = million; brs = branches; amounts in colones)

BANKING

Banco Central de Costa Rica: Apdo 10.058, San José; tel. 334233; telex 2163; f. 1950; cap. 5m., dep. 183,197.1m. (Dec. 1985); Exec. Pres. Dr EDUARDO LIZANO; Gen. Man. CARLOS HERNÁNDEZ R.

State-Owned Banks

Banco Anglo-Costarricense: Avda 2, Calles 1 y 3, Apdo 10.038, San José; tel. 223322; telex 2132; f. 1863; responsible for servicing commerce; cap. and res 1,091m., dep. 12,168.4m. (Dec. 1986); Pres. ROY MCCORMICK GARCÍA; Gen. Man. JOSÉ MANUEL PERAZA; 10 brs.

Banco de Costa Rica: Avdas Central y Segunda, Calles 4 y 6, Apdo 10.035, 1000 San José; tel. 331100; telex 2103; f. 1877; responsible for industry; cap. and res 1,582.4m., dep. 30,478.7m. (Dec. 1987); Pres. Lic. ROLANDO FERNÁNDEZ S.; Gen. Man. Lic. LUIS ALBERTO SALAZAR Z.; 44 brs.

Banco Crédito Agrícola de Cartago: Calle 5 a 2, Apdo 297, Cartago; tel. 513011; telex 8006; f. 1918; responsible for housing;

cap. 377,049m., dep. 3,341m. (March 1987); Pres. Raúl Morales Vargas; Gen. Man. Roberto Cossani Rivera; 5 brs.

Banco Nacional de Costa Rica: Calles 2 y 4, Avda 1A, Apdo 10.015, San José; tel. 232221; telex 02120; f. 1914; responsible for the agricultural sector; cap. and res 2,957.0m., dep. 38,326.2m. (Dec. 1986); Pres. Oscar Auilas; Gen. Man. Lic. Porfirio Morera Batres; 13 brs.

Banco Popular y de Desarrollo Comunal: Calle 1, Avda 2 y 4, Apdo 10.190, San José; tel. 228122; telex 2844; f. 1969; cap. 260m., res 6m., dep. 940m. (June 1981); Pres. Mario Montenegro Mora; Gen. Man. Alvaro Ureña Alvarez.

Private Banks

Banco de la Construcción, SA: Calle 38, Paseo Colón, Apdo 5.099, 1000 San José; tel. 215811; telex 2473; f. 1974; cap. p.u. 47m. (July 1988); Pres. Carlos A. Urcuyo Barrios; Mans Carlos A. Urcuyo P., Gonzalo G. Coto F.

Banco Latinoamericano (Costa Rica), SA: San José; f. 1974; cap. 5m.; Pres. Fernando Berrocal S.; Man. Fred O'Neill G.

Banco Lyon, SA: Calle 2, No 32 Norte, Apdo 10.184, San José; tel. 212611; telex 2577; f. 1871; res 11.8m. (June 1984); Pres. Jorge Lyon Chavarría; Gen. Man. Jorge Arturo Granados M.

Banco de San José, SA: Calle Central, Avdas 3 y 5, Apdo 5.445, 1000 San José; tel. 219911; f. 1968; fmrly Bank of America, SA; cap. p.u. 184m., res 49m. (Dec. 1987); Pres. Alvaro Sancho Castro; Man. Mario Montealegre Saborío.

Banco de Santander (Costa Rica), SA: Avda 2, Calle Central, Apdo 6.714, San José; tel. 228066; telex 2666; f. 1977; cap. 60m. (1986); Pres. Emilio Botín Sanz de S.; Gen. Man. Luis Mier Abans.

Credit Co-operatives

Federación Nacional de Cooperativas de Ahorro y Crédito y de Servicios Múltiples RL (Fedecrédito): Calle 20, Avdas 8 y 10, Apdo 4.748, San José; tel. 335666; f. 1963; 49 co-operatives, with 121,000 mems; combined cap. US $60m.; Gen. Man. Lic. Manuel A. Araya Barboza.

STOCK EXCHANGE

Bolsa Nacional de Valores, SA: Edif. Cartagena 7°, Calle Central, Avda 1, Apdo 1.736, 1000 San José; tel. 228011; telex 2863; f. 1976; Exec. Pres. Ing. Humberto Pérez Bonilla; Gen. Man. Dr Rodrigo Bolaños Zamora.

INSURANCE

Instituto Nacional de Seguros: Calles 9 y 9B, Avda 7, Apdo 10.061, 1000 San José; tel. 235800; telex 2290; f. 1924; administers the state monopoly of insurance; services of foreign insurance companies may be used only by authorization of the Ministry of Economy and after the Instituto has certified it will not accept the risk; cap. and res 3,389m. colones (Dec. 1983); Pres. Fernando Zumbado Berry; Gen. Man. Víctor Julio Brenes Zúñiga.

Trade and Industry

STATE AGENCIES AND DEVELOPMENT ORGANIZATIONS

Cámara Nacional de Artesanía y Pequeña Industria de Costa Rica: Calle 11, Avda 1, Apdo 8-6.540, San José; tel. 232763; f. 1963; development, marketing and export of small-scale industries and handicrafts; Exec. Dir Rafael Sáenz Sandí.

Centro de Promoción de Exportaciones e Inversiones (CENPRO): Apdo 5.418, San José; tel. 217166; telex 2385; f. 1968 to encourage increased investment in export oriented activities and greater exports of non-traditional products; Exec. Dir Eduardo Alonso.

CINDE: Apdo 7.170, 1000 San José; tel. 331711; telex 3514; coalition for development initiatives to attract foreign investment for production and export of new products; Dir Federico Vargas Peralta.

CODESA: Apdo 10.254, 1000 San José; tel. 224422; telex 2405; f. 1972; development corporation; Pres. Edgar Brenes André.

Consejo Nacional de Producción: Calle 36 a 12, Apdo 2.205, San José; tel. 236033; telex 2273; f. 1948 to encourage agricultural and fish production and to regulate production and distribution of basic commodities; Man. Horacio Zúñiga Chavarría.

Instituto del Café: Calle 1, Avdas 18 y 20, Apdo 37, San José; tel. 332888; telex 2279; f. 1948 to develop the coffee industry, to control production and to regulate marketing; Pres. Lic. Luis Diego Escalante Vargas; Exec. Dir Lic. Mario Fernández Urpi.

Instituto Costarricense de Acueductos y Alcantarillados: Avda Central, Calle 5, Apdo 1.420, San José; tel. 332155; telex 2724; water and sewerage; Exec. Pres. Ing. Eladio Prado.

Instituto Costarricense de Electricidad (ICE): Apdo 10.032, 1000 San José; tel. 207720; telex 2140; state power and telecommunications agency; Exec. Pres. Antonio Cañas Mora; Gen. Man. Ing. Rodrigo Suárez Mejido.

Instituto de Desarrollo Agrícola (IDA): Apdo 5.054, 1000 San José; tel. 246066; Exec. Pres. Ing. Sergio Quirós Maroto.

Instituto de Fomento y Asesoría Municipal: Apdo 10.187, San José; tel. 233714; f. 1970; municipal development institute; Exec. Pres. Jorge Urbina Ortega; Exec. Dir Harry Jager Contreras.

Instituto Mixto de Ayuda Social (IMAS): Calle 29, entre Avdas 2 y 4, Apdo 2.613, San José; tel. 252555; telex 1559; Pres. Carlos Corrales Villalobos.

Instituto Nacional de Fomento Cooperativo: Apdo 10.103, San José; tel. 234355; f. 1973; to encourage the establishment of co-operatives and to provide technical assistance and credit facilities; cap. 11m. (May 1986); Pres. José Walter Orozco Fonseca; Exec. Dir Lic. Rafael A. Rojas Jiménez.

Instituto Nacional de Vivienda y Urbanismo: Apdo 2.534, San José; tel. 215266; telex 2908; housing and town planning institute; Exec. Pres. Minister of Housing and Human Settlement; Representative José Manuel Agüero.

Ministerio de Planificación Nacional y Política Económica: Apdo 10.127, 1000 San José; tel. 232322; telex 2962; f. 1963; formulates and supervises execution of the National Development Plan; main aims: to increase national productivity; to improve distribution of income and social services; to increase citizen participation in solution of socio-economic problems; Dir Minister of National Planning and Economic Policy.

Refinadora Costarricense de Petróleo (Recope): Apdo 4.351, San José; tel. 239611; telex 2215; f. 1961; state petroleum organization; Dir Roberto Dobles.

CHAMBERS OF COMMERCE AND INDUSTRY

Cámara de Comercio de Costa Rica: Urbanización Tournón, Apdo 1.114, 1000 San José; tel. 210005; telex 2646; f. 1915; 1,050 mems; Pres. Antonio López Escarré; Exec. Dir Julio Ugarte.

Cámara de Industrias de Costa Rica: Calles 13–15, Avda 6, Apdo 10.003, San José; tel. 232411; telex 2474; f. 1943; Pres. Ing. Samuel Yankelewitz Berger; Exec. Dir Gustavo Gutiérrez Castro.

Unión de Cámaras: Apdo 539-1.002, Paseo de Estudiantes, San José; tel. 333555; telex 3644; f. 1974; business federation; Pres. Víctor E. Herrera Alfaro.

AGRICULTURAL ORGANIZATIONS

Cámara de Azucareros: Calle 3, Avda Fernández Güell, Apdo 1.577, 1000 San José; tel. 221358; f. 1949; sugar growers; Pres. Rodolfo Jiménez Borbón.

Cámara Nacional de Agricultura: Avda 1, Calles 24 y 28, Apdo 1.671, 1000 San José; tel. 216864; telex 3489; f. 1947; Pres. José R. Brenes; Exec. Dir Lic. Gerardina González M..

Cámara Nacional de Bananeros: Calle 11, Avda 6a, Edif. Urcha, Apdo 10.273, 1000 San José; tel. 227891; f. 1967; banana growers; Pres. Ing. Asdrúbal Carballo Chaves.

Cámara Nacional de Cafetaleros: Calle 3, Avdas 6 y 8, Apdo 1.310, San José; tel. 218207; telex 2525; f. 1948; 300 mems; coffee growers; Pres. Tobías Umaña Parra.

Cámara Nacional de Ganaderos: Edif. Iliflán 4°, Calles 2 y 4, Avda Central Apdo 4.564, San José; tel. 221652; cattle farmers; Pres. Víctor Wolf Fournier.

TRADE UNIONS

Central de Trabajadores Costarricenses (Costa Rican Workers' Union): Calle 20 a 3 y 5, Apdo 4.137, 1000 San José; tel. 217701; telex 3091; Sec.-Gen. Alsimiro Herrera Torres.

Confederación Auténtica de Trabajadores Democráticos (Democratic Workers' Union): Calle 13 a 10 y 12, Solera; tel. 532971; Pres. Luis Armando Gutiérrez; Sec.-Gen. Prof. Carlos Vargas.

Confederación Costarricense de Trabajadores Democráticos (Costa Rican Confederation of Democratic Workers): Calles 3–5, Avda 12, Apdo 2.167, San José; tel. 221981; telex 2167; f. 1966; mem. ICFTU and ORIT; Sec.-Gen. Luis Armando Gutiérrez R.; 50,000 mems.

Confederación Unitaria de Trabajadores (CUT): Calles 1 y 3, Avda 12, Casa No 142, Apdo 186, 1009 San José; tel. 214709; f. 1980 from a merger of the Federación Nacional de Trabajadores

COSTA RICA

Públicos and the Confederación General de Trabajadores; linked to Coalición Pueblo Unido; 53 affiliated unions; Pres. MARIO DEVANDAS; Sec.-Gen. ORLANDO SOLANO MEJÍAS; c. 55,000 mems.

Federación Sindical Agraria Nacional (FESIAN) (National Agrarian Confederation): Apdo 2.167, 1000 San José; tel. 335897; 20,000 member families; Sec.-Gen. JUAN MEJÍA VILLALOBOS.

The **Consejo Permanente de los Trabajadores,** formed in 1986, comprises six union organizations and two teachers' unions.

Transport

Ministerio de Obras Públicas y Transportes: Apdo 10.176, 1000 San José; tel. 272188; telex 2493; the ministry is responsible for setting tariffs, allocating funds, maintaining existing systems and constructing new ones.

Cámara Nacional de Transportes: Calle 20, Avda 7, San José; tel. 225394; national chamber of transport.

RAILWAYS

Instituto Costarricense de Ferrocarriles (INCOFER): Apdo No 1, 1009 FE al P Estación, Zona 3, San José; tel. 260011; telex 2393; government-owned; 647.4 km, of which 280.8 km are electrified; Exec. Pres. Ing. JOSÉ F. NICOLÁS ALVARADO.

INCOFER comprises:

División I: San José to Limón; Río Frío to Limón; several branch lines; f. 1986; 63.9 km of track are electrified.

División II: Alajuela to San José; San José to Puntarenas and Caldera branch; 216.9 km of track are electrified.

Other railways in Costa Rica include 48 km of track, formerly belonging to the United Fruit Company of Boston (USA) which are not presently in use.

ROADS

In 1987 there were 35,343 km of roads, of which 4,374 km were paved, excluding 663 km of the Pan-American Highway.

SHIPPING

Local services operate between the Costa Rican ports of Puntarenas and Limón and those of Colón and Cristóbal in Panama and other Central American ports. The multi-million dollar project at Caldera on the Gulf of Nicoya is now in operation as the main Pacific port; Puntarenas is being used as the second port. The Caribbean coast is served by the port complex of Limón/Moín. International services are operated by various foreign shipping lines.

Cooperativa de Pescadores del Pacífico: Apdo 336, Puntarenas; 2 vessels.

Junta de Administración Portuaria y de Desarrollo Económico de la Vertiente Atlántica (JAPDEVA): Calle 17, Avda 7, Apdo 8-5.330, 1000 San José; tel. 335301; telex 2435; state agency for the development of Atlantic ports; Exec. Pres. Ing. JORGE ARTURO CASTRO HERRERA.

Instituto Costarricense de Puertos del Pacífico (INCOP): Calle 36, Avda 3, San José; tel. 237111; telex 2793; state agency for the development of Pacific ports; Exec. Pres. EDGAR GUARDIOLA MENDOZA.

CIVIL AVIATION

Costa Rica's main international airport is the Juan Santamaría Airport, 16 km from San José at El Coco and there are regional airports at Liberia, Limón and Pavas (Tobías Bolaños Airport).

Líneas Aéreas Costarricenses, SA—LACSA (Costa Rican Airlines): Edif. Lacsa, Apdo 1.531, La Uruca, San José; tel. 323555; telex 2188; f. 1946; operates international services to Colombia, El Salvador, Guatemala, Honduras, Mexico, Panama, Puerto Rico, Venezuela and the USA; Chair. and Chief Exec. Capt. OTTO ESCALANTE W.; fleet: 3 Boeing 727-200, 2 Boeing 727-100, 1 DC-8-55F (cargo).

Servicios Aéreos Nacionales, SA (SANSA): Paseo Colón, Apdo 999, 1.007 Centro Colón, San José; tel. 234179; telex 2914; internal services; Gen. Man. Lic. CARLOS MANUEL DELGADO AGUILAR; fleet: 2 Aviocar C-212, 1 DC-3.

Tourism

The main tourist features are the Irazú and Poás volcanoes, the Orosí valley, the ruins of the colonial church at Orosí and the jungle train to Limón. Tourists also visit San José, the capital, and the Pacific beaches of Guanacaste and Puntarenas. A total of 260,840 tourists visited Costa Rica in 1986. The political instability elsewhere in Central America resulted in an increase in the number of visitors to Costa Rica in 1988.

Instituto Costarricense de Turismo: Edif. Genaro Valverde, Calles 5 y 7, Avda 4a, Apdo 777, San José; tel. 231733; telex 2281; f. 1964; Dir MARIO QUIRÓS.

Atomic Energy

Comisión de Energía Atómica de Costa Rica: Edif. Galerias del Este, 3°, Curridabat, Apdo Postal 6.681, San José; tel. 241591; f. 1967; Pres. Dr ENRIQUE GÓNGORA TREJOS; Dir SOLÓN CONTRERAS GARBANZO.

CÔTE D'IVOIRE

(THE IVORY COAST)

Introductory Survey

Location, Climate, Language, Religion, Flag, Capital

The Republic of Côte d'Ivoire lies on the west coast of Africa, between Ghana to the east and Liberia to the west, with Guinea, Mali and Burkina Faso to the north. The climate is hot and wet, with temperatures varying from 14°C to 39°C (57°F to 103°F). The official language is French, and a large number of African languages are also spoken. Most of the inhabitants follow traditional beliefs, while about 12% are Christians, mainly Roman Catholics, and 23% Muslims. The national flag (proportions 3 by 2) has three equal vertical stripes, of orange, white and green. The process of transferring the capital from Abidjan to Yamoussoukro (the President's birthplace), about 220 km (135 miles) north-west of Abidjan, was begun in March 1983.

Recent History

Formerly a province of French West Africa, Côte d'Ivoire achieved self-government, within the French Community, in December 1958. Dr Félix Houphouët-Boigny, leader of the Parti démocratique de la Côte d'Ivoire (PDCI), became Prime Minister in 1959. The country became fully independent on 7 August 1960.

A new constitution was adopted in October 1960, and Houphouët-Boigny became President in November. The ruling PDCI has been the country's only organized political party since it was founded in 1946. Côte d'Ivoire has retained close links with France, and the country's foreign policy is generally pro-Western. A high rate of economic growth, particularly during the 1970s, and strong support from the French have contributed to the stability of the regime. Political unrest has occurred sporadically, though without strong leadership. Two plots were uncovered in 1963, apparently representing a youthful radical element and northerners who resented southern domination in the Government. The army was reduced in size to reduce the risk of military intervention. The Government responded to criticism by implementing a policy of regional development and increased Ivorian management of commercial enterprises.

In 1977 Houphouët-Boigny replaced the Ministers of Finance, Economic Planning and Foreign Affairs, and legislation was enacted against corrupt trading and speculation in commodities. In May 1978 a significant step towards a relaxation of the PDCI's political dominance was taken when it was decided that, with the exception of Abidjan and Bouaké, the capitals of all the Departments would be administered by elected mayors, rather than by party appointees. Elections to the National Assembly were held in November 1980 and, for the first time, more than one candidate was permitted to contest each seat.

A series of strikes and demonstrations took place in the period from late 1980 to mid-1983, mainly involving students and professional groups. The longest strike, lasting from mid-April to early May of 1983, was staged by teachers protesting against the withdrawal of free housing rights, and was supported by members of the medical profession. The strike was terminated by a presidential decree ordering a return to work, and two education ministers were subsequently dismissed from the Government. In 1984 the Government implemented anti-corruption measures, including the imprisonment of several former government officials in the state housing sector, accused of malpractice. In 1985 a much-publicized court case, concerning debts of US $58m., was brought by the National Bank for Agricultural Development (BNDA) against COGEXIM, a private cocoa- and coffee-exporting company whose chairman was the mayor of Abidjan, Emmanuel Dioulo. The ensuing scandal prompted Dioulo to flee to Belgium in March; he was, however, granted amnesty in December, and returned to Côte d'Ivoire in February 1986.

A government reshuffle in November 1983 reduced the number of ministers from 35 to 28, in an attempt to cut administrative costs. The eighth ordinary congress of the PDCI, held in Abidjan in October 1985, approved the adoption of a constitutional amendment suppressing the post of Vice-President of the Republic and allowing for the president of the National Assembly to succeed the President of the Republic, on an interim basis, in the event of a vacancy. Later that month, Houphouët-Boigny was re-elected President for a sixth five-year term. Municipal and legislative elections were held in November, and in January 1986 Henri Konan-Bédié was re-elected to the presidency of the National Assembly. In July the Council of Ministers was reshuffled, and its membership increased to 40, in response to the apparent easing of the country's economic crisis.

Although the Ivorian Constitution permits the existence of a plurality of political parties, no opposition grouping has so far gained official recognition. The Government continues to deal firmly with obvious dissent. In September 1987 three members of the secondary-schoolteachers' union, SYNESCI, were arrested, following divisions within the union and a disputed transference of leadership. They were subsequently imprisoned after being found guilty of embezzlement, while 11 other union members were sent to a military camp for a period of 're-education'. All those detained were released in July 1988. The unexpected dismissal, in December 1987, of the Minister of Maritime Affairs, Lamine Fadika, together with the removal from office of the Chief of Staff of the Armed Forces and of four officials of the PDCI, was rumoured to be linked to the discovery of a coup plot. In September 1988 Laurent Gbagbo, the leader of the Front populaire ivoirien (FPI), an opposition movement, returned to Côte d'Ivoire after a six-year period of exile in Paris.

In the same month it was announced that the membership of the Council of Ministers was to be reduced to 38, as part of a reshuffle that included the creation of a Ministry of Drug Control.

The presence in Côte d'Ivoire of large numbers of Europeans, Levantines and nationals of neighbouring countries has led to sporadic clashes between Ivorians and immigrant groups. In 1981 more than 1m. foreigners were resident in the country; Côte d'Ivoire's French community, numbering some 35,000, is the largest in Africa. Increasing unemployment among university leavers, a concern for 'Ivorianization' and the need for reductions in public spending, however, led to the Government's decision to reduce the level of foreign assistance in the country; in 1987 there were believed to be some 2,000 French 'coopérants' employed by the Government, including about 1,600 teachers and researchers.

In February 1986 Côte d'Ivoire resumed formal diplomatic relations with Israel, following a 13-year suspension as a result of the Arab–Israeli war in 1973. Diplomatic links with the Soviet Union and several Eastern bloc states were also renewed in 1986–87. Houphouët-Boigny is committed to a policy of dialogue between Black Africa and white-ruled South Africa, for which he has been strongly criticized by other African leaders. President Botha of that country visited Côte d'Ivoire in 1988.

In April 1986 it was announced that the country wished to be known internationally by its French name of Côte d'Ivoire, rather than by translations of it. The request was subsequently endorsed by the UN.

Government

Executive power is vested in the President, who is elected for a five-year term by direct universal suffrage. The Council of Ministers is appointed by, and directly responsible to, the President. In 1980 provision was made for the appointment of a Vice-President, but in 1985 this was rescinded, and a constitutional amendment was adopted to provide for the president of the National Assembly to carry out the functions of the Head of State, in case of the latter's death or incapacitation, until a presidential election can be held. Legislative power is vested in the unicameral National Assembly, which is directly elected (using two ballots if necessary) for five years. The Assembly was expanded from 147 to 175 members following the 1985 elections. Although the Constitution provides for the existence of multiple political parties, the ruling Parti démocratique de la Côte d'Ivoire is the only officially-recognized grouping. It has an executive committee of 13 members, a political bureau of 60 and a guiding committee of 100. The country is divided into 49 Departments, each with its own elected Council.

Defence

Defence matters are the concern of the Regional Defence Council of the Conseil de l'Entente, through which agreements with France have been negotiated. France supplies equipment and training, and maintains a force of 500 men. In June 1988 Côte d'Ivoire had 5,500 men in the army, 900 in the air force and 700 in the navy. In addition, there are paramilitary forces of approximately 7,800 men. The estimated defence budget for 1987 was 36,900m. francs CFA (5.9% of total budget spending).

Economic Affairs

For most of its first 20 years of independence, Côte d'Ivoire achieved rapid economic growth, led by expansion in the agricultural sector, particularly the cultivation of plantation crops for export. In 1980 the country's gross national product (GNP) per head was estimated at US $1,150, one of the highest levels in sub-Saharan Africa. However, the subsequent collapse of world prices for cocoa, coffee and timber (then the country's three main exports) led to a period of severe recession. In 1987, according to estimates by the World Bank, Côte d'Ivoire's GNP, measured at average 1985–87 prices, totalled $8,262m., equivalent to $750 per head. Between 1980 and 1987 GNP per head decreased, in real terms, at an average annual rate of 3.0%.

Following independence, Côte d'Ivoire successfully developed its economy from a largely agricultural base, and an estimated 60% of the labour force still worked in the agricultural sector in 1986. From 1965 to 1980 the country's gross domestic product (GDP) grew at an average annual rate of 6.8%. Between 1980 and 1986, however, real GDP declined by an average of 0.3% annually. Between 1980 and 1984 several development projects were postponed, and widespread reforms of state corporations were implemented, in an effort to curb public expenditure. Real GDP fell by 3.1% in 1987, but was expected to have grown, by just 0.2%, in 1988.

Exports of cocoa, coffee and associated products together accounted for 61% of total export earnings in 1986. In the 1977/78 season Côte d'Ivoire became the world's largest producer of cocoa beans, a position that it continued to maintain in 1986. The country also remained one of the world's largest producers of coffee. Production of both crops was severely affected in the early 1980s by irregular rainfall patterns. Following the return of normal rainfall, record cocoa production was achieved between 1984/85 and 1987/88, with output in the latter year being estimated at 620,000 metric tons. A further record crop, of more than 700,000 tons, was forecast for 1988/89. The decline in world prices for this commodity obliged the Government, at the end of 1987, to suspend its replanting programme, and to abandon its production target of 1m. tons annually. Production of green coffee totalled 276,600 tons in 1984/85, but by 1986/87 had declined slightly, to 264,100 tons. Proposals were announced in 1986 for the extension of the cultivation area to achieve annual production of between 330,000 and 360,000 tons. All cocoa and coffee production in Côte d'Ivoire is traditionally purchased, at guaranteed prices, by the state marketing agency, the Caisse de stabilisation et de soutien des prix des productions agricoles (CSSPPA). Since the mid-1980s, however, the sustained decline in world prices for cocoa and coffee has resulted in a reduction in export revenue from these commodities to a level below the cost of their production and marketing. In 1988 the Côte d'Ivoire Government imposed an embargo on the sale of both crops, in an attempt to bring about an increase in world prices. In October of that year the International Coffee Organization (ICO) agreed new export quotas which would, it was believed, stabilize world prices. Despite pressure from the International Cocoa Organization (ICCO), which had repeatedly failed to achieve a price-stabilization mechanism, the Houphouët-Boigny Government refused to lower the official price payable to cocoa producers. In January 1989 it was confirmed that an agreement had been signed between Côte d'Ivoire and a French commodity broker, Sucres et Denrées, under the terms of which the latter had agreed to buy, at an undisclosed price, 400,000 tons of Ivorian cocoa.

Fluctuations in world prices for cocoa and coffee have emphasized the need for crop diversification. Côte d'Ivoire has become one of the world's largest producers of palm oil and palm-kernel oil, with an estimated output of 195,000 metric tons in 1986/87. A five-year programme to rehabilitate and expand the palm-oil industry began in 1986. Production of seed (unginned) cotton reached 213,500 tons in 1986/87. Rice production was affected by low rainfall in the early 1980s, and in 1984 the Government imposed restrictions on rice imports in an attempt to increase production levels. By 1986/87 the annual crop of paddy rice totalled an estimated 603,800 tons, almost twice the level at the beginning of the decade. A development programme for this sector, to be supported by a grant of US $5.8m. from Japan, was expected to increase annual production to 1.6m. tons by 1990. It was hoped that Côte d'Ivoire would become a net exporter of rice and maize (production of which was estimated at 291,400 tons in 1986/87) by 1990. Production of raw sugar totalled an estimated 143,700 tons in 1986/87. A restructuring scheme, introduced in 1986, aimed to increase annual output to 185,000 tons by 1988/89. The rubber industry has shown considerable success, and annual production was expected to rise to 90,000 tons by 1990. An estimated 55,000 tons of natural rubber were produced in 1986/87. Plantations are being expanded, at an estimated cost of 18,000m. francs CFA (to be provided by France and the World Bank), under a 1987–91 development scheme.

Resources of timber (Côte d'Ivoire's fourth most important export commodity in 1986) have been severely depleted in the years since independence. Despite the announcement, in 1984, of an extensive reafforestation programme, and official restrictions on commercial production (to 4m. cu m per year until 1990), deforestation is occurring at an estimated annual rate of 300,000 ha, while replanting takes place on an average of only 5,000 ha per year. In May 1987 the Government announced its intention to suspend timber exports as soon as the country's external financing situation and budgetary difficulties (see below) had been resolved.

In 1977 Côte d'Ivoire's first significant petroleum deposits were discovered off the coast. The Belier field, 15 km south of Grand Bassam, began production in 1980, and was yielding an estimated 20,000 barrels per day (b/d) by late 1982. In early 1980 the Espoir field was discovered, also off shore, with reserves estimated at 500m. metric tons. In 1986 petroleum products constituted the country's third most important source of export revenue. However, offshore oil production has increased much more slowly than was originally hoped: total petroleum production in 1986 was estimated at just under 1m. tons, compared with an original target of 3m. tons per year by 1985. In 1988 it was announced that a new offshore field had been discovered. However, despite the apparent commercial viability of this field, legislation introduced in the same year, which doubled payments of royalties by foreign petroleum companies to the Côte d'Ivoire Government, together with declining production from existing fields, were likely to act as a disincentive to further exploration. Reserves of offshore natural gas are estimated at 50,000m. cu m, but have not yet been exploited, owing to the high cost of initial investment. There are large quantities of high-quality iron ore at Bangolo. Reserves of gold, copper, nickel, molybdenum, cobalt, bauxite and uranium have also been discovered. Small-scale diamond mining, by private companies, ceased in 1979.

The share of agriculture in GDP declined from 47% in 1965 to 36% in 1986. The contribution of industry was 24% in 1986, compared with 19% in 1965. However, the development of the manufacturing sector has been limited to the processing of primary commodities before export. Most exported palm oil is now refined, and large quantities of fruit (particularly pineapple) are tinned or preserved. In 1984 the Government announced a new investment code, including measures to encourage decentralization and the creation of small and medium-sized enterprises. Throughout the 1980s there have been continued efforts to encourage the 'Ivorianization' of industrial companies, and government participation in the sector is being reduced progressively, with 28 state-controlled organizations being transferred to private ownership between 1980 and 1987. In 1988 the Government adopted an industrial development strategy, with the intention of strengthening the import-substitution sector, while expanding the country's narrow manufacturing base to include more export-oriented industries.

Four of Côte d'Ivoire's five hydroelectric plants, which in 1980 provided 92% of the country's electricity, were brought to a halt during the 1982–84 drought. Plans for a new dam and generating plant at Soubré were postponed indefinitely in 1984, owing to the economic recession and doubts about increased dependence on hydroelectric power.

After 1977 Côte d'Ivoire's trade surplus dwindled, as commodity prices weakened, initially for coffee and, in 1980, for cocoa, while import prices, especially for petroleum, increased. By 1985, however, government measures, aimed at restricting imports, had caused the surplus to expand to 545,073m. francs CFA (compared with just 1,180m. francs CFA in 1978). The overall balance-of-payments deficit amounted to 51,500m. francs CFA in 1987, and was estimated to have risen to 78,200m. francs CFA in 1988, as a result of the stockpiling of cocoa and coffee. Meanwhile, substantial borrowing, to finance the ambitious capital-investment programmes of the 1970s, had increased the debt-service ratio from 6.8% of the country's annual export earnings in 1970 to 32% in 1985. This ratio subsequently fell to 29% in 1986 and to 19.7% in 1987, owing to the moratorium on its external debt repayments (see below). Multi-annual debt reschedulings were organized in 1986 by both the 'Paris Club' of government creditors and the 'London Club' of commercial creditors: Côte d'Ivoire became the first African country to obtain such an accord from the 'Paris Club'. In May 1987, however, the Government suspended payments on its external debt (then estimated to total some US $8,400m.), following the announcement of a projected decline in export revenue in that year, as a result of falling world prices for cocoa and coffee. (The actual decline was subsequently put at 220,000m. francs CFA.)

Owing to Côte d'Ivoire's high standing among African nations in the view of the international financial community, this action highlighted the increasing gravity of the 'African debt crisis', and the Côte d'Ivoire Government began a series of negotiations with its creditors. In October 1987 the World Bank declared itself willing to consider a full rescheduling of the Ivorian debt. In November conditions were agreed for the disbursement of the second tranche of a World Bank structural adjustment loan of $250m., approved in June 1986. This agreement was followed, in December 1987, by a further rescheduling of debt, totalling 165,000m. francs CFA, by the 'Paris Club'. In March 1988 the IMF agreed a credit of $241m., of which $113m. was to be made available immediately to compensate for the fall in export revenues. In May Côte d'Ivoire failed to honour debt-service commitments to the 'London Club', despite an agreement that had been made earlier in the month to reschedule 710,000m. francs CFA of the country's total commercial debt of 758,000m. francs CFA. (Côte d'Ivoire made its first debt-service payment since the announcement of the suspension of repayments, to the World Bank, in November 1988.) The 1989 draft budget made no specific provision for debt-servicing, owing to the uncertainty regarding existing rescheduling agreements. Increases in both current and capital expenditure, compared with 1988 levels, were likely to be offset by inflation, which was estimated to be about 7% per year at the end of 1988.

Social Welfare

Medical services are organized by the State. In 1980 the country had 8,799 hospital beds and 518 physicians. There is a minimum wage for workers in industry and commerce. Projects to increase the social and health services to regional centres and villages are being carried out. Of total budgetary expenditure in 1987, 5,044m. francs CFA (0.8%) was allocated to social security and welfare, and 47,928m. francs CFA (7.6%) to health. A major vaccination programme, introduced in April 1987, aimed to immunize between 75% and 80% of Ivorian children against the six major infant diseases.

Education

In 1985, according to UNESCO estimates, adult illiteracy averaged 57.3% (males 46.9%; females 68.9%). Education at all levels is available free of charge. Primary education begins at seven years of age and lasts for six years. Enrolment at primary schools in 1984 was equivalent to 78% of all children between seven and 12 years of age (92% of boys; 65% of girls). In the towns, however, average attendance is more than 90%. Secondary education, beginning at the age of 13, lasts for up to seven years. In 1984 the total enrolment at secondary schools was equivalent to 20% of children aged 13 and 19 (27% of boys; 12% of girls). The National University at Abidjan has five faculties, and in 1984/85 had 12,755 students. In addition, many students attend French universities. In 1981–85 five technical training institutes were to be built, and the University was to be decentralized. About 1,600 teachers and researchers of French nationality were estimated to be working in Côte d'Ivoire in 1987. Expenditure on education in 1987 was projected at 177,060m. francs CFA (28.2% of total budget spending), the highest allocation to any sector.

Public Holidays

1989: 2 January (for New Year's Day), 24 March (Good Friday), 27 March (Easter Monday), 1 May (Labour Day), 4 May (Ascension Day), 7 May* (Id al-Fitr, end of Ramadan), 15 May (Whit Monday), 14 July* (Id al-Adha, feast of the Sacrifice), 15 August (Assumption), 1 November (All Saints' Day), 7 December (Independence Day), 25 December (Christmas).

1990: 1 January (New Year's Day), 13 April (Good Friday), 16 April (Easter Monday), 27 April* (Id al-Fitr, end of Ramadan), 1 May (Labour Day), 24 May (Ascension Day), 4 June (Whit Monday), 4 July* (Id al-Adha, feast of the Sacrifice), 15 August (Assumption), 1 November (All Saints' Day), 7 December (Independence Day), 25 December (Christmas).

* These holidays are dependent on the Islamic lunar calendar and may vary by one or two days from the dates given.

Weights and Measures

The metric system is in force.

Statistical Survey

Source (unless otherwise stated): Direction de la Statistique, Ministère de l'Economie et des Finances, 01 BP V55, Abidjan 01; tel. 32-15-38.

Area and Population

AREA, POPULATION AND DENSITY

Area (sq km)	322,462*
Population (census of 30 April 1975)†	
Males	3,474,750
Females	3,234,850
Total	6,709,600
Population (official estimates at mid-year)	
1980	8,262,300
1983	9,334,800‡
1984	9,742,900‡
Density (per sq km) at mid-1984	30.2

* 124,503 sq miles. † Provisional result. Revised total is 6,702,866.
‡ Provisional. Figures for 1981–82 are not available.

PROVINCES

	Area (sq km)	Population (1975 census)
Abengourou	6,900	177,692
Abidjan*	14,200	1,389,141
Aboisso	6,250	148,823
Adzopé	5,230	162,837
Agboville	3,850	141,970
Biankouma	4,950	75,711
Bondoukou	16,530	296,551
Bouaflé	8,500	263,609
Bouaké*	23,670	808,048
Bouna	21,470	84,290
Boundiali	10,095	132,278
Dabakala	9,670	56,230
Daloa	15,200	369,610
Danané	4,600	170,249
Dimbokro	14,100	475,023
Divo	10,650	278,526
Ferkessedougou	17,728	90,423
Gagnoa	6,900	259,504
Guiglo	14,150	137,672
Katiola	9,420	77,875
Korhogo	12,500	276,816
Man	7,050	278,659
Odienné	20,600	124,010
Sassandra	25,800	191,994
Séguéla	21,900	157,539
Touba	8,720	77,786
Total	320,633†	6,702,866

* Including commune.
† Other sources give the total area as 322,462 sq km.
Source: *La Côte d'Ivoire en Chiffres*, 1979.

(Note: Following a reorganization of local government in 1985, Côte d'Ivoire comprised a total of 49 provinces.)

PRINCIPAL TOWNS (population at 15 June 1979)
Abidjan 1,423,323; Bouaké 272,640.

BIRTHS AND DEATHS (UN estimates, annual averages)

	1970–75	1975–80	1980–85
Birth rate (per 1,000)	44.5	45.9	45.6
Death rate (per 1,000)	21.0	19.5	15.6

Source: UN, *World Population Prospects: Estimates and Projections as Assessed in 1984*.

ECONOMICALLY ACTIVE POPULATION
(ILO estimates, '000 persons at mid-1980)

	Males	Females	Total
Agriculture, etc.	1,385	928	2,314
Industry	231	62	293
Services	693	248	940
Total	2,309	1,238	3,547

Source: ILO, *Economically Active Population Estimates and Projections, 1950–2025*.
Mid-1986 (estimates, '000 persons): Agriculture, etc. 2,474; Total 4,157 (Source: FAO, *Production Yearbook*).

Agriculture

PRINCIPAL CROPS ('000 metric tons)

	1984	1985	1986
Maize	468	530†	550*
Millet	30	40*	35*
Sorghum	20	25*	20*
Rice (paddy)	490	541†	460†
Potatoes*	24	24	24
Sweet potatoes	12	12*	12*
Cassava (Manioc)	1,230	1,500†	1,500*
Yams	2,600	2,900	2,996*
Taro (Coco yam)	202	235†	235*
Pulses*	8	8	8
Tree nuts	5*	6*	6
Sugar cane*	1,400	1,270	1,500
Palm kernels	33	35	43†
Groundnuts (in shell)	98†	80*	86*
Cottonseed	79	120†	115
Coconuts*	290	300	323
Copra*	42	42	47
Tomatoes*	31	32	35
Aubergines (Eggplants)*	19	19	19
Chillies, peppers*	21	22	23
Other vegetables*	336	369	381
Oranges*	26	27	28
Other citrus fruit*	45	50	50
Bananas	148†	170†	170*
Plantains	1,440	1,400*	1,400*
Pineapples	229	298†	300*
Other fruit*	30	31	32
Coffee (green)	85	260	280
Cocoa beans	550	580	520
Tobacco (leaves)*	3	3	3
Cotton (lint)	58	88	75
Natural rubber (dry weight)	35	41	48*

* FAO estimates. † Unofficial figures.
Source: FAO, *Production Yearbook*.

CÔTE D'IVOIRE

LIVESTOCK
(FAO estimates, '000 head, year ending September)

	1984	1985	1986
Cattle	820	843	881
Pigs	410	430	450
Sheep	1,400	1,450	1,502
Goats	1,400	1,450	1,496

Poultry (FAO estimates, million): 16 in 1984; 16 in 1985; 16 in 1986.
Source: FAO, *Production Yearbook*.

LIVESTOCK PRODUCTS (FAO estimates, '000 metric tons)

	1984	1985	1986
Total meat production	124	127	131
Beef and veal	42	42	44
Mutton and lamb	6	6	7
Goats' meat	7	6	6
Pig meat	16	17	18
Poultry meat	25	27	28
Cows' milk	15	16	17
Hen eggs	12.2	10.1	11.0
Cattle hides	5.5	5.6	5.7
Sheepskins	1.5	1.6	1.6
Goatskins	1.6	1.6	1.6

Source: FAO, *Production Yearbook*.

Forestry

ROUNDWOOD REMOVALS ('000 cubic metres)

	1984	1985	1986
Sawlogs, veneer logs and logs for sleepers	3,947	3,315	2,973
Other industrial wood*	596	619	640
Fuel wood*	7,686	7,972	8,252
Total	12,229	11,906	11,865

* FAO estimates.
Source: FAO, *Yearbook of Forest Products*.

SAWNWOOD PRODUCTION ('000 cubic metres)

	1984	1985	1986
Total (incl. boxboards)	679	753	685

Source: FAO, *Yearbook of Forest Products*.

Fishing
('000 metric tons, live weight)

	1984	1985	1986
Freshwater fishes	15.6	15.6	18.0
Bigeye grunt	1.9	1.6	2.3
West African croakers	1.0	1.5	1.5
Dentex, seabreams, etc.	0.9	1.1	1.2
Threadfins and tasselfishes	1.1	1.1	1.1
Sardinellas	13.7	37.7	36.6
Bonga shad	12.0	12.0	12.0
Atlantic black skipjack	1.6*	1.0*	—
Skipjack tuna	4.7*	2.9*	—
Yellowfin tuna	6.6*	4.0*	—
Bigeye tuna	1.3*	0.8*	—
Other marine fishes (incl. unspecified)	20.5*	20.2*	21.2
Total fish	81.0	99.6	93.8
Crustaceans	2.7*	2.6*	3.4
Total catch	83.7	102.2	97.2

* FAO estimate.
Source: FAO, *Yearbook of Fishery Statistics*.

Mining

	1983	1984	1985
Crude petroleum ('000 metric tons)	1,158*	1,368*	1,410

* UN estimates.
Source: UN, *Industrial Statistics Yearbook*.

Industry

SELECTED PRODUCTS
('000 metric tons, unless otherwise indicated)

	1983	1984	1985
Palm oil and palm-kernel oil	200	244	n.a.
Wheat flour	129	163	n.a.
Biscuits	4.0	4.5	n.a.
Pineapple juice (unconcentrated)	9.1	8.8	10.0*
Salted, dried or smoked fish*	15.0	12.0	15.0
Tinned fish	25.5	35.2	n.a.
Cocoa butter (exports)	16.3	18.6	21.7
Raw sugar	150	130	112*
Beer ('000 hectolitres)	1,400	1,245	n.a.
Soft drinks ('000 hectolitres)	564	400	n.a.
Cigarettes (million)	3,640	3,210	4,000
Cotton woven fabrics (million metres)	107.4	100.8	n.a.
Synthetic textile materials (million metres)	2.3	1.7	1.7*
Footwear—excl. rubber ('000 pairs)	6,380	5,900	n.a.
Plywood ('000 cubic metres)	33	26	26
Motor spirit (Petrol)	250	245	250
Jet fuel	97	96	98
Kerosene	261	318	320
Distillate fuel oils	512	450	475
Cement	636	552	535
Electric energy (million kWh)	1,966	1,644	1,785

* FAO estimates.   † UN estimates.
Source: UN, *Industrial Statistics Yearbook*.

CÔTE D'IVOIRE

Statistical Survey

Finance

CURRENCY AND EXCHANGE RATES

Monetary Units
100 centimes = 1 franc de la Communauté financière africaine (CFA).

Denominations
Coins: 1, 5, 10, 25, 50 and 100 francs CFA.
Notes: 500, 1,000, 5,000 and 10,000 francs CFA.

French Franc, Sterling and Dollar Equivalents
(30 September 1988)
1 French franc = 50 francs CFA;
£1 sterling = 538.6 francs CFA;
US $1 = 318.5 francs CFA;
1,000 francs CFA = £1.857 = $3.140.

Average Exchange Rate (francs CFA per US $)
1985   449.26
1986   346.30
1987   300.54

CURRENT BUDGET (estimates, million francs CFA)

Revenue	1987	1988
Fiscal revenue	478,030	488,700
Direct taxes	107,300	116,870
Indirect taxes	355,310	356,810
Customs duties	255,000	243,100
Registration and stamp duty	12,220	13,200
Revenue from property and services	3,200	1,820
Non-fiscal revenue	2,950	4,800
Total	**480,980**	**493,500**

Expenditure	1987	1988
Public debt servicing	2,330	1,700
Personnel	283,770	300,910
Expenditure on goods and services	78,900	77,080
Subsidies and other current transfers	115,980	113,810
Total	**480,980**	**493,500**

INVESTMENT AND CAPITAL BUDGET
(estimates, million francs CFA)

Revenue	1987	1988
Fiscal receipts	20,710	29,770
Domestic borrowing	15,500	20,500
Other receipts	2,600	7,530
External borrowing	107,070	85,800
Total	**145,880**	**143,600**

Expenditure	1987	1988
Economic development	86,410	87,500
Social development	42,220	34,130
Cultural development	8,950	14,260
Other expenditure	8,300	7,710
Total	**145,880**	**143,600**

Source: *La Zone Franc—Rapport 1987*.

1989 (Draft budget, million francs CFA): Current expenditure 499,478; Capital expenditure 144,954.

CENTRAL BANK RESERVES (US $ million at 31 December)

	1985	1986	1987
Gold*	14.4	18.0	21.0
IMF special drawing rights	0.1	8.5	0.2
Foreign exchange	4.7	11.0	8.7
Total	**19.2**	**37.6**	**29.9**

* Valued at market-related prices.
Source: IMF, *International Financial Statistics*.

MONEY SUPPLY ('000 million francs CFA at 31 December)

	1985	1986	1987
Currency outside banks	307.1	317.7	304.7
Demand deposits at deposit money banks*	311.2	317.1	292.3

* Excluding the deposits of public establishments of an administrative or social nature.
Source: IMF, *International Financial Statistics*.

COST OF LIVING
(Consumer Price Index for Africans in Abidjan. Base: 1980 = 100)

	1984	1985	1986
Food	120.1	122.0	133.7
Fuel, light, water and soap	121.8	125.9	130.9
Clothing	203.0	207.3	214.2
Rent	150.9	152.6	152.9
All items (incl. others)	128.8	131.1	139.8

Source: ILO, *Year Book of Labour Statistics*.
1987: Food 156.1; All items 154.1 (Source: UN, *Monthly Bulletin of Statistics*).

NATIONAL ACCOUNTS
('000 million francs CFA at current prices)
National Income and Product

	1980	1981†	1982†
Compensation of employees	748.2	796.2	873.7
Operating surplus	788.2	910.3	954.1
Domestic factor incomes	**1,536.5**	**1,706.5**	**1,827.9**
Consumption of fixed capital	184.0	211.3	208.5
Gross domestic product (GDP) at factor cost	**1,720.5**	**1,917.8**	**2,036.4**
Indirect taxes, *less* subsidies*	429.4	373.6	450.2
GDP in purchasers' values	**2,149.9**	**2,291.4**	**2,486.5**
Factor income received from abroad	7.3	8.1	10.1
Less Factor income paid abroad	117.5	179.7	225.3
Gross national product	**2,039.7**	**2,119.6**	**2,271.3**
Less Consumption of fixed capital	184.0	211.3	208.5
National income in market prices	**1,855.7**	**1,908.3**	**2,062.8**
Other current transfers from abroad	45.0	55.4	55.8
Less Other current transfers paid abroad	138.8	135.7	160.5
National disposable income	**1,761.9**	**1,828.0**	**1,958.1**

* Includes the profit or loss of the Caisse de stabilisation et de soutien des prix des productions agricoles (CSSPPA).
† Figures are provisional. Revised totals of GDP in purchasers' values (in '000 million francs CFA) are: 2,293.3 in 1981; 2,524.5 in 1982.

1983 ('000 million francs CFA at current prices): GDP in purchasers' values 2,652.7.

Source: mainly UN, *National Accounts Statistics*.

CÔTE D'IVOIRE

Expenditure on the Gross Domestic Product*

	1981	1982	1984†
Government final consumption expenditure	398.0	427.8	470.2
Private final consumption expenditure	1,495.4	1,590.5	1,782.4
Increase in stocks	36.0	37.9	−44.8
Gross fixed capital formation	558.4	538.7	352.6
Total domestic expenditure	2,487.7	2,594.8	2,560.4
Exports of goods and services	826.6	928.7	1,286.4
Less Imports of goods and services	1,022.9	1,036.9	991.0
GDP in purchasers' values	2,291.4	2,486.5	2,855.8

* Figures are provisional. Revised totals of GDP (in '000 million francs CFA) are: 2,293.3 in 1981; 2,524.5 in 1982; 2,858.2 in 1984 (Source: IMF, *International Financial Statistics*).
† Figures for 1983 are not available.

GDP in purchasers' values ('000 million francs CFA): 3,137.8 in 1985; 3,244.3 in 1986 (Source: IMF, *International Financial Statistics*).

Gross Domestic Product by Economic Activity

	1980	1981†	1982†
Agriculture, hunting, forestry and fishing	616.3	657.9	651.1
Mining and quarrying	5.7	27.4	52.2
Manufacturing	241.0	229.1	300.9
Electricity, gas and water	34.4	41.0	52.9
Construction	148.9	128.6	126.3
Trade, restaurants and hotels*	392.1	383.9	456.7
Transport, storage and communication	159.7	181.4	177.6
Finance, insurance, real estate and business services	210.5	273.1	296.0
Community, social and personal services	22.0	24.6	23.2
Domestic product of industries	1,830.7	1,947.0	2,136.9
Producers of government services	213.7	243.3	272.6
Other producers	15.6	16.9	16.4
Sub-total	2,060.0	2,207.2	2,425.9
Less Imputed bank service charges	67.7	81.3	86.8
Import duties	157.6	165.5	147.5
GDP in purchasers' values	2,149.9	2,291.4	2,486.5

* Includes the profit or loss of the CSSPPA (see above).
† Figures are provisional. For revised totals, see footnotes to previous tables.

Source: UN, *National Accounts Statistics*.

BALANCE OF PAYMENTS (US $ million)

	1984	1985	1986
Merchandise exports f.o.b.	2,624.8	2,761.0	3,170.6
Merchandise imports f.o.b.	−1,487.3	−1,409.9	−1,625.2
Trade balance	1,137.4	1,351.1	1,545.5
Exports of services	417.4	438.5	544.6
Imports of services	−1,345.9	−1,468.9	−1,866.0
Balance on goods and services	208.9	320.7	224.0
Private unrequited transfers (net)	−291.1	−278.9	−427.4
Government unrequited transfers (net)	24.0	21.8	64.9
Current balance	−58.2	63.6	−138.4
Direct capital investment (net)	3.0	29.2	107.4
Other long-term capital (net)	185.4	180.6	166.6
Short-term capital (net)	−38.0	−119.3	357.8
Net errors and omissions	−130.6	121.4	−466.5
Total (net monetary movements)	−38.4	275.4	27.0
Valuation changes (net)	38.7	−66.2	−66.0
Exceptional financing (net)	12.2	−248.8	63.0
Official financing (net)	1.8	6.9	−12.7
Changes in reserves	14.3	−32.8	11.3

Source: IMF, *International Financial Statistics*.

External Trade

Source: Banque Centrale des Etats de l'Afrique de l'Ouest.

PRINCIPAL COMMODITIES
(million francs CFA)

Imports c.i.f.	1984	1985	1986
Dairy products	20,691	23,629	23,790
Cereals	49,484	32,962	41,589
Beverages and tobacco	13,667	15,154	16,856
Fuels	116,410	170,142	111,525
Crude petroleum	82,667	156,695	104,058
Machinery and transport equipment	153,941	170,483	160,907
Electrical machinery	40,264	25,294	28,813
Non-electric machinery	50,032	54,147	69,750
Road vehicles	33,534	51,525	59,318
Air transport equipment	1,783	29,466	2,246
Sea and river transport equipment	27,852	9,461	340
Chemicals	82,789	102,167	100,420
Cotton yarn and fabrics	10,780	17,240	18,569
Total (incl. others)	658,569	772,987	709,044

Exports f.o.b.	1984	1985	1986
Bananas	6,961	14,697	10,015
Pineapples	14,081	25,516	25,350
Green coffee	183,382	277,657	233,131
Cocoa beans	396,610	398,409	392,877
Cocoa paste and cocoa butter	70,715	88,617	64,667
Coffee extracts and essences	15,362	20,744	20,371
Canned fish	19,892	18,643	18,783
Canned fruit	5,782	7,078	3,218
Fuels	136,221	118,204	94,005
Latex	15,090	13,693	13,644
Wood	108,668	90,857	76,445
Cotton (ginned)	34,019	33,360	27,665
Fats and oils	35,447	30,774	15,975
Chemicals	17,450	30,297	29,761
Cotton yarn and fabrics	14,843	14,311	15,115
Total (incl. others)	1,184,347	1,318,060	1,160,441

CÔTE D'IVOIRE   *Statistical Survey*

PRINCIPAL TRADING PARTNERS (million francs CFA)

Imports	1984	1985	1986
Belgium/Luxembourg	13,188	17,846	20,848
Cameroon	1,845	21,040	1,737
Canada	6,869	7,890	4,042
China, People's Republic	22,704	13,219	11,838
France	216,540	247,873	219,707
Gabon	11,439	13,655	6,556
Germany, Fed. Republic	33,239	37,466	40,429
Italy	21,148	29,121	30,717
Japan	25,273	38,438	44,170
Netherlands	31,823	36,852	39,567
Nigeria	58,882	86,155	69,864
Pakistan	9,521	6,949	16,048
Senegal	12,697	15,377	11,764
Spain	23,901	27,426	26,275
Switzerland	6,585	8,026	9,845
United Kingdom	16,515	16,533	18,003
USA	43,314	52,984	29,219
Venezuela	10,882	2,835	17,173
Total (incl. others)	658,569	772,987	709,044

Exports	1984	1985	1986
Belgium/Luxembourg	28,678	51,055	52,603
Burkina Faso	29,285	38,121	30,716
France	194,097	218,371	165,256
Germany, Fed. Republic	61,935	70,692	64,269
Ghana	6,425	11,038	12,261
Italy	75,926	120,911	90,001
Japan	23,764	13,590	15,931
Mali	29,254	37,975	32,083
Netherlands	193,725	225,633	216,758
Nigeria	8,416	7,718	25,015
Portugal	14,488	8,903	7,774
Senegal	9,447	20,629	12,010
Spain	25,896	33,901	33,915
Togo	23,312	10,706	9,400
USSR	53,979	57,522	59,027
United Kingdom	40,186	57,312	49,324
USA	178,113	154,055	121,980
Total (incl. others)	1,184,347	1,318,060	1,160,441

Transport

RAILWAYS (including Burkina Faso traffic)

	1982	1983	1984
Passengers ('000)	3,171.8	2,941.0	2,574.9
Passenger-km (million)	892.6	971.8	857.8
Freight ('000 metric tons)	731	601	702
Freight (million net ton-km)	610.6	468.7	530.2

ROAD TRAFFIC (motor vehicles in use at 31 December)

	1981	1982	1984†
Passenger cars	157,076	166,920	182,956
Buses and coaches	10,608	11,417	12,944
Goods vehicles*	66,795	69,467	30,057

* Including vans.   † Figures for 1983 are not available.
Source: International Road Federation, *World Road Statistics*.

INTERNATIONAL SEA-BORNE SHIPPING
(freight traffic, '000 metric tons)

	1983	1984	1985
Goods loaded	4,314	4,830	4,658
Goods unloaded	4,593	4,891	4,874

Source: UN, *Monthly Bulletin of Statistics*.

CIVIL AVIATION (traffic on scheduled services*)

	1982	1983	1984
Kilometres flown ('000)	4,500	4,700	4,700
Passengers carried	385,000	389,000	398,000
Passenger-km ('000)	316,000	316,000	325,000
Freight ton-km ('000)	21,600	19,100	17,800
Mail ton-km ('000)	900	900	800

* Including an apportionment of the traffic of Air Afrique.
Source: UN, *Statistical Yearbook*.

Tourism

	1981	1982	1983
Tourist arrivals	194,869	200,005*	202,000*

* Estimated figures.
Sources: Ministère du Tourisme, Abidjan, and UN, *Statistical Yearbook*.

Communications Media

	1981	1982	1983
Radio receivers ('000 in use)	1,050	1,100	1,200
Television receivers ('000 in use)	330	350	380
Book production:			
Titles	n.a.	n.a.	46*
Copies ('000)	n.a.	n.a.	3,766*
Daily newspapers:			
Number	n.a.	2	n.a.
Average circulation ('000 copies)	n.a.	85	n.a.
Non-daily newspapers:			
Number	n.a.	6	n.a.
Average circulation ('000 copies)	n.a.	145	n.a.
Other periodicals:			
Number	n.a.	12	n.a.
Average circulation ('000 copies)	n.a.	325	n.a.

* Excluding pamphlets.
1984: Daily newspapers 1 (estimated circulation 80,000 copies).
1985: ('000 in use): Radio receivers 1,300; Television receivers 500.
Source: UNESCO, *Statistical Yearbook*.
Telephones (1980): 88,000 in use (Source: UN, *Statistical Yearbook*).

Education

PUPILS ENROLLED

	1982/83	1983/84	1984/85
Primary	1,134,915	1,159,824	1,179,456
Public	1,001,647	1,029,628	1,046,790
Private	133,268	130,196	132,666
Secondary	217,824	230,128	245,342
National University	12,363	12,862	12,755

Teachers: Primary 28,561 in 1984; Secondary (General) 5,192 in 1980; Secondary (Vocational) 1,947 in 1981; Higher education 1,204 in 1981 (Source: UNESCO, *Statistical Yearbook*).

Directory

The Constitution

The Constitution was promulgated on 31 October 1960. It was amended in June 1971, October 1975, August 1980, November 1980, October 1985 and January 1986.

PREAMBLE

The Republic of Côte d'Ivoire is one and indivisible. It is secular, democratic and social. Sovereignty belongs to the people who exercise it through their representatives or through referenda. There is universal, equal and secret suffrage. French is the official language.

HEAD OF STATE

The President is elected for a five-year term by direct universal suffrage and is eligible for re-election. He is Head of the Administration and the Armed Forces and has power to ask the National Assembly to reconsider a Bill, which must then be passed by two-thirds of the members of the Assembly; he may also have a Bill submitted to a referendum. In case of the death or incapacitation of the President, the functions of the Head of State are carried out by the president of the National Assembly, until a presidential election has been held, within 45–60 days.

EXECUTIVE POWER

Executive power is vested in the President. He appoints a Council of Ministers, who are responsible only to him. Any member of the National Assembly appointed minister must renounce his seat in the Assembly, but may regain it on leaving the Government.

LEGISLATIVE POWER

Legislative power is vested in a National Assembly of 175 members, elected for a five-year term of office. Legislation may be introduced either by the President or by a member of the National Assembly.

JUDICIAL POWER

The independence of the judiciary is guaranteed by the President, assisted by a High Council of Judiciary.

ECONOMIC AND SOCIAL COUNCIL

This is an advisory commission of 120 members, appointed by the President because of their specialist knowledge or experience.

The Government

HEAD OF STATE

President: Dr FÉLIX HOUPHOUËT-BOIGNY (took office November 1960, re-elected for sixth term of office October 1985).

COUNCIL OF MINISTERS
(January 1989)

President of the Republic: Dr FÉLIX HOUPHOUËT-BOIGNY.
Ministers of State: AUGUSTE DENISE, MATHIEU EKRA, CAMILLE ALLIALI, MAURICE SÉRI GNOLÉBA, EMILE KÉI BOGUINARD, LAZÉNI N. P. COULIBALY, PAUL GUI DIBO, LAMINE DIABATÉ.
Minister of the Economy and Finance: ABDOULAYE KONÉ.
Minister of Justice and Keeper of the Seals: NOËL NÉMIN.
Minister of Defence and the Navy: JEAN KONAN BANNY.
Minister of the Interior: LÉON KONAN KOFFI.
Minister of Foreign Affairs: SIMÉON AKÉ.
Minister of Public Health and Population: ALPHONSE DJÉDJÉ MADI.
Minister of Water and Forestry Resources: VINCENT-PIERRE LOKROU.
Minister of National Education responsible for Secondary and Higher Education: Dr BALLA KÉITA.
Minister of Social Affairs: YAYA OUATTARA.
Minister of Trade: NICOLAS KOUANDI ANGBA.
Minister of Public Works and Transport: AOUSSOU KOFFI.
Minister of Construction and Town Planning: VAMMOUSSA BAMBA.
Minister of Posts and Telecommunications: VINCENT TIEKO DJÉDJÉ.
Minister of Labour: ALBERT VANIÉ BI TRA.
Minister of Information: LAURENT DONA-FOLOGO.
Minister of Mining: YED ESAÏE ANGORAN.
Minister of Internal Security: Gen. IOUSSOUF KONÉ.
Minister in charge of Relations with the National Assembly: EMILE BROU.
Minister of Agriculture and Rural Development: DENIS BRA KANON.
Minister of Women's Promotion: HORTENSE AKA ANGHUI.
Minister of Scientific Research: ALHASSANE SALIF N'DIAYE.
Minister of the Budget: MOÏSE KOUMOUÉ KOFFI.
Minister of Primary Education: ODETTE KOUAMÉ N'GUESSAN.
Minister of Animal Husbandry: CHRISTOPHE GBOHO.
Minister of Technical Education and Professional Training: ANGE-FRANÇOIS BARRY-BATTESTI.
Minister of Industry and Planning: OUMAR DIARRA.
Minister of Youth and Sports: BERNARD EHUI KOUTOUA.
Minister of Culture: DUON SADIA.
Minister of Drug Control: Gen. OUMAR N'DAW.

MINISTRIES

Ministry of Agriculture and Rural Development: BP V82, Abidjan; telex 23612.
Ministry of Animal Husbandry: 01 BP 1249, Abidjan 01.
Ministry of the Budget: Abidjan.
Ministry of Culture: Abidjan.
Ministry of Defence and the Navy: BP V11, Abidjan; telex 22855.
Ministry of Drug Control: Abidjan.
Ministry of the Economy and Finance: Immeuble SCIAM, ave Marchand, BP V163, Abidjan; tel. 32-05-66; telex 23747.
Ministry of Foreign Affairs: BP V109, Abidjan; telex 23752.
Ministry of Industry and Planning: BP V65, Abidjan; tel. 29-14-68; telex 22638.
Ministry of Information: BP V138, Abidjan; telex 23501.
Ministry of the Interior: BP V241, Abidjan; telex 22296.
Ministry of Internal Security: BP V241, Abidjan; telex 23873.
Ministry of Justice: BP V107, Abidjan.
Ministry of Labour: BP V119, Abidjan.
Ministry of Mining: BP V50, Abidjan; telex 22262.
Ministry of National Education: BP V120, Abidjan; telex 23377.
Ministry of Public Health and Population: BP V4, Abidjan; telex 42213.
Ministry of Public Works, Transport, Construction, Posts and Telecommunications: ave Jean Paul II, BP V6, Abidjan 01; tel. 29-13-67; telex 22108.
Ministry of Social Affairs: BP V124, Abidjan; telex 23480.
Ministry of Trade: BP V142, Abidjan; telex 23704.
Ministry of Water and Forestry: BP V82, Abidjan; telex 23612.
Ministry of Women's Promotion: Abidjan.
Ministry of Youth and Sports: Abidjan.

Legislature

ASSEMBLÉE NATIONALE

At elections in November 1985, a total of 546 candidates, all of whom were members of the Parti démocratique de la Côte d'Ivoire, contested the 175 seats in the National Assembly.

President: HENRI KONAN-BÉDIÉ (re-elected January 1986).
Vice-Presidents: GLADYS ANOMA, MARIE-BERNARD KOISSY, CLÉMENT ANET BILÉ, GON COULIBALY, MAURICE OULATÉ.

Political Organizations

Parti démocratique de la Côte d'Ivoire (PDCI): Maison du Parti, Abidjan; f. 1946 as the local section of the Rassemblement démocratique africain; leadership comprises an exec. cttee of 13 mems, a

CÔTE D'IVOIRE

political bureau of 60 and a guiding cttee of 100; Chair. Dr FÉLIX HOUPHOUËT-BOIGNY.

The following groups, although not officially recognized, were also in existence in 1988:

Front Populaire Ivoirien: Leader LAURENT GBAGBO.

Parti Républicain de la Côte d'Ivoire: Abidjan; f. 1975 in Lyon, France; Pres. ROBERT GBAI TAGRO.

Diplomatic Representation

EMBASSIES IN CÔTE D'IVOIRE

Algeria: 53 blvd Clozel, 01 BP 1015, Abidjan 01; tel. 32-23-40; telex 23243; Ambassador: DJAMAL-EDDINE GHERNATI.

Argentina: 08 BP 860, Abidjan 08; tel. 44-41-78; telex 26100; Ambassador: FEDERICO MIRRE.

Austria: 70 bis ave Jean-Mermoz, Cocody, 01 BP 1837, Abidjan 01; tel. 44-03-02; telex 26102; Ambassador: Dr WOLFGANG KRIECHBAUM.

Belgium: Immeuble Alliance, ave Terrasson de Fougères, 01 BP 1800, Abidjan 01; tel. 32-20-88; telex 23633; Ambassador: JACQUES DE MONTJOYE.

Benin: rue des Jardins, 09 BP 238, Abidjan 09; tel. 41-44-14; telex 23922; Ambassador: JONAS GBOGBOHOUNDADA.

Brazil: Immeuble Alpha 2000, rue Gourgas, 01 BP 3820, Abidjan 01; tel. 22-23-41; telex 23443; Chargé d'affaires: Mrs RUJIZA ANDREYEVICH.

Burkina Faso: 2 ave Terrasson de Fougères, 01 BP 908, Abidjan 01; tel. 32-13-13; telex 23453; Ambassador: (vacant).

Cameroon: 01 BP 2886, Abidjan 01; Ambassador: PAUL KAMGA NJIKE.

Canada: Immeuble Trade Centre, 01 BP 4104, Abidjan 01; tel. 32-20-09; telex 23593; Ambassador: JEAN-GUY SAINT-MARTIN.

Central African Republic: rue des Combattants, 01 BP 3387, Abidjan 01; tel. 32-36-46; telex 22102; Ambassador: ANTOINE KEZZA.

Chile: 06 BP 380, Abidjan 06; tel. 41-56-15; telex 22173; Ambassador: FÉLIX CABEZAS.

China, People's Republic: 01 BP 3691, Abidjan 01; tel. 41-32-48; telex 22104; Ambassador: CAI ZAIDU.

Colombia: 01 BP 3874, Abidjan 01; tel. 33-12-44; telex 22576; Ambassador: OCTAVIO GALLÓN RESTREPO.

Czechoslovakia: Immeuble Tropique III, 01 BP 1349, Abidjan 01; tel. 32-20-30; telex 22110; Chargé d'affaires: JIŘÍ VACHA.

Denmark: Immeuble Le Mans, blvd Boitreau Roussel, angle ave Noguès, Plateau, 01 BP 4569, Abidjan 01; tel. 33-17-65; telex 23871; Chargé d'affaires: MOGENS HOLM PEDERSEN.

Egypt: Immeuble El Nasr, ave du Général de Gaulle, 01 BP 2104, Abidjan 01; tel. 32-79-25; telex 23537; Ambassador: AHMADEIN KHALIL.

Ethiopia: Immeuble Nour Al-Hayat, 01 BP 3712, Abidjan 01; tel. 32-33-65; telex 23848; Ambassador: MAHMOUD SEYOUM.

France: rue Lecoeur, quartier du Plateau, 17 BP 175, Abidjan 17; tel. 32-67-49; telex 23699; Ambassador: MICHEL DUPUCH.

Gabon: Immeuble Les Hévéas, 14 ave du docteur Crozet/blvd Carde, 01 BP 3765, Abidjan 01; tel. 33-23-12; telex 23561; Ambassador: ABOUBAKAR BOKOKO.

Germany, Federal Republic: Immeuble Le Mans, blvd Boitreau Roussel, 01 BP 1900, Abidjan 01; tel. 32-47-27; telex 23642; Ambassador: Dr MICHAEL SCHMIDT.

Ghana: résidence de la Corniche, blvd du Général de Gaulle, 01 BP 1871, Abidjan 01; tel. 33-11-24; Ambassador: J. E. A. KOTEI.

Guinea: Immeuble Crosson Duplessis, 08 BP 2280, Abidjan 08; tel. 32-86-00; telex 22865; Ambassador: RICHARD HABA.

Holy See: 08 BP 1347, Abidjan 08; tel. 44-38-35; telex 26182; Apostolic Nuncio: Archbishop ANTONIO MATTIAZZO.

India: Lot 36, Impasse, Ablaha Pokou, Cocody Danga Nord, 06 BP 318, Abidjan 06; tel. 44-52-31; telex 28103; Ambassador: (vacant).

Israel: Immeuble Nour Al-Hayat, 01 BP 1877, Abidjan 01; tel. 32-49-53; Ambassador: MENAHEM CARMON.

Italy: 16 rue de la Canebière, Cocody, 01 BP 1905, Abidjan 01; tel. 44-61-70; telex 26123; Ambassador: CARLO CALIA.

Japan: Immeuble Alpha 2000, rue Gourgas, 01 BP 1329, Abidjan 01; tel. 33-28-63; telex 23400; Ambassador: MASAKI YAGI.

Korea, Democratic People's Republic: BP V48, Abidjan; tel. 44-22-75.

Korea, Republic: Immeuble Le Général, 01 BP 3950, Abidjan 01; tel. 32-22-90; telex 23638; Ambassador: JOUNG-SOO LEE.

Lebanon: 01 BP 2227, Abidjan 01; tel. 33-28-24; telex 22245; Ambassador: (vacant).

Liberia: Immeuble La Symphonie, 30 ave du Général de Gaulle, Abidjan; tel. 22-23-59; telex 23535; Ambassador: HAROLD TARR.

Mali: Maison du Mali, rue du Commerce, 01 BP 2746, Abidjan 01; tel. 32-31-47; telex 23429; Ambassador: MODIBO DIARRA.

Mauritania: 01 BP 2275, Abidjan 01; tel. 35-20-68; telex 22371; Ambassador: Col AHMEDOU OUM ABDALLAH.

Morocco: 24 rue de la Canebière, Cocody, 01 BP 146, Abidjan 01; tel. 44-58-78; telex 26147; Ambassador: (vacant).

Netherlands: Immeuble Les Harmonies, blvd Carde, 01 BP 1086, Abidjan 01; tel. 22-77-12; telex 23694; Ambassador: GUY N. WESTEROUEN VAN MEETEREN.

Niger: 01 BP 2743, Abidjan 01; tel. 35-50-98; telex 43185; Ambassador: MAGAGI GOUROUZA.

Nigeria: 35 blvd de la République, 01 BP 1906, Abidjan 01; tel. 22-30-82; telex 23532; Ambassador: Dr LAWRENCE B. EKPEBU.

Norway: Immeuble N' Zarama, blvd du Général de Gaulle, 01 BP 607, Abidjan 01; tel. 22-25-34; telex 23355; Ambassador: KJELL ØSTREM.

Poland: 04 BP 308, Abidjan 04; tel. 44-12-25; telex 26114; Chargé d'affaires: STANISŁAW SMYSLO.

Rwanda: 01 BP 3905, Abidjan 01; tel. 41-38-31; telex 27152; Ambassador: CALLIXTE HATUNGIMANA.

Senegal: Résidence Nabil, blvd du Général de Gaulle, 08 BP 2165, Abidjan 08; tel. 33-28-76; telex 23897; Ambassador: ABDOURAHMANE TOURÉ.

Spain: 01 BP 2589, Abidjan 01; tel. 44-48-50; telex 28120; Ambassador: FERNANDO CASTILLO.

Sweden: Immeuble Alpha 2000, rue Gourgas, 04 BP 992, Abidjan 04; tel. 33-24-10; telex 23293; Ambassador: ARNE EKFELDT.

Switzerland: Immeuble Alpha 2000, rue Gourgas, 01 BP 1914, Abidjan 01; tel. 32-17-21; telex 23492; Ambassador: JACQUES REVERDIN.

Tunisia: Immeuble Shell, 48 ave Lamblin, 01 BP 3906, Abidjan 01; tel. 32-23-04; telex 23709; Ambassador: ABDEL AZIZ AL-AYADHI.

USSR: ave Dr Crozet, Plateau, 01 BP 7646, Abidjan 01; Ambassador: BORIS MINAKOV.

United Kingdom: Immeuble Les Harmonies, blvd Carde, 01 BP 2581, Abidjan 01; tel. 22-68-50; telex 23706; Ambassador: VERONICA SUTHERLAND.

USA: 5 rue Jesse Owens, 01 BP 1712, Abidjan 01; tel. 32-09-79; telex 23660; Ambassador: DENNIS KUX.

Uruguay: Immeuble ATTA II, 01 BP 4072, Abidjan 01; Chargé d'affaires: OSCAR BENÍTEZ BAEZA.

Zaire: 29 blvd Clozel, 01 BP 3961, Abidjan 01; tel. 22-20-80; telex 23795; Ambassador: LOUYA LONDOALE.

Judicial System

Since 1964 all civil, criminal, commercial and administrative cases have come under the jurisdiction of the Tribunaux de première instance (Magistrates' courts), the assize courts and the Court of Appeal, with the Supreme Court as supreme court of appeal.

The Supreme Court: rue Gourgas, BP V30, Abidjan; has four chambers: constitutional, judicial, administrative and auditing; Pres. ALPHONSE BONI.

Courts of Appeal: Abidjan and Bouaké; hear appeals from courts of first instance; Abidjan: First Pres. CAMILLE HOGUIE, Attorney-Gen. LOUIS FOLQUET; Bouaké: First Pres. AHIOUA MOULARE, Attorney-Gen. ANOMAN OGUIE.

The High Court of Justice: composed of Deputies elected from and by the National Assembly; has jurisdiction to impeach the President or other member of the government; Pres. HENRI KONAN-BÉDIÉ.

State Security Court: composed of a president and six regular judges, all appointed for five years; deals with all offences against the security of the State; Pres. ALPHONSE BONI.

Courts of First Instance: Abidjan, Pres. ROBERT COULOUD NATCHA; Bouaké: Pres. KABLAN AKA EDOUKOU; Daloa: Pres. WOUNE BLEKA; there are a further 25 courts in the principal centres.

Religion

It is estimated that 65% of the population follow traditional animist beliefs, while 23% are Muslims and 12% are Christians, mainly Roman Catholics.

CÔTE D'IVOIRE *Directory*

CHRISTIANITY
The Roman Catholic Church
Côte d'Ivoire comprises one archdiocese and 10 dioceses. At 31 December 1985 there were an estimated 1,015,000 adherents.

Bishops' Conference: Conférence Episcopale de la Côte d'Ivoire, 01 BP 1287, Abidjan 01; tel. 33-22-56; f. 1973; Pres. Cardinal BERNARD YAGO, Archbishop of Abidjan.

Archbishop of Abidjan: Cardinal BERNARD YAGO, Archevêché, ave Jean Paul II, 01 BP 1287, Abidjan 01; tel. 33-12-46.

Protestant Churches
Christian and Missionary Alliance: BP 585, Bouaké 01; tel. 63-23-12; f. 1929; 13 mission stations; Dir Rev. KEVIN D. MCCABE.

Conservative Baptist Foreign Mission Society: BP 109, Korhogo; tel. 86-00-33; f. 1947; active in Abidjan and in the northern area in evangelism, teaching and medical work.

Eglise Protestante Méthodiste: 41 blvd de la République, 01 BP 1282, Abidjan 01; c. 120,000 mems; Pres. Pastor EMMANUEL YANDO.

Mission Evangélique de l'Afrique Occidentale: 08 BP 653, Abidjan 08; tel. 44-02-68; f. 1934; 11 mission centres, 51 missionaries; Field Dir WOLFGANG LIPSCHÜTZ; affiliated church: Alliance des Eglises Evangéliques de Côte d'Ivoire; 80 churches, 23 full-time pastors; Pres. TEHI TIECOURA EMMANUEL.

Union des Eglises Evangéliques du Sud-Ouest de la Côte d'Ivoire and **Mission Biblique:** BP 8020, Abidjan; f. 1927; c. 250 places of worship.

The Press

Abidjan 7 Jours: 01 BP 1965, Abidjan 01; tel. 35-39-39; telex 24317; f. 1964; weekly; local information; circ. 10,000.

Afrique-Sports: Abidjan; weekly.

Bulletin mensuel de Statistiques: Direction de la Statistique, 01 BP V55, Abidjan 01; tel. 32-15-38.

Djeliba—le journal des jeunes Chrétiens: 01 BP 1287, Abidjan 01; tel. 32-69-79; f. 1974; 5 a year; Editor PIERRE TRICHET; circ. 5,500.

Eburnea: Ministry of Information, BP V138, Abidjan; telex 23781; monthly.

Entente Africaine: BP 20991, Abidjan; publ. by Inter Afrique Presse; illustrated; quarterly in French and English; Editor JUSTIN VIEYRA.

Fraternité-Hebdo: 01 BP 1212, Abidjan 01; tel. 33-29-15; organ of the PDCI; weekly; Technical Dir PIERRE CHEYNIER; Editor GUY PIERRE NOUAMA.

Fraternité-Matin: blvd du Général de Gaulle, 01 BP 1807, Abidjan 01; tel. 33-27-27; telex 23718; f. 1964; organ of the PDCI; official journal of record for govt activities; daily; Editor-in-Chief AUGUSTE MIREMONT; circ. 80,000.

Gazette du Centre: Bouaké; weekly.

Le Guido (Abidjan Jour et Nuit): 01 BP 1807, Abidjan 01; tel. 37-06-66; telex 372545; f. 1987; weekly; local information; Dir LAURENT DONA-FOLOGO.

Ivoire-Dimanche: 01 BP 1807, Abidjan 01; f. 1971; weekly; circ. 75,000.

Ivoir 'Soir: blvd du Général de Gaulle, 01 BP 1807, Abidjan 01; f. 1987; organ of the PDCI; aims to reflect social activities, including cultural and sporting events; daily; Dir AUGUSTE MIREMONT; circ. 50,000.

Journal des Amis du Progrès de l'Afrique Noire: Abidjan; 5 a week.

Journal Officiel de la Côte d'Ivoire: Ministry of the Interior, BP V241, Abidjan; telex 22296; weekly.

Le Messager: BP 1776, Abidjan; 6 a year; Editor ANDRÉ LEROUX.

Revue Ivoirienne de Droit: BP 3811, Abidjan; f. 1969; publ. by the Centre ivoirien de recherches et d'études juridiques (CIREJ); circ. 1,500.

Télé-Miroir: Abidjan; monthly.

NEWS AGENCIES
Agence Ivoirienne de Presse (AIP): 04 BP 312, Abidjan 04; telex 23781; f. 1961; Dir KONÉ SEMGUÉ SAMBA.

Foreign Bureaux
Agence France-Presse (AFP): 18 ave du Docteur Crozet, 01 BP 726, Abidjan 01; tel. 32-90-17; telex 22481; Dir BERNARD AUBERT.

Associated Press (AP) (USA): 01 BP 5843, Abidjan 01; tel. 41-37-49; telex 28129; Correspondent ROBERT WELLER.

Reuters (UK): Résidence Les Acacias, 20 blvd Clozel, 01 BP 2338, Abidjan 01; tel. 33-27-01; telex 23921; Chief Correspondent C. REGIN.

Xinhua (New China) News Agency (People's Republic of China): Cocody Danga Nord Lot 46, 08 BP 1212, Abidjan 08; tel. 44-01-24; Chief Correspondent XIONG SHANWU.

Central News Agency (Taiwan) also has an office in Abidjan.

Publishers

Centre d'Edition et de Diffusion Africaines (CEDA): 04 BP 541, Abidjan 04; tel. 22-20-55; telex 22451; f. 1961; general non-fiction; Chair. and Man. Dir VENANCE KACOU.

Centre de Publications Evangéliques: 08 BP 900, Abidjan 08; tel. 44-48-05; f. 1970; religious; Dir ROBERT BRYAN.

Institut africain pour le Développement Economique et Social-Edition (INADES-Edition): 08 BP 8, Abidjan 08; tel. 44-15-94; f. 1975; African studies, philosophy, religion, economics, agriculture, sociology, essays; Man. Dir RAYMOND DENIEL.

Nouvelles Editions Africaines (NEA): 01 BP 3525, Abidjan 01; tel. 32-12-51; telex 22564; f. 1972; bibliography, fiction, poetry, theatre, religion, art, juveniles, history, textbooks; Dir-Gen. Mme K. L. LIGUER-LAUBHOUËT.

Université Nationale de Côte d'Ivoire: 01 BP V34, Abidjan 01; tel. 44-08-59; telex 26138; f. 1964; general non-fiction and periodicals; Publications Dir GILLES VILASCO.

Government Publishing House
Imprimerie Nationale: BP V87, Abidjan; telex 23868.

Radio and Television

In 1985 there were an estimated 1.3m. radio sets and 500,000 television receivers in use.

Radiodiffusion Ivoirienne: BP V191, Abidjan 01; tel. 32-48-00; f. 1962; govt radio station broadcasting in French, English and local languages; MW station at Abidjan, relay at Bouaké; VHF transmitters at Abidjan, Bouaflé, Man and Koun-Abbrosso; Dir MAMADOU BERTÉ.

Télévision Ivoirienne: 08 BP 883, Abidjan 08; tel. 43-90-39; telex 22293; f. 1963; 50 hours a week French broadcasts; colour transmissions since 1973; stations at Abidjan, Bouaflé, Bouaké, Binao, Digo, Dimbokro, Koun, Man, Niangbo, Niangué, Séguéla, Tiémé and Touba; Man. DANIÈLE BONNI-CLAVERIE.

Finance

(br. = branch; cap. = capital; res = reserves; dep. = deposits; m. = million; amounts in francs CFA)

BANKING
Central Bank
Banque Centrale des Etats de l'Afrique de l'Ouest (BCEAO): ave Terrasson de Fougères, 01 BP 1769, Abidjan 01; tel. 32-04-66; telex 3474; headquarters in Dakar, Senegal; bank of issue and central bank for the seven states of the Union monétaire ouest africaine (UMOA), comprising Benin, Burkina Faso, Côte d'Ivoire, Mali, Niger, Senegal and Togo; f. 1955; cap. and res 171,495m. (Dec. 1987); Gov. ALASSANE OUATTARA; Dir in Côte d'Ivoire CHARLES KONAN BANNY; 5 brs.

Other Banks
Banque Atlantique-Côte d'Ivoire: Immeuble El Nasr, ave du Général de Gaulle, 04 BP 1036, Abidjan 04; tel. 32-82-18; telex 23834; f. 1978; cap. 1,000m. (Sept. 1986); Chair. CASIMIR KRA KOUADIO; Man. Dir JEAN-LUC DE LA SERRE.

Banque Internationale pour le Commerce et l'Industrie de la Côte d'Ivoire SA (BICICI): ave Franchet d'Espérey, 01 BP 1298, Abidjan 01; tel. 32-03-79; telex 23651; f. 1962; cap. 5,000m.; 24% state-owned, 21% by Banque Nationale de Paris (BNP), 28% by Société Financière pour les Pays d'Outre-Mer (comprises BNP, Banque Bruxelles Lambert and Dresdner Bank); Chair. JOACHIM RICHMOND; Man. Dir JACK DIEUDÉ; 46 brs.

Banque Ivoirienne de Développement Industriel (BIDI): 13 ave Joseph Anoma, 04 BP 470, Abidjan 04; tel. 32-01-11; telex 23484;

CÔTE D'IVOIRE   *Directory*

f. 1964; cap. 2,100m.; 21% state-owned, 11% by Caisse centrale de coopération économique (France); Man. Dir DAOUDA BAMBA.

Banque Nationale pour le Développement Agricole (BNDA): 11 ave Joseph Anoma, 01 BP 2508, Abidjan 01; tel. 32-07-57; telex 22298; f. 1968; cap. 3,000m.; 61% state-owned, 17% by BCEAO; Chair. LAMINE DIABATÉ; Man. Dir PATRICE KOUAMÉ; 32 brs.

Banque Paribas Côte d'Ivoire: Immeuble Alliance, ave Terrasson de Fougères, 17 BP 09, Abidjan 17; tel. 32-86-86; telex 22870; f. 1984; cap. 1,000m. (Sept. 1986) 40% owned by Paribas International; Chair. DANIEL BÉDIN; Man. Dir ROGER GIBERT.

Banque Real de Côte d'Ivoire SA: Immeuble BAD, ave Joseph Anoma, 04 BP 411, Abidjan 04; tel. 32-84-52; telex 22430; f. 1976; cap. 1,000m. (Sept. 1986); 99.98% owned by Banco Real SA (Brazil); Chair. JUAREZ SOARES; Man. Dir JEAN-MARIE GLEIZES.

BIAO-Côte d'Ivoire: 8/10 ave Joseph Anoma, 01 BP 1274, Abidjan 01; tel. 32-07-22; telex 23641; f. 1980; cap. 5,000m. (Sept. 1986); 35% state-owned, 65% owned by Banque Internationale pour l'Afrique Occidentale (France); Chair. AUGUSTE DAUBREY; Dir-Gen. RAYMOND BIRE; 37 brs in Côte d'Ivoire.

Caisse Autonome d'Amortissement: Immeuble SCIAM, ave Marchand, 01 BP 670, Abidjan 01; tel. 32-06-11; telex 23798; f. 1959; Man. Dir LÉON NAKA; Sec.-Gen. MATHIEU N'GORAN.

Compagnie Financière de la Côte d'Ivoire (COFINCI): Rue Gourgas, 01 BP 1566, Abidjan 01; tel. 32-27-32; telex 22228; f. 1974; cap. 1,100m. (Sept. 1986); 18.5% state-owned, 51% by BICICI; Chair. JOACHIM RICHMOND; Man. Dir JOSEPH ADJOUSSOU.

Crédit de la Côte d'Ivoire (CCI): 22 ave Joseph Anoma, 01 BP 1720, Abidjan 01; tel. 32-03-57; telex 22106; f. 1955; cap. 4,800m.; 58.4% state-owned, 33.3% by BCEAO, 8.3% by CCCE; Man. SOUNGALO TRAORÉ (acting); 5 brs.

Société Générale de Banques en Côte d'Ivoire SA (SGBCI): 5/7 ave Joseph Anoma, 01 BP 1355, Abidjan 01; tel. 32-03-33; telex 23437; f. 1962; cap. 8,000m. (1987); 8.5% state-owned, 37.2% by Société Générale (France); Chair. and Man. Dir TIÉMOKO YADÉ COULIBALY; 48 brs.

Société Générale de Financement et de Participations en Côte d'Ivoire (SOGEFINANCE): 26 ave Jean Delafosse, 01 BP 3904, Abidjan 01; tel. 32-03-33; telex 23502; f. 1978; cap. 1,000m. (Sept. 1987); 15% state-owned, 58% by SGBCI, 12% by Société Générale (France); Chair. and Man. Dir TIÉMOKO COULIBALY; Man. ANTOINE YÉO.

Société Ivoirienne de Banque (SIB): 34 blvd de la République, 01 BP 1300, Abidjan 01; tel. 32-00-00; telex 23751; f. 1962; cap. 6,000m. (Sept. 1986); 41% state-owned, 41% by Crédit Lyonnais (France); Chair. ABOU DOUMBIA; Man. Dir ROBERT PLISSON; 37 brs.

Union de Banques en Côte d'Ivoire (BANAFRIQUE): Résidence Nabil, ave Général de Gaulle, 01 BP 4132, Abidjan 01; tel. 33-15-36; telex 22513; f. 1980; cap. 1,000m. (Sept. 1986); 36% owned by Banque du Liban et d'Outremer (Lebanon); Chair. Dr NAAMAN AZHARI; Dir and Gen. Man. JEAN-PIERRE PARODI; 2 brs.

Bankers' Association

Association Professionnelle des Banques et Etablissements Financiers de Côte d'Ivoire: 01 BP 3810, Abidjan 01; Pres. JEAN PIERRE MEYER.

INSURANCE

Assurances Générales de Côte d'Ivoire (AGCI): Immeuble AGCI, ave Noguès, 01 BP 4092, Abidjan 01; tel. 33-99-32; telex 22502; f. 1979; cap. 1,290m.; Chair. JOACHIM RICHMOND.

Assurmafer: 11 ave Joseph Anoma, 01 BP 62, Abidjan 01; tel. 32-10-52; telex 23231; f. 1941; cap. 700m.; Dir GILBERT HIS.

Compagnie des Assurances Colina SA: 01 BP 3832, Abidjan 01; tel. 32-37-17; telex 20983; f. 1980; cap. 300m.; Chair. MICHEL POUPARD; Dir E. MALARTRE.

Mutuelle Universelle de Garantie (UNIWARRANT): 01 BP 301, Abidjan 01; tel. 32-41-18; telex 22120; f. 1970; cap. 208m.; Chair. and Man. Dir FATIMA SYLLA.

La Nationale d'Assurances (CNA): 30 ave du Général de Gaulle, 01 BP 1333, Abidjan 01; tel. 32-63-63; telex 22176; f. 1972; cap. 400m.; insurance and reinsurance; Chair. LÉON AMON; Man. Dir RICHARD COULIBALY.

La Sécurité Ivoirienne: Immeuble La Sécurité Ivoirienne, blvd Roume, 01 BP 569, Abidjan 01; tel. 32-50-63; telex 23817; f. 1971; cap. 300m.; general; Chair. DIA HOUPHOUËT-BOIGNY; Dir-Gen. CLAVE RAMON.

Société Africaine d'Assurances et de Réassurances en République de Côte d'Ivoire (SAFFARRIV): Résidence Longchamp, 01 BP 1741, Abidjan 01; tel. 32-91-57; telex 22159; f. 1975; cap. 500m.; Pres. TIÉMOKO COULIBALY; Man. Dir JEAN-MARIE COMBES.

Société Ivoirienne d'Assurances Mutuelles (SIDAM): ave Houdaille, 01 BP 1217, Abidjan 01; tel. 32-97-82; telex 22670; f. 1970; cap. 150m.; Dir-Gen. VAKABA KONÉ.

Société Nouvelle d'Assurances de Côte d'Ivoire (SNACI): 9 ave Houdaille, 01 BP 1014, Abidjan 01; tel. 32-10-11; telex 22225; cap. 1,008m.; subsidiary of Axa International; Chair. L. BROSSIER.

Société Tropicale d'Assurances Mutuelles Vie (STAMVIE): 15, ave Joseph Anoma, 01 BP 1337, Abidjan 01; tel. 33-20-24; telex 23774; f. 1969; cap. 150m.; life; Chair. JEAN-BAPTISTE AMETHIER; Dir ALBERT AFFOUE-FAUSTE.

L'Union Africaine: ave de la Fosse Prolongée, 01 BP 378, Abidjan 01; tel. 32-73-81; telex 23568; f. 1980; cap. 1,000m.; insurance and reinsurance; Chair. ERNEST AMOS DJORO; Dir JEAN-KACOU DIAGOU.

Union Africaine Vie: ave de la Fosse Prolongée, 01 BP 2016, Abidjan 01; tel. 32-77-46; telex 22200; f. 1985; cap. 550m., life; Chair. ERNEST AMOS DJORO; Dir JEAN-KACOU DIAGOU.

Trade and Industry

DEVELOPMENT ORGANIZATION

Conseil Economique et Social: 04 BP 301, Abidjan; tel. 32-20-60; reconstituted 1982; govt body overseeing economic development; Pres. PHILIPPE GRÉGOIRE YACÉ; Vice-Pres. F. KONIAN KODJO, B. BEDA YAO, Mme J. CHAPMAN; 120 mems.

DEVELOPMENT AGENCIES

Caisse Centrale de Coopération Economique (France): 01 BP 1814, Abidjan 01; tel. 44-53-05; telex 23439; Dir in Côte d'Ivoire RENÉ MALLORGA.

Mission Française de Coopération: 01 BP 1839, Abidjan 01; tel. 32-60-45; administers bilateral aid from France; Dir ROGER BOURDIL.

STATE COMPANIES

Caisse de Stabilisation et de Soutien des Prix des Productions Agricoles (CSSPPA): BP V132, Abidjan; tel. 32-08-33; telex 23712; f. 1964; cap. 4,000m. francs CFA; controls price, quality and export of agricultural products; offices in Paris, London and New York; Man. Dir RENÉ AMANI.

Compagnie Ivoirienne pour le Développement des Cultures Vivrières (CIDV): 01 BP 2049, Abidjan 01; tel. 32-00-79; telex 23347; f. 1963 as Société pour le Développement de l'Exploitation du Palmier à Huile (SODEPALM), name changed 1988; production of palm oil; Man. Dir N'DRI BROU BENOÎT.

Palmindustrie: 01 BP V239, Abidjan 01; tel. 36-93-88; telex 43100; f. 1969; cap. 3,365m. francs CFA; development of palm, coconut and copra products; Man. Dir BERNARD DOSSONGUI KONÉ.

Société de Développement des Plantations Forestières (SODEFOR): 01 BP 3770, Abidjan 01; tel. 44-36-02; telex 26156; f. 1966; cap. 50m. francs CFA; management of plantations, reafforestation, marketing of timber products; Man. Dir SOUNDELE KONAN.

Société Nationale d'Opérations Pétrolières de la Côte d'Ivoire (PETROCI): BP V194, Abidjan 12; tel. 32-40-58; telex 22135; f. 1975; cap. 20,000m. francs CFA; all aspects of petroleum development; Pres. Minister of Mining; Man. Dir PAUL AHUI.

Société pour le Développement Minier de la Côte d'Ivoire (SODEMI): 31 blvd André Latrille, 01 BP 2816, Abidjan 01; tel. 44-29-94; telex 26162; f. 1962; cap. 65.3m. francs CFA; geological and mineral research; Pres. HACCANDY KOUASSI KOUAKOU; Man. Dir JOSEPH N'ZI.

Société pour le Développement de la Motorisation de l'Agriculture (MOTORAGRI): Km 5, route d'Abobo, 01 BP 3745, Abidjan 01; tel. 37-16-17; telex 23178; f. 1966; cap. 230m. francs CFA; state organization for rationalizing machinery use for agricultural development; Chair. Minister of Agriculture and Rural Development; Man. Dir AMADOU OUATTARA.

Société pour le Développement des Plantations de Canne à Sucre, l'Industrialisation et la Commercialisation du Sucre (SODESUCRE): 16 ave du Docteur Crozet, 01 BP 2164, Abidjan 01; tel. 32-04-79; telex 23451; f. 1971; cap. 30,500m. francs CFA; sugar plantations and refinery; Chair. and Man. Dir JOSEPH KOUAMÉ KRA.

Société pour le Développement des Productions Animales (SODEPRA): c/o Ministry of Animal Husbandry, 01 BP 1249, Abidjan 01; tel. 32-13-10; telex 22123; f. 1970; cap. 404m. francs CFA; livestock cultivation; Chair. CHARLES DONWAHI; Man. Dir PAUL LAMIZANA.

CÔTE D'IVOIRE   *Directory*

Société pour le Développement de la Production des Fruits et Légumes (SODEFEL): 11 ave Barthe, 01 BP 3032, Abidjan 01; tel. 32-63-40; telex 22100; f. 1968; cap. 120m. francs CFA; state organization for fruit and vegetable production and marketing; Chair. FÉLICIEN KONAN KODJO; Man. Dir BOA BOADOU.

CHAMBERS OF COMMERCE

Chambre d'Agriculture de la Côte d'Ivoire: 11 ave Lamblin, 01 BP 1291, Abidjan 01; tel. 32-16-11; Pres. OKA NIANGOIN; Sec.-Gen. GBAOU DIOMANDÉ.

Chambre de Commerce de la Côte d'Ivoire: ave Joseph Anoma, 01 BP 1399, Abidjan 01; tel. 32-46-79; telex 23224; Pres. LAMINE FADIGA; Sec.-Gen. MAURICE DELAFOSSE.

Chambre d'Industrie de la Côte d'Ivoire: 11 ave Lamblin, 01 BP 1758, Abidjan 01; tel. 32-65-34; telex 22291; Pres. LAMBERT KONAN; Sec.-Gen. MAXIME EKRA.

EMPLOYERS' ASSOCIATIONS

Fédération Maritime de la Côte d'Ivoire (FEDERMAR): 01 BP 1546, Abidjan 01; Sec.-Gen. VACABA TOURÉ.

Groupement Interprofessionnel de l'Automobile (GIPA): 01 BP 1340, Abidjan 01; tel. 35-71-42; f. 1953; 30 mems; Pres. D. DUBOIS; Sec.-Gen. P. MEYER.

Syndicat des Commerçants Importateurs, Exportateurs et Distributeurs de la Côte d'Ivoire (SCIMPEX): 01 BP 3792, Abidjan 01; tel. 32-54-27; Pres. JACQUES ROSSIGNOL; Sec.-Gen. PIERRE DE LA MOTTE.

Syndicat des Employeurs Agricoles (SYNDAGRI): Immeuble MGFA (4th Floor), 28 blvd Angoulvant, Plateau, 01 BP 2300, Abidjan 01; tel. 32-26-42; Pres. JEAN-BAPTISTE AMETHIER.

Syndicat des Entrepreneurs et des Industriels de la Côte d'Ivoire (SEICI): 18 ave Joseph Anoma, 01 BP 464, Abidjan 01; tel. 32-11-18; f. 1934; Pres. ABDEL AZIZ THIAM.

Syndicat des Entrepreneurs de Manutention du Port d'Abidjan (SEMPA): 01 BP 172, Abidjan 01; tel. 32-18-82; Vice-Pres. P. SOMICOA.

Syndicat des Exportateurs et Négociants en Bois de Côte d'Ivoire: Immeuble MGFA (4th Floor), 28 blvd Angoulvant, Plateau, 01 BP 1979, Abidjan 01; tel. 32-12-39; Pres. CLAUDE PAINPARAY.

Syndicat des Industriels de la Côte d'Ivoire: 01 BP 1340, Abidjan 01; tel. 35-71-42; Pres. RÉMY LAUBER; Sec.-Gen. PHILIPPE MEYER.

Syndicat des Producteurs Industriels du Bois: Immeuble MGFA (4th Floor), 28 blvd Angoulvant, Plateau, 01 BP 318, Abidjan 01; tel. 32-12-39; f. 1973; Pres. ISIDORO BIANCHI.

Union des Employeurs Agricoles et Forestiers: Immeuble MGFA (4th Floor), 28 blvd Angoulvant, Plateau, 01 BP 2300, Abidjan 01; tel. 32-26-42; f. 1952; Pres. JEAN-BAPTISTE AMETHIER.

Union Patronale de Côte d'Ivoire (UPACI): 01 BP 1340, Abidjan 01; tel. 35-71-42; telex 43280; fmrly Association Interprofessionnelle des Employeurs de la Côte d'Ivoire (AICI); Pres. J. AKA ANGHUI; Sec.-Gen. P. MEYER.

TRADE UNIONS

Union Générale des Travailleurs de Côte d'Ivoire (UGTCI): 05 BP 1203, Abidjan 05; tel. 32-26-65; f. 1962; Sec.-Gen. HYACINTHE ADIKO NIAMKEY; 100,000 individual mems; 190 affiliated unions.

There are also some independent trade unions.

Transport

RAILWAYS

Régie des Chemins de Fer Abidjan-Niger (RAN): 01 BP 1394, Abidjan 01; tel. 32-02-45; telex 23564; f. 1904; 1,156 km of track linking Abidjan to Ouagadougou, in Burkina Faso, and also carrying traffic for Mali and Niger; the co was expected to be reorganized into two independent railways in 1989; Chair. D. BONI; Man. Dir K.-J. BUDIN.

ROADS

There are some 55,000 km of roads, of which 155 km are motorways. A major expansion and rehabilitation programme was announced in 1985, which involved the resurfacing of 5,000 km of existing roads and aimed to construct some 1,500 km of new roads by the late-1980s. Financial constraints have resulted in the postponement of several projects. In 1988, however, it was confirmed that a 56-km road between Bouaké and Béoumi was to be constructed.

Société Ivoirienne de Transports Publics: 01 BP 2949, Abidjan 01; tel. 35-33-68; telex 23685; f. 1964; road transport; Chair. JOSEPH ALLOU BRIGHT; Dir BASILE ABRE.

Société des Transports Abidjanais (SOTRA): 01 BP 2009, Abidjan 01; tel. 36-90-11; telex 43101; f. 1960; 60% state-owned; urban transport; Chair. MAURICE BAHI ZAHIRI; Dir-Gen. ALBERT AKA.

SHIPPING

Côte d'Ivoire has two major ports, Abidjan and San Pedro, both of which are industrial and commercial establishments with financial autonomy. Abidjan, which handles about 90% of the country's external trade, is the largest container and trading port in West Africa, with an overall annual traffic of more than 9m. metric tons, of which containerized goods account for some 1.3m. tons. Access to the port is via the 2.7 km-long Vridi Canal. Rehabilitation works being carried out in 1988 were expected to contribute to a continued increase in Abidjan's traffic. The port at San Pedro remains the main gateway to the south-western region of Côte d'Ivoire.

Port Autonome d'Abidjan: BP V85, Abidjan; tel. 32-01-66; telex 22778; f. 1950; public undertaking supervised by the Ministry of the Navy; Man. Dir JEAN-MICHEL MOULOD.

Port Autonome de San Pedro: BP 339, San Pedro; tel. 71-14-79; f. 1971.

Compagnie Maritime Africaine-Côte d'Ivoire (COMAF-CI): 08 BP 867, Abidjan 08; tel. 32-56-43; telex 23357; f. 1973; navigational equipment and management of ships; Dir STEFANO SOMMARIVA.

Société Agence Maritime de l'Ouest Africain-Côte d'Ivoire (SAMOA-CI): rue des Gallions, 01 BP 1611, Abidjan 01; tel. 33-29-65; telex 23765; f. 1955; agents for Gold Star Line, Lloyd Triestino, Seven Star Line; Man. Dir CLAUDE PERDRIAUD.

Société Ivoirienne de Navigation Maritime (SIVOMAR): 01 BP 1395, Abidjan 01; tel. 32-73-23; telex 22226; f. 1977; services to Mediterranean and Far East; Dir SIMPLICE ZINSOU.

Société Ivoirienne de Transports Maritimes (SITRAM): ave Lamblin, 01 BP 1546, Abidjan 01; tel. 36-92-00; telex 22132; f. 1967, nationalized 1976; services between Europe and west Africa; owns 9 cargo, passenger/cargo and reefer ships; Chair B. PEGAWAGNABA; Dir Commdt FAKO KONE.

Société Ouest-Africaine d'Entreprises Maritimes en Côte d'Ivoire (SOAEM-CI): 01 BP 1477, Abidjan 01; tel. 32-59-69; telex 23654; f. 1978; merchandise handling, transit and storage; Dir JACQUES COLOMBANI.

SOCOPAO-Côte d'Ivoire: 01 BP 1297, Abidjan 01; tel. 32-02-11; telex 23745; agents for Splošna Plovba, K Line, EAL, EAC, Morflot, DSR, POL, Nautilus Line, Gestarma, Westwind, PNSC, CNAN; air and sea freight transport; Dir M. E. VAILLANT.

Transcap-CI-Shipping: 01 BP 1908, Abidjan 01; tel. 32-19-37; telex 23770; f. 1960; agents for Elder Dempster Lines, Barber Line, Guinea Gulf Line, Mitsui-OSK Line, Palm Line, Nautilus Line, Nigerian National Lines, Black Star Lines, Naviera García Minaur (Madrid), Krag Shipping (Denmark), Nigerian Green Lines; Dir GÉRARD DAGOREAU.

CIVIL AVIATION

There is an international airport at Abidjan–Port-Bouët. There are regional airports at Berebi, Bouaké, Daloa, Korhogo, Man, Odienne, San Pedro, Sassandra, Tabou and Yamoussoukro. Facilities at Abidjan were modernized in 1985, but plans for additional expansion were suspended following the introduction of an economic austerity programme.

Air Afrique (Société Aérienne Africaine Multinationale): 3 ave Joseph Anoma, 01 BP 3927, Abidjan 01; tel. 32-09-00; telex 23785; f. 1961; services between 22 African countries and: to Canada, Canary Islands, France, Italy, Saudi Arabia, Switzerland and the USA; Dir-Gen. (Designate) YVES ROLAND-BILLECART; Commercial Dir THÉOPHILE KOMACLO; fleet of 1 DC-8-63F, 1 DC-8-50F, 2 DC-10-30, 3 Airbus A-300 Super B-4, 1 727-200.

Air Afrique was established by an agreement between SODE-TRAF (Société pour le Développement du Transport Aérien en Afrique, a subsidiary of French airline UTA) and 11 states, members of the Organisation Commune Africaine et Mauricienne (OCAM), who each had a 6% share; Togo joined later, Cameroon withdrew in 1971 and Gabon in 1976. SODETRAF has a 28% share and the following states each have a 7.2% holding: Benin, Burkina Faso, the Central African Republic, Chad, the Congo, Côte d'Ivoire, Mauritania, Niger, Senegal, Togo.

Air Ivoire: 13 ave Barthe, 01 BP 1027, Abidjan 01; tel. 32-34-29; telex 23727; f. 1960, govt-owned since 1976; internal flights and services to Bamako (Mali), Conakry (Guinea) and Ouagadougou (Burkina Faso); Man. Dir Col ABDOULAYE COULIBALY; fleet of 2

Fokker F28-4000, 2 F27-600, 1 F27-400, 1 Beech Super King Air 200.

Tourism

The game reserves, forests, lagoons, rich tribal folklore and the lively city of Abidjan are all of interest to tourists. There were some 200,000 visitors in 1985. The 10-km coastal strip along the Lagune Ebrié, to the west of Abidjan, is being developed as a tourist riviera.

Direction de la Promotion Touristique et de l'Artisanat d'Art: BP V184, Abidjan; tel. 32-07-33; telex 23438; Dir Dogo Yao.

CUBA

Introductory Survey

Location, Climate, Language, Religion, Flag, Capital

The Republic of Cuba is an archipelago of two main islands, Cuba and the Isle of Youth (formerly the Isle of Pines), and about 1,600 keys and islets. It lies in the Caribbean Sea, 145 km (90 miles) south of Florida, USA. Other nearby countries are the Bahamas, Mexico, Jamaica and Haiti. The climate is tropical, with the annual rainy season from May to October. The average annual temperature is 25°C (77°F) and hurricanes are frequent. The language is Spanish. Most of the inhabitants are Christians, of whom the great majority are Roman Catholics. The national flag (proportions 2 by 1) has five equal horizontal stripes, of blue, white, blue, white and blue, with a red triangle, enclosing a five-pointed white star, at the hoist. The capital is Havana (La Habana).

Recent History

Cuba was ruled by Spain from the 16th century until 1898, when the island was ceded to the USA after Spain's defeat in the Spanish–American War. Cuba became an independent republic on 20 May 1902, but the USA retained its naval bases on the island and, until 1934, reserved the right to intervene in Cuba's internal affairs. In 1933 an army sergeant, Fulgencio Batista Zaldivar, came to power at the head of a military revolt. Batista ruled the country, directly or indirectly, until 1944, when he retired after serving a four-year term as elected President.

In March 1952, however, Gen. Batista (as he had become) seized power again, deposing President Carlos Prío Socarrás in a bloodless coup. Batista's new regime soon proved to be unpopular and became harshly repressive. In July 1953 a radical opposition group, led by Dr Fidel Castro Ruz, attacked the Moncada army barracks in Santiago de Cuba. Castro was captured, with many of his supporters, but later released. He went into exile and formed a revolutionary movement which was committed to Batista's overthrow. In December 1956 Castro landed in Cuba with a small group of followers, most of whom were captured or killed. However, 12 survivors, including Castro and the Argentine-born Dr Ernesto ('Che') Guevara, escaped into the hills of the Sierra Maestra, where they formed the nucleus of the guerrilla forces which, after a prolonged struggle, forced Batista to flee from Cuba on 1 January 1959. The Batista regime collapsed, and Castro's forces occupied Havana.

The assumption of power by the victorious rebels was initially met with great popular acclaim. The 1940 constitution was suspended in January 1959, being replaced by a new 'Fundamental Law'. Executive and legislative power was vested in the Council of Ministers, with Fidel Castro as Prime Minister and his brother Raúl as his deputy. Guevara reportedly ranked third in importance. The new regime ruled by decree but promised to hold elections within 18 months. When it was firmly established, the Castro Government adopted a radical economic programme, including agrarian reform and the nationalization of industrial and commercial enterprises. These drastic reforms, combined with the regime's authoritarian nature, provoked opposition from some sectors of the population, including former supporters of Castro, and many Cubans went into exile.

All US business interests in Cuba were expropriated, without compensation, in October 1960, and the USA severed diplomatic relations in January 1961. A US-sponsored force of anti-Castro Cuban émigrés landed in April 1961 at the Bahía de Cochinos (Bay of Pigs), in southern Cuba, but the invasion was thwarted by Castro's troops. Later in the year, all pro-Government groups were merged to form the Organizaciones Revolucionarias Integradas (ORI). In December 1961 Fidel Castro publicly announced that Cuba had become a Communist state, and he proclaimed a 'Marxist-Leninist' programme for the country's future development. In January 1962 Cuba was excluded from active participation in the Organization of American States (OAS). The USA instituted a full economic and political blockade of Cuba. Hostility to the USA was accompanied by increasingly close relations between Cuba and the USSR. In October 1962 the USA revealed the presence of Soviet missiles in Cuba but, after the imposition of a US naval blockade, the weapons were withdrawn. The missile bases, capable of launching nuclear weapons against the USA, were dismantled, so resolving one of the most serious international crises since the Second World War. In 1964 the OAS imposed diplomatic and commercial sanctions against Cuba.

The ORI was replaced in 1962 by a new Partido Unido de la Revolución Socialista Cubana (PURSC), which was established, under Fidel Castro's leadership, as the country's sole legal party. Guevara resigned his military and government posts in April 1965, subsequently leaving Cuba to pursue revolutionary activities abroad. In October 1965 the PURSC was renamed the Partido Comunista de Cuba (PCC). Although it is ostracized by most other Latin American countries, the PCC Government has maintained and consolidated its internal authority, with little effective opposition. Supported by considerable aid from the USSR, the regime has made significant progress in social and economic development, including improvements in education and public health. At the same time, Cuba has continued to give active support to left-wing revolutionary movements in Latin America and in many other parts of the world. Guevara was killed in Bolivia, following an unsuccessful guerrilla uprising under his leadership, in October 1967.

In July 1972 Cuba's links with the Eastern bloc were strengthened when the country became a full member of the Council for Mutual Economic Assistance (CMEA, see p. 124), a Moscow-based organization linking the USSR and other communist states. As a result of its admission to the CMEA, Cuba received preferential trade terms and more technical advisers from the USSR and East European countries.

In June 1974 the country's first elections since the revolution were held for municipal offices in Matanzas province. Cuba's first 'socialist' constitution was submitted to the first Congress of the PCC, held in December 1975, and came into force in February 1976, after being approved by popular referendum. The PCC Congress also elected a new Central Committee and an enlarged Politburo. In addition, the existing six provinces were reorganized to form 14. As envisaged by the new constitution, elections for municipal assemblies were held in October 1976. These assemblies later elected delegates to provincial assemblies and deputies to the National Assembly of People's Power, inaugurated in December 1976 as 'the supreme organ of state'. The National Assembly chose the members of a new Council of State, with Fidel Castro as President. The second Congress of the PCC was held in December 1980, when Fidel and Raúl Castro were re-elected First and Second Secretaries respectively. The Politburo and the Central Committee were enlarged, and details of the 1981–85 Plan were announced. Election of candidates to the 169 municipal assemblies took place in October 1981. The National Assembly was inaugurated for a second five-year term in December. Fidel Castro was re-elected by the Assembly as President of the Council of State, and Raúl Castro re-elected as First Vice-President.

Cuba continued to be excluded from the activities of the OAS, although the Organization voted in favour of allowing members to normalize their relations with Cuba in 1975. Relations with the USA worsened because of Cuban involvement in Angola in 1976 and in Ethiopia in 1977. The relaxation of restrictions on emigration in April 1980 resulted in the departure of more than 125,000 Cubans for Florida. Antagonism continued as Cuba's military and political presence abroad increased, threatening US spheres of influence.

In 1981 Cuba expressed interest in discussing foreign policy with the USA, and declared that the shipment of arms to guerrilla groups in Central America had ceased. High-level talks between the two countries took place in November 1981 but US hostility increased. Economic sanctions were tightened, the major air link was closed, and tourism and investment by US nationals were prohibited in April 1982. Cuba's support of Argentina during the 1982 crisis concerning the Falkland Islands improved relations with the rest of Latin America, and the country's legitimacy was finally acknowledged when it was elected to the chair of the UN General Assembly Committee on Decolonization in September 1982, while continuing to play a leading role in the Non-Aligned Movement despite its firm alliance with the Soviet bloc.

In July 1983 President Castro announced his support for the peace initiative of the Contadora group (Colombia, Mexico, Panama and Venezuela), which called for a negotiated settlement to the problems in Central America. In addition, President Castro proposed a reciprocal arrangement between Cuba and the USA to allow for a reduction in the number of military personnel in Central America and for a halt to the supply of armaments to the region. However, an increase in US military activity in Honduras and the Caribbean region led President Castro to declare a 'state of national alert' in August. The US invasion of Grenada in October, and the ensuing short-lived confrontation between US forces and Cuban personnel on the island, severely damaged hopes that the two countries might reach an agreement over Central America, and left Cuba isolated in the Caribbean, following the weakening of its diplomatic and military ties with Suriname in November.

In July 1984 official negotiations were begun with the USA on the issues of immigration and repatriation. In December agreement was reached on the resumption of Cuban immigration to the USA and the repatriation of 2,746 Cuban 'undesirables', who had accompanied other Cuban refugees to the USA in 1980. The repatriation of Cuban 'undesirables' began in February 1985, but, following the inauguration of Radio Martí (a radio station sponsored by the 'Voice of America' radio network, which began to broadcast Western-style news and other programmes to Cuba from Florida, USA), the Cuban Government suspended its immigration accord with the USA. Subsequently, all visits to Cuba by US residents of Cuban origin were banned. The US Government responded by restricting visits to the USA by PCC members and Cuban government officials. In September 1986, as a result of mediation by the Roman Catholic Church, more than 100 political prisoners and their families, were permitted to leave Cuba for the USA.

In 1987 relations with the USA continued to deteriorate when, in February, the US Government launched a campaign to direct public attention to violations of human rights in Cuba. A resolution to condemn Cuba's record on human rights was narrowly defeated at a meeting of the UN Commission on Human Rights in March. In July the Cuban Government retaliated by broadcasting television programmes detailing the alleged espionage activities of officials from the US mission in Havana, who were accused of acting as intelligence agents. Nevertheless, the Cuban Government did allow 348 current and former political prisoners to return to the USA. The restoration of the 1984 immigration accord, in October 1987, led to protests by Cuban exiles detained in US prisons. Rioting in gaols at Oakdale, Louisiana, and Atlanta, Georgia, lasted several days until the US Government assured the exiles that their return to Cuba would be suspended indefinitely and that their cases would be studied individually. The accord allowed for the repatriation of 2,500 Cuban 'undesirables' in exchange for a US agreement to allow 23,000 Cubans to enter the USA annually. The USA continued in its attempts to have Cuba condemned by the UN Commission on Human Rights in March 1988, but the proposal was again vetoed. A resolution was adopted for a human rights' commission to visit Cuba in September.

In May–June 1985 a series of ministerial changes was rumoured to have caused friction within the Government, which resulted in the postponement of a planned PCC Congress from December 1985 to February 1986. The Third Congress of the PCC duly opened in February 1986, and drastic changes were made within the Central Committee. Almost one-third of the 146 full members were replaced. Nine of the 24 members of the new Politburo were elected for the first time, with several senior members, veterans of the 1959 revolution, being replaced by younger persons. A new Council of State was elected in December. However, in 1987, despite the major reorganization of the Politburo, there was little sign that the reforms being advocated in the USSR would be pursued in Cuba; indeed, in a speech made in July 1988, President Castro indicated that changes in policy would not take place in Cuba. There was a limited degree of cultural liberalization, but, as regards the economy, there was further centralization of decision-making and restriction of free enterprise.

Throughout 1984 the number of Cuban personnel in Ethiopia was reduced, from 10,000 to 5,000 men. In Angola, where Cuban troops numbered an estimated 50,000, the peace process gathered momentum in 1988. Cuban representatives were involved for the first time at a meeting in Luanda in February. In May a large Cuban offensive almost succeeded in driving South African forces out of Angola and gave new impetus to the peace negotiations. A cease-fire was implemented, and at discussions held in New York, in October, an agreement was reached for a phased withdrawal of Cuban troops over a period of 24–30 months. By December a timetable for the withdrawal of Cuban troops had been agreed. The first troops were to be withdrawn on 1 April 1989, and all troops were to leave Angola by mid-1991.

Since 1985 Cuba has succeeded in establishing stronger ties with other Latin American countries, notably Argentina, Brazil, Peru and Uruguay. Relations with Spain, however, became more strained in 1986 after the attempted kidnapping in December 1985, by four employees of the Cuban embassy in Madrid, of a Cuban citizen, which led to the expulsion of the four. Relations with the United Kingdom were severely affected in September 1988 by the expulsion of the Cuban ambassador and an envoy at the embassy after a shooting incident in the centre of London. In the same month, however, diplomatic relations were established with the EEC.

Government

Under the 1976 constitution, the first since the 1959 revolution, the supreme organ of state, and the sole legislative authority, is the National Assembly of People's Power, with 499 deputies elected for five years by municipal assemblies. The National Assembly elects 31 of its members to form the Council of State, the Assembly's permanent organ. The Council of State is the highest representative of the State, and its President is both Head of State and Head of Government. Executive and administrative authority is vested in the Council of Ministers, appointed by the National Assembly on the proposal of the Head of State. Municipal, regional and provincial assemblies have also been established. The Partido Comunista de Cuba (PCC), the only authorized political party, is 'the leading force of society and the state'. The PCC's highest authority is the Party Congress, which elects a Central Committee (225 members in February 1986) to supervise the Party's work. To direct its policy, the Central Committee elects a Politburo (24 members in 1986).

Defence

Conscription for military service is for a three-year period from 17 years of age, and conscripts also work on the land. In June 1988, according to Western estimates, the army numbered 145,000, the navy 13,500 and the air force 22,000. Army reserves were estimated to be 130,000. Paramilitary forces include 15,000 State Security troops, 4,000 border guards and a Youth Labour Army of about 100,000. A local militia organization (Milicias de Tropas Territoriales—MTT), comprising 1.3m. men and women, was formed in 1980. Estimated expenditure on defence and internal security for 1987 was 1,300m. pesos. Considerable aid is received from communist countries, notably the USSR. Despite Cuban hostility, the USA maintains a base at Guantánamo Bay, with about 2,000 military (mostly naval) personnel in 1988.

Economic Affairs

The state-controlled Cuban economy is basically agricultural, and is heavily dependent upon the annual output of cane sugar, which provided the country with 77% of its export revenue in 1986. Most of Cuba's sugar exports are sold at fixed prices under long-term agreements, mainly to the USSR and other CMEA countries. Any surplus production for export is sold on the free market. In 1982, however, the international price of raw sugar, at 8 US cents per lb. (down from 28 cents per lb. in 1980), was insufficient to cover production costs. A further set-back for the industry was the devastating rainfall during the first four months of 1983, which reduced the annual output of raw sugar to 7.2m. metric tons. Because of the fall in production, Cuba was unable to fulfil its quota (2.4m. metric tons) of free-market exports under the International Sugar Agreement. In 1985 Cuba was obliged to purchase 500,000 tons of sugar on the open market in order to meet its export commitments. Hurricane Kate, which struck Cuba in November 1985, damaged about 1m. ha of cane plantations

(25% of the country's cultivated land). Despite heavy rains in March 1986 and March 1987 (which severely hampered harvesting), agricultural production was more seriously affected by a four-year drought, which ended in July 1988. The output of raw sugar during the 1987/88 season was estimated at between 7.3m. and 7.5m. metric tons, and it was hoped that 1988/89 would yield the first annual total in excess of 8m. tons since 1984/85. Moreover, there was a significant improvement in the international price of sugar in mid-1988. The USSR provided assistance by underwriting US $200m. in sugar exports for 1989 and pledging aid for the rebuilding of sugar mills.

The annual harvest of Cuba's second most important export crop, tobacco, was also severely damaged by the rains in 1983, and amounted to only 45,000 tons in 1982/83. It declined to 30,200 tons in 1983/84, but increased to an estimated 45,000 tons in 1984/85, and has since remained fairly constant. The financial loss which was caused by the destruction of other crops in 1983 amounted to US $60m. Cuban exports of citrus fruits are of increasing significance. Helped by substantial investment from other CMEA countries, production of citrus fruits had increased to 880,000 metric tons by 1987. Dairy cattle are being introduced on a large scale, and the livestock sector expanded by 6.2% in 1983. As a result of extensive government investment in the fishing industry, Cuba's total catch rose from 27,100 tons in 1959 to a record 244,600 tons in 1986. In 1985 Cuba joined the International Coffee Organization (see p. 223) as an exporting member. In April 1987 Cuba's largest coffee-processing plant in Guantánamo, with an annual processing capacity of 11,000 metric tons, was inaugurated.

Cuba possesses about one-tenth of the world's known nickel reserves, and nickel is Cuba's second most important export commodity. In the 10 years to 1986 the Government invested more than 1,200m. pesos in the development of the industry. Production of nickel and cobalt declined from 39,257 metric tons in 1983 to 33,577 tons in 1984, but recovered to 35,800 tons in 1987. The completion of the Che Guevara plant at Punta Gorda, scheduled for the 1990s, and the overhaul of the plant at Moa will considerably increase nickel output. Compared with the corresponding period of 1987, production increased in the first quarter of 1988 by 22.5%, following the opening of the first production line at Punta Gorda in late 1987. Cuba supplies 35% of the CMEA's nickel requirements under long-term bilateral agreements at preferential prices. There are also deposits of copper, chromite, gold, manganese and iron ore. Projects brought into operation in August 1986 included a chrome-ore dressing plant near Moa, built with Czechoslovak aid, and the Maj.-Gen. Carlos Roloff iron foundry in Guantánamo, built in co-operation with Poland. In late 1987 a gold-processing plant began operation in Holguín.

Cuba is dependent on the USSR for 98% of its petroleum requirements of 206,000 barrels per day. Cuba was guaranteed 61m. tons of petroleum in 1981–85. In 1985 42% of Cuba's total convertible currency earnings of US $1,350m. derived from the re-export of Soviet petroleum. In 1986, however, there was a 53% decline in such revenue from the re-export of oil, following the sharp decline in international petroleum prices. Exploration for petroleum in Cuba is being undertaken with Soviet and Mexican assistance, and discoveries of substantial deposits on the northern coast, near Varadero, have been announced. Domestic production of crude petroleum increased from 253,000 metric tons in 1981 to 938,000 tons in 1986, but declined to 894,500 tons in 1987. As part of an extensive upgrading programme for the petroleum industry, financed by Soviet aid of $1,000m. and aimed at increasing Cuba's refining capacity from 3m. to 7m. tons per year, a new refinery at Cienfuegos (with a capacity of 120,000 barrels per day) was scheduled for completion in 1990. Construction of a 200-km pipeline, to link the Cienfuegos refinery to a new deep-water dock and oil-storage base at Matanzas Bay, was also under way in 1988. A nuclear energy plant is also under construction at Juraguá, Cienfuegos, and will have a generating capacity of 1,668 MW. It is estimated that nuclear power will provide 15% of Cuba's energy requirements in the 1990s. Under the 1986–90 Energy Plan, some 250 small hydroelectricity stations were to be built, principally for irrigation purposes. An eight-unit thermoelectric plant was to be constructed at Habana del Este, with a planned capacity of 1m. kW. In June 1988 a new power plant near Matanzas, with a capacity of 330 MW, was connected to the national grid. In October work was completed on a Czechoslovak-built thermal power station at Nuevitas, with a generating capacity of 567 MW, equivalent to 20% of Cuba's overall power capacity.

The major part of Cuba's industrial capacity comprises plants for processing agricultural produce and for the production of cement, fertilizers, textiles, domestic consumer goods and agricultural machinery. Industrial development is accorded high priority, and under the 1986–90 plan the sector was to be allocated 45% of total projected investment. Cuba's output of crude steel increased from 301,200 metric tons in 1982 to 411,500 tons in 1986. Plans for Cuban-Soviet co-operation, announced in 1981, included an integrated steelmill with an annual capacity of 1.3m. tons. In 1981 the Karl Marx cement factory was completed, and in 1987 domestic output of cement increased to 3.5m. tons. Plans for the development of the motor industry, aided by credits from Spain, were announced in 1987. Industrial production is hampered by Cuba's dependence on Western technology and by a shortage of spare parts for US-made industrial machinery. The gross output of the industrial sector increased by 1.9% in 1986.

In November 1980 an economic exchange agreement was signed, pledging Soviet aid up to the year 2000 at a total value of at least US $35,000m. US trade sanctions have restricted potential trade with Western countries and increased dependence on the USSR, with which Cuba conducts two-thirds of its trade. In 1986 it was estimated that the USSR was supplying Cuba with petroleum, subsidized trade and financial aid amounting to about $4,000m. annually. In October 1987 President Castro requested that the Soviet Government cancel Cuba's debt to the USSR, estimated to be between $8,500m. and $23,000m. Following the signing of four trade and economic co-operation agreements in April 1986, the USSR was to provide the island with new credits totalling 2,500m. roubles between 1986 and 1990, an increase of 50% over the previous five-year period. In 1987 the Government planned to reduce imports from capitalist countries by $600m., and to replace them with goods from socialist countries. Trade with CMEA countries was expected to increase from 86% to more than 90% of total foreign trade. In May 1988, during a session of the joint commission with the USSR, an outline agreement on economic relations between the two countries for a period of 15–20 years was signed.

In January 1983 Cuba announced that there would be no repayments on its foreign debt principal falling due between January 1983 and December 1985. Interest payments would be maintained. Cuba's total debt to the West was US $3,200m. in 1984. In December 1984 agreement was reached on the rescheduling of $100m. of debt. In spite of President Castro's appeals for the repudiation of the foreign debts of all Latin American countries, Cuba continued to reschedule its own debt to Western creditors in 1985. In July 10 Western creditor countries agreed to reschedule some $145m. in debt due for repayment in 1985. In August Cuba's Western creditor banks agreed to reschedule $85m. in debt, also due in 1985.

In 1986, owing partly to the decline in international oil prices and the damage caused by Hurricane Kate, Cuba recorded a trade deficit estimated at US $200m., and earnings of foreign currency declined by almost 50%. To compensate for hurricane damage, the UN World Food Programme and the FAO granted aid to the country. In the same year, while there was a shortage of foreign exchange, Cuba sought to negotiate the rescheduling of the country's $3,500m. debt to Western creditors. In July 1986 Cuba suspended payment on its debt, as a result of financial constraints. No further rescheduling agreement had been reached by the end of 1988, while Cuba's external debt had increased to $5,570m. Owing to the suspension of debt repayments, almost all industrialized nations refused to allow Cuba any new credit.

The 1981–85 Development Plan, based on high projected world prices for sugar, proved to be too ambitious and costly. Although the economy had achieved an overall average growth rate of 7.3% during 1981–85, with industrial output rising by an average of 8.8%, shortcomings were reported in several sectors, particularly in the sugar industry. Consumer prices rose by 10%, and unemployment was estimated to be 3.4% of the labour force. After 1970, financial incentives were introduced to stimulate productivity, and in 1980 a free market for surplus agricultural produce was introduced to undermine the 'black market' which had developed as a result of shortages and rationing. However, the free market was suspended in May 1986, following the discovery of corrupt practices.

CUBA

Under the 1986-90 Development Plan, an annual economic growth rate of 5% was envisaged. Among the measures were a strict austerity programme for state organizations and enterprises, increased investment in the agricultural and industrial sectors, the diversification of export production and a policy of import substitution. Total exports were to increase by an average rate of 5% annually, while the annual rise in imports was to be restricted to 1.5%. The contribution of the industrial sector to overall production was projected to increase to 50%.

In 1987, as in the previous year, the level of economic growth was affected by adverse weather conditions. However, a 20% reduction in imports and an 8.5% increase in non-sugar exports resulted in a US $34.2m. trade surplus in 1987, compared with a $289m. deficit in 1986. Although domestic commercial production fell by 3.2% in 1987, prospects for 1988 were favourable, with the international price of sugar and the forecasts for domestic agricultural production both rising. Economic growth in 1988 was estimated at 2.3%. The number of tourists who visited Cuba in 1988 was 225,000. Tourist receipts totalled $124m. in 1988, a 20% increase over the figure for 1987. Investment in tourism infrastructure is projected to increase hotel accommodation by 60% by 1992, and to make tourism the most important industry after sugar production.

Social Welfare

Through the State Social Security System, employees receive benefits for sickness, accidents, maternity, disability, retirement and unemployment. Health services are available free of charge. In 1986 there were 5.5 hospital beds for every 1,000 inhabitants, and one physician per 401 inhabitants. In 1987 the infant mortality rate was 13.3 per 1,000 live births. The 1986 budget allocation for health and education was 2,626.5m. pesos.

Education

Education is universal and free at all levels. Education is based on Marxist-Leninist principles and combines study with manual work. The 1981-85 Development Plan emphasized improvement of professional and technological education, especially in medicine, economics, accountancy and teaching.

Pre-school national schools are run by the State for children of five years of age, and day nurseries are available for all children after their 45th day. Primary education, from six to 12 years of age, is compulsory, and secondary education lasts from 13 to 16 (to be extended to 18) years of age. In 1985 an estimated 94% of children in the primary school age-group attended primary schools, while 69% of children in the secondary school age-group were enrolled at secondary schools. In 1986/87 there were 256,600 students in higher education. Workers undergoing university courses receive a state subsidy to provide for their dependants. Courses at intermediate and higher levels have an emphasis on technology, agriculture and teacher training. In 1979 the estimated illiteracy rate among persons aged 15 to 49 was only 4.6% (males 4.3%; females 4.9%). Adult education centres gave basic education to 292,067 people in 1984/85.

Public Holidays

1989: 2 January (for Liberation Day), 1 May (Labour Day), 25-27 July (Anniversary of the 1953 Revolution), 10 October (Wars of Independence Day).

1990: 1 January (Liberation Day), 1 May (Labour Day), 25-27 July (Anniversary of the 1953 Revolution), 10 October (Wars of Independence Day).

Weights and Measures

The metric system is in force.

Statistical Survey

Source (unless otherwise stated): Cámara de Comercio de Cuba, Calle 21, No 661, Apdo 4237, Vedado, Havana; tel. 30-3356; telex 51-1752; Comité Estatal de Estadísticas, Havana, Cuba; tel. 31-5171.

Area and Population

AREA, POPULATION AND DENSITY

Area (sq km)	110,860*
Population (census results)	
6 September 1970	8,569,121
11 September 1981	
Males	4,914,873
Females	4,808,732
Total	9,723,605
Population (official estimates at mid-year)	
1985	10,098,000
1986	10,192,000
1987	10,288,000
Density (per sq km) at mid-1987	92.8

* 42,803 sq miles.

PRINCIPAL TOWNS

(estimated population at 31 December 1986)

La Habana (Havana, the capital)	2,036,799		Cienfuegos	112,225
Santiago de Cuba	364,554		Bayamo	108,716
Camagüey	265,588		Pinar del Río	108,109
Holguín	199,861		Matanzas	106,954
Santa Clara	182,349		Las Tunas	96,846
Guantánamo	179,091		Ciego de Ávila	82,942
			Sancti Spíritus	78,154

BIRTHS, MARRIAGES AND DEATHS*

	Registered live births†		Registered marriages‡		Registered deaths	
	Number	Rate (per 1,000)	Number	Rate (per 1,000)	Number	Rate (per 1,000)
1980	136,900	14.1	68,941	7.1	55,707	5.7
1981	136,211	14.0	72,824	7.5	57,814	5.9
1982	159,759	16.3	80,295	8.2	56,485	5.8
1983	165,284	16.7	75,920	7.7	58,334	5.9
1984	166,281	16.6	75,524	7.6	59,895	6.0
1985	182,067	18.0	80,407	8.0	64,430	6.4
1986	166,049	16.3	84,274	8.3	63,140	6.2
1987	179,477	17.4	n.a.	7.7	64,680	6.3

* Data are tabulated by year of registration rather than by year of occurrence.
† Births registered in the National Consumers Register, established on 31 December 1964.
‡ Including consensual unions formalized in response to special legislation.

CUBA

ECONOMICALLY ACTIVE POPULATION (1981 census)

	Males	Females	Total
Agriculture, hunting, forestry and fishing	677,565	113,304	790,869
Mining and quarrying			
Manufacturing	472,399	195,941	668,340
Electricity, gas and water			
Construction	279,327	33,913	313,240
Trade, restaurants and hotels	170,192	135,438	305,630
Transport, storage and communications	205,421	43,223	248,644
Financing, insurance, real estate and business services	541,387	544,665	1,086,052
Community, social and personal services			
Activities not adequately defined	87,778	40,139	127,917
Total labour force	2,434,069	1,106,623	3,540,692

1986 (sample survey): Total labour force 4,342,280 (males 2,786,597; females 1,555,683).

Source: ILO, *Year Book of Labour Statistics*.

CIVILIAN EMPLOYMENT IN THE STATE SECTOR
(annual averages, '000 persons)

	1984	1985	1986
Industry*	683.5	709.3	725.9
Construction	308.5	314.7	322.0
Agriculture	563.9	552.0	572.3
Forestry	26.9	29.2	29.4
Transport	187.2	190.0	197.2
Communications	25.5	26.2	27.0
Trade	367.2	367.2	371.4
Social services	108.0	111.7	114.8
Science and technology	25.5	27.1	27.6
Education	380.1	381.2	381.6
Arts and culture	38.0	40.8	41.8
Public health	184.9	196.8	210.7
Total (incl. others)	3,114.8	3,169.9	3,262.7

* Fishing, mining, manufacturing, electricity, gas and water.

Agriculture

PRINCIPAL CROPS ('000 metric tons)

	1984	1985	1986
Sugar cane	73,794.7	68,927.5	72,921.3
Maize	29.0	32.4	36.0
Cassava (Manioc)*	300†	300‡	304‡
Potatoes	259.4	307.3	316.5
Sweet potatoes	162.3	178.1	150.0
Plantains	171.9	143.5	170.2
Rice (paddy)	554.8	524.3	575.8
Tobacco (leaves)	44.6	44.6	45.6
Tomatoes	228.4	270.8	254.0
Oranges	371.0	406.4	447.3
Lemons	48.2	60.4	59.1
Grapefruit	154.7	241.4	250.0
Bananas	220.5	201.1	147.0
Mangoes	37.6	86.0	61.0
Coffee (green)	22.1	23.8	22.8

* Source: FAO, *Production Yearbook*.
† Unofficial figures. ‡ FAO estimate.

LIVESTOCK ('000 head at 31 December; state enterprises only)

	1984	1985	1986
Cattle*	5,115.2	5,019.5	5,007.1
Horses*	792.0	774.2	752.9
Pigs	1,009.4	1,038.0	1,100.8
Sheep	440.8	494.6	618.2
Poultry	26,734.5	25,859.3	25,677.9

* State and private sectors.

LIVESTOCK PRODUCTS ('000 metric tons)

	1984	1985	1986
Beef and veal	301.8	298.9	302.3
Pig meat	85.6	94.8	100.2
Poultry meat	106.7	113.0	113.3
Cows' milk	945.2	928.7	926.3
Hen eggs (million)	2,557.1	2,523.6	2,518.9

Forestry

ROUNDWOOD REMOVALS
('000 cubic metres, excluding bark)

	1983	1984	1985
Sawlogs, veneer logs and logs for sleepers	166	171	175
Other industrial wood*	350	350	350
Fuel wood	2,747	2,747*	2,753*
Total	3,263	3,268	3,278

* FAO estimates.
1986: Output as in 1985 (FAO estimates).
Source: FAO, *Yearbook of Forest Products*.

SAWNWOOD PRODUCTION ('000 cubic metres)

	1983	1984	1985
Total (incl. railway sleepers)	104	108	104

1986: Production as in 1985 (FAO estimate).
Source: FAO, *Yearbook of Forest Products*.

Fishing

('000 metric tons, live weight)

	1984	1985	1986
Inland waters	16.2	16.9	16.1
Atlantic Ocean	149.2	156.1	165.2*
Pacific Ocean	34.1	46.9	63.3*
Total catch	199.6	219.8	244.6

* FAO estimate.
Source: FAO, *Yearbook of Fishery Statistics*.
1987 ('000 metric tons): Total catch 214.3.

CUBA

Mining

('000 metric tons, unless otherwise indicated)

	1984	1985	1986
Crude petroleum	770.4	867.6	938.0
Natural gas (million cu metres)	3.4	6.9	5.7
Copper concentrates*	2.7	3.1	3.3
Nickel and cobalt*	33.2	33.6	35.1
Refractory chromium	37.9	37.7	50.0
Salt (unrefined)	184.5	220.9	266.0
Silica and sand ('000 cu metres)	5,461	5,636.5	5,619.9
Crushed stone ('000 cu metres)	10,680.7	11,788.3	11,358.3

* Figures refer to the metal content of ores and concentrates.
1987 ('000 metric tons): crude petroleum 894.5; Copper concentrates 3.5; Nickel and Cobalt 35.8.

Industry

SELECTED PRODUCTS
('000 metric tons, unless otherwise indicated)

	1985	1986	1987
Crude steel	401.4	411.5	401.5
Corrugated steel bars	300.2	312.0	312.9
Grey cement	3,182.3	3,305.2	3,535.3
Mosaics ('000 sq metres)	3,223.7	3,076.5	n.a.
Motor spirit (Gasoline)	953.1	979.0	n.a.
Kerosene	527.9	568.5	n.a.
Sulphuric acid (98%)	374.3	396.2	n.a.
Fertilizers	1,159.7	1,045.2	996.4
Tyres ('000)	472.2	436.0	324.7
Woven textile fabrics ('000 sq metres)	205,400	220,800	258,200
Cigarettes (million)	17,961	16,800	15,397.6
Cigars (million)	366.3	340.3	278.6
Raw sugar*	7,603.4	7,203.8	n.a.
Leather footwear ('000 pairs)	12,394	13,400	14,200
Electric energy (million kWh)	12,199.4	13,167.1	13,583.1

* Corresponding to calendar year.

Finance

CURRENCY AND EXCHANGE RATES

Monetary Units:
100 centavos = 1 Cuban peso.

Denominations:
Coins: 1, 5, 20 and 40 centavos; 1 peso.
Notes: 1, 3, 5, 10, 20 and 50 pesos.

Sterling and Dollar Equivalents (30 September 1988)
£1 sterling = 1.305 pesos;
US $1 = 77.2 centavos;
100 Cuban pesos = £76.60 = $129.53.

STATE BUDGET (million pesos)

	1986	1987*
Total revenue	11,699.1	11,272.9
Total expenditure	11,887.4	11,797.9
Productive sector	4,419.8	4,455.2
Housing and community services	717.6	744.4
Education and public health	2,693.1	2,709.2
Other social, cultural and scientific activities	1,830.3	1,857.2
Government administration and judicial bodies	639.4	565.4
Defence and public order	1,268.4	1,241.8
Other	319.0	224.3

* Preliminary.
Source: State Committee for Finance, Havana.

INTERNATIONAL RESERVES
(million pesos at 31 December)

	1986	1987
Gold and other precious metals	17.5	17.5
Cash and deposits in foreign banks (convertible currency)	89.7	34.4
Sub-total	107.2	51.9
Deposits in foreign banks (in transferable roubles)	134.4	142.5
Total	241.6	194.4

NATIONAL ACCOUNTS

Net Material Product (NMP) by Economic Activity*
(million pesos at current prices)

	1984	1985	1986
Agriculture and fishing	1,281.2	1,268.5	1,320.5
Forestry	88.4	93.7	94.5
Industry†	4,734.4	5,071.8	4,822.9
Construction	1,321.0	1,312.6	1,192.1
Trade, restaurants, etc.	5,124.5	5,080.9	4,333.7
Transport	890.0	871.8	823.0
Communications	161.2	167.8	163.2
Other activities of the material sphere	94.3	84.6	103.9
Total	13,695.0	13,951.7	12,853.9
NMP at constant 1981 prices	13,696.2	14,260.6	13,990.7

* NMP is defined as the total net value of goods and 'productive' services, including turnover taxes, produced by the economy. This excludes economic activities not contributing directly to material production, such as public administration, defence and personal and professional services.
† Principally manufacturing, mining, electricity, gas and water.

CUBA

External Trade

PRINCIPAL COMMODITIES (million pesos)

Imports	1984	1985	1986
Food and live animals	822.5	889.2	704.4
Beverages and tobacco	7.7	7.8	8.5
Animal and vegetable fats and oils	79.2	81.6	76.2
Crude materials (inedible) except fuels	270.2	324.3	302.8
Mineral fuels, lubricants, etc.	2,219.1	2,655.6	2,537.6
Chemicals and related products	441.6	409.8	428.4
Basic manufactures	967.9	989.2	921.4
Machinery and transport equipment	2,201.1	2,419.3	2,329.3
Miscellaneous manufactured articles	218.2	258.1	260.4
Total	7,227.5	8,035.0	7,569.0

Exports	1984	1985	1986
Sugar and sugar products	4,123.2	4,462.8	4,099.5
Minerals and concentrates	300.9	307.5	313.4
Tobacco and tobacco products	56.6	92.0	77.8
Fish and fish preparations	91.8	119.6	124.6
Other agricultural products	156.9	203.5	218.8
Total (incl. others)	5,476.5	5,991.5	5,325.0

PRINCIPAL TRADING PARTNERS ('000 pesos)

Imports c.i.f.	1985	1986	1987*
Argentina	193,339	162,250	124,400
Bulgaria	192,110	189,389	183,800
Canada	58,802	53,400	32,900
China, People's Republic	227,876	120,595	97,300
Czechoslovakia	197,194	178,422	190,600
France	93,943	54,394	46,800
German Democratic Republic	282,459	305,334	339,100
Germany, Federal Republic	81,611	85,455	52,600
Hungary	168,048	103,671	69,000
Italy	43,169	54,868	46,000
Japan	219,201	264,484	107,500
Mexico	77,125	29,708	71,200
Poland	75,802	60,757	79,100
Romania	133,354	82,605	183,200
Spain	176,889	147,437	163,300
Switzerland	22,655	23,572	36,800
USSR	5,418,944	5,313,864	5,495,500
United Kingdom	105,078	78,829	70,100
Total (incl. others)	8,034,976	7,568,995	7,611,500

* Preliminary.

Exports f.o.b.	1985	1986	1987*
Bulgaria	185,497	147,011	169,100
Canada	32,185	37,242	36,800
China, People's Republic	157,826	60,277	85,500
Czechoslovakia	119,222	122,944	144,000
France	63,017	47,903	57,600
German Democratic Republic	233,728	257,579	281,900
Hungary	20,639	21,037	66,600
Italy	21,758	28,150	36,100
Japan	78,620	110,442	77,700
Poland	74,477	53,861	43,600
Romania	38,319	83,805	108,900
Spain	101,750	88,158	84,800
Switzerland	68,686	53,849	48,900
USSR	4,481,636	3,933,522	3,867,500
Total (incl. others)	5,991,477	5,325,012	5,401,000

Transport

RAILWAYS

	1984	1985	1986
Passengers ('000)	24,600.0	23,100.0	23,400.0
Passenger-kilometres (million)	2,359.8	2,257.2	2,200.0
Freight carried ('000 metric tons)	18,434.7	18,368.5	16,143.3
Freight ton-kilometres (million)	2,809.0	2,935.1	2,459.8

ROAD TRAFFIC ('000 motor vehicles in use)

	1982	1983	1984
Passenger cars	182.2	190.4	200.1
Commercial vehicles	152.4	158.9	164.5

Source: UN, *Statistical Yearbook*.

INTERNATIONAL SEA-BORNE SHIPPING
(freight traffic, '000 metric tons)

	1984	1985	1986
Goods loaded	8,307.0	8,930.1	8,377.0
Goods unloaded	17,817.8	18,866.9	18,444.6

CIVIL AVIATION

	1984	1985	1986
Passengers carried ('000)	1,000.0	1,000.0	1,000.0
Passenger-kilometres (million)	2,514.2	2,417.0	2,614.3
Freight ton-kilometres (million)	37.6	33.6	34.8

Tourism

	1986	1987	1988
Foreign visitors	194,531	207,000	225,000

Source: Instituto Nacional de Turismo—INTUR.

Education

(1986/87)

	Schools	Teachers	Pupils
Pre-primary	n.a.	5,772	111,600
Primary	9,837	75,273	1,001,000
Secondary: general	1,293	67,122	800,700
Technical and professional	634	27,023	317,600
Higher	35	21,573	256,600

Directory

The Constitution

Following the assumption of power by the Castro regime on 1 January 1959, the Constitution was suspended and a Fundamental Law of the Republic was instituted with effect from 7 February 1959. In February 1976 Cuba's first socialist Constitution came into force after being submitted to the first Congress of the Communist Party of Cuba in December 1975 and to popular referendum in February 1976.

POLITICAL, SOCIAL AND ECONOMIC PRINCIPLES

The Republic of Cuba is a socialist state in which all power belongs to the working people. The Communist Party of Cuba is the leading force of society and the state. The socialist state carries out the will of the working people and guarantees work, medical care, education, food, clothing and housing. The Republic of Cuba is part of the world socialist community. It bases its relations with the Union of Soviet Socialist Republics and with other socialist countries on socialist internationalism, friendship, co-operation and mutual assistance. It hopes to establish one large community of nations within Latin America and the Caribbean.

The State organizes and directs the economic life of the nation in accordance with a central social and economic development plan. Foreign trade is the exclusive function of the State. The State recognizes the right of small farmers to own their lands and other means of production and to sell that land. The State guarantees the right of citizens to ownership of personal property in the form of earnings, savings, place of residence and other possessions and objects which serve to satisfy their material and cultural needs. The State also guarantees the right of inheritance.

Cuban citizenship is acquired by birth or through naturalization.

The State protects the family, motherhood and matrimony.

The State directs and encourages all aspects of education, culture and science.

All citizens have equal rights and are subject to equal duties.

The State guarantees the right to medical care, education, freedom of speech and press, assembly, demonstration, association and privacy. In the socialist society work is the right and duty, and a source of pride for every citizen.

GOVERNMENT

National Assembly of People's Power

The National Assembly of People's Power is the supreme organ of the State and is the only organ with constituent and legislative authority. It is composed of deputies over the age of 18 elected by the Municipal Assemblies of People's Power, for a period of five years. All Cuban citizens over the age of 16, except those who are mentally incapacitated or who have committed a crime, are eligible to vote. The National Assembly of People's Power holds two ordinary sessions a year and a special session when requested by one-third of the deputies or by the Council of State. More than half the total number of deputies must be present for a session to be held.

All decisions made by the Assembly, except those relating to constitutional reforms, are adopted by a simple majority of votes. The deputies may be recalled by their electors at any time.

The National Assembly of People's Power has the following functions:

to reform the Constitution;

to approve, modify and annul laws;

to supervise all organs of the State and government;

to decide on the constitutionality of laws and decrees;

to revoke decree-laws issued by the Council of State;

to discuss and approve economic and social development plans, the state budget, monetary and credit systems;

to approve the general outlines of foreign and domestic policy, to ratify and annul international treaties, to declare war and approve peace treaties;

to approve the administrative division of the country;

to elect the President, First Vice-President, the Vice-Presidents and other members of the Council of State;

to elect the President, Vice-President and Secretary of the National Assembly;

to appoint the members of the Council of Ministers on the proposal of the President of the Council of State;

to elect the President, Vice-President and other judges of the People's Supreme Court;

to elect the attorney-general and the deputy attorney-generals;

to grant amnesty;

to call referendums.

The President of the National Assembly presides over sessions of the Assembly, calls ordinary sessions, proposes the draft agenda, signs the Official Gazette, organizes the work of the commissions appointed by the Assembly and attends the meetings of the Council of State.

Council of State

The Council of State is elected from the members of the National Assembly and represents that Assembly in the period between sessions. It comprises a President, one First Vice-President, five Vice-Presidents, one Secretary and 23 other members. Its mandate ends when a new Assembly meets. All decisions are adopted by a simple majority of votes. It is accountable for its actions to the National Assembly.

The Council of State has the following functions:

to call special sessions of the National Assembly;

to set the date for the election of a new Assembly;

to issue decree-laws in the period between the sessions of the National Assembly;

to decree mobilization in the event of war and to approve peace treaties when the Assembly is in recess;

to issue instructions to the courts and the Office of the Attorney General of the Republic;

to appoint and remove ambassadors of Cuba abroad on the proposal of its President, to grant or refuse recognition to diplomatic representatives of other countries to Cuba;

to suspend those provisions of the Council of Ministers that are not in accordance with the Constitution;

to revoke the resolutions of the Executive Committee of the local organs of People's Power which are contrary to the Constitution or laws and decrees formulated by other higher organs.

The President of the Council of State is Head of State and Head of Government and for all purposes the Council of State is the highest representative of the Cuban state.

Head of State

The President of the Council of State is the Head of State and the Head of Government and has the following powers:

to represent the State and Government and conduct general policy;

to call and preside over the sessions of the Council of State and the Council of Ministers;

to supervise the ministries and other administrative bodies;

to propose the members of the Council of Ministers to the National Assembly of People's Power;

to receive the credentials of the heads of foreign diplomatic missions;

to sign the decree-laws and other resolutions of the Council of State;

to assume command of the Revolutionary Armed Forces.

In the case of absence, illness or death of the President of the Council of State, the First Vice-President assumes the President's duties.

The Council of Ministers

The Council of Ministers is the highest-ranking executive and administrative organ. It is composed of the Head of State and Government, as its President, the First Vice-President, the Vice-Presidents, the Ministers and the President of the Central Planning Board. Its Executive Committee is composed of the President, the First Vice-President and the Vice-Presidents of the Council of Ministers.

The Council of Ministers has the following powers:

to conduct political, economic, cultural, scientific, social and defence policy as outlined by the National Assembly;

to approve international treaties;

to propose projects for the general development plan and, if they are approved by the National Assembly, to supervise their implementation;

to conduct foreign policy and trade;

to draw up bills and submit them to the National Assembly;

CUBA
Directory

to draw up the draft state budget;

to conduct general administration, implement laws, issue decrees and supervise defence and national security.

The Council of Ministers is accountable to the National Assembly of People's Power.

LOCAL GOVERNMENT

The country is divided into 14 provinces and 169 municipalities. The provinces are: Pinar del Río, Habana, Ciudad de la Habana, Matanzas, Villa Clara, Cienfuegos, Sancti Spíritus, Ciego de Avila, Camagüey, Las Tunas, Holguín, Granma, Santiago de Cuba and Guantánamo.

Voting for delegates to the municipal assemblies is direct, secret and voluntary. All citizens over 16 years of age are eligible to vote. The number of delegates to each assembly is proportionate to the number of people living in that area. A delegate must obtain more than half the number of votes cast in the constituency in order to be elected. The Municipal Assemblies are elected for a period of two-and-a-half years and are headed by Executive Committees elected from the members of the Municipal Assemblies. The members of the Executive Committees form five Regional Assemblies and the members of the Regional Assemblies in turn form Provincial Assemblies also headed by Executive Committees. Membership of regional and provincial executive committees is proposed by a commission of Communist Party members and youth and trade union representatives. The President and Secretary of each of the regional and the provincial assemblies are the only full-time members, the other delegates carrying out their functions in addition to their normal employment.

The regular and extraordinary sessions of the local Assemblies of People's Power are public. More than half the total number of members must be present in order for agreements made to be valid. Agreements are adopted by simple majority.

JUDICIARY

Judicial power is exercised by the People's Supreme Court and all other competent tribunals and courts. The People's Supreme Court is the supreme judicial authority and is accountable only to the National Assembly of People's Power. It can propose laws and issue regulations through its Council of Government. Judges are independent but the courts must inform the electorate of their activities at least once a year. Every accused person has the right to a defence and can be tried only by a tribunal.

The Office of the Attorney-General is subordinate only to the National Assembly and the Council of State and is responsible for ensuring that the law is properly obeyed.

The Constitution may be totally or partially modified only by a two-thirds majority vote in the National Assembly of People's Power. If the modification is total, or if it concerns the composition and powers of the National Assembly of People's Power or the Council of State, or the rights and duties contained in the Constitution, it also requires a positive vote by referendum.

The Government
(December 1988)

Head of State: Dr FIDEL CASTRO RUZ (took office 2 December 1976; re-elected December 1981 and December 1986).

COUNCIL OF STATE

President: Dr FIDEL CASTRO RUZ.

First Vice-President: Gen. RAÚL CASTRO RUZ.

Vice-Presidents:
JUAN ALMEIDA BOSQUE.
OSMANY CIENFUEGOS GORRIARÁN.
JOSÉ RAMÓN MACHADO VENTURA.
PEDRO MIRET PRIETO.
Dr CARLOS RAFAEL RODRÍGUEZ RODRÍGUEZ.

Secretary: Dr JOSÉ M. MIYAR BARRUECO.

Members:
JOSÉ RAMÓN BALAGUER CABRERA.
Dr ARMANDO HART DÁVALOS.
PEDRO CHÁVEZ GONZÁLEZ.
MERCEDES DÍAZ HERRERA.
LÁZARO TRENCILO FIS.
RAMIRO VALDÉS MENÉNDEZ.
FELIX VILLAR BENCOMO.
GUILLERMO GARCÍA FRIAS.
CARLOS LANGE DÁVILA.
ROBERTO VEIGA MENÉNDEZ.
VILMA ESPÍN GUILLOLS DE CASTRO.
JOSÉ RAMÍREZ CRUZ.
ARMANDO ACOSTA CORDERO.
SEVERO AGUIRRE DEL CRISTO.
ORLANDO LUGO FONTE.
ROBERTO ROBAINA GONZÁLEZ.
JOSÉ RAMÓN FERNÁNDEZ ALVAREZ.
PEDRO CANISIO SAEZ JOVA.
ZEIDA SUÁREZ PREMIER.
Gen. SENÉN CASAS REGUEIRO.
Gen. ABELARDO COLOMÉ IBARRA.
LIDIA TABLADA ROMERO.

COUNCIL OF MINISTERS

President: Dr FIDEL CASTRO RUZ.

First Vice-President: Gen. RAÚL CASTRO RUZ.

Vice-Presidents:
Dr CARLOS RAFAEL RODRÍGUEZ RODRÍGUEZ.
RAMIRO VALDÉS MENÉNDEZ.
JOEL DOMENECH BENÍTEZ.
ANTONIO ESQUIVEL YEDRA.
DIOCLES TORRALBA GONZÁLEZ.
JOSÉ RAMÓN FERNÁNDEZ ALVAREZ.
JOSÉ A. LÓPEZ MORENO.
OSMANY CIENFUEGOS GORRIARÁN.
PEDRO MIRET PRIETO.
ANTONIO RODRÍGUEZ MAURELL.

Secretary: OSMANY CIENFUEGOS GORRIARÁN.

Minister of Agriculture: ADOLFO DÍAZ SUÁREZ.

Minister of Foreign Trade: RICARDO CABRISAS RUIZ.

Minister of Internal Trade: MANUEL VILA SOSA.

Minister of Communications: MANUEL CASTILLO RABASA.

Minister of Construction: RAÚL CABRERA NÚÑEZ.

Minister of Culture: Dr ARMANDO HART DÁVALOS.

Minister of Education: JOSÉ RAMÓN FERNÁNDEZ ÁLVAREZ.

Minister of Higher Education: FERNANDO VECINO ALEGRET.

Minister of the Revolutionary Armed Forces: Gen. RAÚL CASTRO RUZ.

Minister of the Food Industry: ALEJANDRO ROCA IGLESIAS.

Minister of the Sugar Industry: JUAN HERRERA MACHADO.

Minister of the Construction Materials Industry: LEVI FARAH BALMASEDA.

Minister of Light Industry: ANTONIO ESQUIVEL YEDRA.

Minister of the Fishing Industry: Capt. JORGE A. FERNÁNDEZ-CUERVO VINENT.

Minister of the Iron and Steel and Metallurgical Industries: Ing. MARCOS LAGE COELLO.

Minister of Basic Industries: MARCOS PORTAL LEÓN.

Minister of the Interior: JOSÉ ABRAHANTES FERNÁNDEZ.

Minister of Justice: Dr JUAN ESCALONA REGUERA.

Minister of Foreign Affairs: ISIDORO MALMIERCA PEOLI.

Minister of Public Health: JULIO TEJAS PÉREZ.

Minister of Transport: DIOCLES TORRALBA GONZÁLEZ.

Minister, President Central Planning Board: JOSÉ LÓPEZ MORENO.

Minister, State Committee for Technical and Material Supplies: SONIA RODRÍGUEZ CARDONA.

Minister, State Committee for Economic Co-operation: ERNESTO MELÉNDEZ BACH.

Minister, State Committee for Statistics: FIDEL VASCOS GONZÁLEZ.

Minister, State Committee for Finance: RODRIGO GARCÍA LEÓN.

Minister, State Committee for Standardization: RAMÓN DARIAS RODÉS.

Minister, State Committee for Prices: ARTURO GUZMÁN PASCUAL.

Minister, State Committee for Labour and Social Security: FRANCISCO LINARES CALVO.

Minister, President of the Banco Nacional de Cuba: HÉCTOR RODRÍGUEZ LLOMPART.

Minister, President of the Academy of Sciences of Cuba: ROSA ELENA SIMEÓN.

Minister without Portfolio: JOSÉ A. NARANJO MORALES.

MINISTRIES

Ministry of Agriculture: Avda Independencia, entre Conill y Sta Ana, Havana; tel. 70-8091; telex 511966.

Ministry of Basic Industries: Avda Salvador Allende, No 666, Havana; tel. 70-7711; telex 511183.

Ministry of Communications: Plaza de la Revolución 'José Martí', Havana; tel. 70-5581; telex 511657.

Ministry of Construction: Avda Carlos M. de Céspedes y Calle 35, Havana; tel. 70-9411; telex 511275.

Ministry of the Construction Materials Industry: Calle O esq. 17, Vedado, Havana; tel. 32-2541; telex 51-1517.

Ministry of Culture: Calle 2, entre 11 y 13, Vedado, Havana; tel. 30-3124; telex 511400.

Ministry of Education: Obispo No 160, Havana; tel. 62-4011; telex 511188.

Ministry of the Fishing Industry: Barlovento, Santa Fe, Havana; tel. 22-7333; telex 51-1444.

Ministry of the Food Industry: Calle 41, No 4455, Playa, Havana; tel. 2-6801; telex 511163.

Ministry of Foreign Affairs: Calzada No 360, Vedado, Havana; tel. 32-3279; telex 511122.

Ministry of Foreign Trade: Infanta No 16, Vedado, Havana; tel. 70-9341; telex 511174.

Ministry of Higher Education: Calle 23, No 565 esq. a F, Vedado, Havana; tel. 3-6655; telex 511253.

Ministry of the Interior: Plaza de la Revolución, Havana.

Ministry of Internal Trade: Calle Habana, No 258, Havana; tel. 6-6984; telex 511171.

Ministry of the Iron and Steel and Metallurgical Industries: Avda Rancho Boyeros y Calle 100, Havana; tel. 44-2211; telex 511179.

Ministry of Justice: Calle 0, No 216, Vedado, Havana; tel. 32-4526; telex 511331.

Ministry of Light Industry: Empedrado No 302, Havana; tel. 61-7971; telex 511141.

Ministry of Public Health: Calle 23, No 201, Vedado, Havana; tel. 32-2561; telex 511149.

Ministry of the Revolutionary Armed Forces: Plaza de la Revolución, Havana.

Ministry of the Sugar Industry: Calle 23, No 171, Vedado, Havana; tel. 30-5061; telex 511664.

Ministry of Transport: Rancho Boyeros y Tulipán, Havana; tel. 70-7751; telex 511181.

Central Planning Board: 20 de Mayo y Ayestarán, Plaza de la Revolución, Havana; tel. 79-7501; telex 511158.

State Committee for Economic Co-operation: Calle 1a, No 201, Vedado, Havana; tel. 3-6661; telex 511297.

State Committee for Finance: Obispo esq. Cuba, Havana; tel. 61-1691; telex 511101.

State Committee for Labour and Social Security: Calle 23, esq. Calle P, Vedado, Havana; tel. 70-4571; telex 511225.

State Committee for Prices: Amistad No 552, Havana; tel. 6-7050.

State Committee for Standardization: Egido No 610 entre Gloria y Apodaca, Havana; tel. 6-7901; telex 511422.

State Committee for Statistics: Almendares No 156, Havana; tel. 79-6506; telex 511257.

State Committee for Technical and Material Supplies: Monserrate No 261, Havana; tel. 6-8881; telex 511757.

Legislature

ASAMBLEA NACIONAL DEL PODER POPULAR

The National Assembly of People's Power was constituted on 2 December 1976. The Assembly's third five-year term began in December 1986. It consists of 510 deputies.

President: SEVERO AGUIRRE DEL CRISTO.

Secretary: LUIS MÉNDEZ MOREJÓN.

Political Organization

Partido Comunista de Cuba (PCC) (Communist Party of Cuba): Havana; f. 1961 as the Organizaciones Revolucionarias Integradas (ORI) from a fusion of the Partido Socialista Popular (Communist), Fidel Castro's Movimiento 26 de Julio and the Directorio Revolucionario 13 de Marzo; became the Partido Unido de la Revolución Socialista Cubana (PURSC) in 1962; renamed as the Partido Comunista de Cuba in 1965; 225-member Central Committee (146 full mems and 79 candidate mems were elected in February 1986), Political Bureau (14 full mems and 10 candidate mems in 1986), Secretariat and 5 Commissions; 523,639 mems (1986).

Political Bureau: Full mems Dr FIDEL CASTRO RUZ, Gen. RAÚL CASTRO RUZ, JUAN ALMEIDA BOSQUE, Dr ARMANDO HART DÁVALOS, JOSÉ RAMÓN MACHADO VENTURA, CARLOS RAFAEL RODRÍGUEZ RODRÍGUEZ, PEDRO MIRET PRIETO, JORGE RISQUET VALDÉS-SALDAÑA, JULIO CAMACHO AGUILERA, OSMANY CIENFUEGOS GORRIARÁN, VILMA ESPÍN GUILLOIS DE CASTRO, ESTEBAN LAZO HERNÁNDEZ, Gen. ABELARDO COLOMÉ IBARRA, ROBERTO VEIGA MENÉNDEZ.

Secretariat: Dr FIDEL CASTRO RUZ (First Sec.), Gen. RAÚL CASTRO RUZ (Second Sec.), JORGE RISQUET VALDÉS-SALDAÑA, JOSÉ RAMÓN MACHADO VENTURA, LIONEL SOTO PRIETO, JULIÁN RIZO ALVAREZ, JAIME CROMBET HERNÁNDEZ-BAQUERO, JOSÉ RAMÓN BALAGUER CABRERA, SIXTO BATISTA SANTANA, CARLOS ALDANA ESCALANTE, PEDRO ROSS LEAL.

Diplomatic Representation

EMBASSIES IN CUBA

Afghanistan: Calle 24, No 3414, entre 43 y 45, Miramar, Havana; tel. 22-5444; Ambassador: ABDUL MAJID SARBULAND.

Albania: Calle 13, No 851, Vedado, Havana; tel. 30-2788; Ambassador: CLIRIM CEPANI.

Algeria: 5a Avda, No 2802 esq. 28, Miramar, Havana; tel. 2-6538; Ambassador: HOCINE ZATOUT.

Angola: Avda 5, No 1012, entre 10 y 12, Miramar, Havana; tel. 29-2205; Ambassador: (vacant).

Argentina: Calle 36, No 511, entre 5a y 7a, Miramar, Havana; tel. 22-5540; telex 511138; Ambassador: LUIS RAÚL CLARASO DE LA VEGA.

Austria: Calle 4, No 101 entre 1 y 3, Miramar, Havana; tel. 22-4394; telex 511415; Ambassador: Dr CHRISTOPH PARISINI.

Belgium: Avda 5a, No 7408, Miramar-Playa, Havana; tel. 29-6440; telex 511482; Ambassador: WILLY VERRIEST.

Benin: Calle 20, No 119, Miramar, Havana; tel. 2-3595; Chargé d'affaires a.i.: APOLLINAIRE HACHEME.

Bolivia: 5a Avda, No 3608, entre 36 y 36A, Miramar, Havana; tel. 2-4426; Chargé d'affaires a.i.: MIGUEL ANGEL FLORES ALORAS.

Brazil: Calle 16, No 503, Miramar, Havana; tel. 22-7476; Ambassador: ITALO ZAPPA.

Bulgaria: Calle B, No 252, Vedado, Havana; tel. 30-0256; Ambassador: NIKOLA NENOV.

Burkina Faso: Calle 14, No 125 entre 1 y 3, Miramar; tel. 22-8295; Ambassador: (vacant).

Canada: Calle 30, No 518, esq. a 7a, Miramar, Havana; tel. 2-6421; telex 511586; Ambassador: MICHAEL KERGIN.

Cape Verde: Calle 98, No 508, entre 5 y 5B, Miramar, Havana; tel. 21-8912; Chargé d'affaires a.i.: ARMINDO SANTOS CRUZ.

China, People's Republic: Calle 13, No 551, Vedado, Havana; tel. 32-5205; Ambassador: TANG YONGGUI.

Congo: Avda 5, No 1003, Miramar, Havana; tel. 2-6513; Ambassador: WILSON-ABEL NDESSABEKA.

Czechoslovakia: Avda Kohly, No 259, Nuevo Vedado, Havana; tel. 30-0024; Ambassador: STANISLAV SVOBODA.

Denmark: Paseo de Martí No 20, Apto 4-C, Havana; tel. 61-6610; telex 511100; Chargé d'affaires a.i.: NIELS NEUSTRUP.

Ecuador: Avda 5a-A, No 4407, Miramar, Havana; tel. 29-6839; telex 511770; Ambassador: MANUEL ARAUJO HIDALGO.

Egypt: Avda 5, No 1801, Miramar, Havana; tel. 22-2541; telex 511551; Ambassador: MUHAMMAD E. A. ABBOUDA.

Ethiopia: Calle 6, No 318, Miramar, Havana; tel. 22-1260; Ambassador: NADEW ZEKARIAS.

Finland: Avda 5a, No 9202, Miramar, Playa, Apdo. 3304, Havana; tel. 22-4098; telex 511485; Ambassador: TEPPO TAKALA.

France: Calle 15, No 607, Miramar, Havana; tel. 3-5335; telex 511195; Ambassador: JEAN-LOUIS MARFAING.

German Democratic Republic: Calle 13, No 652, entre A y B, Vedado, Havana; tel. 3-6626; telex 511127; Ambassador: KARLHEINZ MÖBUS.

Germany, Federal Republic: Calle 28, No 313, entre 3a y 5a, Miramar, Havana; tel. 22-2560; telex 511433; Ambassador: ROLAND ZIMMERMANN.

Ghana: Avda 5a, No 1808, esq. Calle 20, Miramar, Havana; tel. 29-3513; Ambassador: KOJO AMOO-GOTTFRIED.

Greece: Havana; Ambassador: ELISABETH PAPAZOI.

CUBA — Directory

Guinea: Calle 20, No 504, Miramar, Havana; tel. 2-6428; Ambassador: LAMINE SOUGOULÉ.
Guinea-Bissau: Calle 14, No 313 entre 3 y 5, Miramar, Havana; tel. 29-6689; Ambassador: CONSTANTINO LOPES DA COSTA.
Guyana: Calle 18, No 506, Miramar, Havana; tel. 22-1249; telex 511498; Ambassador: HAROLD SAKADEO.
Holy See: Calle 12, No 514, Miramar, Havana (Apostolic Nunciature); tel. 29-5700; Apostolic Pro-Nuncio: Bishop FAUSTINO SÁINZ MUÑOZ.
Hungary: Calle 19, No 407, Vedado, Havana; tel. 32-6526; telex 511368; Ambassador: ISTVÁN BOGNÁR.
India: Calle 21, No 202, Vedado, Havana; tel. 32-5777; telex 511414; Ambassador: MADHAV KESHAV MANGALMURTI.
Iran: Avda 5a, No 3002, esq. a 30, Miramar, Havana; tel. 29-4575; telex 512186; Ambassador: MAHMOUD SADRI TABAIE.
Iraq: Avda 5a, No 8201, Miramar, Havana; tel. 2-6461; telex 511413; Ambassador: SABAH TALAT KADRAT.
Italy: Paseo No 606 (altos), Vedado, Havana; tel. 30-0378; telex 511352; Ambassador: VINCENZO MANNO.
Japan: Calle 62, esq. 15, Vedado, Havana; tel. 32-5554; telex 511260; Ambassador: RYO KAWADE.
Kampuchea: Avda 5a, No 7001, Miramar, Havana; tel. 29-6779; Ambassador: ROS KONG.
Korea, Democratic People's Republic: Calle 17, No 752, Vedado, Havana; tel. 30-5132; telex 511553; Ambassador: PAK CHUNG-KUK.
Laos: Avda 5a, No 2808, esq. 30, Miramar, Havana; tel. 2-6198; Ambassador: SAMLITH CHOULA.
Lebanon: Calle 5a, No 11004 entre 110 y 112, Miramar, Havana; tel. 22-8382; Chargé d'affaires a.i.: ZOUHAIR KAZZAZ.
Libya: Calle 8, No 309, Miramar, Havana; tel. 2-4892; telex 511570; Ambassador: ALI MUHAMMAD AL-EJILI.
Malta: Calle 20, No 712, 1°, entre 7a y 9a, Miramar, Havana; tel. 2-6978; Chargé d'affaires a.i.: Dr MAURO CASAGRANDI.
Mexico: Calle 12, No 518, Miramar, Havana; tel. 2-8634; telex 511298; Ambassador: ENRIQUE OLIVARES SANTANA.
Mongolia: Calle 66, No 505, Miramar, Havana; tel. 2-5080; Ambassador: BAYARJUUGUIN NANZAD.
Mozambique: 7a Avda, No 2203 entre 22 y 24, Miramar, Havana; tel. 26445; Ambassador: ESPERANZA MACHAVILA.
Netherlands: Calle 8, No 307, Miramar, Havana; tel. 2-6511; telex 511279; Ambassador: COENRAAD FREDRICK STORK.
Nicaragua: Avda 7a, No 1402, Miramar, Havana; tel. 2-6810; Ambassador: GUSTAVO MORENO.
Nigeria: Avda 5a, No 1401, Apdo 6232, Miramar, Havana; tel. 29-1091; telex 1589; Ambassador: PETER OCHALA OSUMAN.
Panama: Calle 26, No 109, Miramar, Havana; tel. 22-4096; Ambassador: MANUEL ORESTES NIETO DE ICAZA.
Peru: Calle 36, No 109 entre 3 y 5, Miramar, Havana; tel. 29-4477; telex 511289; Ambassador: CARLOS ALBERTO HIGUERAS RAMOS.
Philippines: Calle 28, No 705 entre 7 y 9, Miramar, Havana; tel. 2-6870; Ambassador: OPHELIA GONZALES Y SAN AGUSTIN.
Poland: Avda 5, No 4405, Miramar, Havana; tel. 29-1015; Ambassador: CZESŁAW DEGA.
Portugal: Avda 5a, No 6604, Miramar, Havana; tel. 2-6871; telex 511411; Ambassador: CONSTANTINO RIBEIRO VAZ.
Romania: Calle 21, No 307, Vedado, Havana; tel. 32-4303; Ambassador: VICTOR BOLOJAN.
Sierra Leone: Calle 36, No 718 entre 7 y 9, Miramar, Havana; tel. 29-1897; Ambassador: ALIMAMY YAMBA KOMEH.
Spain: Cárcel No 51, esq. Zulueta, Havana; tel. 6-4741; telex 511367; Ambassador: ANTONIO SERRANO DE HARO MEDIALDES.
Sri Lanka: Calle 32, No 307 entre 5 y 7, Miramar, Havana; tel. 22-7992; Ambassador: APPU HENNEDIGE ASOKA DE SILVA.
Sweden: Avda 31, No 14A, Miramar, Havana; tel. 29-8871; telex 511208; Ambassador: JAN STÅHL.
Switzerland: Calzada, Calle L y M, Vedado, Havana; tel. 2-6452; telex 511194; Ambassador: PETER HOLLENWEGER.
Syria: Avda 5, No 7402, Miramar, Havana; tel. 22-5266; telex 511394; Ambassador: MUHAMMAD NAJDY AL-JAZZAR.
Turkey: Avda 1a A, No 4215, entre 42 y 44, Miramar, Havana; tel. 22-3933; telex 511724; Ambassador: KEMAL GIRGIN.
USSR: Calle 13, No 651, Vedado, Havana; tel. 3-3657; Ambassador: YURIY VLADIMIROVICH PETROV.
United Kingdom: Edif. Bolívar, Capdevila No 101–103, e Morro y Prado, Apdo 1069, Havana; tel. 61-5681; telex 511656; Ambassador: DAVID BRIGHTY.
USA: (Relations broken off in 1961); Interests Section: Calzada entre L y M, Vedado, Havana; tel. 32-9551; Counsellor: JOHN TAYLOR.
Uruguay: Calle 14, No 506 entre 5 y 7, Miramar, Havana; tel. 22-7942; Ambassador: BERNARDO R. PIÑEYRUA PARDIÑAS.
Venezuela: 5A Avda, No 7802, Playa, Havana; tel. 29-4631; telex 511384; Ambassador: FRANCISCO CHACIN MEDINA.
Viet-Nam: Avda 5a, No 1802, Miramar, Havana; tel. 2-3367; Ambassador: HOANG LUONG.
Yemen, People's Democratic Republic: Avda 7a, No 2207 esq. 24, Miramar, Havana; tel. 22-2594; telex 511488; Ambassador: MUHAMMAD ABDULRAHMAN HUSSEIN.
Yugoslavia: Calle 42, No 115, Miramar, Havana; tel. 2-4982; Ambassador: MIHAJLO POPOVIĆ.
Zaire: Calle 36, No 716 entre 7 y 9, Miramar, Havana; tel. 29-1580; Ambassador: SIMBA NDOMBE.
Zimbabwe: Hotel Riviera, habitaciones 1713-1715, Havana; tel. 31-8451; Ambassador: AMOS BERNARD MUVENGWA MIDZI.

Judicial System

The judicial system comprises the People's Supreme Court, the People's Provincial Courts and the People's Municipal Courts. The People's Supreme Court exercises the highest judicial authority.

PEOPLE'S SUPREME COURT

The People's Supreme Court comprises the Plenum, the five Courts of Justice in joint session and the Council of Government. When the Courts of Justice are in joint session they comprise all the professional and lay judges, the Attorney-General and the Minister of Justice. The Council of Government comprises the President and Vice-President of the People's Supreme Court, the Presidents of each Court of Justice and the Attorney-General of the Republic. The Minister of Justice may participate in its meetings.

President: Dr JOSÉ RAÚL AMARO SALUP.
Vice-President: (vacant).

Criminal Court:
President: Dr JOSÉ GARCÍA ALVAREZ.
Eight professional judges and 12 lay judges.

Civil and Administrative Court:
President: Dr LUIS M. BUCH RODRÍGUEZ.
Two professional judges and 12 lay judges.

Labour Court:
President: (vacant).
Three professional judges and 12 lay judges.

Court for State Security:
President: Dr EVERILDO DOMÍNGUEZ DOMÍNGUEZ.
Three professional judges and 12 lay judges.

Military Court:
President: JUAN F. GARCÍA GARCÍA.
Three professional judges and 12 lay judges.

Attorney-General: Dr RAMÓN DE LA CRUZ OCHOA.

Religion

There is no established Church, and all religions are permitted, though Roman Catholicism predominates.

CHRISTIANITY

Consejo Ecuménico de Cuba (Ecumenical Council of Cuba): Calle 6, No 273, entre 12 y 13, Vedado, Havana 4; tel. 3-7404; f. 1941; 13 mem. churches; Pres. Dr ADOLFO HAM REYES; Gen. Sec. RAÚL SUÁREZ RAMOS.

The Roman Catholic Church

Cuba comprises two archdioceses and five dioceses. At 31 December 1985, according to diocesan estimates, there were 4,142,000 adherents in the country, representing about 40% of the total population. The number of practising Roman Catholics was estimated at only 100,000 in 1986.

Bishops' Conference: Conferencia Episcopal de Cuba, Calle Habana 152, Apdo 594, Havana; tel. 80-3005; f. 1983; Pres. JAIME

CUBA

Lucas Ortega y Alamino, Archbishop of San Cristóbal de la Habana.
Archbishop of San Cristóbal de la Habana: Jaime Lucas Ortega y Alamino, Calle Habana 152, Apdo 594, Havana; tel. 6-8463.
Archbishop of Santiago de Cuba: Pedro Meurice Estiu, Sánchez Hechevarría 607, Apdo 26, Santiago de Cuba; tel. 5-4801.

The Anglican Communion
Anglicans are adherents of the Iglesia Episcopal de Cuba (Episcopal Church of Cuba).
Bishop of Cuba: Rt Rev. Emilio J. Hernández Albalate, Calle 13, No 874, entre 4 y 6, Vedado, Havana 4.

Protestant Churches
Convención Bautista de Cuba Oriental (Baptist Convention of Eastern Cuba): Apdo 581, Calle 1, No 101, Rpto Fomento, Santiago; tel. 6643; f. 1905; Pres. Rev. Víctor Ruiz Victores; Sec. Rev. Félix Santos Perrand.
Iglesia Metodista en Cuba (Methodist Church in Cuba): Calle 58, No 4305, Havana; tel. 32-0770; autonomous since 1968; 10,000 mems; Bishop Armando Rodríguez Borges.
Iglesia Presbiteriana-Reformada en Cuba (Presbyterian-Reformed Church in Cuba): Apdo 154, Matanzas; autonomous since 1967; 8,000 mems; Gen. Sec. Rev. Dr Sergio Arce.

Other denominations active in Cuba include the Apostolic Church of Jesus Christ, the Bethel Evangelical Church, the Christian Pentecostal Church, the Church of God, the Church of the Nazarene, the Free Baptist Convention, the Holy Pentecost Church, the Pentecostal Congregational Church and the Salvation Army.

The Press

DAILIES

Havana

Granma: Avda General Suárez y Calle Territorial, Plaza de la Revolución José Martí, Apdo 6260, Havana; tel. 70-3521; f. 1965 to replace *Hoy* and *Revolución;* official Communist Party organ; morning and weekly editions; also weekly editions in Spanish, English, French and Portuguese; Editor Enrique Román; circ. 700,000.
Juventud Rebelde: Territorial esq. Gen. Suárez, Plaza de la Revolución, Apdo 6344, Havana; tel. 79-0744; telex 511168; f. 1965; organ of the Young Communist Union; evening; Dir José R. Vidal Valdés; circ. 300,000.
Trabajadores: Territorial esq. Gen. Suárez, Plaza de la Revolución, Havana; tel. 79-0819; telex 511402; f. 1970; organ of the trade-union movement; daily; Dir Jorge Luis Canela Ciurana; circ. 150,000.
Tribuna de la Habana: Territorial esq. Gen. Suárez, Plaza de la Revolución, Havana; tel. 79-0050; f. 1980; Dir Marta Esplugas Arean; circ. 60,000.

Provinces

Adelante: Goyo Benítez 19, Camagüey; f. 1959; morning; Dir Armando Boudet; circ. 32,000.
Ahora: Frexes y Rastro, Holguín; f. 1962; Dir Ezequiel Hernández; circ. 20,000.
Cinco de Septiembre: Calle 35, No 5609, entre 56 y 58, Cienfuegos; f. 1980; Dir Enrique Román Hernández; circ. 6,000.
La Demajagua: Calle Martí 68, Bayamo; f. 1978; Dir José Fernández Vega; circ. 14,000.
Escambray: Adolfo del Castillo 10, Sancti Spíritus; f. 1979; Dir Rafael García Ruiz; circ. 9,300.
Girón: San Juan de Díos 3, Matanzas; f. 1960; Dir Othoniel González Quevedo; circ. 25,000.
Guerrillero: Colón esq. Delicias y Adela Azcuy, Pinar del Río; f. 1969; Dir Ronald Suárez; circ. 21,000.
Invasor: Marcial Gómez 401 esq. Estrada Palma, Ciego de Avila; Dir Digno Rolando Cedeño; circ. 6,000.
Sierra Maestra: Santa Lucía 356, Santiago de Cuba; f. 1959; Dir Orlando Guevara Núñez; circ. 25,000.
Vanguardia: Matanzas; f. 1962; Dir Pedro Hernández Soto; circ. 24,000.
Venceremos: Cuartel 715 entre Narciso López y J. del Sol, Guantánamo; f. 1962; Dir Roberto Torres; circ. 3,000.
Ventiseis: Calle Colón 157 entre Francisco Vega y Julián Santana, Las Tunas; Dir José Infantes Reyes; circ. 4,500.
Victoria: Calle 41 entre 24 y 26, Nueva Gerona, Isla de la Juventud; f. 1967; Dir Nieve Varona Puente; circ. 9,400.

PERIODICALS

ANAP: Línea 351, Vedado, Havana; f. 1961; monthly; information for small farmers; Dir Ricardo Machado; circ. 90,000.
Bohemia: Avda Independencia y San Pedro, Apdo 6000, Havana; tel. 7-2833; telex 511256; f. 1908; weekly; politics; Dir Caridad Miranda Martínez; circ. 312,000.
El Caimán Barbudo: Paseo 613, Vedado, Havana; f. 1966; monthly; cultural; Dir Paquita Armas; circ. 40,000.
Casa de las Américas: Calle 3a y Avda G, Vedado, Havana; tel. 32-3587; telex 511019; f. 1960; every 2 months; literary; Dir Roberto Fernández Retamar; circ. 15,000.
Con la Guardia en Alto: Avda Salvador Allende 601, Havana; tel. 79-4443; f. 1961; monthly; for mems of the Committees for the Defence of the Revolution; Dir Aurelio Alvarez; circ. 60,000.
Cuba Internacional: Avda Simón Bolívar 352, Apdo 3603, Havana; tel. 6-5323; f. 1959; monthly; political; in Spanish and Russian; Dir Luis Suardíaz; circ. 30,000.
Cubatabaco: Amargura 103, 10100 Havana; tel. 61-8453; telex 511123; f. 1972; quarterly; tobacco industry; Dir Zoila Couceyro; circ. 10,000.
Cubatabaco International: Amargura 103, 10100 Havana; tel. 61-8453; telex 511123; f. 1979; 2 a year; tobacco industry; Dir Zoila Couceyro; circ. 3,000 (in English).
Dedeté: Territorial esq. a Gen. Suárez, Plaza de la Revolución, Havana; tel. 79-0952; f. 1969; 2 a month; Dir Carlos Villar; circ. 150,000.
El Deporte, Derecho del Pueblo: Vía Blanca y Boyeros, Havana; tel. 40-6838; telex 511583; f. 1968; monthly; sport; Dir Manuel Vaillant Carpente; circ. 15,000.
Industria Alimenticia: Amargura 103, 10100 Havana; tel. 61-8453; telex 511123; f. 1977; quarterly; food industry; Dir Zoila Couceyro; circ. 10,000.
Juventud Técnica: O'Reilly 251, Havana; tel. 62-5288; f. 1965; monthly; scientific-technical; Dir Nora Rodríguez; circ. 100,000.
Mar y Pesca: San Ignacio 303, Havana; tel. 80-4569; f. 1965; monthly; fishing; Dir Arnaldo Núñez; circ. 44,000.
El Militante Comunista: Calle 11, No 160, Vedado, Havana; tel. 32-7581; f. 1967; monthly; Communist Party publication; Dir Manuel Menéndez; circ. 200,000.
Moncada: Belascoaín esq. Zanja, Havana; tel. 79-7109; f. 1966; monthly; Dir Ricardo Martínez; circ. 70,000.
Muchacha: Galiano 264 esq. Neptuno, Havana; tel. 61-5919; f. 1980; monthly; young women's magazine; Dir Adelina Vázquez; circ. 84,000.
Mujeres: Galiano 264 esq. Neptuno, Havana; tel. 61-5919; f. 1961; monthly; women's magazine; Dir Adelina Vázquez; circ. 250,000.
Opina: Edif. Focsa, M entre 17 y 19, Havana; f. 1979; 2 a month; consumer-orientated; published by Institute of Internal Demand; Dir Eugenio Rodríguez Balari; circ. 500,000.
Palante: Calle 21, No 954, entre 8 y 10, Vedado, Havana; tel. 3-5098; f. 1961; weekly; humorous; Dir Rosendo Gutiérrez Román; circ. 235,000.
Pionero: Calle 17, No 354, Havana 4; tel. 32-4571; f. 1961; weekly; children's magazine; Dir Pedro González (Péglez); circ. 225,000.
Prima Latinoamericano: Reina 352, Havana; tel. 6-5323; f. 1979; monthly; Man. Dir Luis Suardíaz; circ. 25,000 (Spanish), 20,000 (English), 15,000 (Portuguese).
Revolución y Cultura: Ministerio de Cultura, Avda 47, No 2822 esq. 28 y 34, Reparto Kohly, Municipio Playa, Havana; tel. 22-2161; f. 1972; monthly; cultural; Dir Gilda Betancourt Roa; circ. 20,000.
RIL: O'Reilly 358, Havana; tel. 62-0777; telex 511592; f. 1972; bi-monthly; technical; Dir Exec. Council of Publicity Dept, Ministry of Light Industry; Chief Officer Mireya Crespo; circ. 8,000.
Sol de Cuba: Calle 19, No 60 entre M y N, Vedado, Havana 4; tel. 32-9881; telex 511955; f. 1983; every 3 months; Spanish, English and French editions; Gen. Dir Alcides Giro; Editorial Dir Doris Vélez; circ. 50,000.
Somos Jóvenes: Calle 17, No 354, esq. H, Vedado, Havana; tel. 32-4571; f. 1977; monthly; Dir Guillermo Cabrera; circ. 200,000.
Verde Olivo: Avda de Rancho Boyeros y San Pedro, Havana; tel. 79-8373; f. 1959; monthly; organ of the Revolutionary Armed Forces; Dir Eugenio Suárez Pérez; circ. 100,000.

PRESS ASSOCIATIONS

Unión de Periodistas de Cuba: Calle 23, No 452, Vedado, Apdo 6646, Havana; tel. 325561; f. 1963; Sec.-Gen. Ernesto Vera Méndez.

CUBA

Unión de Escritores y Artistas de Cuba (Union of Writers and Artists): Calle 17, No 351, Vedado, Havana; tel. 32-4551; Pres. NICOLÁS GUILLÉN; Exec. Vice-Pres. LISANDRO OTERO.

NEWS AGENCIES

Agencia de Información Nacional (AIN): Calle 23, No 358 esq. a J, Vedado, Havana; tel. 32-1269; national news agency; Dir ROBERTO PAVÓN TAMAYO.

Prensa Latina (Agencia Informativa Latinoamericana, SA): Calle 23, No 201 esq. a N, Vedado, Havana; tel. 32-5561; telex 511132; f. 1959; Dir PEDRO MARGOLLES VILLANUEVA.

Foreign Bureaux

Agence France-Presse (AFP): Calle O, No 202, esq. 23, 5°, Depto 18, Vedado, Havana; tel. 32-0949; telex 511191; Bureau Chief (vacant).

Agencia EFE (Spain): Calle 36, No 110, entre 1a y 3a, Apdo 5, Miramar, Havana; tel. 22-4958; telex 511395; Bureau Chief JUAN J. AZNARES MOZAS.

Agentstvo Pechati Novosti (APN) (USSR): Calle 28, No 510, entre 5a y 7a, Miramar, Havana; tel. 22-4129; Bureau Chief YURI GOLOVIATENKO.

Agenzia Nazionale Stampa Associata (ANSA) (Italy): Calle Paseo 158, Apto 403, Vedado, Havana; tel. 3-7447; telex 511903; Correspondent GIANNINA BERTARELLI.

Allgemeiner Deutscher Nachrichtendienst (ADN) (German Democratic Republic): Edif. M. Fajardo, Calle 17 y M, Apdo 27A, Vedado, Havana; tel. 32-9247; Bureau Chief ROLF HEMPEL.

Bulgarska Telegrafna Agentsia (BTA) (Bulgaria): Edif. Focsa, Calle 17 esq. M, Apdo 22-E, Vedado, Havana; tel. 32-4779; Bureau Chief VASIL MIKOULACH.

Československá tisková kancelář (ČTK) (Czechoslovakia): Edif. Fajardo, Calle 17, Apto 3-A, Vedado, Havana; tel. 32-6101; telex 511397; Bureau Chief PAVEL ZOVADIL.

Inter Press Service (IPS) (Italy): Calle 36A No 121, Bajos, esq. 3a, Apto 1, Miramar, Havana; tel. 22-1981; telex 512247; Correspondent JESÚS GARCÍA CANOURA.

Korean Central News Agency (Democratic People's Republic of Korea): Calle 10, No 613 esq. 25, Apdo 6, Vedado, Havana; tel. 31-4201; Bureau Chief CHANG YON CHOL.

Magyar Távirati Iroda (MTI) (Hungary): Calle 21, 5° esq. 21 y 4, Vedado, Havana; tel. 32-8353; Correspondent TAMÁS SIMÁRDI.

Novinska Agencija Tanjug (Yugoslavia): Calle 5a F, No 9801 esq. 98, Miramar, Havana; tel. 22-7671; Bureau Chief DUSAN DAKOVIĆ.

Polska Agencja Prasowa (PAP) (Poland): Calle E, entre Línea y Calzada, No 158, Apdo 11-A, Vedado, Havana; tel. 32-5930; Bureau Chief RYSZARD RYMASZEWSKI.

Reuters (UK): Edif. Altamira, Apto 116, Calle O, No 58, Vedado, Havana 4; tel. 32-4345; telex 511584; Bureau Chief GILLES TREQUESSER.

Telegrafnoye Agentstvo Sovetskovo Soyuza (TASS) (USSR): Calle 96, No 317, entre 3a y 5a, Miramar, Havana 4; tel. 29-2528; Bureau Chief ALEXANDER VOROPAEV.

Viet-Nam Agency (VNA): Calle 16, No 514, 1°, entre 5a y 7a, Miramar, Havana; tel. 2-4455; Bureau Chief NGUYEN DUY CUONNG.

Xinhua (New China) News Agency (People's Republic of China): Calle G, No 259, esq. 13, Vedado, Havana; tel. 32-4616; telex 511692; Bureau Chief YAN WEIMIN.

Publishers

Casa de las Américas: Calle 3a y Avda G, Vedado, Havana; tel. 32-3587; telex 511019; f. 1960; Latin American literature and social sciences; Dir ARTURO ARANGO.

Ediciones Unión: Calle 17, No 351, Vedado, Havana; tel. 32-8114; publishing arm of the Unión de Escritores y Artistas de Cuba; Cuban literature, art; Dir PEDRO JUAN RODRÍGUEZ.

Editora Política: Belascoaín No 864, esq. a Desagüe, Havana; publishing institution of the Partido Comunista Cubano; Dir HUGO CHINEA.

Editorial Arte y Literatura: Calle O'Reilly, No 4, esq. Tacón, Habana Vieja, Patrimonio de la Humanidad, Havana; tel. 62-3708; telex 512417; f. 1967; attached to the Ministry of Culture; world literature and art; Dir ELIZABETH DÍAZ.

Editorial Abril: Virtudes 257, entre Aguila y Galiano, Centro Habana, Havana; tel. 61-7038; attached to the Union of Young Communists; children's literature; Dir ERNESTO PADRÓN.

Editorial Academia: Industria No 452, esq. a San José, Habana Vieja, Havana; tel. 6-7171; attached to the Cuban Academy of Sciences; scientific and technical; Dir MIRIAM RAYA.

Directory

Editorial Ciencias Médicas: Calle E No 454. esq. a 19, Vedado, Havana; tel. 32-2004; attached to the Ministry of Public Health; books and magazines specializing in the medical sciences; Dir Dr JORGE ALDEREGUÍA.

Editorial Ciencias Sociales: Calle 14, No 4104, entre 41 y 43, Miramar, Playa, Havana; tel. 2-3959; f. 1967; attached to the Ministry of Culture; social and political literature, history, philosophy, juridical sciences and economics; Dir RICARDO GARCÍA PAMPÍN.

Editorial Científico-Técnica: Calle 2, No 58, entre 3a y 5a, Vedado, Havana; tel. 3-9417; attached to the Ministry of Culture; technical and scientific literature; Dir ISIDRO FERNÁNDEZ.

Editorial Gente Nueva: Palacio del Segundo Cabo, Calle O'Reilly No 4, esq. a Tacón, Havana; tel. 6-8341; books for children; Dir ELENIA RODRÍGUEZ.

Editorial José Martí: Apdo 4208, Havana; tel. 32-9838; f. 1983; attached to the Ministry of Culture; foreign language publishing; Dir FÉLIX SAUTIÉ MEDEROS.

Editorial Oriente: José A. Saco, No 356 entre Harman y Río Rosado, Santiago de Cuba; publishes works from the Eastern provinces; general; Dir REINALDO CUESTA.

Editorial Pablo de la Torriente Brau: Calle 23, esq. a I, Plaza de la Revolución, Havana; tel. 32-2965; attached to the Cuban Union of Journalists; specialized texts and the works of Cuban journalists; Dir IRMA ARMAS.

Editorial Pueblo y Educación: Calle 3a A, No 4605, entre 46 y 60, Playa, Havana; tel. 22-1490; textbooks; Dir CATALINA LAJUD HERRERO.

Letras Cubanas: Calle O'Reilly, No 4, Habana Vieja, Havana; attached to the Ministry of Culture; general, particularly classic and contemporary Cuban literature and arts; Dir ALBERTO BATISTA REYES.

Government Publishing Houses

Instituto Cubano del Libro: Palacio del Segundo Cabo, Calle O'Reilly, No 4, esq. a Tacón, Havana; tel. 6-8341; state printing and publishing organization attached to the Ministry of Culture which combines several publishing houses and has direct links with others; presides over the National Editorial Council (CEN); Pres. PABLO PACHECO LÓPEZ.

Oficina de Publicaciones: Calle 17 No 552, esq. a D, Vedado, Havana; tel. 32-1883; attached to the Council of State; speeches and other texts of state and party leaders; Dir PEDRO ALVAREZ TABÍO.

Radio and Television

In 1986 there were an estimated 1,656,000 radio receivers. In 1987 there were an estimated 2,000,000 television receivers in use.

Ministerio de Comunicaciones: Plaza de la Revolución José Martí, Havana; tel. 70-0911; Tech. Dir CARLOS MARTÍNEZ ALBUERNE.

Empresa Cubana de Radio y Televisión (INTERTV): Calle K, No 352, esq. 19, Vedado, Havana; tel. 32-1746; telex 511600; Dir ENRIQUE SOTO RODRÍGUEZ.

Instituto Cubano de Radio y Televisión: Televisión Nacional, Calle 23, No 258 entre L y M, Vedado, Havana 4; tel. 32-7511; telex 511613; f. 1962; Pres. ISMAEL GONZÁLEZ GONZÁLEZ; Vice-Pres. SERGIO CORRIERI HERNÁNDEZ.

RADIO

In 1986 there were 5 national networks and 1 international network; 17 provincial radio stations and 31 municipal radio stations, with a total of 188 transmitters.

Radio Enciclopedia: Calle N, entre 21 y 23, Vedado, Havana; tel. 32-3502; instrumental music programmes; 24 hours daily; Dir MERCEDES DELGADO BARCELÓ.

Radio Habana Cuba: Avda Menocal, No 105, Apdo 7026, Havana; tel. 7-4954; f. 1961; shortwave station; broadcasts in Spanish, English, French, Portuguese, Arabic, Esperanto, Quechua, Guaraní and Creole; Dir PEDRO ROJAS LORENZO.

CMBF—Radio Musical Nacional: Avda Menocal No 105, Havana; tel. 70-4561; telex 1766; f. 1948; national network; classical music programmes; 17 hours daily; Dir JUAN ANTONIO POLA PEDROSA.

Radio Progreso: Avda Menocal, No 105, Havana; tel. 70-4561; national network; mainly entertainment and music; 24 hours daily; Dir PEDRO MANUEL PÉREZ ROQUE.

Radio Rebelde: Calle M entre 23 y 21, Vedado, Havana; Apdo 6277, Havana; tel. 32-7511; telex 511777; f. 1984 (after merger of former Radio Rebelde and Radio Liberación); national network; 24-hour news programmes, music and sports; Dir-Gen. JUAN B. HERNÁNDEZ.

CUBA
Directory

Radio Reloj: Edif. Radiocentro, Calle 23 No 258 entre L y M, Vedado, Havana; tel. 32-9689; telex 511349; f. 1947; national network; 24-hour news service; Dir FAUSTO SUÁREZ TORRES.

TELEVISION

In 1986 there were two national networks with 73 transmitters.

Canal 6: Calle M, No 213 entre 21 y 23, Vedado, Havana; tel. 32-5000; broadcasts in colour; Dir OMAR GONZÁLEZ.

Canal Tele Rebelde: Calle M, No 213 entre 21 y 23, Vedado, Havana; tel. 32-3369; telex 511661; broadcasts in colour; Dir RODOBALDO DÍAZ OLIVERA.

Finance

Comité Estatal de Finanzas: Obispo esq. a Cuba, Havana; tel. 61-1691; f. 1976; charged with the direction and control of the State's financial policy, including preparation of the budget.

BANKING

All banks were nationalized in October 1960. Legislation establishing the national banking system was approved by the Council of State in October 1984.

Central Bank

Banco Nacional de Cuba (National Bank of Cuba): Cuba 402, esq. a Lamparilla, Apdo 736, Havana 1; tel. 62-5361; telex 511822; f. 1950, reorganized 1984; total assets 12,176.8m. pesos (Dec. 1986); sole bank of issue; arranges short- and long-term credits, finances investments and operations with other countries, and acts as the clearing and payments centre; 162 brs throughout the country; Pres. HÉCTOR RODRÍGUEZ LLOMPART; First Vice-Pres OSVALDO FUENTES TORRES (Domestic), LUIS GUTIÉRREZ (International).

Commercial Bank

Banco Financiero Internacional, SA: Calle Línea, No 1, Vedado, Havana; tel. 32-5972; telex 512405; f. 1984; autonomous; capital 10m. pesos (1985); promotes Cuban exports and banking relations; Chair. EMILIO ARAGONÉS; Gen. Man. ARNALDO ALAYÓN.

Savings Bank

Banco Popular del Ahorro: Calle 16, No 306, entre 5a y 3a Avda, Playa, Havana; tel. 22-8240; telex 511608; f. 1983; savings bank; cap. US $30m., dep. $1,678m.; Pres. OSCAR E. ALCALDE; 474 brs.

INSURANCE

State Organizations

Empresa del Seguro Estatal Nacional (ESEN): Obispo No 257, 3°, Apdo 109, 10100 Havana; tel. 62-2963; f. 1981; Man. Dir PEDRO M. ROCHE ALVAREZ.

Seguros Internacionales de Cuba—Esicuba: Cuba No 314, Apdo 79, Havana; tel. 61-8906; telex 511616; f. 1963, reorganized 1986; Chair. and Chief Exec. SALVADOR OROZCO JHONES.

Trade and Industry

IMPORT-EXPORT BOARDS

Alimport (Empresa Cubana Importadora de Alimentos): Infanta 16, 3°, Apdo 7006, Havana; tel. 7-4971; telex 511454; controls import of foodstuffs and liquors; Man. Dir BADITH SAKER.

Autoimport (Empresa Central de Abastecimiento y Venta de Equipos de Transporte Ligero): Galiano 213, entre Concordia y Virtudes, Havana; tel. 62-5926; telex 511417; imports cars, light vehicles, motor cycles and spare parts; Man. Dir RAFAEL LÓPEZ MARTÍNEZ.

Aviaimport (Empresa Cubana Importadora y Exportadora de Aviación): Calle 182, No 126 entre la y 5a, Reparto Flores, Havana; tel. 21-8656; telex 511174; import of aircraft and components; Man. Dir MANUEL GONZÁLEZ FERNÁNDEZ.

Caribex (Empresa Exportadora del Caribe): Edif. No 7, Barlovento, Santa Fe, Playa La Habana, Havana; tel. 22-7498; telex 511471; import and export of seafood and marine products; Man. Dir PEDRO SUÁREZ GAMBE.

Construimport (Empresa Central de Abastecimiento y Venta de Equipos de Construcción y sus Piezas): Carretera de Varona, Km. 1½, Capdevila, Havana; tel. 44-2111; telex 511213; controls the import and export of construction machinery and equipment; Man. Dir JESÚS SERRANO.

Consumimport (Empresa Cubana Importadora de Artículos de Consumo General): Calle 23, No 55, Apdo 6427, Vedado, Havana; tel. 70-3571; telex 511174; imports and exports general consumer goods; Dir EVELIO LASTRA.

Copextel (Corporación Productora y Exportadora de Tecnología Electrónica): Calle 194 y 7a, Siboney, Havana; tel. 20-5818; telex 512459; exports LTEL personal computers and micro-computer software; Man. Dir LUIS J. CARRASCO.

Coprefil (Empresa Comercial y de Producciones Filatélicas): Calle Infanta No 58 esq. P, Vedado, Apdo 1000, Havana 1; tel. 7-8812; telex 512479; imports and exports postage stamps, postcards, calendars, handicrafts, communications equipment, electronics, watches, etc.; Man. Dir JOAQUÍN PÉREZ FERNÁNDEZ.

Cubaelectrónica (Empresa Importadora y Exportadora de Productos de la Electrónica): Calle 22, No 510 entre 5 y 7, Miramar, Havana; tel. 22-7316; imports and exports electronic equipment and devices; Man. Dir LUIS BLANCA.

Cubaequipos (Empresa Cubana Importadora de Productos Mecánicos y Equipos Varios): Calle 23, No 55, Vedado, Havana; tel. 70-2546; telex 511371; imports of mechanical goods and equipment; Man. Dir JORGE DOMÍNGUEZ.

Cubaexport (Empresa Cubana Exportadora de Alimentos y Productos Varios): Calle 23, No 55, Vedado, Apdo 6719, Havana; tel. 70-4521; telex 511178; export of foodstuffs; Man. Dir JOSÉ M. BARROS.

Cubafrutas (Empresa Cubana Exportadora de Frutas Tropicales): Calle 23, No 55, Vedado 4, Apdo 6683, Havana; tel. 70-4521; telex 511849; f. 1979; controls export of fruits, vegetables and canned foodstuffs; Man. Dir JORGE AMARO.

Cubaindustria (Empresa Cubana Exportadora de Productos Industriales): Calle 15, No 410, entre F y G, Vedado, Havana; tel. 32-5522; telex 511677; controls export of industrial products; Man. Dir JORGE REYES.

Cubametales (Empresa Cubana Importadora de Metales, Combustibles y Lubricantes): Infanta 16, 4°, Apdo 6917, Vedado, Havana; tel. 70-2561; telex 511452; controls import of metals (ferrous and non-ferrous), crude oil and oil products; also engaged in the export of oil products and ferrous and non-ferrous scrap; Dir JUAN L. LOZANO.

Cubaniquel (Empresa Cubana Exportadora de Minerales y Metales): Calle 23, No 55, Apdo 6128, Havana; tel. 7-8460; telex 511178; sole exporter of minerals and metals; Man. Dir WALTER S. LEO.

Cubatabaco (Empresa Cubana del Tabaco): O'Reilly No 104, Apdo 6557, Havana; tel. 62-1403; telex 511760; f. 1962; controls export of leaf tobacco, cigars and cigarettes; Man. Dir FRANCISCO PADRÓN.

Cubatécnica (Empresa de Contratación de Asistencia Técnica): Avda 1a, No 4, entre 0 y 2, Hotel Sierra Maestra, Miramar, Havana; tel. 22-2574; telex 511360; controls export and import of technical assistance; Man. Dir JUAN NUIRY SÁNCHEZ.

Cubatex (Empresa Cubana Importadora de Fibras, Tejidos, Cueros y sus Productos): Calle 23, No 55, Vedado, Apdo 7115, Havana; tel. 70-2531; telex 511175; controls import of fibres, textiles, hides and by-products and export of fabric and clothing; Dir SILVIA ORTA.

Cubazucar (Empresa Cubana Exportadora de Azúcar y sus Derivados): Calle 23, No 55, Vedado, Apdo 6647, Havana; tel. 70-3526; telex 511147; f. 1962; controls export of sugar, molasses and alcohol; Man. Dir EMILIANO LEZCANO VIQUEIRA.

Ecimact (Empresa Comercial de Industrias de Materiales, Construcción y Turismo): Avda Independencia y 19 de Mayo, Plaza de la Revolución, Apdo 6039, Havana; tel. 79-5282; telex 511926; controls import and export of engineering services and plant for industrial construction and tourist complexes; Man. Dir JOSÉ FALERO JURE.

Ecimetal (Empresa Comercial para la Industria Metalúrgica y Metal mecánica): Avda Independencia y 19 de Mayo, Havana; tel. 7-5648; telex 511555; f. 1977; controls import of plant for shaping and milling metals; Dir Lic. ERNESTO RAMÍREZ.

Ediciones Cubanas (Empresa de Comercio Exterior de Publicaciones): Obispo 527, Apdo 605, Havana; tel. 6-9174; telex 511424; controls import and export of books and periodicals; Man. Dir JOSÉ MANUEL CASTRO RODRÍGUEZ.

Egrem (Empresa de Grabaciones y Ediciones Musicales): Campanario No 315, entre San Miguel y Neptuno, Apdo 2217, Havana; tel. 62-2998; telex 512171; controls the import and export of records, tapes, printed music and musical instruments; Man. Dir MIGUEL COMAS.

Emexcon (Empresa Exportadora de la Construcción): Calle 25, No 2606, Miramar, Havana; tel. 2-4093; telex 511693; f. 1978; consulting engineer services, contracting, import and export of building materials and equipment; Pres. Lic. ELIODORO PÉREZ.

Emidict (Empresa Especializada Importadora, Exportadora y Distribuidora para la Ciencia y la Técnica): Calle 16, No 102, Miramar,

Havana 13; tel. 2-5782; telex 512233; controls import and export of scientific and technical products and equipment, live animals and ornamental fishes; Man. Dir ABELARDO IGLESIAS.

Empi (Empresa de Promoción e Intercambio): Muralla No 462, entre Cristo y Villegas, Havana; tel. 62-0301; telex 512347; controls import and export of various surplus produce and export of Cuban handicrafts; Man. Dir JUAN FELAIFEL.

Empoft (Empresa Operadora de Fuerza de Trabajo—UNECA): Calle 9a, No 614, entre 6 y 10, Miramar, Havana; tel. 29-4576; telex 511678; manages specialized personnel for building projects; Man. Dir ALEJANDRO GAUBECA.

Empresa Cubana de Acuñaciones: Calle 18 No 306, entre 3 y 5, Miramar, Havana; tel. 20-5921; telex 511146; f. 1977; controls export of coins, base and precious metals; Man. Dir GUILLERMO TRIANA AGUIAR.

Energoimport (Empresa Importadora de Objetivos Electro-energéticos): Calle 7a No 2602, esq. a 26, Miramar, Havana; tel. 2-8156; telex 511812; f. 1977; controls import of equipment for electricity generation; Dir LÁZARO HERNÁNDEZ.

Eprob (Empresa de Proyectos para las Industrias de la Básica): Calle 184 No 129, entre Avda 1 y 5, Avda Rpto Flores, Playa, Apdo 12100, Havana; tel. 21-8074; telex 0511404; f. 1967; exports consulting services and processing of engineering construction projects, consulting services and supplies of complete industrial plants and turn-key projects; Man. Dir ANTONIO RONDA.

Eproyiv (Empresa de Proyectos para Industrias Varias): Avda Independencia y 19 de Mayo, Plaza de la Revolución, Havana; tel. 7-7092; telex 515004; exports consulting services to third-world countries for plant acquisition, tender analysis and tender application; industrial design; Man. Dir RIGOBERTO RAMÍREZ.

Fecuimport (Empresa Cubana Importadora y Exportadora de Ferrocarriles): Avda 7a, No 6209, entre 62 y 66, Miramar, Havana; tel. 2-3764; telex 511174; imports and exports railway equipment; Man. Dir ANTONIO CONEJO MESA.

Ferrimport (Empresa Cubana Importadora de Artículos de Ferretería): Calle 23, No 55, 2°, Apdo 6258, Vedado, Havana; tel. 70-2531; telex 511144; import of ironware; Man. Dir MIGUEL SOSA.

Fondo Cubano de Bienes Culturales: Muralla No 107, esq. S. Ignacio, Havana; tel. 62-0085; telex 512278; controls export of fine handicraft and works of art; Man. Dir NISIA AGÜERO.

ICAIC (Instituto Cubano del Arte e Industria Cinematográficos): Calle 23, No 1155, Vedado, Havana 4; tel. 30-5041; telex 511419; f. 1959; imports and export films and newsreel; Pres. JULIO GARCÍA ESPINOSA.

Imexin (Empresa Importadora y Exportadora de Infraestructura): Avda 5a, No 1007, esq. a 12, Miramar, Havana; tel. 29-2700; telex 511404; f. 1977; controls import and export of infrastructure; Man. Dir RAÚL BENCE.

Imexpal (Empresa Importadora y Exportadora de Plantas Alimentarias, sus Completamientos y Derivados): Calle 22, No 313, entre 3a y 5a, Miramar, Havana; tel. 29-1671; telex 511404; controls import and export of food processing plants and related items; Man. Dir Ing. CONCEPCIÓN BUENO.

Maprinter (Empresa Cubana Importadora y Exportadora de Materias Primas y Productos Intermedios): Infanta 16, Apdo 2110, Havana; tel. 70-0975; telex 511453; controls import and export of raw materials and intermediate products; Man. Dir CARLOS DANTÍN ACOSTA.

Maquimport (Empresa Cubana Importadora de Maquinarias y Equipos): Calle 23, No 55, Vedado, Apdo 6052, Havana; tel. 70-2546; telex 511371; controls import of machinery and equipment; Man. Dir ARMANDO VERA GIL.

Marpesca (Empresa Cubana Importadora y Exportadora de Buques Mercantes y de Pesca): Conill No 580, esq. Avda 26, Nuevo Vedado, Havana; tel. 30-1971; telex 511687; imports and exports ships and port and fishing equipment; Man. Dir REYNALDO LUIS CABRERA.

Medicuba (Empresa Cubana Importadora y Exportadora de Productos Médicos): Máximo Gómez 1, esq. a Egido, Havana; tel. 6-7936; telex 511658; enterprise for the export and import of medical and pharmaceutical products; Man. Dir ORLANDO ROMERO.

Quimimport (Empresa Cubana Importadora de Productos Químicos): Calle 23, No 55, Vedado, Apdo 6088, Havana; tel. 70-8066; telex 511283; controls import of chemical products; Man. Dir LESLIE E. PATTERSON.

Tecnoimport (Empresa Cubana Importadora y Exportadora de Productos Técnicos): Infanta 16, Apdo 7024, Havana; tel. 22-3861; telex 511572; imports technical products; Man. Dir MANUEL GARCÍA ROBÉS.

Tractoimport (Empresa Central de Abastecimiento y Venta de Maquinaria Agrícola y sus Piezas): Avda Rancho Boyeros y Calle 100, Apdo 6301, Havana; tel. 203473; telex 511162; f. 1960 for the import of tractors and agricultural equipment; also exports pumps and agricultural implements; Man. Dir MANUEL CASTRO DEL AGUILA.

Transimport (Empresa Central de Abastecimiento y Venta de Equipos de Transporte Pesados y sus Piezas): Calle 102 y Avda 63, Marianao, Apdo 6665, 11500 Havana; tel. 20-0325; telex 511150; f. 1962; controls import and export of vehicles and transportation equipment; Man. Dir LORENZO ORTEGA.

UNECA (Unión de Empresas Constructoras Caribe): Avda 9a, No 614, entre 6 y 10, Miramar, Havana; tel. 29-4576; telex 511678; undertakes construction work abroad; Man. Dir ANGEL GÓMEZ TRUEBA.

CHAMBER OF COMMERCE

Cámara de Comercio de la República de Cuba: Calle 21, No 661, Apdo 4237, Vedado, Havana; tel. 30-3356; telex 511752; f. 1963; mems include all Cuban foreign trade enterprises and the most important agricultural and industrial enterprises; Pres. JULIO GARCÍA OLIVERAS.

AGRICULTURAL ORGANIZATION

Asociación Nacional de Agricultores Pequeños—ANAP (National Association of Small Farmers): Calle 1, No 206, Vedado, Havana; tel. 32-4541; telex 511294; f. 1961; 201,000 mems (July 1984); Pres. JOSÉ RAMÍREZ CRUZ; Vice-Pres. PEDRO MANUEL ROCHE.

TRADE UNIONS

All workers have the right to become members of a national trade union according to their industry and economic branch.

The following industries and labour branches have their own unions: Agriculture, Chemistry and Energetics, Civil Workers of the Revolutionary Armed Forces, Commerce and Gastronomy, Communications, Construction, Culture, Education and Science, Food, Forestry, Health, Light Industry, Merchant Marine, Mining and Metallurgy, Ports and Fishing, Public Administration, Sugar, Tobacco and Transport.

Central de Tradajadores de Cuba—CTC (Confederation of Cuban Workers): Palacio de los Trabajadores, San Carlos y Peñalver, Havana; tel. 7-4901; telex 511403; f. 1939; affiliated to WFTU and CPUSTAL; 17 national trade unions affiliated; Gen. Sec. ROBERTO VEIGA MENÉNDEZ; 2,936,457 mems (1987).

Transport

The Ministry of Transport controls all public transport.

RAILWAYS

The total length of railways in 1988 was 12,563 km, of which 7,743 km were used by the sugar industry. The remaining 4,820 km (of which 151 km are electrified) are public service railways operated by Ferrocarriles de Cuba. All railways were nationalized in 1960.

Ferrocarriles de Cuba: Ministerio del Transporte, Avda Independencia y Tulipán, Havana; tel. 70-7751; f. 1960; operates public services; under direct management of the Minister of Transport; divided as follows:

División Occidente: serves Pinar del Río, Ciudad de la Habana, Havana Province and Matanzas.

División Centro: serves Villa Clara, Cienfuegos and Sancti Spíritus.

División Centro-Este: serves Camagüey, Ciego de Avila and Tunas.

División Oriente: serves Santiago de Cuba, Granma, Guantánamo and Holguín.

División Camilo Cienfuegos: serves part of Havana Province and Matanzas.

ROADS

The total length of paved roads in 1987 was 13,112 km, of which 575 km were motorway. The Central Highway runs from Pinar del Río in the west to Santiago, for a length of 1,144 km. In addition to this paved highway, there are a number of secondary and 'farm-to-market' roads. A small proportion of these secondary roads is paved, but in 1985 33,443 km of roads were unpaved, and many can be used by motor vehicles only during the dry season.

SHIPPING

Cuba's principal ports are Havana (which handles 60% of all cargo), Santiago de Cuba, Cienfuegos, Nuevitas, Matanzas, Antilla, Guayabal and Mariel. Maritime transport has developed rapidly since 1959, and in 1988 there was a merchant fleet of 118 ships. In 1988 there was a coastal trading and deep-sea fleet of 82 ships. Cuba's merchant fleet had a total capacity of 1,394,203 dwt in 1988. A supertanker port is under construction at Matanzas, with co-operation from Soviet and French enterprises. A major development of the port of Nuevitas has been planned.

Empresa Consignataria Mambisa: Lamparilla No 2, 2°, Apdo 1785, Havana; tel. 6-8311; telex 511197; shipping agent, shipchandlers, bunker suppliers; Man. Dir JULIO AIRA PRADO.

Empresa Cubana de Fletes (Cuflet): Calle Oficios No 170, entre Teniente Rey y Amargura, Apdo 6755, Havana; tel. 6-7355; telex 512181; freight agents for Cuban cargo; Man. Dir ISAAC CAMACHO AGUILERA.

Empresa de Navegación Caribe (Navecaribe): Lamparilla 2, 4°, Apdo 1784, Havana; tel. 62-3605; telex 511262; f. 1965; operates Cuban coastal fleet; Dir Lic. OTTO ROCA MORALOBOS.

Empresa de Navegación Mambisa: San Ignacio No 104, Apdo 543, Havana; tel. 61-7901; telex 51578; operates dry cargo, reefer and bulk carrier vessels; Gen. Man. GUMERSINDO GONZÁLEZ FELIÚ.

Flota Cubana de Pesca: Ensenada de Pote y Atarés, Havana; tel. 9-4360; telex 51189; fishing fleet; Dir EMIGDIO BÁEZ VIGO.

There are regular passenger and cargo services by Cuban vessels between Cuba and northern Europe, the Baltic, the Mediterranean, the Black Sea and Japan and by Soviet, Bulgarian and Czechoslovak vessels between Cuba and the Baltic and the Black Sea. A regular Caribbean service is maintained by Empresa Multinacional del Caribe (Namucar). The Cuban fleet also runs regular container services to northern Europe, the Mediterranean and the Black Sea.

CIVIL AVIATION

There are international airports at Havana, Santiago de Cuba, Camagüey and Varadero. Improvements to Havana and Santiago de Cuba airports are scheduled for completion in 1990.

Empresa Cubana de Aviación (Cubana): Calle 23 y P, No 64, Apdo 4299, La Rampa, Vedado, Havana; tel. 74961; telex 512273; f. 1929; international services to Angola, Argentina, Barbados, Belgium, Canada, Czechoslovakia, Dominican Republic, France, German Democratic Republic, Grenada, Guinea-Bissau, Guyana, Jamaica, Mexico, Moscow, Mozambique, Nicaragua, Panama, Peru, Spain, Switzerland and Trinidad; internal services from Havana to 11 other cities; Gen. Man. (vacant); fleet: 11 Ilyushin 62, 3 Ilyushin 18, 5 Tupolev B-2, 3 Tupolev 154M, 2 Ilyushin 76, 18 Antonov 24, 20 Antonov An-26 and 8 YAK 40.

Tourism

Tourism began to develop after 1977, with the repeal of travel restrictions by the USA, and Cuba subsequently attracted European tourists. An estimated 225,000 tourists visited Cuba in 1988, compared with only 4,000 in 1973. Under the 1986–90 Development Plan, some 500m. pesos were to be invested in the sector, which was expected to become one of the principal sources of foreign exchange by 1990.

Empresa de Turismo Internacional (Cubatur): Calle 23, No 156, entre N y O, Apdo 6560, Vedado, Havana; tel. 32-4521; telex 511212; Dir BERNARDO BARRERA HERNÁNDEZ.

Empresa de Turismo Nacional (Viajes Cuba): Calle 20, No 352, entre 21 y 23, Vedado, Havana; tel. 30-0587; telex 511366; f. 1981; Dir ELEUTERIO GUERRA GÓMEZ.

Instituto Nacional de Turismo (INTUR): Avda de Malecón y G, Vedado, Apdo 4239, Havana 4; tel. 32-0571; telex 511238; f. 1959; Pres. RAFAEL SED PÉREZ; Vice-Pres ENRIQUE RODRÍGUEZ, OROSMÁN QUINTERO.

Atomic Energy

Cuba's first nuclear power station is under construction at Juraguá, Cienfuegos, with help from the USSR and will have a capacity of 1,668 MW. The first 417-MW reactor is due to begin operations in 1990/91. In 1983 plans were announced to modernize the national research institute. The institute will also receive a 10 MW reactor.

Comisión de Energía Atómica Cuba (CEAC): Apdo 6795, Havana 6; f. 1980; concerned with the peaceful uses of atomic energy; Pres. JOSÉ R. FERNÁNDEZ; Exec. Sec. FIDEL CASTRO DÍAZ-BALART.

Instituto de Investigaciones Nucleares: Managua, Havana; Dir Ing. RAIMUNDO FRANCO PARELLADA.

CYPRUS

Introductory Survey

Location, Climate, Language, Religion, Flag, Capital

The Republic of Cyprus is an island in the eastern Mediterranean Sea, about 100 km south of Turkey. The climate is mild, although snow falls in the mountainous south-west between December and March. Temperatures in Nicosia are generally between 5°C (41°F) and 36°C (97°F). About 75% of the population speak Greek and almost all of the remainder speak Turkish. The Greek-speaking community is overwhelmingly Christian, and almost all Greek Cypriots adhere to the Orthodox Church of Cyprus, while most of the Turks are Muslims. The national flag (proportions 3 by 2) is white, with a gold map of Cyprus, garlanded by olive leaves, in the centre. The capital is Nicosia.

Recent History

A guerrilla war against British rule in Cyprus was begun in 1955 by Greek Cypriots seeking unification (*Enosis*) with Greece. Their movement, the National Organization of Cypriot Combatants (EOKA), was led politically by Archbishop Makarios III, head of the Greek Orthodox Church in Cyprus, and militarily by Gen. George Grivas. Archbishop Makarios was suspected by the British authorities of being involved in EOKA's campaign of violence, and in March 1956 he and three other leaders of the *Enosis* movement were deported. They were released in 1957 but not allowed to return to Cyprus. After a compromise agreement between the Greek and Turkish communities, a constitution for an independent Cyprus was finalized in 1959. Following his return from exile, Makarios was elected the country's first President in December 1959. Cyprus became independent on 16 August 1960, although the United Kingdom retained sovereignty over two military base areas.

Following a constitutional dispute, the Turks withdrew from the central government in December 1963 and serious intercommunal fighting occurred. In 1964 a UN peace-keeping force was established to keep Greeks and Turks apart. The effective exclusion of the Turks from political power led to the creation of separate administrative, judicial and legislative organs for the Turkish community. Discussions concerning the establishment of a more equitable constitutional arrangement began in 1968, and continued sporadically for six years, never producing an agreement, as the Turks favoured some form of federation, while the Greeks advocated a unitary state. Each community received military aid from its mother country, and the Greek Cypriot National Guard was controlled by officers of the Greek Army.

In 1971 Gen. Grivas returned to Cyprus, revived EOKA, and began a terrorist campaign for *Enosis*, directed against the Makarios Government and apparently supported by the military regime in Greece. Grivas died in January 1974, and in June Makarios ordered a purge of EOKA sympathizers from the police, National Guard and civil service, accusing the Greek regime of subversion. On 15 July President Makarios was deposed by a military coup, led by Greek officers of the National Guard, who appointed Nicos Sampson, an extremist Greek Cypriot politician and former EOKA terrorist, to be President. Makarios escaped from the island on the following day and travelled to the UK. At the invitation of Rauf Denktaş, the Turkish Cypriot leader, the Turkish army intervened to protect the Turkish community and to prevent Greece from using its control of the National Guard to take over Cyprus. Turkish troops landed on 20 July and rapidly occupied the northern third of Cyprus, dividing the island along what became the Attila Line, which runs from Morphou through Nicosia to Famagusta. President Sampson resigned on 23 July, and Glavkos Klerides, the President of the House of Representatives, became acting Head of State. The military regime in Greece collapsed on the same day. In December Makarios returned to Cyprus and resumed the presidency. However, the Turkish Cypriots' effective control of northern Cyprus enabled them to establish a *de facto* government, and in February 1975 to declare the establishment of the 'Turkish Federated State of Cyprus' ('TFSC'), with Denktaş as President.

President Makarios died in August 1977. He was succeeded by Spyros Kyprianou, a former Minister of Foreign Affairs, who had been President of the House of Representatives since 1976. In September 1980 a ministerial reshuffle by President Kyprianou caused the powerful communist party, AKEL, to withdraw its support from the ruling Democratic Party. Kyprianou therefore lost his overall majority in the House of Representatives. At the next general election, held in May 1981, AKEL and the Democratic Rally each won 12 seats in the House. The Democratic Party, however, won only eight seats, so the President still depended on the support of AKEL.

In the 'TFSC' a new cabinet was formed in December 1978 under Mustafa Çağatay of the National Unity Party (NUP), a former minister. In the elections held in June 1981, President Rauf Denktaş was returned to office, but his party, the NUP, lost its previous majority, and the government that was subsequently formed by Çağatay was defeated in December. In March 1982 a coalition government, comprising the NUP, the Democratic People's Party and the Turkish Unity Party, was formed by Çağatay.

In September 1980 the intermittent UN-sponsored intercommunal peace talks were resumed. In August 1981 the Turkish Cypriots offered to hand back 3%-4% of the 35% of the area of Cyprus which they controlled, and also to resettle 40,000 of the 200,000 refugees who fled from northern Cyprus in 1974. The constitutional issue remained the main problem: the Turkish Cypriots want equal status for the two communities, with equal representation in government and strong links with the mother country, while the Greeks, although they agree to the principle of an alternating presidency, favour a strong central government, and object to any disproportionate representation for the Turkish community, who form less than 20% of the population. In November 1981 a UN plan (involving a federal council, an alternating presidency and the allocation of 70% of the island to the Greek community) was presented, but talks faltered in February 1982, when the Greek Prime Minister, Andreas Papandreou, called for the withdrawal of all Greek and Turkish troops and an international conference, rather than the continuation of intercommunal talks.

In February 1983 Kyprianou was re-elected President, with the support of AKEL, gaining 56.5% of the votes. In May the UN General Assembly voted in favour of the withdrawal of Turkish troops from Cyprus, whereupon President Denktaş of the 'TFSC' threatened to boycott any further intercommunal talks and to seek recognition for the 'TFSC' as a sovereign state; simultaneously it was announced that the Turkish lira was to replace the Cyprus pound as legal tender in the 'TFSC'. UN proposals for a summit meeting between Denktaş and Kyprianou in late 1983 were unsuccessful.

On 15 November 1983 the 'TFSC' made a unilateral declaration of independence as the 'Turkish Republic of Northern Cyprus' ('TRNC'), with Denktaş continuing as President. An interim government was formed in December, led by Nejat Konuk (Prime Minister of the 'TFSC' from 1976 to 1978 and President of the Legislative Assembly from 1981), pending elections in 1984. Like the 'TFSC', the 'TRNC' was recognized only by Turkey, and the declaration of independence was condemned by the UN Security Council. Conciliatory proposals by the 'TRNC', including the resettlement of 40,000 Greek Cypriot refugees in Famagusta, under UN administration, were rejected by the Cyprus Government in January 1984, while the 'TRNC', in turn, refused to accept Kyprianou's proposal that the Turkish Cypriots should be allowed to administer 25% of the island, on condition that the declaration of independence be withdrawn. The establishment of diplomatic links between the 'TRNC' and Turkey in April 1984 was followed by a formal rejection by the 'TRNC' of UN proposals for a suspension of its declaration of independence prior to further talks. In August and September the Greek and Turkish Cypriots conferred (separately) with the UN Secretary-General, whose aim was to bring the two sides together for direct negotiations. The Turkish Cypriots reiterated that they would accept the proposed creation of a two-zone federation only if power were to be shared equally between the north and the south. In December 1984, after a third round of negotiations, the leaders of the two communities, Spyros Kyprianou and Rauf Denktaş, agreed to hold a summit meeting in January 1985. No agreement was reached, despite some concessions by the Turkish Cypriots. Kyprianou came under severe criticism from some members of the House of Representatives over the failure of the talks.

In July 1985 the UN Secretary-General presented further proposals, which the Greek Cypriots accepted. The proposals envisaged a bi-zonal federal Cyprus (in which the Turkish Cypriots would occupy 29% of the land), with a Greek Cypriot president and a Turkish Cypriot vice-president, both having limited power of veto over federal legislation. Ministers would be appointed in a ratio of seven Greek Cypriots to three Turkish Cypriots, and one important ministry would always be held by a Turkish Cypriot. There would be two assemblies: an upper house, with a 50:50 community representation, and a lower house, weighted 70:30 in favour of the Greek Cypriots. A tripartite body, including one non-Cypriot voting member, would have the final decision in constitutional disagreements. However, serious problems remained over the crucial questions of a timetable for the withdrawal of Turkey's troops and of the nature of international guarantees for a newly-united Republic of Cyprus. This plan was given the guaranteed support of foreign governments (in effect the USA), which were to provide financial help. The Turkish Cypriots rejected these proposals, as they wanted Turkish troops to remain on the island indefinitely, in order to protect their interests, and they felt that any peace settlement should include Turkey as a guarantor.

In November 1985, following a debate on President Kyprianou's leadership, the House of Representatives was dissolved. A general election for an enlarged House was held in December. The Democratic Rally won 19 seats, President Kyprianou's Democratic Party won 16 seats and AKEL won 15 seats. AKEL and the Democratic Rally therefore failed to secure the two-thirds majority required to amend the Constitution and thus challenge the President's tenure of power. The election result was seen as a vindication of President Kyprianou's policies.

During 1984 a 'TRNC' constituent assembly, comprising the members of the Legislative Assembly and 30 nominated members, drew up a new constitution, which was approved by a referendum in May 1985. At the 'TRNC' presidential election on 9 June, Rauf Denktaş was returned to office with over 70% of the vote. A general election followed on 23 June, with the NUP, led by Dr Derviş Eroğlu, winning 24 of the 50 seats in the Legislative Assembly. In July Dr Eroğlu became Prime Minister of the 'TRNC', leading a coalition Government formed by the NUP and the Communal Liberation Party. In July 1986 Turgut Özal, the Prime Minister of Turkey, made his first visit to the 'TRNC', thus increasing Greek Cypriot fears of further international recognition of the Turkish Cypriot state.

Further meetings to discuss the draft peace plan were held in March 1986. On this occasion the Turkish Cypriots accepted the plan (which was, as before, based on the idea of establishing a bi-zonal federal republic, with specified posts and ratios for the Greek and Turkish Cypriot participants in the federal government), while the Greek Cypriots did not. Their principal objections were that the plan failed to envisage: the withdrawal of the Turkish troops in Cyprus prior to implementation of the plan; the removal from Cyprus of settlers from the Turkish mainland; the provision of suitable international guarantors for the settlement, with the exclusion of Turkey; and the assurance of the 'three basic freedoms', namely the right to reside, move and work anywhere in Cyprus. The Greek Cypriot leaders, as well as Prime Minister Papandreou of Greece, still favoured a 'summit' meeting between Kyprianou and Denktaş, or an international conference. President Denktaş, however, stated that he would not accept an international conference that treated the Greek Cypriots as the official government of Cyprus and the Turkish Cypriots as a minority population. He declared that, should such a conference be arranged, he would seek international recognition of the 'TRNC'. By 1986 the UN Secretary-General had presented three sets of peace proposals in less than two years, to no avail, and in 1987 the problems appeared to remain intractable. Moreover, the increase in the number of Turkish forces deployed in northern Cyprus gave rise to growing concern. In June 1987, shortly before the UN Security Council voted to extend the mandate of the UN Peace-keeping Force, Sweden announced that, with effect from January 1988, it was to withdraw its troops from the island, owing to lack of financial support. In July 1987 it was reported that the Cyprus Government had proposed to the UN Secretary-General that the Cypriot National Guard be dissolved, and orders for military equipment cancelled, in exchange for the withdrawal of Turkish forces from the island. In an address to the UN General Assembly in October, President Kyprianou proposed the creation of an international peace-keeping force to replace the armed forces of both the Greek and Turkish Cypriots. President Denktaş of the 'TRNC', however, maintained that negotiations on the establishment of a federal bi-zonal republic should precede any demilitarization.

The first round of voting in the presidential election took place in the Greek Cypriot zone on 14 February 1988. There were four principal candidates, including the incumbent President Kyprianou, who was seeking his third consecutive term. The three other main candidates were: Georghios Vassiliou, who presented himself as an independent, but who was unofficially supported by the communist party, AKEL; Glavkos Klerides, the president of the conservative DISY; and Dr Vassos Lyssarides, the president of the socialist EDEK. Since no candidate obtained more than 50% of the total votes cast, a second poll was held a week later, to decide between the two candidates who had received the most votes—Glavkos Klerides and Georghios Vassiliou. In the second round of voting, Vassiliou was elected as the new President by a narrow margin. President Vassiliou took office later in February and quickly expressed his willingness to enter into direct informal dialogue with the Turkish Cypriot leader. He also promised to re-establish the National Council, which was to include representatives from all the main Greek Cypriot political parties, to discuss plans for the settlement of the Cyprus problem. The only member of Kyprianou's Council of Ministers to retain his post in Vassiliou's new administration, which was sworn in at the end of February, was Georghios Iakovou, the Minister of Foreign Affairs.

In April 1988 the Prime Minister of the 'TRNC', Dr Derviş Eroğlu, and the other members of the Council of Ministers resigned from their posts, following a disagreement between the NUP and its coalition partner (since September 1986), the New Dawn Party, which was demanding greater representation in the Government. At the request of President Denktaş, however, Eroğlu resumed his post and formed a new Council of Ministers in May, comprising mainly NUP members but also including independents. The new Government received a vote of confidence from the Legislative Assembly in the following month.

In March 1988 President Vassiliou rejected various goodwill proposals, which were submitted, via the UN, by President Denktaş of the 'TRNC', and which included a plan to form committees to study the possibilities of intercommunal co-operation. Following a meeting with the newly-revived National Council in June, however, President Vassiliou agreed to a proposal by the UN Secretary-General to resume intercommunal talks, without pre-conditions, with President Denktaş of the 'TRNC', in the capacity of the leaders of two communities. After consulting the Turkish Government in July, Denktaş also approved the proposal. Consequently, the impasse between the two sides was ended, and a Cyprus 'summit' meeting took place in Geneva on 24 August, under the auspices of the UN. At this 'summit', which was the first such meeting between Greek and Turkish Cypriot leaders since January 1985, President Vassiliou and President Denktaş resumed direct talks on a settlement of all aspects of the Cyprus problem. As a result of this meeting, the two leaders began the first round of substantive direct negotiations, under UN auspices, in Nicosia on 15 September. A target date of 1 June 1989 was agreed for the conclusion of a comprehensive political settlement. By November 1988, however, it was apparent that no real progress had been achieved as a result of the discussions. A second round of direct negotiations between the two leaders commenced in Nicosia in December.

Government

The 1960 Constitution provided for a system of government in which power would be shared by the Greek and Turkish communities in proportion to their numbers. This Constitution remains in force officially but since the ending of Turkish

CYPRUS

Introductory Survey

participation in the Government in 1963, and particularly since the creation of a separate Turkish area in northern Cyprus in 1974, each community has administered its own affairs, refusing to recognize the authority of the other's Government. The Greek Cypriot administration claims to be the Government of all Cyprus, and is generally recognized as such, although it has no Turkish participation. The northern area is under the *de facto* control of the 'Turkish Republic of Northern Cyprus' (for which a new constitution was drawn up in 1984 by a constituent assembly, and approved by a referendum in May 1985). Each community has its own President, Council of Ministers, legislature and judicial system.

Defence

The formation of the National Guard was authorized by the House of Representatives in 1964, after the withdrawal of the Turkish members. Men between the ages of 18 and 50 are liable to 29 months' conscription. In June 1988 it comprised an army of 13,000 regulars, mainly composed of Cypriot conscripts but with some seconded Greek Army officers and NCOs, and 60,000 reserves. There is also a Greek Cypriot paramilitary force of 3,666 armed police. In June 1988 the 'TRNC' had an army of about 3,000 regulars and 15,000 reserves. Men between the ages of 18 and 50 are liable to 24 months' conscription. In 1988 it was estimated that the 'TRNC' forces were being supported by about 27,000 Turkish troops. Cyprus also contains the UN Peace-keeping Force (UNFICYP, see p. 45) of 2,125 (May 1988) and the British military bases at Akrotiri, Episkopi and Dhekelia.

Economic Affairs

In 1987, according to estimates by the World Bank, Cyprus's gross national product (GNP) measured at average 1985–87 prices, was US $3,532m., equivalent to $5,210 per head. The Cypriot economy was gravely affected by the events of 1974. However, despite the loss of 80% of the island's citrus fruit groves, 30% of its factories, 60% of the tourist installations and the main port of Famagusta, the economy of the southern (Greek Cypriot) part of the island made a remarkable recovery. The northern third of the island, under Turkish Cypriot control, is closely linked to the economy of Turkey (the source of about 46% of the area's imports), and has almost no economic contacts with the south of the island. The unilateral declaration of independence by the Turkish Cypriots in November 1983 reinforced the international economic embargo which has caused serious problems for the northern sector. The northern economy continues to rely heavily on aid from Turkey: the estimated annual budget expenditure for 1988 was set at TL 170,121.1m., of which TL 57,000m. (about 33%) was to come from Turkey. Grants from the Greek Government to the Greek Cypriot sector amounted to C£7.4m., or 2% of budget revenue, in 1987.

The southern economy is basically agricultural, with potatoes, grapes, barley and citrus fruit as the principal crops. Although citrus and cereal production has remained low because of reduced areas of cultivation, production of other fruits and vegetables, particularly potatoes, has expanded. Vegetables and fruit accounted for 21.8% of domestic exports in 1987, compared with 25.8% in 1986. Export earnings from citrus fruit were C£15.5m. in 1987, compared with C£14.1m. in 1986, while exports of potatoes, the single most important crop, increased from C£20.2m. in 1986 to C£22.2m. in 1987.

The construction sector developed rapidly in the Greek Cypriot area after the 1974 Turkish invasion, with the need to rehouse refugees and to re-establish the tourist industry. The tourist sector became the fastest growing industry in the 1980s, and revenue from tourism was equivalent to 24.7% of total GDP in 1985. In 1986 the tourist industry became the Republic of Cyprus's largest source of income, with receipts totalling C£257m. Manufacturing also recovered strongly after 1974. Clothing and footwear accounted for 38.1% of domestic exports in 1987. Although manufacturing has gradually declined as a proportion of GDP, the sector continues to expand in real terms. The value of the output of manufactured goods increased from C£132.2m. in 1980 to C£168m. in 1987. The restructuring of industry created a large demand for imports, and this, combined with a parallel decline in exports, brought the trade deficit, which was C£60m. in 1976, to C£460m. in 1984. The trade deficit remained at a high level, despite a reduction in the cost of visible imports (including a 39% reduction in the value of petroleum imports), and totalled C£398.9m. in 1986. Because of an 8% increase in the cost of imports, however, the trade deficit rose to C£413.4m. in 1987. An increase in revenues from tourism helped to reduce the current-account deficit by 96%, to C£3.5m., in 1986. In 1987 a surplus of C£50m. was recorded. This was the first current-account surplus for 20 years, and was largely due to a 14% increase in exports and the continuing growth in tourism. The rate of economic growth remained stable at around 3% in 1986, and increased to 7.2% in 1987. Unemployment has increased, but from only 1.8% of the labour force in 1979 to 3.4% in 1987. The rate of inflation fell from 5% in 1985 to 1.2% in 1986 (the lowest rate for 20 years). It increased, however, to 2.8% in 1987, owing to a higher level of economic activity.

In the Turkish-controlled north, emphasis has been laid on restoring the production and export of citrus fruit from damaged groves, relying on seasonal labour from the Turkish mainland, on expanding the tourism and industrial sectors, and on improving the communications network. Exports from the Turkish Cypriot area totalled US $52.0m. in 1986, compared with $45.8m. in 1985. The two largest sources of export revenue are citrus fruit and textiles and clothing. Imports were worth $141.6 in 1985 and $153.2m. in 1986. Inflation exceeded 100% in 1984, compared with 33.8% in 1983, but it stood at 60% in 1987. In 1985 GNP per head was estimated at US $1,620 (compared with $1,350 in 1977), but this was still less than one-third of the level in the south of the island. The third Five-Year Plan, covering 1988–92, envisages an average annual growth rate of 7% in GDP. In 1987 the Turkish Electricity Authority announced that preliminary work had started on the construction of the 'TRNC's' first thermal power station.

There was a significant alteration in the Greek Cypriot trading pattern in the mid-1980s, with EEC countries assuming the dominant role from Arab countries (chiefly Lebanon, Egypt, the states of the Arabian peninsula, and Libya). The Arab countries' share of total Greek Cypriot exports declined from C£102m. (48% of total export revenue) in 1985 to C£79.7m. (35.3%) in 1987, whereas Greek Cypriot exports to EEC countries increased from C£68.4m. (32.4% of total export revenue), in 1985 to C£104.4m. (46.2%) in 1987. EEC countries are also Cyprus's main suppliers, providing 57% (C£405m.) of total imports in 1987. The United Kingdom is the single main trading partner of both the government-controlled and the Turkish-occupied areas, although in recent years this trade has been threatened by EEC regulations. Since 1972, Cyprus has been linked with the European Community by an association agreement (see p. 147), although the initial lifting of Community restrictions on most Cypriot industrial products was not followed, as planned, by the removal of barriers to agricultural produce. In November 1985 the EEC Council of Ministers approved the admission of Cyprus to a full customs union with the Community. In October 1987, after concluding an agreement covering the terms of such a union, the two sides signed a protocol, which came into effect on 1 January 1988. This protocol envisaged the attainment by Cyprus of a full customs union with the EEC, in two stages, within 15 years. The agreement covers the whole of the island, despite President Denktaş's opposition to it. There has been strong disagreement with the EEC, however, over the recognition of the Turkish Cypriot north in trade agreements. Trade between the Greek Cypriots and the EEC is expected to increase as a result of the signing of the customs union protocol, providing new opportunities for local industries, but, simultaneously, presenting them with the challenge of competing with EEC exports to Cyprus.

Social Welfare

A comprehensive social insurance scheme, covering every working male and female and their dependants, is in operation. It includes provisions for protection against arbitrary and unjustified dismissal, for industrial welfare and for tripartite co-operation in the formulation and implementation of labour policies and objectives. Benefits and pensions from the social insurance scheme cover unemployment, sickness, maternity, widows, orphans, injury at work, old age and death. An improved scheme, involving income-related contributions and benefits, was introduced in October 1980. The provision of health services to Greek Cypriots in 1981 included 134 hospital establishments, with a total of 3,535 beds, and 601 physicians. Of total expenditure by the central Government in the Greek Cypriot area in 1986, C£30.9m. (6.8%) was for health services, and a further C£97.8m. (21.6%) for social security and welfare.

In 1986 the state health service in the Turkish Cypriot zone included 16 hospital establishments, with a total of 758 beds and 132 physicians.

Education

Greek Cypriot education, under the control of the Greek communal chamber until 31 March 1965, is now organized by the Ministry of Education. Elementary education, which is compulsory and available free of charge, is provided in six grades for children between five and 11 years of age. In the towns and certain large villages there are separate junior schools consisting of the first three grades. Secondary education is free for all years of study and lasts six years, with three years at the Gymnasiun being followed by three years at a technical school or a Lyceum. There are three types of Lyceum: classical, science, and economic. There are no universities in southern Cyprus, but in 1988 there were plans to construct a new university in Nicosia by the end of 1990. In 1986/87 about 10,500 Cypriot students were studying in universities abroad. Higher education for teachers, technicians, engineers, hoteliers and caterers, foresters, nurses and health inspectors is provided by technical and vocational colleges. Expenditure on education by the central Government in the Greek Cypriot area was C£51.4m. (11.4% of total spending) in 1986.

Education in the Turkish Cypriot zone is controlled by the 'TRNC'. It is divided into two sections formal (nursery, primary, secondary and higher) and adult education. A university, the Eastern Mediterranean University, was opened in November 1986 near Famagusta. It has three faculties: engineering, arts and sciences, and business and economics. There is also a Teachers' Training College. A total of 2,023 students (991 from Turkey) enrolled at the university for the academic year 1988/89.

Public Holidays

1989: 2 January (for New Year's Day), 6 January (Epiphany)*, 19 January (Name Day)*, 13 March (Green Monday)*, 25 March (Greek Independence Day)*, 23 April (National Sovereignty and Children's Day)†, 28 April-1 May (Easter)*, 1 May (Workers' Day and Spring Day)†, 7 May (Ramazam Bayram—end of Ramadan)†, 19 May (Youth and Sports Day)†, 14 July (Kurban Bayram—Feast of the Sacrifice)†, 20 July (Peace and Freedom Day, anniversary of the Turkish invasion in 1974)†, 1 August (Communal Resistance Day)†, 30 August (Victory Day)†, 1 October (Independence Day)*, 13 October (Birth of the Prophet)†, 28 October (Greek National Day)*, 29 October (Turkish Republic Day)†, 15 November (TRNC Day)†, 25-26 December (Christmas)*.

1990: 1 January (New Year's Day), 6 January (Epiphany)*, 19 January (Name Day)*, 26 February (Green Monday)*, 25 March (Greek Independence Day)*, 13-16 April (Easter)*, 23 April (National Sovereignty and Children's Day)†, 27 April (Ramazam Bayram—end of Ramadan)†, 1 May (Workers' Day and Spring Day)†, 19 May (Youth and Sports Day)†, 4 July (Kurban Bayram—Feast of the Sacrifice)†, 20 July (Peace and Freedom Day, anniversary of the Turkish invasion in 1974)†, 1 August (Communal Resistance Day)†, 30 August (Victory Day)†, 1 October (Independence Day)*, 2 October (Birth of the Prophet)†, 28 October (Greek National Day)*, 29 October (Turkish Republic Day)†, 15 November (TRNC Day)†, 25-26 December (Christmas)*.

* Greek and Greek Orthodox.
† Turkish and Turkish Muslim.

Weights and Measures

Although the imperial and the metric systems are understood, Cyprus has a special internal system:

Weights: 400 drams = 1 oke = 2.8 lb (1.27 kg.).
44 okes = 1 Cyprus kantar.
180 okes = 1 Aleppo kantar.

Capacity: 1 liquid oke = 2.25 pints (1.28 litres).
1 Cyprus litre = 5.6 pints (3.18 litres).

Length and Area: 1 pic = 2 feet (61 cm).

Area: 1 donum = 14,400 sq ft (1,338 sq m).

Statistical Survey

Source: Department of Statistics and Research, Ministry of Finance, Nicosia; tel. (02) 303286; telex 3399.

Note: Since July 1974 the northern part of Cyprus has been under Turkish occupation, so some of the statistics relating to subsequent periods may not cover the whole island. Some separate figures for the 'TRNC' are given on p. 823.

AREA AND POPULATION

Area: 9,251 sq km (3,572 sq miles), incl. Turkish-occupied region.

Population: 612,851 (males 306,144; females 306,707), incl. estimate for Turkish-occupied region, at census of 30 September 1976; 642,731 (males 319,562; females 323,169), incl. estimate for Turkish-occupied region, at census of 1 October 1982; 680,400 (estimate for mid-1987).

Ethnic Groups (estimates for mid-1987): Greeks 544,700, Turks 126,900, others 8,800; Total 680,400.

Principal Towns (population at 1 October 1982): Nicosia (capital) 149,100 (excl. Turkish-occupied portion); Limassol 107,200; Larnaca 48,300; Famagusta (Gazi Mağusa) 39,500 (mid-1974); Paphos 20,800.

Births and Deaths (provisional estimates, 1987): Live births 12,600 (birth rate 18.5 per 1,000); Deaths 6,100 (death rate 8.9 per 1,000).

Employment (government-controlled area, 1986): Agriculture, hunting, forestry and fishing 35,400; Manufacturing 43,800; Construction 21,800; Trade, restaurants and hotels 48,600; Other services 68,100; Total (incl. others) 220,100.

AGRICULTURE, ETC.

Principal Crops (provisional, government-controlled area, '000 metric tons, 1987): Wheat 13, Barley 120, Potatoes 150, Carobs 7, Olives 7, Grapes 173, Oranges 47, Grapefruit 65, Lemons 36.

Livestock (government-controlled area, '000 head, December 1987): Cattle 45, Sheep 330, Goats 232, Pigs 266, Chickens 2,400.

Fishing (government-controlled area, metric tons, live weight, 1987): Total catch 2,650.

MINING

Exports (government-controlled area, metric tons, 1987): Asbestos 22,340, Iron pyrites 21,905, Gypsum 11,749, Terra umbra 8,150.

INDUSTRY

Selected Products (government-controlled area, 1987): Cement 853,699 metric tons, Bricks 47.9 million, Mosaic tiles 1,612,000 sq metres, Cigarettes 3,718 million, Footwear (excluding plastic and semi-finished shoes) 7,797,000 pairs, Beer 27.1 million litres, Wines 22.3 million litres, Intoxicating liquors 3.9 million litres.

FINANCE

Currency and Exchange Rates: 100 cents = 1 Cyprus pound (Cyprus £). *Coins:* ½, 1, 2, 5, 10, 20, 50 cents; 1 pound. *Notes:* 50 cents; 1, 5 and 10 pounds. *Sterling and US Dollar Equivalents* (30 September 1988): £1 sterling = 82.75 Cyprus cents; US $1 = 48.94 Cyprus cents; Cyprus £100 = £120.85 sterling = $204.35. *Average exchange rate* (US $ per Cyprus £): 1.6407 in 1985; 1.9353 in 1986; 2.0802 in 1987.

Budget (estimates, Cyprus £, government-controlled area, year ending 31 December 1987): *Revenue:* Direct taxes 118,065,000, Indirect taxes 161,559,990, Sale of goods and services 23,201,125, Interest, dividends, rents and royalties 14,350,700, Transfers 16,602,640, Greek government grants 7,400,000, Loan proceeds 27,432,174, Other 7,266,480, Total 375,878,109; *Expenditure:* Agriculture and forests 5,449,395, Water development 5,070,448, Public works 6,047,601, Cyprus army and tripartite agreement 4,827,034, Customs and excise 11,063,678, Public debt charges 116,188,447, Pensions and grants 14,099,330, Medical 28,940,701, Police 26,873,747, Subsidies, subventions and contributions 72,222,900,

CYPRUS

Education grants 50,479,293, Other 91,925,510, Total 433,188,079. **1988** (estimates, Cyprus £ million, government-controlled area): Revenue 386.8; Expenditure 483.2.

Development Budget (Cyprus £'000, government-controlled area, 1987): Water development 26,598, Road network 11,335, Harbours 11, Agriculture 2,836, Commerce and industry 1,193, Airports 1,343. **1988** (Cyprus £ '000): Total estimated expenditure 68,394.

International Reserves (US $ million at 31 December 1987): Gold 16.4; Reserve position in IMF 6.6, Foreign exchange 904.2; IMF special drawing rights 0.4; Total 927.6.

Money Supply (government-controlled area, Cyprus £ million at 31 December 1987): Currency outside banks 142.6, Demand deposits at deposit money banks 172.3; Total money 314.9.

Cost of Living (Retail Price Index, government-controlled area; base: 1981 = 100): 124.47 in 1985; 126.00 in 1986; 129.52 in 1987.

Gross Domestic Product in Purchasers' Values (government-controlled area, Cyprus £ million at current prices): 1,480.7 in 1985; 1,607.9 in 1986; 1,791.6 in 1987.

Balance of Payments (Cyprus £ million, government-controlled area, 1987): Merchandise exports f.o.b. 271.2, Merchandise imports f.o.b. −638.5, Trade balance −367.3; Receipts from services and transfers 685.9, Payments for services and transfers −268.6, Current balance 50.0; Long-term loans (net) −9.7, Other long-term capital (net) 23.5, Short-term capital (net) −2.0, Net errors and omissions −48.8. Total (net monetary movements) 13.0.

EXTERNAL TRADE

Principal Commodities (Cyprus £ '000, government-controlled area only, distribution by SITC, 1987): Imports c.i.f.: Food and live animals 73,913 (Cereals and cereal preparations 21,733); Petroleum, petroleum products, etc. 82,049 (Crude petroleum oils, etc. 40,618, Refined petroleum products 41,431); Chemicals and related products 68,444; Basic manufactures 198,138 (Textile yarn, fabrics, etc. 74,533); Machinery and transport equipment 174,218 (Road vehicles and parts, excl. tyres, engines and electrical parts, 62,450); Miscellaneous manufactured articles 60,851; Total (incl. others) 711,419. Exports f.o.b.: Fresh or simply preserved vegetables 27,377 (Fresh or chilled potatoes 22,223); Fresh or dried fruit and nuts 21,004 (citrus fruit 15,525); Beverages and tobacco 10,947 (Beverages 4,394); Basic manufactures 15,172; Machinery and transport equipment 7,759; Clothing and accessories (excl. footwear) 68,621 (Men's and boys' outer garments of non-knitted textile fabrics, excl. headgear, gloves, stockings, etc., 14,102, Women's, girls' and infants' outer garments of non-knitted textile fabrics, excl. headgear, gloves, stockings, etc., 31,323); Footwear 16,018; Total (incl. others) 222,306. Figures for exports exclude (Cyprus £ '000): Re-exports 50,016; Stores for ships and aircraft 25,670.

Principal Trading Partners (Cyprus £'000, government-controlled area, 1987): Imports c.i.f.: France 35,290; Federal Republic of Germany 65,237; Greece 54,483; Iraq 31,498; Italy 81,519; Japan 72,403; Spain 17,123; Syria 1,146; USSR 13,483; United Kingdom 101,646; USA 32,248; Total (incl. others) 711,419. Exports f.o.b.: Egypt 11,764; Federal Republic of Germany 12,552; Greece 19,284; Kuwait 5,024; Lebanon 22,307; Libya 24,081; Saudi Arabia 17,305; USSR 9,238; United Arab Emirates 8,957; United Kingdom 66,541; USA 5,412; Total (incl. others) 271,701. Figures for exports exclude (Cyprus £'000): Stores for ships and aircraft 25,670; Unspecified items sent by parcel post 621.

TRANSPORT

Road Traffic (licensed motor vehicles, government-controlled area, 1987): Private cars 137,804, Taxis and self-drive cars 4,205, Lorries and buses 56,091, Motor cycles 43,437, Tractors, etc. 9,933, Total 251,470.

Shipping (government-controlled area, 1987): Freight traffic ('000 metric tons, excluding goods loaded and unloaded at Larnaca and Paphos airports): Goods loaded 2,241, Goods unloaded 3,939; Vessels (steam or motor vessels and sailing vessels entered, '000 net regd tons): 12,839.

Civil Aviation (Cyprus Airways, 1987): Kilometres flown 14,361,224, Passenger arrivals 418,462, Passenger departures 419,085, Freight landed (metric tons) 2,338, Freight cleared (metric tons) 8,193.

TOURISM

Foreign Visitors by Country of Origin (excluding one-day visitors and visitors to the Turkish-occupied zone, 1987): Federal Republic of Germany 77,188, Greece 47,668, Israel 6,020, Lebanon 47,750, Scandinavian countries 195,163, United Kingdom 309,150, USA 11,031; Total (incl. others) 948,551.

EDUCATION

1987/88 (government-controlled area): Kindergarten: 396 institutions, 14,401 pupils; Primary schools: 373 institutions, 54,612 pupils; Secondary schools (Gymnasia and Lyceums): 73 institutions, 2,758 teachers, 33,662 pupils; Technical: 11 institutions, 344 teachers, 3,485 pupils; Teacher-training: 1 institution, 76 teachers, 637 students; Other post-secondary: 15 institutions, 243 teachers, 2,782 students.

'Turkish Republic of Northern Cyprus'*

Sources: Office of the London Representative of the 'Turkish Republic of Northern Cyprus', 28 Cockspur St, London SW1 (tel. (01) 839-4577; telex 8955363); K. Rüstem and Brother, North Cyprus Almanack, 1987; Kıbrıs (Northern Cyprus Weekly); Prime Ministry, State Planning Organization, Statistics and Research Department.

AREA AND POPULATION

Area: 3,355 sq km (1,295 sq miles).

Population (official estimate): 162,679 (mid-1986).

Ethnic Groups (estimates, 1985): Turks 158,225, Greeks 733, Maronites 368, Others 961; Total 160,287.

Principal Towns (estimated population within the municipal boundary, mid-1985): Lefkoşa (Nicosia) 37,400 (Turkish-occupied area only); Gazi Mağusa (Famagusta) 19,428; Güzelyurt (Morphou) 10,179; Girne (Kyrenia) 6,902; Lefka 3,785.

Births and Deaths (provisional, 1985): Birth rate 21.0 per 1,000; Death rate 8.8 per 1,000.

Employment (1986): Agriculture, forestry and fishing 20,320; Industry 6,497; Construction 4,581; Trade and tourism 5,923; Transport and communications 4,554; Financial institutions 1,564; Business and personal services 4,932; Public Services 14,881; Total 63,252. **Total unemployed:** 1,556.

AGRICULTURE, ETC.

Principal Crops ('000 metric tons, 1986): Wheat 9.9, Barley 66.2, Chick-peas 1.5, Potatoes 22.2, Tomatoes 1.3, Artichokes 1.0, Water melons 5.4, Sweet melons 2.3, Carobs 12.3, Olives 3.9, Lemons 20.1, Grapefruit 37.2, Oranges 122.2, Tangerines 1.3.

Livestock ('000 head, 1986): Cattle 14.1, Sheep 201.6, Goats 63.1, Chickens 1,582.5.

Livestock Products ('000 metric tons, 1986): Sheep's and goats' milk 12.3, Cows' milk 20.1, Mutton and lamb 2.2, Goats' meat 0.8, Beef 1.2, Poultry meat 2.2, Wool 0.3.

Fishing (metric tons, 1985); Total catch 300.

FINANCE

Currency and Exchange Rates: Turkish currency: 100 kuruş = 1 Turkish lira (TL) or pound. Coins: 1, 5, 10, 25 and 50 kuruş; 1, 2½, 5 and 10 liras. Notes: 5, 10, 20, 50, 100, 500, 1,000 and 5,000 liras. Sterling and Dollar Equivalents (30 September 1988): £1 sterling = 2,791.3 liras; US $1 = 1,650.7 liras; 10,000 Turkish liras = £3.583 = $6.058. Average Exchange Rate (liras per US dollar): 522.0 in 1985; 674.5 in 1986; 857.2 in 1987.

Draft Budget (estimates, million Turkish liras, year ending 31 December 1988): Revenue: Internal revenue 76,300.0, Aid from Turkey 57,000.0, Loans 36,821.1, Total 170,121.1; Expenditure: Personnel 61,954.5, Other current expenditure 9,033.5, Investment projects 50,925.0, Transfers 39,708.1, Defence 8,500.0, Total 170,121.1.

Development Budget (estimate, million Turkish liras, 1986): Total expenditure 11,196.

Cost of Living (Retail Price Index; base: December 1984 = 100): 143.04 in 1985.

Gross Domestic Product (GDP) by Economic Activity (million Turkish liras, 1986): Agriculture, forestry and fishing 28,016.0; Mining and quarrying 1,425.1; Manufacturing 17,814.0; Electricity and water 1,274.3; Construction 15,892.6; Wholesale and retail trade 34,729.4; Restaurants and hotels 9,281.4; Transport and communications 13,407.6; Finance 8,512.4; Ownership of dwellings 5,407.0; Business and personal services 10,443.8; Government services 34,107.8; Sub-total 180,311.4; Import duties 11,465.0; GDP in purchasers' values 191,776.4.

Balance of Payments (US$ million, 1986): Merchandise exports f.o.b. 52.0; Merchandise imports c.i.f. −153.2; *Trade balance* −101.2; Services and unrequited transfers (net) 79.6; *Current balance* −21.6; Capital movements (net) 34.9; Net errors and omissions −9.2; *Total* (net monetary movements) 4.1.

EXTERNAL TRADE

Principal Commodities (US $ million, 1986): *Imports c.i.f.:* Food and live animals 17.1, Beverages and tobacco 7.3, Crude materials (inedible) except fuels 3.3, Mineral fuels, lubricants, etc. 11.3, Chemicals 13.2, Basic manufactures 49.3, Machinery and transport equipment 37.8, Miscellaneous manufactured articles 13.9; Total 153.2. *Exports f.o.b.:* Citrus fruits 28.5, Potatoes 3.8, Live animals 2.3, Other agricultural products 2.3, Industrial products 14.7, Minerals 0.4; Total 52.0.

Principal Trading Partners (US $ million, 1986): *Imports:* Turkey 70.1, EEC 51.3, Total (incl. others) 153.2; *Exports:* Turkey 7.7, EEC 34.7, Total (incl. others) 52.0.

TRANSPORT

Road Traffic (licensed motor vehicles, 1986): Cars (incl. taxis and self-drive cars) 23,749, Lorries and buses 8,243, Motor cycles 8,403, Tractors, etc. 4,978; Total 45,373.

Shipping (1986): Freight traffic ('000 metric tons): Goods loaded 194.7, Goods unloaded 437.5; Vessels entered 1,375.

Civil Aviation (Turkish Cypriot Airlines Co, Ltd, 1985): Kilometres flown 1,126,848, Passenger arrivals 67,693, Passenger departures 68,392, Freight landed (metric tons) 351, Freight cleared (metric tons) 207.

TOURISM

Visitors (1987): 184,337 (incl. 147,965 from Turkey); **Accommodation** (1986): Hotels 25, Hotel beds 4,200; **Receipts** (US $ million, 1987) 56.1.

EDUCATION

1986/87: Secondary schools and lycées 35 institutions, 706 teachers, 11,103 pupils; Technical lycées and technical secondary schools 10 institutions, 192 teachers, 1,748 pupils; Higher education 3 institutions (including one university), 74 teachers, 1,623 students.

* Note: Following a unilateral declaration of independence in November 1983, the 'Turkish Federated State of Cyprus' became known as the 'Turkish Republic of Northern Cyprus'.

Directory

The Constitution

The Constitution, summarized below, entered into force on 16 August 1960, when Cyprus became an independent republic.

THE STATE OF CYPRUS

The State of Cyprus is an independent and sovereign Republic with a presidential regime.

The Greek Community comprises all citizens of the Republic who are of Greek origin and whose mother tongue is Greek or who share the Greek cultural traditions or who are members of the Greek Orthodox Church.

The Turkish Community comprises all citizens of the Republic who are of Turkish origin and whose mother tongue is Turkish or who share the Turkish cultural traditions or who are Muslims.

The official languages of the Republic are Greek and Turkish.

The Republic shall have its own flag of neutral design and colour, chosen jointly by the President and the Vice-President of the Republic.

The Greek and the Turkish Communities shall have the right to celebrate respectively the Greek and the Turkish national holidays.

THE PRESIDENT AND VICE-PRESIDENT

Executive power is vested in the President and the Vice-President, who are members of the Greek and Turkish Communities respectively, and are elected by their respective communities to hold office for five years.

The President of the Republic as Head of the State represents the Republic in all its official functions; signs the credentials of diplomatic envoys and receives the credentials of foreign diplomatic envoys; signs the credentials of delegates for the negotiation of international treaties, conventions or other agreements; signs the letter relating to the transmission of the instruments of ratification of any international treaties, conventions or agreements; confers the honours of the Republic.

The Vice-President of the Republic, as Vice-Head of the State, has the right to be present at all official functions; at the presentation of the credentials of foreign diplomatic envoys; to recommend to the President the conferment of honours on members of the Turkish Community, which recommendation the President shall accept unless there are grave reasons to the contrary.

The election of the President and the Vice-President of the Republic shall be direct, by universal suffrage and secret ballot, and shall, except in the case of a by-election, take place on the same day but separately.

The office of the President and of the Vice-President shall be incompatible with that of a Minister or of a Representative or of a member of a Communal Chamber or of a member of any municipal council including a Mayor or of a member of the armed or security forces of the Republic or with a public or municipal office.

The President and Vice-President of the Republic are invested by the House of Representatives.

The President and the Vice-President of the Republic in order to ensure the executive power shall have a Council of Ministers composed of seven Greek Ministers and three Turkish Ministers. The Ministers shall be designated respectively by the President and the Vice-President of the Republic who shall appoint them by an instrument signed by them both. The President convenes and presides over the meetings of the Council of Ministers, while the Vice-President may ask the President to convene the Council and may take part in the discussions.

The decisions of the Council of Ministers shall be taken by an absolute majority and shall, unless the right of final veto or return is exercised by the President or the Vice-President of the Republic or both, be promulgated immediately by them.

The executive power exercised by the President and the Vice-President of the Republic conjointly consists of:

Determining the design and colour of the flag.

Creation or establishment of honours.

Appointment of the members of the Council of Ministers.

Promulgation by publication of the decisions of the Council of Ministers.

Promulgation by publication of any law or decision passed by the House of Representatives.

Appointments and termination of appointments as in Articles provided.

Institution of compulsory military service.

Reduction or increase of the security forces.

Exercise of the prerogative of mercy in capital cases.

Remission, suspension and commutation of sentences.

Right of references to the Supreme Constitutional Court and publication of Court decisions.

Address of messages to the House of Representatives.

The executive powers which may be exercised separately by the President and Vice-President include: designation and termination of appointment of Greek and Turkish Ministers respectively; the right of final veto on Council decisions and on laws concerning foreign affairs, defence or security; the publication of the communal laws and decisions of the Greek and Turkish Communal Chambers respectively; the right of recourse to the Supreme Constitutional Court; the prerogative of mercy in capital cases; and addressing messages to the House of Representatives.

THE COUNCIL OF MINISTERS

The Council of Ministers shall exercise executive power in all matters, other than those which are within the competence of a Communal Chamber, including the following:

General direction and control of the government of the Republic and the direction of general policy.

Foreign affairs, defence and security.

Co-ordination and supervision of all public services.

Supervision and disposition of property belonging to the Republic.

Consideration of Bills to be introduced to the House of Representatives by a Minister.

Making of any order or regulation for the carrying into effect of any law as provided by such law.

Consideration of the Budget of the Republic to be introduced to the House of Representatives.

THE HOUSE OF REPRESENTATIVES

The legislative power of the Republic shall be exercised by the House of Representatives in all matters except those expressly reserved to the Communal Chambers.

The number of Representatives shall be 50, subject to alteration by a resolution of the House of Representatives carried by a majority comprising two-thirds of the Representatives elected by the Greek Community and two-thirds of the Representatives elected by the Turkish Community.

Out of the number of Representatives 70% shall be elected by the Greek Community and 30% by the Turkish Community separately from amongst their members respectively, and, in the case of a contested election, by universal suffrage and by direct and secret ballot held on the same day.

The term of office of the House of Representatives shall be for a period of five years.

The President of the House of Representatives shall be a Greek, and shall be elected by the Representatives elected by the Greek Community, and the Vice-President shall be a Turk and shall be elected by the Representatives elected by the Turkish Community.

THE COMMUNAL CHAMBERS

The Greek and the Turkish Communities respectively shall elect from amongst their own members a Communal Chamber.

The Communal Chambers shall, in relation to their respective Community, have competence to exercise legislative power solely with regard to the following:

All religious, educational, cultural and teaching matters.

Personal status; composition and instances of courts dealing with civil disputes relating to personal status and to religious matters.

Imposition of personal taxes and fees on members of their respective Community in order to provide for their respective needs.

THE PUBLIC SERVICE AND THE ARMED FORCES

The public service shall be composed as to 70% of Greeks and as to 30% of Turks.

The Republic shall have an army of 2,000 men, of whom 60% shall be Greeks and 40% shall be Turks.

The security forces of the Republic shall consist of the police and gendarmerie and shall have a contingent of 2,000 men. The forces shall be composed as to 70% of Greeks and as to 30% of Turks.

OTHER PROVISIONS

The following measures have been passed by the House of Representatives since January 1964, when the Turkish members withdrew:

The amalgamation of the High Court and the Supreme Constitutional Court (see Judicial System section).

The abolition of the Greek Communal Chamber and the creation of a Ministry of Education.

The unification of the Municipalities.

The unification of the Police and the Gendarmerie.

The creation of a military force by providing that persons between the ages of 18 and 50 years can be called upon to serve in the National Guard.

The extension of the term of office of the President and the House of Representatives by one year intervals from July 1965 until elections in February 1968 and July 1970 respectively.

New electoral provisions; abolition of separate Greek and Turkish rolls; abolition of post of Vice-President, which was re-established in 1973.

The Government*

HEAD OF STATE

President: GEORGHIOS VASSILIOU (took office 28 February 1988).

COUNCIL OF MINISTERS
(January 1989)

Minister of Foreign Affairs: GEORGHIOS IAKOVOU.
Minister of Finance: GEORGHIOS SYRIMIS.
Minister of the Interior: CHRISTODOULOS VENIAMIN.
Minister of Defence: ANDREAS ALONEFTIS.
Minister of Agriculture and Natural Resources: ANDREAS GAVRIELIDES.
Minister of Health: PANIKOS PAPAGEORGHIOU.
Minister of Education: ANDREAS PHILIPPOU.
Minister of Commerce and Industry: TAKIS NEMITSAS.
Minister of Communication and Works: NAKOS PROTOPAPAS.
Minister of Labour and Social Insurance: TAKIS CHRISTOFIDES.
Minister of Justice: CHRISTODOULOS CHRYSANTHOU.

* Under the Constitution of 1960, the vice-presidency and three posts in the Council of Ministers are reserved for Turkish Cypriots. However, there has been no Turkish participation in the Government since December 1963. In 1968 President Makarios announced that he considered the office of vice-president in abeyance until Turkish participation in the Government is resumed, but the Turkish community elected Rauf Denktaş vice-president in February 1973.

MINISTRIES

All Ministries are in Nicosia.

Ministry of Agriculture and Natural Resources: Loukis Akritas Ave, Nicosia; tel. (02) 402171; telex 4660.
Ministry of Commerce and Industry: 6 Andreas Araouzos St, Nicosia; tel. (02) 403441; telex 2283.
Ministry of Communications and Works: Dem. Severis Ave, Nicosia; tel. (02) 402161; telex 3678.
Ministry of Defence: tel. (02) 403595; telex 3553.
Ministry of Education: Greg. Afxentiou St, Nicosia; tel. (02) 403331; telex 5760.
Ministry of Finance: tel. (02) 403201; telex 3399.
Ministry of Foreign Affairs: 18-19 Dem. Severis Ave, Nicosia; tel. (02) 402307; telex 2366.
Ministry of Health: tel. (02) 403243.
Ministry of the Interior: tel. (02) 402423.
Ministry of Justice: 1 Dioghenous St, Engomi, Nicosia; tel. (02) 402355.
Ministry of Labour and Social Insurance: Byron Ave, Nicosia; tel. (02) 403481.

PRESIDENT

Election, 14 February 1988* and 21 February 1988

Candidates	Votes	%
GEORGHIOS VASSILIOU (Independent)	167,834 (100,748)	51.6 (30.1)
GLAVKOS KLERIDES (Democratic Rally)	157,228 (111,504)	48.4 (33.3)
SPYROS KYPRIANOU (Democratic Party)	— (91,335)	— (27.3)
Dr VASSOS LYSSARIDES (EDEK-Socialist Party)	— (30,685)	— (9.2)
THRASSOS GEORGHIADES (Independent)	— (189)	— (0.1)
Total	325,062 (334,461)	100.0 (100.0)

*Figures from the first round of voting appear in brackets.

House of Representatives

The House of Representatives originally consisted of 50 members, 35 from the Greek community and 15 from the Turkish community, elected for a term of five years. In January 1964 the Turkish members withdrew and set up the 'Turkish Legislative Assembly of the Turkish Cypriot Administration' (see p. 827). The Greek membership of the House was expanded from 35 to 56 members at the 1985 elections.

Elections for the Greek Representatives, 8 December 1985

Party	Votes	% of Votes	Seats
Democratic Rally	107,223	33.56	19
Democratic Party	88,322	27.65	16
AKEL (Communist Party)	87,628	27.43	15
EDEK (Socialist Party)	35,371	11.07	6
Independents	923	0.29	—
Total	319,467	100.00	56

Political Organizations

Anorthotiko Komma Ergazomenou Laou (AKEL) (Progressive Party of the Working People): POB 1827, 6 Akamas St, Nicosia; tel. (02) 441121; f. 1941; successor to the Communist Party of Cyprus (f. 1926); pro-Moscow; supports demilitarized, non-aligned and independent Cyprus; over 14,000 mems; Sec.-Gen. DEMETRIS CHRISTOFIAS.

Demokratiko Komma (DIKO) (Democratic Party): 16 Stasikratou St, Balmona Bldg, Nicosia; tel. (02) 472002; f. 1976; supports settlement of the Cyprus problem based on UN resolutions; Pres. SPYROS KYPRIANOU; Sec.-Gen. ALEXIS GALANOS.

Demokratikos Synagemos (DISY) (Democratic Rally): 7 Stasandrou St, Nicosia; tel. (02) 449791; f. 1976; opposition party; absorbed Democratic National Party (DEK) in 1977 and New Democratic Front (NEDIPA) in 1988; advocates greater active involvement by the West in the settlement of the Cyprus problem; 10,000 mems; Pres. GLAVKOS KLERIDES; Gen. Sec. ALEKOS MARKIDIS.

Enosi Kentrou (EK) (Centre Union): 12 Diagorou St, Nicosia; tel. (02) 461961; f. 1981; Pres. TASSOS PAPADOPOULOS.

Ethniki Demokratiki Enosi Kyprou (EDEK)—Socialistiko Komma (Cyprus National Democratic Union): POB 1064, 2 Bouboulinas St, Nicosia; tel. (02) 450121; telex 3181; f. 1969; the Socialist Party of Cyprus; supports independent, non-aligned, unitary, demilitarized Cyprus; advocates the establishment of a socialist structure; Pres. Dr VASSOS LYSSARIDES.

Komma Phileleftheron (Liberal Party): POB 7289, Flat 202/203, 95 Archbishop Makarios III Ave, Nicosia; tel. (02) 452117; telex 2483; f. 1986; supports settlement of the Cyprus problem based on UN resolutions; Pres. NIKOS A. ROLANDIS.

Diplomatic Representation

EMBASSIES AND HIGH COMMISSIONS IN CYPRUS

Australia: 4 Annis Komninis St, 2nd Floor, Nicosia; tel. (02) 473001; telex 2097; High Commissioner: E. J. STEVENS.

Bulgaria: 15 St Paul St, Nicosia; tel. (02) 472486; telex 2188; Ambassador: MILAN MARINOV.

China, People's Republic: POB 4531, 27 Clementos St, Nicosia; tel. (02) 473041; Ambassador: LUO YISU.

Cuba: 29 Regas Phereos St, Acropolis, Nicosia; tel. (02) 427211; telex 2306; Ambassador: GUILLERMO GÓMEZ.

Czechoslovakia: POB 1165, 7 Kastorias St, Nicosia; tel. (02) 311683; telex 2490; Ambassador: EMIL KEBLUŠEK.

Egypt: POB 1752, 3 Egypt Ave, Nicosia; tel. (02) 465144; Ambassador: M. K. RIFAAT.

France: POB 1671, 6 Ploutarchou St, Engomi, Nicosia; tel. (02) 465258; telex 2389; Ambassador: DANIEL HUSSON.

German Democratic Republic: 115 Prodromos St, Nicosia; tel. (02) 444193; telex 2291; Ambassador: KURT MEIER.

Germany, Federal Republic: POB 1795, 10 Nikitaras St, Nicosia; tel. (02) 444362; telex 2460; Ambassador: Dr THILO RÖTGER.

Greece: POB 1799, 8/10 Byron Ave, Nicosia; tel. (02) 441880; telex 2286; Ambassador: CHRISTOS MACHARITSAS.

Holy See: POB 1964, Paphos Gate, Paphos St, Nicosia; tel. (02) 462132; Apostolic Pro-Nuncio: Archbishop CARLO CURIS.

India: POB 5544, 4th Floor, Anemomylos Bldg, 8 Michael Karaolis St, Nicosia; tel. (02) 461741; telex 4146; High Commissioner: R. ABHYANKAR.

Israel: POB 1049, 4 I. Gryparis St, Nicosia; tel. (02) 445195; telex 5978; Ambassador: AHARON LOPEZ.

Italy: POB 1452, Margarita House, 15 Themistoklis Dervis St, Nicosia; tel. (02) 473183; telex 3847; Ambassador: PAOLO VALFRÈ DI BONZO.

Lebanon: POB 1924, 1 Vasilissis Olga St, Nicosia; tel. (02) 442216; telex 3056; Ambassador: ZAIDAN ZAIDAN.

Libya: POB 3669, 14 Estias St, Nicosia; tel. (02) 496511; Secretary of People's Bureau: AHMED A. SHAHATI.

Romania: 37 Tombazis St, Nicosia; tel. (02) 445845; telex 2431; Chargé d'affaires a.i.: I. BISTREANU.

Syria: POB 1891, Corner Androcleous and Thoukidides Sts, Nicosia; tel. (02) 474481; telex 2030; Chargé d'affaires a.i.: ABD AL-FATAH AMMOURAH.

USSR: POB 1845, 4 Gladstone St, Nicosia; tel. (02) 472141; Ambassador: YURI E. FOKINE.

United Kingdom: POB 1978, Alexander Pallis St, Nicosia; tel. (02) 473131; telex 2208; High Commissioner: HUMPHREY MAUD.

USA: Dositheon St, and Therissos St, Lykavitos, Nicosia; tel. (02) 465151; telex 4160; Ambassador: BILL K. PERRIN.

Yemen, People's Democratic Republic: Nicosia; Ambassador: MUHAMMAD ABDO SHOFTA.

Yugoslavia: 2 Vasilissis Olgas St, Nicosia; tel. (02) 445511; Ambassador: VESELIN POPOVAĆ.

Judicial System

Supreme Council of Judicature: Nicosia. The Supreme Council of Judicature is composed of the President and Judges of the Supreme Court. It is responsible for the appointment, promotion, transfer, etc., of the judges exercising civil and criminal jurisdiction in the District Courts and the Assize Courts.

Attorney-General: M. A. TRIANTAFYLLIDES.

SUPREME COURT

Supreme Court: Char. Mouskos St, Nicosia; tel. (02) 402398. The Constitution of 1960 provided for a separate Supreme Constitutional Court and High Court but in 1964, in view of the resignation of their neutral presidents, these were amalgamated to form a single Supreme Court.

The Supreme Court is the final appellate court in the Republic and the final adjudicator in matters of constitutional and administrative law, including recourses on conflict of competence between state organs on questions of the constitutionality of laws, etc. It deals with appeals from Assize Courts and District Courts as well as from the decisions of its own judges when exercising original jurisdiction in certain matters such as prerogative orders of *habeas corpus, mandamus, certiorari*, etc., and in admiralty cases.

President: A. N. LOIZOU.

Judges: ANTONIS KOURRIS, Y. CH. MALACHTOS, D. GR. DEMETRIADES, L. G. SAVVIDES, D. STYLIANIDES, G. PIKIS, I. PAPADOPOULLOS, CHR. HADJITSANGARIS, I. BOYADJIS, Y. CHRYSOSTOMIS, S. NIKITAS, CHR. ARTEMIDES.

OTHER COURTS

Assize Courts and District Courts: As required by the Constitution a law was passed in 1960 providing for the establishment, jurisdiction and powers of courts of civil and criminal jurisdiction, i.e. of six District Courts and six Assize Courts.

Ecclesiastical Courts: There are seven Orthodox Church tribunals having exclusive jurisdiction in matrimonial causes between members of the Greek Orthodox Church. Appeals go from these tribunals to the appellate tribunal of the Church.

'Turkish Republic of Northern Cyprus'

The Turkish intervention in Cyprus in July 1974 resulted in the establishment of a separate area in northern Cyprus under the control of the Autonomous Turkish Cypriot Administration with a Council of Ministers, and separate judicial, financial, police, military and educational machinery serving the Turkish community.

On 13 February 1975 the Turkish-occupied zone of Cyprus was declared the 'Turkish Federated State of Cyprus', and Rauf Denktaş declared President. At the second joint meeting held by the Executive Council and Legislative Assembly of the Autonomous Turkish Cypriot Administration, it was decided to set up a Constituent Assembly which would prepare a constitution for the 'Turkish Federated State of Cyprus' within 45 days. This Constitution, which was approved by the Turkish Cypriot population in a referendum held on 8 June 1975, was regarded by the Turkish Cypriots as a first step towards a federal republic of Cyprus. The main provisions of the Constitution are summarized below:

The 'Turkish Federated State of Cyprus' is a democratic, secular republic based on the principles of social justice and the rule of

CYPRUS

law. It shall exercise only those functions which fall outside the powers and functions expressly given to the (proposed) Federal Republic of Cyprus. Necessary amendments shall be made to the Constitution of the 'Turkish Federated State of Cyprus' when the Constitution of the Federal Republic comes into force. The official language is Turkish.

Legislative power is vested in a Legislative Assembly, composed of 40 deputies, elected by universal suffrage for a period of five years. The President is Head of State and is elected by universal suffrage for a period of five years. No person may be elected President for more than two consecutive terms. The Council of Ministers shall be composed of a prime minister and 10 ministers. Judicial power is exercised through independent courts.

Other provisions cover such matters as the rehabilitation of refugees, property rights outside the 'Turkish Federated State', protection of coasts, social insurance, the rights and duties of citizens, etc.

On 15 November 1983 a unilateral declaration of independence brought into being the 'Turkish Republic of Northern Cyprus', which, like the 'Turkish Federated State of Cyprus', was not granted international recognition.

The Constituent Assembly, established after the declaration of independence, prepared a new constitution, which was approved by the Turkish Cypriot electorate on 5 May 1985. The new Constitution is very similar to the old one, but the number of deputies in the Legislative Assembly was increased to 50.

Rauf Denktaş was re-elected President on 9 June 1985, and elections to the Legislative Assembly were held on 23 June 1985.

HEAD OF STATE

President of the 'Turkish Republic of Northern Cyprus': RAUF R. DENKTAŞ (assumed office as President of the 'Turkish Federated State of Cyprus' 13 February 1975; became President of the 'TRNC' 15 November 1983; re-elected for a five-year term 9 June 1985).

COUNCIL OF MINISTERS
(January 1989)

Prime Minister: Dr DERVIŞ EROĞLU.

Minister of Foreign Affairs and Defence: Dr KENAN ATAKOL.

Minister of the Economy and Finance: MEHMET BAYRAM.

Minister of Public Works, Communications and Tourism: NAZIF BORMAN.

Minister of Trade and Industry: TAŞKENT ATASAYAN.

Minister of the Interior, Rural Affairs and Environment: OLGUN PAŞALAR.

Minister of Health and Social Welfare: Dr MUSTAFA ERBILEN.

Minister of Labour, Youth and Sport: GÜNAY CAYMAZ.

Minister of Housing: MUSTAFA ADAOĞLU.

Minister of Agriculture and Forestry: AYTAÇ BEŞEŞLER.

Minister of National Education and Culture: SALIH COŞAR.

MINISTRIES

All Ministries are in Nicosia (Lefkoşa), Mersin 10, Turkey.

Prime Minister's Office: tel. (020) 72141; telex 57444.

Ministry of Agriculture and Forestry: tel. (020) 73709; telex 57221.

Ministry of Trade and Industry: tel. (020) 71341; telex 57174.

Ministry of the Economy and Finance: tel. (020) 73626; telex 57268.

Ministry of Foreign Affairs and Defence: tel. (020) 72241; telex 57178.

Ministry of Health and Social Welfare: tel. (020) 75229.

Ministry of Housing: tel. (020) 73213.

Ministry of the Interior, Rural Affairs and Environment: tel. (020) 73645.

Ministry of Labour, Youth and Sport: tel. (020) 73611; telex 57178.

Ministry of National Education and Culture: tel. (020) 72136.

Ministry of Public Works, Communications and Tourism: tel. (020) 75051; telex 57174.

PRESIDENT

Election, 9 June 1985

Candidates	Votes	%
RAUF R. DENKTAŞ (Independent)	55,352	70.47
OSKER ÖZGÜR (Republican Turkish Party)	14,413	18.35
ALPAY DURDURAN (Communal Liberation Party)	7,221	9.19
ARIF T. DESEM (Independent)	693	0.88
SERVET S. DEDECAY	528	0.67
AYHAN KAYMAK	335	0.43
Total	**78,542**	**100.00**

LEGISLATIVE ASSEMBLY

Speaker: HAKKI ATUN.

Election, 23 June 1985

Party	Seats
National Unity Party	24
Republican Turkish Party	12
Communal Liberation Party	10
New Dawn Party	4
Total	**50**

POLITICAL ORGANIZATIONS

Atilimci Halk Partisi (Progressive People's Party): 15A Şerif Arzik St, Nicosia; tel. (02) 73222; telex 57244; f. 1979; based on social democratic principles; nationalist and secular; aims at a bi-zonal, bi-communal and non-aligned federal republic of Cyprus; Leaders İSMET KOTAK and İRSEN KÜCÜK.

Çalişan Halkin Partisi (Working People's Party): 2F Müftü Ziyai Efendi St, Nicosia; tel. (02) 76179; f. 1983; extreme left-wing; Leader BEKIR AZGIN.

Cumhuriyetçi Türk Partisi (Republican Turkish Party): 99A Şehit Salahi, Sevket St, Nicosia; tel. (02) 73300; f. 1970 by members of the Turkish community in Cyprus; socialist principles with anti-imperialist stand; district organizations at Famagusta, Kyrenia, Morphou and Nicosia; Leader ÖSKER ÖZGÜR; Gen. Sec. NACI TALAT USAR.

Kıbrıs Demokrasi Partisi (Cyprus Democratic Party): POB 534, Nicosia; tel. (02) 79053; f. 1984 by fmr mems of the Toplumcu Kurtuluş Partisi; left of centre; believes in social justice and a mixed economy; Leader EKREM URAL.

Kuzey Kıbrıs Sosyalist Partisi (Northern Cyprus Socialist Party): 44 Alay Bey St, Nicosia; tel. (02) 79245; f. 1985; favours absolute independence; Gen. Sec. DOĞAN HARMAN.

Sosyal Demokrat Partisi (Social Democratic Party): 10 Mahmut Paşa St, Nicosia; tel. (02) 75250; f. 1982; aims at a bi-zonal, bi-communal federal republic of Cyprus; Gen. Sec. HASAN NIDAI MESUTOĞLU.

Toplumcu Kurtuluş Partisi (Communal Liberation Party): 13 Mahmut Paşa St, Nicosia; tel. (02) 72555; f. 1976; left of centre; social democratic principles, social justice; believes in the leading role of organized labour; wants a solution of Cyprus problem as an independent, non-aligned, bi-zonal and bi-communal federal state; Leader MUSTAFA AKINCI; Gen. Sec. ERDAL SÜREÇ.

Ulusal Birlik Partisi (National Unity Party): 9 Atatürk Meydanı, Nicosia; tel. (02) 73972; f. 1975; right of centre; based on Atatürk's reforms, social justice, political equality and peaceful co-existence in an independent, bi-zonal, bi-communal, federal state of Cyprus; Leader Dr DERVIŞ EROĞLU; Gen. Sec. OLGUN PAŞALAR.

Yeni Doğuş Partisi (New Dawn Party): 1 Cengiz Han St, Nicosia; tel. (02) 72558; f. 1984; right of centre; supports a mixed economy; Leader ORHAN ÜÇOK; Gen. Sec. VURAL ÇETIN.

DIPLOMATIC REPRESENTATION
Embassy in the TRNC

Turkey: Bedreddin Demirel Ave, Nicosia, Mersin 10, Turkey; tel. (020) 72314; Ambassador: ERTUĞRUL KUMCUOĞLU.

Turkey is the only country to have recognized the 'Turkish Republic of Northern Cyprus'.

JUDICIAL SYSTEM

Supreme Council of Judicature: The Supreme Council of Judicature, composed of the President and Judges of the Supreme Court, a retired member of the Supreme Court, the Attorney-General of

CYPRUS

the 'Turkish Republic of Northern Cyprus' and the elected President of the Cyprus Turkish Bar, is responsible for the appointment, promotion, transfer, leave and discipline of all judges in accordance with the powers vested by the Constitution of the 'Turkish Federated State of Cyprus'. The appointment of the President and judges of the Supreme Court must be approved by the President of the 'Turkish Republic of Northern Cyprus'.

Attorney-General: AKIN SAIT.

Supreme Court: The Supreme Court functions as the Constitutional Court, the Court of Appeal and the Supreme Administrative Court.

President: ŞAKIR SIDKI İLKAY.

Judges: SALIH SAMI DAYIOGLU, NAZIM ERGIN SALÂHI, NIYAZI FAZIL KORKUT, AZIZ ALTAY, HAMDI ATALAY, CELÂL KARABACAK, TANER ERGINEL.

Subordinate Courts: Judicial power other than that exercised by the Supreme Court is exercised by the Assize, District and Family Courts.

Religion

Greeks form 77% of the population and most of them belong to the Orthodox Church. Most Turks (about 18% of the population) are Muslims. At the 1960 census, religious adherence was:

Greek Orthodox	441,656
Muslims	104,942
Armenian Apostolic	3,378
Maronite	2,752
Anglican	
Roman Catholic	18,836
Other	

CHRISTIANITY

The Orthodox Church of Cyprus

The Autocephalous Orthodox Church of Cyprus, founded in AD 45, is part of the Eastern Orthodox Church; the Church is independent, and the Archbishop, who is also the Ethnarch (national leader of the Greek community), is elected by representatives of the towns and villages of Cyprus. The Church comprises six dioceses, and in 1985 had an estimated 442,000 members.

Archbishop of Nova Justiniana and all Cyprus: Archbishop CHRYSOSTOMOS, POB 1130, Nicosia; tel. (02) 474411.

Metropolitan of Paphos: Bishop CHRYSOSTOMOS.

Metropolitan of Kitium: Bishop CHRYSOSTOMOS.

Metropolitan of Kyrenia: Bishop GREGORIOS.

Metropolitan of Limassol: Bishop CHRYSANTHOS.

Metropolitan of Morphou: Bishop CHRYSANTHOS.

The Roman Catholic Church

Latin Rite

The Patriarchate of Jerusalem covers Israel, Jordan and Cyprus. The Patriarch is resident in Jerusalem (see the chapter on Israel).

Vicar Patriarchal for Cyprus: Father CORMAC MCATEER.

Maronite Rite

Most of the Roman Catholics in Cyprus are adherents of the Maronite rite. The Archbishop of Cyprus resides in Lebanon. At 31 December 1986 the archdiocese contained an estimated 198,370 Maronite Catholics.

Maronite Church of Cyprus: 8 Favieros St, Nicosia; tel. (02) 463212; Archbishop of Cyprus: Mgr JOSEPH MOHSEN BECHARA, Maronite Archbishopric, POB 70400, Antelias, Lebanon (winter); tel. 961-410020; Cornet-Chahouane, Lebanon (summer); tel. 925005; Vicar General for Cyprus: Mgr JEAN FORADARIS.

The Anglican Communion

Anglicans in Cyprus are adherents of the Episcopal Church in Jerusalem and the Middle East, officially inaugurated in January 1976. The Church has four dioceses, and the President is the Bishop in Jerusalem (see Israel). The diocese of Cyprus and the Gulf includes Cyprus, Iraq and the countries of the Arabian peninsula.

Bishop in Cyprus and The Gulf: Right Rev. JOHN EDWARD BROWN, POB 2075, St Paul's Anglican Cathedral Church, Byron Ave, Nicosia; tel. (02) 451220.

Archdeacon of Cyprus: Very Rev. BRYAN G. HENRY, POB 2075, 2 Grigoris Afxentiou St, Nicosia; tel. (02) 442241.

ISLAM

Most of the adherents in Cyprus are Sunnis of the Hanafi Sect. The religious head of the Muslim community is the Mufti.

Mufti of Cyprus: AHMET CEMAL İLKTAÇ (acting), POB 142, Nicosia, Mersin 10, Turkey.

The Press

GREEK CYPRIOT DAILIES

Agon (Struggle): POB 1417, 37 Onassagoras St, Nicosia; tel. (02) 477181; f. 1964; morning; Greek; independent, right of centre; Owner and Dir N. KOSHIS; Chief Editor GEORGE A. LEONIDAS; circ. 8,000.

Alithia (Truth): POB 1695, 5 Pindaros and Androklis St, Nicosia; tel. (02) 463040; f. 1952 as a weekly, 1982 as a daily; morning; Greek; right-wing; Dir FR. N. KOULERMOS; Chief Editor ALEKOS KONSTANTINIDES; circ. 8,500.

Apogevmatini (Afternoon): POB 1094, 5 Aegaleo St, Strovolos, Nicosia; tel. (02) 443858; f. 1972; afternoon; Greek; independent, moderate; Owner and Chief Editor ANTHOS LYKAVGHIS; circ. 9,500.

Apogevmatinos Typos (Afternoon Press): POB 1695, 5 Pindaros and Androklis St, Nicosia; tel. (02) 463505; f. 1988; afternoon; Greek; independent; Owner F. N. KOYLERMOS; Chief Editor ARISTOS MICHAELIDES.

Cyprus Mail: POB 1144, 24 Vassilios Voulgaroktonos St, Nicosia; tel. (02) 462074; telex 2616; f. 1945; English; independent, conservative; Dir. IAKOVOS IAKOVIDES; Chief Editors MIKE WADSWORTH, KYRIACOS IAKOVIDES; circ. 3,100.

Eleftheria Tis Gnomis (Freedom of Opinion): 9 Zinonos Kitieos St, Engomi, Nicosia; tel. (02) 449542; f. 1987; Greek; Dir VASSOS ANDONIADES; Chief Editor ARISTOS MICHAELIDES.

Eleftherotypia (Free Press): POB 3821, 6 Themistoklis Dervis St, Nicosia; tel. (02) 454400; f. 1981; morning; Greek; right of centre; organ of DIKO party; Dir and Chief Editor GEORGE ELIADES; circ. 6,700.

Haravghi (Dawn): POB 1556, ETAK Bldg, 6 Akamas St, Nicosia; tel. (02) 476356; f. 1956; morning; Greek; organ of AKEL (Communist Party); Dir and Chief Editor AND. CHRISTODOULOU; circ. 14,500.

Messimvrini (Midday): POB 1543, 29 Diagoras St, Nicosia; tel. (02) 366230; afternoon; Greek; independent, right-wing; Dir and Chief Editor GEORGE HADJINICOLAOU; circ. 2,000.

Phileleftheros (Liberal): POB 1094, 36 Vyronos Ave, Nicosia; tel. (02) 463922; telex 4999; f. 1955; morning; Greek; independent, moderate; Dir C. PATTICHIS; Chief Editor CHR. KATSAMBAS; circ. 19,684.

Simerini (Today): POB 1836, Solea Court, 4 Annis Komninis St, Nicosia; tel. (02) 448708; telex 3826; f. 1976; morning; Greek; rightwing; Dir KOSTAS HADJICOSTIS; Chief Editor SAVVAS IAKOVIDES; circ. 12,900.

Ta Nea (The News): POB 1064, A. Karyos St, Engomi Industrial Area, Nicosia; tel. (02) 449766; telex 3182; f. 1969; morning; Greek; organ of EDEK party; Dir A. MAVROSKOUFIS; Chief Editor TAKIS KOUNNAFIS; circ. 5,500.

TURKISH CYPRIOT DAILIES

Birlik (Unity): POB 841, 43 Yediler St, Nicosia, Mersin 10, Turkey; tel. (020) 72959; f. 1980; Turkish; organ of National Unity Party; Dir RAMIZ N. MANYERA; Chief Editor OLGUN PAŞALAR; circ. 4,500.

Günaydın Kıbrıs (Good Morning, Cyprus): 23/12 Posta St, Nicosia, Mersin 10, Turkey; tel. (020) 71472; telex 57240; f. 1980; Turkish; Editor REŞAT AKAR; circ. 1,900.

Halkin Sesi (Voice of the People): 172 Kyrenia St, Nicosia, Mersin 10, Turkey; tel. (020) 73141; telex 57173; f. 1942; morning; Turkish; independent Turkish Nationalist; Dir Gen. and Man. Editor PEKER M. TURGUD; circ. 6,000.

Kıbrıs: KKTC Enformasyon Dairesi, Mehmet Akif Cad., Nicosia, Mersin 10, Turkey; tel. (020) 73133; telex 57177; f. 1963 as News Bulletin; renamed 1981; English; publ. by the Public Information Office of the 'TRNC'; circ. 4,000.

Kıbrıs Postasi (Cyprus Post): M. İrfan Bey Sok. 30, Nicosia; tel. (020) 75242; telex 57244; f. 1982; Turkish; independent; Owner and Chief Editor İSMET KOTAK; circ. 4,500.

Ortam (Conditions): 158A Girne St, Nicosia, Mersin 10, Turkey; tel. (020) 74872; Turkish; organ of the Toplumcu Kurtuluş Partisi (Communal Liberation Party); Editor KEMAL AKTUNÇ; circ. 1,250.

Yenidüzen (New System): Yeni Sanayi St, Nicosia, Mersin 10, Turkey; tel. (020) 74906; Turkish; organ of the Cumhuriyetçi Türk

CYPRUS   Directory

Partisi (Republican Turkish Party); Chief Editor ERGÜN VEHBI; circ. 1,000.

GREEK CYPRIOT WEEKLIES

Ammochostos: 44 Egnatias, Plati, Eylenja; tel. 352918; Greek; right-wing; reflects views of Famagusta refugees; Dir and Chief Editor NIKOS FALAS; circ. 2,800.

Anexartitos (Independent): POB 1064, A. Karyos St, Engomi, Nicosia; tel. (02) 449766; f. 1973; Greek; independent; socialist; organ of EDEK party; Chief Editor ANTONIS MAKRIDES; circ. 4,700.

Cyprus Weekly: POB 1992, 216 Mitsis 3 Bldg, Archbishop Makarios Ave, Nicosia; tel. (02) 441433; telex 2260; f. 1979; English; independent; Dirs and Editors GEORGES DER PARTHOGH, ALEX EFTHYVOULOU, ANDREAS HADJIPAPAS; circ. 10,000.

Economiki Kypros: 9 Androcleous St, Nicosia; tel. (02) 472510; f. 1987; Greek; Dir NONTAS METAXAS; Chief Editor TASSOS ANASTASSIADES.

Eleftherotypia Tis Defteras (Monday's Free Press): POB 3821, Hadjisavvas Bldg, Eleftheria Sq, Nicosia; tel. (02) 454400; f. 1980; Greek; right of centre; organ of DIKO party.

Embros (Forward): POB 3739, Nicosia; tel. (02) 451280; f. 1987; Dir and Chief Editor ANDREAS KANNAOUROS.

Enimerossi (Briefing): POB 1417, Flat 28, 37 Onassagoras St, Nicosia; tel. (02) 477181; f. 1982; Greek; Dir NIKOS KOSHIS; Chief Editor PANAYIOTIS PAPADEMETRIS; circ. 9,000.

Epikeri: POB 3786, 8 St Eleni St, Nicosia; tel. (02) 455788; f. 1987; Greek; independent; Dir and Chief Editor LAZAROS MAVROS.

Ergatiki Phoni (Workers' Voice): POB 5018, SEK Bldg, 23 Alkeou St, Engomi, Nicosia; tel. (02) 441142; f. 1946; Greek; organ of Cyprus Workers' Confederation (SEK); Chief Editor GREGORIS GREGORIADES; circ. 9,000.

Ergatiko Vima (Workers' Tribune): POB 1885, 31-35 Archemos St, Nicosia; tel. (02) 473192; f. 1956; Greek; organ of the Pancyprian Federation of Labour; Editor-in-Chief PANTELIS VARNAVAS; circ. 16,517.

Kirykas (Herald): 12 Diagorou St, Nicosia; tel. (02) 461961; f. 1981; Greek; right of centre; organ of Centre Union party; Dir and Chief Editor GEORGE ELIADES; circ. 4,500.

Kyriakatikes Ores (Sunday Hours): POB 1450, 7 Androkleous St, Nicosia; tel. (02) 448548; Dir and Chief Editor PHIVOS MORIDES.

Official Gazette: Printing Office of the Republic of Cyprus, Nicosia; tel. (02) 402202; f. 1960; Greek; published by the Government of the Republic of Cyprus.

Paraskinio (Behind the Scenes): 39 Kennedy Ave, Nicosia; tel. (02) 313334; f. 1987; Dir and Chief Editor D. MICHAEL; cir. 6,000.

To Periodiko: 3rd Floor, 4 Annis Komninis, Nicosia; tel. (02) 474041; telex 3826; f. 1986; Greek; Dir PHILIPPOS STYLIANOU; circ. 14,500.

TURKISH CYPRIOT WEEKLIES

Bozkurt (Grey Wolf): 142 Kyrenia St, Nicosia, Mersin 10, Turkey; tel. (020) 71565; f. 1951 as a daily; Turkish; independent; Editor SADI TOGAN; circ. 3,000.

Demokratik Halk Gazetesi (Democratic People's Gazette): Serif Arzif Sok., Nicosia; tel. (020) 73222; f. 1977; Turkish; Editor AHMET GAZIOGLU; circ. 4,000.

Ekonomi (The Economy): POB 718, Bedrettin Demirel Ave, Nicosia, Mersin 10, Turkey; tel. (020) 78760; telex 57137; f. 1958; Turkish; published by the Turkish Cypriot Chamber of Commerce; Editor-in-Chief SAMI TAŞARKAN; circ. 3,000.

Ekspres: Nicosia, Mersin 10, Turkey; f. 1987; Editor-in-Chief ONDER ASLITURK.

Haber: Nicosia, Mersin 10, Turkey; tel. (020) 78188; Turkish; Chief Editor MEHMET AKAR.

Northern Cyprus Weekly: Mehmet Akif Cad., Nicosia, Mersin 10, Turkey; tel. (020) 73498; telex 57177; f. 1963 as *Special News Bulletin*, under present name 1981; English; Turkish edition under name of *Kuzey Kıbrıs* (Northern Cyprus) f. 1976; publ. by Public Information Office of the 'TRNC'; Man. Editor OKTAY OKSUZOĞLU; Chief Editor ESER BIREY (English), SABAHATTIN ISMAIL (Turkish); circ. 5,000 (English), 5,000 (Turkish).

Olay: 5 Hükümet St, Famagusta; tel. (036) 66111; telex 57244; Turkish.

Söz (Word): Sabri Orient Otel Alti, Nicosia, Mersin 10, Turkey; tel. (020) 76179; f. 1985; Turkish; Chief Editor ARIF H. TAHSIN.

Special News Bulletin-Digest: Nicosia, Mersin 10, Turkey; tel. (020) 75773; telex 57169; English; publ. by the 'TRNC' Public Relations Office.

Sportmence: Nicosia, Mersin 10, Turkey; tel. (020) 72212; Turkish; Chief Editor ERTAN BIRINCI.

Super Spor: Nicosia, Mersin 10, Turkey; tel. (020) 74471; Turkish; Chief Editor IBRAHIM ÖZSOY.

Yön (Direction): Selen Otopark, Nicosia, Mersin 10, Turkey; tel. (020) 75250; f. 1983; Editor AYDIN ARIF AKKURT; circ. 1,000.

OTHER WEEKLIES

Lion: British Forces Post Office 53; tel. (052) 21021; British Sovereign Base Areas weekly with Services Sound and Vision Corpn programme guide; Editor Maj. T. BEVAN; circ. 2,600.

Middle East Economic Survey: Middle East Petroleum and Economic Publications (Cyprus), POB 4940, Nicosia; tel. (02) 445431; telex 2198; f. 1957 (in Beirut); weekly review and analysis of petroleum, economic and political news; Publr BASIM W. ITAYIM; Editor IAN SEYMOUR.

GREEK CYPRIOT PERIODICALS

Apostolos Varnavas: Archbishopric of Cyprus, POB 1130, Nicosia; monthly; Greek; organ of the Orthodox Church of Cyprus; Dir Dr ANDREAS N. MITSIDES; circ. 1,200.

Countryman: Nicosia; f. 1943; quarterly; Greek; published by the Cyprus Press and Public Information Office; circ. 6,000.

Cypria (Cypriot Woman): Flat 11, 56 Kennedy Ave, Nicosia; f. 1984; every 2 months; Greek; Owner CHRISTINA VALANIDES; circ. 5,500.

Cyprus Bulletin: Nicosia; tel. (02) 451001; f. 1964; fortnightly; Arabic, English, French, German, Greek, Russian, Spanish; published by the Cyprus Press and Information Office; circ. 28,000.

Cyprus Life: Flat 21, 24 Evagorou St, Nicosia; f. 1987; monthly; English; Chief Editor GARY LAKES; circ. 2,500.

Cyprus Time Out: POB 3697, 4 Pygmalion St, Nicosia; tel. (02) 452079; f. 1978; monthly; English; Chief Editor ELLADA SOPHOCLEOUS; circ. 4,000.

Cyprus Today: c/o Ministry of Education, Nicosia; f. 1963; quarterly; English; cultural and informative review of the Ministry of Education; published and distributed by Press and Information Office; free of charge; Chair. Editorial Board YIANNIS KATSOURIS; circ. 15,000.

Dimosios Ypallilos (Civil Servant): 2 Andreas Demetriou St, Nicosia; tel. (02) 442393; fortnightly; published by the Cyprus Civil Servants' Association; circ. 11,000.

Endoskopissi: 6th Floor, 4 Annis Komninis, Nicosia; tel. (02) 458474; f. 1984; every 2 months; Greek; Chief Editor NICOS HADJICOSTIS; circ. 1,600.

Eso-Etimos (Ever Ready): POB 4544, Nicosia; tel. (02) 443587; f. 1913; quarterly; Greek; publ. by Cyprus Scouts' Assen; Editor C. CONSTANTINOU; circ. 2,500.

Flash: POB 4626, 11 Kolokotronis St, Kaimakli, Nicosia; tel. (02) 437887; f. 1978; fortnightly; Greek; Chief Editor PAMBIS VATIS; circ. 7,000.

Katanalotis (Consumer): POB 4874, 20 Gladstone St, Nicosia 162; tel. (02) 451092; f. 1977; every 2 months; Greek.

Nea Epochi (New Epoch): 6 Akamantos St, Nicosia; tel. (02) 476356; f. 1959; every 2 months; Greek; literary; Editor ACHILLEAS PYLIOTIS; circ. 1,500.

Nicosia This Month: POB 1015, Nicosia; tel. (02) 473124; f. 1984; monthly; English; Chief Editor ELLADA SOPHOCLEOUS; circ. 3,000.

O Kosmos Tou Kypriakou Vivliou (The World of Cypriot Books): POB 1722, Nicosia; tel. (02) 472744; Greek; journal of the book trade; publ. by MAM (see Publishers).

Oikogeneia Kai Scholeio (Family and School): 18 Archbishop Makarios III Ave, 2nd Floor, Nicosia; tel. (02) 454466; f. 1970; every 2 months; Greek; for parents and teachers; publ. by the Pancyprian School for Parents; Editor A. D. CHRISTODOULIDES; circ. 7,000.

Paediki Hara (Children's Joy): 18 Archbishop Makarios III Ave, Nicosia; tel. (02) 442638; monthly; for pupils; publ. by the Pancyprian Union of Greek Teachers; Editor GEORGHIOS LOUKA; circ. 13,000.

Pnevmatiki Kypros (Cultural Cyprus): Nicosia; tel. (02) 659001; f. 1960; monthly; Greek; literary; Owner Dr KYPROS CHRYSANTHIS.

Radio Programme: POB 4824, Cyprus Broadcasting Corpn, Broadcasting House, Nicosia; tel. (02) 422231; telex 2333; fortnightly; Greek and English; published by the CyBC; radio and TV programme news; circ. 20,000.

Success: POB 4706, Nicosia; tel. (02) 472510; f. 1985; monthly; English; Chief Editor SAVVAS SPYRIDES; circ. 4,000.

Synergatiko Vima (The Co-operative Rostrum): Shanteclair Bldg, 4th Floor, No. 401, 2 Sofoulis St, Nicosia; tel. (02) 458757; f. 1982;

CYPRUS

fortnightly; Greek; official organ of the Pancyprian Co-operative Confederation Ltd; circ. 7,000.

Trapezikos (Bank Employee): POB 1235, Nicosia; tel. (02) 449900; f. 1960; bank employees' magazine; Greek; monthly; Editor L. HADZICOSTIS; circ. 3,000.

TURKISH CYPRIOT PERIODICALS

Çengel: Nicosia, Mersin 10, Turkey; tel. (020) 75225; Turkish; Owner and Publr ERDAL ANDIZ.

Eğitim Bülteni (Education Bulletin): Ministry of Education, Nicosia, Mersin 10, Turkey; tel. (020) 72136; f. 1972; monthly; Turkish; published by Ministry of Education of the 'Turkish Republic of Northern Cyprus'; circ. 3,000.

Kooperatif (Co-operative): Dept. of Co-operative Devt, Nicosia, Mersin 10, Turkey; tel. (020) 71207; f. 1970; monthly; Turkish; published by Department of Co-operative Development of the 'Turkish Republic of Northern Cyprus', circ. 2,000.

New Cyprus: POB 327, Nicosia, Mersin 10, Turkey; tel. (020) 72592; telex 2585; English; publ. by the North Cyprus Research and Publishing Centre; Editor AHMET C. GAZIOĞLU.

Öğretmen (Teacher): Nicosia, Mersin 10, Turkey; tel. (020) 472802; f. 1972; monthly; Turkish; organ of Cyprus Turkish Secondary Schools' Teachers' Assen; circ. 1,200.

Özgürlük: POB 327, Nicosia, Mersin 10, Turkey; Turkish; Owner and Publr HÜRREM TOLGA.

Uluslararasi Kuzey Kıbrıs Magazin (International Northern Cyprus Magazine): Cengiz Han St, Yuva Appt, Köşklüçiftlik, Nicosia, Mersin 10, Turkey; f. 1987; quarterly; Turkish and English; publ. by YORUM Publishing House; Editor TANSU KONURALP.

Yeni Kıbrıs: Nicosia, Mersin 10, Turkey; tel. (020) 72592; Editor AHMET C. GAZIOĞLU.

OTHER PERIODICALS

The Blue Beret: POB 1642, HQ UNFICYP, Nicosia; tel. (02) 464000; monthly; English; circ. 2,200.

International Crude Oil and Product Prices: Middle East Petroleum and Economic Publications (Cyprus), POB 4940, Nicosia; tel. (02) 445431; telex 2198; f. 1971 (in Beirut); 2 a year; review and analysis of oil price trends in world markets; Publisher BASIM W. ITAYIM.

NEWS AGENCIES

Cyprus News Agency: POB 3947, 97 Ay. Omoloyitae Ave, Nicosia; tel. (02) 458413; telex 4787; f. 1976; English and Greek; Dir IOANNIS SOLOMOU.

Kuzey Kıbrıs Haber Ajansi (Northern Cyprus News Agency): 11 Hasene Ilgaz St, Nicosia, Mersin 10, Turkey; tel. (020) 73892; telex 57254; f. 1977; Dir-Gen. M. ALI AKPINAR.

Pan Basin Yayin Ajansi (Pan Press Agency): ATO Apt 4, Sht. Ibrahim Yusuf Sok., Nicosia, Mersin 10, Turkey; tel. (020) 77831; f. 1980; Dir ARMAN RATIP.

Türk Ajansı Kıbrıs (TAK) (Turkish News Agency of Cyprus): Süleyman Uluçamgil St, Nicosia, Mersin 10, Turkey; tel. (020) 71818; telex 57448; f. 1973; Dir KEMAL ÂŞIK.

Foreign Bureaux

Agence France-Presse (AFP) (France): POB 7242, Helenium Estates Bldg, 7th Floor, 36 Kypranoros St, Nicosia; tel. (02) 365050; telex 2824; Bureau Chief XAVIER BARON; Correspondent DIMITRI ANDREOU.

Agencia EFE (Spain): 10 Katsonis St, Nicosia; tel. (02) 461311; telex 6126; Bureau Man. MARÍA SAAVEDRA.

Agentstvo Pechati Novosti (APN) (USSR): POB 4051, 5A Dinokratous St, Nicosia; tel. (02) 462287; telex 2379; Rep. VADIM VASILYEVICH LEONOV.

Agenzia Nazionale Stampa Associata (ANSA) (Italy): 10 Katsonis St, Aye Omoloyitae, Nicosia; tel. (02) 446882; telex 4796; Rep. ALBERTO PIAZZA.

Associated Press (AP) Middle East Ltd (USA): POB 4853, Neoelen Marina, 10 Katsonis St, Nicosia; tel. (02) 447086; telex 2459; Rep. NICHOLAS LUDINGTON; Correspondent ALEX EFTY.

Athinaikon Praktorion Eidiseon (Greece): 4 Andreas Patsalides St, Engomi, Nicosia; tel. (02) 441110; Rep. GEORGE LEONIDAS.

Československá tisková kancelář (ČTK) (Czechoslovakia): 30 Evagoros Pallikarides St, Strovolos, Nicosia; Rep. STAVROS ANGELIDES.

Deutsche Presse Agentur (dpa) (Federal Republic of Germany): 9 Deadalou St, Nicosia; tel. (02) 463922; Rep. ANTHOS LYKAVGIS.

Iraqi News Agency: POB 1098, 11 Ippocratous St, Nicosia; tel. (02) 472095; telex 2197; Correspondent AHMED SULEIMAN.

Jamahiriya News Agency (JANA) (Libya): 93 Kennedy Ave, Nicosia; tel. (02) 498937; Rep. MUHAMMAD ALI SHEWEIHDI.

Kyodo Tsushin (Japan): 10 Katsonis St, Nicosia; tel. (02) 365267; telex 4968; Bureau Chief JUNO KONDO.

Novinska Agencija Tanjug (Yugoslavia): 26 Methonis St, Nicosia; tel. (02) 450212; telex 3087; Rep. NADA DUGONJIĆ.

Polska Agencja Prasowa (PAP) (Poland): POB 2373, Prodromos St 24, Nicosia; Rep. MICHALAKIS PANTELIDES.

Prensa Latina (Cuba): 12 Demophon St, 5th Floor, Apt 501, Nicosia; tel. (02) 464131; telex 4505; Rep. LEONEL NODAL.

Reuters (UK): POB 5725, 5th and 6th Floors, George and Thelma Foundation Bldg, 36 Grivas Dhigenis Ave, Nicosia; tel. (02) 475030; telex 4922; f. 1984; Bureau Chief KATHY McELROY.

Syrian Arab News Agency (SANA): POB 1891, Nicosia; tel. (02) 474481; Correspondent SAMIR AL-KHATIB.

Tanjug (Yugoslavia): 26 Methonis St, Lycavitos, Nicosia; tel. (02) 450212; Correspondent NADA DUGONJIĆ.

Telegrafnoye Agentstvo Sovetskovo Soyuza (TASS) (USSR): 3 Philellinon St, Nicosia; tel. (02) 475375; telex 2368; Rep. MIKHAIL MASHKOV.

United Press International (UPI) (USA): 16 Zena de Tyras St, Nicosia; tel. (02) 455998; telex 2260; Rep. GEORGES DER PARTHOGH.

Xinhua (New China) News Agency (People's Republic of China): POB 7024, Flat 32, 6 Nafpactos St, Nicosia; tel. (02) 456703; telex 5265; Rep. ZHANG SHENPING.

Publishers

GREEK CYPRIOT PUBLISHERS

Action Publications: POB 4076, Nicosia; tel. (02) 444104; telex 4455; f. 1971.

Andreou Publications: POB 2298, Nicosia; tel. (02) 476105; f. 1979.

MAM (The House of Cyprus Publications): POB 1722, Nicosia; tel. (02) 472744; f. 1965.

Nicodes Publishing House: POB 3656, Nicosia; tel. (02) 452089.

TURKISH CYPRIOT PUBLISHERS

Bozkurt Basimevi: 142 Kyrenia Ave, Nicosia, Mersin 10, Turkey; tel. (020) 71565; Turkish Cypriot.

Devlet Basimevi (Turkish Cypriot Government Printing House): Şerif Arzik St, Nicosia, Mersin 10, Turkey; tel. (020) 72010; Dir SABRI ERTÜRK.

Radio and Television

In December 1986, in the government-controlled areas, it was estimated that there were 171,500 radio receivers and 88,800 television receivers (including about 50,000 colour receivers) in use; while, in December 1985, in the Turkish sector of Cyprus there were an estimated 42,170 radio receivers and 75,000 television receivers in use.

Cyprus Broadcasting Corporation (CyBC): POB 4824, Broadcasting House, Nicosia; tel. (02) 422231; telex 2333; Chair. CHRYSSES DEMETRIADES; Dir-Gen. D. KYPRIANOU.

Radio: f. 1952; Programme I in Greek, Programme II in Greek, Turkish, English, Arabic and Armenian; two medium wave transmitters of 20 kW in Nicosia with relay stations at Paphos and Limassol; two 30 kW ERP VHF FM stereo transmitters on Mount Olympus; international service in English and Arabic.

Television: f. 1957; one Band III 200/20 kW transmitter on Mount Olympus with 35 transposer stations.

Bayrak Radio and TV Corpn (BRTK): Atatürk Square, Nicosia, Mersin 10, Turkey; tel. (020) 76159; telex 57264; in July 1983 it became an independent Turkish Cypriot Corpn partly financed by the govt; Chair. and Dir-Gen. D. ÖZER BERKEM.

Radio Bayrak: f. 1963; home service in Turkish, overseas services in Turkish, Greek, English, Arabic, Swedish and German; broadcasts 31 hours a day; Dir of Broadcasting HÜSEYIN ÇOBANOĞLU.

Bayrak TV: f. 1976; transmits programmes in Turkish, Greek, English and Arabic on six channels; Dir of Programmes HÜSEYIN ÇOBANOĞLU.

Services Sound and Vision Corpn, Cyprus: Dhekelia, British Forces Post Office 58, Cyprus; tel. (041) 53000; telex 2853; incorporates the British Forces Broadcasting Service, Cyprus; broadcasts a 24-hour radio service in English VHF and medium wave and a four-hour TV service; Gen. Man. JOHN M. CAMPBELL; Engineering Man. ROGER DUNN.

CYPRUS   Directory

Türkiye Radyo Televizyon (TRT): Turkish television programmes are transmitted to the Turkish sector of Cyprus.

Finance

(brs = branches; cap. = capital; p.u. = paid up; auth. = authorized; dep. = deposits; res = reserves; m. = million; amounts in Cyprus pounds)

BANKING
Central Bank

Central Bank of Cyprus: POB 5529, 36 Metochiou Ave, Nicosia; tel. (02) 445281; telex 2424; f. 1963; became the Bank of Issue in 1963; cap. p.u. 100,000, res 460.6m., dep. 437m. (Aug. 1988); Gov. A. C. AFXENTIOU.

Greek Cypriot Banks

Bank of Cyprus Ltd: POB 1472, 86-90 Phaneromeni St, Nicosia; tel. (02) 464064; telex 2451; f. 1899, reconstituted 1943 by the amalgamation of Bank of Cyprus, Larnaca Bank Ltd and Famagusta Bank Ltd; cap. p.u. 14m., res 17.2m., dep. 587.6m. (July 1988); Chair. SOLON A. TRIANTAFYLLIDES; Gov. ANDREAS C. PATSALIDES; 132 brs throughout Cyprus.

Co-operative Central Bank Ltd: POB 4537, Gregoris Afxentiou St, Nicosia; tel. (02) 442921; telex 2313; f. 1937 under the Co-operative Societies Law; banking and credit facilities to member societies, importer and distributor of agricultural requisites, insurance agent; dep. 143.6m. (July 1988); Chair B. BALTAYIAN; Gen. Man. D. PITSILLIDES; 5 brs.

The Cyprus Popular Bank Ltd: POB 2032, Popular Bank Bldg, 39 Archbishop Makarios III Ave, Nicosia; tel. (02) 450000; telex 2272; f. 1901; cap. p.u. 13.4m., res 17m., dep. 366.7m. (July 1988); Chair. EVAGORAS C. LANITIS; Group Chief Exec. KIKIS N. LAZARIDES; 108 brs.

Hellenic Bank Ltd: POB 4747, 92 Dhigenis Akritas Ave, Nicosia; tel. (02) 447000; telex 3311; f. 1974; cap. p.u. 4m., res 2m., dep. 113m. (Nov. 1988); Chair. PASCHALIS L. PASCHALIDES; Gen. Man. PANOS CHR. GHALANOS; 46 brs.

Housing Finance Corpn: POB 3898, 41 Themistoklis Dervis St, Hawaii Tower, Nicosia; tel. (02) 452777; telex 4134; f. 1980; provides long-term loans for home buying; cap. p.u. 500,000, dep. 20m., total assets 25m. (Nov. 1988); Chair. A. MOUSKOS; Gen. Man. A. PAPAGEORGIOU; 6 brs.

Mortgage Bank of Cyprus Ltd: POB 1472, 86-90 Phaneromenis St, Nicosia; tel. (02) 464064; telex 2451; f. 1944; wholly owned subsidiary of Bank of Cyprus Ltd; cap. p.u. 1m., res 7m., dep. 61.4m. (July 1988); Chair. SOLON A. TRIANTAFYLLIDES; Gov. ANDREAS C. PATSALIDES; 132 brs.

Turkish Cypriot Banking Association

Northern Cyprus Bank Association: Nicosia, Mersin 10, Turkey; f. 1987; 9 mems.

Turkish Cypriot Banks
(amounts in Turkish liras)

Asbank Ltd: 23B Sarayönü Sok., POB 448, Nicosia, Mersin 10, Turkey; tel. (020) 77023; telex 57305; f. 1986; cap. and res 2,000m., dep. 750m. (Dec. 1986); Chair. Dr C. A. ADADEMIR; Gen. Man. DERVIŞ TÜRKER; 6 brs.

Inter Overseas Bank Ltd: Nicosia, Mersin 10, Turkey; 3 brs.

Kıbrıs Endüstri Bankası (Cyprus Industrial Bank): 3 Memduh Asaf Sok., Nicosia, Mersin 10, Turkey; tel. (020) 71830; telex 57257.

Kıbrıs Kredi Bankası Ltd (Cyprus Credit Bank Ltd): POB 347, İplik Pazari St, Nicosia, Mersin 10, Turkey; tel. (020) 75026; telex 57246; f. 1978; cap. p.u. 936.0m., res 2,597.2m., dep. 55,623.6m. (Dec. 1987); Chair. SALIH BOYACI; Gen. Man. YÜKSEL YAZGIN (acting); 10 brs.

Kıbrıs Ticaret Bankası Ltd (Cyprus Commercial Bank Ltd): 53 Girne Cad., Nicosia, Mersin 10, Turkey; tel. (020) 75180; telex 57197; f. 1982; cap. p.u. 818m., dep. 11,285m. (Nov. 1988); Chair. YÜKSEL AHMET RAŞIT; Gen. Man. Dr ERDAL ONURHAN; 8 brs.

Kıbrıs Vakıflar Bankası Ltd: POB 212, Evkaf Dairesi Binaları, Nicosia, Mersin 10, Turkey; tel. (020) 75109; telex 57122; f. 1982; cap. 1,500m., dep. 10,100m. (June 1988); Chair. TANSEL LISANI İNANÇ; Gen. Man. NEJAT MANER; 4 brs.

Turkish Bank Ltd: POB 242, 92 Girne Cad., Nicosia, Mersin 10, Turkey; tel. (020) 71313; telex 57138; f. 1901; cap. p.u. and res 10,567m., dep. 151,873m. (1987); Chair. and Gen. Man. M. TANJU OZYOL; 15 brs.

Turkish Cypriot Co-operative Central Bank Ltd: POB 1861, 49-55 Mahmout Pasha St, Nicosia, Mersin 10, Turkey; tel. (020) 64257; telex 57216; cap. and res 4,589m., dep. 19,493m. (Dec. 1987); banking and credit facilities to member societies and individuals; Gen. Man. Dr TUNCER ARIFOĞLU.

Investment Organization

Cyprus Investment and Securities Corpn: POB 597, Ghinis Bldg, 4th Floor, 58-60 Dhigenis Akritas Ave, Nicosia; tel. (02) 451535; telex 4449; f. 1982 to encourage industrial investment; auth. cap. 1m., cap. p.u. 500,000 (1988); Chair. J. CL. CHRISTOPHIDES; Gen. Man. SOCRATES R. SOLOMIDES.

Development Bank

The Cyprus Development Bank Ltd: POB 1415, 50 Archbishop Makarios III Ave, Alpha House, Nicosia; tel. (02) 457575; telex 2797; f. 1963; cap. p.u. 2m.; res 708,000 (July 1988); provides medium- and long-term loans for productive projects, particularly in manufacturing and processing industries, tourism and agriculture, and technical, managerial and administrative assistance and advice; performs related economic and technical research; Chair. RENOS SOLOMIDES; Gen. Man. JOHN G. JOANNIDES; 1 br.

Foreign Banks

Arab Bank Ltd: POB 5700, 85 Dhigenis Akritas Ave, Nicosia; tel. (02) 457111; telex 5717; f. 1983; commercial; Area Exec. C. C. STEPHANI; 9 brs.

Barclays Bank PLC: POB 1022, Nicosia; tel. (02) 461861; telex 3400; f. 1937; Local Dir D. G. BEECHAM; Chief Man. D. VASILIOU; 31 brs.

National Bank of Greece SA: POB 1191, 36 Archbishop Makarios III Ave, Nicosia; tel. (02) 441412; telex 2445; f. 1907; Regional Man. DEMETRIOS YIAKOUMELLOS; 20 brs.

Türkiye İş Bankası AŞ: 9 Girne Cad., Nicosia, Mersin 10, Turkey; tel. (020) 71133; telex 57123; f. 1924; Man. BULENT NISANCIOGLU.

Türkiye Cumhuriyeti Ziraat Bankası: İplik Pazari, Dr Semsi Kazim Pasaji, Bitisigi, Nicosia, Mersin 10, Turkey; tel. (020) 72050; telex 57110.

Türkiye Halk Bankası AŞ: Osman Paşa Cad., Umit Office, Nicosia, Mersin 10, Turkey; tel. (020) 72145; telex 57241.

Offshore Banking Units

An Offshore Banking Unit (OBU) is not permitted to provide local banking services, but is allowed to accept deposits from governments and large financial organizations in the area, and to make medium-term loans for local and regional capital projects (with the approval of the Central Bank). In 1988 OBUs were permitted to extend credit facilities to residents of Cyprus, on condition that the income accruing from such activities is taxed at the normal rate of tax applicable to onshore/domestic activities. In September 1988 there were 16 OBUs operating in Cyprus.

Allied Business Bank SAL: POB 4232, 3rd Floor, Flat 31, Lara Court, 276 Archbishop Makarios III Ave, Limassol; tel. (051) 63759; telex 6040.

Bank of Beirut and the Arab Countries SAL: POB 6201, Emelle Bldg, 1st Floor, 135 Archbishop Makarios III Ave, Limassol; tel. (051) 81290; telex 5444.

*Bank of Credit and Commerce International SA: POB 1963, 256 Leontiou I St, Maximos Court, Limassol; tel. (051) 38336; telex 4255.

*Banque du Crédit Populaire SAL: POB 3493, P. Lordos Centre, Block C, Byron St, Limassol; tel. (051) 76433; telex 4424.

Banque Européenne pour le Moyen-Orient SA: POB 6232, Doma Court, 1st-2nd Floors, 227 Archbishop Makarios III Ave, Limassol; tel. (051) 68628; telex 5575.

Banque Nationale de Paris 'Intercontinentale' SA: POB 4286, Steffel Court, 3 J. F. Kennedy St, Limassol; tel. (051) 60166; telex 5519.

*Barclays Bank PLC: POB 2383, Barclays House, 2nd Floor, Dhigenis Akritas Ave, Nicosia; tel. (02) 464777; telex 5200.

*Byblos Bank SAL: POB 5130, 1 Archbishop Kyprianou St/St Andrew St, Limassol; tel. (051) 41433; telex 5203.

*Crédit Libanais SAL (COBU): POB 3492, Chrysalia Court, 1st Floor, 206 Archbishop Makarios III Ave, Limassol; tel. (051) 76444; telex 4702.

*Federal Bank of the Middle East Ltd: POB 5566, Megaron Lavinia, Santa Rosa Ave and Mykinon St, Nicosia; tel. (02) 461619; telex 4677; f. 1983; cap. US $25m. (1988).

*Générale de Crédit (Cyprus) Ltd: POB 8560, 7-9 Grivas Dhigenis Ave, Nicosia; tel. (02) 824455; telex 5342.

*Jordan National Bank SA: POB 3587, Araouzos Castle Court, 2nd Floor, 12 Richard and Berengaria St, Limassol; tel. (051) 56669; telex 5471.

Lebanon and Gulf Bank SAL: POB 2078, Akamia Center, 3rd Floor, corner of G. Afxentiou and Archbishop Makarios III Ave, Larnaca; tel. (041) 20500; telex 5779; Man. MOUNIB M. HAMMOUD.

Société Bancaire Arabe SA: POB 4405, Bacchus House, 241E Kanika Enaerios Complex, corner of 28th October St and Archbishop Makarios III Ave, Limassol; tel. (051) 68650; telex 3569.

Udružena Beogradska Banka: Ambrosia Bldg, 1st Floor, 92 Archbishop Makarios III Ave, Nicosia; tel. (02) 453493; telex 6413.

*Wardley Cyprus Ltd: POB 5718, Laiki Tower, 3rd Floor, 11–13 Archbishop Makarios III Ave, Nicosia; tel. (02) 477515; telex 4980; Man. Dir R. I. SHIPLEY.

* Restricted licence banks, authorized only to deal with non-residents of Cyprus, excluding nationals, and only in currencies other than the Cyprus pound.

INSURANCE

Office of the Superintendent of Insurance: Treasury Department, Ministry of Finance, Nicosia; tel. (02) 403256; telex 2366; f. 1969 to control insurance companies, insurance agents, brokers and agents for brokers in Cyprus.

Greek Cypriot Insurance Companies

Albedo Insurance Co Ltd: 4th Floor, Block 'B', Fortuna Bldg, 284 Archbishop Makarios III Ave, Limassol 225; tel. (051) 62818; telex 2948; f. 1986; Chair. and Gen. Man. COSTAS KOUTSOKOUMNIS.

Allied Assurance & Reinsurance Co Ltd: POB 5509, 12 Themistoklis Dervis St, Ivory Tower, Nicosia 136; tel. (02) 457311; telex 4265; f. 1982; offshore company operating outside Cyprus; Chair. RONALD J. CLELAND; Man. Dir EDOUARD PAPASIAN.

Apac Ltd: POB 5403, Apt 1, 5 Mourouzi St, Nicosia 133; tel. (02) 455186; telex 2766; f. 1983; captive offshore company operating outside Cyprus; Chair. KYPROS CHRYSOSTOMIDES; Principal Officer GEORGHIOS POYATZIS.

Asfalistiki Eteria I 'Kentriki' Ltd: POB 5131, Flat 201, 2nd Floor, Margarita House, 15 Themistoklis Dervis St, Nicosia 136; tel. (02) 473981; telex 4987; f. 1985; Chair. NESTOR KAKOYIANNIS; Principal Officer GEORGE GEORGALLIDES.

Atlantic Insurance Co Ltd: POB 4579, 34 Theophanis Theodotou St, Nicosia 136; tel. (02) 444052; telex 2535; f. 1983; Chair. and Man. Dir ZENIOS PYRISHIS; Gen. Man. N. MARATHOVOUNIOTIS.

Commercial Union Assurance (Cyprus) Ltd: POB 1312, 4th Floor, Lavinia Bldg, Corner of Santa Rosa Ave and Mykinon St, Nicosia; tel. (02) 445045; telex 2547; f. 1974; Chair. J. CHRISTOPHIDES; Gen. Man. KONSTANTINOS P. DEKATRIS.

Compass Insurance Co Ltd: POB 7501, 48 Kyriacos Matsis St, Engomi, Nicosia 161; tel. (02) 462492; telex 2270; f. 1981; Chair. P. LOUCAIDES; Gen. Man. PHAEDON MAKRIS.

Cosmos) Insurance Co Ltd: POB 1770, 1st Floor, Flat 12, 6 Ayia Eleni St, Nicosia 135; tel. (02) 441235; telex 3433; f. 1982; Chair. ELIZABETH PLAKIDOU; Gen. Man. KYRIACOS TYLLIS.

Fli-Cy Life Insurance Ltd: POB 1612, Julia House, 3 Themistoklis Dervis St, Nicosia 136; tel. (02) 448278; telex 2863; f. 1986; captive offshore company operating outside Cyprus; Chair. and Gen. Man. KYPROS CHRYSOSTOMIDES.

General Insurance Co of Cyprus Ltd: POB 1668, 2–4 Themistoklis Dervis St, Nicosia; tel. (02) 450444; telex 2311; f. 1951; Chair. A. PATSALIDES; Gen. Man. S. SOPHOCLEOUS.

Granite Insurance Co Ltd: POB 613, 2nd Floor, Block 'A', Fortuna Bldg, 284 Archbishop Makarios III Ave, Limassol 255; tel. (051) 62818; telex 2948; captive offshore company operating outside Cyprus; Chair. and Gen. Man. COSTAS KOUTSOKOUMNIS.

Greene Insurances Ltd: POB 132, 284 Archbishop Makarios III Ave, Fortuna Bldg, Block B, 2nd Floor, Limassol 255; tel. (051) 62424; telex 2566; f. 1987; Chair. GEORGHIOS CHRISTODOULOU; Principal Officer JOSIF CHRISTOU.

Hermes Insurance Co Ltd: POB 4828, 1st Floor, Office 101-103, 8 Michalakis Karaolis St, Nicosia; tel. (02) 448130; telex 3466; f. 1980; Chair. and Man. Dir P. VOGAZIANOS.

Iris Insurance Co Ltd: POB 4841, Flat H1, 8th Floor, 'Aspelia' Bldg, 20 Costis Palamas St, Nicosia 136; tel. (02) 448302; telex 3675; Chair. and Gen. Man. PAVLOS CL. GEORGHIOU.

Juniper Insurance Ltd: POB 1121, 'Stasinos' Bldg, 2 Ayias Elenis St, Nicosia 135; tel. (02) 448700; telex 2973; captive offshore company operating outside Cyprus; Chair. YUEN HONG WONG; Gen. Man. STALO ANDREOU.

Laiki Insurance Co Ltd: POB 2069, Laiki Tower, 11–39 Archbishop Makarios III Ave, Nicosia 136; tel. (02) 449900; telex 5916; f. 1981; Chair. E. K. LANITIS; Man. Y. E. SOLOMONIDES.

L.U. Lifestyle Underwriters Ltd: POB 1612, 3 Themistoklis Dervis St, Julia House, Nicosia 136; tel. (02) 453053; telex 2046; f. 1984; Chair. LELLOS DEMETRIADES; Principal Officer NIKOS AVRAAMIDES.

Merehurst (Europe) Ltd: POB 3585, Julia House, 3 Themistoklis Dervis St, Nicosia 136; tel. (02) 453053; telex 2046; f. 1985; captive offshore company operating outside Cyprus; Chair. L. DEMETRIADES; Principal Officer N. AVRAAMIDES.

Minerva Insurance Co Ltd: POB 3554, 8 Epaminondas St, Nicosia 137; tel. (02) 445134; telex 2608; f. 1970; Chair. and Gen. Man. K. KOUTSOKOUMNIS.

North Global Insurance and Reinsurance Co Ltd: POB 1553, Apt 21, 2nd Floor, Block 'B', Fortuna Bldg, 284 Archbishop Makarios III Ave, Limassol 255; tel. (051) 62424; telex 2566; f. 1984; offshore company operating outside Cyprus; Chair. JAMIL BIN NASSER; Principal Officer CHRIS GEORGHIADES.

Pacmag Insurance Ltd: POB 1121, Stasinos Bldg, 2 Ayias Elenis St, Nicosia 135; tel. (02) 448700; telex 2973; f. 1986; captive offshore company operating outside Cyprus; Chair. YUEN HONG WONG; Gen. Man. STALO ANDREOU.

Paneuropean Insurance Co Ltd: POB 3506, 4th and 5th Floor, 95 Archbishop Makarios III Ave, Nicosia 137; tel. (02) 449960; telex 3419; f. 1980; Chair. N. K. SHACOLAS; Gen. Man. ZENIOS DEMETRIOU.

Philiki Insurance Co Ltd: POB 2274, 1st Floor, 2 Demokritos Bldg, Corner Archbishop Makarios III Ave and J. Clerides St, Nicosia; tel. (02) 444433; telex 2353; f. 1982; Chair. LOUKIS PETRIDES; Gen. Man. DOROS ORPHANIDES.

Sage Insurance Ltd: POB 1121, Stasinos Bldg, 2 Ayias Elenis St, Nicosia 135; tel. (02) 448700; telex 2973; captive offshore company operating outside Cyprus; Chair. YUEN HONG WONG; Principal Officer STALO PAPAIOANNOU.

Saudi Stars Insurance Co Ltd: POB 1493, No. 2, Corner Archbishop Makarios III Ave and Methonis St, Nicosia; tel. (02) 445874; telex 3156; f. 1979; offshore company operating outside Cyprus; Chair. M. F. AL-HAJRI; Principal Officer PAN. MEGALEMOS.

Saviour Insurance Co Ltd: POB 3957, 8 Michalakis Karaolis St, Anemomylos Bldg, Flat 204, Nicosia 162; tel. (02) 365085; telex 4351; f. 1987; Chair. CLIVE ANTONY HOLME NICHOLSON; Principal Officer KONSTANTINOS KITTIS.

Seven Stars Insurance Co Ltd: 11A Rega Fereou St, Limassol 251; tel. (051) 445045; telex 2547; f. 1983; offshore company operating outside Cyprus; Chair. KYPROS CHRYSOSTOMIDES.

Universal Life Insurance Company Ltd: POB 1270, Universal Tower, 85 Dhigenis Akritas Ave, Nicosia 135; tel. (02) 461222; telex 3116; f. 1970; Chair. J. CHRISTOPHIDES; Gen. Man. ANDREAS GEORGHIOU.

Warwick Insurance Co Ltd: POB 1612, 3 Themistoklis Dervis St, Julia House, Nicosia 136; tel. (02) 453053; telex 2046; f. 1987; Chair. NIKOS AVRAAMIDES.

WOB Insurances Ltd: 2nd Floor, Block 'A', Fortuna Bldg, 284 Archbishop Makarios III Ave, Limassol 255; tel. (051) 62818; telex 2948; captive offshore company operating outside Cyprus; Chair. and Gen. Man. KOSTAS KOUTSOKOUMNIS.

Turkish Cypriot Insurance Companies

Genel Sigorta: 11 Cumhuriyet Sok., Nicosia, Mersin 10, Turkey; tel. (020) 72658.

Güneş Sigorta: 42–46 Girne Cad., Nicosia, Mersin 10, Turkey; tel. (020) 71132; telex 57139.

Şeker Sigorta: POB 823, K.T. Kooperatif Merkez Bankasi, 49–55 Mahmout Pasha Sok., Nicosia, Mersin 10, Turkey; tel. (020) 71207; telex 57216.

There were 33 foreign insurance companies operating in Cyprus in 1987.

Trade and Industry

GREEK CYPRIOT CHAMBERS OF COMMERCE AND INDUSTRY

Cyprus Chamber of Commerce and Industry: POB 1455, 38 Grivas Dhigenis Ave, Nicosia; tel. (02) 449500; telex 2077; Pres. ANDREAS AVRAAMIDES; Sec.-Gen. PANAYIOTIS LOIZIDES; 4,000 mems, 58 affiliated trade ascns.

Famagusta Chamber of Commerce and Industry: POB 3124, Stylianides Bldg, 3rd Floor, 1 Koumandarias St, Limassol; tel. (051) 70165; telex 4519; f. 1952; Pres. DEMETRIOS P. IOANNOU; Vice-Pres. T. KYRIAKIDES; 300 mems.

Larnaca Chamber of Commerce and Industry: POB 287, 12 Gregoris Afxentiou St, Apt 43, 4th Floor, Skouros Bldg, Larnaca; tel. (041) 55051; telex 3187; Pres. ANDREAS MOUSKOS; Vice-Pres. K. LEFKARITIS; 350 mems.

CYPRUS
Directory

Limassol Chamber of Commerce and Industry: POB 347, 25 Spyrou Araouzou St, Veregaria Bldg, 3rd Floor, Limassol; tel. (051) 62556; telex 2890; Pres. CHRISTAKIS GEORGIADES; Vice-Pres. KYRIACOS PATTICHIS.

Nicosia Chamber of Commerce and Industry: POB 1455, Hajisavvas Bldg, Evagoras Ave, Nicosia; tel. (02) 449500; telex 2077; Pres. LEANDROS ZACHARIADES; Vice-Pres. KOSTAS KONSTANTINIDES.

Paphos Chamber of Commerce and Industry: POB 62, Grivas Dhigenis Ave, Demetra Court, Paphos; tel. (061) 35115; telex 2888; Pres. MICHALAKIS E. KONIOTIS; Vice-Pres. ANDREAS DEMETRIADES.

TURKISH CYPRIOT CHAMBERS OF COMMERCE AND INDUSTRY

Turkish Chamber of Industry: Müftü Racı St, Ontaş İşhanı B24, Nicosia, Mersin 10, Turkey; tel. (020) 71870; Pres. Dr ALI ATUN.

Turkish Cypriot Chamber of Commerce: POB 718, Bedrettin Demirel Cad., Nicosia, Mersin 10, Turkey; tel. (020) 78760; telex 57137; f. 1958; more than 4,000 regd mems; Chair. MUSTAFA YILDIRIM; Sec.-Gen. JANEL BURCAN.

EMPLOYERS' ORGANIZATIONS

Greek Cypriot Employers' Organizations

At 31 December 1980 there were 28 employers' associations, including 14 independent associations, with a total membership of 4,115.

Cyprus Employers' & Industrialists' Federation: POB 1657, 30 Grivas Dhigenis Ave, Nicosia; tel. (02) 445102; telex 4834; f. 1960; 26 member trade associations, 400 direct and 1,600 indirect members; Dir-Gen. ANT. PIERIDES; Chair. PHAEDROS EKONOMIDES. The largest of the trade association members are: Cyprus Building Contractors' Association; Cyprus Hotel Keepers' Association; Clothing Manufacturers' Association; Cyprus Shipping Association; Shoe Makers' Association; Cyprus Metal Industries Association; Cyprus Bankers Employers' Association; Motor Cars, Tractors & Agricultural Machinery Importers' Association.

Turkish Cypriot Employers' Organizations

Kıbrıs Türk İşverenler Sendikasi (Turkish Cypriot Employers Association): POB 674, Nicosia, Mersin 10, Turkey; tel. (020) 76173; Chair. ALPAY ALI RIZA GÖRGÜNER.

TRADE UNIONS

At 31 December 1980 there were 97 trade unions with 240 branches, six union federations and five confederations.

Greek Cypriot Trade Unions

Pankypria Ergatiki Omospondia—PEO (Pancyprian Federation of Labour): POB 1885, 31-35 Archermos St, Nicosia; tel. (02) 473192; f. 1946, registered 1947; previously the Pancyprian Trade Union Committee f. 1941, dissolved 1946; 11 unions and 122 brs with a total membership of 71,000; affiliated to the World Federation of Trade Unions; Pres. PAVLOS DHINGLIS.

Synomospondia Ergaton Kyprou (Cyprus Workers' Confederation): POB 5018, 23 Alkaiou St, Engomi, Nicosia; tel. (02) 441142; f. 1944, registered 1950; 7 Federations, 5 Labour Centres, 47 unions, 12 brs with a total membership of 50,770; affiliated to the ICFTU and the ETUC; Gen. Sec. MICHAEL IOANNOU; Deputy Gen. Sec. DEMETRIS KITTENIS.

Pankyprios Omospondia Anexartition Syntechnion (Pancyprian Federation of Independent Trade Unions): 1 Menadrou St, Nicosia; tel. (02) 442233; f. 1956, registered 1957; has no political orientations; 8 unions with a total membership of 798; Pres. KOSTAS ANTONIADES; Gen. Sec. KYRIACOS NATHANAEL.

Demokratiki Ergatiki Omospondia Kyprou (Democratic Labour Federation of Cyprus): POB 1625, 25 Constantinou Paleologou Ave, Nicosia; tel. (02) 456506; f. 1962; 4 unions with a total membership of 4,250; Gen. Sec. RENOS PRENTZAS.

Cyprus Civil Servants' Trade Union: 2 Andreas Demetriou St, Nicosia; tel. (02) 442278; f. 1949, registered 1966; restricted to persons in the civil employment of the government and public authorities; 6 brs with a total membership of 13,030; Pres. A. PAPANASTASSIOU; Gen. Sec. G. IAKOVOU.

Union of Cyprus Journalists: c/o Andreas Kannaouros, Embros newspaper, Haravghi, Nicosia; tel. (02) 428844; Chair. ANDREAS KANNAOUROS.

Turkish Cypriot Trade Unions

In 1986 trade union membership totalled 20,627.

Kıbrıs Türk İşçi Sendikaları Federasyonu (TÜRK-SEN) (Turkish Cypriot Trade Union Federation): POB 829, 7-7A Sehit Mehmet R. Hüseyin Sok., Nicosia, Mersin 10, Turkey; tel. (020) 72444; f. 1954, regd 1955; 15 unions with a total membership of 9,307 (1986); affiliated to ICFTU, ETUC, CTUC and the Confederation of Trade Unions of Turkey (Türk-İş); Pres. HÜSEYIN CURCIOĞLU; Gen. Sec. (vacant).

Devrimci İşçi Sendikaları Federasyonu (Dev-İş) (Revolutionary Trade Unions' Federation): 30 Beliğ Paşa Sok., Nicosia, Mersin 10, Turkey; tel. (020) 72640; f. 1976; two unions with a total membership of 4,586 (1986); affiliated to WFTU; Pres. HASAN SARICA; Gen.-Sec. BAYRAM ÇELIK.

TRADE FAIRS

Cyprus International (State) Fair: POB 3551, Makedonitissa, Nicosia; tel. (02) 352918; telex 3344; 14th Fair scheduled for 27 May-4 June 1989.

Transport

There are no railways in Cyprus.

ROADS

In December 1987 there were 8,966 km of roads in the government-controlled areas, of which 4,427 km were paved and 4,539 km were earth or gravel roads. The construction of the Nicosia-Limassol four-lane dual carriageway was completed in 1985. A project is under way to link the Nicosia-Limassol highway with another four-lane highway to Larnaca. The construction of the new Nicosia-Kyrenia highway was due to be completed by the end of 1987. Bus and taxi services between Nicosia and the principal towns and villages, which were severely disrupted by the Turkish invasion, have since been restored, but the north and south are now served by separate transport systems, and there are no services linking the two sectors. In 1984 the road network in the Turkish Cypriot area consisted of about 5,278 km of paved and 838 km of unpaved roads. The 'TRNC' Government allocated TL 3,500m. to road construction projects in 1988.

SHIPPING

Until 1974 Famagusta was the island's most important harbour, handling about 83% of the country's cargo. Famagusta is a natural port capable of receiving ships of a maximum draught of 9.2 m. Since its capture by the Turkish army in August 1974 the port has been officially declared closed to international traffic. However, it continues to serve the Turkish-occupied region.

The main ports which serve the island's maritime trade at present are Larnaca and Limassol, which were constructed in 1973 and 1974 respectively. Both ports have been expanded: the quay of the new Limassol port is 1,280 m long and 11 m deep, while the port of Larnaca has a quay length of 866 m and a depth of 10 m. There is also an industrial port at Vassiliko, with a quay 555 m long and 9 m deep, and there are three specialized petroleum terminals, at Larnaca, Dhekelia and Moni.

In 1987, 4,420 vessels with a total net registered tonnage of 12,800,000 visited Cyprus. Limassol handled approximately three-quarters of ships entered and cleared.

Both Kyrenia and Karavostassi are under Turkish occupation and have been declared closed to international traffic. Karavostassi used to be the country's major mineral port dealing with 76% of the total mineral exports. However, since the war minerals have been passed through Vassiliko and Limni which are open roadsteads. In 1977 a hydrofoil service was started between Kyrenia and Mersin on the Turkish mainland. A new car-ferry harbour was opened at Kyrenia in November 1987. This was designed to relieve the congestion at the commercial harbour of Famagusta. Car ferries sail from Kyrenia to Taşucu and Mersin, in Turkey.

The number of merchant vessels registered in Cyprus rose from 1,803 (with a total displacement of 13,948,452 grt) in 1986 to 1,981 (17,890,061 grt) in December 1987.

Cyprus Ports Authority: POB 2007, Nicosia; tel. (02) 450100; telex 2833; f. 1973; Chair. MICHAEL ZAMPELAS; Gen. Man. JOSEPH BAYADA.

Greek Cypriot Shipping Companies

Brasal Offshore Services Ltd: POB 1518, Limassol; tel. (051) 73086; telex 2105; salvage craft, survey launch, suction dredger; Man. Dir E. BRANCO.

Columbia Shipmanagement Ltd: POB 1624, Columbia House, Dodekanison St, Limassol; tel. (051) 20900; telex 3206; f. 1978; 90 ships; Man. Dir H. SCHOELLER.

A. Elias (Overseas) Co Ltd: POB 1165, 104 Archbishop Makarios III Ave, Limassol; tel. (051) 38025; telex 2108; two cargo ships; Chair. A. ELIAS; Man. Dir I. ELIAS.

Hanseatic Shipping Co Ltd: POB 127, 102 St Andrews St, Limassol; tel. (051) 78108; telex 3282; f. 1972; 90 ships; Man. Dir Capt. JOACHIM MEYER; Fleet Man. Capt. B. BEHRENS.

Interorient Navigation Co Ltd: POB 1309, 229 Archbishop Makarios III Ave, Meliza Court, Limassol; tel. (051) 52047; telex 3142; Man. Dir Capt. LISSOW.

Lefkaritis Bros Marine Ltd: POB 162, 1 Kilkis St, Larnaca; tel. (041) 52142; telex 2224; f. 1974; three tankers; Chair. and Man. Dir TAKIS C. LEFKARITIS.

Marlow Navigation Co Ltd: POB 4077, Fortuna Court, Block B, 224 Archbishop Makarios III Ave, Limassol; tel. (051) 67029; telex 2019; Man. Dir H. EDEN.

Navigo Management Co: POB 3087, 111 Spyrou Araouzou Ave, Limassol; tel. (051) 42922; telex 5415; Gen. Man. Capt. L. NEUBAUER.

Northern Marine Management Ltd Cyprus: POB 597, Pareas Arcade, 57 Anexartissias St, Limassol; tel. (051) 76006; telex 4653; Man. Dir H. DONKER.

Josef Roth (Cyprus) Shipping Co Ltd: POB 1536, 28 Archbishop Makarios III Ave, 6th Floor, Limassol; telex 2848; six cargo ships.

Sol Maritime Services Ltd: POB 1682, 1st and 2nd Floor, 140B Franklin Roosevelt St, Limassol; tel. (051) 69000; telex 2882; f. 1977; three car ferries, one roll-on/roll-off ferry; Man. Dir TAKIS SOLOMONIDES.

Uniteam Marine Ltd: POB 4086, Fortuna Court, 284–286 Archbishop Makarios III Ave, Limassol; tel. (051) 52101; telex 2848; Man. Dir G. RUETHER.

Turkish Cypriot Shipping Companies

Denizyolları (Shipping) Co Ltd: 92 Girne Cad., Nicosia, Mersin 10, Turkey; tel. (020) 71313; telex 57138.

Orion Navigation Ltd: Seagate Court, Famagusta, Mersin 10, Turkey; tel. (036) 62006; telex 57228; f. 1976; shipping agents; Dir O. LAMA; Shipping Man. L. LAMA.

Savarona Maritime Ltd: 8 Bekiroğlu İşhani, Müftü Ziya Efendi Sok., Nicosia, Mersin 10, Turkey; tel. (020) 75179; telex 57246.

Traverway Maritime Ltd: Onar Ishani, Mahkemeler Önü, Nicosia, Mersin 10, Turkey; tel. (020) 72323; telex 57249.

Turkish Cypriot Maritime Co Ltd: Girne Cad., Adem Kaner İshanu, Nicosia, Mersin 10, Turkey.

CIVIL AVIATION

There is an international airport at Nicosia, which can accommodate all types of aircraft, including jets. It has been closed since July 1974 following the Turkish invasion. A new international airport was constructed at Larnaca, from which flights operate to Europe, the Middle East and the Gulf. Another international airport at Paphos began operations in November 1983.

In 1975 the Turkish authorities opened Ercan (formerly Tymbou) airport, and a second airport was opened at Geçitkale (Lefkoniko) in 1986.

Cyprus Airways: POB 1903, 21 Alkeou St, Engomi, Nicosia; tel. (02) 443054; telex 2225; f. 1947; jointly owned by Cyprus government and local interests; wholly-owned charter subsidiary Cyprair Tours Ltd; Chair. STAVROS GALATARIOTIS; Man. Dir S. NATHANAEL; services to Athens, Bahrain, Birmingham, Cairo, Damascus, Dubai, Frankfurt, Geneva, Jeddah, Kuwait, London, Manchester, Munich, Paris, Riyadh, Tel-Aviv and Zürich from Larnaca and Paphos Airports; fleet of 3 Airbus A310-200, 3 Boeing 707-123B and 3 BAC 1-11-500.

Turkish Cypriot Airlines Co, Ltd: Bedreddin Demirel Ave, Nicosia, Mersin 10, Yenisehir, Turkey; tel. (020) 71901; telex 57133; f. 1974; jointly owned by the 'TRNC' and Turkish Airlines Ltd.; Gen. Man. FIKRET GÜMÜŞDERE; routes from Ercan Airport, Nicosia, to Ankara, Adana, Antalya, Istanbul, İzmir, Munich and London; fleet of 1 Boeing 727-200, 1 DC9-30, 1 DC10 and 1 A310.

Tourism

In 1987 there were 948,551 foreign visitors to the Greek Cypriot area. Receipts from tourism totalled C£257m. in 1986. The number of visitors to the Turkish Cypriot area reached 184,337 in 1987, when revenue totalled US $56.1m.

Cyprus Tourism Organization: POB 4535, Zena Bldg, 18 Th. Theodotou St, Nicosia; tel. (02) 443374; telex 2165; Chair. STELIOS GARANIS; Dir-Gen. ANTONIOS ANDRONIKOU.

Turkish Cypriot Tourist Board: Kordon Boyu, Kyrenia, Mersin 10, Turkey; tel. 52165; telex 57128.

CZECHOSLOVAKIA

Introductory Survey

Location, Climate, Language, Religion, Flag, Capital

The Czechoslovak Socialist Republic lies in central Europe. Its neighbours are Poland to the north, the German Democratic Republic to the north-west, the Federal Republic of Germany to the west, Austria to the south-west, Hungary to the south-east and the USSR to the extreme east. The state is composed of two main population groups, the Czechs (63.5% of the total population in 1986) and the Slovaks (31.2%). The climate is continental, with warm summers and cold winters. The average mean temperature is 9°C (49°F). The official languages, which are mutually understandable, are Czech and Slovak, members of the west Slavonic group. There is a Hungarian-speaking minority in Slovakia. Most of the country's inhabitants profess Christianity: about 70% are Roman Catholics, and 15% Protestants. The national flag (proportions 3 by 2) has two equal horizontal stripes, of white and red, on which is superimposed a blue triangle (half the length) at the hoist. The capital is Prague (Praha).

Recent History

At the end of the First World War, in 1918, the Austro-Hungarian Empire was dissolved, and its former western Slavonic provinces became Czechoslovakia. The boundaries of the new republic, fixed by treaty in 1919, included the Sudetenland, an area in northern Bohemia that was inhabited by about 3m. German-speaking people. After the Nazis, led by Adolf Hitler, came to power in Germany in 1933, there was increased agitation in the Sudetenland for autonomy within, and later secession from, Czechoslovakia. In 1938, to appease German demands, the British, French and Italian Prime Ministers made an agreement with Hitler, by which the Sudetenland was ceded to Germany, while other parts of Czechoslovakia were transferred to Hungary and Poland. The remainder of Czechoslovakia was invaded and occupied by Nazi Germany in March 1939.

After Germany's defeat in the Second World War (1939–45), the pre-1938 frontiers of Czechoslovakia were restored, although a small area in the east was ceded to the USSR in June 1945. Almost all of the German-speaking inhabitants of Czechoslovakia were expelled, and the Sudetenland was settled by Czechs from other parts of Bohemia. At elections in 1946 the Communists emerged as the leading party, gaining 38% of the votes. The Communist Party's leader, Klement Gottwald, became Prime Minister in a coalition government. After Ministers of other parties resigned, Communist control became complete on 25 February 1948. A People's Republic was established on 9 June 1948. Gottwald replaced Edvard Beneš as President, a position that he held until his death in 1953. The country aligned itself with the Soviet-led East European bloc, joining the Council for Mutual Economic Assistance (CMEA) and the Warsaw Pact (see pp. 124 and 207 respectively).

Under Gottwald, government followed a rigid Stalinist pattern, and in the early 1950s there were many political trials. Although these ended under Gottwald's successors, Antonín Zápotocký and, from 1956, Antonín Novotný, 'de-Stalinization' was late in coming to Czechoslovakia, and there was no relaxation until 1963, when a new government, with Jozef Lenárt (hitherto President of the Slovak National Council) as Prime Minister, was formed. Meanwhile, the country was renamed the Czechoslovak Socialist Republic, under a new constitution, proclaimed in July 1960.

In January 1968 Alexander Dubček succeeded Novotný as Party Secretary, and in March Gen. Ludvík Svoboda succeeded him as President. Oldřich Černík became Prime Minister in April 1968. The policies of the new government were more independent and liberal, and envisaged widespread reforms. These were seen by other members of the East European bloc as endangering their unity, and in August 1968 Warsaw Pact forces occupied Prague and other major cities. The Soviet Government exerted heavy pressure on Czechoslovak leaders to suppress their reformist policies, and in April 1969 Dubček was replaced by Dr Gustáv Husák as First (subsequently General) Secretary of the Communist Party. Although Dr Husák resisted some pressure for stricter control and political trials, there was a severe purge of Communist Party membership, and most of Dubček's supporters were removed from the Government. The first elections since 1964 were held in November 1971 and showed a 99.81% vote in favour of National Front candidates.

In May 1975 Dr Husák was appointed President of the Republic while still holding the positions of Chairman of the National Front and General Secretary of the Communist Party. Dr Husák was re-elected Party leader in April 1976 and again in April 1981, and was re-elected President in May 1980 and May 1985. The 17th Communist Party Congress was held in March 1986. Dr Husák was re-elected General Secretary of the Party's 195-member Central Committee. Legislative elections were held in May 1986. Changes in the Federal Government, appointed in June, included the creation of the new post of First Deputy Prime Minister. In March 1987 Josef Korčák resigned as Prime Minister of the Czech State Government and was replaced by Ladislav Adamec. In April Mikhail Gorbachev, General Secretary of the Soviet Communist Party, paid a three-day visit, which was interpreted by some observers as an attempt to persuade the Czechoslovak Government to pursue Soviet-style political and economic reform. Disappointing results in industry fuelled speculation that a restructuring of the system of economic management was imminent, and Dr Husák duly announced a limited plan for economic reform, which he likened to that initiated by the Dubček Government in 1968.

In December 1987 Dr Husák resigned as General Secretary of the Central Committee of the Communist Party and was replaced by Miloš Jakeš, an economist and member of the Presidium of the Party's Central Committee. However, it was announced that Dr Husák would retain the largely ceremonial post of President of the Republic. Jakeš affirmed his commitment to the moderate programme of reform, initiated by his predecessor, but in his first year of office there was little indication of a policy more liberal than that of Dr Husák, as repressive measures towards the Roman Catholic Church and dissidents continued.

A new programme of economic restructuring (přestavba) was, however, instigated by Jakeš, with 1 January 1991 as the date set for the effective transition to a new economic structure. In this connection, a 30% reduction of employees in federal offices was proposed, and in a major government reshuffle in April 1988 (the first in two decades) the number of ministers was substantially reduced, while five ministries were merged into two. The Czech and Slovak Governments were also reorganized. Further government changes followed in October. Lubomír Štrougal, widely regarded as an advocate of reform, resigned as Federal Prime Minister and was replaced by Ladislav Adamec, hitherto Prime Minister of the Czech Government. Adamec was, in turn, replaced by František Pitra, and Ivan Knotek was appointed Prime Minister of the Slovak Government. During 1988 numerous changes were also made in the Communist Party leadership. An extensive reorganization of the Presidium of the Central Committee was carried out. In February Jakeš replaced Dr Husák as Chairman of the National Front.

Meanwhile, in January 1977 a manifesto known as Charter 77, protesting against the lack of civil rights in Czechoslovakia, was published in the West. Many of the hundreds of Czechoslovak intellectuals and former politicians who signed the Charter were arrested, tried on various charges and imprisoned, but, despite attempts by the Government to suppress the activists, the civil rights campaign continued. A purge of Party members began in 1979 and, although almost all of those protesters who were originally detained had been released by 1983, sporadic arrests and harassment continued. By 1985 the movement's field of comment had broadened, and in that year spokesmen for the signatories issued appeals for the dissolution of NATO and the Warsaw Pact alliance, for the withdrawal of Soviet troops and nuclear weapons from Czechoslovakia, and for the Czechoslovak Government to adopt an attitude in favour of economic reforms, such as was developing in other

CZECHOSLOVAKIA

Introductory Survey

East European countries. In August 1987 representatives of Charter 77 met members of Solidarity, the illegal Polish trade union. On the 20th anniversary of the Warsaw Pact intervention in Czechoslovakia, in August 1988, about 10,000 people demonstrated in Prague against the Government, the largest manifestation of public discontent since 1968. On 28 October 1988 (the 70th anniversary of the republic's independence) several thousand Czechoslovaks held demonstrations in Prague, Brno and Bratislava, in support of demands for political reform. Large numbers were arrested, including leading human rights activists and Charter 77 members. In December 1988 the first officially-authorized human rights demonstration for 20 years was held in Prague. The rally, organized to commemorate the 40th anniversary of the UN General Assembly's adoption of the Universal Declaration of Human Rights, was attended by about 5,000 people, including prominent members of Charter 77, and coincided with a visit to Prague by President Mitterrand of France.

Relations between the Czechoslovak Government and the Roman Catholic Church, which had long been strained, did not improve in spite of a series of discussions with representatives of the Vatican in late 1983 and 1984. The discussions mainly concerned the Government's desire to fill vacant bishoprics with politically acceptable incumbents, and its objection to a Vatican decree of 1982, forbidding priests to join, among other 'political' bodies, the peace organization Pacem in Terris, which was supported by the Czechoslovak Government. Several foreign Roman Catholic dignitaries, including Pope John Paul II, were refused visas to attend celebrations, which took place in Czechoslovakia in July 1985, to mark the 1,100th anniversary of the death of St Methodius. In 1987 a 17-point statement, entitled the 'Charter of Believers in Czechoslovakia', demanding an end to the persecution of Christians, was circulated around the country. In 1988 about 600,000 Czechoslovak Roman Catholics (including the Primate, Cardinal František Tomášek, the Archbishop of Prague) signed a petition appealing for greater autonomy and freedom for the Church. In March demonstrations involving thousands of Czech and Slovak believers took place in both Prague and Bratislava, the latter prompting police action and arrests. In May, however, after protracted negotiations between Church and State over 10 vacant bishoprics, three new bishops were appointed (the first in Czechoslovakia for 15 years), and in June they were consecrated. None was a member of the Pacem in Terris movement.

In September 1986 seven members of the Jazz Section of the Czechoslovak Musicians' Association, including the chairman, Karel Srp, and the secretary, Vladimír Kouřil, were arrested for illegal commercial activity. Since its inception in 1971, the Jazz Section had grown into an unofficial forum for disaffected intellectuals and musicians of all genres to express dissatisfaction at state control of cultural life. At their trial in March 1987, Srp was sentenced to 16 months in prison, and Kouřil to 10 months, while three other members received suspended sentences. The trial was widely considered in the West to be the most important political case in Czechoslovakia since the Charter 77 trial in 1979, particularly in the light of the more liberal cultural policies being pursued in the USSR under Gorbachev. The lenient sentences were regarded as an indication that the Czechoslovak Government was prepared to follow the Soviet example. Srp was released in January 1988.

In February 1988 the Soviet Union began withdrawing nuclear missiles from Czechoslovak territory, in accordance with provisions of the Intermediate-Range Nuclear Forces Treaty, signed by US President Reagan and General Secretary (subsequently President) Gorbachev in December 1987. The withdrawal of 39 missiles prior to the ratification of the treaty was regarded as a positive move towards the establishment of a nuclear-weapon-free 'corridor' in Central Europe.

Government

Czechoslovakia is a federal state of two nations of equal rights, the Czechs and the Slovaks, and composed of two republics, each having its own government. The supreme organ of state power is the Federal Assembly, elected for a five-year term by all citizens over the age of 18 years, and having two chambers, the House of the People and the House of Nations. Membership of the former is proportional to the population of the country. In May 1986, 134 deputies were elected from the Czech Socialist Republic and 66 from the Slovak Socialist Republic. The House of Nations has 150 members: 75 from each of the republics. The Federal Assembly elects the President for a five-year term of office. The President, in turn, appoints the Federal Government, led by the Prime Minister, to hold executive authority. Ministers are responsible to the Assembly.

Each of the two constituent republics has its own government (responsible for all matters except external relations, defence, overseas trade, transport and communications) and its own elected National Council or parliament.

Political power is held by the Communist Party of Czechoslovakia, which dominates the National Front (including four other minor parties). All candidates for representative bodies are sponsored by the Front. The Communist Party's highest authority is the Party Congress, which elects the Central Committee (133 full members and 62 candidate members were elected in March 1986) to supervise Party work. The Committee elects a Presidium (13 full and three alternate members in December 1988) to direct policy.

Defence

Czechoslovakia is a member of the Warsaw Pact. Military service is compulsory and lasts for two years in the army and three years in the air force. Service with the reserve lasts until the age of 50. In June 1988, according to Western estimates, the army numbered 145,000 (100,000 conscripts) and the air force 52,000 (18,000 conscripts); border troops numbered 11,000. The People's Militia comprises 120,000 part-time personnel. The defence budget for 1988 was 29,500m. korunas. Since the invasion of 1968, Soviet forces have occupied permanent positions on the frontier with the Federal Republic of Germany.

Economic Affairs

Although Czechoslovakia depends on the USSR for many raw materials, it is a highly industrialized country. In 1986 industrial activity contributed 59.8% of net material product (NMP), and construction 10.7%. Industry is state-owned. Output of motor cars and cycles is important, and other manufactures are glass, beer, ceramics, footwear and textiles. Mining of coal and lignite is an important activity, output totalling 128.4m. tons in 1986. Other minerals, such as copper and zinc, are also extracted. In 1985 large gold deposits were confirmed to exist near Prague.

In the mid-1980s a long-term programme to develop the generation of electricity by means of nuclear and hydroelectric power was being implemented. In 1986 two new power units at the nuclear station at Dukovany were built, and in October 1987 a further reactor, the fourth, was put into full operation. Construction of two more units, at Mochovce and Temelin, was scheduled for completion in 1989 and 1992 respectively. In 1986 nuclear power stations generated 20% of the total output of electricity; this proportion was expected to rise to 29.4% by the end of 1988 (with a projected output of 22.7m. MWh in that year), and to reach 50% by the year 2000. In 1984 hydroelectric power stations generated 3.7m. MWh, and the country's hydroelectric power potential was to be increased from 36% in 1986 to 63% by the year 2000. In 1988 construction work on the Gabčíkovo-Nagymaros Danube barrage scheme (a joint project with Hungary) continued, despite mounting pressure exerted on the Government by environmentalists to abandon the project. The decision, in February 1988, to suspend plans to build a smaller dam near Prague prompted speculation about the Government's commitment to the larger project. As a consequence of the rapid development of nuclear power plants, the extraction of coal and lignite was projected to decline to 119m. tons in 1990 (accounting for the generation of 63.4% of the total output of electricity). In 1987 an estimated 12,000m. cu m of natural gas were imported from the USSR. Imports of Soviet oil in 1988 were expected to cost 2,200m. roubles.

Agriculture has been collectivized and about 95% of the land is under agricultural co-operatives, state farms or communal enterprises. Agriculture and forestry accounted for 7.8% of NMP in 1986. Important crops are wheat, barley, potatoes, hops and sugar beet. In 1984 a record harvest of 12m. metric tons of cereals was achieved. Cereal production fell in subsequent years, however, to an estimated 10.8m. tons in 1986, but in 1988 output reached 11.8m. tons, slightly in excess of the projected total. Storm damage to hop fields, which cover some 12,000 ha, in 1986 led to a shortfall in the production of beer, which is exported to 70 countries and is an important source of foreign exchange earnings. Forestry is also significant; in 1985 there were 4.6m. ha of forests, covering about 36% of the territory. In 1986 timber production totalled 18.8m. cu m, 4.3% less than in 1985. Afforestation work was carried out on 52,300 ha. Export earnings from coniferous timber declined, however, from 500m. korunas in 1985 to 298m. korunas in 1987.

The targets of the fifth Five-Year Plan (1971-75) were exceeded. NMP rose by 31.7%, 3.7% above the target, and investment went up by 44.1%. Gross output of goods and material services increased by 38%, and industrial output grew by 37.5%. During the period of the sixth Five-Year Plan (1976-80) gross output rose by 20%. Industrial output grew by 25% (the engineering sector by 38%), and agricultural production by 9%. After 1977, however, Czechoslovakia experienced an economic slowdown, owing to adverse weather conditions, poor harvests (necessitating large imports of grain), labour shortages, energy problems and less favourable terms of trade.

The seventh Five-Year Plan (1981-85) envisaged a 10-14% increase in NMP; the increase was 3.2% in 1984 and 3.3% in 1985, bringing the overall increase for 1981-85 to 11.3%. The development of industry (particularly the engineering sector, which increased production by 28.7% in 1981-85) was given priority, resulting in a steady rise in exports. Industrial production during the seventh Five-Year Plan rose by 14.8%, and agriculture by 9.7%, compared with 1976-80.

The Government has sought to resolve the current economic problems through internal measures rather than by external borrowing, and has urged stringent economies, particularly with regard to imported fuels, and increased efficiency and quality in production. Wide-ranging adjustments in the retail prices of food products were made in January 1982, and increases in the wholesale price of energy and raw materials, which averaged 6.4% and were not to be passed on to consumers, took effect in January 1984. A proposed new planning system for enterprises was to create scope for material incentives with the aim of raising production. In 1988 plans were approved for the establishment of self-financing enterprises, following economic reforms introduced in 1987. The new legislation also permitted the establishment of joint ventures with foreign enterprises, with limited supervision by state bodies. Investment, which amounted to 150,000m. korunas in 1980, was reduced in subsequent years to stand at 147,900m. korunas in 1984. The 1988 federal budget proposals balanced total projected revenue and expenditure at 394,000m. korunas, 3.3% more than in 1987.

The eighth Five-Year Plan (1986-90) envisaged a 19% increase in NMP. Increased labour productivity was projected to account for 92% of this increase, and the growth of employment was to contribute only 8%. Industrial production was to increase by 15.8%, and agricultural production by 6.8%, while total investment was to amount to almost 900,000m. korunas (compared with 811,000m. korunas in 1981-85). The proportion of the applied NMP intended for the internal use of the population, society and the economy was to increase from 3.1% to 15.9%, while a further 3.9% was to be allocated to scientific and technological development. Compared with a projected annual increase of 3.5%, NMP rose by 2.8% in 1986 and by 2.2% in 1987. In the first two years of the eighth Five-Year Plan, therefore, economic growth was below expectations. The projected gross national product (GNP) for 1988 was revised downwards to 662,000m. korunas, which, if achieved, would represent an increase of only 2.7% over the 1987 total of 644,300m. korunas. Industrial production increased by 3% in 1986 and by 2.3% in 1987. Output rose by 2% in 1988. In 1986 production in the electrical engineering and engineering industries grew by 4.8%, and electricity generation was 5.1% more than in 1985. Output by the electrical engineering sector increased by 10% in 1987. Agricultural output in 1986 went up by only 0.5%. Although production in the livestock sector exceeded the projected increase, production of crops fell short of the target. In 1987 agricultural production increased by only 0.9%. In 1988 output was hampered by a drought (necessitating imports of grain and fodder), but nevertheless rose by 2.2%.

Czechoslovakia is a member of the Council for Mutual Economic Assistance (CMEA) (see p. 124). In 1987 43.4% of trade was with the USSR. During 1981-85 exports increased by 50% and imports by 48%. Principal exports include machinery and equipment, chemicals and fuels, and glass and other manufactured goods. There is considerable trade with Western European countries, notably the Federal Republic of Germany, Austria and the United Kingdom. However, Czechoslovakia's share in world trade fell from 1.5% in 1965 to 0.9% in 1980. A determined attempt is now being made to increase this share, particularly through the export of industrial products and especially those of the engineering sector, which were planned to rise by 47% in 1986-90. In 1986 the country's trade deficit was 3,672m. korunas, with the value of imports totalling 125,449m. korunas and that of exports 121,777m. korunas. In 1987 total exports increased by 1.4% and imports by 3.4%. Exports to other CMEA countries, however, rose by 8%. Trade with other socialist countries accounted for nearly 80% of total foreign trade. Trade with non-socialist countries grew by 3.9% in 1986. In 1987 exports to those countries declined by 4.4%. In July 1988 representatives of the EEC and the Czechoslovak Trade Ministry held discussions aimed at increasing mutual trade exchanges. Czechoslovakia's gross external debt stood at US $3,700m. in January 1988. Following agreement on a new US $150m. loan from a consortium of Western banks in July 1988, Czechoslovakia's net convertible-currency debt stood at $1,000m., one of the lowest in Eastern Europe. The first stage of a plan to introduce a uniform exchange rate for the koruna was to be implemented in January 1989. From April 1988 Czechoslovak citizens were allowed to open bank accounts in freely convertible currencies; the declared objective of this new regulation was to enhance the prospects of Czechoslovaks for foreign travel.

Social Welfare

A single and universal system of social security was established in Czechoslovakia after the Second World War. All workers and employees benefit equally from the insurance scheme. Protection of health is stipulated by law, with particular emphasis on the prevention of illness rather than treatment and cure. Medical care, treatment, medicines, etc. are available free of charge to the entire Czechoslovak population, and in 1985 28,400m. korunas were spent on the health service. There were almost 55,000 physicians in 1985 and 196,000 hospital beds in 1988, while the number of inhabitants per physician had fallen to 272. The National Health Insurance Scheme is administered by the Revolutionary Trade Union Movement, which also supervises other aspects of social welfare. Sickness benefit is paid for a maximum period of two years, after which time disablement pension applies. Social security is guaranteed for all persons by means of various schemes: for wage-earners, members of co-operative societies, members of agricultural co-operatives, pensioners and members of the armed forces. Benefits and rights are identical for all these groups. Great importance is attached to maternity benefits and family allowances.

Education

Education at all levels is provided free of charge. Almost all children between the ages of three and six years attend kindergarten (mateřská škola). Education is compulsory between the ages of six and 16 years, when children attend the basic school (základní škola). A general curriculum is followed by more specialized subjects. Most Czechoslovak children continue their education after the basic school. Secondary grammar schools provide four years of general education, and prepare students for university. Education of the same level is provided by working people's secondary schools. Four-year secondary vocational schools train young people as specialists in the fields of economics, administration and culture, or prepare them for studies at institutes of higher learning. Courses at the specialized apprentice training centres last from two to four years, and prepare young people for workers' professions. In the 1986/87 school year 659,592 children attended kindergarten, 2,088,750 attended elementary schools, 803,459 the different types of secondary school and 169,011 students were in higher education.

Public Holidays

1989: 2 January (for New Year's Day), 27 March (Easter Monday), 1 May (Labour Day), 9 May (National Day, Anniversary of Liberation), 28 October (National Day, Anniversary of Independence), 25-26 December (Christmas).

1990: 1 January (New Year's Day), 16 April (Easter Monday), 1 May (Labour Day), 9 May (National Day, Anniversary of Liberation), 28 October (National Day, Anniversary of Independence), 25-26 December (Christmas).

Weights and Measures

The metric system is in force.

Statistical Survey

Source: mainly Federal Statistical Office, Sokolovská 142, 180 00 Prague 8; tel. (2) 814; telex 121197.

Area and Population

AREA, POPULATION AND DENSITY

Area (sq km)	127,905*
Population (census results)	
1 November 1980	15,283,095
December 1985	
Males	7,558,152
Females	7,961,150
Total	15,519,302
Population (official estimates at mid-year)	
1986	15,533,526
1987	15,572,852
1988	15,588,177
Density (per sq km) at mid-1988	121.9

* 49,384 sq miles.

POPULATION BY NATIONALITY
(estimates, 31 December 1985)

	Czech Socialist Republic		Slovak Socialist Republic		Total	
	'000	%	'000	%	'000	%
Czech	9,747	94.3	58	1.1	9,805	63.2
Slovak	397	3.8	4,491	86.7	4,888	31.5
Magyar (Hungarian)	21	0.2	572	11.0	593	3.8
German	53	0.5	3	0.1	56	0.4
Polish	69	0.7	3	0.1	72	0.5
Ukrainian and Russian	15	0.1	39	0.7	54	0.3
Others and unspecified	38	0.4	13	0.3	51	0.3
Total	10,340	100.0	5,179	100.0	15,519	100.0

REGIONS

	Area (sq km)	Population (1 Jan. 1987)	Density (per sq km)
Czech Socialist Republic:			
Central Bohemia	10,994	1,131,032	103
Southern Bohemia	11,345	695,300	61
Western Bohemia	10,875	871,280	80
Northern Bohemia	7,819	1,185,526	151
Eastern Bohemia	11,240	1,242,553	111
Southern Moravia	15,028	2,056,786	137
Northern Moravia	11,067	1,961,533	177
Prague (city)	496	1,200,266	2,409
Total	78,864	10,344,276	131
Slovak Socialist Republic:			
Western Slovakia	14,492	1,719,259	118
Central Slovakia	17,986	1,590,611	88
Eastern Slovakia	16,196	1,474,126	91
Bratislava (city)	367	424,378	1,147
Total	49,041	5,208,374	106
Grand total	127,905	15,552,650	121

PRINCIPAL TOWNS
(estimated population at 1 January 1987)

Praha (Prague, capital)	1,200,266	Liberec	102,685
Bratislava	424,378	Hradec Králové	99,757
Brno	385,965	České Budějovice	95,418
Ostrava	328,373	Pardubice	94,805
Košice	225,841	Žilina	92,990
Plzeň (Pilsen)	174,765	Havířov	92,115
Olomouc	105,969	Nitra	86,458
Ústí nad Labem	104,752	Gottwaldov (Zlín)	86,443

BIRTHS, MARRIAGES AND DEATHS

	Registered live births		Registered marriages		Registered deaths	
	Number	Rate (per 1,000)	Number	Rate (per 1,000)	Number	Rate (per 1,000)
1980	248,901	16.3	117,921	7.7	186,116	12.2
1981	237,728	15.5	116,805	7.6	180,039	11.8
1982	234,356	15.2	117,376	7.6	181,158	11.8
1983	229,484	14.9	120,547	7.8	186,907	12.1
1984	226,595	14.7	121,340	7.8	182,351	11.8
1985	225,193	14.5	119,176	7.7	182,581	11.8
1986	220,494	14.2	119,979	7.7	185,718	12.0
1987*	214,505	13.8	n.a.	7.8	179,042	11.5

* Provisional.

CIVILIAN LABOUR FORCE EMPLOYED
('000 persons, excluding apprentices)

	1984	1985	1986
Agriculture	867	865	861
Forestry	93	95	93
Mining, manufacturing, gas and electricity	2,865	2,882	2,922
Construction	752	758	783
Trade, restaurants, etc.	683	693	703
Other commerce	180	181	173
Transport	388	391	395
Communications	108	108	106
Services	278	289	290
Education and culture	551	563	577
Science and research	171	175	177
Health and social services	366	373	383
Civil service, jurisdiction	119	118	117
Others	113	115	125
Total in employment	7,534	7,606	7,705
Women on maternity leave	339	344	350
Total labour force	7,873	7,950	8,055

CZECHOSLOVAKIA

Agriculture

PRINCIPAL CROPS ('000 metric tons)

	1984	1985	1986
Wheat and spelt	6,170	6,023	5,305
Rye*	710	620	547
Barley	3,677	3,538	3,530
Oats†	479	473	419
Maize	940	1,114	992
Sugar beet	7,513	7,747	7,135
Potatoes	3,978	3,450	3,512
Dry peas	181	164	176
Dry broad beans	30	28	21
Grapes	234	236	158
Linseed	12	15	12
Rapeseed	300	285	306
Sunflower seed	43	42	57
Hops	11	13	10
Tobacco	6	6	5
Carrots	180	152	152
Onions	168	151	129
Garlic	12	10	10
Tomatoes	79	122	111
Cabbages	377	261	249
Cauliflowers	86	77	65
Lettuce	19	18	18
Cucumbers and gherkins	78	39	102
Apples	378	379	468
Pears	46	41	40
Plums	47	50	46
Sweet cherries	25	23	22
Sour cherries	10	9	7
Peaches	16	5	19
Apricots	24	13	23
Strawberries	21	27	21
Currants	37	35	35
Walnuts	14	6	12
Flax fibre	27	25	22

* Including mixed crops of rye and wheat.
† Including mixed crops of oats and barley.
Source: mainly FAO, *Production Yearbook*.

1987 ('000 metric tons): Wheat and spelt 6,154; Rye 496; Barley 3,551; Oats 406; Maize 1,160; Sugar beet 6,698; Potatoes 3,072; Dry peas 175; Grapes 102; Rapeseed 337; Sunflower seed 62; Onions 146; Tomatoes 123; Apples 308. Source: FAO, *Quarterly Bulletin of Statistics*.

LIVESTOCK ('000 head at end of year)

	1984	1985	1986
Cattle	5,150	5,065	5,073
Pigs	6,743	6,651	6,833
Sheep	1,068	1,087	1,104
Goats	54	53	52
Horses	46	46	46

Chickens (million): 47 in 1984; 45 in 1985; 47 in 1986.
Source: mainly FAO, *Quarterly Bulletin of Statistics*.

LIVESTOCK PRODUCTS ('000 metric tons)

	1985	1986	1987
Beef and veal	413	412	420
Pig meat	823	832	859
Poultry meat	196	201	205
Edible offals	91	92	92
Cows' milk	6,882.9	7,015.0	6,921.4
Sheep's milk	41	41	41
Goats' milk	18	19	19
Butter	152.0	156.1	149.2
Cheese	195	202	215
Hen eggs	275.0	277.9	277
Wool:			
greasy	5.4	5.4	6
clean	3.2	3.3	3
Cattle hides	58.8	58.0	n.a.

Source: FAO, mainly *Quarterly Bulletin of Statistics*.

Forestry

ROUNDWOOD REMOVALS ('000 cubic metres, excluding bark)

	1984	1985	1986
Planned	19,229	19,173	18,598
Unplanned	222	479	205
Production	19,451	19,652	18,803
Deliveries	18,913	19,002	18,679
of which:			
Industrial	17,607	17,620	17,205
Fuel wood	1,306	1,382	1,476

SAWNWOOD PRODUCTION ('000 cubic metres, including boxboards)

	1984	1985	1986
Coniferous	4,300	4,303	4,334
Broadleaved	800	794	797
Total	5,100	5,097	5,131

Fishing*

(metric tons)

	1984	1985	1986
Carp	15,700	16,089	17,030
Others	3,988	3,914	4,221
Total catch	19,688	20,003	21,251

* Figures refer only to fish caught by the State Fisheries and members of the Czech and Slovak fishing unions.

Mining

('000 metric tons, unless otherwise indicated)

	1984	1985	1986
Hard coal	26,421	26,223	25,658
Brown coal	101,084	98,633	99,131
Lignite	3,659	3,682	3,607
Kaolin	668	679	687
Iron ore:			
gross weight	1,869	1,859	1,754
metal content	494	489	472
Crude petroleum	91	123	142
Salt (refined)	243	243	237
Magnesite	660	654	666
Antimony ore (metric tons)*	763	782	795
Copper concentrates (metric tons)*	29,608	29,296	24,657
Lead concentrates (metric tons)*	5,129	5,244	5,700
Mercury (metric tons)	152	158	168
Tin concentrates (metric tons)*	425	507	240
Zinc concentrates (metric tons)*	14,370	14,441	13,265

* Figures refer to the metal content of ores and concentrates.

CZECHOSLOVAKIA

Industry

SELECTED PRODUCTS
('000 metric tons, unless otherwise indicated)

	1984	1985	1986
Wheat flour	1,305	1,334	1,355
Refined sugar	936	969	985
Margarine (metric tons)	34,898	34,123	35,407
Wine ('000 hectolitres)	1,563	1,763	1,402
Beer ('000 hectolitres)	23,768	22,354	22,787
Cigarettes (million)	24,603	23,840	24,998
Cotton yarn—pure and mixed (metric tons)	140,003	142,166	143,363
Woven cotton fabrics ('000 metres)*	597,932	606,355	600,457
Wool yarn—pure and mixed (metric tons)	57,467	57,711	58,273
Woven woollen fabrics ('000 metres)*	61,786	60,161	59,186
Chemical fibres	188.8	193.2	192.7
Chemical wood pulp	789.4	840.3	869.0
Newsprint	72.2	72.0	67.6
Other paper	866.8	891.5	892.6
Leather footwear ('000 pairs)	58,312	57,887	56,011
Rubber footwear ('000 pairs)	6,140	6,119	5,619
Other footwear ('000 pairs)	66,132	67,316	62,839
Synthetic rubber (metric tons)	70,900	69,600	76,100
Rubber tyres ('000)	5,095	5,015	5,208
Sulphuric acid	1,246	1,298	1,292
Hydrochloric acid	228.0	236.2	245.5
Caustic soda	328.6	331.1	334.6
Soda ash	101.3	112.0	113.3
Nitrogenous fertilizers(a)†	575.8	582.1	614.3
Phosphate fertilizers(b)†	343.7	353.3	307.0
Plastics and synthetic resins	1,039	1,100	n.a.
Liquefied petroleum gas	138	138	n.a.
Motor spirit (petrol)	1,500	1,500	1,500
Kerosene and jet fuel	404	426	371
Distillate fuel oils	3,688	3,648	3,628
Residual fuel oils	7,357	7,363	7,110
Petroleum bitumen (asphalt)	1,074	1,086	n.a.
Coke-oven coke	10,302	10,237	10,091
Cement	10,530	10,265	10,298
Pig iron‡	9,561	9,562	9,573
Crude steel	14,831	15,036	15,112
Rolled steel products	10,910	11,040	11,180
Aluminium—unwrought (metric tons)	31,635	31,725	33,078
Refined copper—unwrought (metric tons)	26,068	26,414	26,182
Lead—unwrought (metric tons)	21,134	21,437	23,602
Radio receivers (number)§	259,137	242,348	240,066
Television receivers (number)	383,636	432,338	434,450
Passenger cars (number)	180,471	183,701	185,010
Goods vehicles (number)	46,872	47,956	50,199
Motor cycles (number)‖	123,628	157,257	151,483
Electric locomotives (number)	131	126	124
Diesel locomotives (number)	517	530	502
Trams (number)	901	955	883
Tractors (number)	34,160	35,184	36,960
Electric energy (million kWh)	78,388	80,627	84,774
Manufactured gas (million cu metres)	7,694	7,500	7,245
Construction: New dwellings completed (number)	91,863	104,524	78,659

* After undergoing finishing processes.
† Production of fertilizers is measured in terms of (a) nitrogen or (b) phosphoric acid. The figures for phosphate fertilizers include ground rock phosphate.
‡ Including blast furnace ferro-alloys.   § Excluding radiograms.
‖ Engine capacity of 100 cubic centimetres and over.

Finance

CURRENCY AND EXCHANGE RATES

Monetary Units
100 haléřů (singular: halér—heller) = 1 koruna (Czechoslovak crown or Kčs.).

Denominations
Coins: 5, 10, 20 and 50 haléřů; 1, 2 and 5 Kčs.
Notes: 10, 20, 50, 100, 500 and 1,000 Kčs.

Sterling and Dollar Equivalents (30 September 1988)
£1 sterling = 16.031 Kčs.;
US $1 = 9.480 Kčs. (non-commercial rates);
1,000 Kčs. = £62.38 = $105.49.

Note: The rates quoted above are applicable to tourism. Foreign trade transactions are valued according to the commercial exchange rate. On this basis, the average value of the koruna was: 14.65 US cents in 1985; 16.79 US cents in 1986; 18.29 US cents in 1987.

BUDGET (million Kčs.)

Revenue	1984	1985	1986
State budget	222,446	233,473	235,238
From socialist economy	246,384	258,183	265,810
Taxes and rates	45,891	47,245	33,990
Other receipts	1,702	2,064	1,906
Minus grants and subsidies to local administrative organs	71,531	74,019	66,468
Budgets of local administrative organs	121,359	126,219	133,458
Total	343,805	359,692	368,696

1987 (provisional): Total revenue 381,900m. Kčs.
1988 (provisional): Total revenue 394,000m. Kčs.

Expenditure	1984	1985	1986
State budget	222,373	233,402	235,226
National economy	87,090	90,179	88,469
Science and technology	8,306	9,133	9,156
Money-order and technical services	5,972	6,432	6,535
Culture and social welfare	90,819	96,121	98,444
Defence	26,276	27,393	28,300
Administration	3,910	4,144	4,302
Budgets of local administrative organs	119,819	124,626	130,726
Total	342,192	358,028	365,949

1987 (provisional): Total expenditure 381,900m. Kčs.
1988 (provisional): Total expenditure 394,000m. Kčs.

COST OF LIVING
(Consumer Price Index. Base: 1 January 1977 = 100)

	1984	1985	1986
Food	117.9	121.0	122.1
Industrial goods	117.1	118.0	119.6
Public catering	124.0	135.3	137.2
Services	118.2	118.2	120.5
All items	118.2	120.9	122.7

CZECHOSLOVAKIA

Statistical Survey

NATIONAL ACCOUNTS
Net Material Product*
('000 million Kčs. at current market prices)

Activities of the material sphere	1984	1985	1986
Agriculture, hunting and fishing	40.8	37.1	39.5
Forestry and logging	4.3	5.0	4.8
Industry†	318.0	334.1	341.0
Construction	59.5	62.9	61.2
Trade, restaurants, etc.	87.5	90.2	76.5
Transport and storage	24.3	23.6	24.1
Communications	4.7	4.9	5.2
Others	1.9	2.1	2.3
Total	**541.1**	**560.0**	**570.1**

* Defined as the total net value of goods and 'productive' services, including turnover taxes, produced by the economy. This excludes economic activities not contributing directly to material production, such as public administration, defence and personal and professional services.

† Principally manufacturing, mining, electricity, gas and water supply.

External Trade

PRINCIPAL COMMODITIES
(distribution by SITC, million Kčs.)

Imports f.o.b.	1984	1985	1986
Food and live animals	6,500.0	6,925.2	6,985
Vegetables and fruit	1,868.7	2,265.5	2,312
Crude materials (inedible) except fuels	9,741.1	9,927.5	9,394
Cotton fibres and waste	1,548.9	1,677.3	1,340
Metalliferous ores and metal scrap	3,538.4	3,546.8	2,357
Mineral fuels, lubricants, etc. (incl. electric current)	35,252.8	36,941.1	38,216
Coal, coke and briquettes	1,888.5	1,936.0	1,731
Petroleum, petroleum products, etc.	23,375.4	24,372.3	25,109
Gas (natural and manufactured)	9,219.7	9,474.5	10,480
Chemicals and related products	7,445.8	8,214.7	8,457
Organic chemicals	1,147.3	1,236.9	1,331
Manufactured fertilizers	1,312.7	1,335.8	1,319
Basic manufactures	10,143.7	10,749.6	11,419
Iron and steel	2,647.2	2,781.4	3,161
Non-ferrous metals	3,536.7	3,586.9	3,340
Machinery and transport equipment	36,261.0	37,464.6	40,286
Power generating machinery and equipment	2,298.1	2,397.6	2,316
Machinery specialized for particular industries	8,629.3	9,025.6	9,995
Agricultural machinery (excl. tractors) and parts	2,324.8	2,345.8	2,246
Civil engineering and contractors' plant, equipment and parts	1,637.4	1,798.1	n.a.
Metalworking machinery	2,303.5	2,077.9	2,405
Machine-tools for working metal	932.8	631.3	1,740
General industrial machinery, equipment and parts	11,584.4	11,499.4	12,487

Imports f.o.b.—*continued*	1984	1985	1986
Office machines and automatic data processing equipment	2,317.1	3,012.0	3,235
Automatic data processing machines and units	1,631.6	2,080.0	2,450
Road vehicles and parts*	3,657.8	3,493.9	1,105
Parts and accessories for cars, buses, lorries, etc.*	2,608.9	2,594.4	2,717
Miscellaneous manufactured articles	4,824.2	5,758.3	5,936
Total (incl. others)	**113,737**	**120,323**	**125,449**

* Excluding tyres, engines and electrical parts.

1987: Total imports 127,259 million Kčs.

Exports f.o.b.	1984	1985	1986
Food and live animals	2,857.1	2,954.1	2,811
Crude materials (inedible) except fuels	3,678.5	3,925.0	3,839
Mineral fuels, lubricants, etc. (incl. electric current)	5,292.2	5,179.8	4,310
Coal, coke and briquettes	2,155.9	2,288.6	2,309
Coal, lignite and peat	1,291.8	1,442.8	1,492
Petroleum, petroleum products, etc.	2,468.4	1,978.6	1,435
Chemicals and related products	6,612.6	7,147.1	7,294
Organic chemicals	1,663.1	1,888.1	1,807
Artificial resins, plastic materials, etc.	1,555.1	1,545.4	1,492
Basic manufactures	19,486.4	20,089.1	20,762
Textile yarn, fabrics, etc.	3,780.8	3,780.1	4,026
Non-metallic mineral manufactures	3,348.8	3,326.0	3,512
Iron and steel	7,847.4	8,276.2	8,263
Bars, rods, angles, shapes, etc.	2,237.4	2,379.8	2,503
Universals, plates and sheets	1,677.4	1,766.2	1,831
Tubes, pipes and fittings	2,234.8	2,181.9	2,083
Machinery and transport equipment	60,608.3	64,220.7	66,034
Power generating machinery and equipment	3,974.0	4,271.1	4,337
Steam power units, steam engines and parts	1,240.2	1,245.0	1,407
Machinery specialized for particular industries	16,981.7	17,429.8	17,520
Agricultural machinery (excl. tractors) and parts	1,685.2	1,658.7	1,874
Civil engineering and contractors' plant, equipment and parts	2,064.2	2,459.1	n.a.
Textile and leather machinery and parts	5,433.1	5,662.1	5,388
Metalworking machinery	4,447.6	4,417.3	4,308
Machine-tools for working metal	3,276.2	3,377.1	3,527
General industrial machinery, equipment and parts	14,808.0	16,038.3	16,562
Office machines and automatic data processing equipment	1,510.0	1,607.6	1,688
Telecommunications and sound equipment	1,783.4	1,867.0	1,806
Other electrical machinery, apparatus, etc.	3,374.8	3,585.3	3,628

CZECHOSLOVAKIA

Statistical Survey

Exports f.o.b.—*continued*	1984	1985	1986
Road vehicles and parts*	10,026.1	10,601.8	11,382
Motor vehicles for goods transport and special purposes	3,998.1	4,302.8	4,481
Parts and accessories for cars, buses, lorries, etc.*	3,794.0	3,995.2	4,525
Railway vehicles and associated equipment	3,334.6	3,872.4	4,252
Miscellaneous manufactured articles	13,050.2	13,529.8	14,242
Furniture and parts	1,484.8	1,581.5	1,675
Footwear	3,251.6	3,281.2	3,298
Total (incl. others)	114,230	119,818	121,777

* Excluding tyres, engines and electrical parts.

1987: Total exports 125,875 million Kčs.

PRINCIPAL TRADING PARTNERS
(million Kčs., country of consignment)

Imports f.o.b.	1984	1985	1986
Austria	2,251	2,680	3,458
Belgium	461	489	567
Brazil	484	448	210
Bulgaria	3,226	3,858	4,002
China, People's Republic	825	1,431	1,978
Cuba	1,061	1,184	992
France	882	802	1,045
German Democratic Republic	11,783	11,469	12,030
Germany, Federal Republic*	4,731	5,091	6,149
Hungary	6,387	6,952	6,844
Iran	904	452	563
Italy	836	1,095	1,302
Japan	455	379	499
Netherlands	740	844	809
Poland	8,193	9,609	10,954
Romania	2,320	2,525	2,670
Switzerland	2,342	n.a.	n.a.
USSR	53,230	55,345	56,794
United Kingdom	1,376	1,472	1,484
USA	305	285	300
Yugoslavia	3,866	3,845	2,278
Total (incl. others)	113,737	120,323	125,449

* Excluding imports from West Berlin.

Exports f.o.b.	1984	1985	1986
Austria	2,917	3,107	2,857
Bulgaria	3,186	3,612	3,994
China, People's Republic	1,056	1,412	1,317
Cuba	1,438	1,296	1,254
France	942	1,010	1,092
German Democratic Republic	10,107	10,992	10,873
Germany, Federal Republic†	5,365	5,401	5,655
Hungary	5,688	5,666	6,247
Iran	302	470	237
Iraq	964	721	926
Italy	1,084	1,117	1,200
Libya	1,219	n.a.	n.a.
Netherlands	904	904	1,008
Poland	8,134	9,169	10,632
Romania	1,981	2,456	2,630
Switzerland	1,066	n.a.	n.a.
Syria	1,873	2,402	943
Turkey	667	n.a.	n.a.
USSR	49,606	52,305	52,948
United Kingdom	1,256	1,237	1,269
Yugoslavia	4,683	4,250	3,563
Total (incl. others)	114,230	119,818	121,777

† Excluding exports to West Berlin.

Transport

	1984	1985	1986
Railway transport:			
Freight ('000 tons)	299,021	293,235	296,561
Passengers (million)	422	419	422
Public road transport:			
Freight ('000 tons)	349,979	339,275	346,460
Passengers (million)	2,260	2,274	2,300
Waterway transport:			
Freight ('000 tons)	13,374	13,331	14,217
Air transport:			
Freight (tons)	23,054	25,190	24,747
Passengers ('000)	1,139	1,220	1,251

ROAD TRAFFIC (vehicles in use at 30 June)

	1982	1983	1984
Passenger cars	2,441,472	2,511,269	2,639,564
Buses and coaches	32,363	33,072	34,747
Goods vehicles	357,868	362,544	378,113
Motorcycles and scooters	662,987	636,281	612,487

Tourism

	1984	1985	1986
Foreign tourist arrivals*	17,510,459	16,505,659	19,030,469

* Including excursionists and visitors in transit. Visitors spending at least one night in the country totalled 3,370,000 in 1982.

Communications Media

	1984	1985	1986
Telephones in use	3,499,022	3,591,045	3,706,718
Radio receivers in use	4,208,538	4,233,702	3,935,233
Television receivers in use	4,346,022	4,368,050	4,387,144
Book production: titles*	7,128	6,956	6,962
Newspapers (dailies)	30	30	30
Periodicals	1,072	1,077	1,080

* Figures include pamphlets, and refer to titles produced by centrally managed publishing houses only; the total number of titles produced was: 9,911 in 1984; 9,844 in 1985; 10,020 in 1986.

Education

(1986/87)

	Institutions	Teachers	Students
Nursery	11,445	50,669	659,592
Primary (classes 1–8)	6,274	97,733	2,088,750
Secondary (classes 9–12)			
Universal	343	9,675	134,103
Special (technical, etc.)	561	15,152	257,968
Continuation schools	940	16,464	411,388
Higher	36	6,080	169,011

Directory

The Constitution

A new constitution was proclaimed on 11 July 1960. It was amended in October 1968, July 1971 and May 1975. A summary of the main provisions of the Constitution follows:

The Czechoslovak Socialist Republic is a Federal State of two fraternal nations possessing equal rights, the Czechs and the Slovaks.

According to the Constitution, work in the interests of the community is a primary duty and the right to work a primary right of every citizen. All citizens have equal rights and equal duties without regard to nationality and race. Remuneration for work done is based on its quantity, quality and social importance. Men and women have equal status. All citizens have the right to health protection, education and leisure after work including paid holidays. Other rights include: freedom of expression, assembly, inviolability of the person, the home, mail, etc. Everyone has the right to profess any religious faith or to be without religious conviction.

The economic foundation of the State is the Socialist economic system which excludes every form of exploitation of man by man. The means of production are socially owned and the entire national economy is directed by plan. Socialist ownership includes both national property such as mineral wealth, the means of industrial production, banks, etc., and co-operative property. The land of members of agricultural co-operatives remains the personal property of the individual members, but is jointly farmed by the co-operative. Small private enterprises based on the labour of the owner himself and excluding exploitation of another's labour power are permitted. Personal ownership of consumer goods, family houses and savings derived from labour is inviolable. Inheritance of such personal property is guaranteed.

The Czechoslovak Constitution does not restrict itself to laying down a system of state organs but also sets forth the principles by which the life of society is to be guided. It is not just a Constitution of the State but a constitution for the whole of society. In economic, political and cultural life, in questions of social security and many other spheres it emphasizes the participation of citizens in the administration of public affairs and even transfers a number of functions that have hitherto pertained to state organs to the working people and their voluntary organizations.

The guiding force in society and in the State is the Communist Party of Czechoslovakia, a voluntary militant alliance of the most active and politically conscious citizens. It is associated with the other political parties, the Trade Union Movement and other people's organizations in the National Front of Czechs and Slovaks.

FEDERAL ASSEMBLY

The supreme organ of state power in the Czechoslovak Socialist Republic is the Federal Assembly (Parliament) which is elected for a five-year term and elects the President of the Republic. The President may be relieved of his or her duties by the Assembly in the event of having been unable to fulfil them for over a year. The Federal Assembly consists of two chambers of equal rights: the House of the People and the House of Nations. The composition of the House of the People, which has 200 deputies, corresponds to the composition of the population of the Czechoslovak Socialist Republic. The House of Nations has 150 deputies on parity basis: 75 are elected in the Czech Socialist Republic and 75 in the Slovak Socialist Republic.

PRESIDENT

The President, elected by the Federal Assembly, appoints the Federal Government. The Government is the supreme executive organ of State power in Czechoslovakia; it consists of a Prime Minister, six Deputy Prime Ministers (including a First Deputy Prime Minister, a new post created in 1986) and 13 Ministers. The Ministries of Foreign Affairs, of National Defence, of Foreign Trade, of Transport and of Posts and Telecommunications, are within the exclusive competence of the Federation, i.e. there are no corresponding portfolios in the governments of the republics. The second group of Federal Government organs share authority with organs of the two republics, i.e. there are corresponding portfolios in the national governments.

ELECTORAL SYSTEM

All representative bodies are elected, and the right to elect is universal, equal and by secret ballot. Every citizen has the right to vote on reaching the age of 18, and is eligible for election on reaching the age of 21. Deputies must maintain constant contacts with their constituents, heed their suggestions and be accountable to them for their activity. A member of any representative body may be recalled by his or her constituents at any time.

For election purposes, the country is divided into electoral districts; there are 200 electoral districts in the Czechoslovak Socialist Republic, each represented by one deputy in the House of the People, and 75 electoral districts each in the Czech and Slovak Socialist Republics, which send one deputy each to the House of Nations.

All candidates are National Front candidates, put forward by the Communist Party of Czechoslovakia and by the other political parties and social organizations associated in the National Front. One or more candidates can be nominated for one electoral district. Appropriate National Front organs select the candidates from the list of nominees, and submit their names for registration.

The principle of simple majority obtains in the elections: the candidate is elected when he obtains more than 50% of the votes cast, provided that the majority of all voters in his electoral district exercise their right to vote. When either of the two conditions is not met, new elections are held in the electoral district concerned within two weeks. When a seat becomes vacant, the Presidium of the Federal Assembly calls a by-election in the constituency; this is not mandatory in the last year of the deputies' term of office.

NATIONAL COUNCILS

Each of the republics has its own parliament: the Czech National Council and the Slovak National Council. The members are elected for a five-year term of office. The Czech National Council has 200 deputies, the Slovak National Council 150 deputies. There are also separate Czech and Slovak Governments, each consisting of a Prime Minister, a First Deputy Prime Minister (a new post created in 1986), three Deputy Prime Ministers and up to 15 other Ministers.

NATIONAL COMMITTEES

National committees are the organs of popular self-government in the regions, districts and localities. The members are elected for a five-year term of office. They rely on the active participation of the working people of their area and co-operate with other organizations of the people. They direct local economic and cultural development, ensure the protection of socialist ownership and the maintenance of socialist order in society, see to the implementation and observance of laws, etc. They take part in drafting and carrying out the State plan for the development of the national economy and draw up their own budgets which form a part of the State budget. Commissions elected by the national committees are charged with various aspects of public work and carry out their tasks with the aid of a large number of citizens who need not be elected members of the national committees.

JUDICIAL SYSTEM

The execution of justice is vested in elected and independent courts. Benches are composed of professional judges and of judges who carry out their function in addition to their regular employment. Both categories are equal in making decisions. Judges are independent in the discharge of their office and bound solely by the legal order of the socialist State. The supervision of the observance of the laws and other legal regulations by public bodies and by individual citizens rests with the Office of the Procurator. The Procurator-General is appointed and recalled by the President of the Republic and is accountable to the Federal Assembly.

Note: In January 1989 work began on the drafting of a new constitution.

The Government

(January 1989)

HEAD OF STATE

President of the Republic: Dr GUSTÁV HUSÁK (elected 29 May 1975; re-elected 22 May 1980 and 22 May 1985).

FEDERAL GOVERNMENT

Prime Minister: LADISLAV ADAMEC.
First Deputy Prime Ministers: PAVOL HRIVNÁK, BOHUMIL URBAN.

CZECHOSLOVAKIA

Deputy Prime Ministers: Karel Juliš, Ivan Knotek, Matej Lúčan, Jaromír Obzina, František Pitra.
Minister of Foreign Affairs: Jaromír Johanes.
Minister of National Defence: Gen. Milán Václavík.
Minister of the Interior: František Kincl.
Minister of Finance: Jan Stejskal.
Minister of Foreign Trade: Jan Sterba.
Minister of Labour and Social Affairs: Miloslav Boďa.
Minister of Fuel and Energy: Antonín Krumnikl.
Minister of Agriculture and Food: Jaromír Algayer.
Minister of Transport and Communications: František Podlena.
Minister of Metallurgy, Machine Building and Electrical Engineering: Karel Juliš.
Minister, Chairman of the Federal Prices Office: Jaromír Žák.
Minister, Chairman of the People's Control Committee: František Ondřich.
Minister, Chairman of the State Commission for Scientific-Technological and Investment Development: Pavol Hrivnák.
Chairman of the State Planning Commission: Bohumil Urban.
Minister without Portfolio: Prof. Marian Calfa.

MINISTRIES
All Ministries are in Prague.

STATE GOVERNMENTS
Czech Government
Prime Minister: František Pitra.
First Deputy Prime Minister: Miroslav Toman.
Deputy Prime Minister: Jaroslav Tlapak.
Minister of Agriculture and Food: Ondrej Vanek.
Minister of Construction and the Building Industry: Jaroslav Vávra.
Minister of Culture: Milan Kymlička.
Minister of Education, Youth and Physical Training: Jana Synková.
Minister of Finance, Prices and Wages: Jiří Nikodým.
Minister of Forestry, Water Management and the Wood-Processing Industry: Jaroslav Bocek.
Minister of Health and Social Affairs: Jaroslav Prokopec.
Minister of Industry: Petr Hojer.
Minister of the Interior and Environment: Václav Jireček.
Minister of Justice: Antonín Kašpar.
Minister of Trade and Tourism: Josef Ráb.
Minister, Chairman of the People's Control Committee: Jan Motl.
Ministers without Portfolio: Karel Löbl, Erich Sýkora.
Chairman of the Czech Commission for Planning and Scientific-Technological Development: Miroslav Toman.

Slovak Government
Prime Minister: Ivan Knotek.
Deputy Prime Ministers: Pavol Bahyl, Štefan Murín.
Minister of Agriculture and Food: Július Varga.
Minister of Construction and the Building Industry: Ivan Steis.
Minister of Culture: Pavol Koys.
Minister of Education, Youth and Physical Training: Ľudovít Kilár.
Minister of Finance, Prices and Wages: František Mišeje.
Minister of Forestry, Water Management and the Wood-Processing Industry: Vladimír Margetin.
Minister of Health and Social Affairs: Anton Molnár.
Minister of Industry: Štefan Urban.
Minister of the Interior and Environment: Štefan Lazar.
Minister of Justice: Milan Cic.
Minister of Labour and Social Affairs: Kazimír Nagy.
Minister of Trade and Tourism: Kazimír Nagy.
Minister, Chairman of the People's Control Committee: Štefan Ferencei.
Chairman of the Slovak Commission for Planning and Scientific-Technological Development: Pavol Bahyl.

PRESIDIUM OF THE CENTRAL COMMITTEE OF THE COMMUNIST PARTY OF CZECHOSLOVAKIA
Secretary-General: Miloš Jakeš.
Full Members: Ladislav Adamec, Ján Fojtík, Karel Hoffmann, Dr Gustáv Husák, Alois Indra, Miloš Jakeš, Ignác Janák, Ivan Knotek, Jozef Lenárt, František Pitra, Miroslav Štěpán, Karel Urbánek, Miroslav Zavadil.
Alternate Members: Josef Haman, Vladimír Herman, Miloslav Hruškovič.

Legislature

FEDERÁLNÍ SHROMÁŽDĚNÍ
(Federal Assembly)

The Federal Assembly consists of 350 deputies elected for a five-year term. The Assembly is bicameral, comprising the House of the People (200 members) and the House of Nations (150 members). General elections to both chambers were held on 23–24 May 1986. All the members, nominated by the National Front, were elected unopposed.
Chairman: Alois Indra.

Sněmovna lidu
(House of the People)
This House has 200 members. At the May 1986 elections, 134 were from the Czech Socialist Republic, and 66 from the Slovak Socialist Republic.
Chairman: Vladimír Vedra.

Sněmovna národů
(House of Nations)
This House has 150 members: 75 each from the Czech and Slovak Socialist Republics.
Chairman: Ján Janík.

NATIONAL COUNCILS
Czech National Council: Prague; 200 deputies elected for a five-year term; Chair. Josef Kempný.
Slovak National Council: Bratislava; 150 deputies elected for a five-year term; Chair. Viliam Šalgovič.

Political Organizations

National Front of the Czechoslovak Socialist Republic (Národní fronty ČSR): Skrétova 6, 120 59 Prague 2; a political organization embracing all political parties and mass organizations; Chair. of Central Cttee Miloš Jakeš.

National Front of the Czech Socialist Republic: Prague; Chair. of Central Cttee Josef Kempný.

National Front of the Slovak Socialist Republic: Bratislava; Chair. of Central Cttee Ignác Janák.

Communist Party of Czechoslovakia—CPCZ (Komunistická Strana Československa—KSČ): nábř. Ludvíka Svobody 12, 125 11 Prague 1; f. 1921; incorporating the former Czechoslovak Social Democratic Party and the Slovak Labour Party; the leading political force in the National Front; 1,717,016 mems (1988); Gen. Sec. of Central Cttee Miloš Jakeš; Secretaries of Central Cttee Ján Fojtík, František Hanus, Karel Hoffmann, Dr Gustáv Husák, Miloš Jakeš, Josef Lenárt.

Communist Party of Slovakia—CPSL (Komunistická Strana Slovenska—KSS): Hlboká 2, 883 33 Bratislava; First Sec. of Central Cttee Ignác Janák.

Czechoslovak People's Party: Revoluční 5, 110 15 Prague 1; f. 1919; Christian Party; Chair. Zbyněk Žalman; Central Sec. Josef Andrš.

Czechoslovak Socialist Party: nám. Republiky 7, 111 49 Prague 1; tel. (2) 313051; telex 121432; f. 1948; Chair. Dr Bohuslav Kučera; Exec. Sec. Jan Škoda.

Revolutionary Trade Union Movement (Revoluční odborové hnutí—ROH): nám. A. Zápotockého 2, 113 59 Prague 3; f. 1945; 7,600,074 mems; is a member of the National Front and is headed by the Central Council of Trade Unions (see below); federated to WFTU; Pres. Miroslav Zavadil.

Slovak Freedom Party (Strana Slobody): Obrancov mieru 8, 816 18 Bratislava; f. 1946 as a splinter party from the Slovak Democratic Party; Chair. Kamil Brodziansky; Sec.-Gen. Ján Pampúch.

Slovak Reconstruction Party (Strana Slovenskej Obrody): Malinovského 70, 897 16 Bratislava; f. 1948 from the Slovak Democratic Party; Chair. Jozef Šimúth; Sec.-Gen. Dalibor Laborecký.

CZECHOSLOVAKIA

Socialist Union of Youth (Socialistický svaz mládeže): nám. M. Gorkého 24, 116 47 Prague 1; f. 1970; a united mass youth movement; 1.6m. mems; Chair. VASIL MOHORITA; Chair. of Czech Central Cttee ZDENKA TESAŘOVÁ; Chair. of Slovak Central Cttee JOZEF DURICA.

Diplomatic Representation

EMBASSIES IN CZECHOSLOVAKIA

Afghanistan: V Vorlíku 17, 125 01 Prague 6; tel. (2) 381532; Ambassador: ABDUL BAGI SAMANDARI.

Albania: Pod Kaštany 22, 160 00 Prague; Chargé d'affaires a.i.: IDRIZ DHRAMI.

Algeria: Korejská 16, 125 21 Prague; tel. (2) 322021; Ambassador: ABDELHAMID LATRECHE.

Argentina: Washingtonova 25, 125 22 Prague 1; Ambassador: JULIO BARBOZA.

Austria: Viktora Huga 10, 125 43 Prague 5; tel. (2) 546550; telex 121849; Ambassador: KARL PETERLIK.

Belgium: Valdštejnská 6, 125 24 Prague 1; tel. (2) 534051; telex 122362; Ambassador: Baron HENRY BEYENS.

Bolivia: Ve Smečkách 25, 125 59 Prague; tel. (2) 263209; Chargé d'affaires a.i.: TEODOSIO IMAÑA-CASTRO.

Brazil: Bolzanova 5, 125 01 Prague 1; tel. (2) 229254; telex 122292; Ambassador: CARLOS EDUARDO DE AFFONSECA ALVES DE SOUZA.

Bulgaria: Krakovská 6, 125 00 Prague 1; tel. (2) 264310; telex 121381; Ambassador: TONCHO CHAKUROV.

Burma: Romaina Rollanda 3, 125 23 Prague 6; Ambassador: U MIN NAUNG.

Canada: Mickiewiczova 6, 125 33 Prague 6; tel. (2) 326941; telex 121061; Ambassador: BARRY M. MAWHINNEY.

China, People's Republic: Majakovského 22, 160 00 Prague 6; Ambassador: WANG XINGDA.

Colombia: Prícna 1, 110 00 Prague 1; tel. (2) 291330; Ambassador: ENRIQUE PAREJO GONZÁLEZ.

Costa Rica: Konevova 192, 130 00 Prague 3; tel. 820706; Ambassador: (vacant).

Cuba: Sibiřské nám. I, 125 35 Prague 6; tel. (2) 341341; telex 93184; Ambassador: MARIO RODRÍGUEZ MARTÍNEZ.

Denmark: U Havlíčkových sadů I, 120 21 Prague 2; tel. (2) 254715; telex 122209; Ambassador: VIGAND LOSE.

Ecuador: Opletalova 43, 125 01 Prague 1; tel. (2) 261258; telex 123286; Ambassador: ARTURO LECARO BUSTAMANTE.

Egypt: Majakovského 14, 125 46 Prague 6; tel. (2) 341051; telex 123552; Ambassador: OMAR GAD.

Ethiopia: nám. M. Gorkého 16, 125 01 Prague 1; tel. (2) 359481; Ambassador: WONDWOSSEN HAILU.

Finland: Dřevná 2, 125 01 Prague 2; tel. (2) 205541; telex 121060; Ambassador: EERO YRJÖLÄ.

France: Velkopřevorské nám. 2, 118 00 Prague 1; tel. (2) 533042; Ambassador: JACQUES ALEXANDRE HUMANN.

German Democratic Republic: Gottwaldovo nábřeží 32, 110 00 Prague 1; tel. (2) 299551; telex 121528; Ambassador: HELMUT ZIEBART.

Germany, Federal Republic: Vlašska 19, 125 60 Prague 1; tel. (2) 532351; telex 122814; Ambassador: (vacant).

Ghana: V Tisine 4, 160 00 Prague 6; tel. (2) 373058; telex 122263; Ambassador: MOSES KWASI AHMAD AGYEMAN.

Greece: Na Ořechovce 19, 125 45 Prague 6; tel. (2) 354279; Ambassador: CONSTANTIN POLITIS.

Hungary: Mičurinova I, 125 37 Prague; tel. (2) 365041; telex 123535; Ambassador: MIKLÓS BARITY.

India: Valdštejnská 6, 125 28 Prague 1; tel. (2) 532642; telex 121901; Ambassador: BHUPATRAY OZA.

Indonesia: Nad Buďánkami II/7, 125 29 Prague 5; tel. (2) 526041; telex 121443; Ambassador: H. R. ENAP SURATMAN.

Iran: Na Zátorce 18, 125 30 Prague 6; tel. (2) 371480; telex 122732; Ambassador: HAMID REZA HOSSEINI.

Iraq: Na Zátorce 10, 125 01 Prague 6; Ambassador: MUNTHER AHMED AL-MUTLAK.

Italy: Nerudova 20, 125 31 Prague 1; tel. (2) 530666; telex 122704; Ambassador: GIOVANNI CASTELLANI PASTORIS.

Japan: Maltézské nám. 6, 125 32 Prague 1; tel. (2) 535751; telex 121199; Ambassador: HARUYUKI MABUCHI.

Kampuchea: Na Hubálce 1, 169 00 Prague 6; tel. 352603; Ambassador: CHIM NGUON.

Korea, Democratic People's Republic: R. Rollanda 10, 160 00 Prague 6; tel. 373953; Ambassador: KIM KWANG SOP.

Lebanon: Gottwaldovo nábřeží 14, 110 00 Prague 1; tel. (2) 293633; telex 123583; Ambassador: SLEIMAN YOUNES.

Libya: Na baště sv. Jiří 7, 160 00 Prague 6; Secretary of People's Cttee: MUHAMMAD MUSBAH KHALIFA.

Mexico: Karlovo nám. 19, 125 49 Prague 2; tel. (2) 299918; telex 121947; Ambassador: ALFONSO HERRERA SALCEDO.

Mongolia: Korejská 5, 160 00 Prague 6; tel. (2) 328992; telex 121921; Ambassador: DJAMSRAGIYN DULMA.

Morocco: Petrska 24, 125 47 Prague 1; tel. (2) 310935; Ambassador: TAJEDDINE BADDOU.

Netherlands: Maltézské nám. 1, 110 00 Prague 1; tel. (2) 531378; telex 122643; Ambassador: Count LAMBERT D'ANSEMBOURG.

Nicaragua: Na Baště sv. Jiří 3, 125 46 Prague 6; tel. 324410; telex 123336; Ambassador: BAYARDO ALTAMIRANO LÓPEZ.

Nigeria: Před Bateriemi 18, 160 00 Prague 6; tel. (2) 354294; telex 123575; Ambassador: Dr MUSA OTIGBA.

Norway: Na Ořechovce 69, 162 00 Prague 6; tel. (2) 354526; telex 122200; Ambassador: KNUT TARALDSET.

Peru: Hradecká 18, 125 01 Prague 3; tel. 733272; telex 123345; Ambassador: IGOR VELÁZQUEZ RODRÍGUEZ.

Poland: Valdštejnská 8, 125 42 Prague 1; tel. (2) 536951; telex 121841; Ambassador: WŁODZIMIERZ MOKRZYSZCZAK.

Portugal: Bubenská 3, 170 00 Prague 7; tel. (2) 878472; telex 121354; Ambassador: (vacant).

Romania: Nerudova 5, 125 44 Prague; tel. 533059; Ambassador: ION PĂTAN.

Spain: Pevnostní 9, 162 00 Prague 6; tel. (2) 327124; telex 121974; Ambassador: CARLOS DE LA FIGUERA Y JAGOU.

Sudan: Malostranské nábřeží 1, 110 00 Prague 1; tel. (2) 536547; Ambassador: SAYYID ABD AL-MUTASIM.

Sweden: Úvoz 13, 125 52 Prague 1; tel. (2) 533344; telex 121840; Ambassador: KARL-WILHELM WÖHLER.

Switzerland: Pevnostní 7, 162 00 Prague 6; tel. (2) 320406; Ambassador: SERGE F. SALVI.

Syria: Pod Kaštany 16, 125 01 Prague 6; tel. 326231; telex 121532; Ambassador: SUBHI HADDAD.

Tunisia: Štěpanská 18, Prague 2; tel. (2) 360901; telex 122512; Ambassador: MONGI KOOLI.

Turkey: Pevnostní 3, 160 00 Prague 6; tel. 320597; Ambassador: ORHAN AKA.

USSR: Pod Kaštany I, 160 00 Prague 6; tel. 381943; Ambassador: VIKTOR PAVLOVICH LOMAKIN.

United Kingdom: Thunovská 14, 125 50 Prague 1; tel. (2) 533347; telex 121011; Ambassador: P. LAWRENCE O'KEEFFE.

USA: Tržiště 15, 125 48 Prague; tel. (2) 536641; telex 121196; Ambassador JULIAN M. NIEMCZYK.

Uruguay: Václavské nám. 64, 111 21 Prague 1; tel. (2) 351989; telex 121291; Ambassador: ADOLFO LINARDI MONTERO.

Venezuela: Janáčkovo nábřeží 49, 150 00 Prague 5; tel. (2) 536051; telex 122146; Ambassador: JOSÉ DE JESÚS OSÍO.

Viet-Nam: Holeckova 6, 125 55 Prague 5; tel. 536127; telex 121824; Ambassador: NGUYEN PHU SOAI.

Yemen Arab Republic: Washingtonova 17, 125 22 Prague 1; tel. (2) 222411; telex 123300; Ambassador: ABD AL-LATIF MUHAMMAD DHAIF ALLAH.

Yemen, People's Democratic Republic: Hradešínská 58, 100 00 Prague 10; tel. 738016; telex 123541; Ambassador: SAIF MOHSIN HUSSAIN.

Yugoslavia: Mostecká 15, 118 00 Prague; tel. (2) 531443; telex 123284; Ambassador: DUSAN RODIĆ.

Judicial System

Justice is executed through elected courts which consist of three ranks of law courts: the Supreme Court of the Czechoslovak Socialist Republic (together with Supreme Courts of the Czech and Slovak Socialist Republics), Regional and District Courts. There are also Military Courts which are subject to special regulations. Judges of the Czechoslovak Supreme Court are elected by the Federal Assembly; judges of the Czech and Slovak Supreme Courts and of the Regional and District Courts are elected by the National Councils of the respective republics. Judges are of two kinds, professional and lay judges, the latter having other occupations, but both types have equal authority. Lay judges are elected by District National Committees. Supervision of the

CZECHOSLOVAKIA

observance of laws and legal regulations rests with the Procurator-General who is appointed by the President of the Republic and accountable to the Federal Assembly.

Chairman of the Supreme Court: Dr JOSEF ONDŘEJ.
Procurator-General: Prof. Dr JÁN PJEŠČAK.

Religion

Secretariat for Ecclesiastical Affairs: f. 1949; controls church affairs; Dir VINCENT MACOVSKY.

CHRISTIANITY

Ekumenická rada Církví v Československé Socialistické republice (Czechoslovak Ecumenical Council of Churches): Vitkova 13, 186 00 Prague 8; tel. 227581; f. 1955, present name since 1984; 11 mem. churches; Chair. FRANTIŠEK HALAMA; Gen. Sec. Rev. Prof. Dr ANEZKA EBERTOVÁ.

The Roman Catholic Church

Czechoslovakia comprises three archdioceses and 10 dioceses, including one (directly responsible to the Holy See) for Catholics of the Slovak (Byzantine) rite.

Latin Rite
Bohemia

Archbishop of Prague: Cardinal FRANTIŠEK TOMÁŠEK, Hradčanské nám. 16, 119 02 Prague 1; tel. (2) 539548; 1,190,000 adherents; 578 parishes.

Moravia

Archbishop of Olomouc: (vacant), Wurmova 9, 771 01 Olomouc; tel. (68) 25726; 1,950,400 adherents; 731 parishes; Apostolic Administrator Prof. FRANTIŠEK VYMĚTAL (acting).

Slovakia

Archbishop of Trnava: (vacant), Svätoplukovo 3, 917 66 Trnava; tel. (805) 26235; 1,329,000 adherents; 435 parishes; Apostolic Administrator Bishop JÁN SOKOL.

Slovak Rite

Bishop of Prešov: (vacant), Greckokatolícky biskupský úrad, Slovenskej Republiky rád 8, Prešov; tel. 34622; 358,860 adherents (January 1988); 199 parishes.

The Orthodox Church

Pravoslavaná Církev v ČSSR (Orthodox Church of Czechoslovakia): V Jámě, 6, 111 21 Prague 1; divided into four eparchies: Prague, Olomouc, Prešov, Michalovce; Head of the Autocephalous Church, Metropolitan of Prague and of all Czechoslovakia DOROTEJ; 150,000 mems; 127 parishes; Theological Faculty in Prešov.

Protestant Churches

Brethren Church: Soukenická 15,110 00 Prague 1; 10,000 mems, 35 congregations, 190 preaching stations; Pres. JAROSLAV KUBOVÝ; Sec. K. TASCHNER.
Christian Corps: Bratislavská 21, 602 00 Brno; 3,200 mems; 123 brs; Rep. Ing. PETR ZEMAN.
Czechoslovak Baptists: Na Topolce 10, 140 00 Prague 4; tel. (2) 430974; f. 1919; 4,000 mems; Pres. Rev. Dr PAVEL TITĚRA; Sec. Rev. Ing. JAN POSPÍŠIL.
Evangelical Church of Czech Brethren (Presbyterian): Jungmannova 9, 111 21 Prague 1; united since 1918; activities extend over Bohemia, Moravia, and Silesia; 236,000 adherents and 272 parishes; Pres. JOSEF HROMADKA; Gen. Sec. MIROSLAV BROŽ.
Methodist Evangelical Church: Ječná 19, 120 00 Prague 2; 4,500 mems; 19 parishes; Supt Dr VILÉM SCHNEEBERGER.
Reformed Christian Church in Slovakia: V Jokaího 34, 945 01 Komárno; tel. 2788; 100,000 mems and 380 parishes; Bishop EUGEN MIKO; Sec. BARTOLOMEJ GÖÖZ.
Silesian Evangelical Church of the Augsburg Confession in the Czech Socialist Republic (Silesian Lutheran Church): Na Nivách 7, 737 01 Český Těšín; tel. 56656; founded in the 16th century during the Luther reformation, reorganized in 1948; 46,800 mems; Bishop Dr VLADISLAV KIEDROŇ.
Slovak Lutheran Church (Evangelical Church of the Augsburg Confession in Czechoslovakia); 326 parishes in 14 seniorates; 40,000 baptized mems; 327 parishes; Bishop-Gen. Prof. Dr JÁN MICHALKO, Palisády 46, 811 06 Bratislava; Eastern District Bishop Dr JÚLIUS FILLO, Jesenského 1, 040 01 Košice; Bishop of the Western District RUDOLF KOŠTIAL, Námestie SNP 17, 960 01 ZVOLEN.
Unitarians: Karlova 8, 110 00 Prague 1; tel. (2) 266730; f. 1923; 5,000 mems; 4 parishes; Presiding Officer Dr D. J. KAFKA.

Unity of Brethren (Jednota bratrská) (Moravian Church): Hálkova, 5, 120 00 Prague 2; tel. (2) 361340; f. 1457; 5,000 mems; 17 parishes; Pres. Rev. JINDŘICH HALAMA.

Other Christian Churches

Church of the Seventh-day Adventists: Zálesí 50, 142 00 Prague 4; tel. (2) 4723745; 12,000 mems; 106 preaching stations; Pres. OLDŘICH SLÁDEK.
Czechoslovak Hussite Church: Kujbyševa 5, 166 26 Prague 6; tel. (2) 320041; f. 1920; 300,000 mems; 331 parishes divided into five dioceses; Bishop-Patriarch Dr MIROSLAV NOVÁK.
Old Catholic Church: Blodkova 4, 130 00 Prague 3; tel. (2) 278777; 1,500 mems, 3 parishes; Bishop Gen. Dr MILOŠ PULEC.

JUDAISM

The present community is estimated at approximately 6,000 people, and is divided under two central organizations:

Council of Jewish Communities in the Czech Socialist Republic (Rada židovských náboženských obcí v České socialistické republice): Maiselova 1, 110 01 Prague 1; tel. (2) 318559; 2,700 mems; Chair. BOHUMIL HELLER; Sec.-Gen. FRANTIŠEK KRAUS; Chief Rabbi of Prague DANIEL MEYER.
Union of the Jewish Religious Communities in the Slovak Socialist Republic (Ústredný zväz židovských náboženských obcí ve Slovenskej socialistickej republike): Šmeralova ul. 29, 800 00 Bratislava; 3,300 mems; Chair. BEDŘICH GRÜNWALD; Chief Rabbi SAMUEL GROSSMANN (Košice).

The Press

Although the Czechoslovak press was considerably affected by the events of 1968, its basic purpose is still as defined in the October 1966 Press Law: 'to give as far as possible complete information...to advance the interest of socialist society...to promote the people's socialist awareness of the policy of the Communist Party as the leading force in society and state'.

This law, which codified previous legislation on the rights and duties of journalists and publishers states that 'freedom of expression and of the press is guaranteed by the fact that publishers and press organizations... have been placed at the disposal of the working people and their organizations'. Hence, only political parties and such social institutions associated with the National Front as trade unions, youth unions, cultural associations and rural co-operatives may own newspapers and periodicals. Private ownership is forbidden. Even collective ownership rests upon official approval; papers must be registered with the Federal Office for Press and Information and the Czech or Slovak Office for Press and Information, and when the editor fails to observe the conditions under which approval was given, the paper may be suspended.

During 1968 there was freedom of publication and Western books circulated in large editions. Censorship was abolished in June, but restored in September. In 1969 censorship was again abolished, but the necessity for official approval has since prevented the publication of ideologically dissenting journals. The editor of a paper or periodical bears full responsibility for its contents.

The Czechoslovak people far exceed other East European nations in their consumption per head of newspapers and magazines. There are 30 daily newspapers (with a combined circulation of 5m. copies per issue in 1987), including nine in Prague and nine (one in Hungarian and the rest in Slovak) in Bratislava. In 1987 there were 1,080 magazines and newspapers published in Czechoslovakia, as well as numerous less frequent periodicals. In addition, farms and factories produce their own daily or weekly news-sheets, dealing mainly with local issues. All registered periodicals receive an allocation of newsprint.

Political speeches and articles on social and economic development are given special prominence. In contrast with much of the East European press, which is often characterized as dull and lacking in popular appeal, the Czechoslovak press is relatively lively and colourful and allows a qualified scope for criticism. There is no tabloid press as the policy is to play down such items as constitute the sort of sensationalism familiar to the West. Advertising is now more common than formerly, and although mainly concerned with state enterprises, it includes some material from abroad. Sales are mainly by subscription.

The most widely read and influential papers are the Prague dailies, headed by *Rudé právo*. This paper is the chief organ of the Czechoslovak Communist Party. It is eight pages long and has a nation-wide circulation of 1,018,000 copies. Its sister paper, the Slovak CP's *Pravda* (407,500), is the leading provincial daily. The Czech and the Slovak trade-union organs are *Práce* and *Práca* in their respective cities. Three other important metropolitan dailies are *Lidová demokracie* and *Svobodné slovo* produced respectively by the People's Party and the Socialist Party, and *Mladá Fronta*,

CZECHOSLOVAKIA

published by the Central Committee of the Socialist Union of Youth.

There are also many small circulation periodicals—often of very high quality—dealing with specialized subjects. One should also note several very popular and colourful women's magazines, such as *Vlasta* (820,000), and the satirical *Dikobraz*, famous for its political cartoons.

The national news agency, Československá tisková kancelář (ČTK), receives a state subsidy and is controlled by the federal government through its presidium.

PRINCIPAL DAILIES
Prague

Československý sport (Czechoslovak Sport): Na poříčí 30, 115 23 Prague 1; tel. 2322528; telex 121514; central organ of the Czech Union of Physical Education; Editor JAROMÍR TOMÁNEK; circ. 195,000.

Lidová demokracie (People's Democracy): Karlovo nám. 5, 120 78 Prague 2; tel. 291505; telex 121403; f. 1945; morning; official organ of the Czechoslovak People's Party (Catholic); Editor Dr STANISLAV TOMS; circ. 210,000.

Mladá fronta (Youth Front): Panská 8, 112 22 Prague 1; tel. 221661; telex 122468; f. 1945; morning; organ of the Central Cttee of the Socialist Union of Youth; Editor-in-Chief CTIRAD FRČKA; circ. 325,000.

Práce (Labour): Václavské nám. 15, 112 58 Prague 1; tel. 266039; telex 121134; f. 1945; morning; published by the Central Council of Trade Unions; Editor-in-Chief FRANTIŠEK COŇK; circ. 345,000.

Rudé právo (Red Right): Na poříčí 30, 112 86 Prague 1; tel. (2) 249851; telex 121184; f. 1920; morning; central organ of the Czechoslovak Communist Party; Editor-in-Chief ZDENĚK HOŘENÍ; circ. 1,018,000.

Svoboda (Freedom): Na Florenci 3, 113 29 Prague 1; tel. 2321634; telex 121856; organ of the Central Bohemian Regional Cttee of the Communist Party of Czechoslovakia; Editor-in-Chief JIŘÍ NOVOTNÝ; circ. 58,000.

Svobodné slovo (Free Word): Václavské nám. 36, 112 12 Prague 1; tel. 226253; telex 121432; f. 1907; organ of the Czechoslovak Socialist Party; Editor-in-Chief JAROMÍR MAŠEK; circ. 220,000.

Večerní Praha (Evening Prague): Na poříčí 30, 112 86 Prague 1; tel. 232345; telex 121883; f. 1955; evening; edited by the Prague Municipal Cttee of the Communist Party; Editor-in-Chief MILOŠ KOLÍSKO; circ. 170,000.

Zemědělské noviny (Farmer's News): Václavské nám. 47, 113 78 Prague 1; tel. 265951-9; telex 121435; f. 1945; organ of the Ministry of Agriculture and Food; Editor-in-Chief VLADIMÍR KULHÁNEK; circ. 370,000.

Banská Bystrica

Smer (Course): Čs. armády 10, 975 43 Banská Bystrica; tel. 22154; organ of the Central Cttee of the Communist Party of Slovakia; Editor-in-Chief ANTON KAMAS; circ. 40,000.

Bratislava

Hlas l'udu (Voice of the People): Žabotova 2, 812 69 Bratislava; tel. 425446; telex 93398; f. 1949; morning; West Slovakia Regional Cttee of the Communist Party of Slovakia; Editor-in-Chief Dr IZIDOR LEDNÁR; circ. 49,000.

Ľud (People): Gorkého 5/1, 812 78 Bratislava; tel. 58854; telex 93254; f. 1948; organ of the Slovak Reconstruction Party; Editor-in-Chief ENGELBERT MERKL; circ. 13,000.

Práca (Labour): Odborárské nám. 3, 812 71 Bratislava; tel. 64547; telex 93283; f. 1946; organ of the Slovak Trades Union Council; Editor-in-Chief JÁN VIŠVÁDER; circ. 238,000.

Pravda (Truth): Štúrova 4, 815 80 Bratislava; tel. 52503; telex 93386; f. 1920; organ of Slovak Communist Party; Editor-in-Chief ŠTEFAN BACHÁR; circ. 407,500.

Rol'nícke noviny (Farmer's News): Fučíkova 6, 813 41 Bratislava; tel. 54449; f. 1946; organ of the Slovak Ministry of Agriculture and Food and the Slovak Cttee of the Co-operative Farmers' Union; Editor-in-Chief JURAJ ŠESTÁK; circ. 78,000.

Smena (Shift): Dostojevského rad 1, 812 84 Bratislava; tel. 54255; telex 93341; f. 1947; organ of Slovak Central Cttee of the Socialist Union of Youth; Editor-in-Chief HELMUT VÁCHA; circ. 121,000.

Šport (Sport): Volgogradská 1, 812 02 Bratislava; tel. 58092; organ of the Slovak Central Cttee of the Czechoslovak Union of Physical Education; Editor-in-Chief IGOR MRÁZ; circ. 65,000.

Új Szó (New World): Gorkého 10, 815 81 Bratislava; tel. 53220; telex 92308; f. 1948; midday; Hungarian-language paper of the Communist Party of Slovakia; Editor-in-Chief ZOLTÁN RABAY; circ. 93,000.

Directory

Večerník (Evening Paper): Októbrové nám. 7, 816 33 Bratislava; tel. 311231; telex 92296; f. 1956; evening; organ of the City Cttee of the Slovak Communist Party; Editor-in-Chief Dr FRANTIŠEK BARTOŠEK; circ. 80,400.

Brno

Brněnský večerník (Brno Evening News): Jakubské nám. 7, 658 44 Brno; tel. 228446; f. 1968; organ of the Brno City Cttee of the Communist Party; Editor-in-Chief Dr DANUŠE ŠKLÍBOVÁ; circ. 33,000.

Rovnost (Equality): nám. Rudé armády 13, 658 22 Brno; tel. 75700; f. 1885; published by South Moravian Regional Cttee of the Communist Party; morning; Editor KAMIL KUSTEK; circ. 126,000.

České Budějovice

Jihočeská Pravda (Truth of Southern Bohemia): Vrbenská 23, 370 45 České Budějovice; tel. 22081; published by the South Bohemian Regional Cttee of the Communist Party; Editor-in-Chief VLADIMÍR DOLEŽAL; circ. 65,000.

Hradec Králové

Pochodeň (Torch): Škroupova 695, 501 72 Hradec Králové; tel. 613511; published by the East Bohemian Regional Cttee of the Communist Party; Editor-in-Chief OLDŘICH ENGE; circ. 72,000.

Košice

Východoslovenské noviny (East Slovak News): Šmeralova 18, 042 66 Košice; tel. 33261; organ of the East Slovakia Regional Cttee of the Communist Party of Slovakia; Editor-in-Chief ŠTEFAN KOČUTA; circ. 57,580.

Ostrava

Nová Svoboda (New Freedom): Novinářská 3, 709 07 Ostrava; tel. 52141; f. 1945; morning; published by the North Moravian Regional Cttee of the Communist Party; Editor-in-Chief JAN HŘÍBEK; circ. 212,000.

Ostravský večerník (Ostrava Evening News): Zeyerova 11, 728 85 Ostrava; tel. 232023; published by the City Cttee of the Communist Party and the Municipal National Cttee; Editor-in-Chief JOSEF ZLOMEK; circ. 28,000.

Plzeň

Pravda (Truth): Leninova 15, 304 83 Plzeň; tel. 222000; telex 154302; f. 1919; published by the West Bohemian Regional Cttee of the Communist Party; Editor-in-Chief JAROSLAV PÁV; circ. 80,000.

Ústí nad Labem

Průboj (Forward): Švermova 83, 400 90 Ústí nad Labem; tel. 23274; published by the North Bohemian Regional Cttee of the Communist Party; Editor-in-Chief JAN NOVÁK; circ. 98,000.

PRINCIPAL PERIODICALS
Czech language

100+1ZZ: Žirovnická 2389, 106 00 Prague 10; tel. 7192248; monthly foreign press digest of the Czechoslovak News Agency (ČTK); Editor-in-Chief JAN BLAŽÍK; circ. 155,000.

Ahoj na sobotu (Hallo Saturday): Václavské nám. 36, 112 12 Prague 1; tel. 264663; illustrated family weekly published by the Czechoslovak Socialist Party; Editor-in-Chief SLAVOMIL OLŠÁK; circ. 178,000.

Československá fotografie: Mrštíkova 23, 100 00 Prague 10; tel. 781553; f. 1946; monthly; photographic; Editor EVA HORSKÁ; circ. 57,500.

Československý architekt (Czechoslovak Architect): Letenská 5, 118 45 Prague 1; f. 1955; fortnightly; Editor Dr JAN NOVOTNÝ.

Československý život (Czechoslovak Life): Vinohradská 46, 120 41 Prague 2; tel. 257741; telex 122948; f. 1946; illustrated monthly magazine; political, economic, social, cultural and sports; published by Orbis Press Agency in English, French, German, Italian and Spanish; Editor (vacant).

Chatař (Weekend House Owner): Václavské náměstí 47, 113 11 Prague 1; tel. 264592; monthly; published by State Agricultural Publishing House; Editor-in-Chief Ing. JIŘÍ TRNAVSKÝ; circ. 100,000.

Chovatel (Breeder): Václavské náměstí 47, 113 11 Prague 1; tel. 266943-9; monthly; published by the Czech Union of Breeders; Editor-in-Chief Ing. OLGA MAKARIUSOVÁ; circ. 100,000.

Čtení (Reading): Národní tř. 25, 110 000 Prague 1; tel. 268011; monthly; about life in the USSR; published by the Union of Czechoslovak-Soviet Friendship; Editor-in-Chief EMILIE HORÁKOVÁ; circ. 275,000.

CZECHOSLOVAKIA

Dikobraz (The Porcupine): Na Florenci 3, 112 86 Prague 1; tel. 2323451; telex 121184; f. 1945; satirical weekly; published by *Rudé právo*; Editor-in-Chief Jindřich Bešta; circ. 531,000.

Film a doba (Film and Time): Slavíčkova 5, 160 00 Prague 6; tel. 2375062; monthly; Editor Vladimír Kolár; circ. 7,000.

Hospodářské noviny (Economic News): Na Florenci 3, 112 86 Prague 1; tel. 2323451; telex 121184; weekly; published by Communist Party of Czechoslovakia; Editor-in-Chief Ing. Rudolf Kostka; circ. 125,000.

Hudební rozhledy (Musical Review): Valdštejnské nám. 1, 118 00 Prague 1; tel. 2536206; f. 1948; monthly review; published by the Union of Czech Composers and Concert Artists; Editor Jan Vičar; circ. 4,200.

Katolické noviny (Catholic News): Sněmovní 9, 118 01 Prague 1; tel. 513717; weekly; published by Czech Catholic Charity; Editor-in-Chief Vendelín Šimeček; circ. 110,000.

Kino (Cinema): Slavíčkova 5, 160 00 Prague 6; tel. 375063; an illustrated film magazine published by Central Management of Czechoslovak Film; fortnightly; Editor-in-Chief Jaromíra Sitařová; circ. 153,000.

Květy (Flowers): Na Florenci 3, 112 86 Prague 1; tel. 2323451; telex 12184; f. 1834; illustrated weekly; published by Czechoslovak Communist Party; Editor-in-Chief Dr Milan Codr; circ. 401,000.

Magazín Co vás zajímá (What Interests You ?): Na Florenci 3, 112 86 Prague 1; tel. 2323451; monthly; published by Rudé právo Publishing House; Editor-in-Chief Dr Miroslava Papežová; circ. 165,000.

Mladý svět (Young World): Panská 8, 112 22 Prague 1; tel. 223726; telex 121510; illustrated weekly for young people published by the Central Cttee of the Socialist Union of Youth; Editor-in-Chief Olga Čermáková; circ. 500,000.

Motoristická současnost (Motoring Today): Jungmannova 24, 113 66 Prague 1; tel. (2) 260651; f. 1969; monthly; published by State Cttee for Road Traffic Security; Editor-in-Chief Miloš Kovářík; circ. 117,000.

Naše rodina (Our Family): Karlovo nám. 5, 120 00 Prague 2; tel. 294196; f. 1968; Christian and cultural weekly published by Czechoslovak People's Party; Editor-in-Chief Dr Libuše Daňková; circ. 179,000.

Obrana lidu (People's Defence): Jungmannova 24, 113 66 Prague 1; tel. 246886; weekly; published by the Political Administration of the People's Army; Editor-in-Chief Miroslav Procházka; circ. 58,000.

Odborář (Trade Unionist): nám. M. Gorkého 23, 112 82 Prague 1; tel. 242610; fortnightly; published by the Central Trade Unions Council; Editor-in-Chief Ing. Helena Mandová; circ. 121,000.

Ohníček (Little Flame): Radlická 61, 150 00 Prague 5; tel. 536523; fortnightly magazine for Czechoslovak children; published by Czech Central Council of the Pioneer Organization of the Socialist Youth Union; Editor-in-Chief Dr Svatava Hirschová; circ. 265,000.

Prager Volkszeitung (Prague's People's Newspaper): Helénská 4, 120 00 Prague 2; weekly; general politics and culture; published by *Rudé právo* Publishing House, the Central Cttee of the Czechoslovak National Front and the Cultural Union of the German citizens in Czechoslovakia; Editor Heribert Panster; circ. 17,000.

Praktická žena (Practical Woman): Na rybníčky 7, 120 00 Prague 2; tel. 224642; monthly; published by the Czechoslovak Union of Women; Editor-in-Chief Božena Kollmanová; circ. 252,000.

Právník (The Lawyer): Národní třída 18, 116 91 Prague 1; tel. (2) 201620; f. 1861; monthly; law; published by Czechoslovak Academy of Sciences (Institute of State and Law); Editor Josef Blahož; circ. 4,700.

Rozhlas (Radio): Vinohradská 12, 120 99 Prague 2; telex 121100; f. 1923; weekly; cultural and sound radio journal; published by the *Rudé právo* Publishing House; Editor Vladimír Pánek; circ. 276,000.

Sedmička Pionýrů (Pioneers' Seven): Radlická 61, 150 00 Prague 5; tel. 540013; weekly; published by Czech Central Council of the Pioneer Organization of the Socialist Youth Union; Editor-in-Chief Rudolf Parenica; circ. 220,000.

Signál (Signal): Hybernská 7, 110 00 Prague 1; tel. 240758; weekly; military; published by Federal Ministry of the Interior; Editor-in-Chief Ing. Pavel Minařík; circ. 281,000.

Stadion (Stadium): Klimentská 1, 115 88 Prague 1; tel. 2312898; illustrated sport weekly published by the Czech Central Cttee for Physical Education; Editor-in-Chief Zvonimír Šupich; circ. 166,000.

Svět motorů (World of Motors): Jungmannova 24, 113 66 Prague 1; tel. 240280; f. 1947; weekly; published by the Union for Cooperation with the army of the ČSSR; motoring; Editor-in-Chief Miroslav Erb; circ. 359,000.

Svět práce (The World of Labour): Václavské nám. 15, 112 58 Prague 1; telex 121134; f. 1946, reorganized 1968; political, economic and cultural weekly; published by Central Council of Trade Unions; Editor František Říha; circ. 65,000.

Svět socialismu (The World of Socialism): Smetanovo nábř. 18, 110 00 Prague 1; tel. 241216; illustrated weekly; published by the Union of Czechoslovak-Soviet Friendship; Editor-in-Chief Miloš Prošek; circ. 115,000.

Svět v obrazech (World in Pictures): Pařížská 9, 110 00 Prague 1; tel. 2314771; illustrated weekly published by the Odeon Publishing House; Editor-in-Chief Dr Zdeněk Hrabica; circ. 150,000.

Světová literatura (World Literature): Na Florenci 3, 115 86 Prague 1; f. 1956; published by Odeon, bi-monthly; contemporary foreign literature; Editor Václav Falada; circ. 12,000.

Tribuna (Tribune): Olšanská 1, 130 00 Prague 3; tel. 260259; f. 1956; published by Odeon; politics weekly of the Czechoslovak Communist Party; Editor-in-Chief Karel Horák; circ. 90,000.

Tvorba (Creation): Na poříčí 30, 112 86 Prague 1; tel. (2) 323935; telex 121184; weekly; political, scientific and cultural; published by the *Rudé právo* Publishing House; Editor-in-Chief Jaroslav Čejka; circ. 80,000.

Týdeník Československé televize (Czechoslovak Television Weekly): nám. Lidových milicí 5, 190 00 Prague 9; tel. 839856; telex 121184; f. 1965; weekly cultural and television journal; published by *Rudé právo*; Editor-in-Chief Jana Kolárová; circ. 510,000.

Věda a život (Science and Life): POB 395, 659 95 Brno; f. 1954; monthly; published by Czech Central Cttee of Socialist Academy; Editor Jiří Cicvárek; circ. 15,000.

Vesmír (Universe): Jungmannova 12, 110 00 Prague 1; f. 1871; a monthly popular science magazine of the Czechoslovak Academy of Science; Editor Prokop Málek; circ. 22,000.

Vlasta: Jindřišská 5, 116 08 Prague 1; tel. (2) 366326; f. 1946; illustrated weekly for women; published by the Union of Czech Women; concerned with the status of women in society, problems of family and education; Editor-in-Chief Alena Šloufová; circ. 820,000.

Zahrádkář (Gardener): Čkalova 22, 160 41 Prague 6; tel. 323105; monthly; published by Czech Union of Gardeners; Editor-in-Chief Dr František Hrdlička; circ. 320,000.

Zápisník (Notebook): Vlastina 23, 160 65 Prague 6; tel. 368866; monthly; army-related topics; published by the Political Administration of the People's Army; Editor-in-Chief Col. Ing. Miroslav Linka; circ. 225,000.

Zdraví (Health): Thunovská 18, 118 04 Prague 1; tel. 532342; monthly; published by the Czechoslovak Red Cross; Editor-in-Chief Karel Průša; circ. 123,000.

Žena a móda (Women and Fashion): Na příkopě 27, 113 49 Prague 1; tel. 261187; monthly; published by the Czech Union of Women; Editor-in-Chief Dr Vladimíra Kvěchová; circ. 257,000.

Zlatý máj (Golden May): Na Perštýně 1, 110 01 Prague 1; telex 121605; magazine on literature for children; 10 a year; published by Albatros Publishing House; Editor Dr Jiří Lapáček; circ. 3,500.

Slovak language

Dievča (Girl): Leninovo náměstí 12, 812 03 Bratislava; tel. 334171; every 2 months; published by the Slovak Union of Women; Editor-in-Chief Dr Elena Girenthová; circ. 163,000.

Družba (Friendship): Sasinkova 5, 815 60 Bratislava; tel. 60303; 14 a year; activities of the Union of Czechoslovak-Soviet Friendship; published by the Slovak Ministry of Education; Editor-in-Chief Viera Labuzová; circ. 235,000.

Eva: Gorkého 13, 811 01 Bratislava; tel. 52271; every 2 months; magazine for women; published by the Slovak Ministry of the Interior; Editor-in-Chief Dr Gita Pechová; circ. 140,000.

Expres: Martanovičova, 815 80 Bratislava; tel. 334209; f. 1969; weekly digest of the foreign press; published by the Pravda Publishing House; Editor-in-Chief Karol Hulman; circ. 80,000.

Horizont: Banskobystrická 18, 815 85 Bratislava; tel. 331117; f. 1965; monthly; magazine of the Union of Czechoslovak-Soviet Friendship; Editor Vojtech Kondel; circ. 32,000.

Kamarát (Friend): Pražská 11, 812 84 Bratislava; tel. 48541-5; weekly for Pioneers; published by the Slovak Central Cttee of the Socialist Youth Union; Editor-in-Chief Anna Hološková; circ. 130,000.

Katolícke noviny (Catholic News): Kapitulská 20, 815 21 Bratislava; tel. 331717; f. 1849; weekly; published by the St Adalbert Association; Editor-in-Chief Ladislav Belás; circ. 130,000.

Krásy Slovenska (Beauty of Slovakia): Vajnorská 100, 832 58 Bratislava; illustrated monthly; published by Sport, publishing house of the Slovak Physical Culture Organization; Editor Dr Milan Kubiš; circ. 18,000.

CZECHOSLOVAKIA

Móda (Fashion): Leninova náměstí 12, 815 05 Bratislava; tel. 334172; monthly; published by the Slovak Union of Women; Editor-in-Chief EMILIA SÁNDOROVÁ; circ. 130,000.

Nové Slovo (New Word): Štúrova 3, 815 80 Bratislava; tel. 50334; f. 1944; weekly; politics, culture, economy; organ of the Central Cttee of the Communist Party of Slovakia; Editor-in-Chief EMIL POLÁK; circ. 65,000.

Ohník (Little Flame): Karpatská 2, 812 84 Bratislava; tel. 44598; fortnightly; youth; published by Slovak Central Cttee of the Socialist Youth Union; Editor-in-Chief GABRIELA ROTHMAYEROVÁ; circ. 130,000.

Roháč (Stag-Beetle): Obráncov mieru 47, 816 06 Bratislava; tel. 40517; f. 1948; humorous, satirical weekly; published by Pravda, publishing house of the Communist Party of Slovakia; Editor-in-Chief PETER BÁN; circ. 120,000.

Slovenka (Slovak Woman): Štúrova 12, 814 92 Bratislava; tel. 55061; f. 1949; weekly pictorial published by the Slovak Women's Union; Editor-in-Chief LÝDIA BRABCOVÁ; circ. 235,000.

Svet socializmu (World of Socialism): Bezručova 9, 815 87 Bratislava; tel. 52959; f. 1951; weekly pictorial of the Union of Czechoslovak-Soviet Friendship; Editor MILOŠ BELUŠ; circ. 140,000.

Štart (Start): Vajnorská 100/A, 832 58 Bratislava; tel. 64666; f. 1956; illustrated weekly; organ of the Slovak Central Cttee of the Czechoslovak Union of Physical Education; Editor-in-Chief JOZEF MAZÁG; circ. 81,000.

Technické noviny (Technology News): Obráncov mieru 19, 812 71 Bratislava; tel. 333028; f. 1953; weekly of the Slovak Council of Trade Unions; Editor-in-Chief MICHAL KIMLIK; circ. 80,000.

Televízia (Television): nám. SNP 33, 814 54 Bratislava; tel. 335242; weekly; published by Pravda Publishing House; Editor-in-Chief KAROL HEDERLING; circ. 190,000.

Tip: Vajnorská 100A, 832 58 Bratislava; tel. 69634; telex 93330; f. 1969; weekly; football and ice-hockey; published by the Slovak Physical Training Organization; Editor FERDINAND KRÁLOVIČ; circ. 50,000.

Výber (Digest): Októbrové nám. 7, 814 76 Bratislava; tel. 316640; f. 1968; weekly; digest of home and foreign press; in Czech and Slovak; published by the Union of Slovak Journalists; Editor-in-Chief VERONIKA TÖKÖLYOVÁ; circ. 30,000.

Život (Life): Martanovičova 23, 812 38 Bratislava; tel. 53046; f. 1951; illustrated weekly; political, economic, social and cultural matters; published by the Pravda Publishing House; Editor-in-Chief Ing. LADISLAV TOMÁŠEK; circ. 200,000.

Foreign languages

Czechoslovak Foreign Trade: ul. 28 října 13, 112 79 Prague 1; tel. (2) 139447; telex 121142; f. 1961; monthly; journal of the Czechoslovak Chamber of Commerce and Industry; published in English, German, Spanish, Russian and French by Rapid, Czechoslovak Advertising Agency; Editor-in-Chief Dr PAVLA PODSKALSKÁ; circ. 11,330.

Czechoslovak Trade Unions: Václavské nám. 17, 112 58 Prague 1; tel. (2) 356107; telex 121134; review of the Central Trades Union Council; 6 a year; English, French, German, Russian, Italian, Swedish, Portuguese and Spanish; Editor-in-Chief HANA SEMÍNOVÁ; circ. 32,000.

The Democratic Journalist: Roosveltova 18, 160 00 Prague 6; tel. (2) 326806; telex 122631; f. 1953; monthly; press organ of the International Organization of Journalists; English, French and Spanish; Editor-in-Chief RUDOLF PŘEVRÁTIL; circ. 11,000.

For You from Czechoslovakia: ul. 28 října 13, 112 79 Prague 1; tel. (2) 139393; telex 121142; quarterly; published by Rapid in English, German, Russian, Spanish and French; Editor-in-Chief MARIE SŮVOVÁ; circ. 15,200.

Neue Prager Presse: Vinohradská 46, 120 41 Prague 2; tel. 256165; telex 122948; weekly; politics, culture, economy, tourism; published by Orbis in German; Editor-in-Chief JOSEF SKÁLA; circ. 15,000.

World Student News: ul. 17 listopadu 58, 110 00 Prague 1; tel. 2312812; published by the International Union of Students in English, French, German and Spanish; Editor-in-Chief ANDREAS HERGER; circ. 20,000.

NEWS AGENCIES

Československá tisková kancelář (ČTK) (Czechoslovak News Agency): Opletalova 5–7, 111 44 Prague 1; tel. (2) 2147; telex 122841; f. 1918; news and photo exchange service with all international and many national news agencies; maintains wide network of foreign correspondents; English, Russian, French and Spanish news service for foreign countries; publishes weekly bulletin in Russian, English, Spanish, French and German; publs specialized economic bulletins and documentation surveys in Czech; Gen. Dir Dr OTAKAR SVĚRČINA.

Orbis Press Agency: Vinohradská 46, 120 41 Prague 2; tel. 257145; telex 122948; f. 1977; supplies information about Czechoslovakia to the foreign press and foreign publishing houses on a commercial basis; Dir Dr VLADIMÍR VIPLER.

ČTK—Made in . . . publicity: Kotorská 16, 140 00 Prague 4; tel. (2) 422151; telex 122501; f. 1964; organization of the Czechoslovak News Agency for advertising foreign products and services in Czechoslovakia; Gen. Dir Dr JOSEF SEDA.

Foreign Bureaux

Agence France-Presse (AFP): Zitná 10, 120 00 Prague 2; tel. 296927; telex 121124; Bureau Chief MICHEL CONRATH.

Agentstvo Pechati Novosti (APN) (USSR): Italská 36, 120 00 Prague 3; tel. 2354459; telex 122235; Bureau Chief VLADIMIR FEDOROV; also br. in Bratislava.

Agenzia Nazionale Stampa Associata (ANSA) (Italy): Smečkách 2, 110 00 Prague 1; tel. (2) 247434; telex 122734; Bureau Chief FLAMINIA BUSSOTTI.

Allgemeiner Deutscher Nachrichtendienst (ADN) (German Democratic Republic): Milevska 835, 140 00 Prague 4; Bureau Chief STEFFI GENSICKE.

Associated Press (AP) (USA): Růžová 7, 110 00 Prague 1; tel. (2) 364838; telex 121987; Correspondent IVA DRÁPALOVÁ.

Bulgarska Telegrafna Agentsia (BTA) (Bulgaria): Ždanova 46, 160 00 Prague 6; telex 121066; Bureau Chief VIOLETA MICEVA.

Deutsche Presse-Agentur (dpa) (Federal Republic of Germany): Želivského 11/4/13, 130 31 Prague 3; tel. (2) 276595; telex 122706; Bureau Chief LADISLAV VALEK.

Inter Press Service (IPS) (Italy): Opletalova 5, 114 40 Prague 1; tel. (2) 2147; telex 122885; Correspondent BARNO FERMIN.

Kyodo Tsushin (Japan): Brevnov Liborova 24, Prague 6; tel. (2) 356797; Bureau Chief KIYOSHI HASUMI.

Magyar Távirati Iroda (MTI) (Hungary): Smaltovný 17, Prague 7; Bureau Chief JUDIT LÁNG.

Prensa Latina (Cuba): Petrské nám. 1, 110 00 Prague 1; telex 121083; Bureau Chief GERADO CÉSAR PROENZA.

Telegrafnoye Agentstvo Sovetskovo Soyuza (TASS) (USSR): Pevnostní 5, 162 00 Prague 6; Bureau Chief LEONID LATYSEV.

Xinhua (New China) News Agency (People's Republic of China): Majakovského 22, Prague 6; tel. (2) 326144; telex 121561; Correspondent YU JUNMIN.

The following are also represented: Agerpres (Romania), PAP (Poland) and Tanjug (Yugoslavia).

PRESS ASSOCIATIONS

Czechoslovak Union of Journalists: Pařížská 9, 116 30 Prague 1; f. 1946; 7,296 mems; Chair. JÁN RIŠKO.

Czech Union of Journalists: Pařížská 9, 116 30 Prague 1; tel. (2) 328015; f. 1877; 4,660 mems; Pres. Dr JOSEF VALENTA.

Slovak Union of Journalists: Októbrové nám. 7, 893 46 Bratislava; f. 1968; 2,206 mems; Pres. Dr ŠTEFAN BACHÁR.

Publishers

In May 1949 legislation was passed making the publication, printing, illustration, and distribution of all books and music the prerogative of the State. These activities are now restricted to the Government, political parties, trade unions, and national and communal bodies. However, churches and religious bodies are permitted to publish if the State will accept their work for printing.

CZECH PUBLISHING HOUSES

Academia: Vodičkova 40, 112 29 Prague 1; tel. (2) 363065; f. 1953; publishing house of the Czechoslovak Academy of Sciences; scientific books, periodicals; Dir RADOSLAV ŠVEC.

Albatros: Na Perštýně 1, 110 01 Prague 1; telex 121605; f. 1949; literature for children and young people; Dir VÁCLAV MIKEŠ.

Artia: Ve Smečkách 30, 111 27 Prague 1; telex 121065; f.1953; part of the Artia Foreign Trade Corporation; children's books, art books and encyclopaedias; Dir MIROSLAV NOVÁK.

Avicenum: Malostranské nám. 28, 118 02 Prague 1; f. 1953; medical books and periodicals; Dir VÁCLAV CIPRA.

Blok: Rooseveltova 4, 657 00 Brno; regional literature, fiction, general; Dir IVO ODEHNAL.

Československý spisovatel (Czechoslovak Writer): Národní 19, 111 47 Prague 1; telex 122645; publishing house of the Czech Literary

Fund; poetry, fiction, literary theory and criticism; Dir Dr JAN PILAŘ.

Horizont: Nekázanka 7, 111 21 Prague 1; f. 1968; publishing house of the Czech Socialist Academy; general; Dir STEFAN SZERYNCKI.

Kartografie: Fr. Křižíka 1, 170 20 Prague 7; state map publishing house; Dir Ing. MIROSLAV MIKŠOVSKÝ.

Kruh: Dlouhá 108, 500 21 Hradec Králové; regional literature, fiction and general; Dir VLADIMÍR BRANDEJS.

Lidové nakladatelství: Václavské nám. 36, 115 65 Prague 1; f. 1968; formerly Svět Sovětů; publishing house of the Union of Czechoslovak-Soviet Friendship; classical and contemporary fiction, general, magazines; Dir Dr KORNEL VAVRINČÍK.

Melantrich: Václavské nám. 36, 112 12 Prague 1; telex 121432; f. 1919; publishing house of the Czechoslovak Socialist Party; general, fiction, newspapers and magazines; Dir Ing. JIŘÍ KRÁTKÝ.

Merkur: Gorkého nám. 11, 115 69 Prague 1; telex 121648; commerce, tourism, catering; Dir JIŘÍ LINHART.

Mladá fronta: Panská 8, 112 22 Prague 1; telex 121510; f. 1945; publishing house of the Central Committee of the Socialist Union of Youth; literature for young people, fiction and non-fiction, newspapers and magazines; Dir MARIE KOŠKOVÁ.

Nakladatelství dopravy a spojů: Hybernská 5, 115 78 Prague 1; state publishing house for transport and communications; Dir Dr OLDŘICH BREJCHA.

Naše vojsko: Na Děkance 3, 128 12 Prague 1; publishing house of the Czechoslovak Army; fiction, general; Dir Dr STANISLAV MISTR.

Odeon: Národní třída 36, 115 87 Prague 1; telex 123055; tel. (2) 366885; f. 1953; literature, poetry, fiction (classical and modern), literary theory, art books, reproductions; Dir JOSEF KULÍČEK.

Olympia: Klimentská 1, 115 88 Prague 1; tel. (2) 2314861; telex 121717; f. 1954; sports, tourism, illustrated books; Dir Ing. KAREL ZELNÍČEK.

Panorama: Hálkova 1, Prague 2; Dir FRANTIŠEK HANZLÍK.

Panton: Říční 12, 118 39 Prague 1; tel. (2) 538151; f. 1958; publishing house of the Czech Musical Fund; books on music, sheet music, records; Dir. JAROSLAV HRABA.

Práce: Václavské nám. 17, 112 58 Prague 1; tel. (2) 266151; telex 121134; f. 1945; publishing house of the Trade Union Movement; trade union movement, fiction, general, periodicals; Dir Dr JURAJ HIMAL.

Profil: Ciklářská 51, 702 00 Ostrava 1; regional literature, fiction and general; Dir IVAN ŠEINER.

Rapid: ul. 28 října 13, 112 79 Prague 1; tel. (2) 139111; telex 121142; foreign trade; Dir Dr Ing. MIROSLAV HEDBÁVNÝ.

Růže: Žižkovo nám. 5, 371 96 České Budějovice; regional literature, fiction and general; Dir FRANTIŠEK PODLAHA.

Severočeské nakladatelství: Velká Hradební 33, 400 21 Ústí nad Labem; regional literature, fiction and general; Dir JIŘÍ ŠVEJDA.

Státní nakladatelství technické literatury: Spálená 51, 113 02 Prague 1; state publishing house of technical literature; technology, applied sciences, dictionaries, periodicals; Dir Ing. STANISLAV KÁNSKÝ.

Státní pedagogické nakladatelství: Ostrovní 30, 113 01 Prague 1; tel. (2) 203787; f. 1775; state publishing house; school and university textbooks, dictionaries, literature; Dir Dr JULIUS JANOVSKÝ.

Státní zemědělské nakladatelství: Václavské nám. 47, 113 11 Prague 1; state publishing house; agriculture; periodicals; Dir Ing. KAREL KOUKAL.

Středočeské nakladatelství a knihkupectví: U Prašné brány 3, 116 29 Prague 1; regional literature, fiction, general; Dir Dr VLADIMÍR PÍŠA.

Supraphon: Palackého 1, 122 99 Prague 1; tel. (2) 268141; telex 121218; f. 1946; publishing house for gramophone records, musicassettes and music; Gen. Dir JAN KVÍDERA.

Svoboda: Revoluční 15, 113 03 Prague 1; publishing house of the Central Committee of the Communist Party of Czechoslovakia; politics, history, philosophy, fiction, general; Dir Dr STANISLAV MAREŠ.

Ústřední církevní nakladatelství: Ječná 2, 120 00 Prague 2; f. 1952; religion; Dir Dr JIŘÍ KAFKA.

Vyšehrad: Karlovo nám. 5, 120 78 Prague 2; tel. 297726; publishing house of the Czechoslovak People's Party; general fiction, newspapers and magazines; Dir JOSEF DANĚK.

Západočeské nakladatelství: Moskevská 36, 301 35 Plzeň; regional literature, fiction, general; Dir VLADIMÍR SLONEK.

SLOVAK PUBLISHING HOUSES

Alfa: Hurbanovo nám. 3, 815 89 Bratislava; previously the Slovak Publishing House of Technical Literature; technical and economic literature, dictionaries; Dir ANNA FLOCHOVÁ.

Církevné vydavatel'stvo: Palisády 64, 801 00 Bratislava; religious literature; ŠTEFÁNIA HREBÍKOVÁ.

Matica Slovenská: Hostihora 2, 036 52 Martin; f. 1863; literary science, bibliography, biography and librarianship; literary archives and museums; life of the Slovaks living abroad; Dir ONDREJ KUČERA.

Mladé Letá (Young Years); nám. SNP 11, 815 19 Bratislava; tel. 50475; telex 93421; state publishing house; f. 1950; literature for children and young people; Dir JURAJ KLAUČO.

Obzor (Horizon): ul. ČS armády 35, 893 36 Bratislava; state publishing house; educational, encyclopedias, popular scientific, fiction, textbooks, law; Dir Ing. JÁN PRINC.

Osveta (Education): Osloboditelov 55, 036 54 Martin; tel. 32921; f. 1953; medical, educational, photographic and regional literature; Editor-in-Chief BOHUSLAV KORTMAN.

Práca: Obráncov mieru 19, 897 17 Bratislava; f. 1946; publishing house of the Slovak Trade Unions Council; economics, labour, work safety, etc.; Dir JÁN DUŽI.

Pravda: Gunduličova 12, 882 05 Bratislava; f. 1969; publishing house of the Central Committee of the Communist Party of Slovakia; politics, philosophy, history, economics, fiction, children's literature; Dir JÁN HANZLÍK.

Príroda: Križkova 7, 894 17 Bratislava; agricultural literature, gardening books; Dir Ing. VINCENT SUGÁR.

Slovenské pedagogické nakladatelstvo: Sasinková 5, 891 12 Bratislava; pedagogical literature, educational, school texts, dictionaries; Dir Dr SERGEJ TROŠCÁK.

Slovenský spisovatel': Leningradská 2, 897 28 Bratislava; publishing house of the Union of Slovak Writers; fiction, poetry; Dir VLADIMÍR DUDÁŠ.

Smena: Pražská 11, 812 84 Bratislava; publishing house of the Slovak Central Committee of the Socialist Union of Youth; fiction, literature for young people; Dir JAROSLAV ŠIŠOLÁK.

Šport: Vajnorská 100, 893 44 Bratislava; telex 93330; publishing house of the Central Committee of the Slovak Physical Culture Organization; sport, physical culture, guide books, periodicals; Dir Ing. JÚLIUS CHVALNÝ.

Tatran: Michalská 9, 815 82 Bratislava; f. 1949; fiction, art books; Dir Dr ANTON MARKUŠ.

Veda (Science): Klemensova 19, 814 30 Bratislava; tel. 56321; f. 1953; publishing house of the Slovak Academy of Science; scientific and popular scientific books and periodicals; Dir Ing. MIROSLAV MURÍN.

Východoslovenské vydavatelstvo: Alejová 3, 040 11 Košice; regional literature, fiction, general; Dir MIKULÁŠ JÁGER.

WRITERS' UNIONS

Svaz československých spisovatelů (Union of Czechoslovak Writers): Národní třída 11, 110 47 Prague 1; Chair. Dr JAN KOZÁK.

Svaz českých spisovatelů (Union of Czech Writers): Národní třída 11, 111 47 Prague 1; f. 1972; 165 mems; Chair. MICHAL ČERNÍK.

Zväz slovenských spisovatel'ov (Union of Slovak Writers): 890 08 Bratislava; f. 1949; Chair. JÁN SOLOVIČ.

Radio and Television

In 1986 there were 3,935,233 radio receivers and 4,387,144 television receivers in use.

RADIO

There are five national networks in Czechoslovakia: Radios Prague and Bratislava (long and medium wave), Radio Hvězda (long, medium and VHF—popular and youth programmes), and Radios Vltava and Děvín (VHF from Prague and Bratislava respectively—programmes on Czech, Slovak, socialist and progressive western culture).

Local stations broadcast from Prague (Central Bohemian Studio), Banská Bystrica, Brno, České Budějovice, Hradec Králové, Košice, Ostrava, Plzeň, Prešov, Ústí nad Labem and other towns.

Foreign broadcasts are made in Arabic, English, French, German, Greek, Hungarian, Italian, Portuguese, Spanish, Ukrainian, and Czech and Slovak.

Československý rozhlas (Czechoslovak Radio): Vinohradská 12, 120 99 Prague 2; tel. 2115; telex 121100; f. 1923; Dir-Gen. Dr JÁN RIŠKO.

Český rozhlas (Czech Radio): Vinohradská 12, 120 99 Prague 2; telex 121100; Dir Dr KAREL KVAPIL.

CZECHOSLOVAKIA

Československý rozhlas na Slovensku (Czechoslovak Radio in Slovakia): Mýtna 1, 812 90 Bratislava; tel. (7) 47697; telex 93353; f. 1926; Dir VASIL BEJDA.

Československé zahraniční vysílání (Czechoslovak Foreign Broadcasts): Vinohradská 12, 120 99 Prague 2; telex 121189; Dir Dr HELENA LANDOVSKÁ.

TELEVISION

There are television studios in Prague, Brno, Ostrava, Bratislava and Košice.

Československá televize (Czechoslovak Television): Jindrisska 16, 111 50 Prague 1; tel. (2) 221247; telex 121800; f. 1953; Dir-Gen. Dr JAN ZELENKA.

Československá televízia na Slovensku (Czechoslovak TV in Slovakia): Asmolovova 28, 845 45 Bratislava; telex 092277; Dir Dr JAROSLAV HLINICKÝ.

Finance

(cap. = capital; dep. = deposits; res = reserves; m. = million; Kčs. = korunas)

BANKS

The Czechoslovak banking system is to be reorganized. In January 1990 the functions of issue and credit of the State Bank were to be separated. An independent central bank and independent credit banks were to be established.

Československá obchodní banka a.s. (Commercial Bank of Czechoslovakia): Na Příkopě 14, 115 20 Prague 1; tel. (2) 2132; telex 122201; f. 1965; commercial and foreign exchange transactions; cap. 1,000m. Kčs. (Dec. 1984), res 6,563.9m. Kčs., dep. 56,678.3m. Kčs. (Dec. 1987); Man. Dir Ing. KVĚTOSLAV BRDIČKA.

Státní banka československá (State Bank of Czechoslovakia): Na Příkopě 28, 110 03 Prague 1; tel. (2) 2112; telex 121831; the State Monetary Agency; f. 1950; bank of issue, a bank for granting long-term and short-term credits, maintaining payments relations, financing and control of capital construction, and buying and selling securities; a deposit centre; a central bank for directing and securing banking economic relations with foreign countries; and a cash clearing centre of the ČSSR. Statutory Funds 5,000m. Kčs.; General Reserve 2,014m. Kčs. (Dec. 1984); Pres. Ing. SVATOPLUK POTAČ; Vice-Pres. Ing. MIROSLAV ZÁMEČNÍK.

Živnostenská banka: Na Příkopě 20, 113 80 Prague 1; tel. (2) 224346; telex 122313; f. 1868; cap. 250m. Kčs., res 168.8m. Kčs., dep. 3,583m. Kčs. (Dec. 1985); Gen. Man. Ing JIŘÍ KUNERT.

SAVINGS BANKS

Česká státní spořitelna (Czech State Savings Bank): Václavské nám. 42, 113 98 Prague 1; telex 121010; accepts deposits and issues loans; 13,373,128 depositors (June 1983); Gen. Dir Ing. VĚRA NEPIMACHOVÁ.

Slovenská státní spořitelna (Slovak State Savings Bank): Leningradská 24, 801 00 Bratislava; telex 93133; Dir Ing. JOZEF CIPOV.

INSURANCE

Česká státní pojišťovna (Czech State Insurance and Reinsurance Corporation): Spálená 16, 113 04 Prague 1; tel. (2) 2148111; telex 121112; many home branches and some agencies abroad; controls all insurance; issues life, accident, fire, aviation and marine policies, all classes of reinsurance; Lloyd's agency; Gen. Man. Ing. JOSEF VEČEŘA.

Slovenská štátna poisťovňa (Slovak State Insurance Corporation): Strakova 1, 815 74 Bratislava; telex 93375; Gen. Dir RASTISLAV HAVERLIK.

Trade and Industry

CHAMBER OF COMMERCE

Československá obchodní a průmyslová komora (Czechoslovak Chamber of Commerce and Industry): Argentinská 38, 170 05 Prague 7; tel. (2) 8724111; telex 121862; f. 1949; its 921 mems are all Czechoslovak foreign trade corporations and the majority of the industrial enterprises, banks and research institutes; Pres. Ing. JAROSLAV JAKUBEC.

FOREIGN TRADE CORPORATIONS

Artia: Ve Smečkách 30, 111 27 Prague 1; imports and exports cultural commodities; Gen. Dir Ing. FRANTIŠEK KAJNÁK.

Centrotex: nám. Hrdinů 3/1634, 140 61 Prague 4; imports and exports textiles; Gen. Dir Ing. JIŘÍ KOUTNÍK.

Čechofracht: Na Příkopě 8, 111 83 Prague 1; tel. (2) 129111; telex 122221; f. 1949; shipping and international forwarding corporation; Gen. Dir JIŘÍ KADANÍK.

Chemapol: Kodaňská 46, 100 10 Prague 10; tel. (2) 715; telex 122021; f. 1948; imports and exports chemical and pharmaceutical products and raw materials; Gen. Dir Ing. VÁCLAV VOLF.

Czechoslovak Ceramics: V Jámě 1, 111 91 Prague 1; exports and imports ceramics; Gen. Dir Ing. MIROSLAV DOBEŠ.

Czechoslovak Filmexport: Václavské nám. 28, 111 45 Prague 1; import and export of films; Gen. Dir JIŘÍ JANOUŠEK.

Drevounia: Dr V. Clementisa 10, 826 10 Bratislava; tel. (7) 229962; telex 93291; imports and exports wood and furniture; Gen. Dir Ing. JIŘÍ JIRAVA.

Exico: Panská 9, 111 77 Prague 1; tel. (2) 246941; telex 122211; f. 1966; exports and imports leather, shoes, skins; Gen. Dir Ing. FRANTIŠEK FREMUND.

Ferromet: Opletalova 27, 111 81 Prague 1; imports and exports metallurgical products; Gen. Dir Ing. BŘETISLAV SEDLÁK.

Inspekta: Na Strži 63, 140 62 Prague 4; control of goods in foreign trade; Gen. Dir Ing. JAN ŠVIHEL.

Jablonex: Palackého 41, 466 37 Jablonec nad Nisou; tel. 428510; telex 186463; f. 1949; imports and exports of imitation jewellery and decorations; Gen. Dir Ing. VÍT RYŠÁNEK.

Koospol: Leninova 178, 160 67 Prague 6; imports and exports foodstuffs; Gen. Dir JAROSLAV ŘÍHA.

Kovo: Jankovcova 2, 170 88 Prague 7; imports and exports precision engineering products; Gen. Dir JOSEF KUDRHALT.

Ligna: Vodičkova 41, 112 09 Prague 1; imports and exports timber, wood products, musical instruments and paper; Gen. Dir Ing. MILOŠ ŠVACH.

Merkuria: Argentinská 38, 170 05 Prague 7; exports and imports tools and consumer goods; Gen. Dir Ing. JOSEF ANDĚL.

Metalimex: Štěpánská 34, 112 17 Prague 1; imports and exports metals, natural gas and solid fuels; Gen. Dir Ing. MIROSLAV HLAVIČKA.

Motokov: Na Strži 63, 140 62 Prague 4; imports and exports vehicles and light engineering products; Gen. Dir Ing. ANDREJ BARČÁK.

Omnipol: Nekázanka 11, 112 21 Prague 1; import and export of sports and civil aircraft; Gen. Dir Ing. LUDĚK SKOČDOPOLE.

Pragoexport: Jungmannova 34, 112 59 Prague 1; imports and exports consumer goods; Gen. Dir JAROMÍR ORŠEL.

Pragoinvest: Českomoravská 23, 180 56 Prague 9; tel. (2) 822741; telex 122379; import and export of machinery and complete plant equipment; Gen. Dir Ing. MILOSLAV KOČÁREK.

Skloexport: tř. 1. máje 52, 461 74 Liberec; exports glass; Gen. Dir Ing. JAROSLAV KŘIVÁNEK.

Škodaexport: Václavské nám. 56, 113 32 Prague 1; tel. (2) 2131; telex 122413; exports and imports power engineering and metallurgical plants, engineering works, electrical locomotives and trolleybuses, tobacco machines; Gen. Dir Ing. MILOSLAV MIKEŠ.

Strojexport: POB 662, Václavské nám. 56, 113 26 Prague 1; tel. (2) 2131; telex 121753; f. 1953; imports and exports machines and machinery equipment; Gen. Dir Ing. JOSEF LEVORA.

Strojimport: Vinohradská 184, 130 52 Prague 3; tel. (2) 713; telex 122241; imports and exports machines and industrial plant; Gen. Dir Ing. IVAN ČAPEK.

Technoexport: Václavské nám. 1, 113 34 Prague 1; tel. (2) 369065; telex 121268; imports and exports chemical and foodstuff engineering plant; Gen. Dir Ing. OLDŘICH KUCHTA.

Tuzex: Rytířská 13, 113 43 Prague 1; retail goods for foreign currency; Gen. Dir Ing. ANTONÍN RAČANSKÝ.

TRADE UNIONS

Ústřední rada odborů (ÚRO) (Central Council of Trade Unions): nám. A. Zápotockého 2, 113 59 Prague 3; f. 1945; governing body of Revoluční odborové hnutí–ROH (Revolutionary Trade Union Movement); Chair. Ing. MIROSLAV ZAVADIL.

Česká odborová rada (ČOR) (Czech Trade Union Council): nám. A. Zápotockého 2, 113 59 Prague 3; Chair. Ing. VÁCLAV BEŽEL.

Slovenská odborová rada (SOR) (Slovak Trade Union Council): Odborárske nám. 3, 897 17 Bratislava; Chair. IVAN GOŇKO.

Odborový svaz civilních pracovníků Československé lidové armády (Civil Employees of the Czechoslovak People's Army): nám. Svobody 471, 160 00 Prague 6; Chair. VLADIMÍR CHRASTIL.

CZECHOSLOVAKIA

Odborový svaz pracovníků chemického, papírenského a sklářského průmyslu a tisku (Chemical, Paper, Glass and Printing Industry): nám. A. Zápotockého 2, 113 59 Prague 3; Chair. LADISLAV ŠANOVSKÝ; 336,386 mems.

Odborový svaz pracovníků dopravy a silničního hospodářství (Transport and Roads): Vinohradská 10, Prague 2; Chair. MIROSLAV VALOUŠEK; 247,667 mems.

Odborový svaz pracovníků dřevoprůmyslu, lesního a vodního hospodářství (Woodwork Industry, Forestry and Water Conservancy): nám. A. Zápotockého 2, 113 59 Prague 3; tel. (2) 350848; telex 121484; Chair. LADISLAV BARNINEC; 284,000 mems.

Odborový svaz pracovníků hornictví a energetiky (Mining and Power Generating Industries): nám. A. Zápotockého 2, 113 59 Prague 3; Chair. VLADIMÍR POLEDNÍK; 398,843 mems.

Odborový svaz pracovníků kovoprůmyslu (Metal): nám. A. Zápotockého 2, 113 59 Prague, 3; Chair. JOSEF TREJBAL; 1,236,374 mems.

Odborový svaz pracovníků místního hospodářství (Communal Enterprises): nám. M. Gorkého 23, 112 82 Prague 1; Chair. RICHARD ŠTĚCH; 359,755 mems.

Odborový svaz pracovníků obchodu (Commerce): nám. M. Gorkého 23, 112 82 Prague 1; tel. (2) 1142728; Chair. DÁRIA ZACHEROVÁ; 730,000 mems.

*Odborový svaz pracovníků potravinářského průmyslu (Food Industry): nám. A. Zápotockého 2, 113 59 Prague 3; Chair. EVA UŠÁKOVÁ; 231,357 mems.

Odborový svaz pracovníků školství a vědy (Education and Science): nám. M. Gorkého 23, 112 82 Prague 1; tel. (2) 1142512; telex 122410; f. 1945; Chair. Dr DRAHOMÍRA HANZALOVÁ; 530,000 mems.

Odborový svaz pracovníků spojů (Post and Telecommunications): nám. A. Zápotockého 2, 113 59 Prague 3; f. 1972; Chair. DARINA PRISTACHOVÁ; 134,626 mems.

Odborový svaz pracovníků státních orgánů, peněžnictví a zahraničního obchodu (Government and Financial Institutions and Foreign Trade): nám. M. Gorkého 23, 118 82 Prague 1; Chair. BOHUMIL HANUŠ; 281,515 mems.

Odborový svaz pracovníků stavebnictví a ve výrobě stavebních hmot (Building and Building Materials Industry): nám. M. Gorkého 23, 118 82 Prague 1; Chair. JAROMÍR KOLLMANN; 641,466 mems.

Odborový svaz pracovníků textilního, oděvního, a kožedělného průmyslu (Textile, Clothing and Leather Industry): nám. A. Zápotockého 2, 113 59 Prague 3; Chair. MÁRIA TRVALOVÁ; 438,518 mems.

Odborový svaz pracovníků umění, kultury a společenských organizací (Art, Cultural and Social Organizations): nám. M. Gorkého 23, 112 82 Prague 1; f. 1945; Chair. Dr JIŘÍ NEUŽIL; 167,803 mems.

Odborový svaz pracovníků zdravotnictví (Health Workers): nám. A. Zápotockého 2, 113 59 Prague 3; Chair. EVA VOHRYZKOVÁ; 389,345 mems.

Odborový svaz pracovníků železnic (Railway Workers): nám. A. Zápotockého 2, 113 59 Prague 3; Chair. JIŘÍ DIVIŠ; 296,736 mems.

*Odborový svaz pracovníků zemědělství (Agricultural Workers): nám. A. Zápotockého 2, 113 59 Prague 3; Chair. VLADISLAV TŘEŠKA; 442,049 mems.

* These two unions merged in January 1989.

TRADE FAIR

BVV Trade Fairs and Exhibitions: Výstaviště 1, 602 00 Brno; tel. (5) 3141111; telex 62239; f. 1959; international engineering fair yearly in September; international consumer goods fair yearly in April; Gen. Dir Dr JAROSLAV KUČERA.

Transport

RAILWAYS

In 1988 the total length of the Czechoslovak railways was 13,116 km; of this total, 3,530 km were electrified, including the connection Prague–Warsaw via Bohumín. The densest section of the network links the north with the south, and there is a direct rail link between the west and east of the country.

Československé státní dráhy (Czechoslovak State Railways): Na Příkopě 33, 110 05 Prague 1; tel. (2) 2122; telex 121096; Dir LADISLAV STROS.

Prague Metropolitan Railway: Dopravní podniky hlavního města Prahy, Bubenská 1, 170 26 Prague 7; the Prague underground railway opened in 1974, and by Nov. 1988 34.7 km were operational; Gen. Dir Ing. LADISLAV SLEPIČKA.

ROADS

In January 1988 there were 73,112 km of roads in Czechoslovakia, including 489 km of motorways. More than 90% of the total road network is hard-surfaced. The Prague–Brno–Bratislava motorway was opened in 1980.

Československá státní automobilová doprava—ČSAD (Czechoslovak State Road Transport): Hybernská 32, 111 21 Prague 1; f. 1949; the organization has 11 regional head offices.

Sdružení československých mezinárodních automobilových dopravců (ČESMAD) (Czechoslovak International Road Transport Enterprises Association): Perucká 5, 120 67 Prague 2; f. 1966; Chair. MIROSLAV JUŘENA.

INLAND WATERWAYS

The total length of navigable waterways in Czechoslovakia is 480 km. The Elbe and its tributary the Vltava connect the country with the North Sea via the port of Hamburg. The Oder provides a connection with the Baltic Sea and the port of Szczecin. The Danube provides a link with Western Germany, Austria, Hungary, Yugoslavia, Bulgaria, Romania and the USSR. Czechoslovakia's river ports are Prague, Mělník, Ústí nad Labem and Děčín on the Vltava and Elbe, and Bratislava and Komárno on the Danube; in 1983, work began on a new port at Praha Radotin, which is to be the largest on the Vltava and Elbe.

Československá plavba dunajská národný podnik (Czechoslovak Danube River Shipping): Červenej armády 35, 890 24 Bratislava; telex 92338; Man. Dir Ing. PAVOL CIBÁK.

Československá plavba labsko-oderská (ČSPLO) (Czechoslovak Elbe-Oder River Shipping): K. Čapka 1, 405 02 Děčín; telex 184241; carries out transport of goods on the Vltava, Elbe and Oder rivers as well as other waterways; transfer and storage of goods in Czechoslovak ports; operates the river ports of Prague, Mělník, Kolín, Ústí nad Labem and Děčín; Man. Dir Ing. KAREL ADAMOVSKÝ.

SHIPPING

Československá námořní plavba, mezinárodní akciová společnost (Czechoslovak Ocean Shipping, International Joint-Stock Company): Počernická 168, 100 99 Prague 10; tel. (2) 778940; telex 122137; f. 1959; shipping company operating the Czechoslovak seagoing fleet; 15 ships totalling 260,066 dwt; Man. Dir ANTONIN SOKOLÍK.

Czechoslovak Danube Navigation: Červenej armády 35, 890 24 Bratislava; telex 92338; five ships totalling 8,954 grt; Man. Dir Ing. PAVOL CIBÁK.

CIVIL AVIATION

There are civil airports at Prague (Ruzyně), Brno, Bratislava, Gottwaldov (Holešov), Karlovy Vary, Košice, Mariánské Lázně, Lucenec, Ostrava, Pieštany, Poprad-Tatry, Sliač (Banská Bystrica), Uherske Hradiste and Zilina, served by ČSA's internal flights. International flights serve Prague, Bratislava and Poprad-Tatry.

ČSA (Československé aerolinie, Czechoslovak Airlines): Head Office: Ruzyně Airport, 160 08 Prague; telex 120338; f. 1923; external services to most European capitals, the Near, Middle and Far East, North and Central America and North Africa; Gen. Dir Ing. JINDŘICH KOPŘIVA; fleet of 4 Ilyushin Il-62, 6 Ilyushin Il-62M, 13 Tupolev TU-134A, 1 Tupolev TU-154-M, 2 Ilyushin Il-18 and 6 Yakovlev Yak-40.

Slov-Air: Ivanka Airport, 823 12 Bratislava; tel. 226172; telex 93270; f. 1969; domestic scheduled and charter services; Dir ONDREJ HUDOBA; fleet of small turboprop aircraft including four Let L-410 and two An-2.

Tourism

Czechoslovakia has magnificent scenery, with winter sports facilities. Prague is the best known of the historic cities, and there are famous castles and cathedrals, numerous resorts and 57 spas with natural mineral springs. In 1987 foreign visitor arrivals totalled 22m., including excursionists. Most visitors came from Poland and the German Democratic Republic. Receipts from tourism totalled US $120m. in 1987.

Čedok (Travel and Hotels Corporation): Na Příkopě 18, 111 35 Prague 1; tel. (2) 127111; telex 121109; the official Czechoslovak Travel Agency; 146 travel offices; branches throughout Europe and the USA; Dir Václav Pleskot.

Atomic Energy

Nuclear power accounted for more than 20% of total electricity production in 1986.

Czechoslovak Atomic Energy Commission (ČSKAE): Slezská 9, 120 29 Prague 2; tel. 254624; responsible for the peaceful utilization of atomic energy and for co-ordinating the atomic energy programme; Chair. Ing. Stanislav Havel.

Federal Ministry of Fuel and Energy: Vinohradská 8, 120 70 Prague 2; tel. 262698; telex 122083; responsible for development and functioning of Czechoslovakia's fuel and energy complex; nuclear power station construction plants at Jaslovské Bohunice (1,760 MW in operation), Dukovany (1,760 MW in operation), Mochovce (1,760 MW under construction), Temelín (4,000 MW under construction); Minister Antonín Krumnikl.

Ústav jaderného výzkumu (Institute of Nuclear Research): CS-250 68 Řež; tel. (2) 896231; telex 122626; f. 1955; Dir Jan Mrkos.

DENMARK

Introductory Survey

Location, Climate, Language, Religion, Flag, Capital

The Kingdom of Denmark is situated in northern Europe. It consists of the peninsula of Jutland, the islands of Zealand, Funen, Lolland, Falster and Bornholm, and 401 smaller islands. The country lies between the North Sea, to the west, and the Baltic Sea, to the east. Denmark's only land frontier is with the Federal Republic of Germany, to the south. Norway lies to the north of Denmark, across the Skagerrak, while Sweden, whose most southerly region is separated from Zealand by a narrow strait, lies to the north-east. Outlying territories of Denmark are Greenland and the Faeroe Islands in the North Atlantic Ocean. Denmark is low-lying and the climate is temperate, with mild summers and cold, rainy winters. The language is Danish. Almost all of the inhabitants profess Christianity: the Evangelical Lutheran Church, to which 91% of the population belong, is the established Church, and there are also small communities of other Protestant groups and of Roman Catholics. The national flag (proportions 37 by 28) displays a white cross on a red background, the upright of the cross being to the left of centre. The capital is Copenhagen (København).

Recent History

In 1945, following the end of German wartime occupation, Denmark recognized the independence of Iceland, which had been declared in the previous year. In 1947 King Frederik IX succeeded to the throne on the death of his father, Christian X. Home rule was granted to the Faeroe Islands in 1948 and to Greenland in 1979. Denmark was a founder member of NATO in 1949 and of the Nordic Council in 1952. Denmark's Constitution was radically revised in 1953: new provisions allowed for female succession to the throne, abolished the upper house of parliament and amended the franchise. King Frederik died in January 1972, and his eldest daughter, Margrethe, became the first queen to rule Denmark for nearly 600 years. Following a referendum, Denmark entered the EEC in January 1973.

The system of proportional representation which is embodied in the 1953 Constitution makes it difficult for a single party to gain a majority in the Folketing (Parliament), and the tendency of Danish parties to fragment has, in recent years, produced a series of coalition and minority governments, all of which have had to face economic problems and popular discontent with Denmark's EEC membership. The Liberal Party's minority Government, led by Poul Hartling and formed in 1973, was followed in 1975 by a minority Social Democratic Government under the leadership of Anker Jørgensen. Jørgensen led various coalitions and minority governments until 1982. There were general elections in 1977, 1979 and 1981, against a background of growing unemployment and attempts to tighten control of the economy. By September 1982 Jørgensen's economic policy, including attempts to reduce the budget deficit by imposing new taxation, had once more led to disagreements within the Cabinet, and the Government resigned.

The Conservatives, who had been absent from Danish coalitions since 1971, formed a centre-right four-party government (with the Liberals, the Centre Democrats and the Christian People's Party), led by Poul Schlüter, who became Denmark's first Conservative Prime Minister since 1894. Holding only 66 of the Folketing's 179 seats, the coalition narrowly avoided defeat in October 1982, when it introduced stringent economic measures (including a six-month 'freeze' on wages), and again in September 1983, when larger reductions in public spending were proposed. In December the anti-tax Progress Party withdrew its support for further spending cuts, and the Government was defeated. A general election to the Folketing was held in January 1984, and Schlüter's Government remained in office, with its component parties holding a total of 77 seats, and relying on the support of the Radical Liberal members.

A general election took place in September 1987 and was contested by 16 political parties, nine of which won seats in the Folketing. Schlüter's coalition retained only 70 seats, and the Radical Liberals gained one seat, while the opposition Social Democratic Party lost two of its 56 seats. Jørgensen later resigned as leader of the latter party. Several of the smaller and extremist parties made considerable gains, with the result that the outgoing coalition was weakened, while the main opposition parties were unable to command a working majority. Schlüter eventually formed a new cabinet which comprised representatives of the former four-party governing coalition. However, the Radical Liberals had earlier declared that they would not support any administration that depended on the support of the Progress Party. This therefore left a precarious balance of power within the Folketing.

In the Folketing a government is expected to resign only if its defeated proposals have been presented as a 'vital element' of policy. This practice enabled the coalition to survive a series of defeats on foreign policy during the early 1980s, including several attempts by the Folketing to dissociate itself from particular aspects of NATO defence strategy. In November 1984 the Government ignored a Folketing decision in favour of a ban on any first use of nuclear weapons by the Western alliance. In March 1985 the Folketing voted against any inclusion of nuclear power stations in public energy plans, and in May a majority approved a motion opposing Danish involvement in research connected with the US Government's 'Strategic Defense Initiative' (a plan, first announced by President Ronald Reagan in March 1983, to test the feasibility of creating a space-based defensive 'shield' against attack by ballistic missiles). This vote was a further defeat for Schlüter's Government. The left-wing parties also committed the Government to work actively towards the creation of a nuclear-free zone in the Nordic region.

In April 1988, however, the Folketing adopted an opposition-sponsored resolution requiring the Government to inform visiting warships of the country's ban on nuclear weapons. The British and US Governments were highly critical of the resolution. Schlüter therefore announced an early general election for May 1988, on the issue of Denmark's membership of NATO and defence policy. Twelve political parties contested the elections in metropolitan Denmark, and eight won seats in the Folketing. The Common Course party lost parliamentary representation, and the right-wing Progress Party increased its number of seats from nine to 16. For the main parties, however, the election result was inconclusive, and three weeks of negotiations took place before Schlüter was appointed to seek a basis for viable government. At the beginning of June a new minority coalition formed a cabinet under Schlüter. The Conservatives retained nine cabinet positions, but the Liberals secured only seven (instead of their former eight) posts, although they gained the defence portfolio. Their new partners, the Radical Liberals, provided five cabinet members. One of the first acts of the new Government was to restore good relations with its NATO allies. This was done with a formula that requested all visiting warships to respect Danish law in its territorial waters, while making no specific reference to nuclear weapons.

Later in 1988, however, NATO criticisms resumed when Schlüter's draft budget proposed a 'freeze' on defence spending. The Government also proposed large reductions in social welfare provision, and attacked Progress Party demands for less taxation as unrealistic but, with polls indicating a massive growth in that party's support since the general election, Schlüter promised some reductions in the rate of taxation for 1990. In January 1989 Schlüter offered to lower income tax rates if unions and employers agreed to negotiate reductions in salaries.

In January 1986 tension arose between Denmark and the other members of the EEC when the left-wing parties in the Folketing combined to defeat proposals for a programme of EEC reforms. These reforms had been designed to accelerate decision-making by the EEC's Council of Ministers, by removing the need for unanimity, and to lift internal trade barriers within the Community. The Social Democrats, who led the opposition, argued that the adoption of the reforms would lead to a diminution of Denmark's powers to protect its own environmental standards, forcing the country to alter its stringent import controls. The reform proposals were rejected in the Folketing by a narrow majority, making any amendment to the EEC's Treaty of Rome impossible, since a positive vote by the legislatures of all member states was required. Schlüter announced that a national referendum on the issue would take place in February, arguing that Danish rejection of the proposals would be the first stage towards Denmark's withdrawal from the EEC, and all parties agreed to respect the referendum result: 56.2% of the votes cast were in favour of the reforms, which were formally approved by the Folketing in May.

De-oxygenization of the Kattegat, the strait between Denmark and Sweden, resulted in the destruction of lobster colonies in the latter part of 1986. This caused widespread concern about ecological matters, and the Folketing responded by enacting legislation that set the world's most rigorous standards of environmental protection. Many of the requirements were expensive for farmers and industrialists, and some measures conflicted with EEC regulations. Environmental concerns, however, were heightened in 1988 by two ecological disasters, both attributed to pollutants. A massive increase in the concentration of algae devastated marine life around Denmark and southern Scandinavia, and this was followed by a virulent outbreak of a canine distemper virus that reduced the seal population of the North and Baltic Seas by two-thirds.

In 1985 a series of bomb explosions, for which an organization of Iranian origin claimed responsibility, heightened social unrest. The Folketing expressed concern at the large numbers of Middle Eastern refugees arriving in Denmark. A law aimed at reducing the flow of arrivals in Denmark by at least one-half was adopted in October 1986.

In May 1986 the Folketing approved the implementation of a total ban on trade in goods and services with South Africa, to take effect from December 1986, in protest at that country's racial policies.

In August 1988 the Danish Government decided to submit a dispute with Norway, concerning maritime economic zones between Greenland and Jan Mayen island, to the International Court of Justice at The Hague.

Government

Denmark is a constitutional monarchy. Under the 1953 constitutional charter, legislative power is held jointly by the hereditary monarch (who has no personal political power) and the unicameral Folketing (Parliament), with 179 members, including 175 from metropolitan Denmark and two each from the Faeroe Islands and Greenland. Members are elected for four years (subject to dissolution) on the basis of proportional representation. A referendum in September 1978 reduced the age of suffrage from 20 to 18. Executive power is exercised by the monarch through a Cabinet, led by the Prime Minister, which is responsible to the Folketing. Denmark comprises 14 counties (amtskommuner), one city and one borough, all with elected councils.

Defence

In June 1988 Denmark maintained an army of some 17,000 (6,800 conscripts), a navy of 5,400 (900 conscripts) and an air force of 6,900 (700 conscripts). There were, in total, about 74,700 reservists, and a volunteer Home Guard numbering 75,000. Military service is for nine–12 months. Denmark abandoned its neutrality after the Second World War and has been a member of NATO since 1949. In 1988 it became the first NATO country to include women in front-line units. The defence budget for 1988 was 13,500m. kroner.

Economic Affairs

Denmark's economy is based mainly on agriculture and manufacturing, with small enterprises predominant in both sectors. The country has a high standard of living, with well-developed social services. In 1987, according to estimates by the World Bank, Denmark's gross national product (GNP), measured at average 1985–87 prices, was US $76,640m., equivalent to $15,010 per head. Denmark's level of GNP per head is one of the highest among industrialized countries. It was estimated that GNP per head increased at an average rate of 2.4% per year, in real terms, between 1980 and 1987, although in 1987 it decreased by 0.3%.

Danish agriculture is internationally competitive and is organized on a co-operative basis. The co-operatives are united in national federations. Denmark exports 63% of its total agricultural production, and cheese, beef and bacon are the main exports. In 1986 agricultural exports accounted for 28% of total exports, and in 1987 for 24%, worth 43,700m. kroner. The proportion of the working population employed in agriculture declined from 21% in 1950 to 4.3% in 1986, although in the latter year over 67% of the land surface was cultivated. Intensive farming and subsidies from the EEC have led to an increase in total production of more than 40% since Denmark joined the EEC in 1973, although rising mortgage interest rates caused many farms to close in the early 1980s, and in 1986 the number of farms being worked full-time was 42,500, compared with 56,000 in 1979. In 1988 the Government estimated that nearly 15% of the country's farms were too indebted to be saved. Legislation planned for April 1989 was to provide assistance to other indebted farmers, and a government commission recommended a politically sensitive course, allowing the formation of larger farming units and encouraging investment.

In the early 1980s pig farming had experienced particular difficulties, owing to an outbreak of foot-and-mouth disease, but it was hoped that a five-year investment plan, begun in 1984, would increase the annual value of pig production by 1989. However, although pig production in 1987 reached a record 16.2m. pigs, export revenue from pig meat had declined in 1986 by 7%. The rate of increase in the number of pigs had slowed, and by 1989 the number of pigs was expected to have fallen. This decline was due to a fall in prices for pig meat, to pressures, such as high interest rates, experienced by all farmers, and to strict environmental legislation, introduced by the Government in early 1987, which required substantial investments by farmers to reduce pollution of coastal waters by nitrates and phosphates. This legislation, combined with EEC proposals to reform its Common Agricultural Policy (thus reducing prices and farm subsidies), was expected to lead to substantial declines in revenue from agricultural exports, in particular from non-EEC countries, where some 37% of Danish agricultural exports are sold. Agricultural products account for almost 25% of Denmark's merchandise exports. In 1986 the value of fish exports was 10,218m. kroner, with a total catch of 1,871,349 metric tons. In 1987, when fish exports earned about 9,000m. kroner, fishermen protested against low prices and quota restrictions on the catches.

Denmark's industrial sector is one of the smallest in the industrialized world, although it has developed considerably since 1945. In 1986 the manufacturing sector accounted for about 67% of the country's exports. Between 1982 and 1986 manufacturing output increased by 25% and exports increased by 41%. In spite of a shortage of raw materials, the iron and metal industry is now the most important producing group. The other major branches of manufacturing include food-processing and beverages, engineering and chemicals. The pharmaceuticals industry exports 88% of its output, and earned 5,520m. kroner in 1987. The manufacturing of electronic goods is one of Denmark's fastest-growing industries, exporting 90% of its output. Exports were estimated at 11,000m. kroner in 1985, an increase of 1,500m. kroner on the 1984 total. However, total manufacturing exports declined by 4% in the final four months of 1986, and the growth of the sector slowed during 1987, owing mainly to a reduction in export demand, as a result of the high rate of exchange of the krone, and to a lack of domestic demand. Manufacturing exports in 1987 earned 118,300m. kroner, or 65% of total exports. In August 1986 it was announced that the Danish shipbuilding industry was to receive state help in the form of loans and more flexible investment rules. Several shipyards had been in danger of closure, owing to the lack of new orders since the end of 1984. The Government plans to reduce the subsidy between 1989 and 1992. In 1988 the Danish International Shipping Registry was established to prevent the use of 'flags of convenience' by the merchant fleet, and before the end of the year more than one-half of the merchant fleet had registered under the new flag. Some ships were transferring back from foreign flags also.

Denmark's economy suffers from the country's dependence on petroleum for most of its energy needs (63% in 1985); it was decided in 1980 not to develop nuclear energy. However, exploration for hydrocarbon reserves in the Danish sector of the North Sea proved successful, and development proceeded. There was great emphasis on developing natural gas reserves. In 1973 Denmark was importing 95% of the petroleum that it consumed, but by 1985 this proportion had been reduced to 48%. A 1988 estimate assessed domestic energy production at 40% of total requirements, including two-thirds of petroleum and gas consumption. It was hoped that by 1990 the level of self-sufficiency would have increased to 70%. Production of crude petroleum increased from 2.2m. metric tons in 1984 to 4.6m. tons in 1987. Since 1981 Danish oil and gas fields have gradually been brought under state control. All exploration groups are required to have a Danish interest of at least 20%.

Denmark's reliance on imported petroleum contributed to current deficits on the balance of payments after 1963, and these were financed by large loans contracted abroad. In their 'programme for the restoration of the Danish economy', aiming principally to eliminate the deficit on the current account by 1988, the Conservative-led coalition imposed a six-month 'freeze' on wages in October 1982, together with a longer-term ban on inflation-linked indexation, and reductions in welfare and unemployment benefits. Nevertheless, unemployment in that year reached 9.5% of the labour force, the annual rate of inflation 10.1%, and external indebtedness was 32% of gross domestic product (GDP). The austerity measures achieved some success in lowering inflation and unemployment, and at the end of the financial year 1985/86 a budget surplus (of 7,800m. kroner) was recorded for the first time in 12 years. The deficit on the current account of the balance of payments, however, had risen to 34,500m. kroner, or 5.2% of GDP, by 1986. Further austerity measures, in 1985 and 1986, increased popular dissatisfaction, but, as a result of the measures, a 9.2% reduction in imports was achieved in 1987. In that year there was a trade surplus of 1,200m. kroner and the current account deficit was reduced to 20,100m. kroner, but plans to eliminate the deficit by 1988 were abandoned. In the first nine months of 1988 the current account deficit reached only 9,900m. kroner. Improvements in the trade balance, however, were countered by rising interest payments on the foreign debt, which normally absorb more than 13% of export earnings. At the end of 1987 the external debt stood at 272,000m. kroner, equivalent to some 40% of annual GDP.

GDP actually declined by 1% in 1987, however, after a high rate of growth had been maintained in the mid-1980s (3.3% in 1986). Predictions for 1988 were that GDP would remain static, but unemployment and inflation rates had begun to rise again. In 1986 and 1987 the unemployment rate had fallen to just under 8%, but in 1988 it was about 8.5% and was expected to rise further. The rate of inflation, 3.7% in 1986 and 4% in 1987, rose to about 4.5% in 1988, owing to the wage agreements of 1987. These had involved a reduction of the hours in a working week and pay increases that were high compared with the stringent 2% limit imposed in the previous two years. At the beginning of 1989 the Government urged trade unions and employers to agree upon a reduction in salaries, and, in return, offered to lower the income tax rate. Further reforms of the tax system had been promised already (see Recent History), and there was pressure to reduce the high levels of indirect taxation before the completion of the EEC internal market in 1992 (or experience a massive rise in the current account deficit), despite the serious loss of revenue that this would involve.

Social Welfare

Denmark was one of the first countries to introduce state social welfare schemes. Principal services cover unemployment, sickness, old age and disability, and are financed largely by state subventions. In 1985 Denmark had 120 hospital establishments, with 36,000 beds. In 1984 there were 12,980 physicians working in the country, and in the same year the Government introduced a new system whereby social benefits are regulated according to the individual's means. In 1988 32% of proposed budget expenditure was allocated to social services.

Education

Education is compulsory for nine years between seven and 16 years of age, though exemption may be granted after seven years. The State is obliged to offer a pre-school class and a tenth voluntary year. State-subsidized private schools are available, but about 90% of pupils attend municipal schools. The 1975 Education Act, with effect from August 1976, increased parental influence, introduced a comprehensive curriculum for the first 10 years and offered options on final tests or a leaving certificate thereafter.

Primary and lower secondary education begins at six or seven years of age and lasts for nine (optionally 10) years. At the age of 16 or 17, pupils may transfer to an upper secondary school (Gymnasium), leading to the Upper Secondary School Leaving Examination (Studentereksamen) after three years, or they may take a two-year course, leading to the Higher Preparatory Examination; both courses give admission to university studies. Students may transfer to vocational courses or apprenticeship training at this point. Enrolment at primary and secondary schools is equivalent to virtually 100% of school-age children.

There are three universities, two university centres, and several other institutions of further and higher education. The traditional folk high schools offer a wide range of further education opportunities, which do not confer any professional qualification. In 1988 government expenditure on education represented 9% of total budget spending.

Public Holidays

1989: 2 January (for New Year's Day), 23–27 March (Easter), 21 April (General Prayer Day), 4 May (Ascension Day), 15 May (Whit Monday), 5 June (Constitution Day), 25–26 December (Christmas).

1990: 1 January (New Year's Day), 12–16 April (Easter), 11 May (General Prayer Day), 24 May (Ascension Day), 4 June (Whit Monday), 5 June (Constitution Day), 25–26 December (Christmas).

Weights and Measures

The metric system is in force.

Statistical Survey

Note: The figures in this survey relate only to metropolitan Denmark, excluding the Faeroe Islands and Greenland, which are dealt with in separate chapters (see pp. 875 and 877 respectively).
Source (unless otherwise stated): Danmarks Statistik, Sejrøgade 11, POB 2550, 2100 Copenhagen Ø; tel. (01) 29-82-22.

Area and Population

AREA, POPULATION AND DENSITY

Area (sq km)	43,092*
Population (census results)	
9 November 1970	4,937,579
1 January 1981	
Males	2,528,225
Females	2,595,764
Total	5,123,989
Population (official estimates at 1 January)	
1986	5,116,273
1987	5,124,794
1988	5,129,254
Density (per sq km) at 1 January 1988	119.0

* 16,638 sq miles.

PRINCIPAL TOWNS (population at 1 January 1986)

København (Copenhagen, the capital)	1,351,999*	Horsens		46,735
		Vejle		44,253
		Helsingør (Elsinore)		43,696
Århus (Aarhus)	195,152	Kolding		43,692
Odense	137,286	Roskilde		39,606
Ålborg (Aalborg)	113,650	Næstved		38,159
Esbjerg	71,112			
Randers	55,563			

* Copenhagen metropolitan area.

BIRTHS, MARRIAGES AND DEATHS

	Registered live births		Registered marriages		Registered deaths	
	Number	Rate (per 1,000)	Number	Rate (per 1,000)	Number	Rate (per 1,000)
1980	57,293	11.2	26,448	5.2	55,939	10.9
1981	53,089	10.4	25,411	5.0	56,359	11.0
1982	52,658	10.3	24,330	4.8	55,368	10.8
1983	50,822	9.9	27,096	5.3	57,156	11.2
1984	51,800	10.1	28,624	5.6	57,109	11.2
1985	53,749	10.5	29,322	5.7	58,378	11.4
1986	55,370	10.8	30,773	6.0	58,139	11.7
1987	56,221	11.0	31,132	6.1	58,136	11.3

Expectation of life at birth: Males 71.6 years; females 77.5 years (1984–85).

CIVILIAN LABOUR FORCE EMPLOYED
(ISIC Major Divisions, '000 persons)

	1985	1986	1987
Agriculture, forestry and fishing	174.9	171.0	165.2
Mining and quarrying	2.3	2.5	2.6
Manufacturing	529.1	540.8	533.3
Electricity, gas and water	15.7	16.0	16.1
Construction	170.1	179.8	183.6
Trade, restaurants and hotels	336.7	343.0	348.3
Transport, storage and communications	176.2	181.5	184.9
Financing, insurance, real estate and business services	221.2	240.2	253.6
Community, social and personal services	916.2	926.9	943.3
Total	**2,542.3**	**2,601.8**	**2,631.0**

Agriculture

PRINCIPAL CROPS ('000 metric tons)

	1985	1986	1987
Wheat	1,972	2,177	2,285
Barley	5,251	5,134	4,292
Rye	565	546	512
Oats	152 }	111	94
Mixed grain	16		
Potatoes	1,100	1,129	957
Pulses	542	553	519
Rapeseed	544	618	556
Sugar beet	3,515	3,195	2,632

LIVESTOCK ('000 head at June-July)

	1985	1986	1987
Horses	31.9	30.5	32.8
Cattle	2,617.7	2,495.4	4,350.8
Pigs	9,089.0	9,320.6	9,266.4
Sheep	70.4	88.8	100.8
Chickens	14,066.9	14,008.5	14,619.1
Turkeys	392.8	488.5	345.3
Ducks	703.0	651.6	525.6
Geese	56.4	71.1	50.2

LIVESTOCK PRODUCTS ('000 metric tons)

	1985	1986	1987
Beef and veal	252.1	264.4	254.9
Pig meat	1,132.0	1,195.1	1,198.5
Poultry meat	114.7	115.4	113.0
Cows' milk	5,099	5,111	4,860
Butter	109.7	112.0	96.2
Cheese	255.5	254.0	272.3
Eggs	79.7	81.3	76.5

DENMARK
Statistical Survey

Forestry

ROUNDWOOD REMOVALS ('000 cu m, excl. bark)

	1984	1985	1986
Sawlogs, veneer logs and logs for sleepers	1,233	941	941*
Pulpwood	639	612	500
Other industrial wood	356	356*	356*
Fuel wood	351	394	394*
Total	2,579	2,303	2,191

* FAO estimate.
Source: FAO, *Yearbook of Forest Products*.

SAWNWOOD PRODUCTION ('000 cu m, incl. boxboards)

	1983	1984*	1985
Coniferous (softwood)	400	400	450
Broadleaved (hardwood)	400	400	400*
Total	800	800	850

* FAO estimates.
1986: Production as in 1985 (FAO estimates).
Railway sleepers ('000 cu m): 29 per year (1981–86).
Source: FAO, *Yearbook of Forest Products*.

Fishing*

('000 metric tons, live weight)

	1984	1985†	1986
Trouts	22.3	24.0	27.8
European plaice	35.2	33.4	41.1
Atlantic cod	193.4	183.3	154.1
Haddock	24.2	22.9	20.3
Norway pout	276.7	262.2	194.5
Blue whiting (Poutassou)	95.1	90.2	69.8
Whiting	32.8	31.1	10.0
Sandeels (Sandlances)	642.4	608.9	847.5
Atlantic horse mackerel	24.8	23.5	52.6
Atlantic herring	117.5	111.4	150.5
European sprat (brisling)	162.0	153.6	105.0
Atlantic mackerel	20.5	19.5	25.0
Other fishes (incl. unspecified)	106.0	93.2	51.0
Total fish	1,753.0	1,657.1	1,749.1
Crustaceans	11.8	11.3	17.3
Blue mussel	81.5	84.1	105.0
Other aquatic animals	0.1	0.1	0.0
Total catch	1,846.4	1,752.6	1,871.3
Inland waters	22.7	24.0	24.2
Atlantic Ocean	1,823.7	1,728.6	1,847.1

* Data include quantities landed by Danish fishing craft in foreign ports and exclude quantities landed by foreign fishing craft in Danish ports.
† Figures for individual species are nearly all FAO estimates.
Source: FAO, *Yearbook of Fishery Statistics*.

Mining

('000 metric tons)

	1985	1986	1987
Crude petroleum	2,853	3,238	4,552
Salt (unrefined)	574	574	537
Sulphur*	7	13	11
Limestone flux and calcareous stone	2,058	2,115	1,362

* Sulphur of all kinds, other than sublimed sulphur, precipitated sulphur and colloidal sulphur.

Industry

SELECTED PRODUCTS
('000 metric tons, unless otherwise indicated)

	1985	1986	1987
Pig meat:			
Fresh, chilled or frozen	645	713	n.a.
Salted, dried or smoked	167	162	152
Poultry meat and offals	109	105	107
Fish fillets: fresh, chilled, frozen	99	109	108
Salami, sausages, etc	74	74	70
Meat in airtight containers:			
Hams	74	66	58
Other meat	30	25	26
Meat preparations, pâtés, etc	97	91	89
Beet and cane sugar (solid)	533	532	522
Beer ('000 hectolitres)	8,286	9,064	8,755
Flours, meals and pastes of fish	437	442	450
Oil cake and meal	136	113	129
Cigarettes (million)	10,966	11,246	11,162
Cement	1,983	2,029	1,886
Motor spirit (Petrol)	1,175	1,274	1,360
Motor and fuel oils	4,405	5,025	5,002
Powder asphalt	2,307	2,743	3,117
Washing powders, etc	203	203	194
Refrigerators for household use ('000)	219	248	229
New dwellings completed (number)	22,613	28,489	27,250
Electric energy (million kWh)	26,903	28,492	27,227
Manufactured gas ('000 gigajoules)	4,043	2,661	2,337

Finance

CURRENCY AND EXCHANGE RATES

Monetary Units
100 øre = 1 Danish krone (plural: kroner).

Denominations
Coins: 5, 10 and 25 øre; 1, 5 and 10 kroner.
Notes: 20, 50, 100, 500 and 1,000 kroner.

Sterling and Dollar Equivalents (30 September 1988)
£1 sterling = 12.170 kroner;
US $1 = 7.1975 kroner;
1,000 Danish kroner = £82.17 = $138.94.

Average Exchange Rate (kroner per US $)
1985 10.596
1986   8.091
1987   6.840

DENMARK

BUDGET (million kroner)

Revenue	1987*	1988†
Income and property taxes	101,815	106,540
Customs and excise duties	121,677	122,291
Other revenue	—	—
Interest (net)	−24,441	−22,153
Total	199,051	206,678

Expenditure	1987*	1988†
Social services	63,130	66,403
Education	16,886	18,595
Defence	12,671	13,498
Public works	2,458	2,660
Agriculture	2,110	2,115
Justice	4,123	4,062
Finance ministry	1,113	1,165
Greenland	2,059	2,170
Other expenditure	95,365	97,580
Total	199,915	208,248

* Approved.   † Estimates.

NATIONAL BANK RESERVES (million kroner)

	1985	1986	1987
Gold	4,772	4,675	4,858
IMF special drawing rights	1,759	1,862	1,301
European currency units	4,194	392	3,777
Gross foreign assets	41,328	33,561	54,078
Reserve position in IMF	6,993	6,390	6,148
Total official reserves	59,046	46,880	70,162

MONEY SUPPLY ('000 million kroner at 31 December)

	1985	1986	1987
Currency outside banks	28.65	28.71	31.43
Demand deposits with commercial banks and savings banks	174.96	192.81	209.88
Savings deposits with commercial banks and savings banks	102.87	112.22	102.53
Short-term government bills outside banks	14.75	14.07	20.61
Total money	321.23	347.81	364.45

COST OF LIVING
(Consumer Price Index. Base: 1980 = 100)

	1984	1985	1986
Food	142	148	151
Fuel and light	146	151	157
Clothing	126	134	145
Rent	140	147	147
All items	139.8	146.4	151.7

1987: Food 152; All items 157.8.

NATIONAL ACCOUNTS (million kroner at current prices)
National Income and Product

	1985	1986	1987
Compensation of employees	331,921	357,455	391,241
Operating surplus	138,314	140,504	126,915
Domestic factor incomes	470,235	497,959	518,156
Consumption of fixed capital	54,800	58,100	62,000
Gross domestic product at factor cost	525,035	556,059	580,156
Indirect taxes	112,898	130,851	135,506
Less Subsidies	18,358	19,769	22,634
GDP in purchasers' values	619,575	667,141	693,028
Factor income from abroad	17,735	19,119	20,885
Less Factor income paid abroad	43,905	46,479	48,871
Gross national product	593,404	639,782	665,042
Less Consumption of fixed capital	54,800	58,100	62,000
National income in market prices	538,604	581,682	603,042
Other current transfers from abroad	7,311	9,404	9,038
Less Other current transfers paid abroad	11,612	15,090	14,751
National disposable income	534,304	575,996	597,329

Expenditure on the Gross Domestic Product

	1985	1986	1987
Government final consumption expenditure	155,481	160,500	175,754
Private final consumption expenditure	340,077	365,045	376,237
Increase in stocks	7,000	5,000	−2,000
Gross fixed capital formation	114,929	138,070	130,076
Total domestic expenditure	617,486	668,615	680,067
Exports of goods and services	225,570	214,144	220,273
Less Imports of goods and services	223,480	215,618	207,312
GDP in purchasers' values	619,575	667,141	693,028

Gross Domestic Product by Economic Activity (at factor cost)

	1985	1986	1987
Agriculture and hunting	26,947	26,778	24,423
Forestry and logging	1,028	1,103	1,086
Fishing	2,683	2,830	2,766
Mining and quarrying	6,718	4,404	5,053
Manufacturing	102,607	111,690	115,006
Electricity, gas and water	6,436	7,326	6,992
Construction	32,628	37,179	40,405
Wholesale and retail trade	75,242	78,184	77,002
Restaurants and hotels	7,304	8,685	9,776
Transport, storage and communication	44,946	46,715	48,146
Finance and insurance	15,700	21,909	24,711
Owner-occupied dwellings	46,815	49,257	51,740
Business services	28,089	31,443	31,400
Market services of education and health	6,287	6,709	6,944
Recreational and cultural services	5,014	5,400	5,749
Household services (incl. vehicle repairs)	14,456	15,557	18,442
Government services	115,230	120,005	131,916
Other producers	3,410	3,734	3,844
Sub-total	541,539	578,909	605,402
Less Imputed bank service charges	16,504	22,850	25,246
Total	525,035	556,059	580,156

DENMARK

BALANCE OF PAYMENTS (US $ million)

	1985	1986	1987
Merchandise exports f.o.b.	17,116	21,274	25,695
Merchandise imports f.o.b.	−17,887	−22,355	−24,900
Trade balance	−771	−1,081	795
Exports of services	6,975	8,375	10,612
Imports of services	−8,798	−11,288	−14,153
Balance on goods and services	−2,594	−3,994	−2,746
Private unrequited transfers (net)	−55	−112	−56
Government unrequited transfers (net)	−80	−166	−164
Current balance	−2,728	−4,271	−2,966
Direct capital investment (net) } Other long-term capital (net) }	4,451	3,554	8,333
Short-term capital (net)	255	−348	−835
Net errors and omissions	−456	−914	−88
Total (net monetary movements)	1,522	−1,979	4,443
Valuation changes (net)	888	865	1,370
Official financing (net)	10	650	−712
Changes in reserves	2,420	−464	5,102

Source: IMF, *International Financial Statistics*.

External Trade

PRINCIPAL COMMODITIES
(distribution by SITC, million kroner)

Imports c.i.f.	1984	1985	1986*
Food and live animals	16,430.3	16,653.4	18,061.7
Fish, crustaceans and molluscs	3,281.3	3,881.6	4,729.1
Animal feeding-stuff (excl. cereals)	4,530.1	3,920.6	3,786.1
Oil-cake, etc.	3,798.5	n.a.	n.a.
Crude materials (inedible) except fuels	8,340.3	8,282.0	7,888.3
Mineral fuels, lubricants, etc.	31,305.9	33,152.2	16,409.4
Coal, coke and briquettes	4,237.0	6,016.1	4,088.1
Coal, lignite and peat	4,141.3	n.a.	n.a.
Coal (not agglomerated)	4,121.7	n.a.	n.a.
Petroleum, petroleum products, etc.	25,863.7	26,325.1	11,972.8
Crude petroleum oils, etc.	11,610.4	n.a.	n.a.
Refined petroleum products	13,341.4	n.a.	n.a.
Gas oils (distillate fuels)	5,910.5	n.a.	n.a.
Chemicals and related products	19,520.9	20,436.9	19,759.0
Artificial resins and plastic materials, etc.	5,931.8	6,327.4	6,436.2
Products of polymerization, etc.	4,191.9	n.a.	n.a.
Basic manufactures	35,636.6	36,720.9	37,412.2
Paper, paperboard and manufactures	5,814.7	6,351.7	6,776.2
Textile yarn, fabrics, etc.	6,119.5	6,723.0	6,641.9
Iron and steel	7,743.8	8,557.2	8,214.0
Machinery and transport equipment	41,086.5	50,734.1	58,292.2
Machinery specialized for particular industries	5,130.5	6,772.5	8,343.2
General industrial machinery, equipment and parts	5,938.0	7,193.5	7,842.9

Imports c.i.f.—continued	1984	1985	1986*
Office machines and automatic data processing equipment	5,704.1	6,583.0	6,922.9
Automatic data processing machines, etc.	3,433.0	n.a.	n.a.
Telecommunications and sound equipment	3,219.1	3,703.0	4,325.1
Other electrical machinery, apparatus, etc.	6,205.5	7,210.8	7,544.1
Road vehicles and parts (excl. tyres, engines and electrical parts)	10,530.4	12,428.2	16,398.8
Passenger motor cars (excl. buses)	5,189.0	n.a.	n.a.
Miscellaneous manufactured articles	16,777.5	19,451.2	21,754.8
Clothing and accessories (excl. footwear)	4,386.7	5,317.8	5,979.9
Total (incl. others)	171,825.8	191,562.6	184,639.5

* Provisional figures.

1987: Total imports 173,457 million kroner.

Exports f.o.b.	1984	1985	1986*
Food and live animals	45,961.2	48,153.4	47,256.3
Meat and meat preparations	19,758.9	20,560.8	19,338.6
Fresh, chilled or frozen meat	10,888.2	11,622.3	11,931.0
Pig meat	6,906.6	n.a.	n.a.
Salted, dried or smoked meat	3,550.7	3,244.9	2,655.0
Other prepared or preserved meat	5,320.0	5,693.5	4,752.6
Dairy products and birds' eggs	7,656.9	7,387.8	6,877.7
Cheese and curd	4,080.2	3,877.6	3,583.6
Fish, crustaceans and molluscs	7,886.8	8,973.4	10,217.6
Fresh, chilled or frozen fish	4,470.3	4,872.4	5,401.4
Cereals and cereal preparations	4,181.9	4,495.0	4,279.4
Crude materials (inedible) except fuels	9,935.2	11,538.9	10,856.6
Hides, skins and furskins	3,256.3	3,646.5	3,405.8
Mineral fuels, lubricants, etc.	8,540.5	9,719.3	5,281.6
Petroleum, petroleum products, etc.	7,689.7	8,190.7	4,097.8
Refined petroleum products	5,615.2	n.a.	n.a.
Chemicals and related products	14,954.9	16,001.3	15,599.5
Medicinal and pharmaceutical products	4,706.8	5,259.6	5,429.1
Medicaments (incl. veterinary medicaments)	3,181.3	n.a.	n.a.
Basic manufactures	20,388.5	19,468.2	19,500.7
Textile yarn, fabrics, etc.	3,726.7	3,886.6	3,792.4
Machinery and transport equipment	37,774.3	43,538.9	41,308.0
Power generating machinery and equipment	3,506.8	4,262.6	3,201.6
Machinery specialized for particular industries	5,990.2	6,843.8	6,796.1
General industrial machinery, equipment and parts	11,106.0	12,221.2	12,734.3
Telecommunications and sound equipment	2,957.5	3,425.6	3,755.3
Other electrical machinery, apparatus, etc.	5,171.5	5,706.5	5,884.9
Transport equipment	7,102.0	8,438.4	6,010.4
Ships, boats and floating structures	4,070.4	n.a.	n.a.
Miscellaneous manufactured articles	23,980.3	26,852.1	27,851.2
Furniture and parts	5,991.3	6,652.7	6,403.0
Clothing and accessories (excl. footwear)	4,373.0	4,962.4	5,122.0
Professional, scientific and controlling instruments, etc.	3,520.1	3,846.7	4,028.9
Total (incl. others)	165,346.4	179,577.1	171,613.9

* Provisional figures.

1987: Total exports 174,508 million kroner.

DENMARK

PRINCIPAL TRADING PARTNERS* (million kroner)

Imports c.i.f.	1984	1985	1986
Belgium/Luxembourg	5,051.7	6,363.7	6,738.8
Finland	6,013.3	6,337.7	5,631.7
France (incl. Monaco)	7,655.8	8,527.4	9,318.7
Germany, Fed. Rep.	35,002.1	40,383.6	43,563.8
Italy	6,181.3	6,840.9	7,837.7
Japan	6,705.3	7,724.8	10,473.1
Netherlands	9,208.2	10,023.4	9,577.3
Norway	7,066.9	7,747.2	6,744.5
Sweden	23,944.7	24,991.3	22,777.9
Switzerland	3,176.1	3,589.0	3,956.4
USSR	3,424.1	3,012.6	1,658.1
United Kingdom	15,458.6	18,009.6	14,005.2
USA	8,930.3	11,339.4	9,744.1
Total (incl. others)	171,825.8	191,562.6	184,639.5

* Imports by country of production; exports by country of consumption.

Exports f.o.b.	1984	1985	1986
Belgium/Luxembourg	2,803.5	3,253.8	3,307.5
Canada	1,545.2	1,789.7	1,441.7
Finland	3,230.8	3,711.5	3,837.7
France (incl. Monaco)	7,317.2	7,924.5	8,911.7
Germany, Fed. Rep.	26,644.4	28,460.1	28,870.8
Italy	6,450.6	7,129.5	7,846.7
Japan	4,696.6	5,532.9	5,893.8
Netherlands	5,545.3	6,520.7	6,168.9
Norway	10,515.9	12,071.3	13,068.3
Sweden	18,874.4	21,692.1	19,474.6
Switzerland	3,067.6	3,412.3	3,565.0
United Kingdom	21,228.4	21,908.2	20,076.7
USA	15,914.5	18,148.7	14,542.2
Total (incl. others)	165,346.4	179,577.1	171,613.9

Transport

RAILWAYS ('000)

	Private railways 1986	State railways 1985	State railways 1986
Number of journeys	10,939	145,482	145,241
Passenger-kilometres	190,161	4,716,000	4,707,000
Ton-kilometres	12,694	1,756,000	1,800,000

ROAD TRAFFIC (motor vehicles in use at 31 December)

	1985	1986	1987
Private cars	1,487,888	1,544,284	1,574,251
Taxis, hire cars, etc.	13,058	13,596	13,168
Buses, coaches	8,010	8,105	8,110
Vans, lorries	259,397	274,991	286,415
Tractors	143,570	142,649	141,022
Trailers	221,781	248,372	269,378
Motor cycles	41,395	41,868	42,456

SHIPPING
Danish Merchant Marine
(vessels exceeding 100 gross registered tons, at 31 December)

	1986 Number	1986 Gross tonnage	1987 Number	1987 Gross tonnage
Dry cargo	578	2,483,038	546	2,421,596
Tankers	94	2,262,744	72	2,090,559
Total	672	4,745,782	618	4,512,155

Sea-borne Freight Traffic at Danish Ports*
('000 metric tons loaded and unloaded)

	1985	1986	1987
Ålborg	2,967	3,356	3,268
Århus	5,738	6,091	5,890
Copenhagen	6,790	6,619	6,163
Fredericia	5,779	6,123	6,676
Kalundborg	3,456	4,220	4,072
Skaelskør	4,443	4,888	5,046
Others	33,043	34,756	33,353
Total	62,216	66,053	64,468

* Including domestic traffic, excluding international ferry traffic.

International Sea-borne Shipping*
(freight traffic, '000 metric tons)

	1985	1986	1987
Goods loaded	11,007	11,273	12,020
Goods unloaded	33,324	33,092	32,317

* Excluding international ferry traffic.
Source: *Danmarks skibe og skibsfart* (all shipping tables).

CIVIL AVIATION (Scandinavian Airlines System)

	1984/85	1985/86
Kilometres flown ('000)	125,000	136,000
Passengers carried ('000)	10,735	11,708
Passenger-kilometres (million)	11,964	12,471
Cargo and mail ton-kilometres (million)	448	464

Tourism

(income from visitors, million kroner)

	1985	1986	1987
Scandinavian visitors	4,849	5,269	5,731
German visitors	3,333	3,334	3,345
All other visitors	5,869	5,629	6,110
Total	14,051	14,232	15,185

OVERNIGHT STAYS (foreign visitors)

	1985	1986	1987
In hotels	4,590,800	4,338,300	4,480,315
At camping sites	3,986,300	3,779,600	3,289,595
Total	8,577,100	8,117,900	7,769,910

DENMARK

Communications Media

	1985	1986	1987
Radio licences*	174,000	n.a.	86,000
Television licences (black and white)	383,000	n.a.	243,000
Television licences (colour)	1,622,000	1,626,000	1,698,000
Telephones in use	4,005,000	4,011,000	n.a.
Number of newspapers	47	47	47
Total circulation (weekdays)	1,855,000	1,880,000	n.a.
Books published	9,554	10,957	11,129

* Radios only, excluding combined radio and television licences.

Education

(1986/87)

	Institutions	Teachers	Students
Pre-primary			
Primary	3,069	68,000	710,034
Secondary: first stage			
Secondary: second stage			
General	162	n.a.	70,257
Vocational			
Teacher-training	343	n.a.	181,483
Technical education			
Universities	5	3,196*	55,633
Other university-level	93	n.a.	38,181

* January 1986, full-time equivalents.

Directory

The Constitution

The constitutional charter (*Grundlov*), summarized below, was adopted on 5 June 1953.

GOVERNMENT

The form of government is a limited (constitutional) monarchy. The legislative authority rests jointly with the Crown and Parliament. Executive power is vested in the Crown, and the administration of justice is exercised by the courts. The Monarch can constitutionally 'do no wrong'. She exercises her authority through the Ministers appointed by her. The Ministers are responsible for the government of the country. The Constitution establishes the principle of Parliamentarism under which individual Ministers or the whole Cabinet must retire when defeated in Parliament by a vote of no confidence.

MONARCH

The Monarch acts on behalf of the State in international affairs. Except with the consent of the Parliament, she cannot, however, take any action which increases or reduces the area of the Realm or undertake any obligation, the fulfilment of which requires the co-operation of the Parliament or which is of major importance. Nor can the Monarch, without the consent of the Parliament, terminate any international agreement which has been concluded with the consent of the Parliament.

Apart from defence against armed attack on the Realm or on Danish forces, the Monarch cannot, without the consent of the Parliament, employ military force against any foreign power.

PARLIAMENT

The Parliament is an assembly consisting of not more than 179 members, two of whom are elected in the Faeroe Islands and two in Greenland. It is called the Folketing. Danish nationals, having attained 18 years of age, with permanent residence in Denmark, have the franchise and are eligible for election. The members of the Folketing are elected for four years. Election is by a system of proportional representation, with direct and secret ballot on lists in large constituencies. A bill adopted by the Folketing may be submitted to referendum, when such referendum is claimed by not less than one-third of the members of the Folketing and not later than three days after the adoption. The bill is void if rejected by a majority of the votes cast, representing not less than 30% of all electors.

The Government

HEAD OF STATE

Queen of Denmark: HM QUEEN MARGRETHE II (succeeded to the throne 14 January 1972).

THE CABINET
(January 1989)

A coalition of the Conservative People's Party (KF), the Liberal Party (V) and the Radical Liberal Party (RV).

Prime Minister: POUL SCHLÜTER (KF).
Minister of Finance: PALLE SIMONSEN (KF).
Minister of Foreign Affairs: UFFE ELLEMANN-JENSEN (V).
Minister of Labour: HENNING DYREMOSE (KF).
Minister of Housing: AGNETE LAUSTSEN (KF).
Minister of Energy: JENS BILGRAV-NIELSEN (RV).
Minister of Fisheries: LARS P. GAMMELGAARD (KF).
Minister of Defence: KNUD ENGAARD (V).
Minister of the Interior and for Nordic Affairs: THOR PEDERSEN (V).
Minister of Justice: HANS PETER CLAUSEN (KF).
Minister of Health: ELSEBETH KOCK-PETERSEN (V).
Minister of Industry: NILS WILHJELM (KF).
Minister of Economic Affairs: NIELS HELVEG PETERSEN (RV).
Minister of Fiscal Affairs: ANDERS FOGH RASMUSSEN (V).
Minister for Ecclesiastical Affairs and Communications: TORBEN RECHENDORFF (KF).
Minister for Cultural Affairs: OLE VIG JENSEN (RV).
Minister of Agriculture: LAURITS TØRNÆS (V).
Minister of the Environment: LONE DYBKJÆR (RV).
Minister for Social Affairs: AESE OLESEN (RV).
Minister of Transport: KNUD ØSTERGAARD (KF).
Minister of Education and Research: BERTEL HAARDER (V).

MINISTRIES

Office of the Prime Minister: Christiansborg, Prins Jørgens Gaard 11, 1218 Copenhagen K; tel. (01) 92-33-00; telex 27027.
Ministry of Agriculture: Slotsholmsgade 10, 1216 Copenhagen K; tel. (01) 92-33-01; telex 27157.
Ministry of Cultural Affairs: Nybrogade 2, 1203 Copenhagen K; tel. (01) 92-33-70; telex 27385.
Ministry of Defence: Slotsholmsgade 10, 1216 Copenhagen K; tel. (01) 92-33-20.
Ministry of Ecclesiastical Affairs: Frederiksholms Kanal 21, 1220 Copenhagen K; tel. (01) 14-62-63.
Ministry of Economic Affairs: Slotsholmsgade 12, 1216 Copenhagen K; tel. (01) 92-32-22; telex 16833.
Ministry of Education and Research: Fredriksholms Kanal 21-25, 1220 Copenhagen K; tel. (01) 92-50-00; telex 16243.
Ministry of Energy: Slotsholmsgade 1, 1216 Copenhagen K; tel. (01) 92-75-00; telex 15505.
Ministry of the Environment: Slotsholmsgade 12, 1216 Copenhagen K; tel. (01) 92-33-88; telex 31209.
Ministry of Finance: Christiansborg Slotsplads 1, 1218 Copenhagen K; tel. (01) 92-33-33; telex 16140.
Ministry of Fiscal Affairs: Slotsholmsgade 12, 1216 Copenhagen K; tel. (01) 92-33-66; telex 16939.

Note on telephone numbers: from May 1989 Denmark's area codes commencing with '0' (given here in parentheses) were to change.

DENMARK

Ministry of Fisheries: Stormgade 2, 1470 Copenhagen K; tel. (01) 92-65-00; telex 16144.
Ministry of Foreign Affairs: Asiatisk Plads 2, 1448 Copenhagen K; tel. (01) 92-00-00; telex 31292.
Ministry of Housing: H. C. Andersens Boulevard 40, 1553 Copenhagen V; tel. (01) 92-61-00; telex 31401.
Ministry of Industry: Slotsholmsgade 12, 1216 Copenhagen K; tel. (01) 92-33-50; telex 22373.
Ministry of the Interior: Christiansborg Slotsplads 1, 1218 Copenhagen K; tel. (01) 92-33-80; telex 16140.
Ministry of Justice: Slotsholmsgade 10, 1216 Copenhagen K; tel. (01) 92-33-40; telex 15530.
Ministry of Labour: Laksegade 19, 1063 Copenhagen K; tel. (01) 92-59-00; telex 19320.
Ministry of Social Affairs: Slotsholmsgade 6, 1216 Copenhagen K; tel. (01) 12-25-17; telex 27343.
Ministry of Transport and Communications: Frederiksholms Kanal 25–27, 1220 Copenhagen K; tel. (01) 12-62-42; telex 22275.

Legislature

FOLKETING

President of the Folketing: ERIK NINN-HANSEN.
Secretary-General: HELGE HJORTDAL.
Clerk of the Folketing: L. E. HANSEN-SALBY.

General Election, 10 May 1988
(metropolitan Denmark only)

	% of votes	Seats
Social-Democratic Party	29.9	55
Conservative People's Party	19.3	35
Socialist People's Party	13.0	24
Liberals	11.8	22
Radical Liberals	9.0	16
Centre Democrats	5.6	10
Progress Party	4.7	9
Christian People's Party	2.0	4
Common Course	1.9	—
Others	2.7	—
Total	**100.0**	**175**

The Folketing also contains two members from Greenland and two from the Faeroe Islands.

Political Organizations

Centrum-Demokraterne (Centre Democrats): Folketinget, Christiansborg, 1240 Copenhagen K; tel. (01) 11-66-00; f. 1973; opposes extreme ideologies, supports EEC and NATO; Leader ERHARD JACOBSEN, Sec.-Gen. YVONNE HERLØV ANDERSEN.
Danmarks Kommunistiske Parti (Danish Communist Party): Dr Tværgade 3, 1302 Copenhagen K; f. 1919; Chair. OLE SOHN.
Danmarks Retsforbund (Justice Party): Landssekretariatet, Lyngbyvej 42, 2100 Copenhagen Ø; tel. (01) 20-44-88; f. 1919; programme is closely allied to Henry George's teachings (single tax, free trade); Chair. POUL GERHARD C. KRISTIANSEN.
Europæiske Centrum-Demokrater (European Centre Democrats): Christiansborg, 1240 Copenhagen K; tel. (01) 11-66-00; f. 1974; supports co-operation within EEC and provides information about the workings of the EEC; Chair. ERHARD JACOBSEN.
Fælles Kurs (Common Course): Copenhagen.
Fremskridtspartiet (Progress Party): Folketinget, Christiansborg, 1218 Copenhagen K; tel. (01) 11-66-00; telex 19461; f. 1972; movement whose policies include gradual abolition of income tax, disbandment of most of the civil service, and abolition of diplomatic service and about 90% of legislation; Chair. ANNETTE JUST.
De Grønne (Green Environmentalists' Party): Landssekretariatet, Sterrebyvej 6, 5762 Vester Skerning, Fyn; International Secretariat, Slugten 10, 3300 Frederiksvaerk; tel. (02) 34-89-19; f. 1983.
Det Humanistiske Parti (Humanistic Party): Ryesgade 110, 2100 Copenhagen Ø.
Internationalen-Socialistiisk Arbejderparti (Socialist Workers' Party): Blegdamsvej 28C, 2200 Copenhagen N.
Kommunistik Arbejderparti (Communist Workers' Party): Studiestræde 24, 1455 Copenhagen K; tel. (01) 15-21-33; f. 1968.

Konservative Folkeparti (Conservative People's Party): Tordenskjoldsgade 21, 1055 Copenhagen K; tel. (01) 13-41-40; f. 1916; advocates free initiative and the maintenance of private property, but recognizes the right of the State to take action to keep the economic and social balance; Chair. POUL SCHLÜTER; Sec.-Gen. JOHN WAGNER.
Kristeligt Folkeparti (Christian People's Party): Bernhard Bangs Alle 23, 2000 Frederiksberg; tel. (38) 88-31-15; f. 1970; interdenominational grouping opposed to pornography and abortion; favours social-liberal economic policy, and emphasizes significance of cultural and family policy; Chair. FLEMMING KOFOD-SVENDSEN; Sec.-Gen. NIELS CHRESTEN ANDERSEN.
Marxistisk-Leninistisk Parti (Marxist-Leninist Party): Griffenfeldsgade 26, 2200 Copenhagen N; tel. (01) 35-60-69; Sec.-Gen. CLAUS RIIS.
Det Radikale Venstre (Radical Liberal Party): Det Radikale Venstres sekretariat, Christiansborg, 1240 Copenhagen K; tel. (01) 12-72-51; telex 16485; f. 1905; supports international détente and co-operation within regional and world organizations, social reforms without socialism, incomes policy, workers' participation in industry, state intervention in industrial disputes, state control of trusts and monopolies, strengthening private enterprise; Chair. THORKILD MØLLER; Leader MARIANNE JELVED; Gen. Sec. JENS CLAUSAGER.
Slesvigske Parti (Schleswig Party): Vestergade 30, 6200 Åbenrå.
Socialdemokratiet (Social Democratic Party): Thorvaldsensvej 2, 1998 Frederiksberg C; tel. (01) 39-15-22; telex 22309; f. 1871; finds its chief adherents among workers, employees and public servants; 100,000 members; Leader SVEND AUKEN; Gen. Sec. STEEN CHRISTENSEN.
Socialistisk Folkeparti (Socialist People's Party): Folketinget, Christiansborg, 1218 Copenhagen K; tel. (01) 12-70-11; telex 1458; f. 1958, with socialist aims, by Aksel Larsen; Chair. GERT PETERSEN; Sec. LILLIAN UBBESEN.
Venstre (Liberal Party): Søllerødvej 30, 2840 Holte; tel. (02) 80-22-33; telex 37783; f. 1870; supports free trade, a minimum of state interference, and the adoption, in matters of social expenditure, of a modern general social security system; Chair. UFFE ELLEMANN-JENSEN; Sec.-Gen. CLAUS HJORT FREDERIKSEN.
Venstresocialisterne (Left Socialist Party): Rosenørns Allé 44, 1970 Frederiksberg C; tel. (01) 35-60-99; f. 1967 as a result of a split from the Socialist People's Party; non-dogmatic Marxist party of the post-1968 'New Left'; collective leadership.

Diplomatic Representation

EMBASSIES IN DENMARK

Argentina: Store Kongensgade 45, 1264 Copenhagen K; tel. (01) 15-80-82; telex 27182; Ambassador: JORGE H. MAUHOURAT.
Australia: Kristianiagade 21, 2100 Copenhagen Ø; tel. (01) 26-22-44; telex 22308; Ambassador: JEFFREY A. BENSON.
Austria: Grønningen 5, 1270 Copenhagen K; tel. (01) 12-46-23; telex 27023; Ambassador: Dr GERHARD GMOSER.
Belgium: Øster Allé 7, 2100 Copenhagen Ø; tel. (01) 26-03-88; telex 22624; Ambassador: ERIK BAL (designate).
Brazil: Ryvangs Allé 24, 2100 Copenhagen Ø; tel. (01) 20-64-78; telex 19322; Ambassador: SERGIO PAULO ROUANET.
Bulgaria: A. N. Hansens Allé 5, 2900 Hellerup; tel. (01) 62-11-20; telex 27020; Ambassador: IVAN D. SPASSOV.
Burkina Faso: Svanemøllevej 20, 2100 Copenhagen Ø; tel. (01) 18-40-22; telex 19375; Ambassador: BRUNO NONGOMA ZIDOUEMBA.
Canada: Kr. Bernikowsgade 1, 1105 Copenhagen K; tel. (01) 12-22-99; telex 27036; Ambassador: DOROTHY J. ARMSTRONG.
Chile: Kastelsvej 15^3, 2100 Copenhagen Ø; tel. (01) 38-58-34; telex 15099; Chargé d'affaires: GERMÁN MEZA.
China, People's Republic: Øregårds Allé 25, 2900 Hellerup; tel. (01) 62-58-06; Ambassador: ZHANG LONGHAI.
Colombia: Esplanaden 7, 1263 Copenhagen K; tel. (01) 11-26-03; telex 16587; Ambassador Dr PEDRO LÓPEZ MICHELSEN.
Costa Rica: Svend Trøsts Vej 6, 1912 Frederiksberg C: tel. (01) 24-03-30; Chargé d'affaires: FRANCISCO GONZÁLEZ CRUZ.
Côte d'Ivoire: Gersonsvej 8, 2900 Hellerup; tel. (01) 62-88-22; telex 22351; Ambassador: EMILE ZOHORÉ BLÉHOUAN.
Cuba: Dag Hammarskjölds Allé 42^2, 2100 Copenhagen Ø; tel. (01) 42-05-15; telex 16852; Ambassador: Sra MARTA JIMÉNEZ MARTÍNEZ.
Czechoslovakia: Ryvangs Allé 14, 2100 Copenhagen Ø; tel. (01) 29-18-88; telex 19188; Ambassador: LUDOVIT PEZLAR.
Egypt: Nyropsgade 47, 1602 Copenhagen V; tel. (01) 12-76-41; telex 19892; Ambassador: ADEL MOHAMED ABBAS ZAKI.

DENMARK

Finland: Hammerensgade 5, 1267 Copenhagen K; tel. (01) 13-42-14; telex 27084; Ambassador: Dr EVA-CHRISTINA MÄKELÄINEN.

France: Kongens Nytorv 4, 1050 Copenhagen K; tel. (01) 15-51-22; telex 27029; Ambassador: MICHEL DRUMETZ.

German Democratic Republic: Svanemøllevej 48, 2100 Copenhagen Ø; tel. (01) 29-22-77; telex 19677; Ambassador: NORBERT JAESCHKE.

Germany, Federal Republic: Stockholmsgade 57, 2100 Copenhagen Ø; tel. (01) 26-16-22; telex 27166; Ambassador: RÜDIGER VON PACHELBEL.

Ghana: Egebjerg Allé 13, 2900 Hellerup; tel. (01) 62-82-22; telex 19471; Ambassador: THOMAS BENJAMIN SAM.

Greece: Borgergade 16, 1300 Copenhagen K; tel. (01) 11-45-33; telex 27279; Ambassador: EVANGELOS GEORGIOU.

Holy See: Immortellevej 11, 2950 Vedbæk; tel. (02) 89-35-36; Apostolic Pro-Nuncio: HENRI LEMAÎTRE, Titular Archbishop of Tongeren.

Hungary: Strandvejen 170, 2920 Charlottenlund; tel. (01) 63-16-88; telex 27186; Ambassador: Mrs PIROSKA KIRÁLY.

Iceland: Dantes Plads 3, 1556 Copenhagen V; tel. (01) 15-96-04; telex 15954; Ambassador: HÖRDUR HELGASON.

India: Vangehusvej 15, 2100 Copenhagen Ø; tel. (01) 18-28-88; telex 15964; Ambassador: RAMESH CHANDRA SHUKLA.

Indonesia: Ørehøj Allé 1, 2900 Hellerup; tel. (01) 62-44-22; telex 16274; Ambassador: SUTADI SUKARYA.

Iran: Grønningen 5, 1270 Copenhagen K; tel. (01) 14-12-38; Ambassador: (vacant).

Ireland: Østbanegade 21, 2100 Copenhagen Ø; tel. (01) 42-32-33; telex 22995; Ambassador: LIAM RIGNEY.

Israel: Lundevangsvej 4, 2900 Hellerup; tel. (01) 62-62-88; telex 27136; Ambassador: AMOS GANOR.

Italy: Gammel Vartov Vej 7, 2900 Hellerup; tel. (01) 62-68-77; telex 27078; Ambassador: ALESSANDRO CORTESE DE BOSIS.

Japan: Oslo Plads 14, 2100 Copenhagen Ø; tel. (01) 26-33-11; telex 27082; Ambassador: MICHIO MIZOGUCHI.

Korea, Democratic People's Republic: Skelvej 2, 2900 Hellerup; tel. (01) 62-50-70; Ambassador: TAK KWAN CHOL.

Korea, Republic: Dronningens Tværgade 8, 1302 Copenhagen K; tel. (01) 14-31-23; Ambassador: MIN-GIL CHUNG.

Lesotho: Østerkildevej 14, 2820 Gentofte; tel. (01) 65-14-42; telex 16687; Ambassador: BISHOP AUSTIN TLELASE.

Libya: Rosenvængets Hovedvej 4, 2100 Copenhagen Ø (People's Bureau); tel. (01) 26-36-11; telex 22652; Chargé d'affaires: El Hadj OMAR EL-HERIK.

Mexico: Gammel Vartov Vej 18, 2900 Hellerup; tel. (01) 20-86-00; telex 27503; Ambassador: SERGIO MOTA MARÍN.

Morocco: Øregårds Allé 19, 2900 Hellerup; tel. (01) 62-45-11; telex 22913; Ambassador: OMAR BELKORA.

Netherlands: Toldbodgade 95, 1253 Copenhagen K; tel. (01) 15-62-93; telex 27093; Ambassador: Jonkheer EDUARD BEELAERTS VAN BLOKLAND.

Norway: Trondhjems Plads 4, 2100 Copenhagen Ø; tel. (01) 38-89-85; telex 27114; Ambassador: OLE ÅLGÅRD.

Pakistan: Valeursvej 17, 2900 Hellerup; tel. (01) 62-11-88; Chargé d'affaires: QAZI HUMAYUN.

Poland: Richelieus Allé 12, 2900 Hellerup; tel. (01) 62-72-44; telex 19264; Ambassador: LUCJAN PIATKOWSKI.

Portugal: Hovedvagtsgade 6, Mezz., 1103 Copenhagen K; tel. (01) 13-13-01; telex 16586; Ambassador: ANTÓNIO CASCAIS.

Romania: Strandagervej 27, 2900 Hellerup; tel. (01) 62-42-04; telex 27017; Ambassador: Mrs CORNELIA FILIPAŞ.

Saudi Arabia: Lille Strandvej 27, 2900 Hellerup; tel. (01) 62-12-00; telex 15931; Ambassador: (vacant).

Spain: Upsalagade 26, 2100 Copenhagen Ø; tel. (01) 42-47-00; telex 27145; Ambassador: MARIANO ÚCELAY DE MONTERO.

Sweden: Skt. Annæ Plads 15A, 1250 Copenhagen K; tel. (01) 14-22-42; telex 22960; Ambassador: ANDERS FERM.

Switzerland: Amaliegade 14, 1256 Copenhagen K; tel. (01) 14-17-96; telex 16239; Ambassador: GAUDENZ VON SALIS.

Thailand: Norgesmindevej 18, 2900 Hellerup; tel. (01) 62-50-10; telex 16216; Ambassador: SATHIT SATHIRATHAYA.

Turkey: Vestagervej 16, 2100 Copenhagen Ø; tel. (01) 20-55-00; telex 27476; Ambassador: ONUR ÖYMEN.

Uganda: Sofievej 15, 2900 Hellerup; tel. (01) 62-05-40; telex 15689; Ambassador: Mrs EDITH GRACE SSEMPALA.

USSR: Kristianiagade 5, 2100 Copenhagen Ø; tel. (01) 42-55-85; Ambassador: BORIS NIKOLAYEVICH PASTUKHOV.

United Kingdom: Kastelsvej 36-40, 2100 Copenhagen Ø; tel. (01) 26-46-00; telex 27106; Ambassador: NIGEL C. R. WILLIAMS.

USA: Dag Hammarskjölds Allé 24, 2100 Copenhagen Ø; tel. (01) 42-31-44; telex 22216; Ambassador: (vacant).

Uruguay: Kastelsvej 15^2, 2100 Copenhagen Ø; tel. (01) 42-79-80; telex 19064; Chargé d'affaires: Dr VILMA VEIDA.

Venezuela: Hammerensgade 3, 2nd Floor, 1267 Copenhagen K; tel. (01) 93-63-11; telex 15309; Ambassador: RAMÓN DELGADO-VALDERRAMA (designate).

Yugoslavia: Svanevænget 36, 2100 Copenhagen Ø; tel. (01) 29-71-61; Ambassador: Mrs ANA JOVANOVIĆ.

Judicial System

In Denmark the judiciary is independent of the Government. Judges are appointed by the Crown on the recommendation of the Minister of Justice and cannot be dismissed except by judicial sentence.

The ordinary courts are divided into three instances, the Lower Courts, the High Courts and the Supreme Court. There is one Lower Court for each of the 84 judicial districts in the country. These courts must have at least one judge trained in law and they hear the majority of minor cases. The two High Courts serve Jutland and the islands respectively. They serve as appeal courts for cases from the lower courts, but are also used to give first hearing to the more important cases. Each case must be heard by at least three judges. The Supreme Court, at which at least five judges must sit, is the court of appeal for cases from the Higher Courts. Usually only one appeal is allowed from either court, but in special instances the Minister of Justice may give leave for a second appeal, to the Supreme Court, from a case which started in a lower court.

There is a special Maritime and Commercial Court in Copenhagen, consisting of a President and two Vice-Presidents with legal training and a number of commercial and nautical assessors; and also a Labour Court, which deals with labour disputes.

An Ombudsman is appointed by Parliament, after each general election, and is concerned with defects in the laws or administrative provisions. He must present an annual report to Parliament.

President of the Supreme Court: P. M. CHRISTENSEN.

President of the East High Court: K. HAULRIG.

President of the West High Court: O. AGERSNAP.

President of the Maritime and Commercial Court: EMIL FRANK POULSEN.

President of the Labour Court: P. HØEG.

Ombudsman: HANS GAMMELTOFT-HANSEN.

Religion

CHRISTIANITY

Det Økumeniske Fællesraad i Danmark (Ecumenical Council of Denmark): Nørregade 11, 1165 Copenhagen K; tel. (01) 15-59-27; f. 1939; seven mem. churches, one observer; Chair. HENRIK CHRISTIANSEN (Lutheran Bishop of Ålborg); Gen. Sec. PETER LODBERG.

The Protestant Churches

Den evangelisk-lutherske Folkekirke i Danmark (Evangelical Lutheran Church of Denmark): Nørregade 11, 1165 Copenhagen K; tel. (01) 13-35-08; telex 16217; the established Church of Denmark, supported by the State; membership in 1985 was 4,684,060 (91% of the population).

Bishop of Copenhagen: OLE BERTELSEN.

Bishop of Helsingør: JOHS JOHANSEN.

Bishop of Roskilde: B. WIBERG.

Bishop of Nykøbing: TH. GRAESHOLT.

Bishop of Odense: V. LIND.

Bishop of Ålborg: HENRIK CHRISTIANSEN.

Bishop of Viborg: GEORG S. GEIL.

Bishop of Århus: H. ERIKSEN.

Bishop of Ribe: H. SKOV.

Bishop of Haderslev: O. LINDEGAARD.

Church of Jesus Christ of Latter-day Saints (Mormons): Informationstjenesten, Annexgårdsvej 37, 2610 Rødovre; tel. (01) 70-90-43; f. (in Denmark) 1850; 4,500 mems.

Det Danske Baptistsamfund (Baptist Union of Denmark): Købnerhus, Lärdalsgade 5.1, 2300 Copenhagen S; tel. (01) 59-07-08; f. 1839; 6,400 mems; Pres. LEIF DAMKIER; Gen. Sec. Rev. OLE JÖRGENSEN.

DENMARK

First Church of Christ Scientist: Nyvej 7, 1851 Frederiksberg C; also in Århus.

German Lutheran Church: Sankt Petri Church, Nørregade, Copenhagen; Hauptpastorat: Larslejsstræde 11, 1451 Copenhagen K; tel. (01) 13-38-34.

Methodist Church: Centralmissionen, Stokhusgade 2, 1317 Copenhagen K; tel. (01) 93-25-96.

Moravian Brethren: The Brethren Community, 6070 Christiansfeld; Pastor HELGE RØNNOW, Lindegade 26, 6070 Christiansfeld; tel. (04) 56-14-20.

Norwegian Lutheran Church: Kong Haakons Kirke, Ved Mønten 9, 2300 Copenhagen S; tel. (01) 57-11-03.

Reformed Church: Reformed Synod of Denmark, Gothersgade 109³, 1123 Copenhagen K; tel. (01) 13-87-53; Rev. ULRICH DUSSE.

Seventh-day Adventists: Adventistsamfundet, Concordiavej 16, 2850 Nærum; tel. (02) 80-56-00.

Society of Friends: Danish Quaker Centre, Vendersgade 29, 1363 Copenhagen K; tel. (01) 11-82-48.

Swedish Lutheran Church: Svenska Gustafskyrkan, Folke Bernadottes Allé, 2100 Copenhagen Ø; tel. (01) 15-54-58; also V. Strandvej 24, 9990 Skagen; tel. (08) 44-23-11.

Unitarians: Unitarernes Hus, Dag Hammarskjölds Allé 30, 2100 Copenhagen Ø; Chair. P. BOVIN; mems: 100 families.

Other denominations active in the country include the Apostolic Church, the Danish Mission Covenant Church and the Salvation Army.

The Roman Catholic Church

Denmark comprises a single diocese, directly responsible to the Holy See. At 31 December 1987 there were an estimated 26,616 adherents in the country. The Bishop participates in the Scandinavian Episcopal Conference (based in Norway).

Bishop of Copenhagen: HANS LUDVIG MARTENSEN, Katolsk Bispekontor, Bredgade 69A, 1260 Copenhagen K; tel. (01) 11-60-80.

Other Christian Churches

Church of England: St Alban's House, Stigårdsvej 6, 2900 Hellerup; f. 1728; Chaplain Rev. DENNIS R. CAPES.

Russian Orthodox Church: Alexander Nevski Church, Bredgade 53, 1260 Copenhagen K.; tel. (01) 13-60-46.

BAHÁ'Í FAITH

Bahá'í: Det Nationale Åndelige Råd, Sofievej 28, 2900 Hellerup; tel. (01) 62-35-18; National Centre for the Bahá'í faith in Denmark.

ISLAM

The Muslim Community: Nusrat Djahan Mosque (and Ahmadiyya Mission), Eriksmunde Allé 2, 2650 Hvidovre, Copenhagen; tel. (01) 75-35-02; telex 16600.

JUDAISM

Jewish Community: The Synagogue, Krystalgade 12, Copenhagen; Mosaisk Trossamfund, Ny Kongensgade 6, 1472 Copenhagen K; tel. (33) 12-88-68; 8,000 mems; Chief Rabbi BENT MELCHIOR.

The Press

Denmark's long press history dates from the first newspaper published in 1666, but it was not until press freedom was introduced by law in 1849 that newspapers began to assume their present importance. The per caput circulation of Danish newspapers is one of the highest in the world. There are over 220 separate newspapers, and over 40 main dailies.

The freedom of the press is embodied in the 1953 Constitution and all censorship laws have been abolished. The legal limits to press comment are wide, legislation on defamation being chiefly concerned to protect the reputation of the individual. The Law of 1938 included provision for a Board of Denials and Corrections to be established to guard the individual's right to require a newspaper to correct factual errors. This Press Law makes editors legally responsible for the contents of a paper with the exception of signed articles for which the author is responsible.

Most newspapers and magazines are privately owned and published by joint concerns, co-operatives or limited liability companies. The main concentration of papers is held by the Berlingske Tidende Group which owns *Berlingske Tidende*, *Weekendavisen*, *B.T.*, the provincial *Jydske Tidende* and *Amtsavisen*, and three weekly magazines. Another company, Politiken A/S, owns several dailies, including *Politiken* and *Ekstra Bladet*, one weekly and a large publishing house. De Bergske Blade owns a group of six Liberal papers.

There is no truly national press. Copenhagen accounts for 16% of the national dailies and about half the total circulation. The provincial press has declined since the last war, but still tends to be more politically orientated than the majority of Copenhagen dailies. The Communist Party's *Land og Folk* is the only paper to be directly owned by a political party, although all papers show a fairly pronounced political leaning. The three Social Democrat papers, headed by Copenhagen's *Aktuelt*, are owned and subsidized by the trade unions.

The major Copenhagen dailies are *Berlingske Tidende*, *Ekstra Bladet*, *B.T.*, *Politiken* and *Aktuelt*. The serious evening paper *Information* and the weekly *Weekendavisen* are also influential. The *Aalborg Stiftstidende*, published at Ålborg, the *Aarhuus Stiftstidende* (Århus), the *Jyllands-Posten*, *Morgenavisen* (Viby), and the *Fyens Stiftstidende* (Odense), are the largest provincial papers.

PRINCIPAL DAILIES

Aabenraa

Jydske Tidende: Storetorv 10, 6200 Aabenraa; tel. (04) 62-62-11; telex 51340; morning; independent; circ. 38,064 weekdays; 53,689 Sundays; Chief Editor ERIK RANDEL; Man. FLEMMING CHRISTENSEN.

Ålborg

Aalborg Stiftstidende: Nytorv 7, 9000 Ålborg; tel. (08) 12-58-00; telex 69747; f. 1767; weekday evenings; Saturday and Sunday mornings; independent Liberal; Publisher and Chief Editor ERLING BRÖNDUM; approx. circ. weekdays 73,964, Sundays 100,496.

Århus

Aarhuus Stiftstidende: Kannikegade 14, Århus; tel. (06) 12-40-00; telex 64321; f. 1794; evening; independent Liberal; Editors AAGE HOLM-PEDERSEN, AAGE LUNDGAARD; circ. 70,862 weekdays, 89,098 Sundays.

Copenhagen

Berlingske Tidende: Pilestræde 34, 1147 Copenhagen K; tel. (01) 15-75-75; telex 27094; f. 1749; morning; independent Conservative; Chief Editor HANS DAM; circ. weekdays 128,815, Sundays 165,341.

Børsen: Møntergade 19, 1116 Copenhagen K; tel. (33) 32-01-02; telex 22903; f. 1896; morning; independent; business news; Chief Editor JAN CORTZEN; circ. 43,041.

B.T.: Kr. Bernikowsgade 6, 1147 Copenhagen K; tel. (01) 14-12-34; f. 1916; morning; independent; Chief Editor PETER DALL; circ. weekdays 202,750, Sundays 171,679.

Ekstra Bladet: Rådhuspladsen 37, 1585 Copenhagen V; tel. (01) 11-85-11; telex 16885; f. 1904; evening; Liberal; Editor-in-Chief SV. O. GADE; Man. Dir E. SONDAL; circ. weekdays 229,509, Sundays 175,960.

Erhvervs-Bladet: Vesterbrogade 12, 1620 Copenhagen V; tel. (01) 21-36-36; telex 19890; circ. 104,386.

Det Fri Aktuelt: Rådhuspladsen 45-47, 1595 Copenhagen V; tel. (01) 32-40-01; telex 19785; f. 1871; morning; Social Democratic; Editors JØRGEN FLINDT PEDERSEN, ERIK STEPHENSEN; Dir LUDVIG BRAMSEN; circ. 66,661 weekdays, 79,484 Sundays.

Information: Store Kongensgade 40, POB 188, 1006 Copenhagen K; tel. (01) 14-14-26; telex 22658; f. (underground during occupation) 1943, legally 1945; morning; independent; Chief Editor PETER WIVEL; circ. 31,084.

Kristeligt Dagblad: Fanøgade 15, 2100 Copenhagen Ø; tel. (01) 27-12-35; f. 1896; morning; independent; Editors GUNNAR RYTGAARD, JENS RAVN OLESEN; Dir IB NORDLAND; circ. 15,922.

Politiken: Politikens Hus, Rådhuspladsen 37, 1585 Copenhagen V; tel. (01) 11-85-11; telex 16885; f. 1884; morning; Liberal; Editors HERBERT PUNDIK, AGNER AHM, JØRGEN GRUNNET; Man. Dir E. SONDAL; circ. weekdays 152,215, Sundays 186,391.

Esbjerg

Vestkysten: Banegårdspladsen, 6700 Esbjerg; tel. (05) 12-45-00; telex 54123; f. 1917; evening; Liberal; Editors THYGE MADSEN, EGON HANSEN; circ. 55,765.

Fredericia

Fredericia Dagblad: Gothersgade 37, 7000 Fredericia; tel. (05) 92-26-00; evening; independent; Editor MØGENS SØRENSEN; Man. GUNNAR CHRISTIANSEN; circ. 10,629.

Herning

Herning Folkeblad: Østergade 25, 7400 Herning; tel. (07) 12-37-00; f. 1869; evening; Liberal; Chief Editor GORM ALBRECHTSEN; circ. 17,222.

Hillerød

De Bergske Blade: Milnersvej 44, 3400 Hillerød; tel. (02) 26-27-00; morning; circ. 109,230.

DENMARK

Frederiksborg Amts Avis: Milnersvej 44-46, 3400 Hillerød; tel. (02) 26-31-00; f. 1874; morning; Liberal; Editor SEJR CLAUSEN; circ. weekdays 34,341, Sundays 45,583.

Hjørring
Vendsyssel Tidende: Frederikshavnsvej 79–81, 9800 Hjørring; tel. (08) 92-17-00; f. 1872; evening; Liberal; Editor MOGENS LORENTSEN; circ. weekdays 26,707, Sundays 41,702.

Holbæk
Holbæk Amts Venstreblad: Ahlgade 1C, 4300 Holbæk; tel. (03) 43-20-48; telex 44148; f. 1905; evening; Radical Liberal; Editor ALFRED HANSEN; circ. 22,519.

Holstebro
Dagbladet Holstebro-Struer-Herning: Lægårdvej 86, 7500 Holstebro; tel. (07) 42-17-22; evening; Liberal independent; Editor ERIK MOELLER; circ. 14,082.

Horsens
Horsens Folkeblad: Søndergade 47, 8700 Horsens; tel. (05) 62-45-00; telex 61626; f. 1866; evening; Liberal; Editor MOGENS AHRENKIEL; circ. 24,265.

Kalundborg
Kalundborg Folkeblad: Skibbrogade 40–42, 4400 Kalundborg; tel. (03) 51-24-60; telex 44351; f. 1917; evening; Liberal Democrat; Editor JØRGEN JENSEN; circ. 10,779.

Kolding
Kolding Folkeblad Sydylland: Jernbanegade 33–35, 6000 Kolding; tel. (05) 52-20-00; telex 51362; f. 1871; evening; Liberal; Editor (vacant); circ. 19,813.

Naskov
Ny Dag: Højevej 15, 4900 Naskov; tel. (03) 92-14-00; telex 47551; evening; Social Democrat; Editor JØRGEN MATHIESEN; circ. 11,378.

Næstved
Næstved Tidende: Ringstedgade 13, 4700 Næstved; tel. (03) 72-45-11; telex 46243; f. 1866; Liberal; Editor POUL KRISTENSEN; circ. 23,730.

Nykøbing
Lolland-Falsters Folketidende: Tværgade 14, 4800 Nykøbing F; tel. (03) 85-20-66; f. 1873; evening; Liberal; Editor PALLE BRANDT; circ. 24,464.

Odense
Fyens Stiftstidende: Jernbanegade 1, 5000 Odense C; tel. (09) 11-11-11; telex 59858; f. 1772; evening; independent; Editors BENT A. KOCH, EGON TØTTRUP; circ. weekdays 72,335, Sundays 109,901.

Randers
Amtsavisen: Nørregade 7, 8900 Randers; tel. (06) 42-75-11; telex 65173; f. 1810; evening; independent; Chief Editor OLE C. JØRGENSEN; circ. 32,373.

Ringkøbing
Ringkøbing Amts Dagblad: St Blichersvej 5, 6950 Ringkøbing; tel. (07) 32-07-22; evening; Editor KRISTIAN SAND; circ. 15,636.

Ringsted
Dagbladet: Søgade 4–12, 4100 Ringsted; tel. (03) 61-25-00; telex 45111; evening; Liberal; Editor TORBEN DALBY LARSEN; circ. 33,552.

Rønne
Bornholms Tidende: Nørregade 11-13, 3700 Rønne; tel. (03) 95-14-00; evening; Liberal; Chief Editor THOMAS E. JENSEN; circ. 11,018.

Silkeborg
Midtjyllands Avis: Vestergade 30, 8600 Silkeborg; tel. (06) 82-13-00; f. 1857; daily except Sundays; Chief Editor VIGGO SØRENSEN; circ. 22,667.

Skive
Skive Folkeblad: Slotsgade 3, 7800 Skive; tel. (07) 52-34-11; f. 1880; Left Socialist; Editor HANS LARSEN; circ. 14,581.

Slagelse
Sjællands Tidende: Korsgade 4, 4200 Slagelse; tel. (03) 52-37-00; telex 45372; f. 1815; evening; Liberal; for western part of Zealand; Editor POVEL UTZON BUCH; circ. 21,946.

Svendborg
Fyns Amts Avis: Sct Nicolaigade 3, 5700 Svendborg; tel. (09) 21-46-21; telex 58118; f. 1863; Liberal; Editor UFFE RIIS SØRENSEN; circ. 24,587.

Thisted
Thisted Dagblad: Jernbanegade 15-17, 7700 Thisted; tel. (07) 92-33-22; Liberal independent; Editor HANS PETER KRAGH; circ. 11,857.

Vejle
Vejle Amts Folkeblad: Kirketorvet 10-16, 7100 Vejle; tel. (05) 82-80-00; f. 1865; evening; Liberal; Editor VAGN NYGAARD; circ. 27,301.

Viborg
Viborg Stifts Folkeblad: Sct Mathiasgade 7, 8800 Viborg; tel. (06) 62-68-00; f. 1877; Liberal Democrat; evening; also published: *Viborg Nyt*, *Skive Bladet* (weekly); *Aktuel Jordbrug* (monthly); Editor PER SUNESEN; circ. 13,501.

Viby
Jyllands-Posten, Morgenavisen: Grøndalsvej, 8260 Viby J; tel. (06) 14-66-77; telex 68747; independent; Man. Editors A. NØRGAARD LARSEN, N. THOSTRUP, T. TOLSTRUP; circ. weekdays 128,601, Sundays 215,231.

OTHER NEWSPAPERS

Den Blå Avis (East edition): Meinungsgade 6-8, 2200 Copenhagen N; tel. (01) 37-72-91; 2 a week; circ. 73,000.

Den Blå Avis (West edition): Frederiksgade 45, 8100 Århus C; tel. (06) 19-14-11; Thursday; circ. 55,500.

Weekendavisen Berlingske Aften: Gammel Mønt 1, 1147 Copenhagen K; tel. (01) 15-75-75; telex 27143; f. 1749; independent Conservative; Friday; Chief Editor TØGER SEIDENFADEN; circ. 25,497.

POPULAR PERIODICALS

Alt for Damerne: Vognmagergade 11, 1148 Copenhagen K; tel. (01) 15-19-25; telex 16705; f. 1946; weekly; women's magazine; Editor EBBA EILERTZEN; circ. 118,754.

Anders And & Co: Vognmagergade 11, 1148 Copenhagen K; tel. (01) 15-19-25; telex 21143; weekly; children's magazine; Editor NANCY DEJGAARD; circ. 155,822.

Arte-Nyt: Hvidkildevej 64, 2400 Copenhagen NV; tel. (01) 10-16-22; 3 a year; arts; circ. 39,959.

Basserne: Krogshøjvej 32, 2880 Bagsværd; tel. (02) 44-32-33; telex 22426; 26 a year; children and youth; circ. 89,000.

Det Bedste fra Reader's Digest A/S: Jagtvej 169B, 2100 Copenhagen Ø; tel. (01) 18-12-13; telex 27357; monthly; Danish *Reader's Digest*; Editor OLE KNUDSEN; circ. 138,000.

Bilen Motor og Sport: Nørre Farimagsgade 49, 1375 Copenhagen K; tel. (01) 12-66-12; telex 15712; monthly; cars, motor sport; Editor FLEMMING HASLUND; circ. 64,000.

Billed-Bladet: Vesterbrogade 16, 1506 Copenhagen V; tel. (01) 23-16-11; telex 27094; f. 1938; weekly; family picture magazine; Editor ANDERS THISTED; circ. 232,400.

Bo Bedre: Strandboulevarden 130, 2100 Copenhagen K; tel. (01) 29-55-00; telex 15712; monthly; homes and gardens; Editor-in-Chief JAN SCHIWE NIELSEN; circ. 118,184.

Bo & Fritid: Munkehatten 17, 5220 Odense SØ; tel. (09) 93-00-80; 4 a year; leisure; circ. 203,021.

Camping: Gammel Kongevej 74, 1850 Copenhagen; tel. (01) 21-06-04; telex 22611; monthly; circ. 50,000.

Eva: Stranboulevarden 130, 2100 Copenhagen C; tel. (01) 29-55-00; telex 15712; 8 a year; fashion, beauty; Editor KAREN LYAGER HORVE; circ. 36,504.

Familie Journalen: Vigerslev Allé 18, 2500 Valby, Copenhagen; tel. (01) 30-33-33; f. 1877; weekly; Editor ANKER SVENDSEN-TUNE; circ. 360,500.

Femina: Vigerslev Allé 18, 2500 Valby, Copenhagen; tel. (01) 30-33-33; f. 1873; weekly; Editor JUTTA LARSEN; circ. 109,471.

Gør det selv: Strandboulevarden 130, 2100 Copenhagen Ø; tel. (01) 29-55-00; telex 15712; monthly; do-it-yourself; circ. 78,000.

Helse—Familiens Lægeblad: Classensgade 36, 2100 Copenhagen Ø; tel. (01) 26-79-00; 8 a year; family health; circ. 420,000.

Hendes Verden: Vognmagergade 11, 1148 Copenhagen K; tel. (01) 15-19-25; telex 16705; f. 1937; weekly; for women; Editor EVA RAVN; circ. 115,835.

Hjemmet (The Home): Vognmagergade 11, 1148 Copenhagen K; tel. (01) 15-19-25; telex 16705; weekly; Chief Editor KAJ DORPH-PETERSEN; circ. 266,835.

DENMARK

Ide-nyt: Gl. Klausdalsbrovej 482, 2730 Herlev; tel. (02) 94-60-40; telex 35148; 4 a year; free magazine; homes and gardens; circ. 2,300,000.

IN: Vigerslev Allé 18, 2500 Valby; women's magazine; tel. (01) 30-33-33; Editor CAMILLA LINDEMANN.

Landbrugsmagasinet: Vester Farimagsgade 6, 1606 Copenhagen V; tel. (01) 12-99-50; weekly; farming; circ. 30,588.

Landsbladet: Vester Farimagsgade 6, 1606 Copenhagen V; tel. (01) 11-22-22; farmer's weekly; Man. Dir NIKO WIEGMAN; circ. 88,661.

Mit Livs Novelle: Krogshøjvej 32, 2880 Bagsværd; tel. (02) 44-32-33; young women's magazine; fortnightly; circ. 35,493.

Motor: Blegdamsvej 124, 1200 Copenhagen Ø; tel. (01) 38-21-12; telex 15857; fortnightly; cars and motor-tourism; circ. 190,000.

Praxis: Gl. Bjert 22, 6092 Varmark; tel. (05) 57-27-00; 10 a year; health; circ. 70,000.

Samvirke: Roskildevej 65, 2620 Albertslund; tel. (02) 64-88-11; telex 33311; f. 1928; consumer monthly; Publr and Chief Editor AA. BÜCHERT; circ. 667,000.

Se og Hør: Vigerslev Allé 18, 2500 Valby, Copenhagen; tel. (01) 30-33-33; telex 22390; f. 1940; news and TV; Editor MOGENS E. PEDERSEN; circ. 298,000.

Sofus' Lillebror: Krogshøjvej 32, 2880 Bagsværd; tel. (02) 98-52-27; monthly; children and youth; circ. 54,000.

Søndags-B.T.: Vesterbrogade 16, POB 424, 1505 Copenhagen V; tel. (01) 23-16-11; f. 1921; weekly; family magazine; Editor JØRGEN BJERRE; circ. 124,000.

TV Bladet: Gl. Mønt 1, 1147 Copenhagen K; tel. (01) 15-20-55; telex 27094; weekly; television and radio programmes; circ. 287,730.

Ude og Hjemme: Vigerslev Allé 18, 2500 Valby, Copenhagen; tel. (01) 30-33-33; f. 1926; family weekly; Editor JØRN BAUENMAND; circ. 227,000.

Ugen Rundt: Vognmagergade 11, 1148 Copenhagen K; tel. (01) 15-19-25; TV and radio; Editor LAILA MOHR.

Ugens Rapport: Skt. Annæ Plads 8, 1250 Copenhagen K; tel. (01) 13-60-60; f. 1971; men's weekly; Editor-in-chief HANS-ULRIK BUCHWALD; circ. 71,717.

Vi på Landet: Købmagergade 58, 1150 Copenhagen K; tel. (01) 91-12-24; 4 a year; farming life; circ. 278,000.

Vi Unge: Hellerupvej 66, 2900 Hellerup; tel. (01) 62-32-22; telex 622446; f. 1958; teenagers' monthly; Editor CARL W. BAERENTZEN; circ. 32,000.

SPECIALIST PERIODICALS

ABF-Nyt: Istedgade 1, 1650 Copenhagen V; tel. (01) 24-75-02; 6 a year; Editor JAN HANSEN; circ. 24,350.

Aktuel Elektronik: Skelbækgade 4, 1717 Copenhagen V; tel. (01) 21-68-01; 37 a year; computing and information technology; circ. 22,016.

Alt om Data: St. Kongensgade 72, 1264 Copenhagen K; tel. (01) 91-28-33; f. 1983; monthly; Chief Editor KLAUS NORDFELD; circ. 22,400.

Amt- og Kommunebladet: Tordenskjoldsgade 27, 1055 Copenhagen K; tel. (01) 14-00-10; telex 21317; monthly; public works and administration; circ. 20,653.

Arbejde og Daginstitution: Pædagogisk Medhjælper Forbund, St Kongensgade 79, 1264 Copenhagen K; tel. (01) 11-03-43; 41 a year; teaching; circ. 26,224.

Arbejdsgiveren: Vester Voldgade 113, 1503 Copenhagen V; tel. (01) 93-40-00; telex 16464; 20 a year; management; Editor SVEND BIE; circ. 50,963.

Arbejdslederen: Vermlandsgade 67, 2300 Copenhagen S; tel. (01) 57-56-22; 15 a year; circ. 66,888.

Automatik: Egebjergvej 13, POB 80, 4500 Nykøbing sj; tel. (03) 41-23-10; engineering; monthly; circ. 37,500.

Bankstanden: Esplanaden 8, 1014 Copenhagen K; tel. (01) 15-83-11; 20 a year; bank employees; circ. 36,000.

Beboerbladet: Studiestræde 50, 1554 Copenhagen V; tel. (01) 11-11-22; 4 a year; home-renting; circ. 420,721.

Bil Snak: Park Allé 355, 2605 Brøndby; tel. (02) 63-11-22; 4 a year; cars; circ. 180,000.

Byg-tek: Hovedvejen 182, 2600 Glostrup; tel. (02) 45-10-63; 11 a year; building and construction; circ. 30,200.

Chef Nyt: Sydvestvej 49, 2600 Glostrup; tel. (02) 63-02-22; 25 a year; managers; circ. 72,682.

Civilforsvar: Datavej 18, 3460 Birkerød; tel. (02) 82-00-66; 6 a year; defence; circ. 20,000.

Computerworld: Torvegade 52, 1400 Copenhagen K; tel. (01) 95-56-95; telex 31566; f. 1981; weekly; computing; Chief Officers JENS MICHAEL DAMM, LARS OLSEN; circ. 20,094.

Cope: Dybensgade 21, 1071 Copenhagen K; tourist magazine; circ. 50,000.

Cyklister: Dansk Cyklist Forbund, Kjeld Langes Gade 14, 1367 Copenhagen K; tel. (01) 14-42-12; f. 1905; 6 a year; organ of Danish Cyclists' Assen; circ. 22,000.

Danmark Idag/Denmark Today/Thema Dänemark: Scandinavian News Information Aps, Hellerupvej 76, 2900 Hellerup; tel. (01) 62-70-1; 2 a year; news for business, exports, etc.; circ. 35,000.

Dansk Jagt: Einer-Jensens Vænge 1, 2000 Frederiksberg; tel. (01) 33-29-11; monthly; hunting; circ. 50,000.

Effektivt Landbrug: Skelbækgade 4, 1717 Copenhagen V; tel. (01) 21-68-01; 23 a year; farming; circ. 38,667.

Eleven: Ryesgade 105 st., 2100 Copenhagen Ø; tel. (01) 42-39-01; 4 a year; organ of secondary school students' union; circ. 90,000.

Folkeskolen: Vandkunsten 12, 1467 Copenhagen K; tel. (01) 11-82-55; weekly; teaching; Editor THORKILD THEJSEN; circ. 80,250.

Forbrugsforeningsbladet: Knabrostræde 12, 1210 Copenhagen K; tel. (01) 13-88-22; monthly; for civil servants and doctors; circ. 30,000.

Gymnasie-eleven: Pilevænget 3, 5620 Glamsbjerg; tel. (09) 72-35-22; 6 a year; for secondary school pupils; circ. 24,600.

Havebladet: Frederikssundsvej 308B, 2700 Brønshøj; tel. (01) 28-87-50; 4 a year; gardening; circ. 44,000.

Haven: Åby Bækgardsvej 6, 8230 Åbyhøj; tel. (06) 15-56-88; monthly; horticulture and gardening; circ. 89,445.

High Fidelity: St. Kongensgade 72, 1264 Copenhagen K; tel. (01) 11-25-47; f. 1968; 11 a year; Chief Editor MICHAEL MADSEN; circ. 22,500.

Hjemmeværnsbladet: Kastellet 82, 2100 Copenhagen Ø; tel. (01) 93-32-10; 10 a year; organ of the Home Guard; circ. 86,000.

Hunden: Parkvej 1, Jersie Strand, 2680 Solrød Strand; tel. (03) 14-15-66; 10 a year; organ of the kennel club; circ. 31,000.

Ingeniøren: Skelbækgade 4, 1717 Copenhagen V; tel. (01) 21-68-01; weekly engineers' magazine; circ. 60,912.

Jagt og Fiskeri: Jørgensvej 4, 5620 Assens; tel. (64) 71-40-31; monthly; hunting, fishing, sport; Editor VILLY ANDERSEN; circ. 60,000.

Jern- og Maskin Industrien: Tordenskjoldsgade 27, 1055 Copenhagen K; tel. (01) 14-00-10; 42 a year; iron and metallic industries; circ. 24,617.

Jyllands Ringens program: Vilvordevej 102, 2920 Charlottenlund; tel. (01) 64-46-92; 5 a year; cars and motor cycles; circ. 270,000.

Kamera: Hellerupvej 66, 2900 Hellerup; tel. (01) 62-32-22; f. 1960; 2 a year; photography; Editor FINN NESGAARD; circ. 55,000.

Kontor/Bladet: Sydvestvej 49, 2600 Glostrup; tel. (02) 63-02-22; monthly; management in trade and industry; circ. 85,596.

Kvinder i Danmark: Virringvej 11, Virring, 8900 Randers; tel. (06) 48-02-17; 6 a year; home management; circ. 25,000.

LLO-bladet: Vesterbrogade 29, 1620 Copenhagen V; tel. (01) 23-81-33; 5 a year; for apprentices; circ. 40,000.

Metal: Nyropsgade 38.2, 1602 Copenhagen V; tel. (01) 12-82-12; 22 a year; iron and metal industries; circ. 144,000.

ny elektronik: St Kongensgade 72, 1264 Copenhagen K; tel. (01) 11-25-47; f. 1977; 11 a year; electronics; Chief Editor JANN KALF LARSEN; circ. 21,500.

MC-Revyen: Nørre Farimagsgade 49, 1375 Copenhagen K; tel. (01) 12-66-12; annually; motorcycling and mopeds; circ. 24,500; Editor FLEMMING HASLUND.

Produktion: Vester Farimagsgade 3, 1606 Copenhagen V; tel. (01) 12-14-19; 8 a year; farming; circ. 140,000.

Samtid: Nordkysvej, 8961 Allingåbro; tel. (06) 49-51-53; 17 a year; for school pupils aged 14–18; circ. 25,000.

Spejd/Broen: Broen Ekstra Lundsgade 6, 2100 Copenhagen Ø; tel. (01) 26-12-11; 8 a year; organ of the Scout Movement; circ. 12,500.

Sundhedsmagasinet Praxis: Gl. Bjert 22, 6091 Bjert; tel. (05) 57-27-00; 8 a year; health; circ. 70,000.

Sygeplejersken: Vimmelskaftet 38, 1008 Copenhagen K; tel. (01) 15-15-55; 50 a year; nursing; circ. 62,232.

Tidernes Tegn: Børstenbindervej 4, 5230 Odense M; tel. (09) 15-88-43; telex 155743; every 2 months; religion; Editor AAGE ANDERSEN; circ. 17,000.

Tidsskrift for Sukkersyge—Diabetes: Filosofgangen 24, 5000 Odense C; tel. (09) 12-90-06; f. 1940; 5 a year; diabetes; Gen.-Sec. OSCAR JENSEN; circ. 27,000.

Uafhængigt Computer Commodore Magasin: St Kongensgade 72, 1264 Copenhagen K; tel. (01) 91-28-33; f. 1985; 11 a year;

DENMARK

also publishes Swedish edition; computing; Chief Editor IVAN SØLVERSON, circ. 23,000.

Ugeskrift for Læger: Trondhjemsgade 9, 2100 Copenhagen Ø; tel. (01) 38-55-00; weekly; medical; circ. 20,300.

NEWS AGENCY

Ritzaus Bureau I/S: Mikkel Bryggersgade 3, 1460 Copenhagen K; tel. (01) 12-33-44; telex 22362; f. 1866; general, financial and commercial news; works in conjuction with Reuters, Agence France-Presse, Deutsche Presse-Agentur and European national agencies; owned by all Danish newspapers; Chair. of Board of Dirs AAGE DELEURAN; Gen. Man. and Editor-in-Chief PER WINTHER.

Foreign Bureaux

Agence France-Presse (AFP): Mikkel Bryggersgade 5, 1460 Copenhagen K; tel. (01) 13-23-31; telex 19584; Bureau Chief SLIM ALLAGUI.

Agencia EFE (Spain): c/o Intl Press Centre, Snaregade 14, 1205 Copenhagen K; Correspondent MARÍA CAMINO SÁNCHEZ.

Agentstvo Pechati Novosti (APN) (USSR): Vestagervej 7, 2100 Copenhagen Ø; tel. (01) 20-04-44; telex 15618; Chief Editor S. SEREBRIAKOV.

Agenzia Nazionale Stampa Associata (ANSA) (Italy): Hvalsoevej 6, 2700 Brønshøj; tel. (01) 80-04-13; telex 19315; Agent VITTORIO SPADANUDA.

Allgemeiner Deutscher Nachrichtendienst (ADN) (German Democratic Republic): 2660 Bröndbystrand, Kisumparken 65 st. th., Copenhagen; Bureau Chief HERBERT HANSCH.

Associated Press (AP) (USA): Kristen Bernikowsgade 4, 2nd floor, 1105 Copenhagen K; tel. (01) 11-15-04; telex 22381; Bureau Chief LARRY GERBER.

Deutsche Presse-Agentur (dpa) (Federal Republic of Germany): Mikkel Bryggersgade 5, 1460 Copenhagen K; tel. (01) 14-22-19; Chief Correspondent THOMAS BORCHERT.

Reuters (UK): Badstuestræde 18, 1209 Copenhagen K; tel. (01) 93-21-42; telex 16846.

Telegrafnoye Agentstvo Sovetskovo Soyuza (TASS) (USSR): Uraniavej 9B, 1, 1878 Copenhagen; tel. (01) 24-04-03; telex 19304; Correspondent YEVGENI KISELYEV.

United Press International (UPI) (USA): Store Strandstræde 8, Copenhagen; Bureau Chief BØRGE MORS.

PRESS ASSOCIATIONS

Danske Dagblades Forening (Danish Newspapers Association): The House of the Press, Skindergade 7, 1159 Copenhagen K; tel. (01) 12-21-15; telex 27183; comprises managers and editors-in-chief of all newspapers; general spokesman for the Danish press.

Illustrated Press Publishers' Association: Copenhagen; publishers of magazines.

Københavnske Dagblades Samraad (Copenhagen Newspaper Publishers' Association): c/o Det Berlingske Hus, Pilestræde 34, 1147 Copenhagen K; Chair. CHR. W. REVES.

Publishers

Forlaget ålökke A/S: 26 Tulinpanparken, 8700 Horsens; tel. (05) 65-77-84; educational, audio-visual and other study aids; Dir BERTIL TOFT HANSEN.

Akademisk Forlag AmbA: Store Kannikestræde 6-8, POB 54, 1002 Copenhagen K; tel. (01) 11-98-26; f. 1962; history, philosophy, psychology, engineering, general science, linguistics, university textbooks, educational materials; Man. Dir PER HOLM RASMUSSEN; Chief Editor NIELS PERSSON.

Alrune Forlaget: Snertinge Markvej 57, 4760 Vordingborg; tel. (03) 78-25-73; children's books.

Apostrof Forlaget: Berggreensgade 24, 2100 Copenhagen Ø; tel. (01) 20-84-20; telex 16600; Dirs MIA TIMM, OLE THESTRUP.

Arnkrone Publishers Ltd: Fuglebækvej 4, 2770 Kastrup; tel. (01) 50-70-00; f. 1941; popular medicine, art and cultural history; children's fiction and non-fiction, psychotherapy, contemporary fiction and humour; Man. Dir J. JUUL RASMUSSEN.

Aschehoug Dansk Forlag A/S: Klosterrisvej 7, 2100 Copenhagen Ø; tel. (01) 29-44-22; telex 16987; f. 1914; school and textbooks; Man. Dir ERIK IPSEN.

    J. Fr. Clausens Forlag: popular specialist literature.

    Grafisk Forlag: textbooks, handbooks, children's books.

    H. Hagerups Forlag: school and textbooks.

    H. Hirschsprungs Forlag: textbooks.

Directory

Peter Asschenfeldt's Stjernbøger A/S: Gerdasgade 37, 2500 Valby; tel. (01) 44-11-20; telex 19387; bestseller paperbacks; Dir BENNY FREDERIKSEN.

Bibelselskabets Forlag og Vajsenhusets Forlag: Frederiksborggade 50, 1360 Copenhagen K; tel. (01) 12-78-35; religious works; Man. Dir NIELS JÖRGEN CAPPELÖRN.

Bibliotekscentralens Forlag: 7–11 Tempovej, 2750 Ballerup; tel. (02) 97-40-00; telex 35730; f. 1939; bibliographies, indexes and library literature; Man. Dir ASGER HANSEN.

Thomas Bloms Forlag A/S: Rudolph Berghsgade 18, 2100 Copenhagen Ø; tel. (01) 29-17-49; non-fiction, children's books; Owners CONNIE and THOMAS BLOM.

Bierman og Bierman A/S: Vestergade 120, 7200 Grindsted; tel. (05) 32-02-88; f. 1968; fiction, non-fiction, children's books, general culture, magazines; Man. Dirs B. LORENTZEN, T. SELMER-PETERSEN.

Bogans Forlag: Kastaniebakken 8, POB 39, 3540 Lynge; tel. (02) 18-80-55; f. 1974; general paperbacks, popular science and occult; Owner EVAN BOGAN.

Bonniers Specialmagasiner A/S: Strandboulevarden 130, 2100 Copenhagen Ø; tel. (01) 29-55-00; telex 15712; f. 1960 as Fogtdals Blade A/S; handbooks, part-works and magazines; Man. Dir STEEN HAU.

Borberg Forlagsbureau: Nørregade 43, 1165 Copenhagen K; tel. (01) 32-88-48; non-fiction, computer software packaging; Man. Dir HENRIK BORBERG.

Borgens Forlag A/S: Valbygårdsvej 33, 2500 Valby; tel. (01) 46-21-00; f. 1948; fiction, non-fiction, handicrafts, religion, children's, computer books, large-print books and textbooks; Man. Dir JARL BORGEN; Dirs ERIK CRILLESEN, NIELS BORGEN.

Börnegudstjeneste-Forlaget: Korskærvej 25, 7000 Fredericia; tel. 05-93-44-55; religion, children's books; Man. Dir CURT GRAVEN NIELSEN.

Børsen Forlaget A/S: Møntergade 19, 1116 Copenhagen K; tel. (33) 32-01-02; telex 22903; business information (daily news, magazines, newsletters and books), electronic publishing; Man. Dir PREBEN SCHACK.

Branner og Korchs Forlag A/S: H.C. Örstedsvej 7B, 1879 Frederiksberg C; tel. (01) 22-45-11; f. 1949; handbooks, fiction, juveniles; Dir TORBEN SCHUR.

Carit Andersens Forlag A/S: Malmögade 3, 2100 Copenhagen Ø; tel. (01) 26-06-21; telex 16121; illustrated books, non-fiction, fiction, science fiction; Dir ERIK ALBRECHTSEN.

Centrum, Jyllands-Posten Forlag: Gunnar Clausensvej 66, 8260 Viby J; tel. (06) 29-69-77; fiction, handbooks, children's, school books; Dir SVEN BEDSTED.

Dansk Historisk Håndbogsforlag A/S: Klintevej 25, 2800 Lyngby; tel. (02) 80-72-00; f. 1976; genealogy, heraldry, culture and local history, facsimile editions, microfilms produced by subsidiary co; Owners and Man. Dirs RITA JENSEN, HENNING JENSEN.

Dansklærerforeningens Forlag: Nørre Søgade 49c, 1370 Copenhagen K; tel. (01) 15-04-99; f. 1885; school books, Danish literature, educational slides and videos; Man. Dir ASGER UHD JEPSEN.

Delta Forlag A/S: Kroghsgade 5, 2100 Copenhagen Ø; tel. (01) 26-38-01; fiction, non-fiction, juveniles, educational, feminist; Dir JÖRGEN MARTENS.

Christian Ejlers' Forlag A/S: Brolæggerstræde 4, POB 2228, 1018 Copenhagen K; tel. (01) 12-21-14; f. 1967; general, art, social and political science; Dir CHRISTIAN EJLERS.

Chr. Erichsens Forlag A/S: Gersonsvej 33, 2900 Hellerup; tel. (01) 61-15-33; f. 1902; fiction, quality paperbacks.

Forlaget Europa: Nyhavn 40, 1051 Copenhagen K; tel. (01) 15-62-73; telex 19280; school and university texts, tourist and restaurant guides; Dir LARS KVISTSKOV LARSEN.

FADL's Forlag A/S (Foreningen af danske Lægestuderendes Forlag): Prinsesse Charlottesgade 29, 2000 Copenhagen N; tel. (31) 35-62-87; f. 1962; medicine, biology; Man. Dir HANS JESPERSEN.

Forlaget for Faglitteratur A/S: Vandkunsten 6, 1467 Copenhagen K; tel. (01) 13-79-00; medicine, technology.

Forlaget Forum A/S: Snaregade 4, 1205 Copenhagen K; tel. (01) 14-77-14; f. 1940; history, fiction, quality paperbacks and children's books; Dir CLAUS BRØNDSTED.

Forlaget Fremad af 1979 A/S: Rentemestervej 45-47, 2400 Copenhagen NV; tel. (01) 33-40-40; f. 1912; fiction, non-fiction, popular science, textbooks, juveniles, reissues; Man. Dir PETER JOHANSEN.

FSRS Forlag: Kronprinsessegade 8, 1306 Copenhagen K; tel. (33) 93-91-91; telex 22491; textbooks, legal, economic, financial, business; Man. Dir VIBEKE CHRISTIANSEN.

J. Frimodts Forlag: Korskærvej 25, 7000 Fredericia; tel. (05) 93-44-55; religion, fiction, devotional; Man. Dir CURT GRAVEN NIELSEN.

DENMARK

G.E.C. Gads Forlag: Vimmelskaftet 32, 1161 Copenhagen K; tel. (01) 15-05-58; university and school books, legal and reference; Man. AXEL KIELLAND.

Gjellerup og Gad Forlagsaktieselskab: Vimmelskaftet 32, 1161 Copenhagen K; tel. (01) 15-05-58; textbooks, school books, audio-visual aids; Mans GRETHE BRYNER, KARSTEN BLAUERT.

Forlaget GMT: Meilgård, 8585 Glæsborg; tel. (06) 31-75-11; f. 1971; history, philosophy, politics, social sciences, general fiction, textbooks; Publrs HANS JØRN CHRISTENSEN, ERIK BJØRN OLSEN.

Grevas Forlag: Auningvej 33, Sdr. Kastrup 8544 Mørke; tel. (06) 16-83-87; f. 1966; novels, debate; Dir LUISE HEMMER PIHL.

Gyldendalske Boghandel-Nordisk Forlag A/S: Klareboderne 3, 1001 Copenhagen K; tel. (01) 11-07-75; telex 15887; f. 1770; fiction, non-fiction, reference books, paperbacks, children's books, textbooks; Dirs PER HEDEMAN, KURT FROMBERG, KLAUS RIFBJERG, EGON SCHMIDT.

P. Haase & Søns Forlag A/S: Lövstræde 8, 1152 Copenhagen K; tel. (01) 11-59-99; f. 1877; Man. Dir N. J. HAASE; educational books, audio-visual aids, children's books, fiction, non-fiction.

Forlaget Hamlet A/S: 25 Linnésgade, 1361 Copenhagen K; tel. (01) 13-16-50; handbooks, art books.

Hekla Forlag: Store Kongensgade 61A and B, POB 9011, 1022 Copenhagen K; tel. (01) 91-19-33; f. 1979; general trade fiction and non-fiction; Owner HELGA W. LINDHARDT.

Hernovs' Forlag: Bredgade 14-16, 1260 Copenhagen K; tel. (01) 15-62-84; f. 1941; fiction, memoirs, children's; Owner JOHS. G. HERNOV; Dir PER LESLIE HOLST.

Forlag Hønsetryk: Rosenørns Allé 18, 1970 Copenhagen V; tel. (01) 54-81-51; Owner Gjellerup Forlags-Aktieselskab.

Høst & Søns Forlag: Dronningens Tværgade 5, POB 9019, 1022 Copenhagen K; tel. (01) 15-30-31; f. 1836; crafts and hobbies, languages, books on Denmark, children's books; Dir ERIK C. LINDGREN.

Forlaget Hovedland: POB 1953, Elsdyrvej 4, 8270 Højberg; tel. (06) 27-44-70; Owner STEEN PIPER.

Finn Jacobsens Forlag: Gothersgade 56, 1123 Copenhagen K; tel. (01) 14-36-32; non-fiction, science, cultural history; Owner FINN JACOBSEN.

Forlaget Kaleidoscope A/S: Njalsgade 19-21, 2300 Copenhagen S; tel. (01) 95-83-33; educational, audio-visual, fiction for youth; Man. Dir JENS BENDTSEN.

Forlaget Per Kofod A/S: Krystalgade 7, 1172 Copenhagen K; tel. (01) 15-03-47.

Forlaget Komma A/S: Frederiksborggade 26, Israels Plads, POB 2163, 1016 Copenhagen K; tel. (01) 14-55-83; telex 19149; f. 1977; reference, sport, maritime, cookery, instructional; Man. Dir LISBETH ANDERSEN SKOV.

Morten A. Korch's Forlag: Aurehøjvej 2, 2900 Hellerup; tel. (01) 62-08-59; children's books; Owner MORTEN KORCH.

Krak: Nytorv 17, 1450 Copenhagen K; tel. (01) 12-03-08; telex 16652; f. 1770; reference works, maps and yearbooks; Dir IB LE ROY TOPHOLM.

Lademann Ltd, Publishers: Linnésgade 25, POB 2163, 1016 Copenhagen K; tel. (01) 13-16-50; telex 19149; f. 1954; novels, history, text books, reference books, encyclopaedias, paperbacks; Man. Dir JØRGEN LADEMANN.

Lindhardt og Ringhof, Forlag A/S, og Jespersen og Pio's Forlag: Studiestræde 14, 1455 Copenhagen K; tel. (01) 11-19-55; f. 1971; general fiction and non-fiction, paperbacks; Owners OTTO B. LINDHARDT, GERT RINGHOF.

Lohses Forlag: Korskærvej 25, 7000 Fredericia; tel. (05) 93-44-55; f. 1868; religion, memoirs, travel; Man. Dir CURT GRAVEN NIELSEN.

Mallings Forlag A/S: Gammel Kongevej 3-5, 1610 Copenhagen V; tel. (01) 24-35-55; telex 15817; f. 1975; Dir HANNAH MALLING.

Martins Forlag: Thorsbjerggård L1 Fjellenstrupvej 25, 3250 Gilleleje; tel. (02) 30-11-00; telex 19203; fiction, non-fiction, juveniles; Man. Dir JENS ERIK HALKIER.

Medicinsk Forlag A/S: Tranevej 2, 3650 Ölstykke; tel. (02) 17-65-92; medical and scientific books; Man. Dir ANNI LINDELÖV.

Forlaget Melgaard A/S: Storegade 5, 4171 Glumsø; tel. 03-64-63-30; travel, general fiction, non-fiction; Owner SØREN MELGAARD.

Modtryk-Socialistisk forlag AmbA: Anholtsgade 4, 8000 Århus C; tel. (06) 12-79-12; telex 4556785; f. 1972; politics, children's and school books, fiction, thrillers and poetry; Man. Dir PREBEN BACH.

Münksgaard International Publishers Ltd: POB 2148, Nørre Søgade 35, 1016 Copenhagen K; tel. (01) 12-70-30; telex 19431; f. 1917; agents to Royal Danish Academy, and various learned societies; specializing in medical and natural science, international scientific journals, humanities, school books and computer software; Man. Dir JOACHIM MALLING.

Forlaget Natur og Harmoni: Lövstræde 8, 1152 Copenhagen K; tel. (01) 11-59-99; alternative health books; Owner P. Haase & Søns Forlag A/S.

Nordiske Landes Bogforlag; Mariendalsvej 33, 2000 Frederiksberg; tel. (01) 34-80-76; illustrated books, travel, fiction books about Greenland; Owner JØRGEN FISKER.

Nyt Nordisk Forlag-Arnold Busck A/S: Koebmagergade 49, 1150 Copenhagen K; tel. (01) 11-11-03; f. 1896; textbooks, school books, non-fiction; Dir OLE ARNOLD BUSCK.

Det Schønbergske Forlag A/S: Landemærket 5, 1119 Copenhagen K; tel. (01) 11-30-66; f. 1857; fiction, travel, history, biography, paperbacks, textbooks; Mans OLE STENDER, OLE THESTRUP.

Forlaget Optima A/S: Møllevænget 16, 7800 Skive; tel. (07) 53-55-80; education; Dir INGRID CHRISTIANSEN.

Jørgen Paludans Forlag A/S: Fiolstræde 16, 1171 Copenhagen K; tel. (01) 15-06-75; ext. 38; language teaching, natural sciences, psychology, history, sociology, politics, economics, reference; Man. Dir JØRGEN PALUDAN.

Politikens Forlag A/S: Vestergade 26, 1456 Copenhagen K; tel. (01) 11-21-22; f. 1947; dictionaries, reference books, handbooks, yearbooks, collected works and maps; Man. Dir JOHANNES RAVN.

Rasmus Navers Forlag: Lövstræde 8, 1152 Copenhagen K; tel. (01) 11-59-99; humour, poetry, fiction; Owner P. Haase & Søns Forlag A/S.

Hans Reitzel Publishers Ltd: Dronningens Tværgade 5, 1302 Copenhagen K; tel. (01) 14-04-51; f. 1949; reference and textbooks, psychology, sociology, Hans Christian Andersen; Man. Dir ERIK C. LINDGREN; Editors PETER THIELST, OLE GAMMELTOFT.

C.A. Reitzels Booksellers and Publishers Ltd: Nørregade 20, 1165 Copenhagen K; tel. (01) 12-24-00; f. 1819; Owner and Man. Dir SVEND OLUFSEN.

Rhodos, International Science and Art Publishers: Niels Brocks Gård, Strandgade 36, 1401 Copenhagen K; tel. (01) 54-30-20; telex 31502; f. 1959; science, art, literature, politics, professional, criticism; Man. Dir NIELS BLAEDEL.

Rosenkilde og Baggers Forlag: POB 2184, 1017 Copenhagen K; tel. (01) 15-70-44; f. 1941; manuals, cultural history, facsimiles; Owner HANS R. BAGGER.

Forlaget Rosinante: POB 5, Kirkevej 15, 2920 Charlottenlund; tel. (01) 63-39-99; f. 1984; general trade books, non-fiction, fiction; Owner and Man. Dir MERETE RIES.

Samlerens Forlag A/S: Snaregade 4, 1205 Copenhagen K; tel. (01) 13-10-23; telex 15887; general fiction, contemporary history and politics, psychology, biographies; Man. Dir JOHANNES RIIS.

A/S J. H. Schultz Forlag: Møntergade 21 (1), 1116 Copenhagen K; tel. (01) 12-11-95; f. 1661; printers, publishers, booksellers; printers to the Danish Government and the Copenhagen University; subsidiary: Schultz Medical Information; Publishing Man. POUL BAY.

Semic Forlagene A/S: Krogshøjvej 32, 2880 Bagsværd; tel. (02) 44-32-33.

Forlaget Sesam A/S: Frederiksborggade 26A, 1360 Copenhagen K; tel. (01) 15-37-00; telex 19149; history, educational, children's; Dir GEORG VEJEN.

Skarv A/S: Kongevejen 45B, 2840 Holte; tel. (02) 42-47-45; children's, educational, general; Owner and Man. Dir SÖREN KOUSTRUP.

A/S Skattekartoteket: Informationskontor, Palægade 4, 1261 Copenhagen K; tel. (01) 11-78-74; books on taxation; Man. Dir P. TAARNHØJ.

Sommer & Sörensen Forlag A/S: Mynstersvej 19, 1827 Frederiksberg C; tel. (01) 23-25-55; Dirs AAGE BÖRGLUM SÖRENSEN, ERIK SOMMER.

Forlaget Spektrum A/S: Snaregade 4, 1205 Copenhagen K; tel. (01) 14-77-14; general literature, paperbacks; Dir CLAUS BRØNSTED.

Strandbergs Forlag A/S: Vedbæk Strandvej 475, 2950 Vedbæk; tel. (02) 89-47-60; cultural history, computer science, travel, humour; Owner HANS JØRGEN STRANDBERG.

Strubes Forlag A/S: POB 827, 2100 Copenhagen Ø; tel. (01) 42-07-16; psychic, occult, philosophy, art, naval; Man. Dir POUL STRUBE.

Teaterforlaget Drama: Ladegårdsskov 14, 6300 Gråsten; tel. (74) 65-11-41; theatrical literature, drama; Man. Dir OVE KIRKETERP.

Teknisk Forlag A/S: Skelbækgade 4, 1717 Copenhagen V; tel. (01) 21-68-01; telex 16368; f. 1948; technical books and periodicals; Man. Dir PETER MÜLLER.

Teknologisk Institus Forlag: POB 141, 2630 Taastrup; tel. (02) 99-66-11; technical, crafts, industries.

DENMARK

Tellerup Forlagsaktieselskab: POB 109, 2900 Hellerup; tel. (01) 62-37-00; f. 1972; children's, young adults fiction, science fiction, fiction; Dir K. TELLERUP.

Thaning & Appels Forlag A/S: H.C. Ørstedsvej 7B, 1879 Frederiksberg C; tel. (01) 22-45-11; f. 1866; fiction, art, popular sciences; Dir AKSEL PEDERSEN.

Forlaget Tiderne Skifter A/S: Skt. Peder Stræde 28B, 1453 Copenhagen K; tel. (01) 13-65-03; fiction, sexual and cultural politics, psychology, criticism, arts, children's books; Man. Dir CLAUS CLAUSEN.

Forlaget Tommeliden: Odensevej 92, Herrested, 5853 Ørbæk; tel. (09) 98-23-74; fiction, school books, handbooks, juveniles; Man. Dir JES TRØST JØRGENSEN.

Unitas Forlag, De Unges Forlag: Valby Langgade 19, 2500 Valby; tel. (01) 16-60-33; religion, fiction, education; Man. Dir LORENS HEDELUND.

Vandrer mod Lysets Forlag A/S: Ellevadsvej 3, 2920 Charlottenlund; tel. (01) 63-22-26; religion, science, philosophy, ethics; Dir BØRGE BRØNNUM.

Forlaget Vindrose A/S: Nybrogade 24, 1203 Copenhagen K; tel. (01) 13-50-00; f. 1980; general trade, fiction and non-fiction; Dir ERIK VAGN JENSEN.

Vitafakta A/S: Kohavevej 28, 2950 Vedbæk; tel. (02) 89-21-03; health books, school books; Dir INGER MARIE HAUT.

Wangels Forlag A/S: Gerdasgade 37, 2500 Valby; tel. (01) 44-11-20; telex 19387; f. 1946; fiction, book club; Gen. Man. BENNY FREDERIKSEN.

Edition Wilhelm Hansen A/S: 9-11 Gothersgade, 1123 Copenhagen K; tel. (01) 11-78-88; telex 19912; educational books, books on music; Owners HANNE WILHELM HANSEN, LONE WILHELM HANSEN, TINE BIRGER CHRISTENSEN.

Winthers Forlag A/S: Gerdasgade 37, 2500 Valby; tel. (01) 44-11-20; telex 19387; f. 1945; general fiction, paperbacks; Man. Dir JOHS. VILSØE.

Forlaget Wøldike K/S: Stægers Allé 13, 2000 Frederiksberg; tel. (01) 86-39-54; fiction and non-fiction; Publr OVE MØLBECK.

Government Publishing House

Statens Informationstjeneste (State Information Service): Bredgade 20, POB 1103, 1009 Copenhagen K; tel. (01) 92-92-00; acts as press, public relations and information body for the government in all media; publishes Official Gazette, etc.

PUBLISHERS' ASSOCIATION

Den danske Forlæggerforening: Købmagergade 11, 1150 Copenhagen K; tel. (01) 15-66-88; f. 1837; 78 mems; Chair. OLE A. BUSCK; Dir ERIK V. KRUSTRUP.

Radio and Television

In 1986 there were 2,061,000 current licences for radio receivers and 1,953,000 licences for television receivers.

Radio Denmark: TV-Byen, 2860 Søborg; tel. (01) 67-12-33; telex 22695; Dir-Gen. HANS JØRGEN JENSEN; Dir of Radio Programmes HANS JØRGEN SKOV; Dir of Television Programmes HENRIK ANTONSEN.

TV 2: Odense; began broadcasts in October 1988; Denmark's first national commercial TV station; only a third of its finances come from licence fees, the rest from advertising.

Finance

The first Danish commercial bank was founded in 1846. In January 1975 restrictions on savings banks were lifted, giving commercial and savings banks equal rights and status. Several foreign banks have representative offices in Copenhagen, and in January 1975 restrictions on the establishment of full branches of foreign banks were removed. In October 1988 all remaining restrictions on capital movements were ended. In 1988 there were about 225 banks, considerably fewer than 20 years earlier. All banks are under government supervision, and public representation is obligatory on all bank supervisory boards.

BANKING

(cap. = capital; p.u. = paid up; res = reserves; dep. = deposits; m. = million; brs = branches; amounts in kroner)

Supervisory Authority

Tilsynet med Banker og Sparekasser (Government Supervision of Banks and Savings Banks): Nørre Voldgade 94, 1358 Copenhagen K; tel. (01) 15-56-46; telex 19457; agency of the Ministry of Industry; Dir EIGIL MOELGAARD.

Central Bank

Danmarks Nationalbank: Havnegade 5, 1093 Copenhagen K; tel. (01) 14-14-11; telex 27051; f. 1818; self-governing; sole right of issue; administers foreign exchange rates and regulations; regulates govt credit policy; capital fund 50m.; gold in coin and bullion 4,858m.; notes in circ. 21,093m. (1987); brs in Århus and Odense; Govs E. HOFFMEYER, O. THOMASEN, R. MIKKELSEN.

Commercial Banks

Århus Discontobank A/S: Søndergade 9, 8100 Århus C; tel. (06) 12-01-88; telex 64518; f. 1894; cap. 25m., res 51.7m., dep. 443m. (1985); Gen. Man. PREBEN ANDERSEN; 7 brs.

Aktivbanken A/S: POB 2350, Ladegaardsvej 3, 7100 Vejle; tel. (05) 85-71-00; telex 61113; f. 1971; cap. 150m., res 658m., dep. 4,478m. (1987); Gen. Man E. K. LARSEN; 61 brs.

Amagerbanken A/S: Amagerbrogade 25, 2300 Copenhagen S; tel. (01) 95-60-90; telex 31262; f. 1903; cap. 125m., res 571m., dep. 8,379m. (Dec. 1987); Chief Gen. Man. KNUD CHRISTENSEN; 28 brs.

Andelsbanken Danebank: Staunings Plads 1-3, 1643 Copenhagen V; tel. (01) 14-51-14; telex 27086; f. 1925; cap. (p.u.) 730.1m., dep. 24,690m. (1987); Chief Gen. Mans Mrs BODIL NYBOE ANDERSEN, A. C. JACOBSEN, H. LUNDAGER, A. KASTBJERG; 248 brs.

Arbejdernes Landsbank A/S: Vesterbrogade 5, 1502 Copenhagen V; tel. (01) 14-88-77; telex 15633; f. 1919; cap. (p.u.) 300m. (1987); Man. Dirs S. NIBELIUS, J. CHRISTENSEN, E. MIDTGAARD, P. E. LETH, E. CASTELLA; 57 brs.

Banken for Årup og Omegn A/S: Bredgade 95, 5560 Årup; tel. (09) 43-12-34; telex 59675; f. 1911; cap. 20m., res 61.6m., dep. 315.6m. (Dec. 1987); Chair. N. H. GULDAGER; Gen. Man. P. E. JENSEN; 4 brs.

Bikuben: Silkegade 8, 1113 Copenhagen K; tel. 12-01-33; telex 19832; f. 1877; cap. 1,293.6m., res 1,903.5m., dep. 28,639.1m. (Dec. 1986); Gen. Mans HANS ERIK BALLE, KNUD BRANDENBORG, BOERGE MUNK EBBESEN, PEDER ELKJAER; 294 brs.

Bonusbanken A/S: Dalgasgade 30, 7400 Herning; tel. (07) 12-11-14; telex 62314; f. 1958; total assets 400m. (1988); Gen. Man. I. ØSTERBY HANSEN; 1 br.

Bornholmerbanken A/S: St. Torv 15, 3700 Rønne, Bornholm; tel. (03) 95-00-61; telex 48117; f. 1966; cap. 22.5m., res 78.3m., dep. 482.7m. (Dec. 1987); Man. SØREN ANDERSEN; 8 brs.

Copenhagen Handelsbank A/S: Holmens Kanal 2, 1091 Copenhagen K; tel. (01) 12-86-00; telex 19177; f. 1873; cap. and res 5,994m., dep. 47,696m. (Dec 1986); Chair. B. GOMARD; Chief Exec. BENDT HANSEN; 350 brs.

Den Danske Bank af 1871 A/S: Holmens Kanal 12, 1092 Copenhagen K; tel. (01) 15-65-00; telex 27000; f. 1871; cap. 1,822.5m., res 7,187.1m., dep. 122,014.9m. (Dec. 1987); Chair. POUL J. SVANHOLM; Pres. TAGE ANDERSEN; 284 brs.

Djurslands Bank: 5 Torvet, 8500 Grenå; tel. (06) 32-15-55; telex 63488; f. 1965; cap. and res 146m., dep. 1,109m. (1986); Gen. Mans F. JUHL KRISTENSEN, H. STEENBERG; 32 brs.

Egnsbank Fyn A/S: Vestergade 33, POB 60, 5100 Odense C; tel. (09) 11-46-11; telex 59876; f. 1902; cap. 18m., res 67.6m., dep. 461.3m. (Dec. 1987); Chair LEIF LADBYE-HANSEN; 12 brs.

Egnsbank Nord A/S: Jernbanegade 4-6, POB 701, 9900 Frederikshavn; tel. (08) 42-04-33; telex 67102; f. 1970; cap. 281m., dep. 1,792m. (Dec. 1987); Gen. Mans B. WAMMEN, JENS OLE JENSEN, OLE KRISTENSEN; 28 brs.

Esbjerg Bank A/S: Kongensgade 70, 6700 Esbjerg; tel. (05) 12-82-00; telex 54161; f. 1917; total assets 1,037m. (June 1988); Man. B. HAABER CHRISTIANSEN; 6 brs.

Forstædernes Bank A/S: Malervangen 1, 2600 Glostrup; tel. (02) 96-17-20; telex 33261; f. 1902; total assets 3,600m. (Sept. 1988); Chair. V. B. CHRISTENSEN; Gen. Man. F. MARCUSSEN; 16 brs.

Haandværker-, Handels- og Landbrugsbanken A/S: Jernbanegade 9, 4700 Næstved; tel. (53) 72-45-55; telex 46255; f. 1901; cap. and res 84m., dep. 443m. (1987); Man. OLE MEYER; 8 brs.

Hafnia Erhversbank A/S (Hafnia Merchant Bank Ltd): Borgergade 24, 1347 Copenhagen K; tel. (01) 11-27-33; telex 22396; f. 1940 as Fællesbanken for Danmarks Sparekasser; a subsidiary of Hafnia Invest since Dec. 1987; cap. 401.1m., dep. 1,579m. (1987); Dirs HANS LINDEGAARD, HANS JENSEN, GRETHE KRISTENSEN; 9 brs.

A/S H & L Banken (Handels- og Landbrugsbanken i Thisted): Jernbanegade 7A, 7700 Thisted; tel. (07) 92-21-11; telex 66699; f. 1915; res 32.8m., dep. 521.2m. (1987); Gen. Man NIELS JENSEN; 5 brs.

Hellerup Bank A/S: Strandvejen 159, 2900 Hellerup; tel. (01) 61-12-00; f. 1922; a subsidiary of Andelsbanken Danebank since January 1988.

DENMARK

Himmerlandsbanken A/S: Adelgade 31, 9500 Hobro; tel. (08) 52-10-00; telex 65864; f. 1892; cap. 37m., res 91m., dep. 1,132m. (1987); Man. BENT HANSEN; 13 brs.

Holstebro Bank A/S: Torvet 1, 7500 Holstebro; tel. (07) 41-21-44; telex 66433; f. 1871; cap. 190.8m., dep. 1,207.6m. (1987); Man. N. K. NIELSEN; 9 brs.

Horsens Landbobank A/S: Jessensgade 6–8, 8700 Horsens; tel. (05) 62-42-22; telex 61680; f. 1925; cap. 15m., res. 74.3m., dep. 685.3m. (Dec. 1986); Gen. Mans SØREN PETER HANSEN, OLE POULSEN; 19 brs.

Jyske Bank: Vestergade 8-16, 8600 Silkeborg; tel. (06) 82-11-22; telex 63231; f. 1855, amalgamated in 1967; dep. 21,960.7m. (Dec. 1986); Chief Exec. POUL NORUP; 139 brs.

Landbobanken i Skive, Salling Bank A/S: Frederiksgade 6, 7800 Skive; tel. (07) 52-33-66; telex 66726; f. 1926; cap. 18m., dep. 877m. (1987); Chair. LARS E. ANDERSEN; Man. P. E. BASTRUP; 12 brs.

Langelands Bank A/S: Øsrtedsgade 6, 5900 Rudkøbing; tel. (09) 51-10-22; telex 50594; f. 1872; cap. and res 64m., dep. 275.7m. (1986); Man. TORBEN RASMUSSEN; 17 brs.

Lokalbanken i Hjørring A/S: Østergade 4, POB 39, 9800 Hjørring; tel. (08) 92-12-33; telex 67881; f. 1929; cap. 12.5m., res 33.8m., dep. 497.1m. (Dec. 1987); Pres. JØRGEN SKOVEN; Chair. THORKIL BECK; 2 brs.

Lollands Bank A/S: Nybrogade 3, 4900 Nakskov, Lolland; tel. (03) 92-11-33; telex 47542; f. 1907; cap. 18.3m., res 54.7m., dep. 348.3m. (1987); Man. MOGENS NIELSEN; 6 brs.

Midtbank A/S: Østergade 2, 7400 Herning; tel. (07) 12-48-00; telex 62142; f. 1965; cap. and res 271m., dep. 3,652m. (Dec. 1987); Gen. Mans KJELD FREDERIKSEN, JØRN ASTRUP HANSEN; 39 brs.

Morsø Bank A/S: Algade, 7900 Nykøbing M.; tel. (07) 72-14-00; telex 60714; f. 1876; cap. 21m., res 52m., dep. 637m. (July 1988); Man. Dir H. J. CHRISTENSEN; 11 brs.

Næstved Diskontobank A/S (Diskonto Banken): Axeltorv 4, 4700 Næstved; tel. (03) 72-15-00; telex 46227; f. 1871; cap. and res 181.7m., dep. 1,218.5m. (Dec. 1987); Gen. Man. A. HOVE ANDREASEN; 9 brs.

Nordvestbank A/S: Torvet 4-5, 7620 Lemvig; tel. (07) 82-07-77; telex 66536; f. 1874; cap. and res 182m., dep. 688m. (1987); Chair. P. GRANKÆR; Gen. Man. J. HOLT; 9 brs.

Nørresundby Bank A/S: Torvet 4, 9400 Nørresundby; tel. (08) 17-33-33; telex 69776; f. 1898; cap. and res 307m., dep. 1,598m. (1987); Man. H. WORMSLEV; 15 brs.

Østjydsk Bank AS: Østergade 6–8, 9550 Mariager; tel. 08-54-14-44; telex 65872; f. 1897; cap. 12m., res. 7.1m., dep. 357.9m. (Dec. 1986); Chair. Mrs LIZZIE ANDERSEN; Gen. Man. POUL BERTELSEN.

Privatbanken A/S: Torvegade 2, POB 1000, 2300 Copenhagen S; tel. (01) 11-11-11; telex 27196; f. 1857; mem. of Scandinavian Banking Partners group; cap. and res 5,183m., dep. 81,227m. (June 1988); Chair. of Board HUGO SCHRØDER; Man. Dirs S. RASBORG, L. JOHANSEN, E. LUNDERSKOV, B. PEDERSEN; 213 brs.

Provinsbanken A/S: Kannikegade 4-6, 8100 Århus C; tel. (06) 12-25-22; telex 64403; regional offices in Odense, Copenhagen and Ålborg; f. 1967 by merger; cap. 920m., res 2,293m., dep. 53,411m. (June 1988); Gen. Mans HANS-VERNER LARSEN, B. DALSGAARD, MOGENS GANTRIIS, JENS OTTO VEILE; 220 brs.

Ringkjøbing Bank: Torvet 2, POB 19, 6950 Rinkjøbing; tel. (07) 32-03-22; telex 62442; f. 1872; cap. and res 186m., dep. 918m. (Dec. 1987); Man. Dir MOGENS SVENSSON; 8 brs.

Ringkjøbing Landbobank A/S: Torvet 1, 6950 Ringkjøbing; tel. (07) 32-11-66; telex 60385; f. 1886; cap. and res 249m., dep. 1,195m. (1987); Chair. HENRY KJELDSEN; Gen. Man. BENT NAUR KRISTENSEN; 12 brs.

Roskilde Bank A/S: Algade 14, POB 39, 4000 Roskilde; f. 1884; tel. (02) 35-17-00; telex 43122; cap. and res 286m., dep. 1,900m. (1988); Man. N. VALENTIN HANSEN; 17 brs.

SJL-Banken A/S: Jarmers Plads 7, 1551 Copenhagen V; tel. (01) 13-11-88; telex 16858; f. 1983; cap. 75m., res 37.9m., dep. 1,296.4m. (Dec. 1986); Chair. JENS LUNDØE POULSEN; Gen. Man. OLE VAGNER.

Skælskør Bank A/S: Algade 18, 4230 Skælskør; tel. (03) 59-60-70; telex 40139; f. 1876; total assets 663m. (Aug. 1988); Man. P. W. OLSEN; 6 brs.

Sparekassen SDS: 8 Kongens Nytorv, 1050 Copenhagen K; tel. (01) 13-13-39; telex 15745; f. 1973; mem. of Norden Banking Group; cap. and res 4,812m., dep. 39,775m. (1987); Chair. L. RINGAARD; 347 brs.

Sydbank A/S: Kirkeplads 2, POB 169, 6200 Åbenrå; tel. (04) 62-12-22; telex 52114; f. 1970; cap. and res 1,083m., dep. 7,007m., total assets 19,480m. (1987); Gen. Mans C. ANDERSEN, N. JAKOBSEN, S. OLSEN, J. ANDERSEN; 68 brs.

Varde Bank A/S: Kongensgade 62-64, 6701 Esbjerg; tel. (05) 12-68-11; telex 54138; f. 1872; cap. 150m., res 714m., dep. 4,988m. (1987); Chair. JENS M. KRISTENSEN; Man. Dirs C. K. HANSEN, ALEX HOLM JENSEN, KAJ THOMSEN; 50 brs.

Vestfyns Bank A/S: Østergade 42, 5610 Assens; tel. (09) 71-21-74; f. 1896; cap. 15m., res 55.8m., dep. 561.8m. (1988); Chair. GEORG GUNDERSEN; Gen. Man./Man. Dir N. J. FORD; 3 brs.

Vestjysk Bank (Hostelbro Landmandsbank): Vestergade 1, 7500 Holstebro; tel. (07) 42-26-11; telex 66412; f. 1887; total assets 1,649m. (Aug. 1985); Mans FRANK HOMAA, GUNNAR V. MOLLER; 3 brs.

Bankers' Organizations

Den Danske Bankforening (Danish Bankers' Association): Bankernes Hus, Amaliegade 7, 1256 Copenhagen K; tel. (01) 12-02-00; telex 16102; f. 1950; 78 mem. banks; Man. Dir KARSTEN HILLESTRØM.

Danmarks Sparekasseforening (Danish Savings Banks Association): Købmagergade 62, POB 2189, 1017 Copenhagen K: tel. (01) 15-18-11; telex 15965; Chair. SVEND JAKOBSEN.

STOCK EXCHANGE

Københavns Fondsbørs (Copenhagen Stock Exchange): Nikolaj Plads 2, 1067 Copenhagen K; tel. (01) 93-33-66; telex 16496; f. 1861; Pres. BENT MEBUS; Chair. CHRISTEN SØVENSEN.

INSURANCE
State Insurance Company

Statsanstalten for Livsforsikring: Kampmannsgade 4, 1645 Copenhagen V; tel. (01) 15-15-15; telex 15283; f. 1842; Gen. Dir ERIK BONNERUP.

Principal Private Companies

Alm. Brand af 1792 gs: Lyngby Hovedgade 4, POB 1792, 2800 Lyngby; tel. (02) 87-33-22; telex 37512; f. 1792; subsidiaries: workers' liabilities, life, international; Chief Gen. Man. BENT KNIE-ANDERSEN.

Baltica Holding A/S: Bredgade 40, 1299 Copenhagen K; tel. (01) 32-56-22; telex 16322; f. 1985; Chief Gen Mans PETER CHRISTOFFERSEN, JØRGEN HAAGEN HANSEN.

Baltica Forsikring A/S: Bredgade 40, 1299 Copenhagen K; tel. (01) 12-24-36; telex 16322; f. 1915 by merger; all classes; subsidiaries: pensions, workers' liabilities, life; Gen. Mans STEEN HEMMINGSEN, JØRGEN SØLTOFT, HOLGER FOGED, MICHAEL PRAM RASMUSSEN.

Forsikringsselskabet Kompas A/S: Raadhuspladsen 14, 1583 Copenhagen V; tel. 01-15-06-42; telex 16375; Gen. Man. JØRGEN DAMM.

Max Levig & Co Eft. A/S: Frederiksborggade 34, 1360 Copenhagen K; tel. 01-14-67-00; telex 27519; Gen. Man. ERNST KAAS WILHJELM.

Forsikringsselskabet Codan A/S: Codanhus, Gl. Kongevej 60, Frederiksberg C; tel. (01) 21-21-21; telex 15469; f. 1915; all classes except life; subsidiaries: workers' liability, life; Gen. Man. PETER ZOBEL.

Hafnia Invest A/S: Holbergsgade 3, 1010 Copenhagen K; tel. (01) 32-45-11; telex 16193; f. 1984; subsidiaries: all classes of insurance and reinsurance; Chair. E. J. B. CHRISTENSEN; Chief Gen. Man. PER VILLUM HANSEN.

A/S Det Kjøbenhavnske Reassurance-Compagni: Amaliegade 39, POB 2093, 1013 Copenhagen K; tel. (01) 14-30-63; telex 19617; f. 1915; reinsurance; Gen. Mans JENS TARP, PETER JERVING.

Købstædernes almindelige Brandforsikring: Grønningen 1, 1270 Copenhagen K; tel. (01) 14-37-48; f. 1761; fire; Chair. INGVARDT PEDERSEN; Gen. Man. ALF TORP-PEDERSEN.

Det kongelige octroierede almindelige Brandassurance-Co. A/S (The Royal Chartered General Fire Insurance Co. Ltd): Hojbro Plads 10, 1248 Copenhagen K; tel. (01) 14-15-16; telex 16016; f. 1798; all branches; subsidiaries: workers' liability, life; Gen. Man. JENS VISSING.

Nordisk Reinsurance Company A/S: Groenningen 25, 1270 Copenhagen K; tel. (01) 14-13-67; telex 15367; Gen. Man. KAJ AHLMAN.

PFA Pension: Marina Park, Sundkrogsgade 4, 2100 Copenhagen Ø; tel. (01) 20-77-11; telex 16183; f. 1917; life; Gen. Mans ANDRE LUBLIN, A. KÜHLE.

Top-Danmark A/S: Borupvang 4, 2750 Ballerup; tel. (02) 65-33-11; telex 35107; f. 1985; all classes, with subsidiaries; Man. Dir HENNING BIRCH.

Tryg Forsikring gs: Forsikringshuset, Parallelvej, POB 300, 2800 Lyngby; tel. (02) 87-88-11; telex 37449; f. 1973 by merger; all classes, with subsidiaries; Chief Gen. Man. STEEN RODE.

DENMARK

Insurance Association

Assurandør-Societetet: Amaliegade 10, 1256 Copenhagen K; tel. (01) 13-75-55; telex 12208; Chair. BENT MØLLER HANSEN; Dir STEEN LETH JEPPESEN; 123 mems.

Trade and Industry

ADVISORY BODIES

Det Økonomiske Råd (Economic Council): Kampmannsgade 1, IV, 1604 Copenhagen V; tel. (01) 13-51-28; f. 1962, under the Economic Co-ordination Act, to watch national economic development and help to co-ordinate the actions of economic interest groups; 27 members representing both sides of industry, the government and independent economic experts; Co-Chair. Prof. ARNE LARSEN, Prof. PEDER J. PEDERSEN, Prof. C. VASTRUP; Sec.-Gen. J. SØNDERGAARD.

Industrirådets Industriregister (Federation of Danish Industries' Register of Industries): H. C. Andersens Blvd 18, 1596 Copenhagen V; tel. (01) 15-22-33; telex 12217.

Landsforeningen Dansk Arbejde (National Association for Danish Enterprise): Telegrafvej 5, 2750 Ballerup; tel. 02-68-16-22.

CHAMBERS OF COMMERCE

Danish National Committee of International Chamber of Commerce: Børsen, 1217 Copenhagen K; Chair. KNUD OLESEN; Sec.-Gen. H. SEJER-PETERSEN.

Det Danske Handelskammer (Danish Chamber of Commerce): Børsen, 1217 Copenhagen K; tel. (01) 91-23-23; telex 19520; f. 1742; approx. 12,000 mems.; Man. Dir H. SEJER-PETERSEN; Pres. KLAVS OLSEN.

EMPLOYERS' ORGANIZATIONS

Brancheforeningen af Farmaceutiske Industrivirksomheder i Danmark (Danish Pharmaceuticals Industry Association): Dir JØRGEN REUMERT, c/o A/S Rosco, Tåstrupgårdsvej 30, 2630 Tastrup; tel. (02) 99-33-77.

Bryggeriforeningen (Danish Brewers' Association): Frederiksberggade 11, 1459 Copenhagen K; f. 1899; Chair. Poul J. Svanholm; Dir POUL ANTONSEN; 15 mems.

Danmarks Textiltekniske Forening (Textile Technical Society): Fredericiavej 99, 7100 Vejle; f. 1942; Pres. AAGE JESPERSEN; Vice-Pres. MOGENS NISSEN; 500 mems.

Dansk Arbejdsgiverforening (Danish Employers' Confederation): Vester Voldgade 113, 1503 Copenhagen V; tel. (01) 93-40-00; telex 16464; f. 1896; Chair. POUL HEDEGAARD; Dir-Gen. HANS SKOV CHRISTENSEN; 23,747 mems.

Danske Husmandsforeninger (Family Farmers' Association): Landbrugsmagasinet, Vester Farimagsgade 6, 1606 Copenhagen V; tel. (01) 12-99-50; f. 1906; Chair. CHR. SØRENSEN; Sec.-Gen. KURT LÆNKHOLM; 30,000 mems.

De danske Mejeriers Fællesorganisation (Danish Dairy Board): Frederiks Allé 22, 8000 Århus; f. 1912; Chair. THOMAS JØRGENSEN; Sec. A. TIRSGAARD; 100 mems.

Dansk Pelsdyravlerforening (DPF) (Danish Fur Breeders' Association): Copenhagen; co-operative of 5,000 mems.

Fællesforeningen for Danmarks Brugsforeninger (Co-op of Denmark): Roskildevej 65, 2620 Albertslund; f. 1896; Chair. BJARNE MØGELHØJ; Chief Exec. Mem BERT J. LE FÈVRE; 975,000 mems.

Foreningen af danske Cementfabrikker (Association of Cement Manufacturers): N. Voldgade 34, Copenhagen; f. 1898; Chair. POUL SKOVGAARD; Sec. PER LAURENTS; 4 mems.

Foreningen af Fabrikanter i Jernindustrien i Provinserne (Manufacturers' Federation of the Provincial Iron Industry): N. Voldgade 34, Copenhagen; tel. (01) 12-22-78; telex 16068; f. 1895; Chair. VAGN-AAGE JENSEN; Sec. GLENN SØGAARD; 435 mems.

Håndværksrådet (Federation of Crafts and Smaller Industries): Amaliegade 15, 1256 Copenhagen K; tel. (01) 12-36-76; telex 16600; f. 1879; comprises about 450 asscns with 57,000 mems; Chair. KLAUS BONDE LARSEN; Man. LAUE TRABERG SMIDT.

Industrirådet (Federation of Danish Industries): H. C. Andersens Blvd 18, 1596 Copenhagen V; tel. (01) 15-22-33; telex 12217; f. 1910; Pres. OTTO CHRISTENSEN; Dir OVE MUNCH; 2,400 mems.

Jernindustrielle Arbejdsgivere i København (Copenhagen Metal Industry Employers' Federation): Nørre Voldgade 34, 1358 Copenhagen K; Chair. P. WERNER HANSEN; Sec. H. ENGELHARDT; 475 mems.

Det kongelige danske Landhusholdningsselskab (The Royal Agricultural Society of Denmark): Rolighedsvej 26, 1958 Frederiksberg C; tel. (01) 35-02-27; f. 1769 to promote agricultural progress; Pres JENS N. HENRIKSEN, A. NEIMANN-SØRENSEN, PETER SKAK OLUFSEN; Dir JENS WULFF; 3,000 mems.

De danske Landboforeninger (Farmers' Unions): Axelborg, Vesterbrogade 4A, 1620 Copenhagen V; tel. (01) 12-75-61; telex 327662; f. 1893; Pres. H. O. A. KJELDSEN; Chief Sec. JØRGEN SKOVBAK; 85,000 mems.

Landbrugsrådet (Agricultural Council): Axelborg, Axeltorv 3, 1609 Copenhagen V; tel. (01) 14-56-72; telex 16772; f. 1919; Pres. HANS O. A. KJELDSEN; Dir KJELD EJLER; 32 mems.

Sammenslutningen af Arbejdsgivere indenfor den keramiske Industri (Federation of Employers of the Ceramic Industry): N. Voldgade 34, Copenhagen; tel. (01) 15-17-00; f. 1918; Chair. L. LAUTRUP LARSEN; Sec. K. MAXEN; 22 mems.

Sammenslutningen af Landbrugets Arbejdsgiverforeninger (SALA) (Federation of Agricultural Employers' Associations): Magstræde 6, 1204 Copenhagen K; tel. (01) 13-46-55.

Skibværftsforeningen (Association of Danish Shipbuilders): St Kongensgade 128, 1264 Copenhagen K; tel. (01) 13-24-16; telex 19582.

Textilindustrien (Federation of Textile Industries): Bredgade 41, POB 300, 7400 Herning; tel. (07) 12-13-66; telex 62199; f. 1895; Pres. C. WICHMANN MADSEN; Man. Dirs J. BOLLERUP JENSEN, S. HOLM PEDERSEN; 310 mems.

TRADE UNIONS

Landsorganisationen i Danmark (LO) (Danish Federation of Trade Unions): Rosenørns Allé 12, 1634 Copenhagen V; tel. (01) 35-35-41; telex 16170; Pres. FINN THORGRIMSON; Vice-Pres. HANS JENSEN; Treas. ERIK HEMMINGSEN; 1,419,984 mems (on 1 January 1988); 1,371 brs.

Principal Affiliated Unions

Blik- og Rørarbejderforbundet i Danmark (Metal and Steel Workers): Ålholmvej 55, 2500 Valby; tel. (01) 71-30-22; Pres. HANS JENSEN; 8,988 mems.

Dansk Beklædnings- og Tekstilarbejderforbund (Textile and Garment Workers); Nyropsgade 14, 1602 Copenhagen V; tel. (01) 11-67-65; f. 1978 by merger of Garment Workers' Union and Textile Workers' Union; Pres. and Gen. Sec. TOVE STENKJÆR; 30,474 mems.

Dansk Bogbinder- og Kartonnagearbejder Forbund (Bookbinders and Cardboard Box Workers): Grafisk Forbundshus, Lygten 16, 2400 Copenhagen NV; tel. (01) 81-42-22; Pres. SVEND MAABJERG; 8,782 mems.

Dansk El-Forbund (Electricians' Union): Vodroffsvej 26, 1900 Frederiksberg C; tel. (01) 21-14-00; Pres. FREDDY ANDERSEN; 25,175 mems.

Dansk Funktionærforbund (Service Trade Employees); Upsalagade 20, 2100 Copenhagen Ø; tel. (01) 38-65-95; Pres. HANS JØRGEN JENSEN; 23,187 mems.

Dansk Jernbaneforbund (Railway Workers); Bredgade 21, 1260 Copenhagen K; tel. (01) 14-33-00; f. 1899; Pres. E. NYGAARD JESPERSEN; 11,095 mems.

Dansk Kommunal Arbejderforbund (Municipal Workers); Nitivej 6, 2000 Frederiksberg; tel. (01) 19-90-22; telex 27481; Pres. POUL WINCKLER; 118,653 mems.

Dansk Metalarbejderforbund (Metalworkers): Nyropsgade 38, 1602 Copenhagen V; tel. (01) 12-82-12; telex 16526; f. 1888; Pres. GEORG POULSEN; 137,532 mems.

Dansk Postforbund (Postmen): Vodroffsvej 13A, 1900 Frederiksberg C; tel. (01) 21-41-24; f. 1908; Pres. JOHAN OVERGAARD; 15,267 mems.

Dansk Tele Forbund (Telecommunications): Rolfsvej 37¹, 2000 Frederiksberg; tel. (01) 88-00-55; Pres. H. C. HANSEN; 9,787 mems.

Dansk Typograf-Forbund (Printers): Grafisk Forbundshus, Lygten 16, 2400 Copenhagen NV; tel. (01) 81-42-22; Pres. KAJ PEDERSEN; 9,735 mems.

Handels- og Kontorfunktionærernes Forbund i Danmark (Commercial and Clerical Employees): H. C. Andersens Blvd 50, POB 268, 1501 Copenhagen V; tel. (01) 12-43-43; f. 1900; Pres. JØRGEN EIBERG; 314,745 mems.

Hotel- og Restaurationspersonalets Forbund i Danmark (Catering Workers): Uplandsgade 52A, 2300 Copenhagen S; tel. (01) 57-14-00; Chair. BENT MOOS; 8,365 mems.

Husligt Arbejder Forbund (Domestic Workers): Rådhuspladsen 77, 1550 Copenhagen V; tel. (01) 13-40-00; Pres. MARGIT VOGNSEN; 71,845 mems.

Kvindeligt Arbejderforbund (Unskilled Women Workers); Ewaldsgade 3-9, 2200 Copenhagen N; tel. (01) 39-31-15; f. 1901; Pres. LILLIAN KNUDSEN; 99,813 mems.

DENMARK

Malerforbundet i Danmark (Housepainters): Tomsgårdsvej 23C, 2400 Copenhagen NV; tel. (01) 34-75-22; f. 1890; Pres. FINN ANDERSEN; 13,829 mems.

Murerforbundet i Danmark (Bricklayers): Mimersgade 47, 2200 Copenhagen N; tel. (01) 81-99-00; Pres. BENDT JENSEN; 13,140 mems.

Nærings- og Nydelsesmiddelarbejder Forbundet (Food, Sugar Confectionery, Chocolate, Dairy Produce and Tobacco Workers): C.F. Richsvej 103, 2000 Frederiksberg; tel. (01) 87-15-22; Pres. E. ANTON JOHANNSEN; 43,025 mems.

Pædagogisk Medhjælper Forbund (Teachers' Assistants): St Kongensgade 79, 1264 Copenhagen K; tel. (01) 11-03-43; f. 1974; Pres. JAKOB SØLVHØJ; 24,482 mems.

Snedker- og Tømrerforbundet i Danmark (Joiners, Cabinet-makers and Carpenters): Mimersgade 47, 2200 Copenhagen N; tel. (01) 81-99-00; Pres. BENT LARSEN; 48,275 mems.

Socialpædagogernes Landsforbund (Social Workers): Brolæggerstræde 9, 1211 Copenhagen K; tel. (01) 14-00-58; Pres. JENS ASGER HANSEN; 15,767 mems.

Specialarbejderforbundet i Danmark (General Workers' Union in Denmark): Nyropsgade 30, POB 392, 504 Copenhagen V; tel. (01) 14-21-40; telex 19596; Pres. HARDY HANSEN; 310,133 mems.

Træindustriforbundet i Danmark (Woodworkers); Mimersgade 47, 2200 Copenhagen N; tel. (01) 81-99-00; Pres. ERIK NIELSEN; 21,183 mems.

Other Unions

Akademikernes Centralorganisation (Academic employees): Nørre Voldgade 29, 1358 Copenhagen K; tel. (01) 12-85-40.

Den Almindelige Danske Lægeforening (Danish Medical Association): Trondhjemsgade 9, 2100 Copenhagen Ø; tel. (01) 38-55-00.

Dansk Journalistforbund (Journalists): Gammel Strand 46, 1202 Copenhagen K; tel. (01) 14-23-88; f. 1961; Pres. Ms TOVE HYGUM JAKOBSEN; 6,200 mems.

Funktionærernes og Tjenestemændenes Fællesråd (Federation of Civil Servants' and Salaried Employees' Organizations): Niels Hemmingsensgade 12, 1010 Copenhagen K; tel. (01) 15-30-22; telex 913022; f. 1952; Chair. MARTIN RØMER; 360,000 mems.

Transport

In June 1986 government plans were announced for a 20-km combined tunnel-and-bridge link across the Great Belt, linking the islands of Zealand and Funen. Work began in 1987; the bridge was due to be completed in 1993, the tunnel in 1996. A meeting between the Governments of Denmark and Sweden was held in October 1986 to discuss plans for a bridge link between the two countries. However, in 1987 the Swedish Government decided to delay its decision and to conduct an inquiry into plans for a tunnel link.

RAILWAYS

DSB (Danish State Railways): Sølvgade 40, 1349 Copenhagen K; tel. (01) 14-04-00; telex 22225; controls 2,471 km of line, of which 145 km in the Copenhagen suburban area are electrified; Dir-Gen. OLE ANDRESEN.

A total of 514 km, mostly branch lines, is run by 13 private companies.

ROADS

At 31 December 1987 Denmark had 70,488 km (43,799 miles) of paved roads, including 599 km (372 miles) of motorways and 3,984 km (2,476 miles) of other national roads.

FERRIES

DSB (Danish State Railways): Sølvgade 40, 1349 Copenhagen K; tel. (01) 14-04-00; telex 22225; operates passenger train and motor car ferries between the mainland and principal islands. Train and motor car ferries are also operated between Denmark, Sweden and Germany in co-operation with German Federal Railways, and German and Swedish State Railways; Gen. Man. PETER LANGAGER.

Other services are operated by private companies.

SHIPPING

The Port of Copenhagen is the largest port in Denmark and the only one including a Free Port Zone. The other major ports are Århus, Ålborg, Fredericia and Esbjerg, which provides daily services to the United Kingdom. There are oil terminals at Kalundborg, Fredericia and Skælskør.

Farvandsdirektoratet (National Administration of Shipping and Navigation): Overgaden oven Vandet 62B, 1001 Copenhagen K; tel. (01) 57-40-50; telex 31319.

Principal Shipping Companies

(Figures for the number of ships and their displacement refer only to Danish flag vessels at 1 July 1988.)

Rederiet Otto Danielsen: Kongevejen 40, 2840 Holte; tel. (02) 42-32-55; telex 15704; 11 vessels of between 2,300 dwt and 3,700 dwt; general tramp trade, chartering, ship sales; Man. Dirs ULLA DANIELSEN, OTTO DANIELSEN, Jr.

Dannebrog Rederi A/S: Rungsted Strandvej 113, 2960 Rungsted Kyst; tel. (02) 86-65-00; telex 37204; f. 1883; owners of tankers and roll-on, roll-off vessels; 5 vessels of 20,900 grt; Liner service Europe–West Africa, US Gulf–Caribbean, Mediterranean; Man. Owner E. WEDELL-WEDELLSBORG.

DFDS A/S—DFDS Seaways: Skt Annæ Plads 30, 1295 Copenhagen; tel. (01) 15-63-00; telex 19435; f. 1866; 11 vessels of 104,300 grt; passenger and car ferry services between Denmark, Sweden, the UK, Germany and Norway, liner trade to Spain, Portugal and South America; Lauritzen owns majority share; Man. Dir NIELS BACH.

The East Asiatic Co Ltd A/S: Holbergsgade 2, 1099 Copenhagen K; tel. (01) 11-83-00; telex 12100; f. 1897; 6 vessels of 189,300 grt; trading, industry, plantations, shipping; Totally owned and managed tonnage: 32 vessels of 788,000 grt; partners in ScanDutch, ScanCarriers, Johnson ScanStar, NedScans and EAC-PNSL Service; other liner services: Europe–West Africa, trans-Pacific service; Chair. T. W. SCHMITH; Board of Management H. H. SPARSØ, J. A. HANSEN, O. F. ANDREASEN, F. HASLE.

Graasten Shipping Company A/S: POB 49, 6300 Gråsten; tel. (04) 65-00-19; telex 52814; 6 livestock carriers of 7,600 grt; shipowners, managers, chartering agents; worldwide; Man. Dir B. CLAUSEN.

Kosan Tankers A/S: Studiestræde 61, 1581 Copenhagen V; tel. (01) 14-34-00; telex 22214; f. 1951; 19 gas carriers of 31,000 grt; Gen. Man. GUNNER NIELSEN.

Knud I. Larsen: Århusgade 129, Frihavnen, 2100 Copenhagen Ø; tel. (01) 18-00-44; telex 22251; f. 1983; 20 vessels of 44,615 grt; general cargo and container ships; Man. Owners KNUD I. LARSEN, FINN SAKSØ LARSEN.

J. Lauritzen A/S: Skt Annæ Plads 28, 1291 Copenhagen K; tel. (01) 11-12-22; telex 15522; f. 1884; world-wide service with refrigerated vessels, product tankers and bulk carriers; drilling rigs; 10 reefers of 96,400 grt, and 18 long-term chartered reefers of 144,000 grt; Man. Dir PETER WEITMEYER.

Mercandia Rederierne: Amaliegade 27, 1256 Copenhagen K; tel. (01) 12-01-55; telex 19762; f. 1964; 20 roll-on, roll-off vessels totalling 234,600 grt; tramp and liner services; Owner and Man. PER HENRIKSEN.

A. P. Møller: Esplanaden 50, 1098 Copenhagen K; f. 1904; 74 ships of 2,753,000 grt; it owns about 80,000 containers, and operates another 20,000 worldwide; car carriers, gas and oil tankers, bulk-carriers, supply-ships and anchor-handling vessels, drilling rigs; principal services under the name of **Maersk Line:** services between Europe, USA, West Africa, Middle East, Far East; Chair. MAERSK MCKINNEY MØLLER.

Mortensen + Lange: Strandvejen 32D, POB 2703, 2100 Copenhagen Ø; tel. (31) 29-55-33; telex 15100; 11 vessels of 12,600 grt; worldwide tramping; Dirs STEEN OLSEN, FINN OLLENDORFF.

Dampskibsselskabet Norden A/S: Amaliegade 49, 1256 Copenhagen K; tel. (01) 15-04-51; telex 22374; f. 1871; 8 bulk carriers and product tankers of 267,500 grt; tramp; Man. Dir STEEN KRABBE.

Ove Skou Rederiaktieselskab: Nytorv 11, 1450 Copenhagen K; tel. (01) 15-36-00; telex 19900; 3 ships totalling 45,200 grt; worldwide tramping; Man. Dir LARS OREBY HANSEN.

A/S Em. Z. Svitzer Bjergnings-Enterprise: Kvæsthusgade 1, 1251 Copenhagen K; tel. (01) 15-51-95; telex 15983; f. 1833; 25 tugs and salvage vessels; worldwide salvage, towage and offshore services; Gen. Man. JØRN HANSEN.

A/S D/S Torm: Holmens Kanal 42, 1060 Copenhagen K; tel. (01) 12-24-37; telex 22315; f. 1889; 1 bulk carrier and 5 product tankers of 165,300 grt; liner services USA–West Africa; Man. Dir ERIK BEHN.

Association

Danmarks Rederiforening (Danish Shipowners' Asscn): Amaliegade 33, 1256 Copenhagen K; tel. (01) 11-40-88; telex 16492; f. 1884; representing 4,125,000 grt (October 1987); Chair. of the Board ERIK BEHN; Man. Dir KNUD PONTOPPIDAN.

DENMARK

CIVIL AVIATION

The International Airport is about 10 km from the centre of Copenhagen. Domestic airports include Roskilde in Sjælland (Zealand), Tirstrup at Århus, Ålborg, Billund, Esbjerg, Karup, Skrydstrup, Stauning, Sønderborg and Thisted in Jutland, Rønne in Bornholm and Odense in Fyn (Funen).

Statens Luftfartsvæsen (Civil Aviation Administration): Luftfartshuset, POB 744, 2450 Copenhagen SV; tel. (01) 44-48-48; telex 27096; Dir-Gen. V. K. H. EGGERS.

Det Danske Luftfartselskab A/S—DDL (Danish Airlines): Industriens Hus, H. C. Andersens Blvd 18, 1553 Copenhagen V; tel. (01) 14-13-33; telex 22437; f. 1918; Danish parent company of the designated national carrier, Scandinavian Airline Systems—SAS (see under Sweden) and SCANAIR; Chair. HALDOR TOPSØE; Man. Dir R. SØKILDE.

National Airlines

Cimber Air A/S: Sonderborg Airport, 6400 Sonderborg; tel. (04) 42-22-77; telex 52315; operates own service from Esbjerg to Humberside, operates services between Copenhagen and Sonderborg for Danair, operates charter flights and total route systems for other companies; Pres. I. L. NIELSEN; Man. Dir H. I. NIELSEN; fleet of 2 Fokker F.28-3000, 2 Aérospatiale 262, 3 ATR-42-300, 1 King Air 200.

Conair A/S (Consolidated Aircraft Corporation): Hangar 276, Copenhagen Airport, 2791 Dragør; tel. (01) 53-17-00; telex 31423; f. 1964; operates charter and inclusive-tour flights to the Mediterranean and Africa for Spies Travel Organization, which owns the airline; Chair. JANNI SPIES; Man. Dir VERNER MOLLER; fleet of 3 Airbus A300 B4-120.

Danair A/S: Kastruplundgade 13, 2770 Kastrup; f. 1971; owned by SAS (see under Sweden), Maersk Air and Cimber Air; operates domestic services between Copenhagen and Ålborg, Billund, Esbjerg, Karup, Odense, Rønne, Skrydstrup, Sønderborg, Thisted, Århus and the Faeroe Islands; f. 1971; Chair. F. ÅHLGREEN ERIKSEN; Man. Dir GUNNAR TIETZ; fleet of DC-9, B-737, Fokker 50 and ATR-42 on lease from parent companies.

Maersk Air: Copenhagen Airport South, 2791 Dragør; tel. (01) 53-44-44; telex 31126; f. 1969; provides charter flights for Scandinavian tour operators, operates scheduled services in Denmark, and between Billund and Southend, England and in 1983 acquired the commuter airline Air Business, linking the oil centres of Esbjerg and Stavanger; Chair. KARSTEN BORCH; Exec. Vice-Pres. OLE DIETZ; fleet of 3 Boeing 737-200, 4 737-300, 5 Dash 7, 2 Shorts 360, 1 BAe.125-700B, 3 Bell 212, 2 Aérospatiale Super Puma; on order: 4 Fokker 50, 3 Boeing 737-300.

Sterling Airways: Hangar 144, Copenhagen Airport, 2791 Dragør; tel. (01) 53-53-53; telex 31231; f. 1962; owned by Tjæreborg International Holdings A/S, operates inclusive-tour flights to Europe, North Africa, North America and Sri Lanka; Chair. NIELS HEERING; Man. Dir EJNAR LUNDT; fleet of 10 Boeing 727-200, 1 DC-8-63, 6 Caravelle 10B.

Tourism

Tourists visit Denmark for the peaceful charm of its countryside and old towns, or the sophistication of Copenhagen. There were an estimated 2,042,908 tourist arrivals at accommodation establishments in 1986. Revenue from tourism totalled 15,185m. kroner in 1987.

Danmarks Turistråd (Tourist Board): Vesterbrogade 6D, 1620 Copenhagen V; tel. (01) 11-14-15; telex 27586; Information Bureau, H. C. Andersens Blvd 22, 1553 Copenhagen V; tel. (01) 11-13-25; telex 27586; f. 1967; Dir JØRGEN BERTELSEN.

Atomic Energy

Danish Energy Agency: Landemærket 11, 1119 Copenhagen K; tel. (01) 92-67-00; telex 22450; f. 1976; under Ministry of Energy; Dir HANS VON BÜLOW.

Risø National Laboratory: Forskningscenter Risø, POB 49, 4000 Roskilde; tel. (02) 37-12-12; telex 43116; f. 1958; environmental and energy research centre; Man. Dir H. BJERRUM MØLLER; Technical Dir K. SINGER; Research Dirs J. KJEMS, S. P. STRANDDORF.

DANISH EXTERNAL TERRITORIES

THE FAEROE ISLANDS

Introductory Survey

Location, Climate, Language, Religion, Flag, Capital

The Faeroe (Faroe) Islands are a group of 18 islands (of which 16 are inhabited) in the Atlantic Ocean, between Scotland and Iceland. The main island is Streymoy, where more than one-third of the population resides. The climate is mild in winter and cool in summer, with a mean temperature of 7°C (45°F). Most of the inhabitants profess Christianity: the majority of Faeroese belong to the Evangelical Lutheran Church of Denmark. The principal language is Faeroese, but Danish is a compulsory subject in all schools. The flag (proportions 22 by 16) displays a red cross, bordered with blue, on a white background, the upright of the cross being to the left of centre. The capital is Tórshavn, which is situated on Streymoy.

History and Government

The Faeroe Islands have been under Danish administration since Queen Margrethe of Denmark inherited Norway in 1380. The islands were occupied by the United Kingdom while Denmark was under German occupation during the Second World War, but they were restored to Danish control immediately after the war. The Home Rule Act of 1948 gave the Faeroese control over all their internal affairs. There is a local parliament (the Løgting), but the Danish Folketing, to which the Faeroese send two members, is responsible for defence and foreign policy, constitutional matters and the judicial and monetary systems. The Faeroes control fishing resources within their territorial waters, but jurisdiction over resources beneath the bed of the sea in the area adjacent to the islands has yet to be settled with Copenhagen. Until the dispute is resolved, and until Faeroese fears of being overwhelmed by an 'oil culture' can be allayed, exploration for petroleum cannot begin. Any further independence from Denmark is unlikely before the size of the Danish subsidy is reduced. The Faeroe Islands did not join the EEC with Denmark in 1973.

The centre-left coalition government of the Social Democratic Party (SDP), Republicans and the People's Party, formed in 1978, collapsed in 1980 over a plan, opposed by the conservative People's Party, to extend through the winter months a government-owned ferry service linking the islands with Denmark, Norway and Scotland. At a general election, held in November, conservative political groups slightly increased their share of the popular vote. Although there was no material change in the balance of party representation in the Løgting, the Union Party formed a centre-right coalition with the People's Party and the Home Rule Party in January 1981. A general election was held in November 1984, and in December a four-party, centre-left coalition government was formed under the premiership of Atli Dam, comprising his SDP, the Home Rule Party, the Republican Party and the Christian People's Party combined with the Progressive and Fishing Industry Party (CPP-PFIP).

Elections in 1988 demonstrated a shift to the right in the Faeroes, to the benefit of the People's Party. Its one member in the Danish Folketing increased his support in the national elections of September 1987 and May 1988. At a Faeroese general election in November 1988 the incumbent Government lost its majority, and the People's Party became the largest party in the Løgting. In January 1989, after 10 weeks of various negotiations, a centre-right coalition comprising the People's Party, the Republican Party, the Home Rule Party and the CPP-PFIP, led by Jógvan Sundstein (Chairman of the People's Party), was formed. The coalition was committed to economic austerity and support for the fishing industry.

In international affairs, the Faeroe Islanders earned opprobium for their traditional slaughter of pilot whales for food. After foreign journalists first publicized the whaling in 1986, the manner in which it is practised has been even more strictly regulated. Whale meat, however, accounted for one-half of the meat produced, and one-quarter of the meat eaten, in 1986. Responsibility for foreign policy lies in Copenhagen, but in 1983 the Løgting unanimously declared the Faeroe Islands a 'nuclear-free zone', and in 1987, as a consequence of this policy, requested the Danish Government to curtail a US naval visit. There have also been several declarations of 'non-aligned' status, notwithstanding NATO membership as part of the Kingdom of Denmark. When the People's Party changed its policy, however, to advocate closer co-operation with the NATO alliance, the party ended political unanimity on the issue and made gains in the elections of 1987 and 1988.

Economic Affairs

The islands have a high standard of living. In 1986, according to estimates by the World Bank, gross national product (GNP), measured at average 1984–86 prices, was US $549m., equivalent to $11,930 per head. Between 1973 and 1986, it was estimated, GNP increased, in real terms, at an average rate of 4.3% per year, with real GNP per head rising by 3.2% annually.

Only about 6% of the land surface is cultivated. As the summers are too cool for cereal production, the main crops are potatoes and vegetables. In 1984 649 ha were planted with potatoes, which yielded a crop of 1,282 metric tons. Grass is also an important crop and is used for the large number of sheep raised on the islands (estimated at 65,029 in December 1984). Coal is mined on Suderoy, and 25% of the islands' electric energy is supplied by a hydroelectric power plant. About one-fifth of the working population is engaged in handicrafts. In 1987 manufacturing output accounted for only 9% of exports. The most important sector of the Faeroese economy is fishing, which employed 26% of the labour force in 1987, contributed 27% of the total gross domestic product (GDP) and accounted for 94% of the islands' exports. In January 1974 the Løgting decided not to join the EEC but to negotiate a special trade agreement which would protect the fishing industry. Following Faeroese pressure, an agreement was reached on limiting the annual catch of cod and haddock by foreign trawlers from January 1974. In March 1977, despite protests from the EEC, the Faeroes imposed stringent conservation measures, curbing fishing within a limit of 200 nautical miles (370 km) from the coast. The Faeroese themselves, however, encountered restrictions in other waters. As a result, there has been a massive investment (of at least 1,000m. kroner) in developing the fishing fleet, and the markets, for blue whiting as the principal catch. There has also been great interest in investing in fish-farming of salmon and trout, although by October 1987 only 52 licences had been granted. By 1990 it was hoped that production would exceed 10,000 metric tons per year. In 1986 production had risen by 800 tons, to 1,900 tons, worth 66m. kroner. In that year the Faeroes' total catch of fish was 357,000 metric tons, and exports of fish and fish products (three-quarters of which went to the EEC) totalled 192,500 tons, valued at 1,830m. kroner. In an attempt to shield the economy from changing market conditions in fishing, tourism has been developed, with a luxury hotel being built at Tórshavn in 1984. There are three shipyards on the islands, which produce fishing and freight vessels for domestic use and for export. In 1986 total turnover at the shipyards was 244m. kroner. Danish subsidies are an important source of income and accounted for about 16% of the Faeroese GDP in 1986.

In 1986 the deficit on the current account of the balance of payments was 496m. kroner, equivalent to 8% of GDP. In the same year the net foreign debt was equivalent to some 67% of GDP, but most of it is owed in Denmark and is therefore not a foreign currency debt. Personal savings, however, were at a very high level, at some 28% of GDP. There is an acute labour shortage in the islands, and in 1987 immigrant workers formed 5% of the labour force.

In 1940 the Faeroese krona was introduced. It must, however, always be freely interchangeable with the Danish krone at the rate of 1: 1. For exchange rate, see under Denmark.

Education and Social Welfare

The education system is similar to that of Denmark, except that Faeroese is the language of instruction. Danish is, however, a compulsory subject in all schools. Plans for the upgrading of the Faeroese Academy to university status were under way in 1986.

In 1984 government medical services included three hospitals, with a total of 352 beds, and 75 physicians.

In the 1985/86 financial year, government expenditure on social welfare represented 15.7% of total budget spending, while education received a further 8.6% of the total.

DANISH EXTERNAL TERRITORIES   The Faeroe Islands

Statistical Survey

Sources: Føroya Landsstýri (Faeroese Government), Tinganes, 3800 Tórshavn, Faeroe Islands; *Statistisk årbog*, Danmarks Statistik, Sejrøgade 11, 2100 Copenhagen Ø.

AREA AND POPULATION

Area: 1,398.9 sq km (540.1 sq miles).
Population: 41,969 (males 21,997, females 19,972) at census of 22 September 1977; 47,000 (official estimate for mid-1987).
Principal Town: Tórshavn (capital), estimated population 15,300 in 1986.
Births and Deaths (1987): Registered live births 780 (birth rate 16.7 per 1,000); Deaths 370 (death rate 7.9 per 1,000) (Source: UN, *Population and Vital Statistics Report*).
Labour Force (census of 22 September 1977): Males 12,808; Females 4,777; Total 17,585.

AGRICULTURE, ETC.

Livestock (FAO estimates, '000 head, year ending September 1986): Cattle 2; Sheep 72 (Source: FAO, *Production Yearbook*).
Fishing ('000 metric tons, live weight, 1986): Atlantic cod 63.7, Haddock 14.9, Saithe (Pollock) 39.9, Norway pout 24.2, Blue whiting (Poutassou) 81.6, Golden redfish 15.8, Capelin 65.4, Other fishes 35.0 (FAO estimates), Northern prawn 11.0, Other crustaceans and molluscs 2.1; total catch 353.7 (FAO estimate). Figures include quantities landed by Faeroes fishing craft in foreign ports but exclude quantities landed by foreign fishing craft in Faeroes ports. Number of whales caught (1986): 1,910 (Source: FAO, *Yearbook of Fishery Statistics*).

FINANCE

Government Accounts ('000 kroner, 1986): Revenue 1,582,385; Danish state subsidy 749,463; Expenditure 2,312,747.
Cost of Living (consumer price index at 1 January; base: 1 January 1983 = 100): 105.4 in 1984; 112.8 in 1985; 117.6 in 1985.
Gross Domestic Product (million kroner at current factor cost): 4,359 in 1984; 4,761 in 1985; 5,460 in 1986.

EXTERNAL TRADE

Principal Commodities (million kroner, 1986): *Imports c.i.f.:* Food and live animals 290.3; Mineral fuels, lubricants, etc. 257.2 (Petroleum products 256.9); Chemicals and related products 127.1; Basic manufactures 266.9; Machinery and transport equipment 1,025.3 (Machinery for special industries 165.8, General industrial machinery 150.6, Electric machinery, apparatus, etc. 84.5, Road vehicles and parts 214.3); Miscellaneous manufactured articles 343.1; Total (incl. others) 2,664.4. *Exports f.o.b.:* Fish and fish preparations 1,682.0; Animal feeding-stuff (excl. cereals) 95.5; Crude animal and vegetable materials 44.4; Transport equipment 122.6; Total (incl. others) 1,960.3.
Principal Trading Partners (million kroner, 1986): *Imports c.i.f.:* Denmark 1,212.4; Japan 127.8; Fed. Repub. of Germany 235.8; Norway 348.9; Sweden 210.7; United Kingdom 113.7; Total (incl. others) 2,664.4. *Exports f.o.b.:* Canada 45.0; Denmark 351.8; France (incl. Monaco) 198.5; Fed. Repub. of Germany 264.1; Greenland 48.0; Italy 128.1; Norway 36.1; Spain 39.6; Sweden 44.5; United Kingdom 261.2; USA 274.9; Total (incl. others) 1,960.3.

TRANSPORT

Road Traffic (registered vehicles, 1986): Private motor cars 13,211; Goods vehicles 3,041; Buses and coaches 105; Motor cycles 119.
Shipping (1986): Merchant fleet (displacement) 112,000 gross registered tons (fishing vessels 64,000 grt); International sea-borne freight traffic ('000 metric tons): Goods loaded 201, Goods unloaded 444 (excluding landings of raw fish).

Directory

The Government

The legislative body is the Løgting, elected on a basis of proportional representation. All Faeroese over the age of 18 years have the right to vote. Based on the strength of the parties in the Løgting, a small Government, the Landsstýri, is formed. This is the administrative body in certain spheres, chiefly relating to Faeroese economic affairs. The Løgmadur (Prime Minister) has to ratify all Løgting laws. The Ríkisumboðsmaður, or High Commissioner, represents the Danish Government.
Ríkisumboðsmaður: BENT KLINTE.

LANDSSTÝRI
(January 1989)

Prime Minister (Løgmadur): JÓGVAN SUNDSTEIN (People's Party*).
Deputy Prime Minister: SIGNAR HANSEN (Republican Party†).
Minister of Finance: FINNBOGI ÍSAKSON (Republican Party†).
Minister of Fisheries: ANFINN KALLSBERG (People's Party*).
Minister of Health, Social Affairs and Agriculture: TORDUR NICLASSEN (CPP-PFIP).
Minister of Transport, Communications, Church and Cultural Affairs: KARL HERI JØNSEN (Home Rule Party).

* The People's Party Ministers are also responsible for the portfolios of Administrative, Foreign, Social (Pensions), Industrial and Municipal Affairs.

† The Republican Party Ministers are also responsible for the portfolios of Education, Broadcasting, the Environment, Tourism, Energy, Legal Affairs, Commerce and Labour.

Government Offices

Føroya Landsstýri (Faeroese Government): POB 64, 110 Tórshavn; tel. (298) 11080; telex 81310.
Føroya Tollstova (Faeroese Customs Authority): POB 3, 110 Tórshavn; tel. (298) 14660; telex 81310.
Fisheries Administration: POB 87, 110 Tórshavn; tel. (298) 13098; telex 81310.

LØGTING

The Løgting has 32 members, elected by universal adult suffrage.
Speaker: HERGEIR NIELSEN (Republican Party).

Election, 8 November 1988

	Votes	Seats
Fólkaflokkurin (People's Party)	6,592	8
Javnaðarflokkurin (Social Democratic Party)	6,233	7
Sambandsflokkurin (Union Party)	6,116	7
Tjóveldisflokkurin (Republican Party)	5,520	6
Sjálvstýrisflokkurin (Home Rule Party)	2,033	2
CPP-PFIP (Christian People's Party, Progressive and Fishing Industry Party)	1,582	2
Framsóknarflokkurin (Progress Party)	516	0

Political Organizations

The address of each of the following organizations is Løgtingid, Aarvegi, 3800 Tórshavn.

Fólkaflokkurin (People's Party): f. 1940; conservative-liberal party, favours free enterprise and wider political and economic autonomy for the Faeroes within the Kingdom of Denmark; Chair. JÓGVAN SUNDSTEIN.

Framburds- og Fiskivinnuflokkurin (Progressive and Fishing Industry Party–CPP-PFIP): combined with the Christian People's Party; non-socialist, social, anti-communist centre party.

Framsóknarflokkurin (Progress Party): f. 1987.

Javnaðarflokkurin (Social Democratic Party–SDP): f. 1928; Chair. ATLI P. DAM.

Sambandsflokkurin (Union Party): f. 1906; favours the maintenance of close relations between the Faeroes and the Kingdom of Denmark; conservative in internal affairs; Chair. PAULI ELLEFSEN.

Sjálvstýrisflokkurin (Home Rule Party): f. 1906; social-liberal party advocating eventual political independence for the Faeroes within the Kingdom of Denmark; Leader HILMAR KASS.

Tjodveldisflokkurin (Republican Party): f. 1948; left-wing party, advocates the secession of the Faeroes from Denmark; Chair. SIGNER HANSEN.

Religion

CHRISTIANITY

The Faeroes Church comes under the jurisdiction of the Lutheran Bishop of Copenhagen, who exercises control through a suffragan bishop. The largest independent group is the 'Plymouth Brethren'. There is also a small Roman Catholic community.

The Press

There are no daily papers in the Faeroe Islands.

Dagbladið: POB 23, 3800 Tórshavn; tel. (042) 17600; telex 81338; 3 a week; People's Party; circ. 5,500.

Dimmalætting: POB 19, 110 Tórshavn; tel. (298) 11212; telex 81222; 3 a week; Union Party; circ. 12,500.

Fríu Føroyar: POB 2055, 165 Argir; tel. (298) 16444; f. 1983; weekly; socialist.

Nordlýsid: POB 58, 3870 Klaksvík; tel. (042) 56285; weekly; circ. 2,000.

Oyggjatídindi: POB 312, 3800 Tórshavn; tel. (042) 14411; 2 a week; circ. 5,000.

Tídindabladid Sosialurin: POB 76, 110 Tórshavn; tel. (042) 11820; f. 1927; 3 a week; Editor JAN MÜLLER; Social Democratic Party; circ. 6,000.

Tingakrossur: Dr Jacobsengøta 16, POB 193, 110 Tórshavn; tel. (298) 15474; f. 1901; 2 a week; Home Rule Party; circ. 2,500.

14 September: POB 62, 3800 Tórshavn; tel. (042) 14412; 2 a week; circ. 4,000.

NEWS AGENCY

Faeroe Press Agency: P/f Salvará, Tjarnardeild 12, Tórshavn; f. 1980; covers Ritzaus Bureau of Copenhagen, Danmarks Radio and Morgunbladid of Reykjavík, Iceland; Man. JÓGVAN ARGE.

Publisher

Útvarp Føroya: Nordari Ringvegur, POB 328, 3800 Tórshavn; tel. (042) 16568; telex 81226; f. 1957; fiction and periodicals; Man. NIELS JUEL ARGE.

Radio and Television

In 1986 there were an estimated 10,000 television receivers, and 18,000 radio receivers in use.

Sjónvarp Føroya (Faeroese Television): POB 21, 3800 Tórshavn; tel. (042) 17780; telex 81391; f. 1982; Man. J. A. SKAALE.

Útvarp Føroya (Faeroese Broadcasting Corporation): POB 328, 3800 Tórshavn; tel. (042) 16566; telex 81226; f. 1957; Man. N. J. ARGE.

Finance

BANKS

(cap. = capital; res = reserves; dep. = deposits; m. = million; amounts in kroner; brs = branches)

Føroya Banki AS: Niels Finsensgøta 15, POB 14, 110 Tórshavn; tel. (298) 11350; telex 81227; f. 1906; total assets 5,635m. (Dec. 1987); Chair. POUL JOHS. JOHANSEN; Gen. Mans HANS-JÓRGEN LAURSEN, JOHAN SIMONSEN, NIELS JOEL NATTESTAD; 32 brs.

Føroya Sparikassi (Faeroese Savings Bank): POB 34, 110 Tórshavn; tel. (298) 14800; telex 81318; f. 1832.

Fossbankin: Niels Finsensgøta 37, POB 1120, 3800 Tórshavn; tel. (298) 12400; telex 81306; f. 1986; cap. 30m., res. 10m., dep. 238m. (1987); Chair. HJARNAR DJURHUUS; Gen. Man. HELGI FOSSADAL.

Sjóvinnubankin PF (Fisheries Bank): POB 48, 110 Tórshavn; tel. (298) 14900; telex 81229; f. 1932; total assets 3,832m. (Dec. 1986); Chair. BIRGIR DANIELSEN; Mans STEINGIRM NIELSEN, REGIN OLSEN; 30 brs.

INSURANCE

Tryggingarsambandid Føroyar: Kongabrúgvin, 3800 Tórshavn; tel. (042) 14590; marine, fire, accident and life.

Trade and Industry

ASSOCIATIONS

L/F Føroya Fiskasøla (Faeroe Seafood): POB 68, 110 Tórshavn; tel. (298) 14960; telex 81224; f. 1948; union of co-operative fish producers; markets approx. 80% of fish product exports; Chair. BIRGIR DANIELSON.

Føroya Reidarafelag (Faeroe Fishing Vessel-Owners' Association): POB 179, 110 Tórshavn; tel. (298) 11864; telex 81388.

TRADE UNION

Føroya Arbeidarafelag (Faeroese Labour Organization): Tjarndeild 5, POB 56, 110 Tórshavn; tel. (298) 12101; telex 82416.

Transport

There are about 400 km of roads in the Faeroe Islands. The main harbour is at Tórshavn; the other ports are at Fuglafjordur, Klaksvík, Skálafjordur, Tvøroyri, Vágur and Vestmanna. Between mid-May and mid-September, a summer roll-on, roll-off ferry service links the Faeroe Islands with Iceland, Shetland, Denmark and Norway.

There is an airport on Vágar. Danair operates services to Bergen and Copenhagen, Maersk Air to Copenhagen, and Icelandair operates a service between Reykjavík and Glasgow via the Faeroes.

Tourism

Ferdamannamidstød Føroya (Faeroese Tourist Board): Skansvegur 1, 100 Tórshavn; tel. (298) 16055; telex 81385.

GREENLAND

Introductory Survey

Location, Climate, Language, Religion, Flag, Capital

Greenland (Kalaallit Nunaat) is the world's largest island, with a total area of 2,175,600 sq km, and lies in the North Atlantic Ocean, east of Canada. Most of it is permanently covered by ice, but 341,700 sq km of coastland are habitable. Danish and Greenlandic are the official languages. The majority of the population profess Christianity and belong mainly to the Evangelical Lutheran Church of Denmark. There are also small communities of other Protestant groups and of Roman Catholics. The flag displays a circular rising sun, set against a red and white background. Nuuk (Godtháb) is the capital.

History, Government, Defence

Greenland first came under Danish rule in 1380. In the revision of the Danish Constitution in 1953, Greenland became part of the Kingdom. The island sends two members to the Danish Folketing, and the Danish authorities are represented in Greenland by the High Commissioner (Rigsombudsmanden).

In October 1972 the Greenlanders voted by 9,658 to 3,990 against joining the European Community but, as part of Denmark, were bound by the Danish decision to join. Resentment of Danish domination of the economy, education and the professions continued, taking expression in 1977 in the formation of a nationalist left-wing party, the Siumut. In 1975 the Minister for Greenland appointed a commission to devise terms for Greenland home rule. Its proposals for a Parliament (Landsting) and Executive (Landsstyre), with several responsibilities, including foreign policy and defence, remaining under Danish control, were approved by 73.1% to 26.9% in a referendum among the Greenland electorate in January 1979. The Siumut, led by a Lutheran pastor, Jonathan Motzfeldt, secured 13 seats in the 21-member Landsting at a general election in April, and a five-member Landsstyre, with Motzfeldt as Prime Minister, took office in May. Since 1979 the island has been gradually assuming full administration of its internal affairs.

In February 1982 a referendum was held to decide Greenland's continued membership of the European Community. This resulted in a 53% majority in favour of withdrawal. Negotiations were begun in May 1982, with the Danish Government acting on Greenland's behalf, and were concluded in March 1984 (with effect from 1 February 1985): Greenland was accorded the status of an overseas territory in association with the Community, with preferential access to EEC markets (see below).

DANISH EXTERNAL TERRITORIES   *Greenland*

At the April 1983 general election to the Landsting (enlarged, by measures adopted in 1982, to between 23 and 26 seats, depending on the proportion of votes cast), the Siumut and Atassut parties won 12 seats each, while the Inuit Ataqatigiit (IA) won two seats. The Siumut party once again formed a government, led by Motzfeldt, dependent on the support of the IA members in the Landsting: this support was withdrawn in March 1984, when the IA members voted against the terms of withdrawal from the European Community, and Motzfeldt resigned. In the ensuing general election, held in June, the Siumut and Atassut parties won 11 seats each while the IA won three. Motzfeldt once again formed a coalition government, comprising the Siumut party and the IA.

In March 1987 the coalition Government collapsed, following a dispute between the Siumut party and the IA over policy towards the modernization of the US radar facility at Thule, which was claimed by the IA to be in breach of the 1972 US-Soviet Anti-Ballistic Missile Treaty. A general election was held in May. The Siumut party lost its status as the largest party, obtaining 39.8% of the total votes, but the proportion of votes won by the Atassut party also declined, to 40.1%. Each party retained 11 seats in the Landsting; the IA won three seats, and the remaining seat was won by the newly-formed Issittup-partii-a, which was demanding the privatization of the trawler fleet. Motzfeldt eventually formed a new coalition government with the IA, although his candidacy for head of government was challenged by left-wing members of the Siumut, after he had attempted to negotiate a coalition with the Atassut party.

In February 1988 a massive vaccination programme attempted to control a virulent outbreak of canine distemper among the island's estimated 30,000 husky sledge-dogs. Despite this, most of the dogs in the northern area of Thule perished. The husky sledge-dogs are important to the economy of Greenland, with one-fifth of the local Inuit (Eskimo) population dependent on them for hunting. This activity, however, probably accounts for the spread of the canine distemper virus to the seal population of the North Sea, with the devastating results apparent later in 1988 (see chapter on Denmark).

Denmark remains responsible for Greenland's foreign relations and defence. Under the 1981 Danish-American agreement on the defence of Greenland, two US radar bases were established on Greenland, at Thule and at Kangerlussuaq (Søndre Strømfjord). An agreement between the USA and Denmark for the reduction of the bases from 325,000 ha to 160,000 ha took effect from 1 October 1986, and the land thus becoming available was returned to the Inuit (Eskimos). In June 1980 the Danish Government declared an economic zone extending 200 nautical miles (370 km) off the east coast of Greenland. This, however, caused a dispute with Norway over territorial waters, owing to the existence of the small Norwegian island of Jan Mayen, 460 km off the east coast of Greenland. In 1988 Denmark requested the International Court of Justice to arbitrate on the issue of conflicting economic zones.

Economic Affairs

Seal-hunting has traditionally been the main occupation in Greenland and it is still important in the northern districts. Sealskins, and also foxskins, are valuable exports. In the south, sheep-rearing is the principal occupation, although difficulties resulting from the climate have caused many of the smaller sheep farms to close, reducing the total number of farms from 153 in 1970 to 69 in 1985. In the central coastal areas fishing is of prime importance, and it constitutes the most important sector of Greenland's economy. It was helped by the 1980 declaration of the maritime economic zone (see above). Under the terms of Greenland's withdrawal from the European Community, which took effect in February 1985, Community member countries retained fishing rights in Greenland waters, in return for an annual payment of 26.5m. ECUs (US $21.2m.) for an initial period of five years: a proportion of the total catch was to be reserved for Greenland, and preferential access to EEC markets for Greenland fish products was to be maintained. It was decided in 1988 to extend this agreement to 1995. In 1987 the fishing industry accounted for some 83% of exports, totalling about 1,973m. kroner. In the mid-1980s, the industry employed about one-sixth of the working population. In 1985 the Landsstyre assumed responsibility for the Royal Greenland Trade Department (KGH), as part of the gradual transfer of internal autonomy. The KGH was replaced by a Greenlandic company, Greenland Trade (Kalaallit Niuerfiat), which subsequently assumed control of most of the territory's fish-processing plants and has developed a new trawler fleet, which totalled 12 vessels in 1986.

The exploitation of mineral resources and of hydroelectric power is subject to agreement between the Danish Government and the Greenland Home Rule Authorities. In 1987 the only exploitation of mineral resources was at a lead and zinc mine in Marmorilik. In 1975 exploration began of three potential petroleum-producing areas off the western shores, but no oil was discovered, and the concessions were terminated in 1978. A concession for onshore exploration for petroleum in East Greenland was issued in 1984, and geological testing was started in 1985.

The economy continues to be dependent on large subsidies, of about 2,500m. kroner per year, from Denmark. Since 1985 a substantial proportion of the subsidies has been used to finance the areas of responsibility that have progressively been transferred from Denmark to the Landsstyre. As an EEC member, Greenland received assistance from the European Regional Development Fund; the total in 1983 was 19.24m. ECUs for 92 investment projects, including airport improvements and energy supply projects. It was hoped that the loss of such assistance, incurred through leaving the Community, would be offset by income from the sale of fishing rights. In 1986, according to estimates by the World Bank, Greenland's gross national product (GNP), measured at average 1984-86 prices, was US $465m., equivalent to $8,780 per head. Between 1973 and 1986, it was estimated, GNP increased, in real terms, at an average annual rate of only 0.5%, with real GNP per head declining by 0.2% per year. In 1986, however, GNP per head rose by about 8% in real terms.

Until 1950 Denmark had a monopoly of trade and industry in Greenland. The abolition of this monopoly opened the market to other European countries, particularly Sweden, Norway and Finland. However, Denmark still took about 82% of exports in 1986, and provided 65% of imports, thereby maintaining a substantial control over trade. Other members of the EEC took 10% of exports in 1986.

Education and Social Welfare

The educational system is based on that of Denmark, except that the main language of instruction is Greenlandic. Danish is, however, quite widely used. There is a school in every settlement. In 1986/87 there were about 100 primary and lower secondary schools, with 9,488 pupils and 1,136 teachers. There is a teacher training college in Nuuk, and a university centre opened in 1987. In 1986 government expenditure on education represented 14.3% of total budget spending.

There is a free health service for all residents, administered by the Danish Government, with a total of 16 hospitals. In 1984 there were 59 physicians working in Greenland. Government expenditure on health in 1986 represented 9.7% of total budget spending.

Statistical Survey

Source: Ministry for Greenland, *Annual Report*.

AREA, POPULATION AND DENSITY

Area: Total 2,175,600 sq km (840,000 sq miles); Ice-free portion 341,700 sq km (131,930 sq miles).

Population: 49,630 (males 26,856; females 22,774) at census of 26 October 1976; (official estimate for 1 January 1988): 54,524 (incl. 44,952 born in Greenland).

Density (1988): 0.025 per sq km.

Capital: Nuuk (Godthåb), population 11,615 (1988).

Births and deaths (1987): Registered live births 1,104 (birth rate 20.4 per 1,000); Deaths 450 (death rate 8.3 per 1,000) (Source: UN, *Population and Vital Statistics Report*). **Marriages** (1986): Registered marriages 349 (marriage rate 6.4 per 1,000).

Labour Force (census of 26 October 1976): Males 14,234; Females 7,144; Total 21,378.

AGRICULTURE, ETC.

Livestock (1985): Sheep 21,443, Reindeer 5,980.

Hunting (1985): 1,182 Fox skins, 24 Polar bears, 50,526 Seals.

Fishing ('000 metric tons, live weight, 1986): Greenland halibut 8.9, Atlantic cod 7.1, Greenland cod 4.0, Atlantic redfishes 12.3, Capelin 55.4, other fishes 3.2, Northern prawn 64.1, Clams 0.4; Total catch 155.4 (Source: FAO, *Yearbook of Fishery Statistics*). The total excludes seals, which are recorded by number rather than by weight (see Hunting, above).

MINING

Production (concentrates, '000 metric tons, 1987): Lead 28; Zinc 114.

FINANCE

Danish currency is in use

Government Accounts (million kroner, 1986): *Revenue:* Landsstyre and local authority revenue 1,689 (Income taxes and import duties

1,379); EEC vocational training 32; State, EEC and other grants 2,583; Total 4,422. *Expenditure:* Health 431; Education 633; Personal social services 662; Housing 546; Administration 552; Traffic and communications 235; Trade and industry 617 (Fisheries and sheep farming 614); Total (incl. others) 4,422.

Cost of Living (consumer price index at 1 January; base: January 1981 = 100): 160.2 in 1986; 164.8 in 1987; 177.4 in 1988.

Gross Domestic Product (million kroner at current factor cost): 4,092 in 1984; 4,104 in 1985; 4,594 in 1986.

EXTERNAL TRADE

Principal Commodities (million kroner, 1987): *Imports c.i.f.:* Food and live animals 390.7 (Meat and meat preparations 111.8); Beverages and tobacco 310.0 (Beverages 280.0); Mineral fuels, lubricants etc. 129.8 (Petroleum products 126.6); Chemicals 136.8; Basic manufactures 653.0; Machinery and transport equipment 1,133.6 (Machinery 642.4, Transport equipment 491.2); Miscellaneous manufactured articles 307.1; Total (incl. others) 3,471.5. *Exports f.o.b.:* Fresh, chilled or frozen fish 247.5; Salted, dried or smoked fish 29.1; Crustaceans and molluscs 1,680.4; Other tinned and prepared fish 16.0; Crude materials (inedible) except fuels 285.3 (Lead ores and concentrates 70.3, Zinc ores and concentrates 202.2); Total (incl. others) 2,369.1.

Principal Trading Partners (million kroner, 1986): *Imports c.i.f.:* Denmark 1,907.0, France and Monaco 37.2, Federal Republic of Germany 138.4, Japan 134.0, Norway 160.0, Sweden 159.7, USA 77.9; Total (incl. others) 2,911.8. *Exports f.o.b.:* Denmark 1,708.0, Federal Republic of Germany 64.3, Finland 52.4, France and Monaco 128.0; Total (incl. others) 2,078.5.

Directory

The Government

The legislative body is the Landsting, with 27 members elected on a basis of proportional representation. Greenlanders and Danes resident in Greenland over the age of 18 years have the right to vote. Based on the strength of the parties in the Landsting, a seven-member executive, the Landsstyre, is formed. During a transitional period the Landsstyre will gradually assume control of the administration of Greenland's internal affairs. Jurisdiction in constitutional matters, foreign affairs and defence remains with Denmark.

LANDSSTYRE
(January 1989)

Prime Minister and Secretary for Administration: JONATHAN MOTZFELDT.
Secretary for Fisheries and Industry: MOSES OLSEN.
Secretary for the Economy: HANS-PAVIA ROSING.
Secretary for Social Affairs, Housing and Environment: ARQALUK LYNGE.
Secretary for the Development of Settlements, for Outlying Districts and for Agriculture: KAJ EGEDE.
Secretary for Trade, Traffic and Youth: JOSEF MOTZFELDT.
Secretary for Schools, Education and Labour: JENS LYBERTH.

Government Offices

Grønlands Hjemmestyre (Greenland Home Rule Government): POB 1015, 3900 Nuuk; tel. (009) 299-2-30-00; telex 90613; Denmark office Sjæleboderne 2, 1122 Copenhagen K; tel. (01) 13-42-24.

LANDSTING
Election, 27 May 1987

	Percentage of Votes	Seats
Atassut (Feeling of Community Party)	40.1	11
Siumut (Forward Party)	39.8	11
Inuit Ataqatigiit (Eskimo Brotherhood)	15.3	4
Issittup-partii-a (Polar Party)	4.5	1

Political Organizations

Atassut (Feeling of Community Party): POB 399, 3900 Nuuk; formed as a national organization in 1978; moderate, non-socialist party; Leader OTTO STEENHOLDT.

Inuit Ataqatigiit (Eskimo Brotherhood): POB 321, 3900 Nuuk; f. 1978; Marxist-Leninist organization, calling for Greenland citizenship to be restricted to those of Inuit parentage; advocates Greenland's eventual independence from Denmark; Chair. ARQALUK LYNGE.

Issittup-partii-a (Polar Party): 3900 Nuuk; f. 1987; aims to improve the status of private tradesmen, private fishermen and other private organizations; Leader NICOLAJ HEINRICH.

Siumut (Forward Party): POB 357, 3900 Nuuk; tel. (299) 22077; f. 1977; aims to improve the status of hunters, fishermen and workers, to promote collective ownership and co-operation, and to develop greater reliance on Greenland's own resources; Chair. LARS EMIL JOHANSEN.

Judicial System

The island is divided into 18 court districts and these courts all use lay assessors. For most cases these lower courts are for the first instance and appeal is to the Landsret, the higher court in Nuuk, which is the only one with a professional judge. This court hears the more serious cases in the first instance and appeal in these cases is to the High Court (Østre Landsret) in Copenhagen.

Religion
CHRISTIANITY

The Greenlandic Church comes under the jurisdiction of the Landsstyre and of the Lutheran Bishop of Copenhagen, who exercises control through a suffragan bishop.

The Press

There are no daily newspapers in Greenland.

Atuagagdliutit/Grønlandsposten: POB 39, 3900 Nuuk; tel. (01) 347070; weekly; Editor PHILIP LAURITZEN.

Niviarsiaq: POB 357, 3900 Nuuk; organ of Siumut (Forward Party); monthly.

Sermitsiaq: POB 150, 3900 Nuuk; weekly; Editor HAGEN HØJER CHRISTENSEN.

Publisher

Atuakkiorfik/Det Grønlandske Forlag: Hans Egedesvej 21, POB 840, 3900 Nuuk; tel. (299) 22122; f. 1956; general, children's and textbooks; public relations; Man. P. P. PÉRONARD; Chief Editor SVEND MØLLER.

Radio and Television

In 1984 there were an estimated 18,000 radio receivers and 12,000 television receivers in use.

Kalaallit Nunaata Radioa/Grønlands Radio: POB 1007, 3900 Nuuk; tel. (299) 21172; telex 90606; 5 AM stations, 38 FM stations, 1 Short Wave station; bilingual programmes in Greenlandic and Danish, 17 hours a day; TV in most habitable areas of Greenland, distributed by cable and transmitters, fed from Nuuk by microwave link; Man. Dir PETER F. ROSING; Admin. Dir PETER RAAHØJ; Dir of TV MIKE SIEGSTAD.

American Forces Radio and Television Service (AFRTS)—Air Force Arctic Broadcasting Squadron (AFABS): Station Manager, OL-A Det 1 AFABS, APO New York, NY 09121, USA; station at Søndre Strømfjord; 2 FM radio stations broadcast 24 hours a day; television transmissions 16 hours daily.

Finance
BANKS
(cap. = capital; dep. = deposits; m. = million; amounts in kroner; br. = branch)

Grønlandsbanken A/S: POB 1033, 3900 Nuuk; tel. (009 299) 21380; telex 90611; f. 1967; cap. 221m., dep. 1,040m. (1985); Man. S. E. DANIELSEN; 5 brs.

Nuna Bank A/S (commercial bank): POB 1031, 3900 Nuuk; tel. (009 299) 21360; Man. JØRGEN ULRICHSEN; 5 brs.

Transport

Inland traffic is mainly by aircraft (fixed-wing and helicopter), boat and dog-sled. There are airports or heliports in all towns for

DANISH EXTERNAL TERRITORIES
Greenland

domestic flights. Flights to Copenhagen are operated by Scandinavian Airline Systems (SAS) from Kangerlussuaq (Søndre Strømfjord), and by Greenlandair from Narsarsuaq via Iceland. There are international flights from Nuuk (Godthåb) to Frobisher Bay in Canada, and to Reykjavik, Iceland, which also receives flights from Constable Pynt, on the east coast. In summer, two Icelandic air companies operate passenger services between Iceland and Kulusuk (Ammassalik; on the east coast).

The main port is at Nuuk; there are also all-year ports at Paamiut (Frederikshåb), Maniitsoq (Sukkertoppen) and Sisimiut (Holsteinborg). Coastal motor vessels operate passenger services along the west coast from Upernavik to Nanortalik.

Grønlandsfly A/S (Greenlandair Inc.): POB 1012, 3900 Nuuk; tel. (009 299) 24488; telex 90602; f. 1960; air services to all towns and main settlements in Greenland, and to Copenhagen (Denmark), Reykjavík and Keflavík (Iceland) and Frobisher Bay (Northwest Territories, Canada); Chair. LARS EMIL JOHANSEN; Pres. JAN K. RASMUSSEN; fleet of 3 Dash 7, 3 Twin Otter, 4 S-61N, 5 Jet Ranger, 7 Bell-212, 1 Super Cub, 1 Beechcraft King Air E-90 and 1 Cessna 172 Spyhawk.

DJIBOUTI

Introductory Survey

Location, Climate, Language, Religion, Flag, Capital

The Republic of Djibouti is in the Horn of Africa, at the southern entrance to the Red Sea. It is bounded on the north, west and south-west by Ethiopia, and on the south-east by Somalia. The land is volcanic desert and the climate hot and arid. There are two main ethnic groups, the Issa, who are of Somali origin and comprise 50% of the population, and the Afar, who comprise 40% of the population and are of Ethiopian origin. Both groups are Muslims, and they speak related Cushitic languages. The official languages are Arabic and French. The flag has two equal horizontal stripes, of blue and green, with a white triangle, enclosing a five-pointed red star, at the hoist. The capital is Djibouti.

Recent History

French involvement in the territory began in 1859 and centred on the port of Djibouti, whose position at the entrance to the Red Sea invests the country with its strategic importance and economic potential. In 1945 the area (then known as French Somaliland) was proclaimed an overseas territory, and in 1967 was renamed the French Territory of the Afars and the Issas. The Afars and the Issas have strong connections with Ethiopia and Somalia respectively.

In the late 1950s divisions between the two communities were not marked, the Issas dominating local politics through their greater numbers in the port, but in the 1960s conflicting interests in the Horn of Africa and the French policy of favouring the minority Afar community combined to reveal tensions in the Territory. Demands for independence were growing, and the violence which had been sporadic since 1967 brought matters to a head in 1975, when Ali Aref Bourhan, Vice-President of the Council of Ministers, lost the support of 13 of his deputies. International assurances to respect the rights of a free Djibouti ushered in negotiations for its independence.

Ali Aref resigned in July 1976, and it was finally agreed that a referendum on independence and elections to a new Chamber of Deputies would be held simultaneously in May 1977, and that independence would follow in June; all parties united to form the Rassemblement Populaire pour l'Indépendance, which became the Rassemblement Populaire pour le Progrès (RPP) in 1979.

The Territory voted overwhelmingly for independence in the referendum, while in the parallel elections to the Chamber of Deputies 77% of votes cast were in support of a single list of candidates. Hassan Gouled Aptidon was elected President and on 27 June 1977 Djibouti became independent.

The most important task facing the new state was that of resolving tensions between Afar and Issa. The first administration attempted to balance all ethnic and political interests, but the Afars soon complained of discrimination and attacked the Government's pro-Somali policies; following the arrest of 600 Afars in December 1977, Ahmed Dini, the Prime Minister, and four other Afar Ministers resigned. A special Commission of Afars was created, and the President agreed to its demands for more Afar representation in the Government, the civil service and the armed forces, and the release of most Afar detainees. In February 1978 a new Council of Ministers, with a careful tribal balance, was announced, and in September Barkad Gourad Hamadou, a former Minister of Health, became Prime Minister and declared a policy of 'rapid detribalization'.

In February 1981 a law providing for the election of the President by universal suffrage was passed; President Gouled, the sole candidate, was subsequently re-elected in June. Other laws, passed in October, led to the establishment of a one-party state. Legislative elections were held in May 1982, when candidates were chosen from a single list approved by the RPP, with 91% of the electorate voting. The new Government, formed in June, differed little from its predecessor. In October 1986 President Gouled announced a ministerial reshuffle, in which three newcomers joined the Government. Tension was renewed within Djibouti during the weeks preceding the presidential and legislative elections of April 1987. In March a bomb exploded at a Djibouti café used by French soldiers, killing 11 people, including eight Europeans. The attack, however, was discovered to have been carried out by an extremist Middle Eastern group protesting against the French military presence in Djibouti, and not by Djiboutian dissidents. At the presidential election, President Gouled, the sole candidate, was re-elected with the endorsement of about 90% of the registered electorate. At the same time, 65 candidates for the Chamber of Deputies, presented on a single list approved by the RPP, were elected unopposed by 87% of the electorate. In November President Gouled announced the dissolution of the Government. The new Council of Ministers was enlarged to comprise 16 members. The success of a presidential tour of remote areas of Djibouti in February 1988 was claimed to have demonstrated national unity. In the same month, however, an attack on the border town of Balho was attributed to the Mouvement Populaire de Libération (MPL) and regarded as a sign of increasing clan tensions.

Separate treaties of friendship and co-operation were signed in 1981 with Ethiopia, Somalia, Kenya and Sudan in an effort to begin the peace process in East Africa. In August 1984 the Minister of Foreign Affairs reaffirmed Djibouti's policy of maintaining a neutral stance in the conflict between its neighbours in the Horn of Africa, and expressed his Government's willingness to act as a mediator. A joint ministerial committee has been formed between Djibouti and Ethiopia, to strengthen existing relations and co-operation between the two countries, and at the first session, held in July 1985, it was agreed to improve technical and scientific co-operation in the agricultural sector. Relations deteriorated in 1986, however, after Aden Robleh Awalleh (a former Minister of Commerce, Transport and Tourism), charged with conducting 'massive propaganda campaigns' against the RPP, fled to Ethiopia, where he was granted asylum and subsequently formed a new opposition group, the Mouvement National Djiboutien pour l'Instauration de la Démocratie (MNDID).

Djibouti's role in promoting regional co-operation was illustrated by the creation, in February 1985, of the six-nation Inter-Governmental Authority on Drought and Development (IGADD, see p. 219); Djibouti was chosen as the site of the new organization's permanent secretariat, and President Gouled became the first chairman. At IGADD's inaugural session, in January 1986, the heads of state of Ethiopia and Somalia met for the first time in 10 years. In March 1988 President Gouled was elected chairman of IGADD for a second term of office.

Djibouti suspended air and sea links with the People's Democratic Republic of Yemen in August 1986, following an incident in which an Air Djibouti aircraft was intercepted by Yemeni fighter aircraft and forced to land at Aden. Djibouti had played a prominent part in the evacuation of foreign nationals from Aden during the fighting there in January 1986. Communications were restored in November.

In April 1984 a new scheme for repatriating Ethiopian refugees (estimated to number 35,000), under the aegis of the UNHCR, was begun. By December 1984 it was estimated that around 16,000 had returned to Ethiopia. However, the recurrence of drought and the political situation in Ethiopia caused some refugees to return, and by June 1987 the number of 'official' refugees in Djibouti was 17,200. In August 1986 a new repatriation programme was announced by the Djibouti Government, in consultation with the Ethiopian Government and the UNHCR. According to Djiboutian sources, the number of voluntary repatriations under this programme had reached 2,000 by the end of March 1987. The burden that 'official' refugees have imposed on the economy has been exacerbated by an influx of illegal immigrants from Somalia and Ethiopia, and in June 1987 the Government announced tighter controls on border crossings and identity papers. Following discussions in February 1988, Djibouti and Ethiopia agreed to control movements across their common border and to curb the influx of refugees into Djibouti.

DJIBOUTI

In December 1987 President Mitterrand visited Djibouti, the first visit by a French President since 1977.

Government

Executive power is vested in the President, who is directly elected by universal adult suffrage for a six-year term. Legislative power is held by the Chamber of Deputies, consisting of 65 members elected for five years. The Council of Ministers, presided over by a Prime Minister, is responsible to the President. The Republic forms a single electoral district. Djibouti became a one-party state in October 1981. The Political Bureau of the ruling party, the Rassemblement Populaire pour le Progrès, is appointed by the President.

Defence

Since French withdrawal, a large portion of the annual budget has been set aside for military expenditure, and defence costs were estimated at US $34.5m. in 1987. In June 1988 there were about 4,000 French troops stationed in Djibouti. The total armed forces of Djibouti itself, in which all services form part of the army, numbered 2,870 (including 60 naval and 100 air force personnel), and there was a paramilitary force of 1,200 gendarmes.

Economic Affairs

There is little arable farming in Djibouti. The land is mainly volcanic desert, one of the least hospitable and productive terrains in Africa. More than one-half of the population are pastoral nomads, herding goats, sheep and camels. The agricultural sector contributed only 5.2% of gross domestic product (GDP) in 1983. The development of underground water supplies for irrigation is being studied, and deep-water wells have been sunk in an attempt to alleviate the effects of periodic drought. In May 1987 the African Development Bank agreed to lend US $16.1m. to Djibouti to finance a project to supply water to the towns of Djibouti, Ali-Sabieh, Tadjourah and Obock. A two-phase fisheries development programme had helped to triple catches by 1985, and aims to raise the per caput income of fishers to $400 per year, from $285.

Industry is limited to a few small-scale enterprises. A mineral-bottling factory was opened in 1981, and a dairy plant came into operation in 1985. Manufacturing accounted for 10% of GDP in 1983. There were plans for a small-scale fodder mill and slaughterhouse to be built, with finance provided by the Arab Fund for Economic and Social Development. In 1983 several contracts, worth more than US $80m., were awarded for the development of industry and infrastructure in Djibouti, including one for the construction of a cement works in the capital, with an expected output of 100,000 metric tons per year. In 1986 work commenced on a major geothermal exploration project, funded by foreign aid and the World Bank, in the Hanle Gaggade area. Conditions in the area proved to be unsuitable for the project, but more promising results were reported after tests in the Gouber-Lac-Assal region in 1987. Work on a second 'construction' phase of the programme has been delayed, however. In June 1986 Saudi Arabia gave a grant of $21.4m. for the purchase and installation of three electricity generators, with a capacity of 15 MW.

Political uncertainty in the Horn of Africa has discouraged the creation of new industries, despite the existence of a free zone, and almost all consumer goods are imported (mainly from France, which supplied almost 19% of Djibouti's imports in 1985). Imports totalled 33,106m. Djibouti francs in 1986 (a decline of 7.2% from 1985), while exports rose to 3,628m. Djibouti francs, 46% higher than in 1985. Somalia is the main export market, taking almost 34% of Djibouti's total exports in 1985. Despite the country's development problems, some economic diversification has taken place, and GDP expanded, in real terms, at an average rate of 3% annually in 1979–82, reversing the annual 2.7% decline in 1977–79. In 1984 GDP rose by less than 1%, after an increase of 1.03% in 1983. In 1987 Djibouti's gross national product per head was estimated at US $600. The refugees from the Ogaden region of Ethiopia who remain in Djibouti represent a huge burden on the economy.

Djibouti's economic potential depends, at present, on its developing service sector, which provided 71.6% of GDP in 1983. The sector is based on the expanding seaport, the modern airport, the Djibouti–Addis Ababa railway and the growing activity in banking, which is aided by the freely convertible Djibouti franc and the absence of exchange controls. The war between Ethiopia and Somalia temporarily closed the railway, which carried about one-half of Ethiopia's foreign trade, thus threatening Djibouti's economic viability. Having been adversely affected by the closure of the Suez Canal (1967–75), the port has also found it difficult to compete with the rising Arab ports nearby: total traffic decreased by 10.4% in 1984 and by 20.5% in 1985. There was a substantial recovery in 1986, however, when traffic almost doubled compared with 1985. Djibouti was established as a free port in 1981. Landlocked African countries, including Uganda and Zaire, airfreight their goods to Djibouti for export. The main hope for the future is to develop Djibouti as a major entrepôt for trade between East Africa and the Arab countries. An international container terminal, capable of handling 40,000 metric tons per year, was inaugurated in 1985. The terminal includes 'roll-on, roll-off' facilities, and a refrigerated warehouse. Work on a project to rehabilitate two of the port's berths was reported to be close to completion in September 1988, and the second phase of the project, which included dredging and reclamation works, was due to begin before the end of the year. An undersea telecommunications cable, linking Djibouti with Saudi Arabia, was inaugurated in September 1986. Djibouti also has two earth satellite stations, forming part of the network of the Arab Satellite Communication Organization (see p. 172).

Djibouti is dependent on foreign aid, which, owing to the country's strategic position, is readily forthcoming, particularly from France and the oil-rich states of the Persian Gulf, as well as from the USA and from other European countries. This assistance, along with a surplus in services and transfers, means that Djibouti usually achieves a positive balance of payments (US $5.3m. in 1981). In 1986, however, Djibouti's budgetary deficit was expected to reach US $560,000 (equivalent to 8.5% of GDP), having reached $360,000 in 1985. The national treasury reserves were reported to have fallen from 10,000m. Djibouti francs in December 1981 to 500m. francs in July 1986. In an attempt to reduce the deficit, planned expenditure in the 1987 budget was projected at 22,198m. Djibouti francs, a reduction of 3.14% from the previous year. Budgetary aid for 1988, totalling 85m. French francs (compared with 82.5m. French francs in 1987), was promised by the French Government. Additional assistance has also been forthcoming from Saudi Arabia, and the EEC granted 58m. ECUs in aid to Djibouti, under the terms of the third Lomé convention (see p. 149). In November 1987 the Government projected expenditure in the 1988 budget at 23,267m. Djibouti francs, a rise of 4.8% over 1987, owing to an increase in provisions for external public debt, personnel and administrative costs. In order to boost its revenue, the Government planned in January 1988 to introduce a tax on profits from public industrial and commercial establishments and on companies; and a surtax on qat (a narcotic shrub), alcohol and tobacco.

The Djibouti Government's first Development Plan (1982–84) aimed to direct foreign aid into a co-ordinated development strategy. The 1984–89 Development Plan envisaged total expenditure of $570m.; a high proportion (62%) of the funds necessary for the implementation of this Plan was raised following a successful conference of aid donors, held in November 1983. In June 1987 Abu Dhabi agreed to provide a loan of $5m. to finance the upgrading of Ambouli airport, work on which was under way in late 1988. Other development plans under way include the modernization of the communications network. In January 1988 a French company was contracted to provide Djibouti with a numerical telephone exchange, the purchase and installation of which was to be financed by France's Central Fund for Economic Co-operation. In March the French Ministry of Co-operation granted Djibouti 2.5m. French francs for the purchase of news-gathering equipment, and to fund a study on the development of broadcasting facilities. In 1980 Djibouti became a member of the World Bank and of its affiliate, the International Finance Corporation.

Social Welfare

The social insurance scheme in Djibouti is divided into three categories, according to whether the worker is employed in the private sector, the civil service or the army. Employees receive benefits in case of accidents at work, and are allocated retirement pensions after the age of 55 years. Budgetary expenditure on health in 1986 was 1,631m. Djibouti francs. In 1987 there were 18 hospital establishments, with a total of 1,285 beds, and more than 700 medical personnel, including 89 physicians.

DJIBOUTI

Education

Since independence, the Government has assumed overall responsibility for education. Primary education generally begins at seven years of age and lasts for six years. Secondary education, usually starting at the age of 13, lasts for seven years. Budgetary expenditure on education in 1986 was 1,651m. Djibouti francs. In 1987/88 there were 26,173 primary school pupils and 6,327 pupils at secondary schools.

Public Holidays

1989: 1 January (New Year's Day), 1 May (Workers' Day), 7 May* (Id al-Fitr, end of Ramadan), 27 June (Independence Day), 14 July* (Id al-Adha, Feast of the Sacrifice), 4 August* (Muharran, Islamic New Year), 13 October* (Mouloud, Birth of the Prophet), 25 December (Christmas Day).

1990: 1 January (New Year's Day), 27 April* (Id al-Fitr, end of Ramadan), 1 May (Workers' Day), 27 June (Independence Day), 4 July* (Id al-Adha, Feast of the Sacrifice), 24 July* (Muharran, Islamic New Year), 2 October* (Mouloud, Birth of the Prophet), 25 December (Christmas Day).

* These holidays are dependent on the Islamic lunar calendar and may vary by one or two days from the dates given.

Weights and Measures

The metric system is in force.

Statistical Survey

Source (unless otherwise stated): Ministère du Commerce, de l'Industrie, des Transports et du Tourisme, BP 1846, Djibouti; tel. 35331.

AREA AND POPULATION

Area: 23,200 sq km (8,958 sq miles).

Population: 220,000 (1976 estimate), including Afars 70,000, Issas and other Somalis 80,000, Arabs 12,000, Europeans 15,000, other foreigners 40,000; 483,000 (including refugees and resident foreigners) at mid-1987 (official estimate).

Principal Towns (1981): Djibouti (capital), population 200,000; Dikhil; Ali-Sabieh; Tadjourah; Obock.

AGRICULTURE, ETC.

Principal Crops ('000 metric tons, 1986): Vegetables 13.

Livestock (FAO estimates, '000 head, year ending September 1986): Cattle 47, Sheep 410, Goats 500, Asses 8, Camels 57.

Livestock Products: (FAO estimates, metric tons, 1986): Meat 6,000, Goatskins 438.

Fishing (metric tons, live weight): Total catch 409 in 1984; 380 in 1985; 385 in 1986 (FAO estimate) (Source: FAO, *Yearbook of Fishery Statistics*).

INDUSTRY

Electric energy (million kWh): 146 in 1984; 164 in 1985; 175 in 1986.

FINANCE

Currency and Exchange Rates: 100 centimes = 1 Djibouti franc. *Coins:* 1, 2, 5, 10, 20, 50 and 100 Djibouti francs. *Notes:* 500, 1,000 and 5,000 Djibouti francs. *Sterling and Dollar Equivalents* (30 September 1988): £1 sterling = 300.53 Djibouti francs; US $1 = 177.72 Djibouti francs; 1,000 Djibouti francs = £3.327 = $5.627. *Exchange Rate:* Fixed at US $1 = 177.721 Djibouti francs since February 1973.

Budget (million Djibouti francs, 1986): *Revenue:* Taxation 17,041, Non-tax current revenue 1,727, Grants 1,662, Repayment of loans 254, Transfers from reserve fund 3,639, Advances from the Treasury 170, Total 24,494; *Expenditure:* General administration 9,908, Defence 4,632, Education 1,651, Health 1,631, Economic services 1,341, Debt servicing 968, Other current expenditure 1,694, Total 23,133.

Gross Domestic Product (million Djibouti francs at current prices): 59,997 in 1983; 60,234 in 1984.

Balance of Payments (million Djibouti francs, 1982): Exports f.o.b. (incl. re-exports) 20,830, Imports c.i.f. −38,523, *Trade Balance* −17,693; Services, port 847, Unrequited transfers (net) 8,909, *Current Balance* −4,366; Capital movements 1,942, Changes in reserves −2,424.

EXTERNAL TRADE

Principal Commodities (million Djibouti francs, 1983): *Imports:* Machinery and electrical equipment 4,301, Textiles 4,713, Food 7,488, Qat 3,550, Petroleum and derivatives 3,708, Road vehicles 4,749; Total (incl. others) 39,307. *Exports:* Live animals 592, Food 356; Total (incl. others) 1,919.

Total imports (million Djibouti francs): 39,425 in 1984; 35,670 in 1985; 33,106 in 1986.

Total exports (million Djibouti francs): 2,362 in 1984; 2,488 in 1985; 3,628 in 1986.

Principal Trading Partners (million Djibouti francs, 1984): *Imports:* Benelux 2,214, Ethiopia 4,926, France and Monaco 22,044, Italy 2,915, United Kingdom 1,592; Total (incl. others) 47,832. *Exports:* France and Monaco 1,704, Italy 89, Somalia 179, Spain and Portugal 2, United Kingdom 23; Total (incl. others) 3,306.

TRANSPORT

Railways (Djibouti-Ethiopian Railway, 1987): Freight traffic ('000 metric tons): 291.7; Passengers 1.3m.

Shipping (Djibouti port, 1986): Vessels entered 1,723; Goods loaded 155,000 metric tons; Goods unloaded 466,000 metric tons.

Civil Aviation (Djibouti airport, 1987): Freight loaded 1,612 metric tons; Freight unloaded 6,036 metric tons; Passenger arrivals 67,856; Passenger departures 61,518.

COMMUNICATIONS MEDIA

Radio Receivers (1985): 30,000 in use.

Television Receivers (1985): 10,000 in use.

Telephones (1987): 4,452 in use.

EDUCATION

Primary (1986/87): 59 schools (52 state schools, 7 private schools); 27,136 pupils (24,606 at state schools, 2,530 at private schools); 559 teachers (state schools only).

Secondary and Technical (1986/87): 21 schools (8 state schools, 13 private schools); 7,895 pupils (6,203 at state schools, 1,692 at private schools); 302 teachers (state schools only).

Teacher Training (1987/88): 117 pupils; 13 teachers.

Directory

The Constitution

In February 1981 the National Assembly approved the first constitutional laws controlling the election and terms of office of the President, who is elected by universal suffrage for six years and may serve for no more than two terms. Candidates for the presidency must be presented by a regularly constituted political party and represented by at least 25 members of the Chamber of Deputies.

Deputies are elected for five years from a single list of candidates proposed by the Rassemblement populaire pour le progrès.

In October 1984 a new constitutional law was proposed, specifying that, when the office of President falls vacant, the President of the Supreme Court will assume the power of Head of State for a minimum of 20 days and a maximum of 35 days, during which period a new President shall be elected.

Laws approving the establishment of a single-party system were adopted in October 1981.

The Government

HEAD OF STATE

President and Commander-in-Chief of the Armed Forces: HASSAN GOULED APTIDON (took office 27 June 1977; re-elected June 1981 and April 1987).

COUNCIL OF MINISTERS
(January 1989)

Prime Minister and Minister of Planning and Land Development: BARKAD GOURAD HAMADOU.

Minister of the Interior, Posts and of Telecommunications: KHAIREH ALLALEH HARED.

Minister of Justice and Islamic Affairs: ELAF ORBISS ALI.

Minister of Foreign Affairs and Co-operation: MOUMIN BAHDON FARAH.

Minister of Defence: HUSSEIN BARKAD SIRAJ.

Minister of Commerce, Transport and Tourism: MOUSSA BOURALE ROBLE.

Minister of Finance and National Economy: MUHAMMAD DJAMA ELABE.

Minister of the Civil Service and Administrative Reform: ISMAIL ALI YOUSSOUF.

Minister of Industry and Industrial Development: SALEM ABDOU.

Minister of Labour and Social Welfare: AHMED IBRAHIM ABDI.

Minister of Education: SULEIMAN FARAH LODON.

Minister of Public Works and Housing: AHMED ADEN YOUSSOUF.

Minister of Agriculture and Rural Development: MUHAMMAD MOUSSA CHEHEM.

Minister of Health and Social Affairs: OUGOURE HASSAN IBRAHIM.

Minister of Ports and Maritime Affairs: BOURHAN ALI WARKI.

Minister of Youth, Sports and Cultural Affairs: OMAR CHIRDON ABASS.

MINISTRIES

Office of the Prime Minister: BP 2086, Djibouti; tel. 351494; telex 5871.

Ministry of Agriculture and Rural Development: BP 453, Djibouti; tel. 351297; telex 5871.

Ministry of the Civil Service: BP 155, Djibouti; tel. 351464; telex 5871.

Ministry of Commerce, Transport and Tourism: BP 121, Djibouti; tel. 352540; telex 5871.

Ministry of Defence: BP 42, Djibouti; tel. 352034; telex 5871.

Ministry of Education, Youth and Sports: BP 2102, Djibouti; tel. 351689; telex 5871.

Ministry of Finance and National Economy: BP 13, Djibouti; tel. 353331; telex 5871.

Ministry of Foreign Affairs and Co-operation: BP 1863, Djibouti; tel. 352471; telex 5871.

Ministry of Health and Social Affairs: BP 296, Djibouti; tel. 353331; telex 5871.

Ministry of Industry and Industrial Development: BP 175, Djibouti; tel. 350137; telex 5871.

Ministry of the Interior: BP 33, Djibouti; tel. 350791; telex 5871.

Ministry of Justice and Islamic Affairs: BP 12, Djibouti; tel. 351506; telex 5871.

Ministry of Labour and Social Welfare: BP 170, Djibouti; tel. 350497; telex 5871.

Ministry of Ports and Maritime Affairs: BP 2107, Djibouti; tel. 350105; telex 5871.

Ministry of Public Works and Housing: BP 11, Djibouti; tel. 350006; telex 5871.

Ministry of Telecommunications: Djibouti; tel. 350971; telex 5871.

Legislature

CHAMBRE DES DÉPUTÉS

Elections for the 65-seat Chamber of Deputies were held on 24 April 1987. A single list of candidates, which was claimed to reflect the traditional balance between different ethnic groups and clans, was presented by the Rassemblement populaire pour le progrès. All candidates were elected unopposed.

President of the Chamber: ABDOULKADER WABERI ASKAR.

Political Organizations

Rassemblement populaire pour le progrès (RPP): Djibouti; f. 1979 to succeed the Ligue populaire africaine pour l'indépendance; sole legal party since 1981; 15-mem. Political Bureau; Pres. HASSAN GOULED APTIDON; Sec.-Gen. MOUMIN BAHDON FARAH.

The following organizations are banned:

Front de Libération de la Côte des Somalis (FLCS): f. 1963; Issa-supported; headquarters in Mogadishu, Somalia; Chair. ABDULLA WABERI KHALIF; Vice-Chair. OMAR OSMAN RABEH.

Front démocratique pour la libération de Djibouti (FDLD): f. 1979 by merger of the fmr Mouvement populaire de libération and Union nationale pour l'indépendance; Afar-supported; Sec. MUHAMMAD KAMIL ALI.

Mouvement national djiboutien pour l'instauration de la démocratie (MNDID): f. 1986; headquarters in Ethiopia; seeks restoration of multi-party system; Leader ADEN ROBLEH AWALLEH.

Mouvement populaire de libération (MPL): Afar-supported; headquarters in Ethiopia; reported to have resumed activities in 1988, following attack on border post.

Mouvement pour la libération de Djibouti (MLD): f. 1964; Afar-supported; headquarters in Dire Dawa, Ethiopia; Leader SHEHEM DAOUD.

Parti populaire djiboutien: f. 1981; mainly Afar-supported; Leader MOUSSA AHMAD IDRIS.

Diplomatic Representation

EMBASSIES IN DJIBOUTI

China, People's Republic: Djibouti; tel. 352246; telex 5926; Ambassador: XU CHENGHUA.

Egypt: BP 1989, Djibouti; tel. 351231; telex 5880; Ambassador: (vacant).

Ethiopia: BP 230, Djibouti; tel. 350718; Ambassador: BERHANU DINKA.

France: 45 blvd du Maréchal Foch, BP 2039, Djibouti; tel. 350963; telex 5861; Ambassador: CLAUDE SOUBESTE.

Iraq: BP 1983, Djibouti; tel. 353469; telex 5877; Ambassador: ABDEL AZIZ AL-GAILANI.

Libya: BP 2073, Djibouti; tel. 353339; telex 5874; Ambassador: JALAL MUHAMMAD AL-DAGHELY.

Oman: BP 1996, Djibouti; tel. 350852; telex 5876; Ambassador: SAOUD SALEM HASSAN AL-ANSI.

Saudi Arabia: BP 1921, Djibouti; tel. 351645; telex 5865; Chargé d'affaires: MOWAFFAK AL-DOLIGANE.

DJIBOUTI   *Directory*

Somalia: BP 549, Djibouti; tel. 353521; telex 5815; Ambassador: MUHAMMAD SHEK MUHAMMAD MALINGUR.
Sudan: Djibouti; tel. 351483; Ambassador: TAG EL-SIR MUHAMMAD ABASS.
USSR: BP 1913, Djibouti; tel. 352051; telex 5906; Ambassador: VIKTOR ZHURAVLEV.
USA: Villa Plateau du Serpent, blvd Maréchal Joffré, BP 185, Djibouti; tel. 353995; Ambassador: ROBERT S. BARRETT.
Yemen Arab Republic: BP 194, Djibouti; tel. 352975; Ambassador: MUHAMMAD ABDOUL WASSI HAMID.
Yemen, People's Democratic Republic: BP 1932, Djibouti; tel. 353704; Chargé d'affaires: AWAD SALEM BAABAD.

Judicial System

The cour suprême was established in October 1979. There is a tribunal supérieur d'appel and a tribunal de première instance in Djibouti; each of the five administrative districts has a tribunal coutumier.

Religion

ISLAM

Almost the entire population are Muslims.
Qadi of Djibouti: MOGUE HASSAN DIRIR, BP 168, Djibouti; tel. 352669.

CHRISTIANITY

The Roman Catholic Church

Djibouti comprises a single diocese, directly responsible to the Holy See. There were an estimated 9,000 adherents in the country at 31 December 1985.
Bishop of Djibouti (vacant): Apostolic Administrator: Fr GEORGES PERRON, Evêché, blvd de la République, BP 94, Djibouti; tel. 350140.

The Anglican Communion

Within the Episcopal Church in Jerusalem and the Middle East, Djibouti lies within the jurisdiction of the Bishop in Egypt.

Other Christian Churches

Eglise Protestante: blvd de la République, BP 416, Djibouti; tel. 351820; f. 1957; Pastor PASCAL VERNIER.
Greek Orthodox Church: blvd de la République, Djibouti; tel. 351325; c. 350 adherents; Archimandrite STAVROS GEORGANAS.
The Ethiopian Orthodox Church is also represented in Djibouti.

The Press

Carrefour Africain: BP 393, Djibouti; fortnightly; publ. by the Roman Catholic mission; circ. 500.
Djibouti Aujourd'hui: Djibouti; f. 1977; monthly; Editor ISMAEL OMAR GUELLEH.
La Nation de Djibouti: place du 27 juin, BP 32, Djibouti; tel. 352201; weekly; Dir ISMAEL H. TANI; circ. 4,000.

NEWS AGENCIES

Agence Djiboutienne de Presse (ADP): BP 32, Djibouti; tel. 350201; telex 5871.

Foreign Bureau

Agence France-Presse (AFP): BP 97, Djibouti; tel. 352294; telex 5863; Correspondent HAIDAR KHALID ABDULLAH.

Radio and Television

There were an estimated 30,000 radio receivers and 10,000 television receivers in use in 1985. In 1980 Djibouti became a member of the Arab Satellite Communication Organization, and opened an earth station for radio, television and telecommunications; a second earth station was inaugurated in June 1985.

Radiodiffusion-Télévision de Djibouti (RTD): BP 97, Djibouti; tel. 352294; telex 5863; f. 1956; state-controlled; programmes in French, Afar, Somali and Arabic; 24 hours radio and 5 hours television daily; Dir MUHAMMAD DJAMA ADEN.

Finance

(cap. = capital; p.u. = paid up; dep. = deposits; m. = million; res = reserves; br. = branch; amounts in Djibouti francs)

BANKING

Banque Nationale de Djibouti: BP 2118, Djibouti; tel. 352751; telex 5838; f. 1981; will eventually take over some of the functions carried out by the Trésor National; Gov. LUC A. ADEN.
Trésor National de la République de Djibouti: blvd de la République, BP 2119, Djibouti; in charge of monetary issue.

Commercial Banks

Bank of Credit and Commerce International: 10 ave Pierre Pascal, BP 2105, Djibouti; tel. 351741; telex 5810; Dir NASIM AHMED.
Banque de Djibouti et du Moyen Orient SA: 6 rue de Marseille, BP 2471, Djibouti; tel. 351133; telex 5943; f. 1983; 55% owned by Middle East Bank; cap. 125m.; Chair. MAJID MUHAMMAD AL-FUTTAIM; Man. Dir T. M. SHETH.
Banque Indosuez (Mer Rouge) (France): 10 place Lagarde, BP 88, Djibouti; tel. 353016; telex 5829; f. 1908; cap. 1,500m., res 150m., dep. 19,858m. (Dec. 1985); Chair. and Man. Dir GEORGES LOUBEYNE; 5 brs.
Banque pour le Commerce et l'Industrie (Mer Rouge): place Lagarde, BP 2122, Djibouti; tel. 350857; telex 5821; f. 1977; 51% of shares owned by Banque Nationale de Paris Intercontinentale; cap. and res. 2,500m., dep. 19,258m. (Dec. 1985); Pres. MARCEL RINAUDO; 4 brs.
British Bank of the Middle East (Hong Kong): place Lagarde, BP 2112, Djibouti; tel. 353291; telex 5826; Man. CHRISTOPHER REDDINGTON.
Commercial and Savings Bank of Somalia: BP 2004, Djibouti; tel. 351282; telex 5879; Man. ALI NOUR ISSAK HOUSSEIN.
Commercial Bank of Ethiopia: BP 187, Djibouti; tel. 352101; telex 5835; f. 1980; Man. ASSEBEWORK ZEGEYE.

Development Bank

Caisse de Développement de Djibouti: rue de l'Ethiopie, BP 520, Djibouti; tel. 353391; f. 1983; national development bank; 51% govt-owned; cap. 500m.; Chair. LUC ADEN; Man. Dir NOUH OMAR MIGUIL.

Banking Association

Association Professionnelle des Banques: c/o Banque pour le Commerce et l'Industrie (Mer Rouge), place Lagarde, BP 2122, Djibouti; tel. 350857; Pres. MUHAMMAD ADEN.

INSURANCE

Assurances Générales de France (AGF): 3 rue Marchand, Djibouti; tel. 352339.
State Insurance Co of Somalia (SICOS): BP 50, Djibouti; tel. 352707; telex 5819; all classes of insurance.
About 10 European insurance companies maintain agencies in Djibouti.

Trade and Industry

Chambre Internationale de Commerce et d'Industrie: place Lagarde, BP 84, Djibouti; tel. 351070; telex 5957; f. 1906; 24 mems; 12 assoc. mems; Pres. SAID ALI COUBECHE; First Vice-Pres. MUHAMMAD ADEN.
Djibouti Labour Federation: Pres. IDRIS OMAR.

Transport

RAILWAYS

Compagnie du chemin de fer Djibouti-Ethiopien: BP 2116, Djibouti; tel. 350353; telex 5953; POB 1051, Addis Ababa; tel. 447250; telex 21414; f. 1908; adopted present name in 1981; jtly-owned by govts of Djibouti and Ethiopia; plans to grant autonomous status were announced by the two govts in July 1985; 781 km of track, 100 km in Djibouti, linking Djibouti with Addis Ababa; Pres. MOUSSA BOURALE ROBLE; Gen. Man. CHANNIE TAMIRU.

ROADS

In 1987 there were 3,037 km of roads, of which over 400 km were bitumen-surfaced, including the 185-km road along the Ethiopian frontier. Of the remainder, 1,000 km are serviceable throughout the year, the rest only during the dry season. Half the roads are usable only by lorries. In 1981 the 40-km Grand Bara road was opened, linking the capital with the south.

SHIPPING

Djibouti was established as a free port in 1981.

Compagnie Générale Maritime: Immeuble Plein Ciel, BP 182, Djibouti; tel. 353825; telex 5817; agents for Mitsui OSK, CGM/Svedel, CGM, SNC, Hapaglloyd and Seal Lines.

Compagnie Maritime Auxiliaire d'Outre-Mer: ave des Messageries Maritimes, BP 89, Djibouti; tel. 352022; telex 5825; agents for Adriatic Red Sea Line, British Petroleum, Compagnie Générale Maritime, Comp. Navale des Pétroles, Deutsche Ost Afrika Line, Djakarta Lloyd, Hapaglloyd, Hungarian Shipping Line, Jadranska Line, Nedlloyd Line, Scandinavian East Africa Line, Shell International, Sovinflot; Gen. Man. L. J. HUGHES.

Gellatly Hankey et Cie (Djibouti) SA: rue de Genève, BP 81, Djibouti; tel. 352012; telex 5860; f. 1942; Lloyd's agents, and shipping agents for Nippon Yusen Kaisha, Waterman Line, P & O, Cosco, Sinochart and others.

J. J. Kothari & Co Ltd: BP 171, rue de Soleillet, Djibouti; tel. 350219; telex 5860; agents for Bangladesh Shipping Corpn, Pacific International Line, Ratnakar Shipping Co, Shipping Corpn of Saudi Arabia, United Thai Shipping Co, Shipping Corpn of India, Mogul Line, United Arab Maritime, Sudan Shipping Line, Finnland Steamship Co; also ship managers, stevedores, freight forwarders; Dirs S. J. KOTHARI, N. KOTHARI.

Mitchell Cotts Djibouti SARL: blvd de la République, BP 85, Djibouti; tel. 351204; telex 5812; agents for Clan Line, Ellerman City Liners, Fearnley and Eger, Harrison Line, Iraqi Maritime Transport Co, Maldivian National Trading Corpn, Farell Lines, Central Gulf, Yemen Gulf Lines, Société Navale Caennaise, OCL, Beacon and other shipping and forwarding cos; Dir FAHMY SAID CASSIM.

Société d'Armement et de Manutention de la Mer Rouge (SAMER): BP 10, Djibouti; agents for Pacific International Line, Cunard Brocklebank, Wilhelm Wilhelmsen Co, Pakistan Shipping Lines, Aktiebolaget Svenska Östasiatiska Kompaniet, Texaco, Chevron Shipping Co, Kie Hock Shipping Co, Barber Lines, Supreme Shipping Co, Scandutch; Chair. JOHN COLLINS; Man. Dir VINCENT DELL'AQUILLA.

Société Maritime L. Savon et Ries: ave Saint-Laurent du Var, BP 2125, Djibouti; agents for Chargeurs Réunis, NCHP, Sudcargos, Svedel Line, Lloyd Triestino, Hellenic Lines, Messina, Polish Ocean Lines; Dir M. AARSTAD.

CIVIL AVIATION

The international airport is at Ambouli, 6 km from Djibouti, and there are six internal airports.

Air Djibouti (Red Sea Airlines): BP 505, rue Marchand, Djibouti; telex 5820; f. 1971, when Air Somalie took over the fmr Air Djibouti (f. 1963); the Djibouti govt holds 62.5% of shares, and Air France 32.3%; internal flights connecting the six major centres and international services to the Yemen Arab Republic, Somalia, the United Arab Emirates, France, Italy, Egypt, Ethiopia and Saudi Arabia; Gen. Man. PAUL BOTBOL; fleet of 2 Twin Otter and 1 Boeing 727.

Tourism

Djibouti's principal attraction is the desert scenery of the interior. In 1987 a total of 21,790 tourists stayed in hotels in Djibouti.

Office National du Tourisme et de l'Artisanat: place du 27 juin, BP 1938, Djibouti; tel. 352800; telex 5938.

DOMINICA

Introductory Survey

Location, Climate, Language, Religion, Flag, Capital

The Commonwealth of Dominica is situated in the Windward Islands group of the West Indies, lying between Guadeloupe, to the north, and Martinique, to the south. The climate is tropical, though tempered by sea winds which sometimes reach hurricane force, especially from July to September. The average temperature is about 27°C (80°F), with little seasonal variation. Rainfall is heavy, especially in the mountainous areas, where the annual average is 6,350 mm (250 inches), compared with 1,800 mm (70 inches) along the coast. English is the official language but a local French patois is widely spoken. Almost all of the inhabitants profess Christianity, and about 80% are Roman Catholics. The national flag has a green field, with equal stripes of yellow, white and black forming an upright cross, on the centre of which is superimposed a red disc containing a parrot surrounded by ten five-pointed green stars (one for each of the island's parishes). The capital is Roseau.

Recent History

A British possession since the 18th century, Dominica formed part of the Leeward Islands federation until 1939. In 1940 it was transferred to the Windward Islands and remained attached to that group until the federal arrangement was ended in December 1959. Under a new constitution, effective from January 1960, Dominica (like each other member of the group) achieved a separate status, with its own Administrator and an enlarged Legislative Council. Dominica was a member of the West Indies Federation between 1958 and its dissolution in 1962.

At the January 1961 elections to the Legislative Council, the ruling Dominica United People's Party was defeated by the Dominica Labour Party (DLP), formed from the People's National Movement and other groups. Edward LeBlanc, leader of the DLP, became Chief Minister. In March 1967 Dominica became one of the West Indies Associated States, gaining full autonomy in internal affairs, with the United Kingdom retaining responsibility for defence and foreign relations only. The Legislative Council was replaced by a House of Assembly, the Administrator became Governor and the Chief Minister was restyled Premier. At elections to the House in October 1970, the Premier was returned to power.

In July 1974 LeBlanc retired, being replaced as DLP leader and Premier by Patrick John, formerly Deputy Premier and Minister of Finance. Elections to an enlarged House of Assembly were held in March 1975, when the DLP was returned again, winning 16 of the 21 elective seats. Following a decision in 1975 by the Associated States to seek independence separately, Dominica became an independent republic within the Commonwealth on 3 November 1978. Patrick John became Prime Minister, and Frederick Degazon, formerly Speaker of the House of Assembly, was eventually elected President.

In May 1979 two people were killed by the defence force at a demonstration against the Government's attempts to introduce legislation which would restrict the freedom of the trade unions and the press. The killings fuelled increasing popular opposition to the Government, and a Committee for National Salvation (CNS) was formed to press for John's resignation. On his refusal, opponents of the Government organized a general strike which lasted 25 days, with John relinquishing power only after all his Cabinet ministers had resigned and President Degazon had gone into hiding abroad (there was a succession of Acting Presidents; Degazon finally resigned in February 1980). Oliver Seraphin, the candidate proposed by the CNS, was elected Prime Minister, and an interim government was then formed to prepare for elections in six months.

Elections were eventually held in July 1980, when the Dominica Freedom Party (DFP) gained a convincing victory, winning 17 of the 21 elective seats in the House of Assembly. Eugenia Charles, the party's leader, became the Caribbean's first woman Prime Minister. Both Patrick John, who contested the elections as leader of the DLP, and Oliver Seraphin, who stood as leader of the newly formed Democratic Labour Party (DEMLAB), lost their seats. The DFP's victory was attributed to its continued integrity, while the DLP and DEMLAB had suffered from major political scandals.

Fears for the island's security dominated 1981. In January the Government disarmed the defence force as a result of reports that weapons were being traded for marijuana. Against a background of increasing violence and the declaration of a state of emergency, however, there were two coup attempts involving former defence force members. Patrick John, the former Prime Minister, was also implicated and imprisoned. In June 1982 John and his fellow prisoners were tried and acquitted but the Government secured a retrial in October 1985, when John and the former deputy defence force commander each received a prison sentence of 12 years. In 1986 the former commander of the defence force was hanged for the murder of a policeman during the second coup attempt. The death sentences on five other soldiers were commuted to life imprisonment.

After his release in June 1982, John attempted to form a new left-wing coalition party, and in 1983 a new DLP was formed upon its reunification with DEMLAB. In January 1985 agreement was reached between the DLP, the United Dominica Labour Party and the Dominica Liberation Movement, to form a united left-wing grouping, known as the Labour Party of Dominica (LPD), to contest the next general election, with Michael Douglas, a former Minister of Finance, as leader. During the election campaign, Eugenia Charles stressed the economic achievements of her administration and accused members of the LPD of having 'pro-Communist' links. At the general election, held on 1 July, the DFP was returned to power, winning 15 of the 21 elective seats in the House of Assembly. The opposition LPD won five seats, with the remaining seat being won by Rosie Douglas, the brother of the LPD leader, whose candidature was not officially endorsed by the LPD. Following the election, the LPD began an 18-month boycott of the House, in protest at the Government's decision to curtail live broadcasts of parliamentary proceedings. By July 1987, the DFP's strength in the House had increased to 17 seats, with four seats still being held by the LPD.

Dissatisfaction at continued government austerity measures was offset by the success of the land reform programme. Since independence, the Government had acquired nearly all the large estates, often in an attempt to forestall violence. In 1986 the first of the estates was divided, and tenure granted to the former workers. This process was continued and, with the accompanying development programme, received widespread support. Plans to reform extensively Roseau's sanitation and environmental services in 1989, however, were cited as the reason for postponing for a year elections to the city council, originally scheduled for November 1988. The opposition DLP and the newly-formed Dominica United Workers' Party bitterly denounced the decision and Prime Minister Charles' style of government.

In foreign policy, Dominica has close links with France and the USA. France helped in putting down the coup attempts against the DFP government, and Dominica was the first Commonwealth country to benefit from the French aid agency, FAC. In October 1983 Dominica, as a member of OECS (see p. 107), contributed forces to the US-backed invasion of Grenada. Since the mid-1980s, the OECS has discussed the possible formation of a political union, although some islands displayed considerable reluctance. Nevertheless, in 1988 four countries, Dominica, Grenada, Saint Lucia and Saint Vincent and the Grenadines, decided to proceed with plans for a political union. Dominica is also a member of CARICOM (see p. 106), and secured limited protection for some of its industries when the organization removed its internal trade barriers in October 1988.

Government

Legislative power is vested in the unicameral House of Assembly, containing 30 members (nine nominated and 21

DOMINICA

elected for five years by universal adult suffrage). Executive authority is vested in the President, elected by the House, but in most matters the President is guided by the advice of the Cabinet and acts as a constitutional Head of State. He appoints the Prime Minister, who must be able to command a majority in the House, and (on the Prime Minister's recommendation) other Ministers. The Cabinet is responsible to the House.

Defence

The Dominican Defence Force was officially disbanded in April 1981. There is a police force of about 300, which includes a coastguard service. A patrol boat was received from the USA in 1983.

Economic Affairs

In 1987, according to estimates by the World Bank, Dominica's gross national product (GNP), measured at average 1985–87 prices, was US $115m., equivalent to $1,440 per head. Between 1980 and 1987, it was estimated, GNP per head increased, in real terms, at an average rate of 3.0% per year, with growth in 1987 reaching 3.3%.

Agriculture is the principal economic activity, accounting for 28% of gross domestic product (GDP) in 1987, and bananas are the main crop. They are, however, a vulnerable crop, and hurricane damage in 1979, and again in 1980, virtually stopped all production. Since 1981, production and export revenue have gradually increased, and the Dominica Banana Marketing Corporation (DBMC) has improved efficiency and management. By 1986, when production reached a record 55,000 metric tons, all bananas were field-packed; exports for the year totalled some 51,000 tons, earning EC $67.1m. in export revenue. Virtually all of Dominica's banana crop is exported to the UK. Production rose to nearly 67,000 tons in 1987, and was estimated to reach 74,000 tons in 1988. Exports in 1987 totalled 60,640 tons, and earned EC $85.3m., owing to favourable exchange rates. Concern about the continuation of preferential access to the UK after the completion of the EEC's internal market in 1992 was largely allayed by negotiations in 1988. Nevertheless, plans were instituted to improve fruit quality, and productivity from four to 10 metric tons per acre. In 1987 bananas and soaps together accounted for 87.3% of total domestic exports, and the number of active banana farmers had increased by 18% compared with the previous year, to 5,998.

Other important crops include coconuts (which provide copra for export as well as edible oil and soap), avocados, limes and other citrus fruits. In an effort to reduce the country's dependence on the banana industry, plans were made in 1983 to revitalize the lime industry, with a grant from the Caribbean Food Corporation. By 1988, however, the Citrus Growers' Association had recorded losses of EC $600,000. Incentives to diversify did continue, and the UK gave a loan of EC $1.7m. in 1988, to the tree crop programme. The plan was to increase production of citrus fruits, mangoes and avocados. Furthermore, a French company planned to export eight tons per week of agricultural products for sale in Europe. There were also renewed plans to attempt to revive the troubled coconut industry, which had been in decline since the sharp fall in exports of coconut oil in 1985. In the first half of 1988, coconut oil exports earned EC $1.9m., having earned EC $1.4m. in the whole of 1987. Dominica also exports bay oil, and there are plans to develop coffee as a major export crop.

The land reforms that were implemented on the large estates acquired by the Government following independence (see above) not only gave rise to social benefits, but were also intended to increase agricultural production and exports. Under the scheme, the Government guaranteed a minimum holding, with security of tenure, to small farmers and landless farm workers. It also promised to provide services and equipment, and to develop communications. The improvement of the country's infrastructure is regarded by the Government as being an important part of its efforts to encourage private investment in the economy. In the budget proposals for the financial year 1987/88, 70% of total capital expenditure was allocated to the Ministry of Communications and Works. Heavy rain in late 1988, however, caused damage costing about EC $3m. to the road system. At the same time, Dominica became the first beneficiary of a Caribbean Development Bank structural adjustment loan, worth more than US $12m. over three years. The plan included development of the economic diversification programme, as well as an improvement in public-sector efficiency, and a reform of the tax system.

There is a small amount of livestock but this is reared mainly for domestic consumption. Fishing is a traditional occupation for the islanders, and several co-operatives have been established to provide vessels and equipment to fishermen on a hire basis. Taiwan has made important contributions, since 1985, to the development of the fishing industry, as did Canada in 1988. In 1987, following four years of negotiations, Dominica and the EEC signed a fisheries agreement which provided for reciprocal fishing activities by vessels registered in Dominica and by EEC member-countries' vessels registered in the French overseas possessions of Martinique and Guadeloupe. Over the first three years of the agreement, the EEC was to pay Dominica US $1.2m. for the use of its territorial waters. There is some quarrying of pumice, and attempts are being made to exploit Dominica's extensive timber reserves. More than 40% of Dominica's land area consists of forest and woodland, according to the FAO, which, with the UN Development Programme, granted EC $1m. in 1988 for training in the development of a balanced timber industry.

Diversification of the island's economic base also includes the development of industry. In 1987 manufacturing accounted for 8% of GDP. There are factories for the manufacture and refining of crude and edible vegetable oils and for the production of cigarettes, canned juices and soaps. Soaps accounted for 38% of domestic products in 1982 and export earnings totalled EC $23.4m. Exports declined, however, and by 1984 had fallen to EC $14.9m., but by 1987 had increased to EC $21.3m., from production of 6,571 metric tons (98% is exported). During 1985 the output of the manufacturing sector expanded by 14%, but in 1986 the rate of growth slowed to 3%. The main constraint on expansion is that of transportation difficulties. Dominica is now using its own plentiful reserves of water to export to other, drier Caribbean islands, such as Aruba. Investment is then made in improving Dominica's water supply infrastructure and the supply of electricity, about one-half of which is generated by hydroelectric power stations. The final stage of the hydroelectricity development began in 1988 and, in order to help finance the EC $52m. project, charges to electricity consumers were increased by 25% and were expected to contribute EC $8m. The new rates were to remain in force until the completion of the scheme in 1991. It is anticipated that by 1992 the country's power requirements will be met entirely by hydroelectric generation.

Tourism is not as developed as in many of the other Caribbean islands, and depends more on the scenery and natural environment. Dominica's first overseas tourist bureau opened in the UK in 1988. Hitherto, the biggest increases in visitors have been among cruise-ship passenger arrivals, particularly the rises of 105% in 1985 and 74% in 1986. From the early 1980s, the number of visitors increased gradually to a total of 35,864 (including 24,410 stop-over tourists) in 1986. Earnings from tourism totalled EC $7.1m. in 1986, compared with EC $5.9m. in 1985. In 1987 tourist arrivals increased moderately, to 26,593 stop-over visitors and 12,080 on cruise-ships. It was hoped that stop-over arrivals, who contribute more to the economy, would increase by up to 20% in 1988. To keep pace with such expansion, the Government announced plans to increase the number of hotels from 12 to 15, and of tourist rooms from 400 to 520 by the end of 1989, helped by an EEC grant of ECU 1.6m.

Before 1980, the Government had a growing budget deficit on its current transactions. However, the funding of capital expenditure projects by means of foreign aid and loans, and the imposition of fiscal restraint, helped to convert the current balance from a deficit of EC $17.3m. in 1980/81 to a surplus of EC $400,000 in 1984/85. The budget proposals for 1988/89 envisaged that the surplus would rise to EC $4.5m., despite an 18% increase in current expenditure, to EC $101.4m., and EC $1.6m. in tax concessions. The Government did express concern at the size of the public external debt in 1988, US $69.3m. Previously, the most recent available official figure, for 1982, was US $32.9m. As a result of IMF support, the current account deficit on the balance of payments, of EC $38.6m. in 1980, was converted into a surplus by 1986 (of EC $13.8m.). In 1987, however, this surplus was only EC $1.5m., owing mainly to an increase in imports and a consequent rise in the trade deficit, to more than EC $37m.

DOMINICA

GDP expanded, in real terms, by 6.2% in 1984, but by only 1.2% in 1985. In 1986/87 the Government aimed for an annual GDP growth rate of at least 4% over three years under a structural adjustment programme assisted by the IMF and the World Bank, and in 1986 GDP growth rate of 4% was achieved. In 1987 the growth rate was 4.6%. The rate of inflation fell from 32.7% in 1980 to 2.1% in 1985. It rose slightly in 1986, to 3.0%, and stabilized at 2.9% in 1987, before showing signs of falling in the first two quarters of 1988. Unemployment fell from 23% of the labour force in 1980 to 13% by 1986. In 1988 it was announced that, since the 1981 census, net migration from Dominica had been more than 3,000.

Social Welfare

There are main hospitals at Roseau and Portsmouth, with 242 and 50 beds respectively, and two cottage hospitals, at Marigot and Grand Bay. A loan was received from France in 1986 for the construction of a polyclinic at the Princess Margaret Hospital, Roseau. There are 44 health centres, located throughout the island. In 1986 there were 27 physicians working in Dominica.

Education

Education is free and is provided by both government and denominational schools. There are also a number of schools for the mentally and physically handicapped. Education is compulsory for 10 years between five and 15 years of age. Primary education begins at the age of five and lasts for seven years. Secondary education, beginning at 12 years of age, also lasts for seven years, comprising a first cycle of five years and a second of two years. A teacher training college provides further education, and there is also a branch of the University of the West Indies on the island. The rate of adult illiteracy was only 5.6% in 1986.

Public Holidays

1989: 2 January (for New Year's Day), 6-7 February (Carnival), 24-27 March (Easter), 1 May (Labour Day), 15 May (Whit Monday), 2 July (Caricom Day), 7 August (August Monday), 3-4 November (Independence Days), 25-26 December (Christmas).

1990: 1 January (New Year's Day), 14-15 February (Carnival), 13-16 April (Easter), 7 May (for Labour Day), 4 June (Whit Monday), 2 July (Caricom Day), 6 August (August Monday), 3-4 November (Independence Days), 25-26 December (Christmas).

Weights and Measures

The imperial system is in use, although the metric system is to be introduced.

Statistical Survey

Sources (unless otherwise stated): Ministry of Finance, Roseau; OECS Economic Affairs Secretariat, *Annual Digest of Statistics*.

AREA AND POPULATION

Area: 750.6 sq km (289.8 sq miles).

Population: 70,513 at census of 7 April 1970; 73,795 (males 36,754, females 37,041) at census of 7 April 1981; 81,200 (estimate, 1988).

Principal Towns (population at 1981 census): Roseau (capital) 8,279; Portsmouth 2,200.

Births and Deaths (registrations, 1984): Live births 1,716 (birth rate 20.8 per 1,000); Deaths 432 (death rate 5.2 per 1,000).

Economically Active Population (1981 census): Agriculture, hunting, forestry and fishing 7,843; Mining and quarrying 8; Manufacturing 1,417; Electricity, gas and water 245; Construction 2,306; Trade, restaurants and hotels 1,613; Transport, storage and communications 914; Financing, insurance, real estate and business services 257; Community, social and personal services 4,980; Activities not adequately defined 1,004; Total employed 20,587 (males 14,057; females 6,530); Unemployed 4,746 (males 2,641; females 2,105); Total labour force 25,333 (males 16,698, females 8,635) (Source: ILO, *Year Book of Labour Statistics*).

AGRICULTURE, ETC.

Principal Crops ('000 metric tons, 1986): Bananas 55, Coconuts 13*, Taro (Dasheen) 11*, Grapefruit 7*, Limes 6*.

* Estimates from FAO, *Production Yearbook*.

Livestock (FAO estimates, year ending September 1986): Cattle 4,000, Pigs 9,000, Sheep 4,000, Goats 6,000 (Source: FAO, *Production Yearbook*).

Fishing (metric tons, live weight): Total catch 500 (FAO estimate) in 1984; 446 in 1985; 450 (FAO estimate) in 1986 (Source: FAO, *Yearbook of Fishery Statistics*).

MINING

Pumice ('000 metric tons, 1985): Estimated production 109 (Source: US Bureau of Mines).

INDUSTRY

Production (1984): Soap 4,068 metric tons; Electricity (1985) 18 million kWh.

FINANCE

Currency and Exchange Rates: 100 cents = 1 East Caribbean dollar (EC $). *Coins:* 1, 2, 5, 10, 25 and 50 cents. *Notes:* 1, 5, 20 and 100 dollars. *Sterling and US Dollar Equivalents* (30 September 1988): £1 sterling = EC $4.566; US $1 = EC $2.700; EC $100 = £21.90 = US $37.04. *Exchange Rate:* Fixed at US $1 = EC $2.70 since July 1976.

Budget (government estimates, EC $ million, year ending 30 June 1989): Revenue 105.9; Recurrent Expenditure 101.4.

International reserves (US $ million at 31 December 1987): Reserve position in IMF 0.01; Foreign exchange 17.42; IMF special drawing rights 0.99; Total 18.43.

Money Supply (EC $ million at 31 December 1987): Currency outside banks 20.77; Demand deposits 37.89; Total money 58.67.

Cost of Living (Retail Price Index, base: 1980 = 100): All items 128.5 in 1985; 132.3 in 1986; 138.7 in 1987.

National Accounts (EC $ million in current prices): Gross domestic product 193.6 in 1982; 211.0 in 1983; 230.7 in 1984.

Balance of Payments (US $ million, 1987): Merchandise exports f.o.b. 46.5, Merchandise imports f.o.b. −60.3; *Trade balance* −13.8; Exports of services 11.8, Imports of services −15.5; *Balance on goods and services* −17.5; Unrequited transfers (net) 18.0; *Current balance* 0.6; Long-term capital (net) 9.9, Short-term capital (net) −11.2; Net errors and omissions 9.4; *Total* (net monetary movements) 8.6; Valuation changes (net) −0.8; Exceptional financing (net) 0.1; *Changes in reserves* 7.9.

(Source: IMF, *International Financial Statistics*.)

EXTERNAL TRADE

Principal Commodities (EC $ million, 1985): *Imports c.i.f.:* Food and live animals 28.8 (cereals and cereal preparations 8.8); Mineral fuels, lubricants, etc. 16.4 (Petroleum and petroleum products 15.1); Chemicals and related products 17.0; Basic manufacturers 30.7 (Paper, paperboard and manufactures 10.3); Machinery and transport equipment 33.6 (Road vehicles and parts 12.5); Miscellaneous manufactured articles 9.6; Total (incl. others) 149.4. *Exports f.o.b.:* Food and live animals 41.7 (Bananas 37.0); Chemicals and related products 22.0 (Soaps 19.2); Machinery and transport equipment 4.2; Total (incl. others) 76.8.

Principal Trading Partners (EC $ million, 1985): *Imports:* Canada 7.1; Guadeloupe 6.1; Japan 11.0; Netherlands 5.1; Saint Lucia 8.5; Saint Vincent and the Grenadines 4.9; Trinidad and Tobago 14.6; United Kingdom 24.9; USA 40.6; Total (incl. others) 149.4. *Exports:* Barbados 3.3; Guadeloupe 2.8; Guyana 2.7; Jamaica 11.3; Saint Vincent and the Grenadines 2.2; Trinidad and Tobago 3.3; United Kingdom 38.5; USA 3.4; Total (incl. others) 76.8.

TRANSPORT

Road Traffic (registered motor vehicles, 1983): 2,261 passenger vehicles; 1,616 commercial vehicles (incl. jeeps); 156 motor cycles; Total (incl. others) 6,552.

DOMINICA

Shipping (international sea-borne freight traffic, '000 metric tons, estimates, 1985): Goods loaded 33; Goods unloaded 51 (Source: UN, *Monthly Bulletin of Statistics*).
Civil Aviation (1981): Aircraft arrivals 3,670.

EDUCATION
Primary and Secondary Schools (1983/84): 56 primary schools, 584 primary teachers, 17,456 primary pupils; 9 secondary schools, 157 teachers, 3,443 secondary pupils; 1 sixth form college, 13 teachers, 113 pupils.
Further Education (1982): 1 teacher training college; 15 teachers; 60 students; 1 technical college, 18 teachers, 120 students.

TOURISM
Tourist arrivals: 28,036 in 1985; 35,864 in 1986; 38,673 (26,593 stop-overs, 12,080 cruise ship passengers) in 1987.

Directory

The Constitution

The Constitution came into effect at the independence of Dominica on 3 November 1978. Its main provisions are summarized below:

FUNDAMENTAL RIGHTS AND FREEDOMS
The Constitution guarantees the rights of life, liberty, security of the person, the protection of the law and respect for private property. The individual is entitled to freedom of conscience, of expression and assembly and has the right to an existence free from slavery, forced labour and torture. Protection against discrimination on the grounds of sex, race, place of origin, political opinion, colour or creed is assured.

THE PRESIDENT
The President is elected by the House of Assembly for a term of five years. A presidential candidate is nominated jointly by the Prime Minister and the Leader of the Opposition and on their concurrence is declared elected without any vote being taken; in the case of disagreement the choice will be made by secret ballot in the House of Assembly. Candidates must be citizens of Dominica aged at least 40 who have been resident in Dominica for five years prior to their nomination. A President may not hold office for more than two terms.

PARLIAMENT
Parliament consists of the President and the House of Assembly, composed of 21 elected Representatives and nine Senators. According to the wishes of Parliament, the latter may be appointed by the President—five on the advice of the Prime Minister and four on the advice of the Leader of the Opposition—or elected. The life of Parliament is five years.

Parliament has the power to amend the Constitution. Each constituency returns one Representative to the House who is directly elected in accordance with the Constitution. Every citizen over the age of 18 is eligible to vote.

THE EXECUTIVE
Executive authority is vested in the President. The President appoints as Prime Minister the elected member of the House who commands the support of a majority of its elected members, and other Ministers on the advice of the Prime Minister. Not more than three Ministers may be from among the appointed Senators. The President has the power to remove the Prime Minister from office if a resolution of 'no confidence' in the Government is passed by the House and the Prime Minister does not resign within three days or advise the President to dissolve Parliament.

The Cabinet consists of the Prime Minister, other Ministers and the Attorney-General in an ex officio capacity.

The Leader of the Opposition is appointed by the President as that elected member of the House who, in the President's judgement, is best able to command the support of a majority of the elected members who do not support the Government.

The Government

HEAD OF STATE
President: Sir CLARENCE SEIGNORET (assumed office 19 December 1983; second term began 20 December 1988).

CABINET
(January 1989)

Prime Minister and Minister of Finance, Defence, Foreign and Economic Affairs: MARY EUGENIA CHARLES.
Attorney-General and Minister of Legal Affairs, Immigration and Labour: BRIAN G. K. ALLEYNE.
Minister of Community Development and Social Affairs: HESKEITH ALEXANDER.
Minister of Health, Water and Sewage: RONAN DAVID.
Minister of Agriculture, Industry, Tourism, Trade, Lands and Surveys: CHARLES MAYNARD.
Minister of Housing, Communications and Works: ALLEYNE CARBON.
Minister of Education and Sports: HENRY GEORGE.

MINISTRIES
Office of the President: Morne Bruce, Roseau; tel. 82054.
Office of the Prime Minister: Government Headquarters, Kennedy Ave, Roseau; tel. 82406.
All other Ministries are at Government Headquarters, Kennedy Ave, Roseau; tel. 82401.

Legislature

HOUSE OF ASSEMBLY
Speaker: MARIE DAVIS PIERRE.
Clerk: ALBERTHA JNO BAPTISTE.
Senators: 9.
Elected Members: 21.

Election, 1 July 1985

Party	Seats
Dominica Freedom Party	15
Labour Party of Dominica	5
United Dominica Labour Party*	1†

* Represented by a single candidate, not officially endorsed by the Labour Party of Dominica.
† At a by-election in May 1986 the seat was won by the Dominica Freedom Party. In July 1987 a former member of the Labour Party of Dominica joined the DFP, increasing the DFP's seats to 17 and reducing the LPD's seats to four.

Political Organizations

Dominica Freedom Party (DFP): Cross St, Roseau; tel. 82104; Leader MARY EUGENIA CHARLES.
Dominica United Workers' Party: Roseau; f. 1988; Chair. EDISON JAMES.
Labour Party of Dominica (LPD): Roseau; f. 1985; a reunification of left-wing groups; Leader MICHAEL A. DOUGLAS; Gen. Sec. JEROME BARZEY; consists of:

Dominica Labour Party (DLP): 19 Federation Drive, Roseau; tel. 82321; f. 1961; split into two factions in 1979: the DLP, under the leadership of PATRICK JOHN, and the Democratic Labour Party (DEMLAB), under OLIVER SERAPHIN; remerged in 1983.

Dominica Liberation Movement (DLM): 69 Queen Mary St, Roseau; tel. 84256; f. 1979 from alliance of four leftist groupings; Leader ATHERTON MARTIN; Gen. Sec. BILL RIVIERE.

United Dominica Labour Party (UDLP): Roseau; f. 1981 after a split in DEMLAB; Leader MICHAEL A. DOUGLAS.

DOMINICA

Diplomatic Representation

EMBASSIES IN DOMINICA

China (Taiwan): Morne Daniel, Roseau; tel. 91385; Chargé d'affaires: THOMAS CHENG.
Venezuela: 37 Cork St, 3rd Floor, Roseau; tel. 83348; telex 8643; Chargé d'affaires: VASCOALTUVE FEBRES.

Judicial System

Justice is administered by the Eastern Caribbean Supreme Court, consisting of a Court of Appeal and a High Court. One of the six puisne judges of the High Court is resident in Dominica and presides over the Court of Summary Jurisdiction. The District Magistrate Courts deal with summary offences and civil offences involving sums of not more than EC $500.

Religion

CHRISTIANITY

The Roman Catholic Church

Dominica comprises the single diocese of Roseau, suffragan to the archdiocese of Castries (Saint Lucia). At 31 December 1985 there were an estimated 65,000 adherents in the country, representing a large majority of the inhabitants. The Bishop participates in the Antilles Episcopal Conference (based in Kingston, Jamaica).

Bishop of Roseau: Rt Rev. ARNOLD BOGHAERT; Bishop's House, 20 Virgin Lane, Roseau; tel. 82837.

The Anglican Communion

Anglicans in Dominica are adherents of the Church in the Province of the West Indies. The country forms part of the diocese of the North Eastern Caribbean and Aruba. The Bishop, who is also Archbishop of the Province, is resident in Antigua.

Other Christian Churches

There are churches of various denominations, including Methodist, Pentecostal, Baptist, Church of Christ and Seventh-day Adventists.

The Press

New Chronicle: 7 Queen Mary St, POB 124, Roseau; tel. 82121; telex 8625; f. 1909; Friday; progressive independent; Gen. Man. J. A. WHITE; Editor MYRTLE SOLOMON; circ. 4,000.

Official Gazette: Government Printery, Roseau; tel. 82401, ext. 330; telex 8613; weekly; circ. 550.

Radio and Television

There were an estimated 28,000 radio receivers in use in 1986. There is no national television service, although there is a cable television network serving one-third of the island.

Dominica Broadcasting Corporation: Victoria St, Roseau; tel. 83283; government station; daily broadcasts in English; 2 hrs daily in French patois; 10 kW transmitter on the medium wave band; programmes received throughout Caribbean excluding Jamaica and Guyana.

Voice of Life Radio—ZGBC: POB 205, Roseau; tel. 84391; linked to the US Christian Reformed Church; 126 hrs weekly; Man. Dir WAYNE K. DEBOER.

Voice of the Islands Radio: Pte Michel; tel. 84042; religious; 126 hrs weekly; Man. Father RAYMOND CONNARD.

Finance

BANKS

Agricultural, Industrial and Development (AID) Bank: 64 Hillsborough St, POB 215, Roseau; tel. 82853; telex 8620; f. 1971; state-owned; cap. EC $5m. (1982); Man. VANS T. LEBLANC.

Banque Française Commerciale: corner of Queen Mary St and Gt Marlborough St, POB 166, Roseau; tel. 84040; telex 8629; Man. P. INGLISS.

Barclays Bank plc: Old St, POB 4, Roseau; tel. 82571; telex 8618; sub-branch in Portsmouth; Man. R. L. SHIPMAN.

International Bank of Roseau: 14 Cork St, Roseau; tel. 88106.

National Commercial Bank of Dominica: 64 Hillsborough St, POB 271, Roseau; tel. 84401/5; telex 8620; public-owned; share cap. EC $10m. (1978); Chair. FRANK A. BARON; Gen. Man. LAMBERT V. LEWIS.

Royal Bank of Canada: Bay St, POB 144, Roseau; tel. 82771; telex 8637; Man. H. PINARD.

INSURANCE

Several British and US companies have agents in Roseau. Local companies include the following:

J. B. Charles and Co. Ltd: POB 121, Roseau; tel. 82876.

Insurance Services Ltd: 8 Castle St, Roseau; tel. 83079.

Tonge Inc: 19 King George V St, Roseau; tel. 84027; telex 8631.

Windward Islands Crop Insurance Co. (Wincrop): Roseau; f. 1987; regional; coverage for weather destruction of, mainly, banana crops; total assets (1988) EC $6.2m.; brs in Grenada and Saint Lucia.

Trade and Industry

Co-operative Citrus Growers' Association: 21 Hanover St, Roseau; tel. 82062; telex 8615; f. 1954; processing and marketing of citrus fruits; Pres. P. NORMAN ROLLE.

DOMLEC: Castle St, POB 13, Roseau; tel. 82681; telex 8655; state-owned national electricity service.

Dominica Association of Industry and Commerce (DAIC): 15 King George V St, POB 85, Roseau; tel. 82874; f. 1972 by a merger of the Manufacturers' Association and the Chamber of Commerce; represents the business sector, liaises with the Government, and stimulates commerce and industry; 91 mems; Pres. EDWARD LAMBERT; Exec. Sec. FERDINAND A. AZILLE.

Dominica Banana Marketing Corporation (DBMC): corner of Queen Mary St and Turkey Lane, Roseau; tel. 82671; telex 8648; f. 1934 as Dominica Banana Growers' Associaton; restructured 1982; state-supported; Chair. VANOULST JNO CHARLES; Exec. Sec. E. M. ANGOL; Gen. Man. LEONARD JAMES.

Dominica Employers' Federation: 14 Church St, Roseau; tel. 82314; Pres. DERMOT SOUTHWELL; Exec. Dir SHIRLEY GUYE.

Dominica Export-Import Agency (Dexia): POB 173, Roseau; tel. 82780; telex 8626; f. 1986; replaced the Dominica Agricultural Marketing Board and the External Trade Bureau.

Dominica Industrial Development Corporation (DIDC): POB 293, Bath Estate, Roseau; tel. 82045; telex 8642; f. 1974; in 1988 it was announced that the DIDC and the Tourist Board (see below) would be merged to form a National Development Corporation; promotes local and foreign investment to increase employment, production and exports; Chair. DERMOT SOUTHWELL; Gen. Man. KENNETH ALLEYNE.

MARKETING AND CO-OPERATIVE ORGANIZATIONS

At the end of 1986 there were 22 registered credit unions, with 39,218 members and share capital of EC $29.5m. There were also 36 other registered co-operatives, of which 19 were agricultural (citrus, fisheries, craft, poultry, vegetables, bay oil, bananas and sugar cane), with 1,861 members and share capital of approximately EC $72,000.

TRADE UNIONS

Civil Service Association: Valley Rd/Windsor Lane, Roseau; tel. 82102; f. 1940 and registered as a Trade Union in 1960, representing all grades of civil servants, including firemen, prison officers, nurses, teachers and postal workers; Pres. JOHN ALEXIS; Sec. ARTHUR R. SMITH; 2,700 mems.

Dominica Amalgamated Workers' Union (DAWU): 40 Kennedy Ave, POB 137, Roseau; tel. 83048; f. 1960; Gen. Sec. DARRYL D. GAGE; 3,500 mems.

Dominica Trade Union: 70–71 Queen Mary St, Roseau; tel. 82903; f. 1945; Pres. CHRISTIAN FREDERICK; Gen. Sec. NEVILLE DARROUX; 650 mems.

National Workers Union: corner of Church St and Old St, Roseau; tel. 84465; f. 1977; Pres. RAWLINS JEMMOTT; Gen. Sec. MARILYN ANTHONY; 600 mems.

Waterfront and Allied Workers' Union: 43 Hillsborough St, Roseau; tel. 82343; f. 1965; Pres. LOUIS BENOIT; Gen. Sec. CURTIS AUGUSTUS; 1,500 mems.

Transport

ROADS

At the end of 1976 there were 327 km (231 miles) of first-class, 262 km (163 miles) of second-class and 117 km (73 miles) of third-class motorable roads, as well as 282 miles (454 km) of tracks. Extensive road development was completed in 1986, at a cost of US $39m., and further improvements were in progress in 1987, although at the end of that year heavy rains caused damage, estimated at over US $1m., to the road system.

SHIPPING

A deep-water harbour at Woodridge Bay serves Roseau, which is the principal port. Several foreign shipping lines call at Roseau. In 1988 a ferry company, Caribbean Link, started a high-speed service from Antigua to Guadeloupe, via Montserrat and Dominica. Ships of the Geest Line call at Portsmouth to collect bananas. There are other specialized berthing facilities on the west coast.

CIVIL AVIATION

Melville Hall Airport, 64 km (40 miles) from Roseau, and Canefield Airport, 5 km (3 miles) from Roseau, are the two airports on the island. An improvement scheme at Canefield, which included a new terminal building, was completed in 1988. The regional airline, LIAT, provides daily services and, with Air Guadeloupe, Air Martinique, Air BVI and Winlink (Saint Lucia), connects Dominica with all the islands of the Eastern Caribbean, including the international airports of Puerto Rico, Antigua, Guadeloupe and Martinique.

Tourism

The Government has designated areas of the island as nature reserves, to preserve the beautiful and lush scenery that is Dominica's main tourist attraction. Tourism is not as developed as it is among Dominica's neighbours. There were 38,673 visitors in 1987.

Dominica Tourist Board: Valley Rd, POB 73, Roseau; tel. 82351; telex 8649; in 1988 it was announced that the Tourist Board would be merged with the DIDC (see above) to form a National Development Corporation; Chair. GERRY AIRD; Dir of Tourism MARIE-JOSE EDWARDS.

Dominica Hotel Association: POB 384, Roseau; tel. 96244; telex 8619.

THE DOMINICAN REPUBLIC

Introductory Survey

Location, Climate, Language, Religion, Flag, Capital

The Dominican Republic occupies the eastern part of the island of Hispaniola, which lies between Cuba and Puerto Rico in the Caribbean Sea. The country's only international frontier is with Haiti, to the west. The climate is sub-tropical, with an average annual temperature of 27°C (80°F). In Santo Domingo, temperatures are generally between 19°C (66°F) and 31°C (88°F). The west and south-west of the country are arid. Hispaniola lies in the path of tropical cyclones. The official language is Spanish. Almost all of the inhabitants profess Christianity, and more than 90% are Roman Catholics. There are small Protestant and Jewish communities. The national flag (proportions 23 by 15) is blue (upper hoist and lower fly) and red (lower hoist and upper fly), quartered by a white cross. The state flag has, in addition, the national coat of arms, showing a quartered shield in the colours of the flag (on which are superimposed national banners, a cross and an open Bible) between scrolls above and below, at the centre of the cross. The capital is Santo Domingo.

Recent History

The Dominican Republic became independent in 1844, although it was occupied by US military forces between 1916 and 1924. General Rafael Leonidas Trujillo Molina overthrew the elected President, Horacio Vázquez, in 1930 and dominated the country until his assassination in May 1961. The dictator ruled personally from 1930 to 1947 and indirectly thereafter. His brother, Héctor Trujillo, was President from 1947 until August 1960, when he was replaced by Dr Joaquín Balaguer, hitherto Vice-President. After Rafael Trujillo's death, President Balaguer remained in office, but in December 1961 he permitted moderate opposition groups to participate in a Council of State, with legislative and executive powers. Balaguer resigned in January 1962, when the Council of State became the Provisional Government. A presidential election in December 1962, the country's first free election for 38 years, was won by Dr Juan Bosch Gaviño, the founder and leader of the Partido Revolucionario Dominicano (PRD), who had been in exile since 1930. President Bosch, a left-of-centre democrat, took office in February 1963 but was overthrown in the following September by a military coup. The leaders of the armed forces transferred power to a civilian triumvirate, led by Emilio de los Santos. In April 1965 a revolt by supporters of ex-President Bosch overthrew the triumvirate. Civil war broke out between pro-Bosch forces and military units headed by Gen. Elías Wessin y Wessin, who had played a leading role in the 1963 coup. The violence was eventually suppressed by the intervention of some 23,000 US troops, who were formally incorporated into an Inter-American peace force by the Organization of American States after they had landed. The peace force withdrew in September 1965.

Following a period of provisional government under Héctor García Godoy, a presidential election in June 1966 was won by ex-President Balaguer, the candidate of the Partido Reformista Social Cristiano (PRSC), who won 57% of the votes cast, while ex-President Bosch won 39%. The PRSC, founded in 1964, also won a majority of seats in both houses of the National Congress. President Balaguer took office in July. A new constitution was promulgated in November 1966. Despite his association with the Trujillo dictatorship, Balaguer initially proved to be a popular leader, and in May 1970 he was re-elected for a further four years. In February 1973 a state of emergency was declared when guerrilla forces landed on the coast. Captain Francisco Caamaño Deñó, the leader of the 1965 revolt, and his followers were killed. Bosch and other opposition figures went into hiding. Bosch later resigned as leader of the PRD (founding the Partido de la Liberación Dominicana—PLD), undermining hopes of a united opposition in the May 1974 elections, when President Balaguer was re-elected with a large majority. In June 1975 guerrilla forces of Dominican émigrés from Cuba landed on the island in an unsuccessful attempt to overthrow Balaguer.

In the May 1978 presidential election, Dr Balaguer was defeated by the PRD candidate, Silvestre Antonio Guzmán Fernández. This was the first occasion in the country's history when an elected President yielded power to an elected successor. An attempted military coup in favour of Dr Balaguer was prevented by pressure from the US Government. On assuming office in August, President Guzmán undertook to professionalize the armed forces by removing politically ambitious high-ranking officers. In June 1981 he declared his support for Jacobo Majluta Azar, his Vice-President, as his successor but in November the PRD rejected Majluta's candidacy in favour of Dr Salvador Jorge Blanco, a left-wing senator, who was elected President in May 1982. In the Congressional elections, held at the same time, the PRD gained a majority in both the Senate and the Chamber of Deputies. President Guzmán committed suicide in July after allegations of fraud were made against his government and members of his family. Vice-President Majluta was immediately sworn in as interim President until Dr Blanco assumed office in August. Although a member of the Socialist International, Blanco maintained good relations with the USA (on which the country is economically dependent) and declared that he would not resume relations with Cuba. In December 1982 the Government revealed that it would not nationalize foreign property, including extensive holdings owned by oil companies, in the Dominican Republic.

In 1983 popular discontent with the Government's austerity programme led to the occupation of the Ministry of Agriculture by peasants, and calls for agrarian reform. In August 1983 a two-week purge of subversives took place on the orders of President Blanco. Two visiting Cuban academics were deported, and Socialist and Communist Party sympathizers were arrested. The Government's move came in response to a report which implicated Cuban and Nicaraguan involvement in the increased left-wing activity in the country.

In April 1984 a series of public protests against substantial increases in the cost of essential items erupted into violent confrontations between government forces and demonstrators in Santo Domingo and four other cities, which lasted for three days. In the course of the protests, more than 50 people were killed, some 200 injured and over 4,000 arrested. The Government held opposition groups of the extreme right and left responsible for the unrest. In May the Government responded to the prospect of further demonstrations by ordering the arrest of more than 100 trade union and left-wing leaders. In August, in anticipation of civil unrest at the announcement of new price increases, more arrests were made among trade union and opposition leaders. Rumours of a plot against the Government by left-wing sympathizers caused serious disquiet throughout the country. In November a new Secretary of State for Finance was named for the second time in 1984, the previous change having been made in May. Further demonstrations, including one attended by 40,000 people in Santo Domingo, were held in protest at the continuing economic decline.

In February 1985 a further series of substantial price increases led to violent clashes between demonstrators and police, during which four people died and more than 50 were injured. Public unrest was exacerbated by the Government's decision, in April, to accept the IMF's terms for further financial aid. In June a 24-hour general strike was organized by trade unions, in protest at the Government's economic policy and its refusal to increase the minimum wage. In July, however, the threat of a 48-hour general strike prompted the Government to order an immediate increase in the minimum wage.

Further violence preceded the presidential and legislative elections of May 1986. Several people were killed, and many more injured, in clashes between rival political supporters. The three principal candidates in the presidential election were all former Presidents: Dr Joaquín Balaguer of the PRSC; Jacobo Majluta, who, having registered La Estructura, his right-wing faction of the PRD, as a separate political party in July 1985, nevertheless secured the candidacy of the ruling PRD; and Dr Juan Bosch of the PLD. The counting of votes was suspended twice, following allegations by Majluta of fraud by the PRSC and by the Central Electoral Board, two of the three members of which then resigned. Dr Balaguer was finally declared the winner by a narrow margin of votes over Majluta, his nearest rival. In the simultaneous legislative elections, the PRSC won 21 of the 30 seats in the Senate and 56 of the 120 seats in the Chamber of Deputies.

Upon taking office as President (for the fifth time) in August 1986, Dr Balaguer initiated an investigation into alleged corrupt practices by members of the outgoing administration. The former President was charged with embezzlement and the illegal purchase of military vehicles. The financial accounts of the armed forces were examined, and the former Secretary of State for the Armed Forces was subsequently imprisoned. In July 1987 a general strike was organized by the trade unions, in support of a demand for an increase of 62% in the minimum wage. In September the Cabinet resigned, at the request of the President, to enable him to restructure the Government. Some 35,000 government posts were abolished in an attempt to reduce public spending, and the money thus becoming available was to be used to finance a programme of public works projects which were expected to create almost 100,000 new jobs. Nevertheless, strike action continued. The situation worsened in February 1988, when demonstrations took place throughout the country, to protest against the high cost of living, after the price of staple foods was increased. Six people were killed as the police intervened to quell the protests. Subsequently, the Roman Catholic Church mediated between the opposing sides, and President Balaguer agreed to stabilize prices of staple foods and to increase the minimum wage by 33%, to 700 pesos per month. However, prices continued to rise, provoking a new wave of strikes in June.

Relations with Haiti remained tense in 1988. Dominican soldiers were accused of arresting immigrant Haitians in order to use them as cutters during the sugar harvest. The problem was eased somewhat when the deposed Haitian leader, Gen. Henri Namphy, was refused permission to remain in the Dominican Republic. Subsequently, however, Gen. Namphy was unable to find a country willing to accept him as a political exile, and the Dominican Government was obliged to allow him to stay.

In November 1988 the former President, Dr Salvador Jorge Blanco, was convicted, in his absence, of corruption during his presidency. He returned to the country from the USA in December, and was sentenced to 20 years' imprisonment.

Government

The Dominican Republic comprises 26 provinces, each administered by an appointed governor, and a Distrito Nacional (DN) containing the capital. Under the 1966 Constitution, legislative power is exercised by the bicameral National Congress, with a Senate of 30 members and a Chamber of Deputies (120 members). Members of both houses are elected for four years by universal adult suffrage. Executive power lies with the President, who is also elected by direct popular vote for four years. He is assisted by a Vice-President and a Cabinet containing Secretaries of State.

Defence

Military service is voluntary and lasts for four years. In June 1988 the armed forces totalled 20,800 men: army 13,000, air force 3,800 and navy 4,000. Paramilitary forces number 1,000. Defence expenditure for 1986 was estimated at RD $255.3m.

Economic Affairs

Between 1965 and 1980 the annual increase in the Dominican Republic's gross domestic product (GDP) averaged 7.3% in real terms, one of the highest growth rates in the world. However, the country is dependent on fuel imports to meet its energy requirements, and in the early 1980s, following sharp rises in the world price of petroleum, its economic progress was slower. Between 1980 and 1986 GDP expanded, in real terms, by only 1.1% per year. Having expanded by 1.3% in 1986, GDP increased by 8% in 1987. In 1987, according to estimates by the World Bank, the Dominican Republic's gross national product (GNP) at average 1985–87 prices, was US $4,930m., equivalent to $730 per head, the latter figure having decreased, in real terms, at an average rate of 1.4% per year since 1980. In 1987, however, GNP per head increased by 5.2% compared with the previous year.

In 1985 agriculture employed 41.2% of the working population, and agricultural products provided about 50% of export earnings. The contribution of the agricultural sector to GDP was 17% in 1986. The principal commercial crop is sugar cane. The USA's decision to reduce its sugar import quota by 44% in 1985, however, led to a crisis within the industry. Export earnings from raw sugar fell from $272m. in 1984 to an estimated $134m. in 1986 (18.5% of the value of total exports, compared with 34.6% in 1982). The USA's quota for sugar imports from the Dominican Republic was reduced from 302,016 short tons in 1986 to 160,160 tons in 1987. The US quota for 1988 was cut to 123,200 tons. However, the USSR agreed to purchase 150,000 metric tons of sugar between 1987 and 1990. Output of raw sugar in the 1987/88 season was estimated at 700,000 tons. This was below the expected level, as a result of labour problems and adverse weather. Total sugar exports in 1987 were estimated at $145.2m.

The Government has encouraged the cultivation of coffee and cocoa in order to diversify exports. In 1987 exports of coffee and cocoa totalled an estimated $61.4m. and $72.4m. respectively. Other crops include rice, maize, beans, bananas, other fruit and tobacco. In 1980 the Sabana Yegua dam, designed to irrigate 600,000 ha of land, was inaugurated. The Government also undertook to develop the Madrigal water supply project for Santo Domingo, and the Río Nizao irrigation project. Loans from the Inter-American Development Bank (IDB) have aided agricultural producers and small commercial enterprises, and have enabled a programme for industrial recovery to be implemented. The agricultural sector is highly vulnerable, suffering from the loss of the entire pig population after an outbreak of African swine fever in 1978, from damage inflicted by adverse weather conditions, including Hurricane David in 1979 and Hurricane Emily in 1987, and from declines in world prices for coffee, cocoa and tobacco in 1980 and for sugar in 1981 and 1984–85. An $8m. donation was received from Italy after Hurricane Emily, together with the promise of a further $150m. in concessionary loans and donations over the subsequent three years.

The manufacturing sector contributed 16% of GDP in 1986. The textile industry is of increasing importance, with exports of garments to the USA becoming a significant source of foreign exchange earnings. The mining sector accounted for 2.4% of GDP in 1984, compared with 5.3% in 1980. The principal mineral resources are bauxite (with reserves of 18m. tons at Cabo Rojo), gold, silver and ferro-nickel. Production of bauxite, however, ceased in early 1984, when the US company Alcoa announced withdrawal from the country. The value of ferro-nickel exports rose from an estimated $77.8m. in 1986 to $115.2m. in 1987. In December 1987 a dispute between the Government and Falconbridge, the Canadian company responsible for the mining of ferro-nickel, developed when a special duty was placed on nickel exports. The dispute lasted until May 1988, by which time the international price of nickel had reached record levels, and production had ceased in the Dominican Republic. The new agreement linked taxes payable to profits accruing from nickel sales, and was estimated to yield $60–70m. in 1988. Earnings from the gold-silver alloy, doré, declined from $163.6m. in 1982 to $111.8m. in 1986, rising to $120m. in 1987. Foreign oil companies have been granted concessions to undertake exploratory drilling, and in 1981 a petroleum deposit was discovered at Charco Largo, Barahona. Its potential output was estimated at 20,000 barrels per day (b/d). National consumption is estimated at 28,000 b/d. In 1985 the cost of imports of petroleum and petroleum products was an estimated $426.8m., compared with $504.8m. in 1984. Substantial savings were anticipated from 1986, following the decline in international petroleum prices. In 1984 the IDB provided financing of US $11m. for petroleum exploration. Attempts were being made to find alternative energy sources, and hydroelectricity is now being developed. In 1983 a hydroelectric generator with a capacity of 40,000 kW became operational at the Tavera dam. The hydroelectric plant, Niza II, was due to start operations in the mid-1980s, with an annual production capacity of 28m. kWh. Two further plants are to be built on the Yaque de Norte river. The first coal-fired plant in the Caribbean region, the 125 MW Haina station, was under construction in the mid-1980s. In June 1988 the World Bank granted a loan of $105m. for the improvement of the electricity grid, aimed at increasing efficiency.

In 1986 budget expenditure was estimated at 2,250m. pesos. Government investment has been concentrated on agriculture, energy and tourism. Revenue from tourism totalled about US $580m. in 1986. The number of tourist arrivals continued to increase, as did investment in the tourist infrastructure. In 1987 an estimated 1m. tourists entered the country, and several new tourist complexes were planned. Remittances from Dominicans resident in the USA are also significant, totalling an estimated $400m. in 1987.

In 1983 a three-year loan of $466m. was agreed with the IMF. In early 1984 the disbursement of some US $70m. (including $40m. from the IMF) was halted, pending the Dominican Republic's fulfilment of the IMF's conditions, principally the introduction of a unified exchange rate for the peso. In May, however, negotiations with the IMF were suspended after the Government rejected the IMF's proposed austerity programme, and refused to comply with the IMF's insistence upon an immediate transfer of all imports to the 'parallel' exchange rate of 2.97 pesos per US dollar, to allow for an increase of between 20% and 300% in the cost of petroleum products and electricity. Negotiations were resumed, and in August agreement was reached on an interim loan. In January 1985 the long-standing parity of the currency with the US dollar was ended, and a new exchange rate of about 3 pesos per dollar was established. In April 1985 the Government obtained a stand-by credit of SDR 78.5m. from the IMF. Consequently, the Government was able to reach provisional agreement on the renegotiation of US $360m. of debts with creditor governments and of $787m. of debts with creditor banks. In November 1985 the IMF approved a loan of SDR 15.5m., under its compensatory financing facility, to offset the decline in the Dominican Republic's earnings from sugar exports. In 1988 the country's total external debt was estimated at $4,000m. No agreement had been concluded with the IMF, which was a precondition for the renegotiation of the external debt.

In 1985 unemployment affected 29.8% of the labour force, not including 30% under-employment. Inflation increased from an annual average of 6.9% in 1983 to 24.4% in 1984. Following two years of austerity measures, the economy was showing signs of recovery in 1986. Inflation fell to an annual average of only 9.7%, compared with 37.5% in 1985. The economic growth of 1986 (3.2%) and 1987 (8.1%) was based on recovery in the tourism, construction, finance and communications sectors. The trade deficit, however, rose from $389.1m. in 1984 to $544.1m. in 1986. In 1987 President Balaguer's economic reforms, especially the programme of public works, stimulated the expansion of industrial output, but had a detrimental effect on inflation and the strength of the peso, which continued into the following year. In 1988 the annual rate of inflation remained substantially above 20%, while the peso depreciated further in relation to the US dollar. Industrial growth of 9.8% in 1987 led to a 20% rise in imports. Much of this increase was attributed to President Balaguer's public works programme. The cost of imports reached US $1,550.0m. in 1987, while export earnings totalled only $711.3m., leaving a trade deficit of $838.7m. The current account deficit was estimated at almost $300m. in 1987. When the value of the peso declined to 8 per US dollar in June 1988, all independent exchange houses were closed, and responsibility for money-changing was left solely to the commercial banks, under the supervision of the Central Bank. The official rate was set at 6.35 pesos per US dollar.

Owing to the depreciation of the peso and to low labour costs, many foreign companies established themselves in the Republic's 'free zones'. Companies in these zones are exempt from paying taxes or export duties. By 1988 nine 'free zones' were already in operation, with another 15 in the planning stage; in late 1988 the 190 companies operating in these zones employed 79,000 people.

In July 1984 the Dominican Republic was granted observer status in CARICOM (see p. 106).

Social Welfare

A voluntary national contributory scheme, introduced in 1947, provides insurance cover for sickness, unemployment, accidental injury, maternity, old age and death. Only 42% of the population are thought to benefit from the system. In 1980 there were 571 hospitals and clinics, 2,142 physicians and 8,953 hospital beds under the auspices of the public health and welfare department and the Institute of Social Security. Of total expenditure by the central Government in 1985, 177.1m. pesos (8.8%) was for health services, and a further 138.8m. pesos (6.9%) for social security and welfare.

Education

Education is, where possible, compulsory for children between seven and 14 years of age. Primary education begins at the age of seven and lasts for six years. Secondary education, starting at 13 years of age, also lasts for six years, comprising a first cycle of two years and a second of four years. In 1985 the total enrolment at primary and secondary schools was equivalent to 88% of the school-age population. However, primary enrolment included only 68% of children in the relevant age-group. In 1983/84 there were an estimated 5,864 primary schools and 1,664 secondary schools. There are eight universities. Expenditure on education by the central Government in 1985 was 253.1m. pesos, representing 12.5% of total spending. In 1985, according to UNESCO estimates, the average rate of adult illiteracy was 22.7%.

Public Holidays

1989: 2 January (for New Year's Day), 6 January (Epiphany), 21 January (Our Lady of Altagracia), 26 January (Duarte), 27 February (Independence), 24 March (Good Friday), 14 April (Pan-American Day), 1 May (Labour Day), 16 July (Foundation of Sociedad la Trinitaria), 16 August (Restoration Day), 24 September (Our Lady of Mercedes), 12 October (Columbus Day), 24 October (United Nations Day), 1 November (All Saints' Day), 25 December (Christmas Day).

1990: 1 January (New Year's Day), 6 January (Epiphany), 21 January (Our Lady of Altagracia), 26 January (Duarte), 27 February (Independence), 13 April (Good Friday), 14 April (Pan-American Day), 1 May (Labour Day), 16 July (Foundation of Sociedad la Trinitaria), 16 August (Restoration Day), 24 September (Our Lady of Mercedes), 12 October (Columbus Day), 24 October (United Nations Day), 1 November (All Saints' Day), 25 December (Christmas Day).

Weights and Measures

The metric system is officially in force but the imperial system is often used.

Statistical Survey

Source (unless otherwise stated): Oficina Nacional de Estadísticas, Edif. de Oficinas Públicas, Avda México esq. Leopoldo Navarro, Santo Domingo; Banco Central de la República Dominicana, Santo Domingo; tel. 689-8141; telex 346-0052.

Area and Population

AREA, POPULATION AND DENSITY

Area (sq km)	
Land	48,072
Inland water	350
Total	48,422*
Population (census results)	
9 January 1970	4,009,458
12 December 1981	
Males	2,832,454
Females	2,815,523
Total	5,647,977
Population (official estimates at mid-year)	
1984	6,101,775
1985	6,244,500
1986	6,416,000
Density (per sq km) at mid-1986	132.5

* 18,696 sq miles.

Births and Deaths: Registered live births 162,774 (birth rate 26.7 per 1,000) in 1984; Registered deaths 26,589 (death rate 4.6 per 1,000) in 1982.

PRINCIPAL TOWNS (Population at 12 December 1981)

Santo Domingo, DN (capital)	1,313,172
Santiago de los Caballeros	278,638
La Romana	91,571
San Pedro de Macorís	78,562
San Francisco de Macorís	64,906
Concepción de la Vega	52,432
San Juan	49,764
Barahona	49,334
San Felipe de Puerto Plata	45,348

ECONOMICALLY ACTIVE POPULATION (1981 census)*

	Males	Females	Total
Agriculture, hunting, forestry and fishing	378,274	42,189	420,463
Mining and quarrying	4,304	439	4,743
Manufacturing	166,748	57,689	224,437
Electricity, gas and water	12,090	1,801	13,891
Construction	77,880	2,970	80,850
Trade, restaurants and hotels	131,634	60,547	192,181
Transport, storage and communications	36,577	3,893	40,470
Financing, insurance, real estate and business services	14,944	7,425	22,369
Community, social and personal services	157,398	205,727	363,125
Activities not adequately defined	284,822	136,806	421,628
Total	**1,264,671**	**519,486**	**1,784,157**

* Figures exclude persons seeking work for the first time, totalling 131,231 (males 96,438; females 34,793), but include other unemployed persons, totalling 220,163 (males 144,823; females 75,340).

Source: ILO, *Year Book of Labour Statistics*.

Agriculture

PRINCIPAL CROPS ('000 metric tons)

	1984	1985	1986
Rice (paddy)	507	494	298
Maize	76	62	47
Sorghum	47	47	46
Potatoes	14	11	12†
Sweet potatoes	58	42	35
Cassava (Manioc)	129	114	107
Yams	7	11	5
Other roots and tubers	40	47	50
Dry beans	67	40	28
Groundnuts (in shell)	42	27	18
Coconuts	95†	95*	95†
Copra*	14	14	15
Tomatoes	162	165	165†
Sugar cane	10,995	8,217	7,300*
Oranges†	75	75	80
Lemons and limes†	14	14	n.a.
Avocados†	140	142	137
Mangoes†	195	200	186
Pineapples	26	32	33†
Bananas	330†	314*	422*
Plantains	615†	600*	650*
Coffee (green)	72	72	55*
Cocoa beans	33	35	37*
Tobacco (leaves)	28	21	12

* Unofficial figures.   † FAO estimates.
Source: FAO, *Production Yearbook*.

LIVESTOCK ('000 head, year ending September)

	1984	1985	1986
Horses*	204	204	205
Mules*	99	99	100
Asses*	120	120	122
Cattle	2,020	1,922	2,055
Pigs	1,000	1,850	2,500*
Sheep*	78	80	80
Goats*	465	465	468

* FAO estimates.

Chickens (FAO estimates, million): 14 in 1984; 15 in 1985; 20 in 1986.

Source: FAO, *Production Yearbook*.

LIVESTOCK PRODUCTS ('000 metric tons)

	1984	1985	1986
Beef and veal	58*	60†	65†
Poultry meat	74*	73	97
Cows' milk*	495	498	500
Butter*	1.5	1.5	1.6
Cheese	3.0*	3.0*	1.3
Hen eggs†	16.8	17.8	18.6
Cattle hides (fresh)*	7.5	7.6	8.2

* FAO estimates.   † Unofficial figures.
Source: FAO, *Production Yearbook*.

THE DOMINICAN REPUBLIC

Fishing

('000 metric tons, live weight)

	1984	1985	1986
Inland waters	1.8	2.5	0.8
Atlantic Ocean	12.8	15.8	16.3
Total catch	14.6	18.3	17.2

Source: FAO, *Yearbook of Fishery Statistics*.

Mining

(metric tons, unless otherwise indicated)*

	1984	1985	1986
Ferro-nickel	63,966	66,828	57,565
Gold (troy oz)	338,272	328,547	285,458
Silver (troy oz)	1,207,472	1,581,250	1,356,240

* Provisional.

Industry

SELECTED PRODUCTS
('000 metric tons, unless otherwise indicated)

	1983	1984*	1985*
Wheat flour	387.4	373.7	466.4
Refined sugar	104.2	108.5	89.1
Molasses ('000 US gallons)*	58,454.9	65,903.8	49,520.4
Cotton and cellulosic fabrics (million metres)	9.6	10.5	n.a.
Fertilizers	188.4	n.a.	n.a.
Cement ('000 sacks)	25,976.0	26,894.0	23,460.0
Beer ('000 litres)	99.9	94.5	103.8
Spirits ('000 litres)	22.4	26.4	24.5
Cigars (million)	13.3	n.a.	n.a.
Cigarettes (million)	4,176.5	3,683.3	3,925.0
Electricity (million kWh)	2,825.4	2,932.4	3,081.3
Cardboard boxes (million units)	369.1	n.a.	n.a.

* Provisional.

Finance

CURRENCY AND EXCHANGE RATES

Monetary Units
100 centavos = 1 Dominican Republic peso (RD $ or peso oro)

Denominations
Coins: 1, 5, 10, 25 and 50 centavos; 1 peso.
Notes: 1, 5, 10, 20, 50, 100, 500 and 1,000 pesos.

Sterling and Dollar Equivalents (30 September 1988)
£1 sterling = 10.907 pesos;
US $1 = 6.450 pesos;
1,000 Dominican Republic pesos = £91.68 = US $155.04.

Average Exchange Rate (RD $ per US $)
1985   3.1126
1986   2.9043
1987   3.8448

CENTRAL BANK RESERVES
(US $ million at 31 December)

	1985	1986	1987
Gold*	5.9	7.1	n.a.
IMF special drawing rights	31.6	—	—
Foreign exchange	308.5	376.3	182.2
Total	346.0	383.4	n.a.

* Valued at market-related prices.
Source: IMF, *International Financial Statistics*.

MONEY SUPPLY (RD $ million at 31 December)

	1985	1986	1987
Currency outside banks	677.2	937.4	1,312.8
Demand deposits at commercial banks	657.8	1,040.2	1,288.6

Source: IMF, *International Financial Statistics*.

BUDGET (RD $ million)

Revenue	1984	1985*	1986*
Tax revenue	1,067.5	1,548.0	2,034.0
Non-tax revenue	81.4	80.1	99.3
Other receipts†	167.6	282.3	382.1
Total	1,316.5	1,910.4	2,515.4

* Preliminary.
† Including loans from domestic banks and from abroad (RD $ million): 265.9 in 1982.

Expenditure	1984	1985*	1986*
Presidency	157.7	493.6	718.4
Interior and police	122.2	132.9	144.5
Armed forces	163.9	190.8	201.8
Education	174.4	213.0	223.4
Health	119.5	141.1	154.1
Others	540.9	715.4	808.4
Total	1,278.6	1,886.8	2,250.6

* Preliminary.

COST OF LIVING
(Consumer Price Index. Base: Year ending April 1977 = 100)

	1984	1985	1986
Food, beverages and tobacco	196.61	282.20	315.85
Housing	224.46	271.97	297.11
Clothing, shoes and accessories	266.84	419.71	484.63
Others	212.19	289.99	295.23
All items	210.27	289.18	317.35

THE DOMINICAN REPUBLIC

Statistical Survey

NATIONAL ACCOUNTS
(RD $ million at current prices, provisional estimates)

National Income and Product

	1982	1983	1984
Domestic factor incomes*	7,017.7	7,535.9	8,949.9
Consumption of fixed capital	473.9	513.1	616.1
Gross domestic product (GDP) at factor cost	7,491.6	8,049.0	9,566.0
Indirect taxes, *less* subsidies	472.8	574.2	789.3
GDP in purchasers' values	7,964.4	8,623.2	10,355.3
Net factor income from abroad	−254.8	−297.1	−241.4
Gross national product (GNP)	7,709.6	8,326.1	10,113.9
Less Consumption of fixed capital	473.9	513.1	616.1
National income in market prices	7,235.7	7,813.0	9,497.8

* Compensation of employees and the operating surplus of enterprises.

1985 (RD $ million): GDP in purchasers' values 13,869; GNP 13,643.
1986 (RD $ million): GDP in purchasers' values 15,664; GNP 15,414.
1987 (RD $ million): GDP in purchasers' values 19,427.

Expenditure on the Gross Domestic Product

	1982	1983	1984
Government final consumption expenditure	779.4	786.3	870.8
Private final consumption expenditure*	5,982.1	6,347.8	7,463.5
Increase in stocks†	99.3	62.4	33.5
Gross fixed capital formation	1,496.4	1,762.5	2,174.6
Total domestic expenditure	8,377.5	8,959.0	10,542.3
Exports of goods and services	1,141.8	1,241.8	1,369.6
Less Imports of goods and services	1,534.6	1,577.6	1,556.6
GDP in purchasers' values	7,964.4	8,623.2	10,355.3
GDP at constant 1970 prices	3,069.2	3,209.4	3,217.7

* Obtained as a residual.
† Including only mining, manufacturing, groundnuts, raw tobacco and beans.

Gross Domestic Product by Economic Activity

	1982	1983	1984
Agriculture	952.0	973.2	1,227.3
Livestock	410.5	461.7	627.2
Forestry and fishing	49.4	50.0	61.2
Mining	206.3	229.2	243.6
Manufacturing	1,454.8	1,527.5	1,707.6
Construction	535.1	669.0	881.6
Wholesale and retail trade	1,350.3	1,450.6	1,781.9
Transport	350.5	364.1	377.0
Communications	69.3	98.8	145.7
Electricity	82.4	77.5	94.1
Finance	335.8	367.6	442.4
Owner-occupied dwellings	693.4	722.7	799.7
Government services	663.7	704.2	812.3
Other services	810.9	927.1	1,153.7
Total	7,964.4	8,623.2	10,355.3

BALANCE OF PAYMENTS (US $ million)

	1984	1985	1986
Merchandise exports f.o.b.	868.1	738.5	722.1
Merchandise imports f.o.b.	−1,257.1	−1,285.9	−1,351.7
Trade balance	−389.0	−547.4	−629.6
Exports of services	507.3	605.9	700.1
Imports of services	−546.7	−522.4	−542.1
Balance of goods and services	−428.4	−463.9	−471.6
Private unrequited transfers (net)	205.0	242.0	309.1
Government unrequited transfers (net)	60.0	114.3	64.0
Current balance	−163.4	−107.6	−98.5
Direct capital investment (net)	68.5	36.2	50.0
Other long-term capital (net)	225.6	149.3	220.0
Short-term capital (net)	−70.0	−110.0	−7.7
Net errors and omissions	29.7	155.7	−28.3
Total (net monetary movements)	90.4	123.6	135.5
Monetization of gold (net)	−22.1	0.1	—
Valuation changes (net)	7.7	−29.2	−32.1
Exceptional financing (net)	−1.1	−49.0	−25.5
Official financing (net)	7.8	−31.9	−49.0
Changes in reserves	82.7	13.6	28.9

Source: IMF, *International Financial Statistics*.

External Trade

PRINCIPAL COMMODITIES (US $ '000)

Imports	1983	1984*	1985*
Cars and other vehicles (incl. spares)	44,350	65,300	84,633
Chemical and pharmaceutical products	70,339	59,649	64,436
Cotton and manufactures	10,829	9,660	15,212
Foodstuffs	103,388	112,295	171,793
Petroleum and petroleum products	461,296	504,842	426,782
Iron and steel manufactures (excl. building materials)	57,594	56,874	43,500
Machinery (incl. spares)	104,285	83,360	119,311
Total (incl. others)	1,279,020	1,257,134	1,285,910

* Figures are provisional.

1986: Total imports US $1,357.1 million.

Exports	1984	1985*	1986*
Raw sugar	271,886	158,477	133,850
Molasses	14,217	9,693	11,040
Cocoa beans	70,064	58,078	58,873
Coffee (green)	95,073	86,149	112,833
Tobacco (unmanufactured)	24,228	17,612	18,581
Ferro-nickel	108,522	120,715	77,820
Alloy of gold and silver	131,810	113,611	111,804
Furfural	19,854	16,505	21,343
Total (incl. others)	868,076	738,548	722,144

THE DOMINICAN REPUBLIC

PRINCIPAL TRADING PARTNERS (US $ '000)

Imports	1983	1984*	1985*
Belgium and Luxembourg	10,736	7,540	9,334
Brazil	20,131	21,537	22,514
Canada	29,684	19,222	17,507
France	13,741	9,351	8,598
Germany, Federal Republic	40,405	33,396	48,611
Italy	11,221	9,745	13,073
Japan	55,032	58,621	78,357
Mexico	151,816	147,660	101,795
Netherlands	10,145	14,752	11,789
Netherlands Antilles (incl. Aruba)	45,611	23,159	6,715
Puerto Rico	24,640	21,869	19,378
Spain	43,886	27,942	21,712
United Kingdom	12,619	11,661	13,462
USA	438,353	407,646	452,786
Venezuela	271,547	332,726	332,250
Total (incl. others)	1,279,020	1,257,134	1,285,910

* Estimates.

Exports	1984	1985*	1986*
Belgium and Luxembourg	11,737	19,971	23,826
Canada	20,542	17,686	12,568
France	417	2,008	931
Haiti	6,339	5,623	5,557
Italy	2,587	3,901	4,430
Japan	15,146	13,229	9,294
Morocco	8,905	758	4,297
Netherlands	60,430	53,023	31,224
Puerto Rico	43,087	52,129	76,148
Spain	12,770	10,897	12,172
Switzerland	111	200	1,823
United Kingdom	561	670	520
USA	625,977	508,569	504,919
Venezuela	12,950	1,810	1,032
Total (incl. others)	868,076	738,548	722,144

Transport

ROAD TRAFFIC (motor vehicles in use at 31 December)

	1982	1983	1984
Passenger cars	94,601	87,605	101,979
Trucks and lorries	50,883	52,197	54,571
Buses	4,463	4,814	6,736

INTERNATIONAL SEA-BORNE SHIPPING
(freight traffic, '000 metric tons)

	1983	1984	1985†
Goods loaded*	1,750	1,777	2,234
Goods unloaded	3,560	3,649	3,844

* Not including exports to duty-free zones.
† Source: UN, *Monthly Bulletin of Statistics*.

CIVIL AVIATION (traffic on scheduled services)

	1982	1983	1984
Kilometres flown (million)	5.5	4.8	4.4
Passengers carried ('000)	414	447	605
Passengers-km (million)	481	429	479
Freight ton-km (million)	9.0	7.1	9.7

Source: UN, *Statistical Yearbook*.

Tourism

	1983	1984	1985
Total visitors	601,314	658,324	753,005

Education

1985

	Institutions	Teachers	Students
Primary	6,299*	27,952*	1,219,681
Secondary	n.a.	11,754	438,922

* Provisional.
Source: UNESCO, *Statistical Yearbook*.

Directory

The Constitution

The present Constitution of the Dominican Republic was promulgated on 28 November 1966. Its main provisions are summarized below:

The Dominican Republic is a sovereign, free, independent state; no organizations set up by the State can bring about any act which might cause direct or indirect intervention in the internal or foreign affairs of the State or which might threaten the integrity of the State. The Dominican Republic recognizes and applies the norms of general and American international law and is in favour of and will support any initiative towards economic integration for the countries of America. The civil, republican, democratic, representative Government is divided into three independent powers: legislative, executive and judicial.

The territory of the Dominican Republic is as laid down in the Frontier Treaty of 1929 and its Protocol of Revision of 1936.

The life and property of the individual citizen are inviolable; there can be no sentence of death, torture nor any sentence which might cause physical harm to the individual. There is freedom of thought, of conscience, of religion, freedom to publish, freedom of unarmed association, provided that there is no subversion against public order, national security or decency. There is freedom of labour and trade unions; freedom to strike, except in the case of public services, according to the dispositions of the law.

The State will set about agrarian reform, dedicating the land to useful interests and gradually eliminating the latifundios (large estates). The State will do all in its power to support all aspects of family life. Primary education is compulsory and all education is free. Social security services will be developed. Every Dominican has the duty to give what civil and military service the State may require. Every legally entitled citizen must exercise the right to vote, i.e. all persons over 18 years of age and all who are or have been married even if they are not yet 18.

GOVERNMENT

Legislative power is exercised by Congress which is made up of the Senate and Chamber of Deputies, elected by direct vote. Senators, one for each of the 26 Provinces and one for the Distrito Nacional, are elected for four years; they must be Dominicans in

THE DOMINICAN REPUBLIC

full exercise of their citizen's rights, and at least 25 years of age. Their duties are to elect judges, the President and other members of the Electoral and Accounts Councils, and to approve the nomination of diplomats. Deputies, one for every 50,000 inhabitants or fraction over 25,000 in each Province and the Distrito Nacional, are elected for four years and must fulfil the same conditions for election as Senators.

Decisions of Congress are taken by absolute majority of at least half the members of each house; urgent matters require a two-thirds majority. Both houses normally meet on 27 February and 16 August each year for sessions of 90 days, which can be extended for a further 60 days.

Executive power is exercised by the President of the Republic, who is elected by direct vote for a four-year term. The President must be a Dominican citizen by birth or origin, over 30 years of age and in full exercise of citizen's rights. The President must not have engaged in any active military or police service for at least a year prior to election. The President takes office on 16 August following the election. The President of the Republic is Head of the Public Administration and Supreme Chief of the armed forces and police forces. The President's duties include nominating Secretaries and Assistant Secretaries of State and other public officials, promulgating and publishing laws and resolutions of Congress and seeing to their faithful execution, watching over the collection and just investment of national income, nominating, with the approval of the Senate, members of the Diplomatic Corps, receiving foreign Heads of State, presiding at national functions, decreeing a State of Siege or Emergency or any other measures necessary during a public crisis. The President may not leave the country for more than 15 days without authorization from Congress. In the absence of the President, the Vice-President will assume power, or failing him, the President of the Supreme Court of Justice.

LOCAL GOVERNMENT

Government in the Distrito Nacional and the Municipalities is in the hands of local councils, with members elected proportionally to the number of inhabitants, but numbering at least five. Each Province has a civil Governor, designated by the Executive.

JUDICIARY

Judicial power is exercised by the Supreme Court of Justice and the other Tribunals; no judicial official may hold another public office or employment, other than honorary or teaching. The Supreme Court is made up of at least nine judges, who must be Dominican citizens by birth or origin, at least 35 years old, in full exercise of their citizen's rights, graduates in law and have practised professionally for at least 12 years. There are also five Courts of Appeal, a Lands Tribunal and a Court of the First Instance in each judicial district; in each Municipality and in the Distrito Nacional there are also Justices of the Peace.

Elections are directed by the Central Electoral Board. The armed forces are essentially obedient and apolitical, created for the defence of national independence and the maintenance of public order and the Constitution and Laws.

The artistic and historical riches of the country, whoever owns them, are part of the cultural heritage of the country and are under the safe-keeping of the State. Mineral deposits belong to the State. There is freedom to form political parties, provided they conform to the principles laid down in the Constitution. Justice is administered without charge throughout the Republic.

This Constitution can be reformed if the proposal for reform is supported in Congress by one-third of the members of either house or by the Executive. A special session of Congress must be called and any resolutions must have a two-thirds majority. There can be no reform of the method of government, which must always be civil, republican, democratic and representative.

The Government

HEAD OF STATE

President: Dr Joaquín Balaguer (took office 16 August 1986).
Vice-President: Carlos Morales Troncoso.

CABINET
(January 1989)

Secretary of State to the Presidency: Dr Rafael Bello Andino.
Secretary of State for External Relations: Joaquín Ricardo García.
Secretary of State for Defence, the Interior and Police: Gen. (retd) Elías Wessin y Wessin.
Secretary of State for Finance: Roberto Martínez Villanueva.
Secretary of State for Education and Culture: Dr Pedro C. Pichardo.
Secretary of State for Agriculture: Manuel de Jesús Viñas Román.
Secretary of State for Public Works and Communications: Ing. Marcos Subero Sajuín.
Secretary of State for Health and Social Welfare: Dr Ney Arias Lora.
Secretary of State for Industry and Commerce: Juan Valerio Sánchez.
Secretary of State for Labour: Rafael Emiliano Agramonte.
Secretary of State for Tourism: Lic. Fernando Rainieri Marranzini.
Secretary of State for Sport, Physical Education and Recreation: Temistocles Metz.
Secretaries of State without Portfolio: Ing. Manuel Guaroa Liranzo, Simón Tomás Fernández, Dr Donald Reid Cabral.
Administrative Secretary to the Presidency: Luis Toral.
Technical Secretary to the Presidency: Dr Guillermo Caram.
Governor of the Central Bank: Dr Roberto Saladín.

SECRETARIATS OF STATE

Secretariat of State for Agriculture: Centro de los Héroes de Constanza, Santo Domingo, DN; tel. 533-7171; telex 346-0393.
Secretariat of State for Defence: Plaza de la Independencia, Avda 27 de Febrero, Santo Domingo, DN; tel. 533-5131; telex 346-0652.
Secretariat of State for Education and Culture: Avda Máximo Gómez, Santo Domingo, DN; tel. 689-9161.
Secretariat of State for External Relations: Avda Independencia, Santo Domingo, DN; tel. 533-4121; telex 326-4192.
Secretariat of State for Finance: Avda México, Santo Domingo, DN; telex 346-0437.
Secretariat of State for Health and Social Welfare: Santo Domingo, DN.
Secretariat of State for Industry and Commerce: Edif. de Oficinas Gubernamentales 7°, Avda México, Santo Domingo, DN; tel. 685-5171.
Secretariat of State for the Interior and Police: Edif. de Oficinas Gubernamentales 3°, Avda Leopoldo Navarro a esq. México, Santo Domingo, DN; tel. 689-1979.
Secretariat of State for Labour: Santo Domingo, DN.
Secretariat of State for the Presidency: Santo Domingo, DN.
Secretariat of State for Public Works and Communications: Ensanche La Fé, Santo Domingo, DN; tel. 567-4929.
Secretariat of State for Sport, Physical Education and Recreation: Calle Pedro Henríquez Ureña, Santo Domingo, DN; tel. 688-0126; telex 346-0471.
Secretariat of State for Tourism: Avda George Washington, Apdo 497, Santo Domingo, DN; tel. 682-8181; telex 346-0303.

President and Legislature

PRESIDENT

Election, 16 May 1986

Candidates	Votes
Dr Joaquín Balaguer (PRSC)	857,942
Lic. Jacobo Majluta Azar (PRD*)	814,716
Dr Juan Bosch Gaviño (PLD)	379,269

There were three other candidates.

* Although Majluta had registered La Estructura, his right-wing faction of the PRD, as a separate political party in July 1985, he succeeded in securing the PRD candidacy.

CONGRESO NACIONAL

President: Luis José González Sánchez.
Vice-President: Maximo Antonio Nova Zapata.

The National Congress comprises a Senate and a Chamber of Deputies.

THE DOMINICAN REPUBLIC

General Election, 16 May 1986

	Senate	Chamber
Partido Reformista Social Cristiano (PRSC)	21	56
Partido Revolucionario Dominicano (PRD)	7	48
Partido de la Liberación Dominicana (PLD)	2	16
Total	**30**	**120**

Political Organizations

La Estructura: f. 1985; right-wing dissident faction of PRD (see below); formed by JACOBO MAJLUTA AZAR; Pres. ANDRÉS VAN DER HORST.

Movimiento de Conciliación Nacional (MCN): Calle Pina 207, Santo Domingo, DN; f. 1969; centre party; 659,277 mems; Pres. Dr JAIME M. FERNÁNDEZ; Sec. VÍCTOR MENA.

Movimiento de Integración Democrática (MIDA): Las Mercedes 607, Santo Domingo, DN; tel. 687-8895; centre-right; Leader Dr FRANCISCO AUGUSTO LORA.

Movimiento Popular Dominicano: Santo Domingo, DN; left-wing; Leader JULIO DE PEÑA VALDÉS.

Partido Comunista Dominicano: Avda Independencia 89, Santo Domingo, DN; tel. 685-3540; f. 1944; Leader JOSÉ ISRAEL CUELLO; Sec.-Gen. NARCISO ISA CONDE.

Partido Demócrata Popular: Arz. Meriño 259, Santo Domingo, DN; tel. 685-2920; opposition party; Leader LUIS HOMERO LÁJARA BURGOS.

Partido de la Liberación Dominicana (PLD): Avda Independencia 401, Santo Domingo, DN; tel. 685-3540; f. 1973 by breakaway group of PRD; left-wing; Leader Dr JUAN BOSCH GAVIÑO; Sec.-Gen. LIDIO CADET.

Partido Quisqueyano Demócrata (PQD): 27 de Febrero 206, altos, Santo Domingo, DN; tel. 567-7970; f. 1968; right-wing; 600,000 mems; Pres. Gen. (retd) ELÍAS WESSIN Y WESSIN; Sec.-Gen. Lic. JUAN MANUEL TAVERAS.

Partido Reformista Social Cristiano (PRSC): Avda San Cristóbal, Ensanche La Fe, Apdo 1332, Santo Domingo, DN; tel. 566-7089; f. 1964; centre-right party; Leader Dr JOAQUÍN BALAGUER; Sec.-Gen. (vacant).

Partido Revolucionario Dominicano (PRD): Espaillat 118, Santo Domingo, DN; tel. 687-2193; f. 1939; democratic socialist; mem. of Socialist International; split in 1985 when right-wing faction, led by JACOBO MAJLUTA AZAR, formed La Estructura; 400,000 mems; Pres. JOSÉ FRANCISCO PEÑA GÓMEZ; Sec.-Gen. HATUEY DECAMPS.

Partido Revolucionario Social Cristiano (PRSC): Las Mercedes 141, Santo Domingo, DN; tel. 688-3511; f. 1961; left-wing; Pres. Dr CLAUDIO ISIDORO ACOSTA; Sec.-Gen. Dr ALFONSO LOCKWARD.

Partido de los Trabajadores Dominicanos: Avda Duarte No 69, altos, Santo Domingo, DN; tel. 685-7705; f. 1979; workers' party; Sec.-Gen. JOSÉ GONZÁLEZ ESPINOZA.

Other parties include Unión Cívica Nacional (UCN), Partido Alianza Social Demócrata (ASD—Leader Dr JOSÉ RAFAEL ABINADER), Movimiento Nacional de Salvación (MNS—Leader LUIS JULIÁN PÉREZ), Partido Comunista del Trabajo de la República Dominicana (Sec.-Gen. RAFAEL CHALJUB MEJÍA), Partido de Veteranos Civiles (PVC), Partido Acción Constitucional (PAC), Partido Unión Patriótica (PUP—Leader ROBERTO SANTANA), Partido de Acción Nacional (right-wing) and Movimiento de Acción Social Cristiana (ASC). The Partido Comunista Dominicano, outlawed in 1962, was authorized again in 1977.

An opposition front, the Frente Izquierda Dominicana, has been formed by 53 political organizations and trade unions.

Diplomatic Representation

EMBASSIES IN THE DOMINICAN REPUBLIC

Argentina: Avda Máximo Gómez 10, Santo Domingo, DN; tel. 682-2977; telex 346-0154; Ambassador: JORGE VÁSQUEZ.

Brazil: Avda Winston Churchill 32, Edif. Franco-Acra y Asociados, 2°, Apdo 1655, Santo Domingo, DN; tel. 532-0868; telex 346-0155; Chargé d'affaires: RUY CASÃES.

Chile: Avda Anacaona 11, Santo Domingo, DN; telex 346-0395; Ambassador: GASTÓN LLANEX FERNÁNDEZ.

China (Taiwan): Avda Abraham Lincoln, Santo Domingo, DN; tel. 566-1277; telex 346-0267; Ambassador: MICHAEL T. S. TUNG.

Colombia: Avda Abraham Lincoln 502, 2°, Santo Domingo, DN; tel. 567-6836; telex 346-0448; Ambassador: Dr ERNESTO TORRES DÍAZ.

Costa Rica: Andrés Julio Aybar 15, Santo Domingo, DN; tel. 565-7294; Chargé d'affaires: ODALISCA AUED RODRÍGUEZ.

Ecuador: Gustavo M. Ricart 90, Santo Domingo, DN; tel. 565-0822; telex 326-4556; Ambassador: ADAIBERTO ORTIZ Q.

El Salvador: Avda Abraham Lincoln 167, Santo Domingo, DN; tel. 567-6084; Ambassador: Dr JOSÉ R. JOVEL PINEDA.

France: Avda Jorge Washington 353, Santo Domingo, DN; tel. 689-2161; telex 346-0392; Ambassador: CLAUDE FOUQUET.

Germany, Federal Republic: Mejía y Cotes 37, Santo Domingo, DN; tel. 565-8811; telex 326-4339; Ambassador: ULRICH SCHOENING.

Guatemala: Z No 8, Naco, Santo Domingo, DN; tel. 566-8881; Ambassador: (vacant).

Haiti: Cub Scouts 11, Naco, Santo Domingo, DN; tel. 567-2511; telex 346-0851; Ambassador: MELIÈRE DUPLAN.

Holy See: Máximo Gómez No 27, Apdo 312, Santo Domingo, DN; tel. 682-3773; Apostolic Nuncio: BLASCO COLLAÇO.

Honduras: Calle Porfirio Herrera No 9 esq. Respaldo Federico Geraldino Ensanche Piantini, Santo Domingo, DN; tel. 566-5707; telex 346-4104; Ambassador: IVÁN ROMERO MARTÍNEZ.

Israel: Pedro Henríquez Ureña 80, Santo Domingo, DN; tel. 686-7359; telex 346-0139; Ambassador: SHMUEL TEVET.

Italy: Rodríguez Objío 4, Santo Domingo, DN; tel. 689-3684; telex 346-0543; Ambassador: (vacant).

Japan: Torre BHD, 8°, Avda Winston Churchill esq. Luis F. Thomén, Santo Domingo, DN; tel. 567-3365; Ambassador: SUKETARO ENOMOTO.

Korea, Republic: Avda Sarasota 98, Santo Domingo, DN; tel. 532-4314; telex 326-4368; Ambassador: KIM SUNG-SHIK.

Mexico: Rafael Hernández 11, Ensanche Naco, Santo Domingo, DN; tel. 565-2744; telex 326-4187; Ambassador: HUMBERTO LIRA MORA.

Nicaragua: El Recodo, Santo Domingo, DN; tel. 532-8846; telex 326-4542; Ambassador: Dr DANILO VALLE MARTÍNEZ.

Panama: E de Marchena 36, Santo Domingo, DN; tel. 685-6950; Chargé d'affaires a.i.: Lic. CRISTÓBAL SARMIENTO.

Peru: Cancillería, Winston Churchill, Santo Domingo, DN; tel. 565-5851; Ambassador: RAÚL GUTIÉRREZ.

Romania: Santo Domingo, DN; Ambassador: (vacant).

Spain: Independencia 1205, Santo Domingo, DN; tel. 533-1425; telex 346-0158; Ambassador: (vacant).

USA: César Nicolás Pensón, esq. Leopoldo Navarro, Santo Domingo, DN; tel. 541-2171; telex 346-0013; Ambassador: PAUL D. TAYLOR.

Uruguay: Avda México 169, Santo Domingo, DN; tel. 565-2669; telex 346-0442; Ambassador: JAIME WOLFSON KOT.

Venezuela: Cancillería, Avda Bolívar 832, Santo Domingo, DN; tel. 687-5066; telex 326-4279; Ambassador: Lic. ABEL CLAVIJO OSTOS.

Judicial System

The Judicial Power resides in the Supreme Court of Justice, the Courts of Appeal, the Tribunals of the First Instance, the municipal courts and the other judicial authorities provided by law. The Supreme Court is composed of nine judges and the Attorney-General and exercises disciplinary authority over all the members of the judiciary. The Attorney-General of the Republic is the Chief of Judicial Police and of the Public Ministry which he represents before the Supreme Court of Justice. All judges are elected by the Senate.

Corte Suprema: Centro de los Héroes de Constanza, Santo Domingo, DN; tel. 533-3522.

President: NÉSTOR COYTÍN AYBAR.

Attorney-General: SEMÍRAMIS OLIVO DE PICHARDO.

Religion

More than 90% of the inhabitants belong to the Roman Catholic Church, but freedom of worship exists for all denominations. The Baptist, Evangelist, Seventh-day Adventist and Jewish churches are also represented.

CHRISTIANITY
The Roman Catholic Church
The Dominican Republic comprises one archdiocese and eight dioceses.

Bishops' Conference: Conferencia del Episcopado Dominicano, Apdo 186, Santo Domingo, DN; tel. 685-3141; f. 1985; Pres. Mgr. NICOLÁS DE JESÚS LÓPEZ RODRÍGUEZ, Archbishop of Santo Domingo.

Archbishop of Santo Domingo: NICOLÁS DE JESÚS LÓPEZ RODRÍGUEZ, Arzobispado, Apdo 186, Isabel la Católica No 55, Santo Domingo, DN; tel. 685-3141.

Episcopal Church
Bishop of the Dominican Republic: Rt Rev. TELÉSFORO A. ISAAC, Apdo 764, Santo Domingo, DN.

BAHÁ'Í FAITH
National Spiritual Assembly of the Bahá'ís of the Dominican Republic: Cambronal 152 esq. Beller, Santo Domingo, DN; f. 1961; tel. 687-1726; 392 localities.

The Press

DAILIES
Santo Domingo, DN

El Caribe: Autopista Duarte, Km 7½, Apdo 416, Santo Domingo, DN; tel. 566-8161; f. 1948; morning; Dir GERMÁN E. ORNES; circ. 28,000.

Diario Las Américas: Avda Tiradentes, Santo Domingo, DN; tel. 566-4577.

Listín Diario: Calle 19 de Marzo 59, Apdo 1455, Santo Domingo, DN; tel. 689-7171; f. 1889; morning; Dir RAFAEL HERRERA; circ. 55,000.

El Nacional: Avda San Martín 236, Santo Domingo, DN; tel. 565-5581; f. 1966; evening and Sunday; Dir MARIO ALVAREZ DUGAN; circ. 45,000.

La Noticia: Julio Verne 14, Santo Domingo, DN; tel. 687-3131; f. 1973; evening; Pres. JOSÉ A. BREA PEÑA; Dir SILVIO HERASME PEÑA.

El Sol: Carrera Sánchez, Km 6½, Santo Domingo, DN; tel. 532-9511; morning; Pres. QUITERIO CEDEÑO; Dir-Gen. MIGUEL ANGEL CEDEÑO.

Ultima Hora: Paseo de los Periodistas 52, Ensanche Miraflores, Santo Domingo, DN; tel. 688-3361; f. 1970; evening; Dir ANÍBAL DE CASTRO; circ. 50,000.

Puerto Plata
El Porvenir: Calle Imbert No 5, Apdo 614, Puerto Plata; f. 1872; Dir CARLOS ACEVEDO.

Santiago de los Caballeros
La Información: Las Carreras 157, Santiago de los Caballeros; tel. 685-2225; f. 1915; morning; Editor LUIS E. FRANCO; circ. 15,000.

PERIODICALS AND REVIEWS
Santo Domingo, DN

Agricultura: Santo Domingo, DN; organ of the State Secretariat of Agriculture and Colonization; f. 1905; monthly; Dir MIGUEL RODRÍGUEZ, Jr.

Agroconocimiento: Apdo 345-2, Santo Domingo, DN; monthly; agricultural news and technical information; Dir DOMINGO MARTE; circ. 10,000.

¡Ahora!: Avda San Martín 236, Apdo 1402, Santo Domingo, DN; tel. 565-5581; telex 346-0423; f. 1962; weekly; Dir MARIO ALVAREZ DUGAN.

La Campiña: San Martín 236, Apdo 1402, Santo Domingo, DN; f. 1967; Dir Ing. JUAN ULISES GARCÍA B.

Carta Dominicana: Avda Tiradentes 56, Santo Domingo, DN; tel. 566-0119; f. 1974; monthly; economics; Dir JUAN RAMÓN QUIÑONES M.

Deportes: San Martín 236, Apdo 1402, Santo Domingo, DN; f. 1967; sports; fortnightly; Dir L. R. CORDERO; circ. 5,000.

Eva: San Martín 236, Apdo 1402, Santo Domingo, DN; f. 1967; fortnightly; Dir MAGDA FLORENCIO.

Horizontes de América: Alexander Fleming 2, Santo Domingo, DN; tel. 565-9717; f. 1967; monthly; Dir ARMANDO LEMUS CASTILLO.

Letra Grande, Arte y Literatura: Leonardo de Vinci 13, Mirador del Sur, Santo Domingo, DN; tel. 533-4522; f. 1980; monthly; art and literature; Dir JUAN RAMÓN QUIÑONES M.

Renovación: Calle José Reyes esq. El Conde, Santo Domingo, DN; fortnightly; Dir OLGA QUISQUEYA Viuda MARTÍNEZ.

FOREIGN PRESS BUREAUX

Agencia EFE (Spain): Avda 27 de Febrero, Galerías Comerciales 5°, Of. 507, Santo Domingo, DN; tel. 567-7617; telex 02024176; Bureau Chief ANTONIO CASTILLO URBERUAGA.

Agenzia Nazionale Stampa Associata (ANSA) (Italy): Calle Navarro 79, 3°, Sala 17, Apdo 20324, Huanca, Santo Domingo, DN; tel. 685-8765; telex 201-4537; Bureau Chief HUMBERTO ANDRÉS SUAZO.

Inter Press Service (IPS) (Italy): Edif. Palamara, El Conde 407, Apto 202, Santo Domingo, DN; tel. 689-6449; Correspondent ANGELA HERNÁNDEZ.

United Press International (UPI) (USA): Carrera A. Manoguaybo 16, Manoguaybo, DN; tel. 689-7171; telex 346-0206; Chief Correspondent SANTIAGO ESTRELLA VELOZ.

Publishers

Santo Domingo, DN

Arte y Cine, C por A: Isabel la Católica 42, Santo Domingo, DN.

Editora Alfa y Omega: José Contreras 69, Santo Domingo, DN; tel. 532-5577.

Editora de las Antillas: Calle Pedro Henríquez Ureña, Santo Domingo, DN; tel. 685-2197.

Editora Colonial, C por A: Calle Moca 27-B, Apdo 2569, Santo Domingo, DN; tel. 688-2394; Pres. DANILO ASENCIO.

Editora Dominicana, SA: 23 Oeste, No 3 Lup., Santo Domingo, DN; tel. 688-0846.

Editora El Caribe, C por A: Autopista Duarte, Km 7½, Apdo 416, Santo Domingo, DN; tel. 566-8161; f. 1948; Dir Dr GERMÁN E. ORNES.

Editora El País: Carretera Sánchez, Km 6½, Santo Domingo, DN; tel. 532-9511.

Editora Hoy, C por A: Avda San Martín, 236, Santo Domingo, DN; tel. 566-1147; telex 346-0423.

Editora Listín Diario, C por A: Paseo de los Periodistas 52, Ensanche Miraflores, Santo Domingo, DN; tel. 689-7171; f. 1889; Pres. Dr ROGELIO A. PELLERANO.

Editorama, SA: Avda Tiradentes 56, Apdo 2074, Santo Domingo, DN; tel. 566-0119.

Editorial Padilla: San F. de Macorís 14, Santo Domingo, DN; tel. 682-3101.

Editorial Santo Domingo: Santo Domingo, DN; tel. 532-9431.

Editorial Stella: 19 de Marzo, Santo Domingo, DN; tel. 682-2281.

Julio D. Postigo e Hijos: Mercedes 49, Santo Domingo, DN; f. 1949; fiction; Man. J. D. POSTIGO.

Publicaciones América: Arz. Meriño, Santo Domingo, DN; Dir PEDRO BISONÓ.

Santiago de los Caballeros
Editora el País, SA: Carrera Sánchez, Km 6½, Santiago de los Caballeros, SD; tel. 532-9511.

Radio and Television

In 1986 there were about 800,000 radio receivers and 500,000 television receivers in use.

Dirección General de Telecomunicaciones: Isabel la Católica 203, Santo Domingo, DN; tel. 689-4161; government supervisory body; Dir-Gen. LEOPOLDO NUEÑEZ SANTOS.

RADIO
There were more than 100 commercial stations in 1987. The government-owned broadcasting network Radio Televisión Dominicana operates 10 radio stations.

TELEVISION
Radio Televisión Dominicana: Dr Tejada Florentino 8, Apdo 969, Santo Domingo, DN; tel. 689-2121; government station; two channels, two relay stations; Dir-Gen. R. A. FONT BERNARD; Gen. Man. AGUSTÍN MERCADO.

THE DOMINICAN REPUBLIC

Rahintel Televisión: Centro de los Héroes de Constanza, Apdo 1220, Santo Domingo, DN; tel. 533-3151; telex 3460213; commercial station; two channels; Pres. LEONEL ALMONTE V.

Color-Visión (Corporación Dominicana de Radio y Televisión): Calle Emilio A. Morel esq. Luis E. Pérez, Ensanche La Fé, Apdo 30043, Santo Domingo, DN; tel. 566-5875; telex 326-4327; commercial station; two channels: Channel 2 (Santiago) and Channel 9 (Santo Domingo, Puerto Plata, La Romana, San Juan); Dir-Gen. M. QUIROZ.

Teleantillas: Autopista Duarte, Km 7½, Apdo 30404, Santo Domingo, DN; tel. 567-7751; telex 3460863; Gen. Man. MARITZA DE LOS SANTOS.

Tele-Inde Canal 13: 30 de Marzo, No 80, Santo Domingo, DN; commercial station; Proprietor JOSÉ A. SEMORILE.

Telesistema Dominicana: Calle El Vergel 88, Ensanche El Vergel, Santo Domingo; tel. 567-5151; Dir OCTAVIO A. BERAS-GOICO.

Finance

(cap. = capital; dep. = deposits; m = million; p.u. = paid up; res = reserves; amounts in pesos)

BANKING

Supervisory Body

Superintendencia de Bancos: Avda México esq. Leopoldo Navarro, Apdo 1326, Santo Domingo, DN; tel. 685-8141; telex 346-0653; f. 1947; Superintendent Lic. ÉMILIO DE LUNA P.

Central Bank

Banco Central de la República Dominicana: Calle Pedro Henríquez Ureña esq. Leopoldo Navarro, Santo Domingo, DN; tel. 689-7121; telex 346-0052; f. 1947; cap. and res 51.1m., total assets 8,447.6m. (Jan. 1987); Gov. Dr ROBERTO SALADÍN; Man. CÉSAR RAMÍREZ GARRIDO.

Commercial Banks

Banco del Comercio Dominicano: Avda 27 de Febrero, esq. Winston Churchill, Apdo 1440, Santo Domingo, DN; tel. 567-8871; telex 346-0621; f. 1980; cap. and res. 57.7m., dep. 418.1m. (June 1986); Pres. JOSÉ UREÑA ALMONTE; 22 brs.

Banco Dominico-Hispano, SA: Avda 27 de Febrero 102, Santo Domingo, DN; tel. 567-8211; f. 1948; cap. and res 6.4m., dep. 1.5m. (June 1985); Exec. Vice-Pres. Lic. AUGUSTO PEIGNAND.

Banco Fiduciario Dominicano, SA: Avda San Martín 122, Apdo 1101, Santo Domingo, DN; tel. 565-9971; f. 1983; cap. and res 5.1m., dep. 17.8m. (June 1985); Exec. Vice-Pres. GEORGE MANUEL HAZOURY PEÑA.

Banco Metropolitano: Avda Lope de Vega esq. Gustavo Mejía Ricart, Apdo 1872, Santo Domingo, DN; tel. 562-2442; telex 346-0419; f. 1974; cap. and res 17.1m., dep. 196.4m. (Dec 1986); Gen. Dir ADALBERTO PÉREZ PERDOMO; 7 brs.

Banco Nacional de Crédito: Avda Lope de Vega 95, Apdo 1502, Santo Domingo, DN; tel. 542-7556; telex 326-4522; f. 1981; cap. and res 24.2m., dep. 192.4m. (June 1987); Dir FREDERICH BERGÉS; 11 brs.

Banco Popular Dominicano: Isabel la Católica 251, Apdo 1441, Santo Domingo, DN; tel. 682-9141; telex 346-0105; f. 1963; cap. and res 57.7m., dep. 765.7m. (Dec. 1986); Pres. ALEJANDRO E. GRULLÓN E.; 28 brs.

Banco del Progreso Dominicano, SA: Avda John F. Kennedy 3, Santo Domingo, DN; tel. 566-7171; telex 346-0181; f. 1975; cap. and res 6.1m., dep. 62.6m. (June 1985); Exec. Vice-Pres. MICHAEL A. KELLY; 6 brs.

Banco Regional Dominicano, SA: Restauración esq. San Luis, Apdo 308, Santiago; tel. 583-8311; f. 1982; cap. and res 9.5m., dep. 41.2m. (March 1987); Pres. LORENZO GARCÍA T.; 5 brs.

Banco de Reservas de la República Dominicana: Isabel la Católica 201, Apdo 1353, Santo Domingo, DN; tel. 687-5366; telex 346-0012; f. 1941; cap. and res 101.9m., dep. 685.6m. (June 1985); Gen. Man. JOSÉ RAFAEL ESTÉVEZ S.; 36 brs.

Banco de Santander Dominicano: Avda John F. Kennedy, Santo Domingo, DN; tel. 566-5811; telex 346-0321; f. 1949 as Banco de Crédito y Ahorros; cap. and res 8.9m., dep. 94.6m. (June 1985); Pres. EMILIO BOTÍN; 12 brs.

Banco de los Trabajadores de la República Dominicana: El Conde esq. Arz. Meriño, Apdo 1446, Santo Domingo, DN; tel. 688-0181; telex 346-4500; f. 1972; state-controlled; cap. and res 9.4m., dep. 16.7m. (June 1987); Pres. Lic. JOSÉ A. RODRÍGUEZ ESPAILLAT; 4 brs.

Banco Universal, SA: El Conde 105, Apdo 2065, Santo Domingo, DN; tel. 688-6666; f. 1982; cap. and res 5.0m., dep. 13.1m. (June 1985); Pres. LEONEL ALMONTE.

Development Banks

Banco Agrícola de la República Dominicana: Avda G. Washington 601, Apdo 1057, Santo Domingo, DN; tel. 533-1171; telex 346-0026; f. 1945; government agricultural development bank; cap. and res 230.9m., dep. 115.5m. (Dec 1985); Gen. Administrator PEDRO BRETUN; 31 brs.

Banco de Crédito Hipotecario, SA: Avda Bolívar esq. Socorro Sánchez, Apdo 497-2, Santo Domingo, DN; tel. 682-3191; telex 346-0820; f. 1983; cap. and res 6.4m., dep. 9.0m. (Oct 1988); Pres. Lic. ENRIQUE DALET LOZANO.

Banco Hipotecario Mercantil, SA: Juan I. Jiménez 1, Santo Domingo, DN; tel. 689-8005; f. 1983; cap. and res 10.6m., dep. 11.7m. (Aug 1988); Exec. Vice-Pres. Lic. JOSÉ MANUEL LÓPEZ VÁLDEZ.

Banco Hipotecario de la Construcción, SA (BANHICO): Avda Tiradentes (Altos Plaza Naco), Santo Domingo, DN; tel. 562-1281; f. 1977; cap. and res 8.4m., dep. 0.4m. (June 1985); Man. Dr JAIME ALVAREZ DUGAN.

Banco Hipotecario Dominicano, SA: Avda 27 de Febrero esq. Winston Churchill, Apdo 266-2, Santo Domingo, DN; tel. 567-7281; telex 4546; f. 1972; housing development bank; cap. and res 20.3m., (June 1985); Pres. SAMUEL CONDE; 5 brs.

Banco Hipotecario Financiero, SA: Avda 27 de Febrero esq. Avda Tiradentes, Apdo 385-2, Santo Domingo, DN; tel. 566-5151; f. 1978; cap. and res 2.6m., dep. 12.9m. (June 1985); Pres. Dr LUCAS T. GUERRA C.

Banco Hipotecario Horizontes, SA: Avda Rómulo Betancourt 1410, Santo Domingo, DN; tel. 532-2527; telex 346-0782; f. 1984; cap. and res 3.5m., dep. 4.5m. (Aug. 1987); Pres. HÉCTOR MARTÍNEZ CASTRO.

Banco Hipotecario Miramar, SA: Avda John F. Kennedy 10, Apdo 2424, Santo Domingo, DN; tel. 566-5681; telex 326-4202; f. 1976; cap. and res 12.0m., dep. 8.2m. (June 1985); Pres. Ing. GUILLERMO ARMENTEROS; 5 brs.

Banco Hipotecario Popular, SA: Avda 27 de Febrero 261, Santo Domingo, DN; tel. 567-5511; f. 1978; cap. and res 33.4m., dep. 110.6m. (June 1987); Pres. MANUEL E. JIMÉNEZ F.

Banco Hipotecario Unido, SA: Calle Del Sol 42, Apdo 290, Santiago; tel. 583-0401; f. 1983; cap. and res 1.8m., dep. 0.7m. (June 1985); Exec. Pres. LUIS MARTÍNEZ VILCHEZ.

Banco Hipotecario Universal, SA: Avda Santa Rosa esq. Gregorio Luperón, Apdo 259, La Romana; tel. 556-2183; f. 1979; cap. and res 3.9m., dep. 0.1m. (June 1985); Pres. LEONEL ALMONTE; 2 brs.

Banco Inmobiliario Dominicano, SA: Calle El Sol 10, Santiago; tel. 583-4331; telex 346-1111; f. 1979; cap. and res 13.6m., dep. 0.5m. (June 1985); Dir Dr J. MANUEL PITTALUGA NIVAR; 3 brs.

Banco Nacional de la Construcción: Avda Alma Mater esq. Pedro Henríquez Ureña, Santo Domingo, DN; tel. 685-9776; f. 1977; cap. and res 3.7m., dep. 0.9m. (June 1985); Gen. Man. LUIS MANUEL PELLERANO.

There were 18 development finance societies and 18 savings and lending associations in 1985.

Foreign Banks

Bank of Nova Scotia (Canada): Avda John F. Kennedy esq. Lope de Vega, Santo Domingo, DN; tel. 566-5671; telex 346-0067; f. 1920; cap. and res 9.5m., dep. 101.1m. (June 1985); Gen. Man. IVAN L. LESSARD; 12 brs.

Chase Manhattan Bank (USA): Avda John F. Kennedy, Apdo 1408, Santo Domingo, DN; tel. 565-4441; telex 346-0096; f. 1962; cap. and res 8.6m., dep. 396.7m. (June 1987); Man. VÍCTOR M. CAÑAS; 7 brs.

Citibank NA (USA): Avda John F. Kennedy 1, Apdo 1492, Santo Domingo, DN; tel. 566-5611; telex 346-0083; f. 1962; cap. and res 14.1m., dep. 97.2m. (June 1985); Vice-Pres. MICHAEL CONTRERAS; 5 brs.

INSURANCE

Supervisory Body

Superintendencia de Seguros: Secretaría de Estado de Finanzas, Leopoldo Navarro esq. Avda México, Santo Domingo, DN; tel. 688-1245; Superintendent Dr JUAN ESTEBAN OLIVERO FELIZ.

National Companies

La Americana, SA: Edif. La Cumbre, Avda Tiradentes, Apdo 25241, Santo Domingo, DN; tel. 567-0181; telex 346-0185; f. 1975; life; Pres. MARINO GINEBRA H.

THE DOMINICAN REPUBLIC   *Directory*

Centro de Seguros La Popular, C por A: Gustavo Mejía Ricart 61, Santo Domingo, DN; tel. 566-1988; general except life; Pres. Lic. FABIO A. FIALLO.

Citizens Dominicana, SA: Avda Winston Churchill esq. Paseo de los Locutores 4°, Santo Domingo, DN; tel. 562-2705; f. 1978; Pres. MIGUEL E. SAVIÑÓN TORRES.

Cía Dominicana de Seguros, C por A: Edif. Buenaventura, Avda Independencia 201, Dr Delgado esq., Apdo 176, Santo Domingo, DN; tel. 689-6127; general except life; Pres. Lic. HUGO VILLANUEVA.

Cía Nacional de Seguros, C por A: Avda Máximo Gómez 31, Apdo 916, Santo Domingo, DN; tel. (809) 685-2121; telex 346-0117; general; Pres. Dr MÁXIMO A. PELLERANO.

Cía de Seguros Quisqueyana, SA: Edif. Galerías Comerciales, 6a Planta, Avda 27 de Febrero, Apdo 21-443, Santo Domingo, DN; tel. 567-0133; telex 346-0637; general; Pres. POLIBIO DÍAZ.

La Colonial, SA: Edif. Haché 2°, Avda John F. Kennedy, Santo Domingo, DN; tel. 565-9926; f. 1971; general; Pres. Dr MIGUEL FERIS IGLESIAS.

El Condor Seguros, SA: Avda 27 de Febrero No 12, Apdo 20077, Santo Domingo, DN; tel. 689-4146; telex 346-0210; f. 1977; general; Pres. JUAN PABLO REYES.

General de Seguros, SA: Avda Bolívar 805, 2-6, Apdo 2183, Santo Domingo, DN; tel. 685-9102; f. 1981; general; Pres. Dr FERNANDO A. BALLISTA.

La Intercontinental de Seguros, SA: Plaza Naco, Avda Tiradentes, Apdo 825, Santo Domingo, DN; tel. 562-1211; general; Pres. Lic. RAMÓN BÁEZ ROMANO.

Latinoamericana de Seguros, SA: Plaza Naco, Avda Tiradentes 2a, Apdo 1215, Santo Domingo, DN; tel. 562-2959; life; Pres. RAFAEL CASTRO MARTÍNEZ.

La Metropolitana de Seguros, C por A: Edif. Alico, 4a, Avda Abraham Lincoln, Apdo 131, Santo Domingo, DN; tel. (809) 532-0541; telex 346-0366; managed by American International Underwriters (AIU); Gen. Man. RAFAEL ARMANDO PICHARDO.

La Mundial de Seguros, SA: Edif. Mella 5°, Avda George Washington, Santo Domingo, DN; tel. 688-4477; telex 346-0466; general except life and financial; Pres. JOHN RICHARDS.

Patria, SA: Avda 27 de Febrero 10, Santo Domingo, DN; tel. 687-3151; general except life; Pres. Dr MIGUEL ANGEL LUNA MORALES.

La Real de Seguros, SA: Avda 27 de Febrero 80, Santo Domingo, DN; tel. 566-5195; general; Pres. Lic. HÉCTOR MARTÍNEZ.

Reaseguradora Internacional, SA: Avda Pasteur 17, Santo Domingo, DN; tel. 685-3903; general; Pres. Lic. FABIO A. FIALLO.

Reaseguradora Nacional, SA: Avda Máximo Gómez 31, Apdo 916, Santo Domingo, DN; tel. 685-3177; f. 1971; general; Pres. MÁXIMO A. PELLERANO.

Reaseguradora Profesional, SA: Edif. Concordia 2°, Avda Abraham Lincoln esq. José Amado Soler, Santo Domingo, DN; tel. (809) 562-5291; telex 346-0385; f. 1981; Pres. ALEJANDRO GRULLÓN.

Reaseguradora Santo Domingo, SA: Centro Comercial Jardines del Embajador, 2a Planta, Avda Sarasota, Apdo 25005, Santo Domingo, DN; tel. (809) 533-5874; telex 346-0566; general; Man. DOUGLAS HARMAND.

Seguros San Rafael, C por A: Leopoldo Navarro 61, esq. San Francisco de Macorís, Santo Domingo, DN; tel. 688-2231; telex 346-0169; general; Pres. DANILO GONZÁLEZ CAMILO.

Seguros La Alianza: Padre Fantino Falcó, Plaza Naco, Avda Tiradentes, Santo Domingo, DN; tel. 562-6361; general; Pres. VIRGILIO ALVAREZ BONILLA.

Seguros América, C por A: Edif. La Cumbre 4°, Avda Tiradentes, Santo Domingo, DN; tel. 567-0181; telex 346-0185; f. 1966; general except life; Pres. Dr LUIS GINEBRA HERNÁNDEZ.

Seguros La Antillana, SA: Avda Abraham Lincoln No 708, Apdo 146 y 27, Santo Domingo, DN; tel. 567-4481; telex 346-0411; general; Pres. ANDRÉS A. FREITES V.

Seguros del Caribe, SA: Edif. Galerías Comerciales 5°, Avda 27 de Febrero, Santo Domingo, DN; tel. 567-0242; general; Pres. EDUARDO GONZÁLEZ.

Seguros Horizontes, SA: Avda Lope de Vega 50 (altos), Santo Domingo, DN; tel. 562-6591; telex 346-0812; f. 1974; general and life; Man. ANTONIO HERNÁNDEZ.

Seguros Pepín, SA: Mercedes 470 esq. Palo Hincado, Santo Domingo, DN; tel. 689-8171; general; Pres. Dr BIENVENIDO COROMINAS.

Unión de Seguros, C por A: Avda 27 de Febrero 263, Santo Domingo, DN; tel. 566-2191; f. 1964; general; Pres. BELARMINIO CORTINA.

La Universal de Seguros, C por A: Edif. Motorámbar 2° y 3°, Avda Abraham Lincoln 1054, Santo Domingo, DN; tel. 562-3011; general; Pres. ERNESTO IZQUIERDO.

Insurance Association

Cámara Dominicana de Aseguradores y Reaseguradores, Inc.: Edif. Central 1°, Avda Winston Churchill esq. Max Henríquez Ureña, Santo Domingo, DN; Pres. MARINO GINEBRA HURTADO.

Trade and Industry

TRADE AND DEVELOPMENT ORGANIZATIONS

Asociación Dominicana de Hacendados y Agricultores Inc.: Avda Sarasota No 20, Santo Domingo, DN; tel. 533-2717; farming and agricultural organization; Pres. Lic. SILVESTRE ALBA DE MOYA.

Asociación de Industrias de la República Dominicana Inc.: Avda Sarasota 20, Apdo 850, Santo Domingo, DN; tel. 532-5523; f. 1962; industrial organization; Pres. Ing. GEORGE ARZENO BRUGAL.

Centro Dominicano de Promoción de Exportaciones (CEDOPEX): Plaza de la Independencia, Sección de Herrera, Apdo 199-2, Santo Domingo, DN; tel. 566-9131; telex 346-0351; organization for the promotion of exports; Dir JOSÉ CARLOS ISAÍAS.

Consejo Estatal del Azúcar (CEA) (State Sugar Council): Calle de los Héroes, PO Box 1256/1258, Santo Domingo, DN; tel. 533-1161; telex 346-0043; f. 1966; autonomous administration for each of the 12 state sugar mills; Dir Ing. CARLOS MORALES TRONCOSO.

Consejo Promotor de Inversiones (Investment Promotion Council): Avda Abraham Lincoln, 2°, Santo Domingo; tel. 532-3281; Pres. Arq. ANTONIO CÁCERES TRONCOSO.

Corporación Dominicana de Electricidad: Avda Independencia, Santo Domingo, DN; tel. 533-1131; state electricity company; Man. Ing. CÉSAR NEWMAN TORRES.

Corporación Dominicana de Empresas Estatales (CORDE) (Dominican State Corporation): Avda General Antonio Duvergé, Apdo 1378, Santo Domingo, DN; tel. 533-5171; telex 346-0311; f. 1966 to administer, direct and develop 26 state enterprises; auth. cap. RD $25m.; Exec. Dir RAÚL BARRIENTOS.

Corporación de Fomento Industrial (CFI): Avda 27 de Febrero, Apdo 1472, Santo Domingo, DN; tel. 547-3328; telex 346-0049; f. 1962 to promote agro-industrial development; auth. cap. RD $25m.; Dir Lic. JULIO CÉSAR PINEDA.

Dirección General de Minería e Hidrocarburos: Edif. de Oficinas Gubernamentales 10°, Avda México esq. Leopoldo Navarro, Santo Domingo, DN; tel. 685-8191; f. 1947; government mining and hydrocarbon organization; Dir-Gen. Ing. FRANCISCO AMEZQUITA.

Fondo de Inversión para el Desarrollo Económico—FIDE (Economic Development Investment Fund): c/o Banco Central de la República Dominicana, Avda Pedro Henríquez Ureña esq. Leopoldo Navarro, Santo Domingo, DN; tel. 689-7121; f. 1965; associated with AID, IDB; resources RD $255.38m.; encourages economic development in productive sectors of economy, excluding sugar; authorizes complementary financing to private sector for establishing new industrial and agricultural enterprises and developing existing ones; Dir Lic. VIRGILIO MALAGON ALVAREZ.

Fundación Dominicana de Desarrollo (Dominican Development Foundation): Calle Mercedes No 4, Apdo 857, Santo Domingo, DN; f. 1962 to mobilize private resources for collaboration in financing small-scale development programmes; 384 mems; assets US $10.7m.; Dir EDUARDO LA TORRE.

Instituto Agrario Dominicano (IAD): Avda 27 de Febrero, Santo Domingo, DN; tel. 566-0141; Dir Ing. CÉSAR SANDINO DE JESÚS.

Instituto Azucarero Dominicano (INAZUCAR): Avda Jiménez Moya, Apdo 667, Santo Domingo, DN; tel. 532-5571; sugar institute; f. 1965; Dir Lic. MIGUEL GUERRERO.

Instituto de Desarrollo y Crédito Cooperativo (IDECOOP): Centro de los Héroes, Santo Domingo, DN; tel. 533-8131; f. 1963 to encourage the development of co-operatives; cap. 100,000 pesos; Dir Dr NELSON EDDY CARRASCO.

Instituto de Estabilización de Precios (INESPRE): Avda Luperón, Santo Domingo, DN; tel. 547-4442; price commission; Dir Lic. KATIUSCA BOBEA DE BRENES.

Instituto Nacional de la Vivienda: Antiguo Edif. del Banco Central, Avda Pedro Henríquez Ureña esq. Leopoldo Navarro, Apdo 1506, Santo Domingo, DN; tel. 685-4181; f. 1962; low-cost housing institute; Dir Ing. MIGUEL PIMENTEL.

CHAMBERS OF COMMERCE

Cámara de Comercio y Producción del Distrito Nacional: Arz. Nouel 206, Apdo Postal 815, Santo Domingo, DN; tel. 689-2688; telex 346-0877; f. 1910; 1,500 active mems; Pres. Lic. FELIPE AUFFANT NAJRI; Sec.-Gen. Lic. ARSENIO JIMÉNEZ P.

Cámara Americana de Comercio de la República Dominicana: Avda Independencia, Hotel Santo Domingo, Apdo 95-2, Santo

Domingo, DN; tel. 533-8171; telex 346-0958; Pres. GUILLERMO AMORE.

There are official Chambers of Commerce in the larger towns.

EMPLOYERS' ASSOCIATIONS

Confederación Patronal de la República Dominicana: Edif. Mella, Cambronal/G. Washington, Santo Domingo, DN; tel. 688-3017; Pres. Ing. HERIBERTO DE CASTRO.

Consejo Nacional de Hombres de Empresa Inc.: Edif. Motorámbar 7°, Avda Abraham Lincoln 1056, Santo Domingo, DN; tel. 562-1666; Pres. Ing. JOSÉ DEL CARMEN ARIZA.

Federación Dominicana de Comerciantes: Carretera Sánchez Km 10, Santo Domingo, DN; tel. 533-2666; Pres. JUAN VALERIO SÁNCHEZ.

TRADE UNIONS

It is estimated that 13% of the total work-force belong to trade unions.

Central General de Trabajadores—CGT: Calle Juan Erazo No 133, Santo Domingo, DN; tel. 688-3932; f. 1972; 13 sections; Sec.-Gen. FRANCISCO ANTONIO SANTOS; 65,000 mems.

Central Unitaria de Trabajadores—CUT: Avda Vicente Noble No 14, Santo Domingo, DN; tel. 686-2807; f. 1978; left-wing; Sec. EFRAÍN SÁNCHEZ SORIANO.

Confederación Autónoma de Sindicatos Clasistas—CASC (Autonomous Confederation of Trade Unions): J. Erazo 39, Santo Domingo, DN; tel. 687-8533; f. 1962; supports PRSC; Sec.-Gen. GABRIEL DEL RÍO.

*****Confederación de Trabajadores Dominicanos—CTD** (Confederation of Dominican Workers): Santo Domingo, DN; f. 1920; 11 provincial federations totalling 150 unions are affiliated; Sec.-Gen. JULIO DE PEÑA VÁLDEZ; 188,000 mems (est.).

*****Unión General de Trabajadores Dominicanos—UGTD:** Santo Domingo, DN; f. 1978; supports PRD; Pres. MATEO VÁLDEZ.

*These two unions announced that they had merged in 1988.

Transport

RAILWAYS

Dirección General de Tránsito Terrestre: Avda San Cristóbal, Santo Domingo, DN; tel. 567-4610; f. 1966; run by Secretary of State for Public Works and Communications; Dir-Gen. Ing. ARIF ABUD ABREU.

Ferrocarril Unidos Dominicanos: Santo Domingo; government-owned; 142 km of track from La Vega to Sánchez principally used for the transport of exports.

There are also a number of semi-autonomous and private railway companies for the transport of sugar cane, including:

Ferrocarril de Central Romana: La Romana; 375 km open; Pres. C. MORALES.

Ferrocarril Central Río Haina: Apdo 1258, Haina; 113 km open.

ROADS

In 1985 there were 17,120 km of roads. There is a direct route from Santo Domingo to Port-au-Prince in Haiti. In 1980 a project to improve the main road between Santo Domingo and Santiago de los Caballeros, at a cost of US $61m., was launched.

SHIPPING

The Dominican Republic has 14 ports, of which Santo Domingo is by far the largest, handling about 80% of imports. In 1983 the country's merchant fleet had a total displacement of 11,963 grt.

A number of foreign shipping companies operate services to the island.

Armadora Naval Dominicana, SA: Calle Isabel la Católica 165, Apdo 2677, Santo Domingo, DN; tel. 689-6191; telex 346-0465; Man. Dir Capt. EINAR WETTRE.

Líneas Marítimas de Santo Domingo, SA: José Gabriel García 8, Apdo 1148, Santo Domingo, DN; tel. 689-9146; telex 326-4274; Pres. C. LLUBERES; Vice-Pres. JUAN T. TAVARES.

CIVIL AVIATION

There are international airports at Santo Domingo (Aeropuerto Internacional de las Américas) and Puerto Plata. The airport at La Romana is authorized for international flights, providing that three days' notice is given. Most main cities have domestic airports.

Aerolíneas Argo: Avda 27 de Febrero 409, Santo Domingo, DN; tel. 566-1844; telex 346-0531; f. 1971; cargo and mail services to USA, Puerto Rico and US Virgin Islands; fleet: 1 L-749 Constellation, 1 Curtiss C-46.

Dominicana de Aviación C por A: Avda Jiménez de Moya esq. José Contreras, Apdo 1415, Santo Domingo, DN; tel. 532-8511; telex. 346-0438; f. 1944; operates on international routes connecting Santo Domingo with the Netherlands Antilles, Aruba, the USA, Haiti, Panama and Venezuela; charter flights in USA, Canada and Europe; Chair. Ing. MANUEL ALSINA PUELLO; fleet: 1 Boeing 727-100, 1 727-100C, 1 727-200, 1 707-320C, 2 DC-6B.

Alas del Caribe, C por A: Avda Luperón, Aeropuerto de Herrera, Santo Domingo, DN; tel. 566-2141; f. 1968; internal routes; Pres. JACINTO B. PEYNADO; Dir MANUEL PÉREZ NEGRÓN.

Tourism

In 1987 tourists receipts totalled US $580m. and nearly 1m. tourists visited the country. Strenuous efforts to improve the tourist infrastructure are being made, with 100m. pesos to be spent on road improvements, and a new development, costing 160m. pesos, planned at Bahía de Manzanillo.

Secretaría de Estado de Turismo: Avda George Washington, Santo Domingo, DN; tel. 682-8181; telex 346-0303; Sec. of State for Tourism Lic. FERNANDO RAINIERI MARRANZINI.

Asociación Dominicana de Agencias de Viajes: Carrera Sánchez 201, Santo Domingo, DN; tel. 687-8984; Pres. RAMÓN PRIETO.

Atomic Energy

Comisión Nacional de Asuntos Nucleares: Edif. de la Defensa Civil, Dr Delgado 58, Santo Domingo, DN; tel. 565-5090; telex 346-0461; Pres. Dr ABEL GONZÁLEZ MASSENET.

ECUADOR

Introductory Survey

Location, Climate, Language, Religion, Flag, Capital

The Republic of Ecuador lies on the west coast of South America. It is bordered by Colombia to the north, by Peru to the east and south, and by the Pacific Ocean to the west. The Galapagos Islands, about 1,000 km (600 miles) off shore, form part of Ecuador. The climate is affected by the Andes mountains, and the topography ranges from the tropical rain forest on the coast and in the eastern region to the tropical grasslands of the central valley and the permanent snowfields of the highlands. The official language is Spanish, but Quechua and other indigenous languages are very common. Almost all of the inhabitants profess Christianity, and about 90% are Roman Catholics. The national flag (proportions 2 by 1) has three horizontal stripes, of yellow (one-half of the depth), blue and red. The state flag has, in addition, the national emblem (an oval cartouche, showing Mt Chimborazo and a steamer on a lake, surmounted by a condor) in the centre. The capital is Quito.

Recent History

Ecuador was ruled by Spain from the 16th century until 1822, when it achieved independence as part of Gran Colombia. In 1830 Ecuador seceded and became a separate republic. A long-standing division between Conservatives (Partido Conservador), whose support is generally strongest in the highlands, and Liberals (Partido Liberal, subsequently Partido Liberal Radical), based in the coastal region, began in the 19th century. Until 1948 Ecuador's political life was characterized by a rapid succession of presidents, dictators and juntas. Between 1830 and 1925 the country was governed by 40 different regimes. From 1925 to 1948 there was even greater instability, with a total of 22 heads of state.

Dr Galo Plaza Lasso, who was elected in 1948 and remained in power until 1952, was the first President since 1924 to complete his term of office. He created a climate of stability and economic progress. Dr José María Velasco Ibarra, who had previously been President in 1934–35 and 1944–47, was elected again in 1952 and held office until 1956. A 61-year-old tradition of Liberal Presidents was broken in 1956, when a Conservative candidate, Dr Camilo Ponce Enríquez, was elected in June (though with only 29% of the votes cast) and took office in September. He was succeeded in September 1960 by ex-President Velasco, who campaigned as a non-party Liberal. In November 1961, however, President Velasco was deposed by a coup, and was succeeded by his Vice-President, Dr Carlos Julio Arosemena Monroy. The latter was himself deposed in July 1963 by a military junta, led by Capt. (later Rear-Adm.) Ramón Castro Jijón, the Commander-in-Chief of the Navy, who assumed the office of President. In March 1966 the High Command of the Armed Forces dismissed the junta and installed Clemente Yerovi Indaburu, a wealthy businessman and a former Minister of Economics, as acting President. Yerovi was forced to resign when the Constituent Assembly, elected in October 1966, proposed a new constitution which prohibited the intervention of the armed forces in politics. In November he was replaced as provisional President by Dr Otto Arosemena Gómez, who held office until the elections of June 1968, when Dr Velasco returned from exile to win the Presidency for the fifth time. He took office in September.

In June 1970 President Velasco, with the support of the army, suspended the Constitution, dissolved the National Congress and assumed dictatorial powers to cope with a financial emergency. In February 1972 he was overthrown for the fourth time by a military coup, led by Brig.-Gen. Guillermo Rodríguez Lara, the Commander-in-Chief of the Army, who proclaimed himself Head of State. In January 1976 President Rodríguez resigned, and power was assumed by a three-man military junta, led by Vice-Adm. Alfredo Poveda Burbano, the Chief of Staff of the Navy. The new junta announced its intention to lead the country to a truly representative democracy. A national referendum approved a newly-drafted constitution in January 1978 and presidential elections took place in July. No candidate achieved an overall majority, and a second round of voting was held in April 1979, when a new Congress was also elected. Jaime Roldós Aguilera of the Concentración de Fuerzas Populares (CFP) was elected President and he took office in August, when the Congress was inaugurated and the new constitution came into force. President Roldós promised social justice and economic development, and guaranteed freedom for the press, but he met antagonism from both the conservative sections of the Congress and the trade unions. In May 1981 the President died in an air crash and was replaced by the Vice-President, Dr Osvaldo Hurtado Larrea, who faced opposition from left-wing politicians and unions for his efforts to cut government spending. He was also opposed by right-wing and commercial interests, which feared encroaching state intervention in the private economic sector.

A dispute between Hurtado and Vice-President León Roldós Aguilera in January 1982 led to the resignation of two Ministers belonging to Roldós' party, Pueblo, Cambio y Democracia (PCD), which then went into opposition. Hurtado replaced the Ministers with members of the CFP, creating a new pro-government majority with a coalition of members of Democracia Popular-Unión Demócrata Cristiana, CFP, Izquierda Democrática and seven independents. The heads of the armed forces resigned and the Defence Minister was dismissed in January 1982, when they opposed Hurtado's attempts to settle amicably the border dispute with Peru (see below). In August Hurtado lost his majority again when two CFP Ministers resigned over energy policy. A state of emergency was declared in October, after a general strike and violent demonstrations against price rises, but it was lifted in November.

In March 1983 the Government introduced a series of austerity measures, which encountered immediate opposition from the trade unions and workers in the private sector. Three Ministers resigned in July, and a new Cabinet was appointed in August. Discontent with the Government's performance was reflected in the results of the concurrent presidential and general elections of January 1984, when the ruling party, Democracia Popular-Unión Demócrata Cristiana, lost support. Seventeen political parties contested the elections. Of the nine presidential candidates competing for votes, the two leading contenders were León Febres Cordero, leader of the Partido Social Cristiano (PSC) and candidate of the conservative Frente de Reconstrucción Nacional (FRN), and Dr Rodrigo Borja Cevallos, representing the left-wing Izquierda Democrática (ID). As neither candidate won an absolute majority, a second round of voting was held in May 1984. After an often acrimonious campaign, Febres Cordero unexpectedly won the second round, securing 52.2% of the votes cast. He took office in August.

In September 1984 a serious constitutional dispute developed between the Government and Congress over the appointments procedure for the Supreme Court. The dispute was finally settled in December, after violent confrontations in Congress and fears of a coup, when Congress agreed to allow the Government to appoint the new Supreme Court justices.

In March 1984 a state of emergency was declared for 11 days in two northern provinces, following unrest and acts of sabotage by workers in the petroleum industry. In October a 24-hour general strike was called by the Frente Unitario de Trabajadores (FUT) and opposition groups, to protest against the restrictions on press freedom and the austerity measures that had been imposed by the new Government. In January 1985 a 48-hour general strike was called by the opposition after the Government announced increases in the cost of petroleum products and public transport fares. In the course of public demonstrations, seven people were killed and more than 100 were arrested. The trade unions staged another 24-hour general strike in September 1986, aimed at doubling the minimum wage. In October 1987 a general strike was called in protest at the Government's decision to reject a resolution, approved by Congress, accusing the Minister of the Interior, Luis Robles Plaza, of violations of human rights, and demanding his resignation. The Government imposed a state of emergency for two days. Further unrest in May 1988 led to the

ECUADOR

implementation of a state of emergency, prior to a one-day general strike, organized by the FUT. In early June President Febres Cordero appeared before the Court of Constitutional Guarantees, accused of contravening Article 78 of the Constitution by imposing the state of emergency in anticipation of the forthcoming strike.

The dismissal of the Chief of Staff of the Armed Forces, Lt-Gen. Frank Vargas Pazzos, brought about a military crisis in March 1986. Lt-Gen. Vargas and his supporters barricaded themselves inside the Mantas military base until they had forced the resignation of both the Minister of Defence, Gen. Luis Piñeiros, and the army commander, Gen. Manuel Albuja, who had been accused by Lt-Gen. Vargas of embezzlement. Lt-Gen. Vargas then staged a second rebellion at the military base where he had been detained. Troops loyal to the President made an assault on the base, captured Lt-Gen. Vargas and arrested his supporters. In January 1987 President Febres Cordero was abducted and, after he had been held for 11 hours, was released in exchange for Lt-Gen. Vargas, who was granted an amnesty. In July 58 members of the air force were sentenced to up to 16 years' imprisonment for involvement in the abduction of the President.

In June 1986, after unfavourable results in mid-term elections in 59 provincial seats, President Febres Cordero lost the majority that his coaliton of parties had held in the Congress. The President retained enough support, however, to survive a vote in the Congress on a resolution demanding his resignation. A total of 10 candidates (including Lt-Gen. Vargas) contested the presidential election of January 1988. The most successful candidates, Dr Rodrigo Borja Cevallos (of the ID) and Abdalá Bucaram Ortiz of the Partido Roldosista Ecuatoriano (PRE), received 20% and 15% respectively of the total votes cast, and advanced to the second round of voting. Sixto Durán Ballén, the PSC candidate, finished third, with 13% of the votes, and was eliminated from the presidential contest. In the second round of voting, held in May, Rodrigo Borja secured 46% of the votes cast, thus defeating Abdalá Bucaram, who won 41%. The President-elect promised to act promptly to address Ecuador's increasing economic problems and to change the country's isolationist foreign policy. Meanwhile, Abdalá Bucaram had fled to Panama, following accusations of corruption when in office as mayor of Guayaquil. During his inauguration in August, President Borja re-established Ecuador's diplomatic relations with Nicaragua, which had been severed in October 1985. He also pledged to join the Contadora group of countries (Colombia, Mexico, Panama and Venezuela). In September there were large demonstrations in protest against the rise in the price of fuel and against other economic measures which had been implemented to combat inflation. In October the guerrilla organization, Montoneros Patria Libre (MPL), proposed the establishment of dialogue between the Government and the rebels. In the same month the President of the Supreme Court of Justice, Ivan Martínez Vela, was murdered in Quito by unknown assassins.

The long-standing border dispute with Peru over the Cordillera del Cóndor erupted into war in January 1981. A cease-fire was declared a few days later under the auspices of the guarantors of the Rio Protocol of 1942 (Argentina, Brazil, Chile and the USA). The Protocol was not recognized by Ecuador as it awarded the area, which affords access to the Amazon river system, to Peru. Further clashes occurred along the border with Peru in December 1982 and January 1983. In addition, skirmishes between Ecuadorean and Colombian forces were reported to have taken place in the border zone in December 1982. Following his inauguration in August 1988, President Borja stated that he wished to negotiate a settlement with Peru over the disputed border areas.

Government

Ecuador comprises 20 provinces, including the Galapagos Islands. Each province has a Governor, who is appointed by the President. Executive power is vested in the President, who is directly elected by universal adult suffrage for a four-year term. The President is not eligible for re-election. Legislative power is held by the 71-member unicameral Congress, which is also directly elected: 12 members are elected on a national basis and serve a four-year term, while 59 members are elected on a provincial basis and are replaced every two years, being ineligible for re-election. In April 1980 the future formation of an upper chamber was agreed.

Defence

Military service, which lasts two years, is selective for men at the age of 20. In June 1988 there were 40,000 men in the armed forces: army 33,000, navy 4,000 (including 1,000 marines) and air force 3,000. Defence expenditure for 1987 was estimated to be 32,000m. sucres.

Economic Affairs

Despite a rapid increase in population (estimated at 2.9% in each year from 1977 to 1986), Ecuador experienced significant economic growth in the 1970s, owing mainly to the development of the country's petroleum resources. In 1987, according to estimates by the World Bank, Ecuador's gross national product (GNP) measured at average 1985–87 prices, was US $10,333m., equivalent to $1,040 per head. Between 1980 and 1987, it was estimated, GNP per head decreased, in real terms, at an average rate of 1.9% per year. Compared with the previous year, GNP per head declined by 7.9% in 1987. The average annual increase in overall gross domestic product (GDP), measured in constant prices, was 8.7% in 1965–80, slowing to 1.8% in 1980–86. In terms of employment, the most important sector of the economy is agriculture. According to census results, however, the proportion of the working population engaged in agriculture, forestry and fishing declined from 54% in 1974 to 35% in 1982. Until the exploitation of petroleum in 1972, Ecuador's main source of income was agriculture. In 1987 the leading agricultural exports were bananas (of which Ecuador is the world's leading exporter), coffee and cocoa. African palm, rice and other grains are also grown. The output of the agricultural sector was projected to expand by 3.9% in 1987. Exports of bananas rose from 864,000 metric tons in 1984 to 1.3m. tons in 1985. In 1987 banana exports were 1.4m. tons, valued at an estimated $267m., accounting for 13% of total exports. Earnings from coffee exports, which fell from $299m. in 1986 to $192m. in 1987 (partly owing to a decline in international prices), accounted for 9.5% of the total. Ecuador's production of coffee declined from 120,861 metric tons in 1985 to about 118,000 tons in 1986. Despite a refining capacity of 130,000 metric tons, Ecuador's annual production of cocoa beans decreased from 89,913 tons in 1986 to 57,529 tons in 1987. Production of raw sugar reached an estimated 285,000 metric tons in 1986.

Fishing has benefited considerably from official development programmes. However, the industry has been particularly badly affected by the adverse presence in the Pacific Ocean of the warm water current known as El Niño. Nevertheless, the total catch reached a record 1,019,304 metric tons in 1986. The shrimp industry continued to thrive in 1987, when export earnings reached US $379m. (compared with $288m. in 1986), despite a crisis within the industry in 1986, owing primarily to a lack of larvae, which emphasized the need for new investment and technology to build new larva hatcheries and so secure the future of the industry. Seafood exports totalled $419m. in 1987. The value of output in the fishing sector expanded, in real terms, by 21.7% in 1986. Ecuador's extensive forests yield valuable hardwoods, and Ecuador is the world's principal producer of balsawood.

In January 1987 proven reserves of petroleum amounted to 1,148m. barrels. With the completion in 1972 of the trans-Andean pipeline (capacity 400,000 barrels per day), linking the oilfields of Oriente Province with the tanker-loading port of Esmeraldas, Ecuador became a petroleum-exporting nation. The Corporación Estatal Petrolera Ecuatoriana (CEPE), founded in 1972 as the state petroleum corporation, bought a 25% share in Texaco-Gulf's operations in Ecuador in 1974, and bought Gulf's 37.5% holding in 1977. In September 1988 the newly-elected Government announced that the State was assuming total control of the country's oil industry. Petroleum exploration would continue to be financed by foreign capital, but CEPE would be responsible for the administration of extraction and transport facilities, such as the trans-Ecuador pipeline, the CEPE-Texaco consortium and two coastal refineries. Between 1984 and 1989 the Government planned to invest $1,590m. to increase the industry's refining and petrochemical capacity, and $883m. was to be spent on the Atahualpa refinery, on the Guayaquil coast, which was projected to have an eventual capacity of 75,000 barrels per day (b/d). In September 1987 a new refinery at Shushufindi, in the Amazon region, was opened, bringing the country's installed refining capacity to 140,550 b/d. In January 1988 plans were announced for the investment of $150m. in petroleum exploration and the drilling of 19 new wells. In March a joint exploration programme with Colombia yielded a high-production well in the border region.

Economic difficulties in 1985 led to Ecuador's temporary withdrawal from OPEC (see p. 196), as the country's production was expanded far in excess of the OPEC quota, in order to increase export revenue. Petroleum accounted for about two-thirds of Ecuador's total export revenue in 1985, but substantial losses were incurred in 1986, following the sharp decline in international oil prices. In 1986 the value of petroleum exports was only $912m., compared with $1,825m. in 1985. Ecuador's quota for the first six months of 1987 was fixed at 210,000 b/d. In 1987 the petroleum sector underwent a crisis with the destruction of more than 30 km of the trans-Ecuadorean pipe-line by the earthquake which struck the country in March. The production of crude petroleum was suspended while reconstruction work was undertaken. Total output of petroleum in 1987 was 62.7m. barrels, 41.4% lower than the 1986 total. This reduction resulted in a further serious decline, to $739m., in the value of petroleum exports in that year. During 1987 OPEC temporarily raised Ecuador's oil quota to 311,000 b/d, in order to compensate for reductions resulting from the earthquake and to enable repayment of borrowed oil. Ecuador's quota for the first six months of 1989 was set at 230,000 b/d.

In the mid-1980s 52% of energy generation was by thermo-electric plants. The capacity of Ecuador's electric generating plants was 1,511,700 kW in 1986. An estimated 61% of the population had access to electricity in 1986. In 1982 electricity provided about one-quarter of energy generation. The Government hopes to expand the hydroelectric sector into the principal source of energy. A series of projects includes the Paute scheme, with a planned capacity of 500,000 kW. By the mid-1980s the first two stages of the Paute scheme were in operation. The inauguration of the Agoyan project in May 1987 increased Ecuador's hydroelectric power generation capacity to 700,000 kW. Ecuador saved $350m. in foreign exchange in 1987 as a result of increasing use of hydroelectric power. Production of natural gas declined from a peak of 40m. cu m in 1978 to 31m. cu m in 1980, when total reserves were estimated at 58,000m. cu m. Production rose to 33m. cu m in 1981. The Amistad field contained 209m. cu m of proven reserves and up to 537m. cu m of possible reserves. There are plans to construct pipelines from Esmeraldas and Shushufindi to Quito. A plant for the production of liquefied petroleum gas at Shushufindi was opened in 1982. Ecuador's other mineral resources include gold, silver, copper, sulphur, titanium, antimony, lead and zinc, all mined in small quantities. The contribution of the petroleum and mining sectors to GDP (at constant 1975 prices) declined from 14.8% in 1986 to 7.6% in 1987.

Manufacturing, mainly consisting of textiles, food processing, cement and pharmaceuticals, developed rapidly in the 1970s, despite shortages of electric energy. Between 1980 and 1986, however, manufacturing output increased by an average annual rate of only 0.2%. In 1987 manufacturing production expanded by 0.8%. There is little heavy industry but some sectors, such as petrochemicals, steel and the assembly of motor vehicles, are being developed through the Andean Group (see p. 90). An $800m. petrochemical complex was completed in 1983, and a $180m. integrated steel mill was expected to be functioning by the mid-1980s.

In July 1983 Ecuador obtained US $170m. in special drawing rights (SDRs) from the IMF, and reached agreement with a consortium of international banks on the rescheduling of $269m. of debt. In November 1984 the Government and the IMF reached agreement, in general terms, on further financing. Following this accord, the Government and commercial bank creditors concluded in December the renegotiation of Ecuador's foreign debt until 1989 (amounting to $4,629m.). Under the terms of the agreement, Ecuador secured additional financing of $2,000m. In March 1985 Ecuador obtained a one-year stand-by credit, amounting to 105.5m. SDRs, from the IMF. In April Ecuador's creditor governments agreed to reschedule debt that was due to be repaid in 1985–87. In August Ecuador secured a further loan of $200m. from its creditor banks, and in December 1985 an agreement to reschedule payment of $4,600m. of Ecuador's foreign debt was signed. In January 1986 the World Bank granted two loans amounting to $106m. to aid Ecuador's economic recovery. This was followed by two further loans, totalling $145m., in April. In early 1986 Ecuador also secured loans and grants totalling $196m. from the IDB.

In 1985 a trade surplus of $1,294m. was achieved. The annual rate of inflation declined from 28% in 1984 to 23.5% in 1985, and unemployment decreased from 13% of the labour force in 1984 to 9% in 1985. In 1986, however, the fall in oil prices resulted in a serious shortfall in export earnings. By mid-1986 foreign exchange reserves had declined to $145m., and in September a surcharge of up to 30% was imposed on imported goods. The trade surplus fell to $555m. in 1986. Following a surplus of $148.6m. on the current account of the balance of payments in 1985, there was a deficit of $613.0m. in 1986. To offset the losses in petroleum revenues, Ecuador obtained further assistance from the IMF. By early 1987, Ecuador's total external debt was approaching $8,300m. In 1986 the annual average rate of inflation was 23%, and the unemployment rate was about 11%. Budget expenditure for 1987 was projected at US $1,800m., of which 19% was to be used to service Ecuador's foreign debt. In January 1987, however, the country suspended payments of interest (estimated at $920m. per year) on its foreign debt in order to seek rescheduling. Following the earthquake in March, the Government cancelled all debt repayments for the rest of the year, and appealed for international aid. The earthquake was expected to cost the country an estimated $1,000m. In May the World Bank granted a loan of $80m. to finance emergency reconstruction. In 1987, owing mainly to the decline in earnings from petroleum exports, there was a trade deficit of $33m. GDP fell by an estimated 5.2%, as the other sectors were unable to compensate for the shortfall in oil production.

At the end of 1988 the disruption to the economy resulting from the 1987 earthquake was still evident. No agreement had been reached with the 'Paris Club' of government creditors over the rescheduling of Ecuador's foreign debt, which had risen to $11,000m. The new administration of President Borja, which took office in August 1988, therefore inherited a severe economic crisis. The annual rate of inflation exceeded 60%, and the number of unemployed had reached 500,000. In September the first stage of a three-part economic programme was implemented. This programme was designed to save $450m. in foreign exchange, to reduce inflation to 30% and to achieve a 7% growth in GDP in 1988. The sucre was devalued to 390 per US dollar, and it was announced that depreciation would continue at a weekly rate of 2.5 sucres per dollar. Import restrictions were tightened, and prices for petrol and electricity were doubled, although the prices of some staple foods were 'frozen'. In January 1989 a debt restructuring arrangement was approved, enabling Ecuador to defer repayments on $197m. that the country had borrowed through the Governments of Italy, Japan and Belgium.

The Government's determination to encourage foreign investment in Ecuador was demonstrated by the liberalization of foreign trade laws in May 1985. The Government's strategy for foreign trade included the establishment of two free-trade zones and the revision of the tariff system. In support of its policy, the Government threatened to withdraw from the Andean Group if the Group's rules on trading were not liberalized. The level of foreign investment in Ecuador rose sharply in 1987, when it totalled 16,665m. sucres, compared with 9,774m. sucres in 1986.

Social Welfare

Social insurance is compulsory for all employees. Benefits are available for sickness, industrial accidents, disability, maternity, old age, widowhood and orphanhood. In 1980 about 125,000 peasants were integrated into social security schemes; the 1980–84 Development Plan aimed to increase the number to 335,000. Hospitals and welfare institutions are administered by Central Public Assistance Boards. In 1973 Ecuador had 221 hospital establishments, with a total of 13,594 beds, and in 1977 there were 4,660 physicians working in the country. Budgetary expenditure on health by the central Government was 12,245m. sucres (7.4% of total spending) in 1985.

Education

Education is compulsory for six years, to be undertaken between six and 14 years of age, and all public schools are free. Private schools continue to play a vital role in the educational system. Primary education begins at six years of age and lasts for six years. Secondary education, in general and specialized technical or humanities schools, begins at the age of 12 and lasts for up to six years, comprising two equal cycles of three years each. In 1975 the enrolment ratios for

ECUADOR

the respective age-groups were 78% in primary schools and 28% in secondary schools. By 1979 primary enrolment had risen to 87%. In 1984 the total enrolment at primary and secondary schools was equivalent to 86% of the school-age population. University courses extend for up to six years, and include programmes for teacher training. A number of adult schools and literacy centres have been built, aimed at reducing the rate of adult illiteracy, which averaged 25.8% in 1974 and 19.8% (males 15.8%; females 23.8%) in 1982. There are 16 universities. Budgetary expenditure on education by the central Government was 40,957m. sucres (24.9% of total spending) in 1985. In many rural areas, Quechua and other indigenous Indian languages are used in education.

Public Holidays

1989: 2 January (for New Year's Day), 6 January (Epiphany), 6–7 February (Carnival), 23 March (Holy Thursday), 24 March (Good Friday), 25 March (Easter Saturday), 1 May (Labour Day), 24 May (Battle of Pichincha), 24 July (Birth of Simón Bolívar), 10 August (Independence of Quito), 9 October (Independence of Guayaquil), 12 October (Discovery of America), 1 November (All Saints' Day), 2 November (All Souls' Day), 3 November (Independence of Cuenca), 6 December (Foundation of Quito), 25 December (Christmas Day).

1990: 1 January (New Year's Day), 6 January (Epiphany), 26–27 February (Carnival), 12 April (Holy Thursday), 13 April (Good Friday), 14 April (Easter Saturday), 1 May (Labour Day), 24 May (Battle of Pichincha), 24 July (Birth of Simón Bolívar), 10 August (Independence of Quito), 9 October (Independence of Guayaquil), 12 October (Discovery of America), 1 November (All Saints' Day), 2 November (All Souls' Day), 3 November (Independence of Cuenca), 6 December (Foundation of Quito), 25 December (Christmas Day).

Weights and Measures

The metric system is in force.

Statistical Survey

Sources (unless otherwise stated): Banco Central de Ecuador, Quito; Ministerio de Industrias, Comercio e Integración, Quito; Instituto Nacional de Estadística y Censos, 10 de Agosto 229, Quito; tel. 519-320.

Area and Population

AREA, POPULATION AND DENSITY

Area (sq km)	
Land	263,950
Inland water	6,720
Total	270,670*
Population (census results)†	
8 June 1974	6,521,710
28 November 1982	
Males	4,021,034
Females	4,039,678
Total	8,060,712
Population (official estimates at mid-year)†	
1986	9,647,107
1987	9,922,514
1988	10,203,722
Density (per sq km) at mid-1988	37.7

* 104,506 sq miles.
† Figures exclude nomadic tribes of indigenous Indians. Census results also exclude any adjustment for underenumeration, estimated to have been 5.6% in 1982.

PROVINCES (estimated population at mid-1988)*

	Population	Capital
Azuay	537,622	Cuenca
Bolívar	166,372	Guaranda
Cañar	205,703	Azogues
Carchi	147,042	Tulcán
Cotopaxi	322,651	Latacunga
Chimborazo	376,413	Riobamba
El Oro	435,217	Machala
Esmeraldas	315,901	Esmeraldas
Guayas	2,661,209	Guayaquil
Imbabura	290,638	Ibarra
Loja	415,255	Loja
Los Ríos	561,947	Babahoyo
Manabí	1,081,950	Portoviejo
Morona Santiago	92,257	Macas
Napo	170,793	Tena
Pastaza	41,361	Puyo
Pichincha	1,844,943	Quito
Tungurahua	388,817	Ambato
Zamora Chinchipe	65,024	Zamora
Archipiélago de Colón (Galápagos)	8,796	Puerto Baquerizo (Isla San Cristóbal)
Total	**10,129,917**	

* Figures exclude persons in unspecified areas, totalling 73,805.

PRINCIPAL TOWNS (estimated population at mid-1986)

Guayaquil	1,509,108	Portoviejo		134,393
Quito (capital)	1,093,278	Manta		129,578
Cuenca	193,012	Ambato		122,139
Machala	137,321	Esmeraldas		115,138

ECUADOR

BIRTHS, MARRIAGES AND DEATHS*
(excluding nomadic Indian tribes)

	Registered live births		Registered marriages		Registered deaths	
	Number	Rate (per 1,000)	Number	Rate (per 1,000)	Number	Rate (per 1,000)
1979	267,372	33.9	46,278	5.9	59,951	7.6
1980	262,778	32.4	48,306	5.9	57,020	7.0
1981	264,963	31.7	49,936	6.0	54,910	6.6
1982	262,102	30.5	49,341	5.7	53,009	6.2
1983	253,990	28.7	49,571	5.6	55,202	6.2
1984	257,044	28.2	54,038	5.9	53,118	5.8
1985	262,260	28.0	56,560	6.0	51,134	5.5
1986	205,797	21.3	60,205	6.2	50,957	5.3

* Registration is incomplete. For the period 1980–85 the average annual rates are estimated to have been: births 36.8 per 1,000; deaths 8.1 per 1,000.

ECONOMICALLY ACTIVE POPULATION*
(ISIC Major Divisions, 1982 census)

	Males	Females	Total
Agriculture, hunting, forestry and fishing	727,880	59,092	786,972
Mining and quarrying	6,912	494	7,406
Manufacturing	214,063	72,467	286,530
Electricity, gas and water	11,946	1,237	13,183
Construction	154,683	3,326	158,009
Trade, restaurants and hotels	185,127	86,787	271,914
Transport, storage and communications	96,345	4,976	101,321
Financing, insurance, real estate and business services	29,865	14,251	44,116
Community, social and personal services	343,627	211,288	554,915
Activities not adequately described	28,567	10,027	38,594
Total	**1,799,015**	**463,945**	**2,262,960**

* Figures refer to persons aged 12 years and over, excluding those seeking work for the first time, totalling 83,103 (males 62,637; females 20,466).

Agriculture

PRINCIPAL CROPS ('000 metric tons)

	1985*	1986†	1987†
Wheat	18.4	33.0	31.4
Rice (paddy)	397.3	575.9	780.8
Barley	26.7	43.8	43.5
Maize	371.4	401.7	376.3
Potatoes	423.2	388.6	353.9
Cassava (Manioc)	228.8	118.0	131.2
Dry beans	24.9	21.5	21.8
Soybeans (Soya beans)	62.9	76.3	146.1
Seed cotton	18.9	36.9	20.1
Coconuts	38.3	55‡	34.6
Pumpkins, squash and gourds	96‡	96‡	n.a.
Sugar cane	4,995	5,398	5,200‡
Oranges	230.7	69.2	77.6
Pineapples	70	72‡	75‡
Bananas	1,969.5	2,316.4	2,386.5
Plantains	945.5	755.8	848.4
Coffee (green)	120.9	118	118
Cocoa beans	130.8	89.9	57.5

* Source: mainly Ministerio de Agricultura y Ganadería.
† Source: mainly Sistema Estadístico Agropecuario Nacional.
‡ FAO estimate.

LIVESTOCK ('000 head)

	1985*	1986†	1987†
Cattle	3,730.4	3,764.8	3,884.3
Sheep	1,080.3	1,194.6	1,619.8
Pigs	2,464.3	1,442.5	1,293.2

* Source: Ministerio de Agricultura y Ganadería.
† Source: Sistema Estadístico Agropecuario Nacional.

Poultry (million, year ending September): 33 in 1984; 41 in 1985; 45 (FAO estimate) in 1986.

Source: FAO, *Production Yearbook*.

LIVESTOCK PRODUCTS ('000 metric tons)

	1984	1985	1986
Beef and veal	85	85	95†
Mutton and lamb*	9	9	7
Pig meat*	62	65	68
Poultry meat*	37	37	46
Cows' milk	1,020	988†	989†
Butter*	4.4	4.4	4.4
Cheese*	14.2	14.2	13.8
Hen eggs	39.6	43.1	41.3
Wool: greasy*	3.4	2.9	2.8
clean*	1.7	1.5	1.2
Cattle hides (fresh)*	12.7	12.8	14.0

* FAO estimate. † Unofficial figure.
Source: FAO, *Production Yearbook*.

Forestry

ROUNDWOOD REMOVALS ('000 cubic metres, excluding bark)

	1984	1985	1986
Sawlogs, veneer logs and logs for sleepers	2,077	2,350	2,285
Pulpwood	73	260	78
Other industrial wood	82	82*	86
Fuel wood	6,002	5,879	6,238
Total	**8,234**	**8,571**	**8,687**

* FAO estimate.
Source: FAO, *Yearbook of Forest Products*.

SAWNWOOD PRODUCTION ('000 cubic metres)

	1984	1985	1986
Total (incl. boxboards)	1,210	1,213	1,256

Source: FAO, *Yearbook of Forest Products*.

Fishing

('000 metric tons, live weight)

	1984	1985	1986
Freshwater fishes	1.0	0.9	0.9
Herrings, sardines, anchovies, etc.	461.4	734.7	688.6
Chub mackerel	291.7	114.1	107.5
Other marine fishes	43.7	52.2	162.6
Other sea creatures	48.0	45.1	59.7
Total catch	**845.8**	**947.0**	**1,019.3**

Source: FAO, *Yearbook of Fishery Statistics*.

ECUADOR

Mining

	1981	1982	1983
Gold (troy oz)	1,286.0	1,601.1	607.6
Silver (troy oz)	32,146.4	10,076.0	3,137.6
Copper (kg)	825,000	25,370	7,960
Zinc (kg)	742,000	47,320	14,820
Petroleum ('000 barrels)	77,062.1	77,072.2	86,691.3

Petroleum ('000 barrels): 93,879.7 in 1984; 102,415.9 in 1985; 106,994.7 in 1986; 62,679 (provisional) in 1987.

Industry

SELECTED PRODUCTS
('000 metric tons, unless otherwise indicated)

	1983	1984	1985
Jet fuels	117	135	145
Kerosene	265	293	274
Gasoline	720	922	913
Residual fuel oils	1,886	2,131	1,865
Distillate fuel oils	605	749	748
Liquefied natural gas	22	41	42*
Crude steel	23	18	18
Cement	1,530	1,730	1,400*
Electric energy (million kWh)	4,289	4,207	4,490

* Estimate.

Source: UN, *Industrial Statistics Yearbook*.

Finance

CURRENCY AND EXCHANGE RATES

Monetary Units
100 centavos = 1 sucre.

Denominations
Coins: 10, 20 and 50 centavos; 1 sucre.
Notes: 5, 10, 20, 50, 100, 500 and 1,000 sucres.

Sterling and Dollar Equivalents (30 September 1988)
£1 sterling = 676.4 sucres;
US $1 = 400.0 sucres;
1,000 sucres = £1.478 = $2.500.

Average Exchange Rate (sucres per US dollar)
1985   69.556
1986   122.779
1987   170.462

BUDGET (million sucres)

Revenue	1985	1986	1987
Petroleum revenue	113,975.1	73,611.6	89,632.9
Tax revenue	4,970.8	3,166.7	7,539.7
Export tax	324.2	311.6	153.6
Taxes on revenue of petroleum companies	2,377.6	1,179.4	1,689.4
Interest on sale and purchase of foreign currency	852.0	741.0	2,651.2
Taxes on petroleum by-products for internal consumption	1,246.8	634.7	2,970.7
Others	170.2	300.0	74.8
Non-tax revenue	109,004.3	70,444.9	82,093.2
Price increases on exports of petroleum and its by-products	11,161.1	365.6	733.2
Income from CEPE's* petroleum exports	4,875.7	2,128.2	2,082.0
Price increases on petroleum by-products for internal consumption	27,599.6	10,638.0	19,438.5
Fondo de Desarrollo Vialidad Agropecuaria: FONASA and FONAFOR	18,188.3	10,761.1	7,724.1
Surplus on exports of crude petroleum by CEPE	32,376.6	33,587.5	35,286.4
Others	14,803.0	12,964.5	16,829.0
Non-petroleum revenue	74,924.4	117,267.7	150,240.1
Tax revenue	70,829.4	111,374.5	142,063.6
Export tax	15.8	80.4	145.0
Import tax	25,997.2	36,189.4	41,713.5
Income tax	13,783.7	20,359.8	26,519.0
Taxes on financial transactions	5,208.8	5,645.8	6,425.1
Taxes on consumption and production	25,135.2	47,804.1	62,644.4
Others	688.7	1,455.8	4,616.6
Non-tax revenue	4,095.0	5,893.2	8,176.5
Interest rates	945.1	913.1	1,324.5
Other revenue	3,149.9	4,980.1	6,852.0
Less CATs†	1,123.7	5,159.2	4,608.3
Sub-Total	187,775.8	185,720.1	235,264.7
Transfers	1,695.7	1,082.9	1,497.0
Capital revenue	1,309.8	44,128.5	115,312.2
Total	190,781.3	230,931.5	352,073.9

* Corporación Estatal Petrolera Ecuatoriana.
† Certificados de Abono Tributario y Bonos IERAC.

Expenditure	1985	1986	1987
General services	40,878.8	58,113.1	67,000.1
Education and culture	40,956.7	55,911.9	70,411.7
Social welfare and labour	1,532.0	2,628.5	3,761.5
Health and communal development	12,244.6	15,858.5	19,681.0
Farming and livestock development	7,301.5	7,475.4	8,865.1
Natural and energy resources	4,539.8	3,337.0	3,543.2
Industry and commerce	1,000.0	1,481.9	1,906.4
Transport and communications	20,276.9	23,212.0	28,069.4
Public debt	47,744.4	57,069.6	127,357.7
Interest	35,919.4	37,414.3	37,242.3
Debt redemption	11,825.0	19,655.3	90,115.4
General appropriations	1,623.0	8,120.8	18,153.2
Other expenditure	1,530.8	5,036.2	21,834.8
Sub-total	179,628.5	238,244.9	370,584.1
Less Withdrawals	302.5	654.4	1,880.6
Total	179,326.0	237,610.5	368,703.5

ECUADOR

CENTRAL BANK RESERVES (US $ million at 31 December)

	1985	1986	1987
Gold*	124.3	124.3	165.7
IMF special drawing rights	28.8	55.9	0.9
Foreign exchange	689.4	588.2	490.2
Total	842.5	768.4	655.8

* Valued at $300 per troy ounce in 1985 and 1986, and at $400 per ounce in 1987.

Source: IMF, *International Financial Statistics*.

MONEY SUPPLY (million sucres at 31 December)

	1985	1986	1987
Currency outside banks	42,705	54,603	74,781
Private sector deposits at central bank	12,115	17,130	27,682
Demand deposits at private banks	103,298	119,328	163,274
Total money	158,118	191,061	265,737

Source: IMF, *International Financial Statistics*.

COST OF LIVING (Consumer Price Index; annual averages for middle- and low-income families in urban area; base: May 1978–April 1979 = 100)

	1985	1986	1987
Food and drink	516.0	635.7	818.4
Housing	257.1	301.5	378.5
Clothing	337.9	435.8	552.7
Miscellaneous	363.2	453.0	609.6
All items	394.0	484.7	627.7

NATIONAL ACCOUNTS
Expenditure on the Gross Domestic Product
(million sucres at current prices)

	1985	1986	1987
Government final consumption expenditure	127,330	168,565	219,979
Private final consumption expenditure	715,659	925,521	1,283,846
Increase in stocks	23,442	28,478	6,804
Gross fixed capital formation	178,255	254,675	416,082
Total domestic expenditure	1,044,686	1,377,239	1,926,711
Exports of goods and services	296,922	316,800	421,249
Less Imports of goods and services	231,668	311,896	539,585
Gross domestic product in purchasers' values	1,109,940	1,382,143	1,808,375

Gross Domestic Product by Economic Activity
(million sucres at constant 1975 prices)

	1985	1986	1987
Agriculture, hunting, forestry and fishing	24,178	26,631	28,603
Petroleum and other mining*	23,875	25,162	12,210
Manufacturing*	28,710	28,225	28,289
Electricity, gas and water	1,833	2,269	2,498
Construction	6,742	6,514	6,603
Trade, restaurants and hotels	24,268	24,800	25,183
Transport, storage and communications	11,506	12,585	13,246
Finance, insurance, real estate and business services	18,162	18,398	17,922
Community, social and personal services	9,529	9,747	9,927
Sub-total	148,803	154,331	144,481
Less Imputed bank service charge	4,519	4,917	3,990
Domestic product of industries	144,284	149,414	140,491
Government services	14,842	14,908	14,969
Domestic services of households	723	735	756
Sub-total	159,849	165,057	156,216
Customs duties (net of import subsidies)	4,205	4,225	4,265
GDP in purchasers' values	164,054	169,282	160,481

* Petroleum-refining is included in mining and excluded from manufacturing.

BALANCE OF PAYMENTS (US $ million)

	1985	1986	1987
Merchandise exports f.o.b.	2,905.0	2,186.0	2,021.0
Merchandise imports f.o.b.	−1,611.0	−1,631.0	−2,054.0
Trade balance	1,294.0	555.0	−33.0
Exports of services	418.0	431.0	444.0
Imports of services	−1,643.4	−1,644.0	−1,674.0
Balance on goods and services	68.6	−658.0	−1,263.0
Private unrequited transfers (net)	80.0	45.0	75.0
Government unrequited transfers (net)			
Current balance	148.6	−613.0	−1,188.0
Direct capital investment (net)	62.0	70.0	75.0
Other long-term capital (net)	−752.0	−339.0	85.0
Short-term capital (net)	−287.0	−89.0	22.0
Net errors and omissions	77.3	−178.5	−27.6
Total (net monetary movements)	−751.1	−1,149.5	−1,033.6
Valuation changes (net)	−27.4	−29.4	−61.6
Exceptional financing (net)	881.0	1,025.0	936.0
Official financing (net)	−107.0	−47.0	−1.0
Changes in reserves	−4.4	−200.9	−160.3

Source: IMF, *International Financial Statistics*.

ECUADOR   Statistical Survey

External Trade

PRINCIPAL COMMODITIES (US $ million)

Imports c.i.f.	1985	1986	1987
Durable consumer goods	58.2	67.5	83.6
Non-durable consumer goods	94.2	102.1	124.8
Fuels and lubricants	198.3	113.4	387.9
Raw material for agriculture	71.7	62.9	52.7
Raw material for industry	768.9	726.4	791.7
Construction materials	49.8	62.0	73.5
Capital goods for agriculture	34.1	35.0	28.8
Capital goods for industry	338.7	407.5	500.8
Transport equipment	152.7	229.6	202.4
Total	1,766.6	1,806.4	2,246.2

Exports f.o.b.	1985	1986	1987
Bananas	220.0	263.4	266.9
Coffee	190.8	298.9	192.3
Cocoa	138.4	71.0	82.8
Seafood	168.5	315.0	419.3
Petroleum	1,824.7	912.4	739.4
Cocoa products	78.8	77.2	57.1
Seafood products	97.2	72.5	58.6
Petroleum derivatives	101.9	70.1	78.2
Total (incl. others)	2,904.9	2,185.8	2,021.3

PRINCIPAL TRADING PARTNERS (US $ million)

Imports c.i.f.	1985	1986	1987
Brazil	144.5	110.0	117.4
Chile	33.8	37.2	38.1
Colombia	38.0	45.8	43.3
Germany, Federal Republic	145.9	172.0	172.3
France	21.0	30.4	41.3
Italy	45.4	57.0	80.6
Japan	189.1	250.4	282.4
Mexico	47.1	58.9	22.0
Peru	73.6	36.5	24.1
Spain	43.3	61.6	65.3
Switzerland	30.5	44.6	51.3
United Kingdom	36.4	45.0	48.8
USA	620.2	547.2	558.8
Total (incl. others)	1,766.6	1,806.4	2,246.2

Exports f.o.b.	1985	1986	1987
Chile	46	47	33.7
China, People's Republic	112	55	2.5
Colombia	65	30	35.6
Germany, Federal Republic	54	78	66.8
Hungary	29	21	10.3
Italy	13	18	15.1
Japan	33	57	47.1
Netherlands	28	28	20.0
Panama	136	58	53.2
USA	1,659	1,332	1,128.9
Total (incl. others)	2,905	2,186	2,021.3

Transport

RAILWAYS (traffic)

	1980	1981	1982
Passenger-kilometres	70	58	50
Net ton-kilometres	14	15	14

Source: UN, *Statistical Yearbook*.

ROAD TRAFFIC (motor vehicles in use at 31 December)

	1984	1985	1986
Passenger cars	248,575	261,267	256,812
Buses and coaches	9,964	12,885	14,270
Goods vehicles	22,450	23,818	22,421

Source: International Road Federation, *World Road Statistics*.

INTERNATIONAL SEA-BORNE SHIPPING (freight traffic, '000 metric tons)

	1983	1984	1985
Goods loaded	9,291	10,019	13,543
Goods unloaded	2,266	2,420	2,458

Source: UN, *Monthly Bulletin of Statistics*.

CIVIL AVIATION (traffic on scheduled services)

	1982	1983	1984
Passengers carried ('000)	676	618	634
Passenger-km (million)	862	762	893
Freight ton-km (million)	36.4	33.0	42.6

Source: UN, *Statistical Yearbook*.

Tourism

	1980	1981	1982
Foreign visitors	244,485	226,297	217,008

1985: 250,000 foreign visitors (estimate).

Education

(1983/84*)

	Institutions	Teachers	Pupils
Primary	11,480	41,973	1,407,898
Middle	1,099	27,289	477,829
Basic	338	3,287	50,772
Specialized	415	15,565	279,159
Technical	346	8,437	147,898
Higher†	12	8,854	227,233

* Provisional.   † 1980 figures.

Directory

The Constitution

The 1945 Constitution was suspended in June 1970. In January 1978 a referendum was held to choose between two draft Constitutions, prepared by various special constitutional committees. In a 90% poll, 43% voted for a proposed new Constitution and 32.1% voted for a revised version of the 1945 Constitution. The new Constitution came into force on 10 August 1979. Its main provisions are summarized below:

CHAMBER OF REPRESENTATIVES

The Constitution of 1979 states that legislative power is exercised by the Chamber of Representatives which sits for a period of 60 days from 10 August. The Chamber is required to set up four full-time Legislative Commissions to consider draft laws when the House is in recess. Special sessions of the Chamber of Representatives may be called.

Representatives are elected for four years from lists of candidates drawn up by legally-recognized parties. Twelve are elected nationally; two from each Province with over 100,000 inhabitants, one from each Province with fewer than 100,000; and one for every 300,000 citizens or fractions of over 200,000. Representatives are eligible for re-election.

In addition to its law-making duties, the Chamber ratifies treaties, elects members of the Supreme and Superior Courts, and (from panels presented by the President) the Comptroller-General, the Attorney-General and the Superintendent of Banks. It is also able to overrule the President's amendment of a bill which it has submitted for Presidential approval. It may reconsider a rejected bill after a year or request a referendum, and may revoke the President's declaration of a state of emergency. The budget is considered in the first instance by the appropriate Legislative Commission and disagreements are resolved in the Chamber.

PRESIDENT

The presidential term is four years, and there is no re-election. The President appoints the Cabinet, the Governors of Provinces, diplomatic representatives and certain administrative employees, and is responsible for the direction of international relations. In the event of foreign invasion or internal disturbance, the President may declare a state of emergency and must notify the Chamber, or the Tribunal for Constitutional Guarantees if the Chamber is not in session.

As in other post-war Latin-American Constitutions, particular emphasis is laid on the functions and duties of the State, which is given wide responsibilities with regard to the protection of labour; assisting in the expansion of production; protecting the Indian and peasant communities; and organizing the distribution and development of uncultivated lands, by expropriation where necessary.

Voting is compulsory for every Ecuadorean citizen who is literate and over 18 years of age. An optional vote has been extended to illiterates (under 15% of the population by 1981). The Constitution guarantees liberty of conscience in all its manifestations, and states that the law shall not make any discrimination for religious reasons.

The Government

HEAD OF STATE

President: Dr RODRIGO BORJA CEVALLOS (took office 10 August 1988).
Vice-President: Ing. LUIS PARODÍ VALVERDE.

THE CABINET
(January 1989)

Minister of the Interior: Lic. ANDRÉS VALLEJO ARCO.
Minister of Foreign Affairs: Dr DIEGO CORDÓVEZ ZÉGERS.
Minister of Finance and Public Credit: Ing. JORGE GALLARDO ZAVALA.
Minister of Industry, Trade, Integration and Fisheries: Ing. JUAN JOSÉ PONS ARÍZAGA.
Minister of Agriculture and Livestock: Dr ENRIQUE DELGADO COPIANO.
Minister of Energy and Mines: Ing. DIEGO TAMARIZ SERRANO.
Minister of Labour and Human Resources: Econ. CÉSAR VERDUGA VÉLEZ.
Minister of Education and Culture: ALFREDO VERA ARRATA.
Minister of Defence: Gen. (retd) JORGE FÉLIX MENA.
Minister of Public Health: Dr PLUTARCO NARANJO VARGAS.
Minister of Social Welfare: Ing. RÁUL BACA CARBO.
Minister of Public Works and Communications: Ing. JUAN NEIRA CARRASCO.
Secretary-General for Public Administration: Econ. WASHINGTON HERRERA.
Secretary-General for Public Information: Dr GONZALO ORTIZ CRESPO.
President of the National Monetary Board: Econ. ABELARDO PACHANO BERTERO.
General Manager of the Central Bank: Lic. JOSÉ MORILLO BATLLE.

MINISTRIES

Office of the President: Palacio Nacional, García Moreno 1043, Quito; tel. 216-300; telex 23751.
Office of the Vice-President: Manuel Larrea y Arenas, Edif. Consejo Provincial de Pichincha, 21°, Quito; tel. 521-045; telex 22058.
Ministry of Agriculture and Livestock: Avda Eloy Alfaro y Amazonas, Quito; tel. 554-122; telex 2291.
Ministry of Defence: Exposición 208, Quito; tel. 216-150; telex 2703.
Ministry of Education, Culture and Sport: Mejía 348, Quito; tel. 216-224.
Ministry of Energy and Mines: Santa Prisca 223 y Manuel Larrea, Quito; tel. 239-100; telex 2271.
Ministry of Finance and Public Credit: Avda 10 de Agosto 1661 y Jorge Washington, Quito; tel. 544-500; telex 2358.
Ministry of Foreign Affairs: Avda 10 de Agosto y Carrión, Quito; tel. 230-500; telex 2441.
Ministry of Industry, Trade, Integration and Fisheries: Juan León Mera y Roca, Quito; tel. 524-666; telex 2166.
Ministry of the Interior: Espejo y Benalcázar, Quito; tel. 216-080; telex 2354.
Ministry of Labour and Human Resources: Ponce y Luis Felipe Borja, Quito; tel. 524-666; telex 2898.
Ministry of Public Health: Juan Larrea 444, Quito; tel. 521-114.
Ministry of Public Works and Communications: Avda 6 de Diciembre y Wilson, Quito; tel. 242-666; telex 2353.
Ministry of Social Welfare: Robles 6, Quito; tel. 540-750; telex 2898.

President and Legislature

PRESIDENTIAL ELECTION

In the first round of voting, held on 31 January 1988, there were 10 candidates, among whom RODRIGO BORJA CEVALLOS (ID) polled an estimated 20% of the votes cast and ABDALÁ BUCARAM ORTIZ (PRE) polled 15%. In the second round of voting, held on 8 May, RODRIGO BORJA CEVALLOS received 46% of the votes cast and ABDALÁ BUCARAM ORTIZ polled 41%. RODRIGO BORJA CEVALLOS was thus elected President.

CONGRESO NACIONAL

Cámara Nacional de Representantes

President of Congress: Dr WILFRIDO LUCERO BOLAÑOS.
Vice-President of Congress: Lic. NICOLÁS ISSA OBANBO.

Party	Seats after elections*	
	1 June 1986	31 January 1988
Izquierda Democrática (ID)	17	27
Partido Social Cristiano (PSC)	15	6
Democracia Popular (DP)	8	7
Partido Socialista Ecuatoriano (PSE)	6	3
Partido Roldosista Ecuatoriano (PRE)	5	4
Concentración de Fuerzas Populares (CFP)	4	6
Movimiento Popular Democrático (MPD)	4	4
Frente Radical Alfarista (FRA)	3	1
Partido Liberal Radical (PLR)	3	2
Frente Amplio de la Izquierda (FADI)	3	2
Partido Demócrata (PD)	1	—
Partido Conservador (PC)	1	1
Pueblo, Cambio y Democracia (PCD)	1	—
Others	—	9
Total	71	71

* The 59 seats allocated on a provincial basis are renewable after two years. The January 1986 mid-term elections were postponed until June 1986. The remaining 12 deputies, elected on a national basis in January 1984, retained their seats until 1988.

Political Organizations

Concentración de Fuerzas Populares (CFP): Quito; f. 1946; Leader GALO VAYAS; Dir Dr AVERROES BUCARAM SAXIDA.

Democracia Popular-Unión Demócrata Cristiana (DP-UDC): Calle Luis Saá No 153 y Hnos Pazmiño, Casilla 2300, Quito; tel. 547-388; f. 1978; Christian democrat; Pres. JAMIL MAHUAD.

Frente Progresista Democrático: f. 1984 to succeed Convergencia Democrática; regrouped June 1986; also known as Bloque Progresista; left-wing coalition comprising the following parties:

Frente Amplio de la Izquierda (FADI): Quito; f. 1977; left-wing alliance comprising the following parties: Partido Comunista Ecuatoriano, Partido Socialista Revolucionario, Movimiento para la Unidad de la Izquierda, Movimiento Revolucionario de la Izquierda Cristiana; Dir Dr RENÉ MAUGÉ M.

Izquierda Democrática (ID): Juan León Mera 268 y Jorge Washington, Quito; f. 1977; Leader RODRIGO BORJA CEVALLOS; Dir XAVIER LEDESMA.

Movimiento Popular Democrático (MPD): Maoist; Leader Dr JAIME HURTADO GONZÁLEZ.

Partido Demócrata (PD): Quito; Leader Dr FRANCISCO HUERTA MONTALVO.

Partido Socialista Ecuatoriano (PSE): San Luis 340, Of. 105, entre Santa Prisca y Ante, Quito; tel. 570-065; f. 1926; Sec.-Gen. Dr VÍCTOR GRANDA AGUILAR.

Pueblo, Cambio y Democracia (PCD) Popular Roldosista: Quito; f. 1980; centre-left; committed to policies of fmr Pres. Jaime Roldós; Dir LEÓN ROLDÓS AGUILERA; Sec.-Gen. ERNESTO BUENANO CABRERA.

Unión Democrática Popular (UDP): Leader JORGE CHIRIBOGA.

Frente Radical Alfarista (FRA): Quito; f. 1972; Leader IVÁN CASTRO PATIÑO.

Frente de Reconstrucción Nacional (FRN): centre-right coalition comprising the following parties:

Alianza Popular Revolucionaria Ecuatoriana (APRE): centrist.

Coalición Nacional Republicana (CNR): Quito; f. 1986; fmrly Coalición Institucionalista Demócrata (CID).

Partido Conservador (PC): Quito; f. 1855; traditional rightist party; Dir JOSÉ TERÁN VAREA.

Partido Liberal Radical (PLR): Quito; f. 1895; held office from 1895 to 1944 as the Liberal Party which subsequently divided into various factions; carries on the traditions of the old party; Dir CARLOS JULIO PLAZA A.

Partido Nacionalista Revolucionario (PNR): Calle Pazmiño 245, Of. 500, Quito; f. 1969; supporters of fmr President Dr Carlos Julio Arosemena Monroy; Dir Dr MAURICIO GÁNDARA.

Partido Nacional Velasquista (PNV): f. 1952; centre-right; Leader ALFONSO ARROYO ROBELLY.

Partido Social Cristiano (PSC): Quito; f. 1951; centre-right party; Pres. CAMILO PONCE; Leaders SIXTO DURÁN BALLÉN, LEÓN FEBRES CORDERO RIVADENEIRA.

Fuerzas Armadas Populares Eloy Alfaro—Alfaro Vive ¡Carajo! (Eloy Alfaro Popular Armed Forces—Alfaro Lives, Damn it!): f. 1982; left-wing; supports Izquierda Democrática; guerrilla group until Feb. 1989; Leader ROSA MIREYA CÁRDENAS; 3,000 mems.

Partido Comunista Marxista-Leninista de Ecuador: Sec.-Gen. CAMILO ALMEYDA.

Partido Republicano (PR): Quito; 1988 Presidential Candidate GUILLERMO SOTOMAYOR.

Partido Roldosista Ecuatoriano (PRE): Quito; f. 1982; Dir ABDALÁ BUCARAM ORTIZ.

Unión del Pueblo Patriótico (UPP): Quito; 1988 Presidential Candidate Lt-Gen. FRANK VARGAS PAZZOS.

The following guerrilla group is active:

Montoneros Patria Libre (MPL): f. 1986; advocates an end to authoritarianism.

Diplomatic Representation

EMBASSIES IN ECUADOR

Argentina: Avda Amazonas 477, Apdo 2937, Quito; tel. 562-292; telex 2136; Ambassador: RICARDO H. ILLIA.

Austria: Avda Patria y Amazonas, Edif. Cofiec 11°; tel. 545-336.

Belgium: Austria 219 e Irlanda, Quito; telex 2767; Ambassador: F. FRANZ.

Bolivia: Quito; Ambassador: EUSEBIO MOREIRA.

Brazil: Calle Amazonas 1429 y Colón, Apdo 231, Quito; tel. 563-846; telex 22218; Ambassador: ADOLPHO BENEVIDES.

Bulgaria: Calle Colina 331 y Orellana, Quito; tel. 552-553; telex 22047; Chargé d'affaires: LUBOMIR IVANOV.

Canada: Edif. Belmonte 6°, Avda Corea 126 y Amazonas; tel. 458-102.

Chile: Edif. Rocafuerte 4° y 5°, Avda Amazonas 325 y Washington, Quito; telex 2167; Ambassador: GABRIEL VAN SCHOUWEN FIGUEROA.

China, People's Republic: Quito; Ambassador: PANG GANGHUA.

Colombia: Calle San Javier 169, Casilla 2923, Quito; telex 2156; Ambassador: LAUREANO ALBERTO ARELLANO.

Costa Rica: Quito; Ambassador: FÉLIX CÓRTEZ.

Cuba: Quito; Ambassador: CARLOS ZAMORA.

Czechoslovakia: Calle General Salazar 459 y Coruña, Quito; telex 2478; Ambassador: JULIUS STANG.

Dominican Republic: Avda 6 de Diciembre 4629, Quito; Ambassador: MARIO PENA.

Egypt: Edif. Araucaria 9°, Baquedano 222 y Reina Victoria, Apdo 9355, Sucursal 7, Quito; tel. 235-046; telex 2154; Ambassador: ESMAT NAGUIB.

El Salvador: Avda de los Shyris 1240 y Portugal, Edif. Albatros, Apdo 8386, Quito; tel. 433-823; telex 22931; Ambassador: BYRON FERNANDO LARIOS L.

France: Plaza 107 y Avda Patria, Apdo 536, Quito; tel. 560-789; telex 2146; Ambassador: JEAN-MICHEL DASQUE.

German Democratic Republic: Calle Ignacio Bossano 460 y Játiva, Apdo 102, Quito; tel. 453-814; telex 2241; Ambassador: GERALD MÖCKEL.

Germany, Federal Republic: Avda Patria y 9 de Octubre, Edif. Eteco 6°, Quito; tel. 232-660; telex 2222; Ambassador: Dr JOSEF ENGELS.

Guatemala: Avda 6 de Diciembre 2636, Quito; Ambassador: JUAN RENDÓN M.

Holy See: (Apostolic Nunciature), Avda Orellana 692, Apdo 4543-A, Quito; tel. 564-938; telex 2053; Nuncio: Mgr LUIGI CONTI.

Honduras: Cordero 279 y Plaza, Quito; telex 2805; Ambassador: ANTONIO MOLINA O.

Hungary: Avda República de El Salvador 733 y Avda Portugal, Quito; tel. 459-700; telex 2255; Chargé d'affaires: PÁL LANDESZ.

Israel: 12 de Octubre 532, 4°, Quito; telex 2174; Ambassador: NAPHTALI GAL.

Italy: Calle La Isla 111, POB 072-A, Quito; tel. 522-015; telex 2715; Ambassador: SEVERIO CALLEA.

Japan: Avda Amazonas 239 y 18 de Septiembre, Quito; telex 2185; Ambassador: H. NISHAMIYA.

Korea, Republic: Calle Reina Victoria 1539 y Avda Colón, Edif. Banco de Guayaquil 11°, Quito; tel. 560-573; telex 2868; Ambassador: YOUNG JAE HWANG.

ECUADOR

Mexico: Avda 6 de Diciembre 4843, Casilla 6371, Quito; tel. 457-820; telex 2395; Ambassador: CARLOS A. DE ICAZA.
Netherlands: Edif. Club de Leones Central 3°, Avda de las Naciones Unidas entre Avdas 10 de Agosto y Amazonas, Apdo 2840, Quito; telex 2576; Ambassador: Dr J. WEIDEMA.
Panama: Calle Pazmiño 245 y Avda 6 de Diciembre, Quito; Ambassador: ROBERTO SAMUEL FÁBREGA GOYTIA.
Paraguay: Avda Gaspar de Villarroel 2013 y Avda Amazonas, Casilla 139-A, Quito; tel. 245-871; telex 2260; Ambassador: Dr GILBERTO CANIZA SÁNCHIZ.
Peru: Edif. España Pent-House, Avda Colón y Amazonas, Quito; Ambassador: FELIPE VALDIVIESO BELAÚNDE.
Poland: Quito; Chargé d'affaires: CZESŁAW BUGAJSKI.
Romania: Avda República del Salvador 482 e Irlanda, Quito; telex 2230; Ambassador: GHEORGHE DOBRA.
Spain: La Pinta 455 y Amazonas, Casilla 9322, Quito; tel. 564-373; telex 2816; Ambassador: JUAN MANUEL EGEA IBÁÑEZ.
Sweden: Edif. Las Cámaras 2°, Avda República y Amazonas, Apdo 420-A, Quito; tel. 454-872; telex 2396; Ambassador: CHRISTIAN BAUSCH.
Switzerland: Edif. Xerox, Avda Amazonas 3617 y Juan Pablo Sanz, 2°, Casilla 4815, Quito; tel. 434-948; telex 2592; Chargé d'affaires a.i.: FRANCIS COUSIN.
USSR: Reina Victoria 462 y Roca, Quito; Ambassador: GUERMAN E. CHLIAPNIKOVA.
United Kingdom: González Suárez 111 y 197, Casilla 314, Quito; tel. 560-669; telex 2138; Ambassador: MICHAEL W. ATKINSON.
USA: Avda 12 de Octubre y Patria 120, Quito; tel. 562-890; telex 2329; Ambassador: RICHARD N. HOLWILL.
Uruguay: Edif. Sonelsa 2°, Calle Mariscal Foch s/n y Avda 6 de Diciembre, Quito; tel. 237-151; telex 2657; Ambassador: Dr JORGE PÉREZ OTERMIN.
Venezuela: Coruña 1733 y Belo Horizonte, Apdo 688, Quito; tel. 564-626; telex 22160; Ambassador: LUIS RODRÍGUEZ MALASPINA.
Yugoslavia: Gen. Francisco Salazar 958 y 12 de Octubre, Quito; tel. 526-218; telex 2633; Ambassador: SAMUILO PROTIĆ.

Judicial System

Note: In August 1984 an amendment to the Constitution was passed to reduce the term of Supreme Court justices from six to four years. Following the appointment of the 16 Supreme Court justices by Congress, a dispute broke out between Congress and the Government, which opposed the appointments on the grounds that they were 'unconstitutional'. In December 1984 the dispute was resolved when Congress agreed to waive its prerogative to select the 16 Supreme Court justices and allowed the Government to make the new appointments.

Attorney-General: JORGE MALDONADO RENELA.
Supreme Court of Justice: Palacio de Justicia, Avda 6 de Diciembre y Piedrahita, Quito; tel. 230-200; Pres. (vacant); 15 Judges and two Fiscals.
Higher or Divisional Courts: Ambato, Cuenca, Guayaquil, Ibarra, Loja, Portoviejo, Quito, Riobamba, El Oro-Latacunga and Esmeraldas; 44 judges.
Provincial Courts: in 15 towns; 35 Criminal, 42 Provincial, 87 Cantonal, 445 Parochial Judges.
Special Courts: for juveniles and for labour disputes.

Religion

There is no state religion but about 90% of the population are Roman Catholics. There are representatives of various Protestant Churches and of the Jewish faith in Quito and Guayaquil.

CHRISTIANITY
The Roman Catholic Church

Ecuador comprises three archdioceses, 10 dioceses, two territorial prelatures, seven Apostolic Vicariates and one Apostolic Prefecture.

Bishops' Conference: Conferencia Episcopal Ecuatoriana, Apdo 1081, Avenida América 1866 y La Gasca, Quito; tel. 524-568; telex 2427; f. 1939; Pres. ANTONIO J. GONZÁLEZ ZUMÁRRAGA, Archbishop of Quito.

Archbishop of Cuenca: LUIS ALBERTO LUNA TOBAR, Casilla 46, Calle Bolívar 7-64, Cuenca; tel. 827-792.

Archbishop of Guayaquil: BERNARDINO ECHEVERRÍA RUIZ, Arzobispado, Apdo 254, Calle Clemente Ballén 501 y Chimborazo, Guayaquil; tel. 328-872.
Archbishop of Quito: ANTONIO J. GONZÁLEZ ZUMÁRRAGA, Arzobispado, Apdo 106, Calle Chile 1140, Quito; tel. 214-429.

The Baptist Church
The Baptist Convention of Ecuador: POB 3236, Guayaquil; tel. 384-865; Pres. Rev. HAROLT SANTE MATA; Sec. JORGE MORENO CHAVARRÍA.

The Episcopal Church
Bishop of Ecuador: Rt Rev. Dr ADRIÁN D. CÁCERES, Apdo 353-A, Quito.

The Methodist Church
The Methodist Church: Evangelical United Church, Rumipamba 915, Apdo 236-A, Quito; 800 mems, 2,000 adherents.

BAHÁ'Í FAITH
The National Spiritual Assembly of the Bahá'ís: Apdo 869-A, Quito; tel. 231-379; mems resident in 1,121 localities.

The Press

PRINCIPAL DAILIES
Quito

El Comercio: Chile 1345, Apdo 57, Quito; tel. 260-020; telex 2246; f. 1906; morning; conservative; Proprs Compañía Anónima El Comercio; Dir SANTIAGO JERVIS; circ. 130,000.
Hoy: Avda Colón 936, Apdo 9069, Quito; tel. 539-888; telex 22718; f. 1982; liberal; Editor BENJAMÍN ORTIZ; circ. 55,000.
El Tiempo: Avda América y Villalengua, Apdo 3117, Quito; f. 1965; morning; independent; Proprs Editorial La Unión, CA; Pres. ANTONIO GRANDA CENTENO; Editor EDUARDO GRANDA GARCES; circ. 35,000.
Ultimas Noticias: Chile 1345, Apdo 57, Quito; tel. 260-020; telex 2246; f. 1938; evening; independent; commercial; Proprs Compañía Anónima El Comercio; Dir DAVID MANTILLA CASHMORE; circ. 90,000.

Guayaquil

Expreso: Avda 9 de Octubre 427 y Chimborazo, Guayaquil; morning; independent; Dir GALO MARTÍNEZ; circ. 30,000.
La Razón: Frente al Terminal Aéreo, Junto a Canal 10, Casilla 5832, Guayaquil; tel. 280100; evening; independent; f. 1964; Dir RENÉ SALCEDO CASTILLO; circ. 28,000.
El Telégrafo: Avda 10 de Agosto 601 y Boyacá, Apdo 415, Guayaquil; tel. 323-265; telex 3473; f. 1884; morning; independent; commercial; Proprs El Telégrafo CA; Dir-Gen. Gen. EDUARDO AROSEMENA GÓMEZ; Man. ROBERTO YCAZA VEGA; circ. 35,000 (weekdays), 52,000 (Sundays).
El Universo: Escobedo y 9 de Octubre, Apdo 531, Guayaquil; tel. 324-630; telex 435566; f. 1921; morning; independent; Dir CARLOS PÉREZ PERAZO; circ. 174,000 (weekdays), 255,000 (Sundays).

There are local daily newspapers of very low circulation in other towns.

PERIODICALS
Quito

La Calle: Casilla 2010, Quito; f. 1956; weekly; politics; Dir CARLOS ENRIQUE CARRIÓN; circ. 20,000.
Carta Económica del Ecuador: Toledo 1448 y Coruña, Apdo 3358, Quito; f. 1969; weekly; economic, financial and business information; Pres. Dr LINCOLN LARREA B.; circ. 8,000.
El Colegial: Calle Carlos Ibarra No. 206, Quito; tel. 216-541; f. 1974; publ. of Student Press Association; Dir WILSON ALMEIDA MUÑOZ; circ. 20,000.
Comercio Ecuatoriano: Avdas Amazona y República, Casilla 202, Quito; tel. 45-3011; telex 2638; f. 1906; monthly; commerce.
Ecuador Guía Turística: Meja 438, Oficina 43, Quito; f. 1969; tourist information in Spanish and English; Propr Prensa Informativa Turística; Dir JORGE VACA O.; circ. 30,000.
Integración: Solano 836, Quito; quarterly; economics of the Andean countries.
Letras del Ecuador: Casa de la Cultura Ecuatoriana, Avda 6 de Diciembre, Casilla 67, Quito; f. 1944; monthly; literature and art; non-political; Dir Dr TEODORO VANEGAS ANDRADE.
El Libertador: Olmedo 931 y García Moreno, Quito; f. 1926; Pres. Dr BENJAMÍN TERÁN VAREA.

ECUADOR

Mensajero: Benalcázar 562, Apdo 4100, Quito; f. 1884; monthly; religion, culture, economics and politics; Dir José González Poyatos, s.i.; circ. 5,000.

Nueva: Apdo 3224, Quito; monthly; left-wing; Dir Magdalena Jaramillo de Adoum.

Solidaridad: Calle Oriente 725, Quito; tel. 216-541; f. 1982; monthly; publ. of Confederation of Catholic Office Staff and Students of Ecuador; Dir Wilson Almeida Muñoz; Man. Johny Merizalde; circ. 15,000.

This is Ecuador: La Niña 555 y Avda Amazonas, Quito; f. 1968; monthly; English; tourism; Dir Gustavo Vallejo.

Guayaquil

Análisis Semanal: Apdo 4925, Elizalde 119 7°, Guayaquil; weekly; economic and political affairs; Editor Walter Spurrier Baquerizo.

Boletín del Sindicato Médico: Guayaquil; f. 1911; monthly; scientific, literary; independent.

Ecuador Ilustrado: Guayaquil; f. 1924; monthly; literary; illustrated.

Estadio: Aguirre 724 y Boyacá, Apdo 1239, Guayaquil; fortnightly; sport; Dir Xavier Alvarado Roca; circ. 70,000.

Hogar: Aguirre 724 y Boyacá, Apdo 1239, Guayaquil; telex 3423; f. 1964; monthly; Man. Editor Rosa Amelia Alvarado; circ. 35,000.

Vistazo: Aguirre 724 y Boyacá, Apdo 1239, Guayaquil; tel. 327-200; telex 3423; f. 1957; fortnightly; general; Pres. Xavier Alvarado Roca; circ. 85,000.

NEWS AGENCIES
Foreign Bureaux

Agencia EFE (Spain): Palacio Arzobispal, Chile 1178, Apdo 4043, Quito; tel. 512-427; telex 2602; Bureau Chief Emilio Crespo.

Agenzia Nazionale Stampa Associata (ANSA) (Italy): Hernando de la Cruz 470, Apdo 2748, Quito; tel. 260-020; telex 2246; Correspondent Mauricio Montaldo Muñoz.

Associated Press (AP) (USA): Edif. Sudamérica, 4°, Of. 44, Calle Venezuela 1018 y Mejía, Apdo 3056, Quito; tel. 570-235; telex 2296; Correspondent Carlos Cisternas.

Deutsche Presse-Agentur (dpa) (Federal Republic of Germany): Pasaje San Luis 104, Edif. Recalde, Of. 402, Quito; tel. 571-214; Correspondent Jorge Ortiz.

Inter Press Service (IPS) (Italy): Edif. Sudamérica 1°, Of. 14, Calle Venezuela 1018, Quito; tel. 215-616; Correspondent Matilde Wolter.

Prensa Latina (Cuba): Edif. Sudamérica 2°, Of. 24, Venezuela 1018 y Mejía, Quito; tel. 519-333; telex 2625; Bureau Chief Enrique García Medina.

Reuters (UK): Chile 1345, 4°, Casilla 4112, Quito; tel. 510972; telex 22620; Correspondent Jorge Aguirre.

Telegrafnoye Agentstvo Sovetskovo Soyuza (TASS) (USSR): Calle Roca 328 y 6 de Diciembre, 2°, Dep. 6, Quito; tel. 511-631; telex 3566; Correspondent Vladimir Gostev.

United Press International (UPI) (USA): Quito; Correspondent Ricardo Polit.

Xinhua (New China) News Agency (People's Republic of China): Edif. Portugal, Avda Portugal y Avda de la República del Salvador No 730, 10°, Quito; telex 2268; Bureau Chief Lin Minzhong.

Publishers

Artes Gráficas Ltda: Avda 12 de Octubre 1637, Apdo 533, Casilla 456-A, Quito; Man. Manuel de Castillo.

Cromograf, SA: Coronel 2207, Casilla 4285, Guayaquil; tel. 346-400; telex 3387; children's books, paperbacks, art productions.

Editorial Ariel: Avda 10 de Agosto No 504, Guayaquil; tel. 519-282; literature, sociology and history.

Editorial de la Casa de la Cultura Ecuatoriana 'Benjamín Carrión': Avda 6 de Diciembre 794, Apdo 67, Quito; tel. (02) 230-260; f. 1944; general fiction and non-fiction, general science; Dir Dr Teodoro Vanegas Andrade.

Editorial Claridad: Quito; tel. 517-442; economics, history, sociology and politics.

Editorial y Librería Selecciones: Avda 9 de Octubre No 724 y Boyacá, Guayaquil; tel. 305-807; history, geography and sociology.

Libros Técnicos Litesa Cía Ltda: Avda América 542, Apdo 456a, Quito; tel. 528-537; Man. Manuel del Castillo.

Pontificia Universidad Católica del Ecuador: 12 de Octubre 1076 y Carrión, Apdo 2184, Quito; tel. 529-240; literature, natural science, law, anthropology, sociology, politics, economics, theology, philosophy, history and archaeology.

Universidad Central del Ecuador: Departamento de Publicaciones, Servicio de Almacén Universitario, Ciudad Universitaria, Quito.

Universidad de Guayaquil: Departamento de Publicaciones, Biblioteca General, Apdo 3834, Guayaquil; tel. 392-430; f. 1930; general literature, history, philosophy, fiction; Man. Dir Leonor Villao de Santander.

Radio and Television

There were about 1,900,000 radio receivers and 600,000 television sets in use in 1986.

Asociación Ecuatoriana de Radiodifusión: 911–915 Edif. Gran Pasaje, Guayaquil; independent association; Pres. Jorge Aguilar V.

Instituto Ecuatoriano de Telecomunicaciones (IETEL): Casilla 3066, Quito; telex 2202; Gen. Man. Ing. Gonzalo Guerrero Jordán.

RADIO

There are nearly 300 commercial stations, 10 cultural stations and 10 religious stations. The following are some of the most important commercial stations:

CRE, Cadena Radial Ecuatoriana: Edif. El Torreón 8°, Avda Boyacá 642, Apdo 4144, Guayaquil; tel. 307-896; telex 3825; Dir Rafael Guerrero.

Emisoras Gran Colombia: Galapagos 112, Quito; tel. 211-670; f. 1943; Dir Eduardo Cevallos Casteñeda.

Radio Colón: Diguja 327, Quito; tel. 453-288; Dir Atahualpa Ruiz Riva.

Radio Cristal: Luque 1407, Guayaquil; Dir Armando Romero.

Radio Nacional del Ecuador: Chile 1267, Quito.

Radio Quito-La Voz de la Capital: Chile 1347, Quito; tel. 511-228; telex 22043; Dir Alfonso Lasso Bermeo.

Radio Tropicana: Edif. El Torreón 8°, Avda Boyacá 642, Apdo 4144, Guayaquil; tel. 307-900; telex 3825; Dir Rafael Guerrero Valenzuela.

La Voz de los Andes: Villalengua 278, Quito; tel. 241-550; telex 22734; f. 1931; operated by World Missionary Fellowship; programmes in 14 languages including Spanish, English and Quechua; private, non-commercial, cultural, religious; Pres. Dr Ronald A. Cline; Dir of Broadcasting Roger Stubbe.

TELEVISION

Corporación Ecuatoriana de Televisión: C. del Carmen, Casilla 10992, Guayaquil; tel. 300-150; telex 43409; f. 1967; Pres. Xavier Alvarado Roca; Gen. Man. Francisco Arosemena Robles.

Cadena Ecuatoriana de Televisión: Avda de las Américas, frente al Aeropuerto, Casilla 673, Guayaquil; tel. 397-888; telex 3530; f. 1969; commercial; Exec. Pres. Louis R. Hanna.

Canal Universitario Católica: Humbolt 3170, Cuenca; tel. 823-040; telex 048567; Dir. César Cordero Moscoso.

Diario Ediasa: Apdo 50, Portoviejo; Dir Pedro Eduardo Izaguirre.

Teleamazonas: Casilla 4844, Quito; tel. 430-313; telex 2244; commercial; Pres. Antonio Granda Centeno.

Telecuatro Guayaquil, SA: 9 de Octubre 1200, Guayaquil; tel. 308-194; telex 3198; Dir. Francisco Quiroz Moran.

Televisión Esmeraldeña Compañía de Economía Mixta— TESEM: Edif. Mutual V. Torres, Casilla 108, Esmeraldas; tel. 710-090; Dir Héctor Endara E.

Televisión del Pacífico SA (Telenacional): Murgeón 732, Casilla 130-B, Quito; tel. 540-877; telex 2435; commercial; Man. Modesto Luque Benítez.

Televisa Ecuatoriana: Rumipamba 1039, Quito; commercial; Dir. Gerardo Baborich.

Televisora Nacional Cía Ltda—Canal 8: Bellavista, Casilla 3888, Quito; tel. 244-888; telex 2888; commercial; Exec. Pres. Cristina Mantilla de Lara.

Ultravisión: 9 de Octubre y Córdova, Guayaquil; Dir Bolívar Malta A.

ECUADOR

Finance

(cap. = capital; p.u. = paid up; res = reserves; dep. = deposits; m. = million; amounts in sucres)

Junta Monetaria Nacional (National Monetary Board): Quito; tel. 514-833; telex 2182; f. 1927; Pres. Econ. ABELARDO PACHANO BERTERO.

Supervisory Authority

Superintendencia de Bancos y Seguros: Avda 12 de Octubre 1561, Apdo 424, Quito; tel. 541-582; telex 2148; f. 1927; Superintendent Dr GONZALO CÓRDOVA GALARZA.

BANKING
State Banks

Banco Central del Ecuador: Avda 10 de Agosto, Plaza Bolívar, Casilla 339, Quito; tel. 210-340; telex 2165; f. 1927; cap. 929m., res 2,533m., dep. 65,150m. (Dec. 1986); Pres. Ing. FEDERICO ARTETA RIVERA; Gen. Man. JOSÉ MORILLO BATLLE.

Banco de Desarrollo del Ecuador, SA (BEDE): Páez 655 y Ramírez Dávalos, Casilla 373, Quito; tel. 546-404; telex 2655; f. 1979; cap. 39,992m., res 2,001m. (Dec. 1986); Pres. Ing. GUSTAVO ESPINOSA CHIMBO; Gen. Man. Econ. EDUARDO VALENCIA.

Banco Ecuatoriano de la Vivienda: Avda 10 de Agosto 2270 y Cordero, Casilla 3244, Quito; tel. 521-311; telex 2399; f. 1962; cap. 5,006m., res 952m., dep. 7,389m. (Dec. 1986); Pres. Abog. JUAN PABLO MONCAGATTA.; Gen. Man. Dr FAUSTO VÁSQUEZ MORALES.

Banco Nacional de Fomento: Ante 107 y 10 de Agosto, Casilla 685, Quito; tel. 230-010; telex 22256; f. 1928; cap. 3,000m., res 11,749m., dep. 79,552m. (Dec. 1986); Pres. Lcdo ABSALÓN ROCHA ROMERO; Gen. Man. Ing. ALBERTO CEDEÑO DUEÑAS.

Corporación Financiera Nacional CFN: Juan León Mera 130 y Avda Patria, Casilla 163, Quito; tel. 564-900; telex 2193; f. 1964; cap. 2,000m., res 8,417m. (July 1987); Pres. Econ. JORGE NÚÑEZ DAHIK; Gen. Man. Lic. RODRIGO MALO GONZÁLEZ.

Commercial Banks
Quito

Banco Amazonas, SA: Avda Amazonas y Santa María, Casilla 1211, Quito; tel. 545-123; telex 2393; f. 1976; affiliated to Banque Paribas; cap. 800m., res 702.1m., dep. 1,811m. (Dec. 1986); Pres. Dr FRANCISCO PARRA GIL; Gen. Man. CARLOS MOSQUERA.

Banco de los Andes: Avda Amazonas 477, Casilla 3761, Quito; tel. 554-215; telex 2214; f. 1973; affiliated to Banco de Bogotá; cap. 247m., res 57m., dep. 1,298m. (June 1984); Pres. Dr AUGUSTO DEL POZO; Gen. Man. GUILLERMO DUEÑAS ITURRALDE.

Banco Caja de Crédito Agrícola Ganadero, SA: Avda 6 de Diciembre 225 y Piedrahita, Quito; tel. 528-521; telex 2559; f. 1949; cap 132m., res 41m., dep. 592m. (Aug. 1984); Man. HUGO GRIJALVA GARZÓN; Pres. NICOLÁS GUILLÉN.

Banco Consolidado del Ecuador: Avda Patria 724 y 9 de Octubre, Apdo 9150, Quito; tel. 552-044; telex 2634; f. 1981; cap. 150m., res 1m., dep. 401m. (June 1984); Pres. Dr MARCO TULIO GONZÁLEZ; Gen. Man. RAFAEL PAZMIÑO HOLGUÍN.

Banco Co-operativas: Avda 10 de Agosto 937, Casilla 2244, Quito; tel. 551-933; telex 2651; f. 1965; cap. 113m., res 8m., dep. 1,100m. (Sept. 1988); Pres. Dr JACINTO MONTERO; Gen. Man. LUIS G. CORNEJO C.

Banco Internacional: Avda Patria 660 y Avda Amazonas, Casilla 2114, Quito; tel. 546-222; telex 2195; f. 1973; cap. 238m., res 40m., dep. 3,434m. (June 1984); Pres. JORGE PÉREZ SERRANO; Gen. Man. MARCO ANTONIO SUÁREZ CUERVO; 4 brs.

Banco del Pichincha, SA: Avda 10 de Agosto y Bogotá, Casilla 717-A, Quito; tel. 551-088; telex 2618; f. 1906; cap. 1,650m., res 394m., dep. 28,585m. (July 1987); Pres. Dr GONZALO MANTILLA MATA; Gen. Man. JAIME ACOSTA VELASCO; 34 brs.

Banco Popular del Ecuador: Amazonas 648, Casilla 696, Quito; tel. 566-305; telex 2234; f. 1953; cap. 1,200m., res 356m., dep. 10,019m. (June 1988); Pres. Dr FRANCISCO ROSALES RAMOS; Gen. Man. NICOLÁS LANDES.

Banco de Préstamos, SA: Venezuela 659, Casilla 529, Quito; tel. 216-360; telex 2854; f. 1909; cap. 337m., res 210m., dep. 8,064m. (March 1987); Pres. ALFREDO ALBÓRNOZ ANDRADE; Gen. Man. MAURO INTRIAGO DUNN; 2 brs.

Banco de la Producción, SA: Avda Amazonas y Japón, Apdo 38-A, Quito; tel. 454-100; telex 2376; f. 1978; cap. 260m., res 91m., dep. 1,099m. (June 1984); Pres. RODRIGO PAZ DELGADO; Exec. Pres. Econ. ABELARDO PACHANO BERTERO.

Directory

Ambato

Banco de Tungurahua: Montalvo 630, Casilla 173, Ambato; tel. 821-122; telex 02-7186; f. 1979; cap. 50m., res 2m., dep. 329m. (June 1984); Pres. GEORG SONNENHOLZNER; Gen. Man. PEDRO CALVACHE MOYA.

Cuenca

Banco del Austro: Bolívar 547, Casilla 167, Cuenca; tel. 830-222; telex 04-8560; f. 1977; cap. 180m., res 16m., dep. 792m. (June 1984); Pres. JUAN ELJURI ANTÓN; Gen. Man. ANTONIO CHAMOUN JORGGE.

Banco del Azuay, S.A.: Bolívar 797, Casilla 33, Cuenca; tel. 831-811; telex 04-8579; f. 1913; cap. 267m., res 33m., dep. 1,860m. (June 1984); Pres. LUIS ARCENTALES GONZÁLEZ; Gen. Man. DENNIS R. SHEETS.

Guayaquil

Banco Bolivariano: Pichincha 412, Casilla 10184, Guayaquil; tel. 321-420; telex 04-3659; f. 1980; cap. 657.8m., res 131.7m., dep. 4,040m. (June 1987); Pres. Abog. JOSÉ SALAZAR BARRAGÁN; Gen. Man. ANGEL TORRES N.; 10 brs.

Banco Continental: General Cordova 811 y Víctor Manuel Rendón, Casilla 9348, Guayaquil; tel. 303-300; telex 04-3418; f. 1974; cap. 1,275m., res 1,097m., dep. 23,322m. (Dec. 1987); Pres. and Gen. Man. Dr LEÓNIDAS ORTEGA TRUJILLO.

Banco de Crédito e Hipotecario: P. Icaza 302, Casilla 4173, Guayaquil; tel. 310-055; telex 04-3336; f. 1871; cap. 639m., res 15m., dep. 2,468m. (June 1988); Pres. LUIS NOBOA NARANJO; Exec. Vice-Pres. FERNANDO LEÓN BARBA.

FILANBANCO: Avda 9 de Octubre y Pichincha, Apdo 149, Guayaquil; tel. 511-780; telex 04-3173; f. 1908; cap. 920m., res 189m., dep. 7,020m. (June 1984); Chair. Dr LUIS PERE CABANAS; Gen. Man. MIGUEL BADUY AHUAD.

Banco de Guayaquil: P. Ycaza 105, Casilla 1300, Guayaquil; tel. 309-300; telex 04-3671; f. 1923; cap. 3,300m., res 138.6m., dep. 20,535m. (1988); Pres. Dr JOSÉ SANTIAGO CASTILLO; Gen. Man. DANILO CARRERA D.

Banco Industrial y Comercial (Baninco): Pichincha 335 e Illingworth, Casilla 5817, Guayaquil; tel. 323-488; telex 04-3199; f. 1965; cap. and res 2m., dep. 10m. (June 1988); Pres. Ing. CARLOS MANZUR PERES; Gen. Man. GABRIEL MARTÍNEZ INTRIAGO; 2 brs.

Banco del Pacífico: P. Ycaza 200 y Pichincha, Casilla 988, Guayaquil; tel. 311-010; telex 04-3240; f. 1972; cap. 2,597m., res 806m., dep. 42,731m. (June 1987); Chair. VÍCTOR MASPONS Y BIGAS; Exec. Pres. MARCEL J. LANIADO.

Banco del Progreso, SA: Primero de Mayo y P. Moncayo, Casilla 11100, Guayaquil; tel. 312-100; telex 04-3662; f. 1981; cap. and res 1,000m., dep. 3,896m. (March 1987); Pres. ARCADIO AROSEMENA GALLARDO; Gen. Man. FERNANDO ASPIAZU S.

Banco Sociedad General de Crédito: 9 de Octubre 1404 y Machala, Casilla 5501, Guayaquil; tel. 396-700; telex 04-3138; f. 1972; cap. 150m., res 37m., dep. 1,274m. (June 1984); Pres. JOSÉ ANTÓN DÍAZ; Gen. Man. EDUARDO SIMÓN PEREIRA CABRAL.

Banco Territorial: Panamá 814 y V.M. Rendón, Casilla 227, Guayaquil; tel. 305-210; f. 1886; cap. 187.5m., res 116.5m., dep. 373.8m. (Aug. 1988); Pres. FEDERICO GOLDBAUM; Gen. Man. HUGO SUÁREZ BAQUERIZO.

La Previsora Banco Nacional de Crédito: Avda 9 de Octubre 110 y Pichincha, Apdo 44, Guayaquil; tel. 306-100; telex 04-3219; f. 1919; cap. 3,050m., res 13m., dep. 17,317m. (Dec. 1986); Pres. JUAN JOSÉ MEDINA; Gen. Man. ALVARO GUERRERO FERBER.

Loja

Banco de Loja: esq. Bolívar y Rocafuerte, Casilla 300, Loja; tel. 960-381; telex 04-4132; f. 1968; cap. 40m., res 47m., dep. 731m. (June 1984); Pres. Dr VÍCTOR EMILIO VALDIVIESO C.; Gen. Man. OSWALDO BURNEO VALDIVIEZO.

Machala

Banco de Machala: Avda 9 de Mayo y Rocafuerte, Casilla 711, Machala; tel. 920-022; telex 04-4479; f. 1962; cap. 330m., res 121.4m., dep. 2,698m. (June 1986); Pres. Dr JOSÉ UGARTE VEGA; Gen. Man. ESTEBAN QUIROLA FIGUEROLA; 6 brs.

Portoviejo

Banco Comercial de Manabí, SA: 10 de Agosto 600 y 18 Octubre, Portoviejo; tel. 653-888; telex 6180; f. 1980; cap. 117m., res 21m., dep. 720m. (June 1985); Pres. Dr RUBÉN DARÍO MORALES; Gen. Man. ARISTO ANDRADE DÍAZ.

ECUADOR

Foreign Banks

Banco Holandés Unido, SA (Netherlands): Avda 10 de Agosto 911, Casilla 42, Quito; tel. 239-765; telex 2153; f. 1959; cap. 358m., res 138m., dep. 1,335m. (Dec. 1986); Gen. Man. KEES DOEFF; br. at Guayaquil.

Bank of America (USA): Edif. Cofiec, Avda Amazonas y Patria, Casilla 344, Quito; tel. 527-011; telex 2152; f. 1966; cap. 250m., res 180m., dep. 1,500m. (Dec. 1986); Gen. Man. STEPHEN HOTCHKISS; br. at Guayaquil.

Citibank, NA (USA): Juan León Mera 130 y Patria, Casilla 1393, Quito; tel. 563-300; telex 2134; f. 1959; cap. 253m., res 563m., dep. 7,333m. (March 1987); Gen. Man. JAMES V. DEANE; 4 brs.

Lloyds Bank (BLSA) Ltd (UK): Avda Amazonas 580, Casilla 556-A, Quito; tel. 564-177; telex 2215; f. 1988 (in succession to the Bank of London and South America, f. 1936); cap. 301m., res 283m., dep. 3,238m. (June 1987); Man. PETER KNIGHT.

Finance Corporations

COFIEC—Compañía Financiera Ecuatoriana de Desarrollo: Avdas Patria y Amazonas, Casilla 411, Quito; f. 1965; cap. 678m., res 85m. (July 1984); Pres. Dr JOSÉ ANTONIO CORREA E.

Financiera Guayaquil, SA: Carchi 702 y 9 de Octubre, 6°, Casilla 2167, Guayaquil; telex 43431; f. 1976; cap. 900m., res 142m. (June 1987); Gen. Man. Dr MIGUEL BABRA LYON.

FINANSA—Financiera Nacional, SA: Avda 6 de Diciembre 2417, entre Orellana y la Niña, Casilla 6420-CCI, Quito; tel. 546-200; telex 2884; f. 1976; cap. 694m., res 103.6m. (June 1986); Gen. Man. RICHARD A. PEARSE.

FINANSUR—Financiera del Sur, SA: 9 de Mayo y 9 de Octubre, Casilla 7436, Machala; f. 1979; cap. 600m., res 30m. (July 1984); Pres. Econ. DANILO CARRERA DROUET.

Associations

Asociación de Bancos Privados del Ecuador: Edif. Banco de Préstamos, Avdas 10 de Agosto y Patria, Casilla 768A, Quito; f. 1965; 28 mems; Pres. Ing. MARCEL J. LANIADO.

Asociación de Compañías Financieras del Ecuador—AFIN: Robles 653 y Amazonas, 13°, Of. 1310-1311, Casilla 9156, Quito; tel. 550-623; telex 2809; Pres. Dr JOSÉ ANTONIO CORREA.

STOCK EXCHANGE

Bolsa de Valores de Quito CA: Avda Río Amazonas 540 y J. Carrión, Quito; tel. 526-805; telex 2565; f. 1969; volume of operations in 1987 13,000m. sucres; Pres Dr JOSÉ MARÍA RUMAZO ARCOS; Gen. Man. Dr BOLÍVAR CHIRIBOGA VALDIVIESO.

INSURANCE

Instituto Ecuatoriano de Seguridad Social: Avda 10 de Agosto y Bogotá, Apdo 2640, Quito; tel. 547-400; telex 2280; f. 1928; various forms of state insurance provided; the Institute directs the Ecuadorean social insurance system; it provides social benefits, medical service and housing programmes; Dir-Gen. Ing. CARLOS SALVADOR SANTOS.

National Companies

In 1981 there were 27 insurance companies operating in Ecuador. The following is a list of the eight principal companies, selected by virtue of capital.

Amazonas Cía Anónima de Seguros: V. M. Rendón y Córdova, Apdo 3285, Guayaquil; tel. 306-300; telex 3176; f. 1966; cap. 175m. sucres (1988); Exec. Pres. ANTONIO AROSEMENA G.-L.

Cía Reaseguradora del Ecuador, SA: Junín No 105 y Malecón Simón Bolívar, Casilla 6776, Guayaquil; f. 1977; tel. 304-458; telex 04-42960; cap. 40m. sucres (1987); Man. Dir Dr EDUARDO PEÑA TRIVIÑO.

Cía de Seguros Condor, SA: P. Ycaza 302, Apdo 5007, Guayaquil; tel. 312-300; telex 43755; f. 1966; cap. 40m. sucres; Gen. Man. JAIME GUZMÁN ITURRALDE.

Cía de Seguros Ecuatoriano-Suiza, SA: Avda 9 de Octubre 2101 y Tulcán, Apdo 397, Guayaquil; tel. 372-222; telex 3386; f. 1954; cap. 65m. sucres (1986); Gen. Man. Econ. ENRIQUE SALAS CASTILLO.

La Nacional Cía de Seguros Generales, SA: Panamá 809, Apdo 1085, Guayaquil; tel. 307-700; telex 3420; f. 1941; cap. 100m. sucres (1984); Gen. Man. LUCIANO CAGNATO CALIGO.

Panamericana del Ecuador, SA: Avda Amazonas 477 entre Roca y Robles, Edif. Banco de los Andes, 4°, Apdo 3902, Quito; tel. 235-358; telex 22352; f. 1973; cap. 61m. sucres (1987); Gen. Man. JOSÉ ANDINO C.

Seguros Rocafuerte, SA: P. Carbo 505 y 9 de Octubre, Apdo 6491, Guayaquil; f. 1967; cap. 40m. sucres; Gen. Man. Ing. DANIEL CAÑIZARES AGUILAR.

La Unión Cía Nacional de Seguros: Km. 5½ Vía a la Costa, Apdo 1294, Guayaquil; tel. 354-800; telex 3421; f. 1943; cap. 106.5m. sucres; Man. DAVID ALBERTO GOLDBAUM MORALES.

Trade and Industry

CHAMBERS OF COMMERCE AND INDUSTRY

Federación Nacional de Cámaras de Comercio del Ecuador: Avda Olmedo 414, Casilla Y, Guayaquil; tel. 524-928; federation of chambers of commerce; Pres. JORGE BEJARANO ORRANTIA.

Cámara de Comercio de Cuenca: Avda Federico Malo 1-90, Casilla 4929, Cuenca; tel. 827531; telex 04-8630; f. 1919; 5,329 mems; Pres. EDUARDO MALO ABAD.

Cámara de Comercio de Quito: Avdas República y Amazonas, Casilla 202, Quito; tel. 453011; telex 2638; f. 1906; 6,000 mems; Pres. Ing. JUAN BERNARDO LEÓN.

Cámara de Comercio de Guayaquil: Avda Olmedo 414, Guayaquil; tel. 511130; f. 1889; 3,700 mems; Pres. JORGE BEJARANO ORRANTIA.

Federación Nacional de Cámaras de Industrias: Avdas República y Amazonas, Casilla 2438, Quito; tel. 452994; telex 2770; f. 1974; Pres. Abog. RODOLFO KRONFLE.

Cámara de Industrias de Cuenca: Edif. Las Cámaras, Avda Federico Malo 1-90, Casilla 326, Cuenca; tel. 830845; telex 8631; f. 1936; Pres. Arq. GASTÓN RAMÍREZ SALCEDO.

Cámara de Industrias de Guayaquil: Avda 9 de Octubre 910, Casilla 4007, Guayaquil; tel. 302705; telex 3686; f. 1936; Pres. RODOLFO KRONFLE AKEL.

STATE ENTERPRISES AND DEVELOPMENT ORGANIZATIONS

Centro de Desarrollo Industrial del Ecuador—CENDES: Avda Orellana 1715 y 9 de Octubre, Casilla 2321, Quito; tel. 527-100; f. 1962; carries out industrial feasibility studies, supplies technical and administrative assistance to industry, promotes new industries, supervises investment programmes; Gen. Man. Ing. PABLO DURANGO VELA.

Centro Nacional de Promoción de la Pequeña Industria y Artesanía (CENAPIA): Quito; agency to develop small-scale industry and handicrafts; Dir Ing. MAURICIO MIER LUNA.

Centro de Reconversión Económica del Austro (CREA): Bolívar y Cueva, Cuenca; tel. 830799; telex 8610; f. 1959; development organization; Dir Lic. DANIEL TORAL V.

Consejo Nacional de Desarrollo (CONADE): Juan Larrea y Arenas, Quito; formerly Junta Nacional de Planificación y Coordinación Económica; aims to formulate a general plan of economic and social development and supervise its execution; also to integrate local plans into the national; Chair. Dr BLASCO PEÑAHERRERA PADILLA.

Corporación Estatal Petrolera Ecuatoriana (CEPE) (Ecuadorean State Petroleum Corporation): Avda Colón No 1021, 8° piso, Edif. Banco Continental, Casillas 5007/8, Quito; tel. 544-939; telex 2861; f. 1972 to promote exploration for and exploitation of petroleum and natural gas deposits by initiating joint ventures with foreign and national companies and to act as the agency controlling the concession of onshore and offshore exploration rights; began international marketing of crude petroleum in 1974 and took over the domestic marketing and distribution of petroleum products in 1976; Gen. Man. Ing. JAIME SÁNCHEZ (acting).

Empresa de Comercio Exterior (ECE): Quito; f. 1980 to promote non-traditional exports; State owns 33% share in company; share capital 25m. sucres.

Empresa Pesquera Nacional: state fishing enterprise.

Fondo de Desarrollo del Sector Rural Marginal (Foderuma): f. 1978 to allot funds to rural development programmes in poor areas.

FONADE—Fondo Nacional de Desarrollo: f. 1973; national development fund to finance projects as laid down in the five-year plan.

Fondo Nacional de Preinversión—FONAPRE: f. 1974 to undertake feasibility projects before investment is made by FONADE; Gen. Man. Econ. ALBERTO CÁRDENAS DÁVILA.

Fondo de Promoción de Exportaciones—FOPEX: Juan León Mera 130 y Avda Patria, Casilla 163, Quito; tel. 564-900; telex 2193; f. 1972; export promotion; Dir Dr JUAN VILLASIS A.

Instituto de Colonización de la Región Amazónica (INCRAE): f. 1978 to encourage settlement in and economic development of the Amazon region.

Instituto Ecuatoriano de Electrificación (INECEL): f. 1961; state enterprise for the generation, transmission and distribution of electric energy; Gen. Man. Ing. HANS COLLINGS MORALES.

ECUADOR

Instituto Ecuatoriano de Recursos Hidráulicos—INEHRI: undertakes irrigation and hydroelectric projects; Man. Ing. PEDRO ALAVA GONZÁLEZ.

Instituto Ecuatoriano de Reforma Agraria y Colonización (IERAC): f. 1973 to supervise the Agrarian Reform Law under the auspices and co-ordination of the Ministry of Agriculture; Dir Ing. RAFAEL PÉREZ REINA.

Organización Comercial Ecuatoriana de Productos Artesanales—OCEPA: Páez 552 y Carrión, Casilla 2948, Quito; tel. 542-045; telex 22062; f. 1964; to develop and promote national arts and crafts; Gen. Man. CRISTIAN PROAÑO.

Programa Nacional del Banano y Frutas Tropicales: Pichincha 103, Guayaquil; to promote the development of banana and tropical fruit cultivation.

Programa Regional de Desarrollo del Sur del Ecuador (PREDE-SUR): 9 de Octubre 275 y Jorge Washington, Quito; tel. 230-531; f. 1972 to promote the development of the southern area of the country; Dir Econ. JORGE PIEDRA.

Superintendencia de Compañías del Ecuador: Roca 660 y Avda Amazonas, Casilla 1387, Quito; tel. 525-022; telex 2595; responsible for the social and economic development of commercial enterprises; Pres. ERNESTO ANDRADE.

EMPLOYERS' ASSOCIATIONS

Asociación de Cafecultores del Cantón Piñas: García Moreno y Abdón Calderón, Piñas; coffee growers' association.

Asociación de Comerciantes e Industriales: Boyacá 1416, Guayaquil; traders' and industrialists' association.

Asociación de Industriales Textiles del Ecuador—AITE: Avdas República y Amazonas, Edif. Las Cámaras 8°, Casilla 2893, Quito; telex 2770; f. 1938; textile manufacturers' association; 33 mems; Pres. RICHARD C. HANDAL; Sec.-Gen. JOSÉ LUIS ALARCÓN.

Asociación de Productores Bananeros del Ecuador—APROBANA: Malecón 2002, Guayaquil; banana growers' association.

Asociación Nacional de Empresarios—ANDE: Edif. España 6°, Of. 67, Avda Colón y Amazonas, Casilla 3489, Quito; tel. 238-507; national employers' association.

Asociación Nacional de Exportadores de Cacao y Café: Casilla 4774, Manta; cocoa and coffee exporters' association.

Cámara de Agricultura: Casilla 560, Quito; tel. 230-195; Pres. Ing. PATRICIO IZURIETA MORA BOWEN.

Consorcio Ecuatoriano de Exportadores de Cacao y Café: Piñas; cocoa and coffee exporters' consortium.

Corporación Nacional de Exportadores de Cacao y Café: Sucre 106 y Malecón, Guayaquil; cocoa and coffee exporters' corporation.

Federación Nacional de Cooperativas Cafetaleras: Guayaquil 1242, Of. 304, Quito; coffee co-operatives federation.

There are several other coffee and cocoa organizations.

TRADE UNIONS

Frente Unitario de Trabajadores (FUT): f. 1971; left-wing; 300,000 mems; Pres. FAUSTO DUTÁN; comprises:

Confederación Ecuatoriana de Organizaciones Clasistas—CEDOC: POB 3207, Calle Rocafuerte 1477, Quito; tel. 519-351; f. 1938; affiliated to CMT and CLAT; socialist; Pres. DAVID TENESACA; Sec.-Gen. GERMÁN BARRAGÁN; 130,000 mems (est.) organized in 19 provinces.

Confederación Ecuatoriana de Organizaciones Sindicales Libres—CEOSL: Casilla 1373, Quito; tel. 522-511; f. 1962; affiliated to ICFTU and ORIT; Pres. JOSÉ CHÁVEZ CHÁVEZ; Sec.-Gen. JULIO CHANG CRESPO.

Confederación de Trabajadores del Ecuador—CTE (Confederation of Ecuadorean Workers): Olmedo y Benalcázar, 3°, Quito; f. 1944; admitted to WFTU and CSTAL; backed by Communist party; Leaders JUAN VÁSQUEZ, EDGAR PONCE; 55,000 mems (est.) in 200 affiliated unions.

Central Católica de Obreros: Avda 24 de Mayo 344, Quito.

A number of trade unions are not affiliated to the above groups. These include the Federación Nacional de Trabajadores Marítimos y Portuarios del Ecuador—FNTMPE (National Federation of Maritime and Port Workers of Ecuador) and both railway trade unions.

Transport

Ministerio de Obras Públicas y Comunicaciones: Avda 6 de Diciembre y Wilson, Quito; tel. 561-830; telex 2353.

RAILWAYS

All railways are government-controlled. Extensive construction work is being undertaken.

Empresa Nacional de Ferrocarriles del Estado: POB 159, Calle Bolívar 443, Quito; tel. 216-180; Gen. Man. Ing. CÉSAR FELIPE NOBOA URRESTA.

Total length 965 km (1987).

There are divisional state railway managements for the following lines: Guayaquil-Quito, Sibambe-Cuenca and Quito-San Lorenzo.

ROADS

There were 36,382 km of roads in 1988, of which 10,118 km were paved. The Pan-American Highway runs north from Ambato to Quito and to the Colombian border at Tulcán and south to Cuenca and Loja. The severe weather of 1982/83 damaged 1,120 km of roads, which were subsequently repaired. The earthquake of March 1987 resulted in further damage to roads and bridges, but by 1988 these were passable again.

SHIPPING

Some US $160m. is to be invested in the modernization of Ecuador's principal ports: Guayaquil, Esmeraldas, Manta and Puerto Bolívar.

Flota Bananera Ecuatoriana, SA: Edif. Gran Pasaje 9°, P. Icaza 437, Casilla 6883, Guayaquil; tel. 309-333; telex 43218; f. 1967; owned by Government of Ecuador and private stockholders; Pres. DIEGO SÁNCHEZ; Gen. Man. JORGE BARRIGA; 5 vessels.

Flota Mercante Grancolombiana, SA: Calle 2 Aguirre 104 y Malecón Simón Bolívar, Casilla 3714, Guayaquil; tel. 512-791; telex 3210; f. 1946 with Colombia and Venezuela; on Venezuela's withdrawal in 1953, Ecuador's 10% interest was increased to 20%; operates services from Colombia and Ecuador to European ports, US Gulf ports and New York, Mexican Atlantic ports and East Canada; offices in Quito, Cuenca, Bahía, Manta and Esmeraldas; Man. Naval Capt. J. ALBERTO SÁNCHEZ; fleet of 29 vessels (21 owned by it and 8 chartered).

Flota Petrolera Ecuatoriana—FLOPEC: Edif. España 4°, Avda Colón y Amazonas, Casilla 535-A, Quito; tel. 552-100; telex 2211; f. 1973; 7 vessels; Pres. F. ALFARO; Gen. Man. M. VILLALBA.

Transportes Navieros Ecuatorianos—Transnave: Edif. Citibank 6°, Avda 9 de Octubre 416 y Chile, Apdo 4706, Guayaquil; tel. 308-400; telex 43249; 5 vessels; transports general cargo within the European South Pacific Magellan Conference, Japan West Coast South America Conference and Atlantic and Gulf West Coast South America Conference; Pres. Vice-Adm. FERNANDO ALFARO ECHEVERRÍA; Gen. Man. Rear-Adm. RUBÉN LANDÁZURI ZAMBRANO.

Various foreign lines operate between Ecuador and European ports.

CIVIL AVIATION

There are two international airports: Mariscal Sucre, near Quito, and Simón Bolívar, near Guayaquil.

Aerolíneas Nacionales del Ecuador, SA—ANDES: Apdo 3317, Aeropuerto Simón Bolívar, Guayaquil; tel. 284-490; telex 3228; f. 1961; headquarters in Miami, USA; regular cargo services Miami-Panamá-Quito-Guayaquil, Cuenca; Gen. Man. Dr ROBERTO PÓLIT; fleet: 2 DC-6A, 2 CL-44.

Empresa Ecuatoriana de Aviación—EEA: Condominios Almargo, Avda Reina Victoria y Colón Esp., Apdo 505, Quito; tel. 563003; telex 21143; nationalized 1974; international scheduled passenger services and cargo and mail services to Argentina, Brazil, Chile, Colombia, Costa Rica, Mexico, Panama, Peru, USA and Venezuela; Exec. Pres. PATRICIO AVILA; fleet: 1 DC-10-30, 3 Boeing 707-320-B, 1 707-300-C.

Transportes Aéreos Nacionales Ecuatorianos—TAME: Casilla 8736, Suc. Almagro, Quito; tel. 547-304; telex 22567; brs in Guayaquil and 10 other cities; f. 1962; domestic scheduled services for passengers and freight; charter services abroad; Gen. Man. Lt-Gen. (retd.) ARMANDO DURÁN N.; fleet: 1 Electra Jet Prop., 2 Avro, 1 Fokker, 1 Boeing 727-200, 2 727-100.

The following airlines also offer national and regional services:

Aerotaxis Ecuatorianos, SA—ATESA; Cía Ecuatoriana de Transportes Aéreos—CEDTA; Ecuastol Servicios Aéreos, SA; Ecuavia Cía Ltda; Sociedad Ecuatoriana de Transportes Aéreos—SAETA; Servicios Aéreos Nacionales—SAN; Aeroturismo Cía Ltda—SAVAC.

Tourism

The number of tourists visiting Ecuador rose from 172,000 in 1975 to 250,000 in 1985.

Asociación Ecuatoriana de Agencias de Viajes y Turismo—ASECUT: Amazonas 657 y Ramírez Dávalos, Casilla 1210, Quito; Apdo 510, Guayaquil; tel. 529-253; telex 2924; f. 1953; Pres. ANDRÉS PÉREZ ESPINOSA.

Dirección Nacional de Turismo: Reina Victoria 514 y Roca, Quito; f. 1964; tel. 527-002; telex 21158; Exec. Dir Dr NELSON ROBELLY L.

Atomic Energy

Comisión Ecuatoriana de Energía Atómica: San Javier 295 y Avda Orellana, Casilla 2517, Quito; f. 1968; research in nuclear physics radio-isotopes, radio-biology, chemistry and medicine; in 1975 it took over the production and sale of radioactive minerals; Exec. Dir. Ing. LEONARDO MACKLIFF EGÜEZ.

EGYPT

Introductory Survey

Location, Climate, Language, Religion, Flag, Capital

The Arab Republic of Egypt occupies the north-eastern corner of Africa, with an extension across the Gulf of Suez into the Sinai Peninsula, sometimes regarded as lying within Asia. Egypt is bounded to the north by the Mediterranean Sea, to the north-east by Israel, to the east by the Red Sea, to the south by Sudan, and to the west by Libya. The climate is arid, with a maximum annual rainfall of only 200 mm (8 in) around Alexandria. More than 90% of the country is desert, and some 99% of the population live in the valley and delta of the River Nile. Summer temperatures reach a maximum of 43°C (110°F) and winters are mild, with an average day temperature of about 18°C (65°F). Arabic is the official language. Many educated Egyptians also speak English or French. More than 80% of the population are Muslims, mainly of the Sunni sect. The remainder are mostly Christians, principally Copts, who number some 6m. The national flag (proportions 3 by 2) has three equal horizontal stripes, of red, white, and black; the white stripe has, in the centre, the national emblem (a shield superimposed on a hawk, with a scroll beneath) in gold. The capital is Cairo.

Recent History

Egypt, a province of Turkey's Ottoman Empire from the 16th century, was occupied by British forces in 1882. The administration was controlled by British officials, although Egypt remained nominally an Ottoman province until 1914, when a British protectorate was declared. The United Kingdom (UK) granted nominal independence to Egypt on 28 February 1922. Fuad I, the reigning Sultan since 1917, became King of Egypt. He was succeeded in 1936 by his son, King Faruq (Farouk). The Anglo-Egyptian Treaty of 1936 recognized full Egyptian sovereignty and provided for the gradual withdrawal of British troops, while giving the UK the right to maintain a garrison on the Suez Canal, which links the Mediterranean and Red Seas, and to use Alexandria and Port Said as naval bases. The Italian invasion of Egypt in 1940 and the subsequent Libyan campaign postponed the departure of British forces. After the Second World War, British forces withdrew from Egypt, except for a military presence in the Suez Canal Zone. When the British mandate in Palestine was ended in 1948, Arab armies intervened to oppose the newly-proclaimed State of Israel. A cease-fire was agreed in 1949, leaving Egyptian forces occupying the Gaza Strip, a coastal strip, around the town of Gaza, in southern Palestine.

On 23 July 1952 King Farouk's unpopular regime, widely recognized as corrupt, was overthrown by a bloodless military coup. Power was seized by a group of young army officers, the 'Free Officers', led by Lt-Col Gamal Abd an-Nasir (Nasser). Three days later, Farouk abdicated in favour of his infant son, Ahmad Fuad II, and went into exile. After the coup, Gen. Muhammad Nagib (Neguib) was appointed Commander-in-Chief of the Army and Chairman of the Revolution Command Council (RCC), a nine-member military junta. In September 1952 Gen. Neguib was appointed Prime Minister and Military Governor of Egypt, with Col Nasser as Deputy Prime Minister. In December 1952 the 1923 Constitution was abolished, and in January 1953 all political parties were dissolved. On 18 June 1953 the monarchy was abolished and Egypt was proclaimed a republic, with Gen. Neguib as President and Prime Minister. In April 1954 President Neguib was succeeded as Prime Minister by Col Nasser. In October Egypt and the United Kingdom signed an agreement concerning the Suez Canal, providing for the withdrawal of all British forces by June 1956. In November 1954, following a dispute within the military regime, President Neguib was relieved of all his remaining posts, and Col Nasser became acting Head of State.

The establishment of military rule was accompanied by wide-ranging reforms, including the redistribution of land, the promotion of industrial development and the expansion of social welfare services. In foreign affairs, the new regime was strongly committed to Arab unity, and Egypt played a prominent part in the Non-Aligned Movement. In 1955, having failed to secure Western armaments on satisfactory terms, Egypt accepted military assistance from the USSR.

In January 1956 Col Nasser proclaimed a new Egyptian constitution, providing for a strong presidency. On 23 June the Constitution was approved by a national referendum, and Nasser was elected President (unopposed). The RCC was dissolved on the next day. In July 1956, following the departure of British forces, the US and British Governments withdrew their offers of financial assistance for Egypt's construction of the Aswan High Dam on the River Nile. In response, President Nasser announced the nationalization of the Suez Canal Company, so that revenue from Canal tolls could be used to finance the High Dam's construction. The take-over of the Canal was a cause of great concern to Israel, Britain and France, and Israel invaded the Sinai Peninsula on 29 October. Britain and France began military operations against Egypt two days later. Strong pressure from the UN and the US Government resulted in a cease-fire on 6 November, and supervision by the UN of the invaders' withdrawal.

Egypt and Syria, although geographically separate, merged in February 1958 to form the United Arab Republic (UAR), with Nasser as President. The new nation strengthened earlier ties with the USSR and other countries of the East European bloc. In September 1961 Syria seceded from the UAR, and resumed its separate independence, after the army had seized power there. However, Egypt retained the title of UAR until September 1971. Further attempts at federating Egypt, Syria and Iraq during the early 1960s proved unsuccessful. Earlier, in 1958, the UAR and Yemen formed a federation called the United Arab States, but this was dissolved at the end of 1961. Following the death in September 1962 of the Imam Ahmad of Yemen, a military coup deposed his successor, and the rebels proclaimed the Yemen Arab Republic (YAR). Civil war broke out between royalist forces, supported by Saudi Arabia, and republicans, aided by Egyptian troops. The republicans eventually gained control, and Egyptian forces withdrew from the YAR in 1967.

President Nasser enjoyed immense prestige throughout the Arab world and beyond. Internally, he was regarded as the founder of modern Egypt. In December 1962 he established the Arab Socialist Union (ASU) as the country's only recognized political organization. In May 1967 he secured the withdrawal of the UN Emergency Force from Egyptian territory. Egypt subsequently reoccupied Sharm esh-Sheikh, near the southern tip of the Sinai Peninsula, and closed the Straits of Tiran to Israeli shipping. These actions provoked the 'Six-Day War' of June 1967, when Israel quickly defeated neighbouring Arab states, including Egypt. The war left Israel in control of the Gaza Strip and a large area of Egyptian territory, including the whole of the Sinai Peninsula. The Suez Canal was blocked, and remained closed until June 1975.

In December 1969 the office of Vice-President was re-established when Col Anwar Sadat, who had held the post in 1964–66, was reappointed. President Nasser died suddenly in September 1970, and was succeeded by Col Sadat. In September 1971 the UAR was renamed the Arab Republic of Egypt, and a new constitution took effect. In the early years of his rule, Sadat attempted to follow Nasser's aim of unity with other Arab states. The Federation of Arab Republics (Egypt, Libya and Syria) came into being in 1972, but proved ineffective. In March 1976 Egypt terminated its Treaty of Friendship with the USSR. Relations with the USA, on the other hand, became closer as President Sadat came to rely increasingly on US aid.

An uneasy cease-fire with Israel lasted until October 1973, when Egyptian troops crossed the Suez Canal to recover territory which had been lost in 1967. After 18 days of fighting, a cease-fire was arranged. Dr Henry Kissinger, the US Secretary of State, negotiated disengagement agreements in 1974 and September 1975, by which Israel evacuated territory in Sinai, and Israeli and Egyptian forces were separated by a buffer zone under the control of UN forces.

A dramatic peace-making initiative was made by President Sadat in November 1977, when he visited Israel and addressed the Knesset. Many Arab countries opposed the visit on the grounds that it undermined Arab unity. The leaders of Syria, Libya, Algeria, Iraq and the People's Democratic Republic of Yemen, and the Palestine Liberation Organization (PLO), condemned Egypt and met in Tripoli in December to discuss what action they should take, but Egypt pre-empted their decision and broke off diplomatic relations with the five.

In September 1978, after talks at Camp David in the USA (under the guidance of President Carter), President Sadat and Menachem Begin, Prime Minister of Israel, signed two agreements. The first was a 'framework of peace in the Middle East' and the second was a 'framework for the conclusion of a peace treaty between Egypt and Israel'. The first agreement provided for a five-year transitional period during which the inhabitants of the Israeli-occupied West Bank of the Jordan and the Gaza Strip would obtain full autonomy and self-government, and the second agreement provided for the signing of a peace treaty between Egypt and Israel by 17 December 1978. The peace treaty was signed in March 1979, and Israel subsequently made phased withdrawals from the Sinai Peninsula, the last of which took place in April 1982. Syria, Algeria, Libya and the PLO had condemned the Camp David agreements, and in March 1979 the Council of the Arab League expelled Egypt from the League and introduced political and economic sanctions. Oman, Sudan and Somalia were the only Arab countries that did not sever their ties with Egypt. Egypt, however, continued to strengthen relations with Israel, and in February 1980 the two countries exchanged ambassadors for the first time.

In 1974 Sadat began to introduce a more liberal political and economic regime. Political parties (banned since 1953) were allowed to participate in the 1976 elections for the People's Assembly. They were legalized in June 1977 but overshadowed in July 1978, when Sadat formed a new political party, the National Democratic Party (NDP), with himself as leader. In April 1979 the special constitutional status of the ASU was terminated. In October 1981 Sadat was assassinated by members of Islamic Jihad, a group of fundamentalists (belonging to the community of Islamic extremists called gamaat, or 'the (Islamic) groups'), led by Lt Khalid Islambouly, who was later executed. Sadat was succeeded by Lt-Gen. Hosni Mubarak, who had been Vice-President since April 1975 and was previously Commander-in-Chief of the Air Force. The state of emergency was extended for another year in October 1982 and October 1983. In 1983 the Minister of the Interior revealed that 13 terrorist organizations had been discovered in the preceding year.

An electoral law, adopted in July 1983, required parties to receive a minimum of 8% of the total vote to be represented in the People's Assembly. This prompted opposition parties to boycott elections to local councils and to the Shura Council, an advisory assembly. In January 1984 the legality of the re-formed New Wafd Party, perhaps the only opposition party with any prospect of wide popular support, was upheld by the courts after the Government had refused to recognize it on its re-emergence in August 1983. At elections to the People's Assembly on 27 May 1984, the ruling NDP received 72.9% of the total vote, winning 389 of the 448 elective seats in the Assembly. Of the four other participating parties, only the New Wafd, with 15.1% of the vote, crossed the 8% threshold, and won the remaining 59 seats. It was suggested that the New Wafd's electoral alliance with the Muslim Brotherhood cost the party the support of many of Egypt's estimated 6m. Copts. The opposition parties protested that the elections were undemocratic and fraudulent. Dr Ahmad Fuad Mohi ed-Din, who had been Prime Minister since January 1982 and was also Secretary-General of the NDP, died on 5 June 1984. As a result, President Mubarak reshuffled the Council of Ministers, appointing Gen. Kamal Hassan Ali, hitherto a Deputy Prime Minister and the Minister of Foreign Affairs, as Prime Minister.

In foreign affairs, a division in the Arab world between a 'moderate' grouping (including Jordan, Iraq and, less vocally, the Gulf states), which viewed the participation of Egypt as indispensable to any diplomatic initiatives for solving the problems of the region, and a 'radical' grouping, led by Syria (which devoted itself to taking Egypt's place as the leader of the Arab community), became increasingly evident. The PLO leader, Yasser Arafat, visited President Mubarak for discussions in Cairo in December 1983, signifying the end of a six-year period of estrangement between Egypt and the PLO. In September 1984 Jordan decided to resume diplomatic relations with Egypt. In 1984 Egypt proposed two formulas for a peaceful settlement of the Gulf War, but neither was adopted by Iran or Iraq. President Mubarak, accompanied by King Hussein of Jordan, made a surprise visit to Baghdad in March 1985, to demonstrate his support for the Iraqi President, Saddam Hussain, despite the fact that there had been no formal diplomatic relations between Egypt and Iraq since 1979. The division of loyalties in the Gulf War reflected the wider split in the Arab world, with Egypt, Jordan, Saudi Arabia and the remaining Gulf states supporting Iraq, while Libya and Syria backed Iran. (Egypt's remaining diplomatic links with Iran were severed in May 1987.) Owing to alleged Libyan terrorist and espionage activities, and the continued problem of Muslim fundamentalists pursuing Islamic revolution, the Egyptian Government extended the national state of emergency for 18 months from October 1984 and for a further two years from April 1986.

In April 1985 President Nimeri of Sudan was deposed by Lt-Gen. Abd ar-Rahman Swar ad-Dahab, who reaffirmed Sudan's commitment to the 1982 integration agreement, which provided for the acceleration of the integration process in the fields of agriculture and industry. In July 1986 the Government of Sudan formally requested Nimeri's extradition from Egypt.

Relations with Libya, meanwhile, continued to deteriorate. In July 1985 the Libyan leader, Col Qaddafi, barred Egyptian workers (of whom there were some 100,000 in the country at the time) from Libya, in retaliation against a similar Egyptian measure preventing Libyans from working in Egypt. However, in 1988, after the improvement in Egypt's relations with other Arab states following its recognition of the independent Palestinian state (declared in November), Egypt announced that Libyan commercial aircraft would be permitted to operate in Egyptian airspace and to land in Cairo.

The resumption of full diplomatic relations with the USSR was announced in April 1984, and ambassadors were exchanged later in the year. Relations had ceased in 1981, when President Sadat expelled the Soviet Ambassador and 1,000 Soviet experts from Egypt.

President Mubarak, King Hussein of Jordan and Yasser Arafat of the PLO continued their discussions in pursuit of a negotiated settlement of the Palestinian question during 1984 and 1985. Mubarak endorsed the agreement of February 1985, concluded by Arafat and King Hussein, establishing the principle of a joint Jordanian-Palestinian delegation to participate in a proposed Middle East peace conference, to include the permanent members of the UN Security Council.

The credibility of the PLO as a participant in peace negotiations, and of the Jordanian-Palestinian agreement, was further compromised in October 1985, when an Italian cruise liner, the *Achille Lauro*, was hijacked in the eastern Mediterranean by four Palestinians, belonging to one faction of the divided Palestine Liberation Front (PLF). The terrorists murdered an American passenger before surrendering to the Egyptian authorities in Port Said. President Mubarak handed the Palestinians over to Abu al-Abbas, the leader of the PLF faction and a member of the PLO's Executive Committee nominally loyal to Arafat, to be tried, as he thought, by the PLO, but US fighter aircraft intercepted the Egyptian airliner that was taking al-Abbas and the hijackers to Tunis, forcing it to land at a US air force base in Sicily. This action aroused considerable anti-American feeling in Egypt. In November an EgyptAir airliner was hijacked to Malta by Palestinians, whom Egypt immediately linked with the renegade PLO leader, Abu Nidal, and his Libyan supporters. Egyptian special forces were sent to Malta to release the 98 passengers, but their assault on the aircraft resulted in the deaths of 58 hostages and strong criticism of Egypt's handling of the affair.

The campaign by Muslim fundamentalists in Egypt for the legal system fully to adopt the principles of the Shari'a (Islamic holy law) intensified in 1985. An amendment to the Constitution, approved by the People's Assembly in 1980, made Islamic law the basis of Egyptian law, and this provision was largely, although not fully, implemented. In May 1985 the People's Assembly rejected proposals for immediate changes in the legal system, and advocated a thorough study of the small proportion of Egyptian law that does not conform to Islamic precepts before proceeding further. Numerous Muslim fundamentalists, including militant leader Sheikh Hafez Salama, were detained in July for crimes of agitation. Dr Ali Lutfi, a former Minister of Finance under President Sadat, was appointed Prime Minister in September, following the resignation of Gen. Kamal Hassan Ali and his Council of Ministers. The new Council of Ministers contained three members with the rank of Deputy Prime Minister, a post already held by the Minister of Defence, Field Marshal Muhammad Abd al-Halim Abu Ghazalah.

Relations between Egypt and Israel, meanwhile, were strained by the latter's invasion of Lebanon in June 1982, and Israel repeatedly accused Egypt of contraventions of the military provisions of the 1979 peace treaty. In January 1985 Israel and Egypt began a series of negotiations, the first for two years, to determine the sovereignty of the small coastal strip of Taba, on the Red Sea, which Israel did not vacate when it completed its withdrawal from the Sinai Peninsula in 1982. In January 1986 Israel agreed to submit the dispute to international arbitration, on condition that this was preceded by a period of conciliation, during which a compromise solution would be sought before the chosen arbitrators delivered a binding decision. After the appointment of arbitrators (three independent and one each from Egypt and Israel) and the demarcation of the Taba enclave had been agreed, the arbitration document was finally approved by both countries in September. The process of arbitration began in December. In May 1987 each side presented its case for sovereignty to the arbitration panel, and in September a three-member 'conciliation chamber' was established. This was allotted 60 days in which to formulate a compromise. In January 1988 Israel rejected a US plan, whereby Egypt would be given sovereignty over Taba, while Israel was granted access to the area. In September the arbitration panel awarded sovereignty to Egypt, but left an important border undefined. Discussions on the final arrangements for the Taba enclave were held in January 1989.

In September 1986 President Mubarak of Egypt and Prime Minister Peres of Israel met in Alexandria, Egypt, to discuss ways of reviving the Middle East peace process. After the 'summit' meeting (the first between Egypt and Israel since August 1981), and following the signing of the Taba arbitration agreement, President Mubarak appointed Muhammad Bassiouni, Egypt's former chargé d'affaires in Tel-Aviv, as ambassador to Israel. The previous Egyptian ambassador had been recalled from Israel in 1982, after the Israeli invasion of Lebanon.

In November 1986 President Mubarak accepted the resignation of the Prime Minister, Ali Lutfi, and a new Council of Ministers, containing, among 11 changes, a new Minister of Finance and three other new ministers in positions related to the management of the economy, was appointed under a new Prime Minister, Dr Atif Sidqi, hitherto the head of the Central Auditing Agency. President Mubarak was believed to be critical of Ali Lutfi for his indecisive approach to the country's economic problems.

A referendum was held on 12 February 1987 to decide whether the People's Assembly (Majlis ash-Sha'ab) should be dissolved, prior to the holding of a general election on the basis of a new electoral law, whereby 48 of the Assembly's 458 seats would be contested by candidates on an individual, rather than a party-list, basis. An overwhelming vote in the referendum in favour of the dissolution of the People's Assembly enabled the holding of a general election on 6 April. The Socialist Labour Party (SLP), the Liberal Socialist Party (LSP) and the Muslim Brotherhood (which was legally barred from operating as a political party in its own right) formed an electoral alliance, principally in order to overcome the requirement for individual parties to win at least 8% of the total votes to qualify for seats in the People's Assembly. The election campaign was marred by sectarian clashes between Muslims and Christians in several towns in February and March, and the opposition parties accused the Government of electoral corruption. The election resulted in a large, although reduced, majority for the ruling NDP in the People's Assembly. Of the 448 elective seats, the NDP won 346 (compared with 389 at the 1984 election), the opposition parties together won 95, and independents seven. The SLP/LSP/Muslim Brotherhood alliance won a combined total of 60 seats, of which the Brotherhood took 37, thus becoming the largest single opposition group in the new Assembly.

In July 1987 Hosni Mubarak was nominated by the necessary two-thirds majority of the members of the People's Assembly, as the sole presidential candidate, to seek a second six-year term of office, and he was confirmed as President by national referendum on 5 October. Prime Minister Atif Sidqi submitted the resignation of the Government and formed a new Council of Ministers, with only minor changes in personnel. In March 1988 the state of emergency was renewed for a further three years. In August, following disturbances in Cairo, 92 Muslim fundamentalists were remanded in custody, charged with various offences, including attempted murder and illegal possession of weapons. Further anti-Government demonstrations, not only by Muslim fundamentalists but also by striking workers, followed later in the year.

A rift between Egypt and the PLO was precipitated by the reunification of the Palestinian liberation movement that took place at a session of the Palestine National Council (PNC) in Algiers in April 1987. The influence of dissident factions that were returning to the mainstream of the movement, under Yasser Arafat's leadership, resulted in the adoption by the PNC of a resolution urging the reappraisal of PLO links with Egypt, and making future contacts dependent on Egypt's abrogation of the Camp David accords and the 1979 peace treaty with Israel. President Mubarak responded by closing the PLO's offices in Egypt. However, President Mubarak and Yasser Arafat conferred in July in Addis Ababa, Ethiopia, and the PLO's Egyptian offices were subsequently reopened. Both leaders had endorsed proposals for the convening of an international peace conference on the Middle East, under UN auspices, involving the five permanent members of the UN Security Council and all parties to the conflict, including the PLO.

In November 1987, at a 'summit' conference in Amman, Jordan, which was attended by the majority of Arab leaders, the Syrian President, Hafiz Assad, obstructed proposals to readmit Egypt to membership of the League of Arab States. However, recognizing Egypt's support for Iraq in the Gulf War and acknowledging the influence that Egypt (as the most populous and, militarily, the most powerful Arab nation) could bring to bear on the problems of the region, the conference approved a resolution putting the establishment of diplomatic links with Egypt at the discretion of member governments. Such links had previously been prohibited. One week after the end of the conference, nine Arab states (the United Arab Emirates, Iraq, Kuwait, Morocco, the Yemen Arab Republic, Bahrain, Saudi Arabia, Mauritania and Qatar) had re-established full diplomatic relations with Egypt. Of the remaining 12 members of the League, three (Sudan, Somalia and Oman) had maintained diplomatic links with Egypt throughout the period of the boycott, Jordan and Djibouti had re-established them in 1985 and 1986, respectively, and the PLO (to which the League accords nation status) had recently begun to settle its differences with Egypt. In February 1988 the People's Democratic Republic of Yemen re-established full diplomatic relations with Egypt, leaving Algeria, Lebanon, Libya and Syria as the only Arab League members not to have done so. Libya was the most outspoken critic of the change in the League's policy towards Egypt, complaining that the 1979 peace treaty with Israel, the original reason for Egypt's ostracism, remained in force. In November Algeria announced that it would re-establish diplomatic relations with Egypt, and in December there were signs of a *rapprochement* with Syria and Libya. It appeared likely that Egypt would participate in any future Arab 'summit' conference.

Following Jordan's decision, in July 1988, to sever its legal and administrative links with the West Bank region (annexed by Jordan in 1950 but, like the Gaza Strip, under Israeli occupation since 1967), President Mubarak urged the PLO to exercise caution in its plans to declare an independent Palestinian state and to form a government-in-exile. In September, during a tour of Western Europe, he expressed reservations regarding the PLO's commitment to renounce terrorism and recognize Israel. At the same time, he sought support for proposals to convene an international conference on the Middle East. In November Egypt granted full recognition to the newly-declared independent Palestinian state. The refusal of the USA to grant Yasser Arafat an entry visa, in order to address the UN General Assembly, embarrassed Egypt, which had encouraged the PLO to believe that moderate policies would result in diplomatic gains. However, President Mubarak was believed to have persuaded the USA to open contact with

EGYPT

the PLO in December, after Arafat had explicitly renounced terrorism and recognized Israel's right to exist.

Government

Legislative power is held by the unicameral Majlis ash-Sha'ab (People's Assembly), which has 458 members: 10 nominated by the President and 448 directly elected for five years from 48 constituencies. The Assembly nominates the President, who is elected by popular referendum for six years (renewable). The President has executive powers and appoints one or more Vice-Presidents, a Prime Minister and a Council of Ministers. There is also a 210-member advisory assembly, the Shura Council. The country is divided into 26 governorates.

Defence

In June 1988 Egypt had total armed forces of 445,000 (army 320,000, air defence command 80,000, navy 20,000, air force 25,000), with 604,000 reserves. There is a selective three-year period of national service. Defence expenditure for 1988/89 was estimated at £E 3,950m.

Economic Affairs

In 1987, according to estimates by the World Bank, Egypt's gross national product (GNP) was US $36,028m. (at average 1985–87 prices), equivalent to $710 per head, the latter figure having increased at an average rate of 2.6% per year, in real terms, since 1980. The average annual growth of overall gross domestic product (GDP), measured in constant prices, was 6.7% in 1965–80, slowing to 4.7% in 1980–86. The decline in the rate of growth was generally attributed to the accumulation of large surplus stocks of petroleum on international markets, which depressed the economies of countries bordering the Persian Gulf.

Egypt's economy comprises a prosperous, relatively efficient, private sector and a heavily-subsidized, generally inefficient, public sector. During the rule of President Nasser, the Egyptian Government nationalized private industry, closed the economy to Western investment and created a huge public sector. State enterprises provide about 70% of Egypt's industrial output. Under Sadat, the economy was liberalized, and from 1974 an 'open door' policy (*infitah*) was pursued, to encourage foreign investment. In 1988 the Government continued actively to encourage foreign investment, requesting the participation of international organizations in domestic development. Subsidies on foodstuffs and petroleum (the latter not even officially included in the subsidy bill) place a considerable strain on the nation's finances. In 1986/87 expenditure on subsidies for food and basic commodities was projected at £E 1,746m. ($802m.), 12% less than in the previous year. The total declined to £E 1,650m. in 1987/88 and was projected at £E 1,813m. for 1988/89.

In 1984 it was estimated that domestic petroleum consumption was rising at an annual rate of between 12% and 15%, while production was increasing by about 7% annually. Petroleum production in Egypt is small by Middle East standards, averaging about 870,000 b/d in 1984/85, and almost 900,000 b/d in 1985/86, compared with capacity of 1m. b/d. Of the average daily output, about 50% is used locally and about 25% is taken by foreign oil companies under production contracts, leaving only about 25% (200,000 b/d–225,000 b/d) available for export. In 1986 petroleum accounted for about 65% of revenue from merchandise exports. Net revenues from petroleum totalled US $2,276m. in 1984/85, but fell to $1,843m. in 1985/86 and to $1,061m. in 1986/87. It was estimated that revenues from oil would amount to $697m.–$1,520m. in 1988. Egypt, not being a member of OPEC and having been suspended from membership of OAPEC, is able to maintain a flexible pricing policy. During 1986, international prices for crude petroleum, already weakened by a surplus of supplies, declined sharply after OPEC decided to increase production. Egypt was forced to restrict production and to reduce prices in order to remain competitive: average output was reduced by some 300,000 b/d in early 1986, and in April exports were only about 50,000 b/d, compared with more than 250,000 b/d at the end of 1985. From August 1986, however, production was increased, rising to 940,000 b/d at the end of the year. Average output in 1987 was 907,000 b/d. By mid-July 1988, with the world market once more oversupplied with petroleum, the price of Egypt's premium Suez blend had been reduced to $12.75 per barrel, compared with $26.70 in December 1985. In April 1988 Egypt agreed to reduce its output by 5% from May, in accordance with an agreement reached with six other non-OPEC countries.

Revenue from Suez Canal transit tolls and other Canal services was a record $1,222m. in 1987, compared with $1,107m. in 1986. For the fiscal year 1987/88, revenue amounted to about $1,300m. Income in the form of remittances from Egyptians working abroad reached US $3,931m. in 1983/84, making them Egypt's largest source of foreign currency in that year. The value of remittances subsequently declined, to $2,595m. in 1985/86, and in 1986/87 they slumped to less than $600m. In 1987/88, however, remittances from Egyptian expatriate workers through the banking system were expected to reach $4,000m. Many such workers traditionally preferred to remit through the 'black market', where their currency commanded a higher rate of return, but reforms of the exchange rate in May 1987 made the banking system more attractive to expatriate workers. Owing to the recession in the petroleum industry, in 1986 it was estimated that the number of Egyptians working abroad was only about 2m., compared with 3.28m. in 1983. By mid-1987, Egyptian workers returning from abroad had increased the total of the unemployed to 2,011,000, or about 15% of the labour force. Revenue from tourism totalled about $1,000m. in 1984/85. Subsequently, however, an increase in terrorist activity in the Middle East and other problems deterred tourists from visiting Egypt, but the industry made a strong recovery, and by 1988 tourism had become one of the most dynamic sectors of the Egyptian economy. The management of several public-sector hotels was transferred to international groups; legislation to reduce land speculation was enacted; and the aviation industry was liberalized. Earnings from tourism totalled $1,500m. in the first nine months of the fiscal year 1987/88, an increase of 30%–40% over the corresponding period of the previous year.

In 1986 the agricultural sector accounted for 20% of GDP. The proportion of the total labour force involved in agriculture declined from 41.5% in 1977 to 34.6% in 1984/85. The principal crops include maize, rice, wheat, sugar cane and cotton. Compared with a position of self-sufficiency in food during the 1970s, by the mid-1980s Egypt was importing more than one-half of its food requirements (at an estimated cost of $4,100m. in 1984). The expansion of agricultural production has failed to keep pace with the increase in population. Since 1960 annual wheat consumption per head has risen from 80 kg to 180 kg, making Egyptians the world's biggest consumers of wheat. Imports of wheat and wheat flour totalled 5.4m. tons in 1986. In 1988 Australia, one of Egypt's principal suppliers of grain, became concerned at its exposure on the Egyptian market, announcing its intention to reduce the volume of grain sold to Egypt on credit and to accept payment only in cash from 1992.

Egypt's external trade deficit has persisted almost without interruption since before the Second World War. However, the deficit was reported to have fallen to $6,000m. in 1985/86, and to $5,200m. in 1986/87. The decline in imports was largely due to a shortage of convertible currency and to limitations on the importation of luxury consumer items, such as passenger motor cars and sound-reproduction equipment. In discussions with senior IMF officials in mid-1988, regarding the elaboration of a new economic reform programme, the Government cited improvements in the export sector as one of its major economic achievements: non-oil exports increased by 14% in 1986/87 and were expected to rise by a further 30% in 1987/88. The Central Bank estimated that the current account deficit rose to $1,936m. in 1985/86, but preliminary figures for 1986/87 indicated a reduction in the deficit to $933m. In 1987/88 the deficit remained below $1,000m., owing mainly to an increase in earnings from tourism and transfers of expatriate workers' remittances through the banking system. The 1987/88 budget attempted to maintain government subsidies on basic commodities at $1,700m., the same as in 1986/87. The ultimate aim of the reduction in subsidies is to put the public and private sectors on an equal footing with regard to real prices and costs. Budget proposals for 1988/89 included provisions for subsidies on basic commodities of £E1,812m.

The Five-Year Plan for 1982–87 had the aims of increasing total investment (particularly in public-sector industrial and agricultural production) and of limiting the growth of the services sector. Particular emphasis was placed on the development of the hydrocarbons sector. However, these plans had to be revised, owing to the crisis in the world petroleum market. According to the World Bank, in a study published in 1985, Egypt fell considerably short of its targets under the Plan. The study estimated the growth of GDP in the first two years at only about 6%, compared with a real growth rate target of

7.9%, while real investment rose by 2.9%, compared with the target of 10.5%. The next Five-Year Plan, which began in July 1987, required an investment of £E 46,500m. The Plan was designed to encourage public-sector production, to increase the manufacturing of commodities and to raise the level of exports. More resources were to be devoted to the development of the private sector, which was to receive 39% of total investment (£E 18,000m.), compared with 22% under the 1982–87 Plan. It was hoped to achieve annual growth in GDP of 5.8% during the Plan. However, the Government estimated that gross investment declined from 31% of GDP in 1981/82 to less than 20% in 1986/87. The Plan also emphasized the improvement of agricultural output, so as to reduce food imports.

The servicing of foreign debt is the greatest drain on Egypt's resources of foreign currency, accounting for $3,400m. in 1985/86, according to IMF estimates. Combined civil and military debt totalled an estimated $44,000m. in 1986/87. Egypt stands second only to Israel in the amount of aid which it receives from the USA. In 1986/87 total US aid to Egypt was US $2,115m. ($1,300m. in military aid; $815m. in economic support). As a result of IMF pressure, in May 1987 domestic energy prices rose by 60%–85%, thereby reducing the 'hidden' energy subsidy. The exchange rate was allowed partially to 'float', with a daily free rate, competitive with the 'black' market rate, being determined by representatives of commercial banks, in order to attract remittances. Having approved the Egyptian Government's programme of economic reform, the IMF accorded Egypt a stand-by credit of $325m., of which $150m. was made available immediately. At the end of May an agreement was reached with the 'Paris Club' of Western creditor nations to reschedule, over 10 years, payments of $12,000m. in civilian and military debt from Egypt's estimated $44,000m. of foreign debt (Central Bank of Egypt estimate). One month earlier, the USSR had agreed to reschedule, over 25 years and without charging interest, more than $3,000m. in military debt, payment of which had been due since 1977. In February 1988 Egypt's military debt totalled an estimated $13,500m., including $5,550m. owed to the USA.

By the end of 1987 it was apparent that Egypt would be unable to adhere to the programme of economic reform approved by the IMF. By June 1988 the Government's wages bill was estimated to have increased by 25%, and to have contributed greatly to a budget deficit equivalent to 16%–17% of GDP in 1987/88, compared with the IMF's target of 13% of GDP. The Government's public-sector salary commitments were expected to rise by a further 42% in 1988/89. Negotiations between the Government and senior IMF officials, regarding the elaboration of a new economic reform programme, recommenced in mid-1988 and continued intermittently for the remainder of the year. The political obstacles to any new agreement appeared to be insurmountable. While the Government argued that it had made significant achievements in its reform of the exchange rate and prices, the IMF pressed for faster, more wide-ranging reform, including an increase of 30%–40% in energy prices. The urgency of Egypt's need for a new agreement with the IMF, as a precondition for a second rescheduling of its foreign debt, was illustrated in October, when the Government implemented emergency measures to 'freeze' prices and relieve shortages in basic commodities. This action was prompted by fears of civil unrest, the threat of which, the Government consistently maintained, would be increased by compliance with the IMF's conditions. Furthermore, failure to secure an agreement with the IMF would oblige Egypt to resume repayment of its huge military debt in July 1989: debt principal and interest due in 1988/89 were estimated at $700m.

Social Welfare

Great progress has been made in social welfare services in recent years. There are comprehensive state schemes for sickness benefits, pensions, health insurance and training. In 1982 Egypt had 1,521 hospital establishments, with a total of 87,685 beds, and there were 58,761 physicians working in the country. Of total expenditure by the central Government in the financial year 1985/86, £E 420m. (2.4%) was for health services, and a further £E 1,893m. (10.8%) for social security and welfare.

Education

Primary education is officially compulsory for six years between six and 12 years of age. In 1985, however, enrolment at primary schools was equivalent to 85% of children in the relevant age-group (boys 94%; girls 76%). Secondary education, beginning at 12 years of age, lasts for a further six years, comprising two equal cycles of three years each. Enrolment at secondary schools in 1985 was equivalent to 62% of children in this age-group (boys 73%; girls 52%). About 8m. people were receiving state education in the 1980/81 school year. There are 12 universities. Education is free at all levels. In 1976 adult illiteracy averaged 61.8% (males 46.4%; females 77.6%), but by 1985, according to UNESCO estimates, the rate had declined to 55.5% (males 41.4%; females 69.8%).

Public Holidays

1989: 1 January (New Year), 5 March (Leilat al-Meiraj, Ascension of Muhammad), 1 May (Sham an-Nessim), 7 May (Id al-Fitr, end of Ramadan), 18 June (Evacuation Day, proclamation of the republic), 14 July (Id al-Adha, Feast of the Sacrifice), 23 July (Revolution Day), 4 August (Islamic New Year), 6 October (Armed Forces Day), 13 October (Mouloud, Birth of Muhammad), 24 October (Popular Resistance Day), 23 December (Victory Day).

1990: 1 January (New Year), 23 February (Leilat al-Meiraj), 16 April (Sham an-Nessim), 27 April (Id al-Fitr), 18 June (Evacuation Day, proclamation of the republic), 4 July (Id al-Adha), 23 July (Revolution Day), 24 July (Islamic New Year), 2 October (Mouloud), 6 October (Armed Forces Day), 24 October (Popular Resistance Day), 23 December (Victory Day).

Coptic Christian holidays include: Christmas (7 January), Palm Sunday and Easter Sunday.

Weights and Measures

The metric system is in force, but some Egyptian measurements are still in use.

Statistical Survey

Sources (unless otherwise stated): Central Agency for Public Mobilization and Statistics, POB 2086, Nasr City, Cairo; tel. (02) 604632; telex 92395; Research Department, National Bank of Egypt, Cairo.

Area and Population

AREA, POPULATION AND DENSITY

Area (sq km)	997,738.5*
Population (census results)	
22–23 November 1976	36,626,204†
17–18 November 1986 (provisional)‡	
Males	24,655,297
Females	23,549,752
Total	48,205,049
Population (official estimates at mid-year)§	
1985	48,503,000
1986	49,609,000
1987	50,740,000
Density (per sq km) at mid-1987	50.9

* 385,229 sq miles. Inhabited and cultivated territory accounts for 35,189 sq km (13,587 sq miles).
† Excluding Egyptian nationals abroad, totalling 1,572,000.
‡ Including Egyptian nationals abroad, totalling an estimated 2,250,000.
§ Including Egyptian nationals abroad. Data have not been adjusted to take account of the 1986 census results.

GOVERNORATES (population at 1986 census*)

Governorate	Area (sq km)	Population ('000)	Capital
Cairo	214.2	6,052.8	Cairo
Alexandria	2,679.4	2,917.3	Alexandria
Port Said	72.1	399.8	Port Said
Ismailia	1,441.6	544.4	Ismailia
Suez	17,840.4	326.8	Suez
Damietta	589.2	741.3	Damietta
Dakahlia	3,470.9	3,500.5	Mansoura
Sharkia	4,179.5	3,420.1	Zagazig
Kalyubia	1,001.1	2,514.2	Benha
Kafr esh-Sheikh	3,437.1	1,800.1	Kafr esh-Sheikh
Gharbia	1,942.2	2,871.0	Tanta
Menufia	1,532.1	2,227.1	Shibin el-Kom
Behera	10,129.5	1,770.6	Damanhur
Giza	85,153.2	3,700.1	Giza
Beni Suef	1,321.7	1,443.0	Beni Suef
Fayum	1,827.2	1,544.0	Fayum
Menia	2,261.7	2,648.0	Menia
Asyut	1,553.0	2,223.0	Asyut
Suhag	1,547.2	2,455.1	Suhag
Qena	1,850.7	2,252.3	Qena
Aswan	678.5	801.4	Aswan
Al-Bahr al-Ahmar	203,685.0	90.5	Al-Ghaurdaqah
Al-Wadi al-Jadid	376,505.0	113.8	Al-Kharijah
Matruh	212,112.0	160.6	Matruh
North Sinai*	60,714.0	171.5	El-Arish
South Sinai*		29.0	Et-Toor

* Preliminary results.

PRINCIPAL TOWNS (estimated population at 1 July 1983; '000)

El-Qahira (Cairo, the capital)	5,875	Es-Suweis (Suez)	274
El-Iskandariyah (Alexandria)	2,905	Asyut	257
		Zagazig	256
El-Giza	1,640	Ismailia	214
Shoubra el-Kheima	497	El-Fayoum	213
Bur Sa'id (Port Said)	364	Damanhur	203
El-Mahalla el-Koubra	355	El-Minya (Menia)	183
Tanta	344	Aswan	181
El-Mansoura	323	Kafr ed-Dawar	174
		Beni Suef	146

Greater Cairo (November 1976): 6,808,318, (July 1979): 7,258,000, (1984): c. 10,000,000.

BIRTHS AND DEATHS

	Registered live births		Registered deaths	
	Number	Rate (per 1,000)	Number	Rate (per 1,000)
1978	1,479,698	37.2	415,605	10.5
1979	1,633,674	40.0	444,753	10.9
1980	1,569,247	37.3	421,227	10.0
1981	1,593,698	36.8	432,264	9.9
1982	1,601,265	36.0	441,621	9.9
1983*	1,690,000	36.8	412,700	9.0
1984*	n.a.	n.a.	400,600	8.5
1985*	1,817,297	37.5	442,258	9.1

* Figures are provisional.

Marriages (registrations): 442,280 (marriage rate 9.1 per 1,000) in 1985 (provisional).

EMPLOYMENT (Egyptians only, '000 persons)

	1982/83	1983/84	1984/85
Agriculture, forestry and fishing	4,296.4	4,384.9	4,464.2
Manufacturing and mining	1,514.2	1,603.2	1,722.0
Petroleum and petroleum products	25.2	26.5	27.0
Housing and construction	867.3	917.4	982.2
Electricity, gas and water	138.3	139.4	147.0
Transport and communications	446.3	463.8	492.2
Suez Canal	18.9	19.2	19.7
Trade	1,161.2	1,187.8	1,214.2
Finance and insurance	88.4	92.5	96.4
Tourism, hotels and restaurants	144.2	149.7	157.2
Social and private services	942.2	939.9	956.9
Social insurance	31.5	33.0	34.9
Government services	2,436.6	2,511.7	2,576.7
Total	12,110.7	12,469.0	12,890.6

Agriculture

PRODUCTION OF LINT COTTON
(by type of staple; '000 kantars*, year ending 30 June)

	1984	1985	1986
Long†	1,947	1,814	1,914
Medium long‡	4,710	6,782	4,988
Medium§	2	3	—
Total	6,659	8,599	6,902

* 1 metric kantar = 50 kg.   † 1.375 in (3.4925 cm) and longer.
‡ 1.25 in–1.375 in (3.175 cm–3.4925 cm.).
§ 1.125 in–1.25 in (2.8575 cm–3.175 cm)

EGYPT

OTHER PRINCIPAL CROPS ('000 metric tons)

	1985	1986	1987
Wheat	1,872	1,929	2,722
Rice (paddy)	2,311	2,388	2,400*
Barley	158	153	136
Maize	3,699	3,793	4,100*
Millet and sorghum	547	600*	610*
Potatoes	1,478	1,500†	1,550†
Sweet potatoes†	100	100	n.a.
Taro (Coco yam)†	100	105	n.a.
Dry broad beans†	307	310	n.a.
Soybeans (Soya beans)	160*	140*	n.a.
Cottonseed	710	655*	640†
Cabbages	392	414	n.a.
Tomatoes	3,576	3,600†	3,650†
Cauliflower†	105	108	n.a.
Pumpkins, squash and gourds	468	503	n.a.
Cucumbers	308	338	n.a.
Aubergines	323	427	n.a.
Green peppers	192	237	n.a.
Onions (dry)	768	456	395
Garlic†	185	160	n.a.
Green beans†	130	135	n.a.
Carrots†	120	122	n.a.
Watermelons	1,318	1,324	n.a.
Melons	298	289	n.a.
Grapes	395	400†	420†
Dates†	450	460	465
Sugar cane	9,429	9,450†	9,500†
Sugar beets	579	607	741
Oranges	1,168	1,235	1,300
Tangerines, mandarins, clementines and satsumas	106	108*	125
Lemons and limes	120	122*	125*
Mangoes	119	125†	130†
Bananas	203	205†	210†

* Unofficial estimate. † FAO estimate(s).

Source: mainly FAO, *Production Yearbook* and *Quarterly Bulletin of Statistics*.

LIVESTOCK ('000 head, year ending September)

	1984	1985*	1986*
Cattle	2,743*	2,800	2,750
Buffaloes	2,430	2,700	2,600
Sheep	2,450*	2,500	2,550
Goats	2,542*	2,650	2,700
Pigs	50*	55	56
Horses	9	10	11
Asses	1,844	1,850	1,900
Camels	150*	160	170

Chickens (million): 50* in 1984; 52* in 1985; 51* in 1986.
Ducks (million): 7* in 1984, 1985 and 1986.
* FAO estimates.
Source: FAO, *Production Yearbook*.

LIVESTOCK PRODUCTS ('000 metric tons)

	1984	1985	1986
Beef and veal	165†	180*	185*
Buffalo meat	134*	138*	150*
Mutton and lamb	32*	34*	35*
Goats' meat	19†	27*	27*
Pig meat	3*	3*	3*
Poultry meat	185*	205*	196*
Other meat	35*	36*	38*
Edible offals	67*	71*	76*
Cows' milk	955*	960*	965*
Buffaloes' milk	1,320*	1,350*	1,350*
Sheep's milk	21*	22*	23*
Goats' milk	9*	9*	9*
Butter and ghee	78.9*	79.6*	79.4*
Cheese	304.3*	306.3*	303.0*
Hen eggs	115†	115†	106†
Honey	11.2*	11.3*	11.5*
Wool: greasy	1.7	1.7*	1.8*
Cattle and buffalo hides	43.4*	46.0*	49.4*
Sheep skins	3.6*	3.7*	3.8*
Goat skins	3.2*	3.9*	3.9*

* FAO estimates. † Unofficial figure.
Source: FAO, mainly *Production Yearbook*.

Forestry

ROUNDWOOD REMOVALS
(FAO estimates, '000 cubic metres, excluding bark)

	1984	1985	1986
Industrial wood	91	93	95
Fuel wood	1,872	1,918	1,962
Total	1,963	2,011	2,057

Source: FAO, *Yearbook of Forest Products*.

Fishing

('000 metric tons, live weight)

	1981	1982	1983
Marine	33.6	24.6	26.4
Freshwater	108.1	112.6	112.3
Total catch	141.7	137.2	138.8

1984–86: Annual catch as in 1983 (FAO estimates).
Source: FAO, *Yearbook of Fishery Statistics*.

Mining

('000 metric tons, year ending 30 June)

	1983/84	1984/85	1985/86
Crude petroleum	38,700	43,300	42,200
Iron ore*	1,901	1,950	2,135
Salt (unrefined)	865	1,061	1,040
Phosphate rock	946	1,038	1,162
Natural gas	3,280	3,780	5,100

Small quantities of lead and zinc are also mined.
* Figures refer to the metal content of ores.

Industry

SELECTED PRODUCTS ('000 metric tons, unless otherwise indicated; year ending 30 June)

	1983/84	1984/85	1985/86
Wheat flour	3,707*	n.a.	n.a.
Refined sugar	228	291	294
White sugar crystal	416	473	479
Cottonseed oil	238	260	274
Wine ('000 hectolitres)	17.1	n.a.	n.a.
Beer ('000 hectolitres)	360	420	460
Cigarettes (million)	45	48	44
Cotton yarn (pure)	239	243	225
Jute yarn	29	27	24
Jute fabrics	24	23	24
Woollen yarn	16	18	18
Paper	161	161	172
Rubber tyres and tubes ('000)†	3,155	3,246	3,526
Ethyl alcohol ('000 hectolitres)	300	300	270
Sulphuric acid (100%)	55	46	55
Caustic soda (Sodium hydroxide)	50	48	55
Fertilizer nitrates	4,578	4,038	4,482
Fertilizer phosphates	847	930	934
Motor spirit (petrol)	1,723	1,940	1,993
Kerosene	2,029	2,123	2,257
Distillate fuel oils	2,313	2,795	3,187
Residual fuel oil (Mazout)	9,057	9,787	9,501
Petroleum bitumen (asphalt)	531	581	539
Cement	4,600	5,275	7,612
Pig-iron	261	241	n.a.
Gypsum and plaster of Paris	576	1,009	556
Radio receivers ('000)	219	221	180
Television receivers ('000)	900	895	443
Passenger motor cars— assembly (number)	20,290	20,790	19,243
Electric energy (million kWh)	27,900	30,300	32,200

* Estimate for calendar year 1983; International Wheat Council, *World Wheat Statistics*.
† Tyres and inner tubes for road motor vehicles (including motor-cycles) and bicycles.

Finance

CURRENCY AND EXCHANGE RATES

Monetary Units
1,000 millièmes = 100 piastres = 5 tallaris = 1 Egyptian pound (£E).

Denominations
Coins: 1, 2, 5 and 10 piastres.
Notes: 5, 10, 25 and 50 piastres; 1, 5, 10, 20 and 100 pounds.

Sterling and Dollar Equivalents (30 September 1988)
£1 sterling = £E1.184;
US $1 = 700 millièmes;
£E100 = £84.48 sterling = $142.86.

Note: The information on exchange rates refers to the official rate of the Central Bank, fixed at US $1 = 700 millièmes (£E1 = $1.4286) since January 1979. However, a system of multiple exchange rates is in operation, and the official rate is applicable only to a limited range of transactions, including payments for selected imports and exports. At 30 September 1988 the free banks' rate, applicable to most other transactions, was $1 = £E2.323 (£E1 = 43.05 US cents).

BUDGET ESTIMATES (£E million, year ending 30 June)*

	1985/86	1986/87	1987/88
Expenditure	19,910	20,246	23,058.9
Current spending	12,480	11,146	13,745.3
Investment	5,430	7,400	5,800.0
Capital transfer	n.a.	n.a.	3,513.6
Subsidies	2,000	1,700	1,700.0
Revenue	15,010	14,386	18,113.2
Gross deficit	4,900	5,860	4,947.7
Financing	4,000	5,080	4,267.7
Net deficit	900	780	680.0

Source: *Al-Ahram*, Cairo.

* The Government does not provide up-to-date figures on actual spending and income. A number of observers, including the IMF, believe that the actual gross and net deficits since 1982/83 have been higher than budgeted. A major reason for the discrepancy is that the expenditure on subsidies tends to exceed its allocation. Estimates by the IMF assess actual spending on subsidies in 1984/85 at about £E2,600m.

CENTRAL BANK RESERVES (US $ million at 31 December)

	1985	1986	1987
Gold*	578	622	814
Foreign exchange	792	829	1,378
Total	1,370	1,451	2,192

* Valued at market-related prices.
Source: IMF, *International Financial Statistics*.

MONEY SUPPLY (£E million at 31 December)

	1985	1986	1987
Currency outside banks	8,285	8,803	9,537
Demand deposits at deposit money banks	5,606	6,135	7,460

Source: IMF, *International Financial Statistics*.

COST OF LIVING
(Consumer Price Index; base: 1980 = 100)

	1984	1985	1986
Food	180.5	206.1	255.0
Fuel and light	109.9	n.a.	n.a.
Clothing	168.2	193.6	n.a.
Rent	100.0	n.a.	n.a.
All items (incl. others)	172.3	196.4	239.3

Source: ILO, *Year Book of Labour Statistics*.

NATIONAL ACCOUNTS
(£E million at current prices, year ending 30 June)
Expenditure on the Gross Domestic Product

	1984/85	1985/86	1986/87*
Government final consumption expenditure	5,712	6,113	6,330
Private final consumption expenditure	24,433	27,267	34,260
Increase in stocks	200	390	450
Gross fixed capital formation	7,272	7,752	7,700
Total domestic expenditure	37,617	41,522	48,740
Exports of goods and services	6,598	6,034	6,230
Less Imports of goods and services	10,004	9,335	10,920
GDP in purchasers' values	34,211	38,221	44,050

* Provisional.
Source: IMF, *International Financial Statistics*.

EGYPT

Gross Domestic Product by Economic Activity
(at constant 1981/82 factor cost)

	1983/84	1984/85	1985/86
Agriculture	3,965.0	4,078.0	4,205.0
Industry, construction and electricity	4,333.0	4,857.9	5,369.4
Petroleum	3,500.0	3,913.4	4,258.3
Distribution	6,289.0	7,274.9	7,766.3
Services	4,073.0	4,436.0	4,783.5
Total	22,160.0	24,560.2	26,382.5

BALANCE OF PAYMENTS (US $ million)

	1985	1986	1987
Merchandise exports f.o.b.	3,836	2,632	3,115
Merchandise imports f.o.b.	−8,338	−6,643	−7,443
Trade balance	−4,503	−4,011	−4,327
Exports of services	3,442	3,764	4,130
Imports of services	−4,400	−4,139	−3,725
Balance on goods and services	−5,461	−4,386	−3,922
Unrequited transfers (net)	3,216	2,515	3,604
Current balance	−2,245	−1,870	−318
Direct capital investment (net)	1,175	1,211	929
Portfolio investment (net)	20	—	2
Other long-term capital (net)	490	515	125
Short-term capital (net)	−335	168	−1,434
Net errors and omissions	664	−96	965
Total (net monetary movements)	−231	−73	268
Valuation changes (net)	−56	−249	−136
Exceptional financing (net)	350	370	266
Changes in reserves	63	48	398

Source: IMF, *International Financial Statistics*.

External Trade

PRINCIPAL COMMODITIES (£E million)

Imports c.i.f.	1984	1985	1986*
Foodstuffs	2,098.0	1,903.4	2,435.9
Wheat	375.9	342.5	463.7
Wheat flour	271.9	213.3	181.3
Maize	174.2	145.2	135.8
Dairy products	165.7	170.5	158.6
Refined sugar	55.0	43.8	116.6
Base metals and related products	847.5	897.2	971.5
Mineral products	689.4	632.8	647.7
Chemical products	525.1	511.0	592.2
Cement	312.4	328.6	338.4
Paper and paper products	187.8	215.4	183.3
Wood and wood products	323.2	422.7	409.7
Artificial resins, plastics, cellulose and rubber	254.0	249.4	332.0
Textile fibres and products	162.5	156.6	104.0
Machinery and electrical apparatus	1,283.7	1,226.1	1,577.2
Vehicles, aircraft and parts	868.0	510.6	455.6
Watches, clocks, scientific apparatus	145.0	129.5	184.5
Total (incl. others)	7,528.0	6,973.1	8,051.4

* Estimates.

Exports f.o.b.	1984	1985	1986*
Textile fibres and products	571.0	521.6	640.3
Raw cotton	340.1	249.0	308.4
Cotton yarn	154.4	154.6	223.5
Cotton fabrics	37.7	42.2	65.6
Potatoes	25.6	18.9	15.3
Rice	15.8	3.6	11.3
Vegetable products	148.0	129.0	120.3
Oranges	53.5	60.6	30.9
Mineral products	1,267.7	1,774.4	1,054.7
Crude petroleum	1,030.5	1,402.0	798.0
Oil from shale	31.2	130.6	4.0
Chemical products	44.9	17.8	27.3
Base metals and related products	116.8	109.6	138.8
Aluminium bars, rods, etc.	90.8	103.0	114.2
Total (incl. others)	2,197.9	2,599.9	1,243.7

* Estimates.

PRINCIPAL TRADING PARTNERS (£E million)

Imports c.i.f.	1983	1984	1985
Australia	130.2	n.a.	n.a.
Belgium/Luxembourg	133.9	n.a.	n.a.
Czechoslovakia	95.9	67.1	94.8
Finland	83.4	n.a.	n.a.
France	496.6	586.0	490.7
German Dem. Rep.	59.3	65.7	64.9
Germany, Fed. Rep.	763.8	769.2	667.6
Greece	268.8	n.a.	n.a.
India	57.7	n.a.	n.a.
Italy	575.3	644.0	530.1
Japan	357.3	477.9	360.4
Netherlands	251.2	263.3	249.6
Romania	190.1	221.5	258.9
Saudi Arabia	166.8	136.5	50.5
Spain	244.8	n.a.	n.a.
Sudan	53.4	81.7	105.6
Sweden	140.6	n.a.	n.a.
Switzerland	150.6	n.a.	n.a.
Turkey	59.2	n.a.	n.a.
USSR	140.0	150.8	196.2
United Kingdom	257.9	264.0	297.7
USA	1,160.2	858.6	904.8
Yugoslavia	126.6	157.4	150.2
Total (incl. others)	7,192.7	7,536.1	6,973.1

Exports f.o.b.	1983	1984	1985
China, People's Rep.	20.4	25.8	0.2
Czechoslovakia	35.2	28.9	42.4
France	213.3	144.5	301.0
German Dem. Rep.	18.9	24.0	37.1
Germany, Fed. Rep.	49.3	73.7	56.9
Greece	44.6	n.a.	n.a.
Iraq	2.6	15.1	27.6
Italy	408.0	379.0	459.6
Japan	59.0	70.3	79.7
Lebanon	11.1	9.0	15.7
Netherlands	88.8	114.1	106.4
Romania	84.2	183.9	303.9
Saudi Arabia	57.2	50.8	52.1
Sudan	11.3	20.7	12.2
Switzerland	28.1	n.a.	n.a.
USSR	160.5	116.2	124.3
United Kingdom	34.8	38.2	26.1
USA	148.6	121.9	23.6
Yugoslavia	23.0	22.3	19.5
Total (incl. others)	2,250.3	2,197.9	2,599.9

Transport

RAILWAYS (year ending 30 June)

	1983/84	1984/85	1985/86
Total freight (million ton-km)	2,631	2,792	2,927
Total passengers (million passenger-km)	24,104	26,232	28,350
Track length (km)	5,327	5,367	5,355

ROAD TRAFFIC (motor vehicle licences at 31 December)

	1984	1985	1986
Buses	26,029	28,273	28,441
Tractors	267,975	297,204	325,698
Cars	679,425	719,199	757,925
Motor cycles	223,370	247,182	263,389

SHIPPING (Suez Canal traffic)

	1985	1986	1987
Transits (number)	19,791	18,403	17,541
Displacement ('000 net tons)	352,579	366,076	347,038
Northbound goods traffic ('000 metric tons)	151,901	165,048	152,951
Southbound goods traffic ('000 metric tons)	105,695	97,404	103,984
Net tonnage of tankers ('000)	122,794	138,559	126,275

Source: Suez Canal Authority.

CIVIL AVIATION (traffic on scheduled services)

	1982	1983	1984
Kilometres flown (million)	34.9	36.5	35.3
Passengers carried ('000)	2,433	2,618	2,786
Passenger-km (million)	3,648	4,118	4,386
Freight ton-km (million)	53.5	69.7	88.2

Source: UN, *Statistical Yearbook*.

Tourism

TOURIST ARRIVALS BY REGION ('000)

	1984	1985	1986*
Arabs	596	564	554
Europeans	589	599	525
Americans	227	212	95
Others	148	143	137
Total	1,560	1,518	1,311

* Estimates.

Education

(number of pupils, 1985/86)

	General Education			Azhar Education		
	Male	Female	Total	Male	Female	Total
Primary	3,397,779	2,605,071	6,002,850	131,897	79,503	211,400
Preparatory	1,274,137	860,870	2,135,007	73,776	23,977	97,753
Secondary	881,737	565,028	1,446,765	48,791	13,700	62,491
General	355,454	213,912	569,366	—	—	—
Technical	526,283	351,116	877,399	—	—	—
Teacher training	34,113	50,474	84,587	—	—	—
University	445,963	215,384	661,347	—	—	—

Directory

The Constitution

A new constitution for the Arab Republic of Egypt was approved by referendum on 11 September 1971.

THE STATE

Egypt is an Arab Republic with a democratic, socialist system based on the alliance of the working people and derived from the country's historical heritage and the spirit of Islam.

The Egyptian people are part of the Arab nation, who work towards total Arab unity.

Islam is the religion of the State; Arabic is its official language and the Islamic code is a principal source of legislation. The State safeguards the freedom of worship and of performing rites for all religions.

Sovereignty is of the people alone which is the source of all powers.

The protection, consolidation and preservation of the socialist gains is a national duty: the sovereignty of law is the basis of the country's rule, and the independence of immunity of the judiciary are basic guarantees for the protection of rights and liberties.

THE FUNDAMENTAL ELEMENTS OF SOCIETY

Social solidarity is the basis of Egyptian society, and the family is its nucleus.

The State ensures the equality of men and women in both political and social rights in line with the provisions of Muslim legislation.

Work is a right, an honour and a duty which the State guarantees together with the services of social and health insurance, pensions for incapacity and unemployment.

The economic basis of the Republic is a socialist democratic system based on sufficiency and justice in a manner preventing exploitation.

Ownership is of three kinds, public, co-operative and private. The public sector assumes the main responsibility for the regulation and growth of the national economy under the development plan.

Property is subject to the people's control.

Private ownership is safeguarded and may not be sequestrated except in cases specified in law nor expropriated except for the general good against fair legal compensation. The right of inheritance is guaranteed in it.

Nationalization shall only be allowed for considerations of public interest in accordance with the law and against compensation.

Agricultural holding may be limited by law.

The State follows a comprehensive central planning and compulsory planning approach based on quinquennial socio-economic and cultural development plans whereby the society's resources are mobilized and put to the best use.

The public sector assumes the leading role in the development of the national economy. The State provides absolute protection of this sector as well as the property of co-operative societies and trade unions against all attempts to tamper with them.

PUBLIC LIBERTIES, RIGHTS AND DUTIES

All citizens are equal before the law. Personal liberty is a natural right and no one may be arrested, searched, imprisoned or restricted in any way without a court order.

Houses have sanctity, and shall not be placed under surveillance or searched without a court order with reasons given for such action.

The law safeguards the sanctities of the private lives of all citizens; so have all postal, telegraphic, telephonic and other means of communication which may not therefore be confiscated, or perused except by a court order giving the reasons, and only for a specified period.

Public rights and freedoms are also inviolate and all calls for atheism and anything that reflects adversely on divine religions are prohibited.

The freedom of opinion, the Press, printing and publications and all information media are safeguarded.

Press censorship is forbidden, so are warnings, suspensions or cancellations through administrative channels. Under exceptional circumstances as in cases of emergency or in war time, censorship may be imposed on information media for a definite period.

Egyptians have the right to permanent or provisional emigration and no Egyptian may be deported or prevented from returning to the country.

Citizens have the right to private meetings in peace provided they bear no arms. Egyptians also have the right to form societies which have no secret activities. Public meetings are also allowed within the limits of the law.

SOVEREIGNTY OF THE LAW

All acts of crime should be specified together with the penalties for the acts.

Recourse to justice, it says, is a right of all citizens, and those who are financially unable, will be assured of means to defend their rights.

Except in cases of *flagrante delicto*, no person may be arrested or their freedom restricted unless an order authorizing arrest has been given by the competent judge or the public prosecution in accordance with the provisions of law.

SYSTEM OF GOVERNMENT

The President, who must be of Egyptian parentage and at least 40 years old, is nominated by at least one-third of the members of the People's Assembly, approved by at least two-thirds, and elected by popular referendum. His term is for six years and he 'may be re-elected for another subsequent term'. He may take emergency measures in the interests of the State but these measures must be approved by referendum within 60 days.

The People's Assembly, elected for five years, is the legislative body and approves general policy, the budget and the development plan. It shall have 'not less than 350' elected members, at least half of whom shall be workers or farmers, and the President may appoint up to 10 additional members. In exceptional circumstances the Assembly, by a two-thirds vote, may authorize the President to rule by decree for a specified period but these decrees must be approved by the Assembly at its next meeting. The law governing the composition of the People's Assembly was amended in May 1979 (see People's Assembly, below).

The Assembly may pass a vote of no confidence in a Deputy Prime Minister, a Minister or a Deputy Minister, provided three days' notice of the vote is given, and the minister must then resign. In the case of the Prime Minister, the Assembly may 'prescribe' his responsibility and submit a report to the President: if the President disagrees with the report but the Assembly persists, then the matter is put to a referendum: if the people support the President the Assembly is dissolved; if they support the Assembly the President must accept the resignation of the Government. The President may dissolve the Assembly prematurely, but his action must be approved by a referendum and elections must be held within 60 days.

Executive Authority is vested in the President, who may appoint one or more vice-presidents and appoints all ministers. He may also dismiss the vice-presidents and ministers. The President has 'the right to refer to the people in connection with important matters related to the country's higher interests.' The Government is described as 'the supreme executive and administrative organ of the state'. Its members, whether full ministers or deputy ministers, must be at least 35 years old. Further sections define the roles of Local Government, Specialized National Councils, the Judiciary, the Higher Constitutional Court, the Socialist Prosecutor General, the Armed Forces and National Defence Council and the Police.

POLITICAL PARTIES

In June 1977 the People's Assembly adopted a new law on political parties, which, subject to certain conditions, permitted the formation of political parties for the first time since 1953. The law was passed in accordance with Article Five of the Constitution which describes the political system as 'a multi-party one' with four main parties: 'the ruling National Democratic Party, the Socialist Workers (the official opposition), the Liberal Socialists and the Unionist Progressive'. (The legality of the re-formed New Wafd Party was established by the courts in January 1984.)

1980 AMENDMENTS

On 30 April 1980 the People's Assembly passed a number of amendments, which were subsequently massively approved at a referendum the following month. A summary of the amendments follows:

(i) the regime in Egypt is socialist-democratic, based on the alliance of working people's forces.

(ii) the political system depends on multiple political parties; the Arab Socialist Union is therefore abolished.

(iii) the President is elected for a six-year term and can be elected for 'other terms'.

(iv) the President shall appoint a Consultative Council to preserve the principles of the revolutions of 23 July 1952, and 15 May 1971.

(v) a Supreme Press Council shall safeguard the freedom of the press, check government censorship and look after the interests of journalists.

(vi) Egypt's adherence to Islamic jurisprudence is affirmed. Christians and Jews are subject to their own jurisdiction in personal status affairs.

(vii) there will be no distinction of race or religion.

The Government

THE PRESIDENCY

President: MUHAMMAD HOSNI MUBARAK (confirmed as President by referendum, 13 October 1981, after assassination of President Sadat; re-elected and confirmed by referendum 5 October 1987).

Vice-President: (vacant).

COUNCIL OF MINISTERS
(January 1989)

Prime Minister and Minister of International Co-operation: Dr ATIF SIDQI.

Deputy Prime Minister and Minister of Defence and Military Production: Field-Marshal MUHAMMAD ABD AL-HALIM ABU GHAZALAH.

Deputy Prime Minister and Minister of Foreign Affairs: Dr AHMAD ESMAT ABD AL-MEGUID.

Deputy Prime Minister and Minister of Planning: Dr KAMAL AHMAD AL-GANZURI.

Deputy Prime Minister and Minister of Agriculture and Land Reclamation: Dr YOUSUF AMIN WALI.

Minister of Finance: Dr MUHAMMAD AHMAD AR-RAZZAZ.

Minister of Social Insurance and Social Affairs: Dr AMAL ABD AR-RAHIM OSMAN.

Minister of Manpower and Vocational Training: ASIM ABD AL-HAQ SALIH.

Minister of Justice: FAROUK SAYF AN-NASR.

EGYPT

Minister of Transport, Communications and Naval Transport: Eng. SULAYMAN MUTAWALLI SULAYMAN.
Minister of Electricity and Energy: Eng. MUHAMMAD MAHIR ABAZAH.
Minister of Culture: FAROUK HOSNI.
Minister of Information: MUHAMMAD SAFWAT MUHAMMAD YOUSUF ASH-SHARIF.
Minister of Health: Dr MUHAMMAD RAGIB DUWAYDAR.
Minister of Tourism and Civil Aviation: Dr FOUAD SULTAN.
Minister of Economy and Foreign Trade: Dr YUSRI ALI MUSTAFA.
Minister of Supply and Internal Trade: Dr MUHAMMAD JALAL AD-DIN ABU ADH-DHAHAB.
Minister of the Interior: Maj.-Gen. ZAKI BADR.
Minister of Industry: Eng. MUHAMMAD FARAG ABD AL-WAHHAB.
Minister of Petroleum and Mineral Resources: ABD AL-HADI MUHAMMAD KANDIL.
Minister of Works and Water Resources: Eng. ISAM RADI ABD AL-HAMID RADI.
Minister of Cabinet Affairs and Minister of State for Administrative Development: Dr ATIF MUHAMMAD OBEID.
Minister of National Education: Dr AHMAD FATHI SURUR.
Minister of Development, Housing, Utilities and New Communities: Eng. HASABALLAH MUHAMMAD AL-KAFRAWI.
Minister of Awqaf (Islamic Endowments): Dr MUHAMMAD ALI MAHGOUB.
Minister for People's Assembly and Shura (Advisory) Council Affairs: Dr AHMAD SALAMAH MUHAMMAD.
Minister of State for Foreign Affairs: Dr BOUTROS BOUTROS GHALI.
Minister of State for Military Production: Dr GAMAL AS-SAYED IBRAHIM.
Minister of State for Immigration and Egyptian Expatriates: Dr FOUAD ISKANDAR.
Minister of State for Scientific Research: Dr ADEL ABD AL-HAMID IZZ.
Minister of State for International Co-operation: Dr MAURICE MAKRAMALLAH.
Minister of State for People's Assembly and Shura (Advisory) Council Affairs: (vacant).

MINISTRIES

Ministry of Agriculture: Sharia Wizaret az-Ziraa, Dokki, Giza; tel. (02) 702677.
Ministry of Awqaf: Sharia Sabri Abu Alam, Ean el-Luk, Cairo; tel. (02) 746305.
Ministry of Civil Aviation: Sharia Matar, Cairo (Heliopolis); tel. (02) 969555.
Ministry of Communications: 26 Sharia Ramses, Cairo; tel. (02) 909090.
Ministry of Culture: 110 Sharia al-Galaa, Cairo; tel. (02) 971995.
Ministry of Development, New Communities, Housing and Public Utilities: 1 Ismail Abaza, Qasr el-Eini, Cairo; tel.: Development (02) 3540419; New Communities (02) 3540590; Public Utilities (02) 3540110; telex: Development and New Communities 20807; Public Utilities 92188.
Ministry of Economic Co-operation: 9 Sharia Adly, Cairo; telex 348.
Ministry of Economy: 8 Sharia Adly, Cairo; tel. (02) 907344.
Ministry of Education: Sharia el-Falaky, Cairo; tel. (02) 8544805.
Ministry of Scientific Research: 4 Sharia Ibrahim Nagiv, Cairo (Garden City).
Ministry of Electricity and Energy: Cairo (Nasr City); tel. (02) 829565.
Ministry of Finance: Sharia Maglis esh-Sha'ab, Lazoughli Sq., Cairo; tel. (02) 24857; telex 92169.
Ministry of Foreign Affairs: Tahrir Sq., Cairo; telex 92220.
Ministry of Foreign Trade: Lazoghli Sq., Cairo; tel. (02) 25424.
Ministry of Health: Sharia Magles esh-Sha'ab, Cairo; tel. (02) 903939; telex 94107.
Ministry of Industry and Mineral Resources: 2 Sharia Latin America, Cairo (Garden City); tel. (02) 3550641; telex 93112.
Ministry of Information: Radio and TV Bldg, Corniche en-Nil, Cairo (Maspiro); tel. (02) 974216.
Ministry of Irrigation: Sharia Qasr el-Eini, Cairo; tel. (02) 3552120.
Ministry of Justice: Justice Bldg, Cairo (Lazoughli); tel. (02) 31176.

Directory

Ministry of Land Reclamation: Land Reclamation Bldg, Dokki, Giza; tel. 703011.
Ministry of Manpower and Vocational Training: Sharia Yousuf Abbas, Nasr City, Abbasia, Cairo.
Ministry of Military Production: 5 Sharia Ismail Abaza, Kasr el-Eini, Cairo; tel. (02) 3553063; telex 92167.
Ministry of Naval Transport: 4 Sharia el-Bataisa, Alexandria; tel. 35763; telex 54147.
Ministry of Petroleum: 2 Sharia Latin America, Cairo (Garden City); tel. (02) 3545022; telex 92197.
Ministry of Planning: Sharia Salah Salem, Cairo (Nasr City); tel. (02) 837868.
Ministry of Social Affairs: Sharia Sheikh Rihan, Cairo; telex 94105.
Ministry of Social Insurance: 3 Sharia el-Alfi, Cairo; tel. (02) 922717.
Ministry of Supply and Internal Trade: 99 Sharia Qasr el-Eini, Cairo; tel. (02) 3552600; telex 93497.
Ministry of Tourism: Misr Travel Tower, Abbassia Sq., Cairo; tel. (02) 2828450; telex 94040.
Ministry of Transport: Sharia Qasr el-Eini, Cairo; tel. (02) 3557402; telex 92802.

Legislature

MAJLIS ASH-SHA'AB
(People's Assembly)

The law governing election to, and the composition of, the People's Assembly was amended on 20 July 1983. Parties are now required to gain a minimum of 8% of the total vote to be represented in the Assembly. Votes for parties which fail to cross the 8% threshold are transferred to the leading party. There are now 48 constituencies, which each elect between three and 12 members to the Assembly. In 31 constituencies, an extra member, who must be a woman, is automatically added to the list of elected members from the majority party. Ten members are appointed by the President, giving a total of 458 seats.

Speaker: Dr RIFA'AT EL-MAHGOUB.
Deputy Speakers: IHAB MAQLAD (workers), AHMAD MOUSSA (professions).
Leader of the Opposition: IBRAHIM SHUKRI (Socialist Labour Party).

Elections, 6 April 1987

Party	Votes*	%	Seats
National Democratic Party	8,316,000	69.3	346
Socialist Labour Party Coalition	2,040,000	17	60
Socialist Labour Party	n.a.	n.a.	20
Liberal Socialist Party	n.a.	n.a.	3
Muslim Brotherhood	n.a.	n.a.	37
New Wafd Party	1,308,000	10.9	35
National Progressive Unionist Party†	n.a.	n.a.	—
Umma Party†	n.a.	n.a.	—
Independents	n.a.	n.a.	7
Total	12,000,000	100.0	448‡

* Estimates.
† These parties failed to win the minimum of 8% of the total vote required for representation in the People's Assembly, and their votes were transferred to the National Democratic Party.
‡ There are, in addition, 10 members appointed by the President.

MAJLIS ASH-SHURA
(Advisory Council)

In September 1980 elections were held for a 210-member **Shura (Advisory) Council**, which replaced the former Central Committee of the Arab Socialist Union. Of the total number of members, 140 are elected and the remaining 70 are appointed by the President. The National Democratic Party holds all the elected seats. The opposition parties boycotted elections to the Council in October 1983, and again in October 1986, in protest against the 8% electoral threshold.

Speaker: Dr ALI LUTFI.
Deputy Speakers: THARWAT ABAZAH, AHMAD AL-IMADI.

Political Organizations

Ikhwan (Brotherhood): f. 1928; officially illegal, the (Muslim) Brotherhood advocates the adoption of the Shari'a, or Islamic law,

EGYPT

as the sole basis of the Egyptian legal system; leaders include AHMAD EL-BANNA, son of HASSAN EL-BANNA, the founder of the movement.

Liberal Socialist Party: Cairo; f. 1976; advocates expansion of 'open door' economic policy and greater freedom for private enterprise; Leader MUSTAFA KAMEL MURAD.

National Democratic Party: Cairo; f. July 1978; government party established by Anwar Sadat; has absorbed Arab Socialist Party; Leader MUHAMMAD HOSNI MUBARAK; Sec.-Gen. Dr YOUSUF AMIN WALI; Political Bureau: Chair. MUHAMMAD HOSNI MUBARAK; mems: KAMAL HASSAN ALI, Dr MUSTAFA KHALIL, Dr RIFA'AT EL-MAHGOUB, Dr SUBHI ABD AL-HAKIM, Dr MUSTAFA KAMAL HILMI, FIKRI MAKRAM OBEID, Dr ISMAT ABD AL-MEGUID, Dr AMAL OSMAN, SAFWAT ASH-SHARIF, Dr YOUSUF AMIN WALI, HASSAN ABU BASHA, KAMAL HENRY BADIR, Dr AHMAD HEIKAL.

National Progressive Unionist Party (Tagammu): 1 Sharia Karim ed-Dawlah, Cairo; f. 1976; left wing; Leader KHALED MOHI ED-DIN; Sec. Dr RIFA'AT ES-SAID; 160,000 mems.

New Wafd Party: Cairo; original Wafd Party f. 1919; banned 1952; re-formed as New Wafd Party February 1978; disbanded June 1978; re-formed August 1983; Leader FOUAD SERAG ED-DIN; Sec.-Gen. IBRAHIM FARAG.

Socialist Labour Party: 12 Sharia Awali el-Ahd, Cairo; f. September 1978; official opposition party; Leader IBRAHIM SHUKRI.

Umma (National) Party: Islamic religious party, based in Khartoum, Sudan; Leader SADIQ AL-MAHDI (Prime Minister of Sudan).

Diplomatic Representation

EMBASSIES IN EGYPT

Afghanistan: *Interests served by India.*
Albania: 29 Sharia Ismail Muhammad, Cairo (Zamalek); tel. (02) 3415651; Ambassador: ALKYZ CERGA.
Algeria: *Interests served by India.*
Angola: 12 Midan en-Nasr, Cairo (Dokki); tel. (02) 707602; Ambassador: KAMU D'ALMEIDA.
Argentina: 8 Sharia as-Saleh Ayoub, Cairo (Zamalek); tel. (02) 3401501; Ambassador: (vacant).
Australia: 5th Floor, South Bldg, Cairo Plaza Annexe, Corniche en-Nil, Cairo; tel. (02) 777900; telex 92257; Ambassador: KENNETH ROGERS.
Austria: Sharia en-Nil, Cnr of Sharia Wissa Wassef, Cairo (Giza); tel. (02) 737640; telex 92258; Ambassador: FRANZ BOGEN.
Bahrain: *Interests served by Pakistan.*
Bangladesh: 18 Sharia Souris, Madinet el-Mohandessin, Cairo (Dokki); tel. (02) 3490646; Ambassador: HEDAYET AHMAD.
Belgium: 20 Sharia Kamel esh-Shennawi, Cairo (Garden City); tel. (02) 3547494; telex 92264; Ambassador: JACQUES GÉRARD.
Bolivia: Cairo; tel. (02) 3550917; Chargé d'affaires (a.i.): ENRIQUE SORIA NAU.
Brazil: 1125 Corniche en-Nil, 11561 Cairo (Maspiro); tel. (02) 756938; telex 92044; Ambassador: IVAN VELLOSO DA SILVEIRA BATALHA.
Brunei: Room 401, Nile Hilton, Tahrir Sq., Cairo; tel. (02) 750666.
Bulgaria: 141 Sharia Tahrir, Cairo (Dokki); tel. (02) 982691.
Burkina Faso: Ramses Centre, 3 Sharia Abd al-Khawi Ahmad, POB 306, Cairo; tel. (02) 3440301; telex 93871; Ambassador: YAYA GNESSIEN.
Burma: 24 Sharia Muhammad Mazhar, Cairo (Zamalek); tel. (02) 3404176; Ambassador: U AYE THEIN.
Burundi: 13 Sharia el-Israa, Madinet el-Mohandessin, Cairo (Dokki); tel. (02) 3419940; telex 20091; Ambassador: ZACHARIE BANYIYEZAKO.
Cameroon: POB 2061, 42 Sharia Babel, Cairo (Dokki); tel. (02) 704843; telex 92088; Ambassador: MOUCHILI NJI MFOUAYO.
Canada: 6 Sharia Muhammad Fahmy es-Sayed, Cairo (Garden City); tel. (02) 3543110; telex 92677; Ambassador: MARC PERRON.
Central African Republic: 13 Sharia Chehab, Madinet el-Mohandessin, Cairo (Dokki); tel. (02) 713291; Ambassador: PIERRE FIDÈLE BAKRI.
Chad: POB 1869, 31 Sharia Adnan Oumar Sedki, Cairo (Dokki); tel. (02) 703232; telex 92285; Ambassador: MADJIMBANG MBAIDA JOSEPH.
Chile: 5 Sharia Chagaret ed-Dorr, Cairo (Zamalek); tel. (02) 3408711; telex 92519; Ambassador: CARLOS MEIRELLES MULLER.
China, People's Republic: 14 Sharia Bahgat Aly, Cairo (Zamalek); tel. (02) 3417691; Ambassador: ZHAN SHILIANG.

Colombia: Apt 141, 1 Sharia Sad el-Ali, Cairo (Dokki); tel. (02) 713233; Ambassador: VIRGINIA OBREGÓN BORRERO.
Côte d'Ivoire: 39 Sharia el-Kods esh-Sherif, Madinet el-Mohandessin, Cairo (Dokki); tel. (02) 699009; telex 2334; Ambassador: KOUAME KOFFI.
Cuba: 2 Sharia el-Aanab, Madinet el-Mohandessin, Cairo (Dokki); tel. (02) 704507; telex 93966; Ambassador: LUIS KARAKADZE BERRAYARZA.
Cyprus: 23A Sharia Ismail Muhammad, Cairo (Zamalek); tel. (02) 3411288; telex 92059; Ambassador: ALECOS H. SHAMBOS.
Czechoslovakia: 4 Sharia Dokki, Cairo (Giza); tel. (02) 3485531; Ambassador: MILOS VESELY.
Denmark: 12 Sharia Hassan Sabri, Cairo (Zamalek); tel. (02) 3407411; telex 92254; Ambassador: JØRGEN BØJER.
Djibouti: 157 Sharia Sudan, Madinet el-Mohandessin, Cairo (Dokki); tel. (02) 709787; telex 93143.
Ecuador: 8 Sharia Abd ar-Rahman Fahmy, Cairo (Garden City); tel. (02) 3546372; Ambassador: LUCINDO ALMEIDA.
Ethiopia: 12 Midan Bahlawi, Cairo (Dokki); tel. (02) 705372; Ambassador: Ato BETROU KIDANE MARIAM.
Finland: 10 Sharia el-Kamel Muhammad, Cairo (Zamalek); tel. (02) 3411487; Ambassador: ANTTI HYNNINEN.
France: 29 ave en-Nil, Cairo (Giza); tel. (02) 728346; telex 92032; Ambassador: PIERRE HUNT; also looks after Lebanese interests at 5 Sharia Ahmad Nessim, Cairo (Giza); tel. (02) 728454; telex 92227.
Gabon: 15 Sharia Mossadek, Cairo (Dokki); tel. (02) 702963; telex 92323; Ambassador: ALAIN MAURICE MAYOMBO.
German Democratic Republic: 13 Sharia Hussein Wassef, Cairo (Dokki); tel. (02) 3484500; telex 22354; Ambassador: WOLFGANG SCHÜSSLER.
Germany, Federal Republic: 8 Sharia Hassan Sabri, Cairo (Zamalek); tel. (02) 3410015; telex 92023; Ambassador: Dr MARTIN ELSÄSSER.
Ghana: 24 Sharia el-Batal Ahmad Abd al-Aziz, Cairo (Dokki); tel. (02) 704275; Ambassador: Dr W. C. YAW ANOFF.
Greece: 18 Sharia Aicha et-Taimouria, Cairo (Garden City); tel. (02) 3550443; telex 92036; Ambassador: PANDEUS MENGLIDIS.
Guatemala: 29 Sharia Dr Muhammad Mandour Madinet Nasr, Cairo; tel. (02) 600371; telex 93242; Ambassador: Gen. FELIPE DOROTEO MONTERROSO MIRANDA.
Guinea: 46 Sharia Muhammad Mazhar, Cairo (Zamalek); tel. (02) 3411088; Ambassador: AMIROU DIALLO.
Guinea-Bissau: 37 Sharia Lebanon, Madinet el-Mohandessin, Cairo.
Holy See: Apostolic Nunciature, Safarat al-Vatican, 5 Sharia Muhammad Mazhar, Cairo (Zamalek); tel. (02) 3402250; Pro-Nuncio: Mgr GIOVANNI MORETTI.
Hungary: 55 Sharia Muhammad Mazhar, Cairo (Zamalek); tel. (02) 3405091; Ambassador: Dr ERNŐ SIMONYI.
India: 5 Sharia Aziz Abaza, Cairo (Zamalek); tel. (02) 3413051; telex 92081; Ambassador: SUDERSHAN KUMAR BHUTANI; also looks after Afghanistan interests at 39 Sharia Orouba (Heliopolis); tel. (02) 666653), Algerian interests at 14 Sharia Brasil (Zamalek) (tel. (02) 3402466).
Indonesia: POB 1661, 13 Sharia Aicha at-Taimouria, Cairo (Garden City); tel. (02) 3547200; Ambassador: R. ACHMAD DJUMIRIL.
Iraq: *Interests served by Yugoslavia.*
Ireland: POB 2681, 3 Sharia Abu el-Feda, Cairo (Zamalek); tel. (02) 3408264; telex 92778; Ambassador: EAMONN O'TUATHAIL.
Israel: 6 Sharia ibn el-Malek, Cairo (Giza); tel. (02) 729329; telex 93363; Ambassador: SHIMON SHAMIR.
Italy: 15 Sharia Abd ar-Rahman Fahmy, Cairo (Garden City); tel. (02) 3553407; telex 94229; Ambassador: GIOVANNI MIGLIUOLO.
Japan: Immeuble Cairo Centre, 3rd Floor, 2 Sharia Abd al-Kader Hamza, 106 Kasr el-Eini; tel. (02) 3551477; telex 92226; Ambassador: HIROSHI HASHIMOTO.
Jordan: 6 Sharia Juhaini, Cairo; tel. (02) 982766; Ambassador: HUSSEIN HAMAMI.
Kampuchea: 2 Sharia Tahawia, Cairo (Giza); tel. (02) 3489966; Ambassador: IN SOPHEAP.
Kenya: POB 362, Cairo (Dokki), 8 Sharia Medina Mounawara; tel. (02) 704546; telex 92021; Ambassador: OCHIENG ADALA.
Korea, Democratic People's Republic: 6 Sharia es-Saleh Ayoub, Cairo (Zamalek); tel. (02) 650970; Ambassador: O CHANG RIM.
Korea, Republic: 6 Sharia el-Hesn, Cairo (Giza); tel. (02) 729162.
Kuwait: 12 Sharia Nabil el-Wakkad, Cairo (Dokki); tel. (02) 701611.
Lebanon: *Interests served by France.*

EGYPT

Liberia: 11 Sharia Brasil, Cairo (Zamalek); tel. (02) 3419864; telex 92293; Ambassador: GABRIEL FARNGALO.

Malaysia: 7 Sharia Wadi en-Nil, Mohandessin, Cairo (Agouza); tel. (02) 699162; Ambassador: ABDULLAH ZAWAWI BIN HAJI MUHAMMAD.

Mali: 3 Sharia al-Kawsar, Cairo (Dokki); tel. (02) 701641; Ambassador: MUPHTAH AG-HAIRY.

Mauritania: 31 Sharia Syria, Cairo (Dokki); tel. (02) 707229; telex 92274.

Mauritius: 72 Sharia Abd el-Moneim Riad, Cairo (Agouza); tel. (02) 3470929; telex 93631; Ambassador: MAHMOOD EDAH TALLY.

Mexico: 5 Sharia Dar es-Shifa, Cairo; tel. (02) 988457; Ambassador: JORGE PALACIOS TREVINO.

Mongolia: 3 Midan en-Nasr, Cairo (Dokki); tel. (02) 650060; Ambassador: SONOMDORJIN DAMBADARJAA.

Morocco: *Interests served by Senegal.*

Nepal: 9 Sharia Tiba, Cairo (Dokki); tel. (02) 704447; Ambassador: KRISHNA BAHADUR MONANDHAR.

Netherlands: 18 Sharia Hassan Sabri, Cairo (Zamalek); tel. (02) 3408744; telex 92028; Ambassador: L. J. HANRATH.

Niger: 28 Sharia Pahlaw, Cairo (Dokki); tel. (02) 987740; telex 2880; Ambassador: SORY MAMADOU DIALLO.

Nigeria: 13 Sharia Gabalaya, Cairo (Zamalek); tel. (02) 3406042; telex 92038; Ambassador: U. B. WALI.

Norway: 8 Sharia el-Gezireh, Cairo (Zamalek); tel. (02) 3403340; telex 92259; Ambassador: KNUT MORKVED.

Oman: 30 Sharia el-Montazah, Cairo (Zamalek); tel. (02) 3407811; telex 92272; Ambassador: GHALEB ABDULLAH JOUBRAN.

Pakistan: 8 Sharia es-Salouli, Cairo (Dokki); tel. (02) 3487677; Ambassador: MIAN MOHAMMAD ISMAIL QURESHI; also looks after Bahrain interests at 8 Sharia Jamaiat an-Nisr, Cairo (Dokki); tel. (02) 705052; telex 2084.

Panama: Apt 9, 97 Sharia Mirghani, Cairo (Heliopolis); tel. (02) 662547; telex 92776; Ambassador: MARCO OCTAVIO AROSEMENA JAÉN.

Peru: 11 Sharia Brasil, Cairo (Zamalek); tel. (02) 3411754; telex 93663; Ambassador: JORGE PLASENCIA.

Philippines: 5 Sharia ibn el-Walid, Cairo (Dokki); tel. (02) 3480396; telex 92446; Ambassador: KASAN A. MAROHOMBSAR.

Poland: 5 Sharia el-Aziz Osman, Cairo (Zamalek); tel. (02) 3409583; Ambassador: (vacant).

Portugal: 15A Sharia Mansour Muhammad, Cairo (Zamalek); tel. (02) 3405583; telex 20325; Ambassador: JOSÉ DE MATTOS-PARREIRA.

Qatar: 10 Sharia ath-Thamar, Midan an-Nasr, Madinet al-Mohandessin, Cairo; tel. (02) 704537; telex 92287.

Romania: 6 Sharia Kamel Muhammad, Cairo (Zamalek); tel. (02) 3409546; telex 93807; Ambassador: ION COZMA.

Rwanda: 9 Sharia Ibrahim Osman, Mohandessin, Cairo, POB 485; tel. (02) 361079; telex 92552; Ambassador: JEAN NTIGURA.

Saudi Arabia: 12 Sharia al-Kamel Muhammad, Cairo (Zamalek); tel. (02) 819111; Ambassador: ASSAD ABUNASR.

Senegal: 46 Sharia Abd al-Moneim Riad, Mohandessin, Cairo (Dokki); tel. (02) 3458479; telex 92047; Ambassador: SHAMS ED-DINE NDOYE; also looks after Moroccan interests at 10 Sharia Salah ed-Din Ayoub, Cairo (Zamalek), and Tunisian interests at 26 Sharia el-Jazirah, Cairo (Zamalek); tel. (02) 3404940.

Sierra Leone: 6 Sharia Hindawi, Midan Finny, Cairo (Dokki); tel. (02) 700699; Ambassador: (vacant).

Singapore: POB 356, 40 Sharia Babel, Cairo (Dokki); tel. (02) 704744; telex 21353; Ambassador: TAN KENG JIN.

Somalia: 38 Sharia esh-Shahid Abd el-Moneim Riad, Cairo (Dokki); tel. (02) 704038; Ambassador: HUSSEIN HASSAN FAREH.

Spain: 9 Hod el-Laban, Cairo (Garden City); tel. (02) 3547069; telex 92255; Ambassador: CARLOS FERNÁNDEZ-LONGORIA.

Sri Lanka: POB 1157, 8 Sharia Sri Lanka, Cairo (Zamalek); tel. (02) 3417138; telex 23375; Ambassador: T. D. S. A. DISSANAYAKE.

Sudan: 4 Sharia el-Ibrahimi, Cairo (Garden City); tel. (02) 3549661; Ambassador: AL-AMIN ABD AL-LATIF.

Sweden: POB 131, 13 Sharia Muhammad Mazhar, Cairo (Zamalek); tel. (02) 3414132; telex 92256; Ambassador: LARS-OLOF BRILIOTH.

Switzerland: 10 Sharia Abd al-Khalek Saroit, POB 633, Cairo; tel. (02) 758133; telex 92267; Ambassador: CLAUDIO CARATSCH.

Tanzania: 9 Sharia Abd al-Hamid Lotfi, Cairo (Dokki); tel. (02) 704155; telex 23537; Ambassador: MUHAMMAD A. FOUM.

Thailand: 2 Sharia al-Malek el-Afdal, Cairo (Zamalek); tel. (02) 3408356; telex 94231; Ambassador: CHAMRAS CHOMBHUBOL.

Tunisia: *Interests served by Senegal.*

Turkey: ave en-Nil, Cairo (Giza); tel. (02) 726115; Ambassador: BERDUK OLGAÇAY; also looks after United Arab Emirates interests at 4 Sharia ibn Sina, al-Gezira, Cairo; tel. (02) 729955.

Uganda: 9 Midan el-Messaha, Cairo (Dokki); tel. (02) 3485544; telex 92087; Ambassador: DAUDI M. TALIWAKU.

USSR: 95 Sharia Giza, Cairo (Giza); tel. (02) 731416; Ambassador: GENNADI ZHURAVLEV.

United Arab Emirates: *Interests served by Turkey.*

United Kingdom: Sharia Ahmad Raghab, Cairo (Garden City); tel. (02) 3540852; telex 94188; Ambassador: WILLIAM JAMES ADAMS.

USA: 5 Sharia Latin America, Cairo (Garden City); tel. (02) 3557371; telex 93773; Ambassador: FRANK G. WISNER.

Uruguay: 6 Sharia Lotfallah, Cairo (Zamalek); tel. (02) 3415137; telex 92435; Ambassador: RAMIRO PIRIZ BALLÓN.

Venezuela: 15A Sharia Mansour Muhammad, Cairo (Zamalek); tel. (02) 3413517; telex 93638; Ambassador: Dr JOSÉ A. MARTÍNEZ-RAMÍREZ.

Viet-Nam: 47 Sharia Ahmad Hishmat, Cairo (Zamalek); tel. (02) 3402401; Ambassador: VU BACH MAI.

Yemen Arab Republic: Cairo.

Yugoslavia: 33 Sharia Mansour Muhammad, Cairo (Zamalek); tel. (02) 3404061; Ambassador: MILAN ZUPAN.

Zaire: 5 Sharia Mansour Muhammad, Cairo (Zamalek); tel. (02) 3403662; telex 92294; Ambassador: NGANDU MWALBA.

Zambia: POB 253, 10 Gomhouriya Mutahada Sq., Madinet el-Mohandessin, Cairo; tel. (02) 709620; telex 92262; Ambassador: KALENGA KANGWA.

Judicial System

The Courts of Law in Egypt are principally divided into two juridical court systems: Courts of General Jurisdiction and Administrative Courts. Since 1969 the Supreme Constitutional Court has been at the top of the Egyptian judicial structure.

THE SUPREME CONSTITUTIONAL COURT

Is the highest court in Egypt. It has specific jurisdiction over: (i) judicial review of the constitutionality of laws and regulations; (ii) resolution of positive and negative jurisdictional conflicts and determination of the competent court between the different juridical court systems, e.g. Courts of General Jurisdiction and Administrative Courts, as well as other bodies exercising judicial competence; (iii) determination of disputes over the enforcement of two final but contradictory judgments rendered by two courts each belonging to a different juridical court system; (iv) rendering binding interpretation of laws or decree laws in the event of a dispute in the application of said laws or decree laws, always provided that such a dispute is of a gravity requiring conformity of interpretation under the Constitution.

COURTS OF GENERAL JURISDICTION

The Courts of General Jurisdiction in Egypt are basically divided into four categories, as follows: (i) The Court of Cassation (ii) The Courts of Appeal; (iii) The Tribunals of First Instance; (iv) The District Tribunals; each of the above courts is divided into Civil and Criminal Chambers.

(i) Court of Cassation: Is the highest court of general jurisdiction in Egypt. Its sessions are held in Cairo. Final judgments rendered by Courts of Appeal in criminal and civil litigation may be petitioned to the Court of Cassation by the Defendant or the Public Prosecutor in criminal litigation and by any of the parties in interest in civil litigation on grounds of defective application or interpretation of the law as stated in the challenged judgment, on grounds of irregularity of form or procedure, or violation of due process, and on grounds of defective reasoning of judgment rendered. The Court of Cassation is composed of the President, 41 Vice-Presidents and 92 Justices.

President: Hon. ABD AL-BORHAN NOOR.

(ii) The Courts of Appeal: Each has geographical jurisdiction over one or more of the governorates of Egypt. Each Court of Appeal is divided into Criminal and Civil Chambers. The Criminal Chambers try felonies, and the Civil Chambers hear appeals filed against such judgment rendered by the Tribunals of First Instance where the law so stipulates. Each Chamber is composed of three superior judges. Each Court of Appeal is composed of President, and sufficient numbers of Vice-Presidents and Superior Judges.

(iii) The Tribunals of First Instance: In each governorate there are one or more Tribunals of First Instance, each of which is divided into several Chambers for criminal and civil litigations.

Each Chamber is composed of: (a) a presiding judge, and (b) two sitting judges. A Tribunal of First Instance hears, as an Appellate Court, certain litigations as provided under the law.

(iv) District Tribunals: Each is a one-judge ancillary Chamber of a Tribunal of First Instance, having jurisdiction over minor civil and criminal litigations in smaller districts within the jurisdiction of such Tribunal of First Instance.

PUBLIC PROSECUTION

Public prosecution is headed by the Attorney General, assisted by a number of Senior Deputy and Deputy Attorneys General, and a sufficient number of chief prosecutors, prosecutors and assistant prosecutors. Public prosecution is represented at all levels of the Courts of General Jurisdiction in all criminal litigations and also in certain civil litigations as required by the law. Public prosecution controls and supervises enforcement of criminal law judgments.

Attorney General: Hon. RAGGA AL-ARABI.

Prosecutor-General: MUHAMMAD ABD AL-AZIZ EL-GINDI.

ADMINISTRATIVE COURTS SYSTEM
(CONSEIL D'ETAT)

The Administrative Courts have jurisdiction over litigations involving the State or any of its governmental agencies. The Administrative Courts system is divided into two courts: the Administrative Courts and the Judicial Administrative Courts, at the top of which is the High Administrative Court. The Administrative Prosecutor investigates administrative crimes committed by government officials and civil servants.

President of Conseil d'Etat: Hon. MUHAMMAD HILAL QASIM.

Administrative Prosecutor: Hon. RIFA'AT KHAFAGI.

THE STATE COUNCIL

Is an independent judicial body which has the authority to make decisions in administrative disputes and disciplinary cases within the judicial system.

THE SUPREME JUDICIAL COUNCIL

The Supreme Judicial Council was reinstituted in 1984, having been abolished in 1969. It exists to guarantee the independence of the judicial system from outside interference and is consulted with regard to draft laws organizing the affairs of the judicial bodies.

Religion

About 90% of Egyptians are Muslims, and almost all of these follow Sunni tenets. According to government figures from 1986, there are about 2m. Copts (a figure contested by Coptic sources, whose estimates range between 6m. and 7m.), forming the largest religious minority, and about 1m. members of other Christian groups. There is also a small Jewish minority.

ISLAM

Grand Sheikh of al-Azhar: Sheikh JAD AL-HAQ ALI JAD AL-HAQ.

Grand Mufti of Egypt: Dr MUHAMMAD SAYED ATTIYAH TANTAWI.

CHRISTIANITY

Orthodox Churches

Coptic Orthodox Church: POB 9035, Anba Ruess Building, Ramses St, Abbasiya, Cairo; f. AD 61; Leader Pope SHENOUDA III; about 8 million followers in Egypt, Sudan, other African countries, the USA, Canada, Australia, Europe and the Middle East. In September 1981 Pope Shenouda was banished to a monastery by President Sadat, and a committee of five bishops was appointed to administer the Church. This decree was rescinded in April 1982, and the Church's synod was summoned to elect a new pope. However, Pope Shenouda was released from internal exile by President Mubarak and permitted to resume his duties in January 1985.

Greek Orthodox Patriarchate: POB 2006, Alexandria; tel. 36839; f. AD 64; Pope and Patriarch of Alexandria and All Africa His Beatitude PARTHENIOS III; 350,000 mems.

The Roman Catholic Church

Armenian Rite

The Armenian Catholic diocese of Alexandria, with an estimated 1,650 adherents at 31 December 1986, is suffragan to the Patriarchate of Cilicia. The Patriarch is resident in Beirut, Lebanon.

Bishop of Alexandria: RAPHAËL BAYAN, Patriarcat Arménien Catholique, 36 Sharia Muhammad Sabri Abou Alam, Cairo; tel. (02) 758429.

Chaldean Rite

The Chaldean Catholic diocese of Cairo had an estimated 500 adherents at 31 December 1986.

Bishop of Cairo: YOUSUF IBRAHIM SARRAF, Evêché Chaldéen, Sanctuaire Notre Dame de Fatima, 141 Sharia Nouzha, Heliopolis, Cairo; tel. (02) 2455718.

Coptic Rite

Egypt comprises the Coptic Catholic Patriarchate of Alexandria and five dioceses. At 31 December 1985 there were an estimated 150,000 adherents in the country.

Patriarch of Alexandria: His Beatitude STEPHANOS II (ANDREAS GHATTAS), Patriarcat Copte Catholique, 34 Sharia Ibn Sandar, Koubbeh Bridge, Cairo; tel. (02) 2571740.

Latin Rite

Egypt comprises the Apostolic Vicariate of Alexandria (incorporating Heliopolis and Port Said), containing an estimated 7,900 adherents at 31 December 1987.

Vicar Apostolic: Fr EGIDIO SAMPIERI (Titular Bishop of Ida in Mauretania), 10 Sharia Sidi Metwalli, Alexandria; tel. (03) 4836065; also at 2 Sharia Banque Misr, Cairo, and at 30 Sharia Ibrahim, Port Said.

Maronite Rite

The Maronite diocese of Cairo had an estimated 4,500 adherents at 31 December 1986.

Bishop of Cairo: JOSEPH MERHI, Evêché Maronite, 15 Sharia Hamdi, Daher, Cairo; tel. (02) 923327.

Melkite Rite

His Beatitude MAXIMOS V HAKIM (resident in Damascus, Syria) is the Greek-Melkite Patriarch of Antioch, of Alexandria and of Jerusalem.

Patriarchal Vicariate of Egypt and Sudan: Patriarcat Grec-Melkite Catholique, 16 Sharia Daher, Cairo; tel. (02) 905790; 8,000 adherents (31 December 1986); Vicar Patriarchal Mgr PAUL ANTAKI, Titular Archbishop of Nubia.

Syrian Rite

The Syrian Catholic diocese of Cairo had an estimated 2,040 adherents at 31 December 1986.

Bishop of Cairo: BASILE MOUSSA DAOUD, Evêché Syrien Catholique, 46 Sharia Daher, Cairo; tel. (02) 901234.

The Anglican Communion

The Anglican diocese of Egypt, suspended in 1958, was revived in 1974 and became part of the Episcopal Church in Jerusalem and the Middle East, formally inaugurated in January 1976. The Church has four dioceses, and its President is the Bishop in Jerusalem (see the chapter on Israel). The Bishop in Egypt has jurisdiction also over the Anglican chaplaincies in Algeria, Djibouti, Ethiopia, Libya, Somalia and Tunisia.

Bishop in Egypt: Rt Rev. GHAIS ABD AL-MALIK, Diocesan Office, POB 87, Zamalek, Cairo.

Other Christian Churches

Armenian Apostolic Church: 179 ave Ramses, Cairo, POB 48-Faggalah; tel. 901385; Archbishop ZAVEN CHINCHINIAN; 10,000 mems.

Protestant Churches of Egypt: POB 1304, Cairo; tel. (02) 904995; f. 1854, independent since 1926; 200,000 mems (1985); Gen. Sec. Rev. Dr SAMUEL HABIB.

Other denominations active in Egypt include the Coptic Evangelical Church (Synod of the Nile) and the Union of the Armenian Evangelical Churches in the Near East.

JUDAISM

The 1976 census recorded 1,631 Jews in Egypt.

Jewish Community: Office of the Chief Rabbi, Rabbi HAIM DOUEK, 13 Sharia Sebil el-Khazindar, Abbassia, Cairo.

The Press

Despite a fairly high illiteracy rate, the Egyptian Press is well developed. Cairo is the biggest publishing centre in the Middle East.

Legally all newspapers and magazines come under the control of the Supreme Press Council. The four big publishing houses of al-Ahram, Dar al-Hilal, Dar Akhbar al-Yawm and Dar al-Gomhouriya, operate as separate entities and compete with each other commercially. Dar al-Hilal is concerned only with magazines and publishes

EGYPT

Al-Musawar, Hawa'a and *Al-Kawakeb*. Dar Akhbar al-Yawm publishes the daily newspaper *Al-Akhbar*, the weekly newspaper *Akhbar al-Yawm* and the weekly magazine *Akher Saa*.

Dar al-Gomhouriya publishes the daily *Al-Gomhouriya*, the daily English language paper *Egyptian Gazette*, the daily French newspaper *Le Progrès Egyptien* and the afternoon paper *Al-Misaa'*.

The most authoritative daily newspaper is the very old-established *Al-Ahram*. Other popular large circulation magazines are *Rose al-Yousuf, Sabah al-Kheir* and *Al-Iza'a wat-Television*.

In May 1975 President Sadat set up the Supreme Press Council, under the Chairmanship of the First Secretary of the Arab Socialist Union, to supervise the Press.

In November 1978, however, President Sadat abolished the Ministry of Culture and Information, but major papers remained under government ownership. A Press Law of July 1980 liberalized the organization of the major papers and, while continuing to provide for 49% ownership by the employees, arranged for the transfer of the remaining 51% from the defunct Arab Socialist Union to the new Shura (Advisory) Council. The editorial board of a national newspaper should consist of at least five members, headed by an editor-in-chief who is selected by the Shura Council. In June 1984 the Shura Council approved a proposal made by the Supreme Press Council that the posts of chairman of the board and editor-in-chief be held separately and not by one individual.

DAILIES

Alexandria

Barad ach-Charikat (Companies' Post): POB 813, Alexandria; f. 1952; Arabic; evening; commerce, finance, insurance and marine affairs, etc.; Editor S. BENEDUCCI; circ. 15,000.

Al-Ittihad al-Misri (Egyptian Unity): 13 Sharia Sidi Abd ar-Razzak, Alexandria; f. 1871; Arabic; evening; Propr ANWAR MAHER FARAG; Dir HASSAN MAHER FARAG.

Le Journal d'Alexandrie: 1 Sharia Rolo, Alexandria; French; evening; Editor CHARLES ARCACHE.

La Réforme: 8 passage Sherif, Alexandria; f. 1895; French; noon; Propr Comte AZIZ DE SAAB; circ. 7,000.

As-Safeer (The Ambassador): 4 Sharia as-Sahafa, Alexandria; f. 1924; Arabic; evening; Editor MUSTAFA SHARAF.

Tachydromos-Egyptos: 4 Sharia Zangarol, Alexandria; tel. 35650; f. 1879; Greek; morning; liberal; Publr PENY COUTSOUMIS; Editor DINOS COUTSOUMIS; circ. 2,000.

Cairo

Al-Ahram (The Pyramids): Sharia al-Galaa, Cairo; tel. (02) 745666; telex 2001; f. 1875; Arabic; morning, incl. Sundays (international edition published in London, England; North American edition published in New York, USA); Editor and Chair. IBRAHIM NAFEH; circ. 900,000 (weekdays), 1.1m. (Friday).

Al-Akhbar (The News): Dar Akhbar al-Yawm, Sharia as-Sahafa, Cairo; tel. (02) 758888; telex 92215; f. 1952; Arabic; Chair. (vacant); Chief Editor SAID SUNBUL; circ. 789,268.

Arev: 3 Sharia Soliman Halaby, Cairo; tel. 754703; f. 1915; Armenian; evening; official organ of the Armenian Liberal Democratic Party; Editor AVEDIS YAPOUDJIAN.

Egyptian Gazette: 24-26 Sharia Zakaria Ahmad, Cairo; tel. (02) 751511; telex 92475; f. 1880; English; morning; Editor-in-Chief SAMI ESH-SHAHED; circ. 35,000.

Al-Gomhouriya (The Republic): 24 Sharia Zakaria Ahmad, Cairo; tel. (02) 751511; telex 92475; f. 1953; Arabic; morning; Chair. MOHSEN MUHAMMAD; Editor MAHFOUZ AL-ANSARI; circ. 650,000.

Journal d'Egypte, Le: 1 Sharia Borsa Guédida, Cairo; f. 1936; French; morning; Gen. Man. LITA GALLAD; Editor-in-Chief MUHAMMAD RACHAD; circ. 72,000.

Mayo (May): Sharia al-Galaa, Cairo; organ of National Democratic Party; Supervisor MUHAMMAD SAFWAT ASH-SHARIF; circ. 500,000.

Al-Misaa' (The Evening): 24 Sharia Zakaria Ahmad, Cairo; telex 92475; f. 1956; Arabic; evening; Editor-in-Chief HAMDI EN-NAHAS; circ. 105,000.

Misr (Egypt): Cairo; f. 1977; organ of the Arab Socialist Party.

Phos: 14 Sharia Zakaria Ahmad, Cairo; f. 1896; Greek; morning; Editor S. PATERAS; Man. BASILE A. PATERAS; circ. 20,000.

Le Progrès Egyptien: 24 Sharia Zakaria Ahmad, Cairo; tel. (02) 741611; telex 92475; f. 1890; French; morning including Sundays; Editor-in-Chief KHALED ANWAR BAKIR; circ. 21,000.

PERIODICALS

Alexandria

Al-Ahad al-Gedid (New Sunday): 88 Sharia Said M. Koraim, Alexandria; tel. 807874; f. 1936; Editor-in-Chief and Publisher GALAL M. KORAITEM; circ. 60,000.

Alexandria Medical Journal: 4 G. Carducci, Alexandria; f. 1922; English, French and Arabic; quarterly; publ. by Alexandria Medical Assen; Editor AMIN RIDA; circ. 1,500.

Amitié Internationale: 59 avenue Hourriya, Alexandria; tel. 23639; f. 1957; publ. by Assen Egyptienne d'Amitié Internationale; Arabic and French; quarterly; Editor Dr ZAKI BADAOUI.

L'Annuaire des Sociétés Egyptiennes par Actions: 23 Midan Tahrir, Alexandria; f. 1930; annually in December; French; Propr ELIE I. POLITI; Editor OMAR ES-SAYED MOURSI.

L'Echo Sportif: 7 Sharia de l'Archevêché, Alexandria; French; weekly; Propr MICHEL BITTAR.

L'Economiste Egyptien: 11 Sharia de la Poste, Alexandria, POB 847; f. 1901; weekly; Proprs MARGUERITE and JOFFRE HOSNI.

Egypte-Sports-Cinéma: 7 avenue Hourriya, Alexandria; French; weekly; Editor EMILE ASSAAD.

Egyptian Cotton Gazette: POB 433, Alexandria; organ of the Cotton Exporters Association; English; 2 a year; Chief Editor AHMAD H. YOUSSEF.

Egyptian Cotton Statistics: Alexandria; English; weekly.

Egyptian Customs Magazine: 2 Sharia Sinan, Alexandria; deals with invoicing, receipts, etc.; Man. MUHAMMAD ALI EL-BADAWI.

La Gazette d'Orient: 5 Sharia Borsa Guédida, Alexandria; Propr MAURICE BETITO.

Guide des Industries: 2 Sharia Adib, Alexandria; French; annual; Editor SIMON A. BARANIS.

Informateur des Assurances: 1 Sharia Sinan, Alexandria; f. 1936; French; monthly; Propr ELIE I. POLITI; Editor SIMON A. BARANIS.

La Réforme Illustrée: 8 passage Sherif, Alexandria; f. 1925; French; weekly; Propr Comte AZIZ DE SAAB; circ. 20,000.

Répertoire Permanent de Législation Egyptienne: 27 Tariq el-Gaish, Chatby-les-Bains, Alexandria; f. 1932; French and Arabic; Editor V. SISTO.

Sina 'at en-Nassig (L'Industrie Textile): 5 rue de l'Archevêché, Alexandria; Arabic and French; monthly; Editor PHILIPPE COLAS.

Voce d'Italia: 90 Sharia Farahde, Alexandria; Italian; fortnightly; Editor R. AVELLINO.

Cairo

Al-Ahali (The People): 23 Sharia Abd al-Khalek, Tharwat, Cairo; tel. (02) 759114; weekly; published by the National Progressive Unionist Party; Editor-in-Chief MAHMOUD AL-MARAGI.

Al-Ahram al-Iqtisadi (The Economic *Al-Ahram*): Sharia al-Galaa, Cairo; telex 20185; Arabic; weekly; economic and political affairs; owned by Al-Ahram publrs; Chief Editor ISSAM RIFA'AT; circ. 65,000.

Al-Ahrar (The Liberals): Cairo; f. 1977; weekly; published by Liberal Socialist Party; Editor WAHID GHAZI.

Akhbar al-Yaum (Daily News): 6 Sharia as-Sahafa, Cairo; f. 1944; Arabic; weekly (Saturday); Editor-in-Chief IBRAHIM ABU SADAH; Man. Dir TALAAT EZ-ZOHEIRI; circ. 1,087,177.

Akher Sa'a (Last Hour): Dar Akhbar al-Yawm, Sharia as-Sahafa, Cairo; telex 92215; f. 1934; Arabic; weekly (Wednesday); independent; Editor-in-Chief MUHAMMAD WAJDI GANDIL; circ. 97,832.

Al-Azhar: Idarat al-Azhar, Sharia al-Azhar, Cairo; f. 1931; Arabic; Islamic monthly; supervised by the Egyptian Council for Islamic Research of Al-Azhar University; Dir MUHAMMAD FARID WAGDI.

Al-Bitrul (Petroleum): Cairo; monthly; published by the Egyptian General Petroleum Corporation.

Contemporary Thought: University of Cairo, Cairo; quarterly; Editor Dr Z. N. MAHMOUD.

Ad-Da'wa (The Call): Cairo; Arabic; monthly; organ of the Muslim Brotherhood.

Ad-Doctor: 8 Sharia Hoda Shaarawy, Cairo; f. 1947; Arabic; monthly; Editor Dr AHMAD M. KAMAL; circ. 30,000.

Echos: 1-5 Sharia Mahmoud Bassiouni, Cairo; f. 1947; French; weekly; Dir and Propr GEORGES QRFALI.

The Egyptian Mail: 24-26 Sharia Zakaria Ahmad; telex 92475; weekly; Saturday edition of *The Egyptian Gazette*; English; circ. 35,000.

Études Médicales: Collège de la Ste Famille, Faggalah, Cairo; quarterly; Editor HUBERT DE LEUSSE.

Études Scientifiques: Cairo; scientific and technical quarterly; Editor HUBERT DE LEUSSE.

Al-Fusoul (The Seasons): 17 Sharia Sherif Pasha, Cairo; Arabic; monthly; Propr and Chief Editor MUHAMMAD ZAKI ABD AL-KADER.

Al-Garidat at-Tigariyat al-Misriya (The Egyptian Business Paper): 25 Sharia Nubar Pasha, Cairo; f. 1921; Arabic; weekly; circ. 7,000.

EGYPT

Hawa'a (Eve): Dar al-Hilal, 16 Sharia Muhammad Ezz el-Arab, Cairo; telex 92703; women's magazine; Arabic; weekly; Chief Editor SUAD AHMAD HILMI; circ. 160,837.

Al-Hilal Magazine: Dar al-Hilal, 16 Sharia Muhammad Ezz el-Arab, Cairo; telex 92703; f. 1895; Arabic; literary monthly; Editor Dr HUSSAIN MONES.

Industrial Egypt: POB 251, 26A Sharia Sherif Pasha, Cairo; f. 1924; quarterly bulletin and year book of the Federation of Egyptian Industries in English and Arabic; Editor DARWISH M. DARWISH.

Informateur Financier et Commercial: 24 Sharia Soliman Pasha, Cairo; f. 1929; weekly; Dir HENRI POLITI; circ. 15,000.

Al-Iza'a wat-Television (Radio and Television): 13 Sharia Muhammad Ezz el-Arab, Cairo; f. 1935; Arabic; weekly; Editor and Chair. AHMAD BAHGAT; circ. 80,000.

Al-Kerazeh (The Sermon): Cairo; Arabic; weekly newspaper of the Coptic Orthodox Church.

Al-Kawakeb (The Stars): Dar al-Hilal, 16 Sharia Muhammad Ezz el-Arab, Cairo; tel. (02) 27954; f. 1952; Arabic; weekly; film magazine; Editor KAMEL EN-NAGMI; circ. 86,381.

Kitab al-Hilal: Dar al-Hilal, 16 Sharia Muhammad Ezz el-Arab, Cairo; monthly; Founders EMILE and SHOUKRI ZEIDAN; Editor Dr HUSSAIN MONES.

Al-Liwa' al-Islami (Islamic Standard): 11 Sharia Sherif Pasha, Cairo; f. 1982; Arabic; weekly; government paper to promote official view of Islamic revivalism; Propr AHMAD HAMZA; Editor MUHAMMAD ALI SHETA; circ. 30,000.

Lotus Magazine (Afro-Asian Writings): 104 Sharia Qasr el-Eini, Cairo; f. 1968; quarterly; English, French and Arabic.

Magallat al-Mohandeseen (The Engineer's Magazine): 28 avenue Ramses, Cairo; f. 1945; published by The Engineers' Syndicate; Arabic and English; 10 a year; Editor and Sec. MAHMOUD SAMI ABD AL-KAWI.

Al-Magallat az-Zira'ia (The Agricultural Magazine): Cairo; monthly; agriculture; circ. 30,000.

Medical Journal of Cairo University: Manyal University Hospital, Sharia Qasr el-Eini, Cairo; f. 1933; Kasr el-Eini Clinical Society; English; quarterly.

The Middle East Observer: 8 Sharia Chawarby, Cairo; f. 1954; English; weekly; specializing in economics of Middle East and African markets; also publishes supplements on law, foreign trade and tenders; Man. Owner AHMAD FODA; Chief Editor AHMAD SABRI; circ. 30,000.

Al-Musawar: Dar al-Hilal, 16 Sharia Muhammad Ezz el-Arab, Cairo; tel. (02) 27954; telex 92703; f. 1924; Arabic; weekly; Editor-in-Chief MAKRAM MUHAMMAD AHMAD; circ. 130,423.

October: 1119 Sharia Corniche en-Nil, Cairo; tel. (02) 746834; telex 847031; monthly; Chair. and Editor-in-Chief ANIS MANSUR; circ. 140,500.

Al-Omal (The Workers): Cairo; published by the Egyptian Trade Union Federation; Arabic; weekly.

Progrès Dimanche: 24 Sharia Galal, Cairo; tel. 741611; telex 92475; French; weekly; Sunday edition of *Le Progrès Egyptien*; Editor-in-Chief KHALED ANWAR BAKIR.

Riwayat al-Hilal: Dar al-Hilal, 16 Sharia Muhammad Ezz el-Arab, Cairo; Arabic; monthly; Proprs EMILE and SHOUKRI ZEIDAN; Editor Dr HUSSAIN MONES.

Rose al-Yousuf: 89A Sharia Qasr el-Eini, Cairo; f. 1925; Arabic; weekly; political; circulates throughout all Arab countries, includes monthly English section; Chair. of Board ABD AL-AZIZ KHAMIS; Editor MUHAMMAD TUHAMI; Editor English section IBRAHIM EZZAT; circ. 35,000.

As-Sabah (The Morning): 4 Sharia Muhammad Said Pasha, Cairo; f. 1922; Arabic; weekly; Editor MUSTAFA EL-KACHACHI.

Sabah al-Kheir (Good Morning): 18 Sharia Muhammad Said Pasha, Cairo; Arabic; weekly; light entertainment; Chief Editor LOUIS JIRYIS; circ. 70,000.

Ash-Shaab (The People): Sharia Corniche en-Nil, Cairo; organ of Socialist Labour Party; weekly; Editor-in-Chief HAMED ZAIDAN; circ. 50,000.

At-Tahrir (Liberation): 5 Sharia Naguib, Rihani, Cairo; Arabic; weekly; Editor ABD AL-AZIZ SADEK.

At-Taqaddum (Progress): c/o 1 Sharia Jarim ed-Dawlah, Cairo; f. 1978; organ of National Progressive Unionist Party; replaced Al-Ahali.

Tchehreh Nema: 14 Sharia Hassan el-Akbar (Abdine), Cairo; f. 1904; Iranian; monthly; political, literary and general; Editor MANUCHEHR TCHEHREH NEMA MOADEB ZADEH.

Up-to-Date International Industry: 10 Sharia Galal, Cairo; Arabic and English; monthly; foreign trade journal.

Al-Wafd: Cairo; f. 1984; weekly; organ of the New Wafd Party; Editor-in-Chief MUSTAFA SHARDI; circ. 360,000.

Watani (My Country): Cairo; French; weekly newspaper of the Coptic Orthodox Church; Editor MEGUID ATTAIA.

Yulio (July): July Press and Publishing House, Cairo; f. 1986; weekly; Nasserist; Editor ABDULLAH IMAM; and a monthly cultural magazine, Editor MAHMOUD AL-MARAGHI.

NEWS AGENCIES

Middle East News Agency: 4 Sharia Sherifin, Cairo; tel. (02) 346160; f. 1955; regular service in Arabic, English and French; Chair. MUHAMMAD ABD AL-GAWAD MANSOUR; Dir-Gen. and Editor-in-Chief MUSTAFA NAGUIB.

Foreign Bureaux

Agence France-Presse (AFP): 33 Sharia Qasr en-Nil, Apt 12, Cairo; tel. (02) 767044; telex 92225; Correspondent MICHEL GARIN.

Agencia EFE (Spain): 35a Sharia Abul Feda, 4th Floor, Apt 14, Cairo (Zamalek); Correspondent JOSÉ LUIS VIDAL COY.

Agenzia Nazionale Stampa Associata (ANSA) (Italy): 19 Sharia Abd al-Khalek Sarwat, Cairo; tel. (02) 3930403; telex 93365; Chief VITTORIO FRENQUELLUCCI.

Allgemeiner Deutscher Nachrichtendienst (ADN) (German Democratic Republic): 17 Sharia el-Brazil, Apt 59, Cairo (Zamalek); tel. (02) 3404006; telex 92339; Correspondent RAINER HÖHLING.

Associated Press (AP) (USA): 33 Sharia Qasr en-Nil, POB 1077, Cairo; tel. (02) 779089; telex 92211; Chief WILLIAM C. MANN.

Bulgarska Telegrafna Agentsia (BTA) (Bulgaria): 13 Sharia Muhammad Kamel Morsi, Aguza, Cairo; Chief DIMITER MASLAROV.

Deutsche Presse-Agentur (dpa) (Federal Republic of Germany): 33 Sharia Qasr en-Nil, Apt 13/4, Cairo; tel. (02) 3928019; telex 92054; Chief Dr NORBERT HOYER.

Jiji Tsushin-Sha (Japan): Room 12, 5th Floor, 3 Gezira el-Wosta, Cairo (Zamalek); tel. (02) 3401443; telex 20940; Correspondent KYOSUKE NAITO.

Kyodo Tsushin (Japan): 9 Sharia el-Kamel Muhammad, Flat 2, Cairo (Zamalek); tel. (02) 3406105; telex 20435; Correspondent SHIRO ONISHI.

Magyar Távirati Iroda (MTI) (Hungary): 11 Sharia Ahmad Heshmat, Flat 15, Cairo (Zamalek); Chief KÁROLY PATAK.

Reuters (United Kingdom): 21st Floor, Bank Misr Tower, 153 Sharia Muhammad Farid, Cairo, POB 2040; tel. (02) 3925667; telex 92210; Chief Correspondent J. ROGERS.

Telegrafnoye Agentstvo Sovetskovo Soyuza (TASS) (USSR): 30 Sharia Muhammad Mazhar, Cairo (Zamalek); Correspondent YURI TYSOVSKY.

United Press International (UPI) (USA): 4 Sharia Eloui, POB 872, Cairo; Chief WADIE KIROLOS.

Xinhua (New China) News Agency (People's Republic of China): 2 Moussa Galal Sq., Mohandessin, Cairo; tel. (02) 3448950; telex 93812; Dir MU GUANGREN.

The Iraqi News Agency (INA) reopened its office in Cairo in October 1985.

Publishers

General Egyptian Book Organization: 117 Sharia Corniche en-Nil, Cairo; tel. (02) 775000; telex 93932; f. 1961; affil. to Min. of Culture; Chair. Dr EZZ ED-DIN ISMAIL.

Alexandria

Alexandria University Press: Shatby, Alexandria.

Artec: 10 Sharia Stamboul, Alexandria.

Dar Nashr ath-Thaqata: Alexandria.

Egyptian Book Centre: A. D. Christodoulou and Co, 5 Sharia Adib, Alexandria; f. 1950.

Egyptian Printing and Publishing House: Ahmad es-Sayed Marouf, 59 Safia Zaghoul, Alexandria; f. 1947.

Maison Egyptienne d'Editions: Ahmad es-Sayed Marouf, Sharia Adib, Alexandria; f. 1950.

Maktab al-Misri al-Hadith li-t-Tiba wan-Nashr: 7 Sharia Noubar, Alexandria; also at 2 Sharia Sherif, Cairo; Man. AHMAD YEHIA.

Cairo

Al-Ahram Establishment: Sharia al-Galaa, Cairo; tel. (02) 758333; telex 92001; f. 1875; publishes newspapers, magazines and books, incl. *Al-Ahram*; Chair. ABDALLA ABD AL-BARI.

Akhbar al-Yawm Publishing House: 6 Sharia as-Sahafa, Cairo; f. 1944; publishes *Al-Akhbar* (daily), *Akhbar al-Yawm* (weekly),

EGYPT

and colour magazine *Akher Sa'a*; Pres. MOUSA SABRI; Dir-Gen. AMIN ADLY.

Al-Arab: 28 Sharia Faggalah, Cairo; tel. (02) 908025; f. 1900; fiction, poetry, history, biography, philosophy, religion, Arabic language and literature etc.; Man. Dir Dr SALADIN BOUSTANI.

Argus Press: 10 Sharia Zakaria Ahmad, Cairo; Owners KARNIG HAGOPIAN and ABD AL-MEGUID MUHAMMAD.

Dar al-Gomhouriya: 24 Sharia Zakaria Ahmad, Cairo; affiliate of At-Tahrir Printing and Publishing House; publications include the dailies, *Al-Gomhouriya, Al-Misaa', Egyptian Gazette* and *Le Progrès Egyptien*; Pres. MOHSEN MUHAMMAD.

Dar al-Hilal Publishing Institution: 16 Sharia Muhammad Ezz el-Arab, Cairo; tel. (02) 20610; telex 92703; f. 1892; publishes *Al-Hilal, Riwayat al-Hilal, Kitab al-Hilal, Tabibak al-Khass* (monthlies); *Al-Mussawar, Al-Kawakeb, Hawaa, Samir, Mickey* (weeklies); Chair. MAKRAN MUHAMMAD AHMAD.

Dar al-Kitab al-Arabi: Misr Printing House, Sharia Noubar, Bab al-Louk, Cairo; f. 1968; Man. Dir Dr SAHAIR AL-KALAMAWI.

Dar al-Kitab al-Masri: POB 156, Cairo; tel. (02) 742168; telex 22481; f. 1929; religion, history, geography, poetry, philosophy, science, etc.; Man. Dir EZ-ZEIN HASSAN.

Dar al-Maaref: 1119 Sharia Corniche en-Nil, Cairo; tel. (02) 777077-87; telex 92199; f. 1890; publishing, printing and distribution of all kinds of books in Arabic and other languages; publishers of *October* magazine; Chair. and Man. Dir SALAH MUNTASSAR.

Dar ash-Shorouk: 16 Sharia Gawad Hosni, Cairo; tel. (02) 774814; telex 93091; f. 1968; publishing, printing and distribution; publishers of books on modern Islamic politics, philosophy and art, and books for children; Chair. M. I. EL-MOALLIM.

Documentation and Research Centre for Education (Ministry of Education): 33 Sharia Falaky, Cairo; f. 1956; Dir Mrs ZEINAB M. MEHREZ; bibliographies, directories, information and education bulletins.

Editions Horus: 1 Midan Soliman Pasha, Cairo.

Editions le Progrès: 6 Sharia Sherif Pasha, Cairo; Propr WADI SHOUKRI.

Editions et Publications des Pères Jésuites: 1 Sharia Boustan al-Maksi, Faggalah, Cairo; religious publications in Arabic.

Les Editions Universitaires d'Egypte: 41 Sharia Sherif Pasha, Cairo; university textbooks.

Egyptian Co for Printing and Publishing: 40 Sharia Noubar, Cairo; tel. (02) 21310; Chair. MUHAMMAD MAHMOUD HAMED.

Higher University Council for Arts, Letters and Sciences: University of Cairo, Cairo.

Lagnat at-Taalif wat-Targama wan-Nashr (Committee for Writing, Translating and Publishing Books): 9 Sharia el-Kerdassi (Abdine), Cairo.

Librairie La Renaissance d'Egypte (Hassan Muhammad & Sons): 9 Sharia Adly, POB 2172, Cairo; f. 1930; Man HASSAN MUHAMMAD; religion, history, geography, medicine, architecture, economics, politics, law, philosophy, psychology, children's books, atlases, dictionaries.

Maktabet Misr: POB 16, 3 Sharia Kamal Sidki, Cairo; tel. (02) 908920; f. 1932; pubs wide variety of fiction, biographies and textbooks for schools and universities; Man. AMIR SAID GOUDA ES-SAHHAR.

Muhammad Abbas Sid Ahmad: 55 Sharia Noubar, Cairo.

National Library Press (Dar al-Kutub): Midan Ahmad Maher, Cairo; bibliographic works.

New Publications: J. Meshaka and Co, 5 Sharia Maspiro, Cairo.

The Public Organization for Books and Scientific Appliances: Cairo University, Orman, Ghiza, Cairo; f. 1965; state organization publishing academic books for universities, higher institutes, etc.; also imports books, periodicals and scientific appliances; Chair. KAMIL SEDDIK; Vice-Chair. FATHY LABIB.

Senouhy Publishers: 54 Sharia Abd al-Khalek Sarwat, Cairo; f. 1956; Dirs LEILA A. FADEL, OMAR RASHAD.

At-Tahrir Printing and Publishing House: 24 Sharia Zakaria Ahmad, Cairo; tel. (02) 751511; telex 92475; f. 1953; affil. to Shura (Advisory) Council; Chair. MOHSEN MUHAMMAD; Man. Dir ABD AL-HAMID HAMROUSH.

Radio and Television

In 1985 there were an estimated 12m. radio receivers and 3.86m. television receivers in use.

RADIO

Egyptian Radio and Television Corporation (ERTV): Radio and TV Building, Sharia Maspiro, Corniche en-Nil, POB 1186, Cairo; tel. (02) 757155; telex 92152; f. 1928; 300 hours daily; Pres. HUSSEIN ENAN; Head of Eng. Section Eng. FAROUK IBRAHIM ALI; Head of Int. and Public Relations and Liaison Officer MUHAMMAD EL-KHATIB. Home Service radio programmes in Arabic, English, French, Armenian, German, Greek, Italian and Hebrew; foreign services in Arabic, English, French, Swahili, Hausa, Bengali, Urdu, German, Spanish, Indonesian, Malay, Thai, Hindi, Pushtu, Persian, Turkish, Somali, Portuguese, Fulani, Italian, Zulu, Shona, Sindebele, Lingala, Afar, Amharic, Yoruba, Wolof, Bambara.

Middle East Radio: Société Egyptienne de Publicité, 24–26 Sharia Zakaria Ahmad, Cairo; f. 1964; commercial service with 500-kW transmitter; UK Agents: Radio and Television Services (Middle East) Ltd, 21 Hertford St, London, W1.

TELEVISION

Egyptian Television Organization: Radio and TV Bldg, Sharia Maspiro, Corniche en-Nil, POB 1186, Cairo; tel. (02) 757155; telex 92152; f. 1960; 22.5 hours daily (three channels); Pres. Mrs SAMIA SADIQ.

Finance

(cap. = capital; auth. = authorized; p.u. = paid up;
dep. = deposits; res = reserves; m. = million; brs = branches;
amounts in £ Egyptian unless otherwise stated)

BANKING

The whole banking system was nationalized in 1961. Since 1974 foreign and private sector banks have been allowed to play a role in the economy, and about 72 joint-venture banks, branches of foreign banks and private banks have been established. More than 200 financial institutions are now operating in Egypt.

Central Bank

Central Bank of Egypt: 31 Sharia Qasr en-Nil, Cairo; tel. (02) 751529; telex 92237; f. 1961; State-owned; cap. 5.0m., dep. 13,671m., res 339.5m., total assets 14,530.2m. (June 1987); 3 brs; Gov. and Chair. Dr MAHMOUD SALAH ED-DIN HAMID.

Commercial and Specialized Banks

Agricultural Bank: there are 17 Agricultural Banks in governorates throughout Egypt.

Alexandria Commercial and Maritime Bank: POB 2376, 85 avenue el-Hourriya, Alexandria 2159; tel. (03) 4921556; telex 54553; f. 1981; cap. p.u. US $32.1m., dep. 142.9m., total assets 212.5m. (Dec. 1987); Chair ADEL GHALEB MAHMOUD; Man. Dir MUHAMMAD MAHMOUD FAHMY.

Bank of Alexandria, SAE: 6 Sharia Salah Salem, Alexandria; and 49 Sharia Kasr en-Nil, Cairo; tel. (03) 806212 (Alexandria), (02) 913822 (Cairo); telex 54107 (Alexandria), 92069 (Cairo); f. 1957; State-owned; cap. p.u. 40m., total assets 5,175m. (Dec. 1986); 91 brs; Chair. ES-SAYED FOUAD M. EL-HABASHI (acting).

Bank of Commerce and Development: 13 Midan 26 July, Sphinx, Mohandessin, Cairo; tel. (02) 3479461; telex 21607; f. 1980; cap. 15m., dep. 260m., res 2.6m., total assets 396m. (Dec. 1986); Chair. Dr ABD AL-AZIZ MUHAMMAD HEGAZI; Vice-Chair and Man. Dir SAMIR MUHAMMAD FOUAD EL-QASRI; 4 brs.

Banque du Caire, SAE: 22 Sharia Adly, POB 1495, Cairo; tel. (02) 931641; telex 92022; f. 1952; State-owned; cap. p.u. 40 m., dep. 4,010.3m., res 126.9m., total assets 5,174.7m. (Dec. 1986); 109 brs; Chair. MAHMOUD HASSAN ALI ABDALLA; Gen. Man MAMDOUH EN-NADOURI.

Banque Misr, SAE: 151 Sharia Muhammad Farid, Cairo; tel. (02) 912711; telex 92242; f. 1920; State-owned since 1960; cap. 40m., dep. 6,297.9m., res 92.2m., total assets 10,289.7m. (June 1986); 300 brs; Chair. MUHAMMAD NABIL IBRAHIM.

Crédit Foncier Egyptien: 11 Sharia el-Mashadi, POB 141, Cairo; tel. (02) 910197; telex 93863; f. 1880; State-owned; cap. p.u. 25m.; Chair. ADEL MAHMOUD ABD AL-BAKI; Gen Man. IBRAHIM ABD AL-HALIM KHOR ED-DIN; 7 brs.

Development Industrial Bank: 110 Sharia el-Galaa, Cairo; tel. (02) 779087; telex 92643; f. 1975; cap. p.u. 34m., dep. 30m., total assets 402m. (Dec 1985); 4 brs; Chair. HUSSAIN MAHMOUD ES-SENNARI.

Egyptian Export Development Bank: Evergreen Bldg, 10 Sharia Talaat Harb, Cairo; f. 1983 to replace National Import-Export Bank; tel. (02) 777033; telex 20850; cap. 35.6m., total assets 89.2m. (Dec. 1986); Chair. Dr HAZEM EL-BEBLAWY.

Egyptian Workers Bank: 90 Sharia el-Galaa, Cairo; telex 23520; f. 1983; Workers Union has a 50% interest, Banque Misr and other Egyptians interests 50%.

EGYPT

Hong Kong Egyptian Bank: Abu el-Feda Bldg, 3 Sharia Abu el-Feda, POB 126 D, Zamalek, Cairo; tel. (02) 3409186; telex 20471; f. 1982; the Hongkong and Shanghai Banking Corporation has a 40% shareholding, Egyptian interests 43%, Egyptian Reinsurance Co 8%, other Arab interests 9%; cap. 16.8m., dep. 194.8m. res 2.6m., total assets 281.8m. (Dec. 1987); 2 brs; Chair. Dr HAMID ABD AL-LATIF ES-SAYEH; Gen. Man. MUHAMMAD A. LATIF NOUR.

National Bank for Development: 5 Sharia el-Borsa el-Gedida, POB 647, Cairo; tel. (02) 763528; telex 20878; f. 1980; cap. p.u. 37.5m., dep. 971.2m., res 10.3m., total assets 1,543.9m. (Dec. 1986); 10 brs; Chair. MUHAMMAD ALI Z. EL-ORABI; Dep. Chair. and Gen. Man. MUHAMMAD IBRAHIM FARID; there are affiliated National Banks for Development in 16 governorates.

National Bank of Egypt: 24 Sharia Sherif, Cairo; tel. (02) 744175; telex 92238; f. 1898; nationalized 1960; handles all commercial banking operations; cap. 40m., dep. 7,327m., total assets 10,820m. (June 1987); Chair. MUHAMMAD NABIL IBRAHIM; Senior Exec. Gen. Man. QASIM BARAKAT; 182 brs.

Commercial International Bank (Egypt), SAE: Nile Tower Bldg, 21-23 Sharia Giza, POB 2430, Giza; tel. (02) 726132; telex 92394; f. 1975; National Bank of Egypt has 51% interest, Chase Manhattan Overseas Corpn 49%; fmrly Chase National Bank (Egypt); name changed 1987; cap. 10m., dep. 774.1m., res 84.8m., total assets 1,102.4m. (Dec. 1986); Chair. and Man. Dir AHMAD ISMAIL; 12 brs.

Principal Bank for Development and Agricultural Credit: 110 Sharia Qasr el-Eini, POB 11612, Cairo; tel. (02) 3551204; telex 93045; f. 1976 to succeed former Credit organizations; State-owned; cap. p.u. 55.7m., dep. 706.9m., res 77.8m, total assets 2,490.9m. (June 1986); Chair. ADEL HUSSEIN EZZI; Gen. Man. ABED AR-RAOUF DEKHEL.

Société Arabe Internationale de Banque: 56 Sharia Gamet ed-Dowal al-Arabia, POB 124, Mohandessin, Giza; tel. (02) 3499460; telex 22087; f. 1976; cap. p.u. US $16m., dep. US $176m., res 7.6m., total assets 220.3m. (Dec. 1986); 3 brs; Chair. Dr HASSAN ABBAS ZAKI; Gen. Man. HISHAM ESH-SHIATI.

Social Bank

Nasser Social Bank: 35 Sharia Qasr en-Nil, POB 2552, Cairo; tel. (02) 744377; telex 92754; f. 1971; State-owned; interest-free savings and investment bank for social and economic activities, participating in social insurance, specializing in financing co-operatives, craftsmen and social institutions; cap. p.u. 20m.; Chair. NASSIF TAHOON.

Multinational Banks

Arab African International Bank: 5 Midan es-Saray al-Koubra, POB 60, Garden City, Maglis esh-Shaab, 11516 Cairo; tel. (02) 3545094; telex 93531; f. 1964; auth. cap. US $500m., cap. p.u. US $400m. (Dec. 1987); commercial investment bank; shareholders are governments of Kuwait, Egypt, Algeria, Jordan and Qatar, Bank Al-Jazira (Saudi Arabia), Rafidain Bank (Iraq), individuals and Arab institutions; Chair. ALI R. AL-BADR; Deputy Chair. and Man. Dir MUHAMMAD ABD AL-MONEIM ROUSHDY; Gen. Mans SAMI EL-HALAWANY, SAMIR HELMY, MOHSEN KHALED; brs in Cairo, Alexandria, Heliopolis, Beirut, Dubai, Abu Dhabi, London (2), Nassau, and New York.

Arab International Bank: 35 Sharia Abd al-Khalek Sarwat, POB 1563, Cairo; tel. (02) 391874; telex 92079; f. 1971 as Egyptian International Bank, renamed 1974; cap. p.u. US $150m., res US $94.8m., dep. US $1,715.4m., total assets US $2,026.6m. (June 1987); offshore bank; aims to promote trade and investment in shareholders' countries and other Arab countries; owned by Egypt, Libya, UAE, Oman, Qatar and private Arab shareholders; Chair. Dr MUSTAFA KHALIL; Man. Dir ABD AL-LATIF A. EL-KIB; 4 brs in Egypt, 1 in Bahrain.

Commercial Foreign Venture Banks

Alexandria-Kuwait International Bank: 10 Sharia Talaat Harb, 4th Floor, POB 92, Maglis esh-Shaab, Cairo; tel. (02) 779776; telex 23535; f. 1978; cap. 17.9m., dep. 338m., res 11m., total assets 410m. (Dec. 1986); Egyptian/Kuwaiti businessmen have 48.4% interest, Bank of Alexandria 25%, Principal Bank for Development and Agric. Credit 4.5%, Egyptian cos 8.8%, UAE cos 13.3%; 5 brs; Chair. and Man. Dir (vacant); Gen. Man. MAMDOUH SHABRI ABOU ALAM; 4 brs.

Alwatany Bank of Egypt: 1113 Sharia Corniche en-Nil, POB 750, Cairo; tel. (02) 740705; telex 93268; f. 1980; cap. p.u. 14m., dep. 214m., res 3m., total assets 331.8m. (Dec. 1986); Chair. FAT'HALLAH RIFA'AT MUHAMMAD; Man. Dir TAWFIQ GAMIL YASSIN; 5 brs.

Arab Land Bank: 33 Sharia Abd al-Khalek Sarwat, POB 26, Cairo; tel. (02) 748506; telex 92208; f. 1958; Egyptian/Jordanian joint venture; cap. p.u. 2m.; Chair. HASSOUMA HASSAN HASIB; 1 br in Egypt, 8 brs in Jordan.

Bank of Credit and Commerce (Misr), SAE: Cairo Centre Building, 106 Sharia Qasr el-Eini, POB 788, Garden City, Cairo; tel. (02) 3557321; telex 20679; f. 1981; member of BCC Group; cap. p.u. 20m., dep. 771.4m., total assets 1,375.3m. (Dec. 1987); 19 brs; Chair. Dr ALY ABD AL-MEGUID ABDOU; Man. Dir SAYED MAZHAR ABBAS.

Banque du Caire Barclays International, SAE: 12 Midan esh-Sheikh Yousuf, POB 2335, Garden City, Cairo; tel. (02) 3549422; telex 93734; founded 1975 as Cairo Barclays Int. Bank; name changed 1983; Banque du Caire has 51%, Barclays Bank 49%; cap. 10m., dep. 322.4m., total assets 475.2m. (Dec. 1987); 2 brs; Chair. MAHMOUD HASSAN ABDALLAH; Joint Man. Dirs MUHAMMAD ABD AL-FATH ABD AL-AZIZ and EGIDIO CUTAYAR.

Banque du Caire et de Paris: 3 Sharia Latin America, Garden City, POB 2441, Cairo; tel. (02) 3548323; telex 93722; f. 1977; Banque du Caire has 51% interest and Banque Nationale de Paris 49%; cap. p.u. 10.3m., dep. 110.7m. (Dec. 1987); Chair. MUHAMMAD ES-SABBAGH; Gen. Man. ADEL KHALIFA TANTAWI; 3 brs.

Cairo Far East Bank: 104 Corniche en-Nil, POB 757, el-Agoza, Cairo; tel. (02) 710280; telex 93977; f. 1978; cap. p.u. 7m., dep. 131.4m., res 16.4m., total assets 202.3m. (Dec. 1986); Chair. Dr AHMAD ABU ISMAIL; Gen. Mans SALEH ABD AL-GAWAD, YOO-SEON LEE; 2 brs.

Crédit International d'Egypte: 2 Sharia Talaat Harb, POB 831, Cairo; tel. (02) 759950; telex 93680; f. 1977; National Bank of Egypt has 51% interest, Crédit Commercial de France 39% and Berliner Handels und Frankfurter Bank 10%; cap. 7m., dep. 83.8m., res 4m., total assets 191.9m. (Dec. 1985); Chair. ABD AL-GHANI HAMID GAMEH; Gen. Man. ANIS RIZKALLAH ABD AL-MALIK.

Delta International Bank: Arab Socialist Union Building, 1113 Corniche en-Nil, POB 1159, Cairo; tel. (02) 753484; telex 93833; f. 1978; cap. p.u. 15m., dep. 621.1m., res 10.7m., total assets 739m. (Dec. 1987); Chair. MAHMOUD SEDQI MOURAD; Gen. Man. IBRAHIM SHEHATA MUSTAFA; 11 brs.

Egyptian American Bank: 4 Sharia Hassan Sabri, Zamalek, POB 1825, Cairo; tel. (02) 651043; telex 92683; f. 1976; Bank of Alexandria has 51% interest and American Express Int. Banking Corpn 49%; dep. 927.5m., total assets 1,133.7m. (Dec. 1987); 10 brs; Chair. ES-SAYED EL-HABASHI; Vice-Chair. and Man. Dir Dr FARID W. SAAD.

Egyptian Gulf Bank: 8–10 Sharia Ahmad Nessim, POB 56, el-Orman, Giza; tel. (02) 736181; telex 20214; f. 1981; cap. p.u. 17.8m., dep. 385m., total assets 506m. (Dec. 1987); 5 brs; Chair. KAMAL HASSAN ALI; Gen. Man. GAMIL HUSSAM ED-DIN ABUS-SU'UD.

Faisal Islamic Bank of Egypt: 1113 Corniche en-Nil, POB 2446, Cairo; tel. (02) 753109; telex 93877; f. 1979; all banking operations conducted according to Islamic principles; auth. cap. US $500m., cap. p.u. US $70m., dep. US $1,505m. (Aug. 1987); Chair. Prince MUHAMMAD AL-FAISAL AS-SAOUD; Gov. Dr MAHMOUD MUHAMMAD EL-HELW; 10 brs.

Misr Exterior Bank, SAE: Cairo Plaza Bldg, Corniche en-Nil, POB 272, Cairo; tel. (02) 778552; telex 94061; f. 1981; Banco Exterior de España has a 40% interest, Banque Misr 40%, Egyptian/Saudi Arabian businessmen 20%; cap. p.u. US $14m., dep. 409m., res 3.6m., total assets 529m. (Dec. 1986); 4 brs; Chair. MUHAMMAD NABIL IBRAHIM; Gen. Mans and Man. Dirs ABDULLAH ABD AL-FATAH TAYEL, AURELIO OLAVARRIETA.

Misr International Bank, SAE: 14 Sharia el-Alfy, POB 631, Cairo; tel. (02) 931002; telex 92688; f. 1975; cap. p.u. 10.9m., dep. 910.3m., total assets 2,238.3m. (Dec. 1987); 7 brs; Chair. MAHMOUD MUHAMMAD MAHMOUD; Vice-Chair. and Man. Dir MUHAMMAD EL-HAFEZ.

Misr-America International Bank: 5 Midan es-Saray el-Kobra, POB 1003, Garden City, Cairo; tel. (02) 3554359; telex 23050; f. 1977; Bank of America has 40%, Banque du Caire 17%, National Bank for Development 17%, Misr Insurance Co 17%, Kuwait Real Estate Bank 4.5% and Red Sea Enterprises 4.5%; cap. p.u. 45m., total assets 330.6m. (Dec. 1985); 5 brs; Chair. Dr MUHAMMAD IBRAHIMY DAKROURY; Man. Dir MICHEL ROWIHAB.

Misr-Romanian Bank, SAE: POB 35, 35 Sharia Abu el-Feda, Zamalek, Cairo; tel. (02) 3419275; telex 93653; f. 1977; Banque Misr has 51% interest, Romanian Bank for Foreign Trade (Bucharest) 19%, Bank for Agriculture and Food Industries (Bucharest) 15%, and Investments Bank (Bucharest) 15%; cap. p.u. US $7.6m., dep. 123.8m., res 19.6m. (Dec. 1986); 2 brs in Egypt, 1 in Romania; Chair. HUSSEIN AMER; Gen. Mans IDITOIU GHEORGHE and BAHIR ABD AL-KERIM FAHMY.

Mohandes Bank: 30 Sharia Ramses, POB 2778, Cairo; tel. (02) 751973; telex 93950; f. 1979; cap. p.u. 12.5m., dep. 236.1m., res 14.6m., total assets 464.1m. (Dec. 1986); Chair. AHMAD ALI KAMAL; Gen. Man. MUHAMMAD ABD AS-SALEM BADR ED-DIN.

Nile Bank, SAE: 35 Sharia Ramses, POB 2741, Cairo; tel. (02) 741417; telex 22344; f. 1978; cap. p.u. US $40m., dep. 317.9m., total assets 557.1m. (Dec. 1987); 13 brs; Chair. and Man. Dir ISSA EL-AYOUTY.

Pyramids Bank (El-Ahram Bank): 12 Sharia Itehad el-Mohameen el-Arab, Garden City, Cairo; tel. (02) 3547112; telex 20623; f. 1980;

EGYPT

cap. p.u. 28m. (Dec. 1986); Chair. Dr TAHER AMIN HASSAN; Gen. Man. MUHAMMAD ABD AL-WAHAB.

Suez Canal Bank: 11 Sharia Muhammad Sabry Abu Alam, POB 2620, Cairo; tel. (02) 751066; telex 93852; f. 1978; cap. p.u. 15m., dep. 1,033.8m., res 41m., total assets 1,484m. (Dec. 1986); Chair. and Man. Dir AHMAD FOUAD; 10 brs.

Non-Commercial Banks

Arab Investment Bank (Federal Arab Bank for Development and Investment): 1113 Corniche en-Nil, POB 1147, Cairo; tel. (02) 753301; telex 22553; f. 1978; cap. p.u. 20m., dep. 519.7m., total assets 558m. (Dec. 1987); 6 brs; Chair. Prof. FOUAD HASHEM AWAD.

Banque Nationale Société Générale, SAE: 4 Sharia Talaat Harb, Evergreen Office Bldg, 3rd Floor, Cairo; tel. (02) 770291; telex 93894; National Bank of Egypt has 51% interest, Société Générale, Paris has 49%; f. 1978; cap. 10m.; Chair. MAHMOUD ABD AL-AZIZ; Gen. Man. JEAN DUBOIS.

Egypt Arab African Bank: POB 61, Magli esh-Shaab, 5 Midan es-Saray, el-Koubra, Garden City, Cairo; tel. (02) 3550948; telex 20965; f. 1982; Arab African International Bank has 49% interest, Egyptian businessmen have 16%, Arab African International Bank Pension Fund, Bank of Alexandria, Banque du Caire, Egyptian Reinsurance Co, and Development Industrial Bank each have 7%; cap. p.u. 20m., dep. 439.2m., res 33.6m., total assets 602.6m. (Dec. 1986); merchant and investment bank services; Chair. and Man. Dir ALI GAMAL ED-DIN DABBOUS; Gen. Man. BAHI ED-DIN M. ES-SADIQ; 3 brs.

Egyptian Investment Finance Corporation: Cairo; f. 1985; cap. 17m.; merchant bank services.

Housing and Development Bank: 26 Batal Ahmad Abd al-Aziz, POB 234, Cairo (Dokki); tel. (02) 717170; telex 94075; f. 1979; cap. p.u. 18m., dep. 46.4m., res. 12.9m. (June 1986); 3 brs; Chair. MAHMOUD NABIH EL-MINSHAWI.

Islamic International Bank for Investment and Development: 4 Sharia Addy, Mesaha Sq., Dokki, POB 180, Cairo; tel. (02) 3489973; f. 1980; auth. cap. US $100, cap. p.u. US $12m. (Dec. 1987); Chair. HASSAN AHMAD NAGI; Gen. Man. ADEL KHALIFA TANTAWI; 5 brs.

Misr Iran Development Bank: The Nile Tower, 21 Sharia Giza, POB 219, El-Orman; tel. (02) 727311; telex 22407; f. 1975; cap. p.u. US $40m., res 9.7m. (Dec. 1986); dep. US $339m. (Dec. 1987); Chair. FATHI MUHAMMAD IBRAHIM; Man. Dir AL-MOTAZ MANSOUR; Gen. Man. Dr IBRAHIM MOUKHTAR; 5 brs.

National Investment Bank: 8 Sharia Abd el-Meguid ar-Remaly, Bab el-Louk, Cairo; tel. (02) 541336; telex 23414; State-owned; responsible for government projects; Chair. GAMAL AL-GANZOURI; Sec.-Gen. MUHAMMAD FAHMY.

National Société Générale Bank, SAE: 4 Sharia Talaat Harb, POB 2664, Cairo; tel. (02) 747396; telex 93895; f. 1978; investment and merchant bank; Chair. YOUSUF AHMAD ALLOUBA.

Offshore Bank

Manufacturers Hanover Trust Co: 3 Sharia Ahmad Nessim, Giza, POB 1962, Giza, Cairo; tel. (02) 726703; telex 92297; Vice-Pres. and Man. R. DOLAN.

STOCK EXCHANGES

Capital Market Authority: 26 Sharia Gomhouriya, Cairo; tel. (02) 3902314; telex 94282; f. 1979; Chair. Dr MUHAMMAD HASSAN FAG AN-NOUR.

Cairo Stock Exchange: 4 Sharia esh-Sherifein, Cairo; tel. (02) 748698; f. 1904; Pres. Dr MUHAMMAD HAMED MUHAMMAD.

Alexandria Stock Exchange: 11 Sharia Talaat Harb, Alexandria; tel. (03) 8824015; f. 1861; Chair. EDWARD ANIS GEBRAYIL.

INSURANCE

Arab International Insurance Co: POB 2704, 28 Sharia Talaat Harb, Cairo; tel. (02) 746322; telex 92599; f. 1976; a joint-stock free zone company established by Egyptian and foreign insurance companies; Chair. GAMAL EL-BOROLLOSSI; Gen. Man. HASSAN M. HAFEZ.

Ach-Chark Insurance Co, SAE: 15 Sharia Kasr en-Nil, Cairo; tel. (02) 753333; f. 1931; Chair. AMIN EL-HIZZAWI; general and life.

The Egyptian Reinsurance Co, SAE: 7 Sharia Dar esh-Shifa, Garden City, POB 950, Cairo; tel. (02) 3543354; telex 92245; f. 1957; Chair. ESSAM ED-DIN OMAR.

L'Epargne, SAE: Immeuble Chemla, Sharia 26 July, POB 548, Cairo; all types of insurance.

Al-Iktisad esh-Shabee, SAE: 11 Sharia Emad ed-Din, POB 1635, Cairo; f. 1948; Man. Dir and Gen. Man. W. KHAYAT.

Directory

Misr Insurance Co: 44A Sharia Dokki, Giza; tel. 700158; telex 93320; f. 1934; all classes of insurance and reinsurance; cap. p.u. 12m., res 414.5 m. (June 1987); Chair. FATHI MUHAMMAD IBRAHIM.

Mohandes Insurance Co: 36 Sharia Batal Ahmad Abd al-Aziz, Mohandesin, POB 363, Giza; tel. 701074; telex 93392.

Al-Mottahida: 9 Sharia Soliman Pasha, POB 804, Cairo; f. 1957.

National Insurance Co of Egypt, SAE: 33 Sharia en-Nabi Danial, POB 446, Alexandria; tel. (03) 4923034; telex 54212; f. 1900; Chair. AHMAD FOUAD EL-ANSARI.

Provident Association of Egypt, SAE: 9 Sharia Sherif Pasha, POB 390, Alexandria; f. 1936; Man. Dir G. C. VORLOOU.

Trade and Industry

CHAMBERS OF COMMERCE

Federation of Chambers of Commerce: 4 el-Falaki Sq., Cairo; tel. (02) 3551164; telex 92645.

Alexandria

Egyptian Chamber of Commerce, Alexandria: Sharia el-Ghorfa Altogariya, Alexandria; tel. (03) 808993; Pres. ABD AL-HAMID SERRI; Sec. AHMAD EL-ALFI MUHAMMAD; Gen. Dir MUHAMMAD FATHI MAHMOUD.

Cairo

Cairo Chamber of Commerce: 4 Sharia Midan el-Falaki, Cairo; tel. (02) 22897; f. 1913; Pres. MUHAMMAD EL-BELEDI; Gen. Dir SAID EL-BARRAD.

INVESTMENT ORGANIZATION

General Authority for Investment and Free Zones: 8 Sharia Adly, POB 1007, Cairo; tel. (02) 3906804; telex 92235; Deputy Chair. MOHI ED-DIN EL-GHAREB.

NATIONALIZED ORGANIZATIONS

In November 1975 a Presidential Decree ratified the establishment of Higher Councils for the various sectors of industry. During 1978, however, various government ministries took increasing control of industries. In 1980 it was estimated that the government controlled about 350 companies. The majority of the larger, more important industrial and commercial companies are now either state-owned or operate under government supervision.

MINERALS

Egyptian Geological Survey and Mining Authority (EGSMA): 3 Sharia Salah Salem, Abbassiya, Cairo; tel. (02) 829662; telex 22695; state supervisory authority concerned with planning of policies relating to mining activities in Egypt; Chair. AHMAD ABD AL-HALIM.

PETROLEUM

Egyptian General Petroleum Corporation (EGPC): 20 Sharia Osman Abd al-Hafiz, POB 2130, Nasr City, Cairo; tel. (02) 837388; telex 92049; state supervisory authority generally concerned with the planning of policies relating to petroleum activities in Egypt with the object of securing the development of the oil industry and ensuring its effective administration; Chair. HAMAD AYOUB.

Belayim Petroleum Co (PETROBEL): Sharia Gharb el-Istad, Nasr City, Cairo; tel. (02) 608456; telex 92449; f. 1978; capital equally shared between EGPC and International Egyptian Oil Co, which is a subsidiary of ENI of Italy; oil and gas exploration, drilling and production.

General Petroleum Co (GPC): 8 Sharia Dr Moustafa Abou Zahra, Nasr City, Cairo; f. 1957; wholly owned subsidiary of EGPC; operates mainly in Eastern Desert.

Gulf of Suez Petroleum Co (GUPCO): POB 2400, Cairo; f. 1965; partnership between EGPC and Amoco-Egypt Co, USA; developed the el-Morgan oilfield in the Gulf of Suez, also holds other exploration concessions in the Gulf of Suez and the Western Desert; output was averaging 24.5m. b/d in 1982; Chair. Dr Eng. HAMDI EL-BANBI.

Western Desert Petroleum Co (WEPCO): POB 412, Alexandria; tel. (03) 4928710; telex 54075; f. 1967 as partnership between EGPC (50% interest) and Phillips Petroleum (35%) and later Hispanoil (15%); developed Alamein, Yidma and Umbarka fields in the Western Desert and later Abu Qir offshore gas field in 1978 followed by NAF gas field in 1987; Chair. Eng. MUHAMMAD MOHI ED-DIN BAHGAT.

Arab Petroleum Pipelines Co (SUMED): 431 el-Geish Ave, Loran, Alexandria; tel. (03) 5863139; telex 54295; f. 1974; Suez-Mediterranean crude oil transportation pipeline (capacity: 80m. tons per year) and oil terminal operators; Chair. and Man. Dir Eng. HAFEZ MUHAMMAD EL-SHERBINI.

Numerous foreign oil companies are prospecting for oil in Egypt under agreements with EGPC.

EMPLOYERS' ORGANIZATION

Federation of Egyptian Industries: POB 251, 26A Sharia Sherif Pasha, Cairo, and 65 Gamal Abdel Nasser Ave, Alexandria; tel. (02) 3557642 (Cairo), (03) 28622 (Alexandria); f. 1922; Pres. Dr ADEL GAZAREIN; represents the industrial community in Egypt.

TRADE UNIONS

Egyptian Trade Union Federation (ETUF): 90 Sharia Galaa, Cairo; tel. (02) 740362; telex 93255; f. 1957; 23 affiliated unions; 4m. mems; affiliated to the International Confederation of Arab Trade Unions and to the Organization of African Trade Union Unity; Pres. MUKHTAR ABD AL-HAMID; Gen. Sec. ABD AL-RAHMAN KEDR.

General Trade Union of Agriculture: 31 Sharia Mansour, Bab el-Louq, Cairo; 150,000 mems; Pres. MUKHTAR ABD AL-HAMID; Gen. Sec. MUHAMMAD ABD AL-KHALEK GOUDA.

General Trade Union of Air Transport: 5 Sharia Ahmad Sannan, St Fatima, Heliopolis; 11,000 mems; Pres. ABD AL-MONEM FARAG EISA; Gen. Sec. SHEKATA ABD AL-HAMID.

General Trade Union of Banks and Insurance: 2 Sharia el-Kady el-Fadel, Cairo; 56,000 mems; Pres. MAHMOUD MUHAMMAD DABBOUR; Gen. Sec. ABDOU HASSAN MUHAMMAD ALI.

General Trade Union of Building Workers: 9 Sharia Emad ed-Din, Cairo; 150,000 mems; Pres. HAMID HASSAN BARAKAT; Gen. Sec. SALEM ABD AR-RAZEK.

General Trade Union of Business and Management Services: 2 Sharia Muhammad Haggag, Midan et-Tahrir, Cairo; 100,000 mems; Pres. ABD AR-RAHMAN KHEDR; Gen. Sec. MAHMOUD MUHAMMAD.

General Trade Union of Commerce: 70 Sharia el-Gomhouriya, Cairo; tel. 914124; f. 1903; more than 100,000 mems; Pres. ABD AR-RAZEK ESH-SHERBEENI; Gen. Sec. KAMEL HUSSEIN A. AWAD.

General Trade Union of Food Industries: 3 Sharia Housni, Hadaek el-Koba, Cairo; 111,000 mems; Pres. SAAD M. AHMAD; Gen. Sec. ADLY TANOUS IBRAHIM.

General Trade Union of Health Services: 22 Sharia esh-Sheikh Qamar, es-Sakakiny, Cairo; 56,000 mems; Pres. IBRAHIM ABOU EL-MUTI IBRAHIM; Gen. Sec. AHMAD ABD AL-LATIF SALEM.

General Trade Union of Maritime Transport: 36 Sharia Sharif, Cairo; 46,000 mems; Pres. THABET MUHAMMAD ES-SEFARI; Gen. Sec. MUHAMMAD RAMADAN ABOU TOR.

General Trade Union of Military Production: 90 Sharia el-Galaa, Cairo; 55,000 mems; Pres. MOUSTAFA MUHAMMAD MOUNGI; Gen. Sec. IBRAHIM LUTFI ZANATI.

General Trade Union of Mine Workers: 5 Sharia Ali Sharawi, Hadaek el-Koba, Cairo; 14,000 mems; Pres. ABBAS MAHMOUD IBRAHIM; Gen. Sec. AMIN HASSAN AMER.

General Trade Union of Petroleum and Chemical Industries: 90 Sharia el-Galaa, Cairo; 103,000 mems; Pres. AHMAD AHMAD EL-AMAWI; Gen. Sec. ABD AL-KADER HASSAN ABD AL-KADER.

General Trade Union of Posts, Telegrams and Telephones: 90 Sharia el-Galaa, Cairo; 80,000 mems; Pres. MUHAMMAD KHAIRI HASHEM; Gen. Sec. MUHAMMAD ABD AR-RAUF DIRRAZ.

General Trade Union of Press, Printing and Information: 90 Sharia el-Galaa, Cairo; 43,100 mems; Pres. MUHAMMAD ALI EL-FIKKI; Gen. Sec. ABD AL-AZIZ MUHAMMAD BASUNI.

General Trade Union of Public Utilities: 22 Sharia Sharif, Cairo; 64,000 mems; Pres. MANSOUR ABD AL-MONEM MANSOUR; Gen. Sec. MUHAMMAD TALAAT HASSAN.

General Trade Union of Railway Workers: 15 Sharia Emad ed-Din, POB 84 (el-Fagalah), Cairo; tel. (02) 930305; 89,000 mems; Pres. MUHAMMAD SHARAWI MUHAMMAD; Gen. Sec. SABR AHMAD HUSSEIN.

General Trade Union of Road Transport: 90 Sharia el-Galaa, Cairo; 243,000 mems; Pres. MUHAMMAD MUHAMMAD AHMAD EL-OKALI; Gen. Sec. MUHAMMAD KAMAL LABIB.

General Trade Union of Textile Workers: 327 Sharia Shoubra, Cairo; 244,000 mems; Pres. ALI MUHAMMAD DOUFDAA; Gen. Sec. HASSAN TOULBA MARZOUK.

General Trade Union of Hotels and Tourism Workers: 90 Sharia el-Galaa, Cairo; 35,000 mems; Pres. MUSTAFA IBRAHIM; Gen. Sec. AMIN ABUBAKR.

General Trade Union of Workers in Engineering, Metal and Electrical Industries: 90 Sharia el-Galaa, Cairo; tel. 742519; 130,000 mems; Pres. SAID GOMAA; Gen. Sec. GAMAL TARABISHI.

Transport

RAILWAYS

The area of the Nile Delta is well served by railways. Lines also run from Cairo southward along the Nile to Aswan, and westward along the coast to Sollum.

Egyptian Railways: Station Bldg, Midan Ramses, Cairo; tel. (02) 347600; telex 92616; f. 1851; length 5,355 km; 25 km electrified; a 430-km line to carry phosphate and iron ore from the Bahariya mines, in the Western Desert, to the Helwan iron and steel works in south Cairo, was opened in August 1973; Chair. Dr Eng. MUHAMMAD MAHER EL-MORSI.

Alexandria Passenger Transport Authority: 2 Sharia Aflatone, POB 466, Alexandria; tel. (03) 5975223; telex 54637; f. 1863; controls City Tramways (28 km), Ramleh Electric Railway (16 km), suburban buses (544.5 km); 159 tram cars, 42 light railway three-car sets; Chair. Eng. MUHAMMAD SALEH ED-DIN ABD AL-MONEIM; Tech. Dir Eng. FIKRY AMIN ABD AL-MALEK.

Cairo Metro: National Authority for Tunnels, Ministry of Transport, Sharia Qasr el-Eini, Cairo; construction of the first underground transport system in Africa or the Middle East began in Cairo in 1982; planned to connect existing electrified Helwan line of Egyptian railways with Koubri el-Lamoun to el-Marg line, via a 4.2-km tunnel with six stations beneath central Cairo, making a 42-km regional line with a total of 33 stations; gauge 1,435 mm, electrified; work on the first stage of the system was completed in July 1987, and it was opened in September; the second and final stage was expected to be completed in 1989; Gen. Dir H. ABD ES-SALAM.

Cairo Transport Authority: POB 254, Madinet Nasr, Cairo; tel. (2) 830533; length 78 km (electrified); gauge 1,000 mm; operates 16 tram routes and 24 km of light railway; 441 cars.

Heliopolis Co for Housing and Inhabiting: 28 Sharia Ibrahim el-Lakkany, Heliopolis, Cairo; 50 km, 148 railcars; Gen. Man. ABD AL-MONEIM SEIF.

Lower Egypt Railway: Mansura; f. 1898; length 160 km; gauge 1,000 mm; 20 diesel railcars.

ROADS

There are good metalled main roads as follows: Cairo–Alexandria (desert road); Cairo–Benna–Tanta–Damanhur–Alexandria; Cairo–Suez (desert road); Cairo–Ismailia–Port Said or Suez; Cairo–Fayum (desert road); in 1986 there were over 90,000 km of roads, including 16,191 km of paved main roads. The Ahmad Hamdi road tunnel (1.64 km) beneath the Suez Canal was opened in October 1980. A road from Aswan to Wadi Halfa, in Sudan, was due to be completed in 1985 and a 320-km macadamized road linking Mersa Matruh, on the Mediterranean coast, with the oasis town of Siwa was completed in 1986.

Egyptian General Organization of Inland Transport for Provinces Passengers: Sharia Qasr el-Eini, Cairo; Pres. HASSAN MOURAD KOTB.

SHIPPING

Egypt's principal ports are Alexandria, Port Said and Suez. A port constructed at a cost of £E315m. and designed to handle up to 16m. tons of grain, fruit and other merchandise per year (22% of the country's projected imports by 2000) in its first stage of development, was opened at Damietta in July 1986. The second stage will increase handling capacity to 25m. tons per year. A ferry link between Nuweibeh and the Jordanian port of Aqaba was opened in April 1985.

Alexandria Port Authority: 66 ave Gamal Abd an-Nasser, Alexandria; Head Office: 106 Sharia el-Hourriya, Alexandria; tel. (03) 34321; telex 54147; Chair. Adm. ANWAR HEGAZI.

Major Shipping Companies

Alexandria Shipping and Navigation Co: 557 ave el-Hourriya, POB 812, Alexandria; tel. (03) 62923; telex 54029; services between Egypt, N. and W. Europe, USA, Red Sea and Mediterranean; 9 vessels; Chair. and Man. Dir Eng. MAHMOUD ISMAIL; Man. Dir ABD AL-AZIZ QADRI.

Arab Bridge Maritime Navigation Co: Amman, Jordan; f. 1987; joint venture by Egypt, Iraq and Jordan to improve economic co-operation; an expansion of the company that established a ferry link between the ports of Aqaba, Jordan, and Nuweibeh, Egypt, in 1985; cap. US $6m.; Chair. SULAYMAN MUTAWALLI SULAYMAN (Egyptian Minister of Transport, Communications and Maritime Navigation).

Egyptian Navigation Co: 2 Sharia en-Nasr, POB 82, Alexandria; tel. (03) 800050; telex 4131; f. 1930; owners and operators of Egypt's mercantile marine; services Alexandria/Europe, USA, Black Sea,

EGYPT

Adriatic Sea, Mediterranean Sea, Indian Ocean and Red Sea; 47 vessels; Chair. ADLY ABD AL-MOUTI.

Pan-Arab Shipping Co: 13 Sharia Salah Salem, POB 39, Alexandria; tel. (03) 4825970; telex 54123; f. 1974; Arab League Co; 8 vessels; Gen. Man. Capt. HASSAN SAID MAHMOUD.

THE SUEZ CANAL

In 1987 17,541 vessels, with a net displacement of 347m. tons, used the Suez Canal, linking the Mediterranean and Red Seas.

Length of Canal 195 km; maximum permissible draught: 16.15 m (53 ft); breadth of canal at water level and breadth between buoys defining the navigable channel 365 m and 180 m respectively in the northern section and 305 m and 175 m in the southern section.

Suez Canal Authority (Hay'at Canal as-Suess): Irshad Bldg, Ismailia; tel. (064) 20000; telex 63238; Cairo Office: 6 Sharia Lazoghli, Garden City, Cairo; f. 1956; Chair. MUHAMMAD EZZAT ADEL.

CIVIL AVIATION

The main international airports are at Heliopolis (23 km from the centre of Cairo) and Alexandria (7 km from the city centre). A second terminal was opened at Cairo International Airport in July 1986. An international airport was opened at Nuzhah in December 1983.

EgyptAir: Cairo International Airport, Heliopolis, Cairo; tel. (02) 455099; telex 22221; f. 1932 as Misr Airwork; known as United Arab Airlines 1960–1971; operates internal services in Egypt and external services throughout the Middle East, Far East, Africa, Europe and the USA; Chair. General MUHAMMAD FAHIM RAYAN; fleet of one Boeing 747-100, one Boeing 747-200, two 747-300 Combi, 3 Boeing 767-200 ER, 6 Boeing 707-320C, 7 Boeing 737-200, 8 Airbus A300B4-203, one DC10, 3 Fokker F-27.

Egyptian Civil Aviation Authority: 31 Sharia 26 July, Cairo; tel. (02) 660525; telex 93044; Chair. ALI OSMAN ZIKO.

Zarkani Air Services (ZAS): Cairo; operates internal services and external services to Amsterdam, Belgrade, Kampala, Lisbon, Mogadishu and Valletta, *inter alia*.

Tourism

Ministry of Tourism: Misr Travel Tower, Abbassia Sq., Cairo; tel. (02) 2828450; telex 94040; f. 1965; branches at Alexandria, Port Said, Suez, Luxor and Aswan; Minister of Tourism and Civil Aviation Dr FOUAD SULTAN.

Egyptian General Authority for the Promotion of Tourism: Misr Travel Tower, Abbassia Sq., Cairo; tel. (02) 823570; telex 20799; Chair. SAYED MOUSSA.

Egyptian General Co for Tourism and Hotels: 4 Latin America St, Garden City, Cairo; tel. (02) 32158; telex 92363; f. 1961; affiliated to the Ministry of Tourism.

Authorized foreign exchange dealers for tourists include the principal banks and the following:

American Express of Egypt Ltd: 15 Sharia Qasr en-Nil, POB 2160, Cairo; tel. (02) 750444; telex 92715; f. 1919; 7 brs.

Thomas Cook Overseas Ltd: 5 Sharia Talaat Harb, Cairo; tel. (02) 767420; telex 92413.

Atomic Energy

A 32-member Higher Nuclear Council was formed in August 1975. Work has begun on two of the eight 1,000 MW nuclear power stations to be built by the year 2000, which it is hoped will provide 40% of total energy requirements.

Atomic Energy Organization: 101 Sharia Qasr el-Eini, Cairo; f. 1955; Chair. Dr IBRAHIM HAMOUDA; Vice-Chair. Dr SALEH HASHISH; Dir of Nuclear Research Centre Dr E. ABD AL-AZIZ; Dir of Nat. Centre for Radiation Research and Technology Dr H. R. EL-KADI.

Nuclear Power Plants Authority: POB 8191, Masaken, Nasr City, 108 Abbassia; tel. 608291; telex 20761; f. 1976; Chair. Dr A. F. AS-SAIDI.

EL SALVADOR

Introductory Survey

Location, Climate, Language, Religion, Flag, Capital
The Republic of El Salvador lies on the Pacific coast of Central America. It is bounded by Guatemala to the west and by Honduras to the north and east. The climate varies from tropical on the coastal plain to temperate in the uplands. The language is Spanish. About 80% of the population are Roman Catholics, and other Christian churches are represented. The national flag (proportions 3 by 2) consists of three equal horizontal stripes, of blue, white and blue, with the national coat of arms in the centre of the white stripe. The capital is San Salvador.

Recent History
El Salvador was ruled by Spain until 1821, and became independent in 1839. Since then the country's history has been one of frequent coups and outbursts of political violence. General Maximiliano Hernández Martínez became President in 1931, and ruthlessly suppressed a peasant uprising, with an alleged 30,000 killings, in 1932. President Hernández was deposed in 1944, and the next elected President, Gen. Salvador Castañeda Castro, was overthrown in 1948. His successor as President, Lt-Col Oscar Osorio (1950–56), relinquished power to Lt-Col José María Lemus, who was deposed by a bloodless coup in 1960. He was replaced by a military junta, which was itself supplanted by another junta in January 1961. Under this junta, the conservative Partido de Conciliación Nacional (PCN) was established and won all 54 seats in the elections to the Legislative Assembly in December 1961. A member of the junta, Lt-Col Julio Adalberto Rivera, was elected unopposed to the presidency in 1962. He was succeeded by a former Minister of the Interior, Gen. Fidel Sánchez Hernández, the candidate of the ruling PCN, in 1967.

In the 1972 presidential election Col Arturo Armando Molina Barraza, candidate of the ruling PCN, was elected. His rival, José Napoleón Duarte, the leader of the left-wing coalition party Unión Nacional de Oposición, launched an abortive coup in March, and Col Molina took office in July, despite allegations of massive electoral fraud. These allegations were repeated in the 1977 presidential election, after which the PCN candidate, Gen. Carlos Humberto Romero Mena, took office.

Reports of violations of human rights by the Government were increasingly prevalent in 1979. The polarization of left and right after 1972 became evident in the rise in guerrilla activity. In October 1979 President Romero was overthrown and replaced by a junta of civilians and army officers. The junta promised to install a democratic system and to call elections, declared a political amnesty and invited participation from the guerrilla groups, but violence continued between government troops and guerrilla forces, and elections were postponed. In January 1980 an ultimatum from progressive members of the Government resulted in the formation of a new government, a coalition of military officers and the Partido Demócrata Cristiano (PDC). In March the country moved closer to full-scale civil war with the assassination of the Roman Catholic Archbishop of San Salvador, Oscar Romero y Galdames, an outspoken supporter of human rights.

In December 1980 José Napoleón Duarte, the 1972 presidential candidate and a member of the junta, was sworn in as President. In January 1981 the guerrillas launched their 'final offensive' and, after initial gains, the opposition front, Frente Democrático Revolucionario—FDR (allied with the guerrilla front, the Farabundo Martí de Liberación Nacional—FMLN), proposed negotiations with the USA. The US authorities referred them to the Salvadorean Government, which refused to recognize the FDR while it was linked with the guerrillas. The USA affirmed its support for the Duarte Government and provided civilian and military aid. During 1981 the guerrilla forces unified and strengthened their control over the north and east of the country. They continued their attacks on important economic targets, mainly bridges, electricity pylons and military installations, while the army retaliated by acting indiscriminately against the local population in guerrilla-controlled areas. By December 1981 there were an estimated 300,000 Salvadorean refugees, many of whom had fled to neighbouring countries. Large areas of Morazán, Chalatenango and Cabañas provinces were almost completely depopulated.

At elections to a Constituent Assembly in March 1982 the PDC failed to win an absolute majority against the five right-wing parties which, with 60% of the vote between them, formed a Government of National Unity. Major Roberto D'Aubuisson Arrieta, leader of the extreme right-wing Alianza Republicana Nacionalista (ARENA), emerged as the most powerful figure and became President of the Constituent Assembly. In April a politically independent banker, Dr Alvaro Magaña Borja, was elected interim President of El Salvador, after pressure from the armed forces. However, the Assembly voted itself wide powers over the President. Military leaders then demanded that five ministerial posts be given to members of the PDC, fearing that, otherwise, US military aid would be withdrawn. A presidential election was scheduled for 1983, and a new constitution was to be drafted.

During 1982 about 1,600 Salvadorean troops were trained in the USA, and US military advisers were reported to be actively participating in the conflict. Agrarian reform was suspended in May by the Government, which ruled out negotiation with guerrillas. It was estimated that 4,000 civilians were killed in the first nine months of 1982, making a total of about 35,000 deaths in three years. In November a military coup was forestalled by Gen. José Guillermo García, the Minister of Defence, who removed several right-wingers from key military posts. President Magaña's position was strengthened in December, when a split within the PCN gave the moderates a majority in the Assembly.

The presidential election, originally planned for 1983, was postponed until March 1984 as a result of disagreement in the Constituent Assembly over the new Constitution, which finally entered into force in December 1983. The agrarian reform programme caused a serious dispute between Maj. D'Aubuisson's ARENA party and the PDC, and led to a campaign by right-wing 'death squads' against trade unionists and peasant leaders. In October 1983 the Assembly voted to allow a maximum permissible holding of 262 ha per landowner. This result represented a victory for the ARENA party, which had been isolated in the Assembly following the collapse of its alliance with the PCN in February.

The issue of human rights abuse continued to be a serious problem for the Government throughout 1983. Following a period of intense activity by the death squads in September and October, when the weekly total of murders exceeded 200, the US Government called for the removal of several high-level officials, military officers and political figures who were linked with death squads. The failure of the US-trained 'rapid reaction' battalions and frequent reports of army atrocities (including the murder of the President of the Human Rights Commission, Marianela García Villas, in March 1983) undermined both public confidence in the Government and President Ronald Reagan's efforts to secure further US aid for El Salvador. Following their capture of the strategically important towns of Berlín and San Miguel, the guerrillas struck a crucial blow against the Government with the attack on the garrison at El Paraíso and the destruction of the Cuscatlán bridge in January 1984. In February the FDR-FMLN proposed the formation of a broad-based provisional government, as part of a peace plan without preconditions. The plan was rejected by the Government. The guerrillas refused to participate in the presidential election, due to be held in March 1984, and threatened to prevent voting in various provinces. The election was marked by a low turn-out of voters, resulting partly from chaotic voting conditions and poor organization and partly from disruptions by the guerrillas. As no candidate emerged with a clear majority, a second round of voting was held in May, when the contest was between José Napoleón Duarte, candidate of the PDC, and Maj. D'Aubuisson, candidate of ARENA. Duarte secured a clear majority over D'Aubuisson, obtaining 54% of the votes cast.

Following his inauguration in June, President Duarte ordered a purge of the armed forces, which resulted in several high-ranking officers being sent abroad, and the reorganization of the police force, including the disbanding of the notorious Treasury Police. Both the FDR-FMLN and the President expressed their willingness to commence peace negotiations. Following pressure from the Roman Catholic Church and trade unions, the Government opened discussions with guerrilla leaders in Chalatenango in October. A second round of negotiations was held in November but the talks ended amid accusations of intransigence from both sides.

In August 1984 President Duarte appointed a five-member commission to investigate various crimes against human rights, including the murder of Archbishop Romero y Galdames. The Government had been prompted to act following reports of the massacre of more than 150 peasants by the armed forces in Cabañas and Chalatenango.

Contrary to public predictions, the PDC won a convincing victory over the ARENA-PCN electoral alliance at the legislative and municipal elections in March 1985, thereby securing a clear majority in the new National Assembly. The PDC's victory, coupled with internal divisions within the right-wing grouping, precipitated a decline in the popularity and influence of the alliance, which culminated in the resignation of ARENA's leader, Roberto D'Aubuisson, in September. Following its electoral success, the Government announced plans to introduce extensive social reforms in the spheres of health, education and local government services. Although President Duarte reaffirmed his intention to resume talks with the FDR-FMLN, both parties failed to agree on preconditions for renewing their dialogue.

Public discontent with President Duarte, prompted by his conduct in response to the abduction by guerrillas of his eldest daughter in September 1985, was compounded by the introduction of a series of controversial austerity measures in January 1986. The new policy was intended to revive El Salvador's economy, but it succeeded only in antagonizing the trade unions and the private sector. The trade unions demonstrated their opposition by holding strikes and protests throughout the year. A further problem for the Government was the deterioration in its relations with the Roman Catholic Church, following allegations that the Church was offering assistance to members of the rebel forces.

In October 1986 a severe earthquake caused extensive damage to the capital, San Salvador; some 1,500 people were reported to have died and more than 10,000 people were injured. An estimated 300,000 people were made destitute by the earthquake, which caused damage estimated to be in excess of US $1,500m. The disaster was expected to have calamitous social and economic consequences for El Salvador.

Throughout 1985 and 1986 there was reported to be a noticeable decline in the number of politically-motivated murders and violations of human rights. In April 1986 private discussions were held in Lima, Peru, between representatives of the Salvadorean Government and the guerrillas, and in June President Duarte made a firm offer to the guerrillas to resume negotiations in September, with mediation by the Roman Catholic Church. Although the FDR-FMLN agreed to attend, the negotiations failed to take place, after a dispute between the Government and the guerrillas over the agenda for the meeting and security arrangements. Although these developments enabled President Duarte to affirm his commitment to securing a negotiated settlement with the FDR-FMLN, there was increasing speculation that a military solution would be sought to end the civil war. Such speculation was supported by reports of the armed forces' growing domination of the conflict and by the success of the army's 'Unidos para reconstruir' campaign, a social and economic programme, launched in July 1986, to recover areas that had been devastated by the protracted fighting. Although the guerrillas mounted a successful attack against the army garrison at San Miguel in June, they failed to make any significant gains in 1986.

During the early months of 1987 President Duarte's Government came under severe pressure from all sections of the opposition. As a result of the ARENA-PCN alliance's decision to boycott the legislature, the Government was unable to obtain approval for the reimposition of the state of siege, which subsequently lapsed in January. In February the Government suffered a humiliating defeat when its attempt to introduce a 'War Tax' was ruled unconstitutional by the Supreme Court. Furthermore, in March guerrillas carried out a successful attack on the army garrison at El Paraíso, Chalatenango, which enabled them to take the military initiative in the civil war. Other problems for the Government were posed by the opposition of both trade unions and the business community to its economic policies. When, in June, the Government endeavoured to regain public confidence by submitting some 41 legislative proposals and seven executive decrees to the legislature (including proposals for an amnesty and for reform of the penal code), its opponents remained unconvinced, and the Government's credibility was regarded as very low.

Later in 1987, however, the Salvadorean Government's participation in the peace plan for Central America (see p. 777), which was signed on 7 August in Guatemala City, encouraged hopes that a peaceful solution could be found to the civil war. President Duarte urged the FDR-FMLN to enter into the peace process, and, in spite of an initial reluctance, the guerrillas subsequently agreed to open a dialogue with the Government, but insisted that there should be no preconditions attached to the talks. Discussions between the Government and the FDR-FMLN were eventually held in October; agreement was reached on the formation of two committees to study the possibility of a cease-fire and an amnesty, but no consensus was reached on the crucial issue of a cease-fire. Following further talks in late October, new discussions were scheduled for November. However, the murder, in October, of the President of the Human Rights Commission, Herbert Anaya Sanabria, prompted the guerrillas to withdraw from the talks.

Despite the Government's proclamation, in November 1987, of a unilateral cease-fire, the armed forces launched a new campaign, Operation Concordia, against the guerrillas. Moreover, the guerrillas refused to adhere to the Government's cease-fire and authorized a continuation of guerrilla activities; by December an estimated 1,300–1,500 people had been killed in the conflict during 1987, and, despite the return from exile, in November, of the opposition leaders Guillermo Ungo and Rubén Zamora, it was clear that attempts to implement the peace plan would continue to encounter serious obstacles. In late 1987 the political situation deteriorated further, following President Duarte's public denunciation of Roberto D'Aubuisson's complicity in the murder of Archbishop Romero y Galdames in March 1980.

In early 1988 there were increasing reports of the resurgence of 'death squads', and it was suggested that abuses of human rights were rapidly returning to the level reached at the beginning of the internal conflict. In February the FMLN launched a campaign of bombings and bans on traffic movements, in order to disrupt preparations for the forthcoming legislative and municipal elections, due to be held in March. The elections took place in an atmosphere of public apathy; an early claim of victory was made by ARENA, which was subsequently confirmed as having secured control of more than 200 municipalities, including San Salvador, hitherto held for more than 20 years by the PDC. However, a dispute broke out over the distribution of seats in the legislature, with both ARENA and the PDC claiming the same seat in one region. Following protracted arguments, ARENA was able to resume an overall majority in the Assembly, when a deputy of the PCN changed allegiance to ARENA, thereby giving the party 31 seats against the PDC's 23 seats.

The PDC's poor performance at the elections had been widely anticipated, and was largely attributed to public disenchantment with the party, fuelled by a series of corruption scandals concerning the misappropriation of US funds by high-ranking PDC officials. (By contrast, ARENA had made a concerted attempt to present a more moderate image to the electorate.) Moreover, the PDC was deeply divided over the question of the party's candidate for the next presidential election, scheduled for March 1989. Two former ministers, Julio Rey Prendes and Dr Fidel Chávez Mena, both sought the candidacy. Rey Prendes commanded considerable support within the PDC but was closely linked with the corruption scandal; Dr Chávez Mena enjoyed the support of the US administration. In April 1988, in an attempt to resolve the dispute, President Duarte proposed an alternative PDC candidate for the presidency, but his suggestion was rejected by Rey Prendes, who was subsequently nominated as presidential candidate at the PDC convention. However, his nomination was disallowed by the election commission, and Dr Chávez Mena was named as candidate in August. Rey Prendes responded by establishing his own political movement in October, in order to contest the presidential election. Earlier in the year, in May, the PDC suffered another reverse when it was revealed that President Duarte was suffering from a terminal illness.

In mid-1988 the Convergencia Democrática, a left-wing alliance comprising two of the leading groups within the FDR-FMLN and the Partido Social Demócrata, announced that Dr Guillermo Ungo would be its candidate at the forthcoming presidential election. In September, however, the guerrillas launched a major new offensive, with particular emphasis on targets in residential areas. In November the guerrillas, taking advantage of a transition period following the installation of a new military high command, undertook an audacious attack against the headquarters of the National Guard in San Salvador.

Despite the Government's willingness to participate in negotiations to revive the Central American peace plan, no progress was made in 1988 in resolving the internal conflict. Indeed, an estimated 11,000 Salvadoreans were killed or injured during the year, including 1,750 civilian deaths. By the end of 1988, it was estimated that between 65,000 and 70,000 Salvadoreans had died in the course of the civil war, while the US administration had provided some US $3,000m. in aid to the Government. Moreover, by early 1989 many areas appeared to be without government, following the resignations of some 75 mayors and nine judges, purportedly because of death threats by the FMLN. The resurgence of the 'death squads' and the new guerrilla offensive appeared to confirm that El Salvador's internal crisis had worsened. In late January, however, radical new peace proposals were announced by the FMLN, which, for the first time, expressed its willingness to participate in the electoral process. Nevertheless, it was widely expected that the ARENA candidate, Alfredo Cristiani, would be elected President at the election in March 1989, and that ARENA's victory would result in an attempt to achieve a definitive military solution to the conflict.

El Salvador has a territorial dispute with Honduras over three islands in the Gulf of Fonseca and a small area of land on the joint border. In an attempt to resolve the issue, President Duarte and President Azcona of Honduras submitted the dispute to the International Court of Justice for arbitration in December 1986.

Government

Executive power is held by the President, assisted by the Vice-President and the Council of Ministers. The President is elected for a five-year term by universal adult suffrage. Legislative power is vested in the National Assembly (which replaced the National Constituent Assembly in March 1985), with 60 members elected by universal adult suffrage for a three-year term.

Defence

Military service is by compulsory conscription of men between 18 and 30 years of age for two years. In June 1988 the army totalled 39,000 men, the navy 1,000 and the air force 2,000. Paramilitary forces number 12,600 men, and the territorial civil defence force also 12,000. Defence expenditure in 1987 was estimated at 885m. colones. The US Government granted US $85m. in military aid to El Salvador for the year ending September 1988.

Economic Affairs

El Salvador has experienced economic decline in recent years. In 1987, according to estimates by the World Bank, the country's gross national product (GNP), measured at average 1985–87 prices, was US $4,220m., equivalent to $850 per head. Between 1980 and 1987, it was estimated, GNP declined, in real terms, at an average annual rate of 0.6%, with real GNP per head falling by 1.8% per year.

El Salvador's economy is primarily agricultural; the sector (including forestry and fishing) employs approximately 40% of the work-force, accounts for an estimated 20% of the gross domestic product (GDP), and generates about 80% of export revenues. The principal commercial crop is coffee, which traditionally accounts for between 55% and 65% of export earnings. In recent years a combination of unfavourable climatic conditions and a successful offensive by the guerrilla forces against the agricultural region centred on Usulután has resulted in a decline in production, which fell from 4.1m. quintales (each of 46 kg) in 1980 to 3.8m. quintales in 1981 and to 3.2m. quintales in 1985. Production declined to 3.0m. quintales in 1986, before recovering to an estimated 3.3m. quintales in 1987. The coffee sector has also been adversely affected by the conflict between the Government and coffee producers, caused by the Government's decision, in 1981, to nationalize the export of coffee. Taxes levied on coffee exports represent an important source of revenue for the Government, contributing 15%–30% of tax income per year. Hence, the Government's control of such a profitable sector has prompted considerable resentment among the influential group of some 730 families who produce approximately 75% of El Salvador's coffee. In spite of the destruction of an estimated 80,000 quintales of coffee by the guerrilla forces, foreign exchange earnings from coffee increased substantially in 1986, to an estimated US $549m., as a result of high international prices in the first half of the year. However, the subsequent fall in prices and the earthquake of October 1986 were expected to result in a decline in earnings of some $200m. in 1987. The 1988 coffee crop was reported to have been severely affected by Hurricane Miriam, which caused considerable damage to coastal areas of the country in October 1988.

Other major crops are cotton, sugar cane, maize, beans and rice. The annual output of maize increased from 9m. quintales in 1982 to 11.5m. quintales in 1984 and 10.8m. quintales in 1985. Production declined to 10m. quintales in 1986, but increased to an estimated 12.4m. quintales in 1987. Cotton production has fallen sharply since 1981, when the area planted was reduced by 50% from 1978. The annual harvest of seed (unginned) cotton declined from 1.4m. quintales in 1980 to 0.9m. quintales in 1983, and to 0.7m. quintales in 1984, causing a dramatic fall in export earnings, from US $55m. in 1983 to $9m. in 1984. Output has continued to decline, falling to 0.3m. quintales in 1986 and to an estimated 0.2m. quintales in 1987. The protracted rural warfare and the displacement of population have continued to reduce productivity. Nevertheless, agricultural production increased by 1% in 1984 and by an estimated 2% in 1985. Production in 1987 was adversely affected by severe drought, and output was expected to fall in 1988, as a result of Hurricane Miriam. In 1986 the IDB allocated a loan of $830,000 to El Salvador to finance a programme to improve the use of resources in some 200 farming co-operatives. Development of the agricultural sector has been hampered by a shortage of land for cultivation, the high density of population, uneven rainfall (84% of which occurs between May and October), and the internal conflict. Irrigation is widely regarded as the most beneficial device for expansion and diversification of the sector, and in 1986 the IDB allocated a loan of $10m. for an important irrigation project in the Lempa-Acahuaya region.

The agrarian reform plan, introduced in March 1980 as part of the junta's political and economic programme, provided for land expropriation in three stages: farms of more than 500 ha; farms of between 150 and 500 ha; all rented cultivated land to be turned over to tenant farmers. The complete programme was intended to benefit some 180,000 families, or approximately 50% of the rural poor. Some success was achieved with the first stage: 12% of total arable land was taken over by the government agency, ISTA, and 330 estates were allocated to 30,000 workers in the form of co-operatives. Production fell by 10% in 1980/81 but average yields exceeded those of the private sector. A high proportion of funds was used to compensate landowners, and there were allegations of incompetence and excessive bureaucracy. By December 1982 only 52,000 people had benefited from the redistribution of land, and landowners had begun to reclaim their expropriated land by force. It was estimated that more than 9,000 peasants who were eligible for land had been evicted, either by landowners or the army. In March 1983 the Constituent Assembly approved a 10-month extension of the third phase of the reform programme, which enabled peasants to apply for title to 7 ha of land. Of the 48,000 peasants who had applied for land by September 1983, it was believed that only 2,600 had received their allocations. In December the Assembly voted to allow a maximum permissible holding of 245 ha, extended the third phase by a further six months and blocked the possibility of further reform, owing to the scarcity of land available for redistribution. In June 1984 the Assembly revoked Article 207 of the land reform law, which provided for a third phase of the programme. In mid-1987, however, President Duarte introduced new legislation, primarily to implement the second phase of the agrarian reform programme. Under the proposals, only 80,000 families were expected to benefit from land distribution. However, following ARENA's victory at the legislative elections in March 1988 (see Recent History), the agrarian reform programme was to undergo a full revision.

El Salvador is the most highly industrialized country in the Central American Common Market (CACM). Manufacturing, concentrated in food processing, textiles, clothing, leatherwork and pharmaceuticals, accounted for an estimated 15.6% of GDP in 1986. The sector has been severely affected by the armed conflict: between 1981 and 1986 production was estimated to have declined by an average rate of 0.7% annually. In 1985 underemployment was estimated to be 40% and unemployment was estimated to be 30%. In 1987 the output of the construction industry expanded by 10%, principally as a result of foreign finance to assist with reconstruction projects following the earthquake in October 1986. El Salvador's principal trade unions have consistently opposed the Government's economic policies, and industrial unrest has been a common occurrence in recent years. Real wages were estimated to have declined by 54% between 1980 and 1985. Following the earthquake in 1986, El Salvador's commercial sector was reported to have recorded losses amounting to $192.5m.

In recent years the Salvadorean economy has been devastated by the effects of the civil war. GDP declined, in real terms, by 23.5% between 1978 and 1982. Export earnings fell by 33% over the same period. Private investment in fixed capital fell by 64% in 1981 to US $500m. Reserves of foreign exchange declined from $114m. in 1979 to $71.8m. in 1982. Reserves recovered between 1983 and 1985, and reached $179.6m. in December 1985. Reserves declined to $169.7m. at the end of 1986, but increased to $186.1m. in 1987. The Government has become increasingly dependent on foreign aid, principally from the USA (El Salvador is the third largest recipient of US aid), which allocated funds amounting to an estimated $3,000m. between 1979 and 1988. US economic aid amounted to $365m. in 1987 and $306m. in 1988. It has been estimated that 47% of government revenue is absorbed by the internal conflict, and losses to the economy during the period 1979-87 have been valued at $2,000m. The balance of payments had a current surplus of $30.6m. in 1980, but showed deficits of $37m. in 1983, $53.5m. in 1984, and $28.7m. in 1985. In 1982 El Salvador received $32.2m. in special drawing rights from the IMF and was able to limit the cost of debt-servicing, owing to assistance from the US Government. In September 1983 El Salvador requested loans amounting to $20m. from commercial banks in the USA and Europe, and received $40m. from the IDB. The budget deficit fell from 1,005.3m. colones in 1984 to 368m. colones in 1985. The average annual rate of inflation increased from 13.1% in 1983 to 22.3% in 1985. In January 1984 a 14% value-added tax was introduced. In spite of continuing difficulties, real GDP growth of 2.3% and 2.0% was recorded in 1984 and 1985 respectively.

In January 1986 the Government introduced a programme of austerity measures, in an attempt to reverse the prevailing economic decline. Under the programme, the colón was devalued by 50% and a single exchange rate of 5 colones per US dollar was established; the minimum wage was increased by 15%; a 'freeze' was imposed on the prices of basic foodstuffs; limits were imposed on imports of non-essential goods and cars; public transport fares were increased by 20%; and a temporary tax of 15% was imposed on exceptional profits derived from coffee earnings. The new programme proved to be highly controversial and prompted an increase in protests by trade unions against the Government. In spite of the new economic initiative, the effects of the mid-year drought, the internal conflict and the stabilization programme resulted in GDP growth of only 1% in 1986, while the annual rate of inflation rose to 31.9%. Moreover, the budget deficit increased to 472.8m. colones in 1986.

The Government's problems increased, following the severe earthquake in October 1986, which caused damage estimated at more than US $1,500m. In October 1987 the World Bank approved a loan of $65m. to assist a three-year reconstruction project in the capital. The project formed part of a broader programme with a projected total cost of $600m.

In 1987 the economic situation was exacerbated by further serious drought, which resulted in shortages of food and electricity, and prompted an increase in fuel imports. The decline in international coffee prices in late 1986 and early 1987 adversely affected export earnings, and some US $160m. in US aid was to be used to support the balance of payments and to assist debt-servicing of $90m. on the foreign debt of some $2,250m. As a result of such difficulties, GDP growth of only 2% was recorded in 1987, and the budget deficit increased to 676.4m. colones. However, somewhat optimistically, GDP growth of 3% was planned for 1988, when the annual rate of inflation was to be curbed to a projected 20% and investment was scheduled to increase by 15%. Despite official predictions to the contrary, the annual rate of inflation increased to more than 35% in 1988. Frequent acts of sabotage by the guerrillas, mainly directed against El Salvador's electricity system and agricultural sector, caused extensive damage and financial losses to the economy during the year, and, in view of the lack of progress in resolving the internal conflict, no significant improvement was expected in the Salvadorean economy in 1989.

El Salvador is a member of CACM (see p. 108), SELA (p. 219) and the IDB (p. 156).

Social Welfare

In 1952 the Instituto Salvadoreño del Seguro Social (ISSS) was established. This institute provides hospital facilities, medicines and benefits for industrial injury, sickness, accident, disability, maternity, old age and death. Health and welfare insurance is financed by contributions from workers, employers and the State. In 1981 El Salvador had 46 government-controlled hospital establishments, with a total of 7,375 beds, and there were 1,793 physicians working in the country. The Ministry of Health administers 250 medical units, including 14 hospitals. In 1986 budgetary expenditure by the central Government (excluding the ISSS) included 185.6m. colones on health and a further 89.3m. colones on social security and welfare.

Education

In 1985 there were 4,034 public and private schools. There were 1,137,379 students receiving education in 1985. There is one national university and 33 private universities. State education is free, and there are also numerous private schools. Primary education, beginning at seven years of age and lasting for nine years, is officially compulsory. In 1984, however, only 62% of children in the relevant age-group were enrolled at primary schools. Secondary education begins at the age of 16 and lasts for three years. In 1984 only 14% of children in this age-group attended secondary schools. In 1985, according to estimates by UNESCO, the illiteracy rate among people aged 15 years and over was 27.9% (males 25.0%, females 30.7%). Budgetary expenditure on education by the central Government in 1986 was 431.8m. colones.

Public Holidays

1989: 2 January (for New Year's Day), 24-27 March (Easter), 1 May (Labour Day), 25 May (Corpus Christi), 4-6 August* (San Salvador Festival), 15 September (Independence Day), 12 October (Discovery of America), 2 November (All Souls' Day), 5 November (First Call of Independence), 24-25 December (Christmas).

1990: 1 January (New Year's Day), 13-16 April (Easter), 1 May (Labour Day), 15 June (Corpus Christi), 4-6 August* (San Salvador Festival), 15 September (Independence Day), 12 October (Discovery of America), 2 November (All Souls' Day), 5 November (First Call of Independence), 24-25 December (Christmas).

* 5-6 August in other cities.

Weights and Measures

The metric system is officially in force. Some old Spanish measures are also used, including:
  25 libras = 1 arroba;
  4 arrobas = 1 quintal (46 kg).

EL SALVADOR

Statistical Survey

Sources (unless otherwise stated): Banco Central de Reserva de El Salvador, 1a Calle Poniente y 7a Avda Norte, San Salvador; tel. 22-1144; telex 20088; Dirección General de Estadística y Censos, 1a Calle Poniente y 43a Avda Norte, Apdo 2670, San Salvador; tel. 71-5011.

Area and Population

AREA, POPULATION AND DENSITY

Area (sq km)	
Land	21,073
Inland water	320
Total	21,393*
Population (census results)†	
2 May 1961	2,510,984
28 June 1971	
Males	1,763,190
Females	1,791,458
Total	3,554,648
Population (official estimates at mid-year)	
1985	4,819,000
1986	4,913,000
1987	5,009,000
Density (per sq km) at mid-1987	234

* 8,260 sq miles.
† Excluding adjustments for underenumeration.

Capital: San Salvador (estimated population 462,652 at 1 July 1985).

BIRTHS AND DEATHS (per 1,000)

	1983	1984	1985
Birth rate	30.5	29.8	28.7
Death rate	6.9	6.0	n.a.

ECONOMICALLY ACTIVE POPULATION*
(household survey, January–June 1980)

	Males	Females	Total
Agriculture, hunting, forestry and fishing	520,699	115,918	636,617
Mining and quarrying	4,103	291	4,394
Manufacturing	144,115	103,506	247,621
Electricity, gas and water	8,828	853	9,681
Construction	79,737	352	80,089
Trade, restaurants and hotels	78,785	177,301	256,086
Transport, storage and communication	62,994	2,599	65,593
Financing, insurance, real estate and business services	10,430	5,433	15,863
Community, social and personal services	121,145	129,013	250,158
Activities not adequately defined	112	112	224
Total labour force	**1,030,948**	**535,378**	**1,566,326**

* Excluding persons seeking work for the first time, totalling 27,027 (males 8,498; females 18,529).

Agriculture

PRINCIPAL CROPS (production in '000 quintals*)

	1985	1986	1987†
Coffee (green)	3,235	3,004	3,304
Seed cotton	542	311	239
Maize	10,764	10,000	12,435
Beans	744	1,000	522
Rice (milled)	1,003	1,929	500
Millet	2,883	2,924	565
Sugar cane‡	3,455	3,655	3,269

* Figures are in terms of the old Spanish quintal, equivalent to 46 kg (101.4 lb).
† Provisional.
‡ Figures are in terms of '000 metric tons.

LIVESTOCK ('000 head, year ending September)

	1984	1985	1986
Horses*	90	90	90
Mules*	23	23	23
Cattle	937	980	1,010†
Pigs	379	397	400†
Sheep*	4	4	4
Goats*	14	14	14

* FAO estimates. † Unofficial figure.
Chickens (million): 4 in 1984; 5 in 1985; 4 in 1986 (FAO estimate).
Source: FAO, *Production Yearbook*.

LIVESTOCK PRODUCTS ('000 metric tons)

	1984	1985	1986
Beef and veal	22	21	22*
Pigmeat†	13	13	13
Poultry meat	23	25	25†
Cows' milk	213	290†	283†
Cheese†	14.6	14.6	14.6
Hen eggs	38.5	40.8†	38.7†

* Unofficial figures. † FAO estimates.
Source: FAO, *Production Yearbook*.

Forestry

ROUNDWOOD REMOVALS
(FAO estimates, '000 cubic metres, excluding bark)

	1984	1985	1986
Sawlogs, veneer logs and logs for sleepers	57	57	56
Other industrial wood	25	26	25
Fuel wood	4,530	4,670	4,818
Total	**4,612**	**4,753**	**4,899**

Source: FAO, *Yearbook of Forest Products*.

EL SALVADOR

SAWNWOOD PRODUCTION (FAO estimates, '000 cubic metres)

	1984	1985	1986
Coniferous	30	28	29
Broadleaved	10	9	9
Total	40	37	38

Source: FAO, *Yearbook of Forest Products*.

Fishing

('000 metric tons, live weight)

	1984	1985*	1986*
Freshwater fishes	1.7	1.7	1.7
Marine fishes	1.4	1.4	1.5
Squat lobsters	1.8	1.8	1.9
Pacific seabobs	3.4	3.4	3.5
Other crustaceans	3.7	3.6	3.8
Molluscs	0.2	0.2	0.2
Total catch	12.2	12.1	12.5

* FAO estimates.
Source: FAO, *Yearbook of Fishery Statistics*.

Industry

SELECTED PRODUCTS
('000 metric tons, unless otherwise indicated)

	1983	1984	1985
Raw sugar	259	242	279
Beer ('000 hectolitres)	344	n.a.	n.a.
Cigarettes (million)	2,128	2,500*	2,300*
Motor spirit (petrol)†	120	127	130
Distillate fuel oils	185	181	180
Residual fuel oils	190	196	190
Cement	296	407*	400*
Electric energy (million kWh)	1,600	1,684	1,695

* Estimated production.
† Including aviation gasoline.
Source: UN, *Industrial Statistics Yearbook*.
1986: Electric energy 1,757 million kWh.

Finance

CURRENCY AND EXCHANGE RATES
Monetary Units
100 centavos = 1 Salvadorean colón.

Denominations
Coins: 1, 2, 3, 5, 10, 25 and 50 centavos; 1 colón.
Notes: 1, 2, 5, 10, 25, 50 and 100 colones.

Sterling and Dollar Equivalents (30 September 1988)
£1 sterling = 8.455 colones;
US $1 = 5.000 colones;
100 Salvadorean colones = £11.827 = $20.000.

Exchange Rate
Prior to January 1986, the official exchange rate was fixed at US $1 = 2.50 colones. In January 1986 a new rate of $1 = 5.00 colones was introduced.

BUDGET (million colones)

Current Revenue	1985	1986	1987
Taxes	1,659.4	2,702.3	2,517.1
Non-tax revenue	202.8	272.1	163.1
Current transfers	39.4	28.4	32.1
Other revenue	9.4	4.5	8.6
Total	1,911.0	3,007.3	2,720.9

Expenditure	1985	1986	1987
Remunerations	1,181.8	1,456.9	1,676.6
Purchase of goods and services	207.6	299.0	288.8
Interest on public debt	171.4	261.3	241.2
Private sector transfers	79.4	58.0	58.1
Public sector transfers	201.8	398.3	273.9
Foreign transfers	3.2	5.7	8.3
Expenditure from previous years	35.1	61.0	126.7
Capital investment	246.4	464.8	384.2
Amortization of public debt	152.4	476.1	339.5
Total	2,279.0	3,481.1	3,397.3

CENTRAL BANK RESERVES (US $ million at 31 December)

	1985	1986	1987
Gold*	19.8	19.8	19.8
Foreign exchange	179.6	169.7	186.1
Total	199.4	189.5	205.9

* Valued at US $42.22 per troy ounce.
Source: IMF, *International Financial Statistics*.

MONEY SUPPLY (million colones at 31 December)

	1985	1986	1987
Currency outside banks	1,080	1,157	1,298
Deposits of non-financial public enterprises at central bank	105	134	175
Demand deposits at deposit money banks	1,303	1,756	1,675
Total money	2,488	3,047	3,147

Source: IMF, *International Financial Statistics*.

COST OF LIVING (Consumer Price Index for Urban Areas. Base: December 1978 = 100)

	1985	1986	1987
Food	260.9	343.1	431.5
Clothing	269.7	364.2	427.3
Rent	259.1	338.4	422.0
Miscellaneous	214.7	284.9	363.6
All items	252.8	333.6	416.6

EL SALVADOR

Statistical Survey

NATIONAL ACCOUNTS (million colones at current prices)
National Income and Product

	1984	1985	1986*
Domestic factor incomes†	10,192.8	12,495.1	16,933.9
Consumption of fixed capital	482.0	591.2	815.3
Gross domestic product at factor cost	10,674.8	13,086.3	17,749.2
Indirect taxes, *less* subsidies	982.4	1,244.5	2,013.7
GDP in purchasers' values	11,657.2	14,330.8	19,762.9
Net factor income from abroad	−342.8	−352.7	−580.7
Gross national product	11,314.4	13,978.1	19,182.2
Less Consumption of fixed capital	482.0	591.2	815.3
National income in market prices	10,832.4	13,386.9	18,366.9

* Provisional.
† Compensation of employees and the operating surplus of enterprises. The amount is obtained as a residual.

Expenditure on the Gross Domestic Product

	1984	1985	1986*
Government final consumption expenditure	1,869.4	2,219.9	2,802.6
Private final consumption expenditure†	9,184.1	11,640.3	15,094.7
Increase in stocks	58.5	−168.9	25.7
Gross fixed capital formation	1,335.9	1,723.3	2,593.5
Total domestic expenditure	12,447.9	15,414.6	20,516.5
Exports of goods and services	2,535.9	3,199.2	4,896.1
Less Imports of goods and services	3,236.6	4,283.0	5,649.7
GDP in purchasers' values	11,657.2	14,330.8	19,762.9
GDP at constant 1962 prices	2,935.6	2,993.6	3,012.5

* Provisional.
† Including a statistical discrepancy.

Gross Domestic Product by Economic Activity

	1984	1985	1986*
Agriculture, hunting, forestry and fishing	2,319.8	2,610.6	3,968.9
Mining and quarrying	18.2	20.7	26.7
Manufacturing	1,837.1	2,345.7	3,085.7
Construction	355.3	437.0	547.1
Electricity, gas and water	281.2	335.3	448.1
Transport, storage and communications	480.6	613.3	815.8
Wholesale and retail trade	2,994.8	3,897.8	5,626.5
Finance, insurance, etc.	392.1	442.0	564.0
Owner-occupied dwellings	629.5	747.4	939.3
Public administration	1,366.2	1,602.8	1,976.5
Private services	982.4	1,278.2	1,794.3
Total	11,657.2	14,330.8	19,762.9

* Provisional.

BALANCE OF PAYMENTS (US $ million)

	1983	1984	1985
Merchandise exports f.o.b.	735.4	725.9	679.0
Merchandise imports f.o.b.	−830.9	−914.5	−895.0
Trade balance	−95.5	−188.6	−216.0
Exports of services	172.9	228.3	272.4
Imports of services	−385.8	−400.8	−428.7
Balance on goods and services	−308.4	−361.1	−372.3
Private unrequited transfers (net)	97.4	118.0	129.4
Government unrequited transfers (net)	174.1	189.6	214.2
Current balance	−37.0	−53.5	−28.7
Direct capital investment (net)	28.1	12.4	12.4
Other long-term capital (net)	183.6	21.5	87.0
Short-term capital (net)	−119.1	−14.8	−72.6
Net errors and omissions	−41.3	−52.1	23.0
Total (net monetary movements)	14.3	−86.5	21.0
Valuation changes (net)	15.2	11.7	3.1
Exceptional financing (net)	15.0	79.6	—
Official financing (net)	−5.6	13.6	6.2
Changes in reserves	38.9	18.4	30.3

Source: IMF, *International Financial Statistics*.

Imports c.i.f. (million colones, provisional): 4,424.4 in 1986; 4,970 in 1987.

External Trade

PRINCIPAL COMMODITIES (million colones)

Imports c.i.f.	1983	1984*	1985*
Foodstuffs	341.9	336.4	240.9
Dairy products	53.1	18.9	21.6
Wheat	50.4	61.2	30.8
Other cereals and cereal preparations	23.3	17.3	20.5
Fruits and fruit preparations	33.3	27.4	22.3
Vegetables	45.5	37.6	36.4
Raw materials, inedible	435.9	419.3	439.9
Crude petroleum	337.1	325.8	333.1
Animal and vegetable oils and fats	59.4	80.6	58.7
Chemical products	503.2	561.9	584.1
Chemical elements and compounds	96.8	108.0	102.1
Medicinal and pharmaceutical products	126.4	152.5	159.5
Perfume materials and other toiletries	36.2	44.1	35.8
Manufactured fertilizers	65.4	62.7	98.8
Basic manufactures and miscellaneous manufactured articles	596.3	658.5	613.9
Paper, cardboard and manufactures	83.2	94.4	82.8
Textile yarn and thread	43.8	45.9	46.4
Textile fabrics, other than cotton	22.6	30.5	26.3
Glass and glass manufactures	33.1	32.7	28.0
Iron and steel	68.0	67.4	68.8
Metal manufactures	55.6	66.7	63.3
Clothing (excl. footwear)	18.6	18.4	13.1

EL SALVADOR

Imports c.i.f.—continued	1983	1984*	1985*
Machinery and transport equipment	288.7	376.8	456.7
Mining, construction and industrial machinery	85.2	92.6	96.3
Electrical machinery and apparatus	121.6	131.4	155.9
Road motor vehicles	37.0	82.3	131.7
Total (incl. others)	2,232.0	2,443.6	2,403.4

* Provisional.

Imports c.i.f. (million colones, provisional): 4,424.4 in 1986; 4,970.3 in 1987.

Exports f.o.b.	1983	1984*	1985*
Foodstuffs	1,289.7	1,279.7	1,266.2
Fresh shrimps	32.1	58.3	31.4
Unrefined sugar	100.2	64.7	57.9
Coffee	1,107.0	1,106.9	1,131.4
Raw materials, inedible	152.5	49.0	101.7
Cotton	140.7	25.9	76.9
Chemical products	98.9	100.8	86.6
Miscellaneous manufactures	291.1	300.9	183.7
Clothing (excl. footwear)	23.9	19.0	6.9
Petroleum products	30.9	38.4	33.8
Total (incl. others)	1,894.6	1,793.4	1,697.4

* Provisional.

Exports f.o.b. (million colones, provisional): 3,564.9 in 1986; 2,954.7 in 1987.

PRINCIPAL TRADING PARTNERS ('000 colones)

Imports c.i.f.	1985*	1986*	1987*
Belgium-Luxembourg	14,819	43,585	38,021
Canada	23,346	31,262	75,289
Colombia	20,353	46,508	21,643
Costa Rica	135,338	188,832	194,262
France	12,138	25,838	22,095
Germany, Federal Republic	104,963	212,224	249,415
Guatemala	374,114	543,321	640,447
Honduras	26,487	46,142	51,260
Italy	15,811	36,687	39,969
Japan	124,047	166,474	311,576
Mexico	223,862	306,330	450,727
Netherlands	38,601	64,097	69,294
Panama	76,401	68,561	44,802
Spain	31,137	45,009	40,533
Sweden	10,457	21,678	16,222
Switzerland	10,228	28,723	30,242
Taiwan	23,926	32,472	64,378
USA	813,420	1,771,107	1,810,875
Venezuela	181,784	286,415	338,675
Total (incl. others)	2,403,444	4,424,440	4,970,335

Exports f.o.b.	1985*	1986*	1987*
Belgium-Luxembourg	28,540	62,618	73,963
Canada	37,269	98,523	43,218
Costa Rica	61,697	130,357	160,976
Germany, Federal Republic	356,053	860,339	509,482
Guatemala	153,512	239,163	364,268
Honduras	16,038	37,903	46,516
Japan	85,978	134,306	127,675
Netherlands	2,212	8,082	72,884
Nicaragua	8,114	26,093	26,232
Panama	36,879	53,177	54,241
Puerto Rico	3,249	6,509	11,316
Spain	37,628	61,869	77,199
Taiwan	4,782	528	3,399
USA	811,515	1,752,222	1,320,034
Total (incl. others)	1,697,420	3,564,850	2,954,705

* Provisional.

Transport

RAILWAYS (traffic)

	1985	1986	1987
Passengers ('000)	307.7	322.2	364.0
Freight ('000 metric tons)	324.4	322.3	353.3

Source: Comisión Ejecutiva Portuaria Autónoma.

ROAD TRAFFIC (motor vehicles in use at 31 December)

	1985	1986	1987
Passenger cars	136,163	136,927	138,276
Buses and coaches	6,073	6,463	6,774
Goods vehicles	13,388	16,463	16,607

Source: IRF, *World Road Statistics*.

SHIPPING

	1985	1986	1987
Vessels entered ('000 tons)	4,015	4,049	3,820
Freight ('000 metric tons)			
Loaded	345.9	255.1	175.0
Unloaded	993	1,038.1	971.6

Source: Comisión Ejecutiva Portuaria Autónoma.

CIVIL AVIATION (traffic on scheduled services)

	1985	1986	1987
Passengers arriving	161,368	167,186	180,469
Passengers leaving	171,666	168,457	165,828
Freight loaded (tons)	4,428	3,160	4,747
Freight unloaded (tons)	6,174	5,677	6,784

Source: Comisión Ejecutiva Portuaria Autónoma.

Tourism

	1985	1986	1987
Tourist arrivals ('000)	133	134	125

Communications Media

	1984	1985	1986
Radio receivers ('000 in use)	n.a.	1,900	n.a.
Television receivers ('000 in use)	n.a.	350	242
Telephones ('000 in use)	89	94	n.a.
Daily newspapers	6	6	6

Source: mainly UNESCO, *Statistical Yearbook*.

Education

(1985)

	Institutions	Teachers	Students
Pre-Primary	916	1,561	62,500
Primary	2,799	24,295	923,597
Secondary	285	3,880	90,288
Higher	34	3,404	60,994

Directory

The Constitution

The Constitution of the Republic of El Salvador came into effect on 20 December 1983.

The Constitution provides for a republican, democratic and representative form of government, composed of three Powers—Legislative, Executive, and Judicial—which are to operate independently. Voting is a right and duty of all citizens over 18 years of age. Presidential and congressional elections may not be held simultaneously.

The Constitution binds the country, as part of the Central American Nation, to favour the total or partial reconstruction of the Republic of Central America. Integration in a unitary, federal or confederal form, provided that democratic and republican principles are respected and that basic rights of individuals are fully guaranteed, is subject to popular approval.

LEGISLATIVE ASSEMBLY

The Legislative Power is vested in a single Chamber, the Legislative Assembly, whose members are elected every three years and are eligible for re-election. The Assembly's term of office begins on 1 May. The Assembly's duties include the choosing of the President and Vice-President of the Republic from the two citizens who shall have gained the largest number of votes for each of these offices, if no candidate obtains an absolute majority in the election. It also selects the members of the Supreme and subsidiary courts; of the Elections Council; and the Accounts Court of the Republic. It fixes taxes; ratifies treaties concluded by the Executive with other States and international organizations; sanctions the Budget; regulates the monetary system of the country; determines the conditions under which foreign currencies may circulate; and suspends and reimposes constitutional guarantees. The right to initiate legislation may be exercised by the Assembly (as well as by the President, through the Council of Ministers, and by the Supreme Court). The Assembly may override, with a two-thirds majority, the President's objections to a Bill which it has sent for presidential approval.

PRESIDENT

The President is elected for five years, the term beginning and expiring on 1 June. The principle of alternation in the presidential office is established in the Constitution, which states the action to be taken should this principle be violated. The Executive is responsible for the preparation of the Budget and its presentation to the Assembly; the direction of foreign affairs; the organization of the armed and security forces; and the convening of extraordinary sessions of the Assembly. In the event of the President's death, resignation, removal or other cause, the Vice-President takes office for the rest of the presidential term; and, in case of necessity, the Vice-President may be replaced by one of the two Designates elected by the Legislative Assembly.

JUDICIARY

Judicial Power is exercised by the Supreme Court and by other competent tribunals. The Magistrates of the Supreme Court are elected by the Legislature, their number to be determined by law. The Supreme Court alone is competent to decide whether laws, decrees and regulations are constitutional or not.

The Government

HEAD OF STATE

President: Ing. JOSÉ NAPOLEÓN DUARTE (sworn in 1 June 1984).
Vice-President: Lic. RODOLFO ANTONIO CASTILLO CLARAMOUNT.

COUNCIL OF MINISTERS
(February 1989)

Minister of the Interior: Dr EDGAR ERNESTO BELLOSO FUNES.
Minister of the Presidency: Col REYNALDO LÓPEZ NUILA.
Minister of Justice: Dr JULIO ALFREDO SAMAYOA.
Minister of Public Health and Social Welfare: Dr BENJAMÍN VÁLDEZ H.
Minister of Finance: RICARDO J. LÓPEZ.
Minister of Economy: Ing. JOSÉ RICARDO PERDOMO.
Minister of Foreign Trade: Ing. CARLOS AQUILINO DUARTE FUNES.
Minister of Foreign Affairs: Dr RICARDO ACEVEDO PERALTA.
Minister of Defence and Public Security: Gen. CARLOS EUGENIO VIDES CASANOVA.
Minister of Education: Prof. CARLOS CRUZ AVALOS.
Minister of Agriculture and Livestock: Dr JUAN ANTONIO MORALES EHRLICH.
Minister of Planning and Co-ordination of Economic and Social Development: Ing. REMO BARDI CEVALLOS.
Minister of Labour and Social Welfare: Dr LÁZARO TADEO BERNAL LIZAMA.
Minister of Public Works: Ing. LUIS LÓPEZ CERÓN.
Minister of Culture and Communications: Ing. ROBERTO EDMUNDO VIERA.

MINISTRIES

Ministry of the Presidency: Casa Presidencial, San Salvador; telex 20245.
Ministry of Agriculture and Livestock: Blvd de Los Héroes y 21a Calle Poniente, San Salvador; telex 20228.
Ministry of Culture and Communications: 17 Avda Sur 430, San Salvador; tel. 22-9152.
Ministry of Defence and Public Security: Palacio Nacional, San Salvador; telex 30345.
Ministry of Economy: Centro de Gobierno, 4a Avda Norte 233, San Salvador.
Ministry of Education: Calle Delgado y 8a Avda Norte, San Salvador.
Ministry of Finance: 3a Avda Norte y 13 Calle Poniente, San Salvador.
Ministry of Foreign Affairs: Blvd Dr Manuel Enrique Araújo, Km 6, San Salvador; telex 20179.
Ministry of Foreign Trade: Paseo Gral Escalón 4122, Apdo 0119, San Salvador; tel. 24-3000; telex 20269.
Ministry of the Interior: Palacio Nacional, San Salvador.
Ministry of Justice: Avda Masferrer 612B, Colonia Escalón, San Salvador; tel. 24-0326.
Ministry of Labour and Social Welfare: Edif. Ministerio del Interior, Palacio Nacional, San Salvador; telex 20016.
Ministry of Planning and Co-ordination of Economic and Social Development: 10 Avda Sur, Costado Noroeste de Casa Presidencial, San Salvador; telex 30309.
Ministry of Public Health and Social Welfare: Calle Arce 827, San Salvador.
Ministry of Public Works: Palacio Nacional, San Salvador.

President

In the second round of voting in the presidential election, held on 6 May 1984 (following an inconclusive first round on 25 March), JOSÉ NAPOLEÓN DUARTE, candidate of the Partido Demócrata Cristiano (PDC), received 752,625 (53.6%) of the votes cast, while Maj. ROBERTO D'AUBUISSON ARRIETA, candidate of the Alianza Republicana Nacional (ARENA), received 651,741 (46.4%) of the votes. The next presidential election was to be held on 19 March 1989.

Legislature

ASAMBLEA NACIONAL

President: Lic. RICARDO ALVARENGA VALDIVIESO (ARENA).
First Vice-President: ALFONSO ARÍSTEDES ALVARENGA.

General Election, 20 March 1988

Party	Seats
Alianza Republicana Nacionalista (ARENA)	31
Partido Demócrata Cristiano (PDC)	23
Partido de Conciliación Nacional (PCN)	6
Total	**60**

EL SALVADOR

Political Organizations

OFFICIALLY RECOGNIZED PARTIES

Alianza Republicana Nacionalista (ARENA): San Salvador; f. 1981; right-wing; Leader and 1989 Presidential Candidate Alfredo Cristiani; Sec.-Gen. Mario Repdaelli.

Movimiento Estable Republicano Centrista (MERECEN): San Salvador; f. 1982; centre party; Sec.-Gen. Juan Ramón Rosales y Rosales.

Partido Acción Democrática (AD): Apdo 01124, San Salvador; f. 1981; centre-right; observer mem. of Liberal International; Leader Ricardo González Camacho.

Partido Acción Renovadora (PAR): San Salvador; f. 1944; advocates a more just society; Leader Ernesto Oyarbide.

Partido Auténtico Institucional Salvadoreño (PAISA): San Salvador; f. 1982; formerly right-wing majority of the PCN; Sec.-Gen. Dr Roberto Escobar García.

Partido de Conciliación Nacional (PCN): Calle Arce 1128, San Salvador; f. 1961; right-wing; Pres. Hugo Carrillo; Leader Francisco José Guerrero; Sec.-Gen. Raúl Molina Martínez.

Partido Demócrata Cristiano (PDC): 3a Calle Poniente 836, San Salvador; f. 1960; 150,000 mems; anti-imperialist, advocates self-determination and Latin American integration; Sec.-Gen. Lic. Rodolfo Antonio Castillo Claramount; 1989 Presidential Candidate Dr Fidel Chávez Mena; factions include:

Movimiento Auténtico Demócrata Cristiano (MADC): f. 1988; 1989 Presidential Candidate Julio Adolfo Rey Prendes.

Partido de Orientación Popular (POP): San Salvador; f. 1981; extreme right-wing.

Partido Popular Salvadoreño (PPS): POB (01) 425, San Salvador; tel. 23-2265; f. 1966; right-wing; represents business interests; Sec.-Gen. Francisco Quiñónez Ávila.

Partido Unionista Centroamericana (PUCA): San Salvador; advocates reunification of Central America; Pres. Dr Gabriel Pilopa Araújo.

Parties awaiting legal recognition are Partido Centrista Salvadoreño (f. 1985; Leader Tomás Chafoya Martínez); Partido de Empresarios, Campesinos y Obreros (ECO, Leader Dr Luis Rolando López) and Partido Independiente Democrático (PID, f. 1985; Leader Eduardo García Tobar).

Other parties include: Partido de la Revolución Salvadoreña (Sec.-Gen. Joaquín Villalobos); Patria Libre (f. 1985; right-wing; Leader Hugo Barrera) and Partido Social Demócrata—PSD (f. 1987; left-wing; Sec.-Gen. Mario Reni Roldán).

OPPOSITION GROUPING

Frente Democrático Revolucionario-Farabundo Martí de Liberación Nacional (FDR-FMLN): San Salvador; f. 1980 as a left-wing opposition front to the PDC-military coalition government; the FDR is the political wing and the FMLN is the guerrilla front; military operations are co-ordinated by the Dirección Revolucionaria Unida (DRU); Pres. (FDR) Dr Guillermo Manuel Ungo; Vice-Pres (FDR) Ing. Eduardo Calles, Rubén Zamora Rivas; General Command (FMLN) Fermán Cienfuegos, Roberto Roca, Joaquín Villalobos, Leonel González, Shafik Jorge Handel; the front comprises c. 20 groups, of which the principal are:

Bloque Popular Revolucionario (BPR): guerrilla arm: Fuerzas Populares de Liberación (FPL; Leader 'Commander Gerónimo'); based in Chalatenango; First Sec. Leonel González; Second Sec. Dimas Rodríguez.

Frente de Acción Popular Unificado (FAPU): guerrilla arm: Fuerzas Armadas de la Resistencia Nacional (FARN); Leaders Fermán Cienfuegos, Saúl Villalta.

Frente Pedro Pablo Castillo: f. 1985.

Ligas Populares del 28 de Febrero (LP-28): guerrilla arm: Ejército Revolucionario Popular (ERP); Leaders Joaquín Villalobos, Ana Guadalupe Martínez.

Movimiento Nacional Revolucionario (MNR): San Salvador; Leader Dr Guillermo Manuel Ungo.

Movimiento Obrero Revolucionario Salvado Cayetano Carpio (MOR).

Movimiento Popular Social Cristiano (MPSC): formed by dissident members of PDC; Leader Rubén Zamora Rivas.

Partido Comunista Salvadoreño (PCS): guerrilla arm: Fuerzas Armadas de Liberación (FAL); Leader Jorge Schafik Handal; Deputy Leader Américo Araújo Ramírez.

Partido Revolucionario de los Trabajadores Centroamericanos (PRTC): Leaders Roberto Roca, María Concepción de Valladares (alias Commdr Nidia Díaz).

Directory

Unión Democrática Nacionalista (UDN): f. 1969; left-wing; Sec.-Gen. Mario Aguinada Carranza (in exile).

In November 1987 the PSD, MNR and MPSC united to form a left-wing alliance, the **Convergencia Democrática** (1989 Presidential Candidate Dr Guillermo Manuel Ungo; Gen. Co-ordinator Rubén Zamora Rivas). The MNR and MPSC were, however, to remain as members of the FDR-FMLN.

OTHER GROUPS

Partido de Liberación Nacional (PLN): political-military organization of the extreme right; the military wing is the Ejército Secreto Anti-comunista (ESA); Sec.-Gen. and C-in-C Aquiles Baires.

The following guerrilla groups are dissident factions of the Fuerzas Populares de Liberación (FPL):

Frente Clara Elizabeth Ramírez: f. 1983; Marxist-Leninist group.

Movimiento Laborista Cayetano Carpio: f. 1983.

There are also several right-wing guerrilla groups and 'death squads' not officially linked to any of the right-wing parties.

Diplomatic Representation

EMBASSIES IN EL SALVADOR

Argentina: 79 Avda Norte 704, Colonia Escalón, Apdo 01-384, San Salvador; tel. 24-4238; telex 20221; Ambassador: Juan Carlos Ibáñez.

Brazil: Edif. la Centroamericana, Alameda Roosevelt 3107 5°, San Salvador; tel. 23-1214; telex 20096; Ambassador: Mario Loureiro Dias Costa.

Chile: Pasaje Belle Vista No 121, Entre 9a C.P. y 9a C.P. bis, Colonia Escalón, San Salvador; tel. 23-7132; telex 20377; Ambassador: René Pérez Negrete.

China (Taiwan): 89a Avda Norte 335, Colonia Escalón, San Salvador; tel. 23-6920; telex 20152; Ambassador: Gen. Lo Yu-lum.

Colombia: Edif. Inter-Capital 2°, Paseo Gral Escalón y Calle La Ceiba, Colonia Escalón, San Salvador; tel. 23-0126; telex 20247; Ambassador: Dr Luis Guillermo Vélez Trujillo.

Costa Rica: Edif. la Centroamericana 3°, Alameda Roosevelt 3107, San Salvador; tel. 23-8283; telex 20171; Ambassador: Lic. Jesús M. Fernández.

Dominican Republic: San Salvador; tel. 23-6636; Ambassador: Alberto Emilio Despradel Cabral.

Ecuador: Blvd Hipódromo 803, Colonia San Benito, San Salvador; tel. 24-5921; telex 20445; Ambassador: Jaime Sánchez Lemos.

France: Colonia La Mascota, Pasaje A 41-46, Casilla 474, San Salvador; tel. 23-0728; telex 20243; Ambassador: Jean-Claude Fortuit.

Germany, Federal Republic: 3a Calle Poniente 3831, Colonia Escalón, Apdo 693, San Salvador; tel. 23-6173; telex 20149; Ambassador: Guido Heymer.

Guatemala: 15 Avda Norte 135, San Salvador; tel. 21-6097; Ambassador: Brig.-Gen. Luis Federico Fuentes Corado.

Holy See: 87a Avda Norte y 7a Calle Poniente, Colonia Escalón, Apdo 01-95, San Salvador; tel. 23-2454; Apostolic Nuncio: Mgr Francesco de Nittis.

Honduras: 9a Calle Poniente 4612 y 89a Avda Norte, Colonia Escalón, San Salvador; tel. 24-6662; telex 20524; Ambassador: Mario Maldonado Muñoz.

Israel: 85 Avda Norte, No 619, Colonia Escalón, Apdo 1776, San Salvador; tel. 23-8770; telex 20777; Ambassador: Aryeh Amir.

Italy: 1a Calle Poniente y 71a Avda Norte 204, San Salvador; tel. 23-7325; telex 20418; Ambassador: Dr Teodoro Fuxa (also represents the interests of Somalia).

Japan: Avda La Capilla 615, Colonia San Benito, San Salvador; tel. 24-4597; Chargé d'affaires: Hiroyuki Kimoto.

Mexico: Paseo Gral Escalón 3832, San Salvador; tel. 23-4243; telex 20070; Ambassador: Federico Uruchúa Durand.

Nicaragua: 27a Avda Norte 1134, Colonia Layco, San Salvador; tel. 25-7281; telex 20546; Chargé d'affaires: Francisco Tenorio Mora.

Panama: Edif. Balam Quitzé 68-1, Calle Circunvalación y 89a Avda Sur, Colonia Escalón, San Salvador; tel. 23-7893; Ambassador: David Samuel Peré Ramos.

Paraguay: Avda La Capilla 414, Colonia San Benito, San Salvador; tel. 23-5951; Ambassador: Juan Alberto Llánez.

Peru: Edif. La Centroamericana 2°, Alameda Roosevelt 3107, San Salvador; tel. 23-0008; Ambassador: Alberto Montagne.

EL SALVADOR
Directory

Spain: 51 Avda Norte 138, San Salvador; tel. 23-7961; telex 20372; Ambassador: Fernando Alvarez de Miranda.

United Kingdom: Edif. Inter Inversión, Paseo Gral Escalón 4828, Apdo 1591, San Salvador; tel. 24-0473; telex 20033; Chargé d'affaires: Iain R. Murray.

USA: 25 Avda Norte 1230, San Salvador; tel. 26-7100; telex 20648; Ambassador: William Waller.

Uruguay: Edif. Intercapital, Calle La Ceiba y Paseo Gral Escalón 1°, San Salvador; tel. 24-6661; telex 20391; Ambassador: Alfredo Lafone.

Venezuela: 93 Avda Norte 619, Colonia Escalón, San Salvador; tel. 23-5809; telex 20388; Ambassador: Dr Pedro E. Coll.

Judicial System

Supreme Court of Justice: Centro de Gobierno José Simeón Cañas, San Salvador; tel. 71-3511; composed of 14 Magistrates, one of whom is its President. The Court is divided into four chambers: Constitutional Law, Civil Law, Penal Law and Litigation.

President: Dr Francisco José Guerrero.

Chambers of 2nd Instance: 14 chambers composed of two Magistrates.

Courts of 1st Instance: 87 courts in all chief towns and districts.

Courts of Peace: 193 courts throughout the Republic.

Attorney-General: Roberto García Alvarado.

Religion

Roman Catholicism is the dominant religion, but other denominations are also permitted. In 1982 there were about 200,000 Protestants. Seventh-day Adventists, Jehovah's Witnesses, the Baptist Church and the Church of Jesus Christ of Latter-day Saints (Mormons) are represented.

CHRISTIANITY
The Roman Catholic Church

El Salvador comprises one archdiocese and eight dioceses. About 90% of the country's inhabitants are adherents.

Bishops' Conference: Conferencia Episcopal de El Salvador, 15 Avda Norte 1420, Colonia Layce, Apdo 1310, San Salvador; tel. 25-8997; f. 1974; Pres. Mgr Marco René Revelo Contreras, Bishop of Santa Ana.

Archbishop of San Salvador: Mgr Arturo Rivera y Damas, Arzobispado, 1a Calle Poniente 3412, Seminario San José de la Montaña, Colonia Escalón, San Salvador; tel. 24-4427.

The Baptist Church

Baptist Association of El Salvador: Apdo 347, San Salvador; tel. 26-6287; f. 1933; Exec. Sec. Rev. Carlos Isidro Sánchez.

The Press

DAILY NEWSPAPERS
San Salvador

El Diario de Hoy: 11a Calle Oriente 271, Apdo 495, San Salvador; tel. 21-5340; telex 20291; f. 1936; independent; Dir Enrique Altamirano Madriz; Man. Francisco Marchesini; circ. 87,260 (weekdays), 84,090 (Sundays).

Diario Latino: 23a Avda Sur 225, Apdo 96, San Salvador; tel. 21-3240; f. 1890; evening; Editor Miguel Angel Pinto; circ. 20,000.

Diario Oficial: 4a Calle Poniente 829, San Salvador; tel. 21-9101; f. 1875; Dir Alonso Mira; circ. 2,100.

El Mundo: 2a Avda Norte 211, Apdo 368, San Salvador; tel. 71-4400; f. 1967; evening; Dir Cristóbal Iglesias; circ. 58,032 (weekdays), 61,822 (Sundays).

La Prensa Gráfica: 3a Calle Poniente 130, San Salvador; tel. 71-3333; f. 1915; general information; conservative, independent; Editor Rodolfo Dutriz; circ. 97,312 (weekdays), 115,564 (Sundays).

Santa Ana

Diario de Occidente: 1a Avda Sur No. 3, Santa Ana; tel. 41-2931; f. 1910; Editor Alex E. Montenegro; circ. 6,000.

PERIODICALS

Anaqueles: 8a Avda Norte y Calle Delgado, San Salvador; review of the National Library.

Cultura: Ministerio de Cultura y Comunicaciones, 17 Avda Sur No 430, San Salvador; tel. 22-9152; quarterly; educational; Dir Dr David Escobar Galindo.

El Salvador Filatélico: Avda España 207, Altos Vidrí Panades, San Salvador; f. 1940; publ. quarterly by the Philatelic Society of El Salvador.

Orientación: Palacio Arzobispal, 1a Calle Poniente 3462, San Salvador; tel. 24-5099; Catholic weekly; Dir Roberto Torroella.

Proceso: Apdo (01) 575, San Salvador; tel. 24-0011; f. 1980; weekly newsletter, published by the Documentation and Information Centre of the Universidad Centroamericana José Simeón Cañas.

Revista del Ateneo de El Salvador: 13a Calle Poniente, Centro de Gobierno, San Salvador; tel. 22-9686; f. 1912; 3 a year; official organ of Salvadorean Athenaeum; Pres. Dr Manuel Luis Escamilla; Sec.-Gen. Dr Carlos Rivas Tejada.

Revista Judicial: Centro de Gobierno, San Salvador; tel. 22-4522; organ of the Supreme Court; Dir Dr Manuel Arrieta Gallegos.

PRESS ASSOCIATION

Asociación de Periodistas de El Salvador (Press Association of El Salvador): Edif. Casa del Periodista, Paseo Gral Escalón 4130, San Salvador; tel. 23-8943; Pres. José Luis Urrutia.

FOREIGN NEWS AGENCIES

Agencia EFE (Spain): Edif. OMSA 2°, 1, 21 Calle Poniente, San Salvador; tel. 26-0110; telex 20455, Bureau Chief Ricardo Chacón.

Agenzia Nazionale Stampa Associata (ANSA) (Italy): Acaxual 30, San Salvador; tel. 26-6427; telex 20083; Bureau Chief René Alberto Contreras.

Associated Press (AP) (USA): Hotel Camino Real, Suite 201, Blvd de Los Héroes, San Salvador; tel. 24-4885; telex 20463; Correspondent Bryna Brennan.

Deutsche Presse-Agentur (dpa) (Federal Republic of Germany): Avda España 225, 2°, Of. 1, San Salvador; tel. 22-2640; Correspondent Jorge Armando Contreras.

Inter Press Service (IPS) (Italy): San Salvador; tel. 26-6814; telex 20523; Correspondent Virginia Aguirre.

Reuters (UK): Hotel Camino Real, Suite 220, Camino de Los Héroes, San Salvador; tel. 23-4736; telex 20634; Bureau Chief Adrian R. Aldana.

United Press International (UPI) (USA): Calle y Pasaje Palneral, Col. Toluca, Apdo 05-185, San Salvador; tel. 25-2885; telex 30131; Correspondent Raúl Bethran.

Publishers

Editorial Universitaria: Ciudad Universitaria, Universidad de El Salvador, Apdo 1703, San Salvador; tel. 25-6604; f. 1923; Dir Alfredo Montti.

Dirección de Publicaciones e Impresos: Ministerio de Cultura y Comunicaciones, 17 Avda Sur 430, San Salvador; tel. 22-9152; f. 1953; educational and general; Dir Lic. Cristóbal Humberto Ibarra.

UCA Editores: Apdo 01-575, San Salvador; tel. 24-0011; f. 1975; social science, religion, economy, literature and textbooks; Dir Rodolfo Cardenal.

PUBLISHERS' ASSOCIATIONS

Asociación Salvadoreña de Agencias de Publicidad: San Salvador; f. 1962.

Cámara Salvadoreña del Libro: Calle Arce No 423, Apdo 2296, San Salvador; tel. 21-7206; f. 1974; Pres. Otto Kurt Wahn Cabrales.

Radio and Television

In 1986 there were an estimated 1,200,000 radio receivers in use, and in 1987 there were an estimated 425,000 television receivers in use.

Administración Nacional de Telecomunicaciones (ANTEL): Edif. Administrativo ANTEL, Centro de Gobierno, San Salvador; tel. 71-7171; telex 20252; f. 1963; Pres. Ing. Julio César Gómez; Man. Dr Maurico Daniel Vides Casanova.

RADIO

Asociación Salvadoreña de Radiodifusores (ASDER): 4a Calle Oriente 528, Apdo 210, San Salvador; tel. 22-0872; Pres. Manuel Antonio Flores Barrera.

EL SALVADOR

YSS Radio El Salvador: Dirección General de Medios, Ministerio de Cultura y Comunicaciones, San Salvador; tel. 21-4376; telex 20145; non-commercial cultural station; Dir-Gen. (vacant).

There are 75 commercial radio stations. The guerrilla group, ERP, operates its own station, Radio Venceremos, and the FPL operate Radio Farabundo Martí.

TELEVISION

Canal 2, SA: Apdo 720, San Salvador; tel. 23-6744; telex 20443; commercial; Pres. B. Eserski; Gen. Man. Eduardo Anaya.

Canal 4, SA: Carretera de San Salvador a Santa Tecla, Apdo 444, San Salvador; tel. 24-4555; commercial; Pres. Boris Eserski; Man. Ronald Calvo.

Canal 6, SA: Alameda Dr Manuel E. Araújo Km. 6, Apdo (06) 1801, San Salvador; tel. 23-5122; commercial; Pres. José A. González L.; Man. Dr Pedro Leonel Moreno Monge.

Canal 8 and 10: Avda Robert Baden Powell, Apdo 4, Nueva San Salvador; tel. 28-0973; telex 21046; f. 1965; government station; Dir Carlos Díaz Chapetón.

Canal 12: 5a Avda las Acacias 130, Col. San Benito, San Salvador; tel. 246171.

Finance

(cap. = capital; p.u. = paid up; res = reserves; dep. = deposits; m. = million; brs = branches; amounts in colones unless otherwise stated)

BANKING

The banking system was nationalized in March 1980.

Supervisory Body

Superintendencia del Sistema Financiero: 79a Avda Norte y Pasaje Los Pinos, 134 Colonia Escalón, San Salvador; tel. 24-0773; Superintendent Lic. Héctor Edmundo Cuellar.

Central Bank

Banco Central de Reserva de El Salvador: 1a Calle Poniente y 7a Avda Norte, San Salvador; tel. 22-1144; telex 20088; f. 1934; nationalized Dec. 1961; sole right of note issue; cap. p.u. 2.5m., res 351.1m., dep. 2,300.28m. (March 1988); Pres. Ing. Maurice Choussy Rusconi; Man. Lic. Armando Barrios; 7 brs.

Commercial and Mortgage Banks

Banco Agrícola Comercial de El Salvador: Blvd del Hipódromo No 803, Colonia San Benito, San Salvador; tel. 71-6126; telex 20395; f. 1955; cap. 30m., res 13.1m., dep. 1,113.8m. (June 1987); Pres. Rodolfo Santos Morales; 17 brs.

Banco Capitalizador, SA: Alameda Roosevelt y 43 Avda Norte Frente Hotel Alameda, San Salvador; tel. 23-1761; telex 20254; f. 1955; cap. 14m., res 4.8m., dep. 839.7m. (June 1987); Pres. Dr Ernesto Arbizú Mata; 17 brs.

Banco de Comercio de El Salvador: Calle y Casa Loma Linda No 104, Colonia San Benito, San Salvador; tel. 23-4130; telex 20124; f. 1949; cap. 35m., res 5.7m., dep. 839.7m. (June 1987); Pres. Lic. Salvador Veliz; Gen. Man. Eusebio Martell; 21 brs.

Banco de Crédito Popular: Avda Olímpica y Pasaje 3, San Salvador; tel. 23-2590; telex 20208; f. 1957; cap. 23m., res 5.2m., dep. 415.7m. (June 1987); Pres. José Alberto Cerna; 12 brs.

Banco Cuscatlán: 6a Avda Sur 118, San Salvador; tel. 71-1233; telex 20220; f. 1972; cap. p.u. 31.5m., res 31.1m., dep. 1,344m. (June 1987); Pres. Lic. Rafael Edmundo Girón Carballo; Man. José Antonio Manzano; 12 brs.

Banco de Desarrollo e Inversión, SA: 67a Avda Norte y Blvd San Antonio Abad, Plaza las Américas, San Salvador; tel. 23-7888; telex 20261; f. 1978; cap. 17m., res 7.5m., dep. 265.1m. (June 1988); Pres. Lic. Xóchitl Tirza de Merino; 7 brs.

Banco Financiero: 67A Avda Sur No 121, San Salvador; tel. 23-6066; telex 20319; f. 1977; cap. 5m., res 0.3m., dep. 86.9m. (June 1987); Pres. Oscar Alfredo Hinds; 3 brs.

Banco Hipotecario de El Salvador: 4a Calle Oriente y 2a Avda Sur, San Salvador; tel. 22-2122; telex 20309; f. 1934; mortgage bank; cap. p.u. 0.9m., res 21.6m., dep. 954.6m. (June 1987); Pres. Lic. Arturo Muysshondt; Man. Lic. Arturo Francisco Guzmán Trigueros; 16 brs.

Banco Mercantil, SA: 1a Calle Poniente y 7a Avda Norte, frente al Banco Central de Reserva, San Salvador; tel. 23-3022; telex 20723; f. 1978; cap. 10m., res 4.6m., dep. 187.8m. (June 1987); Pres. Maximino Belloso; 4 brs.

Banco Salvadoreño, SA: Calle Rubén Darío No 1236, Apdo 01-101, San Salvador; tel. 22-2144; telex 20172; f. 1885; res 4.6m. (Dec. 1986), cap. 25m., dep. 598m. (Dec. 1987); Pres. Lic. Angela Lelany Bigueur; 17 brs.

Public Institutions

Banco de Fomento Agropecuario: Km 10, Carretera a la Libertad, San Salvador; tel. 71-3011; telex 20027; f. 1973; cap. 82m., res 8.7m., dep. 59.2m. (July 1987); Pres. Ing. Joaquín Guevara Morán; Man. Rafael Antonio Alvarenga López; 27 brs.

Banco Nacional de Fomento Industrial (BANAFI): 1a Calle Poniente No 2310, San Salvador; tel. 24-6677; telex 20285; f. 1982; Pres. Lic. Ernesto Allwoods Lagos; Man. Lic. Juan José Manzanares.

Financiera Nacional de la Vivienda (FNV): San Salvador; tel. 23-8822; national housing finance agency; f. 1963 to improve housing facilities through loan and savings associations; cap. 5.2m., res 20.8m. (June 1987); Pres. Ing. Remo Pardi Cevallos; Man. Armando Estrada Valdez.

Financiera Nacional de Tierras Agrícolas (FINATA): San Salvador; tel. 71-2444; Pres. Orlando Arévalo; Man. Lic. Ernesto Torres Chico.

Savings and Loan Associations

Asociación de Ahorro y Préstamo, SA (ATLACATL): Blvd de Los Héroes y 25 Calle Poniente, Apdo 1100, San Salvador; tel. 25-5555; f. 1964; savings and loan association; cap. 19.2m., dep. 305.4m. (June 1987); Pres. Oscar Argueta; 17 brs.

Ahorro, Préstamos e Inversiones, SA (APRISA): Calle San Jerónimo Emiliani No 3, Colonia La Sultana, Antiguo Cuscatlán, San Salvador; tel. 78-9401; f. 1977; cap. 3.1m., res 0.7m., dep. 105.8m. (June 1987); Pres. Dr Napoleón Arnoldo Monterrosa Valle; 9 brs.

Ahorros Metropolitanos, SA (AHORROMET): Edif. Continental, Inicio Paseo Escalón, frente Salvador del Mundo, San Salvador; tel. 23-6337; f. 1972; cap. 4.5m., res 0.5m., dep. 187.9m. (June 1987); Pres. Lic. Efraín Fuentes Alvarenga; 12 brs.

La Central de Ahorros, SA: Alameda Roosevelt y 43 Avda Sur, San Salvador; tel. 24-4840; f. 1979; cap. 5m., res 0.9m., dep. 42.3m. (June 1987); Pres. Ismael Escobar; 5 brs.

Construcción y Ahorro SA (CASA): 75 Avda Sur 126, Colonia Escalón, Apdo 2215, San Salvador; tel. 78-9121; f. 1964; saving and building finance; cap. 8.0m., res 11m., dep. 306m. (Aug. 1988); Pres. José Oscar Medina; 15 brs.

CRECE, SA: Alameda Roosevelt y 59 Avda Norte, Apdo (05) 25, San Salvador; tel. 23-8299; f. 1973; cap. 5.5m., res 0.7m., dep. 122.3m. (June 1987); Pres. Lic. Mauricio Ernesto Martínez; 8 brs.

Crédito Inmobiliario, SA (CREDISA): Edif. CREDISA, Alameda Juan Pablo II, San Salvador; tel. 23-4111; f. 1964; cap. 9m., res 2.8m., dep. 240.2m. (June 1987); Pres. Dr Ing. Rinaldo Galdámez de León; 14 brs.

Foreign Banks

Banco de Santander y Panamá, SA: Alameda Roosevelt 3425, Apdo (01) 231, San Salvador; tel. 24-1099; telex 20003; Pres. Maximino Belloso; Man. Laura Baires Rivas.

Bank of America NT and SA (USA): Edif. San José, Planta Alta, 29 Avda Norte 1223, San Salvador; tel. 26-7391; telex 20072; Pres. Dr Armando Peña Quezada.

Banking Associations

Federación de Asociaciones Cooperativas de Ahorro y Crédito de El Salvador de Responsabilidad Limitada (FEDECACES): 23 Avda Norte y 25 Calle Poniente, No. 1301, Colonia San Jorge, Apdo 156, San Salvador; tel. 26-8925; f. 1966; Pres. Carlos Alberto Baires; Gen. Man. Héctor David Córdova.

Federación de Cajas de Crédito (FEDECREDITO): 25a Avda Norte y 23 Calle Poniente, San Salvador; tel. 25-5922; telex 20392; f. 1943; Pres. Lic. Oscar Raymundo Melgar; Man. Víctor Nosthas Mena.

STOCK EXCHANGE

Bolsa de El Salvador: San Salvador; tel. 23-8342; f. 1964.

INSURANCE

American Life Insurance Co.: Edif. Omnimotores, 2a Planta, Km 4½, Carretera a Santa Tecla, Apdo (06) 169, San Salvador; tel. 23-4925; telex 20627; f. 1963; cap. 1m.; Man. Carlos F. Pereira.

Aseguradora Agrícola Comercial, SA: Alameda Roosevelt 3104, Apdo 1855, San Salvador; tel. 23-8200; telex 20288; f. 1973; cap. 1.5m.; Pres. Jean Paul Bolens.

Aseguradora Popular, SA: 4a Calle Oriente y 2a Avda Sur No 212, Apdo 1991, San Salvador; tel. 71-6033; telex 20531; f. 1975; cap. 2m.; Man. Lic. Roberto José Cantón.

Aseguradora Suiza Salvadoreña, SA: Alameda Dr Manuel Enrique Araújo y Calle La Reforma, Plaza Suiza, San Salvador; tel. 23-2111; telex 20581; f. 1969; cap. 2.5m.; Pres. ROBERTO SCHILDKNECHT.

La Auxiliadora, SA: Avda Olímpica y 63 Avda Sur, Colonia Escalón, Apdo 665, San Salvador; tel. 23-7736; telex 20753; f. 1958; cap. 1.5m., dep. 9m.; Pres. MARÍA EUGENIA BRIZUELA DE AVILA.

La Centro Americana, SA, Cía Salvadoreña de Seguros: Alameda Roosevelt 3107, Apdo 527, San Salvador; tel. 23-6666; telex 20176; f. 1915; cap. 5m.; Gen. Man. Lic. RUFINO GARAY.

Compañía Anglo Salvadoreña de Seguros, SA: Paseo General Escalón 3848, San Salvador; tel. 24-2399; telex 20466; f. 1976; cap. 2m.; Pres. SALVADOR HIDALGO; Exec. Vice-Pres. Dr JOSÉ LUIS URRUTIA ESCOBAR.

Compañía General de Seguros, SA: 7 CP No 4623, entre 89 y 91 Avda Norte, Colonia Escalón, Apdo CC-1004, San Salvador; tel. 23-6413; telex 20218; f. 1955; cap. 6m.; Exec. Chair. Dr RAFAEL CÁCERES VIALE.

La Seguridad Salvadoreña: Km 4½, Carretera a Santa Tecla, Apdo 1527, San Salvador; tel. 23-4100; telex 20626; f. 1974; cap. 2m.; Pres. CARLOS F. PEREIRA.

Seguros Desarrollo, SA: Calle Loma Linda No. 265, Colonia San Benito, Apdo 05-92, San Salvador; tel. 24-3800; telex 20773; f. 1975; cap. 2m.; Exec. Pres. ISMAEL WARLETA FERNÁNDEZ.

Seguros e Inversiones, SA (SISA): Alameda Dr Manuel Enrique Araújo 3530, Apdo 1350, San Salvador; tel. 23-1200; telex 20772; f. 1962; cap. 3m.; Man. MAURICIO SAMAYOA R.

Unión de Seguros, SA: 73 Avda Sur No. 135 Colonia Escalón, San Salvador; tel. 23-4825; telex 20533; f. 1974; cap. 2m.; Vice-Pres. FEDERICO DENIS BADGEROW.

Trade and Industry

CHAMBER OF COMMERCE

Cámara de Comercio e Industria de El Salvador: 9a Avda Norte y 5a Calle Poniente, Apdo (06) 1640, San Salvador; tel. 71-2055; telex 20753; f. 1915; 1,300 mems; Pres. VÍCTOR A. STEINER; Sec. Ing. RICARDO FLORES CENA.

TRADE ORGANIZATIONS

Asociación Cafetalera de El Salvador—ACES: Edif. Instituto del Café 4°, San Salvador; tel. 21-3580; f. 1930; coffee growers' asscn; Pres. Dr FRANCISCO GARCÍA ROSSI.

Asociación de Ganaderos de El Salvador: 1a Avda Norte 1332, San Salvador; tel. 25-7208; telex 20213; f. 1932; livestock breeders' asscn; Pres. Lic. CARLOS ARTURO MUYSHONDT.

Asociación Salvadoreña de Beneficiadores y Exportadores de Café (ABECAFE): 87a Avda Norte 720, Apdo A, Colonia Escalón, San Salvador; tel. 23-3292; telex 20231; coffee producers' and exporters' asscn; Pres. MIGUEL ANGEL SALAVARRÍA.

Asociación Salvadoreña de Industriales: Calles Roma y Liverpool, Colonia Roma, Apdo Postal 06-48, San Salvador; tel. 23-7788; telex 20235; f. 1958; 400 mems; manufacturers' asscn; Pres. Ing. ROBERTO VILANOVA M.; Exec. Dir Lic. ROBERTO ORTIZ AVALOS.

Co-operativa Algodonera Salvadoreña Ltda: 7a Avda Norte 418, Apdo (06) 616, San Salvador; tel. 22-0399; telex 20112; f. 1940; 414 mems; cotton growers' asscn; Pres. JOSÉ ANTONIO LÓPEZ ECHEVERRÍA; Gen. Man. GUSTAVO ADOLFO PÁRRAGA SUAY.

Instituto Nacional del Azúcar: Paseo Gral Escalón y 87a Avda Norte, San Salvador; tel. 24-6044; telex 30024; national sugar institute; Pres. Dr RAMÓN AVALOS NAVARRETE.

Instituto Nacional del Café (INCAFE): 6a Avda Sur 133, San Salvador; tel. 71-3311; telex 20138; f. 1942; national coffee institute; Pres. ROBERT SUÁREZ SUAY; Gen. Man. Lic. MIGUEL ANGEL AGUILAR.

UCAFES: San Salvador; union of coffee-growing co-operatives; Pres. FRANCISCO ALFARO CASTILLO.

STATE AND DEVELOPMENT ORGANIZATIONS

Comisión Ejecutiva Hidroeléctrica del Río Lempa (CEL): 9a Calle Poniente 950, San Salvador; tel. 71-0855; telex 20303; state energy agency dealing with electricity generation, transmission, distribution and non-conventional energy sources; Pres. Gen. JAIME ABDUL GUTIÉRREZ.

Comisión Nacional del Petróleo (CONAPE): 9a Calle Poniente 950, San Salvador; telex 20301; state petroleum enterprise.

Corporación de Exportadores de El Salvador (COEXPORT): Condomínios del Mediterráneo, Edif. A No 23, Colonia Jardines de Guadalupe, San Salvador; tel. 23-1888; telex 20235; f. 1973 to promote Salvadorean exports; Man. Lic. SILVIA CUÉLLAR SICILIA.

Corporación Salvadoreña de Inversiones (CORSAIN): 1a Calle Poniente entre 43 y 45 Avda Norte, San Salvador; tel. 24-4242; telex 20257; Pres. Lic. JULIO RIVAS GALLONT.

Fondo de Financiamiento y Garantía para la Pequeña Empresa (FIGAPE): Diagonal Principal y 1a Diagonal, Apdo 1990, San Salvador; tel. 25-9466; f. 1973; government body to assist small-sized industries; Pres. LEOPOLDO SAMAYOA.

Fondo de Garantía para el Crédito Educativo (EDUCREDITO): Avda España 726, San Salvador; tel. 22-2181; f. 1973; Pres. Ing. JUAN JOSÉ INTERIANO; Dir Lic. ERASMO SERMEÑO.

Fondo Social para la Vivienda (FSV): Edif. Torre Roble, Blvd de Los Héroes, San Salvador; tel. 26-3011; f. 1973; Pres. BALTASAR PERLA.

Instituto Salvadoreño de Transformación Agraria (ISTA): Km 5, Carretera a Santa Tecla, San Salvador; tel. 24-6000; f. 1976 to promote rural development; empowered to buy inefficiently cultivated land; Pres. CARLOS RAMÍREZ SALEGIO.

Instituto de Vivienda Urbana (IVU): Centro Urbano Libertad, San Salvador; tel. 23-3011; government housing agency; Pres. Arq. RENÉ G. LÓPEZ CANANA; Man. CRISTOBAL A. HUEZO NATIVI.

EMPLOYERS' ORGANIZATIONS

There are several business associations, the most important of which is the Alianza Nacional de Empresa Privada (National Private Enterprise Alliance; Pres. JUAN MALDONADO), which has a political organization, the Alianza Productiva.

TRADE UNIONS

Asociación de Sindicatos Independientes—ASIES (Association of Independent Trade Unions).

Confederación General de Sindicatos—CGS (General Confederation of Unions): 3a Calle Oriente 226, San Salvador; f. 1958; admitted to ICFTU/ORIT; 27,000 mems.

Confederación General de Trabajadores Salvadoreños —CGTS (General Confederation of Salvadorean Workers): San Salvador; f. 1957; 10 affiliated unions; Sec.-Gen. JOSÉ LUIS GRANDE PREZA; 3,500 mems.

Coordinadora de Solidaridad de los Trabajadores (CST): f. 1985; conglomerate of independent left-wing trade unions.

Federación Campesina Cristiana de El Salvador-Unión de Trabajadores del Campo (FECCAS-UTC): allied illegal Christian peasants' organizations; Universidad Nac., Apdo 4000, San Salvador.

Federación Revolucionaria de Sindicatos (Revolutionary Federation of Unions): Sec.-Gen. SALVADOR CHÁVEZ ESCALANTE.

Federación Unitaria Sindical de El Salvador (Unitary Federation of Unions): San Salvador.

MUSYGES (United Union and Guild Movement): labour federation previously linked to FDR; 50,000 mems (est.).

UCS: pro-government peasant association; 100,000 mems; Gen. Sec. GUILLERMO BLANCO.

Unidad Nacional de Trabajadores Salvadoreños—UNTS: San Salvador; f. 1986; largest trade union conglomerate; Leader MARCO TULIO LIMA; affiliated unions include:

    Unidad Popular Democrática (UPD): San Salvador; f. 1980; led by a committee of 10; 500,000 mems.

Unión Nacional Obrera-Campesina—Unoc: San Salvador; f. 1986; centre-left labour organization; 500,000 mems.

Some unions, such as those of the taxi drivers and bus owners, are affiliated to the Federación Nacional de Empresas Pequeñas Salvadoreñas—Fenapes, the association of small-scale business.

Transport

Comisión Ejecutiva Portuaria Autónoma—CEPA: Edif. Torre Roble, Blvd de Los Héroes, Apdo 2667, San Salvador; tel. 24-1133; telex 20194; f. 1952; operates and administers the ports of Acajutla (on Pacific coast) and Cutuco (on Gulf of Fonseca) and the El Salvador International Airport, as well as Ferrocarriles Nacionales de El Salvador; Chair. Arq. MARCELO SUÁREZ BARRIENTOS; Gen. Man. Ing. JOSÉ RICARDO HERNÁNDEZ PLATERO.

RAILWAYS

There are about 600 km of railway track in the country. The main track links San Salvador with the ports of Acajutla and Cutuco and with San Jerónimo on the border with Guatemala. The International Railways of Central America run from Anguiatú on the

EL SALVADOR

El Salvador–Guatemala border to the Pacific ports of Acajutla and Cutuco and connect San Salvador with Guatemala City and the Guatemalan Atlantic ports of Puerto Barrios and Santo Tomás del Castillo.

Ferrocarriles Nacionales de El Salvador—FENADESAL: Avda Peralta 903, Apdo 2292, San Salvador; tel. 22-9000; telex 20194; 600 km open; in 1975 Ferrocarril de El Salvador and the Salvadorean section of International Railways of Central America (429 km open) were merged and are administered by the Railroad Division of CEPA (see above); Man. Ing. OSCAR E. CALLES.

ROADS

The country's highway system is well integrated with its railway services. There are some 12,164 km of roads, including: the Pan-American Highway: 306 km; paved highways: 1,700 km; improved roads: 2,827 km; dry-weather roads: 3,872 km. A coastal highway, with interconnecting roads, was under construction in the late 1980s.

SHIPPING

The ports of Acajutla and Cutuco are administered by CEPA (see above). Services are also provided by foreign lines.

CIVIL AVIATION

AESA Aerolíneas de El Salvador, SA de CV: Centro Comercial Beethoven sobre Paseo Gen. Escalón, Apdo (06) 1830, San Salvador; tel. 24-6166; cargo and mail service between San Salvador and Miami; Pres. E. CORNEJO LÓPEZ; Gen. Man. JOSÉ ROBERTO SANTANA.

TACA International Airlines: Edif. Caribe 2°, San Salvador; tel. 23-2244; telex 30156; f. 1939; passenger and cargo services to Belize, Guatemala, Honduras, Mexico, Nicaragua, Panama and the USA; Pres. Dr ENRIQUE BORGO BUSTAMANTE; Exec. Pres. FEDERICO BLOCH; fleet: 2 BAC One Eleven 400, 4 Boeing 737-200, 1 Boeing 767-200.

Tourism

El Salvador was one of the centres of the ancient Mayan civilization, and the ruined temples and cities are of great interest. The volcanoes and lakes of the uplands provide magnificent scenery, while there are fine beaches along the Pacific coast. The civil war, in progress since 1979, has severely affected the tourist industry. The number of tourist arrivals declined from 293,000 in 1978 to 82,000 in 1981, although the total rose to 133,944 in 1986 and reached 124,687 in 1987.

Buró de Convenciones y Visitantes de la Ciudad de San Salvador: Suite 221-222, Hotel Presidente, Avda La Revolución, Col. San Benito, Apdo 2124, San Salvador; tel. (503) 24-0508; telex 20037; f. 1973; assists in organization of national and international events; Pres. Dr RODOLFO MENDOZA; Exec. Dir ROSA MEJÍA DE MARCHESINI.

Cámara Salvadoreña de Turismo: Hotel Sheraton, 89 Avda Norte y 11 Calle Poniente, Colonia Escalón, San Salvador; tel. 24-2222; represents more than 100 hotels, travel agents, restaurants and airlines; Pres. RAÚL SOLER.

Instituto Salvadoreño de Turismo (ISTU) (National Tourism Institute): Calle Rubén Darío 619, Apdo 01-115, San Salvador; tel. 22-8000; telex 20775; f. 1950; Pres. PEDRO DALMAU Y GORRITA; Man. Dir FÉLIX RICARDO ALFONSO TRUJILLO.

Atomic Energy

Comisión Salvadoreña de Energía Nuclear (COSEN): c/o Ministerio de Economía, 4a Avda Norte 233, San Salvador; f. 1961; atomic energy research institute.

EQUATORIAL GUINEA

Introductory Survey

Location, Climate, Language, Religion, Flag, Capital

The Republic of Equatorial Guinea consists of the islands of Bioko (formerly Fernando Póo and subsequently renamed Macías Nguema Biyogo under the regime of President Macías), Corisco, Great Elobey, Small Elobey and Annobón (previously known also as Pagalu), and the mainland territory of Río Muni (Mbini) on the west coast of Africa. Cameroon lies to the north and Gabon to the east and south of Río Muni, while Bioko lies off shore from Cameroon and Nigeria. The small island of Annobón lies far to the south, beyond the islands of São Tomé and Príncipe. The climate is hot and humid, with average temperatures higher than 26°C (80°F). The official language is Spanish. In Río Muni the Fang language is spoken, as well as those of coastal tribes such as the Combe, Balemke and Bujeba, while in Bioko the principal local language is Bubi, although pidgin English and Ibo are also widely understood. An estimated 96% of the population are adherents of the Roman Catholic Church. The national flag (proportions 3 by 2) has three equal horizontal stripes, of green, white and red, with a light blue triangle at the hoist. The state flag has, in addition, the national coat of arms (a white shield, containing a tree, with six yellow stars above and a scroll beneath) on the white stripe. The capital is Malabo (formerly Santa Isabel).

Recent History

Portugal ceded the territory to Spain in 1778. The mainland region and the islands were periodically united for administrative purposes. In July 1959 Spanish Guinea, as the combined territory was known, was divided into two provinces: Río Muni, on the African mainland, and Fernando Póo (with other nearby islands). From 1960 the two provinces were represented in the Spanish legislature. In December 1963 they were merged again, to form Equatorial Guinea, with a limited measure of self-government.

After 190 years of Spanish rule, independence was declared on 12 October 1968, following a referendum on the proposed constitution. At a presidential election, held in September 1968, the Prime Minister of the autonomous government, Bonifacio Ondo Edu, was defeated by Francisco Macías Nguema. President Macías formed a coalition government from all the parties represented in the new National Assembly. Relations with Spain became strained in early 1969, following a series of anti-European incidents and an attempted coup in March by the Minister for Foreign Affairs, Atanasio Ndongo Miyone, who was killed.

In February 1970 the President outlawed all existing political parties and formed the Partido Unico Nacional (PUN), which later became the Partido Unico Nacional de los Trabajadores (PUNT). Macías appointed himself Life President in July 1972. A new constitution, giving absolute powers to President Macías and abolishing the provincial autonomy previously enjoyed by Fernando Póo (then renamed Macías Nguema Biyogo), was adopted in July 1973. President Macías controlled both radio and press and all citizens were forbidden to leave the country, although many fled during his rule. During 1975–77 there were many arrests and executions. Nigerian workers were repatriated in 1976, following reports of maltreatment and forced labour. Foreign affairs were dominated by close relations with the Soviet bloc.

In August 1979 President Macías was overthrown in a coup, led by his nephew, Lt-Col (later Brig.-Gen.) Teodoro Obiang Nguema Mbasogo, hitherto the Deputy Minister of Defence. Macías was later captured, tried on charges of treason, genocide, embezzlement and violation of human rights, and executed by a military firing squad. The Spanish Government, which admitted prior knowledge of the coup, was the first to recognize the new regime, and remains a major supplier of financial and technical aid. Obiang Nguema appointed civilians to the Government for the first time in December 1981. In August 1982 he was reappointed President for a further seven years, and later that month a new constitution, which provided for an eventual return to civilian government, was approved by 95% of voters in a referendum. Equatorial Guinea held its first legislative elections in more than 19 years in August 1983, when an estimated 50,000 voters elected 41 candidates (unopposed) to a new House of Representatives. Further legislative elections were held in July 1988, when it was reported that 99.2% of voters endorsed a single list of candidates who had been nominated by Obiang Nguema.

Obiang Nguema's rule has been threatened on a number of occasions. Attempted coups were reported in April 1981, May 1983 and November 1983. In January 1986, following rumours of discontent among the Río Muni armed forces, the President reshuffled the Government and reinforced his control by assuming the post of Minister of Defence, previously held by his uncle, Deputy Prime Minister Fructuoso Mba Oñana Nchama, who was instead made responsible for public works. In July 1986 an attempt to occupy the presidential palace in Malabo was quelled by loyalist forces, and in August a military tribunal passed sentence upon 13 senior civilian and military officials accused of complicity in the coup attempt. The alleged leader, Eugenio Abeso Mondu (a former diplomat and a member of the House of Representatives), was sentenced to death and executed by firing squad, while prison sentences were passed on 12 others, including Fructuoso Mba Oñana, Planning Minister Marcos Mba Ondo and the national director of the Banque des Etats de l'Afrique Centrale (BEAC), Damian Ondo Mañe. Mba Oñana and Mba Ondo were replaced in a further reallocation of portfolios in September.

The persistence of economic depression during the early 1980s and the existence, between 1979 and 1987, of a ban on organized political activity within Equatorial Guinea contributed towards continued opposition to Obiang Nguema's regime from Equato-Guineans living in exile (estimated to number around 130,000 in 1983). In April 1983 representatives of five opposition groups met at Zaragoza, in Spain, and formed a Junta Coordinadora de las Fuerzas de Oposición Democrática (Co-ordinating Board of Democratic Opposition Forces), and in the following year the Convergencia Social Democrática was formed in Paris by two further groups. In August 1987, on the eighth anniversary of his accession to power, Obiang Nguema ended the ban on political formations by announcing the establishment of a 'governmental party', the Partido Democrático de Guinea Ecuatorial (PDGE), and suggesting that other political parties could be created at a later date. In June 1988 representatives of the Junta Coordinadora de las Fuerzas de Oposición Democrática visited Equatorial Guinea, in order to establish local opposition groups, in preparation for the presidential election scheduled to be held in 1989. However, Obiang Nguema rejected their demands for the legalization of opposition parties. In September 1988, following the discovery of a plot to overthrow Obiang Nguema, seven civilians, including the Secretary-General of the Partido del Progreso de Guinea Ecuatorial, José Luis Jones, were given severe prison sentences. Two army officers were sentenced to death for their part in the plot, but these sentences were subsequently commuted, by Obiang Nguema, to life imprisonment. In January 1989 it was announced that Jones, who had received a 17-year prison sentence, was to be released.

While Spain remains a major trading and aid-giving partner, Equatorial Guinea's entry into the Customs and Economic Union of Central Africa (UDEAC, see p. 154) in December 1983 represented a significant move towards a greater integration with neighbouring francophone countries. In January 1985 the country joined the Franc Zone (see p. 154), with financial assistance from France, which also applied pressure on the 'Paris Club' of creditor nations to achieve a rescheduling of Equatorial Guinea's debts in July of that year. In January 1988 French became a compulsory subject in Equato-Guinean schools. In September Obiang Nguema made an official visit to France, during which Equatorial Guinea's formal entry into the francophone bloc was discussed. In January 1989, however, Obiang Nguema visited Spain, where the continuation of bilateral links between Equatorial Guinea and Spain was confirmed.

Despite Equatorial Guinea's close military links with Nigeria, relations between the two countries underwent some strain in

EQUATORIAL GUINEA

1988, when it became clear that Equatorial Guinea, anxious to attract foreign investment, had formed links with South Africa. The Nigerian Government claimed that contracts between the Governments of Equatorial Guinea and South Africa, for the construction of a satellite-tracking station on Bioko and for the extension and modernization of the airport at Malabo, constituted a threat to Nigerian security, and demanded that all South African nationals be expelled from Equatorial Guinea. Following a visit to Malabo by the Nigerian Minister of External Affairs, it was announced that all South African personnel had been expelled from Equatorial Guinea. However, the Nigerian Government subsequently provided evidence that a number of South African workers (whom the Obiang Nguema Government claimed to be agricultural advisers) had returned to Equatorial Guinea.

Government

After the coup of August 1979, the Supreme Military Council ruled by decree. In August 1982 a new constitution was approved in a referendum, making provision for presidential and legislative elections by universal suffrage, a State Council of 11 members and a House of Representatives of the People (elected for a five-year term).

Defence

In June 1988 there were 1,100 men in the army, 200 in the navy and 100 in the air force. There were also paramilitary forces of 2,000. Military service is voluntary. The estimated defence expenditure for 1982 was US $6m. Spain has provided military advisers and training since October 1979, and the presidential guard is staffed by Morocco, which maintains about 360 troops in the country. Foreign military aid totalled $1.1m. in 1986.

Economic Affairs

The economy is based mainly on agriculture, the principal products being cocoa, coffee, palm oil, bananas, cassava and okoumé timber. About 90% of all cocoa production comes from Bioko. Coffee and timber are produced mainly in Río Muni. Between 1970 and 1975, according to World Bank estimates, Equatorial Guinea's gross national product (GNP) per head declined at an average rate of 6% annually. With the departure of the Nigerian workers in 1976, the economic situation deteriorated further. According to estimates by the UN Economic Commission for Africa, the country's gross domestic product (GDP) in 1976 was 54% lower, in real terms, than in 1974. Real GDP continued to fall, with declines in each of the four years 1977–80. Over the six-year period 1974–80, there was a cumulative fall of 66% in real GDP. Thereafter, some recovery was achieved, with estimated GDP growth of 2.3% in 1981 and 3.8% in 1982. GDP declined by 2.9% in 1983, but increased by 2.2% in 1984. In 1985, however, according to estimates by the UN Statistical Office, Equatorial Guinea's GDP increased by 32.4%, to US $90m. (equivalent to $230 per head). By 1987, according to preliminary figures for that year, GDP per head had increased to $430.

Agricultural production was severely affected by the political upheavals under President Macías. Between 1966/67 and 1979/80 the annual cocoa crop declined from 38,207 metric tons to 5,409 tons. Production rose to 8,998 tons in 1982/83, before declining to 5,657 tons in 1986/87. Favourable climatic conditions, together with increases in incentives for producers (as part of a rehabilitation project for this sector), were expected to lead to a substantial increase in output in 1987/88, to a projected 7,000 tons. Exports of cocoa in 1987 were valued at 3,520m. francs CFA (42.1% of total export earnings). Coffee production declined from 8,450 tons in 1968 to only 108 tons in 1979/80. Production increased to 765 tons by 1985/86, before declining again, to 309 tons, in 1986. However, most of the crop is smuggled out of the country. Timber production, which had totalled 337,438 metric tons in 1967, underwent a period of severe decline, with exports totalling just 796 cu m in 1978. By 1987, however, exports had recovered to 127,487 tons. Equatorial Guinea's total area of exploitable forests is estimated at 800,000 ha. Output of bananas, palm oil and cassava is gradually increasing, and the country has achieved self-sufficiency in most food products. The total fish catch was estimated at 4,400 tons in 1986.

At the time of the overthrow of President Macías, in 1979, the economy was effectively in ruins. Under President Obiang Nguema, aid has been secured, principally from Spain, France, the EEC, the IMF, Japan, the USA and the People's Republic of China. An international aid conference, held in Geneva in April 1982, aimed to provide US $140m. for projects in agriculture, transport and communications, water resources, housing and urbanization, and industry, mining and energy. A second such conference (also held in Geneva), in November 1988, pledged a total of $63m. in support of Equatorial Guinea's medium-term (1988–91) programme for economic development, which aimed to improve the efficiency of the agricultural, transport infrastructure, welfare and administrative sectors. In July 1985 Equatorial Guinea received its first IMF stand-by credit, totalling SDR 9.2m., and in May 1986 the World Bank approved a $10.5m. loan to finance imports of goods needed to boost agricultural production. In December 1988 the IMF granted a structural adjustment facility (SAF) of SDR 11.7m. A rescheduling of $28m. of debt was agreed with the 'Paris Club' of Western creditor governments in July 1985. A further rescheduling, by the 'Paris Club', of the country's public external debt (which was estimated at $160m. at the end of 1988) was expected in early 1989.

In an attempt to further its economic development, Equatorial Guinea joined the Communauté Economique des Etats de l'Afrique Centrale (CEEAC, see p. 218), which was formed in October 1983 and became operational in January 1985. In December 1983 Equatorial Guinea was admitted to the Customs and Economic Union of Central Africa (UDEAC, see p. 154), and in January 1985 the franc CFA was introduced as the unit of currency, to replace the epkwele, which had been linked to the Spanish peseta. It was hoped that Equatorial Guinea's entry into the Franc Zone (which was financed by France) would bring the country out of economic isolation by encouraging foreign trade and investment. A UDEAC technical assistance programme was agreed in September 1984, designed to help to strengthen Equatorial Guinea's administrative structures.

In June 1982 there were 350 Spanish development workers in Equatorial Guinea, working mainly in education and health. Spanish aid between 1979 and 1986 totalled 17,000m. pesetas, and credits in 1989 were expected to amount to some 2,000m. pesetas. Banco Exterior de España's announcement, in 1987, of its withdrawal from the failing joint-venture commercial bank GUINEXTEBANC caused speculation that Spanish aid was to be reduced as a consequence of Equatorial Guinea's entry into the Franc Zone. This was, however, denied by Spain. Obiang Nguema made an official visit to Spain in January 1989, as a result of which it was announced that one-third of Equatorial Guinea's public debt to that country was to be cancelled. France has increased its aid considerably, following Equatorial Guinea's entry into UDEAC: French aid to Equatorial Guinea totalled 8,800m. francs CFA in 1987. France was expected to give 780m. francs CFA in budgetary aid in 1988. French interests are participating in a number of important development projects, including a major telecommunications programme, announced in 1987.

Industrial activity in Equatorial Guinea is minimal. There are offshore and onshore reserves of petroleum, and preliminary surveys have indicated that oil reserves are adequate to meet Equatorial Guinea's domestic demand. Natural gas has been discovered off shore, but the viability of the deposits has yet to be determined. The existence of deposits of gold, iron, manganese, tantalum and uranium has been detected, but prospecting is difficult because of the equatorial forest and the near-total absence of a road network. A law was announced in 1981 that declared all mineral deposits to be state property. A 3.6-MW hydroelectric power station, constructed with French financial and technical assistance, was expected to become operational by mid-1989. A further installation, to be constructed with aid from the People's Republic of China, is planned for Bikomo, near Bata. These developments and the country's considerable agricultural resources are indicative of Equatorial Guinea's potential for a return to economic viability, and possibly to future prosperity. In the early 1980s Spain was by far the largest trading partner. By the end of the decade, however, Equatorial Guinea had established significant trading links with France: in 1987 imports from that country were valued at 1,650m. francs CFA, while exports to France totalled 750m. francs CFA (representing increases of 16% and 160%, respectively, on figures for the previous year). Equatorial Guinea's overall balance of payments showed a deficit of 6,700m. francs CFA in 1985, compared with 4,000m. francs CFA in 1984. The trade deficit totalled just 790m. francs CFA

EQUATORIAL GUINEA

in 1986, compared with 1,860m. francs CFA in 1985 and 7,350m. francs CFA in 1984. The effects on the economy of declines in world prices for Equatorial Guinea's principal commodities obliged the Government to limit expenditure in 1988. Provisional budget figures for that year envisaged revenue of 7,147m. francs CFA (compared with 8,276m. francs CFA in 1987) and expenditure of 7,894m. francs CFA (compared with 8,283m. francs CFA in the previous year).

Social Welfare

Health services are extremely limited, and diseases such as malaria, infectious hepatitis, whooping cough and dysentery are endemic. In 1975 Equatorial Guinea had only five physicians, compared with 25 in 1971. There were 65 hospital establishments, with a total of 3,577 beds, in 1977.

Education

The 1982 Constitution made education the State's first priority, and free and compulsory basic education was to be provided. Education is officially compulsory for eight years between six and 14 years of age. Primary education starts at six years of age and normally lasts for six years. Secondary education, beginning at the age of 12, also spans a six-year period, comprising a first cycle of four years and a second cycle of two years. In 1982 the total enrolment at primary and secondary schools was equivalent to 56% of the school-age population. In 1986 primary education in nine grades was provided for 65,000 pupils in 550 schools. More advanced education for 3,013 pupils took place in 14 centres, with 288 teachers, in 1980/81. A major programme of restructuring was planned for the primary-education sector in 1987, with the IDA providing funds of US $5.1m.

Since 1979, assistance in the development of the educational system has been provided by Spain, which had 100 teaching staff working in Equatorial Guinea in 1986. Two higher education centres, at Bata and Malabo, are administered by the Spanish Universidad Nacional de Educación a Distancia (UNED) and had 500 students in 1986. In 1980, according to official estimates, the average rate of adult illiteracy was 63%.

Public Holidays

1989: 2 January (for New Year's Day), 5 March (Independence Day), 24-27 March (Easter), 1 May (Labour Day), 25 May (OAU Day), 10 December (Human Rights Day), 25 December (Christmas).

1990: 1 January (New Year's Day), 5 March (Independence Day), 13-16 April (Easter), 1 May (Labour Day), 25 May (OAU Day), 10 December (Human Rights Day), 25 December (Christmas).

Weights and Measures

The metric system is in force.

Statistical Survey

Source (unless otherwise stated): Dirección Técnica de Estadística, Secretaría de Estado para el Plan de Desarrollo Económico y Cooperación, Malabo.

AREA AND POPULATION

Area: 28,051 sq km (Río Muni (Mbini) 26,017 sq km, Bioko 2,017 sq km, Annobón 17 sq km).

Population: 246,941 (Río Muni 200,106, Bioko 44,820, Annobón 2,015) at December 1965 census; 300,000 (Río Muni 240,804, Bioko 57,190, Annobón 2,006) at census of July 1983 (Source: Ministerio de Asuntos Exteriores, Madrid).

Provinces (population, census of July 1983): Kié-Ntem 70,202, Litoral 66,370, Centro-Sur 52,393, Wele-Nzas 51,839, Bioko Norte 46,221, Bioko Sur 10,969, Pagalu 2,006.

Principal towns (population at 1983 census): Malabo (capital) 15,253, Bata 24,100.

Births and Deaths (UN estimates, annual averages): Birth rate 42.5 per 1,000 in 1975-80, 42.5 per 1,000 in 1980-85; Death rate 22.7 per 1,000 in 1975-80, 21.0 per 1,000 in 1980-85. (Source: UN, *World Population Prospects: Estimates and Projections as Assessed in 1984*).

Economically Active Population (estimates, '000 at mid-1980): Agriculture, etc. 104 (males 48, females 56); Industry 18 (males 16, females 2); Services 36 (males 28, females 8); Total 159 (males 93, females 65). Source: ILO, *Economically Active Population Estimates and Projections, 1950-2025*. Mid-1986 (estimates, '000): Agriculture, etc. 102; Total 172 (Source: FAO, *Production Yearbook*).

AGRICULTURE, ETC.

Principal Crops (FAO estimates, metric tons, 1986): Sweet potatoes 35,000, Cassava 55,000, Coconuts 8,000, Palm kernels 2,900, Bananas 19,000, Cocoa beans (unofficial estimate) 8,000, Green coffee 7,000 (Source: FAO, *Production Yearbook*).

Livestock (FAO estimates, year ending September 1986): Cattle 4,000, Pigs 5,000, Sheep 35,000, Goats 8,000 (Source: FAO, *Production Yearbook*).

Forestry (1986): Roundwood removals (FAO estimates, '000 cu m): Fuel wood 447, Industrial wood 160, Total 607 (Source: FAO, *Yearbook of Forest Products*).

Fishing (metric tons, live weight): Total catch 4,000 in 1984; 3,600 in 1985; 4,400 in 1986 (Source: FAO, *Yearbook of Fishery Statistics*).

INDUSTRY

Palm oil (FAO estimates, '000 metric tons): 5.2 in 1984; 5.0 in 1985; 5.1 in 1986 (Source: FAO, *Production Yearbook*).

Veneer sheets ('000 cubic metres): 2 (FAO estimate) in 1983; 3 in 1984; 10 in 1985 (Source: FAO, *Yearbook of Forest Products*).

Electric energy (million kWh): 15 in 1983; 15 in 1984; 15 in 1985 (Source: UN, *Industrial Statistics Yearbook*).

FINANCE

Currency and Exchange Rates: 100 centimes = 1 franc de la Coopération financière en Afrique centrale (CFA). *Coins:* 1, 2, 5, 10, 25, 50, 100 and 500 francs CFA. *Notes:* 100, 500, 1,000, 5,000 and 10,000 francs CFA. *French Franc, Sterling and Dollar Equivalents* (30 September 1988): 1 French franc = 50 francs CFA; £1 sterling = 538.6 francs CFA; US $1 = 318.5 francs CFA; 1,000 francs CFA = £1.857 = $3.140. *Average Exchange Rate* (francs CFA per US dollar): 449.26 in 1985; 346.30 in 1986; 300.54 in 1987. *Note:* In January 1985 Equatorial Guinea adopted the franc CFA in place of the epkwele (plural: bipkwele), which had been linked to the Spanish peseta at the rate of 1 peseta = 2 bipkwele since June 1980. Some of the figures in this Survey are still in terms of bipkwele.

Budget (estimates, million francs CFA, 1987): Revenue 8,276 (Fiscal receipts 5,114, Other receipts 3,162); Expenditure 8,283 (Compensation of employees 1,804, Interest payments 1,916, Other goods and services 2,412, Net lending 1,460, Capital expenditure 691). Source: *La Zone Franc—Rapport 1987*.

International Reserves (US $ million at 31 December 1987): IMF special drawing rights 0.21; Foreign exchange 0.36; Total 0.57 (Source: IMF, *International Financial Statistics*).

Money Supply ('000 million francs CFA at 31 December 1987): Currency outside deposit money banks 6.69; Demand deposits at deposit money banks 2.32; Total money 9.00 (Source: IMF, *International Financial Statistics*).

Cost of Living (Consumer price index for Africans in Malabo, January; base: 1985 = 100): 142 in 1987 (Source: BEAC, *Statistiques économiques*).

Gross Domestic Product by Economic Activity (estimates, million bipkwele at current prices, 1983): Agriculture, forestry and fishing 2,150; Manufacturing 270; Electricity, gas and water 20; Construction 280; Trade, restaurants and hotels 530; Transport and communications 120; Finance, insurance, real estate and business services 40; Public administration and defence 1,750; Other services 220; GDP at factor cost 5,380; Indirect taxes (net of subsidies) 650; GDP in purchasers' values 6,030. Source: UN Economic Commission for Africa, *African Statistical Yearbook*.

Balance of Payments (US $'000, 1981): Merchandise exports f.o.b. 16,120.3, Merchandise imports f.o.b. −30,643.6, *Trade balance* −14,523.3; Exports of services 4,616.4, Imports of services −7,282.0, Transfers (net) −400.1, *Current balance* −17,588.9; *Capital balance* −2,120.0; Net errors and omissions −4,250.7; *Total* −23,959.6.

EXTERNAL TRADE

Principal Commodities (million bipkwele, 1981): *Imports:* Food, beverages and tobacco 1,990, Petroleum and petroleum products 1,787, Clothing 478, Iron and steel products 993, Motor vehicles and machinery 1,389; Total (incl. others) 7,982. *Exports:* Cocoa 1,788, Coffee 70, Timber 611; Total (incl. others) 2,502. **1982** (million bipkwele): Total imports 10,857; Total exports 3,837. **1986** (exports, million francs CFA): Cocoa beans 4,110; Wood 3,817; Coffee 434.

Principal Trading Partners (million bipkwele, 1981): *Imports:* Cameroon 574, Spain 6,375; Total (incl. others) 7,982. *Exports:* Federal Republic of Germany 87, Netherlands 81, Spain 2,170; Total (incl. others) 2,502.

TRANSPORT

Shipping (international sea-borne freight traffic, '000 metric tons, 1986): Goods loaded 144, Goods unloaded 51 (Source: BEAC, *Statistiques économiques*).

COMMUNICATIONS MEDIA

Radio receivers 100,000 in use in 1985; Television receivers 2,200 in use in 1985; Daily newspapers 1 in 1984 (Source: UNESCO, *Statistical Yearbook*).

EDUCATION

Primary (1980/81): Schools 511; Teachers 647; Pupils 40,110.

Secondary and Further (1980/81): Schools 14; Teachers 288; Pupils 3,013. There were 175 pupils studying abroad.

Directory

The Constitution

A new constitution was approved by referendum on 15 August 1982.

FUNDAMENTAL PRINCIPLES

Education is the first priority of the State. Civil liberties and basic human rights are guaranteed. The State has sole control of minerals and coal mines, electricity and water supply, posts and telecommunications, and radio and television.

PRESIDENT OF THE REPUBLIC

The President, who is Head of State, leader of the Government and Supreme Commander of the Armed Forces, has the power to appoint and dismiss ministers and to determine and direct national policy. At the expiry of the presidential term of seven years, an election by universal suffrage is to be held. (President Obiang Nguema was appointed for a term of seven years immediately before the publication of this constitution.)

STATE COUNCIL

The State Council has 11 members (including the Chairman of the House of Representatives, the President of the Supreme Tribunal and the Minister of Defence), and is responsible for defending national sovereignty, unity between the territorial units of Equatorial Guinea, peace and justice, and the proper conduct of democracy. The Council acts as an electoral college to approve or reject a presidential candidature, may refuse to accept the resignation of the President of the Republic, and may declare the President physically or mentally unfit to continue in office.

HOUSE OF REPRESENTATIVES

The House of Representatives is elected for a term of five years, and its members should be between 45 and 60 years of age. It sits twice a year, in March and September, for two-month periods, unless an extraordinary session is requested by the President, or by petition of three-quarters of the members of the House.

The Government

HEAD OF STATE

President: Brig.-Gen. TEODORO OBIANG NGUEMA MBASOGO (took office 25 August 1979).

COUNCIL OF MINISTERS
(January 1989)

President and Minister of Defence: Brig.-Gen. TEODORO OBIANG NGUEMA MBASOGO.
Prime Minister: Lt-Col CRISTINO SERICHE BIOKE MALABO.
Deputy Prime Minister, Minister of Territorial Administration and National Security: ISIDORO EYI MONSUY ANDEME.
Minister of Public Works, Housing and Town Planning: ALEJANDRO ENVORO OVONO.
Minister of Education and Sport: FORTUNATO NZAMBI MACHINDE.
Minister of Information and Tourism: LEANDRO MBOMIO NSUE.
Minister of Labour: ANACLETO EJAPA BOLEKIA.
Minister of Communications and Transport: DEMETRIO ELO NDONGO NSEFUMU.
Minister of Agriculture: ALFREDO ABESO OVONO.
Minister of Industry and Commerce: FRANCISCO PASCUAL OBAMA EYEGUE.
Minister of Planning and Economic Development: HILARIO NSUE ALENE.
Minister of Justice and Religion: ANGEL NDONG MICHA.
Minister of the Civil Service: JOSÉ MECHEBA IKAKA MASSOKO.
Minister of Energy: JUAN OLO MBA NSENG.
Minister of Water Resources and Forestry: ANGEL ALOGO NCHAMA.
Minister of Foreign Affairs: MARCELINO NGUEMA ONGUEME.
Minister of Finance: ANTONIO FERNANDO NVE.
Minister of Health: SISINIO MBANA NSORO.
Deputy Minister of Defence: Maj. MELANIO EBENDENG NSOMO.
Minister Secretary-General to the Presidency: ALEJANDRO EVUNA.
Deputy Minister Secretary-General to the Presidency: MARTÍN MKA ESONO.
Minister in charge of Relations with the House of Representatives: ELOY ELO NVE MBENGONO.

MINISTRIES

All Ministries are in Malabo.
Ministry of Finance: Malabo; tel. 20-43.
Ministry of Foreign Affairs and Co-operation: Malabo; tel. 32-20.

Legislature

CÁMARA DE REPRESENTANTES DEL PUEBLO

The 41-member House of Representatives of the People was elected for a five-year term on 28 August 1983. All candidates were nominated by President Obiang Nguema and were elected unopposed. Further legislative elections were held in July 1988.

Political Organizations

Partido Democrático de Guinea Ecuatorial (PDGE): Malabo; f. August 1987 as a 'governmental party'.

EQUATORIAL GUINEA

Movements (in exile in 1988) seeking the restoration of democracy include the following:

Convergencia Social Democrática (CSD): Paris, France; f. 1984; comprises:

Partido Socialista de Guinea Ecuatorial (PSAGE): Oviedo, Spain.

Reunión Democrática para la Liberación de Guinea Ecuatorial (RDLGE): Paris, France: f. 1981; formed 12-mem. provisional govt-in-exile 1983; Pres. MANUEL RUBÉN NDONGO.

Junta Coordinadora de las Fuerzas de Oposición Democrática (Co-ordinating Board of Opposition Forces): Zaragoza, Spain; f. 1983; Pres. TEODORO MACKUANDJI BONDJALE OKO; Sec.-Gen. SEVERO MOTO NSA; comprises:

Alianza Nacional de Restauración Democrática de Guinea Ecuatorial (ANRDGE): BP 335, 1211 Geneva 4, Switzerland; f. 1974; Sec.-Gen. MARTÍN NSOMO OKOMO.

Frente de Liberación de Guinea Ecuatorial (FRELIGE).

Movimiento de Liberación y Futuro de Guinea Ecuatorial (MOLIFUGE).

Partido del Progreso de Guinea Ecuatorial (PPGE): Madrid, Spain; Pres. SEVERO MOTO NSA; Sec.-Gen. JOSÉ LUIS JONES.

Reforma Democrática.

Revolutionary Command Council of Socialist Guinean Patriots and Cadres: f. 1981; Leader DANIEL OYONO.

Diplomatic Representation

EMBASSIES IN EQUATORIAL GUINEA

Cameroon: Malabo; Ambassador: JOHN NCHOTU AKUM.
China, People's Republic: Malabo; Ambassador: DAI SHIQI.
Cuba: Malabo; Ambassador: LOREAL CHOMON MEDIAVILLA.
France: 13 Calle de Argelia, Apdo 326, Malabo; tel. 29-68; Ambassador: MARCEL CAUSSE.
Gabon: Apdo 648, Douala, Malabo; tel. 420; telex 1125; Ambassador: PHILIPPE NDJAVE NDJOY.
Korea, Democratic People's Republic: Malabo; Ambassador: CHI YONG-HO.
Nigeria: 4 Paseo de los Cocoteros, Apdo 78, Malabo; tel. 23-86; Ambassador: Navy Capt. FESTUS PORBENI.
Spain: Malabo; Ambassador: MANUEL ALABART FERNÁNDEZ CABADA.
USSR: Malabo; Ambassador: BORIS KRASNIKOV.
USA: Casilla 597, Malabo; tel. 25-07; Ambassador: CHESTER NORRIS.

Judicial System

The structure of judicial administration was established in February 1981. The Supreme Tribunal in Malabo, consisting of a President of the Supreme Tribunal, the Presidents of the three chambers (civil, criminal and administrative), and two magistrates from each chamber, is the highest court of appeal. There are Territorial High Courts in Malabo and Bata, which are also courts of appeal. Courts of the First Instance exist in Malabo and Bata, and may be convened in the other provincial capitals, and Local Courts may be convened when necessary.

Religion

An estimated 96% of the population are nominally adherents of the Roman Catholic Church. Traditional forms of worship are also followed.

CHRISTIANITY

The Roman Catholic Church

Equatorial Guinea comprises one archdiocese and two dioceses. There were an estimated 319,500 adherents in the country at 31 December 1985.

Bishops' Conference: Arzobispado, Apdo 106, Malabo; f. 1984; Pres. Mgr RAFAEL MARÍA NZE ABUY, Archbishop of Malabo.

Archbishop of Malabo: Mgr RAFAEL MARÍA NZE ABUY, Arzobispado, Apdo 106, Malabo; tel. 21-76.

Protestant Church

Iglesia Evangélica de Guinea Ecuatorial (Evangelical Church of Equatorial Guinea): Apdo 195, Malabo; f. 1960; 8,000 mems (1985); Sec.-Gen. Rev. SAMUEL OKE ESONO ATUGU.

The Press

Africa 2000: Malabo; Spanish; cultural review; quarterly.
Ebano: Malabo; Spanish; irregular; circ. 1,000.
Hoja Parroquial: Malabo; weekly.
Potopoto: Apdo 236, Bata; Fang and Spanish; irregular; Dir FRANCISCO DE ANTA FRANCO.
Unidad de la Guinea Ecuatorial: Malabo; irregular.

FOREIGN NEWS BUREAU

Agencia EFE (Spain): 50 Calle del Presidente Nasser, Malabo; tel. 31-65; Bureau Chief DONATO NDONGO BIDYOGO.

Radio and Television

There were an estimated 100,000 radio receivers and 2,200 television sets in use in 1985.

RADIO

There are three radio stations, all of which are operated by the Government.

Africa 2000: Malabo; f. 1988; cultural station; broadcasts in Spanish.

Radio Ecuatorial Bata: Apdo 749, Bata; tel. 182; commercial station; programmes in Spanish, French and vernacular languages; Dir JESÚS OBIANG NGUEMA NDONG.

Radio Santa Isabel: Apdo 195, Malabo; tel. 382; programmes in Spanish, French, Fang, Bubi, Annobonés and Combe; Dir JUAN EYENE OPKUA NGUEMA.

TELEVISION

Director of Television: MAXIMILIANO MBA.

Finance

(cap. = capital; res = reserves; m. = million; br. = branch; amounts in francs CFA)

BANKING

Central Bank

Banque des Etats de l'Afrique Centrale (BEAC): Apdo 501, Malabo; tel. 20-10; telex 913111; headquarters in Yaoundé, Cameroon; f. 1973 as the central bank of issue for mem. states of the Customs and Economic Union of Central Africa (UDEAC), comprising Cameroon, the Central African Republic, Chad, the Congo, Equatorial Guinea and Gabon; cap. 24,000m., res 148,480m. (Dec. 1986); Gov. CASIMIR OYE MBA; Dir in Equatorial Guinea MARTÍN-CRISANTO EBE MBA; br. in Bata.

Commercial Banks

Banco de Crédito y Desarrollo: 1 Avda de la Libertad, Apdo 39, Malabo; tel. 35-35; cap. 8.75m.; 100% state-owned; br. in Bata; Chair. CARLOS NTUTUMU NENGONO; Man. Dir Dr MANUEL E. KING SOMO.

GUINEXTEBANC: 67 Calle del Presidente Nasser, Apdo 261, Malabo; fmrly Banco Exterior de Guinea Ecuatorial y España (GUINEXTEBANC); 100% state-owned; liquidation announced Jan. 1988.

BIAO-Guinée Equatoriale: 6 Calle de Argelia, Malabo; f. 1986; cap. 300m.; 51% owned by Banque Internationale pour l'Afrique Occidentale (France), 41% state-owned; Chair. FELIPE HINESTROSA IKAKA; Man. Dir JEAN-LOUIS CHAPUIS.

Trade and Industry

Cámara de Comercio, Agrícola y Forestal de Malabo: Apdo 51, Malabo; tel. 151.

Cámaras Oficiales Agrícolas de Guinea: Bioko and Bata; buys cocoa and coffee from indigenous planters, who are partially grouped in co-operatives.

Empresa General de Industria y Comercio (EGISCA): Malabo; f. 1986; parastatal body jtly operated with the French Société pour l'Organisation, l'Aménagement et le Développement des Industries Alimentaires et Agricoles (SOMDIA); import-export agency.

Empresa Guineano-Española de Petróleos (GEPSA): 33 Avda de la Independencia, Apdo 30, Malabo; tel. 23-00; f. 1980; owned equally by the govt and Hispanoil (Spain); legislation governing petroleum production was passed in 1981; wells drilled in early 1982 produced some positive results; also conducts natural gas exploration.

INPROCAO: Malabo; production, marketing and distribution of cocoa.

Oficina para la Cooperación con Guinea Ecuatorial (OCGE): Malabo; f. 1981; administers bilateral aid from Spain.

Sociedad Anónima de Desarrollo del Comercio (SOADECO-Guinée): Malabo; f. 1986; parastatal body jtly operated with the French Société pour l'Organisation, l'Aménagement et le Développement des Industries Alimentaires et Agricoles (SOMDIA); development of commerce.

Total-Guinée Equatoriale: Malabo; f. 1984; cap. 150m. francs CFA; 50% state-owned, 50% by CFP-Total (France); petroleum marketing and distribution; Chair. of Board of Dirs Minister of Public Works, Housing and Town Planning.

TRADE UNIONS

There is no indication of any development of trade unionism in Equatorial Guinea.

Transport

RAILWAYS

There are no railways in Equatorial Guinea.

ROADS

Bioko: a semi-circular tarred road serves the northern part of the island from Malabo down to Batete in the west and from Malabo to Bacake Grande in the east, with a feeder road from Luba to Moka and Bahía de la Concepción; total length of roads: about 160 km.

Río Muni: a tarred road links Bata with Mbini (Río Benito) in the west; another road, partly tarred, links Bata with the frontier post of Ebebiyin in the east and then continues into Gabon; other earth roads join Acurenam, Mongomo de Guadelupe and Nsork; total length of roads: 1,015 km.

SHIPPING

The main ports are Malabo (general cargo), Luba (bananas), Bata (general), Mbini and Kogo (timber). A regular monthly service is operated by the Spanish Compañía Transmediterránea from Barcelona, calling at Malabo and Bata.

CIVIL AVIATION

There is an international airport at Malabo, and a smaller airport at Bata. South Africa is to participate in the modernization of facilities at Malabo, and a US $6m. project, aiming to improve safety facilities at Bata, was announced in 1987. In 1985 discussions took place with the French Government regarding the foundation of a new national airline to provide a regular service between Malabo and Paris.

Aerolíneas Guinea Ecuatorial (ALGESA): Malabo; f. 1982 to operate regular services to Cameroon, Gabon and Nigeria; fleet of 2 HS 748, 1 Cessna 402.

Empresa Ecuato-Guineano de Aviación (EGA): Malabo; f. 1986; 70% state-owned; operates flights to Cameroon and Gabon; fleet of 1 HS 748.

Tourism

Prior to the fall of President Macías Nguema in 1979, few foreigners visited Equatorial Guinea. Tourism remains undeveloped.

ETHIOPIA

Introductory Survey

Location, Climate, Language, Religion, Flag, Capital

The People's Democratic Republic of Ethiopia extends inland from the Red Sea coast of eastern Africa. The country has a long frontier with Somalia near the Horn of Africa. Sudan lies to the west, Djibouti to the east and Kenya to the south. The climate is mainly temperate because of the high plateau terrain, with an average annual temperature of 13°C (55°F), abundant rainfall in most years and low humidity. The lower country and valley gorges are very hot and subject to periodic drought. The official language is Amharic, but many other local languages are also spoken. English is widely used in official and commercial circles, and Arabic is spoken in the province of Eritrea. The Ethiopian Orthodox (Tewahido) Church, an ancient Christian sect, has a wide following in the north and on the southern plateau. In much of the south and east there are Muslims and followers of animist beliefs. The national flag (proportions 3 by 2) has three horizontal stripes, of green, yellow and red. The capital is Addis Ababa.

Recent History

Ethiopia was dominated for more than 50 years by Haile Selassie, who became Regent in 1916, King in 1928 and Emperor in 1930. He ruled the country, except during the Italian occupation of 1936–41, until his deposition by the armed forces in September 1974 in the wake of serious regional famine, inflation and unemployment, and growing demands for democratic reform. The Emperor's rule was highly personal and autocratic, but he consolidated the expansion of Ethiopian territory and the gradual process of national modernization which had been begun by the Emperor Menelik (1865–1913). The former Italian colony of Eritrea was merged with Ethiopia, in a federal arrangement, in September 1952, and annexed to Ethiopia as a province in November 1962. Haile Selassie died, a captive of the military regime, in August 1975.

The revolution of September 1974 was engineered by an Armed Forces Co-ordinating Committee, known popularly as the Dergue ('Shadow'), which controlled ultimate power. The Dergue established a Provisional Military Government (PMG), headed by Lt-Gen. Aman Andom. In November, after a dispute in the military leadership, Gen. Andom was deposed and shot. The PMG was replaced by a Provisional Military Administrative Council (PMAC), led by Brig.-Gen. Teferi Benti; the monarchy was abolished in March 1975. Ethiopia was declared a socialist state in December 1974, and a national programme, called Ethiopia Tikdem (Ethiopia First), was carried out in the following year. Insurance companies, banks, financial institutions, large industrial enterprises, rural and urban land and schools were nationalized, while peasant co-operatives and industrial workers' councils were established.

Widespread unrest continued throughout 1975 and 1976, despite moves by the Dergue to ease tension by releasing some detainees and promising a return to civilian rule, at an unspecified date. Strains within the Dergue were reflected by its reorganization in December 1976. However, in February 1977 Lt-Col Mengistu Haile Mariam executed Brig.-Gen. Teferi Benti and his closest associates, and replaced him as chairman of the PMAC and Head of State.

The Government continued to meet political and armed opposition from various groups, both Marxist and anti-Marxist. During 1977 and 1978 thousands of opponents of the Government were killed or imprisoned in a programme of 'rehabilitation' or 'liquidation'. Until July 1977 the Dergue was assisted by Mei'son (the Marxist All-Ethiopia Socialist Movement) but later formed its own party, Abyot Seded (Revolutionary Flame), which sought to enlist civilian support. However, all political groupings were theoretically swept away in late 1979 when a Commission for Organizing the Party of the Working People of Ethiopia (COPWE) was established.

The Central Committee of COPWE, which was dominated by military personnel, held its first congress in June 1980. It announced in February 1981 that peasant co-operatives were to be encouraged, and that mass organizations for youth, women, peasants and workers were to be strengthened. The third congress and the formal establishment of the Workers' Party of Ethiopia (WPE), which replaced COPWE, took place in September 1984, to coincide with the 10th anniversary of the revolution. Lt-Col Mengistu was unanimously elected Secretary-General of the party, which was modelled on the Communist Party of the Soviet Union. The congress also elected an 11-member Politburo and a 136-member Central Committee.

In June 1986, in preparation for the eventual transfer of power from the PMAC to a civilian government, a draft constitution was published. Following extensive consultative procedures, the draft constitution was endorsed by 81% of the votes cast in a referendum held in February 1987. In June 85% of Ethiopia's registered voters (more than 15.7m.) participated in elections for an 835-seat legislature, the National Shengo (Assembly), to which Lt-Col Mengistu and all members of the Politburo of the WPE were returned as deputies. At the inaugural meeting of the National Shengo in September, the PMAC was abolished and the People's Democratic Republic of Ethiopia (PDRE) was declared. The National Shengo unanimously elected Lt-Col Mengistu as President of the PDRE, while Fisseha Desta, hitherto Deputy Secretary-General of the PMAC Standing Committee, was elected Vice-President. A 24-member Council of State was also elected, to be the Shengo's permanent organ, and Capt. Fikre Selassie Wogderes was appointed Prime Minister.

Numerous separatist movements, encouraged by the confusion resulting from the revolution, seek the secession of their regions from Ethiopia. These movements are strongest in the Ogaden region and Eritrea. Somalia lays claim to the Ogaden, which is inhabited mainly by ethnic Somalis, and regular Somali troops have supported incursions by forces of the Western Somali Liberation Front (WSLF). In 1977 the Somalis made major advances in the Ogaden, but in 1978 were forced to retreat. By the end of 1980 the Ethiopian defence forces were in control of virtually the whole of the Ogaden, but armed clashes have continued in the region. In 1980 an OAU committee declared the Ogaden to be an integral part of Ethiopia.

Secessionist movements have existed in Eritrea since its annexation in 1962, and also in Tigre, claiming to control large tracts of the provinces. The Eritrean Liberation Front (ELF) was originally founded in Egypt in 1958, but the movement subsequently split into numerous factions. In January 1982 the Ethiopian Government announced 'Operation Red Star', to bring the political, social and economic development of Eritrea into line with the rest of the country. However, the accompanying military campaign to allow the implementation of these projects had failed by May. The strongest movement, the Eritrean People's Liberation Front (EPLF), faced a major government offensive outside its stronghold of Nakfa in mid-1983, while a similar campaign was waged against the Tigre People's Liberation Front (TPLF) in western Tigre province. In early 1984 the EPLF launched a major new campaign, and, during heavy fighting, government troops suffered severe losses. The EPLF captured the town of Tessenei, near the Sudanese border, and defeated the army on three fronts in the Eritrean highlands. In January 1985 three of the Eritrean factions agreed to form the Eritrean Unified National Council (EUNC), but the EPLF refused to collaborate with this group. It was revealed that secret talks had been held sporadically between the EPLF and the Ethiopian Government since 1977, aimed at reaching agreement on autonomy for the region, but had so far been unproductive. In March 1985 the Government launched a large-scale offensive in Tigre and Eritrea, and by September had made significant gains, including the recapture of the strategic towns of Barentu and Tessenei. In mid-1986, however, government forces again abandoned the north-east coast, and EPLF attacks on strategic installations continued. In March 1987 it was disclosed that further secret negotiations between the EPLF and the Government had recently taken place. Meanwhile, the EUNC alliance of three Eritrean groups had not proved successful, and it suffered a further set-back upon the death of its chairman in April 1987. The various

ETHIOPIA

factions of the Eritrean movement as a whole remained divided. In September 1987 the newly-elected National Shengo announced that five areas, including Eritrea and Tigre, were to become 'autonomous regions' under the new Constitution. Eritrea was granted the greatest degree of self-government, but the EPLF rejected the new provisions, and in December announced the start of an offensive aiming to expel Ethiopian government troops from Eritrea. In March 1988 the EPLF captured the town of Afabet and claimed to have killed one-third of all Ethiopian troops in Eritrea.

Following the capture of Afabet, the TPLF took immediate advantage of the movement of government forces from Tigre to Eritrea and overran all the garrisons in north-western and north-eastern Tigre. In April the EPLF and the TPLF were reported to have restored contact and to be aiming to co-ordinate their military operations. The expulsion of foreign relief officials from Eritrea and Tigre in April, and the Government's declaration of a state of emergency there in May, emphasized the extent of the rebel forces' military successes. By late July, however, government advances were reported to have displaced the TPLF from some of the captured territory in Tigre Administrative Region. The endorsement by the National Shengo, in January 1989, of a proposal by some elements of the Eritrean Liberation Front (ELF) to divide Eritrea into two autonomous regions (one for the predominantly Muslim-populated lowlands and one for the mainly Christian highlands) was condemned by the EPLF.

The continued fighting in the north during 1984–85 compounded difficulties being experienced in areas of Ethiopia already severely affected by famine. In 1984 the rains failed for the third consecutive crop season, and in May the Relief and Rehabilitation Commission estimated that 7m. people could suffer starvation. Ethiopia received emergency food aid from many Western nations, but distribution of the aid posed a major problem, as the ports rapidly became congested. Some famine relief was airlifted to affected areas, while Western food agencies sent food and medical supplies into Eritrea through Sudan. Some rainfall in 1985 eased the drought in the northern provinces, but Ethiopia remained dependent on foreign aid. Part of the Government's solution to the famine was the controversial plan to resettle more than 1.5m. people from the northern areas to the more fertile lowlands. Initially critics viewed this as an attempt to remove opposition from the disputed areas, but it has since come to be regarded as a possible solution to the problem of recurrent famine in the Ethiopian highlands.

In September 1987, following severe drought and the virtual total failure of all crops in the northern regions of Eritrea, Tigre, Wollo and Northern Shoa, the Ethiopian Government requested about 1m. tons of food aid from Western donors for the estimated 5m. people at risk of starvation (later revised to 1.4m. tons for 5.2m. people). As in 1984-85, the relief campaign that the international community subsequently mounted was hindered by Ethiopia's inadequate infrastructure, which exacerbated the problems of distributing food to the country's inaccessible northern regions. By January 1988, however, sufficient food aid appeared to have been received, or pledged, to avert another major disaster if the problems of distribution could be overcome. In late 1987 the EPLF's attacks on UN convoys, carrying vital food aid to the drought-stricken areas, were universally condemned. The EPLF, however, claimed that the vehicles were transporting military equipment on behalf of the Ethiopian Government. The UN refused to negotiate with the rebels (both the EPLF and the TPLF), but nevertheless resumed relief operations. In April 1988 the government ordered the expulsion of all foreign relief workers from Eritrea and Tigre, claiming that it was about to launch a counter-offensive against the EPLF and the TPLF. This action prompted international condemnation. It was feared that the Government's Relief and Rehabilitation Commission, and the other national agencies which were left in charge of relief operations, would be unable to distribute food on the scale necessary to avert widespread famine. By May, however, there had been no indications of mass starvation, such as had occurred in 1984-85, lending credence to the claims of the EPLF and the TPLF that their own relief operations were capable of reaching large numbers of people. In June 1988 the League of Red Cross and Red Crescent Societies was granted permission to initiate a major famine relief operation in the northern Administrative Regions. The need for another major relief campaign, so soon after the famine of 1984-85, prompted renewed criticism of the Ethiopian Government's commitment to collectivist agricultural policies and its 'villagization' programme.

After Lt-Col Mengistu's coup in February 1977, the USSR supplanted the USA as the principal supplier of armaments to Ethiopia. In 1978 a treaty of friendship and co-operation between Ethiopia and the USSR was signed. Relations with the USA improved slightly in December 1985, however, when Ethiopia agreed to pay compensation to US companies, on claims dating back to the 1975 nationalizations. In August 1981, in response to US military interests in Somalia, Oman and Egypt, a treaty of friendship and co-operation was also signed between Ethiopia, Libya and the People's Democratic Republic of Yemen, which are all Soviet-influenced states. Ethiopia has also developed closer diplomatic links with its neighbours, Kenya and Djibouti, which have attempted to bring about a reconciliation with Somalia. Under the mediation of the President of Djibouti, in January 1986 Mengistu met the Somali President, Mohamed Siad Barre, for the first time since 1977. Talks between the two Ministers of Foreign Affairs took place later in 1986, when the issue of the Ogaden was discussed. Relations between Ethiopia and Somalia deteriorated in 1987, however, following a border clash in February, in which both sides reportedly sustained heavy casualties. In April 1988, after a further meeting between Lt-Col Mengistu and President Siad Barre had taken place in Djibouti, Ethiopia and Somalia agreed to re-establish diplomatic relations, to withdraw troops from their common border and to exchange prisoners of war. Ethiopia had previously insisted that the question of border demarcation be settled before the discussion of other issues. However, it was prompted to seek an improvement in relations with Somalia, owing to its urgent need to redeploy some of its estimated 50,000–70,000 troops in the Ogaden region to reinforce the military presence in the northern Administrative Regions of Eritrea and Tigre. On 25 April the first withdrawal of troops from the common border took place, followed, in August, by an exchange of prisoners who had been in captivity since the Ogaden war of 1978.

Following the military coup in Sudan in April 1985, which displaced President Nimeri, full diplomatic relations were restored between Ethiopia and Sudan. In April 1987 Lt-Col Mengistu paid a four-day visit to Egypt for talks with President Mubarak. In December Sudan's Prime Minister, Sadiq al-Mahdi, met President Mengistu in Uganda. They were believed to have discussed, and possibly sought to end, Ethiopian support for the Sudan People's Liberation Army (SPLA), and Sudanese support for insurgent movements opposed to the Ethiopian Government. Relations between Ethiopia and Sudan were strained by the influx into Ethiopia, in late 1987 and early 1988, of thousands of Sudanese refugees, fleeing from famine and civil war in Southern Sudan. By May 1988 their numbers were estimated to have reached more than 300,000. It was also estimated that, since May 1988, about 400,000 Somalis had fled fighting in northern Somalia and had entered Ethiopia.

Government

Between 1974 and 1987 Ethiopia was ruled by a Provisional Military Administrative Council (PMAC), chaired by the Head of State. Under the new Constitution, adopted in 1987, legislative power is held by the National Shengo, with 835 members elected by universal suffrage for a five-year period. The Constitution provides for the election, by the National Shengo, of a President, who is Head of State and Head of Government. From its members, the National Shengo also elects the Council of State (its permanent organ) and the Council of Ministers, which is headed by a Prime Minister. The President and Vice-President of the country are also, respectively, President and Vice-President of the Council of State. The Marxist-Leninist Workers' Party of Ethiopia (WPE) is the only legal political party. Ethiopia is divided into 24 administrative regions and five autonomous regions, the 1987 Constitution providing for the formation of regional assemblies.

Defence

In June 1988, according to Western estimates, the army (including the People's Militia) numbered 313,000, the air force 4,000 and the navy 1,800. Military service is compulsory, and lasts for 30 months. In addition, all men and women between 18 and 50 years of age undergo six months' reserve training. Ethiopia receives armaments and technical assistance from

ETHIOPIA

Warsaw Pact countries, Cuba, Libya and the People's Democratic Republic of Yemen. In mid-1988 there were an estimated 2,800 Cubans serving in the armed forces. Defence expenditure in 1988/89 was estimated at 1,500m. birr.

Economic Affairs

Ethiopia is, economically, one of the least developed countries in the world, suffering from unfavourable climatic conditions, inadequate infrastructure and a shortage of skilled labour. Economic difficulties have been aggravated by conflict between the central Government and dissident or secessionist groups, while natural disasters have contributed to widespread famine and have increased the already huge refugee problem arising from military hostilities. In April 1987, in a report on recent economic developments and the prospects for recovery in Ethiopia, the World Bank estimated that the country's gross national product (GNP) rose, on average, by 2.5% per year during the period 1976-86. The average annual increase in population, however, was 2.8% over the same period. According to World Bank estimates, Ethiopia's GNP in 1986 (measured at average 1984-86 prices) was US $5,121m., equivalent to $118 per head, and GNP in 1987 (at 1985-87 prices) was $5,537m., equivalent to $124 per head. GNP per head thus remained one of the lowest in the world, having decreased at an average rate of 1.6% per year, in real terms, in 1980-87. In 1987, however, compared with the previous year, real GNP per head rose by 4.0%. The Government forecast that total GNP would increase by 4% in 1988/89. The average annual increase in overall gross domestic product (GDP), in constant prices, was 2.7% in 1965-80, slowing to only 0.8% in 1980-86. The level of investment, which amounted to no more than 10%-11% of GNP during the period 1976-86, remained below the average for low-income African countries. Government expenditure in the 1986/87 fiscal year totalled 5,386m. birr, an increase of 22.5% on the previous fiscal year. The budgetary deficit thus rose to 2,587m. birr, an increase of 34.5% compared with 1985/86. Government expenditure of 6,000m. birr in the 1988/89 fiscal year was approved by the National Shengo. While no detailed figures were made available, it was estimated that this would give rise to a budgetary deficit of 1,600m. birr, a decline of 38.2% compared with 1986/87. However, it was also estimated that military spending would increase the deficit to around 20% of GDP in 1988/89. The average annual rate of inflation was estimated at 3.4% in 1980-86. According to official figures, consumer prices rose by an average of 19.1% in 1985, but declined by 9.8% in 1986 and by a further 2.4% in 1987. Prices rose, however, by 10.5% in the year to May 1988.

The economy is mainly agricultural and pastoral, with agriculture producing almost one-half of GDP in years of normal rainfall (48% in 1986). Agricultural products usually provide about 90% of Ethiopia's export earnings. In 1986 revenue from coffee accounted for 77% of all export receipts. Annual production of coffee generally averages around 200,000 tons, but in 1984/85 it fell to about 150,000 tons, as a result of the drought. In 1985/86, however, quotas were surpassed in several regions, and 74,972 tons of coffee were exported, earning US $277m., according to unofficial sources. In 1987 the decline in international coffee prices was expected to reduce earnings of foreign exchange. In 1988/89 the Government planned to raise coffee exports by 25%, to 1.7m. bags (each of 60 kg). Cotton and sugar cane are also important crops. Agricultural output in general has been devastated by recent drought: the IMF estimated that in 1984/85 domestic food production was reduced by 25%, while export earnings fell by 15% as a result of the drought. Output of food crops totalled 4.6m. metric tons in 1984, compared with a pre-famine total of 7.2m. tons in 1982/83. In 1985/86, however, following improved rainfall in many areas, agricultural production increased by 21.5%, but the good harvests were threatened by a serious plague of locusts in Tigre and Gondar regions. Production of food crops in the 1987/88 crop year (July–June) was estimated at 6m. tons. In 1988/89, however, output was forecast to increase to 7.5m. tons, as a result of abundant rainfall.

Apart from coffee, Ethiopia's major exports include hides and skins, pulses and oilseeds, and refined petroleum products. In recent years the USA has been the largest single export market, taking nearly 20% of total overseas sales in 1984, while the EEC accounts for around one-third of both imports and exports. In 1985, however, the Federal Republic of Germany became Ethiopia's largest single export market. The bulk of Ethiopia's imports come from the USA and the USSR (17.9% and 15.7%, respectively, in 1985). Export earnings consistently fail to pay for imports, and the gap has been widening since 1975: in 1986 the trade deficit totalled 1,339m. birr. Fishing and forestry remain small-scale activities, but international aid is to be sought to develop the fishing industry, which could provide a major long-term solution to the country's food supply problems. In 1975 a radical land reform programme, aimed at stimulating agricultural development by demolishing the feudal system of tenure which existed before the overthrow of the monarchy in 1974, was initiated after all land had been nationalized. In the 1980s the Government introduced a policy of resettlement and 'villagization', moving people from the northern highlands to underpopulated areas in the west and south-west, and grouping them in collective units in order to provide better facilities and to improve production. In 1989 the Government planned to resettle a further 2.7m. people in collective villages, bringing the total number of settlers to almost 15m. By 1994/95 some 50% of farms are scheduled to be organized into co-operatives, compared with 1% in 1984/85. Only about 18% of Ethiopia's total area is cultivated, and in addition only 100,000 ha of land is irrigated, out of a potential of more than 2m. ha. Much of the production of cash crops takes place on state farms, which cover a total of about 300,000 ha. By 1994/95 this area is planned to increase to 500,000 ha. About 45% of agricultural production is at subsistence level. Soil erosion, owing to poor agricultural techniques, deforestation and overgrazing, is an increasing problem, and land is becoming barren at an estimated rate of 200,000 ha per year.

Industrial activity, which contributed about 15% of Ethiopia's GDP in 1986, is confined mainly to food processing and the manufacture of textiles and goods for local consumption. Industrial production increased by 5.1% in 1985/86, and by 4.3% in 1986/87. In 1987/88 the Government planned to invest 342m. birr in nationalized and small-scale industries in order to increase production capacity. The value of production in the state industrial sector amounted to 2,200m. birr in 1988. About one-half of Ethiopia's industry is in Eritrea, although the war there has forced many factories to close. Ethiopia has small reserves of gold, platinum, copper and potash, which are being exploited with the assistance of the USSR. Investment of 188m. birr in the exploitation of these reserves was to be made in 1987/88. There has also been Soviet-led exploration for petroleum, and in 1986 bidding for 25 petroleum-drilling concessions was opened to international companies. The cost of petroleum imports generally accounts for more than 50% of Ethiopia's foreign exchange earnings. The capacity of Ethiopia's only petroleum refinery, at Assab, had reached 800,000 metric tons per year by 1982. Ethiopia has massive hydroelectric power resources, which provide the bulk of electricity generation. In addition, geothermal resources are being assessed, mainly in the Lake Langano area in the Rift Valley. A five-year programme of rehabilitation for the power sector, at a cost of $106.8m., was announced in 1986. Banks, insurance companies and many large industrial concerns, including shipping and maritime services, are all nationalized.

In February 1985 the Government announced an austerity programme, which introduced compulsory contributions for all wage-earners and private companies to an emergency famine relief fund, and also outlined restrictions on petrol consumption and a ban on the import of luxury items, including motor cars and textiles. The problems of drought and famine in 1982-84, and again in 1987-88, were exacerbated by the fighting in Eritrea, the Ogaden and Tigre, which displaced millions of people. Relief attempts were hindered by the continuing conflicts within Ethiopia, the lack of foreign exchange, owing to defence expenditure requirements, and by political differences with the West. These have deterred some sources of aid from funding long-term development projects, which might help to end the cycle of drought and famine. In 1986, in response to strong pressure from the World Bank, the Government intimated at the introduction of agricultural pricing and marketing policies. However, it was not until February 1988 that this took place. It was hoped that the new policies, which included an increase in the official prices payable to farmers and measures to liberalize the marketing of grain, would encourage farmers to produce more grain and facilitate its movement from surplus to deficit regions. In response to these reforms, representatives of the World Bank visited Addis Ababa to discuss the release of a $70m. loan for agricultural development. In October the Government announced plans for a further liberalization of the economy, including an increase in the prices payable to coffee farmers. Further measures were to be incorporated in a new five-year plan, the draft of which was due to be completed in mid-1989. Renewed contact between representatives of the IMF and officials of the National Bank of Ethiopia suggested that these reforms were intended to provide the basis for a new loan agreement.

Economic development is hampered by a lack of adequate transport and communications. However, a port development project, financed by the International Development Association (IDA), is under way at Assab, and will increase the port's capacity, while a railway linking the port with Addis Ababa is to be financed by the CMEA. Other obstacles to the country's development are the lack of trained manpower and financial investment, and the dislocations caused by political change. In 1978 the Government began a series of one-year plans under a National Revolutionary Development Campaign, which resulted in considerable economic recovery in 1978–81. The 10-year plan for 1984/85–1993/94 aims to achieve self-sufficiency in food and to develop the industrial sector. Over the period of the plan, industry's contribution to GDP is projected to increase from 16% to 26%, while agriculture's share is expected to fall to 35%. During the plan period, GDP is expected to grow by around 6% per year in real terms. The State's share of agricultural production is to be significantly expanded, while 216 industrial projects are to be carried out, with the aim of making Ethiopia less dependent on imported capital goods. The plan's success depends largely on foreign assistance (almost 45% of funding is envisaged to come from external sources), and the Government hopes to attract foreign private investment, following the publication of a joint-venture code in 1983. A three-year intermediate plan was announced in 1986, for the period 1986/87–1988/89 (forming part of the 10-year 'perspective' plan). During the plan period, GDP (at 1980/81 prices) was expected to expand by 6.3% per year (from 8,641m. birr in 1985/86 to 10,370m. birr). Agriculture was expected to expand by 6.8% per year, and industry by 8.3%.

Ethiopia's long-term external debt reached US $1,989m. in 1986 (35.7% of GNP), but the country has an excellent record of debt repayment. In addition, Ethiopia's military debt to the USSR was estimated at $2,500m.–$4,000m. in October 1985. In the 1970s the development aid that Ethiopia received was the lowest per head among the UN-designated least developed countries, but by the end of 1984 large amounts of extra emergency aid had been given, following extensive coverage of the drought by foreign media, and by 1985 Ethiopia was the largest recipient of EEC aid. Under the provisions of the Lomé Convention, linking the EEC with African, Caribbean and Pacific countries, the European Development Fund (EDF) granted Ethiopia 230m. ECUs, most of which was allocated to the agricultural sector, followed by development of ports and telecommunications. Loans secured in 1987 included US $7.5m. from the IDA, $12m. from the International Fund for Agricultural Development, and $4m. from the OPEC Fund for International Development towards a $33.7m. project to develop irrigation and soil conservation in mountainous areas, and $76m. (over four years) from the World Food Programme (WFP) to increase agricultural output. The EDF also agreed to release 24m. ECUs of the 230m. ECUs that had been granted to Ethiopia under the Lomé Convention to finance a rural reclamation and development programme in the Northern Shoa region. Following the Ethiopian Government's appeal for famine relief in September 1987, the EEC granted emergency aid of 10m. ECUs to finance the airlifting of food to the country's northern regions.

Folowing a review by the World Bank, in October 1988, of the Government's measures to liberalize the economy, the IDA expected to recommence funding for agriculture. This would include a grant of $85m. towards a $119m. project to develop peasant agriculture. It was also expected that, before the end of 1988, the EDF would agree to the release by the EEC of 39m. ECUs towards a coffee improvement programme costing 60m. ECUs in total.

Social Welfare

The scope of modern health services has been greatly extended since 1960, but they still reach only a small section of the population. In 1980 Ethiopia had 86 hospital establishments. Between 1974 and 1987 26 new hospitals were built. By 1987 there were a total of 11,400 beds, while 1,204 physicians and 3,105 nurses were working in the health service. Relative to the size of the population, the provision of hospital beds and physicians was the lowest among African countries. There were also 2,095 clinics and 159 health centres. With foreign assistance, health centres and clinics are steadily expanding into the rural areas. In times of famine, however, Ethiopian health services are totally inadequate. In 1977 free medical care for the needy was introduced. Of total expenditure by the central Government in the financial year 1980/81, 84.8m. birr (3.6%) was for health, and a further 107.4m. birr (4.6%) for social security and welfare.

Education

Education in Ethiopia is free and, after a rapid growth in numbers of schools, it is hoped to introduce compulsory primary education shortly. Expenditure on education by the central Government in the financial year 1980/81 was 228.3m. birr (9.8% of total spending). A major literacy campaign was launched in 1979. By 1987 more than 20m. people had been enrolled for tuition programmes, and the adult illiteracy rate was reportedly reduced from 93% to 29%.

Since September 1976 most primary and secondary schools have been controlled by local peasant associations and urban dwellers' associations. Primary education begins at seven years of age and lasts for six years. Secondary education, beginning at the age of 13, lasts for a further six years, comprising a first cycle of two years and a second of four years. As a proportion of male children in the relevant age-group, enrolment at primary, junior and senior schools was 35%, 21% and 11%, respectively, in 1988. The corresponding ratios for female children were 27%, 18% and 9%. There are three universities.

Public Holidays

1989: 7 January* (Christmas), 19 January* (Epiphany), 2 March (Battle of Adowa), 6 April (Victory Day), 24 April* (Palm Monday), 1 May* (Easter Monday; also May Day), 7 May (Id al-Fitr, end of Ramadan), 14 July (Id al-Adha/Arafat), 11 September (New Year's Day), 12 September (Popular Revolution Commemoration Day), 27 September* (Feast of the True Cross), 13 October (Mouloud, Birth of the Prophet).

1990: 7 January* (Christmas), 19 January* (Epiphany), 2 March (Battle of Adowa), 6 April (Victory Day), 8 April* (Palm Monday), 15 April* (Easter Monday), 27 April (Id al-Fitr, end of Ramadan), 1 May (May Day), 4 July (Id al-Adha/Arafat), 11 September (New Year's Day), 12 September (Popular Revolution Commemoration Day), 27 September* (Feast of the True Cross), 13 October (Mouloud, Birth of the Prophet).

* Coptic holidays.

Note: Ethiopia uses its own solar calendar; the Ethiopian year 1981 began on 11 September 1988.

Weights and Measures

The metric system is officially in use. There are many local weights and measures.

ated...

Statistical Survey

Source (unless otherwise stated): Central Statistical Office, POB 1143, Addis Ababa; tel. 113010.

Area and Population

AREA, POPULATION AND DENSITY

Area (sq km)	1,251,282*
Population (census of 9 May 1984)†	
Males	21,080,209
Females	21,104,743
Total	42,184,952
Population (official estimates at mid-year)	
1985	43,349,924
1986	44,927,000
1987	46,184,000
Density (per sq km) at mid-1987	36.9

* 483,123 sq miles.
† Including an estimate for areas not covered by the census.

ADMINISTRATIVE REGIONS (census of 9 May 1984)

	Area (sq km)	Population	Density (per sq km)
Arussi	23,674.7	1,662,232	70.2
Bale	127,052.8	1,006,490	7.9
Eritrea	93,679.1	2,614,699	27.9
Gemu Goffa	40,374.8	1,248,033	30.9
Gojam	61,224.3	3,224,881	52.7
Gondar	79,579.4	2,921,124	36.7
Hararge	272,636.9	4,181,167	15.3
Illubabor	46,367.1	963,554	20.8
Kefa (Kaffa)	56,633.6	2,450,468	43.3
Shoa*	85,315.6	9,503,140	111.4
Sidamo	119,760.4	3,790,577	31.7
Tigre	64,921.3	2,409,599	37.1
Wollega	70,481.0	2,477,276	35.1
Wollo	82,143.6	3,642,013	44.3
Assab Administration	27,464.5	89,299	3.3
Total	**1,251,281.9**	**42,184,952**	**33.7**

* Data include the capital, Addis Ababa, which is also a separate Administrative Region (area 222.0 sq km; population 1,412,577).

PRINCIPAL TOWNS (population at 1984 census)

Addis Ababa		Dessie	68,848
(capital)	1,412,577	Harar	62,160
Asmara	275,385	Mekele	61,583
Dire Dawa	98,104	Jimma	60,992
Gondar (incl.		Bahir Dar	54,800
Azeso)	80,886	Akaki	54,146
Nazret	76,284	Debre Zeit	51,143

BIRTHS AND DEATHS (official estimates)

Average annual birth rate 46.0 per 1,000 in 1970–81; death rate 18.1 per 1,000 in 1970–81.

ECONOMICALLY ACTIVE POPULATION
(ILO estimates, '000 persons at mid-1980)

	Males	Females	Total
Agriculture, etc.	8,164	5,877	14,040
Industry	960	422	1,383
Services	1,547	623	2,170
Total	**10,671**	**6,922**	**17,593**

Source: ILO, *Economically Active Population Estimates and Projections, 1950–2025.*

1984 census: Total labour force 18,492,300 (males 11,243,065; females 7,249,235).

Agriculture

PRINCIPAL CROPS ('000 metric tons)

	1984	1985*	1986*
Wheat*	650	700	700
Barley*	800	1,000	1,000
Maize*	1,060	1,300	1,500
Oats*	20	20	20
Millet (Dagusa)*	190	200	200
Sorghum*	515	1,000	1,100
Other cereals*	880	1,100	1,200
Potatoes*	182	210	210
Yams*	212	215	215
Other roots and tubers*	788	850	850
Dry beans*	26	32	33
Dry peas*	113	125	125
Dry broad beans*	450	500	500
Chick-peas	109	135	135
Lentils	25	65	65
Other pulses*	81	87	87
Sugar cane*	1,650	1,600	1,725
Soybeans*	6*	6	6
Groundnuts (in shell)*	28	28	29
Castor beans*	12	12	12
Rapeseed	15	22*	22*
Sesame seed*	36	36	37
Linseed*	30*	30	31
Safflower seed*	32	32	33
Cottonseed†	44	48	48
Cotton (lint)†	20	22	22
Vegetables and melons*	513	533	556
Bananas*	74	74	75
Other fruit (excl. melons)*	136	138	139
Tree nuts*	59	60	61
Coffee (green)†	240	178	225
Tobacco (leaves)*	3	3	3
Fibre crops (excl. cotton)*	17	17	17

* FAO estimates.   † Unofficial estimates.
Source: FAO, *Production Yearbook.*

LIVESTOCK (FAO estimates, '000 head, year ending September)

	1984	1985	1986
Cattle	26,000	26,000	26,300
Sheep	23,450	23,500	23,550
Goats	17,250	17,260	17,280
Asses	3,910	3,915	3,920
Horses	1,570	1,580	1,590
Mules	1,465	1,470	1,480
Camels	1,020	1,030	1,040
Pigs	19	19	19

Poultry (FAO estimates, million): 55 in 1984; 56 in 1985; 56 in 1986.
Source: FAO, *Production Yearbook.*

ETHIOPIA

LIVESTOCK PRODUCTS (FAO estimates, '000 metric tons)

	1984	1985	1986
Beef and veal	214	214	216
Mutton and lamb	86	86	87
Goats' meat	65	66	67
Pig meat	1	1	1
Poultry meat	70	71	72
Other meat	115	118	120
Edible offals	92	92	93
Cows' milk	595	595	600
Goats' milk	95	95	95
Sheep's milk	61	63	64
Butter	8.9	8.9	9.0
Hen eggs	75.9	76.6	77.3
Honey	21.5	21.6	21.9
Wool:			
greasy	12.4	12.5	12.5
clean	6.4	6.5	6.5
Cattle hides	41.0	41.0	41.4
Sheep skins	15.5	15.5	15.6
Goat skins	13.7	14.0	14.2

Source: FAO, *Production Yearbook* and *Monthly Bulletin of Statistics*.

Forestry

ROUNDWOOD REMOVALS
(FAO estimates, '000 cubic metres, excluding bark)

	1984	1985	1986
Sawlogs, etc.*	120	120	120
Other industrial wood*	1,693	1,693	1,693
Fuel wood	35,209	36,083	37,105
Total	37,022	37,896	38,918

* Assumed to be unchanged since 1983.
Source: FAO, *Yearbook of Forest Products*.

SAWNWOOD PRODUCTION ('000 cubic metres)

	1981	1982	1983
Total (including boxboards)	65*	45	45

* FAO estimate.
1984-86: Annual production as in 1983 (FAO estimates).
Source: FAO, *Yearbook of Forest Products*.

Fishing

(FAO estimates, '000 metric tons, live weight)

	1984	1985	1986
Inland waters	3.7	3.5	3.5
Indian Ocean	0.6	0.5	0.6
Total catch	4.3	4.0	4.1

Source: FAO, *Yearbook of Fishery Statistics*.

Mining

(year ending 10 September)

	1983/84	1984/85	1985/86
Gold (kilograms)	661.6	918.1	923.0
Platinum (kilograms)	0.2	0.1	2.4

Industry

SELECTED PRODUCTS ('000 metric tons, unless otherwise indicated; year ending 10 September)

	1981/82	1982/83	1983/84
Wheat flour	164	160	134
Macaroni	11	10	17
Raw sugar	145	178	186
Wine ('000 hectolitres)	86	86	89
Beer ('000 hectolitres)	616	655	613
Soft drinks ('000 hectolitres)	625	650	719
Mineral waters ('000 hectolitres)	177	203	201
Cigarettes (million)	1,741	1,946	2,036
Cotton yarn	9	9	9
Woven cotton fabrics (million sq metres)	92	92	85
Blankets (number)	1,170	1,207	1,233
Woollen carpets ('000 sq metres)	17	19	27
Nylon fabrics (million sq metres)	5.9	5.9	6.1
Footwear ('000 pairs)	7,511	7,985	8,794
Soap	12.2	14.8	14.2
Ethyl alcohol ('000 hectolitres)	5	7	9
Liquefied petroleum gas	5	5	5*
Motor gasoline	92	101	105
Distillate fuel oils	193	209	210
Residual fuel oils	300	303	305
Clay building bricks (million)	20	25	22
Quicklime	4	5	6
Cement	146	120	165
Electric energy (million kWh)	732	757*	829*

1984/85: Electric energy 909m. kWh.*
1985/86: Electric energy 999m. kWh.*
* Provisional.

Finance

CURRENCY AND EXCHANGE RATES
Monetary Units
100 cents = 1 birr.

Denominations
Coins: 1, 5, 10, 25 and 50 cents.
Notes: 1, 5, 10, 50 and 100 birr.

Sterling and Dollar Equivalents (30 September 1988)
£1 sterling = 3.500 birr;
US $1 = 2.070 birr;
100 birr = £28.57 = $48.31.

Exchange Rate
Fixed at US $1 = 2.070 birr since February 1973.

BUDGET ESTIMATES (million birr, year ending 7 July)

Revenue	1981/82	1982/83	1983/84
Direct taxes	506.2	647.2	638.2
Domestic indirect taxes	415.1	448.4	495.5
Taxes on foreign trade	544.8	573.8	572.1
Charges and fees	23.0	23.5	23.9
Sales of goods and services	44.0	42.0	43.0
Property and investment	286.0	320.0	439.1
Miscellaneous	6.0	9.6	7.0
Pension contributions	24.0	25.0	26.0
External assistance	167.5	247.0	219.4
Capital receipts	390.5	441.3	433.4
Total	2,406.9	2,777.9	2,897.6

ETHIOPIA

Expenditure	1981/82	1982/83	1983/84
Current			
National defence	782.5	821.2	869.6
Internal order and justice	140.2	158.1	174.1
Organs of state	127.9	151.6	161.6
Public works and communications	64.3	69.5	64.5
Agriculture, industry, commerce and mining	93.2	106.7	96.9
Education and culture	263.6	302.7	318.9
Public health and social welfare	123.6	135.7	136.3
Pensions	88.3	97.7	100.0
Public debt	117.0	121.2	192.6
Bank charges	2.2	2.5	2.8
Unallocated	35.8	76.6	107.6
Total current	1,838.6	2,043.5	2,224.8
Capital			
Economic development	916.5	1,102.9	1,078.2
Social development	128.7	175.0	148.2
General services	3.9	3.8	8.6
Total capital	1,049.1	1,281.7	1,234.9
Total	2,887.7	3,325.2	3,459.8

NATIONAL BANK RESERVES (US $ million at 31 December)

	1985	1986	1987
Gold*	21.3	21.3	21.3
IMF special drawing rights	0.2	—	1.7
Foreign exchange	147.8	250.5	142.3
Total	169.3	271.8	165.3

* Valued at US $102 per troy ounce.
Source: IMF, *International Financial Statistics*.

MONEY SUPPLY (million birr at 31 December)

	1985	1986	1987
Currency outside banks	1,418	1,640	1,744
Demand deposits at commercial banks	1,285	1,633	1,597
Total money	2,702	3,273	3,341

Source: IMF, *International Financial Statistics*.

COST OF LIVING (General Index of Retail Prices for Addis Ababa, excluding rent; base: 1980 = 100)

	1984	1985	1986
Food	124.0	155.3	131.6
Fuel, light and soap*	118.5	128.2	137.6
Clothing	98.9	97.2	99.0
All items (incl. others)	121.0	144.1	130.0

* Including certain kitchen utensils.
1987: Food 123.6; All items 126.8.

NATIONAL ACCOUNTS
(million birr at current prices, year ending 7 July)

Expenditure on the Gross Domestic Product

	1984/85	1985/86	1986/87
Government final consumption expenditure	1,924	2,045	2,142
Private final consumption expenditure*	8,047	8,308	8,306
Gross fixed capital formation	1,131	1,213	1,297
Total domestic expenditure	11,102	11,566	11,745
Exports of goods and services	1,137	1,421	1,203
Less Imports of goods and services	2,240	2,508	2,089
GDP in purchasers' values	9,999	10,480	10,859

* Including increase in stocks. The figures are obtained as a residual.

Gross Domestic Product by Economic Activity

	1982/83	1983/84*	1984/85*
Agriculture, hunting, forestry and fishing	4,388.7	4,069.8	3,918.6
Mining and quarrying	9.7	12.3	15.1
Manufacturing	655.9	670.1	683.9
Handicraft and small industry	328.3	339.1	339.1
Building and construction	346.0	387.3	374.5
Electricity and water	62.0	67.6	73.6
Wholesale and retail trade	980.4	997.5	962.1
Transport and communications	523.1	564.9	614.0
Banking, insurance and real estate	326.5	286.3	347.1
Public administration and defence	713.5	750.9	770.0
Ownership of dwellings	217.9	223.9	230.3
Educational services			
Medical and health services	348.6	382.8	414.5
Domestic services			
Other services	182.0	190.4	196.2
GDP at factor cost	9,082.7	8,943.1	8,939.0
Indirect taxes, *less* subsidies	948.1	1,057.5	942.3
GDP at market prices	10,030.8	10,000.6	9,881.3

* Figures are provisional. Revised totals for GDP at market prices (in million birr) are: 9,942 in 1983/84; 9,999 in 1984/85.

BALANCE OF PAYMENTS (US $ million)

	1983	1984	1985
Merchandise exports f.o.b.	402.6	416.8	332.9
Merchandise imports f.o.b.	−740.0	−798.4	−840.5
Trade balance	−337.3	−381.5	−507.6
Exports of services	169.6	210.3	313.6
Imports of services	−252.9	−290.1	−310.6
Balance on goods and services	−420.6	−461.4	−504.6
Private unrequited transfers (net)	92.1	144.9	212.9
Government unrequited transfers (net)	158.1	186.1	397.7
Current balance	−170.4	−130.4	105.9
Long-term capital (net)	207.4	192.3	170.8
Short-term capital (net)	−35.9	29.6	49.8
Net errors and omissions	−54.8	−150.6	−168.8
Total (net monetary movements)	−53.6	−59.2	157.6
Valuation changes (net)	7.8	3.9	−9.0
Exceptional financing	0.1	1.2	—
Changes in reserves	−45.8	−54.1	148.6

Source: IMF, *International Financial Statistics*.

ETHIOPIA

External Trade

PRINCIPAL COMMODITIES ('000 birr)

Imports c.i.f.	1982	1983	1984*
Food and live animals	124,320	207,269	170,736
Cereals and cereal preparations	90,259	170,625	122,346
Crude materials (inedible) except fuels	50,229	58,130	43,264
Mineral fuels, lubricants, etc.	399,781	350,231	319,784
Petroleum	357,792	315,344	262,480
Chemicals and related products	173,415	209,275	205,875
Inorganic chemicals	48,115	36,872	36,720
Manufactured fertilizers	13,030	42,040	37,788
Basic manufactures	262,727	263,778	290,167
Textile yarn, fabrics, etc.	45,664	37,375	37,199
Iron and steel	78,620	67,171	76,307
Machinery and transport equipment	513,601	603,434	664,861
General industrial machinery	203,568	229,250	234,439
Electrical machinery, apparatus, etc.	82,729	114,801	86,740
Road vehicles	179,843	187,971	191,535
Miscellaneous manufactured articles	64,579	68,796	59,823
Total (incl. others)	1,623,397	1,813,325	1,813,842

* Figures are provisional. Revised total is 1,921.4 million birr.

Exports f.o.b.	1982	1983	1984
Food and live animals	591,135	596,994	619,090
Coffee	514,388	519,956	545,707
Crude materials (inedible) except fuel	171,640	158,208	164,077
Goatskins	21,119	17,258	18,592
Sheepskins	49,134	52,512	59,746
Cotton lint	21,775	9,342	7,849
Qat	32,862	28,862	32,014
Mineral lubricants, etc.	63,921	68,917	63,851
Furnace and fuel oils	63,919	68,917	63,851
Total (incl. others)	835,983	832,491	861,759

Source: Ethiopian Chamber of Commerce.

1985 (million birr): *Imports:* Total 2,056.4; *Exports:* Coffee 432.7; Hides and skins 103.6; Total (incl. others) 689.4.
1986 (million birr): *Imports:* Total 2,280.4; *Exports:* Coffee 725.6; Hides and skins 109.9; Total (incl. others) 941.6 (Source: IMF, *International Financial Statistics*).

PRINCIPAL TRADING PARTNERS ('000 birr)

Imports	1983	1984	1985
China, People's Rep.	8,775	8,213	8,118
France	51,494	64,231	66,524
German Dem. Rep.	39,086	31,724	29,080
Germany, Fed. Rep.	179,419	201,346	203,791
India	8,098	9,587	9,224
Italy	243,045	190,418	164,184
Japan	168,147	126,042	123,638
Kenya	9,757	9,394	8,098
Korea, Rep.	46,257	20,172	51,378
Netherlands	51,879	37,571	58,201
Saudi Arabia	18,002	9,994	18,142
Sweden	36,108	25,976	63,163
Switzerland	38,798	42,401	40,698
USSR	379,063	452,996	356,339
United Kingdom	137,638	124,589	178,300
USA	83,192	298,219	330,469
Total (incl. others)	1,813,325	1,951,104	2,046,443

Source: Ethiopian Chamber of Commerce.

Exports	1983	1984	1985
Djibouti	65,363	59,856	25,274
Egypt	6	1	2,908
France	63,320	43,720	26,335
Germany, Fed. Rep.	137,809	155,688	129,099
Italy	62,184	63,696	53,809
Japan	62,805	64,510	717,720
Netherlands	16,476	17,471	92,266
Saudi Arabia	47,931	36,440	25,609
Sudan	1,525	10,337	12,690
USSR	3,684	39,074	36,872
United Kingdom	13,435	20,055	22,185
USA	169,665	167,802	73,317
Yemen, People's Dem. Rep.	54,893	49,679	56,819
Yugoslavia	2,204	2,012	3,452
Total (incl. others)	832,973	863,579	698,712

Transport

RAILWAYS (traffic)*

	1981/82	1982/83	1983/84
Addis Ababa–Djibouti:			
Passenger-km ('000)	307,000	360,000	268,000
Freight ('000 net ton-km)	108,000	122,000	117,000

* Excluding Eritrea but including traffic on the portion of the Djibouti–Addis Ababa line which runs through the Republic of Djibouti.

ROAD TRAFFIC (motor vehicles in use at 31 December)

	1983	1984	1985
Cars	43,180	47,470	41,250
Buses and coaches	2,893	2,585	3,622
Goods vehicles	8,385	8,483	15,537
Motorcycles and scooters	1,298	1,292	1,437
Total	58,756	59,830	61,846

SHIPPING (Ports of Assab and Massawa, year ending 7 July)

	1981/82*	1982/83	1983/84
Vessels entered ('000 net reg. tons)	2,681	2,961	3,024
Goods loaded ('000 metric tons)	625	650	711
Goods unloaded ('000 metric tons)	1,753	1,856	1,955

* Provisional figures.

CIVIL AVIATION (traffic on scheduled services)

	1982	1983	1984
Kilometres flown (million)	15.0	14.9	15.9
Passengers carried ('000)	332	346	375
Passenger-km (million)	767	767	785
Freight ton-km (million)	24.5	24.5	32.2

Tourism

	1981	1982	1983
Tourist arrivals ('000)	46	60	64

Source: UN, *Statistical Yearbook*.

ETHIOPIA

Communications Media

	1982	1983	1984
Telephones ('000 in use)	101	110	116
Radio receivers ('000 in use)	3,000	3,000	3,000
Television receivers ('000 in use)	45	45	50
Book production: titles	n.a.	457	349
Daily newspapers:			
Number	3	3	3
Average circulation ('000 copies)	40	n.a.	40
Non-daily newspapers:			
Number	4	n.a.	4
Average circulation ('000 copies)	39	n.a.	40
Other periodicals:			
Number	n.a.	n.a.	3
Average circulation ('000 copies)	n.a.	n.a.	178

Source: Mainly UNESCO, *Statistical Yearbook*.

Education

(1985)

	Teachers	Students
Pre-primary	1,532	69,736
Primary	50,922	2,448,778
Secondary: general	15,218	655,517
Vocational	390	4,969
Universities	1,034	21,601
Other higher	280	5,737

Source: UNESCO, *Statistical Yearbook*.

Directory

The Constitution

The 1931 Constitution was abolished by military decree in September 1974. In June 1986 a draft constitution, prepared by the Workers' Party of Ethiopia (WPE), was published, providing for a unitary state comprising administrative and autonomous regions. The new Constitution was approved by referendum in February 1987. Based on Marxist-Leninist principles, it provides for the election of an 835-seat National Shengo (Assembly), which is the highest organ of government. Candidates for election must either be members of the WPE, or be nominated by representative organizations, such as trade unions, or the armed forces. The term of office of the National Shengo is five years, and its deputies are responsible for the election of the President of the People's Democratic Republic of Ethiopia (PDRE) (established at the inaugural session of the National Shengo in September 1987), and of the Council of State, which oversees state affairs when the National Shengo is not in session. The National Shengo also appoints a Council of Ministers (Cabinet). Under the terms of the Constitution, the President and Vice-President of the PDRE are also President and Vice-President, respectively, of the Council of State.

The Government

(January 1989)

HEAD OF STATE

President: Lt-Col MENGISTU HAILE MARIAM (elected 11 September 1987).
Vice-President: FISSEHA DESTA.

COUNCIL OF STATE

President: Lt-Col MENGISTU HAILE MARIAM.
Vice-Presidents: FISSEHA DESTA, EMANUEL AMDEMIKHAIL, DEBELA DINSA, YUSUF AHMED.
Secretary: EMBIBE AYELE.
Members: Capt. FIKRE SELASSIE WOGDERES, Lt-Gen. TESFAYE GEBRE-KIDAN, Lt-Col BERHANU BAYIH, ADDIS TEDLA, HAILU YIMENU, ALEMU AGEBE, FASIKA SIDELIL, TESFAYE DINKA, SHEWANDAGN BELETE, ENDALLE TESSEMA, ASHAGRE YIGLETU, TEFERA WONDIE, KASAYE ARAGAW, TADESE TAMIRAT, ABDELA SONESA, HAILE GABRIEL DAGNE, ASEGEDECH BIZUNEH, GETACHEW ROBELE.

COUNCIL OF MINISTERS

Prime Minister: Capt. FIKRE SELASSIE WOGDERES.
Deputy Prime Ministers: ADDIS TEDLA, HAILU YIMENU, ALEMU AGEBE, TESFAYE DINKA, TEFERA WONDIE.
Minister of Foreign Affairs: Lt-Col BERHANU BAYIH.
Minister of Internal Affairs: Col TESFAYE WOLDE-SELASSIE.
Minister of Construction: KASSA GEBRE.
Minister of Labour and Social Affairs: SHIMELES ADUGNA.
Minister of Information: ABDUL HAFEZ YUSUF.
Minister of Culture, Sports and Youth Affairs: Maj. GIRAM YILMA.
Minister of Planning: MERSIE EJIGU.
Minister of Defence: Maj.-Gen. HAILE GIORGIS HAPTE MARIAM.
Minister of Industry: FANTA BELAY.
Minister of Coffee and Tea Development: TEKOLA DEJENE.
Minister of Agriculture: GEREMEW DEBELE.
Minister of Finance: WOLE CHEKOL.
Minister of Housing and Urban Development: TESFAYE MARRU.
Minister of Health: Brig.-Gen. Dr GIZAW TSEHAY.
Minister of Mines and Energy: Eng. TEKIZE-SHOA AYITENFISU.
Minister of State Farms: YOSEPH MULETA.
Minister of Foreign Trade: TADESSE GEBRE-KIDAN.
Minister of Law and Justice: WONDAYEN MEHRETU.
Minister of Education: Dr YAYEHRAD KITAW.
Minister of Domestic Trade: MERSHA WODAJO.
Minister of Transport and Communications: ASSEGID WOLDE-AMMANUEL.
Minister for the Co-ordination of Regional Affairs: TSEGAW AYELE.
Minister for the Co-ordination of Religious Affairs: DIBEKULU ZEWDE.
Director of the Institute of Nationalities (with rank of Minister): HAILU WOLDE AMANUEL.
Ministers without Portfolio: Lt.-Gen. TESFAYE GEBRE-KIDAN, BIZUAYEHU ALEMAYEHU.

MINISTRIES AND COMMISSIONS

Office of the Prime Minister: POB 1013, Addis Ababa; tel. 123400.
Ministry of Agriculture: POB 1223, Addis Ababa; tel. 448040.
Ministry of Coffee and Tea Development: POB 3222, Addis Ababa; tel. 448005; telex 21130.
Ministry of Construction: Addis Ababa; tel. 155406.
Ministry of Culture, Sports and Youth Affairs: POB 1902, Addis Ababa; tel. 446338.
Ministry of Defence: POB 125, Addis Ababa; tel. 445555; telex 21261.
Ministry of Domestic Trade: POB 1769, Addis Ababa; tel. 448200.
Ministry of Education: POB 1362, Addis Ababa; tel. 112039.

ETHIOPIA
Directory

Ministry of Finance: POB 1905, Addis Ababa; tel. 113400; telex 21147.
Ministry of Foreign Affairs: POB 393, Addis Ababa; tel. 447345; telex 21050.
Ministry of Foreign Trade: POB 2559, Addis Ababa; tel. 151066; telex 21320.
Ministry of Health: POB 1234, Addis Ababa; tel. 157011.
Ministry of Housing and Urban Development: POB 3386, Addis Ababa; tel. 150000.
Ministry of Industry: POB 704, Addis Ababa; tel. 448025.
Ministry of Information: POB 1020, Addis Ababa; tel. 111124.
Ministry of Internal Affairs: POB 2556, Addis Ababa; tel. 113334.
Ministry of Labour and Social Affairs: POB 2056, Addis Ababa; tel. 447080.
Ministry of Law and Justice: POB 1370, Addis Ababa; tel. 447390.
Ministry of Mines and Energy: POB 486, Addis Ababa; tel. 448250; telex 21448.
Ministry of State Farms: POB 1223, Addis Ababa; tel. 154600.
Ministry of Transport and Communications: POB 1629, Addis Ababa; tel. 155011.
Commission for Hotels and Tourism: POB 2183, Addis Ababa; tel. 447470.
Commission for National Water Resources: POB 486, Addis Ababa; tel. 447597; telex 21219.
Commission for Relief and Rehabilitation: POB 5686, Addis Ababa; tel. 153011; telex 21281.

Legislature

NATIONAL SHENGO

Parliament was suspended by military decree in September 1974. Provision for an elected national assembly was contained in the new Constitution, approved by referendum in February 1987. At elections held on 14 June, 835 members were elected by universal adult suffrage from a list of candidates approved by the Workers' Party of Ethiopia. The National Shengo subsequently elected a 24-member Council of State, which oversees state affairs when the National Shengo is not in session.

Political Organizations

Workers' Party of Ethiopia (WPE): Addis Ababa; f. 1984; sole legal political party; Marxist-Leninist; 50,000 mems; Sec.-Gen. Lt-Col MENGISTU HAILE MARIAM.

Politburo:

11 full members:

Lt-Col MENGISTU HAILE MARIAM
Capt. FIKRE SELASSIE WOGDERES
FISSEHA DESTA
Lt-Gen. TESFAYE GEBRE-KIDAN
Lt-Col BERHANU BAYIH
ADDIS TEDLA
LEGESSE ASFAW
HAILU YIMENU
AMANUEL AMDE-MIKHAIL
ALEMU AGEBE
SHIMELIS MAZENGIA

Alternate members:

TEKA TULU
FASIKA SIDELIL
SHEWANDAGN BELETE
TESFAYE DINKA
TESFAYE WOLDE-SELASSIE
KASSA GEBRE

OPPOSITION GROUPS

The following separatist groups are opposed to the Ethiopian Government:

Afar Liberation Front (ALF): operates in Hararge and Wollo Administrative Regions; Leader ALI MIRAH.

Eritrean Liberation Front (ELF): f. 1958 (in Cairo, Egypt) with aim of achieving autonomy for Eritrea; commenced armed struggle in 1961; subsequently split into numerous factions; mainly Muslim support; Chair. ABDULLAH MUHAMMAD.

Eritrean People's Liberation Front (EPLF): f. 1970 as a breakaway from the Eritrean Liberation Front; Marxist-Leninist; Christian and Muslim support; seeks total independence; maintains Eritrean People's Liberation Army (EPLA) of 25,000–30,000 men; Sec.-Gen. ISSAIAS AFEWERKI.

Oromo Liberation Front (OLF): operates among the Oromo (or Galla) people in Shoa Administrative Region; has received Somali military assistance.

Somali Abo Liberation Front (SALF): operates in Bale Administrative Region; has received Somali military assistance; Sec.-Gen. MASURAD SHU'ABI IBRAHIM.

Tigre People's Liberation Front (TPLF): f. 1975; Marxist; operates in Tigre Administrative Region; seeks autonomy within Ethiopia; 20,000 mems.

Western Somali Liberation Front (WSLF): POB 978, Mogadishu, Somalia; f. 1975; aims to unite the Ogaden region with Somalia; maintains guerrilla forces of c. 3,000 men; has received support from regular Somali forces; Sec.-Gen. ISSA SHAYKH ABDI NASIR ADAN.

Diplomatic Representation

EMBASSIES IN ETHIOPIA

Algeria: POB 5740, Addis Ababa; tel. 441334; Ambassador: HOCINE MESLOUB.
Argentina: Addis Ababa; telex 21172; Ambassador: Dr H. R. M. MOGUES.
Australia: POB 5798; Addis Ababa; tel. 114500; telex 21488; Ambassador: J. P. C. SHEPPARD.
Austria: POB 1219, Addis Ababa; tel. 202144; telex 21060; Ambassador: Dr HORST-DIETER RENNAU.
Belgium: Fikre Mariam St, Higher 16, Kebelo, POB 1239, Addis Ababa; tel. 181813; telex 21157; Ambassador: Baron d' ANETHAN.
Bulgaria: POB 987, Addis Ababa; tel. 153822; Ambassador: G. P. KASSOV.
Burundi: POB 3641, Addis Ababa; tel. 159564; telex 21069; Ambassador: A. SIMBANAIYE.
Cameroon: Bole Rd, POB 1026, Addis Ababa; telex 21121; Ambassador: (vacant).
Canada: African Solidarity Insurance Bldg, Haile Selassie I Sq., POB 1130, Addis Ababa; tel. 151100; telex 21053; Ambassador: W. AGNES.
Chad: Addis Ababa; Ambassador: J. B. LAOKOLE.
China, People's Republic: POB 5643, Addis Ababa; telex 21145; Ambassador: GU JIAJI.
Congo: POB 5571, Addis Ababa; tel. 154331; telex 21406; Ambassador: C. STANISLAS BATHEAS-MOLLOMB.
Côte d'Ivoire: POB 3668, Addis Ababa; tel. 201213; telex 21061; Ambassador: ANTOINE KOUADIO-KIRINE.
Cuba: Jimma Road Ave, POB 5623, Addis Ababa; tel. 202010; telex 21306; Ambassador: ANTONIO PÉREZ HERRERO.
Czechoslovakia: POB 3108, Addis Ababa; tel. 446382; telex 21021; Ambassador: DUŠAN ROVENSKY.
Djibouti: POB 1022, Addis Ababa; tel. 183200; telex 21317; Chargé d'affaires: DJIBRIL DJAMA ELABE.
Egypt: POB 1611, Addis Ababa; tel. 113077; telex 21254; Ambassador: SAMIR AHMED.
Equatorial Guinea: POB 246, Addis Ababa; Ambassador: SALVADOR ELA NSENG ABEGUE.
Finland: Tedla Desta Bldg, Bole Rd, POB 1017, Addis Ababa; tel. 513900; telex 21259; Chargé d'affaires a.i.: ERIK BREHMER.
France: Kabana, POB 1464, Addis Ababa; tel. 110681; Ambassador: FRANÇOIS MICHEL.
Gabon: POB 1256, Addis Ababa; tel. 181075; telex 21208; Ambassador: DENIS DANGUE REWAKA.
German Democratic Republic: POB 5507, Addis Ababa; tel. 181506; telex 21170; Ambassador: WOLFGANG BAYERLACHER.
Germany, Federal Republic: Kabana, POB 660, Addis Ababa; tel. 120433; telex 21015; Ambassador: BERND OLDENKOTT.
Ghana: POB 3173, Addis Ababa; tel. 201402; telex 21249; Ambassador: BONIFACE KWAME ATERPOR.
Greece: Africa Ave, POB 1168, Addis Ababa; tel. 110612; telex 21092; Chargé d'affaires: M. DIAMANTOPOULOS.
Guinea: POB 1190, Addis Ababa; tel. 449712; Ambassador: PIERRE BASSAMBA CAMARA.
Holy See: POB 588, Addis Ababa; tel. 202100; telex 21815; Apostolic Pro-Nuncio: Most Rev. THOMAS A. WHITE, Titular Archbishop of Sabiona.
Hungary: Abattoirs Rd, POB 1213, Addis Ababa; tel. 167610; telex 21176; Ambassador: SÁNDOR ROBEL.
India: Kabana, POB 528, Addis Ababa; tel. 128100; telex 21148; Ambassador: SURENDRA K. ARORA.
Indonesia: POB 1004, Mekanisa Rd, Addis Ababa; tel. 202104; telex 21264; Ambassador: T.M. MOCHTAR MOHAMAD THAJEB.

ETHIOPIA

Directory

Iran: 317/02 Jimma Rd, Old Airport Area, POB 1144, Addis Ababa; tel. 200369; telex 21118; Chargé d'affaires: HASSEN DABIR.

Italy: Villa Italia, POB 1105, Addis Ababa; tel. 113040; telex 21342; Ambassador: SERGIO ANGELETTI.

Jamaica: National House, Africa Ave, POB 5633, Addis Ababa; tel. 183656; telex 21137; Ambassador: R. A. PIERCE.

Japan: Finfinne Bldg, Revolution Sq., POB 5650, Addis Ababa; tel. 448215; telex 21108; Ambassador: SUKETORO ENOMOTO.

Kenya: Fikre Mariam Rd, POB 3301, Addis Ababa; tel. 180033; telex 21103; Ambassador: P. J. NDUNG'U.

Korea, Democratic People's Republic: POB 2378, Addis Ababa; Ambassador: SOK TAE UK.

Korea, Republic: Jimma Rd, Old Airport Area, POB 2047, Addis Ababa; tel. 444490; telex 21140; Ambassador: DEUK PO KIM.

Liberia: POB 3226, Addis Ababa; telex 21083; Ambassador: NATHANIEL EASTMAN.

Libya: POB 5728, Addis Ababa; telex 21214; Secretary of People's Bureau: K. BAZELYA.

Malawi: POB 2316, Addis Ababa; tel. 44829536; telex 21087; Ambassador: D. P. W. KACHIKUWO.

Mexico: Tsige Mariam Bldg 292/21, 4 Piso, Churchill Rd, POB 2962, Addis Ababa; tel. 443456; Ambassador: CARLOS FERRER.

Mozambique: Addis Ababa; Ambassador: ALBERTO SITHOLE.

Netherlands: Old Airport Area, POB 1241, Addis Ababa; tel. 203300; telex 21049; Ambassador: (vacant).

Niger: POB 5791, Addis Ababa; tel. 161175; telex 21284; Ambassador: ABDOURAHAMANE HAMA.

Nigeria: POB 1019, Addis Ababa; tel. 120644; telex 21028; Ambassador: HALIDU HANNANNIYA.

Poland: Bole Rd, POB 1123, Addis Ababa; tel. 180196; telex 21185; Ambassador: ANDRZEJ K. KONOPACKI.

Romania: Africa Ave, POB 2478, Addis Ababa; tel. 181191; telex 21168; Ambassador: BARBU POPESCU.

Rwanda: Africa House, Higher 17 Kelele 20, POB 5618, Addis Ababa; tel. 180300; telex 21199; Ambassador: JEAN-MARIE VIANNEY NDAGIJIMANA.

Saudi Arabia: Old Airport Area, POB 1104, Addis Ababa; tel. 448010; telex 21194; Chargé d'affaires: HASSAN M. ATTAR.

Senegal: Africa Ave, POB 2581, Addis Ababa; tel. 446332; telex 21027; Ambassador: PAPA LOUIS FALL.

Sierra Leone: POB 5619, Addis Ababa; tel. 203210; telex 21144; Ambassador: FRANCIS E. KAREMO.

Spain: Entoto St, POB 2312, Addis Ababa; tel. 115622; telex 21107; Ambassador: A. MARTÍNEZ-MORCILLO.

Sudan: Kirkos, Kabele, POB 1110, Addis Ababa; telex 21293; Ambassador: UTHMAN ADAM.

Sweden: Ras Tesemma Sefer, POB 1029, Addis Ababa; tel. 448110; telex 21039; Ambassador: NILS G. REVELIUS.

Switzerland: Jimma Rd, Old Airport Area, POB 1106, Addis Ababa; tel. 201107; telex 21123; Ambassador: FRANZ BIRRER.

Tanzania: POB 1077, Addis Ababa; tel. 441064; telex 21268; Ambassador: FATUMA TATU NURU.

Turkey: POB 1506, Addis Ababa; tel. 152321; telex 21257; Ambassador: SUPHI MERIÇ.

Uganda: POB 5644, Addis Ababa; tel. 9816945; telex 21143; Chargé d'affaires: ROBERT CANON UCUNGI.

USSR: POB 1500, Addis Ababa; Ambassador: (vacant).

United Kingdom: POB 858, Addis Ababa; tel. 182354; telex 21299; Ambassador: HAROLD WALKER.

USA: Entoto St, POB 1014, Addis Ababa; tel. 110666; Chargé d'affaires: JAMES R. CHEEK.

Venezuela: Dedre Zeit Rd, POB 5584, Addis Ababa; tel. 164790; telex 21102; Chargé d'affaires: ALFREDO HERNÁNDEZ-ROVATI.

Viet-Nam: POB 1288, Addis Ababa; Ambassador: NGUYEN DUY KINH.

Yemen Arab Republic: POB 664, Addis Ababa; Ambassador: Lt-Col HUSSEIN MOHASIN AL-GHAFFARI.

Yemen, People's Democratic Republic: POB 664, Addis Ababa; Ambassador: SALIH ABU BAKR BIN HUSAYNUN.

Yugoslavia: POB 1341; Addis Ababa; tel. 447804; Ambassador: IVAN SENIČAR.

Zaire: Makanisa Rd, POB 2723, Addis Ababa; tel. 204385; telex 21043; Ambassador: WAKU YIZILA.

Zambia: POB 1909; Addis Ababa; tel. 44815; telex 21065; Ambassador: GEORGE CHIPAMPATA.

Zimbabwe: POB 5624, Addis Ababa; tel. 183872; telex 21351; Ambassador: TICHAONA J. B. JOKONYA.

Judicial System

Special People's Courts were established in 1981 to replace the former military tribunals. Judicial tribunals are elected by members of the urban dwellers' and peasant associations. In 1987 the Supreme Court ceased to be administered by the Ministry of Law and Justice and became an independent body.

Procurator-General: BILILIGNE MANDEFRO.

The Supreme Court: Addis Ababa; comprises civil, criminal and military sections; in 1987 its jurisdiction (previously confined to hearing appeals from the High Court) was extended to include supervision of all judicial proceedings throughout the country; the Supreme Court is also empowered, when ordered to do so by the Procurator-General or at the request of the President of the Supreme Court, to review and decide cases upon which final rulings have been made by the courts, including the Supreme Court, but where basic judicial errors have occurred; judges are elected by the National Shengo; Pres. ASEFA LIBEN.

The High Court: Addis Ababa; hears appeals from the Provincial and sub-Provincial Courts; has original jurisdiction.

Awraja Courts: Regional courts composed of three judges, criminal and civil.

Warada Courts: Sub-regional; one judge sits alone with very limited jurisdiction, criminal only.

Religion

About 45% of the population are Muslims and about 40% belong to the Ethiopian Orthodox (Tewahido) Church. There are also significant Evangelical Protestant and Roman Catholic communities. The Pentecostal Church and the Society of International Missionaries carry out mission work in Ethiopia. There are also Hindu and Sikh religious institutions and a small Jewish population.

CHRISTIANITY
Ethiopian Orthodox (Tewahido) Church

The Ethiopian Orthodox (Tewahido) Church is one of the five oriental orthodox churches. It was founded in AD 328, and in 1986 had more than 22m. members, 20,000 parishes and 250,000 clergy. The Supreme Body is the Holy Synod and the National Council, under the chairmanship of the Patriarch. The Church comprises 20 archdioceses and dioceses (including those in Jerusalem, Sudan, Djibouti and the Western Hemisphere). There are 24 Archbishops and Bishops. The Church administers 1,139 schools and 12 relief and rehabilitation centres throughout Ethiopia.

Patriarchate Head Office: POB 1283, Addis Ababa; tel. 116507; telex 21489; Patriarch: Archbishop ABUNE MERKOREWOS; Gen. Sec. L. M. ABEBAW YIGZAW.

Other Christian Churches

Armenian Orthodox Church: Pres. ABEDIS TERZIAN, St George's Armenian Church, POB 116, Addis Ababa; f. 1923.

Ethiopian Evangelical Church (Mekane Yesus): Pres. Ato FRANCIS STEPHANOS, POB 2087, Addis Ababa; tel. 111200; telex 21528; f. 1958; affiliated to Lutheran World Federation; 685,796 mems (1984).

Greek Orthodox Church: Metropolitan of Axum: Most Rev. PETROS GIAKOUMELOS, POB 571, Addis Ababa.

The Roman Catholic Church: At 31 December 1985 there were an estimated 113,000 adherents of the Alexandrian-Ethiopian rite and 158,000 adherents of the Latin rite.

Alexandrian-Ethiopian Rite: There is one archdiocese (Addis Ababa) and two dioceses (Adigrat and Asmara); Archbishop of Addis Ababa: Cardinal PAULOS TZADUA, POB 2109, Addis Ababa; tel. 111667.

Latin Rite: There are five Apostolic Vicariates (Asmara, Awasa, Harar, Nekemte and Soddo-Hosanna) and one Apostolic Prefecture (Meki); Apostolic Administrator of Asmara: Fr LUCA MILESI, 107 National Ave, POB 224, Asmara; tel. 110631.

Seventh-day Adventist Church: Pres. Pastor BEKELE BIRI, POB 145, Addis Ababa; tel. 158300; telex 21549; f. 1907; 46,000 mems.

ISLAM

Leader: Haji MOHAMMED HABIB SANI.

JUDAISM

Following the secret airlifts to Israel in 1984–85 of about 13,000 Falashas (Ethiopian Jews), there were estimated to be some 8,000 Falashas still in the country, living mainly in Gondar and Tigre Administrative Regions.

ETHIOPIA

TRADITIONAL BELIEFS

It is estimated that between 5% and 15% of the population follow animist rites and ceremonies.

The Press

DAILIES

The following three newspapers are published by the Ministry of Information and National Guidance:

Addis Zemen: POB 30145, Addis Ababa; f. 1941; Amharic; Editor-in-Chief Tsehaju Debalkew (acting); circ. 37,000.

Ethiopian Herald: POB 30701, Addis Ababa; tel. 119050; f. 1943; English; Editor-in-Chief Kiflom Hadgoi; circ. 6,000.

Hibret: POB 247, Asmara; Tigrinya; Editor-in-Chief Gurja Tesfa Selassie; circ. 4,000.

PERIODICALS

Al-Alem: POB 30232, Addis Ababa; weekly; Arabic; publ. by the Ministry of Information; Editor-in-Chief Telsom Ahmed; circ. 2,500.

Berisa: POB 30232, Addis Ababa; f. 1976; weekly; Oromogna; publ. by the Ministry of Information; circ. 2,000.

Ethiopia: POB 247, Asmara; weekly; Amharic; publ. by Ministry of Information; Editor-in-Chief Abraha Gebre Hiwot; circ. 2,000.

Ethiopian Trade Journal: POB 517, Addis Ababa; tel. 448240; telex 21213; publ. by the Ethiopian Chamber of Commerce; quarterly; English; Editor-in-Chief Getachew Zicke.

Maedot (Passover): POB 1283, Addis Ababa; tel. 116507; telex 21489; Amharic and English; publ. by the Ethiopian Orthodox Church.

Meskerem: POB 80001, Addis Ababa; quarterly; theoretical politics; circ. 100,000.

Negarit Gazzetta: POB 1031, Addis Ababa; fortnightly; Amharic and English; official gazette of laws, orders and notices.

Nigdina Limat: POB 2458, Addis Ababa; tel. 158039; telex 21213; monthly; Amharic; publ. by the Ethiopian Chamber of Commerce.

Revolutionary Police: POB 40046, Addis Ababa; fortnightly; Amharic; police journal.

Serto Ader (Worker): POB 80123, Addis Ababa; f. 1980; weekly; organ of the WPE; Editor Tesfaye Tadese; Dep. Editor Gezahegn Gebre; circ. 100,000.

Tatek (Get Armed): POB 1901, Addis Ababa; fortnightly; Amharic; army journal.

Tinsae (Resurrection): POB 1283, Addis Ababa; tel. 116507; telex 21489; Amharic and English; publ. by the Ethiopian Orthodox Church.

Trade and Development Bulletin: POB 856, Asmara; tel. 110814; telex 42079; monthly; Amharic and English; publ. by the Ethiopian Chamber of Commerce; Editor Taame Foto.

Yezareitu Ethiopia (Ethiopia Today): POB 30232, Addis Ababa; weekly; Amharic; publ. by the Ministry of Information; Editor-in-Chief Abiye Meizuria (acting); circ. 30,000.

NEWS AGENCIES

Ethiopia News Agency (ENA): Patriots' St, POB 530, Addis Ababa; tel. 120014; telex 21068.

Foreign Bureaux

Agence France-Presse (AFP): POB 3537, Addis Ababa; tel. 511006; telex 21031; Chief Seyoum Ayele.

Agentstvo Pechati Novosti (APN) (USSR): POB 239, Addis Ababa; telex 21237; Chief Vitali Polikarpov.

Allgemeiner Deutscher Nachrichtendienst (ADN) (German Democratic Republic): POB 2387, Addis Ababa; telex 21025; Chief Bernd Hinkelmann.

Agenzia Nazionale Stampa Associata (ANSA) (Italy): POB 1001, Addis Ababa; telex 115704; Chief Brahame Ghebrezghi-Abiher.

Novinska Agencija Tanjug (Yugoslavia): POB 5743, Addis Ababa; telex 21150; Chief Radoslav Jovič.

Prensa Latina (Cuba): 5th Floor, Gen. Makonnen Bldg, nr Ghion Hotel, opposite National Stadium, POB 5690, Addis Ababa; tel. 449299; telex 21151; Chief Roberto Correa Wilson.

Telegrafnoye Agentstvo Sovetskovo Soyuza (TASS) (USSR): POB 998, Addis Ababa; tel. 181255; telex 21091; Chief Gennadi G. Gabrielyan.

Xinhua (New China) News Agency (People's Republic of China): POB 2497, Addis Ababa; tel. 151064; telex 21504; Correspondent Teng Wenqi.

Directory

PRESS ASSOCIATION

Ethiopian Journalists' Association: Addis Ababa; Chair. Imeru Worku (acting).

Publishers

Addis Ababa University Press: POB 1176, Addis Ababa; tel. 119148; telex 21205; f. 1968; educational and reference works in English; Editor Innes Marshall.

Ethiopia Book Centre: POB 1024, Addis Ababa; privately-owned.

Kuraz Publishing Agency: POB 30933, Addis Ababa; state-owned.

Government Publishing House

Government Printing Press: POB 1241, Addis Ababa.

Radio and Television

There were an estimated 3m. radio receivers and 50,000 television receivers in use in 1984.

Board of Telecommunications of Ethiopia: POB 1047, Addis Ababa; Gen. Man. G. Engdayehu.

RADIO

Voice of Revolutionary Ethiopia: POB 1020, Addis Ababa; tel. 121011; f. 1941; Amharic, English, French, Arabic, Afar, Oromigna, Tigrinya and Somali; Gen. Man. Mulugeta Lule.

TELEVISION

Ethiopian Television: POB 5544, Addis Ababa; tel. 16701; telex 21429; f. 1964; state-controlled; commercial advertising is accepted; programmes are transmitted from Addis Ababa to 17 regional stations; broadcasts cover all of Ethiopia except two Administrative Regions; Head of TV Wole Gurmu.

Finance

(cap. = capital; p.u. = paid up; dep. = deposits; m. = million; res = reserves; amounts in birr)

BANKING

On 1 January 1975 all privately-owned banks and other financial institutions were nationalized.

Central Bank

National Bank of Ethiopia: POB 5550, Addis Ababa; tel. 447430; telex 21020; f. 1964; bank of issue; cap. and res 147.1m. (June 1986); Gov. Bekele Tamirat.

Other Banks

Agricultural and Industrial Development Bank: POB 1900, Addis Ababa; tel. 151188; telex 21173; provides development finance for industry and agriculture, technical advice and assists in project evaluation; cap. p.u. 100m.; Gen. Man. Tsegaye Asfaw; 21 brs.

Commercial Bank of Ethiopia: POB 255, Addis Ababa; tel. 155000; telex 21037; f. 1964, reorg. 1980; state-owned; cap. 65m., res 39m. (Dec. 1986); Gen. Man. Alemu Aberra; 146 brs.

Housing and Savings Bank: POB 3480, Addis Ababa; tel. 152300; f. 1975; provides credit for housing construction; cap. p.u. 6m., dep. 212.3m. (June 1984); Gen. Man. Getachew Yifru; 8 brs.

INSURANCE

Ethiopian Insurance Corporation: POB 2545, Addis Ababa; tel. 156348; telex 21120; f. 1976 to undertake all insurance business; Gen. Man. Ayalew Bezabeh.

Trade and Industry

CHAMBER OF COMMERCE

Ethiopian Chamber of Commerce: Mexico Sq., POB 517, Addis Ababa; tel. 518240; telex 21213; f. 1947; city chambers in Addis Ababa, Asmara, Awassa, Bahir Dar, Dire Dawa, Nazret, Jimma, Gondar and Dessie; Pres. Bezabih Ayalew; Sec.-Gen. Workeneh Mengesha.

AGRICULTURAL ORGANIZATION

Ethiopia Peasants' Association (EPA): f. 1978 to promote improved agricultural techniques, cottage industries, education,

ETHIOPIA

public health and self-reliance; comprises 30,000 peasant asscns with c. 7m. mems; Chair. ABDELA SONESA.

TRADE AND INDUSTRIAL ORGANIZATIONS

Ethiopian Beverages Corporation: POB 1285, Addis Ababa; tel. 186185; telex 21373.

Ethiopian Cement Corporation: POB 5782, Addis Ababa; tel. 122323; telex 21308.

Ethiopian Chemical Corporation: POB 5747, Addis Ababa; tel. 184305; telex 21011.

Ethiopian Coffee Marketing Corporation: POB 2591, Addis Ababa; tel. 155330; telex 21174.

Ethiopian Food Corporation: Higher 21, Kebele 04, Mortgage Bldg, Addis Ababa; tel 158522; telex 21292; f. 1975; produces and distributes food items including edible oil, ghee substitute, pasta, bread, maize, wheat flour etc.

Ethiopian Fruit and Vegetable Marketing Enterprise: POB 2374, Addis Ababa; tel. 449192; telex 21106; f. 1980; sole wholesale domestic distributor and exporter of fruit and vegetables, spices and floricultural products; Gen. Man. HAILU BALCHA.

Ethiopian Handicrafts and Small-Scale Industries Development Agency: POB 704, Addis Ababa; tel. 157366.

Ethiopian Import and Export Corporation (ETIMEX): POB 2313, Addis Ababa; tel. 152400; telex 21009; f. 1975; state trading corpn under the supervision of the Ministry of Foreign Trade; import of building materials, foodstuffs, stationery and office equipment, textiles, clothing, chemicals, general merchandise, capital goods.

Ethiopian Livestock and Meat Corporation: POB 5579, Addis Ababa; tel. 159341; telex 21095; f. 1984; state trading organization responsible for management of the meat industry.

Ethiopian Oil Seeds and Pulses Export Corporation: POB 5719, Addis Ababa; tel. 159536; telex 21133; Gen. Man. EPHRAIM AMBAYE.

Ethiopian Petroleum Organization: POB 3375, Addis Ababa; telex 21054; f. 1976; operates Assab petroleum refinery; Gen. Man. MAMO GEBRE MESKEL.

Ethiopian Pharmaceuticals and Medical Supplies Corporation: POB 21904, Addis Ababa; tel. 134511; telex 21248; f. 1976; manufacture, import, export and distribution of pharmaceuticals, chemicals, dressings, surgical and dental instruments, hospital and laboratory supplies; Gen. Man. BERHANU ZELEKE.

Ethiopian Sugar Corporation: POB 133, Addis Ababa; tel. 159700; telex 21038.

National Leather and Shoe Corporation: POB 2516, Addis Ababa; tel. 150832; telex 21096; f. 1975; produces and sells semi-processed hides and skins, finished leather, leather goods and footwear.

National Textiles Corporation: POB 2446, Addis Ababa; tel. 157316; telex 21129; f. 1975; production of yarn, fabrics, knitwear, blankets, bags, etc.; Gen. Man. BEKELE HAILE.

Natural Gums Processing and Marketing Enterprise: POB 62322, Addis Ababa; tel. 159931; telex 21336.

TRADE UNIONS

All trade unions must register with the Ministry of Labour and Social Affairs, and 'subordinate' unions must comply with directives issued by 'higher' unions.

Ethiopian Trade Union (ETU): POB 3653, Addis Ababa; f. 1975 to replace the Confed. of Ethiopian Labour Unions; comprises nine industrial unions and 16 regional unions with a total membership of 320,000 (1987); Chair. TADESSE TAMRAT; Sec.-Gen. ABERA AFFIN.

Transport

RAILWAYS

Ethio-Djibouti Railway Co: POB 1051, Addis Ababa; tel. 447250; telex 21414; f. 1908 as Compagnie du chemin de fer Franco-Ethiopien, renamed 1981; owned jtly by Ethiopian and Djibouti govts; plans to grant autonomous status were announced by the two govts in July 1985; 781 km of track, of which 681 km is in Ethiopia, linking Addis Ababa with Djibouti; Pres. Y. ALI CHIRDON; Man. Dir CHANNIE TAMIRU.

ROADS

In 1985 the total road network comprised 37,871 km of primary, secondary and feeder roads and trails, of which 12,839 km were main roads. A highway links Addis Ababa with Nairobi in Kenya, forming part of the Trans-East Africa Highway.

Ethiopian Transport Construction Authority: POB 1770, Addis Ababa; tel. 447170; telex 21180; f. 1951; constructs roads, bridges, airfields, ports and railways, and maintains roads and bridges throughout Ethiopia; Gen. Man. KELLETTA TESFA MICHAEL.

National Freight Transport Corporation: POB 2538, Addis Ababa; tel. 151841; telex 21238; f. 1974; truck and tanker operations throughout the country.

National Public Transport Authority: POB 5780, Addis Ababa; tel. 156044; telex 21371; f. 1977; urban bus services in Addis Ababa and Jimma, and services between towns.

Road Transport Authority: POB 2504, Addis Ababa; enforcement of road transport regulations, registering of vehicles and issuing of driving licences.

SHIPPING

The Ethiopian merchant shipping fleet totalled 28,409 grt in July 1983. There are irregular services by foreign vessels to Massawa and Assab (the port for Addis Ababa), which can handle over 1m. metric tons of merchandise annually. It has an oil refinery with an annual capacity of 500,000 metric tons. Much trade goes through Djibouti (in the Republic of Djibouti) to Addis Ababa, and Ethiopia has permission to use the Kenyan port of Mombasa. Port and maritime services were nationalized in September 1979.

Ethiopian Shipping Lines Corporation: POB 2572, Addis Ababa; tel. 444205; telex 21045; f. 1964; state-owned; serves Red Sea, Europe and Far East with its own and chartered vessels; Chair. Minister of Transport and Communications; Gen. Man. TESEMA GEZAW; 12 vessels.

Marine Transport Authority: POB 1861, Addis Ababa; tel. 446448; telex 21280; f. 1978; administers and operates the ports of Assab and Massawa, manages inland waterways, handles cargo.

Maritime and Transit Services Corporation: POB 1186, Addis Ababa; tel. 150666; telex 21057; f. 1979; handles cargoes for import and export; operates shipping agency service.

CIVIL AVIATION

Ethiopia has four international airports and around 40 airfields.

Civil Aviation Authority: POB 978, Addis Ababa; tel. 180266; telex 21162; constructs and maintains airports; provides air navigational facilities.

Ethiopian Airlines: Bole International Airport, POB 1755, Addis Ababa; tel. 152222; telex 21012; f. 1945; operates regular domestic services and flights to 31 international destinations in Africa, Europe, Middle East, India and the People's Republic of China; Chair. Minister of Transport and Communications; Gen. Man. Capt. MUHAMMAD AHMAD; fleet of 3 Boeing 767, 2 Boeing 737-200, 3 Boeing 720B, 3 707-320C, 3 727-200, 9 DC-3, 2 ATR-42 (replacing DC-3), 2 Lockheed L-100-30, 2 DHC-5A Buffalo, 6 DHC-6A, 11 Cessna 172, 2 Seneca III, 1 Piper Aztec.

Tourism

The principal tourist attractions are the early Christian monuments and churches, and the ancient capitals of Gondar and Axum. Tourist arrivals in 1983/84 were about 69,000. Tourism provided an estimated 47m. birr in foreign exchange in 1986.

Ethiopian Tourism and Hotels Commission: POB 2183, Addis Ababa; tel. 517470; telex 21067; f. 1961; Commr (vacant).

FIJI

Introductory Survey

Location, Climate, Language, Religion, Flag, Capital

The Republic of Fiji comprises more than 300 islands, of which 100 are inhabited, situated about 1,930 km (1,200 miles) south of the equator in the Pacific Ocean. The four main islands are Viti Levu (on which almost 70% of the country's population lives), Vanua Levu, Tavenui and Kadavu. The climate is tropical, with temperatures ranging from 16° to 32°C (60°-90°F). Rainfall is heavy on the windward side. Fijian and Hindi are the principal languages but English is also widely spoken. In 1986 about 53% of the population were Christians (mainly Methodists), 38% Hindus and 8% Muslims. The national flag (proportions 2 by 1) is light blue, with the United Kingdom flag as a canton in the upper hoist. In the fly is the main part of Fiji's national coat of arms: a white field quartered by a red upright cross, the quarters containing sugar canes, a coconut palm, a bunch of bananas and a dove bearing an olive branch; in chief is a red panel with a yellow lion holding a coconut. The capital is Suva, on Viti Levu.

Recent History

The first Europeans to settle on the islands were sandalwood traders, missionaries and shipwrecked sailors, and in October 1874 Fiji was proclaimed a British possession. In September 1966 the British Government introduced a new constitution for Fiji. It provided for a ministerial form of government, an almost wholly elected Legislative Council and the introduction of universal adult suffrage. Rather than using a common roll of voters, however, the Constitution introduced an electoral system that combined communal (Fijian and Indian) rolls with cross-voting. In September 1967 the Executive Council became the Council of Ministers, with Ratu Kamisese Mara, leader of the multiracial (but predominantly Fijian) Alliance Party (AP), as Fiji's first Chief Minister. Following a constitutional conference in April–May 1970, Fiji achieved independence, within the Commonwealth, on 10 October 1970. The Legislative Council was renamed the House of Representatives, and a second parliamentary chamber, a nominated Senate, was established. The British-appointed Governor became Fiji's first Governor-General, while Ratu Sir Kamisese Mara (as he had become in 1969) took office as Prime Minister.

Fiji was troubled by racial tensions, however. Although the descendants of indentured Indian workers who were brought to Fiji in the late 19th century had grown to outnumber the native inhabitants, they were discriminated against in political representation and land ownership rights. A new electoral system was adopted in 1970 to ensure a racial balance in the legislature.

At the general election held in March and April 1977 the National Federation Party (NFP), traditionally supported by the Indian population, won 26 of the 52 seats in the House of Representatives but was unable to form a government and subsequently split into two factions. The AP governed in a caretaker capacity until another election in September, when it was returned with its largest-ever majority. While these two main parties professed multiracial ideas, the Fijian Nationalist Party campaigned on a 'Fiji for the Fijians' platform in order to foster nationalist feeling.

In 1980 Ratu Sir Kamisese Mara's suggestion that a government of national unity be formed was overshadowed by renewed political disagreement between the AP and the NFP (whose two factions had drawn closer together again) over land ownership. Fijians owned 83% of the land and were strongly defending their traditional rights, while the Indian population was pressing for greater security of land tenure. The July 1982 elections were also dominated by racial issues. The Alliance Party retained power after winning 28 seats, but their majority had been cut from 20 to four. The NFP won 22 seats and the Western United Front (WUF), which professed a multiracial outlook, took the remaining two seats. Allegations by the two major political parties that foreign political and business interests had been involved in each other's election campaign prompted the appointment of a Royal Commission of Inquiry which, however, failed to uncover any conclusive proof of the allegations during its investigations in 1983. The opposition parties in the House of Representatives supported their leader, Jai Ram Reddy, in his boycott of Parliament, which had begun in December 1983 over a point of protocol. The boycott ended in June 1984, after Reddy had resigned his seat in May and had been replaced as parliamentary leader of the NFP, and of the opposition coalition, by Siddiq Koya, whom he had defeated for the leadership in 1977.

In February 1985 the Government held its first economic 'summit conference'; the meeting was boycotted, however, by both the parliamentary opposition and the Fiji Trades Union Congress (FTUC), in protest against a government-imposed 'freeze' on wages, in force since November 1984. A meeting of union leaders in May 1985 marked the beginning of discussions which culminated in the founding of the Fiji Labour Party (FLP), officially inaugurated in Suva in July 1985. Sponsored by the FTUC, and under the presidency of Dr Timoci Bavadra, the new party was formed with the aim of presenting a more effective parliamentary opposition, and declared the provision of free education and a national medical scheme to be among its priorities. The FLP hoped to work through farmers' organizations to win votes among rural electorates, which traditionally supported the NFP.

During 1985 and 1986 disagreements between the Government and the FTUC over economic policies became increasingly acrimonious, and in February 1986, having failed to reach agreement with the labour unions on an acceptable increase in wages for 1986, the Government arbitrarily fixed the increase at 2.25%. This provoked an outbreak of labour unrest, leading to the withdrawal, in June 1986, of government recognition of the FTUC as the unions' representative organization. The FTUC responded by holding public protest rallies and by seeking an international suspension of air and sea links with Fiji. The dispute was finally settled in January 1987, when the FTUC, the Fiji Employers' Consultative Association and the Government signed an agreement whereby a guideline of 5.5% was fixed for pay increases in 1987.

In 1986 representatives from the Fijian Government and the Soviet Union met to discuss trade links, tourism and the possibility of securing a fishing agreement. A ban, imposed in response to Soviet military intervention in Afghanistan, and under which Soviet ships had been prohibited from entering Fiji's ports, was subsequently lifted, although no agreement on Soviet fishing rights was signed. In October 1986 Fiji was one of a group of South Pacific island states to conclude a five-year fishing agreement with the USA, whereby the US tuna fleet was granted a licence to operate vessels within Fiji's exclusive fishing zone.

In early 1986 an NFP working committee was formed to conduct an inquiry into the decline of the party, which had lost a number of parliamentary seats as a result of both by-election defeats and the defection of several of its sitting members (including the former deputy leader, Irene Jai Narayan), who chose to classify themselves as independent. In May Koya resigned from the leadership of the NFP, and was replaced by Harish Chandra Sharma. The party continued to lose internal support, and in August a further three of its parliamentary members transferred their allegiance to the FLP, which, like the NFP, derived its support mainly from the Indian community.

At the general election held in April 1987 a coalition of the FLP and NFP won 28 seats (19 of which were secured by ethnic Indian candidates) in the House of Representatives, thus defeating the ruling AP, which won only 24 seats. The new Government, led by Dr Timoci Bavadra of the FLP, was therefore the first in Fijian history to contain a majority of ministers of Indian, rather than Melanesian, origin, Dr Bavadra himself being of Melanesian descent. On 14 May, however, the Government was overthrown by a military coup, led by Lt-Col (later Maj.-Gen.) Sitiveni Rabuka. The Governor-General, Ratu Sir Penaia Ganilau, responded by declaring a state of

FIJI   Introductory Survey

emergency and appointed a 19-member advisory council, including Bavadra and Rabuka. However, Bavadra refused to participate in the council, denouncing it as unconstitutional and biased in its composition.

Widespread racial violence followed the coup, and there were several public demands for Bavadra's reinstatement as Prime Minister. In July 1987 the Great Council of Fijian Chiefs, comprising the country's 80 hereditary Melanesian leaders, approved plans for constitutional reform, which included a proposal that the Senate be abolished. In September negotiations began, on the initiative of Ganilau, between delegations led by the two former Prime Ministers, Bavadra and Mara, to resolve the political crisis, and on 22 September it was announced that the two factions had agreed to form an interim bipartisan government.

However, on 25 September 1987, before the new plan could be implemented, Rabuka staged a second coup and announced his intention to declare Fiji a republic. Despite Ganilau's refusal to recognize the seizure of power, Rabuka revoked the Constitution on 1 October and proclaimed himself Head of State, thus deposing the Queen. Ganilau conceded defeat and resigned as Governor-General. At a meeting in Canada, Commonwealth Heads of Government formally declared that Fiji's membership of the Commonwealth had lapsed. An interim Council of Ministers, comprising mainly Melanesians, was installed by Rabuka. Senior judges who had opposed the coup were removed from office. Australia and New Zealand refused to recognize the Rabuka regime, although France, Indonesia and the People's Republic of China indicated that they were prepared to expand trade links with Fiji. In late October Rabuka announced that he would resign as Head of State as soon as he had appointed a new President of the Republic. Several cases of violations of human rights by the Fijian army were reported as the regime assumed powers of detention without trial and suspended all political activity.

On 6 December 1987 Rabuka resigned as Head of State. Although he had previously refused to accept the post, Ratu Sir Penaia Ganilau, the former Governor-General, became the first President of the Fijian Republic. Ratu Sir Kamisese Mara was reappointed Prime Minister, and Rabuka became Minister of Home Affairs. A new Cabinet was announced on 9 December, containing 11 members of Rabuka's administration, but no member of Bavadra's deposed government.

In February 1988 Rotuma, an island to the north-west of Suva, declared itself politically independent of Fiji, whose newly-acquired republican status it refused to recognize. Rotuma appealed to the Governments of Australia, New Zealand and the United Kingdom for assistance. However, Fijian troops were dispatched to the island and soon quelled the dissent.

In June 1988 two members of Bavadra's deposed Government were detained, after the discovery by Australian customs officers of a shipment of weapons *en route* to Fiji from the Middle East. Several weeks later, a secret cache of weapons was discovered on the island of Viti Levu, confirming speculation that a similar arms shipment had already reached Fiji. Following the discovery, an internal security decree, granting the armed forces wider powers of arrest, was introduced, as it remained unclear for whom the arms shipment was intended. The decree remained in effect until November 1988.

A new draft constitution was approved by the interim Government in September 1988 and was to be promulgated, subject to endorsement by a multiracial constitutional committee. By the terms of the draft document, both the President of the Republic and the Commander-in-Chief of the Armed Forces were to be appointed by the Great Council of Chiefs, and the Prime Minister was to be invariably of ethnic Melanesian origin. Parliament was to be unicameral and to comprise 71 members, of whom 28 were to be elected by ethnic Fijians, 30 by citizens of other ethnic backgrounds, and one by the inhabitants of Rotuma Island. Of the remaining 12 seats, eight were to be filled by ethnic Fijians, appointed by the Great Council of Chiefs, and the remaining four by nominees of the President. The Commander-in-Chief would automatically be a member of Parliament. The draft Constitution was immediately condemned by many Fijian Indians on the grounds that it would guarantee an ethnic Fijian majority in Parliament, and, if accepted as proposed, it was unlikely to reduce the large-scale emigration of skilled Fijian Indians, which had ensured, in January 1989, that, for the first time since 1946, ethnic Fijians had outnumbered Fijian Indians in the country.

Government

Until October 1987 the Head of State was the British sovereign, represented locally by an appointed Governor-General, who was required to act in accordance with the advice of the Cabinet except in certain constitutional functions. Following two military coups, however, the 1970 Constitution was revoked. A proposed interim constitution vested executive power in the first President of the Republic.

Prior to the coups, legislative power was vested in a bicameral Parliament, comprising the House of Representatives and the nominated Senate. The House of Representatives had 52 members, elected for five years by voting on national and communal rolls, divided into three categories: Fijian, Indian and General (those ineligible for the first two rolls). Twelve Fijians, 12 Indians and three General members were elected on the communal rolls. Ten Fijians, 10 Indians and five General members were elected on the national rolls. The Senate was an appointed Upper House with 22 members: eight were appointed by the Great Council of Fijian Chiefs; seven by the Prime Minister; six by the Leader of the Opposition; and one by the Council of Rotuma (Island). Senators served a six-year term.

A new constitution, the provisions of which included the creation of a unicameral parliament, was awaiting final approval in early 1989 (see Recent History, above).

Defence

The Royal Fiji Military Forces consist of men in the regular army, the Naval Squadron, the conservation corps and the territorials. The conservation corps was created in 1975 to make use of unemployed labour in construction work. In June 1988 the total armed forces numbered 3,500 men: 3,200 in the army and 300 in the navy. The defence budget for 1987 was $F 16.9m.

Economic Affairs

In 1987, according to estimates by the World Bank, Fiji's gross national product (GNP) per head, measured at average 1985–87 prices, was US $1,091m., equivalent to US $1,510 per head. GNP per head was estimated to have decreased at an average annual rate of 2.6%, in real terms, between 1980 and 1987. Compared with the previous year, however, in 1987 real GNP per head declined by an estimated 14.2%.

Fiji's economy is basically agricultural, and the principal cash crop is sugar cane. The instability of the international sugar market seriously affected the Fijian economy in the mid-1970s but, as a member of the group of African, Caribbean and Pacific (ACP) countries which has been linked to the EEC by the Lomé Convention since 1975, Fiji benefits from the Convention's Sugar Protocol, which guarantees that EEC member-states import raw cane sugar from ACP countries at a fixed price. In recent years this price has been far above the prevailing international price of raw sugar on the free market.

The effects of a lengthy drought and a hurricane in March 1983 severely affected the yield of raw sugar in that year, and, with an output of only 275,877 tons, sugar had to be imported for domestic consumption in order that Fiji might meet its export contracts. In 1984 Fiji produced 483,000 tons of raw sugar, just below the record level of 1982, but, as a result of low free-market prices for sugar and reductions in the USA's quota for imports of Fijian sugar, the Fiji Sugar Corporation made the first operating loss in its history. In 1985 production of raw sugar declined to 340,000 tons, owing to cyclone damage. However, long-term trade agreements with New Zealand, the People's Republic of China and Malaysia, negotiated in 1985 and 1986, were expected to increase revenue from sugar sales. The USA increased Fiji's sugar export quota from 12,012 metric tons in 1986 to 25,190 tons in 1987, in order to compensate for previous losses of sugar exports to the USA, due to a statistical error. In 1986 production of raw sugar increased to a record 501,800 tons, with sugar exports earning just under $F 138m. and amounting to nearly 54% of the value of all export earnings. However, owing to a prolonged drought and industrial action by Indian farmers, revenue from sugar sales was expected to fall by nearly $F 60m. in 1987, when output of raw sugar declined to 401,000 tons. Sugar production in 1988 was forecast at only 350,000 tons. In 1978 an Australian aid project, involving an estimated investment of $A 7.5m. over 10 years, was initiated. The project aimed to bring 324,000 ha of hilly and largely undeveloped land into production by establishing 103 individual farm holdings, with an emphasis on livestock and grazing. Fiji's principal trading partners are Australia, Japan, New Zealand, Singapore, the United Kingdom and the USA. After 1982 tourism overtook the sugar industry to become the major source of foreign exchange earnings. Tourist receipts totalled more than $F 190m. in 1986, compared with sugar exports of almost $F 138m. Other important exports are fish, gold and coconut products.

In an effort to diversify the economy, domestic industries such as cement, timber, cigarettes and tuna canning are being encouraged by income tax concessions and export incentive reliefs, and these measures succeeded in reducing the trade deficit from $F 248m. in 1983 to $F 174m. in 1984. The trade deficit was $F 240.2m. in 1985, declining to $F 184m. in 1986. In 1987 it fell still further, to $F 56m. In the first nine months of 1988 the trade deficit increased to $F 108m., the value of exports totalling $F 347m. and imports $F 455m. The annual inflation rate declined from 13.7% in 1975 to 4.4% in the year to December 1985, the lowest rate attained for 14 years. As a result of a wage 'freeze' and price controls, imposed by the Government—in spite of resistance from the trade unions—in November 1984 and remaining in force until February 1986, the country's balance of payments improved to give a current surplus of US $4.5m. in 1986, compared with a deficit of US $12.6m. in 1985. There was another deficit, of US $4.6m., in 1987. A balance-of-payments surplus of US $112m. was anticipated in 1989. The four cyclones that struck Fiji in early 1985, killing 29 people and causing considerable damage to crops, had an adverse effect on the economy: GDP declined by 1.7% in 1985, with agricultural production declining by 8.8% and manufacturing by 4.7%. During 1979–85 GDP grew by an average of only 1.4% per year in real terms, compared with an average growth of 4.6% per year during 1970–78. In 1986 GDP grew, in real terms, by 1.8%, but in 1987, owing to the political upheaval, it contracted by 11%. GDP was forecast to decline by 6.5% in 1988, but it was hoped that it would increase by 4% in 1989.

Under Fiji's eighth Five-Year Development Plan (1981–85), sugar production and tourism remained the dominant industries, but it was hoped that the proposed development of cocoa, ginger, citrus fruits, timber, beef, goats' meat, fish and dairy farming would help to diversify the economy. Moreover, in 1985 plans were formulated to spend $F 6m. on projects to bring more land under rice cultivation and, under the South Pacific Regional Trade and Economic Co-operation Agreement (SPARTECA, see p. 204), which gives access to the Australian and New Zealand markets for manufactured goods, to diversify into the production of items such as washing machines, wheelbarrows and cement mixers. Reliance on imported petroleum products is to be reduced by the development of hydroelectricity (an important scheme, opened in October 1983 at Monasavu, reduced oil imports by 20% in 1984) and by exploring the possibilities of converting coconut oil into fuel. In 1986 construction began of a sawmill and chipmill at Lautoka, on Viti Levu, which was opened in 1987. The new mill cost $F 50m. and was expected to process 215,000 cu m of pine wood per year. Annual export earnings, mainly from sales of sawn timber to Australia and Japan, were projected to be $F 12.5m. Production of timber reached 187,000 cu m in 1986. Following the expansion of the joint Fijian and Australian-owned Vatukoula gold mine, ore capacity was increased, and output raised to 2,856 kg in 1986. Production was estimated at 2,647 kg in 1987. An agreement with Japan, signed in October 1986, secured a grant of more than $A8m. for the construction of a fisheries port at Lautoka.

Fiji's ninth Five-Year Development Plan (1986–90) aimed to achieve an average growth in GDP of 5% per year in real terms. Continuing emphasis was to be placed on resource-based industries, such as sugar, coconut and gold production, and on the development of the tourist industry. A tourist resort under construction at Vunaniu Bay, at an expected cost of US $65m., was due to open in the late 1980s, and $F 40m. of new investment was expected annually during 1986–88. Both a continuing need for wage restraint and a planned shift towards consumption-based taxes were also envisaged.

The 1987 budget proposals envisaged total revenue of $F 400.5m. and expenditure of $F 477.6m., of which some $F 5.2m. was to be used to finance a programme of tax relief for low-paid workers, by establishing a higher income-tax threshold. The economy was adversely affected by Fiji's political instability in 1987. Foreign aid programmes were suspended, and trade sanctions were imposed. The unemployment level increased to 10% of the labour force, from 7.5% in 1986. Disruption in the sugar industry led to serious losses in export earnings, and receipts from tourism also declined sharply. Tourist arrivals in 1987 fell to 189,866 from their 1986 level of 257,824, and earnings were reduced by nearly $F 40m. However, tourist arrivals increased again in 1988 and were expected to surpass 300,000 per year by 1991. Foreign reserves declined from $F 172m. at the end of 1986 to $F 113m. in mid-1987. The Fiji dollar was devalued several times, and controls on the availability of foreign exchange were imposed, in a bid to prevent flight of capital from the country. The annual rate of inflation stood at 8% in November 1987 and increased to 11% in July 1988. Budget proposals were also affected, and the estimated overall deficit of $F 77m. was predicted in late 1987 to be nearer $F 100m. Budget proposals for 1988 envisaged total expenditure of $F 421m. and revenue of $F 342m. Total revenue was budgeted at $F 390m. for 1989. In December 1987 the Government announced increases in taxes on petrol, tobacco products and alcohol. A duty of 2% was to be imposed on major export items.

Social Welfare

The Fiji National Provident Fund, established in 1966, contains provision for retirement pensions, widows' pensions, an insurance scheme and housing loans. Employers and employees contribute equally. In June 1981 there were 125,441 members. Medical and dental treatment is provided for all at a nominal charge. In 1984 Fiji had 27 hospitals (with a total of 1,736 beds), 48 health centres, 90 nursing centres and 339 physicians. Of total budgetary expenditure by the central Government in 1985, $F 31.7m. (8.5%) was for health services, and a further $F 30.4m. (8.2%) for social security and welfare.

Education

Education in Fiji is not compulsory, but in 1985 about 95% of school-age children were enrolled at the country's schools, and the Government's plan to provide free education covered the first eight years of schooling. Primary education begins at six years of age and lasts for six years. Secondary education, beginning at the age of 12, lasts for a further six years. State subsidies are available for secondary and tertiary education in cases of hardship. In 1984 there were 665 state primary schools (with a total enrolment of 131,221 pupils in 1986), 139 state secondary schools (with an enrolment of 42,200 pupils in 1986), 36 vocational and technical institutions (with 3,603 students), three teacher-training colleges (with 37 students) and a school of medicine (with 82 students). There were 876 holders of Fiji government scholarships at the University of the South Pacific in Fiji in 1981. In 1988 university students on campus totalled 2,138, and extension students totalled 4,404. Budgetary expenditure on education by the central Government in 1985 was $F 82.2m., representing 22.1% of total spending. The adult illiteracy rate in 1976 averaged 21% (males 16%; females 26%), but in 1985, according to estimates by UNESCO, the rate was only 14.5% (males 9.8%; females 19.1%).

Public Holidays

1989: 2 January (for New Year's Day), 24–27 March (Easter), 12 June (for Queen's Official Birthday), 31 July (Bank Holiday), 9 October (for Independence Day), 13 October* (Birth of the Prophet Muhammad), October/November (Diwali), 13 November (for Birthday of the Prince of Wales), 25–27 December (Christmas).

1990: 1 January (New Year's Day), 13–16 April (Easter), 11 June (for Queen's Official Birthday), 30 July (Bank Holiday), 2 October* (Birth of the Prophet Muhammad), 8 October (for Independence Day), October/November (Diwali), 12 November (for Birthday of the Prince of Wales), 25–27 December (Christmas).

* This Islamic holiday is dependent on the lunar calendar and may vary by one or two days from the dates given.

Weights and Measures

The metric system is in force.

Statistical Survey

Source (unless otherwise stated): Bureau of Statistics, POB 2221, Government Bldgs, Suva; tel. 315144; telex 2167.

AREA AND POPULATION

Area (incl. the Rotuma group): 18,376 sq km (7,095 sq miles).

Population: 588,068 (296,950 males, 291,118 females) at census of 13 September 1976; 715,375 (362,568 males, 352,807 females) at census of 31 August 1986.

Principal Town: Suva (capital), population 69,665 at 1986 census.

Ethnic Groups (at census of 31 August 1986): Indians 348,704, Fijians 329,305, Others 37,366, Total 715,375.

Births, Marriages and Deaths (registrations, 1985): Live births 19,464 (birth rate 27.9 per 1,000); Marriages 6,593 (marriage rate 9.5 per 1,000); Deaths 3,680 (death rate 5.3 per 1,000).

Economically Active Population (census of 31 August 1986): Agriculture, hunting, forestry and fishing 106,305; Mining and quarrying 1,345; Manufacturing 18,106; Electricity, gas and water 2,154; Construction 11,786; Trade, restaurants and hotels 26,010; Transport, storage and communications 13,151; Financing, insurance, real estate and business services 6,016; Community, social and personal services 36,619; Total (incl. others and unemployed) 241,160 (males 189,929, females 51,231).

AGRICULTURE, ETC.

Principal Crops (metric tons, 1986): Sugar cane 4,300,000, Coconuts 220,000, Cassava 40,000, Rice (paddy) 28,000, Sweet potatoes 8,000, Bananas 5,000, Yams 10,000, Taro 25,000 (FAO estimates). Source: FAO, *Production Yearbook*.

Livestock ('000 head, year ending September 1986): Cattle 159, Pigs 31, Goats 56, Horses 42 (FAO estimates). Source: FAO, *Production Yearbook*.

Forestry (FAO estimates, 1986): *Roundwood removals* ('000 cu m): Sawlogs and veneer logs 205, Fuel wood and charcoal 37, Other industrial wood 7; Total 249 (Source: FAO, *Yearbook of Forest Products*).

Fishing (metric tons, live weight): Total catch 27,909 in 1984; 27,626 in 1985; 27,002 in 1986. Source: FAO, *Yearbook of Fishery Statistics*.

MINING

Production: Gold 2,856 kg (1986), Silver 774 kg (1986), Crushed metal 133,891 cu m (1984).

INDUSTRY

Production (1986, metric tons unless otherwise stated): Beef 3,644, Sugar 501,800, Copra 22,510, Coconut oil 14,122, Soap 6,131, Cement 92,278, Paint 1,951 ('000 litres), Beer 16,018 ('000 litres), Soft drinks 3,893 ('000 litres), Cigarettes 477,491,650 (number), Timber 187 ('000 cu m), Matches 138 ('000 gross boxes).

FINANCE

Currency and Exchange Rates: 100 cents = 1 Fiji dollar ($F). *Coins:* 1, 2, 5, 10, 20 and 50 cents. *Notes:* 1, 2, 5, 10 and 20 dollars. *Sterling and US Dollar Equivalents* (30 September 1988): £1 sterling = $F 2.483; US $1 = $F 1.468; $F 100 = £40.28 = US $68.11. *Average Exchange Rate* (US $ per $F): 0.8676 in 1985; 0.8834 in 1986; 0.8173 in 1987.

Budget ($F '000, 1986): *Revenue:* Customs duties and port dues 126,370, Income tax and estate and gift duties 143,721, Interest 512, All other income 98,208, Total 368,811; *Expenditure:* Public debt charges 74,652, Pensions and gratuities 14,794, Works annually recurrent 39,605, Departmental expenditure 241,932, Total 370,983. **1988** (estimates): Revenue $F 342m.; Expenditure $F 421m.

International Reserves US $ million at 31 December 1987): Gold (valued at market-related prices) n.a., IMF special drawing rights 14.04, Reserve position in IMF 11.16, Foreign exchange 106.92; Total (excl. gold) 132.13 (Source: IMF, *International Financial Statistics*).

Money Supply ($F million at 31 December 1986): Currency outside banks 63.1; Demand deposits at commercial banks 115.4; Total money 178.6 (173.2 at 31 December 1987) (Source: IMF, *International Financial Statistics*).

Cost of Living (Consumer Price Index; base: 1979 = 100): 159.8 in 1985; (base: 1985 = 100): 101.8 in 1986, 107.6 in 1987.

Gross Domestic Product by Economic Activity (1985, $F million at constant 1977 factor cost): Agriculture, forestry and fishing 156.1, Mining and quarrying 0.8, Manufacturing 79.7, Electricity, gas and water 8.4, Building and construction 41.4, Distribution (incl. tourism) 123.6, Transport and communications 90.0, Finance and insurance 98.0, Government and other services 130.6, Sub-total 728.7; *Less* Imputed bank service charges 23.3; Total 705.4.

Balance of Payments (US $ million, 1987): Merchandise exports f.o.b. 303.7; Merchandise imports f.o.b. −330.6; *Trade balance* −26.8; Exports of services 243.4; Imports of services −210.8; *Balance on goods and services* 5.7; Private unrequited transfers (net) −20.8; Government unrequited transfers (net) 10.5; *Current balance* −4.6; Direct capital investment (net) 27.0; Other long-term capital (net) −43.1; Short-term capital (net) −10.4; Net errors and omissions −17.4; *Total* (net monetary movements) −48.5; Valuation changes (net) 10.8; *Change in reserves* −37.7. Source: IMF, *International Financial Statistics*.

EXTERNAL TRADE

Principal Commodities (1986, $F '000, provisional): *Imports:* Machinery and electrical goods 81,224, Transport equipment 34,975, Textile yarn and fabrics 25,955, Iron and steel 23,024, Food 77,720, Petroleum products 79,372, Clothing 4,284, Tape recorders 422, Watches 2,869, Total imports (incl. others) 496,729. *Exports:* Sugar 133,716, Gold 38,632, Coconut oil 3,909, Molasses 7,913, Green ginger 3,001, Veneer sheets 2,325, Biscuits 1,167, Prepared fish 16,680, Cement 200, Lumber 3,949, Silver 152. *Re-exports:* Petroleum products 47,048, Fish 214, Textile yarns and fabrics 4,624, Clothing 1,091. Total exports (incl. others) 280,141.

Principal Trading Partners (1986, $F '000): *Imports:* Australia 166,501 Canada 4,945, Germany, Federal Republic 10,972, Hong Kong 8,541, India 4,909, Japan 71,303, Netherlands 1,056, New Zealand 82,957, Singapore 16,091, United Kingdom 21,628, USA 23,822. *Exports:* Australia 53,487, Canada 4,938, Germany, Federal Republic 1,902, Japan 5,416, New Zealand 20,935, Singapore 122, Tonga 8,495, United Kingdom 108,709, USA 14,762, Western Samoa 8,332.

TRANSPORT

Road Traffic (motor vehicles registered at 31 December 1986): Passenger cars 33,600, All other vehicles 35,054.

Shipping (international traffic, 1984): Freight loaded 661,000 metric tons; freight unloaded 807,000 metric tons; vessels entered 747 (with a total displacement of 3,554,000 net reg. tons); vessels cleared 747 (with a total displacement of 3,554,000 net reg. tons).

Civil Aviation (1985): Passengers arriving 293,646, Passengers departing 298,039, Transit passengers 208,274.

TOURISM

Foreign Tourist Arrivals: 228,175 (1985), 257,824 (1986), 189,866 (1987).

COMMUNICATIONS MEDIA

Radio receivers (1983): 400,000 in use.

Telephones (1985): 53,228 in use.

Book production (1980): 110 titles (84 books, 26 pamphlets); 273,000 copies (229,000 books, 44,000 pamphlets).

Daily newspapers (1988): 2 (combined circulation 40,000 copies per issue).

Non-daily newspapers (1982): 4 (combined circulation 74,300).

EDUCATION

Pre-primary (1985): 244 schools, 308 teachers, 4,206 pupils.

Primary: 668 schools (1985), 4,396 teachers (1985), 127,286 pupils (1985), 131,221 pupils (1986).

General Secondary: 139 schools (1984), 2,656 teachers (1984), 2,669 teachers (1985), 41,505 pupils (1985), 42,200 pupils (1986).

Vocational and Technical: 36 institutions (1984), 2,941 students (1985), 3,603 students (1986).

Teacher Training: 3 institutions (1984), 34 students (1985), 37 students (1986).

Medical (1986): 1 institution, 82 students.

Directory

The Constitution

The Constitution which came into force on 10 October 1970, when Fiji achieved independence, was formally revoked on 1 October 1987, following the military coup of 25 September 1987. An interim constitution recognized Ratu Ganilau as President of the Republic and vested executive authority in him. The President was empowered to make laws by decree, with the advice of the Prime Minister. A new constitution, drafted in 1988, was approved by the interim government in preparation for its formal promulgation.

The Government

HEAD OF STATE

President: Ratu Sir PENAIA GANILAU (took office 6 December 1987).

THE CABINET
(February 1989)

Prime Minister, Minister of Foreign Affairs and Minister for Public Service: Ratu Sir KAMISESE MARA.
Minister of Home Affairs, National Youth Service and Auxiliary Army Services: Maj.-Gen. SITIVENI RABUKA.
Minister for Fijian Affairs: Col VATILIAI NAVUNISARAVI.
Minister of Finance and Economic Planning: JOSEFATA KAMIKAMICA.
Minister of Education: FILIPE BOLE.
Minister for Primary Industries: VILIAME GONELEVU.
Minister of Trade and Commerce: BERENADO VUNIBOBO.
Minister of Health: APENISA KURISAQILA.
Minister of Communications, Works and Transport: APISAI TORA.
Attorney-General and Minister of Justice: SAILOSI KEPA.
Minister of Tourism, Civil Aviation and Energy: DAVID PICKERING.
Minister of Youth and Sport: Col ILAISA KACISOLOMONE.
Minister of Rural Development and Rural Housing: Col APOLOSI BIUVAKALOLOMA.
Minister of Indian Affairs: IRENE JAI NARAYAN.
Minister of Forests: Ratu Sir JOSAIA TAVAIQIA.
Minister of Employment and Industrial Relations: TANIELA VEITATA.
Minister of Co-operatives and National Marketing Authority: ISHWARI BAJPAI.
Minister of Women's Affairs and Social Welfare: FINAU TABAKAUCORO.
Minister of Housing and Urban Development: TOMASI VAKATORA.
Minister of Lands and Mineral Resources: Ratu WILLIAM TOGANIVALU.
Minister of Information: CHARLES WALKER.

MINISTRIES

All Ministries are in Suva.

Legislature

Parliament was suspended following the military coup of 14 May 1987. A draft constitution, proposed in 1988, provided for a unicameral assembly of 71 seats: 28 to be elected by indigenous Fijians, 30 to be elected by Indians and other races, and 12 to be appointed by the President and Prime Minister. The remaining member would be chosen by the inhabitants of Rotuma Island.

PARLIAMENT

During the coup of 14 May 1987 a group of soldiers forcibly entered the House of Representatives and arrested all 28 members of the ruling coalition.

The Senate

There were 22 appointed members.
President: W. J. CLARK.

House of Representatives
Speaker: MILITONI LEWANIQILA.

General Election, 5–11 April 1987

	Seats
FLP-NFP coalition	28
AP	24

Political Organizations

All political activity was suspended on 24 October 1987.

Alliance Party (AP): 41 Gladstone Rd, POB 688, Suva; f. 1965; mainly indigenous Fijian support; ruling party 1970–87; Pres. Ratu Sir KAMISESE K. T. MARA; Sec.-Gen. (vacant).

Fiji Labour Party (FLP): Suva; f. 1985; formed coalition govt with NFP following April 1987 election; Pres. Dr TIMOCI BAVADRA; Sec.-Gen. KRISHNA DATT.

Fijian Nationalist Party (FNP): POB 1336, Suva; f. 1974; seeks additional parliamentary representation for persons of Fijian ethnic origin and other pro-Fijian reforms; Chair. WAISALE BAKALEVU; Sec. SAKIASI BUTADROKA.

National Federation Party (NFP): POB 228, Suva; f. 1960 by merger of the Federation Party, which was multiracial but mainly Indian and the National Democratic Party; joined FLP in coalition govt following April 1987 election; Leader HARISH CHANDRA SHARMA; Pres. JAI RAM REDDY.

Taukei Solidarity Movement: f. 1988, following merger of Taukei Liberation Front and Domo Ni Taukei; extreme right-wing indigenous Fijian nationalist group; Vice-Pres. MELI VESIKULA.

Western United Front (WUF): POB 263, Sigatoka; f. 1981; mainly Fijian; advocates co-existence and co-operation among all communities; 10,000 mems; Pres. Ratu OSEA GAVIDI; Sec. ISIKELI NADALO.

Diplomatic Representation

EMBASSIES IN FIJI

Australia: Dominion House, POB 214, Suva; tel. 312844; telex 2126; Ambassador: ROBERT COTTON.
China, People's Republic: 147 Queen Elizabeth Drive, Suva; tel. 22425; telex 2136; Ambassador: XU MINGYUAN.
France: 1st Floor, Dominion House, Thomson St, Suva; tel. 312925; telex 2326; Ambassador: DANIEL DUPONT.
India: POB 405, Suva; tel. 312255; telex 2110; Ambassador: THETTALIL PARAMESWARAN PILLAI SREENIVASAN.
Japan: 2nd Floor, Dominion House, Suva; tel. 25631; telex 2253; Ambassador: TOSHIO ISOGAI.
Korea, Republic: 8th Floor, Vanua House, PMB, Suva; tel. 311977; telex 2175; Ambassador: HYON CHIN KIM.
Malaysia: Air Pacific House, Suva; tel. 312166; telex 2295; Ambassador: Miss TING WEN LIAN.
New Zealand: 10th Floor, Reserve Bank of Fiji Bldg, POB 1378, Suva; tel. 311422; telex 2161; Ambassador: BRIAN ABSOLUM.
Papua New Guinea: 6th Floor, Ratu Sukuna House, POB 2447, Suva; tel. 25420; telex 2113; Ambassador: MAIMU RAKA-NOU.
Tuvalu: POB 14449, Suva; tel. 301023; telex 2297; Ambassador: SEMU SOPOAGA TAAFAKI.
United Kingdom: Victoria House, 47 Gladstone Rd, POB 1355, Suva; tel. 311033; telex 2129; Ambassador: ROGER A. R. BARLTROP.
USA: 31 Loftus St, POB 218, Suva; tel. 314466; telex 2255; Ambassador: LEONARD ROCHWARGER.

Judicial System

Justice is administered by the Fiji Court of Appeal, the Supreme Court, the High Court and the Magistrates' Courts. The Supreme Court of Fiji is the superior court of record presided over by the Chief Justice, who is also the President of the Fiji Court of Appeal and the Supreme Court. The Chief Justice and six senior judges were removed from office on 15 October 1987, following the

FIJI

military coup of 25 September. In January 1988 the former Chief Justice, Sir Timoci Tuivaga, resumed his post in a newly-constituted judicial system and a further three High Court judges were appointed.

Chief Justice: Sir TIMOCI TUIVAGA.

Religion

Most ethnic Fijians are Christians, mainly Protestant. The Indians are mostly Hindus, and there are also Muslim and Sikh communities.

CHRISTIANITY

Methodists are the largest Christian group, followed by Roman Catholics.

Fiji Council of Churches: POB 2300, Government Buildings, Suva; tel. (1) 313798; f. 1964; seven mem. churches; Pres. HENRY MANUELI; Gen. Sec. Rev. GERALD MCNICHOLAS (acting).

The Anglican Communion

Anglicans in Fiji are adherents of the Church of the Province of New Zealand. The diocese of Polynesia is based in Fiji but also includes numerous other island groups in the central and southern Pacific Ocean.

Bishop in Polynesia: Rt Rev. JABEZ LESLIE BRYCE, Bishop's House, 7 Disraeli Rd, Suva; tel. 302553; POB 35, Suva; tel. 24357.

The Roman Catholic Church

Fiji comprises a single archdiocese. At 31 December 1986 there were an estimated 59,100 adherents in the country.

Bishops' Conference: Episcopal Conference of the Pacific, POB 289, Suva; tel. 313795; f. 1968; 17 mems; Pres. Rt Rev. FRANCIS LAMBERT, Bishop of Port Vila, Vanuatu.

Archbishop of Suva: Most Rev. PETERO MATACA, Archdiocesan Office, POB 109, Suva; tel. 22851.

Other Christian Churches

Methodist Church in Fiji (Lotu Wesele e Viti): Epworth Arcade, Nina St, POB 357, Suva; tel. 24097; f. 1835; autonomous since 1964; 170,820 mems (1985); Pres. Rev. PAULA NIUKULA; Gen. Sec. Rev. INOKE NABULIVOU.

Other denominations active in the country include the Assembly of God (with c. 7,000 mems), the Baptist Mission, the Congregational Christian Church and the Presbyterian Church.

BAHÁ'Í FAITH

National Spiritual Assembly: POB 639, Suva; tel. 22776; mems resident in 392 localities.

The Press

Sunday newspapers have not been published since the military coup of September 1987.

NEWSPAPERS AND PERIODICALS

Coconut Telegraph: POB 249, Savusavu, Vanua Levu; f. 1975; monthly; serves widely-scattered rural communities; Editor Mrs LEMA LOW.

Fiji Beach Press: Publications (Fiji) Ltd, POB 2193, Govt Bldgs, Suva; tel. 311211; telex 2631; fortnightly in English (circ. 8,000), twice a year in English for overseas (circ. 40,000); tourist information; Editor MERE MOMOIVALU.

Fiji Magic: George Rubine Ltd, POB 12511, Suva; tel. 313944; monthly; English; Editor-in-Chief GEORGE MATAI; circ. 10,000.

Fiji Royal Gazette: Printing Dept, POB 99, Suva; f. 1874; weekly; English.

Fiji Times: 20 Gordon St, POB 1167, Suva; tel. 314111; telex 2124; f. 1869; publ. by Fiji Times Ltd; daily; English; Man. Dir GEOFFREY HUSSEY; circ. 27,000.

Islands: 46 Gordon St, POB 12718, Suva; tel. 312040; telex 2528; f. 1980, present name since 1985; quarterly; English; Publr ROBERT KEITH-REID; Editor PETER LOMAS; circ. 20,000.

Jagriti: POB 9, Nadi; f. 1950; 3 a week; Hindi; circ. 5,500.

Nai Lalakai: 20 Gordon St, POB 1167, Suva; tel. 314111; telex 2124; f. 1962; publ. by Fiji Times Ltd; weekly; Fijian; Editor DALE TONAWAI; circ. 18,000.

Shanti Dut: 20 Gordon St, POB 1167, Suva; f. 1935; publ. by Fiji Times Ltd; weekly; Hindi; Editor M. C. VINOD; circ. 8,000.

Siga Rarama: Newspapers of Fiji Ltd, POB 354, Suva; tel. 311944; telex 2333; f. 1974; weekly; Fijian; Editor MIKA TURAGA; circ. 10,000.

Sunday Times: Fiji Times Ltd, POB 1167, Suva; weekly; English; Gen. Man. REX GARDNER.

Publishers

Fiji Times Ltd: POB 1167, Suva; tel. 314111; telex 2124; f. 1869; largest newspaper publr; also publrs of books and magazines; Man. Dir GEOFFREY HUSSEY.

Government Publishing House

Printing Department: POB 98, Suva.

Radio and Television

There were an estimated 400,000 radio receivers in use in 1983. In 1985 a 12-year contract to establish and operate a commercial television broadcasting service was awarded to Pacific Television Pty Ltd, a subsidiary of an Australian television network, Publishing and Broadcasting Ltd; operations were due to begin in March 1988. The content of all broadcasts has been subject to government control since the military coup of 25 September 1987.

Fiji Broadcasting Commission (Radio Fiji): POB 334, Broadcasting House, Suva; tel. 314333; telex 2142; f. 1954; broadcasts from 10 AM and one FM station on two national networks; programmes in English, Fijian and Hindustani; Chair. Ratu J. TOGANIVALU.

FM96: 23 Stewart St, Suva; tel. 314766; telex 2496; f. 1985; commercial; broadcasts 24 hrs per day; Man. Dir WILLIAM PARKINSON.

Finance

(cap. = capital; res = reserves; dep. = deposits; m. = million; brs = branches; amounts in Fiji dollars)

BANKING

Central Bank

Reserve Bank of Fiji: POB 1220, Suva; tel. 313611; telex 2164; f. 1984 to replace Central Monetary Authority of Fiji; bank of issue; cap. and res 81.7m., dep. 104.9m. (1987); Chair. and Acting Gov. JONE YAVALA KUBUABOLA.

Commercial Bank

National Bank of Fiji: 107 Victoria Parade, POB 1166, Suva; tel. 311999; telex 2135; f. 1974; cap. and res 5.3m., dep. 69m. (1986); Chair. PAUL MANUELI; Chief Man. VISANTI MAKRAVA; 11 brs.

Development Bank

Fiji Development Bank: POB 104, Suva; tel. 25661; telex 2279; f. 1967; finances the development of natural resources, agriculture, transportation and other industries and enterprises; statutory body; cap. and res 41.4m., dep. 86.2m. (1987); Chair. LYLE N. CUPIT; Man. Dir LAISENIA QARASE; 8 brs.

Merchant Bank

Merchant Bank of Fiji Ltd: Suva; tel. 314955; f. 1986; Man. RASIK MASTER.

Foreign Banks

Australia and New Zealand Banking Group Ltd: 4th Floor, Civic House, Town Hall Rd, POB 179, Suva; tel. 314000; telex 2194; Chief Man. (Pacific Islands) L. W. COOKE.

Bank of Baroda (India): POB 57, Suva; telex 2120; Vice-Pres., Fiji brs, K. L. BANSAL.

Bank of New Zealand: PMB, Suva; tel. 302144; telex 2132; Regional Man. E. W. HARTSTONGE; 8 brs.

Westpac Banking Corporation (Australia): Town Hall Rd, POB 238, Suva; tel. 311666; telex 2133; Man. B. H. MUDGE; 11 brs.

INSURANCE

Colonial Mutual Life Assurance Society Ltd: Private Bag, Suva; tel. 314400; telex 2254; f. 1876; Man. T. VUETILOVONI.

Dominion Insurance Ltd: partly owned by Flour Mills of Fiji Ltd.

Panpacific Insurance Co Ltd: POB 119, Suva; tel. 22601; telex 2361; f. 1982; Office Man. SAMSON M. SINGH.

FIJI — *Directory*

Queensland Insurance (Fiji) Ltd: Queensland Insurance Center, Victoria Parade, POB 101, Suva; tel. 315455; telex 2414; Gen. Man. J. Wennerbom.

Trade and Industry

DEVELOPMENT CORPORATIONS

Commonwealth Development Corporation: Office of the Representative for Pacific Islands, Velop House, 371 Victoria Parade, POB 161, Suva; tel. 302577; telex 2412; Rep. C. H. C. Seller.

Fiji Trade and Investment Board: Velop House, Govt Bldgs, POB 2303, Suva; tel. 315988; telex 2355; f. 1980, restyled 1988, to promote and stimulate foreign and local economic development investment; Chair. Prof. Asesela Ravuvu; Dir Surendra Sharma.

Fijian Development Fund Board: POB 122, Suva; tel. 22231; f. 1951; funds derived from payments of $F20 a ton from the sales of copra by indigenous Fijians only; deposits receive interest at 2.5%; funds used only for Fijian development schemes; dep. $F959,500 (1980); Chair. Ratu Sir Kamisese Mara; Sec. N. Morris.

Fiji Development Company Ltd: POB 161, Suva; tel. 25611; telex 2412; f. 1960; subsidiary of the Commonwealth Development Corpn; Man. V. W. Yee.

Land Development Authority: c/o Ministry for Primary Industries, POB 358, Suva; tel. 311233; f. 1961 to co-ordinate development plans for land and marine resources; Chair. Ratu Sir Josaia Tavaiqia.

CHAMBER OF COMMERCE

Suva Chamber of Commerce: 7th Floor, Honson Bldg, Thomson St, POB 337, Suva; f. 1902; Pres. Natwar Vagh; Sec. P. B. Sloan; 94 mems.

MARKETING ORGANIZATIONS

Fiji Pine Commission: POB 521, Lautoka; tel. 61511; telex 5294; f. 1976; development of forest plantations, and marketing of forest products through subsidiary joint venture Forestry Development Service Ltd; Gen. Man. P. J. Drysdale; Sec. S. D. Sharma.

Fiji Sugar Cane Growers' Council: 4th Floor, Dominion House, Thomson St, Suva; tel. 314855; telex 2271; f. 1985; aims to develop the sugar industry and protect the interests of registered growers; CEO Kalu Karan Singh; Chair. S. M. Koya; Sec. Ratu John D. V. Cavalevu.

Fiji Sugar Corporation Ltd: 5th Floor, Dominion House, Thomson St, POB 283, Suva; tel. 313455; telex 2119; nationalized 1974; buyer of sugar cane and raw sugar mfrs; Chair. Lyle N. Cupit; Man. Dir Rasheed A. Ali.

Fiji Sugar Marketing Co Ltd: 5th Floor, Dominion House, Thomson St, POB 1402, Suva; tel. 311588; telex 2271; Man. Dir John May.

National Marketing Authority: POB 5085, Raiwaqa, Suva; tel. 385888; telex 2413; f. 1971; a statutory body set up to develop markets for agricultural and marine produce locally and overseas; exporters of fresh fruit and vegetables, fish, fresh, syruped and crystallized ginger; Chair. G. Blakeney; CEO Solomone Makasiale.

Sugar Commission of Fiji: 4th Floor, Dominion House, Thomson St, Suva; tel. 315488; Chair. Gerald Barrack.

CO-OPERATIVES

In 1986 there were 1,203 registered co-operatives.

EMPLOYERS' ORGANIZATIONS

Fiji Employers' Consultative Association: 7th Floor, Honson Bldg, Thomson St, POB 575, Suva; tel. 25688; represents 127 major employers; Pres. Col P. F. Manueli; Dir Kenneth A. J. Roberts.

Fiji Manufacturers' Association: 7th Floor, Honson Bldg, Thomson St, POB 1308, Suva; f. 1902; Pres. Chandu Raniga; Sec. P. B. Sloan; 108 mems.

TRADE UNIONS

Fiji Trades Union Congress (FTUC): 32 Des Voeux Rd, POB 1418, Suva; tel. 315377; f. 1951; affiliated to ICFTU and ICFTU–APRO; 39 affiliated unions; more than 40,000 mems; Pres. Jale Toki; Nat. Sec. Mahendra Chaudhary. Principal affiliated unions:

Fiji Public Service Association: 298 Waimanu Rd, POB 1405, Suva; tel. 311922; 7,285 mems; Pres. D. P. Singh; Gen. Sec. M. P. Chaudhry.

Fiji Registered Ports Workers' Union: f. 1947; Gen. Sec. Taniela Veitata.

Fiji Sugar and General Workers' Union: POB 330, Lautoka; tel. 60746; 2,500 mems; Pres. Shiu Lingam; Gen. Sec. Wilfred Sugrim.

Fiji Teachers' Union: 211 Edinburgh Drive, POB 3582, Samabula; tel. 381585; f. 1930; 2,700 mems; Pres. Anil Sudhakar; Gen. Sec. Pratap Chand.

Mineworkers' Union of Fiji: Vatukoula; f. 1986.

National Union of Factory and Commercial Workers: POB 989, Suva; 3,800 mems; Pres. Cama Tuilevuka; Gen. Sec. James R. Raman.

Public Employees' Union: POB 781, Suva; tel. 313744; 6,752 mems; Pres. James Samujh; Gen. Sec. Joveci Gavoka.

Transport and Oil Workers' Union: f. 1988; following merger of Oil and Allied Workers' Union and Transport Workers' Union; Gen. Sec. Michael Columbus.

Other important unions include the Building Workers' Union, the Fijian Teachers' Asscn, the National Union of Hotel and Catering Workers, the Fiji Bank Employees' Union, the National Union of Electricity Workers and the Fiji Sugar and Tradesmen's Union. There were 42 registered trade unions in October 1984.

Transport

RAILWAYS

Fiji Sugar Corporation Railway: Rarawai Mill, POB 155, Ba; tel. 74044; telex 6248; 595 km of permanent track and 225 km of temporary track, serving cane-growing areas at Ba, Lautoka and Penang on the island of Viti Levu; also Labasa on the island of Vanua Levu.

In 1985 the Asian Development Bank sponsored a feasibility study of the potential for the creation of a major passenger railway system.

ROADS

At the end of 1982 there were 4,295 km of roads in Fiji, of which 1,250 km were main or national roads and 563 km secondary roads. A 500-km highway circles the main island of Viti Levu. Of the total road network, 13% is paved.

SHIPPING

There are ports of call at Suva, Lautoka and Levuka. The main port, Suva, handles more than 800 ships a year, including large passenger liners. Lautoka handles more than 300 vessels and liners and Levuka mainly handles commercial fishing vessels.

Inter-Ports Shipping Corpn Ltd: 25 Eliza St, Walu Bay; POB 152, Suva; tel. 313638; telex 2703; f. 1984; Man. Dir Leo B. Smith.

Transcargo Express Fiji Ltd: POB 936, Suva; f. 1974; Man. Dir Leo B. Smith.

Williams Taoniu Shipping Co Ltd: POB 1270, Suva; inter-island shipping.

The main foreign companies serving Fiji are: Karlander (Aust.) Pty Ltd, Sofrana-Unilines (Fiji Express Line), Pacific Forum Line, and Pacific Navigation of Tonga operating cargo services between Australia and Fiji; Union Steam Ship Co of New Zealand from New Zealand; Blue Star Line Ltd and Crusader Shipping Co Ltd calling at Fiji between North America and New Zealand, and P & O between the USA and Australia; Nedlloyd operates to Fiji from New Zealand, the UK and Northern Europe; Bank Line Ltd from the UK and the Netherlands; NYK Line and Daiwa Lines from Japan; Marshall Islands Maritime Co from Honolulu and Tonga; Kyowa Shipping Co Ltd from Hong Kong, Taiwan, the Republic of Korea and Japan; and Jebsen Line from various Asian ports.

CIVIL AVIATION

There is an international airport at Nadi (about 210 km from Suva), a domestic airport at Nausori and 13 other airfields.

Air Coral Coast: Korolevu; telex 3241; domestic airline; Man. Dir Gordon Oliver; fleet of 1 Britten Norman Islander, 1 Cessna 206.

Air Pacific Ltd: Air Pacific Centre, 263–269 Grantham Rd, Raiwaqa; tel. 386444; telex 2131; f. 1951; domestic services from Nausori Airport (serving Suva) to Nadi and Labasa, and international services to Tonga, Solomon Islands, Vanuatu, Western Samoa, Japan, Australia and New Zealand; in December 1984 management was taken over by the Australian airline Qantas, initially for three years, with an option for renewal for a further two years; in 1989 Qantas owned 19.5% of shares in the airline;

Chair. GERALD BARRACK; CEO ANDREW DRYSDALE; fleet of 1 Boeing 747, 1 Boeing 737, 2 Bandeirante, 2 ATR 42.

Fiji Air Ltd: 219 Victoria Parade, POB 1259, Suva; tel. 22666; telex 2258; domestic airline operating 46 scheduled services a week to 10 destinations; international service to Tuvalu; charter operations, aerial photography and surveillance also conducted; partly owned by the Fijian govt; CEO M. C. D. TYLER; fleet of 2 DHC6 Twin Otters, 2 Britten Norman Islander, 1 Beech Baron C55, 2 Riley Heron DH114.

Sunflower Airlines Ltd: POB 9452, Nadi Airport, Nadi; tel. (679) 73555; telex 5183; f. 1980; domestic airline; Man. Dir DON IAN COLLINGWOOD; fleet of 4 Britten Norman Islander, 1 Riley Heron, 1 Piper Chieftain, 1 Queenair Excalibur.

Tourism

Scenery, climate and fishing attract visitors to Fiji, where tourism is an important industry. In 1984 there were 235,227 visitors, but a series of cyclones in 1985 reduced visitor arrivals for that year to 228,175. Owing to the considerable political unrest in 1987, the number of visitors declined to 189,866. Arrivals increased again in 1988, and the total was expected to surpass 300,000 per year by 1991.

Fiji Visitors Bureau: POB 92, Suva; tel. 22867; telex 2180; f. 1923; Chair. DAVID L. WILLIAMS; Gen. Man. ISIMELI BAINIMARA.

FINLAND

Introductory Survey

Location, Climate, Language, Religion, Flag, Capital

The Republic of Finland lies in northern Europe, bordered to the far north by Norway and to the north-west by Sweden. The USSR adjoins the whole of the eastern frontier. Finland's western and southern shores are washed by the Baltic Sea. The climate varies sharply, with warm summers and cold winters. The mean annual temperature is 5°C (41°F) in Helsinki and −0.4°C (31°F) in the far north. There are two official languages: 93.5% of the population speak Finnish and 6.3% speak Swedish. Finnish is a member of the small Finno-Ugrian group of languages, which includes Hungarian. There is a small Lapp population in the north. Almost all of the inhabitants profess Christianity, and nearly 90% belong to the Evangelical Lutheran Church. The Orthodox Church has the status of a second national church, while there are small groups of Roman Catholics, Methodists, Jews and other religious sects. The national flag (proportions 18 by 11) displays an azure blue cross (the upright to the left of centre) on a white background. The state flag has, at the centre of the cross, the national coat of arms (a yellow-edged red shield containing a golden lion and nine white roses). The capital is Helsinki.

Recent History

Finland was formerly an autonomous part of the Russian Empire. During the Russian revolution of 1917 the territory proclaimed its independence. Following a brief civil war, a democratic constitution was adopted in 1919. The Soviet regime which came to power in Russia attempted to regain control of Finland but acknowledged the country's independence in 1920.

Demands by the USSR for military bases in Finland and for the cession of part of the Karelian isthmus, in south-eastern Finland, were rejected by the Finnish Government in November 1939. As a result, the USSR attacked Finland, and the two countries fought the 'Winter War', a fiercely contested conflict lasting 15 weeks, before Finnish forces were defeated. Following its surrender, Finland ceded an area of 41,880 sq km (16,170 sq miles) to the USSR in March 1940. In the hope of recovering the lost territory, Finland joined Nazi Germany in attacking the USSR in 1941. However, a separate armistice between Finland and the USSR was concluded in 1944.

In accordance with a peace treaty signed in February 1947, Finland agreed to the transfer of about 12% of its pre-war territory (including the Karelian isthmus and the Petsamo area on the Arctic coast) to the USSR, and to the payment of reparations which totalled about US $570m. when completed in 1952. Meanwhile, in April 1948, Finland and the USSR signed the Finno-Soviet Pact of Friendship, Co-operation and Mutual Assistance (the YYA treaty), which was extended for periods of 20 years in 1955, 1970 and again in 1983. A major requirement of the treaty is that Finland repel any attack made on the USSR by the Federal Republic of Germany, or its allies, through Finnish territory. Finnish policy, however, is one of neutrality in foreign affairs.

Since becoming independent in 1917, the politics of Finland have been characterized by premature elections, a rapid succession of coalition governments (including numerous minority coalitions) and the development of consensus. The Social Democratic Party (SDP) and the Centre Party (KP) have been the dominant participants in government. The conservative opposition gained significant support at a general election in March 1979, following several years of economic crises. A new centre-left coalition government was formed in May, however, by Dr Mauno Koivisto, a Social Democratic economist and former Prime Minister. This four-party Government, comprising the KP, the SDP, the Swedish People's Party (SFP) and the Finnish People's Democratic League (SKDL—an electoral alliance which includes the Communists), continued to pursue deflationary economic policies, although crises arose within the Council of State (Cabinet) in 1981 because of disagreements over social welfare policy and budgetary matters.

Dr Urho Kekkonen, President since 1956, resigned in October 1981. Dr Koivisto was elected President in January 1982. He was succeeded as head of the coalition by a former Prime Minister, Kalevi Sorsa, a Social Democrat, who reshuffled the Council of State in January and again in July. Towards the end of 1982 the SKDL refused to support austerity measures (adopted to counteract the effects on the Finnish economy of a Swedish currency devaluation) or an increase in defence spending. This led to the re-formation of the coalition in December, without the SKDL, until the general election of March 1983.

At this election the SDP won 57 (compared with 52 in the 1979 election) of the 200 seats in the Eduskunta (Parliament), while the conservative opposition National Coalition Party (Kok) lost three seats. In May Sorsa formed another centre-left coalition, comprising the SDP, the SFP, the KP and the Rural Party (SMP): the coalition parties had a total of 122 parliamentary seats. The aims of the new Government, which retained office throughout 1984 and 1985 without any major disruption, were to reduce inflation and unemployment, to curb the rise in gross taxation, to limit state borrowing, and to expand trade with Western countries. In May 1985 the coalition was threatened when the Government announced that it would resign if an anti-nuclear parliamentary motion, introduced by the SMP and the SFP, was not withdrawn. The motion, which demanded the dismantling of Finland's four nuclear reactors, was subsequently withdrawn by both parties. The Government also survived a motion of 'no confidence', proposed by the conservative opposition, for its alleged failure to provide accurate information following the accident in April 1986 at the Chernobyl nuclear power station in the USSR, which resulted in radioactive fall-out over Finland.

In 1985 relations between Finland and the USSR were threatened when the Communist Party of Finland (SKP) expelled several groups of pro-Soviet dissidents. This 'Stalinist' minority formed a separate electoral organization, and eventually registered as a distinct political party, known as the Democratic Alternative (later, the SKP–Y).

At a general election held in March 1987, the combined non-socialist parties gained a majority in the Eduskunta for the first time since the election of 1945. Although the SDP remained the largest single party, losing one seat and retaining 56, the system of modified proportional representation enabled the Kok to gain nine seats, winning a total of 53, while increasing its share of the votes cast by only 1%. The Communist parties suffered a decline in popularity: although the SKDL retained all of its 16 seats, the number of seats held by the Democratic Alternative fell from 10 to four. President Koivisto eventually invited Harri Holkeri, a former chairman of the Kok, to form a coalition government comprising the Kok, the SDP, the SFP and the SMP, thus avoiding a polarization of the political parties within the Eduskunta. The four parties controlled 131 of the 200 seats. Holkeri became the first conservative Prime Minister since 1946, and the Centre Party joined the opposition for the first appreciable length of time since independence. Sorsa resigned as SDP chairman, but retained office as Deputy Prime Minister and Minister for Foreign Affairs.

The arrival of the Kok in government represented a major change in Finnish politics, but did not destroy the long-established consensus. The success of the basic Kok-SDP alliance was tested in two elections in 1988. In February Koivisto retained the Presidency after an election that involved direct popular vote for the first time. He campaigned for a reduction in presidential power. He did not win the required absolute majority, however, and the electoral college was convened. Koivisto was re-elected after an endorsement by Prime Minister Holkeri, who was third in terms of direct votes (behind Paavo Väyrynen, leader of the KP).

Local elections in October 1988, however, confirmed the continuing strength of the ruling coalition, with very little change in the balance of support for the parties. This was despite a dispute between some unions and Holkeri, who was accused of condoning the regime of President Pinochet of Chile by guaranteeing a state-owned company's mining operations

FINLAND

Introductory Survey

in that country. The SDP was affected by internal disputes, with none of the Social Democratic ministers willing to resign in order to allow the party chairman, Pertti Paasio, to join the Council of State. In January 1989, however, Sorsa resigned in an attempt to solve the problem. This threatened the Kok's agreement to the coalition, and SDP support for planned austerity measures. The extreme left also continued to experience internal problems. In 1988 the communists suffered financial losses and scandals within the SKP, and further fragmentation following a split in the SKP—Y.

In foreign affairs, Finland is neutral, but President Koivisto continued the Passiviki-Kekkonen policy (named after the two post-war Presidents) of pursuing friendly relations with the USSR. Other relations have been developed, particularly since Mikhail Gorbachev came to power in the USSR in 1985, and with the approach of the EEC's proposed single market in 1992. Finland joined the United Nations and the Nordic Council (see p. 176) in 1955 but decided to become a full member of EFTA (see p. 152) only in 1985, and to apply for full membership of the Council of Europe (see p. 128) in 1988. However, Koivisto excluded the possibility of Finnish membership of the European Communities (a trade agreement between Finland and the EEC has been in effect since 1974). Also in 1988, the USSR agreed to proposals for reforms in trading arrangements, and to halve sulphur emissions from the Kola Peninsula by 1993 (the pollution was seriously affecting Finland's forests and waterways).

Government

Finland has a republican constitution which combines a parliamentary system with a strong presidency. The unicameral Parliament (Eduskunta) has 200 members, elected by universal adult suffrage for four years (subject to dissolution by the President) on the basis of proportional representation. The President, entrusted with supreme executive power, is elected for six years by direct popular vote. If no candidate wins an absolute majority, a 301-member electoral college is convened. Legislative power is exercised by Parliament in conjunction with the President. For general administration, the President appoints a Council of State (Cabinet), which is headed by a Prime Minister and is responsible to Parliament. Finland has 12 provinces, each administered by an appointed Governor. The province of Ahvenanmaa (the Åland Islands) has, in addition, a local parliament (landsting), elected by the predominantly Swedish-speaking residents of the islands, which has independent rights of legislation in internal affairs.

Defence

The armed forces of Finland are restricted by treaty to 41,900, and in June 1988 numbered 35,200 (of whom 25,000 were conscripts serving up to 11 months), comprising an army of 30,000 (22,300 conscripts), an air force of 2,500 and a navy of 2,700 (1,300 conscripts each). There were also 926 serving abroad with UN forces, some 700,000 reserves and 4,400 frontier guards. The estimated defence budget for 1988 was 6,063m. markkaa.

Economic Affairs

Apart from extensive forests and large reserves of copper ore, Finland has few natural resources. The country also has a harsh climate (no port is ice-free throughout the year) and a rugged terrain. Nevertheless, the people of Finland enjoy a high standard of living and the benefits of a modern welfare state. In 1987, according to estimates by the World Bank, Finland's gross national product (GNP), measured at average 1985–87 prices, was US $71,084m., equivalent to US $14,370 per head. It was estimated that GNP per head increased at an average rate of 2.2% per year, in real terms, between 1980 and 1987, with growth reaching 2.8% in 1987.

Forests cover 70% of Finland's land area, and forestry products (mainly wood, pulp and paper) provided more than 38% of export earnings in 1987. Finland's share of the world market in forestry products fell from 25% in the 1960s to just under 10% in 1986. However, the country's share of the market in some sectors, particularly in Europe, is very much higher. Finland has the largest share, 25%, of world trade in printing and writing papers. Investment in higher-quality grades increased, following contraction of the industry in the early 1980s and major restructuring in the mid-1980s. Owing to high production costs and the approach of the EEC single market, Finnish companies have acquired production units within the EEC.

The total arable area in Finland covers only 2.4m. ha, and agricultural production is limited by the shortness of the growing season. In 1985 agriculture (excluding forestry and fishing) contributed 4.4% of the gross domestic product (GDP), compared with more than 10% in 1960. During the same period the number of farms declined, from some 285,000 to 186,000. Animal husbandry is the predominant form of farming, accounting for 70% of total production. Cereal and dairy farming are highly mechanized, and the output of several commodities exceeds domestic consumption. A system of quotas, levies and subsidies is designed to curb over-production, but there are also state subsidies to encourage exports. Severe weather conditions during 1987 led to widespread crop failure. Cereals, sugar beet and potatoes were particularly affected, and total losses were estimated at 2,700m. markkaa. With the exception of the potato harvest, yields in 1988 remained below average.

The metal and engineering sector (particularly shipbuilding and the manufacture of machinery for the paper industry) accounted for 37% of total exports in 1987. Shipbuilding suffered a severe decline in export orders, particularly from the USSR, in 1985 and in the following years. Restructuring was extensive, but investment was high, with a 19% increase in the sector in 1986 alone. The reform of trading practices with the USSR in 1988 led to hopes of renewed orders from a Soviet market that received two-thirds of Finnish production in the early 1980s. In January 1989 the Government announced the introduction of a subsidy of about 15% on ships built for export. Exports of electrical goods and electronic equipment expanded by more than 16% during 1987. During the first eight months of 1987 Finland's total industrial production increased by 4.6%. The capacity for expansion in Finland's industry is limited by a lack of skilled labour and by the need to import energy and some raw materials. There is a small mining sector in Finland, with gold being the most important product.

Apart from hydroelectric power and peat, there are no indigenous forms of energy, and all of Finland's gas, coal and petroleum requirements must be imported. Energy accounted for around 24% of total imports in 1985, but the fall in the price of petroleum helped to reduce the proportion to 13.5% in 1987. Two-thirds of Finland energy requirements are dependent on imports. Finland annually imports about 4,000m. kWh of electricity and 85% of its crude petroleum from the USSR. A natural gas pipeline links Finland (since 1986 as far as Helsinki) with the USSR. Imports of gas from the USSR totalled 1,200m. cu m in 1986. In 1985 41% of electricity was generated by nuclear power, and four nuclear power stations were in operation. Following the accident at the USSR's nuclear power station at Chernobyl in 1986, the Government responded to public opinion by abandoning plans to construct Finland's fifth nuclear plant. Imports of coal, which were to be used for electricity generation, increased from 0.5m. metric tons in 1985 to 1.4m. tons in 1986. By 1987 the Government had committed itself to the use of fossil fuels in a planned expansion of the country's electric generating capacity by 1,000 MW.

Finland's economy has become increasingly dependent on foreign trade, with export earnings constituting some 26.5% of GDP in 1986. A trade agreement between Finland and the EEC countries came into effect in 1974, leading to the abolition of tariffs on most goods by 1977. The abolition of all trade restrictions on industrial goods between the EEC and EFTA, with effect from 1 January 1984, increased Finland's trade with western Europe, exports rising by 27% in that year. In 1987 EEC member-states together provided 44% of Finnish imports and took 42% of exports; EFTA countries accounted for nearly 19% of imports and 23% of exports.

Finland has also participated in a trade agreement with the CMEA (see p. 124) since 1973, and in 1987 CMEA countries in Europe accounted for a share of about 17% of both exports and imports (from about 28% in 1983). The USSR accounted for over 90% of Finland's CMEA trade, and its bilateral trade agreement with Finland has sheltered the latter from the most severe effects of world recessions ever since the 1948 YYA treaty. A revival in world trade in the mid-1980s led to a significant expansion in exports, particularly to Western countries. In 1984 exports to the USSR fell by 16%, but during 1985 exports to CMEA countries increased in value by 16%. A sharp fall in the price of petroleum in December 1985 caused a disruption in trade with the USSR during 1986. The steadily increasing surplus on Finland's trade with the USSR subse-

increasing surplus on Finland's trade with the USSR subsequently led to several attempts to balance it. In 1986 300m. roubles were transferred to an interest-bearing account. The account was to be repaid by the end of 1991. Finally, in 1988, the barter principle was compromised, and it was agreed to finance any trade surplus over 100m. roubles by interest payments, and eventually convertible currency, after 1990. By mid-1988 the surplus had grown to 5,000m. markkaa. With petroleum products constituting 80% of the USSR's exports to Finland, the fall in petroleum prices had caused the value of those exports to decline from 38,000m. markkaa in 1983 to 26,000m. markkaa in 1987.

From 1986 trade with western Europe increased steadily. During 1988 the Federal Republic of Germany replaced the USSR (for the first time since 1948) as the largest market for Finnish exports. Trade with the USSR remains vital to the economy, however, and closely affects growth in GDP. Between 1982 and 1985 the average annual growth rate was 3%. In 1986 it was only 1.8%. GDP increased by about 4% per year in both 1987 and 1988, but the growth rate was expected to slow in 1989.

Despite government efforts since the late 1970s, the average rate of unemployment in 1984 still stood at 6.2% of the labour force. In 1985 a works and employment programme costing an estimated 7,100m. markkaa was approved, with employment projects being focused particularly on areas of high unemployment, such as northern Finland. Total employment rose by 1% but labour supply also increased and the unemployment rate rose slightly, to 6.3%. The average rate of unemployment in 1986 was 7.0%, but at the end of October 1987 the rate stood at 5.3%, and by October 1988 had fallen further, to 4.8%. The budget for 1989 envisaged a rise in government spending of 2%, in real terms, with total expenditure (including debt repayments) projected to reach 124,175m. markkaa.

High wage settlements in 1986 and 1987 (a strike in 1986 had secured a reduction in the average working week from 40 to 37½ hours by 1990) contributed to an increase in imports and in the rate of inflation, with increased domestic spending. Inflation fell from 11.8% in 1981 to 5.9% in 1985, and to 3.4% in 1986. In 1987, however, it rose to 3.7% and was expected to reach 5.5% in 1988. Devaluations of the markka (the most recent by about 2% in 1986) and national wage agreements have been used extensively to counter inflation. In September 1988 a 'stabilization' plan was negotiated, aimed at limiting real rises in pay to 2.5% in 1989. The Government promised reductions in levels of income tax (major reforms of taxation were also planned), while the Bank of Finland made an unprecedented offer of a reduction in base interest rates, dependent upon the agreement of the unions, which was by no means certain.

By 1988 Finland's international debt was about 53,000m. markkaa, or 15.5% of annual GDP, and the State's share was 49%. Government policy of borrowing to sustain economic growth had increased its share from only 15% in 1977, although foreign debt was equivalent to some 20% of GDP. Finland's reserves of foreign exchange totalled 22,650m. markkaa in December 1985, but they fell during 1986, to below 8,000m. markkaa during August, owing to a devaluation of the markka. Reserves of foreign exchange increased from US $1,417m. at the end of 1986 to $6,797m. at mid-1988.

Social Welfare

Social policy covers social security (national pensions, disability insurance, sickness insurance), social assistance (maternity, child, housing, education and other allowances and accident compensation) and social welfare (care of children, the aged, disabled and maladjusted, including residential services). Sickness insurance covers a considerable part of the costs of medical care outside hospital, while the general hospitals charge moderate fees. The National Health Act of 1972 provided for the establishment of health centres in every municipality, and the abolition of doctors' fees. In 1985 Finland had 61,082 hospital beds. In the same year there were 10,193 physicians working in the country. Of total expenditure by the central Government in 1985, 10,707m. markkaa (10.6%) was for health, and a further 34,218m. markkaa (33.9%) for social security and welfare.

Education

Compulsory education, introduced in 1921, lasts for nine years between seven and 16 years of age. By the 1977/78 school year, the whole country had transferred to a new comprehensive education system. Tuition is free and instruction is the same for all students. The compulsory course comprises six years at primary school, beginning at the age of seven, followed by three years at secondary school, beginning at the age of 13. After completing compulsory education, the pupil may transfer to an upper secondary school or other vocational school or institute for a further three years. In 1985 the total enrolment at all primary and secondary schools was equivalent to 103% of the school-age population. After three years in upper secondary school, a student takes a matriculation examination. Students who pass this examination are entitled to seek admission at one of the 22 universities and colleges of further education. Expenditure on education by the central Government in 1985 was 13,795m. markkaa (13.7% of total spending).

Public Holidays

1989: 2 January (for New Year's Day), 7 January (for Epiphany), 24 March (Good Friday), 27 March (Easter Monday), 29 April (for Ascension Day), 1 May (May Day, Labour Day), 13–14 May (Whitsun), 24 June (Midsummer Day, Flag Day), 4 November (for All Saints' Day), 6 December (Independence Day), 25–26 December (Christmas).

1990: 1 January (New Year's Day), 6 January (Epiphany), 13 April (Good Friday), 16 April (Easter Monday), 1 May (May Day, Labour Day), 19 May (for Ascension Day), 2–3 June (Whitsun), 24 June (Midsummer Day, Flag Day), 3 November (for All Saints' Day), 6 December (Independence Day), 25–26 December (Christmas).

Weights and Measures

The metric system is in force.

Statistical Survey

Sources (unless otherwise specified): Central Statistical Office of Finland, POB 504, 00101 Helsinki; *Maataloustilastollinen Kuukausikatsaus* (Monthly Review of Agricultural Statistics), Board of Agriculture Statistical Office, Mariankatu 23, 00170 Helsinki; and *Bank of Finland Monthly Bulletin*.

Note: Figures in this Survey include data for the autonomous Åland Islands, treated separately on pp 1005–1006.

Area and Population

AREA, POPULATION AND DENSITY

Area (sq km)	
Land	304,623
Inland water	33,522
Total	338,145*
Population (census results)	
1 November 1980	
Males	2,313,165
Females	2,471,545
Total	4,784,710
17 November 1985	4,910,619
Population (official estimates at 31 December)	
1985	4,910,664
1986	4,925,644
1987	4,938,602
Density (per sq km) at 31 December 1987	14.6

* 130,559 sq miles.

PROVINCES (estimated population at 31 December 1987)

	Land Area (sq km)*	Population
Uudenmaan (Nylands)	9,898	1,214,775
Turun-Porin (Åbo-Björneborgs)	22,169	714,196
Ahvenanmaan (Åland)	1,527	23,761
Hämeen (Tavastehus)	17,010	681,550
Kymen (Kymmene)	10,783	337,254
Mikkelin (St Michels)	16,343	207,927
Kuopion (Kuopio)	16,511	255,705
Pohjois-Karjalan (Norra Karelens)	17,782	176,699
Vaasan (Vasa)	26,447	444,405
Keski-Suomen (Mellersta Finlands)	16,230	248,441
Oulun (Uleåborgs)	56,866	433,715
Lapin (Lapplands)	93,057	200,174
Total	**304,623**	**4,938,602**

* Excluding inland waters, totalling 33,522 sq km.

PRINCIPAL TOWNS
(estimated population at 31 December 1987)

Helsinki (Helsingfors) (capital)	490,034
Tampere (Tammerfors)	170,533
Espoo (Esbo)	164,569
Turku (Åbo)	160,456
Vantaa (Vanda)	149,063
Oulu (Uleåborg)	98,582
Lahti	93,671
Kuopio	78,619
Pori (Björneborg)	77,395
Jyväskylä	65,719
Kotka	57,745
Vaasa (Vasa)	53,780
Lappeenranta (Villmanstrand)	53,737
Joensuu	47,099
Hämeenlinna (Tavastehus)	42,486

BIRTHS, MARRIAGES AND DEATHS

	Registered live births*		Registered marriages†		Registered deaths*	
	Number	Rate (per 1,000)	Number	Rate (per 1,000)	Number	Rate (per 1,000)
1980	63,064	13.2	29,388	6.1	44,398	9.3
1981	63,469	13.2	30,100	6.3	44,404	9.3
1982	66,106	13.7	30,459	6.3	43,408	9.0
1983	66,892	13.8	29,474	6.1	45,388	9.3
1984	65,076	13.3	28,550	5.8	45,098	9.2
1985	62,796	12.8	25,794	5.3	48,198	9.8
1986	60,799	12.4	25,866	5.3	47,117	9.6
1987	59,241	12.0	26,391	5.4	47,968	9.7

* Including Finnish nationals temporarily outside the country.
† Data relate only to marriages in which the bride was domiciled in Finland.

ECONOMICALLY ACTIVE POPULATION*
('000 persons aged 15 to 74 years)

	1985	1986	1987
Agriculture, forestry and fishing	279	266	251
Mining and quarrying	9	9	7
Manufacturing	557	550	534
Electricity, gas and water	31	30	28
Construction	178	185	184
Trade, restaurants and hotels	355	355	348
Transport, storage and communications	186	183	182
Finance, insurance, real estate and business services	156	160	177
Community, social and personal services	681	690	710
Activities not adequately described	5	3	3
Total employed	**2,437**	**2,431**	**2,423**
Unemployed	129	138	130
Total labour force	**2,566**	**2,569**	**2,554**

* Excluding persons on compulsory military service (30,000 in 1985; 27,000 in 1986; 29,000 in 1987).

Agriculture

PRINCIPAL CROPS
('000 metric tons; farms with arable land of 1 hectare or more)

	1985	1986	1987
Wheat	472.1	529.1	281.1
Barley	1,853.8	1,713.8	1,089.2
Rye	71.8	70.6	74.2
Oats	1,217.8	1,174.5	723.2
Mixed grain	26.5	32.0	14.8
Potatoes	707.7	773.2	490.5
Rapeseed	89.3	123.9	89.7
Sugar beet	739.4	792.2	466.2

FINLAND

LIVESTOCK ('000 head at 1 June; farms with arable land of 1 hectare or more)

	1986	1987	1988
Horses	18.5	19.9	15.1
Cattle	1,567.3	1,497.9	1,443.4
Sheep	116.1	126.2	119.0
Reindeer	366.0	366.0	364.0
Pigs*	1,322.7	1,341.9	1,305.1
Chickens }	7,037.5	6,790.7	6,678.2
Other poultry			
Beehives†	40.0	42.0	47.0

* Including piggeries of dairies.   † '000 hives.

LIVESTOCK PRODUCTS ('000 metric tons)

	1985	1986	1987
Beef	124.6	123.6	122.0
Veal	0.6	0.5	0.7
Pig meat	171.4	172.9	174.8
Poultry meat	20.5	22.0	26.6
Cows' milk*	2,808.0	2,803.1	2,692.0
Butter	72.5	65.6	60.7
Cheese	79.1	83.4	85.2
Hen eggs	85.4	81.4	78.0
Cattle hides	15.9	15.4	15.2

* Million litres.

Forestry

ROUNDWOOD REMOVALS ('000 cu m, excl. bark)

	1984	1985	1986
Sawlogs, veneer logs and logs for sleepers	17,606	16,878	17,021
Pulpwood	18,364	19,284	19,869
Other industrial wood	1,414	1,517	1,213
Fuel wood	3,160	3,071	3,186
Total	40,544	40,750	41,289

Source: FAO, *Yearbook of Forest Products*.

SAWNWOOD PRODUCTION ('000 cu m, incl. boxboards)

	1984	1985	1986
Coniferous (softwood)	8,146	7,240	7,035
Broadleaved (hardwood)	86	60	75
Total	8,232	7,300	7,110

Railway sleepers ('000 cu m): 33 per year (1984–86).
Source: FAO, *Yearbook of Forest Products*.

Fishing

('000 metric tons, live weight)*

	1983	1984	1985
Freshwater fishes	28.6	26.9	26.7
Diadromous fishes	20.0	22.4	22.4
Atlantic herring	95.9	97.3	99.0
Other marine fishes	12.7	11.9	10.5
Total catch	157.1	158.5	158.6
Inland waters	33.7	33.1	32.4
Atlantic Ocean	123.4	125.4	126.2

1986: Catch as in 1985 (FAO estimates).

* Figures include recreational fishing, estimated to account for 5% of the total catch.

Source: FAO, *Yearbook of Fishery Statistics*.

Mining

('000 metric tons, unless otherwise indicated)

	1985	1986	1987
Copper ore*	26.6	24.1	17.8
Lead ore*	2.4	2.0	2.4
Zinc ore*	60.6	60.3	55.0
Silver (metric tons)	31.0	37.1	44.2
Gold (kilograms)	595	1,172	1,776

* Metal content.

Industry

SELECTED PRODUCTS
('000 metric tons, unless otherwise indicated)

	1985	1986*	1987*
Cellulose	4,578	4,686	5,000
Machine pulp (for sale)	2,410	2,381	n.a.
Newsprint	1,613	1,315	1,309
Other paper, boards and cardboards	5,061	6,176	6,910
Plywoods and veneers ('000 cubic metres)	591	568	586
Cement	1,695	1,261	1,426
Pig iron and ferro-alloys	1,901	1,979	2,064
Electricity (million kWh)	48,629	46,659	51,912
Cotton yarn (metric tons)	6,570	3,345	4,315
Cotton fabrics (metric tons)	13,043	8,086	7,677
Sugar (metric tons)	219,710	176,591	172,864
Rolled steel products (metric tons)	2,063	1,996	2,024
Copper cathodes (metric tons)	58,766	64,232	59,538
Cigarettes (million)	8,185	8,156	9,030

* Provisional figures.

FINLAND

Finance

CURRENCY AND EXCHANGE RATES

Monetary Units
100 penniä (singular: penni) = 1 markka (Finnmark).

Denominations
Coins: 5, 10, 20 and 50 penniä; 1, 5 and 10 markkaa.
Notes: 5, 10, 50, 100, 500 and 1,000 markkaa.

Sterling and Dollar Equivalents (30 September 1988)
£1 sterling = 7.471 markkaa;
US $1 = 4.431 markkaa;
100 markkaa = £13.38 = $22.57.

Average Exchange Rate (markkaa per US $)
1985 6.1979
1986 5.0695
1987 4.3956

BUDGET (million markkaa)

Revenue	1985	1986	1987
Direct taxes	25,750	28,079	29,454
Indirect taxes	47,454	52,051	57,538
Social security	671	4	—
Other	22,533	26,641	21,658
Total	96,408	106,775	108,650

Expenditure	1985	1986	1987
Education	15,173	16,439	18,363
Social security	16,570	17,460	20,191
Health	8,149	8,515	9,420
Agriculture and forestry	8,530	9,110	9,501
Transport and communications	7,947	8,860	9,578
Defence	5,214	5,528	5,772
Public debt	11,955	14,769	4,987
Other	22,265	26,093	29,176
Total	95,803	106,774	106,988

Budget Estimates (million markkaa): 1988: Revenue 113,838, Expenditure 113,815; 1989: Revenue 124,177, Expenditure 124,175.

INTERNATIONAL RESERVES (US $ million at 31 December)

	1985	1986	1987
Gold*	384.2	434.1	539.3
IMF special drawing rights	171.8	204.6	227.7
Reserve position in IMF	143.1	165.2	200.8
Foreign exchange	3,435.0	1,417.4	5,989.0
Total	4,134.1	2,221.3	6,956.8

* Valued at market-related prices.
Source: IMF, *International Financial Statistics*.

MONEY SUPPLY (million markkaa at 31 December)

	1985	1986	1987
Currency outside banks	6,143	6,357	7,259
Demand deposits at deposit money banks	21,483	21,425	23,047
Total money*	27,694	27,838	30,342

* Including private-sector deposits at the Bank of Finland.
Source: IMF, *International Financial Statistics*.

COST OF LIVING (Consumer Price Index. Base: 1981 = 100)

	1985	1986	1987
Food	139	144	147
Beverages and tobacco	140	146	155
Clothing and footwear	126	132	135
Rent, heating and lighting	131	135	135
Furniture, household equipment	130	135	140
All items	135	139	145

NATIONAL ACCOUNTS (million markkaa at current prices)
National Income and Product

	1985	1986	1987*
Compensation of employees	184,061	197,329	215,379
Operating surplus	66,106	68,627	74,399
Domestic factor incomes	250,167	265,956	289,778
Consumption of fixed capital	49,198	53,169	57,924
Gross domestic product at factor cost	299,365	319,125	347,702
Indirect taxes	47,806	52,502	57,607
Less Subsidies	10,347	11,308	11,701
GDP in purchasers' values	336,824	360,319	393,608
Factor income received from abroad	6,221	4,976	5,573
Less Factor income paid abroad	12,930	12,560	13,545
Gross national product	330,115	352,735	385,636
Less Consumption of fixed capital	49,198	53,169	57,924
National income in market prices	280,917	299,566	327,712

Expenditure on the Gross Domestic Product

	1985	1986	1987*
Government final consumption expenditure	68,218	74,001	81,158
Private final consumption expenditure	181,664	195,174	213,568
Increase in stocks	−440	−2,211	563
Gross fixed capital formation	80,052	83,512	92,078
Statistical discrepancy	4,050	4,107	4,718
Total domestic expenditure	333,544	354,583	392,085
Exports of goods and services	98,173	95,634	99,208
Less Imports of goods and services	94,893	89,898	97,685
GDP in purchasers' values	336,824	360,319	393,608

FINLAND

Gross Domestic Product by Economic Activity

	1985	1986	1987*
Agriculture, hunting, forestry and fishing	24,136	23,754	22,538
Mining and quarrying	1,193	1,128	1,029
Manufacturing	74,588	76,644	83,897
Electricity, gas and water	8,768	9,344	10,197
Construction	22,880	24,714	27,233
Trade, restaurants and hotels	35,179	36,944	40,493
Transport, storage and communication	24,279	26,314	29,138
Finance, insurance and business services	30,643	35,579	41,676
Owner-occupied dwellings	19,267	21,049	21,368
Public administration and defence	14,106	15,047	16,553
Other community, social and personal services	51,609	56,859	63,045
Sub-total	306,648	327,376	357,167
Less Imputed bank service charge	7,976	8,721	10,230
GDP in basic values	298,672	318,655	346,937
Commodity taxes	45,358	49,609	54,537
Less Commodity subsidies	7,206	7,945	7,866
GDP in purchasers' values	336,824	360,319	393,608

* Provisional figures.

BALANCE OF PAYMENTS (US $ million)

	1985	1986	1987
Merchandise exports f.o.b.	13,351	16,005	19,026
Merchandise imports f.o.b.	−12,473	−14,363	−17,703
Trade balance	878	1,642	1,323
Exports of services	3,427	3,725	4,717
Imports of services	−4,894	−5,706	−7,524
Balance on goods and services	−589	−339	−1,484
Private unrequited transfers (net)	−7	−157	−162
Government unrequited transfers (net)	−169	−236	−304
Current balance	−766	−731	−1,949
Direct capital investment (net)	−280	−430	−813
Other long-term capital (net)	1,301	1,164	1,150
Short-term capital (net)	526	−2,700	6,219
Net errors and omissions	−194	418	−585
Total (net monetary movements)	586	−2,280	4,022
Valuation changes (net)	475	320	609
Official financing (net)	−3	−3	11
Changes in reserves	1,058	−1,963	4,642

Source: IMF, *International Financial Statistics*.

External Trade

PRINCIPAL COMMODITIES
(distribution by SITC, million markkaa)

Imports c.i.f.	1985	1986	1987
Food and live animals	4,026.8	4,375.3	4,435.4
Coffee, tea, cocoa and spices	1,389.2	1,663.9	1,274.9
Crude materials (inedible) except fuels	5,018.6	4,308.7	4,798.5
Mineral fuels, lubricants, etc.	19,887.1	11,887.7	11,676.8
Coal, coke and briquettes	2,119.4	1,843.9	1,341.1
Petroleum, petroleum products, etc.	16,457.3	8,761.8	9,061.9
Crude petroleum oils, etc.	12,301.7	6,168.3	6,368.6
Refined petroleum products	3,978.2	2,498.2	2,592.1
Gas oils (distillate fuels)	1,676.0	1,199.9	1,141.6

Imports c.i.f.—*continued*	1985	1986	1987
Chemicals and related products	7,919.1	7,928.3	9,009.2
Chemical elements and compounds	2,420.6	2,071.0	2,419.7
Plastic materials, etc.	2,368.2	2,496.7	2,873.0
Basic manufactures	12,326.8	12,516.6	14,161.1
Textile yarn, fabrics, etc.	3,048.0	3,171.0	3,283.2
Woven textile fabrics (excl. narrow or special fabrics)	1,370.0	1,468.1	2,203.9
Iron and steel	2,852.4	2,656.5	3,040.4
Non-ferrous metals	1,319.6	1,185.8	1,361.5
Other metal manufactures	1,847.1	1,996.3	2,327.5
Machinery and transport equipment	24,246.1	27,568.5	31,746.7
Non-electric machinery	11,945.4	12,995.6	14,893.5
Electrical machinery, apparatus, etc.	5,722.0	6,293.7	7,271.0
Transport equipment	6,578.8	8,279.3	9,582.2
Road vehicles and parts*	5,493.7	6,807.9	8,250.8
Passenger motor cars (excl. buses)	2,587.5	3,257.1	4,026.1
Miscellaneous manufactured articles	7,122.7	8,090.9	9,751.5
Scientific instruments, watches, etc.	2,130.9	2,335.2	2,609.0
Total (incl. others)	81,520.2	77,601.5	86,696.4

* Excluding tyres, engines and electrical parts.

Exports f.o.b.	1985	1986	1987
Food and live animals	2,489.9	1,927.1	1,711.4
Crude materials (inedible) except fuels	10,331.3	9,692.2	11,155.6
Wood, lumber and cork	4,531.8	4,260.8	4,686.6
Shaped or simply worked wood	3,999.8	3,698.6	4,130.2
Shaped coniferous lumber	3,979.1	3,678.9	4,110.1
Sawn coniferous lumber	3,685.7	3,333.0	3,737.0
Pulp and waste paper	3,427.5	3,223.8	3,993.6
Chemical wood pulp	3,342.9	3,093.4	3,836.9
Mineral fuels, lubricants, etc.	3,599.8	1,999.2	1,940.3
Petroleum, petroleum products, etc.	3,451.8	1,929.3	1,880.0
Refined petroleum products	3,344.5	1,576.4	1,831.7
Chemicals and related products	4,887.3	4,500.5	4,738.2
Basic manufactures	33,031.6	32,832.6	35,807.8
Wood and cork manufactures (excl. furniture)	1,865.2	2,406.8	2,571.3
Veneers, plywood boards, etc.	1,513.2	1,642.4	1,851.4
Paper, paperboard and manufactures	21,067.3	20,766.8	22,533.6
Paper and paperboard	19,155.4	18,786.2	20,699.7
Newsprint paper	3,683.2	3,300.1	3,270.3
Other printing and writing paper in bulk	8,978.6	8,819.1	10,111.7
Kraft paper and paperboard	1,694.2	1,632.4	1,766.9
Articles of paper pulp, paper or paperboard	1,911.9	1,980.6	1,833.9
Iron and steel	3,908.2	3,839.2	4,191.3
Non-ferrous metals	2,492.7	2,005.1	2,139.3
Other metal manufactures	1,586.9	1,580.9	1,885.0

FINLAND

Exports f.o.b.—continued	1985	1986	1987
Machinery and transport equipment	21,127.7	22,792.2	23,520.2
Non-electric machinery	9,717.9	9,871.6	11,474.2
Electrical machinery, apparatus, etc.	3,765.8	4,840.8	5,394.0
Transport equipment	7,643.8	8,079.8	6,651.5
Ships and boats	5,506.4	4,736.7	2,446.4
Miscellaneous manufactured articles	8,119.4	8,470.7	8,241.6
Clothing (excl. footwear)	3,233.4	3,331.4	2,956.2
Clothing not of fur	2,927.0	3,073.1	2,714.1
Non-knitted textile clothing (excl. accessories and headgear)	2,202.4	2,297.3	1,985.4
Total (incl. others)	84,027.9	82,579.3	87,564.1

PRINCIPAL TRADING PARTNERS (million markkaa)*

Imports c.i.f.	1985	1986	1987
Austria	961.4	1,015.2	1,116.5
Belgium/Luxembourg	1,632.4	1,898.6	2,234.5
Denmark	2,036.2	2,180.9	2,453.5
France	2,763.9	3,458.8	3,719.5
Germany, Federal Republic	12,180.0	13,159.3	15,130.4
Iran	984.6	192.1	17.5
Italy	2,754.0	3,256.0	3,789.5
Japan	4,308.9	5,021.8	6,136.8
Netherlands	2,400.4	2,369.0	2,675.8
Norway	1,955.2	1,713.5	1,904.8
Poland	1,211.4	954.9	847.5
Saudi Arabia	1,332.7	731.0	703.7
Sweden	9,620.5	10,558.5	11,205.4
Switzerland	1,364.1	1,579.1	1,743.1
USSR	17,152.6	11,933.0	12,461.9
United Kingdom	5,848.0	5,055.6	6,192.4
USA	4,401.0	3,721.7	4,539.4
Total (incl. others)	81,520.2	77,601.5	86,696.4

Exports f.o.b.	1985	1986	1987
Belgium/Luxembourg	1,267.2	1,409.6	1,566.4
Denmark	3,402.6	3,321.4	3,407.7
France	3,298.3	3,690.7	4,615.3
Germany, Federal Republic	7,779.0	8,016.0	9,580.9
Iraq	264.8	197.5	30.4
Italy	1,687.6	1,741.2	2,239.7
Netherlands	2,779.1	2,854.6	3,141.0
Norway	3,518.8	3,714.9	4,132.0
Sweden	11,084.6	12,228.3	13,090.4
Switzerland	1,210.6	1,331.4	1,564.7
USSR	18,099.4	16,773.8	13,522.5
United Kingdom	9,076.0	8,667.1	9,990.1
USA	5,308.2	4,479.6	4,523.4
Total (incl. others)	84,027.9	82,579.3	87,564.1

* Imports by country of production; exports by country of consumption.

Transport

RAILWAYS (traffic)

	1985	1986	1987
Passenger-km (million)	3,224	2,676	3,106
Freight ton-km (million)	8,066	6,952	7,402

ROAD TRAFFIC (registered motor vehicles at 31 December)

	1985	1986	1987
Passenger cars	1,546,094	1,619,848	1,698,671
Lorries and vans	179,637	187,465	198,175
Buses	9,017	9,166	9,233
Special purpose vehicles	11,867	12,470	13,640

SHIPPING
Merchant Fleet (1987)

	Ships	Displacement ('000 gross reg. tons)
Passenger vessels	170	253
Tankers	28	242
Others	217	346
Total	415	841

International Sea-borne Freight Traffic

	1985	1986	1987
Vessels ('000 net reg. tons):			
Entered	55,740	65,098	68,203
Cleared	55,713	65,509	68,807
Goods ('000 metric tons):			
Loaded	20,307	20,246	22,437
Unloaded	31,648	29,946	31,285

CANAL TRAFFIC

	1985	1986	1987
Vessels in transit	58,835	65,781	64,194
Timber rafts in transit	10,581	8,564	7,287
Goods carried ('000 tons)	8,620	7,152	6,106
Passengers carried ('000)	201	244	267

CIVIL AVIATION (scheduled services, '000)

	1985	1986	1987
Kilometres flown	38,418	38,119	43,362
Passenger-kilometres	2,940,269	2,935,896	3,588,000
Cargo ton-kilometres	84,305	92,923	97,938

Tourism

NUMBER OF NIGHTS AT ACCOMMODATION FACILITIES
(excl. camping sites)

Country of Domicile	1985	1986	1987
Denmark	55,555	53,875	62,202
France	67,854	54,377	61,888
Germany, Federal Republic	273,417	250,083	280,953
Netherlands	47,021	40,577	41,743
Norway	157,566	147,183	142,211
Sweden	535,169	532,664	523,418
Switzerland	69,692	68,286	70,306
USSR	248,192	252,386	262,115
United Kingdom	108,258	103,347	116,553
USA	184,798	159,467	199,655
Total (incl. others)	2,097,101	2,021,663	2,207,484

FINLAND

Communications Media

	1985	1986	1987
Telephones in use	2,189,677	2,271,535	2,365,486
Television receivers*	1,784,000	1,822,000	1,843,000
Book production: titles†	8,930	8,694	9,106
Newspapers and periodicals	4,693	4,965	5,228‡

* Number of licensed sets.
† Including pamphlets (1,886 in 1986; 2,098 in 1987).
‡ Comprising 68 daily newspapers, 311 non-daily newspapers and 4,849 other periodicals.

Education

(1986/87)

	Institutions	Staff*	Students
First level	5,334	46,000	388,465
Secondary, general			289,998
Secondary vocational			113,117
Universities and other education at the third level	574	22,869	133,933

* Excluding part-time teachers paid by the hour.

Directory

The Constitution

The Constitution (summarized below) was adopted on 17 July 1919. The first report of the Constitutional Committee on possible reforms of the fundamental laws was presented in April 1974. The multi-party system and the constitutional checks on revision of the fundamental laws are likely to delay any major changes until later in the 1980s, but several issues have emerged as potential areas for reform. Generally, the right-wing parties are suspicious of reform, but the left has won some support from the centre.

Three main topics have been discussed by the Committee: the respective powers of the President, the Council of State (Cabinet) and Parliament (Eduskunta); legislative procedure, particularly the strength of the protection to be given to parliamentary minorities; the basic economic, social and cultural rights of the individual and security of ownership. The Committee has also recommended the implementation of employee participation in decision-making. The most basic reform under discussion is the left's proposal that Parliament should be the supreme state organ, and that much of the President's power should be transferred to the Council of State. Proposals that citizens vote directly for a presidential candidate were implemented in February 1988. If no candidate wins an absolute majority, the 301-member electoral college is convened.

GOVERNMENT

For the general administration of the country, there is a Council of State, appointed by the President, and composed of the Prime Minister and the Ministers of the various Ministries. The members of the Council, who must enjoy the confidence of the Parliament, are collectively responsible to it for their conduct of affairs, and for the general policy of the administration, while each member is responsible for the administration of his own Ministry.

To this Council the President can appoint supernumerary Ministers, who serve either as assistant Ministers or as Ministers without portfolio. The President also appoints a Chancellor of Justice, who must see that the Council and its members act within the law. If, in the opinion of the Chancellor of Justice, the Council of State or an individual Minister has acted in a manner contrary to the law, the Chancellor must report the matter to the President of the Republic or, in certain cases, to the Parliament. In this way Ministers are rendered legally as well as politically responsible for their official acts.

THE PRESIDENT

The President is elected for a term of six years by direct popular vote. The 301 members of the electoral college, which convenes if no presidential candidate wins an absolute majority, are chosen by public vote in the same manner as members of Parliament.

The President of the Republic is entrusted with supreme executive power. The President's decisions are made known in meetings of the Council of State on the basis of the recommendation of the minister responsible for the matter. The President has the right to depart even from a unanimous opinion reached by the Council of State. Legislative power is exercised by the Parliament in conjunction with the President. Both the President and the Parliament have the right of initiative in legislation. Laws passed by the Parliament are submitted to the President, who has the right of veto. If the President has not within three months assented to a law, this is tantamount to a refusal of assent. A law to which the President has not given assent will nevertheless come into force, if the Parliament elected at the next general election adopts it without alteration.

The President has also the right to issue decrees in certain events, to order new elections to the Parliament, to grant pardons and dispensations, and to grant Finnish citizenship to foreigners.

The President's approval is necessary in all matters concerning the relations of Finland with foreign countries. The President is Supreme Commander of the Defence Forces of the Republic.

Such decisions as are arrived at by the President are made in the Council of State, except in matters pertaining to military functions and appointments.

THE PARLIAMENT

The Parliament is an assembly of one chamber with 200 members elected for four years by universal suffrage on a system of proportional representation, every man and woman aged 18 years or over being entitled to vote and everyone over 20 being eligible. It assembles annually at the beginning of February. The ordinary duration of a session is 120 days but the Parliament can, at its pleasure, extend or shorten its session. The opposition of one-third of the members can cause ordinary legislative proposals to be deferred until after the next elections. Discussion of questions relating to the constitutional laws belongs also to Parliament, but for the settlement of such questions certain delaying conditions (fixed majorities) are prescribed. The Parliament, besides taking part in legislation, has the right to determine the estimates, which, though not technically a law, are published as a law.

Furthermore, the Parliament has the right, in a large measure, to supervise the administration of the Government. For this purpose it receives special reports (the Government also submitting an account of its administration every year) and a special account of the administration of national finances. The Chancellor of Justice submits a yearly report on the administration of the Council of State. The Parliament elects five auditors, who submit to it annual reports of their work, to see that the estimates have been adhered to. The Parliament also appoints every four years a Parliamentary Ombudsman (Judicial Delegate of Parliament) who submits to it a report, to supervise the observance of the laws.

The Parliament has the right to interrogate the Government. It can impeach a member of the Council of State or the Chancellor of Justice for not having conformed to the law in the discharge of his duties. Trials are conducted at a special court, known as the Court of the Realm, of 13 members, six of whom are elected by Parliament for a term of four years.

The Government

(February 1989)

HEAD OF STATE

President: Dr MAUNO KOIVISTO (assumed duties 10 September 1981; elected 26 January 1982; re-elected 15 February 1988).

COUNCIL OF STATE
(Valtioneuvosto)

A coalition of the National Coalition Party (Kok), Social Democratic Party (SDP), Swedish People's Party (SFP) and Finnish Rural Party (SMP), formed in April 1987.

Prime Minister: HARRI HOLKERI (Kok).

Deputy Prime Minister and Minister for Foreign Affairs: PERTTI PAASIO (SDP).

Minister in the Cabinet: ILKKA KANERVA (Kok).

FINLAND

Minister of Foreign Trade: PERTTI SALOLAINEN (Kok).
Minister of Justice: MATTI LOUEKOSKI (SDP).
Minister of the Interior: JARMO RANTANEN (SDP).
Minister of Defence: OLE NORRBACK (SFP).
Minister of Finance: ERKKI LIIKANEN (SDP).
Second Minister of Finance: ULLA PUOLANNE (Kok).
Minister of Education: CHRISTOFFER TAXELL (SFP).
Second Minister of Education: ANNA-LIISA PIIPARI (SDP).
Minister of Agriculture and Forestry: TOIVO T. POHJOLA (Kok).
Minister of Transport and Communications: PEKKA VENNAMO (SMP).
Minister of Trade and Industry: ILKKA SUOMINEN (Kok).
Minister of Social Affairs and Health: HELENA PESOLA (Kok).
Second Minister of Social Affairs and Health: TARJA HALONEN (SDP).
Minister of Labour: MATTI PUHAKKA (SDP).
Minister of the Environment: KAJ BÄRLUND (SDP).

MINISTRIES

Prime Minister's Office: Aleksanterinkatu 3D, 00170 Helsinki; tel. (90) 1601; telex 124636.

Ministry of Agriculture and Forestry: Hallituskatu 3A, 00170 Helsinki; tel. (90) 1601; telex 125621.

Ministry of Defence: Et. Makasiinikatu 8A, 00130 Helsinki; tel. (90) 625801; telex 124667.

Ministry of Education: Meritullinkatu 10, POB 293, 00171 Helsinki; tel. (90) 134171; telex 122079.

Ministry of the Environment: POB 399, 00121 Helsinki; tel. (90) 19911; telex 123717.

Ministry of Finance: Snellmaninkatu 1A, 00170 Helsinki; tel. (90) 1601; telex 123241.

Ministry of Foreign Affairs: Merikasarmi, POB 176, 00161 Helsinki; tel. (90) 134151; telex 124636.

Ministry of the Interior: Kirkkokatu 12, 00170 Helsinki; tel. (90) 1601; telex 123644.

Ministry of Justice: Eteläesplanadi 10, 00130 Helsinki; tel. (90) 18251.

Ministry of Labour: Eteläesplanadi 4, 00130 Helsinki; tel. (90) 18561; telex 121441.

Ministry of Social Affairs and Health: Snellmaninkatu 4-6, 00170 Helsinki; tel. (90) 1601; telex 125073.

Ministry of Trade and Industry: Aleksanterinkatu 10, 00170 Helsinki; tel. (90) 1601; telex 124645.

Ministry of Transport and Communications: Eteläesplanadi 16, 00130 Helsinki; tel. (90) 17361; telex 125472.

President and Legislature

PRESIDENT
Elections of 31 January–1 February and 15 February 1988

	Popular vote (%)	Electoral College First Ballot	Electoral College Second Ballot
MAUNO KOIVISTO	47.92	144	189
PAAVO VÄYRYNEN	20.15	68	68
HARRI HOLKERI	18.06	63	18
KALEVI KIVISTÖ	10.45	26	26
JOUKO KAJANOJA	1.41	—	—

EDUSKUNTA
(Parliament)

Speaker: MATTI AHDE (SDP).
First Deputy Speaker: ELSI HETEMÄKI-OLANDER (Kok).
Second Deputy Speaker: MIKKO PESÄLÄ (KP).
Secretary-General: ERKKI KETOLA.

General Election, 15–16 March 1987

	Votes	%	Seats
Social Democratic Party	694,666	24.14	56
National Coalition Party	665,477	23.13	53
Centre Party	507,384	17.63	40
Finnish People's Democratic League	269,678	9.37	16
Swedish People's Party	153,141	5.32	12
Finnish Rural Party	181,557	6.31	9
Finnish Christian Union	74,011	2.57	5
Democratic Alternative*	122,115	4.24	4
Green Party	115,830	4.03	4
Others	93,661	3.25	1†
Total	**2,877,520**	**100.00**	**200**

* The party subsequently adopted the title of Communist Party of Finland–Unity (SKP–Y).
† Åland delegate.

Political Organizations

Kansallinen Kokoomus (Kok) (National Coalition Party): Kansakoulukuja 3, 00100 Helsinki; tel. (90) 6942611; telex 124591; f. 1918; moderate conservative political ideology; 80,000 mems; Chair. ILKKA SUOMINEN; Sec.-Gen. AARNO KAILA; Chair. Parliamentary Group TAPANI MÖRTTINEN.

Keskustapuolue (KP) (Centre Party): Pursimiehenkatu 15, Helsinki; tel. (90) 170311; f. 1906; a radical centre party founded to promote the interests of the rural population, especially that of the numerous small farmers, on the lines of individual enterprise; also favours decentralization; 304,000 mems; Chair. PAAVO VÄYRYNEN; Sec. SEPPO KÄÄRIÄNEN; Chair. Parliamentary Group KAUKO JUHANTALO.

Liberaalinen Kansanpuolue (LKP) (Liberal People's Party): Fredrikinkatu 58A 6, Helsinki; tel. (90) 440227; f. 1965 as a coalition of the Finnish People's Party and the Liberal Union; in 1982 became mem. organization of the Centre Party; 8,000 mems; Chair. KYÖSTI LALLUKKA; Sec.-Gen. JARI P. HAVIA.

Perustuslaillinen Oikeistopuolue-Konstitutionella högerpartiet r.p. (Constitutional Party of the Right): Mannerheimintie 146A, 00270 Helsinki; tel. (90) 419063; f. 1973; conservative; seeks to protect constitutional rights and parliamentary democracy; Chair. GEORG C. EHRNROOTH; Sec. PANU TOIVONEN.

Suomen Eläkelästen Poulue (Finnish Pensioners' Party): Helsinki; f.1986; represents the interests of pensioners; Chair. YRJOE VIRTANEN.

Suomen Kansan Demokraattinen Liitto r.p. (SKDL) (Finnish People's Democratic League): Kotkankatu 11, 00510 Helsinki; tel. (90) 77081; f. 1944 by social democrats, socialists and communists; co-operative organization of leftist groups; member organizations: Finnish Communist Party, Women's, Youth and Student Leagues; 1988 reforms aimed to create broader leftist alliance; 120,000 mems; Chair. REIJO KÄKELÄ; Sec.-Gen. SALME KANDOLIN; Chair. Parliamentary Group ESKO HELLE.

Suomen Kommunistinen Puolue (SKP) (Communist Party of Finland): Sturenkatu 4, Helsinki; tel. (90) 77081; f. 1918; proscribed until 1944 after the signing of the Armistice with USSR; controlled by Eurocommunists; Chair. JARMO WAHLSTRÖM; Sec.-Gen. HELJÄ TAMMISOLA.

Suomen Kommunistinen Puolue–Yhdenäisyys (SKP–Y) (Communist Party of Finland–Unity): Kornetintie 4, 00380 Helsinki; tel. (90) 5653155; f. 1986 as the Democratic Alternative (still the parliamentary title), by a minority, Stalinist faction of the Communist Party of Finland; Chair. KRISTIINA HALKOLA; Sec.-Gen. SEPPO TIMONEN.

Suomen Kristillinen Liitto (SKL) (Finnish Christian Union): Töölönkatu 50 D, 00250 Helsinki 25; f. 1958; 18,000 mems; Chair. E. ALMGREN; Sec. JOUKO JÄÄSKELÄINEN; Chair. Parliamentary Group C. P. EEVA-LIISA MOILANEN.

Suomen Maaseudun Puolue (SMP) (Finnish Rural Party): Hämeentie 157, 00560 Helsinki; tel. (90) 790299; f. 1959; non-socialist programme; represents lower-middle-class elements, small farmers, small enterprises etc.; Chair. PEKKA VENNAMO; Sec. TINA MAEKELAE (acting); Chair. Parliamentary Group HEIKKI RÜHIJÄRUI.

Suomen Sosialidemokraattinen Puolue (SDP) (Finnish Social Democratic Party): Saariniemenkatu 6, 00530 Helsinki; f. 1899; constitutional socialist programme; mainly supported by the working and middle classes and small farmers; approx. 97,000 mems; Chair. PERTTI PAASIO; Gen.-Sec. ULPU IIVARI; Chair. Parliamentary Group PERTTI HIETALA.

FINLAND

Svenska Folkpartiet (SFP) (Swedish People's Party): Gräsviksgatan 14, POB 282, 00181 Helsinki; tel. (90) 6942322; f. 1906; a liberal party representing the interests of the Swedish-speaking minority; 50,000 mems; Chair. CHRISTOFFER TAXELL; Sec. PETER STENLUND; Chair. Parliamentary Group ELISABETH REHN.

Vihreä Eduskuntaryhmä (Green Parliamentary Group): Eduskunta 00102, Helsinki; tel. (90) 4321; telex (Parliament) 4322274; Chair. ERKKI PULLIAINEN.

Vihreä Liitto (Green Association): Helsinki; f. 1988; Leader HEIDI HAUTALA.

Diplomatic Representation

EMBASSIES IN FINLAND

Argentina: Bulevardi 10A 14, 00120 Helsinki; tel. (90) 607630; telex 122794; Ambassador: NEREO MELO FERRER.

Austria: Eteläesplanadi 18, 00130 Helsinki; tel. (90) 634255; Ambassador: HANS GEORG RUDOFSKY.

Belgium: Kalliolinnantie 5, 00140 Helsinki; tel. (90) 170412; Ambassador: PAUL JANSSENS.

Brazil: Mariankatu 7A 3, 00170 Helsinki; tel. (90) 177922; Ambassador: CARLOS LUZILDE HILDEBRANDT.

Bulgaria: Itäinen puistotie 10, 00140 Helsinki; tel. (90) 661707; Ambassador: VALERI PCHELINTSHEV.

Canada: Pohjoisesplanadi 25B, 00100 Helsinki; tel. (90) 171141; telex 121363; Ambassador: MARY VANDENHOFF.

China, People's Republic: Vanha Kelkkamäki 9-11, 00570 Helsinki; tel. (90) 688371; Ambassador: YU LIXUAN.

Colombia: Fredrikinkatu 61, 00100 Helsinki; tel. (90) 6931255; telex 126210; Ambassador: NICOLAS SALOM-FRANCO.

Cuba: Paasivuorenkatu 3, 00530 Helsinki; tel. (90) 766199; telex 121017; Ambassador: MAGALY T. GOZÁ LEÓN.

Czechoslovakia: Armfeltintie 14, 00150 Helsinki; tel. (90) 171169; Ambassador: PAVEL ŠTULRAJTER.

Denmark: Yrjönkatu 9, POB 178, 00121 Helsinki; tel. (90) 641948; telex 124782; Ambassador: PETER MEYER MICHAELSEN.

Egypt: Stenbäckinkatu 22A, 00250 Helsinki; tel. (90) 413288; telex 124216; Ambassador: AHMED AMIN WALY.

France: Itäinen puistotie 13, 00140 Helsinki; tel. (90) 171521; Ambassador: MARCEL MATYRE.

German Democratic Republic: Vähäniityntie 9, 00570 Helsinki; tel. (90) 688138; telex 12643; Ambassador: ROLF BÖTTCHER.

Germany, Federal Republic: Fredrikinkatu 61, 00100 Helsinki; tel. (90) 6943355; telex 124568; Ambassador: Dr KLAUS TERFLOTH.

Greece: Lönnrotinkatu 15C 26, 00120 Helsinki; tel. (90) 645202; Ambassador: ANASTÁSSIOS SIDERIS.

Holy See: Bulevardi 5 as. 12, 00120 Helsinki; tel. (90) 644664; Apostolic Nuncio: HENRI LEMAÎTRE.

Hungary: Kuusisaarenkuja 6, 00340 Helsinki; tel. (90) 484144; Ambassador: ÁRPÁD HARGITA.

India: Satamakatu 2A 8, 00160 Helsinki; tel. (90) 608927; telex 125202; Ambassador: KALARICKAL PRANCHU FABIAN.

Indonesia: Eerikinkatu 37, 00180 Helsinki; tel. (90) 6947744; Ambassador: PONGKY SOEPARDJO.

Iran: Bertel Jungintie 4, 00570 Helsinki; tel. (90) 687133; Ambassador: (vacant).

Iraq: Lars Sonckintie 2, 00570 Helsinki; tel. (90) 689177; Ambassador: PETER YOUSIF JAJONI.

Israel: Vironkatu 5A, 00170 Helsinki; tel. (90) 175177; Ambassador: MORDECHAI LADOR.

Italy: Fabianinkatu 29C 4, 00100 Helsinki; tel. (90) 175144; telex 121753; Ambassador: GIANCARLO CARRARA CAGNI.

Japan: Yrjönkatu 13, 00120 Helsinki; tel. (90) 644206; Ambassador: WATARU MIYAKAWA.

Korea, Democratic People's Republic: Kulosaaren puistotie 32, 00570 Helsinki; tel. (90) 688195; Ambassador: LI NAM-KYU.

Korea, Republic: Mannerheimintie 76A 7, 00250 Helsinki; tel. (90) 498955; Ambassador: SANG JIN CHOI.

Mexico: Pohjoisranta 14A 16, 00170 Helsinki; tel. (90) 640637; telex 122021; Ambassador: CARLOS GONZALES PARRODI.

Netherlands: Raatimiehenkatu 2A 7, 00140 Helsinki; tel. (90) 661737; telex 121779; Ambassador: H. CH. G. CARSTEN.

Norway: Rehbinderintie 17, 00150 Helsinki; tel. (90) 171234; Ambassador: KJELL COLDING.

Peru: Fredrikinkatu 16A 22, 00120 Helsinki; tel. (90) 631354; telex 123650; Ambassador: AUGUSTO SALAMANCA REGALADO.

Poland: Armas Lindgrenintie 21, 00570 Helsinki; tel. (90) 688077; Ambassador: HENRYK BURCZYK.

Portugal: Itäinen puistotie 11B, 00140 Helsinki; tel. (90) 171717; Ambassador: ANTÓNIO CABRAL DE MONCADA.

Romania: Stenbäckinkatu 24, 00250 Helsinki; tel. (90) 413624; Ambassador: CORNELIA TEODORESCU.

South Africa: Rahapajankatu 1A 5, 00160 Helsinki; tel. (90) 658288; Ambassador: J. J. VENTER.

Spain: Bulevardi 10A 8, 00120 Helsinki; tel. (90) 647351; telex 122193; Ambassador: FERNANDO SARTORIUS Y ALVAREZ DE BOHORQUES.

Sweden: P. Esplanadi 7B, 00170 Helsinki; tel. (90) 651255; Ambassador: KNUT THYBERG.

Switzerland: Uudenmaankatu 16A, 00120 Helsinki; tel. (90) 649422; Ambassador: MARIANNE VON GRUENIGEN.

Turkey: Topeliuksenkatu 3B A 1-2, 00260 Helsinki; tel. (90) 406058; Ambassador: OKTAY AKSOY.

USSR: Tehtaankatu 1B, 00140 Helsinki; tel. (90) 661876; Ambassador: BORIS IVANOVICH ARISTOV.

United Kingdom: Uudenmaankatu 16-20, 00120 Helsinki; tel. (90) 647922; telex 121122; Ambassador: H. A. JUSTIN STAPLES.

USA: Itäinen puistotie 14A, 00140 Helsinki; tel. (90) 171931; telex 121644; Ambassador: ROCKWELL A. SCHNABEL.

Venezuela: Mannerheimintie 14B, 00100 Helsinki; tel. (90) 641522; Ambassador: GERMÁN DE PÉREZ CASTILLO.

Yugoslavia: Kulosaarentie 36, 00570 Helsinki; tel. (90) 688522; telex 122099; Ambassador: IVAN TOŠEVSKI.

Judicial System

The administration of justice is independent of the Government and judges can be removed only by judicial sentence.

SUPREME COURT

Korkein oikeus: Consists of a President and 21 Justices appointed by the President of the Republic. Final court appeal in civil and criminal cases, supervises judges and executive authorities, appoints judges.

President: CURT OLSSON.

SUPREME ADMINISTRATIVE COURT

Korkein hallinto oikeus: Consists of a President and 21 Justices appointed by the President of the Republic. Highest tribunal for appeals in administrative cases.

President: ANTTI SUVIRANTA.

COURTS OF APPEAL

There are Courts of Appeal at Turku, Vaasa, Kuopio, Helsinki, Kouvola, and Rovaniemi, consisting of a President and an appropriate number of members.

DISTRICT AND MUNICIPAL COURTS

Courts of first instance for almost all suits. Appeals lie to the Court of Appeal, and then to the Supreme Court. District Courts consist of a judge and from five to seven jurors. The decision rests with the judge, but the jurors may overrule him if they are unanimous. Municipal Courts are the municipal equivalent of District Courts, consisting of three judges of whom one or two may be lay judges, and presided over by the burgomaster.

CHANCELLOR OF JUSTICE

The Oikeuskansleri is responsible for seeing that authorities and officials comply with the law. He is the chief public prosecutor, and acts as counsel for the Government.

Chancellor of Justice: JORMA S. AALTO.

PARLIAMENTARY SOLICITOR-GENERAL

The Eduskunnan Oikeusasiamies is the Finnish Ombudsman appointed by Parliament to supervise the observance of the law.

Parliamentary Solicitor-General: OLAVI E. HEINONEN.

Religion

CHRISTIANITY

Suomen ekumeeninen neuvosto/Ekumeniska Rådet i Finland (Ecumenical Council of Finland): Luotsikatu 1A, POB 185, 00161 Helsinki; tel. (90) 18021; telex 122357; f. 1919; 10 mem. churches;

FINLAND

Pres. Dr JOHN VIKSTRÖM (Archbishop, Evangelical Lutheran Church of Finland); Gen. Sec. Rev. Dr JAAKKO RUSAMA.

National Churches

Suomen Evankelisluterilainen Kirkko (Evangelical Lutheran Church of Finland): Office of Foreign Affairs, Satamakatu 11, POB 185, 00161 Helsinki; tel. (90) 18021; telex 122357; about 88% of the population are adherents; Archbishop Dr JOHN VIKSTRÖM.

Suomen Ortodoksinen Kirkko (Orthodox Church of Finland): Karjalankatu 1, 70300 Kuopio; tel. (Admin.) (971) 122611; 56,762 mems; Leader JOHANNES, Archbishop of Karelia and All Finland.

Protestant Churches

Finlands Svenska Baptistmission (Baptists, Swedish-speaking): Rådhusgatan 44A, 65100 Vaasa; tel. (961) 118559; f. 1856; 1,742 mems.

Finlands Svenska Kyrkan (Church of Sweden in Finland): Minervagatan 6, 00100 Helsinki; f. 1919; 1,779 mems; Rector Dr JARL JERGMAR.

Jehovan Todistajat (Jehovah's Witnesses): Kuismatie 58, 01300 Vantaa; tel. (90) 826488; 16,700 mems.

Myöhempien Aikojen Pyhien Jeesuksen Kristuksen Kirkko (Church of Jesus Christ of Latter-day Saints—Mormon): Neitsytpolku 3A, 00140 Helsinki; tel. (90) 177311; 4,245 mems.

Suomen Adventtikirkko (Adventist Church of Finland): Uudenmaantie 50, 20720 Turku; tel. (921) 365100; f. 1894; 6,195 mems; Pres. OLAVI ROUHE; Sec. JOEL NIININEN.

Suomen Baptistiyhdyskunta (Baptists, Finnish-speaking): Vasamatie 18, 33450 Siivikkala; 1,834 mems; Pres. Rev. JOUKO NEULANEN.

Suomen Metodistikirkko (Methodist Church of Finland): Punavuorenkatu 2, 00120 Helsinki; 1,967 mems; Moderators Rev. TAPANI RAJAAMA (Finnish-speaking), BJÖRN ELFVING, KAIJA-RIIKA WÄXBY (Swedish-speaking).

Suomen Vapaakirkko (Evangelical Free Church of Finland): Sibeliuksenkatu 17, 13100 Hämeenlinna; tel. (917) 122150; f. 1923; 13,192 mems; Moderator ERKKI VERKKONEN.

Other Christian Churches

Anglican Church in Finland: Putouskuja 5B 7, 01600 Vantaa; tel. (90) 5634829; telex 121122; chaplaincy founded 1921; part of diocese of Gibraltar in Europe; Chaplain Rev. ALAN M. COLE.

Katolinen kirkko Suomessa (Roman Catholic Church in Finland): Rehbinderintie 21, 00150 Helsinki; tel. (90) 637907; Finland comprises the single diocese of Helsinki, directly responsible to the Holy See; 4,000 mems; Bishop of Helsinki PAUL M. VERSCHUREN; Vicar-Gen. Rev. JOHANNES AARTS.

JUDAISM

Helsingin Juutalainen Seurakunta (Jewish Community of Helsinki): Synagogue and Community Centre, Malminkatu 26, 00100 Helsinki; tel. (90) 6941302; 1,309 mems; Pres. GIDEON BOLOTOWSKY.

ISLAM

Suomen Islam-Seurakunta (Islamic Community of Finland): Fredrikinkatu 33A, 00120 Helsinki; tel. (90) 643579; 926 mems.

The Press

The 1919 Constitution provided safeguards for press freedom in Finland, and in the same year the Freedom of the Press Act developed and qualified this principle by defining the rights and responsibilities of editors and the circumstances in which the Supreme Court may confiscate or suppress a publication. In practice there are few restrictions. The most notable offences for newspapermen concern libel and copyright. Two notable features of the press are the public's legal right of access to all official documents (with important exceptions), and since 1966 the right of the journalist to conceal his source of news.

Almost all daily newspapers are independent companies, most of which are owned by large numbers of shareholders. Newspaper chains are virtually unknown, but the Finnish press is a party press. The small number of papers that are generally considered left-orientated are usually owned by the political parties concerned, by trade unions, or by other workers' associations (the Social Democratic Party's chief organ is *Demari* and the Finnish Communist Party publishes *Kansan Uutiset*). Most of the right-wing newspapers are owned by private shareholders, and some belong to private endowments. The leading organ of the National Coalition Party is *Aamulehti* in Tampere. The left-wing papers are subject to considerably closer influence from the parties to which they are affiliated than their right-wing counterparts. Privately owned newspapers—including some of the largest such as *Helsingin Sanomat* and *Turun Sanomat*—are usually independent of political parties.

Helsinki is the only large press centre, with a large number of daily papers. Several large dailies are produced in provincial towns, as are a number of weekly and twice-weekly papers. In 1987 there were 101 daily newspapers in Finland, with a total circulation of about 3,253,000. Twelve of these dailies are printed in Swedish. A further 148 small local non-daily papers were also registered.

The most popular daily papers are *Helsingin Sanomat, Aamulehti, Turun Sanomat, Ilta-Sanomat, Uusi Suomi* and *Savon Sanomat*. Those most respected for their standard of news coverage and commentary are *Helsingin Sanomat*, an independent paper, and the smaller *Uusi Suomi*.

The total circulation of periodicals amounts to about 23m. copies per issue, of which the business and trade press contribute 11.5m. The largest publishers are Kustannusosakeyhtiö Apulehti, Yhtyneet Kuvalehdet Oy, Lehtimiehet Oy and Sanoma Osakeyhtiö. Consumer co-operatives use their periodicals as information media for both their members and their customers. *Pirkka*, *YV*, *Me* and *Yhteishyvä* are among the most important.

There are about 1,100 periodicals, of which some 200 are in the nation's second language, Swedish. Among the leading weekly periodicals are the general interest *Seura*, *Apu* and the illustrated news magazine *Suomen Kuvalehti*. The publications of the consumer co-operatives enjoy large circulations, as do the chief women's magazines *Anna*, *Me naiset* and *Kotiliesi*. The more popular serious magazines include the fortnightly *Pellervo* specializing in agricultural affairs, and *Valitut Palat*, the Finnish *Reader's Digest*.

PRINCIPAL DAILIES

Helsinki

Demari: Paasivuorenkatu 3, 00530 Helsinki; tel. (90) 701041; telex 124433; f. 1918; chief organ of the Social Democratic Party; Editor-in-Chief JUKKA HALONEN; circ. 32,669.

Helsingin Sanomat: Ludviginkatu 6-8, POB 975, 00101 Helsinki; tel. (90) 1221; telex 124897; f. 1889; independent; Editors-in-Chief HEIKKI TIKKANEN, SEPPO KIEVARI, SIMOPEKKA NORTAMO, KEIJO K. KULHA; circ. 453,597 weekdays, 538,370 Sunday.

Hufvudstadsbladet: Mannerheimvägen 18, 00100 Helsinki; tel. (90) 12531; telex 124402; f. 1864; Swedish language; independent; Editor HÅKAN HELLBERG; circ. 66,065 weekdays, 69,179 Sunday.

Iltalehti: POB 139, 00101 Helsinki; tel. (90) 50771; f. 1981; independent; Editor-in-Chief VELI-AUTTI SAVOLAINEN; circ. 83,760 afternoon, 106,842 Saturday.

Ilta-Sanomat: Korkeavuorenkatu 34, POB 375, 00101 Helsinki; tel. (90) 1221; telex 124897; f. 1932; afternoon; independent; Editors-in-Chief VESA-PEKKA KOLJONEN, LAURI HELVE; circ. 208,655 weekdays, 241,021 weekend.

Insinööriuutiset—Tekniika ja Talous: Ratavartijankatu 2, 00520 Helsinki; tel. (90) 15901; daily; technology and economy; Editor-in-Chief RISTO TUOMAINEN.

Kansan Uutiset: Niitaajankatu 8, 00810 Helsinki; tel. (90) 75881; telex 12663; f. 1957; organ of the Finnish Communist Party and People's Democratic League of Finland; Editor ERKKI KAUPPILA; circ. 45,731 weekdays, 57,262 Sunday.

Kauppalehti (The Commercial Daily): POB 189, 00101 Helsinki; tel. (90) 50781; telex 125827; f. 1898; morning; Editor-in-Chief ARTO TUOMINEN; circ. 80,274.

Suomenmaa: Kansakoulukatu 8A, 00100 Helsinki; tel. (90) 6942755; f. 1908; Centre; Editor SEPPO SARLUND; circ. 32,998.

Uusi Suomi: POB 139, 00101 Helsinki; tel. (90) 53031; telex 124898; f. 1847; morning; independent; Editors JOHANNES KOROMA, JYRKI VESIKANSA; circ. 154,794 morning, 96,457 Sunday.

Hämeenlinna

Hämeen Sanomat: Vanajantie 7, POB 530, 13111 Hämeenlinna; tel. 23011; f. 1879; independent; Man. JUSSI ALA-NIKKOLA; Editor-in-Chief ALLAN LIUHALA; circ. 32,253.

Hyrylä

Keski-Uusimaa: Klaavolantie 5, 04300 Hyrylä; tel. (90) 255255; independent; circ. 22,238.

Joensuu

Karjalainen: Torikatu 33, POB 99, 80101 Joensuu; tel. (973) 1551; telex 46126; f. 1874; National Coalition; Editor SEPPO VENTO; circ. 55,261.

Jyväskylä

Keskisuomalainen: Aholaidantie 3, POB 159, 40101 Jyväskylä; tel. (0941) 201211; telex 28211; f. 1871; Centre; Editor ERKKI LAATIKAINEN; circ. 77,905 weekdays, 68,268 Sunday.

FINLAND

Kajaani
Kainuun Sanomat: Viestitie 2, POB 150, 87700 Kajaani; tel. (986) 1661; telex 33172; f. 1918; Centre; Editor Otso Kukkonen; circ. 30,301.

Kemi
Pohjolan Sanomat: POB 17, 94101 Kemi; tel. (80) 2911; telex 3643; f. 1915; Centre; Editors Matti Lammi, Reijo Alatörmänen; circ. 38,123.

Kokkola
Keskipohjanmaa: Kosila, POB 45, 67101 Kokkola; tel. (968) 28511; telex 76118; f. 1917; Centre; Editor Pentti Pulakka; circ. 34,432.

Kotka
Eteenpäin: POB 140, 48101 Kotka; tel. (952) 181515; telex 53143; Social Democratic; circ. 20,647.

Etelä-Suomi: POB 40, 45101 Kotka; tel. (952) 183666; circ. 18,089.

Kouvola
Kouvolan Sanomat: Tommolankatu 2, POB 40, 45101 Kouvola; tel. (951) 16911; telex 52210; f. 1909; Editor Martti Turtola; circ. 33,464.

Kuopio
Savon Sanomat: Vuorikatu 21, POB 68, 70101 Kuopio; tel. (71) 303111; telex 42111; f. 1907; Centre; Dir Risto Suhonen; Editor Reino Myöhänen; circ. 84,712.

Lahti
Etelä-Suomen Sanomat: Ilmarisentie 7, POB 80, 15101 Lahti; tel. (918) 57511; telex 16132; f. 1900; independent; Dir Jaakko Ukkonen; Editors-in-Chief Kauko Mäenpää, Pentti Vuorio; circ. 66,608.

Lappeenranta
Etelä-Saimaa: POB 3, 53101 Lappeenranta; tel. 15600; telex 58217; f. 1885; Centre; Man. Dir Esa Lavender; Editor Lauri Sarhimaa; circ. 32,567.

Mikkeli
Länsi-Savo: POB 6, 50101 Mikkeli; tel. (955) 10555; telex 55154; circ. 26,437.

Oulu
Kaleva: POB 70, 90101 Oulu; tel. (981) 326111; telex 32112; f. 1899; Liberal independent; Editor Teuvo Mällinen; circ. 90,013.

Kansan Tahto: POB 61, 90101 Oulu; tel. (981) 221722; f. 1906; organ of the People's Democratic League; circ. 16,936.

Liitto: Lekatie 4, 90150 Oulu; tel. (981) 336333; morning; Centre; circ. 18,135.

Pori
Satakunnan Kansa: POB 58, 28101 Pori; tel. (939) 328111; telex 66102; f. 1873; National Coalition; Editor Erkki Teikari; circ. 61,482.

Rauma
Länsi-Suomi: Kaivopuistontie 1, 26100 Rauma; tel. 3361; telex 65160; National Coalition Party; circ. 20,000.

Rovaniemi
Lapin Kansa: Veitikantie 6-8, 96100 Rovaniemi; tel. 2911; telex 37213; f. 1928; independent; Editor Heikki Tuomi-Nikula; circ. 41,533.

Salo
Salon Seudun Sanomat: Örninkatu 14, POB 117, 24101 Salo; tel. (924) 30021; circ. 20,949.

Savonlinna
Itä-Savo: POB 35, 57101 Savonlinna; tel. (957) 29171; telex 5611; Centre; circ. 20,841 weekdays, 20,122 Sunday.

Seinäjoki
Ilkka: POB 60, Kouluk, 60101 Seinäjoki; tel. (964) 141100; telex 72130; f. 1906; organ of Centre Party; Editor Kari Hokkanen; circ. 53,465.

Tampere
Aamulehti: Patamäenkatu 7, Tampere; tel. (931) 666111; telex 22111; f. 1881; National Coalition; Editors Prof. Pertti Pesonen, Sakari Kumpulainen, Raimo Seppälä; circ. 141,896 weekdays, 148,215 Sunday.

Turku
Turun Sanomat: Kauppiaskatu 5, 20100 Turku; tel. (921) 693311; telex 62213; f. 1904; independent; Man. Dir Keijo Ketonen; Editor Jarmo Virmavirta; circ. 131,731 weekdays, 140,475 Sunday.

Vaasa
Pohjalainen: Pitkäkatu 37, POB 37, 65101 Vaasa; tel. (961) 111411; telex 74212; f. 1903; National Coalition; Editor Erkki Malmivaara; circ. 63,149.

Vasabladet: Sandögatan 6, POB 52, 65101 Vaasa; tel. (961) 121866; telex 74269; f. 1856; Swedish language; Liberal independent; Editor Birger Thölix; circ. 27,407.

PRINCIPAL PERIODICALS

Aku Ankka (Donald Duck): POB 113, 00381 Helsinki; tel. (90) 1201; telex 125848; f. 1951; weekly; children's; Editor Kirsti Toppari; circ. 281,251.

Anna: Maistraatinportti 1, 00240 Helsinki; tel. (90) 15661; telex 1482025; f. 1963; weekly; women's; Editor-in-Chief Riitta Tulonen; circ. 157,340.

Apu: Hitsaajankatu 7, 00810 Helsinki; tel. (90) 782311; telex 124698; f. 1933; weekly; family journal; Editor-in-Chief Matti Saari; circ. 276,660.

Eeva: Hitsaajankatu 10, 00810 Helsinki; tel. (90) 782311; telex 124732; f. 1933; monthly; women's; Editor-in-Chief Ulla Leskinen; circ. 119,259.

et-lehti: POB 113, 00381 Helsinki; tel. (90) 1201; telex 125848; pensioners' magazine; Editor Marjukka Luomala; circ. 133,461.

Hymy: Puutarhakatu 16, 33210 Tampere; tel. (931) 33333; telex 122730; monthly; family journal; Editor-in-Chief Raimo Toivonen; circ. 119,538.

Kalamies: Svinhufvudintie 11, 00570 Helsinki; tel. (90) 689022; 10 a year; fishing; Editor-in-Chief Timo Seppälä; circ 69,705.

Kameralehti: Eerikinkatu 7c 8, 00100 Helsinki; tel. (90) 6944051; f. 1950; 11 a year; photographic; Editor Pekka Punkari; circ. 14,426.

Katso: Hitsaajankatu 7, 00810 Helsinki; weekly; tel. (90) 782311; telex 124732; TV, radio and video; Editor-in-Chief Anja Tuomi; circ. 61,693.

Kauppa ja Koti: Kalevankatu 6, 00100 Helsinki; tel. (90) 6191; telex 121722; free to customers of retail stores; Editor-in-Chief Tapani Lehmusvaara; circ. 389,743.

Kodin Kuvalehti: POB 113, 00381 Helsinki; tel. (90) 1201; telex 125848; fortnightly; family magazine; Editor Eija Ailasmaa; circ. 165,300.

Koiramme–Våra Hundar: Kamreerintie 8, 02770 Espoo; tel. (90) 8057722; monthly; dogs; circ. 59,976.

Koneviesti: Simonkatu 6, 00100 Helsinki; tel. (90) 463316; bi-monthly; farming and forestry; Editor Risto Knaapi; circ. 51,479.

Kotilääkäri: Maistraatinportti 1, 00240 Helsinki; tel. (90) 15661; telex 122772; f. 1889; monthly; health and beauty; Editor-in-Chief Irma Heydemann; circ. 54,631.

Kotiliesi: Maistraatinportti 1, 00240 Helsinki; tel. (90) 15661; telex 121364; f. 1922; fortnightly; home journal; Editor-in-Chief Elina Simonen; circ. 190,773.

Kotimaa: Norrsväng 15, 00200 Helsinki; tel. (90) 6922591; 3 a week; circ. 77,898.

Koululainen: Maistraatinportti 1, 00240 Helsinki; tel. (90) 15661; telex 121364; 17 a year; for pupils of comprehensive schools; Editor-in-Chief Anneli Ruokonen; circ. 66,322.

Look at Finland: POB 53, 00521 Helsinki; tel. (90) 144511; quarterly; tourist information, travel and general articles; publ. by Finnish Tourist Board and Ministry for Foreign Affairs; Editor-in-Chief Bengt Pihlström; circ. 32,000.

Maita ja Me: POB 440, 00101 Helsinki; tel. (90) 131151; telex 122474; f. 1989; 10 a year; dairy farming; Editor-in-Chief Antti Luhtala; circ. 70,000.

Me naiset: POB 113, 00381 Helsinki; tel. (90) 1201; telex 125848; f. 1952; weekly; women's; Editor Ulla-Maija Paavilainen; circ. 108,482.

Metsälehti: Maistraatinportti 4a, 00240 Helsinki; tel. (90) 1562333; f. 1933; fortnightly; forestry; Editor Paavo Seppänen; circ. 80,276.

Nykyposti: Puutarhakatu 16, 33210 Tampere; tel. (931) 33333; telex 122730; f. 1977; monthly; family journal; Editors-in-Chief Lasse Askolin, Annamaija Kataja; circ. 162,429.

Opettaja: Rautatieläisenkatu 6, 00520 Helsinki; tel. (90) 15021; weekly; teachers; Editor-in-Chief Hannu Laaksola; Man. Editor Jouni Tarjamo; circ. 49,982.

FINLAND

Seura: Maistraatinportti 1, 00240 Helsinki; tel. (90) 15661; telex 121364; f. 1934; weekly; family journal; Editors-in-Chief HANNU PARPOLA, HEIKKI PARKKONEN; circ. 284,060.

Sosiaalinen Aikakauskirja: Snellmaninkatu 4–6, 00170 Helsinki; tel. (90) 1605411; telex 125073; 6 a year; social policy; summaries in English; Editor KARI PURO.

Suomen Kuvalehti: Maistraatinportti 1, 00240 Helsinki; tel. (90) 15661; telex 121364; f. 1916; weekly; illustrated news; Editor-in-Chief PEKKA HYVÄRINEN; circ. 110,116.

Suosikki: Eerikinkatu 3B, 00100 Helsinki; tel. (90) 6943311; telex 122730; 16 a year; youth, music; Editor-in-Chief JYRKI HÄMÄLÄINEN; circ. 110,439.

Suuri Käsityökerho: POB 107, 00381 Helsinki; tel. (90) 1201; telex 125848; f. 1974; monthly; needlework and clothing magazine; Editor KRISTINA TÖTTERMAN; circ. 111,079.

Sydän: Hjärtsjukdomsförbundet i Finland, POB 196, 00121 Helsinki; tel. (90) 650288; 8 a year; hospital news; circ. 93,279.

Tekniikan Maailma: Eerinkatu 3B, 00100 Helsinki; tel. (90) 6943311; telex 122730; 20 a year; technical review; Editors RAUNO TOIVONEN, MAURI J. SALO; circ. 125,667.

Tekniset: POB 146, 00131 Helsinki; tel. (90) 658611; telex 122728; 16 a year; industrial technology; Editor LAURI TUOMINEN; circ. 72,236.

Tuulilasi: Hitsaajankatu 7, 00810 Helsinki; monthly; motoring; Editor-in-Chief ERKKI RAUKKO; circ. 82,387.

Työ Terveys Turvallisuus: Topeliuksenkatu 41A, 00250 Helsinki; tel. (90) 47471; 16 a year; occupational health; Editor-in-Chief THELMA ARO; circ. 97,554.

Valitut Palat: Halsuantie 4, 00420 Helsinki; tel. (90) 5632011; telex 122489; monthly; Finnish Reader's Digest; Editor-in-Chief RAIMO MÖYSÄ; circ. 330,662.

Vene: Melkonkatu 10C, POB 116, 00101 Helsinki; tel. (90) 68261; telex 122730; monthly; sailing; Editor-in-Chief MATTI MURTO; circ. 30,193.

CO-OPERATIVE JOURNALS

Elanto, Elanto-Tidningen: Hämeentie 11, 00530 Helsinki; tel. (90) 7341; monthly magazine of Elanto Co-operative Society; circ. 137,000.

Kymppi: Korkeavuorenkatu 45, POB 42, 00131 Helsinki; tel. (90) 18511; f. 1954; 8 a year; publ. by Finnish Savings Banks Asscn, free to customers; Editor-in-Chief VELI-MATTI HEPOLUHTA; circ. 194,426.

Me: Hameentie 19A, 00500 Helsinki; tel. (90) 7331; telex 124454; monthly; organ of Finnish consumers' societies; Editor-in-Chief HILKKA KEMPPINEN; circ. 329,132.

Meidän Liike: POB 72, 00501 Helsinki; tel. (90) 7331; 6 a year; management and elected officials of co-operative societies; Editor KALEVI SUOMELA; circ. 7,818.

Pellervo: POB 77, 00101 Helsinki; tel. (90) 6955203; f. 1899; monthly; agricultural and co-operative journal; organ of the Central Union of Agricultural Co-operative Societies; Editor-in-Chief MARTTI SEPPÄNEN; circ. 94,718.

Pirkka: Rauhankatu 15, 00170 Helsinki; tel. (90) 175566; monthly; Swedish; free to customers of retail stores; Editor-in-Chief OSMO LAMPINEN; circ. 1,616,881.

Samarbete: Vilhelmsgatan 7, 00100 Helsinki; tel. (90) 1881; telex 121341; f. 1909; monthly; circ. 40,044.

Yhteishyvä: Vilhonkatu 7, 00100 Helsinki; tel. (90) 1881; telex 121341; f. 1905; monthly; free to customers of co-operative shops; Editor-in-Chief JOUKO TYYRI; circ. 477,204.

YV: Arkadiankatu 23, POB 480, 00101 Helsinki; tel. (90) 4041; monthly; free to customers of co-operative banks; Editor-in-Chief MATTI PAAVONSALO; circ. 513,090.

NEWS AGENCIES

Oy Suomen Tietotoimisto-Finska Notisbyrån Ab (STT-FNB): Yrjönkatu 22C, 00100 Helsinki; tel. (90) 646224; telex 124534; f. 1887; six provincial branches; independent national agency distributing domestic and international news in Finnish and Swedish; Pres. KEIJO KETONEN; Gen. Man. and Editor-in-Chief PER-ERIK LÖNNFORS.

Foreign Bureaux

Agence France-Presse (AFP) (France): c/o FNB, Mannerheimintie 18, 00100 Helsinki; tel. (90) 646800; Correspondent ILMARI SUNBLAD.

Agencia EFE (Spain): Mariankatu 7B 8, 00170 Helsinki; Correspondent HANNU VUORI.

Agentstvo Pechati Novosti (APN) (USSR): Lönnrotinkatu 25A, 5 Kerros, 00180 Helsinki; tel. (90) 6942022; telex 124662; Correspondent L. LAASKO.

Agenzia Nazionale Stampa Associata (ANSA) (Italy): Iso Roobertinkatu 46B 31, 00120 Helsinki; tel. (90) 639799; Agent MATTI BROTHERUS.

Allgemeiner Deutscher Nachrichtendienst (ADN) (German Democratic Republic): Aarholmankuja 4C 27, 00840 Helsinki; Correspondent BRUNO STORM.

Associated Press (AP) (USA): 2nd floor, Yrjönkatu 27A, 00100 Helsinki; tel. (90) 646883; Correspondent MATTI HUUHTANEN.

Inter Press Service (IPS) (Italy): c/o Ylioppilaslenti, 5th floor, Mannerheimintie 5C, 01000 Helsinki; tel. 176616; Editor ANTTI ANTIO.

Reuters (UK): c/o STT-FNB, POB 550, 00101 Helsinki.

Telegrafnoye Agentstvo Sovetskovo Soyuza (TASS) (USSR): Ratakatu 1A 10, 00120 Helsinki; Correspondent ALEXANDER GORBUNOV.

United Press International (UPI) (USA): Ludviginkatu 3-5, 00130 Helsinki; tel. (90) 605701; telex 124403; Bureau Man. SIRKA LIISA KANKURI.

Xinhua (New China) News Agency (People's Republic of China): Hopeasalmentie 14, 00570 Helsinki; tel. (90) 687587; telex 122552; Correspondent ZHENG HUANGING.

PRESS ASSOCIATIONS

Aikakauslehtien Liitto (Periodical Publishers' Association): Lönnrotinkatu 33A 1, 00180 Helsinki; tel. (90) 603311; f. 1946; protects the interests of periodical publishers and liaises with the authorities, postal services and advertisers; organizes training courses to improve the quality of periodicals; Man. Dir OLLI KINNUNEN.

Suomen Sanomalehtimiesten Liitto (Union of Journalists): Yrjönkatu 11A, 00120 Helsinki; f. 1921; 7,600 mems; Pres. ANTERO LAINE; Sec.-Gen. EILA HYPPÖNEN.

Sanomalehtien Liitto—Tidningarnas Förbund (Newspaper Publishers' Association): Kalevankatu 4, 00100 Helsinki; tel. (90) 607786; telex 123990; f. 1908; negotiates newsprint prices, postal rates; represents the press in relations with government and advertisers; undertakes technical research; 107 mems; Man. Dir VEIKKO LÖYTTYNIEMI.

Publishers

Gummerus Publishers: Mannerheimintie 6A, POB 479, 00101 Helsinki; tel. (90) 644301; telex 123727; f. 1872; fiction, non-fiction, juvenile and reference books; Man. Dir RISTO LEHMUSOKSA.

Holger Schildts Förlagsaktiebolag: Nylandsgatan 17, 00120 Helsinki; tel. (90) 604892; f. 1913; all subjects in Swedish only; Man. Dir STIG-BJÖRN NYBERG.

Karisto Oy: Paroistentie 2, POB 102, 13101 Hämeenlinna; tel. (917) 161551; telex 2348; f. 1900; non-fiction and fiction; Man. Dir SIMO MOISIO.

Kirjayhtymä Oy: Eerikinkatu 28, 00180 Helsinki; tel. (90) 6944522; f. 1958; fiction, non-fiction, textbooks; Man. Dir OLLI ARRAKOSKI; Publishing Dir K. IMMONEN.

Kustannusosakeyhtiö Kansanvalta: Paasivuorenkatu 3, 00530 Helsinki; tel. (90) 701041; telex 124433; f. 1918; Social Democratic publishing company; publishes newspaper *Demari*; Dir RISTO UOSUKAINEN.

Kustannusosakeyhtiö Otava: Uudenmaankatu 10, 00120 Helsinki; tel. (90) 19961; telex 124560; f. 1890; non-fiction, fiction, science, juvenile, textbooks and encyclopaedias; Chair. HEIKKI A. REENPÄÄ; Man. Dir OLLI REENPÄÄ.

Kustannusosakeyhtiö Tammi: Eerikinkatu 28, 00180 Helsinki; tel. (90) 6942700; telex 125482; f. 1943; fiction, non-fiction, juvenile; Man. Dir OLLI ARRAKOSKI.

Sanoma Corporation: POB 240, 00101 Helsinki; tel. (90) 1221; telex 122772; f. 1889; publishes daily newspapers *Helsingin Sanomat* and *Ilta-Sanomat*; also magazines and books, cable television and electronic publishing; Chair. AATOS ERKKO; Man. Dir JAAKKO RAURAMO.

Söderström & Co. Förlags Ab: Wavulinsvägen 4, 00210 Helsinki; tel. (90) 6923681; f. 1891; all subjects in Swedish only; Man. Dir CARL APPELBERG.

Weilin ja Göös: Ahertajantie 5, 02100 Espoo; tel. 43771; telex 122597; f. 1872; fiction, non-fiction, reference books, juvenile, textbooks, software; Dir OLLE KOSKINEN.

Werner Söderström Osakeyhtiö: Bulevardi 12, 00120 Helsinki; tel. (90) 61681; telex 122644; f. 1878; fiction and non-fiction, science,

FINLAND

juvenile, textbooks, movies, graphic industry; Man. Dir ANTERO SILJOLA.

Government Printing Centre

Valtion Painatuskeskus: Hakuninmaantie 2, POB 516, 00101 Helsinki; tel. (90) 56601; telex 123458; f. 1859; Man. Dir OLAVI PERILÄ.

PUBLISHERS' ASSOCIATION

Suomen Kustannusyhdistys: Merimiehenkatu 12A 6, 00150 Helsinki; tel. (90) 179185; f. 1858; Chair. ANTERO SILJOLA; Sec. VEIKKO SONNINEN; 57 mems.

Radio and Television

In 1987 there were an estimated 3,500,000 radio receivers in use, and 1,842,922 television licences. Some 130,000 homes are linked to cable television in Finland.

Office of the Director-General of Posts and Telecommunications: POB 1001, 00101 Helsinki; tel. (90) 1954004; telex 122695; Dir-Gen. P. TARJANNE.

Oy Yleisradio Ab (YLE) (Finnish Broadcasting Company): Kesäkatu 2, 00260 Helsinki; tel. (90) 441141; telex 124735; f. 1926; state controlled since 1934, with management appointed according to the political character of Parliament; Dir-Gen. SAKARI KIURU (from 1990, REINO PAASILINNA); Dir of Admin. and Deputy Dir-Gen. JOUNI MYKKÄNEN; Dir of Radio KEIJO SAVOLAINEN; Dir of TV Programme 1 ARNE WESSBERG; Dir of TV Programme 2 TAPIO SIIKALA; Dir of Swedish Radio and TV BENGT BERGMAN; Dir of Regional Programming OLAVI PELTOLA; Dir of Engineering ERKKI LARKKA.

RADIO

Oy Yleisradio Ab (YLE) (Finnish Broadcasting Company): POB 10, 00241 Helsinki; tel. (90) 418811; telex 124735; Finnish main programme: both light and serious programmes; Finnish second programme: mainly musical and educational; Swedish programme: Swedish language and music; also regional stations, belonging to a local radio union; Foreign Service: broadcasts to Europe, Africa, the Middle and Far East and America in Finnish, Swedish, German and English.

Experimental Finnish local radio began operations in 1984, and by October 1987 38 such licences had been granted.

TELEVISION

The state operates three television channels, and broadcasting time is leased from them by commercial companies. A co-operation project between Yleisradio and the Nokia electronics company for a third television channel was approved by the Government in 1986. Regular transmissions began in September 1987. A teletext news service is operated in co-operation with Sweden and Denmark.

TV Programme 1: about 45 hours per week (commercial programmes included).
TV Programme 2: about 40 hours per week (commercial programmes included).
TV Programme 3: about 50 hours per week (commercial).

Oy Yleisradio Ab (YLE) (Finnish Broadcasting Company): Programme 1: POB 10, 00241 Helsinki; tel. (90) 418811; telex 121270; Programme 2: Tohlopinranta 12, 33270 Tampere; tel. 445445; telex 22176.

MTV Oy: Ilmalantori 2, 00240 Helsinki; tel. (90) 15001; telex 125144; f. 1957; independent commercial TV company producing programmes on both channels; about 21 hours per week; Pres. EERO PILKAMA.

Finance

The Bank of Finland is the country's central bank and the centre of Finland's monetary and banking system. It functions 'under guarantee and supervision of Parliament and the Bank supervisors delegated by Parliament'.

There are four deposit bank groups in Finland: commercial banks, savings banks, co-operative banks and Postipankki Ltd. The total number of branches in 1987 was more than 3,500.

The commercial banks constitute the most important group of deposit banks. At the end of 1987 there were 10 commercial banks, with a total of 940 offices. Two of these banks are national, and four are foreign-owned.

The savings banks and co-operative banks are regional, providing mainly local banking services. At 31 December 1987 there were 230 savings banks, with 1,315 branch offices, and 369 co-operative banks, with 1,223 branch offices. Postipankki had 57 branch offices. In addition, 2,930 post offices handled certain Postipankki operations.

There are eight mortgage banks operating in Finland, and several special credit institutions. The insurance institutions, of which 56 are private companies, granted credits in 1985. Finance companies, development companies and other special institutions have also joined the money-market.

BANKING

(cap. = capital; p.u. = paid up; dep. = deposits; m. = million; res = reserves; brs = branches; amounts in markkaa)

Central Bank

Suomen Pankki/Finlands Bank (The Bank of Finland): Snellmaninaukio, POB 160, 00171 Helsinki; tel. (90) 1831; telex 121224; f. 1811; Bank of Issue under the guarantee and supervision of Parliament; cap. and res 6,335m. (Aug. 1987); Gov. ROLF KULLBERG; 12 brs.

Commercial and Mortgage Banks

Kansallisluottopankki Oy (Kansallis Mortgage Bank Ltd): Erottajankatu 19B, 00130 Helsinki; tel. (90) 1631; f. 1985; cap. and res 110m. (1987); Chair. JAAKKO LASSILA; Man. Dir EERO HERTTOLA.

Kansallis-Osake-Pankki: Aleksanterinkatu 42, POB 10, 00101 Helsinki; tel. (90) 1631; telex 124412; f. 1889; cap. and res 6,639m., dep. 53,077m. (Aug. 1988); Chair. AATOS ERKKO; Chief Gen. Man. JAAKKO LASSILA; 468 brs.

Midland Montagu Osakepankki: Eteläesplanadi 22A, 00130 Helsinki; tel. (90) 601766; telex 124210; f. 1986; owned by Midland Bank Group; cap. p.u. 70m.; Chair. ANTHONY ARFWEDSON; Man. Dir JUSSI OSOLA.

Mortgage Bank of Finland Ltd: Eteläesplanadi 8, 00130 Helsinki; tel. (90) 650066; telex 121840; f. 1956; subsidiary of Postipankki Ltd; cap. 285m. (Dec. 1987); Chair. SEPPO LINDBLOM; Man. Dir ILPO NIITTI.

OKO—Investointipankki Oy (OKO—Mortgage Bank Ltd): Malminkatu 30, 00100 Helsinki; tel. (90) 4041; telex 124714; f. 1916; cap. and res 221m. (Dec. 1987); Chair. PAULI KOMI; Man. Dir. OSSIAN ANTSON.

Okobank (Osuuspankkien Keskuspankki Oy) (Central Bank of the Co-operative Banks of Finland Ltd): Arkadiankatu 23, 00100 Helsinki; tel. (90) 4041; telex 124714; f. 1902; cap. and res 1,934m., dep. 1,689m. (Aug. 1988); Chair. of Board of Admin. ESA TIMONEN; Chair. of Board of Management PAULI KOMI; 1,224 brs.

Postipankki Oy: Unioninkatu 20, 00007 Helsinki; tel. (90) 1641; telex 121698; f. 1886, a limited company 1988; operates through its head office, 57 branches and the 2,930 local post offices; assets 63,548m., dep. 50,106m. (Dec. 1987); Chair. of Supervisory Board MATTI JAATINEN; Pres. and Chief Exec. SEPPO LINDBLOM.

PSP—Kuntapankki Oy (PSP Municipality Bank Ltd): Unioninkatu 20, 00007 Helsinki; tel. (90) 1641; telex 121428; cap. and res 36m. (Dec. 1987); Chair. SEPPO LINDBLOM; Man. Dir PERTTI MATTILA.

Skopbank (Säästöpankkien Keskus-Osake-Pankki) (Central Bank of the Finnish Savings Banks): Mikonkatu 4, POB 400, 00101 Helsinki; tel. (90) 13341; telex 122284; f. 1908; cap. and res 2,734m., dep. 1,211m. (Dec. 1987); Chair. and Chief Gen. Man. MATTI ALI-MELKKILÄ; Man. Dir CHRISTOPHER WEGELIUS.

Suomen Hypoteekkiyhdistys (Mortgage Society of Finland): Yrjönkatu 9, POB 509, 00101 Helsinki; tel. (90) 647401; telex 123646; f. 1860; cap. and res 82m. (Dec. 1987); Pres. RISTO PIEPPONEN.

Suomen Kiinteistöpankki Oy (Finnish Real Estate Bank Ltd): Erottajankatu 7A, POB 428, 00101 Helsinki; tel. (90) 13341; telex 122284; f. 1907; cap. 70m., res 4m. (Aug. 1988); Pres. PAAVO PEKKANEN; Man. Dir TOIVO IHO.

Suomen Teollisuuspankki Oy (Industrial Bank of Finland Ltd): Fabianinkatu 8, 00130 Helsinki; tel. (90) 177521; telex 121839; f. 1924; cap. and res 371m. (Dec. 1987); Chair. AHTI HIRVONEN; Man. Dir JUHANI ERMA.

Suomen Yhdyspankki Oy/Föreningsbanken i Finland Ab (Union Bank of Finland Ltd): Aleksanterinkatu 30, POB 868, 00101 Helsinki; tel. (90) 1651; telex 124407; f. 1862; mem. of Scandinavian Banking Partners; cap. and res 7,596m., dep. 92,766m. (Dec. 1987); Chair. and Chief Exec. MIKA TIIVOLA; 449 brs.

Banking Associations

Osuuspankkien Keskusliitto r.y. (Central Union of the Co-operative Banks): Arkadiankatu 23, 00100 Helsinki; tel. (90) 4041; f. 1928; in 1988 there were 367 co-operative banks (1,221 offices) with a membership of 630,000; Man. Dir TAISTO JOENSUU.

Pankkien neuvottelukunta (Joint Delegation of Finnish Banks): POB 319, 00131 Helsinki; tel. (90) 629712; Chair. MATTI ALI-MELKKILÄ.

FINLAND

Suomen Pankkiyhdistys r.y. (Finnish Bankers' Association): Kansakoulukatu 1A, POB 1007, 00101 Helsinki; tel. (90) 6948422; f. 1914; Chair. MIKA TIIVOLA; Man. Dir MATTI SIPILÄ.

Suomen Säästöpankkiliitto (Finnish Savings Bank Association): Pohjoisesplanadi 35A, 00100 Helsinki; tel. (90) 13341; telex 125768; f. 1906; 230 mems; 1,315 offices; Chair. MATTI ALI-MELKKILÄ; Man. Dir KALEVI KAUNISKANGAS.

STOCK EXCHANGE

Helsinki Stock Exchange: Fabianinkatu 14, POB 429, 00101 Helsinki; tel. (90) 624161; telex 123460; f. 1912; Chair. of Supervisory Bd MIKA TIIVOLA; Chair of Bd of Dirs VESA VAINIO; Pres. MATTI MÄENPÄÄ.

INSURANCE

EFFOA-yhtymän Keskinäinen Vakuutusyhtiö (Effoa Gp Mutual Insurance Co): Eteläranta 8, POB 290, 00131 Helsinki; tel. (90) 179933; telex 121410; f. 1942; insurance for Effoa-Finland Steamship Co; marine; Chair. MAX OKER-BLOM.

Finnish Marine Insurance Co Ltd/Suomen Merivakuutus Osakeyhtiö: Melkonkatu 22A, 00210 Helsinki; tel. (90) 6927166; telex 121013; f. 1898; Man. Dir CARL-HENRIK LUNDELL.

Kansa Group: Hämeentie 33, POB 78, 00501 Helsinki; tel. (90) 73161; telex 122209; f. 1919; insurance, reinsurance, pensions, finance; Pres. and Chief Exec. MATTI PACKALÉN.

Keskeytysvakuutusosakeyhtiö Otso (Otso Loss of Profits Insurance Co Ltd): Bulevardi 10, POB 00121 Helsinki; tel. (90) 68071; telex 121061; f. 1939; non-life; Gen. Man. MAGNUS NORDLING.

Keskinäinen Vakuutusyhtiö Palonvara (Palonvara Mutual Insurance Co): Rautatienkatu 19, 15110 Lahti; tel. (918) 52261; f. 1912; non-life; Man. Dir JUHANI SORRI.

Keskinäinen Vakuutusyhtiö Tulenvara (Tulenvara Mutual Insurance Co): Porkkalankatu 3, 00180 Helsinki; tel. (90) 13211; telex 124633; f. 1947; non-life; Man. Dir YRJÖ PESSI.

Keskinäinen yhtiö Yrittäjäinvakuutus-Fennia (Enterprise-Fennia Mutual Insurance Co): Asemamiehenkatu 3, 00520 Helsinki; tel. (90) 15031; telex 121280; f. 1928; non-life; Man. Dir KARI ELO.

Lähivakuutus Keskinäinen Yhtiö (Local Mutual Insurance Co): Annankatu 25, 00100 Helsinki; tel. (90) 12941; f. 1917; Gen. Man. SIMO CASTRÉN.

Meijerien Keskinäinen Vakuutusyhtiö (Dairies' Mutual Insurance Co): Meijeritie 6, POB 68, 00371 Helsinki; tel. (90) 5681; f. 1920; Gen. Man. KEIJO RAUTIO.

Osuuspankkien Keskinäinen Vakuutusyhtiö (Mutual Insurance Co of the Co-operative Banks): Temppelikatu 6B, POB 308, 00101 Helsinki; tel. (90) 4041; f. 1964; non-life; Gen. Man. ASKO KUTVONEN.

Patria Group: Vattuniemenkuja 8A, POB 12, 00211 Helsinki; tel. (90) 69611; telex 124832; f. 1881; non-life, reinsurance; Man. Dir CARL-OLAF HOMÉN.

Pohjola Group: Lapinmäentie 1, 00300 Helsinki; tel. (90) 5591; telex 124556; marine, life and non-life insurance, reinsurance; Chair. and Man. Dir PENTTI TALONEN.

Sampo Group: Yliopistonkatu 27, POB 216, 20101 Turku; tel. (921) 663311; telex 62242; life, non-life, pensions, reinsurance; Man. Dir KAUKO PIHLAVA.

Svensk-Finland Ömsesidiga Försäkringsbolaget (Svensk-Finland Mutual Insurance Co): Malminkatu 20, POB 549, 00101 Helsinki; tel. (90) 6944122; telex 125093; f. 1925; non-life; Man. Dir PER-IVAR GUSTAFSSON.

Säästöpankkien Keskinäinen Vakuutusyhtiö (Savings Banks' Mutual Insurance Co): Iso Roobertinkatu 4-6, POB 154, 00121 Helsinki; tel. (90) 18271; f. 1971; Gen. Man. JUHANI LAINE.

Tapiola Insurance Group: Revontulentie 7, POB 30, 02101 Espoo; tel. (90) 4531; telex 121073; life, non-life, livestock, pensions, reinsurance; Chair. and Man. Dir ASMO KALPALA.

Vakuutusosakeyhtiö Pankavara (Pankavara Insurance Co Ltd): Kanavaranta 1, POB 309, 00101 Helsinki; tel. (90) 16291; telex 121438; f. 1943; non-life; Man. Dir VELI KORPI.

Varma Group: Annankatu 18A, POB 175, 00121 Helsinki; tel. (90) 61651; telex 125415; f. 1919; pensions, life, non-life, reinsurance; Man. Dir JUHANI KOLEHMAINEN.

Verdandi Group: Olavintie 2, POB 133, 20101 Turku; tel. (921) 690011; telex 62601; life, pensions, reinsurance; Man. Dir KURT LJUNGMAN.

Wärtsilän Keskinäinen Vakuutusyhtiö (Wärtsilä Mutual Insurance Co): John Stenbergin ranta 2, 00530 Helsinki; tel. (90) 70951; telex 124623; f. 1943; non-life; Gen. Man. MARTTI ALOPAEUS.

Insurance Associations

Federation of Accident Insurance Institutions: Bulevardi 28, 00120 Helsinki; tel. (90) 19251; telex 123511; f. 1920; Man. Dir TAPANI MIETTINEN.

Federation of Employment Pension Institutions: Lastenkodinkuja 1, 00180 Helsinki; tel. (90) 6940122; f. 1964; Man. Dir PENTTI KOSTAMO.

Federation of Finnish Insurance Companies: Bulevardi 28, 00120 Helsinki; tel. (90) 19251; telex 123511; f. 1942; Chair. PENTTI TALONEN; Man. Dir MATTI L. AHO; 49 mems.

Finnish Atomic Insurance Pool, Finnish Pool of Aviation Insurers, Finnish General Reinsurance Pool: Bulevardi 10, 00120 Helsinki; tel. (90) 61691; telex 121061; Man. Dir K.-M. STRÖMMER.

Finnish Marine Underwriters' Association: Bulevardi 28, 00120 Helsinki; tel. (90) 19251; telex 123511; f. 1956; Man. Dir LARS BECKMAN.

Finnish Motor Insurers' Bureau: Bulevardi 28, 00120 Helsinki; tel. (90) 19251; telex 123511; f. 1938; Man. Dir PENTTI AJO.

Insurance Rehabilitation Agency: Asemamiehenkatu 3, 00520 Helsinki; tel. (90) 15041; f. 1964; joint bureau of the Finnish carriers of employment accident insurance, motor insurance and pension insurance, to carry out vocational rehabilitation as part of the insurance compensation; Man. Dir RISTO SEPPÄLÄINEN.

Trade and Industry

CHAMBERS OF COMMERCE

Central Chamber of Commerce (Keskuskauppakamari): Fabianinkatu 14, POB 1000, 00101 Helsinki; tel. (90) 650133; telex 123814; f. 1918; Pres. JAAKKO LASSILA; Gen. Man. MATTI AURA; 23 local chambers of commerce represented by 8 mems each on Board.

Finnish Foreign Trade Association: Arkadiankatu 4-6B, POB 908, 00101 Helsinki; tel. (90) 69591; telex 121696; f. 1919; Chair. KARI KAIRAMO; Chair. of Board TIMO RELANDER; Man. Dir PERTTI HUITU.

Helsinki Chamber of Commerce: Kalevankatu 12, 00100 Helsinki; tel. (90) 644601; f. 1917; Pres. PENTTI KIVINEN; Man. Dir HEIKKI HELIÖ; 3,600 mems.

TRADE AND INDUSTRIAL ORGANIZATIONS

E-osuuskunta Eka (Eka Co-operative Society): Hämeentie 19, 00500 Helsinki; tel. (90) 7331; telex 124454; f. 1983 as a merger of 40 co-operatives; Pres. EINO MALINEN.

Enigheten Centrallaget (Butter and Cheese Export): Päiväläisentie 2, 00390 Helsinki; tel. (90) 5624188; telex 122835; Chair. and Man. Dir B. LEMBERG; 10 mems.

Finnish Cabinet Makers' and Wood Turners' Association: P. Esplanadikatu 25A, Helsinki; f. 1944; Man. Dir JUHO SAVIO.

Finnish Joinery Association: P. Esplanadikatu 25A, Helsinki; Man. Dir JUHO SAVIO.

Hankkija Group: POB 80, 00101 Helsinki; tel. (90) 7291; telex 124660; f. 1905; agricultural produce and supplies, farm machinery, engineering, food technology, construction, automobiles; Chair. and Chief Exec. PERTTI TUOMALA.

Kalatalouden Keskusliitto (Federation of Fisheries Associations): Köydenpunojankatu 7B 23, 00180 Helsinki; tel. (90) 640126; f. 1891; Sec. H. HOKKA; 398,000 mems.

Kaukomarkkinat Oy: Kutojantie 4, 02631 Espoo; tel. (90) 5211; telex 124469; f. 1947; international trade; Pres. JUHANI RIUTTA.

Kesko Oy (Retailers' Wholesale Co): Satamakatu 3, 00160 Helsinki; tel. (90) 1981; telex 124748; f. 1941; retailer-owned wholesale corporation, trading in foodstuffs, textiles, shoes, consumer goods, agricultural and builders' supplies, and machinery; Pres. ECRO UTTER.

Kotimaisen Työn Liitto (Association for Domestic Work): Bulevardi 5A, POB 177, 00121 Helsinki; tel. (90) 645733; f. 1978; public relations for Finnish products and for Finnish work; Chair. of Council ILKKA SUOMINEN; Chair. of Board of Dirs TIMO PELTOLA; Man. Dir RAUNO BISTER; about 1,500 mems.

Kulutusosuustoiminnan Keskusliitto (KK) r.y. (Central Union of Consumer Co-operation): Hämeentie 19, POB 72, 00501 Helsinki; tel. (90) 7331; telex 124454; f. 1916; Chair. VÄINÖ HAKALA; Sec.-Gen. KALEVI SUOMELA; 65 mem. societies with 640,000 individuals.

Oy Labor Ab (Agricultural Machinery): Mikkolantie 1, 00640 Helsinki; tel. (90) 7291; telex 124660; f. 1898; Gen. Man. KIMMO VARJOVAARA.

Maataloustuottajain Keskusliitto (Central Union of Agricultural Producers): Simonkatu 6, 00100 Helsinki; tel. (90) 131151; telex 122474; f. 1917; Chair. of Board of Dirs HEIKKI HAAVISTO; Sec.-Gen. ESKO LINDSTEDT; 310,652 mems.

FINLAND

Munakunta (Co-operative Egg Producers' Association): POB 43, 00721 Helsinki; tel. (90) 372755; telex 1001079; f. 1921; Chair. and Man. Dir TUOMO YLI-KETOLA; 4,920 mems.

Pellervo-Seura (Pellervo Society): Simonkatu 6, 00100 Helsinki; tel. (90) 69551; f. 1899; central organization of farmers' co-operatives; Man. Dir AARNE HAKALA; 780 mem. societies (incl. 8 central co-operative societies).

Suomen Betoniteollisuuden Keskusjärjestö r.y. (Association of the Concrete Industry of Finland): Iso Roobertinkatu 30, 00120 Helsinki; tel. (90) 648212; telex 121394; f. 1929; Chair. EERO NIEMINEN; Man. Dir ERKKI ANTTILA; 66 mems.

Suomen Metsäteollisuuden Keskusliitto r.y. (Central Association of Finnish Forest Industries): Eteläesplanadi 2, 00130 Helsinki; tel. (90) 13261; telex 121823; f. 1918; Chair. CARL G. BJÖRNBERG; Man. Dir MATTI PEKKANEN; mems: 61 companies in the forestry industry and the following sales or trade associations:

Converta (Finnish Paper and Board Converters' Association): Fabianinkatu 9, POB 35, 00131 Helsinki; tel. (90) 661316; telex 124622; f. 1944; Man. Dir ANTTI RISLAKKI; 9 mems.

Finnboard (Finnish Board Mills Association): Eteläesplanadi 2, POB 36, 00131 Helsinki; tel. (90) 13251; telex 121460; f. 1943; Man. Dir JARL H. F. KÖHLER; 12 mems.

Finncell (Finnish Pulp Exporters' Association): Eteläesplanadi 2, POB 60, 00101 Helsinki; tel. (90) 18051; telex 124459; f. 1918; Man. Dir T. NYKOPP; 8 mems.

Finnpap (Finnish Paper Mills' Association): Eteläesplanadi 2, POB 380, 00101 Helsinki; tel. (90) 13241; telex 124429; f. 1918; marketing organization for the paper industry; Man. Dir THOMAS NYSTÉN; 10 mems.

Suomen Kuitulevy-yhdistys (Finnish Wood Fibre Panel Association—FFA): Opastinsilta 8B B, 00520 Helsinki; tel. (90) 141122; telex 124858; f. 1953, reorganized 1960; Man. Dir A. PENTINSAARI; 4 mems.

Suomen Lastulevy-yhdistys (Finnish Particle Board Association): Opastinsilta 8B B, 00520 Helsinki; tel. (90) 141122; telex 124858; Man. Dir PENTTI SAARRO; 5 mems.

Suomen Sahanomistajayhdistys (Finnish Sawmill Owners' Association): Fabianinkatu 29C, 00100 Helsinki; tel. (90) 661801; telex 121851; f. 1895; Man. Dir PEKKA SNÄLL; 27 mems.

Suomen Vaneriyhdistys (Association of Finnish Plywood Industry): Opastinsilta 8B B, 00520 Helsinki; f. 1939; Man. Dir ERIK LINDSTRÖM; 7 mems.

Suomen Osuuskauppojen Keskusliitto (SOKL) (Finnish Co-operative Union): Vilhonkatu 7, 00100 Helsinki; tel. (90) 1881; telex 121341; f. 1908; Chair. SEPPO TÖRMÄLÄ; 79 mems.

Suomen Teknillinen Kauppaliitto (Finnish Technical Traders Association): Mannerheimintie 14B, 00100 Helsinki; f. 1918; organization of the main importers dealing in iron, steel, and non-ferrous metals, machines and equipment, heavy chemicals and raw materials; Chair. K. KUOSMANEN; Man. Dir KLAUS VARTIOVAARA; 67 mems.

Svenska Lantbruksproducenternas Centralförbund (Union of Swedish Agricultural Producers): Fredriksgatan 61, 00100 Helsinki; f. 1945; Swedish-speaking producers; Chair. O. ROSENDAHL; 21,472 mems.

Teknisen Tukkukaupan Keskusliitto (TTK) (Central Federation of Technical Wholesale Traders): Mannerheimintie 14B, 00100 Helsinki; 10 branch asscns with 250 mems.

Tukkukaupan Keskusliitto (Federation of Wholesalers and Importers): Mannerheimintie 76A, 00250 Helsinki; f. 1988 to replace previous Association (f. 1920); Man. Dir GUY WIRES; 24 mem. asscns with over 800 firms.

Tuottajain Lihakeskuskunta (Farmers' Central Meat Administration): Vanha talvitie 5, 00500 Helsinki; tel. (90) 717911; telex 124813; f. 1936; Pres. VOITTO KOSKENMÄKI; 7 mem. co-operatives.

Valio Finnish Co-operative Dairies' Association: POB 390, 00101 Helsinki; tel. (90) 5681; telex 123-427; f. 1905; Man. Dir IIKKA HAKA; 134 mems (dairies).

EMPLOYERS' ORGANIZATIONS

Liiketyönantajain Keskusliitto (LTK) r.y. (Confederation of Service Industries): Eteläranta 10, POB 30, 00131 Helsinki; tel. (90) 17281; f. 1945; seven mem. asscns consisting of about 7,100 enterprises with about 300,000 employees; Chair. PENTTI KIVINEN; Man. Dir JARMO PELLIKKA.

Suomen Työnantajain Keskusliitto (STK) (Finnish Employers' Confederation): Eteläranta 10, POB 30, 00131 Helsinki; tel. (90) 17281; telex 124635; f. 1907 to safeguard the interests of its member enterprises by negotiating and signing collective agreements and by influencing general decisions which affect business life; comprises 28 branch asscns consisting of about 6,300 enterprises employing about 625,000 employees. Chair. KRISTER AHLSTRÖM; Dir-Gen. TAPANI KAHRI.

Autoalan Työnantajaliitto r.y. (Federation of Motor Vehicle Trade Employers): Liisankatu 21B 11, 00170 Helsinki; tel. (90) 171410; Chair. ROLF EHRNROOTH; Man. Dir LEO GYLDÉN; 407 mems.

Autoliikenteen Työnantajaliitto r.y. (Employers' Federation of Road Transport): Nuijamiestentie 7A, 00400 Helsinki; tel. (90) 585022; Chair. JUHANI HEIKKILÄ; Man. Dir HANNU PARVELA; 526 mems.

Autonrengasliitto r.y. (Tyre Federation): Nordenskiöldinkatu 6A 1, 00250 Helsinki; tel. (90) 492054; f. 1944; Chair. HEIKKI HELENIUS; Man. Dir AIMO WASENIUS; 61 mems, 12 assoc. mems.

Elintarviketeollisuuden Työnantajiliitto r.y. (Food Industry Employers' Association): Eteläranta 10, 00130 Helsinki; tel. (90) 172841; Chair. PETER FAZER; Man. Dir PEKKA HÄMÄLÄINEN; 462 mems.

Graafisen Teollisuuden Työnantajaliitto (Employers' Association of the Graphic Arts Industries): Lönnrotinkatu 11A, 00120 Helsinki; tel. (90) 602911; Chair. JAAKKO RAURAMO; Man. Dir MATTI SUTINEN; 430 mems.

Kemianteollisuuden Työnantajalitto r.y. (Chemical Industry Employers' Association): Eteläranta 10, 00130 Helsinki; tel. (90) 172841; Chair. YRJÖ PESSI; Man. Dir MARTTI NISKANEN; 200 mems.

Kenkäteollisuuden Työnantajaliitto r.y. (Employers' Association of the Footwear Industry): Eteläranta 10, 00130 Helsinki; tel. (90) 172841; Chair. ESKO HEINO; Man. Dir JUHANI SALONIUS; 50 mems.

Konttorikoneliikkeiden Yhdistys r.y. (Association of Office Machine Traders): Mariankatu 26B 5, 00170 Helsinki; tel. (90) 656667; Chair. TOM HYNNINEN; Man. Dir KALLE-VEIKKO HAVAS; 133 mems.

Kultaseppien Työnantajaliitto r.y. (Employers' Association of Goldsmiths): Eteläranta 10, 00130 Helsinki; tel. (90) 172841; Chair. and Man. Dir JORMA NURMI; 31 mems.

Metalliteollisuuden Työnantajaliitto (Metal Industries Employers' Association): Eteläranta 10, 00130 Helsinki; tel. (90) 19231; telex 124997; f. 1903; Chair. REIJO KAUKONON; Man. Dir HARRI MALMBERG; 850 mems.

Metsäteollisuuden Työnantajaliitto r.y. (Employers' Association of Forest Industries): Fabianinkatu 9A, POB 5, 00131 Helsinki; tel. (90) 174877; telex 122986; Chair. OLLI PAROLA; Man. Dir MAURI MOREN; 116 mems.

Nahkateollisuuden Työnantajaliitto r.y. (Employers' Association of the Leather Industry): Eteläranta 10, 00130 Helsinki; tel. (90) 172841; Chair. PERTTI HELLEMAA; Man. Dir JUHANI SALONIUS; 37 mems.

Puhelinlaitosten Työnantajaliitto (Employers' Association of Telephone Companies): Yrjönkatu 13A V, 00120 Helsinki; tel. (90) 642811; telex 124845; Chair. ERKKI RIPATTI; 51 mems.

Puusepänteollisuuden Liitto r.y. (Employers' Association of the Furniture and Joinery Industries): Fabianinkatu 9A, 00130 Helsinki; tel. (90) 174877; f. 1917; Chair. RAIMO VAARA; Man. Dir ARTO TÄHTINEN; 125 mems.

Rannikko- ja Sisävesiliikenteen Työnantajaliitto (RASILA) r.y. (Employers' Federation of Coastal and Inland Waterways Transportation): see under Shipping.

Sähkötyönantajain Liitto r.y. (Employers' Association of Electrical Contractors): Yrjönkatu 13A, 00120 Helsinki; tel. (90) 642811; telex 124845; Chair. MARKKU JÄRVINEN; Man. Dir MATTI HÖYSTI; 220 mems.

Suomen Kiinteistöliitto r.y. (Finnish Real-Estate Association): Annankatu 24, 00100 Helsinki; tel. (90) 641331; f. 1907; Chair. SEPPO HIETA; Man. Dir UKKO LAURILA; 41 mems.

Suomen Konsulttitoimistojen Liitto (SKOL) r.y. (Finnish Association of Consulting Firms—SKOL): Pohjantie 12A, 02100 Espoo; tel. (90) 460122; Chair. ANTTI SÄÄSKILAHTI; Man. Dir TIMO MYLLYS; 200 mems.

Suomen Lasitus- ja Hiomoliitto r.y. (Finnish Glass Dealers' and Glaziers' Association): P. Hesperiankatu 11B 10, 00260 Helsinki; tel. (90) 441100; Chair. and Man. Dir MARTTI LINDBLOM; 153 mems.

Suomen Lastauttajain Liitto (SLL) r.y. (Finnish Association of Stevedores): Köydenpunojankatu 8, 00180 Helsinki; tel. (90) 6949800; telex 122977; f. 1906; Chair. JUHANI FORSS; Man. Dir JAN-ERIK EHRSTRÖM; 38 mems.

Suomen Rakennusteollisuusliitto r.y. (Federation of the Finnish Building Industry): Unioninkatu 14 VI, 00130 Helsinki; tel. (90) 12991; telex 125321; f. 1946; Chair. HANNO ISOTALO; Man. Dir MATTI LOUKOLA; 1,974 mems.

FINLAND

Suomen Tiiliteollisuusliitto r.y. (Finnish Brick Industry Association): Laturinkuja 2, 02600 Espoo; tel. (90) 519133; Chair. Leo Seppälä; Man. Dir Jukka Suonio; 13 mems.

Suomen Varustamoyhdistys r.y. (Finnish Shipowners' Association): see under Shipping.

Tekstiiliteollisuusliitto (Association of Textile Industries): Aleksis Kiven katu 10, 33210 Tampere; tel. (931) 32277; f. 1905; Chair. Matti Vainio; Man. Dir Matti Järventie; 140 mems.

Työnantajain Yleinen Ryhmä (Employers' General Group): Eteläranta 10, 00130 Helsinki; tel. (90) 172841; telex 124665; Chair. Harry Mildh; Gen. Dir Juhani Salonius; 540 mems.

Vaatetusteollisuuden Työnantajaliitto r.y. (Clothing Industry Employers' Federation): Eteläranta 10, 00130 Helsinki; tel. (90) 172841; Chair. Seppo Hyyppä; Man. Dir Juhani Salonius; 169 mems.

Voimalaitosrakentajain Liitto (Association of Power Plant Builders): Yrjönkatu 13A V, 00120 Helsinki; tel. (90) 642811; telex 124845; Chair. Erkki Laasko; Man. Dir Matti Höysti; 18 mems.

Voimalaitosten Työnantajaliitto r.y. (Employers' Association of Electrical Contractors): Yrjönkatu 13A V, 00120 Helsinki; tel. (90) 642811; telex 124845; f. 1945; Chair. Kalevi Numminen; Man. Dir Matti Höysti; 93 mems.

TRADE UNIONS

Suomen Ammattiliittojen Keskusjärjestö (SAK) r.y. (Central Organization of Finnish Trade Unions): Siltasaarenkatu 3A, 00530 Helsinki; tel. (90) 77211; telex 122346; f. 1907; 27 affiliated unions; 1,066,790 mems (1986); Pres. Pertti Viinanen; Vice-Pres Aarno Aitamurto, Raimo Kantola; Secs Pekka Ahmavaara, Lauri Ihalainen.

Principal affiliated unions (membership of over 5,000):

Auto- ja Kuljetusalan Työntekijäliitto (AKT) r.y. (Transport Workers): Haapaniemenkatu 7-9B, 00530 Helsinki; tel. (90) 70911; f. 1948; Pres. Risto Kuisma; Secs Kauko Lehikoinen, Leo Roppola; 43,148 mems.

Hotelli- ja Ravintolahenkilökunnan Liitto (HRHL) r.y. (Hotel and Restaurant Workers): Toinen Linja 3, 00530 Helsinki; tel. (90) 77561; f. 1933; Pres. Matti Haapakoski; Sec. Jorma Kallio; 46,890 mems.

Kemian Työntekijäin Liitto r.y. (Chemical Workers): Haapaniemenkatu 7-9B, 00530 Helsinki; tel. (90) 70911; f. 1970; Pres. Heikki Pohja; Sec. Mikko Kulmala; 20,828 mems.

Kiinteistötyöntekijäin Liitto r.y. (Caretakers): Viherniemenkatu 5A, 00530 Helsinki; tel. (90) 750075; f. 1948; Pres. Matti Sikanen; Sec. Tauno Rosten; 12,000 mems.

Kumi- ja Nahkatyöväen Liitto (KNL) r.y. (Rubber and Leather Workers): Siltasaarenkatu 4, 00530 Helsinki; tel. (90) 750044; f. 1897; Pres. Hilkka Häkkilä; Sec. Kalevi Urpelainen; 14,804 mems.

Kunnallisten työntekijäin ja viranhaltijain liitto (KTV) r.y. (Municipal Workers and Employees): Kolmas linja 4, 00530 Helsinki; tel. (90) 77031; f. 1931; Pres. Pekka Salonen; 200,000 mems.

Lasi- ja Posliinityöväen Liitto r.y. (Glass and Porcelain Workers): Haapaniemenkatu 7-9B, POB 319, 00531 Helsinki; tel. (90) 70911; f. 1906; Pres. Risto Sainio; Sec. Toivo Partanen; 5,025 mems.

Liikealan ammattiliitto r.y. (Commercial Employees): Siltasaarenkatu 6, 00530 Helsinki; f. 1987; Pres. Maj-Len Remahl; Secs Nils Komi, Jarmo Koski; 120,000 mems.

Maaseututyöväen Liitto r.y. (Forest and Agricultural Workers): Haapaniemenkatu 7-9B, 00530 Helsinki; tel. (90) 70911; f. 1945; Pres. Matti Putkonen; Secs Raimo Lindleöf, Lauri Ainasto; 21,797 mems.

Metallityöväen Liitto r.y. (Metalworkers): Siltasaarenkatu 3A, 00530 Helsinki; tel. (90) 77071; telex 122571; f. 1899; Pres. Per-Erik Lundh; Secs Osmo Isoviita, Erik Lindfors; 149,104 mems.

Paperiliitto r.y. (Paperworkers): Pl.326, 00531 Helsinki; tel. (90) 70891; f. 1906; Pres. Antero Mäki; Gen. Sec. Artturi Pennanen; 51,373 mems.

Puutyöväen Liitto r.y. (Woodworkers): Haapaniemenkatu 7-9B, 00530 Helsinki; tel. (90) 70911; f. 1973; Pres Heikki Peltonen, Timo Rautarinta; Secs Onni Kuutsa, Kalevi Hölttä; 40,000 mems.

Rakennustyöläisten Liitto r.y. (Construction Workers): Siltasaarenkatu 4, 00530 Helsinki; tel. (90) 77021; telex 121394; f. 1930; Pres. Pekka Hynönen; Sec. Hannu Alanoja; 102,000 mems.

Suomen Elintarviketyöläisten Liitto r.y. (Food Workers): Siltasaarenkatu 6, POB 213, 00531 Helsinki; tel. (90) 717877; f. 1905; Pres. Jarl Sund; Sec. Arto Talasmäki; 39,817 mems.

Suomen Kirjatyöntekijäin Liitto r.y. (Bookworkers): Ratakatu 9, 00120 Helsinki; tel. (90) 649717; f. 1894; Pres. Pentti Levo; Sec. Pekka Lahtinen; 28,916 mems.

Suomen Merimies-Unioni r.y. (Seamen): Siltasaarenkatu 6, 00530 Helsinki; tel. (90) 716177; telex 124795; f. 1916; Pres. Reijo Anttila; Vice-Pres. Risto Ahola; Sec. Per-Erik Nelin; 9,161 mems.

Suomen Sähköalantyöntekijäin Liitto r.y. (Electricity Workers): Hämeenkatu 17A, 33200 Tampere; tel. (931) 34700; f. 1955; Pres. Seppo Salisma; Secs Paavo Talala, Heikki Varjonen; 28,909 mems.

Tekstiili- ja Vaatetustyöväen Liitto r.y. (Textile and Garment Workers): POB 87, 33101 Tampere; tel. (931) 593111; f. 1970; Pres. Tuulikki Kannisto; Secs Pirkko Oksa, Toivo Keränen; 34,000 mems.

Virkamiesten ja Työntekijäin Yhteisjärjestö (VTY) r.y. (Joint Organization of Civil Servants and Workers): Haapaniemenkatu 7-9B, 00530 Helsinki; tel. (90) 70911; f. 1946; Pres. Raimo Rannisto; Sec.-Gen. Pertti Ahonen; 106,550 mems.

Toimihenkilö- ja Virkamiesjärjestöjen Keskusliitto (TVK) r.y. (Confederation of Salaried Employees): Asemamiehenkatu 4, 00520 Helsinki; tel. (90) 1551; telex 122505; f. 1922; 14 affiliates; Chair Matti Kinnunen, Riitta Prusti; approx. 365,000 mems.

Principal affiliated unions (membership of over 5,000):

Auto- ja Konekaupan Toimihenkilöliitto (Car and Machine Commerce Employees): Hämeentie 10A, 00530 Helsinki; tel. (90) 716433; f. 1985; Chair. Erkki Mäkelä; 5,500 mems.

Erityisalojen Toimihenkilöliitto (ERTO) (Special Service and Clerical Employees): Asemamiehenkatu 2, 00520 Helsinki; tel. (90) 1551; f. 1968; Chair. Matti Hellsten; 10,000 mems.

Kunnallisvirkamiesliitto r.y. (KVL) (Municipal Officers): Asemamiehenkatu 4, 00520 Helsinki; tel. (90) 1551; f. 1918; Chair. Taisto Mursula; 58,000 mems.

Pankkitoimihenkilöliitto (Bank Employees): Ratamestarinkatu 12, 00520 Helsinki; tel. (90) 141066; f. 1931; Pres. Pauli Salmio; Sec.-Gen. Raimo Pohjaväre; 38,000 mems.

Suomen Perushoitajaliitto (Nursing Auxiliaries): Asemamiehenkatu 2, 00520 Helsinki; tel. (90) 141833; f. 1948; Chair. Salme Pihl; 31,000 mems.

Suomen Poliisien Liitto (Police): Haapaniemenkatu 7-9B, 00530 Helsinki; tel. (90) 739091; f. 1923; Chair. Timo Mikkola; 7,000 mems.

Suomen Teollisuustoimihenkilöiden Liitto (Salaried Employees in Industry): Asemamiehenkatu 4, 00520 Helsinki; tel. (90) 1551; f. 1917; Chair. Tuulikki Väliniemi; Exec. Dir Tarmo Hyvärinen; 45,000 mems.

Terveydenhuoltoalan ammattijärjestö Tehy (Health Professionals): Asemamiehenkatu 4, 00520 Helsinki; tel. (90) 1551; f. 1982; Chair. Aila Jokinen; 75,000 mems.

Vakuutusväen Liitto (Insurance Employees): Asemamiehenkatu 2, 00520 Helsinki; tel. (90) 1551; telex 122505; f. 1945; Chair. Raila Männistö; Exec. Dir Pekka Porttila; 10,000 mems.

Valtion Laitosten ja Yhtiöiden Toimihenkilöliitto (Employees in State-owned Institutions and Companies): Topparikuja 5, 00520 Helsinki; f. 1945; Chair. Eila Salminen; 14,700 mems.

Virkamiesliitto (Civil Servants): Ratamestarinkatu 11, 00520 Helsinki; tel. (90) 1551; f. 1917; Chair. Keijo Rantala; 64,000 mems.

STATE-OWNED INDUSTRIES

It has never been government policy in Finland to nationalize industries. Occasionally, however, it has been found necessary for various reasons to give substantial state aid in setting up a company and the State has retained a majority of shares in these companies. All are administered as limited companies, the State being represented on the Board of Management and at the General Meeting of Shareholders by either the relevant Minister or an official of the relevant Ministry.

Alko Ltd: Salmisaarenranta 7, POB 350, 00101 Helsinki; tel. (90) 60911; telex 121045; f. 1932; production, import, export and sale of alcoholic beverages and spirits; has monopoly of retail sale of all alcoholic beverages except medium beer; 99.9% state-owned; Chair. of Board of Dirs Heikki Koski; 2,900 employees.

Enso-Gutzeit Oy: Kanavaranta 1, 00160 Helsinki; tel. (90) 16291; telex 124438; f. 1872; wood processing, paper, chemicals, forestry, acquiring and installing hydro-electric power; 55.2% state-owned; Chair. of Board of Dirs Pentti Salmi; Pres. and Chief Exec. Jukka Härmälä; 13,444 employees.

FINLAND   *Directory*

Finnair Oy: see Civil Aviation.

Imatran Voima Oy: POB 138, 00101 Helsinki; tel. (90) 6944811; telex 124608; f. 1932; electric power, including nuclear energy; 95.6% state-owned; Pres. KALEVI NUMMINEN; Chair. of Admin. Council TAPANI MÖRTTINEN; 4,700 employees.

Kemijoki Oy: POB 457, 00101 Helsinki; tel. (90) 6944811; telex 124608; f. 1954; electric power; 77.08% state-owned; Chair. of Supervisory Board PAAVO VÄYRYNEN; Chair. of Board of Management PERTTI KIVINEN; 468 employees.

Kemira Group: Porkkalankatu 3, POB 330, 00101 Helsinki; tel. (90) 13211; telex 121191; f. 1920; 15 plants in Finland, 25 overseas; fertilizers, agricultural and industrial chemicals, biotechnical products, explosives, safety equipment, man-made fibres, paints, filters and autocatalysts; Chair. of Supervisory Board HEIKKI PERHO; Chair. of Board of Management YRJÖ PESSI; 14,000 employees.

Neste Oy: Keilaniemi, 02150 Espoo; tel. (90) 4501; telex 124641; f. 1948; oil refining, petrochemicals, plastics, industrial chemicals and lubricants, shipping, natural gas, batteries; 97.96% state-owned; (see also under Shipping); Chair. of Supervisory Board ULF SUNDQVIST; Chair. of Board of Management JAAKKO IHAMUOTILA; 5,370 employees.

Outokumpu Oy: POB 280, 00101 Helsinki; tel. (90) 4031; telex 124441; f. 1932; exploration, mining, mineral processing, metal refining and processing, equipment manufacture, engineering contracting; 81% state-owned; Chair. of Supervisory Board ERKKI LIIKANEN; Chair. of Board of Dirs and Pres. PERTTI VOUTILAINEN; 15,000 employees.

Rautaruukki Oy: Kiilakiventie 1, POB 217, 90101 Oulu; tel. (81) 327711; telex 32109; f. 1960; steel processing; 99.1% state-owned; Chair. of Supervisory Board AHTI PEKKALA; Chair. of Board of Management, Pres. MIKKO KIVIMÄKI; 7,500 employees.

Oy Sisu-Auto Ab: Ristipellontie 19, 00390 Helsinki; tel. (90) 542011; telex 121245; f. as private company in 1931; in 1975 the State bought 70% of the shares; 99.9% state-owned (1986); manufacture, marketing and maintenance of trucks, terminal tractors and defence vehicles; Chair. of Supervisory Board MATTI LUTTINEN; Chair. of Board of Management and Chief Exec. JORMA S. JERKKU; 1,200 employees.

Valmet Oy: Punanotkonkatu 2, POB 155, 00131 Helsinki; tel. (90) 13291; telex 124427; f. 1946; engineering, automation; 79.8% state-owned; Chair. of Admin. Council HARRI HOLKERI; Chair. of Board of Dirs MATTI KANKAANPÄÄ; 17,372 employees.

Valvilla Oy: POB 108, 20101 Turku; telex 62156; f. 1978; wool and cotton spinning, weaving and sales; 99.4% state-owned; Chair. of Supervisory Board BROR WAHLROOS; Chair. of Board of Management MATTI VAINIO; 850 employees.

Veitsiluoto Oy: 94830 Kemi; tel. (980) 8141; f. 1932; wood processing; 88.8% state-owned; Chair. of Supervisory Board JAAKO PAJULA; Chair. of Board of Management PENTTI O. RAUTALAHTI; 5,119 employees.

TRADE FAIRS

Osuuskunta Suomen Messut (Finnish Fair Corporation): Helsinki Fair Centre, POB 21, 00521 Helsinki; tel. (90) 15091; telex 121119; f. 1919; principal annual events: Helsinki International Boat Show, Medicine, Caravan, Skiexpo (skiing and winter tourism), Matka (Finnish International Travel Fair), Finnish Chemical Congress; biannually: Business Machines and Equipment, Elkom (professional electronics), FinnConsum (Helsinki International Trade Fair), Habitare (furniture and interior decoration), FinnBuild (Helsinki International Building Fair); every 3 years: FinnTec (Helsinki International Technical Fair), PacTec (packaging), FinnTexMa (textile industry machines and accessories), Educa (education), Transportation; every 4 years: Hepac (heating), Maxpo (construction machinery), Eltek (electrical technology); Chair. of Supervisory Board RAIMO ILASKIVI; Chair. of Admin. Board KARI O. SOHLBERG; Man. Dir MATTI HURME.

Transport

RAILWAYS

There are 5,883 km of railways, providing internal services and connections with Sweden and the USSR, and 1,445 km of track are electrified. An underground railway service has been provided by Helsinki City Transport since 1982.

Karhula Railway: Ratakatu 8, 48600 Karhula; tel. (952) 298221; f. 1937; goods transport; Man. PERTTI HONKALA; Man. of Traffic OLLI KOKKOMÄKI.

Valtionrautatiet (State Railways): Finnish State Railways' Board of Administration, Vilhonkatu 13, POB 488, 00101 Helsinki; tel. (90) 7071; telex 301151; began operating 1862; operates 5,863 km of railways; wide gauge (1,524 mm); privately-owned total 6 km; 1,636 km of route are electrified; Dir-Gen. EINO SAARINEN; Vice Dir-Gen. PANU HAAPALA.

ROADS

At 31 December 1986 there were 76,223 km of public roads, of which 205 km were motorways, 11,386 km other main roads (I and II class), 26,319 km other highways and 35,251 km local roads (excluding urban streets). In addition, there are about 53,023 km of private roads, the maintenance of which is subsidized.

Tie- ja vesirakennushallitus (Roads and Waterways Administration): POB 33, 00521 Helsinki; tel. (90) 1541; telex 124589; f. 1799; central office and 13 road and waterways districts; in charge of developing road and water traffic, including planning, constructing and maintaining roads, bridges and ferries, water channels, canals, ports and piers; Dir-Gen. JOUKO LOIKKANEN; Dir-in-Chief VÄINÖ SUONIO.

INLAND WATERWAYS

Lakes cover 31,500 sq km. The inland waterway system comprises 6,100 km of buoyed-out channels, 40 open canals and 25 lock canals. The total length of canals is 76 km. In 1986 the waterways carried about 1,766m. ton-km of goods and 0.6m. domestic passengers.

In 1963 the USSR agreed to lease to Finland the right to use the southern part of the Saimaa Canal. In the summer of 1968 the rebuilt Saimaa Canal was opened for vessels. In 1986 a total of 1,464,000 tons of goods were transported along the canal.

Tie- ja vesirakennushallitus (Roads and Waterways Administration): see Roads.

Suomen Uittajainyhdistys r.y. (Association of Finnish Floaters): POB 33, 70501 Kuopio; tel. (971) 116701; 332 mems; Chair. RISTO HYTÖNEN; Sec. ILKKA PURHONEN.

SHIPPING

The chief port of export is Kotka, where construction of a new deep harbour was due to start in the late 1980s; the main port of import is Helsinki, which has five specialized harbours. The West Harbour handles most of the transatlantic traffic, the East Harbour coastal and North Sea freight, and the South Harbour passenger traffic. North Harbour deals only in local launch traffic. Sörnäinen is the timber and coal harbour; Herttoniemi specializes in oil. Other important international ports are Turku (Åbo), Rauma and Hamina.

Associations

Rannikko- ja Sisävesiliikenteen Työnantajaliitto (RASILA) r.y. (Employers' Federation of Coastal and Inland Waterways Transportation): Satamakatu 4A, 00160 Helsinki; tel. (90) 170485; telex 122751; branch of STK (see Trade and Industry); Chair. TIMO SAARINEN; Man. Dir ILMO RINKINEN; 15 mems.

Suomen Varustamoyhdistys (Finnish Shipowners' Association): Satamakatu 4, POB 155, 00161 Helsinki; tel. (90) 170401; telex 122751; f. 1932; Chair. BO ÅBERG; Man. Dir PER FORSSKÅHL; 14 mems.

Principal Companies

Oy Bore Line Ab: Pohjoisranta 2D, Norra kajen, POB 151, 00171 Helsinki; tel. (90) 135311; telex 123503; f. 1897; routes: Baltic and North Sea cargo services; Man. Dir JARMO SALONEN.

Effoa—Finland Steamship Co Ltd: POB 290, 00130 Helsinki; tel. (90) 179933; telex 121410; f. 1883; liner and contract services: see Finncarriers; passenger services operated by Silja Line; Man. Dir ROBERT G. EHRNROOTH; fully-owned: 6 cargo vessels, 3 cruise ferries.

Etelä-Suomen Laiva Oy: Hitsaajankatu 12, 00810 Helsinki; tel. (90) 782655; telex 124453; world-wide tramp services; Man. Dir K. MERISALO; 4 cargo vessels.

Oy Finnlines Ltd: Lönnrotinkatu 21, POB 406, 00121 Helsinki; tel. (90) 16221; telex 12441; f. 1947; cargo traffic, chartering; ship management, marine consulting; member of freight pools; Pres. RAIMO ROOS; 34 cargo vessels (10 general cargo carriers, 9 barges, 9 roll-on roll-off ships, 2 pushers, 2 bulk carriers, 1 ore carrier, 1 car/passenger ferry).

Oy Finncarriers Ab: Eteläranta 8, POB 185, 00130 Helsinki; tel. (90) 1781; telex 122822; f. 1975; liner and contract services between Finland and other European countries, the Mediterranean, North Africa, the Middle East and South and Central America; Man. Dir BO ÅBERG.

Neste Oy: Keilaniemi, 02150 Espoo 15; tel. (90) 4501; telex 124641; f. 1948; (see also under State-owned Industries); Pres. JAAKKO IHAMUOTILA; Corporate Vice-Pres. Shipping RAIMO ROOS; 17 tankers, 3 LPG carriers, 4 tugs; 942,241 dwt.

FINLAND

Oy Henry Nielsen Ab: Lönnrotinkatu 18, POB 199, 00120 Helsinki; tel. (90) 17291; telex 122519; f. 1923; managing owners for about 119,815 dwt tanker and dry cargo; shipbrokers, liner- and forwarding-agents; Man. BERNDT NIELSEN.

CIVIL AVIATION

An international airport is situated at Helsinki-Vantaa, 19 km from Helsinki. Internal flights connect Helsinki to Ivalo, Joensuu, Jyväskylä, Kajaani, Kemi, Kittilä, Kokkola/Pietarsaari, Kuopio, Kuusamo, Lappeenranta, Mariehamn, Mikkeli, Oulu, Pori, Rovaniemi, Savonlinna, Tampere, Turku, Vaasa and Varkaus.

In 1985 7.3m. passengers passed through Finnish airports.

Finnair Oy: Head Office: Mannerheimintie 102, 00250 Helsinki; tel. (90) 81881; telex 124404; f. 1923; 76.1% state-owned; 21 domestic services and services to 34 cities in Europe, the Middle East, South-East Asia and North America; Chair. ANTTI POTILA; Pres. RISTO OJANEN; fleet of 5 ATR 42-300, 18 DC-9, 4 DC-10, 3 MD-87, 7 MD-80, 2 Airbus A300B4-203.

Finnaviation Oy (FA): POB 39, 01531 Vantaa; tel. (90) 822055; telex 122635; f. 1979; 60% owned by Finnair Oy; scheduled domestic services, also to Trollhätan and Stockholm in Sweden; Man. Dir PEKKA VÄLIMÄKI; fleet of 3 SF.340, 1C441, 1 DA-20 and 1 E-110.

Karair Oy: 01530 Vantaa, tel. (90) 81851; telex 124769; f. 1957; internal services and charter flights abroad; Man. Dir TUOMAS KARHUMÄKI; fleet of 1 EMB-110-P1 Bandeirante, 1 DHC-6-300 Twin Otter, 2 Airbus A300B4.

Tourism

Europe's largest inland water system, vast forests, magnificent scenery and the possibility of holiday seclusion are Finland's main attractions. Most visitors come from other Nordic countries, the Federal Republic of Germany and the USSR. In 1987 the estimated number of arrivals (including excursionists) was 2,207,000, and tourist receipts totalled 3,729m. markkaa.

Matkailun edistämiskeskus (Tourist Board): Asemapäällikönkatu 12B, 00520 Helsinki; tel. (90) 144511; telex 122690; f. 1973; Chair. KALERVO HENTILÄ; Dir BENGT PIHLSTRÖM.

Atomic Energy

Atomic Energy Commission: Ministry of Trade and Industry, Aleksanterinkatu 10, 00170 Helsinki; tel. (90) 1605226; telex 125452; advises the government; the Ministry of Trade and Industry is the administrative and licensing authority; Chair. Prof. JORMA ROUTTI; Sec.-Gen. S. IMMONEN; Admin. Sec. M. HOVI.

Finnish Centre for Radiation and Nuclear Safety: POB 268, 00101 Helsinki; tel. (90) 61671; telex 122691; f. 1958; responsible for the supervision of radiation protection and nuclear safety.

Finnish Nuclear Society: c/o Technical Research Centre of Finland, Nuclear Engineering Laboratory, Lönnrotinkatu 37, 00180 Helsinki; tel. (90) 648931; telex 122972.

Lappeenranta University of Technology: Dept of Energy Technology, POB 20, 53851 Lappeenranta; tel. (953) 5711; telex 58290; f. 1969.

Technical Research Centre of Finland: Vuorimiehentie 5, 02150 Espoo; tel. (90) 4561; telex 122972; six divisions.

Teknillinen korkeakoulu (Helsinki University of Technology): Department of Technical Physics, 02150 Espoo; tel. (90) 4512458; telex 125161; the Department provides engineering education in experimental and theoretical solid-state and atomic physics, semiconductor physics and technology, optoelectronics, materials science, nuclear engineering and energy technology, biophysics and medical engineering, optics and laser technology; Dir Dr T. TUOMI, Dep. Dir Dr R. SALOMAA.

Imatran Voima Oy: see State-Owned Industries.

Teollisuuden Voima Oy (Industrial Power Co Ltd): Fredrikinkatu 51-53, 00100 Helsinki; tel. (90) 605022; telex 122065.

FINNISH EXTERNAL TERRITORY

THE ÅLAND ISLANDS

Introductory Survey

Location, Language, Religion, Flag, Capital

The Åland Islands (Ahvenanmaa) are a group of about 6,500 islands (of which some 50 are inhabited) in the Gulf of Bothnia, between Finland and Sweden. About 95% of the inhabitants are Swedish-speaking; the majority profess Christianity and belong to the Evangelical Lutheran Church of Finland. The flag displays a red cross, bordered with yellow, on a blue background, the upright of the cross being to the left of centre. The capital is Mariehamn (Maarianhamina), which is situated on Åland, the largest island in the group.

History and Government

For geographical and economic reasons, the Åland Islands were traditionally associated closely with Sweden. In 1809, when Sweden was forced to cede Finland to Russia, the islands were incorporated into the Finnish Grand Duchy. However, following Finland's declaration of independence from the Russian Empire, in 1917, the Ålanders demanded the right to self-determination and sought to be reunited with Sweden. Their demands were supported by the Swedish Government and people. In 1920 Finland granted the islands autonomy but refused to acknowledge their secession, and in 1921 the Åland question was referred to the League of Nations. In June the League granted Finland sovereignty over the islands, while directing that certain conditions pertaining to national identity be included in the autonomy legislation offered by Finland and that the islands should be a neutral and non-fortified region. Elections were held in accordance with the new legislation, and the new provincial parliament (Landsting) held its first plenary session on 9 June 1922.

The revised Autonomy Act of 1951 provides for independent rights of legislation in internal affairs and for autonomous control over the islands' economy. This Act cannot be amended or repealed by the Finnish Eduskunta without the consent of the Åland Landsting. At a general election to the Landsting, held on 18–19 October 1987, the Centre Party secured nine of the 30 seats, and the Liberal Party won eight. The Moderates and the Social Democrats won five and four seats respectively, while the Green Party and the Independents each won two.

In 1988 constitutional reform introduced the principle of a majority parliamentary government. Previously the executive council (Landskapsstyrelsen) of the province consisted of the six members of the Landsting who had received the most votes from the 30-member parliament. Thus, any party with at least five members in the Landsting could secure a representative on the Landskapsstyrelsen. From April 1988, however, this system was to function only if a majority government could not be formed by the Lantrådskandidat, the member of the Landsting nominated to conduct negotiations. This nominee must first try to form a government consisting of representatives from all the larger parties, before proceeding to an attempt to form a majority coalition.

When these reforms had been effected, Åland had its first formal parliamentary government and opposition. The governing coalition consisted of the three largest parties in the Landsting (the Centre Party, the Liberals and the Moderates), which together held 22 seats in the legislature.

Economic Affairs

In 1960 some 60% of the working population were employed in agriculture, fishing and shipping. Since then, the economy of the islands has expanded and become more diversified, and fishing has declined as a source of income. Shipping, trade and tourism have come to dominate the economy.

The islands are heavily wooded, and only 7% of the total land area is arable. However, the mild climate and fertile soil enable small, highly-mechanized farms to produce high crop yields of cereals, onions and cucumbers, and there are a number of fruit orchards. Dairy farming and sheep-rearing are also important areas of activity.

The political autonomy of the islands and their strategic location between Sweden and Finland have contributed to an expanding banking and finance sector.

Education and Social Welfare

The education system is similar to that of Finland, except that Swedish is the language of instruction. In 1985 government medical services included two hospitals, with a total of 240 beds, and 34 physicians.

Statistical Survey

Source: Ålands Landsting, POB 69, 22101 Mariehamn; tel. (928) 15000.

AREA, POPULATION AND DENSITY

Area: 1,552 sq km (599 sq miles), of which 25 sq km (9.7 sq miles) is inland waters.
Population (estimate, 31 December 1987): 23,745.
Density (1987): 15.3 per sq km.
Births and Deaths (1987): Registered live births 267 (birth rate 11.2 per 1,000); Deaths 214 (death rate 9.0 per 1,000).
Labour Force (census of 17 November 1985): Males 6,299; Females 5,345; Total 11,644.

FINANCE

Currency: Finnish currency: 100 penni (penniä) = 1 mark (markka).
Government Accounts ('000 marks, 1987): Revenue 491,310; Expenditure 502,393.
Cost of Living (consumer price index; base: 1985 = 100): 102.2 in 1986; 106.1 in 1987.
Gross Domestic Product (million marks at current prices): 1,519.9 in 1983; 1,621.8 in 1984.

EXTERNAL TRADE

1984 (million marks): Imports 1,433.9; Exports 967.9.

TRANSPORT

Shipping (1986): Merchant fleet 42 vessels; total displacement 200,000 grt (Source: *Yearbook of Nordic Statistics*).

TOURISM

Tourist Arrivals (1987): 1,241,898.

Directory

Government and Legislature

The legislative body is the Landsting, comprising 30 members, elected every four years on a basis of proportional representation. All Ålanders over the age of 18 years resident in the islands have the right to vote. An executive council (Landskapsstyrelsen) is either formed by parties with the support of a majority in the Landsting, or it is directly elected by the Landsting. The Provincial Governor (Lantråd), is Chairman of the Landskapsstyrelsen and is appointed by the President of Finland after consultation with the Speaker (Talman) of the Åland Landsting. The President has the right to veto Landsting decisions only when the Landsting exceeds its legislative competence, or when there is a threat to the security of the country.

LANDSKAPSSTYRELSEN

Governor (Lantråd): JOHN SUNE ERIKSSON.
Deputy Governor: MAY VALBORG FLODIN.
Members: GÖRAN BENGTZ, HOLGER ERIKSSON, KARL-GÖRAN ERIKSSON, RAGNAR ERLANDSSON, MAGNUS LUNDBERG.

The governing coalition comprises members of the Centre Party, the Liberal Party and the Moderate Party.

LANDSTINGET

Speaker (Talman): SVEN OLOF JANSSON.
Deputy Speaker: JAN-ERIK H. T. LINDFORS.

FINNISH EXTERNAL TERRITORY

The Åland Islands

Election, 18–19 October 1987

	Seats
Åländsk Center (Centre Party)	9
Liberalerna på Åland (Liberal Party)	8*
Frisinnad samverkan (Moderate Party)	5*
Ålands socialdemokrater (Social Democratic Party)	4
Gröna på Åland (Green Party)	2
Independents	2
Total	**30**

* A Liberal member subsequently joined the Moderate Party.

Political Organizations

The address of each of the following organizations is Ålands Landsting, POB 69, 22101 Mariehamn:

Åländsk Center (Centre Party): Chair. OLOF SALMÉN; Leader ANDERS ERIKSSON; Sec.-Gen. MARIANNE GRÖNHOLM.

Ålands socialdemokrater (Social Democratic Party): Chair. LASSE WIKLÖF; Leader BARBO SUNDBACK; Sec.-Gen. OLA ANDERSSON.

Frisinnad samverkan (Moderate Party).

Gröna på Åland (Green Party): Chair. and Leader CHRISTINA HEDMAN-JAAKKOLA.

The Independents: Chair. and Leader BERT HAGGBLOM.

Liberalerna på Åland (Liberal Party): Chair. GUNNEVI NORDMAN; Leader KARL-GUNNAR FAGERHOLM; Sec.-Gen. LISBETH ERIKSSON.

The Press

Läsarägda Nya Åland: POB 21, 22101 Mariehamn; tel. (928) 23444; 3 a week; circ. 7,047.

Tidningen Åland: POB 50, 22101 Mariehamn; tel. (928) 26026; 5 a week; circ. 11,100.

Radio and Television

Radio Åland: POB 46, 22101 Mariehamn; tel. (928) 26060; broadcasts 10 hours a week.

Finance

BANKS

(cap. = capital; res = reserves; dep. = deposits; m. = million; amounts in marks; brs = branches)

Ålandsbanken Ab (Bank of Åland Ltd): Nygatan 2, POB 3, 22101 Mariehamn; tel. (928) 29011; telex 63119; f. 1919; cap. and res 184m., dep. 790m. (Dec. 1987); 21 brs; Chair. FOLKE WOIVALIN; Chief Gen. Man. FOLKE HUSELL.

Ålands Hypoteksbank Ab: Nygatan 2, 22100 Mariehamn; tel. (928) 29011; telex 63119; f. 1986; cap. and res 5m. (Dec. 1987); Chair. GÖRAN FAGERLUND; Chief Man. Dir LARS DONNER.

Ålands Sparbank: POB 7, 22101 Mariehamn; tel. (928 16200; telex 63154; Dirs ERLING GUSTAVSSON, ERIK SUNDBERG, JAN-ERIK RASK.

Andelsbanken för Åland: POB 34, 22101 Mariehamn; tel. (928) 26000; Dirs HÅKAN CLEMES, ROLAND KARLSSON.

Lappo Andelsbank: 22840 Lappo; tel. (928) 56621; Dir TORSTEN NORDBERG.

INSURANCE

Alandia Group: Ålandsvägen 31, 22100 Mariehamn; tel. (928) 29000; telex 63117; f. 1938; life, non-life and marine; comprises three subsidiaries; Gen. Man. JOHAN DAHLMAN.

Ålands Ömsesidiga Försäkringsbolag: Köpmansgatan 6, POB 64, 22101 Mariehamn; tel. (928) 15100; telex 63191; f. 1866; property; subsidiary: Hamnia Reinsurance; Man. Dir BJARNE OLOFSSON.

Trade and Industry

CHAMBER OF COMMERCE

Ålands Handelskammare: Nygatan 9, 22100 Mariehamn; tel. (928) 29029; f. 1945; brs in Helsinki and Stockholm; Chair. THORVALD ERIKSSON; Man. Dir HARRY JANSSON.

EMPLOYERS' ORGANIZATIONS

Ålands arbetsgivareförening (Åland Employers' Asscn): Ringvägen 19, 22100 Mariehamn; f. 1969; Chair. INGMAR JANSSON; Sec. ROLF BERGMAN.

Ålands företagareförening (Åland Business Asscn): Nygatan 9, 22100 Mariehamn; f. 1957; Chair. GÖRAN FAGERLUND; Sec. BIRGER BLOMQVIST.

Ålands köpmannaförening (Åland Businessmen's Asscn): Nygatan 9, 22100 Mariehamn; f. 1927; Chair. ROLF NORDLUND; Sec. VIKING GRANSKOG.

Ålands producentförbund (Åland Agricultural Producers' Asscn): Styrmansgatan 1B, 22100 Mariehamn; f. 1946; Chair. GÖRAN HELLING; Sec. JAN KARLSSON.

TRADE UNIONS

AKAVA-Åland (Professional Asscn): Styrmansgatan 1B, 22100 Mariehamn; Chair. KARL-JOHAN EDLUND; Gen. Sec. TOR-BJÖRN CARLSSON.

FFC/SAK: s Lokalorganisation på Åland (SAK's Regional Trade Union in Åland): POB 22, 22101 Mariehamn; Chair. FJALAR KARLSSON; Gen. Sec. STIG ENGSTRÖM.

Fackorgan för offentliga arbetsomraden på Åland (FOA-Å) (Joint Organization of Civil Servants and Workers (VTY) in Åland): Styrmansgatan 1B, 22100 Mariehamn; Chair. ÅKE WIRTANEN; Gen. Sec. ANITA RUNDBERG.

TOC/TVK: s Tjänstemannaorganisationer på Åland (TOC-TÅ) (TVK's Union of Salaried Employees in Åland): Styrmansgatan 6, 22100 Mariehamn; Chair. KJELL MATTSSON; Gen. Sec. TUULA MATTSSON.

Transport

The islands are linked to the Swedish and Finnish mainlands by ferry services and by air services from Mariehamn airport.

SHIPPING

Ålands Redarförening r.f. (Åland Shipowners' Association): Ålandsvägen 31, 22100 Mariehamn; tel. (928) 13430; telex 63117; f. 1934; Chair. NILS-ERIK EKLUND; Man. Dir JUSTUS HARBERG.

Principal Companies

Birka Line Ab: Storagatan 11, 22100 Mariehamn; tel. (928) 27027; telex 63163; f. 1971; passenger service; Chair. BENGT WILJANEN; Man. Dir GUNNAR LUNDBERG.

Lundqvist Rederierna: N. Esplanadgt. 9, 22100 Mariehamn; tel. (928) 16411; telex 63115; f. 1927; liner services; Pres. STIG LUNDQVIST; 3 vessels; total tonnage 15,883 dwt.

Rederiaktiebolaget Gustaf Erikson: POB 49, 22101 Mariehamn; tel. (928) 27070; telex 63112; f. 1913; Chair. SUNE LUNDBERG; Man. Dir BO LIMNELL; 10 dry cargo and refrigerated vessels.

Rederiaktiebolaget Sally: Hamngatan 8, 22100 Mariehamn; tel. (928) 16711; telex 63115; ferry services to Sweden, England, France; Caribbean cruises; Man. Dir INGMAR INGVESGÅRD; 6 ferries and 2 cruisers; total tonnage 71,571 grt.

SF Line Ab: Norra Esplanadgt. 3, 22100 Mariehamn; tel. (928) 14120; telex 63151; f. 1963; 3 car/passenger vessels; Chair. STIG LUNDQVIST; Man. Dir GUNNAR EKLUND; total tonnage 59,151 grt.

Tourism

Ålands turistförening r.f. (Åland Tourist Asscn): Storagatan 18, 22100 Mariehamn; tel. (928) 16575; f. 1933; Chair. HENRIK GUSTAFSSON; Man. Dir ANDERS INGVES.

FRANCE

Introductory Survey

Location, Climate, Language, Religion, Flag, Capital

The French Republic is situated in Western Europe. It is bounded to the north by the English Channel, to the east by Belgium, Luxembourg, the Federal Republic of Germany, Switzerland and Italy, to the south by the Mediterranean Sea and Spain, and to the west by the Atlantic Ocean. The island of Corsica is part of metropolitan France, while four overseas departments, two overseas 'collectivités territoriales' and four overseas territories also form an integral part of the Republic. The climate is temperate throughout most of the country, but in the south it is of the Mediterranean type, with warm summers and mild winters. Temperatures in Paris are generally between 0°C (32°F) and 24°C (75°F). The principal language is French, which has numerous regional dialects, and small minorities speak Breton and Basque. Almost all French citizens profess Christianity, and about 80% are adherents of the Roman Catholic Church. Other Christian denominations are represented, and there are also Muslim and Jewish communities. The national flag (proportions three by two) has three equal vertical stripes, of blue, white and red. The capital is Paris.

Recent History

In September 1939, following Nazi Germany's invasion of Poland, France and the United Kingdom declared war on Germany, thus entering the Second World War. In June 1940, however, France was forced to sign an armistice, following a swift invasion and occupation of French territory by German forces. After the liberation of France from German occupation in 1944, a provisional government was set up under Gen. Charles de Gaulle, leader of the 'Free French' forces during the wartime resistance. The war in Europe ended in May 1945, when German forces surrendered at Reims. In 1946, following a referendum, the Fourth Republic was established and Gen. de Gaulle retired from public life.

France had 26 different governments from 1946 until the Fourth Republic came to an end in 1958 with an insurrection in Algeria (then an overseas department) and the threat of civil war. In May Gen. de Gaulle was invited by the President, René Coty, to form a government. In June he was invested as Prime Minister by the National Assembly, with the power to rule by decree for six months. A new constitution was approved by referendum in September 1958 and promulgated in October; thus the Fifth Republic came into being, with Gen. de Gaulle taking office as its first President in January 1959. The new system provided a strong, stable executive. Real power rested in the hands of the President, who strengthened his authority through direct appeals to the people in national referendums.

The early years of the Fifth Republic were overshadowed by the Algerian crisis. De Gaulle suppressed a revolt of French army officers and granted Algeria independence in 1962, withdrawing troops and repatriating French settlers. A period of relative tranquillity was ended in 1968, when dissatisfaction with the Government's authoritarian policies on education and information, coupled with discontent at low wage rates and lack of social reform, fused into a serious revolt of students and workers. For a month the republic was threatened, but the student movement collapsed and the general strike was settled by large wage rises. In April 1969 President de Gaulle resigned after defeat in a referendum on regional reform.

Georges Pompidou, who had been Prime Minister between April 1962 and July 1968, was elected President in June 1969. He attempted to continue Gaullism, while also responding to the desire for change. The Gaullist hold on power was threatened, however, by the Union of the Left, formed in 1972 by the Parti Socialiste (PS) and the Parti Communiste Français (PCF). Leaders of the PS and the PCF agreed a common programme for contesting legislative elections. At a general election for the National Assembly in March 1973, the Government coalition was returned with a reduced majority.

President Pompidou died in April 1974. Valéry Giscard d'Estaing, formerly leader of the Républicains Indépendants (RI), supported by the Gaullist Union des Démocrates pour la République (UDR) and the centre parties, was elected President in May, narrowly defeating François Mitterrand, the First Secretary of the PS and the candidate of the Union of the Left (which was abandoned in 1977). A government was formed from members of the RI, the UDR and the centre parties. In August 1976 Jacques Chirac resigned as Prime Minister and was replaced by Raymond Barre, hitherto Minister of External Trade. Chirac undertook the transformation of the UDR into a new Gaullist party, the Rassemblement pour la République (RPR). In February 1978 the non-Gaullist parties in the Government formed the Union pour la Démocratie Française (UDF), to compete with RPR candidates in the National Assembly elections held in March, when the governing coalition retained a working majority.

In the April/May 1981 presidential elections, Mitterrand, the candidate of the PS, defeated Giscard d'Estaing, with the support of Communist voters. Pierre Mauroy was appointed Prime Minister and formed France's first left-wing Council of Ministers for 23 years. At elections for a new Assembly, held in June, the PS and associated groups, mainly the Mouvement des Radicaux de Gauche (MRG), won an overall majority of the seats. The Government was reshuffled to include four members of the PCF in the Council of Ministers. The new Government introduced a programme of reforms: social benefits and working conditions were substantially improved; several major industrial enterprises and financial institutions were brought under state control; and administrative and financial power was transferred from government-appointed Préfets to locally-elected departmental assemblies.

By 1983 the effects of economic recession had led to the adoption of deflationary policies, including reductions in public expenditure. Following a decline in support for the PS and other left-wing parties at nationwide municipal elections held in March 1983, Mauroy resigned, but was immediately requested to form a new administration by President Mitterrand. Elections for one-third of the seats in the newly-enlarged Senate in September 1983 resulted in an overall majority for the opposition right-wing and centre parties. In the June 1984 elections to the European Parliament, the PS suffered a serious set-back, taking only 20 of the 81 seats allocated to France, while the RPR-UDF opposition alliance won 41 seats. The extreme right-wing Front National (FN) and the PCF each took 10 seats.

Dissension between the PCF and the PS over the Government's continued programme of economic austerity became increasingly bitter as plans for further 'industrial restructuring' were revealed. After forceful protest by opposition politicians and Roman Catholic pressure-groups, a government proposal to introduce a unified, state-run secular education system was abandoned in July 1984, and the Minister of Education, Alain Savary, resigned. President Mitterrand accepted Mauroy's subsequent resignation, and appointed Laurent Fabius, the former Minister for Industry, as Prime Minister. Following Fabius's declared intention to continue policies of economic rigour, the PCF refused to participate in the new Council of Ministers.

A general election for an enlarged National Assembly (increased from 491 to 577 seats) was held in March 1986. In accordance with legislation introduced in 1985, the voting, except in three small overseas possessions, was based on a system of proportional representation (with voters choosing from party lists in each department or territory), rather than under the previous system of single-member constituencies. As in the 1981 general election, the PS and the MRG formed a left-wing alliance, while the RPR and the UDF formed a centre-right alliance. Although the PS remained the largest single party in the new Assembly, the RPR-UDF was able to control a majority of seats, with the support of 14 deputies from minor right-wing parties. The PCF suffered a severe decline in support, whereas the FN won seats in the Assembly for the first time. President Mitterrand invited Jacques Chirac, the leader of the RPR (the dominant party in the centre-right alliance), to become Prime Minister (Chirac, the Mayor of Paris since 1977, had previously been Prime Minister in 1974–76). A new Council of Ministers, comprising RPR-UDF politicians and a few non-party members, was formed. This resulted in an unprecedented situation in France: a right-wing Government 'cohabiting' with a Socialist President, as Mitterrand remained in office until the expiry of his presidential term in 1988. On the same day as the election for the National Assembly, voting took place throughout France for regional councils, using direct suffrage in all areas for the first time (the councils in metropolitan France had previously been chosen by indirect election, except in Corsica—see below). The regional elections also resulted in a swing to the right, although in nine regional councils right-wing parties had to form coalitions with the FN in order to maintain their control.

In April 1986 Chirac introduced highly controversial enabling legislation to allow his Government to legislate by decree on economic and social issues, and on the proposed reversion to the single-seat majority voting system for elections to the National Assembly. However, President Mitterrand insisted on his presidential right to refuse to sign decrees that undermined the previous Government's achievements on social reform. Chirac was therefore forced to use the 'guillotine' procedure (setting a time-limit for parliamentary consideration of legislative proposals) to gain parliamentary approval for contentious legislation, which the President would be constitutionally obliged to sign within 15 days, following its approval by the Senate (with a large right-wing majority) and the Constitutional Council. In July 1986 the 'guillotine' procedure was used to enact legislation which provided for the 'privatization' of 65 state-owned companies (by November 1987 shares in 11 major companies and their subsidiaries had been offered for sale to private investors—see Economic Affairs). From 1986 the Government implemented its programme of deregulation of the French broadcasting system and established a new broadcasting authority, the Commission Nationale de la Communication et des Libertés (CNCL), to oversee the reforms. Stringent legislation to control immigration was adopted by the National Assembly in July 1986, and in September tough anti-terrorism measures were implemented, following a series of bombings in Paris, which were carried out by the Committee of Solidarity with Arab and Middle Eastern Political Prisoners (CSPPA). In elections for one-third of the seats in the enlarged Senate in late September, the right-wing parties consolidated their majority.

By the end of 1986 the Government's popularity had slumped, owing to two consecutive crises. In December 1986 the Minister Delegate attached to the Minister of National Education resigned, and the Government was forced to withdraw proposed legislation on education, which aimed to introduce selection procedures for university places, to increase registration fees, and to reform the degree and baccalauréat systems, after large student demonstrations took place throughout France. Following widespread strikes by the transport unions, the Government abandoned plans to introduce merit-linked salaries in January 1987, but remained determined that increases in wages should not exceed the limit of 2%–3% per year, set by the austerity policy.

By 1987 the RPR-UDF coalition had become increasingly divided, as the UDF resented the RPR's domination of major ministries. In April 1987 Chirac attempted to unify the RPR-UDF coalition by seeking a vote of confidence in the Government's past and future policies. In June François Léotard, the Minister for Culture and Communication and Secretary-General of the Parti Républicain (PR), affiliated to the UDF, announced that he would not support Chirac's presidential candidacy in 1988. In the following month Raymond Barre, a prominent member of the UDF and a former Prime Minister (1976–81), announced that he would be a candidate for the presidency and would base his campaign on criticism of Chirac's economic and foreign policies. Further splits developed in the right-wing coalition, as Chirac reintroduced proposals, previously introduced in 1986, to remove the right of automatic French citizenship from children of foreign parents, with the aim of attracting FN support for his candidacy in the second round of the presidential election. However, UDF and moderate RPR members of the coalition rejected any accommodation with the FN, and the RPR hastily distanced itself from the FN, after Le Pen described the Nazi gas chambers as 'un point de détail' in the history of the Second World War, during a television interview in mid-September.

Towards the end of 1987, scandals relating to the PS term of government were revealed. In October the National Assembly withdrew parliamentary immunity from Christian Nucci, the former PS Minister of Co-operation, thus enabling him to be examined by five special magistrates over his alleged role in the embezzlement of about 5m. francs of development aid during his tenure of office. In November a secret report was disclosed on illegal shipments of French-made weapons to Iran, with the alleged complicity of senior defence officers, under the Socialist Government. Following further allegations that the PS had received commissions from the illegal sales of armaments, President Mitterrand declared his support for a series of proposals which would oblige politicians to declare their incomes, and presidential candidates to declare their sources of funding.

During the last session of the National Assembly in December 1987, Chirac sought a vote of confidence in his Government's policies, in an attempt to deflect widespread criticism over the alleged means by which relations had been normalized with Iran (see below). The National Assembly also adopted 16 legislative proposals, including the reduction of the powers of examining magistrates, the reform of the Bourse and the introduction of a new statute for the French overseas territory of New Caledonia. During an extraordinary session in February 1988, the Assembly adopted legislation requiring elected office-holders to be financially accountable, and regulating the financing of political parties and electoral campaigns.

In early 1988, in the months leading up to the presidential election, President Mitterrand gained a tactical advantage over the other presidential candidates by delaying the announcement of his intention to seek a second five-year term of office until just five weeks before the first round of voting was due to take place, whereas Jacques Chirac of the RPR and Raymond Barre of the UDF had declared their candidacies many weeks in advance. In the first round of the election on 24 April, Mitterrand established a lead, with 34.1% of the votes, while right-wing support was split between Chirac and Barre, who gained 19.9% and 16.5% of the votes respectively. There was an unexpected resurgence in support for the extreme right-wing candidate, Jean-Marie Le Pen, who won 14.4% of the votes, while the PCF official candidate, André Lajoinie, received only 6.8% of the votes. The rate of abstention was 18.6%. Mitterrand and Chirac proceeded to the second round of the election. The PCF recommended its supporters to vote for Mitterrand, while the UDF urged its supporters to vote for Chirac. Le Pen, however, refused to endorse Chirac's candidacy. On 8 May Mitterrand was re-elected President, with 54% of the votes, while Chirac received 46%. Of the total electorate, 15.9% failed to participate. Chirac subsequently resigned as Prime Minister, and Mitterrand appointed Michel Rocard, who had been the Minister of Agriculture in the previous Socialist Government, as his successor. However, Rocard's Government failed to command a reliable majority in the National Assembly, which was promptly dissolved by Mitterrand.

A general election for a new National Assembly was held on 5 and 12 June 1988. The voting was based on the single-seat majority system, which had been reintroduced by Chirac after the 1986 elections. The PS formed a left-wing alliance with the MRG, while the RPR and the UDF decided to contest the elections jointly as the Union du Rassemblement et du Centre (URC). The first round of the election, on 5 June, was characterized by an unusually high abstention rate of 34.3%. The PS-MRG alliance received 37.6% of the votes cast, while the URC received 37.7%. The PCF recovered support, winning 11.3% of the votes, while the FN's share of the votes was 9.7%, as in the 1986 general election. The second round of voting, on 12 June 1988, was restricted to constituencies where no candidate had won an absolute majority. The election was contested by candidates who had received at least 12.5% of the votes in the first round. The PCF agreed not to contest the same constituencies as the PS, and a similar, but controversial, pact was reached between URC and FN candidates in Marseille and the surrounding Bouches-du-Rhône département. Although the PS won the most seats, it failed to win an overall majority: the PS-MRG alliance received 48.7% of the second-round votes and won a total of 276 seats, and the URC secured 46.8% and won 272 seats (the RPR received 23.1% and took 127 seats, the UDF won 21.2% and took 129 seats, while the other right-wing candidates, who campaigned as URC candidates in the second round, won 2.6% of the votes and secured 16 seats).

The PCF, with 3.4%, won 27 seats, while the FN received 1.1% and won only 1 seat. The abstention rate remained high, at 30.1%. After the election, Mitterrand announced that he would form a minority government and seek parliamentary majorities on a case-by-case basis. Meanwhile, Pierre Méhaignerie, the leader of the Centre des Démocrates Sociaux (CDS, a party affiliated to the UDF), announced the formation of a new independent centrist group comprising 40 deputies, the Union du Centre (UDC), with the aim of establishing effective opposition to the Government. Barre subsequently announced that he was allying himself with the UDC.

In late June Rocard was reappointed Prime Minister, and he formed a new Council of Ministers. Although members of the previous Government held the main portfolios, six members of the new Council of Ministers were drawn from the UDF and 13 were independent 'technocrats', thus demonstrating the new Government's wish to attract centrist support in the National Assembly. However, the Government's attempt to gain reliable PCF support, in preparation for the introduction of a potentially controversial series of measures later in the year, received a set-back in July, when a clause of the Amnesty Law (traditionally introduced after the presidential election) that had been proposed by the PCF, seeking to reinstate dismissed trade union officials, was rejected by the Constitutional Council, following an appeal by the RPR. In the cantonal elections on 25 September and 2 October, the PS made a gain of 89 additional seats, but the abstention rate reached its highest post-war levels (50.9% in the first round and 53.0% in the second round).

In October 1988 the Government introduced a series of legislative proposals which aimed to encourage an 'everyday democracy' by protecting the underprivileged. A major proposal, to introduce a minimum guaranteed income, was approved almost unanimously (the FN subsequently expelled its one deputy from the party for supporting the measure), although, to ensure right-wing support, the Government had to introduce a clause whereby those benefiting from the measure would have their allowances suspended if they failed to accept job-training or social employment. A proposal to introduce a 'wealth and solidarity' tax, along with a series of other tax reforms (see Economic Affairs) was also approved, owing to abstentions by the PCF and the UDC. However, legislation to replace the broadcasting authority, the CNCL (which had been criticized for alleged right-wing bias), with a 'more impartial' Conseil Supérieur de l'Audiovisuel provoked much opposition, and Rocard subsequently invoked a procedure whereby a measure was automatically accepted if opposition parties failed to achieve the adoption of a motion of censure.

However, the Government's success in implementing its programme was overshadowed by a series of strikes in protest against its attempts to restrict public-sector wages and thus reduce the budgetary deficit. In September 1988 nurses went on strike, and in the following month the unrest spread to most other public sectors, including schools, urban transport, railways and the civil service. Eventually the Government was forced to concede to the strikers' demands, and by early December most trade unions had reached a settlement. Although the PCF had been criticized by the Government during the unrest for encouraging union discontent, it refused to vote for a motion of censure against the Government which was presented by the RPR in mid-December, in response to the unrest. In January 1989 the PCF agreed not to combine with right-wing deputies to defeat the Government, and formed an electoral alliance with the PS in preparation for the municipal elections in March.

In early 1989, however, details emerged of two 'insider trading' scandals which involved individuals close to President Mitterrand and the Ministry of the Economy, Finance and the Budget. The first scandal focused on the purchase of American Can from the US company, Triangle Holding, by the French state-owned aluminium and packaging company, Péchiney, in November 1988. A few individuals, including a close friend of President Mitterrand and a left-wing financier, bought large amounts of Triangle shares before the Péchiney bid and subsequently made substantial profits. It was suspected that these investors might have received insider information, and it was noted that, as Péchiney was a state-owned company, senior officials in the Ministries of the Economy, Finance and the Budget, and of Industry and Regional Planning, as well as in the Prime Minister's and the President's Offices would have known about the bid beforehand. The second scandal focused on attempts by Pierre Bérégovoy, the Minister of the Economy, Finance and the Budget, to oust the controlling groups of right-wing shareholders created by the Chirac Government during its privatization programme (see Economic Affairs). In October 1988 hostile bidders, financed by a state savings bank (with the alleged implicit support of the Ministry of the Economy, Finance and the Budget), unsuccessfully attempted to acquire a controlling interest in a major privatized bank, the Société Générale. During the attempted takeover, several individuals, including one person who was later implicated in the Péchiney scandal, made substantial profits. In January 1989, in an attempt to contain these scandals, Rocard announced new proposals to increase the powers of the Commission des Opérations de Bourse (COB), the supervisory body of the stock exchange. The head of Bérégovoy's private office resigned, in order to 'defend his honour' against accusations of irregular conduct in the Péchiney takeover. At the end of the month the COB, which had been investigating the Péchiney takeover, presented a dossier on the affair to the Public Prosecutor. In February the COB opened investigations into the Société Générale affair.

As a result of the decentralization legislation of 1982, Corsica was elevated from regional status to that of a 'collectivité territoriale', with its own directly-elected 61-seat Assembly, and an administration with greater executive powers in economic, social and other spheres. This measure failed to pacify the pro-independence Front de Libération Nationale de la Corse (FLNC) and the Consulte des Comités Nationalistes (CCN), which were banned in 1983, following a terrorist campaign. A new independence movement, the Mouvement Corse pour l'Autodétermination (MCA), was immediately formed by members of the banned CCN, and terrorist activities continued from 1984. In January 1987 the MCA, which had six members in the Corsican Assembly in alliance with the Union du Peuple Corse (UPC), was banned after police investigations revealed alleged links with the FLNC, and the UPC later suspended the alliance. In October the police seized an FLNC article, published in a Corsican nationalist newspaper, which advocated the 'physical elimination' of French mainlanders on Corsica and new terrorist operations to be directed against the police. One gendarme was killed, and five were injured, in a series of terrorist attacks in March and April 1988. At the end of May, the FLNC announced a suspension of violent operations, with the aim of achieving a dialogue with the newly-elected Socialist Government. In November the Government proposed that discussions be held with MCA councillors and announced proposals to redress some of the nationalists' grievances. The proposals included measures to introduce the teaching of the Corsican language in all Corsican schools and to encourage economic development on the island. In January 1989, however, the MCA councillors rejected an invitation to meet the Minister of the Interior, Pierre Joxe, although they stressed that this did not imply an end to the dialogue or to the FLNC truce.

From 1984 the French Government faced growing terrorist activity in the Pacific overseas territory of New Caledonia, where Kanak (indigenous Melanesian) separatists were campaigning for independence from metropolitan France. In September 1987 the French Government held a referendum in New Caledonia, with voters choosing between total independence and adoption of a statute to incorporate the territory firmly as part of the French Republic. The FLNKS advocated a boycott of the referendum, as it had not been consulted by the Government over the issue, and instigated a campaign of civil disobedience in the period preceding the referendum. In a low turn-out of 58.9% of the electorate (owing mainly to the FLNKS boycott), 98.3% of voters chose to remain part of France. In December a new statute, granting greater autonomy to the territory by establishing four elected regional councils, was adopted. However, the FLNKS urged a boycott of the elections for the new regional councils, which were to be held concurrently with the first round of the French presidential elections on 24 April 1988. Several days before the elections were held, 30 Kanak separatists killed four gendarmes and took 27 gendarmes hostage. (See p. 1077 for further details.) In May the new French Prime Minister, Michel Rocard, dispatched a six-member mission to New Caledonia to re-establish a dialogue with the Kanaks and to formulate proposals for the territory's future. Meanwhile, controversy arose over the release of the hostages, when a 'leaked' report by the commander of the French paratroopers sent to the hostages' rescue seemed to imply that the Chirac Government had favoured a military solution, rather than a negotiated settlement, to the crisis. After a series of discussions between Rocard and the leaders of the FLNKS and the anti-independence party, the Rassemblement pour la Calédonie dans la République, agreement was reached in August to transfer the administration of New Caledonia to the central Government in Paris for 12 months, and then to appoint a High Commissioner to administer the territory, along with three elected regional councils, for 10 years, prior to a referendum on self-determination, to be held in 1998. The programme was presented to the French electorate in a referendum on 6 November 1988. Out of the 36.9% of the electorate who voted, 80% approved the Government's plan.

Terrorist attacks in the Basque region of south-western France escalated in 1983 and 1984, as violence between Spanish right-wing extremists and members of the Basque separatist movement, ETA, spread across the border from Spain. In 1984 the French Government agreed to stop granting refugee status to ETA members seeking asylum in France, and in July 1986 the Government agreed to increase collaboration with the Spanish authorities to curb ETA. Many ETA members were subsequently deported, detained, or expelled to other countries. In July 1987 the French Government banned another Basque separatist group, Ipparretarrak (IK), which had been responsible for terrorist operations since 1973 and had renewed a bombing campaign in 1986, in protest against the expulsions of ETA members. In September and October French and Spanish police conducted the largest ever series of arrests of suspected members of ETA and IK, and in January 1989 French police arrested the leader of the military wing of ETA and other suspected ETA members.

France is a founder-member of the European Communities. In 1966 it withdrew from the integrated military structure of NATO, but remained a member of the alliance. In 1986 France agreed with the Federal Republic of Germany to intensify military links and to play a more active joint role in international affairs. In January 1988 France and the Federal Republic of Germany signed new agreements on defence and economic co-operation, to commemorate the 25th anniversary of the Franco-German Treaty, the original aims of which had never been realized. In October a joint Franco-German military brigade was formed, which was intended to strengthen the European element within NATO and the French commitment to use conventional forces to defend the Federal Republic of Germany. However, French relations with NATO in 1988 were uneasy. In February other NATO states expressed a wish for closer French co-operation with the Alliance. In March Mitterrand became the first French President to attend a NATO 'summit' meeting since 1966, owing to French concern over the implications of the Intermediate-Range Nuclear Forces Treaty, signed by the USA and the USSR in December 1987. In the same month Mitterrand criticized NATO's plans to modernize its short-range nuclear weapons, arguing that European security would be better served by disarmament. In July Mitterrand welcomed Soviet proposals for the convening of a Soviet-European 'summit' meeting on conventional disarmament, in contrast with NATO's response. In November France incurred NATO's disapproval for its insistence on linking the issue of disarmament with that of human rights in Eastern bloc countries, and for proposing that neutral and non-aligned European countries be given a decisive role in negotiations on conventional forces, thus repudiating NATO's decision that only NATO and Warsaw Pact states should be directly involved in such negotiations.

Meanwhile, President Mitterrand placed a new emphasis on improving France's relations with the USSR and Eastern European countries. In January 1988 Mitterrand met Erich Honecker, thus becoming the first leader of a Western signatory to the Berlin Agreement of 1945 to meet the leader of the German Democratic Republic. In early November the French Government withdrew charges against three people who had been arrested in 1987 for allegedly spying for the USSR. Franco-Soviet relations had deteriorated following the arrests, with the two countries engaging in retaliatory expulsions of diplomatic personnel. Later in November 1988, Mitterrand visited the USSR and attended the launch of the second joint Franco-Soviet space mission. During his visit, Mitterrand signed an agreement allowing for the creation of a line of credit from a French banking consortium to the USSR and for the establishment of a joint venture to construct an aluminium plant in Armenia. He also agreed in principle to the holding of a human rights conference in Moscow in 1991. Mitterrand visited Czechoslovakia in the following month and planned to visit other East European countries in 1989, except Romania, in protest against that country's domestic policies.

France has been conducting tests of nuclear weapons on the South Pacific atoll of Mururoa, in French Polynesia, since 1966, despite protests from countries in the region, particularly Australia and New Zealand. In mid-1985 France's relations with these countries were further damaged by the discovery that French secret service agents had been responsible for the sinking of the trawler *Rainbow Warrior* (flagship of the international environmental protection group, Greenpeace) in the New Zealand port of Auckland. In September 1985 the head of the secret service, Adm. Pierre Lacoste, was dismissed, and the Minister of Defence, Charles Hernu, was forced to resign. In December the French Government agreed to compensate Greenpeace, and in July 1986 the new right-wing French Government issued a formal apology and paid US $7m. compensation to New Zealand, and approved New Zealand butter quotas, while New Zealand returned the secret service agents, whom the New Zealand authorities had imprisoned on charges of manslaughter, on the condition that they were confined to Hao Atoll, a French military base in the Pacific, for three years. There was renewed tension between France and New Zealand, after the two secret service agents were flown back to France on humanitarian grounds in December 1987 and in May 1988, without New Zealand's consent, thus breaking the terms of the 1986 agreement. In November 1988 it was announced that a tribunal, chaired by a Uruguayan national, would arbitrate between France and New Zealand over the fate of the two agents.

France granted independence to most of its former colonies after the Second World War. In Indo-China, after prolonged fighting, Laos, Cambodia (now Kampuchea) and Viet-Nam became fully independent in 1954. In Africa most of the French colonies in the West and Equatorial regions attained independence in 1960, but have retained their close economic and political ties with France. In 1983, under the terms of a co-operation agreement, a large contingent of French troops was sent to Chad as a result of continuing hostilities between government forces and Libyan-backed rebels. France became increasingly involved in the conflict between Chad and Libya (see p. 674 for further details), and in 1987 increased its military presence by 1,000 men. In September, however, Chad and Libya accepted the OAU's proposal for a ceasefire.

In 1986 the Chirac Government changed the direction of French foreign policy in the Middle East. From 1978 France had the largest contingent of soldiers in the UN Interim Force in Lebanon (UNIFIL), but in November 1986 the Government announced the withdrawal of more than one-half of the French contingent from Lebanon, owing to increasing numbers of casualties among French soldiers. In 1986 the French Government reached a settlement with Iran over the repayment of a US $1,000m. loan from the Iranian Government of the late Shah in 1974, expelled leaders of the Mujaheddin resistance (opposed to the Iranian regime of Ayatollah Khomeini) from France and closed the Mujaheddin headquarters in Paris. Improved relations between France and Iran resulted in the release of five French hostages being detained by a pro-Iranian group in Lebanon. In 1987, however, French relations with Iran deteriorated after a series of arrests of suspected members of a pro-Iranian terrorist network in Paris, and an incident involving an interpreter at the Iranian embassy in Paris, who was implicated in the bombing campaign carried out by the CSPPA in 1986 (see above). In July France severed diplomatic relations with Iran. France subsequently reinforced its naval fleet in the Persian (Arabian) Gulf and announced a ban on imports of Iranian crude petroleum. By late November relations between France and Iran had improved, after secret negotiations resulted in the release of two out of five French hostages being detained by a pro-Iranian group in Lebanon. The French Government was widely criticized in France and in Europe, after allegations that it had paid a ransom of US $5m. for the return of the hostages. In early December 17 members of the Mujaheddin resistance (14 Iranians and three Kurdish nationalists from Turkey) were expelled from France to Gabon, in a move which intensified suspicions of a secret French deal with Iran. Following protests in France and abroad, seven of the Iranians were allowed to return to France in January 1988. In May, before the second round of the French presidential election, the three remaining French hos-

FRANCE

tages being held by a pro-Iranian group in Lebanon were released, prompting speculation that a further secret agreement between France and Iran had been made. Later that month, diplomatic relations between France and Iran were restored, and in December the French Government revoked its ban on imports of Iranian crude petroleum.

Government

Under the 1958 constitution, legislative power is held by the bicameral Parliament, comprising a Senate and a National Assembly. The Senate has 319 members (296 for metropolitan France, 13 for the overseas departments, 'collectivités territoriales' and territories, and 10 for French nationals abroad). Senators are elected for a nine-year term by an electoral college composed of the members of the National Assembly, delegates from the Councils of the Departments and delegates from the Municipal Councils. One-third of the Senate is renewable every three years. The National Assembly has 577 members, with 555 for metropolitan France and 22 for overseas departments, 'collectivités territoriales' and territories. In the June 1988 general election, members of the Assembly were elected by universal adult suffrage, under the reintroduced single-member constituency system of direct election, using a second ballot if the first ballot failed to produce an absolute majority for any one candidate. The Assembly's term is five years, subject to dissolution. Executive power is held by the President. Since 1962 the President has been directly elected by popular vote (using two ballots if necessary) for seven years. The President appoints a Council of Ministers, headed by the Prime Minister, which administers the country and is responsible to Parliament.

Metropolitan France comprises 21 administrative regions containing 96 departments. Under the decentralization law of March 1982, administrative and financial power in metropolitan France was transferred from the Préfets, who became Commissaires de la République, to locally-elected departmental assemblies (Conseils généraux) and regional assemblies (Conseils régionaux). The special status of a 'collectivité territoriale' was granted to Corsica, which has its own directly-elected legislative Assembly. There are four overseas departments (French Guiana, Guadeloupe, Martinique and Réunion), two overseas 'collectivités territoriales' (Mayotte and St Pierre and Miquelon) and four overseas territories (French Polynesia, the French Southern and Antarctic Territories, New Caledonia and the Wallis and Futuna Islands), all of which are integral parts of the French Republic (see p. 1051). Each overseas department is administered by an elected Conseil général and Conseil régional, each 'collectivité territoriale' by an appointed government commissioner, and each overseas territory by an appointed high commissioner.

Defence

French military policy is decided by the Supreme Defence Council. Military service is compulsory and lasts for 12–18 months. In June 1988 the total armed forces numbered 456,900 (including 238,500 conscripts), comprising an army of 280,900, a navy of 66,500, an air force of 95,000, inter-service central staffs of 3,600, a Service de Santé of 8,700 and a service des Essences of 2,200. In addition, there was a paramilitary gendarmerie of 87,400 (including 10,100 conscripts). Total reserves stood at 356,000 (army 270,000; navy 28,000; air force 58,000). The defence budget for 1989 was 221,800m. francs. France is a member of NATO, but withdrew from its integrated military organization in 1966, and possesses its own nuclear weapons.

Economic Affairs

France is one of the world's leading industrial countries, with extensive and diversified industrial and commercial activity. Much of the country's industrial base was acquired after the Second World War, while the role in the economy of state-controlled enterprises increased. Since the late 1950s France has experienced significant economic growth, and its people enjoy a high standard of living. In 1987, according to estimates by the World Bank, France's gross national product (GNP), measured at average 1985–87 prices, was US $714,994m., equivalent to $12,860 per head. Between 1980 and 1987 GNP per head increased at an average annual rate of 0.7% in real terms. The average annual increase in overall gross domestic product (GDP), measured in constant prices, was 4.3% in 1965–80, slowing to 1.6% in 1980–86.

France remains Western Europe's leading agricultural nation, with 31.2m. ha, or 57.2% of its area, used for farming. The number of workers engaged in agriculture, however, declined as a proportion of the total employed population from 15% in 1968 to 6.4% in 1986. The agricultural sector registered a trade surplus of 33,128m. francs in 1985. The surplus declined to 27,500m. francs in 1986, but rose to 29,200m. francs in 1987 and to a record 39,400m. francs in 1988. Agriculture accounted for 13.4% of total exports in 1985: the principal commodities were cereals, dairy produce, wine and livestock. Revenue from agriculture declined by 3.8% in 1988 (compared with an increase of 4.1% in 1987), and farmers' debts reached more than 200,000m. francs. In 1988, in accordance with EEC measures to curb overproduction, the French Government announced proposals to make 300,000–400,000 ha of arable land fallow in 1989, with the aim of having 3m. ha of fallow land in the 1990s and 6m. ha of fallow land by the year 2000. Farmers who would be affected by these proposals were to be granted compensation of 2,000 francs per ha. In 1988 the Government also agreed to provide 3,000m. francs in aid to farmers, most of which was to be directed to mountainous or disadvantaged regions. The agricultural sector also absorbed 3,000m. francs accruing from the sale in 1988 of the state-owned agricultural co-operative bank, the Caisse Nationale de Crédit Agricole, to its 94 regional branches. About 1,000m. francs was used to increase interest rate subsidies for farmers, and the remaining 2,000m. francs was reserved for unspecified agricultural purposes. In November 1988 the Government introduced legislation enabling farmers to file for bankruptcy.

French industrial production expanded rapidly between 1945 and 1973. In the late 1970s, however, the rate of growth slowed, and production virtually stagnated during 1979–86. Meanwhile, France's share of world production declined from 5.5% in 1979 to 4.9% in 1985. Industrial production began to recover in 1987, when it increased by 1.8%. In 1988 production grew by 5.6%, and during the first half of 1989 it was expected to increase by 1.9%. The major branches of the manufacturing sector are steel, motor vehicles, aircraft, mechanical and electrical engineering, textiles, chemicals and food processing.

In 1986 the Government of Jacques Chirac introduced a five-year programme to 'privatize' 65 state-owned industrial, banking and financial holding companies, including companies that had been nationalized by the Socialist Government in 1982. The Chirac Government hoped to obtain about 200,000m. francs from the sale of state assets, at a rate of 40,000m. francs per year. By April 1988 the Government had privatized 29 companies, providing a total of 83,740m. francs. The newly-privatized companies remained 10% government-owned, with company employees holding a further 10% of shares and foreign groups holding a maximum of 20% of shares. In order to protect newly-privatized companies from hostile acquisitions, controlling interests in them were sold to shareholders chosen by the Government. These shareholders were required to retain 10% of their shares during the two years following privatization, and had to gain the permission of the board of the privatized company before they could sell their shares during the following three years. In 1988 the newly-elected Socialist Government announced that it would not seek to renationalize any of the privatized companies, nor would it continue to implement the previous Government's privatization programme. Legislation was also introduced to allow the controlling shareholders to dispose freely of their shares in privatized companies, with the aim of reshaping the controlling interests, which had been criticized by the Socialist Government for being composed largely of supporters of the previous Government.

In response to the accumulation of financial losses in the nationalized sector, the Chirac Government appointed new heads of state-owned companies to introduce rationalization programmes in 1986. These programmes continued to be implemented under the Socialist Government, which aimed to make state-controlled companies subject to normal market conditions. Government grants to nationalized industries, excluding the coal sector, were projected to reach 15,000m. francs in 1988 and 4,100m. francs in 1989. In 1989 Charbonnages de France (CdF), the state-controlled coal-mining company, was to receive a subsidy of 7,191m. francs, compared with 7,089m. francs in 1988. Losses by the coal industry fell from 8,900m. francs in 1985 to 200m. francs in 1987, before rising to 1,700m. francs in 1988. Net output of coal was reduced from 15m. metric tons in 1986 to 13.5m. tons in 1987, and was expected to fall to 13.1m. tons in 1989. Under its 1987–92 rationalization plan, CdF aimed to reduce its work-force by 5,000–6,000 per year and to close less profitable mines at a rate of one per year. The French steel industry incurred losses of 56,000m. francs over the period 1980–87, but a profit of 4,000m. francs was envisaged for 1988. As part of a rationalization programme initiated in 1986, the two state-owned steel companies were merged in 1987, and it was proposed that annual steel production be reduced to 16m. tons by 1990, and that the work-force be decreased from 58,000 (at the end of 1987) to 45,000 by 1990.

After a steady decline in the early 1980s, France's share in the market for road vehicles, both at home and abroad, recovered in 1986–88. In the first four months of 1988 exports increased by 8.1%, compared with the corresponding period of 1987. In 1987 exports rose by 7.5%, compared with 1986. Meanwhile, domestic sales increased, owing to a reduction of 5.3% in the value-added tax (VAT) payable on purchases of passenger cars and motor cycles, introduced in September 1987. The performance of the Régie Nationale des Usines Renault, the state-owned vehicle manufacturer, improved dramatically in 1987–88: it achieved a profit of 3,700m. francs in 1987, after accumulating 32,500m. francs in losses since 1981, and a profit of more than 6,000m. francs was envisaged for 1988. Sales grew by 6.6% in 1987, but declined by 2.1% in the first 11 months of 1988. In 1987 the Chirac Government proposed to change Renault's status from a state enterprise, or régie, to a state-owned limited company, or société anonyme, and thus entitle Renault to obtain up to 50% of its capital from the public and to operate without an unlimited state guarantee. This proposal was opposed by the Parti Communiste Français and the trade unions, and in 1988 the newly-elected Socialist Government introduced measures to retain Renault's status as a régie, while making the company subject to the same conditions as a société anonyme. The Government also agreed to cancel Renault's state debt of 12,000m. francs, thus reducing the company's overall debt for 1988 to an estimated 28,000m. francs. In early 1989 Renault proposed to reduce its work-force from 70,400 to 67,647 by early 1990, in order to stimulate productivity. In 1986 the Government reduced aid to the five major shipbuilding yards, and proposed rationalization plans whereby only one of the five yards would remain operational. In 1987 three corporate-tax-free zones were established near the three Normed shipbuilding operations, in order to attract industrial investments to France. State aid to the shipbuilding industry was reduced from 3,590m. francs in 1987 to about 1,000m. francs in 1988.

France was the world's fourth largest exporting country in 1987. There were, however, heavy trade deficits, as France's market share of world trade in manufactured goods had declined from 11.1% in 1980 to 6.8% in 1986. The deficit reached a record 93,300m. francs in 1982, but declined to 600m. francs in 1986. In 1987 the trade deficit increased to 31,600m. francs, as the balance in manufactured products moved into deficit for the first time since 1969. The deficit in manufactured goods was maintained by an increase in industrial investment spending, and the overall trade deficit reached 33,000m. francs in 1988. The trade balance was expected to improve in 1989. France was the world's third largest exporter of armaments in 1987. In that year French sales of armaments totalled 27,300m. francs, compared with 25,000m. francs in 1986. In 1988, however, sales were expected to be adversely affected by the sharp decline of France's traditional military export markets in the Middle East. France also plays a leading part in the European aerospace industry. In 1988 sales of aerospace equipment increased by 30%, compared with the previous year, reaching 38,000m. francs. At the end of 1988, it was forecast that sales would rise to 64,000m. francs per year in 1989–90, on the basis of contracts already signed. France's principal trading partners are the other members of the EEC, especially the Federal Republic of Germany, Italy and Belgium. There has been a significant improvement in the balance of payments in recent years: the current account registered a surplus of US $3,002m. in 1986, compared with a deficit of $12,082m. in 1982. However, there was a deficit of $5,091m. in 1987, although the total was reduced in 1988. Tourism is one of France's largest sources of foreign exchange earnings, contributing 31,500m. francs to the country's current account in 1985, but revenue fell sharply, to 19,927m. francs, in 1987, as the industry suffered from US fears of terrorism. Revenue from tourism totalled an estimated 23,000m. francs in 1988.

France's GDP (in constant prices) increased by 1.3% per year, on average, in 1980–86. In 1987 GDP grew by 2.2%, and in 1988 it expanded by 3.5%, the highest growth rate since 1976. The growth rate for 1989 was projected at 3%. The foreign medium- and long-term debt rose from 187,000m. francs at the end of 1981 to 528,000m. francs at the end of 1984, but fell to 382,100m. francs by the end of 1988. The average annual rate of inflation declined from 13.4% in 1981 to 2.1% in 1986. Inflation reached 3.1% per year in 1987 and 1988, but it was expected to fall to 2.5% in 1989.

Industrial stagnation and the effects of restructuring nationalized industries led to increased unemployment, particularly among young people. The Chirac Government attempted to reduce unemployment by initiating job-creation schemes and by introducing legislation to encourage more flexible working patterns. In 1986 about 50,000 jobs were created on job-creation schemes, although it was estimated that a similar number of jobs had been lost in French industry in the same year. In July 1987 there was a 3.9% increase in unemployment over the 1986 mid-year figure, with an estimated 2.64m. unemployed (some 11% of the total labour force), although by August 1988 unemployment had declined to 2.61m., or 10.4% of the total labour force. In December unemployment fell by 2.7%, compared with August, to 2.54m. The number of unemployed under 25 years of age totalled 961,000 at the end of 1987, a reduction of 1.5% compared with the previous year. The number of long-term unemployed totalled 774,974 in April 1988, a fall of 10.4% compared with mid-1987. However, the numbers of young and long-term unemployed were expected to rise during the second half of 1988, as the training programmes and job-creation schemes that had been initiated in 1986 began to expire. In 1988 the Socialist Government introduced incentives for businesses to expand and create more jobs. Low-interest loans were extended to small businesses, and five-year tax exemptions were to be granted to companies starting between October 1988 and December 1993. Companies reinvesting their profits would have their liability to corporation tax reduced from 42% to 39%. Individuals employing workers for the first time were granted a two-year tax exemption from social security contributions, while other businesses had their social security contributions reduced. Nevertheless, owing to demographic factors, it would be necessary to create about 70,000 new jobs per year in 1988–90, in order to restrict unemployment to 10% of the labour force in 1990.

Following the general election in March 1986, the new right-wing Government introduced a series of economic measures aiming to limit the annual rate of inflation to 2.3% and to reduce the budgetary deficit by 1,300m. francs per year. The Government also proposed to obtain an estimated 200,000m. francs over five years by the disposal of state assets through its privatization programme (see above). Taxation was reduced, owing to the abolition of the Socialist-sponsored wealth tax and to an increase in the level of minimum earnings liable to taxation, although this was offset by an increase in social security and pension fund contributions. The effect of new reductions in corporation tax was balanced by cuts of 10% in government aid to industry. In May 1987, to reduce the social security budgetary deficit of 24,000m. francs, the Government introduced emergency measures, including the extension, into 1988, of an income tax levy of 0.4%. The budget proposals for 1988 reduced direct taxation, although the effect of the reductions was offset by the emergency measures. VAT on passenger motor cars, motor cycles, video-cassette recorders and gramophone records was to be decreased, in an attempt to reduce inflation by encouraging consumption. Companies were to benefit from reductions in rates of taxation, but state subsidies to industries were to be reduced by 9%. Expenditure was to be increased by 2.8%, and was to benefit training schemes for the unemployed, education, research and overseas aid. The budget deficit was projected at 114,983m. francs, or 2.1% of expected annual GDP. In June 1988 the newly-elected Socialist Government increased the minimum wage by 1%, in order to maintain the purchasing power of earnings among low-paid workers. Owing to the unexpectedly high level of tax receipts for the first half of 1988, the Socialist Government's budget proposals for 1989 increased expenditure by 4.7% and reduced the budget deficit to 100,342m. francs, or 1.7% of projected annual GDP. Education, training, research, job creation and overseas aid were designated spending priorities. The Government proposed to establish a minimum income for the poor, which would be partly financed by a new wealth and

FRANCE

Introductory Survey

solidarity tax, to be paid by persons with annual incomes of more than 4m. francs. The Government also introduced reductions in corporation tax (see above), and proposed to reorganize rates of VAT and to reduce the highest rate of VAT from 33.3% to 28%. In 1989 the Government published France's 10th National Plan (for the period 1989-92). The Plan envisaged an annual economic growth rate of at least 2.5%, in order to restrict the rise in unemployment, and increases in investment and exports, with the aim of achieving a trade surplus by 1992. During the period of the Plan, the fiscal system was to be reformed, in order to attract capital to France and to develop Paris as a financial centre, in the context of the EEC's proposed Single European Market, due to take effect at the end of 1992.

Social Welfare

France has evolved a comprehensive system of social security, which is compulsory for all wage-earners and self-employed people. State insurance of wage-earners requires contributions from both employers and employees, and provides for sickness, unemployment, maternity, disability through industrial accident, and substantial allowances for large families. The self-employed must make these contributions in full. War veterans receive pensions and certain privileges, and widows the equivalent of three months' salary and pension. About 95% of all medical practitioners adhere to the state scheme. The patient pays directly for medical treatment and prescribed medicines, and then obtains reimbursement for all or part of the cost. Sickness benefits and pensions are related to the insured person's income, age and the length of time for which he or she has been insured. In 1985 expenditure by the central Government included 394,047m. francs for health, and a further 1,395,600m. francs for social security and welfare. In 1987 France had 3,560 hospital establishments, with a total of 499,326 beds in 1985, equivalent to one for every 92 inhabitants. In 1986 there were 128,000 physicians registered in France. A national minimum hourly wage is in force, and is periodically adjusted in accordance with fluctuations in the cost of living.

Education

France is divided into 27 educational districts, called Académies, each responsible for the administration of education, from primary to higher levels, in its area. Education is compulsory and free for children aged six to 16 years. Primary education begins at six years of age and lasts for five years. At the age of 11 all pupils enter the first cycle of the Enseignement secondaire, with a four-year general course. At the age of 15 they may then proceed to the second cycle, choosing a course leading to the baccalauréat examination after three years or a course leading to the brevet d'études professionnelles after two years, with commercial, administrative or industrial options. In 1963 junior classes in the Lycées were gradually abolished in favour of new junior comprehensives, called Collèges. Alongside the collèges and lycées, technical education is provided in the Lycées professionnels and the Lycées techniques. About 17% of children attend France's 10,000 private schools, most of which are administered by the Roman Catholic Church. The Socialist Government's plans to merge private schools into the state system were abandoned in 1984, following strong public protest; compromise measures were introduced, however, involving continued government financial assistance and greater involvement in the appointment of teachers at private schools.

Educational reforms, introduced in 1980, aimed to decentralize the state school system: the school calendar now varies according to three zones, and the previously rigid and formal syllabus has been replaced by more flexibility and choice of curricula. Further decentralization measures have included, from 1986, the transfer of financial responsibility for education to the local authorities. In January 1989 the Socialist Government initiated a series of reforms aiming to 'develop, diversify and renovate' the education system. The legislation identified four targets for the system: no one should leave school without a recognized form of qualification; 80% of all schoolchildren should achieve the baccalauréat, or its equivalent; everyone who passes the baccalauréat examination should have the right to continue to higher education; and teaching methods should be reformed.

The minimum qualification for entry to university faculties is the baccalauréat. There are three cycles of university education. The first level, the Diplôme d'études universitaires générales (DEUG), is reached after two years of study, and the first degree, the Licence, is obtained after three years. The master's degree (Maîtrise) is obtained after four years of study, while the doctorate requires six or seven years' study and the submission of a thesis. The prestigious Grandes Ecoles complement the universities; entry to them is by competitive examination, and they have traditionally supplied France's administrative élite. The 1968 reforms in higher education aimed to increase university autonomy and to render teaching methods less formal. Several new diploma courses were instituted in 1982 and 1984, and more directly vocational and professional qualifications are planned. However, Government plans to revise the baccalauréat, to introduce further selection procedures for entry to the universities, to restrict places on courses and to award separate degrees in each university were abandoned in December 1986, following student protests.

Expenditure on education by central and local government in 1989 was projected at 209,000m. francs. Different forms of financial aid are available to university students, but in 1985/86 only 16% of French students obtained a grant.

Primary teachers are trained in Ecoles Normales. Secondary teachers must hold either the Certificat d'Aptitude au Professorat d'Enseignement Général des Collèges (CAPEGC), the Certificat d'Aptitude au Professorat de l'Enseignement du Second Degré (CAPES) or the Agrégation.

Public Holidays

1989: 2 January (for New Year's Day), 27 March (Easter Monday), 1 May (Labour Day), 4 May (Ascension Day), 8 May (Liberation Day), 15 May (Whit Monday), 14 July (National Day, Fall of the Bastille), 15 August (Assumption), 1 November (All Saints' Day), 11 November (Armistice Day), 25 December (Christmas Day).

1990: 1 January (New Year's Day), 16 April (Easter Monday), 1 May (Labour Day), 8 May (Liberation Day), 24 May (Ascension Day), 4 June (Whit Monday), 14 July (National Day, Fall of the Bastille), 15 August (Assumption), 1 November (All Saints' Day), 11 November (Armistice Day), 25 December (Christmas Day).

Weights and Measures

The metric system is in force.

Statistical Survey

Unless otherwise indicated, figures in this survey refer to metropolitan France, excluding Overseas Departments and Territories.

Area and Population

AREA, POPULATION AND DENSITY

Area (sq km)	543,965*
Population (census results, *de jure*)†	
20 February 1975	52,655,802
4 March 1982	54,334,871
Population (official estimates at mid-year)	
1985	55,170,000
1986	55,392,000
1987	55,632,000
Density (per sq km) at mid-1987	102.3

* 210,026 sq miles.
† Excluding professional soldiers and military personnel outside the country with no personal residence in France. These were estimated at 44,000 in 1975.

NATIONALITY OF THE POPULATION (1982 census*)

Country of citizenship	Population	%
France	50,593,100	93.22
Algeria	795,920	1.47
Belgium	50,200	0.09
Germany	43,840	0.08
Italy	333,740	0.61
Morocco	431,120	0.79
Poland	64,820	0.12
Portugal	764,860	1.41
Spain	321,440	0.59
Tunisia	189,400	0.35
Turkey	123,540	0.23
Yugoslavia	64,420	0.11
Others	496,800	0.93
Total	**54,273,200**	**100.00**

* Figures based on a 5% sample of census returns.

REGIONS (1982 census*)

	Area (sq km)	Population	Density (per sq km)
Ile-de-France	12,012.3	10,064,840	837.9
Champagne-Ardennes	25,605.8	1,344,820	52.5
Picardie (Picardy)	19,399.5	1,740,460	89.7
Haute-Normandie	12,317.4	1,659,520	134.7
Centre	39,150.9	2,265,340	57.9
Basse-Normandie	17,589.3	1,350,480	76.8
Bourgogne (Burgundy)	31,581.9	1,592,300	50.4
Nord-Pas-de-Calais	12,414.1	3,919,240	315.7
Lorraine	23,547.1	2,334,740	99.2
Alsace	8,280.2	1,553,740	187.6
Franche-Comté	16,202.4	1,078,700	66.6
Pays de la Loire	32,081.8	2,937,980	91.6
Bretagne (Brittany)	27,207.9	2,703,440	99.4
Poitou-Charentes	25,809.5	1,567,600	60.3
Aquitaine	41,308.4	2,655,800	64.3
Midi-Pyrénées	45,347.9	2,308,740	50.9
Limousin	16,942.3	736,340	43.5
Rhône-Alpes	43,698.2	5,022,800	114.9
Auvergne	26,012.9	1,329,180	51.0
Languedoc-Roussillon	27,375.8	1,929,520	70.5
Provence-Alpes-Côte d'Azur	31,397.9	3,942,980	125.6
Corse (Corsica)	8,681.5	234,640	27.0
Total	**543,965.4**	**54,273,200**	**99.8**

* Figures for population are based on a 5% sample of census returns.

PRINCIPAL TOWNS
(population at 1982 census)

Paris (capital)	2,188,918	Le Mans	150,331	
Marseille (Marseilles)	878,689	Dijon	145,569	
		Limoges	144,082	
Lyon (Lyons)	418,476	Angers	141,143	
Toulouse	354,289	Tours	136,483	
Nice	338,486	Amiens	136,358	
Strasbourg	252,264	Nîmes	129,924	
Nantes	247,227	Aix-en-Provence	124,550	
Bordeaux	211,197	Besançon	119,687	
Saint-Etienne	206,688	Metz	118,502	
Montpellier	201,067	Villeurbanne	118,330	
Le Havre	200,411	Caen	117,119	
Rennes	200,390	Mulhouse	113,794	
Reims (Rheims)	181,985	Perpignan	113,646	
Toulon	181,405	Orléans	105,589	
Lille	174,039	Rouen	105,083	
Brest	160,355	Boulogne-Billancourt	102,595	
Grenoble	159,503			
Clermont-Ferrand	151,092	Roubaix	101,886	

BIRTHS, MARRIAGES AND DEATHS*

	Registered live births		Registered marriages		Registered deaths	
	Number	Rate (per 1,000)	Number	Rate (per 1,000)	Number	Rate (per 1,000)
1980	800,376	14.9	334,377	6.2	547,107	10.2
1981	805,483	14.9	315,117	5.8	554,823	10.3
1982	797,223	14.6	312,405	5.7	543,104	10.0
1983	748,525	13.7	300,513	5.5	559,655	10.2
1984	759,939	13.8	281,402	5.1	542,490	9.9
1985	768,431	13.9	269,419	4.9	552,496	10.0
1986†	778,940	14.1	265,990	4.8	546,880	9.9
1987†	768,040	13.8	n.a.	4.8	527,280	9.5

* Including data for national armed forces outside the country.
† Provisional figures.

Expectation of Life at Birth (1983–85): Males 71.04 years; Females 79.19 years.

IMMIGRATION AND EMIGRATION

	1984	1985	1986
Algerian workers and their families:			
Arriving from Algeria in France	1,564,460	1,834,617	1,261,955
Returning from France to Algeria	1,573,090	1,919,124	1,308,440
Other immigrants:			
Permanent	51,426	43,426	38,370
Seasonal	93,220	86,180	81,670

FRANCE

Statistical Survey

ECONOMICALLY ACTIVE POPULATION

	1982 Census*			Official estimate 1985†
	Males	Females	Total	
Agriculture, hunting, forestry and fishing	1,162,840	598,356	1,761,196	1,582,600
Mining and quarrying	123,340	10,636	133,976	114,700
Manufacturing	3,635,104	1,596,440	5,231,544	4,837,800
Electricity, gas and water	165,440	36,652	202,092	210,900
Construction	1,648,380	125,984	1,774,364	1,517,400
Trade, restaurants and hotels	1,871,744	1,576,664	3,448,408	3,483,700
Transport, storage and communications	1,004,752	324,772	1,329,524	1,368,500
Finance, insurance, real estate and business services	861,980	762,496	1,624,476	1,688,900
Community, social and personal services	2,524,804	3,441,400	5,966,204	6,388,200
Total employed	12,998,384	8,473,400	21,471,784	21,192,700
Unemployed	934,860	1,144,532	2,079,392	2,425,900
Total labour force	13,933,244	9,617,932	23,551,176	23,618,600

* Based on a 25% sample of census returns. Figures include all members of the armed forces.
† Data are rounded to the nearest 100. The total labour force comprised 13,630,800 males (12,482,500 employed; 1,148,300 unemployed) and 9,987,900 females (8,710,300 employed; 1,277,600 unemployed). Figures include regular members of the armed forces, totalling 303,900 (males 286,400; females 17,500), but exclude persons on compulsory military service.

1986 (official estimate): Total labour force 24,317,500 (males 14,109,200; females 10,208,300).

Source: ILO, *Year Book of Labour Statistics*.

Agriculture

PRINCIPAL CROPS ('000 metric tons)

	1985	1986	1987
Wheat	28,890	26,570	27,434
Rye	297	229	299
Barley	11,440	10,120	10,490
Oats	1,770	1,066	1,122
Maize*	12,409	11,641	12,052
Sorghum	206	172	209
Rice (paddy)	62	60	n.a.
Sugar beet	29,977	25,830	26,471
Potatoes	7,787	6,021†	7,200‡
Pulses	1,062	1,263	1,955
Soybeans	56	98	n.a.
Sunflower seed	1,514	1,869	2,315
Rapeseed	1,418	1,043	2,669
Tobacco (leaves)	36	38	38
Artichokes	83	100†	n.a.
Cabbages	287	270‡	n.a.
Carrots	644	500	n.a.
Cauliflowers	526	411	n.a.
Cucumbers and gherkins	103	108‡	n.a.
Melons	254	269	n.a.
Onions (dry)	193	172	184
Peas (green)	460	450	n.a.
Tomatoes	940	712	685
Apples	2,349	2,739	2,424
Apricots	103	115	n.a.
Grapes	10,226†	10,800‡	10,300‡
Peaches and nectarines	488	472	n.a.
Pears	435	370	n.a.
Plums	197	200	n.a.

* Figures refer to main, associated and catch crops.
† Unofficial estimate.
‡ FAO estimate.

Source: FAO, *Production Yearbook* and *Quarterly Bulletin of Statistics*.

LIVESTOCK ('000 head at 31 December)

	1984	1985	1986
Cattle	23,099*	23,102	22,803
Pigs	10,975	10,956*	12,002*
Sheep*	10,824	10,790	10,580
Goats	962	969†	976†
Horses	310†	310†	n.a.
Asses	23†	23†	n.a.
Mules	12†	12†	n.a.

Chickens* (million): 188 in 1984; 188 in 1985.
Ducks* (million): 10 in 1984; 11 in 1985.
Turkeys* (million): 17 in 1984; 18 in 1985.

* Unofficial figure.
† FAO estimate.

Source: FAO, *Production Yearbook* and *Quarterly Bulletin of Statistics*.

LIVESTOCK PRODUCTS ('000 metric tons)

	1985	1986	1987
Beef and veal	1,893	1,910	1,955
Mutton and lamb	176†	167	n.a.
Goats' meat	8†	8*	n.a.
Pig meat	1,662	1,677	1,730*
Horse meat	28	24	n.a.
Poultry meat	1,272	1,322	1,384
Other meat	295	295	n.a.
Edible offals*	413	412	415
Cows' milk*	33,000	33,700	32,400
Sheep's milk†	1,061	1,118	1,061
Goats' milk*	350	454	500
Butter	606	640	558†
Cheese	1,277	1,283	1,315*
Hen eggs	915	925	900*
Wool:			
greasy†	24	24	24
clean*	12	12	12

* FAO estimate.
† Unofficial figure.

Source: FAO, *Production Yearbook* and *Quarterly Bulletin of Statistics*.

FRANCE

Forestry

ROUNDWOOD REMOVALS
('000 cubic metres, excluding bark)

	1984	1985	1986
Sawlogs, veneer logs and logs for sleepers	18,639	18,722	18,920
Pulpwood	9,320	9,159	9,159*
Other industrial wood	616	606	606*
Fuel wood*	10,424	10,424	10,430
Total	38,999	38,911	39,115

* FAO estimate.
Source: FAO, *Yearbook of Forest Products*.

SAWNWOOD PRODUCTION
('000 cubic metres, including boxboards)

	1984	1985	1986
Coniferous (softwood)	5,617	5,694	5,700
Broadleaved (hardwood)	3,273	3,199	3,190
Total	8,890	8,893	8,890

Railway sleepers ('000 cubic metres): 185 in 1984; 188 in 1985.
Source: FAO, *Yearbook of Forest Products*.

Fishing*

('000 metric tons, live weight)

	1984	1985	1986†
Atlantic cod	56.4	58.8	58.4
Ling	15.2	14.0	13.9
Blue ling	8.2	15.8	15.7
Haddock	17.9	19.4	19.3
Saithe (Pollock)	68.2	70.0	69.6
Whiting	34.2	33.5	33.3
European hake	21.0	27.9	27.7
Angler (Monk)	22.7	22.8	22.7
Atlantic herring	22.4	14.7	14.6
European sardine (pilchard)	24.3	29.3	29.1
Skipjack tuna	36.5	39.9	56.7
Yellowfin tuna	40.3	43.6	41.0
Atlantic mackerel	13.3	18.2	18.1
Sharks, rays, skates, etc.	21.2	21.9	21.8
Other fishes (incl. unspecified)	143.1	128.1	121.9
Total fish	544.7	557.9	563.7
Crustaceans	27.8	27.6	26.9
Oysters	112.4	139.8	137.0
Blue mussel	49.3	55.0	60.6
Other molluscs	31.2	34.1	32.0
Other marine animals	0.3	0.1	0.1
Total catch	765.7	814.5	820.4
Mediterranean and Black Sea	47.5	49.4	47.3
Atlantic Ocean	656.6	696.0	686.1
Indian Ocean	61.6	69.1	87.0

* Figures include quantities landed by French craft in foreign ports and exclude quantities landed by foreign craft in French ports. Data exclude aquatic plants ('000 metric tons): 64.2 in 1984; 72.2 in 1985; 68.8 in 1986. Also excluded is the catch from inland waters ('000 metric tons): 29.8 in 1985; 29.6 (FAO estimate) in 1986.
† FAO estimates.
Source: FAO, *Yearbook of Fishery Statistics*.

Mining

('000 metric tons, unless otherwise indicated)

	1984	1985	1986
Hard coal	18,278	17,103	16,342
Brown coal (incl. lignite)	2,426	1,839	2,142
Iron ore:			
gross weight	14,840	14,374	12,072
metal content	4,680	4,539	3,717
Bauxite	1,522	1,454	1,238
Crude petroleum	2,065	2,642	2,948
Potash salts	1,873	1,884	1,617
Native sulphur	1,773	1,940	1,170
Salt (unrefined)	7,160	7,111	7,083
Lead concentrates (metric tons)†	2,000	1,800	1,700
Zinc concentrates (metric tons)†	36,000	40,300	47,800
Natural gas (million cu m)	6,580	5,781	4,388

* Figures refer to recovered quantities of K_2O.
† Figures refer to the metal content of concentrates.
Source: Ministère de l'Industrie, des Postes et Télécommunications et du Tourisme; and Institut national de la statistique et des études économiques.

Industry

SELECTED PRODUCTS
('000 metric tons, unless otherwise indicated)

	1984	1985	1986
Wheat flour*	4,632	4,284	4,922
Raw sugar	4,305	4,324	3,734†
Margarine	154	153	152
Wine ('000 hectolitres)	64,148	70,291	74,220
Beer ('000 hectolitres)	20,287	19,305	18,850
Cigarettes (million)	60,729	67,376	59,122
Cotton yarn—pure and mixed (metric tons)[1]	146,863	133,600	n.a.
Woven cotton fabrics—pure and mixed (metric tons)	126,123	119,716	116,988
Wool yarn—pure and mixed (metric tons)	113,644	111,566	n.a.
Woven woollen fabrics—pure and mixed (metric tons)	47,237	49,709	48,375
Rayon and acetate continuous filaments (metric tons)	7,523	7,000†	n.a.
Rayon and acetate discontinuous fibres (metric tons)[2]	20,980	15,000†	n.a.
Non-cellulosic continuous filaments (metric tons)	63,513	62,000	n.a.
Non-cellulosic discontinuous fibres (metric tons)	146,060	137,036	122,838
Woven fabrics of non-cellulosic (synthetic) fibres (metric tons)[3]	66,751	60,828	n.a.
Mechanical wood pulp	454	452	n.a.
Chemical wood pulp	1,455.7	1,390.3	1,445
Newsprint	264.5	263.6	304
Other printing and writing paper	2,254.5	2,127.3	2,196
Other paper and paperboard	3,046.5	2,952.4	3,085
Synthetic rubber	555	548	675
Rubber tyres ('000)[4]	47,817	47,742	52,524
Sulphuric acid	4,531	4,322	3,954
Caustic soda (Sodium hydroxide)	1,497	1,590	1,517
Nitrogenous fertilizers (a)[5]	1,600	1,695	1,690
Phosphate fertilizers (b)[5]	1,230	1,168	1,023
Potash fertilizers (b)[5]	1,685	1,729	1,719
Plastics and synthetic resins	3,319	n.a.	n.a.
Liquefied petroleum gas[6]	2,291	2,515	2,411
Motor spirit (petrol)	16,009	17,210	16,326
Jet fuel	4,479	4,344	4,244
Distillate fuel oils	10,330	10,961	10,364
Residual fuel oil	34,057	31,130	29,716
Petroleum bitumen (asphalt)	2,310	2,413	2,572

FRANCE — *Statistical Survey*

—continued	1984	1985	1986
Coke-oven coke	8,999	8,691	8,258
Cement	22,724.2	22,219.8	n.a.
Pig-iron	15,039	15,072	14,003
Crude steel	19,000	18,808	17,440
Rolled steel products	16,543	15,438	15,165
Aluminium (unwrought):			
primary	342	368	386
secondary (incl. alloys)	159	162	173
Refined copper—unwrought (metric tons)	40,701	43,704	41,294
Lead (unwrought):			
primary	118	133	132
secondary	85	73	72
Zinc (unwrought)[7]	257.6	247.2	257
Radio receivers ('000)	2,128	2,633	n.a.
Television receivers ('000)	2,001	1,913	1,868
Merchant ships launched ('000 gross reg. tons)	290	186	185
Passenger motor cars ('000)	2,713.3	2,632.4	2,773.1
Lorries and vans ('000)	327.8	373.7	409.3
Mopeds and motorcycles ('000)	450	448	n.a.
Construction: dwellings completed ('000)[8]	270.8	254.7	237.3
Electric energy (million kWh)	307,155	326,400	n.a.

* Deliveries.
† Estimate.
[1] Including tyre-cord yarn. [2] Including cigarette filtration tow.
[3] Including fabrics of natural silk.
[4] Tyres for road motor vehicles other than bicycles and motor cycles.
[5] Twelve months ending (a) 30 June or (b) 30 April of year stated. Production is in terms of plant nutrients: nitrogen, phosphoric acid and K_2O.
[6] Excluding production in natural gas processing plants ('000 metric tons): 256 in 1984; 239 in 1985.
[7] Primary production only.
[8] Including restorations and conversions but excluding single rooms without kitchens.

Source: Ministère de l'Industrie, des Postes et Télécommunications et du Tourisme; and Institut national de la statistique et des études économiques.

Finance

CURRENCY AND EXCHANGE RATES

Monetary Units:
100 centimes = 1 French franc.

Denominations:
Coins: 1, 5, 10, 20 and 50 centimes; 1, 2, 5, 10 and 100 francs.
Notes: 10, 50, 100, 200 and 500 francs.

Sterling and Dollar Equivalents (30 September 1988)
£1 sterling = 10.77 francs;
US $1 = 6.37 francs;
1,000 French francs = £92.83 = $156.99.

Average Exchange Rate (francs per US $)
1985 8.985
1986 6.926
1987 6.011

BUDGET (million francs)

Revenue	1984	1985	1986
Tax revenue	950,037	1,009,104	1,062,332
Income tax	203,397	204,155	210,507
Corporation tax	89,290	93,720	99,930
Value-added tax	415,800	444,624	470,895
Stamp duty, etc.*	49,980	53,167	56,024
Other customs revenue	10,455	11,256	12,031
Petroleum revenue	67,396	85,291	90,915
Other taxes	113,719	116,981	122,030
Non-tax revenue	54,002	60,475	63,746
Special accounts	10,623	11,649	11,980
Tax relief and reimbursements	−73,620	−98,570	−107,400
Other deductions, e.g. EEC	−107,912	−115,284	−129,088
Total	833,130	867,374	901,570

* Including registration duties and tax on stock exchange transactions.

Expenditure	1984	1985	1986
Public authorities, general administration	108,694	116,114	128,704
Education and culture	223,084	238,566	246,505
Social services, health and employment	199,688	200,859	199,042
Agriculture and rural areas	24,365	25,179	25,726
Housing and town planning	42,765	46,939	48,023
Transport and communications	42,795	42,920	43,052
Industry and services	46,490	50,853	51,301
Foreign affairs	27,479	26,150	26,236
Defence	150,769	159,531	167,834
Others	94,671	111,060	117,355
Total	960,800	1,018,171	1,053,778

Source: Ministère de l'Economie et des Finances.

BANK OF FRANCE AND EXCHANGE FUND RESERVES*
(US $ million at 31 December)

	1985	1986	1987
Gold†	27,580	33,932	41,496
IMF special drawing rights	900	1,290	1,502
Reserve position in IMF	1,370	1,736	1,914
Foreign exchange	24,319	28,428	29,634
Total	54,169	65,386	74,546

* Excluding deposits made with the European Monetary Co-operation Fund.
† Valued at market-related prices.
Source: IMF, *International Financial Statistics*.

CURRENCY IN CIRCULATION
('000 million francs at 31 December)

	1985	1986	1987
Currency outside banks	207.4	214.2	223.8

Source: Banque de France, Paris.

COST OF LIVING (Consumer Price Index for Urban Households, average of monthly figures; base: 1980 = 100)

	1984	1985	1986
Food	151.4	158.9	164.4
Fuel and light	162.8	176.2	153.9
Clothing and household linen	145.7	157.8	168.0
Rent	146.5	155.9	164.5
All items (incl. others)	149.3	158.0	162.2

1987: Food 167.3; All items 167.3.
Source: ILO, mainly *Year Book of Labour Statistics*.

FRANCE

NATIONAL ACCOUNTS
National Income and Product (million francs at current prices)*

	1983	1984	1985
Compensation of employees	2,188,954	2,343,837	2,476,196
Operating surplus	764,250	832,204	1,001,965
Domestic factor incomes	2,953,204	3,176,041	3,478,161
Consumption of fixed capital	487,800	513,335	572,785
Gross domestic product at factor cost	3,441,004	3,689,376	4,050,946
Indirect taxes	578,065	695,948	639,749
Less Subsidies	84,062	102,481	105,357
GDP in purchasers' values	3,935,007	4,282,843	4,585,338
Factor income received from abroad	−2,709	200,910	219,577
Less Factor income paid abroad		216,206	234,816
Gross national product	3,932,298	4,267,547	4,570,099
Less Consumption of fixed capital	487,800	513,335	572,785
Less Net indirect taxes paid to supranational organizations	6,657	7,927	4,914
National income in market prices	3,437,841	3,746,085	3,992,400

* Figures are provisional. Revised totals of GDP in purchasers' values (in '000 million francs) are: 4,006.5 in 1983; 4,361.9 in 1984; 4,695.0 in 1985.

Source: Ministère de l'Economie et des Finances.

Expenditure on the Gross Domestic Product
('000 million francs at current prices)

	1985	1986	1987
Government final consumption expenditure	924.2	978.6	1,018.1
Private final consumption expenditure	2,856.3	3,032.2	3,202.9
Increase in stocks*	−19.4	12.1	27.6
Gross fixed capital formation*	902.9	960.1	1,017.3
Total domestic expenditure	4,664.0	4,983.0	5,265.9
Exports of goods and services	1,123.9	1,074.6	1,104.2
Less Imports of goods and services	1,093.0	1,022.6	1,091.2
GDP in purchasers' values	4,695.0	5,034.9	5,279.0
GDP at constant 1980 prices	3,021.7	3,084.6	3,154.3

* Construction of non-residential buildings is included in 'Increase in stocks'.

Source: IMF, *International Financial Statistics*.

Gross Domestic Product by Economic Activity
(provisional, million francs at current prices)

	1982	1983	1984
Agriculture and hunting	140,509	142,177	152,651
Forestry and logging	8,937	10,349	10,884
Fishing	3,232	3,640	4,057
Mining and quarrying	28,313	29,061	31,481
Manufacturing	898,268	992,224	1,087,590
Electricity, gas and water	77,150	96,970	109,480
Construction	227,553	236,219	240,918
Wholesale and retail trade	354,890	387,075	409,119
Restaurants and hotels	76,616	87,620	95,005
Transport, storage and communications	187,397	206,051	222,704
Finance, insurance, real estate and business services*	605,820	684,396	772,640
Government services	455,085	505,720	552,620
Other community, social and personal services	292,664	330,539	360,427
Private non-profit services to households / Domestic services of households	25,932	28,166	29,768
Sub-total†	3,382,370	3,740,210	4,079,340
Value-added tax and import duties	331,619	360,160	387,428
Less Imputed bank service charges	147,003	165,360	189,606
Total†	3,566,980	3,935,010	4,277,160

* Including imputed rents of owner-occupied dwellings.
† Rounded to the nearest 10 million francs.

Source: UN, *National Accounts Statistics*.

BALANCE OF PAYMENTS (US $ million)*

	1985	1986	1987
Merchandise exports f.o.b.	95,927	117,988	138,893
Merchandise imports f.o.b.	−101,203	−120,343	−148,713
Trade balance	−5,276	−2,354	−9,820
Exports of services	58,356	69,218	79,648
Imports of services	−50,488	−59,547	−70,090
Balance on goods and services	2,592	7,317	−261
Private unrequited transfers (net)	−1,312	−1,465	−1,715
Government unrequited transfers (net)	−1,315	−2,850	−3,116
Current balance	−35	3,002	−5,091
Direct capital investment (net)	353	−2,147	−4,067
Other long-term capital (net)	3,493	−5,001	6,030
Short-term capital (net)	−1,721	4,905	−6,646
Net errors and omissions	290	662	1,445
Total (net monetary movements)	2,380	1,420	−8,330
Valuation changes (net)	2,981	3,682	4,230
Official financing (net)	316	−237	5,727
Changes in reserves	5,677	4,865	1,627

* Figures refer to transactions of metropolitan France, Monaco and the French overseas departments and territories with the rest of the world.

Source: IMF, *International Financial Statistics*.

FRANCE

FINANCIAL FLOWS TO DEVELOPING COUNTRIES
(US $ million)

	1982	1983	1984*
Official development assistance:			
To individual countries	3,312	3,145	3,170
To multilateral institutions	716	670	618
Other official capital flows	429	467	1,246
Private capital	9,123	5,052	3,862
Total flow of resources	13,580	9,334	8,896

* Provisional.

FINANCIAL FLOWS BY RECEIVING COUNTRIES
(US $ million)

	1982	1983	1984*
Overseas Departments and Overseas Territories (DOM-TOM)	1,560	1,497	1,422
African and Malagasy States	4,146	3,015	1,611
Algeria	−107	379	449
Morocco and Tunisia	613	351	559
Other countries	6,389	3,002	3,715
International organizations	843	906	828
Total	13,444	9,150	8,584

* Provisional.
Source: Ministère des Relations Extérieures, Paris.

External Trade

Note: Figures refer to the trade of metropolitan France and Monaco with the rest of the world, excluding trade in war materials, goods exported under the off-shore procurement programme, war reparations and restitutions and the export of sea products direct from the high seas. The figures include trade in second-hand ships and aircraft, and the supply of stores and bunkers for foreign ships and aircraft.

PRINCIPAL COMMODITIES
(distribution by SITC, million francs)

Imports c.i.f.	1985	1986	1987
Food and live animals	86,338.8	89,648.4	90,857.7
Meat and meat preparations	16,700.3	17,080.2	17,019.1
Fresh, chilled or frozen meat	15,207.0	15,409.2	15,182.2
Vegetables and fruit	21,878.7	22,334.3	23,968.0
Coffee, tea, cocoa and spices	14,274.1	13,972.9	10,921.2
Beverages and tobacco	10,526.9	8,864.3	9,134.0
Crude materials (inedible) except fuels	47,893.7	40,287.6	41,637.6
Mineral fuels, lubricants, etc. (incl. electric current)	215,516.9	112,504.4	102,021.3
Petroleum, petroleum products, etc.	169,506.5	77,637.0	79,135.5
Crude petroleum oils, etc.	126,539.1	51,619.5	50,389.1
Refined petroleum products	40,024.3	23,920.2	26,797.2
Gas (natural and manufactured)	33,083.6	24,813.1	15,712.6
Animal and vegetable oils, fats and waxes	6,628.0	3,879.9	3,127.1
Chemicals and related products	96,649.9	94,879.2	101,083.8
Organic chemicals	24,233.7	22,047.9	23,894.5
Inorganic chemicals	14,665.4	13,649.6	12,976.5
Artificial resins, plastic materials, etc.	21,524.9	22,678.1	25,286.4
Products of polymerization, etc.	13,834.1	14,373.6	16,445.8

Imports c.i.f.—continued	1985	1986	1987
Basic manufactures	155,297.3	157,846.0	164,745.8
Paper, paperboard and manufactures	19,552.5	21,272.4	23,128.1
Paper and paperboard	14,675.8	15,973.9	17,476.7
Textile yarn, fabrics, etc.	31,419.0	32,666.4	33,344.7
Non-metallic mineral manufactures	15,258.4	15,946.0	17,437.0
Iron and steel	32,562.6	31,096.6	30,429.6
Non-ferrous metals	22,692.6	20,581.1	20,541.9
Other metal manufactures	18,983.0	20,580.1	22,849.5
Machinery and transport equipment	239,238.4	261,608.9	298,366.0
Power generating machinery and equipment	21,733.0	21,929.9	24,348.7
Machinery specialized for particular industries	24,350.3	26,647.4	30,695.1
General industrial machinery, equipment and parts	30,233.0	32,276.6	35,743.8
Office machines and automatic data processing equipment	36,519.4	37,759.4	42,007.2
Automatic data processing machines and units	21,269.9	22,064.8	24,832.3
Telecommunications and sound equipment	12,793.4	15,827.0	18,801.9
Other electrical machinery, apparatus, etc.	38,849.3	41,730.8	47,182.0
Road vehicles and parts*	61,914.9	70,397.3	83,333.1
Passenger motor cars (excl. buses)	33,611.9	37,825.3	45,008.9
Parts and accessories for cars, buses, lorries, etc.*	13,977.7	15,428.6	18,016.1
Miscellaneous manufactured articles	102,128.8	114,835.7	130,870.0
Clothing and accessories (excl. footwear)	24,168.8	28,442.9	33,570.6
Professional, scientific and controlling instruments, etc.	14,162.8	14,506.5	16,518.5
Other commodities and transactions†	2,527.5	3,182.1	3,201.2
Total	962,746.4	887,536.5	945,044.5

* Excluding tyres, engines and electrical parts.
† Including items not classified according to kind (million francs): 340.1 in 1985; 365.6 in 1986; 421.5 in 1987.

Exports f.o.b.	1985	1986	1987
Food and live animals	105,566.3	98,900.6	98,336.3
Dairy products and birds' eggs	15,339.4	14,785.9	14,875.9
Cereals and cereal preparations	41,281.3	34,608.7	31,331.5
Wheat and meslin (unmilled)	20,878.5	15,334.9	13,202.8
Beverages and tobacco	27,362.3	28,423.7	30,356.2
Beverages	26,583.9	27,664.5	29,615.1
Alcoholic beverages	25,288.1	26,214.8	27,823.4
Crude materials (inedible) except fuels	36,171.7	30,038.7	33,666.5
Mineral fuels, lubricants, etc. (incl. electric current)	34,533.4	22,758.1	19,541.4
Petroleum, petroleum products, etc.	24,949.6	13,506.2	10,463.6
Refined petroleum products	23,321.8	12,336.0	9,372.9
Animal and vegetable oils, fats and waxes	3,692.9	2,046.0	1,802.4
Chemicals and related products	122,290.2	115,933.1	122,280.6
Organic chemicals	29,022.5	26,460.6	28,247.8
Hydrocarbons and their derivatives	17,805.6	16,622.0	17,714.7
Inorganic chemicals	20,940.9	18,602.9	18,583.3
Medicinal and pharmaceutical products	13,696.9	13,890.9	14,206.4
Essential oils, perfume materials and cleansing preparations	16,009.6	15,846.6	17,100.2
Artificial resins, plastic materials, etc.	21,907.9	21,424.9	23,884.0
Products of polymerization, etc.	15,486.8	15,029.8	16,089.2

FRANCE

Statistical Survey

Exports f.o.b.—*continued*	1985	1986	1987
Basic manufactures	165,745.3	153,299.9	154,274.7
Rubber manufactures	13,010.9	13,653.4	14,142.1
Paper, paperboard and manufactures	14,460.3	14,658.0	16,168.2
Textile yarn, fabrics, etc.	27,886.4	26,966.1	27,195.3
Non-metallic mineral manufactures	17,635.5	16,204.2	16,990.0
Iron and steel	49,353.6	42,483.2	39,710.9
Universals, plates and sheets	14,316.6	13,010.7	12,693.1
Non-ferrous metals	15,778.4	13,697.8	14,120.5
Other metal manufactures	21,856.0	20,326.6	19,826.2
Machinery and transport equipment	285,751.4	286,276.9	303,642.5
Power generating machinery and equipment	24,055.9	23,562.4	25,005.0
Machinery specialized for particular industries	24,674.3	25,193.7	25,220.6
General industrial machinery, equipment and parts	35,980.2	33,931.7	33,513.0
Office machines and automatic data processing equipment	22,900.3	25,293.7	28,902.2
Automatic data processing machines and units	9,593.1	12,554.8	14,377.1
Telecommunications and sound equipment	14,050.7	13,088.2	14,919.7
Other electrical machinery, apparatus, etc.	43,153.4	42,939.9	44,814.4
Road vehicles and parts*	87,652.8	93,354.2	100,872.2
Passenger motor cars (excl. buses)	44,868.0	48,128.2	50,847.3
Parts and accessories for cars, buses, lorries, etc.*	28,890.0	32,142.6	37,944.6
Other transport equipment	28,790.6	24,479.8	26,213.7
Aircraft, etc., and parts*	21,673.9	15,819.9	18,590.8
Miscellaneous manufactured articles	83,517.1	81,928.9	87,936.6
Clothing and accessories (excl. footwear)	17,246.1	17,316.4	18,260.7
Professional, scientific and controlling instruments, etc.	15,503.1	12,932.5	14,590.1
Other commodities and transactions†	6,180.8	5,596.8	5,943.7
Total	870,811.5	825,202.7	857,781.1

* Excluding tyres, engines and electrical parts.
† Including items not classified according to kind (million francs): 2,997.0 in 1985; 2,906.1 in 1986; 3,143.0 in 1987.

PRINCIPAL TRADING PARTNERS (million francs)*

Imports c.i.f.	1985	1986	1987
Algeria	20,754.0	11,547.5	8,535.1
Australia	5,505.3	5,217.8	5,695.4
Austria	6,396.1	7,113.6	7,709.3
Belgium and Luxembourg	82,288.4	83,913.9	88,679.9
Brazil	10,094.4	8,396.8	7,502.2
Cameroon	7,233.7	3,162.2	2,411.4
Canada	6,990.3	6,715.0	6,539.2
China, People's Republic	4,452.9	4,890.3	6,589.8
Côte d'Ivoire	5,241.1	4,139.5	3,456.0
Denmark	6,625.4	7,485.9	8,400.9
Finland	5,546.7	5,805.8	6,978.1
Gabon	5,606.8	3,874.7	3,067.5
Germany, Federal Republic	159,056.7	172,329.4	186,648.1
Iran	7,099.4	2,223.0	3,833.3
Iraq	12,366.2	3,997.8	5,954.9
Ireland	6,850.7	6,955.5	7,374.3
Italy	96,796.3	103,279.1	110,810.2
Japan	26,887.2	32,207.8	36,056.5
Korea, Republic	4,037.4	4,467.0	6,650.6
Libya	6,858.2	2,378.9	2,850.5
Mexico	5,268.0	2,497.7	3,999.5
Morocco	6,052.8	5,749.5	6,380.4
Netherlands	58,538.9	50,996.9	53,271.0
Nigeria	15,320.3	5,624.0	3,466.3
Norway	15,046.7	9,474.8	10,807.8
Portugal	6,797.3	7,807.1	9,282.9
Saudi Arabia	10,841.3	13,173.5	7,448.4
South Africa	5,749.0	3,376.2	3,489.4
Spain (excl. Canary Is.)	36,535.3	36,938.7	41,238.9
Sweden	14,361.3	14,612.5	15,684.3
Switzerland and Liechtenstein	20,275.3	22,167.7	23,625.4
Taiwan	3,551.9	4,920.0	7,405.7
USSR	22,079.0	18,144.6	15,348.3
United Arab Emirates	5,336.9	1,091.5	1,756.2
United Kingdom	78,991.6	57,696.6	67,179.0
USA and Puerto Rico	73,245.8	66,988.9	67,586.9
Total (incl. others)	962,746.4	887,536.5	945,044.5

* Imports by country of production; exports by country of last consignment.

Source: Direction Générale des Douanes et Droits Indirects.

Exports f.o.b.	1985	1986	1987
Algeria	21,798.0	15,850.8	11,755.3
Austria	6,349.5	6,850.0	7,146.1
Belgium and Luxembourg	73,931.1	74,894.3	79,864.9
Brazil	3,563.3	5,237.7	5,249.2
Cameroon	5,389.9	4,955.5	3,835.2
Canada	9,506.7	8,125.7	8,741.3
China, People's Republic	6,976.0	4,596.9	5,086.3
Denmark	7,160.8	7,907.1	7,734.0
Egypt	8,953.1	6,440.1	5,360.9
Germany, Federal Republic	130,513.2	133,045.9	142,699.3
Greece	6,813.7	6,620.3	6,714.4
India	5,267.7	6,605.1	5,148.7
Iraq	6,140.6	3,398.0	2,199.3
Italy	95,322.1	97,014.0	103,597.8
Japan	10,735.8	11,156.3	13,210.3
Morocco	9,178.5	7,300.1	6,475.9
Netherlands	42,608.3	40,661.8	43,600.7
Norway	5,011.6	5,622.9	5,378.3
Portugal	6,153.0	6,724.8	9,328.6
Réunion	4,168.7	4,545.0	5,367.7
Saudi Arabia	10,973.4	8,282.0	6,663.8
Spain (excl. Canary Is.)	29,339.6	33,777.7	45,491.3
Sweden	12,969.0	11,297.0	11,830.5
Switzerland and Liechtenstein	36,498.7	37,719.7	36,786.1
Tunisia	6,454.5	5,508.8	5,040.8
USSR	16,935.0	10,528.7	10,482.9
United Kingdom	71,553.3	72,614.6	75,512.5
USA and Puerto Rico	75,349.0	61,082.5	62,525.0
Total (incl. others)	870,811.5	825,202.7	857,781.1

FRANCE

Transport

RAILWAYS (traffic)

	1985	1986	1987
Paying passengers ('000 journeys)	825,000	794,330	799,400
Freight carried ('000 metric tons)	171,000	145,860	142,290
Passenger-km (million)	61,900	59,860	59,970
Freight ton-km (million)*	55,780	51,690	51,300

* Including passengers' baggage.
Source: Société Nationale des Chemins de Fer Français, Paris.

ROAD TRAFFIC ('000 motor vehicles in use at 31 December)

	1985	1986	1987
Passenger cars	21,090	21,500	21,970
Goods vehicles	3,779	3,895	3,917
Buses and coaches	64	65	65
Motor cycles and mopeds	4,030	3,675	3,370

Source: International Road Federation, *World Road Statistics*.

INLAND WATERWAYS

	1984	1985	1986
Freight carried ('000 metric tons)	68,892	64,120	63,118
Freight ton-km (million)	8,880	8,394	7,767

SHIPPING

Merchant Fleet (vessels registered at 30 June)

	Displacement ('000 gross reg. tons)		
	1982	1983	1984
Oil tankers	6,557	5,443	4,785
Total (incl. others)	10,771	9,868	8,945

Source: UN, *Statistical Yearbook*.

Sea-borne Freight Traffic ('000 metric tons)

	1985	1986	1987
Goods loaded (excl. stores)	75,175.9	75,271	77,782
International	64,997.1	64,732	66,680
Coastwise	10,178.8	10,539	11,182
Goods unloaded (excl. fish)	199,081.2	206,071	203,253
International	186,492.5	194,022	190,014
Coastwise	12,588.7	12,049	13,239

Source: Direction des Ports et de la Navigation Maritimes, Ministère délégué chargé de la Mer.

CIVIL AVIATION (revenue traffic on scheduled services)

	1982	1983	1984
Kilometres flown (million)	270.7	275.2	270.4
Passengers carried ('000)	22,372	23,278	23,646
Passenger-km (million)	37,916	38,599	38,687
Freight ton-km (million)	2,185.2	2,483.7	2,797.7
Mail ton-km (million)	112.1	112.9	112.8
Total ton-km (million)	5,670	6,027	6,347

Source: UN, *Statistical Yearbook*.

Tourism

FOREIGN TOURIST ARRIVALS BY COUNTRY ('000)

	1985	1986	1987*
Belgium and Luxembourg	3,117	3,099	3,111
Canada	477	386	349
Germany, Federal Republic	8,723	8,417	8,915
Italy	2,646	2,798	3,157
Latin America	590	696	780
Netherlands	3,655	4,012	3,936
Spain	995	1,043	1,223
Switzerland	3,603	3,524	3,372
United Kingdom and Ireland	5,862	6,299	6,368
USA	2,778	1,668	1,802
Total (incl. others)	36,748	36,080	36,974

* Provisional figures.
Estimated revenue from tourism: 19,927 million francs in 1987.
Source: Ministère du Tourisme.

Communications Media

	1984	1985	1986
Radio receivers ('000 in use)	n.a.	48,000	49,000
Television receivers ('000 in use)	n.a.	21,500	22,000
Telephones ('000 in use)	33,002	n.a.	n.a.
Book production (titles):			
Books	25,448	37,860	n.a.
Pamphlets	11,741		

Source: mainly UNESCO, *Statistical Yearbook*.
Newspapers (1983): 101 dailies (combined circulation 11,598,000 copies per issue).

Education

(1986)

	Teachers	Schools	Students
Pre-primary	73,192	18,069	2,539,895
Primary	239,438	47,047	4,118,403
Secondary	313,433*	11,589†	5,490,866

* 1984.
† 1985.
Universities: 983,483 students enrolled in 1985/86.
Source: Ministère de l'Education Nationale.

Directory

The Constitution

The Constitution of the Fifth Republic was adopted by referendum on 28 September 1958 and promulgated on 6 October 1958.

PREAMBLE

The French people hereby solemnly proclaims its attachment to the Rights of Man and to the principles of national sovereignty as defined by the Declaration of 1789, confirmed and complemented by the Preamble of the Constitution of 1946.

By virtue of these principles and that of the free determination of peoples, the Republic hereby offers to the Overseas Territories that express the desire to adhere to them, new institutions based on the common ideal of liberty, equality and fraternity and conceived with a view to their democratic evolution.

Article 1. The Republic and the peoples of the Overseas Territories who, by an act of free determination, adopt the present Constitution thereby institute a Community.

The Community shall be based on the equality and the solidarity of the peoples composing it.

I. ON SOVEREIGNTY

Article 2. France shall be a Republic, indivisible, secular, democratic and social. It shall ensure the equality of all citizens before the law, without distinction of origin, race or religion. It shall respect all beliefs.

The national emblem shall be the tricolour flag, blue, white and red.

The national anthem shall be the 'Marseillaise'.

The motto of the Republic shall be 'Liberty, Equality, Fraternity'.

Its principle shall be government of the people, by the people, and for the people.

Article 3. National sovereignty belongs to the people, which shall exercise this sovereignty through its representatives and through the referendum.

No section of the people, nor any individual, may attribute to themselves or himself the exercise thereof.

Suffrage may be direct or indirect under the conditions stipulated by the Constitution. It shall always be universal, equal and secret.

All French citizens of both sexes who have reached their majority and who enjoy civil and political rights may vote under the conditions to be determined by law.

Article 4. Political parties and groups may compete for votes. They may form and carry on their activities freely. They must respect the principles of national sovereignty and of democracy.

II. THE PRESIDENT OF THE REPUBLIC

Article 5. The President of the Republic shall see that the Constitution is respected. He shall ensure, by his arbitration, the regular functioning of the public powers, as well as the continuity of the State.

He shall be the guarantor of national independence, of the integrity of the territory, and of respect for Community agreements and for treaties.

Article 6. The President of the Republic shall be elected for seven years by direct universal suffrage. The method of implementation of the present article shall be determined by an organic law.

Article 7. The President of the Republic shall be elected by an absolute majority of the votes cast. If such a majority is not obtained at the first ballot, a second ballot shall take place on the second following Sunday. Those who may stand for the second ballot shall be only the two candidates who, after the possible withdrawal of candidates with more votes, have gained the largest number of votes on the first ballot.

Voting shall begin at the summons of the Government. The election of the new President of the Republic shall take place not less than 20 days and not more than 35 days before the expiration of the powers of the President in office. In the event that the Presidency of the Republic has been vacated for any reason whatsoever, or impeded in its functioning as officially declared by the Constitutional Council, after the matter has been referred to it by the Government and which shall give its ruling by an absolute majority of its members, the functions of the President of the Republic, with the exception of those covered by Articles 11 and 12 hereunder, shall be temporarily exercised by the President of the Senate and, if the latter is in his turn unable to exercise his functions, by the Government.

In the case of vacancy or when the impediment is declared to be final by the Constitutional Council, the voting for the election of the new President shall take place, except in case of force majeure officially noted by the Constitutional Council, not less than 20 days and not more than 35 days after the beginning of the vacancy or of the declaration of the final nature of the impediment.

If, in the seven days preceding the latest date for the lodging of candidatures, one of the persons who, at least 30 days prior to that date, publicly announced his decision to be a candidate dies or is impeded, the Constitutional Council can decide to postpone the election.

If, before the first ballot, one of the candidates dies or is impeded, the Constitutional Council orders the postponement of the election.

In the event of the death or impediment, before any candidates have withdrawn, of one of the two candidates who received the greatest number of votes in the first ballot, the Constitutional Council shall declare that the electoral procedure must be repeated in full; the same shall apply in the event of the death or impediment of one of the two candidates standing for the second ballot.

All cases shall be referred to the Constitutional Council under the conditions laid down in paragraph 2 of article 61 below, or under those determined for the presentation of candidates by the organic law provided for in Article 6 above.

The Constitutional Council can extend the periods stipulated in paragraphs 3 and 5 above provided that polling shall not take place more than 35 days after the date of the decision of the Constitutional Council. If the implementation of the provisions of this paragraph results in the postponement of the election beyond the expiry of the powers of the President in office, the latter shall remain in office until his successor is proclaimed.

Articles 49 and 50 and Article 89 of the Constitution may not be put into application during the vacancy of the Presidency of the Republic or during the period between the declaration of the final nature of the impediment of the President of the Republic and the election of his successor.

Article 8. The President of the Republic shall appoint the Premier. He shall terminate the functions of the Premier when the latter presents the resignation of the Government.

At the suggestion of the Premier, he shall appoint the other members of the Government and shall terminate their functions.

Article 9. The President of the Republic shall preside over the Council of Ministers.

Article 10. The President of the Republic shall promulgate the laws within 15 days following the transmission to the Government of the finally adopted law.

He may, before the expiration of this time limit, ask Parliament for a reconsideration of the law or of certain of its articles. This reconsideration may not be refused.

Article 11. The President of the Republic, on the proposal of the government during [Parliamentary] sessions, or on joint motion of the two Assemblies published in the *Journal Officiel*, may submit to a referendum any bill dealing with the organization of the public powers, entailing approval of a Community agreement, or providing for authorization to ratify a treaty that, without being contrary to the Constitution, might affect the functioning of the institutions.

When the referendum decides in favour of the bill, the President of the Republic shall promulgate it within the time limit stipulated in the preceding article.

Article 12. The President of the Republic may, after consultation with the Premier and the Presidents of the Assemblies, declare the dissolution of the National Assembly.

General elections shall take place 20 days at the least and 40 days at the most after the dissolution.

The National Assembly shall convene by right on the second Thursday following its election. If this meeting takes place between the periods provided for ordinary sessions, a session shall, by right, be opened for a 15 day period.

There may be no further dissolution within a year following these elections.

Article 13. The President of the Republic shall sign the ordinances and decrees decided upon in the Council of Ministers.

He shall make appointments to the civil and military posts of the State.

Councillors of State, the Grand Chancellor of the Legion of Honour, Ambassadors and Envoys Extraordinary, Master Councillors of the Audit Office, prefects, representatives of the Government in the Overseas Territories, general officers, rectors of academies [regional divisions of the public educational system] and directors of central administrations shall be appointed in meetings of the Council of Ministers.

An organic law shall determine the other posts to be filled in meetings of the Council of Ministers, as well as the conditions under which the power of the President of the Republic to make appointments to office may be delegated by him to be exercised in his name.

Article 14. The President of the Republic shall accredit Ambassadors and Envoys Extraordinary to foreign powers; foreign Ambassadors and Envoys Extraordinary shall be accredited to him.

Article 15. The President of the Republic shall be commander of the armed forces. He shall preside over the higher councils and committees of national defence.

Article 16. When the institutions of the Republic, the independence of the nation, the integrity of its territory or the fulfilment of its international commitments are threatened in a grave and immediate manner and the regular functioning of the constitutional public powers is interrupted, the President of the Republic shall take the measures required by these circumstances, after official consultation with the Premier and the Presidents of the Assemblies, as well as with the Constitutional Council.

He shall inform the nation of these measures in a message.

These measures must be prompted by the desire to ensure to the constitutional public powers, in the shortest possible time, the means of accomplishing their mission. The Constitutional Council shall be consulted with regard to such measures.

Parliament shall meet by right.

The National Assembly may not be dissolved during the exercise of exceptional powers.

Article 17. The President of the Republic shall have the right of pardon.

Article 18. The President of the Republic shall communicate with the two Assemblies of Parliament by means of messages, which he shall cause to be read, and which shall not be the occasion for any debate.

Between sessions, the Parliament shall be convened especially to this end.

Article 19. The acts of the President of the Republic, other than those provided for under Articles 8 (first paragraph), 11, 12, 16, 18, 54, 56 and 61, shall be counter-signed by the Premier and, should circumstances so require, by the appropriate ministers.

III. THE GOVERNMENT

Article 20. The Government shall determine and conduct the policy of the nation.

It shall have at its disposal the administration and the armed forces.

It shall be responsible to the Parliament under the conditions and according to the procedures stipulated in Articles 49 and 50.

Article 21. The Premier shall direct the operation of the Government. He shall be responsible for national defence. He shall ensure the execution of the laws. Subject to the provisions of Article 13, he shall have regulatory powers and shall make appointments to civil and military posts.

He may delegate certain of his powers to the ministers.

He shall replace, should the occasion arise, the President of the Republic as the Chairman of the councils and committees provided for under Article 15.

He may, in exceptional instances, replace him as the chairman of a meeting of the Council of Ministers by virtue of an explicit delegation and for a specific agenda.

Article 22. The acts of the Premier shall be counter-signed, when circumstances so require, by the ministers responsible for their execution.

Article 23. The functions of Members of the Government shall be incompatible with the exercise of any parliamentary mandate, with the holding of any office, at the national level, in business, professional or labour organizations, and with any public employment or professional activity.

An organic law shall determine the conditions under which the holders of such mandates, functions or employments shall be replaced.

The replacement of the members of Parliament shall take place in accordance with the provisions of Article 25.

IV. THE PARLIAMENT

Article 24. The Parliament shall comprise the National Assembly and the Senate.

The deputies to the National Assembly shall be elected by direct suffrage.

The Senate shall be elected by indirect suffrage. It shall ensure the representation of the territorial units of the Republic. Frenchmen living outside France shall be represented in the Senate.

Article 25. An organic law shall determine the term for which each Assembly is elected, the number of its members, their emoluments, the conditions of eligibility, and the system of ineligibilities and incompatibilities.

It shall likewise determine the conditions under which, in the case of a vacancy in either Assembly, persons shall be elected to replace the deputy or senator whose seat has been vacated until the holding of new complete or partial elections to the Assembly concerned.

Article 26. No Member of Parliament may be prosecuted, searched for, arrested, detained or tried as a result of the opinions or votes expressed by him in the exercise of his functions.

No Member of Parliament may, during parliamentary session, be prosecuted or arrested for criminal or minor offences without the authorization of the Assembly of which he is a member except in the case of *flagrante delicto*.

When Parliament is not in session, no Member of Parliament may be arrested without the authorization of the Secretariat of the Assembly of which he is a member, except in the case of *flagrante delicto*, of authorized prosecution or of final conviction.

The detention or prosecution of a Member of Parliament shall be suspended if the assembly of which he is a member so demands.

Article 27. Any compulsory vote shall be null and void.

The right to vote of the members of Parliament shall be personal.

The organic law may, under exceptional circumstances, authorize the delegation of a vote. In this case, no member may be delegated more than one vote.

Article 28. Parliament shall convene by right in two ordinary sessions a year.

The first session shall begin on the first Tuesday of October and shall end on the third Friday of December.

The second session shall open on the last Tuesday of April; it may not last longer than three months.

Article 29. Parliament shall convene in extraordinary session at the request of the Premier or of the majority of the members comprising the National Assembly, to consider a specific agenda.

When an extraordinary session is held at the request of the members of the National Assembly, the closure decree shall take effect as soon as the Parliament has exhausted the agenda for which it was called, and at the latest 12 days from the date of its meeting.

Only the Premier may ask for a new session before the end of the month following the closure decree.

Article 30. Apart from cases in which Parliament meets by right, extraordinary sessions shall be opened and closed by decree of the President of the Republic.

Article 31. The members of the Government shall have access to the two Assemblies. They shall be heard when they so request.

They may call for the assistance of Commissioners of the Government.

Article 32. The President of the National Assembly shall be elected for the duration of the legislature. The President of the Senate shall be elected after each partial re-election [of the Senate].

Article 33. The meetings of the two Assemblies shall be public. An *in extenso* report of the debates shall be published in the *Journal Officiel*.

Each Assembly may sit in secret committee at the request of the Premier or of one-tenth of its members.

V. ON RELATIONS BETWEEN PARLIAMENT AND THE GOVERNMENT

Article 34. Laws shall be voted by Parliament.

They shall establish the regulations concerning:

Civil rights and the fundamental guarantees granted to the citizens for the exercise of their public liberties; the obligations imposed by the national defence upon the person and property of citizens;

Nationality, status and legal capacity of persons; marriage contracts, inheritance and gifts;

Determination of crimes and misdemeanours as well as the penalties imposed therefor; criminal procedure; amnesty; the creation of new juridical systems and the status of magistrates;

The basis, the rate and the methods of collecting taxes of all types; the issue of currency.

They likewise shall determine the regulations concerning:

The electoral system of the Parliamentary Assemblies and the local assemblies;

The establishment of categories of public institutions;

The fundamental guarantees granted to civil and military personnel employed by the State;

The nationalization of enterprises and the transfers of the property of enterprises from the public to the private sector.

Laws shall determine the fundamental principles of:
The general organization of national defence;
The free administration of local communities, of their competencies and their resources;
Education;
Property rights, civil and commercial obligations;
Legislation pertaining to employment unions and social security.

The financial laws shall determine the financial resources and obligations of the State under the conditions and with the reservations to be provided for by an organic law.

Laws pertaining to national planning shall determine the objectives of the economic and social action of the State.

The provisions of the present article may be detailed and supplemented by an organic law.

Article 35. Parliament shall authorize the declaration of war.

Article 36. Martial law shall be decreed in a meeting of the Council of Ministers.

Its prorogation beyond 12 days may be authorized only by Parliament.

Article 37. Matters other than those that fall within the domain of law shall be of a regulatory character.

Legislative texts concerning these matters may be modified by decrees issued after consultation with the Council of State. Those legislative texts which shall be passed after the entry into force of the present Constitution shall be modified by decree only if the Constitutional Council has stated that they have a regulatory character as defined in the preceding paragraph.

Article 38. The Government may, in order to carry out its programme, ask Parliament for authorization to take through ordinances, during a limited period, measures that are normally within the domain of law.

The ordinances shall be enacted in meetings of Ministers after consultation with the Council of State. They shall come into force upon their publication but shall become null and void if the bill for their ratification is not submitted to Parliament before the date set by the enabling act.

At the expiration of the time limit referred to in the first paragraph of the present article, the ordinances may be modified only by the law in those matters which are within the legislative domain.

Article 39. The Premier and the Members of Parliament alike shall have the right to initiate legislation.

Government bills shall be discussed in the Council of Ministers after consultation with the Council of State and shall be filed with the secretariat of one of the two Assemblies. Finance bills shall be submitted first to the National Assembly.

Article 40. The bills and amendments introduced by the Members of Parliament shall be inadmissible when their adoption would have as a consequence either a diminution of public financial resources or an increase in public expenditure.

Article 41. If it shall appear in the course of the legislative procedure that a Parliamentary bill or an amendment is not within the domain of law or is contrary to a delegation granted by virtue of Article 38, the Government may declare its inadmissibility.

In case of disagreement between the Government and the President of the Assembly concerned, the Constitutional Council, upon the request of one or the other, shall rule within a time limit of eight days.

Article 42. The discussion of bills shall pertain, in the first Assembly to which they have been referred, to the text presented by the Government.

An Assembly given a text passed by the other Assembly shall deliberate on the text that is transmitted to it.

Article 43. Government and Parliamentary bills shall, at the request of the Government or of the Assembly concerned, be sent for study to committees especially designated for this purpose.

Government and Parliamentary bills for which such a request has not been made shall be sent to one of the permanent committees, the number of which is limited to six in each Assembly.

Article 44. Members of Parliament and of the Government have the right of amendment.

After the opening of the debate, the Government may oppose the examination of any amendment which has not previously been submitted to committee.

If the Government so requests, the Assembly concerned shall decide, by a single vote, on all or part of the text under discussion, retaining only the amendments proposed or accepted by the Government.

Article 45. Every Government or Parliamentary bill shall be examined successively in the two Assemblies of Parliament with a view to the adoption of an identical text.

When, as a result of disagreement between the two Assemblies, it has been impossible to adopt a Government or Parliamentary bill after two readings by each Assembly, or, if the Government has declared the matter urgent, after a single reading by each of them, the Premier shall have the right to bring about a meeting of a joint committee composed of an equal number from both Assemblies charged with the task of proposing a text on the matters still under discussion.

The text elaborated by the joint committee may be submitted by the Government for approval of the two Assemblies. No amendment shall be admissible except by agreement with the Government.

If the joint committee does not succeed in adopting a common text, or if this text is not adopted under the conditions set forth in the preceding paragraph, the Government may, after a new reading by the National Assembly and by the Senate, ask the National Assembly to rule definitively. In this case, the National Assembly may reconsider either the text elaborated by the joint committee, or the last text voted by it, modified when circumstances so require by one or several of the amendments adopted by the Senate.

Article 46. The laws that the Constitution characterizes as organic shall be passed and amended under the following conditions:

A Government or Parliamentary bill shall be submitted to the deliberation and to the vote of the first Assembly notified only at the expiration of a period of 15 days following its introduction;

The procedure of Article 45 shall be applicable. Nevertheless, lacking an agreement between the two Assemblies, the text may be adopted by the National Assembly on final reading only by an absolute majority of its members;

The organic laws relative to the Senate must be passed in the same manner by the two Assemblies;

The organic laws may be promulgated only after a declaration by the Constitutional Council on their constitutionality.

Article 47. The Parliament shall pass finance bills under the conditions to be stipulated by an organic law.

Should the National Assembly fail to reach a decision on first reading within a time limit of 40 days after a bill has been filed, the Government shall refer it to the Senate, which must rule within a time limit of 15 days. The procedure set forth in Article 45 shall then be followed.

Should Parliament fail to reach a decision within a time limit of 70 days, the provisions of the bill may be enforced by ordinance.

Should the finance bill establishing the resources and expenditures of a fiscal year not be filed in time for it to be promulgated before the beginning of that fiscal year, the Government shall urgently request Parliament for the authorization to collect the taxes and shall make available by decree the funds needed to meet the Government commitments already voted.

The time limits stipulated in the present article shall be suspended when the Parliament is not in session.

The Audit Office shall assist Parliament and the Government in supervising the implementation of the finance laws.

Article 48. The discussion of the bills filed or agreed upon by the Government shall have priority on the agenda of the Assemblies in the order determined by the Government.

One meeting a week shall be reserved, by priority, for questions asked by Members of Parliament and for answers by the Government.

Article 49. The Premier, after deliberation by the Council of Ministers, shall make the Government responsible, before the National Assembly, for its programme or, should the occasion arise, for a declaration of general policy.

When the National Assembly adopts a motion of censure, the responsibility of the Government shall thereby be questioned. Such a motion is admissible only if it is signed by at least one-tenth of the members of the National Assembly. The vote may not take place before 48 hours after the motion has been filed. Only the votes that are favourable to a motion of censure shall be counted; the motion of censure may be adopted only by a majority of the members comprising the Assembly. Should the motion of censure be rejected, its signatories may not introduce another motion of censure during the same session, except in the case provided for in the paragraph below.

The Premier may, after deliberation by the Council of Ministers, make the Government responsible before the National Assembly for the adoption of a vote of confidence. In this case, this vote of confidence shall be considered as adopted unless a motion of censure, filed during the twenty-four hours that follow, is carried under the conditions provided for in the preceding paragraph.

The Premier shall have the right to request the Senate for approval of a declaration of general policy.

Article 50. When the National Assembly adopts a motion of censure, or when it disapproves the programme or a declaration of general policy of the Government, the Premier must hand the resignation of the Government to the President of the Republic.

Article 51. The closure of ordinary or extraordinary sessions shall by right be delayed, should the occasion arise, in order to permit the application of the provisions of Article 49.

VI. ON TREATIES AND INTERNATIONAL AGREEMENTS

Article 52. The President of the Republic shall negotiate and ratify treaties.

He shall be informed of all negotiations leading to the conclusion of an international agreement not subject to ratification.

Article 53. Peace treaties, commercial treaties, treaties or agreements relative to international organization, those that commit the finances of the State, those that modify provisions of a legislative nature, those relative to the status of persons, those that call for the cession, exchange or addition of territory may be ratified or approved only by a law.

They shall go into effect only after having been ratified or approved.

No cession, no exchange, no addition of territory shall be valid without the consent of the populations concerned.

Article 54. If the Constitutional Council, the matter having been referred to it by the President of the Republic, by the Premier, or by the President of one or the other Assembly, shall declare that an international commitment contains a clause contrary to the Constitution, the authorisation to ratify or approve this commitment may be given only after amendment of the Constitution.

Article 55. Treaties or agreements duly ratified or approved shall, upon their publication, have an authority superior to that of laws, subject, for each agreement or treaty, to its application by the other party.

VII. THE CONSTITUTIONAL COUNCIL

Article 56. The Constitutional Council shall consist of nine members, whose mandates shall last nine years and shall not be renewable. One-third of the membership of the Constitutional Council shall be renewed every three years. Three of its members shall be appointed by the President of the Republic, three by the President of the National Assembly, three by the President of the Senate.

In addition to the nine members provided for above, former Presidents of the Republic shall be members *ex officio* for life of the Constitutional Council.

The President shall be appointed by the President of the Republic. He shall have the deciding vote in case of a tie.

Article 57. The office of member of the Constitutional Council shall be incompatible with that of minister or Member of Parliament. Other incompatibilities shall be determined by an organic law.

Article 58. The Constitutional Council shall ensure the regularity of the election of the President of the Republic.

It shall examine complaints and shall announce the results of the vote.

Article 59. The Constitutional Council shall rule, in the case of disagreement, on the regularity of the election of deputies and senators.

Article 60. The Constitutional Council shall ensure the regularity of the referendum procedure and shall announce the results thereof.

Article 61. Organic laws, before their promulgation, and regulations of the parliamentary Assemblies, before they come into application, must be submitted to the Constitutional Council, which shall rule on their constitutionality.

To the same end, laws may be submitted to the Constitutional Council, before their promulgation, by the President of the Republic, the Premier, the President of the National Assembly, the President of the Senate, or any 60 deputies or 60 senators.

In the cases provided for by the two preceding paragraphs, the Constitutional Council must make its ruling within a time limit of one month. Nevertheless, at the request of the Government, in case of urgency, this period shall be reduced to eight days.

In these same cases, referral to the Constitutional Council shall suspend the time limit for promulgation.

Article 62. A provision declared unconstitutional may not be promulgated or implemented.

The decisions of the Constitutional council may not be appealed to any jurisdiction whatsoever. They must be recognised by the public powers and by all administrative and juridical authorities.

Article 63. An organic law shall determine the rules of organization and functioning of the Constitutional Council, the procedure to be followed before it, and in particular of the periods of time allowed for laying disputes before it.

VIII. ON JUDICIAL AUTHORITY

Article 64. The President of the Republic shall be the guarantor of the independence of the judicial authority.

He shall be assisted by the High Council of the Judiciary.

An organic law shall determine the status of magistrates.

Magistrates may not be removed from office.

Article 65. The High Council of the Judiciary shall be presided over by the President of the Republic. The Minister of Justice shall be its Vice-President *ex officio*. He may preside in place of the President of the Republic.

The High Council shall, in addition, include nine members appointed by the President of the Republic in conformity with the conditions to be determined by an organic law.

The High Council of the Judiciary shall present nominations for judges of the Court of Cassation [Supreme Court of Appeal] and for First Presidents of courts of appeal. It shall give its opinion under the conditions to be determined by an organic law on proposals of the Minister of Justice relative to the nominations of the other judges. It shall be consulted on questions of pardon under conditions to be determined by an organic law.

The High Council of the Judiciary shall act as a disciplinary council for judges. In such cases, it shall be presided over by the First President of the Court of Cassation.

Article 66. No one may be arbitrarily detained.

The judicial authority, guardian of individual liberty, shall ensure the respect of this principle under the conditions stipulated by law.

IX. THE HIGH COURT OF JUSTICE

Article 67. A High Court of Justice shall be instituted.

It shall be composed, in equal number, of members elected, from among their membership, by the National Assembly and by the Senate after each general or partial election to these Assemblies. It shall elect its President from among its members.

An organic law shall determine the composition of the High Court, it rules, as well as the procedure to be applied before it.

Article 68. The President of the Republic shall not be held accountable for actions performed in the exercise of his office except in the case of high treason. He may be indicted only by the two Assemblies ruling by identical vote in open balloting and by an absolute majority of the members of said Assemblies. He shall be tried by the High Court of Justice.

The members of the Government shall be criminally liable for actions performed in the exercise of their office and rated as crimes or misdemeanours at the time they were committed. The procedure defined above shall be applied to them, as well as to their accomplices, in case of a conspiracy against the security of the State. In the cases provided for by the present paragraph, the High Court shall be bound by the definition of crimes and misdemeanours, as well as by the determination of penalties, as they are established by the criminal laws in force when the acts are committed.

X. THE ECONOMIC AND SOCIAL COUNCIL

Article 69. The Economic and Social Council, at the referral of the Government, shall give its opinion on the Government bills, ordinances and decrees, as well as on the Parliamentary bills submitted to it.

A member of the Economic and Social Council may be designated by the latter to present, before the Parliamentary Assemblies, the opinion of the Council on the Government or Parliamentary bills that have been submitted to it.

Article 70. The Economic and social council may likewise be consulted by the Government on any problem of an economic or social character of interest to the Republic or to the Community. Any plan, or any bill dealing with a plan, of an economic or social character shall be submitted to it for advice.

Article 71. The composition of the Economic and Social Council and its rules of procedure shall be determined by an organic law.

XI. ON TERRITORIAL UNITS

Article 72. The territorial units of the Republic shall be the communes, the Departments, and the Overseas Territories. Any other territorial unit shall be created by law.

These units shall be free to govern themselves through elected councils and under the conditions stipulated by law.

In the Departments and the Territories, the Delegate of the Government shall be responsible for the national interests, for administrative supervision, and for seeing that the laws are respected.

Article 73. Measures of adjustment required by the particular situation of the Overseas Departments may be taken with regard to the legislative system and administrative organization of those Departments.

Article 74. The Overseas Territories of the Republic shall have a particular organization, taking account of their own interests within the general interests of the Republic. This organization shall be defined and modified by law after consultation with the Territorial Assembly concerned.

Article 75. Citizens of the Republic who do not have ordinary civil status, the only status referred to in Article 34, may keep their personal status as long as they have not renounced it.

Article 76. The Overseas Territories may retain their status within the Republic.

If they express the desire to do so by decision of their Territorial Assemblies taken within the time limit set in the first paragraph of Article 91, they shall become either Overseas Departments of the Republic or, organized into groups among themselves or singly, member States of the Community.

XII. ON THE COMMUNITY

Article 77. In the Community instituted by the present Constitution, the States shall enjoy autonomy; they shall administer themselves and, democratically and freely, manage their own affairs.

There shall be only one citizenship in the Community.

All citizens shall be equal before the law, whatever their origin, their race and their religion. They shall have the same duties.

Article 78. The Community shall have jurisdiction over foreign policy, defence, the monetary system, common economic and financial policy, as well as the policy on strategic raw materials.

In addition, except by special agreement, control of justice, higher education, the general organization of external and common transport, and telecommunications shall be within its jurisdiction.

Special agreements may establish other common jurisdictions or regulate the transfer of jurisdiction from the Community to one of its members.

Article 79. The member States shall benefit from the provisions of Article 77 as soon as they have exercised the choice provided for in Article 76.

Until the measures required for implementation of the present title go into force, matters within the common jurisdiction shall be regulated by the Republic.

Article 80. The President of the Republic shall preside over and represent the Community.

The Community shall have, as organs, an Executive Council, a Senate and a Court of Arbitration.

Article 81. The member States of the Community shall participate in the election of the President according to the conditions stipulated in Article 6.

The President of the Republic, in his capacity as President of the Community, shall be represented in each State of the Community.

Article 82. The Executive Council of the Community shall be presided over by the President of the Community. It shall consist of the Premier of the Republic, the heads of Government of each of the member States of the Community, and of the ministers responsible for the common affairs of the Community.

The Executive Council shall organize the co-operation of members of the Community at Government and administrative levels.

The organization and procedure of the Executive Council shall be determined by an organic law.

Article 83. The Senate of the Community shall be composed of delegates whom the Parliament of the Republic and the legislative assemblies of the other members of the Community shall choose from among their own membership. The number of delegates of each State shall be determined, taking into account its population and the responsibilities it assumes in the Community.

The Senate of the Community shall hold two sessions a year, which shall be opened and closed by the President of the Community and may not last more than one month each.

The Senate of the Community, upon referral by the President of the Community, shall deliberate on the common economic and financial policy, before laws in these matters are voted upon by the Parliament of the Republic, and, should circumstances so require, by the legislative assemblies of the other members of the Community.

The Senate of the Community shall examine the acts and treaties or international agreements, which are specified in Articles 35 and 53, and which commit the Community.

The Senate of the Community shall take enforceable decisions in the domains in which it has received delegation of power from the legislative assemblies of the members of the Community. These decisions shall be promulgated in the same form as the law in the territory of each of the States concerned.

An organic law shall determine the composition of the Senate and its rules of procedure.

Article 84. A Court of Arbitration of the Community shall rule on litigations occurring among members of the Community.

Its composition and its competence shall be determined by an organic law.

Article 85. By derogation from the procedure provided for in Article 89, the provisions of the present title that concern the functioning of the common institutions shall be amendable by identical laws passed by the Parliament of the Republic and by the Senate of the Community.

The provisions of the present title may also be revised by agreements concluded between all states of the Community: the new provisions are enforced in the conditions laid down by the Constitution of each state.

Article 86. A change of status of a member State of the Community may be requested, either by the Republic, or by a resolution of the legislative assembly of the State concerned confirmed by a local referendum, the organization and supervision of which shall be ensured by the institutions of the Community. The procedures governing this change shall be determined by an agreement approved by the Parliament of the Republic and the legislative assembly concerned.

Under the same conditions, a Member State of the Community may become independent. It shall thereby cease to belong to the Community.

A Member State of the Community may also, by means of agreement, become independent without thereby ceasing to belong to the Community.

An independent State which is not a member of the Community may, by means of agreements, adhere to the Community without ceasing to be independent.

The position of these States within the Community is determined by the agreements concluded for that purpose, in particular the agreements mentioned in the preceding paragraphs as well as, where applicable, the agreements provided for in the second paragraph of Article 85.

Article 87. The particular agreements made for the implementation of the present title shall be approved by the Parliament of the Republic and the legislative assembly concerned.

XIII. ON AGREEMENTS OF ASSOCIATION

Article 88. The Republic or the Community may make agreements with States that wish to associate themselves with the Community in order to develop their own civilisations.

XIV. ON AMENDMENT

Article 89. The initiative for amending the Constitution shall belong both to the President of the Republic on the proposal of the Premier and to the Members of Parliament.

The Government or Parliamentary bill for amendment must be passed by the two Assemblies in identical terms. The amendment shall become definitive after approval by a referendum.

Nevertheless, the proposed amendment shall not be submitted to a referendum when the President of the Republic decides to submit it to Parliament convened in Congress; in this case, the proposed amendment shall be approved only if it is accepted by a three-fifths majority of the votes cast. The Secretariat of the Congress shall be that of the National Assembly.

No amendment procedure may be undertaken or followed if it is prejudicial to the integrity of the territory.

The republican form of government shall not be the object of an amendment.

XV. TEMPORARY PROVISIONS

Article 90. The ordinary session of Parliament is suspended. The mandate of the members of the present National Assembly shall expire on the day that the Assembly elected under the present Constitution convenes.

Until this meeting, the Government alone shall have the authority to convene Parliament.

The mandate of the members of the Assembly of the French Union shall expire at the same time as the mandate of the members of the present National Assembly.

Article 91. The institutions of the Republic, provided for by the present Constitution, shall be established within four months counting from the time of its promulgation.

This period shall be extended to six months for the institutions of the Community.

The powers of the President of the Republic now in office shall expire only when the results of the election provided for in Articles 6 and 7 of the present Constitution are proclaimed.

The Member States of the Community shall participate in this first election under the conditions derived from their status at the date of the promulgation of the Constitution.

The established authorities shall continue in the exercise of their functions in these States according to the laws and regulations applicable when the Constitution goes into force, until the establishment of the authorities provided for by their new regimes.

Until its definitive constitution, the Senate shall consist of the present members of the Council of the Republic. The organic laws

FRANCE

that shall determine the definitive constitution of the Senate must be passed before 31 July 1959.

The powers conferred on the Constitutional Council by Articles 58 and 59 of the Constitution shall be exercised, until the establishment of this Council, by a committee composed of the Vice-President of the Council of State, as Chairman, the First President of the Court of Cassation, and the First President of the Audit Office.

The peoples of the member States of the Community shall continue to be represented in Parliament until the entry into force of the measures necessary to the implementation of Chapter XII.

Article 92. The legislative measures necessary to the establishment of the institutions and, until they are established, to the functioning of the public powers, shall be taken in meetings of the Council of Ministers, after consultation with the Council of State, in the form of ordinances having the force of law.

During the time limit set in the first paragraph of Article 91, the Government shall be authorized to determine, by ordinances having the force of law and passed in the same way, the system of elections to the Assemblies provided for by the Constitution.

During the same period and under the same conditions, the Government may also adopt measures, in all domains, which it may deem necessary to the life of the nation, the protection of citizens or the safeguarding of liberties.

ELECTORAL LAW, 1985

At the elections of March 1986, the 577 Deputies of the National Assembly for Metropolitan France and for the Overseas Possessions (except Mayotte, St Pierre and Miquelon and the Wallis and Futuna Islands) were elected under a system of proportional representation, the increase from 491 to 577 giving a ratio of approximately one deputy per 108,000 inhabitants. Within each department, seats were allocated to candidates in the order in which they appeared on party lists, and the votes for any party receiving less than 5% of the total vote were reapportioned among the remaining lists.

ELECTORAL LAW, JULY 1986

The 577 Deputies of the National Assembly are to be directly elected under the former single-member constituency system. Participating parties can nominate only one candidate and designate a reserve candidate, who can serve as a replacement if the elected Deputy is appointed a Minister or a member of the Constitutional Council, or is sent on a government assignment scheduled to last more than six months, or dies. A candidate must receive an absolute majority and at least one-quarter of registered votes in order to be elected to the National Assembly. If these conditions are not fulfilled, a second ballot will be held a week later, for voters to choose between all candidates receiving 12.5% of the total votes on the first ballot. The candidate who receives a simple majority of votes on the second ballot will then be elected. Candidates polling less than 5% of the votes will lose their deposit.

The Government

HEAD OF STATE

President: FRANÇOIS MITTERRAND (took office 21 May 1981, re-elected May 1988).

COUNCIL OF MINISTERS
(February 1989)

A coalition of the Parti Socialiste (PS), Mouvement des Radicaux de Gauche (MRG), members of the Union pour la Démocratie Française (UDF) and its affiliated parties—the Parti Républicain (PR), the Parti Républicain Radical et Radical-Socialiste (Rad.) and the Centre des Démocrates Sociaux (CDS)—and non-party representatives.

Prime Minister: MICHEL ROCARD (PS).
Minister of State for the Economy, Finance and the Budget: PIERRE BÉRÉGOVOY (PS).
Minister of State for National Education, Youth and Sports: LIONEL JOSPIN (PS).
Minister of State for Equipment and Housing: MAURICE FAURE (MRG).
Minister of State for Foreign Affairs: ROLAND DUMAS (PS).
Minister of Justice and Keeper of the Seals: PIERRE ARPAILLANGE.
Minister of Defence: JEAN-PIERRE CHEVÈNEMENT.
Minister of the Interior: PIERRE JOXE (PS).
Minister of Industry and Territorial Development: ROGER FAUROUX.
Minister of European Affairs: EDITH CRESSON (PS).
Minister of Transport and the Sea: MICHEL DELEBARRE (PS).
Minister of the Civil Service and Administrative Reform: MICHEL DURAFOUR (UDF/Rad.).
Minister of Labour, Employment and Professional Training: JEAN-PIERRE SOISSON (UDF/PR).
Minister of Co-operation and Development: JACQUES PELLETIER (UDF).
Minister of Culture and Communications, Major Public Works and Bicentenary: JACK LANG (PS).
Minister of Overseas Departments and Territories: LOUIS LE PENSEC (PS).
Minister of Agriculture and Forests: HENRI NALLET (PS).
Minister of Postal Services, Telecommunications and Space: PAUL QUILÈS (PS).
Minister for Relations with Parliament: JEAN POPEREN (PS).
Minister of Solidarity, Health, Social Protection and Government Spokesman: CLAUDE EVIN (PS).
Minister of Research and Technology: HUBERT CURIEN (PS).
Minister of Foreign Trade: JEAN-MARIE RAUSCH (UDF/CDS).
Minister Delegate attached to the Minister for the Economy, Finance and the Budget:
  Budget: MICHEL CHARASSE (PS).
Ministers Delegate attached to the Minister for Foreign Affairs:
  Francophone Countries: ALAIN DECAUX.
  Foreign Affairs: EDWIGE AVICE (PS).
Ministers Delegate attached to the Minister of Industry and Territorial Development:
  Territorial Development: JACQUES CHÉRÈQUE.
  Commerce and Crafts: FRANÇOIS DOUBIN (MRG).
  Tourism: OLIVIER STIRN (PS).
Minister Delegate attached to the Minister of Culture and Communications:
  Communications: CATHERINE TASCA.
Minister Delegate attached to the Minister of Solidarity, Health and Social Protection:
  Old People: THÉO BRAUN.
Minister Delegate attached to the Minister of Transport:
  The Sea: JACQUES MELLICK (PS).

SECRETARIES OF STATE

Attached to the Prime Minister:
  Planning: LIONEL STOLÉRU (UDF).
  Environment: BRICE LALONDE.
  Without Portfolio: TONY DREYFUS (PS).
  Humanitarian Action: BERNARD KOUCHNER.
Attached to the Minister of National Education:
  Technical Education: ROBERT CHAPUIS (PS).
  Youth and Sports: ROGER BAMBUCK.
Attached to the Minister for the Economy:
  Consumer Affairs: VÉRONIQUE NEIERTZ (PS).
Attached to the Minister of Foreign Affairs:
  International Cultural Relations: THIERRY DE BEAUCÉ.
Attached to the Minister of the Interior:
  Territorial Communities: JEAN-MICHEL BAYLET (MRG).
Attached to the Minister of Transport:
  Road Transport and Waterways: GEORGE SARRE (PS).
Attached to the Minister of Labour:
  Professional Training: ANDRÉ LAIGNEL (PS).
Attached to the Minister of Culture:
  Large Projects: EMILE BIASINI.
Attached to the Minister of Solidarity:
  Family Affairs: HÉLÈNE DORLHAC (UDF).
  Handicapped People: MICHEL GILLIBERT.
Secretary of State for Women's Rights: MICHÈLE ANDRÉ (PS).
Secretary of State for War Veterans: ANDRÉ MÉRIC (PS).
Secretary of State for the Prevention of Technological and Natural Disasters: GÉRARD RENON.

MINISTRIES

Office of the President: Palais de l'Elysée, 55–57 rue du Faubourg Saint Honoré, 75008 Paris; tel. (1) 42-92-81-00; telex 650127.

FRANCE

Office of the Prime Minister: 57 rue de Varenne, 75700 Paris; tel. (1) 42-75-80-00; telex 200724.

Ministry of Agriculture and Forests: 78 rue de Varenne, 75700 Paris; tel. (1) 45-55-95-50; telex 200814.

Ministry of the Civil Service and Administrative Reform: Paris.

Ministry of Co-operation and Development: 20 rue Monsieur, 75700 Paris; tel. (1) 47-83-10-10; telex 202363.

Ministry of Culture and Communications, Major Public Works and Bicentenary: 3 rue de Valois, 75042 Paris Cedex 01; tel. (1) 40-15-80-00; telex 210293.

Ministry of Defence: 14 rue Saint Dominique, 75700 Paris; tel. (1) 45-55-95-20; telex 201375.

Ministry of the Economy, Finance and the Budget: 246 blvd St-Germain, 75700 Paris; tel. (1) 42-60-33-00; telex 217068.

Ministry of Equipment and Housing: 45 ave Georges-Mandel, 75016 Paris; tel. (1) 46-47-31-32.

Ministry of European Affairs: Paris.

Ministry of Foreign Affairs: 37 quai d'Orsay, 75700 Paris; tel. (1) 45-55-95-40; telex 202329.

Ministry of Foreign Trade: Paris.

Ministry of Industry and Territorial Development: 101 rue de Grenelle, 75700 Paris; tel. (1) 45-56-36-36.

Ministry of the Interior: place Beauvau, 75800 Paris; tel. (1) 45-22-90-90; telex 290922.

Ministry of Justice: 13 place Vendôme, 75042 Paris Cedex 01; tel. (1) 42-61-80-22; telex 211320.

Ministry of Labour, Employment and Professional Training: 127 rue de Grenelle, 75700 Paris; tel. (1) 45-67-55-44.

Ministry of National Education, Youth and Sports: 110 rue de Grenelle, 75700 Paris; tel. (1) 45-50-10-10; telex 201244.

Ministry of Overseas Departments and Territories: 27 rue Oudinot, 75700 Paris; tel. (1) 47-83-01-23.

Ministry of Postal Services, Telecommunications and Space: Paris.

Ministry for Relations with Parliament: 72 rue de la Varenne, 75700 Paris; tel. (1) 42-75-80-00.

Ministry of Research and Technology: 1 rue Descartes, 75005 Paris; tel. (1) 46-34-33-33.

Ministry of Solidarity, Health and Social Protection: 127 rue de Grenelle, 75700 Paris; tel. (1) 45-67-55-44.

Ministry of Transport and the Sea: 3 place de Fontenoy, 75700 Paris.

President and Legislature

PRESIDENT

Elections of 24 April and 8 May 1988

	First ballot	Second ballot
RAYMOND BARRE (Union pour la Démocratie Française)	5,031,849	—
PIERRE BOUSSEL IMBERT (Mouvement pour un Parti des Travailleurs)	116,823	—
JACQUES CHIRAC (Rassemblement pour la République)	6,063,514	14,218,970
PIERRE JUQUIN (Independent Communist)	639,084	—
ARLETTE LAGUILLER (Lutte Ouvrière)	606,017	—
ANDRÉ LAJOINIE (Parti Communiste Français)	2,055,995	—
JEAN-MARIE LE PEN (Front National)	4,375,894	—
FRANÇOIS MITTERRAND (Parti Socialiste)	10,367,220	16,704,279
ANTOINE WAECHTER (Les Verts)	1,149,642	—

Figures published by Ministry of the Interior, after corrections by the Conseil Constitutionnel (see p. 1025).

PARLEMENT
(Parliament)

Assemblée Nationale
(National Assembly)

President: LAURENT FABIUS.

General election, 5 and 12 June 1988

Parties and Groups	% of votes cast in first ballot	% of votes cast in second ballot*	Seats
Parti Socialiste (PS)	34.76	45.31	276†
Mouvement des Radicaux de Gauche (MRG)	1.14	1.28	
Affiliated to PS	1.65	2.08	
Union pour la Démocratie Française (UDF)‡	18.50	21.18	129
Rassemblement pour la République (RPR)‡	19.18	23.09	127
Parti Communiste Français (PCF)	11.32	3.43	27
Various right-wing parties‡	2.85	2.58	16
Front National (FN)	9.66	1.07	1§
Others	0.93	—	1‖
Total	100.00	100.00	577¶

* Held where no candidate had won the requisite overall majority in the first round of voting, between candidates who had received at least 12.5% of the votes in that round.
† Of which: PS 260, MRG 9, various left-wing affiliates 7.
‡ The UDF and the RPR contested the elections jointly as the Union du Rassemblement et du Centre (URC). The various right-wing parties joined the URC prior to the second ballot.
§ Subsequently expelled from the FN.
‖ Seat held by centre-left candidate.
¶ Including two representatives from French Polynesia, where elections took place on 12 and 26 June 1988.

Note: On 15 June 1988 the formation of a new centrist group, the Union du Centre (UDC), was announced. This separate grouping was led by the president of the CDS, hitherto part of the UDF. In September 1988 the composition of the National Assembly was as follows: PS and associates 275, RPR and associates 132, UDF and associates 90, UDC and associates 40, PCF and associates 25, unattached 15 (including one FN).

Sénat
(Senate)

President: ALAIN POHER.

Members of the Senate are indirectly elected for a term of nine years, with one-third of the seats renewable every three years.

After the most recent election, held on 28 September 1986, the Senate had 319 seats: 296 for metropolitan France; 13 for the overseas departments and territories; and 10 for French nationals abroad. The strength of the parties was as follows:

	Seats
Groupe communiste	15
Groupe de la Gauche démocratique	35
Groupe de l'Union centriste des Démocrates de Progrès	70
Groupe de l'Union des Républicains et des Indépendants	54
Groupe du Rassemblement pour la République	77
Groupe socialiste	64
Non-attached	4
Total	319

Note: Until the September 1986 election, the Senate had 317 seats. The two additional members represent French nationals abroad.

Political Organizations

Centre National des Indépendants et Paysans (CNIP): 106 rue de l'Université, 75007 Paris; tel. (1) 47-05-49-64; f. 1949; right-wing; Pres. JACQUES FÉRON; Sec.-Gen. YVON BRIANT.

Fédération des Socialistes Démocrates (FSD): 8 rue Saint Marc, 75002 Paris; Pres. CHRISTIAN CHAUVEL; Sec.-Gen. GILBERT PÉROT.

Front National (FN): 8 rue du Général Clergerie, 75116 Paris; tel. (1) 47-27-56-66; f. 1972; extreme right-wing nationalist; Pres. JEAN-MARIE LE PEN; Sec.-Gen. CARL LANG.

Ligue Communiste Révolutionnaire (LCR): c/o Rouge, 2 rue Richard Lenoir, 93108 Montreuil; tel. (1) 48-59-23-00; f. 1974; Trotskyist; French section of the Fourth International; Leader ALAIN KRIVINE.

Lutte Ouvrière (LO): BP 233, 75865 Paris Cedex 18; Trotskyist; Leaders ARLETTE LAGUILLER, F. DUBURG, J. MORAND.

FRANCE

Mouvement des Démocrates: 71 rue Ampère, 75017 Paris; tel. (1) 47-63-99-40; f. 1974; Leader MICHEL JOBERT.

Mouvement gaulliste populaire (MGP): Paris; f. 1982 by merger of Union démocratique du travail and Fédération des républicains de progrès; Gaullist party; Leaders JACQUES DUBU-BRIDEL, PIERRE DABEZIES.

Mouvement des Radicaux de Gauche (MRG): 3 rue la Boétie, 75008 Paris; tel. (1) 47-42-22-41; f. 1973; formed by splinter group from Parti Radical; left-wing; Pres. YVON COLLIN, EMILE ZUCCARELLI.

Nouvelle Gauche: Paris; f. 1988 by 'renovators' expelled from the PCF; Leader PIERRE JUQUIN.

Parti Communiste Français (PCF): 2 place du Colonel Fabien, 75940 Paris Cedex 19; tel. (1) 42-38-66-55; telex 650818; subscribed to the common programme of the United Left (with the Parti Socialiste) until 1977 when the United Left split over nationalization issues; aims to follow the democratic path to socialism and advocates an independent foreign policy; mems 702,800 (1979); Sec.-Gen. GEORGES MARCHAIS.

Parti Socialiste (PS): 10 rue de Solférino, 75007 Paris; tel. (1) 45-56-77-00; telex 200174; f. 1971; subscribed to the common programme of the United Left (with the Parti Communiste) until 1977, when the United Left split over nationalization issues; advocates a planned economy, full employment and the eventual attainment of socialism through the nationalization of key industries; 200,000 mems; First Sec. PIERRE MAUROY.

Parti Socialiste Unifié (PSU): 40 rue de Malte, 75011 Paris; tel. (1) 43-57-44-80; f. 1960; left-wing party; 3,000 mems; National Sec. JEAN-CLAUDE LE SCORNET.

Rassemblement pour la République (RPR): 123 rue de Lille, 75007 Paris; tel. (1) 45-50-32-19; telex 260820; f. 1976 from the Gaullist party Union des Démocrates pour la République (UDR) after the resignation of Jacques Chirac as Prime Minister in Giscard d'Estaing's Government; joined UDF to campaign as Union du Rassemblement et du Centre (URC) at 1988 legislative elections; Pres. JACQUES CHIRAC; Sec.-Gen. ALAIN JUPPÉ.

Union Centriste et Radicale (UCR): f. 1984 after dissolution of Mouvement des Sociaux Libéraux; Pres. OLIVIER STIRN; Sec.-Gen. FRANÇOIS GARCIA.

Union pour la Démocratie Française (UDF): 42 bis, blvd de Latour Maubourg, 75007 Paris; tel. (1) 45-50-34-20; formed in 1978 to unite for electoral purposes non-Gaullist 'majority' candidates; joined RPR to campaign as Union du Rassemblement et du Centre (URC) at 1988 legislative elections; Chair. VALÉRY GISCARD D'ESTAING; Sec.-Gen. MICHEL PINTON.

Affiliated parties:

Centre des Démocrates Sociaux (CDS): 205 blvd Saint Germain, 75007 Paris; tel. (1) 45-44-72-50; f. 1976 by merger of Centre Démocrate and Centre Démocratie et Progrès; formed independent group in National Assembly known as Union du Centre after 1988 election; Pres. PIERRE MÉHAIGNERIE; Sec.-Gen. JACQUES BARROT.

Parti Républicain (PR): 1 rue Villersexel, 75007 Paris; tel. (1) 45-44-44-20; formed May 1977 as a grouping of the Fédération Nationale des Républicains Indépendants (FNRI) and three smaller 'Giscardian' parties; Hon. Pres. MICHEL PONIATOWSKI; Sec.-Gen. FRANÇOIS LÉOTARD.

Parti Républicain Radical et Radical-Socialiste: BP 649, 75162 Paris Cedex 04; tel. (1) 42-33-47-46; f. 1901; Pres. YVES GALLAND; Sec.-Gen. DIDIER BARIANI.

Parti social-démocrate (PSD): 110 rue de Sèvres, 75015 Paris; tel. (1) 45-66-74-73; f. 1973 as Mouvement des démocrates socialistes de France, name changed 1982; Pres. MAX LEJEUNE; Sec.-Gen. CHARLES BAUR.

Les Verts: 90 rue Vergniaud, 75013 Paris; tel. (1) 45-89-99-11; telex 202293; f. 1984; ecologist party; National Sec. GUY MARIMOT.

Small left-wing parties include Organisation Communiste Internationale, Communistes Démocrates et Unitaires, Révolution, Parti communiste révolutionnaire (marxiste-léniniste), and Union des communistes de France (marxiste-léniniste). Small right-wing parties include Nouvelle Action Française (f. 1971), Oeuvre Française (f. 1968), Parti Démocrate Française (f. 1982), Parti des Forces Nouvelles (f. 1974), Restauration Nationale (f. 1947), Travail et Patrie (f. 1987) and Rassembler, Agir pour la France (f. 1988). There are also regional movements in Brittany, the Basque country, Corsica and Occitania (Provence-Languedoc).

Diplomatic Representation

EMBASSIES IN FRANCE

Afghanistan: 32 ave Raphaël, 75016 Paris; tel. (1) 45-27-66-09; Chargé d'affaires a.i.: M. WAHIDULLAH.

Albania: 131 rue de la Pompe, 75116 Paris; tel. (1) 45-53-51-32; telex 611534; Ambassador: KSENOFON NUSHI.

Algeria: 50 rue de Lisbonne, 75008 Paris; tel. (1) 42-25-70-70; Ambassador: ABDELHAMID MEHRI.

Angola: 19 ave Foch, 75116 Paris; tel. (1) 45-01-58-20; telex 649847; Ambassador: LUIS JOSÉ DE ALMEIDA.

Argentina: 6 rue Cimarosa, 75116 Paris; tel. (1) 45-53-14-69; telex 613819; Ambassador: CARLOS ORTIZ DE ROZAS.

Australia: 4 rue Jean Rey, 75724 Paris Cedex 15; tel. (1) 40-59-33-00; telex 202313; Ambassador: EDWARD ROBERT POCOCK.

Austria: 6 rue Fabert, 75007 Paris; tel. (1) 45-55-95-66; telex 200708; Ambassador: WOLFGANG SCHALLENBERG.

Bahrain: 15 ave Raymond Poincaré, 75116 Paris; tel. (1) 45-53-01-19; telex 620924; Ambassador: SALMAN MOHAMED AL-SAFFAR.

Bangladesh: 5 sq. Pétrarque, 75016 Paris; tel. (1) 45-53-41-20; telex 630868; Ambassador: Dr A. MAJEED KHAN.

Belgium: 9 rue de Tilsitt, 75840 Paris Cedex 17; tel. (1) 43-80-61-00; telex 650484; Ambassador: LUC SMOLDEREN.

Benin: 87 ave Victor Hugo, 75116 Paris; tel. (1) 45-00-98-82; telex 610110; Ambassador: SOULER ISSIFOU IDRISSOU.

Bolivia: 12 ave Président Kennedy, 75016 Paris; tel. (1) 42-24-93-44; telex 611879; Ambassador: GASTÓN ARAOZ.

Brazil: 34 cours Albert 1er, 75008 Paris; tel. (1) 42-25-92-50; telex 650063; Ambassador: JOÃO HERMES PEREIRA DE ARAÚJO.

Bulgaria: 1 ave Rapp, 75007 Paris; tel. (1) 45-51-85-90; Ambassador: GUEORGUI YOVKOV.

Burkina Faso: 159 blvd Haussmann, 75008 Paris; tel. (1) 43-59-90-63; telex 201058; Ambassador: EMMANUEL SALEMBERE.

Burma: 60 rue de Courcelles, 75008 Paris; tel. (1) 42-25-56-95; telex 642190; Ambassador: U THEIN HAN.

Burundi: 3 rue Octave Feuillet, 75016 Paris; tel. (1) 45-20-60-61; telex 611463; Chargé d'affaires a.i.: SEBASTIEN NTAHUGA.

Cameroon: 73 rue d'Auteuil, 75016 Paris; tel. (1) 47-43-98-33; telex 620312; Ambassador: SIMON NKO'O ETOUNGOU.

Canada: 35 ave Montaigne, 75008 Paris; tel. (1) 47-23-01-01; telex 280806; Ambassador: CLAUDE T. CHARLAND.

Central African Republic: 29 blvd de Montmorency, 75016 Paris; tel. (1) 42-24-42-56; telex 611908; Ambassador: GABRIEL M'BANGAS.

Chad: 65 rue des Belles Feuilles, 75116 Paris; tel. (1) 45-53-36-75; telex 610629; Ambassador: AHMED ALLAM-MI.

Chile: 2 ave de la Motte-Piquet, 75007 Paris; tel. (1) 45-51-46-68; telex 260075; Ambassador: EDUARDO CISTERNAS.

China, People's Republic: 11 ave George V, 75008 Paris; tel. (1) 47-23-34-45; telex 270114; Ambassador: ZHOU JUE.

Colombia: 22 rue de l'Elysée, 75008 Paris; tel. (1) 42-65-46-08; telex 640935; Chargé d'affaires a.i.: OCTAVIO GALLÓN.

Comoros: 13-15 rue de la Néva, 75008 Paris; tel. (1) 47-63-81-78; telex 642390; Ambassador: ALI MLAHAILI.

Congo: 37 bis rue Paul Valéry, 75116 Paris; tel. (1) 45-00-60-57; telex 611954; Ambassador: JEAN-MARIE EWENGUÉ.

Costa Rica: 74 ave Paul-Doumer, 75116 Paris; tel. (1) 45-04-50-93; telex 648046; Ambassador: ENRIQUE CASTILLO.

Côte d'Ivoire: 102 ave Raymond Poincaré, 75116 Paris; tel. (1) 45-01-53-10; telex 611915; Ambassador: EUGÈNE AIDARA.

Cuba: 16 rue de Presles, 75015 Paris; tel. (1) 45-67-55-35; telex 200815; Ambassador: FERNANDO FLÓREZ IBARRA.

Cyprus: 23 rue Galilée, 75116 Paris; tel. (1) 47-20-86-28; telex 610664; Ambassador: GEORGES LYCOURGOS.

Czechoslovakia: 15 ave Charles Floquet, 75007 Paris; tel. (1) 47-34-29-10; telex 611032; Ambassador: PETER COLOTKA.

Denmark: 77 ave Marceau, 75116 Paris; tel. (1) 47-23-54-20; telex 620172; Ambassador: GUNNAR RIBERHOLDT.

Djibouti: 26 rue Emile Ménier, 75116 Paris; tel. (1) 47-27-49-22; telex 614970; Chargé d'affaires a.i.: Mme FOUDHA ABDOULATIF.

Dominican Republic: 2 rue Georges-Ville, 75116 Paris; tel. (1) 45-00-77-71; telex 615333; Chargé d'affaires a.i.: Sra VIVIAN ALBA-LUNA.

Ecuador: 34 ave de Messine, 75008 Paris; tel. (1) 45-61-10-21; telex 641333; Ambassador: PATRICIO F. AVELLÁN.

Egypt: 56 ave d'Iéna, 75116 Paris; tel. (1) 47-20-97-70; telex 611691; Ambassador: ALI SAMIR SAFOUAT.

El Salvador: 12 rue Galilée, 75116 Paris; tel. (1) 47-20-42-02; telex 612572; Chargé d'affaires a.i.: JOAQUÍN RODEZNO.

Equatorial Guinea: 6 rue Alfred de Vigny, 75008 Paris; tel. (1) 47-66-44-33; Ambassador: FAUSTINO NGUEMA ESONO.

Ethiopia: 35 ave Charles Floquet, 75007 Paris; tel. (1) 47-83-83-95; telex 260008; Chargé d'affaires a.i.: (vacant).

FRANCE

Finland: 2 rue Fabert, 75007 Paris; tel. (1) 47-05-35-45; telex 200054; Ambassador: MATTI HÄKKÄNEN.
Gabon: 26 bis ave Raphaël, 75016 Paris; tel. (1) 42-24-79-60; telex 610146; Ambassador: (vacant).
German Democratic Republic: 24 rue Marbeau, 75116 Paris; tel. (1) 45-00-00-10; telex 620569; Ambassador: ALFRED MARTER.
Germany, Federal Republic: 13–15 ave Franklin D. Roosevelt, 75008 Paris; tel. (1) 42-99-78-00; telex 280136; Ambassador: Dr FRANZ PFEFFER.
Ghana: 8 Villa Said, 75116 Paris; tel. (1) 45-00-09-50; telex 611020; Ambassador: THERESE STRIGGNER SCOTT.
Greece: 17 rue Auguste Vacquerie, 75116 Paris; tel. (1) 47-23-72-28; telex 612747; Ambassador: STATHIS MITSOPOULOS.
Guatemala: 73 rue de Courcelles, 75008 Paris; tel. (1) 42-27-78-63; telex 650850; Ambassador: GUILLERMO PUTZEIS-ALVAREZ.
Guinea: 24 rue Emile Ménier, 75116 Paris; tel. (1) 45-53-72-25; telex 611748; Ambassador: SEKOU DECAST CAMARA.
Haiti: 10 rue Théodule Ribot, 75017 Paris; tel. (1) 47-63-47-78; Chargé d'affaires a.i.: ANTONIO RODRIGUE.
Holy See: 10 ave du Président Wilson, 75116 Paris; tel. (1) 47-23-58-34; Apostolic Nuncio: Most Rev. LORENZO ANTONETTI, Titular Archbishop of Roselle.
Honduras: 6 place Vendôme, 75001 Paris; tel. (1) 42-61-34-75; telex 215535; Ambassador: RAFAEL LEIVA VIVAS.
Hungary: 5 bis sq. de l'Avenue Foch, 75116 Paris; tel. (1) 45-00-41-59; telex 610822; Ambassador: Dr REZSŐ PALOTAS.
Iceland: 124 blvd Haussmann, 75008 Paris; tel. (1) 45-22-81-54; telex 290314; Ambassador: HARALDUR KRÖYER.
India: 15 rue Alfred Dehodencq, 75016 Paris; tel. (1) 45-20-39-30; telex 610621; Ambassador: SOONU KOCHAR.
Indonesia: 49 rue Cortambert, 75016 Paris; tel. (1) 45-03-07-60; telex 648031; Ambassador: BACHTIAR RIFAI.
Iran: 4 ave d'Iéna, 75116 Paris; tel. (1) 47-23-61-22; telex 610600; Ambassador: Dr ALI AHANI. (Relations restored in June 1988.)
Iraq: 53 rue de la Faisanderie, 75116 Paris; tel. (1) 45-01-51-00; telex 613706; Ambassador: ABD AR-RAZZAK AL-HACHEMI.
Ireland: 12 ave Foch, 75116 Paris; tel. (1) 45-00-20-87; telex 620557; Ambassador: TADHG O'SULLIVAN.
Israel: 3 rue Rabelais, 75008 Paris; tel. (1) 42-56-47-47; telex 650831; Ambassador: OVADIA SOFER.
Italy: 51 rue de Varenne, 75007 Paris; tel. (1) 45-44-38-90; telex 270827; Ambassador: WALTER GARDINI.
Japan: 7 ave Hoche, 75008 Paris; tel. (1) 47-66-02-22; telex 660493; Ambassador: MORIYUKI MOTONO.
Jordan: 80 blvd Maurice Barrès, 92200 Neuilly-sur-Seine; tel. (1) 46-24-51-38; telex 630084; Chargé d'affaires a.i.: MOHAMED AFANA.
Kenya: 3 rue Cimarosa, 75116 Paris; tel. (1) 45-53-35-00; telex 620825; Ambassador: SIMEON B. ARAP BULLUT.
Korea, Republic: 125 rue de Grenelle, 75007 Paris; tel. (1) 47-53-01-01; Ambassador: HAN WOO-SUK.
Kuwait: 2 rue de Lubeck, 75116 Paris; tel. (1) 47-23-54-25; telex 620513; Ambassador: ISSA AL-HAMAD.
Laos: 74 ave Raymond Poincaré, 75116 Paris; tel. (1) 45-53-70-74; telex 610711.
Lebanon: 3 villa Copernic, 75116 Paris; tel. (1) 45-00-22-25; telex 611087; Ambassador: FAROUK ABILLAMA.
Liberia: 8 rue Jacques Bingen, 75017 Paris; tel. (1) 47-63-58-55; telex 290288; Ambassador: EDITH BOWEN CARR.
Libya (People's Bureau): 2 rue Charles Lamoureux, 75116 Paris; tel. (1) 47-04-71-60; telex 620643; Sec. of People's Bureau: HAMED EL HOUDERI.
Luxembourg: 33 ave Rapp, 75007 Paris; tel. (1) 45-55-13-37; telex 204711; Ambassador: HENRI ROEMER.
Madagascar: 4 ave Raphaël, 75016 Paris; tel. (1) 45-04-62-11; telex 610394; Ambassador: FRANÇOIS DE PAULE RABOTOSON.
Malaysia: 2 bis rue Bénouville, 75116 Paris; tel. (1) 45-53-11-85; Ambassador: Datuk ISMAIL AMBIA.
Mali: 89 rue du Cherche-Midi, 75006 Paris; tel. (1) 45-48-58-43; telex 260002; Ambassador: MAMADOU DIAWARA.
Malta: 92 ave des Champs Elysées, 75008 Paris; tel. (1) 45-62-53-01; telex 641023; Ambassador: ALBERT BORG OLIVIER DE PUGET.
Mauritania: 5 rue de Montévidéo, 75116 Paris; tel. (1) 45-04-88-54; telex 620506; Ambassador: (vacant).
Mauritius: 68 blvd de Courcelles, 75017 Paris; tel. (1) 42-27-30-19; telex 660233; Ambassador: Mme GHISLAINE HENRY.
Mexico: 9 rue de Longchamp, 75116 Paris; tel. (1) 45-53-76-43; telex 610332; Ambassador: JORGE CASTAÑEDA Y ALVAREZ DE LA ROSA.
Monaco: 22 blvd Suchet, 75016 Paris; tel. (1) 45-04-74-54; telex 611088; Ambassador: CHRISTIAN ORSETTI.
Mongolia: 5 ave Robert Schuman, 92100 Boulogne-Billancourt; tel. (1) 46-05-23-18; telex 200656; Ambassador: (vacant).
Morocco: 3–5 rue Le Tasse, 75016 Paris; tel. (1) 45-20-69-35; telex 611025; Ambassador: Dr YOUSSEF BEN ABBES.
Mozambique: 82 rue Laugier, 75017 Paris; tel. (1) 47-64-91-32; telex 641527; Ambassador: ISAAC MURARGY.
Nepal: 7 rue Washington, 75008 Paris; tel. (1) 43-59-28-61; telex 643929; Ambassador: DILLY RAJ UPRETY.
Netherlands: 7–9 rue Eblé, 75007 Paris; tel. (1) 43-06-61-88; telex 200070; Ambassador: MAX VEGELIN VAN CLAERBERGEN.
New Zealand: 7 ter rue Léonard de Vinci, 75116 Paris; tel. (1) 45-00-24-11; telex 611929; Ambassador: Mrs JUDITH C. TROTTER.
Nicaragua: 11 rue de Sontay, 75116 Paris; tel. (1) 45-00-35-42; telex 612017; Ambassador: ROBERTO ARGÜELLO HURTADO.
Niger: 154 rue de Longchamp, 75116 Paris; tel. (1) 45-04-80-60; telex 611080; Ambassador: ABDOU GARBA.
Nigeria: 173 ave Victor Hugo, 75116 Paris; tel. (1) 47-04-68-65; telex 620106; Ambassador: OLUYEMI ADENIJI.
Norway: 28 rue Bayard, 75008 Paris; tel. (1) 47-23-72-78; telex 280947; Ambassador: ASBJØRN SKARSTEIN.
Oman: 50 ave d'Iéna, 75116 Paris; tel. (1) 47-23-01-63; telex 613765; Ambassador: MOHAMED HASSAN ALI.
Pakistan: 18 rue Lord Byron, 75008 Paris; tel. (1) 45-62-23-32; telex 644000; Ambassador: SHAHID AMIN.
Panama: 145 ave de Suffren, 75015 Paris; tel. (1) 47-83-23-32; telex 205970; Ambassador: GASPAR WITTGREEN.
Paraguay: 8 ave Charles Floquet, 75007 Paris; tel. (1) 47-83-54-77; Ambassador: Dr JORGE HAMUY-DACAK.
Peru: 50 ave Kléber, 75116 Paris; tel. (1) 47-04-46-63; telex 611081; Ambassador: HUGO OTERO.
Philippines: 39 ave Georges Mandel, 75116 Paris; tel. (1) 47-04-65-50; telex 218458; Ambassador: FELIPE MABILANGAN.
Poland: 1–3 rue Talleyrand, 75007 Paris; tel. (1) 45-51-60-80; telex 611029; Ambassador: RYSZARD FIJALKOWSKI.
Portugal: 3 rue de Noisiel, 75116 Paris; tel. (1) 47-27-35-29; telex 620905; Ambassador: LUÍS GASPAR DA SILVA.
Qatar: 57 quai d'Orsay, 75007 Paris; tel. (1) 45-51-90-71; telex 270074; Ambassador: ABDUL RAHMAN BIN HAMAD.
Romania: 5 rue de l'Exposition, 75007 Paris; tel. (1) 47-05-49-54; Ambassador: PETRE GIGEA.
Rwanda: 12 rue Jadin, 75017 Paris; tel. (1) 42-27-36-31; telex 650930; Ambassador: DENIS MAGIRA-BIGIRIMANA.
San Marino: 6 ave Franklin Roosevelt, 75008 Paris; tel. (1) 43-59-22-28; telex 643445; Minister: CAMILLO DE BENEDETTI.
Saudi Arabia: 5 ave Hoche, 75008 Paris; tel. (1) 47-66-02-06 and 42-27-81-12; telex 641508; Ambassador: JAMIL AL-HEJAILAN.
Senegal: 14 ave Robert Schuman, 75007 Paris; tel. (1) 47-05-39-45; telex 611563; Ambassador: MASSAMBA SARRE.
Seychelles: 53 bis rue François 1er, 75008 Paris; tel. (1) 47-23-98-11; telex 649634; Ambassador: (vacant).
Singapore: 12 sq. de l'Avenue Foch, 75116 Paris; tel. (1) 45-00-33-61; telex 630994; Ambassador: DAVID SAUL MARSHALL.
Somalia: 26 rue Dumont d'Urville, 75116 Paris; tel. (1) 45-00-76-51; telex 611828; Ambassador: AHMED SHIRE MAHMOUD.
South Africa: 59 quai d'Orsay, 75007 Paris; tel. (1) 45-55-92-37; telex 200280; Ambassador: HENDRIK GELDENHUYS.
Spain: 13 ave Georges V, 75008 Paris; tel. (1) 47-23-61-83; telex 280689; Ambassador: JUAN DURÁN-LÓRIGA RODRIGÁÑEZ.
Sri Lanka: 15 rue d'Astorg, 75008 Paris; tel. (1) 42-66-35-01; telex 642337; Chargé d'affaires a.i.: Dr A. W. P. GURUGÉ.
Sudan: 56 ave Montaigne, 75008 Paris; tel. (1) 47-20-07-34; telex 660268; Ambassador: AWAD EL-KARIM FADULALLA.
Sweden: 17 rue Barbet de Jouy, 75007 Paris; tel. (1) 45-55-92-15; telex 204740; Ambassador: CARL LIDBOM.
Switzerland: 142 rue de Grenelle, 75007 Paris; tel. (1) 45-50-34-46; telex 270969; Ambassador: FRANÇOIS DE ZIEGLER.
Syria: 20 rue Vaneau, 75007 Paris; tel. (1) 45-50-24-90; Ambassador: YOUSSEF CHAKKOUR.
Tanzania: 70 blvd Péreire, 75017 Paris; tel. (1) 47-66-21-77; telex 643968; Ambassador: TATU NURU.
Thailand: 8 rue Greuze, 75116 Paris; tel. (1) 47-04-32-22; telex 611626; Ambassador: WICHIAN WATANAKUN.
Togo: 8 rue Alfred Roll, 75017 Paris; tel. (1) 43-80-12-13; telex 290497; Ambassador: BOUMBÉRA ALASSOUNOUMA.

FRANCE

Tunisia: 25 rue Barbet de Jouy, 75007 Paris; tel. (1) 45-55-95-98; telex 200639; Ambassador: IBRAHIM TURKI.
Turkey: 16 ave de Lamballe, 75016 Paris; tel. (1) 45-24-52-24; telex 610850; Ambassador: FAIK MELEK.
Uganda: 13 ave Raymond Poincaré, 75116 Paris; tel. (1) 47-27-46-80; telex 630028; Ambassador: Mrs FREDA BLICK.
USSR: 40–50 blvd Lannes, 75016 Paris; tel. (1) 45-04-05-50; telex 611761; Ambassador: YAKOV RIABOV.
United Arab Emirates: 3 rue de Lota, 75116 Paris; tel. (1) 45-53-94-04; telex 620003; Chargé d'affaires a.i.: HILAL SAEED ALZAABI.
United Kingdom: 35 rue du Faubourg Saint Honoré, 75383 Paris Cedex 08; tel. (1) 42-66-91-42; telex 650264; Ambassador: Sir EWEN FERGUSSON.
USA: 2 ave Gabriel, 75008 Paris; tel. (1) 42-96-12-02; telex 650221; Ambassador: WALTER J. P. CURLEY, Jr (designate).
Uruguay: 15 rue Lesueur, 75116 Paris; tel. (1) 45-00-91-50; telex 610564; Ambassador: HORACIO TERRA GALLINAL.
Venezuela: 11 rue Copernic, 75016 Paris; tel. (1) 45-53-29-98; telex 610683; Ambassador: RAMÓN ESCOVAR SALÓM.
Viet-Nam: 62 rue Boileau, 75116 Paris; tel. (1) 45-24-50-63; telex 613240; Ambassador: HA VAN LAU.
Yemen Arab Republic: 21 ave Charles Floquet, 75007 Paris; tel. (1) 43-06-66-22; telex 200076; Ambassador: SALEH ALI AL-ASHWAL.
Yemen, People's Democratic Republic: 25 rue Georges Bizet, 75116; tel. (1) 47-23-61-76; telex 610231; Ambassador: ALI MOUTANA HASSAN.
Yugoslavia: 54 rue de la Faisanderie, 75116 Paris; tel. (1) 45-04-05-05; telex 610846; Ambassador: BOZIDAR GAGRO.
Zaire: 32 cours Albert 1er, 75008 Paris; tel. (1) 42-25-57-50; telex 280661; Ambassador: SAKOMBI INONGO.
Zambia: 76 ave d'Iéna, 75016 Paris; tel. (1) 47-23-43-52; telex 610483; Ambassador: HENRY KOSAM MATIPA.
Zimbabwe: 5 rue de Tilsit, 75008 Paris; tel. (1) 47-63-48-31; telex 643505; Ambassador: BEN KUFAKUNESU JAMBGA.

Judicial System

The Judiciary is independent of the Government. Judges of the Court of Cassation and the First President of the Court of Appeal are appointed by the executive from nominations of the High Council of the Judiciary.

Subordinate cases are heard by Tribunaux d'instance, of which there are 471, and more serious cases by Tribunaux de grande instance, of which there are 181. Parallel to these Tribunals are the Tribunaux de commerce, for commercial cases, composed of judges elected by tradesmen and manufacturers among themselves. These do not exist in every district. Where there is no Tribunal de commerce, commercial disputes are judged by Tribunaux de grande instance.

The Conseils de Prud'hommes (Boards of Arbitration) consist of an equal number of workers or employees and employers ruling on the differences which arise over Contracts of Work.

The Tribunaux correctionnnels (Correctional Courts) for criminal cases correspond to the Tribunaux de grande instance for civil cases. They pronounce on all graver offences (délits), including those involving imprisonment. Offences committed by juveniles of under 18 years go before specialized tribunals for children.

From all these Tribunals appeal lies to the Cours d'appel (Courts of Appeal).

The Cours d'assises (Courts of Assize) have no regular sittings, but are called when necessary to try every important case, for example, murder. They are presided over by judges who are members of the Cours d'appel and composed of elected judges (jury). Their decision is final, except where shown to be wrong in law, and then recourse is had to the Cour de Cassation (Court of Cassation). The Cour de Cassation is not a supreme court of appeal but a higher authority for the proper application of the law. Its duty is to see that judgments are not contrary either to the letter or the spirit of the law; any judgment annulled by the Court involves the trying of the case anew by a court of the same category as that which made the original decision.

COUR DE CASSATION

Palais de Justice, 5 quai de l'Horloge, 75001 Paris; tel. (1) 43-29-12-55.
First President: PIERRE DRAI.
Presidents of Chambers: JEAN-MICHEL AUBOUIN (2ème Chambre Civile), JACQUES BAUDOUIN (Chambre Commerciale), CHRISTIAN LE GUNEHEC (Chambre Criminelle), PIERRE FRANCON (3ème Chambre Civile), ANDRÉ PONSARD (1ère Chambre Civile), JEAN COCHARD (Chambre Sociale).

Solicitor-General: PIERRE BEZIO.
There are 84 Counsellors, one First Attorney-General and 19 Attorneys-General.
Chief Clerk of the Court: DANIEL AUTIÉ.
Council of Advocates at Court of Cassation: Pres. CHARLES CHOUCROY.

COUR D'APPEL DE PARIS

Palais de Justice, blvd de Palais, 75001 Paris.
First President: MYRIAM EZRATTY.
There are also 57 Presidents of Chambers.
Solicitor-General: PIERRE TRUCHE.
There are also 128 Counsellors, 21 Attorneys-General and 37 Deputies.

TRIBUNAL DE GRANDE INSTANCE DE PARIS

Palais de Justice, blvd de Palais, 75001 Paris.
President: ROBERT DIET.
Solicitor of Republic: MICHEL RAYNAUD.

TRIBUNAL DE COMMERCE DE PARIS

1 quai de Corse, 75181 Paris Cedex 04.
President: JACQUES BON.

TRIBUNAUX ADMINISTRATIFS

Certain cases arising between civil servants (when on duty) and the government, or between any citizen and the government are judged by special administrative courts.

The Tribunaux Administratifs, of which there are 22, are situated in the capital of each area; the Conseil d'Etat (see below) has its seat in Paris.

TRIBUNAL DES CONFLITS

Decides whether cases shall be submitted to the ordinary or administrative courts.
President: The Minister of Justice.
Vice-President: PIERRE NICOLAI.
There are also four Counsellors of the Cour de Cassation and three Counsellors of State.

COUR DES COMPTES

13 rue Cambon, 75100 Paris; tel. (1) 42-98-95-00.
An administrative tribunal charged with judging the correctness of public accounts. It is the judge of common law of all public accounts laid before it. The judgments of the Court may be annulled by the Conseil d'Etat.
First President: ANDRÉ CHANDERNAGOR.
Presidents: JUSTIN ROHMER, RENÉ VACQUIER, CHARLES DE VILLAINES, MAURICE BERNARD, FRANCIS RAISON, FRANÇOIS MOSES, GÉRARD DUCHER, JEAN PRADA, PAUL THERRE.
Attorney-General: JEAN RAYNAUD.
Deputy Attorneys-General: JEAN-PIERRE GASTINEL, JEAN-LOUIS BEAUD DE BRIVE.
Secretary-General: ALAIN PICHON.
Deputy Secretaries-General: Alain Lefoulon, Alain Hespel.

CHAMBRES RÉGIONALES DES COMPTES

In 1983 jurisdiction over the accounts of local administrations (Régions, Départements and Communes) and public institutions (hospitals, council housing, etc.) was transferred from the Cour des Comptes to local Chambres Régionales. The courts are autonomous but under the jurisdiction of the State. Appeals may be brought before the Cour des Comptes.

CONSEIL D'ETAT

Palais-Royal, 75100 Paris; tel. (1) 42-61-52-29.
A council of the central power and an administrative tribunal. As the consultative organ of the government, it gives opinions in the legislative and administrative domain (interior, finance, public works and social sections). In administrative jurisdiction it has three functions: to judge in the first and last resort such cases as appeals against excess of power laid against official decrees or individuals; to judge appeals against judgments made by Tribunaux Administratifs and resolutions of courts of litigation; and to annul decisions made by various specialized administrative authorities which adjudicate without appeal, such as the Cour des Comptes.
President: The Prime Minister.

FRANCE

Directory

Vice-President: MARCEAU LONG.

Presidents of Sections: Jacques Boutet, Fernand Grevisse, Suzanne Grevisse, Guy Braibant, Michel Combarnous, Michel Bernard.

General Secretary: JEAN-PIERRE AUBERT.

In 1987 the Government introduced proposals to create five Cours Administratives d'Appel (at Paris, Lyon, Bordeaux, Nancy and Nantes) in 1989. These courts would judge appeals against judgments made by Tribunaux Administratifs on any case with the given facts already supplied. The new courts were to be headed by a Conseiller d'Etat and to be composed of members of the Tribunaux Administratifs, which would be renamed Corps des Tribunaux Administratifs et des Cours Administratives d'Appel. However, the Conseil d'Etat would retain its power to judge appeals against excess of power and the application of the law, and to pronounce on electoral disputes. The Conseil d'Etat would also be empowered to quash judgments made by the Cours Administratives d'Appel.

Religion

CHRISTIANITY

Conseil des Eglises Chrétiennes en France: 106 rue de Bac, 75341; Paris Cedex 07; tel. (1) 42-22-57-08; f. 1987; ecumenical organization comprising representatives from all Christian denominations to express opinions on social issues; 21 mems; Secs Pastor FREYCHET, Fr DAMIEN SICARD, Fr MICHEL EVDOKIMOV.

The Roman Catholic Church

For ecclesiastical purposes, France comprises nine Apostolic Regions, together forming 18 archdioceses (of which one, Marseille, is directly responsible to the Holy See), 77 dioceses (including two, Metz and Strasbourg, directly responsible to the Holy See) and one Territorial Prelature. The Archbishop of Paris is also the Ordinary for Catholics of Oriental Rites. An estimated 80% of the population of France are adherents of the Roman Catholic Church.

Bishops' Conference: Conférence Episcopale Française, 106 rue de Bac, 75341 Paris Cedex 07; tel. (1) 42-22-57-08; telex 260757; f. 1975; Pres. Cardinal ALBERT DECOURTRAY, Archbishop of Lyon and Primate of Gaul.

Latin Rite

Archbishop of Lyon and Primate of Gaul: Cardinal ALBERT DECOURTRAY, Archevêché, 1 place de Fourvière, 69321 Lyon Cedex 05; tel. 78-25-12-27; telex 380835.

Archbishop of Aix: Mgr BERNARD PANAFIEU.

Archbishop of Albi: (vacant).

Archbishop of Auch: Mgr GABRIEL VANEL.

Archbishop of Avignon: Mgr RAYMOND BOUCHEX.

Archbishop of Besançon: Mgr LUCIEN DALOZ.

Archbishop of Bordeaux: Mgr MARIUS MAZIERS.

Archbishop of Bourges: Mgr PIERRE PLATEAU.

Archbishop of Cambrai: Mgr JACQUES DELAPORTE.

Archbishop of Chambéry: Mgr CLAUDE FEIDT.

Archbishop of Marseille: Mgr ROBERT COFFY.

Archbishop of Paris: Cardinal JEAN-MARIE LUSTIGER.

Archbishop of Reims: Mgr JEAN BALLAND.

Archbishop of Rennes: Mgr JACQUES JULLIEN.

Archbishop of Rouen: Mgr JOSEPH DUVAL.

Archbishop of Sens: Mgr EUGÈNE ERNOULT.

Archbishop of Toulouse: Mgr ANDRÉ COLLINI.

Archbishop of Tours: Mgr JEAN HONORÉ.

Armenian Rite

Bishop of Sainte-Croix-de-Paris: KRIKOR GHABROYAN, 10 bis rue Thouin, 75005 Paris; tel. (1) 43-26-50-43; 30,000 adherents (1987).

Ukrainian Rite

Apostolic Exarch of France: MICHEL HRYNCHYSHYN (Titular Bishop of Zygris), 186 boulevard Saint-Germain, 75006 Paris; tel. (1) 45-48-48-65; 16,000 adherents (1985).

Protestant Churches

There are some 850,000 Protestants in France.

Fédération Protestante de France: 47 rue de Clichy, 75009 Paris; tel. (1) 48-74-15-08; telex 642380; f. 1906; Pres. JACQUES STEWART; Vice-Pres. M. HOEFFEL, J. P. MONSARRAT, N. SELORON, A. THOBOIS; Gen. Sec. LOUIS SCHWEITZER.

The Federation comprises the following Churches:

Alliance Nationale des Eglises Luthériennes de France: 1A quai Saint Thomas, Strasbourg; tel. 88-32-45-86; f. 1945; 250,000 mems; groups the two Lutheran churches below; Pres. Mme PIERRETTE RICHARD.

Eglise de la Confession d'Augsbourg d'Alsace et de Lorraine: 1A quai Saint Thomas, 67081 Strasbourg Cedex; tel. 88-32-45-86; Pres. MICHEL HOEFFEL; Gen. Secs Pastor W. JURGENSEN, P. ISSLER.

Eglise Evangélique Luthérienne de France: 13 rue Godefroy, 75013 Paris; tel. (1) 45-82-19-99; 65 parishes grouped in 2 directorates: Paris and Montbéliard; Pres. JEAN-MICHEL STURM; Sec. Pastor MICHEL DAUTRY.

Eglise Méthodiste: 3 rue Paul Verlaine, 30100 Alès; the total Methodist community was estimated at 2,900 mems in 1982.

Eglise Réformée d'Alsace et de Lorraine: 2 rue du Bouclier, 67000 Strasbourg; 45,000 mems; Pres. Pastor ANTOINE PFEIFFER.

Eglise Réformée de France: 47 rue de Clichy, 75009 Paris; tel. (1) 48-74-90-92; Pres. National Council Pastor JEAN-PIERRE MONSARRAT.

Fédération des Eglises Evangéliques Baptistes de France: 48 rue de Lille, 75007 Paris; tel. (1) 42-61-13-96; Pres. Pastor ROBERT SOMERVILLE.

Union Nationale des Eglises Réformées Evangéliques Indépendantes: 7 rue Godin, 30000 Nîmes; Pres. Pastor MAURICE LONGEIRET.

The Orthodox Churches

Administration of Russian Orthodox Churches in Europe (Jurisdiction of the Oecumenical Patriarchate): 12 rue Daru, 75008 Paris; presided over by His Eminence the Most Reverend GEORGES, Archbishop of Russian Orthodox Churches in Europe.

Greek Orthodox Cathedral of St Etienne: 7 rue Georges Bizet, 75116 Paris; tel. (1) 47-20-82-35; Superior The Most Rev. MELETIOS CARABINIS, Greek Archbishop of France, Spain and Portugal.

The Anglican Communion

Within the Church of England, France forms part of the diocese of Gibraltar in Europe.

Archdeacon of Northern France: Ven. M. B. LEA, 5 rue d'Aguesseau, 75008 Paris; tel. (1) 47-42-70-88.

Archdeacon of the Riviera: Ven. J. M. LIVINGSTONE, 11 rue de la Buffa, 06000 Nice; tel. 93-87-19-83.

Other Christian Churches

Société Religieuse des Amis (Quakers) et Centre Quaker International: 114 rue de Vaugirard, 75006 Paris; tel. (1) 45-48-74-23.

ISLAM

Islam is the second most important religion in France; in 1985 there were about 2.5m. adherents, of whom more than 750,000 resided in the Marseille area.

Fédération Nationale des Musulmans de France (FNMF): Paris; f. 1985; 20 asscns; Pres. DANIEL YOUSSOF LECLERQ.

Muslim Institute of the Paris Mosque: place du Puits de l'Ermite, 75005 Paris; tel. (1) 45-35-97-33; f. 1923; cultural, diplomatic, social, judicial and religious sections; research and information and commercial annexes; Dir Cheikh EL ABBAS BENCHEIKH EL HOCINE.

JUDAISM

Consistoire Central—Union des Communautés Juives de France: 17 rue Saint Georges, 75009 Paris; tel. (1) 45-26-02-56; f. 1808; 120 asscns; Chief Rabbi of France JOSEPH SITRUK; Pres. JEAN PAUL ELKANN; Exec. Dir LÉON MASLIAH.

Consistoire Israélite de Paris (Jewish Consistorial Association of Paris): 17 rue Saint Georges, 75009 Paris; tel. (1) 42-85-71-09; Pres. EMILE TOUATI; Chief Rabbi ALAIN GOLDMANN; Sec.-Gen. SERGE GUEDJ.

BUDDHISM

World Federation of Buddhists, French Regional Centre: 98 chemin de la Calade, 06250 Mougins; Sec. Mme TEISAN PERUSAT STORK.

Association Zen Internationale: 17 rue des Cinq Diamants, 75013 Paris; tel. (1) 45-80-10-00; Sec. JANINE MANNOT.

The Press

The legislation under which the French press operates mostly dates back to an Act of 1881, which established very liberal

FRANCE

conditions for journalism, asserting the right of individuals to produce newspapers without any prior authorization. At the same time the law defined certain offences which the press might commit, such as incitement to crime, disturbance of the peace by the publication of false information, libel and defamation, the publication of material offensive to the President and revealing official secrets. Further legislation in the 1940s extended these restrictions, particularly with regard to children's literature. A law to prevent the concentration of newspaper and magazine ownership in the hands of a small number of press conglomerates was adopted in 1984. However, by June 1986 the new right-wing Government had abrogated the 1984 law and a 1944 ordinance, thus increasing the proportion of the total circulation of daily newspapers that an individual was permitted to control. The Constitutional Council added amendments which attempted to prevent the use of 'front' companies and intermediaries to increase an individual company's holdings in the French press.

In 1984 504 newspapers and 2,378 periodicals were published in France. In 1983 there were 11 daily newspapers published in Paris with a national circulation and 80 provincial dailies covering all the French regions. The circulations of the two groups in 1983 were 2.7m. for the Parisian press and 7.5m. for the provincial press. These figures showed a remarkable decline from the situation in 1946, when 28 Parisian dailies had a circulation of 5m. and 175 provincial dailies shared 9m. circulation. In recent years sharply rising costs and falling advertising revenue have increased the difficulties caused by declining circulation. The prestigious daily, *Le Monde*, issued shares to avoid a financial crisis in late 1985. In January 1988 the left-wing daily, *Le Matin de Paris*, was declared bankrupt and published its last edition.

The provincial press, already strong under the Third Republic, achieved a leading role during the German occupation (1940–44), when Paris was cut off from the rest of France. Since the war, it has proved more adept than the national press at dealing with the fall in revenue and rising costs. The best-selling provincial dailies can now almost match the most popular Paris dailies for circulation and they have initiated various rationalization schemes. Groups of provincial papers have been formed to pool advertising and, in some cases, copy and printing facilities. In an attempt to prevent the domination of the press in Lyon by the Hersant Group (following its take-over of *Le Progrès* in January 1986), two national dailies, *Le Monde* and *Libération*, started to produce regional editions in Lyon. By late 1986 the Hersant Group had launched a regional edition of *Le Figaro* in Lyon, which was merged with *Le Journal Rhône-Alpe*, another publication owned by the Hersant Group, to become *Journal Rhône-Alpes-Lyon-Figaro* in 1987.

The weekly news magazines have expanded in recent years; the two best examples of this are *L'Express* and *Le Nouvel Observateur*. Radio and TV magazines have greatly increased in popularity, and were estimated to reach 40% of French homes in 1987. Both national and regional newspapers have started to launch weekly TV supplements and, in response to increased competition in 1987, the Hachette Group, the owner of *Télé-7-Jours*, proposed the creation of another weekly, *Télé Couleur*, to sell as a supplement to regional publications.

The only major daily which acts as the organ of a political party is the Communist paper, *L'Humanité*. All others are owned by individual publishers or by the powerful groups which have developed round either a company or a single personality. The major groups are as follows:

Amaury Group: 25 ave Michelet, 93408 Saint-Ouen Cedex; tel. (1) 42-52-82-15; telex 66041; owns *Le Parisien*, the provincial dailies *Le Courrier de l'Ouest*, *Le Maine Libre* and *Liberté Dimanche*, the sports daily *L'Equipe*, and the monthly, *Tennis de France*; Man. Dir PHILIPPE AMAURY.

Bayard Presse: 3 rue Bayard, 75008 Paris; tel. (1) 45-62-51-51; telex 641868; important Catholic press group; owns the national *La Croix-L'Evénement*, *Pèlerin Magazine*, *Panorama Aujourd'hui*, *Notre Temps*, important magazines for young people and several specialized religious publications; Pres. BERNARD PORTE.

Editions Mondiales: 2 rue des Italiens, 75009 Paris; telex 643932; formerly Del Duca Group; owns several popular weekly magazines, incl. *Nous Deux*, *Intimité*, *Modes de Paris*, *Télé-Poche* and also specialized magazines; Man. Dir JEAN MAMERT.

Expansion Group: 67 ave de Wagram, 75017 Paris; tel. (1) 47-63-12-11; telex 650242; f. 1967; owns a number of magazines, incl. *L'Expansion*, *L'Entreprise*, *Architecture d'Aujourd'hui*, *Harvard L'Expansion*, *Voyages*, *Agefi*, *La Vie Française*, *La Tribune*; Chair. and Man. Dir JEAN-LOUIS SERVAN-SCHREIBER.

Filipacchi Group: 63 ave des Champs Elysées, 75008 Paris; tel. (1) 42-56-72-72; telex 290294; controls a number of large-circulation magazines incl. *Paris-Match, Salut, 7 à Paris, OK!, Podium, Top 50, Newlook, Penthouse, Union, Echo des Savanes, Les Grands Ecrivains, Femme, Pariscope, Jazz Magazine, Lui, Les Grands Peintres, Les Grands Personnages, Jeune et Jolie, Fortune* and *Photo*; Pres. DANIEL FILIPACCHI.

Hachette Groupe Presse: 6 rue Ancelle, 92525 Neuilly-sur-Seine Cedex; tel. (1) 47-38-43-21; telex 611462; f. 1826; publs incl. *Le Journal du Dimanche, France-Dimanche, Elle, Télé-7-Jours, Parents, Le Provençal, Le Méridional, Var Matin, Les Dernières, Nouvelles d'Alsace*; has 36% holding in *Le Parisen Libéré* and *l'Equipe*; Chair. JEAN-LUC LAGARDÈRE; Man. Dir DANIEL FILIPACCHI.

Hersant Group: one of the largest of the provincial daily press groups; owns 20 dailies, numerous weeklies, fortnightlies and periodicals; dailies incl. *Le Progrès, L'Eclair, Le Dauphiné Libéré, Nord-Matin* and *Nord-Eclair*; has a majority holding in *Le Figaro, France-Soir, l'Aurore* and *Paris-Turf*; Chair. and Man. Dir ROBERT HERSANT.

Among the metropolitan dailies, the outstanding papers are *Le Monde* (circulation 362,443) and *Le Figaro* (433,496). Also popular are *France-Soir* and *Le Parisien Libéré*. The English language *International Herald Tribune* (174,200) is also important. The major provincial dailies are *Ouest-France* (Rennes), *Sud-Ouest* (Bordeaux), *Le Dauphiné Libéré* (Grenoble), *La Voix du Nord* (Lille), *Le Progrès* (Lyon), and *L'Est Républicain* (Nancy). Many provincial dailies cater for rural readership by producing local subsidiary editions.

Metropolitan weekly papers range from the popular press, such as *France-Dimanche* (721,000) and *L'Humanité-Dimanche* (360,000), through to the more serious current affairs magazines like *L'Express*, *Le Nouvel Observateur* and the satirical *Canard Enchaîné*. Among the popular periodicals must be mentioned the weekly illustrated *Paris-Match* (690,000) and the women's journals *Marie-Claire* (599,362), *Elle* (395,007) and *Marie-France* (522,284).

DAILY PAPERS (PARIS)

L'Aurore: 133 Champs-Elysées, 75008 Paris; telex 220310; f. 1944; Dir ROGER ALEXANDRE; circ. 35,000 (1983).

La Croix l'Evénement: 3-5 rue Bayard, 75008 Paris; tel. (1) 45-62-51-51; telex 280626; f. 1883; Catholic; Dir BERNARD PORTE; Editors-in-Chief JEAN POTIN, ANDRÉ GÉRAUD, NOËL COPIN; circ. 113,028.

Les Echos: 67 ave des Champs Elysées, 75381 Paris Cedex 08; tel. (1) 45-62-19-68; telex 290275; f. 1908; economic and financial; Chair. FRANK BARLOW (acting); circ. 72,992.

L'Equipe: 4 rue Rouget de Lisle, 92137 Issy-les-Moulineaux; f. 1946; sport; Man. Dir JEAN-PIERRE COURCOL; circ. 239,632.

Le Figaro: 25 ave Matignon, 75398 Paris Cedex 08; tel. (1) 42-56-80-80; telex 211112; f. 1828; morning; news and literary; magazine on Saturdays; Chair. ROBERT HERSANT; Editor-in-Chief FRANZ-OLIVIER GIESBERT; circ. 433,496.

France-Soir: rue de Bercy, 75112 Paris; tel. (1) 45-08-28-00; f. 1941 as *Défense de la France*, present title 1944; merged with *Paris-Presse L'Intransigeant* 1965; magazine on Saturdays, merged with *TV-France-Soir*, 1987; Chair. and Man. Dir PHILIPPE VILLIN; circ. 410,679.

L'Humanité: 5 rue du Faubourg Poissonière, 75440 Paris Cedex 09; tel. (1) 42-46-82-69; f. 1904 by Jean Jaurès; organ of the French Communist Party; morning; Dir ROLAND LEROY; Editor-in-Chief CLAUDE CABANES; circ. 117,005.

International Herald Tribune: 181 ave Charles de Gaulle, 92521 Neuilly-sur-Seine Cedex; tel. (1) 46-37-93-00; telex 612718; f. 1887; English language; Co-Chairs W. S. PALEY, K. GRAHAM, A. O. SULZBERGER; circ. 174,200.

Le Journal Officiel de la République Française: 26 rue Desaix, 75727 Paris Cedex 15; tel. (1) 45-75-62-31; telex 201176; f. 1870; official journal of the Government; publishes laws, decrees, parliamentary proceedings, and economic bulletins; Dir ROBERT BOUQUIN.

Libération: 11 rue Béranger, 75154 Paris Cedex 03; tel. (1) 42-76-17-89; telex 217656; f. 1973; non-conformist; Dir-Gen. JEAN-LOUIS PÉNINOU; circ. 165,539.

Le Monde: 5 rue des Italiens, 75427 Paris Cedex 09; tel. (1) 42-47-97-27; telex 650572; f. 1944; liberal; independent; week-end supplements; Dir ANDRÉ FONTAINE; Editor-in-Chief DANIEL VERNET; circ. 362,443.

Paris-Turf/Sport Complet: 100 rue de Richelieu, 75002 Paris; racing, sport; Dir PIERRE JANROT; circ. 150,000.

Le Parisien Libéré: 25 ave Michelet, 93400 Saint Ouen; tel. (1) 42-52-88-00; telex 660041; f. 1944; morning; Chair. and Man. Dir PHILLIPE AMAURY; Man. Dir MARTIN DESPREZ; circ. 339,271.

Le Quotidien du Médecin: Le France, 2 rue Ancelle, 92200 Neuilly-sur-Seine; medical journal; Dir Dr MARIE CLAUDE TESSON MILLET; Editor RICHARD LISCIA; circ. 62,000.

FRANCE

Le Quotidien de Paris: 2 rue Ancelle, 92521 Neuilly-sur-Seine Cedex; tel. (1) 47-47-12-32; telex 610806; f. 1974, relaunched 1979; Man. Dir JEAN-MICHEL SAINT-OUEN; Editor PHILIPPE TESSON; circ. 75,000 (1987).

La Tribune de l'Economie: 12 rue Béranger, 75003 Paris; tel. (1) 48-04-99-99; telex 230735; f. 1986; economic and financial; Dir JACQUES JUBLIN; circ. 59,000.

SUNDAY PAPERS (PARIS)

France-Dimanche: 6 rue Ancelle, 92525 Neuilly-sur-Seine Cedex; tel. (1) 47-38-43-12; telex 611462; Dir GUY GOUJON; circ. 721,000.

L'Humanité-Dimanche: 5 rue du Faubourg Poissonnière, 75440 Paris Cedex 09; tel. (1) 42-46-82-69; f. 1946; weekly magazine of the French Communist Party; Dir ROLAND LEROY; Editor Mme BULARD; circ. 360,000.

PRINCIPAL PROVINCIAL DAILY PAPERS

Amiens

Le Courrier Picard: 14 rue Alphonse Paillaet, 80010 Amiens Cedex; f. 1944; Chair. DANIEL MARCOURT; Man. Dir JACQUES BENESSE; circ. 86,000.

Angers

Courrier de l'Ouest: blvd Albert Blanchoin, BP 728, 49005 Angers Cedex; tel. 41-66-21-31; telex 720997; f. 1944; Chair. and Man. Dir J. M. DESGREES DU LOU; circ. 107,431.

Angoulême

La Charente Libre: Zone Industrielle no. 3, BP 106, 16001 Angoulême Cedex; tel. 45-69-33-33; telex 791950; Dir LOUIS-GUY GAYAN; circ. 38,869.

Auxerre

L'Yonne Républicaine: 8-12 ave Jean Moulin, BP 399, 89006 Auxerre Cedex; f. 1944; Gen. Man. J. F. COMPÉRAT; circ. 41,606.

Besançon

Le Comtois: 60 rue Grande, 25000 Besançon; f. 1914; Dir. PIERRE BRANTUS; circ. 15,532.

Bordeaux

La France—Nouvelle République de Bordeaux et du Sud-Ouest: 9 rue Guiraude, 33000 Bordeaux; f. 1944; Dir JEAN-MICHEL BLANCHY; circ. 10,270.

Sud-Ouest: 8 rue de Cheverus, BP 521, 33000 Bordeaux; tel. 56-90-92-72; telex 570670; f. 1944; independent; Man. Dir HENRI DE GRANDMAISON; Chief Editor PIERRE VEILLETET; circ. 356,989.

Calais

Nord Littoral: 39 blvd Jacquard, 62100 Calais; tel. 21-34-41-00; f. 1944; Editor JEAN-JACQUES BARATTE; circ. 9,819.

Chalon-sur-Saône

Courrier de Saône-et-Loire: 9 rue des Tonneliers, 71104 Chalon-sur- Saône; f. 1826; Dir RENÉ PRÉTET; circ. 46,021.

Charleville-Mézières

L'Ardennais: 36 cours Aristide Briand, 08102 Charleville-Mézières; tel. 24-32-91-51; f. 1944; Man. Dir PIERRE DIDRY; circ. 29,872.

Chartres

L'Echo Républicain: 39 rue de Châteaudun, 28004 Chartres; f. 1929; Chair. and Man. Dir ALAIN GASCON; Editor-in-Chief ALAIN BOUZY; circ. 31,817.

Chaumont

La Haute-Marne Libérée: 1B rue Chambrulard, 52200 Langres; f. 1944; Editor JEAN BLETNER; circ. 10,100.

Cherbourg

La Presse de la Manche: 14 rue Gambetta, 50104 Cherbourg; tel. 33-94-16-16; telex 171623; f. 1944; Chair. and Man. Dir DANIEL JUBERT; circ. 27,605.

Clermont-Ferrand

La Montagne (Centre-France): 28 rue Morel Ladeuil, 63003 Clermont-Ferrand; tel. 73-93-22-91; telex 990588; f. 1919; independent; Dir RENÉ BONJEAN; circ. 252,457.

Dijon

Le Bien Public: 7 blvd Chanoine Kir, 21015 Dijon Cedex; f. 1850; Pres. and Dir-Gen. A. THÉNARD; Dir-Gen. L. DE BROISSIA; circ. 53,383.

Les Dépêches du Centre-Est: 17 rue de Colmar, BP 570, 21015 Dijon; tel. 80-65-17-45; f. 1936; Chair. FRANCIS BOILEAU; Man. Dir MICHEL-YVES LAURENT; circ. 34,030.

Epinal

Liberté de l'Est: 40 quai des Bons Enfants, 88001 Epinal Cedex; tel. 29-82-98-00; f. 1945; Man. SERGE CLÉMENT; Editor-in-Chief JACQUES DALLÉ; circ. 31,319.

Grenoble

Le Dauphiné Libéré: Les Iles Cordées, 38113 Veurey-Voroize; tel. 76-88-71-00; telex 320822; f. 1944; Chair. CHARLES DEBBASCH; circ. 360,000.

Le Havre

Havre Libre: 25 rue Jules Siegfried, BP 138, 76066 Le Havre; f. 1944; Editor-in-Chief RENÉ LENHOF; circ. 28,268.

Lille

Nord-Matin: 15 rue du Caire, Lille Cedex; f. 1944; Gen. Man. ROGER GRUSS; circ. 73,798.

La Voix du Nord: 8 place du Général de Gaulle, 78167 Lille; f. 1944; Chair. and Man. Dir RENÉ DECOCK; circ. 377,219.

Limoges

L'Echo du Centre: 46 rue Turgot, 87000 Limoges; tel. 55-34-46-35; f. 1943; five editions; Communist; Dir CHRISTIAN AUDOUIN; Chief Editor JEAN SAVARY; circ. 65,000.

Le Populaire du Centre: 9 place Fontaine-des-Barres, Limoges Cedex; f. 1905; four editions; Chair and Man. Dir RENÉ BONJEAN; Editor-in-Chief ROGER QUEYROI; circ. 56,493.

Lyon

Le Progrès: 93 chemin de Saint-Priest, 69680 Chassieu; tel. 78-90-81-18; f. 1859; Chair. DENIS HUERTAS; circ. Mon.–Sat. 353,608, Sun. 447,289.

Marseille

La Marseillaise: 17 cours Honoré d'Estienne d'Orves, BP 1862, 13222 Marseille Cedex 1; tel. 91-54-92-13; f. 1944; Communist; Dir PAUL BIAGGINI; Editor-in-Chief ALAIN FABRE; circ. 159,039.

Le Méridional-La France: 4 rue Cougit, 13316 Marseille Cedex 15; f. 1944; independent; 12 regional editions; Chair. RENÉ MERLE; circ. 72,750.

Le Provençal: 248 ave Roger Salengro, BP 100, 13316 Marseille; tel. 90-84-45-45; f. 1944; the biggest daily paper in the south-east (evening edition **Le Soir**); Chair. and Man. Dir ANDRÉ POITEVIN; circ. 178,502.

Metz

Le Républicain Lorrain: 3 rue de St Eloy, BP 89, 57104 Metz-Woippy; tel. 87-33-22-00; telex 860346; f. 1919; independent; Pres. Mme MARGUERITE PUHL-DEMANGE; Dir-Gen. CLAUDE PUHL; circ. 214,280.

Montpellier

Midi-Libre: Le Mans de Grille, route de Sète, Saint-Jean de Vedas, 34063 Montpellier Cedex; tel. 67-42-00-44; f. 1944; Dir CLAUDE BUJON; circ. 189,283.

Morlaix

Le Télégramme de Brest et de l'Ouest: rue Anatole Le Braz, BP 243, 29205 Morlaix Cedex; tel. 98-62-11-33; telex 940652; f. 1944; Dir JEAN-PIERRE COUDURIER; circ. 201,963 (1985).

Mulhouse

L'Alsace: 25 ave du Président Kennedy, 68053 Mulhouse; tel. 89-43-99-44; telex 881818; f. 1944; Editor GILBERT KLEIN; circ. 136,297.

Nancy

L'Est Républicain: rue Theophraste Renaudot Houdemont, 54185 Heillecourt Cedex; tel. 83-56-80-54; telex 850019; f. 1889; Dir GÉRARD LIGNAC; circ. 267,588.

Nantes

L'Eclair: 5 rue Santeuil, BP 1116, 44010 Nantes Cedex 01; f. 1945; Gen. Man. ROLANDE HERSANT; Dir-Gen. JEAN LUCAS; circ. 20,230.

Presse Océan: 7-8 allée Duguay Trouin, BP 1142, 44024 Nantes Cedex 01; tel. 40-44-24-00; telex 700439; f. 1944; independent; Chair. and Man. Dir PHILIPPE MESTRE; Editor-in-Chief JEAN-MARIE GAUTIER; circ. 93,180.

Nevers

Journal du Centre: 3 rue du Chemin de Fer, BP 14, 58000 Nevers; f. 1943; Editor PAUL BERTHELOT; circ. 37,834.

FRANCE

Nice
Nice-Matin: 214 route de Grenoble, BP 4, 06200 Nice Cedex; tel. 93-21-71-71; telex 460788; f. 1944; Chair. and Man. Dir MICHEL BAVASTRO; circ. 261,980.

Orléans
La République du Centre: 45 rue de la Halte, Saran, BP 35, 45403 Fleury les Aubrais Cedex; tel. 38-86-37-68; telex 780702; f. 1944; Chair. and Man. Dir MARC CARRÉ; Editor JACQUES RAMEAU; circ. 67,144.

Pau
Eclair-Pyrénées: 40 rue Emile Guichenné, 64006 Pau; f. 1944; Dir HENRI LOUSTALAN; circ. 9,801.

Perpignan
L'Indépendant: 4 rue Emmanuel Brousse, 66004 Perpignan; tel. 68-35-51-51; f. 1846; also **Indépendant-Dimanche** (Sunday); Dir DOMINIQUE PRETET; circ. 84,072.

Poitiers
Centre Presse: 5 rue Victor Hugo, BP 299, 86007 Poitiers; f. 1958; Man. Dir CYRILLE DUVAL; Editor-in-Chief ROLAND BARKAT; circ. 20,000.

Reims
L'Union: 87–91 place Drouet d'Erlon, 51052 Reims Cedex; f. 1944; telex 830751; Dir PHILIPPE HERSANT; Editor-in-Chief JACQUES RICHARD; circ. 117,812.

Rennes
Ouest-France: Zone Industrielle Rennes-Chantepie, 35051 Rennes Cedex; tel. 99-03-62-22; telex 730965; f. 1944; Chair. FRANÇOIS-RÉGIS HUTIN; circ. 803,701 (1985).

Roubaix
Nord-Eclair: 21 rue du Caire, 59052 Roubaix Cedex 1; tel. 20-75-92-56; telex 160740; f. 1944; Chair. A. DILIGENT; Man. Dir A. FARINE; circ. 102,773.

Rouen
Paris-Normandie: 19 place du Général de Gaulle, BP 563, 76004 Rouen; f. 1944; tel. 35-14-56-56; telex 771507; Publr Société Normande de Presse Républicaine; Chair. and Man. Dir JEAN ALLARD; circ. 129,030.

Saint-Etienne
La Tribune: 14 place d'Aygu, 26201 Montelimar; tel. (Montelimar) 01-69-66; Editor JEAN-JACQUES AYZEC; circ. 23,352.

La Tribune—Le Progrès: 16 place Jean Jaurès, 42000 Saint-Etienne; tel. 77-32-45-45; Editor DENIS HUERTAS; circ. 130,000.

Strasbourg
Dernières Nouvelles d'Alsace: 17-19-21 rue de la Nuée Bleue, BP 406/R1, 67000 Strasbourg; tel. 88-23-31-23; telex 880445; f. 1877; non-party; Dir JACQUES PUYMARTIN; circ. 220,082.

Le Nouvel Alsacien: 6 rue Finkmatt, 67000 Strasbourg; tel. 88-32-37-14; f. 1885; Man. BERNARD DECK; circ. 15,245.

Tarbes
La Nouvelle République des Pyrénées: 48 ave Bertrand Barère, 65001 Tarbes; tel. (Tarbes) 93-90-90; f. 1944; Man. JEAN GAITS; circ. 17,765.

Toulon
Var Matin: route de la Seyne à Ollioules, 83190 Toulon; f. 1946; Man. Dir CHRISTIAN DE BARBARIN-PAQUET; circ. 80,604.

Toulouse
Dépêche du Midi: 57 rue Bayard, 31003 Toulouse; f. 1870; radical; Gen. Man. Mme EVELYNE-JEAN BAYLET; circ. 247,533.

Tours
La Nouvelle République du Centre-Ouest: 232 ave de Grammont, 37048 Tours Cedex; tel. 47-31-70-00; telex 750693; f. 1944; non-party; Chair JACQUES SAINT-CRICQ; circ. 271,504 (1987).

Troyes
L'Est-Eclair: 55 rue Urbain IV, 10000 Troyes; tel. 25-79-90-10; f. 1945; Dir ANDRÉ BRULEY; circ. 33,000.

Libération-Champagne: 126 rue Général de Gaulle, BP 713, 10003 Troyes Cedex; tel. 25-73-11-55; Dir GILBERT BOUTSOQUE; circ. 21,074.

SELECTED PERIODICALS

The following is a selection from the total of 2,378 periodicals (1984) published in France.

General, Political and Literary

Annales—Economies, sociétés, civilisations: 54 blvd Raspail, 75006 Paris; tel. (1) 45-48-25-64; f. 1929; every 2 months; eight Dirs.

Arts: 3 rue de Valois, 75001 Paris; f. 1987; 10 a year; published by the Ministry for Culture and Communications; arts magazine; Editor-in-Chief ANDRÉ-MARC DELOCQUE-FOURCARD.

Aspects de la France: 10 rue Croix des Petits Champs, 75001 Paris; tel. (1) 42-96-12-06; f. 1947; weekly; monarchist; organ of L'Action Française; Dir PIERRE PUJO.

Autre Journal: 7 rue d'Argout, 75002 Paris; tel. (1) 42-36-33-86; f. 1984, fmrly *Nouvelles Littéraires*; monthly; literature, medicine, science, technology, news; Dir MICHEL BUTEL; circ. 220,000.

Le Canard Enchaîné: 173 rue Saint Honoré, Paris 75001; tel. (1) 42-60-31-36; f. 1915; weekly; political satire; Chair. and Man. Dir ANDRÉ RIBAUD; circ. 450,000.

Carrefour: 114 ave des Champs Elysées, 75008 Paris; f. 1944; weekly; moderate; Dir JEAN DANNENMULLER; circ. 100,000.

Le Crapouillot: 49 ave Marceau, 75016 Paris; f. 1915; satire and humorous; Man. Dir J.-C. GOUDEAU; Editor PATRICE BOIZEAU.

Critique: Editions de Minuit, 7 rue Bernard Palissy, 75006 Paris; tel. (1) 45-44-23-16; f. 1946; monthly; general review of French and foreign literature; Editor JEAN PIEL.

Croissance des Jeunes Nations: 163 blvd Malesherbes, 75017 Paris; tel. (1) 47-66-01-86; f. 1961; monthly on developing nations; circ. 35,000.

Diogène: Unesco House, 1 rue Miollis, 75732 Paris Cedex 15; tel. (1) 45-68-27-34; f. 1951; quarterly; international review of human sciences; four editions, in Arabic, English, French and Spanish; anthologies in Chinese, Hindi, Japanese and Portuguese; Editor JEAN D'ORMESSON.

Les Ecrits de Paris: 9 passage des Marais, 75010 Paris; tel. (1) 42-01-40-51; f. 1944; monthly; current affairs; circ. 15,000.

Esprit: 212 rue St-Martin, 75003 Paris; tel. (1) 48-04-92-90; f. 1932; monthly; Dir OLIVIER MONGIN; circ. 10,000.

Europe: 146 rue du Faubourg Poissonnière, 75010 Paris; tel. (1) 42-81-91-03; f. 1923; monthly; literary review; Chair. PIERRE GAMARRA; Editors CHARLES DOBZYNSKI, JEAN-BAPTISTE PARA.

L'Evénement du Jeudi: 2 rue Christine, 75006 Paris; tel. (1) 43-54-84-80; f. 1984; weekly; current affairs; Editorial Dir JEAN-MARCEL BOUGUEREAU; circ. 240,000.

L'Express: 61 ave Hoche, 75008 Paris; tel. (1) 40-54-30-00; telex 280805; f. 1953; weekly; Head of Publication WILLY STRICKER; Editor-in-Chief YANN DE L'ECOTAIS; circ. 669,600.

Le Hérisson: 2-12 rue de Bellevue, 75019 Paris; f. 1936; weekly; humorous; Dir J. P. VENTILLARD; Editor A. MOREUIL; circ. 270,000.

Ici-Paris: 29 rue Galilée, 75116 Paris; tel. (1) 47-23-78-77; f. 1941; weekly; Editor LOUIS BALAYÉ; circ. 372,386.

Jours de France: 49 ave Marceau, 75116 Paris; tel. (1) 40-70-15-15; f. 1954; weekly; news and fashion magazine; Chief Editor MARCEL DASSAULT; circ. 673,000.

Lire: 61 ave Hoche, 75380 Paris Cedex 08; tel. (1) 42-67-97-98; monthly; literary review; Editor BERNARD PIVOT; circ. 125,070.

Lutte Ouvrière: BP 233, 75865 Paris Cedex 18; f. 1968; weekly; Editor MICHEL RODINSON.

Minute: 11 rue de Clichy, 75009 Paris; tel. (1) 42-85-54-54; f. 1962; right-wing weekly; Pres. and Dir-Gen. J. C. GOUDEAU; Editor-in-Chief J. ROBERTO; circ. 220,000.

Le Monde Diplomatique: 7 rue des Italiens, 75427 Paris Cedex 09; tel. (1) 42-47-98-20; telex 650572; f. 1954; monthly; political and cultural; Dir CLAUDE JULIEN; Editors MICHELINE PAUNET, IGNACIO RAMONET; circ. 165,000.

Le Nouvel Observateur: 14 rue Dussoubs, 75081 Paris; telex 680729; f. 1964; weekly; left-wing political and literary; Dir CLAUDE PERDRIEL; Editorial Dir LAURENT JOFFRIN; circ. 324,200.

La Nouvelle Revue Française (NRF): 5 rue Sébastien Bottin, 75007 Paris; tel. (1) 45-44-39-19; telex 204121; f. 1909; monthly; literary; Editor JACQUES REDA.

Parents: 6 rue Ancelle, 92521 Neuilly-sur-Seine; tel. (1) 47-38-43-21; magazine for parents; circ. 367,571.

Paris-Match: 63 ave des Champs Elysées, 75008 Paris; telex 290294; f. 1949; weekly; magazine of French and world affairs; Dir ROGER THÉROND; circ. 690,000.

FRANCE

Passages: 17 rue Simone Weil, 75013 Paris; f. 1987; monthly; Jewish current affairs, humour and literary review; Dir EMILE MALET; Editor BERNARD ULMANN; circ. 75,000.

Le Peuple: 263 rue de Paris, Case 432, 93516 Montreuil Cedex; tel. 48-51-83-06; telex 213060; f. 1921; fortnightly; official organ of the Confédération Générale du Travail (trade union confederation); Dir JEAN-CLAUDE LAROZE; Editor-in-Chief LUCIEN POSTEL.

Poétique: Editions du Seuil, 27 rue Jacob, 75261 Paris Cedex 06; tel. (1) 40-46-50-50; telex 600605; f. 1970; quarterly; literary review.

Le Point: 140 rue de Rennes, 75006 Paris; tel. (1) 45-44-39-00; telex 202784; f. 1972; politics and current affairs; Man. Dir OLIVIER CHEVRILLON; Editor CLAUDE IMBERT; circ. 329,658.

Point de Vue-Images du Monde: 116 bis ave des Champs Elysées, 75008 Paris; weekly; Dir C. GIRON; circ. 370,311.

Politique Hebdo: 14–16 rue des Petits Hotels, 75010 Paris; weekly; review of world socialist studies and practice.

Politique Internationale: 11 rue du Bois de Boulogne, 75116 Paris; 4 a year.

Quinzaine Littéraire: 43 rue du Temple, 75004 Paris; tel. (1) 48-87-48-58; f. 1966; fortnightly; Dir MAURICE NADEAU; circ. 40,000.

Révolution: 15 rue Montmartre, 75001 Paris; tel. (1) 42-33-61-26; f. 1980; weekly; political and cultural; Dir GUY HERMIER; Chief Editors JEAN-PAUL JOUARY, GÉRARD STREIFF.

Revue des Deux Mondes: 15 rue de l'Université, 75007 Paris; tel. (1) 42-61-21-49; f. 1829; monthly; current affairs; Dir JEAN JAUDEL.

Revue d'Histoire Littéraire de la France: 112 rue Monge, 75005 Paris; f. 1894; 6 a year; Editor RENÉ POMEAU.

Rivarol: 9 passage des Marais, 75010 Paris; tel. (1) 42-06-40-51; f. 1951; weekly; political, literary and satirical; circ. 45,000.

Rouge: 2 rue Richard Lenoir, 93100 Montreuil; tel. 48-59-00-80; f. 1969; weekly; extreme left; circ. 10,000.

Sélection du Reader's Digest: 212 blvd Saint Germain, 75007 Paris; tel. (1) 46-64-16-16; telex 200882; monthly; Chair. HENRI CAPDEVILLE; circ. 1,130,000.

Les Temps Modernes: 26 rue de Condé, 75006 Paris; tel. (1) 43-29-08-47; f. 1945 by J.-P. Sartre; monthly; literary review; publ. by Les Presses d'Aujourd'hui.

Art

L'Architecture d'Aujourd'hui: 67 ave de Wagram, 75017 Paris; tel. (1) 47-63-12-11; telex 650242; f. 1930; publ. by Groupe Expansion; Editor-in-Chief FRANÇOIS CHASLIN; circ. 25,791.

Art et Décoration: 2 rue de l'Echelle, 75001 Paris; tel. (1) 42-60-30-05; f. 1897; 8 a year; Dir JEAN MASSIN; circ. 451,443.

Gazette des Beaux-Arts: 140 Faubourg Saint Honoré, 75008 Paris; tel. (1) 42-89-08-04; f. 1859; monthly; the oldest review of the history of art; Dir DANIEL WILDENSTEIN.

L'Oeil: 10 rue Guichard, 75116 Paris; tel. (1) 45-25-85-60; f. 1955; monthly; Vice-Chair. FRANÇOIS DAULTE; Gen. Sec. and Editor SOLANGE THIERRY.

Bibliography

Bulletin des Bibliothèques de France: 3-5 blvd Pasteur, 75015 Paris; tel. (1) 45-39-25-75; f. 1956; 6 a year; circ. 2,200.

Livres-Hebdo: 30 rue Dauphine, 75006 Paris; tel. (1) 43-29-73-50; f. 1979; 46 a year; Dir JEAN-MARIE DOUBLET.

Livres de France: 30 rue Dauphine, 75006 Paris; tel. (1) 43-29-73-50; f. 1979; 11 a year; Dir JEAN-MARIE DOUBLET.

Economic and Financial

L'Assureur-Conseil: 31 rue d'Amsterdam, 75008 Paris; tel. (1) 48-74-19-23; monthly; review produced by Syndicat National des Courtiers d'Assurances; Editor-in-Chief ALAIN FARSHIAN; circ. 2,000.

L'Expansion: 67 ave de Wagram, 75017 Paris; tel. (1) 47-63-12-11; telex 650242; f. 1967; every 2 weeks; economics and business; Pres. JEAN-LOUIS SERVAN-SCHREIBER; Dir JEAN BOISSONNAT; Editor-in-Chief ALBERT DU ROY; circ. 200,565.

Le Nouvel Economiste: 22 rue de la Tremoille, 75008 Paris; tel. (1) 47-23-01-05; telex 613572; f. 1975 by merger of *l'Entreprise* and *Les Informations*; weekly; Chair. and Man. Dir FRANK TENOT; circ. 117,090.

Revue Economique: 54 blvd Raspail, 75006 Paris; tel. (1) 45-44-39-79; f. 1950; every 2 months; Chair. J. M. PARLY.

Science et Vie Economie: 5 rue de la Baume, 75008 Paris; tel. (1) 40-74-48-71; telex 641866; f. 1984; monthly; economics; Dir PAUL DUPUY; Editor-in-Chief JEAN-MARIE GISCLARD; circ. 160,000.

L'Usine Nouvelle: 59 rue du Rocher, 75008 Paris; tel. (1) 43-87-37-88; telex 640485; f. 1945; weekly with monthly supplements; technical and industrial journal; Chair. and Man. Dir JACQUES MONNIER; circ. 60,000.

Valeurs Actuelles: 14 rue d'Uzès, 75081 Paris Cedex 02; tel. (1) 42-33-21-84; f. 1967; weekly; politics, economics, international affairs; Editor R. BOURGINE; circ. 150,000.

La Vie Française: 2 rue Béranger, 75003 Paris; tel. (1) 48-04-99-99; telex 670092; f. 1945; weekly; economics and finance; Dir and Editor-in-Chief BRUNO BERTEZ; Editorial Dir FRANÇOIS DE WITT; circ. 125,000.

History and Geography

Acta geographica: 184 blvd Saint Germain, 75006 Paris; tel. (1) 45-48-54-62; f. 1821; quarterly; Chair. JACQUELINE BEAUJEU-GARNIER.

Annales de géographie: 103 blvd Saint Michel, 75005 Paris; tel. (1) 46-34-12-19; telex 201269; f. 1891; every 2 months; seven Dirs.

Cahiers de civilisation médiévale: 24 rue de la Chaine, 86022 Poitiers; tel. 49-41-03-86; f. 1958; quarterly; Dirs PIERRE BEC, ROBERT FAVREAU.

XVIIe siècle: c/o Collège de France, 11 place Marcelin Berthelot, 75231 Paris Cedex 05; tel. (1) 45-48-85-24; f. 1948; quarterly; Dir R. ZUBER; Pres. J. TRUCHET; circ. 1,500.

Historia: 61 rue de la Tombe-Issoire, 75104 Paris; f. 1946; monthly; Dirs JACQUES JOURQUIN, CHRISTIAN MELCHIOR-BONNET; circ. 104,097.

Revue d'histoire diplomatique: 13 rue Soufflot, 75005 Paris; f. 1887; quarterly; Dir GEORGES DETHAN.

Revue Historique: Archives Nationales, 60 rue des Francs-Bourgeois, 75003 Paris; f. 1876; quarterly; Dirs JEAN FAVIER, RENÉ RÉMOND.

Revue de synthèse: Centre International de Synthèse, 12 rue Colbert, 75002 Paris; tel. (1) 42-97-50-68; f. 1900; quarterly; Dir JACQUES ROGER.

Law

Propriété Immobilière: 17 rue d'Uzès, 75002 Paris; f. 1945; monthly; Chair. MARC N. VIGIER; Man. Dir JEAN-MARC PILPOUL; circ. 5,846.

Revue Critique de Droit International Privé: 22 rue Soufflot, 75005 Paris; f. 1905; quarterly; publ. by Editions Sirey; Dirs Prof H. BATIFFOL, Prof PH. FRANCESCAKIS.

Leisure

Cahiers du Cinéma: 9 passage de la Boule Blanche, 75012 Paris; tel. (1) 43-43-92-20; telex 220064; f. 1951; monthly; film reviews; Dir and Editor SERGE TOUBIANA; circ. 80,000.

France-Football: 10 rue du Faubourg Montmartre, 75009 Paris; tel. (1) 42-46-92-33; telex 280390; weekly; owned by Amaury Group; circ. 158,553.

Le Miroir du Cyclisme: 10 rue des Pyramides, 75010 Paris; tel. (1) 42-60-31-06; telex 640067; monthly; cycling; circ. 87,536.

Photo: 65 ave des Champs-Elysées, 75360 Paris; tel. (1) 42-56-75-72; telex 29294; f. 1960; monthly; specialist photography magazine; circ. 191,908.

Télé-Magazine: 88 rue du Château, 92600 Asnières; f. 1955; weekly; circ. 273,958.

Télé-Poche: 2 rue des Italiens, 75009 Paris; f. 1966; weekly; television magazine; Pres. and Dir-Gen. FRANCIS MOREL; circ. 1,800,000.

Télérama: 129 blvd Malesherbes, 75017 Paris; f. 1972; weekly; radio, TV, film, literature and music; circ. 450,000.

Télé 7 Jours: 2 rue Ancelle, 92525 Neuilly-sur-Seine Cedex; tel. (1) 47-38-43-21; telex 611462; f. 1960; weekly; television; Dir PAUL GIANOLLI; Chief Editor ALAIN LAVILLE; circ. 3,335,000.

Military

Armées d'Aujourd'hui: 19 blvd de Latour Maubourg, BP 11307, 75326 Paris Cedex 07; 10 a year; military and technical; produced by the Service d'information et de relations publiques des armées (SIRPA); circ. 130,000.

Revue 'Défense Nationale': Ecole Militaire, 1 place Joffre, 75700 Paris; tel. (1) 45-55-92-30; f. 1939; monthly; publ. by Committee for Study of National Defence; military, economic, political and scientific problems; Chair. Gen. JEAN RICHARD; Editor Adm. JACQUES HUGON.

Music

Diapason-Harmonie: 2 rue des Italiens, 75009 Paris; tel. (1) 48-24-16-21; telex 643932; f. 1956; monthly; Pres. and Dir-Gen. JEAN-PIERRE ROGER; Chief Editor YVES PETIT DE VOIZE; circ. 70,000.

Revue de Musicologie: 2 rue Louvois, 75002 Paris; f. 1917; 2 a year; publ. by Société française de musicologie; Editors CHRISTIAN MEYER, GEORGIE DUROSOIR; circ. 1,000.

FRANCE *Directory*

Overseas and Maritime

Le Droit Maritime Français: 190 blvd Haussmann, 75008 Paris; tel. (1) 45-63-11-55; telex 290131; f. 1949; monthly; maritime law; Pres. SERGE MARPAUD.

Europe Outremer: 178 Quai Louis Blériot, 75016 Paris; tel. (1) 46-47-78-44; f. 1923; monthly; Dir R. TATON; circ. 17,800.

Industries et Développement International: 190 blvd Haussmann, 75008 Paris; tel. (1) 45-63-11-55; telex 290131; f. 1953; monthly; analysis and information on developing economies; Pres. SERGE MARPAUD.

Le Journal de la Marine Marchande et du Transport Multimodal: 190 blvd Haussmann, 75008 Paris; tel. (1) 45-63-11-55, telex 290131; f. 1919; weekly shipping publication; Pres. SERGE MARPAUD.

Marchés Tropicaux et Méditerranéens: 190 blvd Haussmann, 75008 Paris; tel. (1) 45-63-11-55; telex 290131; f. 1945; weekly; African trade review; Pres. SERGE MARPAUD.

Navires, Ports et Chantiers: 190 blvd Haussmann, 75008 Paris; tel. (1) 45-63-11-55; telex 290131; f. 1950; monthly; international shipbuilding and harbours; Pres. SERGE MARPAUD.

La Pêche Maritime: 190 blvd Haussmann, 75008 Paris; tel. (1) 45-63-11-55; telex 290131; f. 1919; monthly; fishing industry; Pres. SERGE MARPAUD.

Philosophy, Psychology

Bibliographie de la Philosophie: Librairie J. Vrin, 6 place de la Sorbonne, 75005 Paris; f. 1937; quarterly.

Psychologie française: 28 rue Serpente, 75006 Paris; f. 1956; quarterly; revue of the Société Française de Psychologie; Editor C. BONNET.

Revue d'Esthétique: 162 rue Saint Charles, 75740 Paris Cedex 15; tel. (1) 61-23-09-26; telex 521001; f. 1948; 2 a year; Dirs OLIVIER REVAULT D'ALLONNES, MIKEL DUFRENNE; circ. 2,500.

Revue des sciences philosophiques et théologiques: Librairie J. Vrin, 6 place de la Sorbonne, 75005 Paris; f. 1907; quarterly.

Revue philosophique de la France et de l'étranger: 12 rue Jean de Beauvais, 75005 Paris; f. 1876; quarterly; Dir YVON BRÉS; circ. 1,200.

Religion

L'Actualité Religieuse dans le Monde: 163 blvd Malesherbes, 75017 Paris; tel. (1) 47-66-01-86; telex 649333; f. 1983; Editor JOSÉ DE BROUCKER; circ. 30,000.

Etudes: 14 rue d'Assas, 75006 Paris; tel. (1) 45-48-52-51; f. 1856; monthly; general interest; Editor R. P. PAUL VALADIER.

France Catholique: 12 rue Edmond Valentin, 75007 Paris; tel. (1) 47-05-43-31; weekly; Dir A. CHABADEL; circ. 20,000.

Pèlerin Magazine: 3 rue Bayard, 75008 Paris; tel. (1) 45-62-51-51; f. 1873; weekly; Dir GUY BAUDRILLART; Editors-in-Chief HENRY CARO, GUY MAURATILLE; circ. 445,862.

Prier: 163 blvd Malesherbes, 75017 Paris; tel. (1) 47-66-01-86; telex 649333; f. 1978; monthly; review of modern prayer and contemplation; circ. 85,000.

Témoignage Chrétien: 49 rue du Faubourg Poissonnière, 75009 Paris; tel. (1) 42-46-37-50; telex 290562; f. 1941; weekly; cultural; Dir GEORGES MONTARON; circ. 52,000.

La Vie Catholique: 163 blvd Malesherbes, 75017 Paris; tel. (1) 47-66-01-86; telex 649333; f. 1945; weekly; Chair. and Man. Dir ANDRÉ SCHAFTER; Dir JOSÉ DE BROUCKER; circ. 400,000.

Science and Mathematics

Annales de Chimie—Science des Matériaux: 120 blvd Saint Germain, 75280 Paris Cedex 06; tel. (1) 46-34-21-60; f. 1789; every 2 months; chemistry.

Astérisque: BP 126-05, 75226 Paris Cedex 05; tel. (1) 46-34-27-88; f. 1973; monthly; Dir M. HERMAN; Sec. D. BOLLOT.

L'Astronomie: 3 rue Beethoven, 75016 Paris; tel. (1) 42-24-13-74; f. 1887; monthly; publ. by Société Astronomique de France; Chair. P. DE LA COTARDIÈRE.

Biochimie: 120 blvd Saint Germain, 75280 Paris Cedex 06; tel. (1) 46-34-21-60; telex 260946; f. 1914; monthly; bio-chemistry; Scientific Editor Mme M. GRUNBERG-MANAGO; Editor YVES RAOUL.

Bulletin de la Société mathématique de France: BP 126-05, 75226 Paris Cedex 05; tel. (1) 46-34-27-88; f. 1872; quarterly; Dir P. SCHAPIRA; Sec. D. BOLLOT.

Bulletin des sciences mathématiques: Centrale des Revues, 11 rue Gossin, 92543 Montrouge Cedex; telex 260776; f. 1870; quarterly; circ. 800.

Science et vie: 5 rue de la Baume, 75382 Paris; f. 1913; monthly; Pres. PAUL DU PUY.

Technical and Miscellaneous

L'Argus de l'Automobile: 1 place Boieldieu, 75002 Paris; tel. (1) 42-61-83-03; telex 214633; f. 1927; motoring weekly.

Aviation Magazine International: 15-17 quai de l'Oise, 75019 Paris; tel. (1) 40-34-22-07; telex 211678; f. 1950; fortnightly; circ. 30,000.

Bureaux d'Études Automatismes: 60-62 rue d'Hauteville, 75010 Paris; tel. (1) 48-24-82-82; telex 280274; 9 issues a year; industrial design and CAD; publ. by CEP Information Technologie.

L'Echo de la Presse: 19 rue des Prêtres Saint-Germain l'Auxerrois, 75039 Paris Cedex 01; f. 1945; weekly; journalism, advertising; Editor NOEL JACQUEMART; circ. 8,100.

Ingénieurs de l'Automobile: 3 ave Président-Wilson, 75116 Paris; tel. (1) 47-20-93-23; f. 1927; monthly; formerly *Journal de la S.I.A.*; technical automobile review; Dir PAUL BARDEZ.

Machine Moderne: 2 cité Bergère, 75009 Paris; tel. (1) 48-24-23-24; telex 650702; f. 1906; monthly; technical magazine; Dir J. P. PONCIER; circ. 10,000.

Matériaux et Techniques: 76 rue de Rivoli, 75004 Paris; tel. (1) 42-78-52-20; f. 1913; monthly; review of engineering research and progress on industrial materials; Chief Editor R. DROUHIN.

Le Monde de l'Education: 5 rue des Italiens, 75427 Paris; tel. (1) 42-47-97-10; telex 650572; f. 1974; monthly; circ. 115,000.

Le Moniteur des Travaux Publics et du Bâtiment: 17 rue d'Uzès, 75002 Paris; tel. (1) 42-96-15-50; telex 680876; f. 1903; weekly; Editor-in-Chief JEAN MARCHAND; Gen. Man. JACQUES GUY; circ. 75,952.

La Revue Générale des Chemins de Fer: C.D.R., 11 rue Gossin, 92543 Montrouge Cedex; telex 260776; f. 1878; monthly; Chief Editor J. P. BERNARD; circ. 4,000.

Revue Pratique du Froid et du Conditionnement de l'Air: 254 rue de Vaugirard, 75740 Paris Cedex 15; tel. (1) 45-32-27-19; telex 202639; f. 1945; fortnightly; industrial and technical review on cold storage, heat pumps and heat recovery and air-conditioning; Dir P. BENICHOU; Editor-in-Chief MICHÈLE LERY; circ. 5,079.

Technologies et Formations: 254 rue de Vaugirard, 75740 Paris Cedex 15; tel. (1) 45-32-27-19; telex 202639; f. 1945; every 2 months; review intended for vocational schools and training managers; Dir P. BENICHOU; circ. 3,900.

Traitement Thermique: 254 rue de Vaugirard, 75740 Paris Cedex 15; tel. (1) 45-32-27-19; telex 202639; f. 1963; 9 a year; technical review for engineers and technicians of heat treatment; Dir PIERRE BENICHOU; circ. 2,420.

La Vie des Métiers: Z.A. 34630 St Thibéry; tel. 67-77-80-35; monthly; Man. Editor YVES JEAN.

Women's and Fashion

Bonne Soirée Télé: 8 rue Bellini, 75782 Paris Cedex 16; tel. (1) 47-27-72-80; f. 1922; weekly; French and Belgian; Chief Editor M. H. ADLER; circ. 234,637.

Echo de la Mode: 9 rue d'Alexandrie, 75002 Paris; f. 1890; weekly; publ. by Editions de Montsouris; Chair. and Man. Dir ALBERT DE SMAELE; circ. 405,000.

Elle: 6 rue Ancelle, 92521 Neuilly-sur-Seine Cedex; tel. (1) 47-38-43-21; telex 290294; f. 1945; weekly; Dir PAUL GIANOLLI; circ. 395,007.

Femme d'Aujourd'hui: 73 rue Pascal, 75013 Paris; tel. (1) 43-36-11-11; telex 649964; f. 1933; weekly; circ. 850,000.

Femme Pratique: 34 rue Eugène-Flachat, 75017 Paris; tel. (1) 42-27-49-49; telex 649964; f. 1958; monthly; French and Belgian; circ. 380,000.

Intimité: 2 rue des Italiens, 75009 Paris; f. 1949; weekly; illustrated stories; Dir ANTOINE DE CLERMONT-TONNERRE; circ. 509,622.

Jardin des Modes: 80 ave du Maine, 75014 Paris; tel. (1) 43-20-13-11; telex 615142; f. 1921; monthly; Publr and Editor ALICE MORGAINE; circ. 80,000.

La Maison de Marie-Claire: 11 bis rue Boissy d'Anglas, 75008 Paris; tel. (1) 42-66-88-88; telex 240387; f. 1967; home interest; Dir EVELYNE PROUVOST; circ. 200,801.

Maison et Jardin: 10 blvd du Montparnasse, 75724 Paris Cedex 15; tel. (1) 45-67-35-05; telex 204191; f. 1950; 10 a year, 2 special issues (*Maison Magazine*); associated with *House and Garden*, New York and London, *Casa Vogue*, Italy; Publr PATRICK DELCROIX; circ. 89,477.

Marie-Claire: 11 bis rue Boissy d'Anglas, 75008 Paris; tel. (1) 42-66-93-64; telex 240387; f. 1954; monthly; Dir EVELYNE PROUVOST; circ. 599,362.

Marie-France: 114 ave des Champs Elysées 75008 Paris; tel. (1) 43-59-23-15; f. 1944; monthly; Man. Dir MAURICE BRÉBART; Chief Editor DANIÈLE BOTT; circ. 522,284.

FRANCE

Modes et travaux: 10 rue de la Pépinière, 75380 Paris Cedex 08; tel. (1) 45-22-78-05; telex 280286; f. 1919; monthly; Dir PHILIPPE CHOPIN; circ. 1,500,000.

Nous Deux: 2 rue des Italiens, 75009 Paris; f. 1947; illustrated stories; Dir ANTOINE DE CLERMONT-TONNERRE; circ. 823,397.

Vogue: 4 place de Palais Bourbon, 75007 Paris; tel. (1) 45-50-32-32; telex 260752; f. 1921; 10 a year, plus 10 a year of *Vogue Hommes* and 2 a year of *Vogue Enfants*; Dirs JEAN PONIATOWSKI (*Vogue*), BERNARD CHAPUIS (*Vogue Hommes*).

NEWS AGENCIES

Agence France-Presse: 11–15 place de la Bourse, 75002 Paris; tel. (1) 40-41-46-46; telex 210064; f. 1944; 24-hour service of world political, financial, sporting news, and photographs; 150 agencies and 2,000 correspondents all over the world; Chair. and Man. Dir JEAN-LOUIS GUILLAUD; Sec.-Gen. PIERRE JEANTET.

Agence Parisienne de Presse: 18 rue Saint Fiacre, 75002 Paris; f. 1949; Man. Dir MICHEL RAVELET.

Agence Républicaine d'Information: 22 rue de Châteaudun, 75009 Paris; French domestic and foreign politics; Dir ALBERT LEBACQZ.

Presse Services: 111 ave Victor Hugo, 75116 Paris; f. 1929; Chair. and Man. Dir C. CAZENAVE DE LA ROCHE.

Science-Service—Agence Barnier: 10 rue Notre Dame de Lorette, 75009 Paris; medical, scientific, technical, recreation news; Man. Dir DENISE BARNIER.

Foreign Bureaux

Agencia EFE (Spain): 60 rue de la Chaussée d'Antin, 75009 Paris; tel. (1) 40-16-90-72; telex 660829; Delegate FERNANDO CASARES.

Agentstvo Pechati Novosti (APN) (USSR): 14 place du Général Catroux, 75017 Paris; tel. (1) 42-27-79-21; telex 650673; Bureau Chief V. NEDBAEV.

Agenzia Nazionale Stampa Associata (ANSA) (Italy): 29 rue Tronchet, 75008 Paris; tel. (1) 42-65-55-16; telex 290120; Bureau Chief ADA PRINCIGALLI.

Allgemeiner Deutscher Nachrichtendienst (ADN) (German Democratic Republic): 23 rue Erlanger, 75016 Paris; Bureau Chief JOACHIM SONNENBERG.

Associated Press (AP) (USA): 162 rue du Faubourg Saint-Honoré, 75008 Paris; tel. (1) 43-59-86-76; telex 280770; Bureau Chief HARRY DUNPHY.

Československá tisková kancelář (ČTK) (Czechoslovakia): 6 rue du Dr Finlay, 75015 Paris; tel. (1) 45-79-00-24; telex 201735; Bureau Man. KAREL BARTAK.

Deutsche Presse-Agentur (dpa) (Federal Republic of Germany): 30 rue Saint Augustin, 75002 Paris; tel. (1) 47-42-95-02; telex 212995 (Hamburg, Fed. Republic of Germany); Bureau Chief PEER MEINERT.

Inter Press Service (Italy): 2 ème étage, 39 rue Volta, 75003 Paris; tel. 42-74-47-12; telex 217511; Correspondent JOSÉ A. VERA.

Jiji Tsushin-sha (Japan): 27 blvd des Italiens, 75002 Paris; tel. (1) 42-66-96-57; telex 660616; Bureau Chief JOJI HARANO.

Kyodo Tsushin (Japan): 19 rue Paul Lelong, 75002 Paris; tel. (1) 42-60-13-16; telex 680516; Bureau Chief HIROSHI SASAKI.

Magyar Távirati Iroda (MTI) (Hungary): 8 rue Octave Feuillet, 75116 Paris; Correspondent LÁSZLÓ BALÁZS.

Middle East News Agency (Egypt): 6 rue de la Michodière, 75002 Paris; tel. (1) 47-42-16-03; telex 230011; f. 1956; Dir ESSAM SALEH.

Prensa Latina (Cuba): 22 ave de l'Opéra, 75001 Paris; tel. (1) 42-60-22-18; telex 213688; Bureau Chief RAMÓN MARTÍNEZ CRUZ.

Reuters (UK): 101 rue Réaumur, 75080 Paris Cedex 02; tel. (1) 42-21-50-00; telex 214078; Chief Correspondent J. MORRISON.

Telegrafnoye Agentstvo Sovetskovo Soyuza (TASS) (USSR): 27 ave Bosquet, 75007 Paris; telex 201807; Correspondent YURI LOPATIN.

United Press International (UPI) (USA): 2 rue des Italiens, 75009 Paris; tel. (1) 47-70-91-70; telex 650547; Correspondents JOHN PHILLIPS, BRENDAN MURPHY.

Wikalat al-Maghreb al-Arabi/Agence Maghreb Arabe Presse (Morocco): 4 place de la Concorde, 75008 Paris; tel. (1) 42-65-40-45; telex 214759; f. 1959; Correspondent CHAKIB LAROUSSI.

Xinhua (New China) News Agency (People's Republic of China): 148 rue Petit Leroy, Chevilly-Larue, 94150 Rungis; tel. (1) 46-87-12-08; telex 204398; Correspondent WANG WEN.

The following Agencies are also represented: Jamahiriya News Agency (Libya) and Central News Agency (Taiwan).

PRESS ASSOCIATIONS

Comité de Liaison Professionnel de la Presse: Paris; liaison organization for press, radio and cinema; mems. Fédération Nationale de la Presse Française, Confédération de la Presse Française, Chambre Syndicale de la Presse Filmée, Fédération Française des Agences de Presse; Gen. Sec. CHRISTIAN LOYAUTÉ.

Confédération de la Presse Française: 17 place des Etats Unis, 75116 Paris; tel. (1) 47-23-36-36; Chair. PIERRE ARCHAMBAULT; Dir JEAN-CLAUDE GATINEAU.

Fédération Française des Agences de Presse et d'Informations Audiovisuelles (FFAPA): 32 rue de Laborde, 75008 Paris; tel. (1) 42-93-42-57; Pres. MICHEL BURTON.

Fédération Nationale de la Presse d'Information Spécialisée: 6 bis rue Gabriel Laumain, 75484 Paris Cedex 10; tel. (1) 47-70-93-86; telex 642473; Chair. CLAUDE CHERKI; Dir MAURICE VIAU.

Fédération Nationale de la Presse Française: 6 bis rue Gabriel Laumain, 75010 Paris; tel. (1) 48-24-98-30; f. 1944; mems. Syndicat de la Presse Parisienne, Syndicat de la Presse Hebdomadaire Parisienne, Syndicat des Quotidiens Régionaux, Syndicat des Quotidiens Départementaux, Fédération de la Presse Hebdomadaire et Périodique, Union Nationale de la Presse Périodique d'Information, Fédération Nationale de la Presse d'Information Spécialisée; Chair. CLAUDE PUHL; Dir MICHEL CABART.

Fédération Nationale des Syndicats et Associations Professionnelles de Journalistes Français: Paris; tel. (1) 48-24-65-71; f. 1888, under present title since 1937; 7,000 mems; Chair. ARMAND MACÉ.

Union de la Presse Française à Diffusion Nationale et Internationale: 6 bis rue Gabriel Laumain, 75010 Paris; tel. (1) 48-24-98-30; mems Syndicat de la Presse Parisienne, Fédération Nationale de la Presse Hebdomadaire et Périodique, Syndicat des Publications d'Informations Générales, Syndicat des Publications d'Informations Spécialisées, Syndicat des Publications Economiques et Techniques; Chair. ANDRÉ LOUIS DUBOIS.

Union Nationale de la Presse Périodique d'Information: 6 bis rue Gabriel Laumain, 75010 Paris; tel. (1) 48-24-98-30; f. 1978; mems Syndicat National de la Presse Hebdomadaire Régionale d'Information, Syndicat National des Publications Régionales, Syndicat de la Presse Judiciaire de Province, Fédération de la Presse Agricole; Chair. ALBERT GARRIGUES.

PRESS INSTITUTE

Institut Français de Presse et des Sciences de l'Information: 83 bis rue Notre Dame Des Champs, 75006 Paris; tel. (1) 43-20-12-24; f. 1953; studies and teaches all aspects of communication and the media; maintains research and documentation centre; open to research workers, students, journalists; Dir PIERRE ALBERT.

Publishers

Editions Albin Michel: 22 rue Huyghens, 75014 Paris Cedex 14; tel. (1) 43-20-12-20; telex 203379; f. 1901; general, fiction, history, classics; Chair. and Man. Dir FRANCIS ESMÉNARD.

Editions Arthaud: 20 rue Monsieur-le-Prince, 75006 Paris; tel. (1) 43-29-12-20; telex 205641; f. 1870; literature, arts, history, travel books, reference, sports; Chair. and Man. Dir CHARLES-HENRI FLAMMARION; Dir ROSELYNE DE AYALA.

Assimil: 13 rue Gay Lussac, BP 25, Z.I. 94430 Chennevières-sur-Marne; tel. (1) 45-76-87-37; telex 232775; f. 1929; self-study language methods; Man. Dir JEAN-LOUP CHEREL.

Editions Aubier: 13 quai de Conti, 75006 Paris; tel. (1) 43-26-55-59; telex 205641; f. 1934; literature, philosophy and religion, history and sociology; Chair and Man. Dir CHARLES-HENRI FLAMMARION; Dir PATRICE MENTHA.

J. B. Baillière: 10 rue Thénard, 75005 Paris; tel. (1) 46-34-21-10; telex 201326; f. 1814; science, medicine, agriculture and technical books; Chair. and Man. Dir JACQUELINE BEYTOUT; Dir-Gen. GÉRARD DONGRADI, CHRISTOPHE POUTHIER.

Editions André Balland: 33 rue Saint André des Arts, 75006 Paris; tel. (1) 43-25-74-40; telex 270840; f. 1967; fine art, literature, history, humanities; Chair. and Man. Dir ANDRÉ BALLAND.

Bayard-Presse: 3–5 rue Bayard, 75008 Paris; tel. (1) 45-62-51-51; telex 280626; f. 1873; children's books, religion, literature; owns *La Croix*, *Le Pèlerin*, *Notre Temps*, *Panorama d'Aujourd'hui*, *Grain de Soleil*, etc.; Chair. BERNARD PORTE; Dir NICHOLAS BARDINET.

Beauchesne Editeur: 72 rue des Saints Pères, 75007 Paris; tel. (1) 45-48-80-28; f. 1900; scripture, religion and theology, philosophy, religious history, politics, encyclopaedias, periodicals; Dir MONIQUE CADIC.

Editions Belfond: 216 blvd Saint Germain, 75007 Paris; tel. (1) 45-44-38-23; telex 260717; f. 1963; fiction, poetry, documents, history, arts; Chair. PIERRE BELFOND; Dir-Gen. FRANCA BELFOND.

Berger-Levrault SA: 5 rue Auguste-Comte, 75006 Paris; tel. (1) 46-34-12-35; telex 270797; f. 1976; architecture, art, social and

FRANCE

De Boccard, Edition-Diffusion: 11 rue de Médicis, 75006 Paris; tel. (1) 43-26-00-37; f. 1866; history, archaeology, religion, orientalism, medievalism; Dir DOMINIQUE CHAULET.

Bordas: 17 rue Rémy Dumoncel, BP 50, 75661 Paris Cedex 14; tel. (1) 43-20-15-50; telex 260776; f. 1946; encyclopaedic, scientific, history, geography, arts, children's and educational; Chair. and Man. Dir JEAN MANUEL BOURGOIS.

Editions Bornemann: 15 rue de Tournon, 75006 Paris; tel. (1) 43-26-05-88; f. 1829; art, fiction, sports, nature, easy readers; Chair. and Man. Dir PIERRE C. LAHAYE.

Buchet-Chastel: 18 rue de Condé, 75006 Paris; tel. (1) 43-26-06-20; f. 1929; dietetics, religion, sociology, history, music, literature, biographies, documents; Dir GUY BUCHET.

Calmann-Lévy, SA: 3 rue Auber, 75009 Paris; tel. (1) 47-42-38-33; telex 290993; f. 1836; fiction, history, social sciences, economics, sport, religion; Chair. and Man. Dir JEAN-ETIENNE COHEN-SÉAT; Dir ALAIN OULMAN.

Casterman: 66 rue Bonaparte, 75006 Paris; tel. (1) 43-25-20-05; telex 200001; f. 1780; juvenile, comics, fiction, education, leisure interests; Chair. and Man. Dir ROBERT VANGÉNEBERG.

Les Editions du Cerf: 29 blvd de Latour Maubourg, 75340 Paris Cedex 07; tel. (1) 45-50-34-07; telex 200684; f. 1929; juvenile, religion, social science; Dir-Gen. PASCAL MOITY.

Chiron (Editions): 40 rue de Seine, 75006 Paris; tel. (1) 46-33-18-93; telex 200233; f. 1907; technical, sport, education, leisure; Chair. and Man. Dir DENYS FERRANDO-DURFORT.

Armand Colin: 103 blvd Saint Michel, 75240 Paris Cedex 05; tel. (1) 46-34-12-19; telex 201269; f. 1870; philosophy, history, law, geography and science, pedagogy, music, poetry, maps and textbooks; Chair. and Man. Dir JÉROME TALAMON.

Editions du CNRS (Centre National de la Recherche Scientifique): 15 quai Anatole-France, 75700 Paris Cedex; tel. (1) 45-55-92-25; telex 260034; f. 1946; public institution under the Ministry of Research; science and social science; Dir GÉRARD LILAMAND.

Dalloz: 11 rue Soufflot, 75240 Paris Cedex 05; tel. (1) 43-29-50-80; telex 206446; f. 1824; law, philosophy, political science, business and economics; Chair. and Man. Dir PATRICE VERGÉ.

Dargaud: 12 rue Blaise Pascal, BP 155, 92200 Neuilly-sur-Seine; tel. (1) 47-47-11-33; telex 620631; f. 1943; juvenile, cartoons, music, science-fiction; Chair. and Man. Dir GEORGES DARGAUD.

La Découverte: 1 place Paul Painlevé, 75005 Paris; tel. (1) 46-33-41-16; f. 1959; economic and political science, literature, history, pedagogy; Man. Dir FRANÇOIS GÈZE.

Librairie Delagrave (SARL): 15 rue Soufflot, 75240 Paris Cedex 05; tel. (1) 43-25-88-66; telex 204252; f. 1865; textbooks; Man. FABRICE DELAGRAVE.

Editions Denoël: 30 rue de l'Université, 75007 Paris; tel. (1) 42-61-50-85; f. 1930; general literature, sport, politics, economics; Dir HENRY MARCELLIN.

Editions Des Femmes: 6 rue de Mézières, 75006 Paris; tel. (1) 42-22-60-74; telex 202397; f. 1973; mainly women authors; fiction, essays, art, history, politics, psychoanalysis, talking books; Dirs ANTOINETTE FOUQUE, MARIE-CLAUDE GRUMBACH.

Desclée De Brouwer: 76 bis rue des Saints Pères, 75007 Paris; tel. (1) 45-44-07-63; telex 202098; f. 1875; religion, reference, textbooks, arts, psychiatry; Chair. and Man. Dir MICHEL HOUSSIN.

Deux Coqs d'Or: 28 rue la Boétie, 75008 Paris; tel. (1) 45-62-10-52; telex 650780; f. 1949; children's books, encyclopaedias; Chair. and Man. Dir JEAN-MICHEL AZZI; Dir FRANÇOIS MARTINEAU.

Didot-Bottin SA: 28 rue Docteur Finlay, 75738 Paris Cedex 15; tel. (1) 45-78-61-66; telex 204286; f. 1796; publs *Bottin Mondain* and other commercial registers and directories, encyclopaedias, business and administration; Chair. and Man. Dir VINCENT HOLLARD.

La Documentation Française: 29–31 quai Voltaire, 75340 Paris Cedex 07; tel. (1) 40-15-70-00; telex 204826; f. 1945; government publs; political, economical, topographical, historical, sociological documents and audio-visual material; Dir JEAN JENGER.

Editions ESF/Entreprise Moderne d'Edition: 17 rue Viète, 75854 Paris Cedex 17; tel. (1) 47-63-68-76; f. 1947; business and technical books, humanities, social sciences; Chair. GÉRARD DIDIER; Man. Dir FRANÇOISE DAUZAT.

Eyrolles: 61 blvd Saint Germain, 75240 Paris Cedex 05; tel. (1) 46-34-21-99; telex 203385; f. 1918; scientific, technical; Chair. and Man. Dir SERGE EYROLLES.

Fayard: 75 rue des Saints Pères, 75278 Paris Cedex 06; tel. (1) 45-44-38-45; telex 240918; f. 1850; general fiction, literature, biography, history, religion, essays, philosophy, geography, music, science; Chair. and Man. Dir CLAUDE DURAND.

Librairie Ernest Flammarion: 26 rue Racine, 75278 Paris Cedex 06; tel. (1) 43-29-12-20; telex 205641; f. 1875; general literature, art, human sciences, history, children's books, medicine; Chair. CHARLES-HENRI FLAMMARION.

Fleuve Noir: 6 rue Garancière, 75278 Paris Cedex 06; tel. (1) 46-34-12-80; telex 204870; f. 1949 (Presses de la Cité); crime and science fiction, paperbacks; Dir Gen. CHRISTIAN CHALMIN.

Foucher: 128 rue de Rivoli, 75038 Paris Cedex 01; tel. (1) 42-36-38-90; telex 240231; f. 1935; science, economics, law, medicine; Chair. and Man. Dir BERNARD FOULON.

Editions Gallimard: 5 rue Sébastien-Bottin, 75007 Paris; tel. (1) 45-44-39-19; telex 204121; f. 1911; general fiction, literature, history, poetry, philosophy; Chair. and Man. Dir ANTOINE GALLIMARD.

Librairie Générale de Droit et de Jurisprudence: 26 rue Vercingétorix, 75014 Paris; tel. (1) 43-35-01-67; telex 203918; f. 1836; law and economy; Pres. and Man. Dir G. DE LA ROCHEFOUCAULD; Dir V. MARTY.

Librairie Générale Française—Le Livre de Poche: 79 blvd Saint Germain, 75006 Paris; tel. (1) 46-34-86-34; telex 204434; *Livres de Poche* paperback series, general literature, dictionaries, encyclopaedias; f. 1953; Pres. ANTOINE DI ZAZZO.

Librairie Orientaliste Paul Geuthner SA: 12 rue Vavin, 75006 Paris; tel. (1) 46-34-71-30; f. 1901; philology, travel books, studies and learned periodicals concerned with the Orient; Dir MARC F. SEIDL-GEUTHNER.

Editions Grasset et Fasquelle: 61 rue des Saints Pères, 75006 Paris; tel. (1) 45-44-38-14; f. 1907; contemporary literature, criticism, general fiction and children's books; Chair. and Man. Dir JEAN CLAUDE FASQUELLE.

Groupe de la Cité: 8 rue Garancière, 75285 Paris Cedex 06; tel. (1) 46-34-12-80; telex 204807; f. 1942 as Presses de la Cité; renamed 1988; general fiction, history, paperbacks; group comprises Bordas, Garancière, Garnier, Plon, G.P. Rouge et Or, Solar, Librairie Académique Perrin, Julliard, Presses Pocket, Editions Fleuve Noir, Messageries Centrales du Livre, Editions Christian Bourgois, le Rocher, UGE 10/18, Olivier Orban, M. A.-Edition, OCI; Pres. and Dir-Gen. CHRISTIAN BREGOU.

Librairie Gründ: 60 rue Mazarine, 75006 Paris; tel. (1) 43-29-87-40; telex 204926; f. 1880; art, natural history, children's, books, guides; Chair. ALAIN GRÜND.

Hachette Groupe Livre: 24 blvd Saint Michel, 75006 Paris; tel. (1) 46-34-86-34; telex 204434; f. 1826; general; all types of book, especially text-books; Editorial Dir JEAN-CLAUDE LATTÈS.

Librairie A. Hatier, SA: 8 rue d'Assas, 75006 Paris; tel. (1) 45-44-38-38; telex 202732; f. 1880; text books, art, audio-visual materials, dictionaries, general literature, geographical maps, books for young people, computer software; Pres. MICHEL FOULON.

Hermann: 293 rue Lecourbe, 75015 Paris; tel. (1) 45-57-45-40; telex 200595; f. 1870; sciences and art, humanities; Chair. and Man. Dir PIERRE BERÈS.

I.D. Music: 42–44 rue du Fer à Moulin, 75005 Paris; tel. (1) 45-35-15-68; telex 201947; f. 1972; music; Dir PHILIPPE AGEON.

J'ai Lu: 27 rue Cassette, 75006 Paris; tel. (1) 45-44-38-76; telex 202765; f. 1958; fiction, paperbacks; subsidiary of Flammarion et Cie; Chair. CHARLES-HENRI FLAMMARION; Literary Dir JACQUES SADOUL.

Editions René Julliard: 8 rue Garancière, 75285 Paris Cedex 06; tel. (1) 46-34-12-80; telex 204807; f. 1931; general literature, history, political science, biographies and documents; Chair. and Man. Dir JEAN-MANUEL BOURGOIS; Man. Dir CATHERINE BLANCHARD.

Editions Klincksieck: 11 rue de Lille, 75007 Paris; tel. (1) 42-60-38-25; f. 1842; human sciences, architecture, literature, history, fine art, philosophy, music; Chair. and Man. Dir Mme ANDRÉE LAURENT-KLINCKSIECK; Dir MICHEL PIERRE.

Jeanne Laffitte: 25 Cours d'Estienne d'Orves, BP 1903, 13225 Marseille Cedex 02; tel. 91-54-14-44; f. 1972; art, geography, culture, medicine, history; Chair. and Man. Dir JEANNE LAFFITTE.

Editions Robert Laffont: 6 place Saint Sulpice, 75279 Paris Cedex 06; tel. (1) 43-29-12-33; telex 270607; f. 1941; literature, history, art, translations; Chair. and Man. Dir ROBERT LAFFONT.

Librairie Larousse SA: 17 rue du Montparnasse, 75298 Paris Cedex 06; tel. (1) 45-44-38-17; telex 250828; f. 1852; general, specializing in dictionaries, illustrated books on scientific subjects, encyclopaedias, classics, textbooks and periodicals; Pres. and Dir-Gen. CHRISTIAN BRÉGOU.

Editions Jean-Claude Lattès: 17 rue Jacob, 75006 Paris; tel. (1) 46-34-03-10; telex 205652; f. 1968; general fiction and non-fiction, biography, music; Man. Dir PIERRE-ANTOINE ULLMO.

Letouzey et Ané: 87 blvd Raspail, 75006 Paris; tel. (1) 45-48-80-14; f. 1885; biblical exegesis; history and archaeology of Catholic Church; history of religions; ecclesiastical encyclopaedias and

FRANCE *Directory*

dictionaries, biography; Dirs JEAN LETOUZEY, FLORENCE LETOUZEY-DUMONT.

Editions Magnard: 122 blvd Saint Germain, 75264 Paris Cedex 06; tel. (1) 43-26-39-52; telex 202294; f. 1933; children's and educational books; Man. Dir LOUIS MAGNARD.

Maloine, SA: 27 rue de l'Ecole-de-Médecine, 75006 Paris; tel. (1) 43-25-60-45; telex 203215; f. 1881; medical textbooks, sciences and humanities; Chair. and Man. Dir DANIEL VIGOT.

Editions Maritimes et d'Outre-mer: 17 rue Jacob, 75006 Paris; tel. (1) 46-34-03-10; telex 205652; f. 1839; yachting, marine, maritime history, navigation; Chair. and Man. Dir PIERRE GUTELLE.

Masson: 120 blvd Saint Germain, 75280 Paris Cedex 06; tel. (1) 46-34-21-60; telex 260946; f. 1804; medicine and science, books and periodicals; publrs for various academies and societies; Chair. and Man. Dir JÉROME TALAMON.

Mercure de France, SA: 26 rue de Condé, 75006 Paris; tel. (1) 43-29-21-13; f. 1890; general fiction, history, psychology, sociology; Chair. and Man. Dir SIMONE GALLIMARD.

Les Editions de Minuit: 7 rue Bernard Palissy, 75006 Paris; tel. (1) 42-22-37-94; f. 1945; general literature; Chair. and Man. Dir JÉRÔME LINDON.

Fernand Nathan Editeur: 9 rue Méchain, 75676 Paris Cedex 14; tel. (1) 45-87-50-00; telex 204525; f. 1881; affiliated to Librairie Larousse; school, and children's books, encyclopaedias, educational journals and games, fine arts, literature; Chair. and Man. Dir BERTRAND EVENO.

Les Editions d'Organisation (Editions Hommes et Techniques): 26 ave Emile-Zola, 75015 Paris; tel. (1) 45-78-61-81; f. 1952; management and business economy; Chair. SERGE EYROLLES; Man. DOMINIQUE BIDART.

Editions Ouvrières: 12 ave Soeur-Rosalie, 75621 Paris Cedex 13; tel. (1) 43-37-93-85; f. 1929; religious, educational, political and social, including labour movement; Dir ANDRÉ JONDEAU.

Payot-Paris: 106 blvd Saint Germain, 75006 Paris; tel. (1) 43-29-74-10; telex 203246; f. 1912; general science, biography, philosophy, religion, education, history; Chair. and Man. Dir JEAN-FRANÇOIS LAMUNIÈRE.

Librairie Académique Perrin: 8 rue Garancière, 75285 Paris Cedex 06; tel. (1) 46-34-12-80; telex 204807; f. 1884; historical and literary biographies, fine arts, humanities, trade books; Dir FRANÇOIS-XAVIER DE VIVIE.

A. et J. Picard: 82 rue Bonaparte, 75006 Paris; tel. (1) 43-26-97-78; telex 305551; f. 1869; archaeology, architecture, history of art, history, pre-history, auxiliary sciences, linguistics, musicological works, antiquarian books, *Catalogue Varia* (old and rare books, documentary books, quarterly); Chair. and Man. Dir CHANTAL PASINI-PICARD.

Plon: 8 rue Garancière, 75285 Paris, Cedex 06; tel. (1) 46-34-12-80; telex 204807; f. 1844; fiction, travel, history, anthropology, science, trade books; Dir-Gen. JEAN-LUC PIDOUX-PAYOT.

Présence Africaine: 25 bis rue des Ecoles, 75005 Paris; tel. (1) 43-54-13-74; telex 200891; f. 1949; general books; Dir-Gen. YANDÉ CHRISTIANE DIOP.

Presses de la Fondation Nationale des Sciences Politiques: 27 rue Saint Guillaume, 75341 Paris Cedex 07; tel. (1) 45-49-50-50; f. 1975; history, politics, linguistics, economics, sociology; Chair. and Man. Dir LOUIS BODIN.

Presses Universitaires de France: 108 blvd Saint Germain, 75279 Paris Cedex 06; tel. (1) 46-34-12-01; telex 600474; f. 1921; philosophy, psychology, psychoanalysis, psychiatry, education, sociology, theology, history, geography, economics, law, linguistics, literature, science, the 'Que Sais-Je?' series, and official pubs of universities; Chair. PIERRE ANGOULVENT.

Presses Universitaires de Grenoble: Domaine Universitaire, BP 47 X, 38040 Saint Martin d'Hères, 38040 Grenoble Cedex; tel. 76-44-43-78; telex 980910; f. 1972; architecture, anthropology, law, economics, management, history, statistics, literature, medicine, science, politics; Dir CHRISTIAN AUGUSTE.

Privat, SA: 14 rue des Arts, 31068 Toulouse Cedex; tel. 61-23-09-26; telex 521001; f. 1839; regional pubs, history, medicine, philosophy, religion, tourism, education; Pres. JEAN LISSARRAGUE.

Librairie Aristide Quillet: 3 ave de Garlande, 92220 Bagneux; tel. (1) 47-46-50-00; f. 1898; general; specializes in dictionaries and encyclopaedias; Chair. and Man. Dir JACQUES SOYER.

Editions Seghers, SA: 6 place Saint Sulpice, 75279 Paris Cedex 06; tel. (1) 43-29-12-33; telex 270607; f. 1939; poetry, novels, politics, philosophy, biographies; Dir DANIEL RADFORD.

Editions du Seuil: 27 rue Jacob, 75261 Paris Cedex 06; tel. (1) 40-46-50-50; telex 600605; f. 1936; modern literature, fiction, illustrated books, non-fiction; Chair. and Man. Dir CLAUDE CHERKI.

Slatkine-France: 7 quai Malaquais, 75006 Paris; tel. (1) 46-34-07-29; telex 204689; f. 1973; medieval literature, music, law, history, psychology, comics, ethnology, linguistics; Dir MICHEL SLATKINE.

Editions Stock: 103 blvd St Michel, 75005 Paris; tel. (1) 46-34-89-34; telex 206023; f. 1708; subsidiary of Librairie Hachette; foreign literature, novels, general literature, law, science, philosophy, sport; Dir ALAIN CARRIÈRE.

Editions de la Table Ronde: 40 rue du Bac, 75007 Paris; tel. (1) 42-22-28-91; f. 1944; history, leisure, medicine, children's books; Pres. JEAN PICOLLEC.

Editions Tallandier: 61 rue de la Tombe Issoire, 75677 Paris Cedex 14; tel. (1) 43-20-14-33; telex 210311; f. 1865; literature, history, magazines, popular editions, book club edition; Chair. and Man. Dir JACQUES JOURQUIN.

Editions Vigot: 23 rue de l'Ecole de Médecine, 75006 Paris; tel. (1) 43-29-54-50; telex 201708; f. 1890; medicine, pharmacology, languages, tourism, veterinary science, sport, architecture; Chair. and Man. Dir CHRISTIAN VIGOT; Dir DANIEL VIGOT.

Vilo: 25 rue Ginoux, 75015 Paris; tel. (1) 45-77-08-05; telex 200305; f. 1950; non-fiction, art, history, geography, tourism, sport, architecture; Chair. and Man. Dir M. LARFILLON.

Librairie Philosophique J. Vrin: 6 place de la Sorbonne, 75005 Paris; tel. (1) 43-54-03-47; f. 1911; university textbooks, philosophy, education, science, law, religion; Chair. and Man. Dir A. PAULHAC-VRIN.

Librairie Vuibert: 63 blvd Saint Germain, 75006 Paris; tel. (1) 43-25-61-00; telex 201005; f. 1877; economics, business, mathematics, physics, science; Chair. JEAN ADAM.

CARTOGRAPHERS

Blondel La Rougery: 7 rue Saint Lazare, 75009 Paris; tel. (1) 48-78-95-54; f. 1902; maps; specialized prints of maps and charts; Chair. J. BARBOTTE.

Girard et Barrère: 2 place du Puits de l'Ermite, 75005 Paris; f. 1780; maps and globes; Mans MM BARRY, GOURIER, VUILLERET.

Institut Géographique National: 136 bis rue de Grenelle, 75700 Paris; tel. (1) 45-50-34-95; telex 204989; f. 1940; surveying and mapping of France and many other countries; Dir CLAUDE MARTINAND.

Cartes Taride: 2 bis place du Puits de l'Ermite, 75005 Paris; f. 1852; tourists' maps, guides and maps of the world, globes; Mans MM BARRY, GOURIER, VUILLERET.

PUBLISHERS' ASSOCIATIONS

Cercle de la Librairie (Syndicat des Industries et Commerces du Livre): 35 rue Grégoire de Tours, 75006 Paris Cedex; tel. (1) 43-29-21-01; telex 270838; f. 1847; a syndicate of the book trade, grouping the principal asscns of publishers, booksellers and printers; Chair. MARC FRIEDEL; Man. Dir JEAN-MARIE DOUBLET.

Fédération Française des Syndicats de Libraires: 259 rue Saint Honoré, 75001 Paris; tel. (1) 42-60-93-93; f. 1892; booksellers' asscn; 2,000 mems; Chair. PATRICE VAN MOE; Gen. Man. MICHÈLE BOURGUIGNON.

Syndicat National de l'Edition: 35 rue Grégoire de Tours, 75279 Paris Cedex 06; tel. (1) 43-29-21-01; f. 1892; c. 350 mems; publishers' asscn; Chair. ALAIN GRUND; Man. Dir P. FREDET.

Chambre Syndicale des Editeurs de Musique de France: 175 rue Saint Honoré, 75040 Paris Cedex 01; tel. (1) 42-96-89-11; telex 212740; f. 1873; music publishers' asscn; Chair. FRANÇOIS LEDUC; Sec. DIDIER DUCLOS.

Syndicat Professionnel Annuaires, Télématique, Communication (ATC): 35 rue Grégoire de Tours, 75279 Paris Cedex 06; tel. (1) 43-29-55-03; f. 1984; Pres. HUBERT MOULET.

Chambre Syndicale de l'Edition Musicale (CSDEM): 62 rue Blanche, 75009 Paris; music publishers; Chair. RENÉ BOYER.

Syndicat Général des Imprimeries de Paris et de la Région Parisienne: 46 rue de Bassano, 75008 Paris; tel. (1) 47-20-45-90; f. 1970; printers' asscn; 600 mems; Chair. GEORGES AIMÉ.

Union Parisienne des Syndicats Patronaux de l'Imprimerie: 46 rue de Bassano, 75008 Paris; tel. (1) 47-20-45-90; f. 1923; Chair. JACQUES NOULET.

Union Syndicale des Libraires de France (USLF): 40 rue Grégoire de Tours, 75006 Paris; tel. (1) 46-34-74-20; Pres. RAYMOND PÉJU; Sec.-Gen. ROBERT BOISTEAU.

Radio and Television

From 1964 to 1974 broadcasting was administered by the Office de Radiodiffusion-Télévision Française (ORTF), under the tutelage of the Ministry of Information. The ORTF was replaced by seven

FRANCE

independent state-financed companies and, in 1982, their functions were taken over by a nine-member committee. In 1986 the right-wing Government replaced the committee with a 13-member Commission Nationale de la Communication et des Libertés (CNCL), and in December the CNCL announced a series of new three-year appointments to the chairs of television and radio networks. The creation of the CNCL provoked criticism from the opposition parties, which alleged that the commission was an instrument for the Government to extend its influence over broadcasting. In 1989 the new Socialist Government replaced the CNCL with a nine-member Conseil Supérieur de l'Audiovisuel.

In 1987 there were an estimated 58m. radio receivers and 25m. television receivers in use.

Conseil Supérieur de l'Audiovisuel (CSA): 56 rue Jacob, 75272 Paris Cedex 06; tel. (1) 42-61-83-18; telex 214214; f. 1989; supervises all French broadcasting, allocates concessions for privatized channels, distributes cable networks and frequencies, appoints heads of state-owned radio and television companies, oversees telecommunications sectors, monitors programme standards; consists of nine members, of whom three are appointed for eight years, three for six years and three for four years: three nominated by the Pres. of the Republic; three by the Pres. of the National Assembly; and three by the Pres. of the Senate; Pres. JACQUES BOUTET.

Institut National de la Communication Audiovisuelle: Tour Gamma A, 193-197 rue de Bercy, 75582 Paris Cedex 12; tel. (1) 43-47-64-00; telex 214422; f. 1975; research and professional training in the field of broadcasting; radio and TV archives; Chair. JANINE LANGLOIS-GLANDIER.

Radio Télévision Française d'Outre-Mer (RFO): 5 ave du Recteur Poincaré, 75016 Paris; tel. (1) 45-24-71-00; controls broadcasting in the French overseas territories; Chair. JEAN-CLAUDE MICHAUD; Dir of DOM-TOM CLAUDE LEFÈVRE; Dir of Foreign Affairs ANDRÉ BRIÈRE.

Société Française de Production et de Création Audiovisuelles (SFP): 36 rue des Alouettes, 75935 Paris; tel. (1) 42-03-99-04; telex 240888; f. 1975; production of major programmes for cinema and TV; Chair. PHILIPPE GUILHAUME; Dir FRANCIS BRUN-BUISSON.

Société France Media International (FMI): 78 ave Raymond Poincare, 75116 Paris; tel. (1) 45-01-55-90; telex 614186; f. 1983 and privatized in 1987; distribution and merchandising in France and abroad for all TV programmes except news and sport, co-productions with foreign TV companies: Chair. GÉRARD PRUVOST; Man. Dir ANDRÉ HARRIS.

Télédiffusion de France (TDF), SA: 21-27 rue Barbès, 92542 Montrouge Cedex; tel. (1) 46-57-11-15; telex 25738; f. 1975, partly privatized in 1987; responsible for broadcasting programmes produced by the production companies (Radio France, A2, FR3), for the organization and maintenance of the networks; for study and research into radio and television equipment; administrative council comprising 16 members, of which six are representatives of the State; Pres. XAVIER GOUYOU-BEAUCHAMPS; Man. Dir PASCAL MANCHUEL.

RADIO

Société Nationale de Radiodiffusion (Radio France): 116 ave Président Kennedy, 75786 Paris Cedex 16; tel. (1) 42-30-22-22; telex 200002; f. 1975; production of radio programmes; Chair. and Man. Dir JEAN MAHEU; Dir JEAN IZARD; Dir. France Inter JÉRÔME BELLAY; Information Dir MICHEL MEYER; Dir France Culture JEAN-MARIE BORZEIX; Dir of programmes and musical services ANDRÉ JOUVE; Radio France Internationale HENRI TÉZENAS DU MONTZEL.

Radio France Home Services

France-Inter: Entertains and informs. Broadcasts transmitted for 24 hours a day; they can be received by 98% of the population and by listeners outside France. There are two main programmes, France-Inter and France-Inter Variétés. Other specialized and regional items are also produced. France-Inter is broadcast on long, medium and short waves and France-Inter Variétés is broadcast on medium wave and high fidelity (frequency modulated) transmitters.

France Culture: Serious programme on art, culture and thought; broadcasts can be received by 95% of the population.

France Musique: Transmission on frequency modulation transmitters. Nearly 95% of the programme is devoted to music; there are regular stereophonic transmissions.

Radio Bleue: medium-wave transmission for the elderly.

Radio-Sorbonne: Low-power transmission of educational programmes. Only available in the Paris region.

There are 52 regional and local radio stations, which relay Parisian programmes as well as transmitting their own broadcasts.

Radio France International

Home Service: Broadcasts in France for foreign workers in African-French, Arabic, Cambodian, Lao, Portuguese, Serbo-Croat, Spanish, Turkish, Vietnamese (on France-Culture network).

Foreign Service: Broadcasts 24 hours daily to Europe (in French, German, Portuguese, Polish, Romanian and Spanish), Eastern Europe (in French and Russian), Africa/Indian Ocean (in French, English and Portuguese), North America (in French), Latin America (in French, Portuguese and Spanish) and Asia (in French).

Private Radio

A number of radio stations based in countries on France's perimeter have very large French audiences. These include notably RTL (Luxembourg), Europe No. 1 (Saarbrücken), Radio Monte Carlo (Monaco). The state monopoly of broadcasting was ended in 1982, and in 1986 the French Government sold its controlling stake in Europe No. 1 to Hachette, the largest publishing group in France, and planned to sell its 83% shareholding in Radio Monte Carlo after the presidential election in 1988.

By August 1986 1,527 private radio stations ('radios libres') had been authorized. Advertising on private radio was legalized in 1984. In 1987 the CNCL introduced new regulations for local private radio stations, which stipulated that stations had to provide at least 84 hours of programmes per week, of which a minimum of 20% had to be produced by the owners of the stations. In July the CNCL authorized 96 radio stations to broadcast on the FM airwaves in Paris, which had previously been open to any station.

TELEVISION

In 1989 there were two state-run channels. A2 is on a 625-line system in colour and 96.5 per cent of the population can receive it. FR3, introduced in 1973, is on a 625-line system in colour and 70% of the population can receive it. Government approval was granted in 1984 for the transmission of France's first early-morning television, and by 1986 free videotex data screens had been installed in millions of homes.

Télé-Luxembourg, Télé-Belge and Télé-Monte-Carlo have large regional audiences in France. German-speaking inhabitants of Alsace watch programmes transmitted from the Federal Republic of Germany.

Société Nationale de Télévision en Couleur—Antenne 2 (A2): 22 ave Montaigne, 75387 Paris Cedex 08; tel. (1) 42-99-42-42; telex 204068; f. 1975; production of programmes on the second TV channel; Chair. CLAUDE CONTAMINE; Sec.-Gen. LOUIS BÉRIOT.

Société Nationale de Programmes—France Régions 3 (FR3): 116 ave du Président-Kennedy, 75790 Paris Cedex 16; tel. (1) 42-30-22-22; telex 630720; f. 1975; production of programmes on the third TV channel; responsible for regional and overseas TV; Chair. and Man. Dir RÉNÉ HAN; Dir-Gen. JACQUES GOUJAT.

Private Television

There were four national private television channels in 1989. Canal Plus, the first private channel (introduced in 1984), transmits on a 625-line system in colour, and provides 20 hours of daily broadcasts, mainly films and sport, to 1.5m. subscribers. The channel is financed mainly by subscription, and carries a limited amount of advertising. In 1987 Canal + attempted to raise further revenue by offering shares to the public. In 1985 the Socialist Government approved the formation of two new commercial networks, La 5 and TV6, and both channels started broadcasting in February 1986. In late 1986 the new right-wing Government introduced restrictions on the ownership of media outlets, with the aim of preventing a single communications company from owning more than 25% of a national television channel, and subsequently cancelled the contracts of La 5 and TV6. In 1987 the CNCL reallocated the contract for La 5 to the Hersant consortium, chaired by Robert Hersant, a right-wing National Assembly deputy and newspaper owner. La 5 broadcasts mainly foreign light entertainment programmes and films. In late 1987 the channel faced a financial crisis, owing to low audience figures and a subsequent decline in revenue from advertising. The contract for TV6, the music and video channel, was allocated to the Métropole TV consortium, which renamed the channel M6 and started to broadcast general interest programmes. In 1987 the state-run first channel, TF1, was privatized: the CNCL awarded 50% ownership and a 10-year initial contract to the Bouygues consortium, and the remaining 50% of shares were sold to small investors and TF1 employees. TF1 transmits on a 819-line system, and 98.5% of the population can receive it. In 1987 the CNCL approved the formation of Télé-Toulouse, a private local television channel, and offered to other potential private local channels the right to broadcast on the La 5 and M6 systems.

Canal +: 78 rue Olivier de Serres, 75015 Paris; tel. (1) 45-33-74-74; telex 201141; f. 1984; 25% owned by Havas, 21.4% by Compagnie Générale des Eaux, 10.4% by L'Oréal, 10% by Geneval and 5% by

FRANCE

Sopaclin; coded programmes financed by audience subscription and commercial sponsoring; uncoded programmes financed by advertising sold by Canal +; Pres. ANDRÉ ROUSSELET.

La 5: 241 blvd Péreire, 75017 Paris; tel. (1) 40-55-55-55; telex 640635; f. 1986; 25% owned by Groupe Hersant, 25% by Groupe Berlusconi, 15.8% by Mutuelles Agricoles and 34.2% by other corporate shareholders; financed by advertising sold by La 5; Pres. ROBERT HERSANT.

M6: 91 ave des Champs Elysées, 75008 Paris; tel. (1) 47-23-01-22; telex 648248; f. 1986 as TV6, re-formed as M6 in 1987; owned by Métropole TV consortium, of which 25% is owned by Compagnie Luxembourgeoise de Télédiffusion, 25% by Lyonnaise des Eaux, 10% by Groupe Amaury, 2.5% by Marin Karmitz and 37.5% by financial institutions; Pres. and Dir-Gen. JEAN DRUCKER.

Télévision Française 1 (TF1): 17 rue de l'Arrivée, 75015 Paris; tel. (1) 42-75-12-34; telex 250878; f. 1975 as a state-owned channel, privatized 1987; 25% owned by Bouygues SA, 10% by Pergamon Media Trust, 15% by various French companies, 40% by individual shareholders and 10% by TF1 employees; Pres. and Dir-Gen. PATRICK LE LAY.

Satellite Television

In 1984 TV5 began broadcasting programmes relayed from French, Belgian and Swiss television stations by satellite. In the same year, the French Government reached an agreement with Luxembourg to finance jointly a communal direct-broadcasting satellite television system (TDF-1). TDF-1 was to operate four television channels and 16 sound channels, thus enabling each television channel to broadcast in four different languages. In late 1986 the Government cancelled concessions which had been granted to a European consortium to operate two of the channels, and offered them to the general market on new financial terms. One channel was allocated to La SEPT, a projected French state cultural channel, and in 1987 the CNCL examined applications for the remaining three channels. TDF-1 was inaugurated in October 1988, after a series of technical problems, and another satellite television system, TDF-2 (to be financed by private investors), was planned to be launched in September 1989.

Société d'Edition de Programmes de Télévision (La SEPT): Paris; f. 1986; Franco-German cultural channel to be launched in 1990; Pres. GEORGES DUBY.

TV5: 21 rue Jean Goujon, 75008 Paris; communal channel for francophone European countries, transmitted by EUTEL satellite; Chair. PAUL PEYRE.

Cable Television

After two years of controversy, government approval was given in 1984 to plans to develop a national cable television network. In 1986 the responsibility for the construction of the network was opened to private communications companies, rather than to the state-owned postal and telecommunications service. In 1987 the Government announced that the cable network would be initially developed in 52 towns, and in October new regulations were introduced, which extended contracts for the networks from five to 20 years and applied the conditions governing national television channels to services transmitted by cable television. Foreign transmissions being broadcast by cable were allocated a maximum of 50% of the channels on a cable network, and were obliged to conform to the French regulations, if broadcasting in the French language. Private cable operators have announced their interest in providing local services and specialist cable television channels, such as Canal J, a channel specializing in children's programmes, which was launched in 1985. However, by October 1987 cable television was received by only 13,170 subscribers in France, and in December a campaign was launched to publicize the medium.

Finance

(cap. = capital; p.u. = paid up; dep. = deposits; res = reserves; m. = million; Frs = Francs)

BANKING

In 1982 the Socialist Government nationalized 36 banks, bringing 95% of all deposits under state control. These banks are marked * in the following list. Those marked † had previously been nationalized and became wholly nationalized in 1982. The banking law of July 1984 strengthened government control of local banks. Most banks, including foreign-controlled banks, became unified 'credit establishments', supervised by the Association française des établissements de crédit. A 'credit establishment' is defined as a company whose main business is conducting banking operations, which comprise accepting funds from the public, lending, and managing the payments system. The 'credit establishments' consist of banks that are authorized to accept demand deposits and time deposits with maturities of less than two years. These include banks authorized to conduct all banking operations and banks that conduct only the banking operations permitted by their statutes, such as mutual and co-operative banks (Crédit Agricole, Crédit Mutuel, Crédit Co-opératif and the Banques Populaires), savings banks (caisses d'épargne et de prévoyance) and caisses de crédit municipal. Other 'credit establishments' may accept demand deposits or time deposits with maturities of less than two years with authorization by an additional order. These comprise finance companies (hire purchase, mortgage or leasing companies) and specialized financial institutions (Crédit National and Crédit Foncier de France) which conduct only those banking operations that are necessary for fulfilling their particular functions. The 1984 law did not apply to the public accounts system, to the postal and telecommunications (PTT) financial services, nor to the Caisse des Dépôts et Consignations. In 1985 the banks were deprived of their monopoly of issuing short-term loans, after a market for 'commercial paper' (negotiable instruments) was inaugurated (see below). In 1986 the right-wing Government adopted a Privatization Law, and produced a plan to denationalize 65 state-owned companies including banks, in the following three years. Banks that have been denationalized are marked ‡ in the following list. The Government also introduced proposals to reduce state control over banking operations. In late 1986 quantitative controls on bank lending were ended, although banks were required to maintain a minimum level of reserves to cover at least 60% of long-term borrowing. Banks were allowed to open, close, or transfer their branches without government authorization, and could establish their own interest rates on deposits lasting over three months. Non-banking activities were limited to 10% of a bank's operations. From 1988 banks were to be allowed to hold capital in, and eventually gain control of, official stockbroking firms operating on the Bourse, during the gradual deregulation of the French financial markets (see below).

Central Bank

Banque de France: 39 rue Croix des Petits Champs, BP 140, 75001 Paris; tel. (1) 42-61-56-72; telex 220932; f. 1800; cap. and res 262,569.8m. Frs (Dec. 1987); nationalized from 1946; acts as banker to the Treasury, issues bank notes, controls credit and money supply and administers France's gold and currency assets; the Governor and two Deputy Governors are nominated by decree of the President of the Republic; the bank has 234 offices or brs throughout France; Gov. JACQUES DE LAROSIÈRE; Dep. Govs JACQUES WAITZENEGGER, PHILIPPE LAGAYETTE.

Commercial Banks

Al Saudi Banque: 49/51 ave George V, 75008 Paris; tel. (1) 47-23-00-55; telex 648629; f. 1976; cap. 350m. Frs, dep. 8,152.1m. Frs, res 34.5m. Frs (1986); Chair. CHAFIC AKHRAS; merged with Société de Thomson in 1988.

American Express Bank (France) SA: 12-14 Rond Point des Champs Elysées, 75008 Paris; tel. (1) 42-25-15-16; telex 643177; f. 1957; cap. 150m. Frs, dep. 2,600.3m. Frs, res 41.3m. Frs (1986); Chair. FRANÇOIS GISCARD D'ESTAING; 4 brs.

Bank of Credit and Commerce International (Overseas) Ltd: 125 ave des Champs Elysées, 75008 Paris; tel. (1) 47-23-90-19; telex 611710; Dir NAZIZ CHINOY.

Banque Arabe et Internationale d'Investissement (BAII): 12 place Vendôme, 75001 Paris; tel. (1) 42-60-34-01; telex 680330; investment bank; cap. 1,000m. Frs (April 1988); subsidiary of Baii Holdings, Luxembourg; Chair. and CEO YVES LAMARCHE.

Banque Centrale des Coopératives et des Mutuelles: 12 place de la Bourse, 75002 Paris; tel. (1) 42-21-88-88; telex 211038; f. 1922; cap. 72m. Frs, dep. 11,305.2m. Frs, res 11m. Frs (Dec. 1986); two-thirds of shares are held by 136 co-operative socs; Chair. JEAN LOUIS PETRIAT; 95 brs.

Banque Commerciale pour l'Europe du Nord (Eurobank): 79-81 blvd Haussmann, 75382 Paris Cedex 08; tel. (1) 40-06-43-21; telex 280200; f. 1921; cap. 720m. Frs, res 249.7m. Frs (Dec. 1987); dep. 39,531.9m. Frs (Dec. 1985); Chair. and Man. Dir BERNARD DUPUY.

Banque Courtois: 33 rue de Rémusat, 31000 Toulouse; tel. 61-29-61-29; telex 531580; f. 1760; cap. 46.3m. Frs, dep. 1,924.2m. Frs, res 29m. Frs (Dec. 1986); Chair. and Gen. Man. GILBERT COURTOIS DE VIÇOSE.

*****Banque de Bretagne:** 283 ave du Général Patton, 35000 Rennes Cedex; tel. 99-28-36-89; telex 730094; f. 1909; cap. 65.9m. Frs, dep. 5,783.1m. Frs, res 72m. Frs (1986); Chair. XAVIER HENRY DE VILLENEUVE; 100 brs.

Banque de la Méditerranée-France, SA: 49 ave Hoche, 75008 Paris; tel. (1) 47-66-51-56; telex 648528; f. 1976; cap. 70m. Frs, dep. 3,553.2m. Frs, res 25.6m. Frs (1986); Chair. and Man. Dir JOSEPH GHOLAM.

FRANCE

Banque de Neuflize, Schlumberger, Mallet: 3 ave Hoche, 75008 Paris; tel. (1) 47-66-61-11; telex 640653; f. 1966; subsidiary of Algemene Bank Nederland NV; cap. 672m. Frs, dep. 26,246m. Frs, res 180.6m. Frs (Dec. 1987); Chair. Supervisory Bd JEAN-PIERRE MALLET; Chair. Man. Bd ANTOINE DUPONT-FAUVILLE.

*****Banque de l'Union Européenne:** 4 rue Gaillon, BP 89, 75107 Paris Cedex 02; tel. (1) 42-66-70-00; telex 210942; f. 1920; merged with CIC group April 1984; cap. 500m. Frs, dep. 37,290.7m. Frs, res 471.9m. Frs (1986); Chair. and CEO PAUL ALIBERT; 6 brs.

Banque Européenne de Tokyo: 4–8 rue Sainte Anne, 75001 Paris; tel. (1) 42-61-58-55; telex 210436; f. 1968; cap. 75m. Frs, dep. 776.1m. Frs, res 149.3m. Frs (Dec. 1987); Pres. and Gen. Man. KAORU HAGIWARA.

Banque Fédérative du Crédit Mutuel SA: 34 rue du Wacken, 67000 Strasbourg; tel. 88-35-90-35; telex 880034; f. 1895; cap. 300m. Frs, dep. 32,721.7m. Frs, res 182m. Frs (1986); Chair. Supervisory Board ETIENNE PFIMLIN; Chair. Management Board RAYMOND CROMBECQUE; 11 brs.

Banque Française Commerciale, SA: 74 rue Saint-Lazare, 75428 Paris 09; tel. (1) 42-80-62-03; telex 280833; f. 1922; cap. 92.8m. Frs, dep. 2,709.2m. Frs, res 27.9m. Frs (1986); Pres. THIERRY DE LA BOUILLERIE; 18 brs.

Banque Française de l'Agriculture et du Crédit Mutuel, SA: 21 blvd Malesherbes, 75008 Paris; tel. (1) 42-66-31-40; telex 641040; f. 1933; cap. 100m. Frs, dep. 9,292.5m. Frs, res 26.3m. Frs (1986); Chair. ALAIN ROSTAND.

Banque Française de Crédit Coopératif: parc de la Défense, 33 rue des Trois Fontanot, BP 211, 592002 Nanterre Cedex; tel. (1) 47-24-85-00; telex 620496; f. 1969; cap. 30m. Frs, dep. 6,359m. Frs; Chair. Supervisory Board JACQUES MOREAU; 35 brs.

Banque Française du Commerce Extérieur: 21 blvd Haussmann, 75009 Paris; tel. (1) 42-47-47-47; telex 660370; f. 1947; cap. 1,000m. Frs, dep. 99,806.9m. Frs, res 621.5m. Frs (1986); Chair. MICHEL FREYCHE; Man. Dir PIERRE ANTONI.

*****Banque Hervet SA:** 127 ave Charles de Gaulle, 92201 Neuilly-sur-Seine; tel. 46-40-90-00; telex 620433; f. 1830; cap. 142.4m. Frs, dep. 7,380.3m. Frs, res 211.4m. Frs (1986); Chair. JEAN BAPTISTE PASCAL.

‡**Banque Indosuez:** 96 blvd Haussmann, 75008 Paris; tel. (1) 45-61-20-20; telex 650409; f. 1975; cap. 2,275m. Frs, dep. 246,922.7m. Frs, res 5,055.3m. Frs (Dec. 1987); Chair. ANTOINE JEANCOURT-GALIGNANI; 12 brs.

‡**Banque Industrielle et Mobilière Privée, SA:** 22 rue Pasquier, 75383 Paris Cedex 08; tel. (1) 42-66-91-52; telex 640586; f. 1967; cap. 31.4m. Frs, dep. 3,845.8m. Frs, res 61.5m. Frs (1986); Chair. JEAN-CLAUDE POUJOL.

Banque Intercontinentale Arabe: 67 ave Franklin Roosevelt, 75008 Paris; tel. (1) 43-59-61-49; telex 660630; f. 1975; cap. 310m. Frs, res 18m. Frs, dep. 1,438m. Frs (1984); Chair. MOURAD KHELLAF.

Banque Internationale de Commerce, SA: 62 ave Marceau, 75008 Paris; tel. (1) 47-20-57-39; telex 630151; f. 1919; cap. 13m. Frs, res 5.3m. Frs (1987); Chair. EROL AKSOY.

Banque Libano-Française (France), SA: 33 rue Monceau, 75008 Paris; tel. (1) 43-59-51-88; telex 640820; f. 1976; cap. 100m. Frs, dep. 5,035.8m. Frs, res 4.2m. Frs (1986); Chair. FARID RAPHAËL.

Banque Louis-Dreyfus, SA: 6 rue Rabelais, BP 285, 75384 Paris Cedex 08; tel. (1) 43-59-07-59; telex 290063; f. 1905; cap. 240m. Frs (1987); dep. 2,343m. Frs (Dec. 1986); Chair. JEAN-CLAUDE SEYS.

†**Banque Nationale de Paris, SA:** 16 blvd des Italiens, 75009 Paris; tel. (1) 42-44-45-46; telex 280605; f. 1966; cap. 2,672.4m. Frs, dep. 887,204.8m. Frs, res 22,717.8m. Frs (1986); Chair. and Man. Dir RENÉ THOMAS.

Banque Nationale de Paris 'Intercontinentale', SA: 20 blvd des Italiens, BP 315-09, 75009 Paris; tel. (1) 42-44-22-11; telex 641419; f. 1940; cap. 125m. Frs, dep. 6,613.3m. Frs, res 441.3m. Frs (1986); Chair. RENÉ THOMAS.

‡**Banque Odier Bungener Courvoisier, SA:** 57 ave d'Iéna, BP 195, 75783 Paris Cedex 16; tel. (1) 45-01-50-00; telex 630889; f. 1960; cap. 65.4m. Frs (Dec. 1987); dep. 2,112.6m. Frs, res 53m. Frs (Dec. 1984); Chair. and Man. Dir FRANÇOIS PROPPER.

‡**Banque Paribas:** 3 rue d'Antin, 75002 Paris; tel. (1) 42-98-12-34; telex 210041; f. 1872; cap. 2,223m. Frs, dep. 59,749m. Frs (1986); Chair. MICHEL FRANÇOIS-PONCET; Dirs-Gen. FRANÇOIS MORIN, HUBERT DE SAINT-AMAND, PHILIPPE DULAC.

‡**Banque Parisienne de Crédit:** 56 rue de Châteaudun, 75009 Paris; tel. (1) 42-80-68-68; telex 280179; f. 1920; cap. 70.5m. Frs, dep. 13,006.6m. Frs, res 494m. Frs (Dec. 1986); Chair. GUY CHARTIER; 68 brs.

*****Banque Régionale de l'Ain, SA:** 2 ave Alsace-Lorraine, 01001 Bourg-en-Bresse; tel. 74-32-50-00; telex 310435; f. 1849; mem. of Crédit Industriel et Commercial Group; cap. 60m. Frs; dep. 3,623.6m. Frs, res 34.9m. Frs (1986); Pres. JEAN-NOËL RELIQUET; 50 brs.

*****Banque Régionale de l'Ouest, SA:** 7 rue Gallois, 41003 Blois Cedex; tel. 54-78-96-28; telex 750408; f. 1913; mem. of Crédit Industriel et Commercial Group; cap. 60m. Frs, dep. 5,331.1m. Frs, res 71m. Frs (1986); Chair. JEAN DE LA CHAUVINIÈRE.

Banque Rivaud: 13 rue Notre Dame des Victoires, 75002 Paris; tel. (1) 42-61-52-43; telex 680231; f. 1906; cap. 90m. Frs, dep. 3,798.4m. Frs, res 28.4m. Frs (Dec. 1986); Chair. Comte DE RIBES.

Banque Scalbert-Dupont: 37 rue du Molinel, BP 322, 59020 Lille Cedex; tel. 20-06-92-52; telex 820650; f. 1838; cap. 82.7m. Frs, dep. 10,923m. Frs, res 255m. Frs (Dec. 1987); Chair. and Man. Dir CLAUDE LAMOTTE.

Banque Sudameris: 4 rue Meyerbeer, 75009 Paris; tel. (1) 45-23-72-22; telex 641669; f. 1910; cap. 395.6m. Frs, dep. 26,061.7m. Frs, res 730.2m. Frs (1987); Chair. and Pres. G. RAMBAUD.

Banque Transatlantique, SA: 17 blvd Haussmann, 75428 Paris Cedex 09; tel. (1) 42-47-13-00; telex 650729; f. 1881; cap. 58.3m. Frs, dep. 3,570.9m. Frs, res 103m. Frs (1986); Chair. FRANÇOIS DE SIÈYES.

‡**Banque Vernes et Commerciale de Paris, SA:** 52 ave Hoche, 75008 Paris; tel. (1) 47-54-40-40; telex 290322; f. 1971; cap. 233m. Frs, dep. 8,076m. Frs (1985); Chair. GILBERT LASFARGUES; 25 brs.

*****Banque Worms SA:** Le Voltaire, 1 place des Degrés Cedex 58, 92059 Paris La Défense; tel. (1) 49-07-50-50; telex 616023; f. 1928; cap. 450m. Frs, dep. 48,507.1m. Frs, res 375.8m. Frs (Dec. 1986); Chair. JEAN-MICHEL BLOCH-LAINÉ; 22 brs.

Barclays Bank SA: 33 rue du Quatre Septembre, BP 24X, 75002 Paris; tel. (1) 40-06-85-85; telex 210015; cap. 650m. Frs, dep. 26,390.6m. Frs, res 130.4m. Frs (1986); Chair. and Gen. Man. PIERRE DE LALANDE; 34 brs.

Caisse Centrale des Banques Populaires: 115 rue Montmartre; 75002 Paris; tel. (1) 40-39-00-00; telex 210993; f. 1921; the central banking institution of 33 co-operative regional Banques Populaires; cap. 600m. Frs, dep. 96,187.7m. Frs, res. 539.6m. Frs (1987); Chair. JEAN MARTINEAU; Gen. Man. PAUL LORIOT.

Caisse Nationale de Crédit Agricole (CNCA), SA: 91–93 blvd Pasteur, 75015 Paris; tel. (1) 43-23-52-02; telex 250971; f. 1920; central institution for 94 regional co-operative banks; the Crédit Agricole group is the densest banking network in France, with 9,993 domestic branch offices; broad range of banking services with special emphasis on agribusiness; international network includes brs in Chicago, Frankfurt, London, New York, Milan, Hong Kong and Madrid, rep. offices in Barcelona, Rio de Janeiro, San Francisco, Beijing, Cairo, Tokyo, Singapore, Bangkok, Jakarta and Caracas; total assets 1,144,798.7m. Frs, cap. and res 46,678m. Frs, dep. 871,320m. Frs (Dec. 1987); Chair. YVES BARSALOU.

*****Centrale de Banque, SA:** 5 blvd de la Madeleine, 75001 Paris; tel. (1) 42-61-51-30; telex 680014; f. 1880; cap. 168.7m. Frs, dep. 5,787.8m. Frs, res 12.7m. Frs (Dec. 1986); Chair. PIERRE PICHOT.

Compagnie Parisienne de Réescompte, SA: 59–61 rue La Fayette, 75009 Paris; tel. (1) 42-80-62-28; telex 290942; f. 1928; discount bank; cap. 299.2m. Frs, dep. 33,259.5m. Frs, res 498.5m. Frs (Dec. 1986); Chair. and Gen. Man. RENÉ CASSOU; 2 brs.

*****Crédit Chimique SA:** 20 rue Treilhard, 75008 Paris; tel. (1) 45-61-94-00; telex 650838; f. 1889; cap. 150m. Frs, dep. 13,650.6m. Frs, res 159.2m. Frs (1986); Chair. and Man. Dir JEAN-LUC JAVAL; 2 brs.

‡**Crédit Commercial de France (CCF) SA:** 103 ave des Champs Elysées, 75008 Paris; tel. (1) 40-70-70-40; telex 630300; f. 1894; cap. 1,033m. Frs, dep. 156,204.5m. Frs, res 1,441.6m. Frs (1987); Pres. GABRIEL PALLEZ; Chair. and CEO MICHEL PÉBEREAU; 220 brs.

‡**Crédit du Nord:** 28 place Rihour, 59000 Lille (reg. office); tel. 20-30-61-61; telex 120342; 6–8 blvd Haussmann, 75009 Paris (administrative headquarters); tel. (1) 42-47-12-34; telex 641379; f. 1974; cap. 792.6m. Frs, dep. 85,153.8m. Frs, res 783.5m. Frs (1985); Chair. BRUNO DE MAULDE; 501 brs.

Crédit Foncier de France, SA: 19 rue des Capucines, 75050 Paris; tel. (1) 42-44-80-00; telex 230079; f. 1852; cap. 1,997m. Frs, dep. 282,725.7m. Frs, res 5,024.5m. Frs (Dec. 1986); Gov. GEORGES BONIN.

*****Crédit Industriel d'Alsace et de Lorraine (CIAL):** 31 rue Jean Wenger-Valentin, 67000 Strasbourg; tel. 88-37-61-23; telex 890167; f. 1919; cap. 143.7m. Frs, dep. 13,935m. Frs (1987); res 486m. Frs (1984); Chair. GASTON ZERR; 151 brs.

*****Crédit Industriel de l'Ouest, SA:** 4 rue Voltaire, 44040 Nantes Cedex; tel. 40-35-91-91; telex 700590; f. 1957; cap. 130m. Frs, dep. 12,547m. Frs (Dec. 1987); Chair. BERNARD MADINIER; Man. Dir JEAN-LOUIS RUSTERHOLTZ.

*****Crédit Industriel de Normandie, SA:** 15 place de la Pucelle d'Orléans, 76000 Rouen; tel. 35-08-64-00; telex 770950; f. 1932; cap.

FRANCE

75m. Frs, dep. 5,979.7m. Frs, res 19.5m. Frs (1986); Chair. and Man. Dir ANDRÉ LECOMTE.

***Crédit Industriel et Commercial de Paris, SA:** 66 rue de la Victoire, 75009 Paris; tel. (1) 42-80-80-80; telex 290692; f. 1859; cap. 1,609.9m. Frs, dep. 92,171.6m. Frs, res 515m. Frs (1986); Chair. JEAN-RENÉ BERNARD; 118 brs.

†**Crédit Lyonnais, SA:** Head Office: 18 rue de la République, 69002 Lyon; Central Office: 19 blvd des Italiens, 75002 Paris; tel. (1) 42-95-70-00; telex 615310; f. 1863; cap. 3,278m. Frs, dep. 825,761.8m. Frs, res 11,913.2m. Frs (1986); Chair. J. M. LEVÊQUE; 2,500 brs.

‡**L'Européenne de Banque:** 21 rue Lafitte, 75428 Paris Cedex 09; tel. (1) 42-47-82-47; telex 280952; f. 1817; affiliated to Crédit Commercial de France 1984; cap. 209m. Frs, dep. 14,826.6m. Frs, res 441.8m. Frs (Dec. 1986); Chair. and Man. Dir ROGER PRAIN; 16 brs.

Grindlays Bank SA: 96 ave Raymond Poincaré, 75116 Paris; tel. (1) 45-01-51-61; telex 614193; f. 1969; cap. 60m. Frs, res 7m. Frs, dep. 15,495m. Frs (Dec. 1984); Chair. HUBERT MARTIN; 13 brs.

Midland Bank, SA: 6 rue Piccini, BP 4416, 75761 Paris Cedex 16; tel. (1) 45-02-80-80; telex 658022; f. 1978; cap. 337.1m. Frs, dep. 20,784.7m. Frs, res 321.1m. Frs (Dec. 1986); Chair. HERVÉ DE CARMOY; 14 brs.

National Bank of Kuwait (France), SA: 90 ave des Champs Elysées, 75008 Paris; tel. (1) 43-59-99-49; telex 642528; f. 1969 as Frab-Bank International; cap. 150m. Frs, res 25m. Frs (March 1988); Chair. MUHAMMAD ABDUL MOSHIN AL-KHARAFI; Gen. Man. DAVID M. LOWREY.

Société Bancaire de Paris: 24 rue Murillo, 75008 Paris; tel. (1) 47-66-02-00; telex 643203; f. 1927; cap. 50m. Frs, dep. 674.8m. Frs, res 5.3m. Frs (1987); Chair. MANUEL RICARDO ESPIRITO SANTO SILVA.

***Société Bordelaise de Crédit Industriel et Commercial, SA:** 42 cours du Chapeau Rouge, 33001 Bordeaux; tel. 56-48-52-90; telex (Foreign Dept) 550850; f. 1880; cap. 126.6m. Frs, dep. 5,617m. Frs, res 3.1m. Frs (1987); Chair. and Man. Dir BRUNO MOSCHETTO.

Société de Banque Occidentale (SDBO): 8 rue de la Rochefoucauld, 75009 Paris; tel. (1) 42-81-91-61; telex 650159; f. 1969; wholly-owned subsidiary of Crédit Lyonnais; cap. 260m. Frs, dep. 7,114.9m. Frs, res 133m. Frs (Dec. 1986); Chair. MICHEL GALLOT; 5 brs.

‡**Société Générale, SA:** 29 blvd Haussmann, 75009 Paris; tel. (1) 42-98-20-00; telex 290842; f. 1864; cap. 1,375m. Frs, dep. 727,123.8m. Frs, res 17,698.6m. Frs (1986); Chair. MARC VIÉNOT; 2,200 brs.

‡**Société Générale Alsacienne de Banque (SOGENAL):** 8 rue du Dôme, 67000 Strasbourg; tel. 88-32-99-27; telex 870720; f. 1881; cap. 263m. Frs, dep. 47,953.4m. Frs, res 376.4m. Frs (1986); Chair. RENÉ GERONIMUS; 126 brs.

***Société Lyonnaise de Banque SA:** 8 rue de la République, 69001 Lyon; tel. 78-92-02-12; telex 330532; f. 1865; cap. 400m. Frs, dep. 41,810.6m. Frs, res 326.3m. Frs (Dec. 1986); Chair. and Man. Dir HENRI MOULARD; 300 brs.

***Société Marseillaise de Crédit, SA:** 75 rue Paradis, 13006 Marseille; tel. 91-54-91-12; telex 430232; f. 1865; cap. 100m. Frs, dep. 11,495m. Frs (1987); Chair. and CEO JEAN-PAUL ESCANDE; 190 brs.

***Société Nancéienne Varin-Bernier (SNVB):** 4 place André Maginot, 5400 Nancy; tel. 83-37-65-45; telex 960205; f. 1881; cap. 115m. Frs, dep. 17,858.4m. Frs, res 274.3m. Frs (1986); Pres. BERNARD YONCOURT; 176 brs.

Standard Chartered Bank: 4 rue Ventadour, BP 43, 75001 Paris; tel. (1) 42-61-82-20; telex 213097; 2 brs.

‡**Union de Banques à Paris, SA:** 22 place de la Madeleine, 75008 Paris; tel. (1) 45-30-44-44; telex 206791; f. 1935; cap. 86m. Frs, dep. 9,426.6m. Frs, res. 151.1m. Frs. (Dec. 1986); Chair. ROGER PUJOL; 49 brs.

Union de Banques Arabes et Françaises (UBAF): 190 ave Charles de Gaulle, 92523 Neuilly Cedex; tel. 47-38-01-01; telex 610334; f. 1970; cap. 925m. Frs, dep. 50,379m. Frs (1988); res 206.6m. Frs (1985); Chair. ALY NEGM; Vice-Chairs ABOUBAKER A. AL-SHERIF, BERNARD THIOLON; 5 brs.

Union Française de Banques: 43 quai de Grenelle, 75738 Paris Cedex 15; tel. (1) 45-71-60-60; telex 200015; f. 1950; cap. 428.2m. Frs, dep. 13,252.3m. Frs, res 244.4m. (Dec. 1986); Pres. J. M. BOSSUAT; 64 brs.

Supervisory Body

Association Française des Etablissements de Crédit: 36 rue Taitbout, 75009 Paris; tel. (1) 48-24-34-34; f. 1983; advises government on monetary and credit policy and supervises the banking system; Pres. BERNARD AUBERGER; Gen. Man. ROBERT PELLETIER.

Banking Association

Association Française des Banques: 18 rue La Fayette, 75009 Paris; tel. (1) 42-46-92-59; telex 660282; f. 1941; 407 mems; Chair. DOMINIQUE CHATILLON; Delegate-Gen. JEAN-JACQUES BURGARD.

STOCK EXCHANGES

Since 1808 there have been 45 broking houses operating on the Paris Bourse, and 16 in the six provincial exchanges (at Bordeaux, Lille, Lyon, Marseille, Nancy and Nantes). In 1987 the Government introduced proposals to allow French and foreign banks to hold up to 30% of the capital of a broking house from 1988, increasing to 49% in 1989 and to 100% by 1990. By 1992 the limit of 45 broking houses operating on the Bourse was to be removed, and brokers would be able to extend their activities into investment banking operations. The Conseil des Bourses de Valeur would then examine new broking houses.

In 1985 a market for 'commercial paper' (negotiable instruments) was inaugurated. This allowed companies to borrow directly from each other and from other lenders, and in 1987 the first French market in financial 'futures', the Marché à Terme des Instruments Financiers (MATIF), and the first options exchange, the Marché des Options Négociables sur Actions (MONA), were opened. The Government later announced plans to merge the markets for commodities and financial futures under the authority of MATIF, and thus enable brokers dealing in commodities futures to deal in the financial futures markets.

La Bourse de Paris: Palais de la Bourse, 4 place de la Bourse, 75080 Paris Cedex 02; tel. (1) 40-26-85-90; f. 1808; run by:

Conseil des Bourses de Valeur: Chambre Syndicale des Agents de Change, 4 place de la Bourse, 75080 Paris Cedex 02; tel. (1) 42-61-85-90; telex 230844; undertakes the organization and management of French stock exchanges; 103 mems; Chair. RÉGIS ROUSSELLE.

Stock Exchange Association

Commission des Opérations de Bourse (COB): Tour Mirabeau 39-43 quai André Citroën, 75739 Paris Cedex 15; tel. (1) 45-78-33-33; telex 205238; f. 1967; 150 mems; Chair. JEAN FARGE; Sec.-Gen. PATRICK MORDACQ.

INSURANCE

A list is given below of some of the more important insurance companies:

L'Alsacienne: 1 chemin du Wacken, 67000 Strasbourg; tel. 88-37-15-75; telex 870039; f. 1898; Chair. ROBERT MATT (Leader of Groupe des Mutuelles Alsaciennes, composed of: L'Alsacienne, La Cité, Hisal, La Cité Européenne, Le Comptoir).

Assurances Mutuelles de France: 7 ave Marcel-Proust, 28032 Chartres Cedex; tel. 37-28-82-28; telex 760511; f. 1819; Chair. CHRISTIAN SASTRE.

Caisse Industrielle d'Assurance Mutuelle (CIAM): 7 rue de Madrid, 75383 Paris Cedex 08; tel. (1) 42-94-37-37; telex 290679; f. 1891; Chair. MICHEL LEONET; Gen. Man. HENRI DORON.

Compagnie du Midi SA: 78 rue de l'Université, 75007 Paris; tel. (1) 45-49-18-78; telex 206807; Pres. BERNARD PAGEZY; Dir-Gen. ETIENNE BENEZECH.

La Concorde: 5 rue de Londres, 75439 Paris Cedex 09; tel. (1) 42-80-66-00; telex 650734; f. 1905; Chair. ANDRÉ ROSA; Gen. Man. GASTON ALEXANDRE.

La France IARD: 7-9 blvd Haussmann, 75439 Paris Cedex 09; tel. (1) 42-47-13-29; telex 660272; f. 1837; Pres. and Dir-Gen. ANTOINE BERNHEIM; Dir-Gen. GEORGES SOLEILHAVOUP.

Garantie Mutuelle des Fonctionnaires: 76 rue de Prony, 75857 Paris Cedex 17; tel. (1) 47-54-10-10; telex 640377; f. 1934; Pres. and Dir-Gen. JEAN-LOUIS PETRIAT; Dir ANDRÉ RIALS.

Groupe de Paris: 21 rue de Châteaudun, 75447 Paris Cedex 09; tel. (1) 42-82-82-12; telex 280-638; composed of La Paternelle R.D., La Paternelle Vie, Seine et Rhône, La Défense Civile, Trans Expansion-Vie, Prévoyance Mutuelle MACL, Mutuelle de Marseille; Chair. PIERRE YVES SOLEIL.

Groupe des Assurances Générales de France: 87 rue de Richelieu, 75060 Paris Cedex 02; tel. (1) 42-44-04-44; telex 210697; f. 1968 by merger of Assurances Générales and Phénix, both f. 1819; insurance and reinsurance; cap. 407m. Frs; Chair. and Man. Dir M. DUBOIS DE MONTREYNAUD.

Groupe des Assurances Nationales (GAN): 2 rue Pillet Will, 75448 Paris Cedex 09; tel. (1) 42-47-50-00; telex 280006; f. 1820 (fire), 1830 (life), 1865 (accident), reorganized 1968; Chair. FRANÇOIS HEILBRONNER; Dir-Gen. JEAN-JACQUES BONNAUD.

Groupement Français d'Assurances (GFA): 38 rue de Châteaudun, 75439 Paris Cedex 09; tel. (1) 42-80-63-72; telex 660418; Chair. and Man. Dir G. MASSOUD.

FRANCE

Directory

Groupe Victoire (Abeille Assurances): 52 rue de la Victoire, 75009 Paris; tel. (1) 42-80-75-75; cap. 850.2m. Frs; Chair. PHILIPPE CHAREYRE; CEO JEAN ARVIS.

Mutuelle Centrale d'Assurances (MCA): 65 rue de Monceau, 75008 Paris; tel. (1) 45-63-08-00; telex 280343; Pres. PAUL ARNAUD; Dir-Gen. ANDRÉ JANNIN.

La Mutuelle du Mans: 37 rue Chanzy, 72035 Le Mans Cedex; tel. 43-41-72-72; telex 720664; f. 1828 (fire); Chair. and Man. Dir J. PERROUD.

Les Mutuelles du Mans, Groupe des Sociétés: 19–21 rue Chanzy, 72030 Le Mans Cedex; tel. 43-41-72-72; telex 720764; life and general insurance; f. 1883; Chair. JEAN CLAUDE JOLLAIN; Gen. Man. MICHEL COSSON.

Mutuelles Unies Assurances: 3037x, 76029 Rouen Cedex, and 10 rue de Londres, 75440 Paris Cedex 09; tel. 35-80-40-40 (Rouen), (1) 42-80-62-19 (Paris); telex 180559 (Rouen), 640584 (Paris); f. 1817; comprises Mutuelles Unies Assurances IARD, Mutuelles Unies Assurances-Vie, La Mutualité Générale Risques Divers; Chair. and Gen. Man. C. BEBEAR.

Preservatrice Foncière d'Assurances (PFA): 92076 Paris la Défense Cedex 43; tel. (1) 42-91-10-10; telex 615030; Chair. GUY VERDEIL; Gen. Man. GÉRARD BOUCHER.

Présence Assurances: 56 rue de la Victoire, 75308 Paris Cedex 09; tel. (1) 40-23-56-09; telex 660191; f. 1986 from merger between Présence-Vie, La Providence IARD and Le Secours; Pres. and Dir-Gen. VICTOR-CLAUDE ROSSET; Dir-Gen. CLAUDE TENDIL.

La Réunion Française: 5 rue Cadet, 75009 Paris; tel. (1) 48-24-03-04; telex 648083; f. 1899; insurance and reinsurance; Chair. ALAIN DU COUËDIC; Gen. Man. FRANÇOIS DROUAULT.

Rhin et Moselle-Assurances Françaises: 1 rue des Arquebusiers, BP 52, 67002 Strasbourg Cedex; tel. 88-25-31-31; telex 890332; f. 1881; comprises Compagnie Générale d'Assurances et de Réassurances (cap. 120m. Frs), Compagnie d'Assurances sur la Vie (cap. 60m. Frs); Chair. and Man. Dir MICHEL LEONET.

Société Anonyme Française de Réassurances (SAFR): 34–36 blvd de Courcelles, 75849 Paris Cedex 17; tel. (1) 42-27-86-82; telex 650493; reinsurance; Chair. and Gen. Man. J. BOURTHOUMIEUX.

Société Commerciale de Réassurance (SCOR): Immeuble SCOR, 1 ave du Président Wilson, 92074 Paris la Défense Cedex 39; tel. (1) 42-91-04-32; telex 614151; f. 1969; reinsurance; Chair. PATRICK PEUGEOT; Gen. Man. FRANÇOIS NEGRIER.

Société de Réassurance des Assurances Mutuelles Agricoles (SOREMA): 20 rue Washington, 75008 Paris; tel. (1) 45-61-99-50; telex 640774; f. 1978; reinsurance; Chair. and Man. Dir L. BORDEAUX MONTRIEUX.

UAP Réassurances: 372 rue Saint-Honoré, 75022 Paris Cedex 01; tel. (1) 42-61-50-77; telex 680567; f. 1919; reinsurance; Chair. and Man. Dir ROBERT POUPART-LAFARGE; Man. Dir GÉRARD FRANÇOIS.

L'Union des Assurances de Paris (UAP): Tour Assur, Cedex 14, 92083 Paris La Défense; tel. (1) 47-79-10-02; telex 630998; includes L'UAP-Vie, L'UAP-Incendie-Accidents and L'UAP-Capitalisation; Chair. JEAN PEYRELEVADE.

Via Assurances IARD: 20 rue Le Peletier, 75439 Paris Cedex 09; tel. (1) 45-23-60-00; telex 660918; Chair. EMMANUEL GAUTIER; Man. Dir JACQUES LEFÈVRE.

Insurance Associations

Fédération Française des Sociétés d'Assurances: 26 blvd Haussmann, 75311 Paris Cedex 09; tel. (1) 42-47-90-00; telex 640477; f. 1925; Chair. JACQUES LALLEMENT.

Fédération Nationale des Syndicats d'Agents Généraux d'Assurances de France: 104 rue Jouffroy, 75017 Paris; tel. (1) 47-66-04-25; Chair. DANIEL ORLUC.

Syndicat Français des Assureurs-Conseils: 14 rue de la Grange Batelière, 75009 Paris; tel. (1) 45-23-25-26; Chair. GILBERT BAYOU.

Syndicat National des Courtiers d'Assurances et de Réassurances: 31 rue d'Amsterdam, 75008 Paris; tel. (1) 48-74-19-12; f. 1896; Chair. PATRICK LUCAS; c. 900 mems.

Trade and Industry

CHAMBERS OF COMMERCE

There are Chambers of Commerce in all the larger towns for all the more important commodities produced or manufactured.

Chambre de Commerce et d'Industrie de Paris: 27 ave de Friedland, 75382 Paris Cedex 08; tel. (1) 42-89-70-00; f. 1803; Chair. PHILIPPE CLEMENT; Man. Dir FRANÇOIS ESSIG.

DEVELOPMENT ORGANIZATION

Institut de Développement Industriel (IDI): 4 rue Ancelle, 92203 Neuilly-sur-Seine; tel. (1) 47-58-14-11; telex 630006; f. 1970 as a state agency assisting small and medium-sized businesses by taking equity shares in enterprises and offering advisory services; Chair. CLAUDE MANDIL.

TRADE COUNCIL

Conseil National du Commerce: 53 ave Montaigne, 75008 Paris; tel. (1) 42-25-01-25; Chair. J. DERMAGNE.

EMPLOYERS' ORGANIZATION

Conseil National du Patronat français (CNPF): 31 ave Pierre Ier de Serbie, 75016 Paris; tel. (1) 47-23-61-58; f. 1946; an employers' organization grouping some 900,000 industrial, trading and banking concerns; Chair. FRANÇOIS PÉRIGOT; Vice-Pres. MICHEL MAURY-LARIBIÈRE.

INDUSTRIAL AND TRADE ASSOCIATION

Syndicat Général du Commerce et de l'Industrie—Union des Chambres Syndicales de France: 163 rue Saint Honoré, 75001 Paris; tel. (1) 42-60-66-83; Pres. MAGDELEINE THÉNAULT-MONDOLONI.

INDUSTRIAL ORGANIZATIONS

Assemblée Permanente des Chambres d'Agriculture (APCA): 9 ave George V, 75008 Paris; tel. (1) 47-23-55-40; telex 280720; f. 1929; Chair. LOUIS PERRIN; Gen. Sec. PIERRE CORMORECHE.

Association Nationale des Industries Agro-alimentaires (ANIA): 52 rue Faubourg Saint Honoré, 75008 Paris; tel. (1) 42-66-40-14; telex 641784; f. 1971; food and agricultural produce; Chair. FRANCIS LEPATRE; 43 affiliated federations.

Centre de Liaisons Intersyndicales des Industries et des Commerces de la Quincaillerie: 91 rue du Miromesnil, 75008 Paris; tel. (1) 45-61-99-44; telex 650680; f. 1913; hardware; Chair. MM. BLANC; Pres. OLIVIER BLONDET; Sec.-Gen. M. PASSEBOSC; mems 14 syndicates.

Centre des Jeunes Dirigeants d'Entreprise (CJD): 13 rue Duroc, 75007 Paris; tel. (1) 47-83-42-28; telex 200298; junior management; Pres. JACQUES CHAIZE; Sec.-Gen. JEAN-LUC POTHET; 3,000 mems.

Chambre Syndicale de la Sidérurgie Française: Elysées la Défense, 19 le Parvis Cedex 35, 92072 Paris la Défense; tel. (1) 47-67-85-88; telex 611672; f. 1945; steel-making; Chair. FRANCIS MER; Delegate-Gen. YVES PIERRE SOULÉ.

Chambre Syndicale de l'Ameublement, Négoce de Paris et de l'Ile de France: 15 rue de la Cerisaie, 75004 Paris; tel. (1) 42-72-13-79; f. 1860; furnishing; Chair. GEORGES GIDOIN; Sec.-Gen. CHRISTINE ERRANT; 407 mems.

Chambre Syndicale de l'Amiante: 10 rue de la Pépinière, 75008 Paris; tel. (1) 45-22-12-34; f. 1898; asbestos; Chair. CYRIL X. LATTY; 17 mems.

Chambre Syndicale des Céramistes et Ateliers d'Art: 62 rue d'Hauteville, 75010 Paris; tel. (1) 47-70-95-83; telex 660005; f. 1937; ceramics and arts; Chair. M. BLIN; 1,200 mems.

Chambre Syndicale des Constructeurs d'Automobiles: 2 rue de Presbourg, 75008 Paris; tel. (1) 47-23-54-05; telex 610-446; f. 1909; motor manufacturing; Chair. RAYMOND RAVENEL; 10 mems.

Chambre Syndicale des Constructeurs de Navires: 47 rue de Monceau, 75008 Paris; tel. (1) 45-61-99-11; telex 280756; shipbuilding; Chair. ALAIN GRILL; Gen. Man. BERTRAND VIEILLARD-BARON.

Comité Central de la Laine et des Fibres Associées (Groupement Général de l'Industrie et du Commerce Lainiers Français): 37–39 rue de Neuilly, 92110 Clichy; telex 212591; f. 1922; manufacture of wool and associated textiles; Chair. JEAN ARPENTINIER; Vice-Chair. ROBERT SERRES; 510 mems.

Comité Central des Armateurs de France: 73 blvd Haussmann, 75008 Paris; tel. (1) 42-65-36-04; telex 660532; f. 1903; shipping; Pres. CLAUDE ABRAHAM; Delegate-Gen. AGNÉS DE FLEURIEU; 120 mems.

Confédération des Commerçants-Détaillants de France et d'Outre-Mer: 21 rue du Château d'Eau, 75010 Paris; tel. (1) 42-08-17-15; retailers; Chair. M. FOUCAULT.

Confédération des Industries Céramiques de France: 44 rue Copernic, 75116 Paris; tel. (1) 45-00-18-56; telex 611913; f. 1937; ceramic industry; Chair. FRÉDÉRIC LEBOUCHARD; Man. Dir ROBERT BOUCHET; 300 mems, 12 affiliates.

Confédération Générale des Petites et Moyennes Entreprises: 1 ave du Général de Gaulle, Terrasse Bellini, 92806 Puteaux Cedex; tel. (1) 47-62-73-73; telex 630358; f. 1945; small and medium-sized enterprises; Chair. RENÉ BERNASCONI; 3,000 affiliated asscns.

FRANCE

Fédération des Chambres Syndicales de l'Industrie du Verre: 3 rue de la Boétie, 75008 Paris; tel. (1) 42-65-60-02; f. 1874; glass industry; Chair. PIERRE BREITENSTEIN.

Fédération des Chambres Syndicales des Minerais et Métaux non-Ferreux: 30 ave de Messine, 75008 Paris; tel. (1) 45-63-02-66; telex 650438; f. 1945; minerals and non-ferrous metals; Chair. JEAN-SEBASTIEN LETOURNEUR; Delegate-Gen. G. JOURDAN; 16 affiliated syndicates.

Fédération des Exportateurs des Vins et Spiritueux de France: 95 rue de Monceau, 75008 Paris; tel. (1) 45-22-75-73; telex 280695; f. 1921; exporters of wines and spirits; Pres. JACQUES SAINT MARTIN; Delegate-Gen. LOUIS RÉGIS AFFRE; 450 mems.

Fédération des Industries Electriques et Electroniques (FIEE): 11 rue Hamelin, 75783 Paris Cedex 16; tel. (1) 45-05-70-70; telex 611045; f. 1925; electrical and electronics industries; Chair. A. MERCIER; Delegate-Gen. PAUL ROGER SALLEBERT; c. 1,000 mems.

Fédération des Industries Mécaniques et Transformatrices des Métaux: BP 3515, 11 ave Hoche, 75382 Paris Cedex 08; tel. (1) 45-63-02-00; telex 280900; f. 1840; mechanical and metal-working; Chair. ROLAND KOCH; Man. Dir G. IMBERT.

Fédération des Industries Nautiques: Port de la Bourdonnais, 75007 Paris; tel. (1) 45-55-10-49; telex 203963; Chair. MICHEL RICHARD.

Fédération Française de la Bijouterie, Joaillerie, Orfèvrerie du Cadeau, Diamants, Pierres et Perles et Activités qui s'y rattachent (BJOC): 58 rue du Louvre, 75002 Paris; tel. (1) 42-33-61-33; telex 214351; jewellery, gifts and tableware; Chair. M. ARTHUS-BERTRAND; 1,500 mems.

Fédération Française de la Tannerie-Mégisserie: 122 rue de Provence, 75008 Paris; tel. (1) 45-22-96-45; telex 290785; f. 1885; leather industry; Pres. MICHEL BOUDIN; 250 mems.

Fédération Française de l'Imprimerie et des Industries graphiques (FFIIG): 115 blvd Saint Germain, 75006 Paris; tel. (1) 46-34-21-15; printing; Pres. DOMINIQUE HARLEY; Delegate-Gen. ALAIN COURTIAL.

Fédération Française du Commerce du Bois: 8 rue du Colonel Moll, 75017 Paris; tel. (1) 42-67-64-75; telex 640438; timber trade; Chair. GÉRARD LEMAIGNEN; Man. Dir DENIS SPIRE.

Fédération Nationale de la Musique: 62 rue Blanche, 75009 Paris; tel. (1) 48-74-09-20; f. 1946; includes Chambre Syndicale de la Facture Instrumentale, Syndicat National de l'Édition Phonographique and other groups; musical instruments and recordings; Chair. LUCIEN ADES; Sec.-Gen. PIERRE CHESNAIS.

Fédération Nationale de l'Industrie Hôtelière (FNIH): 22 rue d'Anjou, 75383 Paris Cedex 08; tel. (1) 42-65-04-61; telex 640033; Chair. J. BLAT.

Fédération Nationale des Entreprises à Commerces Multiples: 11 rue Saint Florentin, 75008 Paris; tel. (1) 42-60-36-02; f. 1937; Chair. M. LANIER; Vice-Chair. JACQUES DU CLOSEL.

Fédération Nationale des Industries Électrométallurgiques, Électrochimiques et Connexes: 30 ave de Messine, 75008 Paris; tel. (1) 45-61-06-63; Chair. BRUNO ANGLÈS D'AURIAC.

Fédération Nationale du Bâtiment: 33 ave Kléber, 75784 Paris Cedex 16; tel. (1) 47-20-10-20; f. 1906; building trade; Chair. JACQUES BRUNIER; Dir-Gen. CHRISTIAN MAURETTE; 55,000 mems.

Fédération Nationale du Bois: 1 place André Malraux, 75001 Paris; tel. (1) 42-60-30-27; telex 215409; timber and wood products; Chair. J. NANTY; Dir JEAN FAHYS; 4,000 mems.

Groupement des Industries Françaises Aéronautiques et Spatiales: 4 rue Galilée, 75782 Paris Cedex 16; tel. (1) 47-23-55-56; aerospace industry; Pres. JACQUES BENICHOU; Chair. J. MITTERRAND.

Syndicat Général de l'Industrie Cotonnière Française: 10 rue d'Anjou, 75008 Paris; tel. (1) 42-66-11-11; telex 281187; f. 1902; cotton manufacturing; Chair. JEAN-FRANÇOIS VIRLET; Vice-Chair. DENIS CHAIGNE; mems 79 (spinning), 171 (weaving).

Syndicat Général des Cuirs et Peaux Bruts: Bourse de Commerce, 2 rue de Viarmes, 75040 Paris Cedex 01; tel. (1) 45-08-08-54; f. 1977; untreated leather and hides; Chair. PIERRE DUBOIS; 60 mems.

Syndicat Général des Fabricants de Papiers, Cartons et Celluloses de France: 154 blvd Haussmann, 75008 Paris; tel. (1) 45-62-87-07; telex 290544; f. 1864; paper, cardboard and cellulose; Chair. PAUL BRETON; Gen. Man. JEAN-FRANÇOIS HEMON-LAURENS; 133 firms affiliated.

Syndicat Général des Fabricants d'Huile et de Tourteaux de France: 10 rue de la Paix, 75002 Paris; tel. (1) 42-61-57-21; f. 1928; edible oils; Pres. PIERRE RINGENBACH; Sec.-Gen. J. C. BARSACQ.

Syndicat Général des Fondeurs de France et Industries Connexes: 2 rue Bassano, 75783 Paris Cedex 16; tel. (1) 47-23-55-50; telex 620617; f. 1897; metal smelting; Chair. GILLES CURTI; Delegate-Gen. GÉRARD CORNET; 500 mems.

Syndicat National de l'Industrie Pharmaceutique (CSNIP): 88 rue de la Faisanderie, 75782 Paris Cedex 16; tel. (1) 45-03-21-01; telex 612828; pharmaceuticals; Chair. RENÉ SAUTIER.

Union des Armateurs à la Pêche de France: 59 rue des Mathurins, 75008 Paris; tel. (1) 42-66-32-60; telex 660143; f. 1945; fishing-vessels; Chair. CLAUDE SENECHAL; Delegate-Gen. A. PARRES.

Union des Chambres Syndicales de l'Industrie du Pétrole: 16 ave Kléber, 75116 Paris; tel. (1) 45-02-11-20; telex 630545; petroleum industry; Chair. JEAN-LOUIS BREUIL-JARRIGE.

Union des Fabricants de Porcelaine de Limoges: 7 bis rue du Général Cérez, 87000 Limoges; tel. 55-77-29-18; porcelain manufacturing; Chair. ANDRÉ RAYNAUD; Sec.-Gen. MARIE-THÉRÈSE PASQUET.

Union des Industries Chimiques: 64 ave Marceau, 75008 Paris; tel. (1) 47-20-56-03; telex 630611; f. 1860; chemical industry; Chair. J.-C. ACHILLE; Dir-Gen. C. MARTIN; 58 affiliated unions.

Union des Industries Métallurgiques et Minières: 56 ave de Wagram, 75017 Paris; tel. (1) 40-54-20-20; metallurgy and mining; Chair. JEAN LEENHARDT; Vice-Pres. JEAN D'HUART.

Union des Industries Textiles (Production): 10 rue d'Anjou, 75008 Paris; tel. (1) 42-66-11-11; telex 640969; f. 1901; Chair. LOUIS-CHARLES BARY; 3,000 mems.

TRADE UNIONS

There are three major trade union organizations:

Confédération Générale du Travail (CGT): Complexe Immobilier Intersyndical CGT, 263 rue de Paris, 93516 Montreuil Cedex; tel. (1) 48-51-80-00; telex 214182; f. 1895; a founder member of the World Federation of Trade Unions since 1945; National Congress is held every three years; Sec.-Gen. HENRI KRASUCKI; approx. 1.6m. mems.

Affiliated unions:

Agroalimentaire et Forestière (FNAF): 263 rue de Paris, 93100 Montreuil Cedex; Sec.-Gen. FREDDY HUCK.

Bois (Woodworkers): 171/3 ave Jean Jaurès, 75940 Paris Cedex 10; Sec.-Gen. GEORGES LHERICEL.

Cheminots (Railway Workers): 263 rue de Paris, 93100 Montreuil Cedex; Sec.-Gen. GEORGES LANOUE.

Construction (Building): 263 rue de Paris, 93100 Montreuil Cedex; Sec.-Gen. ROBERT BRUN.

Eclairage (Lighting): 16 rue de Candale, 93057 Pantin Cedex; Sec.-Gen. FRANÇOIS DUTEIL.

Education, Recherche et Culture: 263 rue de Paris, 93100 Montreuil Cedex; Sec.-Gen. JOËL HEDDE.

Employés: 263 rue de Paris, 93100 Montreuil Cedex; Sec.-Gen. PIERRE BLANCHARD.

Energie Atomique: Bâtiment 38, Centre d'Etudes Nucléaires de Saclay, 91191 Gif-sur-Yvette Cedex; Sec.-Gen. J. TRELIN.

Enseignements Techniques et Professionnels (Technical and Professional Teachers): 12 promenade Venise Gosnat, 94200 Ivry-sur-Seine; tel. (1) 46-70-01-59; Sec.-Gen. MICHÈLE BARACAT.

Equipements (Outfitters): 263 rue de Paris, Case 543, 93515 Montreuil Cedex; tel. (1) 48-51-82-81; Sec.-Gen. JEAN-CLAUDE BOUAL.

Finances: 263 rue de Paris, 93100 Montreuil Cedex; tel. (1) 48-51-82-21; Sec.-Gen. JEAN-CHRISTOPHE LE DUIGOU.

Fonctionnaires (Civil Servants): Bourse Nationale du Travail, 263 rue de Paris, 93515 Montreuil Cedex; tel. (1) 48-51-82-31; telex 218912; groups National Education, Finance, Technical and Administrative, Civil Servants, Police, etc.; mems about 70 national unions covered by six federations; Sec.-Gen. THÉRÈSE HIRSZBERG.

Industries Chimiques (Chemical Industries): 263 rue de Paris, 93100 Montreuil Cedex; Sec.-Gen. JEAN VINCENT.

Industries du Livre du Papier et de la Communication (FILPAC) (Printing and Paper Products): Case 426, 263 rue de Paris, 93514 Montreuil Cedex; tel. (1) 48-51-80-45; Sec.-Gen. JACQUES PIOT.

Ingénieurs, Cadres et Techniciens (Engineers, Managerial Staff and Technicians): 263 rue de Paris, 93514 Montreuil Cedex; tel. (1) 48-51-81-25; Sec.-Gen. ALAIN OBADIA.

Journalistes: 50 rue Edouard Pailleron, 75019 Paris; tel. (1) 42-09-23-00; Sec.-Gen. GÉRARD GATINOT.

Marine Marchande (Merchant Marine): Fédération des Officiers CGT, Cercle Franklin, Cours de la République, 76600 Le Havre; tel. 35-25-04-81; Sec.-Gen. D. LEFÈVRE.

Métaux (Metal): 263 rue de Paris, 93100 Montreuil Cedex; Sec.-Gen. JEAN DEMAISON.

FRANCE — *Directory*

Personnels du Commerce, de la Distribution et des Services: Case 425, 263 rue de Paris, 93514 Montreuil Cedex; tel. (1) 48-51-83-11; Sec.-Gen. MICHELLE COMMERGNAT.

Police: 26 rue Saint Félicité, 75015 Paris; Sec.-Gen. PASCAL MARTINI.

Ports et Docks: 263 rue de Paris, 93100 Montreuil Cedex; Sec.-Gen. GÉRARD LECLERCQ.

Postes et Télécommunications: 263 rue de Paris, 93100 Montreuil Cedex; Sec.-Gen. MARYSE DUMAS.

Santé et l'Action Sociale (Health and Social Services): Case 583, 263 rue de Montreuil, 93515 Montreuil Cedex; tel. (1) 48-51-80-91; f. 1907; Sec.-Gen. BERNARD DESORMIÈRE.

Services Publics (Community Services): 263 rue de Paris, 93100 Montreuil Cedex; Sec.-Gen. ALAIN POUCHOL.

Sous-sol (Miners): Case 535, 263 rue de Paris, 93515 Montreuil Cedex; Sec.-Gen. AUGUSTIN DUFRESNE.

Spectacle, Audio-Visuel et Action Culturelle (Theatre, Media and Culture): 14-16 rue des Lilas, 75017 Paris; tel. (1) 46-07-62-22; Sec.-Gen. CLAUDE QUEMY.

Syndicats Maritimes (Seamen): Case 420, 263 rue de Paris, 93514 Montreuil Cedex; tel. (1) 48-51-84-21; Sec.-Gen. F. LAGAIN.

Tabac et Allumettes (Tobacco and Matches): 263 rue de Paris, 93100 Montreuil Cedex; Sec.-Gen. BERTRAND PAGE.

THC (Textiles): 263 rue de Paris, 93100 Montreuil Cedex; Sec.-Gen. CHRISTIAN LAROSE.

Transports: 263 rue de Paris, 93100 Montreuil Cedex; Sec.-Gen. SYLVIE SALMON; 50,000 mems.

Travailleurs de l'Etat (State Employees): 263 rue de Paris, 93100 Montreuil Cedex; Sec.-Gen. HENRI BERRY.

Verre et Céramique (Glassworkers and Ceramics): Case 417, 263 rue de Paris, 93514 Montreuil Cedex; tel. (1) 48-51-80-13; Sec.-Gen. JACQUES BEAUVOIR.

Voyageurs-Représentants, Cadres et Techniciens de la Vente (Commercial Travellers): 67 rue de Turbigo, 75003 Paris; tel. (1) 42-72-96-99; Sec.-Gen. ALAIN SERRE.

Force Ouvrière: 198 ave du Maine, 75680 Paris Cedex 14; tel. (1) 45-39-22-03; telex 203405; f. 1947 by breakaway from the CGT (above); Force Ouvrière is a member of ICFTU and the European Trade Union Confederation; Sec.-Gen. MARC BLONDEL; approx. 1.1m. mems (1985).

Affiliated federations:

Action Sociale: 8 rue de Hanovre, 75002 Paris; tel. (1) 42-68-08-01; Sec. MICHEL PINAUD.

Agriculture et Alimentation (Food and Agriculture): 198 ave du Maine, 75680 Paris Cedex 14; tel. (1) 45-39-22-03; Secs-Gen. GÉRARD FOSSE, ALAIN KERBRIAND, DANIEL DREUX.

Bâtiment, Travaux Publics, Bois, Céramiques, Papier-Carton et Matériaux de Construction (Building and Building Materials, Public Works, Wood, Ceramics and Pasteboard): 170 ave Parmentier, 75010 Paris; tel. (1) 42-01-30-00; Sec.-Gen. MARCEL HUPEL.

Cadres et Ingénieurs (UCI) (Engineers): 2 rue de la Michodière, 75002 Paris; tel. (1) 47-42-39-69; Sec.-Gen. HUBERT BOUCHET.

Cheminots (Railway Workers): 60 rue Vergniaud, 75640 Paris Cedex 13; tel. (1) 45-80-22-98; f. 1948; Sec.-Gen. JEAN JACQUES CARMENTRAN; 16,350 mems.

Coiffeurs, Esthétique et Parfumerie (Hairdressers, Beauticians and Perfumery): 2 rue Gléchiel, 75009 Paris; tel. (1) 42-80-18-94; Sec.-Gen. MICHEL BOURLON.

Cuirs-Textiles-Habillement (Leather and Textiles): 8 rue de Hanovre, esc. B., 75002 Paris; tel. (1) 47-42-92-70; Sec. FRANCIS DESROUSSEAUX.

Education et Culture: 155 rue de Vaugirard, 75015 Paris; tel. (1) 45-67-94-49; Sec.-Gen. FRANÇOIS CHAINTRON; 20,000 mems.

Employés et Cadres (Managerial Staff): 28 rue des Petits Hôtels, 75010 Paris; tel. (1) 42-46-46-64; Sec.-Gen. YVES SIMON.

Energie Electrique et Gaz (Gas and Electricity): 60 rue Vergniaud, 75640 Paris Cedex 13; tel. (1) 45-88-91-51; f. 1947; Sec.-Gen. GABRIEL GAUDY; 22,000 mems.

Finances: 46 rue des Petites Ecuries, 75010 Paris; tel. (1) 42-46-75-20; Sec. ANDRÉ ROULET.

Fonctionnaires (Civil Servants): 46 rue des Petites Ecuries, 75010 Paris; tel. (1) 42-46-48-56; Sec. ROLAND GAILLARD.

Industries Chimiques (Chemical Industries): 60 rue Vergniaud, 75640 Paris Cedex 13; tel. (1) 45-80-14-90; Sec.-Gen. F. GRANDAZZI.

Livre (Printing Trades): 198 ave du Maine, 75014 Paris Cedex 14; tel. (1) 45-40-69-44; Sec.-Gen. ROGER CARPENTIER.

Métaux (Metals): 9 rue Baudoin, 75013 Paris; tel. (1) 45-82-01-00; Sec.-Gen. MICHEL HUC.

Mineurs, Miniers et Similaires (Mine Workers): 169 ave de Choisy, 75624 Paris Cedex 13; tel. (1) 45-87-10-98; Sec.-Gen. RENÉ MERTZ.

Défense des Industries, de l'Armement et des Secteurs Assimilés (National Defence): 46 rue des Petites Ecuries, 75010 Paris; tel. (1) 42-46-00-05; Sec.-Gen. JACQUES PE.

Personnels des Services des Départements et des Régions: 46 rue des Petites Ecuries, 75010 Paris; tel. (1) 42-46-50-52; Sec.-Gen. MICHÈLE SIMONNIN.

Pharmacie (Chemists): 198 ave du Maine, 75680 Paris Cedex 14; tel. (1) 45-39-97-22; Sec.-Gen. MARGUERITE ADENIS.

Police: 6 rue Albert Bayet, 75013 Paris; tel. (1) 45-82-28-08; f. 1948; Sec. JEAN-LOUIS CERCEAU; 11,000 mems.

PTT (Post, Telegraphs and Telephones): 60 rue Vergniaud, 75640 Paris Cedex 13; tel. (1) 40-78-31-50; telex 200644; Sec.-Gen. JACQUES MARÇOT.

Services d'Administration Générale de l'État: 46 rue des Petites Ecuries, 75010 Paris; tel. (1) 42-46-40-19; f. 1948; Sec.-Gen. FRANCIS LAMARQUE; 20,000 mems.

Services Publics et de Santé (Health and Public Services): 153–155 rue de Rome, 75017 Paris; tel. (1) 46-22-26-00; f. 1947; Sec.-Gen. RENÉ CHAMPEAU; 130,000 mems.

Spectacles, Presse et Audiovisuel (Theatre and Cinema Performers, Press and Broadcasting): 2 rue de la Michodière, 75002 Paris; tel. (1) 47-42-35-86; Sec.-Gen. GEORGES DONAUD.

Transports: 198 ave du Maine, 75680 Paris Cedex 14; tel. (1) 45-40-68-00; Sec. GILBERT DORIAT.

Travaux Publics et Portuaires de la Marine et des Transports (Transport and Public Works): 46 rue des Petites Ecuries, 75010 Paris; tel. (1) 42-46-36-63; telex 643115; f. 1932; Sec.-Gen. RENÉ VALLADON; 50,000 mems.

Voyageurs-Représentants-Placiers (Commercial Travellers): 6-8 rue Albert-Bayet, 75013 Paris; tel. (1) 45-82-28-28; f. 1930; Sec. HENRY DUPILLE.

Confédération Française Démocratique du Travail (CFDT): 4 blvd de la Villette, 75955 Paris Cedex 19; tel. (1) 42-03-80-00; telex 240832; constituted in 1919 as Confédération Française des Travailleurs Chrétiens—CFTC, present title and constitution adopted in 1964; co-ordinates 2,500 trade unions, 102 departmental and overseas unions and 22 affiliated professional federations, all of which are autonomous. There are also 22 regional orgs; in 1985 its membership was estimated at 900,000; affiliated to European Trade Union Confederation; Sec.-Gen. JEAN KASPAR.

Principal affiliated federations:

Agroalimentaire (FGA): 26 rue de Montholon, 75439 Paris Cedex 09; tel. (1) 42-47-73-32; f. 1980; Sec.-Gen. MARC GAGNAIRE.

Anciens Combattants (War Veterans): 37 rue Bellechasse, 75007 Paris Cedex 09; tel. (1) 45-50-32-55; Sec.-Gen. NICOLE DELVAUX.

Banques (Banking): 26 rue de Montholon, 75439 Paris Cedex 09; tel. (1) 42-47-76-25; Sec.-Gen. JEAN-LUC WABANT.

Construction-Bois: 26 rue de Montholon, 75439 Paris Cedex 09; tel. (1) 42-47-73-02; f. 1934; Sec.-Gen. JEAN AUBOEUF.

EDF-GDF (Electricity and Gas of France): 5 rue Mayran, 75439 Paris Cedex 09; tel. (1) 42-85-39-31; f. 1946; Sec.-Gen. ALAIN CHUPIN.

Education Nationale (SGEN-CFDT) (National Education): 5 rue Mayran, 75009 Paris; tel. (1) 42-47-74-01; f. 1937; Sec.-Gen. JEAN MICHEL BOULLIER.

Enseignement Privé (Non-State education): 26 rue de Montholon, 75439 Paris Cedex 09; tel. (1) 48-78-32-72; Sec.-Gen. JACQUES ANDRÉ.

Etablissements et Arsenaux de l'Etat: 26 rue de Montholon, 75439 Paris Cedex 09; tel. (1) 42-47-75-74; Sec.-Gen. ALAIN PETITJEAN.

Finances et Affaires Economiques (Finance): 26 rue de Montholon, 75439 Paris Cedex 09; tel. (1) 40-16-92-83; f. 1936; civil servants and workers within government financial departments; Sec.-Gen. JEAN-MARIE PERNOT.

Fonctionnaires et Assimilés (UFFA-CFDT) (Civil Servants): 26 rue de Montholon, 75439 Paris Cedex 09; tel. (1) 42-47-76-50; f. 1972; Sec.-Gen. ROSELYNE VIEILLARD.

Habillement, Cuir et Textile (HACUITEX): 26 rue de Montholon, 75439 Paris Cedex 09; tel. (1) 42-47-75-60; f. 1963; Sec.-Gen. DANIEL TORQUEO.

Industries Chimiques (FUC—CFDT) (Chemicals): 26 rue de Montholon, 75439 Paris Cedex 09; tel. (1) 42-47-73-30; telex 660154; Sec.-Gen. JACQUES KHELIFF.

FRANCE

Information, Livre, Audiovisuel et Culture (FILAC): 43 rue du Faubourg Montmartre, 75009 Paris; tel. (1) 42-46-50-64; Sec.-Gen. MICHEL MORTELETTE.

Ingénieurs et Cadres (UCC-CFDT): 26 rue de Montholon, 75439 Paris Cedex 09; tel. (1) 42-80-01-01; Sec.-Gen. DANIEL CROQUETTE.

Justice: 25 rue de la Fontaine au Roi, 75011 Paris; tel. (1) 48-05-70-56; Sec.-Gen. JEAN-MARIE PILLARD.

Mines et Métallurgie (Miners and Metal Workers): 5 rue Mayran, 75009 Paris; tel. (1) 42-47-74-00; telex 660154; Sec.-Gen. GÉRARD DANTIN.

Personnel du Ministère de l'Intérieur et des Collectivités Locales (INTERCO): 3 cité d'Hauteville, 75010 Paris; tel. (1) 48-24-23-36; telex 660154; Sec.-Gen. JACQUES NODIN.

Protection Sociale, Travail-Emploi (Social Security): 26 rue de Montholon, 75439 Paris Cedex 09; tel. (1) 42-47-75-67; Sec.-Gen. GILBERT CLAUDEL.

PTT (Post, Telegraph and Telephone Workers): 26 rue de Montholon, 75439 Paris Cedex 09; tel. (1) 42-85-13-20; telex 650346; Sec.-Gen. JEAN-CLAUDE DESRAYAUD.

Santé et Services Sociaux (Hospital Workers): 26 rue de Montholon, 75439 Paris Cedex 09; tel. (1) 42-47-73-31; Sec.-Gen. MARC DUPONT.

Services: 26 rue de Montholon, 75439 Paris Cedex 09; tel. (1) 42-47-76-20; Sec.-Gen. MARGUERITE BERTRAND.

Transports et Equipement: 26 rue de Montholon, 75439 Paris Cedex 09; tel. (1) 42-47-73-33; f. 1977; Sec.-Gen. MICHEL PERNET.

Union Confédérale des Retraités (UCR): 26 rue de Montholon, 75439 Paris Cedex 09; tel. (1) 42-47-76-88; Sec.-Gen. MARCEL GONIN.

Confédération Française de l'Encadrement (CGC): 30 rue de Gramont, 75002 Paris; tel. (1) 42-61-81-76; telex 215116; f. 1944; organizes managerial staff, professional staff and technicians; co-ordinates unions in every industry and sector; Pres. PAUL MARCHELLI; Delegate-Gen. JEAN DE SANTIS; 300,000 mems.

Confédération Française des Travailleurs Chrétiens (CFTC): 13 rue des Ecluses Saint Martin, 75483 Paris Cedex 10; tel. (1) 42-05-79-66; telex 214046; f. 1919; present form in 1964 after majority CFTC became CFDT (see above); absorbed Confédération Générale des Syndicats Indépendants 1977; Chair. JEAN BORNARD; Gen. Sec. GUY DRILLEAUD; 250,000 mems in 1985.

Confédération des Syndicats Libres (CSL) (formerly Confédération française du Travail): 13 rue Péclet, 75015 Paris; tel. (1) 45-33-62-62; telex 201390; f. 1959; right-wing; Sec.-Gen. AUGUSTE BLANC; 250,000 mems.

Fédération de l'Education Nationale (FEN): 48 rue La Bruyère, 75440 Paris Cedex 09; tel. (1) 42-85-71-01; telex 648356; f. 1948; federation of teachers' unions; Sec.-Gen. YANNICK SIMBRON; 451,447 mems in 1985.

Fédération Nationale des Syndicats Autonomes: 19 blvd Sébastopol, 75001 Paris; f. 1952; groups unions in the private sector; Sec.-Gen. MICHEL-ANDRÉ TILLIÈRES.

Fédération Nationale des Syndicats d'Exploitants Agricoles (FNSEA) (National Federation of Farmers' Unions): 11 rue de la Baume, 75008 Paris; tel. (1) 45-63-11-77; telex 660587; f. 1946; divided into 92 departmental federations and 30,000 local unions; Chair. RAYMOND LACOMBE; Sec.-Gen. LUC GUYAU; 700,000 mems.

PRINCIPAL STATE-CONTROLLED COMPANIES

Aerospatiale: 37 blvd de Montmorency, 75781 Paris Cedex 16; tel. (1) 45-24-43-21; manufacturer of aircraft, helicopters, strategic missiles, space and ballistic systems; 35,222 employees; Chair. and Gen. Man. HENRI MARTRE.

Avions Marcel Dassault—Breguet Aviation: 33 rue du Professeur Victor Pauchet, 92420 Vaucresson; tel. (1) 47-41-79-21; telex 203944; f. 1967 by merger; state took 46% of shares in 1982; design and production of civil and military aircraft; 14,676 employees; turnover 15,545m. Frs (1987); Pres. SERGE DASSAULT.

Charbonnages de France (CdF): Tour Albert 1er, 65 ave de Colmar, 92507 Rueil Malmaison; tel. (1) 47-52-92-52; telex 631450; established under the Nationalization Act of 1946; responsible for coal mining, sales and research in metropolitan France; there are also engineering and informatics divisions; 60,000 employees; Pres. and Dir-Gen. BERNARD PACHE.

Electricité de France: 32 rue de Monceau, 75008 Paris; tel. (1) 47-55-94-10; telex 280098; established under the Electricity and Gas Industry Nationalization Act of 1946; responsible for generating and supplying electricity for distribution to consumers in metropolitan France; 123,000 employees; Chair. PIERRE DELAPORTE; Man. Dir JEAN BERGOUGNOUX.

Société Nationale Elf Aquitaine (SNEA): Tour Elf, 2 place de la Coupole, Paris la Défense 6, Courbevoie; tel. (1) 47-44-45-46; telex 615400; 67% owned by ERAP—Entreprise de Recherches et d'Activités Pétrolières, a state enterprise; undertakes exploration for and production of petroleum and natural gas, chiefly in France, Africa (Cameroon, the Congo, Gabon and Nigeria), the North Sea and the USA; in 1987 it produced 17.8m. metric tons of crude petroleum and 14,400m. cu m of natural gas; has four refineries in France and a share in four others, with total capacity of 34.8m. tons per year. Elf Aquitaine also exploits uranium and non-energy minerals, and has subsidiaries in petrochemicals (ATOCHEM) and pharmaceuticals (SANOFI); 76,100 employees; Chair. and CEO MICHEL PECQUEUR.

Gaz de France: 23 rue Philibert Delorme, 75840 Paris Cedex 17; tel. (1) 47-54-20-20; telex 650483; established under the Electricity and Gas Industry Nationalization Act of 1946; responsible for distribution of gas in metropolitan France; about 17.5% of gas is produced in France (Aquitaine) and the rest imported from Algeria, the Netherlands, Norway and the USSR; Chair. FRANCIS GUTMANN; Dir-Gen. PIERRE GADONNEIX.

Orkem: Tour Albert 1er, 65 ave de Colmar, 92507 Rueil Malmaison; f. 1986, originally part of CdF; chemicals; 15,000 employees; turnover 20,000m. Frs (1987); Chair. SERGE TCHURUK.

Péchiney: 23 rue Balzac, 75008 Paris; tel. (1) 45-61-61-61; telex 290503; nationalized 1982; aluminium, fine metallurgy and advanced materials, ferroalloys and carbon products, copper fabrication; 49,160 employees; turnover 29,009m. Frs (1983); Chair. and CEO JEAN GANDOIS.

Régie Nationale des Usines Renault: 34 quai du Point du Jour, BP 103, 92109 Boulogne-Billancourt; tel. (1) 46-09-15-30; telex 205677; nationalized in 1945; in 1987 1.6m. passenger cars and small vans were manufactured; sales totalled 115,744m. Frs; Chair. RAYMOND LÉVY.

Rhône-Poulenc: 25 quai Paul Doumer, 92408 Courbevoie Cedex; tel. (1) 47-68-12-34; f. 1858; nationalized 1982; chemicals, pharmaceuticals, animal foodstuffs, film, textiles, communications; 80,000 employees (of whom 48,000 in France); turnover 56,000m. Frs (1984); Chair. and CEO JEAN-RENÉ FOURTOU; Man. Dir JEAN-MARC BRUEL.

Société Nationale d'Etude et de Construction de Moteurs d'Avion (SNECMA): 2 blvd Victor, 75724 Paris Cedex 15; tel. (1) 45-54-92-00; telex 202834; f. 1905; nationalized 1945; manufactures engines for civil and military aircraft, electronic and meteorological equipment; Chair. and Man. Dir Gen. BERNARD CAPILLON.

Société Nationale d'Exploitation Industrielle des Tabacs et des Allumettes (SEITA): 53 quai d'Orsay, 75340 Paris Cedex 07; tel. (1) 45-55-91-50; telex 250604; responsible for the production and marketing of tobacco and matches in France; sales totalled 32,454m. Frs in 1984; 8,000 employees; Chair. and Man. Dir F. EYRAUD.

Thomson, SA: 173 blvd Haussmann, 75379 Paris Cedex 08; tel. (1) 45-61-96-00; telex 204680; f. 1893 as Compagnie Française Thomson-Houston; nationalized 1982; holding company for Thompson group; electrical and electronics industry; 105,000 employees; turnover 62,600m. Frs (1986); Chair. ALAIN GOMEZ.

Usinor Sacilor: Immeuble 'Ile de France', Cedex 33, 92070 Paris la Défense; tel. (1) 49-00-60-10; telex 614730; f. 1948 as two companies, Sacilor and Usinor; Usinor nationalized 1981; Sacilor nationalized 1982; two companies merged as Usinor Sacilor 1987; steel; 90,082 employees (1987); Chair. and Man. Dir FRANCIS MER.

Transport

RAILWAYS

Most of the French railways are controlled by the Société Nationale des Chemins de fer Français (SNCF) which took over the activities of the five largest railway companies in 1937. The SNCF is divided into three réseaux (systems) which are further subdivided into régions (areas), all under the direction of a general headquarters in Paris. In 1988 the SNCF operated 34,680 km of track, of which 11,692 km were electrified. The Parisian transport system is controlled by a separate authority, the Régie Autonome des Transports Parisiens (RATP, see below). A number of small railways in the provinces are run by independent organizations. In 1987 the French and British Governments signed a treaty to construct a rail link between the two countries, under the English Channel, which would be completed by 1993. The rail link was to be constructed and operated by the Anglo-French Eurotunnel Consortium. Further plans were proposed to link the Channel tunnel to towns in the Netherlands, Belgium and the Federal Republic of Germany, by building a railway network in northern France.

Société Nationale des Chemins de fer Français (SNCF): 88 rue Saint Lazare, 75436 Paris Cedex 09; tel. (1) 42-85-60-00; telex

FRANCE

290936; f. 1937; formerly 51% state-owned, wholly nationalized 1982; Dir-Gen. JEAN COSTET; Pres. JACQUES FOURNIER.

Réseau du Nord-Est: 13 rue d'Alsace, 75475 Paris Cedex 10; tel. (1) 42-03-96-31; Dir JEAN CASTILLE.

Réseau Atlantique: 20 rue de Rome, 75008 Paris; tel. (1) 42-85-88-00; Dir DIDIER SAUTTER.

Réseau du Sud-Est: place Louis Armand, 75571 Paris Cedex 12; tel. (1) 43-46-12-12; Dir CLAUDE ARNOLD.

Metropolitan Railways

Régie Autonome des Transports Parisiens (RATP): 53 ter quai des Grands Augustins, BP 70-06, 75271 Paris Cedex 06; tel. (1) 40-46-41-41; telex 200000; f. 1948; state-owned; operates the Paris underground and suburban railways, and buses; Chair. CHRISTIAN BLANC; Gen. Man. MICHEL ROUSSELOT.

Three provincial cities also have underground railway systems: Marseille (first section opened 1977), Lyon and Lille.

ROADS

At 31 December 1987 there were 6,440 km of motorways (autoroutes). There are also about 28,500 km of national roads (routes nationales), 350,000 km of secondary roads, 420,000 km of other urban roads and 700,000 km of rural roads. In 1987 the Government introduced a programme to construct 2,700 km of motorways by 1995, which would be partly financed by 2,000m. francs of receipts from the privatization programme.

Fédération Nationale des Transports Routiers: Paris; tel. (1) 45-63-16-00; road transport; Chair. MAURICE VOIRON.

INLAND WATERWAYS

In 1987 there were 8,500 km of navigable waterways, of which 1,647 km were accessible to craft of 3,000 tons. In 1987 the Government initiated a programme, with a projected cost of 2,800m. francs, to modernize navigable waterways and construct a canal linking the Rivers Rhône and Rhine.

SHIPPING

At 30 June 1984 the French merchant shipping fleet had a total displacement of 8,945,000 grt, of which oil tankers accounted for 4,785,000 grt. In 1986 the Government announced a two-year scheme, costing 1,400m. francs, to revitalize the merchant fleet. In 1965 control of the six major seaports (Marseille, Le Havre, Dunkerque, Rouen, Nantes–Saint-Nazaire and Bordeaux) was transferred from the State to autonomous authorities. The State retains supervisory powers. An independent consultative body, the Conseil National des Communautés Portuaires, was established in 1987 as an umbrella organization for ports and port authorities.

Conseil National des Communautés Portuaires: f. 1987; central independent consultative body for ports and port authorities; over 50 mems including 10 trade union mems; Pres. JACQUES DUPUY-DAUBY.

Principal Shipping Companies

CETRAMAR, Consortium Européen de Transports Maritimes: 87 ave de la Grande Armée, 75782 Paris Cedex 16; tel. (1) 45-00-23-97; telex 611234; tramping; Man. Dir ANDRÉ MAIRE; displacement 149,021 grt.

Chargeurs Réunis: 3 blvd Malesherbes, BP 9808, 75360 Paris Cedex 08; tel. (1) 42-68-44-44; telex 280034; f. 1964; Europe to and from West Africa, South Africa and Far East-North America (east coast) to and from West Africa and Far East to West Africa; Chair. G. ROY; displacement 235,344 grt.

Compagnie Générale Maritime et Financière: Tour Winterthur, 102 Quartier Boieldieu, 92085 Paris la Défense, Cedex 18; tel. (1) 47-76-70-00; telex 630387; f. 1976 from merger of Compagnie Générale Transatlantique and Compagnie des Messageries Maritimes; holding co. Compagnie Générale Maritime et Financière (CGMF); 99.9% state-owned; freight services to USA, Canada, West Indies, Central and South America, Northern Europe, USSR, the Middle East, India, Australia, New Zealand, Indonesia and other Pacific and Indian Ocean areas; Chair. CLAUDE ABRAHAM; Man. Dir JACQUES RIBIÈRE; capacity of fleet 1,819,555 dwt.

Compagnie Nationale de Navigation: 50 blvd Haussmann, 75441 Paris Cedex 09; tel. (1) 42-85-19-00; telex 290673; f. 1930 as Compagnie Navale Worms; merged with Compagnie Nationale de Navigation and Société Française de Transports Maritimes, and changed name to Compagnie Nationale de Navigation in 1986; holding co. with subsidiaries: Société Française de Transports Maritimes (Navale et Commerciale Havraise Péninsulaire, Société Française de Transports Pétroliers, Société Nantaise des Chargeurs de l'Ouest, Cie Morbihannaise de Navigation, Truckline Ferries France), Feronia International Shipping (FISH) and other subsidiaries

Directory

abroad; Pres. and Dir-Gen. GILLES BOUTHILLIER; Dir-Gen. PIERRE DE DEMANDOLX.

Esso SAF: 6 ave André Prothin, 92093 Paris la Défense Cedex 2; tel. (1) 43-34-60-00; telex 620031; ocean-going tankers; Chair. M. KOPFF; Marine Man. A. CALVARIN; fleet of 4 cargo carriers (1m. grt) and 2 coasters.

Gazocéan: Tour Fiat, 1 place de la Coupole, 92084 Paris la Défense Cedex 16; tel. (1) 47-96-60-60; telex 615234; f. 1957; fleet with a capacity of about 240,000 cu m of liquefied gas; world-wide gas sea transportation; Chair. JACQUES PETITMENGIN.

Louis-Dreyfus et Cie: 87 ave de la Grande Armée, 75782 Paris Cedex 16; tel. (1) 45-01-54-45; telex 611234; tramping; Chair. C. BOQUIN; Man. Dir P. D'ORSAY; displacement of fleet 630,000 grt.

Mobil Oil Française: Tour Septentrion, 92081 Paris la Défense Cedex 09; tel. (1) 47-73-42-41; telex 610412; bulk petroleum transport; refining and marketing of petroleum products; Chair. MARC CASANOVA.

Nouvelle Compagnie de Paquebots: 33 rue J. F. Leca, Marseille; tel. 91-91-91-21; telex 440003; f. 1965; cap. 10,229,100 Frs; passenger cruise services; Chair. and Man. Dir BERNARD MAURIAC; displacement 27,658 grt.

Sealink Voyages: 16 blvd des Capucines, 75009 Paris; tel. (1) 47-42-86-87; telex 281710; cross-Channel passenger, accompanied motorcar, freight and roll on/roll off on train-ferries and car-ferries; Chair. P. ESSIG; Man. Dir A. TOUBOL; displacement 45,000 grt.

Société Maritime des Pétroles BP et Cie: 10 quai Paul Doumer, 92412 Courbevoie Cedex; tel. (1) 47-68-40-00; telex 630546; oil tankers; Man. Dir YVES METGE; capacity of fleet 809,341 dwt.

Société Maritime Shell: 29 rue de Berri, 75397 Paris Cedex 08; tel. (1) 45-61-82-82; telex 644487; oil tankers; Man. Dir M. JOLIVET.

Société Nationale Maritime Corse-Méditerranée: 61 blvd des Dames, 13002 Marseille; tel. 91-56-32-00; telex 440068; passenger and roll on/roll off ferry services between France and Corsica, Sardinia, North Africa; Pres. J. RIBIÈRE; Man. Dir J. P. ISOARD; 13 vessels.

Société Navale Caennaise: 58 ave Pierre Berthelot, BP 6183, 14061 Caen Cedex; tel. 31-82-21-76; telex 170122; f. 1901; regular lines; Chair. JEAN-MICHEL BLANCHARD; Man. Dir Y. LENEGRE; displacement 43,501 grt.

Société Navale et Commerciale Delmas-Vieljeux: 16 ave Matignon, 75008 Paris; tel. (1) 42-56-44-33; telex 290354; f. 1867; cargo service from North and South European ports to West and North Africa; Chair. TRISTAN VIELJEUX; Vice-Pres. PATRICE VIELJEUX; capacity of fleet 444,114 dwt.

Soflumer Van Ommeren (France): 5 ave Percier, 75008 Paris; tel. (1) 45-62-50-50; telex 650252; coastal tankers and tramping; Chair. F. VALLAT; Man. Dir P. DECAVELE; displacement 120,718 grt.

Total Compagnie Française de Navigation: Tour Mirabeau, 39-43 quai André Citroen, 75739 Paris Cedex 15; tel. (1) 45-78-33-33; telex 201604; f. 1931; cap. 120m. Frs; oil tankers; Chair. LOUIS BOUZOLS; capacity of fleet 2,516,747 dwt.

Union Industrielle et Maritime: 6 rue Anatole de la Forge, 75017 Paris; tel. (1) 47-66-00-02; telex 649383; cargo services, continental, North Africa, transatlantic; Chair. J. M. CANGARDEL; displacement 105,642 grt.

CIVIL AVIATION

There are international airports at Orly, Roissy and Le Bourget (Paris), Bordeaux, Lille, Lyon, Marseille, Nice, Strasbourg and Toulouse.

National Airlines

Air France: 1 sq Max Hymans, 75757 Paris Cedex 15; tel. (1) 43-23-81-81; telex 200666; f. 1933; international, European and intercontinental services; flights to Africa, Madagascar, Americas, Middle and Far East and West Indies; Chair. BERNARD ATTALI; Pres. JEAN-DIDIER BLANCHET; Sec.-Gen. MARC MAUGARS; fleet (1988) 7 Concorde, 27 Boeing 747, 16 Boeing 737, 16 Airbus A300, 26 Boeing 727, 7 Airbus A310, 4 Airbus A320.

Air Inter: 1 ave du Maréchal Devaux, 91550 Paray Vieille Poste; tel. (1) 46-75-12-12; telex 250932; f. 1954; operates internal services within metropolitan France; service to Madrid; Air France, UTA and the SNCF are the part owners; Chair and Man. Dir PIERRE EELSEN; fleet (1988) 18 Airbus A300, 4 Airbus A320, 11 Mercure, 12 Super 12.

Private Airlines

Union de Transports Aériens (UTA): 3 blvd Malesherbes, 75008 Paris; tel. (1) 42-66-30-30 and 776-41-33; telex 610692; f. 1963; services to West and South Africa, Middle and Far East, Australia, New Caledonia, New Zealand, Japan, Tahiti, Guadeloupe, Martinique and the west coast of the USA; Chair. RENÉ LAPAUTRE;

FRANCE
Directory

Vice-Pres. DANIEL-CHARLES RICHON; fleet of 4 Boeing 747-300, 1 Boeing 747-200F, 2 Boeing 747-400.

Nineteen small private companies provide regional air services. Small private airlines flying services outside France include:

Euralair: 93350 Aéroport du Bourget, Paris; tel. (1) 48-35-95-22; telex 230662; f. 1964; Chair. ALEXANDRE COUVELAIRE; fleet of 4 Boeing 737-200, 1 BAe 146, 1 Citation I, 2 Citation II, 1 Citation III, 2 Mystère 20, 2 Mystère 10, 1 Baron.

Europe Aéro Service SA: Aérodrome de Perpignan-Rivesaltes, 66028 Perpignan; telex 500084; f. 1965; internal passenger and cargo services and services to Spain; Chair. GEORGES MASUREL; fleet of 8 Caravelle 10B.

Transport Aérien Transrégional (TAT): Aérogare Civile, BP 0237, 37100 Tours Cedex; tel. 47-54-21-45; telex 750876; f. 1968; took over Air Alpes 1981; took over Air Alsace routes following its demise in 1982; Chair. and Man. Dir MICHEL MARCHAIS; fleet of 7 Fokker F.28-1000, 4 F.28-2000, 5 F.28-4000, 15 Fairchild FH-227B, 4 Twin Otter, 8 Beech 99.

Airlines Association

Chambre Syndicale du Transport Aérien (CSTA): 43 blvd Malesherbes, 75008 Paris; tel. (1) 47-42-11-00; telex 281491; f. 1946 to represent French and foreign airlines at national level; Chair. PIERRE EELSEN; Delegate-Gen. JEAN-LOUIS GASCHET; 17 mems.

Tourism

France draws tourists from all over the world. Paris is famous for its boulevards, historic buildings, theatres, art treasures, fashion houses and restaurants, and for its many music halls and night clubs. The Mediterranean and Atlantic coasts and the French Alps are the most popular tourist resorts. Among other attractions are the many ancient towns, the châteaux of the Loire, the fishing villages of Brittany and Normandy, and spas and places of pilgrimage, such as Vichy and Lourdes. There were 36,974,000 tourist arrivals in 1987, when tourist receipts totalled 19,927m. francs. Most visitors are from the Federal Republic of Germany, Belgium, the United Kingdom, the Netherlands and Switzerland.

Ministère de l'Industrie et du Développement Territorial: 101 rue de Grenelle, 75007 Paris; Minister Delegate for Tourism OLIVIER STIRN.

Direction de l'Industrie Touristique: 2 rue Linois, 75740 Paris Cedex 15; tel. (1) 45-75-62-16; Dir FRANCESCO FRANGIALLI.

Maison de la France: 8 ave de l'Opéra, Paris; tel. (1) 42-96-10-23; Pres. CHRISTIAN BLANKAERT.

There are Regional Tourism Committees in the 23 regions and 4 overseas départements. There are over 5,000 Offices de Tourisme and Syndicats d'Initiative (tourist offices run by the local authorities) throughout France.

Atomic Energy

In 1986 France had 49 nuclear reactors in operation, with a total generating capacity of 44,693 MW.

Commissariat à l'Energie Atomique (CEA) (Atomic Energy Commissariat): 31–33 rue de la Fédération, 75752 Paris Cedex 15; tel. (1) 40-56-10-00; telex 200671; f. 1945; Gen. Administrator JEAN-PIERRE CAPRON; High Commissioner JEAN TEILLAC; Sec.-Gen. JEAN MARMOT.

The CEA is an establishment of scientific, industrial and technological character. Its function is to promote the uses of nuclear energy in science, industry and national defence; the fields in which it is active, either directly or through its own subsidiaries and participation in private companies, are: production of nuclear materials; reactor development; fundamental research; innovation and transfer of technologies; military applications; bio-technologies; robotics; electronics; new materials; radiological protection and nuclear safety.

Administration is in the hands of a 15-member Comité de l'Energie Atomique (Atomic Energy Committee), presided over by the Prime Minister and consisting of government officials and representatives of sciences and industry.

Institutes and Administrative Bodies:

Direction des Applications Militaires (Military Applications Division): Dir ALAIN VIDART.

Groupe ORIS: BP 6, 91192 Gif-sur-Yvette; tel. 69-08-27-08; telex 692431; f. 1987, fmrly Compagnie ORIS Industrie; Pres. and Dir-Gen. YVES LE GALLIC.

Institut de Protection et de Sûreté Nucléaire (Institute for Nuclear Protection and Security): CEN/Fontenay-aux-Roses, BP 6, 92260 Fontenay-aux-Roses; Dir FRANÇOIS COGNE.

Institut de Recherche Fondamentale (Fundamental Research Institute): Orme des Merisiers, 91191 Gif-sur-Yvette Cedex; Dir DANIEL CRIBIER.

Institut de Recherche Technologique et de Développement Industriel (Institute of Technological Research and Industrial Development): 31 rue de la Fédération, 75752 Paris Cedex 15; tel. (1) 40-56-10-00; Dir MICHEL RAPIN.

Agence Nationale pour la Gestion des Déchets Radioactifs: 31–33 rue de la Fédération, 75752 Paris Cedex 15; tel. (1) 40-56-15-15; Dir JEAN CHATOUX.

Institut National des Sciences et Techniques Nucléaires (National Institute of Nuclear Science and Technology): CEN Saclay-INSTN, 91191 Gif-sur-Yvette Cedex; f. 1956; Dir. Y. CHELET.

Research Centres:

Centre d'Etudes Nucléaires de Cadarache (CEN-Ca) (Cadarache Nuclear Research Centre): 13108 Saint-Paul-les-Durance Cedex, Bouches-du-Rhône; tel. 42-25-70-00; telex 440678; f. 1960; Dir JEAN MEGY.

Centre d'Etudes Nucléaires de Fontenay-aux-Roses (Fontenay-aux-Roses Nuclear Research Centre): BP 6, 92265 Fontenay-aux-Roses Cedex; tel. (1) 46-54-70-80; f. 1945; Dir G. VIAL.

Centre d'Etudes Nucléaires de Grenoble (CEN-G) (Grenoble Nuclear Research Centre): BP 85, 38041 Grenoble Cedex; tel. 76-88-44-00; telex 320323; f. 1955; 40 laboratories; Dir FRANÇOIS DECOOL.

Centre d'Etudes Nucléaires de Saclay (CENS) (Saclay Nuclear Research Centre): 91191 Gif-sur-Yvette Cedex; tel. 69-08-60-00; telex 604641; f. 1949; Dir PAUL DELPEYROUX.

Centre d'Etudes Nucléaires de la Vallée du Rhône (CEN-VALRHO): BP 171, 30205 Bagnols-sur-Cèze Cedex; tel. 66-79-60-00; telex 480816; Dir ALBERT TEBOUL.

Société des Participations du CEA: CEA-Industrie: 31–33 rue de la Fédération, 75752 Paris Cedex 15; tel. (1) 40-56-10-00; telex 200671; principal affiliates CISI, COGEMA, FRAMATOME, TECHNICATOME, Groupe ORIS, INTERCONTROLE STMT, etc.; Pres. JEAN-PIERRE CAPRON; Dir-Gen. DENIS MORTIER.

Centre National de la Recherche Scientifique (CNRS): 15 quai Anatole France, 75700 Paris; tel. (1) 45-55-92-25; telex 260-034; there are nuclear research centres attached to this institution in Strasbourg, Grenoble and Orsay.

Groupe de Laboratoires de Strasbourg-Cronenbourg: rue du Loess, BP 20 CRO, 67037 Strasbourg Cedex; tel. 88-28-63-00; telex 890032; f. 1957; Dirs P. DEJOURS, C. GAILLARD, R. SELTZ, J. J. VOGT.

FRENCH OVERSEAS POSSESSIONS

Ministry of Overseas Departments and Territories: rue Oudinot 27, 75700 Paris, France; tel. 47-83-01-23.
Minister: Louis Le Pensec.
The national flag of France, proportions three by two, with three equal vertical stripes, of blue, white and red, is used in the Overseas Possessions.

French Overseas Departments

The four Overseas Departments (départements d'outre-mer) are French Guiana, Guadeloupe, Martinique and Réunion. They are integral parts of the French Republic, and the administrative structure is similar to that of the Departments of metropolitan France. Overseas Departments, however, have their own Courts of Appeal. Until 1982 each Overseas Department was administered by a Prefect, with elected General Councils, indirectly-elected Regional Councils and with elected representatives in the French National Assembly and Senate of the Republic in Paris. Under the decentralization law of March 1982, the appointed Prefect in each Overseas Department was restyled Commissaire de la République (Government Commissioner). The former executive power of the Prefect was transferred to the General Council. A proposal to replace the General and Regional Councils by a single assembly was rejected by the French Constitutional Council in December 1982. As a compromise between autonomy and complete assimilation into France, the Regional Councils' powers were increased in 1983. In February the first direct elections for the Regional Councils were held. Their wider powers included responsibility for economic, social and cultural affairs. The Overseas Departments continue to send elected representatives to the French National Assembly and to the Senate in Paris.

FRENCH GUIANA

Introductory Survey

Location, Climate, Language, Religion, Capital

French Guiana (Guyane) lies on the north coast of South America, with Suriname to the west and Brazil to the south and east. The climate is humid, with a season of heavy rains from April to July and another short rainy season in December and January. Average temperature at sea-level is 27°C (85°F), with little seasonal variation. French is the official language but a creole patois is also spoken. The majority of the population belong to the Roman Catholic Church, although other Christian churches are represented. The capital is Cayenne.

Recent History

French occupation commenced in the early 17th century. After brief periods of Dutch, English and Portuguese rule, the territory was finally confirmed as French in 1817. The colony steadily declined, after a short period of prosperity in the 1850s as a result of the discovery of gold in the basin of the Approuague river. French Guiana, including the notorious Devil's Island, increasingly became used as a penal colony, and as a place of exile for convicts and political prisoners, before the practice was stopped in 1937. The colony became a department of France in 1946.

French Guiana's reputation as an area of political and economic stagnation was dispelled by the growth of pro-independence sentiments, and the use of violence by a small minority, compounded by tensions between the Guyanais and large numbers of immigrant workers. In 1974 demonstrations against unemployment, the worsening economic situation, and French attitudes towards the department, led to the detention of leading trade unionists and pro-independence politicians. In 1975 the French Government announced plans to improve the economic situation through increasing investment and interest in French Guiana. However, these were unsuccessful, owing partly to the problems of developing French Guiana's interior. As a result of growing industrial and political unrest in the late 1970s, there were increased demands for greater autonomy for the department by the Parti Socialiste Guyanais (PSG), the strongest political party. In 1980 there were several bomb attacks against 'colonialist' targets by an extremist group known as Fo nou Libéré la Guyane (FNLG). Reforms, introduced by the French Socialist Government in 1982 and 1983, succeeded in decentralizing some power over local affairs to a new Regional Council. The French Government, however, has refused to countenance any change in French Guiana's departmental status.

In the February 1983 elections to the Regional Council, the left-wing parties gained a majority of votes, but not of seats, and the balance of power was held by the separatist Union des Travailleurs Guyanais (UTG), which was restyled the Parti National Populaire Guyanais (PNPG) in November 1985. In May 1983 French Guiana was the target for bombings by the Alliance Révolutionnaire Caraïbe (ARC), an extremist independence movement based in Guadeloupe, another French Overseas Department in the West Indies. At elections to the General Council, held in March 1985, the PSG and left-wing independents succeeded in increasing their representation to 13 seats out of a total of 19.

For the general election to the French National Assembly in March 1986, French Guiana's representation was increased from one to two deputies. The incumbent member, Elie Castor of the PSG, received 48.1% of the total votes (voting at this election being based on a system of proportional representation), and was re-elected. The other seat was won by Paulin Bruné of the right-wing Rassemblement pour la République (RPR). On the same day as the elections to the Assembly, direct elections were held for the 31 seats on the Regional Council. The PSG, with 42.1% of the votes, increased its strength on the Council from 14 to 15 members, and Georges Othily of the PSG was re-elected president of the Council. The RPR won nine seats, and the centrist Union pour la Démocratie Française (UDF) three, while four seats were secured by Action Démocratique Guyanaise.

A French presidential election was held in April and May 1988. Of the votes cast in French Guiana, the incumbent President Mitterrand of the Parti Socialiste (PS) obtained 52% in the first round, and 60% in the second round against Jacques Chirac of the RPR. Nevertheless, in the legislative elections held in June (when the former constituency system was reintroduced), the RPR succeeded in retaining one of the two seats in the National Assembly in Paris. In September–October the left-wing parties consolidated their control of local government by winning 14 of the 19 seats at elections to the General Council.

In 1986–87 French Guiana's relations with neighbouring Suriname deteriorated as increasing numbers of Surinamese refugees fled across the border to escape rebel uprisings in their own country. In late 1986 additional French troops were brought in to patrol the border, as a result of which the Surinamese Government accused the French Government of preparing an invasion into Suriname via French Guiana. It was also reported that Surinamese rebels were using French Guiana as a conduit for weapons and supplies.

Government

France is represented in French Guiana by an appointed Government Commissioner. There are two Councils with local powers: the General Council, with 19 members, and the Regional Council, with 31 members. Both are elected by universal adult suffrage for a period of six years. French Guiana elects two representatives to the French National Assembly in Paris, and sends one elected representative to the French Senate.

Defence

In 1988 France maintained a military force of about 8,000 in French Guiana and the Antilles.

FRENCH OVERSEAS DEPARTMENTS — French Guiana

Economic Affairs

The economy of French Guiana is heavily dependent on France for budgetary aid and imports of food and manufactured goods. Local production is mainly in the agricultural sector, particularly forestry and fisheries. In 1982, according to estimates by the World Bank, the gross national product (GNP), measured at average 1980–82 prices, was US $210m. ($3,230 per head).

Fishing, especially for shrimps, has grown in importance since 1965, and in 1985 exports of fish products were worth 220m. francs and accounted for almost two-thirds of total export earnings. Most of the catch is made by foreign vessels and landed in French Guiana for processing, prior to export, mainly to the USA. Exports of shrimps totalled 2,308 metric tons, valued at 151.8m. francs (59.4% of total export earnings), in 1986, compared with 2,078 tons, worth 177.0m. francs (53.5% of total exports), in 1985. Forests cover 90% of the territory's area and contain valuable reserves of tropical hardwoods, such as rosewood, mahogany and satinwood. However, poor communications, lack of development and the difficulties involved in working in the tropical rain forest have prevented these vast reserves from being exploited to any significant extent. Between 1973 and 1986, the annual output of sawlogs increased from 30,100 cu m to 83,945 cu m. Local sawmills provide finished products for export, including plywoods and veneers. Rosewood oil is also extracted. Exports of wood (excluding finished products) declined from 21,615 metric tons in 1982 to 7,992 tons in 1984, but rose to 11,084 tons in 1985, when wood provided 7.9% of total export earnings. In 1986, however, wood exports were only 5,822 tons, valued at US $2.2m. (5.9% of export earnings). Agricultural cultivation is confined to the coastal strip, where 90% of the population is concentrated. Rice, cassava, bananas and vegetables are grown for local consumption, while sugar cane is cultivated for use in the production of rum, which totalled 872 hl in 1986. The rearing of livestock has been developed since 1975 by stock farms on the coastal plain. In 1987 the French Government allocated 17m. francs in grants to improve local agriculture.

Mineral resources have been shown to exist, but their exploitation at the present time does not seem to be economically viable, considering the huge investment needed. An estimated 42m. tons of bauxite exists on the Kaw plateau, and 40m. tons of kaolin near Saint-Laurent-du-Maroni. Other minerals are present in smaller quantities, but only gold is mined with any success, with production totalling 514 kg in 1987.

Tourism is growing, but improvements are needed in transport and hotel facilities. Unemployment is high, affecting more than 15% of the labour force in 1987, and is a particularly serious problem among young people. In 1982 a new investment bank, the Société financière de développement de la Guyane (SOFIDEG), was created to encourage agricultural development. In 1968 a rocket-launching base was established at Kourou, where *Ariane*, the European Space Agency's communications satellite launcher, was developed. After initial set-backs, successful launches between 1983 and 1986 confirmed the centre's future commercial prospects. A new town was created to accommodate the resident engineers and technicians. A second launch pad was constructed at Kourou, and the first rocket was launched from the new site in March 1986. However, following the mid-air destruction of a rocket in June, the Arianespace company announced that, pending the report of an independent commission of inquiry into the causes of the failure, no further rockets would be launched. The next launch successfully took place in September 1987. By June 1988 the new *Ariane 4* rocket was in service, and all the available capacity on scheduled future flights had already been allocated.

There has been a steady flow of emigrants away from French Guiana, while the Government has tried to attract up to 30,000 immigrants to boost the labour force. These have included civil servants from France, and members of the Hmong tribe from Laos. There are also large numbers of illegal immigrants, estimated at over 20,000, from Haiti, other Caribbean islands, and from French Guiana's neighbours. Although French Guiana is underpopulated and suffering from a shortage of skilled labour, most immigrants remain in Cayenne, and impose a strain on the city's resources. In 1983 46% of births were to immigrant parents. The high proportion of immigrants is a source of racial imbalance and tensions.

French Guiana, in common with other French Overseas Departments, is heavily dependent on imports of food and energy. The cost of imports rose from US $248.8m. in 1984 to $297.7m. in 1986, while the value of French Guiana's exports remained low ($37.0m. in 1986), producing a trade deficit of $260.7m. in that year. The deficit increased to about $340m. in 1987. By September 1988 French Guiana's external debt had reached $1,200m. The Government was endeavouring to arrange a moratorium on debt repayments. Furthermore, restrictions on the import of foreign goods were relaxed in order to reduce bureaucracy and to appease the IMF in preparation for a possible balance-of-payments agreement.

Social Welfare

In 1984 there were two hospitals, with a total of 611 beds, a health centre and three private clinics. The Institut Pasteur undertakes research into malaria and other tropical diseases. There is a system of social security similar to the French model. In 1984 there were 154 physicians working in French Guiana.

Education

Education is modelled on the French system, and is compulsory for 10 years between the ages of six and 16 years. Primary education begins at six years of age and lasts for five years. Secondary education, beginning at 11 years of age, lasts for up to seven years, comprising a first cycle of four years and a second of three years. Education at state schools is provided free of charge. There are also a number of private denominational schools. Between 1974 and 1986 the number of children attending primary schools increased from 6,465 to 16,916 (including 1,711 pupils at six private schools). Over the same period, the total enrolment at secondary (including technical) schools rose from 5,251 to 10,429. This expansion has placed a strain on the education system. Higher education in law is provided by a branch of the Université Antilles-Guyane in Cayenne.

Public Holidays

1989: 2 January (for New Year's Day), 7–8 February (Lenten Carnival), 24–27 March (Easter), 1 May (for Labour Day), 4 May (Ascension Day), 15 May (Whit Monday), 14 July (National Day), 11 November (Armistice Day), 25 December (Christmas Day).

1990: 1 January (New Year's Day), 27–28 February (Lenten Carnival), 13–16 April (Easter), 1 May (Labour Day), 24 May (Ascension Day), 4 June (Whit Monday), 14 July (National Day), 11 November (Armistice Day), 25 December (Christmas Day).

Weights and Measures

The metric system is in use.

Statistical Survey

Sources (unless otherwise stated): Institut national de la statistique et des études économiques, 1 rue Maillard Dumesle, BP 6017, 97306 Cayenne; tel. 311279; telex 910344; Service de Presse et d'Information, Ministère des départements et territoires d'outre-mer, 27 rue Oudinot, 75700 Paris; tel 47-83-01-23.

AREA AND POPULATION

Area: 90,000 sq km (34,750 sq miles).

Population: 73,012 (males 38,448; females 34,564) at census of 9 March 1982; 90,240 (estimate for 1 January 1988); *Capital:* Cayenne, population 38,200 (1987). *Other towns* (population at 1982 census): Kourou 7,061; Saint-Laurent-du-Maroni 6,971.

Births and Deaths (1986): Registered live births 2,392 (birth rate 27.9 per 1,000); Registered deaths 491 (death rate 5.7 per 1,000).

Economically Active Population (persons aged 16 years and over, 1982 census): Agriculture, hunting, forestry and fishing 3,706; Mining and quarrying 163; Manufacturing 1,359; Electricity, gas and water 380; Construction 2,837; Trade, restaurants and hotels 2,025; Transport, storage and communications 1,347; Financing, insurance, real estate and business services 3,662; Community, social and personal services 8,931; Activities not adequately defined 2,013; Total civilians employed 26,423 (males 17,205, females 9,218); Unemployed 4,760 (males 2,389, females 2,371); Armed Forces 1,192 (all males); Total labour force 32,375 (males 20,786, females 11,589).

AGRICULTURE, ETC.

Principal Crops (metric tons, 1986): Sugar cane 2,500, Cassava (Manioc) 8,350, Rice (paddy) 8,880.

Livestock (1986): Cattle 17,530, Pigs 8,100, Goats 2,000, Poultry 105,000.

Forestry (cu m, 1986): Sawlogs 83,945, Sawnwood 35,294.

Fishing (landings in metric tons, 1986): Fish 2,944; Shrimps 2,356; Total 5,300.

MINING

Production (1987): Gold 514 kg. Source: Le Secrétariat du Comité Monétaire de la Zone Franc: *La Zone Franc, Rapport 1987.*

INDUSTRY

Production (1986): Rum 872 hl, Electricity 223.3 million kWh.

FRENCH OVERSEAS DEPARTMENTS   *French Guiana*

FINANCE

Currency and Exchange Rates: 100 centimes = 1 French franc. *Coins:* 1, 5, 10, 20 and 50 centimes; 1, 2, 5 and 10 francs. *Notes:* 10, 50, 100, 200 and 500 francs. *Sterling and Dollar Equivalents* (30 September 1988): £1 sterling = 10.77 francs; US $1 = 6.37 francs; 1,000 French francs = £92.83 = $156.99. *Average Exchange Rate* (French francs per US dollar): 8.985 in 1985; 6.926 in 1986; 6.011 in 1987.

Budget (estimates, 1987): Revenue and expenditure to balance at 441.5 million francs 1987. Source: Le Secrétariat du Comité Monétaire de la Zone Franc: *La Zone Franc, Rapport 1987*.

Aid from France (1976): US $81 million.

Cost of Living (Consumer Price Index for Cayenne; base: 1980 = 100): 170.4 in 1985; 174.1 in 1986; 181.2 in 1987. Source: UN, *Monthly Bulletin of Statistics*.

EXTERNAL TRADE

Principal Commodities (US $ million, 1986): *Imports c.i.f.:* Food and live animals 56.3 (Fish and fish preparations 14.5); Beverages and tobacco 14.4; Petroleum and petroleum products 24.3 (Refined petroleum products 23.7); Chemicals and related products 19.4; Basic manufactures 41.4; Machinery and transport equipment 98.0 (General industrial machinery, equipment and parts 14.6; Electrical machinery, apparatus, etc. 26.0; (Road vehicles and parts 29.2); Miscellaneous manufactured articles 39.3; Total (incl. others) 297.7. *Exports f.o.b.:* Fish and fish preparations 23.8 (Fresh and frozen shellfish 22.0); Cork and wood 2.2 (Non-coniferous lumber 2.2); Machinery and transport equipment 1.9; Non-monetary gold 2.7; Total (incl. others) 37.0.

Principal Trading Partners (US $ million, 1986): *Imports c.i.f.:* France 187.4; Federal Republic of Germany 10.1; Japan 12.6; Trinidad and Tobago 22.9; USA 13.5; Total (incl. others) 297.7. *Exports f.o.b.:* France 6.2; Guadeloupe 4.8; Japan 5.8; Martinique 3.3; USA 13.2; Total (incl. others) 34.3.

Source: UN, *International Trade Statistics Yearbook*.

1987 (million francs): Imports 2,372; Exports 324.

TRANSPORT

Road Traffic (vehicles in use, 31 December 1986): Passenger cars 27,010; Buses and coaches 1,120; Goods vehicles 7,208. Source: IRF, *World Road Statistics*.

International Sea-borne Shipping (freight traffic, '000 metric tons, 1985): Goods loaded 27; Goods unloaded 249. Source: UN, *Monthly Bulletin of Statistics*.

Civil Aviation (1986): Freight carried 3,867 metric tons, Passengers carried 207,154.

EDUCATION

Primary (1986): 73 schools; 16,916 pupils (incl. 1,711 pupils at 6 private schools).

Secondary (1986): Secondary and technical schools 22; 10,429 pupils.

Higher (1986): The Université Antilles-Guyane comprises, in French Guiana, a College of Law. In 1986 it was attended by 202 students. There is also an Ecole Normale for teacher-training and an agricultural college.

Directory

The Government

(February 1989)

Government Commissioner (Prefect): JEAN-PIERRE LACROIX.

President of the General Council: ELIE CASTOR (PSG).

Deputies to the French National Assembly: ELIE CASTOR (PSG), LÉON BERTRAND (RPR).

Representative to the French Senate: RAYMOND TARCY (PSG).

REGIONAL COUNCIL

President: GEORGES OTHILY (PSG).

Election, 16 March 1986

	Votes	%	Seats
PSG	6,704	43.00	15
RPR	4,319	27.69	9
ADG	1,906	12.22	4
UDF	1,390	8.91	3
FN	571	3.66	—
PNPG	533	1.41	—
Others	490	3.14	—
Total	15,913	100.00	31

Political Organizations

Action Démocratique Guyanaise (ADG): ave d'Estrées, Cayenne; Leader ANDRÉ LECANTE.

Front National: BP 478, 97384 Kourou Cedex; tel. 321034; f. 1984; extreme right-wing; Leader GUY MALON.

Parti National Populaire Guyanais (PNPG): ave d'Estrées, Cayenne; f. 1985; independence party; Leader CLAUDE ROBO.

Parti Socialiste Guyanais (PSG): Cité Césaire, Cayenne; f. 1956; Sec.-Gen. GÉRARD HOLDER.

*Rassemblement pour la République (RPR): 84 ave Léopold Héder, 97300 Cayenne; tel. 316660; f. 1946; right-wing (Gaullist); Pres. PAULIN BRUNÉ.

*Union pour la Démocratie Française (UDF): 111 bis rue Christophe Colomb, BP 472, 97331 Cayenne; tel. 311710; f. 1979; centrist; Leader CLAUDE HO A CHUCK.

* The RPR and the UDF allied to contest the 1988 legislative elections as the Union du Rassemblement du Centre (URC).

Judicial System

See: Judicial System, Martinique.

Religion

The majority of the population belong to the Roman Catholic Church.

CHRISTIANITY

The Roman Catholic Church

French Guiana comprises the single diocese of Cayenne, suffragan to the archdiocese of Fort-de-France, Martinique. At 31 December 1986 there were an estimated 65,000 adherents in French Giuana, representing almost 75% of the total population.

Bishop of Cayenne: FRANÇOIS-MARIE MORVAN, Evêché, BP 378, 24 rue Madame-Payé, 97328 Cayenne; tel. 310118.

The Anglican Communion

Within the Church in the Province of the West Indies, French Guiana forms part of the diocese of Guyana. The Bishop is resident in Georgetown, Guyana.

Other Christian Churches

The Seventh-day Adventist, Evangelist, Assembly of God, and Jehovah's Witnesses Churches are also represented.

The Press

France-Guyane: 28 rue Félix Eboué, Cayenne; telex 910552; 2 a week; Dir LUC GERMAIN; circ. 4,000.

Guyane-Matin: 42 blvd Jubelin, Cayenne; tel. 313524; daily; Dir FABIEN ROUBAUD; circ. 1,000.

La Presse de Guyane: 26 rue Lieutenant Brassé, 97300 Cayenne; daily; Dir JEAN SERGE; circ. 16,000.

Radio and Television

In 1986 there were an estimated 60,000 radio receivers and 14,000 television receivers in use.

FRENCH OVERSEAS DEPARTMENTS

Cayenne FM: Hôtel PLM Montabo, BP 581, 97334 Cayenne; tel. 313938; 120 hours weekly.
Radio-Télévision Française d'Outre-mer (RFO): rue du Dr Devèze, BP 336, 97305 Cayenne; tel. 311500; telex 910526; Radio-Guyane Inter: 16 hours broadcasting daily; Téléguyane: 2 channels, 32 hours weekly; Dir MAURICE GRIMAUD.
Radio Antipa: 1 place Schoëlcher, Cayenne; tel. 310037; 126 hours weekly.
Radio Tout Moune: route de Montabo, BP 74, Cayenne; tel. 318074; 24 hours a day; Dir HECTOR JEAN-LOUIS.

Finance

(cap. = capital; dep. = deposits; m. = million; frs = French francs; brs = branches)

BANKING

Central Bank
Caisse Centrale de Coopération Economique: 13 rue Louis Blanc, Cayenne; tel. 314133; telex 910570; Dir HERVÉ MAURICE.

Commercial Banks
Banque Française Commerciale: 8 place Palmistes, Cayenne; tel. 303577; telex 910559; Dir ANDRÉ GEROLIMATOS; 2 brs.
Banque Nationale de Paris-Guyane (BNP Guyane): 2 place Victor Schoëlcher, BP 35, Cayenne; tel. 303866; telex 910522; f. 1855; cap. 40m. frs (July 1987); Dir M. BLONDEL; 5 brs.
Crédit Populaire Guyanais: Caisse de Crédit Mutuel, 93 rue Lallouette, BP 818, 97338 Cayenne; tel. 301523; Dir LEI-SAN ELIANE.

Development Bank
Société financière de développement de la Guyane (SOFIDEG): 25 rue F. Arago, Cayenne; tel. 300418; telex 910556; f. 1982; Dir PATRICE PIN.

Trade and Industry

Chambre de Commerce de la Guyane: 8 ave Général de Gaulle, Cayenne; tel. 303000; telex 910537; Pres. JEAN-PIERRE PRÉVÔT.
Jeune Chambre Economique de Cayenne: 2 bis rue Docteur Saint-Rose, BP 1094, Cayenne; Pres. MADELEINE GEORGES.

TRADE UNIONS
Centrale Démocratique des Travailleurs de la Guyane (CDTG): 113 rue Christophe Colomb, BP 383, Cayenne; tel. 310232; Sec.-Gen. RENÉ SYDALZA.
Fédération de l'Education Nationale: 68 rue Justin Catayee, BP 807, Cayenne; Sec.-Gen. ELIANE NIEL.
Force Ouvrière (FO): 107 rue Barthélemy, Cayenne; Sec.-Gen. M. XAVERO.
Syndicat National des Instituteurs (SNI): Ecole Maximilien Sabas, BP 265, Cayenne; Sec.-Gen. CLAUDE LEONARDI.
Union des Travailleurs Guyanais (UTG): 7 ave Ronjon, Cayenne; tel. 312642; Sec.-Gen. PAUL CÉCILIEN.

Transport

RAILWAYS
There are no railways in French Guiana.

ROADS
In 1986 there were 480 km (300 miles) of Routes Nationales and 8,410 km (5,256 miles) of other roads; 836 km (522 miles) of roads were paved.

SHIPPING
The new port of Dégrad-des-Cannes, on the estuary of the river Mahury, has become the major port. There are other ports at Le Larivot, Saint-Laurent-du-Maroni and Kourou. Saint-Laurent is used primarily for the export of timber. There are river ports on the Oyapock and on the Approuague. There is a ferry service across the Maroni river between Saint-Laurent and Albina, Suriname. The rivers provide the best means of access to the interior, although numerous rapids prevent navigation by large vessels.

CIVIL AVIATION
Rochambeau International Airport, situated 17.5 km (11 miles) from Cayenne, is equipped to handle the largest jet aircraft. Air Guyane operates internal air services.
Guyane Air Transport (GAT): Aéroport de Rochambeau, 97307 Matoury; tel. 356555; telex 910619; f. 1980; Dir-Gen. GUY MALIDOR.

Tourism

The main attractions are the natural beauty of the tropical scenery and the Amerindian villages of the interior. There were 800 hotel rooms in 1988.
Délégation Régionale au Tourisme pour la Guyane: BP 7008, 97307 Cayenne; tel. 318491; telex 910532.

GUADELOUPE

Introductory Survey

Location, Climate, Language, Religion, Capital

Guadeloupe is the most northerly of the Windward Islands group in the West Indies. Dominica lies to the south, and Antigua and Montserrat to the north-west. Guadeloupe is formed by two large islands, Grande-Terre and Basse-Terre, separated by a narrow sea channel, with a smaller island, Marie-Galante, to the south-east, and another, La Désirade, to the east. There are also a number of small dependencies, mainly Saint-Barthélemy and the northern half of Saint-Martin (the remainder being part of the Netherlands Antilles, among the Leeward Islands. The climate is tropical, with an average temperature of 26°C (79°F), and a more humid and wet season between June and November. French is the official language, but a creole patois is widely spoken. The majority of the population profess Christianity, and belong to the Roman Catholic Church. The capital is the town of Basse-Terre; the other main town and principal commercial centre is Pointe-à-Pitre on Grande-Terre.

Recent History

Guadeloupe was first occupied by the French in 1635, and has remained French territory, apart from a number of brief occupations by the British in the 18th and early 19th century. It gained departmental status in 1946. Economic and political power has been the monopoly of the white Creole population who wish to maintain the country's relationship with France, and the right-wing and centre parties have traditionally been the strongest political force on the islands. Most Guadeloupeans, however, are dissatisfied with the economic results of departmentalization and with the attitudes of central government towards Guadeloupe's own identity, and they have sought greater internal autonomy for the department. The principal left-wing party, the Parti Communiste Guadeloupéen (PCG), was reorganized as an autonomous body in 1955, in response to greater nationalist feeling. The PCG has rejected attempts to attain independence at any cost, preferring to seek internal autonomy.

The deterioration of the economy and an increase in unemployment provoked industrial and political unrest during the 1960s and 1970s, including outbreaks of serious rioting in 1967. Pro-independence parties have rarely won more than 5% of the total vote at elections in Guadeloupe, but their activities have served to increase tension on the islands. Several have turned to violence as a means of expressing their opposition to what they see as French colonialism. In 1980 and 1981 there was a series of bomb attacks on hotels, government offices and other targets by a group called the Groupe Libération Armée (GLA), and in 1983 and 1984 there were further bombings by a group called the Alliance Révolutionnaire Caraïbe (ARC). The Government responded by outlawing the ARC and reinforcing the military and police presence on the islands. In 1984, however, the ARC merged with the Mouvement populaire pour une Guadeloupe indépendante (MPGI) in order to continue its campaign. Further sporadic acts of violence continued into 1985, but in October the ARC suspended its bombing campaign, prior to the holding of legislative elections. In November 1986, however, a further series of bomb attacks began. In January

1988 a series of bomb explosions occurred in various parts of the island. Responsibility was claimed by a previously unknown pro-independence group, the Organisation Révolutionnaire Armée.

In June 1985 the leader of the ARC, Luc Reinette, escaped from prison for the second time. He was eventually recaptured in July 1987, on Saint Vincent, after he and four other members of the separatist movement had been refused political asylum in Suriname. The five were extradited to Paris to face charges of involvement in terrorist activities.

In 1974 Guadeloupe was granted the status of a region, and an indirectly-elected Regional Council was formed. In direct elections to a new Regional Council in February 1983, held as a result of the decentralization reforms that were introduced by the Socialist Government of President Mitterrand, the centre-right coalition succeeded in gaining a majority of the seats and control of the administration. In January 1984 Lucette Michaux-Chevry, the president of the General Council, formed a new conservative centre party, Le Parti de la Guadeloupe (LPG), to provide a more Guadeloupean approach to continued relationships with France, although the LPG remained in alliance with the right-wing Rassemblement pour la République (RPR). However, at the elections for the General Council, held in March 1985, the left-wing combination of the Parti Socialiste (PS) and the PCG gained a majority of seats on the enlarged Council, and Dominique Larifla of the PS was elected its president. In July demonstrations and a general strike, organized by pro-separatist activists in order to obtain the release of a leading member of the MPGI, quickly intensified into civil disorder and rioting in the main town, Pointe-à-Pitre.

For the general election to the French National Assembly in March 1986, Guadeloupe's representation was increased from three to four deputies. The local branches of the RPR and the Union pour la Démocratie Française (UDF), which had campaigned jointly at the 1981 general election and the 1983 regional elections, presented separate candidates (voting for the 1986 election being based on a system of proportional representation). In February 1986 the president of the Regional Council, José Moustache, resigned from the RPR and joined the UDF. As a result of this split, the incumbent PCG and PS members of the Assembly (Ernest Moutoussamy and Frédéric Jalton respectively) were re-elected, but the other deputy seeking re-election, Marcel Esdras of the UDF, was defeated, and the two remaining seats were won by RPR candidates (Lucette Michaux-Chevry and Henri Beaujean).

In the concurrent elections for the 41 members of the Regional Council, the two left-wing parties together received 52.4% of the total votes (compared with 43.1% in 1983) and won a majority of seats, increasing their combined strength from 20 to 22 members (PS 12, PCG 10). As a result, Moustache was replaced as president of the Council by Félix Proto of the PS. The elections were boycotted by the Union Populaire pour la Libération de la Guadeloupe. In September the publication of a report (prepared at Proto's request) criticizing the management of finances by the former RPR/UDF majority on the Regional Council, led by Moustache, caused disruption within the Council and, as expected, had repercussions on the indirect elections for the two Guadeloupe members of the French Senate later in the month: there was a decline in support for centre-right candidates, and, as before, two left-wing Senators were elected (one from the PCG and one from the PS).

In the French presidential elections held in April and May 1988, the incumbent President Mitterrand of the PS received 55% of the votes cast in Guadeloupe in the first round, and 69% in the second round against Jacques Chirac of the RPR. At legislative elections in June, the constituency system was reintroduced. Dominique Larifla of the PS defeated Henri Beaujean of the RPR, while the three other deputies to the National Assembly retained their seats. In September–October the left-wing parties won 26 of the 42 seats at elections to the General Council.

Government

France is represented in Guadeloupe by an appointed Government Commissioner. There are two councils with local powers: the 42-member General Council and the 41-member Regional Council. Both are elected by universal adult suffrage for a period of up to six years. Guadeloupe elects four deputies to the French National Assembly in Paris, and sends two indirectly elected representatives to the Senate.

Defence

In 1987 France maintained a military force of about 8,000 in French Guiana and the Antilles.

Economic Affairs

Guadeloupe's economy is based on agriculture, tourism and light industry, but is heavily dependent on French aid and imports. In 1985, according to estimates by the World Bank, the gross domestic product (GDP), measured at average 1983–85 prices, was US $1,100m. ($3,300 per head).

Agricultural production has traditionally been dominated by the sugar industry, but this sector of the economy has declined in recent years. In 1983 less than 35% of available agricultural land was planted with sugar cane. The annual harvest of cane declined from 1.8m. metric tons in 1962 to 500,000 tons in 1984. Output rose to 623,000 tons in 1985, and to an estimated 773,000 tons in 1986. Production of raw sugar consequently decreased from 184,812 tons in 1965 to about 41,000 tons in 1984. Production increased to 53,000 tons in 1985, and to 65,589 tons in 1986. Exports of raw sugar increased from 29,953 tons, valued at $7.7m. (10.3% of total export earnings), in 1985 to 63,661 tons, worth $22.2m. (20.5% of total exports), in 1986. Only four sugar factories remain in operation, and these suffer from inefficiency, lack of investment and large financial deficits. The production of rum, derived from sugar cane, has also declined: 67,015 hectolitres were distilled in 1986, compared with more than 90,000 hectolitres in 1982. Government attempts to revitalize the sugar industry by encouraging smallholders have been less successful than was hoped. However, in 1982 a plan was agreed which provides a fixed price for sugar and subsidies for small-scale farmers. A three-year replantation scheme was launched in 1983, and it was intended that 10,000 ha would be replanted during that period.

Bananas are the other major crop, and provide more than 40% of Guadeloupe's export earnings. Exports of bananas had declined since 1984, but in 1986 there was a slight increase in banana exports, earning $53m. in export revenue Attempts have been made to diversify agricultural production by developing the cultivation of tropical fruits and vegetables, but Guadeloupe still relies heavily on imported food, which cost 917.2m. francs in 1984. In spite of a high level of unemployment (affecting 38% of the labour force in 1988), there is an acute shortage of agricultural labour, caused by the reluctance of young people to accept less than the minimum wage (earnings are linked to those of metropolitan France). This has led to a large influx of immigrant workers from Haiti and Dominica, and to tensions in some areas of the towns. In September 1988 agricultural production was severely affected by Hurricane Gilbert. Damage was estimated at 132m. francs, with approximately one-third of the banana plantations destroyed.

Tourism is an important sector of the economy, but it employs only about 9% of the working population. Adverse publicity from the terrorist attacks in 1983 and 1984 led to many cancellations from tourists, and tourist arrivals at hotels declined in 1984 by more than 15%, to 163,469. The number declined still further in 1986, to 148,021. However, it was hoped that the deregulation of air transport to the island, which ended Air France's monopoly on flights to Guadeloupe in November 1986, would help to reverse this trend.

The development of industrial activity has been promoted by the Government, and 36 companies were created between 1980 and 1982, involving an investment of 120m. francs. However, the industrial sector employs fewer than 4,000 people, and contributes only about 9% of GDP. Development of domestic industries has been hindered by the large volume of imports from France. There is an industrial zone and free port at Jarry. The 65% of the active population engaged in the administrative and service sector produce about 80% of GDP. Civil servants from France receive a 40% bonus on their basic earnings, and other incentives, for working in the French Antilles. Local investment is concentrated in the import/export business, and in the discount stores which sell imported goods.

France provides more than 85% of Guadeloupe's imports, which totalled US $108.6m. in 1986. Imports of energy, 83% of which are provided by the other French Overseas Departments, increased by around 50% between 1982 and 1984. This dependence on imported fuel, combined with the rapid rise in prices and the growth in demand for transport equipment, contributed to a massive trade deficit, which rose from $512.5m. in 1984 to $683.5m. in 1986 and to about $947m. in 1987. Between 1981 and 1986, the annual rate of inflation declined from 14% to 2.8%.

Social Welfare

There are two main public hospitals, a psychiatric hospital and 10 private clinics, with a total of 2,314 beds in 1978. In 1979 there were 373 physicians and 78 dentists working in Guadeloupe.

Education

Education is free and compulsory in state schools between the ages of six and 16 years. The system is similar to that of France, with primary, junior and secondary academic and technical education. Primary education begins at six years of age and lasts for five years. Secondary education, beginning at the age of 11, lasts for up to seven years, comprising a first cycle of four years and a second of three years. Higher education is provided by a branch of the Université Antilles-Guyane, containing faculties of law, economics and science.

FRENCH OVERSEAS DEPARTMENTS — Guadeloupe

Public Holidays

1989: 2 January (for New Year's Day), 6–7 February (Lenten Carnival), 24–27 March (Easter), 1 May (Labour Day), 4 May (Ascension Day), 15 May (Whit Monday), 14 July (National Day), 21 July (Victor Schoëlcher Day), 11 November (Armistice Day), 25 December (Christmas Day).

1990: 1 January (New Year's Day), 26–27 February (Lenten Carnival), 13–16 April (Easter), 1 May (Labour Day), 24 May (Ascension Day), 4 June (Whit Monday), 14 July (National Day), 21 July (Victor Schoëlcher Day), 11 November (Armistice Day), 25 December (Christmas Day).

Weights and Measures

The metric system is in use.

Statistical Survey

Sources (unless otherwise stated): Institut national de la statistique et des études économiques, ave Paul Lacavé, BP 96, 97102 Basse-Terre; tel. 990250; Service de Presse et d'Information, Ministère des départements et territoires d'outre-mer, 27 rue Oudinot, 75700 Paris; tel. 47-83-01-23.

AREA AND POPULATION

Area: 1,780 sq km (687.3 sq miles), of which dependencies (La Désirade, Les Saintes, Marie-Galante, Saint-Barthélemy, Saint-Martin) 269 sq km.

Population: 327,002 (males 160,112; females 166,890) at census of 9 March 1982; 336,538 (estimate for 30 June 1987): *Principal Towns* (population at 1982 census): Les Abymes 56,165; Pointe-à-Pitre 25,310; Basse-Terre (capital) 13,656.

Births and Deaths (1986): Registered live births 6,374 (birth rate 19.1 per 1,000); Registered deaths 2,238 (death rate 6.7 per 1,000).

Economically Active Population (persons aged 16 years and over, 1982 census): Agriculture, forestry and fishing 12,997; Manufacturing, mining and quarrying 6,643; Electricity, gas and water 703; Construction 9,997; Wholesale and retail trade 10,062; Transport, storage and communications 4,819; Financing, insurance, real estate and business services 15,109; Community, social and personal services (incl. restaurants and hotels) 26,106; Activities not adequately defined 5,963; Total employed 92,399 (males 54,529, females 37,870); Unemployed 29,427 (males 14,629, females 14,798); Civilian labour force 121,826 (males 69,158, females 52,668); Armed forces 2,062 (all males); Total labour force 123,888.

AGRICULTURE, ETC.

Principal Crops (FAO estimates, '000 metric tons, 1986): Sugar cane 773, Bananas 157, Aubergines 6, Coconuts 3, Pineapples 3. Source: FAO, *Production Yearbook*.

Livestock (1986): Cattle 75,177, Pigs 42,000, Goats 31,500, Sheep 3,900.

Forestry (1979): Roundwood removals 17,000 cubic metres.

Fishing (metric tons, live weight): Total catch 8,940 in 1984; 8,390 in 1985; 8,500 (FAO estimate) in 1986.

INDUSTRY

Production (1986): Raw sugar 65,589 metric tons, Rum 67,015 hl, Electricity 545.9 million kWh.

FINANCE

Currency and Exchange Rates: French currency is used (see French Guiana).

Budget (estimates, 1987): Revenue and expenditure to balance at 1,510.1 million francs.

Aid from France (1981): US $215 million.

Cost of Living (Consumer Price Index for urban areas; base: 1980 = 100): 160.8 in 1985; 165.4 in 1986; 170.3 in 1987. Source: UN, *Monthly Bulletin of Statistics*.

Gross Domestic Product (million francs at current prices): 8,427 in 1983; 9,049 in 1984; 9,650; in 1985; Source: Le Secrétariat du Comité Monétaire de la Zone Franc: *La Zone Franc, Rapport 1987*.

EXTERNAL TRADE

Principal Commodities (US $ million, 1986): *Imports c.i.f.*: Food and live animals 146.0 (Meat and meat preparations 35.9; Cereals and cereal preparations 32.4); Beverages and tobacco 33.0; Petroleum and petroleum products 56.6 (Refined petroleum products 54.6); Chemicals and related products 73.1; Basic manufactures 122.8; Machinery and transport equipment 211.4 (Electrical machinery, apparatus, etc. 46.6; Road vehicles and parts 74.9); Miscellaneous manufactured articles 122.4; Total (incl. others) 792.1. *Exports f.o.b.*: Food and live animals 85.3 (Wheat meal or flour 6.9; Bananas and plantains 53.0; Raw sugar 22.2); Beverages 7.3 (Distilled alcoholic beverages 6.8); Machinery and transport equipment 6.6 (Ships and boats 3.7); Total (incl. others) 108.6; Source: UN, *International Trade Statistics Yearbook*.

Principal Trading Partners (US $ million, 1986): *Imports c.i.f.*: France 517.9; Fed Repub. of Germany 24.2; Italy 34.6; Japan 19.8; Martinique 45.5; USA 18.5; Total (incl. others) 792.0. *Exports f.o.b.*: France 78.6; French Guiana 2.3; Martinique 15.1; Portugal 6.1; USA 2.5; Total (incl. others) 108.6. Source: UN, *International Trade Statistics Yearbook*.

1987 (million francs): Imports 6,229; Exports 564.

TRANSPORT

Road Traffic (vehicles in use, 1986): Passenger cars 69,200, Buses and coaches 500, Goods vehicles 500. Source: IRF, *World Road Statistics*.

Shipping (international sea-borne traffic, '000 metric tons, 1985): Freight loaded 297; Freight unloaded 929. Source: UN, *Monthly Bulletin of Statistics*.

Civil Aviation (commercial traffic, 1984): Number of flights 31,687; Passengers carried 1,168,670, Freight carried 11,213 metric tons.

TOURISM

Visitors (1986): 148,021.

EDUCATION

Primary (1986): Schools 304; Students 57,198.

Secondary (1986): Schools 75; Students 47,086.

Higher (1986): The Université Antilles-Guyane comprises, in Guadeloupe, a College of Arts, a College of Law and Economics and a College of Physical and Natural Sciences. In 1986 it was attended by an estimated 2,404 students. There is also an Ecole Normale for teacher-training.

Directory

The Government
(February 1989)

Government Commissioner (Prefect): BERNARD SARAZIN.
President of the General Council: DOMINIQUE LARIFLA (PS).
President of the Economic and Social Council: GUY FRÉDÉRIC.
Deputies to the French National Assembly: ERNEST MOUTOUSSAMY (PCG), FRÉDÉRIC JALTON (PS), LUCETTE MICHAUX-CHEVRY (RPR), DOMINIQUE LARIFLA (PS).
Representatives to the French Senate: HENRI BANGOU (PCG), FRANÇOIS LOUISY (PS).

REGIONAL COUNCIL

President: FÉLIX PROTO (PS).

Election, 16 March 1986

	Votes	%	Seats
RPR	25,371	33.09	15
PS	21,969	28.65	12
PCG	18,229	23.77	10
UDF	8,217	10.71	4
Others	2,876	3.78	—
Total	76,662	100.00	41

Political Organizations

Fédération Guadeloupéenne du Parti Socialiste (PS): Avenue de Général de Gaulle, Cité Jardin du Raizet, 97110 Abymes; in March 1987 the PS announced plans to become autonomous party, while maintaining links with PS in France; First Sec. DOMINIQUE LARIFLA.

*****Fédération Guadeloupéenne du Rassemblement pour la République (RPR):** 1 rue Baudot, Basse-Terre; tel. 811069; Gaullist; Pres. MARLÈNE CAPTANT.

FRENCH OVERSEAS DEPARTMENTS   *Guadeloupe*

*Fédération Guadeloupéenne de l'Union pour la Démocratie Française (UDF): Pointe-à-Pitre; centrist; Pres. MARCEL ESDRAS.
Mouvement populaire pour une Guadeloupe indépendante (MPGI): Pointe-à-Pitre; f. 1982; extremist independence party; Sec.-Gen. SIMONE FAISANS-RENAC.

Alliance Révolutionnaire Caraïbe (ARC): Pointe-à-Pitre; f. 1983; illegal pro-independence alliance; left-wing; supports armed struggle; officially dissolved, but merged with MPGI in 1984 and continued activities; Leader LUC REINETTE (arrested July 1987).
Mouvement Socialiste Départmentaliste Guadeloupéen: Mairie de Morne-à-l'Eau, 97111 Morne-à-l'Eau; Sec.-Gen. ABDON SAMAN.
Parti Communiste Guadeloupéen (PCG): 119 rue Vatable, 97110 Pointe-à-Pitre; f. 1944; Sec.-Gen. CHRISTIAN CELESTE.
Le Parti de la Guadeloupe (LPG): Pointe-à-Pitre; f. 1984; centre party; Leader LUCETTE MICHAUX-CHEVRY.
Union Populaire pour la Libération de la Guadeloupe (UPLG): Basse-Terre; f. 1978; semi-clandestine pro-independence movement; Pres. Dr CLAUDE MAKOUKÉ.
*The RPR and the UDF allied to contest the 1988 legislative elections as the Union du Rassemblement du Centre (URC).

In June 1987 three leaders of the separatist movement, Luc Reinette, Henri Amédien and Henri Bernard, announced the formation of the Conseil National de la Résistance Guadeloupéene (CNRG), which was to organize a provisional government whose aim was to establish conditions for the creation of a future Republic of Guadeloupe.

Judicial System

Cour d'Appel: Palais de Justice, 97100 Basse-Terre; First Pres. JEAN THIERRY; Procurator-Gen. JERRY SAINTE-ROSE; two Tribunaux de Grande Instance, four Tribunaux d'Instance.

Religion

The majority of the population belong to the Roman Catholic Church.

CHRISTIANITY
The Roman Catholic Church

Guadeloupe comprises the single diocese of Basse-Terre, suffragan to the archdiocese of Fort-de-France, Martinique. At 31 December 1986 there were an estimated 301,720 adherents, representing more than 90% of the total population. The Bishop participates in the Antilles Episcopal Conference, based in Kingston, Jamaica.

Bishop of Basse-Terre: Mgr ERNEST MESMIN LUCIEN CABO, Evêché, place Saint-François, BP 50, 97101 Basse-Terre; tel. 813669.

The Press

Combat Ouvrier: Valette, 97180 St Anne; monthly; trade union publ.
L'Etincelle: 119 rue Vatable, 97110 Pointe-à-Pitre; weekly; organ of the Communist Party; Dir ROBERT BARON; circ. 5,000.
France-Antilles: 1 rue Hincelin, BP 658, 97159 Pointe-à-Pitre; telex 919728; daily; Dir CLAUDE PROVENÇAL; circ. 25,000.
Guadeloupe 2000: Résidence Massabielle, 97110 Pointe-à-Pitre; fortnightly; right-wing extremist; Dir EDOUARD BOULOGNE; circ. 4,000.
Information Caraïbe (ICAR): BP 958, Pointe-à-Pitre; tel. 825606; f. 1973; weekly; Dir P. FERTIN.
Jakata: 18 rue Condé, 97110 Pointe-à-Pitre; f. 1977; fortnightly; Dir FRANTZ SUCCAB; circ. 6,000.
Magwa: Résidence Vatable, Bâtiment B, BP 1286, 97178 Pointe-à-Pitre; tel. 917698; monthly; independent; Editor DANIK ZANDWONIS; circ. 4,000.
Match: 33 rue St John Perse, 97110 Pointe-à-Pitre; tel. 820187; fortnightly; Dir CAMILLE JABBOUR; circ. 6,000.
Moun: BP 128, 97184 Pointe-à-Pitre; quarterly; culture; circ. 3,500.
Le Progrès social: rue Toussaint L'Ouverture, 97100 Basse-Terre; tel. 811041; weekly; Dir HENRI RODES; circ. 5,000.
Télé Sept Jours: Agence Promoventa, Immeuble Lagland Bergevin, 97110 Pointe-à-Pitre; weekly; TV.

NEWS AGENCIES
Agence Centrale Parisienne de Presse (ACP): BP 1105, 97181 Pointe-à-Pitre; tel. 821476; telex 919728; Rep. RENÉ CAZIMIR-JEANON.

Foreign Bureaux

Agencia EFE (Spain): BP 1016, 97178 Pointe-à-Pitre; Correspondent DANNICK ZANDRONIS.
United Press International (UPI) (USA): BP 658, 97159 Pointe-à-Pitre; Rep. STÉPHANE DELANNOY.

Radio and Television

In 1987 there were an estimated 100,000 radio receivers and 70,000 television receivers (of which 28,000 were colour) in use. The establishment of a private local television channel was approved in 1987.

Société nationale de radio-télévision française pour l'Outre-Mer (RFO): BP 402, 97163 Pointe-à-Pitre Cedex; tel. 902424; 24 hours radio and 14 hours television broadcast daily; Dir JACQUES BARBIER-DECROZES.
Radio Antilles: 55 rue Henri IV, 97110 Pointe-à-Pitre.
Radio Caraïbes International: Tour Cecid, Blvd Legitimus, 97110 Pointe-à-Pitre; tel. 821746; telex 019083. Dir OLIVIER GARON.

Finance

(cap. = capital; dep. = deposits; m. = million;
frs = French francs; brs = branches)

BANKING
Central Bank

Caisse Centrale de Coopération Economique: Faubourg Frébault, BP 160, 97154 Pointe-à-Pitre; tel. 833272; telex 919074.

Commercial Banks

Banque des Antilles Françaises: place de la Victoire, 97110 Pointe-à-Pitre; tel. 268007; telex 919866; rue de Cours Nolivos, 97100 Basse-Terre; f. 1853; cap. 32,583m. frs (1986); Dir d'Agence MICHEL MEYNIAL; Dir-Gen. MICHEL GENADINOS; 4 brs.
Banque Française Commerciale: 21 rue Gambetta, 97110 Pointe-à-Pitre; tel. 821201; telex 919764; f. 1977; cap. 21m. frs (Dec. 1981); Dir RENÉ MOUTTET; 7 brs.
Banque Nationale de Paris: place de la Rénovation, 97110 Pointe-à-Pitre; tel. 829696; telex 919706; Dir HENRI BETBEDER; 13 brs.
Banque Populaire de la Guadeloupe—Crédit Guadeloupéen: 10 rue Achille René-Boisneuf, 97110 Pointe-à-Pitre; f. 1926; tel. 914560; telex 919713; dep. 550m. frs (1983); Pres. CHRISTIAN RIMBAUD; Dir RICHARD NALPAS; 6 brs.
Caisse Régionale de Crédit Agricole Mutuel de la Guadeloupe: BP 134, Zone artisanale de petit perou, 97154 Pointe-à-Pitre; tel. 906565; telex 919708; Dir THÉLÈME GEDEON; 5 brs.
Crédit Martiniquais: Angle des rues P. Lacavé et Cités Unies, 97100 Pointe-à-Pitre; tel. 831859; f. 1987, in succession to Chase Manhattan Bank (USA).
Société Générale de Banque aux Antilles (SGBA): 30 rue Frébault, POB 630, 97110 Pointe-à-Pitre; tel. 825423; telex 919735; f. 1979; cap. 15m.; Pres. JACQUES DE MALEVILLE; Dir HENRI GILLES; 6 brs.

INSURANCE

Mutuelle Antillaise d'Assurances, Société d'Assurances à forme mutuelle: 12 rue Gambetta, BP 409, 97110 Pointe-à-Pitre; tel. 832332; telex 919945; f. 1937; Dir-Gen. FÉLIX CHERDIEU D'ALEXIS; Man. A. ZOGG; Dir ALAIN BUFFON.

Foreign Companies

Some 30 of the principal European insurance companies are represented in Pointe-à-Pitre, and another six companies have offices in Basse-Terre.

Trade and Industry

Agence pour la promotion industrielle de la Guadeloupe (APRIGA): BP 1229, 97184 Pointe-à-Pitre; tel. (590) 834897; telex 919780; f. 1979; development agency; Pres. MARIUS BADE; Dir CHARLY BLONDEAU.
Centre Technique de la Canne et du Sucre: Morne l'Epingle, 97139 Les Abymes; tel. 829470; Pres. ANTOINE ANDREZE-LOUISON; Dir PHILIPPE DOUCHEL.
Chambre de Commerce et d'Industrie de Pointe-à-Pitre: rue F. Eboué, BP 64, 97152 Pointe-à-Pitre; tel. 900808; telex 919780; Pres. GEORGES MARIANNE; Dir-Gen. JEAN-CLAUDE PARIS.

FRENCH OVERSEAS DEPARTMENTS

Chambre de Commerce et d'Industrie de Basse-Terre: 6 rue Victor Hugues, BP 17, 97100 Basse-Terre; tel. 811656; telex 919781; f. 1832; 24 mems; Pres. Gérard Penchard; Sec.-Gen. Germain William.

Chambre d'Agriculture de la Guadeloupe: 27 rue Sadi-Carnot, 97110 Pointe-à-Pitre; tel. 821130; telex 919286; Pres. Christian Flereau; Dir Victorien Lurel.

Société d'Intérêt Collectif Agricole (Sica-Assobag): Desmarais, 97100 Basse-Terre; tel. 810552; telex 919727; f. 1967; banana producers; Pres. François le Metayer; Dir Jean-Claude Petrelluzzi.

Syndicat des Producteurs-Exportateurs de Sucre et de Rhum de la Guadeloupe et Dépendances: Zone Industrielle de la Pointe Jarry, 97122 Baie-Mahault, BP 2015, 97191 Pointe-à-Pitre; tel. 266212; telex 919824; f. 1937; 4 mems; Pres. Amédée Huyghues-Despointes.

TRADE UNIONS

Confédération Générale du Travail de la Guadeloupe (CGTG): 4 cité Artisanale de Bergevin, 97173 Pointe-à-Pitre; tel. 823461; telex 919061; f. 1973; Sec.-Gen. Claude Morvan; 15,000 mems.

Union Départementale de la Confédération Française des Travailleurs Chrétiens: Pointe-à-Pitre; f. 1937; Sec.-Gen. E. Democrite; about 3,500 mems.

Union Départementale des Syndicats CGT-FO: 59 rue Lamartine, Pointe-à-Pitre; Gen. Sec. Clotaire Bernos; about 1,500 mems.

Union Générale des Travailleurs de la Guadeloupe: 5 Immeuble Diligenti, 97110 Pointe-à-Pitre; tel. 900539; confederation of pro-independence trade unions.

Union Interprofessionnelle de la Guadeloupe (UIG): Logement TEFT, Bergevin, 97181 Pointe-à-Pitre; tel. 831650; (affiliated to the Confédération Française Démocratique du Travail (CFDT) of France); Institut National de la Recherche Agronomique (INRA), Domaine de Duclos, 97170 Petit-Bourg; Sec.-Gen. A. Mephon.

Transport

RAILWAYS

There are no railways in Guadeloupe.

ROADS

In 1986 there were 2,087 km of roads in Guadeloupe, of which 328 km were Routes Nationales.

SHIPPING

The major port is at Pointe-à-Pitre, and a new port for the export of bananas has been built at Basse-Terre.

CIVIL AVIATION

Raizet International Airport is situated 3 km (2 miles) from Pointe-à-Pitre and is equipped to handle jet aircraft.

Air Guadeloupe: Raizet Airport, 97110 Abymes; tel. 903737; telex 919008; f. 1970; regular flights to Antigua, Dominica, St Martin, St Thomas; connects the various dependent islands; fleet of 2 Fairchild F-27-J, 4 Twin Otters, 2 ATR 42, 1 Dornier 228.

Tourism

Guadeloupe is a popular tourist destination, especially for visitors from France and the USA. The main attractions are the beaches, the mountainous scenery and the unspoilt beauty of the island dependencies. In 1986 there were more than 80 hotels providing a total of 4,109 rooms, and the number of visitors totalled 148,021.

Office du Tourisme: 5 square de la Banque, POB 1099, 97181 Pointe-à-Pitre; tel. 820930; telex 919715; Dir-Gen. Erick W. Rotin; Pres. Philippe Chaulet.

Bureau Industrie et Tourisme: Préfecture de la Guadeloupe, rue de Lardenoy, 97109 Basse-Terre; tel. 817681; telex 919707; Dir François Vosgien.

Syndicat d'Initiative de la Guadeloupe: 28 rue Sadi-Carnot, 97110 Pointe-à-Pitre; Pres. Dr Edouard Chartol.

MARTINIQUE

Introductory Survey

Location, Climate, Language, Religion, Capital

Martinique is one of the Windward islands in the West Indies, with Dominica to the north and Saint Lucia to the south. The island is dominated by the volcanic peak of Mont Pelée. The climate is tropical, but tempered by easterly and north-easterly breezes. The more humid and wet season runs from July to November, and the average temperature is 26°C (80°F). French is the official language, but a creole patois is widely spoken. The majority of the population profess Christianity and belong to the Roman Catholic Church. The capital is Fort-de-France.

Recent History

Martinique has been a French possession since 1635. The prosperity of the island was based on the sugar industry, which was dealt a devastating blow by the volcanic eruption of Mont Pelée in 1902. Martinique became a department of France in 1946, when the Governor was replaced by a Prefect, and an elected General Council was created.

The French Government's policy of assimilation since 1946 has created a strongly French society, bound by linguistic, cultural and economic ties to metropolitan France. The island enjoys a better infrastructure and a higher standard of living than its immediate Caribbean neighbours but, in consequence, it has also become heavily dependent on France. In 1960 the French Government granted the island's General Council the power to discuss political, as well as administrative, questions, partly in response to civil disturbances, and partly to the growth of nationalist feeling in the 1950s, as expressed by Aimé Césaire's Parti Progressiste Martiniquais (PPM), and the Parti Communiste Martiniquais (PCM). However, economic power remained concentrated in the hands of the *békés* (descendants of white colonial settlers), who own most of the agricultural land, and control the lucrative import/export market. This led to little incentive for innovation or self-sufficiency, and resentment at lingering colonial attitudes.

In 1974 Martinique, together with Guadeloupe and French Guiana, was given regional status as part of France's governmental reorganization. An indirectly-elected Regional Council was created, with some control over the local economy. In 1982 and 1983 the Socialist Government of President François Mitterrand, which had pledged itself to decentralizing power in favour of the overseas departments, made further concessions towards autonomy by giving the local councils greater control over taxation, local police and the economy. In the first direct elections to the new Regional Council, held in February 1983, left-wing parties gained a small majority of votes and seats. This success, and the election of Aimé Césaire as the Council's President, strengthened his influence against the pro-independence elements in his own party. Full independence for Martinique is supported by only a small minority of the population, while the majority seek reforms that would bring greater autonomy within French control. The Mouvement Indépendantiste Martiniquais (MIM), the most vocal of the separatist parties, fared badly in the elections, gaining less than 3% of the total vote. Late in 1983, and in 1984, Martinique became a target for the terrorist activities of the outlawed Alliance Révolutionnaire Caraïbe (ARC), which claimed responsibility for a number of bombings on the island. In August 1987 an explosion outside the main post office in Fort-de-France was attributed to pro-independence groups avenging the arrests in July of Luc Reinette and Henri Amédien of the ARC. At elections to an enlarged General Council, held in March 1985, the left-wing parties increased their representation, but the coalition of right-wing and centre parties maintained their control of the administration.

For the general election to the French National Assembly in March 1986, Martinique's representation was increased from three to four deputies. Martinique was the only French department in which the major left-wing parties presented a unified list of candidates (voting for the 1986 election being based on a system of proportional representation). The left-wing alliance received 51.2% of the votes, and two of its candidates were elected: Aimé Césaire (who retained his seat) and Louis-Joseph Dogué of the Fédération Socialiste de la Martinique (FSM), the local branch of the Parti Socialiste. The joint list of the right-wing Rassemblement pour la République (RPR) and the centrist Union pour la Démocratie Française (UDF) obtained 42.4% of the votes, and each party won one seat. For the concurrent elections to the Regional Council, the Union of the Left (including the PPM, the FSM and the PCM) similarly campaigned with a joint programme, winning 21 of the 41 seats (as the three parties had together won in 1983), although with a reduced share (41.3%) of the votes. The RPR and the UDF together obtained 49.8% of the votes and won the 20 remaining seats. Aimé Césaire retained the presidency of the Council until June 1988, when he relinquished the post to Camille Darsières.

In September 1986 indirect elections were held for the two Martinique seats in the French Senate. As in the March elections, the left-wing parties united, and, as a consequence, Martinique acquired a left-wing Senator for the first time since 1958: Rodolphe Désiré of the PPM was elected, while the other successful candidate was an incumbent Senator, Roger Lise of the UDF.

Following the recent trend in Martinique, the incumbent Socialist President won a decisive majority of the island's votes at the 1988 presidential election. President Mitterrand obtained 71% of the votes cast in Martinique in the second round of voting against Jacques Chirac of the RPR. Left-wing candidates secured all four seats at elections to the National Assembly in June (when the former single-member constituency system was reintroduced). Furthermore, in September–October, for the first time in 40 years the parties of the left achieved a majority at elections to the General Council, winning 23 of the 45 seats.

Government

France is represented in Martinique by an appointed Government Commissioner. There are two councils with local powers: the 45-member General Council and the 41-member Regional Council. Both are elected by universal adult suffrage for a period of up to six years. Martinique elects four deputies to the French National Assembly in Paris, and sends two indirectly elected representatives to the Senate.

Defence

In 1988 France maintained a military force of about 8,000 in French Guiana and the Antilles.

Economic Affairs

Martinique's economic development, in common with that of Guadeloupe, has created a society that combines a relatively high standard of living, and the benefits of a developed island, with a weak economic base in agricultural and industrial production, and a chronic trade deficit. This has contributed to problems such as high unemployment, emigration and social unrest. In 1985, according to estimates by the World Bank, Martinique's gross domestic product (GDP), measured at average 1983–85 prices, was US $1,400m., equivalent to $4,280 per head.

Sugar cane is the main agricultural crop, but the plantations have been allowed to decline in order to protect growers of sugar beet in France and other EEC countries. Martinique's annual output of raw sugar fell from 12,500 metric tons in 1968 to 2,000 tons in 1982, while only one sugar mill remained in production on the island. Martinique's sugar production now fails to satisfy one-quarter of local demand, and sugar is imported from Guadeloupe. Production increased in 1983, and reached 8,379 tons in 1986, although the level of output was expected to decline in subsequent years. Most of the cane crop is used in the production of rum for export. Total output of rum was 97,245 hl in 1986. In the 1970s local investment was diverted from sugar cane towards the development of banana plantations. Bananas are the second major crop, but the plantations suffered damage from Hurricane Allen in 1980. Total production of bananas in 1986 was an estimated 203,000 metric tons. Exports of bananas increased from 161,799 tons in 1984 to an estimated 178,000 tons in 1988. The Government is attempting to diversify agricultural products by developing underused areas of the country, and encouraging smallholders. Pineapples, aubergines, avocados and other tropical fruits are produced for the export market. However, the agricultural sector provides only about 6% of GDP, and the island still remains dependent on imported food supplies. A large proportion of the island's meat requirements has to be imported, and virtually all the vegetables. This contributes to the massive trade deficit, which increased from US $532.2m. in 1984 to $670.5m. in 1986 and to about $926m. in 1987. The fishing sector has received substantial investment, but the total catch declined from an estimated 5,500 tons in 1982 to 4,038 tons in 1986.

Light industry and small businesses have been encouraged by specialist government agencies in an attempt to fill the gap left by the decline in agriculture. Two industrial zones have been established, tax incentives are in operation, and 154m. francs were invested between 1980 and 1983. However, industry provides only about 10% of GDP and employs 6,000 of the workforce. Between 1960 and 1980 the percentage of the working population employed in agricultural and industrial production declined from 62% to 29%. The majority of workers are employed in services and administration, and investment by the white landowners has been redirected into the more profitable food import and tourism sectors. There is also a large community of white civil servants, and other immigrants from France, attracted by the high standard of living and the close links with France.

Tourism is a major activity on the island and one of the most important sources of foreign exchange. The numbers of tourists have fallen since 1981, partly owing to the recession, and partly as a result of the terrorist campaign in which bombs were planted outside hotels. In 1986 there were 150,316 visitors to Martinique. A new two-berth cruise ship terminal is to be built at Baie des Flamands, near Fort-de-France, at a projected cost of 20m. francs. This should reverse the trend of cruise ships' ceasing to call at Martinique, which has led to a decline in the number of tourists. In 1985 stop-over arrivals totalled 190,255, and the number of cruise-ship passengers increased by almost 13%.

Unemployment is high, especially in the under-25 age group; in 1985 it was estimated to affect between 25% and 30% of the labour force. There is extensive emigration to France and, to a lesser extent, French Guiana, at a rate of about 15,000 annually. The linking of wage levels to those of metropolitan France, despite the island's lower level of productivity, has increased labour costs and restricted development. France supports Martinique's economy by providing large amounts of government aid. Jacques Chirac's 'social parity' plan, approved by the French National Assembly in 1987, aimed to improve infrastructure and housing, and to reactivate the economy with the establishment of free-trade zones to encourage exports.

Social Welfare

Martinique has a system of social welfare similar to that of metropolitan France. In 1981 there were 14 hospitals, with a total of 4,117 beds, and 361 physicians.

Education

There is free and compulsory education in government schools for children aged six to 16 years. Higher education in law, science and economics is provided by a branch of the Université Antilles-Guyane.

Public Holidays

1989: 2 January (for New Year's Day), 24–27 March (Easter), 1 May (Labour Day), 4 May (Ascension Day), 15 May (Whit Monday), 14 July (National Day), 11 November (Armistice Day), 25 December (Christmas Day).

1990: 1 January (New Year's Day), 13–16 April (Easter), 1 May (Labour Day), 24 May (Ascension Day), 4 June (Whit Monday), 14 July (National Day), 11 November (Armistice Day), 25 December (Christmas Day).

Weights and Measures

The metric system is in use.

Statistical Survey

Source: Institut national de la statistique et des études économiques, Pointe de Jaham Schoëlcher, BP 605, 97261 Fort-de-France; tel. 717179.

AREA AND POPULATION

Area: 1,100 sq km (424.7 sq miles).

Population: 326,717 (males 158,415, females 168,302) at census of 9 March 1982; 335,130 (estimate for 1 January 1988); *Capital:* Fort-de-France, population 110,000 (1987). *Other towns* (population at 1982 census): Le Lamentin 26,367; Saint-Marie 18,094; Le François 14,383.

Births and Deaths (1987): Registered live births 6,388 (birth rate 19.0 per 1,000); Registered deaths 2,152 (death rate 6.5 per 1,000).

Economically Active Population (persons aged 16 years and over, 1982 census): Agriculture, hunting, forestry and fishing 9,844; Mining and quarrying 1,853; Manufacturing 4,001; Electricity, gas and water 1,006; Construction 7,832; Trade, restaurants and hotels 9,864; Transport, storage and communications 5,197; Financing, insurance, real estate and business services 17,878; Community, social and personal services 29,382; Activities not adequately defined 7,707; Total employed 94,564 (males 54,121, females 40,443); Unemployed 35,936 (males 18,086, females 17,850); Total labour force 130,500 (males 72,207, females 58,293).

1986: Total employed 94,800 (males 48,300, females 46,500); Unemployed 42,800 (males 19,600, females 23,000); Total labour force 137,400 (males 68,900, females 69,500).

Martinique

AGRICULTURE, ETC.

Principal Crops (FAO estimates, '000 metric tons, 1986): Roots and tubers 40, Sugar cane 232, Bananas 203, Pineapples 26. Source: FAO, *Production Yearbook*.

Livestock (FAO estimates, year ending September 1986): Cattle 41,000, Pigs 45,000, Sheep 87,000, Goats 45,000. Source: FAO, *Production Yearbook*.

Forestry (1978): Roundwood removals 11,000 cubic metres.

Fishing (metric tons, live weight): Total catch 5,174* in 1984; 4,604* in 1985; 4,038 in 1986.

*FAO estimate (Source: FAO, *Yearbook of Fishery Statistics*).

INDUSTRY

Production (1986): Raw sugar 8,379 metric tons, Rum 97,245 hl, Cement 191,000 metric tons (1985), Refined petroleum products 603,270 tons (1984), Electricity 415 million kWh.

FINANCE

Currency and Exchange Rates: French currency is used (see French Guiana).

Budget (estimates, 1987): Revenue and expenditure to balance at 1,340.5 million francs.

Aid from France (1982): 5,150 million francs.

Cost of Living (consumer price index; base: 1979=100): 190.8 in 1985; 195.8 in 1986; 202.9 in 1987.

Gross Domestic Product (million francs at current prices): 10,114 in 1983; 11,020 in 1984; 12,577 in 1985. Source: Le Secrétariat du Comité Monétaire de la Zone Franc: *La Zone Franc, Rapport 1987*.

EXTERNAL TRADE

Principal Commodities (US $ million, 1986): *Imports c.i.f.:* Food and live animals 162.5 (Meat and meat preparations 40.3); Petroleum and petroleum products 84.9 (Crude petroleum oils 63.8); Chemicals and related products 90.0; Basic manufactures 133.6; Machinery and transport equipment 204.1 (Electrical machinery, apparatus, etc. 54.6; Road vehicles and parts 79.5); Miscellaneous manufactured articles 145.9; Total (incl. others) 879.4. *Exports f.o.b.:* Food and live animals 115.6 (Bananas and plantains 102.5); Beverages 22.9 (Distilled alcoholic beverages 21.7); Refined petroleum products 37.7 (Gas oils 13.4; Residual fuel oils 16.2); Total (incl. others) 208.9. Source: UN, *International Trade Statistics Yearbook*.

Principal Trading Partners (US $ million, 1986): *Imports c.i.f.:* France 559.7; Fed. Repub. of Germany 24.2; Italy 36.1; Japan 22.9; United Kingdom 65.1; USA 21.5; Total (incl. others) 879.1. *Exports f.o.b.:* France 136.0; Fed. Repub. of Germany 8.3; Guadeloupe 53.8; Total (incl. others) 208.9. Source: UN, *International Trade Statistics Yearbook*.

TRANSPORT

Road Traffic (motor vehicles in use at 31 December 1984): Passenger cars 140,000; Buses and coaches 700; Goods vehicles 2,000. Source: IRF, *World Road Statistics*.

Shipping (freight traffic in '000 metric tons, 1984): Goods loaded 542.7; Goods unloaded 1,241.8.

Civil Aviation (1984): Passengers carried 949,700, Freight 10,373 metric tons.

TOURISM

Tourist Arrivals (1986): 150,316.

EDUCATION

Primary (1983): 224 schools, 2,004 teachers 43,287, 49,920 students (1986).

Secondary (1986): 75 schools, 3,065 teachers (1983), 43,287 students.

Higher (1986): 2,606 students at the Université Antilles-Guyane which, in Martinique, comprises a College of Economic Science and a College of Law. There is also a teacher-training college.

Directory

The Government
(February 1989)

Government Commissioner (Prefect): Jean Jouandet.
President of the General Council: Emile Maurice (RPR).

Deputies to the French National Assembly: Aimé Césaire (PPM), Louis-Joseph Dogué (FSM), Guy Lordinot (PPM/PCM/FSM), Claude Lise (PPM).

Representatives to the French Senate: Roger Lise (UDF), Rodolphe Désiré (PPM).

REGIONAL COUNCIL

President: Camille Darsières (PPM).
Vice-President: Georges de Vassoigne (PPM).

Election, 16 March 1986

	Votes	%	Seats
Union de la Gauche*	50,372	41.34	21
RPR	37,573	30.83	11
UDF	23,087	18.94	9
Others	5,807	8.89	—
Total	121,839	100.00	41

* Including the PPM, the FSM and the PCM.

Political Organizations

Fédération Socialiste de la Martinique (FSM): Cité la Meynard, 97200 Fort-de-France; tel. 503477; local branch of the Parti Socialiste; Leader Michel Yoyo.

Groupe Révolution Socialiste (GRS): 40 rue Pierre Semar, 97200 Fort-de-France; tel. 703649; f. 1973; Trotskyist; Leader Gilbert Pago.

Mouvement Indépendantiste Martiniquais (MIM): Fort-de-France; pro-independence party; also known as La Parole au peuple; Leader Alfred Marie-Jeanne.

Parti Communiste Martiniquais (PCM): Fort-de-France; f. 1957; Leader Armand Nicolas.

Parti Progressiste Martiniquais (PPM): Fort-de-France; f. 1957; Pres. Aimé Césaire; Sec.-Gen. Camille Darsières.

*Rassemblement pour la République (RPR):** BP 448, 97205 Fort-de-France; Gaullist; Sec. Stephen Bagoe.

*Union pour la Démocratie Française (UDF):** Fort-de-France; centrist; Pres. Jean Maran.

Parti Républicain (PR): Fort-de-France; Leader Jean Bally.

*The RPR and the UDF allied to contest the 1988 legislative elections as the Union du Rassemblement du Centre (URC).

Judicial System

Cour d'Appel de Fort-de-France: Fort-de-France; tel. 706262; telex 912525; highest court for Martinique and French Guiana; Pres. Robert Bosc; Procurator-Gen. Henri Jacquemin.

Two Tribunaux de Grande Instance at Fort-de-France and Cayenne (French Guiana) and three Tribunaux d'Instance, two in Fort-de-France and one in Cayenne.

Religion

The majority of the population belong to the Roman Catholic Church.

CHRISTIANITY
The Roman Catholic Church

Martinique comprises a single archdiocese, with an estimated 290,000 adherents (nearly 90% of the total population) at 31 December 1985. The Archbishop participates in the Antilles Episcopal Conference, based in Kingston, Jamaica.

Archbishop of Fort-de-France: Maurice Marie-Sainte, Archevêché, Route du Viet-Nâm héroïque, BP 586, 97207 Fort-de-France; tel. 637070.

The Press

Antilla: BP 46, Lamentin; tel. 500868; weekly; Dir Alfred Fortune.

L'Arbalète: Cité Saint-Georges, Fort-de-France; weekly.

Aujourd'hui Dimanche: presbytère de Bellevue, Fort-de-France; tel. 714897; weekly; Dir Père Gauthier; circ. 12,000.

FRENCH OVERSEAS DEPARTMENTS *Martinique*

Carib Hebdo: 23 rue Yves Goussard, Fort-de-France; Dir MAURICE TAÏLAMÉ.

Combat Ouvrier: BP 386, 97258 Fort-de-France; weekly; Dir M. G. BEAUJOUR.

France-Antilles: place Stalingrad, 97200 Fort-de-France; tel. 710883; telex 912677; f. 1964; daily; Dir PIERRE LENÔTRE; circ. 30,000 (Martinique edition).

Information Caraïbe (ICAR): 18 allée des Perruches, 97200 Fort-de-France; tel. 643740; weekly; Editor DANIEL COMPÈRE; circ. 1,500.

Justice: rue E. Zola, Fort-de-France; weekly; organ of the PPM; Dir G. THIMOTÉE; circ. 8,000.

Le Naif: voie no 7, route du Lamentin, Fort-de-France; weekly; Dir R. LAOUCHEZ.

Le Progressiste: rue de Tallis Clarière, Fort-de-France; weekly; organ of the PPM; Dir PAUL GABOURG; circ. 13,000.

Révolution Socialiste: BP 1031, 97200 Fort-de-France; tel. 703649; f. 1973; weekly; organ of the GRS; Dir PHILIPPE PIERRE CHARLES; circ. 2,500.

L'Union: weekly; organ of l'Union Departmentaliste Martiniquaise; Fort-de-France; Dir JEAN MARAN.

Radio and Television

In 1986 there were an estimated 58,000 radio receivers and 45,000 television receivers in use. The establishment of a private local television channel was approved in 1987.

Radio-Télévision Française d'Outre-mer (RFO): La Clairère, BP 662, Fort-de-France; tel. 711660; Dir PIERRE GIRARD.

Radio Caraïbe Internationale (RCI): BP 1111, 97248 Fort-de-France; tel. 636555; telex 912579; Dir-Gen. OLIVIER GARON.

Finance

(cap. = capital; dep. = deposits; m. = million; frs = French francs; brs = branches)

BANKING

Central Bank

Caisse Centrale de Coopération Economique: 12 blvd du Général de Gaulle, BP 804, 97200 Fort-de-France; Dir JEAN BRUTOT.

Major Commercial Banks

Banque des Antilles Françaises: 34 rue Lamartine, 97200 Fort-de-France; tel. 719344; f. 1853; cap. 32.5m. frs (1983); Pres. Dir BERNARD NOGRET.

Banque Française Commerciale: 6–10 rue Ernest Deproge, 97200 Fort-de-France; telex 912526; cap. 50m. frs (1983); Dir HENRI DE MALEZIEUX.

Banque Nationale de Paris: 72 ave des Caraïbes, 97200 Fort-de-France; tel. 737111; telex 912619; Dir MICHEL MASSE.

Caisse Nationale d'Epargne et de Prévoyance: 82 rue Perrinon, 97200 Fort-de-France; telex 912435; Dir Mme M. E. ANDRE.

Caisse Régionale de Crédit Agricole Mutuel: 106 blvd Général de Gaulle, BP 583, 97207 Fort-de-France; tel. 717607; telex 912657; f. 1950; 9,500 mems; Pres. M. SAINTE-ROSE; Dir MAURICE LAOUCHEZ; 27 brs.

Crédit Maritime Mutuel: 45 rue Victor Hugo, 97200 Fort-de-France; tel. 730093; telex 912477.

Crédit Martiniquais: rue de la Liberté, Fort-de-France; tel. 701240; telex 029612; f. 1922; associated with Crédit Lyonnais (France), Banque Paribas (France) and, since 1987, with Chase Manhattan Bank (USA); cap. 113.4m. frs (1987); Pres. (vacant); Gen. Man. PIERRE MICHAUX; 10 brs.

Crédit Ouvrier: 30 rue Franklin Roosevelt, Fort-de-France; Dir ALAIN LOUTOBY.

Crédit Populaire: ave Jean Jaurès, 97200 Fort-de-France; Dir M. L. ASSELIN DE BEAUVILLE.

Crédit Social des Fonctionnaires: 63 rue Perrion, 97200 Fort-de-France; Dir FRED AUGUSTIN.

Société Générale de Banque aux Antilles: 19 rue de la Liberté, BP 408, 97200 Fort-de-France; tel. 716983; telex 912545; f. 1979; cap. 15m. frs; Dir MICHEL SAMOUR.

Société Martiniquaise de Financement (SOMAFI): route de Saint Thérèse, 97200 Fort-de-France; Dir JEAN MACHET.

INSURANCE

Cie Antillaise d'Assurances: 19 rue de la Liberté, 97205 Fort-de-France; tel. 730450.

Caraïbe Assurances: 11 rue Victor Hugo, BP 210, 97202 Fort-de-France; tel. 639229; telex 912096.

Groupement Français d'Assurances: 46–48 rue Ernest Deproge, 97205 Fort-de-France; tel. 605455; telex 912403.

La Nationale (GAN): 30 blvd Général de Gaulle, BP 185, Fort-de-France; tel. 713007; Reps MARCEL and ROGER BOULLANGER.

La Protectrice: 27 rue Blénac, 97205 Fort-de-France; tel. 702545; Rep. RENÉ MAXIMIN.

Le Secours: 74 ave Duparquet, 97200 Fort-de-France; tel. 700379; Dir Y. ANGANI.

L'Union des Assurances de Paris: 28 rue de la République, Fort-de-France; tel. 700470; Rep. R. DE REYNAL.

Trade and Industry

CHAMBER OF COMMERCE

Chambre de Commerce et d'Industrie de la Martinique: 50–56 rue Ernest Deproge, Fort-de-France; tel. 630008; telex 912633; f. 1907; Pres. ALEX HUYGHUES-DESPOINTES; Dir-Gen. HENRI TITINA; 26 mems.

DEVELOPMENT

Agence pour le Développement Economique de la Martinique: 26 rue Lamartine; BP 803, 97244 Fort-de-France; tel. 734581; telex 912946; f. 1979; promotion of industry.

Bureau de l'Industrie de l'Artisanat: Préfecture, 97262 Fort-de-France; tel. 713627; telex 029650; f. 1960; government agency; research, documentation and technical and administrative advice on investment in industry and tourism; Dir RAPHAËL FIRMIN.

Société de Crédit pour le Développement de la Martinique (SODEMA): 12 blvd du Général de Gaulle, BP 575, 97242 Fort-de-France; tel. 605578; telex 91402; f. 1970; cap. 22.8m. frs; medium- and long-term finance.

Société de Développement Régional Antilles-Guyane (SODERAG): 109 rue Ernest Deproge, 97200 Fort-de-France; tel. 635978; telex 912343; Dir-Gen. FERNAND LERYCHARD; Sec.-Gen. OLYMPE FRANCIL.

ASSOCIATIONS

Chambre Départementale d'Agriculture: 55 rue Isambert, BP 432, Fort-de-France; tel. 715146; Pres. MARCEL FABRE.

Chambre de Métiers de la Martinique: Morne Tartenson, 97200 Fort-de-France; tel. 713222; f. 1970; 40 mems; Pres. MAURICE TAILAME.

Groupement de Producteurs d'Ananas de la Martinique: BP 12, 97201 Fort-de-France; f. 1967; Pres. C. DE GRYSE.

Société Coopérative d'Intérêt Collectif Agricole Bananière de la Martinique (SICABAM): Domaine de Montgéralde, Dillon, 97200 Fort-de-France; telex 912617; f. 1961; 1,000 mems; Pres. ALEX ASSIER DE POMPIGNAN; Dir GÉRARD BALLY.

Syndicat des Distilleries Agricoles: Immeuble Clément, rive droite Levassor, Fort-de-France; tel. 712546.

Syndicat des Producteurs de Rhum Agricole: Dillon, 97200 Fort-de-France.

Union Départementale des Coopératives Agricoles de la Martinique: Fort-de-France; Pres. M. URSULET.

TRADE UNIONS AND PROFESSIONAL ORGANIZATIONS

Centrale Démocratique Martiniquaise des Travailleurs: BP 21, 97201 Fort-de-France; Sec.-Gen. LINE BEAUSOLEIL.

Chambre Syndicale des Hôtels de Tourisme de la Martinique: Entrée Montgéralde, Route de Chateauboeuf, BP 1011, Fort-de-France; tel. 702780.

Confédération Générale du Travail: Maison des Syndicats, Jardin Desclieux, Fort-de-France; tel. 712589; f. 1936; affiliated to WFTU; Sec.-Gen. VICTOR LAMON; about 12,000 mems.

Ordre des Médecins de la Martinique: 35 rue Victor-Sévère, 97200 Fort-de-France; tel. 632701; Pres. Dr RENÉ LEGENDRI.

Ordre des Pharmaciens de la Martinique: Zone Industrielle de la Lézarde, 97232 Lamentin; tel. 511356.

Syndicat National des Instituteurs: 3 rue de la Mutualité, Fort-de-France.

Union Départementale des Syndicats—FO: BP 1114, 97209 Fort-de-France; affiliated to ICFTU; Sec.-Gen. R. FABIEN; about 2,000 mems.

Transport

RAILWAYS

There are no railways in Martinique.

FRENCH OVERSEAS DEPARTMENTS *Martinique, Réunion*

ROADS
There are 267 km of autoroutes and first class roads, and 615 km of secondary roads.

SHIPPING
Alcoa Steamship Co, Alpine Line, Agdwa Line, Delta Line, Raymond Witcomb Co, Moore MacCormack, Eastern Steamship Co: c/o Ets René Cottrell, 48 rue Ernest Deproge, Fort-de-France.

Compagnie Générale Maritime: BP 574, ave Maurice Bishop, 97206 Fort-de-France; tel. 630040; telex 912049; also represents other passenger and freight lines; Rep. GUY ADAM.

Compagnie de navigation Mixte: Immeuble Rocade, La Dillon, BP 1023, 97209 Fort-de-France; Rep. R. M. MICHAUX.

Compagnie Maritime des Chargeurs Réunis: 34 rue Ernest Deproge, 97200 Fort-de-France; Rep. M. G. PLISSONNEAU.

CIVIL AVIATION
Martinique's international airport is at Lamentin, 6 km from Fort-de-France, and is served by the following airlines: Air Canada, American Airlines (USA), Air France, LIAT (Antigua) and Air Martinique. A new terminal is to be built at Lamentin at a cost of 300m. francs, and should be completed in 1993.

Air Martinique: Aéroport du Lamentin, 97232 Le Lamentin; tel. 510990; telex 912048; f. 1981; scheduled and charter services within the lesser Antilles; Chair. MICHEL ZEIGLER; Dir-Gen. MICHEL GOUZE; fleet of 2 Twin Otters and 2 ATR 42.

Tourism

Martinique's tourist attractions are its beaches and coastal scenery, its mountainous interior, and the historic towns of Fort-de-France and St Pierre. Tourist arrivals totalled 150,316 in 1986.

Délégation Régionale au Tourisme: 41 rue Gabriel Péri, 97200 Fort-de-France; tel. 631861; Dir GILBERT LECURIEUK.

Office du Tourisme: Pavillon du Tourisme, blvd Alfassa, BP 520, 97206 Fort-de-France; tel. 637960; telex 912678; f. 1938; Pres. JEAN-BAPTISTE EDMOND; Dir JACQUES GUANNEL.

Syndicat d'Initiative: BP 299, 97203 Fort-de-France; Pres. M. R. ROSE-ROSETTE.

RÉUNION

Introductory Survey

Location, Climate, Language, Religion, Capital

Réunion is an island in the Indian Ocean, lying about 800 km (500 miles) east of Madagascar. The climate varies greatly according to altitude: at sea-level it is tropical, with average temperatures between 20°C (68°F) and 28°C (82°F), but in the uplands it is much cooler, with average temperatures between 8°C (46°F) and 19°C (66°F). Rainfall is abundant, averaging 4,714 mm annually in the uplands, and 686 mm at sea-level. The population is of mixed origin, including people of European, African, Indian and Chinese descent. The official language is French. A large majority of the population are Christians belonging to the Roman Catholic Church. The capital is Saint-Denis.

Recent History

Réunion was first occupied by France in 1642, and was ruled as a colony until 1946, when, in common with certain Caribbean territories, it received full departmental status. In 1974 it became an Overseas Department with the status of a region.

In June 1978 the liberation committee of the OAU adopted a report recommending measures to hasten the independence of the island, and condemned its occupation by a 'colonial power'. However, this view seems to have little support among the people of Réunion themselves. Although the left-wing political parties on the island advocate increased autonomy (amounting to virtual self-government), few people are in favour of complete independence.

In 1982 the French Government proposed a decentralization scheme, envisaging the dissolution of the General and Regional Councils in the Overseas Departments and the creation in each territory of a single assembly, to be elected on the basis of proportional representation. However, this plan met with considerable opposition in Réunion and the other Overseas Departments, and the Government was eventually forced to abandon the project. Revised legislation on decentralization in the Overseas Departments was approved by the French National Assembly in December 1982. Elections for the new Regional Council were held in Réunion in February 1983, when left-wing candidates won 50.77% of the votes cast.

For the general election to the French National Assembly in March 1986, Réunion's representation was increased from three to five deputies. At this election voting was based on a system of proportional representation. The Parti Communiste Réunionnais (PCR) won two seats, while the Union pour la Démocratie Française (UDF), the Rassemblement pour la République (RPR) and a newly-formed right-wing party, France-Réunion-Avenir (FRA), each secured one seat. In the concurrent elections to the Regional Council, the centre-right RPR-UDF alliance and FRA together received 54.1% of the votes cast, winning respectively 18 and eight of the 45 seats, while the PCR won 13 seats. Pierre Lagourgue of FRA was elected President of the Regional Council.

In September 1986 the French Government's plan to introduce a programme of economic reforms (see Economic Affairs) provoked criticism from the left-wing parties, who claimed that the proposals should grant the Overseas Departments social equality with metropolitan France through similar levels of taxation and benefits. In October Paul Vergès, the PCR Secretary-General and a deputy to the French National Assembly, accused France of instituting 'social apartheid' in the Overseas Departments, and presented his case to the European Parliament in Strasbourg. In October 1987 Vergès and the other PCR deputy, Elie Hoarau, resigned from the National Assembly, in protest against the Government's proposals, and Laurent Vergès, Paul Vergès's son, and Claude Hoarau, the PCR mayor of Saint-Louis, filled the vacated seats.

In January 1988 a French government proposal to redraw the boundaries of Réunion's administrative districts (cantons) was rejected by the General Council. The proposal was initiated by Auguste Legros, the RPR President of the General Council and mayor of Saint-Denis, and Michel Debré, the island's RPR deputy (and a former French Prime Minister), and was opposed by the Parti Socialiste (PS), the PCR, and by UDF councillors from the RPR-UDF alliance, who resented the extent of power held by Legros, and believed that the proposed boundary changes would, if implemented, be detrimental to the rural districts.

In the second round of the French presidential election on 8 May 1988, François Mitterrand, the incumbent President and PS candidate, received 60.3% of the votes cast in Réunion, whereas Jacques Chirac, the RPR Prime Minister, obtained only 39.7%. Mitterrand won an absolute majority of votes in all five electoral districts in Réunion, including the RPR stronghold of Saint-Denis, owing partly to the transfer of votes from supporters of the PCR and the centre-right parties. Following his re-election, Mitterrand called a general election for the French National assembly in June, when the system of single-member constituencies was reintroduced. As in the previous general election, the PCR won two seats, while the UDF, the RPR (these two parties allying to form the Union du Rassemblement du Centre—URC) and the FRA each won one seat. Following the election, however, relations between the PCR and then PS deteriorated, as the PCR accused the PS of failing to encourage its supporters to transfer their support to the PCR candidate for Saint-André in the second round of the election, thus ensuring that the rival UDF candidate won the seat. The PS counterclaimed that the PCR had advised its supporters not to vote for the PS candidate for Saint-Denis in the second round. In July the PCR criticized the Socialist Government for continuing to allocate lower levels of benefits and revenue to the Overseas Departments, despite President Mitterrand's promise, made during his visit to Réunion in February, to grant these departments social equity with metropolitan France.

In the elections for the newly-enlarged 44-member General Council in September and October 1988, the PCR and the PS won nine and four seats respectively, while other leftist candidates won two seats. The UDF secured six seats and other right-wing candidates took 19, but the RPR, which had previously held 11 seats, won only four. Later in October, Eric Boyer, a right-wing independent, was elected to succeed Legros as President of the General Council. In the same month, the PCR deputy, Laurent Vergès was killed in a road accident. His seat was subsequently taken by Alexis Pota, another member of the PCR. However, Paul Vergès, the PCR Secretary-General, asked Pota to resign, with the apparent intention of taking the seat himself upon the expiry of his term of office as a member of the European Parliament in 1989. Pota refused, and in December he announced that he would not support a list of PCR candidates for Saint-Paul, to be drawn up by Vergès in preparation for the municipal elections in March 1989, as Vergès had excluded him from the electoral campaign.

FRENCH OVERSEAS DEPARTMENTS

Réunion

In December 1988 the French Government announced that a regional development programme for the Overseas Departments would be implemented in 1989. The Government also proposed to establish a commission in January 1989 to determine how the newly-introduced guaranteed minimum income (see France) should be applied in the Overseas Departments.

In January 1986 France was admitted to the Indian Ocean Commission (IOC, see p. 219), on account of its sovereignty over Réunion. Réunion was given the right to host ministerial meetings of the IOC, but would not be allowed to occupy the presidency, owing to its status as a non-sovereign state.

Government
France is represented in Réunion by an appointed Government Commissioner. There are two councils with local powers: the 44-member General Council and the 45-member Regional Council. Both are elected for up to six years by direct universal suffrage. Réunion sends five directly elected deputies to the National Assembly in Paris and three indirectly elected representatives to the Senate.

Defence
Réunion is the headquarters of French military forces in the Indian Ocean. In June 1988 there were 3,300 French troops stationed on Réunion and Mayotte.

Economic Affairs
The economy has traditionally been based on agriculture, which employed 13.7% of the working population in 1986. Sugar cane is the principal crop and has formed the basis of the economy for over a century. Only 26% of the land area can be cultivated because of the volcanic origin of the soil, but over 70% of the arable land is used for sugar cane. Annual production of raw sugar declined from 246,400 tons in 1984 to 229,000 tons in 1985. Production of raw sugar recovered in 1986, reaching 243,800 tons, but output fell to 225,576 tons in 1987, owing to severe damage to the cane crop, resulting from a cyclone in February 1987. In 1986 state aid totalling 45 francs per ton of sugar was given directly to farmers for the first time, and in 1987 aid was increased to 48 francs per ton. In 1987 sugar exports accounted for 77.4% of total exports by value. The volume of sugar exports increased by 3.8%, although their value fell by 6.9%, compared with 1986. Other crops include vanilla, tobacco and geraniums, vetiver and ylang-ylang, which are grown for the production of tropical essences. Réunion is far from self-sufficient in food, and substantial imports are necessary. The only industry of importance is the processing of sugar and rum.

France remains the major trading partner, supplying 67.9% of imports and buying 71.4% of exports in 1987. However, Réunion suffers from a substantial trade deficit: in 1987 receipts from exports covered only 11.2% of the import bill. The deficit is partly offset by financial support from France and by receipts from expatriate workers. Tourism is becoming more important, and it is hoped that increased investment in this sector will lead to higher receipts and will help to reduce the trade deficit, as well as providing new jobs. In 1988 Réunion received an EEC loan to stimulate the sector. The rate of population growth has dropped sharply since 1973, from 3% per year to around 1.7%, but the population density remains extremely high (228 per sq km in 1988). Réunion has a high level of unemployment. The 1982 census recorded 54,338 people, or 31.4% of the labour force, as unemployed, and by the end of 1987 the number of unemployed had exceeded 73,000, or 35% of the labour force. Unemployment was expected to reach 80,000 in 1988. Since 1980 the Government has invested heavily in a series of public works projects in an effort to create jobs and to alleviate the high level of seasonal unemployment following the sugar cane harvest. In 1987 about 5,600 new jobs were created, mainly in the construction sector. However, large numbers of workers still emigrate in search of employment, principally to France.

In October 1986 the French Government introduced a programme of reforms to enhance the Overseas Departments' economic status by 1991. The reforms included a removal of taxation from investments in all economic sectors of the Overseas Departments for a renewable period of 10 years. The Integrated Development Operation (OID) for the Overseas Departments, initiated in 1979 by local assemblies in conjunction with the French Government, would be continued, and 400m. francs was to be provided for Réunion (over a five-year period) from various sources, including the French Government, the EEC, and from revenue resulting from the implementation of the 1986 programme of reforms. In December 1988 the French Government announced that it would instigate a regional development programme in the Overseas Departments in 1989, to be financed partly by EEC aid. The annual rate of inflation decreased from 13.9% in 1981 to 7.2% in 1985 and to 2.6% in 1986, before increasing slightly, to 2.8%, in 1987. In 1986, according to estimates by the World Bank, Réunion's gross domestic product (GDP), measured at average 1984–86 prices, was US $2,120m., equivalent to $3,940 per head. Between 1973 and 1986, it was estimated, GDP per head increased, in real terms, at an average rate of only 1.0% per year. Measured at current prices, Réunion's GDP totalled 16,337m. francs in 1985, 18,069m. francs in 1986 and an estimated 20,363m. francs in 1987. Réunion's economic future is largely dependent on France's willingness to continue the subsidies implicit in the island's status as a department, despite the low tax yield from its generally unprosperous citizens.

Social Welfare
In 1988 Réunion had 3,275 hospital beds, 837 physicians, 185 nurses and 212 dentists.

Education
Education is compulsory for children aged six to 16 years, and consists of five years' primary and five years' secondary schooling. In 1987 there were 505 primary schools and 69 secondary schools, comprising 59 junior comprehensives, or collèges, and 10 lycées, on the island. There is a university, with several faculties, a teacher training college, a technical institute and an agricultural college. In 1982 the illiteracy rate among the population over 15 years of age averaged 21.4% (males 23.5%; females 19.5%).

Weights and Measures
The metric system is in use.

Statistical Survey

Source: Institut National de la Statistique et des Etudes Economiques, Service Régional de la Réunion, Saint-Denis.

AREA AND POPULATION

Area: 2,512 sq km (970 sq miles).

Population: 515,798 (males 252,997, females 262,801) at census of 9 March 1982; 571,600 (estimate for 1 January 1988).

Principal Towns (population at 1982 census): Saint-Denis (capital) 109,068; Saint-Paul 58,410; Saint-Pierre 50,081.

Births and Deaths (1987): Registered live births 12,599 (birth rate 22.3 per 1,000); Registered deaths 3,090 (death rate 5.5 per 1,000). Figures exclude live-born infants dying before registration of birth.

Labour Force (1982 census): Employed 118,490 (males 77,270, females 41,220); Unemployed 54,338 (males 33,548, females 20,790).

AGRICULTURE, ETC.

Principal Agricultural Products (metric tons, 1987): Sugar cane 2,203,037, Raw sugar 225,576, Maize 10,450, Oil of geranium 15.3, Oil of vetiver root 12.1, Vanilla 132.8 Tobacco 209.0.

Livestock (FAO estimates, '000 head, year ending September 1986): Cattle 20, Pigs 72, Goats 44, Sheep 3.

Fishing (landings, metric tons): 2,180 (1985); 1,706 (1986); 1,554 (1987).

FINANCE

Currency and Exchange Rates: French currency is used (see French Guiana).

Budget (million francs, 1988): Revenue 3,326.6m.; Expenditure 3,326.6m.

Cost of Living (Consumer Price Index, average of monthly figures; base: 1980 = 100): 158.1 in 1985; 162.2 in 1986; 166.9 in 1987.

Expenditure on the Gross Domestic Product (million francs at current prices, 1987): Government final consumption expenditure 6,503; Private final consumption expenditure 16,811; Increase in stocks 125; Gross fixed capital formation 4,560; *Total domestic expenditure* 27,999; Exports of goods and services 1,115; *Less* Imports of goods and services 8,751; *GDP in purchasers' values* 20,363.

Gross Domestic Product by Economic Activity (million francs at current prices, 1982): Agriculture, hunting, forestry and fishing 828.2; Mining and manufacturing 1,125.8; Electricity, gas and water 225.1; Construction 638.5; Trade, restaurants and hotels 1,751.2; Transport, storage and communications 561.0; Finance, insurance, real estate and business services 1,340.7; Government services 3,495.7; Other community, social and personal services 1,558.6; Other services 301.5; *Sub-total* 11,826.3; Import duties 488.1; Value-added tax 510.6; *Less* Imputed bank service charge 538.7; *Total* 12,286.2.

FRENCH OVERSEAS DEPARTMENTS   *Réunion*

EXTERNAL TRADE

Principal Commodities (million francs): *Imports* (1987): Agricultural, fishing and forestry products 1,250, Processed agricultural products 550, Fuels 400, Intermediate goods 1,500, Capital goods 2,900, Consumer goods 2,150; Total 8,750. *Exports* (1987): Sugar 761.3, Rum 28.3, Oil of geranium 10.0, Vanilla 6.2, Oil of vetiver root 5.8, Spiny lobsters 25.9; Total (incl. others) 983.9.

Principal Trading Partners (million francs): *Imports* (1987): Bahrain 259.5, France 5,939.0, Federal Republic of Germany 252.7, Italy 305.6, Japan 229.8, South Africa 204.6; Total (incl. others) 8,751.2. *Exports* (1987): France 702.5, Others 281.4.

TRANSPORT

Road Traffic (1987): Motor vehicles in use 114,600.

Shipping (1987): Vessels entered 412; Freight unloaded 1,465,600 metric tons; Freight loaded 325,100 metric tons; Passenger arrivals (1986) 496; Passenger departures (1986) 478.

Civil Aviation (1987): Passenger arrivals 273,072; Passenger departures 277,411; Freight unloaded 9,499 metric tons; Freight loaded 3,207 metric tons.

COMMUNICATIONS MEDIA

Radio receivers (1986): 123,000 in use.

Television receivers (1987): 91,700 in use.

Telephones (1987): 122,000 in use.

Book production (1985): 73 titles (41 books; 32 pamphlets).

Daily newspapers (1984): 2 (average circulation 51,000 copies).

Non-daily newspapers (1982): 2 (average circulation 9,000 copies).

EDUCATION

Pre-primary: Teachers 1,336 (1986), Pupils 39,391 (1987/88), Schools 151 (1987).

Primary: Teachers 3,917 (1986), Pupils 74,714 (1987/88), Schools 354 (1987).

Secondary: Teachers 3,982 (1986), Pupils 72,753 (1987/88), Schools 69 (1987).

University: Teaching Staff 90 (1986/87), Students 3,564 (1987/88). There is also a teacher training college, a technical institute and an agricultural college.

Directory

The Government

(February 1989)

Government Commissioner (Prefect): JEAN ANCIAUX.
President of the General Council: ERIC BOYER (Independent).
Economic and Social Councillor: GUY JARNAC.
Deputies to the French National Assembly: AUGUSTE LEGROS (RPR), ALEXIS POTA (PCR), ELIE HOARAU (PCR), JEAN-PAUL VIRAPOULLÉ (UDF/CDS), ANDRÉ THIEN AH KOON (FRA).
Representatives to the French Senate: JOSEPH SINIMALÉ (RPR-UDF), ALBERT RAMASSAMY (PS), LOUIS VIRAPOULLÉ (Independent).

REGIONAL COUNCIL

Place Barachois, 97405 Saint-Denis.

President: PIERRE LAGOURGUE (FRA).

Election, 16 March 1986

Party	% of Votes	Seats
RPR-UDF	36.8	18
PCR	28.2	13
FRA and other right-wing	17.3	8
PS	14.1	6
Others	3.6	—
Total	100.0	45

Political Organizations

France-Réunion-Avenir (FRA): Saint-Denis; f. 1986; right-wing; Leader ANDRÉ THIEN AH KOON.

Front National (FN): Saint-Denis; f. 1972; extreme right-wing; Leader ALIX MOREL.

Mouvement des Radicaux de Gauche (MRG): BP 991, 97479 Saint-Denis; f. 1977; advocates full independence and an economy separate from, but assisted by, France; Pres. JEAN-MARIE FINCK.

Mouvement pour l'Indépendance de la Réunion (MIR): f. 1981 from Mouvement pour la libération de la Réunion; groups all those favouring autonomy.

Parti Communiste Réunionnais (PCR): Saint-Denis; f. 1959; Sec.-Gen. PAUL VERGÈS.

Parti Socialiste (PS)—Fédération de la Réunion: 85 rue d'Après, 97400 Saint-Denis; tel. 21-77-95; telex 916445; left-wing; Sec.-Gen. JEAN-CLAUDE FRUTEAU.

Rassemblement des Démocrates pour l'Avenir de la Réunion (RADAR): BP 866, 97477 Saint-Denis Cedex; f. 1981; centrist.

Rassemblement des Socialistes et des Démocrates (RSD): Saint-Denis; Sec.-Gen. DANIEL CADET.

Rassemblement pour la République (RPR): 25 rue Labourdonnais, 97400 Saint-Denis; tel. 20-21-18; telex 916080; Gaullist; Sec. for Réunion FRANÇOIS MAS.

Union pour la Démocratie Française (UDF): Saint-Denis; f. 1978; centrist; Sec.-Gen. GILBERT GÉRARD.

   Centre des Démocrates Sociaux (CDS).

   Parti Républicain (PR).

Judicial System

Cour d'appel: Palais de Justice, 166 rue Juliette Dodu, 97488 Saint-Denis; tel. 21-75-39; telex 916149; Pres. HENRI VRAY.

There are two **Tribunaux de grande instance,** one **Cour d'assises,** four **Tribunaux d'instance,** two **Tribunaux pour enfants** and two **Conseils de prud'hommes.**

Religion

A substantial majority of the population are adherents of the Roman Catholic Church.

CHRISTIANITY

The Roman Catholic Church

Réunion comprises a single diocese, directly responsible to the Holy See. At 31 December 1986 there were an estimated 488,000 adherents, representing about 90% of the population.

Bishop of La Réunion: Mgr GILBERT AUBRY, Evêché, 36 rue de Paris, BP 55, 97462 Saint-Denis; tel. 21-28-49.

The Press

DAILIES

Journal de l'Ile de la Réunion: 42 rue Alexis de Villeneuve, BP 98, 97463 Saint-Denis; tel. 21-32-64; telex 916453; f. 1956; Dir PHILIPPE BALOUKJY; circ. 26,000.

Quotidien de la Réunion: BP 303, 97467 Saint-Denis Cedex; tel. 28-10-10; telex 916183; f. 1976; Dir MAXIMIN CHANE KI CHUNE; circ. 23,000.

Témoignages: 21 bis rue de l'Est, BP 192, 97465 Saint-Denis; f. 1944; organ of the Parti Communiste Réunionnais; Dir ELIE HOARAU; circ. 6,000.

PERIODICALS

Al-Islam: 31 rue M. A. Leblond, BP 437, 97410 Saint-Pierre; tel. 25-19-65; publ. by the Centre Islamique de la Réunion; monthly; Dir SAÏD INGAR.

Cahiers de la Réunion et de l'Océan Indien: 24 blvd des Cocotiers, 97434 Saint-Gilles-les-Bains; monthly; Man. Dir CLAUDETTE SAINT-MARC.

Les Cahiers du Centre Universitaire de la Réunion: ave de la Victoire, 97400 Saint-Denis; Dir ANNE JACQUEMIN.

L'Economie de la Réunion: c/o INSEE, 15 rue de l'Ecole, Le Chaudron, 97490 Ste-Clothilde; tel. 29-51-57; 6 a year; Dir M. JACOD.

Gazette de l'Ile de la Réunion: angle rues Bouvet/Monthyon, Saint-Denis; weekly.

Le Memento Industriel et Commercial Réunionnais: 80 rue Pasteur, 97400 Saint-Denis; tel. 21-94-12; Dir CATHERINE LOUAPRE POTTIER; circ. 10,000.

FRENCH OVERSEAS DEPARTMENTS   *Réunion*

974 Ouest: Montgaillard, 97400 Saint-Denis; monthly; Dir DENISE ELMA.

Les Nouvelles Economiques: 5 bis rue de Paris, BP 120, 97463 Saint-Denis; tel. 21-53-66; telex 916278; monthly; Dir JEAN-PIERRE FOURTOY.

La Réunion Agricole: Chambre d'Agriculture, 24 rue de la Source, BP 134, 97464 Saint-Denis Cedex; tel. 21-25-88; monthly; Dir MARCEL BOLON; Chief Editor RENÉ BOUISSEAU; circ. 8,000.

Télé 7 Jours Réunion: BP 405, 9469 Saint-Denis; weekly; Dir MICHEL MEKDOUD; circ. 25,000.

Témoignage Chrétien de la Réunion: 21 bis rue de l'Est, 97465 Saint-Denis; weekly; Dir RENÉ PAYET; circ. 2,000.

Visu: BP 3000, 97402 Saint-Denis; tel. 29-10-10; weekly; Editor-in-Chief J. J. AYAN; circ. 53,000.

Radio and Television

There were an estimated 120,000 radio receivers in use in 1983 and 91,200 television receivers (including 49,400 colour receivers) in use in 1986. Since 1985 there has been a growth in the number of private local radio stations. In 1987 the French national broadcasting commission approved the formation of a private local television channel.

Radio France d'Outre-Mer (RFO): place Sarda Garriga, BP 309, 97405 Saint-Denis; tel. 21-34-56; home radio and television relay services in French; a second TV channel was opened in 1983; Dir ALAIN QUINTRIE-LAMOTHE.

Télé Free-DOM: Saint-Denis; f. 1986; privately-owned TV service; Dir Dr CAMILLE SUDRE.

Other privately-owned television services include TVB, RTV and TV-Run.

Finance

(cap. = capital; res = reserves; dep. = deposits; brs = branches; amounts in French francs)

BANKING

Central Bank

Institut d'Emission des Départements d'Outre-mer: 1 cité du Retiro, 75008 Paris, France; Office in Réunion: 4 rue de la Compagnie, 97487 Saint-Denis Cedex; tel. 21-18-96; Dir JACQUES PIERRAT.

Commercial Banks

Banque Française Commerciale: 60 rue Alexis de Villeneuve, 97400 Saint-Denis; tel. 21-82-50; telex 916162; affiliated to Banque Indosuez; Dir ROGER VINCENTI; 8 brs.

Banque Nationale de Paris Intercontinentale: 67 rue Juliette Dodu, BP 113, 97463 Saint-Denis; telex 916133; Man. Dir SERGE NICOLAOUI; 13 brs.

Banque de la Réunion, SA: 27 rue Jean-Chatel, 97400 Saint-Denis; tel. 21-32-20; telex 916134; f. 1849; affiliated to Crédit Lyonnais; cap. and res 159.3m., dep. 2,599.8m. (1986); Pres. TANNEGUY DE F. DE CHAUVIN; Man. Dir JEAN-FRANÇOIS MAULANDI; 12 brs.

Caisse Régionale de Crédit Agricole Mutuel de la Réunion: cité des Lauriers 'les Camélias', BP 84, 97462 Saint-Denis; f. 1949; affiliate of Caisse Nationale de Crédit Agricole; Chair. HENRY ISAUTIER; Dir HENRI PAVIE.

Development Bank

Banque Populaire Fédérale de Développement: 33 rue Victor MacAuliffe, 97400 Saint-Denis; tel. 21-18-11; telex 916582; Dir OLIVIER DEVISME; 3 brs.

INSURANCE

More than 20 major European insurance companies are represented in Saint-Denis.

Trade and Industry

Association pour le Développement industriel de la Réunion: 18 rue Milius, 97468 Saint-Denis Cedex; f. 1975; 154 mems; Pres. RAPHAËL CHANE-NAM.

Chambre de Commerce et d'Industrie de la Réunion: 25 bis rue de Paris, BP 120, 97463 Saint-Denis; telex 916278; f. 1830; Pres. ALEX HOW-CHOONG; Man. Dir JEAN-PIERRE FOURTOY.

Direction de l'Action Economique: Secrétariat Général pour les Affairs Economiques, ave de la Victoire, 97405 Saint-Denis; tel. 21-86-10; telex 916111.

Jeune Chambre Economique de Saint-Denis de la Réunion: 25 rue de Paris, BP 1151, 97483 Saint-Denis; f. 1963; 30 mems; Chair. OLIVIER MOREAU.

Société de Développement Economique de la Réunion (SODERE): 26 rue Labourdonnais, 97469 Saint-Denis; tel. 20-01-68; telex 916471; f. 1964; Chair. PIERRE PEYRON; Man. Dir ALBERT TRIMAILLE.

Syndicat des Exportateurs d'Huiles Essentielles, Plantes Aromatiques et Medicinales de Bourbon: 38 bis rue Labourdonnais, 97400 Saint-Denis; tel. 20-10-23; exports oil of geranium, vetiver and vanilla; Pres. RICO PLOENIÈRES.

Syndicat des Fabricants de Sucre de la Réunion: BP 57, 97462 Saint-Denis; tel. 21-67-00; telex 916138; Chair. ARMAND BARAU.

Syndicat des Producteurs de Rhum de la Réunion: BP 57, 97462 Saint-Denis; tel. 21-67-00; telex 916138; Chair. ARMAND BARAU.

Syndicat Patronal du Bâtiment de la Réunion: BP108, 97463 Saint-Denis; tel. 21-03-81; telex 916393; Pres. B. LENFANT; Sec.-Gen. Mlle C. D'HANENS.

TRADE UNIONS

Confédération Générale du Travail de la Réunion (CGTR): 104 rue Maréchal Leclerc, 97400 Saint-Denis; Sec.-Gen. BRUNY PAYET.

Réunion also has its own sections of the major French trade union confederations, **Confédération Française Démocratique du Travail (CFDT)**, **Force Ouvrière (FO)**, **Confédération Française de l'Encadrement** and **Confédération Française des Travailleurs Chrétiens (CFTC)**.

Transport

ROADS

A route nationale circles the island, generally following the coast and linking all the main towns. Another route nationale crosses the island from south-west to north-east linking Saint-Pierre and Saint-Benoît. In 1982 there were 345.7 km of routes nationales, 731.5 km of departmental roads and 1,602.9 km of other roads. Many roads were damaged by a cyclone in February 1987.

SHIPPING

In 1986 work started on the expansion of the Port de la Pointe des Galets.

Compagnie Générale Maritime (CGM): 2 rue de l'Est, BP 10, 97420 Le Port; tel. 42-00-88; agents for Mitsui OSK Lines, Unicorn Lines, Black Sea Shipping, Marine Chartering, Taiyo Shipping, Unigas Oceangas; Dir HENRI-PIERRE SIGNEUX.

Navale et Commerciale Havraise Péninsulaire: rue de St Paul, BP 29, 97420 Le Port; freight only.

Société de Manutention et de Consignation Maritime (SOMACOM): BP 7, Le Port; agents for Scandinavian East Africa Line, Bank Line, Clan Line, Union Castle Mail Steamship Co and States Marine Lines.

CIVIL AVIATION

There is an international airport at Saint-Denis Gillot.

Air Réunion: BP 611, 97473 Saint-Denis; tel. 28-22-60; telex 916236; f. 1975; subsidiary of Air France; scheduled services to Madagascar and the Comoros; Gen. Man. Mme B. POPINEAU; fleet of 1 HS748, 1 Navajo Chieftain, 1 Cherokee Six, 2 SA315B Lama, 1 Alouette II, 1 Alouette III, 1 Dauphin C2, 1 Fokker F28/1000.

Tourism

Tourism is being extensively developed. Several new hotels have been built, and a 'holiday village' has been opened in Saint-Gilles. In 1987 a total of 135,233 tourists stayed in the island's hotels.

L'Agence Régionale du Tourisme et des Loisirs (ARTL): 2 rue de la Victorie, 97400 Saint-Denis; Pres. BERTHO AUDIFAX.

Délégation Régionale au Commerce, à l'Artisanat et au Tourisme: Préfecture/Commissariat de la République, 97405 Saint-Denis; tel. 21-86-10; telex 916068; Dir JEAN-FRANÇOIS DESROCHES.

Office du Tourisme: rue Rontaunay 97400 Saint-Denis; tel. 21-24-53; telex 916486; Chair. S. PERSONNÉ.

French Overseas Collectivités Territoriales

The two Overseas Collectivités Territoriales are Mayotte and St Pierre and Miquelon. Their status is between that of an overseas department and that of an overseas territory. They are integral parts of the French Republic and are both administered by a Government Commissioner (Prefect), appointed by the French Government. The Government Commissioner is assisted by an elected General Council. The collectivités territoriales are represented in the French National Assembly and in the Senate in Paris.

MAYOTTE

Introductory Survey

Location, Climate, Language, Religion, Capital

The island of Mayotte forms part of the Comoro archipelago, which lies between the island of Madagascar and the east coast of the African mainland. The climate is tropical. The official language is French, and Islam is the main religion. The capital is Dzaoudzi.

Recent History

Since the Comoros unilaterally declared independence in July 1975, Mayotte (Mahoré) has been administered separately by France. The independent Comoran state claims Mayotte as part of its territory and officially represents it in international organizations, including the United Nations. In December 1976 France introduced the special status of collectivité territoriale for the island. Following the coup in the Comoros in May 1978, Mayotte rejected the new government's proposal that it should rejoin the other islands under a federal system, and reaffirmed its intention of remaining linked to France. In December 1979 the French National Assembly approved legislation to prolong Mayotte's special status for another five years, during which the islanders were to be consulted. However, in October 1984 the National Assembly further prolonged Mayotte's status, and the referendum on the island's future was postponed indefinitely. The UN General Assembly has adopted several resolutions reaffirming the sovereignty of the Comoros over the island, and urging France to come to an agreement with the Comoran Government as soon as possible. The main political party on Mayotte, the Mouvement populaire mahorais (MPM), demands full departmental status for the island, but France has been reluctant to grant this in view of Mayotte's undeveloped condition.

Following the general election to the French National Assembly in March 1986, the RPR-UDF alliance formed a new government in mainland France. At the election, a UDF/CDS candidate was elected as deputy for Mayotte. In October Jacques Chirac became the first French Prime Minister to visit Mayotte, and he assured the islanders that they would remain French citizens for as long as they wished. Meanwhile, the French Government prepared a five-year Development Plan (see Economic Affairs) which included the reform of laws relating to land, labour, town-planning, public markets and penal procedure, to be implemented by decree if necessary. In March 1987 there were clashes between islands and illegal Comoran immigrants. Order was eventually restored, following the arrival of gendarmes from Réunion. In August the Comoros boycotted the Indian Ocean's first 'Youth Games', in protest against the participation of Mayotte. Relations between the MPM and the French Government rapidly deteriorated after the Franco-African summit in November, when Chirac expressed his reservations to the Comoran President concerning the elevation of Mayotte to the status of an overseas department, and thus seemed to contradict his statement, made during the RPR-UDF alliance's election campaign in early 1986, that he shared the MPM's aim to upgrade Mayotte's status.

In the first round of the 1988 French presidential election, on 24 April, the islanders favoured the candidacy of Raymond Barre, from the centre-right, to that of Chirac, the RPR candidate. In the second round of the election on 8 May, which was contested by Chirac and the incumbent Socialist President, François Mitterrand, supporters of Barre on Mayotte transferred a large proportion of their votes to Mitterrand, rather than to Chirac. Mitterrand received 50.3% of the votes cast on Mayotte in the second round, compared with only 4% in the first round. At the general election for the French National Assembly, which was held in June after Mitterrand's re-election as President, the UDF/CDS deputy for Mayotte retained his seat. (Later that month, he joined the newly-formed centrist group in the French National Assembly, the Union du Centre (UDC), which aimed to provide constructive opposition to the newly-elected Socialist Government.) In the cantonal election in September and October, the MPM retained the majority of seats in the General Council. In November the General Council urged the French Government to introduce measures to curb immigration to Mayotte from neighbouring islands, particularly from the Comoros.

(For further details of the recent history of the island, see the chapter on the Comoros, p. 760.)

Government

The French Government is represented in Mayotte by an appointed Government Commissioner. There is a General Council, with 17 members, elected by universal adult suffrage. Mayotte elects one deputy to the French National Assembly, and one representative to the Senate.

Defence

There were 300 French troops stationed on Mayotte in 1984.

Economic Affairs

The economy of the island is entirely agricultural. Vanilla, ylang-ylang, coffee and copra are the main products. In 1987 Mayotte exported 19.6 metric tons of ylang-ylang, worth 3.6m. francs. In the same year 5.9 tons of vanilla, worth 2.2m. francs were exported. In 1985 about 500 ha of forest were planted. Livestock rearing and fishing are secondary agricultural activities. Mayotte is not self-sufficient, and has to import substantial quantities of foodstuff, at a cost of 53.3m. francs in 1987.

France is Mayotte's major trading partner: France supplied imports to the value of 154.9m. francs in 1987 and bought exports worth 4.4m. francs in 1983. Mayotte has a large trade deficit, owing to its reliance on imports, which cost 247.1m. francs in 1987, compared with export earnings of 17.8m. francs. The island is dependent on French aid, which totalled 84m. francs in 1983. In 1986 Mayotte's external assets totalled 203.8m. francs, and banking aid reached 6.3m. francs. In 1988 Mayotte's provisional budget expenditure was an estimated 301.7m. francs.

In 1986 the French Government announced a five-year Development Plan for Mayotte, involving projected expenditure of 100m. francs. The island has invested in public works, including roads, ports and buildings: during the period 1978–85 a total of 22 administrative buildings and 600 dwellings were constructed. In March 1987 France agreed to provide 850m. francs in aid, over five years, to finance the construction of a deep-water port at Longoni and an airport to accommodate large aircraft. There is considerable potential for tourism, although any economic progress in Mayotte is largely dependent on French aid.

Statistical Survey

Source: mainly Office of the Prefect/Government Commissioner, Dzaoudzi.

AREA AND POPULATION

Area: 376 sq km (145 sq miles).

Population: 67,167 (census of August 1985); *Principal towns:* Dzaoudzi (capital) 5,865, Mamoudzou 12,026, Pamanzi-Labattoir 4,106.

FINANCE

Currency and Exchange Rates: French currency is used (see French Guiana).

Budget (estimates, million francs): Total expenditure 197 in 1986; 221 in 1987; 301.7 in 1988.

EXTERNAL TRADE

Principal Commodities ('000 francs, 1987): *Imports:* Machinery 55,595, Foodstuffs 53,268, Mineral products 28,268, Transport equipment 22,966, Metals 22,644, Total (incl. others) 247,117; *Exports:* Oil of ylang-ylang 3,614, Vanilla 2,178, Total (incl. others) 17,811.
Principal Trading Partners ('000 francs): *Imports* (1987): France 154,932, South Africa 29,839, Thailand 12,628, Bahrain 11,000. *Exports* (1983): France 4,405.
Source: Secrétariat du Comité Monétaire de la Zone Franc: *La Zone Franc, Rapport 1987*.

TRANSPORT

Roads (1984): 93 km of main roads, of which 72 km are tarred, 137 km of local roads, of which 40 km are tarred, and 54 km of tracks unusable in the rainy season; 1,528 vehicles.
Civil Aviation (1984): *Arrivals:* 7,747 passengers, 120 metric tons of freight; *Departures:* 7,970 passengers, 41 metric tons of freight.

EDUCATION

Primary (1986): 28 schools, 366 teachers, 15,632 pupils.
Secondary (1986): 2 schools, 65 teachers, 1,392 pupils.

Directory

The Constitution

In a referendum in April 1976, the population of Mayotte voted to renounce the status of an overseas territory. They expressed their desire for departmental status, but this has been rejected by the French Government. The change in status of the island to a collectivité territoriale involved the election of a General Council with 17 members to assist the Government Commissioner (Prefect) in the administration of the island. In December 1979 the French National Assembly voted to extend this status for five years. A further referendum was due to be held in 1984, but was postponed indefinitely in December of that year.

The Government

(February 1989)

Government Commissioner (Prefect): AKLI KHIDER.
Secretary-General: PHILIPPE SCHAEFER.
Deputy to the French National Assembly: HENRY JEAN-BAPTISTE (UDC).
Representative to the French Senate: MARCEL HENRY (MPM).

GENERAL COUNCIL

The General Council has 17 members, of whom nine represent the Mouvement populaire mahorais (MPM). Elections were last held in September and October 1988.
President of the General Council: YOUSSOUF BAMANA.

Political Organizations

Fédération de Mayotte du Rassemblement pour la République: Dzaoudzi; Mayotte branch of the French (Gaullist) RPR; holds six seats in the General Council; Sec.-Gen. MANSOUR KAMARDINE.
Mouvement populaire mahorais (MPM): Dzaoudzi; seeks departmental status for Mayotte; Leader YOUSSOUF BAMANA.
Parti pour le rassemblement démocratique des mahorais (PRDM): Dzaoudzi; f. 1978; seeks unification with the Federal Islamic Republic of the Comoros; Leader DAROUÈCHE MAOULIDA.
Union pour la Démocratie Française (UDF): centrist.
Centre des Démocrates Sociaux (CDS).

Prior to the French general election of June 1988, the two major French right-wing political parties, the **Rassemblement pour la République** and the **Union pour la Démocratie Française**, formed an electoral alliance, the **Union du Rassemblement du Centre (URC)**. After the election, 40 UDF deputies, including the deputy from Mayotte, formed a new centrist parliamentary group, the **Union du Centre (UDC)**.

Judicial System

Tribunal Supérieur d'Appel: Pres. CLAUDE BAURAIN.
Procureur de la République: JEAN JACQUES LECOMTE.
Tribunal d'Instance: Pres. JEAN-PASCAL MARTRES.

Religion

Muslims comprise about 98% of the population. Most of the remainder are Christians, mainly Roman Catholics.

The Press

Le Journal de Mayotte: BP 108, 97610 Dzaoudzi; daily.

Radio and Television

In 1983 there were an estimated 13,800 radio receivers in use.
Société Nationale de Radio-Télévision Française d'Outre-mer (RFO)—Mayotte: BP 103, Dzaoudzi, 97610 Mayotte; tel. 60-10-17; telex 915822; f. 1977; govt-owned; radio broadcasts in French and Mahorian; television transmissions began in December 1986; Regional Dir YVES RAMBEAU; Technical Dir J. BIASCO.

Finance

BANKS

Institut d'Emission d'Outre-mer: Dzaoudzi, 97610 Mayotte.
Banque Française Commerciale: Mamoudzou, 97600 Mayotte; br. at Dzaoudzi.

Transport

ROADS

The main road network totals approximately 93 km, of which 72 km are bituminized. There are 137 km of local roads, of which 40 km are tarred, and 54 km of minor tracks which are unusable during the rainy season.

SHIPPING

Coastal shipping is provided by locally-owned small craft. A deep-water port is under construction at Longoni.

CIVIL AVIATION

There is an airfield at Dzaoudzi, serving four-times weekly commercial flights to Réunion and twice-weekly services to Njazidja, Nzwani and Mwali.

Tourism

Office du Tourisme de Mayotte: 10 rue de Presbourg, 75116 Paris, France; tel. (1) 45-01-28-30.

St Pierre and Miquelon

ST PIERRE AND MIQUELON

Introductory Survey

Location, Climate, Language, Religion, Capital

The territory of St Pierre and Miquelon (Iles Saint-Pierre-et-Miquelon) consists of a number of small islands which lie about 25 km (16 miles) from the southern coast of Newfoundland, Canada, in the North Atlantic Ocean. The climate is cold and wet, with temperatures falling to −20°C (−4°F) in winter, and averaging between 10° and 20°C (50°–68°F) in summer. The islands are often shrouded in mist and fog. The language is French, and the majority of the population profess Christianity and belong to the Roman Catholic Church. The capital is Saint-Pierre, on the island of St Pierre.

Recent History

The islands of St Pierre and Miquelon are the remnants of the once extensive French possessions in North America. They were confirmed as French territory in 1816, and gained departmental status in July 1976. The departmentalization proved unpopular with many of the islanders, since it incorporated the territory's economy into that of the EEC, and other institutions of metropolitan France, neglecting the islands' isolation and their dependence on Canada for supplies and transport links. In March 1982 Socialist and other left-wing candidates, campaigning for a change in the islands' status, were elected unopposed to all seats in the department's General Council. St Pierre and Miquelon was excluded from the Mitterrand Government's decentralization reforms.

In 1976 Canada imposed an economic interest zone extending to 200 nautical miles (370 km) around its shores. As a result of French fears over the loss of traditional fishing areas, and the threat to the livelihood of the fishermen of St Pierre, the Government claimed a similar zone around the islands. The possibility of discovering valuable reserves of petroleum and natural gas in the area has heightened the tension between France and Canada. In December 1984 legislation was approved to help solve both the internal and external problems by giving the islands the status of a collectivité territoriale with effect from June 1985. This would allow St Pierre and Miquelon to receive the investment and development that are suitable for its position, and would allay Canadian fears of EEC exploitation of its offshore waters. Local representatives, however, remained apprehensive about the outcome of negotiations between the French and Canadian Governments to settle the dispute over coastal limits. (France has been claiming a 200-mile fishing and economic zone around St Pierre and Miquelon, while Canada wants the islands to have only a 12-mile zone.) In February 1985 the Government Commissioner was expelled from St Pierre by striking workers during the course of an industrial dispute, while in June disagreements between members of the General Council led to the temporary resignations of four council members.

In January 1987 it was decided that the dispute over the maritime border around St Pierre and Miquelon should be taken to the International Court of Justice in an attempt to resolve the issue. Discussions were scheduled to take place in March, and negotiations to determine quotas for France's catch of Atlantic cod over the period 1988-91 were to take place simultaneously. In the mean time, Canada and France agreed on an interim fishing accord which would allow France to increase its cod quota by about 15,000 metric tons in 1987. In October, however, the discussions collapsed, and French trawlers were prohibited from fishing in Canadian waters. In February 1988 Albert Pen and Gérard Grignon, St Pierre's elected representatives (see below), went on hunger strike for 10 days to protest at the continuing deadlock between Canada and France. In April Pen and Grignon, together with two members of the St Pierre administration and 17 sailors, were arrested for fishing in Canadian waters. This episode, and the arrest of a Canadian trawler captain in May for fishing in St Pierre's waters, led to a resumption of negotiations in September. However, the discussions collapsed again, with no prospect of agreement. In November Enrique Iglesias, the President of the Inter-American Development Bank, was appointed as mediator in the dispute. In January 1989 the dispute re-emerged after two French factory fishing ships from St Malo sailed to the area to catch the fish allowed by government quotas. Two military aircraft were also sent, but encountered hostility from the islanders, who feared that damage might be caused to fishing stocks by the factory ships. Albert Pen warned the new Government Commissioner (Prefect), Jean-Pierre Marquie, that France must change its stance on the dispute in order to avoid further conflict with the islanders. It was subsequently agreed with the French Prime Minister, Michel Rocard, that one of the factory ships would return to France.

A general election to the French National Assembly was held in March 1986. The islands' incumbent deputy, Albert Pen (representing the Parti Socialiste), was re-elected. Pen was also the sole candidate at the indirect election to choose the islands' representative in the French Senate in September. A fresh election for a deputy to the National Assembly was held in November, when Gérard Grignon, representing the Union pour la Démocratie Française, was elected. In the 1988 French presidential election Jacques Chirac received 56% of the votes cast by the islanders in the second round against the successful incumbent, President Mitterrand. In June Gérard Grignon was re-elected to the National Assembly. However, in September–October, the parties of the left won a majority at elections to the General Council, taking 13 of the 19 seats.

Government

The French Government is represented in St Pierre by an appointed Government Commissioner (Prefect). There is a General Council, with 19 members (15 for St Pierre and four for Miquelon) elected by adult universal suffrage for a period of six years. St Pierre and Miquelon elects one deputy to the French National Assembly and one representative to the Senate in Paris.

Economic Affairs

The islanders have traditionally earned their living by fishing, and by acting as a supply base for fishing fleets operating in the rich seas off Newfoundland. However, the economy has been experiencing a long decline. The number of French and foreign ships coming to fish, and calling at St Pierre, declined from 1,290 in 1976 to 917 in 1986. An agreement with Canada, signed in 1972, which expired in 1986, limited the amounts of fish caught by French ships in the Gulf of Saint Lawrence to 20,500 metric tons per year. The agreement also granted permanent fishing rights to fishing vessels from St Pierre, provided that they fished 'on an equal footing' with Canada. Disagreements arose in 1984 over St Pierre's right to use a modern vessel that enabled fish to be treated on board and thus exported immediately, while Canadian fishermen were obliged to return to port with their catch. Discussions between France and Canada were opened in Geneva in 1986 to decide the terms of a new fishing agreement. The Canadian Government accused France of overfishing, and of causing a depletion in the supplies of cod in the local seas. In March 1987 French trawlers were barred from Canadian ports. It was feared that this action would have a disastrous effect on the economy of St Pierre and Miquelon. Interpêche, the primary company in the fishing sector on the islands (and a major employer), has been in financial difficulties, and required government subsidy. Owing to the ban on fishing in Canadian waters (implemented in October 1987), one of St Pierre's fish-processing plants was on the verge of bankruptcy, while the other had incurred losses of 8m. francs by April 1988; 350 workers were laid off until a settlement could be reached with Canada over fishing rights. Unemployment affected 13.3% of the labour force in 1987.

Around 70% of imported goods, including fuel and building materials, come from Canada. Items such as clothing and consumer goods are imported from France via Nova Scotia. The proximity of Canada, and the islands' reliance on imported goods, caused an increase in the annual rate of inflation, which rose to 18% in 1983. However, the decline in value of the US dollar resulted in reduced import costs, producing a subsequent decline in inflation. In 1986 average prices decreased by 1%. In 1987 the inflation rate stood at 1%.

Social Welfare

In 1981 there was one general hospital, with 68 beds, and maternity and hospice establishments. In 1977 there were six physicians working in the islands.

Education

The education system is modelled on the French system, and education is compulsory for children between the ages of six and 16 years. There are nine primary schools (of which five are privately-run), three secondary schools (of which two are private) and six technical schools.

Public Holidays

1989: 2 January (for New Year's Day), 24–27 March (Easter), 1 May (Labour Day), 4 May (Ascension Day), 15 May (Whit Monday), 14 July (National Day), 11 November (Armistice Day), 25 December (Christmas Day).

FRENCH OVERSEAS COLLECTIVITÉS TERRITORIALES *St Pierre and Miquelon*

1990: 1 January (New Year's Day), 13–16 April (Easter), 1 May (Labour Day), 24 May (Ascension Day), 4 June (Whit Monday), 14 July (National Day), 11 November (Armistice Day), 25 December (Christmas Day).

Weights and Measures
The metric system is in use.

Statistical Survey

Source (unless otherwise stated): Préfecture, 97500 Saint Pierre; tel. 412801; telex 914410.

AREA AND POPULATION

Area: 242 sq km (93.4 sq miles).
Population: 6,041 (census of 9 March 1982); Saint-Pierre 5,415, Miquelon 626.
Births and Deaths (1987): Live births 85; Deaths 50.
Labour Force (1982 census): Employed 2,145 (males 1,483, females 662); Unemployed 235 (males 141, females 94).

AGRICULTURE, ETC.

Agriculture and Livestock: Vegetables are grown, and some cattle, sheep and pigs are kept for local consumption.
Fishing (metric tons, live weight): Total catch 14,752 (incl. Atlantic cod 10,739) in 1986. Source: Ministère des Départements et Territoires d'Outre Mer. Fishing is the only industry of consequence, and fish products are the main exports.

FINANCE

Currency and Exchange Rates: French currency is used (see French Guiana).
Aid from France (1987): 224 million francs.
Budget (estimates, 1988): Expenditure 83 million francs. Source: Secrétariat du Comité Monétaire de la Zone Franc: *La Zone Franc, Rapport 1987*.

EXTERNAL TRADE

Total ('000 francs, 1986): *Imports:* 348,300 (Fuel, meat, clothing, electrical equipment and machinery); *Exports:* 161,100 (Fish, marine equipment). Most trade is with Canada, France and the USA.

TRANSPORT

Road Traffic (1987): 2,694 motor vehicles in use.
Shipping (1982): Ships entered 917 (1986), Freight entered 58,656 metric tons, Freight cleared 3,688 metric tons.
Civil Aviation (1987): Passengers carried 18,985, Freight carried 97 metric tons.

TOURISM

Tourist Arrivals (1982): 11,293.

EDUCATION

Primary (1982): 9 schools, 50 teachers, 983 students (1986).
Secondary (1982): 3 schools, 55 teachers, 745 students (1986).
There are also 6 technical schools.

Directory

The Government
(February 1989)

Government Commissioner (Prefect): JEAN-PIERRE MARQUIE.
Representative to the Social and Economic Council: RÉMY BRIAND.
Deputy to the French National Assembly: GÉRARD GRIGNON (UDF/CDS).
Representative to the French Senate: ALBERT PEN (PS).

GENERAL COUNCIL

The General Council has 19 members (St Pierre 15, Miquelon four). At the most recent election, held in September–October 1988, 13 seats were won by the Parti Socialiste (PS) and other left-wing candidates, the remaining six being taken by the Union pour la Démocratie Française (UDF) and right-wing candidates.
President of the General Council: MARC PLANTEGENEST (PS).

Political Organizations

Parti Socialiste (PS).
Rassemblement pour la République (RPR): Gaullist.
Union pour la Démocratie Française (UDF): centrist.
Centre des Démocrates Sociaux (CDS).

Judicial System

Tribunal Supérieur d'Appel at Saint-Pierre (Pres. FRANÇOIS DENEAUVE); Tribunal de Première Instance (Pres. LIONEL RINUY).

Religion

Almost all of the inhabitants are adherents of the Roman Catholic Church.

CHRISTIANITY
The Roman Catholic Church

The islands form the Apostolic Vicariate of the Iles Saint-Pierre et Miquelon. At 31 December 1985 there were an estimated 6,090 adherents (about 99% of the total population).
Vicar Apostolic: FRANÇOIS JOSEPH MAURER (Titular Bishop of Chimaera), Vicariat Apostolique, BP 4245, 97500 Saint-Pierre; tel. 412035.

The Press

Journal Officiel: Saint-Pierre; published by the Government Printer; f. 1886; fortnightly.

Radio and Television

In 1986 there were an estimated 4,000 radio receivers and 4,000 television receivers in use.
Radio-Télévision Française d'Outre-mer (RFO): BP 4227, 97500 Saint-Pierre; tel. 413824; telex 914443; the government station, broadcasts 16 hours of radio programmes daily, and 50 hours of television programmes weekly on two channels; Dir CLAUDE ESPERANDIEU.

Finance

MAJOR BANKS

Banque des Iles Saint-Pierre-et-Miquelon: rue Jacques-Cartier, Saint-Pierre; tel. 412217; telex 914435; f. 1889; cap. 7.5m. francs; Pres. and Gen. Man. GEORGES LANDRY; Man. GUY ROULET.
Crédit Saint Pierrais: 20 place du Général de Gaulle, BP 4218, Saint-Pierre; tel. 412249; telex 914429; Pres. MARCEL GIRARDIN; Man. G. COQUELIN.

PRINCIPAL INSURANCE COMPANIES

Comité Central des Assureurs Maritimes de France: 16 rue M. Georges Lefèvre, BP 4222, 97500 Saint-Pierre; tel. 414355; telex 914420; Reps GUY PATUREL, BERNARD HARAN.
Mutuelle Générale Française: Saint-Pierre; Rep. J. ANDRIEUX.

Trade and Industry

Chambre de Commerce, d'Industrie et de Métiers: blvd Constant Colmay, BP 4207, 97500 Saint-Pierre; tel. 414512; telex 914437; Pres. LOUIS E. HARDY.

TRADE UNION

Force Ouvrière (FO): 15 rue Dr Dunan, 97500 Saint-Pierre; tel. 412522; Sec.-Gen. MAX OLAÏSOLA.

Transport

SHIPPING

Packet boats run to Halifax, Sydney and Louisbourg in Canada, and there are container services between Saint-Pierre and Halifax, Nova Scotia. The seaport at Saint Pierre has three jetties and 1,200 metres of quays.

CIVIL AVIATION

There is an airport at St Pierre, served by airlines linking the territory with France and Canada.

Air Saint-Pierre: 18 rue Albert Briand St Pierre, POB 4225, 97500 Saint-Pierre; tel. 412720; telex 914422; f. 1961; connects the territory with Sydney (Canada) and directly with Halifax, Nova Scotia, and Montréal, Québec; Pres. RÉMY L. BRIAND; fleet of 1 HS. 748, 1 Navajo Chieftain, 1 Aztec, and 1 Apache.

Tourism

Office du Tourisme: 97500 Saint-Pierre; tel. 412222; telex 914437; f. 1959; Pres. ANDRÉ PATUREL; Man. JEAN-CHARLES GIRARDIN.

There were 11,293 tourist arrivals in 1982.

French Overseas Territories

The four Overseas Territories (territoires d'outre-mer) are French Polynesia, the French Southern and Antarctic Territories, New Caledonia, and the Wallis and Futuna Islands. They are integral parts of the French Republic. Each is administered by a High Commissioner or Chief Administrator, who is appointed by the French Government. Each Territory also has a Territorial Assembly or Congress, elected by universal adult suffrage. Certain members of the Territorial Assembly or Congress sit in the French National Assembly and the Senate of the Republic in Paris. The Territories have varying degrees of internal autonomy.

FRENCH POLYNESIA

Introductory Survey

Location, Climate, Language, Religion, Flag, Capital

French Polynesia comprises several scattered groups of islands in the south Pacific Ocean, lying about two-thirds of the way between the Panama Canal and New Zealand. Its nearest neighbours are the Cook Islands, to the east, and the Line Islands (part of Kiribati), to the north-east. French Polynesia consists of the following island groups: the Iles du Vent (including the islands of Tahiti and Moorea) and the Iles Sous le Vent (located about 160 km north-west of Tahiti) which, together, constitute the Society Archipelago; the Tuamotu Archipelago, which comprises 78 islands scattered east of the Society Archipelago in a line stretching north-west to south-east for about 1,500 km; the Gambier Islands, located 1,600 km south-east of Tahiti; the Austral Islands, lying 640 km south of Tahiti; and the Marquesas Archipelago, which lies 1,450 km north-east of Tahiti. There are 120 islands in all. The average monthly temperature throughout the year varies between 20°C (68°F) and 29°C (84°F), and most rainfall occurs between November and April, the average annual precipitation being 1,625 mm. The official language is French, and Polynesian languages are spoken by the indigenous population. The principal religion is Christianity, 55% of the population being Protestant and 24% Roman Catholic. Provision was made in a statute of 6 September 1984 for the adoption of a French Polynesian flag, to fly alongside the French tricolour. The capital is Papeete, on the island of Tahiti.

Recent History

Tahiti, the largest of the Society Islands, was declared a French protectorate in 1842, and became a colony in 1880. The other island groups were annexed during the last 20 years of the 19th century. The islands were governed from France under a decree of 1885 until 1957, when French Polynesia became an Overseas Territory, administered by a Governor in Papeete. A Territorial Assembly and a Council of Government were elected to advise the Governor.

Between May 1975 and May 1982 a majority in the Territorial Assembly sought independence for French Polynesia. Following pressure by Francis Sanford, leader of the largest autonomist party in the Assembly, a new constitution for the Territory was negotiated with the French Government and approved by a newly-elected Assembly in 1977. Under the provisions of the new statute, France retained responsibility for foreign affairs, defence, monetary matters and justice, but the powers of the territorial Council of Government were increased, especially in the field of commerce. The French Governor was replaced by a High Commissioner, who was to preside over the Council of Government and was head of the administration, but had no vote. The Council's elected Vice-President, responsible for domestic affairs, was granted greater powers. An Economic and Social Council, responsible for all development matters, was also created, and French Polynesia's economic zone has been extended to 200 nautical miles (370 km) from the islands' coastline.

Following elections to the Territorial Assembly in May 1982, the Tahoeraa Huiraatira Party of Gaston Flosse, with 13 of the 30 seats, formed successive ruling coalitions, first with the Ai'a Api Party and in September with John Teariki's Pupu Here Ai'a Party. Seeking greater (but not full) independence from France, especially in economic matters, elected representatives of the Assembly held discussions with the French Government in Paris in 1983. In spite of feelings expressed by the Assembly, that the French proposals for increased internal autonomy did not go far enough, a new statute was approved by the French National Assembly in September 1984. This allowed the territorial government greater powers, mainly in the sphere of commerce and development; the Council of Government was replaced by a Council of Ministers, whose President was to be elected from among the members of the Territorial Assembly. Gaston Flosse became the first President of the Council of Ministers.

In February 1985 Flosse and his New Caledonian counterpart, Dick Ukeiwé, signed an anti-independence alliance protocol, calling for closer economic, cultural and political co-operation within the French Republic; it was immediately described as 'illegal' and 'unconstitutional' by France's High Commissioner to New Caledonia, and subsequently annulled by a French administrative tribunal in that territory.

The testing of nuclear devices by the French Government began in 1966 at Mururoa Atoll, in the Tuamotu Archipelago. In 1983, in spite of strong protests by many Pacific nations, the Government indicated that tests would continue for a number of years. In October 1983 Australia, New Zealand and Papua New Guinea accepted a French invitation jointly to send scientists to inspect the test site, but the team's subsequent report was widely criticized for being inconclusive with regard to the problem of nuclear waste disposal, and, although the French test programme appeared to present no immediate health hazards, there was definite evidence of environmental damage, resulting from the underground explosions, which had caused subsidence by weakening the rock structure of the atoll. This was confirmed by a further inspection in 1988.

A series of tests in May and June 1985, involving bigger explosions than hitherto, prompted a renewed display of opposition. In July the trawler *Rainbow Warrior*, the flagship of the anti-nuclear environmentalist group, Greenpeace, which was to have led a protest flotilla to Mururoa, was sunk in Auckland Harbour, New Zealand, in an explosion that killed one crew member. Two agents of the French secret service, the Direction générale de sécurité extérieure (DGSE), were subsequently convicted of manslaughter and imprisoned in New Zealand. In July 1986, however, they were transferred to Hao Atoll, in the Tuamoto Archipelago, after a ruling by the UN Secretary-General (acting as mediator), which effectively reduced the agents' sentences from 10 to three years' imprisonment, in return for a French payment of $NZ 7m. in compensation to the New Zealand Government. Relations between France and New Zealand worsened still further in 1987, when the French Prime Minister, Jacques Chirac, approved the removal of one of the prisoners to Paris, owing to illness. By the terms of the UN ruling, 'mutual consent' by both Governments was to be necessary for any such repatriation. An exchange of letters between the Prime Ministers of the two countries failed to resolve the issue, and in 1988 the other prisoner was also flown back to Paris when she became pregnant. In November 1988 it was announced that France and New Zealand had agreed to accept a three-member arbitration panel. In September 1985 the French President, François Mitterrand, had visited the test site to reaffirm France's nuclear policy and its strategic interests in the Pacific, and had declared that the tests at Mururoa would continue for as long as necessary. In October the Greenpeace yacht, *Vega*, was seized by French naval commandos, as it sailed into the prohibited zone around the atoll, in an unsuccessful attempt to disrupt further scheduled tests; although the protest as a whole ended in deadlock, it succeeded in attracting world-wide attention. Further tests were conducted, and in January 1989 the total number of underground tests since 1975 had risen to 101.

At elections held in March 1986, the Tahoeraa Huiraatira Party/Rassemblement pour la République (RPR) gained the first outright majority to be achieved in the territory, winning 24 of the 41 seats in the Territorial Assembly, after a recount in one constituency, and the decision of two successful independent candidates to join the ruling party. Leaders of opposition parties subsequently expressed dissatisfaction with the election result, claiming that the Tahoeraa Huiraatira Party's victory had been secured only as a result of one of the five constituencies' having been allocated a disproportionately large number of seats in the Territorial Assembly, whereby the weight carried by its constituents' votes was effectively increased. The constituency at the centre of the dispute was that comprising the Mangareva and Tuamotu islands, where the two French army bases at Hao and Mururoa constituted a powerful body of support for Flosse and the Tahoeraa Huiraatira Party, which, in spite of winning a majority of seats, had obtained a minority of individual votes in the election (30,571, compared with the opposition parties' 43,771). At the concurrent elections for French Polynesia's two seats in the National Assembly in Paris, Flosse and Alexandre Léontieff, the candidates of the RPR, were elected, Flosse subsequently ceding his seat to Edouard Fritch. At the June 1988 elections to the Assembly, Léontieff retained his seat, while the other was won by Emile Vernaudon, the leader of Ai'a Api.

In April 1986 Flosse was re-elected President of the Council of Ministers, supported by the votes of 25 of the 41 members of the Territorial Assembly. Meanwhile, in March, the incoming French Prime Minister, Jacques Chirac, appointed Flosse to a post in the French Council of Ministers, assigning him the portfolio of Secretary of State for South Pacific Problems. Flosse faced severe criticism from leaders of the opposition for his allegedly inefficient and extravagant use of public funds, and was accused, in particular, of corrupt electoral practice, through having distributed government-financed gifts of construction materials, food and clothing, in an attempt to influence voters during his pre-election campaign. In September 1986 a formal complaint against Flosse was made by Enrique ('Quito') Braun-Ortega, one of the leaders of the Amuitahiraa Mo Porinesia (a coalition of opposition parties), who accused Flosse of appropriating public funds for his own personal and political purposes. Flosse resigned as President of the Territory's Council of Ministers in February 1987, and was replaced by Jacques Teuira.

Unrest among dock-workers led to serious rioting in October 1987. More than 100 people were arrested, and 27 injured, as arson and looting broke out across Papeete. Paramilitary police and French Legionnaires were flown in from Paris and Mururoa Atoll, with the Government declaring a state of emergency and imposing a dusk-to-dawn curfew in Papeete and four neighbouring districts. Daniel Millaud, French Polynesia's representative to the French Senate, demanded the holding of a public inquiry into the rioting, and in November the French High Commissioner, Pierre Angéli, was recalled and replaced by Jean Montpezat.

In December 1987, amid growing discontent over his policies, Teuira resigned as President of the Council of Ministers, along with the seven remaining ministers (the three other ministers, including Alexandre Léontieff, having resigned a few days previously). Léontieff was elected President of the Council of Ministers by a new alliance of 28 of the Territorial Assembly's 41 members. Jean Juventin, the Mayor of Papeete, replaced Roger Doom as President of the Territorial Assembly. The new Council of Ministers included only two members of the previous administration. However, several members of the realigned Assembly had refused to resume their seats, in protest at the alleged illegitimacy of the new Government, as the outgoing administration, which had continued on a caretaker basis, had announced the dissolution of the Assembly, in preparation for the holding of new elections, shortly before the appointment of Léontieff. In 1988 three members of Léontieff's Council of Ministers resigned, including Quito Braun-Ortega, who, it was speculated, intended to form a new political grouping.

Government

The French Government is represented in French Polynesia by its High Commissioner to the territory, and controls various important spheres of government, including defence, foreign diplomacy and justice. A local Territorial Assembly, with 41 members, is elected for a five-year term by universal adult suffrage. The Assembly may elect a President of an executive body, the territorial Council of Ministers, who, in turn, submits a list of between five and 10 members of the Assembly to serve as Ministers, for approval by the Assembly.

In addition, French Polynesia elects two deputies to the French National Assembly in Paris, one representative to the French Senate and one Economic and Social Councillor, all chosen on the basis of universal adult suffrage.

Defence

France has been testing nuclear weapons at Mururoa Atoll, in the Tuamotu Archipelago, since 1966 and was maintaining a force of 5,000 military personnel in the territory in June 1988.

Economic Affairs

In 1985, according to estimates by the World Bank, the territory's gross domestic product (GDP), measured at average 1983–85 prices, was US $1,370m. ($7,840 per head). The influx of large numbers of French military personnel, in connection with the testing of nuclear weapons in the territory since the mid-1960s, has, by creating new opportunities for employment, distorted the economy, to the extent that many islanders believe that a French withdrawal from Tahiti would mean economic disaster. The initial demand for labour diverted large numbers of the work-force from the coconut and vanilla plantations to construction work for the French, causing a steady migration from outer islands into Tahiti and the military bases. However, the gradual decline of this demand has led to the existence of a large group of people who no longer possess the agricultural subsistence skills of previous generations, and has resulted in a growth in the rate of unemployment. Coconuts are the principal cash crop, and copra the major export commodity, but the territory's total earnings from exports were less than 25% of the cost of imports in the mid-1980s, compared with 83% before the nuclear tests began. Other export commodities include vanilla, black pearls and, since 1986, shark meat. In 1986 13,707 metric tons of copra and 8,522 metric tons of coconut oil were produced.

Tourism is an important and developed industry, particularly on Tahiti, and helps to offset a persistent trade deficit, which in 1985 was 82,375m. francs CFP. In 1986 the deficit rose to 87,556m. francs CFP, an increase of 6.3% on the previous year, but fell to 81,493m. francs CFP in 1987. This was followed by a further reduction in the first six months of 1988. The tourist industry accounts for some 7% of the territory's GDP, and its contribution to the economy is estimated to be at least three times that of total exports. In 1985 an extensive programme for expansion in this sector included a huge combined tourism and agriculture project at Aimaono, on the south coast of Tahiti, involving an investment of 20,000m. francs CFP, and plans for a luxury hotel on the island of Huahine, to be built with private US investment of 1,400m. francs CFP. The total number of hotel rooms in the territory was expected to increase from 2,100 in 1985 to 4,000 by 1989. Tourist arrivals numbered 142,820 in 1987, a drop of 11% on the figure for 1986, but were not expected to exceed 140,000 in 1988.

The annual rate of inflation declined from 16% in 1982 to only 1.2% in the year to August 1987. A five-year development plan (1984–88) stressed increased primary production, especially in agriculture, forestry and fishing, the development of hydroelectric schemes, improved social services and the expansion of the tourist industry. In 1988 it was announced that six hydroelectric power dams were to be constructed by 1991, with the capacity to generate 45% of Tahiti's electricity requirements. Proposed budget expenditure for 1985, totalling 45,189m. francs CFP, was to be financed mainly by indirect taxation, which was to account for 78% of the projected revenues, with income tax being levied only on commercial firms. Customs duties payable on materials imported in connection with the nuclear tests were to be the only direct contribution from France; in an attempt to increase the territory's economic independence, 700m. francs CFP was to be allocated to the promotion of tourism, and 590m. francs CFP to exploration of the sea-bed. The 1986 budget envisaged total revenue of 52,100m. francs CFP and expenditure of 50,500m. francs CFP. Imports totalled 555,400 metric tons in 1987, a drop of 2.7% on the figure for 1986. Exports, however, increased by 61.8% to reach 18,006 tons. In 1986 rich, exploitable deposits of cobalt were discovered on the outer slopes of several atolls in the Tuamotu Archipelago.

Social Welfare

In 1980 there were 31 hospitals in French Polynesia, with a total of 982 beds, and there were 143 physicians working in the territory.

Education

Education is compulsory for eight years between six and 14 years of age. It is free of charge for day pupils in government schools. Primary education, lasting six years, is financed by the territorial budget, while secondary and technical education are supported by state funds. In 1985/86 there were 254 kindergartens and primary schools (237 public, 17 private), while secondary education is provided by both government and church schools. There were 12,700 pupils attending kindergartens, 28,707 at primary schools, 13,372 at secondary schools, and 3,944 at technical institutions. In 1986 France announced plans to create a university on Tahiti. In the 1988/89 budget the territory envisaged expenditure of US $226m. on its 311 schools. The French Government was to contribute about 68% of the total expenditure on education.

Public Holidays

1989: 2 January (for New Year's Day), 27 March (Easter Monday), 1 May (Labour Day), 4 May (Ascension Day), 8 May (Liberation Day),15 May (Whit Monday), 14 July (Fall of the Bastille), 11 November (Armistice Day), 25 December (Christmas Day).

1990: 1 January (New Year's Day), 16 April (Easter Monday), 7 May (for Labour Day), 8 May (Liberation Day), 24 May (Ascension Day), 4 June (Whit Monday), 14 July (Fall of the Bastille), 11 November (Armistice Day), 25 December (Christmas Day).

FRENCH OVERSEAS TERRITORIES   French Polynesia

Weights and Measures
The metric system is in force.

Statistical Survey

Source (unless otherwise indicated): Institut Territorial de la Statistique, BP 395, Papeete; tel. 37196.

AREA AND POPULATION

Area: 4,200 sq km (1,622 sq miles).

Population: 188,814 (census of 6 September 1988); *Towns* (population estimates for 1983): Papeete 23,496, Faaa 21,927, Pirae 12,023, Uturoa 2,733.

Births and Deaths (1987): Live births 5,130 (birth rate 30.8 per 1,000 in 1985); Deaths 933 (death rate 5.5 per 1,000 in 1985).

Employment (census of 15 October 1983): Civilians 54,599 (males 36,392, females 18,207); Police and armed forces 3,264 (males 3,166, females 98).

AGRICULTURE, ETC.

Principal Crops (metric tons, 1986): Vegetables 4,833, Fresh fruit 7,657, Coconuts 150,000 (1985), Vanilla 25, Coffee 14.

Livestock (FAO estimates, year ending September 1985): Cattle 9,907 (1986), Horses 2,000, Pigs 22,942 (1986), Goats 3,000, Sheep 2,000. Source: mainly FAO, *Production Yearbook*.

Livestock Products (1986): Milk 214,900 litres, Beef 143 metric tons, Pork 855 tons, Poultry meat 277 tons, Rabbit meat 12 tons, Eggs 158,400.

Fishing (metric tons, live weight): Total catch 2,378 in 1984; 2,028 in 1985; 1,915 in 1986. Source: FAO, *Yearbook of Fishery Statistics*.

INDUSTRY

Production: Coconut oil 8,522 metric tons (1986), Copra 14,998 metric tons (1987), Beer 100,000 hectolitres (1980), Printed cloth 200,000 m (1979), Japanese sandals 600,000 pairs (1979), Electric energy (Tahiti) 244.7m. kWh (1987).

FINANCE

Currency and Exchange Rates: 100 centimes = 1 franc des Comptoirs français du Pacifique (franc CFP or Pacific franc). *Coins:* 50 centimes; 1, 2, 5, 10, 20 and 50 francs CFP. *Notes:* 100, 500, 1,000 and 5,000 francs CFP. *Sterling, Dollar and French Franc Equivalents* (30 September 1988): £1 sterling = 195.86 francs CFP; US $1 = 115.82 francs CFP; 1 French franc = 18.182 francs CFP; 1,000 francs CFP = £5.106 = $8.634 = 55 French francs.

Budget (million francs CFP, 1986 estimates): *Revenue:* Ordinary receipts 41,200, Extraordinary receipts 10,800, Total 52,100; *Expenditure:* Ordinary expenditure 40,500, Extraordinary expenditure 10,000, Total 50,500.

Aid from France (1981, million francs CFP): 37,300; also subsidies to local authorities, of which 660 to general expenses, 381 to FIDES, 2,500 (1978) to public funds; loans at low interest rates 2,500.

Cost of Living (Consumer Price Index for December; base: December 1980 = 100): 168.1 in 1984; 181.1 in 1985; 179.9 in 1986.

Gross Domestic Product (million francs CFP at current prices): 270,000 in 1986.

EXTERNAL TRADE

Principal Commodities (million francs CFP, 1986): *Imports:* Flour 588; Hydraulic cement 1,128; Petroleum products 6,546; Total (incl. others) 92,667. *Exports:* Copra oil 327 (1987); Cultured pearls 2,252 (1987); Total (incl. others) 9,094 (1987).

Principal Trading Partners (million francs CFP, 1987): *Imports:* France (metropolitan) 47,249; USA 9,360; New Zealand 4,489; Total (incl. others) 90,587. *Exports:* France (metropolitan) 2,870; USA 1,374; Total (incl. others) 9,094.

TRANSPORT

Road Traffic (1987): Total vehicles registered 54,979.

Shipping (1986): *International traffic:* passengers carried 1,014, freight handled 684,100 (1987) metric tons. *Domestic traffic:* passengers carried 416,335, freight handled 347,000 (1987) metric tons.

Civil Aviation (1987): *International traffic:* passengers carried 391,519, freight handled 8,535 metric tons. *Domestic traffic:* passengers carried 384,604, freight handled 586 metric tons.

TOURISM

Visitors (1987): 142,820, excluding cruise passengers and excursionists. Of which: 69,909 from USA, 21,351 from France.

EDUCATION

1985/86: Pupils: Kindergarten 12,700; Primary 28,707; Secondary 13,372; Technical 3,944; Teachers (total, 1982/83): 3,215.
Source: Service de l'Education, Papeete.

Directory

The Government
(February 1989)

High Commissioner: JEAN MONTPEZAT.
Secretary-General: ROGER MOSER.

COUNCIL OF MINISTERS

The Council of Ministers is formed of a President, who is elected by the Territorial Assembly (see below) from among its members, and between six and 10 other members of the Assembly, chosen by the President and approved by the Assembly, to serve as Ministers.

President: ALEXANDRE LÉONTIEFF.
Vice-President and Minister for Agriculture, Traditional Crafts and the Cultural Heritage: GEORGES KELLY.
Minister for Social Affairs, Housing and Unity: Mme HUGUETTE HONG-KIOU.
Minister for Employment, Tourism and Sports: NAPOLÉON SPITZ.
Minister for the Sea, Equipment and Energy: BORIS LÉONTIEFF.
Minister for Finance and the Economy: LOUIS SAVOIE.
Minister for Financial Affairs and Island Development: IOANE TEMAURI.
Minister for Health, the Environment and Scientific Research: JACKY DROLLET.
Minister for Education and Teaching: RAYMOND VAN BASTOLAER.
Minister for Regionalization, Island Administration and Posts and Telecommunications: EMILE VERNAUDON.
Minister for Urbanization, Ground Transport and General Administration: FRANÇOIS NANAI.

MINISTRIES

All Ministries are in Papeete.

Legislature

ASSEMBLÉE TERRITORIALE

The Territorial Assembly is elected for a five-year term on the basis of universal adult suffrage. It has 41 members.

President: JEAN JUVENTIN.
Vice-President: HENRI MARERE.

Election, 16 March 1986

Party	Seats
Tahoeraa Huiraatira/RPR	24*
Amuitahiraa Mo Porinesia†	6
Pupu Here Ai'a	4
Ia Mana Te Nunaa	3
Front de Libération	2
Others	2
Total	**41**

* Increased from preliminary result of 21 seats, following a recount in one constituency and the decision of two members, elected as independents, to join the ruling party.
† A coalition of parties under the leadership of EMILE VERNAUDON and ENRIQUE ('QUITO') BRAUN-ORTEGA.

Deputies to the French National Assembly: ALEXANDRE LÉONTIEFF (RPR), EMILE VERNAUDON (Ai'a Api).
Representative to the French Senate: DANIEL MILLAUD (Union centriste des Démocrates de Progrès).

FRENCH OVERSEAS TERRITORIES

French Polynesia

Economic and Social Councillor: RAYMOND DESCLAUX.

Political Organizations

Ai'a Api (New Land): BP 11055, Mahina, Tahiti; tel. 481135; f. 1982 after split in Te E'a Api; Leader EMILE VERNAUDON.

Free Tahiti Party: Pres. CHARLIE CHING.

Front de Libération de la Polynésie (FLP)/Tavini Huiraatira: independence movement; Leader OSCAR TEMARU.

Ia Mana Te Nunaa: rue du Commandant Destrémau, BP 1223, Papeete; tel. 426699; f. 1976; advocates 'socialist independence'; Sec.-Gen. JACQUES DROLLET.

Maohi Nui: Leader MARIUS RAAPOTO.

Pupu Here Ai'a Te Nunaa Ia Ora: BP 3195, Papeete; tel. 420766; f. 1965; advocates autonomy; 8,000 mems; Pres. JEAN JUVENTIN.

Pupu Taina/Rassemblement des Libéraux: rue Cook, BP 169, Papeete; tel. 429880; f. 1976; seeks to retain close links with France; associated with the French Union pour la Démocratie Française (UDF); Leader MICHEL LAW.

Taatiraa Polynesia: BP 283, Papeete; tel. 428619; f. 1976; Leader ARTHUR CHUNG.

Tahoeraa Huiraatira/Rassemblement pour la République—RPR: rue du Commandant Destrémeau, BP 471, Papeete; tel. 429898; telex 249; f. 1958; supports links with France, with internal autonomy; Pres. GASTON FLOSSE.

Te E'a Api (United Front Party): Papeete; tel. 420366; advocates increased autonomy; Leader FRANCIS SANFORD.

Judicial System

Court of Administrative Law: BP 4522, Papeete; tel. 422482; Pres. JEAN LAVOIGNAT; Cllrs BERNARD LEPLAT, JEAN BRENIER, MICHEL AUBERT.

Court of Appeal: Papeete; tel. 420117; telex 308; Pres. HENRI DE LABRUSSE; Attorney-General PAUL MARCHAUD.

Court of the First Instance: Papeete; tel. 420116; telex 308; Pres. ALAIN LE GALL; Procurator JEAN-YVES DUVAL; Clerk of the Court DANIEL SALMON.

Religion

About 55% of the population are Protestant Christians.

CHRISTIANITY
Protestant Church

L'Eglise évangélique de Polynésie française (Ekalesia Evanelia no Polynesia Farani): BP 113, Papeete; tel. 420029; f. 1884; autonomous since 1963; c. 80,000 mems; Pres. of Council Rev. JACQUES TERAI IHORAI; Sec.-Gen. JOHN DOOM.

The Roman Catholic Church

French Polynesia comprises the archdiocese of Papeete and the suffragan diocese of Taiohae o Tefenuaenata. At 31 December 1986 there were an estimated 55,000 adherents in the territory, representing about 31% of the total population. The Archbishop and the Bishop participate in the Episcopal Conference of the Pacific, based in Fiji.

Archbishop of Papeete: Most Rev. MICHEL-GASPARD COPPENRATH, Archevêché, BP 94, Papeete; tel. 420251.

Other Churches

There are small Sanito, Church of Jesus Christ of Latter-day Saints (Mormon), and Seventh-day Adventist missions.

The Press

Le Canard Tahitien: rue Clapier, Papeete; weekly; French; satire.

La Dépêche de Tahiti: Société Polynésienne de Presse, BP 50, Papeete; tel. 424343; f. 1964; daily; Dir MICHEL ANGLADE; Man. PHILIPPE MAZELLIER; circ. 15,000.

Le Journal de Tahiti: BP 6000, Papeete; daily; French.

Les Nouvelles: BP 629, Papeete; tel. 429556; f. 1956; daily; French; Editor MICHEL FRANÇOIS.

Sports Tahiti: rue des Ramparts, BP 600, Papeete; 2 a week.

Tahiti Bulletin: BP 912, Papeete; daily; French and English.

Tahiti Sun Press: BP 887, Papeete; tel. 426850; f. 1980; weekly; English; Man. Editor AL PRINCE; circ. 4,000.

Te Ve'a Porotetani: BP 113, Papeete; tel. 420029; monthly; French and Tahitian; publ. by the Evangelical Church.

Foreign Bureaux

Agence France-Presse (AFP): BP 2679, Papeete; tel. 482121; Correspondent JEAN-PAUL PERÉA.

Associated Press (AP) (USA): BP 912, Papeete; tel. 437562; telex 537; Correspondent AL PRINCE.

Reuters (UK): BP 6144, Faaa, Tahiti; tel. Papeete 424343; Correspondent PHILIPPE MAZELLIER.

United Press International (UPI) (USA): BP 50, Papeete; tel. 424343; Correspondent MICHEL ANGLADE.

Publisher

Haere Po No Tahiti: BP 1958, Papeete; tel. 422469; f. 1981; travel, history, botany, linguistics and local interest.

Radio and Television

In 1985 there were an estimated 80,000 radio receivers and 26,000 television receivers in use, of which about 1,500 were colour receivers.

Radio-Télé-Tahiti: 410 rue Dumont d'Urville, BP 125, Papeete; tel. 439212; telex 200; f. 1951 as Radio-Tahiti; television service began 1965; operated by Société Nationale de Radio-Télévision Française d'Outre-Mer (RFO), Paris; daily programmes in French and Tahitian; Dir MARCEL BEAUBZA.

Finance

(cap. = capital; res = reserves; dep. = deposits; m. = million; brs = branches; amounts in CFP francs)

BANKING
Commercial Banks

Banque Indosuez (France): 2 place Notre-Dame, Papeete; tel. 427526; telex 395; Dir YVES CEVAERT; brs in Papeete, Faaa, Pirae and Uturoa.

Banque Paribas (France): Papeete; telex 392.

Banque de Polynésie SA: blvd Pomare, BP 530, Papeete; tel. 428688; telex 230; f. 1973; cap. and res 810m., dep. 24,219m. (Dec. 1985); Pres. JEAN-MICHEL LE PETIT; Gen. Man. GÉRARD CAVOLI; 13 brs.

Banque de Tahiti SA: 18 rue Paul Gauguin, BP 1602, Papeete; tel. 425389; telex 237; f. 1969; affil. to Bank of Hawaii, Honolulu, and Crédit Lyonnais, Paris; cap. 600m., dep. 28,077m. (Dec. 1987); Pres. JEAN-CLAUDE DUCCINI; Dirs MICHEL DUPIEUX, FRANCIS FORTLACROIX, GÉRARD E. SEIDL; 12 brs.

Trade and Industry

Chambre de Commerce et d'Industrie de la Polynésie Française: BP 118, Papeete; tel. 420344; telex 274; f. 1880; 27 mems; Pres. CHARLES T. POROÏ.

Chambre d'Agriculture et d'Elevage (CAEP): route de l'Hippodrome, BP 5383, Pirae; tel. 425393; f. 1886; 10 mems; Pres. SYLVAIN MILLAUD.

EMPLOYERS' ORGANIZATIONS

Chambre Syndicale des Entrepreneurs du Bâtiment et des Travaux Publics: BP 2218, Papeete; tel. 425309; Pres. CLAUDE GUTIERREZ.

Conseil des Employeurs: Immeuble FARA, rue E. Ahnne, BP 972, Papeete; tel. 438898; f. 1983; Pres. GILBERT BESNARD; Sec.-Gen. ASTRID PASQUIER.

Fédération Polynésienne de l'Agriculture et de l'Elevage: Papara, Tahiti; Pres. MICHEL LEHARTEL.

Fédération Polynésienne de l'Hôtellerie et des Industries Touristiques: BP 118, Papeete; tel. 423596; f. 1967; Pres. MICHEL AGID.

Syndicat des Importateurs et des Négociants: BP 1607, Papeete; Pres. JULES CHANGUES.

Union Interprofessionnelle du Tourisme de la Polynésie Française: BP 4560, Papeete; tel. 439114; f. 1973; 1,200 mems; Pres. PAUL MAETZ; Sec.-Gen. JEAN CORTEEL.

FRENCH OVERSEAS TERRITORIES — *French Polynesia, French Southern and Antarctic Territories*

Union Patronale: BP 317, Papeete; tel. 420257; f. 1948; 63 mems; Pres. Dominique Auroy.

TRADE UNIONS

Confédération des Syndicats Indépendants de Polynésie: Papeete; Sec.-Gen. Stanley Cross.

Fédération des Syndicats de la Polynésie Française: BP 1136, Papeete; Pres. Marcel Ahini.

Fédération Inter-Iles des Syndicats des Travailleurs de Polynésie Française: Papeete; Pres. Charles Taufa.

Syndicat de la Solidarité des Travailleurs Polynésiens: Papeete; Pres. Jean-Marc Pambrun.

Syndicat des Cadres de la Fonction Publique: Papeete; Pres. Pierre Allain.

Syndicat Territorial des Instituteurs et Institutrices de Polynésie: BP 3007, Papeete; Sec.-Gen. Willy Urima.

Union des Syndicats Autonomes des Travailleurs de Polynésie: BP 1201, Papeete; tel. 426049; Pres. Coco Teraiefa Chang; Sec.-Gen. Théodore Céran Jérusalemy.

Union des Syndicats de l'Aéronautique: Papeete; Pres. Joseph Conroy.

Union des Syndicats des Dockers Polynésiens: BP 3366, Papeete; Pres. Felix Colombel.

Union des Travailleurs de Tahiti et des Iles: rue Albert Leboucher, BP 3366, Papeete; tel. 437369; Pres. John Tefatua-Vaiho.

Transport

ROADS

French Polynesia has 792.2 km of roads, of which about one-third are bitumen-surfaced and two-thirds stone-surfaced.

SHIPPING

The principal port is Papeete, on Tahiti.

Agence Tahiti Poroi: Fare Ute, BP 83, Papeete; tel. 420070; telex 211; f. 1956; travel agents, tour operators.

Blue Star Line: Agents: Agence Maritime Internationale de Tahiti, BP 274, Papeete; tel. 428972; telex 227; monthly services to USA and New Zealand.

Compagnie Générale Maritime: ave du Général de Gaulle, BP 96, Papeete; tel. (689) 420890; telex 259; shipowners and agents; freight services between Europe and many international ports; agents in French Polynesia for Shell, Chevron, Total, Morflot, Cunard Line, Holland America Line and Sitmar Cruises, Norwegian American Cruises, Arcalia Shipping, Deilmann Reederei, Dilmun Navigation and Hapag Lloyd; Dir (vacant).

Other companies operating services to, or calling at, Papeete are: Daiwa Line, Karlander, Hamburg-Sued, China Navigation Co, Nedlloyd, Shipping Corpn of New Zealand Ltd, Bank Line and Kyowa Line.

CIVIL AVIATION

There is one international airport, Faaa airport, on Tahiti and there are about 40 smaller airstrips.

Air Moorea: BP 6019, Papeete; tel. 424834; telex 314; f. 1968; operates internal services between Tahiti and Moorea Island and some inter-territorial services; since 1985 the airline has been 90% govt-owned; Dir-Gen. Jean Gillot; fleet of 6 Britten Norman Islander, 2 Piper Aztec, 2 Twin Otter.

Air Tahiti: Blvd Pomare, BP 314, Papeete; tel. 422333; f. 1953; inter-islands services to Anaa, Apataki, Arutua, Bora Bora, Fakahina, Fakarava, Fangatau, Gambier-Mangareva, Hao, Hiva-oa, Huahine, Kaukura, Makemo, Manihi, Mataiva, Maupiti, Moorea, Napuka, Nuku Hiva, Nukutavake, Pukapuka, Pukarua, Raiatea, Rangiroa, Reao, Rurutu, Takapoto, Takaroa, Tatakoto, Tikehau, Tubuai, Tureia, Ua-Huka, Ua Pou and Vahitahi; since 1985 the company has been 24% govt-owned, with 10% being retained by the French airline UTA; Chair. Christian Vernaudon; Gen. Man. Marcel Galenon; fleet of 4 ATR-42, 1 Twin Otter DHC-6.

Tourism

Tourism is an important and developed industry in French Polynesia, particularly on Tahiti, and 161,200 people visited the territory in 1986, excluding cruise passengers and excursionists. In 1987 visitor arrivals declined to 142,820.

Office de Promotion et d'Animation Touristiques de Tahiti et ses Iles: Fare Manihini, blvd Pomare, BP 65, Papeete; tel. (689) 429626; telex 254; f. 1966; Dir Christian Vernaudon.

Service du Tourisme: Fare Manihini, blvd Pomare, BP 4527, Papeete; tel. (689) 429330; telex 254; Dir Gérard Vanizette.

Syndicat d'Initiative de la Polynésie Française: BP 326, Papeete; Pres. Mme Piu Bambridge.

FRENCH SOUTHERN AND ANTARCTIC TERRITORIES

The French Southern and Antarctic Territories (Terres Australes et Antarctiques françaises) form an Overseas Territory but are administered under a special statute. The territory comprises Adélie Land, a narrow segment of the mainland of Antarctica, and several islands (the Kerguelen and Crozet Archipelagos, St Paul and Amsterdam) in the southern Indian Ocean.

In 1987 certain categories of vessels were allowed to register under the flag of the Kerguelen Archipelago if 25% of their crew were French, including the captain and at least two officers. In January 1989 work began on the construction of a 1,100m airstrip in Adélie Land, which aimed to improve access to research facilities. However, violent clashes took place between construction workers and members of Greenpeace, the international environmental protection group, who occupied the site in protest against the project, which, they claimed, would involve the destruction of large penguin-breeding colonies. The French authorities subsequently agreed to allow Greenpeace to conduct an independent assessment of the environmental impact of the airstrip, before resuming work several days later.

Statistical Survey

Area (sq km): Kerguelen Archipelago 7,000, Crozet Archipelago 500, Amsterdam Island 60, St Paul Island 7, Adélie Land (Antarctica) 500,000.

Population (the population, comprising members of scientific missions, fluctuates according to season, being higher in the summer; the figures given are approximate): Kerguelen Archipelago, Port-aux-Français 100; Amsterdam Island at Martin de Viviès 40; Adélie Land at Base Dumont d'Urville 30; the Crozet Archipelago at Alfred-Faure 40; St Paul Island is uninhabited. Total population (January 1985): 210.

Fishing: (catch in metric tons): Crayfish in Amsterdam and St Paul: 330 (1988); fishing by French and foreign fleets in the Kerguelen Archipelago: 10,000 annually.

Currency: French currency is used (see French Guiana).

Budget: Balanced at approx. 160m. francs annually.

External Trade: Exports consist mainly of crayfish and other fish going to France and Réunion.

Directory

Government: Chief Administrator Claude Corbier; there is a Central Administration in Paris (34 rue des Renaudes, 75017 Paris, France; telex 640980).

Consultative Council: composed of 7 members appointed by the Secrétariat d'Etat aux Départments et Territoires d'Outre-Mer, Ministries of National Education, Scientific Research, Merchant Marine, National Meteorology, National Defence and scientists; Pres. Claude Frejacques.

Transport: Shipping: A charter vessel calls five times a year in the Antarctic islands, and another calls twice a year in Adélie Land. Civil Aviation: a landing strip of 1,100 m is being built, at a cost of 100m. francs, to serve the research station on Adélie Land.

Research Stations: There are meteorological stations and geophysical research stations on Kerguelen, Amsterdam, Adélie Land and Crozet.

… FRENCH OVERSEAS TERRITORIES — New Caledonia

NEW CALEDONIA

Introductory Survey

Location, Climate, Language, Religion, Capital

The territory of New Caledonia comprises one large island and several smaller ones, lying in the south Pacific Ocean, about 1,500 km (930 miles) east of Queensland, Australia. The main island, New Caledonia, is long and narrow, and has a total area of 16,750 sq km; rugged mountains divide the west of the island from the east, and there is little flat land. The nearby Loyalty Islands, which are administratively part of the territory, are 2,353 sq km in area, and a third group of islands, the uninhabited Chesterfield Islands, lies about 400 km north-west of the main island. The climate is generally a mild one, with an average temperature of about 23°C (73°F) and a rainy season between December and March. The average rainfall in the east of the main island is about 2,000 mm (80 in) per year, and in the west about 1,000 mm (40 in). French is the official language, but Polynesian and Melanesian languages are also spoken by the indigenous population. New Caledonians are almost all Christians; about 65% are Roman Catholics, and there is a substantial Protestant minority. The capital is Nouméa, on the main island.

Recent History

New Caledonia became a French possession in 1853, when the island was annexed as a dependency of Tahiti. In 1884 a separate administration was established, and in 1946 it became an overseas territory of the French Republic. Early European settlers on New Caledonia, supported by legislation, quickly assumed possession of Melanesian land, which provoked a number of rebellions by the indigenous population.

In 1956 the first Territorial Assembly, with 30 members, was elected by universal adult suffrage, although the French Governor effectively retained control of the functions of government. New Caledonian demands for a measure of self-government were answered in December 1976 by a new statute, which gave the Council of Government, elected from the Territorial Assembly, responsibility for certain internal affairs. The post of Governor was replaced by that of French High Commissioner to the territory. In 1978 the pro-independence parties obtained a majority of the posts in the Council of Government but, in March 1979, the French Government dismissed the Council, following its failure to support a proposal for a 10-year 'contract' between France and New Caledonia, because the plan did not acknowledge the possibility of New Caledonian independence. The territory was then placed under the direct authority of the High Commissioner. A general election was held in July, but a new electoral law, which affected mainly the Melanesian-supported, pro-independence parties, ensured that minor parties were not represented in the Assembly. Two parties loyal to France together won 22 of the 36 seats.

Tension grew sharply in September 1981 after the assassination of Pierre Declercq, Secretary-General of the pro-independence party Union calédonienne, and in November President Mitterrand of France called an urgent meeting of ministers in Paris to discuss the situation. Recognizing the need for major reforms, Henri Emmanuelli, the Secretary of State for Overseas Departments and Territories, outlined in December the immediate aims of the French Government, including fiscal reform, equal access for all New Caledonians to positions of authority, land reforms, the wider distribution of mining revenue and the fostering of Melanesian cultural institutions. To assist in effecting these reforms, the French Government simultaneously announced that it would rule by decree for a period of at least one year. In June 1982, accusing its partner in the ruling coalition of 'active resistance to evolution and change' in New Caledonia, the Fédération pour une nouvelle société calédonienne (FNSC) joined with the opposition Front indépendantiste (FI) to form a government which was more favourable to the proposed reforms.

In July 1983 the French Government held a meeting in Paris with representatives of the territory's main political groupings, and drew up a statute, providing for a five-year period of increased autonomy from July 1984 and a referendum in 1989 to determine New Caledonia's future, with independence as one of the options to be offered. The statute was opposed in New Caledonia, both by parties in favour of earlier independence and by those against, and it was rejected by the Territorial Assembly in April 1984. However, it was approved by the French National Assembly in September 1984. Under the provisions of the statute, the territorial Council of Ministers was responsible for many internal matters of government, its President henceforth being an elected member instead of the French High Commissioner; a second legislative chamber, with the right to be consulted on development planning and budgetary issues, was created at the same time. All of the main parties seeking independence, except the Libération kanake socialiste (LKS) party, which left the FI, boycotted elections for a new Territorial Assembly in November 1984 and, following the dissolution of the FI, formed a new movement called the Front de libération nationale kanake socialiste (FLNKS), whose congress instituted a 'provisional government', headed by Jean-Marie Tjibaou, on 1 December. The elections to the Territorial Assembly attracted only 50.12% of electors, and the anti-independence party Rassemblement pour la Calédonie dans la République (RPCR) won 34 of the 42 seats and 70.9% of the total vote. An escalation of violence by both Kanaks (Melanesians) and Caldoches (French settlers) began in November but, after a number of deaths had resulted, political leaders successfully appealed for peace.

In January 1985 Edgard Pisani, the new High Commissioner, announced a plan by which the territory might become independent 'in association with' France on 1 January 1986, subject to the result of a referendum in July 1985, in which all adults resident in the territory for at least three years would have the right to vote. A major obstacle to the success of such a plan was the fact that Melanesians constituted only 43% of the population of the territory, with people of European (37%) and other, mainly Asian and Pacific, origin accounting for the balance; Melanesian groups seeking independence had hitherto insisted that the indigenous population be allowed to determine its own fate. A resurgence of violence followed the announcement of Pisani's plan for a referendum on independence, and a state of emergency was declared after Eloi Machoro, a leading member of the FLNKS, was shot dead by police in an incident at La Foa, 65 km west of Nouméa. The renewed violence prompted President Mitterrand to make a brief visit to the territory later in the month.

In April 1985 the French Prime Minister, Laurent Fabius, announced a new plan for the future of New Caledonia, whereby the referendum on independence, formerly scheduled for July 1985, was deferred until an unspecified date not later than the end of December 1987. Meanwhile, the territory was to be divided into four regions, each to be governed by its own elected autonomous council, which would have extensive powers in the spheres of planning and development, education, health and social services, land rights, transport and housing. The elected members of all four councils together would serve as regional representatives in a territory-wide Congress (to replace the Territorial Assembly).

The new set of proposals (known as the 'Fabius plan') was well received by the FLNKS, which, at its third Congress in May 1985, voted in favour of participating in the regional elections, although it reaffirmed the ultimate goal of independence. It was also decided to maintain the 'provisional government' under Tjibaou at least until the end of December. The RPCR, however, condemned the plan, pointing out that the envisaged distribution of seats would give a more favourable ratio of seats to voters in the pro-independence regions, and the proposals were rejected by the predominantly anti-independence Territorial Assembly at the end of May. However, the necessary legislation was approved by the French National Assembly in Paris in July, and the Fabius plan came into force.

The elections were held in September 1985, and, as expected, only in the Centre region around Nouméa, where the bulk of the population is non-Melanesian, was an anti-independence majority recorded. However, the pro-independence Melanesians, in spite of their majorities in the three non-urban regions, would be in a minority in the Territorial Congress. Although the elections took place without disruption, there were subsequent fears that the feelings that had been aroused by right-wing anti-independence campaigners might result in resistance to the new political arrangements.

The FLNKS boycotted the general election to the French National Assembly in March 1986, in which the Socialists were defeated by a conservative alliance, including the Rassemblement pour la République (RPR), led by Jacques Chirac, who became Prime Minister of France. Only about 50% of the eligible voters in New Caledonia participated in the election, at which the territory's two seats in the Assembly were won by RPR candidates.

In May 1986 the French Council of Ministers approved a draft law providing for a referendum to be held in New Caledonia within 12 months, whereby a choice would be offered between independence and a further extension of regional autonomy. Chirac indicated that he was confident that the populace would vote to remain part of the French Republic. The proposal was opposed by the Socialist President, François Mitterrand, but was approved by the French National Assembly.

Chirac visited New Caledonia in August 1986, when he outlined a proposed development programme, costing an estimated $A80m., to be implemented during 1986/87. He also indicated to the New Caledonian political groups that the conduct of the referendum was open to negotiation.

At the 17th meeting of the South Pacific Forum in Suva, Fiji, in September 1986, representatives of the 13 member countries condemned the Chirac programme and expressed support for measures to hasten New Caledonia's independence from France, voting to refer the issue to the UN Committee on Decolonization.

Discussions on the question of self-determination were resumed in Nouméa in December, when the French Minister for Overseas Departments and Territories, Bernard Pons, acceded to the request of the FLNKS that the electorate eligible to participate in the referendum on independence be limited to those who had been resident in New Caledonia for at least three years. Subsequently, however, the discussions reached a deadlock. In December, in spite of strong French diplomatic opposition, the UN General Assembly voted to reinscribe New Caledonia on the UN list of non-self-governing territories.

At the sixth FLNKS Congress, held in May 1987, Tjibaou announced the movement's decision to advocate an 'active but peaceful' boycott of the referendum, which, a month later, the French Government officially fixed for 13 September. In August six Kanaks were arrested during protests against the proposed referendum, which occurred despite a French ban on demonstrations in the territory. President Mitterrand condemned his Government's handling of the affair, criticizing, in particular, the brutality with which police units had dispersed the protesters.

At the referendum on 13 September 1987, 48,611 votes were cast in favour of New Caledonia's continuation as part of the French Republic (98.3% of the total) and only 842 (1.7%) were cast in favour of independence. Of the registered electorate, almost 59% voted, a higher level of participation than was expected, although 90% of the electorate abstained in constituencies inhabited by a majority of Melanesians.

In November 1987 Pons submitted a plan, designed to give the territory a limited administrative independence, to New Caledonia's Territorial Assembly. The plan received 24 votes (out of 46 cast), although FLNKS members refused to participate. The plan provided for a slight modification to three of New Caledonia's administrative regions, with the fourth, the Loyalty Islands, remaining unaffected. It was also envisaged that the Territorial Assembly would be replaced by an Executive Council, composed of the four regional Presidents, an elected President of the Council and five other elected members. However, the plan was sharply criticized by FLNKS leaders, who claimed that it would reduce New Caledonia to a position of 'economic slavery'.

In October 1987 seven pro-French loyalists were acquitted on a charge of murdering 10 Kanak separatists in 1984. Tjibaou, who reacted to the ruling by declaring that his followers would have to abandon their stance of pacifism, and his deputy, Yeiwéné Yeiwéné, were indicted for 'incitement to violence'. In December Yeiwéné was arrested and formally charged, but was soon released.

In April 1988, however, four gendarmes were killed, and 27 held hostage in a cave, on the island of Ouvéa by supporters of the FLNKS. Days later, Kanak separatists prevented about one-quarter of the territory's polling stations from opening, when local elections, scheduled to coincide with the French presidential election, were held. The FLNKS boycotted the elections. Although 12 of the gendarmes taken hostage were subsequently released, six members of a French anti-terrorist squad were captured. French security forces immediately laid siege to the cave and, in the following month, made an assault upon it, leaving 19 Kanaks and two gendarmes dead. Following the siege, allegations that three Kanaks had been executed or left to die, after being arrested, led to an announcement by the new French Government that a judicial inquiry into the incident was to be opened.

At the elections to the French National Assembly in June 1988, both seats were retained by the RPCR. Michel Rocard, the new French Prime Minister, chaired negotiations in Paris between the President of the RPCR, Jacques Lafleur, and the President of the FLNKS, Jean-Marie Tjibaou, which reached agreement to transfer the administration of the territory to Paris for 12 months. Under the provisions of the agreement, the territory was to be divided into three administrative regions (of which two would almost certainly be under Kanak rule) until 1998, when a territorial plebiscite was to be held. Only people resident in the territory in 1988, and their direct descendants, would be allowed to vote in the plebiscite. The programme was presented to the French electorate in a referendum, held on 6 November 1988, and approved by a majority of 80%, although an abstention rate of 63%, the largest in French electoral history, was recorded. The programme was approved by a 57% majority in New Caledonia, where the rate of absention was 37%. In November, under the terms of the agreement, 51 separatists were released from prison, including 26 Kanaks implicated in the incident on Ouvéa. Elections to the three newly-constituted provincial assemblies were scheduled to take place in June 1989.

Government

The French Government is represented in New Caledonia by its High Commissioner to the territory, and controls a number of important spheres of government, including defence, foreign diplomacy and justice. Pending the implementation in July 1989 of proposed administrative reforms, whereby the territory was to be divided into three regions—North, South and the Loyalty Islands, New Caledonia was to be administered by the French Government directly from Paris. Each region would be governed by a council, which would be elected by direct universal suffrage and have its own elected President. The three regional councils together would form the Territorial Congress, which, in turn, would have its own elected President. Members of the three regional councils were to be subject to re-election every six years. The French High Commissioner was to retain overall executive power.

In 1988 an executive council, comprising the Presidents of the regional councils and headed by the President of the Territorial Congress, had a consultative role in the discussion of proposals submitted to the Congress. In each region there was a 'customary' consultative council, charged with giving an opinion on all matters submitted to it by the regional authorities, while the members of all four consultative councils together constituted a territorial 'customary' council, which had an advisory role in the consideration of all questions submitted to it by the High Commissioner.

In addition, New Caledonia elects two deputies to the French National Assembly in Paris, one representative to the French Senate and one Economic and Social Councillor, all chosen on the basis of universal adult suffrage.

Defence

France was maintaining a force of 9,500 military personnel in New Caledonia in June 1988.

Economic Affairs

New Caledonia possesses about 30% of the world's known reserves of nickel, and is one of the largest producers of the metal. Production of nickel ore totalled 86,592 metric tons (metal content) in 1980, declining to 46,162 tons in 1983, but rising to 58,326 tons in 1984. Industrial production of ferro-nickel and nickel matte increased from 37,000 metric tons in 1987 to 47,000 tons in 1988. Other metals present in the territory include chromium cobalt, iron, manganese, lead and zinc, but these are mined only spasmodically.

Nickel is the principal export commodity, accounting for 87% of total export revenue in 1986, the main customers being France (which took 56.5% of total exports in 1986) and Japan. Exports for that year totalled 1,286,840 metric tons, earning 26,249m. francs CPF, and imports amounted to 768,018 tons, incurring expenditure of 62,939m. francs CFP. Copra and coffee are also exported, and other important crops are cereals, potatoes, sweet potatoes, bananas and other fruits and vegetables. Cattle-farming is often able to satisfy entirely the territory's demand for beef.

New Caledonia's considerable dependence on the nickel industry has led to periods of economic depression, such as occurred in 1973, when demand for the product is low. Political unrest during 1984 and 1985 led to enormous financial losses; sabotage and strike action at New Caledonia's main nickel mine, at Thio, in early 1985 stopped production for three months, and resulted in a reduction in output of more than 40%.

In an effort to diversify the economy, the production of import substitutes, together with other enterprises not based on nickel, are being encouraged by grants, subsidies and tax concessions, and the territory's 1984 budget provided for considerable expenditure on regional development, with particular emphasis on agriculture, forestry and fishing. In January 1985 the French President, François Mitterrand, announced plans to strengthen French military bases in New Caledonia and to build a major naval base in Nouméa.

In mid-1985 a million-dollar campaign was launched in an attempt to revive the tourist industry, one of the mainstays of the territory's economy, which had also been severely affected by the recent political strife. The French Government agreed to subsidize the wages of staff at hotels and restaurants that would otherwise have been faced with the prospect of closure, and to provide funding for a large-scale development programme to improve tourist facilities. Large-scale promotional campaigns, aimed at encouraging tourists, were also launched, and by the end of 1986 the number of visitors to the territory had risen to 57,396 from the 1985 total of 51,190. However, outbreaks of violence in mid-1988 between local French settlers and Kanak separatists seriously affected tourist arrivals in 1988.

With business interests and overseas investment in New Caledonia growing, the economy was showing signs of recovery in

1987. About one-third of budget expenditure was financed by France, and it was announced in August that France's exceptional aid to the territory was to continue, with 2,500m. Franch francs being contributed towards the 1988 budget.

The annual rate of inflation averaged 12.3% in 1983, falling to 8.7% in 1984, 5.5% in 1985 and 1.5% in 1986. Inflation was only 0.1% in the year ending April 1987. According to estimates by the World Bank, the territory's gross national product (at average 1983–85 prices) was US $860m. ($5,760 per head) in 1985.

Social Welfare
In 1981 there were 38 hospitals in New Caledonia, with a total of 1,536 beds, and there were 168 physicians working in the territory.

Education
Education is compulsory for 10 years between six and 16 years of age. Schools are operated by both the State and churches, under the supervision of the Department of Education. The French Government finances the state secondary system. In 1984 there were 278 primary schools (with 33,884 pupils), 41 secondary schools (with 12,481 pupils), 32 technical institutions (with 5,264 students) and five institutions of higher education (with 660 students). About 100 students attend universities in France. Part of a new regional university, planned by France, is to be based in New Caledonia.

Public Holidays
1989: 2 January (for New Year's Day), 27 March (Easter Monday), 1 May (Labour Day), 4 May (Ascension Day), 8 May (Liberation Day), 15 May (Whit Monday), 14 July (Fall of the Bastille), 11 November (Armistice Day), 25 December (Christmas Day).
1990: 1 January (New Year's Day), 16 April (Easter Monday), 7 May (for Labour Day), 8 May (Liberation Day), 24 May (Ascension Day), 4 June (Whit Monday), 14 July (Fall of the Bastille), 11 November (Armistice Day), 25 December (Christmas Day).

Weights and Measures
The metric system is in force.

Statistical Survey

Source (unless otherwise stated): Direction Territoriale de la Statistique et des Etudes Economiques, BP 823, Nouméa; tel. 275481.

AREA AND POPULATION
Area: 19,103 sq km (7,376 sq miles).
Population: 145,368 (census of April 1983); 154,000 (official estimate, mid-1986); *Capital:* Nouméa, population 60,112 (1983 census).
Ethnic Groups (census of 1983): Melanesians 61,870, Europeans 53,974, Wallisians 12,174, Polynesians 5,570, Others 11,780.
Births and Deaths (1986): Live births 3,779, deaths 851.
Economically Active Population (census of 1983, excluding 3,497 unemployed): Agriculture 4,727, Total (incl. others) 44,842.

AGRICULTURE, ETC.
Principal Crops (FAO estimates, metric tons, 1985): Maize 1,156 (1986), Wheat 572 (1986), Sorghum 443 (1986), Taro 3,000, Potatoes 2,000, Sweet potatoes 4,000, Yams 11,000, Coconuts 11,000, Cassava 3,000, Vegetables and melons 5,000, Fruit 9,000. Source: mainly FAO, *Production Yearbook*.
Livestock ('000 head, 1986): Horses 9, Cattle 121, Pigs 35, Sheep 2, Goats 18.
Forestry (FAO estimate, '000 cu m): Roundwood removals: 12 in 1986. Source: FAO, *Yearbook of Forest Products*.
Fishing (FAO estimates, metric tons): 3,508 in 1984; 3,027 in 1985; 4,156 in 1986. Source: FAO, *Yearbook of Fishery Statistics*.

MINING
Production (metric tons): Nickel ore (metal content) 60,101 in 1982; 46,162 in 1983; 58,326 in 1984. Source: UN, *Industrial Statistics Yearbook*.

INDUSTRY
Production ('000 metric tons, 1986): Ferro-nickel 33; nickel matte 9.2; Electric energy 1,050.2m. kWh.

FINANCE
Currency and Exchange Rates: see French Polynesia.
Budget (1986, million francs CFP): Expenditure: Ordinary expenditure 36,023, Extraordinary expenditure 3,232, Total 39,255; Revenue: Ordinary receipts 36,023, Extraordinary receipts 3,232, Total 39,255. Direct aid from France in 1986 amounted to 13,640m. francs CFP.

Aid from France (francs CFP, FIDES 1982): Local section 153m.; General section 1,018m.
Cost of Living (Consumer Price Index for Nouméa; base: 1980 = 100): 160.2 in 1984; 169.0 in 1985; 171.6 in 1986. Source: International Labour Office.
Gross Domestic Product (million francs CFP at current prices): 96,304 in 1981; 108,093 in 1982; 114,161 in 1983.

EXTERNAL TRADE
Principal Commodities (million francs CFP, 1986): *Imports:* Petroleum products 7,373; Solid mineral fuels 1,291; Wine 842; Rice 276; Total (incl. others) 62,939. *Exports:* Ferro-nickel 14,125; Nickel ore 3,146; Nickel matte 3,245; Total (incl. others) 26,249.
Principal Trading Partners (million francs CFP, 1986): *Imports:* France (metropolitan) 31,648; USA 3,107; Australia 4,669; Oman 2,417; Total (incl. others) 62,939. *Exports:* France (metropolitan) 13,732; Japan 4,142; India 1,478; USA 1,673; Total (incl. others) 26,249.

TRANSPORT
Road Traffic (1986): Motor vehicles (incl. tractors) 44,551.
Shipping (1986): Vessels entered 363; Freight unloaded 813,000 metric tons, Freight loaded 1,334,900 metric tons.
Civil Aviation (La Tontouta airport, Nouméa, 1986): Passengers arriving 101,584, Passengers departing 101,736; Freight unloaded 3,828 metric tons, Freight loaded 1,594 metric tons.

TOURISM
Visitors (1986): 57,396. (Source: Police de l'Air et des Frontières.)

EDUCATION
Primary (1986): 271 schools, 31,875 pupils, 1,560 teachers.
Secondary (1986): 45 schools, 13,193 pupils, 1,382 teachers (secondary and technical).
Technical (1986): 29 institutions, 5,721 students, 1,382 teachers (secondary and technical).
Higher (1986): 5 institutions, 859 students, 66 teachers.

Directory
The Government
(February 1989)

High Commissioner: BERNARD GRASSET.
Secretary-General: JACQUES IÉKAWÉ.

Legislature

Before late 1988 the territory was administered by a Territorial Congress, comprising four autonomous elected regional councils. However, following prolonged civil unrest in 1988, an agreement among contending factions within the territory provided for the transfer of power to metropolitan France for 12 months, pending the creation of three new regional councils. Elections for the new councils were due to take place in June 1989. The three regions were to be the North (with 15 members), the South (with 32 members), and the Loyalty Islands (with 7 members). As part of the agreement, a referendum on self-determination was scheduled for 1998.

Pending the creation of councils, the territory was to be administered by a French high commissioner, assisted by a consultative committee. The members of the committee were: JACQUES LAFLEUR (RPCR), MAURICE NÉNOU-PWATAHO (RPCR), DICK UKEIWÉ (RPCR), JEAN LÈQUES (RPCR), JEAN-MARIE TJIBAOU (FLNKS), CHENEPA BOWÉ (UPM), LOUIS KOTRA UREGEÏ (USTKE), JEAN-PIERRE AÏFA (Independent).

FRENCH OVERSEAS TERRITORIES

Election, 24 April 1988*

Party	Votes	%	Seats
RPCR	31,235	64.46	35
FN	10,899	22.49	8
FC	2,916	6.01	2
UPC†	1,475	3.04	2
Others	1,924	3.97	1
Total	48,449	100.00	48

* The election was boycotted by pro-independence groups, including the FLNKS and LKS. The abstention rate was 43.6%.
† The Union pour construire (UPC) was established specially for the election by dissidents from the LKS who disagreed with their party's decision to refuse to participate.

Until 1988 a 'customary' consultative council (conseil consultatif coutumier) from each region was charged with giving an opinion on all matters submitted to it by the regional authorities. A territorial 'customary' council (conseil coutumier territorial), composed of all four consultative councils, gave advice on all questions submitted to it by the High Commissioner.

Deputies to the French National Assembly: JACQUES LAFLEUR (RPCR), MAURICE NÉNOU-PWATAHO (RPCR).

Representative to the French Senate: DICK UKEIWÉ (RPCR).

Economic and Social Councillor: GUY MENNESSON.

Political Organizations

Parties in favour of retaining the status quo or of New Caledonia's becoming a department of France:

Front calédonien (FC): extreme right-wing.

Front national (FN): Nouméa; extreme right-wing; Leader GUY GEORGE.

Rassemblement Pour la Calédonie dans la République (RPCR): 8 avenue Foch, BP 306, Nouméa; tel. 282620; f. 1977; Leader JACQUES LAFLEUR; a coalition of the following parties:

   Centre des démocrates sociaux (CDS): Nouméa; f. 1971; Leader JEAN LÈQUES.

   Parti républicain (PR): BP 3002, Nouméa; tel. 282620; Leader PIERRE MARESCA.

Parties in favour of internal autonomy:

Fédération pour une nouvelle société calédonienne (FNSC): Nouméa; f. 1979; Leader JEAN-PIERRE AÏFA; a coalition of the following parties:

   Mouvement wallisien et futunien: f. 1979; Pres. FINAU MELITO.

   Parti républicain calédonien (PRC): 8 rue Gagarine, Nouméa; tel. 252395; f. 1979; Leader LIONEL CHERRIER.

   Union démocratique (UD): Nouméa; f. 1968; Leader GASTON MORLET.

   Union nouvelle calédonienne (UNC): Nouméa; f. 1977; Leader JEAN-PIERRE AÏFA.

Parties in favour of independence:

Front de libération nationale kanake socialiste (FLNKS): BP 3553, Nouméa; tel. 274033; f. 1984 (following dissolution of Front indépendantiste); Leaders JEAN-MARIE TJIBAOU, YEIWÉNÉ YEIWÉNÉ; a grouping of the following parties:

   Front uni de libération kanak (FULK): Nouméa; f. 1974; Leader YANN CÉLÉNÉ UREGEI.

   Parti de libération kanak (PALIKA): Cité Pierre L'enquête, Nouméa; f. 1975; 5,000 mems; Leaders PAUL NEAOUTYINE, ELIE POIGOUNE.

   Parti socialiste calédonien (PSC): Nouméa; f. 1975; Leader M. VIOLETTE.

   Union calédonienne (UC): 8 rue Gambetta, 1° Vallée du Tir, Nouméa; f. 1952; 5,000 mems; Leader JEAN-MARIE TJIBAOU; Sec.-Gen. LÉOPOLD JORÉDIÉ.

   Union progressiste mélanésienne (UPM): Nouméa; f. 1974 as the Union progressiste multiraciale; 2,300 mems; Leader CHENEPA BOWÉ.

Libération kanake socialiste (LKS): Nouméa; Leader NIDOÏSH NAISSELINE.

Union pour construire (UPC): f. 1988, by mems of the LKS who opposed their party's decision to boycott regional elections; Leader FRANCIS POADOUY.

New Caledonia

Judicial System

Court of Appeal: Palais de Justice, BP F4, Nouméa; First Pres. C. HANOTEAU; Procurator-Gen. GILLES LUCAZEAU.

Court of the First Instance: Nouméa; Pres. JEAN-LOUIS SIBAND; Procurator of the Republic ROBERT FINIELZ.

Religion

The population is overwhelmingly Christian, with Roman Catholics comprising about 65% of the total. About 3% of the inhabitants are Muslims.

CHRISTIANITY

The Roman Catholic Church

The territory comprises a single archdiocese, with an estimated 93,500 adherents in 1986. The Archbishop participates in the Episcopal Conference of the Pacific, based in Fiji.

Archbishop of Nouméa: Most Rev. MICHEL-MARIE-BERNARD CALVET, Archevêché, BP 3, 4 rue Mgr-Fraysse, Nouméa; tel. 273149.

The Anglican Communion

Within the Church of the Province of Melanesia, New Caledonia forms part of the diocese of Vanuatu (q.v.). The Archbishop of the Province is the Bishop of Central Melanesia (resident in Honaira, Solomon Islands).

Protestant Churches

Eglise évangelique en Nouvelle-Calédonie et aux Iles Loyauté: BP 277, Nouméa; f. 1960; Pres. Rev. SAILALI PASSA; Gen. Sec. Rev. TELL KASARHEROU.

Other churches active in the territory include the Assembly of God, the Free Evangelical Church, the Presbyterian Church and the Tahitian Evangelical Church.

BAHÁ'Í FAITH

National Spiritual Assembly: BP 1564, Nouméa; tel. 275624; mems resident in 27 localities in New Caledonia and 11 localities in the Loyalty Is.

The Press

L'Avenir Calédonien: 10 rue Gambetta, Nouméa; organ of the Union calédonienne; Dir PAÏTA GABRIEL.

Le Devenir Calédonien: 7 rue Mascart, Rivière Salée, BP 4481, Nouméa; monthly; social, cultural and economic news.

Dixit: BP 370, Nouméa; tel. 286631; telex 3078; f. 1984; annual; French (circ. 12,000) and English (circ. 8,000); Dir HUBERT CHAVELET.

Eglise de Nouvelle-Calédonie: BP 170, Nouméa; f. 1976; fortnightly; official publ. of the Roman Catholic Church; circ. 450.

La France Australe: 5 rue de la Somme, BP 25, Nouméa; tel. 274444; daily.

Le Journal Calédonien: BP 3002, Nouméa; weekly.

Les Nouvelles Calédoniennes: 41–43 rue de Sébastopol, BP 179, Nouméa; tel. 272584; telex 3812; f. 1971; daily; Publr HENRI MORNY; Dir MAXIME BRIANÇON; Editor HENRI PERRON; circ. 18,000.

La Presse Calédonienne: 14 rue de Sebastopol, BP 4034, Nouméa; tel. 285055; daily; circ. 8,000.

NEWS AGENCY

Agence France-Presse (AFP): 29 rue Tindale, Nouméa; tel. 263033; telex 3826; Correspondent (vacant).

Publisher

Editions d'Art Calédoniennes: 40 rue de Paris, BP 1626, Nouméa; tel. 261184; telex 3048; art, reprints, travel.

Radio and Television

In 1985 there were an estimated 80,000 radio receivers and 32,000 television receivers in use, of which about 21,000 were colour receivers.

RADIO

Radiodiffusion Française d'Outre-mer (RFO): BP G3, Nouméa; tel. 274327; telex 3052; f. 1942; 20 hours of daily programmes in French; Dir ALAIN LE GARREC.

Radio Djiido: Dir OCTAVE TOGNA.

Radio Rythme Bleu: BP 1390, Nouméa; tel. 283357.

TELEVISION

Télé Nouméa: Société Nationale de Radio-Télévision Française d'Outre-mer, BP G3, Nouméa; tel. 274327; telex 3052; f. 1965; transmits 10 hours daily; Dir ALAIN LE GARREC.

Finance

(cap. = capital; res = reserves; m. = million; brs = branches; amounts in CFP francs)

BANKING

Banque Indosuez (France): angle rue de l'Alma et ave Foch, BP G5, Nouméa; tel. 272212; telex 3023.

Banque Nationale de Paris Nouvelle Calédonie (France): 37 R.T. 13, BP K3, Nouméa; tel. 275555; telex 3022; f. 1969 as Banque Nationale de Paris; present name adopted in 1978; cap. and res 70m., dep. 920m. (Dec. 1986); Pres. JEAN-LOUIS HAUTCOEUR; Gen. Man. JACQUES LOBINGER; 8 brs.

Banque de Nouvelle-Calédonie (BNC)/Crédit Lyonnais: 25 ave de la Victoire, BP L3, Nouméa; tel. 285069; telex 3091; f. 1984; cap. 285m. (Oct. 1988); Pres. BERNARD THIOLON; Dir ROBERT SABATIER.

Banque Paribas Pacifique (Nouvelle-Calédonie): 33 rue de l'Alma, BP 777, Nouméa; tel. 275181; telex 3086; cap. and res 740m., dep. 9,636m. (Dec. 1986); Chair. PIERRE MARTINAUD; Gen. Man. CHRISTIAN DE BERNEDE.

Société Générale Calédonienne de Banque: 56 ave de la Victoire, BP G2, Nouméa; tel. 272264; telex 3067; f. 1981; cap. 275m. (1985); Gen. Man. RAYMOND CLAVIER; 6 brs.

Trade and Industry

Chambre d'Agriculture: BP 111, Nouméa; tel. 272056; f. 1909; 46 mems; Pres. ROGER PENE.

Chambre de Commerce et d'Industrie: BP 10, Nouméa; tel. 272551; telex 3045; f. 1879; 20 mems; Pres. ARNOLD DALY; Gen. Man. GEORGES GIOVANNELLI.

EMPLOYERS' ORGANIZATION

Fédération Patronale de Nouvelle-Calédonie et Dépendances: 13 rue de Verdun, BP 466, Nouméa; tel. 273525; telex 3045; f. 1936; represents the leading companies of New Caledonia in the defence of professional interests, co-ordination, documentation and research in socio-economic fields; Pres. DIDIER LEROUX; Sec.-Gen. ANNIE BEUSTES.

TRADE UNIONS

Confédération des Travailleurs Calédoniens: Nouméa; Sec.-Gen. R. JOYEUX; grouped with:

    Fédération des Fonctionnaires: Nouméa; Sec.-Gen. GILBERT NOUVEAU.

Syndicat Général des Collaborateurs des Industries de Nouvelle Calédonie: Sec.-Gen. H. CHAMPIN.

Union des Syndicats des Travailleurs kanak exploités (USTKE): Nouméa, BP 4372; affiliated to FLNKS; Leader LOUIS KOTRA UREGEÏ.

Union des Syndicats Ouvriers et Employés de Nouvelle-Calédonie: Nouméa; Sec.-Gen. GUY MENNESSON.

Union Territoriale Force Ouvrière: 13 rue Jules Ferry, BP 4773, Nouméa; tel. 274950; f. 1982; Sec.-Gen. BERNARD CHENAIE.

Transport

ROADS

In 1983 there was a total of 5,980 km of roads in New Caledonia; 766 km were bitumen-surfaced, 589 km unsealed, 1,618 km stone-surfaced and 2,523 km tracks in 1980. The outer islands had a total of 470 km of roads and tracks in 1980.

SHIPPING

Most traffic is through the port of Nouméa. Passenger and cargo services, linking Nouméa to other towns and islands, are regular and frequent.

Shipping companies operating cargo services include Hamburg-Sued, Nedlloyd and Bank Line (which connect Nouméa with European ports), Kyowa Line (with Hong Kong, Taiwan, the Republic of Korea and Japan), Somacal (with Sydney, Australia), Sofrana-Unilines (with various Pacific islands and ports on the west coast of Australia), Daiwa Line (with Sydney, Australia, Japan, and various Pacific Islands), Compagnie des Chargeurs Calédoniens (with Sydney, Australia, and European and Mediterranean ports) and the China Navigation Co (with New Zealand, Fiji and Japan).

CIVIL AVIATION

There is an international airport at Nouméa, and an internal network provides air services linking Nouméa to other towns and islands.

Air Calédonie: BP 212, Nouméa; tel. 252339; telex 3112; f. 1955; services throughout New Caledonia and to the Loyalty Islands; Chair. ROBERT PAOUTA; Gen. Man. CHRISTIAN LIAUDET; fleet of 3 Twin Otter, 1 ATR 42-300, 1 Cessna 310P.

Air Calédonie International: POB 3736, Nouméa; tel. 283333; telex 3177; f. 1983; services to Sydney, Brisbane and Melbourne (Australia), Auckland (New Zealand), Fiji, Wallis Island and Vanuatu; CEO JEAN-PIERRE VARNIER.

Tourism

New Caledonia earned almost $A40m. from tourism in 1983, when 91,775 people visited the territory. The total increased to 92,982 in 1984, but fell to 51,190 in 1985, owing to the political unrest. Although a slight improvement was recorded in 1986 (to 58,732), further political unrest in 1988 seriously affected the total of visitor arrivals.

Office Territorial du Tourisme de Nouvelle-Calédonie: 25 ave Maréchal Foch, BP 688, Nouméa; tel. 272632; telex 3063; f. 1960; Dir MICHEL DOPPLER.

WALLIS AND FUTUNA ISLANDS

Introductory Survey

Location, Climate, Language, Religion, Capital

The territory of Wallis and Futuna comprises two groups of islands: the Wallis Islands, including Wallis Island (also known as Uvea) and 22 islets on the surrounding reef, and, to the south-east, Futuna (or Hooru), comprising the two small islands of Futuna and Alofi. The islands are located north-east of Fiji and west of Western Samoa. Temperatures are generally between about 23°C (73°F) and 30°C (86°F), and there is a cyclone season between October and March. French and Wallisian, the indigenous Polynesian language, are spoken in the territory, and the entire population is nominally Roman Catholic. The capital is Mata-Utu, on Wallis Island.

Recent History

A French protectorate since 1888, the islands chose by referendum in December 1959 to become an overseas territory. In July 1961 they were granted this status. Although there is no movement in Wallis and Futuna seeking secession of the territory from France (in contrast with the situation in the other French Pacific territories, French Polynesia and New Caledonia), the two kings whose kingdoms share the island of Futuna requested in November 1983, through the Territorial Assembly, that the island groups of Wallis and Futuna become separate overseas territories of France, arguing that the administration and affairs of the territory had become excessively concentrated on Wallis Island.

At elections to the 20-member Territorial Assembly in March 1982, the Rassemblement pour la République (RPR) and its allies won 11 seats, while the remaining nine went to candidates belonging to, or associated with, the Union pour la Démocratie Française (UDF). Later in 1982 one member of the Lua kae tahi, a group affiliated to the metropolitan UDF, defected to the RPR group, thereby strengthening the RPR's majority. In November 1983, however, three of the 12 RPR members joined the Lua kae tahi, forming a new majority. In the subsequent election for President of the Territorial Assembly, this 11-strong block of UDF-associated members supported the ultimately successful candidate, Falakiko Gata, even though he had been elected to the Territorial Assembly in 1982 as a member of the RPR.

In April 1985 Gata formed a new political party, the Union populaire locale (UPL), which was committed to giving priority to local, rather than metropolitan, issues. At a meeting with the French Prime Minister in Paris in June, Gata reaffirmed that it was in the territory's interests to remain French and not to seek independence.

In March 1986 Benjamin Brial, the candidate of the RPR, was re-elected as the territory's deputy to the French National Assembly, obtaining 2,798 votes (44.4%) of the total 6,302 votes cast in the second ballot. On 29 October 1986 the islands' Chief Administrator, Jacques Le Hénaff, declared a state of emergency in the territory, following a stone-throwing incident during a display of unrest among some local chiefs. The latter had expressed dissatisfaction with the French Secretary-General of the territory, Georges Jaymes, and requested his removal and repatriation, owing to his transfer of a number of highly-respected French civil servants from their posts in the territory. As a precautionary measure, 30 gendarmes were brought in from New Caledonia to restore order, but the disturbance was not renewed, and the state of emergency was lifted on the following day.

At elections to the Territorial Assembly held in March 1987, the UDF (together with affiliated parties) and the RPR each won seven seats. However, by forming an alliance with the UPL, the RPR maintained its majority, and Gata was subsequently re-elected President, receiving 13 of the 20 votes cast in the Territorial Assembly, the remaining seven being in favour of Basil Tui, an affiliate of the UDF. In October 1987 Gérard Lambotte replaced Jacques Le Hénaff as the islands' Chief Administrator, and in July 1988 was himself replaced by Roger Dumec. At elections for the French National Assembly in June 1988, Benjamin Brial was re-elected deputy. However, when the result was contested by an unsuccessful candidate, Kamilo Gata, the election was investigated by the French Constitutional Council and the result declared invalid, owing to electoral irregularities. When the election was held again in Janaury 1989, Gata was elected deputy, obtaining 3,390 votes, or 57.4% of the total.

In 1987 a dispute broke out between two families both laying claim to the throne of Sigavé, one of the two kingdoms on the island of Futuna. The conflict arose following the deposition of the former King, Sagato Keletaona, and his succession by Sosepho Vanaï. The intervention of the island's administrative authorities, who attempted to ratify Vanaï's accession to the throne, was condemned by the Keletaona family as an interference in the normal course of local custom, according to which such disputes are traditionally settled by a fight between the protagonists.

Government

The territory of Wallis and Futuna is administered by a representative of the French Government, the Chief Administrator, who is assisted by a Territorial Assembly. The Assembly has 20 members and is elected for a five-year term. The three traditional kingdoms, from which the territory was formed, one on Wallis and two sharing Futuna, have equal rights, although the kings' powers are limited. In addition, the territory elects one deputy to the French National Assembly in Paris and one representative to the French Senate.

Economic Affairs

Most monetary income in Wallis and Futuna is derived from government employment and remittances sent home by islanders employed in New Caledonia. Copra and handicrafts are the only significant export commodities. Yams, taro, bananas, coconuts, cassava and other food crops are also cultivated.

During his visit to Paris in June 1985, Falakiko Gata, the President of the Territorial Assembly, told the French Prime Minister that the policies relating to agricultural and fisheries development since 1960 had been a complete failure. It was hoped that these areas of the economy could be improved through new administrative arrangements, whereby development funding would be channelled through traditional chiefs.

In December 1986 almost all the cultivated vegetation on the island of Futuna, notably the banana plantations, was destroyed by a cyclone. In response to the cyclone damage, the French Government announced, in February 1987, that it was to provide exceptional aid of 55m. French francs to alleviate the situation.

Social Welfare

In 1981 there were three state hospitals in Wallis and Futuna, with a total of 93 beds, and there were four physicians working in the islands.

Education

In 1983 there were 13 state-financed primary and lower-secondary schools in Wallis and Futuna, with a total of 3,962 pupils.

Public Holidays

1989: 2 January (for New Year's Day), 27 March (Easter Monday), 1 May (Labour Day), 4 May (Ascension Day), 8 May (Liberation Day), 15 May (Whit Monday), 14 July (Fall of the Bastille), 11 November (Armistice Day), 25 December (Christmas Day).

1990: 1 January (New Year's Day), 16 April (Easter Monday), 7 May (for Labour Day), 8 May (Liberation Day), 24 May (Ascension Day), 4 June (Whit Monday), 14 July (Fall of the Bastille), 11 November (Armistice Day), 25 December (Christmas Day).

Weights and Measures

The metric system is in force.

Statistical Survey

AREA AND POPULATION

Area (sq km): Wallis Island 159, Futuna Island and Alofi Island 115, total of all islands 274.

Population (1985): 12,408; Wallis Island 8,084 (chief town Mata-Utu), Futuna Island 4,324; Alofi Island uninhabited; about 12,000 Wallisians and Futunians live in New Caledonia and in Vanuatu.

AGRICULTURE, ETC.

Principal Crops (FAO estimates, '000 metric tons, 1985): Cassava 2, Yams 1, Taro (Coco yam) 2, Coconuts 3, Bananas 4, Other fruit 5, Vegetables and melons 1. Source: FAO, *Production Yearbook*.

Livestock (FAO estimates, year ending September 1985): Pigs 26,000, Goats 7,000. Source: FAO, *Production Yearbook*.

FINANCE

Currency and Exchange Rates: see French Polynesia.

Budget (1983): 20,350,000 French francs.

Aid from France (1982): 55,000,000 French francs.

EXTERNAL TRADE
1984: *Imports:* 1,302m. francs CFP. *Exports:* n.a.

TRANSPORT
Civil Aviation: Wallis Island (1980): aircraft arrivals and departures 581; freight handled 171 metric tons; passenger arrivals 4,555, passenger departures 4,300; mail loaded and unloaded 72 metric tons.

EDUCATION
Primary and Lower Secondary (1987): 13 state-financed schools, 4,622 pupils.

Directory

The Government
(February 1989)

The territory is administered by a French-appointed Chief Administrator who is assisted by a Territorial Assembly.
Chief Administrator: ROGER DUMEC.
All government offices are in Mata-Uta, Wallis Island.

Legislature

ASSEMBLÉE TERRITORIALE
The Territorial Assembly is elected for a five-year term on the basis of universal adult suffrage. It has 20 members. The members (like the representative to the French Senate and the deputy to the French National Assembly) are elected locally on a common roll. At the election of 15 March 1987 the Rassemblement pour la République (RPR) won seven seats, the Union populaire locale (UPL) won six seats and the Union pour la Démocratie Française (UDF) and its affiliates won seven seats.
President of the Territorial Assembly: FALAKIKO GATA (UPL).
Deputy to the French National Assembly: KAMILO GATA (MRG).
Representative to the French Senate: SOSEFO MAKAPE PAPILIO (RPR).

Political Organizations

Lua kae tahi: affiliated to UDF.
Mouvement des Radicaux de Gauche (MRG): left-wing.
Rassemblement pour la République (RPR): Gaullist.
Union populaire locale (UPL): f. 1985; emphasizes importance of local issues; Leader FALAKIKO GATA.
Union pour la Démocratie Française (UDF): centrist.

Religion

Almost all of the inhabitants profess Christianity and are adherents of the Roman Catholic Church.

CHRISTIANITY
The Roman Catholic Church

The territory comprises a single diocese, suffragan to the archdiocese of Nouméa (New Caledonia). In 1985 an estimated 99.5% of the population were adherents. The Bishop participates in the Episcopal Conference of the Pacific, based in Fiji.
Bishop of Wallis and Futuna: Mgr LOLESIO FUAHEA, Evêché, Lano, BP 6, Mata-Utu, Wallis Island; tel. 722783.

Radio and Television

Radiodiffusion Française d'Outre-mer (RFO): BP 102, Mata-Utu, Iles de Wallis et Futuna (par Nouméa); tel. 722020; telex 250500; transmitters at Mata-Utu (Wallis) and Alo (Futuna); programmes in Wallisian, Futunian and French; a television service, transmitting for four and a half hours daily, began operation in September 1986; Man. RENÉ DENIS.

Transport

ROADS
Wallis Island has a few kilometres of road, one route circling the island, and there is also a road circling the island of Futuna; the only surfaced roads are in Mata-Utu.

SHIPPING
Mata-Utu serves as the seaport of Wallis Island, while Sigave is the only port on Futuna. Services to Nouméa (New Caledonia), Suva (Fiji), Port Vila and Santo (Vanuatu), are operated by the Compagnie Wallisienne de Navigation.

CIVIL AVIATION
There is an international airport on Wallis Island. Air Calédonie (New Caledonia) operates three flights a week from Wallis to Futuna, and one flight a week from Wallis to Nouméa; Air Calédonie International also serves Wallis Island.

Tourism

Tourism remains undeveloped. There are three small hotels on Wallis Island.

GABON

Introductory Survey

Location, Climate, Language, Religion, Flag, Capital

The Gabonese Republic is an equatorial country on the west coast of Africa, with Equatorial Guinea and Cameroon to the north and the Congo to the south and east. The climate is tropical, with an average annual temperature of 26°C (79°F) and an average annual rainfall of 2,490 mm (98 in). The official language is French, but Fang (in the north) and Bantu dialects (in the south) are also widely spoken. About 60% of the population are Christians, mainly Roman Catholics. Most of the remainder follow animist beliefs. The national flag (proportions 4 by 3) has three equal horizontal stripes, of green, yellow and blue. The capital is Libreville.

Recent History

Formerly a province of French Equatorial Africa, Gabon gained internal autonomy in 1957. It achieved self-government, within the French Community, in November 1958 and attained full independence on 17 August 1960.

At the time of independence, there were two main political parties: the Bloc démocratique gabonaise (BDG), led by Léon M'Ba, and the Union démocratique et sociale gabonaise (UDSG), led by Jean-Hilaire Aubame. The two parties were almost evenly matched in support and neither had a majority in the National Assembly. However, with the backing of independent deputies, M'Ba became Prime Minister in 1958 and Head of State at independence. He favoured close relations with France, and his rule was generally conservative. Members of the UDSG joined the Council of Ministers after independence, and the two parties agreed on a joint list of candidates for elections in February 1961, when a new constitution came into effect. In that month M'Ba was elected Gabon's first President, with 99.6% of the votes cast, and Aubame, his long-standing rival, was appointed Minister for Foreign Affairs. The BDG wanted the two parties to merge but the UDSG resisted this proposal. As a result, all the UDSG ministers were forced to resign in February 1963. President M'Ba dissolved the National Assembly in January 1964, in preparation for new elections.

In February 1964, five days before the date set for the elections, President M'Ba was deposed by a military coup, staged by army supporters of Aubame. However, French forces immediately intervened, and the M'Ba Government was restored. Aubame was found guilty of treason, and sentenced to 10 years' imprisonment. At the elections, held in April, the BDG won 31 of the 47 seats in the National Assembly. The UDSG was formally outlawed and, over the next two years, almost all of the opposition members in the Assembly joined the BDG.

In February 1967, with President M'Ba in poor health, the Constitution was revised to provide for the succession of a Vice-President if the President died or resigned. At the next elections, in March, there were no opposition candidates and the BDG was returned to power. President M'Ba was re-elected for a seven-year term, with Albert-Bernard Bongo, previously Deputy Prime Minister, as Vice-President. M'Ba died in November 1967 and was succeeded by Bongo, then aged 31. On 12 March 1968 the Parti démocratique gabonais (PDG) was established, and one-party government was formally instituted.

In February 1973 Bongo was re-elected President. In September he announced his conversion to Islam, adopting the forename Omar. In April 1975 President Bongo abolished the Vice-Presidency, appointing Léon Mébiame, who had been Vice-President since 1968, to the new post of Prime Minister. At the same time, local administration was reorganized to confer considerable autonomous powers on the provinces.

In 1977 President Kerekou of Benin accused Gabon of having aided an airborne mercenary attack on Cotonou. President Bongo strongly denied these accusations, and ordered the expulsion of all nationals of Benin from Gabon. In May 1981 several thousand Cameroonians resident in Gabon were airlifted back to Cameroon following violence against the Cameroonian communities in Libreville and Port-Gentil.

At a meeting of the PDG Congress in January 1979, elections were held to the party's Central Committee, thus introducing the first element of democracy into Gabon's political system. Following his nomination by the PDG, President Bongo stood as the sole candidate in the presidential election held in December 1979, and was re-elected for another seven-year term, receiving 99.96% of the votes cast. In early 1980 legislative and municipal elections were held, in which, for the first time since 1960, independents were free to stand against party candidates. All seats in the National Assembly were, none the less, won by members of the PDG. In a government reshuffle in August 1981, Bongo relinquished the title of Head of Government (thereafter conferred upon the Prime Minister, Léon Mébiame) and his ministerial portfolios. PDG candidates received 99.5% of the total votes at a general election in March 1985 for an enlarged National Assembly, and at the party's third ordinary congress, held in September 1986, the memberships of the Central Committee and Political Bureau were also increased. At the next presidential election, held in November, Bongo (the sole candidate) received an estimated 99.97% of the votes. In January 1987, in response to a steadily worsening economic situation, the Council of Ministers was reshuffled, and its membership was reduced. Elections to assemblies in the country's nine provinces, 37 prefectures and 12 municipal districts were held in June. Further reallocations of ministerial portfolios occurred in August and October 1988. In the latter month measures were also taken to improve the efficiency of administrative structures.

President Bongo has adopted stern measures against any form of protest or dissent in the country. An illegal opposition group, the Mouvement de redressement national (MORENA), emerged in November 1981, advocating the establishment of a multi-party system in Gabon. In November 1982 a total of 29 MORENA sympathizers, including a former government minister, were found guilty of endangering state security, and received prison sentences, some with hard labour. Although they were all subsequently released, with the last group being granted clemency in May 1986, Bongo's firm line against any opposition movement has been maintained. When MORENA announced the formation of a government-in-exile in Paris during August 1985, Bongo applied pressure on the French Government to deny any form of recognition to the new grouping. An air-force captain was executed in the same month, following his conviction on charges of plotting a coup. Although a MORENA candidate stood against Bongo in the November 1986 presidential election, he was prevented from organizing a campaign.

Under Gabon's liberal economic system, efforts have been made to attract foreign companies and investors to the country. However, since January 1974 all companies operating in Gabon are required to have their headquarters there, and the State must be given a 10% share in all new foreign enterprises setting up in the country. Deteriorating economic conditions led to the imposition of controls on immigrant workers in May 1986. In June 1988 about 3,500 foreign nationals, described by the Government as illegal immigrants, were arrested by the Gabonese security forces. This action was followed by the announcement of new nationality regulations. Bongo has pursued a policy of close co-operation with France in the fields of economic and foreign affairs. Relations with France became strained in October 1983, however, as a result of the publication in Paris of a book which was critical of the Bongo regime, and a six-week ban on news pertaining to France was imposed on the Gabonese media. Tension was reduced following a visit to Libreville in April 1984 by the French Prime Minister, Pierre Mauroy, and relations between the two countries were finally restored in October 1984, when Bongo paid a three-day state visit to Paris. In early 1988, however, copies of three French newspapers were seized, following the publication of allegations concerning Bongo's misuse of French financial aid. President Bongo maintains that Gabon does not have an exclusive relationship with any country, and in recent years he has attempted to diversify Gabon's external relations. During 1987 he paid visits to the People's Republic of China and to the USA, as well as to France. Bongo has also acted as an intermediary in regional disputes, chairing the OAU *ad hoc* committee charged with solving the border conflict between Chad and Libya, and encouraging a dialogue between Angola and the USA.

Government

The 1961 Constitution, as subsequently revised, vests executive power in the President, directly elected by universal suffrage for seven years. The President appoints the Prime Minister, who is Head of Government; he also appoints, and presides over, a Council of Ministers. The legislative organ is the unicameral National Assembly, with a term of five years. The Assembly has 120 members, of whom 111 are chosen by election and nine by nomination. Voting is compulsory for all citizens aged 21 years or over. Gabon became a one-party state in 1968. The Parti démocratique gabonais (PDG) is the only legal party. The PDG's highest authority is the Party Congress which, in September 1986, elected 186 of the 297 members of the Central Committee, the remaining members being appointed by the President, to supervise Party work. To direct its policy, the Central Committee has a Political Bureau of 44 members. The country is divided into nine provinces, each under an appointed Governor, and 37 prefectures. Elections to local councils were held in June 1987.

Defence

In June 1988 the army consisted of 1,900 men, the air force of 600 men, and the navy of 500 men. Paramilitary forces numbered at least 4,800. Military service is voluntary. France maintains a military detachment of 550 in Gabon. Estimated defence expenditure for 1988 was 40,000m. francs CFA (22% of total administrative spending).

Economic Affairs

With abundant mineral resources and a relatively small population, Gabon is the richest country in sub-Saharan Africa, measured in terms of average income. In 1987, according to estimates by the World Bank, Gabon's gross national product (GNP), measured at average 1985–87 prices, was US $2,890m. (equivalent to $2,750 per head). Between 1980 and 1987, it was estimated, GNP per head declined, in real terms, at an average annual rate of 3.5%.

More than one-half of the working population are engaged in subsistence agriculture, largely untouched by the expansion of the market economy. There is a little commercial agricultural production, the main crops being the oil palm, coffee, cocoa and bananas. The agricultural sector contributed about 10% of Gabon's gross domestic product (GDP) in 1986, compared with 26% in 1965. Government plans to develop the rural sector are intended to halt the drift of population to urban areas and to reduce Gabon's dependence on imported foodstuffs, which in 1987 supplied about 88% of the country's needs. Imports of food and agricultural products in 1985, which were valued at 61,000m. francs CFA, represented an estimated 15.8% of the total import bill in that year. Following heavy flooding in late 1988, the Gabonese Government appealed for international food-aid.

Forests cover some 75% of Gabon's land area, and for many years the economy was largely dependent upon forestry, particularly production of okoumé, a tropical softwood used in the making of plywood. The total volume of timber exports in 1984 was 1.3m. cu m. Although wood remains Gabon's second most important export commodity (providing 6.2% of total export earnings in 1985), the country's production of timber underwent a period of decline between 1977 and 1983, with several forestry companies incurring financial losses. The lack of internal outlets, and international competition, as well as transport difficulties, mean that the wood industry is underdeveloped.

The economy is heavily dependent on petroleum: in 1987 Gabon was the third largest producer of crude petroleum in sub-Saharan Africa. The petroleum price rises of 1974 coincided with peak production from Gabon's oilfields, but in 1977 the level of output began to stabilize and the country experienced recession, as economic expansion had proceeded more rapidly than the availability of finance. Gabon's annual output of crude petroleum attained its highest level, of 11.3m. metric tons, in 1976, but subsequently declined, reaching a low of 7.6m. tons in 1981. Production recovered following a period of increased exploration, to more than 8m. tons per year in 1985 and 1986, before declining again, to about 7.9m. tons annually, in the following two years. The entry into production of the Obando Marin concession (estimated to contain recoverable reserves of 24m. tons) in late 1987, and of the major Rabi-Kounga onshore field (believed to contain recoverable reserves of 47m. tons) in January 1989, was to have the effect of increasing Gabon's annual production capacity to 8.5m. tons in 1989. However, output was likely to be restricted to 8.3m. tons in that year, in accordance with the country's commitment to OPEC production quotas. Earnings from the petroleum sector were sharply reduced as a result of the coincidence of a sharp decline in world oil prices with a fall in the value of the US dollar in early 1986. The petroleum industry provided 66% of export earnings in that year, compared with 83% in 1985, and 58% of government revenue, compared with 63% in the previous year. The value of the Government's oil receipts declined from 399,700m. francs CFA in 1985 to an estimated total of only 85,000m. francs CFA in 1988.

Gabon is the world's fourth largest producer of manganese, and it has been estimated that the deposits at Moanda constitute around one-quarter of the world's known reserves (excluding the USSR). An estimated 1.17m. tons of manganese (figures refer to the metal content of the ore) were produced in 1980, but output fell to less than 800,000 tons per year in 1981 and 1982, following the recession in the world's steel industries, which utilize 95% of world manganese production in the manufacture of various alloys. Production increased to almost 1.2m. tons in 1985. Commencing in December 1988, the direct export of more than one-half of Gabon's manganese production was facilitated by the inauguration of a minerals terminal at Owendo. (All exports of the country's manganese output had previously been directed through the Congo.) There are plans for the eventual exploitation of major iron-ore deposits at Belinga, in the north-east. The deposits contain an estimated 850m. tons of ore, with a metal content of 64.5%.

The exploitation of uranium deposits at Mounana began in 1961. Known reserves amount to around 35,000 tons, or 40 years' output at recently-achieved rates, and new deposits have been discovered at Boyindzi and Oklo. Annual output of uranium metal totalled more than 1,000 tons between 1978 and 1981, before declining slightly to total 918 tons in 1985. Output recovered again, to about 1,000 tons, in 1987. The ore is extracted and concentrated by the Compagnie des Mines d'Uranium de Franceville (COMUF), a consortium largely controlled by French interests but with a 25% interest held by the Gabonese Government. A geological survey of the interior, conducted as part of a mineral development project, has confirmed the existence of deposits of niobium (columbium), barytes, talc, lead, zinc, copper, phosphates, gold and diamonds.

Gabon's manufacturing sector is relatively restricted, though it is being expanded, and accounted for 4.8% of GDP in 1986. However, shortage of labour and a high minimum wage, together with inadequate infrastructure, have prevented further expansion. There are petroleum refineries at Port-Gentil and tanker facilities for vessels of up to 25,000 tons. Since July 1972 the 'Gabonization' of the economy has been undertaken. Foreigners have been replaced by Gabonese in positions of authority, and the state has taken a share in the capital of foreign companies.

An ambitious five-year plan was launched in 1976, of which the most important part was the Transgabon railway. The 340-km first stage, from Owendo to Booué, was opened in 1983, and the second stage, a line of 330 km from Booué to Franceville, was inaugurated in December 1986, ahead of schedule. The cost of the entire Transgabon project was estimated at US $3,000m. in late 1986. It was hoped that the railway would permit the efficient exploitation of mineral deposits inland (uranium, manganese and iron ore) should petroleum reserves become exhausted. The development of both forestry and mining has been hampered by a lack of transport facilities. However, the construction of a third section, from Booué to Belinga, has been suspended indefinitely, owing to the Government's policy of investing in projects that will be financially viable in the short-term. There is considerable potential for hydroelectric power in Gabon: three hydroelectric power stations are currently in operation, while feasibility studies for the construction of a further installation commenced in 1988. An electricity- and water-supply programme was launched in 1984, with financial assistance from France and Canada. Proposals for the construction of a 300-MW nuclear power station, to be financed by France, were abandoned in May 1986, following the nuclear accident at Chernobyl in the USSR.

Gabon's economic difficulties during the mid-1980s were compounded by the existence of a large foreign debt, which was estimated to total US $1,200m. at the end of 1986 and which exacerbated the need for budgetary restraint. Following the implementation of an IMF-supported stabilization plan in 1978, the total debt, then estimated at 1,600m. French francs, fell by 15.5% in 1979: the cost of debt servicing has remained heavy, however, and was assigned 154,000m. francs CFA out of total planned expenditure of 450,000m. francs CFA in 1987. Following the collapse of world oil prices in 1985 and 1986, and the subsequent decline in Gabon's total export revenue, rescheduling agreements were reached with both the 'Paris Club' of creditor governments and the 'London Club' of commercial creditors during 1987. A further rescheduling of debt was agreed by the 'Paris Club' in 1988. In 1987 the balance of payments showed an estimated current deficit of $443.3m., compared with deficits of $162.5m. and $1,057.6m., respectively, in 1985 and 1986. The total nominal value of annual imports increased by almost 40% over the period 1983–85, while that of petroleum exports increased by only 17% over the same period. The trade surplus totalled $1,096.7m. in 1985, declining to $95.1m. in 1986, before recovering to $554.5m. in 1987. A further surplus, of $650m., was forecast for 1988. Gabon's GDP totalled 1,535,800m. francs CFA in 1984, increasing to 1,645,800m. francs CFA in 1985, before declining by 30%, in nominal terms, to 1,148,000m. francs CFA in 1986.

The fifth Plan (originally formulated to cover the years 1984–88, but later extended to 1990) aimed to stabilize growth under a liberal but planned economy. Almost one-half of the proposed investment of 1,228,478m. francs CFA over the Plan period was allocated to infrastructure projects. Several projects were subsequently suspended, owing to reductions in the availability of investment capital. In December 1986 the IMF granted Gabon a medium-term stand-by arrangement worth SDR 98.7m. in support of a new three-year economic adjustment programme, which aimed primarily to diversify the country's productive activities while re-examining both the efficacy of the price system and the performance of the parastatal sector. A structural adjustment programme, announced in April 1988, aimed to reverse the economic decline that had resulted from the collapse in petroleum prices, by encouraging a diversification of the economy away from its dependence on that sector. The programme, which was to be supported by credits from the IMF, the African Development Bank (ADB) and France, envisaged improvements in the efficiency of the public sector, in parallel with the development of private-sector activities. Small- and medium-scale enterprises were to be encouraged, especially in the agriculture and forestry sectors. Wage reductions were imposed in the 1987 budget, and in June of that year it was announced that a compulsory 'solidarity loan' of 27,000m. francs CFA was to be raised from wage-earners and commercial enterprises by means of a levy on salaries and turnover. Employment legislation, introduced in 1988, imposed reductions in the work-force, in salaries and in the length of the working week.

The 1989 budget proposals envisaged revenue of 271,000m. francs CFA, compared with 260,000m. francs CFA in 1988, and total expenditure of 358,000m. francs CFA, compared with 318,000m. francs CFA in the previous year. However, these increases were expected to be offset by inflation, which was estimated to be about 5% per year at the end of 1988.

Social Welfare

There is a national Fund for State Insurance, and a guaranteed minimum wage. In January 1985 Gabon had 28 hospitals, 87 medical centres and 312 dispensaries, with a total of 5,156 hospital beds. In 1984 there were 300 physicians in the country. Maternal and infant health is a major priority. The 1988 budget allocated 18,000m. francs CFA (10% of total administrative spending) to health expenditure.

Education

Education is officially compulsory for 10 years between six and 16 years of age: in 1984 an estimated 75% of children in the relevant age-group attended primary and secondary schools (78% of boys; 72% of girls). Primary and secondary education is provided by state and mission schools. Primary education begins at the age of six and lasts for six years. Secondary education, beginning at 12 years of age, lasts for up to seven years, comprising a first cycle of four years and a second of three years. The Université Omar Bongo, at Libreville, had 2,505 students in 1985. In addition, many students go to France for university and technical training. In 1985, according to estimates by UNESCO, adult illiteracy averaged 38.4% (males 29.8%; females 46.6%). Education is a major priority, and the 1988 budget allocated 47,000m. francs CFA (26% of total administrative spending) to expenditure on education and culture.

Public Holidays

1989: 2 January (for New Year's Day), 12 March (Anniversary of Renovation, foundation of the Parti démocratique gabonais), 27 March (Easter Monday), 1 May (Labour Day), 7 May* (Id al-Fitr, end of Ramadan), 15 May (Whit Monday), 14 July* (Id al-Adha, feast of the Sacrifice), 17 August (Anniversary of Independence), 13 October* (Mouloud, birth of Muhammad), 1 November (All Saints' Day), 25 December (Christmas).

1990: 1 January (New Year's Day), 12 March (Anniversary of Renovation, foundation of the Parti démocratique gabonais), 16 April (Easter Monday), 27 April* (Id al-Fitr, end of Ramadan), 1 May (Labour Day), 4 June (Whit Monday), 4 July* (Id al-Adha, feast of the Sacrifice), 17 August (Anniversary of Independence), 2 October* (Mouloud, birth of Muhammad), 1 November (All Saints' Day), 25 December (Christmas).

* These holidays are dependent on the Islamic lunar calendar and may vary by one or two days from the dates given.

Weights and Measures

The metric system is in official use.

Statistical Survey

Source (unless otherwise stated): Direction Générale de l'Economie, Ministère de la Planification et de l'Economie, Libreville.

Area and Population

AREA, POPULATION AND DENSITY

Area (sq km)	267,667*
Population (census results)†	
8 October 1960–May 1961	
Males	211,350
Females	237,214
Total	448,564
Population (official estimate at mid-year)	
1985‡	1,206,000
Density (per sq km) at mid-1985	4.5

* 103,347 sq miles.

† The results of a census in August 1980 were officially repudiated and a decree in May 1981 declared a population of 1,232,000, including 122,000 Gabonese nationals resident abroad.

‡ Both the World Bank and the UN dispute Gabonese official population estimates. For mid-1987 the World Bank assumes a population of 1,047,000, while the UN estimates a population of 1,058,000.

REGIONS

Region	Population (1976 estimate)	Chief town
Estuaire	311,300	Libreville
Haut-Ogooué	187,500	Franceville
Moyen-Ogooué	50,500	Lambaréné
N'Gounié	122,600	Mouila
Nyanga	89,000	Tchibanga
Ogooué-Ivindo	56,500	Makokou
Ogooué-Lolo	50,500	Koulamoutou
Ogooué-Maritime	171,900	Port-Gentil
Woleu-N'Tem	162,300	Oyem
Total	**1,202,100**	

PRINCIPAL TOWNS (population in 1975)

Libreville (capital)	251,400		Lambaréné	22,682
Port-Gentil	77,611			

BIRTHS AND DEATHS (UN estimates, annual averages)

	1970–75	1975–80	1980–85
Birth rate (per 1,000)	31.0	30.8	33.8
Death rate (per 1,000)	20.2	18.9	18.1

Source: UN, *World Population Prospects: Estimates and Projections as Assessed in 1984*.

ECONOMICALLY ACTIVE POPULATION
(ILO estimates, '000 persons at mid-1980)

	Males	Females	Total
Agriculture, etc.	205	174	379
Industry	49	5	54
Services	50	19	69
Total	**305**	**198**	**502**

Source: ILO, *Economically Active Population Estimates and Projections, 1950–2025*.

Mid-1986 (estimates, '000 persons): Agriculture, etc. 370; Total 522 (Source: FAO, *Production Yearbook*).

Agriculture

PRINCIPAL CROPS (FAO estimates, '000 metric tons)

	1984	1985	1986
Maize	10	10	11
Cassava (Manioc)	245	250	255
Yams	90	80	85
Taro (Coco yam)	60	51	55
Vegetables	26	28	28
Bananas	8	8	8
Plantains	170	165	170
Cocoa beans*	2	2	2
Coffee (green)	1	1	1
Groundnuts (in shell)	8	8	8
Sugar cane	155	155	130

* Unofficial estimates.

Source: FAO, *Production Yearbook*.

LIVESTOCK
(FAO estimates, '000 head, year ending September)

	1984	1985	1986
Cattle	7	8	8
Pigs	150	150	152
Sheep	80	80	82
Goats	60	60	62

* Unofficial estimates.

Poultry (FAO estimates, million): 2 in 1984; 2 in 1985; 2 in 1986.

Source: FAO, *Production Yearbook*.

LIVESTOCK PRODUCTS
1986 (FAO estimates, '000 metric tons): Meat 22; Hen eggs 1.

Forestry

ROUNDWOOD REMOVALS ('000 cubic metres)

	1984	1985*	1986*
Industrial wood	1,484†	1,484	1,484
Fuel wood*	2,482	2,522	2,572
Total	**3,966**	**4,006**	**4,056**

* FAO estimates.
† Unofficial estimate.

Source: FAO, *Yearbook of Forest Products*.

Production of logs (official estimates, '000 cubic metres): 1,470 in 1984; 1,380 in 1985; 1,310 in 1986.

SAWNWOOD PRODUCTION ('000 cubic metres)

	1983	1984	1985
Total	**88***	**97**	**106**

* FAO estimate.

Railway sleepers ('000 cubic metres): 20 per year in 1983–85 (FAO estimates).

1986: Output as in 1985 (FAO estimates).

Source: FAO, *Yearbook of Forest Products*.

GABON

Fishing

('000 metric tons, live weight)

	1984	1985	1986
Freshwater fishes	1.8	1.8	1.8
West African croakers	3.4	2.7	2.5*
Lesser African threadfin	1.7	1.8	1.7*
Bonga shad	8.5	9.8	9.8*
Other marine fishes (incl. unspecified)	3.9	3.3	3.1*
Total fish	19.4	19.3	18.8*
Southern pink shrimp	1.6	1.7	1.6*
Total catch	21.0	21.0	20.4*

* FAO estimates.

Source: FAO, *Yearbook of Fishery Statistics*.

Mining

('000 metric tons, unless otherwise indicated)

	1983	1984	1985
Crude petroleum	7,842*	8,725*	8,201*
Natural gas (petajoules)	8	8	8
Uranium ore (metric tons)†	1,006	918	940
Manganese ore†	947.1*	1,077.6	1,199.2*
Gold (kilograms)	17	41	31

* Provisional or estimated data.
† Figures refer to the metal content of ores and concentrates.

Source: UN, *Industrial Statistics Yearbook*.

Crude petroleum ('000 metric tons): 8,000 in 1986; 7,920 in 1987 (Source: UN, *Monthly Bulletin of Statistics*).
Uranium ore (metric tons): 917 in 1986.

Industry

PETROLEUM PRODUCTS ('000 metric tons)

	1983	1984	1985
Liquefied petroleum gas*	5	6	6
Motor spirit (petrol)	110	113	110
Kerosene	25	26	26
Jet fuel	87	90	90
Distillate fuel oils	345	355	350
Residual fuel oil	491	535	510
Bitumen (asphalt)	12	14	13

* Provisional or estimated data.

Source: UN, *Industrial Statistics Yearbook*.

SELECTED OTHER PRODUCTS
(metric tons, unless otherwise indicated)

	1984	1985	1986*
Palm oil	2,655	4,697	8,400
Flour	25,957	25,857	28,240
Refined sugar	10,474	15,162	18,000
Soft drinks ('000 hectolitres)	369	447	480
Beer ('000 hectolitres)	769	827	820
Cement ('000 metric tons)	208	245	210
Electric energy (million kWh)	792	861	886

* Estimated figures.

Plywood ('000 cu metres): 110 in 1984; 131 in 1985 (Source: FAO, *Yearbook of Forest Products*).
Veneer sheets ('000 cu metres): 97 per year (FAO estimates) in 1984–86 (Source: FAO, *Yearbook of Forest Products*).

Finance

CURRENCY AND EXCHANGE RATES

Monetary Units
100 centimes = 1 franc de la Coopération financière en Afrique centrale (CFA).

Denominations
Coins: 1, 2, 5, 10, 25, 50 and 100 francs CFA.
Notes: 100, 500, 1,000, 5,000 and 10,000 francs CFA.

French Franc, Sterling and Dollar Equivalents (30 September 1988)
1 French franc = 50 francs CFA;
£1 sterling = 538.6 francs CFA;
US $1 = 318.5 francs CFA;
1,000 francs CFA = £1.857 = $3.140.

Average Exchange Rate (francs CFA per US $)
1985 449.26
1986 346.30
1987 300.54

BUDGET ('000 million francs CFA)

Revenue	1986	1987	1988*
Income from petroleum	285.2	64.5	85.0
Ordinary receipts	214.5	163.8	175.0
Exceptional receipts	3.0	35.0	—
Total	502.7	263.3	260.0

Expenditure	1986	1987	1988*
Current expenditure	277.2	247.0	236.0
Administrative expenditure	230.0	194.8	173.0
Interest payments	47.2	52.2	63.0
Capital expenditure	298.6	97.2	73.0
Extra-budgetary expenditure	92.4	11.7	9.0
Total	668.2	355.9	318.0

* Provisional figures.

Source: *La Zone Franc-Rapport 1987*.

1989 (estimates, '000 million francs CFA): Total revenue 271.0; Total expenditure 358.0 (Debt servicing 74.0, Capital expenditure 96.0).

CENTRAL BANK RESERVES
(US $ million at 31 December)

	1985	1986	1987
Gold*	4.16	5.03	6.19
IMF special drawing rights	2.28	12.29	11.62
Reserve position in IMF	0.03	0.04	0.04
Foreign exchange	190.23	114.02	0.34
Total	196.71	131.38	18.19

* Valued at market-related prices.

Source: IMF, *International Financial Statistics*.

MONEY SUPPLY ('000 million francs CFA at 31 December)

	1985	1986	1987
Currency outside banks	55.78	47.39	49.47
Demand deposits at commercial and development banks	119.33	103.91	82.91
Checking deposits at post office	1.45	1.08	0.89
Total money	176.55	152.39	133.26

Source: IMF, *International Financial Statistics*.

GABON

Statistical Survey

FIFTH DEVELOPMENT PLAN, 1984-88*
(proposed expenditure, million francs CFA at 1983 prices)

Productive sector	239,054
Infrastructure	595,662
Social services and education	213,972
General investments	162,520
Total	**1,228,478**

Source: *Annuaire National de la République Gabonaise 1983-84*.
* The Plan was later extended until 1990.

COST OF LIVING
(Retail Price Index for African families in Libreville; base: 1980 = 100)

	1985	1986	1987
All items	159.1	169.1	167.5

Source: IMF, *International Financial Statistics*.

NATIONAL ACCOUNTS
('000 million francs CFA at current prices)

Expenditure on the Gross Domestic Product

	1984	1985	1986
Government final consumption expenditure	284.4	306.3	286.0
Private final consumption expenditure	430.7	501.2	509.0
Increase in stocks	36.7	16.8	25.0
Gross fixed capital formation	476.6	596.8	517.0
Total domestic expenditure	**1,228.4**	**1,421.1**	**1,337.0**
Exports of goods and services	934.4	935.7	430.0
Less Imports of goods and services	628.9	711.0	619.0
Statistical discrepancy	1.9	—	—
GDP in purchasers' values	**1,535.8**	**1,645.8**	**1,148.0**

1987 (forecast, '000 million francs CFA): GDP in purchasers' values 986.0.

Gross Domestic Product by Economic Activity

	1984	1985	1986
Agriculture, stock-breeding and fishing	64.0	71.1	66.0
Forestry	16.0	15.5	14.0
Petroleum exploitation and research	738.0	733.4	236.0
Mining and quarrying	55.0	53.0	40.0
Timber industry	10.7	9.0	8.0
Refining	7.5	14.2	10.8
Processing industries	38.0	37.8	36.9
Electricity, water, gas and steam	22.3	26.2	26.2
Construction	101.2	125.0	103.0
Trade	91.5	106.5	130.0
Hotels, cafés and restaurants	12.4	17.9	24.0
Transport	55.5	61.3	60.0
Financial institutions	7.9	10.7	12.8
Public administration and services to households	132.1	148.7	157.3
Other services	97.0	110.6	131.0
Sub-total	**1,449.1**	**1,540.9**	**1,056.0**
Import duties	86.7	104.9	92.0
Total	**1,535.8**	**1,645.8**	**1,148.0**

BALANCE OF PAYMENTS (US $ million)

	1985	1986	1987
Merchandise exports f.o.b.	1,951.4	1,074.2	1,286.4
Merchandise imports f.o.b.	−854.7	−979.1	−731.8
Trade balance	**1,096.7**	**95.1**	**554.5**
Exports of services	167.7	141.7	125.6
Imports of services	−1,331.1	−1,147.5	−998.7
Balance on goods and services	**−66.7**	**−910.7**	**−318.5**
Private unrequited transfers (net)	−109.2	−169.1	−146.4
Government unrequited transfers (net)	13.5	22.3	21.6
Current balance	**−162.5**	**−1,057.6**	**−443.3**
Direct capital investment (net)	11.1	103.7	84.8
Other long-term capital (net)	201.5	485.3	426.4
Short-term capital (net)	−48.4	322.0	−191.1
Net errors and omissions	−50.6	−47.9	−13.5
Total (net monetary movements)	**−48.9**	**−194.5**	**−136.5**
Valuation changes (net)	43.6	32.7	57.3
Exceptional financing (net)	—	63.0	−63.1
Official financing (net)	−1.6	−0.9	1.3
Changes in reserves	**−6.9**	**−99.7**	**−141.1**

Source: IMF, *International Financial Statistics*.

External Trade

Source: *La Zone Franc—Rapport 1986*.

Note: Figures exclude trade with other countries in the Customs and Economic Union of Central Africa (UDEAC): Cameroon, the Central African Republic, Chad (since January 1984), the Congo and Equatorial Guinea (since January 1985).

PRINCIPAL COMMODITIES ('000 million francs CFA)

Imports	1983	1984	1985*
Machinery and apparatus	60.3	61.8	80.7
Transport equipment	30.5	36.5	52.2
Food products	39.4	43.5	50.0
Metals and metal products	32.6	34.1	44.6
Chemical products	9.5	11.7	15.0
Vegetable and animal products (non-food)	6.7	8.4	11.0
Precision instruments	9.8	11.6	13.7
Textiles and textile products	10.4	11.3	15.0
Hygiene and cleaning products	8.2	11.0	12.7
Vehicles	6.8	9.1	11.0
Mineral products	6.2	5.7	8.5
Total (incl. others)	**276.5**	**320.4**	**387.0**

Exports	1983	1984	1985*
Petroleum and petroleum products	629.5	735.7	735.0
Manganese	43.4	51.7	55.0
Timber	55.0	57.1	55.0
Uranium	26.7	26.9	27.0
Total (incl. others)	**762.2**	**881.7**	**887.0**

* Estimated figures.

GABON

PRINCIPAL TRADING PARTNERS ('000 million francs CFA)

Imports	1983	1984	1985*
Belgium/Luxembourg	4.7	10.1	15.1
France	141.5	172.5	176.2
Germany, Fed. Republic	13.3	18.0	22.2
Italy	8.2	14.9	16.1
Japan	19.3	22.1	24.5
Netherlands	9.9	9.4	8.8
Spain	6.5	7.5	6.1
United Kingdom	9.4	11.7	16.0
USA	28.8	25.1	38.9
Total (incl. others)	276.5	320.4	387.0

Exports	1983	1984	1985*
Canada	24.9	54.6	34.3
France	171.0	271.8	295.3
Germany, Fed. Republic	6.3	33.2	6.0
Italy	30.8	9.9	20.1
Netherlands	26.9	20.3	30.0
Spain	37.6	60.6	62.8
United Kingdom	22.9	16.2	37.1
USA	144.1	195.5	164.8
Total (incl. others)	762.2	881.7	887.0

* Estimated figures.

Transport

RAILWAYS (traffic)

	1984	1985	1986*
Passengers carried	135,913	137,111	125,816
Freight carried (metric tons)	664,605	723,034	666,412

* Estimated figures.

ROAD TRAFFIC (motor vehicles in use)

	1983	1984	1985
Passenger cars	15,150	15,650	16,093
Buses and coaches	479	508	546
Goods vehicles	9,240	9,590	9,960

Source: the former Ministère des Transports Terrestres, Ferroviaires, Fluviaux et Lagunaires.

INTERNATIONAL SEA-BORNE SHIPPING
(freight traffic at Libreville and Port-Gentil, '000 metric tons)

	1984	1985	1986
Goods loaded	8,179	8,291	5,868
Goods unloaded	827	857	968

CIVIL AVIATION (traffic on scheduled services)

	1982	1983	1984
Kilometres flown ('000)	5,800	6,100	5,800
Passengers carried	421,000	428,000	436,000
Passenger-kilometres ('000)	430,000	435,000	468,000
Freight ton-kilometres ('000)	27,300	30,900	31,800
Mail ton-kilometres ('000)	800	1,000	600

Source: UN, *Statistical Yearbook*.

Tourism

	1985	1986	1987
Tourist arrivals	5,248	4,917	3,454

Source: Ministère du Tourisme, de la Communication Sociale et des Loisirs.

Communications Media

	1985	1986
Radio receivers ('000 in use)	110	117
Television receivers ('000 in use)	22	23

Daily newspapers (1984): 1 (average circulation 15,000).
Source: UNESCO, *Statistical Yearbook*.

Telephones (1983): 14,000 in use (Source: UN, *Statistical Yearbook*).

Education

(1984)

	Schools	Teachers	Pupils Males	Pupils Females	Pupils Total
Primary	940	3,837	90,465	88,348	178,813
Secondary:					
General	n.a.	1,490	14,610	11,195	25,805
Vocational	n.a.	454	5,527	2,323	7,850
Teacher-training	n.a.	266	2,817	2,862	5,679
University*	1	359	1,455	604	2,059
Other higher*	n.a.	257	900	269	1,169

* 1983 figures.

1986: University: 364 teachers, 2,741 pupils (males 1,888, females 853); Other higher: 1,348 pupils (males 1,033, females 315).
Source: UNESCO, *Statistical Yearbook*.

Directory

The Constitution

The Constitution of the Gabonese Republic was adopted on 21 February 1961. It was revised in February 1967, April 1975, August 1981 and September 1986.

PREAMBLE

Upholds the Rights of Man, liberty of conscience and of the person, religious freedom and freedom of education. Sovereignty is vested in the people, who exercise it through their representatives or by means of referenda. There is direct, universal and secret suffrage.

HEAD OF STATE

The President is elected by universal direct suffrage for a seven-year term and is eligible for re-election without limit. He is Head of State and of the Armed Forces. The President may, after consultation with his Ministers and leaders of the National Assembly, order a referendum to be held. The President appoints the Prime Minister, who is Head of Government and who is accountable to the President.

EXECUTIVE POWER

Executive power is vested in the President and the Council of Ministers, who are appointed by the President and are responsible to him. The President presides over the Council.

LEGISLATIVE POWER

The National Assembly is elected by direct universal suffrage for a five-year term and normally holds two sessions a year. It may be dissolved or prorogued for up to 18 months by the President, after consultation with the Council of Ministers and President of the Assembly. The President may return a Bill to the Assembly for a second reading, when it must be passed by a majority of two-thirds of the members. If the President dissolves the Assembly, elections must take place within 40 days.

JUDICIAL POWER

The President guarantees the independence of the Judiciary and presides over the Conseil Supérieur de la Magistrature. There is a Supreme Court and a High Court of Justice. The High Court, which is composed of deputies of the National Assembly elected from among themselves, has power to try the President or members of the government.

The Government

HEAD OF STATE

President: El Hadj OMAR (ALBERT-BERNARD) BONGO (took office 2 December 1967, elected 25 February 1973, re-elected December 1979 and November 1986).

COUNCIL OF MINISTERS
(February 1989)

Prime Minister: LÉON MÉBIAME.

First Deputy Prime Minister, Minister of Forest Resources, National Parks and Fisheries, in charge of Office du Chemin de Fer Transgabonais: GEORGES RAWIRI.

Second Deputy Prime Minister, Minister of Mines, Industry and Consumption: GUY-ETIENNE MOUVAGHA.

Third Deputy Prime Minister, Minister of Tourism, Social Communication and Leisure: EMILE KASSA MAPSI.

Fourth Deputy Prime Minister, Minister of Town Planning, Housing and Habitation: SIMON ESSIMENGANE.

Minister of State for Foreign Affairs and Co-operation: MARTIN BONGO.

Minister of State for Public Land, Land Registration and the Law of the Sea: HENRI MINKO.

Minister of State, Secretary-General at the Presidency: RENÉ RADEMBINO CONIQUET.

Minister of State for Higher Education, Scientific Research and Technology: JULES BOURDÈS OGOULIGUENDE.

Minister of State for Transport and Civil Aviation: ETIENNE MOUSSIROU.

Minister of State for the Civil Service, Administrative Reform and Redeployment: RICHARD NGUEMA BEKALE.

Minister of State for Trade, Transfer of Technologies and Rationalization: JEAN-FRANÇOIS NTOUTOUME-EMANE.

Minister of State for Culture, Arts, Popular Education and Francophone Affairs: FRANÇOIS OWONO-NGUEMA.

Minister of State for the Environment and Nature Protection: ALEXANDRE SAMBAT.

Minister of National Defence, Veterans' Affairs, Public Security and Hydrocarbons: JULIEN MPOUHO-EPIGAT.

Minister of Justice and Keeper of the Seals: SOPHIE NGWA-MASSANA.

Minister of Information, Posts and Telecommunications, in charge of Relations with the National Assembly: ZACHARIE MYBOTO.

Minister of Finance, the Budget and State Shareholdings: JEAN-PIERRE LEMBOUMBA LEPANDOU.

Minister of Public Works, Equipment, Construction and Territorial Development: Gen. JEAN-BONIFACE ASSELE.

Minister of Planning and Economy: PASCAL NZÉ.

Minister of Agriculture, Livestock and Rural Development: MICHEL ANCHOUEY.

Minister of National Education: GUY NZOUBA NDAMA.

Minister of Labour, Employment, Human Resources and Professional Training: LOUIS-GASTON MAYILA.

Minister of Public Health and Population: Dr JEAN-PIERRE OKIAS.

Minister of Social Affairs, Social Security, Natural Disasters and National Solidarity: SILVESTRE OYOUOMI.

Minister of Youth and Sports: VICTOR AFFENE.

Minister of State Control and Contracts: EMILE MBOT.

Minister of Territorial Administration, Local Communities and Immigration: JOSÉ-JOSEPH AMIAR NGANGA.

Minister of Energy and Hydraulic Resources: LIDJOB DIVUNGI DI DINGE.

Minister of Small- and Medium-sized Enterprises, in charge of Rural Investment: EMMANUEL NZÉ-BEKALE.

Minister of the Merchant Navy: MATHIEU NGUEMA.

Minister-delegate to the First Deputy Prime Minister: Dr PAULIN OBAME-NGUEMA.

Minister-delegate to the Second Deputy Prime Minister: BON-JEAN FRANÇOIS ONDO.

Minister-delegate to the Third Deputy Prime Minister: ANTOINE MBOUMBOU-MIYAKOU.

Minister-delegate to the Fourth Deputy Prime Minister: ALBERT YANGARI.

There are 10 Secretaries of State.

MINISTRIES

Office of the Prime Minister: BP 546, Libreville; telex 5409.

Ministry of Agriculture, Livestock and Rural Development: BP 551, Libreville; tel. 76-29-43; telex 5587.

Ministry of the Civil Service, Administrative Reform and Redeployment: Libreville.

Ministry of Culture, Arts, Popular Education and Francophone Affairs: Libreville; telex 5625.

Ministry of Energy and Hydraulic Resources: Libreville; tel. 72-31-96; telex 5629.

Ministry of the Environment and Nature Protection: Libreville.

Ministry of Finance, the Budget and State Shareholdings: BP 165, Libreville; tel. 72-12-10; telex 5238.

Ministry of Foreign Affairs and Co-operation: BP 2245, Libreville; tel. 76-22-70; telex 5255.

Ministry of Forest Resources, National Parks and Fisheries: Libreville.

Ministry of Higher Education, Scientific Research and Technology: BP 496, Libreville; tel. 72-21-75.

Ministry of Information, Posts and Telecommunications: BP 2280, Libreville; tel. 76-16-92; telex 5361.

Ministry of Justice: Libreville; tel. 72-26-95.

GABON

Ministry of Labour, Employment, Human Resources and Professional Training: Libreville.

Ministry of Mines, Industry and Consumption: Libreville; tel. 74-06-00; telex 5499.

Ministry of National Defence, Veterans' Affairs, Public Security and Hydrocarbons: Libreville; tel. 76-25-95; telex 5453.

Ministry of National Education: BP 6, Libreville; tel. 72-17-41; telex 5501.

Ministry of Planning and Economy: Libreville.

Ministry of Public Health and Population: Libreville; tel. 76-30-32; telex 5385.

Ministry of Public Land, Land Registration and the Law of the Sea: Libreville; tel. 72-10-39; telex 5545.

Ministry of Public Works, Equipment, Construction and Territorial Development: BP 371, Libreville; tel. 76-14-87.

Ministry of Small- and Medium-sized Enterprises: Libreville.

Ministry of Social Affairs, Social Security, Natural Disasters and National Solidarity: Libreville; tel. 72-42-22.

Ministry of State Control and Contracts: Libreville.

Ministry of Territorial Administration, Local Communities and Immigration: Libreville; tel. 74-00-21; telex 5638.

Ministry of Tourism, Social Communication and Leisure: BP 403, Libreville.

Ministry of Town Planning, Housing and Habitation: Libreville.

Ministry of Trade, Transfer of Technologies and Rationalization: BP 3906, Libreville; tel. 76-30-55; telex 5347.

Ministry of Transport and Civil Aviation: BP 3974, Libreville; tel. 72-11-62; telex 5479.

Ministry of Youth and Sports: Libreville; tel. 76-35-76; telex 5642.

Legislature

ASSEMBLÉE NATIONALE

At the most recent general election, held in March 1985, all 111 elective seats were won by candidates selected by the sole legal political organization, the Parti démocratique gabonais. A further nine members of the Assembly are appointed by the Head of State.

President: AUGUSTIN BOUMAH.

Secretary-General: PIERRE N'GUEMA-MVÉ.

Political Organizations

Parti démocratique gabonais (PDG): Libreville; f. 1968; sole political party; comprises a supreme congress, a perm. cttee of 13 mems, a political bureau of 44 mems and a cen. cttee of 297 mems; the political bureau may issue decrees without reference to the govt; the cen. cttee acts in an advisory capacity; there are nine regional delegates, numerous local cttees and four specialized organs: Ecole des cadres du parti, Union des jeunes (UJPDG), Union des femmes du PDG (UFPDG) and Fédération des syndicats gabonais (FESYGA); Founding Chair. El Hadj OMAR BONGO; First Sec. LÉON MÉBIAME.

Mouvement de redressement national (MORENA): Paris, France; f. 1981; advocates a multi-party democracy; formed government-in-exile in August 1985; Pres. MAX ANICET KOUMBA MBADINGA; Gen. Sec. MARCEL OGOULA RENOUMBO.

Diplomatic Representation

EMBASSIES IN GABON

Algeria: BP 4008, Libreville; tel. 73-23-18; telex 5313; Ambassador: SAMIR IMALHAYEN.

Angola: BP 4884, Libreville; tel. 73-04-26; telex 5565; Ambassador: BERNARDO DOMBELE M'BALA.

Argentina: BP 4065, Libreville; tel. 74-05-49; telex 5611; Chargé d'affaires: JOSÉ H. LEDESMA.

Belgium: BP 4079, Libreville; tel. 73-29-92; telex 5273; Ambassador: JACQUES-BENOÎT FOBE.

Brazil: BP 3899, Libreville; tel. 76-05-35; telex 5492; Ambassador: JAIME VILLA-LOBOS.

Cameroon: BP 14001, Libreville; tel. 73-28-00; telex 5396; Ambassador: DOMINIQUE YONG.

Canada: BP 4037, Libreville; tel. 72-41-54; telex 5527; Ambassador: BERNARD DUSSAULT.

Central African Republic: BP 2096, Libreville; tel. 72-12-28; telex 5323; Ambassador: FRANÇOIS DIALLO.

China, People's Republic: BP 3914, Libreville; tel. 72-44-11; telex 5376; Ambassador: TIAN YIMING.

Congo: BP 269, Libreville; tel. 73-29-06; telex 5541; Ambassador: ROGER ISSOMBO.

Côte d'Ivoire: BP 3861, Libreville; tel. 72-05-96; telex 5317; Ambassador: JEAN-OBEO COULIBALY.

Egypt: BP 4240, Libreville; tel. 73-25-38; telex 5425; Ambassador: EFFAT REDA.

Equatorial Guinea: BP 14262, Libreville; tel. 76-30-15; Ambassador: NDONG HIBA OBONO.

France: BP 2125, Libreville; tel. 74-04-75; telex 5249; Ambassador: LOUIS DOMINICI.

Germany, Federal Republic: BP 299, Libreville; tel. 72-27-90; telex 5248; Ambassador: GERMAN HAUPTMANN.

Guinea: BP 4046, Libreville; Chargé d'affaires: El Hadj SOULEYMANE DIALLO.

Iran: BP 2158, Libreville; tel. 73-05-33; telex 5502; Ambassador: Dr ABBASSE SAFARIAN.

Italy: Immeuble Personnaz et Gardin, rue de la Mairie, PB 2251, Libreville; tel. 72-10-93; telex 5287; Ambassador: ALFREDO MATACOTTA.

Japan: BP 2259, Libreville; tel. 73-22-97; telex 5428; Ambassador: HIDEO KAKINUMA.

Korea, Democratic People's Republic: BP 4012, Libreville; tel. 73-26-68; telex 5486; Ambassador: TCHA-SUN GON.

Korea, Republic: BP 2620, Libreville; tel. 72-36-44; telex 5356; Ambassador: NAM-CHA HWANG.

Lebanon: BP 3341, Libreville; tel. 73-14-77; telex 5547; Ambassador: MAMLOUK ABDELLATIF.

Mauritania: BP 3917, Libreville; tel. 72-32-38; telex 5570; Ambassador: El Hadj THIAM.

Morocco: BP 3983, Libreville; tel. 73-31-03; telex 5434; Ambassador: MOULAYE DRISS ALAOUI.

Nigeria: BP 1191, Libreville; tel. 73-22-03; telex 5605; Ambassador: JOE-EFFIONG UDOH EKONG.

Philippines: BP 1198, Libreville; tel. 72-34-80; telex 5279; Chargé d'affaires: MARCIANO A. PAYNOR.

São Tomé and Príncipe: BP 409, Libreville; tel. 72-15-46; telex 5557; Ambassador: CARLOS ALBERTO MENEZES BRANGANÇA GÓMEZ.

Senegal: BP 3856, Libreville; tel. 74-11-36; telex 5332; Ambassador: OUMAR WELE.

Spain: BP 1157, Libreville; tel. 77-30-68; telex 5258; Ambassador: GERMÁN ZURITA Y SÁENZ DE NAVARRETE.

Togo: BP 14160, Libreville; tel. 72-40-81; telex 5490; Chargé d'affaires a.i.: ADOMAYAKPON YAWO.

Tunisia: Libreville; Ambassador: EZZEDINE KERKENI.

USSR: BP 3963, Libreville; tel. 73-27-46; Ambassador: YURI SHMANEVSKY.

United Kingdom: Immeuble CK2, blvd de l'Indépendance, BP 476, Libreville; tel. 74-07-07; telex 5538; Ambassador: MARK AUBREY GOODFELLOW.

USA: BP 4000, Libreville; tel. 76-20-03; telex 5250; Ambassador: WARREN CLARK, Jr.

Uruguay: BP 5556, Libreville; tel. 74-30-44; telex 5646; Ambassador: Dr ALVARO ALVAREZ.

Venezuela: BP 3854, Libreville; tel. 73-31-18; telex 5264; Ambassador: VÍCTOR CROQUER-VEGA.

Yugoslavia: BP 930, Libreville; tel. 73-30-05; telex 5329; Ambassador: NIKOLA SKRELJI.

Zaire: BP 2257, Libreville; tel. 72-02-56; telex 5335; Ambassador: BOMINA-N'SONI LANGANGE N'GOMBA.

Judicial System

Supreme Court: BP 1043, Libreville; tel. 76-09-68; has four chambers: constitutional, judicial, administrative, and accounts; Pres. (vacant).

High Court of Justice: Libreville; mems appointed by and from the deputies of the National Assembly; Pres. MARCEL SANDOUNGOUT.

Court of Appeal: Libreville-Franceville.

Cour de Sûreté de l'Etat: Libreville; 13 mems; Pres. VICTOR DIEUDONNÉ MOUCKEYTOU.

GABON

Conseil Supérieur de la Magistrature: Libreville; Pres. El Hadj OMAR BONGO; Vice-Pres. Minister of Justice (ex officio).

There are also Tribunaux de Première Instance (County Courts) at Libreville-Port-Gentil, Franceville, Lambaréné, Mouila, Oyem, Koulamoutou, Makokou and Tchibanga.

Religion

About 60% of Gabon's population are Christians, mainly adherents of the Roman Catholic Church. About 40% are animists, and fewer than 1% are Muslims.

CHRISTIANITY
The Roman Catholic Church

Gabon comprises one archdiocese and three dioceses. At 31 December 1985 there were an estimated 564,000 adherents in the country.

Bishops' Conference: Conférence Episcopale du Gabon, BP 230, Franceville; tel. 67-71-83; f. 1973; Pres. Mgr FÉLICIEN-PATRICE MAKOUAKA, Bishop of Franceville.

Archbishop of Libreville: Mgr ANDRÉ-FERNAND ANGUILÉ, Archevêché, Sainte-Marie, BP 2146, Libreville; tel. 72-20-73.

Protestant Churches

Christian and Missionary Alliance: active in the south of the country; 16,000 mems.

Eglise Evangélique du Gabon: BP 10080, Libreville; tel. 72-41-92; f. 1842; independent since 1961; 120,000 mems; Pres. Pastor SAMUEL NANG ESSONO; Sec. Rev. EMILE NTETOME.

The Evangelical Church of South Gabon and the Evangelical Pentecostal Church are also active in the country.

The Press

Bulletin Evangélique d'Information et de Presse: BP 80, Libreville; monthly; religious.

Bulletin Mensuel de la Chambre de Commerce, d'Agriculture, d'Industrie et des Mines: BP 2234, Libreville; tel. 72-20-64; telex 5554; monthly.

Bulletin Mensuel de Statistique de la République Gabonaise: BP 179, Libreville; monthly; publ. by Direction Générale de l'Economie.

Dialogue: Maison du PDG, BP 213, Libreville; f. 1969; publ. by the PDG; monthly; Man. ELOIE CHAMBRIEN; circ. 3,000.

L'Economiste Gabonais: BP 3906, Libreville; quarterly; publ. by the Centre gabonais du commerce extérieur.

Gabon d'Aujourd'hui: BP 750, Libreville; weekly; publ. by the Ministry of Information, Posts and Telecommunications.

Gabon-Matin: BP 168, Libreville; daily; publ. by Agence Gabonaise de Presse; Man. HILARION VENDANY; circ. 18,000.

Journal Officiel de la République Gabonaise: BP 563, Libreville; f. 1959; fortnightly; Man. EMMANUEL OBAMÉ.

Ngondo: BP 168, Libreville; monthly; publ. by Agence Gabonaise de Presse.

Promex: BP 3906, Libreville.

Sept Jours: BP 213, Libreville; weekly.

L'Union: BP 3849, Libreville; f. 1975; daily; official govt publication; 75% state-owned; Man. Dir ALBERT YANGARI; Dir RENÉ KOUPANGOYE; circ. 15,000.

NEWS AGENCIES

Agence Gabonaise de Presse (AGP): BP 168, Libreville; tel. 21-26; telex 5628.

Foreign Bureau

Agence France-Presse (AFP): Villa 32, Borne 2, Cité du 12 mars, BP 788, Libreville; tel. 76-14-36; telex 5239; Correspondents BERNARD APFELDORFER, LAURENT MENNELET.

Publishers

Imprimerie Centrale d'Afrique (IMPRIGA): BP 154, Libreville; tel. 70-22-55; f. 1973; Chair. ROBERT VIAL; Dir FRANCIS BOURQUIN.

Multipress Gabon: blvd Président-Léon-M'Ba, BP 3875, Libreville; tel. 73-22-33; telex 5389; f. 1973; Chair. PAUL BORY.

Société Imprimerie de l'Ogooué (SIMO): BP 342, Port-Gentil; f. 1977; Man. Dir URBAIN NICOUE.

Société Nationale de Presse et d'Edition (SONAPRESSE): BP 3849, Libreville; tel. 73-21-84; telex 5391; f. 1975; Pres. and Man. Dir JOSEPH RENDJAMBE.

Radio and Television

In 1983 there were an estimated 102,000 radio receivers and 20,000 television receivers in use.

RADIO

The national network, 'La Voix de la Rénovation', and a provincial network broadcast for 24 hours each day in French and local languages. Proposals for the construction of 13 new FM radio stations were announced in 1986.

Africa No. 1: BP 1, Libreville; tel. 76-00-01; telex 5588; f. 1980; 35% state-controlled; international commercial radio station; broadcasts began in February 1981; daily broadcasts in French and English; Pres. LOUIS BARTHÉLEMY MAPANGOU; Mans MICHEL KOUMBANGOYE, RENAUD LAFARGUE.

Radiodiffusion-Télévision Gabonaise (RTG): Libreville; Man. Dir LUC MVOUAMBA; Dir of Radio JOSEPH TSOMO.

TELEVISION

Television transmissions can be received as far inland as Kango and Lambaréné; in 1986, proposals were announced for the extension and modernization of the network to cover the whole of Gabon, including the construction of 13 new TV broadcasting stations. Programmes are also transmitted by satellite to other African countries. Colour broadcasts began in December 1975. Negotiations began in 1988 with Canal Plus Afrique, a subsidiary of Canal Plus (France), for the establishment of a private television channel in Gabon.

Radiodiffusion-Télévision Gabonaise (RTG): BP 10150, Libreville; tel. 73-27-84; telex 5342; state-controlled; Man. Dir JACQUES ADIAHENOT; Dir of Television R. MOUBOUYI.

Télé-Africa: Libreville; tel. 76-20-33; private channel.

Finance

(cap. = capital; res = reserves; dep. = deposits; brs = branches; m. = million; amounts in francs CFA)

BANKING
Central Bank

Banque des Etats de l'Afrique Centrale (BEAC): BP 112, Libreville; tel. 76-13-52; telex 5215; headquarters in Yaoundé, Cameroon; f. 1973 as central bank of issue for mem. states of the Customs and Economic Union of Central Africa (UDEAC), comprising Cameroon, the Central African Republic, Chad, the Congo, Equatorial Guinea and Gabon; cap. 24,000m., res 148,480m. (Dec. 1986); Gov. CASIMIR OYE MBA; Dir in Gabon JEAN-PAUL LEYIMANGOYE; 2 brs.

Commercial Banks

Banque du Gabon et du Luxembourg: blvd de l'Indépendance, BP 3879, Libreville; tel. 72-28-62; telex 5344; f. 1974; cap. 1,200m.; activities temporarily suspended by the govt.

Banque Intercontinentale du Gabon (INTERBANQUE): BP 4013, Libreville; tel. 76-11-13; telex 5482; f. 1979; cap. 750m.; Chair. GEORGES RAWIRI; Man. Dir MAXIMILIAN J. SEYNI.

Banque Internationale pour le Commerce et l'Industrie du Gabon SA (BICIG): ave du Colonel Parant, BP 2241, Libreville; tel. 76-26-13; telex 5526; f. 1973; cap. 6,000m. (July 1986); 27.7% state-owned, 26% Société Financière pour les Pays d'Outre-Mer, 25% Banque Nationale de Paris; Pres. ETIENNE-GUY MOUVAGHA TCHIOBA; Man. Dir EMILE DOUMBA; 9 brs.

Banque Internationale pour le Gabon (BIPG): immeuble Concorde, blvd de l'Indépendance, BP 106, Libreville; tel. 76-26-26; telex 5221; f. 1975; cap. 900m. (Dec. 1986); 10% state-owned, 90% owned by Banque Internationale pour l'Afrique Occidentale (France); Pres. PAUL BIYOGHE MBA; Man. Dir SAMSON NGOMO; 6 brs.

Banque Paribas Gabon: BP 2253, blvd de l'Indépendance, Libreville; tel. 76-40-35; telex 5265; f. 1971; cap. and res 5,099m.; 32.2% state-owned; Pres. ETIENNE MOUSSIROU; Man. Dir HENRI CLAUDE OYIMA; br. at Port-Gentil.

Crédit Foncier du Gabon (CREFOGA): BP 3905, Libreville; tel. 72-47-45; telex 5450; f. 1976; cap. 1,500m.; 67% state-owned; Man. Dir ADRIEN NKOGHE ESSINGONE.

Union Gabonaise de Banque SA (UGB): BP 315, ave du Colonel Parant, Libreville; tel. 76-15-14; telex 5232; f. 1962; cap. and res

GABON
Directory

2,696m., dep. 53,340m. (Dec. 1984); Pres. MATHIEU NGUEMA; Gen. Man. MARCEL DOUPAMBY MATOKA; 6 brs.

Development Banks

Banque Gabonaise de Développement (BGD): rue Alfred Marche, BP 5, Libreville; tel. 76-24-29; telex 5430; f. 1960; cap. 7,000m. (Dec. 1986); 69% state-owned; Pres. MICHEL ANCHOUEY; Man. Dir JEAN-FÉLIX MAMALEPOT; brs in Franceville, Port-Gentil.

Banque Nationale de Crédit Rurale (BNCR): ave Bouet, BP 1120, Libreville; f. 1986; cap. 200m. (Dec. 1987); 91.5% state-owned; Pres. PASCAL NZÉ BIE; Man. Dir JACQUES DIOUF.

Société Gabonaise de Participations et de Développement (SOGAPAR): blvd de l'Indépendance, BP 2253, Libreville; tel. 76-23-26; telex 5265; f. 1971; cap. 2,063m. (Dec. 1986); 27% state-owned, 70% owned by Paribas International; studies and promotes projects conducive to national economic development; Pres. DANIEL BÉDIN; Man. Dir HENRI-CLAUDE OYIMA.

Société Nationale d'Investissements du Gabon (SONADIG): BP 479, Libreville; tel. 72-09-22; f. 1968; cap. 100m.; state-owned investment co; Pres. ANTOINE OYIEYE; Dir-Gen. SIMON EDOU-EYENNE.

INSURANCE

Assurances Générales Gabonaises (AGG): BP 2148, Libreville; tel. 76-09-73; telex 5473; cap. 26.5m.; Chair. and Man. Dir JEAN DENDE.

Assureurs Conseils Franco-Africains du Gabon (ACFRA-GABON): BP 1116, Libreville; tel. 72-32-83; telex 5485; cap. 43.4m.; Chair. EMILE CASALEGNO; Dir M. GARNIER.

Assureurs Conseils Gabonais-Faugère, Jutheau et Cie: Immeuble Shell-Gabon, rue de la Mairie, BP 2138, Libreville; tel. 72-04-36; telex 5435; cap. 10m.; represents foreign insurance cos; Dir GÉRARD MILAN.

Mutuelle Gabonaise d'Assurances: ave du Colonel Parant, BP 2225, Libreville; tel. 72-13-91; telex 5240; Sec.-Gen. M. YENO-OLINGOT.

Omnium Gabonais d'Assurances et de Réassurances (OGAR): blvd Triomphal Omar Bongo, BP 201, Libreville; tel. 76-15-96; telex 5505; f. 1976; cap. 340m.; 10% govt-owned; general; Pres. MARCEL DOUPAMBY-MATOKA; Man. Dir EDOUARD VALENTIN; brs in Oyem, Port-Gentil, Franceville.

Société Nationale Gabonaise d'Assurances et de Réassurances (SONAGAR): ave du Colonel Parant, BP 3082, Libreville; tel. 76-28-97; telex 5366; f. 1974; cap. 300m.; business taken over in June 1987 by l'Union des Assurances de Paris (France), following liquidation; Dir-Gen. JEAN-LOUIS MESSAN.

SOGERCO-Gabon: BP 2102, Libreville; tel. 76-09-34; telex 5224; f. 1975; cap. 10m.; general; Dir M. RABEAU.

L'Union des Assurances du Gabon (UAG): ave du Colonel Parant, BP 2141, Libreville; tel. 72-22-52; telex 5404; f. 1976; cap. 280.5m.; 72% owned by l'Union des Assurances de Paris; Chair. ALBERT ALEVINA-CHAVIHOT; Dir FRANÇOIS SIMON.

Trade and Industry

GOVERNMENT ADVISORY BODY

Conseil Economique et Social de la République Gabonaise: BP 1075, Libreville; tel. 76-26-68; comprises representatives from salaried workers, employers and govt; commissions on economic, financial and social affairs and forestry and agriculture; Pres. EDOUARD ALEXIS M'BOUY-BOUTZIT; Vice-Pres. M. RICHEPIN EYOGO-EDZANG.

CHAMBER OF COMMERCE

Chambre de Commerce, d'Agriculture, d'Industrie et des Mines du Gabon: BP 2234, Libreville; tel. 72-20-64; telex 5554; f. 1935; regional offices at Port-Gentil and Franceville; Pres. EDOUARD ALEXIS M'BOUY-BOUTZIT; Sec.-Gen. DOMINIQUE MANDZA.

EMPLOYERS' FEDERATIONS

Confédération Patronale Gabonaise: BP 84, Libreville; tel. 76-02-43; f. 1959; represents the principal industrial, mining, petroleum, public works, forestry, banking, insurance, commercial and shipping concerns; Pres. M. ANDRÉ DIEUDONNÉ BERRE; Sec.-Gen. ERIC MESSERSCHMITT.

Conseil National du Patronat Gabonais (CNPG): Libreville; Pres. RAHANDI CHAMBRIER; Sec.-Gen. THOMAS FRANCK EYA'A.

Syndicat des Entreprises Minières du Gabon (SYNDIMINES): BP 260, Libreville; telex 5388; Pres. ANDRÉ BERRE; Sec.-Gen. SERGE GREGOIRE.

Syndicat des Importateurs Exportateurs du Gabon (SIMPEX): BP 1743, Libreville; Pres. ALBERT JEAN; Sec.-Gen. R. TYBERGHEIN.

Syndicat des Producteurs et Industriels du Bois du Gabon: BP 84, Libreville; tel. 72-26-11; Pres. CLAUDE MOLENAT.

Syndicat Professionnel des Usines de Sciages et Placages du Gabon: BP 417, Port-Gentil; f. 1956; Pres. PIERRE BERRY.

Union des Représentations Automobiles et Industrielles (URAI): BP 1743, Libreville; Pres. M. MARTINENT; Sec. R. TYBERGHEIN.

Union Nationale du Patronat Syndical des Transports Urbains, Routiers et Fluviaux du Gabon (UNAPASYFTUROGA): BP 1025, Libreville; f. 1977 as Syndicat National des Transporteurs Urbains et Routiers du Gabon (SYNTRAGA); Pres. LAURENT BELLAL BIBANG-BI-EDZO; Sec.-Gen. MARTIN KOMBILA-MOMBO.

PRINCIPAL DEVELOPMENT ORGANIZATIONS

Agence Nationale de Promotion de la Petite et Moyenne Entreprise (PROMO-GABON): BP 3939, Libreville; tel. 74-31-16; f. 1964; state-controlled; promotion of and assistance to small and medium-sized industries; Pres. SIMON BOULAMATARI; Man. Dir JEAN-FIDÈLE OTANDO.

Caisse Centrale de Coopération Economique (CCCE) (France): BP 64, Libreville; tel. 72-23-89; telex 5362; Dir JACQUES ALBUGUES.

Centre Gabonais de Commerce Extérieur (CGCE): BP 3906, Libreville; tel. 76-11-67; telex 5347; promotion of foreign trade and investment; Man. Dir MICHEL LESLIE TEALE.

Commerce et Développement (CODEV): BP 2142, Libreville; tel. 76-06-73; telex 5214; f. 1976; cap. 2,000m. francs CFA; 95% state-owned, privatization plans announced 1986; import and distribution of capital goods and food products; Chair. and Man. Dir JÉRÔME NGOUA-BEKALE.

Mission Française de Coopération: BP 2105, Libreville; administers bilateral aid from France; Dir FRANÇOIS CHAPPELLET.

Office Gabonais d'Amélioration et de Production de Viande (OGAPROV): BP 245, Moanda; tel. 66-12-67; f. 1971; development of private cattle farming; manages ranch at Lekedi-Sud; Pres. PAUL KOUNDA KIKI; Dir-Gen. VINCENT EYI-NGUI.

Palmiers et Hévéas du Gabon (PALMÉVÉAS): BP 75, Libreville; f. 1956; cap. 145m. francs CFA; govt-owned; palm-oil development.

Société de Développement de l'Agriculture au Gabon (AGROGABON): BP 2248, Libreville; tel. 76-40-82; telex 5468; f. 1976; cap. 7,356m. francs CFA; 96% state-owned; Man. Dir ANDRÉ LE ROUX.

Société de Développement de l'Hévéaculture (HÉVÉGAB): BP 316, Libreville; tel. 70-03-48; telex 5615; f. 1981; cap. 4,098m. francs CFA; 99.9% state-owned; development of rubber plantations; Chair. EMMANUEL ONDO-METHOGO; Man. Dir PIERRE-YVES WINTREBERT.

Société Gabonaise de Recherches et d'Exploitations Minières (SOGAREM): blvd de Nice, Libreville; state-owned; research and development of gold mining; Chair. ARSÈNE BOUNGUENZA; Man. Dir SERGE GASSITA.

Société Gabonaise de Recherches Pétroliers (GABOREP): BP 564, Libreville; tel. 77-23-86; telex 5829; exploration and exploitation of hydrocarbons; Man. Dir P. F. LECA.

Société Nationale de Développement des Cultures Industrielles (SONADECI): BP 256, Libreville; tel. 76-33-97; telex 5362; f. 1978; cap. 600m. francs CFA; state-owned; agricultural development; Chair. PAUL KOUNDA KIKI; Man. Dir GEORGES BEKALE.

TRADE UNIONS

Confédération Syndicale Gabonaise (COSYGA): BP 14017, Libreville; telex 5623; f. 1969 by the govt as a specialized organ of the PDG to organize and educate workers, to contribute to social peace and economic development and to protect the rights of trade unions; Pres. GASTON INDASSY-GNAMBAULT.

Transport

RAILWAYS

The Transgabon railway, which will eventually open up the densely-forested interior, was begun in 1974. The first phase, from Owendo (the port of Libreville) to Booué (340 km), was inaugurated in January 1983, and the second phase, from Booué to Franceville (330 km), in December 1986. The construction of a 235-km spur from Booué to Belinga, to serve future iron-ore mines in the north-east, was planned for the 1990s, but has been postponed indefinitely, owing to reductions in public investment expenditure and to a lack of private finance. At present, the manganese mine at Moanda is connected with Pointe-Noire (Congo) by a 76-km cableway and a 296-km railway.

GABON

Office du Chemin de Fer Transgabonais (OCTRA): BP 2198, Libreville; tel. 70-24-78; telex 5307; f. 1972; cap. 231,243m. francs CFA; state-owned; Man. Dir CHARLES TSIBAH.

ROADS

In late 1987 there were 6,898 km of roads, of which 735 km were surfaced. A large-scale programme of road development is in progress.

Société Africaine de Transit et d'Affrètement Gabon (SATA-GABON): blvd de l'Indépendance, BP 2258, Libreville; tel. 76-11-28; telex 5439; f. 1961; cap. 300m. francs CFA; freight; Man. Dir YVES LERAYS.

INLAND WATERWAYS

The most important river is the Ogooué, navigable from Port-Gentil to Ndjolé (310 km) and serving the towns of Lambaréné, Ndjolé and Sindara.

Compagnie de Navigation Intérieure (CNI): BP 3982, Libreville; tel. 72-39-28; telex 5289; f. 1978; cap. 500m. francs CFA; state-owned; inland waterway transport; agencies at Port-Gentil, Mayumba and Lambaréné; Dir MATHURIN ANOTHO-ONANGA.

SHIPPING

The principal deep-water ports are Port-Gentil, which handles chiefly petroleum exports, and Owendo, 15 km from Libreville, which handles mainly barge traffic. Facilities for handling timber came into operation at Owendo in 1979. There are also timber ports at Mayumba and Nyanga, and a fishing port at Libreville. A new terminal for the export of minerals at Owendo, was inaugurated in December 1988. The terminal has an annual handling capacity of 2.5m. metric tons of manganese ore. The construction of a deep-water port at Mayumba is planned. At mid-1984 the merchant shipping fleet had a total displacement of 97,000 grt, of which 74,000 grt were oil tankers.

Compagnie de Manutention et de Chalandage d'Owendo (COMACO): BP 2131, Libreville; tel. 70-26-35; telex 5208; f. 1974; cap. 1,500m. francs CFA; Pres. GEORGES RAWIRI; Dir in Libreville M. HERBUEL.

Office des Ports et Rades du Gabon (OPRAG): BP 1051, Libreville; tel. 70-17-97; telex 8312; state-owned; Pres. JEAN-FELIX ONTALA M'BAYE; Man. Dir MARIUS FOUNGUES.

Société Nationale d'Acconage et de Transit (SNAT): BP 3897, Libreville; tel. 72-04-04; telex 5420; f. 1976; cap. 600m. francs CFA; 51% state-owned; freight transport; Chair. M. MASSALA-MALONGA; Man. Dir ERNEST REDOMBO.

Société Nationale de Transports Maritimes (SONATRAM): BP 3841, Libreville; tel. 76-39-51; telex 5289; f. 1976; cap. 1,500m. francs CFA; 51% state-owned; river and ocean cargo transport; Man. Dir LUDOVIC OGNAGNA OCKOGHO.

Société Ouest Africaine d'Entreprises Maritimes (SOAEM-GABON): BP 518, Port-Gentil; tel. 75-21-71; telex 5205; freight shipping; Chair. RENÉ KOLOWSKI; Man. Dir T. DE PONTBRIAND.

Société du Port Mineralier d'Owendo: f. 1987; cap. 4,000m. francs CFA; majority holding by COMILOG; management of new terminal for minerals at Owendo.

SOCOPAO-Gabon: BP 4, Libreville; tel. 70-21-40; telex 5212; f. 1963; cap. 120m. francs CFA; Dir H. LECORDIER.

CIVIL AVIATION

There are international airports at Libreville, Port-Gentil and Franceville, 65 other public and 50 private airfields linked mostly with forestry and oil industries. The second phase of a project to modernize and extend Libreville's Léon M'Ba airport was completed in early 1988. A third phase, to expand the airport's passenger-handling capacity, was to be financed by France.

Air Affaires Gabon: BP 3962, Libreville; tel. 73-20-10; telex 5360; f. 1975; domestic passenger and cargo chartered and scheduled flights; Chair. RAYMOND BELLANGER; Man. Dir D. BOMPARD; fleet of 2 King Air 90, 2 Super King 200, 2 Bandeirante E110, 1 Lear 35, 1 HS 125-600, 4 B-58.

Air Service Gabon (ASG): BP 2232, Libreville; tel. 73-24-07; telex 5522; f. 1965; cap. 50m. francs CFA; charter flights; Chair. JÉRÔME OKINDA; Gen. Man. FRANCIS LASCOMBES.

Compagnie Nationale Air Gabon: BP 2206, Libreville; tel. 73-21-97; telex 5213; f. 1977 following Gabon's withdrawal from Air Afrique (see under Côte d'Ivoire); cap. 6,500m. francs CFA; 80% state-owned; internal and international cargo and passenger services; Chair. JEAN-LOUIS MESSAN; Dir-Gen. JEAN-CLAUDE LABOURA; fleet of 1 Boeing 747-200B, 1 Boeing 737-200C, 2 Fokker F28-2000, 1 F28-1000, 1 F28-1000C, 1 Lockheed C-130.

Société de Gestion de l'Aéroport de Libreville (ADL): Libreville; f. 1988; cap. 340m. francs CFA; 26.5% state-owned; management of airport at Libreville.

Tourism

Tourism is being extensively developed, with new hotels and several important projects, including a 'holiday village' near Libreville (opened in 1973), reorganization of Pointe-Denis tourist resort, and the promotion of national parks. In 1987 there were 74 hotels, with a total of 3,077 rooms.

Centre de Promotion Touristique du Gabon (GABONTOUR): Libreville.

Ministère du Tourisme, de la Communication Sociale et des Loisirs: BP 403, Libreville.

Office National Gabonais du Tourisme: BP 161, Libreville; tel. 72-21-82.

THE GAMBIA

Introductory Survey

Location, Climate, Language, Religion, Flag, Capital

The Republic of The Gambia is a narrow territory around the River Gambia on the west coast of Africa. The country has a short coastline on the Atlantic Ocean but is otherwise surrounded by Senegal. The climate is tropical and, away from the river swamps, most of the terrain is covered by savanna bush. The average annual temperature in the capital, Banjul, is 27°C (80°F). English is the official language, while the principal vernacular languages are Mandinka, Fula and Wolof. About 85% of the inhabitants are Muslims, and most of the remainder are Christians, with some adherents of animism. The national flag (proportions 3 by 2) has red, blue and green horizontal stripes, with two narrow white stripes bordering the central blue band. The capital is Banjul (formerly called Bathurst).

Recent History

The Gambia was formerly a British dependency. It became a separate colony in 1888, having previously been united with Sierra Leone. The principle of election was introduced for the first time in the 1946 constitution. Political parties were formed in the 1950s, and another constitution was adopted in 1960. This was amended in April 1962, when the office of Premier was created. Following elections in May, the leader of the People's Progressive Party (PPP), Dr (later Sir) Dawda Kairaba Jawara, took office as Premier in June 1962. Full internal self-government followed in October 1963.

On 18 February 1965 The Gambia became an independent country within the Commonwealth, with Dr Jawara as Prime Minister. On 24 April 1970 the country became a republic, with Sir Dawda Jawara (as he had become in 1966) taking office as President. He was re-elected in 1972 and again in April 1977, as a result of PPP victories in legislative elections. In September 1978 the only United Party member remaining in the House of Representatives, following a by-election defeat in May 1977, joined the PPP, leaving only the five members of the National Convention Party (NCP) as opposition.

In October 1980 the Government was obliged to ask neighbouring Senegal to dispatch troops to The Gambia to assist in maintaining internal security under the terms of a mutual defence pact. A more serious threat was posed in July 1981, when a coup was staged during President Jawara's absence. Left-wing rebels formed a 12-man National Revolutionary Council and proclaimed their leader, Kukoi Samba Sanyang, as Head of State. Senegalese troops again entered Banjul and quickly crushed the rebellion. A state of emergency was announced, and more than 1,000 people were arrested. During the resulting trials, held in subsequent months, more than 60 people were sentenced to death, but by late 1987 the majority of the sentences had been commuted to life imprisonment and no executions had taken place. The state of emergency was finally revoked in February 1985.

Plans were announced in August 1981 for the merger of The Gambia and Senegal, which had always had close links, in a confederation to be called Senegambia. These proposals were approved by the Gambian House of Representatives in December, and came into effect on 1 February 1982 (see chapter on Senegal, Vol. II). The first Confederal Council of Ministers, headed by President Abdou Diouf of Senegal (with President Jawara as his deputy), was announced in November 1982 and held its inaugural meeting in January 1983, as did the new, 60-member, Confederal Assembly. Subsequent meetings have led to agreements on co-ordination of foreign policy, communications, defence and security; negotiations on economic and monetary union continue. There is some disillusion, particularly in Senegal, over President Jawara's apparent reluctance to complete the process of confederation, in the interests of minimizing the economic cost to The Gambia. Meanwhile, Gambian critics have felt that the country's political autonomy has been sacrificed to ensure the Government's survival.

In The Gambia's first presidential election by direct popular vote, held in May 1982, President Jawara was re-elected, obtaining 72% of the votes cast, while the leader of the NCP, Sherif Mustapha Dibba (at that time in detention for his alleged involvement in the abortive coup), received 28%. In the concurrent legislative elections, the PPP won 27 of the 35 elective seats in the House of Representatives. Following the elections, the PPP sought to restore further its public standing by bringing a number of younger, reformist Ministers into the Cabinet. However, the resignation of the Minister of Justice in June 1984, amid unconfirmed reports of financial misconduct, and the dismissal of the Minister of Economic Planning in January 1985, following allegations of abuse of power, served to illustrate that corruption remained a major problem. In 1988 several senior executives in the public sector were suspended or dismissed, and investigations began into administrative irregularities in that sector.

The PPP overcame an intensified challenge from opposition groups in the legislative and presidential elections held in March 1987, winning 31 out of 36 directly-elected seats in the House of Representatives. Three other parties presented candidates: the NCP (which won the remaining five elective seats) and two newly-formed groupings, the Gambia People's Party (GPP) and the People's Democratic Organization for Independence and Socialism (PDOIS). In the presidential election, Dr Jawara was re-elected with 59% of the votes cast, while Sherif Dibba (who had been acquitted and released from detention in June 1982) and the GPP leader, Assan Musa Camara (a former Vice-President), received 27% and 14% of the votes respectively.

In January 1988 10 people, including six Senegalese, were detained following the discovery of a coup plot. Musa Sanneh, Amadou Badjie, Adrien Sambou (both Badjie and Sambou being members of the Senegalese separatist movement, the Mouvement des forces démocratiques de la Casamance) and Ousman Sanneh were brought to trial in April, on charges of high treason and conspiracy to overthrow the Gambian Government. During the trial, it was alleged that false travel documents had been supplied to Gambian and Senegalese citizens, with a view to receiving military training abroad. The involvement in the plot of both Kukoi Samba Sanyang (the leader of the 1981 coup, who was resident in Libya) and the Senegalese opposition leader, Abdoulaye Wade, was suggested by witnesses. Musa Sanneh, Badjie and Ousman Sanneh subsequently received prison sentences, with hard labour, of between nine and 30 years, while Sambou was acquitted.

Government

Legislative power is held by the unicameral House of Representatives, with 50 members: 36 directly elected by universal adult suffrage for five years; five Chiefs' Representatives Members, elected by the Chiefs in Assembly; eight non-voting nominated members; and the Attorney-General. The President is elected by direct universal suffrage for a five-year term. He is Head of State and appoints a Vice-President (who is leader of government business in the House) and a Cabinet consisting of elected members of the House or other nominees.

Defence

In accordance with the Senegambia confederation pact, which came into effect in February 1982, Confederal units were formed, comprising members of the Senegalese and Gambian defence forces. However, both countries also maintain separate armies. Confederal defence expenditure in 1987/88 was 3,030m. francs CFA. In June 1988 the Gambian armed forces comprised 600 men (including a gendarmerie of 400). Military service is mainly voluntary. The Gambia's defence budget for 1985/86 was estimated at 7.8m. dalasi.

Economic Affairs

The Gambia has experienced economic decline in recent years, with output falling while the population has increased rapidly.

THE GAMBIA

In 1987, according to World Bank estimates, the country's gross national product (GNP), measured at average 1985-87 prices, was US $177m.—equivalent to $220 per head. Between 1980 and 1987, it was estimated, GNP per head decreased, in real terms, at an average annual rate of 4.0%.

The economy is based on peasant cultivation of groundnuts, which in 1985/86 provided 78.6% of export earnings. The Gambia is therefore particularly vulnerable to fluctuations in groundnut harvests and to changes in international prices. More than 70% of the working population are engaged in agriculture, and the sector provided 26% of gross domestic product (GDP) in 1985/86. The other major cash crop is cotton, which accounted for 5.7% of export earnings in 1985/86. Industrial activity is based largely on the processing of groundnuts, while beverages and construction materials are also produced. The Government has attempted to diversify the industrial sector in recent years, with particular emphasis on the fishing and livestock industries. 'Gambianization' has gradually been introduced into all sectors of the economy except tourism, which remains largely under foreign control. Since 1981, however, foreign investment has been encouraged in other sectors, particularly horticulture and light industry. Food, machinery and other manufactured goods constitute the country's main import requirements. Seismic surveys have indicated the existence of significant reserves of petroleum.

Between 1977 and 1981 erratic rainfall and pest infestation had an adverse effect on the output of crops, so that foreign aid, in the form of emergency food supplies, was required. By 1980/81 groundnut production had fallen to 46,000 metric tons, its lowest level for 30 years. It recovered again, to 151,000 tons, in 1982, but declined by almost 30%, to 106,000 tons, in 1983, as a result of renewed drought. Output increased slightly, to total 120,000 tons in 1985, before declining again, to an estimated 100,000 tons, in 1986. Food-grain production is consistently below The Gambia's requirements, with a shortfall of some 44,000 tons occurring in 1984/85. The trade deficit in that year totalled 235.1m. dalasi (compared with 132.7m. dalasi in 1982/83), increasing to 594m. dalasi in 1986/87, partly as a consequence of low export prices for groundnuts. Output of paddy rice declined by 20% in 1987/88, while that of seed (unginned) cotton fell by 50%, owing to pest infestation. The cultivation of crops such as citrus fruits, avocados and sesame seed has been encouraged by the Government, and has proved to be commercially viable.

In February 1984 the dalasi was devalued by 25% against the pound sterling, in order to arrest increases in prices of imports from non-sterling sources. A series of austerity measures, including a 'freeze' on wages, reductions in planned government spending and an increase in prices for basic commodities, was implemented in accordance with a 15-month IMF stand-by arrangement, agreed in May 1984 and authorizing purchases by The Gambia of up to 12.8m. SDRs. This was suspended in April 1985, however, after only one instalment had been drawn, because The Gambia owed substantial arrears to the Fund. At the end of 1984 the country's total external public debt was estimated at US $161m. In June 1985 the Government inaugurated an Economic Recovery Programme (ERP), with the aim of achieving sustained economic growth by increasing and diversifying agricultural output, and by stimulating commercial activity, while curtailing the role and size of the public sector. The IMF loan was subsequently restored. A 'floating' exchange rate was adopted in January 1986. The ERP has received substantial support from both bilateral and multilateral aid donors. In August 1986 formal agreement was reached on a structural adjustment credit of SDR 14.1m. from the World Bank, and in September the IMF agreed to provide loans totalling SDR 17.8m., while the 'Paris Club' of Western creditor governments agreed to a rescheduling of The Gambia's debts. Total donor support in 1986/87 was estimated at US $44.5m. Commercial debts totalling US $19.5m. were rescheduled in January 1988. In December of that year existing agreements with the IMF were superseded by a three-year enhanced structural adjustment facility (ESAF) of SDR 20.52m., in support of measures to consolidate the achievements of the ERP.

The 1987/88 budget proposals envisaged a budget surplus for the first time in some years, to be achieved by means of a reduction in the official prices payable to producers of groundnuts. Most producer prices for agricultural commodities were to be 'frozen' or further reduced under the provisions of the 1988/89 budget. Budget estimates for that financial year envisaged revenue of 405.1m. dalasi, compared with 386.7m. dalasi in 1987/88, and recurrent expenditure of 404.6m. dalasi, compared with 380.0m. dalasi in 1987/88. Development expenditure in 1988/89 was projected at 205.0m. dalasi, compared with 169.6m. dalasi in 1987/88.

The annual rate of inflation, estimated at 10.2% in 1982/83, rose to 70% in 1985/86 before falling to 20% in 1986/87. GDP in 1987/88 was estimated at 431.8m. dalasi, compared with 409.9m. dalasi in 1986/87. Real annual GDP growth was in excess of 5.0% in 1986/87 and 1987/88, thereby surpassing the ERP target of GDP growth of 3.5%-4.0% by 1989/90.

Development programmes have been concerned mainly with improving and diversifying The Gambia's infrastructure. A five-year project, begun in 1976, emphasized rural development, irrigation, increased production of subsistence crops, including the Jahaly and Patcharr swamp rice project (which produced one-quarter of The Gambia's rice output in 1984), and the expansion of education and health facilities. Projects to increase cotton, livestock and fish production have come into effect, while the implementation of proposals for a joint desalination bridge-barrage over the River Gambia, at Balingho, were approved in January 1985 by the Heads of State of the Gambia River Basin Development Organization (OMVG, see p. 219). The project was to extend irrigated cultivation in The Gambia to 24,000 ha, and it was hoped that the country would eventually become a net exporter of rice. In 1988 The Gambia received a loan of US $6.8m., in support of a further, five-year, rice development project. In the same year the UN World Food Programme granted $8.9m., as part of a three-year food-aid programme.

The Senegambian Confederation, inaugurated in February 1982 (see Recent History), is intended eventually to produce an economic and monetary union between Senegal and The Gambia, and, possibly, the absorption of The Gambia into the West African Monetary Union (see p. 154). It was anticipated that an agreement regarding the establishment of a free-trade zone would be reached by the two countries in 1989. The 1988/89 Confederal budget was set at 3,423m. francs CFA.

Social Welfare

In 1978 The Gambia had 16 hospital establishments, with a total of 699 beds. At the end of 1980 there were 43 government physicians, 23 private practitioners and five dentists. There were four hospitals and a network of 12 health centres, 17 dispensaries and 68 maternity and child welfare clinics throughout the country. Of total expenditure by the central Government in the financial year 1981/82, about 12.7m. dalasi (8.0%) was for health services, and a further 5.75m. dalasi (3.6%) for social security and welfare. A national health development project, to cost US $19.8m. over five years, was announced in 1987.

Education

Primary education, beginning at eight years of age, is free but not compulsory and lasts for six years. On completion of this period, pupils may sit a common entrance examination, leading either to five years of secondary high school or to four years of secondary technical school. High schools offer an academic-based curriculum leading to examinations at the 'Ordinary' level of the General Certificate of Education (GCE), under the auspices of the West African Examinations Council. Two of the high schools provide two-year courses leading to GCE 'Advanced' level. Gambia College, at Brikama, offers post-secondary courses in teacher-training, agriculture and health; other post-secondary education is provided by technical training schools. Non-formal education services are being expanded to offer increased educational opportunities in rural areas, and to provide for primary-school leavers who are unable to continue their studies. University education must be obtained abroad. In 1985 an estimated 68% of children in the relevant age-group (84% of boys; 53% of girls) were enrolled at primary schools. Secondary enrolment in 1985 was equivalent to only 17% of children aged between 14 and 19 (23% of boys; 10% of girls). According to UNESCO estimates, adult illiteracy in 1985 averaged 74.9% (males 64.4%, females 84.9%). In 1977 The Gambia introduced Koranic studies at all stages of education. Expenditure on education by the central Government in 1981/82 was 27.7m. dalasi (17.4% of total spending).

THE GAMBIA

Public Holidays

1989: 2 January (for New Year's Day), 1 February (Senegambia Confederation Day), 18 February (Independence), 24-27 March (Easter), 1 May (Labour Day), 7 May* (Id al-Fitr, end of Ramadan), 14 July* (Id al-Adha, feast of the Sacrifice), 15 August (Assumption), 13 October* (Mouloud, birth of the Prophet), 25 December (Christmas).

1990: 1 January (New Year's Day), 1 February (Senegambia Confederation Day), 18 February (Independence), 13-16 April (Easter), 27 April* (Id al-Fitr, end of Ramadan), 1 May (Labour Day), 4 July* (Id al-Adha, feast of the Sacrifice), 15 August (Assumption), 2 October (Mouloud, birth of the Prophet), 25 December (Christmas).

* These holidays are dependent on the Islamic lunar calendar and may vary by one or two days from the dates given.

Weights and Measures

Imperial weights and measures are used. Importers and traders also use the metric system.

Statistical Survey

Source (unless otherwise stated): Directorate of Information and Broadcasting, 14 Hagan St, Banjul; tel. 27230.

AREA AND POPULATION

Area: 11,295 sq km (4,361 sq miles).

Population: 493,499 (census of 23-30 April 1973); 698,817 (census of 24 April 1983). *Principal ethnic groups* (April 1963 census): Mandinka (40.8%), Fula (13.5%), Wolof (12.9%), Jola (7.0%), Serahuli (6.7%).

Density: 61.9 per sq km (April 1983).

Principal Towns (1983 census): Serrekunda 68,433, Banjul (capital) 44,188, Brikama 19,584, Bakau 19,309, Farafenni 10,168, Sukuta 7,227, Gunjur 7,115.

Births and Deaths (1983 census): Birth rate 49.0 per 1,000; death rate 21.0 per 1,000.

Economically Active Population (persons aged 10 years and over, 1983 census): Agriculture, hunting, forestry and fishing 239,940; Mining and quarrying 66; Manufacturing 8,144; Electricity, gas and water 1,233; Construction 4,373; Trade, restaurants and hotels 16,551; Transport, storage and communication 8,014; Public administration and defence 8,295; Education 4,737; Medical services 2,668; Personal and domestic services 6,553; Activities not adequately defined 25,044; Total 325,618 (males 174,856, females 150,762); Figures exclude persons seeking work for the first time.

AGRICULTURE, ETC.

Principal Crops (FAO estimates, '000 metric tons, 1986): Millet and sorghum 60, Rice (paddy) 45, Maize 31, Cassava (Manioc) 6, Palm kernels 2, Groundnuts (in shell) 100 (unofficial figure) (Source: FAO, *Production Yearbook*).

Livestock (FAO estimates, '000 head, year ending September 1986): Cattle 290, Sheep 191, Goats 200, Pigs 12, Asses 4 (Source: FAO, *Production Yearbook*).

Livestock Products (FAO estimates, '000 metric tons, 1986): Meat 7, Cows' milk 5 (Source: FAO, *Production Yearbook*).

Forestry (FAO estimates, 1986): *Roundwood removals* ('000 cu m): Sawlogs, veneer logs and logs for sleepers 14, Other industrial wood 7, Fuel wood 835; Total 856 (Source: FAO, *Yearbook of Forest Products*).

Fishing ('000 metric tons, live weight, 1986): Inland waters 2.7; Atlantic Ocean 8.0; Total catch 10.7 (Source: FAO, *Yearbook of Fishery Statistics*).

INDUSTRY

Production ('000 metric tons, unless otherwise indicated, 1985): Palm oil 2.5 (FAO estimate), Salted, dried or smoked fish 3.0 (FAO estimate), Electric energy 42 million kWh (Source: mainly UN, *Industrial Statistics Yearbook*).

FINANCE

Currency and Exchange Rates: 100 butut = 1 dalasi (D). *Coins:* 1, 5, 10, 25 and 50 butut; 1 dalasi. *Notes:* 1, 5, 10 and 25 dalasi. *Sterling and Dollar Equivalents* (30 September 1988): £1 sterling = 12.05 dalasi; US $1 = 7.13 dalasi; 1,000 dalasi = £82.99 = $140.33. *Average Exchange Rate* (US $ per dalasi): 0.2593 in 1985; 0.1464 in 1986; 0.1415 in 1987. Note: On 20 January 1986 a 'floating' rate of exchange was introduced.

Budget ('000 dalasi, year ending 30 June): 1985/86 revised estimates: Recurrent revenue 247,250; Recurrent expenditure 182,100; Development expenditure 83,500. 1986/87 budget proposals: Recurrent revenue 296,700; Recurrent expenditure 262,530; Development expenditure 201,200. 1987/88 revised budget proposals: Recurrent revenue 386,709; Recurrent expenditure 379,954.

Second National Development Plan (proposed investment, '000 dalasi, 1981/82-1985/86): Agriculture and natural resources 131,300, Industry 29,200, Public utilities 67,300, Transport and communications 143,900, Tourism, trade and finance 7,300, Education, youth, sports and culture 37,000, Health, labour and social welfare 15,000, Housing 21,000, Total (incl. others) 475,000 (Source: *National Development Plan, 1981/82-1985/86*).

International Reserves (US $ million at 31 December 1986): IMF special drawing rights 0.72, Reserve position in IMF 0.06, Foreign exchange 12.78, Total 13.56 (Source: IMF, *International Financial Statistics*).

Money Supply (million dalasi at 31 December 1987): Currency outside banks 95.02; Demand deposits at commercial banks 100.32 (Source: IMF, *International Financial Statistics*).

Cost of Living (Consumer price index for Banjul and Kombo St Mary, year ending 30 June; base: 1974 = 100): 351.9 in 1984/85; 475.1 in 1985/86; 693.6 in 1986/87.

Gross Domestic Product by Economic Activity ('000 dalasi at constant prices, year ending 30 June 1986): Agriculture, etc. 108,400; Industry 35,600; Trade 93,600; Other services 141,500; GDP at factor cost 379,100; Indirect taxes, *less* subsidies 35,000; GDP at market prices 414,100.

Balance of Payments (US $ million, year ending 30 June 1987): Merchandise exports f.o.b. 65.45, Merchandise imports f.o.b. -91.24, *Trade Balance* -25.79; Exports of services 44.49, Imports of services -58.12, *Balance on Goods and Services* -39.42; Private unrequited transfers (net) 16.40, Government unrequited transfers (net) 37.06, *Current Balance* 14.04; Long-term capital (net) 46.51, Short-term capital (net) -, Net errors and omissions -6.50, *Total (net monetary movements)* 54.04; Valuation changes (net) 9.10, Exceptional financing (net) -39.19, *Change in Reserves* 23.96. (Source: IMF, *International Financial Statistics*).

EXTERNAL TRADE

Principal Commodities ('000 dalasi, year ending 30 June 1986): *Imports:* Food and live animals 175,280, Beverages and tobacco 27,881, Inedible crude materials (except fuels) 8,167, Mineral fuels, lubricants, etc. 56,630, Animal and vegetable oils and fats 3,146, Chemicals 34,008, Basic manufactured goods 113,916, Machinery and transport equipment 97,850, Miscellaneous and manufactured articles 27,322, Total (incl. others) 567,631. *Exports* (excl. re-exports): Groundnuts (shelled) 33,570, Groundnut cake 4,142, Groundnut oil 15,132, Fish and fish preparations 2,507, Hides and skins 1,652, Cotton (lint) 3,862, Total (incl. others) 67,257. *Re-exports:* 136,938.

Principal Trading Partners ('000 dalasi, year ending 30 June 1986): *Imports:* Belgium 18,998, People's Republic of China 31,157, France 81,457, Federal Republic of Germany 28,835, Japan 22,096, Malawi 6,439, Netherlands 30,135, Thailand 32,409, United Kingdom 64,294, USA 26,633. *Exports:* Belgium 3,334, France 8,123, Guinea 4,654, Guinea-Bissau 16,959, Mali 8,807, Netherlands 30,263, Nigeria 918, Sweden 1,579, Switzerland 46,706, United Kingdom 13,686.

TRANSPORT

Road Traffic (motor vehicles in use, estimates, 31 December 1985): Passenger cars 5,200; Buses and coaches 100; Goods vehicles 600; Tractors and trailers 200; Motorcycles, scooters and mopeds 2,000 (Source: IRF, *World Road Statistics*).

International Shipping (estimated sea-borne freight traffic, '000 metric tons, 1985): Goods loaded 78; Goods unloaded 167.

Civil Aviation (1984/85): 1,576 aircraft landed.

TOURISM

Tourist Arrivals: 80,469 in 1987/88.

COMMUNICATIONS MEDIA

Radio receivers 110,000 in use in 1986; Daily newspapers 1 in 1984 (average circulation 2,000 copies); Book production 72 titles in 1985 (Source: UNESCO, *Statistical Yearbook*).

EDUCATION

Primary (1984/85): 189 schools, 2,640 teachers, 66,257 pupils (25,083 girls).

Secondary Technical (1984/85): 16 schools, 502 teachers, 10,102 pupils (3,119 girls).

Secondary High (1984/85): 8 schools, 235 teachers, 4,348 pupils (1,180 girls).

Post-secondary (1984/85): 8 schools, 179 teachers, 1,489 pupils.

Directory

The Constitution

The Gambia's present Constitution took effect on 24 April 1970, when the country became a republic. Its major provisions are summarized below:

Executive power is vested in the President, who is Head of State and Commander-in-Chief of the armed forces. The President is elected by direct universal suffrage, following a constitutional amendment in March 1982, and serves a five-year term. The President appoints a Vice-President, who is leader of government business in the House of Representatives, and other Cabinet Ministers from members of the House.

Legislative power is vested in the unicameral House of Representatives, with 50 members: 36 elected by universal adult suffrage, five Chiefs (elected by the Chiefs in Assembly), eight non-voting nominated members and the Attorney-General.

The Government

HEAD OF STATE

President: Alhaji Sir DAWDA KAIRABA JAWARA (took office 24 April 1970; re-elected 1972, 1977, 1982 and 1987).

CABINET
(February 1989)

President and Minister of Defence: Alhaji Sir DAWDA KAIRABA JAWARA.
Vice-President and Minister of Education, Youth, Sports and Culture: BAKARY B. DARBO.
Minister of Justice and Attorney-General: HASSAN B. JALLOW.
Minister of External Affairs: Alhaji OMAR SEY.
Minister of the Interior: Alhaji LAMIN KITTY JABANG.
Minister of Finance and Trade: Alhaji SAIHOU SABALLY.
Minister of Information and Tourism: Dr LAMIN SAHO.
Minister of Health, Labour, Social Welfare and the Environment: LOUISE N'JIE.
Minister of Agriculture: Alhaji OMAR AMADOU JALLOW.
Minister of Economic Planning and Industrial Development: MBEMBA JATTA.
Minister of Local Government and Lands: Alhaji LANDING JALLOW-SONKO.
Minister of Works and Communications: MOMODOU CADI CHAM.
Minister of Water Resources, Forestry and Fisheries: SARJO TOURAY.

MINISTRIES

Office of the President: State House, Banjul; tel. 27208; telex 2204.
Ministry of Agriculture: The Quadrangle, Banjul; tel. 2147.
Ministry of Economic Planning and Industrial Development: Central Bank Bldg, Banjul; tel. 28229; telex 2293.
Ministry of Education, Youth, Sports and Culture: Bedford Place Bldg, Banjul; tel. 28231.
Ministry of External Affairs: The Quadrangle, Banjul; tel. 28291; telex 2254.
Ministry of Finance and Trade: The Quadrangle, Banjul; tel. 28291; telex 2264.
Ministry of Health, Labour, Social Welfare and the Environment: The Quadrangle, Banjul; tel. 27223.
Ministry of Information and Tourism: The Quadrangle, Banjul; tel. 28496; telex 2204.
Ministry of the Interior: 71 Dobson St, Banjul; tel. 28611.
Ministry of Justice: Marina Parade, Banjul; tel. 28181.
Ministry of Local Government and Lands: The Quadrangle, Banjul; tel. 28291.
Ministry of Water Resources, Forestry and Fisheries: 5 Marina Parade, Banjul; tel. 27431; telex 2204.
Ministry of Works and Communications: Half-Die, Banjul; tel. 27449.

President and Legislature

PRESIDENT

Presidential Election, 11 March 1987

	Votes	% of total
Alhaji Sir DAWDA JAWARA (PPP)	123,385	58.71
SHERIF MUSTAPHA DIBBA (NCP)	57,343	27.29
ASSAN MUSA CAMARA (GPP)	29,428	14.00
Total	210,156	100.00

HOUSE OF REPRESENTATIVES

Speaker: Alhaji MOMODOU B. N'JIE.

Election, 11 March 1987

	Votes	% of total	Seats
People's Progressive Party	117,599	56.61	31
National Convention Party	57,340	27.60	5
Gambia People's Party	30,606	14.73	0
PDOIS	2,069	1.00	0
Independent	105	0.05	0
Total	207,719	100.00	36

In addition to the 36 members directly elected, the House has 14 other members: the Attorney-General, five Chiefs and eight nominated (non-voting) members.

Political Organizations

Gambia People's Party (GPP): Banjul; f. 1986 by fmr mems of the PPP; socialist; Leader ASSAN MUSA CAMARA.

National Convention Party (NCP): 4 Fitzgerald St, Banjul; f. 1975; advocates social reform and more equitable distribution of national wealth; 50,000 mems; Leader SHERIF MUSTAPHA DIBBA.

People's Democratic Organisation for Independence and Socialism (PDOIS): Banjul; f. 1986; aims to maintain economic and political independence of The Gambia; Leaders HALIFA SALLAH, SAM SARR, SIDIA JATTA.

People's Progressive Party (PPP): 21 Leman St, Banjul; f. 1959; merged in 1965 with Democratic Congress Alliance, and in 1968

THE GAMBIA — Directory

with Gambia Congress Party; ruling party; favours continued membership of the Commonwealth; Nat. Pres. I. A. A. KELEPHA SAMBA; Sec.-Gen. Alhaji Sir DAWDA KAIRABA JAWARA.

The following organizations were banned in November 1980:
Gambia Socialist Revolutionary Party (GSRP).
Movement for Justice in Africa–The Gambia (MOJA-G): Leader KORO SALLAH.

Diplomatic Representation

EMBASSIES AND HIGH COMMISSIONS IN THE GAMBIA

China, People's Republic: 6A Marina Parade, Banjul; tel. 23835; Chargé d'affaires: AN YONGYU.
Nigeria: Garba Jahumpa Ave, Bakau New Town Rd, Banjul; tel. 95805; High Commissioner: (vacant).
Senegal: 10 Cameron St, Banjul; tel. 27469; High Commissioner: SALIOU CISSÉ.
Sierra Leone: 67 Hagan St, Banjul; tel. 28206; High Commissioner: H. R. S. BULTMAN.
United Kingdom: 48 Atlantic Rd, Fajara, POB 507, Banjul; tel. 95133; telex 2211; High Commissioner: ALEC IBBOTT.
USA: Kairaba Ave, Banjul; tel. 92858; telex 2229; Ambassador: HERBERT E. HOROWITZ.

Judicial System

The judicial system of The Gambia is based on English Common Law and legislative enactments of the Republic's Parliament which include an Islamic Law Recognition Ordinance by which an Islamic Court exercises jurisdiction in certain cases between, or exclusively affecting, Muslims.

The Supreme Court consists of the Chief Justice and puisne judges; has unlimited jurisdiction; appeal lies to the Court of Appeal.
  Chief Justice: EMMANUEL OLAYINKA AYOOLA.

The Gambia Court of Appeal is the Superior Court of Record and consists of a president, justices of appeal and other judges of the Supreme Court ex officio. Final appeal, with certain exceptions, to the Judicial Committee of the Privy Council in the United Kingdom.
  President: (vacant).

The Banjul Magistrates Court, the Kanifing Magistrates Court and the **Divisional Courts** are courts of summary jurisdiction presided over by a magistrate or in his absence by two or more lay justices of the peace. In 1974 a system of travelling magistrates was introduced to help promote more effective administration of justice in the provinces. They have limited civil and criminal jurisdiction, and appeal lies from these courts to the Supreme Court.

Islamic Courts have jurisdiction in matters between, or exclusively affecting, Muslim Gambians and relating to civil status, marriage, succession, donations, testaments and guardianship. The Courts administer Islamic Law. A cadi, or a cadi two assessors, preside over and constitute an Islamic Court. Assessors of the Islamic Courts are Justices of the Peace of Islamic faith.

District Tribunals are appeal courts which deal with cases touching on customs and traditions. Each court consists of three district tribunal members, one of whom is selected as president, and other court members from the area over which it has jurisdiction.

Religion

About 85% of the people are Muslims. The remainder are mainly Christians, and there are a few animists, mostly of the Jola and Karoninka tribes.

ISLAM
Imam of Banjul: Alhaji ABDOULIE JOBE, 39 Lancaster St, Banjul.

CHRISTIANITY
The Gambia Christian Council: POB 27, Banjul; f. 1966; seven mems (churches and other Christian bodies); Pres. Rt Rev. MICHAEL J. CLEARY (Roman Catholic Bishop of Banjul); Sec.-Gen. J. TUNDÉ TAYLOR-THOMAS.

The Anglican Communion
The diocese of The Gambia, which includes Senegal and Cape Verde, forms part of the Church of the Province of West Africa. There are about 1,320 adherents in The Gambia.
Bishop of The Gambia: (vacant), Bishop's Court, POB 51, Banjul; tel. 27405.

The Roman Catholic Church
The Gambia comprises a single diocese, directly responsible to the Holy See. At 31 December 1986 there were an estimated 14,300 adherents in the country. The Bishop of Banjul is a member of the Inter-territorial Catholic Bishops' Conference of The Gambia, Liberia and Sierra Leone (based in Freetown, Sierra Leone).
Bishop of Banjul: Rt Rev. MICHAEL J. CLEARY, Bishop's House, POB 165, Banjul; tel. 27439; telex 2201.

Other Christian Churches
Methodist Church: POB 288, Banjul; tel. 27425; Chair. and Gen. Supt Rev. ERNEST B. STAFFORD; Sec. Rev. K. JOHN A. STEDMAN.

The Press

The Gambia News: 14 Hagan St, Banjul; f. 1943 as Gambia News Bulletin, name changed 1988; weekly; govt newspaper; Editor C. A. JALLOW; circ. 2,500.
The Gambia Onward: 48 Grant St, Banjul; Editor RUDOLPH ALLEN.
The Gambia Outlook: 29 Grant St, Banjul; Editor M. B. JONES.
The Gambian: 60 Lancaster St, Banjul; Editor NGAING THOMAS.
The Gambian Times: 21 Leman St, POB 698, Banjul; tel. 445; f. 1981; fortnightly; publ. by the People's Progressive Party; Editor JAY SAIDY.
The Nation: People's Press, 3 Boxbar Rd, POB 334, Banjul; fortnightly; Editor W. DIXON-COLLEY.
The Post: Lancaster St, Banjul; Editor ANNA THOMAS.
The Toiler: 31 Leman St, POB 698, Banjul; Editor PA MODOU FALL.
The Torch: 59 Gloucester St, Banjul; f. 1984; Editor SANA MANNEH.
The Worker: 6 Albion Place, POB 508, Banjul; publ. by the Gambia Labour Congress; Editor PIER SOCK.

NEWS AGENCIES
Gambia News Agency (GAMNA): Information Office, 14 Hagan St, Banjul; tel. 28403; telex 2308.

Foreign Bureau
Agence France-Presse (AFP): 6 Allen St, POB 279/280, Banjul; tel. 28133; Correspondent DEYDA HYDARA.

Associated Press (USA) is also represented in The Gambia.

Publishers

Government Printer: MacCarthy Sq., Banjul; tel. 27399; telex 2204.
Inter Africa Press Inc: Banjul; Pres. PETER ENAHORO.

Radio and Television

There were an estimated 110,000 radio receivers in use in 1986. There is no national television service, but transmissions can be received from Senegal.

Radio Gambia: Mile 7, Banjul; tel. 95101; telex 2204; f. 1962; non-commercial govt service of information, education and entertainment; one transmitting station of two 10-kW transmitters broadcasting about 15 hours daily in English, French, Mandinka, Wolof, Fula, Jola, Serer and Serahuli; Dir MARCEL THOMASI.
Radio Syd: POB 279/280, Banjul; tel. 26490; commercial station broadcasting 20 hours a day, mainly music; programmes in English, French, Wolof, Mandinka, Fula, Jola and Serahuli; tourist information in Swedish; Dir CONSTANCE W. ENHÖRNING.

Finance

(cap. = capital; res = reserves; dep. = deposits; br. = branch; m. = million; amounts in dalasi unless otherwise stated)

BANKING

Central Bank
Central Bank of The Gambia: 1-2 Buckle St, Banjul; tel. 28103; telex 2218; f. 1971; bank of issue; cap. and res 8.5m.; dep. 161m. (June 1983); Gov. MAMOUR IAGNE; Gen. Man. EDWARD FILLINGHAM.

Other Banks
Agricultural Development Bank: 10 Cameron St, Banjul; tel. 8721; telex 2273; cap. 3m. (Dec. 1983); Man. Dir SIDIN SAGUIA.

The Gambia Commercial and Development Bank: 3-4 Buckle St, POB 666, Banjul; tel. 28651; telex 2221; f. 1972; 52% state-owned; cap. and res 3.8m., dep. 136m. (1981); Chair. M. M. DIBBA; Man. Dir BENJAMIN CARR; 3 brs.

Standard Chartered Bank Gambia Ltd: 8 Buckle St, POB 259, Banjul; tel. 28681; telex 2210; f. 1978 to acquire Gambian brs of Standard Bank of West Africa Ltd; 15% state-owned; cap. and res 9.4m., dep. 105.3m. (Dec. 1986); Chair. H. LLOYD-EVANS; Man. Dir M. INMAN; 4 brs.

INSURANCE
Capital Insurance Co. Ltd: 7 Buckle St, POB 485, Banjul; tel. 28544; telex 2320; f. 1986; Man. Dir MOMODOU M. TAAL.

The Gambia National Insurance Corporation: 6 Leman St, POB 750, Banjul; tel. 28412; telex 2268; f. 1979; Man. Dir SANKUNG S. FATTY.

Senegambia Insurance Co Ltd: 23 Buckle St, Banjul; tel. 8866; f. 1984; Gen. Man. BABOU CEESAY.

Trade and Industry

CHAMBER OF COMMERCE
Gambia Chamber of Commerce and Industry: 78 Wellington St, POB 33, Banjul; tel. 765; f. 1961; Exec. Sec. P. W. F. N'JIE.

TRADE AND MARKETING ORGANIZATIONS
Gambia Produce Marketing Board: Marina Foreshore, Banjul; tel. 27572; telex 2205; state-controlled; Chair. M. M. JALLOW; Man. Dir (vacant).

National Trading Corporation of The Gambia Ltd (NTC): 1-3 Wellington St, POB 61, Banjul; tel. 28395; telex 2252; f. 1973; Chair. and Man. Dir ALIEU A. M. MBOGE; 15 brs.

EMPLOYERS' ASSOCIATION
Gambia Employers' Association: POB 333, Banjul; f. 1961; Vice-Chair. G. MADI; Sec. P. W. F. N'JIE.

TRADE UNIONS
Gambia Labour Union: 6 Albion Place, POB 508, Banjul; tel. 641; f. 1935; 25,000 mems; Pres. B. B. KEBBEH; Gen. Sec. MOHAMED CEESAY.

Gambia Workers' Confederation: Banjul; Sec.-Gen. PA MODOU FALL.

The Gambia Trades Union Congress: POB 307, Banjul; Sec.-Gen. SAM THORPE.

The Gambia Workers' Union (GWU): 16 Lancaster St, POB 979, Banjul; f. 1958; 3,000 mems (June 1983); Sec.-Gen. AMADOU ARABA BAH.

Transport

RAILWAYS
There are no railways in The Gambia.

ROADS
In 1985 there were 2,358 km of roads in The Gambia. Of this total, 757 km were main roads, and 452 km were secondary roads. Some roads are impassable in the rainy season, as only 21% of the road network is paved. The South Bank Trunk Road links Banjul with the Trans-Gambian Highway, which intersects it at Mansakonko. The South Bank Trunk Road is bituminized as far as Basse, about 386 km from Banjul. The North Bank Trunk Road connects Barra with Georgetown. A major highways maintenance project was announced in 1986 and aimed to rehabilitate 1,250 km of roads.

Gambia Public Transport Corporation: POB 801, Banjul; tel. 93-2501; telex 2243; f. 1979 as Gambian-Libyan Public Transport Corpn; fleet of 50 buses; Chair. Alhaji A. J. SENGHORE; Man. Dir ISMAILLA CEESAY.

SHIPPING
The River Gambia is well suited to navigation. The port of Banjul receives about 300 ships annually, and there are intermittent sailings to and from North Africa, the Mediterranean and the Far East. A weekly river service is maintained between Banjul and Basse, 390 km above Banjul, and a ferry plies between Banjul and Barra. Construction of a barrage across the river at Balingho is planned. Small ocean-going vessels can reach Kuntaur, 190 km above Banjul, throughout the year.

Gambia Ports Authority: Wellington St, POB 617, Banjul; tel. 27266; telex 2235; administers Banjul port, which was substantially expanded in 1974; further improvements were completed in 1984; Man. Dir MOMODOU GAYE.

The **Organisation de mise en valeur du fleuve Gambie** (Gambia River Basin Development Organization), a joint project with Senegal, Guinea and Guinea-Bissau to develop the river and its basin, was founded in 1978 and is based in Dakar, Senegal (see p. 219).

Regular shipping services to Banjul are maintained by **Elder Dempster Agencies.** Other British and Scandinavian lines run occasional services. The Gambia is also served by **Nigerian National** and **Black Star** (Ghana) Lines.

CIVIL AVIATION
There is an international airport at Yundum, 27 km from Banjul.

Gam-Air: Banjul; f. 1987; 60% owned by private Gambian interests, 10% by Barbican Holdings (UK); scheduled weekly flights to Paris; fleet of 1 Boeing 707.

Gambia Air Shuttle: 32-33 Buckle St, Banjul; telex 2303; f. 1987; 60% owned by private Swedish interests, 40% by private Gambian interests; daily flights to Dakar (Senegal), twice-weekly flights to Guinea-Bissau, weekly flights to Bamako (Mali) and Cape Verde; Chair. LENNART HESSELBERG; Gen. Man. CLAES LAAGE; fleet of 1 Vickers Viscount.

Gambia Airways: City Terminal, Wellington St, POB 268, Banjul; tel. 778; f. 1964; handling agency only; operated by Gambian govt, which holds 60% of shares; owns no aircraft; Gen. Man. S. M. JALLOW.

West African Airways (WAA): Banjul; f. 1987; owned by private Gambian interests; operations temporarily suspended May 1988; Gen. Man. WAFIC AJOUZ; fleet of 1 Boeing 707.

Tourism

More than 80,000 tourists visited The Gambia in 1987/88. Tourists come mainly from the United Kingdom and the Federal Republic of Germany. In 1987/88 there were 4,500 hotel beds in resort areas.

Ministry of Information and Tourism: The Quadrangle, Banjul; tel. 28472; telex 2204.

THE GERMAN DEMOCRATIC REPUBLIC

Introductory Survey

Location, Climate, Language, Religion, Flag, Capital

The German Democratic Republic lies in Eastern Europe. It is bounded to the north by the Baltic Sea, to the west, south-west and south by the Federal Republic of Germany, to the south-east by Czechoslovakia and to the east by Poland along the line of the rivers Oder and Neisse. The climate is temperate. The mean annual temperature is 8.5°C (47.3°F), with an average of −0.7°C (30.7°F) for January and 18.1°C (64.6°F) for July. The official language is German, spoken by an overwhelming majority of the population. There is a small Sorbian-speaking minority. Most of the inhabitants profess Christianity: about 50% are Protestants (mainly belonging to the Evangelical Church) and 8% Roman Catholics. The national flag (proportions 5 by 3) has three equal horizontal stripes, of black, red and gold, bearing, in the centre, the state emblem (a hammer and a pair of compasses, encircled by a wreath of grain). The capital is Berlin (the German Democratic Republic having jurisdiction only in the eastern section of the city).

Recent History

At the Potsdam Conference in July 1945 it was decided that the former German territories east of the Oder and Neisse rivers, with the city of Danzig, should become part of Poland, and that the northern part of East Prussia should become a part of the USSR. Germany was divided into British, French, Soviet and US occupation zones, as was Berlin. The whole country was placed under Allied Administration but, after the failure of negotiations to form a unified German administration, the zones that were occupied by the Western allies merged to form the Federal Republic of Germany in September 1949. On 7 October the Soviet zone proclaimed itself the German Democratic Republic (GDR), with Wilhelm Pieck as President and Otto Grotewohl as Prime Minister. These two men were joint chairmen of the Sozialistische Einheitspartei Deutschlands (SED, Socialist Unity Party of Germany), which had been formed in April 1946 by the merger of the Communist Party and the Social Democratic Party in the Soviet zone. The USSR granted complete sovereignty to the GDR on 27 March 1954.

In the immediate post-war period, the USSR compensated for a small part of its wartime losses with equipment, money and livestock from the Soviet zone. More than 200 industrial concerns became Soviet joint-stock companies and were returned, after reconstruction, to the GDR in 1953. In comparison with the reparations paid by the GDR, the Federal Republic escaped relatively lightly. Soviet policy also involved the creation of a Communist economic and political system. As early as 1945 the large agricultural estates were broken up and nationalized. In July 1946 all large-scale industrial concerns became state-owned. The policy of nationalization was continued by the SED regime as the USSR gradually transferred control. The increasing 'Sovietization' of administrative and economic affairs, coupled with severe food shortages, led to uprisings and strikes in June 1953. These were forcibly suppressed by Soviet troops. In 1960 it was announced that 50% of those farms which remained outside state control were to be nationalized. This measure led to a sudden rush of refugees to West Berlin, which, in turn, was the main reason for the construction by GDR 'shock troops' of a wall between East and West Berlin in August 1961.

The first elections, which were local ones, took place in September 1946, when the SED gained 57.1% of the vote, the Christian Democrat and Liberal Democrat parties together 39.9% and others 3.0%. The composition of the National Front, an umbrella organization formed in January 1950 for the various political parties and mass organizations, effectively gave the SED and its partners an overall majority. The SED has been the dominant political force since that time.

Walter Ulbricht took office as Secretary-General (later restyled First Secretary) of the SED in 1950, and was Chairman of the Council of State (Head of State) from September 1960 until his death in August 1973. He had been replaced by Erich Honecker as First Secretary of the SED in May 1971.

The ninth congress of the SED, held in May 1976, approved a revised party statute, whereby the leader was restyled General (rather than First) Secretary. In October 1976 Honecker was also named Chairman of the Council of State, replacing Willi Stoph, who was reappointed Chairman of the Council of Ministers, the post that he had held from 1964 to 1973.

The 11th SED congress took place in April 1986. It was reported that 63,000 party members had been expelled in the five years preceding the congress. A new Central Committee and Politburo (differing little from their predecessors) were elected, and Honecker was unanimously re-elected General Secretary of the party. The congress endorsed a mandate to continue existing policies, approved the draft of a new five-year economic plan, and reaffirmed the GDR's allegiance to the USSR, whose leader, Mikhail Gorbachev, attended the congress. Elections to the Volkskammer (People's Chamber) were held in June, when the National Front candidates won 99.94% of the vote. The United Kingdom, France, the USA and the Federal Republic of Germany protested at the direct election of 66 deputies to represent East Berlin, which violated the 1971 Quadripartite Agreement on the status of Berlin. Honecker was formally reaffirmed as Head of State on 16 June. In December 1988 it was announced that the 12th SED congress would be brought forward from 1991 to May 1990.

During 1988 the GDR leadership continued to resist the Soviet concepts of *perestroika* and *glasnost* (even banning the distribution of five Soviet films and one Soviet magazine), and there was no visible relaxation in the Government's harsh policy towards dissidents. In January 1988 about 100 supporters of civil rights (many seeking to leave the GDR) were arrested while attempting to participate in an official rally. At the end of the month, several thousand citizens attended services in Protestant churches throughout the country in protest at the arrests. Shortly afterwards, all the dissidents were released, and many were expelled to the West. This incident illustrated the growing influence of the Evangelical Church as an expression of popular dissent. In December, however, the Volkskammer approved legislation granting GDR citizens the right, for the first time, to appeal against arbitrary decisions by administrative bodies. Another law, giving East Germans greater freedom to travel to the West, was also expected to be enacted.

In 1970, with the adoption by the Government of the Federal Republic of a new policy towards Eastern Europe (Ostpolitik), talks were held for the first time since the division of Germany between representatives of the two German states. Further such talks, following a Quadripartite Agreement on West Berlin in September 1971, clarified the details of access rights to West Berlin and also allowed West Berliners to visit the GDR. The two states signed a Basic Treaty in December 1972, agreeing to develop normal good-neighbourly relations with each other, on the basis of equality of rights, and to be guided by the United Nations Charter. In March 1974 a further agreement was signed in Bonn, implementing Article 8 of the Basic Treaty, to set up Permanent Representative Missions in Bonn and East Berlin. As a result, many Western countries were able to establish diplomatic relations with the GDR, and the GDR and the Federal Republic joined the UN in September 1973.

In October 1980 relations with the Federal Republic deteriorated when the GDR Government raised the minimum exchange requirement for foreign visitors and renewed its old demands for recognition as an independent state. In December 1981, however, the first official meeting between the two countries' leaders for 11 years took place, when Chancellor Helmut Schmidt of the Federal Republic travelled to the GDR for talks with Honecker. In April 1983 Honecker cancelled a proposed visit to Bonn, following the death of three West Germans at a border checkpoint. The situation was further threatened by the deployment, in late 1983, of US nuclear missiles in the Federal Republic, and by the subsequent siting of additional Soviet missiles in the GDR. Nevertheless, inter-German relations improved steadily under the new Federal

THE GERMAN DEMOCRATIC REPUBLIC

Introductory Survey

German Chancellor, Dr Helmut Kohl, and in 1983–84 there was a series of meetings between East and West German politicians.

The inter-German *rapprochement* suffered a serious set-back in September 1984, however, when Honecker again abruptly cancelled a scheduled visit to the Federal Republic, apparently under pressure from the USSR. During 1984–85 relations between the two German governments were strained by the issue of the numerous East German refugees who sought asylum in the Federal German permanent mission in East Berlin and in Federal German embassies in Eastern Europe. However, contacts between the two states gradually resumed during 1985; Honecker and Kohl met in Moscow in March, following the funeral of the Soviet President, Konstantin Chernenko, and there were hopes that Honecker's long-awaited visit to the Federal Republic might be rearranged. It did not take place during 1986, but the President of the Volkskammer, Horst Sindermann, did visit Bonn in February. He was the most senior GDR politician to visit the Federal Republic for 15 years, and he confirmed that Honecker still intended to visit Chancellor Kohl 'at a time to be agreed by both'. In May 1986 the two German states signed a wide-ranging cultural agreement, but relations were then strained by the GDR's sudden demand that diplomats who were based in East Berlin should show passports to cross to the West (instead of the previously acceptable identity cards). This demand was seen by the Western powers as an attempt to alter the complex status of Berlin (by implying that the Berlin Wall was an international frontier, a view rejected by the West). Eventually the GDR compromised by agreeing to issue a new type of identity card, not a passport, for the purpose. The Federal Republic also protested at the number of refugees, mainly from developing countries, who were allowed to reach the West via East Berlin. By mid-1986 a total of 60,000 requests for asylum were pending. This was again seen as an attempt by the GDR to compel the FRG to impose border controls, thus implicitly recognizing the border as international. In September 1986, however, the GDR agreed to impose a visa requirement before allowing the refugees to cross into West Berlin. The 25th anniversary of the initial construction of the Berlin Wall, in August 1986, was commemorated by demonstrations and protest rallies in the West of the city, while the GDR organized a parade and speeches to commemorate the erection of the 'anti-fascist protective barrier'.

In September 1987, at the invitation of Chancellor Kohl, Honecker paid a five-day visit to the Federal Republic, the first such visit by a state and party leader of the GDR since 1949. The visit was preceded by the declaration of a general amnesty for prisoners and the abolition of the death penalty in the GDR, with effect from October 1987 (the 38th anniversary of the founding of the GDR). During the visit, Honecker held talks with Chancellor Kohl and was received by Federal President Weizsäcker. The Basic Treaty of December 1972, on which relations between the two states were based, was reaffirmed, and agreements were concluded with regard to environmental protection, radiation protection and scientific and technological co-operation. The establishment of a commission to develop economic and commercial relations was also agreed.

In foreign affairs, the GDR has sought to improve relations with other Western European states, and established a dialogue with ministers from several countries during 1985. Honecker's visit to Italy in April marked his first visit to a NATO country. However, the GDR's celebration in May of the 40th anniversary of the capitulation of Nazi Germany proved to be controversial, owing to the strong emphasis that was placed on the Soviet role in the defeat of Nazism. During 1986 relations with the People's Republic of China were upgraded, apparently with the approval of the USSR. In May a Chinese Government delegation visited Berlin, and in October Honecker visited China (as well as Mongolia and the Democratic People's Republic of Korea), when it was announced that links between the Chinese Communist Party and the SED were to be restored. In 1987 Honecker became the first GDR leader to visit the Netherlands and Belgium, and, in January 1988, the first to pay an official visit to France. In mid-1988 the GDR, together with five other CMEA countries, requested that diplomatic relations with the EEC be initiated, and that an agreement on commercial co-operation be negotiated. This was to be independent of the GDR's existing special trade agreement with the Federal Republic of Germany, and was regarded as a move by the GDR towards achieving an improvement in commercial (and also political) relations with EEC countries.

The GDR became a member of the Council for Mutual Economic Assistance (CMEA, see p. 124) in 1950 and signed the Warsaw Pact (see p. 207) in 1955. A Treaty of Friendship and Mutual Assistance between the GDR and the USSR, concluded in 1964, was renewed for 25 years in 1975. Similar treaties exist between the GDR and other East European countries.

In March 1988 the withdrawal of shorter-range Soviet nuclear missiles from GDR territory was completed, in anticipation of the ratification of the Intermediate-Range Nuclear Forces Treaty, signed by the USA and the USSR in December 1987. In December 1988 the USSR announced that it would also withdraw large numbers of Soviet troops and tanks from the GDR. This was regarded by many GDR citizens as an important step towards greater self-determination for their country. In January 1989 Honecker announced reductions in GDR troop numbers and in defence expenditure.

Government

Under the 1968 Constitution, the supreme organ of state power is the Volkskammer (People's Chamber), a unicameral body of 500 members, including 66 representatives of East Berlin. Since June 1979, when East Berlin was fully incorporated, all members of the Chamber have been directly elected for five years by universal adult suffrage. The Chamber elects a Staatsrat (Council of State) to be its permanent organ. The Council of State functions collectively but its Chairman deals with all foreign relations as effective Head of State. The executive branch of government is the Ministerrat (Council of Ministers), headed by a Chairman (Minister-President) who is appointed by the Chamber, which also approves his appointed Ministers. The Chairman directs the activities of the Council of Ministers and its Presidium. Political power is held by the Socialist Unity (Communist) Party of Germany, the SED, which dominates the National Front of the German Democratic Republic (including four minor parties and four mass organizations). The SED's highest authority is the Party Congress, which elects the Central Committee to supervise Party work. The Central Committee elects a Political Committee (Politbüro) to direct its policy.

For local government, the country is divided into 14 districts (Bezirke) and the city of East Berlin.

Defence

A National People's Army, comprising land, sea and air forces, was created out of the People's Police in 1956. In June 1988, according to Western estimates, the total strength of the armed forces was 172,000, comprising: army 120,000, navy 15,000, air force 37,000. Military service lasts 18 months in the army and air force, and 36 months in the navy. There are also 47,000 border troops, 12,000 special police units and 15,000 combat groups of the Workers' Militia. Defence expenditure for 1988 was estimated at 21,647m. DDR-Marks. The GDR is a member of the Warsaw Pact, and in June 1988 there were some 380,000 Soviet troops stationed in the country. In January 1989 it was announced that the GDR armed forces were to be reduced by 10,000 members, and that defence expenditure was to be cut by 10% by 1990.

Economic Affairs

The GDR has been a member of the CMEA since 1950, and the economy of the country is closely linked with that of the USSR and other CMEA member-states. In 1987, however, it was indicated that the GDR would not be pursuing the reforms being undertaken elsewhere in Eastern Europe. The GDR's economy is one of the most successful in the Soviet bloc, and ambitious economic targets have been set in a series of Five-Year Plans. The 1976–80 Plan achieved an increase of 25.4% in net material product (NMP); industrial production rose by 32%, and foreign trade by 61%. During the 1981–85 Plan, the country's NMP (at 1980 prices) for the five-year period totalled 1,087,000m. DDR-Marks, an increase of around 33% over the comparable total during the previous Plan. Labour productivity was reported to have increased by 38% during 1981–85. In the agricultural sector, crop production increased by 11%, while livestock production rose by 5.4%. Foreign trade turnover increased by 50%. The 1986–90 Five-Year Plan set further ambitious targets in many sectors. The Plan's aim was to improve living standards through continued high growth, increased efficiency and scientific and technological progress. It was envisaged that NMP would increase by 24%–26%, to total more than 1,300,000m. Marks during the Plan period. Net production in the sectors of the industrial ministries was to be increased by 46%–51%, while the production of manufactured goods was to be increased by 22%–24%. Livestock production was to rise by 10%. Proposed investment during the five years was set at 346,000m. Marks, to be concentrated in the area of micro-electronics, computers, automation technology and bio-technology. Exports to socialist countries were projected to increase by 29% (30% to the USSR), and the Plan envisaged that trade with the West would also expand, and would achieve a significant export surplus.

In 1986 NMP increased by 4.3%, while industrial production went up by 4.3% and labour productivity in the industry sector grew by 8.8%. In 1987 NMP rose by less than 4% to total 261,200m. DDR-Marks at 1985 prices. Output of industrial goods went up by 3.7%, and industrial labour productivity increased by 6.6%. In 1988 NMP increased by 3%, net production in industry went up by 7%, and labour productivity in the industrial combines also rose by 7%. As a result of heavy expenditure on imports of industrial machinery during the 1970s, debts to Western countries amounted to US $12,800m. at the end of 1981. By December 1987, however, the GDR's net debt in convertible currencies had been reduced to US $7,600m. Successful debt management since 1983 was reported to have raised significantly the GDR's creditworthiness with international banks. In September 1987 its credits stood at DM 8,160m. In the 1989 state budget, revenue was envisaged at 301,521.0m. DDR-Marks and expenditure at 301,365.6m. (compared with 291,180.4m. and 291,005.4m., respectively, in 1988).

By 1972 99% of the GDR's industry was state-owned. In 1987 industrial activities employed 40.6% of the labour force and contributed 64.2% of NMP. More than 90% of employees working in state-owned industry are concentrated in large Kombinate, which have a degree of autonomy in production and trade. There is, however, a small private sector, mainly limited to trades and services, which, since 1976, has benefited from a relaxation of trade policy and from increased state support for private initiative. The private sector accounted for only 2% of total industrial output in 1983, but represented 11.7% of total retail turnover. The number of private trade establishments totalled 80,000 in 1987. In terms of production, the GDR is one of the world's leading industrial nations. The machine, chemical and heavy engineering industries are leading exporters (with chemical products accounting for almost 20% of national industrial output), but, in addition to these traditional areas, emphasis is being laid on the development of new high-technology industries. The electronics industry has developed rapidly since the 1970s, and priority is being given to the expansion of industrial automation, in an attempt to modernize the manufacturing sector.

All farmers are members of agricultural production co-operatives. The number employed in agriculture and forestry has remained steady and in 1987 was 10.8% of the working population. The economic importance of agriculture is gradually declining. The agricultural and forestry sectors together provided 11.0% of NMP in 1987. The 1986 harvest of grain (cereals and pulses) reached a record 11.7m. tons, and the 1987 harvest totalled 11.5m. tons. In 1988, however, the grain harvest reached only 10m. tons, 1.4m. tons less than planned. Other important crops are potatoes and sugar beet.

The only major natural resource is lignite (a low-grade form of brown coal), which supplies more than 60% of the GDR's basic energy. Annual production is being expanded from 258m. metric tons in 1980 to a long-term target of 315m. tons per year by the year 2000, but in recent years the mining of lignite has become increasingly expensive, owing to less favourable geological conditions. Output of lignite in 1986, at about 311m. tons, fell short of the production target of a record 314m. tons. In 1987 total production of raw brown coal fell by 0.7%. Output of lignite in 1988 was targeted at 317.2m. tons. The GDR relies heavily on coal from Poland and on petroleum from the USSR, which is supplied by pipeline, and which meets about 90% of the country's oil requirements; a five-year trade agreement, signed in 1985, provided for the delivery of 17.1m. metric tons of Soviet oil per year, compared with 19.2m. tons in 1981. The GDR has also had to import petroleum from the Federal Republic of Germany and the Middle East in order to meet its needs. The GDR produces most of its natural gas requirements (13,000m. cu m in 1987), although the USSR agreed to increase supplies of natural gas from 1986, and in 1987 delivered 7,000m. cu m. There are two nuclear power plants in operation, and the GDR is continuing to develop the use of nuclear energy, which generated 9.5% of the country's electricity in 1986; although nuclear power has decreased as a proportion of total generation, it was announced that after 1988 the GDR's rising demand for electricity was to be met only through the development of nuclear power.

The growth of foreign trade turnover was around 14% annually in 1971–76, but declined in subsequent years. In 1986 turnover expanded by only 1% compared with the previous year, and in 1987, when it totalled less than 177,000m. DDR Valuta-Marks, turnover declined by 3%. Nevertheless, in 1987 the GDR achieved a surplus of 3,300m. DDR Valuta-Marks on total trade. Foreign trade turnover was targeted to increase by 2.6% in 1988, but remained at 177,000m. DDR Valuta-Marks, with the export surplus again exceeding 3,000m. DDR Valuta-Marks. In dollar terms, however, trade turnover increased from US $55,142m. in 1986 to $58,657m. in 1987. About 69% of GDR trade in 1987 was with the USSR and other socialist countries. Trade with the USSR accounted for 39% of the total in 1985, and remained at the same level in 1987. Between 1976 and 1983 the GDR had an accumulated trade deficit of about $4,500m. with the USSR. This figure was largely attributable to the increases in the price of petroleum and other raw materials imported from the USSR. In an attempt to counteract this, the GDR agreed to supply goods and technical expertise in return for Soviet supplies of petroleum and natural gas. In 1984 the GDR became the first CMEA country to achieve a surplus in trade with the USSR, thus enabling it to begin reducing its debt. In 1987 the value of trade between the GDR and other CMEA countries declined, owing to lower prices for Soviet petroleum imports. At the same time, the GDR's terms of trade with Western countries worsened, as a result of the fall in the value of the dollar. Imports from the West were reduced to counterbalance the loss of exports, both of which fell by 10%. The Federal Republic of Germany remains the most important trading partner outside the Eastern bloc, accounting for 7.1% of total trade in 1987. In 1984 the GDR achieved a small surplus on its trade with the Federal Republic, but in 1985 and 1986 the Federal Republic achieved surpluses of DM 430m. and DM 500m. respectively. In 1986 intra-German trade fell by 9%, to DM 15,200m. largely owing to the effects of the fall in world petroleum prices. In the following year the turnover fell by 5%, to DM 14,500m., as the GDR reduced its purchases from the Federal Republic. In 1986 the value of the GDR's imports from the Federal Republic fell by 9%, to DM 7,840m., while the value of its exports to the Federal Republic fell by 10%, to DM 7,340m. In 1987, the value of the GDR's imports from the Federal Republic amounted to DM 7,370m., a fall of 6% from the previous year. At the same time, the value of the GDR's exports to the Federal Republic fell by around 5%, to DM 7,120m. In the first 10 months of 1988 the value of the GDR's imports from the Federal Republic was DM 5,580m. (6% less than in the corresponding period of 1987), while exports to the Federal Republic were worth DM 5,560m. (a rise of 3%). Intra-German trade operates under a system of 'swing' loans, providing the GDR with interest-free credit from the Federal Republic; in 1985 this facility was increased from DM 600m. to DM 850m. for the period 1986–90 (although, in practice, the facility is not usually drawn upon to the full amount; in March 1988 it stood at DM 357m.). The Federal Republic is seeking a wider role in the GDR economy, and in 1984 the two states reached agreements on economic co-operation, including one allowing West German companies to process East German steel, and a contract providing for the production, under licence, of Volkswagen engines in the GDR. In 1987 an agreement was concluded to connect the electric power systems of the GDR and the Federal Republic. It was envisaged that by late 1991, after the construction of a new power line, the GDR (and West Berlin) would receive about 1,000m. kWh annually from the Federal Republic.

In 1980 the GDR and France signed a five-year trade agreement, designed to establish France as the GDR's second largest Western trading partner; this was extended by an agreement in 1985 to expand trade between France and the GDR five-fold by 1990.

THE GERMAN DEMOCRATIC REPUBLIC   Introductory Survey, Statistical Survey

Social Welfare
State social insurance is compulsory for all employees. It also covers their dependants and special categories such as students. The scheme is administered by the Confederation of Free German Trades Unions (FDGB; see p. 1119) and provides for medical and dental treatment, sickness benefits, maternity grants and pensions for retirement, disability and bereavement. There are communal medical centres (Poliklinik), all physicians and nurses are employed by the state health service and medical treatment is free. In 1987 the GDR had 167,612 hospital beds (equivalent to one for every 99 inhabitants). In 1988 the number of physicians reached 41,500, and there were 13,000 dentists. There is a comprehensive scheme of family allowances and places in crèches are available for 60% of children under three years of age. Government expenditure on health and social care for 1989 was budgeted at 18,353m. DDR-Marks. A five-day working week is now constitutionally enforced, and the paid annual holiday of 18–24 days may be spent at one of the GDR's 1,200 vacation centres. Youth services and sport receive large state subsidies.

Education
Children attend nursery schools from the age of three to six years. In 1975 the replacement of elementary and secondary schools by comprehensive schools was completed. The 10-year course, beginning at six years of age, is free and officially compulsory. In 1984 the total enrolment at comprehensive schools was equivalent to 98% of all children in the relevant age-group. After attendance at a comprehensive school, a pupil may apply to stay for a further two years to take the advanced level examination (Abitur), which is necessary for admission to higher education. Enrolment in this two-year course in 1984 was equivalent to 87% of children in the appropriate age-group. Those leaving school after 10 years may serve either a two- or a three-year apprenticeship, thus qualifying for enrolment respectively at a technical school or at a university or college. Courses at technical schools are generally of three years' duration and lead to professional qualifications. Courses at institutions of university status (these include colleges of technology, engineering and agriculture, teacher training colleges and art schools as well as seven actual universities) last for either four or five years, the first two years being dedicated to basic and general study, and the remainder to specialization. Day-release, correspondence and evening courses allow people to obtain a degree without interrupting their career. Government expenditure on public education for 1989 was budgeted at 11,241m. DDR-Marks.

Public Holidays
1989: 2 January (for New Year's Day), 24 March (Good Friday), 1 May (May Day), 15 May (Whit Monday), 7 October (National Day), 25–26 December (Christmas), 31 December (half-day, New Year's Eve).

1990: 1 January (New Year's Day), 13 April (Good Friday), 1 May (May Day), 4 June (Whit Monday), 7 October (National Day), 25–26 December (Christmas), 31 December (half-day, New Year's Eve).

Weights and Measures
The metric system is in force.

Statistical Survey

Source (unless otherwise stated): Panorama DDR, Auslandspresseagentur GmbH, 1054 Berlin, Wilhelm-Pieck-Str. 49; tel. 230; telex 114872; and *Statistisches Jahrbuch 1987 der DDR*.

Area and Population

AREA, POPULATION AND DENSITY

Area (sq km)	108,333*
Population (census results)	
1 January 1971	17,068,318
31 December 1981	
Males	7,849,112
Females	8,856,523
Total	16,705,635
Population (official estimates at mid-year)	
1985	16,644,308
1986	16,624,375
1987	16,641,298
Density (per sq km) at mid-1987	153.6

* 41,828 sq miles.

DISTRICTS (each district is named after its capital)

	Area (sq km)	Population at mid-1987 ('000)			Density (per sq km)
		Male	Female	Total	
Berlin (city)	403	588.7	658.2	1,246.9	3,094
Cottbus	8,262	425.9	457.8	883.7	107
Dresden	6,738	830.4	935.7	1,766.0	262
Erfurt	7,349	589.6	647.2	1,236.9	168
Frankfurt (a.d. Oder)	7,186	344.8	366.6	711.4	99
Gera	4,004	351.1	388.7	739.8	185
Halle (a.d. Saale)	8,771	845.3	935.6	1,780.9	203
Karl-Marx-Stadt	6,009	869.8	992.5	1,862.3	310
Leipzig	4,966	640.4	727.9	1,368.3	276
Magdeburg	11,526	594.4	654.6	1,248.9	108
Neubrandenburg	10,948	302.1	318.2	620.3	57
Potsdam	12,568	538.7	583.0	1,121.7	89
Rostock	7,075	443.5	468.1	911.7	129
Schwerin	8,672	285.7	307.5	593.2	68
Suhl	3,856	262.5	286.7	549.2	142
Total	108,333	7,912.9	8,728.4	16,641.3	154

PRINCIPAL TOWNS (estimated population at mid-1987)

East Berlin (capital)	1,246,872		Erfurt	217,961
Leipzig	549,229		Potsdam	141,662
Dresden	519,524		Gera	132,939
Karl-Marx-Stadt (Chemnitz)	313,347		Schwerin	128,821
			Cottbus	127,477
Magdeburg	289,627		Zwickau	120,738
Rostock	250,727		Jena	107,678
Halle an der Saale	235,730		Dessau	103,644

THE GERMAN DEMOCRATIC REPUBLIC

Statistical Survey

BIRTHS, MARRIAGES AND DEATHS

	Registered live births		Registered marriages		Registered deaths	
	Number	Rate (per 1,000)	Number	Rate (per 1,000)	Number	Rate (per 1,000)
1980	245,132	14.6	134,195	8.0	238,254	14.2
1981	237,543	14.2	128,174	7.7	232,244	13.9
1982	240,102	14.4	124,890	7.5	227,975	13.7
1983	233,756	14.0	125,429	7.5	222,695	13.3
1984	228,135	13.7	133,900	8.0	221,181	13.3
1985	227,648	13.7	131,514	7.9	225,353	13.5
1986	222,269	13.4	137,208	8.3	223,536	13.4
1987*	225,959	13.6	142,185	8.5	213,870	12.9

* Provisional figures.

EMPLOYMENT ('000 persons at 30 September each year)*

	1985	1986	1987
Industry†	3,500	3,485.3	3,479.4
Agriculture and forestry	922	926.5	928.5
Construction	578	574.1	568.9
Commerce	869	877.8	881.0
Transport and communications	630	627.4	632.7
Others	2,041	2,056.5	2,080.2
Total	8,539	8,547.6	8,570.7
Males	4,330	4,347.3	4,370.3
Females	4,209	4,200.4	4,200.3

* Excluding apprentices, numbering (at 30 September each year): 398,000 in 1985; 390,600 in 1986; 383,700 in 1987.
† Including fishing and handicraft.

Agriculture

PRINCIPAL CROPS ('000 metric tons)

	1985	1986	1987
Wheat	3,936	4,195	4,040
Rye	2,505	2,406	2,283
Barley	4,366	4,293	4,198
Oats	746	666	637
Sugar beet	7,397	7,747	7,683
Potatoes	12,350	9,997	12,228
Pulses	100	101	90
Rapeseed	380	446	366
Carrots*	359	358	377
Onions (dry)†	125	106	117
Tomatoes†	57	63	n.a.
Cabbages*	473	428	443
Cauliflowers*	150	137	148
Green beans*	33	29	35
Green peas*	21	20	21
Cucumbers and gherkins†	74	69	n.a.
Apples†	797	722	n.a.
Pears†	119	100	n.a.
Plums†	103	41	n.a.
Currants†	27	28	n.a.
Strawberries†	37	30	n.a.

* Production from socialist enterprises only.
† Source: FAO, *Production Yearbook* and *Quarterly Bulletin of Statistics*.

LIVESTOCK ('000 head recorded at December)

	1985	1986	1987
Cattle	5,827	5,804	5,721
Pigs	12,946	12,840	12,503
Sheep	2,587	2,647	2,656
Goats	22	21	n.a.
Horses	105	105	n.a.
Poultry	50,680	50,216	50,719
Beehives	492	514	n.a.

LIVESTOCK PRODUCTS ('000 metric tons)

	1984	1985	1986
Beef and veal	369	380	409*
Mutton and lamb	16	17	16
Pig meat	1,273*	1,332*	1,356*
Poultry meat	157	162	156
Other meat	21	23	24
Edible offals	108	110	111
Cows' milk	8,729	9,044	9,358
Goats' milk†	16	16	17
Butter	309	316	322
Cheese	240	249	268
Condensed and evaporated milk†	130	130	132
Dried milk	165	173	176
Hen eggs	341.0	330.2	332.4
Honey	6.0	6.3	8.8
Wool (clean)	7.5	7.4	7.8
Cattle hides and calf skins†	50.1	50.3	50.7
Sheep skins†	1.8	1.7	1.5

* Unofficial figure. † FAO estimate.
Source: mainly FAO, *Production Yearbook* and *Quarterly Bulletin of Statistics*.

1987 ('000 metric tons): Butter 310; Hen eggs 335.1; Honey 6.5; Wool (clean) 8.2.

Forestry

ROUNDWOOD REMOVALS
('000 cubic metres, excluding private consumption)

	1983	1984	1985
Industrial wood	9,764	9,910	10,306
Fuel wood	669	656	562
Total	10,433	10,566	10,868

1986: Output as in 1985 (FAO estimates).
Source: FAO, *Yearbook of Forest Products*.

SAWNWOOD PRODUCTION ('000 cubic metres)

	1982	1983	1984
Coniferous (softwood)	1,879	1,904	1,903
Broadleaved (hardwood)	447	464	497
Total	2,326	2,368	2,400

1985-86: Annual production as in 1984 (FAO estimates).
Source: FAO, *Yearbook of Forest Products*.

THE GERMAN DEMOCRATIC REPUBLIC   Statistical Survey

Fishing

('000 metric tons, live weight)

	1984	1985	1986
Common carp	12.9	13.6	13.1
Atlantic cod	10.6	7.7	4.7
Atlantic redfishes	6.6	9.5	10.6
Jack and horse mackerels	74.1	42.9	62.5
Atlantic herring	50.1	51.6	53.1
Sardinellas	11.1	7.5	1.8
Atlantic mackerel	5.5	11.0	18.9
Other fishes	45.6	43.9	39.1
Total fish	216.5	187.7	203.9
Crustaceans	0.7	0.9	1.0
Argentine shortfin squid	8.4	11.8	3.9
Other molluscs	0.5	0.1	0.2
Total catch	226.0	200.5	208.9
Inland waters	20.9	22.3	19.7
Atlantic Ocean	204.5	177.3	188.3
Indian Ocean	0.7	0.9	1.0

Source: FAO, *Yearbook of Fishery Statistics*.

Mining

('000 metric tons, unless otherwise indicated)

	1983	1984	1985
Brown coal (incl. lignite)[1]	277,968	296,341	312,156
Iron ore	9	8	9*
Copper ore (metric tons)[2,3]	12,000	12,000	12,000
Tin ore (metric tons)[2,4]	2,000	2,500	2,800
Nickel ore (metric tons)[2,3]	2,200	2,000	2,000
Salt (unrefined)	5,339	5,041	5,104
Potash salts (crude)[5]	3,431	3,465	3,465
Sulphur			
(a)[6,7]	8	n.a.	n.a.
(b)[6]	97	108	109
Silver (metric tons)[7]	43	40	44
Natural gas (million cu m.)[8]	7,650	8,000	7,650
Crude petroleum	53	42	40

* Provisional figure.
[1] Gross weight.
[2] Figures refer to the metal content of ores.
[3] Estimated production (Source: Metallgesellschaft Aktiengesellschaft, Frankfurt am Main).
[4] Estimated production (Source: *World Metal Statistics*).
[5] Figures refer to the K$_2$O content or equivalent of potash salts mined.
[6] Figures refer to (a) the sulphur content of iron and copper pyrites, including pyrite concentrates obtained from copper, lead and zinc ores; and (b) sulphur recovered as by-products in the purification of coal-gas, petroleum refineries, gas plants and from copper, lead and zinc sulphide ores.
[7] Estimated production (Source: Bureau of Mines, US Department of the Interior).
[8] Net calorific value 3,120 kilocalories per cubic metre.

Source: mainly UN, *Industrial Statistics Yearbook*.

1986 ('000 metric tons): Brown coal 311,260; Potash salts 3,485.
1987 ('000 metric tons): Brown coal 308,980; Potash salts 3,510.

Industry

SELECTED PRODUCTS
('000 metric tons, unless otherwise indicated)

	1984	1985	1986
Flour[1]	1,402	1,399	1,383
Refined sugar	870	911	935
Margarine	179.7	180.3	175
Spirits ('000 hectolitres)	2,521	2,601	2,675
Beer ('000 hectolitres)	24,500	24,288	24,316
Non-alcoholic beverages ('000 hectolitres)	14,121	14,409	15,584
Cigarettes (million)	28,018	26,909	27,364
Cigars and cigarillos (million)	521	477	441
Cotton yarn—pure and mixed (metric tons)[2]	138,200	138,000	n.a.
Woven cotton fabrics ('000 sq metres)	294,000	298,000	308,000
Wool yarn—pure and mixed (metric tons)[2]	75,500	75,000	n.a.
Woven woollen fabrics ('000 sq metres)	40,700	41,300	n.a.
Non-cellulosic discontinuous fibres	153.8	157.7	152
Rayon and acetate fabrics ('000 sq metres)	47,400	48,700	n.a.
Leather footwear ('000 pairs)	43,364	43,803	44,300
Other footwear ('000 pairs)	39,061	39,748	41,200
Cellulose wood pulp	511	520	522
Newsprint and other paper	871	860	891
Paperboard and products	422	435	429
Synthetic rubber (metric tons)	152,000	140,000	118,000
Rubber tyres ('000)[3]	7,784	8,362	8,582
Ethyl alcohol ('000 hectolitres)	490	494	n.a.
Sulphuric acid	885	883	883
Caustic soda (metric tons)	694,000	667,000	638,000
Soda ash (metric tons)	890,000	884,000	885,000
Ammonia (metric tons)	1,467,000	1,471,000	1,455,000
Calcium carbide	1,177	1,135	1,080
Nitrogenous fertilizers (metric tons)[4]	959,100	1,078,200	1,252,100
Phosphate fertilizers (metric tons)[4]	308,400	299,200	309,200
Plastics and synthetic resins	1,057	1,048	1,045
Motor spirit (petrol)[5]	4,140	4,302	4,329
Kerosene and distillate fuel oils[5]	6,132	6,350	6,324
Residual fuel oils[5]	9,000	9,000	n.a.
Lubricating oils	462	478	n.a.
Petroleum bitumen (asphalt)	670	681	n.a.
Liquefied petroleum gas	239	252	n.a.
Coke-oven coke (incl. gas coke)	1,179	1,257	n.a.
Brown coal coke	5,790	5,682	5,601
Cement	11,555	11,608	11,988
Pig-iron and ferro-alloys	2,357	2,578	2,738
Crude steel	7,573	7,853	7,967
Radio receivers (number)	1,110,000	1,162,000	1,168,000
Television receivers (number)	639,000	668,000	712,000
Vacuum cleaners (number)	1,248,000	1,267,000	1,311,000
Domestic refrigerators (number)	895,000	973,000	1,018,000
Domestic washing machines (number)	525,000	503,000	495,000

THE GERMAN DEMOCRATIC REPUBLIC

—continued	1984	1985	1986
Merchant ships launched ('000 grt)	362	406	334
Passenger motor cars (number)	202,000	210,000	218,000
Lorries (number)	43,000	45,000	45,000
Motor cycles—all types (number)	84,000	76,000	73,000
Bicycles ('000)	664	672	643
Sewing machines ('000)	292	310	324
Construction:			
New dwellings completed (number)[6]	121,654	120,728	119,335
Electric energy (million kWh)	110,093	113,834	115,291
Manufactured gas (million cu metres)	7,722	7,780	7,958

[1] Flour from wheat, rye and semolina.
[2] Including thread and (for cotton) tyre-cord yarn.
[3] Tyres for passenger motor cars, commercial motor vehicles and motor cycles.
[4] Production of nitrogenous fertilizers is measured in terms of nitrogen, and that of phosphate fertilizers in terms of phosphoric acid. Output of phosphate fertilizers includes ground rock phosphate.
[5] Including products made from coal.
[6] Dwellings in residential buildings only.

Finance

CURRENCY AND EXCHANGE RATES

Monetary Units
100 Pfennige = 1 Mark der Deutschen Demokratischen Republik (DDR-Mark).

Denominations
Coins: 1, 5, 10, 20 and 50 Pfennige; 1, 2, 5, 10 and 20 DDR-Marks.
Notes: 5, 10, 20, 50 and 100 DDR-Marks.

Sterling and Dollar Equivalents (30 September 1988)
£1 sterling = 3.162 DDR-Marks;
US $1 = 1.870 DDR-Marks;
100 DDR-Marks = £31.62 = $53.48.

BUDGET ESTIMATES (million DDR-Marks)*

Revenue	1987	1988	1989
State economy	191,080.6	n.a.	n.a.
Taxes and dues	19,662.4	20,589	21,830
Health care and social care	8,888.4	9,246	9,966
Social insurance, etc.	18,017.3	18,733	19,246
Total (including others)	276,779.1	291,180.4	301,521.0

Expenditure	1987	1988	1989
State economy	76,677.0	n.a.	n.a.
Housing construction	15,834.5	16,326	16,619
Price support	48,820.4	49,483	51,006
Public education	9,280.6	10,389	11,241
Health care and social care	14,889.4	17,153	18,353
Social insurance, etc.	34,985.6	35,934	37,416
National defence	15,140.9	15,654	16,186
Total (including others)	276,614.1	291,005.4	301,365.6

* Figures represent a consolidation of the state budget plan and funds from the profits of state-owned combines and enterprises.

COST OF LIVING
(Index of Retail Prices and Service Charges; base: 1970 = 100)

	1985	1986	1987
Food (incl. drinks)	99.8	99.8	99.8
Fuel, light and water	100.0	100.0	100.0
Clothing (excl. footwear) and household linen	87.6	87.6	87.6
Rent	98.9	98.9	98.9
All items (incl. others)	99.5	99.5	99.5

NATIONAL ACCOUNTS
Net Material Product (NMP)*
(million DDR-Marks at 1985 prices)

Activities of the Material Sphere	1985	1986	1987
Agriculture and forestry	30,204	29,966	29,966
Industry and productive crafts	159,814	167,789	174,360
Construction	17,843	18,925	19,690
Trade, restaurants and hotels	21,984	22,822	23,594
Transport, post and telecommunications	14,035	14,340	14,300
Others	8,733	9,160	9,500
Sub-total	252,613	263,002	271,410
Statistical discrepancy†	−10,750	−10,782	−10,210
Total	241,863	252,220	261,200

* Defined as the total net value of goods and 'productive' services, including turnover taxes, produced by the economy. This excludes economic activities not contributing directly to material production, such as public administration, defence and personal and professional services.
† Relating to intermediate consumption.

External Trade

COMMODITY GROUPS (% of trade in effective prices)

Imports	1985	1986	1987
Machinery, equipment and means of transport	26.8	29.5	34.1
Fuels, mineral raw materials, metals	42.5	39.8	38.0
Other raw materials and semi-manufactured goods for industrial purposes, raw materials and products of the food industry	16.1	15.6	13.1
Durable consumer goods	6.2	6.5	5.7
Chemical products, fertilizers, synthetic rubber, building materials and other goods	8.4	8.6	9.1

Exports	1985	1986	1987
Machinery, equipment and means of transport	46.6	46.7	48.0
Fuels, mineral raw materials, metals	20.0	15.9	16.7
Other raw materials and semi-manufactured goods for industrial purposes, raw materials and products of the food industry	7.7	7.8	6.8
Durable consumer goods	14.1	16.4	16.0
Chemical products, fertilizers, synthetic rubber, building materials and other goods	11.6	13.2	12.5

THE GERMAN DEMOCRATIC REPUBLIC

PRINCIPAL TRADING PARTNERS
(turnover in million DDR Valuta-Marks, valued f.o.b.)*

	1985	1986	1987
Austria	4,264.8	3,147.6	3,136.1
Belgium/Luxembourg	2,378.4	1,552.5	1,360.3
Bulgaria	5,151.4	5,672.1	5,715.0
Cuba	2,098.5	2,340.0	2,550.8
Czechoslovakia	12,999.0	13,316.3	14,250.3
France	2,735.0	2,786.3	2,947.7
Germany, Federal Republic, and West Berlin	14,993.8	13,083.6	12,522.3
Hungary	8,820.6	9,255.1	9,266.2
Japan	1,573.0	1,202.0	1,489.6
Netherlands	1,866.0	1,619.5	1,926.4
Poland	9,773.4	10,979.5	11,436.1
Romania	4,966.4	5,218.9	5,059.3
Sweden	1,682.6	1,433.4	1,983.4
Switzerland†	3,173.7	3,014.7	3,088.2
USSR	69,940.7	70,626.4	68,477.6
United Kingdom	2,752.9	2,139.2	2,152.7
Yugoslavia	2,474.7	2,526.5	2,673.0
Total (incl. others)‡	180,191.3	181,970.2	176,556.3

* For 1985 the exchange rate was US $1 = 3.70 DDR Valuta-Marks; for 1986 it was $1 = 3.30 DDR Valuta-Marks; and for 1987 it was $1 = 3.01 DDR Valuta-Marks.
† Including Liechtenstein.
‡ Separate figures for imports and exports by countries are not available. The totals (in million DDR Valuta-Marks) were: Imports 86,701 in 1985, 90,465 in 1986, 86,646 in 1987; Exports 93,490 in 1985, 91,505 in 1986, 89,910 in 1987.

Transport

RAILWAYS (traffic)

	1985	1986	1987
Passenger journeys (million)	623	609	603
Passenger-km (million)	22,451	22,402	22,563
Freight ton-km (million)	58,668	58,881	58,823

ROAD TRAFFIC (licensed vehicles)

	1985	1986	1987
Passenger cars	3,306,230	3,462,184	3,600,450
Lorries	360,821	367,449	375,619
Omnibuses	55,698	57,600	59,245

SHIPPING
Inland Waterways (traffic)

	1985	1986	1987
Passenger journeys (million)	7	6	7
Passenger-km (million)	188	180	188
Freight ton-km (million)	2,431	2,477	2,361

Merchant Fleet (at 31 December)

	1985	1986	1987
Number of ships	171	174	170
Displacement (grt)	1,222,410	1,344,795	1,332,181

International Sea-borne Freight Traffic ('000 metric tons)

	1985	1986	1987
Goods loaded and unloaded	25,100	25,510	24,805

CIVIL AVIATION (traffic)

	1985	1986	1987
Kilometres flown ('000)	34,173	34,449	37,166
Passengers carried	1,446,000	1,496,000	1,506,000
Passenger-km ('000)	2,541,000	2,649,000	2,846,000
Freight ton-km ('000)*	71,643	70,693	78,805

* Figures refer to both cargo and mail.

Tourism

FOREIGN TOURIST ARRIVALS*

Country of Origin	1985	1986	1987
Bulgaria	11,113	14,498	13,277
Czechoslovakia	123,413	129,946	122,264
Hungary	13,876	16,021	17,977
Poland	46,673	56,200	68,440
Romania	10,721	5,409	8,332
USSR	115,548	130,424	125,908
Total (incl. others)	1,060,219	1,038,866	1,121,737

* Visits arranged by the State Travel Bureau.

Communications Media

	1980	1981	1982
Radio licences	6,409,200	6,459,100	6,439,500
Television licences	5,730,900	5,811,100	5,847,200
Telephones in use	3,155,733	3,251,950	3,344,263
Book production: titles	6,109	6,180	6,130
Newspapers and magazines:			
Number	523	519	521
Circulation (total, million)	255.2	262.3	n.a.

1983: Radio licences 6,415,000; Television licences 5,970,000.

Education
(1987)

	Institutions	Students
Infant schools	13,334	770,300
General polytechnic schools	5,202	1,947,915
Extended polytechnic schools and special schools	n.a.	n.a.
Vocational schools	957	366,300
Technical schools	237	158,777
Universities (incl. technical)	53	132,602

Directory

The Constitution

The Constitution of the German Democratic Republic was promulgated on 9 April 1968, replacing the original Constitution which came into force when the Republic was founded in 1949. It was amended on 7 October 1974. A summary is given below.

I. FOUNDATIONS OF THE SOCIALIST SOCIAL AND STATE ORDER

Political Foundations

Articles 1-8. The German Democratic Republic is a socialist state of workers and farmers. It is the political organization of the working people in towns and countryside who are jointly implementing socialism under the leadership of the working class and its Marxist-Leninist party. The capital is Berlin; the state flag is black, red, and gold, and bears the state coat of arms. All political power in the Republic is exercised by the working people and all power serves their welfare. The National Front of the German Democratic Republic unites all political parties and mass organizations working for the development of the socialist state. Citizens exercise their political power through democratically elected people's representatives. The Republic pursues a peaceful foreign policy and is linked irrevocably and permanently with the USSR and other socialist states.

Economic Foundations, Science, Education and Culture

Articles 9-18. The national economy is based on the socialist ownership of the means of production and is a socialist planned economy. All foreign economic relations are the monopoly of the state. All large industrial enterprises, mineral resources, banks and means of transport are nationally owned and private ownership of these facilities is not allowed. All installations, machinery and livestock in agricultural co-operatives and profits derived from co-operative use of the soil are co-operative property. The personal property of citizens and the right of inheritance are guaranteed. The Republic promotes culture, the arts and science and assures all citizens a high standard of education.

II. CITIZENS AND ORGANIZATIONS IN SOCIALIST SOCIETY

Basic Rights and Basic Duties of Citizens

Articles 19-40. The Republic respects the dignity and freedom of the individual and guarantees to all citizens the exercise of their rights. The conditions for acquiring and losing citizenship of the German Democratic Republic are stipulated by law. All citizens are equal before the law. Men and women have equal rights and the same legal status. Every citizen who has reached the age of 18 on election day has the right to vote and may be elected to the People's Chamber (Volkskammer) and to local people's representative bodies. Every citizen is obliged to serve in defence of his country. The Republic can grant political asylum to citizens of other states in certain circumstances.

Freedom of speech, the press, radio and television are guaranteed, as is the right to peaceful demonstration and assembly. Personal liberty is inviolable and everyone has the right to move freely within the state territory within the framework of the law. Postal and telecommunication privacy is assured and may be limited only for purposes of state security or criminal prosecution. Every citizen has the right to legal protection by the organs of the state when he is abroad.

The right to work is guaranteed and every citizen is free to select his own job. Everyone has the same right to education and attendance at secondary school is obligatory. All citizens are entitled to leisure time and annual paid holidays, to medical and other social welfare benefits. Social care is provided for the elderly and disabled. Housing is under public control and there is legal protection against eviction. Every citizen has the right of the inviolability of his home. Marriage, motherhood and the family have the special protection of the state and provision is made for large families, fatherless families, etc. Religious freedom is assured. Citizens of the German Democratic Republic of Sorb nationality have the right to cultivate their mother tongue and culture.

Enterprises, Towns and Local Communities in Socialist Society

Articles 41-43. Enterprises, towns, villages and communal associations are entities with responsibilities of their own in which citizens work and shape their social relations. They safeguard the basic rights of citizens and are protected by the constitution. The local representative bodies are elected by the people and are responsible for local affairs. The working people also co-operate in the management of enterprises both directly and with the help of their elected organs.

The Trades Unions and Their Rights

Articles 44-45. The free trades unions are united in the Confederation of Free German Trades Unions. They are independent bodies, are represented at all levels of the social system and play a decisive part in the solution of problems. They conclude agreements with government authorities and enterprise managements on all questions concerning the working and living conditions of the people. They take part in the shaping of the socialist legal system and administer the social insurance system of the workers.

Socialist Production Co-operatives and Their Rights

Article 46. These are voluntary associations of farmers for the purpose of joint production and receive government assistance. They are represented in the state organs and take an active part in the state planning. Production co-operatives on the same lines also exist among fishermen, craftsmen and market gardeners.

III. STRUCTURE AND SYSTEM OF STATE MANAGEMENT

Democratic Centralism

Article 47. The structure and activities of the state organs are determined by the aims and tasks of state power, as stipulated in this Constitution. The sovereignty of the working people, which is implemented on the basis of democratic centralism, is the fundamental principle of the state structure.

The People's Chamber (Volkskammer)

Articles 48-65. The People's Chamber is the supreme organ of state power and guarantees the enforcement of its laws. It is composed of 500 deputies elected by the people in a free, general, equal and secret ballot for a period of five years. It is convened not later than the 30th day after the election. It elects its Presidium to conduct the plenary sessions for the legislative period. The People's Chamber can be dissolved before the expiry of the legislative period only on its own decision.

Committees are formed from among the members of the People's Chamber to discuss bills and to co-operate in submitting them to the voters for popular discussion. They then submit their comments to the plenary session of the People's Chamber. Laws passed are proclaimed in the Law Gazette by the Chairman of the Council of State within one month and come into force on the 14th day after their proclamation.

The People's Chamber decides on the proclamation of war and the holding of referenda.

The Council of State (Staatsrat)

Articles 66-75. The Council of State is the organ of the People's Chamber, operating between sessions of the latter, and fulfils all fundamental tasks resulting from its laws and decisions. It is elected by the People's Chamber at its first session and is responsible to it for its activities. It deals with bills to be submitted to the People's Chamber and with all basic tasks arising from its laws and decisions. It makes fundamental decisions on defence matters and exercises control over the constitutionality and legality of the activities of the Supreme Court and the Prosecutor-General. The Council of State represents the GDR internationally and ratifies and abrogates international treaties. It determines military and diplomatic ranks and other special titles and establishes state honours. It also exercises the right of amnesty and pardon.

The Council of Ministers (Ministerrat)

Articles 76-80. The Council of Ministers, the Government of the GDR, is an organ of the People's Chamber. Acting on its behalf, it directs government policy, economic affairs and foreign policy in accordance with the provisions of the Constitution. It prepares international treaties, draws up bills, directs and co-ordinates the Ministries and other government bodies. It is answerable to the People's Chamber.

Local People's Representative Bodies and Their Organs

Articles 81-85. The elected organs of state power in the districts, towns, regions, municipal boroughs and local communities are responsible for deciding on all local issues on the basis of law. The local people's representative bodies draw up and implement the economic plan and budget for their areas, and have their own

THE GERMAN DEMOCRATIC REPUBLIC

income. Their decisions are binding and must be published. All such bodies elect their own councils and committees.

IV. SOCIALIST LEGALITY AND THE ADMINISTRATION OF JUSTICE

Articles 86–104. The Constitution has the force of law and legal regulations may not contradict it. Details of all laws and binding regulations are published. The citizens' participation in the administration of justice is guaranteed and it is the declared aim of socialist society to combat all violations of the law. Laws on the punishment of war crimes and of crimes against peace and humanity correspond to the generally recognized norms of international law.

The administration of justice in the Republic is exercised by the Supreme Court, the District Courts, the Regional Courts and the social (lay) courts. In military matters jurisdiction is exercised by the Supreme Court, military tribunals and military courts. The Supreme Court is the highest organ of the administration of justice and is responsible to the People's Chamber. All judges are democratically elected by the people's representative bodies or by the citizens themselves and must be men of knowledge and experience who are loyally devoted to the socialist state. The public prosecutors' office safeguards socialist legality and ensures that persons who have commmitted crimes are called to account before the court. The public prosecutors' office is directed by the Prosecutor General and the public prosecutors of the districts and regions are appointed by him and subordinate to him.

An act is punishable only if it contravened penal law at the time of its commission, if the offender has acted in a culpable way and if his guilt is proved beyond doubt. Persons under arrest must be brought before a judge within 24 hours of their arrest and only judges are authorized to judge the admissibility of detention on remand. Nobody may be denied the right to appear before his lawful judge and special courts are inadmissible. Every citizen has the right to be heard in court and the right to be defended by a counsel is guaranteed throughout the whole criminal procedure. Any citizen or organization has the right to submit suggestions or grievances to the authorities and may suffer no disadvantages as a result. Damages inflicted on a citizen or his personal property as a result of unlawful measures by government officials are to be compensated by the authority concerned.

CONCLUDING PROVISIONS

Articles 105–106. The Constitution may be amended only through a law of the People's Chamber of the German Democratic Republic which expressly amends or supplements the text of the Constitution.

The Government
(January 1989)

COUNCIL OF STATE

Chairman: ERICH HONECKER.
Vice-Chairmen: WILLI STOPH, HORST SINDERMANN, Dr MANFRED GERLACH, GERALD GÖTTING, Prof. Dr HEINRICH HOMANN, EGON KRENZ, Dr GÜNTHER MALEUDA, Dr GÜNTER MITTAG.
Members: EBERHARD AURICH, FRITZ DALLMANN, Prof. KURT HAGER, BRUNHILDE HANKE, LEONHARD HELMSCHROTT, FRIEDRICH KIND, EVELINE KLETT, Prof. Dr LOTHAR KOLDITZ, PETER MORETH, MARGARETE MÜLLER, ALOIS PISNIK, BERNHARDT QUANDT, Dr KLAUS SORGENICHT, PAUL STRAUSS, ILSE THIELE, HARRY TISCH, Prof. Dr JOHANNA TÖPFER, ROSEL WALTHER, MONIKA WERNER.
Secretary: HEINZ EICHLER.

COUNCIL OF MINISTERS
Presidium

Chairman (Prime Minister): WILLI STOPH.
First Deputy Chairmen: ALFRED NEUMANN, HORST SÖLLE.
Deputy Chairman and Chairman of the National Arbitration Board: MANFRED FLEGEL.
Deputy Chairman and Minister of Justice: HANS-JOACHIM HEUSINGER.
Deputy Chairman and Permanent Representative to the CMEA: GÜNTHER KLEIBER.
Deputy Chairman and Minister for the Supply of Materials: WOLFGANG RAUCHFUSS.
Deputy Chairman and Minister for Environmental Protection and Water Resources: Dr HANS REICHELT.

Deputy Chairman and Chairman of the State Planning Commission: GERHARD SCHÜRER.
Deputy Chairman and Minister for Posts and Telecommunications: RUDOLPH SCHULZE.
Deputy Chairman and Minister for Science and Technology: Dr HERBERT WEIZ.

Members

Minister of Transport: OTTO ARNDT.
State Secretary for Labour and Wages: WOLFGANG BEYREUTHER.
Minister of Geology: Dr MANFRED BOCHMANN.
Minister of Finance: ERNST HÖFNER.
Minister for Higher and Technical Education: Prof. HANS-JOACHIM BÖHME.
Minister of Trade and Supply: GERHARD BRIKSA.
Minister of Light Industry: WERNER BUSCHMANN.
Minister of the Interior and Chief of People's Police: Col-Gen. FRIEDRICH DICKEL.
Minister of Foreign Affairs: OSKAR FISCHER.
Minister of Machine Tools and Processing Machines: Dr RUDI GEORGI.
Minister of the Glass and Ceramics Industry: Prof. Dr KARL GRÜNHEID.
State Secretaries in the State Planning Commission: HEINZ KLOPFER, WOLFGANG GRESS.
Minister and Head of the Price Office: WALTER HALBRITTER.
Minister of Culture: HANS-JOACHIM HOFFMANN.
Minister of National Defence: Gen. HEINZ KESSLER.
Minister of Education: Dr h.c. MARGOT HONECKER.
Minister of Construction: WOLFGANG JUNKER.
President of the State Bank of the German Democratic Republic: HORST KAMINSKI.
Lord Mayor of the GDR Capital, Berlin: ERHARD KRACK.
Minister of Agriculture, Forestry and Food Economy: BRUNO LIETZ.
Minister of General and Agricultural Machinery and Vehicle Construction: GERHARD TAUTENHAHN.
Minister of Health: KLAUS THIELMANN.
Minister of State Security: Gen. ERICH MIELKE.
Minister of Coal and Power: WOLFGANG MITZINGER.
Minister of Ore Mining, Metallurgy and Potash: Dr-Ing. KURT SINGHUBER.
Minister of Foreign Trade: Dr GERHARD BEIL.
Minister of Electrical Engineering and Electronics: FELIX MEIER.
Minister and Chairman of the Committee of the Workers' and Farmers' Inspectorate: Dr ALBERT STIEF.
Minister of County-Controlled and Food Industries: Dr UDO-DIETER WANGE.
Minister of the Chemical Industry: GÜNTHER WYSCHOFSKY.
Minister of Heavy Engineering and Plant Construction: HANS-JOACHIM LAUCK.
State Secretary for Religious Affairs: KURT LOEFFLER.

MINISTRIES

Council of Ministers: 1020 Berlin, Klosterstr. 47; tel. 223; telex 1152337.
Ministry of Agriculture, Forestry and Food Economy: 1157 Berlin, Köpenicker Allee 39-57; tel. 25007; telex 112584.
Ministry of the Chemical Industry: 1086 Berlin, Leipziger Str. 5-7; tel. 232; telex 1152311.
Ministry of Coal and Power: 102 Berlin, Karl-Liebknecht-Str. 34; tel. 235; telex 114528.
Ministry of Construction: 102 Berlin, Scharrenstr. 2-3; tel. 223; telex 61523.
Ministry of County-Controlled and Food Industries: 1086 Berlin, Leipziger Str. 5-7; tel. 232; telex 1152311.
Ministry of Culture: 1020 Berlin, Molkenmarkt 1-3; tel. 230; telex 115230.
Ministry of Education: 1086 Berlin, Unter den Linden 69-73; tel. 232; telex 1152345.
Ministry of Electrical Engineering and Electronics: 102 Berlin, Alexanderplatz 6; tel. 218; telex 1152417.

THE GERMAN DEMOCRATIC REPUBLIC

Directory

Ministry of Environmental Protection and Water Resources: 1026 Berlin, Hans-Beimler-Str. 70–72; tel. 235.

Ministry of Finance: 1086 Berlin, Leipziger Str. 5–7; tel. 232; telex 1152331.

Ministry of Foreign Affairs: 1020 Berlin, Marx-Engels-Platz 2; tel. 220; telex 114621.

Ministry of Foreign Trade: 1080 Berlin, Unter den Linden 44–60; tel. 2330; telex 114437.

Ministry of General and Agricultural Machinery and Vehicle Construction: 1086 Berlin, Leipziger Str. 5–7; tel. 232; telex 1152311.

Ministry of Geology: 104 Berlin, Invalidenstr. 44; tel. 236; telex 1152251.

Ministry of the Glass and Ceramics Industry: 1086 Berlin, Leipziger Str. 5–7; tel. 232; telex 1152311.

Ministry of Health: 102 Berlin, Rathausstr. 3; tel. 235.

Ministry of Heavy Engineering and Plant Construction: 1086 Berlin, Leipziger Str. 5–7; tel. 232.

Ministry of Higher and Technical Education: 1020 Berlin, Marx-Engels-Platz 2; tel. 230; telex 1152415.

Ministry of the Interior: 1086 Berlin, Mauerstr. 29–32; tel. 222; telex 112255.

Ministry of Justice: 108 Berlin, Clara-Zetkin-Str. 93; tel. 237; telex 113155.

Ministry of Light Industry: 1086 Berlin, Leipziger Str. 5–7; tel. 232; telex 1152311.

Ministry of Machine Tools and Processing Machines: 1086 Berlin, Leipziger Str. 5–7; tel. 232; telex 1152311.

Ministry of National Defence: 119 Berlin, Schnellerstr. 1–4; tel. 6352881; telex 112582.

Ministry of Ore Mining, Metallurgy and Potash: 102 Berlin, Karl-Liebknecht-Str. 34; tel. 235; telex 1152371.

Ministry of Posts and Telecommunications: 1066 Berlin, Mauerstr. 69–75; tel. 2312101; telex 112558.

Ministry of Science and Technology: 1170 Berlin, Köpenicker Str. 325A; tel. 65760; telex 113070.

Ministry of State Security: 113 Berlin, Normannenstr. 22; tel. 5509991; telex 112726.

Ministry of Supply of Materials: 1086 Berlin, Leipziger Str. 5–7; tel. 232; telex 1152342.

Ministry of Trade and Supply: 1026 Berlin, Hans-Beimler-Str. 70–72; tel. 235; telex 1152421.

Ministry of Transport: 1086 Berlin, Voss Str. 33; tel. 490; telex 112250.

POLITBÜRO OF THE SOCIALIST UNITY PARTY CENTRAL COMMITTEE

Members: Hermann Axen, Hans-Joachim Böhme, Horst Dohlus, Werner Eberlein, Prof. Kurt Hager, Joachim Herrmann, Erich Honecker (General Secretary of the Central Committee), Dr Werner Jarowinsky, Gen. Heinz Kessler, Günther Kleiber, Egon Krenz, Werner Krolikowski, Siegfried Lorenz, Gen. Erich Mielke, Günter Mittag, Erich Mückenberger, Alfred Neumann, Günter Schabowski, Horst Sindermann, Willi Stoph, Harry Tisch.

Candidate Members: Ingeburg Lange, Gerhard Müller, Margarete Müller, Gerhard Schürer, Werner Walde.

Legislature

VOLKSKAMMER
(People's Chamber)

Presidium

President: Horst Sindermann (SED).

Vice-President: Gerald Götting.

Members: Dr Rudolf Agsten (LDPD), Eberhard Aurich (FDJ), Erwin Binder, Heinz Eichler (SED), Werner Heilemann (FDGB), Wolfgang Heyl (CDU), Ernst Mecklenburg (DBD), Erich Mückenberger (SED), Wolfgang Rösser (NDPD), Rudi Rothe (DBD), Wilhelmine Schirmer-Pröscher (DFD), Dr Karl-Heinz Schulmeister (KB).

The most recent election for the Volkskammer was held on 8 June 1986. The candidates nominated by the National Front obtained 99.94% of the total vote. The Chamber has 500 members, including 66 representatives of East Berlin.

Political Organizations

Nationale Front der Deutschen Demokratischen Republik (National Front): combines the political organizations listed below, which issue a joint programme before elections; Pres. Prof. Dr Lothar Kolditz.

Christlich-Demokratische Union Deutschlands (CDU) (Christian Democratic Union of Germany): 1080 Berlin, Otto-Nuschke-Str. 59–60; tel. 22880; telex 112240; f. 1945; 140,000 mems (1987); Chair. Gerald Götting; Vice-Chair. Wolfgang Heyl, Max Sefrin, Dr Heinrich Toeplitz.

Demokratische Bauernpartei Deutschlands (DBD) (Democratic Farmers' Party): 1080 Berlin, Behrenstr. 47-48; telex 114801; f. 1948; 115,000 mems (1987); Chair. Dr Günther Maleuda; Deputy Chair. Paul Scholz, Dr Hans Reichelt.

Demokratischer Frauenbund Deutschlands (DFD) (Democratic Women's League of Germany): 1080 Berlin, Clara-Zetkin-Str. 16; f. 1947; 1.5m. mems (1987); Chair. Ilse Thiele.

Freie Deutsche Jugend (FDJ) (Free German Youth): 1086 Berlin, Unter den Linden 36-38; f. 1946; 2.3m. mems (1987); First Sec. Eberhard Aurich.

Freier Deutscher Gewerkschaftsbund (FDGB) (Confederation of Free German Trades Unions): see p. 1119.

Kulturbund der DDR (KB) (GDR League of Culture): 1080 Berlin, Otto-Nuschke-Str. 1; tel. 2202991; telex 114630; f. 1945; 275,000 mems (1988); Pres. Prof. Dr Hans Pischner.

Liberal-Demokratische Partei Deutschlands (LDPD) (Liberal Democratic Party of Germany): 1086 Berlin, Johannes-Dieckmann-Str. 48-49; telex 114806; f. 1945; 112,000 mems (1988); Chair. Prof. Dr Manfred Gerlach.

National-Demokratische Partei Deutschlands (NDPD) (National Democratic Party of Germany): 108 Berlin, Friedrichstr. 65; telex 112293; f. 1948; 110,000 mems (1987); Chair. Prof. Dr Heinrich Homann.

Sozialistische Einheitspartei Deutschlands (SED) (Socialist Unity Party of Germany): 1020 Berlin, Am Marx-Engels-Platz 2; tel. 2020; telex 112511; formed in 1946 as a result of a unification of the Social Democratic Party and the Communist Party in Eastern Germany; 2.3m. mems (1987); Gen. Sec. Erich Honecker; Chair. of Central Control Commission Erich Mückenberger; Chair. of Central Auditing Commission Kurt Seibt.

There are no opposition parties.

Diplomatic Representation

EMBASSIES IN THE GERMAN DEMOCRATIC REPUBLIC

Afghanistan: 1080 Berlin, Otto-Grotewohl-Str. 3A/III; tel. 2202071; Ambassador: Jalani Bakhtari.

Albania: 1100 Berlin, Florastr. 94; tel. 4825435; Ambassador: Ilir Boçka.

Algeria: 1100 Berlin, Esplanade 23; tel. 4722043; Ambassador: Youcef Kraïba.

Angola: 1080 Berlin, Clara-Zetkin-Str. 89/II; tel. 2202031; Ambassador: Agostinho André Mendes de Carvalho.

Argentina: 1080 Berlin, Clara-Zetkin-Str. 89, IV/Links; tel. 2202621; telex 113018; Ambassador: Alfredo Cipriano Pons Benítez.

Austria: 1080 Berlin, Otto-Grotewohl-Str. 5; tel. 2291031; telex 114275; Ambassador: Dr Franz Wunderbaldinger.

Bangladesh: 1080 Berlin, Clara-Zetkin-Str. 97/V; tel. 2292434; telex 114272; Ambassador: Ali Kaiser Hasan Morshed.

Belgium: 1100 Berlin, Esplanade 13; tel. 4723102; telex 113153; Ambassador: Theo Lansloot.

Brazil: 1110 Berlin, Esplanade 11; tel. 4723002; telex 113123; Ambassador: Ernesto Alberto Ferreira de Carvalho.

Bulgaria: 1100 Berlin, Berliner Str. 127; tel. 4800171; telex 112907; Ambassador: Peter Meschduretschki.

China, People's Republic: 1110 Berlin, Heinrich-Mann-Str. 9; tel. 4800161; telex 112474; Ambassador: Zhang Dake.

Colombia: 1080 Berlin, Clara-Zetkin-Str. 89/V; tel. 2292669; telex 114221; Ambassador: Dr Luis Villar Borda.

Congo: 1080 Berlin, Clara-Zetkin-Str. 97/III; tel. 2202021; telex 114088; Ambassador: Justin Ballay-Mégot.

Cuba: 1100 Berlin, Berliner Str. 120–121; tel. 4800216; telex 112449; Ambassador: Ramiro del Río Pérez Terán.

Czechoslovakia: 1080 Berlin, Otto-Grotewohl-Str. 21; tel. 2200481; telex 114026; Ambassador: František Langer.

THE GERMAN DEMOCRATIC REPUBLIC

Denmark: 1080 Berlin, Unter den Linden 41; tel. 2202916; telex 114220; Ambassador: Erik Herluf Krog-Meyer.

Ecuador: 1080 Berlin, Clara-Zetkin-Str. 89/V; tel. 2291367; telex 112755; Ambassador: Alfonso Barrera Valverde.

Egypt: 1100 Berlin, Str. 22, 3; tel. 4825095; telex 113014; Ambassador: Mustafa Ahmed Hannafi.

Ethiopia: 1100 Berlin, Arnold-Zweig-Str. 19; tel. 4700117; telex 114286; Ambassador: Lemma Gutema Debel.

Finland: 1080 Berlin, Schadowstr. 6; tel. 2202521; telex 114029; Ambassador: Arto Tanner.

France: 1080 Berlin, Unter den Linden 40; tel. 2202101; Ambassador: Joëlle Timsit.

Germany, Federal Republic: 1040 Berlin, Hannoversche Str. 30; tel. 2805101; telex 113244; Head of Permanent Representation: Franz Bertele.

Ghana: 1110 Berlin, Waldstr. 10; tel. 4827893; telex 112405; Ambassador: Kwame Sanaa-Poku Jantuah.

Greece: 1080 Berlin, Otto-Grotewohl-Str. 3a; tel. 2291922; telex 112464; Ambassador: Antonios J. Coundakis.

Guinea: 1110 Berlin, Heinrich-Mann-Str. 32; tel. 4829488; telex 112473; Ambassador: Tolo Béavogui.

Guinea-Bissau: 1080 Berlin, Clara-Zetkin-Str. 97/11; tel. 2292661; Ambassador: Ensa Mahatma Djandy.

Hungary: 1080 Berlin, Unter den Linden 76; tel. 2202561; telex 114201; Ambassador: István Roska.

India: 1080 Berlin, Clara-Zetkin-Str. 89/VI; tel. 2292213; Ambassador: Jagannath Doddamani.

Indonesia: 1100 Berlin, Esplanade 9; tel. 4722002; telex 112652; Ambassador: Gusti Ngurah Gedhe.

Iran: 1071 Berlin, Stavanger Str. 23; tel. 4720002; telex 113085; Ambassador: Dr Hamid Reza Assefi.

Iraq: 1110 Berlin, Tschaikowskistr. 51; tel. 4800501; telex 114056; Ambassador: Riyadh Ali Saba al-Azzawi.

Italy: 1080 Berlin, Unter den Linden 40; tel. 2202601; telex 113262; Ambassador: Dr Alberto Indelicato.

Japan: 1080 Berlin, Otto-Grotewohl-Str. 5/1; tel. 2202481; telex 114053; Ambassador: Hirokazu Arai.

Kampuchea: 1100 Berlin, Str. 22, 2; tel. 4828853; telex 113228; Ambassador: Meas Sip.

Korea, Democratic People's Republic: 1080 Berlin, Glinkastr. 5–7; tel. 2298013; telex 113039; Ambassador: Pak Yong Chan.

Laos: 1100 Berlin, Esplanade 17; tel. 4722052; telex 113167; Ambassador: Vanheuang Vongvichit.

Lebanon: 1080 Berlin, Clara-Zetkin-Str. 89/V; tel. 2202921; telex 114048; Ambassador: Joseph Akl.

Libya: 1157 Berlin, Hermann-Duncker-Str. 26; tel. 5090951; Secretary of the People's Bureau: Daw Abdullah Kaylani.

Mali: 1110 Berlin, Heinrich-Mann-Str. 22; tel. 4824751; telex 112988; Ambassador: Souleymane Sidibé.

Mexico: 1110 Berlin, Homeyerstr. 40; tel. 4829492; telex 112977; Ambassador: Raúl Valdés Aguilar.

Mongolia: 1157 Berlin, Fritz-Schmenkel-Str. 81; tel. 5090119; telex 112736; Ambassador: Ragtschaabasaryn Shamz.

Morocco: 1110 Berlin, Kuckhoffstr. 116; tel. 4829703; Ambassador: Abdelmajid Bouab.

Mozambique: 1080 Berlin, Clara-Zetkin-Str. 97/IV; tel. 2291751; telex 115074; Ambassador: Júlio Gonçalo Braga.

Netherlands: 1080 Berlin, Otto-Grotewohl-Str. 5/II; tel. 2292057; Ambassador: Carel J. Schneider.

Nicaragua: 1193 Berlin, Puschkinallee 49; tel. 2728761; telex 113292; Ambassador: Rodrigo Cardenal Martínez.

Nigeria: 1100 Berlin, Platanenstr. 98a; tel. 4828321; telex 112741; Ambassador: Edward Martins.

Norway: 1080 Berlin, Otto-Grotewohl-Str. 5/IV; tel. 2292489; Ambassador: Erik Christian Selmer.

Pakistan: 1080 Berlin, Otto-Grotewohl-Str. 3A/II; tel. 2292428; telex 114020; Ambassador: A. A. Chowdhury.

Panama: 1156 Berlin, Ho-Chi-Minh-Str. 2; tel. 3720093; Chargé d'affaires: Dr Humberto Jaén Castillo.

Peru: 1080 Berlin, Schadowstr. 6/IV; tel. 2291455; telex 114274; Ambassador: Jaime Cacho-Sousa Castro.

Philippines: 1080 Berlin, Otto-Grotewohl-Str. 3a; tel. 2202136; telex 112810; Ambassador: Rafael A. Gonzales.

Poland: 1080 Berlin, Unter den Linden 72–74; tel. 2202551; Ambassador: Dr Janusz Obodowski.

Portugal: 1080 Berlin, Otto-Grotewohl-Str. 3A/V; tel. 2291388; telex 112406; Ambassador: Dr Pedro Madeira de Andrade.

Romania: 1100 Berlin, Parkstr. 23; tel. 4825594; Ambassador: Gheorghe Caranfil.

Somalia: 1080 Berlin, Clara-Zetkin-Str. 97/I; tel. 2202006; telex 112411; Ambassador: Dr Ahmed Shire Mohamed.

Spain: 1080 Berlin, Clara-Zetkin-Str. 97/II; tel. 2292586; telex 113296; Ambassador: Alonso Alvarez de Toledo y Merry del Val.

Sudan: 1080 Berlin, Clara-Zetkin-Str. 89/III; telex 114009; Ambassador: Omar Muhammad Babiker Shouna.

Sweden: 1080 Berlin, Otto-Grotewohl-Str. 3a; tel. 2202146; Ambassador: Henrik Liljegren.

Switzerland: 1100 Berlin, Esplanade 21; tel. 4724002; telex 112430; Ambassador: Dr Franz Birrer.

Syria: 1080 Berlin, Otto-Grotewohl-Str. 3a; tel. 2202046; Ambassador: Fayssal Sammak.

Tunisia: 1100 Berlin, Esplanade 12; tel. 4722064; telex 114019; Ambassador: Taoufik Largui.

Turkey: 1080 Berlin, Schadowstr. 6/IV; tel. 2202471; Ambassador: Hikmet Özkan.

USSR: 1080 Berlin, Unter den Linden 63–65; tel. 2291110; telex 114045; Ambassador: Vyacheslav Ivanovich Kochemasov.

United Kingdom: 1080 Berlin, Unter den Linden 32–34; tel. 2202431; telex 113171; Ambassador: Nigel Broomfield.

USA: 1080 Berlin, Neustädtische Kirchstr. 4-5; tel. 2202741; telex 112479; Ambassador: Francis Joseph Meehan.

Uruguay: 1080 Berlin, Clara-Zetkin-Str. 97/V, rechts; tel. 2291424; telex 112413; Ambassador: Leslie Close-Pozzo.

Venezuela: 1080 Berlin, Otto-Grotewohl-Str. 5/IV; tel. 2292111; telex 114058; Ambassador: Dr José Luis Salcedo-Bastardo.

Viet-Nam: 1157 Berlin, Hermann-Duncker-Str. 125; tel. 5098262; telex 112416; Ambassador: Ta Huu Canh.

Yemen Arab Republic: 1110 Berlin, Waldstr. 15; tel. 4800391; telex 112857; Ambassador: Mansoor Abdulgalil Abdulrab.

Yemen, People's Democratic Republic: 1100 Berlin, Str. 22, 1; tel. 4800206; telex 113119; Ambassador: Ali Ismail Sayf.

Yugoslavia: 1040 Berlin, Albrechtstr. 26; tel. 2825446; Ambassador: Milan Predojević.

Zaire: 1080 Berlin, Otto-Grotewohl-Str. 3a; tel. 2292103; telex 112490; Ambassador: Ikolo Bolelama W'Okondola.

Zimbabwe: 1080 Berlin, Otto-Grotewohl-Str. 3a/IV; tel. 2202056; Ambassador: (vacant).

Judicial System

The principles on which the legal system functions are embodied in the Constitution. Jurisdiction is exercised by the Supreme Court, the County Courts (Bezirksgerichte), the District Courts (Kreisgerichte) and the Social Courts. There are also Military Courts. The Supreme Court is the highest organ of justice and supervises the work of the other courts. It is responsible to the People's Chamber.

Cases in the first instance are dealt with in the County and District Courts with one presiding judge and two lay judges. In a District Court one judge may preside and pass sentence. Cases in the second instance are dealt with by three judges in the County Courts and in the Supreme Court. However, cases are handled to an increasing extent by the Social Courts and, in the case of minor civil offences and labour disputes, by the disputes commissions.

All judges and members of the Social Courts are independent in their administration of justice. They can be recalled by their electors only if they violate the Constitution or the law or commit a serious breach of their duties.

According to the Constitution, all judges and members of the Social Courts are elected either by popular representative bodies (People's Chamber, County Parliaments, Town Assembly, etc.) or by direct popular vote. Candidates are submitted by the Minister of Justice after consultations with the relevant committees of the National Front. Candidates for the Labour Courts are submitted to the Minister of Justice by the Confederation of Free German Trades Unions (FDGB). The members of the disputes commissions are elected by the workers in their organizations. The State Prosecutors are appointed by the Prosecutor-General.

Attached to the People's Chamber is the Constitutional and Legislature Commission in which all parties are represented according to their size. All members of the Commission are appointed by the People's Chamber. Three members of the Supreme Court and three State Law Teachers, who may not be members of the People's Chamber, also serve on the Commission.

A new Criminal Code was introduced in January 1968, replacing the German Criminal Code of 1871. Amendments to this were

THE GERMAN DEMOCRATIC REPUBLIC

made in December 1974 and January 1976. Similarly, a new Civil Code of January 1976 replaced the German Civil Code of 1896. A new Labour Code came into force on 1 January 1978.

Oberstes Gericht der Deutschen Demokratischen Republik (Supreme Court of the GDR): 1026 Berlin, Littenstr. 13; Pres. Dr GÜNTER SARGE.

Generalstaatsanwalt der Deutschen Demokratischen Republik (Prosecutor-General of the GDR): GÜNTER WENDLAND; 1040 Berlin, Hermann-Matern-Str. 33–34.

Ministerium der Justiz der Deutschen Demokratischen Republik (Ministry of Justice of the GDR): 108 Berlin, Clara-Zetkin-Str. 93; tel. 237; telex 113155; Minister HANS-JOACHIM HEUSINGER.

Religion

CHRISTIANITY

Protestant Churches

(For the origin, constitutional structure, and recent development of the Evangelical Churches, see the corresponding section in the chapter on the Federal Republic of Germany.)

Bund der Evangelischen Kirchen in der Deutschen Demokratischen Republik (BEKDDR) (Federation of Evangelical Churches): 1040 Berlin, Auguststr. 80; tel. 28860; some 4m. people, about 25% of the population of the GDR, belong to one of the Territorial Churches united in the BEKDDR, compared with an estimated 70% in the 1950s; Pres. of Synod Dr RAINER GAEBLER; Exec. Sec. Oberkirchenrat MARTIN ZIEGLER.

Arbeitsgemeinschaft Christlicher Kirchen in der DDR (Association of Christian Churches in the GDR): 1040 Berlin, Auguststr. 80; tel. 28860; f. 1970; unites member churches of BEKDDR with other churches; 16 full mems, five observers; Chair. EBERHARD NATHO; Gen. Sec. Rev. MARTIN LANGE.

Konferenz der Evangelischen Kirchenleitungen in der DDR (Conference of Evangelical Church Leaders in the GDR): 1040 Berlin, Auguststr. 80; Chair. Landesbischof Dr WERNER LEICH.

Affiliated to the BEKDDR

Evangelische Kirche der Union (EKU): Kirchenkanzlei (Chancellery): 1040 Berlin, Auguststr. 80; tel. 28860; (see the corresponding section in the chapter on the Federal Republic of Germany for details); Pres. Dr FRIEDRICH WINTER.

†**Evangelical Church of Anhalt:** Kirchenpräsident: EBERHARD NATHO (4500 Dessau, Otto-Grotewohl-Str. 22; tel. 7247).

†**Evangelical Church in Berlin-Brandenburg** (in the GDR): 1020 Berlin, Neue Grünstr. 19; tel. 27802200; Bischof Dr GOTTFRIED FORCK (1120 Berlin-Weissensee, Parkstr. 21).

†**Evangelical Church of the Church Region of Görlitz:** 8900 Görlitz, Berliner Str. 62; tel. 5412; formerly Church Province of Silesia; Bischof Prof. Dr JOACHIM ROGGE.

†**Evangelical Church of Greifswald:** 2200 Greifswald, Bahnhofstr. 35–36; tel. 5261; formerly Evangelical Church of Pomerania; Bischof Dr HORST GIENKE.

Evangelical-Lutheran Church of Mecklenburg: 2751 Schwerin, Münzstr. 8; tel. 864165; Landesbischof CHRISTOPH STIER.

†**Evangelical Church of the Church Province of Saxony:** 3010 Magdeburg, Am Dom 2; tel. 31881; Bischof Dr CHRISTOPH DEMKE.

Evangelical-Lutheran Church of Saxony: 8032 Dresden, Lukasstr. 6; tel. 475841; Landesbischof Dr JOHANNES HEMPEL.

Evangelical-Lutheran Church in Thuringia: 5900 Eisenach, Dr-Moritz-Mitzenheim Str. 2A; tel. 5226; Landesbischof Dr WERNER LEICH.

(† Member of the EKU)

Other Protestant Churches

Bund Evangelisch-Freikirchlicher Gemeinden in der DDR (Union of Evangelical Free Church Congregations): 1034 Berlin, Gubener Str. 10; tel. 5891832; Pres. Rev. MANFRED SULT; Gen. Sec. Rev. ROLF DAMMANN.

Bund Freier evangelischer Gemeinden in der DDR (Federation of Free Evangelical Congregations): 1199 Berlin, Handjerystr. 29-31; tel. 6762665; Federal Chair. JOHANNES SCHMIDT.

Evangelische Brüder-Unität, Distrikt Herrnhut (Unitas Fratrum-Moravian Church in the District of Herrnhut); 8709 Herrnhut, Zittauer Str. 20; tel. 258; Pres. Rev. CHRISTIAN MÜLLER.

Evangelisch-Lutherische (altlutherische) Kirche in der DDR (Evangelical Lutheran (Old Lutheran) Church): 1020 Berlin, Annenstr. 53; tel. 2793583; f. 1830; c. 8,000 mems; Sec. Kirchenrat JOHANNES ZELLMER.

Evangelisch-Methodistische Kirche in der DDR (United Methodist Church): 8020 Dresden, Wiener Str. 56; tel. 477441; Bischof Dr RÜDIGER MINOR.

Kirchenbund Evangelisch-Reformierter Gemeinden in der DDR (Church Federation of Evangelical Reformed Congregations): 7010 Leipzig, Tröndlinring 7; tel. 291079; Pastor HANS-JÜRGEN SIEVERS.

Mennonitengemeinde in der DDR (Mennonite Congregation): 1174 Berlin, Donizettistr. 47; tel. 5275028; Dir Pastor KNUTH HANSEN.

The Roman Catholic Church

It is estimated that about 1.1 million people (1987) are Roman Catholics.

Römisch-katholische Kirche in der DDR: 1086 Berlin, Französische Str. 34; tel. 2000281; supervises the activities of Roman Catholic churches in the GDR and organizes the Berlin Bishops' Conference of GDR Bishops.

Bishops' Conference: Berliner Bischofskonferenz, 1086 Berlin, Französische Str. 34; f. 1984; Pres. (vacant).

Bishop of Berlin: (vacant), 1086 Berlin, Französische Str. 34; tel. 2000281.

Bishop of Dresden-Meissen: JOACHIM REINELT, 8053 Dresden, Käthe-Kollwitz-Ufer 84; tel. 34161.

Apostolic Administrator of Görlitz: BERNHARD HUHN (Titular Bishop of Tasaccora), 8900 Görlitz, Carl-von-Ossietzky-Str. 41; tel. 4630.

Apostolic Administrator in Erfurt-Meiningen: Dr JOACHIM WANKE (Titular Bishop of Castellum in Mauretania), 5010 Erfurt, Herrmannsplatz 9; tel. 24595.

Apostolic Administrator in Magdeburg: JOHANNES BRAUN (Titular Bishop of Putia in Byzacena), 3010 Magdeburg, Max-Josef-Metzger Str. 1; tel. 33991.

Apostolic Administrator in Schwerin: THEODOR HUBRICH (Titular Bishop of Auca), 2762 Schwerin, Lankower Str. 14; tel. 44025.

Other Christian Churches

Apostelamt Jesu Christi in der DDR: 7500 Cottbus, Otto-Grotewohl-Str. 57; tel. 713297; Pres. WALDEMAR ROHDE.

Gemeindeverband der Altkatholischen Kirche in der DDR (Union of the Old Catholic Church): 3720 Blankenburg, Georgstr. 7; tel. 2297; Deaconess URSULA BUSCHLÜTER.

Gemeinschaft der Siebenten-Tags-Adventisten in der DDR (Seventh-day Adventist Church): 1160 Berlin, Helmholtzstr. 1; tel. 6351320; Pres. LOTHAR REICHE.

Religiöse Gesellschaft der Freunde (Quäker) in der DDR (Society of Friends): 1086 Berlin, Planckstr. 20; tel. 2071525; f. 1969; 51 mems; Sec. HEINRICH BRÜCKNER.

Russische Orthodoxe Kirche—Mitteleuropäisches Exarchat (Russian Orthodox Church): 1157 Berlin, Wildensteiner Str. 10; tel. 5082024; Archbishop GERMAN.

JUDAISM

It is estimated that the Jewish Community in the Democratic Republic numbers about 5,000.

Verband der Jüdischen Gemeinden in der DDR (Union of Jewish Communities): 806 Dresden, Bautzner Str. 20; tel. 55491; Pres. SIEGMUND ROTSTEIN.

Jüdische Gemeinde Berlin (Jewish Community in Berlin): 1040 Berlin, Oranienburgerstr. 28; tel. 2823327; Pres. Dr PETER KIRCHNER; Chief Rabbi ERNST LORGE.

The Press

The 1968 Constitution of the German Democratic Republic guarantees the freedom of the press, radio and television, and states that every citizen of the GDR has the right, 'in accordance with the spirit and aims of the Constitution, to express his opinion freely and publicly. This right is not limited by any service or employment relationship. No person may be placed at a disadvantage for exercising this right'. There is thus no formal censorship but editors are personally responsible for the content of their papers which are expected to reflect the social and political system of the GDR.

All newspapers and periodicals are owned and managed by political or independent organizations such as party committees, trade unions, cultural associations, youth organizations, etc. Almost all dailies are controlled by or affiliated to a political party, such as *Neues Deutschland* (Socialist Unity party), *Der Morgen* (Liberal Democratic Party), *National-Zeitung* (National Democratic Party) and *Neue Zeit* (Christian Democratic Union). *Tribüne* is the organ of the Confederation of Free German Trades Unions and *Bauern-Echo* of the Democratic Farmers' Party. The Free German Youth

THE GERMAN DEMOCRATIC REPUBLIC

publishes the daily *Junge Welt*. The official news agency, the *Allgemeiner Deutscher Nachrichtendienst*, became a state monopoly in 1946.

In 1987 39 dailies appeared in the GDR, with a total circulation of 9.4m. copies per issue. There are 32 weeklies, with a circulation of 9.4m., and 541 periodicals and illustrated magazines, with a combined average circulation of 21.4m. According to the Press Association of the GDR, each family buys on average at least one daily newspaper, one weekly and three periodicals. In 1987 the GDR ranked second in the world in terms of daily newspaper circulation (550 per 1,000 of population).

The most important and influential dailies are those published by the Socialist Unity Party, headed by *Neues Deutschland* in Berlin, and by the Berlin organs of the other parties mentioned above. Though circulation figures are often not disclosed, a very popular paper is *Berliner Zeitung am Abend* (circulation 198,961 in 1986). Leading dailies outside Berlin are *Freie Presse* (Karl-Marx-Stadt), *Freiheit* (Halle), *Sächsische Zeitung* (Dresden), *Leipziger Volkszeitung* (Leipzig), *Ostsee Zeitung* (Rostock) and *Freies Wort* (Suhl).

The most widely-read periodicals are the weeklies *FF-dabei*, an illustrated radio and television magazine, *Wochenpost*, and the women's magazine *Für Dich*. Other high-circulation weeklies are the illustrated popular magazines *Neue Berliner Illustrierte* and *Freie Welt*, and the satirical weekly *Eulenspiegel*.

PRINCIPAL DAILIES

Bautzen
Nowa Doba: 8600 Bautzen, Tuchmacher Str. 27; tel. 511316; telex 287220; morning; Sorbian language paper; Editor SIEGHARD KOSEL; circ. 1,957.

Berlin
Bauern-Echo: 1040 Berlin, Reinhardtstr. 14; tel. 28930; telex 114424; f. 1948; morning; organ of the DBD; Editor LEONHARD HELMSCHROTT; circ. 93,969.

Berliner Zeitung: 1026 Berlin, Karl-Liebknecht-Str. 29; tel. 2440; telex 114854; f. 1945; morning; SED; Editor DIETER KERSCHEK; circ. 424,949.

Berliner Zeitung (BZ) am Abend: 1026 Berlin, Karl-Liebknecht-Str. 29; tel. 2440; telex 114854; evening; Editor HORST HERTELT; circ. 203,653.

Deutsches Sport-Echo: 1086 Berlin, Neustädtische Kirchstr. 15; sports; Editor DIETER WALES; circ. 184,960.

Junge Welt: 1026 Berlin, Karl-Liebknecht-Str. 29; tel. 2440; telex 114857; f. 1947; morning; FDJ; Editor HANS-DIETER SCHÜTT; circ. 1,380,477.

Der Morgen: 1086 Berlin, Johannes-Dieckmann-Str. 47; tel. 2202181; telex 112704; f. 1945; morning; LDPD; Editor GERHARD FISCHER; circ. 61,682.

National-Zeitung: 1055 Berlin, Prenzlauer Allee 36; tel. 4300215; telex 112714; f. 1948; morning; NDPD; Editor DIETHARD WEND; circ. 55,450.

Neue Zeit: 1080 Berlin, Mittelstr. 2-4; tel. 2000421; telex 112536; f. 1945; morning; CDU; Editor Dr DIETER EBERLE; circ. 113,054.

Neues Deutschland: 1017 Berlin, Franz-Mehring-Platz 1; tel. 5850; telex 112051; f. 1946; morning; SED; Editor HERBERT NAUMANN; circ. 1,092,811.

Tribüne: 1193 Berlin, Am Treptower Park 28-30; tel. 27100; telex 112611; f. 1945; morning; FDGB; Editor GÜNTER SIMON; circ. 414,200.

Cottbus
Lausitzer Rundschau: 7500 Cottbus, Bahnhofstr. 52; tel. 625231; telex 17210; SED; morning; Editor JOACHIM TELEMANN; circ. 291,073.

Dresden
Märkische Union: 8000 Dresden, Str. der Befreiung 21; f. 1948; morning; CDU; Editor FRIEDRICH EISMANN; circ. 3,704.

Sächsische Neueste Nachrichten: 8060 Dresden, Antonstr. 8; morning; NDPD; Editor SIEGMAR HOFMANN; circ. 29,006.

Sächsische Zeitung: 8010 Dresden, Julian-Grimau-Allee; tel. 4864240; telex 2251; f. 1946; morning; SED; Editor JOHANNES SCHULZ; circ. 560,800.

Die Union: 8000 Dresden, Str. der Befreiung 21; f. 1946; morning; CDU; Editor FRIEDRICH EISMANN; circ. 63,010.

Erfurt
Das Volk: 5010 Erfurt, Juri-Gagarin-Ring 113-117; tel. 530316; telex 61212; f. 1946; morning; SED; Editor WERNER HERRMANN; circ. 401,236.

Frankfurt a.d. Oder
Neuer Tag: 1200 Frankfurt a.d. Oder, Karl-Marx-Str. 23; tel. 311211; telex 16288; morning; SED; Editor HERBERT THIEME; circ. 210,507.

Gera
Volkswacht: 6500 Gera, Julius-Fucik-Str. 18; tel. 612262; telex 58227; morning; SED; Editor LOTHAR OBERÜCK; circ. 237,537.

Halle
Freiheit: 4020 Halle, Str. der DSF 76; tel. 38461; telex 4265; f. 1946; morning; SED; Editor Dr HANS-DIETER KRÜGER; circ. 584,505.

Liberal-Demokratische Zeitung: 4020 Halle, Gr. Brauhausstr. 16-17; tel. 38396; telex 04359; f. 1945; morning; LDPD; Editor HANS-HERBERT BIERMANN; circ. 57,000.

Der Neue Weg: 4000 Halle, Klement-Gottwald-Str. 61; telex 4417; f. 1946; morning; CDU; Editor KLAUS-PETER BIGALKE; circ. 37,100.

Karl-Marx-Stadt
Freie Presse: 9010 Karl-Marx-Stadt 1, Karl-Marx Allee 15-19; tel. 656280; telex 7233; SED; morning; Editor DIETMAR GRIESHEIMER; circ. 660,945.

Leipzig
Leipziger Volkszeitung: 7010 Leipzig, Peterssteinweg 19; tel. 7154327; telex 51495; f. 1894; morning; SED; Editor RUDI RÖHRER; circ. 485,000.

Mitteldeutsche Neueste Nachrichten: 7010 Leipzig, Thomasiusstr. 2; morning; NDPD; Editor RAINER DUCLAUD; circ. 20,499.

Sächsisches Tageblatt: 7010 Leipzig, Neumarkt 6; tel. 295251; telex 512236; f. 1946; morning; LDPD; Editor ARMIN HOPF; circ. 65,150.

Magdeburg
Volksstimme: 3010 Magdeburg, Bahnhofstr. 17; tel. 388240; telex 8462; morning; SED; Editor HEINZ WIESE; circ. 450,685.

Neubrandenburg
Freie Erde: 2080 Neubrandenburg, Str. der Befreiung 27; tel. 585440; telex 33211; f. 1945; morning; SED; Editor GERHARD SCHIEDEWITZ; circ. 201,461.

Potsdam
Brandenburgische Neueste Nachrichten: 1500 Potsdam, Leninallee 185; morning; NDPD; Editor GEORG JOPKE; circ. 22,453.

Märkische Volksstimme: 1500 Potsdam, Friedrich-Engels-Str. 24; tel. 3240; telex 15333; morning; SED; Editor WERNER SCHUBERT; circ. 347,495.

Rostock
Der Demokrat: 2500 Rostock, Kröpelinerstr. 44-47; telex 31205; f. 1945; CDU; Editor XAVER KUGLER; circ. 18,160.

Norddeutsche Neueste Nachrichten: 2500 Rostock, Kröpelinerstr. 21; tel. 94161; telex 031105; f. 1953; morning; NDPD; Editor WOLF-DIETRICH GEHRKE; circ. 38,827.

Ostsee-Zeitung: 2500 Rostock, Richard-Wagner-Str. 1A; tel. 3650; telex 31317; f. 1952; morning; SED; Editor Dr SIEGBERT SCHÜTT; circ. 292,469.

Schwerin
Norddeutsche Zeitung: 2751 Schwerin, Graf-Schack-Allee 11; tel. 865091; telex 32238; f. 1946; morning; LDPD; Editor GÜNTER GRASMEYER; circ. 23,000.

Schweriner Volkszeitung: 2791 Schwerin, Hermann-Duncker-Str. 27; tel. 3530; telex 32420; f. 1946; morning; SED; Editor HANS BRANDT; circ. 201,299.

Suhl
Freies Wort: 6000 Suhl, Wilhelm-Pieck-Str. 6; tel. 5130; telex 62205; morning; SED; Editor HELMUT LINKE; circ. 177,460.

Weimar
Thüringer Neueste Nachrichten: 5300 Weimar, Goetheplatz 9A; tel. 4192; telex 618924; f. 1951; NDPD; Editor KLAUS-RAINER LORENZ; circ. 32,055.

Thüringer Tageblatt: 5300 Weimar, Coudraystr. 6; telex 618922; f. 1951; morning; CDU; Editor FRANZ GERTH; circ. 31,671.

Thüringische Landeszeitung: 5300 Weimar, Marienstr. 14; tel. 3201; telex 618937; f. 1945; morning; LDPD; Editor H.-D. WOITHON; circ. 68,000.

THE GERMAN DEMOCRATIC REPUBLIC

SELECTED POPULAR PERIODICALS

Bild und Ton: 7031 Leipzig, Karl-Heine-Str. 16; tel. 49500; telex 51451; f. 1947; special photographic and cinematographic monthly; Editor Dr WALTER.

Deine Gesundheit: 1020 Berlin, Neue Grünstr. 18; tel. 2700516; popular monthly dealing with health and welfare; circ. 242,700.

Einheit: 1020 Berlin, Am Marx-Engels-Platz; tel. 2023860; f. 1946; monthly; theory and practice of scientific socialism; circ. 250,000.

Eulenspiegel: 1026 Berlin, Karl-Liebknecht-Str. 29; tel. 2440; telex 114854; political satirical weekly; Editor GERD NAGEL; circ. 492,568.

FF-dabei: 1026 Berlin, Karl-Liebknecht-Str. 29; tel. 2440; telex 114854; weekly; Editor OSMUND SCHWAB; circ. 1,483,495.

Filmspiegel: 1040 Berlin, Oranienburger Str. 67–68; fortnightly; films and cinematography; circ. 300,000.

Fotografie: 7031 Leipzig, Karl-Heine-Str. 16; tel. 49500; telex 51451; f. 1946; special photographic monthly; Editor Dr WALTER.

Fotokino-Magazin: 7031 Leipzig, Karl-Heine-Str. 16; tel. 49500; telex 51451; f. 1962; popular photographic monthly; Editor Dr WALTER.

Freie Welt: 1026 Berlin, Karl-Liebknecht-Str. 29; tel. 2440; telex 114854; weekly; international politics; Editor BARBARA SCHABLINSKI; circ. 362,164.

Für Dich: 1026 Berlin, Karl-Liebknecht-Str. 29; tel. 2440; telex 114854; women's weekly; Editor Dr FRIEDA JETZSCHMANN; circ. 942,000.

FUWO—Die Neue Fussballwoche: 1086 Berlin, Neustädtische Kirchstr. 15; tel. 2212420; telex 2853; weekly; football; Editor JÜRGEN NÖLDNER; circ. 284,993.

Guter Rat: 7010 Leipzig, Friedrich-Ebert-Str. 76–78; quarterly for women and home; circ. 446,700.

horizont: 1026 Berlin, Karl-Liebknecht-Str. 29; tel. 2440; telex 114854; f. 1968; monthly; international politics and economics; Editor ERNST-OTTO SCHWABE; circ. 130,400.

Illustrierter Motorsport: 1086 Berlin, Neustädtische Kirch-Str. 15; monthly; cars, motorcycles and motor-boats; Editor GÜNTER GRASSMANN.

Jugend + Technik: 1026 Berlin, Postfach 43, Mauerstr. 39–40; tel. 2233427; telex 114483; f. 1953; popular scientific/technological monthly for young people; circ. 205,000.

Die Kirche: 1020 Berlin, Sophienstr. 3; f. 1945; organ of the Protestant Church in Berlin-Brandenburg; Editor Pastor GERHARD JOHANN; circ. 42,000.

Das Magazin: 1026 Berlin, Karl-Liebknecht-Str. 29; tel. 2443435; telex 114854; monthly; Editor MANFRED GEBHARDT; circ. 569,297.

Modische Maschen: 7010 Leipzig, Friedrich-Ebert-Str. 76–78; popular women's quarterly for fashion and knitting.

Neue Berliner Illustrierte: 1026 Berlin, Karl-Liebknecht-Str. 29; tel. 2440; telex 114854; f. 1945; weekly; Editor WOLFGANG NORDALM; circ. 794,102.

neues leben: 1080 Berlin, Mauerstr. 39–40; monthly; youth; circ. 550,111.

Pramo: 7010 Leipzig, Friedrich-Ebert-Str. 76–78; tel. 71790; telex 51733; monthly; practical fashion for women and children; circ. 753,100.

Saison: 7010 Leipzig, Friedrich-Ebert-Str. 76–78; quarterly; fashion; circ. 209,500.

St Hedwigsblatt: 1086 Berlin, Hinter der Katholischen Kirche 3, Postfach 1343; tel. 2071754; f. 1954; weekly; organ of the Catholic Church, Berlin diocese; circ. 25,000.

Sibylle: 7010 Leipzig, Friedrich-Ebert-Str. 76–78; 6 a year; women's fashion magazine.

Sonntag: 1086 Berlin, Niederwallstr. 39; cultural weekly; Editor Dr WILFRIED GEISSLER; circ. 22,598.

Standpunkt: 1190 Berlin, Fennstr. 16; tel. 6350915; f. 1973; Protestant monthly; circ. 3,000.

Urania: 1080 Berlin, Otto-Nuschke-Str. 28; tel. 2000181; popular scientific monthly; circ. 116,000.

Die Weltbühne: 1026 Berlin, Karl-Liebknecht-Str. 29; tel. 2443301; telex 114854; weekly; politics, art, economics; Editor PETER THEEK; circ. 31,551.

Wochenpost: 1026 Berlin, Karl-Liebknecht-Str. 29; tel. 2440; telex 114854; weekly; Editor BRIGITTE ZIMMERMANN; circ. 1,243,264.

SELECTED SPECIALIST PERIODICALS

Ärztliche Jugendkunde: 7010 Leipzig, Salomonstr. 18B, Postfach 109; tel. 70131; f. 1888; 5 a year; medical; Editor Prof. Dr K. JÄHRIG; circ. 750.

Bildende Kunst: 1040 Berlin, Oranienburger Str. 67–68; tel. 2879306; telex 112302; f. 1953; monthly; painting, sculpture and graphics; Editor BERND ROSNER; circ. 20,000.

Biologische Rundschau: 6900 Jena, Villengang 2; tel. 27332; telex 58 86176; f. 1963; 6 a year; all fields of biology; Editor F. W. STÖCKER; circ. 1,300.

Chemische Technik: 7031 Leipzig, Karl-Heine-Str. 27; tel. 474441; monthly; chemistry, chemical engineering.

Deutsche Lehrerzeitung: 1086 Berlin, Krausenstr. 50, Am Spittelmarkt; weekly for teachers; Editor OTTO PFEIFFER; circ. 151,885.

Deutsche Nationalbibliographie und Bibliographie des im Ausland erschienenen deutschsprachigen Schrifttums: 7010 Leipzig, Deutscher Platz 1; tel. 88120; telex 51562; register of all German language publications all over the world; published by the Deutsche Bücherei, Leipzig, in three sections: Series A: New publications of the book trade (weekly); Series B: New publications not for general sale (fortnightly); Series C: Theses and Inaugural Dissertations (monthly).

Elektrie: 1020 Berlin, Postfach 201, Oranienburger Str. 13–14; tel. 28700; telex 112228; f. 1947; monthly for electrical trade; circ. 5,000.

Film und Fernsehen: 1040 Berlin, Oranienburger Str. 67–68; tel. 2879265; telex 112302; f. 1973; monthly; organ of the Union of Film and TV Artists; Editor GÜNTER NETZEBAND; circ. 10,700.

Fremdsprachen: 7010 Leipzig, Gerichtsweg 26, Postfach 130; quarterly dealing with interpreting, translating, etc. in Russian, English, French and Spanish; circ. 3,200.

Handelswoche/Konsum-Genossenschafter: 1055 Berlin, Am Friedrichshain 22; tel. 43870; telex 114566; fortnightly for trade and business.

Das Hochschulwesen: 1080 Berlin, Johannes-Dieckmann-Str. 10; monthly; education; circ. 3,500.

Humanitas: 1020 Berlin, Neue Grünstr. 18; fortnightly for medical and social welfare; circ. 47,707.

Informatik: 1055 Berlin, Am Friedrichshain 22; tel. 43870; telex 114566; 6 a year; scientific journal.

Junge Generation: 1026 Berlin, Postfach 43, Mauerstr. 39–40; tel. 2233321; f. 1947; monthly; youth; circ. 72,000.

Die Mode: 7010 Leipzig, Friedrich-Ebert-Str. 76–78; 2 a year; fashion; circ. 23,300.

Neue Deutsche Bauernzeitung: 1017 Berlin, Franz-Mehring-Platz 1; tel. 58312191; telex 112728; f. 1960; agricultural weekly; Editor Dr UDO AUGUSTIN; circ. 225,066.

Neue Deutsche Literatur: 1086 Berlin, Friedrichstr. 169; tel. 2335059; f. 1953; monthly; review of literature; Editor WALTER NOWOJSKI.

Neue Deutsche Presse: 1086 Berlin, Friedrichstr. 101; tel. 2000106; telex 114947; f. 1946; monthly; journalist affairs, press, radio, television; Editor ERIKA GELHAAR; circ. 5,000.

Das neue Handwerk: 1055 Berlin, Am Friedrichshain 22; tel. 43870; telex 114566; monthly; circ. 236,630.

Neue Werbung: 1055 Berlin, Am Friedrichshain 22; tel. 43870; telex 114566; 6 a year; advertising.

Plaste und Kautschuk: 7031 Leipzig, Karl-Heine-Str. 27; monthly; chemistry, physics, processing and application.

Radio Fernsehen Elektronik: 1020 Berlin, Postfach 201, Oranienburger Str. 13–14; tel. 28700; telex 0112228; f. 1952; monthly; theory and practice of electronics; circ. 90,000.

Sozialistische Finanzwirtschaft: 1055 Berlin, Am Friedrichshain 22; tel. 4387237; telex 0114566; 6 a year; finance and economics; circ. 42,000.

Technische Gemeinschaft: 1080 Berlin, Kronenstr. 18; monthly; technology; circ. 285,000.

Theater der Zeit: 1040 Berlin, Oranienburger Str. 67; tel. 2879259; telex 112302; f. 1946; monthly; theatre, drama, opera, operetta, musical, puppet theatre, ballet; Editor HANS-RAINER JOHN; circ. 12,000.

Wirtschaftswissenschaft: 1055 Berlin, Am Friedrichshain 22; tel. 43870; telex 0114566; monthly; economic science, socialist economy.

Zahntechnik: 1020 Berlin, Neue Grünstr. 18; tel. 2700516; every 2 months; dentistry; circ. 5,200.

ZAMM: 1199 Berlin, Rudower Chaussee 5; monthly; applied mathematics and mechanics; circ. 1,900.

Zeitschrift für Chemie: 7031 Leipzig, Karl-Heine-Str. 27; tel. 474441; monthly; chemistry.

Zeitschrift für Geschichtswissenschaft: 1080 Berlin, Glinkastr. 13–15; f. 1953; monthly; history and historiography; circ. 4,500.

Zeitschrift für Klinische Medizin (Das deutsche Gesundheitswesen): 1020 Berlin, Neue Grünstr. 18; fortnightly for the medical profession.

THE GERMAN DEMOCRATIC REPUBLIC

Zeitschrift für Psychologie mit Zeitschrift für angewandte Psychologie: 7010 Leipzig, Salomonstr. 18B, Postfach 109; tel. 70131; f. 1890; 4 a year; psychology and applied psychology; Editors Prof. Dr F. KLIX, Prof. Dr W. HACKER, Prof. Dr J. HOFFMANN, Prof. Dr E. VAN DER MEER; Dr J. MEHL, Dr F. KUKLA; circ. 1,300.

Zentralblatt für Neurochirurgie: 7010 Leipzig, Salomonstr. 18B, Postfach 109; tel. 70131; f. 1936; 4 a year; neuro-surgery; Editors Prof. Dr H.-G. NIEBELING, Dr W.-E. GOLDHAHN; circ. 850.

NEWS AGENCIES

Allgemeiner Deutscher Nachrichtendienst (ADN): 1026 Berlin, Mollstr. 1; tel. 230; telex 1146010; f. 1946; official news agency of the GDR; has 42 offices and additional correspondents abroad; maintains a press photo dept, 'Zentralbild', and provides daily news service in German as well as radio teletype casts in English, French, Spanish, Portuguese and Arabic, and radio photo services; Dir-Gen. GÜNTER PÖTSCHKE.

Foreign Bureaux

Agence Belga (BRT) (Belgium): 1006 Berlin, Koppenstr. 59, Postfach 37-05; tel. 6816468; Correspondent Dr R. MONDELAERS.

Agence Congolaise d'Information (ACI) (Congo): 1156 Berlin, Rudolf-Seifert-Str. 60; tel. 3729137.

Agence France-Presse (AFP): 1020 Berlin, Karl-Liebknecht-Str. 11; tel. 2123549; telex 114001; Correspondent CHARLES HENRI BAAB.

Agenzia Nazionale Stampa Associata (ANSA) (Italy): 1020 Berlin, Karl-Liebknecht-Str. 11; tel. 2123662; telex 114094; Correspondent RICCARDO EHRMAN.

Bulgarska Telegrafna Agentsia (BTA) (Bulgaria): 1020 Berlin, Alexanderstr. 5; telex 114227.

Československá tisková kancelář (ČTK) (Czechoslovakia): 1100 Berlin, Max-Lingner-Str. 12A; tel. 4721015; telex 114269.

Deutsche Presse Agentur (dpa) (Federal Republic of Germany): 1080 Berlin, Clara-Zetkin-Str. 89; tel. 2291109; telex 114038.

Iraqi News Agency (INA): 1136 Berlin, Dolgenseestr. 21/0602; Correspondent SA'ID AL-SADI.

Magyar Távirati Iroda (MTI) (Hungary): 1020 Berlin, Mollstr. 12; telex 114081; Correspondent LÁSZLÓ DOROGMAN.

Novinska Agencija Tanjug (Yugoslavia): 1017 Berlin, Lichtenbergerstr. 13.

Polska Agencja Prasowa (PAP) (Poland): 1086 Berlin, Neustädtische Kirchstr. 3; telex 114060.

Prensa Latina (Cuba): 1080 Berlin, Mohrenstr. 36-37; tel. 2080257; telex 114284; Correspondent MERCEDES RAMOS CHAVIANO.

Reuters (UK): 1080 Berlin, Mohrenstr. 36-37; tel. (0372) 2071718; telex 115150.

Syrian Arab News Agency (SANA): 1017 Berlin, Karl-Marx-Allee 16.

Telegrafnoye Agentstvo Sovetskovo Soyuza (TASS) (USSR): 1080 Berlin, Mohrenstr. 36-37; Correspondent ANATOLY TUPAEV.

Viet-Nam News Agency (VNA): 1017 Berlin, Leninplatz 27; telex 114008.

Xinhua (New China) News Agency (People's Republic of China): 1110 Berlin, Pfeilstr. 17; tel. 4824396; telex 112231; Correspondent XING GUIMIN.

PRESS ASSOCIATION

Verband der Journalisten der DDR: 1086 Berlin, Friedrichstr. 101; tel. 2000106; telex 114974; f. 1946; Chair. EBERHARD HEINRICH; 9,000 mems.

Publishers

Akademie-Verlag: 1086 Berlin, Leipziger Str. 3-4, Postfach 1233; tel. 22360; telex 114420; f. 1946; books and periodicals on scientific theory and practice; Dir Prof. Dr L. BERTHOLD.

Akademische Verlagsgesellschaft Geest & Portig K.-G.: 7010 Leipzig, Sternwartenstr. 8, Postfach 106; tel. 293158; telex 512381; f. 1906; mathematics, physics, science, engineering, history of science; Dir H. KRATZ.

Altberliner Verlag: 1020 Berlin, Neue Schönhauser Str. 8; tel. 2806634; f. 1945; books for children; Dir Dr G. DAHNE.

Aufbau-Verlag Berlin und Weimar: 1080 Berlin, Französische Str. 32; tel. 2202421; telex 114739; f. 1945; literature, German and foreign, classical literature and criticism; Dir ELMAR FABER.

VEB Johann Ambrosius Barth: 7010 Leipzig, Salomonstr. 18B, Postfach 109; tel. 70131; f. 1780; textbooks, monographs and periodicals, medicine, stomatology, physics, chemistry, astronomy and psychology; Dir K. WIECKE.

VEB Verlag für Bauwesen: 1086 Berlin, Französische Str. 13-14; tel. 20410; telex 112229; building; Dir S. SEELIGER.

VEB Bibliographisches Institut Leipzig: 7010 Leipzig, Gerichtsweg 26; tel. 7801; telex 512773; f. 1826; encyclopaedias, German language books, reference books, bibliographies, biographies, information and documentation; Dir H. BÄHRING.

Hermann Böhlaus Nachf. Verlag: 5300 Weimar, Meyerstr. 50A; tel. 2071; f. 1624; literary history and criticism, history, law; Man. Dir Prof. Dr LOTHAR BERTHOLD.

VEB Breitkopf & Härtel Musikverlag: 7010 Leipzig, Karlstr. 10; tel. 7351; f. 1719; classical music, contemporary and vocal music and literature on music; Dir Dr G. HEMPEL.

VEB F. A. Brockhaus Verlag Leipzig: 7010 Leipzig, Postfach 19; tel. 7846; f. 1805; travel books, reference books, picture books, popular science, calendars; Dir A. NEUMANN.

VEB Deutscher Landwirtschaftsverlag: 1040 Berlin, Reinhardstr. 14; tel. 28930; f. 1960; agriculture, forestry, horticulture; Dir G. HOLLE.

VEB Deutscher Verlag der Wissenschaften: 1080 Berlin, Johannes-Dieckmann-Str. 10; tel. 22900; telex 114390; f. 1954; mathematics, physics, chemistry, philosophy, psychology, history; Dir Dr L. WALTER.

VEB Deutscher Verlag für Grundstoffindustrie: 7031 Leipzig, Karl-Heine-Str. 27; tel. 474441; telex 51451; f. 1960; technical books and journals for science and industry; Dir H. BROMMA.

VEB Deutscher Verlag für Musik: 7010 Leipzig, Karlstr. 10; tel. 7351; f. 1954; classical and contemporary and vocal music and literature on music; Dir Dr G. HEMPEL.

Dieterich'sche Verlagsbuchhandlung: 7022 Leipzig, Mottelerstr. 8; tel. 58726; f. 1766; literature; Dir R. LINKS.

Dietz Verlag Berlin: 1020 Berlin, Wallstr. 76-79; tel. 27030; telex 114741; f. 1945; social science, politics, history, philosophy, political economy, cultural policy, memoirs, periodicals; Dir Dr G. HENNIG.

VEB Domowina-Verlag: 8600 Bautzen, Tuchmacherstr. 27; tel. 511316; telex 287220; f. 1958; Slavonic studies; books in Sorbian and in German on Sorbian culture, children's books, belles-lettres; Dir M. BENAD.

Edition Leipzig—Verlag für Kunst und Wissenschaft: 7030 Leipzig, Karl-Liebknecht-Str. 77; tel. 312412; telex 512918; f. 1960; arts and history of civilization, scientific and bibliophilic reprints, science and technics, general; Dir Prof. Dr D. NADOLSKI.

VEB Edition Peters: 7010 Leipzig, Talstr. 10, Postfach 746; tel. 7721; telex 512381; f. 1800; classical and contemporary music, music books: *Musikwissenschaftliche Studienbibliothek Peters, Peters-Textbücher*; Dir N. MOLKENBUR.

VEB Verlag Enzyklopädie Leipzig: 7010 Leipzig, Gerichtsweg 26; tel. 7801; telex 512773; f. 1956; dictionaries, foreign language text-books, German for foreigners; Dir H. BÄHRING.

Eulenspiegel, Verlag für Satire und Humor: 1080 Berlin, Kronenstr. 73-74; tel. 2202126; f. 1954; humour, satire, caricature, cartoons; Dir W. SELLIN.

Evangelische Haupt-Bibelgesellschaft zu Berlin: 1040 Berlin, Ziegelstr. 30; f. 1814; tel. 2837191; religion; Dir K. WEBER.

Evangelische Verlagsanstalt GmbH: 1040 Berlin, Ziegelstr. 30; tel. 28370; f. 1946; religion; Dir Dr S. BRÄUER.

VEB Fachbuchverlag Leipzig: 7031 Leipzig, Karl-Heine-Str. 16, Postfach 67; tel. 49500; telex 51451; f. 1949; mathematics, physics and technical, basic sciences, textiles, commerce, printing, catering, etc, and technical periodicals; Dir E. WALTER.

VEB Gustav Fischer Verlag: 6900 Jena, Villengang 2; tel. 27332; telex 5886976; f. 1878; biological science, human and veterinary medicine; Dir Dr D. KÜNZEL.

VEB Fotokinoverlag Leipzig: 7031 Leipzig, Karl-Heine-Str. 16, Postfach 67; tel. 49500; telex 51451; f. 1957; books on photography, cinematography and periodicals; Dir Dr E. WALTER.

Verlag für die Frau: 7010 Leipzig, Friedrich-Ebert-Str. 76-78; tel. 71790; telex 51773; f. 1946; women's magazines and books, fashion, household, family, hobby, hand-coloured art prints; Dir E. KONECNY.

Greifenverlag: 6820 Rudolstadt, Heidecksburg, Postfach 142; tel. 22085; f. 1919; belles-lettres; Dir Dr URSULA STEINHAUSSEN.

VEB Harth Musik Verlag: 7010 Leipzig, Karl-Liebknecht-Str. 12; tel. 312612; f. 1946; Dir RITA PREISS.

Henschelverlag Kunst und Gesellschaft: 1040 Berlin, Oranienburgerstr. 67; tel. 28790; telex 112302; f. 1945; stage, music, literature, film, art; Dir K. MITTELSTÄDT.

VEB Hermann Haack Geographisch-Kartographische Anstalt Gotha: 5800 Gotha, Justus-Perthes-Str. 3-9; tel. 3872; telex 6185333; f. 1785; maps, atlases, geographical and cartographical books and periodicals; Dir M. HOFFMANN.

THE GERMAN DEMOCRATIC REPUBLIC

VEB Hinstorff Verlag Rostock: 2500 Rostock, Lagerstr. 7; tel. 34441; f. 1831; German and north European literature, regional literature, maritime literature; Dir H. FAUTH.

S. Hirzel Verlag: 7010 Leipzig, Sternwartenstr. 8; tel. 282263; f. 1853; medicine, veterinary medicine, natural sciences, agronomic sciences, intellectual sciences, periodicals, review, *Deutsches Wörterbuch* von J. und W. Grimm; Dir H. KRATZ.

VEB Friedrich Hofmeister Musikverlag: 7010 Leipzig, Karlstr. 10; tel. 7351; f. 1807; classical, contemporary, vocal and folk music; Dir Dr G. HEMPEL.

Insel-Verlag Anton Kippenberg: 7022 Leipzig, Mottelerstr. 8; tel. 58726; f. 1899; Insel library; world literature, classics, arts; Dir R. LINKS.

Verlag Junge Welt: 1026 Berlin, Postfach 43; tel. 22330; telex 114483; f. 1952; books and periodicals for children and young people; Dir M. RUCHT.

Gustav Kiepenheuer Verlag: 7022 Leipzig, Mottelerstr. 8; tel. 58726; f. 1909; general; Gustav-Kiepenheuer library; literature, history, arts; Dir R. LINKS.

Kinderbuchverlag: 1080 Berlin, Behrenstr. 40–41; tel. 20933200; Postfach 1225; f. 1949; children's books; Dir A. HEMPEL.

Koehler & Amelang: 7010 Leipzig, Hainstr. 2; tel. 282379; f. 1925; history, history of culture and art, literary history, theology; Dir Prof. Dr H. FAENSEN.

VEB Verlag der Kunst: 8019 Dresden, Spenerstr. 21; tel. 34486; f. 1952; art books and reproductions; Dir Dr K. SELBIG.

VEB Lied der Zeit, Musikverlag: 1020 Berlin, Rosa-Luxemburgstr. 41; tel. 2825081; f. 1954; dance, brass band and light music, sheet-music, musical comedies, books on music, children's books, almanacs, posters; autographs; Dir D. PREISS.

Paul List Verlag: 7022 Leipzig, Mottelerstr. 8; tel. 58726; f. 1894; literature; Dir R. LINKS.

Militärverlag der DDR: 1055 Berlin, Storkower Str. 158, Postfach 46 551; tel. 4300618; telex 112673; f. 1956; military topics, fiction.

Mitteldeutscher Verlag Halle-Leipzig: 4010 Halle/Saale, Postfach 295, Thälmannplatz 2; tel. 873544; f. 1946; general fiction and non-fiction; Man. Dir Dr EBERHARD GÜNTHER.

Buchverlag Der Morgen: 1170 Berlin, Seelenbinderstr. 152; tel. 6504151; telex 6504151; f. 1958; belles-lettres, politics; Dir Dr W. TENZLER.

Verlag der Nation: 1040 Berlin, Friedrichstr. 113; tel. 28390; f. 1948; literature, politics, biographies, paperbacks; Dir H.-O. LECHT.

Verlag Das Neue Berlin: 1080 Berlin, Kronenstr. 73–74; tel. 2202126; f. 1946; crime, adventure, science fiction; Dir W. SELLIN.

Verlag Neues Leben: 1080 Berlin, Behrenstr. 40–41; tel. 20932765; telex 114781; f. 1946; books for young people and fiction; Dir RUDOLF CHOWANETZ.

Verlag Neue Musik: 1086 Berlin, Leipziger Str. 26; tel. 2202051; f. 1957; music and literature on music; Dir FERDINAND HIRSCH.

Neumann Verlag: 7010 Leipzig, Salomonstr. 26–28; tel. 7426; f. 1946; books on gardening, forestry, agriculture, fishing, nature.

VEB Postreiter-Verlag: 4020 Halle/Saale, Ernst-Toller-Str. 18; tel. 28097; f. 1947; children's books; Dir CH. KUPFER.

Prisma-Verlag Zenner und Gürchott: 7010 Leipzig, Leibnizstr. 10; tel. 281411; f. 1957; popular science, art history, novels; Dirs KLAUS ZENNER, FRITZ GÜRCHOTT.

VEB Pro Musica Verlag: 7010 Leipzig, Karl-Liebknecht-Str. 12; tel. 312612; f. 1946; Dir RITA PREISS.

VEB Räthgloben-Verlag Leipzig: 7033 Leipzig, Raimundstr. 14; tel. 475169; telex 512923; f. 1917; Dir H. GOESCHEL.

Verlag Philipp Reclam Jun.: 7031 Leipzig, Nonnenstr. 38; tel. 474501; f. 1828; *Reclams Universal-Bibliothek:* pocket-book series (including philosophy, history and culture, language and literature, biographies) and works of world literature in attractive format; Dir Prof. Dr R. OPITZ.

Rütten & Loening Berlin: 1080 Berlin, Französische Str. 32; f. 1844; tel. 2202421; telex 114739; belles-lettres, literary criticism magazines; Dir ELMAR FABER.

VEB E. A. Seemann, Buch- und Kunstverlag: 7010 Leipzig, Jacobstr. 6; tel. 7736; f. 1858; art books and reproductions; Dir Dr R. WINKLER.

St Benno Verlag GmbH: 7033 Leipzig, Thüringerstr. 1–3; tel. 474161; f. 1951; Catholic publications; Dirs F.-J. CORDIER, C. BOCKISCH.

Seven Seas Publishers: 1086 Berlin, POB 1221, Glinkastr. 13–15; tel. 2202851; paperbacks, books by English language writers, and English translations of modern GDR authors.

Sportverlag: 1086 Berlin, Neustädtische Kirchstr. 15, Postfach 1218; tel. 22120; telex 0112853; f. 1947; sports, recreation, technical, sport education, reports; Dir H. SCHUBERT.

VEB Verlag Technik: 1020 Berlin, Oranienburgerstr. 13–14, Postfach 201; tel. 28700; telex 112228; f. 1946; technical books, dictionaries and periodicals; Dir K. HIERONIMUS.

BSB B.G. Teubner Verlagsgesellschaft Leipzig: 7010 Leipzig, Sternwartenstr. 8, Postfach 930; tel. 293158; telex 512381; f. 1811; mathematics, physics, science, technology, classical philology, biography, history of science; Dir H. KRATZ.

VEB Georg Thieme: 7010 Leipzig, Hainstr. 17–19; tel. 27332; telex 5886176; f. 1886; medicine, bioscience; Dir Dr D. KÜNZEL.

VEB Tourist Verlag: 1020 Berlin, Neue Grünstr. 17; tel. 2071018; telex 114488; f. 1977; maps, tourist guides and travel books; Dir Dr R. PUSTKOWSKI.

Transpress VEB Verlag für Verkehrswesen: 1086 Berlin, Französische Str. 13–14; tel. 20410; telex 112229; f. 1960; specialized literature on transport, telecommunications, philately, numismatics; Dir Dr H. BÖTTCHER.

Tribüne, Verlag und Druckereien des FDGB: 1193 Berlin, Am Treptower Park 28–30; tel. 27100; telex 112611; f. 1945; trade union publications, general literature; Dir F. MÖLLER.

Union Verlag: 1080 Berlin, Charlottenstr. 79; tel. 2202711; telex 114767; f. 1951; publications of the Christlich-Demokratische Union Deutschlands; literature, art; Dir KLAUS-PETER GERHARDT.

Urania-Verlag Leipzig/Jena/Berlin: 7010 Leipzig, Salomonstr. 26–28, Postfach 969; tel. 7426; f. 1924; natural and social sciences, cultural history, hobbies; Dir H. BULLAN.

VEB Verlage für Medizin und Biologie, Berlin-Leipzig-Jena: 1020 Berlin, Neue Grünstr. 18; tel. 2700516; telex 114488; f. 1952; medicine, biology and veterinarian medicine; 8 assoc. companies; Dir Dr D. KÜNZEL.

Verlag Volk und Welt: 1086 Berlin, Postfach 1221, Glinkastr. 13–15; tel. 2202851; f. 1947; 20th-century international fiction, drama and poetry; Dir J. GRUNER.

Volk und Wissen Volkseigener Verlag: 1086 Berlin, Krausenstr. 50, Am Spittelmarkt; tel. 20430; telex 112181; f. 1945; adult education; Dir R. WEBER.

Verlag Die Wirtschaft: 1055 Berlin, Am Friedrichshain 22; tel. 43870; telex 114566; f. 1946; specialist books, brochures and periodicals on economics, industrial management, statistics, economic planning, data processing, work study, trade; Dir D. GRÜNEBERG.

Verlag Zeit im Bild: 8012 Dresden, Postfach 61; tel. 48640; telex 2291; f. 1946; periodicals, politics, economics, foreign language; Man. K.-H. KAMENZ.

Zentralantiquariat der DDR, Reprint-Verlag: 7010 Leipzig, Talstr. 29; tel. 295808; telex 512684; f. 1964; reprints; Dir H. KAZIMIREK.

A. Ziemsen Verlag: 4600 Wittenberg Lutherstadt, Lucas-Cranach-Str. 21; tel. 2528; f. 1902; works on biology.

Government Publishing House

Staatsverlag der DDR: 1086 Berlin, Otto-Grotewohl-Str. 17; tel. 2336336; telex 1152344; f. 1963; official publications, law, history, economics, politics; Dir R. TIETZ.

PUBLISHERS' ORGANIZATION

Börsenverein der Deutschen Buchhändler zu Leipzig (Association of German Democratic Republic Publishers and Booksellers in Leipzig): 7010 Leipzig, Gerichtsweg 26, POB 146; tel. 293851; telex 512773; f. 1825; Chair. JÜRGEN GRUNER; Dir H. BAIER.

Radio and Television

Radio licences issued totalled 6,647,000 and television licences 6,079,000 in 1985.

RADIO

Staatliches Komitee für Rundfunk beim Ministerrat der DDR (State Committee for Radio Broadcasting): 1160 Berlin, Nalepastr. 18–50; tel. 6360; telex 112276; Chair. ACHIM BECKER; the co-ordinating body of all radio organizations in the GDR.

Home Service

Berliner Rundfunk: 1160 Berlin, Nalepastr. 18–50; tel. 6360; telex 112276; 16 medium wave and 11 VHF transmitters broadcasting 142 hours a week; Dir HANNES POTTHAST.

Radio DDR: 1160 Berlin, Nalepastr. 18–50; tel. 6360; telex 112276; 11 medium wave and VHF transmitters, broadcasting 168 hours a week on Programme I, 104 hours a week on Programme II and 329 hours a week on regional programmes; Dir ROLF SCHMIDT.

Stimme der DDR: 1160 Berlin, Nalepastr. 18–50; tel. 6360; telex 112276; one long wave, two medium wave, two short wave and 10 VHF transmitters broadcasting 168 hours a week; Dir MARTIN RADMANN.

External Service

Radio Berlin International: 1160 Berlin, Nalepastr. 18–50; tel. 6360; telex 112276; broadcasts in 11 languages (Arabic, Danish, English, French, German, Hindi, Italian, Portuguese, Spanish, Swahili and Swedish) on one medium wave and 11 short wave transmitters; Dir KLAUS FISCHER.

Radio Volga: 15 Potsdam, Menzelstr. 5; operates one 200 kW transmitter on 1141 metres for Soviet forces in the GDR; broadcasts for 18 hours a day with its own Russian language programmes and relays from Radio Moscow.

TELEVISION

About 80% of East Germans live in areas where they can receive television programmes from the Federal Republic. It is estimated that West German current affairs programmes are seen by about 40%, some light entertainment by 70% and news programmes by as many as 80% of East German viewers.

Staatliches Komitee für Fernsehen (State Committee for Television Broadcasting): 1199 Berlin-Adlershof, Rudower Chaussee 3; tel. 6310; telex 112885; Chair. HEINZ ADAMECK; supervises:

Fernsehen der DDR: 1199 Berlin-Adlershof, Rudower Chaussee 3; tel. 6310; telex 112885; member of International Radio and Television Organization since 1960. There are 13 transmitters, which in 1984 broadcast 96 hours a week on Programme I (90 hours in colour) and 61 hours a week on Programme II (54 hours in colour); Programme Dir HORST SAUER; Technical Dir ROLF KRAMER; Dir of International Relations Dr KURT OTTERSBERG.

Finance

(cap. = capital; res = reserves; m. = million; M. = Marks)

BANKS

Central Bank

Staatsbank der Deutschen Demokratischen Republik (State Bank of the GDR): 1086 Berlin, Charlottenstr. 33–33A; tel. 23230; telex 114671; f. 1948; capital stock 1,500m. M.; Pres. HORST KAMINSKY; Vice-Pres. HANS TAUT.

Other Banks

Bank für Landwirtschaft und Nahrungsgüterwirtschaft der DDR: 108 Berlin, Clara-Zetkin-Str. 37; f. 1951; cap. 250m. M.; credits for agricultural and co-operative organizations; Pres. GÜNTHER SCHMIDT; Vice-Pres. HANS WOLFF.

Deutsche Aussenhandelsbank AG: 1080 Berlin, Unter den Linden 24–30; tel. 22870; telex 114411; f. 1966; responsible for the carrying out of all business connected with export, import and transit trade; cap. 1,500m. M., res 1,785m. M., dep. 69,753.6m. M. (Dec. 1987); Pres. Dr WERNER POLZE; Vice-Pres. Prof. Dr FRIEDMAR JOHN.

Deutsche Handelsbank AG: 1080 Berlin, Behrenstr. 22; tel. 2202911; telex 114665; f. 1956; cap. 440m., res 15,670m., dep. 15,072m. M. (Dec. 1987); conducts banking business with regard to import, export and transit trade; Gen. Man. FEODOR ZIESCHE; Deputy Gen. Mans HEINRICH GRAMER, INGEBORG KLEIN.

INSURANCE

Auslands- und Rückversicherungs-AG der DDR (DARAG): 1020 Berlin, Inselstr. 1B; tel. 2700522; telex 114402; f. 1957; marine and general insurances of all kinds, re-insurance, non-payment insurance; Chair. GÜNTER HEIN; Gen. Man. L. THOMAS.

Staatliche Versicherung der DDR: 1026 Berlin, Breite Str. 30–31; tel. 21620; telex 115043; f. 1952; state organization for property, liability, and personal insurance; Gen. Man. GÜNTER HEIN.

Trade and Industry

Foreign trade is a state monopoly. Trade organizations conduct import and export transactions for particular sectors of industry.

Ministerium für Aussenhandel (Ministry of Foreign Trade): 1080 Berlin, Unter den Linden 44/60; tel. 230; telex 1152361.

TRADE CENTRE

Internationales Handelszentrum (International Trade Centre): 1086 Berlin, Friedrichstr.; tel. 20960; telex 114381; opened 1978; offices of foreign enterprises accredited in the GDR; seat of the GDR Association of Foreign Trade Agencies and Brokers and its member organizations; provision of rooms and services for conferences, symposia, exhibitions and negotiations for the promotion of international trade.

CHAMBER OF FOREIGN TRADE

Kammer für Aussenhandel der Deutschen Demokratischen Republik: 1100 Berlin, Schönholzer Str. 10–11; tel. 48220; telex 114840; f. 1952; members of the Chamber are the foreign trade corporations, major industrial enterprises and transport, banking and insurance institutions; Pres. HANS-JOACHIM LEMNITZER.

FOREIGN TRADE ORGANIZATIONS

Baukema Export/Import: 1080 Berlin, Mohrenstr. 53–54; tel. 2240; telex 112248; building machines, cranes, machinery and equipment for the production of building material machines, foundry plant.

Berliner Import-Export-Gesellschaft mbH: 1185 Berlin, Bruno-Taut-Str. 8; tel. 68120; telex 113284; consumer goods, metal processing industry and building industry products.

Buchexport: 7010 Leipzig, Leninstr. 16; tel. 71370; telex 51678; books, periodicals, music, records, reproductions, calendars, globes, maps, atlases, etc.

Chemieanlagen Export/Import: 1055 Berlin, Storkower Str. 120; tel. 43520; telex 112916; export of plant and machinery for the chemical industry, equipment for special fields of foodstuffs sector.

Chemie-Export-Import: 1055 Berlin, Storkower Str. 133; tel. 43220; telex 112171; chemicals, incl. household chemicals and plastics, photographic materials, tyres, etc.

DEFA-Aussenhandel: 1058 Berlin, Milastr. 2; tel. 4400801; telex 114511; films.

Demusa: 9652 Klingenthal, Leninstr. 133; tel. 2341; telex 77920; musical instruments, toys, paint brushes, writing equipment, artists' materials, jewellery, fancy goods, arts and crafts.

Elektronik Export-Import: 1026 Berlin, Alexanderplatz 6; tel. 2180; telex 114721; time-measuring and meteorological instruments, electronic components, freeze drying.

Elektrotechnik Export-Import: 1026 Berlin, Alexanderplatz 6; tel. 2180; telex 115061; electrical installations for industry, radio, railways.

Fischimpex Rostock: 2510 Rostock 5, Postfach 42; tel. 8100; telex 31309; export and import of fish and fish products; commercial relations in all fields of the fishing industry, fishing operations, scientific-technical services, licences.

Fortschritt Landmaschinen Export-Import: 1185 Berlin, Bruno-Taut-Str. 4; tel. 68220; telex 112522-527; agricultural machinery, machines for foodstuffs industry.

Fruchtimex: 1020 Berlin, Schicklerstr. 7; tel. 21480; telex 114684; fresh fruit and vegetables, raw products for children's food.

Genussmittel Import-Export: 1086 Berlin, Mohrenstr. 1; tel. 2202811; telex 112353; exports and imports foodstuffs, spices, brewing malt, wines and spirits; also imports coffee, cocoa, tea, tobacco.

GERMED-export-import: 1199 Berlin, Glienicker Weg 125–127; tel. 6790; telex 112740; medicines, drugs, dressing materials, plaster, chemicals.

Glas-Keramik: 1080 Berlin, Kronenstr. 19–19A; tel. 20570; telex 114661; glass and glass products, porcelain, earthenware.

Heim-Electric Export-Import: 1026 Berlin, Alexanderplatz 6; tel. 2180; telex 0114555; electric household appliances, equipment for engineering, electronics and electric industry, cameras, entertainment electronics, electroceramics, electric installation material, light fittings, electrical equipment for motor vehicles and bicycles.

Holz und Papier Export-Import: 1080 Berlin, Krausenstr. 35–36; tel. 20750; telex 112235; exports furniture and upholstery; imports timber, veneers, wicker, cellulose, paper.

Industrieanlagen-Import: 1086 Berlin, Mauerstr. 83–84; tel. 22890; telex 112214; import of complete plant and processes for chemical industry, metallurgy, power generation, glassware, ceramics, building materials, process instrumentation, control engineering, electronics and telecommunication engineering, automotive industry.

Intercontrol GmbH: 1080 Berlin, Clara-Zetkin-Str. 112–114; tel. 22860; telex 114852; controls commercial goods of all types, inspection, supervision, expert opinions, analyses.

Interpelz: 7010 Leipzig, Nikolaistr. 13–25; tel. 71330; telex 51477; leather goods, shoes, furs and hides.

Interwerbung GmbH: 1157 Berlin, Hermann-Duncker-Str. 89, Postfach 230; tel. 5090981; telex 112106; advisory organization for advertising, including exhibitions for foreigners in the GDR.

THE GERMAN DEMOCRATIC REPUBLIC

Intrac Handelsgesellschaft mbH: 1100 Berlin, Pestalozzistr. 5–8; tel. 4840; telex 114923; metals, ores, mineral oil and oil products.

Isocommerz GmbH: 1115 Berlin, Lindenberger Weg 70; tel. 3400111; telex 113148; f. 1964; export of radioactive and stable isotopes, phosphors, special inorganic chemicals; Dir Dr G. EWALD.

Kali-Bergbau: 1080 Berlin, Otto-Nuschke-Str. 55; tel. 20450; telex 114471; export of fertilizers, agricultural chemicals and mineral salts; imports of barytes, etc.

Kohle-Energie Export-Import: 1080 Berlin, Johannes-Dieckmann-Str. 26; tel. 20450; telex 114470; export and import of coal, natural gas, lignite and mixed fuels, electric energy.

Kunst und Antiquitäten GmbH: 1080 Berlin, Französische Str. 15; tel. 0220682; telex 158538; art and antiquities.

Limex-Bau-Export-Import: 1020 Berlin, Neue Jakobstr. 5–7; tel. 2737; telex 114968; metal and concrete constructions and building material; responsible for scientific-technological co-operation with socialist and developing countries on the basis of state orders.

Metallurgiehandel: 1054 Berlin, Brunnenstr. 188–190; tel. 28920; telex 115123; steel and other metals.

MLW intermed-export-import: 1020 Berlin, Schicklerstr. 5–7; Postfach 17; tel. 21480; telex 114571; medical equipment and supplies (including public health service), technical education equipment, equipment for industrial and agricultural research.

Nahrung Export-Import: 1020 Berlin, Schicklerstr. 5–7; tel. 21480; telex 114892; seeds, sugar, starch, dairy products, meat, fish, live animals.

VEB Philatelie Wermsdorf: 7264 Wermsdorf, Grüner Weg 4A, Postfach; tel. 216; telex 518871; wholesale import and export of stamps, stamp collections and special issues.

Polygraph Export/Import: 1080 Berlin, Friedrichstr. 61; tel. 2000601; telex 112310; machinery for the printing industry.

Robotron Export/Import: 1080 Berlin, Friedrichstrasse 61; tel. 5400130; telex 112311; exports data-processing systems.

Schienenfahrzeuge Export/Import: 1100 Berlin, Ötztalerstr. 5; tel. 48040; telex 114322; passenger coaches, compartment wagons, sleeping-cars, restaurant cars, luggage vans, long distance carriages, etc.

Schiffscommerz: 2500 Rostock, Doberaner Str. 44–47; tel. 3670; telex 31355; cargo vessels, fishing vessels, special ships and marine machinery and equipment.

SKET Export/Import: 1086 Berlin, Johannes-Dieckmann-Str. 7–9; tel. 2240; telex 112693; cement plants and equipment, plants for the production of cables and wire ropes.

Spielwaren und Sportartikel Export-Import: 1080 Berlin, Charlottenstr. 46; tel. 22830; telex 112797; export and import of boats, camping, sports and fishing equipment, arts and craft products, toys and prams.

TAKRAF Export/Import: 1080 Berlin, Mohrenstr. 53–54; tel. 2240; telex 112347; cranes, open-cast mining equipment, small lifting appliances.

Technocommerz: 1086 Berlin, Johannes-Dieckmann-Str. 11–13; tel. 2240; telex 114977; technical equipment including air-conditioning, refrigeration plants, pumps, compressors, diesel engines and diesel-driven generating sets, ventilation, hydraulic sets and equipment, gearings, couplings, fittings and valves for all branches of industry.

Textil Commerz: 1080 Berlin, Unter den Linden 62–68, Postfach 1206; tel. 22610; telex 112816; fabrics, clothing, household linen, carpets, upholstery, haberdashery.

TEXTIMA-Export-Import: 1086 Berlin, Johannes-Dieckmann-Str. 11–13; tel. 2240; telex 114118; machinery and plants for the textile industry.

Transportmaschinen Export-Import: 1086 Berlin, Johannes-Dieckmann-Str. 11–13; tel. 2240; telex 114494; lorries, cars, motor-cycles, scooters, spare parts, components and accessories.

Union Haushaltgeräte Export-Import: 1080 Berlin, Wilhelm-Külz-Str. 46, Postfach 1203; tel. 2200101; telex 115193; f. 1965; tools, metalware, household appliances.

Verpackung und Bürobedarf Export/Import: 7010 Leipzig, Nikolaistr. 15–25, Postfach 806; tel. 7974370; telex 512594; export and import of packing materials, cardboard, paper, foil, wallpapers, labels, stationery, school and office supplies.

WMW-Export-Import: 1040 Berlin, Chausseestr. 111–112; tel. 28900; telex 112804; exports machine tools.

WUNEX Wälzlager und Normteile Export/Import: 9010 Karl-Marx-Stadt, Reichenhainer Str. 31–33, Postfach 1045; tel. 57060; telex 07279; export and import of roller bearings, fasteners and wire products.

Kombinat VEB Carl Zeiss JENA: 6900 Jena, Carl-Zeiss-Str. 1; tel. 832246; telex 587442; f. 1846; exports instruments and instrument systems for industrial research, particularly in optics.

Zellstoff und Papier Export/Import: 1080 Berlin, Mauerstr. 77; tel. 20750; telex 114523; paper, carton, cellulose.

Zentral-Kommerz GmbH: 1100 Berlin, Pestalozzistr. 5–8; tel. 4840; telex 114981; agricultural products, foodstuffs, secondary raw materials.

Zimex GmbH: 7010 Leipzig, Goldschmidtstr. 29; tel. 71870; telex 51492; exports books, brochures, greetings cards, prints, philatelic items, folders, albums, playing cards, etc.

NATIONALIZED INDUSTRY

The greater part of industry is organized in Volkseigene Betriebe (VEBs—nationally-owned enterprises). About 80% of workers are employed in state enterprises, 15% in co-operatives, 1% in semi-state enterprises and less than 5% in private concerns. The following are some of the major industrial combines:

VEB Kombinat Luft- und Kältetechnik: 8080 Dresden; telex 2414; aero-technical plant and equipment.

VEB Kombinat NAGEMA: 8045 Dresden; tel. 22520; telex 2443; food processing machinery; about 30 factories and 21,000 employees.

VEB Leuna-Werke 'Walter Ulbricht': 4220 Leuna; telex 4221; chemicals; about 30,000 employees.

VEB Schwermaschinenbau-Kombinat 'Ernst Thälmann' Magdeburg (SKET): 3011 Magdeburg; telex 8241; rolling mills, cement, wire and cables, vegetable oil, minerals; about 28,000 employees.

VEB Werkzeugmaschinenkombinat 'Fritz Heckert': 9030 Karl-Marx-Stadt, Jagdschänkenstr. 17; tel. 8090; telex 07393; machine tools, machining systems, lubricators, fixtures, castings, industrial plants.

MANUFACTURERS' ASSOCIATIONS

Vereinigungen volkseigener Betriebe der DDR (Associations of Nationally Owned Enterprises): each major industry has its own Association, and the foreign trade enterprises co-operate closely with them. The managements of the Associations share responsibility with the foreign trade enterprises for the export of modern and top quality products, for market research, for advising customers and for organizing a number of services.

TRADE UNIONS

Freier Deutscher Gewerkschaftsbund (FDGB) (Confederation of Free German Trade Unions): 1026 Berlin, Märkisches Ufer 54; tel. 27820; telex 113011; f. 1945; Chair. HARRY TISCH; 9.6m. mems.

The following unions are affiliated to the FDGB:

Agricultural, Food Processing and Forestry Workers' Union: 1086 Berlin, Unter den Linden 15; tel. 2000131; telex 113218; f. 1968; Pres. HORST ZIMMERMANN; 650,000 mems.

Industrial Union of Building and Wood Workers: 1026 Berlin, Fritz-Heckert-Str. 70; tel. 27820; telex 113011; f. 1950; Pres. LOTHAR LINDNER; 950,000 mems.

Union of Central and Local Government Employees and Municipal Workers: 1026 Berlin, Fritz-Heckert-Str. 70; tel. 27820; telex 113011; f. 1945; Pres. ROLF HÖSSELBARTH; 860,000 mems.

Industrial Union of Chemical, Glass and Ceramic Workers: 4020 Halle/Saale, Rudolf-Breitscheid-Str. 9; tel. 38011; f. 1946; Pres. EDITH WEBER; 530,000 mems.

Cultural Workers' Union: 1026 Berlin, Fritz-Heckert-Str. 70; tel. 27820; telex 113011; f. 1949; Pres. HERBERT BISCHOFF; 81,000 mems.

Union of Distributive, Catering, Food and Allied Products Workers: 1086 Berlin, Unter den Linden 15; tel. 2000131; telex 113218; f. 1958; Pres. HANNELORE SCHULZ; 1.2m. mems.

Health Workers' Union: 1026 Berlin, Fritz-Heckert Str. 70; tel. 27820; telex 113011; f. 1949; Pres. Dr ELFRIEDE GERBOTH; 640,000 mems.

Trade Union of Instruction and Education: 1086 Berlin, Unter den Linden 15; tel. 2000131; telex 113218; f. 1946; teachers and educational workers; Pres. HELGA LABS; 570,000 mems.

Industrial Union of Metal Workers: 1026 Berlin, Fritz-Heckert-Str. 70; tel. 27820; telex 113011; f. 1946; Pres. GERHARD NENNSTIEL; 1.8m. mems.

Industrial Union of Mine and Energy Workers: 4073 Halle/Saale, Merseburger Str. 135; tel. 48272; telex 04337; f. 1963; Pres. GÜNTHER WOLF; 471,000 mems.

Industrial Union of Printing and Paper Workers: 1086 Berlin, Unter den Linden 15; tel. 2000131; telex 113218; f. 1946; Pres. WERNER PEPLOWSKI; 153,000 mems.

Scientific Workers' Union: 1086 Berlin, Unter den Linden 15; tel. 2000131; telex 113218; f. 1953; Pres. Dr ROLF RINKE; 185,000 mems.

THE GERMAN DEMOCRATIC REPUBLIC

Industrial Union of Textile, Clothing and Leather Workers: 1026 Berlin, Fritz-Heckert-Str. 70; tel. 27820; telex 113011; f. 1950; Pres. ANNELIE UNGAR; 601,000 mems.

Industrial Union of Transport and Communications Workers: 1086 Berlin, Unter den Linden 15; tel. 2000131; telex 113218; f. 1963; Pres. KARL KALAUCH; 799,000 mems.

TRADE FAIR

International Leipzig Trade Fair: 7010 Leipzig, Leipziger Messeamt, Markt 11-15, Postfach 720; tel. 71810; telex 512294; 9,000 exhibitors from all over the world in spring, 6,000 exhibitors in autumn; 200 issuing offices for Fair tickets in principal cities of the world; capital and consumer goods; twice a year in March and September; Dir-Gen. SIEGFRIED FISCHER.

Transport

Ministerium für Verkehrswesen (Ministry of Transport): Ministerrat der DDR, 1086 Berlin, Vossstr. 33; tel. 2322881; telex 112250; controls all transport.

RAILWAYS

In 1987 the total length of track was 14,008 km, of which some 3,092 km were electrified. There were also 275 km of narrow gauge.

Deutsche Reichsbahn: 1086 Berlin, Vossstr. 33; under the auspices of the Ministry of Transport.

ROADS

In 1987 there were 1,855 km of motorways, 11,265 km of trunk roads, 34,023 km of district roads and 77,400 km of roads in towns and villages (Kommunalstrassen).

Hauptverwaltung Strassenwesen (Dept of Public Roads and Motorways): 1086 Berlin, Vossstr. 33.

Hauptverwaltung des Kraftverkehrs (Dept of Public Passenger and Goods Road Transport): 1086 Berlin, Vossstr. 33.

INLAND WATERWAYS

Hauptabteilung Binnenschiffahrt und Wasserstrassen (Dept of Inland Shipping and Waterways): 1086 Berlin, Vossstr. 33; controls all inland navigation; there were 2,319 km of navigable waterways in 1986.

Wasserstrassenaufsichtsamt der DDR (Supervisory Board of Inland Navigation and Waterways): 1020 Berlin, Poststr. 21-22; telex 114967; Dir ADOLF MEIER.

VE Kombinat Binnenschiffahrt und Wasserstrassen: 1017 Berlin, Alt Stralau 55-58; tel. 55230; telex 112703; Dir-Gen. Dr WOLFGANG HETTLER.

Affiliated:

VEB Binnenreederei im VE Kombinat Binnenschifffahrt und Wasserstrassen (Inland Shipping Company): 1017 Berlin, Alt Stralau 55-58; tel. 55230; telex 112703.

VEB Binnenhäfen 'Mittelelbe': 3010 Magdeburg, Wittenberger Str. 17.

VEB Binnenhäfen 'Oberelbe': 8012 Dresden, Magdeburger Str. 58.

VEB Binnenhäfen 'Oder': 1220 Eisenhüttenstadt, Glashüttenstr.; telex 168444.

VEB Forschungsanstalt für Schiffahrt, Wasser- und Grundbau: 1017 Berlin, Alt Stralau 44; tel. 55230; telex 112703.

VEB Schiffsreparaturwerften: 1017 Berlin, Alt Stralau 55-58.

VEB Wasserstrassenbau: 1160 Berlin, Goethestr. 16; tel. 6352316.

VEB Wasserstrassenbetrieb und -unterhaltung Eberswalde: 1300 Eberswalde/Finow, Hans-Beimler-Str. 1.

VEB Wasserstrassenbetrieb und -unterhaltung Magdeburg: 3010 Magdeburg, Wallstr. 19-20.

SHIPPING

Rostock is the principal seaport. In 1987 the GDR's merchant fleet had 171 ships (excluding passenger vessels), with a total capacity of about 1.8m. dwt.

DDR-Schiffs-Revision und -Klassifikation: 1615 Zeuthen, Eichenallee 12; tel. 2633; telex 158721; f. 1950; registration of shipping, survey of the technical safety of ships and classification; Man. Dir Prof. Dr GÜNTER BOSSOW.

Hauptverwaltung des Seeverkehrs (Dept of Merchant Fleet and Sea-Ports): 1086 Berlin, Vossstr. 33.

Seefahrtsamt der DDR (Board of Navigation and Maritime Affairs of the GDR): 2500 Rostock, Patriotischer Weg 120; telex 31134; Dir Capt. GERD HAUSSMANN.

Seekammer der DDR (Naval Court of the GDR): 2500 Rostock, Patriotischer Weg 120; tel. 3832363; Chair. Capt. DIETER RAPPHAHN.

Tallierungs-GmbH—Ladungskontrollunternehmen der DDR: 2500 Rostock-Überseehafen; tallying, checking, weighing, surveying, draught measurement, inspection and expertise; Dir MARGOT RECKLING.

VE Kombinat Deutrans: 1086 Berlin, Otto-Grotewohl-Str. 25, Postfach 1243; tel. 2200121; telex 114631; international forwarding enterprise; Dir-Gen. RAINER SCHWABE.

VE Kombinat Seeverkehr und Hafenwirtschaft—Deutfracht/Seereederei: 2500 Rostock-Überseehafen; tel. 3660; telex 31381; comprises various shipping and harbour enterprises; Dir-Gen. ARTUR MAUL.

VEB Bagger-, Bugsier- und Bergungsreederei: 2530 Rostock, An der See 14; tel. 8152727; telex 31441318; dredging, towage, salvage; Dir WOLFGANG SOYK.

VEB Deutfracht/Seereederei: 2500 Rostock-Überseehafen; telex 31139; shipping company; 167 ships with about 1.7m. dwt, bulk carriers, liner ships, cargo trailer ships, refrigeration ships, tankers; Dir-Gen. ARTUR MAUL.

VEB Schiffsmaklerei: 2500 Rostock, Strandstr. 25; tel. 383365; telex 31265; f. 1958; international clearing and liner agency; agencies at Rostock, Wismar, Stralsund; branch office in Berlin; Dir EDUARD ZIMMERMANN.

VEB Schiffsversorgung Rostock: 2500 Rostock-Überseehafen; tel. 3667000; telex 31114; f. 1959; general ship supplies, provisions, technical equipment, nautical charts and handbooks, duty-free goods; Dir GERHARD BECKMANN.

VEB Seehafen Rostock (Overseas port, Rostock): 2500 Rostock-Überseehafen; telex 31264; Dir DIETER NOLL.

VEB Seehafen Stralsund (Stralsund seaport): 2300 Stralsund, Hafenstr. 15; tel. 692360; telex 317350; Dir HEINZ HAPP.

VEB Seehafen Wismar (Wismar seaport): 2400 Wismar; telex 318882; Dir KLAUS BODDIN.

CIVIL AVIATION

Interflug, Gesellschaft für internationalen Flugverkehr mbH: 1189 Berlin-Schönefeld; tel. 6720; telex 112891; f. 1955; flights throughout Europe and to the Middle, Near and Far East, Africa and Central America; Pres. Dr KLAUS HENKES; fleet of IL-62, IL-18, and TU-134 aircraft; 3 Airbus A-310-330 on order (2 to be delivered in 1989).

There are international airports at Berlin-Schönefeld, Dresden, Erfurt and Leipzig.

Tourism

Tourism is promoted by the State Travel Bureau. The island of Rügen, off the Baltic coast, has considerable tourist traffic. The mountains of Thuringia and the Erzgebirge, on the Czech frontier, are much visited, both in summer and winter. In 1982 there were 1.5m. tourist arrivals at all accommodation establishments. In 1987 a total of 1,121,737 tourists visited the GDR through the State Travel Bureau.

Reisebüro der Deutschen Demokratischen Republik: 1026 Berlin, Alexanderplatz 5; tel. 2150; telex 114652; f. 1958; 120 branches in different towns; Dir-Gen. HORST DANNAT.

Atomic Energy

In 1986 there were two nuclear power plants in operation and nuclear power accounted for 9.5% of total electricity generation. The German Democratic Republic is a member of the International Atomic Energy Agency (IAEA).

Arbeitsstelle für Molekularelektronik (Institute for Molecular Electronics): 808 Dresden, Königsbrücker Landstr. 159; f. 1961; Dir Prof. Dr-Ing. WERNER HARTMANN.

Institut für Hochenergiephysik der Akademie der Wissenschaften der DDR (Research Institute of High Energy Physics of the GDR Academy of Sciences): 1615 Zeuthen, Platanenallee 6; tel. 6858001; telex 158770; f. 1952; Dir Prof. Dr K. LANIUS.

Isocommerz GmbH (Import and Export of Radioactive and Stable Isotopes): 1115 Berlin, Robert-Rössle-Str. 10; telex 113148; f. 1964; Dir Dr G. EWALD.

Ministerium für Wissenschaft und Technik (Ministry of Science and Technology): 1170 Berlin, Köpenickerstr. 325A; tel. 65760; telex 113070; f. 1955.

Staatliches Amt für Atomsicherheit und Strahlenschutz der DDR (Board of Nuclear Safety and Radiation Protection of the GDR): 1157 Berlin-Karlshorst, Waldowallee 117; tel. 5020; telex 112632; f. 1962; theoretical problems of radiation protection and nuclear safety; medical, biological and technical research; legislation and licensing; radiation protection monitoring in working areas and medical supervision; environmental protection including radioactive waste processing and disposal; nuclear safeguards; training courses for health physicists and physicians; Pres. Prof. Dr Georg Sitzlack.

VEB Kernkraftwerk (VEB Atomic Power Station): Rheinsberg/Mark; telex 318322; f. 1961; Dir Prof. Karl Ramsbusch; Technical Centre: Berlin-Pankow, Görschstr. 45–46; Dir Dipl.-Ing. Gerhard Teichler.

VEB Robotron-Messelektronik 'Otto Schön' Dresden: 8010 Dresden, Postfach 211; tel. 4870; telex 26068; Dir Dr A. Jugel.

Zentralinstitut für Festkörperphysik und Werkstofforschung der Akademie der Wissenschaften (Central Institute for Solid State Physics and Materials Research of the Academy of Sciences): 8027 Dresden, Helmholtzstr. 20; tel. 46590; telex 2131; f. 1969; Dir Prof. Dr Johannes Barthel.

Zentralinstitut für Isotopen- und Strahlenforschung der Akademie der Wissenschaften (Central Institute of Isotope and Radiation Research of the AdW): 7050 Leipzig, Permoserstr. 15; tel. 2392308; telex 512492; f. 1969; Dir Prof. Dr Dr Klaus Wetzel.

Zentralinstitut für Kernforschung der Akademie der Wissenschaften (Central Institute for Nuclear Research of the Academy of Sciences): 8051 Dresden, Postfach 19; tel. 5910; telex 2167; f. 1956; Dir Prof. Dr-Ing. Günter Flach.

THE FEDERAL REPUBLIC OF GERMANY AND WEST BERLIN

Introductory Survey

Location, Climate, Language, Religion, Flag, Capital

The Federal Republic of Germany lies in the heart of Europe. Its neighbours to the west are the Netherlands, Belgium, Luxembourg and France, to the south Switzerland and Austria, to the east Czechoslovakia and the German Democratic Republic, and to the north Denmark. The climate is temperate, with an average annual temperature of 9°C (48°F), although there are considerable variations between the North German lowlands and the Bavarian Alps. The language is German. Almost all citizens of the Federal Republic profess Christianity, and adherents are about equally divided between Protestants and Roman Catholics. The national flag (proportions 5 by 3) consists of three equal horizontal stripes, of black, red and gold. The seat of government is Bonn.

Recent History

After the defeat of the Third Reich in 1945, Germany was divided, according to the Berlin Agreement, into US, Soviet, British and French occupation zones. Berlin was similarly divided. After the failure of negotiations to establish a unified German administration, the three Western-occupied zones were integrated economically in 1948. A provisional constitution, the Grundgesetz (Basic Law), came into force in the three zones (excluding Saarland) in May 1949. The first federal elections were held in August 1949, when the Christlich Demokratische Union Deutschlands/Christlich Soziale Union (CDU/CSU, Christian Democratic Union/Christian Social Union) and the Sozialdemokratische Partei Deutschlands (SPD, Social Democratic Party) emerged as the two largest political parties. The Federal Republic of Germany (FRG) was established on 21 September 1949, although its sovereignty was limited by the continuing Allied military occupation. The first President of the Republic was Theodor Heuss. In October 1949 the Soviet-occupied zone of Germany declared itself the German Democratic Republic (GDR), with the Soviet-occupied zone of Berlin as its capital. This left the remainder of Berlin, known as West Berlin, as an 'island' of the FRG in GDR territory. Following the establishment of the Federal Republic, the military occupation was converted into a contractual defence relationship. The Paris Agreement of 1954 gave full sovereign status to the Federal Republic from 5 May 1955, and also gave it membership of NATO. In 1957 the Bundestag (Federal Assembly) declared Berlin the capital of Germany, and the Federal Republic continues to aim for a united Germany. Until such time, the seat of the Federal Government is Bonn. Saarland, under French occupation, was reunited with the FRG administratively in 1957 and became economically incorporated in 1959. The isolation of West Berlin was increased in August 1961, when the GDR constructed a wall along the boundary between the eastern and western sectors of the city.

Under the chancellorship of Dr Konrad Adenauer (1949–63) and the direction of Economics Minister Dr Ludwig Erhard, who succeeded Adenauer as Chancellor in 1963, the Federal Republic rebuilt itself rapidly to become one of the most affluent and economically dynamic states of Europe, allying itself with the West, to avoid the threat of 'expansionist' communism, and becoming a founder member of the European Communities. Owing to the Government's insistence on reunification, maintaining that the 1937 borders of the Reich remained legally valid until the signing of a peace treaty by the government of a united Germany, the Federal Republic became completely cut off from eastern Europe.

The CDU/CSU, which had formed the government from 1949, ruled in coalition with the SPD from 1966 to 1969, under the chancellorship of Dr Kurt Kiesinger. After the general election of October 1969, a new coalition of the SPD and the Freie Demokratische Partei (FDP, Free Democratic Party) formed the government, under the chancellorship of Willy Brandt, adopting a fresh policy towards eastern Europe (Ostpolitik) and particularly towards the GDR. Following elections in November 1972, the SPD became, for the first time, the largest party in the Bundestag. Chancellor Brandt resigned in May 1974, after the discovery that his personal assistant had been working for the GDR, and was succeeded by Helmut Schmidt, previously Minister of Finance. In the same month Walter Scheel, Brandt's Vice-Chancellor and Foreign Minister, was elected Federal President in place of Gustav Heinemann. A deteriorating economic situation was accompanied by a decline in the popularity of the Government and increasing tension between the coalition partners. In the general election of October 1976 the SPD lost its position as largest party in the Bundestag, but the SPD-FDP coalition retained a slender majority. Traditional partnerships between parties became less certain; the Bavarian CSU split from, and then rejoined, the CDU in 1976. In July 1979 Dr Karl Carstens of the CDU, President of the Bundestag, succeeded Walter Scheel as President of the Federal Republic.

In the general election of October 1980 the SPD-FDP coalition achieved a majority of 45 seats in the Bundestag: the greatest gains were made by the FDP, whereas the SPD made almost negligible gains. At local elections in 1981 and 1982 the SPD-FDP coalition suffered severe set-backs and became increasingly unstable, while disputes over nuclear power, defence policy and economic measures continued to divide the parties. By September 1982 the two parties were disagreeing openly and the FDP eventually withdrew from the coalition, marking the long-expected end of the 13-year partnership. On 1 October, after a 'constructive vote of no confidence', Schmidt was replaced as Chancellor by the CDU leader, Dr Helmut Kohl, and the FDP agreed to form a coalition with the CDU/CSU. This partnership was confirmed by the results of the general election held in March 1983, when the CDU/CSU substantially increased their share of the vote, winning 48.8% of the total, while the SPD, led by Hans-Jochen Vogel after Helmut Schmidt's retirement, gained only 38.8%. The environmentalist Green Party entered the Bundestag for the first time.

During 1983–84 the Government suffered a series of domestic crises. There was disunity between the coalition partners over several questions of policy, while in November 1983 the deployment of US missiles in the FRG provoked a large-scale confrontation with the country's anti-nuclear movement. In May–June 1984 the Government faced the first major industrial conflict since 1978 when trade union demands for a shorter working week led to a seven-week strike in the engineering and metal industry, which brought the country's production of motor cars almost to a standstill. In July Dr Richard von Weizsäcker, the former Governing Mayor of West Berlin, became Federal President, succeeding Dr Karl Carstens.

In November 1984, following continuing differences within the coalition, Dr Kohl appointed Wolfgang Schäuble as Head of the Chancellery. The new post carried responsibility for the co-ordination of government policy, and its creation was seen as an attempt to improve the efficiency of the Government. Three important regional elections, which were considered to be vital mid-term tests for the Government, were held in 1985: in March the SPD won an absolute majority in Saarland, gaining control of the regional government for the first time; an election in West Berlin on the same day, however, led to a disappointing result for the SPD, as the CDU and FDP, the existing coalition partners in the city, increased their representation at the SPD's expense. In May the SPD won an overwhelming victory in the North Rhine-Westphalia local election. This result represented a personal victory for Johannes Rau, the local SPD leader, who in August 1986 was officially confirmed as the SPD's candidate for Chancellor at the 1987 general election.

Investigations into a long-running scandal over allegations of bribery and irregular political campaign funds, obtained from the Flick industrial holding company, led to the resignation in June 1984 of the Minister of Economics, Dr Otto Graf Lambsdorff of the FDP, followed in October by that of Dr Rainer Barzel, President of the Bundestag. Several leading politicians, including Dr Kohl, Willy Brandt and Franz Josef Strauss (Minister-President of Bavaria), appeared before an all-party committee of enquiry, and investigations suggested that the Flick concern had made illegal donations to all parties in the Bundestag, except the Green Party. In May 1986 the last two charges against Chancellor Kohl were withdrawn, because of insufficient evidence. In July 1986 the Federal Constitutional Court revised legislation regarding party political donations and the release of information concerning parliamentary delegates' sources of income. These new rulings were approved by the Bundestag in December 1986. In February 1987 Dr Lambsdorff, together with Dr Hans Friderichs (also of the FDP), his predecessor as Minister of Economics and the former chief executive of the Dresdner Bank, and Eberhard von Brauchitsch (a former senior manager of the Flick concern), were convicted on charges of tax evasion and aiding tax evasion on party political donations. However, all three were cleared of more serious charges of corruption.

Three important local elections were held during 1986. In June the CDU lost its absolute majority in the Lower Saxony assembly, but retained control by forming a coalition with the FDP. This result also meant that the CDU majority in the Bundesrat (Federal Council) was preserved. In October the CSU retained control, as expected, in Bavaria, but the SPD lost some of its support to the Green Party, whose representatives entered the local parliament for the first time. At elections in November, for the city parliament in Hamburg (a traditional SPD stronghold), the SPD's share of the vote fell from 51.3% to 41.4%, while the CDU received 42.4%, the largest proportion of the vote. As in the local elections, the campaign for the general election, scheduled for January 1987, was dominated by environmental issues. The nuclear accident at Chernobyl, in the USSR, in April 1986 had extensive environmental repercussions in the Federal Republic. Anti-nuclear protests took place throughout the country, and in June Chancellor Kohl acknowledged public concern by creating a new ministry, of the Environment, Conservation and Reactor Safety.

Despite disunity between the coalition partners (principally the CSU and FDP) in late 1986, over the issue of proposed new legislation on law and order, the Government faced the forthcoming general election to the Bundestag with confidence, boosted by the strong economy. At the election, held on 25 January 1987, the CDU/CSU received 44.3% of the votes, 4.5% less than in 1983, while the FDP's share rose by 2.1%, to 9.1%. The SPD received 37% of votes cast, while the Green Party increased its share of support from 5.6% to 8.3%. The CDU/CSU/FDP coalition returned to power, although with a reduced majority. In March Dr Kohl's reappointment as Chancellor was approved by the Bundestag, but he received only four more votes than the requisite absolute majority, the worst result for any FRG Chancellor since 1949. The new Government differed little from its predecessor, except that the FDP was allotted four portfolios instead of three, reflecting its improved results at the general election.

The Government was encouraged by the results of the election to the state parliament of Hesse in April 1987, in which the CDU received the largest proportion of the votes cast (42.1%, compared with 39.4% at the previous election in 1983). For the first time in the history of the state, a CDU-FDP government was formed. The decline in support for the SPD (40.2% of the votes, compared with 46.2% in 1983) was attributed, to a large extent, to a crisis within the SPD leadership. In March Willy Brandt had announced his forthcoming resignation as party chairman, prompted by criticism from within the party leadership over his choice of Dr Margarita Mathiopoulos as SPD spokesperson. Hans-Jochen Vogel was elected chairman of the SPD in June, and Brandt was appointed honorary chairman.

At elections to the Hamburg city parliament and the Rhineland-Palatinate state parliament in May, however, the CDU suffered losses which were attributed to the Government's indecisive response to Soviet proposals regarding the withdrawal of short- and medium-range nuclear missiles from Europe (the 'double zero' option). At the election in Hamburg (called because the SPD had failed to negotiate a coalition agreement with either the CDU or the Green Party after the previous election in November 1986), the SPD again received the largest proportion of the votes, but failed to achieve an absolute majority. Protracted negotiations led to the formation, in August, of the first SPD-FDP alliance since the collapse of the SPD-FDP federal coalition in 1982. In the election to the state parliament of Rhineland-Palatinate, the CDU received the largest proportion of the votes, but lost the absolute majority which it had held since 1971. Negotiations resulted in the formation of an alliance with the FDP, whose share of the votes had risen from 3.5% at the previous election in 1983 to 7.3%.

In September 1987 the CDU again suffered heavy losses in elections to the state parliaments of Schleswig-Holstein and Bremen. In Bremen the SPD maintained its absolute majority, winning 50.5% of the total votes, compared with 51.3% at the previous election in 1983. The FDP won 10% of the total votes, compared with 4.6% at the previous election, thus re-entering the state parliament. The CDU, meanwhile, suffered a heavy decline in its share of support, which fell from 33.3% at the previous election to 23.4%. The CDU's poor performance was again attributed to the disunity which the Government had displayed with regard to Soviet proposals concerning the USA's Pershing missiles in the FRG, and to farmers' dissatisfaction with EEC agricultural policies. The CDU lost many votes to the Deutsche Volksunion (DVU), an alliance of right-wing associations, formed in March 1987. The DVU obtained 3.4% of the total votes, winning one seat in the state parliament.

In the election to the state parliament in Schleswig-Holstein, the CDU lost its absolute majority for the first time in 16 years, winning 42.6% of the total votes, compared with 49% at the previous election in 1983. The SPD became the largest single party in the assembly, securing 45.2% of the votes, while the FDP's support rose by 3%, to 5.2%. The SPD won 36 seats in the state parliament, the CDU 33, and the FDP 4. The formation of a CDU-FDP coalition administration thus depended upon the support of the holder of the one remaining seat, Karl-Otto Meyer of the minority Südschleswigscher Wählerverband (SSW). However, the situation was immediately complicated by allegations from a former CDU press aide that the Minister-President of Schleswig-Holstein, Dr Uwe Barschel, had fabricated evidence against his SPD opponent, Björn Engholm, in an attempt to discredit him in the opinion of voters. The ensuing scandal, which subsequently became known as 'Waterkantgate', culminated in Dr Barschel's resignation on 25 September. The FDP, meanwhile, refused to form an administration with the CDU until all the facts of the case had been ascertained by a parliamentary commission. The scandal deepened on 11 October, when Dr Barschel was found dead in a Swiss hotel. Investigations later proved that he had committed suicide. A new state election was held on 8 May 1988, at which the SPD decisively defeated the CDU, winning 54.8% of the total votes, while the CDU's support declined to 33.3%. The SPD's representation in the state parliament rose by 10 seats, to 46 seats, whereas the CDU's share of seats fell by six, to 27. Both the FDP and the Green Party failed to secure the 5% of the vote required to gain representation in the state legislature, as a result of which the FDP lost the four seats that it had won in the election of September 1987. The SPD's overwhelming victory was attributed, in large part, to the CDU's considerable loss of popular support after the 'Waterkantgate' scandal, but was also due to growing dissatisfaction with the Government's plans to reform the tax, health insurance and postal systems.

Meanwhile, at state elections in Baden-Württemberg, held in March 1988, the CDU retained its absolute majority in the state legislature, although, with 49.1% of the votes, its share of support declined by nearly 3% from that achieved at the previous election (in March 1984), and it lost two of its 68 seats. The three other main parties, the SPD, the FDP and the Greens, also suffered a loss in votes, although the SPD and the Greens each gained one seat. The election result was widely regarded as a personal victory for Dr Lothar Späth, the long-standing CDU Minister-President of Baden-Württemberg, who, during the election campaign, had been openly critical of the Government's handling of nuclear and economic issues, and especially its controversial programme of tax reform, scheduled to take effect in 1990. At the CDU party congress, held in

June 1988, there was evidence of growing discontent within the party with the leadership of Chancellor Kohl, and doubts were raised as to Dr Kohl's ability to lead the CDU to success in the next general election (the date of which was later set for December 1990).

At an election for the West Berlin House of Representatives in January 1989, the proportion of votes won by the CDU again declined, from 46.4% in 1985 to 37.8%, compared with the SPD's 37.3%. The FDP, which had ruled in coalition with the CDU in West Berlin since 1983, failed to secure the 5% share of the votes required to win seats in the House, and was thus obliged to withdraw from the coalition. The Republicans, a recently-formed extreme right-wing party, caused considerable alarm by amassing 7.5% of the votes and winning 11 of the 138 seats, their first representatives in an FRG state legislature. The Alternative List, West Berlin's Green party, received 11.8% of the votes, winning 17 seats. The CDU and the SPD each won 55 seats, but the CDU's marginally higher share of the vote meant that the CDU Governing Mayor would retain office until a coalition of parties, holding a majority of seats, might be formed.

In 1988 there was increasing tension between two wings of the Green Party: the *Realos*, who favoured political co-operation with the SPD, and the extreme 'eco-socialist' *Fundis*. At a special party conference held in December 1988, the entire *Fundi*-dominated national executive of the party resigned after a motion expressing 'no confidence' in the leadership was approved by 214 votes to 186. The executive and its supporters had been accused of misappropriation of party funds. New party elections were scheduled for February 1989, when it was expected that the *Realos* would take control of the executive.

During 1970 formal talks were conducted for the first time between the Federal Republic and the GDR, and there was a marked increase in diplomatic contacts between the Federal Republic and the other Communist countries of Europe. Treaties were signed with the USSR on the Renunciation of Force, and with Poland, recognizing the Oder/Neisse Line as the border between Germany (actually the GDR) and Poland. The Federal Republic also renounced German claims on the eastern territories of the old Reich. In 1971 the Quadripartite Agreement of the four powers on the position of West Berlin provided that there should be unimpeded access from the Federal Republic to West Berlin and that citizens of West Berlin should be allowed to visit the GDR. In 1972 the two German states concluded a Basic Treaty governing their relationship, and in September 1973 they became members of the United Nations. Between 1974 and 1979 Permanent Representative Missions were set up in Bonn and East Berlin, and access for West Germans to the GDR was made easier.

In October 1980, however, relations between the two countries deteriorated when the GDR Government raised the minimum exchange requirement for foreign visitors and renewed its demands for full diplomatic recognition by the FRG. The situation has since gradually improved, despite a set-back in August 1985, when a new espionage scandal emerged: several suspected GDR agents, including Bonn's senior counter-intelligence official, defected to the GDR, seriously undermining West German security. In 1986 relations with the GDR were again strained, when a large number of refugees, mainly from developing countries, were allowed by the GDR to cross into West Berlin. The issue was resolved in September, when the GDR agreed to restrict access for the refugees. In 1987, the 750th anniversary of the founding of Berlin, Eberhard Diepgen, the mayor of West Berlin, invited Erich Honecker, the GDR leader, to attend celebrations in the western half of the city, and received a reciprocal invitation from Honecker to attend celebrations in East Berlin. The invitations gave rise to concern that acceptance by either might undermine the four-power status of Berlin, and both were declined. In September, however, Honecker paid his first, and long-awaited, visit to the FRG, after proposed visits had twice been cancelled abruptly in the past. The FRG described this as a 'working' visit, rather than a state visit, since it did not wish to grant *de facto* recognition of the GDR as an independent state. In March 1986 Chancellor Kohl announced his Government's support for the USA's 'Strategic Defense Initiative' (SDI), a plan, first announced by President Ronald Reagan in March 1983, to assess the feasibility of creating a space-based 'shield' against attack by ballistic missiles. However, West German participation in SDI was to be restricted to low-level research, in an attempt to limit any damage to the Federal Republic's Ostpolitik.

During 1988 relations between the FRG and the USSR, which had been strained for several years, showed signs of improvement. In July 1988 the FRG Minister for Foreign Affairs, Hans-Dietrich Genscher, and the Soviet leader, Mikhail Gorbachev, conferred in Moscow, in preparation for Chancellor Kohl's long-delayed visit to the USSR, which took place in October. During the visit, the FRG and the USSR signed several economic accords, including one involving West German help in the construction of nuclear reactors in the USSR, the first such agreement between the USSR and a Western country. The issue of arms control was also discussed. In August 1987 Chancellor Kohl had offered to eliminate the FRG's 72 Pershing 1A missiles (the warheads of which belonged to the USA) in an attempt to facilitate the successful conclusion of US-Soviet negotiations on the elimination of short-range nuclear weapons in Europe. The elimination of the FRG's missiles, which had emerged as the principal obstacle to the success of the negotiations, was conditional upon the satisfactory conclusion of the negotiations and verification provisions acceptable to all concerned, including the FRG. Meanwhile, in September 1988, some of the USA's 108 Pershing-2 medium-range ballistic missiles were withdrawn from FRG territory. This was in accordance with provisions of the US-Soviet Intermediate-Range Nuclear Forces Treaty, ratified in June 1988. In 1987 the FRG strengthened its defence links with France. In September a joint military exercise, involving 75,000 French and West German troops, took place in Bavaria. In January 1988 the French and West German Governments established a joint Council for Defence and Security to conduct regular consultations on military co-operation.

Government

The Federal Republic is composed of 10 Länder (states)—each Land having its own constitution, parliament and government—plus West Berlin, which retains a separate status.

The country has a parliamentary regime, with a bicameral legislature. The Upper House is the Bundesrat (Federal Council), with 45 seats, including 41 members of Land governments (which appoint and recall them) and four representatives, with limited voting rights, appointed by the West Berlin Senate. The term of office of Bundesrat members varies with Land election dates. The Lower House, and the country's main legislative organ, is the Bundestag (Federal Assembly), with 519 deputies, including 497 elected for four years by universal adult suffrage (using a mixed system of proportional representation and direct voting) and 22 members, with limited voting rights, elected by the West Berlin House of Representatives.

Executive authority rests with the Federal Government, led by the Federal Chancellor, who is elected by an absolute majority of the Bundestag and appoints the other Ministers. The Federal President is elected by a Federal Convention (Bundesversammlung) which meets only for this purpose and consists of the Bundestag and an equal number of members elected by Land parliaments. The President is a constitutional Head of State with little influence on government.

Each Land has its own legislative assembly, with the right to enact laws except on matters which are the exclusive right of the Federal Government, such as defence, foreign affairs and finance. Education, police, culture and environmental protection are in the control of the Länder. Local responsibility for the execution of Federal and Land laws is undertaken by the city boroughs and counties.

Defence

The Federal Republic is a member of NATO. Conscription has been in force since 1956 and lasts for 18 months. In June 1988 the armed forces totalled 488,700, including 222,600 conscripts. The strength of the army stood at 332,100, including 175,900 conscripts. The navy numbered 36,400 (including 8,600 conscripts), and there were 108,700 in the air force (38,100 conscripts). The remaining 11,500 were inter-service staff. Defence expenditure for 1988 was estimated at DM51,460m.

Economic Affairs

After the destruction caused by the Second World War, the Federal Republic, containing most of the principal industrial areas of Germany, made a remarkable economic recovery which was sustained over a number of years and has often been described as Germany's 'Wirtschaftswunder' (economic mir-

FEDERAL REPUBLIC OF GERMANY

Introductory Survey

acle). In 1987, according to estimates by the World Bank, the Federal Republic's gross national product (GNP), measured at average 1985–87 prices, was US $879,630m., equivalent to $14,460 per head. Between 1980 and 1987, it was estimated, GNP per head increased, in real terms, at an average rate of 1.9% per year. The average annual increase in overall gross domestic product (GDP), measured in constant prices, was 3.3% in 1965–80, slowing to 1.5% in 1980–86. West Germany is now one of the world's major economic powers, and its people enjoy a high standard of living.

The basis of the country's prosperity has been the industrial sector, which (with mining and construction) provided 42.4% of GDP in 1987, compared with 53.2% in 1960. The principal manufacturing sectors are mechanical engineering, electrical engineering and electronics, vehicles, chemicals and food processing. The mechanical engineering industry is heavily export-oriented, with around two-thirds of output being sold abroad. However, the volume of orders fell sharply in the first half of 1987, owing to the continuing decline in the value of the US dollar in relation to the Deutsche Mark. Industries employing advanced technology are developing rapidly, especially microelectronics, communications and computer industries, and traditional engineering products, such as machine tools and locomotives, have been largely overtaken in importance by the office and information equipment sector, which increased by 350% between 1970 and 1985. The chemical industry (particularly plastics and synthetic fibres) has shown steady growth in recent years, with output from the sector increasing by 5.2% in 1984 and 2.6% in 1985, and has been among the main contributors to the Federal Republic's economic growth since 1983. However, output declined by 0.8% in 1986. After experiencing recession in the early 1980s, the steel industry achieved an export-led recovery in 1984 and 1985, but output fell by 8.3% in 1986, as exports again decreased, and by a further 2.4% in 1987. Nevertheless, steel production in 1988, according to preliminary figures, exceeded 41m. tons, instead of the anticipated 36m. tons. The manufacture of vehicles is very important, the FRG being the world's third largest producer of cars in 1987; in 1986 output of cars increased by 3.5% over 1984, to reach 4.13m. vehicles, of which around 62% were exported. Car production in 1988 was expected to reach 4.34m. vehicles. Industrial output as a whole increased by 3.2% in 1984, despite a protracted strike in the metal-working industry which adversely affected the year's output. In 1985 industrial output rose by 5.1%, but in 1986 it grew by only 2.3%. The agricultural sector (including forestry and fishing) contributed only 1.5% of GDP in 1987 (down from 5.8% in 1960) and employed just over 5% of the working population. In May 1986 the Government announced a new programme of farming subsidies, totalling DM 575m., which were intended partially to offset reductions in the price of some agricultural produce, as agreed by the EEC in April. The contribution of trade and transport to GDP has also declined (from 18.5% to 14.6% between 1960 and 1987).

The Federal Republic has relatively few natural resources; hard coal, lignite (low-grade brown coal) and salt are the only mineral deposits of any size. Mining of hard coal in the Ruhr area has been declining, with production falling from 87.1m. metric tons in 1980 to 76.3m. tons in 1987. Annual output was to be reduced by a further 13m.–15m. tons by 1995. The Government is strongly committed to the nuclear energy programme (which provided 31.3% of total electricity output in 1987), and has shifted its priorities away from coal production. Nuclear energy's share of total electricity output is expected to increase to 34.7% by the year 2000. A trade agreement on supplies of natural gas from the USSR, to satisfy about 30% of gas requirements, was signed in November 1981. Dependence on petroleum was expected to fall from 45% of energy requirements in 1982 to 41% in 1990.

In 1986 the Federal Republic replaced the USA as the world's largest exporter, in US dollar terms, owing to the steep decline in the value of the dollar in relation to the Deutsche Mark. In 1988, according to provisional estimates, the trade surplus reached a record DM 121,330m. (compared with DM 117,735m. in 1987), owing largely to the continuing strength of the Deutsche Mark in relation to the dollar. Since 1970 about 50% of trade has been with other EEC countries (52.7% in 1987), especially the Netherlands and France, but in 1984, as the US dollar rose against the Deutsche Mark, German exports to the USA increased by 42.6%, making the USA West Germany's second most important foreign market (after France). This trend continued in 1985, when total imports rose by 6.8%, while exports increased by 10%. In 1986, however, the renewed strength of the Deutsche Mark was regarded as having had an adverse effect on trade, despite the achievement of a record trade surplus. The decline in the value of the FRG's imports, at 10.8%, was exaggeratedly steep, while the fact that the value of exports also declined, by 2%, suggested that the strength of the Deutsche Mark had reduced the competitiveness of West German goods on world markets. This trend continued in 1987, when the value of exports rose by 0.3%, while the value of imports fell by 1.2%. In 1988 total exports rose by 5.1%, in real terms, and imports by 6.3%. Forecasts for 1989 envisaged exports rising by 4–5% and imports by 4.5–5.5%. The Federal Republic's current account registered a record surplus of DM 85,000m. in 1986, and in 1987 this figure declined only slightly, to DM 81,000m., and was expected to recede only marginally in 1988. The size of the Federal Republic's trade surplus in 1986–88 placed it under increasing pressure from abroad (especially the USA) to adopt a more expansionist economic policy, in order to stimulate growth in the world market. West Germany responded by advancing some of the tax reductions that had originally been scheduled for 1990, and by announcing a programme of subsidized loans, worth DM 21,000m., to accelerate domestic growth.

GNP increased by 2.5% in 1986, by 1.8% in 1987, and, according to preliminary figures, by 3.4% in 1988 (the highest growth rate since 1979, when 4.0% was recorded). GNP was expected to rise by between 2% and 2.5% in 1989. During 1986 the stimulus for economic growth shifted from the export sector to the home market, as domestic demand increased by 4.3%. Domestic demand grew by a further 3% in 1987, but growth in GNP was due mainly to a slight rise in productivity. Domestic demand expanded by 3.7% in 1988, but was expected to rise by an estimated 2.5% in 1989, partly as a result of new consumer taxes. The annual inflation rate averaged 1% in 1987, after having turned negative in 1986 (-0.2%) for the first time since 1953. In 1988 the annual inflation rate averaged 1.2%, although by the end of the year it showed signs of acceleration (1.6% in the 12 months to November) and was expected to rise to as much as 2.5% in 1989. Tax reductions which were introduced in January 1986 further boosted consumer spending, and in June 1988, in a further attempt to promote economic growth, legislation was enacted to reduce projected annual tax revenue by a further DM 37,200m. from January 1990.

Unemployment represents the Government's most pressing problem: the unemployment rate rose from 3.8% of the labour force in 1979 to 9.1% in 1983 and 1984. In 1987 the rate averaged 8.9%, but in 1988 it declined to 8.7% (2.24m. people). It was expected to rise in 1989, partly as a result of the influx of ethnic Germans from abroad (200,000 in 1988). The construction industry, in particular, has been adversely affected by unemployment, owing to large reductions in the public-sector construction programme. In response to the problem, the Government introduced legislation allowing workers to retire at 59 years of age, and encouraging employers to engage temporary workers, and also announced a scheme of repatriation grants to encourage some of the country's 4.7m. foreign workers (Gastarbeiter) to leave the FRG. The shipbuilding industry, faced with increasing competition from the Far East, has also been affected by unemployment: it was estimated in 1986 that one-quarter of the remaining 40,000 people employed in the sector (compared with 54,000 in 1982) would lose their jobs over the next few years. In October 1986 the Government announced a plan to allocate DM 420m. in regional aid to the shipbuilding areas, to provide alternative work on infrastructural projects. The Government and trade unions reached an agreement to reduce jobs in the steel industry by 20,000 by 1990 (representing an 18% cut in the total work-force), and a programme for the closure of coal-mines, announced in December 1987, was expected to lead to the loss of 30,000 jobs in the mining industry by 1995.

Upon taking office, the Kohl Government adopted a stringent fiscal policy, and reduced the federal budget deficit from DM 31,500m. to DM 22,700m. in 1985. In 1986, however, the budget deficit rose to DM 23,000m., and by 1988 it had risen by 26% over the 1987 level, to a record DM 35,300m. (albeit DM 3,300m. less than had been anticipated in the Government's supplementary budget of October 1988). It was hoped that in 1989 the budget deficit would decline to around DM 27,000m. The Government attributed its failure to reduce the budget deficit to the economy's low rate of growth in 1987 and to the

FEDERAL REPUBLIC OF GERMANY

postponement of the sale of the government holding in the motor company Volkswagen, due to the global collapse of stock markets in October 1987 and the company's involvement in a currency fraud. The increase in government expenditure, at 2.9%, nevertheless remained below 3% for the fifth consecutive year in 1987. In 1988 government expenditure rose by 2.3%.

Social Welfare

Social legislation has established comprehensive insurance cover for sickness, accidents, retirement, disability and unemployment. The insurance schemes for disability, retirement and unemployment are compulsory for all employees, and more than 80% of the population is covered. Insurance is administered by autonomous regional and local organizations. Pensions are the highest in Europe; the amount is based on contributions paid, is related to national average earnings and regularly adjusted. Sickness insurance pays for all medical attention and provides a benefit of 85% to 90% of the normal wage. There is no national health service, but in 1986 the country had 3,071 hospital establishments, with a total of 674,384 beds (equivalent to one for every 91 inhabitants). In 1985 there were 160,902 physicians working in the Federal Republic. Of total expenditure by the Federal Government (including social insurance institutions) in 1984, about DM 100,820m. (18.7%) was for health services, and a further DM 270,180m. (50.2%) for social security and welfare.

Education

The Basic Law gives the control of education entirely to the Land governments. They do, however, co-operate quite closely to ensure a large degree of conformity in the system. Education is compulsory for children aged six to 18 years. At least nine years of education must be full-time. Primary education is free, and grants are made for secondary education wherever fees are payable. Attendance at the Grundschule (elementary school) is obligatory for all children during the first four years of their school life, after which they go on to one of three other types of school. Approximately one-half of this age-group attend the Hauptschule (general school) for five or six years, after which they go into employment, but continue their education part-time for three years at a vocational school. Alternatively, pupils may attend the Realschule (intermediate school) for six years, or the Gymnasium (grammar school) for nine years. The Abitur (grammar school leaving certificate) is a necessary prerequisite for university education. All Länder also have experimental Gesamtschulen (comprehensive schools). In 1985 the total enrolment at primary and secondary schools was equivalent to 78% of the school-age population. In the 1970s the Federal Republic's universities and technical universities suffered a severe crisis of space. A university building programme, started in 1971, failed to keep up with demand, as the number of students at universities and colleges rose from 585,000 in 1971 to 1.4m. in 1987. Legislation now limits the length of study and numbers of students. Expenditure on education by all levels of government in 1984 was about DM 73,150m. (7.8% of total public spending).

Public Holidays

1989: 2 January (for New Year's Day), 6 January (Epiphany)*, 24 March (Good Friday), 27 March (Easter Monday), 1 May (Labour Day), 4 May (Ascension Day), 15 May (Whit Monday), 25 May (Corpus Christi)*, 17 June (Day of German Unity, anniversary of 1953 uprising in the GDR), 15 August (Assumption)*, 1 November (All Saints' Day)*, 22 November (Repentance Day), 25-26 December (Christmas).

1990: 1 January (New Year's Day), 6 January (Epiphany)*, 13 April (Good Friday), 16 April (Easter Monday), 1 May (Labour Day), 24 May (Ascension Day), 4 June (Whit Monday), 14 June (Corpus Christi)*, 17 June (Day of German Unity, anniversary of 1953 uprising in the GDR), 15 August (Assumption)*, 1 November (All Saints' Day)*, 21 November (Repentance Day), 25-26 December (Christmas).

* Religious holidays observed in certain Länder only.

Weights and Measures

The metric system is in force.

Statistical Survey

Source (unless otherwise stated): Statistisches Bundesamt, 6200 Wiesbaden 1, Gustav-Stresemann-Ring 11, Postfach 5528; tel. (06121) 7051; telex 4-86511.

(All statistical data relate to the Federal Republic of Germany, including West Berlin, except where indicated.)

Area and Population

AREA, POPULATION AND DENSITY

Area (sq km)	248,709*
Population (census results)	
6 June 1961	56,174,826
27 May 1970	
Males	28,866,724
Females	31,783,875
Total	60,650,599
Population (official estimates at mid-year)	
1985	61,015,300
1986	61,047,700
1987	61,171,000
Density (per sq km) at mid-1987	246.0

* 96,027 sq miles.

PRINCIPAL TOWNS (estimated population at 31 December 1986)

West Berlin	1,879,200	Gelsenkirchen	283,600
Hamburg	1,571,300	Karlsruhe	268,300
München (Munich)	1,274,700	Münster	267,600
Köln (Cologne)	914,300	Wiesbaden	266,500
Essen	615,400	Mönchengladbach	255,100
Frankfurt am Main	592,400	Braunschweig (Brunswick)	247,800
Dortmund	568,200	Augsburg	246,000
Stuttgart	565,500	Kiel	243,600
Düsseldorf	560,600	Aachen (Aix-la-Chapelle)	239,200
Bremen	522,000	Oberhausen	221,500
Duisburg	514,600	Krefeld	216,600
Hannover (Hanover)	505,700	Lübeck	209,200
Nürnberg (Nuremberg)	467,400	Hagen	206,100
Bochum	381,200	Mainz	189,000
Wuppertal	374,200	Freiburg im Breisgau	186,200
Bielefeld	299,400	Kassel	185,400
Mannheim	294,600	Saarbrücken	184,400
Bonn (capital)	291,400		

FEDERAL REPUBLIC OF GERMANY

Statistical Survey

STATES (31 December 1986)

	Area (sq km)	Population ('000)	Density (per sq km)	Capital	Population of capital ('000)
Schleswig-Holstein	15,727.9	2,612.7	166	Kiel	243.6
Hamburg	754.7	1,571.3	2,082	Hamburg	1,571.3
Niedersachsen (Lower Saxony)	47,439.2	7,196.1	152	Hannover (Hanover)	547.8
Bremen	404.2	654.2	1,618	Bremen	522.0
Nordrhein-Westfalen (North Rhine-Westphalia)	34,067.9	16,676.5	490	Düsseldorf	560.6
Hessen (Hesse)	21,113.9	5,543.7	263	Wiesbaden	266.5
Rheinland-Pfalz (Rhineland-Palatinate)	19,847.8	3,611.4	182	Mainz	189.0
Baden-Württemberg	35,751.4	9,326.8	261	Stuttgart	565.5
Bayern (Bavaria)	70,552.9	11,026.5	156	München (Munich)	1,274.7
Saarland	2,569.3	1,042.1	406	Saarbrücken	184.4
West Berlin	480.1	1,879.2	3,914	West Berlin	1,879.2
Total	248,709.3	61,140.5	246	Bonn	291.4

BIRTHS, MARRIAGES AND DEATHS (Federal Republic)

	Registered live births		Registered marriages		Registered deaths	
	Number	Rate (per 1,000)	Number	Rate (per 1,000)	Number	Rate (per 1,000)
1980	620,657	10.1	362,408	5.9	714,117	11.6
1981	624,557	10.1	359,658	5.8	722,192	11.7
1982	621,173	10.1	361,966	5.9	715,857	11.6
1983	594,177	9.7	369,963	6.0	718,337	11.7
1984	584,157	9.5	364,140	5.9	696,118	11.3
1985	586,155	9.6	364,661	6.0	704,296	11.5
1986	625,963	10.3	372,112	6.1	701,890	11.5
1987*	642,010	10.5	382,377	6.3	687,419	11.2

* Provisional figures.

EMPLOYMENT (civilian labour force employed, '000 persons aged 15 years and over)

	1984	1985*	1986*
Agriculture, hunting, forestry and fishing	1,376	1,360	1,345
Mining and quarrying	317	316	316
Manufacturing	7,932	8,007	8,119
Electricity, gas and water	238	236	236
Construction	1,776	1,699	1,662
Trade, restaurants and hotels	3,802	3,812	3,812
Transport, storage and communications	1,506	1,514	1,527
Financing, insurance, real estate and business services	1,618	1,648	1,681
Community, social and personal services	6,269	6,412	6,559
Total	24,835	25,004	25,257
Males	15,178	15,256	15,381
Females	9,657	9,748	9,876

* Provisional.

Source: ILO, *Year Book of Labour Statistics*.

Agriculture

PRINCIPAL CROPS ('000 metric tons)

	1985	1986	1987
Wheat	9,866	10,406	9,932
Rye	1,821	1,768	1,599
Barley	9,691	9,377	8,571
Oats	2,807	2,276	2,008
Maize	1,204	1,302	1,217
Mixed grain	527	460	444
Sugar beets*	20,813	20,260	19,049
Potatoes	7,905	7,390	6,836
Rapeseed	803	969	1,265
Cabbages	602	578	430
Carrots	173	148	139
Grapes	780†	1,450	1,280
Apples	1,410	2,180	1,077
Pears	335	499	294
Plums	481	453	337
Currants	127	131	n.a.

* Deliveries to sugar factories. † Unofficial estimate.

LIVESTOCK ('000 head at December)

	1985	1986	1987
Horses	n.a.	367.6	n.a.
Cattle	15,626.6	15,305.3	14,886.9
Pigs	24,282.1	24,503.0	23,669.6
Sheep	1,295.8	1,382.8	1,413.7
Chickens	71,057.1	72,123.7	n.a.
Geese	346.4	403.1	n.a.
Ducks	1,382.5	1,092.7	n.a.
Turkeys	2,209.5	2,648.7	n.a.

LIVESTOCK PRODUCTS ('000 metric tons)

	1985	1986	1987
Beef and veal	1,575.7	1,695.7	1,680.5
Mutton and lamb	27.2	25.5	29.4
Pig meat	3,242.5	3,335.8	3,364.7
Poultry meat	366	384	396
Edible offals	318	332	340*
Lard	417	432	n.a.
Tallow	79	85	n.a.
Cows' milk	25,676.2	26,350.3	24,436
Butter	515.1	565.8	464.3
Cheese	929	939	979
Hen eggs	789	766	739†

* FAO estimate. † Unofficial figure.

Source: FAO, mainly *Quarterly Bulletin of Statistics*.

FEDERAL REPUBLIC OF GERMANY

Forestry

ROUNDWOOD REMOVALS
('000 cubic metres, excluding bark)

	1984	1985*	1986
Sawlogs, veneer logs and logs for sleepers	16,465	16,465	16,626
Pulpwood	9,000	9,000	8,600
Other industrial wood	1,390	1,390	1,390*
Fuel wood	3,795	3,795	3,795*
Total	30,650	30,650	30,411

* FAO estimates.
Source: FAO, *Yearbook of Forest Products*.

SAWNWOOD PRODUCTION
('000 cubic metres, including boxboards)

	1984	1985	1986
Coniferous (softwood)	8,139	7,896	8,105
Broadleaved (hardwood)	1,593	1,550	1,605
Total	9,732	9,446	9,710

Railway sleepers ('000 cu metres): 93 in 1984; 90 in 1985; 90 in 1986.

Fishing

('000 metric tons, live weight)

	1984	1985	1986
Freshwater fishes	23.9	24.0	24.3
Atlantic cod	78.4	63.6	47.9
Saithe (Pollock)	30.6	25.3	28.2
Alaska pollock	23.8	—	—
Atlantic redfishes	27.9	16.6	15.3
Atlantic herring	25.3	23.9	15.5
Atlantic mackerel	11.0	11.8	9.7
Common shrimp	12.0	17.7	17.0
Blue mussel	59.3	20.8	29.9
Total catch (incl. others)	327.2	225.3	202.4
Inland waters	23.8	24.0	24.2
Atlantic Ocean	279.5	201.3	178.2
Pacific Ocean	23.9	—	—

Source: FAO, *Yearbook of Fishery Statistics*.

Mining

('000 metric tons)

	1985	1986	1987
Hard coal	82,398	80,801	76,300
Brown coal	120,667	114,310	108,799
Iron ore*	309	212	n.a.
Crude petroleum	4,105	4,017	3,800

* Metal content.

Industry

SELECTED PRODUCTS
('000 metric tons, unless otherwise indicated)

	1985	1986	1987
Electricity (million kWh)	408,705	408,266	n.a.
Manufactured gas from gas works (terajoules)	32,508	n.a.	n.a.
Manufactured gas from cokeries (terajoules)	188,177	n.a.	n.a.
Hard coal briquettes	1,511	1,199	1,001
Hard coal coke	22,331	22,254	19,674
Brown coal briquettes	4,068	3,630	3,188
Pig-iron	31,919	29,443	28,918
Steel ingots	40,076	36,737	35,919
Motor spirit (petrol)	20,387	19,536	18,832
Diesel oil	11,637	11,677	10,928
Cement	25,758	26,580	25,268
Potash (K_2O)	2,583	2,161	2,199
Sulphuric acid	3,428	3,351	3,323
Soda ash	1,412	1,442	1,448
Caustic soda	3,697	3,625	3,635
Chlorine	3,493	3,426	3,452
Nitrogenous fertilizers (N)	1,161	1,040	1,056
Phosphatic fertilizers (P_2O_5)	490	384	393
Artificial resins, plastics	7,666	7,941	8,546
Primary aluminium (unwrought)	745.5	765	738
Refined copper (unwrought)	414.4	422	n.a.
Zinc (unwrought)	367.8	n.a.	n.a.
Refined lead (unwrought)*	260.9	273	261
Rubber tyres ('000)	40,475	42,826	47,083
Wool yarn	42	41	40
Cotton yarn	131	128	142
Machine tools	336	372	342
Agricultural machinery	372	351	298
Textile machinery	202	225	225
Passenger cars and minibuses ('000)	3,867	3,952	4,008
Motor cycles ('000)	85	64	60
Bicycles ('000)	2,891	3,209	2,884
Radio receivers ('000)	3,376	3,936	5,141
Television receivers ('000)	3,738	3,895	3,537
Clocks and watches ('000)	33,521	33,689	28,946
Footwear ('000 pairs)	83,504	83,024	74,589
Cameras ('000)	863	1,145	664
Dwellings completed (number)	284,438	227,721	196,115

* Excluding antimonial lead and production from imported bullion.

Finance

CURRENCY AND EXCHANGE RATES

Monetary Units
100 Pfennige = 1 Deutsche Mark (DM).

Denominations
Coins: 1, 2, 5, 10 and 50 Pfennige; 1, 2, 5 and 10 DM.
Notes: 5, 10, 20, 50, 100, 500 and 1,000 DM.

Sterling and Dollar Equivalents (30 September 1988)
£1 sterling = 3.1675 DM;
US $1 = 1.8725 DM;
100 DM = £31.57 = $53.40.

Average Exchange Rate (DM per US $)
1985 2.9440
1986 2.1715
1987 1.7974

FEDERAL REPUBLIC OF GERMANY

BUDGET (million DM)*

Revenue	1985	1986	1987†
Current receipts	530,738	547,069	558,152
Taxes and similar revenue	422,943	435,811	451,291
Income from economic activity	40,884	40,520	34,782
Interest	3,410	3,324	2,937
Allocations and grants for current purposes	100,093	104,525	110,512
Other receipts	54,437	57,574	59,145
Less Deductible payments on the same level	91,029	94,685	100,515
Capital receipts	17,375	19,251	21,012
Sale of property	5,386	6,606	8,149
Loans and grants for investment	25,625	24,798	25,861
Repayment of loans	8,597	9,445	9,615
Public sector borrowing	2,785	3,020	2,621
Less Deductible payments on the same level	25,018	24,618	25,234
Total	548,113	566,320	579,164

Expenditure	1985	1986	1987†
Current expenditure	491,883	511,048	529,760
Personnel expenses	190,708	199,578	208,174
Goods and services	96,947	99,905	102,423
Interest	56,211	58,076	58,852
Allocations and grants for current purposes	239,046	248,174	260,826
Less Deductible payments on the same level	91,029	94,685	100,515
Capital expenditure	94,673	97,584	98,776
Construction	37,219	39,360	40,183
Purchase of property	12,477	13,552	13,790
Allocations and grants for investment	44,418	44,714	45,296
Loans	20,330	19,809	19,879
Sale of shares	3,794	3,341	3,273
Repayment expenses in the public sector	1,454	1,427	1,589
Less Deductible payments on the same level	25,018	24,618	25,234
Total	586,556	608,632	628,536

* Figures represent a consolidation of the accounts of all public authorities, including the Federal Government and state administrations.
† Provisional.

INTERNATIONAL RESERVES* (US $ million at 31 December)

	1985	1986	1987
Gold†	5,562	7,054	8,656
IMF special drawing rights	1,547	2,020	1,964
Reserve position in IMF	3,808	3,848	3,900
Foreign exchange	39,025	45,866	72,893
Total	49,942	58,788	87,413

* Data on gold and foreign exchange holdings exclude deposits made with the European Monetary Co-operation Fund.
† National valuation.
Source: IMF, *International Financial Statistics*.

MONEY SUPPLY (million DM at 31 December)

	1985	1986	1987
Currency outside banks	103,870	112,154	124,092

COST OF LIVING (Consumer Price Index. Base: 1980 = 100)

	1985	1986	1987
Food	116.9	117.6	117.0
Clothes and shoes	118.4	120.6	122.2
Rent	123.9	126.4	128.7
Energy	133.4	116.4	106.1
Furniture, domestic appliances and other household expenses	117.7	119.1	120.5
Transport and communications	123.2	118.3	119.5
Health	119.7	121.5	122.8
Entertainment and culture	116.2	117.8	119.1
Personal expenses	125.7	130.1	132.6
All items	121.0	120.7	121.0

NATIONAL ACCOUNTS
(provisional, million DM at current prices)
National Income and Product

	1985	1986	1987
Compensation of employees	987,230	1,037,230	1,076,300
Operating surplus*	420,350	464,310	484,480
Domestic factor incomes	1,407,580	1,501,540	1,560,780
Consumption of fixed capital	231,790	240,240	249,710
Gross domestic product at factor cost	1,639,370	1,741,780	1,810,490
Indirect taxes	230,290	236,390	245,710
Less Subsidies	37,810	41,220	43,580
GDP in purchasers' values	1,831,850	1,936,950	2,012,620
Factor income from abroad	53,920	56,120	60,570
Less Factor income paid abroad	40,170	44,270	49,990
Gross national product	1,845,600	1,948,800	2,023,200
Less Consumption of fixed capital	231,790	240,240	249,710
National income in market prices	1,613,810	1,708,560	1,773,490
Other current transfers from abroad	12,580	14,840	13,650
Less Other current transfers paid abroad	45,860	45,430	45,030
National disposable income	1,580,530	1,677,970	1,742,110

* Obtained as a residual.

Expenditure on the Gross Domestic Product

	1985	1986	1987
Government final consumption expenditure	365,550	382,140	396,760
Private final consumption expenditure	1,040,970	1,080,140	1,119,640
Increase in stocks	−1,400	−2,100	8,700
Gross fixed capital formation	360,800	376,750	388,330
Total domestic expenditure	1,765,920	1,836,930	1,913,430
Exports of goods and services	593,030	580,160	576,010
Less Imports of goods and services	527,100	480,140	476,820
GDP in purchasers' values	1,831,850	1,936,950	2,012,620
GDP at constant 1980 prices	1,568,010	1,608,500	1,637,020

FEDERAL REPUBLIC OF GERMANY

Gross Domestic Product by Economic Activity

	1985	1986	1987
Agriculture and livestock	27,720	34,080	29,360
Forestry and fishing	4,200		
Mining[1]	17,800	67,010	62,270
Electricity, gas and water	50,170		
Manufacturing[1, 2, 3]	584,020	642,070	664,700
Construction[2]	93,760	98,310	101,640
Wholesale and retail trade	170,300	169,520	174,180
Transport, storage and communications	106,030	107,760	110,170
Finance, insurance and dwellings[4]	225,920	233,540	243,600
Restaurants and hotels	23,940	277,250	299,630
Community, social and personal services[3, 5]	235,440		
Less Imputed bank service charges	84,240	84,530	85,430
Domestic product of industries	1,455,060	1,545,010	1,600,120
Government services	207,310	217,420	226,470
Private non-profit services to households	34,870	37,910	42,200
Domestic services of households	1,550	1,530	
Sub-total	1,698,790	1,801,870	1,868,790
Non-deductible sales tax	116,640	118,100	125,200
Import duties	16,420	16,980	18,630
GDP in purchasers' values	1,831,850	1,936,950	2,012,620

[1] Quarrying is included in manufacturing.
[2] Structural steel erection is included in manufacturing.
[3] Publishing is included in community, social and personal services.
[4] Including imputed rents of owner-occupied dwellings.
[5] Business services and real estate, except dwellings, are included in community, social and personal services.

BALANCE OF PAYMENTS (million DM)

	1984	1985	1986
Merchandise exports f.o.b.	461,250	510,189	502,168
Merchandise imports f.o.b.	−396,166	−425,513	−379,684
Trade Balance	65,084	84,676	122,484
Exports of services	135,263	144,342	142,165
Imports of services	−146,390	−154,740	−156,476
Balance of goods and services	53,957	74,278	108,173
Unrequited transfers:			
Foreign workers' remittances*	−8,350	−7,550	−7,000
Other private transfers (net)	−3,104	−3,652	−3,849
Government transfers (net)	−18,618	−18,560	−16,771
Current balance	23,887	44,516	80,554
Long-term capital (net):			
Private	−25,664	−33,916	−15,681
Government	4,565	15,602	38,003
Short-term capital (net):			
Private	−15,451	−9,549	−44,774
Government	−1,780	131	−1,061
Net errors and omissions	10,039	8,057	−5,624
Total (net monetary movements)	−4,402	24,841	51,416

* Estimates.

DEVELOPMENT AID (public and private development aid to developing countries and multilateral agencies, million DM)

	1985	1986	1987
Public development co-operation	8,657	8,317	8,009
Bilateral	5,826	5,736	5,596
Multilateral	2,831	2,581	2,413
Other public transactions	2,699	2,465	2,613
Bilateral	2,731	2,474	2,616
Multilateral	−32	−9	−3
Private development aid	1,247	1,183	1,100
Other private transactions	4,314	5,162	4,226
Bilateral	3,194	4,141	3,510
Multilateral	1,120	1,021	716
Total	16,917	17,127	15,948

External Trade

Note: Figures include trade in second-hand ships, and stores and bunkers for foreign ships and aircraft. Imports also exclude military supplies under the off-shore procurement programme and exports exclude war reparations and restitutions, except exports resulting from the Israel Reparations Agreement. Official figures exclude trade with the German Democratic Republic, which is compiled separately (see table below).

PRINCIPAL COMMODITIES (distribution by SITC, million DM)

Imports c.i.f.	1985	1986	1987
Food and live animals	44,320.2	42,742.4	40,147.3
Meat and meat preparations	5,845.0	5,420.6	5,533.2
Fresh, chilled or frozen meat	5,063.3	4,639.6	4,734.8
Dairy products and birds' eggs	4,422.5	5,106.9	4,268.7
Cereals and cereal preparations	4,373.9	3,628.6	3,289.7
Vegetables and fruit	13,759.8	13,277.4	14,092.3
Fresh and dried fruit and nuts (excl. oil nuts)	5,447.8	5,290.9	5,742.2
Coffee, tea, cocoa and spices	8,244.9	8,124.7	5,742.2
Coffee and coffee substitutes	4,883.1	5,410.1	3,352.0
Animal feeding stuff (excl. cereals)	3,354.1	2,873.3	2,602.7
Beverages and tobacco	4,602.2	4,495.6	4,472.4
Crude materials (inedible) except fuels	31,881.1	26,502.2	25,111.8
Oilseeds and oleaginous fruit	4,382.2	3,302.0	3,058.2
Cork and wood	2,579.2	2,587.4	2,610.0
Metalliferous ores and metal scrap	9,236.6	6,930.2	5,731.7
Mineral fuels, lubricants, etc.	92,181.9	48,246.7	39,508.4
Petroleum, petroleum products, etc.	70,956.9	34,224.7	30,399.8
Crude petroleum oils, etc.	39,918.3	16,950.6	16,016.9
Refined petroleum products	28,945.7	15,953.1	13,251.2
Motor spirit and other light oils	8,697.1	4,412.6	4,294.4
Gas oils	13,616.0	8,615.6	6,333.4
Gas (natural and manufactured)	18,010.4	11,192.5	6,869.2
Petroleum gases, etc. in the gaseous state	17,370.0	10,883.0	6,562.7
Animal and vegetable oils, fats and waxes	2,754.7	1,519.0	1,173.2
Chemicals and related products	41,259.6	38,313.0	38,512.2
Organic chemicals	11,735.3	9,994.9	10,018.9
Inorganic chemicals	5,697.9	4,594.8	4,275.0
Artificial resins and plastic materials, etc.	10,512.6	10,475.7	10,837.5

FEDERAL REPUBLIC OF GERMANY

Statistical Survey

Imports c.i.f.—*continued*	1985	1986	1987
Basic manufactures	74,921.5	73,404.4	71,642.8
Paper, paperboard and manufactures	8,662.7	9,131.8	9,510.5
Paper and paperboard (not cut to size or shape)	7,189.6	7,576.0	7,856.5
Textile yarn, fabrics, etc.	14,972.5	14,809.8	14,712.2
Non-metallic mineral manufactures	6,189.1	6,420.2	6,653.2
Iron and steel	16,005.6	15,373.5	13,524.6
Non-ferrous metals	12,838.6	10,564.7	9,768.9
Other metal manufactures	7,788.9	8,256.4	8,426.9
Machinery and transport equipment	105,954.4	108,954.0	114,475.5
Power generating machinery and equipment	7,059.8	7,119.7	7,405.2
Machinery specialized for particular industries (excl. metalworking)	7,479.9	7,731.6	7,784.0
General industrial machinery, equipment and parts	10,933.6	11,585.7	11,849.8
Office machines and automatic data processing equipment	16,343.9	15,784.4	16,399.2
Telecommunications and sound equipment	8,282.2	8,958.2	10,169.8
Other electrical machinery, apparatus and appliances	19,329.1	19,212.4	19,702.7
Road vehicles (incl. air-cushion vehicles) and parts[1]	21,838.9	26,282.0	28,718.9
Passenger motor cars (excl. buses)	12,635.2	16,164.3	17,678.4
Motor vehicle parts and accessories	6,270.5	6,813.5	7,347.5
Other transport equipment	11,922.6	8,820.2	9,130.7
Aircraft and associated equipment	10,802.6	8,273.2	8,399.5
Miscellaneous manufactured articles	52,904.4	55,928.8	61,537.6
Furniture and parts	3,634.9	3,810.7	4,333.6
Articles of apparel and clothing accessories (excl. footwear)	20,562.0	22,397.6	25,386.0
Footwear	4,804.4	4,982.9	5,323.2
Professional, scientific and controlling instruments, etc.	6,204.1	6,525.9	6,509.9
Photographic apparatus, optical goods, watches and clocks	5,139.1	5,037.6	5,327.1
Other commodities and transactions[2]	13,031.1	13,638.3	13,060.0
Special transactions[3]	10,201.7	10,531.9	10,813.3
Total[2]	463,811.0	413,744.4	409,641.3

[1] Excluding tyres, engines and electrical parts.
[2] Including monetary gold.
[3] Including government imports. Also included are returns and replacements, not allocated to their appropriate headings.

Exports f.o.b.	1985	1986	1987
Food and live animals	21,540.6	21,712.6	21,103.1
Dairy products and birds' eggs	5,292.5	5,047.6	5,741.9
Beverages and tobacco	3,510.9	3,363.4	3,095.6
Crude materials (inedible) except fuels	10,727.9	9,225.1	9,240.8
Mineral fuels, lubricants, etc.	15,284.1	8,611.4	7,103.9
Coal, coke and briquettes	4,360.1	3,294.8	2,504.2
Petroleum, petroleum products, etc.	6,850.7	3,801.4	3,248.6
Animal and vegetable oils, fats and waxes	2,795.3	1,689.6	1,322.2
Chemicals and related products	71,143.3	67,691.0	68,485.2
Organic chemicals	19,158.0	16,309.0	16,048.3
Inorganic chemicals	6,132.9	5,525.8	5,360.9
Dyeing, tanning and colouring materials	6,619.2	7,020.9	7,303.5
Medicinal and pharmaceutical products	6,938.8	7,111.2	7,268.5
Artificial resins and plastic materials, etc.	17,673.3	17,538.3	18,362.1

Exports f.o.b.—*continued*	1985	1986	1987
Basic manufactures	100,311.3	95,134.3	93,344.3
Rubber manufactures	4,465.8	4,648.0	4,737.6
Paper, paperboard and manufactures	10,152.4	10,079.4	10,673.0
Textile yarn, fabrics, etc.	17,836.3	17,749.1	17,576.9
Non-metallic mineral manufactures	8,858.3	9,190.1	9,103.4
Iron and steel	27,510.2	23,033.4	21,153.0
Bars, rods, angles, shapes and sections	3,758.7	3,198.0	2,767.6
Universals, plates and sheets	7,580.4	6,247.8	6,081.0
Tubes, pipes and fittings	7,212.3	5,979.1	4,887.6
Non-ferrous metals	10,883.2	9,473.1	9,326.5
Other metal manufactures	16,398.2	16,843.9	16,582.1
Machinery and transport equipment	246,715.2	251,332.0	255,132.3
Power generating machinery and equipment	14,796.2	14,861.3	15,161.2
Internal combustion piston engines and parts	7,207.9	7,592.7	7,611.4
Machinery specialized for particular industries (excl. metalworking)	33,127.7	34,633.5	34,238.6
Textile and leather machinery	6,894.8	7,536.7	7,770.5
Metalworking machinery	8,059.9	9,313.2	9,045.5
Machine-tools for working metal, etc.	6,609.5	7,672.8	7,352.4
General industrial machinery and equipment	32,748.5	33,942.6	33,397.0
Mechanical handling equipment	4,646.0	4,892.4	4,728.1
Office machines and automatic data processing equipment	14,168.4	14,451.0	14,066.8
Telecommunications and sound equipment	10,022.7	10,734.6	10,977.6
Other electrical machinery, apparatus and appliances	30,582.1	31,842.5	32,236.6
Switchgear, etc.	8,682.1	8,849.3	8,965.2
Road vehicles (incl. air-cushion vehicles) and parts[1]	86,392.8	89,070.0	92,624.4
Passenger motor cars (excl. buses)	55,927.4	57,907.3	59,518.5
Motor vehicles for goods transport, etc.	7,054.7	7,247.3	7,501.1
Goods vehicles	6,085.6	6,293.1	6,565.3
Motor vehicle parts and accessories	18,918.1	19,641.1	21,264.7
Other transport equipment	12,946.9	8,640.2	9,754.5
Miscellaneous manufactured articles	53,625.2	55,921.2	56,837.4
Furniture and parts	5,396.8	5,863.8	5,997.7
Articles of apparel and clothing accessories (excl. footwear)	8,381.0	9,016.7	9,051.5
Professional scientific and controlling instruments, etc.	12,508.4	12,968.3	12,973.6
Measuring, checking, analysing and controlling instruments	8,687.8	9,112.3	9,386.7
Photographic apparatus, optical goods, watches and clocks	6,138.3	5,994.6	5,924.8
Other commodities and transactions[2]	11,510.3	11,682.4	11,711.9
Special transactions[3]	9,524.6	9,570.9	10,476.0
Total[2]	537,164.2	526,363.0	527,376.7

[1] Excluding tyres, engines and electrical parts.
[2] Including monetary gold.
[3] Including returns and replacements, not allocated to their appropriate headings.

FEDERAL REPUBLIC OF GERMANY

Statistical Survey

PRINCIPAL TRADING PARTNERS*
(million DM, including gold)

Imports c.i.f.	1985	1986	1987
Algeria	4,111.8	1,917.0	1,893.5
Austria	15,350.5	16,383.4	17,292.8
Belgium/Luxembourg	29,112.0	29,249.6	29,129.3
Brazil	6,365.4	4,396.7	3,994.0
Canada	3,845.5	3,372.0	3,366.8
China, People's Repub.	2,556.1	2,703.3	3,455.8
Denmark	8,017.7	7,658.9	7,669.8
Finland	4,295.0	3,940.2	4,259.7
France	49,279.8	47,083.5	47,482.1
Greece	3,259.2	3,281.6	3,369.4
Hong Kong	3,709.6	4,169.9	4,259.6
Ireland	3,141.5	3,101.3	3,520.0
Italy	37,154.8	38,091.7	39,206.4
Japan	20,719.8	24,030.4	25,245.1
Korea, Republic	2,556.7	3,080.4	4,012.5
Libya	6,274.7	2,154.9	2,079.2
Netherlands	58,277.1	47,798.1	44,934.5
Nigeria	6,343.1	2,780.4	1,387.7
Norway	11,006.6	6,598.7	5,534.8
Poland	3,080.4	2,596.4	2,477.1
South Africa	3,162.7	2,881.2	2,242.6
Spain	7,672.1	7,387.5	8,060.2
Sweden	10,870.0	9,984.0	9,979.3
Switzerland	17,164.3	18,494.1	18,968.4
Taiwan	2,968.7	3,274.4	4,284.4
Turkey	2,907.7	3,100.7	3,706.5
USSR	13,628.5	9,298.5	7,260.6
United Kingdom	37,163.9	29,757.7	29,393.6
USA	32,341.5	26,863.5	25,612.9
Venezuela	3,494.2	1,494.5	1,149.0
Yugoslavia	4,773.8	4,906.6	4,887.2
Total (incl. others)	463,811.0	413,744.4	409,641.3

Exports f.o.b.	1985	1986	1987
Australia	4,587.2	4,007.0	3,458.5
Austria	27,394.6	28,118.5	28,410.5
Belgium/Luxembourg	36,967.2	37,171.9	38,845.6
Canada	5,474.6	5,285.4	4,759.9
China, People's Repub.	6,428.8	6,221.1	4,999.6
Denmark	11,810.2	12,214.6	11,165.0
Egypt	3,149.9	2,513.2	1,924.8
Finland	5,547.2	5,506.4	5,827.4
France	64,000.8	62,331.3	63,608.8
Greece	5,454.3	5,212.8	4,950.6
Hungary	3,062.6	2,996.8	2,891.7
India	3,377.3	3,370.6	3,230.7
Iran	4,841.7	3,272.4	2,831.6
Italy	41,794.9	42,878.7	46,056.3
Japan	7,888.4	8,706.7	10,544.5
Netherlands	46,254.5	45,457.7	46,087.5
Norway	6,797.3	7,103.4	5,790.3
Portugal	2,642.0	2,923.1	3,701.2
Saudi Arabia	5,235.4	3,370.1	2,579.6
South Africa	4,997.2	4,191.0	4,554.2
Spain	9,755.8	12,135.5	14,559.4
Sweden	14,733.6	14,746.8	15,841.7
Switzerland	28,855.7	31,033.2	32,126.3
Turkey	4,212.4	4,009.0	4,748.7
USSR	10,527.2	9,373.5	7,845.6
United Kingdom	45,967.4	44,599.6	46,632.4
USA	55,533.4	55,206.1	49,879.0
Yugoslavia	6,215.1	6,422.2	5,783.8
Total (incl. others)	537,164.2	526,363.0	527,376.7

* Imports by country of production; exports by country of consumption. Totals exclude trade with the German Democratic Republic (see below). The distribution by countries excludes stores and bunkers for ships and aircraft (million DM): Imports 280.9 in 1985, 252.0 in 1986, 261.2 in 1987; Exports 1,629.5 in 1985, 1,060.9 in 1986, 839.2 in 1987.

TRADE WITH THE GERMAN DEMOCRATIC REPUBLIC
(million DM)

	1985	1986	1987
Purchases from the GDR	7,636	6,844	6,650
Deliveries to the GDR	7,901	7,454	7,406

Transport

FEDERAL RAILWAYS (traffic)

	1985	1986	1987*
Passengers (million)	1,134	1,108	1,127
Passenger-km (million)	43,451	42,129	46,627
Freight net ton-km (million)	65,451	62,093	60,231

* Provisional figures.

ROAD TRAFFIC ('000 licensed vehicles at July each year)

	1985	1986	1987
Passenger cars	25,844.5	26,917.4	27,908.2
Lorries	1,280.8	1,294.8	1,305.3
Buses	69.4	69.3	70.2
Motor cycles	1,406.9	1,411.7	1,391.1
Trailers	1,763.2	1,854.7	1,940.6

SHIPPING
Inland Waterways

	1984	1985	1986
Freight ton-km (million)	51,996	48,183	52,185

Sea-borne Shipping

	1982	1983	1984
Merchant fleet (gross registered tons)*	6,671,196	6,308,017	5,932,694
Vessels entered ('000 net registered tons)†			
Domestic (coastwise)	16,702	15,189	15,036
International	139,486	135,040	136,819
Vessels cleared ('000 net registered tons)†			
Domestic	16,108	14,907	14,979
International	119,300	115,983	119,243
Freight unloaded ('000 metric tons)‡			
International	88,864	81,178	84,984
Freight loaded ('000 metric tons)‡			
International	42,975	40,855	43,601
Total domestic freight ('000 metric tons)	5,209	4,242	4,105

* Vessels of more than 100 grt at 31 December.
† Loaded vessels only.
‡ Including transhipments.

CIVIL AVIATION (traffic)

	1983	1984	1985
Kilometres flown (million)	551	584	640
Passenger-km (million)	67,072	73,280	80,075
Freight ton-km (milion)	2,884	3,276	3,711
Mail ton-km (million)	246	274	297

Tourism

FOREIGN TOURIST ARRIVALS

Country of Residence	1983	1984	1985
Austria	403,149	426,294	450,574
Belgium and Luxembourg	403,948	454,708	458,593
Canada	129,221	193,400	205,038
Denmark	469,189	550,178	614,839
France	508,761	617,894	651,717
Italy	454,419	512,886	542,130
Japan	354,876	410,296	488,582
Netherlands	1,559,521	1,699,965	1,706,906
Norway	192,007	210,794	266,705
Spain	140,622	166,108	188,199
Sweden	465,355	565,420	611,682
Switzerland	465,690	511,249	544,827
United Kingdom	969,644	1,142,233	1,179,126
USA	1,827,080	2,498,993	2,630,553
Total (incl. others)	9,829,617	11,866,420	12,605,695

Communications Media

	1982	1983	1984
Radio receivers in use	24,158,000	24,299,855	24,856,997
Television receivers in use	21,834,000	21,959,483	22,340,623
Telephones in use	31,370,000	35,137,000	36,582,000
Book production titles	61,332	60,598	51,733
Daily newspaper circulation	25,882,000	25,834,000	26,800,000

1985: Telephones 37,899,000; Book titles 57,623.

Education

	Institutions		Teachers	Students ('000)	
	1986	1987	1986	1986	1987
Primary	20,431	21,072	212,100	3,721.8	3,660.7
General Secondary:					
Intermediate schools	2,609	2,593	57,700	975.5	915.3
Grammar schools	2,469	3,455	120,200	1,655.8	1,596.1
Comprehensive schools	339	365	19,300	238.7	244.3
Special	2,824	2,816	39,800	261.4	254.1
Vocational secondary*	5,252	5,211	89,600	2,510.1	2,410.8
Trade and technical	1,049	1,076		90.6	97.7
Higher:					
Universities, etc.†	94	93	114,088	1,033.2	1,060.0
Colleges of art and music	26	28	5,191	22.0	22.2
Vocational	122	123	22,921	312.5	328.6

* Including part-time students.
† Universities and other institutions of similar standing, including colleges of theology and colleges of education.

Directory

The Constitution

The Basic Law (Grundgesetz), which came into force in the British, French and US Zones of Occupation in Germany (excluding Saarland) on 23 May 1949, was and is intended as a provisional Constitution to serve until a permanent one for Germany as a whole can be drawn up. The Parliamentary Council which framed it set out to continue the tradition of the Constitution of 1848–49, and to preserve some continuity with subsequent German constitutions (with Bismarck's Constitution of 1871, and with the Weimar Constitution of 1919) while avoiding the mistakes of the past. It contains 146 articles, divided into 11 sections, and introduced by a short preamble.

I. BASIC RIGHTS

The opening articles of the Constitution guarantee the dignity of man, the free development of his personality, the equality of all men before the law, and freedom of faith and conscience. Men and women shall have equal rights, and no one may be prejudiced because of sex, descent, race, language, homeland and origin, faith or religion or political opinion.

No one may be compelled against his conscience to perform war service as a combatant (Article 4). All Germans have the right to assemble peacefully and unarmed and to form associations and societies. Everyone has the right freely to express and to disseminate his opinion through speech, writing or pictures. Freedom of the press and freedom of reporting by radio and motion pictures are guaranteed (Article 5). Censorship is not permitted.

The State shall protect marriage and the family, property and the right of inheritance. The care and upbringing of children is the natural right of parents. Illegitimate children shall be given the same conditions for their development and their position in society as legitimate children. Schools are under the supervision of the State. Religion forms part of the curriculum in the State schools, but parents have the right to decide whether the child shall receive religious instruction (Article 7).

A citizen's dwelling is inviolable; house searches may be made only by Court Order. No German may be deprived of his citizenship if he would thereby become stateless. The politically persecuted enjoy the right of asylum (Article 16).

II. THE FEDERATION AND THE LÄNDER

Article 20 describes the Federal Republic (Bundesrepublik Deutschland) as a democratic and social federal state. The colours of the Federal Republic are to be black-red-gold, the same as those of the Weimar Republic. Each Land within the Federal Republic has its own Constitution, which must, however, conform to the principles laid down in the Basic Law. All Länder, districts and parishes must have a representative assembly resulting from universal, direct, free, equal and secret elections (Article 28). The exercise of the power of state is the concern of the Länder, in so far as the Basic Law does not otherwise prescribe. Where there is incompatibility, Federal Law supersedes Land Law (Article 31). Every German has in each Land the same civil rights and duties.

Political parties may be freely formed in all the states of the Federal Republic, but their internal organization must conform to democratic principles, and they must publicly account for the sources of their funds. Parties which seek to impair or abolish the free and democratic basic order or to jeopardize the existence of the Federal Republic of Germany are unconstitutional (Article 21). So are activities tending to disturb the peaceful relations between nations, and, especially, preparations for aggressive war, but the Federation may join a system of mutual collective security in order to preserve peace. The rules of International Law shall form part of Federal Law and take precedence over it and create rights and

FEDERAL REPUBLIC OF GERMANY

duties directly for the inhabitants of the Federal territory (Article 25).

The territorial composition of the Länder may be reorganized by Federal law, subject to plebiscite and with due regard to regional unity, territorial and cultural connections, economic expediency and social structure.

III. THE BUNDESTAG

The Federal Assembly or Bundestag is the Lower House. Its members are elected by the people in universal, free, equal, direct and secret elections, for a term of four years.* Any person who has reached the age of 18 is eligible to vote and any person who has reached the age of 18 is eligible for election (Article 38). A deputy may be arrested for a punishable offence only with the permission of the Bundestag, unless he be apprehended in the act or during the following day.

The Bundestag elects its President and draws up its Standing Orders. Most decisions of the House require a majority vote. Its meetings are public, but the public may be excluded by the decision of a two-thirds majority. Upon the motion of one-quarter of its members the Bundestag is obliged to set up an investigation committee.

IV. THE BUNDESRAT

The Federal Council or Bundesrat is the Upper House, through which the Länder participate in the legislation and the administration of the Federation. The Bundesrat consists of members of the Land governments, which appoint and recall them (Article 51). Each Land has at least three votes; Länder with more than two million inhabitants have four, and those with more than six million inhabitants have five. The votes of each Land may only be given as a block vote. The Bundesrat elects its President for one year. Its decisions are taken by simple majority vote. Meetings are in public, but the public may be excluded. The members of the Federal Government have the right, and, on demand, the obligation, to participate in the debates of the Bundesrat.

V. THE FEDERAL PRESIDENT

The Federal President or Bundespräsident is elected by the Federal Convention (Bundesversammlung), consisting of the members of the Bundestag and an equal number of members elected by the Länder Parliaments (Article 54). Every German eligible to vote in elections for the Bundestag and over 40 years of age is eligible for election. The candidate who obtains an absolute majority of votes is elected, but if such majority is not achieved by any candidate in two ballots, whoever receives most votes in a further ballot becomes President. The President's term of office is five years. Immediate re-election is admissible only once. The Federal President must not be a member of the Government or of any legislative body or hold any salaried office. Orders and instructions of the President require the counter-signature of the Federal Chancellor or competent Minister, except for the appointment or dismissal of the Chancellor or the dissolution of the Bundestag.

The President represents the Federation in International Law and accredits and receives envoys. The Bundestag or the Bundesrat may impeach the President before the Federal Constitutional Court on account of wilful violation of the Basic Law or of any other Federal Law (Article 61).

VI. THE FEDERAL GOVERNMENT

The Federal Government (Bundesregierung) consists of the Federal Chancellor (Bundeskanzler) and the Federal Ministers (Bundesminister). The Chancellor is elected by an absolute majority of the Bundestag on the proposal of the Federal President (Article 63). Ministers are appointed and dismissed by the President upon the proposal of the Chancellor. Neither he nor his Ministers may hold any other salaried office. The Chancellor determines general policy and assumes responsibility for it, but within these limits each Minister directs his department individually and on his own responsibility. The Bundestag may express its lack of confidence in the Chancellor only by electing a successor with the majority of its members; the President must then appoint the person elected (Article 67). If a motion of the Chancellor for a vote of confidence does not obtain the support of the majority of the Bundestag, the President may, upon the proposal of the Chancellor, dissolve the House within 21 days, unless it elects another Chancellor within this time (Article 68).

VII. THE LEGISLATION OF THE FEDERATION

The right of legislation lies with the Länder in so far as the Basic Law does not specifically accord legislative powers to the Federation. Distinction is made between fields of exclusive legislation of the Federation and fields of concurrent legislation of Bund and Länder. In the field of concurrent legislation the Länder may legislate so long and so far as the Federation makes no use of its legislative right. The Federation has this right only in so far as a matter cannot be effectively regulated by Land legislation, or the regulation by Land Law would prejudice other Länder, or if the preservation of legal or economic unity demands regulation by Federal Law. Exclusive legislation of the Federation is strictly limited to such matters as foreign affairs, citizenship, migration, currency, copyrights, customs, railways, post and telecommunications. In most other fields, as enumerated (Article 74), concurrent legislation exists.

The legislative organ of the Federation is the Bundestag, into which Bills are introduced by the Government, by members of the Bundestag or by the Bundesrat (Article 76). After their adoption they must be submitted to the Bundesrat, which may demand, within three weeks, that a committee of members of both houses be convened to consider the Bill (Article 77). In so far as its express approval is not needed, the Bundesrat may veto a law within two weeks. This veto can be overruled by the Bundestag, with the approval of a majority of its members.

An alteration of the Basic Law requires a majority of two-thirds in both houses, but an amendment by which the division of the Federation into Länder and the basic principles contained in Articles 1 and 20 would be affected, is inadmissible (Article 79).

The Federal Government or the Länder Governments may be authorized by law to issue ordinances. A state of legislative emergency for a Bill can be declared by the President on the request of the Government with the approval of the Bundesrat. If then the Bundestag again rejects the Bill, it may be deemed adopted nevertheless in so far as the Bundesrat approves it. An emergency may not last longer than six months and may not be declared more than once during the term of office of any one Government (Article 81).

VIII. THE EXECUTION OF FEDERAL LAWS AND THE FEDERAL ADMINISTRATION

The Länder execute the Federal Laws as their own concern in so far as the Basic Law does not otherwise determine. In doing so, they regulate the establishment of the authorities and the administrative procedure, but the Federal Government exercises supervision in order to ensure that the Länder execute the Federal Laws in an appropriate manner. For this purpose the Federal Government may send commissioners to the Land authorities (Article 84). Direct Federal administration is foreseen for the Foreign Service, Federal finance, Federal railways, postal services, Federal waterways and shipping.

In order to avert imminent danger to the existence of the democratic order, a Land may call in the police forces of other Länder; and if the Land in which the danger is imminent is itself not willing or able to fight the danger, the Federal Government may place the police in the Land, or the police forces in other Länder, under its instructions (Article 91).

IX. THE ADMINISTRATION OF JUSTICE

Judicial authority is invested in independent judges, who are subject only to the law and who may not be dismissed or transferred against their will (Article 97).

Justice is exercised by the Federal Constitutional Court, by the Supreme Federal Courts and by the Courts of the Länder. The Federal Constitutional Court decides on the interpretation of the Basic Law in cases of doubt, on the compatibility of Federal Law or Land Law with the Basic Law, and on disputes between the Federation and the Länder or between different Länder. Supreme Federal Courts are to be established for the spheres of ordinary, administrative, finance, labour and social jurisdiction. If a Supreme Federal Court intends to judge a point of law in contradiction to a previous decision of another Supreme Federal Court, it must refer the matter to a special senate of the Supreme Courts. Extraordinary courts are inadmissible.

The freedom of the individual may be restricted only on the basis of a law. No one may be prevented from appearing before his lawful judge (Article 101). Detained persons may be subjected neither to physical nor to mental ill-treatment. The police may hold no one in custody longer than the end of the day following the arrest without the decision of a court. Any person temporarily

---

* The elections of 1949 were carried out on the basis of direct election, with some elements of proportional representation. In January 1953 the draft of a new electoral law was completed by the Federal Government and passed shortly before the dissolution. The new law represents a compromise between direct election and proportional representation, and is designed to discourage the rise of many small parties.

detained must be brought before a judge who shall either issue a warrant of arrest or set him free, at the latest on the following day. A person enjoying the confidence of the detainee must be notified forthwith of any continued duration of a deprivation of liberty. An act may be punished only if it was punishable by law before the act was committed, and no one may be punished more than once on account of the same criminal act. The death sentence shall be abolished.

X. FINANCE

The Federation has the right of exclusive legislation only on customs and financial monopolies; on most other taxes, especially on income, property and inheritance, it has concurrent legislation rights with the Länder (see VII above).

Customs, financial monopolies, excise taxes (with exception of the beer tax), the transportation tax, the value added tax and property dues serving non-recurrent purposes, are administered by Federal finance authorities, and the revenues thereof accrue to the Federation. The remaining taxes are administered, as a rule, by the Länder and the Gemeinden to which they accrue. The Federation and the Länder shall be self-supporting and independent of each other in their budget economy (Article 109). In order to ensure the working efficiency of the Länder with low revenues and to equalize their differing burden of expenditure, there exists a system of revenue sharing among the Länder; in addition, the Federation may make grants, out of its own funds, to the poorer Länder. All revenues and expenditures of the Federation must be estimated for each fiscal year and included in the budget, which must be established by law before the beginning of the fiscal year. Decisions of the Bundestag or the Bundesrat which increase the budget expenditure proposed by the Federal Government require its approval (Article 113).

XI. TRANSITIONAL AND CONCLUDING PROVISIONS

The Articles 116-146 regulate a number of disconnected matters of detail, such as the relation between the old Reich and the Federation, the Federal Government and Allied High Commission, the expenses for occupation costs which have to be borne by the Federation, and the status of former German nationals who now may regain their citizenship. Article 143 contains the threat of severe punishment to those who attempt to change by force the constitutional order of the Federation or of a Land, or to prevent the Federal President by force or the threat of danger from exercising his powers.

Major Constitutional Amendments

I. SOVEREIGNTY AND RESPONSIBILITY

An amending bill of 1954:

(1) Laid down under an amendment to Article 73 of the Basic Law that the Federal Parliament had full powers to legislate in all matters relating to national defence 'including obligatory national service for men over 18 years of age';

(2) Introduced a new article (142A) which declared that 'the treaties signed in Bonn and Paris on 26 and 27 May 1952 (i.e. the Bonn Conventions and European Defence Community Treaty) were not contrary to the Federal Constitution'.

Until September 1954 the operation of the Basic Law was conditioned by two further instruments: the first, the Occupation Statute of 1949 (with subsequent amendments) defining the rights and obligations of the United States, Great Britain and France with respect to Germany; and the second, the Bonn Conventions, designed to replace the Occupation Statute and to grant almost full sovereignty to the German people.

The Bonn Conventions, 1952

(1) The Occupation Statute was abolished, and the Federal Government inherited full freedom in so far as the international situation permits.

(2) Allied forces in Germany were no longer occupation forces, but part of 'the defence of the free world, of which the Federal Republic and West Berlin form a part'.

(3) A number of problems which would normally be settled by a Peace Treaty were resolved; the Conventions were in effect a provisional treaty to end the war between the Federal Republic and the Three Powers, pending a final treaty between the whole of Germany and the Four. Under this heading the following provisions were made:

(a) The Federal Republic would have full control over its internal and foreign affairs and relations with the Three Powers would be conducted through ambassadors.

(b) Only because of the international situation would the Three Powers claim their rights regarding the stationing of armed forces on German soil, matters concerning Berlin, the reunification of Germany and the final Peace Treaty.

(c) The Federal Republic undertook to conduct its policy according to the principles of the United Nations.

(d) In their negotiations with states with which the Federal Republic has no relations, the Three Powers would consult with the Federal Government.

(e) The Federal Republic would participate in the European Defence Community.

(f) The Three Powers and the Federal Republic agreed that a freely negotiated peace settlement for the whole of Germany was their common aim, and that determination of the final boundaries of Germany must await such a treaty.

The Conventions also included supplementary contractual agreements concerning the rights and obligations of foreign troops in Germany, taxation of the armed forces, a Finance Convention, and a Convention on the settlement of matters arising out of the war and the occupation.

The London and Paris Agreements

The terms of the London Agreement of 1954 were that Germany and Italy should enter an expanded Brussels Treaty Organization; that German sovereignty should be restored and that Germany should, on agreed terms, enter NATO, and that an Agency for the control of armaments on the continent of Europe should be set up. The Paris Agreement later that year established the details of the points agreed in London.

German Sovereignty

On 5 May 1955, with the depositing of the instruments of ratification of the London and Paris Agreements, the Federal Republic of Germany attained its sovereignty. The three-power status continues for the time being in West Berlin, but is modified by a declaration by the American, French and British Commandants.

II. OTHER AMENDMENTS

In June 1968 legislation was finally passed providing for emergency measures to be taken during a time of crisis.

The main provisions of this, the 17th Amendment to the Constitution, were to allow the authorities to place certain restrictions on the secrecy of correspondence and telecommunications, to conscript men into the armed forces and to use the armed forces to fight armed insurgents if the free democratic status of the Federal Republic or of any Land was threatened. A new Article 53A provided for the establishment of a committee of 33 members, two-thirds members of the Bundestag and one-third members of the Bundesrat, which must be informed by the Federal Government of any plans in the event of a defence emergency. The life of parliamentary bodies and the terms of office of the Federal President and his deputy might be extended during a defence emergency.

The Government

(February 1989)

HEAD OF STATE

Federal President: Dr RICHARD VON WEIZSÄCKER (took office 1 July 1984).

THE FEDERAL GOVERNMENT

A coalition of the Christian Democratic Union (CDU)/Christian Social Union (CSU) and the Free Democratic Party (FDP).

Federal Chancellor: Dr HELMUT KOHL (CDU).

Vice-Chancellor and Minister for Foreign Affairs: HANS-DIETRICH GENSCHER (FDP).

Minister of Special Tasks and Head of the Chancellery: Dr WOLFGANG SCHÄUBLE (CDU).

Minister of the Interior: Dr FRIEDRICH ZIMMERMANN (CSU).

Minister of Justice: HANS A. ENGELHARD (FDP).

Minister of Finance: Dr GERHARD STOLTENBERG (CDU).

Minister of Economics: HELMUT HAUSSMANN (FDP).

Minister of Food, Agriculture and Forestry: IGNAZ KIECHLE (CSU).

Minister of Labour and Social Affairs: DR NORBERT BLÜM (CDU).

Minister of Defence: Prof. Dr RUPERT SCHOLZ (CDU).

FEDERAL REPUBLIC OF GERMANY

Minister for Youth, Family, Women and Health Affairs: Prof. Ursula-Maria Lehr (CDU).

Minister of Transport: Dr Jürgen Warnke (CSU).

Minister for the Environment, Conservation and Reactor Safety: Prof. Dr Klaus Töpfer (CDU).

Minister of Posts and Telecommunications: Dr Christian Schwarz-Schilling (CDU).

Minister for Regional Planning, Construction and Urban Development: Dr Oscar Schneider (CSU).

Minister for Intra-German Relations: Dr Dorothee Wilms (CDU).

Minister of Research and Technology: Dr Heinz Riesenhuber (CDU).

Minister for Education and Science: Jürgen W. Möllemann (FDP).

Minister for Economic Co-operation: Dr Hans Klein (CSU).

MINISTRIES

Office of the Federal President: 5300 Bonn 1, Kaiser-Friedrich-Str. 16; tel. (0228) 2001; telex 886393.

Office of the Federal Chancellor: 5300 Bonn 1, Adenauerallee 141; tel. (0228) 561; telex 886750.

Ministry of Defence: 5300 Bonn 1, Hardthöhe, Postfach 1328; tel. (0228) 121; telex 886575.

Ministry of Economic Co-operation: 5300 Bonn 1, Karl-Marx-Str. 4-6; tel. (0228) 5351; telex 8869452.

Ministry of Economics: 5300 Bonn 1, Villemombler Str. 76; tel. (0228) 6151; telex 886747.

Ministry of Education and Science: 5300 Bonn 2, Heinemannstr. 2; tel. (0228) 571; telex (17) 228315.

Ministry of the Environment, Conservation and Reactor Safety: 5300 Bonn 2, Kennedyallee 5; tel. (0228) 30501; telex 885790.

Ministry of Finance: 5300 Bonn 1, Graurheindorfer Str. 108; tel. (0228) 6821; telex 886645.

Ministry of Food, Agriculture and Forestry: 5300 Bonn 1, Rochusstr. 1; tel. (0228) 5291; telex 886844.

Ministry of Foreign Affairs: 5300 Bonn 1, Adenauerallee 99-103; tel. (0228) 170; telex 886591.

Ministry of the Interior: 5300 Bonn 1, Graurheindorfer Str. 198; tel. (0228) 6811; telex 886896.

Ministry for Intra-German Relations: 5300 Bonn 2, Godesberger Allee 140; tel. (0228) 3061; telex 885673.

Ministry of Justice: 5300 Bonn 2, Heinemannstr. 6, Postfach 200365; tel. (0228) 581; telex 8869679.

Ministry of Labour and Social Affairs: 5300 Bonn 1, Rochusstr. 1, Postfach 140280; tel. (0228) 5271; telex 886641.

Ministry of Posts and Telecommunications: 5300 Bonn 2, Heinrich-von-Stephan-Str. 1; tel. (0228) 140; telex 886707.

Ministry of Regional Planning, Construction and Urban Development: 5300 Bonn 2, Deichmannsaue; tel. (0228) 3371; telex 885462.

Ministry of Research and Technology: 5300 Bonn 2, Heinemannstr. 2; tel. (0228) 591; telex 885674.

Ministry of Transport: 5300 Bonn 2, Kennedyallee 72; tel. (0228) 3001; telex 885700.

Ministry of Youth, Family, Women and Health Affairs: 5300 Bonn 2, Kennedyallee 105-107; tel. (0228) 308-0; telex 885517.

Legislature

BUNDESTAG
(Federal Assembly)

President: Prof. Dr Rita Süssmuth (CDU).

Vice-Presidents: Annemarie Renger (SPD), Dieter Julius Cronenberg (FDP), Richard Stücklen (CSU), Heinz Westphal (SPD).

General Election, 25 January 1987

	Votes*	%	Seats†
Social Democratic Party (SPD)	14,025,763	37.04	186
Christian Democratic Union (CDU)	13,045,745	34.45	174
Christian Social Union (CSU)	3,715,827	9.81	49
Free Democratic Party (FDP)	3,440,911	9.09	46
Green Party	3,126,256	8.26	42
National Democratic Party (NPD)	227,054	0.60	—
Ecological Democratic Party (ÖDP)	109,152	0.29	—
Women's Party	62,904	0.17	—
Others	113,707	0.30	—
Total	**37,867,319**	**100.00**	**497**

* Figures refer to valid second votes (i.e. for state party lists). Valid first votes (for individual candidates) totalled 37,742,813.

† In addition to the 497 directly elected members, the Bundestag has 22 members, with limited voting powers, elected by the West Berlin House of Representatives.

BUNDESRAT
(Federal Council)

President: Björn Engholm.

The Bundesrat has 45 members. Each Land has three, four or five votes, depending on the size of its population, and sends as many members to the sessions as it has votes. As in the Bundestag, representatives from West Berlin have no voting power in plenary sessions. The head of government of each Land is automatically a member of the Bundesrat. Ministers and Members of the Federal Government attend the sessions, which are held every two to three weeks.

Länder	Seats
North Rhine-Westphalia	5
Bavaria	5
Baden-Württemberg	5
Lower Saxony	5
Hesse	4
Rhineland-Palatinate	4
Schleswig-Holstein	4
Hamburg	3
Saarland	3
Bremen	3
Berlin (West)	4

The Land Governments

The 10 Länder of the Federal Republic are autonomous but not sovereign states, enjoying a high degree of self-government and wide legislative powers.

SCHLESWIG-HOLSTEIN

The Provisional Constitution was adopted by the Diet on 13 December 1949. The Land Government consists of the Minister-President and the Ministers appointed by him. Following an inconclusive election in September 1987, a new election was held in May 1988.

Minister-President: Björn Engholm (SPD).

The composition of the Diet, as the result of elections held on 8 May 1988, is as follows:

President of Diet: Lianne Paulina-Mürl.

Party	Seats
Social Democratic Party	46
Christian Democratic Union	27
Südschleswigscher Wählerverband	1

HAMBURG

The Constitution of the 'Free and Hanseatic City of Hamburg' was adopted in June 1952. There is complete parity between the Town Assembly and the Land Diet on the one hand and between the Mayor and the President on the other. The members of the Senate are elected by the City Council. The Senate in turn elects the President and his deputy from its own ranks. The President remains in office for one year, but may offer himself for re-election. The Senate has a coalition Government formed by the SPD and the FDP.

FEDERAL REPUBLIC OF GERMANY

President of Senate and First Bürgermeister: Dr HENNING VOSCHERAU (SPD).

The City Council was elected on 17 May 1987, and is composed as follows:

President: HELGA ELSTNER (SPD).

Party	Seats
Social Democratic Party	55
Christian Democratic Union	49
Free Democratic Party	8
Green Alternative List	8

LOWER SAXONY

The Provisional Constitution was adopted by the Diet on 13 April 1951, and came into force on 1 May 1951. The Land Government is formed from a coalition of the CDU and the FDP.

Minister-President: Dr ERNST ALBRECHT (CDU).

As a result of elections held on 15 June 1986, the Diet is composed as follows:

President of the Diet: Dr EDZARD BLANKE (CDU).

Party	Seats
Christian Democratic Union	69
Social Democratic Party	66
Green Party	11
Free Democratic Party	9

Lower Saxony is divided into four governmental districts: Brunswick, Hanover, Lüneburg and Weser-Ems.

BREMEN

The Constitution of the Free Hanseatic City of Bremen was sanctioned by referendum of the people on 12 October 1947. The main constitutional organs are the City Council, the Senate and the Constitutional Court. The Senate is the executive organ elected by the Council for the duration of its own tenure of office. The Senate elects from its own ranks two Bürgermeister, one of whom becomes President of the Senate. The Senators cannot be simultaneously members of parliament. A vote of no-confidence can only be given under special conditions. Decisions of the Council are subject to the delaying veto of the Senate. The Senate is formed from the majority party (SPD).

First Bürgermeister and President of the Senate: KLAUS WEDEMEIER (SPD).

The Council consists of 100 members elected for four years. The election of 13 September 1987 resulted in the following composition:

President of the Bürgerschaft: Dr DIETER KLINK (SPD).

Party	Seats
Social Democratic Party	54
Christian Democratic Union	25
Free Democratic Party	10
Green List	10
German People's Union	1

NORTH RHINE-WESTPHALIA

The present Constitution was adopted by the Diet on 6 June 1950, and was endorsed by the electorate in the elections held on 18 June. The Land Government is presided over by the Minister-President who appoints his Ministers. It is formed from the majority SPD.

Minister-President: JOHANNES RAU (SPD).

The Diet, elected on 12 May 1985, is composed as follows:

President of Diet: KARL-JOSEF DENZER (SPD).

Party	Seats
Social Democratic Party	125
Christian Democratic Union	88
Free Democratic Party	14

The state is divided into five governmental districts: Düsseldorf, Münster, Arnsberg, Detmold and Cologne.

HESSE

The Constitution of this Land dates from 11 December 1946. The Minister-President is elected by the Diet and he appoints and dismisses his Ministers with its consent. The Diet can force the resignation of the State Government by a vote of no-confidence. The Government is formed from a coalition of the CDU and the FDP.

Minister-President: Dr WALTER WALLMANN (CDU).

The Diet, elected on 5 April 1987, is composed as follows:

President of Diet: KLAUS-PETER MÖLLER (CDU).

Party	Seats
Christian Democratic Union	47
Social Democratic Party	44
Green Party	10
Free Democratic Party	9

Hesse is divided into two governmental districts: Kassel and Darmstadt.

RHINELAND-PALATINATE

The three chief agencies of the Constitution of this Land are the Diet, the Government and the Constitutional Court. The Minister-President is elected by the Diet, with whose consent he appoints and dismisses his Ministers. The Government, which is dependent on the confidence of the Diet, is made up from a coalition of the CDU and the FDP.

Minister-President: CARL-LUDWIG WAGNER (CDU).

The members of the Diet are elected according to a system of proportional representation. Its composition, as the result of elections held on 17 May 1987, is as follows:

President of Diet: Dr HEINZ PETER VOLKERT (CDU).

Party	Seats
Christian Democratic Union	48
Social Democratic Party	40
Free Democratic Party	7
Green Party	5

Rhineland-Palatinate is divided into three districts: Koblenz, Rheinhessen-Palatinate and Trier.

BADEN-WÜRTTEMBERG

The Constitution was adopted by the Land Assembly in Stuttgart on 19 November 1953. The Minister-President is elected by the Diet. He appoints and dismisses his Ministers. The Government, which is responsible to the Diet, is formed by the majority party (CDU).

Minister-President: Dr LOTHAR SPÄTH (CDU).

The composition of the Diet, as the result of elections held on 20 March 1988, is as follows:

President of Diet: ERICH SCHNEIDER (CDU).

Party	Seats
Christian Democratic Union	66
Social Democratic Party	42
Green Party	10
Free Democratic Party	7

The Land is divided into four administrative districts: Stuttgart, Karlsruhe, Tübingen and Freiburg.

BAVARIA

The Constitution of Bavaria allows for a two-chamber Parliament and a Constitutional Court. Provision is also made for a popular referendum. The Minister-President is elected by the Diet for four years. He appoints the Ministers and Secretaries of State with the consent of the Diet. The State Government is formed from the majority party (CSU).

Minister-President: Dr MAX STREIBL (CSU).

The composition of the Diet, as a result of elections held on 12 October 1986, is as follows:

President of Diet: Dr FRANZ HEUBL (CSU).

Party	Seats
Christian Social Union	128
Social Democratic Party	61
Green Party	15

FEDERAL REPUBLIC OF GERMANY

The Senate, or second chamber, consists of 60 members, divided into 10 groups representing professional interests, e.g. agriculture, industry, trade, free professions and religious communities. Every two years one-third of the Senate is replaced at elections.

President of the Senate: Dr HANS WEISS.

Bavaria is divided into seven districts: Mittelfranken, Oberfranken, Unterfranken, Schwaben, Niederbayern, Oberpfalz and Oberbayern.

SAARLAND

By the Constitution which came into force on 1 January 1957, Saarland became politically integrated with the Federal Republic as a Land. It became economically integrated with the Federal Republic in July 1959. The Minister-President is elected by the Diet. The Government is formed by the SPD.

Minister-President: OSKAR LAFONTAINE (SPD).

The Diet, elected on 10 March 1985, is composed as follows:
President of the Diet: ALBRECHT HEROLD (SPD).

Party	Seats
Social Democratic Party	27
Christian Democratic Union	19
Free Democratic Party	5

West Berlin

On 4 August 1950, the Berlin City Assembly adopted a constitution defining its special position under technical three-power control. Under German Constitutional Law, Berlin is a Land of the Federal Republic but this law is at present suspended by three-power reservations. Nevertheless, West Berlin sends representatives to the Bundestag and Bundesrat in Bonn, but these representatives have no vote in the plenary sessions of either House. To be valid in West Berlin, Federal Law has to be specially adopted there. The Constitution came into force on 1 October 1950.

The House of Representatives (Abgeordnetenhaus) is the legislative body, and has 138 members. The executive agency is the Senate, which is composed of the Governing Mayor (Regierender Bürgermeister), his deputy, and at the most 16 Senators. The Governing Mayor is elected by a majority of the House of Representatives. The Senate is responsible to the House of Representatives and dependent on its confidence.

Regierender Bürgermeister: EBERHARD DIEPGEN (CDU).

Bürgermeisterin and Senator for Education, Vocational Training and Sport: Dr HANNA-RENATE LAURIEN (CDU).

SENATORS

Economics and Labour: ELMAR PIEROTH (CDU).
Justice and Federal Affairs: LUDWIG A. REBLINGER (CDU).
Finance: Dr GÜNTER REXROTH (FDP).
Cultural Affairs: Dr VOLKER HASSEMER (CDU).
Interior: Dr WILHELM KEWENIG (CDU).
Public Health and Social Affairs: ULF FINK (CDU).
Building and Housing: GEORG WITTWER (CDU).
Urban Development and Environment: Dr JÜRGEN STARNICK (Independent).
Transport and Public Utilities: EDMUND WRONSKI (CDU).
Youth and Family Affairs: CORNELIA SCHMALZ-JACOBSEN (FDP).
Science and Research: Dr GEORGE TURNER (Independent).

The state of parties in the House, as the result of elections held on 29 January 1989, is as follows:

President of House of Representatives: PETER REBSCH (CDU).

Party	Seats
Christian Democratic Union	55
Social Democratic Party	55
Alternative List	17
Republican Party	11

Political Organizations

Christlich Demokratische Union Deutschlands (in Bavaria: **Christlich Soziale Union**) **(CDU/CSU)** (Christian Democratic and Christian Social Union):

CDU: 5300 Bonn 1, Konrad-Adenauer-Haus, Friedrich-Ebert-Allee 73–75; tel. (0228) 5441; telex 886804; f. 1945, became a federal party in 1950; stands for the united action between Catholics and Protestants for rebuilding German life on a Christian basis, while guaranteeing private property and the freedom of the individual and for a 'free and equal Germany in a free, politically united and socially just Europe'; other objectives are to guarantee close ties with allies within NATO and the principle of self-determination; 702,000 mems (1988); Chair. Dr HELMUT KOHL; Sec.-Gen. Dr HEINER GEISSLER.

CSU: 8000 Munich 2, Nymphenburger Str. 64; tel. (089) 1243-0; telex 898666; f. 1946; Christian Democratic party, aiming for a free market economy 'in the service of man's economic and intellectual freedom'; also combines national consciousness with support for a united Europe; 186,000 mems; Chair. Dr THEO WAIGEL; Sec.-Gen. ERWIN HUBER.

Deutsche Kommunistische Partei (DKP) (German Communist Party): 4000 Düsseldorf, Prinz-Georg-Str. 79; telex 8584387; 49,000 mems; Chair. HERBERT MIES.

Freie Demokratische Partei (FDP) (Free Democratic Party): 5300 Bonn, Baunscheidtstr. 15, Thomas-Dehler-Haus; tel. (0228) 5470; telex 886580; f. 1948; represents democratic and social liberalism and makes the individual the focal point of the state and its laws and economy; approx. 65,000 mems (1988); Chair. Dr OTTO GRAF LAMBSDORFF; Deputy Chair. Dr IRMGARD ADAM-SCHWAETZER, GERHART RUDOLF BAUM, Dr WOLFGANG GERHARDT; Chair. in Bundestag WOLFGANG MISCHNICK; Sec.-Gen. CORNELIA SCHMALZ-JACOBSEN.

Die Grünen (Green Party): 5300 Bonn 1, Colmantstr. 36; tel. (0228) 692021; telex 886330; f. 1980; largely comprised of the membership of the Grüne Aktion Zukunft, the Grüne Liste Umweltschutz and the Aktionsgemeinschaft Unabhängiger Deutscher, also includes groups of widely varying political views; essentially left-wing party programme includes ecological issues, dissolution of NATO and Warsaw Pact military blocs, breaking down of large economic concerns into smaller units, 35-hour week and unlimited right to strike; approx. 42,000 mems (1987); Exec. (vacant); Gen. Sec. EBERHARD WALDE.

Nationaldemokratische Partei Deutschlands (NPD) (National Democratic Party of Germany): 7000 Stuttgart 10, Postfach 103528; tel. (0711) 610605; telex 244012; f. 1964; right-wing; 15,000 mems; youth organization Junge Nationaldemokraten (JN), 6,000 mems; Chair. MARTIN MUSSGNUG.

Die Republikaner (REP) (Republican Party): f. 1983; approx. 8,500 mems; extreme right-wing; Chair. FRANZ SCHÖNHUBER.

Sozialdemokratische Partei Deutschlands (SPD) (Social Democratic Party of Germany): 5300 Bonn, Ollenhauerstr. 1; tel. (0228) 5321; telex 886306; f. 1863; the party maintains that a vital democracy can be built only on the basis of social justice; advocates for the economy as much competition as possible, as much planning as necessary to protect the individual from uncontrolled economic interests; a positive attitude to national defence, while favouring controlled disarmament; a policy of religious toleration; rejects any political ties with Communism; approx. 920,000 mems (1988); Chair. of SPD Dr HANS-JOCHEN VOGEL; Deputy Chair. JOHANNES RAU, OSKAR LAFONTAINE, HERTA DÄUBLER-GMELIN; Chair. of Parliamentary Party Dr HANS-JOCHEN VOGEL.

There are also numerous other small parties, none of them represented in the Bundestag, covering all shades of the political spectrum and various regional interests.

Diplomatic Representation

EMBASSIES IN THE FEDERAL REPUBLIC OF GERMANY

Afghanistan: 5300 Bonn 1, Liebfrauenweg 1A; tel. (0228) 251927; Chargé d'affaires: TAHER NANGIALAI.

Albania: Bonn; Ambassador: SHPËTIM CAUSHI.

Algeria: 5300 Bonn 2, Rheinallee 32; tel. (0228) 356054; telex 885723; Ambassador: AMOR BENGHEZAL.

Angola: Bonn; Ambassador: HERMÍNIO ESCORCIO.

Argentina: 5300 Bonn 1, Adenauerallee 50–52; tel. (0228) 222011; telex 886478; Ambassador: HUGO BOATTI OSSORIO.

Australia: 5300 Bonn 2, Godesberger Allee 107; tel. (0228) 81030; telex 885466; Ambassador: RAYMOND JAMES GREET.

Austria: 5300 Bonn 1, Johanniterstr. 2; tel. (0228) 230051; telex 886780; Ambassador: Dr FRIEDRICH BAUER.

Bangladesh: 5300 Bonn 2, Bonner Str. 48; tel. (0228) 352525; telex 885640; Ambassador: Maj.-Gen. MUZAMMEL HUSSAIN.

Belgium: 5300 Bonn 1, Kaiser-Friedrich-Str. 7; tel. (0228) 212001; telex 886777; Ambassador: GEORGES VANDER ESPT.

FEDERAL REPUBLIC OF GERMANY

Benin: 5300 Bonn 2, Rüdigerstr. 10; tel. (0228) 344031; telex 885594; Ambassador: Guy Boukary-Mory.

Bolivia: 5300 Bonn 2, Konstantinstr. 16; tel. (0228) 362038; telex 885785; Ambassador: Carlos Prudencio Pinedo.

Brazil: 5300 Bonn 2, Kennedyallee 74; tel. (0228) 376976; telex 885471; Ambassador: Jorge de Carvalho e Silva.

Bulgaria: 5300 Bonn 2, Auf der Hostert 6; tel. (0228) 363061; telex 885739; Ambassador: Georgi Evtimov.

Burkina Faso: 5300 Bonn 2, Wendelstadtallee 18; tel. (0228) 332063; telex 885508; Ambassador: Gomtirbou Anatole Tiendrebeogo.

Burma: 5300 Bonn 1, Schumann Str. 112; tel. (0228) 210091; telex 8869560; Ambassador: U Maung Maung Than Tun.

Burundi: 5307 Wachtberg-Niederbachem, Drosselweg 2; tel. (0228) 345032; telex 885745; Ambassador: Ildephonse Nkeramihigo.

Cameroon: 5300 Bonn 2, Rheinallee 76; tel. (0228) 356037; telex 885480; Ambassador: Jean Melaga.

Canada: 5300 Bonn 1, Friedrich-Wilhelm-Str. 18; tel. (0228) 231061; telex 886421; Ambassador: Donald S. McPhail.

Central African Republic: 5300 Bonn 2, Dürenstr. 12; tel. (0228) 354077; telex 8861166; Ambassador: Nestor Kombot-Naguemon.

Chad: 5300 Bonn 2, Basteistr. 80; tel. (0228) 356025; telex 8869305; Ambassador: Dr Issa Hassan Khayar.

Chile: 5300 Bonn 2, Kronprinzstr. 20; tel. (0228) 363089; telex 885403; Ambassador: Ricardo Riesco Jaramillo.

China, People's Republic: 5300 Bonn 2, Kurfürstenallee 12; tel. (0228) 361095; telex 885655; Ambassador: Mei Zhaorong.

Colombia: 5300 Bonn 1, Friedrich-Wilhelm-Str. 35; tel. (0228) 234565; telex 886305; Ambassador: Dr Luis González Barros.

Congo: 5300 Bonn 2, Rheinallee 45; tel. (0228) 357085; telex 886690; Ambassador: Gérard-François Yandza.

Costa Rica: 5300 Bonn 1, Borsigallee 2; tel. (0228) 252940; telex 8869961; Ambassador: José Joaquín Chaverri.

Côte d'Ivoire: 5300 Bonn 1, Königstr. 93; tel. (0228) 212098; telex 886524; Ambassador: Lambert Amon-Tanoh.

Cuba: 5300 Bonn 2, Kennedyallee 22–24; tel. (0228) 3091; telex 885733; Ambassador: Luis García Peraza.

Cyprus: 5300 Bonn 2, Kronprinzstr. 58; tel. (0228) 363336; telex 885519; Ambassador: Costas Papademas.

Czechoslovakia: 5300 Bonn 1, Im Rheingarten 7; tel. (0228) 284765; telex 8869322; Ambassador: Dušan Spáčil.

Denmark: 5300 Bonn 1, Pfälzer Str. 14; tel. (0228) 729910; telex 886892; Ambassador: Dr Paul Henning Fischer.

Dominican Republic: 5300 Bonn 2, Burgstr. 87; tel. (0228) 223160; Ambassador: Dr Manuel Rafael García Lizardo.

Ecuador: 5300 Bonn 2, Koblenzer Str. 37; tel. (0228) 352544; telex 8869527; Ambassador: Dr Julio Aníbal Moreno Espinosa.

Egypt: 5300 Bonn 2, Kronprinzstr. 2; tel. (0228) 364008; telex 885719; Ambassador: Abdel Fattah Mohamed Shabana.

El Salvador: 5300 Bonn 1, Burbacherstr. 2; tel. (0228) 221351; Ambassador: Dr Juan Ricardo Ramírez Rauda.

Ethiopia: 5300 Bonn 1, Brentanostr. 1; tel. (0228) 233041; telex 8869498; Ambassador: Tadesse Terrefe.

Finland: 5300 Bonn 2, Friesdorfer Str. 1; tel. (0228) 311033; telex 885626; Ambassador: Antti Karppinen.

France: 5300 Bonn 2, Kapellenweg 1A; tel. (0228) 362031; telex 885445; Ambassador: Serge Boidevaix.

Gabon: 5300 Bonn 2, Kronprinzstr. 52; tel. (0228) 354084; telex 885520; Ambassador: Léon N'Dong.

German Democratic Republic: 5300 Bonn 2, Godesberger Allee 18; tel. (0228) 379051; telex 885645; Head of Permanent Representation: Horst Neubauer; also in Düsseldorf.

Ghana: 5300 Bonn 2, Rheinallee 58; tel. (0228) 352011; telex 885660; Ambassador: Kwame Samuel Adusei-Poku.

Greece: 5300 Bonn 2, Koblenzerstr. 103; tel. (0228) 355036; telex 885636; Ambassador: Leonidas A. Evangelidis.

Guatemala: 5300 Bonn 2, Ziethenstr. 16; tel. (0228) 351579; telex 8869983; Ambassador: Ana Lucrecia Rivera Schwarz.

Guinea: 5300 Bonn 1, Rochusweg 50; tel. (0228) 231097; telex 886448; Ambassador: Alkhaly Bangoura.

Haiti: 5300 Bonn 2, Schlossallee 10; tel. (0228) 340351; Ambassador: Jean-Robert Saget.

Holy See: 5300 Bonn 2, Turmstr. 29; tel. (0228) 376901; Apostolic Nuncio: Mgr Giuseppe Uhač.

Honduras: 5300 Bonn 2, Ubierstr. 1; tel. (0228) 356394; telex 889496; Ambassador: Alex Mayr.

Hungary: 5300 Bonn 2, Turmstr. 30; tel. (0228) 376797; telex 886501; Ambassador: Dr István Horváth.

Iceland: 5300 Bonn 2, Kronprinzstr. 6; tel. (0228) 364021; telex 885690; Ambassador: Pall Asgeir Tryggvason.

India: 5300 Bonn 1, Adenauerallee 262–264; tel. (0228) 54050; telex 8869301; Ambassador: Anantanarayan Madhavan.

Indonesia: 5300 Bonn 1, Bernkasteler Str. 2; tel. (0228) 310091; telex 886352; Ambassador: Ashadi Tjahjadi.

Iran: 5300 Bonn 2, Godesberger Allee 133–137; tel. (0228) 8100521/22; telex 885697; Ambassador: Mehdi Ahari Mostafavi.

Iraq: 5300 Bonn 2, Dürenstr. 33; tel. (0228) 82031; telex 8869471; Ambassador: (vacant).

Ireland: 5300 Bonn 2, Godesberger Allee 119; tel. (0228) 376937; telex 885588; Ambassador: Kester W. Heaslip.

Israel: 5300 Bonn 2, Simrockallee 2; tel. (0228) 8231; telex 885490; Ambassador: Jitzhak Ben-Ari.

Italy: 5300 Bonn 2, Karl-Finkelnburg-Str. 51; tel. (0228) 82006-0; telex 885450; Ambassador: Raniero Vanni d'Archirafi.

Jamaica: 5300 Bonn 2, Am Kreuter 1; tel. (0228) 354045; telex 885493; Ambassador: M. Patricia Durrant.

Japan: 5300 Bonn 1, Bonn-Center, H1 701, Bundeskanzlerplatz; tel. (0228) 5001; telex 886878; Ambassador: Yasushi Miyazawa.

Jordan: 5300 Bonn 2, Beethovenallee 21; tel. (0228) 357046; telex 885401; Ambassador: Fawaz Sharaf.

Kenya: 5300 Bonn 2, Villichgasse 17; tel. (0228) 353066; telex 885570; Ambassador: Maurice Peter Omwony.

Korea, Republic: 5300 Bonn 1, Adenauerallee 124; tel. (0228) 267960; telex 8869508; Ambassador: Chung-Sub Shin.

Kuwait: 5300 Bonn 2, Godesberger Allee 77-81; tel. (0228) 378081; telex 886525; Ambassador: Chalid al-Babtain.

Lebanon: 5300 Bonn 2, Rheinallee 27; tel. (0228) 352075; telex 8869339; Ambassador: Souheil Chammas.

Lesotho: 5300 Bonn 2, Godesberger Allee 50; tel. (0228) 376868; telex 8869370; Ambassador: Mokheseng Reginald Tekateka.

Liberia: 5300 Bonn 1, Hohenzollernstr. 73; tel. (0228) 351810; telex 886637; Ambassador: Nathaniel Eastman.

Libya: 5300 Bonn 2, Beethovenallee 12A; tel. (0228) 362041; telex 885738; Secretary of the People's Committee: Elmahdi M. Imberesh.

Luxembourg: 5300 Bonn 1, Adenauerallee 110; tel. (0228) 214008; telex 886557; Ambassador: Adrien Ferdinand Josef Meisch.

Madagascar: 5300 Bonn 2, Rolandstr. 48; tel. (0228) 331057; telex 885781; Ambassador: Jean Ernest Bezaza.

Malawi: 5300 Bonn 1, Bonn-Center, HI 1103, Bundeskanzlerplatz; tel. (0228) 213050; telex 8869689; Ambassador: Linnaeus Stephen Kauta Msiska.

Malaysia: 5300 Bonn 2, Mittelstr. 43; tel. (0228) 376803; telex 885683; Ambassador: Dato' Zainal Abidin bin Ibrahim.

Mali: 5300 Bonn 2, Bassteistr. 86; tel. (0228) 357048; telex 885680; Ambassador: Sekou Almamy Koreissi.

Malta: 5300 Bonn 2, Viktoriastr. 1; tel. (0228) 363017; telex 885748; Ambassador: Frederick E. Amato-Gauci.

Mauritania: 5300 Bonn 2, Bonnerstr. 48; tel. (0228) 364024; telex 885550; Ambassador: Nalla Oumar Kane.

Mexico: 5300 Bonn 1, Oxfordstr. 12–16; tel. (0228) 631226; telex 886819; Ambassador: Adolfo Hegewisch.

Monaco: 5300 Bonn 1, Zitelmannstr. 16; tel. (0228) 232007; Ambassador: Rene Bocca.

Morocco: 5300 Bonn 2, Gotenstr. 7–9; tel. (0228) 355044; telex 885428; Ambassador: Abdelkader Benslimane.

Nepal: 5300 Bonn 2, Im Hag 15; tel. (0228) 343097; telex 8869297; Ambassador: Gen. Simha Pratap Shah.

Netherlands: 5300 Bonn 1, Strässchensweg 10; tel. (0228) 238091; telex 886826; Ambassador: Jan Gerard van der Tas.

New Zealand: 5300 Bonn 1, Bonn-Center, HI 902, Bundeskanzlerplatz; tel. (0228) 214021; telex 886322; Ambassador: Edward Farnon.

Nicaragua: 5300 Bonn 2, Konstantinstr. 41; tel. (0228) 362505; telex 885734; Ambassador: Hernán Estrada.

Niger: 5300 Bonn 2, Dürenstr. 9; tel. (0228) 356057; telex 885572; Ambassador: Idrissa Arouna.

Nigeria: 5300 Bonn 2, Goldbergweg 13; tel. (0228) 322071; telex 885522; Ambassador: Abba Zoru.

Norway: 5300 Bonn 2, Gotenstr. 163; tel. (0228) 374055; telex 885491; Ambassador: Sverre Julius Gjellum.

Oman: 5300 Bonn 2, Lindenallee 11; tel. (0228) 357031; telex 885688; Ambassador: Saud bin Suliman al-Nabhani.

FEDERAL REPUBLIC OF GERMANY

Pakistan: 5300 Bonn 2, Rheinallee 24; tel. (0228) 352004; telex 885787; Ambassador: MAHDI MASUD.

Panama: 5300 Bonn 2, Lützowstr. 1; tel. (0228) 361036; telex 885600; Ambassador: DAVID SAMUDIO, Jr.

Papua New Guinea: 5300 Bonn 2, Gotenstr. 163; tel. (0228) 376855; telex 886340; Ambassador: ANDREW M. D. YAUIEB.

Paraguay: 5300 Bonn 2, Plittersdorfer Str. 121; tel. (0228) 356727; Ambassador: Dr VÍCTOR MANUEL GODOY.

Peru: 5300 Bonn 2, Godesbergerallee 127; tel. (0228) 373045; telex 886325; Ambassador: GABRIEL GARCÍA PIKE.

Philippines: 5300 Bonn 1, Argelanderstr. 1; tel. (0228) 267990; telex 8869571; Ambassador: Prof. AUGUSTO CAESAR ESPIRITU.

Poland: 5000 Cologne 51, Lindenallee 7; tel. (0221) 380261; telex 8881040; Ambassador: Dr RYSZARD KARSKI.

Portugal: 5300 Bonn 2, Ubierstr. 78; tel. (0228) 363011; telex 885577; Ambassador: FERNANDO MANUEL DA SILVA MARQUES.

Qatar: 5300 Bonn 2, Brunnenallee 6; tel. (0228) 351074; telex 885476; Ambassador: AHMED ABDULLA AL-KHAL.

Romania: 5300 Bonn 1, Legionsweg 14; tel. (0228) 670001; telex 8869792; Ambassador: MARCEL DINU.

Rwanda: 5300 Bonn 2, Beethovenallee 72; tel. (0228) 355058; telex 885604; Ambassador: JUVÉNAL RENZAHO.

Saudi Arabia: 5300 Bonn 2, Godesberger Allee 40–42; tel. (0228) 379013; telex 885442; Ambassador: Sheikh RASAHD MUSSALLAM NUWEILATI.

Senegal: 5300 Bonn 1, Argelanderstr. 3; tel. (0228) 218008; telex 8869644; Ambassador: Gen. JOSEPH LOUIS TAVARES DA SOUZA.

Singapore: 5300 Bonn 2, Südstr. 133; tel. (0228) 312007; telex 885642; Ambassador: TONY K. SIDDIQUE.

Somalia: 5300 Bonn 2, Hohenzollernstr. 12; tel. (0228) 355084; telex 885724; Ambassador: Dr HASSAN SHEIKH HUSSEIN.

South Africa: 5300 Bonn 2, Auf der Hostert 3; tel. (0228) 82010; telex 885720; Ambassador: WILLEM RETIEF.

Spain: 5300 Bonn 1, Schlossstr. 4; tel. (0228) 217094; telex 886792; Ambassador: EDUARDO FONCILLAS.

Sri Lanka: 5300 Bonn 2, Rolandstr. 52; tel. (0228) 332055; telex 885612; Ambassador: Mrs IRANGANI MANEL ABEYSEKERA.

Sudan: 5300 Bonn 2, Koblenzerstr. 99; tel. (0228) 363074; telex 885478; Ambassador: MIRGHANI SULEIMAN KHALIL.

Sweden: 5300 Bonn 1, Allianzplatz, Haus I, Heussallee 2–10; tel. (0228) 260020; telex 886667; Ambassador: LENNART ECKERBERG.

Switzerland: 5300 Bonn 2, Gotenstr. 156; tel. (0228) 810080; telex 885646; Ambassador: ALFRED HOHL.

Syria: 5300 Bonn 2, Am Kurpark 2; tel. (0228) 363091; telex 885757; Ambassador: SULEYMAN HADDAD.

Tanzania: 5300 Bonn 2, Theaterplatz 26; tel. (0228) 353477; telex 885569; Ambassador: AHMED HASSAN DIRIA.

Thailand: 5300 Bonn 2, Ubierstr. 65; tel. (0228) 355065; telex 886574; Ambassador: SOKOL VANABRIKSHA.

Togo: 5300 Bonn 2, Beethovenallee 13; tel. (0228) 355091; telex 885595; Ambassador: NAPO ALI.

Tunisia: 5300 Bonn 2, Godesberger Allee 103; tel. (0228) 376981; telex 885477; Ambassador: HAMED AMMAR.

Turkey: 5300 Bonn 2, Ute Str. 47; tel. (0228) 346052; telex 885521; Ambassador: OKTAY IŞCEN.

Uganda: 5300 Bonn 2, Dürenstr. 44; tel. (0228) 355027; telex 885578; Ambassador: Mrs FREDA BLICK.

USSR: 5300 Bonn 2, Waldstr. 42; tel. (0228) 312086; Ambassador: YULI A. KVITSINSKY.

United Arab Emirates: 5300 Bonn 1, Erste Fährgasse 6; tel. (0228) 267070; telex 885741; Ambassador: Dr SAEED MOHAMMAD AL-SHAMSI.

United Kingdom: 5300 Bonn 1, Friedrich-Ebert-Allee 77; tel. (0228) 234061; telex 886887; Ambassador: Sir CHRISTOPHER MALLABY.

USA: 5300 Bonn 2, Deichmanns Aue 29; tel. (0228) 3391; telex 885452; Ambassador: VERNON A. WALTERS (designate).

Uruguay: 5300 Bonn 2, Gotenstr. 1–3; tel. (0228) 356570; telex 885708; Ambassador: JULIO LACARTE MURÓ.

Venezuela: 5300 Bonn 3, Im Rheingarten 7; tel. (0228) 466057; telex 885447; Ambassador: HUMBERTO ENRIQUE ALCALDE ALVAREZ.

Viet-Nam: 5300 Bonn 2, Konstantinstr. 37; tel. (0228) 357022; telex 8861122; Ambassador: (vacant).

Yemen Arab Republic: 5300 Bonn 2, Godesberger-Allee 125–127; tel. (0228) 376851; telex 885765; Ambassador: MUHAMMAD ABDULLA AL-ERIANI.

Yugoslavia: 5300 Bonn 2, Schlossallee 5; tel. (0228) 344051; telex 885530; Ambassador: Dr MILAN DRAGOVIĆ.

Zaire: 5300 Bonn 2, Im Meisengarten 133; tel. (0228) 346071; telex 885573; Ambassador: MABOLIA INENGO TRA BWATO.

Zambia: 5300 Bonn 2, Mittelstr. 39; tel. (0228) 376811; telex 885511; Ambassador: Lt-Gen. CHRISTON SIFAPI TEMBO.

Zimbabwe: 5300 Bonn 2, Viktoriastr. 28; tel. (0228) 356071; telex 885580; Ambassador: EUBERT PAUL TAYIREVA MASHAIRE.

Judicial System

Judges are not removable except by the decision of a court. Half of the judges of the Federal Constitutional Court are elected by the Bundestag and half by the Bundesrat. A committee for the selection of judges participates in the appointment of judges of the Superior Federal Courts.

FEDERAL CONSTITUTIONAL COURT

Bundesverfassungsgericht (Federal Constitutional Court): 7500 Karlsruhe, Schlossbezirk 3; tel. (0721) 1491; telex 8869679.

President: Prof. Dr ROMAN HERZOG.

Vice-President: Dr ERNST GOTTFRIED MAHRENHOLZ.

Judges: Prof. Dr HERMAN HEUSSNER, Dr KARIN GRASSHOF, Dr EVERHARDT FRANSSEN, KONRAD KRUIS, Prof. Dr ALFRED SÖLLNER, Prof. Dr THOMAS DIETERICH, Prof. Dr PAUL KIRCHOF, Dr GISELA NIEMEYER, ERNST TRÄGER, Dr OTTO SEIDL, Dr JOHANN FRIEDRICH HENSCHEL, Prof. Dr ERNST-WOLFGANG BÖCKENFÖRDE, Prof. Dr HANS HUGO KLEIN, Prof. Dr DIETER GRIMM.

SUPERIOR FEDERAL COURTS

Bundesgerichtshof (Federal Court of Justice): 7500 Karlsruhe, Herrenstr. 45A; tel. (0721) 159-0; telex 07825828.

President: Prof. Dr WALTER ODERSKY.

Vice-President: HANNSKARL SALGER.

Presidents of the Senate: Dr DIETER HOEGEN, Dr OTTO FRIEDRICH Freiherr VON GAMM, HORST HERRMANN, WOLFRAM BRAXMAIER, Dr WOLFGANG GIRISCH, FRIEDRICH LOHMANN, GERHARD HERDEGEN, Dr GÜNTER KROHN, FRANZ MERZ, Dr ERICH STEFFEN, Dr HORST SCHAUENBURG, Dr KARL BRUCHHAUSEN, Dr WOLFGANG RUSS, Prof. Dr HORST HAGEN, HERBERT SCHIMANSKY.

Federal Solicitor-General: Prof. Dr KURT REBMANN.

Federal Prosecutors: RAINER SCHULTE, GERHARD LÖCHNER, Dr RAINER MÜLLER.

Bundesverwaltungsgericht (Federal Administrative Court): 1000 Berlin 12, Hardenbergstr. 31; tel. (030) 3197-1.

President: Prof. Dr HORST SENDLER.

Vice-President: Dr GÜNTER ZEHNER.

Presidents of the Senate: JÜRGEN SAALMANN, Dr HERBERT HEINRICH, Prof. Dr FELIX WEYREUTHER, Dr GÜNTER KORBMACHER, Dr PAUL SCHWARZ, HELMUT HACKER, Prof. Dr OTTO SCHLICHTER, Dr CHARLOTTE ECKSTEIN, Dr ALFRED DICKERSBACH, ERICH BERMEL.

Bundesfinanzhof (Federal Financial Court): 8000 Munich 80, Ismaningerstr. 109; tel. (089) 9231-1.

President: Prof. Dr FRANZ KLEIN.

Vice-President: Dr CLAUS GRIMM.

Presidents of the Senate: Dr KURT MESSMER, Prof. HEINRICH BEISSE, Dr GEORG DÖLLERER, Dr MAX RID, HEINZ SCHELLENBERGER, Dr WILHELM LEINGÄRTNER, Dr LOTHAR WOERNER, Prof. Dr LUDWIG SCHMIDT, Dr KLAUS OFFERHAUS.

Religion

CHRISTIANITY

Arbeitsgemeinschaft christlicher Kirchen in der Bundesrepublik Deutschland und Berlin (West) eV (Association of Christian Churches in the Federal Republic of Germany and West Berlin): 6000 Frankfurt/Main 1, Neue Schlesingergasse 22–24; tel. (069) 20334; f. 1948; 15 Churches are affiliated to this Council, including the Roman Catholic Church and the Greek Orthodox Metropoly; Pres. Rev. HANS-BEAT MOTEL.

The Roman Catholic Church

It is estimated that about 45% of the population of the Federal Republic are adherents of the Roman Catholic Church, which is strongest in the South.

FEDERAL REPUBLIC OF GERMANY

Bishops' Conference: Deutsche Bischofskonferenz, 5300 Bonn, Kaiserstr. 163; tel. (0228) 1030; telex 8869438; Pres. Dr Dr KARL LEHMANN, Bishop of Mainz; Sec. Prälat WILHELM SCHÄTZLER.

Archbishop of Bamberg: Dr ELMAR MARIA KREDEL, Erzbischöfliches Ordinariat, 8600 Bamberg, Domplatz 3, Postfach 4034.

Archbishop of Cologne: Cardinal JOACHIM MEISNER, Generalvikariat, 5000 Cologne 1, Marzellenstr. 32; tel. (0221) 16421.

Archbishop of Freiburg im Breisgau: Dr OSKAR SAIER, 7800 Freiburg im Breisgau, Herrenstr. 35.

Archbishop of Munich and Freising: Cardinal FRIEDRICH WETTER, 8000 Munich 33, Postfach 360; tel. (089) 21371.

Archbishop of Paderborn: Dr JOHANNES JOACHIM DEGENHARDT, Erzbischöfliches Generalvikariat, 4790 Paderborn, Domplatz 3.

Commissariat of German Bishops—Catholic Office: 53 Bonn, Kaiser-Friedrich-Str. 9; tel. 218015; (represents the German Conference of Bishops before the Federal Government on political issues); Leader Prälat PAUL BOCKLET.

Central Committee of German Catholics: 5300 Bonn 2, Hochkreuzallee 246; tel. (0228) 316056; telex (17) 2283 748; f. 1868; summarizes the activities of Catholic laymen and lay-organizations in the Federal Republic; Pres. Prof. Dr HANS MAIER; Gen. Sec. Dr FRIEDRICH KRONENBERG.

Protestant Churches

Until 1969 the Protestant churches in both the Federal and Democratic Republics were united in the Evangelische Kirche in Deutschland (EKD), a federation established at the Conference of Eisenach (Thuringia) in 1948. In 1969, however, the churches in the Democratic Republic declared themselves organizationally independent and established the Bund der Evangelischen Kirchen in der DDR. Consequently the EKD is now restricted to the Federal Republic and Berlin (West) only, but maintains links with the churches in the Democratic Republic.

The Vereinigte Evangelisch-Lutherische Kirche Deutschlands (VELKD), one of the federations within the EKD, also divided in 1968 and is paralleled in the Democratic Republic by the VELKDDR. The Evangelische Kirche der Union (EKU) is partly divided and spans both the Federal and the Democratic Republics (see the chapter on the German Democratic Republic).

About 41.6% of the population of the Federal Republic (25.5m.) are members of the Protestant Church, the great majority belonging to churches forming the EKD. The total membership of the Lutheran churches is almost 10m., of the United Churches about 13.5m., and of the Reformed Churches about 448,000.

Outside the EKD are numerous small Protestant Free Churches, such as the Baptists, Methodists, Mennonites and the Lutheran Free Church, with a membership of approximately 400,000 in all.

Evangelische Kirche in Deutschland (EKD) (Protestant Church in Germany): 3000 Hanover 21, Herrenhäuser Str. 12, Postfach 210120; tel. (0511) 71110; telex 923445; Berlin Office: 1000 Berlin 12, Jebensstr. 3. The governing bodies of the EKD are its Synod of 120 clergy and lay members which meets at regular intervals, the Conference of member churches, and the Council, composed of 15 elected members; the EKD has an ecclesiastical secretariat of its own (the Protestant Church Office), including a special office for foreign relations; Chair. of the Council Bischof Dr MARTIN KRUSE; Pres. of the Office WALTER HAMMER.

Synod of the EKD: 3000 Hanover 21, Herrenhäuserstr. 12; tel. (0511) 71110; telex 923445; Pres. Dr JÜRGEN SCHMUDE.

Deutscher Evangelischer Kirchentag (German Protestant Church Assembly): 6400 Fulda, Magdeburgerstr. 59, Postfach 480; tel. (0661) 601091; Pres. Dr HELMUT SIMON; Gen. Sec. CHRISTIAN KRAUSE.

Churches and Federations within the EKD:

Vereinigte Evangelisch-Lutherische Kirche Deutschlands (VELKD) (The United Evangelical-Lutheran Church of Germany): 3000 Hanover 1, Richard-Wagner-Str. 26; tel. (0511) 62611; telex 922673; f. 1949; mems 9.4m.; a body uniting all but two of the Lutheran territorial Churches within the Protestant Church in Germany; Presiding Bishop Bischof KARLHEINZ STOLL (2380 Schleswig, Plessenstr. 5A).

Evangelische Kirche der Union (EKU) (Protestant Church of the Union): Chancellery, Western Region: 1000 Berlin 12, Jebensstr. 3; Eastern Region: 1040 Berlin, Auguststr. 80; tel. (030) 319001-0; composed of Lutheran and Reformed elements; includes the Protestant Churches of Berlin-Brandenburg, Westphalia and the Rhineland (Western Region), Berlin-Brandenburg, Saxony, Greifswald (Pomerania), Görlitz (Silesia) and Anhalt (Eastern Region); Chair. of Council Präses HANS-MARTIN LINNEMANN (Western Region), Bischof Dr GIENKE (Eastern Region); Chair of Synod Präses MANFRED KOCK (1000 Berlin 12, Jebensstr. 3) (Western Region), Präses DIETRICH AFFELD (Eastern Region); Pres. of Administration WERNER RADATZ (Western Region), Dr FRIEDRICH WINTER (Eastern Region).

Arnoldshainer Konferenz: 1000 Berlin 12, Jebensstr. 3; tel. (030) 319001-0; f. 1967; a loose federation of the church governments of one Lutheran, one Reformed Territorial and all United Churches, aiming at greater co-operation between them; Chair. of Council HELMUT SPENGLER.

Reformierter Bund (Reformed League): 4444 Bad Bentheim, Klapperstiege 13; tel. (05922) 1234; f. 1884; unites the Reformed Territorial Churches and Congregations of Germany. The central body of the Reformed League is the 'Moderamen', the elected representation of the various Reformed Congregations; Moderator Prof. Dr HANS-JOACHIM KRAUS (5600 Wuppertal 23, Zur Gloria 25); Gen. Sec. Pfarrer JOACHIM GUHRT.

Affiliated to the EKD:

Bund Evangelisch-Reformierter Kirchen (Association of Protestant Reformed Churches): 2000 Hamburg 1, Ferdinandstr. 21; tel. (040) 337260; Chair. Präses P. HERMANN KELLER.

Evangelical-Lutheran Church in Brunswick: 3340 Wolfenbüttel, Neuer Weg 88–90; tel. (05331) 8020; Landesbischof Prof. Dr GERHARD MÜLLER DD.

Herrnhuter Brüdergemeine or **Europäisch-Festländische Brüder-Unität** (Moravian Church): f. 1457; there are 24 congregations in the Federal Republic, the Democratic Republic, Switzerland, Denmark and the Netherlands with approximately 30,000 mems; Chair. of Western District Rev. ROLAND BAUDERT (7325 Bad Boll, Badwasen 6; tel. (07164) 2047).

†**Protestant Church in Baden:** 7500 Karlsruhe 1, Blumenstr. 1; tel. (147) 234; Landesbischof Prof. Dr KLAUS ENGELHARDT.

*Protestant-Lutheran Church in Bavaria:** 8000 Munich 2, Meiserstr. 13; tel. (089) 55951; telex 529674; Landesbischof D. Dr phil., Mag. theol. JOHANNES HANSELMANN DD.

†**Protestant Church in Berlin-Brandenburg (Berlin West):** Konsistorium: 1000 Berlin 21, Bachstr. 1–2; tel. (030) 390910; Bischof Dr MARTIN KRUSE.

†**Bremen Evangelical Church:** 2800 Bremen 1, Franziuseck 2–4, Postfach 10 69 29; tel. (0421) 55970; Pres. ECKART RANFT.

*Protestant-Lutheran Church of Hanover:** 3000 Hanover 1, Haarstr. 6; tel. (0511) 12411; Landesbischof HORST HIRSCHLER.

†**Protestant Church in Hesse and Nassau:** 6100 Darmstadt, Paulusplatz 1; tel. (06151) 4050; telex 4197176; Pres. Rev. HELMUT SPENGLER.

†**Protestant Church of Kurhessen-Waldeck:** 3500 Kassel-Wilhelmshöhe, Wilhelmshöher Allee 330; tel. (0561) 30831; Bischof Dr HANS-GERNOT JUNG.

†**Church of Lippe:** 4930 Detmold 1, Leopoldstr. 27; tel. (05231) 74030; Landessuperintendent Dr AKO HAARBECK.

*Protestant-Lutheran Church of North Elbe:** Bischof D. KARLHEINZ STOLL (2380 Schleswig, Plessenstr. 5A; tel. (04621) 24622); Bischof Prof. Dr ULRICH WILCKENS (2400 Lübeck, Bäckerstr. 3–5; tel. (0451) 797176); Bischof Prof. D. PETER KRUSCHE (2000 Hamburg 11, Neue Burg 1; tel. (040) 3689-216); Pres. of North Elbian Church Administration Dr KLAUS BLASCHKE (2300 Kiel, Dänische Str. 21–35; tel. (0431) 991-1).

†**Protestant-Reformed Church in North-West Germany:** 2950 Leer, Saarstr. 6; tel. (0491) 8030; Moderator Rev. HINNERK SCHRÖDER; Synod Clerks Rev. WALTER HERRENBRÜCK, Dr WINIFRIED STOLZ.

†**Protestant-Lutheran Church in Oldenburg:** 2900 Oldenburg, Philosophenweg 1; tel. (0441) 77010; Bischof Dr WILHELM SIEVERS.

†**Protestant Church of the Palatinate:** 6720 Speyer, Domplatz 5; tel. (06232) 1091; Pres. WERNER SCHRAMM.

†**Protestant Church in the Rhineland:** 4000 Düsseldorf 30, Hans-Böckler-Str. 7; tel. (0211) 45620; telex (17) 2114057; Pres. D. GERHARD BRANDT.

*Protestant-Lutheran Church of Schaumburg-Lippe:** 3062 Bückeburg, Herderstr. 27; tel. (05722) 25021; Landesbischof Prof. Dr JOACHIM HEUBACH; Pres. Dr MICHAEL WINCKLER.

†**Protestant Church of Westphalia:** 4800 Bielefeld 1, Altstädter Kirchplatz 5; tel. (0521) 5940; Präses D. HANS-MARTIN LINNEMANN.

†**Protestant-Lutheran Church of Württemberg:** 7000 Stuttgart 1, Gänsheidestr. 4, Postfach 101342; tel. (0711) 2149-0; Landesbischof THEO SORG.

(* Member of the VELKD; † member of the EKU)

Other Protestant Churches

Bund Evangelisch-Freikirchlicher Gemeinden (Union of Protestant Free Church Congregations; Baptists): 6380 Bad Homburg v.

FEDERAL REPUBLIC OF GERMANY

d. H. 1, Friedberger Str. 101; tel. (06172) 80040; f. 1849; Pres. Rev. GÜNTER HITZEMANN; Dirs Rev. MANFRED OTTO, Rev. GERD RUDZIO, Rev. ECKHARD SCHAEFER.

Bund Freier evangelischer Gemeinden (Covenant of Free Evangelical Churches in Germany): 5810 Witten (Ruhr), Goltenkamp 4; tel. (02302) 39901; f. 1854; Pres. KARL H. KNÖPPEL; Administrator JÜRGEN HEDFELD; 25,100 mems.

Evangelisch-methodistische Kirche (United Methodist Church): 6000 Frankfurt/Main 1, Wilhelm-Leuschner-Str. 8; tel. (069) 239373; f. 1968 when the former Evangelische Gemeinschaft and Methodistenkirche united; Bishop HERMANN L. STICHER.

Selbständige Evangelisch-Lutherische Kirche (Independent Evangelical-Lutheran Church): Schopenhauerstr. 7, 3000 Hanover 61; tel. (0511) 557808; f. 1972; Bishop Dr JOBST SCHÖNE, D.D.

Vereinigung der deutschen Mennonitengemeinden (Union of German Mennonite Congregations): 2970 Emden, Brückstr. 74; tel. (04921) 22966; f. 1886; Chair. Dr HEINOLD FAST.

Other Christian Churches

Alt-Katholische Kirche (Old Catholic Church): 5300 Bonn 1, Gregor-Mendelstr. 28; seceded from the Roman Catholic Church as a protest against the declaration of Papal infallibility in 1870; belongs to the Utrecht Union of Old Catholic Churches; in full communion with the Anglican Communion; Pres. Bischof Dr SIGISBERT KRAFT (Bonn); 28,000 mems.

JUDAISM

The Jewish community in Germany is estimated to number about 35,000, of whom more than 30,000 live in the Federal Republic and West Berlin.

Zentralrat der Juden in Deutschland (Central Council of Jews in Germany): 5300 Bonn 2, Rüngsdorfer Str. 6; tel. (0228) 357023; telex 8869230; Pres. Board of Dirs Dr HEINZ GALINSKI; Sec.-Gen. MICHA GUTTMANN.

The Press

Article 5 of the 1949 Basic Law of the Republic stipulates: 'Everyone has the right freely to express or to disseminate his opinion by speech, writing and pictures and freely to inform himself from generally accessible sources. Freedom of the press and freedom of reporting by radio and motion pictures are guaranteed. There shall be no censorship. These rights are limited by the provisions of the general laws, the provisions of the law for the protection of youth, and by the right to inviolability of personal honour.' These last qualifications refer to the Federal law penalizing the sale to young people of literature judged to endanger morality, and to articles in the Penal Code relating to defamation, in particular Article 187A concerning defamation of public figures.

There is no Federal Press Law, all legal action being normally referred back to the Constitution. But the press is subject to general items of legislation, some of which may significantly limit press freedom. Article 353C of the Penal Code, for example, dating from the Nazi period, prohibits the publication of official news supposed to be secret; under it a journalist may be required to reveal his sources. The Code of Criminal Procedure also constitutes a danger in that it authorizes the Government to confiscate objects potentially important as evidence in a legal investigation, which may be construed to include papers, print, etc.

Freedom of the press is stipulated in each of the Constitutions of the individual Länder. Many Länder have enacted laws defining the democratic role of the press and some give journalists access to sources of government information; some authorize the journalist to refuse to disclose his sources; others qualify, and even withhold this right. Some permit printed matter to be confiscated on suspicion of an indictable offence only if authorized by an independent judge; others allow a district attorney or even the police to give this authorization.

The German Press Council was founded in 1956 and is composed of publishers and journalists. It lays down guidelines, investigates complaints against the press and enjoys considerable standing.

The Federal German press is quite free of government control. No daily is directly owned by a political party, and though some 10% of papers support a party line, the majority of newspapers, including all the major dailies, are politically independent.

The political and economic conditions since 1949 have fostered the rapid development of a few large publishing groups.

In 1968 a government commission laid down various limits on the proportions of circulation one group should be allowed to control: (1) 40% of the total circulation of newspapers or 40% of the total circulation of magazines; (2) 20% of the total circulation of newspapers and magazines together; (3) 15% of the circulation in one field if the proportion owned in the other field is 40%. At that time the Springer Group's estimated ownership was 39.2% of newspaper circulation (65–70% in Berlin) and 17.5% of magazine circulation. In June 1968 Springer reduced his share of the periodical market to around 11%.

In 1988 there were 375 daily newspapers, with a combined circulation of 20.6m. copies. There were five Sunday papers, with a circulation of 3.8m., and 44 weekly papers, with a circulation of 1.8m. The most important and influential national dailies include *Frankfurter Allgemeine Zeitung*, *Süddeutsche Zeitung* (Munich) and *Die Welt* (Hamburg). The newspaper with the largest circulation is *Bild Zeitung* (circ. 5.1m.) which is printed in eight different provincial centres. The most influential weekly newspapers include *Die Zeit* and the Sundays *Bild am Sonntag* and *Welt am Sonntag*. In 1983, apart from newspapers, 6,702 periodicals were published, with a total circulation of 255.9m. copies. Those with circulations of over 1m. included the illustrated news weeklies *Der Spiegel*, *Stern* and *Quick*, the TV and Radio magazine *HÖRZU* and women's magazines *Brigitte*, *Burda-moden*, *Frau im Spiegel* and *Für Sie*.

The principal newspaper publishing groups are:

Axel Springer Group: 1000 Berlin 61, Kochstr. 50; tel. (030) 25-91-0; telex 184257; and 2000 Hamburg 36, Kaiser-Wilhelm-Str. 6; tel. (040) 3-47-1; telex 403242; the largest newspaper publishing group in continental Europe; includes five major dailies (*Die Welt*, *Hamburger Abendblatt*, *Bild Zeitung*, *Berliner Morgenpost*, *BZ*), two Sunday papers (*Welt am Sonntag*, *Bild am Sonntag*), three radio, television and family magazines (*HÖRZU*, *Funk Uhr*, *Bildwoche*), two women's journals (*JOURNAL für die Frau*, *Bild der Frau*), the weekly motoring magazine *Auto-Bild*, and the book publishing firm Verlag Ullstein GmbH; Propr Axel Springer Verlag AG.

Gruner und Jahr AG & Co Druck- und Verlagshaus: 2210 Itzehoe, Am Vossbarg, Posfach 1240; telex 28289; and 2000 Hamburg 36, Postfach 302040; telex 2195213; owns *Stern*, *Brigitte*, *Essen und Trinken*, *Geo*, *Capital*, *Eltern*, *Nicole*, *Häuser*, *Yps*, *Schöner Wohnen*, *Hamburger Morgenpost*.

Süddeutscher-Verlag: 8000 Munich 2, Sendlingerstr. 80; tel. (089) 21830; telex 523426; owns *Süddeutsche Zeitung*; 5 Mans.

Jahreszeiten-Verlag GmbH: 2000 Hamburg 60, Possmoorweg 1; tel. (040) 27170; telex 213214; owns amongst others the periodicals *Für Sie* and *Moderne Frau*; Pres. HELMUT GANSKE.

Heinrich-Bauer-Verlag: 2000 Hamburg 1, Burchardtstr. 11 and 8000 Munich 83, Charles-de-Gaulle-Str.; telex 212845; owns 29 popular illustrated magazines, including *Quick* (Munich), *Neue Revue* (Hamburg), *Praline*, *Neue Post*, *Das Neue Platt* and *Bravo*; Pres. HEINRICH BAUER.

Burda GmbH: 7600 Offenburg, Postfach 1230; tel. (0781) 8401; telex 528000; owns *Bunte*, *Bild+Funk*, *Freundin*, *Pan*, *Freizeit Revue*, *Meine Familie und ich*, *Mein Schöner Garten*, *Das Haus*, *Architectural Digest (Deutsch)* and *Ambiente*; 7 Mans.

PRINCIPAL DAILIES

Aachen

Aachener Nachrichten: 5100 Aachen, Dresdner Str. 3, Postfach 110; tel. (0241) 5101-1; telex 832851; f. 1872; Publrs Zeitungsverlag Aachen; Edited by Verlagsanstalt Cerfontaine GmbH & Co., 5100 Aachen, Theaterstr. 24–34; circ. 60,000.

Aachener Volkszeitung: 5100 Aachen, Dresdner Str. 3, Postfach 110; tel. (0241) 51011; telex 832851; f. 1946; Publishers Zeitungsverlag Aachen; Editor-in-Chief Dr ANTON STERZL; circ. 106,000.

Ansbach

Fränkische Landeszeitung: 8800 Ansbach, Nürnberger Str. 9–17, Postfach 1362; tel. (0981) 95000; telex 61815; Editors-in-Chief GERHARD EGETEMAYER, PETER M. SZYMANOWSKI; circ. 50,000.

Aschaffenburg

Main-Echo: 8750 Aschaffenburg (Main), Goldbacher Str. 25–27, Postfach 548; tel. (06021) 3961; telex 4188837; Editors Dr GEROLD MARTIN, FRANZ NIESSNER, Dr HELMUT TEUFEL; circ. 86,000.

Augsburg

Augsburger Allgemeine: 8900 Augsburg 1, Curt-Frenzel-Str. 2, Postfach 100054; tel. (0821) 70071; telex 53837; Editor GÜNTER HOLLAND; circ. 350,000.

Baden-Baden

Badisches Tagblatt: 7570 Baden-Baden, Stefanienstr. 1–3, Postfach 120; tel (07221) 2151; telex 781158; Editor UDO F. A. ROTZOLL; circ. 40,600.

Bamberg

Fränkischer Tag: 8600 Bamberg, Gutenbergstr. 1; tel. (0951) 1880; telex 662426; Publr KARL WEBER; circ. 76,800.

FEDERAL REPUBLIC OF GERMANY

Berlin

Berliner Morgenpost: 1000 Berlin 61, Kochstr. 50, Postfach 110303; tel. (030) 25910; telex 183508; f. 1898; published by Ullstein Verlag GmbH & Co KG; Editor BRUNO WALTERT; circ. 182,000.

BZ (Berliner Zeitung): 1000 Berlin 61, Kochstr. 50; tel. (030) 25910; telex 184589; f. 1877; published by Ullstein GmbH; Editor WILHELM PANNIER; circ. 296,300.

Der Tagesspiegel: 1000 Berlin 30, Potsdamer Str. 87; tel. (030) 26009-0; telex 183773; f. 1945; circ. 125,000.

Bielefeld

Neue Westfälische: 4800 Bielefeld 1, Niedernstr. 23-27, Postfach 26; tel. (0521) 5550; telex 932799; f. 1967; Editors TIM ARNOLD, Dr HEINZ EPPING; circ. 227,850.

Westfalen-Blatt: 4800 Bielefeld, Südbrackstr. 14-18, Postfach 8740; tel. (0521) 5850; f. 1946; Editor CARL-W. BUSSE; circ. 145,000.

Bonn

Bonner Rundschau: 5300 Bonn, Thomas-Mann-Str. 51-53, Postfach 1248; tel. (0228) 651911; telex 886702; f. 1946; Dir Dr HEINRICH HEINEN; circ. 24,300.

General-Anzeiger: 5300 Bonn, Justus von Liebig-Str. 15, Postfach 1609; tel. (0228) 66880; f. 1725; independent; Publrs HERMANN NEUSSER, HERMANN NEUSSER, Jr; Editor FRIEDHELM KEMNA; circ. 85,000.

Die Welt: 5300 Bonn, Godesberger Allee 99; tel. (0228) 3041; telex 885714; f. 1946; published by Axel Springer Verlag; Editor MANFRED SCHELL; circ. 225,000.

Bremen

Bremer Nachrichten: 2800 Bremen, Martinistr. 43; tel. (0421) 36711; telex 244709; f. 1743; Publr HERBERT C. ORDEMANN; Editors DIETRICH IDE, VOLKER WEISE; circ. 44,000.

Weser-Kurier: 2800 Bremen 1, Martinistr. 43, Postfach 107801; tel. (0421) 36711; telex 244709; f. 1945; Publr HERBERT C. ORDEMANN; circ. 185,000.

Bremerhaven

Nordsee-Zeitung: 2850 Bremerhaven 1, Hafenstr. 140; tel. (0471) 597-0; telex 238761; Chief Editor CLAUS PETERSEN; circ. 80,000.

Brunswick

Braunschweiger Zeitung: 3300 Braunschweig, Hamburger Str. 277 (Pressehaus), Postfach 3263; tel. (0531) 39000; telex 952722; Editor Dr ARNOLD RABBOW; circ. 167,000.

Cologne

Express: 5000 Cologne 1, Breite Str. 70, Postfach 100410; tel. (0221) 2240; telex 8881162; f. 1964; Publr ALFRED NEVEN DUMONT; Editor MICHAEL SPRENG; circ. 447,500.

Kölner Stadt-Anzeiger: 5000 Cologne 1, Breite Str. 70, Postfach 100410; tel. (0221) 2240; telex 8881162; f. 1876; Publr ALFRED NEVEN DUMONT; Editor HANS SCHMITZ; circ. 265,800.

Kölnische Rundschau: 5000 Cologne 1, Stolkgasse 25-45, Postfach 101910; tel. (0221) 16320; telex 8882687; f. 1946; Publr Dr HEINRICH HEINEN; Editor-in-Chief JÜRGEN C. JAGLA; circ. 162,000.

Darmstadt

Darmstädter Echo: 6100 Darmstadt, Holzhofallee 25-31, Postfach 110269; tel. (06151) 3871; telex 419363; f. 1945; Publrs MAX BACH, HORST BACH; Editor-in-Chief ROLAND HOF; circ. 100,000.

Dortmund

Ruhr-Nachrichten: 4600 Dortmund 1, Pressehaus, Westenhellweg 68-88, Postfach 282; tel. (0231) 54941; telex 822106; f. 1949; Editor FLORIAN LENSING-WOLFF; circ. 269,000.

Westfälische Rundschau: 4600 Dortmund 1, Brüderweg 9; tel. (0231) 54941; telex 822460; Editor GÜNTER HAMMER; circ. 250,000.

Düsseldorf

Handelsblatt: 4000 Düsseldorf 1, Kasernenstr. 67, Postfach 1102; tel. (0211) 83880; telex 17221391; 5 a week; only economics, business and finance newspaper with national circulation; Man. Dirs Dr KLAUS HATTEMER, Dr GERNOT MARSCH; circ. 112,000.

Rheinische Post: 4000 Düsseldorf, Blumenstr. 16; tel. (0211) 5050; telex 8581901; f. 1946; Dirs Dr J. SCHAFFRATH; Editor Dr JOACHIM SOBOTTA; circ. 401,000.

Westdeutsche Zeitung: 4000 Düsseldorf 1, Königsallee 27, Postfach 1132; tel. (0211) 83820; Editor-in-Chief PAULHEINZ GRUPE; Publisher and Editor Dr M. GIRARDET; circ. 200,000.

Essen

Neue Ruhr Zeitung: 4300 Essen, Sachsenstr. 30, Postfach 6969; tel. (0201) 20640; telex 8579951; Editor-in-Chief JENS FEDDERSEN; circ. 215,000.

Westdeutsche Allgemeine Zeitung: 4300 Essen, Friedrichstr. 34-38, Postfach 104161; tel. (0201) 20640; telex 8579951; Editor RALF LEHMANN; circ. 660,000.

Frankfurt am Main

Frankfurter Allgemeine Zeitung: 6000 Frankfurt a.M., Hellerhofstr. 2-4, Postfach 100808; tel. (069) 75910; telex 41223; f. 1949; Editors BRUNO DECHAMPS, FRITZ ULLRICH FACK, JOACHIM C. FEST, JÜRGEN JESKE, JOHANN GEORG REISSMÜLLER; circ. 360,000.

Frankfurter Neue Presse: 6000 Frankfurt a.M., Frankenallee 71-81, Postfach 100801; tel. (069) 75011; telex 411054; independent; Editor WERNER WIRTHLE; circ. 137,000.

Frankfurter Rundschau: 6000 Frankfurt a.M., Grosse Eschenheimer Str. 16-18, Postfach 100660; tel. (069) 21991; telex 411651; Editor WERNER HOLZER; circ. 196,000.

Freiburg

Badische Zeitung: 7800 Freiburg i. Br., Basler Landstr. 3; tel. (0761) 4961; telex 772660; f. 1946; Editor Dr ANSGAR FÜRST; circ. 194,000.

Göttingen

Göttinger Tageblatt: 3400 Göttingen, Dransfelder Str. 1, Postfach 1953; tel. (0551) 9019; telex 96800; f. 1889; Man. Dir MANFRED DALLMANN; Editor-in-Chief Dr RAINER WIESE; circ. 41,000.

Hagen

Westfalenpost: 5800 Hagen-Bathey, Hohensyburgstr. 67; tel. (02331) 6980; telex 823168; f. 1946; Chief Editor Dr FRITZ HEIMPLÄTZER; circ. 160,000.

Hamburg

Bild Zeitung: 2000 Hamburg 36, Kaiser-Wilhelm-Str. 6; tel. (040) 3471; telex 217001333; f. 1952; published by Axel Springer Verlag; Chief Editor HORST FUST; circ. 5,124,000.

Hamburger Abendblatt: 2000 Hamburg 36, Kaiser-Wilhelm-Str. 6, Postfach 304630; tel. (040) 3471; telex 217001333; published by Axel Springer Verlag; Editor-in-Chief KLAUS KORN; circ. 280,000 (Saturdays 358,000).

Hamburger Morgenpost: 2000 Hamburg 50, Griegstr. 75; tel. (040) 883031; telex 2161168; Editor WOLFGANG CLEMENT; circ. 156,000.

Hanover

Hannoversche Allgemeine Zeitung: 3000 Hanover 1, Bemeroder Str. 58, Postfach 209; tel. (0511) 5180; telex 923911-15; Editor LUISE MADSACK; circ. 220,000.

Heidelberg

Rhein-Neckar-Zeitung: 6900 Heidelberg, Hauptstr. 23, Postfach 104560; tel. (06221) 519-1; telex 461751; f. 1945; Publrs WINFRIED KNORR, RUPRECHT SCHULZE; circ. 100,000.

Heilbronn

Heilbronner Stimme: 7100 Heilbronn, Hochhaus Allee 2, Postfach 1940; tel. (07131) 615-1; telex 728729; f. 1946; Editor-in-Chief WERNER THUNERT; circ. 102,000.

Hof-Saale

Frankenpost: 8670 Hof-Saale, Poststr. 11, Postfach 1320; tel. (09281) 8160; telex 643601; Publr Frankenpost Verlag GmbH; Editor-in-Chief HEINRICH GIEGOLD; circ 75,000.

Ingolstadt

Donau Kurier: 8070 Ingolstadt, Stauffenbergstr. 2, Postfach 340; tel. (0841) 6800; telex 55845; f. 1872; Publr and Dir Dr W. REISSMÜLLER; circ. 80,000.

Karlsruhe

Badische Neueste Nachrichten: 7500 Karlsruhe 1, Linkenheimer Landstr. 133, Postfach 311168; tel. (0721) 7890; telex 7826960; Publr and Editor HANS W. BAUR; circ. 174,000.

Kassel

Hessische/Niedersächsische Allgemeine: 3500 Kassel, Frankfurter Str. 168, Postfach 101009; tel. (0561) 2030; telex 99635; f. 1959; independent; Editor-in-Chief LOTHAR ORZECHOWSKI; circ. 230,000.

Kempten

Allgäuer Zeitung: 8960 Kempten, Kotternerstr. 64, Postfach 1129; tel. (0831) 2060; telex 54871; f. 1968; Publrs GEORG FÜRST VON WALDBURG-ZEIL, GÜNTER HOLLAND; Editor-in-Chief GÜNTER HOLLAND; circ. 111,000.

FEDERAL REPUBLIC OF GERMANY

Kiel
Kieler Nachrichten: 2300 Kiel 1, Fleethörn 1-7, Postfach 1111; tel. (0431) 9030; telex 292768; Chief Editor KARLHEINZ VATER; circ. 128,654.

Koblenz
Rhein-Zeitung: 5400 Koblenz, August-Horch-Str. 28, Postfach 1540; tel. (0261) 89200; telex 862611; Editor HANS PETER SOMMER; circ. 233,000.

Konstanz
Südkurier: 7750 Konstanz, Marktstätte 4, Postfach 4300; tel. (07531) 2820; telex 733231; f. 1945; Publr Dr BRIGITTE WEYL; circ. 140,000.

Leutkirch
Schwäbische Zeitung: 7970 Leutkirch 1, Rudolf-Roth-Str. 18, Postfach 1145; tel. (07561) 800; telex 7321915; f. 1945; Editor HANNS FUNK; circ. 202,000.

Lübeck
Lübecker Nachrichten: 2400 Lübeck, Königstr. 55; tel. (0451) 1441; telex 26801; f. 1945; Chief Editor KLAUS J. GROTH; circ. 113,666.

Ludwigshafen
Die Rheinpfalz: 6700 Ludwigshafen/Rhein, Amtsstr. 5-11, Postfach 211147; tel. (0621) 590201; telex 464822; Dir Dr DIETER SCHAUB; circ. 250,000.

Mainz
Allgemeine Zeitung: 6500 Mainz, Grosse Bleiche 44-50, Postfach 3120; tel. (06131) 144-0; telex (17) 61319832; part of the Zeitungsgruppe Rhein-Main-Nahe; circ. 128,000.

Mannheim
Mannheimer Morgen: 6800 Mannheim 1, Am Marktplatz, Postfach 1503; tel. (0621) 17020; telex 462171; Publrs Dr K. ACKERMANN, R. V. SCHILLING; Chief Editors SIGMAR HEILMANN, HORST-DIETER SCHIELE; circ. 145,618.

Munich
Abendzeitung/8-Uhr-Blatt: 8000 Munich 2, Sendlingerstr. 79; tel. (089) 23770; telex 528011; f. 1948; Publr Dr JOHANNES FRIEDMANN; Editor-in-Chief Dr UWE ZIMMER; circ. 260,000.

Münchner Merkur: 8000 Munich 2, Paul-Heyse-Str. 2-4, Pressehaus; tel. (089) 53060; telex 522100; Publr Dr DIRK IPPEN; Editor ALFONS DÖSER; circ. 171,731.

Süddeutsche Zeitung: 8000 Munich 2, Sendlingerstr. 80, Postfach 202220; tel. (089) 21830; telex 523426; f. 1945; Editor-in-Chief DIETER SCHRÖDER; circ. 378,420.

Münster
Münstersche Zeitung: 4400 Münster, Neubrückenstr. 8-11, Postfach 5560; tel. (0251) 5920; f. 1870; independent; Editor Dr RALF RICHARD KOERNER; circ. 63,934.

Westfälische Nachrichten: ZENO-Zeitungen, 4400 Münster, Soester Str. 13, Postfach 8680; tel. (0251) 6900; telex 892830; Chief Editor BERTRAM VON HOBE; circ. 215,000.

Nuremberg
Nürnberger Nachrichten: 8500 Nuremberg, Marienplatz 1/5; tel. (0911) 2160; telex 622339; f. 1945; Editor BRUNO SCHNELL; circ. 336,175.

Oberndorf-Neckar
Schwarzwälder Bote: 7238 Oberndorf-Neckar, Postfach 1380; tel. (07423) 780; telex 762814; circ. 135,576.

Oelde
Die Glocke: 4740 Oelde, Engelbert-Holterdorf-Str. 4-6; tel. (02522) 73-0; telex 89543; f. 1880; Editors KARL FRIEDRICH GEHRING, ENGELBERT HOLTERDORF; circ. 65,000.

Offenbach
Offenbach-Post: 6050 Offenbach, Grosse Marktstr. 36-44, Postfach 164; tel. (069) 80631; telex 4152864; f. 1947; Publr UDO BINTZ; circ. 54,000.

Oldenburg
Nordwest-Zeitung: 2900 Oldenburg, Peterstr. 28-34, Postfach 2525; tel. (0441) 2391; telex 25878; published by the Druck- und Pressehaus GmbH; Editor B. SCHULTE; circ. 122,000.

Osnabrück
Neue Osnabrücker Zeitung: 4500 Osnabrück, Breiter Gang 11-14 and Grosse Str. 17/19, Postfach 4260; tel. (0541) 3250; telex 944841; f. 1967 from merger of *Neue Tagespost* and *Osnabrücker Tageblatt*; Chief Editor F. SCHMEDT; circ. 289,508.

Passau
Passauer Neue Presse: 8390 Passau, Neuburger Str. 28, Postfach 2040; tel. (0851) 5020; telex 57879; f. 1946; Man. Dir FRANZ XAVER HIRTREITER; Editor-in-Chief ULRICH ZIMMERMANN; circ. 161,000.

Regensburg
Mittelbayerische Zeitung: 8400 Regensburg 1, Kumpfmühler Str. 11; tel. (0941) 2070; telex 65841; f. 1945; Editor KARLHEINZ ESSER; circ. 100,000.

Saarbrücken
Saarbrücker Zeitung: 6600 Saarbrücken, Gutenbergstr. 11-23, Postfach 296; tel. (0681) 5020; telex 4421262; f. 1761; Editors Dr HANS STIFF, UWE JACOBSEN; circ. 205,000.

Stuttgart
Stuttgarter Nachrichten: 7000 Stuttgart 80, Räpplenstr. 17, Postfach 550; tel. (0711) 72051; telex 7255395; f. 1946; Editor-in-Chief JÜRGEN OFFENBACH; circ. 260,000.

Stuttgarter Zeitung: 7000 Stuttgart 80, Plieninger Str. 150, Postfach 141; tel. (0711) 72051; telex 7255384; Chief Editor Dr THOMAS LÖFFELHOLZ; circ. 503,925.

Trier
Trierischer Volksfreund: 5500 Trier, Nikolaus-Koch-Platz 1-3, Postfach 3770; tel. (0651) 45091; telex 472860; Chief Editor ALLRICH EDEN; circ. 95,876.

Ulm
Südwest Presse: 7900 Ulm, Frauenstr. 77, Postfach 3333; tel. (0731) 15601; telex 712461; circ. 361,924.

Weiden
Der Neue Tag: 8480 Weiden, Weigelstr. 16, Postfach 1340; tel. (0961) 851; telex 63880; Editor-in-Chief HORST HOMBERG; circ. 81,500.

Wetzlar
Wetzlarer Neue Zeitung: 6330 Wetzlar, Elsa-Brandström-Str. 18, Postfach 2940; tel. (06441) 7010; telex 483883; f. 1945; Editor JANOS BARDI; circ. 70,000.

Wiesbaden
Wiesbadener Kurier: 6200 Wiesbaden 1, Langgasse 21, Postfach 6029; tel. (06221) 3551; telex 4186841; Chief Editor HILMAR BÖRSING; circ. 65,000.

Würzburg
Main-Post: 8700 Würzburg, Berner Str. 2; tel. (0931) 60010; f. 1883; independent; Publrs JOHANNES VON GUTTENBERG, GERHARD WIESEMANN; Editors-in-Chief REINER F. KIRST, DIETER W. ROCKENMAIER; circ. 152,000.

SUNDAY AND WEEKLY PAPERS

Bayernkurier: 8000 Munich 19, Nymphenburger Str. 64; tel. (089) 120041; weekly; organ of the CSU; Chief Editor W. SCHARNAGL; circ. 161,802.

Bild am Sonntag: 2000 Hamburg 36, Kaiser-Wilhelm-Str. 6, Postfach 566; tel. (040) 3471; telex 403242; f. 1956; Sunday; Published by Axel Springer Verlag; Chief Editor EWALD STRUWE; circ. 2,400,000.

Deutsches Allgemeines Sonntagsblatt: 2000 Hamburg 13, Mittelweg 111; tel. (040) 445440; telex 212973; Sunday; circ. 122,585.

Rheinischer Merkur Christ und Welt: 5300 Bonn 2, Godesberger Allee 157; tel. (0228) 8840; f. 1946; weekly; Editor THOMAS KIELINGER; circ. 133,000.

Welt am Sonntag: 2000 Hamburg 36, Kaiser-Wilhelm-Str. 1; tel. (040) 3471; telex 403242; Sunday; published by Axel Springer Verlag; Editors CLAUS JACOBI, MANFRED GEIST; circ. 336,000.

Die Zeit: 2000 Hamburg 1, Postfach 10 68 20, Speersort 1, Pressehaus; tel. (040) 3280-0; telex 886433; f. 1946; weekly; Publrs HILDE VON LANG, HELMUT SCHMIDT; Editor-in-Chief Dr THEO SOMMER; circ. 468,000.

SELECTED PERIODICALS
Agriculture
Agrar Praxis: 7022 Leinfelden-Echterdingen, Ernst-Mey-Str. 8; tel. (0711) 7594-423; telex 7255421; f. 1882; monthly; Editor-in-Chief KLAUS NIEHÖRSTER; circ. 60,250.

FEDERAL REPUBLIC OF GERMANY

Agrarwirtschaft: 6000 Frankfurt 1, Schumannstr. 27; tel. (069) 7433-1; telex 4170335; f. 1952; monthly; agricultural management, market research and agricultural policy; Publr ALFRED STROTHE; Editor Prof. Dr BUCKHOLZ; circ. 3,000.

Bayerisches Landwirtschaftliches Wochenblatt: 8000 Munich 2, Postfach 400320, Lothstr. 29; f. 1810; weekly; organ of the Bayerischer Bauernverband; Editor LUDWIG M. GAUL; circ. 106,621.

Eisenbahn-Landwirt: 43 Essen 11, Am Ellenbogen 12, Postfach 110664; tel. (0201) 670525; f. 1918; monthly; Dir HANS HÜSKEN; circ. 120,000.

Land und Garten: 3 Hanover, Bemeroder Str. 58, Postfach 3720; f. 1920; weekly; agriculture and gardening; Editor LUISE MADSACK; circ. 80,000.

Das Landvolk: 3000 Hanover, Warmbüchenstr. 3; telex 9230457; fortnightly; issued by Landbuch-Verlag GmbH; Chief Editor GÜNTHER MARTIN BEINE; circ. 104,000.

Die Landpost: 7000 Stuttgart 70, Wollgrasweg 31; tel. (0711) 451091; telex 456603; f. 1945; weekly; agriculture and gardening; Editors Dr KONRAD BINKERT, ERICH REICH.

Art, Drama, Architecture and Music

AIT Architektur, Innenarchitektur, Technischer Ausbau: 7000 Stuttgart 1, Postfach 3081; f. 1890; every two months; Editors E. HOEHN, R. SELLIN; circ. 10,000.

Die Kunst: 8000 Munich 90, Elisenstr. 3; telex 522745; f. 1885; monthly; arts and antiques; published by Karl Thiemig AG München; circ. 6,500.

Das Kunstwerk: 7000 Stuttgart 80, Hessbrühlstr. 69; tel. (0711) 7863-1; telex 7-255820; f. 1946; every two months; modern art.

Musica: 3500 Kassel, Postfach 10 03 29; Editor Prof. Dr CLEMENS KÜHN; circ. 8,000.

Theater heute: 1000 Berlin 30, Lützowplatz 7; tel. (030) 2617003; f. 1960; monthly; Editors Dr HENNING RISCHBIETER, Dr PETER VON BECKER, Dr MICHAEL MERSCHMEIER.

Economics, Finance and Industry

Absatzwirtschaft: 4000 Düsseldorf 1, Kasernenstr. 67, Postfach 1102; tel. 8388493/4; f. 1958; monthly; journal for marketing; Dir UWE HOCH; Editor FRIEDHELM PÄLIKE; circ. 13,000.

Atomwirtschaft-Atomtechnik: 4000 Düsseldorf 1, Kasernenstr. 67, Postfach 1102; tel. (0211) 8388-498; telex 17211308; f. 1956; monthly; technical, scientific and economic aspects of nuclear engineering and technology; Editors Dipl.-Ing. R. HOSSNER, Dipl.-Ing. W.-M. LIEBHOLZ; circ. 5,000.

Baurundschau: 2 Hamburg 11, Gr. Burstah 49; monthly; published by Robert Mölich Verlag; Editor ROBERT MÖLICH.

Der Betrieb: 4000 Düsseldorf 1, Kasernenstr. 67, Postfach 1102; tel. (0211) 83880; telex 11308; weekly; business administration, revenue law, labour and social legislation; circ. 25,000.

Capital: 2000 Hamburg, Postfach 302040; telex 2195213; f. 1956; business and economics; circ. 248,876.

Creditreform: Düsseldorf, Kasernenstr. 67, Postfach 1102; tel. (0211) 16710; telex 17211308; f. 1879; 11 a year; Editor WERNER A. MERKES; circ. 88,000.

Getränketechnik, Zeitschrift für Industrie und Handel: 8500 Nuremberg 1, Breite Gasse 58-60; tel. (0911) 238331; telex 623081; 6 a year; trade journal for the brewing and beverage industries; circ. 205,113.

Der Handelsvertreter und Handelsmakler: 6 Frankfurt a.M., Grosse Eschenheimer Str. 16, Postfach 101937, Siegel-Verlag Otto Müller GmbH; tel. (069) 2999050; telex 411699; f. 1949; fortnightly; Editor ERNST H. HAUMANN; circ. 23,000.

Industrie-Anzeiger: 43 Essen, Girardetstr. 2; tel. (0202) 7996-0; telex 857888; f. 1879; 2 a week; Editor W. GIRARDET; circ. 26,000.

Management International Review: 6200 Wiesbaden, Taunusstr. 54; tel. (06121) 53435; telex 4186567; f. 1960; quarterly; issued by Betriebswirtschaftlicher Verlag Dr Th. Gabler; English; Editor Prof. Dr K. MACHARZINA (Stuttgart-Hohenheim).

VDI Nachrichten: 4000 Düsseldorf 1, Postfach 8228, Heinrichstr. 24; tel. (0211) 61880; telex 8587743; f. 1946; weekly; circ. 135,000.

Versicherungswirtschaft: 7500 Karlsruhe 1, Klosestr. 22; tel. (0721) 30811; telex 7826943; f. 1946; fortnightly; Editor KARL-HEINZ REHNERT; circ. 10,406.

Wirtschaft und Statistik: 6500 Mainz 42, Postfach 421120; tel. (06131) 59094; telex 4187768; monthly; organ of the Federal Statistical Office; published by Verlag W. Kohlhammer GmbH; Editor Dr GERHARD BÜRGIN; circ. 5,000.

Wirtschaftswoche: 4000 Düsseldorf 1, Kasernenstr. 67, Postfach 3734; tel. (0211) 8388-0; telex 8582048; weekly; business; Publrs Dr HEIK AFHELDT, Prof. Dr WOLFRAM ENGELS; Editor WOLFRAM BAENTSCH; circ. 118,882.

Education and Youth

Bravo: 8000 Munich 83, Postfach 201728; telex 524350; weekly; for young people; circ. 1,190,495.

Erziehung und Wissenschaft: 4300 Essen, Goldammerweg 16; tel. (0201) 41757; telex 8579801; f. 1948; monthly; Editor-in-Chief DIRK-PETER ORTH; circ. 187,000.

Geographische Rundschau: 3300 Brunswick, Georg-Westermann-Allee 66; tel. (0531) 75-237; f. 1949; monthly; Man. Editor VERENA PICKART.

Praxis Deutsch: 3016 Seelze, Postfach 100150; tel. (0511) 400040; telex 922923; 6 a year; German language and literature; circ. 28,786.

Rocky-Das Freizeit Magazine: 8000 Munich 19, Arnulfstr. 197; monthly; pop music magazine for young people; circ. 475,662.

Westermanns Pädagogische Beiträge: 3300 Braunschweig, Georg-Westermann-Allee 66, Postfach 3320; telex 952841; f. 1949; monthly; Editors R. TESKE, Prof. Dr H. GUDJONS, Prof. Dr R. WINKEL; circ. 7,320.

Law

Deutsche Richterzeitung: 5300 Bonn-Bad Godesberg, Seufertstr. 27; f. 1909; monthly; circ. 11,000.

Juristenzeitung: 7400 Tübingen, Wilhelmstr. 18, Postfach 2305; tel. (07071) 26064; telex 7262872; fortnightly; circ. 6,000.

Juristische Rundschau: 1000 Berlin 30, Genthiner Str. 13; tel. (030) 26005-0; telex 184027; monthly; Editors Prof. Dr KLAUS SCHREIBER, Prof. Dr HERBERT TRÖNDLE.

Neue Juristische Wochenschrift: 6 Frankfurt a.M. 1, Palmengartenstr. 14, and 8 Munich 40, Wilhelmstr. 5-9; tel. (069) 7560910; telex 412472; f. 1947; weekly; 6 Editors; circ. 55,000.

Rabels Zeitschrift für ausländisches und internationales Privatrecht: 2000 Hamburg 13, Mittelweg 187; tel. 41271; telex 212893; f. 1927; quarterly; Editors ULRICH DROBNIG, HEIN KÖTZ, ERNST-JOACHIM MESTMÄCKER; Man. Editor JÜRGEN THIEME.

Versicherungsrecht: 7500 Karlsruhe 1, Klosestr. 22; tel. (0721) 30811; telex 7826943; f. 1950; 4 a month; Editors Prof. Dr ERNST KLINGMÜLLER, Prof. Dr EGON LORENZ, KARL-HEINZ REHNERT; circ. 7,750.

Zeitschrift für die gesamte Strafrechtswissenschaft: 1000 Berlin 30, Genthiner Str. 13; tel. (030) 26005-0; telex 184027; f. 1881; quarterly; Chief Editor Prof. Dr Dr HANS JOACHIM HIRSCH.

Politics, Literature, Current Affairs

Akzente: 8000 Munich 86, Kolbergerstr. 22; tel. (089) 92694-0; f. 1954; Editor MICHAEL KRÜGER.

Buch Aktuell: 4600 Dortmund 1, Westfalendamm 67, Postfach 1305; tel. (0231) 4344-0; telex 822214; 3 a year.

Europa-Archiv, Zeitschrift für internationale Politik: 5300 Bonn, Adenauerallee 131; tel. (0228) 217021; telex 886822; f. 1946; 2 a month; journal of the German Society for Foreign Affairs; published by the Verlag für Internationale Politik GmbH, Bonn; Editor WOLFGANG WAGNER; Man. Editor JOCHEN THIES; circ. 4,500.

Die Fackel: 5300 Bonn 2, Wurzerstr. 2-4; tel. (0228) 364061; telex 885464; f. 1950; monthly; Publr Verband der Kriegs- und Wehrdienstopfer, Behinderten und Sozialrentner Deutschlands eV; Editor JOACHIM FAUSTMANN; circ. 850,000.

Gegenwartskunde: Leske Verlag + Budrich GmbH, 5090 Leverkusen 3 (Opladen), Postfach 300406; tel. (02171) 2079; quarterly; economics, politics, education; Editors W. GAGEL, H.-H. HARTWICH, B. SCHÄFERS.

Geist und Tat: 6 Frankfurt a.M., Elbestr. 46; Bonn, Postfach 364; monthly; political, cultural; Editor W. EICHLER; circ. 3,500.

Merian: 2000 Hamburg 13, Harvestehuder Weg 45; tel. (040) 441881; telex 214259; f. 1948; monthly; every issue deals with a country or city; Chief Editor FERDINAND RANFT; circ. 250,000.

Merkur (Deutsche Zeitschrift für europäisches Denken): 8000 Munich 2, Angertorstr. 1a; tel. (089) 555681; f. 1947; monthly; literary, political; Editor KARL HEINZ BOHRER; circ. 6,000.

Die Neue Gesellschaft—Frankfurter Hefte: 5300 Bonn 1, Godesberger Allee 143; tel. (0228) 883539; telex 885479; f. 1946; monthly; cultural, political; Editors WALTER DIRKS, EUGEN KOGON, HEINZ KÜHN, JOHANNES RAU, HEINZ O. VETTER, HANS-JOCHEN VOGEL, HERBERT WEHNER; circ. 11,000.

Neue Rundschau: 6000 Frankfurt a.M. 70, Postfach 700335, Hedderichstr. 114; tel. (069) 60620; telex 412877; f. 1890; quarterly; literature and essays; Editors THOMAS BECKERMANN, GÜNTHER BUSCH; circ. 6,000.

Politik und Kultur: 5300 Bonn 1, Remigiusstr. 1; f. 1983; quarterly; Editor Dr W. W. SCHUTZ.

FEDERAL REPUBLIC OF GERMANY

Sozialdemokrat Magazin: 5300 Bonn 2, Am Michaelshof 8; tel. (0228) 361011; telex 885603; Publisher Vorwärts Verlag GmbH; circ. 834,599.

Universitas: 7000 Stuttgart 1, Birkenwaldstr. 44, Postfach 105339; tel. (0711) 2582-0; f. 1946; monthly; scientific, literary and philosophical; Editor Dr CHRISTIAN ROTTA; circ. 7,200; quarterly editions in English and Spanish (circ. 4,800).

Welt des Buches: 53 Bonn 2, Godesberger Allee 99; telex 885714; f. 1971; weekly; literary supplement of *Die Welt*.

Westermanns Monatshefte: 3300 Brunswick, Georg-Westermann-Allee 66; telex 952973; f. 1856; monthly; circ. 100,000.

Wille und Weg: 8000 Munich 34, Schellingstr. 31, Postfach 340144; tel. (089) 2117-0; telex 5212394; f. 1948; monthly; published by Verband der Kriegs- und Wehrdienstopfer, Behinderten und Sozialrentner Deutschlands eV, Landesverband Bayern eV; Editor STEFAN PARENT; circ. 330,000.

Popular

Anna: 7600 Offenburg, Am Kestendamm 2; tel. (0781) 8402; telex 752804; f. 1974; knitting and needlecrafts; Editor AENNE BURDA.

Das Beste aus Readers Digest: 7000 Stuttgart 1, PO Box 178, Augustenstr. 1; tel. (0711) 66020; telex 723539; magazines, books and recorded music programmes; Man. Dir WILFRIED RUSS; circ. 1,300,000.

Bild + Funk: 8000 Munich 81, Arabellastr. 23; tel. (089) 9250-0; telex 522043; radio and television weekly; Editor GÜNTER VAN WAASEN; circ. 1,040,829.

Brigitte: Gruner und Jahr AG, 2 Hamburg 36, Postfach 302040; tel. (040) 41182550; telex 2195228; fortnightly; women's magazine; circ. 1,350,000.

Bunte Illustrierte: 7600 Offenburg, Burda-Hochhaus, Hauptstr. 130; tel. (0781) 8402; telex 528000; f. 1948; weekly family illustrated; circ. 1,140,439.

burdamoden: 7600 Offenburg, Am Kestendamm 2, Postfach 1160; tel. (0781) 8402; telex 752804; f. 1949; Editor AENNE BURDA; circ. 2,300,000.

Eltern: 2000 Hamburg 1, Postfach 302040; Pressehaus Gruner und Jahr; telex 2195213; f. 1966; monthly; for young parents; Editor NORBERT HINZE; circ. 540,274.

Frau aktuell: 4000 Düsseldorf 1, Adlerstr. 22; tel. (0211) 36660; telex 8587669; f. 1965; Editor DIETER ULRICH; circ. 297,395.

Frau im Spiegel: 2000 Hamburg 50, Griegstr. 75; tel. (040) 88303-0; women's magazine; circ. 1,006,846.

Freundin: 8000 Munich 81, Arabellastr. 23; telex 522274; f. 1948; fortnightly for young women; Chief Editor ELISABETH BÄR; circ. 850,743.

Funk Uhr: 2000 Hamburg 36, Kaiser-Wilhelm-Str. 6, Postfach 304630; tel. (040) 3471; telex 403242; radio and television weekly; published by Axel Springer Verlag AG; Editor WERNER PIETSCH; circ. 2,013,072.

Für Sie: 2000 Hamburg 60, Possmoorweg 5; telex 213214; women's magazine; circ. 959,838.

Gong: 8500 Nuremberg, Innere Cramer-Klett-Str. 6; telex 9118134; f. 1948; radio and TV weekly; Editor HELMUT MARKWORT; circ. 1,016,415.

Heim und Welt: 3000 Hanover, Am Jungfernplan 3; tel. (0511) 855757; telex 921158; weekly; Editor H. G. BRÜNEMANN; circ. 300,000.

Hörzu: 2 Hamburg 36, Kaiser-Wilhelm-Str. 6, Postfach 304630; tel. (040) 3471; telex 217001210; f. 1946; radio and television; published by Axel Springer Verlag; Editor FELIX SCHMIDT; circ. 3,238,900.

Kicker-Sportmagazin: 85 Nuremberg 81, Badstr. 4-6; tel. (911) 2160; telex 626244; f. 1946; sports weekly illustrated; published by Olympia Verlag; Man. Dir HERMANN KRAEMER; circ. 240,803.

Meine Familie & ich: 8000 Munich 81, Arabellastr. 23; tel. (089) 9250-0; telex 522802; circ. 769,306.

Neue Post: 2000 Hamburg 1, Burchardstr. 11, Postfach 100444; telex 2163770; weekly; circ. 1,728,750.

Neue Revue: 2000 Hamburg 1, Burchardstr. 11, Postfach 100444; tel. (040) 3019-0; telex 2163770; f. 1946; illustrated weekly; Editor-in-Chief RICHARD MAHKORN; circ. 1,121,184.

Neue Welt: 4000 Düsseldorf 1, Adlerstr. 22; telex 8587669; f. 1932; weekly; Editors PETER PREISS, GÜNTHER GROTKAMP; circ. 499,885.

Pardon: 6000 Frankfurt a.M., Oberweg 157, Postfach 180426; f. 1962; satirical monthly; Editor HANS A. NIKEL; circ. 70,000.

Petra: Jahreszeiten-Verlag, 2000 Hamburg 60, Possmoorweg 1; telex 213214; monthly; circ. 496,305.

Praline: 2000 Hamburg 1, Burchardstr. 11; telex 2163770; weekly; women's magazine; circ. 760,369.

Quick: 8000 Munich 83, Charles-de-Gaulle Str. 8; tel. (089) 67860; telex 2163770; f. 1948; illustrated weekly; Editor GERT BRAUN; circ. 843,908.

Scala: 6000 Frankfurt a.M. 1, Frankenallee 71–81; tel. (069) 75010; telex 411655; 6 a year; independent; Editor WERNER WIRTHLE; circ. 330,000; editions in German, English, French, Spanish, Portuguese.

Schöner Wohnen: 2000 Hamburg 36, Warburgstr. 50, Postfach 302040; telex 2195228; monthly; homes and gardens; Editor ANGELIKA JAHR; circ. 365,000.

7 Tage: 7570 Baden-Baden, Augustaplatz 10; telex 781410; f. 1843; weekly; Editor ERNST-HEINZ BREIL; circ. 234,000.

Der Spiegel: 2000 Hamburg 11, Brandstwiete 19/Ost-West-Str., Postfach 110420; telex 2162477; f. 1947; weekly; political, general; Publr RUDOLF AUGSTEIN; Editors-in-Chief ERICH BOEHME, Dr WERNER FUNK; circ. 957,068.

Stern: Gruner und Jahr AG, 2000 Hamburg 36, Postfach 302040; tel. (040) 41181; telex 2195213; illustrated weekly; Publr Dr PETER SCHOLL-LATOUR; Editors-in-Chief HEINER BREMER, MICHAEL JÜRGS, KLAUS LIEDTKE; circ. 1,478,926.

TV Hören+Sehen: 2000 Hamburg 1, Burchardstr. 11; tel. (040) 3019400; telex 2163770; Chief Editor HAJO PAUS; circ. 2,343,848.

Wochenend: 2000 Hamburg 1, Burchardstr. 11, Postfach 100444; telex 2163770; f. 1948; weekly; Editor GERD ROHLOF; circ. 668,278.

Religion and Philosophy

Christ in der Gegenwart: 7800 Freiburg i. Br., Hermann-Herder-Str. 4; f. 1948; weekly; Editor MANFRED PLATE; circ. 40,000.

Die Christliche Familie: 4300 Essen-Werden, Ruhrtalstr. 52–60; f. 1885; weekly; Publisher Dr ALBERT E. FISCHER; Editor Dr HEINRICH HÖPKER; circ. 85,724.

Der Dom: 4790 Paderborn, Liboristr. 1–3; telex 936807; weekly; Catholic; Publr Bonifatius-Druckerei GmbH; circ. 121,077.

Europa: 8000 Munich 5, Ickstattstr. 7, Postfach 140620; tel. (089) 2015505; telex 5215020; Publr VZV Zeitschriften-Verlags-GmbH; circ. 15,800.

Evangelischer Digest: 7000 Stuttgart 10, Landhausstr. 82, Postfach 104864; tel. (0711) 26863-0; telex 722985; f. 1958; monthly; Publr Verlag Axel B. Trunkel; circ. 9,300.

Evangelische Theologie: 8000 Munich 40, Isabellastr. 20; 6 a year; f. 1934; Editor GERHARD SAUTER; circ. 3,400.

Katholischer Digest: 7000 Stuttgart 10, Landhausstr. 82, Postfach 104864; tel. (0711) 268630; telex 722985; f. 1949; monthly; Publr Verlag Axel B. Trunkel; circ. 28,900.

Katholisches Sonntagsblatt: 7302 Ostfildern 1, Senefelderstr. 12; telex 723556; f. 1848; weekly; Publr Schwabenverlag AG; circ. 120,000.

Kirche und Leben: 4400 Münster, Antoniuskirchplatz 21; tel. (0251) 525379; telex 892888; f. 1945; weekly; Catholic; Chief Editor Dr GÜNTHER MEES; circ. 215,542.

Kirchenzeitung für das Erzbistum Köln: 5 Cologne, Ursulaplatz 1; tel. (0221) 134960; telex 8881128; weekly; Editor Dr HAJO GOERTZ; circ. 120,000.

Philosophisches Jahrbuch: 78 Freiburg i. Breisgau, Hermann-Herder Str. 4; f. 1893; 2 a year; Editors Prof. Dr H. KRINGS, Prof. Dr L. OEING-HANHOFF, Prof. Dr H. ROMBACH, Prof. Dr A. HALDER, Prof. Dr A. BARUZZI.

Der Sonntagsbrief: 7000 Stuttgart 10, Landhausstr. 82, Postfach 104864; tel. (0711) 268630; telex 722985; f. 1974; monthly; Publr AXEL B. TRUNKEL; circ. 81,400.

Der Weg: 4000 Düsseldorf, Postfach 6409; tel. (0211) 3610-1; telex 8582627; weekly; protestant; Editor Dr GERHARD E. STOLL; circ. 70,000.

Weltbild: 89 Augsburg, Frauentorstr. 5; telex 533715; 2 a month; Catholic; Editor EUGEN GEORG SCHWARZ; circ. 310,000.

Science, Medicine

Angewandte Chemie: VCH Verlagsgesellschaft mbH, 6940 Weinheim, Postfach 1260/1280; tel. (06201) 602310; telex 465516; f. 1888; monthly; circ. 4,000; monthly international edition in English, f. 1962, circ. 3,000.

Archiv der Pharmazie: 694 Weinheim/Bergstr., Pappelallee 3; f. 1822; monthly; Editor Prof. Dr J. KNABE; circ. 1,000.

Ärztliche Praxis: 8032 München-Gräfelfing, Hans-Cornelius-Str. 4; tel. (089) 855021; telex 522451; 2 a week; Editor Dr EDMUND BANASCHEWSKI; circ. 52,000.

Berichte der Bunsen-Gesellschaft für physikalische Chemie: VCH Verlagsgesellschaft mbH, 6940 Weinheim/Bergstr., Pappe-

FEDERAL REPUBLIC OF GERMANY

lallee 3; tel. (06201) 6020; telex 465516; f. 1894; monthly; Editors K. G. WEIL, A. WEISS; circ. 2,300.

Chemie-Ingenieur-Technik: VCH Verlagsgesellschaft mbH, 6940 Weinheim, Boschstr. 12, Postfach 1260; tel. (06201) 6020; telex 467155; f. 1928; monthly; Editor G. WELLHAUSEN; circ. 7,807.

Chemische Industrie: 6000 Frankfurt a.M. 1, Karlstr. 21; tel. (69) 2556454; telex 411372; f. 1949; review for chemical engineering and industrial chemistry; Dir UWE HOCH; Editor M. KERSTEN; circ. 5,000.

Der Chirurg: 6900 Heidelberg 1, Postfach 105280; tel. (06621) 487387; telex 461723; f. 1929; monthly; Editors Prof. Dr Ch. HERFARTH, Prof. Dr G. HEBERER, Prof. Dr E. KERN; circ. 6,500.

Deutsche Apotheker Zeitung: 7000 Stuttgart 1, Birkenwaldstr. 44, Postfach 40; tel. (0711) 25820; telex 723636; f. 1861; weekly; Editor Dr WOLFGANG WESSINGER; circ. 22,518.

Deutsche Automobil-Revue: 6 Frankfurt a.M., Städelstr. 19; f. 1926; Editor Dr JÜRGEN CHRIST.

Deutsche Medizinische Wochenschrift: 7000 Stuttgart 30, Rüdigerstr. 14; weekly; Editors F. KÜMMERLE, P. C. SCRIBA, W. SIEGENTHALER, A. STURM, R. AUGUSTIN, W. KUHN; circ. 33,142.

Deutsche Zahnärztliche Zeitschrift: 8000 Munich 2, Kolbergerstr. 22, Postfach 860420; monthly; dental medicine; Editors Prof. Dr A. KRÖNCKE, Dr G. MASCHINSKI.

Deutsche Zeitschrift für Mund-, Kiefer- und Gesichtschirurgie: 4400 Münster, Waldeystr. 30; quarterly; oral and maxillofacial surgery and oral pathology; Editors Dr R. BECKER, Dr H. SCHEUNEMANN, Dr G. SEIFERT.

Elektro-Anzeiger: 7022 Leirnfelden-Echterdingen, Postfach 100252; telex 7255421; f. 1948; monthly; Editor Dipl.-Ing. W. ODO; circ. 18,000.

Europa Chemie: 6000 Frankfurt a.M. 1, Karlstr. 21, tel. (69) 2556464; telex 411372; topical news service of the review *Chemische Industrie;* Dir UWE HOCH; Editor Dipl. Chem. H. SEIDEL; circ. 5,200.

Geologische Rundschau: Geologische Vereinigung eV, 5442 Mendig, Industriestr. 8; tel. (02652) 1508; general, geological; circ. 3,000.

Handchirurgie, Mikrochirurgie, Plastische Chirurgie: 7000 Stuttgart 30, Rüdigerstr. 14; tel. (0711) 89310; telex 7252275; 6 a year; Editors Prof. Dr med. D. BUCK-GRAMCKO, Prof. Dr H. MILLESI, Prof. Dr E. BIEMER.

Historisches Jahrbuch: 78 Freiburg i. Breisgau, Hermann-Herder Str. 4; f. 1879; 2 double vols a year; Editor Prof. Dr J. SPÖRL.

Journal of Neurology: Springer-Verlag, 1000 Berlin 33, Heidelberger Platz 3; tel. (030) 8207-0; telex 0183319; f. 1891; continuation of *Deutsche Zeitschrift für Nervenheilkunde;* Editors-in-Chief Prof. Dr R. A. C. HUGHES, Prof. Dr K. POECK.

Kerntechnik: 8014 Neubiberg, Werner-Heisenberg-Weg 39; tel. (089) 6004-2017; telex 5215800; f. 1958; published by Carl Hanser GmbH; 6 a year; independent journal on nuclear engineering, energy systems and radiation; circ. 1,200.

Kosmos: 7 Stuttgart 1, Pfizerstr. 5-7, Postfach 106011; tel. (0711) 21910; telex 721669; f. 1904; monthly; popular scientific journal; Editor Dr RAINER KÖTHE; circ. 102,925.

Medizinische Klinik: 8000 Munich 2, Lindwurmstr. 95; tel. (089) 514150; telex 521701; f. 1905; fortnightly; Editor Dr HELGA SCHICHTL; circ. 11,827.

Mikrokosmos: 7000 Stuttgart 1, Pfizerstr. 5-7; tel. (0711) 2191304; telex 721669; f. 1906; monthly; microscopical studies; Editor Dr D. KRAUTER; circ. 3,000.

Nachrichten aus Chemie, Technik und Laboratorium: 6940 Weinheim, Boschstr. 12; tel. (06201) 602318; telex 465516; f. 1953; fortnightly; circ. 22,000.

Naturwissenschaftliche Rundschau: 7000 Stuttgart 10, Birkenwaldstr. 44, Postfach 105339; tel. (0711) 2582-0; telex 723636; f. 1948; monthly; scientific; Editors HANS ROTTA, ROSWITHA SCHMID; circ. 7,600.

Planta medica: 7000 Stuttgart 30, Rüdigerstr. 14, Postfach 104853; tel. (0711) 8931-0; telex 7252275; f. 1952; every 2 months; publ. by Society of Medicinal Plant Research; Editor E. REINHARD.

Therapie der Gegenwart: 8000 Munich 15, Lindwurmstr. 95; tel. (089) 51415-0; telex 521701; f. 1890; weekly; Chief Editor Dr TILL UWE KEIL; circ. 36,000.

Zahnärztliche Praxis: 8032 München-Gräfelfing, Hans-Cornelius-Str. 4; monthly; Editor Dr EDMUND BANASCHEWSKI; circ. 12,000.

Zeitschrift für Allgemeinmedizin: 7000 Stuttgart 30, Rüdigerstr. 14; tel. (0711) 89310; f. 1924; 3 a month; general medicine; publ. by Hippokrates Verlag GmbH; Editors Dr W. MAHRINGER, Prof. Dr P. DOENECKE, Dr M. KOCHEN, Dr G. VOLKERT, Dr W. HARDINGHAUS.

Zeitschrift für Kinderchirurgie: 7000 Stuttgart 10, Rüdigerstr. 14, Postfach 102263; f. 1964; 6 a year; Editors Prof. Dr A. M. HOLSCHNEIDER; Dr M. BETTEX.

Zeitschrift für Klinische Psychologie u. Psychotherapie: 78 Freiburg i. Breisgau, Hermann-Herder-Str. 4; f. 1952; quarterly; Editor Dr W. J. REVERS.

Zeitschrift für Metallkunde: 7000 Stuttgart 80, Heisenbergstr. 5; tel. (0711) 6861200; telex 7111576; f. 1911; monthly; metal research; Editors G. PETZOW, P. HAASEN, V. SCHUMACHER.

Zeitschrift für Physik: 6900 Heidelberg 1, Philosophenweg 19; 16 a year; Editors-in-Chief (Atomic Nuclei) Prof. Dr H. A. WEIDENMÜLLER, (Condensed Matter) Prof. Dr H. HORNER, Prof. Dr F. STEGLICH, (Particles and Fields) Prof Dr G. KRAMER, Prof. Dr W. SATZ, (Atoms, Molecules and Clusters) Prof. Dr. I. V. HERTEL.

NEWS AGENCIES

dpa Deutsche Presse-Agentur GmbH: 2000 Hamburg 13, Mittelweg 38; tel. (040) 41131; telex 212995; f. 1949; supplies all the daily newspapers, broadcasting stations and some 1,000 further subscribers in the Federal Republic of Germany and West Berlin with its national and regional news service. English, Spanish, Arabic and German language news is also transmitted regularly to 550 press agencies, newspapers, radio and television stations and ministries of information in over 85 countries. The dpa Television News Service 'e-te-s' delivers news films in several languages to television stations abroad; Dir Gen. Dr WALTER RICHTBERG; Editor-in-Chief Dr HANS BENIRSCHKE.

VWD: 6236 Eschborn 1, Niederurseler Allee 8-10, Postfach 6105; tel. (06196) 405-0; telex 4072895; economic news.

Foreign Bureaux

Agence France-Presse (AFP): 5300 Bonn 1, Friedrich-Ebert-Allee 13; tel. (0228) 225031; telex 886898; Man. PIERRE LEMOINE.

Agencia EFE (Spain): 5300 Bonn 1, Heussallee 2-10, Pressehaus II/12-14; tel. (0228) 214058; telex 886556; Bureau Chief JOAQUÍN RABAGO.

Agenzia Nazionale Stampa Associata (ANSA) (Italy): 5300 Bonn 1, Dahlmannstr. 36; tel. (0228) 214770; telex 886857; Correspondent SANDRO DE ROSA.

Allgemeiner Deutscher Nachrichtendienst (ADN) (German Democratic Republic): 5300 Bonn, Allianzplatz, Pressehaus I/15; Correspondent RALF BACHMANN.

Associated Press (AP) (USA): 6000 Frankfurt am Main 1, Moselstr. 27; tel. (069) 2713-0; telex 412118; also in Hanover, Hamburg, Stuttgart, Wiesbaden, Saarbrücken, Bonn, Berlin, Munich and Düsseldorf; Man. STEPHEN H. MILLER.

Central News Agency (Republic of China): 5307 Wachtberg-Pech, Auf dem Girzen 4; tel. (0228) 324972; Correspondent FRANCIS FINE.

Československá tisková kancelář (ČTK) (Czechoslovakia): 5300 Bonn, Heussallee 2-10, Pressehaus I/207; tel. (0228) 215811; telex 886772.

Inter Press Service (IPS) (Italy): 5300 Bonn 1, Heussallee 2-10, Pressehaus II/205; tel. (0228) 219138; telex 886331; Correspondents RAMESH JAURA, JORGE GILLIES, ROBERTO AMPUERO ESPINOZA.

Jiji Tsushin-sha (Japan): 2000 Hamburg 13, Mittelweg 38; tel. (040) 445553; telex 211470; Correspondent EIICHI NAKAMURA.

Kyodo Tsushin (Japan): 5300 Bonn, Reuterstr. 124-132, Bonn-Center; tel. (0228) 225543; telex 886308; Chief Correspondent MASARU IMAI.

Magyar Távirati Iroda (MTI) (Hungary): 5300 Bonn 1, Heussallee 2-10, Pressehaus I; telex 8869652; Correspondent JÁNOS FOLLINUS.

Prensa Latina (Cuba): 5300 Bonn 1, Heussallee 2-10, Pressehaus II/201; tel. (0228) 211330; telex 886517; Man. FAUSTO TRIANA.

Reuters (UK): 5300 Bonn, Bonn-Center, Bundeskanzlerplatz 2-10, Postfach 120324; tel. (0228) 260970; telex 886677; Chief Correspondent BJÖRN EDLUND.

Telegrafnoye Agentstvo Sovetskovo Soyuza (TASS) (USSR): 5300 Bonn, Heussallee 2-10, Pressehaus I/133; telex 886472; Chief Correspondent ALEKSEY GRIGORIEV.

United Press International (UPI) (USA): 5300 Bonn, Heussallee 2-10, Pressehaus I; tel. (0228) 215031; telex 886538; Bureau Man. EDWARD F. ROBY; Chief Correspondent J. B. FLEMING.

Xinhua (New China) News Agency (People's Republic of China): 5300 Bonn 2, Lyngsbergstr. 33; tel. (0228) 331845; telex 885531; Correspondent XIA ZHIMIAN.

APN (USSR) is also represented.

PRESS AND JOURNALISTS' ASSOCIATIONS

Bundesverband Deutscher Zeitungsverleger eV (Association of Newspaper Publishers): 5300 Bonn 2, Riemenschneiderstr. 10,

FEDERAL REPUBLIC OF GERMANY

Postfach 205002; tel. (0228) 810040; telex 885461; there are 10 affiliated Land Associations; Pres. ROLF TERHEYDEN; Chief Sec. CLAUS DETJEN.

Deutscher Journalisten-Verband (German Journalists' Association): 5300 Bonn, Bennauerstr. 60; tel. (0228) 219093; telex 886567; Chair. WERNER RUDOLPH; Sec. HUBERT ENGEROFF; 12 Land Associations.

Deutscher Presserat (German Press Council): 5300 Bonn 2, Wurzerstr. 46, Postfach 200433; tel. (0228) 361087; 20 mems; Man. DOROTHEE RÜFFER.

Verband Deutscher Zeitschriftenverleger eV (Association of Publishers of Periodicals): 5300 Bonn 2, Winterstr. 50; tel. (0228) 311046; telex 8869391; there are six affiliated Land Associations; Man. Dir Dr WINFRIED RESKE.

Verein der Ausländischen Presse in der BRD (VAP) (Foreign Press Association): 5300 Bonn 1, Heussallee 2–10, Pressehaus I/35; tel. (0228) 210885; f. 1951; Chair. JORGE GILLIES.

Publishers

There are about 1,850 publishing firms in the Federal Republic of Germany, of which nearly 80% produce fewer than 10 books per year. There is no national publishing centre.

ADAC Verlag: 8000 Munich 70, Am Westpark 8; tel. (089) 76760; telex 528404; f. 1958; travel, guidebooks, legal brochures, technical manuals, maps, magazines ADAC-Motorwelt, Deutsches Autorecht; Man. Dir MANFRED M. ANGELE.

Karl Alber Verlag GmbH: 7800 Freiburg i.Br., Hermann-Herder-Str. 4; tel. (0761) 273495; telex 7721440; f. 1939; philosophy, history and theory of science, psychology, sociology, political science, communications; Man. Dir Dr MEINOLF WEWEL.

Arani-Verlag GmbH: 1000 Berlin 31, Kurfürstendamm 126, Postfach 31 0829; tel. (030) 8911008; f. 1947; fiction, general; Man. HORST MEYER.

Arena Verlag GmbH: 8700 Würzburg 1, Rottendorfer Str. 16; tel. (0931) 75011; telex 68833; f. 1949; books for children and juveniles, non-fiction; Dir HANS-GEORG NOACK.

Artemis und Winkler Verlag GmbH: 8000 Munich 40, Martiusstr. 8; tel. (089) 348074; telex 5215517; f. 1957; literature, encyclopaedias; Dir FRANZ EBNER.

Aschendorffsche Verlagsbuchhandlung: 4400 Münster/Westfalen, Soesterstr. 13, Postfach 1124; tel. (0251) 6900; telex 892830; f. 1720; Catholic theology, philosophy, psychology, education, jurisprudence, general and church history, philology; Dirs MAXIMILIAN F. HÜFFER, Dr ANTON WILHELM HÜFFER.

Athenäum Verlag: 6000 Frankfurt a.M., Savignystr. 53, Postfach 170101; tel. (069) 7560950; telex 414531; f. 1973; literary sciences, languages, social sciences, general trade and non-fiction, education, Judaism; Publisher AXEL RÜTTERS.

Aussaat- und Schriftenmissions-Verlag: 4133 Neukirchen-Vluyn, Andreas-Braemstr. 18–20, Postfach 1265; tel. (02845) 392239; f. 1981; religion, juveniles; Man. Dirs Dr RUDOLF WETH, LIESEL RENNSCHEIDT.

Badenia Verlag und Druckerei GmbH: 7500 Karlsruhe 21, Rudolf-Freytag-Str. 6, Postfach 210248; tel. (0721) 578041; telex 7826726; f. 1874; religion, text-books, school books, fiction; Dir Dr HELMUT WALTER.

Friedrich Bahn Verlag GmbH: 7750 Konstanz, Zasiusstr. 8, Postfach 1186; tel. (07531) 23054; f. 1891; religion, literature; Dir HERBERT DENECKE.

Bardtenschlager Verlag GmbH: 8000 Munich 81, Oberfoehringerstr. 105A; tel. (089) 952043; f. 1852; juvenile literature, pedagogics; Dir PETER EISMANN.

Otto Wilhelm Barth Verlag: 8000 Munich 19, Stievestr. 9; tel. (089) 172237; telex 5215282; f. 1924; a division of Scherz Verlag; Far East religions and philosophy, meditation, healing, mysticism, etc.; Dir RUDOLF STREIT-SCHERZ; Editor STEPHAN SCHUHMACHER.

Bastei-Verlag: 5060 Bergisch Gladbach 2, Scheidtbachstr. 23–31; tel. (02202) 1210; telex 887922; f. 1949; paperbacks; Man. Dir GUSTAV LÜBBE.

Bayerische Verlagsanstalt GmbH: 8600 Bamberg, Laubanger 23; tel. (0951) 7902-0; telex 9518118; f. 1949; Dir KURT KIENING.

Bechtle-Verlag: 7300 Esslingen, Zeppelinstr. 116; tel. (0711) 3108-1; telex 7-256487; f. 1868; biography, history, literature, humour, poetry; Man. Dir OTTO W. BECHTLE.

Verlag C. H. Beck: 8000 Munich 40, Wilhelmstr. 9; tel. (089) 381890; telex 5215085; f. 1763; law, science, theology, archaeology, philosophy, philology, history, politics, art, literature; Dirs Dr HANS DIETER BECK, WOLFGANG BECK.

Beltz Verlag: 6940 Weinheim, Am Hauptbahnhof 10, Postfach 1120; tel. (06201) 63071; telex 465500; f. 1841; textbooks; Man. Dir Dr MANFRED BELTZ-RÜBELMANN.

Berghaus Verlag: 8347 Kirchdorf/Inn, Ramerding 18; tel. (08571) 2042; f. 1973; art; Man. Dir URSULA BADER.

Verlagsgruppe Bertelsmann: 8000 Munich 80, Neumarkterstr. 18; tel. (089) 431890; telex 523259; f. 1970; general, reference; Man. Dirs Dr H. BENZING, B. VON MINCKWITZ, O. PAESCHKE, K. PORADA, DR U. WECHSLER.

Beuroner Kunstverlag: 7792 Beuron 1; tel. (07466) 17228; f. 1898; fine art, religion, calendars; Dir LEO P. GABRIEL GAWLETTA.

Bibliographisches Institut und F.A. Brockhaus AG: 6800 Mannheim 1, Dudenstr. 6, Postfach 100311; tel. (0621) 390101; telex 462107; f. (1805/1826) 1984; encyclopaedia, reference books, scientific books, atlases; Man. Dirs HUBERTUS BROCKHAUS, CLAUS W. GREUNER, ANDREAS LANGENSCHEIDT, Dr FLORIAN LANGENSCHEIDT, Dr MICHAEL WEGNER.

Biederstein Verlag: 8000 Munich 40, Wilhelmstr. 9; tel. (089) 381890; telex 05-215085; f. 1946; belles-lettres, non-fiction; Man. Dir WOLFGANG BECK.

Georg Bitter Verlag KG: 4350 Recklinghausen, Herner Str. 24; tel. (02361) 25888; f. 1968; children's books; Dir Dr GEORG BITTER.

Blanvalet Verlag: 8000 Munich 80, Neumarkter Str. 18, Postfach 800 360; tel. (089) 431890; telex 523259; fiction; Man. Dirs WOLFGANG KURTH, MICHAEL MELLER.

BLV Verlagsgesellschaft mbH: 8000 Munich 40, Lothstr. 29; tel. (089) 127050; telex 5215087; f. 1946; cookery, sports, gardening, equitation, technical books, nature, motoring, etc.; Chair. Dr D. IPPEN; Man. Dir HEINZ HARTMANN.

Böhlau-Verlag GmbH: 5000 Cologne 60, Niehlerstr. 272–274; tel. (0221) 769340; f. 1951; history, music, art; Man. Dir Dr GÜNTER J. HENZ.

Boje-Verlag GmbH: 8520 Erlangen, Am Pestalozziring 14, Postfach 2829; tel. (09131) 6060-0; telex 629766; f. 1947; children's books; Man. Dirs Dr RHEINHOLD WEIGAND, NORBERT FRANKE.

Harald Boldt Verlag GmbH: 5407 Boppard am Rhein 1, Postfach 1110; tel. (06742) 2511; f. 1951; history, reference, general and social science, demography; Man. Dirs HARALD BOLDT, PETER BOLDT.

Gebrüder Borntraeger Verlagsbuchhandlung: 7000 Stuttgart 1, Johannesstr. 3A; tel. (0711) 625001; telex 723363; f. 1790; geology, palaeontology, mineralogy, biology, botany, oceanography, meteorology, geophysics, geomorphology, geography, metallography, periodicals; Proprs Dr E. NÄGELE, KLAUS OBERMILLER.

Verlag G. Braun: 7500 Karlsruhe, Karl-Friedrich-Str. 14–18; tel. (0721) 1650; telex 7826904; f. 1813; physics, mathematics, flow mechanics, medicine; Dirs Dr EBERHARD KNITTEL, HELLO Graf VON RITTBERG, Dipl. Ing. FRIEDRICH WERTH.

Braun & Schneider: 8000 Munich 2, Maximiliansplatz 9; tel. (089) 555580; f. 1843; children's literature, fiction; Dirs Dr J. SCHNEIDER, FRIEDRICH SCHNEIDER.

Breitkopf & Härtel: 6200 Wiesbaden, Walkmühlstr. 52, Postfach 1707; tel. (06121) 4903-0; telex 4182647; f. 1719; music and music books; Dirs LIESELOTTE SIEVERS, GOTTFRIED MÖCKEL.

F. A. Brockhaus GmbH: 6800 Mannheim 1, Dudenstr. 6, Postfach 5305; tel. (0621) 390101; telex 462107; f. 1805; encyclopaedias, dictionaries, travel, natural sciences, memoirs, archaeology; Dirs HUBERTUS BROCKHAUS, Dr MICHAEL WEGNER.

Verlag Bruckmann München: 8000 Munich 20, Nymphenburgerstr. 86, Postfach 27; tel. (089) 125701; telex 523739; f.1858; books, calendars, video cassettes, magazines, fine art prints, original prints; Man. Dir Dr JORG D. HIEBNER.

Buchhändler-Vereinigung GmbH: 6000 Frankfurt a.M.1, Grosser Hirschgraben 17-21; tel. (069) 13060; telex 413573; f. 1846; publishing dept of Börsenverein des Deutschen Buchhandels eV (German Book Trade Assoc); Dir W. ROBERT MÜLLER.

Verlag Busse und Seewald GmbH: 4900 Herford, Ahmser Str. 190, Postfach 1344; tel. (05221) 7750; telex 934717; politics, economics, contemporary history, philosophy, sociology, wine, interior decoration, carpets, etc.; Man. HELMUT RUSS.

Butzon & Bercker GmbH: 4178 Kevelaer 1, Postfach 215; tel. (02832) 2906; telex 812207; f. 1870; Catholic religion and theology, meditation, prayers, liturgy, children's books; Dirs KLAUS BERCKER, Dr EDMUND BERCKER.

Verlag Georg D. W. Callwey GmbH & Co: 8000 Munich 80, Streitfeldstr. 35; tel. (089) 436005-0; telex 5216752; f. 1884; history, cultural history, architecture, sculpture, painting, gardens, art restoration; Man. Dirs HELMUTH BAUR-CALLWEY, Dr VERONIKA BAUR-CALLWEY.

Verlag Hans Carl GmbH & Co KG: 8500 Nuremberg 1, Breite Gasse 58–60; tel. (0911) 2383-0; telex 623081; f. 1861; technical, scientific and general literature; Man. Dir GÜNTER SCHMIEDEL.

FEDERAL REPUBLIC OF GERMANY

Carlsen Verlag GmbH: 2057 Reinbek, Dieselstr. 6, Postfach 1169; tel. (040) 727609-0; telex 217879; f. 1953; children's books; Dirs CARL-JOHAN BONNIER, VIKTOR NIEMANN.

Christliche Verlagsanstalt GmbH: 7750 Konstanz, Zasiusstr. 8; tel. (07531) 23054; f. 1892; religion, children's books, literature; Dir HERBERT DENECKE.

Colloquium Verlag GmbH: 1000 Berlin 45, Unter den Eichen 93; tel. (030) 8328085; f. 1948; biography, history, political and social science, Latin-American studies; Dirs OTTO H. HESS, STEFAN HESS; Editor Dr GABRIELE PANGRATZ.

Columbus Verlag Paul Oestergaard GmbH: 7056 Weinstadt 1, Postfach 1180, Columbus Haus; tel. (07151) 68011; telex 724382; f. 1909; maps, globes, atlases; Dir PETER OESTERGAARD.

Cornelsen Hirschgraben-Verlag GmbH & Co: 6000 Frankfurt 1, Fürstenbergerstr. 223, Postfach 180 245; tel. (069) 550491; telex 176997604; f. 1946; school books; Dirs Dr F. LÖFFELHOLZ, WERNER THIELE.

Deutsche Verlags-Anstalt GmbH: 7000 Stuttgart 1, Neckarstr. 121, Postfach 106012; tel. (0711) 26310; telex (17) 7111193; f. 1831; general; Dirs ULRICH FRANK-PLANITZ, Dr HANS GLÜCKER.

Deutscher Apotheker Verlag: 7000 Stuttgart 10, Birkenwaldstr. 44, Postfach 101061; tel. (0711) 25820; telex 723636; f. 1861; pharmacy; Dirs Dr WOLFGANG WESSINGER, VINCENT SIEVEKING, REINHOLD HACK.

Deutscher Instituts-Verlag: 5000 Cologne 51, Gustav-Heinemann-Ufer 84–88, Postfach 510670; tel. (0221) 370801; telex 8882768; f. 1951; economic, literature; attached to Institut der deutschen Wirtschaft, Cologne (German Economics Institute); Man. Dir Prof. Dr GERHARD FELS.

Deutscher Kunstverlag GmbH: 8000 Munich 21, Vohburgerstr. 1; tel. (089) 568145; f. 1921; art books.

Deutscher Verlag für Kunstwissenschaft GmbH: 1000 Berlin 61, Lindenstr. 76; tel. (030) 25913864; telex 183723; f. 1964; German art; Dirs KLAUS MÜLLER-CREPON, Prof. HENNING BOCK, Prof. PETER BLOCH.

Deutscher Taschenbuch Verlag (dtv): 8000 Munich 40, Friedrichstr. 1A; tel. (089) 3817060; telex 5215396; f. 1960; general fiction, history, music, art, reference, children, general and social science, medicine, textbooks; Man. Dir HEINZ FRIEDRICH.

Eugen Diederichs Verlag: 5000 Cologne 1, Merlosstr. 8; tel. (0221) 720672; f. 1896; literature, cultural sciences, psychology, sociology, philosophy; Dirs KLAUS DIEDERICHS, ULF DIEDERICHS.

Verlag Moritz Diesterweg: 6000 Frankfurt a.M. 1, Hochstr. 29–31, Postfach 110651; tel. (069) 13010; telex 413234; f. 1860; text books, economics, social sciences, sciences, pedagogics; Dir DIETRICH HERBST.

Droemersche Verlagsanstalt Th. Knaur Nachf GmbH & Co: 8000 Munich 80, Rauchstr. 9–11; tel. (089) 92710; telex 51933524; f. 1901; general literature, non-fiction, art books, paperbacks; Man. Dirs RÜDIGER HILDEBRANDT, Dr KARL H. BLESSING.

Droste Verlag GmbH: 4000 Düsseldorf 11, Druckzentrum Düsseldorf, Zülpicher Str. 10, Postfach 1135; tel. (0211) 5052604; telex 8582495; f. 1711; fiction, non-fiction, German and foreign literature; Publ. Dir Dr M. LOTSCH.

Duncker & Humblot GmbH: 1000 Berlin 41, Dietrich-Schäfer-Weg 9; tel. (030) 790006-0; f. 1798; economics, sociology, law, science, history, philosophy, political sciences.

Econ Verlagsgruppe: 4000 Düsseldorf 30, Kaiserwertherstr. 282, Postfach 300321; tel. (0211) 439060; telex 8587327; general fiction and non-fiction; Publr Dr HERO KIND; Man. Dir PETER SCHAPER.

Ehrenwirth Verlag GmbH: 8000 Munich 80, Vilshofenerstr. 8; tel. (089) 989025; telex 529667; f. 1945; general literature, fiction, education, textbooks, periodicals; Dirs MARTIN EHRENWIRTH, FRANK AUERBACH.

N. G. Elwert Verlag: 3550 Marburg/Lahn, Reitgasse 7–9; tel. (06421) 25023; f. 1726; history, religion, law, social science; Man. Dir Dr W. BRAUN-ELWERT.

Ferdinand Enke Verlag: 7000 Stuttgart 10, Postfach 101254, and 7000 Stuttgart 30, Rüdigerstr. 14; tel. (0711) 89310; telex 7252275; f. 1837; medicine, veterinary medicine, sciences (geosciences), psychology, social sciences; books and periodicals; Man. Dr MARLIS KUHLMANN.

Wilhelm Ernst & Sohn: 1000 Berlin 31, Hohenzollerndamm 170; tel. (030) 860003-0; telex 184143; f. 1851; architecture, technology.

Europäische Verlagsanstalt GmbH: 6000 Frankfurt a.M. 1, Savignystr. 53; tel. (069) 7560950; telex 414531; f. 1946; social sciences, politics, culture, history, economics, education; Publr AXEL RÜTTERS.

Fackelträger-Verlag GmbH: 3000 Hanover 1, Goseriede 10–12; tel. (0511) 14648; f. 1949; Man. Dirs SIEGFRIED LIEBRECHT, PETER SEIFRIED.

Fackelverlag Fackelversand G. Bowitz GmbH: 7000 Stuttgart 80, Schockenriedstr. 46; tel. (0711) 20171; telex 722875; f. 1919; popular literature; Man. DIETER BOWITZ.

S. Fischer Verlag GmbH: 6000 Frankfurt a.M. 70, Hedderichstr. 114, Postfach 700355; tel. (069) 60620; telex 412410; f. 1886; general, paperbacks; Publr MONIKA SCHOELLER; Man. Dir Dr ARNULF CONRADI.

Fleischhauer & Spohn Verlag: 7000 Stuttgart 30, Maybachstr. 18, Postfach 301160; tel. (0711) 89340; telex 723113; f. 1830; fiction, literature.

Focus-Verlag: 6300 Giessen, Lonystr. 19, Postfach 110328; tel. (0641) 71799; f. 1971; history, reference, literature, ecology, social science; Man. Dir HELMUT SCHMID; Publ. Man. RAYMUND NEUHOFER.

Francké'sche Verlagshandlung, W. Keller & Co: 7000 Stuttgart 1, Pfizerstr. 5–7, Postfach 640; tel. (0711) 21910; telex 721669; f. 1822; science, natural history, railway books, field guides, children's books; Dirs C. KELLER, F. KELLER, E. NEHMANN.

Verlag Frauenoffensive: 8000 Munich 80, Kellerstr. 39; tel. (089) 485102; f. 1976; feminist publs; Dirs INGE JAKOB, SUSANNE KAHN-ACKERMANN, GERLINDE KOWITZKE, REGINA GUCKERT.

Friedrich Frommann Verlag, Günther Holzboog: 7000 Stuttgart 50 (Bad Cannstatt), König-Karl-Str. 27, Postfach 500460; tel. (0711) 569039; telex 7254754; f. 1727; philosophy, theology, sociology, politics, linguistics, mathematics, history of science; Man. GÜNTHER HOLZBOOG.

Dr Th. Gabler Betriebswirtschaftlicher Verlag GmbH: 6200 Wiesbaden 1, Taunusstr. 54, Postfach 1546; tel. (06121) 5341; telex 4186567; f. 1928; business, industry, banking, insurance; Dirs Dr FRANK LUBE, Dr HANS-DIETER HAENEL.

Dr Rudolf Georgi Verlag: 5100 Aachen, Theaterstr. 77; tel. (0241) 477910; telex 832337; f. 1932; history, calendars, art, general science; Man. Dirs WERNER, MANFRED GEORGI.

Wilhelm Goldmann Verlag: 8000 Munich 80, Neumarkter Str. 18; tel. (089) 43189-0; telex 529965; f. 1922; fiction, non-fiction, paperbacks; Man. Dir JÜRGEN KREUZHAGE.

Gräfe und Unzer GmbH: 8000 Munich 40, Isabellastr. 32; tel. (089) 272720; telex 5216929; f. 1722; cookery, health, nature; Man. Dirs KURT PRELINGER, CHRISTIAN STRASSER, DIETER BANZHAF.

Verlag Kurt Gross: 6000 Frankfurt a.M. 1, Zeppelinallee 43, Postfach 970148; tel. (069) 793009-0; telex 4189621; f. 1949; law; Man. Dir NICO DE GIER.

G. Grote'sche Verlagsbuchhandlung KG: 5000 Cologne 40, Max-Planck-Str. 12, Postfach 400263; tel. (02234) 1060; telex 8882662; f. 1861; social and political science, history, law, economics, administration, periodicals; Dir F. PLAGGE.

Matthias-Grünewald-Verlag GmbH: 6500 Mainz-Weisenau 1, Max-Hufschmidt-Str. 4A, Postfach 3080; tel. (06131) 839055; f. 1918; theology, philosophy, history, children's books; Dir Dr JAKOB LAUBACH.

Walter de Gruyter & Co Verlag: 1000 Berlin 30, Genthiner Str. 13; tel. (030) 260050; telex 184027; f. 1919; humanities and theology, law, science, medicine, mathematics, economics, data processing, general; Man. Dirs Dr KURT LUBASCH, Dr KURT-GEORG CRAM, Dr HELWIG HASSENPFLUG.

Gütersloher Verlagshaus Gerd Mohn: 4830 Gütersloh 1, Königstr. 23–25, Postfach 1343; tel. (05241) 862-0; telex 933868; f. 1959; theology, politics, paperbacks; Man. HANS-JÜRGEN MEURER.

Verlag Anton Hain: 6000 Frankfurt a.M., Savignystr. 53, Postfach 170101; tel. (069) 7560950; telex 414531; f. 1946; philosophy, psychology, politics, sociology, economics, quarterly periodicals; Publr AXEL RÜTTERS.

Carl Hanser Verlag: 8000 Munich 80, Kolbergerstr. 22; tel. (089) 92694-0; telex 522837; f. 1928; modern literature, plastics, technology, chemistry, science, dentistry; Man. Dirs JOACHIM SPENCKER, F.-J. KLOCK.

Peter Hanstein Verlag GmbH: 6000 Frankfurt a.M., Savignystr. 53, Postfach 170101; tel. (069) 7560950; telex 414531; f. 1878; religion, economics; Publr AXEL RÜTTERS.

Verlag Otto Harrassowitz: 6200 Wiesbaden 1, Taunusstr. 14, Postfach 2929; tel. (06121) 521046; telex 4186135; f. 1872; oriental studies, linguistics, history of Eastern Europe, education in Eastern Europe, librarianship.

Verlag Gerd Hatje: 7000 Stuttgart 50, Wildungerstr. 83, Postfach 500468; tel. (0711) 561109; f. 1945; modern art, architecture and design, general; Propr GERD HATJE.

Karl F. Haug Verlag: 6900 Heidelberg 1, Fritz-Frey-Str. 21, Postfach 102840; tel. (06221) 49974; telex 461683; f. 1903; medicine; Man. Dir Dr E. FISCHER.

Dr Ernst Hauswedell & Co: 7000 Stuttgart 1, Rosenberg Str. 113; tel. (0711) 638264; f. 1927; bibliographies, book trade, fine arts,

FEDERAL REPUBLIC OF GERMANY

humanities, literature, illustrated periodicals, collecting; Man. Dirs GERD HIERSEMANN, Dr REIMAR W. FUCHS.

Henssel Verlag: 1000 Berlin 39 (West), Glienicker Str. 12; tel. (030) 8051493; f. 1938; poetry, literature, general fiction, travel, humour; Man. Dir KARL-HEINZ HENSSEL.

F. A. Herbig Verlagsbuchhandlung: 8000 Munich 22, Thomas-Wimmer-Ring 11; tel. (089) 2350080; telex 5215045; f. 1821; fine arts, popular sciences, fiction, hobbies; Man. Dir Dr HERBERT FLEISSNER.

Verlag Herder GmbH & Co KG: 7800 Freiburg i. Br., Hermann-Herder-Str. 4; tel. (0761) 27171; telex 7721440; f. 1801; religion, philosophy, history, education, art, music, encyclopaedias, children's books; Propr Dr H. HERDER.

Carl Heymanns Verlag KG: 5000 Cologne 41, Luxemburger Str. 449; tel. (0221) 460100; telex 8881888; brs at Berlin, Bonn and Munich; f. 1815; law, political science and administration; periodicals; Man. Dir BERTRAM GALLUS.

Anton Hiersemann Verlag: 7000 Stuttgart 1, Rosenbergstr. 113, Postfach 102251; tel. (0711) 638264; f. 1884; library, documentation, history, philology, literature, theatre, religion, art, bibliography; Pres. KARL G. HIERSEMANN.

S. Hirzel Verlag GmbH & Co: 7000 Stuttgart 10, Birkenwaldstr. 44, Postfach 102237; tel. (0711) 25820; telex 723636; f. 1853; chemistry, physics, philosophy, psychology; Dirs Dr WOLFGANG WESSINGER, VINCENT SIEVEKING, REINHOLD HACK.

Julius Hoffmann Verlag: 7000 Stuttgart 1, Neckurstr. 121; tel. (0711) 26310; architecture, art, technology, handbooks.

Hoffmann & Campe Verlag: 2000 Hamburg 13, Harvestehuderweg 45; tel. (040) 214259; telex 214259; f. 1781; biography, fiction, history, economics, science, also magazine *Merian*; Man. Dir THOMAS GANSKE.

Insel Verlag: 6000 Frankfurt 1, Lindenstr. 29, Suhrkamp Haus, Postfach 101130; tel. (069) 756010; telex 413972; f. 1899; literature, general; Dir Dr SIEGFRIED UNSELD.

Axel Juncker-Verlag: 8000 Munich 40, Neusser Str. 3; tel. (089) 360960; f. 1902; dictionaries, phrase-books; Man. Dir Dr FLORIAN LANGENSCHEIDT.

Chr. Kaiser Verlag GmbH: 8000 Munich 80, Lilienstr. 70; tel. (089) 483014; f. 1845; theological; Dir MANFRED WEBER.

Hermann Kessler Verlag für Sprachmethodik: 5300 Bonn 2, Plittersdorfer Str. 91; tel. (0228) 363004; f. 1953; German, English and Chinese language; Publr HANS-PETER DÜRR-AUSTER.

Verlag Kiepenheuer & Witsch & Co: 5000 Cologne 51, Rondorferstr. 5; tel. (0221) 376850; telex 8881142; f. 1948; general fiction, biography, history, sociology, politics; Man. Dir Dr REINHOLD NEVEN DU MONT.

Kindler Verlag GmbH: 8000 Munich 40, Leopoldstr. 54; tel. (089) 394041; telex 5215678; f. 1951; biography, literature, psychology, fiction; Man. Dirs Dr KARL BLESSING, RÜDIGER HILDEBRANDT.

Kirchheim & Co GmbH: 6500 Mainz 1, Kaiserstr. 41; tel. (06131) 671081; telex 4187521; f. 1736; science, law, medicine, periodicals; Dir MANUEL ICKRATH.

Verlag Ernst Klett: 7000 Stuttgart 1, Rotebühlstr. 77; tel. (0711) 66720; telex 722225; f. 1844; secondary school and university textbooks (especially German as a foreign language), dictionaries, atlases, teaching aids; Dirs MICHAEL KLETT, ROLAND KLETT, Dr THOMAS KLETT.

Klett-Cotta Verlagsgemeinschaft: 7000 Stuttgart 1, Rotebühlstr. 77; tel. (0711) 66720; telex 722225; f. 1977; literature, linguistics, education, humanities, social sciences, psychology, history, philosophy, fine arts; Dirs MICHAEL KLETT, ROLAND KLETT, Dr THOMAS KLETT.

Erika-Klopp-Verlag GmbH: 1000 Berlin 31, Postfach 310829, Kurfürstendamm 126; tel. (030) 8911008; f. 1925; children's books; Man. HORST MEYER.

Vittorio Klostermann GmbH: 6000 Frankfurt a.M. 90, Frauenlobstr. 22; tel. (069) 774011; f. 1930; bibliography, philosophy, literature, history, law, periodicals; Man. Dirs MICHAEL and VITTORIO E. KLOSTERMANN.

Verlag Josef Knecht: 6000 Frankfurt a.M. 1, Liebfrauenberg 37; tel. (069) 281767; f. 1946; politics, religion, arts; Man. Dirs Dr HERMANN HERDER, Dr MARIANNE REGNIER.

Knorr & Hirth Verlag GmbH: 3167 Burgdorf/Hanover, Alt-Ahrbeck 1; tel. (05136) 5501; f. 1894; art, travel, guide-books, postcards; Dir BERTHOLD FRICKE.

K. F. Koehler Verlag: 7000 Stuttgart 80, Schockenriedstr. 39; tel. (0711) 7860; telex 7255344; f. 1789; biography, history, sociology, political science, law, geography; Publr TILL GRUPP.

Koehlers Verlagsgesellschaft mbH: 4900 Herford, Steintorwall 17, Postfach 2352; tel. (05221) 59910; telex 934801; f. 1789; international shipping, marine reference books.

W. Kohlhammer GmbH: 7000 Stuttgart 80, Hessbrühlstr. 69, Postfach 800430; tel. (0711) 7863-1; telex 7255820; f. 1866; publishers of the Federal Statistical Office; general textbooks; Man. Dirs Dr JÜRGEN GUTBROD, GÜNTER HABERLAND, HANS-JOACHIM NAGEL.

Kommentator Verlag: 6000 Frankfurt a.M. 1, Zeppelinallee 43, Postfach 970148; tel. (069) 793009-0; telex 4189621; f. 1947; mem. of Kluwer Group; law, taxation; Man. Dir NICO DE GIER.

Konradin-Fachzeitschriften-Verlag GmbH: 7022 Leinfelden-Echterdingen, Ernst-Mey-Str. 8; tel. (0711) 7594-0; telex 7255421; f. 1865; technical and agricultural trade journals; Publr KONRAD KOHLKAMMER.

Kösel-Verlag: 8000 Munich 19, Flüggenstr. 2; tel. (089) 179008-0; telex 5215492; f. 1593; philosophy, religion, psychology, esoteric, family and education; Dir Dr CHRISTOPH WILD.

Kreuz Verlag GmbH: 7000 Stuttgart 80, Breitwiesenstr. 30, Postfach 800669; tel. (0711) 788030; f. 1983; theology, psychology, pedagogics; Man. Dir DIETER BREITSOHL.

Alfred Kröner Verlag: 7000 Stuttgart 1, Reinsburgstr. 56, Postfach 102862; tel. (0711) 620221; f. 1904; humanities, handbooks, reference; Man. Dirs ARNO KLEMM, WALTER KOHRS.

Kyrios-Verlag GmbH: 8050 Freising, Luckengasse 8/10; tel. (08161) 5527; f. 1916; religion, meditation, calendars, periodicals; Dir URSULA BLUM.

Lambertus-Verlag: 7800 Freiburg i. Br., Wölflinstr. 4, Postfach 1026; tel. (0761) 31566; f. 1898; social work, social sciences, education, theology, periodicals; Dirs FRITZ BOLL, GERHILD NEUGART.

Landbuch Verlag GmbH: 3000 Hanover 1, Kabelkamp 6; tel. (0511) 67806-0; telex 921169; f.1945; agriculture, animal breeding, forestry, hunting, gardening, nature; Dir FRIEDRICH BUTENHOLZ.

Langenscheidt-Verlag: 1000 Berlin 62, Crellestr. 29–30; 8000 Munich 40, Neusser Str. 3, Postfach 401120; tel. (089) 360960; telex 183175; f. 1856; foreign languages, German for foreigners, dictionaries, textbooks, records, tapes, cassettes; Man. Dir KARL ERNST TIELEBIER-LANGENSCHEIDT.

Karl Robert Langewiesche Nachfolger Hans Köster KG: 6240 Königstein im Taunus, Am grünen Weg 6, Postfach 1327; tel. (06174) 7333; f. 1902; art, literature, music, history, monographs; Owner and Man. HANS-CURT KÖSTER.

Leske Verlag & Budrich GmbH: 5090 Leverkusen 3 (Opladen), Gerhart-Hauptmann-Str. 27, Postfach 300 406; tel. (02171) 2079; f. 1820; economics, politics, psychology, sociology, educational and school books; Man. Dir EDMUND BUDRICH.

Lichtenberg Verlag GmbH: 8000 Munich 40, Leopoldstr. 54; tel. (089) 394041; telex 5215678; f. 1962; popular fiction, non-fiction; Dir PETER NIKEL.

Limes Verlag: 8000 Munich 22, Thomas-Wimmer-Ring 11; tel. (089) 235008-0; telex 5215045; f. 1945; poetry, essays, novels, art, contemporary history, translations; Dir M. SCHLÜTER.

Paul List Verlag und Schroedel Schulbuchverlag GmbH: 8000 Munich 2, Goethestr. 43; tel. (089) 51480; telex 522405; school books, atlases; Man. Dir Dr WOLFGANG REISTER.

Hermann Löffler: 1000 Berlin 49, Schillerstr. 115; tel. (030) 7425818; f. 1903; music; Propr H. LÖFFLER.

Hermann Luchterhand Verlag GmbH & Co: 5450 Neuwied, Heddesdorfer Str. 31, Postfach 1780; tel. (02631) 8010; telex 867853; f. 1924; insurance, law, taxation, labour; Man. N. W. A. DE GIER.

Otto Maier Verlag GmbH: 7980 Ravensburg, Marktstr. 22–26, Postfach 1860; tel. (0751) 861; telex 732926; f. 1883; games, puzzles, hobbies, children's crafts, art, design, educational; Man. Dir CLAUS RUNGE.

Gebr. Mann Verlag GmbH & Co: 1000 Berlin 61, Lindenstr. 76; tel. (030) 25913864; telex 183723; f. 1917; archaeology, art; Dir KLAUS MÜLLER-CREPON.

Maximilian-Verlag: 4900 Herford, Steintorwall 17, Postfach 2352; tel. (05221) 59910; telex 934801; textbooks, history, social sciences, law, administration.

Felix Meiner Verlag GmbH: 2000 Hamburg 76, Richardstr. 47; tel. (040) 294870; f. 1911; re-f. 1951 in Hamburg; humanities, especially philosophy; Dirs R. MEINER, M. MEINER.

J. B. Metzlersche Verlagsbuchhandlung und C.E. Poeschel Verlag GmbH: 7000 Stuttgart 1, Kernerstr. 43, Postfach 529; tel. (0711) 223067; telex 7262891; literature, pedagogics, linguistics, history, economics, commerce, textbooks; Dir GÜNTHER SCHWEIZER.

Alfred Metzner Verlag: 6000 Frankfurt a.M. 1, Postfach 970148, Zeppelinallee 43; tel. (069) 793009-0; telex 4189621; f. 1909; mem. of Kluwer Group; law; Man. Dir NICO DE GIER.

Gertraud Middelhauve Verlag GmbH & Co KG: 5000 Cologne 80, Wiener Platz 2; tel. (0221) 614982; f. 1947; children's and picture books; Dir GERTRAUD MIDDELHAUVE.

FEDERAL REPUBLIC OF GERMANY

Verlag E. S. Mittler & Sohn GmbH: 4900 Herford, Steintorwall 17, Postfach 2352; tel. (05221) 59910; telex 934801; also 5300 Bonn 2, Austr. 19; military sciences, aviation, philosophy, history.

Verlag Moderne Industrie AG: 8910 Landsberg, Justus-von-Liebig-Str. 1; tel. (08191) 125-1; telex 527114; f. 1952; management, investment, technical; Man. Dir Dr REINHARD MÖSTL.

Verlag Modernes Lernen Borgmann KG: 4600 Dortmund, Hohe Str. 39; tel. (0231) 128008; telex (17) 231329; f. 1969; modern learning and educational books; Dir D. BORGMANN.

J. C. B. Mohr (Paul Siebeck): 7400 Tübingen, Wilhelmstr. 18; tel. (07071) 26064; telex 7262872; f. 1801; religion, philosophy, law, economics, sociology, history, political science; Propr G. SIEBECK.

C. F. Müller Juristischer Verlag: 6900 Heidelberg 1, Im Weiher 10, Postfach 102640; tel. (06221) 489250; telex 461727; f. 1973; periodicals, humanities, insurance, law, science, technology; Dir Dr HANS WINDSHEIMER.

Muster-Schmidt-Verlag Christian Hansen-Schmidt: 3400 Göttingen 1, Grünberger Weg 6; tel. (0551) 71741; telex 96720; f. 1905; history, scientific works; Dirs HANS HANSEN-SCHMIDT, Frau E. GERHARDY.

Verlag Neue Wirtschafts-Briefe: 4690 Herne 1, Eschstr. 22; tel. (02323) 141-0; telex 8229870; f. 1947; accountancy, industrial management, political economics; Man. Dir E.-O. KLEYBOLDT.

Verlag Günther Neske: 7417 Pfullingen, Kloster, Postfach 7240; tel. (07121) 71339; telex 729790; f. 1951; poetry, psychiatry, philosophy, theology, jurisprudence, picture books; Propr GÜNTHER NESKE.

Max Niemeyer Verlag: 7400 Tübingen, Pfrondorferstr. 6, Postfach 2140; tel. (07071) 81104; f. 1870; scholarly books on philology, philosophy, history, linguistics; Dir R. HARSCH-NIEMEYER.

Nymphenburger Verlagshandlung: 8000 Munich 22, Thomas-Wimmer-Ring 11; tel. (089) 235008-0; telex 5215045; f. 1946; belles lettres, history, adventure, sports and music; Man. Dir JUGEBORG CASTELL.

R. Oldenbourg Verlag GmbH: 8000 Munich 80, Rosenheimerstr. 145; tel. (089) 41120; telex 529296; f. 1858; technology, science, history, textbooks, mathematics, economics, dictionaries, periodicals; Dirs Dr T. VON CORNIDES, W. DICK, G. OHMEYER, JOHANNES OLDENBOURG.

Paul Parey: 2000 Hamburg 1, Spitalerstr. 12; tel. (040) 339690; telex 2161391; and 1000 Berlin 61, Lindenstr. 44–47; tel. (030) 2599040; telex 184777; f. 1848; biology, botany, zoology, ethology, veterinary science, laboratory animals science, food technology and control, agriculture, starch research and technology, brewing and distilling, forestry, horticulture, phytomedicine, plant and environment protection, water management, hunting, fishing, dogs, equitation; technical and scientific journals; Dirs Dr FRIEDRICH GEORGI, Dr RUDOLF GEORGI.

Pattloch-Bibel Verlags GmbH: 8751 Haibach Unterfranken, Haydnstr. 8; tel. (06021) 68328; telex 4188517; f. 1827; theology; Man. Dirs WOLFGANG LOWITZKI, KLEMENS PATTLOCH.

Paulinus-Verlag: 5500 Trier, Fleischstr. 62/65, Postfach 3040; tel. (0651) 4604-34; telex 472735; f. 1875; religious literature and theology, periodicals; Dir SIEGFRIED FÄTH.

Physik Verlag GmbH: 6940 Weinheim/Bergstr., Pappelallee 3; tel. (06201) 602-0; telex 465516; f. 1947; physics journals; Man. Dirs Prof. Dr H. GRÜNEWALD, HANS DIRK KÖHLER.

R. Piper GmbH & Co KG Verlag: 8000 Munich 40, Georgenstr. 4, Postfach 430120; tel. (089) 381801-0; telex 5215385; f. 1904; literature, philosophy, theology, psychology, natural sciences, political and social sciences, history, biographies, music; Dirs Dr KLAUS PIPER, Dr ERNST R. PIPER.

Polyglott-Verlag: 8000 Munich 40, Neusser Str. 3; tel. (089) 36096-0; telex 5215379; f. 1902; travel and camping guides, menu guides, dictionaries, phrase-books; Man. Dir Dr FLORIAN LANGENSCHEIDT.

Prestel-Verlag: 8000 Munich 40, Mandlstr. 26; tel. (089) 381709-0; telex 5216366; fine arts, arts and crafts, art history, travel; Dirs GEORGETTE CAPELLMANN, GUSTAV STRESOW, JÜRGEN TESCH.

Verlag Friedrich Pustet: 8400 Regensburg 11, Gutenbergstr. 8, Postfach 110441; tel. (0941) 96049; telex 65672; f. 1826; religion, art, liturgical books, folklore; also periodical *Liturgie Konkret;* Man. Dir Dr FRIEDRICH PUSTET.

Quell Verlag: 7000 Stuttgart 1, Furtbachstr. 12A, Postfach 897; tel. (0711) 60100-0; f. 1830; Protestant literature; Dirs Dr WOLFGANG REISTER, WALTER WALDBAUER.

Quelle & Meyer Verlag: 6200 Wiesbaden, Luisenplatz 2, Postfach 4747; tel. (06121) 373071; f. 1906; religion, natural and social science, textbooks; Man. Dirs GÜNTHER FERTIG, GERHARD STAHL.

Walter Rau Verlag: 4000 Düsseldorf 12, Benderstr. 168A, Postfach 120407; tel. (0211) 283095; telex 8586682; literature, magazines, translations, chess; Dirs GISELA RAU, BEATRIX RAU.

Karl Rauch Verlag KG: 4000 Düsseldorf 1, Grafenberger Allee 100; tel. (0211) 16795-0; telex 8586707; history, translations, art; Dir HARALD EBNER.

Ravenstein Verlag: 6232 Bad Soden, Auf der Krautweide 24; tel. (06196) 29040; telex 4072538; f. 1830; maps and atlases; Man. Dirs RÜDIGER BOSSE, HELGA RAVENSTEIN.

Philipp Reclam jun. Verlag GmbH: 7257 Ditzingen bei Stuttgart, Siemensstr. 32, Postfach 1349; tel. (07156) 1630; telex 7266704; f. 1828; literature, literary criticism, fiction, history of culture and literature, philosophy and religion, biography, fine arts, music; Acting Partner Dr DIETRICH BODE.

Regensbergsche Buchhandlung und Buchdruckerei GmbH & Co: 4400 Münster, Daimlerweg 58, Postfach 6748; tel. (0251) 717061; f. 1591; Catholic and scientific books; Dir Dr BERNHARD LUCAS.

Dietrich Reimer Verlag: 1000 Berlin 45, Unter den Eichen 57; tel. (030) 8314081; f. 1845; geography, ethnology, sociology, scientific, archaeology, history of civilization, art; Propr Dr FRIEDRICH KAUFMANN.

Verlag Ernst Reinhardt GmbH & Co: 8000 Munich 19, Kemnatenstr. 46; tel. (089) 1783005; f. 1899; psychology, education, philosophy, psychotherapy, social sciences; Man. KARL MÜNSTER.

Dr Riederer Verlag GmbH: 7000 Stuttgart 1, Gutbrodstr. 9, Postfach 104052; tel. (0711) 639797; f. 1947; technology, metallography; Dir H. SCHNEIDER.

Rowohlt Verlag GmbH and Rowohlt Taschenbuch Verlag GmbH: 2057 Reinbek bei Hamburg, Hamburgerstr. 17; tel. (040) 72721; telex 217854; f. 1908/1953; politics, science, fiction, translations of international literature; Dirs Dr MICHAEL NAUMANN, HORST VARRELMANN, Dr HELMUT DÄHNE, ERWIN STEEN.

K.G. Saur Verlag: 8000 Munich 71, Heilmannstr. 17, Postfach 711009; tel. (089) 791040; telex 5212067; f. 1949; library science, reference, dictionaries, microfiches; brs in New York, London, Oxford and Paris; subsidiary of Butterworths & Co (Publishers) Ltd, London.

Moritz Schauenburg Verlag GmbH & Co: 7630 Lahr 1, Schillerstr. 13, Postfach 2120; tel. (07821) 2783-0; telex 754943; f. 1794; fiction, literature, linguistics, philosophy, music; Dir Dipl.-Kfm. JÖRG SCHAUENBURG.

Fachverlag Schiele & Schön GmbH: 1000 Berlin 61, Markgrafenstr. 11; tel. (030) 2516029; telex 181470; f. 1946; technology, telecommunications, textile and clothing industry, biomedical engineering, optics, reference; Dir PETER SCHÖN.

Schlütersche Verlagsanstalt und Druckerei GmbH & Co: 3000 Hanover 1, Georgswall 4, Postfach 5440; tel. (0511) 12360; telex 923978; f. 1747; non-fiction, periodicals, Yellow Pages; Man. Dir HORST DRESSEL.

Erich Schmidt Verlag GmbH & Co: 1000 Berlin 30, Genthinerstr. 30G; tel. (030) 250085-0; telex 183671; law, economics, philology, technology; Man. CLAUS-MICHAEL RAST.

Wilhelm Schmitz Verlag: 6301 Wettenberg-Wissmar 2, Auf der Heide 5; tel. (06406) 2324; f. 1847; German studies, East European studies, Slavonic folklore; Dir S. SCHMITZ.

Franz Schneekluth Verlag: 8000 Munich 22, Widenmayerstr. 34; tel. (089) 221391; telex 529070; f. 1949; general literature; Publr ULRICH STAUDINGER.

Franz Schneider Verlag: 8000 Munich 40, Frankfurter Ring 150; tel. (089) 381910; telex 5215804; f. 1913; children's books; Publr Dr HUBERTUS SCHENKEL.

Verlag Lambert Schneider GmbH: 6900 Heidelberg, Hausackerweg 16, Postfach 105802; tel. (06221) 21354; f. 1925; literature, philosophy, religion, Judaism (especially the publications of Martin Buber); Dir L. STIEHM.

Verlag Schnell & Steiner: 8000 Munich 60, Paganinistr. 92, Postfach 112; tel. (089) 8112015; f. 1933; art, travel, history; Man. Dir KARL A. STICH.

B. Schott's Söhne: 6500 Mainz 1, Weihergarten, Postfach 3640; tel. (06131) 246-0; telex 4187 821; f. 1770; sheet music, music books, records, music periodicals; Man. Dirs Dr PETER HANSER-STRECKER, LUDOLF Freiherr VON CANSTEIN, JÜRGEN M. LUCZAK.

Verlag J. F. Schreiber: 7300 Esslingen, Postfach 285; tel. (07153) 22011; telex 7266880; f. 1831; children's books, juveniles; Publr JÜRGEN MEISSNER.

Carl Ed. Schünemann KG: 2800 Bremen 1, 2 Schlachtpforte 7, Postfach 106067; tel. (0421) 36903-0; telex 244397; f. 1810; art, periodicals; Dirs CARL SCHÜNEMANN, CARL FRITZ SCHÜNEMANN.

Schwabenverlag AG: 7302 Ostfildern 1; tel. (0711) 4406-0; telex 723556; f. 1848; regional history, literature, theology, picture books; Man. Dir DIETER HIRSMÜLLER.

Pädagogischer Verlag Schwann-Bagel GmbH: 4000 Düsseldorf 1, Postfach 7640, Am Wehrhahn 100; tel. (0211) 360301; telex

FEDERAL REPUBLIC OF GERMANY

8581345; f. 1821; pedagogics, languages, art, history, children's books, textbooks, records; Dir Dr HANS WEYMAR.

J. Schweitzer Verlag: 6000 Frankfurt a.M. 1, Zeppelinallee 43, Postfach 970148; tel. (069) 793009-0; telex 4189621; f. 1949; mem. of Kluwer Group; law, jurisprudence; Man. Dir NICO DE GIER.

E. Schweizerbart'sche Verlagsbuchhandlung: 7000 Stuttgart 1, Johannesstr. 3A; tel. (0711) 625001; telex 723363; f. 1826; geology, palaeontology, mineralogy, hydrobiology, limnology, botany, zoology, fisheries, anthropology; periodicals; Proprs KLAUS OBERMILLER, Dr E. NÄGELE.

Societäts-Verlag: 6000 Frankfurt a.M. 1, Frankenallee 71–81, Postfach 100801; tel. (069) 75010; telex 411655; f. 1921; literature, art, economics; Publr W. WIRTHLE.

Sonnenweg-Verlag: 7750 Konstanz, Raitenaugasse 11, Postfach 1186; tel. (07531) 23054; f. 1922; religion, literature; Dir HERBERT DENECKE.

W. Spemann Verlag: 7000 Stuttgart 1, Pfizerstr. 5/7; tel. (0711) 21910; telex 721669; f. 1873; history, culture, art, military; Dirs C. KELLER, F. KELLER, E. NEHMANN.

Adolf Sponholtz Verlag: 3250 Hameln, Osterstr. 19; tel. (05151) 200310; telex 92859; f. 1894; literature, poetry; Publ. Dir HANS FREIWALD.

Springer-Verlag Berlin, Heidelberg, New York KG: 1000 Berlin 33, Heidelberger Platz 3; tel. (06221) 4870; telex 461723; f. 1842; medicine, biology, mathematics, physics, chemistry, psychology, engineering, geosciences, philosophy, law, economics; Proprs Dr Dres. h.c. HEINZ GÖTZE, Dr KONRAD F. SPRINGER, Dipl.-Kfm. CLAUS MICHALETZ, Prof. Dr DIETRICH GÖTZE, JOLANDA L. VON HAGEN.

Franz Steiner Verlag Wiesbaden GmbH: 7000 Stuttgart, Birkenwaldstr. 44, Postfach 101526; tel. (0711) 25820; telex 723636; f. 1949; archaeology, linguistics and philology, classical and oriental studies, history, geography, history of arts and sciences; periodicals; Man. Dirs WOLFGANG WESSINGER, VINCENT SIEVEKING, REINHOLD HACK.

Dr Dietrich Steinkopff Verlag: 6100 Darmstadt 11, Saalbaustr. 12, Postfach 111442; tel. (06151) 26538; f. 1908; medical, chemical and scientific books and periodicals; Dir BERNHARD LEWERICH.

Lothar Stiehm Verlag: 6900 Heidelberg 1, Hausackerweg 16, Postfach 105802; tel. (06221) 21354; f. 1966; literature, bibliography; Dir L. STIEHM.

Stoytscheff Verlag: 6000 Frankfurt a.M. 1, Zeppelinalle 43, Postfach 970148; tel. (069) 793009-0; telex 4189621; f. 1949; law; Man. Dir NICO DE GIER.

Süddeutscher Verlag: 8000 Munich 2, Goethestr. 43; tel. (089) 51480; telex 522405; f. 1945; fiction, non-fiction, history, art, religion; Man. Dir Dr WOLFGANG REISTER.

Suhrkamp Verlag KG: 6000 Frankfurt a.M. 1, Lindenstr. 29–35, Suhrkamp Haus, Postfach 101945; tel. (069) 756010; telex 413972; f. 1950; modern German and foreign literature, philosophy, poetry; Dir SIEGFRIED UNSELD.

Verlag B. G. Teubner GmbH: 7000 Stuttgart 80, Industriestr. 15, Postfach 801069; tel. (711) 789010; f. 1811; physics, mathematics, computer science, engineering, biology, geography, philology, sociology; Man. Dir HEINRICH KRÄMER.

Georg Thieme Verlag: 7000 Stuttgart 30, Rüdigerstr. 14; tel. (0711) 89310; telex 7252275; f. 1886; medicine and natural science; Man. Dirs Dr GÜNTHER HAUFF, Dr ALBRECHT GREUNER.

K. Thienemanns Verlag: 7000 Stuttgart 1, Blumenstr. 36; tel. (0711) 210550; telex 723933; f. 1849; diet cookery books, picture books, children's books, juveniles; Dirs HANSJÖRG WEITBRECHT, RICHARD WEITBRECHT, GUNTER EHNI.

Jan Thorbecke Verlag: 7480 Sigmaringen, Karlstr. 10; tel. (07571) 3016; telex 732534; f. 1946; reference books; Dir GEORG BENSCH.

Verlag Ullstein GmbH: 1000 Berlin 61, Lindenstr. 76; tel. (030) 25911; telex 183723; f. 1877; belles-lettres, biography, history, art, general and social science, politics; Man. Dir Dr HERBERT FLEISSNER.

Buchverlage Ullstein Langen Müller: 8000 Munich 22, Thomas-Wimmer-Ring 11; tel. (089) 235008-0; telex 5215045; f. 1894; literature, art, music, theatre, contemporary history, biography; Man. Dir Dr HERBERT FLEISSNER.

Verlag Eugen Ulmer GmbH & Co: 7000 Stuttgart 70, Wollgrasweg 41, Postfach 700561; tel. (0711) 45070; telex 723634; f. 1868; agriculture, horticulture, science, periodicals; Dir ROLAND ULMER.

Umschau-Verlag Breidenstein GmbH: 6000 Frankfurt a.M. 1, Stuttgarter Str. 18–24, Postfach 110262; tel. (069) 26001; telex 411964; f. 1850; picture books, non-fiction, biology, chemistry, geography, films, food, military affairs, travel; Man. Dir HANS-JÜRGEN BREIDENSTEIN.

Universitas Verlag: 8000 Munich 22, Thomas-Wimmer-Ring 11; tel. (089) 177041; f. 1920; travel, history, fiction, biography; Dir Dr HERBERT FLEISSNER.

Urban & Schwarzenberg GmbH: 8000 Munich 2, Pettenkoferstr. 18; tel. (089) 5383-0; telex 523864; f. 1866; medicine, natural sciences; Man. Dir MICHAEL URBAN; brs in Munich, Vienna, Baltimore.

VCH Verlagsgesellschaft mbH: 6940 Weinheim, Pappelallee 3, Postfach 101161; tel. (06201) 602-0; telex 465516; f. 1921; natural sciences, especially chemistry, biotechnology and physics, medicine, history, philosophy, history of art, architecture, scientific software, civil engineering; Man. Dirs Prof. Dr HELMUT GRÜNEWALD, HANS DIRK KÖHLER.

Verlag Franz Vahlen GmbH: 8000 Munich 40, Wilhelmstr. 9; tel. (089) 381890; telex 5215085; f. 1870; law, economics; Man. Dir Dr HANS DIETER BECK.

Vandenhoeck & Ruprecht Verlag: 3400 Göttingen, Theaterstr. 13, Postfach 3753; tel. (0551) 54031; telex 965220; f. 1735; Protestant theology, economics, medical psychology, mathematics, philosophy, linguistics, history, classical studies, secondary school books, periodicals; Dirs Dr ARNDT RUPRECHT, Dr DIETRICH RUPRECHT.

Friedr. Vieweg & Sohn VerlagsgmbH: 6200 Wiesbaden 1, Faulbrunnenstr. 13, Postfach 5829; tel. (06121) 16020; telex 4186928; f. 1786; books on mathematics, natural sciences, architecture, medicine, philosophy, microcomputers, technics; scientific and technical periodicals; Man. Dir Dr FRANK LUBE.

Curt R. Vincentz-Verlag: 3000 Hanover 1, Schiffgraben 41–43, Postfach 8247; tel. (0511) 3499944; telex 923846; f. 1893; science, trade, building, social welfare; Dir Dr LOTHAR VINCENTZ.

Verlag Klaus Wagenbach: 1000 Berlin 30, Ahornstr. 4; tel. (030) 2115060; f. 1964; literature, politics, periodicals, paperbacks; Dir Dr KLAUS WAGENBACH.

Ernst Wasmuth Verlag GmbH & Co: 7400 Tübingen, Fürststr. 133; tel. (07071) 33658; f. 1872; architecture, archaeology, art, history of art; Dirs ELSE WASMUTH, KARL-HEINZ SCHATTNER.

A. Weichert Verlag: 3000 Hanover 1, Tiestestr. 14; tel. (0511) 813068; telex 923872; f. 1872; children's books; Man. Dir ALFRED TRIPPO.

Weidmannsche Verlagsbuchhandlung: 3200 Hildesheim, Hagentorwall 7; tel. (05121) 37007; telex 927454; f. 1945; history, art, study of languages and literature, classics, pedagogy, law; Publr W. GEORG OLMS, Dr E. MERTENS.

Weiss Verlag: 6072 Dreieich 3, Wildscheuerweg 1; tel. (030) 7817725; telex 4185381; f. 1945; fiction, popular science, children's books, science fiction, paperbacks; Propr. ABRAHAM MELZER.

Westdeutscher Verlag GmbH: 6200 Wiesbaden 1, Faulbrunnenstr. 13, Postfach 5829; tel. (06121) 160210; telex 4186928; f. 1947; history, economics, sociology, politics, psychology, law, periodicals; Man Dir Dr FRANK LUBE.

Georg Westermann Verlag: 3300 Brunswick, Georg-Westermann-Allee 66, Postfach 3320; tel. (0531) 7081; telex (17) 622153; f. 1838; cartography, education, science, technology, fiction, periodicals; Dir Dr JÜRGEN RICHTER.

Bruno Wilkens Verlag KG: 3000 Hanover 51, Postfach 510308; tel. (0511) 6498811; f. 1922; medicine; Dir HELGA HOFMEISTER-WILKENS.

Carl Winter Universitätsverlag GmbH: 6900 Heidelberg, Lutherstr. 59; tel. (06221) 4149-0; telex 461660; f. 1822; university textbooks; Publr Dr CARL WINTER.

Verlag Wissenschaft und Politik: 5000 Cologne 1, Salierring 14–16; tel. (0221) 312878; f. 1961; politics, sociology, history, law, periodicals; Dirs BEREND VON NOTTBECK, CLAUS-PETER VON NOTTBECK.

Wissenschaftliche Verlagsgesellschaft mbH: 7000 Stuttgart 10, Birkenwaldstr. 44, Postfach 105339; tel. (0711) 25820; telex 723636 daz; science, medicine, pharmacy; Dirs Dr WOLFGANG WESSINGER, VINCENT SIEVEKING, REINHOLD HACK.

Friedrich Wittig Verlag: 2000 Hamburg 61, In der Masch 6; tel. (040) 5535019; f. 1946; religion, children's, art books; Man. Dir FRIEDRICH HOLST.

Rainer Wunderlich Verlag Hermann Leins: 7400 Tübingen 1, Eduard-Haber-Str. 15, Postfach 2740; tel. (0711) 223067; telex 7262891; f. 1926; fiction, biography, music, politics, history, poetry; Man. Dir Dipl. Kfm. GÜNTHER SCHWEIZER.

Paul Zsolnay Verlag GmbH: 6100 Darmstadt 16, Havelstr. 16; tel. (06151) 386301; f. 1948; poetry, non-fiction, fiction; Man. Dir GERHARD BECKMANN.

PRINCIPAL ASSOCIATION OF BOOK PUBLISHERS AND BOOKSELLERS

Börsenverein des Deutschen Buchhandels eV: 6000 Frankfurt a.M. 1, Postfach 100442, Grosser Hirschgraben 17–21; tel. (069)

FEDERAL REPUBLIC OF GERMANY

1306-0; telex 413573; f. 1825; Chair. GÜNTHER CHRISTIANSEN; Man. Dir Dr HANS-KARL VON KUPSCH (see Buchhändler-Vereinigung GmbH under Publishers).

Radio and Television

In June 1986 there were 25,737,837 radio receivers and 22,908,293 television receivers in use in the Federal Republic.

Arbeitsgemeinschaft der öffentlich-rechtlichen Rundfunkanstalten der Bundesrepublik Deutschland (ARD) (Association of Public Law Broadcasting Organizations): 6000 Frankfurt a.M., Bertramstr 8, Postfach 101001; tel. (069) 590607; telex 411127; Chair. Intendant Prof. Dr HARTWIG KELM; the co-ordinating body of the Federal German Radio and Television organizations: Bayerischer Rundfunk, Hessischer Rundfunk, Norddeutscher Rundfunk, Radio Bremen, Saarländischer Rundfunk, Sender Freies Berlin, Süddeutscher Rundfunk, Südwestfunk, Westdeutscher Rundfunk, Deutsche Welle, Deutschlandfunk; RIAS Berlin is represented on the Council by an observer.

RADIO

Each of the members of ARD broadcasts 2-3 channels. Deutsche Welle and Deutschlandfunk broadcast programmes for Europe and overseas.

Deutsche Welle: 5000 Cologne 1, Raderberggürtel 50, Postfach 100444; tel. (0221) 3890; telex 888485; German short-wave service; broadcasts 93 programmes daily in 34 languages; Dir-Gen. Dr HEINZ FELLHAUER; Dir of Programmes JOSEF M. GERWALD; Dir of Television SIEGFRIED BERNDT; Tech. Dir GÜNTER ROESSLER; Dir of Administration GERHARD BRAUN; Dir of Public Relations LOTHAR SCHWARTZ.

Deutschlandfunk: 5 Cologne 51, Raderberggürtel 40; tel. (0221) 3451; telex 8884920; 24 hours daily broadcasting from eight stations for the Federal Republic and Europe; Dir-Gen. EDMUND GRUBER; Administrative Dir KLAUS PRISSOK; Technical Dir W. HINZ.

RIAS Berlin (Rundfunk im amerikanischen Sektor): 1000 Berlin 62, Kufsteiner Str. 69; tel. (030) 85030; telex 183790; Chair. of US Supervisory Board ROBERT C. VOTH; Dir BERNHARD F. RÖHE.

TELEVISION

There are three television channels. The nine autonomous regional broadcasting organizations combine to provide material for the First Programme which is produced by ARD. The Second Programme (Zweites Deutsches Fernsehen/ZDF) is completely separate and is controlled by a public corporation of all the Länder. It is partly financed by advertising. The Third Programme provides a cultural and educational service in the evenings only with contributions from several of the regional bodies.

Zweites Deutsches Fernsehen (ZDF): 6500 Mainz 1, Postfach 4040; tel. (06131) 701; telex 4187661; f. 1961 by the Länder Governments as a second television channel; 90 main transmitters; Dir-Gen. Prof. DIETER STOLTE; Dir of Programmes OSWALD RING; Editor-in-Chief KLAUS BRESSER; Dir, International Affairs HANS KIMMEL.

REGIONAL BROADCASTING ORGANIZATIONS

Bayerischer Rundfunk: 8000 Munich 2, Rundfunkplatz 1; tel. (089) 5900-01; telex 521070; Chair. Dr FRANZ HEUBL; Dir-Gen. REINHOLD VÖTH; Admin. Dir OSKAR MAIER.

Radio Bremen: 28 Bremen 33, Heinrich-Hertz-Str. 13; tel. (0421) 2460; telex 245181; Dir-Gen. KARL-HEINZ KLOSTERMEIER.

Hessischer Rundfunk: 6000 Frankfurt a.M. 1, Bertramstr. 8; tel. (069) 1551; telex 411127; Dir-Gen. Prof. Dr HARTWIG KELM; Chair. Admin. Council EITEL-OSKAR HÖHNE; Chair. Broadcasting Council IGNATZ BUBIS.

Norddeutscher Rundfunk (NDR): 2 Hamburg 13, Rothenbaumchaussee 132-134; tel. (040) 413-0; telex 2198910; Dir-Gen. Dr PETER SCHIWY.

Saarländischer Rundfunk: 6600 Saarbrücken, Funkhaus Halberg, Postfach 1050; tel. (0681) 6021; telex 4428977; Chair. FRANZ SCHLEHOFER; Dir-Gen. Prof. Dr HUBERT ROHDE; Admin. Dir Dr FRIEDRICH FELDBAUSCH.

Sender Freies Berlin: 1 Berlin 19, Masurenallee 8-14; tel. (030) 30310; telex 182813; Chair. HELMUT EICHMEYER; Dir-Gen. Dr GÜNTER HERRMANN; Admin. Dir DIRK JENS RENNEFELD.

Süddeutscher Rundfunk: 7000 Stuttgart 1, Neckarstr. 230, Postfach 837; tel. (0711) 2881; telex 723456; f. 1924; Chair. WALTER AYASS; Dir-Gen. Prof. Dr HANS BAUSCH; Admin. Dir HERMANN FÜNFGELD.

Südwestfunk (SWF): 7570 Baden-Baden, Hans-Bredow-Str., Postfach 820; tel. (07221) 2761; telex 787810; Chair. Admin. Council Dr ROBERT MAUS; Dir-Gen. WILLIBALD HILF; Admin. Dir Dr HANS-JOACHIM LEHMANN.

Westdeutscher Rundfunk (WDR): 5000 Cologne 1, Appellhofplatz 1; tel. (0221) 2201; telex 8882575; Chair. REINHARD GRÄTZ (Broadcasting Council), Dr THEODOR SCHWEFER (Admin. Council); DORIS EMONS (School Broadcasting); Dir-Gen. FRIEDRICH NOWOTTNY; Admin. Dir Dr NORBERT SEIDEL.

Europe 1: Europäische Rundfunk und Fernsehen AG, Europe 1, 6600 Saarbrücken, Postfach 111; tel. (0681) 30782; telex 4421166; broadcasts in French; Dir CLAUDE FABRE.

FOREIGN RADIO STATIONS

American Forces Network: 6000 Frankfurt/Main, Bertramstr. 6; tel. (069) 1156101; telex 413201; f. 1943; 10 stations, 52 AM/FM transmitters and four TV studios; Commanding Officer Lt-Col BRUCE EATON; Programme Dir PAUL D. VAN DYKE.

British Forces Broadcasting Service, Germany: 5 Cologne-Marienburg, Postfach 510526; tel. (0221) 376990; telex 8881329; since April 1982 a division of the newly-formed Services Sound and Vision Corporation; 12 VHF radio transmitters and 45 low-powered TV transmitters; Regional Dir (Broadcasting) COLIN RUGG.

Radio Free Europe/Radio Liberty Inc: Oettingenstr. 67, 8000 Munich 22; tel. (089) 21020; telex 523228; a non-profit-making private corporation, operating under American management and funded by congressional grants supplied through the Board for International Broadcasting, which also oversees the operations of both stations; transmitter facilities in Spain, Portugal and the Federal Republic of Germany. Radio Free Europe broadcasts to Bulgaria, Czechoslovakia, Estonia, Hungary, Latvia, Lithuania, Poland and Romania. Radio Liberty broadcasts to the USSR in Russian, Armenian, Azeri, Byelorussian, Georgian, Kazakh, Kirghiz, Tadzhik, Tatar-Bashkir, Turkestani, Ukrainian, Uzbek; Pres. E. EUGENE PELL; Dirs Dr A. ROSS JOHNSON (RFE Div.), Dr S. ENDERS WIMBUSH (Radio Liberty Div.).

Voice of America (VOA Europe): 8000 Munich 22, Ludwigstr. 2; tel. (089) 286091; telex 523737; f. 1985; controlled by the US Information Agency, Washington, DC; broadcasts in English on MW and VHF to 13 European countries, mainly music, news and features on US life and culture; the Correspondents' Bureau provides VOA Washington headquarters with reports and feature programmes on newsworthy developments in Eastern and Western Europe and the USSR; Dir FRANK SCOTT.

Finance

(cap. = capital; p.u. = paid up; brs = branches; dep. = deposits; DM = Deutsche Mark; m. = million; res = reserves)

The Deutsche Bundesbank, the central bank of the Federal Republic of Germany, consists of the central administration in Frankfurt (considered to be the financial capital of the country), 11 main offices (Landeszentralbanken) in the Länder and Berlin, and over 200 branches. In carrying out its functions as determined by law, the Bundesbank is independent of the Federal Government, but is required to support the government's general economic policy. All other credit institutions are subject to governmental supervision through the Federal Banking Supervisory Office (Bundesaufsichtsamt für das Kreditwesen) in Berlin.

Banks outside the central banking system are divided into three groups: private commercial banks, credit institutions incorporated under public law and co-operative credit institutions. All these commercial banks are 'universal banks', conducting all kinds of customary banking business. There is no division of activities. As well as the commercial banks there are a number of specialist banks, such as private or public mortgage banks.

The group of private commercial banks includes: those known as the 'Big Three' (the Deutsche Bank, the Dresdner Bank and the Commerzbank); all banks incorporated as a company limited by shares (Aktiengesellschaft—AG, Kommanditgesellschaft auf Aktien—KGaA) or as a private limited company (Gesellschaft mit beschränkter Haftung—GmbH) and those which are known as 'regional banks' because they do not usually function throughout the Federal Republic; and the private banks, which are established as sole proprietorships or partnerships and mostly have no branches outside their home town. Foreign banks are classed as regional banks. The main business of all private commercial banks is short-term lending. The private bankers fulfil the most varied tasks within the banking system.

The public law credit institutions are the savings banks (Sparkassen) and the Landesbanken. The latter act as central banks and clearing houses on a national level for the savings banks. Laws governing the savings banks limit them to certain sectors—credits, investments and money transfers—and they concentrate on the areas of home financing, municipal investments and the

FEDERAL REPUBLIC OF GERMANY

trades. In December 1984 there were 591 savings banks and 11 Landesbanken.

The head institution of the co-operative system is the Deutsche Genossenschaftsbank. At the end of 1984 there were 3,707 industrial and agricultural credit co-operatives, with a total of 19,587 offices.

Banking federations were set up in 1948. The federal association for the private commercial banks is the German Bankers' Association (Bundesverband deutscher Banken), which consists of 11 provincial associations, the Association of German Mortgage Banks (Verband deutscher Hypothekenbanken) and the Association of German Shipping Banks (Verband deutscher Schiffsbanken). Other federal banking associations are the German Savings Banks Association (Deutscher Sparkassen- und Giroverband), the Association of German Industrial and Agricultural Credit Co-operatives (Bundesverband der Deutschen Volksbanken und Raiffeisenbanken) and the Association of Public-Law Credit Institutions (Verband öffentlicher Banken).

BANKS

The Central Banking System

Deutsche Bundesbank: 6000 Frankfurt 50, Wilhelm-Epstein-Str. 14; tel. (069) 1581; telex 414431; f. 1957; to issue bank notes, to regulate note and coin circulation and supply of credit; maintains head offices (Hauptverwaltungen) in each Land, known as Landeszentralbanken; required to support government economic policy, although it is independent of instructions from the government. The Bank may advise on important monetary policy, and members of the Federal Government may take part in the deliberations of the Central Bank Council but may not vote; Pres. KARL OTTO PÖHL; Vice-Pres. Dr HELMUT SCHLESINGER.

Landeszentralbank in Baden-Württemberg: 7000 Stuttgart 1, Marstallstr. 3; tel. (0711) 20741; telex 723512; Pres. Board of Management Prof. Dr Dr h.c. NORBERT KLOTEN.

Landeszentralbank in Bayern: 8000 Munich 2, Postfach 20 16 05, Ludwigstr. 13; tel. (089) 23700-1; telex 522890; Pres. Board of Management LOTHAR MÜLLER.

Landeszentralbank in Berlin: 1000 Berlin 12, Leibnizstr. 9-10; tel. (030) 3404-1; telex 181653; Pres. Board of Management Dr DIETER HISS.

Landeszentralbank in Bremen: 2800 Bremen 1, Kohlhökerstr. 29; tel. (0421) 3291-0; telex 244810; Pres. Board of Management Dr KURT NEMITZ.

Landeszentralbank in der Freien und Hansestadt Hamburg: 2000 Hamburg 11, Ost-West-Str. 73; tel. (040) 3707-0; telex 21455450; Pres. Board of Management Dr WILHELM NÖLLING.

Landeszentralbank in Hessen: 6000 Frankfurt a.M. 1, Taunusanlage 5; tel. (069) 2388-0; telex (17) 6997404; Pres. Board of Management Dr ALFRED HÄRTL.

Landeszentralbank in Niedersachsen: 3 Hanover, Georgsplatz 5; tel. (0511) 1233-1; telex 922651; Pres. Board of Management Prof. Dr HELMUT HESSE.

Landeszentralbank in Nordrhein-Westfalen: 4000 Düsseldorf, Berliner Allee 14; tel. (0211) 874-1; telex 8582774; Pres. HANS WERTZ.

Landeszentralbank in Rheinland-Pfalz: 6500 Mainz, Kaiserstr. 50-52; tel. (06131) 602-1; telex 4187544; Pres. Board of Management Dr HEINRICH SCHREINER.

Landeszentralbank im Saarland: 6600 Saarbrücken 1, Keplerstr. 18; tel. (0681) 5802-0; telex 4421258; Pres. HANS GLIEM.

Landeszentralbank in Schleswig-Holstein: 2300 Kiel, Fleethörn 26; tel. (0431) 990-0; telex 299803; Pres. Board of Management Dr JOHANN B. SCHÖLLHORN.

Private Commercial Banks

Baden-Württembergische Bank AG: 7000 Stuttgart 1, Kleiner Schlossplatz, Postfach 142; tel. (0711) 2094-0; telex 721881; f. 1977 by merger of Badische Bank, Handelsbank Heilbronn and Württembergische Bank; cap. DM 120m., dep. DM 11,379m. (Dec. 1987); 7 Mans; 86 brs and 53 agencies.

Bank für Gemeinwirtschaft AG: 6000 Frankfurt a.M. 11, Theaterplatz 2; tel. (069) 2580; telex 4122154; f. 1958; cap. and res DM 2,524m. (Dec. 1986); Chair. Dr HELMUT GIES; over 250 brs.

Bank für Handel und Industrie AG: 1 Berlin 12, Uhlandstr. 9/11; tel. (030) 3196-1; telex 1-83875; f. 1949; subsidiary of Dresdner Bank AG; cap. DM 155m., res DM 684m., dep. DM 10,044m. (Dec. 1987); Man. Dirs Dr JOACHIM MEYER-BLÜCHER, Dr WOLFGANG POECK, RUDI PUCHTA, MANFRED TÜNGLER; 80 brs.

Bankers Trust GmbH: 6000 Frankfurt a.M. 1, Bockenheimer Landstr. 39, Postfach 100345; f. 1889; tel. (069) 71321; telex 411500; formerly Deutsche Unionbank GmbH, name changed in 1980; cap. DM 29.2m., dep. DM 2,824m. (Dec. 1985); Gen. Mans Dr WOLFGANG DIETRICH KUNZ, CECIL Baron VON HAHN, WOLFGANG ARGELANDER; 3 brs.

Bankhaus H. Aufhäuser: 8000 Munich 2, Löwengrube 18; tel. (089) 2393-1; telex 523154; f. 1870; cap. DM 48.4m., res DM 45.4m., dep. DM 928.4m. (Dec. 1987); Chair. Dr LUDWIG HUBER; Partners RUDOLF BAYER, Dr WOLFGANG WUNDER, Dipl.-Kfm. DIRK Freiherr VON DÖRNBERG, RÜDIGER VON MICHAELIS.

Bankhaus Bensel GmbH: 6800 Mannheim 1, Postfach 210; tel. (0621) 180080; telex 463271; f. 1936; cap. DM 10m., dep. DM 141m. (Dec. 1987); Partner and Gen. Man. WOLFGANG KÖHN, Dr HARRO PETERSEN; Partner Baden-Württembergische Bank AG.

Bankhaus Gebrüder Bethmann: 6000 Frankfurt a.M. 1, Bethmannstr. 7-9, Postfach 100349; tel. (069) 2177-0; telex 413033; f. 1748; commercial and investment bank; total assets DM 1,112.3m. (Dec. 1987); Partners WERNER CHROBOK, MATTHIAS VON OPPEN, Dr WALTER SCHORR; 7 brs.

Bankhaus J. A. Krebs: 7800 Freiburg i. Br., Münsterplatz 4; tel. (0761) 31466; telex 772807; f. 1721; Proprs ADOLF KREBS, HEINZ KREBS, Dr WALTER KRÄMER.

Bankhaus Gebr. Martin: 7320 Göppingen (Württemberg), Kirchstr. 35; tel. (07161) 6714-0; telex 727880; f. 1912; Partners Dr RENATE HEES, SUSANNE MARTIN, ANDREAS HEES, WOLF MARTIN.

Bankhaus Neelmeyer AG: 2800 Bremen 1, Am Markt 14/16; tel. (0421) 36030; telex 244866; f. 1907; cap. DM 18m., dep. DM 910.2m. (Dec. 1986); Gen. Mans Dr UWE JANSSEN, Dr ROLF LATTREUTER, Dr HANS EBERHARD MENGES, Dr HELMUT LANDSWEHR; 9 brs.

Bankhaus Carl F. Plump & Co: 2800 Bremen 1, Am Markt 19, Postfach 102507; tel. (0421) 36851; telex 244756; f. 1828; private commercial bank; Partners Fr. HOFFMANN, JAN FREYSOLDT.

Bankverein Bremen AG: 2800 Bremen 1, Wachtstr. 16; tel. (0421) 3684-1; telex 244816; f. 1863; cap. DM 15.5m., dep. DM 716m. (Dec. 1987); Mans GÜNTHER KÜCK, Dr W. J. ROELANTS; 1 br.

Bayerische Hypotheken- und Wechsel-Bank AG (Hypo-Bank): 8000 Munich 2, Theatinerstr. 11, Postfach 200527; tel. (089) 23661; telex 52865-0; f. 1835; cap. and res DM 3,812m., dep. DM 120,216m., total assets 126,284m. (Dec. 1987); Chair. (Supervisory Board) Dr WILHELM ARENDTS; Chair. (Board of Management) Dr EBERHARD MARTINI; 489 brs.

Bayerische Vereinsbank AG: 8000 Munich 2, Kardinal-Faulhaber-Str. 1 and 14, Postfach 1; tel. (089) 21321; telex 529921; f. 1869; cap. DM 574m., dep. DM 81,517m. (Dec. 1987); Chair. (Board of Dirs) Dr WERNER PREMAUER.

Joh. Berenberg, Gossler & Co: 2000 Hamburg 36, Neuer Jungfernstieg 20; tel. (040) 34960; telex 215781; f. 1590; cap. DM 90m., dep. DM 1,606m. (Dec. 1987); Partners JOACHIM H. WETZEL, PETER Freiherr VON KAP-HERR, JOACHIM VON BERENBERG-CONSBRUCH.

Berliner Bank AG: 1000 Berlin 12, Hardenbergstr. 32, Postfach 12 17 09; tel. (030) 3109-0; telex 182010; f. 1950; cap. DM 250m., res 513m., total assets DM 30,681m. (Dec. 1987); Chair. EDZARD REUTER; Man. Dir (International) GÜNTHER BERNT; Chief International Exec. CLAUDIO JARCZYK; 83 brs in West Berlin, brs in Düsseldorf, Frankfurt, Hamburg, Hanover, Stuttgart and Munich, London, subsidiary in Luxembourg.

Berliner Commerzbank AG: 1000 Berlin 30, Potsdamerstr. 125, Postfach 110420; tel. (030) 26971; telex 183862; f. 1949; wholly-owned subsidiary of Commerzbank AG; cap. DM 72.5m., dep. DM 5,579m. (Dec. 1986); Mans SIEGFRIED ERNST, Dr HANS STRATHUS, PETER VON JENA; 60 brs in West Berlin.

Berliner Handels- und Frankfurter Bank (BHF-Bank): 6000 Frankfurt a.M. 1, Bockenheimer Landstr. 10; tel. (069) 718-0; telex 411026; f. 1856; cap. DM 245m., dep. DM 17,647m. (Dec. 1987); Partners Dr W. GRAEBNER, Dr D. OPITZ; Dr W. RUPF, W. STRUTZ, K. SUBJETZKI, R. V. TRESCKOW.

Berliner Volksbank (West) EG: 1000 Berlin 19, Kaiserdamm 86; tel. (030) 303061; telex 182803; f. 1946; cap. DM 54.1m., dep. DM 3,297m. (Dec. 1986); Chair. HANS-DIETER BLAESE; 30 brs in West Berlin.

Commerzbank AG: 6000 Frankfurt a.M., Neue Mainzer Str. 32-36; tel. (069) 13620; telex 4152530; f. 1870; cap. and res DM 6,114m., dep. DM 92,828m. (Dec. 1987); Chair. (Supervisory Board) PAUL LICHTENBERG; Chair. Board of Man. Dirs Dr WALTER SEIPP; 779 domestic and 13 foreign brs.

Delbrück & Co: 1000 Berlin 30, Rankestr. 13; tel. (030) 8842880; 5000 Cologne 1, Gereonstr. 15-23; tel. (0221) 16241; telex 8882605; f. 1854; cap. DM 50m., dep. DM 944m. (Dec. 1987); 9 Man. Partners.

Deutsch-Skandinavische Bank AG: 6000 Frankfurt a.M., Alte Rothofstr. 8; tel. (069) 29830; telex 413413; f. 1976; cap. DM 81m., dep. DM 1,973m. (Dec. 1987); Chair. JACOB PALMSTIERNA.

Deutsch-Südamerikanische Bank AG (Banco Germánico de la América del Sud): 2000 Hamburg 36, Neuer Jungfernstieg 16,

FEDERAL REPUBLIC OF GERMANY

Postfach 301246; tel. (040) 341070; telex 2142360; f. 1906; cap. DM 178m., dep. DM 6,157m. (Dec. 1987); Chair. JÜRGEN SARRAZIN; Gen. Mans ALBRECHT C. RÄDECKE, JAN-GERD EVERSMANN, HELMUT FRÖHLICH, Dr HERBERT MITTENDORFF, KURT ZIMMERLING.

Deutsche Bank AG: Central Office: 6000 Frankfurt a.M., Taunusanlage 12; tel. (069) 71500; telex 417300; f. 1870; cap. DM 1,773m., dep. DM 144,577m. (Dec. 1987); Hon. Pres. HERMANN J. ABS; Chair. Dr WILFRIED GUTH; 1,162 brs.

Deutsche Bank Berlin AG: 1000 Berlin 10, Otto-Suhr-Allee 6/16; tel. (030) 34070; telex 181433; f. 1949; wholly-owned subsidiary of Deutsche Bank AG; cap. DM 100m., dep. DM 7,308m. (Dec. 1987); Chair. Supervisory Board Dr HERBERT ZAPP.

Dresdner Bank AG: 6000 Frankfurt a.M. 11, Jürgen-Ponto-Platz 1; tel. (069) 2630; telex 415240; f. 1872; cap. DM 1,243m., dep. DM 94,699m. (Dec. 1986); Chair. Board of Man. Dirs Dr WOLFGANG RÖLLER; 953 brs.

Grunelius & Co: 6000 Frankfurt a.M. 16, Untermainkai 26; tel. (069) 273905-0; telex 411723; f. 1824; Partners Dr ERNST MAX VON GRUNELIUS, EDMUND KNAPP.

Georg Hauck & Sohn Bankiers KGaA: 6000 Frankfurt a.M. 1, Kaiserstr. 24; tel. (069) 21611; telex 411061; f. 1796; cap. DM 20m., res DM 23.5m. (Dec. 1987); Chair. Dr HEINRICH IRMLER; Partners MICHAEL HAUCK, AXEL SCHÜTZ.

Hesse Newman & Co: 2000 Hamburg 1, Ferdinandstr. 25-27, Postfach 103020; tel. (040) 339620; telex 2161942; f. 1777; cap. DM 25m., dep. DM 197m. (June 1987); Man. PETER C. QUEITSCH.

Von der Heydt-Kersten & Söhne: 5600 Wuppertal-Elberfeld 1, Neumarkt 5-13; tel. (0202) 4871; telex 8591824; f. 1754; wholly-owned subsidiary of Commerzbank AG; Partners ADOLF HEDRICH, GERHARD WICHELHAUS.

Ibero-Amerika Bank AG: 2800 Bremen 1, Domshof 14/15, Postfach 104509; tel. (0421) 36300-0; telex 244899; f. 1949; cap. DM 10m., res DM 33.0m. (Dec. 1987); br. in Hamburg; Gen. Mans KLAUS F. MÜLLER-LEIENDECKER, ROLF E. BEISSER, HERBERT SCHOENNAGEL.

Kleinwort, Benson (Deutschland) GmbH & Co: 2800 Bremen 1, Langenstr. 15-21; tel. (0421) 36660; telex 244812; f. 1872, fmrly Bankhaus Martens & Weyhausen, name changed 1983; cap. DM 35m., res DM 7,037m., dep. DM 576m. (Dec. 1982); Mans WOLFGANG KUNZE, JENS-PETER KNOBLAUCH.

Marcard, Stein & Co: 2000 Hamburg 1, Ballindamm 36; tel. (040) 30990; telex 2165032; f. 1790; cap. DM 74.15m., dep. DM 1,078m. (Jan. 1987); 4 partners.

Merck Finck & Co: 8000 Munich 2, Pacellistr. 4; tel. (089) 21041; telex 522303; f. 1870; cap. DM 75m., dep. DM 3,526m. (Dec. 1986); Partners AUGUST VON FINCK, WILHELM VON FINCK, ADOLF KRACHT, Dr iur. WILHELM WINTERSTEIN, Agricola Verwaltungsgesellschaft KG.

Metallbank GmbH: 6000 Frankfurt a.M. 1, Reuterweg 14, Postfach 101501; telex 416341; f. 1980; cap. DM 36.5m., dep. DM 443.3m. (Sept. 1984); Chair. WERNER BUSCH; 2 brs.

B. Metzler seel. Sohn & Co Bankers: 6000 Frankfurt a.M. 1, Grosse Gallusstr. 18; tel. (069) 21040; telex 412724; f. 1674; cap. DM 100m., dep. DM 664m. (Dec. 1987); Partners CHRISTOPH VON METZLER, FRIEDRICH VON METZLER, HANS HERMANN RESCHKE.

National-Bank AG: 4300 Essen 1, Theaterplatz 8; tel. (0201) 1721; telex 857811; f. 1921; cap. DM 22m., dep. DM 1,453m. (Dec. 1986); Mans GÜNTER EHLEN, Dr HANS BRAUN, GUNTHER LANGE, GERHARD LEPPELMANN.

Norddeutsche Genossenschaftsbank AG: 3000 Hanover, Rathenaustr. 5-6, Postfach 249; tel. (0511) 1227-0; telex 922751; f. 1982 by merger; cap. DM 230m., dep. DM 15,390m. (Dec. 1987); Chair. KARL-HEINZ SCHARMANN.

Oldenburgische Landesbank AG: 2900 Oldenburg, Stau 15; tel. (0441) 2211; telex 25882; f. 1868; cap. DM 52.2m., dep. DM 4,942m. (Dec. 1987); Chair. Dr jur. CARL S. GROSS; Mans HERMANN CONRING, Dr HUBERT FORCH, H.-H. LUDEWIG.

Sal. Oppenheim Jr & Cie: 5 Cologne 1, Unter Sachsenhausen 4; tel. (0221) 145-01; telex 8882547; 6 Frankfurt/M., Bockenheimer Landstr. 20; tel. (069) 7134-0; telex 411016; f. 1789; cap. DM 165m., dep. DM 2,861m. (Dec. 1987); 8 partners.

Reuschel & Co: 8000 Munich 2, Maximiliansplatz 13; tel. (089) 2395-0; telex 523690; f. 1947; cap. DM 35m., dep. DM 2,379m. (Dec. 1986); Partners Dr ERNST THIEMANN, Dr BERND VOSS, THOMAS KLINGELHÖFER.

Karl Schmidt Bankgeschäft: 8670 Hof/Saale, Ernst-Reuter-Str. 119, Postfach 1629, 1649; tel. (09281) 6010; telex 643880; f. 1828; cap. DM 103.2m., dep. DM 2,485.9m. (Dec. 1986); Partners Dr KARL-GERHARD SCHMIDT, GEORG BECHER, WERNER SCHMIDT, Dr REINER SCHMIDT, Dr KLAUS BECHER; 90 brs.

Otto M. Schröder: 2000 Hamburg 36, Alsterarkaden 27; tel. (040) 363141; telex 211119; f.1932; Owner OTTO M. SCHRÖDER.

Schröder, Münchmeyer, Hengst & Co: 2000 Hamburg 1, Postfach 105903, 33 Ballindamm; tel. (040) 32950; telex 2162151; f. 1969 by merger, 1983 became subsidiary of the Lloyds Bank group; cap. DM 140m. (March 1985); CEO JOHN HOBLEY.

Schweizerische Bankgesellschaft (Deutschland) AG: 6000 Frankfurt a.M., Bleichstr. 52, Postfach 102063; tel. (069) 1369-0; telex 412194; f. 1909; merchant bank; frmly Deutsche Länderbank AG; cap. DM 45m., res DM 95m. (Dec. 1987); Chair. Dr JÜRGEN-PETER KAVEN.

Schweizerische Kreditanstalt (Deutschland) AG: 6000 Frankfurt a.M., Kaiserstr. 30; tel. (069) 2691-0; telex 412127; f. 1969; cap. DM 165m., dep. DM 5,545.2m. (March 1988); Mans. K. MIESEL, F. HOYOS, K. J. ZAPF.

Simonbank AG: 4000 Düsseldorf 1, Martin-Luther-Platz 32; tel. (0211) 87930; telex 8587931; f. 1960; cap. DM 34m., dep. DM 1,785.9m. (Dec. 1987); Chair. Dr MAXIMILIAN HACKL; Man. Dirs Dr OTTHEINZ JUNG-SENSSFELDER, PETER KLEVER.

J. H. Stein: 5000 Cologne 1, Unter Sachsenhausen 10-20, Postfach 101748; telex 8882506; f. 1790; Partners JOHANN HEINRICH VON STEIN, Dr GERD HOLLENBERG, Dr HANS KASPAR Freiherr VON RHEINBABEN.

Trinkaus & Burkhardt: 4000 Düsseldorf 1, Königsallee 21-23; tel. (0211) 831-1; telex 8581490; f. 1785; cap. DM 90m., dep. DM 4,241m. (Dec. 1987); Chair. HERBERT H. JACOBI.

Vereins- und Westbank: 2000 Hamburg 11, Alter Wall 22; tel. (040) 3692-01; telex 2151640; f. 1974 by merger; cap. and res DM 594m., dep. DM 10,850m. (Dec. 1987).

M. M. Warburg-Brinckmann, Wirtz & Co: 2000 Hamburg 1, Ferdinandstr. 75; tel. (040) 32820; telex 2162211; f. 1798; cap. DM 130m., dep. DM 2,524m. (Dec. 1987); Partners Dr C. BRINCKMANN, Dr C. OLEARIUS, H.-D. SANDWEG, MAX A. WARBURG.

Westfalenbank AG: 4630 Bochum 1, Huestr. 21-25; tel. (0234) 6160; telex 825825; f. 1921; cap. DM 75m., dep. DM 4,745m. (1987); 4 Dirs.

Public-Law Credit Institutions

Bayerische Landesbank Girozentrale: 8000 Munich 2, Brienner Str. 20; tel. (089) 217101; telex 5286270; f. 1972; cap. DM 1,000m., dep. DM 107,354m. (Dec. 1987).

Deutsche Girozentrale-Deutsche Kommunalbank: 6000 Frankfurt a.M. 1, Taunusanlage 10, Postfach 110542; tel. (069) 26930; telex 414168; and 1000 Berlin 15, Kurfürstendamm 32; tel. (030) 8812096; telex 183353; f. 1918; cap. and res DM 775m. (Dec. 1986); Chair. Board of Management ERNST-OTTO SANDVOSS.

Hamburgische Landesbank-Girozentrale: 2000 Hamburg 1, Gerhart-Hauptmann-Platz 50, Postfach 102820; tel. (040) 3333-0; telex 2161792; f. 1938; cap. DM 570m., res DM 729m. (Dec. 1987); Chair. Dr H. FAHNING.

Hessische Landesbank-Girozentrale: 6000 Frankfurt a.M. 11, Junghofstr. 18-26, Postfach 110833; tel. (069) 132-01; telex 415291-0; cap. and res DM 1,396m. (Dec. 1987); CEO Dr HERBERT KAZMIERZAK.

Landesbank Rheinland-Pfalz Girozentrale: 6500 Mainz, Grosse Bleiche 54-56; tel. (06131) 130; telex 4187858; cap. and res DM 959m., total assets DM 40,500m. (Dec. 1986); Chair. Dr PAUL WIEANDT.

Landesbank Stuttgart Girozentrale: 7000 Stuttgart 10, Lautenschlagerstr. 2; tel. (0711) 2049-0; telex 725190; cap. and res DM 791m., total assets DM 36,201m. (1986); Chair. Dr GERHARD VOLZ; Deputy Chair. WERNER SCHMIDT; Mans ALFRED BAUMANN, Dr CLAUS HELBIG, ROLF LIMBACH.

Norddeutsche Landesbank Girozentrale (NORD/LB): 3000 Hanover 1, Georgsplatz 1; tel. (511) 103-0; telex 921620; f. 1970 by merger of several north German banks; cap. and res DM 2,441m., total assets DM 69,036m. (Dec. 1986); Chair. Dr BERND THIEMANN; 224 brs.

Westdeutsche Landesbank Girozentrale (WestLB): 4000 Düsseldorf 1, Herzogstr. 15, Postfach 1128; tel. (0211) 826-01; telex 8588216; f. 1969; cap. DM 1,815m., res DM 2,421m., dep. DM 141,088m. (1987); Chair. F. NEUBER.

Central Bank of Co-operative Banking System

Deutsche Genossenschaftsbank: 6000 Frankfurt a.M. 1, Am Platz der Republik, Postfach 100651; tel. (069) 744701; telex 412291; f. 1949; cap. and res DM 2,724m., total assets DM 127,416m. (Dec. 1987); supports more than 3,400 local and five regional co-operative banks; Chair. H. GUTHARDT.

Specialist Banks

Deutsche Verkehrs-Kredit-Bank AG: 6000 Frankfurt a.M., Untermainkai 23-25; tel. (069) 2648-0; telex 416925; f. 1923; cap. p.u. DM 75m., res DM 128m., dep. DM 4,992m. (Dec. 1987); Mans A. GRUNHOLD, Dr K. J. MENCHE, Dr F. SCHLOSSNIKL.

FEDERAL REPUBLIC OF GERMANY

Frankfurter Hypothekenbank AG: 6000 Frankfurt a.M., Junghofstr. 5–7; tel. (069) 29898-0; telex 411608; f. 1862; mortgage bank; cap. DM 89.6m.; Gen. Mans Dr DIETER BOSCHERT, Dr BERNT W. ROHRER, Dr HANS SCHUCK.

Industriekreditbank AG-Deutsche Industriebank: 4000 Düsseldorf 1, Karl-Theodor-Str. 6; tel. (0211) 8221-0; telex 8582791; and 1000 Berlin 12, Bismarckstr 105; tel. (030) 31009-0; telex 184376; f. 1949; cap. DM 757.5m. (1987); Chair. (Supervisory Board) Dr DIETER SPETHMANN.

Kreditanstalt für Wiederaufbau: 6000 Frankfurt a.M. 11, Postfach 111141; tel. (069) 74310; telex 4152560; f. 1948; cap. DM 1,000m., total assets DM 96,836m. (Dec. 1987); Chair. Bd of Dirs Dr GERHARD STOLTENBERG; Vice-Chair. Dr MARTIN BANGEMANN.

Bankers' Organizations

Bundesverband deutscher Banken eV: 5000 Cologne 1, Mohrenstr. 35–41, Postfach 100246; tel. (0221) 16631; telex 8882730; f. 1948; Pres. Dr WOLFGANG RÖLLER.

Bundesverband der Deutschen Volksbanken und Raiffeisenbanken eV: 5300 Bonn 1, Heussallee 5, Postfach 120440; tel. (0228) 509-0; telex 886779; f. 1971; Pres. BERNHARD SCHRAMM; 3,600 mems.

Deutscher Sparkassen- und Giroverband eV; 5300 Bonn, Simrockstr. 4, Postfach 1429; tel. (0228) 204-0; telex 886709; Pres. Dr HELMUT GEIGER; Mans GUSTAV SCHRÖDER, WOLFGANG STARKE.

STOCK EXCHANGES

Arbeitsgemeinschaft der Deutschen Wertpapierbörsen (Federation of German Stock Exchanges): 6000 Frankfurt a.M. 1, Biebergasse 6-10; tel. (069) 2999030; f. 1986; supervisory board of regional exchanges; Chair. of Assembly of Members Dr GERNOT ERNST.

Frankfurt-am-Main: 6000 Frankfurt a.M., Wertpapierbörse, Postfach 100811; tel. (069) 21970; telex 411412; f. 1585; mems 198; Chair. MICHAEL HAUCK; 3 Mans.

Berlin: Börse, 1000 Berlin 12, Hardenbergstr. 16–18; tel. (030) 31800; telex 183663; f. 1685; Pres. Dr GERNOT ERNST.

Bremen: Bremer Wertpapierbörse, 2800 Bremen 1, Domshof 12, Postfach 10 07 26; tel. (0421) 323037; telex 246331; mems 24 credit institutes; Pres. Dr ROLAND BELLSTEDT; Man. AXEL H. SCHUBERT.

Düsseldorf: Rheinisch-Westfälische Börse zu Düsseldorf, Ernst-Schneider-Platz 1; tel. (0211) 8621; telex 8582600; f. 1935; 98 mem. firms; Pres. ALFRED Freiherr VON OPPENHEIM.

Hamburg: 2000 Hamburg 11, Börse; tel. (040) 367444; telex 213228; 96 mem. firms; Pres. HANS-DIETER SANDWEG.

Hanover: Niedersächsische Börse zu Hannover, 3000 Hanover 1, Rathenaustr. 2; tel. (0511) 327661; telex 5118444; f. 1787; mems 27; Pres. HORST RISSE; Man. Rechtsanwalt RUDOLF GROMMELT.

Munich: Bayerische Börse, 8 Munich 2, Lenbachplatz 2A/1; tel. (089) 59900; telex 523515; f. 1548; mems 74; Chair. of Council RUDOLF BAYER.

Stuttgart: Baden-Württembergische Wertpapierbörse zu Stuttgart, 7 Stuttgart 1, Hospitalstr. 12; tel. (0711) 290183; telex 721514; f. 1861; mems 46; Pres. GERHARD BURK; Man. Dir Rechtsanwalt HANS-JOACHIM FEUERBACH.

INSURANCE

German law specifies that property- and accident insurance may not be jointly underwritten with life-, sickness-, legal protection- or credit- insurance by the same company. Insurers are therefore obliged to establish separate companies to cover the different classes of insurance.

Aachener und Münchener Lebensversicherung AG: 5100 Aachen, Postfach 26; tel. (0241) 6001-01; telex 832346; f. 1868; Chair. Dr HELMUT GIES; Gen. Man. W. H. BÖRNER.

Aachener und Münchener Beteiligungs-AG: 5100 Aachen, Postfach 10; tel. (0241) 46101; telex 832872; f. 1825; Chair. Prof. Dr jur. Dr-Ing. E.h. R. SCHMIDT; Gen. Man. Dr HELMUT GIES.

Albingia Versicherungs-AG: 2000 Hamburg 1, Ballindamm 39; tel. (040) 30220; telex 2161774; f. 1901; Chair. H. SINGER; Gen. Man. V. BREMKAMP.

Allianz AG Holding: 8000 Munich 44, Postfach 440124; tel (089) 38001; telex 5230110; f. 1890; Chair. Supervisory Bd Prof. Dr H. GRÜNEWALD; Chair. Bd of Mans Dr W. SCHIEREN.

Allianz Lebensversicherungs-AG: 7000 Stuttgart 1, Postfach 534; tel. (0711) 663-0; telex 723571; f. 1922; Chair. Dr W. SCHIEREN; Gen. Man. Dr U. HAASEN.

Colonia Lebensversicherung AG: 5000 Cologne 80, Postfach 805060; tel. (0221) 690-02; telex 881585; f. 1853; Chair. Dr N. Graf STRASOLDO; Gen. Man. D. WENDELSTADT.

Colonia Versicherung AG: 5000 Cologne 80, Postfach 805050; tel. (0221) 69001; telex 8815-0; f. 1838; Chair. Dr N. Graf STRASOLDO; Gen. Man. D. WENDELSTADT.

Continentale Krankenversicherung auf Gegenseitigkeit: 4600 Dortmund 1, Postfach 1343; tel. (0231) 12011; telex 822515; f. 1926; Chair. Dr J. LORSBACH; Gen. Man. Dr H. HOFFMANN.

Debeka Krankenversicherungsverein auf Gegenseitigkeit: 5400 Koblenz, Postfach 460; tel. (0261) 4980; f. 1905; Chair. H. LANGE; Gen. Man. P. GREISLER.

Deutsche Beamten-Versicherung Öffentlichrechtliche Lebens- und Renten-Versicherungsanstalt: 6200 Wiesbaden 1, Postfach 2109; tel. (06121) 3630; telex (17) 6121946; f. 1872; Chair. Dr W. HESSELBACH; Gen. Man. M. BROSKA.

Deutsche Krankenversicherung AG: 5000 Cologne 41, Aachener Str. 300, Postfach 100588; tel. (0221) 5780; telex 8881634; f. 1927; Chair. K. WESSELKOCK; Gen. Man. H. G. TIMMER.

Deutscher Herold Lebensversicherungs-AG: 5300 Bonn 1, Postfach 1448; tel. (0228) 26801; telex 886653; f. 1921; Chair. W. SOBOTA; Speaker H. D. RITTERBEX, W. EWERT.

Frankfurter Versicherungs-AG: 6000 Frankfurt 1, Postfach 100201; tel. (069) 71261; telex 411376; f. 1929; Chair. E. WUNDERLICH; Gen. Man. Dr H. SCHMEER.

Gerling-Konzern Allgemeine Versicherungs-AG: 5000 Cologne 1, Postfach 100808; tel. (0221) 144-1; telex 88110; f. 1918; Chair. G. VOGELSANG; Speaker A. WEILER.

Gothaer Versicherungsbank Versicherungsverein auf Gegenseitigkeit: 5000 Cologne 1, Postfach 108026; tel. (0221) 5746-00; telex 221305; f. 1820; Chair. Dr H. VOSSLOH; Gen. Man. Prof. A. W. KLEIN.

Haftpflicht-Unterstützungs-Kasse kraftfahrender Beamter Deutschlands auf Gegenseitigkeit in Coburg (HUK-Coburg): 8630 Coburg, Postfach 1802; tel. (09561) 96-0; telex 663414; f. 1933; Chair. Dr B. SCHRÖDER; Gen. Mans Dr H.-J. DREWS, Dr G. SCHRAMM, F. BECK, R.-P. HOENEN, W. MICHEL.

Haftpflichtverband der Deutschen Industrie Versicherungsverein auf Gegenseitigkeit: 3000 Hanover 51, Postfach 510369; tel. (0511) 645-1; telex 922678; f. 1903; Chair. Prof. Dr F. THOMÉE; Gen. Man. Dipl. Ing. A. MORSBACH.

Hamburger-Mannheimer Versicherungs-AG: 2000 Hamburg 60, Postfach 601060; tel. (040) 6376-1; telex 2174600; f. 1899; Chair. Dr H. K. JANNOTT; Gen. Man. K. WESSELKOCK.

Iduna Vereinigte Lebensversicherung auf Gegenseitigkeit für Handwerk, Handel und Gewerbe: 2000 Hamburg 36, Postfach 302761; tel. (040) 41240; telex 211397; f. 1914; Chair. G. WÄGER; Gen. Man. H. BECKER.

Landwirtschaftlicher Versicherungsverein Münster AG: 4400 Münster, Kolde-Ring 21, Postfach 6145; tel. (0251) 7020; telex 892650; f. 1896; Chair. H. OSTROP; Gen. Man. K.-A. LOSKANT.

Nordstern Allgemeine Versicherungs-AG: 5000 Cologne 1, Gereonstr. 43-45, Postfach 101368; tel. (0221) 148-1; telex 8882714; f. 1866; direct and indirect underwriting of all classes of private insurance in Germany and abroad; life-, health-, credit- and legal protection-insurance through reinsurance only; Pres. Supervisory Bd Dr N. Graf STRASOLDO; Chair. C. KLEYBOLDT.

R+V Versicherungs-Gruppe: 6200 Wiesbaden, Taunusstr. 1, Postfach 4840; tel. (06121) 533-0; telex 4186803; f. 1922; group consists of 7 companies incl. R+V Allgemeine Versicherung AG, R+V Lebensversicherung AG and R+V Krankenversicherung AG; Chair. W. CROLL; Gen. Man. Dr PETER C. VON HARDER.

SIGNAL Krankenversicherung auf Gegenseitigkeit: 4600 Dortmund 1, Postfach 105052; tel. (0231) 135-0; telex 822231; f. 1907; Chair. PAUL SCHNITKER; Gen. Man. H. FROMMKNECHT.

Vereinte Krankenversicherung AG: 8000 Munich 2, Postfach 202522; tel. (089) 6785-0; telex 5215721; f. 1925; Chair. Dr R. GAMPER; Gen. Man. Dr H. K. JÄKEL.

Victoria Feuer-Versicherungs-AG: 4000 Düsseldorf 1, Postfach 1116; tel. (0211) 82801; telex 8582984; f. 1904; Chair. Dr E. OVERBECK; Gen. Man. Dr E. JANNOTT.

Victoria Lebens-Versicherungs-AG: 4000 Düsseldorf 1, Postfach 1116; tel. (0211) 82801; telex 8582984; f. 1853; Chair. Dr E. OVERBECK; Gen. Man. Dr E. JANNOTT.

Volksfürsorge Deutsche Lebensversicherung AG: 2000 Hamburg 1, Postfach 106420; tel. (040) 2865-0; telex 2112440; f. 1912; Chair. H. MATTHÖFER; Gen. Man. W. SCHWICKART.

Württembergische Feuerversicherung AG; 7000 Stuttgart 10, Postfach 60; tel. (0711) 6620; telex 723553; f. 1828; Chair. O.-J. MAIER; Gen. Man. Dr G. BÜCHNER.

Reinsurance

Aachener Rückversicherungs-Gesellschaft AG: 5100 Aachen, Postfach 25; tel. (0241) 186-0; telex 832629; f. 1853; Chair. Dr jur. HELMUT GIES, Dr A. MORENZ.

Bayerische Rückversicherung AG: 8000 Munich 22, Postfach 220010; tel. (089) 3844-1; telex 5215247; f. 1911; Chair. Prof. Dr B. BÖRNER; Gen Man Dr P. FREY.

Deutsche Rückversicherung AG: 2000 Hamburg 13, Postfach 2622; tel. (040) 4106055; telex 214950; f. 1952; Chair. Dr W. RIEGER; Gen. Man. G. HASSE.

Frankona Rückversicherungs-AG: 8000 Munich 86, Postfach 860380; tel. (089) 9228-1; telex 522531; f. 1886; Chair. Dr H. GERLING; Gen. Man. Dr A. KANN.

Gerling-Konzern Globale Rückversicherungs-AG: 5000 Cologne 1, Postfach 100808; tel. (0221) 144-1; telex 88110; f. 1954; Chair. R. SCHLENKER; Speaker Dr R. WOLTERECK.

Hamburger Internationale Rückversicherung AG: 2000 Hamburg 11, Postfach 111522; tel. (040) 37008-1; telex 2162938; f. 1965; Chair. W. SCHWICKART; Gen. Man. R. SOLL.

Hannover Rückversicherungs-AG: 3000 Hanover 61, Karl-Wiechert-Allee 50, Postfach 610369; tel (0511) 5604-0; telex 922599; f. 1966; Chair. Supervisory Board A. MORSBACH; Chair. Board of Mans R. C. BINGEMER.

Kölnische Rückversicherungs-Gesellschaft AG: 5000 Cologne 1, Theodor-Heuss-Ring 11, Postfach 108016; tel. (0221) 7759-0; telex 8885231-0; f. 1846; Chair. Dr N. Graf STRASOLDO; Gen. Man. Dr J. ZECH.

Münchener Rückversicherungs-Gesellschaft: 8000 Munich 40, Königstr. 107; tel. (089) 3891-0; telex 5215233-0; f. 1880; all classes of reinsurance; Chair. Supervisory Bd Dr D. SPETHMANN; Chair. Bd of Mans Dr H. K. JANNOTT.

Rhein-Main-Rückversicherungs-Gesellschaft AG: 6200 Wiesbaden 1, Sonnenberger Str. 44; tel. (06121) 525001; telex 4186473; f. 1935; all classes of reinsurance; Chair. W. CROLL; Gen. Man. Dr P. C. VON HARDER.

Principal Insurance Association

Gesamtverband der Deutschen Versicherungswirtschaft eV: 5000 Cologne 1, Ebertplatz 1; tel. (0221) 7764-0; telex 8885255; f. 1948; affiliating 5 mem. asscns and 419 mem. companies; Pres. Dr GEORG BÜCHNER (Stuttgart); Vice-Pres. Dr U. HAASEN (Stuttgart), D. WENDELSTADT (Cologne).

Trade and Industry

CHAMBERS OF INDUSTRY AND COMMERCE

Deutscher Industrie- und Handelstag (Association of German Chambers of Industry and Commerce): 5300 Bonn 1, Adenauerallee 148; tel. (0228) 1040; telex 886805; Pres. Dipl. Ing. HANS PETER STIHL; Sec.-Gen. Dr FRANZ SCHOSER; affiliates 69 Chambers of Industry and Commerce.

There are Chambers of Industry and Commerce in all the principal towns and also nine regional associations as follows:

Arbeitsgemeinschaft der Industrie- und Handelskammern in Baden-Württemberg, Vorort: Industrie- und Handelskammer Mittlerer Neckar Sitz Stuttgart: 7000 Stuttgart 1, Jägerstr. 30, Postfach 84; tel. (0711) 2005-0; telex 722031; Chair. Dipl.-Ing. BERTHOLD LEIBINGER; Sec. PETER KISTNER.

Arbeitsgemeinschaft der Bayerischen Industrie- und Handelskammern: 8000 Munich 2, Max-Joseph-Str. 2; tel. (089) 51160; telex 523678; Chair. Prof. Dr ROLF RODENSTOCK; Sec. Dr WILHELM WIMMER; 10 mems.

Arbeitsgemeinschaft Hessischer Industrie- und Handelskammern: 6000 Frankfurt a.M. 1, Börsenplatz; tel. (069) 21970; telex 411255; Chair. Dr HANS MESSER; Sec. RICHARD SPEICH; 12 mems.

Vereinigung der Niedersächsischen Industrie- und Handelskammern: 3000 Hanover 1, Königstr. 19, Postfach 3029; tel. (0511) 3481565; telex 922769; f. 1899; Pres. Senator HORST MÜNZNER; Man. Dir Dr jur. CHRISTIAN AHRENS; 7 mems.

Vereinigung der Industrie- und Handelskammern des Landes Nordrhein-Westfalen: 4000 Düsseldorf 1, Postfach 240120; tel. (0211) 352091; telex 8582363; Chair. Dr ALFRED VOSSSCHULTE; Sec. Ass. HANS G. CRONE-ERDMANN; 16 mems.

Kammergemeinschaft Öffentlichkeitsarbeit der Nordrhein-Westfälischen Industrie- und Handelskammern: 5000 Cologne 1, Unter Sachsenhausen 10–26; tel. (0221) 1640-157; telex 8881400; Chair. Dr HEINZ MALANGRÉ; Sec. GÜNTER BOCK; 14 mems.

Arbeitsgemeinschaft der Industrie- und Handelskammern Rheinland-Pfalz: 6700 Ludwigshafen, Ludwigsplatz 2/3, Postfach 210744; tel. (0621) 59040; telex 176215942; Sec. Dr ANDREAS HERTING; 4 mems.

Verband der Industrie- und Handelskammern des Landes Schleswig-Holstein: 2400 Lübeck 1, Breit Str. 6-8; tel. (0451) 1350; telex 26776; Chair. KONSUL KLAUS RICHTER; Sec. Dr Dr JÜRGEN PRATJE; 3 mems.

Arbeitsgemeinschaft Öffentlichkeitsarbeit der Norddeutschen Industrie- und Handelskammern: 2000 Hamburg 11, Börse; tel. (040) 366382; telex 211250; Chair. GUSTAV G. HEBOLD; Sec. Dr UWE CHRISTIANSEN.

EXPORT AND TRADE ASSOCIATIONS

Arbeitsgemeinschaft Aussenhandel der Deutschen Wirtschaft: 5000 Cologne 51, Gustav-Heinemann-Ufer 84–88; Dir HEINZ TEMBRINK.

Bundesstelle für Aussenhandelsinformation (German Foreign Trade Information Office): 5000 Cologne, Blaubach 13, Postfach 108007; tel. (0221) 2057-1; telex 8882735.

Bundesverband des Deutschen Gross- und Aussenhandels eV: 5300 Bonn, Kaiser-Friedrichstr. 13, Postfach 1349; tel. (0228) 26004-0; telex 886783; Pres. Konsul KLAUS RICHTER; 70 mem. asscns.

Hauptgemeinschaft des Deutschen Einzelhandels eV: 5000 Cologne, Sachsenring 89; tel. (0221) 33980; telex 8881443; f. 1947; Chair. WOLFGANG HINRICHS; Exec. Dir GÜNTHER WASSMANN.

Zentralverband der Genossenschaftlichen Grosshandels- und Dienstleistungsunternehmen eV (Central Association of Co-operative Wholesale and Service Trade): 53 Bonn 1, Postfach 120220; tel. (0228) 210011; Pres. HANS-JURGEN KLUSSMANN; c. 250,000 mems; 880 primary co-operatives; 13 central co-operatives.

INDUSTRIAL ASSOCIATIONS

Bundesverband der Deutschen Industrie eV (Federation of German Industry): 5000 Cologne 51, Gustav-Heinemann-Ufer 84–88; tel. (0221) 3708-1; telex 8882601; Pres. Dr TYLL NECKER; Dir-Gen. Dr SIEGFRIED MANN; mems include some of the following asscns:

Arbeitsgemeinschaft Industriengruppe (General Industry): 7530 Pforzheim, Industriehaus, Postfach 470; tel. (07231) 33041; telex 783855; Chair. JOACHIM KÖHLE; Dir Dr ALFRED SCHNEIDER.

Arbeitsgemeinschaft Keramische Industrie eV (Ceramics): 6000 Frankfurt a.M. 97, Friedrich-Ebert-Anlage 38, Postfach 970171; tel. (069) 756082-0; telex 4189085; Chair. ROLAND DORSCHNER; Dir R. A. REINFRIED VOGLER; 6 mem. asscns.

Bundesverband Bekleidungsindustrie eV (Clothing): 5000 Cologne 1, Mevissenstr. 15; tel. (0221) 77440; telex (17) 22150803; Pres. GERD SOMBERG; Dirs-Gen. Dipl.-Kfm. WALTER F. HERPELL, RAINER MAUER.

Bundesvereinigung der Deutschen Ernährungsindustrie eV (Food): 5300 Bonn 2, Rheinallee 18; tel. (0228) 351051; telex 885679; f. 1949; Chair. Konsul HERMANN BAHLSEN; Chief Gen. Man. Dr GERHARD HEIN; 36 branch-organizations.

Bundesverband der Deutschen Luftfahrt-, Raumfahrt- und Ausrüstungsindustrie eV (BDLI) (Aerospace Industries): 5300 Bonn 2, Konstantinstr. 90; tel. (0228) 330011; telex 885528; Pres. Dr-Ing. HANNS ARNT VOGELS; Dir Dr H. GEORG BRODACH.

Bundesverband Druck eV (Printing): 6200 Wiesbaden 1, Postfach 1869, Biebricher Allee 79; tel. (06121) 8030; telex 4186888; f. 1947; Pres. HANS-OTTO REPPEKUS; Dir Dr WALTER HESSE; 11 mem. asscns.

Bundesverband Glasindustrie und Mineralfaserindustrie eV (Glass): 4000 Düsseldorf 1, Stresemannstr. 26, Postfach 8340; tel. (0211) 16894-0; telex 8587686; Chair. Dr WALTER TRUX; Dir Dipl.-Vw. NORBERT ELL; 6 mem. asscns.

Bundesverband Steine und Erden eV (Building): 6000 Frankfurt a.M., Friedrich-Ebert-Anlage 38, Postfach 970171; tel. (069) 7560820; telex 4189085; f. 1948; Pres. Dipl.-Kfm. PETER SCHUHMACHER; Chief Dir Dipl.-Volksw. HANS-JÜRGEN REITZIG.

Deutscher Giessereiverband (Foundries): 4000 Düsseldorf, Sohnstr. 70, Postfach 8709; tel. (0211) 68711; telex 8586885; Pres. Dipl.-Ing. EBERHARD MÖLLMANN; Man. Dir Dr KLAUS URBAT.

Deutsche Verbundgesellschaft eV (Electricity): 6900 Heidelberg 1, Ziegelhäuser Landstr. 5; tel. (06221) 4037-0; telex 461849; Chair. Dr-Ing. GÜNTER KLÄTTE; Dir-Gen. Dipl.-Ing. HANS-GÜNTER BUSCH.

EBM Wirtschaftsverband (Metal Goods): 4000 Düsseldorf 30, Kaiserswerther Str. 135, Postfach 321230; tel. (0211) 454930; telex 8584985; Pres. GÜNTER BECKER; Gen.-Man. Dipl.-Vw. KLAUS BELLWINKEL.

Gesamtverband kunststoffverarbeitende Industrie eV (GKV) (Plastics): 6000 Frankfurt a.M. 1, Am Hauptbahnhof 12; tel. (069) 271050; telex 411122; f. 1949; Chair. LUDWIG EBERHARDT; Sec.-Gen. Dr REINHARD ACKERMANN; 950 mems.

Gesamtverband der Textilindustrie in der BRD (Gesamttextil) eV (Textiles): 6000 Frankfurt a.M. 70, Schaumainkai 87; tel. (069) 633040; telex 411034; Pres. WOLF DIETER KRUSE; Dir-Gen. Dr KONRAD NEUNDÖRFER.

FEDERAL REPUBLIC OF GERMANY

Hauptverband der Deutschen Bauindustrie eV (Building): 6200 Wiesbaden, Abraham-Lincoln-Str. 30, Postfach 2966; tel. (06121) 7720; telex 4186147; 5300 Bonn 1, Am Hofgarten 9; tel. (0228) 267090; telex 886881; f. 1948; Pres. Dr-Ing. GÜNTHER HERION; Dir-Gen. HORST FRANKE; 16 mem. asscns.

Hauptverband der Deutschen Holzindustrie und verwandter Industriezweige eV (Woodwork): 6200 Wiesbaden 1, An den Quellen 10, Postfach 2928; tel. (06121) 39305; telex 4186631; f. 1948; Pres. Dr Senator HEINZ GOTSCHY; Dir HORST PRIEPNITZ; 28 mem. asscns, 4,000 mems.

Hauptverband der Papier, Pappe und Kunststoffe verarbeitenden Industrie eV (HPV) (Paper, Board and Plastic): 6000 Frankfurt a.M. 1, Arndtstr. 47; tel. (069) 740311; telex 411925; f. 1948; 10 regional groups, 20 production groups; Pres. RICHARD DOHSE; Dirs-Gen. Dr HORST KOHL, DIETER VON TEIN; 1,300 mems.

Mineralölwirtschaftsverband eV (Petroleum): 2000 Hamburg 1, Steindamm 71; tel. (040) 2854-0; telex 2162257; f. 1946; Chair. Dr HELLMUTH BUDDENBERG; Man. Dir Dr FRANK SCHMIDT.

Verband der Automobilindustrie eV (Motor Cars): 6000 Frankfurt a.M. 17, Westendstr. 61, Postfach 170563; tel. (069) 7570-1; telex 411293; Pres. Dr ERIKA EMMERICH.

Verband der Chemischen Industrie eV (Chemical Industry): 6000 Frankfurt a.M. 1, Karlstr. 21; tel. (069) 2556-0; telex 411372; f. 1877; Pres. Dr HELMUT SIHLER; Dir-Gen. Dr WOLFGANG MUNDE; 1,500 mems.

Verband der Cigarettenindustrie (Cigarettes): 2000 Hamburg 13, Harvestehuder Weg 88; tel. (040) 414009-0; telex 215044; Chair. GÜNTER WILLE; Dir-Gen. Dr HARALD KÖNIG.

Verband der deutschen feinmechanischen und optischen Industrie eV (Optical and Precision Instruments): 5000 Cologne 1, Pipinstr. 16; tel. (0221) 219458; telex 8882226; f. 1949; Chair. Dipl.-Ing. GUNTER SIEGLIN; Dir Dipl.-Kfm. HARALD RUSSEGGER.

Verband Deutscher Maschinen- und Anlagenbau eV (VDMA) (Machinery and Plant Manufacture): 6000 Frankfurt a.M. 71 (Niederrad), Lyoner Str. 18, Postfach 710864; tel. (069) 66030; telex 411321; f. 1892; Pres. Dr FRANK PAETZOLD; Gen. Man. Dr JUSTUS FÜRSTENAU.

Verband Deutscher Papierfabriken eV (Paper): 5300 Bonn 1, Adenauerallee 55; tel. (0228) 26705-0; telex 886767; Pres. CARL LUDWIG Graf VON DEYM; Dir-Gen. Dr OSCAR HAUS.

Verband für Schiffbau und Meerestechnik eV (Shipbuilding): 2000 Hamburg 1, An der Alster 1; tel. (040) 246205; telex 2162496; Pres. Dr jur. NORBERT HENKE; Gen. Man. Dipl.-Kfm. WERNER FANTE.

Verein der Zuckerindustrie (Sugar): 5300 Bonn 1, Am Hofgarten 8, Postfach 2545; tel. (0228) 22850; telex 886718; f. 1850; Chair. JASPAR Freiherr VON MALTZAN; Dir-Gen. Dr KONRAD DANKOWSKI.

Wirtschaftsverband der Deutschen Kautschukindustrie eV (W.d.K.) (Rubber): 6000 Frankfurt a.M. 90, Zeppelinallee 69; tel. (069) 79360; telex 411254; f. 1894; Pres. WOLFGANG TRAUTWEIN; Gen. Man. KLAUS MOCKER; 94 mems.

Wirtschaftsverband Erdöl- und Erdgasgewinnung eV (Association of Crude Oil and Gas Producers): 3000 Hanover, Brühlstr. 9; tel. (0511) 327648; telex 921462; f. 1945; Pres. Prof. Dr-Ing. HEINO LÜBBEN; Gen. Man. Dr GÜNTER FUCHS.

Wirtschaftsverband Stahlbau und Energietechnik (SET) (Steel and Energy): 5000 Cologne 1, Ebertplatz 1; tel. (0221) 7731117; Chair. Dipl.-Ing. FRITZ ADRIAN; Dir-Gen. Dr rer. pol. HANS-GEORG KIERA.

Wirtschaftsverband Stahlverformung eV (Steelworks): 5800 Hagen-Emst, Goldene Pforte 1, Postfach 4009; tel. (02331) 51041; telex 823806; Pres. Dr-Ing. JOCHEN F. KIRCHHOFF; Dir-Gen. Dr HERMANN HASSEL.

Wirtschaftsvereinigung Bergbau eV (Mining): 5300 Bonn 1, Zitelmannstr. 9–11, Postfach 120280; tel. (0228) 540020; telex 8869566; Pres. Bergass. a.D. Dr-Ing. E.h. FRIEDRICH CARL ERASMUS; Gen. Mans KARL-HEINRICH JAKOB, Dr-Ing. HARALD KLIEBHAN; 16 mem. asscns.

Wirtschaftsvereinigung Eisen- und Stahlindustrie (Iron and Steel): 4000 Düsseldorf 1, Breitestr. 69, Postfach 8705; tel. (0211) 8291; telex 8582286; Pres. Dr RUPRECHT VONDRAN; Dir ALBRECHT KORMANN.

Wirtschaftsvereinigung Metalle eV (Metal): 4000 Düsseldorf 30, Tersteegenstr. 28, Postfach 8706; tel. (0211) 45471-0; telex 8584721; Pres. Dr JÜRGEN HERAEUS; Dir-Gen. JÜRGEN ULMER.

Wirtschaftsvereinigung Ziehereien und Kaltwalzwerke eV (Metal): 4000 Düsseldorf 30, Drahthaus, Kaiserswerther Str. 137; tel. (0211) 4564-246; Chair. HANS MARTIN WÄLZHOLZ-JUNIUS; Gen.-Man. GÜNTER MÜLLER.

Zentralverband Elektrotechnik- und Elektronik-industrie (ZVEI) eV (Electrical and Electronic Equipment): 6000 Frankfurt a.M. 70, Stresemannallee 19, Postfach 701261; tel. (069) 6302-1; telex 411035; f. 1918; Chair. Dr-Ing. KARLHEINZ KASKE; Dirs Prof. Dr RUDOLF SCHEID, Dr BODO BÖTTCHER (Economic and Commercial), RUDOLF WINCKLER (Technical); 1,200 mems.

CONSULTATIVE ASSOCIATIONS

(See also under Bankers' Organizations, Chambers of Industry and Commerce, etc.)

Gemeinschaftsausschuss der Deutschen gewerblichen Wirtschaft (Joint Committee for German Industry and Commerce): 5300 Bonn 1, Adenauerallee 148; tel. (0228) 1040; telex 886805; f. 1950; a discussion forum for the principal industrial and commercial organizations; Pres. OTTO WOLFF VON AMERONGEN; 15 mem. organizations, including:

Centralvereinigung Deutscher Handelsvertreter- und Handelsmakler-Verbände (CDH): 5000 Cologne 41, Geleniusstr. 1; tel. (0221) 514043; telex 8881743; Pres. NORBERT HOPF; Gen. Sec. ERNST H. HAUMANN; 31,000 mems in all brs.

Deutscher Hotel- und Gaststättenverband eV: 5300 Bonn 2, Kronprinzenstr. 46; tel. (0228) 820080; telex 885489; f. 1949; Pres. LEO IMHOFF; Gen. Sec. Dr EGON HEIDER; over 90,000 mems.

Zentralverband des Deutschen Handwerks: 5300 Bonn 1, Haus des Deutschen Handwerks, Johanniterstr. 1; tel. (0228) 545-0; telex 886338; f. 1949; Pres. Dipl. Ing. HERIBERT SPÄTH; Gen. Sec. Dr KLAUS-JOACHIM KÜBLER; 42 mem. chambers, 57 asscns.

EMPLOYERS' ASSOCIATION

Bundesvereinigung der Deutschen Arbeitgeberverbände (Confederation of German Employers' Associations): 5000 Cologne 51, Postfach 510508, Gustav-Heinemann Ufer 72; tel. (0221) 37950; telex 8881466; Pres. Dr KLAUS MURMANN; Dirs Dr ERNST-GERHARD ERDMANN, Dr FRITZ-HEINZ HIMMELREICH, Dr WERNER DOETSCH; affiliates 12 regional associations, and 46 trade associations, of which some are listed under industrial associations (see above).

Affiliated associations:

Arbeitgeberkreis Gesamttextil im Gesamtverband der Textilindustrie in der Bundesrepublik Deutschland eV (General Textile Employers' Organization): 6000 Frankfurt a.M. 70, Schaumainkai 87; tel. (069) 63304-0; telex 411034; Chair. Dr PETER FROWEIN; Dir Dr KLAUS SCHMIDT; 7 mem. asscns.

Arbeitgeberverband der Cigarettenindustrie (Employers' Association of Cigarette Manufacturers): 2 Hamburg 13, Harvestehuder Weg 88; tel. (040) 4140090; telex 215044; f. 1949; Pres. Prof. Dr ERNST ZANDER; Dir Dr JOACHIM SCHWAHN.

Arbeitgeberverband der Deutschen Binnenschiffahrt eV (Employers' Association of German Inland Waterway Transport): 4100 Duisburg 13, Dammstr. 15–17; tel. (0203) 800060; telex 855692; Pres. Dr G. W. HULSMAN; Dir G. DÜTEMEYER.

Arbeitgeberverband Deutscher Eisenbahnen eV (German Railway Employers' Association): 5000 Cologne, Volksgartenstr. 54A; tel. (0221) 313980; Pres. HANSJÖRG KRAFT; Dir Dr HELMUT DEPENHEUER.

Arbeitgeberverband des Privaten Bankgewerbes eV (Private Banking Employers' Association): 5 Cologne, Mohenstr. 35-41; tel. (0221) 131024; f. 1954; 155 mems; Pres. Dr CHRISTIAN SEIDEL; Dir Dr KLAUS DUTTI.

Arbeitgeberverband der Versicherungsunternehmen in Deutschland (Employers' Association of Insurance Companies): 8000 Munich 22, Bruderstr. 9; tel. (089) 2368080; telex 524713; Pres. Dr PETER VON BLOMBERG; Dir-Gen. Dr JÜRGEN WILLICH.

Bundesarbeitgeberverband Chemie eV (Federation of Employers' Associations in the Chemical Industry): 6200 Wiesbaden, Abraham-Lincoln-Str. 24, Postfach 1280; tel. (06121) 719016; telex 4186646; Pres. Dr DIETER SCHLEMMER; Dir Dr KARL MOLITOR; 12 mem. asscns.

Bundesvereinigung der Arbeitgeber im Bundesverband Bekleidungsindustrie eV (Confederation of Employers of the Clothing Industry): 5 Cologne 1, Mevissenstr. 15; tel. (0221) 77440; telex (17) 22150803; Pres. GUSTAV ADOLF PASS; Dir RAINER MAUER; 10 mem. asscns.

Gesamtverband der Deutschen Land- und Forstwirtschaftlichen Arbeitgeberverbände eV (Federation of Agricultural and Forestry Employers' Associations): 53 Bonn 2, Godesberger Allee 142–148, Postfach 200454; tel. (0228) 376955; telex 885586; Pres. ODAL VON ALTEN-NORDHEIM; Dir Dipl.-Volksw. Dipl.-Landw. MARTIN MALLACH; 13 mem. asscns.

Gesamtverband der metallindustriellen Arbeitgeberverbände eV (Federation of the Metal Trades Employers' Associations): 5000 Cologne 1, Volksgartenstr. 54A; tel. (0221) 33990; telex

FEDERAL REPUBLIC OF GERMANY

8882583; Pres. Dr WERNER STUMPFE; Dir Dr DIETER KIRCHNER; 13 mem. asscns.

Vereinigung der Arbeitgeberverbände der Deutschen Papierindustrie eV (Federation of Employers' Associations of the German Paper Industry): 5300 Bonn, Adenauerallee 55; tel. (0228) 222066; telex 886767; Pres. Dr WOLFGANG FROMEN; Dir RA. ANSGAR PAWELKE; 8 mem. asscns.

Vereinigung der Arbeitgeberverbände energie- und versorgungswirtschaftlicher Unternehmungen (Employers' Federation of Energy and Power Supply Enterprises): 3000 Hanover, Kurt Schumacher-Str. 24; tel. (0511) 323405; f. 1962; Pres. ULRICH HARTMANN; Dir GERHARD M. MEYER; 6 mem. asscns.

Regional employers' associations:

Landesvereinigung Baden-Württembergischer Arbeitgeberverbände eV: 7000 Stuttgart 1, Hölderlinstr. 3A, Postfach 527; tel. (0711) 294753; telex 723651; Pres. HELMUT EBERSPÄCHER; Dir HERFRIED HEISLER; 44 mem. asscns.

Vereinigung Badischer Unternehmerverbände eV (Association of Industry in Baden): 7800 Freiburg i. Br., Lerchenstr. 6; tel. (0761) 31734; telex 772876; Pres. RICHARD H. CLASS; Dir WERNER RUDOLPH; 17 mem. asscns.

Vereinigung der Arbeitgeberverbände in Bayern (Federation of Employers' Associations in Bavaria): 8000 Munich 2, Briennerstr. 7, Postfach 202527; tel. (089) 228211; telex 523457; f. 1949; Pres. HUBERT STÄRKER; Dir KARL BAYER; 80 mem. asscns.

Zentralvereinigung Berliner Arbeitgeberverbände (Federation of Employers' Associations in Berlin): 1000 Berlin 12, Am Schillertheater 2; tel. (030) 310050; telex 184366; Pres. KLAUS OSTERHOF; Dir Dr HARTMANN KLEINER; 50 mem. asscns.

Vereinigung der Arbeitgeberverbände im Lande Bremen eV (Federation of Employers' Associations in the Land of Bremen): 2800 Bremen, Schillerstr. 10; tel. (0421) 36802-0; telex 244577; Pres. Dipl. Ing. PETER KLOESS; Dir EBERHARD SCHODDE; 14 mem. asscns.

Landesvereinigung der Arbeitgeberverbände in Hamburg eV (Federation of Employers' Associations in Hamburg): 2 Hamburg 13, Feldbrunnenstr. 56; tel. (040) 447486; telex (17) 403825; Pres. DIETER BONOW; Gen. Man. JÜRGEN MEINEKE; 23 mem. asscns.

Vereinigung der Hessischen Unternehmerverbände eV (Federation of Employers' Associations in Hesse): 6000 Frankfurt a.M. 90, Lilienthalallee 4; tel. (069) 79050; telex 412136; f. 1947; Pres. HERMANN HABICH; Dir and Sec. Dr HUBERT STADLER; 52 mem. asscns.

Unternehmerverbände Niedersachsen eV (Federation of Employers' Associations in Lower Saxony): 3000 Hanover 1, Schiffgraben 36; tel. (0511) 85050; telex 0929912; Pres. HERMANN BAHLSEN; Mans GERNOT PREUSS, GÜNTER SEIDE, Dr JÜRGEN WOLFSLAST; 58 mem. asscns.

Landesvereinigung der Arbeitgeberverbände Nordrhein-Westfalens eV (North Rhine-Westphalia Federation of Industrial Employers' Associations): 4000 Düsseldorf 30, Uerdingerstr. 58–62; tel. (0211) 45731; telex 8586864; Pres. Dr Ing. JOCHEN F. KIRCHHOFF; 86 mem. asscns.

Landesvereinigung Rheinland-Pfälzischer Unternehmerverbände eV (Federation of Employers' Associations in the Rhineland Palatinate): 6500 Mainz, Schillerplatz 7; tel. (06131) 232715; telex 4187741; f. 1963; Pres. Prof. Dr ROLF FILLIBECK; Man. Dr GÜNTHER HERZOG; 13 mem. asscns.

Vereinigung der Arbeitgeberverbände des Saarlandes eV (Federation of Employers' Associations in Saarland): 6600 Saarbrücken 6, Harthweg 15; tel. (0681) 51061; telex 4421229; Pres. Dipl. Ing. EDGAR STÖBER; Dir Dr KURT PHIELER; 18 mem. asscns.

Vereinigung der Schleswig-Holsteinischen Unternehmensverbände eV (Federation of Employers' Associations in Schleswig-Holstein): 2370 Rendsburg, Adolf-Steckel-Str. 17; tel. (04331) 5232; telex 29640; Pres. Dr DIETRICH SCHULZ; Dir Dr WOLFGANG DE HAAN; 37 mem. asscns.

TRADE UNIONS

Deutscher Gewerkschaftsbund (DGB): 4 Düsseldorf 30, Hans-Böckler-Str. 39, Postfach 2601; tel. (0211) 43010; telex 8584819; f. 1949; Pres. ERNST BREIT; Vice-Pres. GERD MUHR, GUSTAV FEHRENBACH.

The following unions, with a total of 7,757,039 (Dec. 1987) members, are affiliated to the DGB:

Industriegewerkschaft Bau-Steine-Erden (Building and Construction Trade): 6000 Frankfurt a.M., Bockenheimer Landstr. 73–77; tel. (069) 7437-0; telex 412826; Pres. KONRAD CARL; 465,000 mems (Oct. 1988).

Industriegewerkschaft Bergbau und Energie (Mining and Energy): 4630 Bochum, Alte Hattingerstr. 19; tel. (0234) 3190; telex 825809; f. 1889; Pres. HEINZ-WERNER MEYER; 347,528 mems (Dec. 1987).

Industriegewerkschaft Chemie- Papier- Keramik (Chemical, Paper and Ceramics): 3 Hanover, Königswörther Platz 6; telex 922608; Pres. HERMANN RAPPE; 655,776 mems (Dec. 1987).

Industriegewerkschaft Druck und Papier (Printing and Paper): 7000 Stuttgart 1, Friedrichstr. 15, Postfach 102436; tel. (0711) 20181; telex (17) 711292; Pres. ERWIN FERLEMANN; 147,500 mems. (Dec. 1987).

Gewerkschaft der Eisenbahner Deutschlands (Railwaymen): 6 Frankfurt a.M., Beethovenstr. 12–16; tel. 75360; Pres. RUDI SCHÄFER; 340,000 mems (Dec. 1987).

Gewerkschaft Erziehung und Wissenschaft (Education and Sciences): 6 Frankfurt a.M., Unterlindau 58; tel. (069) 720096; telex 412989; Pres. Dr DIETER WUNDER; 188,861 mems (Dec. 1987).

Gewerkschaft Gartenbau, Land- und Forstwirtschaft (Horticulture, Agriculture and Forestry): 3500 Kassel 1, Druselstalstr. 51, Postfach 410180; tel. (0561) 34060; telex 99630; f. 1909; Pres. GÜNTER LAPPAS; 42,253 mems (Dec. 1987).

Gewerkschaft Handel, Banken und Versicherungen (Commerce, Banks and Insurance): 4 Düsseldorf 30, Tersteegenstr. 30; telex 8584653; f. 1973; Pres. LORENZ SCHWEGLER; 385,166 mems (Dec. 1987).

Gewerkschaft Holz und Kunststoff (Wood and Plastic-work): 4000 Düsseldorf, Sonnenstr. 14; tel. (0211) 786461; telex 2114218; f. 1945; Pres. HORST MORICH; 143,272 mems (Oct. 1988).

Gewerkschaft Kunst (Art): 4000 Düsseldorf 30, Hans-Böckler-Str. 39; tel. (0211) 4301-334; Pres. ALFRED HORNE; 29,404 mems (June 1988).

Gewerkschaft Leder (Leather): 7000 Stuttgart 1, Willi-Bleicher-Str. 20; tel. (0711) 295555; Pres. WERNER DICK; 47,800 mems (Dec. 1987).

Industriegewerkschaft Metall (Metal Workers' Union): 6 Frankfurt a.M., Wilhelm-Leuschner-Str. 79–85; tel. (069) 26471; telex 411115; Chair. FRANZ STEINKÜHLER; 2,609,247 mems (Dec. 1987).

Gewerkschaft Nahrung- Genuss- Gaststätten (Food, Delicacies and Catering): 2 Hamburg 1, Gertrudenstr. 9; telex 2161884; f. 1949; Pres. GÜNTER DÖDING; 267,500 mems (Dec. 1987).

Gewerkschaft Öffentliche Dienste, Transport und Verkehr (Public Services and Transport Workers' Union): 7000 Stuttgart 1, Theodor Heuss-Str. 2; telex 723302; Chair. Dr MONIKA WULF-MATHIES; 1,202,629 mems (Dec. 1987).

Gewerkschaft der Polizei (Police Union): 4010 Hilden, Forststr. 3A; tel. (0211) 71040; telex 8581968; f. 1950; Chair. HERMANN LUTZ; Sec. W. DICKE; 158,888 mems (Dec. 1987).

Deutsche Postgewerkschaft (Postal Union): 6000 Frankfurt a.M. 71, Rhonestr. 2; tel. (069) 66951; telex 412112; Pres. KURT VAN HAAREN; 463,757 mems (Dec. 1987).

Gewerkschaft Textil-Bekleidung (Textiles and Clothing): 4 Düsseldorf 30, Ross Str. 94; Pres. BERTHOLD KELLER; 254,417 mems (Dec. 1987).

The following are the largest unions outside the DGB:

Deutsche Angestellten-Gewerkschaft (DAG) (Clerical, Technical and Administrative Workers): 2 Hamburg 36, Karl-Muck-Platz 1; tel. (040) 349150; telex 211642; f. 1945; Chair. ROLAND ISSEN; 494,126 mems (1987).

Deutscher Beamtenbund (Federation of Civil Servants): 5300 Bonn 2, Dreizehnmorgenweg 36; tel. (0228) 8110; f. 1918; Pres. WERNER HAGEDORN; 785,576 mems (1987).

TRADE FAIRS

More than 80 trade fairs take place annually in the Federal Republic. Fair organizers include:

Berlin: AMK Berlin Ausstellungs-Messe-Kongress-GmbH, Messedamm 22, 1000 Berlin 19; tel. (030) 30381; telex 182908; Man. Dirs Dr MANFRED BUSCHE, Dr WOLFGANG WEGMANN.

Cologne: Messe- und Ausstellungs GmbH, 5000 Cologne 21, Postfach 210760; tel. (0221) 821-1; telex 8873426.

Düsseldorf: Düsseldorfer Messe GmbH–NOWEA, Postfach 320203, 4000 Düsseldorf 30; tel. (0211) 456001; telex 8584853.

Essen: Messe Essen GmbH, Norbertstr., Postfach 100165, 4300 Essen 1; tel. (0201) 7244-0; telex 8579647.

Frankfurt: Messe Frankfurt GmbH, Postfach 970126, 6000 Frankfurt a.M. 1; tel. (069) 7575-0; telex 411558; f. 1907; Chair. EIKE MARKAU.

Friedrichshafen: Internationale Bodensee-Messe GmbH, Messegelände, 7990 Friedrichshafen 1; tel. (07541) 708-0; telex 734315.

Hamburg: Hamburg Messe und Kongress GmbH, Jungiusstr. 13, 2000 Hamburg 36; tel. (040) 3569-0; telex 212609; f. 1973; multipurpose congress centre with 17 halls and conference rooms; Dir Conventions Joachim Dieterich.

Hanover: Deutsche Messe- und Ausstellungs-AG, Messegelände, 3000 Hanover 82; tel. (0511) 891; telex 922728.

Karlsruhe: Karlsruher Kongress- und Ausstellungs GmbH, Postfach 1208, 7500 Karlsruhe 1; tel. (0721) 37200.

Munich: Münchener Messe- und Ausstellung GmbH, Messegelände, Postfach 121009, 8000 Munich 12; tel. (089) 51070; telex 5212086.

Nuremberg: NMA Nürnberger Messe- und Ausstellungs GmbH, Messezentrum, 8500 Nuremberg 50; tel. (0911) 8606-0; telex 623613; f. 1974; Dir Dr Hartwig Hauck.

Offenbach: Offenbacher Messe GmbH, Postfach 101423, 6050 Offenbach/M. 1; tel. (069) 817091; telex 411298.

Saarbrücken: Saarmesse GmbH, Messegelände, 6600 Saarbrücken; tel. (0681) 53056.

Stuttgart: Stuttgarter Messe- und Kongress-GmbH, Am Kochenhof 16, Postfach 103252, 7000 Stuttgart 10; tel. (0711) 25890; telex 722584.

Wiesbaden: Heckmann GmbH, Kapellenstr. 47, 6200 Wiesbaden; tel. (06121) 58040; telex 4186518.

Transport

RAILWAYS

In 1986 German Federal Railways controlled 27,484 km of standard gauge track, of which 11,433 km were electrified.

Deutsche Bundesbahn (DB) (German Federal Railways): 6000 Frankfurt a.M., Friedrich-Ebert-Anlage 43–45; tel. (069) 2651; telex 414087; Pres. Dr.-Ing. Reiner Gohlke; Chair. H. Wertz.

Metropolitan Railway

Berliner Verkehrs-Betriebe (Berlin Transport Authority—West Berlin): 1000 Berlin 30, Potsdamer Str. 188; tel. (030) 2561; telex 183329; operates 108.2 km of underground railway and 71.5 km of 'S-Bahn' railway; also runs bus services; Dirs Dipl. Ing. Helmut Döpfer, Willi Diedrich, Harro Sachsse.

Stadtwerke München: 8000 Munich 80, Einsteinstr. 28, Postfach 202222; tel. (089) 2191-1; telex 522063; underground (47 km), tramway (87.7 km), omnibus (401.8 km); Dir Dipl.-Ing. Dieter Buhmann.

Associations

BDE Bundesverband Deutscher Eisenbahnen, Kraftverkehre und Seilbahnen (Union of Non-Federal Railways, Bus-Services and Cable-Ways): 5000 Cologne 1, Hülchrather Str. 17; tel. (0221) 730021; Pres. Dieter Ludwig; Dir Manfred Montada.

Verband Öffentlicher Verkehrsbetriebe eV (VÖV) (Association of Public Transport): 5000 Cologne 1, Kamekestr. 37–39; tel. 525064; telex 8881718; f. 1895; Pres. Dr Sattler; Sec. Prof. Dr-Ing. Girnau.

ROADS

In December 1986 there were 492,478 km of classified roads, including 8,437 km of motorway, 31,368 km of other main roads and 63,382 km of secondary roads.

Zentralarbeitsgemeinschaft des Strassenverkehrsgewerbes eV (ZAV) (Central Association of the Road Transport Industry): 6 Frankfurt a.M. 93, Breitenbachstr. 1, Haus des Strassenverkehrs; tel. (069) 775719; telex 411627; Pres. Heinz Herzig; Gen. Sec. W. Neumann.

INLAND WATERWAYS

There are about 4,430 km of navigable inland waterways, and the Rhine-Main-Danube Canal, linking the North Sea and the Black Sea, is expected to be completed by 1992. Inland shipping accounts for more than 20% of total freight traffic.

Abteilung Binnenschiffahrt und Wasserstrassen (Federal Ministry of Transport, Inland Waterways Dept): 5300 Bonn 2, Kennedyallee 72; tel. (0228) 3001; telex 885700; deals with construction, maintenance and administration of federal waterways and with national and international inland water transport.

Associations

Bundesverband der deutschen Binnenschiffahrt eV: 4100 Duisburg 13, Dammstr. 15–17; tel. (0203) 800060; telex 855692; f. 1948; central Inland Waterway Association to further the interests of operating firms; Pres. Dr Karl Heinz Kühl; 5 Mans.

Hafenschiffahrtverband Hamburg eV: 2000 Hamburg 11, Mattentwiete 2; tel. 36128-0.

Verein für Binnenschiffahrt und Wasserstrassen eV (VBW): 4100 Duisburg 13, Dammstr. 15–17, Postfach 130 960; tel. (0203) 800060; formerly Zentral-Verein für deutsche Binnenschiffahrt eV and Verein zur Wahrung der Rheinschiffahrtsinteressen eV; an organization for the benefit of all branches of the inland waterways; Pres. Dr H. Zünkler; 6 Dirs.

SHIPPING

The principal seaports for freight are Bremen, Hamburg and Wilhelmshaven. Some important shipping companies are:

Christian F. Ahrenkiel GmbH & Co.: 2000 Hamburg 1, An der Alster 45; tel. (040) 28680; telex 2195580; tramp, shipowners and managers; 30 vessels, 523,000 grt.

Argo Reederei Richard Adler & Söhne: 2800 Bremen, Argo-Haus, Postfach 107529; tel. (0421) 3630725; telex 245206; Finland, United Kingdom; Propr Max Adler; 4 vessels, 15,300 grt.

Aug. Bolten Wm. Miller's Nachfolger: 2 Hamburg 11, Mattentwiete 8; tel. (040) 3601-1; telex 211431; tramp; 6 vessels, 105,700 grt.

Bugsier- Reederei- und Bergungs-Gesellschaft mbH: 2 Hamburg 11, Johannisbollwerk 10, Postfach 112273; tel. (040) 31110; telex 211228; salvage, towage, tugs, ocean-going heavy lift cranes, submersible pontoons, harbour tugs; liner services between continent/Denmark and UK and Ireland; Chief Officers B. J. Schuchmann, J. W. Schuchmann, A. Huettmann; 6 vessels, 26,500 grt.

DAL Deutsche Afrika-Linien GmbH & Co: 2000 Hamburg, Palmaille 45, Postfach 500 369; tel. (040) 380160; telex 212897-0; Europe, West, South and East Africa; Man. Dirs R. Brennecke, H. von Rantzau, Dr E. von Rantzau.

Deutsche Shell Tanker GmbH: 2000 Hamburg 60, Ueberseering 35, Postfach 600 520; tel. (40) 6341; telex 21970; 9 vessels; 530,322 grt.

Dohle, Peter, Schiffahrts-KG (GmbH & Co): 2000 Hamburg 50, Palmaille 33, Postfach 500440; tel. (040) 381080; telex 214444; Man. Dirs Peter Dohle, H.-G. Hölck, Jochen Dohle; shipbrokers, chartering agent for about 120 vessels, shipowners.

John T. Essberger: 2000 Hamburg 50, Palmaille 49, Postfach 500429; tel. (040) 380160; telex 212852; f. 1924; Man. Dirs L. v. Rantzau-Essberger, Dr E. von Rantzau, H. von Rantzau; 9 tankers, 12,792 grt.

Esso Tankschiff Reederei GmbH: 2000 Hamburg 60, Postfach 600640, Kapstadtring 2; tel. (040) 6331; telex 2174151; f. 1928; 13 tank barges.

Fisser & v. Doornum: 2 Hamburg 13, Feldbrunnenstr. 43, Postfach 132265; tel. (040) 44186211; telex 212671; f. 1879; tramp; Man. Dirs Dr Frank Fisser, Wulf v. Moltke; 22 vessels, 79,600 grt.

Johs. Fritzen & Sohn GmbH: 2970 Emden 1, Neptunhaus; tel. (04921) 20011; telex 27821; f. 1919; port agents, Lloyd's sub-agents, bunker agents.

Hamburg-Südamerikanische Dampfschiffahrts-Gesellschaft Eggert & Amsinck: 2000 Hamburg 11, Ost-West-Str. 59, Hamburg-Süd-Haus; tel. (040) 37050; telex 21321699; worldwide service; 19 vessels, 342,697 grt.

Hapag-Lloyd AG: 2000 Hamburg 1, Ballindamm 25 and 2800 Bremen, Gustav-Deetjen-Allee 2–6; tel. (040) 3030; telex 217002; f. 1970; USA East Coast, Canada, North Pacific (Euro-Pacific), US Gulf/South Atlantic (Combi Line), West Indies (Carol), Mexico, Venezuela, Colombia and Costa Rica (Euro-Caribbean), Central America/West Coast (German Central America Service), Northern Brazil, South America/West Coast, Far East (Trio Service) and China, Indonesia, Australia, New Zealand (Australia, New Zealand, Europe Container Service), and the Canary Islands; Chair. H.-J. Kruse; 20 vessels, 696,000 grt.

F. Laeisz Schiffahrts gmbH & Co: 2 Hamburg 11, Trostbrücke 1, Postfach 111111; tel. (040) 36881; telex (17) 403143; Dir Nikolaus W. Schües; Dir G. Heyenga; 3 refrigerated vessels, 7 containers, 2 bulk carriers, 2 bulk-container vessels, 250,000 grt.

Moller, Walther & Co: 2000 Hamburg 50, Thedestr. 2; tel. (040) 389931; telex 211523; 30 vessels.

Sloman Neptun Schiffahrts-AG: 2800 Bremen 1, Langenstr. 52+54, Postfach 1014 69; tel. (0421) 17630; telex 244421; f. 1873; Scandinavia, Western Europe, North Africa; gas carriers and heavy-lift vessels; seismic survey vessels; agencies, shiphandling, stevedoring; Mans Jürgen Willhöft, Werner Krieger, Herbert Juniel; 17 vessels, 43,570 grt.

Oldenburg-Portugiesische Dampfschiffs-Rhederei GmbH: 2000 Hamburg 11, Postfach 110869; tel. (040) 361580; telex 211110; f. 1882; Spain, Portugal, Mediterranean, Madeira, Algeria, Tunisia, Morocco, Canary Isles; Man. Dirs P. T. Hansen, J. Bergmann; 3 vessels, 6,000 grt; 2 vessels, 1,599 grt.

FEDERAL REPUBLIC OF GERMANY

Egon Oldendorff: 24 Lübeck, Fünfhausen 1; tel. (0451) 15000; telex 26411; Dirs H. OLDENDORFF, H. E. HELLMANN, G. ARNDT, E. L. GIERMANN, W. SCHARNOWSKI, K. WEIDEMANN; tramp; 29 vessels, 550,000 gross tonnage.

Rhein Maas und See-Schiffahrtskontor GmbH: 4100 Duisburg 13, Krausstr. 1A, Postfach 130780; tel. (0203) 8041; telex 855700; 68 vessels.

Ernst Russ: 2000 Hamburg 36, Alsterarkaden 27; tel. (040) 36840; telex 2150090; f. 1893; Europe, Scandinavia, worldwide; tramps; Dir ERNST-ROLAND LORENZ-MEYER; 7 vessels, 110,856 grt.

Schlüssel Reederei KG: 2800 Bremen 1, Am Wall 58/60, Postfach 10 18 47; tel. (0421) 170561; telex 244520; f. 1950; tramps; 3 vessels, 86,158 grt.

H. Schuldt: 2000 Hamburg 1, Ballindamm 8; tel. (040) 309050; telex 2161900; f. 1868; ship management; services to the USA; Gen. Mans E. SIEH, B. TODSEN; 7 vessels, 88,000 grt.

Seereederei "Frigga" GmbH: 2000 Hamburg 1, Ballindamm 17; tel. (040) 335782; telex 2161345; f. 1921; tramps; Dir E. EBERS; 2 vessels, 79,695 grt.

Hugo Stinnes Transozean Schiffahrt GmbH: 4330 Mülheim (Ruhr), Weseler Str. 60; telex 856714; liner service; Continent–West Africa; 9 vessels; 40,867 grt.

Thode, Johs.: 2000 Hamburg 50, Kohlbrandtreppe 2; tel. (040) 3802040; telex 211375; 50 vessels.

Tietjen, Wilhelm: 2000 Hamburg 50, Palmaille 35; tel. (040) 381171; telex 211342; 43 vessels.

Unterweser Reederei GmbH: 2800 Bremen 1, Blumenthalstr. 16, Postfach 100867; tel. (0421) 340085; telex 244179; f. 1890; Man. Dirs K. ESAU, M. SCHROIFF; 2 reduced draft supply vessels; 25 tugs.

Shipping Organizations

Verband Deutscher Küstenschiffseigner (German Coastal Shipowners Association): 2000 Hamburg-Altona, Grosse Elbstr. 36; tel. (040) 313435; telex 214444; f. 1896; Pres. Dr H. J. STÖCKER; Man. Dipl. sc. pol. KLAUS KÖSTER.

Verband Deutscher Reeder eV (German Shipowners' Association): 2000 Hamburg 36, Esplanade 6, Postfach 305580; tel. (040) 350970; telex 211407; Dir Dr BERND KRÖGER.

Verband für Schiffbau und Meerestechnik eV: 2000 Hamburg 1, An der Alster 1; tel. (040) 246205; telex 2162496; Pres. Dr jur. MICHAEL BUDCZIES; Gen. Man. Dipl.-Kfm. WERNER FANTE.

Zentralverband der Deutschen Seehafenbetriebe eV (Federal Association of German Seaport Operators): 2000 Hamburg 50, Grosse Elbstr. 14; tel. (040) 311561; f. 1932; Chair. HELMUTH KERN; Man. Dr LOTHAR L. V. JOLMES; approx. 850 mems.

CIVIL AVIATION

The major international airports are at Berlin (West), Cologne-Bonn, Düsseldorf, Frankfurt, Hamburg, Hanover, Munich and Stuttgart. Lufthansa has no landing rights at Berlin (West). More than 80 foreign airlines operate scheduled services to the Federal Republic and West Berlin.

Aero Lloyd Flugreisen GmbH & Co: Luftverkehrs KG, 6000 Frankfurt a.M. 1, Wilhelm-Leuschner-Str. 25, Postfach 160152; tel. (069) 25730; telex 4189372; f. 1981; charter services; Man. Dr W. SCHNEIDER; Dir Dr M. AKSMANOVIĆ; fleet of 3 Caravelle SE 210-10, 3 DC 9-32, 3 MD83, 2 MD-87.

Condor Flugdienst GmbH: Hans-Boeckler-Str. 7, 6078 Neu-Isenburg 1; tel. (06102) 2450; telex 417697; f. 1955; wholly-owned subsidiary of Lufthansa; charter and inclusive-tour services; fleet of 3 DC-10-30, 6 727-230, 5 737-230, 4 Airbus A310; Man. Dirs Dr MALTE BISCHOFF, Dr CLAUS GILLMANN, RUDOLF VON OERTZEN.

Deutsche Lufthansa AG: 5000 Cologne 21, Von-Gablenz-Str. 2–6; tel. (0221) 8261; telex 8873531; f. 1953; extensive world-wide network; Chair. Exec. Board HEINZ RUHNAU; Deputy Chair. Exec. Board Dipl. Ing. REINHARDT ABRAHAM; Chair. Supervisory Board GERD LAUSEN; fleet of 1 Airbus A300, 13 A310, 5 Boeing B747E, 14 B747D/G/H, 4 B747C, 22 B727B, 2 B737C, 40 B737D/E, 12 B737X, 5 Douglas DC8-73, 14 DC10-30.

DLT Deutsche Luftverkehrs-GmbH: 6000 Frankfurt a.M. 71, Lyonerstr. 14; tel. (069) 664004-20; telex 411643; scheduled services; Exec. Mans PETER ORLOVIUS, G. H. EBERHARD SCHMIDT; fleet of 6 HS 748, 2 Fokker 50, 10 Embraer 120.

GCS German Cargo Services GmbH: Lufthansa Cargo Centre, Airport, Postfach 750271, 6000 Frankfurt a.M. 75; tel. (069) 6905426; telex 4189142; f. 1977; wholly-owned subsidiary of Lufthansa; freight-charter world-wide; Mans K.-H. KÖPFLE, G. SCHMID; fleet of 5 DC8-73 F.

Germania Flug-GmbH: 5000 Cologne 90, Flughafen; tel. (02203) 401; telex 8873712; f. 1978; charter and inclusive-tour services; Man. Dr BISCHOFF; fleet of 2 Boeing 727-100; 2 737-300.

Hapag-Lloyd Flug-GmbH: 3000 Hanover 42, Flughafen; tel. (0511) 73030; telex 9230136; f. 1972; charter and inclusive-tour services; Man. Dir CLAUS WÜLFERS; fleet of 5 Airbus A 300B4, 1 A300C4, 4 Boeing 737-200, 2 Boeing 727-200, 1 727-100.

LTS Lufttransport-Unternehmen Süd AG & Co Fluggesellschaft: 8000 Munich 87, Flughafen München-Riem; tel. (089) 9211-8950; telex 5214762; f. 1983; charter; Dirs WERNER HÜHN, WOLFGANG PAULUS; fleet of 6 Boeing 757, 3 Boeing 767.

LTU Lufttransport-Unternehmen GmbH & Co KG: 4000 Düsseldorf 30, Flughafen Halle 8; tel. (0211) 41520; telex 8585573; f. 1955; charter; Man. WERNER HÜHN; fleet of 9 TriStar.

Tourism

Germany's tourist attractions include spas, summer and winter resorts, mountains, medieval towns and villages. The North Sea coast, the Rhine Valley, the Black Forest and Bavaria are the most popular areas. In 1985 there were around 1.8m. beds available for tourists. Overnight stays by foreign tourists totalled more than 28m. in 1985, when the total number of foreign tourists visiting the Federal Republic was 12.6m.

Deutsche Zentrale für Tourismus eV (DZT) (German National Tourist Board): 6000 Frankfurt a.M. 1, Beethovenstr. 69; tel. (069) 75720; telex 4189178; f. 1948; Dir-Gen. GÜNTHER SPAZIER.

Atomic Energy

Bundesministerium für Forschung und Technologie (Federal Ministry for Research and Technology): 5300 Bonn 2, Heinemannstr. 2, Postfach 200240; tel. (0228) 591; telex 885674; f. 1955; Minister Dr HEINZ RIESENHUBER.

The Ministry is divided into five departments, the first dealing with administration and establishment, the second with basic research, co-ordination of research, and international co-operation, the third with energy, biology and ecology, the fourth with information and production engineering and research on working conditions, and the fifth with aerospace, raw materials and geosciences.

The Ministry's responsibility in the nuclear energy field is to promote nuclear research and nuclear engineering as well as to plan and co-ordinate the activities of all of these bodies.

Nuclear research and development is carried out by the research centres of the following institutions in co-operation with universities and industry:

1. Kernforschungszentrum Karlsruhe GmbH, Karlsruhe (KfK).
2. Kernforschungsanlage Jülich GmbH, Jülich (KFA).
3. Max-Planck-Institut für Plasmaphysik (IPP) Garching bei München.
4. Gesellschaft für Strahlen- und Umweltforschung mbH, Munich (GSF).
5. GKSS-Forschungszentrum, Geesthacht GmbH.
6. Hahn-Meitner Institut GmbH, Berlin (HMI).
7. Deutsches Elektronen-Synchrotron (DESY), Hamburg.
8. Gesellschaft für Schwerionenforschung mbH, Darmstadt (GSI).

Nuclear power made a contribution of 31.3% to electricity supply in 1987. This proportion is to rise to about 35% by the year 2000. In December 1987 there were 21 nuclear power stations in operation, with a total generating capacity of almost 19m. kW.

Nuclear power stations in operation in 1986 were: the AVR Project at Jülich (North Rhine-Westphalia), with a capacity of 15 MW; the KWO Project at Obrigheim/Neckar (Baden-Württemberg), with a capacity of 345 MW; the KWW Project at Würgassen/Weser (North Rhine-Westphalia), with a capacity of 670 MW; the KKS Project at Stade/Elbe (Lower Saxony), with a capacity of 662 MW; the Biblis A and Biblis B Projects at Biblis/Rhein (Hessen), with respective capacities of 1,204 MW and 1,300 MW; the KKP Project at Philippsburg (Baden-Württemberg), with a capacity of 960 MW; the KKB Project at Brunsbuttel/Elbe (Schleswig-Holstein), with a capacity of 805 MW; the GKN I Project at Neckarwestheim/Neckar (Baden-Württemberg), with a capacity of 855 MW; the KNK II Project at Karlsruhe (Baden-Württemberg), with a capacity of 21 MW; the KKU Project at Esenshamm (Lower Saxony), with a capacity of 1,300 MW; the KKI I Project at Ohu/Isar (Bavaria), with a capacity of 907 MW; the KKK Project at Krümmel (Schleswig-Holstein), with a capacity of 1,316 MW; the KWG Project at Grohnde (Lower Saxony), with a capacity of 1,361 MW; the KKG Project at Grafenrheinfeld (Bavaria), with a capacity of 1,229 MW; the KRB IIB and C Projects at Gundremmingen (Bavaria), with a capacity of 1,310

FEDERAL REPUBLIC OF GERMANY

MW each; and the KBR Project at Brokdorf (Schleswig-Holstein), with a capacity of 1,365 MW.

Construction of the SNR-300 Project at Kalkar (North Rhine-Westphalia), with a capacity of 327 MW, and of the Mulheim-Kärlich Project (Rhineland Palatinate), with a capacity of 1,308 MW, was completed in the mid-1980s, but various problems have prevented their full operation. Four nuclear power plants were under construction in 1987: the THTR-300 Project at Hamm-Uentrop (North Rhine Westphalia), with a capacity of 308 MW; the KKI II Project at Ohu/Isar (Bavaria), with a capacity of 1,369 MW; the KKE Project at Emsland (Lower Saxony), with a capacity of 1,314 MW; and the GKN II Project at Neckarwestheim/Neckar (Baden-Württemberg), with a capacity of 1,300 MW.

In addition, ten more nuclear power plants are due to be constructed and start operation by the year 2000. Sites have been chosen at Biblis, Neupotz (two plants), Wyhl, Hamm, Pfaffenhofen, Vahnum (two plants) and Borken. These will have a total capacity of about 15,600 MW. The following nuclear power stations, which were demonstration plants and started operation in the mid-1960s, have been closed down: the KRB Project at Gundremmingen (Bavaria), with a capacity of 250 MW; the KWL Project at Lingen (Lower Saxony), with a capacity of 268 MW; and the VAK Project at Kohl/Main, with a capacity of 17 MW.

The use of nuclear energy has given rise to much controversy in the Federal Republic and various protest groups have been formed. In 1975 the Government started an information campaign, which aims to provide the public with information on nuclear energy and all related energy questions, including energy conservation. The Government of Chancellor Helmut Kohl is strongly in favour of the continuation of the nuclear energy programme, and several new projects have been proposed.

GHANA

Introductory Survey

Location, Climate, Language, Religion, Flag, Capital

The Republic of Ghana lies on the west coast of Africa, with Côte d'Ivoire to the west and Togo to the east. It is bordered by Burkina Faso to the north. The climate is tropical, with temperatures generally between 21°C and 32°C (70°–90°F) and average annual rainfall of 2,000 mm (80 in) on the coast, decreasing inland. English is the official language, but there are eight major national languages. Many of the inhabitants follow traditional beliefs and customs. Christians make up an estimated 42% of the population. The national flag (proportions 3 by 2) has three equal horizontal stripes, of red, gold and green, with a five-pointed black star in the centre of the gold stripe. The capital is Accra.

Recent History

Ghana was formed by a merger of the Gold Coast, a former British colony, and the British-administered part of Togoland, a UN Trust Territory.

In the Gold Coast a new constitution was issued in 1950. The first general election to the new Legislative Assembly, held in 1951, resulted in an overwhelming victory for the Convention People's Party (CPP), led by Dr Kwame Nkrumah, who became Prime Minister in 1952. In 1956, at a UN-supervised plebiscite, British Togoland voted to join the Gold Coast in an independent state. Ghana was duly granted independence, within the Commonwealth, on 6 March 1957, and thus became the first British dependency in sub-Saharan Africa to achieve independence under majority rule. Dr Nkrumah established an authoritarian regime, aiming to lead Ghana towards 'African socialism', and played a leading role in the Non-Aligned Movement. Ghana became a republic on 1 July 1960, with Dr Nkrumah as President. In 1964 the country became a one-party state, with the CPP as the sole authorized party. President Nkrumah established close relations with the USSR and other communist countries. On 24 February 1966 Nkrumah, whose repressive policies and financial mismanagement had caused increasing resentment, was deposed by the army and police. The coup leaders established the National Liberation Council (NLC), led by Gen. Joseph Ankrah. In April 1969, following disputes within the ruling NLC, Gen. Ankrah was replaced by Brig. (later Lt-Gen.) Akwasi Afrifa, who introduced a new constitution, which established a non-executive presidency. In August an election for a new National Assembly was held, and the Progress Party (PP), led by Dr Kofi Busia, won 105 of the 140 seats. Dr Busia was appointed Prime Minister, and the PP Government took office on 1 October 1969. A three-man commission, formed by NLC members, held presidential power until 31 August 1970, when Edward Akufo-Addo was inaugurated as civilian President.

In the wake of increasing economic and political difficulties, the army seized power again in January 1972. The Constitution was abolished and all political institutions were replaced by a National Redemption Council (NRC) under the chairmanship of Lt-Col (later Gen.) Ignatius Acheampong. In 1975 supreme legislative and administrative authority was transferred from the NRC to a Supreme Military Council (SMC), also led by Gen. Acheampong. In 1976 Gen. Acheampong announced plans for a return to civilian rule without political parties, in the form of 'union' government, in which it was envisaged that the military should continue to play a role, and a programme for return to civilian government by June 1979 was announced. In March 1978 a referendum resulted in a vote of 54% in favour of 'union' government. This result was largely discredited, and in July Acheampong's deputy, Lt-Gen. Frederick Akuffo, assumed power in a bloodless coup. Akuffo declared that the return to a popularly elected government would take place in 1979, as planned, and he introduced a number of civilians into the NRC. The six-year ban on party politics was lifted in January 1979, and 16 new parties were subsequently registered.

Only a fortnight before the elections were due to take place in June 1979, however, a coup was staged by junior officers of the armed forces, led by Flight-Lt Jerry Rawlings. Their main grievance was the fact that Ghana's military leaders would not be held responsible for economic mismanagement and corruption, as the draft constitution granted former rulers immunity from financial investigation. Under Rawlings, an Armed Forces Revolutionary Council (AFRC) took over power and began to eradicate corruption. A 'Revolutionary Court' found Acheampong, Akuffo, Afrifa and six other senior officers guilty of corruption, and they were executed.

Although the return to civilian rule was postponed until September 1979, the elections took place in June. The People's National Party (PNP) gained a majority of parliamentary seats, and its leader, Dr Hilla Limann, was elected President, taking office on 24 September 1979. In 1980 the United National Convention (UNC) ended its alliance with the PNP, leaving the latter with a majority of only one seat in Parliament. In 1981 the UNC joined three other parties to form the All People's Party, a viable alternative to the PNP.

Dissatisfaction with the Government culminated in December 1981, when Flight-Lt Rawlings again took power in a military coup, establishing a Provisional National Defence Council (PNDC), with himself as Chairman. The Council of State was abolished, the Constitution suspended, Parliament dissolved and political parties banned. City and district councils were dissolved in 1982 and replaced by People's Defence Committees (PDCs), designed to give the people a voice in the government of Ghana. They were renamed Committees for the Defence of the Revolution (CDRs) in 1984.

The PNDC's policies initially received strong support, but discontent with the regime and the apparent ineffectiveness of its economic policies took the form of a series of attempted coups, widespread student unrest and alleged anti-Government conspiracies. In December 1985 the chairman of the London-based Ghana Democratic Movement (GDM) was arrested in the USA, and was accused of participating in a conspiracy to purchase weapons for shipment to dissidents in Ghana. In 1986 nine people were sentenced to death for their alleged involvement in a conspiracy to overthrow the Government, and a former minister and presidential candidate, Victor Owusu (leader of the disbanded Popular Front Party), was arrested for alleged subversion. In June 1987 it was announced that several people had been arrested and that weapons had been seized, following the discovery of another plot to overthrow the PNDC. In response to increasing tension, members of trade unions and PNDC organizations were ordered to register their firearms. In November the detention of seven people, including leaders of the pro-PNDC organizations, the New Democratic Movement (NDM) and the Kwame Nkrumah Revolutionary Guards (KNRG), four of whom were former PNDC officials, was authorized in the interests of national security. In the same month two people were sentenced to 25 years' hard labour for their involvement in an attempted coup in 1983. The leader of the NDM was released from detention in December 1988.

In July 1987 the PNDC announced that elections for district assemblies would be held in late 1988. However, one-third of the 7,278 members of the district assemblies were to be selected by the Government, and the ban on political parties was to remain. These assemblies were to be 'the highest district political and administrative authorities', holding deliberative, political and executive power, and were regarded as the first stage in the development of a new political system of national democratic administration. In October and November 87% of eligible voters were registered for the forthcoming elections, and in April 1988 a further 0.4% of voters were registered in a supplementary registration exercise. In that month there was an extensive government reshuffle, in which a new post to co-ordinate the work of the CDRs was created, and new Secretaries for Information, Political Programmes and for the National Commission for Women and Development were appointed. The reshuffle was regarded as a move to prepare for the district assembly elections and as an attempt to assist public acceptance of the Government's Economic Recovery Programme (see Economic Affairs). During 1988 the number of districts was increased from 65 to 110, and in October districts were grouped within three electoral zones. Elections for the district assemblies in each zone were to be held in stages between December 1988 and February 1989. At the elections for district assemblies in the first zone, held on 6 December, an estimated 60% of registered voters participated.

After the 1983 coup in Upper Volta (now Burkina Faso), which brought Capt. Thomas Sankara to power, the Ghanaian Government established close links with the neighbouring state. In 1986 Ghana and Burkina Faso agreed to establish a high-level political body, which would be responsible for preparing a 10-year timetable for the political union of the two countries. The countries also agreed to harmonize their currencies, energy, transport, trade and educational systems, and a joint military exercise, 'Teamwork 1986', was held. Further joint exercises were held in mid-1987. However, Capt. Sankara was overthrown and killed in a military coup in October. This development was condemned by Ghana, but relations with Burkina Faso improved following meetings between Rawlings and Capt. Blaise Compaoré, Sankara's successor, in early 1988.

Relations with Togo deteriorated in 1986, after Ghanaian security forces captured a group of armed dissidents crossing the border from Togo. The Ghanaian Secretary for Foreign Affairs protested over the use of neighbouring territories as bases for subversive activities against Ghana. In September there was an attempted coup in Togo, and the Togolese Government claimed that the plotters came from Ghanaian territory, and were trained in Ghana and Burkina Faso. In Lomé, the Togolese capital, there was growing tension between Ghanaian immigrants and the Togolese, and between October and early December 233 Ghanaians were deported from Togo. The common border between the two countries was closed in October, but was reopened by Togo in February 1987 and by Ghana in May. Relations between the two countries became strained again in January 1989, when Togo expelled 120 Ghanaians.

Government

Upon its accession to power on 31 December 1981, the Provisional National Defence Council (PNDC) dissolved Parliament, abolished the Council of State and suspended the 1979 Constitution. Executive and legislative powers are vested in the PNDC, which rules by decree. Ghana comprises 10 regions, each administered by a Regional Secretary. Within the regions, there is a total of 110 administrative districts. The basic unit of local democracy is the Committee for the Defence of the Revolution (CDR). In December 1988, and in January and February 1989, elections were to be held for district assemblies. Each district assembly was to have an elected chairman, while the District Secretary was to remain responsible for the routine administration of the district and was to continue to be appointed by the PNDC.

Defence

In June 1988 Ghana had total armed forces of 10,600 (army 9,000, navy 800 and air force 800) and a paramilitary force of 5,000. Expenditure on defence in 1986 was 4,605m. cedis. The headquarters of the Defence Commission of the OAU is in Accra.

Economic Affairs

In 1987, according to estimates by the World Bank, Ghana's gross national product (GNP), measured at average 1985–87 prices, was US $5,328m., equivalent to $390 per head. It was estimated that GNP per head declined, in real terms, at an average rate of 2.0% per year between 1980 and 1987. Ghana's overall gross domestic product (GDP), measured in constant prices, increased at an average of 1.4% annually in 1965–80 but declined by 0.7% per year in 1980–86. There is considerable state participation in the major sectors of the economy. In 1986 some state enterprises were reorganized and partly 'privatized', in an attempt to increase efficiency in production and marketing, and legislation was introduced to allow the Government the right to acquire land for mineral exploration. In 1988 the Government sought to withdraw its ownership from 32 enterprises.

Ghana is primarily an agricultural country. In 1986 the agricultural sector (including forestry and fishing) employed an estimated 52.3% of the working population and accounted for about 45% of the country's GDP. In 1985 only 11.8% of the land area was cultivated, half of which was used to grow cocoa, the country's principal commercial crop, which provided 46% of export earnings in 1987. Ghana's harvest of cocoa beans declined from 470,000 metric tons in 1971/72 to 158,000 tons in 1983/84, owing to ageing and diseased trees, poor transport facilities, smuggling and adverse weather conditions. Production increased in subsequent years, and in 1986/87 reached an estimated 225,000 tons, but in 1987/88 output fell to 200,000 tons. Production was expected to rise in 1988/89. Earnings from exports of cocoa beans totalled an estimated US $430m. in 1988, but were expected to fall to only $370m. in 1989. A five-year cocoa rehabilitation programme, inaugurated in mid-1988, aimed to increase cocoa production to 300,000 tons per year by 1990. Incentives to cocoa producers were improved by increasing the official price payable to them for the 1987/88 season by 60%, to 140,000 cedis per ton, with a bonus of 10,000 cedis per ton where production targets were exceeded. The producer price of cocoa was increased to 165,000 cedis per ton for the 1988/89 season. In 1987 the Ghana Cocoa Board (COCOBOD) sold 52 of its 92 plantations, and its responsibility for maintaining rural roads was transferred to the Government. In the long term, COCOBOD's functions were to be confined to purchasing, marketing and providing extension facilities, while the private sector was to acquire its other functions, such as the provision of cocoa transport facilities.

Unfavourable weather conditions and the return, in 1983, of 1m. Ghanaian migrants from Nigeria have necessitated huge imports of staple foodstuffs and have increased Ghana's dependence on international aid. In 1986 imports of rice and maize were banned, following good harvests in 1985 and 1986. In June 1987, however, the ban was revoked, owing to a production shortfall, and external sources were expected to provide about 177,000 tons of foodstuffs. In September 1987 the Government introduced a four-year agricultural programme, which included proposals to 'privatize' certain services provided by the Secretariat for Agriculture and to reorganize its planning and research unit. In 1988 the Government announced higher producer prices for rice and maize, with the aim of increasing productivity.

The timber and mining industries are next in importance after agriculture, with hardwoods, gold, bauxite, manganese and diamonds as major sources of foreign exchange. Earnings from exports of logs and sawn timber increased from US $12.3m. in 1982 to $55m. in 1986, reaching $89.5m. in 1987. Owing to concern over the rapid depletion of Ghana's forest resources, a project aiming to improve the management of the forests, and to protect the environment, was initiated in 1989. In 1981 a project was adopted to revitalize the ailing gold-mining industry, as average monthly production had slumped to 5,000 troy ounces from 15,000 in the 1970s. By 1985 production had recovered to reach 327,000 troy ounces, and in 1987 output totalled 294,830 troy ounces. Export earnings from gold rose from $106m. in 1986 to $140m. in 1987. Ghana is seeking to develop its energy resources: offshore petroleum was discovered in 1970, and natural gas in 1980. Extraction of petroleum began from the Saltpond oilfield in January 1979, and by 1984 production of crude oil had reached 1,200 barrels per day, equivalent to 7% of the country's needs. The Ghana National Petroleum Corporation was established in 1983 to explore areas not covered by agreement with foreign companies. The country's largest petroleum refinery, at Tema, is being rehabilitated and enlarged to handle increased petroleum production.

Political instability and general mismanagement had a disastrous effect on the economy, and by the early 1980s there were large current deficits on the balance of payments, a rapidly increasing money supply, a high rate of inflation, a large external debt, high budget deficits and low reserves of foreign exchange. In late 1982 the Government launched the 1983–85 Economic Recovery Programme (ERP), and in 1983 the IMF agreed to provide financial assistance on condition that the cedi would be devalued within a year of the agreement. The cedi was subsequently devalued by more than 90% in November 1983. Three further devaluations were made in 1984, and three in 1985. The second three-year ERP (1986–88), introduced in 1985, aimed to achieve a significant rate of export growth. In 1986 the Government devalued the cedi by 33.3%, with the exchange rate adjusted from 60 to 90 cedis per US dollar. A weekly auction of foreign exchange to purchase imports was operated from September 1986. However, purchases of crude petroleum and essential drugs, debt servicing and cocoa revenue continued to be traded at the fixed rate of US $1 = 90 cedis. In February 1987 the two-tier market for foreign exchange was abolished, and all transactions were included in the weekly auction. The foreign-exchange market aimed to stimulate exports and domestic production. Between January and September 1987 the value of the cedi fell by 48.7% in relation to the US dollar.

In 1987 the second three-year ERP was supplemented by a medium-term structural adjustment programme (SAP) for 1987–90, which included policies to liberalize trade, to rehabilitate the cocoa sector, to control public expenditure and to reform state-owned enterprises, public-sector management, and the banking and finance sector. The SAP aimed to maintain GDP growth at 5% per year, to reduce the annual rate of inflation to 8% by 1990 and to generate balance-of-payments surpluses to finance external debt obligations. The SAP was partly financed by three World Bank credits (totalling $125.8m.), aid from external donors (totalling about $800m.) and a three-year arrangement, agreed with the IMF in November 1987, comprising an extended Fund facility of SDR 245.4m. and a structural adjustment loan of SDR 129.9m. In November 1988 the IMF agreed to replace the three-year arrangement with a three-year extended structural adjustment facility (ESAF) of SDR 368.1m.

By the late 1980s Ghanaian economic performance had improved, although in 1987 there was a temporary decline, caused by a shortfall in food production. The rate of inflation, which had reached 122.9% in 1983, declined to 25% in 1988 and was expected to fall to 15% in 1989. GDP growth reached 6% in 1988 and was expected to reach 5.5% in 1989. A surplus of US $21.7m. on the balance of payments was projected for 1988. However, in 1987 there was a trade deficit of $124.7m., compared with a surplus of $60.9m. in 1986. Reserves of foreign exchange declined from $541.6m. at mid-1987 to $172.1m. at 31 March 1988. Ghana's external debt stood at an estimated $2,600m. in November 1987.

The 1988 budget proposals projected revenue at 139,898m. cedis and expenditure at 136,296m. cedis. Personal income tax levels were reduced and import duties on small vehicles were abolished, although duties and purchase tax on certain categories of larger vehicles were reintroduced. In order to protect domestic industries, unified rates of sales tax were introduced for locally-made and imported goods. As part of a programme, introduced in 1988, to mitigate the social costs of the SAP, 40,000 new jobs were to be created in road rehabilitation and other public works schemes. According to the 1989 budget proposals, revenue was projected to rise by 34%, to 204,617m. cedis, while expenditure was expected to rise by 31%, to 196,191m. cedis. Revenue was to be increased by improving methods of tax collection and by introducing higher direct taxes on petroleum products, cigarettes and alcohol. Meanwhile, the basic rate of income tax was reduced, tax thresholds were raised and negotiations were initiated on the establishment of a national minimum wage. In accordance with the Government's liberalization policies under the SAP, import licences were abolished and importers were merely required to sign a declaration confirming that their transactions conformed with existing regulations.

Ghana is a member of ECOWAS (see p. 132). Overseas aid comes mainly from the EEC, particularly the United Kingdom and the Federal Republic of Germany, and also from the UN, Japan, the USA, Canada and the People's Republic of China.

Social Welfare

The Government provides hospitals and medical care at nominal rates, and there is a government pension scheme. There were 293 hospitals, health centres and posts and 60 private clinics in 1982. There were 1,665 physicians working in Ghana in 1981, although by 1984 the World Bank estimated that the number of doctors had fallen to 817. Ghana's shortage of foreign exchange has limited imports of medical equipment. Of total expenditure by the central Government in 1986, 5,854m. cedis (8.3%) was for health services, and a further 3,777m. cedis (5.3%) for social security and welfare. The 1986–88 Economic Recovery Programme was to provide 7,126m. cedis to expand health services, and aimed to make these services accessible to all Ghanaians by the year 2000.

Education

In April 1974 the NRC announced the introduction of a new educational structure, consisting of an initial phase of six years' primary education (beginning at six years of age), followed by three years' junior secondary education. All this schooling is free and, officially, compulsory. At the junior secondary schools a selection is made between senior secondary school courses, leading to examinations at the 'Ordinary' level of the General Certificate of Education, and technical and vocational courses. However, this system is being operated on an experimental basis, and more than 90% of children continue to follow the old educational system, consisting of six years' primary education and four years at a middle school. In 1985 enrolment at primary schools was equivalent to 63% of children in the relevant age-group, while the comparable ratio at secondary schools was 35%. In 1984 enrolment at primary schools was equivalent to 67% (75% of boys; 59% of girls), while the comparable ratio at secondary schools was 36% (45% of boys; 27% of girls). There are three universities. Expenditure on education by the central Government in 1986 was 16,905m. cedis (23.9% of total spending). The Programme of Action to mitigate the Social Costs of Adjustment (PAMSCAD), which was introduced in 1988, allocated 1,904m. cedis to education, to be invested in adult literacy programmes and the rehabilitation of school buildings. According to UNESCO estimates, the average rate of adult illiteracy in 1985 was 46.8% (males 35.9%; females 57.2%).

Public Holidays

1989: 2 January (for New Year's Day), 6 March (Independence Day), 24–27 March (Easter), 1 May (Labour Day), 5 June (Anniversary of the 1979 coup), 1 July (Republic Day), 25–26 December (Christmas), 31 December (Revolution Day).

1990: 1 January (New Year's Day), 6 March (Independence Day), 13–16 April (Easter), 1 May (Labour Day), 5 June (Anniversary of the 1979 coup), 1 July (Republic Day), 25–26 December (Christmas), 31 December (Revolution Day).

Weights and Measures

The metric system is in force.

Statistical Survey

Source (except where otherwise stated): Central Bureau of Statistics, POB 1098, Accra; tel. 66512.

Area and Population

AREA, POPULATION AND DENSITY

Area (sq km)	238,537*
Population (census results)	
1 March 1970	8,559,313
11 March 1984	12,205,574†
Population (UN estimates at mid-year)	
1985	12,840,000
1986	13,280,000
1987	13,704,000
Density (per sq km) at mid-1987	57.5

* 92,100 sq miles.   † Preliminary figures.

POPULATION BY REGION (1984 census*)

Western	1,116,930
Central	1,145,520
Greater Accra	1,420,065
Eastern	1,697,483
Volta	1,201,095
Ashanti	2,089,683
Brong-Ahafo	1,179,407
Northern	1,162,645
Upper East	771,584
Upper West	439,161
Total	**12,205,574**

* Preliminary figures.

Principal Ethnic Groups (1960 census, percentage of total population): Akan 44.1, Mole-Dagbani 15.9, Ewe 13.0, Ga-Adangbe 8.3, Guan 3.7, Gurma 3.5.

PRINCIPAL TOWNS (population at 1984 census)

Accra (capital)	964,879
Kumasi	348,880
Tamale	136,828
Tema	99,608
Takoradi	61,527
Cape Coast	57,700
Sekondi	32,355

BIRTHS AND DEATHS (UN estimates, annual averages)

	1970–75	1975–80	1980–85
Birth rate (per 1,000)	47.2	47.1	46.9
Death rate (per 1,000)	17.4	15.9	14.6

Source: UN, *World Population Prospects: Estimates and Projections as Assessed in 1984*.

ECONOMICALLY ACTIVE POPULATION (1970 census*)

	Males	Females	Total
Agriculture, hunting, forestry and fishing	1,038,468	773,634	1,812,102
Mining and quarrying	29,075	2,385	31,460
Manufacturing	168,918	214,761	383,679
Electricity, gas and water	11,984	459	12,443
Construction	73,495	2,708	76,203
Trade, restaurants and hotels	68,496	370,852	439,348
Transport, storage and communications	84,212	2,325	86,537
Financing, insurance, real estate and business services	7,651	1,877	9,528
Community, social and personal services	272,770	52,578	325,348
Total	**1,755,069**	**1,421,579**	**3,176,648**

* Figures exclude persons seeking work for the first time, totalling 154,970 (males 104,326; females 50,644), but include other unemployed persons, numbering 43,601 (males 37,141; females 6,460).

1980 (ILO estimates, '000 persons at mid-year): Agriculture, etc. 2,430; Industry 775; Services 1,148; Total labour force 4,353 (males 2,551, females 1,802). Source: ILO, *Economically Active Population Estimates and Projections, 1950–2025*.

Agriculture

PRINCIPAL CROPS ('000 metric tons)

	1984	1985	1986
Maize	575	411	471†
Millet	106	80*	130†
Sorghum	156	160*	210†
Rice (paddy)	66	90†	95†
Sugar cane*	90	110	110
Cassava (Manioc)	4,083	3,076†	3,692†
Yams*	880	900	937
Taro (Coco yam)	730	650*	650
Onions*	27	28	29
Tomatoes	300*	375	403*
Eggplants (Aubergines)*	20	24	24
Pulses*	11	11	11
Oranges*	35	35	37
Lemons and limes*	30	30	30
Bananas	15*	22	23*
Plantains	650*	677†	677*
Pineapples*	5	6	6
Palm kernels*	30	30	30
Groundnuts (in shell)	90*	128	129*
Coconuts	120*	108	108*
Copra*	7	7	7
Coffee (green)†	2	1	1
Cocoa beans	173†	212†	240
Tobacco (leaves)	2*	3	3*

* FAO estimate.   † Unofficial figure.
Source: FAO, *Production Yearbook*.

GHANA

Statistical Survey

LIVESTOCK ('000 head, year ending September)

	1984	1985	1986
Horses*	4	4	4
Asses*	25	25	25
Cattle	1,078	1,132	1,188
Pigs	407	489	586
Sheep†	1,850	2,100	2,175
Goats†	1,800	2,100	2,400

* FAO estimates.   † Unofficial figures.
Poultry (FAO estimates, million): 8 in 1984; 9 in 1985; 10 in 1986.
Source: FAO, *Production Yearbook*.

LIVESTOCK PRODUCTS (FAO estimates, '000 metric tons)

	1984	1985	1986
Beef and veal	15	16	16
Mutton and lamb	5	6	6
Goat meat	5	6	7
Pig meat	9	11	13
Poultry meat	8	9	11
Other meat	92	90	97
Cows' milk	9	9	10
Hen eggs	8.2	9.4	10.6
Cattle hides	1.9	2.0	2.1

Source: FAO, *Production Yearbook*.

Forestry

ROUNDWOOD REMOVALS ('000 cubic metres)

	1984	1985	1986*
Sawlogs, veneer logs and logs for sleepers	603	794	794
Other industrial wood*	381	381	381
Fuel wood*	7,951	8,212	8,493
Total	8,935	9,387	9,668

* FAO estimates.
Source: FAO, *Yearbook of Forest Products*.

SAWNWOOD PRODUCTION ('000 cubic metres)

	1983	1984	1985
Total (incl. boxboards)	210	220	302

Railway sleepers ('000 cubic metres): 65 per year (1983-85).
1986: Production as in 1985 (FAO estimates).
Source: FAO, *Yearbook of Forest Products*.

Fishing

('000 metric tons, live weight)

	1984	1985	1986
Inland waters*	40.0	40.0	40.0
Atlantic Ocean	232.5	234.2	269.2
Total catch	272.5	274.2	309.2

* Assumed to be unchanged since 1980.
Source: FAO, *Yearbook of Fishery Statistics*.

Mining

('000 metric tons, unless otherwise indicated)

	1985	1986	1987
Gold ore ('000 kg)	9.3	9.0	10.2
Diamonds ('000 carats)	636	599	44.0
Manganese ore	316	259	254
Bauxite	170	204	195

Crude petroleum (estimates, '000 metric tons): 92 in 1984; 94 in 1985 (Source: UN, *Industrial Statistics Yearbook*).

Industry

SELECTED PRODUCTS
('000 metric tons, unless otherwise indicated)

	1985	1986	1987
Wheat flour	45.3	62.8	71.4
Beer ('000 hectolitres)	429	546	589
Soft drinks ('000 crates)	718	658	1,355
Cigarettes (millions)	1,942	1,826	1,734
Motor spirit (petrol)	216.0	200.0	154.7
Kerosene	120.0	112.0	92.2
Diesel and gas oil	278.0	275.0	220.0
Cement	356.0	219.0	294.4
Electric energy (million kWh)	2,996.2	4,435.0	4,676.3

Aluminium (unwrought): 47,500 metric tons (primary metal) in 1985.

Finance

CURRENCY AND EXCHANGE RATES
Monetary Units
100 pesewas = 1 new cedi.

Denominations
Coins: ½, 1, 2½, 5, 10, 20 and 50 pesewas; 1 and 5 cedis.
Notes: 1, 2, 5, 10, 50, 100, 200 and 500 cedis.

Sterling and Dollar Equivalents (30 September 1988)
£1 sterling = 383.86 cedis;
US $1 = 227.00 cedis;
1,000 cedis = £2.605 = $4.405.

Average Exchange Rate (US $ per cedi)
1985   0.0185
1986   0.0112
1987   0.0068

GENERAL BUDGET (million cedis)

Revenue*	1984	1985	1986
Taxation	17,931	31,918	61,923
Taxes on income, profits, etc.	4,060	7,426	13,537
Domestic taxes on goods and services	5,620	8,592	19,778
General sales taxes	441	1,176	3,172
Excises	5,121	7,197	16,449
Taxes on international trade	8,242	15,824	28,467
Import duties	3,159	6 591	14,236
Export duties	4,974	9,172	14,231
Other current revenue	3,797	5,216	7,835
Operating surpluses of departmental enterprises	—	—	2,450
Property income	3,555	2,590	4,427
Fines and forfeits	225	1,009	478
Total	21,728	37,134	69,758

* Excluding grants received from abroad (million cedis): 914 in 1984; 1,620 in 1985; 3,868 in 1986.

GHANA

Statistical Survey

Expenditure†	1984	1985	1986
General public services	5,846	9,180	13,362
Defence	1,605	3,432	4,605
Education	5,387	8,238	16,905
Health	2,291	4,483	5,854
Social security and welfare	1,131	2,288	3,777
Housing and community amenities	571	915	1,366
Other community and social services	598	706	1,192
Economic services	5,053	10,888	11,099
Agriculture, forestry and fishing	1,321	2,831	3,199
Mining, manufacturing and construction	664	1,120	1,094
Roads	1,891	4,533	2,668
Other transport and communications	517	1,302	2,706
Other purposes	4,212	5,633	12,500
Interest payments	3,425	5,086	11,341
Total	26,694	45,763	70,660
Current	23,326	38,461	60,834
Capital	3,368	7,302	9,826

† Excluding net lending (million cedis): 791 in 1984; 2,127 in 1985; 2,667 in 1986.

Source: IMF, *Government Finance Statistics Yearbook*.

1987 (projections, million cedis): Revenue and grants 109,700; Expenditure and net lending 109,400.
1988 (projections, million cedis): Revenue and grants 139,898; Expenditure and net lending 136,296.
1989 (projections, million cedis): Revenue and grants 204,617; Expenditure and net lending 196,191.

INTERNATIONAL RESERVES (US $ million at 31 December)

	1985	1986	1987
Gold*	46.1	76.6	81.5
IMF special drawing rights	18.9	2.0	15.9
Foreign exchange	459.6	511.0	179.2
Total	524.6	589.6	276.6

* National valuation.

Source: IMF, *International Financial Statistics*.

MONEY SUPPLY (million new cedis at 31 December)

	1985	1986	1987
Currency outside banks	21,896.9	31,240.2	46,116.5
Official entities' deposits with monetary authorities	784.5	2,034.5	3,693.5
Demand deposits at commercial banks	20,789.7	31,344.9	42,041.8
Total money	42,686.6	64,619.6	91,851.8

Source: Research Dept, Bank of Ghana.

COST OF LIVING (Consumer Price Index for Accra; average of monthly figures. Base: 1977 = 100)

	1985	1986	1987
Food	2,407.3	2,871.5	4,068.0
Clothing	3,859.2	5,205.8	8,069.6
Rent, fuel and light	1,947.5	3,380.8	5,059.8
All items (incl. others)	3,282.7	4,262.8	6,156.0

NATIONAL ACCOUNTS (million new cedis at current prices)
National Income and Product

	1985	1986	1987
GDP in purchasers' values	343,048.4	511,372.7	745,999.8
Net factor income from abroad	−5,768.5	−12,576.0	−20,458.6
Gross national product	337,279.8	498,796.7	725,541.2
Less Consumption of fixed capital	16,338.8	29,267.1	47,679.8
National income in market prices	320,941.0	469,529.6	677,861.4
Other current transfers from abroad (net)	7,421.5	20,016.0	29,723.1
National disposable income	328,362.5	489,545.6	707,584.5

Expenditure on the Gross Domestic Product

	1985	1986	1987
Government final consumption expenditure	32,241.0	56,595.6	76,331.8
Private final consumption expenditure	284,621.0	421,849.4	608,801.4
Increase in stocks	138.9	340.1	554.1
Gross fixed capital formation	32,688.5	49,087.6	79,969.8
Total domestic expenditure	349,689.4	527,872.7	768,658.1
Exports of goods and services	33,185.0	98,148.0	153,836.7
Less Imports of goods and services	39,826.0	114,648.0	176,494.0
GDP in purchasers' values	343,048.4	511,372.7	745,999.8
GDP at constant 1975 prices	5,420.1	5,701.9	5,975.6

Source: Bank of Ghana.

BALANCE OF PAYMENTS (US $ million)

	1985	1986	1987
Merchandise exports f.o.b.	632.4	773.4	826.8
Merchandise imports f.o.b.	−668.7	−712.5	−951.5
Trade balance	−36.3	60.9	−124.7
Export of services	43.6	45.1	79.3
Import of services	−283.6	−343.6	−376.3
Balance of goods and services	−276.3	−237.6	−421.7
Private unrequited transfers (net)	32.6	72.1	201.6
Government unrequited transfers (net)	109.5	122.5	123.2
Current balance	−134.2	−43.0	−96.9
Direct capital investment (net)	5.6	4.3	4.7
Other long-term capital (net)	32.3	130.8	215.0
Short-term capital (net)	39.8	−82.9	23.3
Net errors and omissions	63.4	−81.3	−18.4
Total (net monetary movements)	6.9	−72.1	127.7
Monetization of gold (net)	−45.6	26.3	4.9
Valuation changes (net)	−71.7	−27.1	−472.5
Exceptional financing (net)	53.5	41.9	−61.9
Changes in reserves	−56.9	−30.9	−401.8

Source: IMF, *International Financial Statistics*.

GHANA

External Trade

PRINCIPAL COMMODITIES ('000 cedis)

Imports	1984	1985	1986
Food and live animals	1,171,275	1,892,025	47,218,134
Beverages and tobacco	249,163	733,592	20,508
Crude materials (inedible) except fuels	472,515	827,424	7,104,389
Mineral fuels, lubricants, etc.	7,603,686	13,786,621	3,158,337
Animal and vegetable oils and fats	268,308	301,553	6,352
Chemicals	1,895,506	5,896,401	42,146
Basic manufactures	2,983,427	5,060,600	7,649,155
Machinery and transport equipment	5,321,655	12,436,517	11,084
Miscellaneous manufactured articles	629,748	4,890,961	114,122
Other commodities and transactions	1,291,977	1,329,592	12,081,922
Total	21,887,260	47,155,286	77,406,149

Exports	1985	1986	1987
Cocoa	19,904,089	41,895,579	67,872,726
Logs	576,116	2,682,012	n.a.
Sawn timber	835,445	1,995,159	n.a.
Bauxite	147,802	547,412	851,442
Manganese ore	487,779	894,811	1,205,743
Diamonds	280,919	561,231	696,996
Gold	5,010,746	11,915,233	24,205,589
Total (incl. others)	33,185,000	76,948,000	147,275,000

PRINCIPAL TRADING PARTNERS ('000 cedis)

Imports	1983	1984*	1985*
Canada	75,958	122,554	384,680
China, People's Republic	54,397	199,847	445,812
France	217,012	395,804	1,036,690
Germany, Federal Republic	1,456,783	2,510,000	5,394,777
Italy	558,702	867,633	1,561,173
Japan	475,059	838,011	2,845,424
Libya	56,085	1,339	7,433
Netherlands	340,383	700,980	1,216,629
Nigeria	529,861	6,964,148	10,601,454
Norway	57,026	75,224	201,533
United Kingdom	2,580,179	3,689,357	11,843,832
USA	1,000,741	1,247,423	2,725,773
Total (incl. others)	11,021,818	20,871,000	39,826,000

Exports	1983	1984	1985*
Germany, Federal Republic	688,173	1,291,156	2,035,879
Japan	6,990,046	1,913,942	3,249,391
Netherlands	932,170	237,472	3,400,444
USSR	813,721	1,917,849	2,156,475
United Kingdom	1,009,065	3,230,081	6,806,297
USA	628,230	883,882	2,743,024
Yugoslavia	n.a.	89,522	328,770
Total (incl. others)	8,851,000	20,161,000	33,185,000

* Provisional figures.

Source: Ghana High Commission, London.

Transport

RAILWAYS (traffic)

	1985	1986	1987
Passengers carried ('000)	2,115	2,908	3,486
Freight carried ('000 metric tons)	509.6	600.2	593.4
Passenger-km (million)	190.3	255.1	566.8
Net ton-km (million)	77.2	100.0	106.2

ROAD TRAFFIC ('000 motor vehicles in use at 31 December)

	1983
Passenger cars	52,864
Buses and coaches	15,995
Goods vehicles	7,380

Source: International Road Federation, *World Road Statistics*.

INTERNATIONAL SEA-BORNE SHIPPING
(estimated freight traffic, '000 metric tons)

	1983	1984	1985
Goods loaded	1,120	1,190	1,036
Goods unloaded	2,522	2,596	2,496

Source: UN, *Monthly Bulletin of Statistics*.

CIVIL AVIATION (traffic on scheduled services)

	1982	1983	1984
Kilometres flown (million)	3.0	3.0	2.5
Passengers carried ('000)	230	271	261
Passenger-km (million)	291	338	276
Freight ton-km (million)	4.6	6.6	7.5
Mail ton-km (million)	0.6	0.4	2.2
Total ton-km (million)	31	37	34

Source: UN, *Statistical Yearbook*.

Tourism

	1985	1986	1987
Tourist arrivals ('000)*	54.3	55.1	41.2

* Excluding arrivals of Ghanaian nationals residing abroad (62,214 in 1987).

Source: Ghana High Commission, London.

Education

(1985)

	Institutions	Teachers†	Students
Pre-primary	2,399	10,218	171,182
Primary	9,004	64,795	1,410,718
Secondary*	5,589†	35,085	718,444
Teacher training	39†	1,011	15,169
Technical and vocational	22†	1,194	16,367
University†	3†	1,041	7,878

* Including Middle and Junior Secondary schools.
† 1984/85 figures.

Source: mainly UNESCO, *Statistical Yearbook*.

Directory

The Constitution

Following the coup in December 1981, the 1979 Constitution was suspended.

The Government

(February 1989)

HEAD OF STATE

Chairman of the Provisional National Defence Council: Flight-Lt JERRY RAWLINGS (took power 31 December 1981).

PROVISIONAL NATIONAL DEFENCE COUNCIL

Flight-Lt JERRY RAWLINGS (Chairman and Chief of Defence Staff).
Justice DANIEL F. ANNAN (Vice-Chair).
Mrs AANAA ENIN.
EBO TAWIAH.
Alhaji IDDRISU MAHAMA.
Capt. (retd) KOJO TSIKATA.
P. V. OBENG.
Lt-Gen. ARNOLD QUAINOO.
Maj.-Gen. W. M. MENSA-WOOD.

COMMITTEE OF SECRETARIES

Chairman of the Committee of Secretaries: P. V. OBENG.
Secretary for Fuel and Power: ATO AHWOI.
Secretary for Trade and Tourism: KOFI DJIN.
Secretary for Local Government and Rural Development: KWAMENA AHWOI.
Secretary for Internal Affairs: NII OKAIJA ADAMAFIO.
Secretary for Education and Culture: K. B. ASANTE.
Secretary for Youth and Sports: K. SAARAH-MENSAH.
Secretary for Foreign Affairs: Dr OBED ASAMOAH.
Secretary for Information: Dr MUHAMMAD BEN ABDALLAH.
Secretary for Transport and Communications: E. O. YAW DONKOR.
Secretary for Works and Housing: CHARLES BOADU (acting).
Secretary for Industry, Science and Technology: Dr FRANCIS ACQUAH.
Secretary for Justice and Attorney General: G. E. K. AIKINS.
Secretary for Agriculture: Cdre (retd) STEVE OBIMPEH.
Secretary for Roads and Highways: Lt-Col (retd) MENSAH GBEDEMAH.
Secretary for Finance and Economic Planning: Dr KWESI BOTCHWEY.
Secretary for Health: NANA AKUODO SARPONG.
Secretary for Lands and Natural Resources: KWAME PEPRAH.
Secretary for Mobilization and Productivity: HUNDO YAHAYA.
Secretary of Chieftaincy Affairs: EMMANUEL TANOH.

PROVISIONAL NATIONAL DEFENCE COUNCIL SECRETARIAT

Secretary responsible for the Committees for the Defence of the Revolution: WILLIAM YEBOAH.
Secretary responsible for the State Committee for Economic Co-operation: E. G. DON-ARTHUR.
Secretary responsible for the Committee of Cocoa Affairs: I. K. ADJEI-MARFO.
Secretary responsible for the National Commission for Democracy: JOYCE ARYEE.
Secretary responsible for the National Commission for Women and Development: SELINA TAYLOR.
Secretaries responsible for Political Programmes: KOFI TOTOBI QUAKYI, ATO DADZIE, YAW AKRASI-SARPONG.

REGIONAL SECRETARIES

Greater Accra: Lt-Col (retd) W. A. THOMSON.
Eastern: F. OHENE-KENA.
Volta: RICHARD SEGLAH.
Brong Ahafo: J. H. OWUSU-ACHEAMPONG.
Ashanti: Col (retd) E. M. OSEI-OWUSO.
Central: ATO AUSTIN.
Northern: JOHN BAWA.
Upper East: KUNDAB MOLBILA.
Upper West: YELIBORA ANTUMINI.
Western Region: J. R. E AMENLEMAH.

SECRETARIATS

Secretariat for Agriculture: POB M37, Accra; tel. 665421.
Secretariat for Defence: Burma Camp, Accra; tel. 777611; telex 2077.
Secretariat for Education and Culture: POB M45, Accra; tel. 665421.
Secretariat for Finance and Economic Planning: POB M40, Accra; tel. 665421; telex 2132.
Secretariat for Foreign Affairs: POB M53, Accra; tel. 665421; telex 2001.
Secretariat for Fuel and Power: POB M212, Accra; tel. 665421.
Secretariat for Health: POB M44, Accra; tel. 665421.
Secretariat for Industry, Science and Technology: POB M47, Accra; tel. 665421.
Secretariat for Information: POB M41, Accra; tel. 228011; telex 2201.
Secretariat for Internal Affairs: POB M42, Accra; tel. 665421.
Secretariat for Lands and Natural Resources: POB M212, Accra; tel. 665421.
Secretariat for Local Government and Rural Development: POB M50, Accra; tel. 665421.
Secretariat for Mobilization and Productivity: POB M84, Accra; tel. 665421.
Secretariat for Roads and Highways: POB M43, Accra.
Secretariat for Trade and Tourism: POB M47, Accra; tel. 665421; telex 2105.
Secretariat for Transport and Communications: POB M38, Accra; tel. 665421.
Secretariat for Works and Housing: POB M43, Accra; tel. 665421.
Secretariat for Youth and Sports: Accra; tel. 665421.

Legislature

Parliament was dissolved following the December 1981 coup.

Political Organizations

Following the coup in December 1981, all political parties were proscribed, as they had been in 1966–69 and 1972–79. Several political groups continue to operate, some mainly from outside Ghana:

Campaign for Democracy in Ghana (CDG): London, England; advocates return to democracy as a conduit to development; Leader Maj. (retd.) BOAKYE DJAN.

The Dawn Group: London, England; socialist.

Ghana Democratic Movement (GDM): London, England; f. 1983; advocates the restoration of a liberal democratic system; Leader JOSEPH H. MENSAH.

Kwame Nkrumah Revolutionary Guards (KNRG): Accra; African socialist; Sec.-Gen. JOHN NDEBUGRE (acting).

New Democratic Movement (NDM): Accra; socialist; Chair. KWAME KARIKARI.

United Revolutionary Front (URF): London, England; coalition of Marxist-Leninist groups.

Diplomatic Representation

EMBASSIES AND HIGH COMMISSIONS IN GHANA

Algeria: House No. F606/1, off Cantonments Rd, Christiansborg, POB 2747, Accra; tel. 776828; Ambassador: HAMID BOURKI.

GHANA

Benin: C175 Odoi Kwao Crescent, POB 7871, Accra; tel. 225701; Chargé d'affaires: L. TONOUKOUIN.

Brazil: 5 Volta St, Airport Residential Area, POB 2918, Accra; tel. 777154; telex 2081; Ambassador: CARLOS NORBERTO DE OLIVEIRA PARES.

Bulgaria: 3 Kakramadu Rd, East Cantonments, POB 3193, Accra; tel. 774231; Ambassador: KOSTADIN GEORGIEV GYAUROV.

Burkina Faso: House No. 772/3, Asylum Down, off Farrar Ave, POB 651, Accra; tel. 221988; telex 2108; Ambassador: EMILE GOUBA.

Canada: No. 46, Independence Ave, POB 1639, Accra; tel. 228555; telex 2024; High Commissioner: SANDELLE SCRIMSHAW.

China, People's Republic: No. 7, Agostinho Neto Rd, Airport Residential Area, POB 3356, Accra; tel. 777073; Ambassador: GU XINER.

Côte d'Ivoire: House No. 9, 8th Lane, off Cantonments Rd, POB 3445, Christiansborg, Accra; tel. 774611; telex 2131; Ambassador: KONAN NDA.

Cuba: 10 Ridge Rd, Roman Ridge, Airport Residential Area, POB 9163 Airport, Accra; tel. 775842; Ambassador: NICOLÁS RODRÍGUEZ.

Czechoslovakia: C260/5, Kanda High Rd No. 2, POB 5226, Accra-North; tel. 223540; Ambassador: LADISLAV SOBR.

Egypt: 3 Jawaharlal Nehru Ave, POB 2508, Accra; Ambassador: MUHAMMAD AHMAD SHELBAYA.

Ethiopia: House No. 6, Adiembra Rd, East Cantonment, POB 1646, Accra; tel. 775928; Chargé d'affaires a.i.: BEIDE MELAKU.

France: 12th Rd, off Liberation Ave, POB 187, Accra; tel. 228571; telex 2101; Ambassador: JEAN MICHEL AUCHÈRE.

German Democratic Republic: House No. 40, Liberation Rd, Airport Residential Area, POB 2348, Accra; tel. 776861; telex 2142; Ambassador: GOTTFRIED BUHRING.

Germany, Federal Republic: Valldemosa Lodge, Plot No. 18, North Ridge Residential Area, 7th Ave Extension, POB 1757, Accra; tel. 221311; telex 2025; Ambassador: BURGHART NAGEL.

Guinea: 11 Osu Badu St, Dzorwulu, POB 5497, Accra-North; tel. 777921; Ambassador: DORE DIALE DRUS.

Holy See: Airport Residential Area, POB 9675, Accra; tel. 777759; Apostolic Pro-Nuncio: Most Rev. GIUSEPPE BERTELLO, Titular Archbishop of Urbisaglia.

Hungary: House No. F582 A/1, Salem Rd, Christiansborg, POB 3027, Accra; tel. 774917; Ambassador: RAYMOND TÓTH.

India: 9 Ridge Rd, Roman Ridge, POB 3040, Accra; tel. 777916; telex 2154; High Commissioner: M. S. MALIK.

Iran: 10 Agbaamo St, Airport Residential Area, POB 1260073, Accra; tel. 74474; telex 2117; Ambassador: SHAMEDDIN KHAREGHANI.

Italy: Jawaharlal Nehru Rd, POB 140, Accra; tel. 775621; telex 2039; Ambassador: MARIO FUGAZZOLA.

Japan: 8 Rangoon Ave, off Switchback Rd, POB 1637, Accra; tel. 775616; telex 2068; Ambassador: SHIGERU KUROSAWA.

Korea, Democratic People's Republic: 139 Roman Ridge, Ambassadorial Estate, Nortei Ababio Estate, POB 13874, Accra; tel. 777825; Ambassador: CHANG DU HO.

Korea, Republic: 3 Abokobi Rd, East Cantonments, POB 13700, Accra; tel. 777533; Ambassador: HONG-WOO NAM.

Lebanon: 2 Rangoon Ave, POB 562, Accra; tel. 776727; telex 2118; Ambassador: Dr MUHAMMAD ISSA.

Liberia: F675/1, off Cantonments Rd, Christiansborg, POB 895, Accra; tel. 775641; telex 2071; Ambassador: T. BOYE NELSON.

Libya: 14 Sixth St, Airport Residential Area, POB 6995, Accra; tel. 774820; telex 2179; Secretary of People's Bureau: (vacant).

Mali: Crescent Rd, Block 1, POB 1121, Accra; tel. 666421; telex 2061; Ambassador: MUPHTAH AG HAIRY.

Netherlands: 89 Liberation Rd, National Redemption Circle, POB 3248, Accra; tel. 221655; telex 2128; Chargé d'affaires a.i.: R. S. BEKINK.

Nigeria: Rangoon Ave, POB 1548, Accra; tel. 776158; telex 2051; High Commissioner: T. A. OLU-OTUNLA.

Pakistan: 11 Ring Rd East, POB 1114, Accra; tel. 776059; telex 2426; Ambassador: IFTIKHAR ALI SHEIKH.

Poland: House No. F820/1, off Cantonments Rd, Christiansborg, POB 2552, Accra; tel. 774711; Ambassador: KLEMENS WALKOWIAK.

Romania: North Labone, Ward F, Block 6, House 262, POB M112, Accra; tel. 774076; telex 2027; Chargé d'affaires: GHEORGHE V. ILIE.

Saudi Arabia: F868/1, off Cantonments Rd, OSU RE, Accra; tel. 776651; Chargé d'affaires: ANWAR ABDUL FATTAH ABDRABBUH.

Spain: Airport Residential Area, Lamptey Ave Extension, POB 1218, Accra; tel. 774004; Ambassador: MANUEL MARÍA GONZÁLEZ-HABA.

Switzerland: 9 Water Rd S.I., North Ridge Area, POB 359, Accra; tel. 228125; telex 2197; Ambassador: H. STRAUCH.

Togo: Togo House, near Cantonments Circle, POB 4308, Accra; tel. 777950; telex 2166; Ambassador: LARBLI TCHINTCHIBIDJA.

USSR: F856/1, Ring Rd East, POB 1634, Accra; tel. 775611; Ambassador: VYACHESLAV M. SEMYONOV.

United Kingdom: Osu Link, off Gamel Abdul Nasser Ave, POB 296, Accra; tel. 221665; telex 2323; High Commissioner: ARTHUR H. WYATT.

USA: Ring Road East, POB 194, Accra; tel. 775346; Ambassador: STEPHEN R. LYNE.

Yugoslavia: 47 Senchi St, Airport Residential Area, POB 1629, Accra; tel. 775761; Ambassador: LAZAR COVIĆ.

Judicial System

The civil law in force in Ghana is based on the Common Law, doctrines of equity and general statutes which were in force in England in 1874, as modified by subsequent Ordinances. Ghanaian customary law is, however, the basis of most personal, domestic and contractual relationships. Criminal Law is based on the Criminal Code, enacted in 1960 and dependent on English Criminal Law, and since amended at intervals. The Superior Court of Judicature consists of the Supreme Court, the Court of Appeal and the High Court of Justice; the Inferior Courts include the Circuit Courts, the District Courts and such other inferior courts as may be provided by law.

Supreme Court: The Supreme Court consists of the Chief Justice and not fewer than four other Justices of the Supreme Court. It is the final court of appeal in Ghana and has jurisdiction in matters relating to the enforcement or interpretation of the Constitution.

Chief Justice: E. N. P. SOWAH.

The Court of Appeal: The Court of Appeal consists of the Chief Justice and not fewer than five Judges of the Court of Appeal. It has jurisdiction to hear and determine appeals from any judgment, decree or order of the High Court.

The High Court: The High Court of Ghana consists of the Chief Justice and not fewer than twelve Justices of the High Court and has an original jurisdiction in all matters, civil and criminal, other than those for offences involving treason. Trial by jury is practised in criminal cases in Ghana and the Criminal Procedure Code, 1960, provides that all trials on indictment shall be by a jury or with the aid of Assessors.

The Circuit Court: Circuit Courts were created in 1960, and the jurisdiction of a Circuit Court consists of an original jurisdiction in civil matters where the amount involved does not exceed C100,000. It also has jurisdiction with regard to the guardianship and custody of infants, and original jurisdiction in all criminal cases, except offences where the maximum punishment is death or the offence, treason. Finally it has appellate jurisdiction from decisions of any District Court situated within its circuit.

District Courts: To each magisterial district is assigned at least one District Magistrate who has original jurisdiction to try civil suits in which the amount involved does not exceed C50,000. District Magistrates also have jurisdiction to deal with all criminal cases, except first-degree felonies, and commit cases of a more serious nature to either the Circuit Court or the High Court. A Grade I Circuit Court can impose a fine not exceeding C1,000 and sentences of imprisonment of up to two years and a Grade II Circuit Court may impose a fine not exceeding C500 and a sentence of imprisonment of up to 12 months. A District Court has no appellate jurisdiction, except in rent matters under the Rent Act.

Juvenile Courts: Empowered to hear charges against juveniles, persons under 17 years, except where the juvenile is charged jointly with an adult. They consist of a Chairman who must be either the District Magistrate or a lawyer, and not fewer than two other members appointed by the Chief Justice in consultation with the Judicial Council. The public is excluded from proceedings of Juvenile Courts which can make orders as to the protection and supervision of a neglected child and can negotiate with parents to secure the good behaviour of a child.

National Public Tribunal: Established by the PNDC in 1984 to consider appeals from the Regional Public Tribunals. Its decisions are final and are not subject to any further appeal. The Tribunal consists of at least three members and not more than five, one of whom acts as Chairman.

Regional Public Tribunals: Formed by the PNDC in 1982 to judge criminal offences relating to prices, rent or exchange control,

GHANA

theft, fraud, forgery, corruption or any offence under any enactment which may be referred to them by the PNDC.

Special Military Tribunal: Formed by the PNDC in 1982 to judge crimes committed by members of the armed forces. It consists of between five and seven members.

Religion

According to the 1960 census, the distribution of religious groups was: Christians 42.8%, traditional religions 38.2%, Muslims 12.0%, unclassified 7.0%.

CHRISTIANITY

Christian Council of Ghana: POB 919, Accra; tel. 776725; f. 1929; advisory body comprising 13 Protestant churches; Chair. Rt Rev. FRANCIS W. B. THOMPSON (Anglican Bishop of Accra); Gen. Sec. Rev. A. K. ZORMELO.

The Anglican Communion

Anglicans are adherents of the Church of the Province of West Africa, with six dioceses in Ghana. The Archbishop of the Province is the Bishop of Liberia.

Bishop of Accra: Rt Rev. FRANCIS W. B. THOMPSON, Bishopscourt, POB 8, Accra; tel. 662292.

Bishop of Cape Coast: (vacant), Bishopscourt, POB 38, Cape Coast.

Bishop of Koforidua: Rt Rev. ROBERT OKINE, POB 980, Koforidua.

Bishop of Kumasi: Rt Rev. EDMUND YEBOAH, Bishop's House, POB 144, Kumasi.

Bishop of Sekondi: Rt Rev. THEOPHILUS ANNOBIL, POB 85, Sekondi.

Bishop of Sunyani and Tamale: Rt Rev. JOSEPH KOBINA DADSON, Bishop's House, POB 110, Tamale.

The Roman Catholic Church

Ghana comprises two archdioceses and seven dioceses. At 31 December 1986 there were 1,935,492 adherents in the country.

Ghana Bishops' Conference: National Catholic Secretariat, POB 9712, Accra; tel. 776491; telex 2471; f. 1980; Pres. Most Rev. PETER POREKU DERY, Archbishop of Tamale.

Archbishop of Cape Coast: Most Rev. JOHN KODWO AMISSAH, Archbishop's House, POB 112, Cape Coast; tel. 2593.

Archbishop of Tamale: Most Rev. PETER POREKU DERY, Gumbehini Rd, POB 42, Tamale; tel. 2425.

Other Christian Churches

African Methodist Episcopal Zion Church: POB 239, Sekondi.

Christian Methodist Episcopal Church: POB 3906, Accra.

Evangelical-Lutheran Church of Ghana: POB 197, Kaneshie; tel. 223487; telex 2134; Pres. Rev. PAUL KOFI FYNN; 6,200 mems.

Evangelical-Presbyterian Church: POB 18, Ho; tel. 755; f. 1847; Moderator Rt Rev. Prof. N. K. DZOBO; 205,000 mems.

Ghana Baptist Convention: POB 1979, Kumas; Pres. L. SARPONG-MENSAH.

Ghana Conference of Seventh-day Adventists: Cape Coast; 24,100 mems.

Mennonite Church: POB 5485, Accra; f. 1957; Moderator Rev. E. A. GALBAH-NUSETOR; Sec. ABRAHAM K. WETSEH; 800 mems.

Methodist Church of Ghana: Liberia Rd, POB 403, Accra; tel. 228120; independent since 1961; Pres. Rt Rev. Prof. K. A. DICKSON; Sec. Rev. Dr EBENEZER H. BREW RIVERSON; 320,000 mems.

Presbyterian Church of Ghana: POB 1800, Accra; tel. 662511; f. 1828; Moderator Rt Rev. D. A. KORANTENG; Sec. Rev. S. K. ABOA; 422,438 mems.

Western African Union Mission of Seventh-day Adventists: POB 1016, Accra; tel. 223720; telex 2119; f. 1943; Pres. P. K. ASAREH; Sec. SETH A. LARYEA.

The African Methodist Episcopal Church, the F'Eden Church, the Salvation Army and the Society of Friends (Quakers) are also active in Ghana.

ISLAM

There are a considerable number of Muslims in the Northern Region. The majority are Malikees.

Chief Imam: Alhaji MUKITAR ABASS.

The Press

NEWSPAPERS

Daily

Daily Graphic: Graphic Rd, POB 742, Accra; tel. 228911; f. 1950; state-owned; Editor SAM CLEGG; circ. 40,000.

The Ghanaian Times: New Times Corpn, Ring Rd West, POB 2638, Accra; tel. 228282; f. 1958; state-owned; Editor CHRISTIAN AGGREY; circ. 40,000.

The Pioneer: Abura Printing Works Ltd, POB 325, Kumasi; tel. 2204; f. 1939; Editor KI OPUKU ACHEAMPONG; circ. 100,000.

Weekly

Business Weekly: Ring Rd, Industrial Area South, POB 2351, Accra; tel. 226037; f. 1966; Man. Editor MARK BOTSIO; circ. 5,000.

The Catholic Standard: POB 765, Accra; tel. 222185; f. 1938; Roman Catholic; Editor ANTHONY BONNAH KOOMSON; circ. 30,400; (licence revoked Dec. 1985).

Champion: POB 6828, Accra-North; tel. 229079; Man. Dir MARK D. N. ADDY; Editor FRANK CAXTON WILLIAMS; circ. 300,000.

Christian Messenger: Presbyterian Book Depot Bldg, POB 3075, Accra; tel. 662415; telex 2525; f. 1883; English, Twi and Ga edns; Editor G. B. K. OWUSU; circ. 60,000.

Echo: POB 5288, Accra; f. 1968; Sundays; Man. Editor J. K. TSIBOE; circ. 30,000.

Evening News: POB 7505, Accra; tel. 229416; Man. Editor OSEI POKU; circ. 30,000.

The Mirror: Graphic Rd, POB 742, Accra; tel. 228911; telex 2475; f. 1953; state-owned; Sundays; Editor E. M. O. PROVINCAL (acting); circ. 60,000.

New Nation: POB 6828, Accra-North; Man. Dir MARK D. N. ADDY; Editor S. N. SASRAKU; circ. 300,000.

The Palaver Tribune: POB 5018, Accra; f. 1970; Editor-in-Chief CHRISTIAN ASHER; Editor BENJAMIN BAAH ARMAH; circ. 100,000; (publication suspended).

Punch: POB 6828, Accra-North; f. 1976; Man. Dir MARK D. N. ADDY; Editor PRINCE K. GOSWIN; circ. 280,000; (publication suspended).

Radio and TV Times: POB 1633, Accra; tel. 221161; telex 2114; f. 1960; Editor ERNEST ASAMOAH; circ. 5,000.

Sporting News: POB 5481, Accra-North; f. 1967; Man. Editor J. OPPONG-AGYARE.

Star: Accra; Editor J. W. DUMOGA.

The Statesman: Accra; Man. Editor W. K. DUMOGA (acting).

Weekly Spectator: New Times Corpn, Ring Road West, POB 2638, Accra; state-owned; f. 1963; Sundays; Editor J. D. ANDOH KESSON; circ. 165,000.

PERIODICALS

Fortnightly

Ideal Woman (Obaa Sima): POB 5737, Accra; tel. 221399; f. 1971; Editor KATE ABBAM.

Legon Observer: POB 11, Legon; f. 1966; publ. by Legon Society on National Affairs; Chair. J. A. DADSON; Editor EBOW DANIEL.

New Ghana: Information Services Dept, POB 745, Accra; English; political, economic and cultural affairs.

Monthly

African Woman: Ring Rd West, POB 1496, Accra.

Armed Forces News: Ghana Armed Forces, Burma Camp, Accra.

Boxing and Football Illustrated: POB 8392, Accra; f. 1976; Editor NANA O. AMPOMAH; circ. 10,000.

Chit Chat: POB 7043, Accra; Editor ROSEMOND ADU.

Drum: POB 1197, Accra; general interest.

Ghana Journal of Science: Ghana Science Asscn, POB 7, Legon; Editor Dr A. K. AHAFIA.

Police News: Police HQ, Accra; Editor S. S. APPIAH; circ. 20,000.

The Scope: POB 8162, Tema; Editor EMMANUEL DOE ZIORKLUI; circ. 10,000.

Students World: POB M18, Accra; tel. 774248; telex 2171; f. 1974; educational; Man. Editor ERIC OFEI; circ. 10,000.

The Teacher: Ghana National Union of Teachers, POB 209, Accra; tel. 221515; f. 1931.

The Ghana Information Services (POB 745, Accra; tel. 228011) publish the following periodicals:

Akwansosem: Akwapim Twi; Editor FOSTER APPIAH.

GHANA

Ghana Digest: UN, OAU and agency reports; Editor S. IKOI-KWAKU; circ. 12,000.

Ghana News Bulletin: f. 1974; Editor E. A. AFRO; circ. 8,000.

Ghana Review: f. 1961; economic, social and cultural affairs; Editor J. OPPONG-AGYARE; circ. 18,000.

Kabaare: f. 1967; edited by ISD; circ. 2,000.

Kakyevole: Nzema; Editor T. E. KWESI; circ. 10,500.

Kasem Labie (Kasem): POB 57, Tamale; Editor A. C. AZIIBA.

Lahabili Tsugu: POB 57, Tamale; Dagbani; Editor T. T. SULEMANA.

Mansralo: Ga; Editor MARTIN NII-MOI.

Motabiala: Ewe; Editor K. GROPONE; circ. 10,000.

Nkwantabisa: Asante, Twi and Fante; Editors FOSTER APPIAH (Twi), E. N. S. EDUFUL (Fante); circ. 20,000.

The Post: f. 1980; state-owned; current affairs and analysis; circ. 25,000.

Volta Review: f. 1976; edited by ISD; circ. 3,000.

Quarterly

Ghana Enterprise: c/o Ghana National Chamber of Commerce, POB 2325, Accra; f. 1961; Editor J. B. K. AMANFU.

Ghana Manufacturer: c/o Asscn of Ghana Industries, POB 8624, Accra-North; tel. 777283; f. 1974; Editor (vacant); circ. 1,500.

Insight and Opinion: POB 5446, Accra; Editorial Sec. W. B. OHENE.

Kpodoga: Tsito; f. 1976; rural community newspaper publ. by the Inst. of Adult Education of Univ. of Ghana; Ewe; Editor YAO ADUAMAH; circ. 2,000.

NEWS AGENCIES

Ghana News Agency: POB 2118, Accra; tel. 665135; telex 2001; f. 1957; Gen. Man. MAWUSI AFELE; 10 regional offices, 30 district offices and 1 overseas office.

Foreign Bureaux

Associated Press (AP) (USA): POB 6172, Accra; Bureau Chief P. K. COBBINAH-ESSEM.

Telegrafnoye Agentstvo Sovetskovo Soyuza (TASS) (USSR): POB 9141, Accra; Agent IGOR AGEBEKOV.

United Press International (UPI) (USA): POB 9715, Accra; tel. 225436; telex 2340; Bureau Chief R. A. QUANSAH.

Xinhua (New China) News Agency (People's Republic of China): 35 Sir Arku Korsah Rd, Airport Residential Area, POB 3897, Accra.

Deutsche Presse-Agentur (Federal Republic of Germany) is also represented.

Publishers

Advent Press: POB 0102, Osu, Accra; tel. 777861; telex 2119; f. 1937; Gen. Man. SETH A. ARMAH.

Adwinsa Publications (Ghana) Ltd: 3rd Floor, Advance Press Bldg, School Rd, POB 92, Accra New Town; tel. 221577; telex 2171; f. 1977; general, educational; Man. Dir KWABENA AMPONSAH.

Afram Publications: 72 Ring Rd East, POB M18, Accra; tel. 774248; telex 2171; f. 1974; textbooks and general; Man. Dir ERIC OFEI.

Africa Christian Press: POB 30, Achimota; tel. 225554; f. 1964; religious, biography, paperbacks; Gen. Man. RICHARD A. B. CRABBE.

Asempa Publishers: POB 919, Accra; tel. 221706; f. 1973; religion, social questions, African music, fiction, children's books; Gen. Man. Rev. EMMANUEL A. B. BORTEY.

Baafour and Co: POB K189, Accra New Town; f. 1978; general; Man. B. KESE-AMANKWAA.

Benibengor Book Agency: POB 40, Aboso; fiction, biography, children's books and paperbacks; Man. Dir J. BENIBENGOR BLAY.

Black Mask Ltd: POB 252, Kumasi; tel. 6454; f. 1979; textbooks, plays, novels; Man. Dir YAW OWUSU ASANTE.

Editorial and Publishing Services: POB 5743, Accra; general, reference; Man. Dir M. DANQUAH.

Educational Press and Manufacturers Ltd: POB 9184; Airport-Accra; tel. 220395; f. 1975; textbooks, children's books; Man. G. K. KODUA.

Emmanuel Publishing Services: POB 5282, Accra; tel. 225238; f. 1978; educational and children's books; Dir EMMANUEL K. NSIAH.

Encyclopaedia Africana Project: POB 2797, Accra; tel. 776939; f. 1962; reference; Dir E. T. ASHONG.

Frank Publishing Ltd: POB M414, Accra; tel. 229510; f. 1976; secondary school textbooks; Man. Dir FRANCIS K. DZOKOTO.

Ghana Publishing Corpn: PMB Tema; tel. 2921; f. 1965; textbooks and general fiction and non-fiction; Man. Dir F. K. NYARKO.

Ghana Universities Press: POB 4219, Accra; tel. 225032; f. 1962; scholarly and academic; Dir A. S. K. ATSU.

Goodbooks Publishing Co: POB 10416, Accra North; tel. 665629; f. 1968; children's books; Man. A. ASIRIFI.

Miracle Bookhouse: POB 7487, Accra North; tel. 226684; f. 1977; general; Man. J. APPIAH-BERKO.

Moxon Paperbacks: Barnes Rd, POB M160, Accra; tel. 665397; f. 1967; travel and guide books, Africana, fiction and poetry; quarterly catalogue of Ghanaian books and periodicals in print; Man. Dir JAMES MOXON.

Sedco Publishing Ltd: Sedco House, Tabon St, North Ridge, POB 2051, Accra; tel. 221332; telex 2456; f. 1975; educational; Man. Dir COURAGE KWAMI SEGBAWU.

Unlit Publishing Co: POB 4432, Accra; tel. 222689; f. 1970; religion, politics, economics, science, fiction; Publr RONALD MENSAH.

Unimax Publishers Ltd: 136 Ringway Crescent, Ringway Estate, POB 10722, Accra-North; tel. 226244; telex 2295; atlases, educational and children's books; Dir EDWARD ADDO.

Waterville Publishing House: POB 195, Accra; tel. 663124; f. 1963; general fiction and non-fiction, textbooks, paperbacks, Africana; Man. Dir A. S. OBUAM.

Woeli Publishing Services: POB K601, Accra New Town; f. 1984; children's books, fiction; Dir W. A. DEKUTSEY.

PUBLISHERS' ASSOCIATIONS

Ghana Book Development Council: POB M430, Accra; tel. 229178; f. 1975; agency of Ministry of Education; promotes and co-ordinates writing, production and distribution of books; Exec. Dir S. A. AMU DJOLETO.

Ghana Book Publishers' Association: c/o Ghana Universities Press, POB 4219, Accra; Sec. W. A. DEKUTSEY.

Radio and Television

In 1988 there were an estimated 2.9m. radio receivers in use. There are internal radio broadcasts in English, Akan, Dagbani, Ewe, Ga, Hausa and Nzema; there is an external service in English and French. There are two sound transmitting stations and 53 relay stations. In 1986 a new radio station was constructed at Bolgatanga.

The television service came into operation in 1965; there are two studios in Accra and four transmission stations: Ajangote about 32 km from Accra, Kissi in the Central Region, Jamasi in Ashanti and Bolgatanga in the Northern Region. In 1987 new colour television equipment was commissioned in Accra. In 1988 there were an estimated 175,000 television receivers in use.

Ghana Broadcasting Corporation: Broadcasting House, POB 1633, Accra; tel. 221161; telex 2114; f. 1935; Dir-Gen. L. W. FIFI-HESSE; Deputy Dir-Gen. DAVID GHARTEY-TAGOE; Dir of TV J. CROMWELL; Dir of Radio FELIX SEDZIATA.

Finance

(cap. = capital; p.u. = paid up; res = reserves; dep. = deposits; m. = million; brs = branches; amounts in cedis)

BANKING
Central Bank

Bank of Ghana: Thorpe Rd, POB 2674, Accra; tel. 666902; telex 2052; f. 1957; cap. 100m., dep. 6,706.7m., res 896.1m. (Dec. 1986); Chair. Dr GODFRIED KPORTUFE AGAMA.

State Banks

Agricultural Development Bank: C288/3 Ring Rd Central, POB 4191, Accra; tel. 228453; telex 2295; f. 1965; state-owned; credit facilities for farmers and commercial banking; cap. p.u. 100m. (1986); Chair. and Man. Dir SAMUEL ODAME-LABI.

Bank of Credit and Commerce Ghana: 4 Graphic Rd, POB 11011, Accra; tel. 220788; telex 2208; cap. 8.2m. (1985); Chair. Dr J. L. S. ABBEY; Man. S. M. K. AIDAM.

Bank for Housing and Construction (BHC): Kwame Nkrumah Ave, POB MI, Adabraka, Accra; tel. 220033; telex 2096; f. 1973; cap. p.u. 20m. (June 1987); Chair. Mrs GLORIA NILOI.

GHANA

Ghana Commercial Bank: POB 134, Accra; tel. 663529; telex 2034; f. 1953; state-owned; cap. 1,200m., dep. 48,266m. (1986); res 264.7m. (1985); 148 brs; Man. Dir KOFI AGYEMAN.

Ghana Co-operative Bank: Kwame Nkrumah Ave, POB 5292, Accra-North; tel. 228735; telex 2446; f. 1970; cap. p.u. 9.9m. (1985); dep. 1,260.4m. (June 1987); Man. Dir Dr A. K. APPIAH; 75 brs.

National Investment Bank: 37 Kwame Nkrumah Ave, POB 3726, Accra; tel. 221312; telex 2161; f. 1963; 75% state-owned; provides long-term investment capital and consultancy, joint venture promotion, consortium finance management and commercial banking services; cap. p.u. 39m.; Chair. JOHN KOBINA RICHARDSON.

National Savings and Credit Bank: Ring Rd Central, Accra; tel. 228322; telex 2383; f. 1972; 75% state-owned; cap. 47.6m., dep. 2,398.6m. (Dec. 1986); Man. Dir J. A. NUAMAH.

National Trust Holding Co: Dyson House, Kwame Nkrumah Ave, POB 9563, Airport, Accra; tel. 229664; f. 1976 to finance acquisitions of indigenous companies by Ghanaians; also assists in their development and expansion, and carries out trusteeship business; cap. p.u. 3.3m.; Chair. JOE DONKOR; Man. Dir WILLIAM COOKE.

Social Security Bank: POB 13119, Accra; tel. 221726; telex 2209; f. 1976; cap. p.u. 360m. (Dec. 1986); Chair. K. O. SACKEY.

Merchant Bank

Merchant Bank (Ghana) Ltd: Swanmill, Kwame Nkrumah Ave, POB 401, Accra; tel. 666331; telex 2191; f. 1972; 30% state-owned; cap. and res 397.9m., dep. 5,712m. (Dec. 1987); Chair. YAW MANU SARPONG; Man. Dir KWAKU AGYEI-GYAMFI; 3 brs.

Foreign Banks

Barclays Bank of Ghana Ltd (UK): High St, POB 2949, Accra; tel. 664901; f. 1971; 40% state-owned; cap. 100m., dep. 11,544m., res 817m. (1986); Chair. Prof. SAMUEL SEY; Man. Dir CHARLES M. MABON; 40 brs.

Standard Chartered Bank Ghana Ltd (UK): Standard Bank Bldg, High St, POB 768, Accra; tel. 664591; f. 1896; cap. 200m., dep. 12,398.9m., res 1,180.3m. (1987); Chair. KWAME A. KWATENG; Man. Dir J. R. GILBERT; 28 brs.

INSURANCE

The State Insurance Corporation of Ghana: POB 2363, Accra; tel. 666961; telex 2171; f. 1962; state-owned; undertakes all classes of insurance; also engages in real estate and other investment.

Social Security and National Insurance Trust: POB M149, Accra; f. 1972; covers over 1.25m. employees; Chief Admin. A. AWUKU.

Vanguard Assurance Co Ltd: Post Office Sq., Insurance Hall, POB 1868, Accra; f. 1975; general accident, marine and motor insurance.

Several foreign insurance companies operate in Ghana.

Trade and Industry

PUBLIC BOARDS AND CORPORATIONS

Bast Fibres Development Board: POB 1992, Kumasi; f. 1970; promotes the commercial cultivation of bast fibres and their processing, handling and grading.

Food Production Corporation: POB 1853, Accra; f. 1971; state corpn providing employment for youth in large scale farming enterprises; controls 76,900 ha of land with 16,200 ha under cultivation; operates 87 food farms on a co-operative and self-supporting basis, and rears poultry and livestock.

Ghana Cocoa Board (COCOBOD): POB 933, Accra; telex 2082; f. 1985 to replace the Cocoa Marketing Board; responsible for purchase, grading and export of cocoa, coffee and shea nuts, and encourages production and scientific research aimed at improving quality and yield of cocoa, coffee and shea nuts; Chief Exec. KWAME NINI OWUSU.

Ghana Consolidated Diamond Co Ltd: POB M108, Accra; telex 2058; f. 1986, to replace Diamond Marketing Corpn, to grade, value and process diamonds, buy all locally won, produced or processed diamonds, promote the industry; responsible for securing the most favourable terms for purchase, grading, valuing, export and sale of local diamonds; Chair. KOFI AGYEMAN.

Ghana Cotton Co Ltd: f. 1986 to replace Cotton Development Board; ownership: govt 70%, private textile cos 30%; 15 regional offices; Chair. HARRY GANDA.

Ghanaian Enterprises Development Commission: Accra; f. 1975; assists the indigenization of the economy; especially small and medium-scale industrial and commercial enterprises, by providing loans and advisory services.

Ghana Food Distribution Corporation: POB 4245, Accra; tel. 228428; f. 1971 by merger of Food Marketing Corpn and Task Force Food Distribution unit; buys, stores, preserves, distributes and sells foodstuffs through 10 regional centres; Man. Dir Dr P. A. KURANCHIE.

Ghana Industrial Holding Corporation (GIHOC): POB 2784, Accra; tel. 664998; telex 2109; f. 1967; manages 26 state enterprises, including the steel, paper, bricks, paint, pharmaceuticals, electronics, metals, canneries, distilleries and boat-building factories; also has three wholly-owned subsidiaries and four joint ventures; in 1979 it was decided to convert all divisions into wholly-owned limited liability companies; Chair. J. E. K. MOSES; Man. Dir J. K. WILLIAMS.

Ghana Investment Centre: Central Ministerial Area, POB M193, Accra; tel. 665125; telex 2229; f. 1981 to replace Capital Investments Board; negotiates new investments, approves projects, registers foreign capital and decides extent of govt participation; Chair. Sec. for Finance and Economic Planning.

Ghana National Manganese Corporation: POB M183, Ministry PO, Accra; telex 2046; f. 1975 following nationalization of African Manganese Co mine at Nsuta; Chair. P. O. AGGREY; Man. Dir Dr A. O. BARNAFO.

Ghana National Petroleum Corporation: Accra; f. 1984; develops petroleum potential; Chair. Alhaji IDDRISU MAHAMA; Man. Dir. Dr A. K. ADDAE (acting).

Ghana National Trading Corporation: POB 67, Accra; tel. 664871; f. 1961; organizes exports and imports of selected commodities; over 500 retail outlets in 14 admin. dists.

Ghana Standards Board: c/o POB M245, Accra; tel. 662606; telex 2289; f. 1967; establishes and promulgates standards; promotes standardization, industrial efficiency and development and industrial welfare, health and safety; operates certification mark scheme; 285 mems; Dir Dr L. TWUM-DANSO; Deputy Dir SAM BOATENG.

Ghana Water and Sewerage Corporation: POB M194, Accra; f. 1966 to provide, distribute and conserve water for public, domestic and industrial use, and to establish, operate and control sewerage systems.

Grains and Legumes Development Board: POB 4000, Kumasi; tel. 4231; f. 1970; state-controlled; promotes and develops grain and legume production.

Minerals Commission: State House, 2nd Floor, 2nd Bay, POB M248, Accra; tel. 662986; telex 2545; f. 1984; fmrly Aluminium Industries Comm.; supervises, promotes and co-ordinates the minerals industry.

Posts and Telecommunications Corporation: Posts and Telecommunications Bldg, Accra-North; tel. 221001; telex 3010; f. 1974; provides both internal and external postal and telecommunication services.

State Construction Corporation: Ring Rd West, Industrial Area, Accra; f. 1966; state corpn with a labour force of 7,000; construction plans are orientated to aid agricultural production; Man. Dir J. A. DANSO, Jr.

State Farms Corporation: Accra; undertakes agricultural projects in all regions but Upper Region; Man. Dir E. N. A. THOMPSON (acting).

State Fishing Corporation: POB 211, Tema; telex 2043; f. 1961; govt-sponsored deep-sea fishing, distribution and marketing (including exporting) org.; owns 12 deep-sea fishing trawlers.

State Gold Mining Corporation: POB 109, Tarkwa; Accra Office, POB 3634; tel. 775376; telex 2348; f. 1961; manages four gold mines; CEO F. AWUA-KYEREMATEN.

State Hotels Corporation: POB 7542, Accra-North; tel. 664646; telex 2113; f. 1965; responsible for all state-owned hotels, restaurants, etc.; provides such facilities in 13 major centres; Man. Dir S. K. A. OBENG; Gen. Man. EBEN AMOAH.

State Housing Construction Co: POB 2753, Accra; f. 1982 by merger of State Housing Corpn and Tema Development Corpn; oversees govt housing programme.

Timber Export Development Board: POB 515, Takoradi; tel. 2921; telex 2189; f. 1985 to replace Ghana Timber Marketing Board; promotes the sale and export of timber; CEO (vacant).

CHAMBER OF COMMERCE

Ghana National Chamber of Commerce: POB 2325, Accra; tel. 662427; f. 1961; promotes trade and commerce, organizes trade fairs; 2,500 individual mems and 13 mem. chambers; Pres. ISAAC D. ADADE; Exec. Sec. JOHN B. K. AMANFU.

COMMERCIAL AND INDUSTRIAL ORGANIZATIONS

Ghana Export Promotion Council: Republic House, POB M146, Accra; tel. 228813; telex 2289; f. 1972; Chair. and mems appointed

GHANA

by Ghana Mfrs' Asscn, Ghana National Chamber of Commerce, Ghana Export Co, Capital Investments Board, Secrs for Agriculture, Foreign Affairs, Information, Industry, Science and Tech., Trade and Tourism, Bank of Ghana, and the Ghana Standards Board.

The Indian Association of Ghana: POB 2891, Accra; tel. 776227; f. 1939; Pres. ATMARAM GOKALDAS.

EMPLOYERS' ASSOCIATION

Ghana Employers' Association: Kojo Thompson Rd, POB 2616, Accra; tel. 228455; f. 1959; 365 mems; Pres. E. DARKO-OWIREDU; Vice-Pres. J. V. L. PHILLIPS.

Affiliated Bodies

Association of Ghana Industries: POB 8624, Accra-North; tel. 777283; telex 3027; f. 1957; Pres. JOHN K. RICHARDSON; Exec. Sec. EDDIE IMBEAH-AMOAKUH.

Ghana Booksellers' Association: POB 10367, Accra-North; tel. 227148; Pres. SAMPSON BRAKO; Gen. Sec. FRED J. REIMMER.

Ghana Chamber of Mines: POB 991, Accra; tel. 662719; telex 2036; f. 1928; promotes mining interests; Exec. Dir SAM POKU.

Ghana Electrical Contractors' Association: POB 1858, Accra.

Ghana National Contractors' Association: c/o J. T. Osei and Co, POB M11, Accra.

Ghana Port Employers' Association: c/o Ghana Cargo Handling Co Ltd, POB 488, Tema.

Ghana Timber Association (GTA): POB 246, Takoradi; f. 1952; promotes, protects and develops timber industry; Pres. NANA YAW OWUSU.

CO-OPERATIVES

The co-operative movement began in Ghana in 1928 among cocoa farmers, and evolved into the country's largest farmers' organization. In 1944 the co-operative societies were placed under government supervision. The movement was dissolved by the Nkrumah government in 1960, but was re-established after the coup in 1966. It is now under the direction of a government-appointed secretary-general. In 1986 there were 8,387 co-operative societies. The structure of the movement places the co-operative associations at the top, co-operative unions in a secondary position of seniority in the towns, and village co-operative societies at the base.

Department of Co-operatives: POB M150, Accra; tel. 666212; f. 1944; govt-supervised body, responsible for registration, auditing and supervision of co-operative socs; Registrar R. BUACHIE-APHRAM; Sec.-Gen. J. M. APPIAH.

Ghana Co-operatives Council Ltd: POB 4034, Accra; f. 1951; co-ordinates activities of all co-operative socs; comprises 15 nat. co-operative asscns and five central socs; Sec.-Gen. JOHN MARTIN APPIAH.

The 15 co-operative associations include the Ghana Co-operative Marketing Asscn Ltd, the Ghana Co-operative Credit Unions Asscn Ltd, the Ghana Co-operative Agricultural Producers and Marketing Asscn Ltd, and The Ghana Co-operative Consumers' Asscn Ltd.

TRADE UNIONS

Ghana Trades Union Congress: Hall of Trade Unions, POB 701, Accra; f. 1945; all chairmen, general secretaries and vice-chairmen of 17 affiliated unions, and the constitution of the TUC were suspended in March 1982; Chair. Interim Man. Cttee D. K. Y. VOMAWOK; Sec.-Gen. AUGUSTUS YANKEY.

The following Unions are affiliated to the Congress (figures refer to membership in 1979):

Construction and Building Workers' Union (46,000); General Agricultural Workers' Union (127,000); General Transport, Petroleum and Chemical Workers' Union (12,504); Private Road Transport Workers' Union (21,700); Health Services Workers' Union (12,000); Industrial and Commercial Workers' Union (115,052); Local Government Workers' Union (38,933); Maritime and Dockworkers' Union (23,720); Mine-workers' Union (22,000); National Union of Seamen (5,000); Post and Telecommunications Workers' Union (11,500); Public Services Workers' Union (45,000); Public Utility Workers' Union (25,000); Railway Enginemen's Union (701); Railway and Port Workers' Union (13,216); Teachers' and Educational Workers' Union (34,000); Timber and Woodworkers' Union (22,000).

Transport

State Transport Corporation: Accra; f. 1901 as Govt Transport Dept, name changed in 1965; Man. Dir Lt-Col AKYEA-MENSAH.

RAILWAYS

There were 947 km of railways in 1986, connecting Accra, Kumasi and Takoradi. In 1988 the Italian Government agreed to provide US $30m., and the World Bank approved a loan of $9.4m., to finance a project to rehabilitate the railway network.

Ghana Railway Corporation: POB 251, Takoradi; tel. 2181; telex 2297; f. 1977; responsible for the operation and maintenance of all railways; Gen. Man. AMPONSAH ABABIO.

ROADS

In 1985 there were about 28,300 km of classified roads in Ghana. Of this total, 14,140 km were trunk roads, managed by the Ghana Highway Authority. A further 14,160 km were feeder roads, managed by the Department of Feeder Roads. These two agencies are under the control of the Secretariat for Roads and Highways. There were also some 6,000 km of tracks, owned and managed by private mining and timber companies. These are not classified. Only roads managed by the Ghana Highway Authority are paved. Of the total length of roads, 5,782 km were paved in 1985, including 150 km of motorway. A major five-year programme of road development and rehabilitation, costing U.S. $828m., was initiated in 1988.

Ghana Highway Authority: POB 1641, Accra; tel. 666591; telex 2359; f. 1974 to plan, develop, classify and maintain roads and ferries; CEO H. O. A. QUAYNOR.

The **Ghana-Burkina Faso Road Transport Commission** was set up to implement the 1968 agreement to improve communications between the two countries. The road between Accra and Abidjan, Côte d'Ivoire, forms part of the planned Trans-African Highway.

SHIPPING

The two main ports are Tema (near Accra) and Takoradi, both of which are linked with Kumasi by rail. In 1988 work began on the rehabilitation of Tema port, at a projected cost of US $73.3m. The port was to be equipped with modern mechanical handling equipment to enable a quicker turn-round of ships. In 1983 goods loaded totalled an estimated 1.12m. metric tons, and goods unloaded an estimated 2.52m. tons.

Alpha (West Africa) Line Ltd: POB 451, Tema; telex 2184; operates regular cargo services to West Africa, the UK, the USA, the Far East and northern Europe; agents for Mercandia (West Africa) Line, Cameroon National Line, Pakistan National Lines, Uiterwyk West Africa Lines and Great South America Line; Man. Dir E. COLLINGWOODE-WILLIAMS.

Black Star Line Ltd: 4th Lane, Kuku Hill Osu, POB 2760, Accra; tel. 776161; telex 2019; f. 1957; state-owned; operates passenger and cargo services to Europe, the UK, Canada, the USA, the Mediterranean and west Africa; agents for Gold Star Line, Woermann Line, Zim West Africa Lines, Compagnie Maritime Belge, Seven Stars (Africa) Line, Société Ivoirienne de Transport Maritime (SITRAM), and Compagnie Maritime Zaïroise (CMZ); fleet of 5 freighters; displacement 59,495 g.r.t.; Man. Dir HERON R. BLAGOGEE.

Holland West-Afrika Lijn N.V.: POB 269, Accra; POB 216, Tema; and POB 18, Takoradi; cargo services to and from North America and the Far East; agents for Royal Interocean Lines and Dafra Line.

Liner Agencies (Ghana) Ltd: POB 66, Accra; tel. 222680; telex 2396; freight services to and from UK, Europe, USA, Canada, Japan and Far East; intermediate services between West African ports; agents for Barber W.A. Line, Elder Dempster Lines, Guinean Gulf Line, Kawasaki Kisen Kaisha, Mitsui OSK Lines, Nigerian National Shipping Line, Marine Chartering of San Francisco, A/S Bulkhandling of Oslo, Botany Bay Shipping Co, SITRAM, CMZ and Palm Line; Man. Dir M. N. ANKUMA.

Remco Shipping Lines Ltd: POB 3898, Accra; tel. 224609; displacement 11,880 g.r.t.

Scanship (Ghana) Ltd: CFAO Bldg, High St, POB 1705, Accra; tel. 664314; telex 2181; agents for Maersk Line, Splosna Plovba Line, Hoegh Line, Jadranska Slobodna Plovidba-Split, Keller Shipping, Prompt Shipping, Polish Ocean Line, DSR Line, EAC Line, Estonian Shipping Co, Shipping Corpn of India, US Africa Line.

CIVIL AVIATION

The main international airport is at Kotoka (Accra). There are also airports at Takoradi, Kumasi, Sunyani and Tamale. In 1988 Ghana received a loan of US $12m. from France to finance the rehabilitation of Kotoka Airport.

Gemini Airlines Ltd: America House, POB 7328, Accra-North; tel. 665785; f. 1974; operates once-weekly cargo flight between Accra and London; fleet of one B-707F; Dir V. OWUSU; Gen. Man. P. F. OKINE.

Ghana Airways Corporation: Ghana House, POB 1636, Accra; tel. 664856; f. 1958; state-owned; operates domestic services and international routes to west African destinations, Italy, the Federal Republic of Germany and the UK; fleet of one DC-10-30, two Fokker F28, one DC 9-50; Chair. W. A. ADDA; Man. Dir Wing-Commdr J. B. AZARIAH.

Tourism

Ghana's tourist sector is expanding. The country's attractions include fine beaches, game reserves, traditional festivals, and old trading forts and castles. In 1987 there were 103,440 tourist arrivals.

Ghana Tourist Board: Kwame Nkrumah Conference Centre, 6th Floor, Bay 2, POB 3106, Accra; tel. 665461; telex 2105; f. 1968; Exec. Dir EDMUND Y. OFOSU-YEBOAH.

Ghana Association of Tourist and Travel Agencies: Ramia House, Kojo Thompson Rd, POB 7140, Accra; Pres. JOSEPH K. ANKUMAH; Sec. JOHNNIE MOREAUX.

Ghana Tourist Development Co Ltd: POB 772084; telex 2140; f. 1974; develops tourist infrastructure, including hotels, restaurants and casinos; operates foreign exchange, duty-free and diplomatic shops; Man. Dir BETTY AKUFFO-AMOABENG.

Atomic Energy

Atomic Energy Commission: POB 80, Legon/Accra; construction of a nuclear reactor at Kwabenya, near Accra, which was begun in 1964, was temporarily halted between 1966 and 1974; the Commission's present activities are mainly concerned with the applications of radio-isotopes in agriculture and medicine; Chair. Dr A. K. AHAFIA.

GREECE

Introductory Survey

Location, Climate, Language, Religion, Flag, Capital

The Hellenic Republic lies in south-eastern Europe. The country consists mainly of a mountainous peninsula between the Mediterranean Sea and the Aegean Sea, bounded to the north by Albania, Yugoslavia and Bulgaria, and to the east by Turkey. To the south, east and west of the mainland lie numerous Greek islands, of which the largest is Crete. The climate is Mediterranean, with mild winters and hot summers. The language is Greek, of which there are two forms—the formal language (katharevoussa) and the language commonly spoken and taught in schools (demotiki). Almost all of the inhabitants profess Christianity, and the Greek Orthodox Church, to which about 97% of the population adhere, is the established religion. The national flag (proportions 3 by 2) displays a white cross on a blue background. The capital is Athens.

Recent History

The liberation of Greece from the German occupation was followed by a civil war which lasted until 1949. The Communist forces were defeated, and the constitutional monarchy re-established. King Constantine came to the throne on the death of his father, King Paul, in 1964. A succession of weak governments and conflicts between the King and his ministers, and an alleged conspiracy involving military personnel who supported the Centre Union Party, resulted in a coup, led by right-wing army officers, in April 1967. An attempted counter-coup, led by the King, failed, and he went into exile. Colonel George Papadopoulos emerged as the dominant personality in the new regime, becoming Prime Minister in December 1967 and Regent in March 1972. The regime produced nominally democratic constitutional proposals, but all political activity was banned and opponents of the regime were expelled from all positions of power or influence.

Following an abortive naval mutiny, said to be supported by the exiled King, Greece was declared a republic in June 1973. Papadopoulos was appointed President in July. Martial law was ended, and a civilian cabinet was appointed in preparation for a general election to be held by the end of 1973. A student uprising at the Athens Polytechnic in November 1973 was bloodily repressed by the army, and another military coup overthrew Papadopoulos. Lieut-Gen. Phaidon Ghizikis was appointed President, and a mainly civilian cabinet, led by Adamantios Androutsopoulos, was installed, but effective power lay with a small group of officers and the military police under Brig.-Gen. Demetrios Ioannides. As a result of the failure of the military junta's attempt to overthrow President Makarios of Cyprus and its inability to prevent the Turkish invasion of the island (see chapter on Cyprus), the Androutsopoulos Cabinet disintegrated in July 1974. President Ghizikis called Constantine Karamanlis, a former Prime Minister, back from exile to form a civilian Government of National Salvation. Martial law was ended, the press was freed from state control, and political parties, including the Communists, were allowed to emerge. A general election in November 1974 resulted in a decisive victory for Karamanlis' New Democracy (ND) party, which gained 54% of the votes cast and won 220 of the 300 seats in Parliament. A referendum in December 1974 rejected proposals for a return to constitutional monarchy, and in June 1975 a new republican constitution, providing for a parliamentary democracy, was promulgated. In the same month Prof. Constantine Tsatsos, a former cabinet minister, was elected President.

In the general election of November 1977 ND was re-elected with a reduced majority. In May 1980 Karamanlis was elected President and resigned as Prime Minister. The new leader of ND, George Rallis, formed a government, reshuffling the previous Cabinet. He faced a growing challenge from the rising Panhellenic Socialist Movement (PASOK). In the general election of October 1981 PASOK gained an absolute majority in Parliament. Its leader, Andreas Papandreou, became Prime Minister of the first socialist government in Greek history, initially committed to withdrawal from the EEC, removal of US military bases, and to implementing a sweeping programme of reform. By the end of 1982 domestic reforms included the lowering of the voting age to 18; legalization of civil marriage and divorce, while adultery was no longer to be a criminal offence; and a restructuring of the university system. Proposed radical 'socialization' of industry encountered widespread opposition and was largely limited to the introduction of worker participation in supervisory councils. Index-linking of wage increases to the rate of inflation, one of the first measures that the PASOK Government had introduced, was modified at the end of 1982 in an attempt to reduce inflation, and a 'freeze' on wages was imposed from January 1983. After a series of strikes in the first half of 1983, a controversial law was adopted in June, increasing worker participation in the public sector, but also limiting the right to strike: this measure was strongly opposed by the Communist Party, which had hitherto generally supported the Government's domestic policy. A prices and incomes policy, announced in December, provided for wage indexation in the public sector in 1984, and for price controls. The unions withdrew their demands for wage indexation in the private sector, and a back-dated general wage increase was agreed in February 1984. In the elections to the European Parliament, held in June 1984, PASOK slightly increased its percentage of the votes in comparison with the 1981 election, winning 10 of the 24 seats, while ND won nine.

In March 1985 Papandreou unexpectedly withdrew support for President Karamanlis' candidature for a further five-year term in office. The Prime Minister planned to amend the 1975 constitution, proposing to relieve the President of all executive power and transfer it to the legislature, thus reducing the head of state to a purely ceremonial figure. President Karamanlis resigned in protest at the proposed changes, and Parliament elected Christos Sartzetakis, a judge, as President, in a vote that was widely considered to be unconstitutional. A general election was held in June to enable the Government to secure support for the proposed constitutional changes. PASOK was returned to power, receiving 45.8% of the total votes (compared with 48% in 1981) and winning 161 seats in the 300-member Parliament. The main opposition party, ND, received 41% of the votes and secured 126 seats.

In October 1985 the Government introduced a stringent two-year programme of economic austerity, including the devaluation of the drachma by 15% and a two-year 'freeze' on wages, to combat inflation and a soaring deficit on the current account of the balance of payments. In response to these measures, a series of strikes took place throughout Greece, culminating in November in a one-day general strike, called by the militant left wing and the majority of the trade unions (a minority remained loyal to the Government). Anti-austerity protests and strikes continued throughout Greece in 1986.

In March 1986 the Greek Parliament approved a series of constitutional amendments (denounced by ND as 'a step towards autocratic rule') limiting the powers of the President, whose executive powers were transferred to the legislature. The amendments limited the President's power to call a referendum and transferred to Parliament the right to declare a state of emergency. The President lost the right to dismiss the Prime Minister, and was to be permitted to dissolve Parliament only if the resignation of two Governments in quick succession demonstrated the absence of political stability. However, the President was still allowed a substantial moderating role by the use of his right to object to legislation and to request Parliament to reconsider it or to approve it with an enlarged majority.

In an extensive government reshuffle in April 1986, Papandreou relinquished the portfolio of National Defence, and the Ministries of the Interior and of Public Order reverted to their separate status. At the local elections held throughout Greece in October 1986, the ruling PASOK lost substantial support to both ND and the Communist Party ('of the Exterior'). Despite Papandreou's attempt to operate a tactical alliance between PASOK and the Communists, three ND candidates were elected as mayors in Greece's three largest cities—Athens,

Piraeus and Thessaloniki. A government reshuffle in October, which reduced the Cabinet from 48 to 36 members, was widely criticized for failing to remove those ministers generally considered to be most responsible for PASOK's decline in popularity.

In February 1987 Papandreou gave the Government a more moderate appearance by dismissing (among others) three outspokenly left-wing senior ministers from their posts in the Cabinet and nominating them as members of PASOK's executive office. These ministers had frequently expressed their disapproval of the Prime Minister's increasingly conservative policies. They were brought back into the Cabinet, however, in a further reshuffle in September. In May, in response to numerous accusations made by ND of mismanagement and corruption on the part of the Government in the public sector, Papandreou sought and won (by 157 votes to 139) a parliamentary vote of confidence in his Government.

In April 1987 the Government came into conflict with the Greek Orthodox Church when Parliament approved legislation allowing the State to expropriate about 140,000 ha of monastic land and to administer the Church's valuable urban assets. The Church (while agreeing in principle to the redistribution of its agricultural land) argued that the new law would destroy its autonomy, and threatened to sever its constitutional links with the State; it held mass public demonstrations in opposition to the proposals. As a result, the Government withdrew the legislation in August, and in November an agreement was reached whereby the monastic land would be jointly administered by the Church and the State, and the Church would retain its urban property.

Opposition to the Government's economic austerity programme continued in 1987, with further strikes and demonstrations (supported by the principal trade union confederation, which had previously been loyal to the Government). The introduction of value-added tax in January was particularly unpopular. Despite the scale of the opposition and the upheaval that the strikes caused in the towns, the Government's sole initial concession was to make a small adjustment of wages at the lower end of the salary scale in February. In November, however, Papandreou, confronted by continuing protests (and, according to some, with a view to regaining public support for PASOK in the forthcoming general election, due in 1989), modified the austerity programme by advancing the payment of 1988 wage increases from May to January; this prompted the resignation of the Minister of National Economy, who had been the main instigator of the programme. Despite the concession on wages, the trade unions organized a one-day general strike in December, but another strike, to be held in January 1988, was cancelled after the unions accepted a wages agreement for the year.

Despite a series of disruptive strikes (in protest against a scarcity of resources and low levels of earnings) by teachers and doctors in early June 1988, a parliamentary motion expressing 'no confidence' in the Government proposed by the opposition parties, was rejected by 157 votes to 123. At the end of the month Papandreou carried out a cabinet reshuffle (which included the appointment of his son, Georgios Papandreou, as the new Minister of Education and Religion) in preparation for the next general election, due to take place in June 1989. However, the Government suffered a serious set-back in November 1988, when several leading members of the Cabinet were implicated in a major financial scandal involving the Bank of Crete. As a result of these allegations, the Minister of Justice and the Minister of Public Order resigned from their posts. In an attempt to suppress opposition demands for the resignation of the entire Cabinet and the holding of an early general election, the Prime Minister carried out a further cabinet reshuffle, including the abolition of the important post of Deputy Prime Minister. Between November and December five more ministers either resigned or were dismissed, after denouncing corruption. In December, however, Parliament approved the Government's 1989 budget proposals. This did not prevent the opposition parties from renewing their demand for immediate elections.

The treaty of accession to the European Communities was signed in May 1979 and Greece became a full member in January 1981. Although originally critical of Greece's membership, the Socialist Government confined itself to seeking modification of the terms of accession, in order to take into account the under-developed Greek economy, and gave qualified assent to concessions proposed by the EEC in April 1983.

In September 1983, despite its pledge to remove US military bases, the Government signed a five-year agreement on defence and economic co-operation with the USA: the four existing US bases were to remain, and Greece was to receive US $300m.–$500m. worth of military aid annually. In November 1986 a Greek-US agreement on defence and industrial co-operation was signed. Under this five-year agreement, the USA agreed to help Greece to modernize its military industry and armed forces. In May 1987 Papandreou announced that a national referendum would be held to decide the future of the bases, when negotiations with the USA on renewal of the 1983 agreement were completed. Negotiations concerning the bases began in September, and there were indications that, in exchange for the retention of the bases, Greece was seeking US support in its various disputes with Turkey. The USA stated, however, that it would allow no specific reference to third countries in any new agreement. In August 1988 the Greek Government announced its intention to close the most conspicuous of the four bases, the Air Force base at Hellenikon, near Athens. Negotiations concerning the future of the remaining US military installations in Greece were resumed in October.

A 10-year economic co-operation agreement with the USSR was signed in 1983. Proposals for the establishment of a Balkan nuclear-free zone were made by Greece in 1983, and in 1987 Greece issued joint appeals, with both the Bulgarian and Romanian Governments, for the elimination of nuclear and chemical weapons from the Balkan region.

Relations with Turkey have been characterized by longstanding disputes concerning Cyprus (q.v.) and sovereignty over the continental shelf beneath the Aegean Sea. Having left the military structure of NATO in 1974, in protest at the Turkish occupation of northern Cyprus, Greece rejoined in 1980, but in 1981 the new Government demanded that NATO should guarantee protection against possible Turkish aggression, as a condition of continuing Greek membership; disputes with Turkey over air-space continued, and talks between the two countries' Ministers of Foreign Affairs made little progress. The difficulties in relations with Turkey were exacerbated by the unilateral declaration of an 'independent' Turkish-Cypriot state in Cyprus in November 1983, together with various minor sovereignty disputes over islands in the Aegean Sea, which led to Greece's withdrawal from NATO exercises in August 1984 and to a boycott of them in subsequent years. In June 1986 another UN peace initiative for Cyprus collapsed, and, despite several efforts by the UN, little progress was made in 1987. The Cyprus problem was exacerbated by the expansion of the Turkish forces on the island in 1987. However, distinct progress was made in September 1988, when the Greek Cypriot and Turkish Cypriot leaders began the first round of substantive direct negotiations, under UN auspices, in Nicosia. In March 1987 a disagreement between Greece and Turkey over petroleum-prospecting rights in disputed areas of the Aegean Sea almost resulted in the outbreak of military conflict. In January 1988, however, the Greek and Turkish Prime Ministers held discussions at Davos, Switzerland, and agreed on measures to reduce tension and to improve bilateral relations. It was agreed that the two countries' Prime Ministers should meet annually (the Davos meeting was the first formal contact between Greek and Turkish Heads of Government for 10 years), and that joint committees should be established to negotiate peaceful solutions to disputes. In April, however, relations between Greece and Turkey deteriorated, when a meeting of the Turkish-EEC Association Council was postponed, following objections by the Turkish delegation to an attempt by the Greek delegates to include the Cyprus issue on the agenda of the meeting. In the following month the 'Davos spirit' was renewed, when the Greek and Turkish Ministers of Foreign Affairs met in Athens and formally pledged to respect each other's sovereignty in the Aegean region. In June Turgut Özal became the first Turkish Prime Minister to visit Greece for 36 years, when he arrived in Athens for a meeting with Papandreou. There was, however, no sign of any significant development of the *rapprochement* between the two countries that resulted from this meeting.

In August 1985 Greece and Albania reopened their borders, which had remained closed since 1940, and Greece formally annulled claims to North Epirus (southern Albania), where there is a sizeable Greek minority. In August 1987 the Greek Government put a formal end to a legal vestige of the Second World War by proclaiming that it no longer considered Greece to be at war with Albania. In April 1988 relations between Greece and Albania improved significantly when the two countries signed an agreement to promote trade between their border provinces.

Government

Under the Constitution of June 1975, the President is Head of State and is elected by Parliament for a five-year term. The President appoints the Prime Minister and, upon his recommendation, the other members of the Cabinet. In March 1986 Parliament approved a series of constitutional amendments, divesting the President of his executive powers and transferring them to the legislature (see Recent History). The unicameral Parliament has 300 members, directly elected by universal adult suffrage for four years. In 1983 measures were introduced to devolve powers of local government (formerly confined almost exclusively to 55 representatives of the central government) to local councils, which were eventually to be directly elected. In January 1987 it was announced that 13 administrative regions were to be created.

Defence

Greece returned to the military structure of NATO in October 1980, after an absence of six years. Military service is compulsory for all men between 18 and 40 years of age, and lasts 21–25 months. In 1978 women were given the right to volunteer for military service of 30–50 days' basic training and for specialized training. In June 1988 the armed forces numbered 214,000, of whom 140,500 were conscripts, and consisted of an army of 170,500, a navy of 19,500 and an air force of 24,000; there was a gendarmerie of 25,000 and also a National Guard of 110,000. The defence budget for 1988 totalled 356,300m. drachmae.

Economic Affairs

Greece has traditionally been an agricultural nation, producing most of its own needs and exporting a considerable amount of produce. The country produces large quantities of wheat, barley, maize, tobacco, sugar beet, tomatoes and dried and fresh fruit. Since 1960, however, there has been a rapid increase in the importance of industry. The annual rate of expansion of agricultural output slowed from about 2.5% in the 1970s to about 1% in 1986. Agricultural products accounted for 91.45% of all exports in 1960, but in 1986 they accounted for only 27%, while manufacturing provided 52%. Agriculture provided an estimated 15.8% of gross domestic product (GDP), and manufacturing an estimated 17.5%, in 1987. In the previous year, however, about 27.4% of the working population were engaged in agriculture, compared with an EEC average of 7.6%. About one-third of the population and 57% of industrial production is situated in the area around Athens, and this creates serious environmental problems. Nevertheless, Greece is generally regarded as only semi-industrialized, and its average income is lower than that of other EEC countries. In 1987, according to estimates by the World Bank, Greece's gross national product (GNP), measured at average 1985–87 prices, was US $43,557m., equivalent to $4,350 per head. Between 1980 and 1987, it was estimated, GNP per head increased, in real terms, at an average rate of 1.6% per year.

Mineral resources are intensively exploited, and a major development has been the processing of an expanding proportion of the ores in Greece, rather than exporting raw materials. In 1985 Greece was dependent on petroleum for about 61% of its energy requirements. Petroleum and petroleum products accounted for 13.3% of the cost of imports in 1987, compared with 16.3% in 1986 and 28.5% in 1985. Hydroelectric power resources are being developed, and in June 1981 the production of crude petroleum began from the Prinos oilfield, off the northern Aegean island of Thassos. In 1987 the average daily output from Prinos was 26,000 b/d (about 1m. metric tons annually). To replace power generated from lignite deposits (which are expected to be exhausted by the 1990s), the Greek Government had planned to construct nuclear power stations, but the project was temporarily halted in 1981, owing partly to a series of unusually severe and widespread earthquakes. Industry is being encouraged to convert from petroleum to alternative sources of power, principally coal. In 1979 uranium deposits were discovered in northern Greece, and in 1981 a small natural gas field was discovered off the western Peloponnese. In March 1984 agreement was reached with the USSR on the joint construction of a plant on the Gulf of Corinth for the processing of Greek bauxite, with the aim of exporting 600,000 metric tons of alumina annually to the USSR. The plant was due to be completed in 1992. In 1987 it was announced that, from 1992, Greece would import natural gas from the USSR and Algeria to satisfy part of its energy requirements.

The average annual increase of overall GDP, measured in constant prices, was 5.6% in 1965–80, slowing to 1.5% in 1980–86. The growth of GDP was 1.8% in 1985, but only 0.5% in 1986. GDP declined by 0.6% in 1987, owing mainly to very poor harvests. Unemployment rose from 4.1% of the labour force in 1982 to 7.6% in 1987. Industrialization and the expansion of exports, which increased more than 11-fold between 1970 and 1980, failed to prevent a large deficit on the current account of the Greek balance of payments, exacerbated in 1978–80 by a sharp rise in the cost of petroleum imports. In 1985 the deficit reached a record US $3,276m. (equivalent to about 8% of GDP), reflecting a decline in earnings from tourism, shipping and workers' remittances from abroad. In 1986 the deficit was reduced to $1,676m. This decrease could be ascribed to the combination of the Government's austerity programme (see below), a fall in the cost of petroleum imports, an increase in funds provided by the EEC, and a rise in 'invisible' receipts, particularly from tourism. The deficit declined to $1,298m. in 1987, partly because of the 30% increase in 'invisible' receipts and despite the widening of the trade deficit. In December 1986, according to the Central Bank, Greece's debt to foreign institutions was $17,127m. (virtually treble the figure in 1978). The level of foreign debt repayment over the period 1986–90 was expected to average $1,700m. per annum. The trade deficit rose from 212,582m. drachmae in 1979 to 877,966m. drachmae in 1987, despite a continuing decrease in the cost of petroleum imports. The public-sector deficit has also risen because of mismanagement and indirect financing of consumption. In 1986 the Ministry of National Economy established a 50-member secretariat to monitor public-sector bodies, with the aim of improving their efficiency and ensuring that they adhere to the Government's stringent targets for wage levels and public spending. In 1987 the Government was planning to 'privatize' about 20 state-owned companies, which had accumulated heavy debts. In 1986 the public-sector borrowing requirement was reduced to 13.7% of GDP, from 17.8% in 1985. It fell marginally, to 13.5% of GDP, in 1987, compared with a target of 10%. The worsening economic crisis fuelled inflation, which averaged 20.3% annually in the years 1980–86. In 1987 inflation fell to 16.4%, which was, however, still much higher than that of other EEC members. In the 12 months to November 1988 the rate of inflation declined to 14.1%.

In October 1985 the Papandreou Government introduced a programme of austerity measures, aiming to reduce the current account deficit. The main measures were a 15% devaluation of the drachma; a two-year 'freeze' on wages, with extensive deregulation of the system of wage indexation; an import deposit scheme on about 40% of total imports (lifted in February 1987); higher taxes and prices; and reductions in planned government spending. Plans to stimulate Greece's deteriorating economy, announced by the Government in August 1986, included the linking of wages to productivity rather than to inflation (effective from January 1988) and, in an effort to reduce unemployment, the introduction of strict controls on the holding of second jobs by workers in both the public and private sectors. In 1986, as part of the move towards the full liberalization of capital movement in Greece (demanded by the EEC), the Government ended restrictions on the repatriation of foreign capital brought into the country by foreigners, and profits deriving from it. In 1987 Papandreou appealed for more foreign investment in Greece, and stressed that he was not opposed to free market forces in the economy. On 1 January 1987 value-added tax (VAT) was introduced. In November the two-year austerity programme was officially ended (although few of the 1987 economic targets appeared likely to be met). It was simultaneously announced, however, that the Government would continue to apply austere monetary and economic policies for at least another year. The wage 'freeze' was lifted on 1 January 1988, as promised, and free collective bargaining was restored.

Despite the relative success of the stabilization programme in 1986–87, the budget deficit remained a major problem. In 1987 budget expenditure reached 2,593,000m. drachmae and revenue totalled 2,214,000m. drachmae, leaving a deficit of 379,000m. drachmae. The budget maintained high levels of expenditure on defence and social welfare, while seeking to reduce the inflation rate. The proposed budget for 1988 envisaged a deficit of 957,000m. drachmae (equivalent to about 13% of projected annual GDP). The actual deficit, however, was expected to reach 1,167,000m. drachmae (equivalent to 15.6% of GDP). Budget estimates for 1989 envisaged expenditure of 4,050,000m. drachmae and revenue of 2,660,000m. drachmae, with a record deficit of 1,390,000m. drachmae (equivalent to 16.2% of projected annual GDP). The increases in expenditure in the 1989 budget were mainly directed towards education, health and social welfare.

The major part of Greece's external trade is with other members of the EEC (which together provided about 58% of imports and took 63% of exports in 1986). Under the transitional arrangements, subsequent to joining the EEC in January 1981, Greece agreed to remove all remaining tariffs and quantitative controls by 1986. Greek agriculture was to be aligned with EEC policy over a period of seven years, with farm prices being raised gradually to meet the higher levels prevailing in other EEC countries. In March 1982 the Government requested special arrangements, complaining that EEC rules on competition, subsidies and the protection of new industries were hindering Greek development, while the EEC's common agricultural policy, designed to assist the more advanced northern members, had brought no benefit to Greece. In response, the European Commission offered special assistance in the areas of transport, agriculture, employment, pollution and taxation reform, while Greece's share of Community aid under the 1985–91 Integrated Plan for the Mediterranean Region was to amount to 2,542m. ECUs (US $2,460m. at December 1982 values), of which 49% was for the development and diversification of agriculture. The Commission insisted, however, that Greece should operate within existing Community rules, and refused to allow more than one-half of the import restrictions which had been proposed by Greece in January 1983.

In November 1985 the EEC approved a loan of ECU 1,750m. (US $1,535m. at November 1985 values) for Greece, to help the country to overcome its balance-of-payments problems, but linked the two-part loan to the implementation of strict economic conditions. The first instalment was made available immediately, and the second instalment was released in December 1986, on condition that Greece would progressively eliminate import deposits in 1987 and export subsidies by 1990.

Social Welfare

There is a state social insurance scheme for wage-earners, while voluntary or staff insurances provide for salaried staff. Every citizen is entitled to an old-age pension and sickness benefit. In 1981 Greece had 688 hospital establishments, with a total of 59,914 beds (equivalent to one for every 162 inhabitants), and there were 24,724 physicians working in the country. Of total expenditure by the central Government in 1981, about 86,700m. drachmae (10.1%) was for health, and a further 251,900m. drachmae (29.3%) for social security and welfare.

Education

Education is available free of charge at all levels, and is officially compulsory for all children between the ages of six and 15 years. Primary education begins at the age of six and lasts for six years. Secondary education, beginning at the age of 12, is generally for six years, divided into two equal cycles. In 1983 the total enrolment at primary and secondary schools was equivalent to 95% of the school-age population. Primary enrolment in that year included 91% of children in the relevant age-group, while the comparable ratio at secondary schools was 77%. In 1985/86 there were 13,878 pre-primary and primary schools, with a total estimated enrolment of 1,047,814 pupils, and 3,134 secondary schools, with an estimated 813,534 pupils. There was a total of 181,901 students in 89 higher education institutions (including 16 universities) in 1985/86. Between 1951 and 1981 the average rate of adult illiteracy declined from 72% to 10%. In 1985, according to estimates by UNESCO, the rate was only 7.7% (males 2.9%; females 12.2%).

The vernacular language (demotiki) has replaced the formal version (katharevoussa) in secondary education.

Public Holidays

1989: 2 January (for New Year's Day), 6 January (Epiphany), 13 March (Clean Monday), 25 March (Independence Day), 28 April–1 May (Greek Orthodox Easter, and Labour Day), 19 June (Holy Spirit Day), 15 August (Assumption of the Virgin Mary), 28 October ('Ochi' Day, anniversary of Greek defiance of Italy's 1940 ultimatum), 25–26 December (Christmas).

1990: 1 January (New Year's Day), 6 January (Epiphany), 26 February (Clean Monday), 25 March (Independence Day), 13–16 April (Greek Orthodox Easter), 1 May (Labour Day), 4 June (Holy Spirit Day), 15 August (Assumption of the Virgin Mary), 28 October ('Ochi' Day, anniversary of Greek defiance of Italy's 1940 ultimatum), 25–26 December (Christmas).

Weights and Measures

The metric system is in force.

Statistical Survey

Source (unless otherwise stated): National Statistical Service of Greece, Odos Lycourgou 14–16, Athens; tel. (21) 3249302; telex 216734.

Area and Population

AREA, POPULATION AND DENSITY

Area (sq km)	131,957*
Population (census results)	
14 March 1971	8,768,641
5 April 1981	9,740,417
Population (official estimates at mid-year)	
1985	9,934,294
1986	9,963,604
1987†	9,990,000
Density (per sq km) at mid-1987†	75.7

* 50,949 sq miles.
† Provisional.

PRINCIPAL TOWNS (population at 1981 census)

Athinai (Athens, the capital)	885,737	Larissa	102,426
Thessaloniki (Salonika)	406,413	Iraklion	102,398
		Volos	71,378
Piraeus	196,389	Kavala	56,705
Patras	142,163	Canea	47,451
		Serres	46,317

GREECE

BIRTHS, MARRIAGES AND DEATHS

	Registered live births		Registered marriages		Registered deaths	
	Number	Rate (per 1,000)	Number	Rate (per 1,000)	Number	Rate (per 1,000)
1980	148,134	15.4	62,352	6.5	87,282	9.1
1981	140,953	14.5	71,178	7.3	86,261	8.9
1982	137,275	14.0	67,784	6.9	86,345	8.8
1983	132,608	13.5	71,143	7.2	90,586	9.2
1984	125,724	12.7	54,793	5.6	88,397	8.9
1985	116,481	11.7	63,709	6.4	92,886	9.3
1986	112,810	11.3	58,091	5.9	91,783	9.2
1987	105,899	10.6	62,899	6.3	95,232	9.5

ECONOMICALLY ACTIVE POPULATION
('000 persons, 1987*)

	Males	Females	Total
Agriculture, hunting, forestry and fishing	536.3	439.5	975.7
Mining and quarrying	23.9	2.2	26.1
Manufacturing	529.8	220.4	750.1
Electricity, gas and water	31.2	5.2	36.4
Construction	247.4	1.6	249.0
Trade, restaurants and hotels	379.5	232.8	612.4
Transport, storage and communications	234.8	26.5	261.3
Finance, insurance, real estate and business services	92.1	57.5	149.7
Community, social and personal services	354.8	293.5	648.3
Activities not adequately defined	19.8	31.4	51.2
Total	2,449.6	1,310.6	3,760.2

* Figures are based on a labour force survey. The data exclude persons seeking work for the first time, numbering 123,400 (males 39,800; females 83,600), and other unemployed persons, numbering 162,800 (males 88,100; females 74,700).

LIVESTOCK ('000 head at December)

	1983	1984	1985
Asses	199	188	177
Buffaloes	1	1	1
Cattle	755	725	722
Goats	4,744	4,816	4,936
Horses	80	74	67
Mules	94	89	84
Pigs	1,065	1,061	1,009
Sheep	8,252	8,258	8,343
Chickens	29,082	29,123	28,030
Ducks	105	107	99
Geese	44	44	48
Turkeys	158	149	147

LIVESTOCK PRODUCTS (metric tons)

	1983	1984	1985
Beef, veal and buffalo meat	95,404	91,206	84,398
Mutton, lamb and goat meat	123,686	126,619	126,478
Pig meat	146,896	148,174	138,273
Poultry meat*	124,137	120,968	113,023
Edible pig fat	4,760	4,237	3,158
Cows' milk	610,072	574,836	570,409
Buffaloes' milk	191	159	132
Sheep's milk	612,160	621,987	624,592
Goats' milk	456,103	462,833	464,657
Butter	5,462	5,285	4,699
Cheese:			
hard	34,942	34,989	34,623
soft	107,320	106,756	107,002
Fresh cream	3,410	3,466	3,670
Hen eggs	124,608	117,657	123,857
Honey	10,902	11,786	10,405
Raw silk	65	53	61
Wool: greasy	9,286	9,331	9,400
Hides and skins ('000 pieces):			
from small animals	7,565	7,559	7,649
from large animals	280	258	232

* Including meat from other small animals.

Agriculture

PRINCIPAL CROPS ('000 metric tons)

	1985	1986*	1987*
Wheat	1,806	2,390	2,213
Rice (paddy)	103	121	136
Barley	583	681	573
Maize	1,908	1,994	2,156
Oats	65	70	70
Potatoes	1,009	971	948
Dry beans	29	38	27
Other pulses	27	28	26
Sunflower seed	96	160	140
Cottonseed	336	412	589
Cotton (lint)	157	194	
Olives	1,440	1,205	1,100†
Cabbages	167	156	n.a.
Tomatoes	2,264	1,700	1,665
Cucumbers and gherkins	159	145	n.a.
Onions (dry)	140	156	141
Watermelons	617	610	627
Melons	131	130	150
Grapes	1,673	1,712	1,500
Sugar beet	2,515	2,458	2,025
Apples	262	306	303
Pears	140	129	120
Peaches and nectarines	548	605	575
Oranges	630	837	579
Lemons and limes	204	200	119
Apricots	131	97	107
Nuts	86	78	57
Tobacco (leaves)	150	161	155

* Estimates. † FAO estimate.

Forestry

ROUNDWOOD REMOVALS ('000 cubic metres, excl. bark)

	1984	1985	1986
Sawlogs, veneer logs and logs for sleepers	407	577	617
Pulpwood	142	142*	142*
Other industrial wood	219	219*	219*
Fuel wood	1,915	1,915*	1,915*
Total	2,683	2,853*	2,893*

* FAO estimate.

Source: FAO, *Yearbook of Forest Products*.

SAWNWOOD PRODUCTION
('000 cubic metres, incl. boxboards)

	1984	1985	1986*
Coniferous (softwood)	191	200	200
Broadleaved (hardwood)	130	105	105
Total	321	305	305

* FAO estimates.

Source: FAO, *Yearbook of Forest Products*.

GREECE

Fishing

('000 metric tons, live weight)

	1984	1985	1986
Inland waters	8.6	7.8	10.2
Atlantic Ocean	9.0	11.4	11.3
Mediterranean Sea*	88.1	94.1	101.5
Total catch*	105.7	113.3	123.0

* Excluding catches from vessels of less than 19 hp, estimated at 24,500 metric tons in 1986.

Mining

('000 metric tons, unless otherwise indicated)

	1983	1984	1985
Lignite	30,705.5	32,467.1	35,875.1
Crude petroleum	1,176	1,251	1,250
Iron ore*	1,330	n.a.	n.a.
Bauxite	2,435.2	2,286.2	2,341.1
Zinc concentrates†	21.4	21.9	n.a.
Lead concentrates†	19.4	21.2	n.a.
Chromium ore†	9	21	n.a.
Magnesite	858.8	1,057.0	884.4
Kaolin (raw)	42.4	75.1	75.6
Perlite (raw)	32.0	17.7	54.7
Bentonite (raw)	144.1	54.0	182.7
Salt (unrefined)	147.7	126.5	195.1
Marble ('000 cu m)	207.4	229.9	279.2
Natural gas (million cu m)	3‡	66	62

* The estimated iron content is 43%.
† Figures refer to the metal content of ores and concentrates.
‡ '000 terajoules.
Crude petroleum ('000 metric tons): 1,254 in 1986; 1,131 in 1987.
Natural gas (million cu m): 85 in 1986; 96 in 1987.

Industry

SELECTED PRODUCTS
('000 metric tons, unless otherwise indicated)

	1983	1984	1985
Edible fats	42.8	40	40
Olive oil (crude)	268	305	409
Raw sugar	297.5	218	318
Wine	305	312	308
Beer ('000 hectolitres)	2,847	2,969	3,262
Cigarettes (million)	24,286	25,699	27,635
Cotton yarn (pure)	128.7	125.3	127
Woven cotton fabrics—pure and mixed (metric tons)	39,693	37,188	40,949
Flax, hemp and jute yarn—pure and mixed (metric tons)	1,801	1,328	994
Wool yarn—pure (metric tons)	11,068	10,076	9,223
Woven woollen fabrics—pure and mixed (metric tons)[1]	3,256	2,816	2,959
Yarn of artificial material (metric tons)	9,330	9,580	9,814
Fabrics of artificial fibres (metric tons)	1,616	1,459	1,529
Footwear—excl. rubber and plastic ('000 pairs)	12,599	11,180	11,305
Rubber footwear ('000 pairs)	1,338	410	394
Paper and paperboard	273	325	365

—continued	1983	1984	1985
Sulphuric acid	1,016	1,155	1,086
Hydrochloric acid (21° Bé)	40.5	49	54
Nitric acid (54% or 36.3° Bé)	440	478	501
Ammonia (anhydrous)	276	305	296
Caustic soda (Sodium hydroxide)	30	31	34
Nitrogenous fertilizers (single)	717	581	583
Superphosphatic fertilizers (single)	105	80	79
Polyvinyl chloride	50.7	57.2	57
Liquefied petroleum gas	180	248	215
Naphthas	830.5	645	497
Motor spirit (petrol)	1,575	1,745	1,840
Jet fuels	1,608	1,341	1,364
Distillate fuel oils	3,901	3,687	3,310
Residual fuel oils	5,456	5,167	5,222
Cement	14,196.3	13,521	12,855
Crude steel (incl. alloys)	868	915	979
Aluminium (unwrought)	157.9	189	175
Refined lead (unwrought)	—	12	14
Refrigerators—household ('000)	149.8	118	139
Washing machines—household ('000)	88	78	85
Television receivers ('000)	177	158	183
Lorries (number)[2]	7,552	4,685	3,081
Electric energy (million kWh)	22,048	22,820	25,344

[1] After undergoing finishing processes.
[2] Assembled wholly or mainly from imported parts.

Finance

CURRENCY AND EXCHANGE RATES

Monetary Units
100 leptae (singular: lepta) = 1 drachma.

Denominations
Coins: 10, 20 and 50 leptae; 1, 2, 5, 10 and 20 drachmae.
Notes: 50, 100, 500 and 1,000 drachmae.

Sterling and Dollar Equivalents (30 September 1988)
£1 sterling = 256.90 drachmae;
US $1 = 152.30 drachmae;
1,000 drachmae = £3.893 = $6.566.

Average Exchange Rate (drachmae per US $)
1985   138.12
1986   139.98
1987   135.43

BUDGET ESTIMATES (million drachmae)

Revenue	1986	1987	1988
Ordinary budget:			
Direct taxes	481,780	492,400	616,440
Excise duties	2,470	2,050	500
Indirect taxes	870,300	1,194,730	1,369,430
European Community	30,100	53,020	52,900
Credit receipts	—	—	656,530
Other	104,850	96,900	105,730
Sub-total	1,489,500	1,840,000	2,801,530
Extraordinary budget:			
Revenue from investments	6,000	6,000	6,500
Aid and loans from abroad	172,000	258,000	200,000
Revenue from NATO works	7,300	10,000	12,800
Increase in national debt	140,000	100,000	100,500
Receipts from EEC	—	—	63,000
Total	1,814,800	2,214,000	3,184,330

GREECE

Statistical Survey

Expenditure	1986	1987	1988
Ordinary budget:			
Political ministries	1,386,400	1,758,757	2,259,790
Defence	235,337	278,823	344,100
European Community	74,607	70,100	80,000
Police and other sectors	59,956	61,320	72,640
Sub-total	1,756,300	2,169,000	2,756,530
Provision for increase	20,000	50,000	45,000
Sub-total	1,776,300	2,219,000	2,801,530
Extraordinary budget:			
Expenditure on NATO works	5,700	10,000	12,800
Investments	318,000	364,000	370,000
Total	2,100,000	2,593,000	3,184,330

INTERNATIONAL RESERVES (US $ million at 31 December)

	1985	1986†	1987†
Gold*	862.8	841.3	1,057.2
Reserve position in IMF	82.4	85.8	99.5
Foreign exchange	785.6	1,432.9	2,581.9
Total	1,730.8	2,360.0	3,738.6

* Beginning in December 1985, gold reserves are valued at market-related prices.
† Beginning in January 1986, figures exclude deposits made with the European Monetary Co-operation Fund.
Source: IMF, *International Financial Statistics*.

MONEY SUPPLY ('000 million drachmae at 31 December)

	1985	1986	1987
Currency outside banks	513.5	550.1	641.4
Private sector deposits at Bank of Greece	31.3	123.5	120.1
Demand deposits at commercial banks	174.6	202.1	238.5
Total money	719.4	875.6	1,000.0

Source: IMF, *International Financial Statistics*.

COST OF LIVING (Consumer Price Index. Base: 1982 = 100)

	1985	1986	1987
Foodstuffs	166.8	200.6	225.9
Alcohol, beverages and tobacco	162.4	196.4	227.2
Clothing and footwear	188.4	236.2	287.5
Housing	152.8	184.6	211.6
Household equipment	180.1	233.9	278.6
Medical and personal care	166.7	201.1	242.3
Education and recreation	188.7	230.1	284.3
Transport and communications	157.8	199.9	222.7
Miscellaneous	199.0	251.4	296.1
All items	169.9	209.0	243.3

NATIONAL ACCOUNTS (million drachmae at current prices)

	1985	1986*	1987†
Gross domestic product at factor cost	4,135,387	4,894,781	5,539,100
of which:			
Agriculture	713,824	791,915	875,000
Manufacturing	752,500	907,415	971,000
Wholesale and retail trade (incl. banking, insurance, etc.)	647,420	802,934	893,100
Public administration and defence	476,324	541,948	2,800,000
Other activities	1,543,319	1,850,576	
Income from abroad	−33,784	−67,846	−63,332

—continued	1985	1986*	1987†
Gross national product (GNP) at factor cost	4,101,603	4,826,935	5,475,768
Less depreciation allowances	−403,045	−505,238	−583,984
National income at factor cost	3,698,558	4,321,697	4,891,784
Indirect taxes, less subsidies	480,964	648,426	850,400
National income in market prices	4,179,522	4,970,123	5,742,184
Depreciation allowances	403,045	505,238	583,984
GNP in market prices	4,582,567	5,475,361	6,326,168
Balance of exports and imports of goods and services, and borrowing‡	569,690	538,002	486,100
Available resources	5,152,257	6,013,363	6,812,268
of which:			
Private consumption expenditure§	3,228,027	3,876,046	4,471,043
Government consumption expenditure	942,050	1,075,040	1,246,500
Fixed capital formation‡	880,370	1,024,370	1,113,525
Change in stocks	101,810	37,907	−18,800

* Provisional. † Estimates.
‡ Excluding ships operating overseas.
§ Including statistical discrepancies (million drachmae): 202,535 in 1985; 187,069 in 1986; 180,271 in 1987.

BALANCE OF PAYMENTS (US $ million)

	1985	1986	1987
Merchandise exports f.o.b.	4,293	4,513	5,613
Merchandise imports f.o.b.	−9,346	−8,936	−11,111
Trade balance	−5,053	−4,423	−5,498
Exports of services	2,818	3,392	4,528
Imports of services	−2,707	−3,012	−3,364
Balance on goods and services	−4,942	−4,043	−4,334
Private unrequited transfers (net)	797	975	1,371
Government unrequited transfers (net)	869	1,392	1,665
Current balance	−3,276	−1,676	−1,298
Direct capital investment (net)	447	471	683
Other long-term capital (net)	2,319	1,680	703
Short-term capital (net)	158	257	587
Net errors and omissions	637	150	1,417
Total (net monetary movements)	285	882	2,092
Valuation changes (net)	80	127	−229
Exceptional financing (net)	255	−380	−168
Changes in reserves	620	629	1,695

Source: IMF, *International Financial Statistics*.

External Trade

PRINCIPAL COMMODITIES (million drachmae)

Imports c.i.f.	1985	1986	1987
Food and live animals	161,844	235,147	292,486
Meat and meat preparations	60,961	79,108	105,838
Fresh, chilled or frozen meat	58,173	76,046	101,002
Crude materials (inedible) except fuels	80,708	97,834	104,949
Textile fibres and waste	23,948	25,323	22,659
Mineral fuels, lubricants, etc.	416,522	275,686	242,864
Petroleum and petroleum products	402,538	258,539	233,127
Crude petroleum	363,927	228,601	203,311
Petroleum products*	34,986	25,981	27,321

GREECE

Statistical Survey

Imports c.i.f.—continued	1985	1986	1987
Chemicals	121,036	166,071	193,226
Chemical elements and compounds	35,181	46,967	54,522
Plastic materials, etc.	29,913	41,021	48,366
Basic manufactures	224,365	301,970	361,986
Textile yarn, fabrics, etc.	15,128	21,276	29,023
Iron and steel	59,268	73,918	69,786
Machinery and transport equipment	333,852	409,826	429,849
Non-electric machinery	114,411	143,280	164,803
Electrical machinery, apparatus, etc.	33,367	46,839	48,666
Transport equipment	165,351	187,239	188,081
Road motor vehicles and parts (excl. tyres, engines and electrical parts)	79,893	98,208	109,399
Ships and boats	77,321	79,534	75,797
Miscellaneous manufactured articles	56,555	71,572	98,281
Total (incl. others)	1,412,797	1,582,298	1,758,951

Exports f.o.b.	1985	1986	1987
Food and live animals	134,142	174,471	183,285
Fruit and vegetables	95,824	113,332	116,959
Fresh fruit and nuts (excl. oil nuts)†	30,946	34,472	31,494
Dried fruit†	16,947	18,847	19,317
Dried grapes (raisins)	14,839	17,722	16,059
Preserved or prepared vegetables	22,933	26,193	30,033
Beverages and tobacco	28,651	40,108	49,245
Tobacco and manufactures	21,202	30,589	38,435
Unmanufactured tobacco	20,792	29,856	37,251
Crude materials (inedible) except fuels	46,666	46,367	58,143
Mineral fuels, lubricants, etc.	75,780	51,833	58,905
Petroleum products*	62,231	51,027	48,097
Chemicals	25,469	26,021	27,434
Basic manufactures	180,991	216,488	230,777
Textile yarn, fabrics, etc.	57,407	76,813	85,043
Textile yarn and thread	37,159	46,190	51,067
Non-metallic mineral manufactures	31,254	33,822	34,035
Lime, cement, etc.	27,545	28,472	27,430
Cement	22,414	22,488	21,148
Iron and steel	40,576	43,444	35,725
Non-ferrous metals	24,125	25,335	35,015
Aluminium and aluminium alloys	19,718	18,361	27,688
Machinery and transport equipment	18,351	23,100	23,890
Miscellaneous manufactured articles	104,471	173,372	215,871
Clothing (excl. footwear)	87,052	151,855	194,981
Total (incl. others)	629,085	789,994	880,985

* Including partly refined petroleum.
† Dried citrus fruit and dried tropical fruit are included with 'fresh fruit and nuts'.

PRINCIPAL TRADING PARTNERS* (million drachmae)

Imports c.i.f.	1985	1986	1987
Austria	14,864	15,986	23,422
Belgium/Luxembourg	39,532	53,799	60,403
Brazil	9,678	11,882	15,280
Denmark	15,324	21,639	21,820
Egypt	9,454	16,717	5,145
France	90,925	127,885	137,574
German Democratic Republic	8,857	6,542	6,003
Germany, Federal Republic	240,360	335,592	389,888
Iran	7,705	7,046	4,053
Iraq	66,049	18,345	17,213
Italy	131,963	182,787	215,569
Japan	89,734	96,417	73,488
Netherlands	82,409	106,010	123,752
Romania	7,796	7,532	9,049
Saudi Arabia	113,583	102,460	66,879
Spain	17,929	20,042	25,162
Sweden	14,149	22,068	22,449
Switzerland	18,601	27,353	32,643
USSR	73,545	39,824	43,998
United Kingdom	53,412	65,735	85,790
USA	44,437	47,912	48,451
Yugoslavia	14,712	19,251	27,247
Total (incl. others)	1,412,797	1,582,299	1,758,951

* Imports by country of first consignment; exports by country of consumption.

Exports f.o.b.	1985	1986	1987
Belgium/Luxembourg	11,792	22,018	24,562
Bulgaria	6,092	8,229	5,689
Cyprus	11,650	11,938	13,037
Denmark	n.a.	7,571	8,579
Egypt	19,802	18,909	16,447
France	50,227	74,872	75,909
Germany, Federal Republic	126,293	186,925	214,452
Hungary	2,141	2,581	2,541
Iraq	6,283	8,424	2,299
Italy	71,196	106,528	142,298
Japan	5,891	5,843	8,056
Lebanon	5,759	4,897	4,188
Libya	6,534	7,990	5,483
Netherlands	25,534	39,188	33,407
Romania	5,419	6,645	6,431
Saudi Arabia	24,990	22,162	17,521
Spain	n.a.	7,194	12,234
Sweden	5,048	7,022	10,702
Switzerland	n.a.	10,347	11,637
Syria	4,982	3,877	3,005
USSR	19,528	10,874	10,279
United Kingdom	43,603	53,772	75,522
USA	51,268	56,102	59,862
Yugoslavia	10,304	10,313	8,682
Total (incl. others)	629,085	789,995	880,985

Transport

RAILWAYS (estimated traffic)

	1985	1986	1987
Passenger-kilometres (million)	1,501.8	1,667.2	1,658.2
Net ton-kilometres (million)	733.0	702.4	598.8

ROAD TRAFFIC (motor vehicles in use at 31 December)

	1985	1986	1987*
Passenger cars	1,263,366	1,359,173	1,432,577
Buses and coaches	18,237	18,485	18,748
Goods vehicles	600,955	627,231	656,144
Motorcycles, etc.	167,882	179,281	188,840

* Provisional.

GREECE

SHIPPING
Merchant fleet (at 1 July)

	1987		1988	
	Vessels	Gross reg. tons	Vessels	Gross reg. tons
Cargo boats	1,057	12,588,061	974	12,114,894
Passenger boats	355	614,307	378	686,448
Tankers	343	9,944,081	331	9,015,348
Others	334	97,020	360	109,596

Freight traffic

	1985	1986	1987†
Vessels entered ('000 net reg. tons)	151,530	173,315	192,330
Goods loaded ('000 metric tons)*	20,111	22,146	24,256
Goods unloaded ('000 metric tons)*	24,773	27,998	30,699

* International sea-borne shipping.   † Provisional.

CIVIL AVIATION
(domestic and foreign flights of Olympic Airways)

	1985	1986	1987
Kilometres flown ('000)	52,918	48,501	51,317
Passenger-kilometres ('000)	7,468,306	6,382,020	7,121,478
Freight ton-kilometres ('000)	103,246	91,671	104,283
Mail ton-kilometres ('000)	11,744	9,617	9,810

Tourism

FOREIGN TOURIST ARRIVALS

	1985	1986*	1987*
Cruise passengers	465,435	n.a.	n.a.
Other tourists	6,573,993	n.a.	n.a.
Total	7,039,428	7,400,000	8,053,000
Earnings (US $'000)	1,428,030	1,834,218	2,191,700

* Estimates.

TOURISTS BY COUNTRY OF ORIGIN
(foreign citizens, excluding cruise passengers)

Country	1983	1984	1985
Australia	83,230	96,953	121,894
Austria	195,381	237,918	282,468
Canada	72,540	82,226	102,552
Denmark	148,626	124,037	160,792
France	299,506	405,907	441,141
German Democratic Republic / Germany, Federal Republic	728,478	864,000	1,050,078
Italy	327,610	328,598	364,177
Netherlands	153,672	192,879	280,309
Sweden	189,921	194,356	223,956
Switzerland	173,830	156,995	205,662
United Kingdom	888,991	1,043,363	1,329,259
USA	406,887	474,845	466,155
Yugoslavia	55,375	263,209	350,735
Others	1,050,767	1,055,746	1,194,319
Unspecified	3,663	2,160	496
Total	4,778,477	5,523,192	6,573,993

Communications Media

	1985	1986	1987
Radio receivers ('000 in use)	4,000	n.a.	n.a.
Television receivers ('000 licensed)	1,715	n.a.	n.a.
Telephones ('000 in use)	3,714.8	3,915.3	4,122.3
Newspapers:			
Daily	n.a.	143	142
Non-daily	n.a.	962	962
Other periodicals	n.a.	778	777

Book production: 4,651 titles (incl. pamphlets) in 1985.

Education
(1985/86)

	Institutions	Teachers	Students
Pre-primary	5,203	7,617	160,079
Primary	8,675	37,994	887,735
Secondary:			
General	2,654	41,782	704,119
Vocational	480	8,138	109,415
Higher:			
Universities	16	6,934	110,917
Other	73	4,944	70,984

Directory

The Constitution

A new constitution for the Hellenic Republic came into force on 11 June 1975. The main provisions of this Constitution, as subsequently amended, are summarized below.

Greece shall be a parliamentary democracy with a President as Head of State. All powers are derived from the people and exist for the benefit of the people. The established religion is that of The Eastern Orthodox Church of Christ.

EXECUTIVE AND LEGISLATIVE

The President

In March 1986 a series of amendments to the Constitution was approved by a majority vote of Parliament, which relieved the President of his executive power and transferred such power to the legislature, thus reducing the Head of State to a largely ceremonial figure.

The President is elected by Parliament for a period of five years. The re-election of the same person shall be permitted only once. The President represents the State in relations with other nations, is Supreme Commander of the armed forces and may declare war and conclude treaties. The President shall appoint the Prime Minister and, on the Prime Minister's recommendation, the other members of the Government. The President shall convoke Parliament once every year and in extraordinary session whenever he deems it reasonable. In exceptional circumstances the President may preside over the Cabinet, call the Council of the Republic, and suspend Parliament for a period not exceeding 30 days. In the amendment of March 1986, the President lost the right to dismiss the Prime Minister, his power to call a referendum was limited, and the right to declare a state of emergency was transferred to Parliament. The President can now dissolve Parliament only if the resignation of two Governments in quick succession demonstrates the absence of political stability. If no party has a majority in Parliament, the President must offer an opportunity to form a government to the leader of each of the four biggest parties in turn, strictly following the order of their parliamentary strengths. If no party leader is able to form a government, the President may try to assemble an all-party government; failing that, the President must appoint a caretaker cabinet, led by a senior judge, to hold office until a fresh election takes place. The Constitution continues to reserve a substantial moderating role for the President, however, in that he retains the right to object to legislation and may request Parliament to reconsider it or to approve it with an enlarged majority.

The Government

The Government consists of the Cabinet which comprises the Prime Minister and Ministers. The Government determines and directs the general policy of the State in accordance with the Constitution and the laws. The Cabinet must enjoy the confidence of Parliament and may be removed by a vote of no confidence. The Prime Minister is to be the leader of the party with an absolute majority in Parliament, or, if no such party exists, the leader of the party with a relative majority.

The Council of the Republic

The Council of the Republic shall be composed of all former democratic Presidents, the Prime Minister, the leader of the Opposition and the parliamentary Prime Ministers of governments which have enjoyed the confidence of Parliament, presided over by the President. It shall meet when the largest parties are unable to form a government with the confidence of Parliament and may empower the President to appoint a Prime Minister who may or may not be a member of Parliament. The Council may also authorize the President to dissolve Parliament.

Parliament

Parliament is to be unicameral and composed of not fewer than 200 and not more than 300 deputies elected by direct, universal and secret ballot for a term of four years. Parliament shall elect its own President, or Speaker. It must meet once a year for a regular session of at least five months. Bills passed by Parliament must be ratified by the President and the President's veto can be nullified by an absolute majority of the total number of deputies. Parliament may impeach the President by a motion signed by one-third and passed by two-thirds of the total number of deputies. Parliament is also empowered to impeach present or former members of the Government. In these cases the defendant shall be brought before an *ad hoc* tribunal presided over by the President of the Supreme Court and composed of 12 judges. Certain legislative work, as specified in the Constitution, must be passed by Parliament in plenum, and Parliament cannot make a decision without an absolute majority of the members present, which under no circumstances shall be less than one-quarter of the total number of deputies. The Constitution provides for certain legislative powers to be exercised by not more than two Parliamentary Departments. Parliament may revise the Constitution in accordance with the procedure laid down in the Constitution.

THE JUDICIAL AUTHORITY

Justice is to be administered by courts of regular judges, who enjoy personal and functional independence. The President, after consultations with a judicial council, shall appoint the judges for life. The judges are subject only to the Constitution and the laws. Courts are divided into administrative, civil and penal and shall be organized by virtue of special laws. They must not apply laws which are contrary to the Constitution. The final jurisdiction in matters of judicial review rests with a Special Supreme Tribunal.

Certain laws, passed before the implementation of this constitution and deemed not contrary to it, are to remain in force. Other specified laws, even if contrary to the Constitution, are to remain in force until repealed by further legislation.

INDIVIDUAL AND SPECIAL RIGHTS

All citizens are equal under the Constitution and before the law, having the same rights and obligations. No titles of nobility or distinction are to be conferred or recognized. All persons are to enjoy full protection of life, honour and freedom, irrespective of nationality, race, creed or political allegiance. Retrospective legislation is prohibited and no citizen may be punished without due process of law. Freedom of speech, of the Press, of association and of religion are guaranteed under the Constitution. All persons have the right to a free education, which the state has the duty to provide. Work is a right and all workers, irrespective of sex or other distinction, are entitled to equal remuneration for rendering services of equal value. The right of peaceful assembly, the right of a person to property and the freedom to form political parties are guaranteed under the Constitution. The exercise of the right to vote by all citizens over 18 years of age is obligatory. No person may exercise his rights and liberties contrary to the Constitution.

MOUNT ATHOS

The district of Mount Athos shall, in accordance with its ancient privileged status, be a self-governing part of the Greek State and its sovereignty shall remain unaffected.

The Government

HEAD OF STATE

President: CHRISTOS SARTZETAKIS (took office 30 March 1985).

THE CABINET
(February 1989)

Prime Minister: ANDREAS PAPANDREOU.
Minister to the Prime Minister: AGAMEMNON KOUTSOGIORGAS.
Minister of National Defence: IOANNIS KHARALAMBOPOULOS.
Minister of Foreign Affairs: KAROLOS PAPOULIAS.
Minister of the Interior: APOSTOLOS TSOKHATZOPOULOS.
Minister of the National Economy: PANAYIOTIS ROUMELIOTIS.
Minister of Finance: DHIMITRIOS TSOVOLAS.
Minister of Agriculture: IOANNIS POTTAKIS.
Minister of Labour: GEORGIOS GENNIMATAS.
Minister of Health, Welfare and Social Services: APOSTOLOS KAKLAMANIS.
Minister of Justice: VASILIOS ROTIS.
Minister of Education and Religion: GEORGIOS PAPANDREOU.
Minister of Public Order: GEORGIOS PETSOS.
Minister of Macedonia and Thrace: STILIANOS PAPATHEMELIS.
Minister of Culture: MELINA MERCOURI.
Minister of the Aegean: EVANGELOS YIANNOPOULOS.
Minister of the Environment and Town Planning and of Public Works: VASILIS KEDHIKOGLOU.

GREECE — Directory

Minister of Industry: ANASTASIOS PEPONIS.
Minister of Commerce: NIKOLAOS AKRITIDHIS.
Minister of Transport and Communications: IOANNIS KHARALAMBOUS.
Minister of Merchant Marine: VASILIOS SARANDITIS.
Ministers without Portfolio: ATHANASIOS FILIPPOPOULOS, KHRISTOS MARKOPOULOS, KONSTANDINOS LALIOTIS.

MINISTRIES

Ministry to the President: Odos Zalokosta 10, Athens; tel. (01) 3630911; telex 216325.
Ministry to the Prime Minister: Leoforos Vassilissis Sophias 15, 106 74 Athens; tel. (01) 3646350; telex 214333.
Ministry of Agriculture: Odos Aharnon 2–6, Athens; tel. (01) 3291206; telex 215308.
Ministry of Commerce: Kanningos Sq., Athens; tel. (01) 3616251; telex 215282.
Ministry of Culture: Odos Aristidou 14, 101 86 Athens; tel. (01) 3243015; telex 216412.
Ministry of Education and Religion: Odos Metropoleos 15, Athens; tel. (01) 3230461; telex 216059.
Ministry of the Environment and Town Planning: Odos Amaliados 17, Athens; tel. (01) 6431461; telex 216374.
Ministry of Finance: Odos Karageorgi Servias 10, Athens; tel. (01) 3224071; telex 216373.
Ministry of Foreign Affairs: Odos Zalokosta 2, Athens; tel. (01) 3610581.
Ministry of Health, Welfare and Social Services: Odos Zalokosta 10, Athens; tel. (01) 3630911; telex 21625.
Ministry of Industry, Energy and Technology: Odos Zalokosta 10, Athens; tel. (01) 3630911; telex 216325.
Ministry of the Interior: Odos Stadiou 27, Athens; tel. (01) 3223521; telex 215776.
Ministry of Justice: Odos Zinonos 12, Athens; tel. (01) 5225903; telex 216352.
Ministry of Labour: Odos Pireos 40, Athens; tel. (01) 5233110; telex 216608.
Ministry of Merchant Marine: Odos Vassilissis Sophias 150, Piraeus; tel. (01) 4121211; telex 211232.
Ministry of National Defence: Holargos, Athens; tel. (01) 6465201.
Ministry of National Economy: Syntagma Sq., Athens; tel. (01) 3230911; telex 221086.
Ministry of Northern Greece: Odos El. Venizelou 48, Thessaloniki; tel. (031) 264321.
Ministry of Public Order: Katehaki 1, 101 77 Athens; tel. (01) 6928510; telex 216353.
Ministry of Public Works: Odos Har Trikoupi 182, Athens; tel. (01) 3618311; telex 216353.
Ministry of Transport and Communications: Leoforos Syngrou 49, Athens; tel. (01) 9233941; telex 216369.

Legislature

VOULI

President of Parliament: IOANNIS ALEVRAS.

General Election, 2 June 1985

	Votes	%	Seats
Panhellenic Socialist Movement (PASOK)	2,916,450	45.82	161
New Democracy (ND)	2,599,949	40.85	126
Communist Party (KKE—'Exterior')	629,518	9.89	12
Communist Party (KKE—'Interior')*	117,050	1.84	1
Others	102,072	1.60	—

* Renamed New Hellenic Left Party in May 1986, and became a founding member of the Greek Left Party in April 1987.

Political Organizations

Communist Party of Greece (Kommunistiko Komma Elladas—KKE) ('Orthodox', 'of the Exterior'): Leoforos Irakliou 145, 142 31 Athens; tel. (01) 2523543; telex 225402; f. 1918; banned 1947, reappeared 1974; Moscow-line communist party; Gen. Sec. CHARILAOS FLORAKIS.

Democratic Centre Union (Enosi Demokratikou Kentrou—EDIK): Odos Charilaou Trikoupi 18, 106 79 Athens; tel. (01) 3612792; telex 216689; f. 1974; democratic socialist party, merging Centre Union (f. 1961 by GEORGIOS PAPANDREOU) and New Political Forces (f. 1974 by Prof. IOANNIS PESMAZOGLOU and Prof. G. A. MANGAKIS); favours membership of the EEC; Leader Dr IOANNIS G. ZIGHDIS.

Democratic Initiative Party: Athens; f. 1987; democratic socialist party; advocates decentralization, a mixed economy, and the removal of foreign military bases from Greece; at least 60% of its mems are ex-PASOK mems; Leader GERASIMOS ARSENIS.

Democratic Renewal: Athens; f. 1985 by former ND deputies; populist; advocates a moderate centre-right policy on economic and social matters and a pro-Western position on foreign affairs; Leader KOSTIS STEFANOPOULOS.

Democratic Socialist Party (KODISO): Odos Mavromichali 9, Athens; tel. (01) 3600724; f. March 1979 by former EDIK deputies; favours membership of the EEC and political wing of NATO, decentralization and a mixed economy; Sec.-Gen. CH. PROTOPAPAS.

Greek Left Party (Elliniki Aristera—EAR): 1 Eleftherias Sq. and Odos Pireos, 105 53 Athens; tel. (01) 3219908; telex 224555; f. 1987; broadly-based socialist party comprising the former Greek Communist Party of the Interior, splinter groups from the KKE ('Exterior') and PASOK, minority groups and independents; 15,000 mems; Sec.-Gen. LEONIDAS KYRKOS.

Greek National Political Society (EPEN): Athens; f. 1984; right-wing; Leader GEORGIOS PAPADOPOULOS.

Hellenic Liberal Party: Vissarionos 1, 106 72 Athens; tel. (01) 3606111; telex 214886; f. 1910; aims to revive political heritage of fmr Prime Minister, Eleftherios Venizelos; 6,500 mems; Pres. NIKITAS VENIZELOS.

New Democracy Party (Nea Demokratia—ND): Odos Rigillis 18, 106 74 Athens; tel. (01) 7290071; telex 210856; f. 1974 by CONSTANTINE KARAMANLIS; a broadly-based centre-right party that advocates social reform in the framework of a liberal economy; favours membership of the EEC and NATO; Leader CONSTANTIN MITSOTAKIS; Dir-Gen. ANGELOS BRATAKOS.

Panhellenic Socialist Movement (Panellinion Socialistikon Kinema—PASOK): Odos Charilaou Trikoupi 50, Athens; tel. (01) 3232049; telex 218763; f. 1974; incorporates Democratic Defence and Panhellenic Liberation Movement resistance organizations; favours socialization of the means of production, decentralization and self-management, aims at a Mediterranean socialist development through international co-operation; 500 local organizations, 30,000 mems; Leader ANDREAS PAPANDREOU.

Other parties include the People's Militant Unity Party (f. 1985 by PASOK splinter group), the Progressive Party (f. 1979, right-wing), the (Maoist) Revolutionary Communist Party of Greece (EKKE) and the left-wing United Socialist Alliance of Greece (ESPE, f. 1984).

Diplomatic Representation

EMBASSIES IN GREECE

Albania: Odos Karachristou 1, Kolonaki, 115 21 Athens; tel. (01) 7234412; telex 210351; Ambassador: IZEDIN HAJDINI.
Algeria: Leoforos Vassileos Konstantinou 14, Athens; tel. (01) 7513560; telex 219992; Ambassador: SÉLIM BENKHELIL.
Argentina: Leoforos Vassilissis Sofias 59, Athens; tel. (01) 7224753; telex 215218; Ambassador: HIPÓLITO JESÚS PAZ.
Australia: Odos Dimitriou Soutsou 37/Odos Tsoha, Athens; tel. (01) 6447303; telex 215815; Ambassador: KEVIN IAN GATES.
Austria: Leoforos Alexandras 26, 106 83 Athens; tel. (01) 8211036; telex 215938; Ambassador: Dr HELLMUTH STRASSER.
Belgium: Odos Sekeri 3, Athens; tel. (01) 3617886; Ambassador: ROGER MARTIN.
Brazil: Platia Philikis Etairias 14, Athens; tel. (01) 7213039; telex 216604; Ambassador: ALARICO SILVEIRA JUNIOR.
Bulgaria: Odos Akademias 12, Athens; tel. (01) 3609411; Ambassador: PETAR ILIEV SLAVTCHEV.
Canada: Odos Ioannou Ghennadiou 4, 115 21 Athens; tel. (01) 7239511; Ambassador: ANDRÉ COUVRETTE.
Chile: Leoforos Vasilissis Sofias 96, Athens; tel. (01) 7775017; Chargé d'affaires a.i.: MANUEL ATRIA.
China, People's Republic: Odos Krinon 2A, Palaio Psychico, Athens; tel. (01) 6723282; Ambassador: ZHU YOUWAN.
Cuba: Odos Davaki 10, Athens; tel. (01) 6925367; Ambassador: M. F. ALFONSO RODRÍGUEZ.

GREECE

Cyprus: Odos Herodotou 16, Athens; tel. (01) 7232727; telex 215642; Ambassador: DEMOS HADJIMILTIS.
Czechoslovakia: Odos Georges Seferis 6, Palaio Psychico, Athens; tel. (01) 6713755; Ambassador: JOZEF NALEPKA.
Denmark: Platia Philikis Etairias 15, 106 73 Athens; tel. (01) 7249315; telex 215586; Ambassador: SKJ_LD G. MELLBIN.
Egypt: Leoforos Vassilissis Sofias 3, Athens; tel. (01) 3618612; Ambassador: AHMAD KADRY SALAMAH.
Ethiopia: Odos Davaki 10, Erythros, 115 26 Athens; tel. (01) 6920483; telex 218548; Ambassador: SAMUEL TEFERRA.
Finland: Odos Eratosthenous 1, 116 35 Athens; tel. (01) 7011775; Ambassador: ERKKI TIILIKAINEN.
France: Leoforos Vassilissis Sofias 7; tel. (01) 3611683; Ambassador: FRANÇOIS PLAISANT.
German Democratic Republic: Vassileos Pavlou 7, Palaio Psychico, Athens; tel. (01) 6725160; telex 214544; Ambassador: HORST BRIE.
Germany, Federal Republic: POB 61011, Leoforos Vassilissis Sofias 10, 151 24 Athens; tel. (01) 36941; telex 215441; Ambassador: RÜDIGER VON PACHELBEL.
Holy See: Odos Mavili 2, Palaio Psychico, 154 52 Athens; tel. (01) 6473598; Apostolic Pro-Nuncio: Most Rev. GIOVANNI MARIANI, Titular Archbishop of Missua.
Honduras: Leoforos Vassilissis Sofias 86, 115 28 Athens; tel. (01) 7775802; telex 241890; Chargé d'affaires a.i.: TEODOLINDA DE MAKRIS.
Hungary: Odos Kalvou 16, Palaio Psychico, 154 52 Athens; tel. (01) 6714889; Ambassador: LÁSZLÓ KINCSES.
India: Odos Meleagrou 4, Athens; tel. (01) 7216481; Ambassador: HARCHARAN SINGH DHODY.
Iran: Odos Kalari 16, Palaio Psychico, Athens; tel. (01) 6471436; Ambassador: AHMAD AJALLOOEIAN.
Iraq: Odos Mazaraki 4, Palaio Psychico, Athens; tel. (01) 6715012; Ambassador: NABIL NAJIM.
Ireland: Leoforos Vassileos Konstantinou 7, Athens; tel. (01) 7232771; telex 218111; Ambassador: EAMON RYAN.
Israel: Odos Marathonodromou 1, Palaio Psychico, 154 52 Athens; tel. (01) 6719530; Chargé d'affaires a.i.: ARIE TENNE.
Italy: Odos Sekeri 2, Athens; tel. (01) 3611722; Ambassador: MARCO PISA.
Japan: 21st Floor, Athens A Tower, Leoforos Messoghion 2-4, Ambelokipi, 115 27 Athens; tel. (01) 7758101; telex 214460; Ambassador: (vacant).
Jordan: Odos Palaio Zervou 30, Palaio Psychico, 154 52 Athens; tel. (01) 6474161; telex 219366; Ambassador: SAMIR KHALIFEH.
Korea, Republic: Odos Eratosthenous 1, Athens; tel. (01) 7012122; telex 216202; Ambassador: SHIM KI-CHUL.
Kuwait: Odos Alex. Papanastassiou 55, Athens; tel. (01) 6473593; Ambassador: SALEH MOHAMED AL-MOHAMED.
Lebanon: Leoforos Kifissias 26, Athens; tel. (01) 7785158; Ambassador: CHAWKI CHOUERI.
Libya: Odos Vironos 13, Palaio Psychico, Athens; tel. (01) 6472120; Ambassador: ABDALLA ABUMAHARA.
Mexico: Leoforos Vassileos Konstantinou 5-7, Zappio, 106 74 Athens; tel. (01) 7230754; telex 216172; Ambassador: OLGA PELLICER.
Morocco: Odos Mousson 14, Palaio Psychico, 154 52 Athens; tel. (01) 6474209; telex 210925; Ambassador: LARBI MOULINE.
Netherlands: Leoforos Vassileos Konstantinou 5-7, 106 74 Athens; tel. (01) 7239701; telex 215971; Ambassador: G. W. VAN BARNEVELD KOOY.
New Zealand: An. Tsoha 15-17, Ambelokipi, 115 21 Athens; tel. (01) 6410311; telex 216630; Ambassador: DONALD HARPER.
Norway: Leoforos Vassileos Konstantinou 7, 106 74 Athens; tel. (01) 7246173; telex 215109; Ambassador: TANCRED IBSEN.
Pakistan: Odos Loukianou 6, Athens; tel. (01) 7290122; Ambassador: MOHAMMAD RAWAL VERYAMANI.
Panama: Leoforos Vassilissis Sofias 21, Athens; tel. (01) 3631847; Ambassador: MARÍA LAKAS BAHAS.
Poland: Odos Chryssanthemon 22, Palaio Psychico, Athens; tel. (01) 6716917; Ambassador: JÓZEF TEJCHMA.
Portugal: Odos Karneadou 44, Athens; tel. (01) 7290096; Ambassador: JOÃO MORAIS DA CUNHA MATOS.
Romania: Odos Emmanuel Benaki 7, Palaio Psychico, Athens; tel. (01) 6718008; Ambassador: NICOLAE ECOBESCU.
Saudi Arabia: Odos Marathonodromou 71, Palaio Psychico, 154 52 Athens; tel. (01) 6716911; Ambassador: Sheikh ABDULLAH ABDUL-RAHMAN AL-MALHOOQ.
South Africa: Leoforos Kifissias 124, Athens; tel. (01) 6922125; telex 218165; Ambassador: JOHN FRANS JOHANNES CRONJE.
Spain: Leoforos Vassilissis Sofias 29, Athens; tel. (01) 7214885; telex 215860; Ambassador: ENRIQUE MAHOU STAUFFER.
Sweden: Leoforos Vassileos Konstantinou 7, 106 74 Athens; tel. (01) 7290421; telex 215646; Ambassador: HANS COLLIANDER.
Switzerland: Odos Iassiou 2, 115 21 Athens; tel. (01) 7230364; telex 216230; Ambassador: CHARLES STEINHÄUSLIN.
Syria: Odos Marathonodromou 79, Palaio Psychico, Athens; tel. (01) 6725577; Ambassador: SHAHIN FARAH.
Thailand: Odos Taygetou 23, Palaio Psychico, 154 52 Athens; Ambassador: S. C. M. SUCRI GAJASENI.
Tunisia: Odos Ethnikis Antistaseos 91, Chalandri, Athens; tel. (01) 6717590; Ambassador: SALAH LADGHAM.
Turkey: Odos Vassileos Gheorghiou 118, Athens; tel. (01) 7245915; Ambassador: NAZMI AKIMAN.
USSR: Odos Nikiforou Litra 28, Palaio Psychico, Athens; tel. (01) 6725235; Ambassador: ANATOLY A. SLIUSAR.
United Kingdom: Odos Ploutarchou 1, 106 75 Athens; tel. (01) 7236211; telex 216440; Ambassador: Sir JEREMY CASHEL THOMAS.
USA: Leoforos Vassilissis Sofias 91, Athens; tel. (01) 7212951; Ambassador: ROBERT VOSSLER KEELEY.
Uruguay: Odos Licavitou I G, 106 72 Athens; tel. (01) 3613549; Ambassador: CARLOS MARÍA ROMERO.
Venezuela: Leoforos Vassilissis Sofias 112, Athens; tel. (01) 7708769; Ambassador: JOSÉ MARÍA MACHIN.
Yugoslavia: Leoforos Vassilissis Sofias 106, Athens; tel. (01) 7774344; Ambassador: VLADIMIR SULTANOVIĆ.
Zaire: Odos Vassileos Constantinou 2, 116 35 Athens; tel. (01) 7016171; telex 215994; Ambassador: BOMOLO LOKOKA.

Judicial System

The Constitution of 1975 provides for the establishment of a Special Supreme Tribunal. Other provisions in the Constitution provided for a reorganization of parts of the judicial system to be accomplished through legislation.

SUPREME ADMINISTRATIVE COURTS

Special Supreme Tribunal: Odos Patision 30, Athens; this court has final jurisdiction in matters of constitutionality.

Council of State: Old Palace Bldg, Athens; the Council of State has appellate powers over acts of the administration upon application by civil servants or other civilians.

SUPREME JUDICIAL COURT

Supreme Court: Leoforos Alexandros 121, Athens; this is the supreme court in the State, having also appellate powers. It consists of six sections, four Civil and two Penal, and adjudicates in quorum; Pres. Supreme Court GEORGE KONSTAS.

COURTS OF APPEAL

These are 12 in number. They have jurisdiction in cases of Civil and Penal Law of second degree, and, in exceptional penal cases, of first degree.

COURTS OF FIRST INSTANCE

There are 59 Courts of First Instance with jurisdiction in cases of first degree, and in exceptional cases, of second degree. They function both as Courts of First Instance and as Criminal Courts. For serious crimes the Criminal Courts function with a jury.

In towns where Courts of First Instance sit there are also Juvenile Courts. Commercial Tribunals do not function in Greece, and all commercial cases are tried by ordinary courts of law. There are however, Tax Courts in some towns.

OTHER COURTS

There are 360 Courts of the Justice of Peace throughout the country. There are 48 Magistrates' Courts (or simple Police Courts).

In all the above courts, except those of the Justice of Peace, there are District Attorneys, In Courts of the Justice of Peace the duties of District Attorney are performed by the Public Prosecutor.

Religion

CHRISTIANITY

The Eastern Orthodox Church

The Orthodox Church of Greece: Odos Ioannou Gennadiou 14, 115 21 Athens; tel. (01) 7218381; f. 1850; 78 dioceses, 8,335 priests, 84 bishops, 9,025,000 adherents (1985).

GREECE

The Greek branch of the Holy Eastern Orthodox Church is the officially established religion of the country, to which nearly 97% of the population profess adherence. The administrative body of the Church is the Holy Synod of 12 members, elected by the bishops of the Hierarchy.

Primate of Greece: Archbishop SERAPHIM of Athens.

Within the Greek State there is also the semi-autonomous Church of Crete, composed of seven Metropolitans and the Holy Archbishopric of Crete. The Church is administered by a Synod consisting of the seven Metropolitans under the Presidency of the Archbishop; it is under the spiritual jurisdiction of the Oecumenical Patriarchate of Constantinople, which also maintains a degree of administrative control.

Archbishop of Crete: Archbishop TIMOTHEOS (whose See is in Heraklion).

There are also four Metropolitan Sees of the Dodecanese, which are spiritually and administratively dependent on the Oecumenical Patriarchate and, finally, the peninsula of Athos, which constitutes the region of the Holy Mountain (Mount Athos) and comprises 20 monasteries. These are dependent on the Oecumenical Patriarchate of Constantinople, but are autonomous and are safeguarded constitutionally.

The Roman Catholic Church

Latin Rite

Greece comprises four archdioceses (including two directly responsible to the Holy See), four dioceses and one Apostolic Vicariate. In December 1986 there were an estimated 47,759 adherents in the country.

Archdiocese of Athens: Archbishopric, Odos Omirou 9, 106 72 Athens; tel. (01) 3624311; Archbishop Most Rev. NICOLAOS FOSCOLOS.

Archdiocese of Rhodes: Archbishopric, Odos Dragoumi 5A, 891 00 Rhodes; tel. (0241) 21845; Apostolic Administrator Fr MICHEL PIERRE FRANZIDIS.

Metropolitan Archdiocese of Corfu, Zante and Cefalonia: Catholic Archbishopric, 491 00 Kerkyra; tel. (0661) 30277; Archbishop Mgr ANTONIO VARTHALITIS.

Metropolitan Archdiocese of Naxos, Andros, Tinos and Myconos: Archbishopric, 842 00 Tinos (summer residence); tel. (0283) 22382; Naxos (winter residence); also responsible for the suffragan dioceses of Candia (Crete), Chios, Santorini and Syros and Milo; Archbishop Mgr GIOVANNI PERRIS.

Apostolic Vicariate of Salonika (Thessaloniki): Leoforos Vassilissis Olgas 120B, 546 45 Thessaloniki; tel. (031) 835780; Apostolic Administrator Fr DEMETRIOS ROUSSOS.

Byzantine Rite

Apostolic Exarchate for the Byzantine Rite in Greece: Odos Acharnon 246, 112 53 Athens; tel. (01) 8677039; 2 parishes (Athens and Jannitsa, Macedonia); 12 secular priests, 18 religious sisters, 2,300 adherents (1986 est.); Exarch Apostolic Mgr ANARGHYROS PRINTESIS, Titular Bishop of Gratianopolis.

Armenian Rite

Episcopacy of the Armenian Rite in Greece: Odos René Piot 2, 117 44 Athens; tel. (01) 9014089; 650 adherents (1985); Bishop HOVANNES KOYOUNIAN.

Protestant Church

Greek Evangelical Church (Presbyterian): Odos Markon Botsari 24, 117 41 Athens; f. 1858; comprises 30 organized churches; 5,000 adherents (1985); Moderator Rev. NIC. LANDROU.

ISLAM

The law provides as religious head of the Muslims a Chief Mufti; the Muslims in Greece possess a number of mosques and schools.

JUDAISM

The Jewish population of Greece, estimated in 1943 at 75,000 people, was severely reduced as a result of the German occupation. In 1988 there were about 5,000 Jews in Greece.

Central Board of the Jewish Communities of Greece: Odos Sourmeli 2, 104 39 Athens; tel. (01) 8839953; telex 225110; f. 1945; officially recognized representative body of the communities of Greece; Pres. JOSEPH LOVINGER.

Jewish Community of Athens: Odos Melidoni 8, 105 53 Athens; tel. (01) 3252823; Rabbi JACOB D. ARAR.

Jewish Community of Thessaloniki: Odos Tsimiski 24, 546 24 Thessaloniki; tel. (031) 275701; Pres. LEON BENMAYOR.

The Press

In 1983 total newspaper circulation for the year was 276.2m. in Athens and 30.7m. in Thessaloniki. Afternoon papers are more popular than morning ones; in the Athens area in 1983 about 141,071 papers were sold each morning and up to 771,516 each afternoon.

PRINCIPAL DAILY NEWSPAPERS

Morning papers are not published on Mondays, nor afternoon papers on Sundays.

Athens

Acropolis: Odos Fidiou 12, 106 78 Athens; tel. (01) 3618811; telex 215733; f. 1881; morning; Independent-Conservative; Acropolis Publications SA; Publr G. LEVIDES; Dir MARNIS SKOUNDRIDAKIS; circ. 50,819.

Apogevmatini (The Afternoon): Odos Fidiou 12, 106 78 Athens; tel. (01) 3618811; telex 215733; f. 1956; independent; Publr GEORGIOS HATZIKONSTANTINOU; Editor J. MOSCHOVITIS; circ. 130,000.

Athens Daily Post: Odos Stadiou 57, Athens; tel. (01) 3249504; f. 1952; morning; English; Owner G. SKOURAS.

Athens News: Odos Lekka 23–25, 105 62 Athens; tel. (01) 3224253; f. 1952; morning; English; Publr-Propr JOHN HORN; circ. 10,000.

Athlitiki Icho (Athletics Echo): Odos Voulgari 11, 104 37 Athens; tel. (01) 5222524; f. 1945; morning; Editors and Proprs ATHAN SEMBOS, G. GEORGALAS; circ. 24,117.

Avghi (Dawn): Ag. Constantiou 12, 104 31 Athens; tel. (01) 5231831; telex 222671; f. 1952; morning; publ. by the Greek Left Party; Dir GRIGORIS GIANNAROS; Editor L. VOUTSAS; circ. 55,000.

Avriani: Odos Dimitros 11, 177 78 Athens; tel. (01) 3424090; telex 218440; f. 1980; evening; Dir JOHN GAVRIELATOS; Publr and Editor G. A. COURIS; circ. 115,000.

Dimokratikos Logos: Odos Dimitros 11, 177 78 Athens; tel. (01) 3424090; telex 218440; f. 1986; morning; Dir KOSTAS GERONIKOLOS; PUBLR AND EDITOR G. A. COURIS; circ. 12,000.

Eleftheri Ora: Odos Akadimias 32, 106 72 Athens; tel. (01) 3644128; f. 1981; evening; Publr J. MICHALOPOULOS; Dir G. MICHALOPOULOS; circ. 5,239.

Eleftherotypia: Odos Panepistimiou 57, Athens; f. 1974; evening; Publr CHR. TEGOPOULOS; Dir S. FYNTANIDIS; circ. 85,000.

Estia (Vesta): Odos Anthinou Gazi 7, 105 61 Athens; tel. (01) 3220631; f. 1898; afternoon; Publr and Editor ADONIS K. KYROU; circ. 7,978.

Ethnos (Nation): Odos Benaki, Metamorfosi Chalandriou, 152 35 Athens; tel. (01) 6580640; telex 2104415; f. 1981; evening; Publr GEORGE BOBOLAS; Dir G. LEVENTOYIANNIS; circ. 150,500.

Express: Halandriou 39, Paradissos Amaroussiou, 125 15 Athens; tel. (01) 6827582; telex 219746; morning, financial; Publr Hellenews Publications; Gen. Dir D. G. KALOFOLIAS; Editor-in-Chief T. MATSOUKIS; circ. 22,000.

Filathlos: Odos Dimitros 11, 177 78 Athens; tel. (01) 3424090; telex 218440; f. 1982; morning; Dir NICK KARAGIANNIDIS; Publr and Editor G. A. COURIS; circ. 40,000.

Imerissia: Odos Geraniou 7A, 105 52 Athens; tel. (01) 5232159; f. 1947; morning; Publr A. MOTHONIOS and Co; circ. 11,000.

Kathmerini: Odos Marathon National 18, 153 44 Pallini, Attica; telex 226692; f. 1919; morning; Conservative; Editor DIMITRIS PAPANAGIOTOU; circ. 80,000.

Mesimvrini (Midday): Odos Panepistimiou 10, 106 71 Athens; tel. (01) 3646010; telex 216495; f. 1980; evening; Publr ATHAN SEKERIS; Dir CH. PASSALARIS; circ. 24,701.

Naftemboriki (Daily Journal): Odos Piraeus 9–11, Athens; tel. (01) 5246711; f. 1923; morning; non-political journal of finance, commerce and shipping; Dir N. ATHANASSIADIS; circ. 33,000.

Rizospastis (Radical): Leoforos N. Ionias 13B, Perissos, Athens; tel. (01) 2526434; telex 216156; morning; pro-Soviet Communist; Dir GRIGORIS FARAKOS; Editor G. TRIKALINOS; circ. 48,513.

Ta Nea (News): Odos Christou Lada 3, 102 39 Athens; tel. (01) 3230221; telex 210608; f. 1944; Liberal; evening; Publr CHRISTOS LAMBRAKIS; Dir L. KARAPANAGIOTIS; circ. 155,000.

Vradyni (Evening Press): Odos Piraeus 9–11, 105 52 Athens; tel. (01) 5231001; telex 215354; f. 1923; evening; right-wing; Gen. Man. H. ATHANASIADOU; circ. 71,914.

Patras

Peloponnesos: Odos Alex. Ipsilandou 177, 262 25 Patras; tel. (061) 272452; f. 1886; independent conservative; Publr and Editor S. DOUCAS; circ. 6,000.

GREECE   *Directory*

Thessaloniki

Ellinikos Vorras (Greek North): Odos Grammou-Vitsi 19, 551 34 Thessaloniki; tel. (031) 416621; telex 412213; f. 1935; morning; Publr TESSA LEVANTIS; Dir N. MERGIOS; circ. 14,467.

Makedonia: Odos Monastiriou 85, 546 27 Thessaloniki; tel. (031) 521621; f. 1911; morning; Propr Publishing Co of Northern Greece SA; Dir K. DIMADIS; Editor KATERINA VELIDES; circ. 47,989.

Thessaloniki: Odos Monastiriou 85, 546 27 Thessaloniki; tel. (031) 521621; f. 1963; evening; Propr Publishing Co of Northern Greece SA; Editor KATERINA VELIDES; circ. 36,040.

SELECTED PERIODICALS

Aktines: Odos Karytsi 14, 105 61 Athens; tel. (01) 3235023; f. 1938; monthly; current affairs, science, philosophy, arts; aims to promote a Christian civilization; Publr Christian Union; circ. 10,000.

The Athenian: Odos Daedalou 20, 105 58 Athens; f. 1974; monthly; English; Publr and Editor SLOANE ELLIOTT; circ. 13,200.

Cosmopolitan: Leoforos Marathonas 14, Pallini, 153 00 Athens; tel. (01) 6665706; f. 1979; monthly; women's magazine; Publr P. ROKANAS; Dir K. KOSTOULIAS.

Deltion Diikiseos Epichiriseon (Business Administration Bulletin): Odos Rigilis 26, 106 74; Athens; tel. (01) 7235736; telex 29006; monthly; Editor J. PAPAMICHALAKIS; circ. 26,000.

Demosiografiki (Journalism): Armatolon Klefton 5, 114 71 Athens; monthly; Dir EFI ANGELAKOS.

Economicos Tachydromos (Financial Courier): Odos Christou Lada 3, 102 37 Athens; tel. (01) 3230221; telex 210608; f. 1926; weekly; Dir JOHN MARINOS; circ. 17,000.

Embros (Forward): Odos Christou Lada 7, Athens; tel. (01) 3228656; f. 1896; weekly; independent; Editor A. E. PARASCHOS.

Epikaira: Odos Voulis 17, Athens; Amaroussion Papyros Press Ltd; weekly; circ. 35,274.

Gynaika (Women): Fragoklissias 7, Marousi, 151 25 Athens; tel. (01) 6826680; f. 1950; fortnightly; fashion, beauty, handicrafts, cookery, social problems, fiction, knitting, embroidery; Publr EVANGELOS TERZOPOULOS SA; circ. 94,654.

Hellenews: Halandriou 39, Paradissos Amaroussiou 151 25 Athens; tel. (01) 6827582; telex 219746; weekly; English; finance and business; Publr Hellenews Publications; Editor G. V. PAVLIDES.

Ikogeniakos Thesavros (Family Treasure): Athens; tel. (01) 5231033; f. 1967; weekly; women's and social matters; Publr COSTANTINOS PAPACRISTOPHILOU; Editor TAKIS AGELOPOULOS; circ. 31,180.

Makedoniki Zoi (Macedonian Life): Odos Mitropoleos 70, 546 22 Thessaloniki; tel. (031) 277700; monthly; Editor N. J. MERTZOS.

Pantheon: Odos Anaksagora 5, Athens; tel. (01) 5245433; fortnightly; Publr and Dir N. THEOFANIDES; circ. 74,141.

Politica Themata: Odos Ipsilantou 25, 106 75 Athens; tel. (01) 7218421; weekly; Publr J. CHORN; Dir C. KYRKOS; circ. 2,544.

Tachydromos (The Courier): Odos Christou Lada 3, 102 37 Athens; tel. (01) 3250810; telex 215904; f. 1953; weekly; illustrated magazine; Publr C. LAMBRAKIS SA; Dir ROULA MITROPOULOU; circ. 177,182.

Technika Chronika (Technical Times): Odos Carageorgi Servias 4, 105 62 Athens; tel. (01) 3234751; f. 1952; monthly; general edition on technical and economic subjects; Editor D. ROKOS; circ. 12,000.

To Vima (Tribune): Odos Christou Lada 3, 107 32 Athens; tel. (01) 3230221; telex 215904; f. 1922; weekly; Liberal; Dir and Editor STAVROS P. PSYCHARIS; circ. 35,000.

Viomichaniki Epitheorissis (Industrial Review): Odos Zalokosta 4, 106 71 Athens; f. 1934; monthly; industrial and economic review; Publr S. VOVOLINIS; Editor D. KARAMANOS; circ. 25,000.

NEWS AGENCIES

Athenagence (ANA): Odos Pindarou 6, 106 71 Athens; tel. (01) 3639816; telex 215300; f. 1896; correspondents in leading capitals of the world and towns throughout Greece; Gen. Dir ANDREAS CHRISTODOULIDES.

Foreign Bureaux

Agence France-Presse (AFP): POB 3392, Odos Voukourestiou 18, 106 71 Athens; tel. (01) 3633388; telex 215595; Bureau Chief JEAN-PIERRE ALTIER.

Agencia EFE (Spain): Odos Zalokosta 4, 106 71 Athens; tel. (01) 3635826; telex 219561; Bureau Chief D. MARÍA-LUISA RUBIO; Correspondent JUAN JOSÉ FERNÁNDEZ ELORRIAGA.

Agentstvo Pechati Novosti (APN) (USSR): Odos Irodotou 9, 138 Athens; tel. (01) 7291016; telex 219601; Bureau Chief BORIS KOROLYOV; Correspondent J. KURIZIN.

Agenzia Nazionale Stampa Associata (ANSA) (Italy): Odos Valaoritou 9B, 106 71 Athens; tel. (01) 3605285; telex 221860; Correspondent NICOLA RIENZI.

Allgemeiner Deutscher Nachrichtendienst (ADN) (German Democratic Republic): Patriarchou Ioakim 58, Kolonaki, 106 76 Athens; Correspondent HANS-JOACHIM THEBUD.

Associated Press (AP) (USA): Odos Akadimias 27A, 106 71 Athens; tel. (01) 3602755; telex 215133.

Deutsche Press-Agentur (dpa) (Federal Republic of Germany): Odos Achaeou 8, 106 75 Athens; tel. (01) 7230290; telex 215839; Correspondent URSULA DIEPGEN.

Reuters News Agency (Hellas) SA (UK): 3rd Floor, Odos Voukourestiou 15, 106 71 Athens; tel. (01) 3647610; telex 215912.

Telegrafska Agencija Nova Jugoslavija (Tanjug) (Yugoslavia): Evrou 94–96, Ambelokipi, Athens; tel. (01) 7791545.

Telegrafnoye Agentstvo Sovetskovo Soyuza (TASS) (USSR): Odos Gizi 44, Palaio Psychico, Athens; Correspondent ANATOLI TKACHUK.

United Press International (UPI) (USA): Odos Valaoritou 12, 106 71 Athens; tel. (01) 3633807; telex 215572; Correspondent RALPH JOSEPH.

Xinhua (New China) News Agency (People's Republic of China): Odos Amarilidos 19, Palaio Psychico, Athens; tel. (01) 6724997; telex 216235; Bureau Chief XIE CHENGHAO.

PRESS ASSOCIATIONS

Enossis Syntakton Imerission Ephimeridon Athinon (Journalists' Union of the Athens Daily Newspapers): Odos Akademias 20, Athens; f. 1914; Pres. VAS. KORAHAIS; Gen. Sec. DIMITRIOS MATHIOPOULOS; 918 mems.

Enossis Syntakton Periodikou Typou (Journalists' Union of the Periodical Press): Odos Valaoritou 9, Athens; Pres. ANDREAS KALOMARIS; 220 mems.

Foreign Press Association of Greece: Odos Academias 23, 134 Athens.

Publishers

Angyra Publications: Kifisou 85, Egaleo, 122 41 Athens; tel. (01) 3455276; telex 210804; f. 1932; general; Man. Dir DIMITRIOS PAPADIMITRIOU.

John Arsenidis Ekdotis: Odos Akademias 57, 106 79 Athens; tel. (01) 3629538; biography, literature, chidren's books, history, philosophy, social sciences; Man. Dir JOHN ARSENIDIS.

Ekdotike Athenon SA: Vissariones 1, 106 72 Athens; tel. (01) 3608911; f. 1961; history, archaeology, art; Man. Dirs GEORGE A. CHRISTOPOULOS, JOHN C. BASTIAS.

Bergadi Editions: Odos Mavromichali 4, Athens; tel. (01) 3614263; academic, children's books; Dir MICHAEL BERGADIS.

Boukoumanis Editions: Odos Mavromichali 1, 106 79 Athens; tel. (01) 3618502; f. 1967; history, politics, sociology, psychology, belles lettres, educational, arts, children's books, ecology; Man. ELIAS BOUKOUMANIS.

G. C. Eleftheroudakis SA: Odos Nikis 4, 105 63 Athens; tel. (01) 3222255; telex 219410; f. 1915; general, technical and scientific; Man. Dir VIRGINIA ELEFTHEROUDAKIS-GREGOU.

Etairia Ellinikon Ekdoseon: Odos Akademias 84, 142 Athens; tel. (01) 3630282; f. 1958; fiction, academic, educational; Man. Dir STAVROS TAVOULARIS.

Gnosis Publishing Co: Odos Zoodochou Pigis 29, 106 81 Athens; history, literature, art, children's books.

Hellenic Editions Co SA: Odos Akadimias 84, 106 78 Athens; tel. (01) 3607343; encyclopaedias; Editor-in-Chief J. ZAFIROPOULOS.

Kassandra M. Grigoris: Odos Solonos 71, 106 79 Athens; tel. (01) 3629684; f. 1967; Greek history, Byzantine archaeology, literature, theology; Man. Dir MICHEL GRIGORIS.

Denise Harvey and Co: Lambrou Fotiadi 6, Mets, 116 36 Athens; tel. (01) 9233547; f. 1972; modern Greek literature and poetry, translations, selected general list (English and Greek); Man. Dir DENISE HARVEY.

I.D. Kollaros & Co SA: Odos Solonos 60, 106 72 Athens; tel. (01) 3635970; f. 1885; literature, history, textbooks, general; Gen. Dir MARINA KARAITIDIS.

Papazissis Publishers: Nikitara 2, 106 78 Athens; tel. (01) 3622496; telex 219807; f. 1929; economics, politics, law, history, school books; Man. Dir VICTOR PAPAZISSIS.

Patakis Editions: Odos Nikitara 3, 106 78 Athens; tel. (01) 3638362; literature, educational, philosophy, psychology, children's books.

GREECE

D. and B. Saliveros: Arcadias and Teftidos 1, Peristeri, Athens; f. 1893; general and religious books, maps, diaries and calendars; Chair. D. SALIVEROS.

John Sideris: Odos Stadiou 44, Athens; tel. (01) 3229638; f. 1898; school textbooks, general; Man. J. SIDERIS.

J. G. Vassiliou: Odos Hippocratous 15, 106 79 Athens; tel. (01) 3623382; f. 1913; fiction, history, philosophy, dictionaries and children's books.

Government Publishing House

Government Printing House: Odos Kapodistriou 34, 104 32 Athens; tel. (01) 5248320.

PUBLISHERS' FEDERATIONS

Athens Federation of Publishers and Booksellers: Odos Themistocleus 54, 106 81 Athens; tel. (01) 3630029; Pres. D. PANTELESKOS; Sec. THANASSIS KASTANIOTIS.

Hellenic Federation of Publishers and Booksellers: Odos Arachovis 61, 106 81 Athens; tel. (01) 3625458; f. 1961; Pres. STELIOS HALKIADAKIS; Gen. Sec. GEORGE DARDANOS.

Radio and Television

A television network of 17 transmitters is in operation. In 1985 there were an estimated 4m. radio receivers and 1,715,000 television receivers in use. The Constitution of June 1975 placed radio and television under the direct supervision of the State. In 1987, however, 10 new municipal radio stations began to transmit programmes.

Elliniki Radiophonia Tileorassi (Hellenic National Radio-Television): POB 19, Aghia Paraskevi 153 10, near Athens; tel. (01) 6595970; telex 216066; state-controlled since 1939; Pres. of Admin. Council K. BEIS; Dir-Gen. G. ROMEOS; Dir Radio I. KAMBANELLIS.

ERA 4 (Hellenic Radio—4th Programme): Odos Messogion 136, 115 27 Athens; radio broadcasts from Athens, Thessaloniki, Serres, Orestias, Kavala, Florina, Larissa, Kojani, Ioannina, Heraklion, Pyrgos and Tripolis; Pres. (vacant); Dir S. A. VERGOS.

E.T. 2 (Hellenic Television—Channel 2): Odos Messogion 136, 115 27 Athens; tel. (01) 7701911; telex 214439; f. 1967; television broadcasts from Athens; Pres. (vacant); Dir-Gen. DIMITRI A. PALEOTHODOROS.

Finance

(cap. = capital; p.u. = paid up; res = reserves; dep. = deposits; drs = drachmae; m. = million; br. = branch)

BANKING

Central Bank

Bank of Greece: Odos El. Venizelou 21, 102 50 Athens; tel. (01) 3201111; telex 215102; f. 1928; State Bank of Issue; cap. drs 3,876.9m., res drs 7,894.1m., dep. drs 816,128.8m. (Dec. 1987); Gov. DEMETRIOS CHALIKIAS; 27 brs.

Commercial Banks

Agricultural Bank of Greece: Odos Panepistimiou 23, 105 64 Athens; tel. (01) 3230521; telex 222160; f. 1929; a state agricultural bank; cap. and res drs 53,000m., dep. drs 540,000m. (April 1987); Gov. and Chair. VASSILIS A. KAFIRIS; 420 brs.

Bank of Attica: Odos Omirou 23, 106 72 Athens; tel. (01) 3646910; telex 223344; f. 1925; affiliated to Commercial Bank of Greece; cap. drs 432.5m., res drs 463.9m., dep. drs 16,018.7m. (Dec. 1986); Chair. and Gen. Man. COSTAS KALYVIANAKIS; Vice-Chair. PANAYIOTIS POULIS; 12 brs.

Bank of Crete, SA: Odos Voukourestiou 22, 106 71 Athens; tel. (01) 3606511; telex 218633; f. 1924 (reformed 1973); cap. drs 3,037.8m., res drs 902.3m., dep. drs 60,074.8m. (Dec. 1986); Chair. and Man. Dir GEORGE KOSKOTAS; First Vice-Chair. and Gen. Man. PANAYIOTIS VAKALIS; 36 brs.

Bank of Piraeus: Odos Stadiou 34, 132 Athens; f. 1916; cap. drs 83.2m., res drs 193.5m., dep. drs 2,694.6m. (Dec. 1979); Chair. of Bd, Pres. and Gen. Man. KOSTAS LAMBRAKIS; Man. PETROS S. GREGOROPOULOS; 8 brs.

Commercial Bank of Greece: POB 16, Odos Sophocleous 11, 102 35 Athens; tel. (01) 3210911; telex 216545; f. 1907; cap. drs 4,203.2m., res drs 22,304.5m., dep. drs 656,083m. (Dec. 1987); Chair. ADAMANTIOS PEPELASSIS; Gen. Man. PANAYOTIS POULIS; 280 brs.

Credit Bank: Odos Stadiou 40, 102 52 Athens; tel. (01) 3245111; telex 218691; f. 1879, renamed 1972; cap. drs 2,640m., res drs 3,690m., dep. drs 281,004m. (Dec. 1986); Chair. and Gen. Man. YANNIS S. COSTOPOULOS; 97 brs.

Ergobank, SA: Odos Panepistimiou 36, 106 79 Athens; tel. (01) 3601011; telex 218826; f. 1975; cap. drs 1,034.4m., res drs 8,565.1m., dep. drs 108,961.5m. (June 1988); Chair. C. S. CAPSASKIS; Gen. Man. Dr P. P. HAGGIPAVLOU; 47 brs.

General Hellenic Bank, SA: Odos Panepistimiou 9, 102 29 Athens; tel. (01) 3241283; telex 215702; f. 1937 as Bank of the Army Share Fund, renamed 1966; cap. drs 1,375.1m., res drs 1,142.4m., dep. drs 106,419.9m. (Dec. 1986); Chair. DIMOSTHENIS DIMOSTHENOPOULOS; Gen. Man. PANAGIS A. BENETATOS; 76 brs.

Investment Bank, SA: Odos Korai 1, 105 64 Athens; tel. (01) 3230214; telex 214239; f. 1962; cap. drs 1,707.3m., res drs 1,701.3m., dep. drs 18,239.2m. (Dec. 1986); Chair. PANAYIOTIS B. POULIS; Gen. Man. NIKOS P. THEODOSSIADES.

Ionian Bank (Ionian and Popular Bank of Greece): Odos Panepistimiou 45, 102 43 Athens; tel. (01) 3225501; telex 215269; f.1839; cap. drs 2,301.4m., res drs 9,398.9m., dep. drs 306,800.2m. (Dec. 1986); Chair. Prof. PANAYOTIS KORLIRAS; Gen. Man. EUGENE CALAFATIS; 162 brs.

National Bank of Greece, SA: Odos Aeolou 86, Cotzia Sq., 102 32 Athens; tel. (01) 3210411; telex 214931; f. 1841; cap. drs 19,635.9m., res drs 56,358.0m., dep. drs 2,159,575.5m. (Dec. 1986); Gov. STELIOS PANAGOPOULOS; 472 brs in Greece, 22 abroad.

National Mortgage Bank of Greece: POB 667, Odos El. Venizelou 40, POB 667, Athens; tel. (01) 7799301; telex 215026; f. 1927; cap. drs 2,349m., res drs 12,744.2m., dep. drs 300,948.3m. (Dec. 1986); Gov. GEORGE D. ANOMERITIS; 42 brs.

Traders' Credit Bank, SA: Odos Santaroza 3, 131 Athens; tel. (01) 3212371; telex 215481; f. 1924, renamed 1952; cap. drs 565.5m., res drs 901.7m., dep. drs 26,343.9m. (Dec. 1986); Chair. CONSTANTINE SIETOS; Gen. Man. JOHN PAPALEVENTIS; 14 brs.

Development Banks

Hellenic Industrial Development Bank, SA: Odos El. Venizelou 18/20, 106 72 Athens; tel. (01) 3237981; telex 215203; f. 1964; cap. drs 38,394.9m., res drs 7,373.6m., dep. drs 241,196.3m. (Dec. 1986); state-owned limited liability banking company; the major Greek institution in the field of industrial investment; Gov. and Chair. SOPHOULIS COSTAS.

National Investment Bank for Industrial Development, SA: Leoforos Amalias 14, 102 36 Athens; tel. (01) 3242651; telex 216113; f. 1963; cap. drs 1,359.4m., res drs 9,933.3m., dep. drs 55,877.1m. (Dec. 1986); long-term loans, equity participation, promotion of co-operation between Greek and foreign enterprises; Chair. STYLIANOS PANAGOPOULOS; Man. Dir KLEON ANTONARAS.

STOCK EXCHANGE

Athens Stock Exchange: Odos Sophocleous 10, 105 59 Athens; tel. (01) 3211301; telex 215820; f. 1876; Pres. NIKITAS A. NIARCHOS.

PRINCIPAL INSURANCE COMPANIES

Alfa: Leoforos Kifissias 252–254, 152 31 Halandri; tel. (01) 6472411; telex 222693; f. 1977; Gen. Man. DEM. ATHINEOS.

Apollon: Leoforos Syngrou 39, 117 43 Athens; tel. (01) 9236362; Gen. Man. A. M. APOSTOLATOS.

Aspis Pronia: Odos Othonos 4, 105 57 Athens; tel. (01) 3224023; telex 215350; f. 1945; Man. Dir A. TAMBOURAS.

Astir: Odos Merlin 6, 106 71 Athens; tel. (01) 3604111; telex 215383; f. 1930; Gen. Man. G. PAIPETIS.

Athinaiki: Odos Panepistimiou 34, 106 79 Athens; tel. (01) 3615774; f. 1917; Dir C. PAPACONSTANTIOU.

Atlantiki Enosis: Odos Messoghion 71, 115 26 Athens; tel. (01) 7799211; telex 216822; f. 1970; Gen. Man. N. LAPATAS.

Atlas: Odos Stadiou 24, 105 64 Athens; tel. (01) 3254971; telex 216635; f. 1941; Gen. Man. A. COOK.

Cigna Insurance Co Hellas SA: Odos Phidippidou 2, 115 26 Athens; tel. (01) 7754731; telex 218339; Gen. Man. DEMOSTHENES PIPEROPOULOS.

Continental Hellas: Leoforos Syngrou 253, 171 22 Athens; tel. (01) 9429021; telex 222746; f. 1942; incorporating Plioktitai SA; Man. Dir MANOLIS VALAVANIS.

Cosmos: Odos Panepistimiou 25, 105 64 Athens; tel. (01) 3229273; f. 1942; Gen. Man. N. PLACIDIS.

Crete Life Insurance Co SA: Odos Karageorghi Servias 4, 105 62 Athens; tel. (01) 3230981; telex 215379; f. 1940; Gen. Man. V. PLYTA.

Diana: Odos Tsimiski and I. Dragoumi 6, 546 24 Thessaloniki; tel. (031) 263729; telex 412526; f. 1975; Gen. Man. D. SPYRTOS.

Doriki: Odos Panepistimiou 58, 106 78 Athens; tel. (01) 36358121; telex 214326; f. 1972; Gen. Man. SPYROS NIKOLAIDES.

GREECE

Directory

Dynamis SA: Leoforos Syngrou 106, 117 41 Athens; tel. (01) 9227255; telex 216678; f. 1977; Man. Dir NICOLAS STAMATOPOULOS.

Economiki: Odos Capodistriou 38, 104 32 Athens; tel. (01) 5243374; Rep. D. NICOLAYDIS.

Emporiki: Odos Philhellinon 6, 105 57 Athens; tel. (01) 3240093; telex 219218; f. 1940; Chair. PHOTIS P. COSTOPOULOS; Exec. Dir MICHAEL P. PSALIDAS.

Estia Insurance and Reinsurance Co SA: Leoforos Syngrou 255, 171 22 Nea Smyrni, Athens; tel. (01) 9425513; telex 215833; f. 1943; Chair. ALKIVIADIS CHIONIS; Gen. Man. STAVROULA VAVAS-POLYCHRONOPOULOS.

Ethniki: Odos Karageorgi Servias 8, 105 62 Athens; tel. (01) 3222121; telex 215400; f. 1891; Man. Dir P. NICOLAIDIS.

Ethnikon Idrima Asphalion tis Ellados: Odos Agiou Constantinou 6, 101 Athens; f. 1933; Gen. Man. J. KYRIAKOS.

Europa Insurance Co SA: Leoforos Syngrou 70, 117 42 Athens; tel. (01) 9226077; telex 215268; Rep. I. MORFINOS.

Evropaiki Enosis: Odos Nikis 10, 105 63 Athens; tel. (01) 3249234; telex 214392; f. 1973; Gen. Man. PANOS MINETTAS.

Galaxias: Odos Panepistimiou 56, 106 78 Athens; tel. (01) 3639370; f. 1967; Gen. Man. I. TSOUPRAS.

Geniki Epagelmatiki: Odos Panepistimiou 56, 106 78 Athens; tel. (01) 3636910; f. 1967; Gen. Man. G. GIATRAKOS.

Gothaer Hellas: Odos Michalakopoulou 174, 115 27 Athens; tel. (01) 7750801; Gen. Man. S. GALANIS.

Halkyon: Odos Philonos 107-109, Piraeus; Man. Dir K. MARTINOS.

Hellas: Leoforos Kifissias 119, 151 24 Marousi; tel. (01) 8068501; telex 215226; f. 1973; Gen. Man. N. ADAMANTIADIS.

Hellenic Reliance Insurances S.A.: Odos Mavromichali 3, 185 03 Piraeus; tel. (01) 4115311; telex 212679; f. 1972; Gen. Man. M. N. LOURIDAS.

Hellinoelvetiki: Odos Hermou 6, 105 63 Athens; tel. (01) 3252106; telex 216936; f. 1943; Gen. Man. J. DELENDAS.

Hellinokypriaki A.E.G.A.: Leoforos Syngrou 102, 117 41 Athens; tel. (01) 9226094; telex 218722; Rep. PANOS PAPAYANNOPOULOS.

Hellinovretanniki: Odos Messoghion 2-4, 115 27 Athens; tel. (01) 7755301; telex 216448; f. 1974; Gen. Man. J. PALEOLOGOS.

Hermes: Odos Christou Lada 2, 105 61 Athens; tel. (01) 3225602; f. 1940; general insurance; Gen. Man. N. NEGAS.

Horizon Insurance Co SA: Leoforos Amalias 26A, 105 57 Athens; tel. (01) 3227932; telex 216158; f. 1965; Gen. Mans THEODORE ACHIS and CHR. ACHIS.

Hydrogios: Odos Lagoumigi 6, 176 71 Athens; tel. (01) 9222749; Gen. Man. A. CASCARELIS.

Ikonomiki: Odos Kapodistriou 38, 102 Athens; f. 1968; Gen. Man. D. NIKOLAIDIS.

Ikostos Aion: Odos Kapodistriou 38, 104 32 Athens; tel. (01) 5243544; f. 1972; Gen. Man. N. KYLPASIS.

Ilios: Odos Mavromichali 10, 106 79 Athens; tel. (01) 3606410; telex 215834; f. 1941; Gen. Man. M. N. LOURIDAS; Chair J. PSOMAS.

Imperial Hellas SA: Odos Veranzerou 5, 106 77 Athens; tel. (01) 3630600; f. 1971; Gen. Man. SAVVAS TZANNIS.

Interamerican Insurance Co: Interamerican Tower, Leoforos Syngrou 350, 176 74 Kallithea; tel. (01) 9421222; telex 214685; f. 1971; Gen. Man. DIMITRI KONTOMINAS.

Interamerican Property and Casualty Insurance Co: Odos Agiou Constantinou 59-61 and Leoforos Kifissias 117, 151 24 Maroussi, Athens; tel. (01) 9421222; telex 226177; f. 1975; Man. Dir G. ANTONIADIS.

Ioniki: Odos Korai 1, 105 64 Athens; tel. (01) 3236901; f. 1939; Gen. Man. N. CRONTIRAS.

Kykladiki: Odos Panepistimiou 59, 105 64 Athens; tel. (01) 3219184; telex 218560; f. 1919; Gen. Man. PAN. KATSICOSTAS.

Laiki: Leoforos Syngrou 135, 171 21 N. Smyrni; tel. (01) 9332911; telex 215403; f. 1942; Gen. Man. N. MOURTZOUKOS.

Lloyd Hellenique SA: Odos Psaron 2 and Odos Agiou Constantinou, 104 37 Athens; tel. (01) 5237168; telex 225397; f. 1942; Dir DOMINIQUE PRIGENT.

Makedonia Insurance Co: Odos Egnatia 1, 546 30 Thessaloniki; tel. (031) 526133; Gen. Man. K. EFTHIMIADIS.

Merimna: Odos Voulis 45-47, 105 57 Athens; tel. (01) 3235553; f. 1943; Man. Dir E. BALA-HILL.

Messoghios: Leoforos Syngrou 165, Athens; f. 1942; Gen. Man. E. TSAOUSIS.

National Insurance Institution of Greece: Odos Agiou Constantinou 6, 104 31 Athens; tel. (01) 5223300; Rep. J. KYRIAKOS.

Olympic Ins. Co SA: Odos Tsimiski 21, 546 24 Thessaloniki; tel. (31) 239331; telex 415251; f. 1962; Man. Dir G. TARNATOROS-ANAGNOSTOU.

Omonia: Odos Agiou Constantinou 2, Athens; Pres. F. TSOUKALAS.

Pagosmios Insurance SA: Leoforos Syngrou 194, 176 71 Athens; tel. (01) 9581341; telex 219319; f. 1975; Chair. L. FRANGOS; Gen. Man. G. FRANGOS.

Panellinios: Leoforos Syngrou 171, 171 21 Athens; tel. (01) 9352003; f. 1918; Gen. Man. A. VALYRAKIS.

Pegasus Insurance Co: Odos Stadiou 5, 105 62 Athens; tel. (01) 3227357; telex 214188; Gen. Man. M. PARASKAKIS.

Phoenix-General Insurance Co of Greece SA: Odos Omirou 2, 105 64 Athens; tel. (01) 322951; telex 215608; f. 1928; general insurance; Chair. P. I. LAMBROU; Gen. Man. Y. G. LINOS.

Piraiki: Odos Georges 10, 106 77 Athens; tel. (01) 3624868; telex 225921; f. 1943; Dir Gen. K. PAPAGEORGIOU.

Poseidon: Odos Karaiskou 163, 185 35 Piraeus; tel. (01) 4522685; f. 1972; Gen. Man. THANOS J. MELAKOPIDES.

Promitheus: Odos 3rd September 84, 104 Athens; tel. (01) 8827085; f. 1941; Gen. Man. C. GHONIS.

Proodos: Leoforos Syngrou 196, 176 71 Kallithea; tel. (01) 9593302; telex 214364; f. 1941; Gen. Man. N. DOIMAS.

Propontis: Odos Agiou Constantinou 6, 104 31 Athens; tel. (01) 522300; f. 1917; Gen. Man. J. KYRIAKOS.

Prostasia: Leoforos Syngrou 253, 176 72 Athens; tel. (01) 9427091; Rep. A. PALMOS.

Scourtis GH: Odos Panepistimiou 58, 106 78 Athens; tel. (01) 3626081; Gen. Man. G. SCOURTIS.

Syneteristiki: Odos Gennadiou and Akadimias 8, 115 24 Athens; tel. (01) 3642611; Gen. Man. N. GEORGAKOPOULOS.

A large number of foreign insurance companies also operate in Greece.

Insurance Associations

Insurers' Union of Greece: Odos Voulis 22, 105 63 Athens; tel. (01) 3229395; 39 mems; Pres. J. KYRIAKOS; Man. CH. TSOUPIS.

Association of Greek Insurance Companies: Odos Solonos 14, 106 73 Athens; tel. (01) 3610287; f. 1907; 26 mems; Chair. P. NICOLAIDES.

Association of Insurance Companies: Odos Xenophontos 10, 105 57 Athens; tel. (01) 3236733; telex 223522; 94 mems.

Trade and Industry

CHAMBERS OF COMMERCE

Athens Chamber of Commerce & Industry: Odos Akademias 7, 106 71 Athens; tel. (01) 3604815; telex 215707; f. 1919; Pres. LAZAROS EFRAIMOGLOU; Sec.-Gen. DIM. DANILATOS; 37,500 mems.

Handicraft Chamber of Athens: Odos Akademias 18, 106 71 Athens; tel. (01) 3630253; Pres. G. KYRIOPOULOS; Sec.-Gen. S. PAPAGELOU; c. 60,000 mems.

Handicraft Chamber of Piraeus: Odos Karaiscou 111, 185 32 Piraeus; tel. (01) 4174152; f. 1925; Pres. EVAG. MYTILINEOS; Sec.-Gen. ATHAN. MYSTAKIDIS; 18,500 mems.

Piraeus Chamber of Commerce & Industry: Odos Loudovicou, 185 31 Piraeus; tel. (01) 4177241; telex 212970; f. 1919; Pres. MANOLIS NIADAS; Sec.-Gen. GEORGE KASSIMATIS.

Thessaloniki Chamber of Commerce and Industry: Odos Tsimiski 29, 546 24 Thessaloniki; tel. (031) 220920; telex 412115; f. 1919; Pres. PANTELIS CONSTANTINIDIS; Sec.-Gen. JOHN MITATOS; 11,500 mems.

INDUSTRIAL ASSOCIATIONS

Association of Industries of Northern Greece: POB 10709, 1 Morihovou Sq., 541 10 Thessaloniki; tel. (031) 539817, telex 418310; f. 1914; Pres. ALEXANDROS BAKATSELOS.

Federation of Greek Industries (SEB): Odos Xenophontos 5, 105 57 Athens; f. 1907; Pres. STELIOS ARGYROS; 950 mems.

Hellenic Cotton Board: Leoforos Syngrou 150, 176 71 Athens; tel. (01) 9225011; telex 214556; f. 1931; state organization; Pres. ANASTASIOS LEKKAS.

Hellenic Organization of Small and Medium-size Industries and Handicrafts: Odos Xenias 16, 115 28 Athens; tel. (01) 7715002; telex 218819.

TRADE UNIONS

There are about 5,000 registered trade unions, grouped together in 82 federations and 86 workers' centres, which are affiliated to the Greek General Confederation of Labor (GSEE).

Greek General Confederation of Labor (GSEE): Odos Patission 69, Athens; tel. (01) 8834611; f. 1918; Pres. GEORGE RAFTOPOULOS; Gen. Sec. GEORGE PAVLIDAKIS; 700,00 mems.

GREECE
Directory

Pan-Hellenic Seamen's Federation: Livaros Building, Akti Miaouli 47–49, Piraeus; tel. (01) 4523589; f. 1920; confederation of 14 marine unions; Gen. Sec. MICHEL ZENZEFILIS.

TRADE FAIR

Helexpo: Odos Egnatia 154, 546 36 Thessaloniki; tel. (031) 239221; telex 412291; f. 1926; official organizer of international fairs, exhibitions, festivals and congresses (most notably the annual General Trade Fair of Thessaloniki, which takes place over two weeks starting on the first Sunday in September); Pres. VASSILIS DOLMAS.

Transport

RAILWAYS

Ilektriki Sidirodromi Athinon–Pireos (ISAP) (Athens–Piraeus Electric Railways): Odos Athinas 67, 105 52 Athens; tel. (01) 3248311; telex 219998; Gen. Dir G. BOUSBOURAS.

Organismos Sidirodromon Ellados (OSE) (Hellenic Railways Organization Ltd): Odos Karolou 1, 104 37 Athens; tel. (01) 5240996; telex 215187; f. 1971; state railways. Total length of track: 2,577 km (1987); Pres. A. LAMBRINOPOULOS; Dir-Gen. CHR. PAPAGEORGIOU.

ROADS

In 1985 there were 34,492 km of roads in Greece. Of this total, 8,700 km were main roads, and 92 km were motorways.

INLAND WATERWAYS

There are no navigable rivers in Greece.

Corinth Canal: built 1893; over six km long, links the Corinthian and Saronic Gulfs. The Canal shortens the journey from the Adriatic to the Piraeus by 325 km; it is spanned by three single-span bridges, two for road and one for rail. The canal can be used by ships of a maximum draught of 22 ft and a width of 60 ft. During 1976, 9,438 ships with a total tonnage of 4,616,852 nrt passed through the Corinth Canal.

SHIPPING

In June 1987 the Greek merchant fleet totalled 2,089 vessels compared with 3,922 ships in 1980. The principal ports are Piraeus, Patras and Thessaloniki.

Union of Greek Shipowners: Karageorgis Bldg, Akti Kondyli, Piraeus; Pres. STATHIS GOURDOMICHALIS.

Among the largest shipping companies are:

Anangel Shipping Enterprises SA: Akti Miaouli 25, 185 35 Piraeus; tel. (01) 4112511; telex 212567; Dir A. ANGELICOUSIS; 48 vessels.

Ceres Hellenic Shipping Enterprises Ltd: Akti Miaouli 69, 185 37 Piraeus; tel. (01) 4523612; telex 212257; Dir D. C. HADJIANTONIOU; 68 vessels.

Chandris Cruise Lines: Akti Miaouli 95, 185 38 Piraeus; tel. (01) 4120932; telex 212327; Man. Dirs M. A. FOROS and CH. SYNODINOS; 6 cruise liners.

Comninos Brothers' Shipping Co SA: Odos Filonos 61–65, 185 35 Piraeus; tel. (01) 4132612; telex 212915; Man. Dirs CONSTANTINE E. COMNINOS, ANTHONY E. COMNINOS; 18 vessels.

Golden Union Shipping Co SA: Odos Kolokotroni 126, 185 35 Piraeus; tel. (01) 4114511; telex 211190; Man. Dir THEODORE VENIAMIS; 35 vessels.

Hellenic Mediterranean Lines Co Ltd: Electric Railway Station Building, POB 80057, 185 10 Piraeus; tel. (01) 4174341; telex 212517; f. 1929; Chair. CONST. A. RINGAS; Man. Dir A. G. YANNOULATOS; 4 passenger and car ferries.

Mayamar Marine Enterprises SA: POB 80161, 185 10 Piraeus; tel. (01) 4115931; telex 213107; Dir J. C. MAVRAKAKIS; 22 vessels.

John S. Latsis: POB 203, Odos Othonos 8–10, 105 57 Athens; tel. (01) 3230151; telex 215456; passenger and cargo services; Pres. J. S. LATSIS; fleet of 50 vessels, including 28 tankers.

Tsakos Shipping and Trading SA: Akti Miaouli 85, 185 38 Piraeus; tel. (01) 4182111; telex 212670; Dirs P. N. TSAKOS, E. N. TSAKOS, P. N. EFTHIMIADES; 23 vessels.

United Shipping and Trading Co of Greece, SA: Odos Iassonos 6, 185 37 Piraeus; tel. (01) 4522511; telex 213014; Dir M. ZARBIS; 14 vessels.

Varnima Corporation International SA: Marine Enterprises Bldg, Akti Miaouli 53–55, 185 36 Piraeus; tel. (01) 4522911; telex 212461; worldwide oil transportation; Chair. VARDIS J. VARDINOYANNIS; Man. Dir G. J. VARDINOYANNIS; 16 vessels.

CIVIL AVIATION

There are international airports at Athens, Thessaloniki, Alexandroupolis, Corfu, Lesbos, Andravida, Rhodes, Kos and Heraklion/Crete, and 25 domestic airports. There are plans for a new international airport to be built at Spatsa, 48 km east of Athens.

Olympic Airways SA: Leoforos Syngrou 96–100, 117 41 Athens; tel. (01) 9292111; telex 215134; f. 1957; state-owned; domestic services linking principal cities and islands in Greece, and international services to Albania, Australia, Austria, Belgium, Canada, Cyprus, Denmark, Egypt, France, Germany, Israel, Italy, Jordan, Kenya, Kuwait, Libya, the Netherlands, Saudi Arabia, Singapore, South Africa, Spain, Switzerland, Syria, Turkey, the United Kingdom, the United Arab Emirates and the USA; fleet of 4 Boeing 747-200B, 4 Boeing 707-320C, 2 Boeing 707-320B, 6 Boeing 727-200, 11 Boeing 737-200, 8 Airbus A300B4, and 2 Airbus A300B2. Chair. and Dir-Gen. ALEXANDROS D. AKRIVAKIS; Vice-Chair. Dr DIMITRIU BAIRAKTARIS.

Tourism

The sunny climate, the natural beauty of the country and its great history and traditions attract tourists to Greece. There are numerous islands and other sites of archaeological interest. Tourism is expanding rapidly, with the improvement of transport and accommodation facilities. The number of tourists visiting Greece increased from 1m. in 1968 to an estimated 8.1m. in 1987. Earnings from tourism, which totalled US $120m. in 1968, reached $2,191.7m. in 1987.

Ellinikos Organismos Tourismou (National Tourist Organization of Greece): Odos Amerikis 2B, 101 10 Athens; tel. (01) 3223111; telex 215832; Pres. K. KYRIAZIS; Dir Prof. P. LAZARIDIS.

Atomic Energy

Elliniki Epitropi Atomikis Energias (Greek Atomic Energy Commission): POB 60228, 153 10 Aghia Paraskevi, near Athens; tel. (01) 6513111; telex 216199; f. 1954; seven-member administrative cttee; Pres. Prof. MICH. ANTONOPOULOS-DOMIS; Vice-Pres. Prof. L. KAMARINOPOULOS.

'Demokritos' National Research Center for Physical Sciences: POB 60228, 153 10 Aghia Paraskevi, near Athens; tel. (01) 6513111; telex 216199; institutes for: materials science, microelectronics, nuclear technology, radiation protection, nuclear physics, biology, physical chemistry, informatics and telecommunications, radio-isotopes and radiodiagnostic products.

GRENADA

Introductory Survey

Location, Climate, Language, Religion, Flag, Capital

Grenada, a mountainous, heavily-forested island, is the most southerly of the Windward Islands, in the West Indies. The country also includes some of the small islands known as the Grenadines, which lie to the north of Grenada. The largest of these is the low-lying island of Carriacou. The climate is semi-tropical, with an average annual temperature of 28°C (82°F) in the lowlands. Annual rainfall averages about 1,500 mm (60 in) in the coastal area and 3,800 mm to 5,100 mm (150–200 in) in mountain areas. Most of the rainfall occurs between June and December. The majority of the population speak English, although a French patois is also spoken. Most of the population profess Christianity, and the main denomination is Roman Catholicism. The national flag (proportions 2 by 1) consists of a diagonally-quartered rectangle (yellow in the upper and lower segments, green in the right and left ones) surrounded by a red border bearing six five-pointed yellow stars (three at the upper edge of the flag, and three at the lower edge). There is a red disc, containing a large five-pointed yellow star, in the centre, and a representation of a nutmeg (in yellow and red) on the green segment near the hoist. The capital is St George's.

Recent History

Grenada was initially colonized by the French but was captured by the British in 1762. British control was recognized in 1783 by the Treaty of Versailles. Grenada continued as a British colony until 1958, when it joined the Federation of the West Indies, remaining a member until the dissolution of the Federation in 1962. Full internal self-government and statehood in association with the United Kingdom were achieved in March 1967. During this period, the political life of Grenada was dominated by Eric Gairy, a local trade union leader, who in 1950 founded the Grenada United Labour Party (GULP), with the support of an associated trade union. In 1951 GULP won a majority of the elected seats on the Legislative Council but in 1957 it was defeated by the Grenada National Party (GNP), led by Herbert Blaize. Gairy was Chief Minister in 1961–62 but was removed from office by the British, and the Constitution suspended, after allegations of corruption. In the subsequent elections the GNP gained a majority of the elected seats, and Blaize became Chief Minister again. Gairy became Premier after the elections of 1967 and again after those of 1972, which he fought chiefly on the issue of total independence. Grenada became independent, within the Commonwealth, on 7 February 1974, with Gairy as Prime Minister. Opposition to Gairy within the country was expressed in demonstrations and a general strike, and the formation, by the three opposition parties, of the People's Alliance, which contested the 1976 general elections and reduced GULP's majority in the Lower House. The alliance comprised the GNP, the United People's Party and the New Jewel Movement (NJM).

The rule of Sir Eric Gairy, who was knighted in June 1977, was regarded by the opposition as increasingly autocratic and corrupt, and on 13 March 1979 he was replaced in a bloodless coup by the leader of the left-wing NJM, Maurice Bishop. The new People's Revolutionary Government (PRG) suspended the 1974 Constitution and announced the imminent formation of a People's Consultative Assembly to draft a new constitution. Meanwhile, Grenada remained a monarchy, with the British Queen as Head of State, represented in Grenada by a Governor-General. During 1980 and 1981 there was an increase in repression, against a background of mounting anti-Government violence and the PRG's fears of an invasion by US forces.

By mid-1982 relations with the USA, the United Kingdom and the more conservative members of CARICOM were becoming increasingly strained: elections had not been arranged, restrictions against the privately-owned press had been imposed, many detainees were still awaiting trial, and Grenada was aligning more closely with Cuba and the USSR. Cuba was supplying about 40% of the funds, and several hundred construction workers, for the airport at Point Salines, a project which further fuelled the USA's insistence that Grenada was to become a major staging-post for Soviet manoeuvres in the area.

In March 1983 the PRG reiterated its fears that the USA was planning an invasion, and the armed forces were put on alert. The USA strenuously denied these allegations. In June Maurice Bishop sought to improve relations with the USA, and announced the appointment of a commission to draft a new constitution. This attempt at conciliation was not popular with the more left-wing members of the PRG regime, who regarded Bishop's actions as an ideological betrayal. This division within the Government erupted in October into a power struggle between Bishop and his deputy, Bernard Coard, the Minister of Finance and Planning. On 13 October Bishop was placed under house arrest, allegedly for his refusal to share power with Coard. Four days later, Gen. Hudson Austin, the commander of the People's Revolutionary Army (PRA), announced that Bishop had been expelled from the NJM. On 19 October thousands of Bishop's supporters, incensed by this news, stormed the house, freed Bishop from imprisonment, and demonstrated outside the PRA headquarters. Violence ensued, with PRA forces firing into the crowd. Later in the day, Bishop, three of his ministers and two trade union spokesmen were all executed by the PRA. A military coup had taken place, and the Government was replaced by a 16-man Revolutionary Military Council (RMC), led by Gen. Austin and supported by Coard and one other minister. The remaining NJM ministers were arrested and imprisoned, and a total curfew was imposed.

Regional and international outrage at the assassination of Bishop, plus fears of a US military intervention, were so intense that, after four days, the RMC relaxed the curfew, reopened the airport and promised to return to civilian rule as soon as possible. However, the Organization of Eastern Caribbean States (OECS, see p. 107) decided to intervene in an attempt to restore democratic order, and asked for help from the USA, which readily complied. (It is unclear whether the decision to intervene preceded or followed a request for help to the OECS by the Grenadian Governor-General, Sir Paul Scoon.) On 25 October 1983 about 1,900 US military personnel invaded the island, accompanied by 300 troops from Jamaica, Barbados and member-countries of the OECS. Fighting continued for some days, and the USA gradually increased its troop strength, with further reinforcements waiting off shore with a US naval task force. The RMC's forces were defeated, while Coard, Gen. Austin and others who had been involved in the coup were captured and imprisoned on the island, to await trial.

On 9 November 1983 Sir Paul Scoon appointed a non-political interim council to assume responsibility for the government of the country until elections could be held. Nicholas Braithwaite, a former Commonwealth official, was appointed chairman of this council in December. The 1974 Constitution was reinstated, and an electoral commission was created to prepare for elections. By mid-December the USA had withdrawn all its forces except 300 support troops, military police and technicians who were to help the 430 members of Caribbean forces who remained on the island. These numbers were maintained throughout 1984. A 550-member police force, trained by the USA and the United Kingdom, was established, including a paramilitary element which was to be the new defence contingent.

Several political parties, which had gone underground or into exile during the rule of the PRG, re-emerged and announced their intention of contesting the elections for a new House of Representatives. Sir Eric Gairy returned to Grenada in January 1984 to lead his GULP, although he stated that he would not stand as a candidate himself. In May three former NJM ministers formed the Maurice Bishop Patriotic Movement (MBPM) to contest the elections. A number of centre parties emerged, including the Grenada National Party (GNP), led by Herbert Blaize, the former Premier; the Grenada Democratic Movement (GDM), led by Dr Francis Alexis; the National Democratic Party (NDP), led by George Brizan; and the Chris-

GRENADA

tian Democratic Labour Party (CDLP). Fears that a divided opposition would allow GULP to win a majority of seats in the new House led to negotiations between the centre parties to form an electoral alliance. After the failure of one attempt, and in response to US apprehension over growing support for GULP, a meeting between the GNP, GDM, NDP and CDLP was arranged at the end of August 1984 on Union Island, and attended by the Prime Ministers of Barbados, Saint Lucia and Saint Vincent and the Grenadines. The result was the agreed merger of the parties to form the New National Party (NNP), to be led by Herbert Blaize. The CDLP, however, soon left the new party, and there were some fears over the cohesion of the new grouping.

At the general election, held on 3 December 1984, the NNP achieved a convincing victory over its opponents by winning 14 of the 15 seats in the House of Representatives, and 59% of the popular vote. Both Sir Eric Gairy and the MBPM claimed that the poll had been fraudulent, and the one successful GULP candidate, Marcel Peters, initially refused to take his seat in protest. He subsequently accepted the seat, but was expelled from the party and formed the Grenada Democratic Labour Party (GDLP). Blaize became Prime Minister, and appointed a seven-member Cabinet, which included Brizan and Alexis. He also asked the remaining US and Caribbean troops on the island to stay, at least until March 1985, and stressed the need for national reconciliation. The last contingents of US and Caribbean troops left the island in September 1985.

The trial before the Grenada High Court of 19 detainees (including Coard, his wife and Austin), accused of murder and conspiracy against Bishop and six of his associates, had opened in November 1984. However, repeated adjournments prevented the start of proceedings. The approval by the House of Representatives of all the legislation that had been enacted during the rule of the PRG prevented an appeal by the detainees to the judicial committee of the British Privy Council, and, in response to requests from the defence lawyers, further adjournments postponed the trial of 18 of the detainees until April 1986. One of the detainees agreed to give evidence for the State in return for a pardon. Eventually, verdicts on 196 charges of murder and conspiracy to murder were returned by the jury in December. Fourteen of the defendants were sentenced to death, three were given prison sentences of between 30 and 45 years, and one was found not guilty. Appeals by the accused were expected to be considered during 1988, but were delayed by procedural challenges and criticisms, and by the death of the president of the Appeal Court in December.

A recurring feature of the NNP's administration has been the divisions between the different groupings that comprise the party, which have been expressed in frequent disagreements between cabinet members and in resentment at Blaize's style of leadership. In particular, the issue of leadership has assumed greater importance following successive visits by Blaize to the USA for medical treatment. In 1986 the Junior Minister of Education, Kenny Lalsingh, withdrew from the party; he was later followed by the Deputy Speaker of the House of Representatives, Phinsley St Louis, thereby reducing the NNP's parliamentary strength to 12 seats. St Louis and Lalsingh subsequently formed the Democratic Labour Congress. In April 1987 the parliamentary strength of the NNP was reduced to nine seats, and the coalition collapsed, when Alexis and Brizan (the former leaders of the GDM and NDP) resigned, together with the Junior Minister of Legal Affairs, Tillman Thomas, stating that they could not support Blaize's decision to make 1,800 government employees redundant.

In July 1987 the three joined forces with St Louis, Lalsingh and Marcel Peters (leader of the GDLP) to form a 'shadow cabinet'. In October they formally launched a new political party, the National Democratic Congress (NDC). Brizan, who had earlier been appointed parliamentary opposition leader (following St Louis' resignation from that post in September), was elected leader of the party. However, in November 1988, after months of speculation, Nicholas Braithwaite, former head of the Interim Government of 1983–84, joined the NDC and was adopted as its candidate to contest the constituency of Prime Minister Blaize, Carriacou and Petit Martinique, at the next general election, due to be held in 1989. (In early 1989 Braithwaite replaced Brizan as leader of the NDC.) Furthermore, in November 1988 the Junior Minister for Carriacou and Petit Martinique Affairs, John De Roche, resigned from the Government and as an NNP senator, in order to join the NDC.

In December he was followed by another senator, Norton Noel, the Minister of State for Labour, who cited divisions within the Cabinet as the motive for his resignation.

A deterioration in Prime Minister Blaize's health coincided with a growing challenge to his administration from within the NNP throughout 1988. In addition, the NNP's popularity suffered from Grenada's continuing economic problems, as well as Blaize's authoritarian style of leadership. Moreover, during 1988 the actions of the Government also gave rise to concerns among both regional neighbours and the opposition, when various deportation orders and bans were enforced by the administration against prominent left-wing politicians and journalists from the region, under provisions of the controversial 1987 Emergency Powers Act. In January 1989 Blaize was replaced as leader of the ruling party by his cabinet colleague, Dr Keith Mitchell, but he remained Prime Minister.

Government

Grenada has dominion status within the Commonwealth. The British monarch is Head of State and is represented locally by a Governor-General. Executive power is held by the Cabinet, led by the Prime Minister. Parliament comprises the Senate, made up of 13 Senators appointed by the Governor-General on the advice of the Prime Minister and the Leader of the Opposition, and the 15-member House of Representatives, elected by universal adult suffrage. The Cabinet is responsible to Parliament.

Defence

A police force was set up in late 1983, modelled on the British system and trained by British officers. A paramilitary element, known as the Special Service Unit and trained by US advisers, acts as the defence contingent and participates in the regional defence pact with other East Caribbean states.

Economic Affairs

In 1987, according to estimates by the World Bank, Grenada's gross national product (GNP), measured at average 1985–87 prices, was US $134m., equivalent to US $1,340 per head. Between 1980 and 1987, it was estimated, the country's GNP per head increased, in real terms, by an average of 3.0% annually. In 1987 it increased by an estimated 3.9%.

The economy of Grenada is essentially agricultural and centres on the traditional production of spices, particularly nutmeg. The principal exports are nutmeg, cocoa and bananas, although mace (the dried outer covering of nutmeg), cotton, coffee, coconuts, citrus fruit and minor spices are also significant. Agriculture contributed about 22% of gross domestic product (GDP) and accounted for more than 40% of export earnings in 1987. Since the early 1970s, however, Grenada's agricultural exports have been seriously affected by a combination of natural disasters and low international commodity prices. The banana plantations have been extensively damaged by the ravages of the banana disease, moko, since 1978, and adverse weather conditions between 1979 and 1981, while export shipments were suspended in 1983 because of the political crisis. Exports of bananas declined steadily from 12,200 metric tons in 1980 to 7,942 tons in 1986, while the value of earnings fell from EC $11m. to $8.2m. in 1984, but subsequently increased to about $10m. by 1986, owing to an improvement in international prices. In 1987 production of bananas increased by 6.3%, to 8,665 tons, helped by an upgrading of agronomic practices and the extended use of field-packing techniques to improve fruit quality. Exports increased to 8,130 tons, earning $11.1m. Earnings from cocoa exports fell from EC $18m. in 1981 to $11m. in 1983, although there was a modest recovery in production during 1984, when export earnings rose to $12.1m. The recovery continued during 1985, and it was announced that the Canadian International Development Agency (CIDA) was to help to finance a multi-year rehabilitation project. Production declined during 1986, but export earnings increased slightly, to $12.2m. Production increased by nearly 9% in 1987 to 1,793 metric tons, of which 1,714 tons were exported, earning only an estimated EC $11m. The EEC announced in 1988 that it would give the industry EC $1.8m. as compensation for earnings lost in 1987.

Nutmeg has traditionally been Grenada's main export, although the political troubles of 1983 caused considerable disruption to the industry. Low prices and the Indonesian monopoly of the market led to the stockpiling of 6m. lb (about 2,700 metric tons) during 1984, representing six months' production. Nutmeg exports earned only EC $5.8m. in 1984, but in the following year, although exports declined in volume, a rise in world prices increased export earnings to EC $11.4m. In 1986 exports increased to about 2,500 tons, earning EC $26.2m. In 1987 the Grenada Co-operative Nutmeg Association and the Indonesian Nutmeg Association signed a three-year cartel agreement covering prices and production levels of nutmeg and mace, and providing for co-operation in marketing and research. In that year production of nutmeg increased by more than 20%, to 2,788 tons, and of mace by 35%, to 313 tons. Export volumes remained at a similar level to those of 1986, but earnings increased to EC $39.4m. for nutmeg, and by almost $2m., to $7.3m., for mace (243 tons). Preliminary data for the first half of 1988 indicated a slight decline in the production, export and earnings of nutmeg, but mace production was reported to have increased. Plans to build a nutmeg-oil factory were announced in 1988.

Sugar cane and a wide variety of fruit and vegetables are also grown for local consumption, and exports of fresh fruit and vegetables increased steadily during 1984 and 1985, only to remain fairly static until 1987, when exports again increased significantly. In 1988 exports fell by almost 50%, owing to the decline of the market in Trinidad and Tobago. There are extensive forested areas in the interior of the country. Land tenure is based on privately-owned smallholdings and local co-operative ventures, and a number of the loss-making state-run farms are being returned to private ownership. Carriacou is significant for its livestock production, which is important for local consumption, although meat and milk still have to be imported. In the early 1980s Cuba and the USSR provided some equipment and expertise to develop Grenada's fishing industry. In 1980 a fish-processing plant was established, and in 1981 the Government formed a National Fishing Company.

The development of manufacturing industries has not kept pace with other activities, owing mainly to the limited local market. Industry centres on the processing of agricultural products, and cottage industries producing garments and spice-based goods for the export market. It was announced in mid-1986 that a consortium of 18 international companies was to invest more than US $70m. in a series of projects, including an aircraft repair station, a hotel and an electricity-generating plant. In July 1987 Venezuela and Grenada began work on a joint-venture project in garment manufacturing. Although 134 projects in manufacturing, tourism and agri-business were approved in 1986 by the Industrial Development Corporation, only 42 had started operating by April 1987, and anticipated investment by US-based corporations in light industry on the island, taking advantage of the benefits of the US Government's Caribbean Basin Initiative (CBI), had failed to materialize. Taxes on company profits and customs duties remain high when compared with rates of taxation in other Caribbean islands, and Grenada's infrastructure is poor. The 1986 reform of the taxation system, however, was claimed by the Government to have led to growth in the manufacturing sector of 16.5% in 1987. Nevertheless, the sector accounted for only 5.3% of GDP in 1987, and suffered a decline in the first half of 1988.

Tourism is an important sector of the economy but, because of political upheaval, the number of tourist arrivals declined dramatically between 1978 and 1983. Only 82,676 tourists arrived in 1983, compared with 148,667 in 1978. However, the completion of the new Point Salines Airport, opened in 1984, and the refurbishment and expansion of the island's hotels stimulated a revival in the tourist trade. Although the number of cruise-ship passenger arrivals declined by 32% during 1984, the number of stop-over arrivals increased by 21%, to a total of 39,503, and earnings from tourism totalled EC $45m. In 1985 the number of stop-over arrivals increased by a further 32%, and there was an increase of 165.5% in the number of cruise-ship passengers. Total tourist arrivals increased by 20% in 1986, to 171,200, and tourist expenditure totalled $72m., an increase of 12% on the 1985 figure. In 1987 growth in the tourist sector was minimal, although it still accounted for some 70% of GDP. The number of tourist arrivals increased to 184,620 in that year.

The level of unemployment declined from 49% of the labour force in 1979 to 22% by 1982, mainly as a consequence of the PRG's expansion of the armed forces, and the development of youth and community projects. The disbanding of the army, and the suspension of the projects by the Interim Government, helped to cause a rise in unemployment, which was estimated to be between 25% and 30% in 1986. The trade deficit rose from EC $105.1m. in 1984 to EC $126.2m. in 1985. In 1986 the deficit increased still further, to $149.2m., but in 1987 it fell slightly, to $143.2m. Total national debt had reached EC $218.3m. by the end of 1987 (more than one-half of the debt was owed to foreign creditors). In 1988 the Government sought to reschedule debt repayments, and the total public debt was expected to reach almost EC $300m. by the end of the year.

The construction of roads, buildings and other infrastructural necessities, and the development of the agricultural and industrial sectors, is heavily dependent on foreign aid and loans. In 1983 the IMF agreed to loan US $14.1m. but this was withdrawn because of political instability in late 1983. Heavy expenditure on the new airport resulted in an increase in the level of capital expenditure to EC $145m. in the 1983 budget, and funds for recurrent expenditure were diverted towards the airport project, producing an increased burden of debt and interest payments, which rose from the equivalent of 16.5% of GDP in 1980 to 42% by the end of 1983. Expenditure was reduced by 17% in the 1984/85 budget, introduced by the Interim Government. The projected budget deficit of EC $31.8m., however, was largely offset by US aid, totalling US $57.2m. for the 1984/85 financial year. In addition, US $3m. was provided in November 1983 as emergency aid, and $6m. as compensation for war damage. The 1986/87 budget proposals envisaged total expenditure of EC $236.2m., or EC $13.5m. less than in 1985/86. A total of 17 taxes were abolished, the most significant of which was income tax. A value-added tax (VAT) of 20% was introduced and was expected to yield EC $50m. during the financial year. However, in September 1986 the Government was forced to reduce planned expenditure in its capital budget by more than EC $10m., to postpone debt repayments of EC $13.4m. and to reduce recurrent expenditure, owing to a shortfall in revenue from the new tax system and a reduction in US budgetary support. In early 1987 pressure from the industrial sector forced the Government to exempt several items from VAT. The budget deficit for the financial year totalled EC 37.3m. The 1987/88 budget proposed total expenditure of EC $226.3m. Fiscal problems of collection and administration continued to affect revenue, although VAT provided EC $43.3m., or nearly one-half of total tax revenue, in 1987. Despite improved efficiency in the administration of public finances, recurrent expenditure increased by 18%. In 1988 a surcharge of 10% was imposed on all imports from countries outside CARICOM, thereby increasing receipts from import duties by more than 20%. The controversial redundancy programme for government employees, however, was halted. The annual rate of inflation averaged only 0.5% in 1986, and prices fell by 1.4% in 1987.

Canada, the United Kingdom, the EEC and the USA have been among those aid donors contributing to Grenada's reconstruction and development, by financing various projects. US aid during 1984 and 1985 totalled US $74m. However, aid was reduced in 1986 to US $10.8m., and was reduced to about $10m. in 1987. In February 1984 the US Government agreed to provide US $21m. towards the completion of the Point Salines Airport, and further sums for the repair of roads and the telephone system, damaged during the fighting. External budgetary support ended in 1987.

Social Welfare

There was no system of social security payments in Grenada prior to 1979. New initiatives launched in that year included the Youth for Reconstruction Programme, to provide basic paramedical services and assistance to the elderly and disabled, a national milk distribution programme and the establishment of community-directed day care centres. A National Insurance Scheme began in 1983, and in 1988 had a total investment portfolio of EC $58m. In 1987 there were 38 physicians working in Grenada and the country had three hospitals, with a total of about 360 beds. There are local health centres in the main towns. A mental hospital, destroyed by military action in 1983, was rebuilt with US financial aid.

Education

Education is free and compulsory for children between the ages of six and 14 years. The standard of education is high;

GRENADA

primary education begins at five years of age and lasts for seven years. Secondary education, beginning at the age of 12, lasts for a further seven years, comprising a first cycle of five years and a second of two years. In 1986 a total of 19,984 children received primary education in 59 schools. There were 20 secondary schools, with 6,462 pupils registered at the end of 1986. In 1970 only 2.2% of the adult population had received no schooling. Technical Centres have been set up in each parish, and there is a Technical and Vocational Institute in St George's. The Extra-Mural Department of the University of the West Indies has a branch in St George's, and there is also a Teachers' Training College. A School of Medicine has been established at St George's, a School of Agriculture at Mirabeau and a School of Fishing at Victoria.

Public Holidays

1989: 1–2 January (New Year), 7 February (Independence Day), 24–27 March (Easter), 1 May (Labour Day), 15 May (Whit Monday), 27 May (Corpus Christi), 7–8 August (Emancipation Holidays), 25 October (Thanksgiving Day), 25–26 December (Christmas).

1990: 1–2 January (New Year), 7 February (Independence Day), 13–16 April (Easter), 1 May (Labour Day), 4 June (Whit Monday), 14 June (Corpus Christi), 6–7 August (Emancipation Holidays), 25 October (Thanksgiving Day), 25–26 December (Christmas).

Weights and Measures

The metric system is in use.

Statistical Survey

Source (unless otherwise stated): Central Statistical Office, Government of Grenada, Church Street, St George's; tel. (440) 3034.

AREA AND POPULATION

Area: 344 sq km (133 sq miles).

Population: 93,858 at census of 7 April 1970; 89,088 (males 42,943; females 46,145) at census of 30 April 1981; 98,000 (UN estimate) at mid-1987.

Principal Town: St George's (capital), population 7,500 (1980 estimate).

Births and Deaths (1982): Registered live births 2,614; Registered deaths 721.

AGRICULTURE, ETC.

Principal Crops (FAO estimates, '000 metric tons, 1986): Roots and tubers 4, Bananas 8, Coconuts 8, Sugar cane 6, Cocoa beans 3, Mangoes 2, Avocados 2 (Source: FAO, *Production Yearbook*).

Livestock (FAO estimates, year ending September 1986): Cattle 4,000, Pigs 11,000, Sheep 17,000, Goats 14,000, Asses 1,000 (Source: FAO, *Production Yearbook*).

Fishing (metric tons, live weight): Total catch 1,507 in 1984; 1,584 in 1985; 2,328 in 1986 (Source: FAO, *Yearbook of Fishery Statistics*).

INDUSTRY

Production (1985): Rum 4,000 hectolitres; Beer 14,000 hectolitres; Cigarettes 118 metric tons; Electric energy 25 million kWh (Source: UN, *Industrial Statistics Yearbook*).

FINANCE

Currency and Exchange Rates: 100 cents = 1 East Caribbean dollar (EC $). *Coins:* 1, 2, 5, 10, 25 and 50 cents. *Notes:* 1, 5, 20 and 100 dollars. *Sterling and US Dollar Equivalents* (30 September 1988): £1 sterling = EC $4.566; US $1 = EC $2.700; EC $100 = £21.90 = US $37.04. *Exchange Rate:* Fixed at US $1 = EC $2.70 since July 1976.

Budget (estimates, EC $ million, 1988): Expenditure 249 (current 147, capital 102).

International Reserves (US $ million at 31 December 1987): Foreign exchange 23.33; Total 23.33 (Source: IMF, *International Financial Statistics*).

Money Supply (EC $ million at 31 December 1987): Currency outside banks 33.07; Demand deposits at deposit money banks 41.37; Total money 74.43 (Source: IMF, *International Financial Statistics*).

Cost of Living (Consumer Price Index; base: 1980 = 100): 147.2 in 1985; 148.0 in 1986; 146.7 in 1987 (Source: IMF, *International Financial Statistics*).

Gross Domestic Product (EC $ million in current purchasers' values): 311.2 in 1985; 347.6 in 1986; 375.7 in 1987 (Source: IMF, *International Financial Statistics*).

Balance of Payments (US $ million, 1987): Merchandise exports f.o.b. 31.60; Merchandise imports f.o.b. −77.70; *Trade balance* −46.10; Exports of services 33.40; Imports of services −32.40; *Balance on goods and services* −45.10; Private unrequited transfers (net) 11.80; Government unrequited transfers (net) 7.60; *Current balance* −25.70; Long-term capital (net) 26.75; Short-term capital (net) −0.04; Net errors and omissions 0.42; *Total* (net monetary movements) 1.42; Valuation changes (net) −0.18; Exceptional financing (net) 1.90; *Changes in reserves* 3.14 (Source: IMF, *International Financial Statistics*).

EXTERNAL TRADE

Principal Commodities (EC $ million, 1983): *Imports:* Food and live animals 35.4; Beverages and tobacco 3.3; Crude materials (inedible) except fuels 8.4; Mineral fuels, lubricants, etc. 17.2; Chemicals 12.1; Basic manufactures 39.2; Machinery and transport equipment 17.1; Total (incl. others) 154.5. *Exports:* Food and live animals 46.6 (Cocoa 11.0, Nutmeg 9.5, Bananas 8.7, Mace 2.3, Fresh fruit 12.8); Clothing 3.5; Total (incl. others) 50.7 (excl. re-exports 1.1).

Principal Trading Partners (EC million, 1984): *Imports:* Japan 10.4; Trinidad and Tobago 22.5; United Kingdom 27.6; USA 37.2; Total (incl. others) 151.1. *Exports* (incl. re-exports): Federal Republic of Germany 4.5; Netherlands 3.5; Trinidad and Tobago 16.7; United Kingdom 15.6; USA 2.4; Total (incl. others) 46.0.

TRANSPORT

Road Traffic (1984): Vehicles registered 7,741.

International Sea-borne Shipping (estimated freight traffic, '000 metric tons, 1985): Goods loaded 27; Goods unloaded 52 (Source: UN, *Monthly Bulletin of Statistics*).

TOURISM

Visitor Arrivals (1987): 184,620 (incl. 127,214 cruise-ship passengers).

COMMUNICATIONS MEDIA

Radio Receivers (estimate, 1986): 50,000 in use.

Telephones (1984): 3,432 in use.

Book Production (1979): 10 titles (11,000 copies).

EDUCATION

Primary (1986): 59 schools; 735 teachers (1984); 19,984 pupils.

Secondary (1986): 20 schools; 311 teachers (1984); 6,462 pupils.

Higher* (1983): 53 teachers; 535 students.

* Source: UNESCO, *Statistical Yearbook* (figures exclude Grenada Teachers' College).

Directory

The Constitution

The 1974 independence Constitution was suspended in March 1979, following the coup, and restored in November 1983 after the overthrow of the People's Revolutionary Government. The main provisions of this Constitution are summarized below:

The Head of State is the British monarch, represented in Grenada by an appointed Governor-General. Legislative power is vested in the bicameral Parliament, comprising a Senate and a House of Representatives. The Senate consists of 13 Senators, seven of whom are appointed on the advice of the Prime Minister, three on the advice of the Leader of the Opposition and three on the advice of the Prime Minister after he has consulted interests which he considers Senators should be selected to represent. The House of Representatives consists of 15 members elected from single-member constituencies on the basis of universal adult suffrage.

The Cabinet consists of a Prime Minister, who must be a member of the House of Representatives, and such other Ministers as the Governor-General may appoint on the advice of the Prime Minister.

There is a Supreme Court and, in certain cases, a further appeal lies to Her Majesty in Council.

The Government

Head of State: HM Queen ELIZABETH II.
Governor-General: Sir PAUL SCOON (took office 1978).

THE CABINET
(February 1989)

Prime Minister and Minister of Finance, Trade, Industry, Planning, Carriacou and Petit Martinique Affairs, Security, Information and Energy: HERBERT BLAIZE.
Deputy Prime Minister and Minister of External Affairs, Tourism, Agriculture, Land and Forestry: BEN JONES.
Attorney-General and Minister of Legal Affairs, Health, Housing and Physical Planning: DANNY WILLIAMS.
Minister of Communications, Works, Public Utilities, Co-operatives, Community Development, Women's Affairs and Civil Aviation: Dr KEITH MITCHELL.
Minister of Education, Social Security, Labour, Culture, Youth Affairs, Sports, Local Government and Fisheries: GEORGE McGUIRE.
Minister of State for Agriculture and Tourism: PAULINE ANDREWS.
Minister of State for Women's Affairs and Community Development: GRACE DUNCAN.
Minister of State for Works and Co-operatives: ALLEYNE WALKER.
Minister of State in the Prime Minister's Ministry, with special responsibility for Information, Finance, Trade, Industry and Energy: FELIX ALEXANDER.
Minister of State for Legal Affairs and National Security: Senator LAWRENCE JOSEPH.
Minister of State for Education, Culture, Youth Affairs and Fisheries: Senator BEN ANDREWS.
Minister of State for Social Security, Local Government and Labour: (vacant).

MINISTRIES

All Ministries are in St George's.

Office of the Prime Minister: St George's; tel. (440) 2255; telex 3457.

Legislature

PARLIAMENT

Senate

President: JOHN WATTS.
There are 13 appointed members.

House of Representatives

Speaker: Sir HUDSON SCIPIO.

General Election, 3 December 1984

Party	Votes	%	Seats
New National Party (NNP)	23,984	58.64	14*
Grenada United Labour Party (GULP)	14,677	35.88	1†
Maurice Bishop Patriotic Movement (MBPM)	2,022	4.94	—
Others	220	0.54	—
Total	40,903	100.00	15

* In 1987 the NNP's strength was reduced to nine seats, following the resignations of two members in 1986 and of a further three members in April 1987. In October the five former members of the NNP established the National Democratic Congress (NDC).
† The Grenada United Labour Party member at first refused to take his seat. When he did so, however, he was expelled from the party. He subsequently formed his own party, the Grenada Democratic Labour Party, which, in turn, merged with the NDC in October 1987.

Political Organizations

Christian Democratic Labour Party (CDLP): St George's; f. 1984; Leader WINSTON WHYTE.
Grenada United Labour Party (GULP): St George's; f. 1950; right-wing; Leader Sir ERIC GAIRY.
Maurice Bishop Patriotic Movement (MBPM): St George's; f. 1984 by former members of the New Jewel Movement; socialist; Leader TERRENCE MARRYSHOW.
National Democratic Congress (NDC): St George's; f. 1987 by former members of the NNP and merger of Democratic Labour Congress and Grenada Democratic Labour Party; centrist; Chair. KENNY LALSINGH; Leader NICHOLAS BRAITHWAITE; Gen. Sec. JEROME JOSEPH.
New National Party (NNP): St George's; f. 1984; merger of Grenada Democratic Movement, Grenada National Party and National Democratic Party; centrist; Chair. LAWRENCE JOSEPH; Leader Dr KEITH MITCHELL; Gen. Sec. JOHN MUNROE.

Diplomatic Representation

EMBASSIES AND HIGH COMMISSION IN GRENADA

United Kingdom: British High Commission, 14 Church St, St George's; tel. (440) 3222; telex 3419 (High Commissioner resident in Barbados).
USA: Belmont, POB 54, St George's; tel. (440) 1731; Chargé d'affaires: JAMES FORD COOPER.
Venezuela: Archibald Ave, POB 201, St George's; tel. (440) 1721; telex 3414; Ambassador: EFRAIN SILVA MÉNDEZ.

Judicial System

Justice is administered by the Grenada Supreme Court, composed of a High Court of Justice and a two-tier Court of Appeal. The Court of Magisterial Appeals is presided over by the Chief Justice. The Itinerant Court of Appeal consists of three judges and sits twice a year; it hears appeals from the High Court and is the final court of appeal. There are also Magistrates' Courts which administer summary jurisdiction.

In 1988 the OECS excluded the possibility of Grenada's readmittance to the East Caribbean court system until after the conclusion of appeals by the defendants in the Maurice Bishop murder trial (see Recent History).

Chief Justice: Sir SAMUEL GRAHAM.
Puisne Judge: LYLE C. PAUL.
Registrar of the Supreme Court: DENISE CAMPBELL.

Religion

CHRISTIANITY

The Roman Catholic Church

Grenada comprises a single diocese, suffragan to the archdiocese of Castries (Saint Lucia). The Bishop participates in the Antilles Episcopal Conference (based in Kingston, Jamaica).

Bishop of St George's in Grenada: Rt Rev. SYDNEY CHARLES, Bishop's House, Morne Jaloux, POB 375, St George's; tel. (443) 5299.

The Anglican Communion

Anglicans in Grenada are adherents of the Church in the Province of the West Indies. The country forms part of the diocese of the Windward Islands (the Bishop resides in Kingstown, Saint Vincent).

Other Christian Churches

The Presbyterian, Methodist, Plymouth Brethren, Baptist and Seventh-day Adventist faiths are also represented.

The Press

NEWSPAPERS

Grenada Guardian: St George's; weekly; organ of GULP.

The Grenadian Voice: POB 3, St George's; tel. (440) 1498; weekly; Editor LESLIE PIERRE.

Government Gazette: St George's; weekly; official.

The Indies Times: Grenville St, St George's.

The Informer: Young St, St George's; tel. (440) 1530; weekly; Editor CARLA BRIGGS.

The West Indian: 45 Hillsborough St, St George's.

PRESS ASSOCIATION

Press Association of Grenada: St George's; f. 1986; Pres. LESLIE PIERRE.

Publishers

Grenada Publishers Ltd: Torchlight Melville St, St George's; tel. (440) 2305.

West Indian Publishing Co Ltd: Hillsborough St, St George's; tel. (440) 2118; government-owned.

Radio and Television

In 1986 there were an estimated 50,000 radio receivers in use.

The radio station, known as Radio Free Grenada between 1979 and 1983, was destroyed during the military intervention in October 1983, and is at present housed in temporary studios.

Radio Grenada: POB 34, St George's; tel. (440) 3033; f. 1983; state-owned; Man. JEROME M. BARNETTE.

Between 1980 and 1983 television broadcasts were provided by Free Grenada Television, which was owned and operated by the Government. In 1986 a small television station was opened, financed by the US Discovery Foundation. Television programmes from Trinidad and from Barbados can be received on the island.

Finance

BANKING

Grenada Bank of Commerce Ltd: Corner of Cross and Halifax Sts, POB 4, St George's; tel. (440) 3521; telex 3467; Man. M. MATHLIN.

Grenada Co-operative Bank Ltd: 8 Church St, St George's; tel. (440) 2111; f. 1932; Man. Dir and Sec. G. V. STEELE; brs in St Andrew's and St Patrick's.

Grenada Development Bank: Halifax St, St George's; tel. (440) 2382; f. 1976 after merger of the Grenada Agricultural Bank and the Grenada Development Corpn; Chair. SAMUEL GRAHAM; Man. RONALD CHARLES.

National Commercial Bank of Grenada Ltd: Corner of Halifax and Hillsborough Sts, POB 57, St George's; tel. (440) 3566; telex 3413; f. 1979; state-owned; Gen. Man. M. B. ARCHIBALD; 5 brs.

People's Bank (Grenada) Ltd: St George's; f. 1988; cap. EC $34m.; Chair. GEORGE DE BOURG.

Foreign Banks

Bank of Nova Scotia (Canada): Halifax St, POB 194, St George's; tel. (440) 3274; telex 3452; Man. FITZROY O'NEALE.

Barclays Bank PLC (UK): Church and Halifax Sts, POB 37, St George's; tel. (440) 3232; telex 3421; Man. L. E. POLLARD; 2 sub-brs in Carriacou and Grenville.

INSURANCE

Several foreign insurance companies operate in Grenada and the other islands of the group. Principal locally-owned companies include the following:

Grenada Insurance and Finance Co Ltd: Young St, POB 139, St George's; tel. (440) 3004.

Grenada Insurance Services Ltd: 12-14 Young St, POB 47, St George's; tel. (440) 2434.

Grenada Motor and General Insurance Co Ltd: Scott St, St George's; tel. (440) 3379.

Trade and Industry

Grenada Chamber of Industry and Commerce, Inc: POB 129, St George's; tel. (440) 2937; telex 3469; f. 1921, incorporated 1947; 189 mems; Pres. HUGH DOLLAND; Exec. Dir ADRIAN REDHEAD.

Grenada Cocoa Board: Scott St, St George's; tel. (440) 2234; telex 3444; f. 1987 (permanent from 1989) as merger of Cocoa Assen. and Govt's Cocoa Rehabilitation Project.

Grenada Co-operative Banana Society: Scott St, St George's; tel. (440) 2486; f. 1955; a statutory body to control production and marketing of bananas; Chair. R. M. BHOLA.

Grenada Co-operative Nutmeg Association: POB 160, St George's; tel. (440) 2117; telex 3454; f. 1947; processes and markets all the nutmeg and mace grown on the island; Chair. NORRIS JAMES; Gen. Man. ROBIN S. RENWICK.

Grenada Electricity Services Ltd (Grenlec): POB 381, St George's; tel. (440) 2097; telex 3472; Man. G. C. BOWEN.

Grenada Industrial Development Corporation: Archibald Ave, St George's; tel. (440) 2857; f. 1985; Chair. ALBERT XAVIER.

Grenada Manufacturers' Association: St George's; f. 1986; Pres. OSLYN WILLIAMS; Sec. ANN CAMPBELL.

Marketing and National Importing Board: Young St, St George's; tel. (440) 3191; telex 3435; f. 1974; state-owned; imports basic food items, incl. sugar, rice and milk; Chair. FINTON GEORGE DE BOURG; Gen. Man. STEPHEN JOHN.

EMPLOYERS' ORGANIZATION

Employers' Federation: Mt Gay, St George's; tel. (440) 1832.

TRADE UNIONS

Grenada Trade Union Council (GTUC): Green St, POB 405, St George's; Pres. A. DE BOURG.

Commercial and Industrial Workers' Union: St George's; tel. (440) 3423; 492 mems; Pres. A. DE BOURG.

Grenada Union of Teachers (GUT): Marine Villa, St George's; f. 1913; Pres. (vacant); 1,300 mems.

Seamen and Waterfront Workers' Union: Carenage St, POB 154, St George's; tel. (440) 2573; f. 1952; Pres. ARTHUR RAMSEY; Gen. Sec. ERIC PIERRE; 350 mems.

Technical and Allied Workers' Union (TAWU): Green St, POB 405, St George's; tel. (440) 2231; f. 1958; Pres. (vacant).

Agricultural and General Workers' Union: St George's; Pres. GODWIN THOMAS.

Bank and General Workers' Union: St George's; tel. (440) 3563; Pres. DEREK ALLARD.

Grenada Manual, Maritime and Intellectual Workers' Union: St George's; Pres. Sir ERIC GAIRY.

Public Workers' Union (PWU): POB 420, St George's; tel. (440) 2203; f. 1931; Pres. CHARLES FRANCIS; Exec. Sec. GARTH D. GEORGE.

Transport

RAILWAYS

There are no railways in Grenada.

ROADS

In 1983 there were approximately 980 km (610 miles) of roads, of which 766 km (476 miles) were suitable for motor traffic. Many of these were severely damaged by military action in October 1983, and US aid was provided in 1984 for their repair. The 1986/87 budget allocated EC $29m. for road repair and construction. In 1984 there were 7,741 vehicles registered. Public transport is provided by small private operators, with a system covering the entire country.

SHIPPING

The main port is St George's, with accommodation for two ocean-going vessels of up to 500 ft. A number of shipping lines call at St George's. Grenville, on Grenada, and Hillsborough, on Carriacou, are used mostly by small craft.

Grenada Ports Authority: St George's; tel. (440) 3013; telex 3418.

CIVIL AVIATION

The Point Salines International Airport, 10 km (6 miles) from St George's, was opened in October 1984, and has scheduled flights to most East Caribbean destinations, including Venezuela, and to the United Kingdom and North America. There is an airfield at Pearls, 30 km (18 miles) from St George's, and Lauriston Airport, on the island of Carriacou, offers regular scheduled services to Grenada, Saint Vincent and Palm Island (Grenadines of Saint Vincent).

Grenada is a shareholder in LIAT (see under Antigua and Barbuda). In 1987 Air Antilles (based in Saint Lucia) was designated as the national carrier.

Tourism

In 1987 there were 184,620 tourist arrivals, of which about 70% were cruise-ship passengers. There were approximately 2,080 hotel beds in 1988.

Grenada Hotel Association: POB 440, St George's; tel. (440) 1590; telex 3425; f. 1961; Pres. ANDRÉ CHERMAN.

Grenada Tourist Department: POB 293, St George's; tel. (440) 2001; telex 3422; Dir of Tourism DIANA TAYLOR (acting).

GUATEMALA

Introductory Survey

Location, Climate, Language, Religion, Flag, Capital

The Republic of Guatemala lies in the Central American isthmus, bounded to the north and west by Mexico, with Honduras and Belize to the east and El Salvador to the south. It has a long coastline on the Pacific Ocean and a narrow outlet to the Caribbean Sea. The climate is tropical in the lowlands, with an average temperature of 28°C (83°F), and more temperate in the central highland area, with an average temperature of 20°C (68°F). The official language is Spanish, but more than 20 indigenous languages are also spoken. Almost all of the inhabitants profess Christianity: the majority are Roman Catholics, while about 25% are Protestants. The national flag (proportions 3 by 2) has three equal vertical stripes, of blue, white and blue, with the national coat of arms (depicting a quetzal, the 'bird of freedom', and a scroll, superimposed on crossed rifles and sabres, encircled by a wreath) in the centre of the white stripe. The capital is Guatemala City.

Recent History

Under Spanish colonial rule, Guatemala was part of the Viceroyalty of New Spain. Independence was obtained from Spain in 1821, from Mexico in 1824 and from the Federation of Central American States in 1838. Subsequent attempts to revive the Federation failed and, under a series of dictators, there was relative stability, tempered by periods of disruption. A programme of social reform was begun by Juan José Arévalo (President in 1944–50) and his successor, Col Jacobo Arbenz Guzmán, whose policy of land reform evoked strong opposition from landowners. In 1954 President Arbenz was overthrown in a coup led by Col Carlos Castillo Armas, who invaded the country with US assistance. Castillo became President but was assassinated in July 1957. The next elected President, Gen. Miguel Ydígoras Fuentes, took office in March 1958 and ruled until he was deposed in March 1963 by a military coup, led by Col Enrique Peralta Azurdia. He assumed full powers as Chief of Government, suspended the Constitution and dissolved the legislature. A Constituent Assembly, elected in 1964, produced a new constitution in 1965. Dr Julio César Méndez Montenegro was elected President in 1966, and in 1970 the candidate of the Movimiento de Liberación Nacional (MLN), Col (later Gen.) Carlos Araña Osorio, was elected President. Despite charges of fraud in the elections of March 1974, Gen. Kjell Laugerud García of the MLN took office as President in July.

President Laugerud sought to discourage extreme right-wing violence and claimed some success, although in September 1979 Amnesty International estimated the number of lives lost in political violence since 1970 at 50,000–60,000. In March 1978 Gen. Fernando Romeo Lucas García was elected President. The guerrilla movement increased in strength in 1980–1981, while the Government was accused of the murder and torture of civilians and, particularly, persecution of the country's indigenous Indian inhabitants, who make up 60% of the population. An estimated 11,000 civilians were killed in 1981.

In the presidential and congressional elections of 7 March 1982, from which the left-wing parties were absent, the largest number of votes was awarded to the Government's candidate, Gen. Angel Aníbal Guevara, who was later confirmed as President by Congress. The other presidential candidates denounced the elections as fraudulent. Guevara was prevented from taking office in July by a coup on 23 March, in which a group of young right-wing military officers installed Gen. Efraín Ríos Montt (a candidate in the 1974 presidential elections) as leader of a three-man junta. Congress was closed, and the Constitution and political parties suspended. In June Gen. Ríos Montt dissolved the junta and assumed the Presidency. He attempted to fight corruption, reorganized the judicial system and disbanded the secret police. The number of violent deaths diminished. However, after initially gaining the support of the national university, the Roman Catholic Church and the labour unions and hoping to enter into dialogue with the guerrillas, who refused to respond to an amnesty declaration in June, President Ríos Montt declared a state of siege, and imposed censorship of the press, in July. In addition, the war against the guerrillas intensified, and a civil defence force of Indians was established. The efficiency of the army increased. Whole villages were burnt, and many inhabitants killed, in order to deter the Indians from supporting the guerrillas. President Ríos Montt's increasingly corporatist policies alienated all groups, and his fragile hold on power was threatened in 1982 by several attempted coups, which he managed to forestall.

The US administration was eager to renew sales of armaments and the provision of economic and military aid to Guatemala, which had been suspended in 1977 as a result of serious violations of human rights. Several sales of spare parts for military equipment were made to Guatemala in 1982, despite restrictions by the US Congress. In January 1983 the US Government, satisfied that there had been a significant decrease in the abuse of human rights during Gen. Ríos Montt's presidency, announced the resumption of arms sales to Guatemala. However, independent reports claimed that the situation had deteriorated, and revealed that 2,600 people had been killed during the first six months of President Ríos Montt's rule. An estimated 100,000 refugees fled to Mexico during early 1983, and relations between Guatemala and Mexico were strained, following further incursions into Mexican territory by Guatemalan security forces, which resulted in the deaths of several refugees. In March the army was implicated in the massacre of 300 Indian peasants at Nahulá, and there was a resurgence in the activity of both left- and right-wing 'death squads'. The President declared a 30-day amnesty for guerrillas and political exiles, and lifted the state of siege which had been imposed in July 1982. Furthermore, he announced the creation of an electoral tribunal to organize and oversee a proposed transfer from military rule to civilian government. In April the army launched a new offensive, which made significant gains against the guerrillas, principally in the rebel stronghold of Petén and the province of El Quiché. In response, the Unidad Revolucionaria Nacional Guatemalteca (URNG), the main guerrilla grouping (formed in February 1982 in a new initiative seeking to end repression by the Government), announced a major change in tactics, which gave priority to attacks on economic targets instead of to direct confrontation with the army. The Government's pacification programme comprised three phases of aid programmes, combined with the saturation of the countryside by anti-guerrilla units. The 'guns and beans' policy provided food and medicine in exchange for recruitment to the PAC, a pro-Government peasant militia. The 'roofs, bread and work' phase involved the development of 'model villages', and the 'Aid Programme for Areas in Conflict' (PAAC) was an ambitious rural development scheme.

By June 1983 opposition to the President was widespread, and several attempted coups were reported. On 29 June the air force and four army garrisons rebelled against the President. They demanded a return to constitutional rule and the dismissal of the President's advisers. Gen. Ríos Montt agreed to both demands but remained unconvincing on the issue of electoral reform. On 8 August 1983 Gen. Oscar Humberto Mejía Victores, the Minister of Defence, led a successful coup against President Ríos Montt.

The new President announced the abolition of the secret tribunals and ended press censorship. In addition, the Council of State was abolished. A 90-day amnesty for guerrillas was announced in October. The amnesty was extended throughout 1984. Urban and rural terrorism continued to escalate, however, and in November 1983 the Government was accused of directing a campaign of kidnappings against the Roman Catholic Church. Following the murder in northern Guatemala of six workers from the US Agency for International Development, the US House of Representatives suspended the US $50m. in aid which President Reagan had requested for Guatemala in 1984. Israel continued to supply weapons to Guatemala, and Israeli military advisers were reported to be active in the country. In October Gen. Mejía Victores acted to strengthen his position after rumours of his unpopularity among high-ranking officers. Supporters of Gen. Ríos Montt were sent into exile, and in January 1984 new army reforms were introduced. In accordance with the President's assurance of electoral reform, elections for a Constituent Assembly were scheduled for July 1984.

Under Gen. Mejía Victores, it was estimated that more than 100 political assassinations and 40 abductions occurred each month. The start of campaigning for elections to the Constituent Assembly heralded a new wave of political violence. Fifteen political parties planned to contest the election in July. Contrary to public forecasts, the centre groups, including the newly formed Unión del Centro Nacional (UCN), obtained the greatest number of votes. Under the system of proportional representation, however, the right-wing coalition of the MLN and the Central Auténtica Nacionalista (CAN) together obtained a majority of seats in the Assembly. In August a directive board, composed of representatives from the three major political parties, began drafting the Constitution.

In 1984 the Government continued to develop its controversial strategy of 'model villages', which entailed the construction of new settlements in isolated locations for Indian communities. Relations with neighbouring Mexico deteriorated in 1984, following an attack in April on a Guatemalan refugee camp situated in Mexico, during which six people were killed. By August 1984 the Organización del Pueblo en Armas (ORPA) had emerged as the most active of the guerrilla groups, operating in San Marcos and Quezaltenango.

Guatemala's new constitution was promulgated in May 1985. In June President Mejía Victores confirmed that elections for the presidency, the National Congress and 331 mayoralties would be held in November. Prior to the elections, there was a substantial increase in rebel activity and political assassinations by 'death squads'. However, the principal threat to internal security before the elections occurred in September, when violent protests, led by students and trade unionists, broke out in reaction to a series of price increases which had been authorized by the Government in August. During the protests, several people were reported to have been killed and hundreds of demonstrators were arrested. The University of San Carlos in Guatemala City was temporarily occupied by soldiers.

Eight candidates participated in the presidential election in November 1985, but the main contest was between Jorge Carpio Nicolle, candidate of the Unión del Centro Nacional, and Mario Vinicio Cerezo Arévalo, candidate of the Partido Democracia Cristiana Guatemalteca (PDCG). As neither of the leading candidates obtained the requisite majority, a second round of voting was held in December, when Vinicio Cerezo secured 68% of the votes cast. The PDCG formed the majority party in the new National Congress and won the largest proportion of mayoralties. Vinicio Cerezo was believed to enjoy the support of the US administration, which increased its allocation of economic aid to $104.4m. in 1986, and resumed military aid (of $5.1m.) to Guatemala, in support of the new civilian Government. In December 1986 the Guatemalan Government denied that Nicaraguan Contra rebels (supported by the USA) were being trained on Guatemalan territory. In 1987 only $3m. of non-lethal military aid was granted to Guatemala by the USA, and the amount was to be reduced to $2m. in 1988.

Immediately prior to the transfer of power in January 1986, the outgoing military Government decreed a general amnesty to encompass those suspected of involvement in murders and other abuses of human rights since March 1982. In February 1986, however, in an attempt to curb the continuing violence and to improve the country's bad record for the observance of human rights, the Department of Technical Investigations (DIT), which had been accused of numerous kidnappings and murders of citizens, was dissolved and replaced by a new criminal investigations unit. Cerezo's action was welcomed by the Grupo Apoyo Mutuo (GAM), a grouping of the relatives of victims of repression, and by Amnesty International. Violence continued unabated, however, with 700 killings being recorded by human rights groups in the first six months of 1986 alone. President Cerezo claimed that not all murders were politically motivated, while his relations with the armed forces remained precarious. Meanwhile, the GAM attracted increasing support, and in August about 3,000 demonstrators took part in a protest to demand information on the fate of the thousands of 'disappeared'. In April 1987 the creation of a government commission to investigate disappearances was announced, and in May Amnesty International appealed to the President to fulfil his pledge to investigate abuses of human rights. Nevertheless, by mid-1988 there were frequent reports of torture and killings by right-wing 'death squads' as discontent with the Government's liberal policies increased.

Until the return to civilian government in 1986, Guatemala remained steadfast in its claims to the neighbouring territory of Belize, a former British dependency. In protest at the United Kingdom's decision to grant independence to Belize, in accordance with a UN resolution of November 1980, Guatemala severed diplomatic relations with the United Kingdom. Guatemala's new constitution, promulgated in May 1985, did not include Belize in its delineation of Guatemalan territory. In August 1986 consular links between Guatemalan and the United Kingdom were restored. In December full diplomatic relations were resumed, and in 1987 a British Embassy was opened in Guatemala City. In May 1988 discussions were held in Miami, USA, between representatives of Guatemala, Belize and the United Kingdom. The participants decided to establish a permanent Joint Commission to formulate a draft treaty to resolve Guatemala's claims to Belize. In October the Commission announced the establishment of three subcommissions, to be responsible for drafting the treaty; the delimitation of the border; and the creation of a joint development zone, with the co-operation of the United Kingdom and the EEC. Approval of the treaty was to be decided by referendums, to be held in both Guatemala and Belize. Since the mid-1970s the United Kingdom has retained a garrison in Belize, numbering 1,500 soldiers in June 1988.

The lifting of economic sanctions and trade restrictions from Belize in late 1986 opened the way to Guatemalan investment in that territory and to the possibility of joint development projects. As much of Guatemala's foreign debt is owed to EEC members, President Cerezo was anxious to remain on good terms with the EEC countries. A settlement of the dispute over Belize is also important for Guatemala's Central American policy and for hopes of achieving peace in the region. Neighbouring countries did not support Guatemala in its claims to Belize. In June 1987 Guatemala was the site of a meeting of Central American Presidents to discuss a peace proposal for the region. The country was a signatory of the agreed peace plan, signed in Guatemala City in August by the Presidents of Costa Rica, El Salvador, Guatemala, Honduras and Nicaragua. Although the plan was principally concerned with the conflicts in Nicaragua and El Salvador, it also referred to the long-standing guerrilla war in Guatemala. Subsequently, a Commission of National Reconciliation was formed in compliance with the terms of the accord. In October representatives of the Guatemalan Government and URNG guerrillas met in Spain to discuss the question of peace in Guatemala. Although the negotiations ended without agreement, the two sides did not exclude the possibility of holding further talks. The Government also presented to Congress legislation for an amnesty applicable to members of the URNG. Congress approved the amnesty law in November. Further talks between the two sides would be dependent on the guerrillas' acceptance of this amnesty. In December it was announced that an extreme right-wing coup attempt against President Cerezo had been foiled.

Right-wing pressure on the Government continued to force President Cerezo to postpone negotiations with the URNG, scheduled for March 1988. In May a further attempted coup, involving both civilians and members of the army, was foiled without incident, but led to a further postponement of negotiations with the URNG. Despite evident right-wing opposition to the policies of President Cerezo, the PDCG won 140 mayoralties out of 272 at municipal elections held in April. These were Guatemala's first elections in which voting was not compulsory, and, consequently, the level of participation was low (only an estimated 40% of the electorate). Despite his party's success, President Cerezo remained wary of discontent within the army. After another coup plot was discovered in July, President Cerezo rejected the URNG's proposal for a truce.

Government

Guatemala is a republic comprising 22 departments. (In December 1986 Congress approved a preliminary law whereby the country was to be divided into eight regions.) Under the new Constitution, which took effect in January 1986, legislative power is vested in the unicameral National Congress, with 100 members elected for five years by universal adult suffrage. Of the total seats, 75 are filled by direct election and 25 on the

GUATEMALA

basis of proportional representation. Executive power is held by the President (also directly elected for five years), assisted by a Vice-President and an appointed Cabinet.

Defence

In June 1988 the armed forces totalled 42,000, of whom 40,000 were in the army, 1,200 in the navy (including 650 marines) and 850 in the air force. There were paramilitary forces of 9,500. Military service is by conscription for at least two years. In the early 1980s the Patrullas de Autodefensa Civil (PAC), an anti-guerrilla peasant militia, was established. By 1985 these self-defence patrols numbered 900,000 men. Defence expenditure in 1987 was budgeted at 265.8m. quetzales.

Economic Affairs

The economy is predominantly agricultural, with more than one-half of the country's working population engaged in agriculture, forestry and fishing. The agricultural sector usually provides more than 25% of Guatemala's gross domestic product (GDP) and over 60% of export earnings. In 1987, according to estimates by the World Bank, the country's gross national product (GNP), measured at average 1985–87 prices, was US $6,839m., equivalent to $940 per head. Between 1980 and 1987, it was estimated, GNP declined, in real terms, at an average annual rate of 0.9%, with real GNP per head falling by 3.7% per year. Overall GDP, in constant prices, was estimated to have increased at an average annual rate of 5.9% in 1965–80, and to have decreased by 1.2% per year in 1980–86. Guatemala is Central America's second most important coffee producer. Coffee is the country's leading export commodity, generating 35% of total export earnings in 1987. In 1987 production increased by 3.5% from the 1986 level of 197,000 metric tons. Export earnings increased from US $361m. in 1984 to $502.3m. in 1986, but, as a result of a sharp fall in the world price for coffee, revenue declined to $345.5m. in 1987. Other major crops are sugar cane, bananas, cardamom and cotton. Production of sugar cane declined from a record 6.2m. metric tons in 1982 to 5.5m. tons in 1983. Unfavourable weather conditions during 1985 depressed production (estimated at 5.5m. tons), but a new record level of 7.0m. tons was achieved in 1987. Exports of sugar were worth an estimated $51.3m. in 1987, compared with $71.3m. in 1984. The USA reduced its import quota of Guatemalan sugar from 82,388 tons in 1985/86 to 43,680 tons in 1986/87, although it was increased slightly, to 48,200 tons, in 1987/88. Cotton provided 13.3% of export income in 1981 but less than 2% in 1986, owing to high costs, low world prices, lack of domestic credit and the guerrilla war. Production of cotton lint declined from 67,000 metric tons in 1985 to 45,000 tons in 1987, when exports of cotton were valued at only $16m. In March 1983 high winds caused $60m. worth of damage to banana plantations. Agricultural production declined by 6% in 1983. A further threat to the agricultural sector was the guerrilla campaign against economic targets, launched in 1983. Attempts to diversify agricultural production initially resulted in increased exports of tobacco, vegetables, fruit and beef. Between 1981 and 1986, however, Guatemala's exports of fresh meat declined from $29.3m. to $4m., owing to the suspension of sales to Mexico and a fall in domestic beef production. In 1987, however, exports of fresh meat increased to $14.5m. Additional funding for agricultural development projects has been provided by the IMF and the IDB. Extensive forests provide timber and chicle.

Guatemala's industrial sector is the largest in Central America. Manufacturing contributed 15.7% of GDP, and provided employment for 13.6% of the working population, in 1987. The main branches of industry are food processing, rubber, textiles, paper and pharmaceuticals. Exports of manufactured goods more than trebled between 1972 and 1978, but in 1982 the Central American market declined sharply. Subsequently, priority has been given to trade with the USA, which is Guatemala's principal trading partner. A shortage of domestic credit and low level of external demand, principally from other CACM members, have reduced the sector's growth rate. Both public and private investment declined because of social unrest and austerity measures. By the mid-1980s the industrial sector was operating at only 50% of capacity. In 1987 an estimated 15% of the labour force were unemployed.

Commercial quantities of petroleum were discovered in 1974 and 1975, and the Rubelsanto and West Chinajá fields have reserves estimated at 127m. barrels. Further deposits were found in 1981 in Alta Verapaz and the Petén Basin: these are being exploited by Texaco, Amoco and Hispanoil. A pipeline with a capacity of 50,000 barrels per day (b/d), linking Rubelsanto and the Caribbean coastline, was completed in 1981. Guatemala's earnings from exports of petroleum declined from US $60m. in 1983 to $12m. in 1985, but recovered to an estimated $19.3m. in 1987. New oilwells were located in 1981 and 1982, and the discovery at Tierra Blanca is expected to produce as much as 6,000–6,500 b/d. Domestic consumption averaged 25,000 b/d in 1987. A new oilwell in Petén, which started producing 2,000 b/d, increased Guatemala's oil production by 30% in 1986. Guatemala remains a marginal producer; average output declined from over 6,000 b/d in 1982 to 2,000 b/d in 1988. Proven reserves total 22m. barrels, while potential reserves are believed to be 800m.–1,000m. barrels. New legislation, introduced in October 1983, has encouraged investment in exploration for petroleum by foreign companies. There were plans to build a state-owned petroleum refinery with a capacity of 30,000 b/d, despite an existing surplus of refining capacity. In 1985 Guatemala experienced severe fuel shortages as a result of its inability to raise foreign exchange to pay for imports of petroleum, costing an estimated $22m. per month. In July the Government sold one-fifth of Guatemala's reserves of gold in order to finance petroleum imports. However, the cost of such imports in 1986 was considerably lower, owing to the fall in world oil prices and to increased domestic production. A 300-MW hydroelectric project at Chixoy was inaugurated in 1986. There were plans to construct a geothermal generating plant, to be known as Zunil 1.

The Exmibal consortium has invested 224m. quetzales in exploiting the deposits of nickel ore, estimated at 60m. tons, near Lake Izabal at Chalac-El Estor. In mid-1977 a refining plant began operating, but in November 1981 the mine was closed down indefinitely, as falling sales, the rising cost of fuel and new taxation had made the venture financially unviable. In July 1986 plans to revive the small-scale mining industry were announced. Minas de Guatemala was expected to reopen small lead, antimony and tungsten mines.

Between 1980 and 1986 GDP per head fell by 20.5% in real terms. Total export earnings declined from US $1,519.8m. in 1980 to $977.9m. in 1987, owing partly to reductions in world commodity prices. However, the current deficit on the balance of payments, which had been $573m. in 1981, declined to only $17.6m. in 1986. The fall in the world price for coffee in 1987 contributed to a deficit of $469.8m. in that year. Official reserves of foreign exchange fell from $653.5m. at the end of 1979 to only $65m. in April 1983 (owing to a flight of capital and an increase in service payments on Guatemala's external debt), but had increased to $362m. by the end of 1986, owing partly to the devaluation of the quetzal (see below) and to a sharp rise in coffee prices. However, reserves declined to $170.8m. in August 1988. In 1983, in response to increasing economic difficulties, the Government implemented a series of austerity measures. In September the Government reached agreement with the IMF on a stand-by arrangement. In order to fulfil the terms of the agreement, a programme of tax reforms was introduced to reduce the budget deficit. Following protests at the 10% rate of value-added tax (VAT), the rate was reduced to 7% in October. This decision prompted the IMF to suspend its agreement with the Government. Further credit amounting to $360m. was withdrawn by international financing agencies. The existing tax programme was regarded as a failure, having yielded only 40% of the expected revenue. In July 1984 the IMF suspended disbursement of $60m. from the original credit. In November, after many years of being at parity with the US dollar, the quetzal was partially devalued, when a 'parallel' exchange rate of 1.60 quetzales per US dollar, applicable to non-essential imports and to some exports, was introduced. Following the introduction of a 'parallel' rate, the cost of importing basic foods and other goods increased by between 25% and 50%. In June 1986 a regulated market rate of US $1 = 2.5 quetzales was introduced.

In early 1986 President Cerezo outlined plans to improve the standard of living in Guatemala, where an estimated 63% of the population were living in conditions inferior to the officially-defined level of poverty. A programme of road-building and improvement to the water system was expected to generate 3,000–4,000 new jobs. A World Bank loan of $81m. was secured in 1986 to finance the expansion of electric services and the improvement of power distribution, a project costing an estimated $133.2m. in total. A further loan of $23m. was granted to finance a water supply rehabilitation project.

GUATEMALA

Following the transfer of power to a civilian government in January 1986, a programme of austerity measures and financial reform was implemented, and, as a result, the economy started to show signs of revival after several years of decline. By 1986 Guatemala's foreign debt had fallen to about $2,400m., and inflation fell to an annual average of 25%. Guatemala's economic revival continued in 1987, and brought increased stability. Although a slight fall in total export earnings was registered, non-traditional exports increased by 20%, to $180m., in 1987. Internal demand rose by 5.2%, while the annual rate of inflation remained stable, at approximately 10%.

In September 1987 President Cerezo announced a programme of tax reforms. However, his proposal encountered hostility from the business and private sectors, which refused to accept the proposed changes. In February 1988 President Cerezo's announcement of an increase in electricity prices provoked the threat of strike action by the Unidad de Acción Sindical y Popular (UASP), a co-ordinating group of popular organizations (formed in January 1988). President Cerezo subsequently suspended the increases and agreed to confer with the UASP's leaders. In March electricity prices were increased for major consumers, while the prices of 10 'essential' commodities were 'frozen', subject to periodic review. In July President Cerezo finally succeeded in unifying the exchange rate for the Guatemalan currency. After an 8% devaluation, the rate for the quetzal was fixed at 2.70 per US dollar. At the same time, the 'freeze' on prices of food and fuel was revoked, producing immediate price rises of 10%–15% and, consequently, vigorous protests from popular organizations. In August the unions arranged a one-day general strike, and met President Cerezo to discuss their opposition to the Government's policy, and to attempt to establish a social pact, also involving the business sector, with the administration. In October, however, both the representatives of the business sector and the UASP withdrew from the discussions with President Cerezo.

In October 1988 Guatemala reached agreement with the IMF on the final requirements for a stand-by loan of SDR 75.6m. Targets of economic growth of 4% and a budget deficit of less than 3% of GDP were set for 1989. At the end of 1987 Guatemala's foreign debt was estimated at $2,720m. In December 1988 the 1989 budget proposals, envisaging total expenditure of 3,640m. quetzales, were approved by congress.

Social Welfare

Social security is compulsory, and all employers with five or more workers are required to enrol with the State Institute of Social Security. Benefits are available to registered workers for industrial accidents, sickness, maternity, disability, widowhood and hospitalization. In 1978 Guatemala had 107 hospitals, with a total of 12,217 beds, and in 1979 there were 819 physicians working in the government health service. A $51m. project to improve health services, including two new hospitals in Guatemala City and one in Antigua, was announced in 1980. In 1986 a vaccination programme to benefit more than 1m. children was announced, in a campaign to combat infant mortality

Education

Elementary education is free and, in urban areas, compulsory between seven and 14 years of age. Primary education begins at the age of seven and lasts for six years. Secondary education, beginning at 13 years of age, lasts for up to six years, comprising two cycles of three years each. In 1984 the total enrolment at primary and secondary schools was equivalent to 50% of the school-age population. In 1983 an estimated 62% of children in the relevant age-group (boys 65%; girls 58%) attended primary schools. The comparable figure for secondary education in 1982 was 14%. In 1986 there were 7,979 primary schools and 1,390 secondary schools. In December 1988 the World Bank approved a loan of US $30m., which was intended to finance a programme to increase primary school enrolment to 80% by 1993. There are five universities. In 1981 a 'national literacy crusade' was launched by the Government, but in 1985, according to estimates by UNESCO, the average rate of adult illiteracy was 45% (males 37.4%; females 52.9%), the second highest level in the Western hemisphere.

Public Holidays

1989: 2 January (for New Year's Day), 6 January (Epiphany), 24–27 March (Easter), 1 May (Labour Day), 30 June (Anniversary of the Revolution), 15 August (Assumption, Guatemala City only), 15 September (Independence Day), 12 October (Columbus Day), 20 October (Revolution Day), 1 November (All Saints' Day), 24–25 December (Christmas), 31 December (New Year's Eve).

1990: 1 January (New Year's Day), 6 January (Epiphany), 13–16 April (Easter), 1 May (Labour Day), 30 June (Anniversary of the Revolution), 15 August (Assumption, Guatemala City only), 15 September (Independence Day), 12 October (Columbus Day), 20 October (Revolution Day), 1 November (All Saints' Day), 24–25 December (Christmas), 31 December (New Year's Eve).

Weights and Measures

The metric system is in official use.

GUATEMALA

Statistical Survey

Sources (unless otherwise stated): Banco de Guatemala, 7a Avda 22-01, Zona 1, Apdo 365, Guatemala City; Dirección General de Estadística, Edif. América 4°, 8a Calle 9-55, Zona 1, Guatemala City; tel. 26136.

Area and Population

AREA, POPULATION AND DENSITY

Area (sq km)	
Land	108,429
Inland water	460
Total	108,889*
Population (census results)†	
26 March 1973	5,160,221
26 March 1981	
Males	3,015,826
Females	3,038,401
Total	6,054,227
Population (official estimates at mid-year)	
1985	7,963,355
1986	8,195,000
1987	8,434,339
Density (per sq km) at mid-1987	77.5

* 42,042 sq miles.
† Excluding adjustments for underenumeration, estimated to have been 13.7% in 1981.

DEPARTMENTS (estimated population at mid-1987)

Alta Verapaz	522,901	Jutiapa	325,382	
Baja Verapaz	165,863	Quezaltenango	499,148	
Chimaltenango	306,701	Retalhuleu	212,284	
Chiquimula	232,336	Sacatepéquez	160,080	
El Petén	203,747	San Marcos	626,851	
El Progreso	100,054	Santa Rosa	246,733	
El Quiché	507,123	Sololá	213,801	
Escuintla	481,323	Suchitepéquez	324,717	
Guatemala	1,800,076	Totonicapán	265,445	
Huehuetenango	629,494	Zacapa	150,114	
Izabal	287,479			
Jalapa	172,687	**Total**	**8,434,339**	

PRINCIPAL TOWNS (population at 1981 census)

Guatemala City (capital)	754,243	Puerto Barrios	46,882
Escuintla	75,442	Retalhuleu	46,652
Quezaltenango	72,922	Chiquimula	42,571
		Mazatenango	38,181

Source: CELADE.

BIRTHS, MARRIAGES AND DEATHS

	Registered live births		Registered marriages		Registered deaths	
	Number	Rate (per 1,000)	Number	Rate (per 1,000)	Number	Rate (per 1,000)
1982	311,978	42.6	31,233	4.3	76,267	10.4
1983	288,502	38.3	30,422	4.0	74,462	9.9
1984	302,961	39.1	31,351	4.1	75,462	9.7
1985	322,994	40.6	38,199	4.8	68,955	8.7
1986	319,321	38.9	45,755	5.6	69,275	8.4
1987	324,784	38.5	44,440	5.3	66,703	7.9

ECONOMICALLY ACTIVE POPULATION
(official estimates for 1987)

	Males	Females	Total
Agriculture, forestry, hunting and fishing	1,474,793	26,585	1,500,378
Mining and quarrying	2,545	37	2,582
Manufacturing	271,381	79,826	351,207
Construction	105,278	581	105,879
Electricity, gas, water and sanitary services	7,529	218	7,747
Commerce	127,067	61,449	188,516
Transport, storage and communications	62,962	1,598	64,560
Services	128,990	180,899	309,889
Activities not adequately described	39,663	11,985	51,648
Total	**2,219,228**	**363,178**	**2,582,406**

Agriculture

PRINCIPAL CROPS ('000 metric tons)

	1985	1986	1987
Sugar cane	6,054	6,192	6,971
Cotton (lint)	69	38	45
Maize	1,029	1,258	1,313
Rice	42	40	48
Dry beans	126	132	105
Wheat	49	57	50
Coffee	195	197	204
Bananas ('000 stems)	15,068	15,617	15,790

Source: *Cuentas Nacionales*, Banco de Guatemala.

LIVESTOCK ('000 head, year ending September)

	1984	1985	1986
Horses*	100	100	100
Cattle†	2,224	2,254	2,284
Sheep*	660	670	680
Pigs	806	834	862
Goats*	76	76	76

Chickens (million): 15* in 1984; 15* in 1985; 15* in 1986.
* FAO estimates.   † Unofficial figures.
Source: FAO, *Production Yearbook*.

LIVESTOCK PRODUCTS ('000 metric tons)

	1984	1985	1986
Beef and veal	50	55*	45*
Pig meat	16	16	14*
Poultry meat†	50	52	50
Cheese†	15.3	15.6	15.6
Butter and ghee†	4.7	4.9	4.9
Hen eggs†	40.5	41.2	42.2
Cattle hides†	12.5	11.6	11.4

* Unofficial figure.   † FAO estimates.
Source: FAO, *Production Yearbook*.

GUATEMALA

Forestry

ROUNDWOOD REMOVALS
('000 cubic metres, excluding bark)

	1984	1985	1986
Sawlogs, veneer logs and logs for sleepers	146	185	104
Other industrial wood	10*	10	10
Fuel wood*	6,489	6,674	6,869
Total	6,645	6,869	6,983

* FAO estimates.

Source: FAO, *Yearbook of Forest Products*.

SAWNWOOD PRODUCTION ('000 cubic metres)

	1984	1985	1986
Coniferous (soft wood)	77	98	75
Broadleaved (hard wood)	26	33	8
Total	103	131	83

Source: FAO, *Yearbook of Forest Products*.

Fishing

(metric tons, live weight)

	1984	1985	1986
Total catch	2,963	2,707	2,119

Source: FAO, *Yearbook of Fishery Statistics*.

Mining

SELECTED PRODUCTS (metric tons)

	1985	1986	1987
Antimony ore	2,106	3,173	3,083
Petroleum	143,384	242,003	179,640
Iron ore	2,334	6,950	10,706
Lead ore	70	100	92

Source: Ministry of Energy and Mines.

Industry

SELECTED PRODUCTS
('000 metric tons, unless otherwise indicated)

	1985	1986	1987
Cement	526	585	703
Sugar	597	691	679
Electricity (million kWh)	1,568	1,769	1,911
Cigarettes (million)	1,936	1,828	2,000

Source: *Cuentas Nacionales*, Banco de Guatemala.

Statistical Survey

Finance

CURRENCY AND EXCHANGE RATES

Monetary Units
100 centavos = 1 quetzal.

Denominations
Coins: 1, 5, 10 and 25 centavos.
Notes: 50 centavos; 1, 5, 10, 20, 50 and 100 quetzales.

Sterling and Dollar Equivalents (31 August 1988)
£1 sterling = 4.555 quetzales;
US $1 = 2.705 quetzales;
100 quetzales = £21.95 = $36.97.

Note: A multiple exchange rate system was introduced in November 1984. This system was modified in June 1986, since which time the official rate of US $1 = 1 quetzal has been applicable mainly to debt-service payments. There is also a banking market rate (introduced in 1984) and a regulated market rate. The banking market rate, applicable to private capital inflows and to 'invisible' transactions, was US $1 = 2.71 quetzales at 31 August 1988. The regulated market rate, which applies to most trade and capital transactions, was fixed at $1 = 2.50 quetzales from June 1986, when it replaced the previous auction market rate, until June 1988, when the rate was adjusted to $1 = 2.705 quetzales.

BUDGET (million quetzales)

Revenue	1985	1986	1987
Taxation	679.3	1,111.4	1,430.7
Treasury bills and foreign loans	441.3	602.0	472.2
Other receipts	187.1	355.6	427.1
Total	1,307.7	2,069.0	2,330.0

Expenditure	1985	1986	1987
Education	138.0	226.4	397.3
Health	78.8	159.7	201.3
Agriculture	34.0	74.0	91.1
Defence	196.9	219.0	351.8
Communications and public works	93.4	84.0	71.9
Transportation	72.9	121.0	131.7
Other items	572.6	1,214.9	1,095.8
Total	1,186.6	2,099.0	2,340.9

Source: Ministry of Finance.

INTERNATIONAL RESERVES
(US $ million at 31 December)

	1985	1986	1987
Gold*	22.1	22.1	22.1
IMF special drawing rights	—	—	1.7
Foreign exchange	300.9	362.1	286.1
Total	323.0	384.2	309.9

* Valued at US $42.22 per troy ounce.

Source: IMF, *International Financial Statistics*.

MONEY SUPPLY (million quetzales at 31 December)

	1985	1986	1987
Currency outside banks	697.8	804.6	931.2
Private sector deposits at Bank of Guatemala	34.2	55.2	26.5
Demand deposits at deposit money banks	614.5	748.6	807.9
Total money	1,346.5	1,608.4	1,765.6

Source: IMF, *International Financial Statistics*.

GUATEMALA

COST OF LIVING
(Consumer Price Index; base: March–April 1983 = 100)

	1985	1986*	1987
Food and beverages	130.3	181.5	209.8
Domestic living expenses	111.5	129.8	141.6
Furniture, maintenance and equipment for the home	135.2	191.3	198.4
Clothing and footwear	137.1	203.6	224.4
Medical assistance	130.7	166.4	232.7
Education	126.2	147.3	146.8
Transport and communications	126.4	178.1	192.7
Reading and recreation	121.2	166.3	182.4
Others	154.2	203.6	218.7
All items	129.1	176.8	198.6

NATIONAL ACCOUNTS

Expenditure on the Gross Domestic Product
(million quetzales at current prices)

	1985	1986	1987*
Government final consumption expenditure	777.4	1,123.9	1,373.8
Private final consumption expenditure	9,295.9	12,846.7	14,931.8
Increase in stocks	60.5	43.3	280.4
Gross fixed capital formation	1,224.9	1,593.2	2,150.3
Total domestic expenditure	11,358.8	15,607.1	18,736.2
Exports of goods and services	2,068.0	2,542.1	2,807.0
Less Imports of goods and services	2,246.8	2,311.1	3,948.5
GDP in purchasers' values	11,180.0	15,838.1	17,594.7

* Preliminary.

Gross Domestic Product by Economic Activity
(million quetzales at constant 1958 prices)

	1985	1986	1987*
Agriculture, hunting, forestry and fishing	759.3	753.0	780.1
Mining and quarrying	6.5	8.4	8.4
Manufacturing	464.8	467.9	475.6
Electricity, gas and water	56.3	63.2	68.1
Construction	49.7	51.3	56.6
Trade, restaurants and hotels	747.0	730.9	749.3
Transport, storage and communications	209.8	210.6	220.0
Finance and insurance	108.1	111.1	115.0
Real estate	155.0	158.2	161.1
General government services	192.0	199.5	208.8
Other community, social and personal services	187.6	186.1	189.1
Total	2,936.1	2,940.2	3,032.1

* Preliminary.

BALANCE OF PAYMENTS (US $ million)

	1985	1986	1987
Merchandise exports f.o.b.	1,059.7	1,043.8	981.1
Merchandise imports f.o.b.	−1,076.7	−875.7	−1,363.8
Trade balance	−17.0	168.1	−382.7
Exports of services	131.6	159.4	189.5
Imports of services	−380.6	−420.2	−469.8
Balance on goods and services	−266.0	−92.7	−663.0
Private unrequited transfers (net)	18.9	50.6	101.0
Government unrequited transfers (net)	0.8	24.5	92.3
Current balance	−246.3	−17.6	−469.8
Direct capital investment (net)	61.8	68.8	150.2
Other long-term capital (net)	−133.1	−371.0	−302.6
Short-term capital (net)	−57.1	−31.0	339.1
Net errors and omissions	43.7	67.5	−45.3
Total (net monetary movements)	−331.0	−283.3	−328.4
Valuation changes (net)	−14.2	−11.1	−9.1
Exceptional financing (net)	438.2	392.2	274.4
Official financing (net)	4.0	4.0	1.0
Changes in reserves	97.0	101.8	−62.1

Source: IMF, *International Financial Statistics*.

External Trade

PRINCIPAL COMMODITIES (US $ '000)

Imports c.i.f.	1983	1984	1985
Food products	77,107	84,142	81,883
Crude materials (inedible) except fuels	31,939	28,687	29,642
Mineral fuels, lubricants, etc.	256,651	303,123	271,296
Chemicals and products	257,436	297,292	269,840
Basic manufactures	232,591	236,195	195,288
Machinery and transport equipment	167,291	210,258	222,831
Total (incl. others)	1,134,995	1,278,496	1,174,811

1986 (US $ million, preliminary): Total imports 959.5.
1987 (US $ million, preliminary): Total imports 1,447.2.

Exports f.o.b.	1985	1986	1987
Coffee (incl. soluble)	451.5	502.3	354.5
Cotton	73.1	24.3	16.2
Fresh meat	10.0	4.3	14.5
Bananas	70.9	73.4	74.6
Sugar	46.5	51.7	51.3
Shellfish	9.1	8.1	12.9
Cardamom	60.7	47.7	45.1
Petroleum	12.0	27.0	19.3
Total (incl. others)	1,059.7	1,043.8	977.9

Source: *Balanza de Pagos*, Banco de Guatemala.

GUATEMALA

PRINCIPAL TRADING PARTNERS (US $ '000)

Imports c.i.f.	1985	1986	1987
Costa Rica	31,150	27,960	43,504
El Salvador	47,717	46,045	73,557
Germany, Federal Republic	86,550	69,956	92,764
Honduras	4,198	4,105	11,489
Italy	12,084	10,123	50,621
Japan	67,835	54,205	94,836
Mexico	124,273	60,120	108,920
Netherlands	14,676	11,483	11,747
Netherlands Antilles	53,978	7,963	5,163
United Kingdom	22,076	13,858	28,306
USA	435,097	414,455	557,958
Venezuela	78,726	53,420	60,141
Total (incl. others)	1,174,811	959,496	1,447,178

Exports f.o.b.	1985	1986	1987
Costa Rica	45,208	52,955	60,583
El Salvador	120,239	100,869	133,934
Germany, Federal Republic	59,161	87,334	71,677
Honduras	26,538	21,800	24,903
Italy	47,717	32,257	35,498
Japan	35,522	41,189	18,418
Mexico	10,979	6,185	11,090
Netherlands	19,858	29,857	26,812
Nicaragua	15,772	9,419	11,137
United Kingdom	4,368	8,564	9,203
USA	406,586	483,183	399,081
Total (incl. others)	1,059,671	1,043,755	977,917

Source: *Balanza de Pagos*, Banco de Guatemala.

Transport

ROAD TRAFFIC ('000 motor vehicles in use)

	1983	1984	1985
Passenger cars	188.1	n.a.	207.6
Commercial vehicles	58.5	n.a.	65.1

Source: Ministerio de Finanzas Públicas.

SHIPPING (freight traffic, '000 metric tons)

	1985	1986	1987
Goods loaded	1,158	1,425	1,381
Goods unloaded	1,800	1,833	2,307

* Preliminary.

CIVIL AVIATION (traffic on scheduled services)

	1982	1983	1984
Passengers carried ('000)	115	100	124
Passenger-km (million)	160	156	168
Freight ton-km (million)	5.2	6.3	8.1

Tourism

	1985	1986	1987
Tourist arrivals	251,946	287,460	352,741
Expenditure (US $ million)	67.2	76.9	102.9

Source: Instituto Guatemalteco de Turismo (INGUAT).

Education

(1987*)

	Schools	Teachers	Pupils
Pre-primary	2,992	5,029	144,312
Primary	8,636	32,100	1,123,305
Secondary	1,448	16,332	241,053

* Preliminary.

Source: Instituto Nacional de Estadística/USIPE, Ministerio de Educación.

Directory

The Constitution

In December 1984 the Constituent Assembly drafted a new constitution (based on that of 1965), which was approved in May 1985 and came into effect in January 1986. Its main provisions are summarized below:

Guatemala has a republican representative democratic system of government and power is exercised equally by the legislative, executive and judicial bodies. The official language is Spanish. Suffrage is universal and secret, obligatory for those who can read and write and optional for those who are illiterate. The free formation and growth of political parties whose aims are democratic is guaranteed. There is no discrimination on grounds of race, colour, sex, religion, birth, economic or social position or political opinions.

The State will give protection to capital and private enterprise in order to develop sources of labour and stimulate creative activity.

Monopolies are forbidden and the State will limit any enterprise which might prejudice the development of the community. The right to social security is recognized and it shall be on a national, unitary, obligatory basis.

Constitutional guarantees may be suspended in certain circumstances for up to 30 days (unlimited in the case of war).

CONGRESS

Legislative power rests with Congress, which is made up of 100 deputies, 75 of whom are elected directly by the people through universal suffrage. The remaining 25 deputies are elected on the basis of proportional representation. Congress meets on 15 June each year and ordinary sessions last four months; extraordinary sessions can be called by the Permanent Commission or the Executive. All Congressional decisions must be taken by absolute majority of the members, except in special cases laid down by law. Deputies are elected for five years; they may be re-elected after a lapse of one session, but only once. Congress is responsible for all matters concerning the President and Vice-President and their execution of their offices; for all electoral matters; for all matters concerning the laws of the Republic; for approving the budget and decreeing taxes; for declaring war; for conferring honours, both civil and military; for fixing the coinage and the system of weights

GUATEMALA

and measures; for approving, by two-thirds majority, any international treaty or agreement affecting the law, sovereignty, financial status or security of the country.

PRESIDENT

The President is elected by universal suffrage, by absolute majority for a non-extendable period of five years. Re-election or prolongation of the presidential term of office are punishable by law. The President is responsible for national defence and security, fulfilling the Constitution, leading the armed forces, taking any necessary steps in time of national emergency, passing and executing laws, international policy, nominating and removing Ministers, officials and diplomats, co-ordinating the actions of Ministers of State. The Vice-President's duties include presiding over Congress and taking part in the discussions of the Council of Ministers.

ARMY

The Guatemalan Army is intended to maintain national independence, sovereignty and honour, territorial integrity and peace within the Republic. It is an indivisible, apolitical, non-deliberating body and is made up of land, sea and air forces.

LOCAL ADMINISTRATIVE DIVISIONS

For the purposes of administration the territory of the Republic is divided into Departments and these into Municipalities, but this division can be modified by Congress to suit interests and general development of the Nation without loss of municipal autonomy.

JUDICIARY

Justice is exercised exclusively by the Supreme Court of Justice and other tribunals. Administration of Justice is obligatory, free and independent of the other functions of State. The President of the Judiciary, judges and other officials are elected by Congress for four years. The Supreme Court of Justice is made up of at least seven judges. The President of the Judiciary is also President of the Supreme Court. The Supreme Court nominates all other judges. Under the Supreme Court come the Court of Appeal, the Administrative Disputes Tribunal, the Tribunal of Second Instance of Accounts, Jurisdiction Conflicts, First Instance and Military, the Extraordinary Tribunal of Protection. There is a Court of Constitutionality presided over by the President of the Supreme Court.

The Government

HEAD OF STATE

President: Mario Vinicio Cerezo Arévalo (took office 14 January 1986).
Vice-President: Roberto Carpio Nicolle.

THE CABINET
(January 1989)

Minister of Foreign Affairs: Alfonso Cabrera Hidalgo.
Minister of the Interior: Roberto Valle Valdizán.
Minister of National Defence: Gen. Héctor Gramajo Morales.
Minister of Economy: Lizardo Arturo Sosa López.
Minister of Finance: Rodolfo Paiz Andrade.
Minister of Public Health and Social Assistance: Carlos Armando Soto.
Minister of Communications, Transport and Public Works: Mario López Estrada.
Minister of Agriculture: Rodolfo Estrada.
Minister of Education: Eduardo Meyer Maldonado.
Minister of Labour and Social Welfare: Catalina Soberanis.
Minister of Energy and Mines: Roland Castillo Contoux.
Minister of Culture and Sport: Isabel Prera de Lobo.
Minister of Urban and Rural Development: René Armando de León Schlotter.

MINISTRIES

All Ministries are situated in the Palacio Nacional, Guatemala City.

President and Legislature

PRESIDENT
Election, 3 November 1985

	Votes cast	Percentage of votes cast
Mario Vinicio Cerezo Arévalo (PDCG)	648,681	38.65
Jorge Carpio Nicolle (UCN)	339,552	20.23
Jorge Serrano Elías (PDCN/PR coalition)	231,397	13.78
Mario Sandóval Alarcón (MLN/PID coalition)	210,806	12.56
Mario David García (CAN)	105,473	6.28
Mario Solórzano Martínez (PSD)	57,362	3.41
Alejandro Maldonado Aguirre (PNR)	52,941	3.15
Leonel Sisniega Otero (PUA/FUN/MEC coalition)	32,118	1.91

Since no candidate achieved the required overall majority, a second round of voting was held on 8 December 1985. At this election, Mario Vinicio Cerezo Arévalo (PDCG) received 68% of the valid votes cast, while Jorge Carpio Nicolle (UCN) won the remaining 32%.

CONGRESO NACIONAL

President: José Ricardo Gómez Gálvez.

At elections on 3 November 1985 the PDCG secured an absolute majority in the National Congress by winning 51 of the 100 seats. The National Congress took office on 14 January 1986, replacing the previous legislative body, the Asamblea Nacional Constituyente.

Political Organizations

Following the introduction of new legislation in 1983, all political parties were required to disband and reapply for registration. All political parties were legalized in May 1985.

Alianza Democrática: Guatemala City; f. 1983; centre party; Leader Leopoldo Urrutia.

Central Auténtica Nacionalista (CAN): Guatemala City: f. 1980 from the CAO (Central Arañista Organizado); Leader Héctor Mayora Dawe.

Comité Guatemalteca de Unidad Patriota (CGUP) (Guatemalan Committee of Patriotic Unity): f. 1982; opposition coalition consisting of:

Frente Democrático contra la Represión (FDCR): Leader Rafael García.

Frente Popular 31 de Enero (FP-31): f. 1980; left-wing amalgamation of student, peasant and trade union groups; seized Brazilian Embassy, May 1982.

Frente Cívico Democrático (FCD): Guatemala City; Leaders Danilo Barillas, Jorge González del Valle; formed electoral alliance with PDCG, January 1985.

Frente Demócrata Guatemalteco: Leader Clemente Marroquín Rojas.

Frente de Trabajadores: workers' front.

Frente Unido Revolucionario (FUR): f. 1985; electoral alliance formed by parties of the democratic left and consisting of:

Fuerza Nueva: Leader Carlos Rafael Soto.

Movimiento Humanista de Integración Demócrata: Guatemala City; f. 1983; Leader Victoriano Alvarez.

Movimiento 20 de Octubre: Leader Marco Antonio Villamar Contreras.

Partido Socialista Democrático (PSD): Guatemala City; Pres. Carlos Gallardo Flores; Sec.-Gen. Mario Solórzano Martínez.

Frente de Unidad Nacional (FUN): 7a Avda Sta Cecilia 27-51, Zona 8, Guatemala City; tel. 714048; f. 1971; nationalist group; Leaders Col Enrique Peralta Azurdia, Gabriel Girón Ortiz.

Fuerza Democrática Popular: 11a Calle 4-13, Zona 1, Guatemala City; f. 1983; democratic popular force; Sec. Lic. Francisco Reyes Ixcamey.

Fuerza Popular Organizada: popular organized force.

GUATEMALA

Movimiento Emergente de Concordia (MEC): Guatemala City; f. 1983; Leaders DARÍO CHÁVEZ, ARTURO RAMÍREZ.

Movimiento de Liberación Nacional (MLN): 5a Calle 1–20, Zona 1, Guatemala City; f. 1960; extreme right-wing; 95,000 mems; Leader Lic. MARIO SANDÓVAL ALARCÓN.

Pantinamit: f. 1977; represents interests of Indian population; Leader FERNANDO TEZAHUIC TOHÓN.

Partido Democracia Cristiana Guatemalteca (PDCG): 8a Avda 14-53, Zona 1, Guatemala City; f. 1968; 89,000 mems; Sec.-Gen. and 1989 Presidential Candidate ALFONSO CABRERA; right-wing faction led by Dr FRANCISCO VILLAGRÁN KRAMER.

Partido Democrático de Cooperación Nacional (PDCN): 4a Avda 4-05, Zona 1, Guatemala City; tel. 24848; f. 1985; Sec.-Gen. Lic. ROLANDO BAQUIAX GÓMEZ.

Partido Institucional Democrático (PID): 2a Calle 10–73, Zona 1, Guatemala City; f. 1965; 60,000 mems; moderate conservative; Leader OSCAR HUMBERTO RIVAS GARCÍA; Dir DONALDO ALVAREZ RUIZ.

Partido Nacionalista Renovador (PNR): Guatemala City; first granted legal status in August 1979; 72,000 mems; Leader ALEJANDRO MALDONADO AGUIRRE; Sec.-Gen. RENÁN QUIÑÓNEZ SAGASTUME.

Partido Petenero: Guatemala City; f. 1983; defends regional interests of El Petén.

Partido Populista: populist party.

Partido Revolucionario (PR): Guatemala City; f. 1957; democratic party; 100,000 mems; Leaders JORGE GARCÍA GRANADOS, MARIO FUENTES PIERUCCINI.

Partido Revolucionario de los Trabajadores Centro-americanos (PRTC): Guatemala City.

Partido Socialista: Guatemala City; f. 1980.

Partido Social Cristiano: Guatemala City; f. 1983.

Partido de Unificación Anticomunista (PUA): Guatemala City; right-wing party; Leader LEONEL SISNIEGA OTERO.

Unidad Revolucionaria Demócrata (URD).

Unión del Centro Nacional (UCN): f. 1984; centre party; Leader JORGE CARPIO NICOLLE; Sec.-Gen. RAMIRO DE LEÓN CARPIO.

Unión Popular: popular union.

In February 1982 the principal guerrilla groups unified to form the **Unidad Revolucionaria Nacional Guatemalteca (URNG)** (Guatemalan National Revolutionary Unity), which has links with the PSD. The political wing of the URNG is the **Representación Unitaria de la Oposición Guatemalteca (RUOG):** Leader RAÚL MOLINA MEJÍA. The URNG seeks a guarantee of basic human rights, truly representative government, and an end to repression and racial discrimination; the grouping consists of:

Ejército Guerrillero de los Pobres (EGP): f. 1972; draws main support from Indians of western highlands; works closely with the **Comité de Unidad Campesina (CUC)** (Committee of Peasant Unity) and radical Catholic groups; mems 4,000 armed, 12,000 unarmed.

Fuerzas Armadas Rebeldes (FAR): formed early 1960s; originally military commission of CGT; associated with the CNT and CONUS trade unions; based in Guatemala City, Chimaltenango and El Petén; Commander NICOLÁS SIS.

Organización del Pueblo en Armas (ORPA): f. 1979; military group active in San Marcos province; originally part of FAR; Leader RODRIGO ASTURIAS ('Commdt GASPAR ILOM').

Partido Guatemalteco del Trabajo (PGT): communist party; divided into three armed factions: PGT-Camarilla (began actively participating in war in 1981); PGT-Núcleo de Conducción y Dirección; PGT-Comisión Nuclear; Gen. Sec. CARLOS GONZÁLEZ.

Other guerrilla groups are:

Comando de las Fuerzas Populares: f. 1981; left-wing.

Comando Guerrilleros del Pueblo (CGP): f. 1985; left-wing.

Comando Popular Revolucionario: f. 1988; frmly part of URNG.

Ejército Secreto Anticomunista (ESA): right-wing guerrilla group.

Escuadrón de la Muerte (EM): right-wing death squad.

Frente Central de Resistencia-Partido Guatemalteco del Trabajo (FCR-PGT): f. 1988; left-wing.

Fuerza de Guerrilleros de los Pobres (FGP).

Diplomatic Representation

EMBASSIES IN GUATEMALA

Argentina: 2a Avda 11-04, Zona 10, Guatemala City; telex 5285; Ambassador: Dr ANGEL FERNANDO GIRARDI.

Austria: 6a Avda 20-25, Zona 10, Guatemala City; telex 5224; Chargé d'affaires a.i.: Dr HANS KAUFMANN.

Belgium: Avda Reforma 13-70, Apdo 687-A, Zona 9, Guatemala City; tel. 315608; telex 5137; Ambassador: PAUL VERMEIRSCH.

Bolivia: 12 Avda 15-37, Zona 10, Guatemala City; Chargé d'affaires a.i.: Dr JOSÉ GABINA VILLANUEVA G.

Brazil: 18 Calle 2-22, Zona 14, Guatemala City; tel. 370949; telex 5200; Ambassador: HEITOR PINTO DE MOURA.

Canada: Galería España, 7 Avda y 12 Calle, Zona 9, Guatemala City; telex 5206; Ambassador: PIERRE TANGUAY.

Chile: 13 Calle 7-85, Zona 10, Guatemala City; telex 6162; Ambassador: SILVIO SALGADO RAMÍREZ.

China (Taiwan): Edif. Torrecafe, Of. 1030, 7a Avda 1-20, Zona 4, Guatemala City; telex 5107; Ambassador: MAO CHI-HSIEN.

Colombia: Edif. Gemini 10, 12 Calle, 1 Avda, Zona 10, Guatemala City; tel. 320604; Ambassador: LAURA OCHOA DE ARDILLA.

Costa Rica: Edif. Galerías Reforma, Of. 320, Avda Reforma 8-60, Zona 9, Guatemala City; tel. 325768; Chargé d'affaires: ROBERTO CHÁVEZ LIZANO.

Dominican Republic: 7a Calle 'A' 4-28, Zona 10, Guatemala City; Ambassador: PEDRO PABLO ALVAREZ BONILLA.

Ecuador: Avda Reforma 12-01, Zona 10, Apdo 46-A, Guatemala City; tel. 63296; telex 6218; Ambassador: MAGDALENA FEGAN PÓLIT.

Egypt: 12a Calle 6-15, Zona 9, Guatemala City; telex 5157; Ambassador: MAHMOUD ABBAS.

El Salvador: 12 Calle 5-43, Zona 9, Guatemala City; tel. 629385; telex 5418; Ambassador: AGUSTÍN MARTÍNEZ VARELA.

France: 14 Calle 5-52, Zona 9, Guatemala City; tel. 66336; telex 5963; Ambassador: JEAN MAZEO.

Germany, Federal Republic: Edif. Plaza Maritima, 6 Avda 20-25, Zona 10, Guatemala City; tel. 370028; telex 5209; Ambassador: Dr PETER BENSCH.

Holy See: 10a Calle 4-47, Zona 9, Guatemala City; tel. 324274; Apostolic Nuncio: Mgr ORIANO QUILICI.

Honduras: 15 Avda 9-16, Zona 13, Guatemala City; tel. 373921; Ambassador: OSCAR COLINDRES COARRALES.

Israel: 13a Avda 14-07, Zona 10, Guatemala City; telex 5218; Ambassador: ELIEZER ARMON.

Italy: 5 Avda 8-59, Zona 14, Guatemala City; tel. 374557; telex 5129; Ambassador: FRANCESCO MARCELLO RUGGIRELLO.

Japan: Ruta 6, 8-19, Apdo 531, Zona 4, Guatemala City; telex 5926; Ambassador: KEISHIRO MATSURA.

Korea, Republic: 16a Calle 3-38, Zona 10, Guatemala City; telex 5369; Ambassador: MOON CHANG-HWA.

Mexico: 16a Calle 0-51, Zona 14, Guatemala City; tel. 680769; telex 5961; Ambassador: ABRAHAM TALAVERA LÓPEZ.

Nicaragua: 10 Avda 14-72, Zona 10, Guatemala City; telex 5653; Ambassador: RICARDO ZAMBRANA.

Paraguay: 7 Avda 7-78 8°, Zona 4, Guatemala City.

Peru: 2a Avda 9-58, Zona 9, Guatemala City; Ambassador: ANDRÉS ARAMBURU ALVAREZ-CALDERÓN.

Portugal: 5 Avda 12-60, Zona 9, Guatemala City.

South Africa: 6 Avda 14-75, Zona 9, Guatemala City.

Spain: 10 Calle 6-20, Zona 9, Guatemala City; telex 5393; Ambassador: JUAN PABLO DE LA IGLESIA.

Sweden: 8a Avda 15-07, Zona 10, Guatemala City; tel. 680621; telex 5916; Ambassador: PETER LANDELIUS.

Switzerland: 4a Calle 7-73, Apdo 1426, Zona 9, Guatemala City; tel. 65726; telex 5257; Ambassador: (vacant).

United Kingdom: Centro Financiero, Torre II 7°, 7A Avda 5-10, Zona 4, Guatemala City; tel. 321601; telex 5686; Ambassador: BERNARD J. EVERETT.

USA: Avda La Reforma 7-01, Zona 10, Guatemala City; tel. 311541; Ambassador: JAMES MICHEL.

Uruguay: 20a Calle 8–00, Apdo 2b, Zona 10, Guatemala City; Chargé d'affaires: HÉCTOR L. PEDETTI A.

Venezuela: 8a Calle 0-56, Zona 9, Guatemala City; telex 5317; Ambassador: Dr ROGELIO ROSAS GIL.

Judicial System

Corte Suprema: Centro Cívico, 21 Calle y 7a Avda, Guatemala City; tel. 84323.

President of the Supreme Court: EDMUNDO VÁSQUEZ MARTÍNEZ.

GUATEMALA

Civil Courts of Appeal: 10 courts, 5 in Guatemala City, 2 in Quezaltenango, 1 each in Jalapa, Zacapa and Antigua. The two Labour Courts of Appeal are in Guatemala City.

Judges of the First Instance: 7 civil and 10 penal in Guatemala City, 2 civil each in Quezaltenango, Escuintla, Jutiapa and San Marcos, 1 civil in each of the 18 remaining Departments of the Republic.

Religion

Almost all of the inhabitants profess Christianity, with a majority belonging to the Roman Catholic Church. In recent years the Protestant Churches have attracted a growing number of converts.

CHRISTIANITY

The Roman Catholic Church

For ecclesiastical purposes, Guatemala comprises one archdiocese, eight dioceses, the Territorial Prelature of Escuintla, the Apostolic Vicariate of El Petén and the Izabal region, under the jurisdiction of an Apostolic Administrator.

Bishops' Conference: Conferencia Episcopal de Guatemala, Secretariado General del Episcopado, Apdo 1698, 26a Calle 8-90, Zona 12, Guatemala City; tel. 764171; f. 1973; Pres. Víctor Hugo Martínez Contreras, Bishop of Huehuetenango.

Archbishop of Guatemala City: Próspero Peñados del Barrio, Arzobispado, Apdo 723, 7a Avda 6-21, Zona 1, Guatemala City; tel. 29707.

Protestant Churches

The Baptist Church: Convention of Baptist Churches of Guatemala, 12a Calle 9-54, Zona 1, Apdo 322, Guatemala City; tel. 24227; Pres. Lic. José Angel Samol González.

The Episcopal Church: Avda Castellana 40-06, Zona 8, Guatemala City; tel. 720764; diocese founded 1967; Bishop of Guatemala: Rt Rev. Armando Guerra Soria (Apdo 58a, Guatemala City); Cathedral Church of St James and six missions in Guatemala City, three missions in Quezaltenango, three missions in El Quiché and 13 rural missions in the Departments of Izabal and Zacapa.

Church of Jesus Christ of Latter-day Saints: 12a Calle 3-37, Zona 9, Guatemala City; 17 bishoprics, 9 chapels; Regional Rep. Guillermo Enrique Rittscher.

The Lutheran Church: Consejo Nacional de Iglesias Luteranas, Apdo 1111, Guatemala City; tel. 23401; 3,077 mems; Pres. Rev. David Rodríguez U.

The Presbyterian Church: Iglesia Evangélica Presbiteriana Central, 6a Avda 'A' 4-68, Zona 1, Apdo 655, Guatemala City; tel. 538532; f. 1882; 36,000 mems; Pastors: Rev. Samuel Reinoso de León, Rev. Mardoqueo Muñoz C., Rev. Julio César Paz Portillo, Rev. David Velásquez.

The Union Church: 12 Calle 7-37, Plazuela España, Zona 9, Apdo 150a; Guatemala City; tel. 316904; f. 1943; Pastor Rev. Philip Truesdale.

BAHÁ'Í FAITH

National Spiritual Assembly of the Bahá'ís: 3a Calle 4-54, Zona 1, Guatemala City; tel. 29673; mems resident in 411 localities.

The Press

PRINCIPAL DAILIES

Diario de Centroamérica: 18a Calle 6-72, Zona 1, Guatemala City; tel. 24418; f. 1880; morning; official; Dir Luis Mendizábal; circ. 15,000.

El Gráfico: 14a Avda 9-18, Zona 1, Guatemala City; tel. 510021; f. 1963; morning; Dir Jorge Carpio Nicolle; circ. 60,000.

La Hora: 9a Calle 'A' 1-56, Zona 1, Guatemala City; tel. 26864; f. 1944; evening; independent; Dir Oscar Marroquín Rojas; circ. 20,000.

Prensa Libre: 13a Calle 9-13, Zona 1, Guatemala City; tel. 511838; f. 1951; morning; independent; Dir and Gen. Man. Pedro Julio García; circ. 68,500.

PERIODICALS

AGA: 9a Calle 3-43, Zona 1, Guatemala City; monthly; agricultural.

Gerencia: 10a Calle 3-17, Zona 10, Guatemala City; tel. 311564; fmrly Otra Revista; official organ of the Association of Guatemalan Managers; Dir Richard Aitkenhead Castillo.

El Industrial: Ruta 6 No 9-21, Zona 4, Guatemala City; monthly; official organ of the Chamber of Industry.

Directory

Inforpress Centroamericana: 9a Calle 'A' 3-56, Zona 1, Guatemala City; tel. 29432; f. 1972; weekly; published in Spanish and English; regional political and economic news and analysis; Dir Ricardo Wilson-Grau.

PRESS ASSOCIATIONS

Asociación de Periodistas de Guatemala (APG): 14 Calle 3-29, Zona 1, Guatemala City; tel. 21813; Pres. Alvaro Contreras Vélez.

Cámara Guatemalteca de Periodismo (CGP): Guatemala City; Pres. Eduardo Díaz Reina.

Círculo Nacional de Prensa (CN): Guatemala City; Pres. Jesús Abalcázar López.

NEWS AGENCIES

Inforpress Centroamericana: 9a Calle 'A' 3-56, Zona 1, Guatemala City; tel. 29432; f. 1972; independent news agency.

Foreign Bureaux

ACAN-EFE (Central America): Edif. El Centro, 9a Calle y 7a Avda, Zona 1, Guatemala City; tel. 519484; Dir Alberto Flores.

Agencia EFE (Spain): Edif. El Centro, 7a Avda 8-56, Zona 1, Guatemala City; tel. 519454; Bureau Chief (vacant).

Agenzia Nazionale Stampa Associata (ANSA) (Italy): 2a Avda 3-36, Zona 10, Guatemala City; tel. 320346; telex 5251; Chief Alfonso Anzueto López.

Deutsche Presse-Agentur (dpa) (Federal Republic of Germany): 5a Calle No 4-30, Apdo 2333, Zona 1, Guatemala City; tel. 517505; telex 5227; Correspondent Julio César Anzueto.

Inter Press Service (IPS) (Italy): 6a Avda 1-27, Edif. Muni, Zona 4, Guatemala City; tel. 517271; telex 9246; Correspondent Carlos Rodolfo Mobil.

United Press International (UPI) (USA): 7a Calle 10-54, Zona 1, Guatemala City; tel. 535815.

Publishers

Editorial del Ministerio de Educación: 15a Avda 3-22, Zona 1, Guatemala City.

Editorial Universitaria: Universidad de San Carlos de Guatemala, Edif. de Recursos Educativos, Ciudad Universitaria, Zona 12, Guatemala City; tel. 760790; literature, social sciences, health, pure and technical sciences, humanities, secondary and university educational textbooks; Editor Lic. Oscar Guillermo López.

Piedra Santa: 7a Avda 4-45, Zona 1, Guatemala City; tel. 510231; telex 9225; f. 1947; children's literature, incl. the magazine *Chiquirín*; Man. Dir Oralia Díaz de Piedra Santa.

Seminario de Integración Social Guatemalteco: 11a Calle 4-31, Zona 1, Guatemala City; tel. 29754; f. 1956; sociology, anthropology, social sciences, educational textbooks.

Radio and Television

In 1985 there were an estimated 350,000 radio receivers and 207,000 television receivers in use.

Dirección General de Radiodifusión y Televisión Nacional: Edif. Tipografía Nacional, 3°, 18 de Septiembre 6-72, Zona 1, Guatemala City; tel. 532539; f. 1931; government supervisory body; Dir-Gen. Ricardo Gómez Flor.

RADIO

There are five government and six educational stations, including:

La Voz de Guatemala: 18 Calle 6-70, Zona 1, Guatemala City; Government station; Dir Arturo Soto Echeverría.

Radio Cultural TGN: 4a Avda 30-09, Zona 3, Apdo 601, Guatemala City; tel. 714378; f. 1950; religious and cultural station; programmes in Spanish and English, Cakchiquel, Kekchí and Mam; Dir Esteban Sywulka; Man. A. Wayne Berger.

There are 84 commercial stations of which the most important are:

Emisoras Unidas de Guatemala: 7a Avda 6-45, Zona 9, Guatemala City; tel. 321654; Pres. Jorge Edgardo Archila; Vice-Pres. Rolando Archila.

La Voz de las Américas: 11a Calle 2-43, Zona 1, Guatemala City; Dir Augusto López S.

Radio Cinco Sesenta: 8a Calle 1-11, Zona 11, Guatemala City; Dir Edna Castillo Obregón.

Radio Continental: 15a Calle 3-45, Zona 1, Guatemala City; Dir R. Vizcaíno R.

GUATEMALA

Radio Nuevo Mundo: 6a Avda 10-45, Zona 1, Apdo 281, Guatemala City; Man. ALFREDO GONZÁLEZ G.

Radio Panamericana: 1a Calle 35-48, Zona 7, Guatemala City; Dir MARÍA V. DE PANIAGUA.

TELEVISION

Canal 3—Radio-Televisión Guatemala, SA: 30a Avda 3-40, Zona 11, Apdo 1367, Guatemala City; tel. 922491; telex 5253; f. 1956; commercial station; Pres. Lic. MAX KESTLER FARNÉS; Vice-Pres. J. F. VILLANUEVA.

Tele Once: 20a Calle 5-02, Zona 10, Guatemala City; tel. 682165; commercial; Dir A. MOURRA.

Televisiete, SA: 3a Calle 6-24, Zona 9, Apdo 1242, Guatemala City; tel. 62216; f. 1964; commercial station channel 7; Dir Dr J. VILLANUEVA P.

Televisión Cultural Educativa: 4a Calle 18-38, Zona 1, Guatemala City; tel. 531913; government station.

Trecevisión SA: 3a Calle 10-70, Zona 10, Guatemala City; tel. 63266; telex 6070; commerical; Dir Ing. PEDRO MELGAR R.; Gen. Man. GILDA VALLADARES ORTIZ.

Finance

(cap. = capital; p.u. = paid up; res = reserves; dep. = deposits; m. = million; brs = branches; amounts in quetzales)

A Stock Exchange was established in Guatemala City in April 1987. The Exchange was to be commonly owned (one share per associate) and was to trade stocks from private companies, government bonds, letters of credit and other securities.

BANKING

Superintendencia de Bancos: 7a Avda 22-01, Zona 1, Apdo 2306, Guatemala City; tel. 534243; telex 5231; f. 1946; Superintendent Lic. GUSTAVO AYESTAS ESCOBAR; Gen. Sec. Lic. DOUGLAS BORJA VIELMAN.

Central Bank

Banco de Guatemala: 7a Avda 22-01, Zona 1, Apdo 365, Guatemala City; tel. 534053; telex 5231; f. 1946; guarantee fund 94.8m. (Sept. 1987); Pres. (vacant); Man. ÓSCAR ALVAREZ MARROQUÍN.

State Commercial Bank

Crédito Hipotecario Nacional de Guatemala: 7a Avda 22-77, Zona 1, Apdo 242, 01901, Guatemala City; tel. 82041; telex 5192; f. 1930; government-owned; cap. p.u. 11.5m., res 7.9m., dep. 188.8m. (June 1988); Pres. Lic. VÍCTOR MANUEL MORAGA MIRANDA; Gen. Man. Lic. RICARDO CONTRERAS CRUZ; 2 brs.

Private Commercial Banks

Guatemala City

Banco Agrícola Mercantil, SA: 7a Avda 9-11, Zona 1, Guatemala City; tel. 21601; telex 5347; f. 1946; cap. 5m, res 15.3m., dep. 331.8m. (June 1988); Man. Lic. ARMANDO GONZÁLEZ CAMPO; 2 brs.

Banco del Agro, SA: 9a Calle 5-39, Zona 1, Apdo 1443, Guatemala City; tel. 514026; telex 4167; f. 1958; cap. 7.1m., res 11.0m., dep. 246.8m. (June 1988); Pres. RICARDO RODRÍGUEZ PAÚL; Man. JUAN JOSÉ FALLA SÁNCHEZ.

Banco del Café, SA: Avda La Reforma 9-00, Zona 9, Apdo 831, Guatemala City; tel. 311311; telex 5123; f. 1978; cap. 9.1m., res 1.3m., dep. 259.4m. (June 1988); Pres. EDUARDO M. GONZÁLEZ RIVERA; Gen. Man. Lic. ROBERTO MAZARIEGOS GODOY.

Banco de la Construcción, SA: 12a Calle 4-17, Zona 1, Apdo 999, Guatemala City; tel. 539827; telex 5708; f. 1983; cap. 6.4m., dep. 121.4m. (Sept. 1988); Pres. Arq. HÉCTOR HUMBERTO QUEZADA LEONARDO; Man. Lic. OSCAR ALVAREZ MARROQUÍN.

Banco del Ejército, SA: 5a Avda 6-06, Zona 1, Apdo 1797, Guatemala City; tel. 532146; telex 5574; f. 1972; cap. 9.6m., res 6.1m., dep. 170.5m. (June 1988); Pres. Col MARCO ANTONIO SÁNCHEZ SAMAYOA; Man. Lic. MÁXIMINO RUANO AYALA.

Banco de Exportación, SA: Avda La Reforma 11-49, Zona 10, Guatemala City; tel. 373861; telex 5896; f. 1985; cap. 7.5m., res 4.7m., dep. 97.6m. (June 1988); Pres. VENANCIO BOTRÁN BORJA; Man. Ing. RAFAEL VIEJO RODRÍGUEZ.

Banco Granai y Townson, SA: 7a Avda 1-86, Zona 4, Apdo 654, Guatemala City; tel. 65981; telex 5159; f. 1962; cap. 13.0m., res 6.9m., dep. 403.6m. (June 1988); Pres. MARIO GRANAI ARÉVALO; Gen. Man. Lic. MARIO ASTURIAS ARÉVALO; 22 brs.

Banco Industrial, SA: 7a Avda 5-10, Zona 4, Apdo 744, Guatemala City; tel. 312323; telex 5236; f. 1968 to promote industrial development; cap. 25m., res 16.0m., dep. 500.4m. (June 1988); Pres. Ing. RAMIRO CASTILLO LOVE; Man. Lic. NORBERTO RODOLFO CASTELLANOS DÍAZ.

Banco Inmobilario, SA: 8a Avda 10-57, Zona 1, Apdo 1181, Guatemala City; tel. 519022; telex 6140; f. 1958; cap. 31.0m., res 0.5m., dep. 204.3m. (June 1988); Pres. VALENTÍN VALDERRÁBANO BÁRCENA; Man. MANUEL MÉNDEZ ESCOBAR; 15 brs.

Banco Internacional, SA: 7a Avda 11-20, Zona 1, Apdo 2588, Guatemala City; tel. 538679; telex 4178; f. 1976; cap. 10.0m., res 4.5m., dep. 201.0m. (June 1988); Pres. Lic. JORGE SKINNER-KLÉE; Man. JULIO VIELMAN PINEDA.

Banco Metropolitano, SA: 5a Avda 8-24, Zona 1, Apdo 2688, Guatemala City; tel. 25360; telex 5288; f. 1978; cap. 13.4m., res 0.5m., dep. 162.9m. (Aug. 1988); Pres. Ing. FRANCISCO ALVARADO MACDONALD; Man. EBERTO CÉSAR SIGÜENZA LÓPEZ.

Banco Promotor, SA: 10 Calle 6-47, Zona 1, Apdo 930, Guatemala City; tel. 512928; telex 9238; f. 1986; cap. 4.5m., dep. 75.8m. (June 1988); Pres. Lic. JULIO VALLADARES CASTILLO; Man. Lic. RAÚL MONTERROSO RIVERA.

Banco del Quetzal, SA: Edif. Plaza 6-26, Zona 9, Apdo 1002, Guatemala City; tel. 318333; telex 5893; f. 1984; cap. 4.4m., dep. 71.9m. (June 1988); Pres. Lic. MARIO ROBERTO LEAL PIVARAL; Man. Ing. JUAN CARLOS VERCESI GALEANI.

Banco de los Trabajadores: 8a Avda 9-41, Zona 1, Apdo 1956, Guatemala City; tel. 24341; telex 9212; f. 1966; cap. 19.2m., dep. 61.4m. (June 1988); deals with loans for establishing and improving small industries as well as normal banking business; Pres. Lic. JUAN JOSÉ ALONZO ESTRADA; Man. Lic. OSCAR H. ANDRADE ELIZONDO.

Quezaltenango

Banco de Occidente, SA: 4a Calle 11-38, Zona 1, Apdo 28, Quezaltenango; tel. 0612861; telex 5455; f. 1881; cap. 5.0m., res 23.0m., dep. 503.5m. (June 1988); Pres. Lic. LUIS MIGUEL AGUIRRE FERNÁNDEZ; Man. Lic. MARIO ANTONIO MEJÍA GONZÁLEZ; 1 br.

State Development Banks

Banco Nacional de Desarrollo Agrícola—BANDESA: 9a Calle 9-47, Zona 1, Apdo 350, Guatemala City; tel. 535222; telex 4122; f. 1971; cap. 10.5m., dep. 89.2m. (June 1988); agricultural development bank; Pres. Ing. RODOLFO ESTRADA HURTARTE; Man. Lic. JOSÉ MIGUEL ARGUETA BONE.

Banco Nacional de la Vivienda—BANVI: 6a Avda 1-22, Zona 4, Apdo 2632, Guatemala City; tel. 325777; telex 5371; f. 1973; cap. 30.6m., dep. 50.6m. (June 1988); Pres. Arq. RAFAEL ESCOBAR DONIS.

Finance Corporations

Corporación Financiera Nacional—CORFINA: 8a Avda 10-43, Zona 1, Guatemala City; tel. 83331; telex 5186; f. 1973; provides assistance for the development of industry, mining and tourism; cap. 34.3m., res 0.2m. (June 1988); Pres. Lic. ELIZARDO SOSA; Gen. Man. Lic. SERGIO RENÉ DÍAZ IZQUIERDO.

Financiera Guatemalteca, SA—FIGSA: 1a Avda 11-50, Zona 10, Apdo 2460, Guatemala City; tel. 316051; f. 1962; cap. 4.7m., res 1.3m. (June 1988); Pres. CARLOS GONZÁLEZ BARRIOS; Man. Lic. JOSÉ ROBERTO ORTEGA HERRERA.

Financiera Industrial y Agropecuaria, SA (FIASA): Avda La Reforma 10-00, Zona 9, Guatemala City; tel. 310303; telex 5958; f. 1969; private development bank; medium- and long-term loans to private industrial enterprises in Central America; cap. 2.5m., res 16.7m. (June 1988); Pres. JORGE CASTILLO LOVE; Gen. Man. Lic. J. RODERICO ROSSELL ANZUETO.

Financiera Industrial, SA (FISA): Torre No. 2 Centro Financiero, 7a Avda 5-10, Zona 4, Apdo 744, Guatemala City; tel. 312323; telex 5236; f. 1981; cap. 3m., res 1.1m. (June 1988); Pres. CARLOS ARÍAS MASSELLI; Man. Lic. CARLOS HUMBERTO ALPÍREZ PÉREZ.

Financiera de Inversión, SA: 10a Calle 3-17, Zona 10, Guatemala City; tel. 311266; telex 3155; f. 1981; cap. 2.7m. (June 1988); Pres. Lic. MARIO AUGUSTO PORRAS G.

Foreign Banks

Bank of America, NT & SA: 11a Calle 5-07, Zona 1, Apdo 1335, Guatemala City; tel. 512266; telex 5205; f. 1957; cap. 3m., res 2.9m., dep. 78.6m. (June 1988); Man. MICHAEL SUÁREZ.

Lloyds Bank International Ltd: POB 1106, 8a Avda 10-67, Zona 1, Guatemala City; tel. 24651; telex 5263; f. 1959; cap. 5.2m., res 4.8m., dep. 159.1m. (June 1988); Man. PHILIP COGGINS LONG; 6 brs.

Banking Association

Asociación de Banqueros de Guatemala: Edif. Quinta Montúfar 2°, 12a Calle 4-74, Zona 9, Guatemala City; tel. 318211; f. 1961; represents all state and private banks; Pres. Lic. MANUEL MÉNDEZ ESCOBAR.

GUATEMALA

INSURANCE
National Companies

La Alianza, Cía Anglo-Centroamericana de Seguros, SA: Edif. Etisa 6°, Plazuela España, Zona 9, Guatemala City; tel. 315475; telex 5551; f. 1968; Pres. F. Antonio Gándara García; Man. Ing. Rudy Gándara Merkle.

Aseguradora General, SA: 10a Calle 3-17, Zona 10, Guatemala City; tel. 325933; telex 5441; f. 1968; Pres. Juan O. Niemann; Man. Enrique Neutze.

Aseguradora Guatemalteca de Transportes, SA: 5a Avda 6-06, Zona 1, 01001 Guatemala City; tel. 519794; telex 5574; f. 1978; Pres. Col Marco Antonio Sánchez; Man. César A. Ruano Sandoval.

Cía de Seguros Generales Granai & Townson, SA: 7a Avda 1-82, Zona 4, Guatemala City; tel. 61361; telex 5955; f. 1947; Pres. Ernesto Townson R.; Gen. Man. Mario Asturias Arévalo.

Cía de Seguros Panamericana, SA: Avda La Reforma 9-00, Zona 9, Guatemala City; tel. 325922; telex 5925; f. 1968; Pres. G. Frank Purvis, Jr; Gen. Man. J. Antonio González A.

Cía de Seguros El Roble, SA: 7a Avda 5-10, Zona 4, Guatemala City; tel. 321702; telex 6094; f. 1973; Pres. Federico Köng Vielman; Man. Ing. Ricardo Erales Cóbar.

Comercial Aseguradora Suizo-Americana, SA: 7a Avda 7-07, Zona 9, Apdo Postal 132, Guatemala City; tel. 320666; telex 5502; f. 1946; Pres. Ernesto A. Piñero; Vice-Pres. Lic. Pedro Aycinena B.

Departamento de Seguros y Previsión del Crédito Hipotecario Nacional: 7a Avda 22-77, Zona 1, Guatemala City; tel. 82041; telex 6065; f. 1935; Pres. Lic. Luis M. Montúfar Luna; Man. Lic. Ricardo Contreras Cruz.

La Seguridad de Centroamérica, SA: Avda La Reforma 12-01, Zona 10, Guatemala City; tel. 317566; telex 5243; f. 1967; Pres. Edgardo Wagner D.; Vice-Pres. Marta de Toriello.

Seguros Cruz Azul, SA: Edif. Plaza Marítima 10, 6a Avda 20-25, Zona 10; tel. 372285; telex 5204; Gen. Man. Brian Murphy.

Seguros de Occidente, SA: 7a Calle 'A' 7-14, Zona 9, Guatemala City; tel. 311222; telex 5605; f. 1979; Pres. Ing. Herculano Aguirre Montalvo; Gen. Man. Lic. Pedro Aguirre.

Seguros Universales, SA: 4a Calle 7-73, Zona 9, Guatemala City; tel. 66156; telex 6104; f. 1962; Pres. Francisco Javier Valls Planas; Man. Nolasco Sicilia García.

Insurance Association

Asociación Guatemalteca de Instituciones de Seguros —AGIS: Guatemala City; f. 1953; 8 mems; Pres. Enrique Neutze Aycinena; Man. Lic. Federico Piñol.

Trade and Industry

CHAMBERS OF COMMERCE AND INDUSTRY

Comité Coordinador de Asociaciones Agrícolas, Comerciales, Industriales y Financieras (CACIF): Edif. Cámara de Industria de Guatemala, Ruta 6, No 9-21, Zona 4, Guatemala City; tel. 310651; telex 6133; co-ordinates work on problems and organization of free enterprise; mems: 6 chambers; Pres. Lic. Arturo Pellecer Arellano; Vice-Pres. Arturo Pellecer.

Cámara de Comercio de Guatemala: 10a Calle 3-80, Zona 1, Guatemala City; tel. 82681; telex 5478; f. 1894; Pres. Edgar A. Heinemann; Man. Jonás Vásquez Alvarado.

Cámara de Industria de Guatemala: Ruta 6, 9-21, Zona 4, Apdo 214, Guatemala City; tel. 340849; telex 5402; f. 1958; Pres. Ing. Juan Luis Bosch Gutiérrez; Gen. Man. Ing. Carlos Ramiro García Chiu.

DEVELOPMENT ORGANIZATIONS

Comisión Nacional del Petróleo: Diagonal 17, 29-78, Zona 11, Guatemala City; tel. 460111; f. 1983; awards petroleum exploration licences.

Consejo Nacional de Planificación Económico: Edif. Ministerio de Finanzas 12°, Palacio Nacional, Guatemala City; tel. 80264; f. 1964; prepares and supervises the implementation of the national economic development plan; Sec. Arq. Hermes Marroquín.

Corporación Financiera Nacional (Corfina): see under Finance.

Dirección General de Hidrocarburos: Diagonal 17, 29-78, Zona 11, Guatemala City; tel. 760679; f. 1983; control and supervision of petroleum and gas development.

Empresa Nacional de Fomento y Desarrollo Económico de El Petén (FYDEP): 11a Avda 'B' 32-46, Zona 5, Guatemala City; tel. 316834; telex 6178; f. 1959; attached to the Presidency; economic

Directory

development agency for the Department of El Petén; Dir Francisco Angel Castellanos Góngora.

Instituto de Fomento de Hipotecas Aseguradas (FHA): 6a Avda 0-60, Zona 4, Guatemala City; f. 1961; insured mortgage institution for the promotion of house construction; Pres. Lic. Homero Augusto González Barillas; Man. Lic. José Salvador Samayoa Aguilar.

Instituto Nacional de Administración Pública (INAP): 5a Avda 12-65, Zona 9, Apto 2753, Guatemala City; tel. 66339; f. 1964; provides technical experts to assist all branches of the Government in administrative reform programmes; provides in-service training for local and central government staff; has research programmes in administration, sociology, politics and economics; provides post-graduate education in public administration; Gen. Man. Dr Ariel Rivera Irías.

Instituto Nacional de Transformación Agraria (INTA): 14 Calle 7-14, Zona 1, Guatemala City; tel. 80975; f. 1962 to carry out agrarian reform; current programme includes development of the 'Faja Transversal del Norte'; Pres. Ing. Jaime González; Vice-Pres. Ing. Francisco Morales.

PRODUCERS' ASSOCIATIONS

Asociación de Azucareros de Guatemala (ASAZGUA): Edif. Tívoli Plaza, 6a Calle 6-38, Zona 9, Guatemala City; telex 5248; f. 1957; sugar producers' asscn; 19 mems; Gen. Man. Lic. Armando Boesche.

Asociación de Exportadores de Café: 11a Calle 5-66 3°, Zona 9, Guatemala City; telex 5368; coffee exporters' asscn; 29 mems; Pres. Eduardo González Rivera.

Asociación General de Agricultores: 9a Calle 3-43, Zona 1, Guatemala City; f. 1920; general farmers' asscn; 350 mems; Pres. David Ordoñez; Man. Pedro Arrivillaga Rada.

Asociación Nacional de Avicultores (ANAVI): Avda La Reforma 8-60, Zona 9, Edif. Galerías Reforma, 9°, Of. 904 Torre 2, Guatemala City; tel. 311381; telex 6215; f. 1964; national asscn of poultry farmers; 60 mems; Pres. Ing. Roberto Ordóñez Lacayo; Gen. Man. Dr Mario A. Motta González.

Asociación Nacional de Fabricantes de Alcoholes y Licores (ANFAL): Km 16½ Carretera Roosevelt, Apdo 2065, Zona 10, Guatemala City; tel. 920430; telex 5565; f. 1947; distillers' asscn; Pres. Felipe Botrán Merino; Man. Lic. Juan Guillermo Borja Mogollón.

Asociación Nacional del Café—Anacafé: Edif. Etisa, Plazuela España, Zona 9, Guatemala City; tel. 67531; telex 5915; f. 1960; national coffee asscn; Pres. Lic. Luis E. González Hertzsch; Man. Lic. Oscar G. Zuástegui.

Asociación de Agricultores Productores de Aceites Esenciales: 6a Calle 1-36, Zona 10, Apdo 272, Guatemala City; tel. 314255; telex 5316; f. 1948; essential oils producers' asscn; 40 mems; Pres. José Luis Ralda; Man. Ing. Luis Alberto Asturias.

Cámara del Agro: 15a Calle 'A', No 7-65, Zona 9, Guatemala City; tel. 61473; f. 1973; Man. César Bustamante Araúz.

Consejo Nacional del Algodón: 7a Avda 6-26, Zona 9, Guatemala City; tel. 324540; f. 1964; consultative body for cultivation and classification of cotton; 125 mems; Pres Dieter Keller, Dr Moises Flores Pacheco; Man. Alfredo Gil Spillari.

Gremial de Huleros de Guatemala: 7a Avda 7-78, Zona 4, Edif. Centroamericano, Of. 406, Guatemala City; tel. 314917; telex 5114; f. 1970; union of rubber producers; 125 mems; Pres. José Luis Ralda; Man. Lic. César Soto.

CO-OPERATIVES

The following federations group all Guatemalan co-operatives:

Federación de Cooperativas Artesanales.

Federación Nacional de Cooperativas de Ahorro y Crédito.

Federación Nacional de Cooperativas de Consumo

Federación Nacional de Cooperativas de Vivienda y Servicios Varios.

TRADE UNIONS

Trade union activity can now take place freely, having been severely restricted after repression in 1979 and 1980.

Frente Nacional Sindical—FNS (National Trade Union Front): Guatemala City; f. 1968; to achieve united action in labour matters; affiliated are two confederations and 11 federations, which represent 97% of the country's trade unions and whose General Secretaries form the governing council of the FNS. The affiliated organizations include:

Comité Nacional de Unidad Sindical Guatemalteca (CONUS): Leader Miguel Angel Solís; Sec.-Gen. Gerónimo López Díaz.

GUATEMALA

Confederación General de Sindicatos (General Trade Union Confederation): 18a Calle 5-50, Zona 1, Apdo 959, Guatemala City.

Confederación Nacional de Trabajadores (National Workers' Confederation): Guatemala City; Sec.-Gen. MIGUEL ANGEL ALBIZÚREZ.

Consejo Sindical de Guatemala (Guatemalan Trade Union Council): 18a Calle 5-50, Zona 1, Apdo 959, Guatemala City; f. 1955; admitted to ICFTU and ORIT; Gen. Sec. JAIME V. MONGE DONIS; 30,000 mems in 105 affiliated unions.

Federación Autónoma Sindical Guatemalteca (Guatemalan Autonomous Trade Union Federation): Guatemala City; Gen. Sec. MIGUEL ANGEL SOLIS.

Federación de Obreros Textiles (Textile Workers' Federation): Edif. Briz, Of. 503, 6a Avda 14-33, Zona 1, Guatemala City; f. 1957; Sec.-Gen. FACUNDO PINEDA.

Federación de Trabajadores de Guatemala (FTG) (Guatemalan Workers' Federation): 5a Calle 4-33, Zona 1, Guatemala City; tel. 26515; Promoter ADRIAN RAMÍREZ.

A number of unions exist without a national centre, including the Union of Chicle and Wood Workers, the Union of Coca-Cola Workers and the Union of Workers of the Enterprise of the United Fruit Company.

Central Nacional de Trabajadores (CNT): 9a Avda 4-29, Zona 1, Apdo 2472, Guatemala City; f. 1972; cover all sections of commerce, industry and agriculture including the public sector; clandestine since June 1980; Sec.-Gen. JULIO CELSO DE LEÓN; 23,735 mems.

Unidad de Acción Sindical y Popular (UASP): f. 1988; broad coalition of leading labour and peasant organizations; includes:

Comité de la Unidad Campesina—CUC (Committee of Peasants' Unity).

Confederación General de Trabajadores de Guatemala (CGTG).

Confederatión de Unidad Sindical de Trabajadores de Guatemala (CUSG): 5a Calle 4-33, Zona 1, Guatemala City; tel. 26515; f. 1983; Sec.-Gen. FRANCISCO ALFARO MIJANGOS.

Sindicato de Trabajadores de la Educación Guatemaltecos (STEG).

Sindicato de Trabajadores de la Industria de la Electricidad (STINDE).

Sindicato de Trabajadores del Instituto Guatemalteco de Seguro Social (STIGSS).

Unidad Sindical de Trabajadores de Guatemala (UNSITRAGUA).

Transport

RAILWAYS

Ferrocarriles de Guatemala—FEGUA: 9a Avda 18-03, Zona 1, Guatemala City; telex 5342; f. 1968; government-owned; 953 km open from Puerto Barrios and Santo Tomás de Castilla on the Atlantic coast to Tecún Umán on the Mexican border, via Zacapa, Guatemala City and Santa María. Branch lines: Santa María–San José; Las Cruces–Champerico. From Zacapa another line branches southward to Anguiatú, on the border with El Salvador; owns the ports of Barrios (Atlantic) and San José (Pacific); Chair. of Board J. A. PILONA CORDERO; Gen. Man. F. A. LEAL ESTÉVEZ.

There are 102 km of plantation lines.

ROADS

In 1984 there were 17,315 km of roads, of which 2,887 km were asphalted and 6,576 km gravel. The Guatemala section of the Pan-American highway is 824 km long, including 552 km of paved roads. The construction of a 1,500-km network of new highways, including a four-lane motorway from the capital to San José, began in 1981. A 44-km toll road linking Escuintla with San José was due to be built in the mid-1980s, at a cost of US $18m. In late 1988 a $49.1m. project, supported by a loan of $31.5m. from the World Bank, was begun, under which improvements were to be made to many secondary roads.

SHIPPING

Guatemala's major ports are Puerto Barrios, San José, Santo Tomás de Castilla and Champerico. A major port reconstruction and expansion programme began in 1976, and in March 1983 the extension to the port of San José was opened.

Armadora Marítima Guatemalteca, SA: 14a Calle 8-14, Zona 1, Apdo 1008, Guatemala City; tel. 537243; telex 5214; cargo services; Pres. and Gen. Man. J. L. CORONADO ALVAREZ.

Flota Mercante Gran Centroamericana, SA: Edif. Canella 5°, 1a Calle 7-21, Zona 9, Guatemala City; tel. 316666; telex 5211; f. 1959; services from Europe (in association with WITASS), Gulf of Mexico, US Atlantic and East Coast Central American ports; Pres. R. S. RAMÍREZ; Gen. Man. J. E. A. MORALES.

Líneas Marítimas de Guatemala, SA: 6a Avda 20-25, Edif. Plaza Marítima 8°, Zona 10, Guatemala City; tel. 370166; telex 5174; cargo services; Pres. J. R. MATHEU ESCOBAR; Gen. Man. F. HERRERAS E.

Several foreign lines link Guatemala with Europe, the Far East and North America.

CIVIL AVIATION

In 1982 a new international airport was completed at Santa Elena Petén.

AVIATECA—Empresa Guatemalteca de Aviación: Avda Hincapié, Aeropuerto 'La Aurora', Zona 13, Guatemala City; telex 4160; f. 1945; internal services and external services to the USA; Pres. Ing. JULIO OBOLS GOMES; Vice-Pres. Ing. LARRY ANDRADE LARA; fleet: 2 Boeing 727-100C.

Tourism

As a result of violence in the country, the annual total of tourist arrivals declined from 504,000 in 1979, when tourist receipts were US $201m., to 192,000 in 1984 (receipts $56.6m.). Since 1985, however, the number of arrivals has risen and reached 352,741 in 1987, when receipts increased to $102.9m.

Guatemala Tourist Commission: 7a Avda 1-17, Centro Cívico, Zona 4, Guatemala City; tel. 311333; telex 5532; f. 1967; policy and planning council: 13 mems representing the public and private sectors; Pres. BEATRÍZ ZÚÑIGA-SEIGNÉ.

Asociación Guatemalteca de Agentes de Viajes (AGAV) (Guatemalan Association of Travel Agents): 6a Avda 8-41, Zona 9, Apdo 2735, Guatemala City; tel. 310320; telex 5127; Pres. MARÍA DEL CARMEN FERNÁNDEZ O.

Atomic Energy

Dirección General de Energía Nuclear: Diagonal 17 29-78, Zona 11, Apdo 1421, Guatemala City; tel. 760679; telex 5516; programmes include the application of nuclear energy in agriculture and industry, nuclear medicine and the control of the import of radioactive materials; Dir Ing. RAÚL EDUARDO PINEDA GONZÁLEZ.

GUINEA

Introductory Survey

Location, Climate, Language, Religion, Flag, Capital

The Republic of Guinea lies on the west coast of Africa, with Sierra Leone and Liberia to the south, Senegal to the north, and Mali and Côte d'Ivoire inland to the east. The climate on the coastal strip is hot and moist, with temperatures ranging from about 17°C (62°F) in the dry season to about 30°C (86°F) in the wet season. The interior is higher and cooler. The official language is French, but Soussou, Manika and six other national languages are widely spoken. Most of the inhabitants are Muslims but some still adhere to traditional animist beliefs. Around 1% are Roman Catholics. The national flag (proportions 3 by 2) consists of three equal vertical stripes, of red, yellow and green. The capital is Conakry.

Recent History

Guinea was formerly French Guinea, part of French West Africa. It became the independent Republic of Guinea on 2 October 1958, after 95% of voters had rejected the Constitution of the Fifth Republic under which the French colonies became self-governing within the French Community. The new state was the object of punitive reprisals by the outgoing French authorities: all aid was withdrawn, and the government infrastructure destroyed. The administration was rebuilt on the basis of the Guinean Confédération Général du Travail, which had organized a series of strikes culminating in a general strike in 1953, and the Parti démocratique de Guinée (PDG), which won 58 of the 60 seats in the Territorial Assembly in 1957. Its leader, Ahmed Sekou Touré, became President, and the PDG the sole political party. President Sekou Touré vigorously pursued a policy of socialist revolution, with emphasis on popular political participation.

There were attempted coups in 1961, 1965 and 1967. An abortive invasion by Portuguese troops and Guinean exiles in 1970 was followed by the arrest of prominent Guineans and foreigners, suspected of involvement. Many executions took place, and, as a result, diplomatic relations with Senegal and the Federal Republic of Germany were broken off in 1971, and with Côte d'Ivoire in 1973. This led to the country's virtual isolation, as dealings with the USSR had declined since the early 1960s. Reports of a 'permanent conspiracy' by foreign powers to overthrow the Government continued to circulate, but in 1975 Guinea resumed normal relations with its African neighbours, France and the Western powers, signing the Lomé Convention (see p. 149) and joining ECOWAS (see p. 132).

All private trade was forbidden in 1975, and transactions were conducted through official co-operatives under the supervision of an 'economic police'. In August 1977 demonstrations against the abolition of the traditional market, and the abuse of power by the 'economic police', were held by women in Conakry, and rioting broke out in other towns. Three state governors were killed. As a result, Sekou Touré yielded to many of the demands expressed, disbanded the 'economic police' and allowed private trading to recommence in July 1979.

Under Sekou Touré's regime, opposition was ruthlessly crushed and by 1983 almost 2m. Guineans were estimated to have fled abroad. Allegations of widespread violations of human rights were repeatedly denied by the Government. In November 1978, at the 11th Congress of the PDG, the membership of the central organs of the party was increased, and the merging of the functions of party and state was announced. The country was renamed the People's Revolutionary Republic of Guinea. In December 1978 President Giscard d'Estaing made the first visit by a French President to independent Guinea, and plans for economic co-operation between the two countries were discussed. During 1979 Guinea furthered relations with other countries, and there was a general move away from rigid Marxism.

In legislative elections, held in January 1980, the voters approved the PDG's list of 210 candidates to the National Assembly. Sekou Touré was returned unopposed for a fourth seven-year term of office as President at an election in May 1982, with a reported 100% of the votes cast, and was re-elected Secretary-General of the PDG during the Party Congress of November 1983. A *rapprochement* with France resulted from the President's visit to Paris in 1982, despite protests by various groups of Guinean exiles. Sekou Touré also visited the USA and Canada during that year.

In January 1984 a plot to overthrow the Government was discovered when a group of 20 mercenaries was arrested in southern Senegal. It was reported that thousands of Guineans were subsequently detained, accused of complicity in the coup plot. In March 1984, however, Sekou Touré died while undergoing heart surgery in the USA. On 3 April, before a permanent successor had been chosen by the PDG, the armed forces seized power in a bloodless coup. A Comité Militaire de Redressement National (CMRN) was appointed, headed by Col (later Gen.) Lansana Conté. The PDG and the National Assembly were dissolved, and the Constitution was suspended. The CMRN affirmed Guinea's support for the OAU and the country's principles of non-alignment, and pledged to restore democracy and to respect human rights. Some 250 political prisoners were released, and a lifting of press restrictions was announced. A delegation led by the Prime Minister, Col Diarra Traoré, toured West African states to rally support from Guinea's neighbours. In May the country was renamed the Second Republic of Guinea, and in June Col Traoré visited several European countries in an effort to attract foreign investment and to consolidate relations, particularly with France. By July an estimated 200,000 Guinean exiles had returned to the country.

Trials of former politicians, most of whom had been detained since the coup in April, began in November 1984. In December President Conté extensively reshuffled his government, personally assuming the posts of Head of Government and Minister of Defence. The post of Prime Minister was abolished, and Col Traoré was demoted from that post to Minister of State for National Education. On 4 July 1985, while President Conté was chairing a summit conference of ECOWAS in Togo, Col Traoré staged an attempted coup, seizing the radio station in Conakry. Troops loyal to Conté suppressed the revolt, during which 18 people were killed. Traoré was later arrested, along with many members of his family and more than 200 suspected sympathizers and followers. A series of attacks was subsequently aimed at the Malinke ethnic group, of which both Traoré and the late Sekou Touré were members.

In October 1985 President Conté began to implement the radical economic reforms that the World Bank and IMF had demanded as preconditions for the provision of structural aid. In December the Council of Ministers was reshuffled to include a majority of civilians, and a CMRN Executive Committee was created. In addition, resident ministries were established in Guinea's four main natural regions. In May 1987 it was announced that 58 people, including nine former ministers, had been sentenced to death, following secret trials of more than 200 Guineans who had been detained either for crimes committed during the rule of Sekou Touré or for implication in the July 1985 coup attempt. The fate of Col Diarra Traoré was not mentioned. The announcement did little to allay the beliefs held by international observers (and repeatedly denied by the Government) that many detainees had already been executed in the aftermath of the abortive coup, and in December 1987 President Conté admitted publicly that Traoré had died in the hours following his detention. In January 1988 an amnesty for 67 political prisoners, including Sekou Touré's widow and son, was announced.

Reports of growing unrest within the armed forces caused Conté to postpone a proposed official visit to France in December 1987, and in January 1988, following riots in Conakry as a result of the announcement of sharp increases in retail prices of staple goods, the Government was forced instead to announce a price 'freeze'. Later that month Conté reshuffled the Council of Ministers, removing his second-in-command, Maj. Kerfalla Camara, from the post of permanent secretary of the CMRN and allocating him instead to the resident Ministry for Upper Guinea, based in Kankan. Lt-Col Sory

Doumbouya, previously Minister delegated to the Presidency in charge of defence, was reassigned to the Middle Guinea region, while Maj. Faciné Touré, a former Minister of Foreign Affairs who had been appointed to the Forest Guinea Ministry in December 1985, returned to Conakry as Minister of Transport and Public Works. The dismissal, in July 1988, of the Commander and Deputy Commander of the Presidential Guard was widely interpreted as a further attempt by Conté to consolidate his position. In September four government officials were given prison sentences, while the Norwegian honorary consul was fined, after having been found guilty of facilitating the dumping of toxic waste (which had been removed, at the request of the Conté Government, by a Norwegian cargo vessel) on Guinean territory in February 1988.

In October 1988, in a speech to commemorate the 30th anniversary of the country's independence, Conté announced the establishment of a committee to draft a new constitution. Conté also declared an amnesty for 39 political prisoners, including those who had been implicated in the 1985 coup attempt. Rumours were denied of an attempt, at the time of the anniversary celebrations, to overthrow the Government.

Government

The 1982 Constitution, providing for a National Assembly elected by universal adult suffrage, was suspended following the coup in April 1984. A Comité Militaire de Redressement National (CMRN—Military Committee for National Recovery), with 25 (later 17) members, assumed power. The President of the Republic is assisted by a Council of Ministers. In December 1984 the President also became Head of Government, and in 1985 an eight-member CMRN Executive Committee was created. Local administration is based on eight provinces, each under the authority of a provincial governor; there are 33 provincial prefectures. Provincial administrative councils meet every three months. Elections to district councils in the Conakry area were held in April 1986. The drafting of a new constitution began in late 1988.

Defence

In June 1988 Guinea had an army of 8,500, a navy of 600 and an air force of 800. Paramilitary forces numbered 9,600, including a People's Militia of about 7,000. It was announced in March 1985 that the Militia was to be dissolved and assigned to the army. Military service is compulsory and lasts for two years. Defence expenditure in 1982 was 1,850m. sylis. In August 1986 the Federal German Government agreed a US $2.4m. loan for the purchase of engineering equipment for the Guinean army. In November 1986 a non-aggression pact was signed with Sierra Leone and Liberia, Guinea's partners in the Mano River Union (see Economic Affairs).

Economic Affairs

Following Guinea's independence in 1958, a centralized socialist economy was set up, with direct state control of production and consumption in every sector except mining. However, the loss of French aid, technology and export markets was not easily overcome, and the economy did not perform well during the 1960s and 1970s, with many industrial units operating at below 25% capacity. Under the Lansana Conté Government, extensive efforts have been made to liberalize the economy and to increase participation by both local and foreign private investors.

Guinea's agricultural sector employed about 77% of the labour force in 1986 and contributed an estimated 38% of the gross domestic product (GDP) in 1985. The principal export crops are bananas, groundnuts, oil palm, citrus fruits, pineapples and coffee. The output of major food crops in 1986 was estimated at 480,000 metric tons of paddy rice, 500,000 tons of cassava and 50,000 tons of maize. Imports of food grains averaged around 130,000 tons per year during the early 1980s, covering some 25% of total food requirements and accounting for 30% of export revenue. Since July 1984, the Government has attempted to expand agricultural production by progressively increasing the official prices payable to agricultural producers. Programmes to develop rice-growing have been implemented in the Guéckédou and Siguiri areas. Under the 1987–91 medium-term recovery programme, major rural development schemes were to be implemented in the regions of Maritime Guinea and Upper Guinea. Manufacturing is based mainly on the processing of local raw materials, and in 1985 contributed about 3% of GDP.

Guinea's most important foreign-currency earner is the mining sector, which provided more than 90% of recorded export receipts in the late 1980s. The country possesses large bauxite deposits, accounting for one-third of the world's high-grade reserves. Output of crude bauxite rose from 2.6m. tons in 1972 to an estimated 14.7m. tons in 1986, and was scheduled to reach 20m. tons per year by 1990. The main sites under exploitation in 1987 were Boké, Fria-Kimbo and Kindia-Debélé. Bauxite is processed into alumina by a Fria-based company, Friguia, which is 49% state-owned. Production of alumina rose from 489,000 tons in 1963 to 708,000 tons in 1980, but declined in subsequent years, to an estimated 580,000 tons in 1985. A rehabilitation programme, aided by the European Development Fund and the European Investment Bank and due for completion in the early 1990s, aimed to increase annual capacity to 670,000 tons by 1993 and to reduce operating costs. In January 1987 the Government reached agreement with overseas producers of aluminium on a new pricing formula for bauxite, which was intended to bring about a reduction in export prices, to complement lower international prices for that commodity, with effect from January 1988. At present, Cameroon processes much of Guinea's alumina to produce aluminium.

Following the exhaustion of iron-ore deposits at Kaloum, near Conakry, in 1969, government efforts have been directed towards obtaining international financial support for the exploitation of more than 1,000m. tons of high-grade reserves on the border with Liberia. A revised scheme, developed jointly by the Governments of Guinea and Liberia, was announced in October 1987. At an estimated total cost of US $100m., it aimed to extract some 6m. tons of ore per year (commencing in 1990) from deposits at Pierre Richaud in Guinea. (The original scheme envisaged exploitation of deposits in both countries at a cost of $1,000m.) The ore would be exported through the Liberian port of Buchanan, pending the construction of a railway to connect with the proposed deep-water port at Conakry.

Diamond mining was suspended in the late 1970s, owing to smuggling and theft from the mines, but was resumed in 1980. In May 1984 the Association pour la Recherche et l'Exploitation des Diamants et de l'Or (AREDOR), jointly owned by the Government and private foreign investors, began production at Gbenko, in south-east Guinea. Output by AREDOR totalled 174,916 carats in 1987, increasing to an estimated 200,000 carats in 1988. A second joint-venture company, the Société de Diamant de Guinée, was formed in November 1984. In January 1985 private diamond and gold mining was banned, and land was transferred to AREDOR, while a loan of US $230m. was granted by the USSR towards restoring the diamond mines. Later in the same year, two joint-venture companies, the Association pour la Recherche et l'Exploitation de l'Or de Kouroussa and the Société Aurifère de Guinée (SAG), were formed to conduct exploitation of gold deposits. The production of gold, from gravel processed for diamonds, commenced in September 1987. In November 1988 SAG began exploitation of the gold reserves at Koron. Annual production was forecast at 2–3 metric tons of unrefined gold. In October of the same year an agreement was signed with the Government of Morocco, providing for the establishment of a joint-venture company to prospect for gold, silver, diamonds and other minerals in Mandiana province. Deposits of amber, cobalt, manganese and uranium have been located, and there is offshore exploration for petroleum.

Guinea also has considerable hydroelectric resources. The Yugoslav Government has financed the construction of a dam on the Bafing river, with a hydroelectric generating capacity of 100 MW, and there are plans to build a 350-MW complex on the Konkouré river. In late 1988 it was announced that Guinea's first petroleum refinery was to be built with Yugoslav assistance.

Despite its mineral wealth, Guinea remains one of the world's poorest countries. In 1985, according to World Bank estimates, Guinea's gross national product (GNP), measured at average 1983–85 prices, was US $1,940m., equivalent to $320 per head. GNP per head had increased at an average rate of only 0.8% annually, in real terms, since 1965. Overall GDP, which totalled an estimated $1,980m. (in current prices) in 1985, rose by an average of 3.8% per year between 1965 and 1980, but by just 0.9% annually between 1980 and 1985. The rate of inflation was estimated at 78% in 1986 and 33% in 1987.

GUINEA

The first development plan (1960–64) was largely financed by Eastern bloc countries, but since then more assistance has been given by the West. At the end of 1986 Guinea's total foreign debt was $1,421m. Export earnings were estimated to be $536m. in 1986, while the cost of imports amounted to $472m. in the same year. Annual debt service payments averaged an estimated $83.5m. in 1982–84. In April 1986 the 'Paris Club' of Western creditor nations rescheduled US $200m. of Guinea's official external debt. Discussions on rescheduling were also reported to have begun with Eastern bloc creditors.

Guinea's potential wealth in terms of mineral and agricultural resources has helped the Conté Government to secure substantial overseas financial support for its economic adjustment programme, comprising a 1985–87 Interim Programme for National Recovery and a 1987–91 medium-term recovery programme. In February 1986 the IMF approved a stand-by credit arrangement of SDR 33m. and the World Bank agreed to provide a structural adjustment loan worth $42.6m. Prior to, and as a precondition for, the granting of these loans, a radical restructuring of the banking sector was implemented, with the six principal state-owned banks being dissolved and replaced, in December 1985, by Guinean subsidiaries of French banks. In October 1985 a dual exchange rate for the syli was established, and in January 1986 the currency was further devalued, when the syli was abolished and replaced by a revived Guinea franc, the unit that the syli replaced in 1972. The dual exchange rate was abolished in June 1986. In March 1987, during a meeting in Paris, a special donor consultative group pledged US $670m. in investment aid and $200m. in balance-of-payments support for the 1987–89 investment programme, which allocated 42% of total investment to infrastructure projects and 24% to rural development. The programme formed part of a medium-term (1987–91) recovery programme, which envisaged further liberalization measures, including a radical reduction of the role of the public sector throughout the economy (which had commenced during the previous, three-year, programme). In addition to 'privatization' measures and the progressive withdrawal of state subsidies, it was planned to reduce the size of the public-sector work-force (which totalled around 90,000 employees at the time of Sekou Touré's death) by one-third. A new investment code, designed to encourage foreign investment in almost all sectors of the economy, was promulgated in January 1987, and in July the IMF approved a 13-month stand-by arrangement worth SDR 11.6m. and a structural adjustment facility worth SDR 36.8m. over three years. In June 1988 the International Development Association (IDA) approved a credit of $65m., in support of the second phase of the economic adjustment programme. This phase aimed to maintain average annual GDP growth of 4% over a five-year period, by means of further improvements in the management of public finances and continued retrenchment in the public sector. In November a Reform Monitoring Unit was established, to oversee the Government's economic and institutional reforms, as part of a four-year economic management project. The $27.8m. project was to be financed by both bilateral and multilateral donors. The Government envisaged that expenditure and revenue under the 1989 budget would balance at 377,000m. Guinea francs.

In 1980 Guinea became a member of both the Mano River Union (with Sierra Leone and Liberia) and the Gambia River Development Organization (with Senegal and The Gambia), thus strengthening economic links with the rest of West Africa.

In October 1987 it was announced that the member states of the Organization for the Development of the Senegal River (OMVS, see p. 219) had given their approval to Guinea's joining that organization. Sekou Touré's policy of 'positive neutrality' has been continued by the Conté Government: since 1984, agreements on aid and co-operation have been signed with a number of countries, including the USSR, the People's Republic of China, Morocco and Saudi Arabia. US aid totalled $9m. in 1984, and France provided $75.2m. in 1985, mainly in support of education, agriculture and transport projects. In 1988 the Federal Republic of Germany cancelled Guinean debt arrears to that country of $30.4m.

Social Welfare

Wages are fixed according to the Government Labour Code. A maximum working week of 48 hours is in force for industrial workers. In 1979 there were 248 hospitals and dispensaries, with a total of 6,858 beds. In 1981 there were only an estimated 100 physicians working in official medical services. Private medical care has been legally available since July 1984.

Education

Education is provided free of charge at every level. Primary education, beginning at seven years of age and lasting for six years, is officially compulsory. However, estimated enrolment at primary schools in 1986 was equivalent to only 22% of the relevant age-group (boys 30%; girls 14%). Secondary education, from the age of 13, lasts for a further seven years, comprising a first cycle of four years and a second of three years. In 1985 the estimated enrolment at secondary schools was equivalent to only 7% of children (11% of boys; 4% of girls) in the appropriate age-group. There are universities at Conakry and Kankan. In 1985, according to estimates by UNESCO, the average rate of adult illiteracy was 71.7% (males 60.3%; females 82.8%). Under a six-year transitional education plan, announced in June 1984, ideological education was eliminated and French was adopted as the language of instruction in schools. Teaching of the eight national languages has been suspended. Private schools were legalized in 1984, after 23 years of being banned under the regime of the late President Sekou Touré.

Public Holidays

1989: 1 January (New Year's Day), 27 March (Easter Monday), 1 May (Labour Day), 7 May* (Id al-Fitr, end of Ramadan), 27 August (Anniversary of Women's Revolt), 28 September (Referendum Day), 2 October (Republic Day), 13 October* (Mouloud, birth of Muhammad), 1 November (All Saints' Day), 22 November (Day of 1970 Invasion), 25 December (Christmas).

1990: 1 January (New Year's Day), 16 April (Easter Monday), 27 April* (Id al-Fitr, end of Ramadan), 1 May (Labour Day), 27 August (Anniversary of Women's Revolt), 28 September (Referendum Day), 2 October (Republic Day and Mouloud, birth of Muhammad*), 1 November (All Saints' Day), 22 November (Day of 1970 Invasion), 25 December (Christmas).

* These holidays are determined by the Islamic lunar calendar and may vary by one or two days from the dates given.

Weights and Measures

The metric system is in force.

GUINEA

Statistical Survey

Source (unless otherwise stated): Service de la Statistique Générale, Bureau du Premier Ministre, Conakry; tel. 44-21-48.

Area and Population

AREA, POPULATION AND DENSITY

Area (sq km)	245,857*
Population (census results)	
15 January–31 May 1955	2,570,219†
4–17 February 1983	4,533,240‡
Population (UN estimates at mid-year)§	
1985	6,075,000
1986	6,225,000
1987	6,380,000
Density (per sq km) at February 1983	18.4‡

* 94,926 sq miles.
† Estimates for African population, based on results of sample survey.
‡ Excluding adjustment for underenumeration.
§ Not revised to take account of the 1983 census results.

REGIONS (population at mid-1963)

Region	Area (sq km)	Population ('000)
Beyla	17,542	170
Boffa	6,003	90
Boké*	11,053	105
Conakry	308	172
Dabola	6,000	54
Dalaba	5,750	105
Dinguiraye	11,000	67
Dubréka*	5,676	86
Faranah*	12,397	94
Forécariah	4,265	98
Fria	n.a.	27
Gaoual	11,503	81
Guéckédou	4,157	130
Kankan	27,488	176
Kindia	8,828	152
Kissidougou	8,872	133
Kouroussa	16,405	93
Labé	7,616	283
Macenta	8,710	123
Mali	8,800	152
Mamou	6,159	162
N'Zérékoré	10,183	195
Pita	4,000	154
Siguiri	23,377	179
Télimélé	8,155	147
Tougué	6,200	75
Youkounkoun	5,500	55
Total	**245,857**	**3,360**

* The provinces of Boké, Dubréka and Faranah were abolished by presidential decree in January 1988.

PRINCIPAL TOWNS (population at December 1972)

Conakry (capital) 525,671 (later admitted to be overstated); Kankan 60,000.

BIRTHS AND DEATHS (UN estimates, annual averages)

	1970–75	1975–80	1980–85
Birth rate (per 1,000)	46.9	46.9	46.8
Death rate (per 1,000)	26.8	25.3	23.5

Source: UN, *World Population Prospects: Estimates and Projections as Assessed in 1984*.

ECONOMICALLY ACTIVE POPULATION
(ILO estimates, '000 persons at mid-1980)

	Males	Females	Total
Agriculture, etc.	1,153	966	2,119
Industry	183	54	237
Services	196	74	270
Total	**1,532**	**1,094**	**2,626**

Source: ILO, *Economically Active Population Estimates and Projections, 1950–2025*.

Mid-1986 (estimates in '000): Agriculture, etc. 2,226; Total 2,894 (Source: FAO, *Production Yearbook*).

Agriculture

PRINCIPAL CROPS (FAO estimates, '000 metric tons)

	1984	1985	1986
Maize	42*	40*	50
Sorghum	3*	3*	4
Rice (paddy)*	403	437	480
Other cereals	72*	43*	70
Sweet potatoes	70*	70	70
Cassava (Manioc)	496*	500	500
Yams	60*	61	61
Taro (Coco yam)	32*	32*	32
Pulses	45	47	50
Coconuts	15	15	15
Vegetables	420	420	420
Sugar cane	225	225	200
Citrus fruits	160	160	161
Bananas	104*	105*	105
Plantains	350	350	350
Pineapples	20	20	20
Other fruits	36	35	37
Palm kernels*	40	40	40
Groundnuts (in shell)	82*	74*	75
Coffee (green)	15*	15*	15

* Official estimates.

Source: FAO, *Production Yearbook*.

LIVESTOCK
(FAO estimates, '000 head, year ending September)

	1984	1985	1986
Cattle	1,850	1,800	1,838
Sheep	455	460	465
Goats	450	460	470
Pigs	45	47	49
Asses	3	3	3

Poultry (FAO estimates, million): 10 in 1984; 11 in 1985; 12 in 1986.
Source: FAO, *Production Yearbook*.

LIVESTOCK PRODUCTS (FAO estimates, metric tons)

	1984	1985	1986
Beef and veal	19,000	18,000	18,000
Poultry meat	14,000	15,000	16,000
Other meat	6,000	7,000	7,000
Cows' milk	43,000	42,000	42,000
Goats' milk	4,000	4,000	4,000
Hen eggs	10,710	11,550	12,180
Cattle hides	3,330	3,240	3,321

Source: FAO, *Production Yearbook*.

GUINEA

Statistical Survey

Forestry

ROUNDWOOD REMOVALS
(FAO estimates, '000 cubic metres, excluding bark)

	1984	1985	1986
Sawlogs, veneer logs and logs for sleepers*	180	180	180
Other industrial wood	414	424	434
Fuel wood	3,561	3,645	3,736
Total	4,155	4,249	4,350

* Assumed to be unchanged since 1972.
Source: FAO, *Yearbook of Forest Products*.

SAWNWOOD PRODUCTION
Total (incl. boxboards): 90,000 cubic metres per year in 1972–86 (FAO estimates).

Fishing

(FAO estimates, '000 metric tons, live weight)

	1984	1985	1986
Freshwater fishes	1.8	2.0	2.0
Sardinellas	19.1	20.4	20.4
Other marine fishes	7.1	7.6	7.6
Total catch	28.0	30.0	30.0

Source: FAO, *Yearbook of Fishery Statistics*.

Mining

	1983	1984	1985
Bauxite ('000 metric tons)*	12,986	14,738	13,956
Diamonds ('000 carats)†	40	48	112

* Data from *World Metal Statistics*, London.
† Estimates by the US Bureau of Mines.
Source: UN, *Industrial Statistics Yearbook* and *Monthly Bulletin of Statistics*.
Bauxite ('000 metric tons): 14,656 in 1986 (Source: *World Metal Statistics*, London).

Industry

SELECTED PRODUCTS (estimated production; '000 metric tons, unless otherwise indicated)

	1983	1984	1985
Electric energy (million kWh)	499	499	500
Raw sugar	14	10	5
Palm oil*	45	45	45
Plywood ('000 cubic metres)*	2	2	2
Alumina (calcined equivalent)†	583	508	580

* FAO estimates.
† Estimates by the US Bureau of Mines.
Source: UN, *Industrial Statistics Yearbook*.
Plywood (FAO estimate): 2,000 cubic metres in 1986 (Source: FAO, *Yearbook of Forest Products*).

Finance

CURRENCY AND EXCHANGE RATES
Monetary Units
100 centimes = 1 franc guineén (FG or Guinea franc).
Denominations
Notes: 25, 50, 100, 500, 1,000 and 5,000 francs.
Sterling and Dollar Equivalents (30 September 1988)
£1 sterling = 845.5 Guinea francs;
US $1 = 500.0 Guinea francs;
1,000 Guinea francs = £1.183 = $2.000.

Note: The Guinea franc was reintroduced in January 1986, replacing (at par) the syli. At the same time, the currency was devalued by more than 90%. The syli had been introduced in October 1972, replacing the original Guinea franc (at 10 francs per syli). In June 1975 the syli's value was linked to the IMF special drawing right at an exchange rate of SDR 1 = 24.6853 sylis. This remained in force until the syli's abolition. The average exchange rate of sylis per US dollar was: 22.366 in 1982; 23.095 in 1983; 24.090 in 1984. Some of the figures in this Survey are still in terms of sylis.

BUDGET* (million sylis)

	1975/76	1976/77
Ordinary budget:		
Revenue	4,312	5,283
Expenditure	3,047	3,904
Capital budget	1,614	3,089

*Unofficial estimates.
1979 (million sylis): Balanced at 11,250 (Current Budget 6,790, Capital Budget 4,460).
1982 (million sylis): Revenue 17,013 (Taxation 10,924, Other current receipts 6,089), excluding grants received (585).
1983 (million sylis): Revenue 9,386 (Taxation 6,150, Other current receipts 3,236), excluding grants received (485).
Source (for 1982 and 1983): IMF, *Government Finance Statistics Yearbook*.
1989: Budget balanced at 377,000m. Guinea francs.

NATIONAL ACCOUNTS
(estimates, million sylis at current prices)
Expenditure on the Gross Domestic Product

	1983	1984	1985
Government final consumption expenditure	8,270	9,170	9,860
Private final consumption expenditure	34,460	37,760	40,510
Increase in stocks / Gross fixed capital formation	8,150	9,230	9,120
Total domestic expenditure	50,880	56,160	59,490
Exports of goods and services	11,520	12,350	12,520
Less Imports of goods and services	12,470	14,180	14,240
GDP in purchasers' values	49,930	54,330	57,770
GDP at constant 1980 prices	36,942	37,962	37,552

GUINEA

Gross Domestic Product by Economic Activity

	1983	1984	1985
Agriculture, hunting, forestry and fishing	18,510	20,150	21,820
Mining and quarrying	5,640	6,050	6,180
Manufacturing	1,430	1,610	1,700
Electricity, gas and water	140	160	170
Construction	1,160	1,370	1,380
Trade, restaurants and hotels	6,080	6,660	7,040
Transport, storage and communications	1,160	1,280	1,340
Finance, insurance, real estate and business services	930	1,030	1,080
Public administration and defence	5,770	6,300	6,810
Other services	380	420	430
GDP at factor cost	41,200	45,030	47,950
Indirect taxes, *less* subsidies	8,730	9,300	9,820
GDP in purchasers' values	49,930	54,330	57,770

Source: UN Economic Commission for Africa, *African Statistical Yearbook*.

External Trade

PRINCIPAL COMMODITIES (million sylis)

Imports	1978	1979	1980
Food	123	628	389
Beverages	277	4	n.a.
Petroleum products	3	720	1,173
Building materials	2	106	117
Agricultural equipment	85	197	153
Textiles	291	221	117
Pharmaceutical products	115	99	92
Industrial processing equipment	548	841	1,087
Total (incl. others)	2,411	4,568	3,877

Exports	1978	1979	1980
Bauxite	4,728	7,082	8,571
Alumina	1,740		
Pulses and oilseeds	n.a.	257	253
Fresh fruit	n.a.	27	11
Total (incl. others)	6,567	7,383	8,852

Source: Ministère des Finances et Direction des Douanes.

PRINCIPAL TRADING PARTNERS

Imports (14 months, 1975–76): EEC 2,301 million sylis; USA 743 million sylis.
Exports (1973): EEC 1,260 million sylis, USA 545 million sylis.

Transport

RAILWAYS (traffic)

	1983	1984	1985
Freight ton-km (million)	524	530	534

Source: UN Economic Commission for Africa, *African Statistical Yearbook*.

ROAD TRAFFIC ('000 motor vehicles in use)

	1983	1984	1985
Passenger cars	98	103	106
Commercial vehicles	100	100	113

Source: UN Economic Commission for Africa, *African Statistical Yearbook*.

INTERNATIONAL SEA-BORNE SHIPPING
(estimated freight traffic, '000 metric tons)

	1983	1984	1985
Goods loaded	10,403	10,430	10,106
Goods unloaded	666	630	489

Source: UN, *Monthly Bulletin of Statistics*.

CIVIL AVIATION (traffic on scheduled services, '000)*

	1981	1982
Kilometres flown	3,100	3,100
Passengers carried	128	131
Passenger-km	142,000	144,000
Freight ton-km	600	700

* UN estimates.
Source: UN, *Statistical Yearbook*.

Communications Media

	1981	1982	1983
Radio receivers ('000 in use)	144	153	160
Television receivers ('000 in use)	7	8	8

Daily newspapers (1984): 1 (average circulation 13,000 copies).
1986 ('000 in use): Radio receivers 200; television receivers 10.
Source: UNESCO, *Statistical Yearbook*.

Education

(1987/88)

	Institutions	Teachers	Pupils		
			Males	Females	Total
Primary	2,315	7,239	199,516	89,398	288,914
Secondary General*	225	3,577	57,683	18,810	76,493
Teacher training	9	123	634	552	1,186
Vocational	26	635	3,327	1,347	4,674
Higher	10	1,033	5,220	695	5,915

* 1986/87 figures.
Source: Direction de la Statistique et de la Planification de l'Education, Conakry.

Directory

The Constitution

The Constitution of the People's Revolutionary Republic of Guinea, adopted in May 1982, was suspended in April 1984 by the Military Committee for National Recovery, which had assumed power in a coup. The country's former name, the Republic of Guinea, was subsequently restored. The establishment of a committee to draft a new constitution was announced in October 1988.

The Government

HEAD OF STATE

President: Gen. LANSANA CONTÉ (took office 4 April 1984).

MILITARY COMMITTEE FOR NATIONAL RECOVERY
(February 1989)

Gen. LANSANA CONTÉ (President).
Maj. ABOU CAMARA (Permanent Secretary).
Lt-Col SORY DOUMBOUYA.
Maj. MAMADOU BALDET.
Maj. KEKOURA CAMARA.
Maj. KERFALLA CAMARA.
Maj. SEKOU MANKAN CAMARA.
Maj. ALPHA OUMAR DIALLO.
Maj. ALHOUSSÉNY FOFANA.
Maj. JEAN KOLIPÉ LAMA.
Maj. BABACAR N'DIAYE.
Maj. OUSMANE SOW.
Maj. FACINÉ TOURÉ.
Maj. JEAN TRAORÉ.
Capt. ABDOURAHMANE DIALLO.
Capt. MOHAMED TRAORÉ.
Capt. JOSEPH GBAGO ZOUMANIGUI.

COUNCIL OF MINISTERS
(February 1989)

Head of Government, Minister of Defence, Security and Information: Gen. LANSANA CONTÉ.
Minister and Permanent Secretary of the CMRN in charge of Relations with Non-Governmental Organizations: Maj. ABOU CAMARA.
Minister delegated to the Presidency for National Defence: Maj. BABACAR N'DIAYE.
Minister delegated to the Presidency for Economic and Financial Control: KEMOKO KEITA.
Minister delegated to the Presidency for Missions: Capt. ABDOURAHMANE DIALLO.
Minister delegated to the Presidency for Information, Culture and Tourism: ZAÏNOUL ABIDINÉ SANOUSSI.
Minister of the Interior and Decentralization: Maj. ALI SOFANI.
Minister of Planning and Co-operation: EDOUARD BENJAMIN.
Minister of Justice and Keeper of the Seals: BASSIROU BARRY.
Minister of Foreign Affairs: Maj. JEAN TRAORÉ.
Minister of Economy and Finance: LAMINE BOLIVOGUI.
Minister of Agriculture and Animal Resources: Maj. ALHOUSSÉNY FOFANA.
Minister of Natural Resources and the Environment: Dr OUSMANE SYLLA.
Minister of Industry, Trade and Crafts: Maj. OUSMANE SOW.
Minister of Urban Development and Housing: MBAYA SIDIBE.
Minister of National Education: SALIOU KOUMBASSA.
Minister of Public Health and Population: PATHE DIALLO.
Minister of Transport and Public Works: Maj. FACINÉ TOURÉ.
Minister of Administrative Reform and the Public Service: MAMOUNA BANGOURA.
Minister of Youth and Sports: El Hadj AMADOU BILALI DIALLO.
Minister of Social Affairs and Employment: Maj. JEAN KOLIPÉ LAMA.
Minister of Posts and Telecommunications: HERVÉ VINCENT BANGOURA.
Minister, Secretary-General of the Presidency: ALSENY RENÉ GOMEZ.
Resident Minister for Maritime Guinea (Kindia): Capt. JOSEPH GBAGO ZOUMANIGUI.
Resident Minister for Middle Guinea (Labé): Lt-Col SORY DOUMBOUYA.
Resident Minister for Upper Guinea (Kankan): Maj. KERFALLA CAMARA.
Resident Minister for Forest Guinea (N'Zérékoré): Maj. MAMADOU BALDET.

There are also 5 Secretaries of State.

MINISTRIES

Office of the President: Conakry; tel. 44-11-47; telex 623.
Permanent Secretariat of the CMRN: Conakry.
Ministry of Administrative Reform and the Public Service: Conakry.
Ministry of Agriculture and Animal Resources: BP 576, Conakry; tel. 44-19-66.
Ministry of Economy and Finance: Conakry; tel. 44-21-62; telex 2199.
Ministry of Foreign Affairs: Conakry; tel. 40-50-55; telex 634.
Ministry of Industry, Trade and Crafts: Conakry.
Ministry of the Interior and Decentralization: Conakry; telex 621.
Ministry of Justice: Conakry; tel. 44-16-04.
Ministry of National Education: Conakry; tel. 44-19-01; telex 631.
Ministry of Natural Resources and the Environment: Conakry.
Ministry of Planning and Co-operation: Conakry.
Ministry of Posts and Telecommunications: Conakry.
Ministry of Public Health and Population: Conakry.
Ministry of Social Affairs and Employment: Conakry; tel. 44-33-05.
Ministry of Transport and Public Works: Conakry.
Ministry of Urban Development and Housing: Conakry.
Ministry of Youth and Sports: Conakry.

Legislature

ASSEMBLÉE NATIONALE

The National Assembly was dissolved by the Military Committee for National Recovery on 3 April 1984, following the military coup.

Political Organizations

Following the military coup of April 1984, the country's sole political party, the Parti démocratique de Guinée (PDG), was dissolved. Although no political organizations have been formally active in Guinea since the coup, there still exist several groups, which were originally formed by Guineans in exile to oppose the regime of the late President Sekou Touré:

Mouvement pour le renouveau en Guinée: fmrly the Union du peuple guinéen (UPG); Pres. Maj. DIALLO THIERNO.

Organisation unifiée pour la libération de la Guinée (OULG): based mainly in Côte d'Ivoire; Pres. IBRAHIMA KAKE.

Six other groups are based in France: **Association de la jeunesse guinéenne en France (AJGF); Groupe de réflexion des Guinéens (GRG); Ligue guinéenne des droits de l'homme (LGDHC); Regroupement de Guinéens de l'exterieur (RGE); Solidarité guinéenne (SG); Union des forces patriotiques guinéennes (UFPG).**

Diplomatic Representation

EMBASSIES IN GUINEA

Algeria: BP 1004, Conakry; tel. 44-15-03; Chargé d'affaires a.i.: BOUCHERIT NACEUR.
Benin: BP 787, Conakry; Ambassador: JONAS GBOHOUNDADA.
Canada: Corniche Sud, BP 99, Coleah, Conakry; tel. 46-36-26; telex 2170; Chargé d'affaires a.i.: ANDRÉE DUBOIS.

GUINEA

Directory

China, People's Republic: BP 714, Conakry; Ambassador: YU HUIMIN.
Congo: BP 178, Conakry; Ambassador: Mme C. ECKOMBAND.
Côte d'Ivoire: Conakry; telex 2126; Chargé d'affaires: ATTA YACOUBA.
Cuba: BP 71, Conakry; Ambassador: COLMAN FERREI.
Czechoslovakia: BP 1009 bis, Conakry; tel. 46-14-37; Ambassador: Dr ZDENKO HRČKA.
Egypt: BP 389, Conakry; Ambassador: HUSSEIN EL-NAZER.
France: BP 373, Conakry; tel. 44-16-55; telex 600; Ambassador: ROBERT THOMAS.
German Democratic Republic: Conakry; tel. 44-15-16; Ambassador: Dr WOLFGANG KUBISCH.
Germany, Federal Republic: BP 540, Conakry; telex 779; Ambassador: Dr PETER TRUHART.
Ghana: BP 732, Conakry; Ambassador: LARRY BIMI.
Guinea-Bissau: BP 298, Conakry; Ambassador: ARAFAN ANSU CAMARA.
Iraq: Conakry; telex 2162; Chargé d'affaires: MUNIR CHIHAB AHMAD.
Italy: BP 84, Village Camayenne, Conakry; tel. 46-23-32; telex 636; Ambassador: (vacant).
Japan: BP 895, Conakry; tel. 46-14-38; telex 782; Chargé d'affaires: TERUO OKADA.
Korea, Democratic People's Republic: BP 723, Conakry; Ambassador: KIM CHIN-KI.
Lebanon: BP 342, Conakry; telex 2106; Ambassador: MOHAMED ISSA.
Liberia: BP 18, Conakry; telex 2105; Chargé d'affaires: ANTHONY ZEZO.
Libya: BP 1183, Conakry; telex 645; Chargé d'affaires: MUFTAH MADI.
Mali: Conakry; telex 2154; Ambassador: KIBILI DEMBA DIALLO.
Morocco: BP 193, Conakry; telex 22422; Ambassador: MOHAMED AYOUCH.
Nigeria: BP 54, Conakry; telex 633; Ambassador: GBOKO YOUGH.
Romania: BP 348, Conakry; Ambassador: PETRU DESPOT.
Saudi Arabia: BP 611, Conakry; telex 2146; Chargé d'affaires: WAHEEB SHAIKHON.
Sierra Leone: BP 625, Conakry; Ambassador: Mrs MARIAM KAMARA.
Switzerland: BP 720, Conakry; tel. 46-26-12; telex 22231; Chargé d'affaires: SIEGFRIED BRAZEROL.
Syria: BP 609, Conakry; tel. 46-13-20; Chargé d'affaires: BECHARA KHAROUF.
Tanzania: BP 189, Conakry; tel. 46-13-32; telex 2104; Ambassador: NORMAN KIONDO.
USSR: BP 329, Conakry; Ambassador: VLADIMIR N. RAYEVSKY.
USA: BP 603, Conakry; tel. 44-15-20; Ambassador: SAMUEL E. LUPO.
Viet-Nam: BP 551, Conakry; Ambassador: PHAM VAN SON.
Yugoslavia: BP 1154, Conakry; Ambassador: LJILJANA TODOROVA.
Zaire: BP 880, Conakry; telex 632; Ambassador: B. KALUBYE.

Judicial System

There is a High Court whose jurisdiction extends to political cases. The Cour d'appel, the Chambre des mises en accusation and the Tribunal supérieur de cassation are at Conakry. A Court of State Security and a military tribunal were established in August 1985 to try cases of crime against the internal and external security of the state.

Tribunaux du premier degré exist at Conakry and Kankan and have jurisdiction over civil and criminal cases and also act as industrial courts. A justice of the peace sits at N'Zérékoré.

Président, Cour d'Appel: FODÉ MAMADOU TOURÉ.

Religion

It is estimated that 95% of the population are Muslims and 1.5% Christians. In May 1967 President Sekou Touré ordered that all priests should be Guinea nationals.

ISLAM

Islamic League: Conakry; Sec.-Gen. El Hadj AHMED TIDIANE TRAORÉ.

CHRISTIANITY
The Anglican Communion

Anglicans in Guinea are adherents of the Church of the Province of West Africa, comprising 11 dioceses. The Archbishop of the Province is the Bishop of Liberia. The diocese of Guinea (formerly the Rio Pongas), inaugurated in August 1985, is the first French-speaking diocese in the Province. The Bishop of Guinea also has jurisdiction over Guinea-Bissau.

Bishop of Guinea: Rt Rev. A. WILLIE Y. MACAULEY, BP 105, Conakry.

The Roman Catholic Church

Guinea comprises the archdiocese of Conakry (with an estimated 20,000 adherents at 31 December 1977), the diocese of N'Zérékoré (19,300 adherents at 31 December 1986) and the apostolic prefecture of Kankan (15,040 adherents in 1968), of which the Archbishop of Conakry is Apostolic Administrator.

Bishops' Conference: Conférence Episcopale de la Guinée, BP 1006 bis, Conakry; Pres. Mgr ROBERT SARAH, Archbishop of Conakry.

Archbishop of Conakry: Mgr ROBERT SARAH, Archevêché, BP 1006 bis, Conakry; tel. 44-36-27.

There are also six Protestant mission centres active in Guinea: four run by British and two by US societies.

The Press

Ecole Nouvelle: Conakry; monthly; education.
Fonike: BP 341, Conakry; sport and general; Dir IBRAHIMA KALIL DIARE.
Horoya (Liberty): BP 191, Conakry; weekly; Man. Dir MOHAMED MOUNIR CAMARA.
Journal Officiel de Guinée: BP 156, Conakry; fortnightly; govt.
La Guinéenne: Conakry; monthly; women's interest.
Le Travailleur de Guinée: Conakry; monthly; trade union organ.

NEWS AGENCIES

Agence Guinéenne de Presse: BP 1535, Conakry; tel. 46-54-14; telex 640; f. 1960; Man. Dir MOHAMED CONDÉ.

Foreign Bureaux

Agentstvo Pechati Novosti (APN) (USSR): BP 414, Conakry; Dir VASILI ZUBKOV.
Xinhua (New China) News Agency (People's Republic of China): BP 455, Conakry; tel. 46-13-47; telex 2128; Correspondent ZHANG ZHENYI.

TASS (USSR) is also represented.

Publisher

Editions du Ministère de l'Education Nationale: Secrétariat à la Recherche scientifique, BP 561, Conakry; general and educational.

Radio and Television

In 1986 there were an estimated 200,000 radio receivers and 10,000 television receivers in use.

Radiodiffusion-Télévision Guinéenne (RTG): BP 391, Conakry; telex 640; programmes in French, English, Créole-English, Portuguese, Arabic and local languages; colour transmissions; Man. Dir EMMANUEL KATTY.

Finance

(cap. = capital; m. = million; amounts in Guinea francs unless otherwise stated); br. = branch.

BANKING
Central Bank

Banque Centrale de la République de Guinée: 12 blvd du Commerce, BP 692, Conakry; tel. 44-17-25; telex 22225; f. 1960; controls all banking activity; Gov. KERFALLA YANSANA; 4 brs.

Commercial Banks

As part of the economic reform programme implemented during the latter part of 1985 and in 1986, all existing state-owned

GUINEA

banks were liquidated and replaced by the following joint-venture institutions:

Banque Internationale pour l'Afrique en Guinée (BIAG): blvd du Commerce, BP 1419, Conakry; telex 22180; f. 1985; cap. 500m.; 51% state-owned, 34% owned by Banque Internationale pour l'Afrique de l'Ouest (France); provides 'offshore' banking services; Pres. JEAN TRAORÉ; Man. Dir YVES DURAND.

Banque Internationale pour le Commerce et l'Industrie de la Guinée (BICI-GUI): route du Niger, BP 1484, Carrefour Moukarim, Conakry 1; tel. 44-37-84; telex 22175; f. 1985; cap. US $9m., dep. $28.9m.; 39.6% state-owned, 15.4% by Banque Nationale de Paris (BNP); Pres. JEAN TRAORÉ; Man. Dir JEAN TABARIES.

Société Générale de Banques en Guinée: ave de la République, BP 1514, Conakry 1; tel. 44-25-65; telex 22212; f. 1985; cap. 617.1m. (Dec. 1986); 34% owned by Société Générale (France); Pres. J. M. LE PETIT; Man. Dir H. YON.

Union Internationale de Banque en Guinée (UIBG): Conakry; f. 1987; 51% owned by Crédit Lyonnais (France).

Islamic Bank

Banque Islamique de Guinée: ave de la République, BP 1247, Conakry; tel. 44-50-73; telex 2184; f. 1983; cap. US $1.9m. (Dec. 1986); 51% owned by Dar al-Maal al-Islami (DMI); provides Islamic banking services; Pres. MOHAMED FOUAD EL SARRAF; Man. MOHAMED YAYA KOROMA.

INSURANCE

Société Nationale d'Assurances et de Réassurances de la République de Guinée (SNAR): BP 179, Conakry; Man. Dir OUSMANE SANOKO.

Union Guinéenne d'Assurances et de Réassurances (UGAR): Conakry; f. 1988; cap. 2,000m. 60% state-owned, 40% by Union des Assurances de Paris.

Trade and Industry

DEVELOPMENT AGENCY

Caisse Centrale de Coopération Economique (CCCE): Conakry; telex 780; French agency for economic co-operation; Dir in Guinea GUY LECAMUS.

CHAMBERS OF COMMERCE

Chambre de Commerce, d'Industrie et d'Agriculture de Guinée: BP 545, Conakry; tel. 44-44-95; telex 609; f. 1985; Chair. Capt. THIANA DIALLO; 70 mems.

Chambre Economique de Guinée: BP 609, Conakry.

TRADE ORGANIZATION

Entreprise Nationale Import-Export (IMPORTEX): BP 152, Conakry; tel. 44-28-13; telex 625; state-owned import and export agency; Dir MAMADOU BOBO DIENG.

NATIONALIZED INDUSTRIES

Under the regime of the late President Sekou Touré, a total of 35 state companies, responsible for all sectors of the economy, were established. By the end of 1988, 22 of the 24 state companies whose dissolution, restructuring or 'privatization' had been announced in 1986 (as part of a programme of economic and financial reform) had been transferred to private ownership.

TRADE UNIONS

The Military Committee for National Recovery has announced the legalization of free trade unions.

Confédération des travailleurs de Guinée (CTG): BP 237, Conakry; f. 1984 to replace the Confédération nationale des travailleurs de Guinée, which had formed part of the structure of the Parti démocratique de Guinée; Sec.-Gen. Dr MOHAMED SAMBA KÉBÉ.

Transport

RAILWAYS

There are 662 km of 1-m gauge track from Conakry to Kankan in the east of the country, crossing the Niger at Kouroussa. Three lines for the transport of bauxite link Sangaredi with the port of Kamsar in the west, and Conakry with Kindia and Fria, a total of 376 km. Arrangements have been made with the Liberian authorities for the use of the line linking the Nimba iron ore deposits with the port of Buchanan, and rehabilitation work is being carried out.

Office National des Chemins de Fer de Guinée (ONCFG): BP 581, Conakry; Gen. Man. SEKOU CAMARA.

ROADS

In 1985 there were 29,108 km of roads, including 4,000 km of main roads and 7,608 km of secondary roads; 4,366 km of the road network was paved. An 895-km cross-country road links Conakry to Bamako, in Mali, and the main highway connecting Dakar (Senegal) to Abidjan (Côte d'Ivoire) also crosses Guinea.

The second phase of a rehabilitation and maintenance project, covering 54% of Guinea's paved roads, began in 1984, financed by a loan of US $14m. from the International Development Association (IDA). The construction of a 303-km bituminized road from Guéckédou to N'Zérékoré, scheduled for completion in 1988, will connect the forested south-eastern region to the internal road network. The construction of roads linking Conakry to Mamou, Mamou to Kankan and Dubréka to Yienguissa is also planned. In June 1988 it was announced that 10,000 km of roads were to be improved, with the help of a $55m. credit from the IDA.

Office du Projet Routier: BP 581, Conakry.

Société Générale des Transports de Guinée (SOGETRAG): Conakry; f. 1984; state-owned; bus operator.

SHIPPING

Conakry and Kamsar are the international seaports. In 1987 3.1m. tons of bauxite were exported through Conakry and 9m. tons through Kamsar. A US $38m. port rehabilitation programme, supported by the World Bank and other donor agencies, was carried out in Conakry in 1983–87 and included the upgrading and extension of quays and storage facilities. A naval repair dockyard and deep-water port facilities were also to be constructed at Conakry, at a cost of $60m., as part of a further (1989–92) port extension programme. The merchant fleet (13 vessels in 1981) was also to be expanded. There are 2,450 m of quays providing nine alongside berths for ocean-going ships at Conakry.

Port Autonome de Conakry: BP 715, Conakry; tel. 44-27-37; telex 22276.

Port Autonome de Kamsar: Kamsar.

ENTRAT: BP 315, Conakry; state-owned stevedoring and forwarding co; Dir-Gen. DAOUDA DIAWARA.

Société Navale Guinéenne: BP 522, Conakry; telex 644; f. 1968; state-owned shipping co; agents for Cie Maritime des Chargeurs Réunis, Cie de Navigation Fraissinet et Cyprien Fabre, Delta Steamship Lines, Elder Dempster Line, Hanseatic Africa Line, Leif Hoëgh and Co A/S, Lloyd Triestino, Nouvelle Cie de Paquebots (NCP), Palm Line, Scandinavian West Africa Line, Société Navale de l'Ouest, United West Africa Service; Dir-Gen. NABY SYLLA.

SOTRAMAR: Kamsar; f. 1971; bauxite export from mines at Boké through port of Kamsar.

CIVIL AVIATION

There is an international airport at Conakry-Gbessia, and smaller airfields at Labé, Kankan and Faranah.

Air Guinée: ave de la République, BP 12, Conakry; f. 1960; international and internal services; flights to Bamako, Dakar, Freetown and Monrovia; Dir-Gen. NFA MOUSSA DIANE; fleet of 1 Ilyushin Il-18, 2 Antonov An-12B, 4 An-24, 1 737-200C, 1 Yak-40, 1 Dash-7.

Société de Gestion et d'Exploitation de l'Aéroport de Conakry (SOGEAC): Conakry; f. 1987 to manage Conakry international airport; 51% state-owned.

Tourism

Office National du Tourisme et de l'Hôtellerie (ONATHOL): square des Martyrs, BP 1304, Conakry; tel. 44-26-06; f. 1984; state tourist office.

GUINEA-BISSAU

Introductory Survey

Location, Climate, Language, Religion, Flag, Capital

The Republic of Guinea-Bissau lies on the west coast of Africa, with Senegal to the north and Guinea to the east and south. The climate is tropical, although maritime and Sahelian influences are felt. The average temperature is 20°C (68°F). The official language is Portuguese, of which the locally spoken form is Creole (Crioulo). Other dialects are also widely spoken. The principal religious beliefs are animism and Islam. There is a small minority of Roman Catholics and other Christian groups. The national flag (proportions 2 by 1) has two equal horizontal stripes, of yellow and green, and a red vertical stripe, with a five-pointed black star at its centre, at the hoist. The capital is Bissau.

Recent History

Portuguese Guinea (Guiné) was settled by the Portuguese in the 15th century. Small nationalist groups began to form in the 1950s, and the Partido Africano da Independência da Guiné e Cabo Verde (PAIGC) was formed in 1956. Fighting broke out in the early 1960s, and by 1972 the PAIGC was in control of two-thirds of the country. In 1973 a National People's Assembly was elected in 'liberated' areas, and the independence of the Republic of Guinea-Bissau was proclaimed in September, with Luiz Cabral as President of the State Council. To combat the PAIGC's guerrilla campaign, about 40,000 Portuguese troops were operating in the territory. Portuguese forces began to sustain heavy losses in 1973–74, and this may have been a factor in the military coup in Portugal in April 1974. This coup brought the fighting to an end, and in August the new Portuguese Government and the PAIGC negotiated an agreement to end Portuguese rule. Accordingly, on 10 September 1974, Portugal recognized the independence of Guinea-Bissau.

The PAIGG regime introduced measures to lay the foundations for a socialist state. At elections in December 1976 and January 1977 voters chose regional councils from which a new National People's Assembly was later selected. In 1978 Francisco Mendes, who had been Chief State Commissioner since 1973, died; he was replaced by Commander João Vieira, the former State Commissioner for the Armed Forces and President of the National People's Assembly.

Until 1980 the PAIGC supervised both Cape Verde and Guinea-Bissau, the two constitutions remaining separate, but with a view to eventual unification. However, on 14 November, four days after the Government had approved a new constitution, President Cabral was deposed in a coup and Vieira was installed as Chairman of the Council of the Revolution. The National People's Assembly was dissolved.

At the PAIGC Congress in 1981, it was decided to preserve the single-party status of the PAIGC, with Vieira as Secretary-General, despite Cape Verde's withdrawal from the party. Diplomatic relations between the two countries were restored after the release of Cabral from detention in 1982. Vítor Saúde Maria, Vice-Chairman of the Council of the Revolution and former Minister of Foreign Affairs, was appointed Prime Minister in 1982, the post having been vacant since the 1980 coup; several ministers who were regarded as left-wing lost their portfolios.

In 1983 President Vieira established a commission, headed by the Minister of Justice, to examine plans for the revision of the Constitution and the electoral law. In 1984 President Vieira dismissed Saúde Maria from the premiership. Although the reason given for his dismissal was alleged involvement in a planned coup, it appeared that the principal reason was Saúde Maria's opposition to the proposed constitutional changes, which would concentrate more power in the hands of the President. Several other senior party members were subsequently accused of colluding with Saúde Maria and were expelled from the PAIGC. President Vieira formally assumed the role of Head of Government, and elections to the regional councils were held in April. The National People's Assembly was re-established, its members being chosen from the regional councillors. The Council of the Revolution was replaced by a 15-member Council of State, selected from the members of the National People's Assembly. Vieira was subsequently elected as President of the Council of State and Head of State. The National People's Assembly immediately ratified the new Constitution, and formally abolished the position of Prime Minister.

In August 1985 President Vieira launched a campaign against corruption, and many senior officials were dismissed or arrested. This campaign was apparently the cause of an attempted military coup which took place in November, led by Col Paulo Correia, the First Vice-President of the Council of State, and several senior army officers. By July 1986 six people who had been accused of involvement in the coup attempt had died in prison, leading to claims that they had been murdered. At the trial of the surviving defendants, which concluded in July, 12 alleged plotters were sentenced to death and 41 were sentenced to hard labour. Later in the month, six of those condemned to death, including Correia, were executed, but the six other plotters had their death sentences commuted. In December 1988 four plotters were released, under an amnesty to commemorate the 40th anniversary of the UN General Assembly's adoption of the Universal Declaration of Human Rights.

In July 1986 President Vieira enlarged the Council of Ministers from 15 to 19 members and created the posts of three resident Ministers for the Provinces. During the fourth PAIGC congress, held in November, delegates supported the liberalization of the economy (see Economic Affairs), and re-elected President Vieira as Secretary-General of the PAIGC for a further four years. In February 1987 Vieira appointed Dr Vasco Cabral, the Minister of Justice, as Permanent Secretary of the Central Committee of the PAIGC, in an attempt to ensure that the programme of economic liberalization would receive the PAIGC's support. A minor government reshuffle ensued, which included the appointment of a new Minister of Justice, to replace Cabral, and the creation of two new Secretariats of State with responsibility for justice and foreign affairs. Following the devaluation of the peso in May, political tension increased, and the Government denied reports, published in a Lisbon magazine, that 20 army officers had been arrested for conspiring against Vieira. In August Vieira denied rumours that an attempted coup had been foiled during his visit to France for medical treatment in June and July. In July 1988 Bartolomeu Pereira, the Minister of Planning who had prepared Guinea-Bissau's structural adjustment programme with the IMF and the World Bank (see Economic Affairs), was killed in a road accident. His post was assumed in November by Bernardino Cardoso, the Secretary of State for Economic Affairs and International Co-operation. In February 1989 a further minor government reshuffle was carried out.

Relations with Portugal deteriorated in October 1987, when six Portuguese vessels were seized for alleged illegal fishing in Guinea-Bissau's territorial waters. Portugal retaliated by suspending non-medical aid, but revoked its decision in early November, after the vessels were released. A few days later, however, the head of security at the embassy of Guinea-Bissau in Lisbon requested political asylum and disclosed the presence of explosive devices in the embassy, which, he alleged, were to be used to eliminate members of the opposition movement, Bafata, living in exile in Portugal, France, Senegal and Cape Verde. These allegations were vehemently denied by the Government of Guinea-Bissau. During a one-day visit to Portugal in October 1988, President Vieira discussed the issue of Portuguese-based members of Bafata with President Soares of Portugal. Vieira also invited Soares to visit Guinea-Bissau in early 1989.

Meanwhile, relations with Cape Verde, which had deteriorated after the coup in 1980, began to improve. In January 1988 the two countries signed a bilateral co-operation agreement and agreed to liquidate a joint shipping company, which had been founded before the 1980 coup.

GUINEA-BISSAU

Government

The Constitution of 1984 states that the PAIGC is the leading force in society and in the nation. The PAIGC's highest authority is the Party Congress, convened every five years. The Congress elects a Central Committee (70 members in November 1986) to supervise the Party's work. To direct its policy, the Central Committee elects from its members a Political Bureau (12 full members and four alternate members in November 1986). Legislative power is vested in the National People's Assembly, which has 150 members, chosen by the eight directly-elected regional councils from among their own members. The National People's Assembly, in turn, elects from among its members the 14-member Council of State, which assumes legislative functions between sessions of the National People's Assembly. The regional councils also elect, for a five-year term, the President of the Council of State (a post corresponding to that of President of the Republic), in whom executive power is vested. The President of the Council of State is also Head of Government, and appoints the Ministers and Secretaries of State.

Defence

In June 1988 the armed forces totalled 9,200 men (army 6,800, navy 300, air force 100 and paramilitary gendarmerie 2,000). Expenditure on defence in 1985 was 737.8m. Guinea pesos.

Economic Affairs

In 1987, according to estimates by the World Bank, Guinea-Bissau's gross national product (GNP), measured at average 1985–87 prices, was US $152m., equivalent to $170 per head. Between 1980 and 1987, it was estimated, GNP per head increased, in real terms, at an average rate of 0.8% per year.

Subsistence agriculture is the principal economic activity, and the agricultural sector (including forestry and fishing) provided about 65% of gross domestic product (GDP) in 1987 and engaged an estimated 80.3% of the working population in 1986. Rice is the staple food, and maize, beans, cassava, millet, sorghum and sweet potatoes are also grown. In 1987 there was a shortfall in cereal production of 16,000 metric tons, and a deficit of 23,000 tons was forecast for 1988. Owing to late and insufficient rainfall and locust damage, cereal production again decreased during the 1988/89 season, resulting in an anticipated shortfall of 165,700 tons for 1989. In 1988 the USA financed a crop protection scheme and agreed to construct 12 warning stations to alert the country to the arrival of swarms of locusts. In late 1988 the World Food Programme agreed to provide $13.8m. to finance 21,000 tons of food imports over the next three years. Groundnuts, cashew nuts, cotton and palm kernels are exported, providing 76% of export earnings in 1986. Cattle-breeding is important in the interior. In 1987 a three-year programme was introduced to improve the managerial and technical capacity of the Ministry of Rural Development and Fisheries, financed by a credit from the International Development Association (IDA), totalling US $3.7m. In October 1988 the consumer price of rice was increased by 36%, with the aim of encouraging higher output. The fishing industry is being modernized and has expanded rapidly; in 1986 fish products provided 11.5% of export earnings, and it has been estimated that the potential annual catch in Guinea-Bissau's waters is up to 250,000 tons of fish. The Government has signed fishing agreements with the EEC and Algeria, permitting foreign vessels to fish in Guinea-Bissau's maritime zone in return for aid to the country's own fishing industry. In 1987 the USA financed a fishing patrol programme to prevent illegal fishing. In 1988 Italy agreed to construct a fishing school in Boloma. It has been estimated that Guinea-Bissau's forests could yield 100,000 tons of timber per year. Timber is exported, providing $960,000, or 10% of export earnings, in 1986. Forestry was to be given a high priority in the 1988–91 Development Plan, and a reafforestation programme was to be initiated.

Industry, based on the processing of food and raw materials, is being developed in order to provide employment, to reduce imports and to satisfy consumer demand. The agro-industrial complex at Cumeré is capable of processing 50,000 metric tons of rice and 70,000 tons of groundnuts annually. A sugar refinery that is being built at Gambiel will be capable of producing 10,000 tons of refined sugar per year. Following the Government's encouragement of the private sector in 1986, a car assembly plant was reopened. The factory had opened in 1979, but was forced to close in 1984, owing to a lack of components and low productivity. In 1987 foreign investment was sought for the rehabilitation and expansion of a fish-processing plant, and the establishment of a factory to produce wood laminates and furniture. Feasibility studies were to be undertaken to assess the potential of agro-industrial development and private-sector projects, following an agreement between Guinea-Bissau, Portugal and the USA, in late 1987, to establish an experimental credit fund to encourage private enterprise. In early 1988 Guinea-Bissau signed an agreement to accept 15m. tons of industrial toxic waste from Europe, the USA and Australia over a five-year period. The Government hoped to earn $120m. per year, but in mid-1988 it withdrew from the agreement, following international criticism. The mining sector has still to be developed. In 1987 the Government negotiated for foreign support to exploit reserves of phosphate, estimated at 100m. tons. In 1984 the Government reached agreement with a group of foreign oil companies concerning petroleum-prospecting in an offshore concession covering 4,500 sq km. In 1985, following the relaxation of the country's hydrocarbons law to attract foreign companies, licences for exploration of some 40 offshore blocks were offered on very favourable terms.

There is a serious lack of basic infrastructure and transport facilities. Owing to persistent shortages of foreign exchange, Guinea-Bissau has been unable to import sufficient quantities of petroleum and spare parts. Guinea-Bissau relies heavily on water transport, and in 1984 work began on the modernization of the port of Bissau and the rehabilitation of four river stations. In 1986 construction of a new river port at N'Pangda was initiated, to improve the transport of rice to northern Guinea-Bissau. Other plans include the construction of a dam on the Corrubal river (to supply hydroelectric power for the development of a modern aluminium industry), the renovation of the Bissau thermal power station, the development of a new telecommunications network, the expansion of the international airport at Bissalanca, the rehabilitation of the national airline and a major road rehabilitation project. In 1983 Guinea-Bissau joined the Organisation pour la Mise en Valeur du Fleuve Gambie (OMVG, see p. 219), in the hope of benefiting from integrated development projects in the Gambia river basin.

Since independence, the country has had a serious trade deficit, which has increased since 1977, because of the effects of the drought on crops, rising oil prices and world inflation. In 1986 exports covered only 17% of imports, leaving a trade deficit of $48.8m. In 1987, however, export earnings increased, following the devaluation of the peso in May (see below), and the estimated rate of cover rose to about 34%, while the estimated trade deficit fell to $32.3m. In the same year the deficit on the current account of the balance of payments was an estimated $16m., and in 1986 the budgetary deficit was equivalent to 21% of gross domestic product (GDP). The annual rate of inflation rose from an estimated 9% in 1977 to an estimated 149% in 1987, but deflation of 8.7% was projected for 1988. GDP declined by 1% in 1986, but it increased by an estimated 5.5% in 1987 and was expected to expand by 4% in 1988.

Commander Vieira's Government had originally aimed to downgrade many of the prestigious projects that had been started during the regime of President Cabral, and to emphasize rural development. The need for co-ordination was recognized, and the first development plan (1983–86) was prepared in 1982. In December 1983 the peso was devalued by 50% as part of a programme of economic stabilization, which aimed to liberalize trade and to increase activity in the private sector. In 1986 trade restrictions were relaxed, allowing private traders to import and export goods, although the two state-owned enterprises continued to control trading of rice, petroleum products, pesticides and various other articles.

After consultations with the World Bank, the IMF and other external donors, Guinea-Bissau initiated its first structural adjustment programme (SAP), for 1987–89. The programme was to be wholly financed by external aid totalling $46.4m. In May 1987 the World Bank agreed to provide a structural adjustment loan of $15m., and in October the IMF approved a structural adjustment facility of SDR 4.8m., of which SDR 1.5m. was to be made immediately available. The SAP included proposals to liberalize the economy and to reform public administration and enterprises. It aimed to achieve a real GDP growth rate of at least 3.5% per year, a lower annual inflation rate (of about 8%) and a reduction in the current account and budgetary deficits. In May 1987 the peso was devalued by about 60%, with the official rate set at 650 pesos = US $1, and new taxes and higher tariffs were introduced. Civil servants' salaries were increased by 25% in 1987, and by 50% in 1988, although one-third of the 16,623 state employees were to be gradually made redundant, and redeployed in the agricultural sector and in public works projects. In May 1988 fuel subsidies were reduced, resulting in average price increases of 40%, and in October the price of rice was raised by 36%. The Government also announced a sharp rise in the price of fish. In mid-1988 the IDA provided a loan of $9.7m. to finance a technical assistance project, which aimed to strengthen the Government's capacity to implement reforms under the SAP. In early 1989 the Government introduced higher taxes, and announced increases of 40% and 33% in the respective prices of petrol and bread. The Government also proposed to dissolve loss-making state-owned companies, to 'privatize' more viable ones, and to draw up a revised investment code.

The SAP was introduced to support the proposals of the second Development Plan for 1988–91. The Plan envisaged the reduction of the State's role in the economy and the growth of private investment. The agricultural and fishing sectors were to be given priority as a means of achieving self-sufficiency and reducing the balance-of-payments deficit. Executive training was to form a major part of the Plan, in an attempt to reduce the costs of foreign technical assistance. In mid-1988 the SAP received the endorsement of donor countries, who subsequently agreed to provide most of the $300m. in financing needed for 1989–91.

By the end of 1987, Guinea-Bissau's total foreign debt had reached an estimated $360m. Guinea-Bissau receives many foreign loans and credits, and is a member of ECOWAS (see p. 132). In November 1987 Guinea-Bissau applied to join the Franc Zone.

Social Welfare

Medical services are limited, owing to a severe shortage of facilities. The Government aims to establish one regional hospital in each of the eight regions. In 1981 there were 1,532 hospital beds. In 1982 there were about 100 physicians and 360 nurses working in the country. Of total budgetary expenditure by the central Government in 1985, 753.9m. pesos (5.0%) was for health services, and a further 160.4m. pesos (1.1%) for social security and welfare. In 1987 the IDA approved a credit of US $4.2m. for a health project involving the reorganization of the Ministry of Public Health, the rehabilitation of 25 health centres and the provision of drugs and other facilities, in an attempt to improve the level of primary health care. In 1988 Denmark provided a loan to build 13 health centres. However, in January 1989 the Government announced that hospital treatment would no longer be provided free of charge.

Education

Education is officially compulsory only for the period of primary schooling, which begins at seven years of age and lasts for six years. Secondary education, beginning at the age of 13, lasts for up to five years (a first cycle of three years and a second of two years). In 1984 the total enrolment at primary and secondary schools was equivalent to 40% of the school-age population (males 56%, females 26%), while enrolment at primary schools of children in the relevant age-group was equivalent to 53% (males 71%; females 35%). The comparable figure for secondary schools in 1983 was 3% (males 6%; females 1%). Expenditure on education by the central Government in 1985 was 1,475.6m. pesos (9.8% of total spending). In 1988 the IDA approved a credit of US $4.3m. for a project to expand the primary education system. Mass literacy campaigns have been launched: according to UNESCO estimates, the average rate of adult illiteracy in 1980 was 81.1% (males 75.4%; females 86.6%), but by 1985 the rate had declined to 68.6% (males 53.8%; females 82.7%).

Public Holidays

1989: 1 January (New Year), 20 January (Death of Amílcar Cabral), 1 May (Labour Day), 7 May* (Korité, end of Ramadan), 14 July* (Tabaski, Feast of the Sacrifice), 3 August (Anniversary of the Killing of Pidjiguiti), 24 September (National Day), 14 November (Anniversary of the Movement of Readjustment), 25 December (Christmas Day).

1990: 1 January (New Year), 20 January (Death of Amílcar Cabral), 27 April* (Korité, end of Ramadan), 1 May (Labour Day), 4 July* (Tabaski, Feast of the Sacrifice), 3 August (Anniversary of the Killing of Pidjiguiti), 24 September (National Day), 14 November (Anniversary of the Movement of Readjustment), 25 December (Christmas Day).

* Religious holidays, which are dependent on the Islamic lunar calendar, may differ by one or two days from the dates shown.

Weights and Measures

The metric system is used.

Statistical Survey

AREA AND POPULATION

Area: 36,125 sq km (13,948 sq miles).
Population: 487,448 (census of 15 December 1970, which covered only those areas under Portuguese control); 767,739 (males 370,225; females 397,514) at census of 16–30 April 1979; 943,000 (official estimate for January 1989). *By Region* (1979 census, provisional): Bafatá 116,032, Biombo 56,463, Bissau 109,214, Bolama/Bijagos 25,743, Cacheu 130,227, Gabú 104,315, Oio 135,114, Quinara 35,532, Tombali 55,099.
Density (January 1989): 26.1 per sq km.
Principal Towns: Bissau (capital) 109,214, Bafatá 13,429, Gabú 7,803, Mansôa 5,390, Catió 5,170, Cantchungo 4,965, Farim 4,468 (census of April 1979).
Births and Deaths (UN estimates, annual averages): Birth rate 40.9 per 1,000 in 1975–80, 40.7 per 1,000 in 1980–85; Death rate 21.9 per 1,000 in 1975–80, 21.7 per 1,000 in 1980–85. Source: UN, *World Population Prospects: Estimates and Projections as Assessed in 1984*.
Economically Active Population (ILO estimates, '000 persons at mid-1980): Agriculture, etc. 332 (males 174, females 158); Industry 14 (males 12, females 3); Services 57 (males 46, females 11); Total 403 (males 231, females 172). Source: ILO, *Economically Active Population Estimates and Projections, 1950–2025*.

AGRICULTURE, ETC.

Principal Crops ('000 metric tons, 1986): Rice (paddy) 125, Maize 18, Millet 29, Sorghum 33, Roots and tubers 40*, Groundnuts (in shell) 29, Coconuts 25*, Copra 5*, Palm kernels 14, Palm oil 2.8*, Vegetables and melons 20*, Plantains 25*, Other fruits 15*, Sugar cane 5*.

* FAO estimate.

Livestock ('000 head, year ending September 1986): Cattle 333, Pigs 286, Sheep 200, Goats 205.
Livestock Products (FAO estimates. '000 metric tons, 1986): Beef and veal 3; Pig meat 9; Cow's milk 10; Goat's milk 2.
Forestry (FAO estimates, '000 cubic metres, 1986): Roundwood removals 561 (sawlogs, etc. 40, other industrial wood 99, fuel wood 422); Sawnwood production 16.
Fishing (FAO estimates, metric tons, live weight, 1986): Fishes 2,620; Crustaceans and molluscs 1,000; Total catch 3,620.

INDUSTRY

Electric energy (1985): 14 million kWh.

FINANCE

Currency and Exchange Rates: 100 centavos = 1 Guinea peso. *Coins:* 5, 10, 20 and 50 centavos; 1, 2½, 5, 10 and 20 pesos. *Notes:* 50, 100 and 500 pesos. *Sterling and Dollar Equivalents* (30 June 1988): £1 sterling = 1,683.15 pesos; US $1 = 985.45 pesos; 10,000 Guinea pesos = £5.941 = $10.148. *Average Exchange Rate* (Guinea pesos per US dollar): 39.87 in 1982; 42.10 in 1983; 105.29 in 1984. Note: Between May 1978 and December 1983 the currency was

GUINEA-BISSAU

tied to the IMF's special drawing right at a mid-point exchange rate of SDR1 = 44 Guinea pesos.

General Budget (million Guinea pesos, 1985): *Revenue:* Taxation 1,947.8 (Excises 405.6, Taxes on international trade 1,201.8); Other current revenue 984.9; Capital revenue 7.5; Total 2,940.2. Figures exclude grants received from abroad (million pesos): 5,472.7 (current 896.7, capital 4,576.0). *Expenditure:* General public services 1,539.8; Defence 737.8; Education 1,475.6; Health 753.9; Social security and welfare 160.4; Housing and community amenities 336.8; Other community and social services 737.8; Economic services 7,862.2; Other purposes 1,379.4; Sub-total 14,983.7 (current 5,580.9, capital 9,402.8); Adjustment to cash −464.0; Total 14,519.7. Figures exclude net lending (1,056.0 million pesos). Source: IMF, *Government Finance Statistics Yearbook*.

Gross Domestic Product (estimates, million Guinea pesos at current prices): 11,293 in 1983; 18,802 in 1984; 26,801 in 1985. Source: UN Economic Commission for Africa, *African Statistical Yearbook*.

EXTERNAL TRADE

Principal Commodities (US $ million): *Imports* (1983): Food, beverages and tobacco 11.9, Fuels and lubricants 7.5, Machinery and equipment 2.6, Transport equipment 7.1, Total (incl. others) 54.9. *Exports* (1986): Palm kernels 1.0, Groundnuts (shelled) 0.7, Cashew nuts 5.1, Cotton 0.5, Fish 1.1, Timber 1.0, Total (incl. others) 9.6.

Principal Trading Partners (million pesos): *Imports* (1984): France 232.7, Germany, Fed. Repub. 213.7, Italy 110.4, Netherlands 215.6, Portugal 924.0, Senegal 362.0, Sweden 70.2, USSR 462.7, USA 192.4, Total (incl. others) 3,230.7. Source: Ministry of Planning, Bissau.

Exports (1980): Cape Verde 23.0, China, People's Repub. 14.6, Guinea 10.3, Netherlands 20.9, Portugal 101.3, Senegal 5.5, Spain 95.2, Switzerland 87.5, Total (incl. others) 382.3. Source: Direcção-Geral de Estatística, Bissau.

TRANSPORT

Road Traffic (vehicles in use, 1972): Cars 3,268, Lorries and buses 1,098, Motor cycles 758, Total 5,124.

International Sea-borne Shipping (estimated freight traffic, '000 metric tons, 1985): Goods loaded 33; Goods unloaded 129. Source: UN, *Monthly Bulletin of Statistics*.

Civil Aviation (1979): Passengers embarked 11,916, Passengers disembarked 9,879, Freight loaded 102,406 kg, Freight unloaded 364,276 kg.

COMMUNICATIONS MEDIA

Radio receivers (1986): 33,000 in use.
Telephones (1985): 7,000 in use.

EDUCATION

Pre-School (1984/85): 6 schools, 736 pupils, 38 teachers.
Basic 1st cycle (1984/85): 640 schools, 67,818 pupils, 2,435 teachers.
Basic 2nd cycle (1984/85): 28 schools, 13,626 pupils, 718 teachers.
Secondary (1984/85, *liceus*): 12 schools, 11,710 pupils, 650 teachers.
Teacher Training (1984/85): 2 schools, 594 pupils, 38 teachers.
Technical (1984/85): 2 schools, 433 pupils, 69 teachers.
Source: Ministério da Educação Nacional, Bissau.

Directory

The Constitution

A new constitution for the Republic of Guinea-Bissau was approved by the National People's Assembly on 16 May 1984. Its main provisions are summarized below:

The Constitution defines Guinea-Bissau as an anti-colonialist and anti-imperialist Republic and a State of revolutionary national democracy, based on the people's participation in carrying out, controlling and directing public activities. The Constitution states that the party that fought against Portuguese colonialism, the Partido Africano da Independência da Guiné e Cabo Verde (PAIGC), shall be the leading political force in society and in the State. The PAIGC shall define the general bases for policy in all fields.

The economy of Guinea-Bissau shall be organized on the principles of state direction and planning. The State shall control the country's foreign trade.

The representative bodies in the country are the National People's Assembly and the regional councils. Other state bodies draw their powers from these. The members of the regional councils shall be directly elected. Members of the councils must be more than 18 years of age. The National Assembly shall have 150 members, who are to be elected by the regional councils from among their own members. All members of the National Assembly must be more than 21 years of age.

The National Assembly shall elect a 15-member Council of State, to which its powers are delegated between sessions of the Assembly. The Assembly also elects the President of the Council of State, who is also automatically Head of the Government and Commander-in-Chief of the Armed Forces. The Council of State will later elect two Vice-Presidents and a Secretary. The President and Vice-Presidents of the Council of State form part of the Government, as do Ministers, Secretaries of State and the Governor of the National Bank.

The Constitution can be revised at any time by the National People's Assembly on the initiative of the deputies themselves, or of the Council of State or the Government.

The Government

HEAD OF STATE

Head of Government, President of the Council of State and Commander-in-Chief of the Armed Forces: Commdr JOÃO BERNARDO VIEIRA (assumed power 14 November 1980; elected President of the Council of State 16 May 1984).

COUNCIL OF STATE
(February 1989)

Commdr JOÃO BERNARDO VIEIRA (President).
Col IAFAI CAMARA (Vice-President).
Dr VASCO CABRAL (Secretary).
CARLOS CORREIA.
JOSÉ PEREIRA.
FILINTO BARROS.
TIAGO ALELUA LOPES.
BUATO NA BATCHA.
BENGATE NA BEATE.
JÚLIO SEMEDO.
FRANCISCA PEREIRA.
MÁRIO MENDES.
TEOBOLDO BARBOZA.
BANA MATCH.

COUNCIL OF MINISTERS
(February 1989)

Head of Government, President of the Council of State, Commander-in-Chief of the Armed Forces, Minister of Defence and of the Interior: Commdr JOÃO BERNARDO VIEIRA.

Vice-President of the Council of State and Minister of State for the Armed Forces: Col IAFAI CAMARA.

Minister of State for the Presidency and Minister of Fisheries: TIAGO ALELUIA LOPES.

Minister of State for the Presidency in charge of Social Welfare: Dr FIDELES CABRAL D'ALMADA.

Minister of State for Rural Development and Agriculture: CARLOS CORREIA.

Minister of State for Economic Co-ordination, Trade and Tourism: Col MANUEL MÁRIO MONTEIRO DOS SANTOS.

Minister of Education: MANUEL RAMBOU BARCELOS.

Minister for Justice: NICANDRO PEREIRA BARRETO.

Minister of National Security and Public Order: JOSÉ PEREIRA.

Minister of Natural Resources and Industry: FILINTO DE BARROS.

Minister of Foreign Affairs: JÚLIO SEMEDO.

Minister of Finance: VÍTOR FREIRA MONTEIRO.

Minister of Public Health: ALEXANDRE NUNES CORREIA.

Minister of Trade and Tourism: Col MANUEL MARIA DOS SANTOS.

Minister of Economic Planning: BERNARDINO CARDOSO.

GUINEA-BISSAU

Minister for the Civil Service and Labour: HENRIQUETA GODINHO GOMES.
Minister-Governor of the National Bank: Dr PEDRO A. GODINHO GOMES.
Minister of Information and Telecommunications: MUSSA DJASSI.
Minister for the Northern Province: MÁRIO CABRAL.
Minister for the Eastern Province: MALAM BACAI SANHA.
Minister for the Southern Province: Dr LUÍS OLIVEIRA SANCA.
There are 10 Secretaries of State.

MINISTRIES

All Ministries are in Bissau.
Ministry of Information: Avda do Brasil, CP 248, Bissau.

Legislature

NATIONAL PEOPLE'S ASSEMBLY

A new National People's Assembly was inaugurated on 14 May 1984. Its 150 members were selected from among the members of the eight directly-elected regional councils. All members are nominees of the PAIGC.
President: CARMEN PEREIRA.

Political Organizations

Partido Africano da Independência da Guiné e Cabo Verde (PAIGC): CP 106, Bissau; f. 1956 by Dr Amílcar Cabral; fmrly the ruling party in both Guinea-Bissau and Cape Verde; although Cape Verde withdrew from the PAIGC following the coup in Guinea-Bissau in November 1980, Guinea-Bissau has retained the party name and initials; cen. cttee of 70 mems (60 full and 10 alt. mems) and political bureau of 16 mems (12 full and four alt.); Sec.-Gen. Commdr JOÃO BERNARDO VIEIRA; Perm. Sec. of Cen. Cttee Dr VASCO CABRAL.

In November 1986 an opposition party, the **Guinea-Bissau Bafata Resistance Movement,** advocating a pluralist democratic system and led by DOMINGOS FERNANDES GOMES, was founded in Lisbon. The party maintains offices in Paris, Dakar (Senegal) and Praia (Cape Verde).

Diplomatic Representation

EMBASSIES IN GUINEA-BISSAU

Algeria: Rua 12 de Setembro 12, CP 350, Bissau; tel. 211522; Ambassador: R. BENCHIKH EL FEGOUN.
Brazil: Rua São Tomé Esquina/Avda Francisco Mendes, Bissau; tel. 212648; telex 245; Ambassador: GUY MENDES PINHEIRO DE VASCONCELLOS.
Cape Verde: Bissau; Ambassador: ANTÓNIO LIMA.
China, People's Republic: Rua Eduardo Mondlane 33–35, Bissau; tel. 212908; Ambassador: SHI WUSHAN.
Cuba: Rua Joaquim N'Com 1, Bissau; tel. 213579; Ambassador: Dr ARMANDO TORRES SANTRAYLL.
Egypt: Rua 12 de Setembro, CP 72, Bissau; tel. 213642; Ambassador: FADEL FADEL ATTA.
France: Rua Eduardo Mondlane 67-A, Bissau; tel. 212633; Ambassador: LOUIS BOUROUX.
German Democratic Republic: Avda Osvaldo Vieira 28, Bissau; tel. 212992; Ambassador: ERICH MESKE.
Guinea: Rua 14, no. 9, CP 396, Bissau; tel. 212681; Ambassador: GUIRANE NDIAYE.
Korea, Democratic People's Republic: Avda Domingos Ramos 42, Bissau; tel. 212885; Ambassador: SHIM JAE-DU.
Libya: Rua 16, CP 362, Bissau; tel. 212006; Representative: DOKALI ALI MUSTAFA.
Portugal: Rua de Lisboa, no. 6, Bissau; tel. 213009; telex 248; Ambassador: MANUEL BARREIROS MARTINS.
Senegal: Bissau; tel. 212636; Ambassador: AHMED TIJANE KANE.
USSR: Rua Rui Djassi 17, Bissau; tel. 213535; Ambassador: VLADIMIR ALDOSHIN.
USA: Avda Domingos Ramos, CP 297, Bissau; Ambassador: JOHN BLACKEN.

Judicial System

Under the provisions of the 1984 Constitution, judges of the Supreme Court are appointed by the President of the Council of State.
Attorney-General: JOSEPH TURPIN.

Religion

About 65% of the population are animists, 30% are Muslims and 5% are Christians, mainly Roman Catholics.

CHRISTIANITY

The Roman Catholic Church

Guinea-Bissau comprises a single diocese, directly responsible to the Holy See. At 31 December 1986 there was an estimated 49,500 adherents in the country.
Bishop of Bissau: Mgr SETTIMIO ARTURO FERRAZZETTA, CP 20, Bissau; tel. 212469.

The Anglican Communion

Within the Church of the Province of West Africa, Guinea-Bissau forms part of the diocese of Guinea, inaugurated in August 1985. The Archbishop of the Province is the Bishop of Liberia. The Bishop of Guinea is resident in Conakry, Guinea.

The Press

Nô Pintcha: Bissau; 3 a week; official govt publ.; Dir Sra CABRAL; circ. 6,000.
Voz da Guiné: Bissau; daily; circ. 6,000.

NEWS AGENCIES

Agencia Noticiosa da Guinea (ANG): CP 248, Bissau; tel. 212151; telex 96900.

Foreign Bureau

Agentstvo Pechati Novosti (APN) (USSR): CP 11, Bissau; tel. 213433; Correspondent A. KASSIMOV.

Radio and Television

There were 31,181 radio receivers in use in 1988. An experimental television service, funded by the Portuguese Government, Radiotelevisão Portuguesa and the Gulbenkian Foundation, was due to start broadcasting in 1988.
Radiodifusão Nacional da República da Guiné-Bissau: CP 191, Bissau; govt-owned; broadcasts on short-wave, medium-wave and FM in Portuguese; Dir FRANCISCO BARRETO.

Finance

(cap. = capital; m. = million; brs = branches; amounts in Guinea pesos)

BANKING

Banco Nacional da Guiné-Bissau: Avda Amílcar Cabral, CP 38, Bissau; tel. 215433; telex 969249; central and commercial bank; f. 1976; cap. 100m.; Gov. Dr PEDRO A. GODINHO GOMES; 3 brs.
Caixa de Crédito da Guiné: Bissau; govt savings and loan institution.
Caixa Económica Postal: Avda Amílcar Cabral, Bissau; tel. 212999; telex 979; postal savings institution.

INSURANCE

In June 1979 it was announced that a single state-owned insurer would be set up to replace the Portuguese company Ultramarina.

Trade and Industry

Since independence the Government has been actively pursuing a policy of small-scale industrialization to compensate for the almost total lack of manufacturing capacity. It adopted an elaborate programme of state control, and in late 1976 acquired 80% of the capital of a Portuguese company, **Ultramarina,** a large firm specializing in a wide variety of trading, ship-repairing and agricultural processing. The Government has also acquired major interests in the **CICER** brewery and created a joint-venture company with the Portuguese concern **SACOR** to sell petroleum products, following the construction of new storage facilities. Since 1975 three fishing companies have been formed with foreign participation: **GUIALP** (with Algeria), **Estrela do Mar** (with the USSR) and **SEMAPESCA** (with France). In December 1976 **SOCOTRAM**, an enterprise for the sale and processing of timber, was inaugurated. It operates a new factory in Bissau for the production of wooden tiles and co-ordinates sawmills and carpentry shops throughout the country. In 1979 the **Empresa de Automóveis da Guiné** opened a car-assembly plant at Bissau, capable of producing 500 vehicles per year.

Empresa Nacional de Pesquisas e Exploração Petroliferas e Mineiras (PETROMINAS): Rua Eduardo Mondlane 58, Bissau; tel. 212279; state-owned; regulates all mineral prospecting; Dir-Gen. PIO GOMES CORREIA.

CHAMBER OF COMMERCE

Chamber of Commerce, Industry and Agriculture of Guinea-Bissau: Bissau; f. 1987.

TRADE UNION

União Nacional dos Trabalhadores de Guiné (UNTG): 13 Avda Ovai di Vievra, CP 98, Bissau; tel. 212094; telex 900; Sec.-Gen. MÁRIO MENDES CORREA.

Transport

RAILWAYS

There are no railways in Guinea-Bissau.

ROADS

In 1983 there were 2,500 km of roads, of which 400 km were tarred. A major road rehabilitation scheme is under way, and in 1989 donors provided US $31.3m. for road projects. An international road is planned, which would link Guinea-Bissau with The Gambia and Senegal.

SHIPPING

Under a major port modernization project, the main port at Bissau was to be renovated and expanded, and four river ports were to be upgraded to enable barges to load and unload at low tide. The total cost of the project was estimated at US $47.4m., and finance was provided by the World Bank and Arab funds. In 1986 work began on a new river port at N'Pungda, which will be partly funded by the Netherlands.

Empresa Nacional de Agências e Transportes Marítimos (Guinémar): Sociedade de Agências e Transportes da Guiné Lda, Rua Guerra Mendes, 4-4A, CP 244, Bissau; tel. 212675; telex 240; nationalized 1976; shipping agents and brokers; Gen. Man. MARCOS T. LOPES; Asst Gen. Man. NOËL CORREIA.

CIVIL AVIATION

There is an international airport at Bissalanca, which there are plans to expand, and 10 smaller airports serving the interior.

Transportes Aéreos da Guiné-Bissau (TAGB): Aeroporto Oswaldo Vieira, CP 111, Bissau; telex 268; f. 1977; domestic services and flights to France, Portugal, Guinea and Senegal; Gen. Man. Capt. JOSÉ MARIN CASTRO; fleet of 1 HS-748, 1 DC-3, 1 An-24, 1 Boeing 727, several light aircraft.

Tourism

Centro de Informação e Turismo: CP 294, Bissau; state tourism and information service.

GUYANA

Introductory Survey

Location, Climate, Language, Religion, Flag, Capital

The Co-operative Republic of Guyana lies on the north coast of South America, between Venezuela to the west and Suriname to the east, with Brazil to the south. The narrow coastal belt has a moderate climate with two wet seasons, from April to August and from November to January, alternating with two dry seasons. Inland, there are tropical forests and savannah, and the dry season lasts from September to May. The average annual temperature is 27°C (80°F), with average rainfall of 1,520 mm (60 in) per year inland, rising to between 2,030 mm (80 in) and 2,540 mm (100 in) on the coast. English is the official language but Hindi, Urdu and Amerindian dialects are also spoken. The principal religions are Christianity (which is professed by about 50% of the population), Hinduism (about 33%) and Islam (less than 10%). The national flag (proportions 5 by 3 when flown on land, but 2 by 1 at sea) is green, with a white-bordered yellow triangle (apex at the edge of the fly) on which is superimposed a black-bordered red triangle (apex in the centre). The capital is Georgetown.

Recent History

Guyana was formerly British Guiana, a colony of the United Kingdom, formed in 1831 from territories finally ceded to Britain by the Dutch in 1814. A new constitution, providing for universal adult suffrage, was introduced in 1953. The elections of April 1953 were won by the left-wing People's Progressive Party (PPP), led by Dr Cheddi Jagan. In October, however, the British Government, claiming that a communist dictatorship was threatened, suspended the Constitution. An interim administration was appointed. The PPP split in 1955, and in 1957 some former members founded a new party, the People's National Congress (PNC), under the leadership of Forbes Burnham. The PNC draws its support mainly from the African-descended population, while PPP support comes largely from the (Asian-descended) 'East' Indian community. Both parties adhere to Marxist-Leninist ideology.

A revised constitution was introduced in December 1956 and fresh elections held in August 1957. The PPP won and Dr Jagan became Chief Minister. Another constitution, providing for internal self-government, was adopted in July 1961. The PPP won the elections in August and Dr Jagan was appointed Premier in September. In the election of December 1964, held under the system of proportional representation that had been introduced in the previous year, the PPP won the largest number of seats in the Legislative Assembly, but not a majority. A coalition government was formed by the PNC and the United Force, with Burnham as Prime Minister. This coalition led the colony to independence, as Guyana, on 26 May 1966.

The PNC won elections in 1968 and in 1973, although the results of the latter, and every poll since, have been disputed by the opposition parties. Guyana became a Co-operative Republic on 23 February 1970, and Arthur Chung was elected non-executive President in March. In 1976 the PPP, which had boycotted the National Assembly since 1973, offered the Government its 'critical support'. Following a referendum in July 1978, which gave the Assembly power to amend the Constitution, elections to the Assembly were postponed for 15 months. The legislature assumed the role of a Constituent Assembly, established in November 1978, to draft a new constitution. In October 1979 elections were postponed for a further year. In October 1980 Forbes Burnham declared himself executive President of Guyana, and a new constitution was promulgated. Elections were announced for December.

Internal opposition to the PNC Government had increased after the assassination in June 1980 of Dr Walter Rodney, leader of the Working People's Alliance (WPA). The Government was widely believed to have been involved in the incident (an official inquest into Rodney's death was finally ordered in November 1987, but in 1988 it produced a verdict, rejected by the opposition, of death by misadventure). All opposition parties except the PPP and United Force urged their supporters to boycott the December 1980 elections to the National Assembly. The PNC, under Burnham, received 77.7% of the votes, according to official results, and won 41 of the 53 elective seats, although allegations of substantial electoral malpractice were made. The Government's international reputation was further diminished when an international observer team denounced the elections as fraudulent, but, on the basis of the voting for the Assembly, Burnham was declared to have been elected President. He was formally inaugurated in January 1981.

In 1981 arrests and trials of opposition leaders continued, and in 1982 the Government's relations with human rights groups, and especially the Christian churches, deteriorated further. Editors of opposition newspapers were threatened, political violence increased, and the Government was accused of interference in the legal process. Popular passive resistance to the Government took the form of economic non-co-operation, while the Government gave much publicity to rumours of an imminent invasion by Venezuela, in an attempt to divert attention from the internal crisis. Industrial unrest and public discontent continued in 1983, as Guyana's worsening economic situation increased opposition to the Government, and led to growing disaffection within the trade union movement and the PNC. Food shortages were exacerbated by government attempts to end the 'black market' in banned foodstuffs, which operated between Guyana and its neighbours. There were more strikes in 1984, and in December Burnham announced some concessions, including a rise in the daily minimum wage (virtually the only increase since 1979). There was also speculation about a possible government of national unity, formed by the PNC and the PPP to counter the threat of a right-wing military coup.

Forbes Burnham died in August 1985 and was succeeded as President by Desmond Hoyte, hitherto the First Vice-President and Prime Minister. President Hoyte's former posts were filled by Hamilton Green, previously the First Deputy Prime Minister. At a general election, held in December, the PNC won 78% of the votes and 42 of the elective seats in the National Assembly. Desmond Hoyte was declared elected as President. Opposition groups, including the PPP and WPA, denounced the poll as fraudulent. In January 1986 five of the six opposition parties formed the Patriotic Coalition for Democracy (PCD).

President Hoyte's Government announced that its chief priority would be the revitalization of Guyana's rapidly deteriorating economy. Efforts were to be made to improve investment opportunities in Guyana. In addition, the ban on the import of wheat flour, imposed in 1982, was repealed, and the first shipments of flour from the USA arrived in September, as part of a new agreement on food aid. Further restrictions on several food items were rescinded in November.

The PCD refused to present candidates for the December 1986 municipal elections, and the 91 PNC candidates were declared winners by default. Hoyte reshuffled the Cabinet, and in January 1987 he announced his Government's intention to begin the 'roll-back of co-operative socialism'. Fuel shortages and interruptions to the electric power supply in Georgetown during October and November 1987, however, provoked protests by the opposition, which also demanded the implementation of the recommendations of an integrity commission, published in a report in August, for a legally enforceable code of conduct for persons in public life.

During 1988 the opposition expressed fears about the independence of the judiciary. In February the Government, prompted by a ruling of the Court of Appeal (in 1987) declaring invalid sections of the 1984 Labour (Amendment) Act, enacted a constitutional amendment which rescinded the court's jurisdiction in matters of labour legislation, particularly with regard to the Government's obligation to consult with trade unions and other organizations concerning such legislation. In addition, the amendment established that any legislation to be enacted by the National Assembly, including retrospective legislation, could not be deemed invalid on the grounds of inconsistency with former constitutions. Moreover, in April Keith Massiah

GUYANA

retired as Chancellor of Justice, but, within one day, he was appointed to the Cabinet as Attorney-General, thereby causing controversy both in Guyana and other countries in the region. The opposition also claimed that the Government's continued recourse to the laws of libel against its critics was an abuse of the legal system.

In 1988 President Hoyte continued to hold negotiations with international financial agencies on an economic recovery plan acceptable to potential aid donors and, particularly, to the IMF. The successful implementation of an IMF-sponsored programme was also considered important to Hoyte's own position within the ruling PNC. In September, however, a division in the trade union movement threatened Hoyte's efforts. Seven unions not under the control of the PNC withdrew from the Trades Union Congress (TUC), after Gordon Todd, their candidate for the presidency of the TUC, was defeated. Despite Todd's publicly-stated willingness to co-operate with Hoyte and any economic austerity plans imposed by the Government, it was reported that a faction within the PNC had decided to re-establish the party's dominance in the TUC and to prevent Todd's election. In October 1988 the seven dissident unions formed a separate congress, the Federation of Independent Trade Unions in Guyana (FITUG). In January 1989 FITUG proposed a one-day strike in protest against extensive interruptions to the electricity supply during that month.

Guyana has border disputes with its neighbours, Venezuela and Suriname, although relations with Brazil have continued to improve through trade and military agreements. Suriname restored diplomatic representation in Guyana in 1979, however, and bilateral meetings were resumed at the end of the year. In 1983 relations improved further as a result of increased trade links between the countries. An EEC grant was provided in 1985 for a new ferry service between the two countries.

In 1962 Venezuela renewed its claim to 130,000 sq km (50,000 sq miles) of land west of the Essequibo river (nearly two-thirds of Guyanese territory). The area was accorded to Guyana in 1899, but Venezuela based its claim on a papal bull of 1493, referring to Spanish colonial possessions. The Port of Spain Protocol of 1970 put the issue in abeyance until 1982. Several border incidents were reported in 1982. After the failure of two rounds of negotiations in 1982, Guyana and Venezuela referred the dispute to the UN in 1983, but no further progress was made. A meeting between the Ministers of Foreign Affairs of the two countries in February 1985 led to a series of agreements on trade and the exchange of information and assistance. A UN special envoy was asked to mediate in the border dispute, and, following talks held in March, it was announced that some progress had been made towards a reconciliation.

Guyana officially condemned the US-led invasion of Grenada in October 1983. This attitude, although popular in Guyana, led to rapid deterioration in relations with the USA, which had already been adversely affected by the US Government's veto of anticipated loans to Guyana in September. Guyana's decision to dispense with seeking IMF financial support further compounded the country's increasing isolation among Western nations. To offset the fall in Western aid, Guyana sought to improve relations with socialist countries, such as Cuba, Libya, Yugoslavia and the Democratic People's Republic of Korea. After Hoyte became President, however, Guyana started to improve its relations with the USA and other Western countries. Hoyte sought to encourage investment in Guyana and emphasized policy changes during visits to North America in 1987, and to the United Kingdom and other European countries in 1988.

Government

Under the 1980 Constitution, legislative power is held by the unicameral National Assembly, with 65 members: 53 elected for five years by universal adult suffrage, on the basis of proportional representation, and 12 regional representatives. Executive power is held by the President, who leads the majority party in the Assembly and holds office for its duration. The President appoints and leads a Cabinet, which includes a Prime Minister, and may include Ministers who are not elected members of the Assembly. The Cabinet is collectively responsible to the National Assembly. Guyana comprises 10 regions, each having a Regional Democratic Council which returns a representative to the National Assembly.

Defence

The armed forces are combined in a single service, the Guyana Defence Force, consisting of 5,450 men (of whom 300 were in the air force and 150 in the navy) in June 1988. Paramilitary forces total 3,500, including 1,500 on National Service (established in 1974). Estimated defence expenditure in 1986 was US $65m.

Economic Affairs

The economy is based mainly on agriculture and the production of bauxite. Bauxite, sugar and rice accounted for 80% of domestic export earnings in 1987. According to estimates by the World Bank, in 1987 Guyana's gross national product (GNP), measured at average 1985–87 prices, was US $310m. Between 1980 and 1987, it was estimated, GNP declined, in real terms, at an average annual rate of 6%. GNP per head, equivalent to $380 in 1987, was estimated to have decreased at an average rate of 6.8% per year, in real terms, between 1980 and 1987. The principal crops are sugar cane and rice; other important agricultural products are citrus fruits, coconuts, groundnuts, oil palms and vegetables. Since 1982 the agricultural sector has suffered from low productivity and the effects of the ending of government price subsidies. The Government has invested US $45m. in the Mahaica-Mahaicony-Abary agricultural development scheme, which will, the Government hopes, enable Guyana to supply both itself and other CARICOM countries with food. A four-year agricultural development plan, announced in October 1985, aimed to achieve a 31% increase in productivity by 1989. Subsequently, there has been some expansion in non-traditional exports, with Barbados as the main recipient in 1988.

By 1979 Guyana had become self-sufficient in sugar, rice, vegetables, fish, meat, poultry and fruit. Sugar accounted for about 31% of export earnings in 1985, but revenue has fallen since 1982, owing to poor harvests. Production of raw sugar was 300,790 metric tons in 1981, but annual output, affected by strikes and adverse weather, fell to 245,731 tons by 1984. Output rose to 246,888 tons in 1985, but was still 9% below the planned target, and the state sugar corporation, Guysuco, recorded operating losses of $ G77.8m. In March 1986 the Government introduced a restructuring plan for the sugar sector, in an effort to improve the efficiency of the industry. One factory was to be closed, the area planted with sugar cane was to be reduced, and production of raw sugar was to be stabilized at 250,000 tons per year. Cane plantations were also to be used for the cultivation of other crops, including rice and fruit. Sugar production increased slightly in 1986, to 249,367 tons, and Guysuco achieved pre-tax profits of $ G20m. In late 1986, however, the USA announced a reduction in its annual import quota for Guyanese sugar, from 18,677 metric tons to 9,904 tons. In spite of a US compensatory grant of US $3.2m., this threatened a considerable decline in earnings of foreign exchange. Production of raw sugar fell in 1987 to 224,538 tons, but exports earned $ G910.8m., compared with $ G348.9m. in 1986. The increase in earnings was mainly due to the devaluation of the currency in January 1987. In November 1988, however, it was announced that production would reach only about 175,000 tons in that year, and that Guyana could not supply its quota for the USA. Furthermore, sugar would have to be imported in order to supply the EEC quota.

The cultivation of rice in Guyana is highly mechanized but the crop is farmed in uneconomic units of an average of 11 acres (4.5 ha). In 1981 only about one-half of the land available for rice was cultivated. Production of milled rice has fluctuated from year to year, and has been affected by disease and weather conditions. Output increased by 24% in 1984, but fell by 13%, to 156,124 metric tons, in 1985, when export sales were only 50% of the planned target, at US $1.8m. Output in 1986 remained below the annual target, but represented a 17% advance on the 1985 total. Increases in the prices payable to farmers, announced in September 1986, stimulated exports, and export earnings for the year totalled US $6.5m. In 1987, however, output fell to 148,545 tons (earning $7.7m.), despite improvements in both yield and milling facilities; electricity shortages and adverse weather conditions had affected production.

More than 80% of Guyana is covered by tropical forest, and the estimated annual volume of marketable timber is 1m. cu m, of which 25% is accessible. In 1985 the Government signed an agreement with private-sector sawmilling companies for the commercial exploitation of around 1m. acres (400,000 ha) of state-owned forest, and in 1986 a separate Ministry of Forestry was established (in January 1989 the Ministry was dissolved, and its responsibilities were assumed by the Guyana National Resources Agency). In 1986 timber production declined by about 30%, to 97,069 cu m, but export earnings remained at about $ G18m. Export receipts increased to $ G43.7m. in 1987, helped by the currency devaluation and by a rise in production, to 173,026 cu m. Guyana's fishing fleet has been improved with the assistance of foreign countries. The total fish catch in 1986 was 44,582 metric tons, of which 3,808 tons of shrimps provided export earnings of $ G14.2m.

Bauxite is Guyana's principal source of export earnings. By the end of 1975 the whole bauxite industry had been nationalized. Annual output declined from 3.6m. metric tons in 1973–74 to 1.7m. tons by 1981, 30% below target. In 1982 the industry began to experience difficulties as the price of bauxite collapsed on the world market, and production fell to 1.25m. tons. Although output recovered slightly in 1983, about 1,700 workers were laid off, and the country's only refinery was closed. Exports of alumina fell in 1982, owing to a reduction in demand, and the alumina plant at Linden was temporarily closed in June. The state-owned mining company, Guymine, registered a loss of $ G131m. in 1983. Production of bauxite in 1984 was 1.33m. tons, achieving target levels. Output continued to increase, and in 1986 reached 1.47m. tons. As part of the Government's plan to achieve a recovery in the bauxite industry, the US company, Reynolds, was invited to return to Guyana in 1985 to provide technical and marketing assistance, and to rehabilitate the country's alumina refinery, which was expected to reopen in 1989. Plans to revitalize the industry by 1989 and to increase the production of calcined bauxite by 40%, at a projected cost of around US $22m., were announced in 1986. Plans were also announced for the marketing of a new refractory-grade bauxite. Production increased slightly in 1987, to 1.48m. tons, and exports earned $ G841.9m. in that year

Agreements to expand the gold-mining industry, with the assistance of companies from North and South America, were announced in February 1986. A US $5m. mining operation was begun at Omai by the Canadian company, Golden Star Resources, and the mine was expected to yield around 20,000 troy ounces of gold per year. Golden Star Resources intended to develop four other mining sites, and in 1987 it announced a joint-venture agreement with an Australian company. The average annual output being declared to the Geology and Mines Commission in the mid-1980s was 10,000 ounces, but officials estimated in 1986 that annual output would increase rapidly. In an effort to prevent the smuggling of gold out of the country, the Government announced in October 1986 that miners would be paid 132% more per ounce of raw gold declared. Declared output of gold was 14,040 ounces in 1986, rising to 26,100 ounces in 1987, when exports earned $ G165.9m. In September 1988 the Guyana Geology and Mines Commission announced the formation of a joint venture with the Brazilian company, Paranapanema, to explore for gold at Tassawini, in north-western Guyana.

Industry is based on mineral processing, agro-industries (such as the production of rum, beer and cigarettes) and light industry, principally textiles and clothing. The manufacture of pharmaceutical products began in June 1988, following Argentine investment of US $20m. in a factory for which Barbados and Trinidad and Tobago were to supply the raw materials. Industrial development depends on the expansion of energy sources, and the 750 MW hydroelectric project on the Upper Mazaruni river, scheduled for completion in the late 1980s, should make possible the construction of a local aluminium smelter. However, energy shortages continued to affect Guyana in 1987 and 1988. In 1986 the results of a petroleum exploration study of Guyana were presented to several foreign oil companies. Information packs were purchased by four major companies, and in August 1987 a Trinidadian company signed a four-year exploration licence; another agreement was signed in 1988, with a British company.

The economy, in a crisis since the mid-1970s, was on the point of collapse by 1982, as inefficiency, corruption and a decline of managerial and technical skills (as a result of emigration, mainly from the Asian sector) were added to low world prices. It has been estimated that 71,000 people emigrated from Guyana between 1976 and 1981. The collapse of popular morale was also widely regarded as a fundamental cause of the country's failure to produce. Guyana's relations with other CARICOM members had deteriorated, following its violation of a CARICOM trade agreement and its failure to repay large debts to the organization. Guyana's gross domestic product (GDP) declined by 12.4%, in real terms, in 1982, and by a further 9.6% in 1983. GDP rose by 5% during 1984, mainly as the result of improved production by the mining sector, and grew by 4% in 1985. Growth of only 0.3% was achieved in 1986, and of 0.7% in 1987. At the end of 1985 the total public external debt, excluding repayment arrears of US $753.6m., was $721m., equivalent to 156% of annual GDP, and was expected to rise still further to finance the growing budget deficit, which totalled $ G308.5m. in 1986, $ G752m. in 1987 and was estimated to be $ G1,202m. in 1988. In August 1986 foreign exchange dealings by the Guyana Central Bank were suspended, owing to a shortage of convertible currency. In January 1987 commercial banks were authorized to purchase convertible currency. By September, however, reserves of foreign exchange had dwindled to US $2.47m. (Reserves increased to $8.43m. in December, but they had declined to $4.21m. by June 1988.) The acute shortage of foreign currency provoked an extension of import controls and a thriving illegal trade in the smuggling of foodstuffs and other goods from neighbouring countries. In 1982 the official inflation rate was 25%, but 100% increases of prices on the 'parallel' market occurred between January and June alone. Illegal trading in foreign currency was widely practised in order to pay rapidly-increasing prices. The restriction of imports was initially successful in curbing the trade deficit, which totalled $ G407m. in 1982, but by the end of 1986 it had increased to $ G526m., owing to the decline in bauxite exports and to reductions in output of sugar and rice. The widespread smuggling of goods, both in and out of the country, makes reliable trade statistics impossible to evaluate.

The economy is 80% state-controlled, but in May 1982 the Government began a programme of privatization, although this was officially denied. In 1983 and 1984 co-operation agreements were signed with several foreign companies. In June 1983 the Government expressed its willingness to engage in non-monetary transactions in order to secure vital products. A barter agreement with Trinidad and Tobago, whereby rice had been exchanged for petroleum, was suspended in December 1985, however, because of Guyana's inability to repay debts of TT $400m. Shortages of petroleum led to fuel rationing in February 1986. However, an agreement for the exchange of bauxite for oil was signed with Venezuela, thus easing the fuel shortage, and a further agreement with Trinidad and Tobago was signed in May. Despite these agreements, there were renewed fuel shortages during the final months of 1987 and throughout 1988. In 1986 President Hoyte stressed the need for greater private-sector involvement in the economy and for the restructuring of the public sector. In March he introduced legislation to encourage overseas banks and businesses to invest in the country. Several trade agreements were signed in 1986 and 1987.

The IMF has provided balance-of-payments support and other facilities since 1979, but agreements have lapsed, owing to Guyana's failure to meet IMF conditions. Credits were finally suspended in June 1982. By January 1984 the country's economic crisis had become so severe that the Government was forced to devalue the Guyana dollar by 20%, and a further devaluation of 8.9% occurred in October. In May 1985 the IMF formally declared Guyana ineligible for further assistance until outstanding debts to the Fund had been cleared. Subsequently, an agreement between the Guyanese Government and the IMF has been cited as a pre-condition by many potential investors attracted to Guyana in recent years. Discussions between the Fund and the Government were resumed in 1986, and have taken place each year thereafter. In January 1987 the Guyana dollar was devalued by 56%, with the aim of strengthening the Government's policies for economic readjustment and recovery. The devaluation helped to increase export earnings, but it was estimated that inflation rose to 35.3% in 1987, from about 29.6% in 1986.

In late 1988 the Government announced details of a new economic programme, which envisaged the curtailment of the two-tier exchange rate system, the rescheduling of the foreign debt, and the abolition of price controls. (Prior to this announcement, the Government's intention to liberalize Guyana's import policy had been confirmed in September, when restrictions on imports of many non-food items were repealed. In addition, in mid-1988 the Government disclosed plans to abolish all controls on foreign private ownership and investment.) In 1988

GUYANA

Guyana's total foreign debt was estimated to be US $800m. Economic growth in 1988 was not expected to exceed the 1987 level of 0.7%.

Guyana is a founder member of the Caribbean Common Market (CARICOM, see p. 106) and the International Bauxite Association (p. 221), and in May 1986 joined the Inter-American Investment Corporation (p. 157).

Social Welfare

Improved water supplies, anti-tuberculosis campaigns and the control of malaria have steadily improved general health. A National Insurance scheme, compulsory for most workers and employers, was established in 1969, and was subsequently extended to cover self-employed people. In 1979 there were 85 physicians in government service. In 1981 Guyana had 29 hospitals and 149 health centres. Of total expenditure by the central Government in 1984, $ G51.5m. (3.7%) was for health, and a further $ G36.8m. (2.7%) for social security and welfare.

Education

Education is officially compulsory, and is provided free of charge, for eight years between six and 14 years of age. In 1976 the Government assumed responsibility for all church and private schools. In 1983 Guyana had 368 nursery, 423 primary, 30 secondary and community high, and 58 general secondary schools. Primary education begins at six years of age and lasts for at least six years. Children receive secondary education either in a general secondary school for five years or stay on at primary school for a further three years. Enrolment at all primary and secondary schools in 1981 was equivalent to 80% of the school-age population, but the proportion fell to 73% in 1983. Primary enrolment in 1981 included an estimated 90% of children in the relevant age-group. The total number of pupils in all schools was 233,723 in 1983. There are also 15 technical, vocational, special and higher educational institutions. These include the University of Guyana in Georgetown and three teacher training colleges. A loan of US $14.4m. was received in 1985 for improvements in the higher education system. Expenditure on education by the central Government in 1988 was estimated at $ G114.7m., representing 6.4% of total spending. In 1985, according to estimates by UNESCO, the average rate of adult illiteracy was only 4.1% (males 3.0%; females 5.2%), one of the lowest in the Western hemisphere.

Public Holidays

1989: 2 January (for New Year's Day), 23 February (Republic Day), 24–27 March (Easter), 1 May (Labour Day), 5 May (Indian Heritage Day), 7 May (Id al-Fitr, end of Ramadan), 1 July (Caribbean Day), 14 July (Id al-Adha, feast of the Sacrifice), 7 August (Freedom Day), 13 October (Yum an-Nabi, birth of the Prophet), 25–26 December (Christmas).

1990: 1 January (New Year's Day), 23 February (Republic Day), 13–16 April (Easter), 27 April (Id al-Fitr, end of Ramadan), 1 May (Labour Day), 5 May (Indian Heritage Day), 2 July (for Caribbean Day), 4 July (Id al-Adha, feast of the Sacrifice), 6 August (Freedom Day), 2 October (Yum an-Nabi, birth of the Prophet), 25–26 December (Christmas).

In addition, the Hindu festivals of Holi Phagwah (usually in March) and Divali (October or November) are celebrated. These festivals are dependent on sightings of the moon and their precise date is not known until two months before they take place.

Weights and Measures

The metric system has been introduced.

Statistical Survey

Sources (unless otherwise stated): Bank of Guyana, POB 1003, Georgetown; tel. (02) 63251; telex 2267; Ministry of National Development, Sophia, Georgetown.

AREA AND POPULATION

Area: 214,969 sq km (83,000 sq miles).

Population: 758,619 (males 375,481, females 382,778) at census of 12 May 1980; 790,000 (official estimate for mid-1985).

Density: 3.7 per sq km (mid-1985).

Ethnic Groups (1970 census, *de jure* population): 'East' Indians 362,735, Africans 218,400, Europeans 7,849, Chinese 3,402, Amerindians 34,302, Mixed 72,316, Others 844; Total 699,848.

Capital: Georgetown, population 72,049 (metropolitan area 187,056) at mid-1976 (estimate).

Births and Deaths (1978 registrations, provisional): 23,200 live births (birth rate 28.3 per 1,000); 6,000 deaths (death rate 7.3 per 1,000).

Economically Active Population (persons between 15 and 65 years of age, 1980 census): Agriculture, forestry and fishing 48,603; Mining and quarrying 9,389; Manufacturing 27,939; Electricity, gas and water 2,772; Construction 6,574; Trade, restaurants and hotels 14,690; Transport, storage and communications 9,160; Financing, insurance, real estate and business services 2,878; Community, social and personal services 57,416; Activities not adequately defined 15,260; Total employed 194,681 (males 153,645; females 41,036), Unemployed 44,650 (males 26,439, females 18,211); Total labour force 239,331 (males 180,084, females 59,247).

AGRICULTURE, ETC.

Principal Crops (FAO estimates, '000 metric tons, 1986): Rice (paddy) 357, Maize 1, Roots and tubers 30, Coconuts 41, Sugar cane 3,365, Oranges 11, Bananas 10, Plantains 18 (Source: FAO, *Production Yearbook*).

Livestock (FAO estimates, '000 head, year ending September 1986): Cattle 200, Pigs 180, Sheep 120, Goats 77, Chickens 15,000 (Source: FAO, *Production Yearbook*).

Livestock Products (FAO estimates, '000 metric tons, 1986): Beef and veal 2, Mutton and lamb 1, Pig meat 1, Poultry meat 15, Cows' milk 23, Hen eggs 4.2 (Source: FAO, *Production Yearbook*).

Forestry (FAO estimates, '000 cubic metres, 1986): Roundwood removals: Sawlogs, veneer logs and logs for sleepers 170, Other industrial wood 21, Fuel wood 18, Total 209; Sawnwood production: Total (incl. boxboards) 65 (Source: FAO, *Yearbook of Forest Products*).

Fishing ('000 metric tons, live weight): Total catch 44.9 in 1984; 45.8 in 1985; 44.6 in 1986 (Source: FAO, *Yearbook of Fishery Statistics*).

MINING

Production (official estimates, 1987): Bauxite 1,478,927 metric tons; Gold 812 kg; Diamonds 6,881 metric carats.

INDUSTRY

Selected Products (1985): Raw sugar (1987, official estimate, '000 metric tons) 225, Rum (1984, '000 hectolitres) 154, Beer (1984, estimate, '000 hectolitres) 71, Cigarettes (estimate, million) 600, Electric energy (million kWh) 390 (Source: UN, *Industrial Statistics Yearbook*).

FINANCE

Currency and Exchange Rates: 100 cents = 1 Guyana dollar ($ G). *Coins:* 1, 5, 10, 25 and 50 cents. *Notes:* 1, 5, 10, 20 and 100 dollars. *Sterling and US Dollar Equivalents* (30 September 1988): £1 sterling = $ G16.91; US $1 = $ G10.00; $ G1,000 = £59.14 = US $100.00. *Average Exchange Rate:* ($ G per US $): 4.252 in 1985; 4.272 in 1986; 9.756 in 1987.

Budget (official estimates, $ G million, 1988): *Revenue:* Current revenue 1,642.5, Capital receipts 1.7, External grants 200.2; Total 1844.4. *Expenditure:* Current expenditure on goods and services 2,844.1, Capital expenditure 1,074.2; Total 3,918.3.

International Reserves (US $ million at 31 December 1987): Foreign exchange 8.43; Total 8.43 (Source: IMF, *International Financial Statistics*).

Money Supply ($ G million at 31 December 1987): Currency outside banks 726.2, Demand deposits at commercial banks 599.9; Total money (including also private-sector deposits at the Bank of Guyana) 1,332.6 (Source: IMF, *International Financial Statistics*).

Cost of Living (Urban Consumer Price Index; base: 1980 = 100): 244.7 in 1985; 263.9 in 1986; 339.7 in 1987 (Source: IMF, *International Financial Statistics*).

Gross Domestic Product ($ G million at current prices): 1,964 in 1985; 2,219 in 1986; 3,357 in 1987.

Balance of Payments (US $ million, 1985): Merchandise exports f.o.b. 214.0, Merchandise imports f.o.b. −209.1, *Trade Balance* 4.9; Exports of services 48.0, Imports of services −144.3, *Balance on Goods and Services* −91.4; Private unrequited transfers (net) −2.0, Government unrequited transfers (net) −3.2, *Current Balance* −96.6; Long-term capital (net) −36.0, Short-term capital (net) −1.5, Net errors and omissions −4.3, *Total* (net monetary movements) −138.5; Valuation changes (net) −9.5, Exceptional financing (net) 143.0, *Changes in Reserves* −5.0 (Source: IMF, *International Financial Statistics*).

EXTERNAL TRADE

Principal Commodities ($ G million, 1985): *Imports c.i.f.:* Consumer goods 76.5 (Food 16.0); Intermediate goods 660.6 (Fuels and lubricants 436.4, Chemicals 44.4); Capital goods 307.3 (Machinery 170.6, Transport equipment 92.6, Building materials 30.5); Total (incl. others) 1053.5. *Exports f.o.b.* Bauxite 421.6; Sugar 282.2; Rice 56.6; Shrimps 18.3; Rum 29.6; Gold 17.2; Total (incl. others) 883.6. (Figures exclude re-exports of $ G19.6 million).

Principal Trading Partners (US $ million, 1982): *Imports:* Canada 11.4; Trinidad and Tobago 122.8; United Kingdom 25.5; USA 55.2; Total (incl. others) 290.2. *Exports:* Trinidad and Tobago 27.6; United Kingdom 79.4; USA 93.6; Venezuela 56.0; Total (incl. others) 388.1.

TRANSPORT

Road Traffic ('000 vehicles in use, 1980): Passenger cars 32.5, Commercial vehicles 12.9 (Source: UN, *Statistical Yearbook*).

Shipping (international sea-borne freight traffic, estimates in '000 metric tons, 1985): Goods loaded 1,548; Goods unloaded 636 (Source: UN, *Monthly Bulletin of Statistics*).

Civil Aviation (1975): Passenger arrivals 42,210, departures 59,364; Freight loaded 2,438 tons, unloaded 1,297 tons.

COMMUNICATIONS MEDIA
(Source: UNESCO, *Statistical Yearbook*)

Radio Receivers (1986): 355,000 in use.

Telephones (1 January 1978): 27,000 in use (UN, *Statistical Yearbook*).

Book Production (1983): 55 titles (16 books, 39 pamphlets).

EDUCATION
(Source: UNESCO, *Statistical Yearbook*)

Pre-primary (1981): Institutions 368, Teachers 1,783, Students 29,958.

Primary (1983): Institutions 423, Teachers 3,257, Students 121,869.

Secondary (1983, excluding vocational courses): Teachers 3,334, Students 64,518.

Higher (1985): Teachers 527, Students 2,328.

Directory

The Constitution

Guyana became a republic, within the Commonwealth, on 23 February 1970. A new constitution was promulgated on 6 October 1980. Its main provisions are summarized below:

The Constitution declares the Co-operative Republic of Guyana to be an indivisible, secular, democratic sovereign state in the course of transition from capitalism to socialism. The bases of the political, economic and social system are political and economic independence, involvement of citizens and socio-economic groups, such as co-operatives and trade unions, in the decision-making processes of the State and in management, social ownership of the means of production, national economic planning and co-operativism as the principle of socialist transformation. Personal property, inheritance, the right to work, with equal pay for men and women engaged in equal work, free medical attention, free education and social benefits for old age and disability are guaranteed. Individual political rights are subject to the principles of national sovereignty and democracy, and freedom of expression to the State's duty to ensure fairness and balance in the dissemination of information to the public. Relations with other countries are guided by respect for human rights, territorial integrity and non-intervention.

THE PRESIDENT

The President is the supreme executive authority, Head of State and Commander-in-Chief of the armed forces, elected for a term of office, usually of five years' duration, with no limit on re-election. The successful presidential candidate is the nominee of the party with the largest number of votes in the legislative elections. The President may prorogue or dissolve the National Assembly (in the case of dissolution, fresh elections must be held immediately) and has discretionary powers to postpone elections for up to one year at a time for up to five years. The President may be removed from office on medical grounds, or for violation of the Constitution (with a two-thirds majority vote of the Assembly), or for gross misconduct (with a three-quarters majority vote of the Assembly if allegations are upheld by a tribunal).

The President appoints a First Vice-President and Prime Minister who must be an elected member of the National Assembly, and a Cabinet of Ministers, which includes non-elected members and is collectively responsible to the legislature. The President also appoints a Minority Leader, who is the elected member of the Assembly deemed by the President most able to command the support of the opposition.

THE LEGISLATURE

The legislative body is a unicameral National Assembly of 65 members; 53 members are elected by universal adult suffrage in a system of proportional representation, 10 members are elected by the 10 Regional Democratic Councils and two members are elected by the National Congress of Local Democratic Organs. The Assembly passes bills, which are then presented to the President, and may pass constitutional amendments.

LOCAL GOVERNMENT

Guyana is divided into 10 Regions, each having a Regional Democratic Council elected for a term of up to five years and four months, although it may be prematurely dissolved by the President. Local councillors elect from among themselves deputies to the National Congress of Democratic Organs. This Congress and the National Assembly together form the Supreme Congress of the People of Guyana, a deliberative body which may be summoned, dissolved or prorogued by the President and is automatically dissolved along with the National Assembly.

OTHER PROVISIONS

Impartial commissions exist for the judiciary, the public service and the police service. An Ombudsman is appointed, after consultation between the President and the Minority Leader, to hold office for four years.

Note: In February 1988 the National Assembly approved a constitutional amendment which ended the Government's obligation, as stipulated in the 1980 Constitution, to consult with trade unions and co-operative bodies on matters of labour legislation. The amendment also provided that any law enacted by the National Assembly could not be declared invalid on the grounds of inconsistency with previous constitutions.

The Government

HEAD OF STATE

President: HUGH DESMOND HOYTE (assumed office 6 August 1985; sworn in as elected President 12 December 1985).

CABINET
(February 1989)

President and Minister of Home Affairs and Public Information: HUGH DESMOND HOYTE.

GUYANA

Vice-Presidents

Prime Minister and First Vice-President: HAMILTON GREEN.

Deputy Prime Minister and Vice-President for Culture and Social Development: VIOLA BURNHAM.

Deputy Prime Minister and Vice-President in the Office of the President: RANJI CHANDISINGH.

Senior Ministers

Attorney-General and Minister of Justice: KEITH STANISLAUS MASSIAH.

Deputy Prime Minister and Minister of Planning and Development: WILLIAM HASLYN PARRIS.

Deputy Prime Minister and Minister of Public Utilities: ROBERT CORBIN.

Minister of Agriculture: Dr PATRICK MCKENZIE.

Minister of Communications and Works: JULES RANENBURG.

Minister of Education: DERYCK BERNARD.

Minister of Finance: CARL B. GREENIDGE.

Minister of Foreign Affairs: RASHLEIGH E. JACKSON.

Minister of Health: NOEL BLACKMAN.

Minister of Regional Development: JEFFREY THOMAS.

Minister of Trade and Tourism: WINSTON MURRAY.

Minister in the Ministry of Planning and Development: SEERAM PRASHAD.

Minister in the Office of the President: YVONNE HAREWOOD-BENN.

Ministers

Minister of Agriculture: VIBERT PARVATTAN.

Minister of Home Affairs: STELLA ODIE-ALLI.

Minister of Public Services: Dr FAITH HARDING.

Minister of Labour and Co-operatives: PANDIT CHINTAMAN GOWKARRAN SHARMA.

Minister in the Ministry of Public Utilities: SHARAMDHEO SAWH.

Minister in the Ministry of Regional Development: URMIA E. JOHNSON.

Minister of State

Ministry of Culture and Social Development: JEAN PERSICO.

MINISTRIES

Office of the President: New Garden St, Georgetown; tel. 51330; telex 2205.

Ministry of Agriculture: Regent and Vlissingen Rds, Georgetown; tel. 69154.

Ministry of Communications and Works: Wight's Lane, Kingston, Georgetown; tel. 56510.

Ministry of Co-operatives: Homestretch Ave, D'Urban Park, Georgetown; tel. 60754.

Ministry of Education and Social Development: 26 Brickdam, POB 1014, Georgetown; tel. 54163.

Ministry of Energy and Mines: 41 Brickdam, Georgetown; tel. 66549.

Ministry of Finance: Main and Urquhart Sts, Georgetown; tel. 67241.

Ministry of Foreign Affairs: Georgetown; telex 2220.

Ministry of Health and Public Welfare: Homestretch Ave, D'Urban Park, Georgetown; tel. 65861.

Ministry of Home Affairs: 6 Brickdam, Georgetown; tel. 62444.

Ministry of Internal Trade and Consumer Protection: 95 Carmichael St, Georgetown; tel. 62505; telex 2288.

Ministry of Justice: 95 Carmichael St, Georgetown; tel. 62616.

Ministry of Labour: Homestretch Ave, D'Urban Park, Georgetown; tel. 57070.

Ministry of Regional Planning: Georgetown.

Directory

Legislature

NATIONAL ASSEMBLY

Speaker: SASE NARAIN.

Election, 9 December 1985

Party	Votes	%	Seats
People's National Congress	228,718	78.55	42
People's Progressive Party	45,926	15.77	8
United Force	9,810	3.37	2
Working People's Alliance	4,176	1.43	1
Democratic Labour Movement	2,157	0.74	—
People's Democratic Movement	232	0.08	—
National Democratic Front	156	0.05	—
Total	291,175	100.00	53

In addition to the 53 elected members, the Assembly has 12 regional representatives.

Political Organizations

Patriotic Coalition for Democracy (PCD): Georgetown; f. 1986; comprising:

Democratic Labour Movement (DLM): Lot 88, Alexander St, Lacytown, Georgetown; f. 1983; democratic-nationalist; Leader PAUL NEHRU TENNASSEE.

National Democratic Front (NDF): Georgetown; f. 1985; Leader JOSEPH BACCHUS.

People's Democratic Movement (PDM): Georgetown; tel. 64707; f. 1973; centrist; Leader LLEWELLYN JOHN.

People's Progressive Party (PPP): 41 Robb St, Georgetown; tel. 72095; f. 1950; Marxist-Leninist; Gen. Sec. Dr CHEDDI B. JAGAN.

Working People's Alliance (WPA): Walter Rodney House, 45 Croal St, Stabroek, Georgetown; originally popular pressure group, became political party 1979; independent Marxist; Collective Leadership: EUSI KWAYANA, Dr RUPERT ROOPNARINE.

People's National Congress (PNC): Congress Place, Sophia, POB 10330, Georgetown; tel. 57850; f. 1955 after a split with the PPP; socialist; Leader HUGH DESMOND HOYTE; Deputy Leader and Gen. Sec. RANJI CHANDISINGH.

United Force (UF): 96 Robb St, Bourda, Georgetown; right-wing; advocates rapid industrialization through government partnership and private capital; Leader MARCELLUS FEILDEN SINGH.

Diplomatic Representation

EMBASSIES AND HIGH COMMISSIONS IN GUYANA

Brazil: 308 Church St, Queenstown, POB 10489, Georgetown; tel. 57970; telex 2246; Ambassador: ADERBAL COSTA.

Canada: High and Young Streets, POB 10880, Georgetown; tel. 72081; telex 2215; High Commissioner: JOHN MACLACHLAN.

China, People's Republic: 108 Duke St, Kingston, Georgetown; tel. 71651; tel. 2251; Ambassador: YANG ZENGYE.

Colombia: 306 Church and Peter Rose Sts, Queenstown, Georgetown; tel. 71410; telex 2206; Ambassador: REYNALDO OSPINA CAICEDO.

Cuba: 46 High St, Kingston, Georgetown; tel. 66732; telex 2272; Ambassador: LÁZARO CABEZAS GONZÁLEZ.

German Democratic Republic: 176 Middle St, POB 10308, Georgetown; tel. 66755; telex 2230; Chargé d'affaires a.i.: GÜNTER MÄSER.

Germany, Federal Republic: Georgetown; tel. 61089; Ambassador: (vacant).

India: 10 Ave of the Republic, Georgetown; tel. 63996; telex 3025; High Commissioner: G. D. ATUK.

Jamaica: Camp St, Georgetown; tel. 69517; telex 226; High Commissioner: (vacant).

Korea, Democratic People's Republic: 88 Premniranjan Place, Georgetown; tel. 60266; telex 2228; Ambassador: CHONG JON-GYU.

Libya: 375 Ganges St, Prashad Nagar, Georgetown; tel. 61697; telex 2259; Chargé d'affaires: AHMED IBRAHIM EHIWASS.

Suriname: 304 Church St, POB 10508, Georgetown; tel. 67844; telex 2282; Ambassador: JOHN KOLANDER.

GUYANA

Trinidad and Tobago: 91 Middle St, POB 101029, Georgetown; tel. 72061; telex 2287; High Commissioner: TERRENCE BADEN-SEMPER (acting).

USSR: 48 Chandra Nagar St, Prashad Nagar, Georgetown; tel. 72975; telex 2277; Ambassador: ANATOLY ULANOV.

United Kingdom: 44 Main St, POB 10849, Georgetown; tel. 65881; telex 2221; High Commissioner: DAVID P. SMALL.

USA: 31 Main St, Georgetown; tel. 54900; telex 2213; Ambassador: THERESA ANNE TULL.

Venezuela: 296 Thomas St, Georgetown; tel. 61543; telex 2237; Ambassador: HUGO ALVAREZ PIFANO.

Yugoslavia: 72 Brickdam, POB 10408, Georgetown; tel. 71136; telex 2231; Ambassador: MARIN GERSKOVIĆ.

Judicial System

The Judicature of Guyana comprises the Supreme Court of Judicature, which consists of a Court of Appeal and a High Court (both of which are superior courts of record), and a number of Courts of Summary Jurisdiction.

The Court of Appeal consists of the Chancellor as President, the Chief Justice, and such number of Justices of Appeal as may be prescribed by the National Assembly. This Court came into operation in June 1966.

The High Court of the Supreme Court consists of the Chief Justice as President of the Court and Puisne Judges. Its jurisdiction is both original and appellate. It has criminal jurisdiction in matters brought before it on indictment. A person convicted by the Court has a right of appeal to the Guyana Court of Appeal. The High Court of the Supreme Court has unlimited jurisdiction in civil matters and exclusive jurisdiction in probate, divorce and admiralty and certain other matters. Under certain circumstances, appeal in civil matters lies either to the Full Court of the High Court of the Supreme Court, which is composed of not less than two judges, or to the Guyana Court of Appeal.

A magistrate has jurisdiction to determine claims where the amount involved does not exceed $ G1,500. Appeal lies to the Full Court.

Chancellor of Justice: KENNETH M. GEORGE.
Chief Justice: RUDOLPH H. HARPER.
Attorney-General: KEITH S. MASSIAH.

Religion

CHRISTIANITY

Guyana Council of Churches: 71 Murray St, Georgetown; tel. 66610; f. 1967 by merger of the Christian Social Council (f. 1937) and the Evangelical Council (f. 1960); 15 mem. churches, 1 assoc. mem.; Chair. Rt Rev. RANDOLPH O. GEORGE (Anglican Bishop of Guyana); Sec. MICHAEL MCCORMACK.

The Anglican Communion

Anglicans in Guyana are adherents of the Church in the Province of the West Indies, comprising eight dioceses. The Archbishop of the Province is the Bishop of the North Eastern Caribbean and Aruba, resident in St John's, Antigua. The diocese of Guyana also includes French Guiana and Suriname. In 1986 the estimated membership in the country was 125,000.

Bishop of Guyana: Rt Rev. RANDOLPH OSWALD GEORGE, Austin House, Georgetown; tel. 64183.

The Baptist Church

The Baptist Convention of Guyana: POB 101030, Georgetown; tel. 60428; Chair. Rev. ALFRED JULIEN.

The Lutheran Church

The Lutheran Church in Guyana: 28–29 North and Alexander Sts, Lacytown, Georgetown; tel. 64227; 14,147 mems; Pres. JAMES LOCHAN.

The Roman Catholic Church

Guyana comprises the single diocese of Georgetown, suffragan to the archdiocese of Port of Spain, Trinidad and Tobago. At 31 December 1985 there were an estimated 94,000 adherents in the country. The Bishop participates in the Antilles Episcopal Conference, based in Kingston, Jamaica.

Bishop of Georgetown: G. BENEDICT SINGH, Bishop's House, 27 Brickdam, POB 10720, Georgetown; tel. 64469.

Other Christian Churches

Other denominations active in Guyana include the African Methodist Episcopal Church, the African Methodist Episcopal Zion Church, the Church of God, the Church of the Nazarene, the Ethiopian Orthodox Church, the Guyana Baptist Mission, the Guyana Congregational Union, the Guyana Presbyterian Church, the Hallelujah Church, the Methodist Church in the Caribbean and the Americas, the Moravian Church and the Presbytery of Guyana.

HINDUISM

The Hindu religious centre is Maha Sabha, 162 Lamaha St, Georgetown; tel. 57443; f. 1934; Hindus account for about one-third of the population; Pres. SASE NARAIN.

ISLAM

Guyana United Sad'r Islamic Anjuman: 157 Alexander St, Kitty, POB 10715, Georgetown; tel. 69620; f. 1936; 120,000 mems; Pres. Haji ABDOOL RAHMAN; Sec. Haji S. M. YASEEN.

The Press

The Constitution does not provide for complete freedom of expression, and indirect press censorship is exercised by the state control of newsprint.

DAILY

Guyana Chronicle: 2A Lama Ave, Bel Air Park, POB 11, Georgetown; tel. 67461; f. 1881; state-owned; Editor-in-Chief (vacant); circ. 60,000 (weekdays), 100,000 (Sundays).

WEEKLIES AND PERIODICALS

The Catholic Standard: 293 Oronoque St, Queenstown, POB 10720, Georgetown; tel. 61540; f. 1905; weekly; Editor Rev. ANDREW MORRISON; circ. 10,000.

Diocesan Magazine: 144 Almond and Oronoque Sts, Queenstown, Georgetown; quarterly.

Guyana Business: 156 Waterloo St, POB 10110, Georgetown; tel. 56451; f. 1889; organ of the Georgetown Chamber of Commerce and Industry; quarterly; Editor C. D. KIRTON.

Guymine News: Linden, Georgetown; f. 1971; organ of Guyana Mining Enterprise Ltd; quarterly; Editor LOUIS LONDON; circ. 8,000 (local and overseas).

Guynews: 18 Brickdam, Georgetown; monthly.

Guysuco News: 22 Church St, Georgetown; f. 1955; 7 a year; house journal of the Guyana Sugar Corporation; Editor MCDONALD DASH; circ. 12,750.

Labour Advocate: 61 Hadfield St, Werkenrust, Georgetown; weekly.

Mirror: Lot 8, Industrial Estate, Ruimveldt, Greater Georgetown; tel. 62471; organ of the People's Progressive Party; owned by the New Guyana Co Ltd; Sundays; Editor JANET JAGAN; circ. 20,000.

New Nation: Sophia Exhibition Site, Georgetown; tel. 68520; f. 1955; organ of the People's National Congress; weekly; Editor ADAM E. HARRIS; circ. 26,000.

The Official Gazette of Guyana: Ministry of Information, 18–20 Brickdam, Georgetown; weekly; circ. 1,156.

Ratoon: 215 King St, Georgetown; monthly.

Stabroek News: Georgetown; f. 1986; weekly; independent; Editor CECIL GRIFFITH.

Sunday Chronicle: 2A Lama Ave, Bel Air Park, POB 11, Georgetown; tel. 63243; f. 1881; state-owned; Editor-in-Chief (vacant); circ. 100,000.

Thunder: 41 Robb St, Georgetown; f. 1950; organ of the People's Progressive Party; quarterly; Editor CLINTON COLLYMORE; circ. 10,000.

NEWS AGENCIES

Guyana News Agency: Lama Ave, Bel Air Park, Georgetown; tel. 53105; telex 2210; f. 1981; state-run; Editor-in-Chief COURTNEY E. GIBSON.

Foreign Bureaux

Inter Press Service (Italy): Suites 7 and 8, Federation Bldg, Croal St, Stabroek, Georgetown; tel. 025-3213; Correspondent PETE NINVALLE.

Prensa Latina (Cuba): 19–20 Lama Ave, Bel Air Park, Georgetown; tel. 67026; telex 2247; Chief Correspondent ROBERTO CASIN.

Telegrafnoye Agentstvo Sovetskovo Soyuza (TASS) (USSR): Bo Kaieteur Rd and Eping Ave, Bel Air Park, Georgetown; Correspondent ALEKSANDR KAMISHEV.

GUYANA
Directory

Xinhua (New China) News Agency (People's Republic of China): 52 Brickdam, Stabroek, Georgetown; tel. 69965; Correspondent CHEN JING.

Associated Press (USA) is also represented.

PRESS ASSOCIATION

Guyana Press Association: Georgetown; revived in 1988; Pres. COURTNEY GIBSON.

Publisher

Guyana National Printers Ltd: 1 Public Rd, La Penitence, POB 10256, Greater Georgetown; tel. 53623; telex 2212; state-owned printers and publishers (member of Guystac); Gen. Man. NOVEAR DE FREITAS.

Radio

In 1983 there were an estimated 350,000 radio receivers in use.

Guyana Broadcasting Corporation: St Phillips Green and High Sts, POB 10760, Georgetown; tel. 69231; f. 1979; formed from the Guyana Broadcasting Service and the Broadcasting Co Ltd (Radio Demerara) when the Government took over the assets of the latter; Exec. Chair. J. L. PHILADELPHIA; Gen. Man. AVE BREWSTER.

Plans to set up a national television network have been shelved.

Finance

(dep. = deposits; m. = million; brs = branches; amounts in Guyana dollars)

BANKING

Central Bank

Bank of Guyana: 1 Church St and Ave of the Republic, POB 1003, Georgetown; tel. 63250; telex 2267; f. 1965; assets $ G3,771.0m. (Dec. 1985); central bank of note issue; Gov. PATRICK E. MATTHEWS; Man. IVAN HAMILTON.

Local Banks

Guyana Bank for Trade and Industry Ltd: Water St, POB 10280, Georgetown; tel. 68431; f. 1987; frmly Barclays Bank; Gen. Man. MARGUERITE DA SILVA; 1 br.

Guyana Co-operative Agricultural and Industrial Development Bank: Lot 126, Parade and Barrack Sts, Kingston, Georgetown; tel. 58808; f. 1973; Man. Dir CYRIL K. HUNTE; 10 brs.

Guyana Co-operative Mortgage Finance Bank: 46 Main St, POB 1083, Georgetown; tel. 68415; f. 1973; Man. Dir ALFRED E. O. BOBB.

Guyana National Co-operative Bank: 1 Lombard and Cornhill Sts, POB 242, Georgetown; tel. 57810; telex 2235; f. 1970; dep. $ G132m. (1976); Man. Dir STEPHEN BACKER; 7 brs and 3 agencies.

National Bank of Industry and Commerce: 38–40 Water St, POB 10440, Georgetown; tel. 63231; 1 br.

Republic Bank: Bank of Guyana Bldg, 1 Church St and Ave of the Republic, Georgetown; tel. 63201; telex 2222; fmrly Chase Manhattan Bank; 1 br.

Foreign Banks

Bank of Baroda: 10 Regent St and Ave of the Republic, POB 10768, Georgetown; tel. 64005; telex 2243; f. 1908.

Bank of Nova Scotia: Alico Bldg, Regent and Hincks Sts, POB 10631; Georgetown; tel. 64031; Man. RUBEN R. SALAZAR.

INSURANCE

Demerara Mutual Life Assurance Society Ltd: 61 Ave of the Republic and Robb St, POB 10409, Georgetown; tel. 58991; f. 1891; Chair. RICHARD B. FIELDS; Gen. Man. EAWAN E. DEVONISH.

Guyana Co-operative Insurance Service: 47 Main St, Georgetown; tel. 68421; telex 2255; f. 1976; Chair. B. CLAUDE BONE; Gen. Man. HAROLD WILSON; Sec. D. COLE.

Guyana and Trinidad Mutual Life Insurance Co Ltd: Lots 27–29, Robb and Hincks Sts, Georgetown; tel. 57912; telex 2207; f. 1925; Chair. GEORGE U. JAIKARAN; Man. Dir R. E. CHEONG; affiliated company: Guyana and Trinidad Mutual Fire Insurance Co Ltd.

Hand-in-Hand Mutual Fire Insurance Co Ltd, Hand-in-Hand Mutual Life Assurance Co Ltd: 1–4 Ave of the Republic, Georgetown; tel. 51867; telex 2211; f. 1865; Chair. J. A. CHIN; Gen. Man. F. W. SPOONER.

There are also several foreign companies operating in Guyana.

Insurance Association

Insurance Association of Guyana: Georgetown.

Trade and Industry

CHAMBER OF COMMERCE

Georgetown Chamber of Commerce and Industry: 156 Waterloo St, Cummingsburg, POB 10110, Georgetown; tel. 56451; f. 1889; 104 mems; Pres. WAINWRIGHT MCKENZIE; Chief Exec. G. C. FUNG-ON.

PRODUCERS' ORGANIZATIONS

Consultative Association of Guyanese Industry Ltd: East St, POB 10730, Georgetown; tel. 57170; f. 1962; 6 mem. asscns, 12 assoc. mems; Chair. H. B. DAVIS.

Forest Products Association of Guyana: 6 Croal St and Manget Place, Georgetown; tel. 69848; f. 1944; 43 mems; Pres. DAVID PERSAUD (acting); Exec. Officer F. E. DALZELL.

Guyana Manufacturers' Association Ltd: 8 Church St, Company Path, Georgetown; tel. 66791; Pres. BRIAN GITTENS; Exec. Sec. SEETA A. MAHADEO.

Guyana Rice Producers' Association: Lot 104 Regent St, Lacytown, Georgetown; tel. 64411; f. 1946; c. 35,000 families; Pres. BUDRAM MAHADEO; Gen. Sec. PARIAG SUKHAI.

STATE AGENCIES AND MARKETING ORGANIZATIONS

Guyana's major industrial companies were nationalized during the 1970s, and the state sector predominates in the economy.

Advisory Environmental Council (AEC): Georgetown; f. 1988; to monitor the environmental impact of agricultural and industrial sectors; Dir JAILALL KISSOON.

Bauxite Industry Development Company Ltd: 71 Main St, Georgetown; tel. 57780; telex 2244; f. 1976; holding company of Guyana Mining Enterprise Ltd; Chair. BERNARD CRAWFORD.

Guyana Mining Enterprise Ltd (Guymine): East Bank, Berbice; tel. (03) 22336; telex 2245; f. 1977 by merger of Guyana Bauxite Co (Guybau) and Berbice Mining Enterprises; Chair. W. H. PARRIS.

Guyana Electricity Corporation (GEC): 40 Main St, Georgetown; tel. 62601; telex 2250; Gen. Man. NARVON PERSAUD.

Guyana Fisheries Ltd: Georgetown; tel. 58960; telex 2286; owners of 26 trawlers, landing and processing facilities; Man. Dir MICHAEL ELLIOT DAVIS.

Guyana Liquor Corporation: 8–11 Water and Schumaker Sts, Georgetown; tel. 64404; telex 2284; Exec. Chair. YESU PERSAUD.

Guyana Marketing Corporation: Lombard St, Georgetown; tel. 65846; Chair. Dr P. MCKENZIE; Gen. Man. KELVIN CRAIG.

Guyana National Engineering Corporation: see section on Shipping.

Guyana National Resources Agency: Georgetown; management and development of natural resources; Dir WINSTON KING.

Guyana National Trading Corporation Ltd: see section on Shipping.

Guyana Oil Co Ltd: Providence, East Bank, Demerara; tel. 62877; telex 2291.

Guyana Pharmaceutical Corporation Ltd: 1 Public Rd, La Penitence, Georgetown; tel. 63281; telex 2203; pharmaceuticals, chemicals and cosmetics; Exec. Chair. W. A. LEE.

Guyana Rice Board: 1–2 Water St, Georgetown; tel. 62480; telex 2266; f. 1973 to develop the rice industry and promote the expansion of its export trade, and to engage in industrial, commercial and agricultural activities necessary for the development of the rice industry; Exec. Chair. O. E. CLARKE.

Guyana Stockfeeds Ltd: Ruimveldt, Greater Georgetown; tel. 63402; telex 2203.

Guyana Stores Ltd: 19 Water St, Georgetown; tel. 66171; telex 2212; retailers and wholesalers; Chair. PAUL CHAN-A-SUE.

Guyana Sugar Corporation Ltd (Guysuco): 22 Church St, POB 10547, Georgetown; tel. 66171; telex 2265; f. 1976; Chair. HAROLD B. DAVIS; Sec. C. J. LAWRENCE.

Guyana Transport Services: Lamaha and Carmichael Sts, Georgetown; tel. 67547; due to be 'privatized' in 1989.

Livestock Development Co Ltd: 58 High St, Georgetown; tel. 61601.

DEVELOPMENT AGENCIES

Guyana-Libya Fishing Co: Houston, East Bank, Demerara; tel. 54382; joint venture between the Governments of Guyana and Libya to develop fishing potential; Chair. F. G. DORWAY.

GUYANA

Mahaica-Mahaicony-Abary Agricultural Development Authority: Onverwagt, West Coast, Berbice; tel. (03) 3117; telex 3055; aims to bring Berbice-Abary region into full agricultural production.

CO-OPERATIVE SOCIETIES

Chief Co-operatives Development Officer: Ministry of Co-operatives, Homestretch Ave, Durban Park, Georgetown; tel. 60754; M. G. EDGHILL.

In October 1988 there were 1,459 registered co-operative societies, mainly savings clubs and agricultural credit societies, with a total membership of over 100,000.

TRADE UNIONS

Federation of Independent Trade Unions (FITUG): Georgetown; f. Oct. 1988 by seven independent unions that withdrew from the Trades Union Congress (see below); Pres. GEORGE DANIELS.

Clerical and Commercial Workers' Union (CCWU): 140 Murray St, Georgetown; tel. 52822; Pres. GORDON TODD.

Guyana Agricultural and General Workers' Union (GAWU): 104–106 Regent St, Lacytown, Georgetown; tel. 72091; allied to the PPP; Gen. Sec. KOMAL CHAND; 15,000 mems.

Guyana Bauxite Supervisors' Union: Linden.

Guyana Mine Workers' Union: 784 Determa St, Mackenzie, Linden; tel. (04) 3146; 5,800 mems.

Guyana Public Service Union (GPSU): 160 Regent Rd and New Garden St, Georgetown; tel. 61770; Pres. GEORGE DANIELS; 11,600 mems.

National Association of Agricultural, Commercial and Industrial Employees: Georgetown.

University of Guyana Workers' Union: Georgetown.

Trades Union Congress (TUC): Critchlow Labour College, Woolford Ave, Nonpareil Park, Georgetown; tel. 61493; national trade union body; 16 affiliated unions; Pres. FRANK ANDREWS.

Amalgamated Transport and General Workers' Union: 46 Urquhart St, Georgetown; tel. 66243; Pres. FRANK ANDREWS.

General Workers' Union: 106–107 Lamaha St, North Cummingsburg, Georgetown; tel. 61185; f. 1954; Pres. NORRIS WITTER; Gen. Sec. EDWIN JAMES.

Guyana Labour Union: 198 Camp St, Georgetown; tel. 63275; Pres.-Gen. DESMOND HOYTE; 6,000 mems.

Guyana Postal and Telecommunication Workers' Union: 310 East St, POB 10352, Georgetown; tel. 65255; Pres. SELWYN O. FELIX; Gen. Sec. ANJOU DANIELS.

Transport

RAILWAYS

There are two railways in Guyana. One between Ituni and Linden is used for the transport of bauxite. The other, between Matthews Ridge and Port Kaituma in the north-west of the country, is also used for minerals. Neither caters for passengers.

ROADS

The coastal strip has a well-developed road system. There are more than 3,000 miles (4,830 km) of paved and good-weather roads and trails. In 1982 a road linking Linden to Mabura was officially opened. A floating two-lane bridge to replace ferry services on the Demerara River to Georgetown was opened in July 1978. A road project linking Guyana with Brazil was resumed in 1986 after being suspended in 1980.

SHIPPING

Guyana's principal ports are at Georgetown and New Amsterdam. A ferry service is operated between Springlands, Guyana, and Nieuw Nickerie, Suriname, and it was hoped that a new ferry service would be in operation by 1988. Communications with the interior are chiefly by river, although access is hindered by rapids and falls. There are 607 miles (1,077 km) of navigable rivers. The main rivers are the Mazaruni, the Potaro, the Essequibo, the Demerara and the Berbice.

John Fernandes Ltd: 24 Water St, Georgetown; tel. 56294; telex 2226; ship agents and stevedore contractors; reps for West Indies Shipping Corpn (WISCO), Bernuth Lines, SMS, Caribbean Liners and Rambarran Shipping; Man. B. A. FERNANDES.

Shipping Association of Georgetown: 28 Main and Holmes Sts, Georgetown; tel. 62632; f. 1952; Chair. F. A. GRIFFITH; Sec. and Man. W. V. BRIDGEMOHAN; members:

Caribbean Molasses Co Ltd: Mud Lots 1–2, Water St, POB 10208, Georgetown; tel. 69238; telex 2274; exporters of molasses in bulk; Man. Dir N. F. COOPER.

Guyana National Engineering Corporation Ltd: 1–9 Lombard St, Charlestown, POB 10520, Georgetown; tel. 63291; telex 2218; metal foundry, ship building and repair, agents for Saguenay Shipping Ltd, Tec Lines Ltd, W.I. Shipping Co Inc, Ivaran Lines, Linhas Brasileiras de Navegação, SA, Shipping Corpn of India Ltd, Flota Mercante Grancolombiana, SA; Exec. Chair. CLAUDE SAUL.

Guyana National Shipping Corporation Ltd: 5–9 Lombard St, La Penitence, Georgetown; tel. 66171; telex 2232; reps for Harrison and Mitsui OSK Lines, Samba and Resolve Maritime Corpn, airline reservations, and Lloyd Agencies; Exec. Chair. P. A. CHAN-A-SUE.

Guyana National Trading Corporation Ltd: 45–47 Water St, POB 10480, Georgetown; tel. 61666; telex 2214; importers and distributors; reps for Nedlloyd Lines, Himmelman Supply Co, Smit-Lloyd, Atlantic Chartering and Trading Co and K-Line; travel agents for BWIA (Trinidad and Tobago) and Guyana Airways; Exec. Chair. F. A. GRIFFITH.

CIVIL AVIATION

The main airport is Timehri International, 42 km (26 miles) from Georgetown. The more important settlements in the interior have airstrips.

Guyana Airways Corporation: 32 Main St, POB 10223, Georgetown; tel. 68195; telex 2242; f. 1939; state-owned; operates internal scheduled services and to the Caribbean, the USA, Brazil and Suriname; Exec. Chair. JOSEPH R. VIEIRA; fleet of 2 Twin Otters, 1 DC-6BF, 1 Boeing 707, 2 HS-748.

A weekly jet service operates between Georgetown and Boa Vista in Brazil.

Tourism

Despite the beautiful scenery in the interior of the country, Guyana does little to encourage tourism.

Guyana Overland Tours: 1st Floor, 6 Avenue of the Republic, Robbstown, POB 10173, Georgetown; tel. 69876; f. 1968.

HAITI

Introductory Survey

Location, Climate, Language, Religion, Flag, Capital

The Republic of Haiti occupies the western part of the Caribbean island of Hispaniola (the Dominican Republic occupies the remaining two-thirds) and some smaller offshore islands. Cuba, to the west, is less than 80 km away. The climate is tropical but the mountains and fresh sea winds mitigate the heat. Temperatures vary little with the seasons, and the annual average in Port-au-Prince is about 27°C (80°F). The rainy season is from May to November. The official languages are French and Creole. About 80% of the population belong to the Roman Catholic Church, the country's official religion, and other Christian churches are also represented. A form of witchcraft, known as voodoo, is the folk religion. The national flag (proportions 2 by 1) has two equal vertical stripes, of blue and red. The state flag has, in addition, a white rectangular panel, containing the national coat of arms (a palm tree, surmounted by a Cap of Liberty and flanked by flags and cannons), in the centre. The capital is Port-au-Prince.

Recent History

Haiti was first colonized in 1659 by the French, who named the island Saint-Domingue. A successful uprising between 1791 and 1803 by African-descended slaves established the country in 1804 as an independent state, ruled by Jean-Jacques Dessalines, who proclaimed himself Emperor of Haiti. Hostility between the negro population and the mulattos continued throughout the 19th century until, after increasing political instability, the USA intervened militarily and ruled the country from 1915 to 1934. Thereafter, mulatto presidents were in power until 1946, when a negro president, Dusmarsais Estimé, was elected. He was overthrown in 1950 by a military coup, led by another negro, Gen. Paul Magloire, who was himself forced to resign in 1956. In 1957 Dr François Duvalier, a country physician, was elected President.

Despite a promising start, the Duvalier administration soon became a dictatorship, maintaining its authority by means of a notorious private army, popularly called the Tontons Macoutes (Creole for 'Bogeymen'), who used extortion and intimidation to crush all possible opposition to the President's rule. In 1964 Duvalier's tenure was changed to that of President-for-Life, and he retained almost total power over the country, by means of violence and voodoo threats, until his death in April 1971. In January 1971 the Constitution was amended to allow Duvalier to nominate his successor. He promptly named his son, Jean-Claude Duvalier, who became President, at 19 years of age, on the day of his father's death.

The release of political prisoners and an amelioration of conditions, including the appointment of more moderate cabinet ministers, indicated that the regime was slightly more humane than its predecessor, with the increasing need for international aid pressuring the Government to be responsive to human rights agencies and critical donor countries. The regime was characterized by frequent cabinet changes and alternating policies of tentative liberalization and subsequent repression. Elections took place in February 1979 for the 58-seat National Assembly. As 57 of the seats were won by the official government party, the Parti de l'Unité Nationale (PUN), demonstrations took place against alleged electoral malpractice.

In mid-1979 three illegal Christian Democratic opposition parties were formed by critics of the Duvalier regime. In October 1979 a new press law was introduced, banning any criticism of the President, or of government or security officials, and any articles or broadcasts deemed to be subversive. The rearrest in October 1980 of Sylvio Claude, the leader of the Parti Démocratique Chrétien d'Haïti (PDCH), for alleged subversion was followed in November and December by more than 400 arrests of opposition politicians, journalists and broadcasters. Leading opponents of the regime were deported. Claude was sentenced to 15 years' hard labour in August 1981. Foreign criticism forced a retrial at which the sentence was reduced to six years, and in September 1982 Claude was released into house arrest, from which he subsequently escaped.

The first municipal elections for 25 years were held in 1983. President Duvalier had promised in April 1982 that they would be 'free, honest and democratic'. In the event, all the opposition candidates for the politically sensitive Port-au-Prince posts were arrested just before the polls. In the provincial constituencies allegations of electoral fraud were made. On 27 August the Assembly was dissolved when the Constitution was amended, reaffirming, however, the Presidency-for-Life and Duvalier's right to name his successor. Elections for the Assembly were held on 12 February 1984. All 59 seats were won by the pro-Duvalier party, PUN, as no opposition candidates were allowed. Respect for human rights deteriorated further, as all political activity and opposition newspapers were banned. Rioting in May and June against government corruption resulted in the dismissal of Ministers who were held responsible for the disturbances, and a further reshuffle in August helped to strengthen the power of uncompromising elements within the Government, especially that of Dr Roger Lafontant, the Minister of State for the Interior and National Defence.

Demonstrations were organized by the Roman Catholic Church and other religious groups to protest at poverty and corruption within the country. In April 1985 Duvalier announced a programme of constitutional reforms, including the eventual appointment of a Prime Minister and the formation of political parties, subject to certain limiting conditions. A popular referendum, held in June, to endorse these changes and the concept of the Life Presidency resulted in a 99.98% vote in favour. Opposition leaders alleged widespread electoral fraud, and denounced the Government's liberalization measures as an insincere gesture, designed for the benefit of foreign aid donors. In September Roger Lafontant, the minister most closely identified with the Government's acts of repression, was dismissed in a cabinet reshuffle. Unrest in the northern areas of Haiti was again reported in December, after the deaths of four students in an anti-Government demonstration in Gonaïves. Duvalier dismissed four of his principal ministers and reduced the prices of basic commodities in an attempt to prevent an escalation of the disturbances. Further measures to curb continued disorder were taken in January 1986. The university and schools were closed indefinitely, and radio stations were forbidden to report on current events. Finally, Duvalier imposed a state of siege and declared martial law.

On 7 February 1986, following intensified public protests, Duvalier and his family fled from Haiti to exile in France, leaving a five-member National Council of Government (CNG), led by the army chief of staff, Gen. Henri Namphy, to succeed him. The interim military-civilian Council announced the appointment of a new cabinet. The National Assembly was dissolved, and the Constitution was suspended. Later in the month, the Tontons Macoutes were disbanded, educational establishments were reopened, the traditional blue and red flag was restored, and plans were made to recover and nationalize Duvalier's vast assets. Prisoners from Haiti's largest gaol were freed under a general amnesty. In March US $26m. of US aid, which had been withheld since January in protest against abuses of human rights, was released.

However, after the initial euphoria following the downfall of Duvalier, renewed rioting occurred to protest against the inclusion in the new Government of known supporters of the former dictatorship. Curfews lasting 16 hours per day were imposed to quell the disturbances. In March there was a cabinet reshuffle, following the resignations of three Duvalierist members of the National Council of Government (only one of whom was replaced). The new three-member National Council of Government comprised Gen. Namphy, Col Williams Régala (Minister of the Interior and National Defence) and Jacques François (then Minister of Finance).

In April Gen. Namphy showed signs of positive action in the announcement, firstly, of a road-building programme, expected to provide 6,000 jobs, and, secondly, of a proposed time-table for elections to restore constitutional government by February 1988. He also announced that he would not be a candidate in the presidential election. The first of these elections, to select 41 people (from 101 candidates) who would form part of the 61-member Constituent Assembly which was to revise the Constitution, took place in October 1986. However, the level of participation at the election was only about 5%, owing to the absence of democratic tradition in Haiti and to the lack of adequate organization and publicity.

The new Constitution was approved by 99.8% of voters in a referendum held on 29 March 1987. An estimated 50% of the electorate voted. An independent Provisional Electoral Council (CEP) was appointed to supervise the presidential and legislative elections, which were scheduled for 29 November.

There was continued unrest in the country, and in June 1987 a wave of general strikes took place in protest at the Government's attempt to dissolve the country's principal trade union, the Centrale Autonome des Travailleurs Haïtiens (CATH), and its decision to limit the authority of the CEP. Violent confrontations continued prior to the elections. Two presidential candidates were murdered, while 12 other potential candidates were barred from taking part in the election because of their connections with the Duvalier regime. On 29 November the elections were cancelled three hours after voting had begun, owing to renewed violence and killings, for which former members of the Tontons Macoutes were believed to be responsible. The Government dissolved the CEP and took control of the electoral process. In December a new CEP was appointed by the Government, and elections were rescheduled for 17 January 1988. In protest at the removal from office of the independent electoral body, four prominent opposition candidates announced that they would boycott the new presidential election, and demanded the resignation of the CNG. Voting took place as planned, however, and a former university professor, Leslie Manigat of the Rassemblement des Démocrates Nationaux Progressistes (RDNP), with 50.3% of the total votes cast, was declared the winner. Legislative and municipal elections were held concurrently. It was officially estimated that 35% of the electorate had voted in the elections, although opposition leaders claimed that only 5% had participated, and alleged that there had been extensive fraud and malpractice. Although the result of the presidential election was widely discredited, Manigat took office on 7 February 1988.

The Cabinet that President Manigat formed did not include any pro-Duvalier members, an omission which led to increasing protests by Duvalier's supporters, as they attempted to regain the political initiative. In June 1988, as a result of a dispute between President Manigat and Gen. Namphy over changes in the military hierarchy, the President dismissed Gen. Namphy from office. However, three days later, on 20 June, President Manigat was overthrown by disaffected members of the army. He was replaced by Gen. Namphy, who appointed a cabinet composed entirely of members of the armed forces, and removed all restrictions on the appointment of Duvalier's supporters to the Government. The legislature was dissolved, and the Constitution of 1987 was formally abrogated; the new administration announced its intention to draft a new constitution. Under the new regime, atrocities involving the Tontons Macoutes became more widespread, culminating, in September, with an attack by a gang of armed civilians on the congregation at a church in Port-au-Prince. Thirteen people died and more than 80 were injured in the attack, which provoked international condemnation.

On 18 September 1988 Gen. Namphy was ousted in a coup, led by Brig.-Gen. Prosper Avril (who became President) and non-commissioned officers from the Presidential Guard, who advocated the introduction of radical reforms. Subsequently, there was a purge of Duvalier's supporters within the armed forces, which included the removal from office of eight generals; only one representative of the armed forces was appointed to the new Cabinet. In October an attempted coup by pro-Duvalier members of the army was thwarted. In November an independent electoral body, the Collège Electoral d'Haïti (CEDA), was established to supervise future elections, to draft an electoral law and to ensure proper registration of voters. In November Col Jean-Claude Paul, the former commander of the Dessalines barracks and a leading figure in the September coup (who had been indicted, in March, for drugs-trafficking offences by a court in the USA), died in mysterious circumstances. Colonel Paul's death removed one of the principal obstacles to the resumption of US aid to Haiti.

In January 1989 the CATH organized a one-day general strike in support of demands for a reduction in the prices of basic products and for an increase in the minimum wage. In addition, the union demanded that persons accused of violations of human rights be put on trial. The strike was declared illegal by the Government.

International relations, although improved after 1971, continued to be strained because of Haiti's unpopular political regimes and government corruption. Relations between Haiti and its neighbour on the island of Hispaniola, the Dominican Republic, have traditionally been tense because of the use of the border area by anti-Government guerrillas, smugglers and illegal emigrants, resulting in the periodic closure of the border. In April 1987 the border was reopened to travellers, but not to trade. Haiti is a member of the OAS (see p. 190).

Government

The Constitution, approved by referendum in March 1987, provided for a bicameral legislature, comprising a 77-member Chamber of Deputies and a 27-member Senate. Executive power was held by the President, who was elected by universal adult suffrage for a five-year term and could not stand for immediate re-election. The President selected a Prime Minister from the political party commanding a majority in the legislature. The Prime Minister chose a cabinet in consultation with the President. There are nine Départements, subdivided into arrondissements and communes. However, the Constitution was rejected by the military Government that was installed after the coup in June 1988. Following a further coup in September 1988, the new President, Brig.-Gen. Prosper Avril, announced that his Government would respect the principles formulated in the 1987 Constitution until legislative elections were held, after which the newly-elected legislature, acting as a Constituent Assembly, would amend the Constitution. During the interim period, President Avril's Government was to rule by decree.

Defence

In June 1988 Haiti had a defence force with a total strength of about 7,600, including a battalion of commando-type troops known as the Léopards. The army of 7,000 men includes a Presidential Guard. The navy comprises a coastguard patrol of 300 men and four vessels, and there is an air force of 300. Estimated defence expenditure in 1985 was US $30.5m.

Economic Affairs

In terms of average income, Haiti is the poorest country in the Western hemisphere. In 1987, according to estimates by the World Bank, Haiti's gross national product (GNP), measured at average 1985–87 prices, was US $2,221m., equivalent to $360 per head, well below the level of any other country in Latin America. Even this low income is unevenly distributed. In the mid-1980s the richest 1% of the population accounted for about 44% of national income. Between 1980 and 1987, it was estimated, GNP declined, in real terms, at an average annual rate of 0.3%, with real GNP per head fallling by 2.1% per year. The overall growth of gross domestic product (GDP) averaged 2.9% per year in 1965–80, but in 1980–86 GDP contracted by an average annual rate of 0.7%. Many sectors of the economy, including agriculture, remained stagnant. GDP grew by only 0.6% in 1985/86, and declined by 0.7% in 1986/87.

In 1982/83 an estimated 65% of the working population were engaged in agriculture, forestry and fishing, although this sector provided only 33.2% of the country's GDP in that year. Agricultural production meets only about 60% of Haiti's domestic needs. The amount spent on food imports increased from US $16m. in 1970 to $76m. in 1986/87. Haiti's principal commercial crop, and its major export commodity, is coffee. However, the yields from coffee have been poor in recent years. Efforts to increase agricultural productivity, through the improvement of power, transportation and irrigation, are hindered by deforestation and soil erosion. Reductions in public spending have caused the suspension of many rural development projects. In 1986/87 Haiti's exports of coffee were valued at $36m., providing 17% of total export earnings.

Drought in 1982 and 1983 affected the production of important staple food crops, such as maize, rice and beans, although the output of sugar cane and sweet potatoes increased. Cocoa and sisal are the other major crops grown for export. Livestock is raised for internal consumption, and for limited export, but the country's entire population of black pigs was destroyed because of infection by African swine fever. Restocking, with the American pink pig (which costs more to feed), has been gradual. In January 1987 the USA reduced its quota for imports of Haitian sugar by 40%. This, combined with increased smuggling of sugar, has greatly affected Haiti's sugar industry, and by April 1987 all of the country's sugar mills had been closed. In July 1988 the USA increased its quota for annual imports of Haitian sugar by 27.5%, to 8,000 short tons. The use of charcoal, which accounts for about 75% of Haiti's energy consumption, is rapidly causing the deforestation of mountain sides, leading to serious problems of soil erosion. Two hydro-electric dams have been been built in the Artibonite valley, but they supply electricity only to Port-au-Prince. A third dam is being built on the Massacre river, at a cost of US $2m., in a joint operation with the Dominican Republic, and was due to become operational from January 1989.

The mining of bauxite in Haiti, which used to produce about 600,000 metric tons annually, ceased in 1983, owing to the low international demand for aluminium. In 1986 the manufacturing sector contributed about 20% of GDP. An industrial zone has been established outside Port-au-Prince, and more than 300 companies, mostly from the USA, have built factories there. Processing industries, attracted by a cheap labour force (minimum daily wage US $3.12) and the lack of legislation to protect workers, include the assembly of sophisticated electronic equipment, toys, sports equipment, clothes and other goods for the US market. Trade is largely with the USA, although the EEC countries, especially France, are now significant trading partners. The benefits for US companies of the US Government's Caribbean Basin Initiative (CBI) have provided an additional incentive: the value of exports of assembled goods to the USA increased from $107m. in 1978/79 to $187.4m. in 1982/83. In 1986/87 the value of exports of manufactured articles totalled $134m., providing 63.5% of total export earnings. In 1986 about 15,000 workers in the export assembly industry lost their jobs as a result of political instability in the country. However, a US-funded investment programme was expected to create some 50,000 new jobs in the assembly industry between 1987 and 1990.

Tourism was formerly a major source of foreign exchange, and an important sector of the economy. In 1985/86 the total number of arrivals, including cruise passengers, was 208,092, following a trend of decline. This decline was partly caused by reports that Haiti was one of the sources of the incurable disease AIDS, and partly because of unrest in the country. Unemployment is widespread, especially in the rural areas, causing migration to the towns, in particular to Port-au-Prince, where the population has doubled in 10 years, placing a severe strain on the capital's resources. In 1987 unemployment was estimated at 60% of the work-force. In October 1986 the Government announced a $40m. emergency development programme, to be financed by foreign aid.

Haiti is a major beneficiary of international aid organizations, and up to 75% of its budget is financed by foreign donors. Between 1981 and 1986 disbursement of aid was increasingly accompanied by demands for an end to administrative corruption and for an improvement in social and political conditions. In 1984/85 the US Government provided US $45m. in aid, a figure which was $9m. less than the amount requested by the Duvalier Government. Foreign aid, with the exception of humanitarian aid, was entirely suspended following the cancellation of the elections in November 1987. Almost one-third of the state budget was lost as a result of these measures. In November 1988, however, the US administration announced the allocation of some $30m. in aid and credit guarantees.

Haiti has recorded a deficit on merchandise trade in every year since 1965. In the year to September 1981 this was extremely high (US $225m.), owing to the fall in exports after Hurricane Allen. The IMF provided compensatory financing, and in 1982 agreed to provide support of SDR 34.5m. over a two-year period. In 1983 this facility was extended to provide a $60m. stand-by loan for a further two years. In December 1986 the IMF approved a three-year structural adjustment facility of SDR 20.7m. Haiti's trade deficit declined to $121.7m. in 1984/85, but rose to $135.4m. in 1985/86 before easing again, to $109.3m., in 1986/87. In the year to September 1987 the current balance of payments registered a deficit of $31.2m., the lowest since 1975/76. In 1987 growth in GDP was estimated at 2.7%.

About one-half of government revenue, which totalled US $169.2m. in 1982/83, derives from customs duties. Haiti's public debt is low in comparison with other Latin American countries, since a large proportion of the budget is provided by grant aid and concessionary loans. The budget proposals for 1988/89 envisaged total expenditure of more than $200m., but did not include provision for foreign aid. The average annual rate of inflation declined from 10.2% in 1983 to 3.3% in 1986, and prices fell by 11.5% in 1987. It has been calculated that remittances from Haitians living and working abroad contribute about $100m. annually to the economy. In recent years one of Haiti's main economic problems has been the shortage of foreign exchange to finance imports of fuel, food and spare parts. The country's reserves of foreign exchange increased from $2.7m. at mid-1986 to $20.6m. at mid-1987, but declined to $11.5m. at mid-1988.

Social Welfare

Industrial and commercial workers are provided with free health care. In 1980 Haiti had 52 hospital establishments, with a total of only 3,964 beds, equivalent to one for every 1,264 inhabitants: the lowest level of provision in any country of the Western hemisphere. In 1979 there were 600 physicians in government service. Public health received an allocation of 89.5m. gourdes for 1984/85. Religious and other voluntary groups provide medical services in rural areas and in Port-au-Prince.

Education

Education is provided by the State, by the Roman Catholic Church and by other religious organizations, but many schools charge for tuition, books or uniforms. Learning is based on the French model, and French is used as the language of instruction. Primary education, beginning at six years of age and lasting for six years, is officially compulsory. Secondary education begins at 12 years of age and lasts for a further six years, comprising two cycles of three years each. In 1984 the total enrolment at primary and secondary schools was equivalent to 50% of the school-age population (54% of boys; 47% of girls). Primary enrolment in that year included only 44% of children in the relevant age-group. Secondary education is provided by 21 public lycées and by a number of private and religious schools. Enrolment at secondary schools in 1984 was equivalent to only 18% of children in the relevant age-group. In 1985, according to estimates by UNESCO, the average rate of adult illiteracy was 62.4% (males 59.9%; females 64.7%), the highest national level in the Western hemisphere. The rate is even higher in rural areas (about 85%), where Creole is the popular language. Some basic adult education programmes, with instruction in Creole, have been created in an attempt to redress this. Higher education is provided by technical, vocational and domestic science schools, and by the Université d'Etat d'Haïti, which has faculties of law, medicine, dentistry, science, agronomy and ethnology. Government expenditure on education in 1985 was 117.6m. gourdes.

Public Holidays

1989: 1 January (Independence Day), 2 January (Heroes of Independence), 6 February (Shrove Monday, half day), 7 February (Shrove Tuesday), 24 March (Good Friday), 14 April (Pan-American Day), 1 May (Labour Day), 18 May (Flag Day), 22 May (National Sovereignty), 15 August (Assumption), 24 October (United Nations Day), 2 November (All Souls' Day, half day), 18 November (Army Day and Commemoration of the Battle of Vertières), 5 December (Discovery Day), 25 December (Christmas Day).

1990: 1 January (Independence Day), 2 January (Heroes of Independence), 26 February (Shrove Monday, half day), 27 February (Shrove Tuesday), 13 April (Good Friday), 14 April (Pan-American Day), 1 May (Labour Day), 18 May (Flag Day), 22 May (National Sovereignty), 15 August (Assumption), 24 October (United Nations Day), 2 November (All Souls' Day, half day), 18 November (Army Day and Commemoration of the Battle of Vertières), 5 December (Discovery Day), 25 December (Christmas Day).

Weights and Measures

Officially the metric system is in force but many US measures are also used.

HAITI

Statistical Survey

Sources (unless otherwise stated): Banque de la République d'Haïti, Angle rue du Magasin d'État et rue des Miracles, Port-au-Prince; tel. 2-4142; telex 2030394; Ministère de l'Economie, des Finances et de l'Industrie, Port-au-Prince.

Area and Population

AREA, POPULATION AND DENSITY

Area (sq km)	27,750*
Population (census results)†	
31 August 1971	4,329,991
30 August 1982	
Males	2,448,370
Females	2,605,422
Total	5,053,792
Population (official estimates at mid-year)	
1985	5,501,000
1986	5,603,000
1987	5,707,000
Density (per sq km) at mid-1987	205.7

* 10,714 sq miles.
† Excluding adjustment for underenumeration.

PRINCIPAL TOWN

Port-au-Prince (capital), estimated population 738,342 (including suburbs) at mid-1984.

BIRTHS AND DEATHS

Average annual birth rate 36 per 1,000; death rate 17 per 1,000 (estimates).

ECONOMICALLY ACTIVE POPULATION*
(official estimates, mid-1983)

	Males	Females	Total
Agriculture, hunting, forestry and fishing	872,220	427,220	1,299,440
Mining and quarrying	9,045	11,329	20,374
Manufacturing	68,485	60,553	129,038
Electricity, gas and water	1,292	972	2,264
Construction	19,383	3,255	22,638
Trade, restaurants and hotels	65,901	237,452	303,353
Transport, storage and communications	14,214	3,897	18,111
Financing, insurance, real estate and business services	2,584	1,944	4,528
Community, social and personal services	67,193	66,373	133,566
Activities not adequately defined	27,136	27,196	54,332
Total labour force	**1,147,453**	**840,191**	**1,987,644**

* Figures exclude unemployed persons not previously employed, totalling 276,188 (males 144,724; females 131,464).
Source: ILO, *Year Book of Labour Statistics*.

Agriculture

PRINCIPAL CROPS ('000 metric tons)

	1984	1985	1986
Rice (paddy)	123	165*	180*
Maize	186	110*	160*
Sweet potatoes	350*	360†	360†
Beans	48	48	48†
Sugar cane†	3,000	3,150	3,150
Bananas	235*	235*	235†
Coffee (green)†	33	33	33
Cocoa beans†	2	3	3

* Unofficial figure.   † FAO estimates.
Source: FAO, *Production Yearbook*.

LIVESTOCK
(FAO estimates, '000 head, year ending September)

	1984	1985	1986
Horses	425	425	425
Mules	83	83	84
Asses	212	212	215
Cattle	1,350	1,350	1,400
Pigs	500	500	700
Sheep	92	92	92
Goats	1,100	1,100	1,100

Chickens (FAO estimates, million): 8 in 1984; 8 in 1985; 8 in 1986.
Source: FAO, *Production Yearbook*.

LIVESTOCK PRODUCTS (FAO estimates, '000 metric tons)

	1984	1985	1986
Beef and veal	33	33	34
Goats' meat	4	4	4
Pig meat	9	9	12
Horse meat	5	5	5
Poultry meat	9	9	9
Cows' milk	22	22	22
Goats' milk	28	28	28
Hen eggs	3.3	3.3	3.8
Cattle hides	4.1	4.1	4.2

Source: FAO, *Production Yearbook*.

Forestry

ROUNDWOOD REMOVALS
(FAO estimates, '000 cubic metres)

	1984	1985	1986
Sawlogs, veneer logs and logs for sleepers*	224	224	224
Other industrial wood*	15	15	15
Fuel wood	5,522	5,663	5,817
Total	**5,761**	**5,902**	**6,056**

* Assumed to be unchanged since 1971.

Sawnwood production (FAO estimates): 12,000 cubic metres per year (1973–86).

Source: FAO, *Yearbook of Forest Products*.

HAITI

Statistical Survey

Fishing

(FAO estimates, '000 metric tons, live weight)

	1984	1985	1986
Freshwater fishes	0.3	0.3	0.3
Marine fishes	6.5	7.0	7.5
Caribbean spiny lobster	0.3	0.3	0.3
Total catch	7.0	7.5	8.0

Source: FAO, *Yearbook of Fishery Statistics*.

Mining

('000 metric tons)

	1980	1981	1982
Bauxite	477	488	431

Note: The mining of bauxite ceased in 1983.
Source: UN, *Industrial Statistics Yearbook*.

Industry

SELECTED PRODUCTS ('000 metric tons, unless otherwise indicated—year ending 30 September)

	1983/84	1984/85	1985/86
Wheat flour	113.8	111.9	127.6
Raw sugar	40.5	57.9	41.3
Cigarettes (million)	938.0	786.3	846.2
Soap	11.8	28.2	29.8
Cement	230.2	262.7	221.4
Electric energy (million kWh)	408.3	425.4*	440.1*

* Provisional.

Finance

CURRENCY AND EXCHANGE RATES

Monetary Units
100 centimes = 1 gourde.

Denominations
Coins: 5, 10, 20 and 50 centimes.
Notes: 1, 2, 5, 10, 50, 100, 250 and 500 gourdes
(US currency notes also circulate).

Sterling and Dollar Equivalents (30 September 1988)
£1 sterling = 8.455 gourdes;
US $1 = 5.000 gourdes;
100 gourdes = £11.827 = $20.000.

Exchange Rate
Fixed at US $1 = 5 gourdes.

BUDGET (million gourdes, year ending 30 September)

Revenue	1983/84	1984/85	1985/86
Tax revenue	883.9	1,074.3	1,023.9
Taxes on income	156.6	180.9	153.3
Excises	184.9	259.7	293.1
Other taxes on goods and services	165	249.7	203.5
Import duties	236.5	251.2	256.0
Export duties	63.2	61.0	55.1
Other revenue*	706.9	855.4	572.9
Total	1,590.8	1,929.7	1,596.8

* Including grants from abroad.

Expenditure	1979/80	1980/81	1981/82
Goods and services		1,191.0	802.4
Interest payments	1,012.5	36.0	58.7
Other current expenditure		72.7	344.3
Capital expenditure	255.7	160.4	144.2
Total	1,268.2	1,460.1	1,349.6

Current expenditure (million gourdes): 1,406.8 in 1982/83; n.a. in 1983/84; 1,798.5 in 1984/85; 1,780.4 in 1985/86.
Source: IMF, *Government Finance Statistics Yearbook*.

INTERNATIONAL RESERVES (US $ million at 31 December)

	1985	1986	1987
Gold*	6.2	7.5	7.5
IMF special drawing rights	—	6.6	—
Reserve position in IMF	0.1	0.1	0.1
Foreign exchange	6.3	9.2	16.9
Total	12.6	23.4	24.5

* Valued at market-related prices.
Source: IMF, *International Financial Statistics*.

MONEY SUPPLY (million gourdes at 31 December)

	1985	1986	1987
Currency outside banks	763.2	829.1	979.5
Demand deposits at commercial banks	n.a.	n.a.	658.6

Source: IMF, *International Financial Statistics*.

COST OF LIVING
(Consumer Price Index for metropolitan area; base: 1980 = 100)

	1985	1986	1987
Food	150.3	155.2	125.9
Clothing	180.8	200.2	184.6
Rent, fuel and light	198.7	192.0	193.4
All items (incl. others)	154.5	159.6	141.3

HAITI

Statistical Survey

NATIONAL ACCOUNTS
(million gourdes at current prices, year ending 30 September)

Expenditure on the Gross Domestic Product

	1984/85	1985/86	1986/87
Final consumption expenditure	9,471	10,513	9,209
Increase in stocks			
Gross fixed capital formation	1,673	1,614	1,509
Total domestic expenditure	11,144	12,127	10,718
Exports of goods and services	2,328	2,063	2,086
Less Imports of goods and services	3,425	2,972	3,052
GDP in purchasers' values	10,047	11,218	9,752
GDP at constant 1979/80 prices	6,828	6,867	6,822

Source: IMF, *International Financial Statistics*.

BALANCE OF PAYMENTS
(US $ million, year ending 30 September)

	1984/85	1985/86	1986/87
Merchandise exports f.o.b.	223.0	190.8	198.4
Merchandise imports f.o.b.	−344.7	−303.2	−307.7
Trade balance	−121.7	−112.5	−109.3
Exports of services	119.3	105.8	115.5
Imports of services	−237.3	−190.4	−220.2
Balance on goods and services	−239.7	−197.1	−214.0
Private unrequited transfers (net)	48.5	52.0	56.2
Government unrequited transfers (net)	96.5	99.8	126.6
Current balance	−94.7	−45.2	−31.2
Direct capital investment (net)	4.9	4.8	4.7
Other long-term capital (net)	16.0	13.0	31.0
Short-term capital (net)	−7.3	−6.4	−4.8
Net errors and omissions	55.2	−1.3	−25.4
Total (net monetary movements)	−25.8	−35.1	−25.7
Exceptional financing (net)	9.8	17.7	1.3
Changes in reserves	−16.0	−17.3	−24.4

Source: IMF, *International Financial Statistics*.

External Trade

PRINCIPAL COMMODITIES
(million gourdes, year ending 30 September)

Imports c.i.f.	1984/85*	1985/86*	1986/87*
Food and live animals	429.4	346.4	380.2
Beverages and tobacco	43.7	39.5	38.5
Mineral fuels, lubricants, etc.	319.4	254.1	237.5
Crude materials (inedible) except fuels	61.2	43.5	41.0
Animal and vegetable oils and fats	156.9	169.7	197.0
Chemicals	210.8	180.2	210.5
Basic manufactures	389.6	300.1	341.8
Machinery and transport equipment	412.7	314.8	372.6
Total (incl. others)	2,245.8	1,836.2	2,034.5

* Provisional.
Source: Administration Générale des Douanes.

Exports f.o.b.†	1984/85	1985/86	1986/87
Coffee	242.9	273.1	179.1
Cocoa	34.5	24.8	21.2
Essential oils	21.7	21.5	14.5
Light industrial products	88.3	57.2	64.0
Manufactured articles	411.6	412.8	669.0
Sisal	1.9	4.0	3.8
Molasses	0.5	6.5	1.9
Rope and cord	10.3	2.8	14.9
Total (incl. others)	910.3	866.5	1,053.2

† Excluding re-exports.

PRINCIPAL TRADING PARTNERS*
(million gourdes, year ending 30 September)

Imports c.i.f.	1984/85	1985/86	1986/87
Belgium	19.0	20.3	24.0
Canada	136.4	106.0	112.8
France	81.7	78.0	92.0
Germany, Federal Republic	67.5	60.4	65.3
Italy	17.0	16.2	18.9
Japan	145.6	121.0	130.1
Netherlands	63.2	52.1	58.4
United Kingdom	34.8	27.8	30.7
USA	1,085.0	892.0	859.1
Total (incl. others)	2,245.8	1,836.2	1,884.3

* Provisional.
Source: Administration Générale des Douanes.

Exports f.o.b.†	1984/85	1985/86	1986/87
Belgium	92.9	79.1	82.0
Canada	19.3	17.1	19.3
France	124.8	104.2	110.7
Germany, Federal Republic	38.2	38.0	36.5
Italy	143.4	117.3	123.0
Japan	4.2	3.5	4.8
Netherlands	22.3	15.7	17.3
United Kingdom	6.1	8.0	9.1
USA	605.7	516.0	531.5
Total (incl. others)	1,132.6	969.3	1,007.9

† Excluding re-exports.

Transport

ROAD TRAFFIC ('000 motor vehicles in use)

	1979	1980	1981
Passenger cars	24.9	21.8	21.8
Commercial vehicles	8.3	11.2	12.4

Source: UN, *Statistical Yearbook*.
1984: 50,000 vehicles.

INTERNATIONAL SEA-BORNE SHIPPING
(freight traffic, '000 metric tons)

	1983	1984	1985
Goods loaded	328	161	169
Goods unloaded	886	806	680

Source: UN, *Monthly Bulletin of Statistics*.

CIVIL AVIATION

International Flights, 1976: Passengers arriving 217,657; Passengers departing 147,668.

Tourism

VISITORS

	1983/84	1984/85	1985/86
Arrivals	136,429	135,103	117,455
Cruise passengers	91,573	95,129	90,637

Source: Office National du Tourisme.

Education

(1986/87)

	Schools	Teachers	Students
Primary	n.a.	24,299	921,500
Secondary	423	7,280	6,900

University of Haiti: c. 4,600 students (1986).

Directory

The Constitution

The Constitution of Haiti was approved by the electorate in a referendum held in March 1987. According to its provisions, a system of power-sharing between a President (who may not serve two consecutive five-year terms), a Prime Minister and a bicameral legislature was to be established. Former supporters of ex-President Jean-Claude Duvalier were to be barred from elective office for 10 years. Authority was to be distributed regionally by investing new powers in local government. The army and the police were no longer to be a combined force. The death penalty was abolished, and there was to be an independent judiciary. Official status was given to the Creole dialect spoken in Haiti and to the folk religion, voodoo. In June 1988 the Constitution was annulled by the military Government that was installed after a coup, but in September Brig.-Gen. Prosper Avril (who took office as President, following a further coup) announced that the principles of the 1987 Constitution would be respected by his administration. Municipal and legislative elections were to be held in late 1989, following which the legislature was to assume the role of a Constituent Assembly, and was to amend various articles of the 1987 Constitution. A presidential election was scheduled to take place by the end of 1990.

The Government

HEAD OF STATE

President: Brig.-Gen. PROSPER AVRIL (took office 18 September 1988).

CABINET
(February 1989)

Minister of the Interior and National Defence: Col ACCEDIUS SAINT-LOUIS.
Minister of Information and Co-ordination: ANTHONY VIRGILIE SAINT-PIERRE
Minister of Economy and Finance: LÉONCE THELUSMA.
Minister of Education, Youth and Sports: Prof. RÉMY ZAMOR.
Minister of Foreign Affairs and Worship: SERGE ELIE CHARLES.
Minister of Justice: AGUSTIN ROMAIN CÈME.
Minister of Agriculture: FRÉDÉRIC AGENOR.
Minister of Health and Housing: Dr SERGE PINTHRO.
Minister of Commerce: JEAN GÉRARD LOUISIAS.
Minister of Public Works, Transport and Communications: FRANCK PAULTRE.
Minister of Social Affairs: LOUIS ARNAULT GUERRIER.
Minister of Administration and Civil Service: WILNER DESSOURCES.
Minister of Planning and External Co-operation: THÉOPHILE ROCHE.

MINISTRIES

Head of Commission for Overseas Haitians: GÉRARD BISSAINTHE.
Office of the President: Palais National, Port-au-Prince; tel. 2-4020; telex 2030068.
Ministry of Agriculture: Damien, Port-au-Prince; tel. 2-3457.
Ministry of Commerce: Port-au-Prince.
Ministry of Economy and Finance: Palais des Ministères, Port-au-Prince; tel. 2-1628; telex 2030207.
Ministry of Education: Port-au-Prince; tel. 2-1036.
Ministry of Foreign Affairs and Worship: Cité de l' Exposition, Port-au-Prince; tel. 2-1647.
Ministry of Health and Housing: Palais des Ministères, Port-au-Prince; tel. 2-1248.
Ministry of Information and Co-ordination: 300 route de Delmas, Port-au-Prince; tel. 6-3229; telex 2030238.
Ministry of the Interior and National Defence: Palais des Ministères, Port-au-Prince; tel. 2-1714.
Ministry of Justice: Cité de l'Exposition, Port-au-Prince; tel. 2-0718.
Ministry of Planning: Port-au-Prince; tel. 2-1027.
Ministry of Public Works, Transport and Communications: Palais des Ministères, Port-au-Prince; tel. 2-3240; telex 2030321.
Ministry of Social Affairs: rue de la Révolution, Port-au-Prince; tel. 2-2450.
Ministry of Youth and Sports: rue Camille Léon, Port-au-Prince; tel. 5-3415.

President and Legislature

PRESIDENT

Election, 17 January 1988

Candidate	Votes	% of Votes
LESLIE MANIGAT (RDNP)	534,080	50.3
HUBERT DE RONCERAY (MDP)	210,526	19.8
GÉRARD PHILIPPE AUGUSTE (MOP)	151,391	14.3
GRÉGOIRE EUGÈNE (PDCH-27 Juin)	97,556	9.2
Others*	68,463	6.4
Total	1,062,016	100.0

* Six other candidates.

Note: President Manigat took office on 7 February 1988, but was deposed by a military coup in June. Brig.-Gen. Prosper Avril was installed as President on 18 September 1988, following another military coup.

LEGISLATURE

Legislative elections were held on 17 January 1988 for the 27-member Senate and the 77-member Chamber of Deputies. Following the coup in September 1988, the new Government was to rule by decree until further elections were held in 1989.

Political Organizations

Many political leaders returned to Haiti from exile, following the downfall of President Duvalier in February 1986. In August 1986 the National Council of Government issued a decree granting legal recognition to political parties on condition that they had at least 20 founding members and 2,000 sponsors. Many new parties were subsequently formed.

Alliance pour la Renouvellement d'Haïti: f. 1987.

Front National de Concertation (FNC): f. 1987 to urge mobilization, organization and unity, while rejecting fascism and violence, in order to achieve democratic elections; consists of the 'Group of 57', 18 provincial co-ordinating committees and sectors

HAITI

Directory

of civilian society; moderate left-wing; Leader GÉRARD GOURGUE; affiliated organizations include:

Comité National du Congrès des Mouvements Démocratiques (Conacom): Leader VICTOR BENOÎT.

Mobilisation pour le Développement National (MDP): Pres. HUBERT DE RONCERAY.

Mouvement pour l'Instauration de la Démocratie en Haïti (MIDH): centre-right; Pres. MARC BAZIN.

Mouvement d'Organisation du Pays (MOP): centre party; Leader GÉRARD PHILIPPE AUGUSTE.

Parti Agricole et Industriel National (PAIN): Sec.-Gen. LOUIS DÉJOIE II.

Parti démocratique Chrétien d'Haïti (PDCH): f. 1979; Christian Democrat party; Leader SYLVIO CLAUDE.

Parti démocratique Chrétien d'Haïti de 27 juin (PDCH-27 juin): f. 1979; also known as Parti Social Chrétien (PSC); Christian Democrat party; Leader GRÉGOIRE EUGÈNE.

Parti National du Travail (PNT): Leader THOMAS DESULMÉ.

Parti Nationaliste Progressiste Démocratique: Left-wing.

Parti Nationaliste Progressiste Révolutionnaire (PANPRA): f. 1986; Leader SERGE GILLES.

Parti Populaire National Haïtien (PPNH): Pres. BERNARD SANSARICQ.

Parti Unifié des Communistes Haïtiens (PUCH): f. 1968; Sec.-Gen. RENÉ THÉODORE.

Parti pour l'Unité Nationale et Développement (PUND): f. 1988; Leader Dr WISLER PIERRE-LOUIS.

Rassemblement des Démocrates Nationaux Progressistes (RDNP): centre party; Sec.-Gen. LESLIE MANIGAT.

Union des Forces Patriotiques et Démocratiques Haïtiennes (UFOPADA): socialist.

Union des Patriotes Démocratiques (UPD): f. 1988; Leader ROCKEFELLER GUERRE.

Diplomatic Representation

EMBASSIES IN HAITI

Argentina: impasse Géraud, 20 Bourdon, Port-au-Prince; tel. 2-2063; telex 0176; Chargé d'affaires: ANTONIO MERI.

Brazil: 387 ave John Brown, Bourdon, BP 808, Port-au-Prince; tel. 56208; telex 2030181; Ambassador: ALOYSIO M. D. GOMIDE.

Canada: 18 route de Delmas, Port-au-Prince; tel. 2358; telex 0069; Ambassador: ANTHONY MALONE.

Chile: 384 route de Delmas entre rues 42 et 44, Port-au-Prince; Ambassador: AGUSTÍN RODRÍGUEZ PULGAR.

China (Taiwan): 2 rue Rivière, Port-au-Prince; Ambassador: LEE NAN HSING.

Colombia: 384 route de Delmas, entre rues 42 et 44, Port-au-Prince; tel. 6-2599; Ambassador: JUAN ZAPATA OLIVELLA.

Dominican Republic: Port-au-Prince; Ambassador: OSCAR PAVILLA MEDRANO.

Ecuador: BP 2531, Port-au-Prince; tel. 2-4576; telex 2030195; Chargé d'affaires: ADOLFO ALVAREZ.

France: 51, Place des Héros de l'Indépendance, Port-au-Prince; tel. 2-0951; telex 0049; Ambassador: JEAN-RAPHAËL DUFOUR.

Germany, Federal Republic: 14 ave Marie Jeanne, Port-au-Prince; tel. 2-0634; telex 0072; Ambassador: Dr KARL-FRIEDRICH GANSÄUER.

Holy See: Morne Calvaire, Pétionville, BP 326, Port-au-Prince; tel. 7-3411; Apostolic Nuncio: Most Rev. PAOLO ROMEO, Titular Archbishop of Vulturia.

Israel: 8 rue Mangones, BP 2456, Berthé, Pétionville; tel. 7-2008; telex 2030096; Ambassador: MOSHE ITAN.

Italy: 18 route de Delmas, BP 886, Port-au-Prince; tel. 2-2649; telex 0447; Ambassador: LUIGI MORRONE.

Japan: Villa Bella Vista, 2 impasse Tulipe, Desprez, Port-au-Prince; tel. 5-3333; telex 0368; Ambassador: MUSSORO OSSADA.

Liberia: Port-au-Prince; tel. 7-0692; Ambassador: HENRY T. HOFF.

Mexico: Maison Roger Esper, 57A route de Delmas, Port-au-Prince; tel. 6-2215; telex 0217; Ambassador: MARIO ARMANDO AMADOR.

Panama: 29 rues Met. and Chavannes, Pétionville; tel. 7-2260; Ambassador: ALEJANDRO CUÉLLAR.

Peru: 38 Débussy, Port-au-Prince; tel. 55-425; Ambassador: JULIO BALBUENA.

Spain: 11 rue Oscar, Desprez, Port-au-Prince; tel. 2-4410; Ambassador: JOSÉ FRANCISCO DE CASTRO.

USA: blvd Harry Truman, Cité de l'Exposition, Port-au-Prince; tel. 2-0200; telex 0157; Ambassador: BRUNSON MCKINLEY.

Venezuela: blvd Harry Truman, Cité de l'Exposition, BP 2158, Port-au-Prince; tel. 2-0973; telex 0413; Ambassador: JOSÉ GREGORIO GONZÁLEZ-RODRÍGUEZ.

Judicial System

Law is based on the French Napoleonic Code, substantially modified during the presidency of Dr François Duvalier.

Courts of Appeal and Civil Courts sit at Port-au-Prince and the three provincial capitals: Gonaïves, Cap Haïtien and Port de Paix. In principle each commune has a Magistrates' Court.

Court of Cassation: Port-au-Prince; Pres. GILBERT AUSTIN.

Courts of Appeal. Civil Courts. Magistrates' Courts. Judges of the Supreme Courts and Courts of Appeal appointed by the President.

Religion

Roman Catholicism is the official religion, followed by 80% of the population. The folk religion is voodoo.

CHRISTIANITY

The Roman Catholic Church

For ecclesiastical purposes, Haiti comprises two archdioceses and five dioceses.

Bishops' Conference: Conférence Episcopale de Haïti, Archevêché, CP 22, Cap Haïtien; tel. 2-0071; f. 1977; Pres. Most Rev. FRANÇOIS GAYOT, Archbishop of Cap Haïtien.

Archbishop of Cap Haïtien: Most Rev. FRANÇOIS GAYOT, Archevêché, CP 22, Cap Haïtien; tel. 2-0071.

Archbishop of Port-au-Prince: Most Rev. FRANÇOIS-WOLFF LIGONDÉ, Archevêché, BP 538, rue Dr Aubry, Port-au-Prince; tel. 2-2043.

The Episcopal Church

Bishop of Haiti: Rt Rev. Dr LUC ANATOLE JACQUES GARNIER, Eglise Episcopale d'Haïti, BP 1309, Port-au-Prince.

Other Christian Churches

Baptist Convention: BP 20, Cap-Haïtien; tel. 2-0567; Pres. Rev. ANDRÉ JEAN.

Lutheran Church: Petite Place Cuzeau, BP 13147, Delmas, Port-au-Prince; tel. 6-3179; f. 1975; Minister RODRIGUE BEN BICHOTTE.

Other denominations active in Haiti include Methodists and the Church of God 'Eben-Ezer'.

The Press

Following the downfall of President Duvalier in 1986, numerous new newspapers were established.

DAILIES

Artibonite Journal: Gonaïves.

Haïti Journal: BP 866, Port-au-Prince; circ. 2,000.

Haïti Libérée: Cité de l'Exposition, Port-au-Prince.

Le Jour: Port-au-Prince.

Le Journal Sud-Ouest: Jacmel.

Le Matin: 88 rue du Quai, Port-au-Prince; tel. 2-2040; f. 1908; French; independent; Dir FRANK MAGLOIRE; circ. 5,000.

Le Nouvelliste: 198 rue du Centre, BP 1013, Port-au-Prince; tel. 2-2114; f. 1896; evening; French; independent; Editor LUCIEN MONTAS; circ. 6,000.

Panorama: 27 rue du Peuple, Port-au-Prince; tel. 2-2625; French; Dir PAUL BLANCHET; circ. 2,500.

PERIODICALS

Haïti Observateur: Port-au-Prince; weekly; Editor RAYMOND JOSEPH.

Haïti Progrès: 11 rue Capois, Port-au-Prince; weekly; Editor BEN DUPUY.

Haiti Times: Port-au-Prince; monthly.

HAITI

Directory

Le Journal de Commerce: 49 rue Traversière, BP 1569, Port-au-Prince; tel. 7-3008; weekly; Dir GÉRARD ALLEN; circ. 4,000.

Le Messager du Nord-Ouest: Port de Paix; weekly.

Le Miroir: Port-au-Prince; weekly.

Le Moniteur: BP 214 bis, Port-au-Prince; tel. 2-1026; 2 a week; French; the official gazette; Dir MARCEL ELIBERT; circ. 2,000.

Optique: French Institute, BP 1316, Port-au-Prince; monthly; arts.

Le Petit Samedi Soir: Fontamara, Port-au-Prince; tel. 4-0144; weekly; French; independent; Editor DIEUDONNÉ FARDIN; circ. 10,000.

Revue l'Educateur: Grande Rue, BP 164, Port-au-Prince; tel. 2-2297; telex 0533; monthly; circ. 8,000.

Le Septentrion: Cap Haïtien; weekly; Editor NELSON BELL; circ. 2,000.

FOREIGN NEWS BUREAUX

Agence France-Presse (AFP): 72 rue Pavée, BP 62, Port-au-Prince; tel. 2-3759; telex 2030379; Bureau Chief DOMINIQUE LEVANTI.

Associated Press (AP) (USA): BP 2443, Port-au-Prince; tel. 2-0062; telex 2030277; Dir (vacant).

United Press International (UPI) (USA) and **Agencia EFE** (Spain): 21 rue Gabart, Pétionville; tel. 7-1628; telex 3490480; Reps SONDRA SINGER BEAULIEU, SERGE BEAULIEU.

Publishers

Editions Caraïbes: Lalue, BP 2013, Port-au-Prince; tel. 2-3179; telex 0198.

Editions Fardin: Fontamara, Port-au-Prince.

Editions du Soleil: BP 2471, rue du Centre, Port-au-Prince; tel. 2-3147; telex 0001; education.

Maison Henri Deschamps: Grand rue, BP 164, Port-au-Prince; tel. 2-2297; telex 0533; f. 1893; education and literature; Man. Dir JACQUES DESCHAMPS.

Theodor: Imprimerie, rue Dantes, Destouches, Port-au-Prince.

Radio and Television

In 1986 there were an estimated 200,000 radio receivers and 25,000 television receivers in use. There are 25 radio stations and one television station.

Conseil National des Télécommunications (CONATEL): Cité de l'Exposition, BP 2002, Port-au-Prince; tel. 24123; telex 2030353; government communications licensing authority; Dir-Gen. LUCIEN ADAM.

Télévision Nationale d'Haïti: Delmas 33, BP 13400, Port-au-Prince; tel. 6-0200; telex 2030416; Dir (vacant).

RADIO

Radio Antilles International: 175 rue du Centre, BP 2325, Port-au-Prince; tel. 2-8797; f. 1984; independent; Dir-Gen. JACQUES SAMPEUR.

Radio Cacique: 5 Bellevue, BP 1480, Port-au-Prince; independent; Dir PATRICK DE LANDSHEER.

Radio Caraïbes: 23 ruelle Chavannes, Port-au-Prince; independent; Dir HARRY K. MULLER.

Radio Haïti Inter: Delmas 66A en face de Delmas 91, BP 737, Port-au-Prince; tel. 7-3111; independent; Dir JEAN L. DOMINIQUE.

Radio Lumière: BP 1050, Port-au-Prince; tel. 4-0330; f. 1959; Protestant; independent; Dir JOSEPH ROBINSON.

Radio MBC: 86 rue Américaine, BP 367, Port-au-Prince; independent; Dir-Gen. F. C. MAGLOIRE.

Radio Métropole: rue Pavée, BP 62, Port-au-Prince; independent; Dir HERBERT WIDMAIER.

Radio Port-au-Prince: Stade Sylvio Cator, BP 81, Port-au-Prince; independent; Dir GEORGES J. HÉRARD.

Radio Soleil: BP 1362, Port-au-Prince; tel. 2-3073; f. 1978; Catholic; independent; educational; broadcasts in Creole; Dir Fr HUGO TRIESTE.

Radio Télédiffusion Nationale: rue du Magasin de l'Etat, BP 1143, Port-au-Prince; tel. 2-2421; government-operated; Dir Dr GEORGES MICHEL.

TELEVISION

Télé Haïti: blvd J. J. Dessalines, BP 1126, Port-au-Prince; telex 0189; f. 1959; independent; pay-cable station with 4 channels; in French and English; Gen. Man. PHILIP BAYARD.

Télévision Nationale d'Haïti: BP 13400, Delmas 31, Port-au-Prince; tel. 6-0200; telex 0416; government-owned; cultural; administered by four-mem. board.

Finance

(cap. = capital; m. = million; dep. = deposits; amounts in gourdes; brs = branches)

BANKING

Banque de la République d'Haïti: Angle rue du Magasin de l'Etat et rue des Miracles, BP 1570, Port-au-Prince; tel. 2-4700; telex 0394; f. 1911; fmrly Banque Nationale de la République d'Haïti; the central bank and bank of issue; cap. 50m. (1987); Dir-Gen. JOSEPH LACROUE; 12 brs.

Banque Nationale de Crédit: rue des Miracles et rue Américaine, BP 1320, Port-au-Prince; tel. 2-0800; telex 0196; f. 1979; cap. 25m., dep. 424.7m. (Sept. 1987); Pres. YVON CÉSAR.

Banque Populaire Haïtienne: Angle rue Américaine et Fort Per, Port-au-Prince; tel. 2-1800; telex 0406; f. 1955; state bank; cap. 5m.; Dir-Gen. SENAT MORTEL.

Banque de l'Union Haïtienne: Angle rue du Quai et rue Bonne Foi, BP 275, Port-au-Prince; tel. 2-1300; telex 0173; f. 1973; cap. 15m.; Pres. and Dir-Gen. CHRISTIAN DUMOULIN; 5 brs.

Foreign Banks

Bank of Nova Scotia (Canada): rue des Miracles, Port-au-Prince; tel. 2-4461; telex 0155; Dir-Gen. CHESTER HINKSON; 3 brs.

Banque Nationale de Paris (France): ave John Brown, Port-au-Prince; tel. 2-2908; telex 0191; Dir-Gen. MARCEL GARCÍA; 2 brs.

Citibank, NA (USA): BP 1688, route de Delmas, Port-au-Prince; tel. 6-0985; telex 0124; Vice-Pres. GLADYS M. COUPET.

First National Bank of Boston (USA): BP 2216, rue des Miracles, Port-au-Prince; tel. 2-1900; telex 0163; Dir-Gen. GUY CUVILLY; 3 brs.

Development Bank

Banque Nationale de Développement Agricole et Industriel: rue de Quai, BP 1313, Port-au-Prince; tel. 2-1969; telex 2030116; Dir-Gen. YVES LEREBOURS.

INSURANCE

North American and European insurance companies have branches in Haiti.

Trade and Industry

Chambre de Commerce et de l'Industrie d'Haïti: BP 982, Port-au-Prince; tel. 2-0281; f. 1907; Pres. GEORGES SICARD; Exec. Dir MICHAELE BERROUET.

Chambre de Commerce et d'Industrie Haïtiano-Américaine (HAMCHAM): Delmas 384, BP 13486, Port-au-Prince; tel. 6-3164; Pres. GLADYS COUPET.

Association des Industries d'Haïti (ADIH): 199 Delmas 31, BP 2568, Port-au-Prince; tel. 6-4509; telex 2030071; Pres. JEAN-EDOUARD BAKER.

Association des Producteurs Agricoles (APA): rue Pavée 86, BP 1139, Port-au-Prince; tel. 2-5848; f. 1985; Pres. CLAUDE MARTIN JR.

DEVELOPMENT ORGANIZATIONS

Fonds de Développement Industriel: 43 rue des Miracles, BP 2597, Port-au-Prince; tel. 2-7852; telex 0432; f. 1981; Dir YVES BLANCHARD.

Société Financière Haïtienne de Développement (SOFIHDES): BP 1399, blvd Harry S. Truman, Port-au-Prince; tel. 2-8628; f. 1983; accounting, data processing, management consultancy; cap. 1m. (1988); Dir-Gen. THIERRY BUNGENER; 1 br.

TRADE UNIONS

Centrale Autonome des Travailleurs Haïtiens: rue Mgr Guilloux 134, Port-au-Prince; f. 1980; Sec. YVES ANTOINE RICHARD.

Fédération Haïtienne de Syndicats Chrétiens (Haitian Federation of Christian Unions): BP 416, Port-au-Prince; Pres. LÉONVIL LEBLANC.

Fédération des Ouvriers Syndiques (FOS): Angle rue des Miracles et rue Dr Aubry 115, Port-au-Prince; tel. 2-0035; Pres. JOSEPH J. SENAT.

HAITI

Organisation Générale Indépendante des Travailleurs Haïtiens: Delmas, Port-au-Prince; admitted to ORIT; Gen. Sec. SCHILLER MARCELIN.

Union Nationale des Ouvriers d'Haïti—UNOH (National Union of Workers of Haiti): BP 276, Port-au-Prince; f. 1951; admitted to ORIT; Pres. MARCEL VINCENT; Sec.-Gen. FRITZNER ST VIL; 3,000 mems from 8 affiliated unions.

A number of unions are non-affiliated and without a national centre, including those organized on a company basis.

Transport

RAILWAYS

The only railway is used to transport sugar cane.

ROADS

There are 4,000 km of roads, of which about 600 km are paved; a construction and repair programme is being undertaken. An all-weather road from Port-au-Prince to Cap Haïtien, on the northern coast, has been completed with finance from the World Bank. Another major road, connecting Port-au-Prince with Jacmel, has been built and financed by France. Haiti has also received a $15m. credit from the IDA towards the reconstruction and upgrading of roads and the rebuilding of two major bridges.

SHIPPING

Many European and American shipping lines call at Haiti. The two principal ports are Port-au-Prince and Cap Haïtien. The development of port facilities at Port-au-Prince and two other ports is being financed by the IDA.

CIVIL AVIATION

The international airport, situated 16 km outside Port-au-Prince, is the country's principal airport, and is served by many international airlines linking Haiti with the USA and other Caribbean islands. There is an airport at Cap Haïtien, and there are smaller airfields at Jacmel, Jérémie and Port-de-Paix.

Air Haiti: 35 ave Marie-Jeanne, Port-au-Prince; f. 1969; began cargo charter operations 1970; scheduled cargo and mail services from Port-au-Prince to Cap Haïtien, San Juan (Puerto Rico), Santo Domingo (Dominican Republic), Miami and New York; Gen. Man. ERNEST CINEAS; fleet of 2 Curtiss C-46 Commando.

Tourism

Tourism was formerly Haiti's second largest source of foreign exchange. In 1985/86 the number of visitors totalled 208,092. As a result of subsequent political instability, the number of cruise ships visiting Haiti has declined considerably, causing a sharp decline in the number of tourist arrivals.

Office National du Tourisme d'Haïti: ave Marie-Jeanne, Port-au-Prince; tel. 2-1729; telex (203) 0206; Dir ANTONIO FENELON.

Association Hotelière et Touristique d'Haïti: BP 2562, Port-au-Prince; tel. 7-1920; telex 2030493; Pres. MARYSE CHANCY; Exec. Dir JOËLLE L. COUPAND.

HONDURAS

Introductory Survey

Location, Climate, Language, Religion, Flag, Capital

The Republic of Honduras lies in the middle of the Central American isthmus. It has a long northern coastline on the Caribbean Sea and a narrow southern outlet to the Pacific Ocean. Its neighbours are Guatemala to the west, El Salvador to the south-west and Nicaragua to the south-east. The climate ranges from temperate in the mountainous regions to tropical in the coastal plains. The rainy season is from May to November. The national language is Spanish. Almost all of the inhabitants profess Christianity, and the overwhelming majority are adherents of the Roman Catholic Church. The national flag (proportions 3 by 2) has three horizontal stripes, of blue, white and blue, with five blue five-pointed stars, arranged in a diagonal cross, in the centre of the white stripe. The capital is Tegucigalpa.

Recent History

Honduras was ruled by Spain from the 16th century until independence in 1821, when the Federation of Central America was formed. Honduras emerged as an independent state in 1838. Between 1939 and 1949 the country was ruled as a dictatorship by Gen. Tiburcio Carías Andino, leader of the Partido Nacional (PN). He was succeeded by Juan Manuel Gálvez. In 1954 the leader of the Partido Liberal de Honduras (PLH), Dr José Ramón Villeda Morales, was elected President but was immediately deposed by Julio Lozano Díaz, himself overthrown by a military junta in 1956. The junta organized elections in 1957, when the PLH secured a majority in Congress and Dr Villeda Morales was re-elected President for a six-year term. He was overthrown in 1963 by Col (later Brig.-Gen.) Oswaldo López Arellano, the Minister of Defence, who, following elections held on the basis of a new constitution, was appointed President in June 1965.

A presidential election in March 1971 was won by Dr Ramón Ernesto Cruz Uclés, the PN candidate, who took office in June. However, popular discontent over government austerity measures and delayed land reforms culminated in a bloodless coup, led by the former President, Gen. López Arellano, in December 1972. A group of young army officers, in favour of social reform, took control of the Supreme Council of the Armed Forces, and in March 1974 replaced President López Arellano as Commander-in-Chief of the Army by Col (later Gen.) Juan Melgar Castro, who was appointed President in April 1975. In 1976 the President postponed the 1977 elections until 1979. He was forced to resign by the Supreme Council of the Armed Forces in August 1978, being replaced by a military junta comprising the commanders-in-chief of the army, air force and national police. The army commander, Gen. Policarpo Paz García, assumed the role of Head of State, and the junta promised that elections would be held.

Military rule was ended officially when, in April 1980, elections to a Constituent Assembly were held. The PLH won 52% of the votes but was unable to assume power. General Paz was appointed interim President for one year and, as the armed forces were allowed to nominate four members of the coalition Cabinet, the PLH was in a minority. A general election in November 1981 resulted in a victory for the PLH, led by Dr Roberto Suazo Córdova, which gained an absolute majority in the National Assembly. Dr Suazo was sworn in as President in January 1982. However, the country's military leaders retained control of security decisions and were able to veto cabinet appointments. Real power rested in the hands of Gen. Gustavo Alvarez, the Commander-in-Chief of the Armed Forces, who rejected the previous policy of neutrality regarding regional conflicts, and engaged his troops in operations against guerrilla forces in El Salvador. His plans for a major offensive against Nicaragua in August 1982 were thwarted by US opposition. In November Gen. Alvarez succeeded in amending the Constitution in order to reduce government control over the armed forces. Political unrest increased, trade union activists and left-wing sympathizers were arrested, and the appearance of 'death squads' was reported. Tension was increased by the presence of about 35,000 refugees from neighbouring countries in 1982. It was thought that Honduran troops were responsible for the deaths of several hundred Salvadorean refugees, and that refugee camps for Miskito Indians from Nicaragua were being used by former Nicaraguan National Guards, regarded by the left-wing Sandinista Government of Nicaragua as counter-revolutionaries ('Contras'), as bases for attacks on Nicaragua. Gen. Alvarez supported US policy in Central America, favouring further Honduran involvement in the conflict along the border with Nicaragua. In September 1983 an air and sea battle with Nicaraguan forces was reported, and there were frequent accusations from both sides of cross-border incursions. In an attempt to eradicate internal dissent, Gen. Alvarez organized a campaign of repression against trade unions and small left-wing parties. In October 100 left-wing guerrillas were killed in an army ambush at Olancho.

Throughout 1983, US involvement in Honduras increased substantially. In February the USA and Honduras began a series of joint manoeuvres, known as 'Big Pine', which were expected to continue until 1990. The manoeuvres enabled the USA to construct permanent military installations in Honduras. A naval base was under construction at Puerto Castilla, while a further two airstrips and radar stations were built in 1983. The US Central Intelligence Agency continued to be active in both covert and overt operations against the Nicaraguan Government, and there was clear evidence that Honduras and the USA provided assistance to Nicaraguan counter-revolutionaries based in Honduras.

In March 1984 Gen. Alvarez was ousted from power by a group of junior officers. He was subsequently sent into exile. His dismissal was thought to be the result of growing disenchantment among the armed forces with the General's authoritarian policies. Several other high-ranking officers were also sent abroad. The appointment of Gen. Walter López Reyes as his successor was approved by the National Assembly. For the US Government, the departure of Gen. Alvarez represented the loss of its main ally within the Honduran administration. In response to mounting public opposition to the US military presence, the Government indicated its intention to examine its role within the US Government's policy towards Central America. In August the Government suspended the training of Salvadorean troops by US military advisers in Honduras, pending agreement with El Salvador on disputed territory. In addition, the Government called for the establishment of a joint US-Honduran commission to review military and economic co-operation, and to revise the 1954 military agreement between the two countries. In December the US Government, prompted by the deterioration in its relations with Honduras, held talks with the Honduran Government. In 1985 the US administration declined to enter into a security pact with Honduras, but confirmed that it would take 'appropriate measures' to defend Honduras against 'Communist aggression'.

Prior to the presidential election in 1985 President Suazo faced opposition even within his own party. In March a constitutional crisis developed over the President's refusal to accept the appointment of five Supreme Court judges, who had been nominated by the National Assembly. At the same time a conflict was taking place within the PLH between President Suazo and Efraín Bu Girón, President of the National Assembly: President Suazo refused to support the latter as PLH candidate in the presidential election. An agreement was reached in May between representatives of the trade unions and the Assembly and members of the armed forces, whereby the judges originally appointed by the Government were permitted to complete their four-year term of office and the President's prerogative to designate the ruling party's presidential candidate was abolished.

Nine candidates contested the presidential election held in November 1985. Elections were also held for 134 seats in the National Assembly and 284 mayoralties. The PLH presented four presidential candidates and the PN presented three. The 1982 Constitution established that the election of the President would be by a simple majority of the voters, but, prior to the

HONDURAS

elections, the electoral tribunal ruled that the presidency would be assumed by the leading candidate of the party receiving the most votes. Although the leading candidate of the PN, Rafael Leonardo Callejas, obtained 42% of the individual votes cast, the leading candidate of the PLH, José Simeón Azcona del Hoyo (who had obtained only 27% of the individual votes cast), was declared the winner because the combined votes of the PLH's candidates secured the requisite majority of 51% of the total votes cast. The result led to some dissent, but the transfer of power took place in January 1986, as planned. The new Cabinet contained two PN members. The powerful Commander-in-Chief of the Armed Forces, Gen. Walter López Reyes, unexpectedly announced his retirement, and was replaced by Brig.-Gen. Humberto Regalado Hernández.

Renewed fighting on the border with Nicaragua occurred during 1986, and the involvement of the USA in the conflict gave rise to concern in the region. The decision by Honduras to curb border violations by Nicaraguan government forces marked a serious escalation in the conflict. Following revelations that the USA had secretly sold weapons to Iran and that the proceeds had been used to finance the activities of the Contras, and fearing the withdrawal of aid from the USA, President Azcona requested the removal of Nicaraguan Contra rebels from Honduras. Their presence in an area that had become known as 'Nueva Nicaragua' (New Nicaragua) was also adversely affecting the Honduran economy, as the region contained important coffee-growing land. In June 1987 the President also announced his intention to prevent Contra leaders from continuing to meet in Tegucigalpa, the long-standing political headquarters of the Contra movement.

Honduras remained the USA's closest ally in the region. Joint US-Honduran military manoeuvres continued on Honduran territory in 1987. In addition, Honduras received 12 F-5 jet aircraft, worth $75m., from the USA.

Honduras was a signatory of the Central American peace plan, the 'Esquipulas agreement', signed in Guatemala by Costa Rica, El Salvador, Guatemala, Honduras and Nicaragua in August 1987 (see p. 777). However, the commitment of the Honduran Government to the accord, the provisions of which included an end to rebel forces' use of foreign territory as a base for attack, appeared to be only partial. The Government was also slow to introduce an amnesty law, as stipulated by the Esquipulas agreement, and delayed the establishment of a national commission for reconciliation until October.

In March 1988 President Azcona requested military support from the USA after an incursion by the Nicaraguan army into the Bocay Valley, and 3,200 US troops were airlifted into Honduras. However, incursions into Honduran territory continued to occur as the Nicaraguan army attempted to drive back the Contras from their bases on the frontier between the two countries. At least 12,000 Contras were forced into Honduras. In October President Reagan declared that the USA would be ultimately responsible for the welfare of the Contras. In November President Azcona declared that the Contras would have to leave Honduran territory, as they had lost international support.

In April 1988 the extradition of an alleged drug-trafficker to the USA (contravening the Honduran Constitution) provided the impulse for violent anti-American demonstrations, and a state of emergency was imposed for several days in Tegucigalpa and the northern town of San Pedro Sula. In November the Honduran Government refused to sign a new protocol on military co-operation with the USA. The protocol would have given US forces virtually free access to Honduran military bases.

In February 1988 a report by Amnesty International gave evidence of an increase in violations of human rights by the armed forces and by right-wing 'death squads'. In the same month three human rights activists were murdered. A Honduran human rights organization reported in 1988 that 263 'extra-judicial executions' had taken place in 1987, and claimed that the armed forces had been responsible for many of these deaths. In August the Inter-American Court of Human Rights found the Honduran Government guilty of the 'disappearance' of one of its citizens in 1981 and ordered that compensation be paid to his family. In January 1989 the former Commander-in-Chief of the Armed Forces, Gen. Gustavo Alvarez, was killed by left-wing guerrillas in Tegucigalpa. General Alvarez was alleged to have been responsible for violations of human rights in the early 1980s.

In October 1988 the Honduran Minister of Foreign Affairs, Carlos López Contreras, proposed that a peace-keeping force be established in Central America to prevent border violations. In December the International Court of Justice ruled that it was within its jurisdiction to consider an application filed by the Nicaraguan Government in 1986, in which Nicaragua held that Honduras had breached international law by allowing the Contras to operate from its territory. In response to this judgment, the Honduran Government threatened to withdraw its support from the Esquipulas agreement. In February 1989 President Azcona held discussions with President Ortega of Nicaragua, who agreed to widen the terms of the amnesty offered to the Contras currently encamped in Honduras, in order to encourage them to return to Nicaragua.

In 1986 the Presidents of Honduras and El Salvador agreed to refer to the International Court of Justice a long-standing dispute concerning the island of Meanguera, in the Gulf of Fonseca, and several small stretches of the land border covering some 400 sq km. In October 1988 an agreement was made with El Salvador to allow the free passage of Salvadorean goods to the Atlantic ports in Honduras and of Honduran goods to the Pacific ports in El Salvador.

Government

Under the provisions of the Constitution approved by the National Assembly in 1982, the President is elected by a simple majority of the voters. However, at the presidential and general elections in November 1985, the leading candidate of the political party that received the most votes was appointed President. The President holds executive power and has a four-year mandate. Legislative power is vested in the National Assembly, with 134 members elected by universal adult suffrage for a term of four years.

Defence

Military service is by conscription. Active service lasts eight months, with subsequent reserve training. In June 1988 the armed forces totalled 18,800 men, of whom 15,400 were in the army, 1,200 in the navy and 2,200 in the air force. Paramilitary forces numbered 5,000 men. Defence expenditure in 1988 was estimated at 150.0m. lempiras. In 1986/87 Honduras was to receive foreign military aid amounting to US $87m.

Economic Affairs

In 1987, according to estimates by the World Bank, the country's total gross national product (GNP) was US $3,627m., equivalent to $780 per head. Apart from Haiti and Bolivia, Honduras had the lowest level of average income in Latin America. Between 1980 and 1987, it was estimated, GNP per head declined, in real terms, at an average rate of 1.9% annually. The overall increase in gross domestic product (GDP) averaged 4.2% per year in 1965–80, slowing to only 0.6% per year in 1980–86. GDP expanded by 2.6% in 1986 and by an estimated 4.2% in 1987 (according to government figures).

Agriculture is the principal sector of the economy and, with forestry and fishing, provided an estimated 22% of total GDP in 1987. The agricultural sector employed an estimated 52.5% of the work-force in 1985. Agriculture is vulnerable to fluctuations in world prices for principal exports. Coffee and bananas are the leading exports and accounted for about 65% of all export earnings in 1987. The banana crop had an export value of US $324m. in 1987. Low world prices and reduced export quotas led to a sharp fall in coffee earnings in the early 1980s. In 1985 earnings from coffee exports were $185m. In 1986, after a rise in international coffee prices, exports of Honduran coffee increased to $322m., However, in 1987 after another fall in prices, revenue from coffee exports declined to an estimated $208m. The sugar industry has been operating at less than 60% of capacity, and export earnings were only $10.4m. in 1985. In 1986–87 the USA halved its quota for imports of Honduran sugar. In October 1988 agricultural production was severely affected by a hurricane, making it necessary to import large quantities of food.

A programme of agrarian reform, aimed at redistributing land, was initially adopted in 1975, and was renewed in 1982, but was hampered by insufficient funding. There are still an estimated 200,000 landless peasant families in Honduras. In 1986 and 1987 peasants staged land invasions in protest at delays in implementation of a land reform programme. In June 1987 the President agreed to establish a commission to consider land redistribution.

Forests cover nearly 45% of the land area, and timber is a significant export. The mining and quarrying sector provided only 1.5% of GDP in 1987. Zinc, lead, gold and silver are mined, and there are deposits of copper and low-grade iron ore. Petroleum output in the mid-1980s averaged about 14,000 barrels per day, and small quantities of petroleum derivatives are exported. In 1987 imports of fuels comprised 12% of total imports. The 292,000 kW hydroelectric plant at El Cajón came into operation in late 1985, but by 1988 it was still not operating at its full capacity.

In 1986 the industrial sector as a whole accounted for about 25% of GDP, while manufacturing accounted for about 14%. Production and exports of industrial goods declined during the early 1980s, with factories operating at well below their full capacity. Industry suffered from insufficient investment, a shortage of foreign exchange, a lack of spare parts, and depressed overall demand from the Central American Common Market (CACM, see p. 108). Honduras joined CACM in 1960, but in 1970 it reintroduced duties on imports from the other member countries. In 1985 Puerto Cortés was designated a free-trade zone. A further free-trade zone was planned at La Ceiba.

During the 1980s political developments in the region eroded the confidence of the private sector and discouraged foreign creditors. The budget deficit increased from $246m. in 1986 to $461m. in 1987, equivalent to 11% of GDP. The current deficit on the balance of payments fell from $317m. in 1984 to $204m. in 1985 and to $105m. in 1986, largely reflecting an increase in earnings from exports of coffee; the deficit increased to $183m. in 1987. The foreign debt was estimated at $3,100m. in 1988. In 1987 debt-servicing costs were estimated to be equivalent to 30% of export earnings. In 1987 unemployment affected about 35% of the labour force. In 1988 the average annual rate of inflation was 5%. A budget envisaging expenditure of 2,171.8m. lempiras was approved for 1989.

A stand-by arrangement, over a period of 14 months, was agreed with the IMF in November 1982. Under the terms of the agreement, strict controls were to be imposed on mismanaged state-owned corporations, and incentives were to be given to the private sector and to attract foreign capital. In May 1984, following further negotiations with the IMF, the Government announced a programme of austerity measures, including increases in direct taxes and reductions in planned expenditure. As a result of the Government's action, the US Government disbursed $65m. in aid. In June, however, public protests at the austerity measures, coupled with the threat of a general strike, prompted the Government to suspend its programme. In March 1985 the Government reached a preliminary agreement with 40 foreign creditor banks on the rescheduling of $220m. of debts. In 1987 Honduras negotiated the rescheduling of $257m. owing to commercial banks. In December 1987 the IMF, the IDB and the World Bank temporarily suspended disbursements of loans, following Honduras' accumulation of $19m. of arrears on repayments. In July 1988 President Azcona announced the implementation of a 29-point austerity plan designed to reduce the fiscal deficit, and to bring about economic stability. The proposed measures included an increase in taxation on consumer goods and non-essential imports, and the privatization of certain state enterprises. In September the World Bank approved two loans totalling $75m. to support the Government's economic adjustment programme and to finance agricultural development. In October a group of donor governments and organizations, convened by the World Bank, agreed to provide $450m. in assistance for Honduras over the next two years, in support of the country's economic reforms.

In December 1988 Honduras agreed to rejoin the free-trade system of the Central American Common Market. In May the United Nations General Assembly approved a $4,300m. plan for economic assistance to the region, to support the peace process and to encourage trade between the Central American countries.

Social Welfare

The state-run system of social security provides benefits for sickness, maternity, orphans, unemployment and accidents. It also provides family and old-age allowances. A Labour Code affords guarantees for employees. In 1980 Honduras had 1,141 physicians and 35 hospitals. In 1979 there were 449 rural health centres. There was a total of 4,723 hospital beds available. The 1988 budget allocated 249.5m. lempiras to the health sector. In July 1988 the USA made a $57.2m. donation to the Honduran health sector. In 1988 five new hospitals were reported to be close to completion.

Education

Primary education, beginning at seven years of age and lasting for six years, is officially compulsory and is provided free of charge. Secondary education, which is not compulsory, begins at the age of 13 and lasts for up to five years, comprising a first cycle of three years and a second of two years. In 1984 the enrolment at primary schools included an estimated 87% of children in the relevant age-group (compared with 76% in 1980), while the comparable ratio for secondary enrolment was only 20%. On completion of the first period of compulsory education, every person is required to teach at least two illiterate adults to read and write. In 1986 there were 6,710 primary schools and 428 secondary and technical schools. There is an autonomous national university in Tegucigalpa, and private universities in San Pedro and Tegucigalpa. In 1985, according to official estimates, adult illiteracy averaged 40.5% (males 39.3%; females 41.6%). In 1988 the education budget was 417m. lempiras.

Public Holidays

1989: 2 January (for New Year's Day), 23–26 March (Easter), 14 April (Pan-American Day/Bastilla's Day), 1 May (Labour Day), 15 September (Independence Day), 3 October (Morazán Day), 12 October (Discovery Day), 21 October (Army Day), 25 December (Christmas).

1990: 1 January (New Year's Day), 12–15 April (Easter), 14 April (Pan-American Day/Bastilla's Day), 1 May (Labour Day), 15 September (Independence Day), 3 October (Morazán Day), 12 October (Discovery Day), 21 October (Army Day), 25 December (Christmas).

Weights and Measures

The metric system is in force, although some old Spanish measures are used, including: 25 libras = 1 arroba; 4 arrobas = 1 quintal (46 kg).

Statistical Survey

Source (unless otherwise stated): Department of Economic Studies, Banco Central de Honduras, 1a Calle, 6a y 7a Avda, Apdo 58-C, Tegucigalpa; tel. 22-2270; telex 1121.

Area and Population

AREA, POPULATION AND DENSITY

Area (sq km)	
Land	111,888
Inland water	200
Total	112,088*
Population (census results)†	
17 April 1961	1,884,765
6 March 1974	
Males	1,317,307
Females	1,339,641
Total	2,656,948
Population (official estimates at mid-year)	
1985	3,826,200
1986	3,937,200
1987	4,051,400
Density (per sq km) at mid-1987	36.1

* 43,277 sq miles.
† Excluding adjustments for underenumeration, estimated to have been 10% at the 1974 census.

PRINCIPAL TOWNS
(Preliminary mid-1987 population estimate, excluding suburbs)

Tegucigalpa	640,900		Tela	27,800
San Pedro Sula	429,300		Siguatepeque	26,400
La Ceiba	66,000		Santa Rosa de	
Choluteca	64,500		Copán	20,600
El Progreso	61,100		Danlí	19,500
Puerto Cortés	42,100		Juticalpa	14,100
Comayagua	31,500		Olanchito	13,500

BIRTHS AND DEATHS

(1983 estimates): Birth rate 44.0 per 1,000; death rate 8.3 per 1,000. Expectation of life at birth: Males 60.2 years; females 63.9 years (1983).

EMPLOYMENT ('000)

	1985	1986	1987*
Agriculture, forestry, hunting and fishing	584.8	605.9	624.2
Mining and quarrying	5.3	4.4	3.8
Manufacturing	146.6	150.9	163.1
Construction	47.9	49.3	51.8
Electricity, gas, water and sanitary services	4.0	4.1	4.4
Transport, storage and communications	44.1	45.4	46.7
Wholesale and retail trade	106.9	110.0	114.3
Banking, insurance, etc.	12.9	13.4	13.5
Other services	152.7	157.2	168.1
Total	1,105.2	1,140.6	1,189.9

* Preliminary.

Agriculture

PRINCIPAL CROPS ('000 quintales*)

	1985	1986	1987†
Maize	9,405	8,943	8,412
Rice	748	887	893
Dry beans	1,115	1,113	963
Sorghum	852	707	800
Cotton	321	197	172
Tobacco	115	104	106
Coffee	1,653	1,677	2,179
Bananas	24,011	22,435	25,354
Sugar cane	65,894	65,888	62,898
Plantains	3,779	3,953	4,024
African palm	7,032	n.a.	7,832

* Figures are in terms of the old Spanish quintal, equal to 46 kg (101.4 lb).
† Preliminary.

LIVESTOCK ('000 head)

	1985	1986	1987*
Cattle	2,494	2,615	2,752
Pigs	717	719	721
Horses and mules	302	300	302
Chickens	9,436	10,290	10,908

* Preliminary.

LIVESTOCK PRODUCTS ('000 metric tons)

	1985	1986	1987*
Beef and veal	66	68	72
Pig meat	9	10	10
Cows' milk ('000 litres)	247	260	272
Hen eggs ('000 eggs)	553	569	586

* Preliminary.

Forestry

ROUNDWOOD REMOVALS ('000 cubic metres, excluding bark)

	1984*	1985	1986
Sawlogs, veneer logs and logs for sleepers	670	836	793
Other industrial wood*	15	15	15
Fuel wood*	4,393	4,538	4,682
Total	5,078	5,389	5,490

* FAO estimates.
Source: FAO, *Yearbook of Forest Products*.

SAWNWOOD PRODUCTION ('000 cubic metres)

	1985	1986	1987*
Coniferous (softwood)	811	762	898
Broadleaved (hardwood)	21	26	38
Total	832	788	936

* Preliminary.

HONDURAS

Fishing

(metric tons, live weight)

	1985	1986	1987*
Fishes	4,367	4,561	4,703
Shrimps and lobsters	3,779	3,730	3,737
Others	166	164	164
Total catch	8,312	8,455	8,604

* Preliminary.

Mining

(metric tons, unless otherwise indicated)

	1985	1986	1987*
Lead	15,601	8,584	2,087
Zinc	36,176	21,334	7,455
Silver	80	44	11
Gold (kg)	16	12	2

* Preliminary.

Industry

SELECTED PRODUCTS

	1985	1986	1987*
Raw sugar ('000 quintales)	4,687	4,892	4,121
Cement ('000 bags of 42.5 kg)	8,177	8,470	10,615
Cigarettes ('000 packets of 20)	115,594	106,718	104,566
Matches ('000 boxes of 50)	65,166	68,243	62,140
Beer ('000 12 oz bottles)	132,204	144,803	153,352
Soft drinks ('000 12 oz bottles)	533,452	510,353	588,455
Wheat flour ('000 quintales)	1,475	1,624	1,644
Fabric ('000 yards)	13,883	11,806	17,837
Rum ('000 litres)	1,555	1,693	1,683
Other alcoholic drinks ('000 litres)	4,272	4,484	4,220
Iron bars ('000 kg)	16,371	11,846	16,598
Pasteurized milk ('000 litres)	46,377	49,935	53,477
Vegetable oil ('000 lb)	4,619	5,776	15,175
Vegetable fat ('000 lb)	65,024	74,644	77,309

*Preliminary.

Finance

CURRENCY AND EXCHANGE RATES

Monetary Units
100 centavos = 1 lempira.

Denominations
Coins: 1, 2, 5, 10, 20 and 50 centavos.
Notes: 1, 2, 5, 10, 20, 50 and 100 lempiras.

Sterling and Dollar Equivalents (30 September 1988)
£1 sterling = 3.382 lempiras;
US $1 = 2.000 lempiras;
100 lempiras = £29.57 = $50.00.

Exchange Rate
The official rate is fixed at US $1 = 2.00 lempiras.

BUDGET (million lempiras)

Revenue	1985	1986	1987*
Current revenue	1,837.5	1,936.2	2,211.0
Taxes	1,023.6	1,035.3	1,155.5
Income tax	240.6	250.2	297.9
Property tax	23.6	23.5	26.6
Tax on production, domestic trade and transactions	349.4	356.0	388.3
Import taxes and duties	316.6	301.2	345.2
Export taxes and duties	92.5	103.5	95.8
Other taxes	0.9	0.9	1.7
Non-tax revenue	615.2	641.4	779.6
Transfers	14.9	1.6	2.8
Other receipts	183.8	257.9	273.1
Capital revenue	1,165.9	1,104.4	1,000.5
Internal borrowing	523.9	628.3	628.0
External borrowing	525.2	345.8	258.5
Capital transfers	116.8	130.3	114.0
Other	74.8	151.5	237.3
Total	3,078.2	3,192.1	3,448.8

Expenditure	1985	1986*	1987*
Current expenditure	1,777.6	1,945.0	2,259.2
Consumption expenditure	1,685.7	1,847.9	2,156.2
of which wages and salaries	851.3	1,009.4	1,060.4
Current transfers	91.9	97.1	103.0
Capital expenditure	666.8	629.1	529.8
Direct investment	648.7	581.6	502.9
of which real investment	577.7	480.7	394.8
Indirect investment	18.1	47.5	26.9
Net allowance on loans	82.4	76.6	104.7
Public debt servicing	551.4	541.4	555.1
Internal	432.5	409.9	445.7
External	118.9	131.5	109.4
Total	3,078.2	3,192.1	3,448.8

* Preliminary.

CENTRAL BANK RESERVES (US $ million at 31 December)

	1985	1986	1987
Gold	1.05	1.05	1.05
Foreign exchange	105.80	111.30	105.80
Total	106.85	112.35	106.85

Source: IMF, *International Financial Statistics*.

MONEY SUPPLY (million lempiras at 31 December)

	1985	1986	1987
Currency outside banks	410.2	425.8	491.5
Private sector deposits at Central Bank	18.6	36.9	44.4
Demand deposits at commercial banks	426.8	492.6	583.2
Total money	855.6	955.3	1,119.1

Source: IMF, *International Financial Statistics*.

HONDURAS

COST OF LIVING
(Consumer Price Index for Urban Centres. Base: 1978 = 100)

	1985	1986	1987*
Food	160.5	164.9	167.0
Housing	198.5	212.0	221.3
Clothing	234.9	240.0	242.6
Medical care	189.9	192.4	197.3
Personal care	178.4	180.1	182.5
Beverages and tobacco	220.3	245.8	247.1
Transport	161.9	167.7	169.5
Miscellaneous	200.6	206.4	215.6
All items	**184.9**	**193.0**	**197.8**

* Preliminary.

NATIONAL ACCOUNTS (million lempiras at current prices)
Expenditure on the Gross Domestic Product

	1985	1986	1987*
Government final consumption expenditure	1,046	1,144	1,289
Private final consumption expenditure	5,033	5,383	5,787
Increase in stocks	19	43	83
Gross fixed capital formation	1,245	1,143	1,155
Total domestic expenditure	**7,343**	**7,713**	**8,314**
Exports of goods and services	1,754	1,971	1,912
Less Imports of goods and services	2,120	2,119	2,183
GDP in purchasers' values	**6,977**	**7,565**	**8,043**

* Preliminary.

Gross Domestic Product by Economic Activity

	1985	1986	1987*
Agriculture, hunting, forestry and fishing	1,328	1,495	1,529
Mining and quarrying	139	141	118
Manufacturing	926	963	1,030
Electricity, gas and water	109	126	133
Construction	366	350	383
Wholesale and retail trade	843	905	952
Transport, storage and communications	408	455	483
Finance, insurance and real estate	419	443	477
Owner-occupied dwellings	504	558	592
Public administration and defence	350	383	433
Other services	743	811	930
GDP at factor cost	**6,135**	**6,630**	**7,060**
Indirect taxes, *less* subsidies	842	935	983
GDP in purchasers' values	**6,977**	**7,565**	**8,043**

* Preliminary.

BALANCE OF PAYMENTS (US $ million)

	1985	1986	1987
Merchandise exports f.o.b.	789.6	891.3	862.6
Merchandise imports f.o.b.	−879.2	−874.1	−893.9
Trade balance	**−89.6**	**17.2**	**−31.3**
Exports of services	128.6	130.9	130.9
Imports of services	−388.8	−411.9	−429.2
Balance on goods and services	**−349.8**	**−263.8**	**−329.6**
Private unrequited transfers (net)	12.4	13.0	16.0
Government unrequited transfers (net)	133.2	145.4	130.3
Current balance	**−204.1**	**−105.5**	**−183.3**
Direct capital investment (net)	27.5	30.0	36.0
Other long-term capital (net)	180.6	37.1	−12.3
Short-term capital (net)	−11.4	17.3	46.5
Net errors and omissions	−55.8	9.9	53.9
Total (net monetary movements)	**−63.2**	**−11.2**	**−59.2**
Valuation changes (net)	−1.3	12.7	−51.4
Exceptional financing (net)	45.8	41.0	136.6
Official financing (net)	—	—	—
Changes in reserves	**−18.6**	**42.5**	**26.0**

Source: IMF, *International Financial Statistics*.

External Trade

PRINCIPAL COMMODITIES (million lempiras)

Imports c.i.f.	1985	1986	1987*
Food and live animals	160.7	165.8	178.8
Mineral fuels, lubricants, etc.	317.1	194.7	208.0
Chemicals	353.8	403.9	406.0
Basic manufactures	387.6	363.5	379.2
Machinery and transport equipment	404.1	406.6	415.9
Miscellaneous manufactured articles	101.4	128.9	129.6
Total (incl. others)	**1,776.2**	**1,750.1**	**1,797.3**

Exports f.o.b.	1985	1986	1987*
Bananas	547.0	513.5	648.5
Coffee	370.4	644.1	416.7
Wood	68.2	64.6	72.6
Lead and zinc	71.8	64.9	27.0
Silver	26.0	25.1	10.8
Frozen meat	36.3	39.9	42.2
Shellfish	81.9	90.9	122.8
Soap	4.7	2.9	1.9
Cotton	13.6	9.3	6.5
Tobacco	17.3	10.6	7.1
Total (incl. others)	**1,529.2**	**1,708.5**	**1,651.4**

* Preliminary.

HONDURAS

PRINCIPAL TRADING PARTNERS (million lempiras)

Imports c.i.f.	1985	1986	1987*
Brazil	29.4	24.7	42.2
Canada	19.4	13.2	15.3
Costa Rica	75.1	65.9	50.1
France	27.1	33.8	41.2
Germany, Federal Republic	70.0	62.5	54.1
Guatemala	88.4	73.6	46.6
Japan	103.5	151.6	205.3
Mexico	82.0	93.8	70.8
Netherlands	41.0	51.8	64.2
Trinidad and Tobago	3.7	—	3.1
United Kingdom	31.0	28.1	34.5
USA	636.0	664.8	701.3
Venezuela	233.4	114.3	105.9

Exports f.o.b.	1985	1986	1987*
Belgium	92.3	115.9	61.8
Costa Rica	14.2	10.9	7.9
Germany, Federal Republic	117.5	182.2	190.1
Guatemala	7.9	16.2	20.1
Italy	118.6	119.6	97.3
Japan	100.8	157.7	98.8
Netherlands	45.2	50.1	42.8
Nicaragua	13.0	5.0	2.3
Spain	40.7	29.4	28.1
Trinidad and Tobago	20.4	11.0	10.1
United Kingdom	33.7	28.8	26.3
USA	734.1	807.3	891.9

* Preliminary.

Transport

ROAD TRAFFIC (motor vehicles in use)

	1984	1985	1986
Passenger cars	24,516	25,031	25,194
Lorries and buses	53,013	56,302	56,916

INTERNATIONAL SEA-BORNE SHIPPING
(freight traffic in '000 metric tons)

	1983	1984	1985*
Goods loaded	1,398	1,428	1,392
Goods unloaded	1,146	1,248	1,138

* Provisional figures.

CIVIL AVIATION (traffic on scheduled services)

	1983	1984	1985*
Passengers ('000)	301	307	313
Passenger-km (million)	329	388	458
Freight-km (million)	13	17	22

* Provisional figures.

Tourism

	1985	1986	1987*
Number of visitors	154,599	170,599	192,426

* Preliminary.

Education

(1987)

	Institutions	Teachers	Pupils
Primary	7,054	21,476	840,057
Secondary	438	7,618	142,679
Teachers' training college	1	271	6,061
Universities	3	2,572	32,107

Directory

The Constitution

Following the elections of April 1980, the 1965 Constitution was revised. The new Constitution was approved by the National Assembly in November 1982. The following are some of its main points:

Honduras is constituted as a democratic Republic. All Hondurans over the age of 18 are citizens.

THE SUFFRAGE AND POLITICAL PARTIES

The vote is direct and secret. Any political party which proclaims or practises doctrines contrary to the democratic spirit is forbidden. A National Electoral Council will be set up at the end of each Presidential term. Its general function will be to supervise all elections and to register political parties. A proportional system of voting will be adopted for the election of Municipal Corporations.

INDIVIDUAL RIGHTS AND GUARANTEES

The right to life is declared inviolable; the death penalty is abolished. The Constitution recognizes the right of habeas corpus and arrests may be made only by judicial order. Remand for interrogation may not last more than six days, and no-one may be held incommunicado for more than 24 hours. The Constitution recognizes the rights of free expression of thought and opinion, the free circulation of information, of peaceful, unarmed association, of free movement within and out of the country, of political asylum and of religious and educational freedom. Civil marriage and divorce are recognized.

WORKERS' WELFARE

All have a right to work. Day work shall not exceed eight hours per day or 44 hours per week; night work shall not exceed six hours per night or 36 hours per week. Equal pay shall be given for equal work. The legality of trades unions and the right to strike are recognized.

EDUCATION

The State is responsible for education, which shall be free, lay, and, in the primary stage, compulsory. Private education is liable to State inspection and regulation.

LEGISLATIVE POWER

Deputies are obliged to vote, for or against, on any measure at the discussion of which they are present. The National Assembly has power to grant amnesties to political prisoners; approve or disapprove of the actions of the Executive; declare part or the whole of the Republic subject to a state of siege; declare war; approve or withhold approval of treaties; withhold approval of the accounts of public expenditure when these exceed the sums fixed in the Budget; decree, interpret, repeal and amend laws, and pass legislation fixing the rate of exchange or stabilizing the national currency. The National Assembly may suspend certain guarantees in all or part of the Republic for 60 days in the case of grave danger from civil or foreign war, epidemics or any other calamity. Deputies are elected in the proportion of one deputy and one substitute for every 35,000 inhabitants, or fraction over 15,000. Congress may amend the basis in the light of increasing population.

EXECUTIVE POWER

The Executive Power is exercised by the President of the Republic, who is elected for four years, by a simple majority of the people. No President may serve more than one term.

JUDICIAL POWER

The Judiciary consists of the Supreme Court, the Courts of Appeal and various lesser tribunals. The nine judges and seven substitute judges of the Supreme Court are elected by the National Assembly for a period of four years. The Supreme Court is empowered to declare laws unconstitutional.

THE ARMED FORCES

The armed forces are declared by the Constitution to be essentially professional and non-political. The President exercises military power through a Commander-in-Chief who is designated for a period of three years by the National Assembly, and may be dismissed only by it by a two-thirds majority. Military service is obligatory.

LOCAL ADMINISTRATION

The country is divided into 18 Departments for purposes of local administration, and these are subdivided into autonomous Municipalities; the functions of local offices shall be only economic and administrative.

The Government

HEAD OF STATE

President: José Simeón Azcona del Hoyo (assumed office 27 January 1986).
Vice-Presidents: Jaime Rosenthal Oliva, Alfredo Fortín Inestroza, José Pineda Gómez.

CABINET
(February 1989)

Minister of the Interior and Justice: Enrique Ortez-Colindres.
Minister of Foreign Affairs: Carlos López Contreras*.
Minister of Public Education: Elisa Estela Valle de Martínez Pavetti.
Minister of Finance: José Efraín Bu Girón.
Minister of Economy and Commerce: Reginaldo Pantin.
Minister of Health and Social Security: Dr Rubén Antonio Villeda Bermúdez.
Minister of Natural Resources: Rodrigo Castillo Aguilar.
Minister of Labour and Social Affairs: Adalberto Discua Rodríguez*.
Minister of Defence and Public Security: Wilfredo Sánchez.
Minister of Communications, Public Works and Transport: Juan Fernando López.
Minister of Culture, Tourism and Information: Arturo Rendón Pineda.
Secretary for Economic Planning: Francisco Figueroa Zúñiga.
Director of the National Agrarian Institute: Raúl Flores Gómez.
Secretary of State to the Presidency: Celeo Arias Moncacada.
* Member of Partido Nacional (PN).

MINISTRIES

Office of the President: Casa Presidencial, 6a Avda, 1a Calle, Tegucigalpa; tel. 22-8287.
Ministry of Communications, Public Works and Transport: Barrio La Bolsa, Comayagüela, Tegucigalpa; tel. 33-7690.
Ministry of Culture, Tourism and Information: Costado Este del Palacio Legislativo, Tegucigalpa; tel. 22-9721.
Ministry of Defence and Public Security: Palacio de los Ministerios, Tegucigalpa; tel. 22-9521.
Ministry of Economy and Commerce: Edif. Salame, 5a Avda, 4a Calle, Tegucigalpa; tel. 22-3251; telex 1396.
Ministry of Finance: Palacio de Hacienda, Avda Cervantes, Tegucigalpa; tel. 22-8452.
Ministry of Foreign Affairs: Avda La Paz, Edif. Atala, Tegucigalpa; tel. 31-4209; telex 1129.
Ministry of Health and Social Security: 4a Avda, 3a Calle, Tegucigalpa; tel. 22-1386.
Ministry of the Interior and Justice: Palacio de los Ministerios 2°, Tegucigalpa; tel. 22-8604.
Ministry of Labour and Social Affairs: 2a y 3a Avda, 7a Calle, Comayagüela, Tegucigalpa; tel. 22-8527.
Ministry of Natural Resources: Blvd Miraflores, Tegucigalpa; tel. 32-3141.
Ministry of Public Education: 1a Avda, 2a y 3a Calle, No 201, Comayagüela, Tegucigalpa; tel. 22-8573.

President and Legislature

PRESIDENT

A presidential election was held on 24 November 1985. Nine candidates contested the election: four candidates of the PLH, three candidates of the PN, one candidate of the PINU and one candidate of the PDC. The two leading candidates, Rafael Leonardo Callejas (PN) and José Simeón Azcona del Hoyo (PLH), obtained 639,000 votes and 416,000 votes respectively. However, as the combined votes for the candidates of the PLH amounted to 51% of the total votes cast, whilst the combined votes for the candidates of the PN were only 45% of the total votes cast, José Simeón Azcona del Hoyo was declared President-elect, in accordance with the new electoral law. The transfer of power took place on 27 January 1986.

ASAMBLEA NACIONAL

President: Carlos Orbín Montoya.

General Election, 24 November 1985

Party	Seats
Partido Liberal de Honduras (PLH)	67
Partido Nacional (PN)	63
Partido Demócrata Cristiano (PDC)	2
Partido de Innovación y Unidad (PINU)	2
Total	134

Political Organizations

Asociación para el Progreso de Honduras (APROH): right-wing grouping of business interests and members of the armed forces; Vice-Pres. Miguel Facussé; Sec. Oswaldo Ramos Soto.

Francisco Morazán Frente Constitucional (FMFC): f. 1988; composed of labour, social, political and other organizations.

Frente Patriótico Hondureño (FPH): left-wing alliance comprising:

    Partido Comunista de Honduras (PCH): f. 1954; gained legal status 1981; linked with DNU; Leader Rigoberto Padilla Rush.

    Partido Comunista Marxista-Leninista.

    Partido Socialista (Paso): Leaders Mario Virgilio Caras, Rogelio Martínez Reina.

Partido Demócrata Cristiano (PDC): legally recognized in 1980; Pres. Efraín Díaz Arrivillaga; Leader Dr Hernán Corrales Padilla.

Partido de Innovación y Unidad (PINU): Apdo 105, Tegucigalpa; f. 1970; legally recognized in 1978; Leader Dr Miguel Andonie Fernández.

Partido Liberal de Honduras (PLH): Tegucigalpa; tel. 32-6049; f. 1980; Liberal Party; factions within the party include the Alianza Liberal del Pueblo, the Movimiento Florista (Leader Ing. Carlos Roberto Flores Facusse), and the Movimiento Liberal Democrático Revolucionario (Pres. Jorge Arturo Reina); Pres. Ing. Carlos Roberto Flores Facusse; Sec.-Gen. Roberto Micheletti Bain; Carlos Flores Facusse was to be the PLH candidate in the 1989 presidential election.

Partido Nacional (PN): Tegucigalpa; f. 1902; traditional right-wing party; internal opposition tendencies include Movimiento Democratizador Nacionalista (Modena), Movimiento de Unidad y Cambio (MUC), Movimiento Nacional de Reivindicación Callejista (MONARCA) and Tendencia Nacionalista de Trabajo; Sec. Abog.

HONDURAS
Mario Aguilar González; Rafael Leonardo Callejas was to be the PN candidate in the 1989 presidential election.

Partido Revolucionario Hondureño (PRH): Apdo 1319, San Pedro Sula; f. 1977; not legally recognized; Sec.-Gen. Francisco Rodolfo Jiménez Caballero.

Unión Revolucionaria del Pueblo (URP): f. 1980 from split in Communist Party; left-wing group, with peasant support.

In 1985 a broad-based opposition alliance, the Coordinadora Opositora Democrática Constitucional—Codeco, was formed by members of the PDC, PLH and PN.

In 1983 the guerrilla forces united to form the Directorio Nacional Unido (DNU), consisting of the following groups:

Fuerzas Populares Revolucionarias (FRP) Lorenzo Zelaya.

Frente Morazanista para la Liberación de Honduras (FMLH).

Froylan Turcios.

Movimiento Popular de Liberación Cinchonero (MPLC).

Movimiento de Unidad Revolucionaria (MUR).

Partido Revolucionario de los Trabajadores Centroamericanos de Honduras (PRTCH).

Diplomatic Representation

EMBASSIES IN HONDURAS

Argentina: Colonia Rubén Darío 2 cuadras al sur del Cenáculo, Apdo 101-C, Tegucigalpa; tel. 32-3376; telex 1120; Ambassador: Luis N. Augusto Sánchez R.

Brazil: Plaza San Martín 501, Colonia Palmira, Apdo 341, Tegucigalpa; tel. 32-2021; telex 1151; Ambassador: Cyro Gabriel do Espirito Santo Cardoso.

Chile: Blvd Morazán, Edif. Interamericana frente Los Castaños, Apdo 222, Tegucigalpa; telex 1195; Ambassador: Hosmán A. Pérez Sepúlveda.

China (Taiwan): Avda República de Panamá 2024, Colonia Palmira, Apdo 6-C, Tegucigalpa; tel. 32-9490; telex 1383; Ambassador: Huang Chuam-li.

Colombia: Edif. Palmira 4°, Colonia Palmira, Apdo 468, Tegucigalpa; tel. 32-9300; telex 1336; Ambassador: (vacant).

Costa Rica: Blvd Morazán, Colonia Palmira, 1a Calle 704, Apdo 512, Tegucigalpa; tel. 32-1768; telex 1154; Ambassador: Maximiliano Oreamuno Brenes.

Dominican Republic: Colonia La Granja 402, 4a Calle entre 4a y 5a Avda Comayagüela, Apdo 1460, Tegucigalpa; Ambassador: Juan Emilio Canó de la Mota.

Ecuador: Colonia Palmira 3a, junto al Parque Benito Juárez, Apdo 358, Tegucigalpa; telex 1471; Ambassador: Rosendo Maridueña Germán.

El Salvador: 2a Avda 205, Colonia San Carlos, Tegucigalpa; tel. 32-1344; telex 1301; Ambassador: Salvador Trigueros.

France: Avda Juan Lindo, Apdo 14-C, Colonia Palmira, Tegucigalpa; tel. 32-1800; telex 1180; Ambassador: Pierre Dumon.

Germany, Federal Republic: Edif. Paysen 3°, Blvd Morazán, Apdo C-38, Tegucigalpa; tel. 32-3161; telex 1118; Ambassador: Dr Eckehard Schober.

Guatemala: Colonia Palmira, Avda Juan Lindo 313, Apdo 34-C, Tegucigalpa; tel. 32-5018; Ambassador: Eunice Lima.

Holy See: Palacio de la Nunciatura Apostólica, Colonia Palmira 412, Apdo 324, Tegucigalpa; tel. 32-8280; Apostolic Nuncio: Mgr Francisco de Nittis.

Israel: Edif. Palmira, Apdo 1187, Tegucigalpa; Ambassador: Shlomo Cohen.

Italy: Avda Principal Colonia Reforma 2062, Apdo 317, Tegucigalpa; telex 1332; Ambassador: Dr Mario Alberto Montecalvo.

Japan: 2a Avda, Colonia Reforma, Plaza del Guanacaste, Apdo 125-C, Tegucigalpa; telex 1141; Ambassador: Kiichi Itabashi.

Mexico: Avda República del Brasil 2028, Apdo 769, Tegucigalpa; tel. 32-4039; telex 1143; Ambassador: Lic. Francisco Correa Villalobos.

Nicaragua: Colonia Tepeyac, Bloque M-1, Apdo 392, Tegucigalpa; tel. 32-1209; telex 1274; Ambassador: Lic. Francisco José Lacayo.

Panama: Edif. Palmira, Apdo 397, Tegucigalpa; Ambassador: Dr Carlos Alberto de Diego Soriano.

Peru: Edif. Palmira 5°, Apdo 64-C, Tegucigalpa; Ambassador: Jaime Castro Mendivil.

Spain: Colonia Matamoros 801, Apdo 114-C, Tegucigalpa; tel. 32-1875; telex 1142; Ambassador: (vacant).

United Kingdom: Edif. Palmira 3°, Colonia Palmira, Apdo 290, Tegucigalpa; tel. 32-5429; telex 1234; Ambassador: David Joy.

USA: Avda La Paz, Apdo 26-C, Tegucigalpa; tel. 32-3120; Ambassador: Everett E. Briggs.

Uruguay: Edif. Palmira 4°, Apdo 329, Tegucigalpa; Ambassador: Alfredo Menini Terra.

Venezuela: Colonia Palmira 2302, 4°, Calle República de Colombia, Apdo 775, Tegucigalpa; telex 1238; Ambassador: Dionssio Teodoro Marcano.

Judicial System

There is a Supreme Court with nine judges. In addition, there are five Courts of Appeal, and departmental courts which have their own local jurisdiction.

Tegucigalpa has two Courts of Appeal which have jurisdiction (1) in the department of Francisco Morazán, and (2) in the departments of Choluteca Valle, El Paraíso and Olancho.

The Appeal Court of San Pedro Sula has jurisdiction in the department of Cortés. That of Comayagua has jurisdiction in the departments of Comayagua, La Paz and Intibucá; that of Santa Bárbara in the departments of Santa Bárbara, Lempira, Copán.

Supreme Court: 10a y 11a Avda, 3a Calle, Tegucigalpa; tel. 22-8790.

President of the Supreme Court of Justice: Salomon Jiménez Castro.

Attorney-General: Rubén Darío Zepeda Gutiérrez.

Religion

The majority of the population are Roman Catholics; the Constitution guarantees toleration to all forms of religious belief.

CHRISTIANITY

The Roman Catholic Church

Honduras comprises one archdiocese, four dioceses and one territorial prelature. At 31 December 1984 an estimated 93% of the population were adherents.

Bishops' Conference: Conferencia Episcopal de Honduras, Arzobispado, Apdo 106, Tegucigalpa; tel. 22-0353; f. 1972; Pres. Héctor Enrique Santos Hernández, Archbishop of Tegucigalpa.

Archbishop of Tegucigalpa: Héctor Enrique Santos Hernández, Arzobispado, Apdo 106, Tegucigalpa; tel. 22-0353.

The Episcopal Church

Bishop of Honduras: Rt Rev. Leo Frade, Apdo 586, San Pedro Sula; tel. 57-4009.

The Baptist Church

Baptist Convention of Honduras: Apdo 868, Tegucigalpa; tel. 22-7392; Pres. Alexis Vides.

BAHÁ'Í FAITH

National Spiritual Assembly: Apdo 273, Tegucigalpa; tel. 33-1182; mems resident in 560 localities.

The Press

DAILIES

El Faro Porteño: Puerto Cortés.

La Gaceta: Tegucigalpa; f. 1830; morning; official government paper; Dir Rodolfo Heriberto Gómez; circ. 3,000.

El Heraldo: Avda los Próceres, Frente Instituto del Tórax, Tegucigalpa; f. 1979; morning; independent; Dir José Francisco Morales Cálix; circ. 25,000.

La Prensa: 3a Avda No 34, Apdo 143, San Pedro Sula; f. 1964; independent; Pres. Amilcar Santamaría; circ. 40,000.

El Tiempo: Altos del Centro Comercial Miramontes, Colonia Miramontes, Tegucigalpa; f. 1970; liberal; Dir Manuel Gamero; circ. 30,000.

El Tiempo: 7a Avda No 6, Calle S.O. 55, Apdo 450, San Pedro Sula; f. 1970; left-of-centre; Dir Edmond L. Bográn; Editor Manuel Gamero; circ. 70,000.

La Tribuna: Apdo 1501, Tegucigalpa; f. 1977; morning; independent; Dir Adán Elvir Flores; circ. 50,000.

HONDURAS

PERIODICALS

El Alfiler: San Pedro Sula; weekly.

Ariel: Tegucigalpa; monthly.

Cambio Empresarial: Apdo 4, Tegucigalpa; monthly; economic, political, social; Editor JOAQUÍN MEDINA OVIEDO.

El Comercio: Cámara de Comercio e Industrias de Tegucigalpa, Bulevar Centroamérica, Apdo 17-C, Tegucigalpa; tel. 32-8210; telex 1537; f. 1970; monthly; commercial and industrial news; Man. JORGE MEJÍA ORTEGA.

Cultura para Todos: San Pedro Sula; monthly.

El Expectador: San Pedro Sula; weekly.

Extra: Apdo 133, Tegucigalpa; tel. 37-2533; f. 1965; monthly; independent; current affairs; Dir VICENTE MACHADO VALLE.

Impacto: Tegucigalpa; weekly; Gen. Man. RAÚL BARNICA LÓPEZ.

Presente: Tegucigalpa; monthly.

Revista Ideas: Tegucigalpa; 6 a year; women's interest.

Revista Prisma: Tegucigalpa; quarterly; cultural; Editor MARÍA LUISA CASTELLANOS.

Semáforo: Tegucigalpa; weekly.

Sucesos: Tegucigalpa; monthly.

Tragaluz: Apdo 1843, Tegucigalpa; every 2 months; cultural and literary review; Editor HELEN UMAÑA; circ. 2,000.

Tribuna Gráfica: Tegucigalpa; fortnightly.

Tribuna Sindical: Tegucigalpa; monthly.

El Trópico: Avda Atlántida, 3a Calle, La Ceiba; f. 1938; weekly; independent; general news; Dir RODOLFO ZAVALA.

PRESS ASSOCIATION

Asociación de Prensa Hondureña: 6a Calle (altos), Barrio Guanacaste, Apdo 893, Tegucigalpa; f. 1930; Pres. GUILLERMO PAGAN SOLÓRZANO.

FOREIGN NEWS AGENCIES

Agence France-Presse (AFP) (France): Tegucigalpa; Correspondent WINSTON CALIX.

Agencia EFE (Spain): Edif. Jiménez Castro, 5°, of. 505, Tegucigalpa; tel. 22-0493; Bureau Chief ARMANDO ENRIQUE CERRATO CORTÉS.

Agenzia Nazionale Stampa Associata (ANSA) (Italy): 2a Avda B 434, Barrio Morazán, Tegucigalpa; tel. 220109; telex 1353; Correspondent RAÚL MONCADA.

Deutsche Presse-Agentur (dpa) (Federal Republic of Germany): Edif. Jiménez Castro, 4a Calle y 5a Avda, Of. 203, Apdo 1501, Tegucigalpa; tel. 22-8883; Correspondent WILFREDO GARCÍA CASTRO.

Inter Press Service (IPS) (Italy): Apdo 228, Tegucigalpa; tel. 32-5342; Correspondent JUAN RAMÓN DURÁN.

Reuters (UK): Edif. Palmira frente Honduras Maya, 5°, Barrio Palmira, Tegucigalpa; tel. 31-5329.

United Press International (UPI) (USA): Tegucigalpa; Correspondents NOEL LEIVA, VILMA GLORIA ROSALES.

Publishers

Compañía Editora Nacional, SA: 5a Calle Oriente No 410, Tegucigalpa.

Editora Cultural: 6a Avda Norte, 7a Calle, Comayagüela, Tegucigalpa.

Editorial Nuevo Continente: Avda Cervantes 123, Tegucigalpa; tel. 22-5073; Dir LETICIA SILVA DE OYUELA.

Editorial Paulino Valladares, Carlota Vda de Valladares: 5a Avda, 5a y 6a Calle, Tegucigalpa.

Guayamuras: Apdo 1843, Tegucigalpa; tel. 37-5433; f. 1980; Dir ISOLDA ARITA MELZER; Admin. ROSENDO ANTÚNEZ.

Industria Editorial Lypsa: Apdo 167-C, Tegucigalpa; tel. 22-9775; Man. JOSÉ BENNATON.

Universidad Nacional Autónoma de Honduras: Oficina de Relaciones Públicas, Tegucigalpa.

Radio and Television

In 1986 there were 251 radio stations, four main television stations, and an estimated 1,600,000 radio receivers and 280,000 television sets in use.

RADIO

Empresa Hondureña de Telecomunicaciones (Hondutel): Apdo 1794, Tegucigalpa; tel. 37-9802; telex 1343; Gen. Man. Col MARIO LEONEL FONSECA.

Radio América: Apdo 259, Tegucigalpa; commercial station; 13 relay stations; Gen. Man. RODRIGO WONG ARÉVALO.

Radio Nacional de Honduras: Apdo 403, Tegucigalpa; tel. 22-8042; telex 1147; f. 1976; official station, operated by the Government; Dir TOMÁS VINDEL.

La Voz de Centroamérica: Apdo 120, San Pedro Sula; commercial station; Gen. Man. JORGE SIKAFFY.

La Voz de Honduras: Apdo 642, Tegucigalpa; commercial station; 23 relay stations; Gen. Man. NAHÚN VALLADARES.

TELEVISION

Compañía Televisora Hondureña, SA: Apdo 642, Tegucigalpa; tel. 32-7835; telex 1126; f. 1959; main station Channel 5; nine relay stations; Gen. Man. JOSÉ RAFAEL FERRARI.

Telesistema Hondureño, SA: Apdo 642, Tegucigalpa; tel. 32-0710; telex 1126; f. 1967; main station Channel 3; four relay stations; Gen. Man. MANUEL VILLEDA TOLEDO; Asst Gen. Man. Lic. ANA MARÍA VILLEDA F.

Voz y Imagen de Centro América: Apdo 120, San Pedro Sula; 2 relay stations; Pres. JORGE SIKAFFY.

Trecevisión: Apdo 393, Tegucigalpa; subscriber TV; one relay station in San Pedro Sula; Gen. Man. F. PON AGUILAR.

Finance

(cap. = capital; p.u. = paid up; res = reserves; dep. = deposits; m. = million; amounts in US dollars unless otherwise stated)

BANKING

Central Bank

Banco Central de Honduras—BANTRAL: 6a y 7a Avda, 1a Calle, Apdo 58-C, Tegucigalpa; tel. 22-2270; telex 1121; f. 1950; cap. and res $91.7m. (July 1985); bank of issue; Pres. GONZALO CARÍAS PINEDA; Man. RIGOBERTO PINEDA S.; 3 brs.

Commercial Banks

Banco de El Ahorro Hondureño, SA (BANCAHORRO): Avda Colón 711, Apdo 78-C, Tegucigalpa; tel. 22-5161; telex 1184; f. 1960; cap. and res $5.3m., dep. $83.3m. (June 1984); Pres. and Gen. Man. FRANCISCO VILLARS; 8 brs.

Banco Atlántida, SA (BANCATLAN): Blvd Miraflores, Plaza Bancatlán, Apdo 57-C, Tegucigalpa; tel. 32-2670; telex 1106; f. 1913; cap. and res $11.8m., dep. $160m. (Dec. 1986); Pres. Dr PAUL VINELLI; 18 brs.

Banco Capitalizadora Hondureña, SA (BANCAHSA): 5a Avda 501, Apdo 344, Tegucigalpa; tel. 22-1171; telex 1162; f. 1948; cap. and res $7.2m., dep. $130.6m. (June 1987); Pres. and Gen. Man. Lic. JORGE ALBERTO ALVARADO; 38 brs.

Banco del Comercio, SA (BANCOMER): 6a Avda, 1-2 Calle SO, Apdo 160, San Pedro Sula; tel. 54-3600; telex 5480; cap. and res $6.5m., dep. $28.3m. (June 1984); Pres. RODOLFO CÓRDOBA PINEDA; 4 brs.

Banco Continental, SA (BANCON): Edif Continental, 3a Avda 50, entre 2 y 3 Calle, Apdo 390, San Pedro Sula, Cortés; tel. 53-2622; telex 5561; f. 1974; cap. and res $10.4m., dep. $42m. (June 1987); Pres. Ing. JAIME ROSENTHAL OLIVA; 3 brs.

Banco de Honduras, SA: 3a Calle, 7a Avda 301, Apdo 7-C, Tegucigalpa; tel. 22-1151; telex 1116; f. 1889; cap. and res $3.8m., dep. $31.3m. (June 1984); Gen. Man. Lic. MARÍA LIDIA SOLANO; 3 brs.

Banco de las Fuerzas Armadas, SA (BANFFAA): Calle Peatonal Costado Catedral, Apdo 877, Tegucigalpa; tel. 22-8131; telex 1245; f. 1979; cap. and res $4m., dep. $40.5m. (June 1984); Pres. Capt. ARMANDO SAN MARTÍN; Vice Pres. Lic. ROBERTO DALA OBANDO.

Banco de Occidente, SA (BANCOCCI): Apdo 208, Santa Rosa de Copán; tel. 62-0232; f. 1951; cap. and res $7.3m., dep. $122m. (Dec. 1987); Pres. and Gen. Man. Lic. JORGE BUESO ARIAS; 14 brs.

Banco Mercantil, SA: 5a Calle, 10 Avda 924, Apdo 116, Tegucigalpa; tel. 22-6280; telex 1260; Pres. JOSÉ LAMAS; Gen. Man. Lic. JACOBO ATALA.

Banco Sogerin, SA: Plaza Sogerin 1, Apdo 440, San Pedro Sula; tel. 53-5948; telex 5526; f. 1969; cap. and res $6.1m., dep. $92.0m. (Dec. 1987); Pres. EDMOND L. BOGRÁN; Gen. Man. SIDNEY JOSÉ PANTING; 28 brs.

HONDURAS

Banco de los Trabajadores, SA (BANCOTRAB): 3a Avda, 13a Calle, El Obelisco, Apdo 139-C, Comayagüela; tel. 22-8723; telex 1202; f. 1967; cap. and res $7.1m., dep. $28.0m. (June 1984); Pres. ROLANDO DEL CID V.; Man. RAÚL SOLÍS DACOSTA; 13 brs.

Development Banks

Banco Centroamericano de Integración Económica: Apdo 772, Tegucigalpa; tel. 22-2230; telex 1103; f. 1961 to finance the economic development of the Central American Common Market and its member countries; mems Guatemala, El Salvador, Honduras, Nicaragua, Costa Rica; cap. and res $436.8m. (Dec. 1986); Pres. Lic. DANTE GABRIEL RAMÍREZ.

Banco Hondureño del Café (BANHCAFE, SA): 6a Avda 501, 5a Calle, Apdo 583, Tegucigalpa; tel. 22-4210; telex 1278; f. 1981 to help finance coffee production; cap. and res $16.9m., dep. $35.0m. (July 1986); owned principally by private coffee producers; Pres. TITO ANTONIO SAGASTUME; Gen. Man. Lic. CARLOS CANIZALES.

Banco Municipal Autónomo (BANMA): 6a Avda, 6a Calle, Tegucigalpa; tel. 22-5963; f. 1963; cap. and res $25.2m., dep. $1.4m. (June 1984); Pres. Lic. JUSTO PASTOR CALDERÓN; 2 brs.

Banco Nacional de Desarrollo Agrícola (BANADESA): 13 Calle, 4–5 Avda Comayagüela, Apdo 212, Tegucigalpa; tel. 22-8505; telex 1105; f. 1980; cap. and res $37.5m., dep. $70m. (Oct. 1987); government development bank; loans to agricultural sector; Pres. Ing. ADOLFO LIONEL SEVILLA G.; 28 brs.

Financiera Centroamericana, SA (FICENSA): Edif. FICENSA, Blvd 'Los Castaños', Apdo 1432, Tegucigalpa; tel. 22-1035; telex 1200; f. 1974; private finance organization giving loans to industry, commerce and transport; cap. and res $3.9m., dep. $41.1m. (Dec. 1984); Pres. OSWALDO LÓPEZ ARELLANO; Gen. Man. JOSÉ ARTURO ALVARADO.

Financiera Nacional de la Vivienda—FINAVI: Apdo 1194, Tegucigalpa; f. 1975; housing development bank; cap. and res $5.3m. (July 1984); Exec. Pres. Lic. ELMAR LIZARDO.

Foreign Banks

Bank of America NT & SA (USA): Edif. Centro Comercial Los Castaños, Blvd Morazán, Apdo 199, Tegucigalpa; tel. 32-7350; telex 1101; cap. and res $1.5m., dep. $10.8m. (July 1983); Gen. Man. VÍCTOR PAZ.

Bank of London and Montreal Ltd (Bahamas): 5a Avda, 4a Calle, Apdo 29-C, Tegucigalpa; tel. 22-5151; telex 1117; Man. JULES P. GENASI; 6 brs.

Banking Association

Asociación Hondureña de Instituciones Bancarias (AHIBA): Edif. Bancahsa 5°, Pieza 505, Apdo 1344, Tegucigalpa; tel. 37-7336; f. 1956; 14 mem. banks; Pres. Gen. OSWALDO LÓPEZ ARELLANO; Vice Pres. Lic. SALDOR GÓMEZ.

INSURANCE

El Ahorro Hondureño, SA, Compañía de Seguros: Edif. Trinidad, 5a Calle, 11a Avda, Tegucigalpa; tel. 22-8219; telex 1122; f. 1917; Pres. Dr ROBERTO RAMÍREZ; Gen. Man. RAÚL A. RAUDALES.

American Home Asssurance Co: Edif. Los Castaños 4°, Blvd Morazán, Apdo 113-C, Tegucigalpa; tel. 32-1849; telex 1228; f. 1933; fmrly Hanover Insurance Co.; Gen. Man. O. REYNALDO RAMÍREZ C.

Aseguradora Hondureña, SA: Centro Comercial Plaza Miraflores 3°, Col. Miraflores, Apdo 312, Tegucigalpa; tel. 32-2729; telex 1246; f. 1954; Pres. and Gen. Man. ALBERTO AGURCIA.

Compañía de Seguros Interamericana, SA: Apdo 593, Colonia Los Castaños, Tegucigalpa; tel. 32-7614; telex 1362; f. 1957; Pres. SALOMÓN D. KAFATI; Gen. Man. RUBÉN ALVAREZ H.

Pan American Life Insurance Co: Edif. PALIC, Avda República de Chile 804, Tegucigalpa; tel. 32-8774; telex 1237; f. 1944; Gen. Man. Lic. FERNANDO RODRÍGUEZ.

Previsión y Seguros, SA: Apdo 770, Colonia Sabana-Grande y Avda Los Próceres, Tegucigalpa; tel. 32-4834; telex 1392; f. 1981; Gen. Man. EDGARDO ZAPATA C.

Seguros Continental, SA: Edif. Continental 4°, 3a Avda SO 7, Apdo 320, San Pedro Sula; tel. 53-1821; telex 5561; f. 1968; Pres. Ing. JAIME ROSENTHAL OLIVA; Man. MARIO R. SOLÍS.

Insurance Association

Cámara Hondureña de Aseguradores (CAHDA): Edif. JS, frente Iglesia la Guadalupe, Blvd Morazán, Apdo 183-C, Tegucigalpa; tel. 32-6020; Pres. Lic. FERNANDO J. RODRÍGUEZ; Sec. Lic. RUBÉN ALVAREZ H.

Directory

Trade and Industry

CHAMBERS OF COMMERCE

Cámara de Comercio e Industrias de Cortés: 17a Avda, 10a y 12a Calle, Apdo 14, San Pedro Sula; tel. 53-0761; f. 1931; 812 mems; Pres. Ing. FELIPE ARGÜELLO C.

Federación de Cámaras de Comercio e Industrias de Honduras (Fedecámara): Blvd Centroamérica, Apdo 17-C, Tegucigalpa; tel. 32-8110; telex 1537; f. 1985; 2,100 mems; Exec. Sec. JORGE MEJÍA ORTEGA.

DEVELOPMENT ORGANIZATIONS

Consejo Hondureño de la Empresa Privada (COHEP): Avda Los Próceres 505, Apdo Postal 133-C, Tegucigalpa; f. 1968; comprises 23 private enterprises; Pres. (vacant); Exec. Sec. Ing. JOAQUÍN LUNA MEJÍA.

Corporación Financiera de Olancho: f. 1977 to co-ordinate and manage all financial aspects of the Olancho forests project; Pres. RAFAEL CALDERÓN LÓPEZ.

Corporación Hondureña del Banano—COHBANA (Banana Corporation of Honduras): Tegucigalpa; tel. 53-2868; f. 1975; autonomous organization in charge of all operations concerned with bananas; privatization announced in 1988; Gen. Man. CARLOS D. CABRERA.

Corporación Hondureña de Desarrollo Forestal (COHDEFOR): Salida Carretera del Norte, Zona El Carrizal, Apdo 1378, Comayagüela; tel. 22-8810; telex 1172; f. 1974; semi-autonomous organization in charge of forestry management and control of the forestry industry; Gen. Man. Ing. JOSÉ SEGOVIA I.

Corporación Nacional de Inversiones (CONADI): Apdo 842, Tegucigalpa; telex 1192; f. 1974; industrial development investment corporation; in 1988 managed 62 public-sector corporations of which 20 were to be sold to private investors by 1990; Exec. Pres. EDUARDO RAMOS; Exec. Vice-Pres. Lic. LEMPIRA BONILLA.

Dirección General de Minas e Hidrocarburos (General Directorate of Mines and Hydrocarbons): Blvd Miraflores, Apdo 981, Tegucigalpa; tel. 32-6227; telex 1404; Dir-Gen. Ing. JOSÉ MAGIN LANZA V.

Instituto Hondureño del Café—IHCAFE: POB 40-C, Tegucigalpa; tel. 37-3131; telex 1167; f. 1970; coffee development programme; Gen. Man. Lic. RAMIRO RODRÍGUEZ LANZA.

Instituto Hondureño de Mercadeo Agrícola (IHMA): POB 727, Tegucigalpa; tel. 321629; telex 1138; Gen. Man. OSCAR ROBERTO GALLARDO.

Instituto Nacional Agrario (INA): Tegucigalpa; telex 1218; agricultural development programmes; Dir RAÚL FLORES GÓMEZ.

Secretaría Técnica del Consejo Superior de Planificación Económica (CONSUPLANE): Edif. Bancatlán 3°, Apdo 1327, Comayagüela; tel. 22-8738; telex 1222; f. 1965; national planning office; Exec. Sec. FRANCISCO FIGUEROA ZÚÑIGA.

PRODUCERS' ASSOCIATIONS

Asociación de Bananeros Independientes—ANBI (National Association of Independent Banana Producers): San Pedro Sula; tel. 22-7336; f. 1964; 62 mems; Pres. Ing. JORGE ALBERTO ALVARADO; Sec. CECILIO TRIMINIO TURCIOS.

Asociación Hondureña de Productores de Café (Coffee Producers' Association): 10a Avda, 6a Calle, Apdo 959, Tegucigalpa.

Asociación Nacional de Exportadores de Honduras (ANEXHON): Tegucigalpa; comprises 104 private enterprises; Pres. Dr RICHARD ZABLAH.

Asociación Nacional de Industriales (ANDI) (National Association of Manufacturers): Blvd Los Próceres No 505, Apdo 20-C, Tegucigalpa; Pres. HÉCTOR BULNES; Exec. Sec. DORCAS DE GONZALES.

Asociación Nacional de Pequeños Industriales (ANPI) (National Association of Small Industries): Apdo 730, Tegucigalpa; Pres. JUAN RAFAEL CRUZ.

Federación Hondureña de Cooperativas Cafetaleras (Fehcocal) (Federation of Coffee Co-operatives of Honduras): Tegucigalpa; f. 1969.

Federación Nacional de Agricultores y Ganaderos de Honduras (FENAGH) (Farmers and Livestock Breeders' Association): Tegucigalpa; Pres. Ing. FERNANDO LARDIZÁBAL.

Federación Nacional de Cooperativas Cañeras (Fenacocal) (National Federation of Sugar Cane Co-operatives): Tegucigalpa.

TRADE UNIONS

Confederación de Trabajadores de Honduras—CTH (Workers' Confederation of Honduras): Barrio La Fuente, Calle Lempira,

HONDURAS

Casa 515, Apdo 720, Tegucigalpa; tel. 22-4243; f. 1964; affiliated to CTCA, ORIT and ICFTU; Pres. Mariano de Jesús González; Sec.-Gen. Andrés Víctor Artiles; 150,000 mems; comprises the following federations:

Federación Central de Sindicatos Libres de Honduras (FECE-SITLIH) (Federation of Free Trade Unions): 1a Avda, 1a Calle, No 102, Apdo 621, Comayagüela; Pres. Emilio Gonzales García.

Federación Sindical de Trabajadores Nacionales de Honduras (FESITRANH) (Honduran Federation of Farmworkers): 9a Avda, 3a Calle SO, No 65, Apdo 245, San Pedro Sula, Cortés; f. 1957; Pres. Francisco Guerrero.

Sindicato Nacional de Motoristas de Equipo Pesado de Honduras (SINAMEQUIP) (National Union of HGV Drivers): Tegucigalpa.

Central General de Trabajadores (CGT) (General Confederation of Labour): Apdo 1236, Tegucigalpa; attached to Partido Demócrata Cristiano; Sec.-Gen. Felicito Avila.

Federación Auténtica Sindical de Honduras (FASH): 1a Avda, 11a Calle No 1102, Comayagüela.

Federación de Trabajadores del Sur (FETRASUR) (Federation of Southern Workers): Choluteca.

Federación Unitaria de Trabajadores de Honduras (FUTH): Avda Cervantes 1219, Apdo 1663, Barrio la Plazuela, Tegucigalpa; tel. 22-6349; f. 1981; linked to left-wing electoral alliance Frente Patriótico Hondureño; Leader Carlos Reyes; 50,000 mems.

Frente de Unidad Nacional Campesino de Honduras (FUNA-CAMH): f. 1980; group of farming co-operatives and six main peasant unions as follows:

Asociación Nacional de Campesinos de Honduras (ANACH) (National Association of Honduran Farmworkers): 8a Avda, 9a Calle SO, No 36, Blvd Lempira, San Pedro Sula, Cortés; f. 1962; affiliated to ORIT; Pres. Antonio Julín Méndez; 80,000 mems.

Federación de Cooperativas Agropecuarias de la Reforma Agraria de Honduras (FECORAH).

Frente Nacional de Campesinos Independientes de Honduras.

Unión Nacional de Campesinos (UNC) (National Union of Farmworkers): Tegucigalpa; linked to CLAT; Leader Adán Palacios; Sec.-Gen. Marcel Caballero; c. 25,000 mems.

Unión Nacional de Campesinos Auténticos de Honduras (UNCAH).

Unión Nacional de Cooperativas Populares de Honduras (UNACOOPH).

Transport

RAILWAYS

In 1986 there were 955 km of railways, all of which are in the north of the country and most of which are used for fruit cargo. A 97-km rail link was reportedly being built between La Ceiba and San Pedro Sula in the mid-1980s.

Ferrocarril Nacional de Honduras (National Railway of Honduras): 1 Calle 0 2, Apdo Postal 496, San Pedro Sula; tel. 53-3230; f. 1870; government-owned; 128 km of track open; Gen. Man. P. R. Romero.

Tela Railroad Co: La Lima; tel. (504) 56-2018; telex 8305; 344 km of track open; Pres. Ronald F. Walker; Gen. Man. John A. Ordman.

Vaccaro Railway: La Ceiba; 390 km of track open; Gen. Man. D. Dehorenzo.

ROADS

In 1986 there were 14,167 km of roads in Honduras, including 2,216 km of main or national roads. Roads have been constructed by the Instituto Hondureño del Café and COHDEFOR in order to facilitate access to coffee plantations and forestry development areas.

Dirección General de Caminos: Tegucigalpa; highways board.

SHIPPING

Empresa Nacional Portuaria (National Port Authority): Apdo 18, Puerto Cortés; telex 8007; f. 1965; has jurisdiction over all ports in Honduras; manages Puerto Cortés, Tela, La Ceiba, Trujillo/Castilla, Roatán, Amapala and San Lorenzo; a network of paved roads connects Puerto Cortés and San Lorenzo with the main cities of Honduras, and with the principal cities of Central America; Gen. Man. Lic. Jerónimo Sandóval.

There are several minor shipping companies. A number of foreign shipping lines call at Honduran ports.

CIVIL AVIATION

Local airlines in Honduras compensate for the deficiencies of road and rail transport, linking together small towns and inaccessible districts. There are three international airports. A new airstrip was opened at Roatán in 1988. In December 1988 the Spanish Government and the IDB approved a loan of US $50m. to aid the construction of a new airport at Tegucigalpa, which would, it was estimated, cost $200m.

Servicio Aéreo de Honduras, SA (SAHSA): Apdo 129, Tegucigalpa; telex 321-1146; f. 1945; private company; operates domestic flights and also to the USA, Colombia, Nicaragua, Guatemala, Belize, Costa Rica and Panama; Pres. Gen. Oswaldo López; Gen. Man. Capt. Rolando Figueroa; fleet: 3 DC-3, 1 Boeing 727-100, 1 Boeing 737-200.

Aerovías Nacionales de Honduras, SA (ANHSA): c/o SAHSA; f. 1950; a local airline which serves the north coast and the east of the country; fleet: 2 DC-3.

Transportes Aéreos Nacionales, SA (TAN): Edif. TAN, Apdo 628, Tegucigalpa; telex 848-5909; f. 1947; operates passenger and cargo services, internal and international to Belize, Mexico and the USA; Pres. Gen. Oswaldo López; Gen. Man. Capt. Rolando Figueroa; fleet: 1 Boeing 737-200, 2 L-188 CF Electra.

Líneas Aéreas Nacionales, SA (LANSA): Apdo Postal 35, La Ceiba; f. 1971; scheduled services within Honduras and to Islas de Bahía; Gen. Man. Oscar M. Elvir; fleet: 1 F27J, 4 DC-3, 1 Cessna 182, 1 Cessna 206.

Tourism

Tourists are attracted by the Mayan ruins, the fishing and boating facilities in Trujillo Bay and Lake Yojoa, near San Pedro Sula, and the beaches on the northern coast. Honduras received an estimated 192,426 tourists in 1987.

Instituto Hondureño de Turismo: Costado este del Palacio Legislativo, Apdo 154-C, Tegucigalpa; tel. 22-1183; telex 1322; f. 1975; department of the Secretaría de Cultura y Turismo; Dir-Gen. Lic. Deborah Mills de Goldner.

Atomic Energy

Comisión Hondureña de Energía Atómica: Apdo 104, Tegucigalpa; Pres. Dr Rafael Torres Fiallos.

HUNGARY

Introductory Survey

Location, Climate, Language, Religion, Flag, Capital

The Hungarian People's Republic lies in Eastern Europe, bounded to the north by Czechoslovakia, to the east by the USSR and Romania, to the south by Yugoslavia and to the west by Austria. Its climate is continental, with long, dry summers and severe winters. Temperatures in Budapest are generally between −3°C (27°F) and 28°C (82°F). The language is Hungarian (Magyar). Most of the inhabitants profess Christianity, and the largest single religious denomination is the Roman Catholic Church, claiming more than 6m. adherents. Other Christian groups are the Hungarian Reformed Church (a Presbyterian sect with about 2m. members), the Lutheran Church and the Hungarian Orthodox Church. The national flag (proportions 3 by 2) consists of three equal horizontal stripes, of red, white and green. The capital is Budapest.

Recent History

Hungary allied itself with Nazi Germany before the Second World War and obtained additional territory when Czechoslovakia was partitioned in 1938 and 1939. Having sought to break the alliance in 1944, Hungary was occupied by German forces. In January 1945 Hungary was liberated by Soviet troops and signed an armistice, restoring the pre-1938 frontiers. It became a republic in February 1946. Meanwhile, land distribution, under the March 1945 land reform, continued. Nationalization measures began in December 1946, despite opposition from the Roman Catholic Church under Cardinal József Mindszenty. In the 1947 elections the Communists became the largest single party, with 22.7% of the vote. By the end of that year the Communist Party had emerged as the leading political force. The Communists merged with the Social Democrats to form the Hungarian Workers' Party in June 1948. A People's Republic was established in August 1949.

Mátyás Rákosi became the leading figure as First Secretary of the Workers' Party. Opposition was subsequently removed by means of purges and political trials. Rákosi became Prime Minister in 1952 but, after the death of Stalin a year later, lost this post to the more moderate Imre Nagy, and a short period of liberalization followed. Rákosi, however, remained as First Secretary of the Party, and in 1955 Nagy was forced to resign. András Hegedüs, sponsored by Rákosi, was appointed Prime Minister. In-fighting between the Rákosi and Nagy factions increased in 1956 after the condemnation of Stalinism at the 20th CPSU Congress in Moscow; in July Rákosi was forced to resign but was replaced by a close associate, Ernő Gerő.

The consequent discontent provoked demonstrations, and in October 1956 fighting broke out. Nagy was reinstated as Prime Minister and headed a series of governments. He promised various controversial reforms, but fighting continued. In November a new Soviet-supported government, led by János Kádár, was installed. Soviet troops, stationed in Hungary under the 1947 peace treaty, were asked to intervene and the uprising was suppressed. In June 1958 Nagy and four associates were executed for their part in the uprising. Kádár also became the leader of the newly-formed Hungarian Socialist Workers' Party (HSWP). He held the premiership until January 1958 and from September 1961 to July 1965 but, even when not formally in the Government, his Party leadership made him dominant in political life.

György Lázár became Chairman of the Council of Ministers (Prime Minister) in May 1975. In April 1978 Béla Biszku, who had been regarded as Kádár's deputy, was retired from the Secretariat of the Central Committee of the HSWP. At the Party Congress in March 1980 Kádár was re-elected First Secretary of the Central Committee; five Politburo members were not reappointed. The June 1980 general election resulted in a 99.3% vote in favour of the Patriotic People's Front (dominated by the HSWP). An extensive government reshuffle followed. Changes included the election of six new members to the Presidential Council and the removal of two Deputy Chairmen from the Council of Ministers. In January 1981 three industrial ministries were merged into a single Ministry of Industry to improve co-ordination. A minor reshuffle took place in June 1982. In July 1983 Péter Várkonyi was appointed as Minister of Foreign Affairs. In December 1984 three new Deputies to the Chairman of the Council of Ministers were appointed. Gen. Ferenc Kárpáti became Minister of Defence in December 1985.

The 13th HSWP Congress was held in March 1985. János Kádár was re-elected leader of the Party, taking the new title of General Secretary of the Central Committee. Károly Németh, a member of the HSWP Politburo and of the Presidential Council, was elected to the newly-created post of Deputy General Secretary of the Party Central Committee. A new Politburo and Central Committee Secretariat were chosen, each containing three members elected for the first time. The Congress also reaffirmed the commitment to the country's economic reforms.

The legislative elections of June 1985 were the first to be held under the revised electoral law, giving voters a wider choice of candidates under the system of mandatory multiple nominations. The National Assembly again re-elected Pál Losonczi as President of the Presidential Council, which included seven new members.

In December 1986 a Deputy Chairman of the Council of Ministers was replaced, and a new Minister of Finance was appointed. In June 1987 Pál Losonczi retired from the largely ceremonial post of President of the Presidential Council, and was replaced by Károly Németh. Károly Grósz, a member of the Politburo and hitherto First Secretary of the Budapest HSWP Committee, was appointed Chairman of the Council of Ministers in place of György Lázár, who succeeded Németh as Deputy General Secretary of the Party Central Committee. Other changes in the HSWP leadership included the appointment of two new Politburo members. In December the Council of Ministers underwent an extensive reorganization. The number of Deputy Chairmen was reduced from five to two. The Ministries of Internal Trade and of Foreign Trade were merged to form a single Trade Ministry, headed by József Marjai, and a new Ministry for the Protection of the Environment and Water Management was established. Other appointments included that of Miklós Villányi as Minister of Finance.

In April 1988 four prominent members of the HSWP, known for their advocacy of radical political and economic reforms, were expelled from the party. All four were associated with an unofficial political group, the Hungarian Democratic Forum, which was formally established in September 1988 to discuss, among other subjects, political reforms. At a special ideological conference of the HSWP, held in May 1988, major changes in party personnel and policy were approved. János Kádár was replaced as General Secretary of the Central Committee by Károly Grósz, the Chairman of the Council of Ministers. Kádár was promoted to the newly-created and purely ceremonial post of HSWP President, but lost his membership of the Politburo. About one-third of the members of the Central Committee (in particular, conservative associates of Kádár) were removed and replaced by younger politicians. The new Politburo included Imre Pozsgay (hitherto the Secretary-General of the Patriotic People's Front), a prominent advocate of reform and political pluralism, and Rezső Nyers, who had been largely responsible for the 'new economic mechanism' (NEM), initiated in 1968, but who had been removed from the Politburo in 1975. Grósz declared his commitment to radical economic and political reforms, although he excluded the immediate possibility of a multi-party political system. In June 1988 several changes were made in the Council of Ministers, including Pozsgay's appointment as a Minister of State, with special responsibility for political development. Also in June 1988, Dr Brunó Ferenc Straub, who was not a member of the HSWP, was elected to the post of President of the Presidential Council, in succession to Károly Németh. It was anticipated that the Presidential Council would be abolished in 1990, in accordance with the planned new constitution. In November 1988 Miklós Németh, hitherto the head of a department of the HSWP Central Committee, replaced Károly Grósz as Chairman of the Council of Ministers.

In the months following Grósz's appointment as leader of the HSWP, there was a relaxation of censorship laws, while a new free trade union, the Democratic Union of Scientific Workers (Hungary's first independent trade union for 40 years), and also a new independent political group, the Hungarian Democratic Forum, were founded. In January 1989 the work-force's right to strike was fully legalized. At a plenary session in July 1988, the Central Committee of the HSWP voted overwhelmingly in favour of an austere economic programme, designed to revitalize the economy within 10 years. The programme would involve immediate reductions in subsidies and a drastic devaluation of the forint, which would, in turn, lead to an increase in unemployment of 100,000 workers in 1989, and to an annual inflation rate of up to 30%. In October 1988 the economic reform programme was given final approval by the National Assembly. In January 1989 the National Assembly enacted two laws guaranteeing Hungarians the right to demonstrate freely, and to form associations and political parties independent of the HSWP. The new law on association, however, granted political parties and new groups the right to exist only. A separate law regulating their operation was expected to be submitted to the National Assembly before August 1989. It was recognized that, as a consequence of the new law, the HSWP might not win a majority of seats in the Assembly at the next general election, scheduled for mid-1990. A new constitution was due to be introduced before the election. In January 1989 a six-member Inner Cabinet was established within the Council of Ministers. In February a special session of the HSWP Central Committee agreed to support the transition to a multi-party system. Another meeting of the Committee, later in the month, agreed to abandon the clause in the Constitution guaranteeing the HSWP's 'leading role'.

In February 1986 up to 100 Hungarian and Austrian environmentalists attempted to stage a demonstration in Budapest to protest against the construction, in northern Hungary, of one of the two dams in the Gabčíkovo-Nagymaros hydroelectric project, involving the diversion of a 222-km stretch of the River Danube (a joint Hungarian-Czechoslovak scheme, with Austrian assistance), but the demonstration was halted by the police. The environmentalists claimed that the project would upset the Danube's ecological balance, destroy wildlife and flood historic sites. In May 1987 nine Austrian protesters, including three 'green' members of the Austrian legislature, were expelled from Hungary for distributing leaflets opposing the project. In September 1988 an estimated 20,000 people gathered in Budapest to protest against further construction work on the dam. In October, however, the National Assembly voted overwhelmingly to continue with the project.

In March 1986 disturbances broke out when hundreds of disenchanted young people took part in a protest march. The police used force to stop the marchers, and the incident was reportedly the worst display of public disorder in the country for many years. Criminal proceedings, on charges of breach of the peace, were instigated against 11 of the demonstrators. The 30th anniversary of the 1956 uprising, in October, passed off peacefully. In March 1987 more than 2,000 protesters marched through Budapest. The demonstration was tolerated by the authorities. In March 1988, on the 140th anniversary of the 1848 Hungarian uprising against Austrian rule, some 10,000 people took part in an unofficial march through Budapest, demanding freedom of the press, freedom of association and the introduction of genuine reforms. The protest was not halted by the authorities, although eight prominent dissidents were prevented by the police from participation. In June 1988 police prevented several hundred people from commemorating publicly the 30th anniversary of the execution of Imre Nagy. In January 1989, however, there was official debate as to whether the events of 1956 had been a 'popular uprising' or (the official designation hitherto) a counter-revolution. The bodies of Imre Nagy and four of his associates, who had also been executed in 1958, were reburied in marked graves in January 1989.

Hungary is closely aligned with the countries of Eastern Europe through its membership of the Warsaw Pact (see p. 207). However, Hungary's relations with Romania and, to a lesser extent, with Czechoslovakia have been strained by the issue of the position of the large Hungarian minorities resident in these countries. In 1987 and 1988 Hungary received thousands of applications from Romanian citizens of Hungarian origin who wished to settle in Hungary, and by November 1988 11,600 such Romanians had received temporary residence permits in Hungary. In June 1988 an estimated 50,000 people protested in Budapest against the Romanian Government's proposed destruction of some 7,000 villages in Romania, including 1,500 inhabited by ethnic Hungarians. Romania, apparently prompted by the officially tolerated demonstration, expelled the staff of the Hungarian consulate in Cluj, Transylvania. In August 1988 Grósz conferred with the Romanian leader, Nicolae Ceauşescu, in an attempt to solve the issue of the 1.7m. ethnic Hungarians in Romania. In January 1989 plans were under discussion in Hungary for the establishment of four refugee camps in Budapest and near the Romanian border.

Hungary pursues an active foreign policy, and relations with the West, particularly Austria, France, the Federal Republic of Germany and the United Kingdom, are improving steadily. In 1988, with the liberalization of passport regulations, a record number of Hungarians travelled to Western countries. During 1987 Kádár paid official visits to Sweden, the People's Republic of China and Belgium. In October 1987 Károly Grósz visited the Federal Republic of Germany, and in 1988, as HSWP General Secretary, he visited the United Kingdom, the USA, Canada, the USSR, Austria, Spain and France. In 1988 contacts were improved with Israel, diplomatic relations having been severed in 1967.

Government

Proposals for a new constitution were under discussion in 1989. Under the 1949 Constitution, the highest organ of state power is the unicameral National Assembly, with 387 members (expanded from 352 in 1985), elected for five years by universal adult suffrage. Since 1971 the electorate has had the right to nominate two or more candidates for a constituency, thus providing wider representation in the National Assembly. At the elections of June 1985 the system of multiple candidacy was extended to all the original 352 constituencies, in 78 of which there were more than two candidates. The additional 35 members were elected unopposed on a new national list of prominent politicians (including nine members of the HSWP Politburo), trade unionists, clergymen, etc. The Assembly elects from its members a Presidential Council (21 members were elected in 1985) to be its permanent organ and the State's executive authority, responsible to the Assembly. The Council, led by a President, collectively acts as the Head of State. The Council of Ministers, the highest organ of state administration, is elected by the Assembly on the recommendation of the Presidential Council.

Political power is held by the Communist HSWP, which dominates the Patriotic People's Front. The Front presents an approved list of candidates, nominated at public meetings, for elections to representative bodies. No other candidates are permitted. Any individual or body may nominate a candidate, but must receive the support of at least one-third of those at the meeting for the nomination to be valid. The HSWP's highest authority is the Party Congress, which elects a Central Committee (108 members were elected in May 1988) to supervise Party work. The Central Committee elects a Political Committee (Politburo) of 11 members to direct policy. For local administration Hungary is divided into 19 counties and the capital city (with 22 districts).

Defence

Hungary was a founder member of the Warsaw Pact in 1955. Military service starts at the age of 18 years and normally lasts for 18 months in the army and 24 months in the air force. In July 1988, however, it was announced that in 1989 an alternative military service for conscientious objectors would be introduced, the first of its kind in Eastern Europe. According to Western estimates, the total regular forces in June 1988 numbered 99,000 (including 64,000 conscripts): army 77,000 (including 45,000 conscripts) and air force 22,000. There is also an armed force of 16,000 border guards and a Workers' Militia with 60,000 members. The 1988 defence budget totalled an estimated 47,000m. forint. In January 1989 it was announced that, during the course of 1989–90, the People's Army would be reduced by about 9%, and that armaments and other military equipment (including 250 tanks) would also be decreased. It was also announced that, during 1989, there would be a partial withdrawal of the 65,000 Soviet troops stationed in Hungary.

Economic Affairs

In 1968 a new system of economic management was introduced, known as the 'new economic mechanism' (NEM). The official definition of the plan was to 'harmonize state planning and market development'. Until then the economy had been based on the standard Soviet central planning system. Under the new scheme, industry has been decentralized to a certain extent, with the aim of evolving a socialist market economy, with emphasis on monetarist policies. The reforms initially brought a rapid improvement in the standard of living in Hungary.

Various measures to encourage the further development of private enterprise have been implemented since 1982. In January 1982 new regulations were introduced to give more scope to small private and co-operative ventures. In 1983, in order to attract foreign investment, new measures permitted the establishment of customs-free zones for joint ventures between Hungarian enterprises and foreign companies. In January 1986 taxes on the profits of joint ventures were reduced and the licensing system was simplified. By December 1988 a total of 255 joint ventures had been agreed with Western companies, mostly from Austria and the Federal Republic of Germany.

In 1985 radical reforms in the system of management, giving enterprises more autonomy, were introduced. In about 80% of companies managers are to be elected: in large and medium companies election will be by newly-formed enterprise councils, representing workers and officials; in small companies managers will be elected directly by employees. New regulations, aimed at improving efficiency and profitability, allow successful enterprises to pay higher wages and to reduce the labour force if necessary, while loss-making companies face the possibility of liquidation. Between 1980 and 1985 the State provided 80,000m. forint in subsidies to unprofitable enterprises. A new bankruptcy law, applicable to both companies and co-operatives, took effect in September 1986. Henceforth, state aid to loss-making organizations will be offered only in exceptional circumstances. In October 1988 the Government introduced a new law allowing full foreign ownership of Hungarian companies and permitting Hungarians to trade shares and to employ up to 500 employees for private profit.

Reforms in the financial sector include the restructuring of the banking system. In 1987 and 1988 several commercial banks were established, in order to improve efficiency in the allocation of financial resources. In 1984 a domestic 'bond market' came into existence, the money raised by the issue of bonds (both to enterprises and to private individuals) being used to finance housing and infrastructural schemes, and in January 1988 a national securities market opened in Budapest. In the same month, new austerity measures included the introduction of value-added tax (VAT) and direct personal income tax, in an attempt to reduce consumption and stimulate production. Revenue from VAT was expected to total 126,000m. forint in 1988. In January 1989 a stock exchange was opened in Budapest.

Various reforms to liberalize the regulations governing Hungarian foreign trade began in 1980. The economy is heavily dependent on foreign trade, which usually accounts for about 50% of net material product (NMP). Higher-quality goods that are competitive on the world market are now being produced, in an attempt to increase exports.

In recent years the population of Hungary has been declining steadily, but the country has experienced economic growth. In 1987, according to estimates by the World Bank, Hungary's gross national product (GNP), measured at average 1985–87 prices, was US $23,757m., equivalent to $2,240 per head. Between 1980 and 1987, it was estimated, GNP expanded, in real terms, at an average rate of 1.5% per year, while real GNP per head rose by 1.6% annually. The average annual growth of overall gross domestic product, in constant prices, was 5.6% between 1965 and 1980, slowing to 1.6% in 1980–86. However, real GNP per head increased by an estimated 3.6% in 1987.

The principal branches of manufacturing in Hungary are engineering and chemicals, the engineering sector employing 32% of those engaged in industry in 1984. However, the value of the Hungarian chemical industry's exports to the convertible currency area declined substantially in 1986, owing to the fall in international prices for petroleum and consequently for petrochemical products. It was hoped to offset this shortfall by increasing exports of other chemical products. With a work-force of about 110,000 people, the chemical industry provided 20% of total industrial production in 1987, and more than one-third of its output was exported. Hungary's newly-established microelectronics industry suffered a major set-back in May 1986, when the industry's main plant in Budapest was destroyed by fire. Hungary is an exporter of engineering products, machine tools, buses, telecommunications and electrical equipment, electronic instruments, pharmaceutical products, rolled steel, clothing and footwear. In 1987, as part of a restructuring programme, the iron and steel industry underwent radical reorganization, the work-force being reduced by 2,400. Owing to the decline in export markets, Hungary's output of iron and steel was to be decreased by as much as 10% in 1988, and during the year the work-force was reduced by 5%. It was envisaged that by the end of 1992 a further 6,000 workers would have been made redundant. Meat, fruit, vegetables, wine and honey are also significant exports, sales of agricultural produce accounting for almost 30% of total exports in 1987. The country's principal imports are crude petroleum, iron ore, copper and copper products, raw materials for the plastics industry, chemical fibres, artificial fertilizers, paper, cotton, animal feeding-stuff and capital and consumer goods.

In 1988 18.8% of the economically active population were employed in agriculture and forestry. More than 50% of the total area is arable land, most of which is state or co-operatively owned. In 1988 there were 131 state and complex farms, cultivating 11% of Hungary's arable land and contributing nearly 20% of total agricultural output. In 1986 the 1,270 co-operative farms cultivated a total of 5.8m. ha and accounted for 70% of the country's agricultural production. Between 1984 and 1988 the number of co-operative members and employees declined by 8.5% (about 30,000 annually). The household plots of co-operative members make a significant contribution to total agricultural output. The principal crops include wheat, maize, sunflowers, sugar beet and potatoes. The severe weather of early 1985 and a decline in international market prices created serious problems in the agricultural sector. These difficulties were compounded in 1986 by the nuclear power station accident at Chernobyl, in the USSR, and the West's introduction of restrictions on agricultural imports from Hungary, and also by drought, which resulted in serious shortfalls in crop production and further export losses. Owing to adverse weather, crop production declined by 4% in 1987, compared with the previous year. The grain harvest reached only 14.1m. metric tons in 1987, but totalled an estimated 14.7m. tons in 1988, including 6.3m. tons of wheat and 5.7m. tons of maize. Vineyards covered a total of 145,000 ha in 1988, but were to be reduced by 20,000–25,000 ha over the subsequent four or five years. For the third consecutive year, viticulture was severely affected by frost damage in early 1987, and the year's wine production fell to an estimated 3.4m. hectolitres. However, output was expected to increase to about 4.0m. hectolitres in 1988. Forests covered a total of 1.7m. ha in 1987, and output in the forestry and timber industry increased by 8% compared with 1986.

With the exception of rich deposits of bauxite (production of which totalled almost 3m. metric tons in 1988), Hungary is not well-endowed with natural resources. Although copper deposits (with an estimated value of $13m.) have been discovered at Recsk, the mines remained undeveloped in 1988, owing to lack of finance and to the low international price for the commodity. In an attempt to limit import costs, the country's oil consumption was reduced from 12.5m. metric tons in 1979 to 9.1m. tons in 1985. The cost of imports of petroleum and petroleum products (mostly from the USSR) declined from 60,572.6m. forint in 1984 to 46,612.6m. forint in 1987. Domestic output of crude petroleum, from the Pannonian Basin, totalled 1.9m. tons in 1987. Petroleum imports from the USSR were to total 6.5m. tons in 1989. Output of hard coal fell from 2.6m. metric tons in 1984 to 2.3m. tons in 1986 and remained at about the same level in 1987. It was envisaged that during 1986–90 total coal production (hard coal, brown coal and lignite) would remain at around 24m. tons annually. Total output was 22.8m. tons in 1987, but fell to 20.9m. tons in 1988. In 1988 it was announced that subsidies to the coal-mining industry were to be reduced. Output of natural gas totalled 7,126m. cu m in 1987, but it was feared that annual output would decline to 5,000m.–6,000m. cu m by the year 2000, unless substantial new deposits could be discovered. Gas imports from the USSR, by pipeline, were to total 5,900m. cu m in 1989. The Paks nuclear power station project was inaugurated in 1983. In 1988 about 31% of Hungary's electricity supply was generated from coal, 30% from hydrocarbons and 39% from nuclear power. It is envisaged that, by the end of the century, nuclear power will provide almost one-half of the country's total energy output. Hungary's uranium reserves are sufficient to supply the Paks station until the year 2020. In 1985 Hungary decided to proceed with the

HUNGARY

Introductory Survey

Gabčíkovo-Nagymaros Danube barrage scheme, a joint project with Czechoslovakia. Austrian participation in the scheme was agreed in 1986. Scheduled for completion in 1993, the project's two hydroelectric power stations are expected to supply a total of 3,600m. kWh per year. The total cost of the project was estimated at 70,000m. forint. By mid-1988 about 20% of the Hungarian share of the construction work had been completed.

During the fourth Five-Year Plan (1971-75) Hungary's NMP rose by 35% over the previous five-year period, industrial production increased by 38%, and agricultural output by 18%. The 1976-80 Plan laid emphasis on the modernization of industry. As a result of higher costs for raw materials and less favourable conditions of trade, the targets of this Plan were scaled down. NMP increased by 20% instead of 30%-32%. Industrial production rose by 18%-19%, and agricultural output by 13%. Investment, originally scheduled to increase by 25%, was severely curtailed.

The sixth Five-Year Plan (1981-85) envisaged a continuation of austerity and stressed the need for greater efficiency and profitability. Over the Plan period, an increase of 14%-17% in NMP was projected, but growth of only 7% was achieved. Industrial production rose by 12%, compared with a target of 19%-22%. The engineering and chemical industries recorded increases in output of 18% and 11.8% respectively over the five-year period. As a percentage of the 1976-80 average, agricultural output went up by 12%. Per caput real income rose by 7%-8% during the 1981-85 period, slightly more than planned. Total exports were set to increase by 37%-39%, and imports by 18%-19%, but went up by 27% and 6%, respectively.

The seventh Five-Year Plan (1986-90) projected growth of 15%-17% in NMP, compared with the level of 1985. Industrial production was planned to increase by 14%-16%. Agricultural output (compared with the 1981-85 period) was expected to rise by 7%-10%. It was envisaged that domestic consumption would go up by 13%-16% and real income per head by 9%-11%. Total exports were planned to grow by 16%-18% and imports by the same percentage. Investments in the socialist sector would approach 1,500,000m. forint.

In 1986 NMP rose by 0.5% over the previous year compared with the target of 2.3%-2.7%. An increase of more than 2% was achieved in 1987. Real income per person rose by 3% in 1986, but remained at the same level in 1987. Industrial production rose by 3.7% in 1987 and by 1.0%-1.5% in 1988. Having risen by only 1% in 1986, agricultural output in 1987 again increased by only 1%, owing to adverse weather. In 1988, however, a 4.2% expansion in agricultural production was achieved (only 0.1% less than planned), and a further increase of 1.2% was anticipated for 1989. Domestic consumption was reduced by 2.5%-3.0% in 1988, reflecting the decline in living standards. In 1989 domestic consumption was to decrease by 1%, and income per caput by 2%. Compared with the previous year, the volume of exports fell by 2% in 1986, while that of imports rose by 2.5%.

A uniform exchange rate for the forint was introduced in 1981. The forint has been successively devalued against major Western currencies. In March 1987 the forint was devalued by an average of 8% against Western currencies. A further devaluation of 5% was made in November 1987, and the forint was again devalued (by 6%) in July 1988.. Consumer prices rose by 39% between 1981 and 1985, and by 5.3% in 1986. During 1987 there were steep rises in the prices of basic foodstuffs and domestic fuels, and further increases, affecting 53% of products and services, were implemented in January 1988. In the same month the Government announced that it would relinquish control of most consumer prices at the end of March 1988. In an effort to counterbalance the price increases (largely caused by the introduction of VAT in January 1988), the Government was to adopt measures relating to welfare policy, to the value of 16,000m. forint. In January 1989 major new price rises were introduced, including an average 16%-17% increase in the price of basic foodstuffs. An annual inflation rate of 8.6% was recorded in 1987 and the rate rose to an estimated 16%-17% in 1988, compared with the planned 15%. An inflation rate of as much as 25% was predicted for 1989. In December 1986 a four-month wage 'freeze' was declared. Real wages were estimated to have fallen by 8%-10% in 1988, and in 1989 a 6% reduction in real wages was envisaged. As a result of the Government's programme to restructure the industrial sector, between January 1987 and January 1988 the number of unemployed doubled to reach 10,500, and had reached 30,000 by the end of 1988. In 1988 the Government planned to introduce an enterprise allowance scheme, which would enable persons leaving the labour market to establish independent private businesses. The 1989 budget deficit was estimated at 20,000m.-22,000m. forint, compared with 18,000m. forint in 1988.

Hungary is a member of the Council for Mutual Economic Assistance (CMEA, see p. 124) and of GATT (p. 56), and in 1982 joined the IMF and the World Bank. In January 1984 the IMF granted Hungary a seven-year credit of US $450m. In December 1985 Hungary made an early repayment to the IMF of SDR88.3m., having been granted a two-year stand-by loan of SDR375m. in 1982 and a one-year stand-by loan of SDR425m. in 1984. In May 1988 the IMF approved a stand-by arrangement of SDR265m. Between 1983 and 1988 the World Bank approved loans totalling $1,496m. towards industrial restructuring to help Hungary to achieve international competitiveness, crop production improvement, the renovation of Hungary's power stations and the energy rationalization programme, and the development of the telecommunications system. In October 1988 it was announced that Hungary would receive an annual loan from the World Bank to the value of $300m.-350m. In 1986 Hungary obtained an eight-year loan of $300m. from an international banking consortium for the financing of foreign trade, and similar loans of $400m. and $200m. were agreed in July 1987 and June 1988. Hungary's gold and convertible-currency reserves stood at $2,100m. at the end of 1988. The country's gross debt in convertible currency increased from $15,085m. in December 1986 to $17,700m. in December 1987. In December 1988 it stood at an estimated $17,500m., the highest level per head in Eastern Europe.

Trade with other socialist countries, mainly the USSR, accounted for 58% of total foreign trade in 1986. In 1987 nearly 18% of Hungary's exports and about 20% of imports were transacted with the EEC. The Federal Republic of Germany is Hungary's second largest trading partner. In 1980 Hungary achieved a surplus in its balance of payments with the West, the first since 1973. In order to maintain this surplus, temporary import quotas for raw materials and industrial components were introduced in 1982. The trade surplus on transactions in convertible currencies fell from US $720m. in 1984 to $303m. in 1985, and in 1986 a trade deficit of more than $400m. was recorded. This deficit fell to $361m. in 1987, and a trade surplus of $515m. was achieved in 1988. A trade surplus of $400m.-450m. was expected for 1989. As a result of strong growth in exports, the current account deficit in convertible currency fell from $847m. in 1987 to an estimated $600m. in 1988. The deficit on trade with CMEA countries was eliminated in 1985. A surplus of 280m. transferable roubles was recorded in 1987. In 1988 the value of exports to the convertible-currency area increased by 16.4%, to $5,837m., while imports declined from $5,392m. in 1987 to $5,322m. in 1988. Exports in transferable roubles rose in 1988 by 1.2%, to R8,003m., and imports increased by 1.2%, to R7,820m. In September 1988 Hungary and the EEC signed a major agreement, designed to promote the expansion of trade in the following 10 years. It was envisaged that by 1995 a wide range of restrictions on Hungarian exports to the EEC would be abolished.

Social Welfare

The national insurance scheme is based largely on non-state contributions. Employees contribute between 3% and 15% of their earnings to the pension fund. Employers usually pay 40% of the earnings of each person employed. Publicly-financed employers pay 10%. The cost of health services and other social services is met by state subsidies and contributions from the place of work. The 1987 state budget allotted 42,200m. forint to health and social welfare, and a further 154,700m. forint to social security.

The implementation of the five-day working week was completed by 1985. A uniform system of retirement pensions was introduced in 1975: workers draw between 33% and 75% of their earnings, according to the number of years of service. Male workers are usually entitled to retirement pensions at the age of 60 and women at 55. In January 1989 unemployment benefit was introduced, following the Government's approval, in October 1988, of an economic austerity plan which, it was envisaged, would result in up to 100,000 redundancies in 1989. There are also invalidity pensions, widows' pensions and orphans' allowances. Social insurance covers sickness benefits. Patients are entitled to sick pay, usually for one year, or two years in the case of tuberculosis, occupational disease and industrial accident. Most medical consultation and treatment is free, although a very small charge is generally made for medicines and between 15% and 50% for medical appliances. In January 1989, however, the price of medicines was increased by an average of 80%. In 1987 there were 33.4 physicians per 10,000 of the population, and the total number of hospital beds was 104,581. The social insurance scheme also covers maternity benefits. Women are entitled to 24 weeks' maternity leave on full pay. A new child-care payment, in addition to the child-care allowance, was made available in 1985. In 1984 there were more than 3,600 private medical practices in Hungary, one-third of which were in Budapest.

Education

Children under the age of three years attend crèches (bölcsődék), and those between the ages of three and six years attend kindergartens (óvodák). They are not compulsory, but in 1986 about 92% of children in this age-group were attending. Compulsory education begins at six years of age, with the basic school (általános iskola). Basic education, comprising general subjects together with some practical training, continues until the child is 14. Provision is made in the basic school for talented children, particularly those who are linguistically inclined. In southern Hungary bilingual schools are being established to promote the languages of the national minorities. Children attend school until the age of 16 years. There are four types of secondary school, excluding special schools for the very gifted or, alternatively, the backward or abnormal child. The majority of children continue with their education after 16 years of age. The most popular types of secondary school are the grammar school (gimnázium) and the secondary vocational schools (technikum). The gimnázium provides a four-year course of mainly academic studies, although some vocational training does figure on the curriculum. The technikum offers full vocational training together with a general education, emphasis being laid on practical work. Apprentice training schools (ipari tanulók gyakorló iskolai) are attached to factories, agricultural co-operatives, etc., and lead to full trade qualifications. General education is less important as part of the curriculum in this type of school. Further education reform is being directed at revising the curricula and the method of assessing pupils. There are about 60 higher institutes, including 10 universities and nine technical universities. Expenditure on education by all levels of government in 1985 was about 50,100m. forint (7.2% of total spending). Hungary's first open university was to begin operating in 1988.

Public Holidays

1989: 2 January (for New Year's Day), 15 March (anniversary of 1848 uprising against Austrian rule), 27 March (Easter Monday), 4 April (Liberation Day), 1 May (Labour Day), 20 August (Constitution Day), 25–26 December (Christmas).

1990: 1 January (New Year's Day), 15 March (anniversary of 1848 uprising against Austrian rule), 4 April (Liberation Day), 16 April (Easter Monday), 1 May (Labour Day), 20 August (Constitution Day), 25–26 December (Christmas).

Weights and Measures

The metric system is in force.

Statistical Survey

Source (unless otherwise stated): Központi Statisztikai Hivatal (Hungarian Central Statistical Office), 1525 Budapest, Keleti Károly u. 5–7; tel. 358-530; telex 22-4308.

Area and Population

AREA, POPULATION AND DENSITY

Area (sq km)	93,033*
Population (census results)	
1 January 1970	10,322,099
1 January 1980	
Males	5,188,709
Females	5,520,754
Total	10,709,463
Population (official estimates at 1 January)	
1986	10,640,000
1987	10,621,000
1988	10,604,000
Density (per sq km) at 1 January 1988	114.0

* 35,920 sq miles.

Languages (1980 Census): Magyar (Hungarian) 98.8%; German 0.3%; Slovak 0.1%; Romany 0.3%; Croatian 0.2%; Romanian 0.1%.

ADMINISTRATIVE DIVISIONS (1 January 1988)

	Area (sq km)	Resident Population ('000)	Density (per sq km)	County Town (with population)
Counties:				
Baranya	4,487	433	97	Pécs (181,356)
Bács-Kiskun	8,362	553	66	Kecskemét (105,107)
Békés	5,632	415	74	Békéscsaba (70,981)
Borsod-Abaúj-Zemplén	7,247	779	107	Miskolc (209,807)
Csongrád	4,263	457	107	Szeged (187,800)
Fejér	4,373	426	97	Székesfehérvár (113,442)
Győr-Sopron	4,012	426	106	Győr (130,703)
Hajdú-Bihar	6,211	549	88	Debrecen (217,364)
Heves	3,637	338	93	Eger (66,953)
Komárom	2,251	320	142	Tatabánya (76,471)
Nógrád	2,544	229	90	Salgótarján (48,922)
Pest	6,394	988	155	Budapest* (2,104,700)
Somogy	6,036	349	58	Kaposvár (73,832)
Szabolcs-Szatmár	5,938	570	96	Nyíregyháza (119,040)
Szolnok	5,607	429	77	Szolnok (81,361)
Tolna	3,704	263	71	Szekszárd (38,757)
Vas	3,337	277	83	Szombathely (87,419)
Veszprém	4,689	387	83	Veszprém (65,927)
Zala	3,784	311	82	Zalaegerszeg (63,088)
Capital City				
Budapest*	525	2,105	4,010	—
Total	93,033	10,604	114	—

* Budapest has separate County status. The area and population of the city are not included in the larger County (Pest) which it administers.

HUNGARY

PRINCIPAL TOWNS (population at 1 January 1988)

Budapest (capital) 2,104,700	Nyíregyháza 119,040
Debrecen 217,364	Székesfehérvár 113,442
Miskolc 209,807	Kecskemét 105,107
Szeged 187,800	Szombathely 87,419
Pécs 181,356	Szolnok 81,361
Győr 130,703	Tatabánya 76,471

BIRTHS, MARRIAGES AND DEATHS

	Registered live births		Registered marriages		Registered deaths	
	Number	Rate (per 1,000)	Number	Rate (per 1,000)	Number	Rate (per 1,000)
1980	148,673	13.9	80,331	7.5	145,355	13.6
1981	142,890	13.3	77,131	7.2	144,757	13.5
1982	133,559	12.5	75,550	7.1	144,318	13.5
1983	127,258	11.9	75,969	7.1	148,643	13.9
1984	125,359	11.8	74,951	7.0	146,709	13.8
1985	130,200	12.2	73,238	6.9	147,614	13.9
1986	128,204	12.1	72,434	6.8	147,089	13.8
1987	125,840	11.9	66,082	6.2	142,601	13.4

ECONOMICALLY ACTIVE POPULATION*
('000 persons at January each year)

	1986	1987	1988
Agriculture and forestry	986.1	942.7	911.5
Manufacturing, mining, electricity and water	1,615.2	1,605.4	1,576.8
Construction	347.5	341.5	345.4
Commerce	508.8	514.2	519.7
Transport and communications	400.5	404.3	400.0
Services (incl. gas and sanitary services)	1,034.4	1,077.1	1,091.4
Total	**4,892.5**	**4,885.2**	**4,844.8**

* Excluding persons seeking work for the first time.

LIVESTOCK ('000 head at December each year)

	1985	1986	1987
Cattle	1,766	1,725	1,664
Pigs	8,280	8,687	8,216
Sheep	2,465	2,337	2,336
Horses	98	95	88
Goats	n.a.	16	n.a.
Chickens	56,686	62,570	61,069
Ducks	1,946	2,011	1,906
Geese	1,402	1,172	1,109
Turkeys	1,536	1,255	1,076
Bee colonies	n.a.	343	n.a.

LIVESTOCK PRODUCTS (metric tons)

	1985	1986	1987
Beef and veal	145,500	124,200	129,300
Mutton and lamb	8,800	8,300	4,800
Pig meat	1,011,100	985,500	1,036,700
Poultry meat	402,000	439,700	463,300
Edible offal	49,000	46,500	48,300
Edible pig fat	346,000	323,900	352,000
Cows' milk	2,710,033	2,760,194	2,813,754
Sheep's milk	7,959	7,607	7,899
Goats' milk	2,995	3,034	3,034
Butter*	31,110	32,992	32,788
Cheese:			
from cows' milk*	35,693	36,412	37,388
from other milk*	1,169	758	849
Dried milk	32,747	31,768	30,681
Hen eggs	235,090	238,548	235,564
Honey	15,388	18,260	15,170
Wool:			
greasy	11,118	10,187	10,050
clean†	4,769	4,600	n.a.
Cattle hides	15,358	12,694	n.a.
Pig skins	15,451	11,967	n.a.

* Factory production only, i.e. butter and cheese produced at milk plants, excluding farm production.
† Source: FAO, *Production Yearbook*.

Agriculture

PRINCIPAL CROPS ('000 metric tons)

	1985	1986	1987
Wheat	6,578	5,793	5,748
Rice (paddy)	38	47	40
Barley	1,046	857	794
Maize	6,818	7,261	7,234
Rye	166	172	186
Oats	133	126	99
Potatoes	1,378	1,264	1,077
Pulses	216	241	272
Sunflower seed	676	862	803
Rapeseed	85	121	108
Sugar beet	4,073	3,760	4,258
Grapes	466	691	512
Apples	954	1,253	1,064
Tobacco (leaves)	21	21	20

Forestry

ROUNDWOOD REMOVALS ('000 cu metres)

	1985	1986	1987
Industrial wood	3,782	3,939	3,731
Fuel wood	2,980	3,014	2,934
Total	**6,762**	**6,953**	**6,665**

SAWNWOOD PRODUCTION ('000 cu metres)

	1985	1986	1987
Coniferous (soft wood)	392	379	361
Broadleaved (hard wood)	327	320	329
Total	**719**	**699**	**690**

Fishing

(metric tons, live weight)

	1985	1986	1987
Total catch	36,927	36,062	36,759

HUNGARY

Mining

('000 metric tons, unless otherwise indicated)

	1985	1986	1987
Hard coal	2,639	2,325	2,360
Brown coal	14,016	13,821	13,261
Lignite	7,387	6,983	7,223
Crude petroleum	2,012	2,005	1,914
Iron ore:			
gross weight	311	—	—
metal content	68	—	—
Bauxite	2,815	3,022	3,101
Natural gas (million cu metres)	7,456	7,022	7,126

Industry

SELECTED PRODUCTS
('000 metric tons, unless otherwise indicated)

	1985	1986	1987
Pig iron	2,095	2,054	2,107
Crude steel	3,646	3,713	3,621
Rolled steel	2,863	2,898	2,831
Aluminium	73.9	73.9	73.5
Cement	3,678	3,846	4,153
Nitrogenous fertilizers*	684.1	654.6	666.7
Phosphatic fertilizers†	252.1	267.4	282.8
Refined sugar	483.2	422.3	447.3
Buses and lorries (number)	13,982	14,408	13,740
Cotton fabrics ('000 sq metres)	309,715	313,648	311,466
Leather footwear ('000 pairs)	45,169	42,324	39,356
Electric power (million kWh)	26,725	28,004	29,693
Woollen cloth ('000 sq metres)	36,100	34,115	30,339
Television receivers ('000)	407	417	446

* Production in terms of nitrogen.
† Production in terms of phosphoric acid.

Finance

CURRENCY AND EXCHANGE RATES

Monetary Units
100 fillér = 1 forint.

Denominations
Coins: 10, 20 and 50 fillér; 1, 2, 5, 10 and 20 forint.
Notes: 20, 50, 100, 500 and 1,000 forint.

Sterling and Dollar Equivalents (30 September 1988)
£1 sterling = 91.510 forint;
US $1 = 54.320 forint;
1,000 forint = £10.93 = $18.41.

Average Exchange Rate (forint per US dollar)
1985 50.107
1986 45.831
1987 46.987

STATE BUDGET ('000 million forint)

Revenue	1985	1986	1987
Payments made by enterprises (co-operatives) and agricultural co-operatives	407.5	434.2	469.4
Consumers' turnover tax	92.2	103.1	122.3
Payments made by the population	61.5	72.9	79.3
Payments made by organizations financed by state budget	51.0	54.3	63.7
Other receipts	20.6	17.5	25.9
Total revenue	632.8	682.0	760.6

Expenditure	1985	1986	1987
Investment	82.4	87.5	99.9
Industrial enterprises (co-operatives) and agricultural co-operatives	119.1	141.7	150.7
Supplement to consumers' prices	50.2	59.8	66.7
Budgetary institutions	204.9	219.2	242.7
Health and social welfare	35.0	38.3	42.2
Culture	62.9	66.8	73.5
Defence	37.6	40.9	45.4
Legal and security order	2.6	2.8	3.2
Administration	8.7	9.2	10.5
Economic tasks	48.9	53.0	54.5
Others	9.2	8.2	13.4
Social security	131.5	142.1	154.7
Others	58.5	77.0	80.3
Total expenditure	646.6	727.3	795.0

INTERNATIONAL RESERVES (US $ million at 31 December)

	1985	1986	1987
Gold*	640	751	525
Foreign exchange	3,119	3,062	2,272
Total	3,759	3,813	2,797

* National valuation.
Source: IMF, *International Financial Statistics*.

MONEY SUPPLY (million forint at 31 December)

	1985	1986	1987
Currency outside banks	116,665	130,695	153,700
Demand deposits at commercial and savings banks	126,286	159,661	161,723

COST OF LIVING (Consumer Price Index; base: 1980 = 100)

	1985	1986	1987
Food	135.7	138.4	151.1
Fuel and light	146.0	151.1	160.9
Clothing	146.3	160.1	175.6
Rent	166.8	190.2	n.a.
All items (incl. others)	139.1	146.5	159.1

BALANCE OF PAYMENTS (US $ million)

	1985	1986	1987
Merchandise exports f.o.b.	8,935	9,140	9,826
Merchandise imports f.o.b.	−8,324	−9,668	−9,659
Trade balance	610	−529	166
Exports of services	1,472	1,831	2,246
Imports of services	−2,203	−2,670	−3,098
Balance on goods and services	−121	−1,367	−686
Unrequited transfers (net)	69	78	106
Current balance	−52	−1,289	−580
Long-term capital (net)	1,709	653	852
Short-term capital (net)	−488	483	−1,087
Net errors and omissions	28	10	−75
Total (net monetary movements)	1,198	−143	−890
Valuation changes (net)	−121	35	—
Changes in reserves	1,077	−108	−890

Source: IMF, *International Financial Statistics*.

HUNGARY

NATIONAL ACCOUNTS
Net Material Product* ('000 million forint at current prices)

Activities of the Material Sphere	1985	1986	1987
Industry†	329.7	335.5	401.8
Construction	86.2	94.0	105.2
Agriculture and forestry	100.3	110.6	112.5
Transport and communications	60.6	67.9	74.9
Wholesale and retail trade	101.1	114.4	114.6
Other material activities	12.8	13.9	15.7
Taxes on commodities (net) and price differences	114.1	103.8	128.5
Non-material services purchases by material sphere	37.5	41.2	46.4
Total	842.3	881.3	999.6

* Defined as the total net value of goods and 'productive' services, including turnover taxes, produced by the economy. This excludes economic activities not contributing directly to material production, such as public administration, defence and personal and professional services.

† Manufacturing, mining, electricity and gas.

External Trade

PRINCIPAL COMMODITIES
(distribution by SITC, million forint)

Imports c.i.f.	1985	1986	1987
Food and live animals	24,017.4	25,417.6	28,600.7
Coffee, tea, cocoa and spices	6,759.9	9,463.9	7,849.6
Animal feeding-stuff (excl. cereals)	9,244.0	7,926.4	9,668.0
Crude materials (inedible) except fuels	28,396.2	30,648.2	31,354.8
Cork and wood	5,349.0	5,481.2	4,857.5
Textile fibres and waste	7,362.3	7,792.8	7,839.5
Mineral fuels, lubricants, etc.	90,363.7	89,573.1	78,707.6
Coal, coke and briquettes	14,410.0	12,293.1	7,374.8
Petroleum, petroleum products, etc.	51,728.4	50,549.5	46,612.6
Gas (natural and manufactured)	14,494.2	16,922.4	15,199.1
Chemicals and related products	54,921.4	60,321.4	69,646.8
Organic chemicals	9,113.4	9,482.7	11,100.4
Inorganic chemicals	8,580.0	8,344.0	10,482.4
Artificial resins and plastic materials, etc.	8,286.0	9,723.6	10,732.4
Basic manufactures	67,580.0	70,654.5	75,979.4
Paper, paperboard and manufactures	6,763.9	7,841.1	8,365.6
Textile yarn, fabrics, etc.	12,662.4	14,315.4	15,547.6
Iron and steel	13,772.0	13,894.5	15,272.7
Non-ferrous metals	11,170.7	13,092.9	12,824.2
Other metal manufactures	6,535.7	7,439.6	7,571.3
Machinery and transport equipment	112,352.8	124,354.7	142,193.2
Machinery specialized for particular industries	30,513.1	35,150.5	39,110.9
Metalworking machinery	5,738.5	6,367.2	8,099.4
Road vehicles and parts (excl. tyres, engines and electrical parts)	25,520.3	30,699.2	31,618.5
Miscellaneous manufactured articles	24,938.1	27,373.7	29,571.6
Total (incl. others)	410,127.5	439,690.7	463,098.7

Exports f.o.b.	1985	1986	1987
Food and live animals	71,354.9	69,814.2	71,920.5
Live animals	8,907.7	7,439.4	8,183.1
Meat and meat preparations	23,586.6	23,014.0	25,964.9
Cereals and cereal preparations	15,497.6	12,866.2	9,276.4
Vegetables and fruit	15,325.8	18,259.5	20,359.5
Beverages and tobacco	10,127.6	7,621.1	7,091.2
Crude materials (inedible) except fuels	17,215.7	16,997.6	19,318.0
Mineral fuels, lubricants, etc.	21,692.6	16,871.0	18,894.1
Petroleum, petroleum products, etc.	19,731.1	15,163.7	17,701.0
Chemicals and related products	48,876.0	45,720.9	52,280.7
Organic chemicals	11,584.8	8,525.8	9,051.2
Medicinal and pharmaceutical products	17,341.4	18,280.3	19,429.0
Basic manufactures	52,195.1	54,783.9	61,678.4
Textile yarn, fabrics, etc.	10,534.1	10,821.6	13,575.3
Iron and steel	14,478.6	13,824.3	14,971.5
Non-ferrous metals	7,496.2	9,042.8	10,124.9
Machinery and transport equipment	142,094.5	147,364.0	152,781.1
Machinery specialized for particular industries	29,855.8	28,849.1	31,513.4
Telecommunications and sound equipment	20,273.0	22,245.3	22,494.1
Other electrical machinery, apparatus, etc.	17,334.5	18,208.4	19,723.8
Road vehicles and parts (excl. tyres, engines and electrical parts)	42,311.2	45,446.0	46,015.0
Miscellaneous manufactured articles	47,849.2	50,255.3	54,156.6
Clothing and accessories (excl. footwear)	14,799.6	15,793.3	17,604.4
Footwear	7,196.3	7,257.9	7,445.6
Professional, scientific and controlling instruments and apparatus	12,414.4	13,302.8	14,356.6
Total (incl. others)	424,600.6	420,303.1	450,142.2

PRINCIPAL TRADING PARTNERS* (million forint)

Imports c.i.f.	1985	1986	1987
Austria	26,313.6	27,225.7	29,414.6
Belgium and Luxembourg	4,391.5	5,541.0	6,981.5
Brazil	6,854.8	5,183.8	5,783.1
Bulgaria	6,080.9	5,979.5	5,847.7
China, People's Republic	3,524.3	7,896.7	10,030.2
Czechoslovakia	20,311.8	22,780.8	24,979.2
Finland	2,542.8	2,488.2	2,772.8
France	7,555.9	8,145.2	8,940.3
German Democratic Republic	26,550.2	29,420.1	29,523.2
Germany, Federal Republic	46,830.0	54,470.3	64,298.5
Indonesia	677.8	2,556.6	2,171.9
Iran	2,978.6	3,022.7	4,903.7
Italy	11,466.6	11,920.7	12,411.2
Japan	6,887.7	6,492.4	7,116.9
Libya	2,430.1	5.9	0.1
Netherlands	5,329.7	6,243.1	6,876.4
Poland	19,209.1	20,766.5	18,385.0
Romania	7,185.8	8,347.2	8,516.9
Spain	2,092.4	2,210.4	1,726.5
Sweden	4,364.9	4,699.9	5,423.9
Switzerland and Liechtenstein	8,098.9	9,014.8	11,874.5
USSR	123,186.1	135,815.3	131,780.0
United Kingdom	7,857.6	7,840.2	7,963.4
USA	12,292.1	8,911.4	11,775.1
Yugoslavia	14,470.5	11,660.7	9,649.5
Total (incl. others)	410,127.5	439,690.7	463,098.7

* Imports by country of production; exports by country of last consignment.

HUNGARY

Statistical Survey

Exports f.o.b.	1985	1986	1987
Algeria	5,372.7	3,804.2	3,186.9
Austria	22,854.6	22,422.7	24,841.0
Belgium and Luxembourg	1,618.9	2,800.0	3,189.8
Bulgaria	6,080.2	6,614.2	6,576.9
China, People's Republic	5,608.4	7,863.6	4,975.0
Cuba	3,807.0	2,388.1	2,280.1
Czechoslovakia	24,039.5	24,758.1	22,623.7
Egypt	3,858.4	3,483.4	3,250.9
Finland	2,269.5	2,145.4	2,925.7
France	5,714.2	6,521.4	8,475.3
German Democratic Republic	25,805.2	26,865.9	25,165.5
Germany, Federal Republic	33,186.6	35,351.5	44,209.5
Greece	2,126.8	1,828.1	2,452.1
Iran	5,342.4	2,370.7	5,265.7
Iraq	5,112.6	2,618.6	1,512.4
Italy	12,496.2	13,431.9	16,244.8
Japan	1,437.5	2,219.3	3,282.4
Libya	4,551.8	3,098.6	1,142.9
Netherlands	3,883.4	4,752.4	4,843.8
Nigeria	3,190.6	1,607.4	2,177.1
Poland	16,289.2	17,770.8	15,452.6
Romania	7,248.8	8,390.0	7,987.1
Sweden	3,127.5	3,457.2	4,484.2
Switzerland and Liechtenstein	8,507.4	7,859.9	8,220.7
Turkey	2,472.0	2,170.7	3,578.4
USSR	142,749.1	142,291.4	147,249.5
United Kingdom	6,154.9	5,571.2	6,793.8
USA	9,830.7	9,836.4	13,526.2
Yugoslavia	15,166.4	13,138.8	11,411.8
Total (incl. others)	424,600.6	420,303.1	450,142.2

Transport

RAILWAYS (traffic)

	1985	1986	1987
Passengers carried (million)	334.4	334.9	332.5
Passenger-kilometres (million)	12,130	12,151	12,259
Net ton-kilometres (million)	22,305	22,598	21,729

ROAD TRAFFIC (motor vehicles in use at 31 December)

	1985	1986	1987
Passenger cars	1,435,937	1,538,877	1,660,258
Goods vehicles	167,136	179,272	191,851
Buses	24,854	25,920	26,893
Motor cycles*	395,622	399,447	405,690

* Excluding mopeds and motor cycles with an engine capacity of less than 125 c.c.

INLAND WATERWAYS (traffic)

	1985	1986	1987
Freight carried ('000 metric tons)	3,300	3,401	3,758
Freight ton-km (million)	1,623	1,914	2,046

CIVIL AVIATION (traffic)

	1985	1986	1987
Kilometres flown	22,287,100	22,097,200	21,711,900
Passengers carried	1,159,773	1,196,622	1,320,311
Passenger-km ('000)	1,134,047	1,142,995	1,285,597
Cargo carried: metric tons	15,391	16,372	11,972
Cargo ton-km	23,097,000	23,689,000	15,880,000

Tourism

('000 arrivals)

	1985	1986	1987
Foreign tourists	9,724	10,613	11,826
Foreign visitors in transit	5,402	6,033	7,127
Total	15,126	16,646	18,953

1988: Total 17,965,000.

TOURISTS BY COUNTRY OF ORIGIN
('000 arrivals, including visitors in transit)

	1985	1986	1987
Austria	2,024.3	2,416	3,264
Bulgaria	462.2	544	575
Czechoslovakia	5,449.2	4,892	4,870
German Democratic Republic	1,314.4	1,431	1,621
Germany, Federal Republic	898.8	862	1,097
Poland	1,892.0	3,086	3,253
Romania	623.5	386	421
USSR	451.2	501	529
Yugoslavia	1,171.0	1,711	2,228
Total (incl. others)	15,126.5	16,646	18,953

Communications Media

	1985	1986	1987
Television receivers*	404	421	414
Radio receivers†	577	591	512
Telephones in use	1,484,508	1,541,409	1,609,465
Books titles (including translations)	8,015	8,206	7,804
Daily newspapers	29	29	29
Average daily circulation	2,992,894	3,045,198	3,078,731

* Estimated number of television receivers per 1,000 inhabitants.
† Estimated number of radio receivers per 1,000 inhabitants.

Education

(1987/88)

	Institutions	Teachers	Students
Nursery	4,786	33,896	398,325
Primary	3,540	90,925	1,277,257
Secondary	608	19,184	321,798
Higher	54	15,302	99,025

Directory

The Constitution

A new constitution was introduced on 18 August 1949, and the Hungarian People's Republic was established two days later. The Constitution was amended in April 1972 and December 1983. A new constitution was due to be introduced in early 1990. The following is a summary of the main provisions of the Constitution as it stood in early 1989:

NATIONAL STATUS

Hungary is a People's Republic, a state of workers and working peasants, in which all power belongs to the working people and is exercised through elected representatives. The Republic defends the power and liberty of the working people and the independence of the country and opposes the exploitation of man.

SOCIAL STRUCTURE

The bulk of the means of production is owned by the State, by public bodies or by co-operative organizations, and state and co-operative ownership enjoy equal status. Means of production may also be privately owned. The national economy is directed by the state power of the people. The economic life of the Republic is determined by a state national economic plan in which the State strives to expand the forces of production, increase national wealth, raise material and cultural standards and strengthen the defences of the country. All natural resources, means of communication, banks, mines and major industrial plants are the property of the State. Foreign trade is carried out both by state trading companies and by companies and enterprises with export-import rights.

The Republic recognizes and guarantees the right of the working peasants to the land and regards it as its duty to assist the socialist development of agriculture. The State supports every genuine co-operative movement of the workers that is directed against exploitation. The Constitution recognizes and protects all property acquired by labour and guarantees the right of inheritance. Private enterprise is not allowed to run counter to the public interest.

Labour is the base of the social order and every able-bodied citizen has the right and the duty to work to the best of his ability. By their labour, the workers serve the cause of socialist construction.

GOVERNMENT

National Assembly

The highest organ of state authority in the Hungarian People's Republic is the National Assembly which exercises all the rights deriving from the sovereignty of the people and determines the organization, direction and conditions of government. The National Assembly enacts laws, determines the state budget, decides the national economic plan, elects the Presidential Council and the Council of Ministers, directs the activities of ministries, decides upon declaring war and concluding peace and exercises the prerogative of amnesty.

The National Assembly is elected for a term of five years and members enjoy immunity from arrest and prosecution without parliamentary consent. It meets at least twice a year and is convened by the Presidential Council or by a written demand of one-third of its members. It elects a President, two Deputy Presidents and six recorders from among its own members, and it lays down its own rules of procedure and agenda. As a general rule, the sessions of the National Assembly are held in public.

The National Assembly has the right of legislation which can be initiated by the Presidential Council, the Council of Ministers or any member of the National Assembly. Decisions are valid only if at least half of the members are present, and they require a simple majority. Constitutional changes require a two-thirds majority. Acts of the National Assembly are signed by the President and the Secretary of the Presidential Council. The National Assembly may set up committees.

The National Assembly may pronounce its dissolution before the expiration of its term, and in the event of an emergency may prolong its mandate or may be reconvened after dissolution. A new National Assembly must be elected within three months of dissolution and convened within one month of polling day. At its first sitting the National Assembly elects from among its members the Presidential Council, consisting of a President, two Vice-Presidents, a Secretary and 17 members. The Chairman of the Council of Ministers, its Deputy Chairmen and its members are ineligible for election to the Presidential Council.

Members of the National Assembly are elected on the basis of universal, equal and direct suffrage by secret ballot, and they are accountable to their constituents, who may recall them. All citizens of 18 years and over have the right to vote, with the exception of those who are unsound of mind, and those who are deprived of their civil rights by a court of law.

Presidential Council

The Presidential Council may issue the writ for a general election, convene the National Assembly, initiate legislation, hold plebiscites, direct local government, conclude international treaties, appoint diplomatic representatives, ratify international treaties, appoint higher civil servants and officers of the armed forces, award orders and titles, and exercise the prerogative of mercy. It may annul or modify by-laws, dissolve local organs of government and, when the National Assembly is not in session, may enact laws. The Presidential Council is responsible to the National Assembly, which can recall it.

Council of Ministers

The highest organ of state administration is the Council of Ministers, responsible to the National Assembly and consisting of a Chairman, Deputy Chairmen, Ministers of State and other Ministers who are elected by the National Assembly on the recommendation of the Presidential Council. The Council of Ministers directs the work of the ministries (listed in a special enactment) and ensures the enforcement of laws and the fulfilment of economic plans; it may issue decrees and annul or modify measures taken by any central or local organ of government.

Local Administration

The local organs of state power are the county, town, borough and town precinct councils, whose members are elected for a term of five years by the voters in each area. Local councils direct economic, social and cultural activities in their area, prepare local economic plans and budgets and supervises their fulfilment, enforce laws, supervise subordinate organs, maintain public order, protect public property and individual rights, direct local economic enterprises and support co-operatives. They may issue regulations and annul or modify those of subordinate councils. Local Councils are administered by an Executive Committee elected by and responsible to them.

JUDICATURE

Justice is administered by the Supreme Court of the Hungarian People's Republic, county and district courts. The Supreme Court exercises the right of supervising in principle the judicial activities and practice of all other courts.

All judicial offices are filled by election; Supreme Court, county and district court judges are all elected for an indefinite period; the President of the Supreme Court is elected by the National Assembly. All court hearings are public unless otherwise prescribed by law, and those accused are guaranteed the right of defence. An accused person must be considered innocent until proved guilty.

Public Prosecutor

The function of the Chief Public Prosecutor is to watch over the observance of the law. He is elected for a period of five years by the National Assembly, to whom he is responsible. The organization of public prosecution is under the control of the Chief Public Prosecutor, who appoints the public prosecutors.

RIGHTS AND DUTIES OF CITIZENS

The Hungarian People's Republic guarantees for its citizens the right to work and to remuneration, the right of rest and recreation, the right to care in old age, sickness or disability, the right to education, and equality before the law; women enjoy equal rights with men. Discrimination on grounds of sex, religion or nationality is a punishable offence. The State also ensures freedom of conscience, religious worship, speech, the Press and assembly. The right of workers to organize themselves is stressed in order to promote democracy, socialist construction, cultural and educational development and international solidarity. The freedom of the individual, and the privacy of the home and of correspondence are inviolable. Freedom for creative work in the sciences and the arts is now guaranteed by the Constitution under the amendments adopted in 1972.

The basic freedoms of all workers are guaranteed and foreign citizens enjoy the right of asylum.

It is the fundamental duty of all citizens to defend the property of the people, consolidate social assets, increase economic strength,

HUNGARY

raise the living standards and cultural levels of the workers, and strengthen the people's democratic system. Military service and the defence of their country are the duties of all citizens.

AMENDMENTS

Amendments to the Constitution were approved by the National Assembly in December 1983. These included the setting up of an independent Council for Constitutional Law to examine legislation; the inclusion of the President of the Central People's Control Commission in the Council of Ministers; and the abolition of administrative districts within the counties, coupled with an increase in the authority of local town councils.

Amendments to the electoral law, approved at the same session, provided for all seats in the National Assembly and local councils to be contested in future elections.

The Government

(February 1989)

HEAD OF STATE

President of the Presidential Council: Dr BRUNÓ FERENC STRAUB (elected 29 June 1988).

PRESIDENTIAL COUNCIL

President: Dr BRUNÓ FERENC STRAUB.
Vice-Presidents: ISTVÁN SARLÓS, Dr REZSŐ TRAUTMANN.
Secretary: IMRE KATONA.
Members: ERZSÉBET BÁNATI, SÁNDOR BARCS, IMRE BIRÓ, REZSŐ BOGNAR, MÁRIA DUSCHEK, JÁNOS ELEKI, ISTVÁN GAJDOCSI, ERZSÉBET HORVÁTH, JÁNOS KÁDÁR, GYULA KÁLLAI, TEREZ KREMER, PÁL LOSONCZI, MARIN MANDITY, GÉZA SZALAI, JÁNOS SZENTAGOTHAY, Dr KÁROLY TÓTH.

COUNCIL OF MINISTERS

Chairman: MIKLÓS NÉMETH*.
Deputy Chairman: PÉTER MEDGYESSY*.
Minister of State: REZSŐ NYERS*.
Minister of State: IMRE POZSGAY*.
Minister of Foreign Affairs: Dr PÉTER VÁRKONYI*.
Minister of the Interior: Dr ISTVÁN HORVÁTH*.
Minister of Defence: Col-Gen. FERENC KÁRPATI.
Minister of Agriculture and Food: JENŐ VÁNCSA.
Minister of Finance: Dr MIKLÓS VILLÁNYI.
Minister of Health and Social Affairs: Dr JUDIT CSEHÁK.
Minister of Culture and National Education: TIBOR CZIBERE.
Minister of Trade: TAMÁS BECK.
Minister of Industry: FRIGYES BERECZ.
Minister of Justice: KÁLMÁN KULCSÁR.
Minister of Construction, Transport and Telecommunications: ANDRÁS DERZSI.
Minister for the Environment and Water Management: Dr LÁSZLÓ MARÓTHY.
President of the National Planning Office: JÁNOS HOÓS.
Chairman of the Central People's Control Commission: LÁSZLÓ BALLAI.

* Member of the Inner Cabinet.

MINISTRIES

Council of Ministers (Secretariat): 1055 Budapest, Kossuth Lajos tér 1/3; tel. 120-600; telex 22-5547.
Ministry of Agriculture and Food: 1055 Budapest, Kossuth Lajos tér 11; tel. 533-000; telex 22-5445.
Ministry of Construction, Transport and Telecommunications: 1400 Budapest, Dob u. 75/81, POB 87; tel. 220-220; telex 22-5729.
Ministry of Culture and National Education: 1055 Budapest, Szalay u. 10/14; tel. 530-600; telex 22-5935.
Ministry of Defence: 1055 Budapest, Pálffy György u. 7/11; tel. 322-500; telex 22-5424.
Ministry for the Environment and Water Management: Budapest.
Ministry of Finance: 1051 Budapest, József Nádor tér 2/4; tel. 182-066.
Ministry of Foreign Affairs: 1027 Budapest, Bem rkp. 47; tel. 350-100; telex 22-5571.
Ministry of Health and Social Affairs: 1051 Budapest, Arany János u. 6/8; tel. 323-100; telex 22-4337.
Ministry of Industry: 1024 Budapest, Mártírok u. 85; tel. 326-570; telex 22-5376.
Ministry of the Interior: 1051 Budapest, József Attila u. 2/4; tel. 121-710; telex 22-5216.
Ministry of Justice: 1055 Budapest, Szalay u. 16; tel. 325-330.
Ministry of Trade: 1055 Budapest, Honvéd u. 13/15; tel. 530-000; telex 22-5578.
National Planning Office: 1051 Budapest, Roosevelt tér 7/8; tel. 110-200; telex 22-4993.
Central People's Control Commission: 1052 Budapest, Apáczai Csere János u. 10; tel. 188-799; telex 22-4308.

POLITICAL COMMITTEE (POLITBURO) OF THE HUNGARIAN SOCIALIST WORKERS' PARTY

KÁROLY GRÓSZ (General Secretary), (vacant—Deputy General Secretary), JÁNOS KÁDÁR (President), JÁNOS BERECZ, Dr JUDIT CSEHÁK, CSABA HÁMORI, PÁL IVÁNYI, JÁNOS LUKÁCS, MIKLÓS NÉMETH, REZSŐ NYERS, IMRE POZSGAY, ISTVÁN SZABÓ, ILONA TATAI.

Legislature

ORSZÁGGYŰLÉS

(National Assembly)

The National Assembly consists of a single chamber of 387 members, elected every five years; 352 members are elected on a territorial basis and the 35 additional members are elected unopposed on a national list which includes leading politicians, trade unionists, clergymen and prominent members of the national minority groups. The national list was introduced at the most recent elections, held on 8 June 1985, when all territorial constituencies were contested. About 7.7m. people were entitled to vote and take part in the nomination meetings; 873 candidates were put forward for the 352 territorial constituencies—795 proposed by the Patriotic People's Front and 78 direct from the floor of the nomination meetings, 43 of whom were elected. There were more than two candidates in 78 constituencies. A total of 244 members were elected for the first time. On 22 June 1985 a second round of voting was held in over 40 constituencies where no candidate had obtained the requisite absolute majority, this time the candidate receiving the largest number of votes being elected. Turn-out was 93.9% at the first round and 83% at the second round of voting.

President of the National Assembly: ISTVÁN STADINGER.
Deputy Presidents: LAJOS HORVÁTH, Mrs ROBERT JAKAB, Dr MIKLÓS VIDA.

Political Organizations

In January 1989 legislation to permit the formation of independent and opposition groups, outside the HSWP, was approved.

Magyar Szocialista Munkáspárt (Hungarian Socialist Workers' Party—HSWP): 1054 Budapest, Széchenyi rkp. 19; f. 1956 to replace the Workers' Party (merger of the Communist and Social Democratic Parties); 108-mem. Cen. Cttee; 816,000 mems (1988); Pres. JÁNOS KÁDÁR; Gen. Sec. of Cen. Cttee KÁROLY GRÓSZ; Deputy Gen. Sec. (vacant); Mems of Secretariat of Cen. Cttee: JÁNOS BERECZ, GYÖRGY FEJTI, PÁL IVÁNYI, JÁNOS LUKÁCS, MÁTYÁS SZÜRÖS.

Hazafias Népfront (Patriotic People's Front): 1056 Budapest, Belgrád rkp. 24; f. 1954; socio-political mass movement formed as a successor to the Hungarian Independent People's Front; composed of Party and non-Party people, and represents mass organizations such as trade unions, peasants, youth movements, the churches and national minorities; compiles the lists of candidates, on the basis of nominations from public meetings, for national and local elections; 3,000 committees with 85,000 elected mems; Pres. GYULA KÁLLAI; Sec.-Gen. ISTVÁN HUSZÁR.

Magyar Kommunista Ifjúsági Szövetség—KISZ (Communist Youth Union of Hungary): 1388 Budapest, Kun Béla rkp. 37–38; tel. 403-940; telex 22-4244; f. 1957 to replace the Union of Working Youth—DISZ; 700,000 mems (1988); First Sec. of Cen. Cttee CSABA HÁMORI.

Magyar Nők Országos Tanácsa—MNOT (National Council of Hungarian Women): 1062 Budapest, Népköztársaság u. 124; tel. 317-529; f. 1957 to replace Hungarian Democratic Women's Union; 32,000 stewards, 160,000 activists; Pres. MÁRIA DUSCHEK.

HUNGARY

In late 1988 and early 1989 various independent groups were revived or formed for the first time. These included: the Hungarian Democratic Forum (10,000 mems), the Smallholders' Party (3,000 mems), the Alliance of Free Democrats and the Social Democratic Party.

Diplomatic Representation

EMBASSIES IN HUNGARY

Afghanistan: 1062 Budapest, Lendvay u. 23; tel. 126-896; Ambassador: ASSAD KESHTMAND.
Albania: Budapest VI, Munkácsy Mihály u. 6; tel. 229-278; Ambassador: ÇLIRIM MUZHA.
Algeria: Budapest I, Disz tér 6; tel. 759-884; telex 22-6916; Ambassador: MUSTAPHA BOUTAIEB.
Argentina: 1068 Budapest, Rippl-Rónai u. 1; tel. 228-467; telex 22-4128; Ambassador: ARNOLDO MANUEL LISTRE.
Australia: 1062 Budapest, Délibáb u. 30; tel. 534-233; telex 22-7708; Ambassador: DOUGLAS TOWNSEND.
Austria: 1068 Budapest VI, Benczúr u. 16; tel. 229-467; telex 22-4447; Ambassador: Dr FRANZ SCHMID.
Belgium: Budapest I, Donáti u. 34; tel. 153-099; telex 22-4664; Ambassador: WILLEM VERKAMMEN.
Bolivia: Budapest II, Mártírok u. 43–45; tel. 163-019; Chargé d'affaires: Dr MARIO PAZ-ZAMORA.
Brazil: Budapest XI, Somlói u. 3; tel. 666-992; telex 22-5795; Ambassador: CELSO DINIZ.
Bulgaria: Budapest V, Népköztársaság u. 115; tel. 220-836; telex 22-5441; Ambassador: VENELIN TODOROV.
Canada: 1121 Budapest, Budakeszi u. 32; tel. 767-312; telex 22-4588; Ambassador: (vacant).
China, People's Republic: Budapest VI, Benczúr u. 17; tel. 224-872; Ambassador: ZU ANKANG.
Colombia: 1024 Budapest, Mártírok u. 43–45; tel. 352-534; telex 22-6012; Ambassador: (vacant).
Cuba: Budapest VI, Benczúr u. 26; tel. 214-039; telex 22-4388; Ambassador: FAUSTINO MANUEL BEATO MOREJÓN.
Czechoslovakia: Budapest XIV, Népstadion u. 22; tel. 636-600; telex 22-4744; Ambassador: ONDREJ DUREJ.
Denmark: 1023 Budapest, Vérhalom u. 12–16B; tel. 152–066; telex 22-4137; Ambassador: HANS KUHNE.
Egypt: Budapest I, Bérc u. 16; tel. 668-060; telex 22-5184; Ambassador: (vacant).
Finland: Budapest XI, Kelenhegyi u. 16a; tel. 850-700; telex 22-4710; Ambassador: ARTO MANSALA.
France: Budapest VI, Lendvay u. 27; tel. 128-268; telex 22-5143; Ambassador: CHRISTIANE MALITCHENKO.
German Democratic Republic: 1143 Budapest, Népstadion u. 101–103; tel. 635-275; telex 22-5954; Ambassador: GERD VEHRES.
Germany, Federal Republic: Budapest XIV, Izsó u. 5; tel. 224-204; telex 22-5951; Ambassador: Dr HANS ALFRED STEGER.
Greece: Budapest VI, Szegfű u. 3; tel. 228-004; telex 22-4113; Ambassador: EMMANUEL KALPADAKIS.
India: 1025 Budapest, Buzavirág u. 14; tel. 153-243; telex 22-6374; Ambassador: SATINDER KUMAR LAMBAH.
Indonesia: Budapest VI, Gorkij fasor 26; tel. 428-508; telex 22-5263; Ambassador: BUSTANUL ARIFIN.
Iran: Budapest VI, Délibáb u. 29; tel. 225-038; telex 22-4129; Ambassador: KEYVAN IMANI.
Iraq: Budapest XIV, Szánto Béla u. 13; tel. 226-418; telex 22-6058; Ambassador: (vacant).
Italy: Budapest XIV, Népstadion u. 95; tel. 225-077; telex 22-5294; Ambassador: JOSEPH NITTI.
Japan: Budapest II, Rómer Flóris u. 58; tel. 150-043; telex 22-5048; Ambassador: RYOZO MOGI.
Kampuchea: Budapest XII, Rath György u. 48; tel. 151-878; Ambassador: CHIM NGUON.
Korea, Democratic People's Republic: Budapest VI, Benczúr u. 31; tel. 425-174; telex 22-6721; Chargé d'affaires: (vacant).
Korea, Republic: Budapest; Ambassador: HAN TAK-CHAE.
Libya: Budapest XIV, Népstadion u. 111; tel. 226-076; Head of People's Bureau: FATHI M. AL-MISRATI.
Mexico: Budapest II, Budakeszi u. 55/D; tel. 767-906; telex 22-6633; Ambassador: JOSÉ CABALLERO BAZÁN.
Mongolia: Budapest XII, Istenhegyi u. 59–61; tel. 151-412; Ambassador: DANGASURENGIN SALDAN.
Netherlands: 1146 Budapest, Abonyi u. 31A; tel. 228-432; telex 22-5562; Ambassador: J. C. FERRINGA.
Norway: 1426 Budapest, Határör u. 35, POB 32; tel. 551-811; telex 22-5867; Ambassador: LEIF EDWARD EDWARDSEN.
Peru: Budapest II, Mártírok u. 43–45; tel. 150-292; Ambassador: JOSÉ PABLO MORÁN VAL.
Poland: Budapest VI, Gorkij fasor 16; tel. 228-437; Ambassador: TADEUSZ CZECHOWICZ.
Portugal: 1024 Budapest, Mártírok u. 43–45; tel. 155-602; telex 22-6509; Ambassador: ZÓZIMO DA SILVA.
Romania: Budapest XIV, Thököly u. 72; tel. 426-944; telex 22-5847; Ambassador: TRAIAN POPOT.
Spain: Budapest VI, Eötvös u. 11B; tel. 428-580; telex 22-4130; Ambassador: FRANCISCO JAVIER RUBIO.
Sweden: Budapest XIV, Ajtósi Dürer sor 27/A; tel. 229-880; telex 22-5647; Ambassador: ANDERS RAGNAR DROMBERG.
Switzerland: Budapest XIV, Népstadion u. 107; tel. 229-491; Ambassador: PAUL WIPFLI; also serves Israeli interests.
Syria: 1026 Budapest, Harangvirág u. 3; tel. 767-186; telex 22-6605; Ambassador: (vacant).
Turkey: Budapest I, Úri u. 45; tel. 161-497; Ambassador: HALIT GUVENER.
USSR: Budapest VI, Bajza u. 35; tel. 320-911; Ambassador: BORIS STUKALIN.
United Kingdom: Budapest V, Harmincad u. 6; tel. 182-888; telex 22-4527; Ambassador: LEONARD APPLEYARD.
USA: 1054 Budapest, Szabadság tér 12; tel. 126-450; telex 22-4222; Ambassador: MARK PALMER.
Uruguay: Budapest II, Vérhalom u. 12–16; tel. 368-333; Ambassador: Dr GUALBERTO TALAMAS.
Venezuela: Budapest II, Vérhalom u. 12–16; tel. 353-562; telex 22-6666; Ambassador: ANTONIO CASAS SALVI.
Viet-Nam: Budapest VI, Benczúr u. 18; tel. 429-943; Ambassador: (vacant).
Yemen, People's Democratic Republic: Budapest II, Budakeszi u. 55/D; tel. 164-259; Ambassador: MUHSIN NAJI BIN NAJI.
Yugoslavia: Budapest VI, Dózsa György u. 92/B; tel. 420-566; Ambassador: RUDOLF-RUDI SOVA.

Judicial System

The system of court procedure in Hungary is based on an Act that was promulgated in 1954 and updated in 1972. The system of jurisdiction is based on the local courts (district courts in Budapest, city courts in other cities), labour courts, county courts, the Metropolitan Court and the Supreme Court. In the legal remedy system of two instances, appeals against the decisions of city and district courts can be lodged with the competent county court and the Metropolitan Court of Budapest respectively. Against the judgment of first instance of the latter, appeal is to be lodged with the Supreme Court. The Chief Public Prosecutor and the President of the Supreme Court have the right to submit a protest on legal grounds against the final judgment of any court.

By virtue of the 1973 Act, effective 1974 and modified in 1979, the procedure in criminal cases is differentiated for criminal offences and for criminal acts. In the first instance, criminal cases are tried, depending on their character, by a professional judge; where justified by the magnitude of the criminal act, by a council composed of three members, a professional judge and two lay assessors, while in major cases the court consists of five members, two professional judges and three lay assessors. In the Supreme Court, second instance cases are tried only by professional judges. The President of the Supreme Court is elected by the National Assembly for a period of five years. Judges are elected by the Presidential Council for an indefinite period. Assessors, in turn, are elected by the local municipal councils.

In the interest of ensuring legality and a uniform application of the Law, the Supreme Court exercises a principled guidance over the jurisdiction of courts. In the Hungarian People's Republic judges are independent and subject only to the Law and other legal regulations.

The Minister of Justice supervises the general activities of courts. The Chief Public Prosecutor is elected by the National Assembly for a period of five years. The Chief Public Prosecutor and the Prosecutor's Office provide for the consistent prosecution of all acts violating or endangering the legal order of society, the safety and independence of the state, and for the protection of citizens.

The Prosecutors of the independent prosecuting organization exert supervision over the legality of investigations and the implementation of punishments, and assist with specific means in

HUNGARY

ensuring that legal regulations should be observed by state, economic and other organs and citizens, and they support the legality of court procedures and decisions.

President of the Supreme Court: Dr JENŐ SZILBEREKY.
Chief Public Prosecutor: Dr KÁROLY SZIJÁRTÓ.

Religion

Állami Egyházügyi Hivatal (State Office for Church Affairs): 1062 Budapest, Lendvay u. 28; f. 1951; deals with Church-State relations; Chair. IMRE MIKLÓS.

CHRISTIANITY

Magyarországi Egyházak Ökuménikus Tanácsa (Ecumenical Council of Churches in Hungary): 1054 Budapest, Szabadság tér 2; tel. 114-862; f. 1943; member churches: Reformed Church, Evangelical Lutheran, Baptist, Methodist, Hungarian Orthodox, Romanian Orthodox and Council of Free Churches; Pres. Bishop Dr KÁROLY TÓTH; Gen. Sec. Rev. LÁSZLÓ LEHEL.

The Roman Catholic Church

Hungary comprises three archdioceses, eight dioceses (including one for Catholics of the Byzantine rite) and one territorial abbacy (directly responsible to the Holy See). In 1985 the Church had 6,365,976 adherents in Hungary. There are 3,250 active churches.

Bishops' Conference: Magyar Püspöki Kar Konferenciája, 6301 Kalocsa, Szabadság tér 1; tel. 155; f. 1969; Pres. Cardinal Dr LÁSZLÓ PASKAI, Archbishop of Esztergom.

Latin Rite

Archbishop of Eger: Dr ISTVÁN SEREGÉLY, 3301 Eger, Széchenyi u. 1; tel. 13-259.

Archbishop of Esztergom: Cardinal Dr LÁSZLÓ PASKAI, Primate of Hungary, 2500 Esztergom, Berenyi Zsigmond u. 2; tel. 330-511.

Archbishop of Kalocsa: Dr LÁSZLÓ DANKÓ, 6301 Kalocsa, Szabadság tér 1; tel. 155.

Byzantine Rite

Bishop of Hajdudorog: SZILÁRD KERESZTES, 4401 Nyiregyháza, Bethlen u. 5, POB 60; tel. 42-12852; about 250,000 adherents; the Bishop is also Apostolic Administrator of the Apostolic Exarchate of Miskolc, with an estimated 22,800 Catholics of the Byzantine rite (Nov. 1988).

Protestant Churches

Evangélikus Egyház (Lutheran Church in Hungary) (Evangelical): 1088 Budapest, Puskin u. 12; tel. 13-86-56; 430,000 mems (1985); Presiding Bishop Dr GYULA NAGY; Gen. Sec. Dr ÁGOSTON KARNER.

Magyarországi Baptista Egyház (Baptist Union of Hungary): 1062 Budapest, Aradi u. 48; tel. 322-332; f. 1846; 12,250 mems; Pres. Rev. JÁNOS VICZIÁN; Sec. Rev. KORNÉL GYŐRI.

Magyarországi Református Egyház (Reformed Church in Hungary) (Presbyterian): 1146 Budapest, Abonyi u. 21; tel. 227-870; 2m. mems (1987); 1,306 churches; Pres. of Gen. Synod Bishop Dr KÁROLY TÓTH.

Magyarországi Szabadegyházak Tanácsa (Council of Free Churches in Hungary): 1062 Budapest, Aradi u. 48; tel. 310-194; f. 1944; co-operative organization of Baptists, Methodists, Adventists, Evangelical Christians, Pentecostalists, and other smaller denominations; 40,000–50,000 mems; Pres. JÁNOS VICZIÁN; Gen. Sec. Rev. OLIVER SZEBENI.

Orthodox Churches

Magyar Orthodox Egyház (Hungarian Orthodox Church): 1052 Budapest, Petőfi tér 2.1.2.; tel. 184-813; Administrator Archpriest Dr FERIZ BERKI.

Görögkeleti Szerb Egyházmegye (Serbian-Orthodox Diocese): Szentendre; Parochus DUSÁN VUJICSICS.

The Russian (6,000 mems), Bulgarian and Romanian Orthodox Churches are also represented.

ISLAM

There are about 3,000 Muslims in Hungary. In 1987 it was announced that an Islamic centre was to be built in Budapest, with assistance from the Muslim World League.

JUDAISM

The first new synagogue to be built in Hungary since 1945 opened at Siofok in 1986.

Magyar Izraeliták Országos Képviselete (Central Board of Hungarian Jews); **Budapesti Izraelita Hitközség** (Jewish Community of Budapest): 1079 Budapest, Síp u. 12; 80,000 mems; 40 active synagogues; Orthodox and Conservative; Pres. Dr ANDRÁS LOSONCI; Gen. Sec. ILONA SEIFERT; Chief Rabbi of Budapest Dr ALFRÉD SCHÖNER.

The Press

The Hungarian Constitution guarantees freedom of the press and freedom of speech, but the press is in fact constrained to promote the ideological aims of the Hungarian Socialist Workers' Party and fundamental criticism of the political system is not permitted. On the other hand, failures in public administration, economic, cultural and other fields, are commonly criticized in editorials and grievances publicized in letters from members of the public. Since 1963 all official institutions so criticized have been legally obliged to investigate the matter promptly.

Conversely, considerable legislation is designed to prevent the abuse of press rights; Article 127 of the penal code penalizes the provoking of hatred of minorities by the press; incitement and libel are similarly dealt with. Since a decree in 1959, persons and institutions victimized by false press reports may claim rectification which a government minister is empowered to enforce.

No organization has the right to exercise censorship. The Government Information Office has nation-wide authority over the press, including the right to grant licences and ensure newsprint distribution, and the task of seeing that all government decrees and decisions are made available to the press. The national news agency, Magyar Távirati Iroda (MTI), handles the bulk of foreign news and has bilateral agreements with the major world agencies.

As in many East European countries most papers are the organs of political parties, trade unions, youth and social organizations. A wide range of specialist periodicals is published by societies, factories, scientific institutions, etc. There is no private ownership of publications but since 1957 independent commercial organizations have received publishing licences.

The high circulation of daily papers enables publishing houses to produce specialized periodicals of a high standard. Moreover, the State gives direct subsidies to certain educational, medical and literary publications, to the religious press and to the four minority language papers. Some 80% of newspapers are sold by subscription.

There are 29 dailies with an average total circulation of 3,045,198 (1986). These include 21 provincial dailies which have a combined daily circulation of about 1,328,000. Budapest dailies circulate nationally. In order of popularity they are: *Népszabadság*, *Népszava*, the evening *Esti Hirlap* and *Magyar Nemzet*. *Népszabadság*, the most important daily, is the central organ of the Socialist Workers' Party. The paper most respected for the quality of its news coverage and commentary is *Magyar Nemzet*.

Weekly newspapers and periodicals number 56; there are 111 fortnightly journals and 490 monthlies. Among the most popular are the illustrated weeklies, which include the satirical *Ludas Matyi*, the women's magazine *Nők Lapja*, the illustrated news journal *Képes Újság* and the political paper *Szabad Föld*. A news magazine giving a high standard of reporting and political discussion is *Magyarország*. Specialized periodicals include 42 cultural publications, 35 medical journals, 108 scientific papers, 24 agricultural and 16 religious publications. Of this last category *Új Ember*, *Evangélikus Élet* and *Új Élet* for Catholic, Lutheran and Jewish congregations respectively, are representative.

PRINCIPAL DAILIES

Daily News: 1016 Budapest, Fém u. 5-7; tel. 756-722; telex 22-4371; f. 1967; published by the Hungarian News Agency; in English and German; Editor-in-Chief TAMÁS KOCSIS; circ. 15,000.

Esti Hirlap (Evening Journal): 1085 Budapest, Blaha Lujza tér 1-3; tel. 336-130; telex 22-7040; Editor ERVIN RETI; circ. 200,000.

Magyar Hirlap (Hungarian Journal): 1393 Budapest, POB 305; tel. 222-400; telex 22-4268; f. 1968; Editor-in-Chief ZSOLT BAJNOK; circ. 89,000.

Magyar Nemzet (Hungarian Nation): 1073 Budapest, Lenin krt 9-11; tel. 222-400; telex 22-4269; organ of the Patriotic People's Front; Editor ISTVÁN SOLTESZ; circ. 132,000.

A Nap (The Sun): Budapest; f. 1988; Editor-in-Chief ISTVÁN HORVÁTH; circ. 80,000.

Népsport (People's Sport): 1085 Budapest, Somogyi Béla u. 6; tel. 130-460; telex 22-5245; Editor JÓZSEF VARGA; circ. 275,000.

Népszabadság (People's Freedom): 1960 Budapest, Blaha Lujza tér 3; tel. 336-130; telex 22-5551; f. 1942; organ of the Hungarian Socialist Workers' Party; Editor-in-Chief GABOR BORBELY; circ. 670,000.

Népszava (Voice of the People): 1964 Budapest, Rákóczi u. 54; tel. 224-810; telex 22-4101; organ of the Hungarian Trades Union Council; Editor LÁSZLÓ FODOR; circ. 276,000.

HUNGARY

WEEKLIES

Élet és Irodalom (Life and Literature); 1054 Budapest, Széchenyi u. 1; tel. 533-122; f. 1957; literary and political; Editor IMRE BATA; circ. 60,000.

Élet és Tudomány (Life and Science): 1073 Budapest, Lenin krt 5; tel. 215-290; f. 1946; popular science; Editor-in-Chief LÁSZLÓ M. LUDAS; circ. 65,000.

Evangélikus Élet: 1088 Budapest, Puskin u. 12; tel. 142-074; f. 1933; Evangelical/Lutheran Church newspaper; Editor LÁSZLÓ LEHEL; circ. 12,000.

Figyelő (Observer): 1355 Budapest, Alkotmány u. 10; tel. 127-664; telex 22-6613; weekly; f. 1957; economic policy and management; Editor-in-Chief Dr GYÖRGY VARGA; circ. 24,000.

Film, Szinház, Muzsika (Films, Theatre, Music): 1073 Budapest, Lenin krt 9–11; tel. 222-400; Editor ZOLTÁN ISZLAI; circ. 70,000.

Heti Világgazdaság (World Economics Weekly): 1133 Budapest, Vág u. 13; tel. 408-776; telex 22-6676; f. 1979; Editor-in-Chief MÁTYÁS VINCE; circ. 141,000.

Képes Újság (Illustrated News): 1085 Budapest, Gyulai Pál u. 14; tel. 137-660; f. 1960; Patriotic People's Front; Editor MIHALY KOVÁCS; circ. 400,000.

Ludas Matyi: 1077 Budapest, Gyulai Pál u. 14; tel. 335-718; satirical; Editor JÓZSEF ÁRKUS; circ. 352,000.

L'udové Noviny: 1065 Budapest, Nagymező u. 49; tel. 319-184; for Slovaks in Hungary; Editor PÁL KONDÁCS; circ. 1,700.

Magyar Ifjúság (Hungarian Youth): 1085 Budapest, Somogyi Béla u. 6; tel. 130-460; telex 22-6423; Editor LAJOS GUBCSI; circ. 207,000.

Magyar Mezőgazdaság (Hungarian Agriculture): 1053 Budapest, Kossuth Lajos tér 11; tel. 122-433; telex 22-5445; f. 1946; Editor KÁROLY FEHÉR; circ. 24,000.

Magyarország (Hungary): 1085 Budapest, Gyulai Pál u. 14; tel. 384-644; telex 22-6351; f. 1964; news magazine; Editor Dr JÓZSEF PÁLFY; circ. 200,000.

Narodne Novine: 1396 Budapest, POB 495; tel. 124-869; f. 1945; for Yugoslavs in Hungary; in Serbo-Croat and Slovene; Chief Editor MARKO MARKOVIĆ; circ. 2,800.

Neue Zeitung: 1391 Budapest, Nagymező u. 49, Pf. 224; tel. 326-334; f. 1957; for Germans in Hungary; Editor PETER LEIPOLD; circ. 4,500.

Nők Lapja (Women's Journal): 1085 Budapest, Blaha Lujza tér 3; tel. 384-828; telex 225554; f. 1949; Editor-in-Chief VALÉRIA RÉVAI; circ. 870,000.

Ország-Világ (Land and World): 1073 Budapest, Lenin krt 9–11; tel. 222-400; f. 1957; Editor ANDRÁS GÁL; circ. 208,000.

Rádió és Televízióújság (Radio and TV News): 1801 Budapest; tel. 387-739; f. 1956; Editor JÁNOS BOROS; circ. 1,350,000.

Reform: Budapest; f. 1988; popular; Editor PÉTER TŐKE; circ. 250,000.

Reformátusok Lapja: 1395 Budapest, POB 424; tel. 176-809; f. 1957; Reformed Church paper for the laity; Editor-in-Chief and Publr ATTILA P. KOMLÓS; circ. 40,000.

Szabad Föld (Free Soil): 1085 Budapest, Somogyi Béla u. 6; tel. 138-821; Patriotic People's Front; Editor GYULA ECK; circ. 600,000.

Szövetkezet (Co-operative): 1054 Budapest, Szabadság tér 14; tel. 313-132; National Council of Hungarian Consumer Co-operative Societies; Editor-in-Chief ATTILA KOVÁCS; circ. 85,000.

Új Ember (New Man): 1053 Budapest, POB 111; tel. 173-638; religious weekly of the Actio Catholica; Editor FERENC MAGYAR; circ. 100,000.

Új Tükör (New Mirror): 1073 Budapest, Lenin krt 9–11; tel. 223-058; illustrated cultural and sociological magazine; Editor-in-Chief SANDOR FEKETE; circ. 101,000.

Vasárnapi Hirek (Sunday News): 1979 Budapest, POB 14; tel. 134-460; telex 22-3174; political; Editor Dr ZOLTÁN LŐKÖS; circ. 320,000.

FORTNIGHTLIES

Foaia Noastra (Our Leaf): 1055 Budapest, Bajcsy Zs. u. 78; for Romanians in Hungary; Editor SÁNDOR HOCOPÁN; circ. 1,500.

Magyar Hirek (Hungarian News): 1068 Budapest, Benczúr u. 15; tel. 225-616; illustrated magazine published by World Asscn of Hungarians; primarily for Hungarians living abroad; Editor GYÖRGY HALÁSZ; circ. 70,000.

Szövetkezeti Hírlap (Co-operative Herald): 1052 Budapest, Pesti Barnabás u. 6; tel. 170-181; National Union of Artisans; Editor MÁRIA DOLEZSÁL; circ. 12,000.

Új Élet (New Life): 1075 Budapest, Síp u. 12; tel. 222-829; for Hungarian Jews; Editor Dr ISTVÁN DOMÁN; circ. 7,000.

OTHER PERIODICALS

(Published monthly unless otherwise indicated)

Állami Gazdaság (State Farming): General Direction of State Farming, 1054 Budapest, Akadémia u. 1–3; tel. 323-934; f. 1946; Editor Mrs P. GÖRGÉNYI.

Business Partner Hungary: 1051 Budapest, Dorottya u. 6; tel. 371-438; f. 1986; quarterly; Hungarian, German and English; economic journal published by Institute for Economic, Market Research and Informatics (KOPINT-DATORG).

Cartactual: 1367 Budapest, POB 76; tel. 126-480; telex 22-4964; f. 1965; every 2 months; map service periodical with supplement *Cartinform* (map bibliography); published in English, French, German and Hungarian; Editor-in-Chief ERNŐ CSÁTI.

Egyházi Krónika (Church Chronicle): 1052 Budapest, Petőfi tér 2.1.2; tel. 184-813; f. 1952; every 2 months; Eastern Orthodox Church journal; Editor Archpriest Dr FERIZ BERKI.

Elektrotechnika (Electrical Engineering): 1055 Budapest, Kossuth Lajos tér 6–8; tel. 530-117; f. 1908; organ of Electrotechnical Association; Editor Dr TIBOR KELEMEN; circ. 3,000.

Élelmezési Ipar (Food Industry): 1361 Budapest, POB 5; tel. 122-859; f. 1947; Scientific Society for Food Industry; Editor Dr ÖDÖN VAJDA.

Energia és Atomtechnika (Energy and Nuclear Technology): 1054 Budapest, Kossuth Lajos tér 6–8; tel. 532-751; Scientific Society for Energy Economy; Editor ISTVÁN VARGA.

Energiagazdálkodás (Energy Economy): 1055 Budapest, Kossuth Lajos tér 6; tel. 532-894; Scientific Society for Energetics; Editor Dr TAMÁS RAPP.

Épitésügyi Szemle (Building Review): 1054 Budapest, Beloiannisz u. 2–4; tel. 313-180; building; Editor Dr JÓZSEF KÁDÁR.

Ezermester (The Handyman): 1066 Budapest, Dessewffy u. 34; tel. 320-542; telex 22-6423; f. 1957; do-it-yourself magazine; Editor J. SZÜCS; circ. 135,000.

Gép (Machinery): 1055 Budapest, Kossuth Lajos tér 6–8; tel. 530-340; telex 22-5792; f. 1949; monthly; Society of Mechanical Engineers; Editor Dr KORNÉL LEHOFER.

Hungarian Book Review: 1051 Budapest, Vörösmarty tér 1.X.1010; tel. 176-222; f. 1958; quarterly review of Hungarian Publishers' and Booksellers' Association; in English, French and German; Editor-in-Chief GYULA KURUCZ.

Hungarian Business Herald: 1075 Budapest, Tanács krt 7.1.3; tel. 417-270; f. 1970; quarterly review published in English and German by the Hungarian Chamber of Commerce; Editor-in-Chief Dr GERD BIRÓ; circ. 4,000.

Hungarian Digest: 1073 Budapest, Lenin krt 9–11; tel. 811-580; f. 1980; illustrated quarterly on political, economic and cultural issues; English; also in French as Revue de Hongrie, and in German as Ungarland; Editor TIBOR ZÁDOR; circ. 50,000.

Hungarian Economy: 1355 Budapest, POB 18; tel. 322-186; telex 22-6613; quarterly; economic and business review; English edn of weekly Figyelő; Editor-in-Chief Dr JÁNOS FOLLINUS.

Hungarian Trade Journal: 1073 Budapest, Lenin krt 9–11; tel. 221-285; telex 22-6207; fmrly New Hungarian Exporter; Hungarian Chamber of Commerce; monthly in English; fortnightly in other languages; technical issues in English, 2 a year; Editor-in-Chief MÁRIA MURAI; circ. 18,000.

Hungarian Trade Union News: 1415 Budapest, Dózsa György u. 84/B; tel. 428-313; f. 1957; in six languages including English; Editor-in-Chief JÁNOS SIKLÓS.

Hungarian Travel Magazine: 1088 Budapest, Múzeum u. 11; tel. 361-384; quarterly in English and German; illustrated journal of the Tourist Board for the visitor to Hungary; Managing Editor JÚLIA SZ. NAGY.

Ipargazdaság (Industrial Economy): 1371 Budapest, POB 433; tel. 354-529; f. 1948; Editor Dr LÁSZLÓ LADÓ; circ. 4,000.

Jogtudományi Közlöny (Law Gazette): 1250 Budapest, Pf. 25, Országház u. 30; tel. 556-894; f. 1866; law; Editor-in-Chief Dr JÓZSEF HALÁSZ; Editor Dr IMRE VÖRÖS; circ. 2,500.

Kortárs (Contemporary): 1054 Budapest, Széchenyi u. 1; tel. 121-240; literary gazette; Editor GYÖRGY SZÁRAZ; circ. 11,000.

Könyvtáros (The Librarian): 1024 Budapest, Mártirok u. 55; tel. 163-495; monthly; Editor LÁSZLÓ BERECZKY; circ. 6,000.

Közgazdasági Szemle (Economic Review): 1112 Budapest, Budaörsi u. 43–45; tel. 850-777; f. 1954; monthly; published by Cttee for Economic Sciences of Academy of Sciences; Editor KATALIN SZABÓ; circ. 15,000.

Look at Hungary: 1906 Budapest, POB 223; tel. 860-133; f. 1980; quarterly photomagazine in English, Arabic, French and Portuguese; Editor-in-Chief GÁBOR VAJDA.

HUNGARY

Made in Hungary: 1426 Budapest, POB 3; every 2 months; economics and business magazine published in English by MTI; Editor GYÖRGY BLASITS.

Magyar Jog (Hungarian Law): 1055 Budapest, Szalay u. 16; tel. 326-170; law; Editor Dr PÉTER BÖÖR.

Magyar Közlöny (Official Gazette): 1055 Budapest, Bajcsy Zs. u. 78; tel. 121-236; Editor Dr ELEMÉR KISS; circ. 90,000.

Magyar Tudomány (Hungarian Science): Hungarian Academy of Sciences, 1051 Budapest, Münnich Ferenc u. 7; tel. 179-524; Editor-in-Chief BÉLA KŐPECZI.

Muzsika: 1073 Budapest, Lenin krt 9–11; tel. 215-440; f. 1958; musical review; Editor-in-Chief MÁRIA FEUER; circ. 7,500.

Nagyvilág (The Great World): 1054 Budapest, Széchenyi u. 1; tel. 321-160; f. 1956; review of world literature; Editor LÁSZLÓ KÉRY; circ. 12,000.

Nemzetközi Szemle (International Review): 1054 Budapest, Steindl u. 6; tel. 110-697; f. 1957; Editor-in-Chief LÁSZLÓ FENCSIK; circ. 32,000.

Népfront (People's Front): 1054 Budapest, Belgrád rkp. 24; published by the Patriotic People's Front; Editor ISTVÁN HAJDUSKA; circ. 18,000.

New Hungarian Quarterly: 1088 Budapest, Rákóczi u. 17; tel. 384-214; f. 1960; illustrated quarterly in English; politics, economics, philosophy, education, culture, poems, short stories, etc.; Editor IVÁN BOLDIZSÁR; circ. 5,400.

Református Egyház: 1146 Budapest, Abonyi u. 21; tel. 227-870; f. 1949; official journal of the Hungarian Reformed Church; Editor-in-Chief FERENC DUSICZA; circ. 1,600.

Statisztikai Szemle (Statistical Review): 1525 Budapest, POB 51; tel. 155-208; f. 1923; monthly; Editor-in-Chief Dr FERENC GYULAY; circ. 3,500.

Társadalmi Szemle (Social Review): 1358 Budapest, Széchenyi rkp. 19; tel. 114-400; theoretical-political review; Editor KATALIN RADICS; circ. 45,000.

Technika (Technology): 1037 Budapest, Kiscelli köz 30; tel. 672-148; f. 1957; general technical review; monthly in Hungarian, annually in English, German and Russian; Editor GYULA SIMON; circ. 20,000.

Turizmus (Tourism): 1088 Budapest, Múzeum u. 11; tel. 138-625; Editor ZSOLT SZEBENI; circ. 8,000.

Új Technika (New Technology): 1014 Budapest, Szentháromság tér 1; tel. 557-122; telex 22-6490; f. 1967; popular industrial quarterly; circ. 35,000.

Vigilia (Vigil): 1364 Budapest, POB 111; tel. 177-246; f. 1935; monthly; Catholic; Editor LÁSZLÓ LUKÁCS; circ. 11,500.

Villamosság (Electricity): 1055 Budapest, Kossuth Lajos tér 6–8; tel. 530-117; organ of Electrotechnical Association; Gen. Editor FERENC KOVÁCS; circ. 3,000.

NEWS AGENCIES

Magyar Távirati Iroda (MTI) (Hungarian News Agency): 1016 Budapest, Fém u. 5–7; tel. 756-722; telex 22-4371; f. 1880; 19 brs in Hungary; 23 bureaux abroad; Pres., Man. Dir TAMÁS PALOS.

Foreign Bureaux

Agence France-Presse (AFP): 1145 Budapest, Korong u. 35; tel. 836-861; telex 22-6030; Correspondent PAL HERSKOVITS.

Agentstvo Pechati Novosti (APN) (USSR): 1075 Budapest VII, Tanács Kőrút 9; tel. 32-05-94; telex 61-224792; Bureau Chief N. ZABELKIN.

Agenzia Nazionale Stampa Associata (ANSA) (Italy): 1024 Budapest, Mártírok u. 43/45; tel. 352-323; telex 22-4711; Bureau Chief ROBERTO PAPI.

Allgemeiner Deutscher Nachrichtendienst (ADN) (German Democratic Republic): 1146 Budapest, Zichy Géza u. 5; telex 22-4675; Bureau Chief BERND RUNGE.

Associated Press (AP) (USA): Budapest II, Riado u. 12; tel. 159-490; Rep. ANDY TIMAR.

Bulgarian Telegraph Agency (BTA): 1016 Budapest, Flat 10, Lisznyai u. 15; Bureau Chief GEORG VEDRODENSZKI.

Československá tisková kancelář (ČTK) (Czechoslovakia): 1146 Budapest, Zichy Géza u. 5; tel. 427-115; telex 22-5367; Correspondent STEFAN NÉMETH.

Inter Press Service (IPS) (Italy): 1026 Budapest, Filler u. 26; tel. 363-903; telex 22-4371; Rep. CATALINA WEINER.

Prensa Latina (Cuba): 1021 Budapest, Budakeszi u. 55/D, 7 p.; tel. 387-474; telex 22-4800; Correspondent HUGO LUIS SÁNCHEZ GONZÁLEZ.

Reuters (UK): c/o Magyar Távirati Iroda, 1426 Budapest, POB 3.

Telegrafnoye Agentstvo Sovetskovo Soyuza (TASS) (USSR): 1023 Budapest, Vérhalom u. 12–16; Correspondent YEVGENI POPOV.

United Press International (UPI) (USA): 1137 Budapest, Pozsonyi u. 14; telex 22-5649; Bureau Chief Dr ANDREW L. SÜMEGHI.

Xinhua (New China) News Agency (People's Republic of China): 1068 Budapest, Benczur u. 39/A.1.4; tel. 228-420; telex 22-5447; Chief Correspondent HOU FENGQING.

PRESS ASSOCIATIONS

Magyar Újságírók Országos Szövetsége (MUOSZ) (National Association of Hungarian Journalists): 1062 Budapest, Népköztársaság u. 101; tel. 221-699; telex 22-5045; Pres. JÓZSEF PÁLFY; Gen. Sec. KÁROLY MEGYERI; 4,700 mems.

Association of Hungarian Newspaper Publishers: Budapest; f. 1986 by four major newspaper publishing companies, MTI and local newspaper publrs; Chair. JÓZSEF BOCZ.

Publishers

PRINCIPAL PUBLISHING HOUSES

Akadémiai Kiadó: 1054 Budapest, Alkotmány u. 21; tel. 111-010; telex 22-6228; f. 1828; Publishing House of the Hungarian Academy of Sciences; humanities, social, natural and technical sciences, dictionaries, encyclopaedias, periodicals of the Academy and other institutions, issued partly in foreign languages; Man. Dir GYÖRGY HAZAI.

Corvina Kiadó: 1051 Budapest, Vörösmarty tér 1; tel. 176-222; telex 22-4440; f. 1955; Hungarian works translated into foreign languages, art and educational books, fiction and non-fiction, tourist guides, cookery books, sport, musicology, juvenile and children's literature; Man. Dir ISTVÁN BART; Editorial Dir BÉLA REVICZKY.

Editio Musica Budapest: 1051 Budapest, Vörösmarty tér 1; tel. 184-228; telex 22-4405; f. 1950; sheet music and books on musical subjects; Dir ISTVÁN HOMOLYA.

Európa Könyvkiadó: 1055 Budapest, Kossuth Lajos tér 13–15; tel. 312-700; telex 22-5645; f. 1945; world literature translated into Hungarian; Man. LEVENTE OSZTOVITS.

Gondolat Könyvkiadó: 1088 Budapest, Bródy Sándor u. 16; tel. 343-380; popular scientific publications on natural and social sciences, art, encyclopaedic handbooks; Dir Dr MARGIT SIKLÓS.

Helikon Kiadó: 1053 Budapest, Eötvös L. u. 8; tel. 174-765; bibliophile books; Dir MAGDA MOLNAR.

Képzömüvészeti Kiadó: 1051 Budapest, Vörösmarty tér 1; tel. 184-981; telex 22-4405; fine arts; Man. PÉTER LÁTKI.

Kossuth Könyvkiadó Vállalat: 1054 Budapest, Steindl u. 6; tel. 117-440; f. 1944; political, historical, economic and philosophical publications; Man. TIBOR ILLÉS.

Közgazdasági és Jogi Könyvkiadó: 1054 Budapest, Nagy Sándor u. 6; tel. 126-430; telex 22-6511; f. 1955; economic, sociological and juridical; Man. VILMOS DALOS.

Magvető Könyvkiadó: 1806 Budapest, Vörösmarty tér 1; tel. 185-109; literature; Man. MIKLÓS JOVÁNOVICS.

Medicina Könyvkiadó: 1054 Budapest, Beloiannisz u. 8; tel. 122-650; f. 1957; books on medicine, sport, tourism; Man. Prof. Dr ISTVÁN ÁRKY.

Mezőgazdasági Könyvkiadó: 1054 Budapest, Báthory u. 10; tel. 116-650; ecology, natural sciences, environmental protection, food industry; Man. Dr CSABA GALLYAS.

Móra Ferenc Gyermek és Ifjúsági Könyvkiadó: 1146 Budapest, Május 1 u. 57–59; tel. 212-390; telex 22-7027; f. 1950; children's books, science fiction; Man. JÁNOS SZILÁDI.

Müszaki Könyvkiadó: 1014 Budapest, Szentháromság tér 6; tel. 557-122; telex 22-6490; f. 1955; scientific and technical, fiction and non-fiction; Man. PÉTER SZÜCS.

Népszava Lap-és Könyvkiadó Vállalat: 1553 Budapest, Rákóczi u. 54; tel. 224-810; Hungarian Trade Union Council Press; Man. Dr JENŐ KISS.

Statisztikai Kiadó Vállalat: 1033 Budapest, Kaszásdülő u. 2; tel. 803-511; telex 22-6699; f. 1954; publications on statistics, system-management and computer science; Dir JÓZSEF KECSKÉS.

Szépirodalmi Könyvkiadó: 1073 Budapest, Lenin krt 9–11; tel. 221-285; telex 22-6754; f. 1950; modern and classical Magyar literature; Man. Dr MÁRTON TARNÓC.

Tankönyvkiadó Vállalat: 1055 Budapest, Szalay u. 10–14; tel. 530-600; f. 1949; school and university textbooks, pedagogical literature and language books; Man. ANDRÁS PETRÓ.

Zrinyi Katonai Kiadó: 1087 Budapest, Kerepesi u. 29; tel. 334-750; military literature; Man. LÁSZLÓ NÉMETH.

HUNGARY

CARTOGRAPHERS

Cartographia (Hungarian Company for Surveying and Mapping): 1443 Budapest, POB 132; tel. 634-639; telex 22-6218; f. 1954; Dir GYÖRGY DOMOKOS.

Országos Földügyi és Térképészeti Hivatal (National Office of Lands and Mapping): 1055 Budapest, Kossuth Lajos tér 11; tel. 311-349; telex 22-5445; f. 1954; Pres. ISTVÁN HOFFER.

PUBLISHERS' ASSOCIATION

Magyar Könyvkiadók és Könyvterjesztők Egyesülése (Hungarian Publishers' and Booksellers' Association): 1051 Budapest, Vörösmarty tér 1; POB 130; tel. 184-758; f. 1878; most Hungarian publishers are members of the Association; Pres. ANDRÁS PETRÓ; Sec.-Gen. FERENC ZÖLD.

WRITERS' UNION

Magyar Írók Szövetsége (Association of Hungarian Writers): 1062 Budapest, Bajza u. 18; tel. 228-840; f. 1945; Pres. TIBOR CSERES; Sec.-Gen. SÁNDOR KOCZKÁS.

Radio and Television

Radio licences (1979): 2,608,000. Radio licences were abolished in 1980. Television licences (1984): 2,895,000. Cable television systems are expanding, and in early 1985 were operating in 12 cities. In 1986 Hungary completed negotiations to receive TV programmes from a Western European satellite network. By the end of 1987 more than 25,000 homes in the city of Szekesfehervar were able to receive experimental satellite transmissions from the British Sky Channel. Programmes from the British-based Super Channel, the French TV-5 and the USA's CNN-Europe service were also available by 1988. In 1988 more than 40 areas (300,000 homes) were able to receive cable and satellite services.

RADIO

Magyar Rádió: 1800 Budapest, Brody Sándor u. 5–7; tel. 388-388; telex 22-5188; f. 1924; stations: Radio Kossuth (Budapest); Radio Petőfi (Budapest); Radio Bartók (Budapest, mainly classical music); 6 regional studios; external broadcasts: in English, German, Hungarian, Italian, Spanish and Turkish; Pres. ISTVÁN HAJDU.

Radio Danubius: f. 1986; commercial station; broadcasts news, music and information in German 11 hours a day in summer to tourists in Lake Balaton region; Dir GYÖRGY VARGA.

TELEVISION

Magyar Televízió: 1810 Budapest, Szabadság tér 17; tel. 533-200; telex 22-5568; f. 1957; first channel broadcasts about 66 hours a week and the second channel about 20 hours a week, mostly colour transmissions; 100 relay stations; no broadcasts on Mondays; Pres. GYULA BERECZKY.

Finance

The Hungarian financial system is being restructured. In January 1985 the functions of issue and credit at the National Bank were separated. Under reforms implemented in January 1987, the central banking and commercial banking functions were separated, and the banking system is now organized on three levels. The National Bank of Hungary, as the bank of issue, continues to participate in the formulation of economic policy. The 1987 reforms did not affect the National Bank's foreign exchange authority, nor alter substantially the Bank's total assets. At the second level are the commercial banks. These institutions have general and nationwide authority, keep the accounts of enterprises, accept their deposits and extend credits to them. The commercial banks may participate in ventures and may provide banking services for their clients. They establish their own business policy and the terms and conditions of their contracts, within the limits of central banking regulations. The commercial banks (established from the units seceding from the National Bank of Hungary, the reorganization of the State Development Bank and the Creditbank of Budapest, and the General Banking and Trust Co Ltd) are: The General Banking and Trust and Co Ltd; Budapest Bank Rt.; Hungarian Creditbank Ltd; Hungarian Foreign Trade Bank; Commercial and Creditbank Ltd. At the third level of the banking system are the so-called specialized financial institutions. These small banks may establish deposit and credit links with economic entities, may participate in ventures and may provide banking services. Unlike the commercial banks, the specialized financial institutions may not keep the accounts of their clients.

Like the National Savings Bank (OTP), the Savings Co-operatives (Takarékszövetkezet) function as banks for the use of the general public, operating at the local level. Their main activity is the collection of deposits and the provision of credit to their members. Since January 1985, these co-operatives have been able to maintain accounts for small enterprises and private entrepreneurs, and can extend credit to them. They are also empowered to provide mortgage facilities to individuals. Minimum registered capital is 2.0m. forint at each co-operative. In early 1987 there were 260 such co-operatives in Hungary. Their interests are represented by SZÖVOSZ (National Council of Consumer Co-operatives—see p. 1279).

Financial institutions with foreign capital shares may be founded with government permission. The first bank in Hungary to be founded with foreign capital involvement was the Central European International Bank (CIB), established in 1979. In 1985 a joint Hungarian-US commercial bank was established by the Central Exchange and Credit Bank of Budapest and Citibank of New York. It began operations in 1986, under the supervision of the National Bank of Hungary. Unicbank Rt., founded with 45% foreign capital, commenced operations in January 1987.

The issue of bonds, in order to finance housing and infrastructural projects, is of increasing significance. Offering a higher rate of interest than that of the National Savings Bank, bonds were first issued on a large scale in early 1983, available initially only to enterprises but later also to private individuals. In September 1984 the State Development Bank (now State Development Institution) began repurchasing and reselling bonds, thus giving rise to the existence of a domestic 'bond market'. By mid-1986 local councils and enterprises had issued 130 bonds to a total value of 8,000m. forint (equivalent to almost 3% of total Hungarian investment in 1985), about 70% of which had been purchased by private citizens. The bond market expanded rapidly in 1987, and by December 200 bonds, worth 24,320m. forint, were in circulation. In January 1988 the state guarantee for bonds was terminated, thus rendering the issue of bonds more difficult for less profitable organizations. The State also began to issue treasury bills in order to finance budget deficits. A national securities market opened in Budapest in January 1988, and a stock exchange in January 1989.

BANKING

(cap. = capital; res = reserves; dep. = deposits; m. = million; Ft = forint; brs = branches)

Central Bank

Magyar Nemzeti Bank (National Bank of Hungary): 1850 Budapest, Szabadság tér 8; tel. 532-600; telex 22-5755; f. 1924; cap. 10,000m. Ft, res 8,403m. Ft, dep. 470,718m. Ft (Dec. 1985); issue of bank notes; transacts international payments business; supervises banking system; 18 brs; Pres. FERENC BARTHA; First Vice-Pres. IMRE TARAFAS.

Commercial Banks

Általános Értékforgalmi Bank Rt. (General Banking and Trust Co Ltd): 1093 Budapest, Szamuely u. 38; tel. 171-255; telex 22-6548; f. 1923; commercial banking activities in Hungarian currency, deposit-taking and account-keeping in foreign currency, services for joint-venture companies; cap. 1,000m. Ft; Dir-Gen. Dr ANTAL BESZEDES.

Befektetési és Forgalmi Leánybank (Bank for Investment and Transactions): 1051 Budapest, József A. u. 8.; tel. 172-011; telex 22-3203; f. 1987; subsidiary of Hungarian Credit Bank Ltd; cap. 250m. Ft; Dir KÁLMÁN DEBRECZENI.

Budapest Bank Rt.: 1052 Budapest, Deák Ferenc u. 5; tel. 181-200; telex 22-3013; f. 1986; cap. 5,332m. Ft; Dir-Gen. OSZKÁR HEGEDŰS.

Középeurópai Hitelbank Rt. (Central European Credit Bank Ltd): 1052 Budapest, Váci u. 16/B; tel. 188-377; telex 22-4759; f. 1988; Dirs Dr LAJOS KOMÁR, Dr MATTHIAS KUNSCH.

Magyar Hitel Bank Rt. (Hungarian Credit Bank Ltd): 1054 Budapest, Szabadság tér 5–6; tel. 361-113; telex 22-3202; f. 1986; cap. 13,983m. Ft; activities include venture financing, securities trading, real estate investments, joint venture promotion and advisory services; Chair and CEO SÁNDOR DEMJÁN.

Magyar Külkereskedelmi Bank Rt. (Hungarian Foreign Trade Bank Ltd): 1821 Budapest, Szt. István tér 11; tel. 329-360; telex 22-6941; f. 1950; cap. 4,374m. Ft; Chair. and Man. Dir GÁBOR ERDÉLY.

Merkantil: 1056 Budapest, Belgrád rkp. 16; tel. 181-222; telex 22-3200; f. 1988; affiliated to Commercial and Creditbank Ltd; cap. 500m. Ft; Dir ÁDÁM KOLOSSVÁRY.

Országos Kereskedelmi és Hitelbank Rt. (Commercial and Creditbank Ltd): 1850 Budapest, Arany János u. 24; tel. 532-052; f. 1986; cap. 10,590m. Ft; Pres.-Gen. Dir Dr GÉZA LENK.

HUNGARY

Development Financial Institution

Állami Fejlesztési Intézet (State Development Institution): 1052 Budapest, Deák F. u. 5; tel. 181-200; telex 22-5672; f. 1987 to succeed the State Development Bank; management and control of development projects financed partly from the state budget; Gen. Dir Dr BORBÁLA BÁGER.

Specialized Financial Institutions

AGROBANK Rt. (Agricultural Innovation Bank Ltd): 1054 Budapest, Széchenyi rkp. 6; tel. 315-995; telex 22-3111; f. 1984; joint-stock company; cap. 1,500m. Ft; 10 brs; Dir MIKLÓS SZIGETHY.

Általános Vállalkozási Bank Rt. (General Bank for Venture Financing Ltd): 1055 Budapest, Stollár B. u. 3A; tel. 326-590; f. 1985; joint-stock company; cap. 2,200m. Ft; Gen. Man. JÁNOS BOROS.

Építőipari Innovációs Bank Rt. (Innovation Bank for Construction Industry Ltd): 1139 Budapest, Teve u. 8-10; tel. 298-044; telex 22-533; f. 1985; joint stock company; cap. 1,126m. Ft; Man. Dir TAMÁS VARGA.

INNOFINANCE—Általános Innovációs Pénzintézet (General Financial Institution for Innovation): 1365 Budapest, POB 718; tel. 383-366; f. 1980; joint-stock company; registered cap. 500m. Ft; Man. Dir ERZSÉBET BIRMAN.

INTERBANK—Külkereskedelmi Fejlesztési Hitelintézet Rt. (INTERBANK Credit Corporation for the Development of Foreign Trade Ltd): 1051 Budapest, Dorottya u. 8; tel. 186-427; telex 22-7879; f. 1980 as INTERINVEST; cap. 2,175m. Ft; Man. Dir GYÖRGY IVÁNYI.

INVESTBANK—Műszaki Fejlesztési Bank (Bank for Technical Development): 1053 Budapest, Képíró u. 9; tel. 184-917; telex 22-3250; f. 1983; cap. 1,233m. Ft; Dir Dr ANNA TEMESI.

Ipari Fejlesztési Bank Rt. (Industrial Development Bank Ltd): 1054 Budapest, Rosenberg u. 25; tel. 320-320; telex 22-7351; f. 1988 (previously Magyar Iparbank Rt., f. 1987); cap. 3,200m. Ft; Gen. Man. Dr GYULA PÁZMÁNDI.

Ipari Szövetkezeti Fejlesztési Bank (Development Bank of Industrial Co-operatives): Budapest, Gerlóczy u. 5; tel. 176-811; telex 22-3042; f. 1984; cap. 1,060.7m. Ft; Dir BÉLA SEYDL.

Kisvállalkozási Bank (Bank for Small Ventures): 1876 Budapest, Münnich F. u. 16; tel. 316-940; telex 22-4280; f. 1986; affiliated to NSB; cap. 3,200m. Ft; Dir ÁRPÁD BACSÓKA.

Konzumbank (Consumer Co-operatives' Bank): 1052 Budapest, Vitkovics M. u. 15; tel. 172-600; telex 22-4671; f. 1986; cap. 850m. Ft; Dir Dr GÁBOR PÁL.

Mezőbank (National Banking Institution of Agricultural Co-operatives Corporation): 1025 Budapest, Áldás u. 5; tel. 359-362; telex 22-7058; f. 1986; cap. 1,166m. Ft; Dir Dr GYULA KABAI.

Consortium Banks

Central-European International Bank Ltd—CIB: 1364 Budapest, Váci u. 16B, POB 170; tel. 188-377; telex 22-4759; f. 1979; shareholders: National Bank of Hungary (34%), Banca Commerciale Italiana, Bayerische Vereinsbank, Creditanstalt Bankverein, Long-Term Credit Bank of Japan, Société Générale, Taiyo Kobe Bank (11% each); an offshore bank conducting international banking business of all kinds; share cap. US $43.071m., dep. $487m., total resources $539.6m. (Dec. 1987); Chair. Dr MARIO ARCARI; Deputy Chair. Dr LAJOS KOMÁR; Man. Dir GYÖRGY ZDEBORSKY.

Citibank Budapest: 1052 Budapest, Váci u. 19-21; tel. 382-666; telex 22-7822; f. 1986; joint-stock company; share cap. 1,000m. Ft; Gen. Man. ROBIN M. WINCHESTER.

Unicbank Rt.: 1052 Budapest, Váci u. 19-21; tel. 182-088; telex 22-3123; f. 1986; cap. 1,000m. Ft; Man. Dir Dr ÁGNES CSERESNYÉS; Deputy Man. Dir Dr RUDOLF PFLETSCHINGER; Shareholders: International Finance Corporation (IFC) (15%); Genossenschaftliche Zentralbank AG (GZB), Vienna (15%); DG Bank (Deutsche Genossenschaftsbank AG), Frankfurt (15%); Central Bank of Exchange and Credit Ltd (20%); National Savings Bank (11%); Association of Agricultural Co-operatives (6%); Association of Industrial Co-operatives (6%); Association of Service Co-operatives (6%); Association of Private Artisans (6%).

Savings Bank

Országos Takarékpénztár—OTP (National Savings Bank—NSB): 1876 Budapest, Münnich Ferenc u. 16; tel. 531-444; telex 22-4280; f. 1949; cap. 1,300m. Ft, dep. 239,000m. Ft (Dec. 1986); savings deposits, credits, foreign transactions, lotteries; acts as estate agent; 598 brs; Gen. Man. Dr LÁSZLÓ TISZA.

Postabank és Takarékpénztár Rt. (Post Bank and Savings Bank Corporation): 1052 Budapest, József nádor tér 2; tel. 180-855; f. 1988; cap. 2,230m. Ft; Dir GÁBOR PRINCZ.

Central Corporation

Pénzintézeti Központ (Central Corporation of Banking Companies): 1431 Budapest, Szamuely u. 38; tel. 171-255; f. 1916; banking, property, rights and interests, deposits, securities, and foreign exchange management; Dir-Gen. MIHÁLY BIRÓ.

STOCK EXCHANGE

In January 1989 a stock exchange was opened in Budapest.

Budapest Stock Exchange: Budapest; f. 1989; Chair. ZSIGMOND JARAI.

INSURANCE

In July 1986 the state insurance enterprise was divided into two companies, one of which retained the name of the former Állami Biztosító. Two further companies were founded in 1988.

Állami Biztosító—ÁB (State Insurance Co): 1813 Budapest, Üllői u. 1; tel. 181-866; telex 22-4550; f. 1949, reorganized 1986; handles life and property insurance, insurance of agricultural plants, co-operatives, foreign insurance, etc.; Gen. Man. ANDREA DEÁK.

Atlasz Utazási Biztosító (Atlasz Travel Insurance Co): 1053 Budapest, Deák F. u. 23; tel. 181-999; f. 1988; cap. 1,000m. Ft; Gen. Man. GYÖRGY BORDÁS.

Garancia Biztosító (Garancia Insurance Co): 1148 Budapest, Martos F. u. 13/D; tel. 630-623; f. 1988; cap. 1,050m. Ft; Gen. Man. OTTÓ GAÁL.

Hungária Biztosító (Hungária Insurance, Reinsurance and Export Credit Insurance Co): 1014 Budapest, Dísz tér 4-5; tel. 759-211; telex 22-3199; f. 1986; handles international insurance, insurance of state companies and motor-car, marine, life, accident and liability insurance; Man. Dir TAMÁS UZONYI.

Trade and Industry

CHAMBER OF COMMERCE

Magyar Gazdasági Kamara (Hungarian Chamber of Commerce): 1389 Budapest, POB 106; tel. 533-333; telex 22-4745; f. 1948; develops trade with other countries; mediates between companies, etc.; mems: 1,500 industrial and foreign trade organizations; Pres. ANDRÁS GÁBOR; Gen. Sec. PETER LŐRINCZE.

SELECTED FOREIGN TRADE ORGANIZATIONS

Since 1980 the foreign trade organizations have been undergoing modernization. By 1987 over 300 enterprises had acquired foreign trade rights. Also, radical reforms in 1985 permitted the foreign trade organizations to become 'trading houses', widening their sphere of activity by extending the range of goods available, supplying capital to producers and commissioning manufacture of the goods required by the foreign market. New regulations, introduced in 1988, permitted all business organizations to export products and to conduct business with foreign partners without the involvement of specialized traders.

AÉV No 31: 1364 Budapest, POB 83; tel. 180-511; telex 22-4928; f. 1951; state building factory; construction of industrial units, power plants, chemical combines, cement plants, etc.; undertakes building work abroad.

Agrária-Bábolna: 2943 Bábolna; tel. 34-11118; telex 22-6555; f. 1789; turn-key poultry and pig farms with breeding stock and feed premixes; hatching eggs, breeding poultry, pigs, sheep and breeding jumping and riding horses; processed chicken, rodent and insect extermination services, etc.

Agrikon: 6001 Kecskemét, POB 43; tel. (76) 27-666; telex 26-493; Budapest office: 1364 Budapest 4, POB 167; tel. 189-557; telex 22-5517; engineering and servicing for agricultural and food processing machines.

Agrimpex: 1392 Budapest, POB 278; tel. 113-800; telex 22-5751; f. 1948; agricultural products; Gen. Dir ANDRÁS VERMES.

Agrober: 1502 Budapest, POB 94; tel. 260-640; telex 22-5868; consulting engineers and contractors for the agriculture and food industry.

Agrotek: 1388 Budapest, POB 66; tel. 530-555; telex 22-5651; import of agricultural machinery, including machinery for livestock breeding, and forestry equipment.

Artex: 1390 Budapest, POB 167; tel. 530-222; telex 22-4951; f. 1949; furniture, carpets, porcelain, ceramics, gold and silver ware, applied arts, household and sports goods.

BHG: 1509 Budapest, POB 2; tel. 453-300; telex 22-5933; telecommunications.

Bivimpex: 1325 Budapest, POB 55; tel. 690-614; telex 22-4279; f. 1971; raw hide and leather; Dir JÓZSEF KEZTYŰS.

HUNGARY

Bőrker: 1391 Budapest, POB 215; tel. 210-760; telex 22-5543; trading company for basic materials and accessories for shoes, fancy leather goods, garments and furniture.

BRG: 1300 Budapest, POB 43; tel. 682-080; telex 22-5928; radio engineering.

Budaprint: 1036 Budapest, POB 111; tel. 889-780; telex 22-4576; textile printing.

Budavox: 1392 Budapest, POB 267; tel. 868-988; telex 22-5077; f. 1956; exports telecommunications equipment and systems; Gen. Man. LÁSZLÓ NYIREDY.

Chemokomplex: 1389 Budapest, POB 141; tel. 329-980; telex 22-5158; machines and equipment for the chemical industry; Man. Dir ISTVÁN KOVÁCS.

Chemolimpex: 1805 Budapest, POB 121; tel. 183-970; telex 22-4351; chemicals, agrochemicals, plastics, paints; Gen. Man. Dr PÉTER DOBROVITS.

Chinoin: 1325 Budapest, POB 110; tel. 690-900; telex 22-4236; pharmaceutical and chemical works.

Compack: 1441 Budapest, POB 42; tel. 211-520; telex 22-4846; trading and packing company.

Datorg Foreign Trade Data Processing and Organizing Co Ltd: 1396 Budapest, POB 479; tel. 184-055; telex 22-5191.

Délker: 1051 Budapest, POB 70; tel. 185-888; telex 22-4428; company for trading of tropical fruits, foodstuffs, cosmetics and household goods.

Elektroimpex: 1392 Budapest, POB 296; tel. 328-300; telex 22-5771; telecommunication and precision articles.

Elektromodul: 1390 Budapest, POB 158; tel. 495-940; telex 22-5154; electro-technical components; Gen. Man. GÁBOR IKLODY.

ERBE: 1361 Budapest, POB 17; tel. 116-460; telex 22-5442; power plant investment company.

Factory and Machinery Erecting Enterprise: 1394 Budapest, POB 384; tel. 327-360; telex 4783.

Fékon: 1475 Budapest, POB 67; tel. 572-447; telex 22-5527; clothing company.

Ferunion: 1829 Budapest, POB 612; tel. 172-611; telex 22-5054; tools, glassware, building materials, hardware.

FMV: 1475 Budapest, POB 215; tel. 640-200; telex 22-4409; precision mechanics.

Folkart: 1364 Budapest, Régiposta u. 12, POB 20; tel. 184-844; telex 22-6814; f. 1983; foreign trade office of the Cooperative Enterprise for Folk Art and Handicraft; Dir Dr JUDITH LENDVAI.

Foreign Trade Company for Industrial Co-operation: 1367 Budapest, POB 111; tel. 424-950; telex 22-4435; foreign trade office for co-operation and purchasing of licences in industry.

Gábor Áron Works: 1440 Budapest, POB 39; tel. 335-986; telex 22-4127; engineering works.

Gamma Művek: 1519 Budapest, POB 330; tel. 850-800; telex 22-4946; f. 1920; medical instruments, deep-bore logging and process control systems, elements for the instrumentation industry; Gen. Dir JÁNOS HENZ.

Ganz Danubius Shipyard and Crane Factory: Budapest XIII, Váci u. 202; tel. 496-370; telex 22-5047; f. 1835.

Ganz Electric Works: 1525 Budapest, POB 63; tel. 753-322; telex 22-5363; f. 1878; electric power generators, transformers, switchgear, electrical vehicles.

Ganz-MÁVAG: 1967 Budapest, POB 136; tel. 335-950; telex 22-5575; f. 1844; railway rolling stock, hydraulic equipment, lifts, compressors, diesel engines, steel structures; to be dissolved into six independent factories under enterprise council management in 1988; railway vehicle factory to remain under state supervision; Gen. Man. Dr ADÁM JUHÁSZ.

Ganz Measuring Instrument Works: 1701 Budapest, POB 58; tel. 271-025; telex 22-4395; all types of electrical measuring instrument.

Generalimpex: 1518 Budapest, POB 168; tel. 260-200; telex 22-6758; f. 1980; permitted to import or export any product; Dir LÁSZLÓ NAGY.

Geominco: 1525 Budapest, POB 92; tel. 354-580; telex 22-4442; geological and mining engineering; undertakes exploration and research.

Hungagent Ltd: 1374 Budapest, POB 542; tel. 886-180; telex 22-4526; foreign representations agency; export-import co-operation.

Hungarian Aluminium Corporation (HUNGALU): 1387 Budapest, POB 30; tel. 494-750; telex 22-5471; Gen. Man. Dr LAJOS DÓZSA.

Hungarian Deepfreezing Industry: 1364 Budapest, POB 12; tel. 183-900; telex 22-4579.

Hungarocoop: 1370 Budapest, POB 334; tel. 531-711; telex 22-4859; Hungarian Co-operative Foreign Trading Company; import and export of consumer goods.

Hungarofilm: 1363 Budapest, POB 39; tel. 116-650; telex 22-5768; f. 1956; films; Sales Man. ISTVÁN VÁRADI.

Hungarofruct: 1394 Budapest, POB 386; tel. 317-120; telex 22-5351; f. 1953; fresh, preserved and dehydrated fruit and vegetables.

Hungarotex: 1804 Budapest, POB 100; tel. 174-555; telex 22-4751; f. 1953; textiles and garments; Gen. Dir ÉVA SZABÓ.

Hungexpo (Hungarian Foreign Trade Company for Fairs and Publicity): 1441 Budapest, POB 44; tel. 225-008; telex 22-4525; advertising, publicity, public relations; printing; fairs, exhibitions.

IDEX: 1011 Budapest, Fő u. 14–18, POB 24; tel. 150-090; telex 22-4541; complete factory equipment.

Ikarus: 1630 Budapest, POB 3; tel. 636-440; telex 22-4766; construction and export of buses in complete state or in sets for assembly; Man. Dir ANDRÁS SEMSEY.

Industria Ltd: 1117 Budapest, POB 272; commercial representation of foreign firms, technical consulting service, market research etc.

Interag Co Ltd: 1390 Budapest, Rajk László u. 11, POB 184; tel. 326-770; telex 22-4776; represents foreign firms; conducts general export/import business, after-sale service, domestic trade; operates filling and service stations.

Intercooperation Co Ltd: 1253 Budapest, POB 53; tel. 152-220; telex 22-4242; establishment and carrying out of co-operation agreements, joint ventures and import and export deals.

IPV (Publishing and Promotion Co for Tourism): 1140 Budapest, POB 164; tel. 633-652; telex 22-6074; publishing, publicity, film-making, exhibitions, advertising; Gen. Man JÓZSEF TESZÁR.

KGyV Metallurgical Engineering Corpn: 1553 Budapest, POB 23; tel. 112-274; telex 22-5920; metallurgical engineering.

Komplex: 1807 Budapest, POB 125; tel. 117-010; telex 22-5957; f. 1953; agricultural machinery, plant and equipment for food industry; Man. Dir ADOLF FÉDERER.

Konsumex: 1441 Budapest, POB 58; tel. 530-511; telex 22-5151; consumer goods, household articles, etc.

Kultura: 1389 Budapest, POB 149; tel. 359-370; telex 22-4441; f. 1950; books, periodicals, posters, calendars, video cassettes, postcards, slides, works of art, sheet music, teaching aids; Gen. Man. JÓZSEF SZABÓ.

Labor MIM: 1450 Budapest, POB 73; tel. 339-708; telex 22-4162; f. 1899; scientific instruments, laboratory equipment and engineering; Gen. Man. M. MÓDI.

Lampart: 1475 Budapest, POB 41; tel. 570-111; telex 22-5365; f. 1883; glass-lined processing equipment.

Lehelex: 5101 Jászberény, POB 64; tel. 12611; telex 02-3341; export of domestic refrigerators.

Licencia: 1368 Budapest, POB 207; tel. 181-111; telex 22-5872; f. 1950; purchase and sale of patents and inventions; Gen. Dir Dr LAJOS VÉKONY; Dir FERENC GEBAUER.

Lignimpex: 1393 Budapest, POB 323; tel. 129-850; telex 22-4251; timber, paper and fuel.

Magnesite Industry: 1475 Budapest, POB 11; tel. 571-378; telex 22-5644; f. 1892; refractory products; Dir B. HAZAI.

Magyar Media Advertising Agency: 1392 Budapest 62, POB 279; tel. 325-176; telex 22-3040.

MAHIR Hungarian Publicity Company: 1818 Budapest, POB 367; tel. 183-444; telex 22-5341; advertising agency.

Masped: 1364 Budapest, Kristóf tér 2, POB 104; tel. 182-922; telex 22-4471; international forwarding and carriage; Gen. Man. KALMAN GELENCSÉR.

Medicor: 1389 Budapest, POB 150; tel. 495-130; telex 22-5051; medical instruments, X-ray apparatus and complete hospital installations; Pres. Dr ISTVÁN MARTOS.

Medimpex: 1808 Budapest; tel. 183-955; telex 22-5477; export and import of pharmaceutical and biological products, veterinary drugs, laboratory chemicals.

Mert: 1397 Budapest, POB 542; tel. 325-300; telex 22-5777; f. 1951; quality control of import and export goods.

Metalimpex: 1393 Budapest, POB 330; tel. 187-611; telex 22-5251; metals and metal products.

Metrimpex: 1391 Budapest, POB 202; tel. 125-600; telex 22-5451; electronic measuring instruments and equipment.

Mineralimpex: 1389 Budapest, POB 130; tel. 116-470; telex 22-4651; oils and mining products; Dir-Gen. Dr JÓZSEF TÓTH.

Modex: 1366 Budapest, POB 53; tel. 383-133; telex 22-7525; ready-made clothing.

Mogürt: 1391 Budapest, POB 249; tel. 184-133; telex 22-5357; f. 1949; motor vehicles; Gen. Man. LÁSZLÓ PÁL TÓTH.

MOM: 1525 Budapest, POB 52; tel. 564-122; telex 22-4151; f. 1876; laboratory and optical instruments.

HUNGARY

Monimpex: 1392 Budapest, POB 268; tel. 531-222; telex 22-5371; wines, spirits, paprika, honey, sweets, ornamental plants.

MVMT: 1251 Budapest, POB 34; tel. 152-600; telex 22-4382; electricity.

Nádex: 1525 Budapest, POB 14; tel. 350-365; telex 22-6767; reed farming.

Nikex: 1016 Budapest, Mészáros u. 48–54; tel. 560-122; telex 22-6406; heavy industry.

Novex: 1364 Budapest, POB 62; tel. 184-022; telex 22-6054; deals with transfer of technology to and from Hungary; Man. Dir JUDITH SALUSINSZKY.

Ofotért: 1917 Budapest; tel. 203-669; telex 22-4418; f. 1949; optical and photographic articles; Gen. Dir JANOS SZILÁGYI.

OMIKK Technoinform: 1428 Budapest, POB 12; tel. 138-247; telex 22-4944; technical and economic information services including translations, studies, conferences, periodicals and documentation, software programmes.

OMKER: 1367 Budapest, POB 91; tel. 123-000; telex 22-4683; f. 1950; medical instruments; Gen. Dir RÓBERT ZENTAI.

ORION: 1475 Budapest, POB 84; tel. 284-830; telex 22-5798; radios, televisions and electrical goods.

Pannonia (Foreign Trade Company of Cespel Works): 1394 Budapest, POB 354; tel. 212-450; telex 22-5128; metallurgical materials, welding electrodes, cast iron fittings, steel tubes and cylinders, bicycles, industrial sewing and pressing machinery and laundry equipment, complete tube manufacturing plants, bottle plants, etc.

Patentbureau Danubia: 1368 Budapest, POB 198; tel. 181-111; telex 22-5872; f. 1951; patent services; Dir Dr L. VÉKONY.

Pharmatrade: 1367 Budapest, POB 126; tel. 185-966; telex 22-6650; medicinal plants, cosmetics, medicinal muds and waters, food and feed additives, radioactive products.

Philatelia Hungarica: 1373 Budapest, POB 600; tel. 316-146; telex 22-6508; stamps; wholesale only.

Phylaxia: 1486 Budapest, POB 23; tel. 575-311; telex 22-4549; vaccines, veterinary products.

Precision Fittings Factory: 3301 Eger, POB 2; tel. 11-911; telex 63-331.

Prodinform: 1372 Budapest, POB 453; tel. 323-770; telex 22-7750; technical and scientific information, technical consultations.

RÁBA (Hungarian Railway Carriage and Machine Works): 9002 Györ, POB 50; tel. 12-111; telex 02-4255; f. 1896; commercial vehicles, diesel engines, agricultural tractors; Gen. Man. EDE HORVÁTH.

Rekard: 9027 Györ, Kandó Kálmán u. 5–7; tel. (96) 13-122; telex 24-360; farm equipment.

Skála-Coop: 1450 Budapest, POB 60; tel. 336-770; telex 22-5135; national co-operative company for purchase and disposal of goods including fine ceramics and glassware, industrial, agricultural and household metal ware, hand tools, electronic games, rubber and plastic products, cosmetics and chemicals, wood and paper industry products, leather and textile industry products, ready-to-wear clothing, vegetables and other foodstuffs; Gen. Man. ISTVÁN IMRE.

Tannimpex: 1395 Budapest, POB 406; tel. 123-400; telex 22-4557; hides, leather shoes, gloves, fancy goods and furs.

Tatabánya Mining Co: 2803 Tatabánya, POB 323; tel. (34) 10-144; telex 22-6206; f. 1894; production of mining equipment and machinery, preparation of industrial and drinking water, purification of waste waters, dewatering of sludges, tunnelling; Gen. Man. LÁSZLÓ VAS.

Taurus Rubber Works: 1440 Budapest, POB 25; tel. 341-140; telex 22-5312; f. 1882; rubber; Chief Exec. Dr ILONA TATAI.

Technoimpex: 1390 Budapest, POB 183; tel. 184-055; telex 22-4171; exports machine tools, specialized machinery, equipment for the oil and gas industry, agricultural equipment; imports machine tools, machines for light industry; organizes barter deals, co-operation, leasing and joint ventures; Gen. Man. ISTVÁN MÁTYÁS.

Temaforg: 1361 Budapest, POB 8; tel. 118-450; telex 22-4663; textile and synthetic wastes, industrial wipers, geotextiles for agriculture, road and railway construction.

Terimpex: 1825 Budapest, POB 251; tel. 175-011; telex 22-4551; cattle and agricultural products; Gen. Man. Dr LÁSZLÓ RÁNKY.

TERTA: 1956 Budapest, POB 16; tel. 634-240; telex 22-4087; telecommunications and data transmission equipment.

Tesco: 1367 Budapest, POB 101; tel. 110-850; telex 22-4642; f. 1962; organization for international technical and scientific co-operation; export and import of technical services world-wide; Gen. Man. IMRE SZEKACS.

Transelektro: 1394 Budapest, POB 377; tel. 320-100; telex 22-4571; generators, power stations, cables, lighting, transformers, household appliances, catering equipment, etc.; Dir-Gen. PÁL KERTÉSZ.

TSZKER (Trading Company for Agricultural Cooperatives): 1445 Budapest, POB 354; tel. 340-900; telex 22-4147; industrial metal constructions, red and white wines, wooden products and toys, charcoal, fancy goods, canned fruits and vegetables, dried and fresh fruits, poppy seeds, walnuts and other nuts, ornamental shrubs, seedlings and stock.

TUNGSRAM Co Ltd: 1340 Budapest, Újpest 4; tel. 692-800; telex 22-5058; f. 1896; light sources, lighting systems, vacuum engineering machinery, vacuum electronics, electronics and components, etc.; Gen. Man. ANDRÁS GÁBOR.

Vegyépszer: 1379 Budapest, POB 540; tel. 666-497; telex 22-6017; building and assembling of chemical plant, supply of complete equipment.

VEPEX Contractor Ltd: 1370 Budapest, POB 308; tel. 425-534; telex 22-4208; vegetable protein extract.

Videoton Rt: 1398 Budapest, POB 557; tel. 210-520; telex 22-4763; TV sets, tape recorders, computer systems and peripherals, software; Man. Dir ISTVÁN PAPP; Gen. Man. JÁNOS KAZSMER.

Volánpack: 1475 Budapest, POB 76; tel. 484-300; telex 22-6935; forwarding and transport, packaging, warehousing, etc.; Gen. Dir MIKLÓS VAJDA.

Vörös Október MGTSZ, Ócsa: 1734 Budapest, POB 26; tel. 473-759; telex 22-6156; agricultural co-operative.

TRADE FAIRS

Budapest International Fairs: Hungexpo, 1441 Budapest, POB 44; tel. 573-555; telex 22-4188; f. 1968; technical goods (spring), consumer goods (autumn), and other specialized exhibitions and fairs; Dir FERENC SCHRIFFERT.

CO-OPERATIVE ORGANIZATIONS

Fogyasztási Szövetkezetek Országos Tanácsa (SZÖVOSZ) (National Council of Consumer Co-operatives): 1054 Budapest, Szabadság tér 14; tel. 534-222; telex 22-4862; safeguards interests of Hungarian consumer, housing and saving co-operative societies, co-owner of co-op foreign trading companies and joint ventures; Pres. JÓZSEF HARTMANN; Gen. Sec. Dr ISTVÁN SZLAMENICKY; 3.5m. mems.

Ipari Szövetkezetek Országos Tanácsa (OKISZ) (National Council of Industrial Co-operatives): 1146 Budapest, Thököly u. 58–60; tel. 415-140; telex 22-7576; Pres. LAJOS KÖVESKUTI.

Országos Szövetkezeti Tanács (OSzT) (National Co-operative Council): 1373 Budapest, Szabadság tér 14; tel. 127-467; telex 22-4862; Pres. JÓZSEF HARTMANN; Sec. Dr JÓZSEF PÁL.

Termelöszövetkezetek Országos Tanácsa (TOT) (National Council of Agricultural Co-operatives): 1054 Budapest, Akadémia u. 1–3; tel. 328-167; telex 22-6810; f. 1967; Pres. ISTVÁN SZABÓ; Gen. Sec. Dr JÁNOS ELEKI; 1,280 co-operatives with 816,000 mems.

TRADE UNIONS

Magyar Szakszervezetek Országos Tanácsa (SZOT) (Central Council of Hungarian Trade Unions): 1415 Budapest, Dózsa György u. 84B; tel. 532-900; telex 22-5861; f. 1898; Pres. (vacant); Gen. Sec. Dr SÁNDOR NAGY; 4,000,000 mems.

Affiliated Unions

Magyar Bányaipari Dolgozók Szakszervezete (Hungarian Union of Mineworkers): 1068 Budapest, Gorkij fasor 46–48; tel. 221-226; telex 22-7499; f. 1913; Pres. ISTVÁN HAVRÁN; Gen. Sec. LÁSZLÓ KOVÁKS; 167,716 mems.

Magyar Böripari Dolgozók Szakszervezete (Hungarian Union of Leather Industry Workers): 1062 Budapest, Bajza u. 24; tel. 429-970; f. 1868; Pres. LÁSZLÓ TURZO; Gen. Sec. TIBOR TRÉBER; 48,518 mems.

Magyar Egészégügyi Dolgozók Szakszervezete (Hungarian Union of Health Service Workers): 1363 Budapest, Münnich F. u. 32; tel. 327-530; f. 1945; Pres. Dr ZOLTÁN SZABÓ; Gen. Sec. Dr ISTVÁN FÜZI; 280,536 mems.

Magyar Élelmezésipari Dolgozók Szakszervezete (Hungarian Union of Food Industry Workers): 1068 Budapest, Gorkij fasor 44; tel. 225-880; f. 1905; Pres. ANDRAS GYENES; Gen. Sec. ERZSEBET BALOGH; 226,243 mems.

Magyar Épitö-, Fa- és Épitöanyagipari Dolgozók Szakszervezete (Hungarian Union of Building, Wood and Building Industry Workers): 1068 Budapest, Dózsa György u. 84A; tel. 425-760; f. 1906; Pres. ROZALIA SOMOGYI; Gen. Sec. GYULA SOMOGYI; 365,561 mems.

Magyar Helyiipari és Városgazdasági Dolgozók Szakszervezete (Hungarian Union of Local Industry and Municipal Workers): 1391

HUNGARY

Directory

Budapest, Benczur u. 43; tel. 116-950; f. 1952; Pres. ZOLTAN FABOK; Gen. Sec. Dr FERENC SALI; 281,073 mems.

Magyar Kereskedelmi, Pénzügyi és Vendéglátóipari Dolgozók Szakszervezete (Hungarian Union of Commercial, Financial and Catering Industry Workers): 1066 Budapest, Jókai u. 6; tel. 318-970; f. 1948; Gen. Sec. JÁNOS VAS; 535,834 mems.

Magyar Közalkalmazottak Szakszervezete (Hungarian Union of Public Employees): 1088 Budapest, Puskin u. 4; tel. 188-900; f. 1945; Pres. BUDA GÁBOR; Gen. Sec. Dr ENDRE SZABÓ; 256,910 mems.

Magyar Közlekedési és Szállítási Dolgozók Szakszervezete (Hungarian Union of Transport Workers): 1081 Budapest, Köztársaság tér 3; tel. 138-468; f. 1898; Gen. Sec. GYULA MOLDOVAN; 190,464 mems.

Magyar Mezőgazdasági, Erdészeti és Vizügyi Dolgozók Szakszervezete (MEDOSZ) (Hungarian Union of Agricultural, Forestry and Water Conservancy Workers): 1066 Budapest, Jókai u. 2-4; tel. 314-550; telex 22-7535; f. 1906; Pres. (vacant); Gen. Sec. Dr FERENC DOBI; 389,569 mems.

Magyar Művészeti Szakszervezetek Szövetsége (Association of Hungarian Artists' Unions): 1068 Budapest, Gorkij fasor 38; tel. 211-120; f. 1957; Pres. IMRE VASS; Gen. Sec. TIBOR SIMÓ; 42,292 mems.

Magyar Nyomda-, a Papiripar, a Sajto és a Könyvkiadás Dolgozóinak Szakszervezete (Hungarian Printing, Paper, Press and Publishing Workers' Union): 1085 Budapest, Kölcsey u. 2; tel. 142-413; f. 1862; Pres. MÁRTON BUZA; Gen. Sec. LAJOS NAGY; 49,436 mems.

Magyar Pedagógusok Szakszervezete (Hungarian Union of Teachers): 1068 Budapest, Gorkij fasor 10; tel. 228-456; f. 1945; Pres. Dr LÁSZLÓ SZÜCS; Gen. Sec. Dr JÓZSEF VOKSÁN; 299,867 mems.

Magyar Postások Szakszervezete (Hungarian Union of Postal Workers): 1146 Budapest, Cházár András u. 13; tel. 428-777; f. 1945; Pres. GÉZÁNÉ BENKE; Gen. Sec. GRICSER ENIKŐ HENSZKY; 88,651 mems.

Magyar Ruházatipari Dolgozók Szakszervezete (Hungarian Union of Clothing Workers): 1077 Budapest, Almássy tér 1; tel. 229-843; f. 1892; Pres. JULIANNA TÓTH; Gen. Sec. Dr MARGIT CZERVÁN; 37,117 mems.

Magyar Textilipari Dolgozók Szakszervezete (Hungarian Union of Textile Workers): 1068 Budapest, Rippl-Rónai u. 2; tel. 123-868; f. 1905; Pres. JÓZSEF APRÓ; Gen. Sec. Dr IREN MARTOS; 135,871 mems.

Magyar Vas- Fém- és Villamosenergiaipari Dolgozók Szakszervezete (Hungarian Union of Iron, Metal and Electricity Workers): 1086 Budapest, Koltói Anna u. 5-7; tel. 135-200; telex 22-4791; f. 1877; Pres. AMBRUS BOROVSZKY; Gen. Sec. LÁSZLÓ PASZTERNÁK; 625,118 mems.

Magyar Vasutasok Szakszervezete (Hungarian Union of Railway Workers): 1068 Budapest, Benczúr u. 41; tel. 221-895; telex 22-6819; f. 1945; Pres. JENŐ GYÓCSI; Gen. Sec. FERENC KOSZORUS; 196,698 mems.

Magyar Vegyipari Dolgozók Szakszervezete (Hungarian Union of Chemical Industry Workers): 1068 Budapest, Benczúr u. 45; tel. 421-778; telex 22-3420; f. 1897; Pres. FERENC DAJKA; Gen. Sec. LAJOS FŐCZE; 158,578 mems.

Tudományos Dolgozók Demokratikus Szakszervezete Szövetsége (TDDSZ) (Democratic Trade Union of Scientific Workers): Budapest; f. 1988; Chair. PÁL FORGACS.

Transport

Raabersped: 1531 Budapest, POB 33; tel. 751-322; telex 22-5919; international forwarding agency (rail, road, air and sea); Dir Dr JÁNOS BERÉNYI.

Other forwarding agencies are Masped and Volánpack (see under Foreign Trade Organizations).

RAILWAYS

Magyar Államvasutak (MÁV) (Hungarian State Railways): 1940 Budapest, Népköztarsaság u. 73-75; tel. 220-660; telex 22-4342; state-owned since 1868; total network 8,500 km, including 1,920 km of electrified lines; in the 1986-90 period 354 km of lines were to be electrified; Dir-Gen. GYÖRGY ONOZO.

Győr–sopron–ebenfurti vasut—Gysev-ROeEE (Railway of Győr–Sopron–Ebenfurt): 1536 Budapest, Szilágyi Dezső tér 1, POB 241; tel. 159-420; telex 22-4249; Hungarian-Austrian-owned railway; 137 km in Hungary, 63 km in Austria, all electrified; transport of passengers and goods; Dir-Gen. LÁSZLÓ OROSZVÁRY.

There is an underground railway in Budapest, with a network of 28 km in 1987; in that year 354m. passengers were carried.

ROADS

In January 1987 the road network totalled 90,696 km, including 324 km of motorways, 6,385 km of main or national roads and 22,987 km of secondary roads. Construction of the Budapest ring motorway began in 1987, with financial assistance from the World Bank, and is scheduled for completion in 1990. There are extensive long-distance bus services. Road passenger and freight transport is provided by the state-owned VOLÁN companies and by individual (own account) operators.

Hungarocamion: 1442 Budapest, POB 108; tel. 573-811; telex 22-5455; international road freight transport company; 18 offices in Europe and the Middle East; fleet of 1,800 lorries; Gen. Man. IMRE TORMA.

Volán Vállalatok Központja (Centre of Volán Enterprises): 1391 Budapest, Lenin krt 96, POB 221; tel. 124-290; telex 22-5177; centre of 25 Volán enterprises for inland and international road freight and passenger transport, forwarding, tourism; fleet of 17,000 lorries, incl. special tankers for fuel, refrigerators, trailers, 8,000 buses for regular passenger transport; 3 affiliates, offices and joint-ventures in Europe; Head KÁLMÁN GARAMI.

SHIPPING AND INLAND WATERWAYS

In 1987 the Hungarian merchant fleet comprised 15 vessels totalling 106,710 dwt.

MAHART—Magyar Hajózási Rt. (Hungarian Shipping Co): 1366 Budapest, POB 58; tel. 181-880; telex 22-5258; carries passenger traffic on the Danube and Lake Balaton; cargo services on the Danube and its tributaries, Lake Balaton, and also Mediterranean and ocean-going services; operates port of Budapest (container terminal, loading, storage, warehousing, handling and packaging services); ship-building and ship-repair services; Dir-Gen. PÉTER MURADIN.

MAFRACHT: 1364 Budapest, Kristóf tér 2, POB 105; tel. 185-276; telex 22-4471; shipping agency.

CIVIL AVIATION

The Ferihegy international airport is 16 km from the centre of Budapest. An expansion and development programme began in 1977, and the reconstruction work on the runway was completed in 1987. Ferihegy-2 opened in 1985. There are no public internal air services.

Légügyi Főigazgatóság (General Directorate of Civil Aviation): 1400 Budapest, Dob u. 75-81, POB 87; tel. 422-544; telex 22-5729; controls civil aviation; Dir-Gen. ENDRE FARKAS.

Légiforgalmi és Repülőtéri Igazgatóság—LRI (Air Traffic and Airport Administration): 1675 Budapest, POB 53; tel. 579-123; telex 22-4054; controls civil air traffic and operates Ferihegy Airport; Dir-Gen. TAMÁS ERDEI.

Magyar Légiközlekedési Vállalat—MALÉV (Hungarian Airlines): 1367 Budapest, Roosevelt tér 2, POB 122; tel. 189-033; telex 22-4954; f. 1946; regular services from Budapest to Europe, North Africa and the Middle East; Gen. Dir LAJOS JAHODA; fleet of 6 TU-134 and 14 TU-154; 3 Boeing 737-200 on lease.

Tourism

Tourism has developed rapidly and is an important source of foreign exchange. In 1988 convertible-currency income from tourism totalled US $668m., 20% more than in 1987. Rouble receipts in 1988 reached 388m., 12% less than in 1987. Lake Balaton is the main holiday centre for boating, bathing and fishing. The cities have great historical and recreational attractions. The annual Budapest Spring Festival is held in March. Budapest has numerous swimming pools watered by thermal springs, which are equipped with modern physiotherapy facilities. The first Budapest Grand Prix, the only Formula-1 motor race to be held in Eastern Europe, took place in August 1986. In 1988 there were almost 18m. foreign visitors (including visitors in transit), 5.2% less than in the previous year. There were 47,317 hotel beds in 1986, and a further 8,000–10,000 were to be created by 1994.

Országos Idegenforgalmi Hivatal—OIH (Hungarian Tourist Board): 1051 Budapest, Dorottya u. 4; tel. 186-354; telex 22-5182; f. 1968; Head Dr JÓZSEF CZEGLÉDI.

Budapest Tourist—Budapesti Idegenforgalmi Vállalat (Budapest Travel Company): 1051 Budapest, Roosevelt tér 5-7; tel. 186-663; telex 22-6448; f. 1972; runs tours, congresses and cultural programmes; provides accommodation; Dir ISTVÁN KOVÁCS.

COOPTOURIST—Co-operative Travel Agency: 1016 Budapest, Derék u. 2; tel. 568-122; telex 22-5399; general tourism services for groups and individuals; branch offices throughout Hungary; Gen. Dir Dr SÁNDOR SIPOS.

HUNGARY

DANUBIUS—Danubius Travels: 1138 Budapest, Margitsziget; tel. 111-000; telex 22-6850; Dir Dr IMRE GELLAI.

Express Ifjúsági és Diák Utazási Iroda (Express Youth and Student Travel Bureau): 1054 Budapest, Szabadság tér 16; tel. 530-660; telex 22-5384; f. 1957; specializes in tours and services for young people; Gen. Man. Dr GYULA TARCSI.

HungarHotels—Hungarian Hotel and Restaurant Company: 1052 Budapest, Petőfi Sándor u. 14, POB 106; tel. 182-033; telex 22-4209; f. 1956; Pres. Dr GYULA GYÖKÖSSY.

IBUSZ—Idegenforgalmi, Beszerzési, Utazási és Szállitási Rt. (Hungarian Travel Agency): 1364 Budapest, Felszabadulás tér 5; tel. 186-866; telex 22-4976; f. 1902; 24-hour service for individual travellers at: 1052 Budapest, Petőfi tér 3; tel. 185-707; telex 22-4941; IBUSZ has 118 brs throughout Hungary; Gen. Man. ERIKA SZEMENKÁR.

Locomotiv Tourist: 1536 Budapest, Szilágyi Dezső tér 1, POB 241; tel. 159-420; telex 22-4249; Dir Dr ADÁM MENYHÁRT.

Malév Air-Tours: 1367 Budapest, Roosevelt tér 2, POB 122; tel. 184-212; telex 22-4954; Dir TAMÁS DÉRI.

Máv Tours (Travel Bureau of Hungarian State Railways): 1378 Budapest, Guszev u. 1, POB 25; tel. 173-723; telex 22-3251; Dir THOMAS LENGYEL.

Pannónia—Hotel and Catering Company: 1088 Budapest, Puskin u. 6, POB 159; tel. 382-187; telex 22-4561; f. 1949; owns 45 hotels; organizes through its Tourist Service Bureau tours, programmes, conferences etc. in Hungary, and Hungarian gastronomic festivals abroad; Gen. Man. JENŐ SOMOGYI.

Pegazus Tours: 1053 Budapest, Károlyi Mihály u. 5; Dir MAUSZ GOTTHARD.

Volántourist Vállalat: 1051 Budapest, Oktober 6 u. 11/13; tel. 123-410; telex 22-6181; f. 1971; Dir LAJOS CSETE.

Atomic Energy

Hungary's first nuclear power station at Paks (on the Danube, south of Budapest), built with Soviet assistance, began trial operations in December 1982, and was formally inaugurated in November 1983. Four units, each of 440 MW, were in operation by 1987. In 1988 a record output of 13,420m. kWh was achieved. Two 1,000-MW blocks are planned on the same site, and construction is scheduled to begin in 1989. Hungary has signed agreements for co-operation in the peaceful uses of atomic energy with Bulgaria, Cuba, Czechoslovakia, France, the German Democratic Republic, India, Italy, Romania and the USSR. Hungary is a member of the International Atomic Energy Agency (based in Vienna), the Joint Institute for Nuclear Research (at Dubna, near Moscow) and the CMEA Standing Committee on the Peaceful Uses of Atomic Energy.

Országos Atomenergia Bizottság (National Atomic Energy Commission): 1374 Budapest, POB 565; tel. 327-172; telex 22-4907; f. 1956; Pres. PÁL TÉTÉNYI.

Budapesti Műszaki Egyetem Nukleáris Technikai Intézet (Institute of Nuclear Technics of the Technical University of Budapest, Training Reactor): 1521 Budapest, POB 91; tel. 812-564; telex 22-5931; f. 1971; Dir Prof. Dr GY. CSOM.

Kossuth Lajos Tudományegyetem Kisérleti Fizikai Intézete (Institute for Experimental Physics of the Kossuth Lajos University): 4001 Debrecen, POB 105; tel. 15-222; telex 72-200; f. 1923; research in low-energy nuclear physics, neutron physics, and application of atomic and nuclear methods; Dir Prof. Dr J. CSIKAI.

Magyar Tudományos Akadémia Atommag Kutató Intézete—ATOMKI (Institute of Nuclear Research of the Hungarian Academy of Sciences): 4026 Debrecen, Bem tér 18/C; tel. 17-266; telex 72-210; f. 1954; research in nuclear structure, reaction, ion-atom collisions, etc.; Dir Prof. Dr D. BERÉNYI.

Magyar Tudományos Akadémia Izotópkutató Intézete (Institute of Isotopes of the Hungarian Academy of Sciences): 1525 Budapest, POB 77, Konkoly Thege u. 29–33; tel. 696-687; telex 22-5360; f. 1959; Dir Dr G. FÖLDIÁK.

Magyar Tudományos Akadémia Központi Fizikai Kutató Intézete—KFKI (Central Research Institute for Physics of the Hungarian Academy of Sciences): 1525 Budapest, POB 49; tel. 698-566; telex 22-4722; f. 1950; 7 organizational units, incl. research in practical and nuclear physics; Dir-Gen. Dr FERENC SZABÓ.

Országos 'Frédéric Joliot-Curie' Sugárbiológiai és Sugáregészségügyi Kutató Intézet (National Research Institute for Radiobiology and Radiohygiene): 1775 Budapest, POB 101; f. 1957; tel. 730-026; telex 22-5103; research on effects of ionizing and non-ionizing radiations; Dir Dr L. B. SZTANYIK.

Paksi Atomerőmű Vállalat—PAV (Paks Nuclear Power Plant): Paks, POB 71; tel. (75) 11-222; telex 14-440; f. 1976; foreign trade org.; training of nuclear power plant specialists, licences and auxiliary equipment for nuclear power plants; exports spent nuclear fuel; imports fresh nuclear fuel, nuclear power plant mountings; Dir JÓZSEF PÓNYA.

Villamosenergiaipari Kutató Intézet—VEIKI (Institute for Electric Power Research) 1368 Budapest, POB 233; tel. 183-233; telex 22-5744; f. 1949; research on technology, safety, structure mechanics, control and instrumentation, water chemistry of nuclear power plants. Scientific divisions; Divisions of Nuclear and Heat Power Engineering, Systemtechnics, Chemical Engineering, Computer Engineering, Electrical Equipment and Combustion Engineering; Dir Dr GYÖRGY VAJDA.

ICELAND

Introductory Survey

Location, Climate, Language, Religion, Flag, Capital

The Republic of Iceland comprises one large island and numerous smaller ones, situated near the Arctic Circle in the North Atlantic Ocean. The main island lies about 300 km (190 miles) south-east of Greenland, about 1,000 km (620 miles) west of Norway and about 800 km (500 miles) north of Scotland. The Gulf Stream keeps Iceland warmer than might be expected, with average temperatures ranging from 10°C (50°F) in the summer to 1°C (34°F) in winter. Icelandic is the official language. Almost all of the inhabitants profess Christianity: the Evangelical Lutheran Church is the established church and embraces 93% of the population. The national flag (proportions 25 by 18) displays a red cross, bordered with white, on a blue background, the upright of the cross being to the left of centre. The capital is Reykjavík.

Recent History

Iceland became independent on 17 June 1944, when the Convention that linked it with Denmark, under the Danish throne, was terminated. Iceland became a founder-member of the Nordic Council (see p. 176) in 1952, and has belonged to both NATO (see p. 179) and the Council of Europe (see p. 128) since 1949.

From 1959 to 1971 Iceland was governed by a coalition of the Independence Party and the Social Democratic Party (SDP). In the general election of June 1971 there was a swing to the left, and Ólafur Jóhannesson, the leader of the Progressive Party, formed a coalition government with the People's Alliance and the Union of Liberals and Leftists. Elections held in June 1974 showed a swing back to the right, and in August the Independence and Progressive Parties formed a coalition led by Geir Hallgrímsson. Loss of popularity through its treatment of Iceland's economic problems, such as the perpetuation of rampant inflation by index-linked wage settlements, led to the Government's resignation in June 1978, following extensive election gains by the left-wing People's Alliance and SDP. Disagreements over economic measures, and over the People's Alliance's policy of withdrawal from NATO, led to two months of negotiations before a new government could be formed. In September 1978 Jóhannesson, the former Prime Minister, formed a coalition of his own Progressive Party with the People's Alliance and the SDP, but this Government, after addressing immediate economic necessities, resigned in October 1979, when the Social Democrats withdrew. An interim administration was formed by Benedikt Gröndal, the SDP leader. The results of a general election held in December were inconclusive, and in February 1980 Gunnar Thoroddsen of the Independence Party formed a coalition with the People's Alliance and the Progressive Party.

In June 1980 Vigdís Finnbogadóttir, a non-political candidate who was favoured by left-wing groups because of her opposition to the US military airbase in Iceland, achieved a narrow victory in the election for the mainly ceremonial office of President. She took office on 1 August 1980, becoming the world's first popularly-elected female Head of State, although her election had no direct effect on government policy. The coalition Government lost its majority in the Lower House of the Althingi in September 1982, and a general election was held in April 1983. The Independence Party received the largest share (38.7%) of the votes, but there was a swing away from traditional parties, with two new parties (the Social Democratic Alliance and the Women's Alliance) together winning nearly 13% of the votes. A centre-right coalition was formed between the Independence and Progressive Parties, with Steingrímur Hermannsson, the Progressive Party leader and former Minister of Fisheries and Communications, as Prime Minister, and Geir Hallgrímsson, Prime Minister from 1974 to 1978 and leader of the Independence Party, as Minister for Foreign Affairs. In an attempt to halt the sharp increase in the rate of inflation, the Government discontinued the indexation of wages to the rate of inflation, extended existing wage agreements and devalued the króna in May 1983. Although these measures reduced inflation in 1984, there was considerable industrial unrest, in that year and in 1985, as a result of which large increases in wages for public-sector employees and fishermen were secured. There was also a further devaluation of the króna. In June 1985, to forestall the threat of further strikes, private-sector employers secured a no-strike agreement with the Icelandic Federation of Labour. In February 1986 a further wage settlement was agreed by the Government, the trade unions and the employers, and in 1987 another agreement, which restricted wage increases to less than the rate of inflation, were negotiated, although several unions chose to negotiate separate agreements.

In March 1987 Albert Guðmundsson resigned as Minister of Energy and Industry and as a member of the Independence Party, following accusations of tax evasion. He subsequently formed the Citizens' Party. A general election for an enlarged, 63-seat Althingi was held in April. Both parties of the outgoing coalition suffered losses: the Independence Party's share of the seats was reduced from 24 to 18, and the Progressive Party lost one of its 14 seats. The newly-formed Citizens' Party won seven seats, while the Women's Alliance increased its number of seats from three to six. Ten seats were won by the SDP, which included former members of the Social Democratic Alliance, disbanded in 1986. Hermannsson tendered the resignation of his Government, but was requested to remain as leader of an interim administration until a new coalition was formed. Protracted negotiations took place, resulting in a coalition of the Independence, Progressive and Social Democratic Parties, formally constituted in July. Thorsteinn Pálsson, the leader of the Independence Party and the Minister of Finance in the outgoing Cabinet, was appointed Prime Minister.

In June 1988 President Finnbogadóttir (who had begun a second term in office in August 1984, no presidential election having been held, as her candidacy was unopposed) was elected for a third term. This was the first occasion on which an incumbent President seeking re-election had been challenged. Supported by all the main political parties, she received more than 90% of the votes and defeated her only rival, who had campaigned for a greater role for the Presidency.

In September 1988 the SDP and the Progressive Party withdrew from Prime Minister Pálsson's Government, following disagreements over economic policy. Later that month, the leader of the Progressives, Steingrímur Hermannsson (a former Prime Minister and the Minister for Foreign Affairs in the outgoing Government), became Prime Minister in a centre-left coalition with the SDP and the People's Alliance. The new Government immediately announced a 3% devaluation of the króna, and committed itself to the introduction of austerity measures, designed to lower inflation and to help the fishing industry.

The importance of fishing to Iceland's economy, and fears of excessive exploitation of the fishing grounds near Iceland by foreign fleets, caused the Icelandic Government to extend its territorial waters to 12 nautical miles (22 km) in 1964 and to 50 nautical miles (93 km) in September 1972. British opposition to these extensions resulted in two 'cod wars'. In October 1975 Iceland unilaterally introduced a fishing limit of 200 nautical miles (370 km), both as a conservation measure and to protect important Icelandic interests. The 1973 agreement on fishing limits between Iceland and the United Kingdom expired in November 1975, and failure to reach a new agreement led to the third and most serious 'cod war'. Casualties occurred, and in February 1976 Iceland temporarily severed diplomatic relations with Britain, the first diplomatic break between two NATO countries. In June 1976 the two countries reached an agreement, and in December the British trawler fleet withdrew from Icelandic waters. In June 1979 Iceland declared its exclusive rights to the 200-mile fishing zone.

In May 1985 the Althingi unanimously approved a resolution declaring the country a 'nuclear-free zone', i.e. banning the entry of nuclear weapons. Iceland was host to a US-Soviet 'summit' meeting in October 1986. The country's membership of NATO is widely supported, although the military air-base

ICELAND

at Keflavík is a cause of political controversy. In September 1988 the new Government declared that there would be no new military projects in Iceland.

Relations between Iceland and the USA were strained during July 1986, when the USA argued that, by approving the catch of 80 fin whales and 40 sei whales, Iceland was acting against a moratorium imposed by the International Whaling Commission (IWC), and the US Government threatened to impose a boycott on Icelandic fish products. Iceland declared that the catch of whales was for scientific purposes only and continued its programme, despite the sinking of two whaling ships in Reykjavík harbour by militant environmentalists. In 1987 Iceland reduced its catch by 20 sei whales, but threats of US sanctions resumed in August. The controversy raised doubts concerning the continuing use by US forces of the NATO base at Keflavík, and led to speculation that Iceland and Japan might withdraw from the IWC. Iceland reduced its catch quota for 1988. International pressure continued, and in 1988 the new centre-left Government of Hermansson considered the termination of whaling in the following year.

Government

According to the Constitution, executive power is vested in the President (elected for four years by universal adult suffrage) and the Cabinet, consisting of the Prime Minister and other Ministers appointed by the President. In practice, however, the President performs only nominally the functions ascribed in the Constitution to this office, and it is the Cabinet alone which holds real executive power. Legislative power is held jointly by the President and the Althingi (Parliament), with 63 members elected by universal suffrage for four years (subject to dissolution by the President), using a mixed system of proportional representation. The Althingi chooses 21 of its members to form the Upper House, the other 42 forming the Lower House. For some purposes the two Houses sit jointly as the United Althingi. Electoral reforms, introduced in 1987, included the lowering of the minimum voting age from 20 to 18 years. The Cabinet is responsible to the Althingi. Iceland has seven administrative districts.

Defence

Iceland has no defence forces of its own but is a member of NATO. There are units of US forces at Keflavík air base, which is used for observation of the North Atlantic Ocean, under an agreement made in 1951 between Iceland and NATO. The airfield at Keflavík is a base for the new US airborne early warning system. In June 1988 a total of 3,100 US military personnel (navy 1,800, air force 1,300) were stationed in Iceland. In July 1983 Iceland agreed to the construction of a military and civilian air-terminal at Keflavík, funded by the USA at a cost of US $120m.

Economic Affairs

Iceland's inhabitants enjoy a high standard of living. In 1987, according to estimates by the World Bank, the country's gross national product (GNP), measured at average 1985–87 prices, was US $4,083m., equivalent to US $16,670 per head, one of the highest national levels in Europe. Between 1980 and 1987, it was estimated, GNP per head, measured in constant prices, increased at an average rate of only 0.7% per year.

The economy is very dependent on fishing, which provided 76% of total visible export receipts in 1987. Iceland is, therefore, very susceptible to movements in world prices of fish products and to fluctuations in the size of its catches. The modernized trawler fleet supplies about 80 freezing plants, which produce white fish fillets, frozen prawns, scallops, Norway lobster (scampi) and capelin. Other fish products, such as oil, meal and salted fish, are major exports. During the 1970s, an increase in fisheries production was made possible by Iceland's exclusive rights over an extended fishing zone (see Recent History). Iceland's total annual catch rose from 680,700 metric tons in 1971 to 1,640,700 tons in 1979. The catch subsequently decreased, to 785,600 tons in 1982 (mainly because of a temporary ban on capelin fishing, to preserve stocks), before beginning to recover. However, 1985 was one of the best years in Icelandic fishing history, with a total catch of 1,672,300 tons (including 322,800 tons of cod, the most valuable part of the total, and 993,000 tons of capelin), an increase of nearly 10% over the 1984 total. In 1986 the total catch was 1,650,900 tons (including 365,900 tons of cod and 894,600 tons of capelin). All fishing was temporarily halted in January 1987, when 5,000 fishermen staged a 15-day strike, demanding a higher share of the catch. Despite an agreement by the fishermen to return to work, exports continued to be delayed by a walk-out of 250 seamen, which prevented cargo ships from leaving the country. The total catch in 1987 declined only slightly, however, to 1,624,800 tons (including 389,800 tons of cod and 803,500 tons of capelin). In the first nine months of 1988 the total catch increased by 9% compared with the corresponding period of the previous year. Higher prices were expected in 1989, after two years of reduced export earnings.

Less than 5% of Iceland is arable land, but good grazing keeps the country self-sufficient in meat and milk products. Production costs are high and exports have to be subsidized. In recent years the wool industry has developed rapidly, a total of 1,533 metric tons being produced in 1983, when exports of woollen products earned 653m. krónur. Export earnings totalled 1,099m. krónur in 1985, 1,005m. krónur in 1986 and 1,066m. krónur in 1987.

Iceland's only significant natural resource, apart from fish, is its potential for cheap hydroelectric and geothermal power production. Geothermal energy is used for home heating (for 80% of the population in 1986) and in the production of diatomite. It may be more fully exploited as a substitute for imported petroleum products, of which 60% come from the USSR. In 1986 Iceland's economically harnessable hydroelectric power was estimated at 45,000 GWh per annum, of which only about 9% was being utilized. Total installed capacity was 950 MW by 1988. In 1987 a British consortium, North Venture Associates, announced plans for the possible purchase of up to 10 GWh of Icelandic geothermal and hydroelectric generating capacity. The power would be supplied to the United Kingdom via a 950-km undersea cable. Cheap hydroelectricity is used by the aluminium plant owned by the Swiss Alusuisse group. At this plant imported ore is processed, producing ingots and rolling slabs for export. Aluminium exports contributed 14.6% of total visible export receipts in 1984 but only 9.9% in 1985, when production fell by 9.5%. By 1987 production had reached 83,500 metric tons (4% more than in 1984), but export receipts contributed only 9.6% of total visible export receipts. Other foreign companies have shown an interest in the establishment of plants in Iceland for energy-intensive processes. Norway owns a 45% share in Iceland's first ferro-silicon plant in Whale Bay, which began production in 1979, when exports earned a total of 33m. krónur. Between 1979 and 1986 the annual output of ferro-silicon increased from 16,900 metric tons to 63,600 tons, but in 1987 production declined to 56,600 tons, although exports increased (earning 1,473m. krónur).

In 1987 the principal sources of imports to Iceland were the Federal Republic of Germany, Denmark, Norway, the United Kingdom and Sweden; its main export markets were the USA, the United Kingdom, the Federal Republic of Germany and Portugal. Iceland joined EFTA in 1970, and negotiated a trade agreement with the EEC in 1972. Tariffs on Icelandic fish exports to the EEC were reduced after the settlement of the fisheries dispute with the United Kingdom. The final abolition of tariffs between Iceland and the EEC and EFTA took place on 1 January 1980. In 1987 EFTA countries took 8.2% of exports and provided 20.6% of imports, while EEC members accounted for 57.4% of exports and 52.1% of imports; the USA took 18.3% of exports.

In recent years the Icelandic economy has experienced the difficulties resulting from severe inflation, which reached an annual average of 46.6% during 1975–84, owing to large pay rises, accompanied by the index-linking of wages to the price level. Government economic policy was mainly directed towards maintaining full employment, reducing inflation and minimizing borrowing abroad. In May 1983 the Government announced that the policy of wage indexation was to be discontinued; the rate of inflation subsequently declined, averaging 31.9% in 1985. A new wage agreement, signed in 1986, provided for an overall pay increase of 13.6%, based on the premise that the exchange rate would be kept stable and that price increases between January and November would be limited to 6.1%. This, combined with improvements in trade, reduced average inflation to 22.2% in 1986, and to 18.3% in 1987, helped by a 'freeze' on wages and prices in the latter half of the year. In the 12 months to November 1988, however, the inflation rate was 22.5%.

Price rises have forced repeated devaluation of the currency to maintain competitive pricing of fish exports. In January 1981 a 'new' króna was introduced, equivalent to 100 'old'

ICELAND

krónur. Declines in prices for fish and fish products led to further devaluations of the króna in 1988: by 6% in March, 10% in May and 3% in September. Efforts to help the fishing industry continued in 1989, with devaluations of 4% in January and 2.5% in February. Controls on interest rates were abolished in August 1984, and rates were subsequently among the highest in the world.

The trade deficit increased from 949m. krónur in 1981 to 3,168m. krónur in 1982, owing to falling fish catches and depressed world demand for aluminium and ferro-silicon. Exports of these metals improved, however, in 1983 and 1984. The trade deficit fell to 1,973m. krónur in 1983, but rose to 3,187m. krónur in 1984. Despite an increase in total export earnings during 1985 (exports of marine products increased in value by 59%, to 25,226m. krónur), the trade deficit also increased, to 3,850m. krónur. The decline in international petroleum prices in 1986 considerably reduced expenditure on imports, and this development, combined with increased demand for exports and record earnings of 34,627m. krónur from exports of marine products, produced a significant improvement in the trade deficit for 1986, which was reduced to 942m. krónur. In 1987, despite an increase of 16% in the value of exports of marine products, there was a significant deterioration in the trade deficit, to 8,184m. krónur, owing to a considerable rise in imports. This trend continued in 1988. In 1986 a current account surplus of 714m. krónur was achieved, compared with a deficit in 1985 of 4,808m. krónur. In 1987 there was a deficit of 7,209m. krónur, equivalent to 3.5% of gross domestic product (GDP), and it was predicted that the deficit would increase in 1988 to some 4.6% of GDP. Real GNP (in 1980 prices) increased by 3.1% in 1985, by a further 6.3% in 1986, and by 6.5% in 1987. Iceland's long-term foreign debt was equivalent to 38.9% of annual GDP at the end of 1982, and had risen to 50.8% of GDP by the end of 1985. However, by the end of 1987 it had declined to 40.6% of GDP. Unemployment averaged 1% of the labour force in 1983, remained below 2% during 1984, in spite of the Government's anti-inflationary measures, and was reduced to an average of 0.9% in 1985, 0.7% in 1986 and 0.5% in 1987.

Social Welfare

There is a comprehensive system of social security, providing a wide range of insurance benefits, including old-age pensions, family allowances, maternity grants, widows' pensions, etc. Contributions to the scheme are compulsory. Pensions and health insurance now apply to the whole population. Accident insurance applies to all wage and salary earners and self-employed persons—unless they request exemption—and unemployment insurance to the unions of skilled and unskilled workers and seamen in all towns and villages of over 300 inhabitants, as well as to several unions in villages of less than 300 inhabitants. In 1980 there were 488 physicians working in Iceland, and the country had 46 hospital establishments, with a total of 3,730 beds, equivalent to one for every 61 inhabitants: one of the best ratios in the world. Of total expenditure by the central Government in 1987, 23,266m. krónur (43.4%) was for health and welfare, including 11,409m. krónur (21.3%) for social security.

Education

Education is compulsory and free for nine years between seven and 16 years of age. Primary education, beginning at the age of seven and lasting for six years, is available in day schools in urban regions, while in the more remote country districts pupils attend a state boarding-school. The total enrolment at primary schools in 1986 was equivalent to 99% of children in the relevant age-group. Secondary education begins at 13 years of age and lasts for up to seven years, comprising a first cycle of three years and a second of four years. Enrolment at secondary schools in 1985 was equivalent to 95% of children in the appropriate age-group. In 1974 the primary and lower secondary schools were formed into basic schools, leading to a national examination which gives access to further education. The matriculation examination at the end of four years at upper secondary school or at comprehensive school provides the qualification for university entrance. Iceland has three institutions of higher learning. Expenditure on education by the central Government in 1987 was 8,683m. krónur, representing 16.2% of total spending.

Public Holidays

1989: 2 January (for New Year's Day), 23 March (Maundy Thursday), 24 March (Good Friday), 27 March (Easter Monday), 4 May (Ascension Day), 15 May (Whit Monday), 17 June (National Day), 7 August (Bank Holiday), 24–26 December (Christmas), 30 December (for New Year's Eve).

1990: 1 January (New Year's Day), 12 April (Maundy Thursday), 13 April (Good Friday), 16 April (Easter Monday), 24 May (Ascension Day), 4 June (Whit Monday), 18 June (for National Day), 6 August (Bank Holiday), 24–26 December (Christmas), 31 December (New Year's Eve).

Weights and Measures

The metric system is in force.

Statistical Survey

Sources (unless otherwise stated): Statistical Bureau of Iceland, Hverfisgata 8-10, 150 Reykjavík; tel. (91) 26699; National Economic Institute of Iceland, Reykjavík; tel. (91) 26699; Séđlabanki Íslands (Central Bank of Iceland), Kalkofnsvegur 1, 150 Reykjavík; tel. (91) 699600; telex 2020.

AREA AND POPULATION

Area: 103,000 sq km (39,769 sq miles).

Population: (official estimate): 247,357 (males 124,232; females 123,125) at 1 December 1987.

Density (per sq km): 2.4 (1987).

Principal Town: Reykjavík (capital), estimated population 87,309 at 1 December 1983.

Births, Marriages and Deaths (1987): Live births 4,193 (birth rate 17.0 per 1,000); Marriage rate 4.7 per 1,000; Deaths 1,725 (death rate 7.0 per 1,000).

Employment* (1986): Agriculture, forestry and fishing 13,495; Mining, quarrying and manufacturing 27,581; Construction 11,322; Trade, restaurants and hotels 19,074; Community, social and personal services 20,994; Total (incl. others) 124,520.

* Figures refer to the working population covered by compulsory social insurance.

AGRICULTURE, ETC.

Principal Crops (metric tons, 1987): Potatoes 18,093; Turnips 1,084.

Livestock (December 1987): Cattle 69,029; Sheep 624,262; Horses 59,218; Pigs 3,351; Poultry 274,210.

Livestock Products (metric tons, 1987): Mutton and lamb 12,153; Milk 119,000; Wool (unwashed) 1,200; Sheep skins 2,400; Eggs 3,300.

Fishing ('000 metric tons, live weight, 1987): Atlantic cod 389.8; Haddock 39.5; Saithe 78.2; Atlantic redfishes 87.8; Capelin 810.0; Atlantic herring 75.4; Crustaceans 41.3; Total (incl. others) 1,624.8.

INDUSTRY

Selected Products ('000 metric tons, unless otherwise indicated, 1987): Frozen fish 138; Salted, dried or smoked fish 95; Cement 127; Ferro-silicon 59.4; Aluminium (unwrought) 83.5; Electric energy 4,157 million kWh.

FINANCE

Currency and Exchange Rates: 100 aurar (singular: eyrir) = 1 new Icelandic króna (plural: krónur). *Coins:* 10 and 50 aurar; 1, 5, 10 and 50 krónur. *Notes:* 100, 500, 1,000 and 5,000 krónur. *Sterling and Dollar Equivalents* (30 September 1988): £1 sterling = 81.47 krónur; US $ = 48.18 krónur; 1,000 krónur = £12.27 = $20.76.

ICELAND

Average Exchange Rate (krónur per US $): 41.508 in 1985; 41.104 in 1986; 38.677 in 1987.

Budget (million krónur, 1987): *Revenue:* Direct taxes 6,381 (taxes on income and wealth 5,846); Indirect taxes 42,017 (sales tax 21,387, taxes on alcohol and tobacco 3,200, excise tax 2,777, import duties 5,798, other indirect taxes 8,855); Non-tax revenue 3,926; Total 52,324. *Expenditure* (excluding net lending): General administration 5,828; Education 8,683; Health and welfare 23,266; Subsidies 1,657; Agriculture 2,000; Fisheries 1,250; Manufacturing 682; Power 1,196; Communications 3,642; Other purposes 5,378; Total 53,582.

International Reserves (US $ million at 31 December 1987): Gold 2.4; IMF special drawing rights 2.7; Reserve position in IMF 5.7; Foreign exchange 302.9; Total 313.7 (Source: IMF, *International Financial Statistics*).

Money Supply (million krónur at 31 December 1987): Currency outside banks 2,243; Demand deposits at commercial and savings banks 32,131; Total money 34,374 (Source: IMF, *International Financial Statistics*).

Cost of Living (consumer price index for Reykjavík; average of monthly figures; base: 1 February 1984 = 100): 141.97 in 1985; 172.17 in 1986; 204.48 in 1987.

Gross Domestic Product in purchasers' values (million krónur at current prices): 119,910 in 1985; 158,907 in 1986; 206,346 in 1987.

Balance of Payments (US $ million, 1987): Merchandise exports f.o.b. 1,376.1, Merchandise imports f.o.b. −1,428.2, *Trade balance* −52.1; Exports of services 569.7, Imports of services −707.8, *Balance of goods and services* −190.2; Private unrequited transfers (net) 0.9, Government unrequited transfers (net) −1.7, *Current balance* −191.0; Direct capital investment (net) 1.7, Other long-term capital (net) 176.4, Short-term capital (net) 53.6, Net errors and omissions −58.8, *Total* (net monetary movements) −18.1; Valuation change (net) 32.8, *Changes in reserves* 14.6 (Source: IMF, *International Financial Statistics*).

EXTERNAL TRADE

Principal Commodities (US $ million, distribution by SITC, 1986): *Imports c.i.f.:* Food and live animals 85.2; Crude materials (inedible) except fuels 52.3; Petroleum, petroleum products, etc. 97.5 (Refined petroleum products 94.5); Chemicals and related products 88.0; Basic manufactures 211.1; Machinery and transport equipment 368.7 (General industrial machinery, equipment and parts 53.6, Electrical machinery, apparatus, etc. 88.4, Road vehicles and parts 91.9); Miscellaneous manufactured articles 177.1 (Clothing and accessories (excl. footwear) 52.0); Total (incl. others) 1,115.5. *Exports f.o.b.:* Fish, crustaceans, molluscs and preparations 769.9 (Fresh, chilled or frozen fish 436.4, Dried, salted or smoked fish 194.8, Crustaceans and molluscs 118.3); Animal feeding-stuff (excl. cereals) 66.6 (fish meal 65.1); Basic manufactures 155.8 (Unwrought aluminium and alloys 100.5); Total (incl. others) 1,095.8 (Source: UN, *International Trade Statistics Yearbook*).

Principal Trading Partners (million krónur, country of consignment, 1987): *Imports c.i.f.:* Belgium 1,602, Denmark 5,623, Finland 1,438, France 2,068, Federal Republic of Germany 9,310, Italy 1,922, Japan 5,013, Netherlands 4,956, Norway 5,053, Sweden 5,032, USSR 2,574, United Kingdom 5,032, USA 4,367; Total (incl. others) 61,232. *Exports f.o.b.:* Denmark 2,050, France 2,854, Federal Republic of Germany 5,301, Italy 1,613, Japan 4,139, Portugal 4,967, Spain 1,576, Switzerland 1,430, USSR 1,923, United Kingdom 10,321, USA 9,678; Total (incl. others) 53,053.

TRANSPORT

Road Traffic (registered motor vehicles at 31 December 1987): Passenger cars 121,694; Buses and coaches 1,238; Goods vehicles 11,846.

Shipping: *Merchant fleet* (registered vessels, 31 December 1987): Fishing vessels 899 (displacement 117,451 grt); Passenger ships, tankers and other vessels 138 (displacement 70,378 grt). *International freight traffic* ('000 metric tons, 1987): Goods loaded 932; Goods unloaded 1,643.

Civil Aviation (scheduled external Icelandic traffic, '000, 1987): Kilometres flown 16,146, Passenger-kilometres 2,467,000, Cargo ton-kilometres 22,064, Mail ton-kilometres 5,035.

TOURISM

Foreign Visitors By Country of Origin (1987): Denmark 16,191, France 5,311, Federal Republic of Germany 14,011, Norway 10,165, Sweden 15,614, United Kingdom 10,579, USA 35,669; Total (incl. others) 129,315.

COMMUNICATIONS MEDIA

Radio Receivers (1987): 83,000 licensed.

Television Receivers (1987): 75,000 licensed.

Telephones (1987): 113,000 in use.

Books (production, 1984): 917 titles (incl. new editions).

Daily Newspapers (1987): 6 (combined circulation 100,000 copies per issue).

EDUCATION

1987: Pre-primary, primary and secondary (lower stage): 211 institutions, 3,200 staff (incl. part-time teachers), 42,200 pupils (pre-primary 4,400, primary 25,100, secondary (lower stage) 12,700); Secondary (higher stage): 54 institutions, 13,900 students; Universities and colleges: 4 institutions, 4,700 students.

Source: Ministry of Education and Culture.

Directory

The Constitution

A new constitution came into force on 17 June 1944, when Iceland declared its full independence. The main provisions of the Constitution are summarized below:

GOVERNMENT

The President is elected for four years by universal suffrage. All those qualified to vote who have reached the age of 35 years are eligible for the Presidency.

Legislative power is jointly vested in the Althingi and the President. Executive power is exercised by the President and other governmental authorities in accordance with the Constitution and other laws of the land.

The President summons the Althingi every year and determines when the session shall close. The President may adjourn meetings of the Althingi but not for more than two weeks nor more than once a year. The President appoints the Ministers and presides over the State Council. The President may be dismissed only if a resolution supported by three-quarters of the Althingi is approved by a plebiscite.

The President may dissolve the Althingi. Elections must be held within two months and the Althingi must reassemble within eight months.

The Althingi is composed of 63 members, elected by eight proportionately represented constituencies for a period of four years. Substitute members are elected at the same time and in the same manner as Althingi members. The Althingi is divided into two houses, the Upper House (efri deild) and the Lower House (nedri deild); but sometimes both Houses work together as a United Althingi. The Upper House consists of 20 of the members, whom the United Althingi chooses from among the representatives, the remaining 43 forming the Lower House. Each House and the United Althingi elects its own Speaker. The minimum voting age, both for local administrative bodies and for the Althingi is 18 years and all citizens domiciled in Iceland may vote, provided they are of unblemished character and financially responsible.

The budget must be introduced in the United Althingi but other bills may be introduced into either House. They must, however, be given three readings in each house and be approved by a simple majority before they are submitted to the President. If the President disapproves a bill, it nevertheless becomes valid but must be submitted to a plebiscite. Ministers may speak in either House, but may vote only in that of which they are members. The Ministers are responsible to the Althingi and may be impeached by that body, in which case they are tried by the Court of Impeachment.

LOCAL GOVERNMENT

For purposes of local government, the country is divided into Provinces, Districts and Municipalities. The eight Urban Municipalities are governed by Town Councils, which possess considerable autonomy. The Districts also have Councils and are further grouped together to form the Provinces, over each of which a

ICELAND

centrally appointed Chief Official presides. The franchise for municipal purposes is universal above the age of 18 years, and elections are conducted on a basis of proportional representation.

The Government

HEAD OF STATE

President: VIGDÍS FINNBOGADÓTTIR (took office 1 August 1980; began a second term 1 August 1984; re-elected for a third term, beginning 1 August 1988).

THE CABINET
(February 1989)

A coalition of the Progressive Party (PP), the Social Democratic Party (SDP) and the People's Alliance (PA).

Prime Minister: STEINGRÍMUR HERMANNSSON (PP).
Minister for Foreign Affairs and Foreign Trade: JÓN BALDVIN HANNIBALSSON (SDP).
Minister of Finance: ÓLAFUR RAGNAR GRÍMSSON (PA).
Minister of Fisheries, Justice and Ecclesiastical Affairs: HALLDÓR ÁSGRÍMSSON (PP).
Minister of Agriculture and Communications: STEINGRÍMUR SIGFÚSSON (PA).
Minister of Commerce, Industry and Nordic Co-operation: JÓN SIGURÐSSON (SDP).
Minister of Education and Culture: SVAVAR GESTSSON (PA).
Minister of Health and Social Security: GUÐMUNDUR BJARNASON (PP).
Minister of Social Affairs: JÓHANNA SIGURÐARDÓTTIR (SDP).

MINISTRIES

Prime Minister's Office: Stjórnarráðshúsið v/Lkæjartorg, 150 Reykjavík; tel. (91) 25000.
Ministry of Agriculture: Rauðarárstíg 25, 150 Reykjavík; tel. (91) 25000.
Ministry of Commerce: Arnarhváli, 150 Reykjavík; tel. (91) 25000; telex 2092.
Ministry of Communications: Hafnarhúsinu við Tryggvagötu, 150 Reykjavík; tel. (91) 621700.
Ministry of Education: Hverfisgötu 6, 150 Reykjavík; tel. (91) 25000; telex 2111.
Ministry of Finance: Arnarhváli, 150 Reykjavík; tel. (91) 25000; telex 2092.
Ministry of Fisheries: Lindargötu 9, 150 Reykjavík; tel. (91) 25000; telex 2342.
Ministry for Foreign Affairs: Hverfisgötu 115, 150 Reykjavík; tel. (91) 623000; telex 2225.
Ministry of Health: Laugavegi 116, 150 Reykjavík; tel. (91) 25000.
Ministry of Industry: Arnarhváli, 150 Reykjavík; tel. (91) 25000.
Ministry of Justice and Ecclesiastical Affairs: Arnarhváli, 150 Reykjavík; tel. (91) 25000.
Ministry of Social Affairs: Hafnarhúsinu við Tryggvagötu, 150 Reykjavík; tel. (91) 25000; telex 3000.

President

Presidential Election, 25 June 1988

	% of Votes
VIGDÍS FINNBOGADÓTTIR	92.7
SIGRÚN THORSTEINSDÓTTIR	5.3

Legislature

ALTHINGI

Speaker of the United Althingi: THORVALDUR G. KRISTJÁNSSON (IP).
Speaker of the Upper House: KARL S. GUÐNASON.
Speaker of the Lower House: JÓN KRISTJANSSON.
Secretary-General (Clerk) of the Althingi: FRIDRIK OLAFSSON.

Directory

General Election, 25 April 1987

	% of Votes	Seats
Independence Party	27.2	18
Progressive Party	18.9	13
Social Democratic Party	15.2	10
People's Alliance	13.3	9
Citizens' Party	10.9	7
Women's Alliance	10.1	6
Others	4.4	1*
Total	**100.0**	**63**

* Independent member elected with 1.2% of the total votes.

Political Organizations

Althýdubandalag (People's Alliance—PA): Hverfisgata 105, 101 Reykjavík; tel. (91) 17500; f. 1956 by amalgamation of a section of the Social Democratic Party and the Socialist Unity Party, reorganized as a socialist party 1968; Chair. ÓLAFUR RAGNAR GRÍMSSON; Parliamentary Leader RAGNAR ARNALDS; Gen. Sec. KRISTJÁN VALDIMARSSON.

Althýduflokkurinn (Social Democratic Party—SDP): Althýduhusid, Hverfisgata 8-10, Reykjavík; tel. (91) 29244; f. 1916 with a moderate socialist programme; Chair. JÓN BALDVIN HANNIBALSSON; Parliamentary Leader EIÐUR GUÐNASON.

Borgaraflokkurinn (Citizens' Party): Reykjavík; f. 1987; adheres to the ideology of the Independence Party but with emphasis on the needs and rights of the individual; Leader ALBERT GUÐMUNDSSON.

Framsóknarflokkurinn (Progressive Party—PP): Noatún 21, POB 5331, 105 Reykjavík; tel. (91) 24480; f. 1916 with a programme of social and economic amelioration and co-operation; Chair. STEINGRÍMUR HERMANNSSON; Parliamentary Leader PÁLL PÉTURSSON; Sec. GUÐMUNDUR BJARNASON.

Samtoek um Kvennalista (Women's Alliance): Laugaveg 17, Reykjavík; f. 1983; feminist movement to promote the interests of women and children; parliamentary leadership rotates.

Sjálfstaedisflokkurinn (Independence Party—IP): Háaleitisbraut 1, Reykjavík; tel. (91) 82900; f. 1929 by an amalgamation of the Conservative and Liberal Parties; its programme is social reform within the framework of private enterprise and the furtherance of national and individual independence; Leader THORSTEINN PÁLSSON.

Diplomatic Representation

EMBASSIES IN ICELAND

China, People's Republic: Viðimelur 29, POB 580, Reykjavík; telex 2148; Chargé d'affaires: ZHAI SHIXIONG.
Czechoslovakia: Smáragata 16, POB 1443, 101 Reykjavík; tel. (91) 19823; Chargé d'affaires a.i.: (vacant).
Denmark: Hverfisgata 29, Reykjavík; telex 2008; Ambassador: HANS ANDREAS DJURHUUS.
Finland: Reykjavík; telex 2373; Ambassador: ANDERS HULDEN.
France: Túngata 22, Reykjavík; tel. (91) 17621; telex 2063; Ambassador: JACQUES MER.
German Democratic Republic: Ægissiða 78, 107 Reykjavík; telex 2162; Chargé d'affaires: KLAUS BREDOW.
Germany, Federal Republic: Túngata 18, POB 400, 101 Reykjavík; tel. (91) 19535; telex 2002; Ambassador: HANS HERMANN HAFERKAMP.
Norway: Fjólugata 17, Reykjavík; telex 2163; Ambassador: NIELS L. DAHL.
Sweden: Lágmúla 7, 108 Reykjavík; telex 2087; Ambassador: PER OLOF FORSHELL.
USSR: Garðastræti 33, Reykjavík; telex 2200; Ambassador: IGOR NIKOLAYEVICH KRASAVIN.
United Kingdom: Laufásvegur 49, POB 460, Reykjavík; tel. (91) 15883; telex 2037; Ambassador: RICHARD BEST.
USA: Laufásvegur 21, Reykjavík; tel. (91) 29100; telex 3044; Ambassador: NICHOLAS RUWE.

Judicial System

All cases are heard in Ordinary Courts except those specifically within the jurisdiction of Special Courts. The Ordinary Courts

ICELAND

include both a lower division of urban and rural district courts presided over by the district magistrates, and the Supreme Court.

Justices of the Supreme Court are appointed by the President and cannot be dismissed except by the decision of a court. The Justices elect the Chief Justice for a period of two years.

SUPREME COURT

Chief Justice: GUÐMUNDUR JÓNSSON.

Justices: BENEDIKT BLÖNDAL, BJARNI K. BJARNASON, GUÐMUNDUR SKAFTASON, GUÐRÚN ERLENDSDÓTTIR, HRAFN BRAGASON, MAGNÚS THORODDSEN, THOR VILHJÁLMSSON.

Religion

There is complete religious freedom in Iceland.

CHRISTIANITY

Protestant Churches

Tjodkirkja Islands: (Evangelical Lutheran Church of Iceland): Biskupsstofa, Suðurgata 22, 150 Reykjavík; tel. (91) 621500; telex 3014; the national Church, endowed by the State; more than 93% of the population are members; Iceland forms one diocese, Reykjavík, with two suffragan sees; 284 parishes and 126 pastors; Bishop PÉTUR SIGURGEIRSSON.

Frikirkjani Reykjavík (Free Church of Reykjavík): POB 1671, 121 Reykjavík; tel. (91) 14579; f. 1899; Free Lutheran denomination; 7,000 mems; Head (vacant).

Óhádi söfnudurinn (Independent Congregation): Reykjavík; Free Lutheran denomination; 1,100 mems; Head Rev. THÓRSTEINN RAGNARSSON.

Seventh-day Adventists: POB 262, 121 Reykjavík.

The Roman Catholic Church

Iceland comprises a single diocese, directly responsible to the Holy See. At 31 December 1987 there were an estimated 2,003 adherents in the country.

Bishop of Reykjavík: Rt Rev. ALFRED JOLSON, Hávallagata 14, POB 489, 121 Reykjavík; tel. (91) 11423.

The Press

PRINCIPAL DAILIES

Althýdubladid (The Labour Journal): Ármúli 38, Reykjavík; tel. (91) 681866; f. 1916; organ of the Social Democratic Party; Editor INGOLFUR MARGEIRSSON; circ. 8,500.

DV (Dagblaðid-Vísir): Thverholt 11, Reykjavík; tel. (91) 27022; telex 3079; f. 1910; independent; Editors JÓNAS KRISTJÁNSSON, ELLERT B. SCHRAM; circ. 39,000.

Dagur (The Day): Strandgata 31, POB 58, Akureyri; f. 1918; organ of the Progressive Party; Editors ÁSKELL THÓRISSON, BRAGI BERGMANN; circ. 6,400.

Morgunbladid (Morning News): Adalstrtæi 6, POB 1555, Reykjavík; tel. (91) 691100; telex 2127; f. 1913; Independent; Editors MATTHÍAS JOHANNESSEN, STYRMIR GUNNARSSON; circ. 50,000.

Thjódviljinn (Will of the Nation): Siðumúla 6, POB 8020, 108 Reykjavík; tel. (91) 681333; f. 1936; organ of socialism, labour movement and national independence; Editor ÁRNI BERGMANN; circ. 12,000.

Timinn (The Times): Lyngháls 9, Box 370, Reykjavík; tel. (91) 686300; f. 1917; organ of the Progressive Party; Editors INDRIDI G. THORSTEINSSON, INGVAR GISLASON; circ. 15,000.

WEEKLIES

Althýdumadurinn (Commoner): Strandgata 9, Akureyri; f. 1931; weekly; organ of Social Democratic Party; Editor (vacant); circ. 3,500.

Einherji: Siglufjörður; weekly; organ of the Progressive Party.

Íslendingur-Isafold (Icelander-Icecountry): Kaupangi v/Mýrarveg, 600 Akureyri; tel. (96) 21500; f. 1915; for North and East Iceland; Editor STEFÁN SIGTRYGGSSON.

Siglfirdingur: Siglufjorður; weekly; organ of the Independence Party.

Skutull: Isafjörður; weekly; organ of the Social Democratic Party.

PERIODICALS

ABC: Ármúla 18, 108 Reykjavík; tel. (91) 82300; f. 1979; 8 a year; children; Editor HRAFNHILDUR VALGARDSDÓTTIR.

Directory

Ægir (The Sea): c/o Fiskifélag Íslands, Reykjavík; f. 1905; published by the Fisheries Asssociation, Reykjavík; monthly; Editor KRISTJÁN R. KRISTJÁNSSON; circ. 2,500.

Æskan (The Youth): POB 523, 121 Reykjavík; f. 1897; 10 a year; children's magazine.

Áfangar: Bildshöfða 18, 112 Reykjavík; tel. (91) 685380; f. 1979; quarterly; travel; Editor VALTHÓR HLÖÐVERSSON; circ. 5,000.

Atlantica: Hoefdabakki 9, POB 128, Reykjavík 112; tel. (91) 84966; telex 2121; quarterly; in-flight magazine of Icelandair; Editor HARALDUR J. HAMAR.

Bíllinn: Bildshöfða 18, 112 Reykjavík; tel. (91) 685380; f. 1982; quarterly; cars and motorsport; Editor LEÓ M. JÓNSSON; circ. 8,000.

Bóndinn: Bildshöfða 18, 112 Reykjavík; tel. (91) 685380; 6 a year; agriculture and farming; Editor LEÓ M. JÓNSSON; circ. 5,000.

Economic Statistics: Central Bank of Iceland, 150 Reykjavík; f. 1980; quarterly; published by the Economic Department of the Central Bank.

Eimreidin (Progress): Síðumúli 12, Reykjavík; f. 1895; quarterly; literary and critical review.

Fiskifréttir: Ármúla 18, 108 Reykjavík; tel. (91) 82300; f. 1983; weekly; fishing; Editor GUÐJÓN EINARSSON; circ. 6,000.

Freyr: POB 7080, 127 Reykjavík; tel. (91) 19200; f. 1904; fortnightly; organ of the Icelandic Agriculture Society and the Farmers' Union; Editors MATTHÍAS EGGERTSSON, JÚLÍUS DANIELSSON; circ. 4,100.

Frjáls verzlun (Free Trade): Ármúla 18, POB 1193, 108 Reykjavík; tel. (91) 82300; f. 1939; 8 a year; business magazine; Editor HELGI MAGNÚSSON; circ. 8,500.

Gestgjafinn: Ármúla 18, 108 Reykjavík; tel. (91) 82300; quarterly; food and drink; Editor IRIS ERLINGSDÓTTIR; circ. 11,200.

Gródur and Gardar: Ármúla 18, 108 Reykjavík; tel. (91) 82300; f. 1984; 2 a year; gardening; Editor EIRÍKUR EIRIKSSON.

Hagtíðindi: published by the Statistical Bureau of Iceland, Hverfisgata 8-10, 150 Reykjavík; tel. (91) 26699; f. 1914; monthly; Dir-Gen. HALLGRÍMUR SNORRASON.

Heima Er Bezt: Tryggvabraut 18-20, Akureyri; f. 1951; monthly; literary; circ. 4,200.

Hús og híbýli: Háaleitisbraut 1, Reykjavík; 6 a year; architecture, family and homes; Editors THÓRARINN J. MAGNÚSSON, FRÍÐA BJÖRNSDÓTTIR; circ. 15,000.

Iceland Review: Hoefdabakki 9, POB 128, 112 Reykjavík; tel. (91) 84966; telex 2121; f. 1963; 4 a year; English; general; Editor HARALDUR J. HAMAR.

Ithróttabladid: Ármúla 18, 108 Reykjavík; tel. (91) 82300; f. 1939; 6 a year; sport; Editor THORGRÍMUR THRÁINSSON.

Mannlif: Ármúla 18, 108 Reykjavík; tel. (91) 82300; general interest; Editor SVANHILDUR KONRADSDÓTTIR.

News from Iceland: Hoefdabakki 9, POB 8576, Reykjavík; tel. (91) 84966; telex 2121; f. 1975; monthly; English; circ. 19,500.

Nýtt Lif: Ármúla 18, 108 Reykjavík; tel. (91) 82300; f. 1978; 8 a year; fashion; Editor GULLVEIG SÆMUNDSDÓTTIR; circ. 17,000.

Rjettur: Reykjavík; monthly; left-wing magazine on politics and social problems; Editor EINAR OLGEIRSSON.

Samúel: Háaleitisbraut 1, 105 Reykjavík; tel. (91) 83122; f. 1968; monthly; entertainment, sport and cars; Editor THÓRARINN J. MAGNÚSSON; circ. 12,700.

Samvinnan: Suðurlandsbraut 32, Reykjavík; monthly; publ. by the Federation of Icelandic Co-operative Societies; Editor GYLFI GRÖNDAL; circ. 6,000.

Sjávarfréttir: Ármúla 18, 108 Reykjavík; tel. (91) 685380; f. 1973; quarterly; fishing and fishing-industry; Editor GUÐJÓN EINARSSON; circ. 5,500.

Sjónvarpsvísir Stöðvar 2: Ármúla 18, 108 Reykjavík; tel. (91) 82300; f. 1987; monthly; Editor KJORTAN STEFÁNSSON; circ. 40,800.

Úrval (Digest): Thverholti 11, Reykjavík; monthly; Editor SIGURÐUR HREIÐAR HREIÐARSSON; circ. 6,500.

A veiðum: Ármúla 18, 108 Reykjavík; tel. (91) 82300; f. 1984; 2 a year; fishing and shooting; Editor STEINAR J. LÚÐVÍKSSON; circ. 6,000.

Við sem fljúgum: Ármúla 18 108 Reykjavík; tel. (91) 82300; f. 1980; 8 a year; Icelandair in-flight magazine; Editor STEINAR J. LÚÐVÍKSSON; circ. 7,000.

Vikan (The Week): Háaleitisbrand 1, Reykjavík; tel. (91) 83122; f. 1938; every 2 weeks; illustrated; Editors THÓRARINN J. MAGNÚSSON, BRYNDÍS KRISTJÁNSDÓTTIR; circ. 14,500.

Víkingur (Seaman): Borgartúni 18, Reykjavík; 10 a year; Editor SIGURJÓN VALDIMARSSON.

ICELAND   Directory

Vinnan (Work): Grensásvegur 16, 108 Reykjavík; tel. (91) 83044; f. 1943; publ. by Icelandic Federation of Labour; Editor SVERRIR ALBERTSSON; circ. 7,000.

NEWS AGENCY
Foreign Bureau

Agence France-Presse (AFP): Bragattagata 3A, 101 Reykjavík; tel. (91) 2066; Correspondent GÉRARD LEMARQUIS.

Publishers

Akranesútgáfan: Deildartúni 8, Akranes.

Almenna Bókafélagid: Austurstræti 18, Reykjavík; tel. (91) 25544; f. 1955; general; book club editions; Man. Dir KRISTJÁN JOHANNSSON.

Bókaforlag Odds Björnssonar: POB 558, Tryggvabraut 18–20, 600 Akureyri; tel. (96) 22500; f. 1897; general; Dir GEIR S. BJÖRNSSON.

Bókaútgáfa Æskunnar: POB 523, 121 Reykjavík; tel. (91) 10248.

Bókaútgáfa Gudjóns O. Gudjónssonar: Thverholti 13, Reykjavík; tel. (91) 27233.

Bókaútgáfa Thorsteins M. Jónssonar: Eskihlid 21, 105 Reykjavík.

Bókaútgáfan Björk: Háholti 7, Akranes; Man. DANIEL AGÚSTÍNUSSON.

Bókaútgáfan Hildur: Fögrubrekku 47, Kópavogi; tel. (92) 76700; Man. GUNNAR THORLEIFSSON.

Bókaútgáfan Hlidskjálf: Ingólfsstraeti 22, 101 Reykjavík; tel. (91) 17520.

Bókaverzlun Sigfúsar Eymundssonar: Austurstræti 18, Reykjavík; f. 1872; educational and general, import and export of books, maps of Iceland; Man. EINAR OSKARSSON.

Fjölvi: Hjallalandi 28, Reykjavík.

Forni: Kleppsvegi 4, 105 Reykjavík.

Fródi, hf: Armúla 21, Reykjavík; Man. GISSUR EGGERTSSON.

Heimskringla: Laugavegi 18, Reykjavík, POB 392; tel. (91) 15199; telex 2265; f. 1932; Man. ARNI EINARSSON.

Hid íslenzka bókmenntafélag: Thingholtsstræti 3, 121 Reykjavík, POB 1252; tel. (91) 21960; f. 1816; general; Pres. SIGURDUR LÍNDAL.

Hörpuútgáfan: Stekkjarholt 8-10, POB 25, 300 Akranes; Dir BRAGI THORDARSON.

Idunn: Brædraborgarstígur 16, POB 294, 121 Reykjavík; tel. (91) 28555; telex 2308; general; f. 1945; Man. Dir JÓN KARLSSON.

Hladbud, hf: Brædraborgarstígur 16, POB 294, 121 Reykjavík; tel. (91) 28555; telex 2308; f. 1944; mainly school books; Dir JÓN KARLSSON.

Ísafoldarprentsmidja, hf: Thingholtsstræti 5, Reykjavík; tel. (91) 17165; f. 1877; Chair. and Gen. Man. LEÓ E. LÖVE.

Íslenzka Fornritafélag, Hid: Austurstræti 18, Reykjavík; f. 1928; Pres. J. NORDAL.

Jonsonn & Co (The English Bookshop): Hafnarstr 4/9, POB 1131, Reykjavík 101; tel. (91) 13133; f. 1927; general; Man. Dir BENEDIKT KRISTJÁNSSON.

Kynning: POB 1238, Reykjavík; tel. (91) 38456; f. 1966; natural science, books on Iceland, art, history; Man. H. HANNESSON.

Leiftur, hf: Höfdatúni 12, Reykjavík; tel. (91) 17554; Man. HJÖRTUR THORDARSON.

Litbrá-Offset: Höfdatúni 12, POB 999, 121 Reykjavík.

Ljódhus Ltd: Laufásvegi 4, POB 1506, Reykjavík; Man. SIGFÚS DADASON.

Mál og Menning (Literary Book Club): Laugavegi 18, Reykjavík; tel. (91) 15199; telex 2265; f. 1937; 4,600 mems; Chair. THORLEIFUR EINARSSON; Man. ARNI EINARSSON; Editor HALLDOR GUDMUNDSSON.

Menningarsjódur og Thjódvinafélag: Skálholtsstíg 7, POB 1398, Reykjavík; tel. (91) 621822; f. 1940; publishing dept of Cultural Fund; Dir EINAR LAXNESS.

Námsgagnastofnun (National Centre for Educational Materials): POB 5192, Reykjavík 125; tel. (91) 28088; telex 3000; f. 1979; Dir (Publishing House) ASGEIR GUDMUNDSSON.

Örn og Örlygur, hf: Sídumúli 11, 108 Reykjavík; tel. (91) 84866; telex 2197; f. 1966; general; book club editions; Owner and Man. Dir ÖRLYGUR HÁLFDANARSON.

Prenthusid: Barónsstíg 11B, Reykjavík.

Prentsmidja Árna Valdimarssonar: Brautarholti 16, Reykjavík.

Prentsmidjan Oddi, hf: Höfdabakka 7, POB 1305, 121 Reykjavík.

Rökkur: Flókagötu 15, Reykjavík; tel. (91) 18768.

Setberg: Freyjugatu 14, POB 619, 121 Reykjavík; tel. (91) 17667; telex 3000; fiction, cookery, juvenile and children's books; Dir ARNBJÖRN KRISTINSSON.

Siglufjardardrentsmidja: Sudurgötu 16, Siglufirdi.

Skjaldborg Ltd: Hólmgardi 34, POB 8427, 128 Reykjavík; tel. (91) 672400.

Skuggsjá: Strandgötu 31, 222 Hafnarfjördur; tel. (01) 50045; general fiction; Dirs JÓHANNES OLIVERSSON, LILJA OLIVERSDÓTTIR.

Snaefell: Álfaskeidi 58, 220 Hafnarfirdi; Man. THORKELL JOHANNESSON.

Stafafell: Laugavegi 1, Reykjavík; Man. MAGNÚS BRYNJÓLFSSON.

Steindórsprent, hf: Ármúla 5, POB 8495, 128 Reykjavík; tel. (91) 685200.

Sudri: Kleppsvegi 2, 105 Reykjavík; tel. (91) 36384; Man. GUDJÓN ELÍASSON.

Thjódsaga: Thingholtsstræti 27, Reykjavík; tel. (91) 13510; Dir HAFSTEINN GUDMUNDSSON.

Vaka-Helgafell: Sidumúla 29, 108 Reykjavík; tel. (91) 16837; Dir ÓLAFUR RAGNARSSON.

Vikingsútgáfan: Veghúsastíg 7, Reykjavík; Dir RAGNAR JONSSON.

Vikurútgáfan: Kleppsvegi 2, Reykjavík.

PUBLISHERS' ASSOCIATION

Félag íslenskra bókaútgefenda: Suduslandsbraut 4, 108 Reykjavík; tel. (91) 38020; Pres. EYJÓLFUR SIGURDSSON; Man. BJÖRN GÍSLASON.

Radio and Television

In 1988 there were 80,600 radio receivers and 73,000 television receivers in use.

Ríkisútvarpid (Icelandic National Broadcasting Service): Broadcasting Centre, Efstaleiti 1, 150 Reykjavík; tel. (91) 693000; telex 2066; f. 1930; Dir-Gen. MARKÚS ÖRN ANTONSSON; Chair. of Programme Board INGA JÓNA THORDARDÓTTIR.

RADIO

Ríkisútvarpid: Radio Division, Efstaleiti 1, 150 Reykjavík; tel. (91) 693000; telex 2066; f. 1930; Dir of Radio ELFA-BJÖRK GUNNARSDÓTTIR.

  Programme 1 has two long wave, 8 medium wave and 65 FM transmitters broadcasting 127 hours a week; Head GUNNAR STEFÁNSSON.

  Programme 2 has 45 FM transmitters broadcasting 168 hours a week; Head THORGEIR ÁSTVALDSSON.

Radio Bylgjan: Snorrabraut 54, 105 Reykjavík; privately-owned.

TELEVISION

Ríkisútvarpid—Sjónvarp (Icelandic National Broadcasting Service—Television): Laugavegur 176, 105 Reykjavík; tel. (91) 693900; telex 2035; f. 1966; covers 99% of the population; broadcasts daily, total 46 hours a week; Dir of Television PÉTUR GUDFINNSSON.

Stöd 2: Krókhálsi 6, 110 Reykjavík; privately-owned.

The US Navy operates a radio station (24 hours a day), and a television service (80 hours a week), on the NATO base at Keflavík.

Finance

(cap. = capital; p.u. = paid up; res = reserves; dep. = deposits; m. = million; kr = krónur; brs = branches)

BANKING
Central Bank

Sedlabanki Íslands (Central Bank of Iceland): Kalkofnsvegur 1, 150 Reykjavík; tel. (91) 699600; telex 2020; f. 1961 to take over central banking activities of Landsbanki Íslands; cap. 1m. kr, res 3,418m. kr, dep. 18,281m. kr (1986); Govs Dr JÓHANNES NORDAL, TÓMAS ARNASON, GEIR HALLGRÍMSSON.

Commercial Banks

Althýdubankinn hf (The Union Bank Ltd): Laugavegur 31, Reykjavík; tel. (91) 621188; telex 4925; f. 1971; cap. and res 315m. kr, dep. 2,264m. kr (1987); Gen. Man. BJÖRN BJÖRNSSON; 3 brs.

Búnadarbanki Íslands (Agricultural Bank of Iceland): Austurstræti 5-7, 101 Reykjavík, POB 1720; tel. (91) 25600; telex 2383; f. 1929; independent state-owned bank; res 1,357m. kr, dep. 13,408m.

ICELAND

kr (1987); Chair. Stefán Valgeirsson; Man. Dirs Stefán Hilmarsson, Stefán Pálsson, Jón Adolf Gudjonsson; 33 brs.

Idnadarbanki Íslands (Industrial Bank of Iceland): Lækjargata 12, 101 Reykjavík; tel. (91) 691800; telex 3003; f. 1953; cap. and res 691m. kr, dep. 5,412m. kr; Gen. Mans Bragi Hannesson, Valur Valsson, Ragnar Önundarson; 9 brs.

Landsbanki Íslands (National Bank of Iceland): Austurstræti 11, POB 170, 101 Reykjavík; tel. (91) 27722; telex 2030; f. 1885; cap. and res 2,682m. kr, dep. 16,902m. kr (1986); Gen. Mans Björgvin Vilmundarson, Jónas H. Haralz, Helgi Bergs; 32 brs.

Samvinnubanki Íslands hf (Co-operative Bank of Iceland Ltd): Bankastræti 7, 101 Reykjavík; tel. (91) 20700; telex 3142; f. 1962; cap. and res 455m. kr, dep. 4,796m. kr; Gen. Man. Geir Magnússon; 22 brs.

Útvegsbanki Íslands hf (Fisheries Bank of Iceland Ltd): POB 190, Austurstræti 19, 101 Reykjavík; tel. (91) 17060; telex 2047; f. 1930; converted into limited company from May 1987; cap. and res 1,000m. new kr, dep. 6,193m. kr (May 1987); Gen. Man Gudmundur Hauksson; 13 brs.

Verslunarbanki Íslands hf: (Iceland Bank of Commerce Ltd): Bankastræti 5, POB 790, 121 Reykjavík; tel. (91) 27200; telex 3027; f. 1961; cap. and res 424m. kr, dep. 3,285m. kr (1987); Chair. Gísli V. Einarsson; Man. Dirs Kristján Oddsson, Tryggvi Pálsson; 8 brs.

INSURANCE

Tryggingastofnun Ríkisins (State Social Security Institution): Laugavegi 114, 105 Reykjavík; tel. (91) 19300; f. 1936; Man. Dir Eggert G. Thorsteinsson; Chair. of Tryggingaráð (Social Security Board) Helga Jónsdóttir.

Private Companies

Almennar Tryggingar Ltd (General Insurance): Síðumúla 39, 108 Reykjavík; tel. (91) 82800; telex 2086; f. 1943; cap. p.u. 56.2m. kr (1987); Gen. Man. Ólafur B. Thors.

Brunabótafélag Íslands (Iceland Fire Insurance Society): Laugavegi 103, Reykjavík; tel. (91) 696000; f. 1915; net assets 185.5m. kr (1987); Man. Dir I. R. Helgason.

Íslenzk Endurtrygging (National Icelandic Reinsurance Co): Suðurlandsbraut 6, 108 Reykjavík; tel. (91) 681444; telex 2153; f. 1939; cap. 60.2m. kr (1987); Gen. Man. Bjarni Thordarson.

Líftryggingafélagið Andvaka (Andvaka Mutual Life Insurance Co): Ármúla 3, 108 Reykjavík; tel. (91) 681411; telex 2103; f. 1949; Chair. V. Arnthorsson; Man. Dir Hallgrímur Sigurðsson.

Samábyrgð Íslands á fiskiskipum (Icelandic Mutual Fishing Craft Insurance): Lágmúli 9, 108 Reykjavík; tel. (91) 681400; telex 3163; f. 1909; Man. Dir Páll Sigurdsson.

Samvinnutryggingar (Mutual Insurance Co): Ármúla 3, 108 Reykjavík; tel. (91) 681411; telex 2103; f. 1946; Chair. V. Arnthorsson; Man. Dir A. Gíslason.

Sjóvátryggingarfélag Íslands hf (Iceland Marine Insurance Co): POB 5300, Suðurlandsbraut 4, 125 Reykjavík; tel. (91) 692500; telex 2051; f. 1918; share cap. 50.2m. kr, res fund 741.9m. kr (1985); Chair. Benedikt Sveinsson; Gen. Man. Einar Sveinsson.

Trade and Industry

CHAMBER OF COMMERCE

Verzlunarráð Íslands (Chamber of Commerce); Hús verslunarinnar, 103 Reykjavík; tel. (91) 83088; telex 2316; f. 1917; Chair. Jóhann J. Ólafsson; Gen. Sec. Vilhjálmur Egilsson; 500 mems.

EMPLOYERS' ORGANIZATIONS

Federation of Icelandic Industries: POB 1407, 121 Reykjavík; tel. (91) 27577; f. 1933; Chair. Viglundur Thorsteinsson; Gen. Man. Olafur Davidsson; 300 mems.

Vinnuveitendasamband Íslands (Employers' Federation): Garðastræti 41, POB 514, 121 Reykjavík; tel. (91) 25455; f. 1934; Chair. G. J. Friðriksson; Man. Dir Thorarinn V. Thorarinsson.

FISHING INDUSTRY ASSOCIATIONS

Félag Íslenzkra Botnvörpuskipæigenda (Steam Trawler Owners' Association): Hafnarhuoll, Tryggvagötu, Reykjavík; tel. (91) 29500; telex 2090; f. 1916; Chair. Thorhallur Helgason; Sec.-Gen. Ágúst Einarsson.

Fiskifélag Íslands (Fisheries Association): Reykjavík; f. 1911; conducts technical and economic research and services for fishing vessels; performs various functions for the fishing industry in accordance with Icelandic law or by arrangement with the Ministry of Fisheries; Man. Már Elísson.

Fiskveidasjódúr Íslands (Fisheries Loan Fund of Iceland): Reykjavík; f. 1905; lends money for construction and purchase of fishing vessels, equipment and plant; financed by interest charges; loans granted 1,121m. kr (1985); Chair. Björgvin Vilmundarson; Gen. Man. Már Elísson.

Landssamband Íslenzkra Utvegsmanna (Fishing Vessel Owners' Federation): POB 893, Reykjavík; f. 1939; Chair. K. Ragnarsson; Man. Kristjan Ragnarsson.

Sölusamband Íslenzkra Fiskframleidenda (Union of Icelandic Fish Producers): Adalstræti 6, POB 889, 121 Reykjavík; tel. (91) 11480; telex 2041; Dir Magnús Gunnarsson.

CO-OPERATIVE ASSOCIATION

Samband Íslenskra Samvinnufélaga (Federation of Icelandic Co-operative Societies): Sölvhólsgata 4, 101 Reykjavík; tel. (91) 698100; telex 2023; f. 1902; links 40 co-operative societies; Chair. Valur Arnthórsson; Dir-Gen. Gudjón B. Ólafsson; 46,368 mems.

TRADE UNIONS

Althýdusamband Íslands (ASÍ) (Icelandic Federation of Labour): Grensásveg 16, 108 Reykjavík; f. 1916; affiliated to ICFTU; Pres. Ásmundur Stefánsson; 63,235 mems.

Menningar- og Frædslusamband Althýdu (MFA) (Workers' Educational Association): Grensásveg 16, 108 Reykjavík; Chair. Helgi Gudmundsson; Gen. Sec. Tryggvi Thór Adalsteinsson.

Bandalag Starfsmanna Ríkis og Bæja (BSRB) (Municipal and Government Employees' Association): Grettisgötu 89, 105 Reykjavík; f. 1942; Chair. Ögmundur Jónasson; 16,174 mems.

Bladamannafélag Íslands (Union of Icelandic Journalists): Síðumúla 23, Reykjavík; tel. (91) 39155; f. 1897; Chair. Ludvík Geirsson; Sec. Frída Björnsdottir; 400 mems.

Landssamband Idnadármanna (Federation of Icelandic Crafts and Industries): Hallveigarstigur 1, Reykjavík; tel. (91) 621590; f. 1932; non-party; Chair. Haraldur Sumarlidason; Gen. Sec. Thórleifur Jónsson; 3,200 mems.

Transport

RAILWAYS

There are no railways in Iceland.

ROADS

Much of the interior is uninhabited and the main road follows the coastline. Regular motor coach services link the main settlements. Development plans provide for new roads and harbour installations. At 31 December 1987 Iceland had 11,373 km of roads, of which 3,805 km were main roads.

Félag Sérleyfishafa (Icelandic Bus Routes Union): BSI bus terminal, Umferðarmiðstöðinni, Vatnsmýrarveg 10, 101 Reykjavík; tel. (91) 22300; telex 3082; f. 1936; scheduled bus services throughout Iceland; also operates sightseeing tours and excursions; Chair. Ágúst Hafberg.

SHIPPING

Heavy freight is carried by coastal shipping. The principal seaport for international shipping is Reykjavík.

Hf Eimskipafélag Íslands (Iceland Steamship Co): POB 220, Pósthússtræti 2, 101 Reykjavík; tel. (91) 697100; telex 2022; f. 1914; transportation service incl. liner trade, general and bulk cargo between Iceland and the UK, Scandinavia, the Continent, the Baltic and the USA; also operates coastal services, warehousing and stevedores; Man. Dir Hörður Sigurgestsson; 17 vessels totalling 33,738 grt.

Nesskip hf: Nesskip's House, 170 Seltjarnarnes; tel. (91) 625055; telex 2256; f. 1974; all shipping services; Man. Dir G. Ásgeirsson; 7 vessels totalling 35,000 dwt (1988).

Skipaútgerd Ríkisins (Icelandic Shipping Dept): Hafnarhúsinu V, Tryggvagötu, Reykjavík 101; tel. (91) 28822; telex 3008; f. 1930; passenger and freight service round Iceland all the year; Gen. Man. Gudmundur Einarsson.

Samband Íslenskra Samvinnufélaga (Samband Line): POB 1480, Sölvholsgata 4, 101 Reykjavík; tel. (91) 698100; telex 2101; Iceland–Europe–USA; Dir Omar Johannsson; 8 cargo vessels, 1 tanker.

CIVIL AVIATION

Air transport is particularly important to Iceland and is used, for example, to transport agricultural produce from remote districts.

ICELAND

There are regular air services between Reykjavík and outlying townships. There is an international airport at Keflavík, 47 km from Reykjavík.

Eagle Air (Arnarflug): POB 1046, Lágmúli 7, 121 Reykjavík; telex 2183; f. 1976; privately owned, approx. 800 shareholders; internal network to 11 domestic airfields; external service to Amsterdam, Hamburg, Milan and Zürich; Chair. of Board HORDUR EINARSSON; Man. Dir KRISTINN SIGTRYGGSSON; fleet of 1 Boeing 737-200C, 2 Cessna 402C, 1 Twin Otter.

Icelandair (Flugleidir hf): Reykjavík Airport, 101 Reykjavík; tel. (91) 690100; telex 2021; f. 1973 as the holding company for the two principal Icelandic airlines Flugfélag Íslands (f. 1937) and Loftleidir (f. 1944); in 1979 all licences, permits and authorizations previously held by Flugfélag Íslands and Loftleidir were transferred to it; network centred on Reykjavík, to 10 domestic airfields, and scheduled external services to Scandinavia, the United Kingdom, Luxembourg and the USA, and summer flights to Austria, France, Greenland and the Federal Republic of Germany; Pres. and CEO SIGURÐUR HELGASON; fleet of 3 DC-8-63, 1 DC-8-63CF, 1 DC-8-55, 1 Boeing 727-100C, 1 Boeing 727-200, 6 Fokker F27-200; 2 737-400 on order.

Tourism

Iceland's main attraction for tourists lies in the ruggedness of the interior, with its geysers and thermal springs. Since the mid-1980s tourist arrivals and receipts have risen steadily. In 1987 there were 129,315 arrivals, and receipts reached 5,379m. krónur (4,122m. in 1986).

Iceland Tourist Board: Laugavegur 3, 101 Reykjavík; tel. (91) 27488; telex 2248; Gen. Man. BIRGIR THORGILSSON.

INDIA

Introductory Survey

Location, Climate, Language, Religion, Flag, Capital

The Republic of India forms a natural sub-continent, with the Himalaya mountain range to the north. Two sections of the Indian Ocean, the Arabian Sea and the Bay of Bengal, lie to the west and east, respectively. India's neighbours are the People's Republic of China, Bhutan and Nepal to the north, Pakistan to the north-west and Burma to the north-east, while Bangladesh is surrounded by Indian territory except for a short frontier with Burma in the east. Near India's southern tip, across the Palk Strait, is Sri Lanka. India's climate ranges from temperate to tropical, with an average summer temperature on the plains of approximately 27°C (85°F). Annual rainfall varies widely, but the summer monsoon brings heavy rain over much of the country in June and July. The official language is Hindi, spoken by about 30% of the population. English is used as an associate language for many official purposes. The Indian Constitution also recognizes 16 regional languages, of which the most widely spoken are Telugu, Bengali, Marathi, Tamil, Urdu and Gujarati. Many other local languages are also used. According to the 1981 census, about 80% of the population are Hindus and 11% Muslims. There are also Christians, Sikhs, Buddhists, Jains and other minorities. The national flag (proportions 3 by 2) has three equal horizontal stripes, of saffron, white and green, with the Dharma Chakra (Wheel of the Law), in blue, in the centre of the white stripe. The capital is New Delhi.

Recent History

After a prolonged struggle against British colonial rule, India became independent, within the Commonwealth, on 15 August 1947. The United Kingdom's Indian Empire was partitioned, broadly on a religious basis, between India and Pakistan (then in two sections, of which the eastern wing became Bangladesh in 1971). The principal nationalist movement opposing British rule was the Indian National Congress (later known as the Congress Party). At independence the Congress leader, Jawaharlal Nehru, became India's first Prime Minister. Sectarian violence, the movement of 12m. refugees, the integration of the former princely states into the Indian federal structure and a dispute with Pakistan over Kashmir presented major problems.

India became independent as a dominion, with the British monarch as Head of State, represented locally by an appointed Governor-General. In November 1949, however, the Constituent Assembly approved a republican constitution, providing for a President (with mainly ceremonial functions) to be Head of State. Accordingly, India became a republic on 26 January 1950, although remaining a member of the Commonwealth. France transferred sovereignty of Chandernagore to India in May 1950, and ceded its four remaining Indian settlements in 1954.

The lack of effective opposition to Congress policies expedited industrialization and social reform. In December 1961 Indian forces overran the Portuguese territories of Goa, Daman and Diu, which were immediately annexed by India. Border disputes with the People's Republic of China escalated into a brief military conflict in October 1962. Nehru died in May 1964 and was succeeded by Lal Bahadur Shastri, a former Minister of Home Affairs. India and Pakistan fought a second war over Kashmir in August–September 1965. Following mediation by the USSR, Shastri and President Ayub Khan of Pakistan signed a joint declaration, aimed at a peaceful settlement of the Kashmir dispute, on 10 January 1966. Shastri died on the next day, however, and Nehru's daughter, Mrs Indira Gandhi, formerly Minister of Information and Broadcasting, became Prime Minister. The Congress Party's majority was reduced at the 1967 general election.

Following the presidential election of August 1969, when two factions of Congress supported different candidates, the success of Indira Gandhi's candidate split the party. The Organization (Opposition) Congress, led by Morarji Desai, a former Deputy Prime Minister, emerged in November, but at the next general election to the Lok Sabha, held in March 1971, Indira Gandhi's wing of Congress won 350 of the 515 elective seats where polling took place.

Border incidents led to a 12-day war with Pakistan in December 1971. The Indian army rapidly occupied East Pakistan, which India recognized as the independent state of Bangladesh. Indira Gandhi and President Zulfiqar Ali Bhutto of Pakistan held a summit conference at Simla, India, in June–July 1972, when the two leaders agreed that their respective forces should respect the cease-fire line in Kashmir, and that India and Pakistan should resolve their differences through bilateral negotiations or other peaceful means. In 1975 the former protectorate of Sikkim became the 22nd state of the Indian Union, leading to tensions in India's relations with Nepal.

In 1975 Indira Gandhi was found guilty of electoral malpractice in 1971, and was barred from holding elective office for six years. She then declared a state of emergency, and arrested more than 900 political opponents. In November 1975 the Supreme Court cleared her of electoral malpractice. A general election to the Lok Sabha was held in March 1977, when the number of elective seats was increased to 542. The election resulted in victory for the Janata (People's) Party, chaired by Morarji Desai, who became Prime Minister. Janata and an allied party, the Congress for Democracy, together received 43.2% of the total votes and won 298 of the 540 seats where polling took place. Congress received 34.5% of the votes and won 153 seats.

In January 1978 Indira Gandhi became leader of a new political group, the Congress (Indira) Party, known as Congress (I). A commission of inquiry, investigating the alleged excesses of her regime, found her guilty of corruption. In June Charan Singh, the Home Minister, and Raj Narain, the Health Minister, were dismissed for their criticism of Desai's Government. In November Indira Gandhi was elected to the Lok Sabha, but the House found her guilty of breach of privilege during the emergency rule, and she was expelled from the Lok Sabha.

In January 1979 Charan Singh returned to the Government as Minister of Finance and Desai's deputy. The Government's ineffectual approach to domestic problems provoked a wave of defections by Lok Sabha members of the Janata Party. Many joined Narain, who formed a new party, the Lok Dal, based on secularism. Congress (I) lost its position as official opposition party after defections from its ranks to the then official Congress party by members who objected to Indira Gandhi's authoritarianism. The resignation of Desai's Government was followed by the resignation from the party of Charan Singh, who became the leader of the Lok Dal and, shortly afterwards, Prime Minister in a coalition with both Congress parties. When Congress (I) withdrew its support in August, Singh's 24-day administration collapsed, and Parliament was dissolved. A general election to the Lok Sabha was held in January 1980, when polling took place in 525 of the 542 elective seats. Two more seats were decided in February. Altogether, Congress (I) received 42.7% of the total votes but won an overwhelming majority (352) of the elective seats. Janata, with 18.9% of the votes, won only 31 seats, while the Lok Dal (9.4%) won 41 seats. Indira Gandhi was reinstated as Prime Minister. Presidential rule was imposed in nine states, ruled by opposition parties, in February. At state elections in June, Congress (I) gained majorities in eight of the nine states.

By-elections in June 1981 for the Lok Sabha and state assemblies were notable because of the landslide victory which Rajiv Gandhi, the Prime Minister's son and a former airline pilot, obtained in the former constituency of his late brother, Sanjay (who had been killed in an air crash in June 1980) and because of the failure of the fragmented Janata party to win any seats. In January 1982 Indira Gandhi reshuffled the Council of Ministers, appointing a new Minister of Defence, a portfolio that she had previously held. In September there was a major reshuffle when Indira Gandhi appointed eight new ministers. In February 1983 Rajiv Gandhi became a General Secretary of Congress (I).

Indira Gandhi's Government faced serious problems, as disturbances in several states, particularly in Assam, continued in 1982 and 1983, with violent protests against the presence of Bengali immigrants. Presidential rule in Assam was replaced by a Congress (I) Government in February 1982, in an effort to quell dissent. To avert a constitutional crisis, further elections were held in Assam (and Meghalaya) in February 1983, amid scenes of great intercommunal violence, leading to several thousand deaths. In an effort to curtail the flow of Bengali immigrants, it was decided in July that the Assam/Bangladesh border should be fenced. Election defeats in Andhra Pradesh, Karnataka and Tripura in January 1983 represented a set-back for Indira Gandhi, who then reshuffled her Council of Ministers. There was also unrest in Jammu and Kashmir during local elections there in June 1983, and in July 1984, when the Chief Minister was deposed. Alleged police corruption and the resurgence of caste violence (notably in Bihar and Gujarat) caused further problems for the Government.

Another major problem was the widespread unrest in the Sikh community of Punjab, despite the election to the Indian presidency in July 1982 of Giani Zail Singh, the first Sikh to hold the position. There were demands for greater religious recognition, for the settlement of grievances over land and water rights, and over the sharing of the state capital at Chandigarh with Haryana, and also demands from a small minority for a separate Sikh state ('Khalistan'). In October 1983 the Punjabi Government was removed, and the state was brought under presidential rule, to prevent an escalation of violence between the Sikh and Hindu populations. However, the violence continued, and followers of an extremist Sikh leader, Jarnail Singh Bhindranwale, established a terrorist stronghold inside the Golden Temple (the Sikh holy shrine) at Amritsar. In June 1984 the Government sent in troops to dislodge the extremists. The armed assault on the Golden Temple resulted in the death of Bhindranwale and hundreds of his supporters, and serious damage to sacred buildings. A curfew was imposed in Punjab, and army personnel blockaded Amritsar. There were mutinies among Sikh troops in various parts of India.

In October 1984 Indira Gandhi was assassinated by militant Sikh members of her personal guard. Her son, Rajiv Gandhi, was immediately sworn in as Prime Minister, despite his lack of previous ministerial experience. There was widespread communal violence throughout India, with more than 2,000 deaths, which was curbed by the prompt action of the Government.

A general election to the Lok Sabha, which was due in January 1985 under the Constitution, was held in December 1984 throughout the country, apart from the states of Assam and Punjab, which were deemed by the Government to be too disturbed, as well as in two snowbound constituencies and five in which voting was postponed until January 1985. Congress (I), aided by the youthfulness of the electorate (68% of whom were between 21 and 40 years of age), the total disunity of the opposition and a large sympathy vote for Rajiv Gandhi, achieved a decisive victory, gaining the largest parliamentary majority in India's history. Including the results of the January 1985 polling, the party received 49.2% of the total votes and won 403 of the 513 contested seats. Rajiv Gandhi pledged to continue most of his mother's policies. At the state assembly elections of March 1985, however, Congress (I) performed less well than expected, suffering heavy defeats in Andhra Pradesh, Karnataka and Sikkim, and reduced majorities in other states.

In January 1986, in an attempt to revitalize Congress (I), Rajiv Gandhi appointed Arjun Singh, a former Governor of Punjab and hitherto Minister of Commerce, to the recently created post of Vice-President of the party (the post being abolished in October 1986), and two other senior Ministers as General Secretaries. In February there were mass demonstrations and strikes throughout India, in protest against government-imposed increases in the prices of basic commodities such as petroleum products, fertilizers, rice and wheat. The opposition parties united against Rajiv Gandhi's policies, and the entire parliamentary opposition boycotted the President's traditional address on the opening day of the budget session in Parliament. Congress (I) suffered considerable set-backs in the indirect elections to the Rajya Sabha in March, when its overall strength in the House declined to considerably less than the two-thirds majority necessary to enable constitutional amendments to be approved without the support of opposition members. In April Rajiv Gandhi expelled one senior member and suspended three others from Congress (I), in an attempt to purge the party of critics calling themselves 'Indira Gandhi loyalists'. In a major government reshuffle in May, the Prime Minister appointed Sikhs to two senior positions. Rajiv Gandhi survived an assassination attempt by three Sikhs in New Delhi in October.

In June 1986 Lal Denga, the leader of the Mizo National Front (MNF), signed a peace agreement with Rajiv Gandhi, thus ending Mizoram's 25 years of rebellion. The accord granted Mizoram limited autonomy in the drafting of local laws, independent trade with neighbouring foreign countries and a general amnesty for all Mizo rebels. Lal Denga led an interim coalition government, formed by the MNF and Congress (I), until February 1987, when the MNF won an absolute majority at elections for the state assembly. In the same month, Mizoram and Arunachal Pradesh were officially admitted as the 23rd and 24th states of India, respectively, and in May the Union Territory of Goa became India's 25th state.

During 1987 the Prime Minister and his party experienced a number of serious political set-backs. Congress (I) lost control of the Kerala state government at elections to the state assembly in March. It sustained further defeats in state elections in West Bengal in the same month, and in Haryana in June, but retained control of the Nagaland legislature at elections in November. For much of the early part of the year, political tensions were intensified by an open dispute between the Prime Minister and the outgoing President, Giani Zail Singh. Serious public concern was also aroused throughout 1987 by various accusations of corruption and financial irregularities, made against senior figures in Congress (I). Notable among these scandals was the 'Bofors affair', in which large payments were allegedly made to Indian agents by a Swedish company in connection with its sales of munitions to the Indian Government. The Prime Minister strongly denied any involvement in these matters, and a committee of inquiry, established by the Government in August 1987, subsequently exonerated him of any impropriety. However, following the electoral defeats, the allegations of corruption and the declining popularity of Congress (I), five ministers and one deputy minister resigned from the Government between March and August. Among them was the Minister of Defence, Vishwanath Pratap Singh, who was also, with three other senior politicians, expelled from Congress (I) for 'anti-party activities'. V. P. Singh soon emerged as the leader of the Congress (I) dissidents, and in October formed a new political group, the Jan Morcha (People's Front), advocating fundamental socialist principles.

In January 1988 Rajiv Gandhi dissolved the administration of Tamil Nadu and placed the state under presidential rule, in response to the outbreak of violent quarrels between rival factions of the ruling party following the death of the Chief Minister in December 1987. Elections for state assemblies were held in the north-eastern states of Tripura and Meghalaya in February 1988. In Tripura the ruling Communist-led Left Front coalition was narrowly defeated by Congress (I) and an allied local party, following a period of extreme separatist violence (see below). In Meghalaya, however, Congress (I) lost its absolute majority, although remaining the largest single party, in the state assembly. Gandhi then effected a major government reshuffle.

Following a considerable number of resignations from the ruling Congress (I) party in Nagaland in August 1988, the state government was dissolved, and presidential rule was declared. The number of states under direct rule increased to four in September, when President's rule was imposed in Mizoram, following a week of political instability. In the same month, the opposition forces attained a degree of unity when four major centrist parties (the Indian National Congress (S), the Jan Morcha, the Janata Party and the Lok Dal) and three major regional parties (the Asom Gana Parishad, the Dravida Munnetra Kazhagam (DMK) and the Telugu Desam) formed a coalition Rashtriya Morcha (National Front), to oppose Congress (I) at the next general election. In October three of the four centrist parties formed a new political grouping, the Janata Dal (People's Party), which was to work in collaboration with the Rashtriya Morcha. V.P. Singh, who was being widely regarded as Rajiv Gandhi's closest rival, was elected as the Janata Dal's president. In January 1989 Congress (I) was decisively defeated by the DMK in the elections to the state assembly in Tamil Nadu, but gained outright majorities over the regional parties in the elections in the less significant states of Nagaland and Mizoram.

Meanwhile, intercommunal violence continued. The violence in Goa, Assam, Karnataka and Tamil Nadu arose as a result of agitation over the official languages, and in Gujarat, Uttar Pradesh and Madhya Pradesh as a result of Hindu-Muslim tension. In May 1987 more than 100 people were killed during intercommunal clashes between Hindus and Muslims at Meerut, in Uttar Pradesh, and in the old sector of Delhi. Caste violence continued to be a problem in Bihar. After its failure to curb the Hindu-Muslim violence, the elected Government of Jammu and Kashmir was dismissed, and the state was placed first under Governor's rule in March 1986, and then under President's rule in September. In November Rajiv Gandhi and Dr Farook Abdullah, the leader of the Jammu and Kashmir National Conference Party (F), reached an agreement whereby an interim government—a coalition of Congress (I) and the National Conference Party (F), with Dr Abdullah as Chief Minister—was installed in the state. This coalition won an absolute majority at state assembly elections, held in March 1987. In 1986 the Gurkhas (of Nepalese stock) resident in West Bengal launched a campaign for a separate autonomous homeland in the Darjeeling region and the recognition of Nepali as an official language. The violent separatist campaign, led by the Gurkha National Liberation Front (GNLF), was activated by the eviction, in March, of about 10,000 Nepalis from the state of Meghalaya, where the native residents had feared that they were becoming outnumbered by immigrants. When violent disturbances and a disruptive general strike were organized by the GNLF in West Bengal in June 1987, the central Government agreed to hold tripartite discussions with the GNLF's leader, Subhas Ghising, and the Chief Minister of West Bengal, Jyoti Basu. At these negotiations, which were held in Delhi in January 1988, the Prime Minister immediately rejected the GNLF's demand for an autonomous Gurkha state. However, the GNLF campaign for an independent homeland was ended in July, when Subhas Ghising agreed to the establishment of a semi-autonomous Darjeeling Hill Development Council, at a meeting with Jyoti Basu and the Minister of Home Affairs in Delhi. Under the formal peace agreement, which was signed in August, the GNLF was to cease all agitation and to surrender weapons, while the state government was to release all GNLF detainees. In addition, the Government agreed to grant Indian citizenship to all Gurkhas born or domiciled in India. Following the surrender of a large number of weapons by Gurkha separatists, elections to the Darjeeling Hill Development Council were held. Although the GNLF won 26 of the 28 elective seats (the 14 remaining members of the 42-member Council were to be nominated), the prospects for the political situation in West Bengal continued to appear unsettled, since, despite the election results, Subhas Ghising (who was elected as Chairman of the Council) and his supporters continued to demand the establishment of a fully autonomous Gurkha state. In the latter half of the 1970s a campaign was launched by the Tribal National Volunteers (TNV), demanding an autonomous state in part of Tripura. After more than 100 murders by TNV guerrillas in 1986, the organization was declared illegal in January 1987. The violence intensified in January 1988, however, when a further 100 people were killed in guerrilla attacks. In an attempt to quell the violence, the central Government dispatched large numbers of paramilitary troops to Tripura and declared the state a disturbed area. Order was restored in the following month, when Congress (I), in alliance with a small local party, ousted the Marxists from power in the state assembly elections. In August the ethnic conflict was ended when an agreement was signed between the central Government and the TNV guerrillas, who agreed to disarm, disband and abandon their demands for an independent homeland. In return, the Government agreed to amend the Constitution to allow an increased participation of tribal representatives in local government and to restore alienated lands. The paramilitary troops were to be withdrawn following the implementation of the agreement.

The situation in Punjab has shown little sign of improvement since 1985, despite various attempts by the Government to curb tensions and to end the violence. In September 1985 Rajiv Gandhi achieved a temporary solution to the unrest when a general election for the state assembly was held, following an agreement, signed in July, between the central Government and Harchand Singh Longowal, the moderate president of the main Sikh party, Shiromani Akali Dal. Despite the assassination of Longowal by Sikh extremists in August, the election was peaceful and resulted in a victory for Shiromani Akali Dal, which assumed power in the state after two years of presidential rule. On the same day as the state election, polling also took place for Punjab's 13 seats in the Lok Sabha, postponed from December 1984. An important element in the agreement that Rajiv Gandhi and Longowal negotiated in July 1985 was the proposed transfer of Chandigarh, since 1966 the joint capital of Punjab and Haryana, to Punjab alone. In return, Haryana was to benefit from the completion of the Sutlej-Yamuna canal, to bring irrigation water from Punjab to the dry south of the state, and the transfer of several Hindi-speaking border villages from Punjab to Haryana. Four commissions were established to organize the transfer, but each one failed to accomplish its task, and by early 1989 the transfer had still not taken place. Hindu-Sikh violence continued throughout 1986 (it was estimated that about 650 people were killed during the year) despite the replacement of the Governor of Punjab, after only three months in office, in April 1986, the dispatch of thousands of paramilitary reinforcements from New Delhi and the considerable improvement in the efficiency of the Punjab police force. A worrying development was that, after years of comparative quiescence among Punjab's Hindu minority, the extremist Hindu Shiv Sena ('Army of Shiva') group began to organize resistance against Sikh terrorism. Many Hindu families, on the other hand, left Punjab for Haryana, to escape the unrest. A steady flow of Sikh families began to enter Punjab from Haryana, where they feared retaliation from the Hindu majority. In January 1986 the Sikh extremist groups re-established a terrorist stronghold inside the Golden Temple complex at Amritsar. In mid-1986 the extremists separated from the ruling moderate Shiromani Akali Dal (Longowal) and formed two militant factions—the United Akali Dal, led by Joginder Singh, and the Akali Dal (B), led by Prakash Singh Badal, a former Chief Minister of the state (these two factions merged to form the Unified Akali Dal in February 1987). In May 1987 Rajiv Gandhi dismissed the Chief Minister, Surjit Singh Barnala, and his government, suspended the state assembly and imposed President's rule in Punjab. Despite an increase in the number of arrests of Sikh terrorists and the resumption of discussions between the Government and the moderate Sikh leaders, the violence in Punjab worsened, and it was estimated that more than 2,700 people were killed during 1987 and 1988.

In December 1985 an election for the state assembly in Assam took place, following an accord, reached after five years of sectarian violence, which limited the voting rights of immigrants to Assam: those foreigners (mainly Bangladeshis) who had arrived before 1966 were to be accorded full voting rights; those who had arrived between 1966 and 1971 were to be disenfranchised for 10 years; and those who had arrived after 1971 (the proclamation date of the independence of Bangladesh) were to be expelled from Assam. The election result was a victory for the Asom Gana Parishad (Assam People's Council), a newly-formed local party, which won a clear majority over its nearest rival, Congress (I). The delayed voting for Assam's 14 seats in the Lok Sabha took place on the same day. Plans were revived in 1985 to erect a fence along the Assam/Bangladesh border, in an attempt to curb illegal immigration from Bangladesh. When the accord was announced in December, Bangladesh stated that it would not take back Bengali immigrants from Assam and denied that it had allowed any illegal refugees to cross its borders into Assam. By early 1988, however, most of the clauses of the accord still awaited implementation.

In foreign affairs, the Janata Government of 1977-80 had embarked on a policy of improving relations with all neighbouring countries, which the Congress (I) Government continued. In 1982 India made an interim agreement with Bangladesh over the sharing of the Ganges waters, and in 1985 an interim agreement was reached which guaranteed Bangladesh's share of the Ganges' dry-season flow. In December 1986 India and Bangladesh signed an agreement on measures aimed at preventing cross-border terrorism. In September 1988 the two countries established a joint working committee to examine methods of averting the annual devastating floods in the Ganges delta.

Relations with Pakistan had deteriorated in the late 1970s and early 1980s, owing to Pakistan's potential capability for the development of nuclear weapons and major US deliveries of armaments to that country. The Indian Government believed that such deliveries would upset the balance of power in the region and would precipitate an arms race. Talks between Pakistan's President, Gen. Mohammad Zia ul-Haq, and Indira Gandhi in November 1982 eased the tension. On the death

INDIA

Introductory Survey

of Indira Gandhi, Pakistan immediately assured India of its continued peaceful intentions. President Zia ul-Haq visited India in December 1985, when he and Rajiv Gandhi announced their mutual commitment not to attack each other's nuclear installations and to negotiate the sovereignty of the disputed Siachin glacier region in northern Kashmir. By March 1986, however, relations had deteriorated again, and the two countries had resumed the exchange of widely-publicized diplomatic attacks (including India's allegations that Pakistan was harbouring and training Sikh extremists to infiltrate Punjab). Pakistan continued to demand a settlement of the Kashmir problem in accordance with earlier UN resolutions, prescribing a plebiscite in the two parts of the state, now divided between India and Pakistan. India, however, argued that the problem should be settled in accordance with the Simla agreement of 1972, which required that all Indo-Pakistani disputes be resolved through bilateral negotiations. Tension increased between December 1986 and February 1987, when both countries conducted extensive military exercises near their common border in the sensitive Punjab region. Measures were rapidly taken to reduce the tension. Pakistan and India conducted phased withdrawals of troops between February and May. In September, however, a clash between Indian and Pakistani troops was reported from Kashmir (Indian army officials claimed that about 150 Pakistanis were killed). The Indian decision to construct a barrage on the River Jhelum, in an alleged violation of the 1960 Indus Water Treaty, has also created concern in Pakistan. In December 1988 relations between India and Pakistan improved when Rajiv Gandhi visited Islamabad for discussions with Pakistan's new Prime Minister, Benazir Bhutto. At this meeting, which constituted the first official visit of an Indian Prime Minister to Pakistan for nearly 25 years, the two leaders signed three agreements, including a formal pledge not to attack each other's nuclear installations.

Since 1983 India's relations with Sri Lanka have been dominated by tensions and conflicts between the island's Sinhalese and Tamil communities, in which India has sought to arbitrate. Negotiations and proposals by Indian mediators proved fruitless until July 1987, when Rajiv Gandhi and the Sri Lankan President, Junius Jayawardene, signed an accord aimed at settling the conflict. To help with the implementation of the accord, a 7,000-strong Indian Peace-Keeping Force (IPKF) was dispatched to Sri Lanka in August (the size of the IPKF had increased to an estimated 50,000 by February 1988). The IPKF has encountered considerable resistance from the Tamil separatist guerrillas, especially during the siege of the Tamil stronghold in Jaffna in October 1987. Following the gradual implementation of the peace accord, however, several thousand IPKF troops were withdrawn from Sri Lanka in the latter half of 1988 and early 1989. An estimated 40,000 IPKF troops remained in Sri Lanka in February 1989.

During 1981 there was a marked improvement in India's relations with the People's Republic of China, which had suffered a set-back after India's recognition of the Heng Samrin Government of Kampuchea in July 1980. Both countries agreed to find an early solution to their Himalayan border dispute (over about 128,000 sq km of land) and to seek to normalize relations. China was displeased, however, when Arunachal Pradesh was granted full statehood in December 1986. In 1987 both sides accused each other of troop concentrations on the disputed frontier and of border violations. No substantial progress was made during the eighth round of Sino-Indian negotiations, held in New Delhi in November. However, during Rajiv Gandhi's visit to China in December 1988 (the first visit to China by an Indian Prime minister for 34 years), the two countries agreed to establish a joint working group to negotiate the border dispute. This group was due to meet in June 1989.

The USSR is a major contributor of economic and military assistance to India (in 1986 it was estimated that about 70% of India's defence equipment was supplied by the USSR). The Indo-Soviet Chamber of Commerce and Industry was formally inaugurated in Delhi, to expand bilateral trade between the two countries, in June 1986, and Rajiv Gandhi held a successful series of meetings during a visit to Moscow in July 1987. There are close ties between the USA and India in economic and scientific affairs, and political ties were further strengthened after Rajiv Gandhi's visit to the USA in October 1987. India remains uneasy, however, over the continued support, in aid and armaments, which is given to Pakistan by the USA, while the USA, in turn, remains worried lest its military or dual-use technology be 'leaked' to the USSR through India, or diverted to an Indian programme to produce nuclear weapons.

Government

India is a federal republic. Legislative power is vested in Parliament, consisting of the President and two Houses. The Council of States (Rajya Sabha) has 245 members, most of whom are indirectly elected by the State Assemblies for six years (one-third retiring every two years), the remainder being nominated by the President for six years. The House of the People (Lok Sabha) has 542 elected members, serving for five years (subject to dissolution). A small number of members of the Lok Sabha may be nominated by the President to represent the Anglo-Indian community, while the 542 members are directly elected by universal adult suffrage in single-member constituencies. The President is a constitutional Head of State, elected for five years by an electoral college comprising elected members of both Houses of Parliament and the state legislatures. The President exercises executive power on the advice of the Council of Ministers, which is responsible to Parliament. The President appoints the Prime Minister and, on the latter's recommendation, other Ministers.

India contains 25 self-governing states, each with a Governor (appointed by the President for five years), a legislature (elected for five years) and a Council of Ministers headed by the Chief Minister. Bihar, Jammu and Kashmir, Karnataka, Maharashtra and Uttar Pradesh have bicameral legislatures, the other 20 state legislatures being unicameral. Each state has its own legislative, executive and judicial machinery, corresponding to that of the Indian Union. In the event of the failure of constitutional government in a state, presidential rule can be imposed by the Union. There are also seven Union Territories, administered by Lieutenant-Governors or Administrators, all of whom are appointed by the President.

Defence

In June 1988 the estimated strength of India's armed forces was 1,367,000: an army of 1,200,000, a navy of 52,000 and an air force of 115,000. Military service has been voluntary but, under the amended Constitution, it is the fundamental duty of every citizen to perform national service when called upon. The proposed defence budget for 1988/89 was 130,000m. rupees.

Economic Affairs

On the basis of aggregate gross national product (GNP), India ranks among the 15 largest economies in the world. However, with its vast population (second only to the People's Republic of China), the country remains among the 20 poorest in terms of average income. In 1987, according to estimates by the World Bank, India's GNP was US $241,305m. (at average 1985–87 prices). GNP per head in that year was about $300, having increased by 2.6% annually, in real terms, since 1980. The average annual growth of overall gross domestic product (GDP), measured in constant prices, was 3.7% in 1965–80, rising to 4.9% in 1980–86. According to government sources, it was estimated that, because of the serious drought in 1987, GDP growth in 1987/88 did not exceed 1.5%. Owing to favourable monsoon conditions and the resultant good harvests in 1988, however, growth was expected to reach about 8% in 1988/89.

About 65% of the working population are engaged in agriculture, which accounted for 29% of GDP in 1987/88. The major part of the sown area is planted with cereals, the staple crops. Extensive plantations produce tea, rubber and coffee, while cotton, jute, sugar, oilseeds, tobacco and other cash crops are also grown. Crops are frequently damaged by drought and floods. Since 1975/76 improved irrigation (in 1987 the total land area under irrigation was about 67m. ha), the increased use of chemical fertilizers and the introduction of high-yield strains of rice and wheat, as well as favourable monsoons, have led to record harvests, enabling India to accumulate surplus stocks of food grains and even to export wheat and rice. The annual output of food grains (cereals and pulses) increased by 14% in the period 1979–84, representing an average annual increase of 2.6%; a rate which exceeded the 2.3% annual population growth. The annual harvest of food grains (including rice on a milled basis) declined from 150.4m. tons in 1985/86 to 143.4m. tons in 1986/87: a reduction of only 4.7%, despite an extremely severe drought (reportedly the worst of the 20th century) in about two-thirds of the country, as well as heavy flooding in the north and east. Total agricultural production in 1986/87 was estimated to have risen by about 1.5%, compared with the previous year, despite the drought and flooding. In 1987/88 the most severe drought since India's independence was estimated to have reduced the country's food output by only 10%. In addition, for the first time in a year of major drought, the Indian economy achieved overall growth rather than overall decline. The output of food grains was 138.4m. tons in 1987/88, and was expected to increase to 166m. tons in 1988/89, following a bountiful monsoon season. Under the seventh Five-Year Plan, it was estimated that India's annual output of food grains would have to reach 175m. tons by 1990, in order that the country's overall economic targets be met. While concentrating on increasing the production of wheat and rice, however, other crops have been neglected, with the result that India continues to require food imports.

India has the fourth largest coal reserves in the world, and in 1987/88 output totalled an estimated 179.8m. metric tons. Coal is India's prime source of commercial energy (providing about 65% of the total energy consumed by Indian industry), and the production target for 1988/89 envisaged output of 196.3m. tons. The Jhanjhar coal mine in West Bengal, when completed in 1995, will be the largest underground mine in the country. There are large reserves of iron ore in Bihar and Orissa, as well as bauxite, titanium ore, manganese, mica and rare metals (including gold). In 1981 the Government negotiated a large foreign loan to finance construction of new aluminium and steel plants in Orissa. A large steel plant at Visakhapatnam, in Andhra Pradesh, was due to be completed in 1990. The state-owned Hindustan Copper Ltd planned to increase copper production at its Malanjkhard copper project in Madhya Pradesh in 1987, and to carry out further exploration. In 1986 the Malanjkhard copper project was India's largest open-cast mine. In 1983 India became the world's leading exporter of cut diamonds, and in 1986/87 placed 7.5m. carats on the international market, representing an increase of nearly 40% over the 1985/86 level. Total output of uncut diamonds reached 17,580 carats in 1987.

Inshore deposits of petroleum have been found in Assam, Arunachal Pradesh, Gujarat, Madhya Pradesh, Tamil Nadu (Cauvery basin) and Nagaland, and offshore oilfields have been discovered in the Western continental shelf off the Maharashtra and Gujarat coasts, off the coast of Tamil Nadu, and in the Bay of Bengal. In 1980 it was announced that foreign oil companies would be allowed to explore for petroleum, both on shore and off shore. In 1986 India invited bids from international oil companies for exploring 27 offshore blocks. In late 1987 the Government signed contracts with a consortium of two US companies for exploration in three of the blocks. Petroleum from India's own resources is playing a growing role in the economy. India produced about 70% of its petroleum requirements in 1986, compared with 50% in 1983 and 34% in 1980. Output of crude petroleum was 27.9m. tons in 1984, and increased to 29.8m. tons in 1985. In 1986, as there was no significant addition to the recoverable reserves, production reached its peak level of about 31.2m. tons. As a result of increased production, imports (in value terms) of crude petroleum and petroleum products declined by around 25% in the fiscal year 1984. The cost of petroleum imports remained low in 1986/87, owing to the collapse of international petroleum prices, but was expected to increase by at least 50% in 1987/88, as a result of rising consumption and stagnating domestic production. The Government aimed to spend Rs 1,272,767m. on the petroleum industry during the seventh Five-Year Plan (1985–90), drilling more than 2,500 new oil wells and increasing annual refining capacity to 45m. tons, in an attempt to become self-sufficient in petroleum by 1990. Discoveries in the 1980s of natural gas deposits have led to the widely-held opinion that India has the potential for natural gas production on a very large scale. Production at the Bassei offshore gas field (one of the largest in the world) began in 1985. In 1985 the Government planned to construct a gas pipeline of 1,800 km, from near Bombay to Bareilly, to exploit the reserves of the Bombay offshore fields. In 1986 an ambitious gas pipeline project was instigated, involving the laying of a 1,730-km pipeline from Hazira, in Gujarat, to Jagdishpur, in Uttar Pradesh, to carry natural gas from two offshore fields to six fertilizer plants in northern India.

India ranks among the 10 leading industrial nations in the world, although manufacturing employs only about 10% of the country's workers. New industries, such as heavy engineering, iron and steel, chemicals and electronics, have expanded rapidly, and in 1986/87 machinery and transport equipment constituted India's fourth-largest earner of foreign currency (with exports worth an estimated Rs 7,451.4m.). Various measures have been introduced to try to improve both power generation and industrial relations, the two main hindrances to increased industrial production. During the sixth Five-Year Plan (1980–85) the average annual increase in industrial output was 5.6%. Industrial growth reached around 8% per year in both 1985/86 and 1986/87, and was expected to remain at about the same level in 1987/88, despite the adverse effects of the drought.

The annual rate of inflation declined steadily from 10% in 1982/83 to 3.8% in 1985/86. It rose again, however, to 5.1% in 1986/87, and to an estimated 9% in drought-affected 1987/88. In 1985/86 the trade deficit (a perennial problem for the Indian economy) increased by about 63%, to a record Rs 87,631m. (imports Rs 196,576.9m., exports Rs 108,945.9m.), owing partly to a drastic decrease in exports of crude petroleum. In 1986/87, however, the trade deficit narrowed to Rs 75,169m. (imports Rs 200,835.3m., exports Rs 125,666.2m.), owing to a deceleration in the rate of increase of imports, a considerable improvement in export growth, and a reduction in the cost of petroleum imports, resulting from the fall in international petroleum prices. The current deficit on the balance of payments fell from $3,950m. (equivalent to 2% of GDP) in 1985/86 to $2,420m. (equivalent to 1.1% of GDP) in 1986/87. In 1988 India secured from its Western aid consortium new financial aid commitments totalling US $6,300m. for 1988/89 (17% higher than the aid commitments granted in 1987).

In 1985 the seventh Five-Year Plan (1985–90) was announced. It envisaged a total investment of Rs 3,200,000m., double that of the sixth Plan, and aimed at an average annual GDP growth rate of around 5% (the sixth Plan achieved its target of an annual growth rate of 5.2%). The Plan projected an average annual growth of 5.8% in imports and of 6.8% in exports. Growth rates of 4% for agriculture and 8% for industry were also envisaged. The main emphasis was on improving the energy sector, which was to receive 30% of the total outlay in an attempt to reduce the crippling power shortages, and on reducing the number of people below the 'poverty line' from 273m. (36% of the total population) in 1985 to 211m. (26%) by 1990. The Plan also aimed to develop the infrastructure and to make more efficient use of existing capital investment while increasing employment. The guidelines for the eighth Five-Year Plan (1990–95) were approved in late 1988. The eighth Plan was to aim at an average annual GDP growth rate of 6%. It was projected, however, that this higher growth rate would require an increase in levels of taxation and a reduction in government expenditure.

A major problem in the Indian economy is a recurrent budget deficit. This deficit increased steadily in the latter half of the 1980s and budgeted expenditure on debt interest rose sharply. In the draft budget for 1988/89, interest payments comprised the largest single item of expenditure (exceeding even defence expenditure), and were equivalent to more than one-half of that year's projected development expenditure. The main features of the 1988/89 budget were the proposed increase in public spending on rural development, together with general measures, which were aimed at benefiting minority sections in society, and incentives for selected industries.

Social Welfare

Health programmes are primarily the responsibility of the State Governments, but the Union Government provides finance for improvements in public health services. The structure of the health system is based on a network of primary health centres. In 1977 there were 5,372 such centres and 37,745 sub-centres in rural areas. In 1981 India had 1,066,164 hospital beds and 268,712 physicians. Various national health programmes aim to combat leprosy, malaria and tuberculosis. Smallpox was declared eradicated in 1977. The family planning programme was launched in 1952 and the emphasis now is on advice and education through Family Welfare Centres. A new approach to family planning was introduced in 1986, with the aim of reducing India's rate of population growth from 2.3% to 1.2% per year, so that the population does not exceed 1,000m. by the year 2000. Expenditure on health by all levels of government in the financial year 1984/85 was about 20,860m. rupees (3.9% of total government spending).

INDIA

Introductory Survey, Statistical Survey

Education

Education is primarily the responsibility of the individual State Governments. Elementary education for children up to 14 years of age is theoretically compulsory in all states except Nagaland and Himachal Pradesh. Lower primary education, for children aged six to 11, is free in all states. Upper primary education, for children aged 11–14, is free in 12 states. Enrolment at the first level of education in 1984 was equivalent to 92% of children aged six to 10 years (107% of boys; 76% of girls). Secondary enrolment in 1984 was 35% of those aged 11 to 17 (45% of boys; 24% of girls). A new pattern of education, consisting of 10 years' elementary education, two years at higher secondary level and three years for the first degree course, had been introduced in the majority of states by 1985/86. It is hoped that universal free and compulsory education up to the age of 14 can be achieved by 1990. In 1978 the National Board for Adult Education launched a massive programme to combat illiteracy. Of the total population, 36.17% were literate in 1981, compared with 15.67% in 1961. However, female literacy was only 24.88% in 1981, and women's education, especially in rural areas, has made few advances. Expenditure on education by all levels of government in 1984/85 was about 76,160m. rupees (14.4% of total government spending).

Public Holidays

The public holidays observed in India vary locally. The dates given below apply to Delhi. As religious feasts depend on astronomical observations, holidays are usually declared at the beginning of the year in which they will be observed. It is not possible, therefore, to indicate more than the month in which some of the following holidays will occur.

1989: January (Pongal), 26 January (Republic Day), 6 March (Maha Shrivratri), 22 March (Holi), 24 March (Good Friday), 14 April (Ram Navami), 18 April (Mahabir Jayanti), 7 May (Id al-Fitr, end of Ramadan), 20 May (Buddha Purnima), 5 July (Rath Yatra), 14 July (Id-uz-Zuha, Feast of the Sacrifice), 4 August (Muharram, Islamic New Year), 15 August (Independence Day), 24 August (Janmashtami), August/September (Onam), 2 October (Mahatma Gandhi's Birthday), 10 October (Dussehra), 29 October (Diwali), 13 November (Guru Nanak Jayanti), 25–26 December (Christmas).

1990: January (Pongal), 26 January (Republic Day), January/February/March (Maha Shrivratri and Holi), March/April (Ram Navami and Mahabir Jayanti), 13 April (Good Friday), 27 April (Id al-Fitr, end of Ramadan), May (Buddha Purnima), June/July (Rath Yatra), 4 July (Id-uz-Zuha, Feast of the Sacrifice), 24 July (Muharram, Islamic New Year), August/September (Janmashtami and Onam), October/November (Dussehra, Diwali and Guru Nanak Jayanti), 2 October (Mahatma Gandhi's Birthday), 25–26 December (Christmas).

Weights and Measures

The metric system has been officially introduced. The imperial system is also still in use, as are traditional Indian weights and measures, including:
1 tola = 11.66 grams
1 seer = 933.1 grams
1 maund = 37.32 kg
1 lakh = (1,00,000) = 100,000
1 crore = (1,00,00,000) = 10,000,000

Statistical Survey

Source (unless otherwise stated): Central Statistical Organization, Ministry of Planning, Sardar Patel, Bhavan, Parliament St, New Delhi 110 001; tel. (11) 353626.

Area and Population

AREA, POPULATION AND DENSITY*

Area (sq km)	3,287,263†
Population (census results)‡	
1 April 1971	548,159,652
1 March 1981§	
Males	354,397,884
Females	330,786,808
Total	685,184,692
Population (official estimates at mid-year)	
1986	766,135,000
1987	781,374,000
1988 (provisional)	796,600,000
Density (per sq km) at mid-1988	242.3

* Including Sikkim (incorporated into India on 26 April 1975) and the Indian-held part of Jammu and Kashmir.
† 1,269,219 sq miles.
‡ Excluding adjustment for underenumeration, estimated at 1.67% in 1971 and 1.7% in 1981.
§ Including estimates for Assam.
Source: Registrar General of India.

STATES AND TERRITORIES

	Capital	Area (sq km)	Population April 1971	Population March 1981
States				
Andhra Pradesh	Hyderabad	275,068	43,502,708	53,549,673
Arunachal Pradesh[1]	Itanagar	83,743	467,511	631,839
Assam	Dispur	78,438	14,625,152	19,896,843*
Bihar	Patna	173,877	56,353,369	69,914,734
Gujarat	Gandhinagar	196,024	26,697,475	34,085,799
Haryana	Chandigarh[2]	44,212	10,036,808	12,922,618
Himachal Pradesh	Simla	55,673	3,460,434	4,280,818
Jammu and Kashmir[3]	Srinagar	222,236	4,616,632	5,987,389
Karnataka	Bangalore	191,791	29,299,014	37,135,714
Kerala	Trivandrum	38,863	21,347,375	25,453,680
Madhya Pradesh	Bhopal	443,446	41,654,119	52,178,844
Maharashtra	Bombay	307,690	50,412,235	62,784,171
Manipur	Imphal	22,327	1,072,753	1,420,953
Meghalaya	Shillong	22,429	1,011,699	1,335,819
Mizoram[4]	Aizawl	21,081	332,390	493,757
Nagaland	Kohima	16,579	516,449	774,930
Orissa	Bhubaneswar	155,707	21,944,615	26,370,271
Punjab	Chandigarh[2]	50,362	13,551,060	16,788,915
Rajasthan	Jaipur	342,239	25,765,806	34,261,862
Sikkim	Gangtok	7,096	209,843	316,385
Tamil Nadu	Madras	130,058	41,199,168	48,408,077
Tripura	Agartala	10,486	1,556,342	2,053,058
Uttar Pradesh	Lucknow	294,411	88,341,144	110,862,013
West Bengal	Calcutta	88,752	44,312,011	54,580,647

INDIA

Statistical Survey

STATES AND TERRITORIES—continued

	Capital	Area (sq km)	Population April 1971	Population March 1981
Territories				
Andaman and Nicobar Islands	Port Blair	8,249	115,133	188,741
Chandigarh[2]	Chandigarh	114	257,251	451,610
Dadra and Nagar Haveli	Silvassa	491	74,170	103,676
Delhi	Delhi	1,483	4,065,698	6,220,406
Goa, Daman and Diu[5]	Panaji	3,814	857,771	1,086,730
Lakshadweep	Kavaratti	32	31,810	40,249
Pondicherry	Pondicherry	492	471,707	604,471

* Estimate.

[1] Arunachal Pradesh was granted statehood in February 1987.

[2] Chandigarh forms a separate Union Territory, not within Haryana or Punjab. As part of a scheme for a transfer of territory between the two states, Chandigarh was due to be incorporated into Punjab on 26 January 1986, but the transfer has been postponed.

[3] The area figure refers to the whole of Jammu and Kashmir State, of which 78,114 sq km is occupied by Pakistan. The population figures refer only to the Indian-held part of the territory.

[4] Mizoram was granted statehood in February 1987.

[5] Goa was granted statehood in May 1987. Daman and Diu remain a Union Territory.

Source: *Census of India*, Part II—B(i) Primary Census Abstract of General Population 1981.

PRINCIPAL TOWNS (population at 1981 census*)

Greater Bombay	8,243,405	Hubli-Dharwar	527,108	
Delhi	4,884,234	Sholapur	514,860	
Calcutta	3,305,006	Jodhpur	506,345	
Madras	3,276,622	Trivandrum	499,531	
Bangalore	2,628,593	Ranchi	489,626	
Hyderabad	2,187,262	Mysore	479,081	
Ahmedabad	2,159,127	Vijaywada (Vijayavada)	461,772	
Kanpur (Cawnpore)	1,486,522	Jamshedpur	457,061	
Nagpur	1,219,461	Rajkot	445,076	
Pune (Poona)	1,203,351	Meerut	417,395	
Jaipur (Jeypore)	977,165	Jalandhar	408,196	
Lucknow	916,954	Bareilly	394,938	
Indore	829,327	Kozhikode (Calicut)	394,447	
Madurai	820,891	Chandigarh	379,660	
Patna	813,963	Ajmer	375,593	
Surat	776,876	Guntur	367,699	
Howrah	744,429	Tiruchirapalli	362,045	
Vadodara (Baroda)	734,473	Salem	361,394	
Varanasi (Banaras)	720,755	Kota	358,241	
Coimbatore	704,514	Kolhapur	340,625	
Agra	694,191	Raipur	338,245	
Bhopal	671,018	Warangal	335,150	
Jabalpur (Jubbulpore)	649,085	Faridabad	330,864	
Allahabad	619,628	Moradabad	330,051	
Ludhiana	607,052	Aligarh	320,861	
Amritsar	594,844	Bhilainagar	319,450	
Srinagar	594,775	Durgapur	311,798	
Visakhapatnam	584,166	Thane	309,897	
Cochin	551,567	Bhavnagar	308,642	
Gwalior	539,015	Gorakhpur	307,501	

* Figures refer to the city proper in each case. For urban agglomerations, the following populations were recorded: Calcutta 9,194,018; Delhi 5,729,283; Madras 4,289,347; Bangalore 2,921,751; Ahmedabad 2,548,057; Hyderabad 2,545,836; Pune (Poona) 1,686,109; Kanpur 1,639,064; Nagpur 1,302,066; Jaipur 1,015,160; Lucknow 1,007,604; Coimbatore 920,355; Patna 918,903; Surat 913,806; Madurai 907,732; Varanasi (Banaras) 797,162; Jabalpur 757,303; Agra 747,318; Vadodara (Baroda) 744,881; Cochin 685,836; Dhanbad 678,069; Jamshedpur 669,580; Allahabad 650,070; Ulhasnagar 648,671; Tiruchirapalli 609,548; Srinagar 606,022; Visakhapatnam 603,630; Gwalior 555,862; Kozhikode (Calicut) 546,058; Vijaywada 543,008; Meerut 536,615; Trivandrum 520,125; Salem 518,615; Sholapur 514,860; Ranchi 502,771.

Capital: New Delhi, population 273,036 in 1981.

BIRTHS AND DEATHS
(estimates, based on Sample Registration Scheme)

	1985	1986	1987
Birth rate (per 1,000)	32.9	32.6	32.0
Death rate (per 1,000)	11.8	11.1	n.a.

ECONOMICALLY ACTIVE POPULATION
(1981 census, excluding Assam)*

	Males	Females	Total
Agriculture, hunting, forestry and fishing	116,482,682	36,532,504	153,015,187
Mining and quarrying	1,100,931	163,158	1,264,089
Manufacturing	21,480,943	3,662,094	25,143,037
Electricity, gas and water	949,663	24,135	973,799
Construction	3,207,287	358,121	3,565,408
Trade, restaurants and hotels	11,356,083	808,674	12,164,757
Transport, storage and communications	5,898,901	170,432	6,069,332
Finance, insurance, real estate and business services	1,656,407	107,830	1,764,237
Community, social and personal services	15,410,505	3,146,217	18,556,722
Activities not adequately defined†	3,536,806	18,551,606	22,088,411
Total	181,080,208	63,524,771	244,604,979

* Figures are based on a 5% sample tabulation of census returns. As each figure is estimated independently, the totals shown may differ from the sum of the component parts.

† The figures refer to marginal workers and persons who were unemployed or seeking work for the first time.

Agriculture

PRINCIPAL CROPS ('000 metric tons, year ending 30 June)

	1985/86	1986/87	1987/88
Rice (milled)	63,825	60,557	56,434
Sorghum (Jowar)	10,197	9,185	11,847
Cat-tail millet (Bajra)	3,664	4,514	3,282
Maize	6,644	7,593	5,629
Finger millet (Ragi)	2,518	2,708	2,325
Small millets	1,217	1,169	1,169
Wheat	47,052	44,323	45,096
Barley	1,962	1,669	1,593
Total cereals	137,079	131,711	127,374
Chick-peas (Gram)	5,788	4,532	3,622
Pigeon-peas (Tur)	2,441	2,272	2,234
Dry beans, dry peas, lentils and other pulses	5,133	4,904	5,184
Total food grains	150,440	143,418	138,414
Groundnuts (in shell)	5,121	5,875	5,673
Sesame seed	501	448	562
Rapeseed and mustard	2,681	2,605	3,370
Linseed	376	317	372
Castor beans	308	230	185
Total oil seeds (incl. others)	10,833	10,723	11,822
Cotton lint*	8,727	6,905	6,432
Jute†	10,886	7,353	5,800
Kenaf (Mesta)†	1,761	1,273	982
Tea (made)	657	624	673
Sugar cane:			
production gur	17,100	18,700	19,700
production cane	170,648	186,090	196,723
Tobacco (leaves)	441	460	n.a.
Potatoes	10,423	12,740	14,138
Chillies (dry)	877	780	n.a.

* Production in '000 bales of 170 kg each.
† Production in '000 bales of 180 kg each.

Source: Directorate of Economics and Statistics, Ministry of Agriculture and Rural Development, and Ministry of Commerce (for tea).

INDIA

LIVESTOCK (FAO estimates, '000 head year ending September)

	1984	1985	1986
Cattle	195,610*	197,950*	200,000
Sheep*	51,130	52,770	54,460
Goats	99,430	99,490*	102,870*
Pigs	8,650	8,700	8,700
Horses	900	910	910
Asses	1,000	1,000	1,001
Mules	130	132	132
Buffaloes*	71,900	73,440	75,010
Camels	1,050	1,100	1,100

* Unofficial figure(s).
Poultry (FAO estimates, million): 160 in 1984; 170 in 1985; 180 in 1986.

Source: FAO, *Production Yearbook*.

LIVESTOCK PRODUCTS ('000 metric tons)

	1984	1985	1986
Beef and veal†	149	150	160
Buffalo meat†	148	152	163
Mutton and lamb†	135	141	147
Goats' meat†	346	358	370
Pig meat†	82	85	86
Poultry meat†	150	161	175
Cows' milk*	17,100	19,000	20,100
Buffaloes' milk*	20,439	22,265	23,180
Goats' milk*	1,161	1,035	1,020
Butter and ghee*	690	700	720
Hen eggs	784†	840*	916.5*
Wool:			
greasy	38.7	39.9	40.7†
clean	25.9*	26.7*	27.3†
Cattle and buffalo hides (fresh)†	817	823	831.1
Sheep skins (fresh)†	37.4	37.6	37.9
Goat skins (fresh)†	73.4	75.6	76.2

* Unofficial figure(s).   † FAO estimate(s).

Source: FAO, *Production Yearbook*.

Forestry

ROUNDWOOD REMOVALS (FAO estimates, '000 cu metres)

	1984	1985	1986
Sawlogs, veneer logs and logs for sleepers	17,518	18,350	18,350
Pulpwood*	1,208	1,208	1,208
Other industrial wood	4,242	4,324	4,400
Fuel wood	218,172	222,437	226,298
Total	241,140	246,319	250,256

* Assumed to be unchanged since 1978.
Source: FAO, *Yearbook of Forest Products*.

SAWNWOOD PRODUCTION (FAO estimates, '000 cu metres)

	1983	1984	1985
Coniferous sawnwood (incl. boxboards)	1,965	2,160	2,374
Broadleaved sawnwood (incl. boxboards)	12,278	13,495	14,834
Sub-total	14,243	15,655	17,208
Railway sleepers*	252	252	252
Total	14,495	15,907	17,460

* Assumed to be unchanged since 1979.
1986: Production as in 1985 (FAO estimates).
Source: FAO, *Yearbook of Forest Products*.

Statistical Survey

Fishing

('000 metric tons, live weight)

	1985	1986	1987
Indian Ocean:			
Bombay-duck (Bummalo)	104.9	95.7	88.9
Marine catfishes	48.8	65.4	59.4
Croakers and drums	151.6	162.2	189.1
Indian oil-sardine (sardinella)	273.0	270.5	244.1
Anchovies	71.4	66.6	58.1
Hairtails and cutlass fishes	84.8	73.5	72.5
Indian mackerel	89.9	62.3	66.6
Other marine fishes (incl. unspecified)	633.7	665.8	648.3
Total sea-fish	1,458.3	1,462.0	1,427.0
Shrimps and prawns	232.5	215.3	206.9
Other marine animals	43.6	39.7	47.6
Total sea catch	1,734.2	1,717.0	1,681.5
Inland waters:			
Freshwater fishes	1,090.1	1,205.0	1,212.0
Total catch	2,824.3	2,922.0	2,893.5

Source: Ministry of Agriculture and Rural Development (Fisheries Division).

Mining

('000 metric tons, unless otherwise indicated)

	1985	1986	1987
Coal	149,259	161,328	173,352
Lignite	7,774	7,104	8,244
Iron ore*	44,184	49,020	49,184
Manganese ore*	1,260	1,212	1,272
Bauxite	2,268	2,340	2,460
Chalk (Fireclay)	696	636	540
Kaolin (China clay)	756	708	696
Dolomite	2,232	2,100	2,160
Gypsum	1,284	1,596	1,728
Limestone	48,384	52,752	56,496
Crude petroleum	29,856	31,149	30,144
Sea salt	9,876	10,116	9,900
Chromium ore*	564	708	612
Phosphorite	912	648	672
Kyanite	30	31.2	38.4
Magnesite	420	444	432
Steatite	348	348	360
Copper ore*	4,200	4,416	5,136
Lead concentrates (metric tons)*	35,448	44,412	47,364
Zinc concentrates (metric tons)*	87,084	89,532	104,808
Mica—crude (metric tons)	4,800	4,800	3,600
Gold (kilograms)	1,848	1,932	1,872
Diamonds (carats)	16,272	16,644	17,580
Natural gas (million cu m)†	4,692	6,624	7,008

* Figures refer to gross weight. For 1985 the estimated metal content (in '000 metric tons) was: Iron 27,837; Manganese 481.9; Chromium 174; Copper 50.3; Lead 26.6; Zinc 53.4.
† Figures refer to gas utilized.
Source: Indian Bureau of Mines.

Industry

SELECTED PRODUCTS
('000 metric tons, unless otherwise indicated)

	1985	1986	1987
Refined sugar*	6,504	7,008	8,508
Cotton cloth (million metres)	9,289	9,294	9,017
Jute manufactures	1,288	1,442	1,238
Paper and paper board	1,463	1,889	1,985
Sulphuric acid	2,709	n.a.	n.a.
Soda ash	826	874	970
Fertilizers	5,580	6,670	7,248
Petroleum products	39,268	41,880	44,688
Cement	37,368	33,672	37,011
Pig iron	9,701	10,460	10,808
Finished steel	7,841	8,864	9,790
Aluminium (metric tons)	260,016	234,650	245,328
Diesel engines (number)	1,945,200	2,065,200	1,911,600
Sewing machines (number)	333,600	338,500	368,400
Radio receivers (number)	1,212,000	1,080,000	1,176,000
Electric fans (number)	6,240,000	6,348,000	5,736,000
Passenger cars and jeeps (number)	117,156	130,090	155,592
Passenger buses and trucks (number)	105,324	94,905	123,921
Motor cycles and scooters (number)	670,464	887,808	1,479,020
Bicycles (number)	5,640,000	5,844,000	7,740,000

* Figures relate to crop year (beginning November) and are in respect of cane sugar only.

Source: Ministry of Industry and Company Affairs.

Finance

CURRENCY AND EXCHANGE RATES

Monetary Units
100 paise (singular: paisa) = 1 Indian rupee.

Denominations
Coins: 5, 10, 20, 25 and 50 paise; 1 and 2 rupees.
Notes: 1, 2, 5, 10, 20, 50 and 100 rupees.

Sterling and Dollar Equivalents (30 September 1988)
£1 sterling = 24.55 rupees;
US $1 = 14.52 rupees;
1,000 Indian rupees = £40.73 = US $68.88.

Average Exchange Rate (rupees per US $)
1985   12.369
1986   12.611
1987   12.962

BUDGET (estimates, million rupees, year ending 31 March)

Revenue	1987/88*	1988/89
Tax revenue	379,884.5	419,858.4
Customs	135,000.0	153,200.0
Union excise duties	165,801.2	179,329.9
Corporation tax	36,500.0	40,500.0
Income tax	33,500.0	36,500.0
Estate duty	90.0	32.5
Wealth tax	1,200.0	1,200.0
Gift tax	100.0	100.0
Expenditure tax	200.0	500.0
Taxes from Union Territories	6,908.9	7,501.6
Other taxes	584.4	994.4
Non-tax revenue	92,298.6	103,161.7
Interest receipts	60,838.5	71,874.1
Dividends and profits	5,539.6	5,719.8
Others	25,920.5	25,567.8
Total	**472,183.1**	**523,020.1**
Less States' share	95,978.1	106,340.0
Less Transfer of Union Territory taxes and duties to local bodies	533.3	480.4
Net Centre's revenue	**375,671.7**	**416,199.7**

Expenditure	1987/88*	1988/89
General services	43,458.4	52,127.9
Interest payments	114,500.0	141,000.0
Defence	120,000.0	130,000.0
Major subsidies	53,700.0	63,910.0
Other subsidies	9,091.2	9,251.9
Postal deficit	1,317.2	1,318.6
Social services	11,420.0	12,504.7
Economic services	17,562.7	18,526.2
Non-Plan capital outlay	5,498.0	7,684.9
Non-Plan loans to public enterprises	5,723.6	7,676.2
Other non-Plan loans	1,663.6	2,104.7
Non-Plan grants to states	17,963.3	21,403.8
Non-Plan loans to states	655.7	390.7
Non-Plan grants to Union Territories	260.8	232.7
Non-Plan loans to Union Territories	67.4	69.8
Non-Plan expenditure on Union Territories without legislature	5,791.8	6,426.0
Grants to foreign governments	1,679.7	1,801.6
Loans to foreign governments	2,002.9	2,528.0
Total	**412,356.3**	**478,957.7**

* Revised budget.

Source: Government of India, Annual Budget Papers, 1988/89.

Seventh Five-Year Plan (1985–90) (estimates, million rupees): total expenditure 3,200,000; public sector outlay 1,800,000; private sector outlay 650,000.

INTERNATIONAL RESERVES (US $ million at 31 December)

	1985	1986	1987
Gold*	203	209	213
IMF special drawing rights	336	356	159
Reserve position in IMF	535	596	691
Foreign exchange	5,549	5,444	5,603
Total	**6,623**	**6,605**	**6,666**

* National valuation, based on cost of acquisition.
Source: IMF, *International Financial Statistics*.

INDIA

Statistical Survey

MONEY SUPPLY (million rupees, last Friday of the year)

	1985	1986	1987
Currency with the public	239,040	267,360	315,320
Demand deposits with banks	186,220	226,890	246,530
Other deposits with reserve bank	2,890	2,860	3,470
Total money	428,150	497,110	565,320

Source: Reserve Bank of India.

COST OF LIVING
(Consumer Price Index for industrial workers; base: 1980 = 100)

	1984	1985	1986
Food	148.8	154.2	168.7
Fuel and light	161.7	178.8	191.3
Clothing	134.1	142.9	150.6
Rent	139.7	157.9	172.2
All items (incl. others)	147.7	155.9	169.5

1987: Food 184.7; All items 184.4.

Source: ILO, mainly *Year Book of Labour Statistics*.

NATIONAL ACCOUNTS
('000 million rupees at current prices, year ending 31 March)
National Income and Product (provisional estimates)

	1984/85	1985/86	1986/87
Compensation of employees	740.02	n.a.	n.a.
Operating surplus*	1,014.87	n.a.	n.a.
Domestic factor incomes	1,754.89	2,068.65	2,304.64
Consumption of fixed capital	153.99	264.40	301.20
Gross domestic product at factor cost	1,908.88	2,333.05	2,605.84
Indirect taxes	306.92 }	284.28	322.03
Less Subsidies	71.95 }		
GDP in purchasers' values	2,143.85	2,617.33	2,927.87
Factor income from abroad	6.02 }		
Less Factor income paid abroad	20.73 }	−14.29	−14.29
Gross national product	2,129.14	2,603.04	2,913.58
Less Consumption of fixed capital	153.99	264.40	301.20
National income in market prices	1,975.15	2,338.64	2,612.38
Other current transfers from abroad	31.16 }		
Less Other current transfers paid abroad	0.15 }	28.21	27.00
National disposable income	2,006.16	2,366.85	2,639.38

* Including mixed income of self-employed ('000 million rupees): 696.24 in 1984/85.

Expenditure on the Gross Domestic Product

	1983/84	1984/85	1985/86*
Government final consumption expenditure	211.41	243.52	292.61
Private final consumption expenditure	1,446.30	1,596.89	1,734.73
Increase in stocks	83.12	94.48	136.28
Gross fixed capital formation	398.66	448.47	545.49
Total domestic expenditure	2,139.49	2,383.36	2,709.11
Exports of goods and services	131.39	159.57	150.68
Less Imports of goods and services	176.75	195.23	218.62
Sub-total	2,094.13	2,347.70	2,641.17
Statistical discrepancy	−21.41	−52.28	−23.84
GDP in purchasers' values	2,072.72	2,295.42	2,617.33

* Provisional.

Gross Domestic Product by Economic Activity
(at current factor cost)

	1985/86*	1986/87*	1987/88*
Agriculture	712.33	694.59	760.10
Forestry and logging	35.74	47.27	50.72
Fishing	20.49	20.58	25.36
Mining and quarrying	65.02	61.14	61.69
Manufacturing	435.58	423.52	486.96
Electricity, gas and water	47.47	25.84	25.49
Construction	118.01	138.93	161.46
Trade, restaurants and hotels	289.97	319.64	355.53
Transport, storage and communications	140.80	115.17	138.14
Banking and insurance	85.25	89.02	102.37
Real estate and business services	120.15	88.49	97.42
Public administration and defence	123.59	136.03	162.25
Other services	138.65	147.93	168.69
Total	2,333.05	2,308.15	2,596.18

* Provisional estimates.

BALANCE OF PAYMENTS (US $ million)

	1984	1985	1986
Merchandise exports f.o.b.	10,192	9,465	10,248
Merchandise imports f.o.b.	−14,216	−15,081	−15,686
Trade balance	−4,025	−5,616	−5,438
Exports of services	3,719	3,913	3,746
Imports of services	−4,808	−5,250	−5,526
Balance on goods and services	−5,114	−6,953	−7,218
Private unrequited transfers (net)	2,278	2,456	2,223
Government unrequited transfers (net)	492	320	399
Current balance	−2,343	−4,178	−4,597
Long-term capital (net)	2,769	3,341	4,373
Short-term capital (net)	275	−60	−503
Net errors and omissions	368	500	196
Total (net monetary movements)	1,069	−397	−531
Monetization of gold (net)	3	13	22
Valuation changes (net)	−196	491	154
Exceptional financing (net)	32	37	30
Changes in reserves	908	145	−326

Source: IMF, *International Financial Statistics*.

External Trade

PRINCIPAL COMMODITIES
(million rupees, year ending 31 March)

Imports c.i.f.	1984/85	1985/86	1986/87*
Wheat	1,295.8	610.3	372.7
Milk and cream	1,287.7	323.1	84.5
Fruit and nuts (excl. cashew nuts)	345.6	380.1	592.1
Textile yarn, fabrics, etc.	1,126.4	1,526.8	1,247.2
Synthetic and regenerated fibres	602.7	686.3	441.1
Crude rubber (incl. synthetic and reclaimed)	872.3	1,006.2	807.4
Crude fertilizers	1,374.7	1,626.2	1,311.0
Manufactured fertilizers	10,065.7	10,528.4	4,951.3
Sulphur and unroasted iron pyrites	2,020.1	2,203.4	1,473.1
Other crude minerals	645.0	254.3	644.6
Metalliferous ores and metal scrap	1,854.7	3,627.4	3,677.1
Iron and steel	9,411.0	13,946.0	14,496.9
Non-ferrous metals	4,117.3	5,418.2	4,149.1
Other metal manufactures	1,408.4	2,014.7	1,991.4
Edible vegetable oil	9,210.7	7,346.6	6,119.6
Mineral fuels, lubricants, etc.	54,090.5	49,893.9	25,795.6
Organic chemicals	4,429.9	5,194.7	5,044.1
Inorganic chemicals	4,136.6	5,699.4	5,312.6
Chemical materials and products	1,354.8	1,439.1	1,196.2
Artificial resins, plastic materials	2,227.9	3,220.2	4,358.9
Medicinal and pharmaceutical products	1,371.4	1,771.5	1,580.3
Paper, paperboard and manufactures	1,954.8	2,259.7	1,948.1
Pulp and waste paper	1,762.3	2,454.7	2,084.3
Pearls, precious and semi-precious stones	10,321.1	10,996.7	14,954.8
Other non-metallic mineral manufactures	821.8	1,017.4	851.3
Non-electric machinery	21,083.6	28,489.8	37,139.0
Electrical machinery	5,498.7	6,662.9	8,774.5
Transport equipment	3,688.5	5,686.9	6,768.4
Professional, scientific and controlling instruments, photographic and optical goods, watches and clocks	2,870.6	3,789.1	4,556.2
Wool (raw)	712.8	975.0	558.7
Total (incl. others)	171,342.0	196,576.9	200,835.3

* Provisional.

Source: Ministry of Commerce, *Annual Report 1985/86, 1986/87, 1987/88*.

Exports f.o.b.	1984/85	1985/86	1986/87*
Fish, crustaceans, molluscs and preparations	3,813.7	4,089.8	4,785.3
Meat and meat preparations	825.0	738.1	759.7
Rice	1,691.9	1,963.2	1,648.4
Wheat	114.8	458.6	338.7
Cashew kernels	1,796.8	2,251.0	3,206.4
Other vegetables and fruit	1,831.3	1,239.7	1,473.9
Crude vegetable materials	1,525.7	1,143.6	n.a.
Sugar and sugar preparations	361.3	158.4	8.7
Coffee and coffee substitutes	2,102.2	2,648.5	3,062.4
Tea and maté	7,666.9	6,262.7	5,496.5
Spices	2,066.7	2,778.1	2,690.6
Oil cakes	1,369.2	1,339.9	1,872.1
Unmanufactured tobacco, tobacco refuse	1,505.4	1,369.4	1,398.3
Cotton (raw)	597.3	681.7	1,820.8
Cotton fabrics	4,505.0	5,736.7	5,620.7
Ready-made garments	9,192.3	10,670.4	12,183.0
Jute manufactures	3,412.6	2,617.7	2,650.4
Carpets (hand-made)	2,586.6	2,327.5	2,873.9
Leather and leather manufactures	6,270.4	7,699.1	7,871.8
Gems and jewellery	11,532.7	15,026.5	20,692.5
Works of art	1,597.4	1,460.4	1,450.2
Iron ore	4,594.4	5,788.0	5,432.2
Other ores and minerals	738.9	1,849.2	1,139.4
Iron and steel	757.3	561.6	568.6
Metal manufactures (excl. iron and steel)	2,170.8	1,944.0	1,298.2
Machinery and transport equipment	6,631.7	7,035.4	7,451.4
Chemicals and allied products	4,650.2	4,685.0	4,377.9
Mineral fuels, lubricants, etc.	2,597.8	5,095.7	4,112.3
Total (incl. others)	117,436.8	108,945.9	125,666.2

* Provisional.

Source: Ministry of Commerce, *Annual Report 1985/86, 1986/87, 1987/88*.

PRINCIPAL TRADING PARTNERS
(million rupees, year ending 31 March)

Imports c.i.f.	1984/85	1985/86	1986/87*
Australia	2,005.5	4,420.9	4,310.3
Belgium	7,938.9	9,505.9	10,897.2
Brazil	3,219.8	3,737.6	2,807.0
Canada	4,993.3	4,511.1	3,803.7
Egypt	n.a.	1,163.1	2,864.5
France	3,576.3	5,825.9	6,694.4
Germany, Democratic Republic	n.a.	852.8	896.5
Germany, Federal Republic	12,891.4	15,436.7	19,366.2
Hong Kong	n.a.	693.9	1,092.0
Iran	4,848.3	8,851.3	1,349.5
Iraq	6,745.8	5,470.4	1,496.7
Italy	2,967.5	3,189.8	4,902.2
Japan	12,400.2	17,739.9	25,579.9
Jordan	n.a.	1,602.4	1,343.7
Korea, Republic	1,664.7	2,711.8	3,223.2
Kuwait	3,700.4	3,397.6	2,861.7
Malaysia	5,397.5	4,076.5	5,521.4
Morocco	n.a.	1,512.1	2,259.3
Netherlands	3,646.9	2,961.0	3,856.6
Poland	n.a.	885.5	1,094.3
Romania	n.a.	1,437.4	1,058.1
Saudi Arabia	12,629.0	7,942.4	6,872.3
Singapore	5,254.1	3,421.6	3,697.2
Spain	n.a.	1,704.3	2,144.4
Sweden	n.a.	1,382.8	3,533.0
Switzerland	1,607.9	1,599.6	3,485.4
USSR	17,881.0	16,775.1	10,722.1
United Arab Emirates	3,445.7	6,443.6	3,328.0
United Kingdom	9,334.7	12,506.2	16,229.9
USA	17,005.7	20,636.8	19,633.0
Yugoslavia	n.a.	741.8	1,022.9
Zambia	n.a.	1,157.4	703.1

* Provisional.

Source: Ministry of Commerce, *Annual Report 1985/86, 1986/87, 1987/88*.

INDIA

Statistical Survey

Exports f.o.b.	1984/85	1985/86	1986/87*
Australia	1,379.8	1,231.2	1,472.8
Bangladesh	n.a.	1,287.5	1,620.1
Belgium	1,932.1	2,247.1	3,534.7
Canada	n.a.	1,320.7	1,494.8
Czechoslovakia	n.a.	700.8	852.6
Egypt	1,175.2	1,096.6	731.8
France	1,914.5	2,027.1	2,745.1
Germany, Democratic Republic	n.a.	953.9	840.1
Germany, Federal Republic	4,878.8	5,129.6	7,403.0
Hong Kong	1,765.2	2,104.2	4,013.5
Iran	1,340.5	948.6	472.9
Italy	2,129.4	2,060.9	3,206.6
Japan	10,293.7	11,643.9	13,436.4
Kuwait	1,071.6	1,213.8	953.8
Malaysia	n.a.	709.9	1,048.5
Nepal	1,064.6	1,017.0	1,428.6
Netherlands	1,946.0	1,583.9	2,263.5
Poland	n.a.	621.7	1,058.2
Romania	702.2	977.5	803.8
Saudi Arabia	2,718.1	2,213.2	2,189.4
Singapore	1,436.4	1,415.0	2,208.1
Sri Lanka	1,268.3	806.2	873.3
Switzerland	1,082.9	1,074.6	1,601.8
USSR	18,796.4	20,056.9	18,728.8
United Arab Emirates	2,544.7	2,652.2	2,874.5
United Kingdom	6,126.0	5,243.8	7,371.1
USA	17,658.3	19,738.0	23,593.2

Transport

RAILWAYS (million, year ending 31 March)

	1984/85	1985/86	1986/87
Passengers	3,333.0	3,433.5	3,580.0
Passenger-km	226,582.0	240,614.0	256,467.6
Freight (metric tons)	264.8	286.4	307.3
Freight (metric ton-km)	182,161.0	205,904.0	223,097.0

Source: Ministry of Railways.

ROAD TRAFFIC ('000 motor vehicles in use at 31 March)

	1985	1986	1987*
Private cars			
Jeeps	1,546	1,710	1,895
Taxis			
Buses and coaches	211	228	247
Goods vehicles	782	878	967
Motor cycles and scooters	5,121	6,264	7,658
Others	1,346	1,401	1,580
Total	9,006	10,481	12,347

* Provisional

Source: Transport Wing, Ministry of Surface Transport.

INTERNATIONAL SEA-BORNE SHIPPING
(year ending 31 March)

	1981/82	1982/83	1983/84
Vessels* ('000 net regd tons):			
Entered	25,913	27,188	24,786
Cleared	24,709	26,614	23,002
Freight† ('000 metric tons):			
Loaded	30,709	21,258	26,983
Unloaded	38,068	36,375	36,693

* Excluding minor and intermediate ports.
† Including bunkers.

Source: Directorate General of Commercial Intelligence and Statistics.

CIVIL AVIATION (traffic)

	1985	1986	1987
Kilometres flown ('000)	104,904	109,392	99,181
Passenger-km ('000)	14,762,304	15,425,592	17,153,340
Freight ton-km ('000)	513,960	538,416	645,480
Mail ton-km ('000)	33,144	27,588	27,516

Source: Directorate General of Civil Aviation.

Tourism

FOREIGN VISITORS BY COUNTRY OF ORIGIN*

	1985	1986	1987
Australia	22,047	33,264	n.a.
Canada	29,022	39,837	37,677
France	44,091	65,948	64,432
Germany, Federal Republic	44,790	61,397	70,697
Iran	23,305	20,697	23,571
Italy	23,187	38,548	41,151
Japan	30,573	36,402	46,240
Malaysia	23,265	26,209	28,480
Saudi Arabia	20,728	27,282	24,475
Singapore	18,485	24,189	26,380
Sri Lanka	69,063	75,631	74,351
Switzerland	14,855	25,850	27,791
USSR	14,202	17,069	27,968
United Arab Emirates	20,784	28,084	31,180
United Kingdom	119,544	160,685	166,590
USA	95,920	125,364	134,876
Total (incl. others)	836,908	1,080,050	1,163,774

* Figures exclude nationals of Bangladesh and Pakistan. Including these, the total was 1,259,384 in 1985 and would have exceeded 1.5m. in 1987.

Source: Ministry of Tourism and Civil Aviation.

Receipts from tourism (million rupees, year ending 31 March): 14,600 in 1985/86; 17,800 in 1986/87; 18,900 in 1987/88.

Communications Media

	1983	1984	1985
Television receivers*	2,783,000	2,723,000	n.a.
Telephones*	3,215,000	3,714,000	4,044,000
Daily newspapers*	1,423	1,609	1,802
Non-daily newspapers*	19,335	20,175	20,846
Other periodicals			

Radio receivers: 50 million in use (estimate, 1985).
* Figures refer to year ending 31 March.

Sources: Ministry of Communications; Registrar of Newspapers for India; Ministry of Information and Broadcasting.

Education

(1986/87)

	Institutions	Teachers	Students
Primary	537,399	1,522,108	89,993,046
Middle	137,196	979,073	28,780,099
Secondary (High School)	53,172	716,997	12,472,932
Higher secondary (Old course)	898	28,832	160,882
Higher secondary (New pattern)	10,170	453,538	2,867,385

Source: Ministry of Human Resources Development.

Directory

The Constitution

The Constitution of India, adopted by the Constituent Assembly on 26 November 1949, was inaugurated on 26 January 1950. The Preamble declares that the People of India solemnly resolve to constitute a Sovereign Democratic Republic and to secure to all its citizens justice, liberty, equality and fraternity. There are 397 articles and nine schedules, which form a comprehensive document.

UNION OF STATES

The Union of India comprises 25 states and seven Union Territories. There are provisions for the formation and admission of new states.

The Constitution confers citizenship on a threefold basis of birth, descent, and residence. Provisions are made for refugees who have migrated from Pakistan and for persons of Indian origin residing abroad.

FUNDAMENTAL RIGHTS AND DIRECTIVE PRINCIPLES

The rights of the citizen contained in Part III of the Constitution are declared fundamental and enforceable in law. 'Untouchability' is abolished and its practice in any form is a punishable offence. The Directive Principles of State Policy provide a code intended to ensure promotion of the economic, social and educational welfare of the State in future legislation.

THE PRESIDENT

The President is the head of the Union, exercising all executive powers on the advice of the Council of Ministers responsible to Parliament. He is elected by an electoral college consisting of elected members of both Houses of Parliament and the Legislatures of the States. The President holds office for a term of five years and is eligible for re-election. He may be impeached for violation of the Constitution. The Vice-President is the ex officio Chairman of the Rajya Sabha and is elected by a joint sitting of both Houses of Parliament.

THE PARLIAMENT

The Parliament of the Union consists of the President and two Houses: the Rajya Sabha (Council of States) and the Lok Sabha (House of the People). The Rajya Sabha consists of 245 members, of whom a number are nominated by the President. One-third of its members retire every two years. Elections are indirect, each state's legislative quota being elected by the members of the state's legislative assembly. The Lok Sahba has 542 members elected by adult franchise; not more than 17 represent the Union Territories. It may also include a number of members nominated by the President.

GOVERNMENT OF THE STATES

The governmental machinery of states closely resembles that of the Union. Each of these states has a governor at its head appointed by the President for a term of five years to exercise executive power on the advice of a council of ministers. The states' legislatures consist of the Governor and either one house (legislative assembly) or two houses (legislative assembly and legislative council). The term of the assembly is five years, but the council is not subject to dissolution.

LANGUAGE

The Constitution provides that the official language of the Union shall be Hindi. (The English language will continue to be an associate language for many official purposes.)

LEGISLATION—FEDERAL SYSTEM

The Constitution provides that bills, other than money bills, can be introduced in either House. To become law, they must be passed by both Houses and receive the assent of the President. In financial affairs, the authority of the Lower House is final. The various subjects of legislation are enumerated on three lists in the seventh schedule of the Constitution: the Union List, containing nearly 100 entries, including external affairs, defence, communications and atomic energy; the State List, containing 65 entries, including local government, police, public health, education; and the Concurrent List, with over 40 entries, including criminal law, marriage and divorce, labour welfare. The Constitution vests residuary authority in the Centre. All matters not enumerated in the Concurrent or State Lists will be deemed to be included in the Union List, and in the event of conflict between Union and State Law on any subject enumerated in the Concurrent List the Union Law will prevail. In time of emergency Parliament may even exercise powers otherwise exclusively vested in the states. Under Article 356, 'If the President on receipt of a report from the government of a state or otherwise is satisfied that a situation has arisen in which the Government of the state cannot be carried on in accordance with the provisions of this Constitution, the President may by Proclamation: (a) assume to himself all or any of the functions of the government of the state and all or any of the powers of the governor or any body or authority in the state other than the Legislature of the state; (b) declare that the powers of the Legislature of the state shall be exercisable by or under the authority of Parliament; (c) make such incidental provisions as appear to the President to be necessary': provided that none of the powers of a High Court be assumed by the President or suspended in any way. Unless such a Proclamation is approved by both Houses of Parliament, it ceases to operate after two months. A Proclamation so approved ceases to operate after six months, unless renewed by Parliament. Its renewal cannot be extended beyond a total period of three years. An independent judiciary exists to define and interpret the Constitution and to resolve constitutional disputes arising between states, or between a state and the Government of India.

OTHER PROVISIONS

Other Provisions of the Constitution deal with the administration of tribal areas, relations between the Union and states, inter-state trade and finance.

AMENDMENTS

The Constitution is flexible in character, and a simple process of amendment has been adopted. For amendment of provisions concerning the Supreme Courts and the High Courts, the distribution of legislative powers between the Union and the states, the representation of the states in Parliament, etc., the amendment must be passed by both Houses of Parliament and must further be ratified by the legislatures of not less than half the states. In other cases no reference to the state legislatures is necessary.

Numerous amendments were adopted in August 1975, following the declaration of a state of emergency in June. The Constitution (39th Amendment) Bill laid down that the President's reasons for proclaiming an emergency may not be challenged in any court. Under the Constitution (40th Amendment) Bill, 38 existing laws may not be challenged before any court on the ground of violation of fundamental rights. Thus detainees under the Maintenance of Internal Security Act could not be told the grounds of their detention and were forbidden bail and any claim to liberty through natural or common law. The Constitution (41st Amendment) Bill provided that the President, Prime Minister and state Governors should be immune from criminal prosecution for life and from civil prosecution during their term of office.

In November 1976 a 59-clause Constitution (42nd Amendment) Bill was approved by Parliament and came into force in January 1977. Some of the provisions of the Bill are that the Indian Democratic Republic shall be named a 'Democratic Secular and Socialist Republic'; that the President 'shall act in accordance with' the advice given to him by the Prime Minister and the Council of Ministers, and, acting at the Prime Minister's direction, shall be empowered for two years to amend the Constitution by executive order, in any way beneficial to the enforcement of the whole; that the term of the Lok Sabha and of the State Assemblies shall be extended from five to six years; that there shall be no limitation on the constituent power of Parliament to amend the Constitution, and that India's Supreme Court shall be barred from hearing petitions challenging Constitutional amendments; that strikes shall be forbidden in the public services and the Union Government have the power to deploy police or other forces under its own superintendence and control in any state. Directive Principles are given precedence over Fundamental Rights: 10 basic duties of citizens are listed, including the duty to 'defend the country and render national service when called upon to do so'.

The Janata Party government, which came into power in March 1977, promised to amend the Constitution during the year, so as to 'restore the balance between the people and Parliament, Parliament and the judiciary, the judiciary and the executive, the states and the centre, and the citizen and the Government that the founding fathers of the Constitution had worked out'. The Constitution (43rd Amendment) Bill, passed by Parliament in December 1977, the Constitution (44th Amendment) Bill, passed by Parliament in December 1977 and later redesignated the 43rd Amendment, and the Constitution (45th Amendment) Bill, passed by Parliament in December 1978 and later redesignated the 44th Amendment, reversed most of the changes enacted by the Constitution (42nd Amendment) Bill. The 44th Amendment is particularly detailed on emergency provisions: An emergency may not be proclaimed unless 'the security of India or any part of its territory was threatened by war or external aggression or by armed rebellion.' Its introduction must be approved by a two-thirds majority of Parliament within a month, and after six months the emergency may be continued only with the approval of Parliament. Among the provisions left unchanged after these Bills were a section subordinating Fundamental Rights to Directive Principles and a clause empowering the central government to deploy armed forces under its control in any state without the state government's consent. In May 1980 the Indian Supreme Court repealed sections 4 and 55 of the 42nd Amendment Act, thus curtailing Parliament's power to enforce directive principles and to amend the Constitution. The death penalty was declared constitutionally valid. The 53rd Amendment to the Constitution, approved by Parliament in August 1986, granted statehood to the Union Territory of Mizoram; the 55th Amendment, approved in December 1986, granted statehood to the Union Territory of Arunachal Pradesh; and the 57th Amendment, approved in May 1987, granted statehood to the Union Territory of Goa (Daman and Diu remain, however, as a Union Territory). The 59th Amendment, approved in March 1988, empowered the Government to impose a state of emergency in Punjab, on the grounds of internal disturbances. The 62nd Amendment, approved in December 1988, lowered the voting age from 21 to 18 years.

THE PANCHAYAT RAJ SCHEME

This scheme is designed to decentralize the powers of the Union and state governments. It is based on the Panchayat (Village Council) and the Gram Sabha (Village Parliament) and envisages the gradual transference of local government from state to local authority. Revenue and internal security will remain state responsibilities at present. By 1978 the scheme had been introduced in all the states except Meghalaya, Nagaland and 23 out of 31 districts in Bihar. The Panchayat operated in all the Union Territories except Lakshadweep, Mizoram (which became India's 23rd state in February 1987) and Pondicherry.

The Government

President: RAMASWAMY VENKATARAMAN (sworn in 25 July 1987).
Vice-President: Dr SHANKAR DAYAL SHARMA (sworn in 3 September 1987).

COUNCIL OF MINISTERS
(February 1989)

Prime Minister and Minister of Science and Technology, of Atomic Energy, and of Space: RAJIV GANDHI.
Minister of Agriculture and Rural Development: BHAJAN LAL.
Minister of Commerce: DINESH SINGH.
Minister of Communications: BIR BAHADUR SINGH.
Minister of Defence: KRISHNA CHANDRA PANT.
Minister of Energy: VASANT SATHE.
Minister of the Environment and Forests: Z. R. ANSARI.
Minister of External Affairs: P. V. NARASIMHA RAO.
Minister of Finance: S. B. CHAVAN.
Minister of Home Affairs: Sardar BUTA SINGH.
Minister of Human Resources Development: P. SHIV SHANKAR.
Minister of Industry: J. VENGAL RAO.
Minister of Labour: BINDESHWARI DUBEY.
Minister of Law and Justice and of Water Resources: B. SHANKARANAND.
Minister of Parliamentary Affairs and of Information and Broadcasting: HAR KISHAN LAL BHAGAT.
Minister of Planning and Programme Implementation: MADHAV SINH SOLANKI.
Minister of Steel and Mines: MAKHAN LAL FOTEDAR.
Minister of Textiles and of Health and Family Welfare: RAM NIWAS MIRDHA.
Minister of Urban Development: MOHSINA KIDWAI.
Minister of State for Civil Aviation and Tourism: SHIV RAJ PATIL.
Minister of State for Food and Civil Supplies: SUKH RAM.
Minister of State for Food Processing: JAGDISH TYTLER.
Minister of State for Petroleum and Natural Gas: BRAHM DUTT.
Minister of State for Railways: MADHAVRAO SCINDIA.
Minister of State for Surface Transport: RAJESH PILOT.
Minister of State for Welfare: Dr RAJENDRA KUMARI BAJPAI.
There are, in addition, 30 Ministers of State (without independent charges) and four Deputy Ministers.

MINISTRIES

President's Office: Rashtrapti Bhavan, New Delhi 110 004; tel. (11) 3015321.
Prime Minister's Office: South Block, New Delhi 110 011; tel. (11) 3012312.
Ministry of Agriculture and Rural Development: Krishi Bhavan, Dr Rajendra Prasad Rd, New Delhi 110 001; tel. (11) 382651; telex 3165423.
Ministry of Atomic Energy: South Block, New Delhi 110 011; tel. (11) 3011773; telex 3166182.
Ministry of Civil Aviation: Sardar Patel Bhavan, New Delhi 110 001; tel. (11) 351700.
Ministry of Commerce: Udyog Bhavan, New Delhi 110 011; tel. (11) 3016664; telex 3165970.
Ministry of Communications: Sanchar Bhavan, 20 Asoka Rd, New Delhi 110 001; tel. (11) 381209; telex 314422.
Ministry of Defence: South Block, New Delhi 110 011; tel. (11) 3012380; telex 3162679.
Ministry of Energy: Shram Shakti Bhawan, Rafi Marg, New Delhi 110 001; tel. (11) 382966.
Ministry of the Environment and Forests: Paryavaran Bhavan, CGO Complex Phase II, Lodi Rd, New Delhi 110 003; tel. (11) 360721.
Ministry of External Affairs: South Block, New Delhi 110 011; tel. (11) 3012318; telex 3161880.
Ministry of Finance: North Block, New Delhi 110 001; tel. (11) 3012611; telex 3166562.
Ministry of Food and Civil Supplies: Krishi Bhavan, New Delhi 110 001; tel. (11) 382349; telex 3166505.
Ministry of Health and Family Welfare: Nirman Bhavan, New Delhi 110 011; tel. (11) 3018863.
Ministry of Home Affairs: North Block, New Delhi 110 001; tel. (11) 3011989.
Ministry of Human Resources Development: Shastri Bhavan, New Delhi 110 001; tel. (11) 381298.
Ministry of Industry: Udyog Bhavan, New Delhi 110 011; tel. (11) 3010221; telex 3166294.
Ministry of Information and Broadcasting: Shastri Bhavan, New Delhi 110 001; tel. (11) 382639; telex 3166349.
Ministry of Labour: Shram Shakti Bhavan, Rafi Marg, New Delhi 110 001; tel. (11) 382945; telex 3161131.
Ministry of Law and Justice: Shastri Bhavan, Dr Rajendra Prasad Rd, New Delhi 110 001; tel. (11) 384777.
Ministry of Ocean Development: Block 12, CGO Complex, Lodi Rd, New Delhi 110 003; tel. (11) 360874.
Ministry of Parliamentary Affairs: Parliament House, New Delhi 110 001; tel. (11) 3017663.
Ministry of Personnel, Public Grievances and Pensions: North Block, New Delhi 110 001; tel. (11) 3014848.
Ministry of Petroleum and Natural Gas: Shastri Bhavan, New Delhi 110 001; tel. (11) 383501; telex 3166235.
Ministry of Planning: Yojana Bhavan, Parliament St, New Delhi 110 001; tel. (11) 386354.
Ministry of Programme Implementation: Sardar Patel Bhavan, New Delhi 110 001; tel. (11) 3012787; telex 3163195.
Ministry of Railways: Rail Bhavan, New Delhi 110 001; tel. (11) 384010.
Ministry of Science and Technology: Technology Bhavan, New Mehrauli Rd, New Delhi 110 016; tel. (11) 661439.
Ministry of Space: 3 Lok Nayak Bhavan, New Delhi 110 003; tel. (11) 698313.
Ministry of Steel and Mines: Udyog Bhavan, New Delhi 110 011; tel. (11) 3014096; telex 3161483.
Ministry of Surface Transport: Transport Bhavan, Sansad Marg, New Delhi 110 001; tel. (11) 384938; telex 3161159.
Ministry of Textiles: Udyog Bhavan, New Delhi 110 011; tel. (11) 3011769.
Ministry of Tourism: Transport Bhavan, Parliament St, New Delhi 110 001; tel. (11) 383816; telex 3165976.
Ministry of Urban Development: Nirman Bhavan, New Delhi 110 011; tel. (11) 3019377.
Ministry of Water Resources: Shram Shakti Bhavan, Rafi Marg, New Delhi 110 001; tel. (11) 383098; telex 3166568.
Ministry of Welfare: Shastri Bhavan, New Delhi 110 001; tel. (11) 382683; telex 3166256.

Legislature

PARLIAMENT

Rajya Sabha
(Council of States)

Most of the members of the Rajya Sabha are indirectly elected by the State Assemblies for six years, with one-third retiring every two years. The remaining members are nominated by the President.

Chairman: Dr SHANKAR DAYAL SHARMA.

Distribution of Seats, January 1989

Party	Seats
Congress (I)	141
Janta Party	20
Communist (CPI—Marxist)	15
Telugu Desam	13
Bharatiya Janata Party	8
Lok Dal	7
All India Anna Dravida Munnetra Kazhagam (I)	6
All India Anna Dravida Munnetra Kazhagam (II)	4
Communist (CPI)	3
Dravida Munnetra Kazhagam	3
Asom Gana Parishad	2
Revolutionary Socialist Party	2
Shiromani Akali Dal (Longowal)	1
Forward Bloc	1
Jammu and Kashmir National Conference (F)	1
Independents and others	5
Nominated	5
Vacant	8
Total	**245**

Lok Sabha
(House of the People)

Speaker: BALRAM JHAKHAR.

General Election, 24, 27 and 28 December 1984*

Party	Percentage of votes	Seats at election	Seats at Jan. 1989
Congress (I)	49.17	400	397
Telugu Desam	4.12	28	29
Communist (CPI—Marxist)	5.80	22	22
All India Anna Dravida Munnetra Kazhagam (AIADMK)	1.72	12	11†
Janata	7.03	10	13
Asom Gana Parishad	—	—	6
Communist (CPI)	2.73	6	6
Congress (S)	n.a.	4	—
Jammu and Kashmir National Conference (F)	n.a.	3	3
Revolutionary Socialist Party	n.a.	3	3
Lok Dal	5.91	3	5
Akali Dal (B)	—	—	3
Shiromani Akali Dal (Longowal)	—	—	2
Forward Bloc	n.a.	2	2
Bharatiya Janata Party	7.71	2	2
Muslim League	—	—	2
Kerala Congress	—	—	2
Dravida Munnetra Kazagam	—	—	2
Unattached, independents and others	15.80‡	12	18
Nominated	—	2§	2§
Vacant	—	35	14
Total	**100.00**	**544**	**544**

* Polling was postponed until 28 January 1985 in two constituencies in Andhra Pradesh, one in Uttar Pradesh, one in Tamil Nadu and also in Bhopal, in Madhya Pradesh. Ladakh, in Jammu and Kashmir, and Mandi, in Himachal Pradesh, went to the polls on 24 April and 24 May respectively. Polling took place in Punjab on 25 September, and in Assam on 16 December 1985.
† Following factional divisions within the parliamentary party, AIADMK (I) held seven seats and AIADMK (II) held four seats.
‡ Including the parties listed above for which voting figures are not available.
§ Nominated by the President to represent the Anglo-Indian community.

State Governments
(February 1989)

ANDHRA PRADESH
(Capital—Hyderabad)

Governor: KUMUDBEN M. JOSHI.
Chief Minister: NANDMURI TARAK RAMA RAO (Telugu Desam).
Legislative Assembly: 294 seats (Telugu Desam Party 201, Congress—I 51, Janata 3, Communist—CPI—M 11, Communist—CPI 10, Majlis-Ittehad-ul-Muslimeen 4, Bharatiya Janata Party 8, independents and others 6).

ARUNACHAL PRADESH
(Capital—Itanagar)

Governor: R. D. PRADHAN.
Chief Minister: GAGONG APANG (Congress—I).
Legislative Assembly: 30 seats (Congress—I 28, People's Party of Arunachal 2.

ASSAM
(Capital—Dispur)

Governor: BHISHMA NARAIN SINGH.
Chief Minister: PRAFULLA KUMAR MAHANTA (Asom Gana Parishad).
Legislative Assembly: 126 seats (Asom Gana Parishad 71, Congress—I 24, United Minorities Front 17, Congress—S 4, Plains Tribal Council of Assam 3, Communist—CPI—M 2, independents and others 4, vacant 1).

BIHAR
(Capital—Patna)

Governor: R. D. PRADHAN.
Chief Minister: BHAGWAT JHA AZAD (Congress—I).
Legislative Assembly: 324 seats (Congress—I 195, Lok Dal 46, Communist—CPI 12, Bharatiya Janata Party 17, Janata 13, Jharkhand Mukti Morcha 9, independents and others 32.
Legislative Council: 96 seats.

GOA
(Capital—Panaji)

Governor: Dr GOPAL SINGH.
Chief Minister: PRATAP SINGH RANE (Congress—I).
Legislative Assembly: 31 seats (Congress—I 20, Maharashtrawadi Gomantak Party 8, others 3).

GUJARAT
(Capital—Gandhinagar)

Governor: R. K. TRIVEDI.
Chief Minister: AMAR SINGH B. CHAUDHARI (Congress—I).
Legislative Assembly: 182 seats (Congress—I 145, Janata 13, Bharatiya Janata Party 12, independents 8, vacant 4).

HARYANA
(Capital—Chandigarh)

Governor: HARA ANAND BARARI.
Chief Minister: DEVI LAL (Lok Dal—B).
Legislative Assembly: 90 seats (Congress—I 5, Lok Dal—B 60, Bharatiya Janata Party 17, independents and others 8).

HIMACHAL PRADESH
(Capital—Simla)

Governor: Vice-Adm. (retd) RUSTOM KHUSRO SHAMPOORJEE GANDHI.
Chief Minister: VIR BHADRA SINGH (Congress—I).
Legislative Assembly: 68 seats (Congress—I 57, Bharatiya Janata Party 7, Lok Dal 1, independents and others 3).

JAMMU AND KASHMIR
(Capitals—Srinagar (Summer), Jammu (Winter))

Governor: JAGMOHAN (MALHOTRA).
Chief Minister: Dr FAROOK ABDULLAH (Coalition of Jammu and Kashmir National Conference Party—F and Congress—I).
Legislative Assembly: 76 seats (National Conference Party 40, Congress—I 26, Muslim United Front 4, Bharatiya Janata Party 2, others 4.
Legislative Council: 36 seats.

INDIA

KARNATAKA
(Capital—Bangalore)
Governor: PONDAKAINTI VENKATASUBBAIAH.
Chief Minister: S. R. BOMMAI (Janata).
Legislative Assembly: 224 seats (Congress–I 66, Janata 139, independents and others 11, Bharatiya Janata Party 2, Communist–CPI 4, Communist–CPI–M 2).
Legislative Council: 75 seats.

KERALA
(Capital—Trivandrum)
Governor: RAM DULARI SINHA.
Chief Minister: EZHAMBALA KRISHNAN NAYANAR (Communist–CPI–M).
Legislative Assembly: 140 seats (Communist–CPI–M 38, Communist–CPI 16, Congress–I 33, Muslim League 15, Kerala Congress 5, Kerala Congress (M) 4, Congress–S 6, Janata 7, Revolutionary Socialist Party 5, independents 10, Lok Dal 1).

MADHYA PRADESH
(Capital—Bhopal)
Governor: Prof. K. M. CHANDY.
Chief Minister: MOTI LAL VORA (Congress–I).
Legislative Assembly: 320 seats (Congress–I 248, Bharatiya Janata 58, Janata 5, independents and others 6, vacant 3).

MAHARASHTRA
(Capital—Bombay)
Governor: K. BRAHMANANDA REDDY.
Chief Minister: SHARAD PAWAR (Congress–I).
Legislative Assembly: 289 seats (Congress–I 210, Congress–S 2, Janata 21, Bharatiya Janata Party 15, independents and others 21, People and Workers' Party 13, Communist–CPI 2, Communist–CPI–M 2, vacant 3).
Legislative Council: 78 seats.

MANIPUR
(Capital—Imphal)
Governor: Gen. (retd) K. V. KRISHNA RAO.
Chief Minister: R. K. JAICHANDRA SINGH (Congress–I).
Legislative Assembly: 60 seats (Congress–I 39, United Democratic Party 10, others 11).

MEGHALAYA
(Capital—Shillong)
Governor: BHISHMA NARAIN SINGH.
Chief Minister: PURNO A. SANGMA (Congress–I).
Legislative Assembly: 60 seats (Congress–I 21, Hill People's Union 18, Hills State People's Democratic Party 4, independent 9, others 5, vacant 3).

MIZORAM
(Capital—Aizawl)
Governor: HITESWAR SAIKIA.
Chief Minister: LALTHANHAWLA (Congress–I).
Legislative Assembly: 40 seats (Mizo National Front 14, Congress–I 22, others 3, vacant 1).

NAGALAND
(Capital—Kohima)
Governor: Gen. (retd) K. V. KRISHNA RAO.
Chief Minister: S. CHUBATOSHI JAMIR (Congress–I).
Legislative Assembly: 60 seats (Congress–I 36, Nagaland People's Council 24).

ORISSA
(Capital—Bhubaneswar)
Governor: SYED NURUL HASSAN.
Chief Minister: JANAKI BALLABH PATNAIK (Congress–I).
Legislative Assembly: 147 seats (Congress–I 115, Janata 22, independents and others 10).

PUNJAB
(Capital—Chandigarh)
Governor: SIDHARTHA SHANKAR RAY.
Chief Minister: (vacant).
Legislative Assembly: 117 seats (Shiromani Akali Dal (Longowal) 50, Congress–I 31, Bharatiya Janata Party 5, Communist 1, Janata 1, others 3, vacant 26).
The Chief Minister and the Cabinet were dismissed, and the Assembly was dissolved, when Punjab was placed under President's rule in May 1987.

RAJASTHAN
(Capital—Jaipur)
Governor: SUKHDEV PRASAD (acting).
Chief Minister: SHIV CHARAN MATHUR (Congress–I).
Legislative Assembly: 200 seats (Congress–I 115, Bharatiya Janata Party 37, Janata 10, Lok Dal 27, Congress–S 3, independents and others 8).

SIKKIM
(Capital—Gangtok)
Governor: T. V. RAJESHWAR.
Chief Minister: NAR BAHADUR BHANDARI (Sikkim Samgram Parishad).
Legislative Assembly: 32 seats (Sikkim Samgram Parishad 30, Congress–I 1, Independent 1).

TAMIL NADU
(Capital—Madras)
Governor: Dr P. C. ALEXANDER.
Chief Minister: Dr K. KARUNANIDHI (DMK).
Legislative Assembly: 234 seats (DMK 148, AIADMK (Jayalalitha) 27, AIADMK (Janaki) 1, Congress–I 26, Communist–CPI–M 15, Communist–CPI 3, Janata 4, others 8, vacant 2).

TRIPURA
(Capital—Agartala)
Governor: Gen. (retd) K. V. KRISHNA RAO.
Chief Minister: SUDHIR RANJAN MAJUMDAR (Congress–I).
Legislative Assembly: 60 seats (Communist–CPI–M 26, Congress–I 24, Tripura Upajati Juba Samity 7, Revolutionary Socialist Party 2, vacant 1).

UTTAR PRADESH
(Capital—Lucknow)
Governor: MOHD USMAN ARIF.
Chief Minister: NARAYAN DUTT TIWARI (Congress–I).
Legislative Assembly: 425 seats (Congress–I 267, Lok Dal (A) 53, Lok Dal (B) 30, Bharatiya Janata Party 16, Janata 20, Communist–CPI 6, Communist–CPI–M 2, Congress–J 3, independents and others 27, vacant 1).
Legislative Council: 108 seats.

WEST BENGAL
(Capital—Calcutta)
Governor: SYED NURUL HASSAN.
Chief Minister: JYOTI BASU (Communist–CPI–M).
Legislative Assembly: 294 seats (Communist–CPI–M 187, Congress–I 40, Forward Bloc 26, Revolutionary Socialist 18, Communist–CPI 11, others 12).

UNION TERRITORIES

Andaman and Nicobar Islands (Headquarters—Port Blair): Lt-Gov.: TIRATH SINGH OBEROI.

Chandigarh (Headquarters—Chandigarh):
Administrator: SIDHARTHA SHANKAR RAY.
Chandigarh was to be incorporated into Punjab state on 26 January 1986, but the transfer was postponed.

Dadra and Nagar Haveli (Headquarters—Silvassa):
Administrator: GOPAL SINGH.

Daman and Diu:
Administrator: Dr GOPAL SINGH.

Delhi (Headquarters—Delhi):
Lt-Gov.: RAMESH BHANDARI.
Metropolitan Council: 61 seats (Congress–I 33, Bharatiya Janata Party 20, Lok Dal 2, Janata 1, nominated 5).

Lakshadweep (Headquarters—Kavaratti):
Administrator: J. SAGAR.

Pondicherry (Capital—Pondicherry):
Lt-Gov.: R. S. DAYAL.
Chief Minister: M. O. H. FAROOK (Congress–I).
Assembly: 30 seats (DMK 5, ADMK 4, Congress–I 16, Janata 1, others 2, vacant 2).

Political Organizations

Prior to independence in 1947, the leading nationalist group was the Congress Party, established in 1885. In 1907 Congress split into two factions: the Extremists and the Moderates. In 1969 Congress again split into two distinct organizations, with Indira Gandhi's Government continuing in office, while the Indian National Congress (Organization) became India's first recognized opposition party. Further splits occurred in January 1978, when Indira Gandhi formed a breakaway group, the Indian National Congress (I), and again in 1981, when the Indian National Congress (Socialist) was formed. In July 1981 a Supreme Court ruling confirmed Congress (I) as the official Congress party. In December 1986 Congress (S) split, the majority faction voting to rejoin Congress (I) while the remaining members decided to continue as Congress (S).

All India Congress Committee (I): 24 Akbar Rd, New Delhi 110 011; tel. (11) 3019080; f. 1978, as Indian National Congress (I), as a breakaway group under Indira Gandhi; Pres. RAJIV GANDHI; Gen. Secs KEDAR NATH SINGH, GHULAM NABI AZAD, JAGANNATH PAHADIA, SHEILA KAUL, VITHAL NARWAL GADGIL, OSCAR FERNANDES.

In September 1988 four national-level centrist opposition parties and three major regional parties announced the formation of a coalition Rashtriya Morcha (National Front), with the intention of competing against Congress (I) at the next general election. Each component party in the Front was to retain its separate political identity. In October 1988 three of the four centrist parties formed a new political party, the Janata Dal (People's Party), which was to work in collaboration with the regional opposition parties in the Rashtriya Morcha.

Asom Gana Parishad (AGP)* (Assam People's Council): Golaghat, Assam; f. 1985; draws support from the All-Assam Gana Sangram Parishad and the All-Assam Students' Union (Pres. KESHAB MAHANTA; Gen. Sec. ATUL BORA); advocates the unity of India in diversity and a united Assam; Leader PRAFULLA KUMAR MAHANTA.

Dravida Munnetra Kazhagam (DMK)*: Royapuram, Madras 600 013; f. 1949; aims at full autonomy for Tamil Nadu within the Union, to establish regional languages as state languages and English as the official language; Pres. Dr K. KARUNANIDHI; Gen. Sec. NANJIL K. MANOGARAN; over 1.6m. mems.

Indian National Congress (S)*: 3 Raisina Rd, New Delhi 110 001; tel. (11) 382478; f. 1981; aims include the establishment by peaceful means of a socialist, co-operative commonwealth; advocates govt control of large-scale industries and services, co-operativism in industry and agriculture, and a neutral foreign policy; 4m. mems; Pres. SARAT CHANDRA SINHA; Gen. Secs K. P. UNNIKRISHNAN, V. KISHORE CHANDRA S. DEO.

Jan Morcha*† (People's Front): f. October 1987 by a breakaway group from Congress (I), led by VISHWANATH PRATAP SINGH; socialist-based programme.

Janata Dal* (People's Party): f. 1988 as a merger of parties within the Rashtriya Morcha; advocates immediate cease-fire and negotiated settlement in Sri Lanka, non-alignment, the eradication of poverty, unemployment and wide disparities in wealth, and the protection of minorities; 136-mem. National Executive; Pres. VISHWANATH PRATAP SINGH; Sec.-Gen. AJIT SINGH.

Janata Party*† (People's Party): 7 Jantar Mantar Rd, New Delhi 110 001; tel. (11) 351833; f. May 1977 by the merger of the Indian National Congress (Organization), the Bharatiya Lok Dal (BLD), the Bharatiya Jan Sangh (People's Party of India) and the Socialist Party, which had combined as the Janata Party to contest the March 1977 general election; Congress for Democracy, a party formed in February 1977, merged with the Janata Party in May 1977; the Rashtriya Sanjay Manch and the Lok Dal (A), one of the two factions in the Lok Dal, merged with the Janata Party in April 1988; aims to achieve by democratic and peaceful means a socialist society, free from social, political and economic exploitation; Leaders Prof. MADHU DANDAVATE (Lok Sabha), M. S. GURUPADASWAMY (Rajya Sabha); Pres. INDU BHAI PATEL (acting); Gen. Secs BAPU KALDATE, RAM NARESH YADAV, RAM BILAS PASWAN, HARIKESH BAHADUR, THAMPAN THOMAS, MANEKA GANDHI; 2m. mems.

Lok Dal*† (People's Party): 15 Windsor Place, New Delhi 110 001; tel. (11) 388925; f. 1984 by merger of the Lok Dal (a splinter group from the Janata Party) with the Democratic Socialist Party and the Janavadi Dal; advocates secularism, the cause of the poor and underprivileged, the primacy of agriculture and small industry; in 1987 split into two factions, of which the larger was Lok Dal (B); Pres. Lok Dal (B) HEMVATI NANDAN BAHUGUNA; Lok Dal (A) merged with the Janata Party in 1988; Lok Dal (B) split into two factions, one led by HEMVATI NANDAN BAHUGUNA and the other by DEVI LAL, in 1988.

Rashtriya Morcha (National Front): f. 1988 as a seven-party united opposition front; Chair. NANDMURI TARAK RAMARAO; Convener and CEO VISHWANATH PRATAP SINGH.

Telugu Desam* (Telugu Nation): 3-5-910, Himayatnagar, Hyderabad 500 029; tel. (842) 227070; f. 1982; state-based party (Andhra Pradesh); campaigns against rural poverty and social prejudice; Founder and Pres. NANDMURI TARAK RAMA RAO; Gen.-Sec. P. UPENDRA; 1,184,595 mems.

* Member of Rashtriya Morcha.
† Member of Janata Dal.

India's other major national political organizations are:

Akhil Bharat Hindu Mahasabha: Hindu Mahasabha Bhavan, Mandir Marg, New Delhi 110 001; tel. (11) 343105; f. 1915; seeks the establishment of a democratic Hindu state; Pres. BALARAO SAVARKAR; Gen. Sec. MADHAV DUTTATRAYA PATHAK; 500,000 mems.

All India Forward Bloc: 28 Gurdwara Rakabganj Rd, New Delhi 110 001; tel. (11) 384576; f. 1940 by Netaji Subhash Chandra Boase; socialist aims, including nationalization of major industries, land reform and redistribution; Chair. P. D. PALIWAL; Gen. Sec. CHITTA BASU; 900,000 mems.

Bharatiya Janata Party (BJP): (Indian People's Party): 11 Ashok Rd, New Delhi 110 001; tel. (11) 383349; f. 1980; breakaway group from Janata Party; radical right-wing Hindu party; Pres. L. K. ADVANI; Vice-Pres. M. M. JOSHI; Gen. Secs KRISHANLAL SHARMA, K. S. THAKRE, K. N. SAHNI.

Communist Party of India (CPI): Ajoy Bhavan, Kotla Marg, New Delhi 110 002; tel. (11) 3315546; f. 1925; advocates the establishment of a socialist society led by the working class, and ultimately of a communist society; Leaders INDRAJIT GUPTA, N. E. BALARAM; Sec.-Gen. C. RAJEESWARA RAO; 445,483 mems.

Communist Party of India–Marxist (CPI–M): 14 Ashoka Rd, New Delhi 110 001; tel. (11) 382870; f. 1964 as pro-Beijing breakaway group from the CPI; declared its independence of Beijing in 1968 and is managed by a politburo of 10 mems; Leaders JYOTI BASU, B. T. RANADIVE, H. K. S. SURJEET; Gen. Sec. E. M. SANKARAN NAMBOODIRIPAD; 464,000 mems.

Indian Communist Party (ICP): f. 1988 by dissident CPI mems; Marxist; Chair. S. A. DANGE; Gen. Sec. MOHIT SEN.

Peasants' and Workers' Party of India: Mahatma Phule Rd, Naigaum, Bombay 400 014; f. 1949; Marxist; seeks to nationalize all basic industries, to promote industrialization, and to create a unitary state with provincial boundaries drawn on a linguistic basis; Gen. Sec. DAJIBA DESAI; c. 10,000 mems.

Republican Party of India (RPI): Azad Maidan, Fort, Bombay 400 001; main aim is to realize the aims and objects set out in the preamble to the 1950 Constitution; Pres. BALA SAHIB PRAKASH; Gen. Sec. Mrs J. ISHWARIBAI.

India's other major regional political organizations are:

All-India Anna Dravida Munnetra Kazhagam (AIADMK) (All-India Anna Dravidian Progressive Asscn): 156 Lloyds Rd, Madras 600 004; f. 1972; breakaway group from the DMK; in 1987 split into two rival factions, one led by VAIKOM NARAYANI JANAKI RAMACHANDRAN and the other by C. JAYALALITHA JAYARAM; a third faction, which emerged in 1988, is led by S. RAMACHANDRAN.

Jammu and Kashmir National Conference (JKNC): Mujahid Manzil, Srinagar 190 002; tel. 71500; fmrly All Jammu and Kashmir National Conference, f. 1931, renamed 1939, reactivated 1975; state-based party campaigning for internal autonomy and responsible self-govt; split into two rival sections in 1984: JKNC (F), led by Dr FAROOQ ABDULLAH, Gen. Sec. SHEIKH NAZIR AHMED, and JKNC (K) led by BEGUM KHALIDA SHAH. (The latter section was not recognized by the Election Commission of India and was dissolved by its leader in 1987.)

Nagaland Regional Council: f. 1988 by Congress (I) dissidents.

Shiromani Akali Dal (Longowal): Baradan Shri Darbar Sahib, Amritsar; f. 1920; merged with Congress Party 1958–62; moderate Sikh party; opposes govt intervention in Sikh affairs; seeks autonomy for all states, equal rights for all and safeguards for minorities; Pres. TOTA SINGH (acting); Sr Vice-Pres. JATHEDAR JIWAN SINGH UMRANANGA; Sec.-Gen. MANJIT SINGH TARNTARANI; 1m. mems. In 1986 the Akali Dal split into three factions: the officially-recognized moderate party and two militant factions—the United Akali Dal, led by JAGDEV SINGH TALWANDI, and the Akali Dal (B), led by PRAKASH SINGH BADAL. In February 1987 the two militant factions merged to form the Unified Akali Dal; Pres. S. S. MANN.

Thamizhaga Munnetra Munnani (TMM) (Tamil Nadu Progressive Front): Madras; f. 1988; socialist; promotes the rights of the working class, campaigns against unemployment and social discrimination, and encourages the advancement of the Tamil language and culture; Leader SIVAJI GANESAN.

INDIA

Diplomatic Representation

EMBASSIES AND HIGH COMMISSIONS IN INDIA

Afghanistan: Shanti Path, Chanakyapuri, New Delhi 110 021; tel. (11) 606625; Ambassador: ABDUL SAMAD AZHAR.

Algeria: 15 Anand Lok, New Delhi 110 049; tel. (11) 6445216; telex 3162258; Ambassador: ABDERRAHMANE BENSID.

Argentina: B-8/9 Vasant Vihar, Paschimi Marg, New Delhi 110 057; tel. (11) 671345; telex 3161110; Ambassador: TERESA HORTENCIA INÉS FLOURET.

Australia: 1/50-G Shanti Path, Chanakyapuri, New Delhi 110 021; tel. (11) 601336; telex 3161156; High Commissioner: GRAHAM BARTON FEAKES.

Austria: EP/13 Chandragupta Marg, Chanakyapuri, New Delhi 110 021; tel. (11) 601555; telex 3161699; Ambassador: Dr CHRISTOPH CONORO.

Bangladesh: 56 Ring Rd, Lajpat Nagar-III, New Delhi 110 024; tel. (11) 6834668; telex 3165218; High Commissioner: FARUQ AHMED CHOUDHURY.

Belgium: 50N, Plot 4, Shanti Path, Chanakyapuri, New Delhi 110 021; tel. (11) 608295; telex 3161487; Ambassador: KAMIEL CRIEL.

Bhutan: Chandragupta Marg, Chanakyapuri, New Delhi 110 021; tel. (11) 609217; telex 3162263; Ambassador: Dasho KARMA LETHO.

Brazil: 8 Aurangzeb Rd, New Delhi 110 011; tel. (11) 3015086; telex 3165277; Ambassador: OCTAVIO RAINHO DO SILVA NEVES.

Bulgaria: 16/17 Chandragupta Marg, Chanakyapuri, New Delhi 110 021; tel. (11) 607411; telex 3161490; Ambassador: ALEXANDER TONEV.

Burma: Burma House, 3/50F Nyaya Marg, Chanakyapuri, New Delhi 110 021; tel. (11) 600251; Ambassador: Dr KHIN MAUNG WIN.

Canada: 7/8 Shanti Path, Chanakyapuri, New Delhi 110 021; tel. (11) 608161; telex 3166346; High Commissioner: JAMES G. HARRIS.

Chile: 1/13 Shanti Niketan, New Delhi 110 021; tel. (11) 671363; telex 3166097; Ambassador: MARCELO PADILLA MINVIELLE.

China, People's Republic: 50D Shanti Path, Chanakyapuri, New Delhi 110 021; tel. (11) 600328; telex 3172210; Ambassador: TU GUOWEI.

Colombia: 82D Malcha Marg, Chanakyapuri, New Delhi 110 021; tel. (11) 3012771; Ambassador: Dr NELLY TURBAY DE MUÑOZ.

Cuba: D-5 South Extension, Part II, New Delhi 110 049; tel. (11) 6442897; telex 3166286; Ambassador: SONIA DÍAZ LLERA.

Cyprus: 52 Jor Bagh, New Delhi 110 003; tel. (11) 697503; telex 3161788; High Commissioner: ANTONIOS J. VAKIS.

Czechoslovakia: 50M Niti Marg, Chanakyapuri, New Delhi 110 021; tel. (11) 608382; telex 312386; Ambassador: Dr MILOSLAV JEZIL.

Denmark: 2 Golf Links, New Delhi 110 003; tel. (11) 616273; telex 3166160; Ambassador: JENS OSTENFELD.

Egypt: 1/50M Niti Marg, New Delhi 110 021; tel. (11) 608904; telex 3162611; Ambassador: MOHAMMED AHMED EL-ZOEIBY.

Ethiopia: 7/50G Satya Marg, Chanakyapuri, New Delhi 110 021; tel. (11) 604407; telex 314429; Ambassador: (vacant).

Finland: Nyaya Marg, Chanakyapuri, New Delhi 110 021; tel. (11) 605409; telex 3165030; Ambassador: JYRKI AIMONEN.

France: 2/50E Shanti Path, Chanakyapuri, New Delhi 110 021; tel. (11) 604004; telex 3166077; Ambassador: ANDRÉ LEWIN.

German Democratic Republic: 2 Nyaya Marg, Chanakyapuri, New Delhi 110 021; tel. (11) 3014204; telex 312245; Ambassador: (vacant).

Germany, Federal Republic: 6 Block 50G, Shanti Path, Chanakyapuri, New Delhi 110 021; tel. (11) 604861; telex 3165670; Ambassador: Dr KONRAD SEITZ.

Ghana: A-42 Vasant Marg, New Delhi 110 057; tel. (11) 670716; High Commissioner: KWAME SAARAH-MENSAH.

Greece: 16 Sundar Nagar, New Delhi 110 003; tel. (11) 617800; telex 3165232; Ambassador: GEORGE SIORIS.

Guyana: 85 Poorvi Marg, Vasant Vihar, New Delhi 110 057; tel. (11) 674194; telex 313246; High Commissioner: S. S. NARAINE.

Holy See: 50C Niti Marg, Chanakyapuri, New Delhi 110 021 (Apostolic Nunciature); tel. (11) 606520; Pro-Nuncio: Most Rev. AGOSTINO CACCIAVILLAN.

Hungary: Plot 2, 50M Niti Marg, Chanakyapuri, New Delhi 110 021; tel. (11) 608414; telex 314718; Ambassador: Dr ANDRÁS BALOGH.

Indonesia: 50A Chanakyapuri, New Delhi 110 021; tel. (11) 602352; telex 3165709; Ambassador: R. TAMTOMO.

Iran: 5 Barakhamba Road, New Delhi 110 001; tel. (11) 385491; telex 3166421; Ambassador: EBRAHIM BENHAM DEHKORDY.

Iraq: 169 Jor Bagh, New Delhi 110 003; tel. (11) 618011; telex 313353; Ambassador: ABDU WADOOD ABDUL AL-SHEIKHLI.

Ireland: 13 Jor Bagh, New Delhi 110 003; tel. (11) 617435; telex 3165546; Ambassador: PAUL DEMPSEY.

Italy: 13 Golf Links, New Delhi 110 003; tel. (11) 618311; telex 3166020; Ambassador: Dr RINIERI PAULUCCI DI CALBOLI BARONE.

Japan: Plots 4-5, 50G Shanti Path, Chanakyapuri, New Delhi 110 021; tel. (11) 604071; Ambassador: EIJIRA NODA.

Jordan: 35 Malcha Marg, Chanakyapuri, New Delhi 110 021; tel. (11) 3013495; telex 3161963; Ambassador: JAMAL KHUTAT.

Kampuchea: E-23 Defence Colony, New Delhi 110 024; tel. (11) 693417; Ambassador: SOK AN.

Kenya: E-66 Vasant Marg, Vasant Vihar, New Delhi 110 057; tel. (11) 672303; telex 3161485; High Commissioner: TIREITO KIMUNAI.

Korea, Democratic People's Republic: 42/44 Sundar Nagar, New Delhi 110 003; tel. (11) 616889; telex 3165059; Ambassador: CHO CHON IL.

Korea, Republic: 9 Chandragupta Marg, Chanakyapuri, New Delhi 110 021; tel. (11) 601602; telex 315537; Ambassador: KIM TAE-JI.

Kuwait: 5A Shanti Path, Chanakyapuri, New Delhi 110 021; tel. (11) 600791; telex 3172211; Ambassador: ALI ZAKARIA AL-ANSARI.

Laos: 20 Jor Bagh, New Delhi 110 003; tel. (11) 616187; telex 3165128; Ambassador: CHANPHENG SIHAPHOM.

Lebanon: 10 Sardar Patel Marg, Chanakyapuri, New Delhi 110 021; tel. (11) 3013174; Ambassador: (vacant).

Liberia: 79 Poorvi Marg, Vasant Vihar, New Delhi 110 057; tel. (11) 602800; Ambassador: RUDOLFF KOLACO.

Libya: 22 Golf Links, New Delhi 110 003; tel. (11) 697717; telex 3162601; Secretary of People's Bureau: OMAR AHMAD JADOLLAH AL-AUKALI.

Malaysia: 50M Satya Marg, Chanakyapuri, New Delhi 110 021; tel. (11) 601291; telex 3165096; High Commissioner: MOHAMMED AMIR JAFFAR.

Maldives: New Delhi; High Commissioner: MOHAMED MUSTHAFA HUSSAIN.

Mauritius: 5 Kautilya Marg, Chanakyapuri, New Delhi 110 021; tel. (11) 3011112; telex 312945; High Commissioner: ANUND PRIYA NEEWOOR.

Mexico: 10 Jor Bagh, New Delhi 110 003; tel. (11) 697991; telex 3166121; Ambassador: LUIS DANTÓN RODRÍGUEZ.

Mongolia: 34 Archbishop Makarios Marg, New Delhi 110 003; tel. (11) 618921; Ambassador: OYUNY HOSBAYAR.

Morocco: 33 Archbishop Makarios Marg, New Delhi 110 003; tel. (11) 611588; telex 3166118; Chargé d'affaires: ALAOUI M'HAMEDI MOUSTAPHA.

Nepal: Barakhamba Rd, New Delhi 110 001; tel. (11) 381384; Ambassador: Ms BINDHESWARI SHAH.

Netherlands: 6/50F Shanti Path, Chanakyapuri, New Delhi 110 021; tel. (11) 609571; telex 3165070; Ambassador: E. MARJOLIJN SCHOO.

New Zealand: 25 Golf Links, New Delhi 110 003; tel. (11) 697592; telex 3165100; High Commissioner: Sir EDMUND HILLARY.

Nicaragua: E-514 Greater Kailash-II, New Delhi 110 048; tel. (11) 6442083; Ambassador: CÉSAR A. AROSTEGUI.

Nigeria: 21 Palam Marg, Vasant Vihar, New Delhi 110 057; tel. (11) 670405; telex 312595; High Commissioner: Rear-Adm. (retd) DENSON ERE OKUJAGU.

Norway: 50C Shanti Path, Chanakyapuri, New Delhi 110 021; tel. (11) 605982; telex 3165397; Ambassador: KAARE DAEHLEN.

Oman: 16 Palam Marg, New Delhi 110 057; tel. (11) 670215; telex 3165689; Ambassador: AHMED YOUSUF AL-HARITHY.

Pakistan: 2/50G Shanti Path, Chanakyapuri, New Delhi 110 021; tel. (11) 600601; telex 3165270; Ambassador: NIAZ A. NAIK.

Panama: D-129 Panchsheel Enclave, New Delhi 110 017; tel. (11) 6438620; telex 3117094; Ambassador: HORACIO J. BUSTAMANTE.

Peru: D-1/39, Vasant Vihar, New Delhi 110 057; tel. (11) 673937; telex 3165274; Ambassador: FERNANDO GUILLÉN.

Philippines: 50N Nyaya Marg, Chanakyapuri, New Delhi 110 021; tel. (11) 608842; Ambassador: ROSALINDA V. TIRONA.

Poland: 50M Shanti Path, Chanakyapuri, New Delhi 110 021; tel. (11) 608321; telex 3161894; Ambassador: JANUSZ SWITOWSKI.

Portugal: A-24 West End Colony, New Delhi 110 021; tel. (11) 674568; telex 313608; Ambassador: ANTÓNIO TELCO DE ALMEIDA DE MAGHALHÃES COLACO.

Qatar: A-3 West End Colony, New Delhi 110 021; tel. (11) 673745; telex 3172304; Ambassador: Dr HASSAN ALI HUSSAIN AL-NI'MAH.

Romania: A-52 Vasant Marg, Vasant Vihar, New Delhi 110 057; tel. (11) 676111; telex 312287; Ambassador: N. Finantu.

Saudi Arabia: S-347 Panchshila Park, New Delhi 110 017; tel. (11) 6445419; Ambassador: Shaikh Fouad S. Moufti.

Senegal: Taj Mahal Hotel, Man Singh Rd, New Delhi 110 011; tel. (11) 3016162; Ambassador: Ahmed el Mansour Diop.

Singapore: E-6 Chandragupta Marg, Chanakyapuri, New Delhi 110 021; tel. (11) 604162; telex 3161494; High Commissioner: Chan Keng Howe.

Somalia: 12A Golf Links, New Delhi 110 003; tel. (11) 619559; telex 3165010; Ambassador: Brig.-Gen. Mohamad Farah Aldid.

Spain: 12 Prithviraj Rd, New Delhi 110 011; tel. (11) 3013834; telex 3161488; Ambassador: Carlos Fernández Espeso.

Sri Lanka: 27 Kautilya Marg, Chanakyapuri, New Delhi 110 021; tel. (11) 3010201; telex 3161162; High Commissioner: Bernard P. Tilakaratna.

Sudan: M-14 NDSE Part II, New Delhi 110 049; tel. (11) 6440434; telex 313728; Ambassador: Abdel Moneim Mustafa.

Sweden: Nyaya Marg, Chanakyapuri, New Delhi 110 021; tel. (11) 604011; telex 3162282; Ambassador: Örjan Berner.

Switzerland: Nyaya Marg, Chanakyapuri, New Delhi 110 021; tel. (11) 604225; telex 3172350; Chargé d'affaires a.i.: Peter A. Schweizer.

Syria: 28 Vasant Marg, Vasant Vihar, New Delhi 110 057; tel. (11) 670233; telex 3166248; Ambassador: Mohammad Khodar.

Tanzania: 27 Golf Links, New Delhi 110 003; tel. (11) 694351; High Commissioner: Mohammed Ramia Abdiwawa.

Thailand: 56N Nyaya Marg, Chanakyapuri, New Delhi 110 021; tel. (11) 607289; Ambassador: Nikorn Praisaengpetch.

Trinidad and Tobago: 131 Jor Bagh, New Delhi 110 003; tel. (11) 618186; telex 3162481; High Commissioner: Premchand Jagdeo Dass.

Tunisia: 23 Palam Marg, Vasant Vihar, New Delhi 110 057; tel. (11) 676174; telex 3172162; Ambassador: Ali Tekaia.

Turkey: 50N Nyaya Marg, Chanakyapuri, New Delhi 110 021; tel. (11) 601921; Ambassador: Yalim Eralp.

Uganda: 61 Golf Links, New Delhi 110 003; tel. (11) 693584; telex 312243; High Commissioner: Dr Chebrot Stephen Chemoiko.

USSR: Shanti Path, Chanakyapuri, New Delhi 110 021; tel. (11) 606026; telex 312802; Ambassador: Viktor Fedorovich Isakov.

United Arab Emirates: A-7 West End, New Delhi 110 021; tel. (11) 670830; telex 3165494; Ambassador: Ahmed Abdullah al-Musally.

United Kingdom: Shanti Path, Chanakyapuri, New Delhi 110 021; tel. (11) 601371; telex 3165125; High Commissioner: Sir David Goodall.

USA: Shanti Path, Chanakyapuri, New Delhi 110 021; tel. (11) 600651; telex 3165269; Ambassador: Prof. John Randolph Hubbard.

Venezuela: 114N Panchshila Park, New Delhi 110 017; tel. (11) 6436783; telex 314674; Ambassador: Bernarde Bricene.

Viet-Nam: 2 Navjivan Vihar, New Delhi 110 017; tel. (11) 663427; Ambassador: Vu Xuan Ang.

Yemen Arab Republic: 55B Paschimi Marg, Vasant Vihar, New Delhi 110 057; tel. (11) 674064; telex 3166246; Ambassador: Yehya Zaid al-Radhi.

Yemen, People's Democratic Republic: B-70 Greater Kailash-I, New Delhi 110 048; tel. (11) 6414623; telex 3165567; Ambassador: Mohamed bin Mohamed al-Hubeishi.

Yugoslavia: 3/50G Niti Marg, Chanakyapuri, New Delhi 110 021; tel. (11) 604313; telex 316354; Ambassador: Zivojin Jazić.

Zaire: 160 Jor Bagh, New Delhi 110 003; tel. (11) 619455; telex 3166275; Ambassador: Beltchika Kalubye.

Zambia: 14 Jor Bagh, New Delhi 110 003; tel. (11) 619115; telex 3166084; High Commissioner: Martin Chibulu Mubanga.

Zimbabwe: B-1/42 Safdarjung Enclave, New Delhi 110 029; tel. (11) 677460; telex 3172289; High Commissioner: Dr N. G. G. Makura.

Judicial System

THE SUPREME COURT

The Supreme Court, consisting of a Chief Justice and not more than 17 judges appointed by the President, exercises exclusive jurisdiction in any dispute between the Union and the states (although there are certain restrictions where an acceding state is involved). It has appellate jurisdiction over any judgment, decree or order of the High Court where that Court certifies that either a substantial question of law or the interpretation of the Constitution is involved.

Provision is made for the appointment by the Chief Justice of India of judges of High Courts as ad hoc judges at sittings of the Supreme Court for specified periods, and for the attendance of retired judges at sittings of the Supreme Court. The Supreme Court has advisory jurisdiction in respect of questions which may be referred to it by the President for opinion. The Supreme Court is also empowered to hear appeals against a sentence of death passed by a State High Court in reversal of an order of acquittal by a lower court, and in a case in which a High Court has granted a certificate of fitness.

The Supreme Court also hears appeals which are certified by High Courts to be fit for appeal, subject to rules made by the Court. Parliament may, by law, confer on the Supreme Court any further powers of appeal.

Chief Justice of India: Raghunandan Swarup Pathak.

Judges of the Supreme Court: G. L. Oza, E. S. Venkataramiah, B. C. Ray, Lalit Mohan Sharma, M. N. Venkatachaliah, S. Ranganathan, Sabyasachi Mukherjee, N. D. Ojha, Manharial Pranlal Thakkar, Ranganath Misra, V. Khalid, Murari Mohan Dutt, Kamal Narain Singh, Sivasankar Natarajan, Madhukar Hiralal Kaniya, Kalmanje Jaggannatha Shetty, Dr Thamarapalli Kochu Thommen, Aziz Mushabber Ahmadi, Kuldip Singh, S. B. Pandian, Khagendra Nath Saikia.

Attorney General: K. Parasaran.

HIGH COURTS

The High Courts are the Courts of Appeal from the lower courts, and their decisions are final except in cases where appeal lies to the Supreme Court.

LOWER COURTS

Provision is made in the Code of Criminal Procedure for the constitution of lower criminal courts called Courts of Session and Courts of Magistrates. The Courts of Session are competent to try all persons duly committed for trial, and inflict any punishment authorized by the law. The President and the local government concerned exercise the prerogative of mercy.

The constitution of inferior civil courts is determined by regulations within each state.

Religion

INDIAN FAITHS

Buddhism: The Buddhists in Ladakh (Jammu and Kashmir) are followers of the Dalai Lama. Head Lama of Ladakh: Kaushak Sakula, Dalgate, Srinagar, Kashmir. In 1981 there were 4.72m. Buddhists in India, representing 0.70% of the population.

Hinduism: 549.8m. Hindus (1981 census), representing 80.25% of the population.

Islam: Muslims are divided into two main sects, Shi'as and Sunnis. Most of the Indian Muslims are Sunnis. At the 1981 census Islam had 75.4m. adherents (11% of the population).

Jainism: 3.2m. adherents (1981 census), 0.46% of the population.

Sikhism: 13.1m. Sikhs (comprising 1.91% of the population at the 1981 census), the majority living in the Punjab.

Zoroastrians: More than 120,000 Parsis practise the Zoroastrian religion.

CHRISTIANITY

National Council of Churches in India: Christian Council Lodge, Civil Lines, Nagpur 440 001, Maharashtra; tel. (712) 31312; f. 1953; mems: 22 reformed and three orthodox churches, 14 regional Christian councils, 15 All-India ecumenical orgs and six related agencies; represents c. 8m. mems; Pres. Rt Rev. S. K. Parmar; Gen. Sec. Mathai Zachariah.

Orthodox Churches

Malankara Orthodox Syrian Church: Catholicate Palace, Devalokam, Kottayam 686 038, Kerala; tel. 8500; c. 1.6m. mems (1985); Catholicos of the East and Malankara Metropolitan: HH Baselius Marthoma Mathews I; Sec. Paul Mathai.

Mar Thoma Syrian Church of Malabar: Mar Thoma Sabha Office, Poolatheen, Tiruvalla 689 101, Kerala; tel. (47811) 2449; c. 700,000 mems (1988); Metropolitan: Most Rev. Dr Alexander Mar Thoma; Sec. Rev. Dr K. V. Mathew.

The Malankara Jacobite Syrian Orthodox Church is also represented.

INDIA

Protestant Churches

Church of North India (CNI): CNI Bhavan, Wesley Lodge, 16 Pandit Pant Marg, New Delhi 110 001; tel. (11) 386513; telex 3166763; f. 1970 by merger of the (Anglican) Church of India, the Council of the Baptist Churches in Northern India, the Methodist Church (British and Australasian Conferences), the United Church of Northern India (a union of Presbyterians and Congregationalists, f. 1924), the Church of the Brethren and the Disciples of Christ; comprises 23 dioceses; c. 1m. mems (1988); Moderator Most Rev. Din Dayal, Bishop of Lucknow; Gen. Sec. Rev. Pritam B. Santram.

Church of South India (CSI): Cathedral Rd, POB 4906, Madras 600 086; tel. (44) 811266; f. 1947 by merger of the Methodist Church in South India, the South India United Church (itself a union of churches in the Congregational and Presbyterian/Reformed traditions) and the four southern dioceses of the (Anglican) Church of India; comprises 21 dioceses (incl. one in Sri Lanka); c. 1.5m. mems (1985); Moderator Most Rev. Dr P. Victor Premasagar, Bishop in Medak; Gen. Sec. Rev. M. Azariah.

Methodist Church in India: Methodist Centre, 21 YMCA Rd, Bombay 400 008; tel. (22) 374137; 473,000 mems (1985); Gen. Sec. Rev. Stanley E. Downes.

Samavesam of Telugu Baptist Churches: C. A. M. Highschool Compound, Nellore 524 003, Andhra Pradesh; f. 1962; comprises 515 independent Baptist churches; 340,000 mems (1985); Gen. Sec. P. Jayachandra Rao.

United Church of North India and Pakistan: Church House, Mhow, Madhya Pradesh; Sec. (vacant).

United Evangelical Lutheran Churches in India: 1 First St, Haddows Rd, Madras 600 006; tel. (44) 471676; telex 416613; f. 1975; nine constituent denominations: Andhra Evangelical Lutheran Church, Arcot Lutheran Church, Evangelical Lutheran Church in Madhya Pradesh, Gossner Evangelical Lutheran Church, India Evangelical Lutheran Church, Jeypore Evangelical Lutheran Church, Northern Evangelical Lutheran Church, South Andhra Lutheran Church and Tamil Evangelical Lutheran Church; c. 1.5m. mems (1985); Pres. Rev. K. Nathaniel; Exec. Sec. Dr K. Rajaratnam.

Other denominations active in the country include the Assembly of the Presbyterian Church in North East India, the Bengal-Orissa-Bihar Baptist Convention (6,000 mems), the Chaldean Syrian Church of the East, the Convention of the Baptist Churches of Northern Circars, the Council of Baptist Churches of North East India, the Council of Baptist Churches of Northern India, the Hindustani Convent Church and the Mennonite Church in India.

The Roman Catholic Church

India comprises 19 archdioceses, 101 dioceses and one Apostolic Prefecture. These include two archdioceses and 19 dioceses of the the Syro-Malabarese rite, and one archdiocese and two dioceses of the Syro-Malankarese rite. The archdiocese of Goa and Damão, the seat of the Patriarch of the East Indies, is directly responsible to the Holy See. The remaining archdioceses are metropolitan sees. In December 1986 there were an estimated 12,075,316 adherents in the country.

Catholic Bishops' Conference of India (CBCI): CBCI Centre, Ashok Place, nr Goldakkhana, New Delhi 110 001; tel. (11) 322064; telex 3161366; f. 1944; Pres. Most Rev. Benedict Mar Gregorios, Archbishop of Trivandrum; Sec.-Gen. Most Rev. Alan Basil de Lastic, Bishop of Lucknow.

Latin Rite

Patriarch of the East Indies: Most Rev. Raul Nicolau Gonsalves (Archbishop of Goa and Damão), Paço Patriarcal, POB 216, Altinho, Pangim, Goa 403 001; tel. 3353.

Archbishop of Agra: Most Rev. Cecil de Sa, Archbishop's House, Wazirpura Rd, Agra 282 003, Uttar Pradesh; tel. (562) 72407.

Archbishop of Bangalore: Most Rev. Alphonsus Mathias, Archbishop's House, 18 Miller's Rd, Bangalore 560 046, Karnataka; tel. (812) 575438.

Archbishop of Bhopal: Most Rev. Eugene D'Souza, Archbishop's House, 33 Ahmedabad Palace Rd, Bhopal 462 001, Madhya Pradesh; tel. (755) 73619.

Archbishop of Bombay: Cardinal Simon Ignatius Pimenta, Archbishop's House, 21 Nathalal Parekh Marg, Bombay 400 039, Maharashtra; tel. (22) 2021093.

Archbishop of Calcutta: Most Rev. Henry Sebastian D'Souza, Archbishop's House, 32 Park St, Calcutta 700 016; tel. (33) 444666.

Archbishop of Cuttack-Bhubaneswar: Most Rev. Raphael Cheenath, Archbishop's House, Satya Nagar, Bhubaneswar 751 007, Orissa; tel. 52234.

Archbishop of Delhi: Most Rev. Angelo Innocent Fernandes, Archbishop's House, Ashok Place, New Delhi 110 001; tel. (11) 343457.

Archbishop of Hyderabad: Most Rev. Saminini Arulappa, Archbishop's House, Sardar Patel Rd, Secunderabad 500 003, Andhra Pradesh; tel. (842) 75545.

Archbishop of Madras and Mylapore: Most Rev. Gnanadickam Casimir, Archbishop's House, 21 San Thome High Rd, Madras 600 004, Tamil Nadu; tel. (44) 71102.

Archbishop of Madurai: Most Rev. Marianus Arokiasamy, Archdiocesan Curia, Madurai 625 008, Tamil Nadu; tel. (452) 41408.

Archbishop of Nagpur: Most Rev. Leobard D'Souza, Archbishop's House, Mohan Nagar, Nagpur 440 001, Maharashtra; tel. (712) 33239.

Archbishop of Pondicherry and Cuddalore: Most Rev. Venmani S. Selvanather, Archbishop's House, POB 2, Pondicherry 605 001; tel. 4748.

Archbishop of Ranchi: Most Rev. Telesphore P. Toppo, Archbishop's House, Purulia Rd, POB 5, Ranchi 834 001, Bihar; tel. 22226.

Archbishop of Shillong-Gauhati: Most Rev. Hubert D'Rosario, Archbishop's House, POB 37, Shillong 793 003, Meghalaya; tel. 23355.

Archbishop of Verapoly: Most Rev. Cornelius Elanjikal, Latin Archbishop's House, POB 2581, Cochin 682 031, Kerala; tel. 352892.

Syro-Malabarese Rite

Archbishop of Changanacherry: Most Rev. Joseph Powathil, Metropolitan Curia, POB 20, Changanacherry 686 101, Kerala; tel. 20040.

Archbishop of Ernakulam: Cardinal Anthony Padiyara, Archdiocesan Curia, POB 2580, Ernakulam, Cochin 682 031, Kerala; tel. 352629.

Syro-Malankarese Rite

Archbishop of Trivandrum: Most Rev. Benedict Mar Gregorios, Archbishop's House, Pattom, Trivandrum 695 004, Kerala; tel. (471) 77642.

BAHÁ'Í FAITH

National Spiritual Assembly: POB 19, New Delhi 110 001; tel. (11) 389326; telex 3163171; c. 1m. mems.

The Press

Freedom of the Press was guaranteed under the 1950 Constitution. A measure giving the Press the right to publish proceedings of Parliament without being subjected to censorship or the fear of civil or criminal action, popularly known as the 'Feroz Gandhi Act', was withdrawn when the government declared a state of emergency in June 1975 and article 19 of the Constitution, which guaranteed the right to freedom of speech and expression, was suspended. In order to facilitate news censorship, the existing news agencies were merged to form Samachar, a state news agency. Although pre-censorship was disallowed by the courts in 1975, and censorship of foreign correspondents ended in 1976, the Prevention of Publication of Objectionable Matter Act, passed by parliament in early 1976, still greatly restricted press freedom.

In April 1977 the government introduced bills to repeal the Prevention of Publication of Objectionable Matter Act and to restore the rights of the 'Feroz Gandhi Act', which were both subsequently approved by parliament. The right to report parliamentary proceedings was further guaranteed under the Constitution (45th amendment) Bill of December 1978, later redesignated the 44th amendment. In April 1978 Samachar was disbanded and the original agencies were re-established.

In March 1979 a Press Council was set up (its predecessor was abolished in 1975). Its function is to uphold the freedom of the Press and maintain and improve journalistic standards. In 1980 a second Press Commission was appointed to inquire into the growth and status of the press since the first commission gave its report.

The growth of a thriving press has been inhibited by cultural barriers caused by religious, social and linguistic differences. Consequently the English-language press, with its appeal to the educated middle-class urban readership throughout the states, has retained its dominance. The English-language metropolitan dailies, such as the *Times of India* (published in seven cities), *Indian Express* (published in 11 cities), the *Hindu* (published in six cities) and the *Statesman* (published in two cities), are some of the widest circulating and most influential newspapers. In December 1987 there were 27,685 newspapers and magazines. The readership of daily newspapers is just over 21 per thousand, and in 1985 they were published in 85 languages.

The main Indian language dailies, such as the *Navbharat Times* (Hindi), *Malayala Manorama* (Malayalam), the *Jugantar* (Bengali) and *Ananda Bazar Patrika* (Bengali), by paying attention to rural

INDIA

affairs, cater for the increasingly literate non-anglophone provincial population. Most Indian-language papers have a relatively small circulation.

The more popular weekly and fortnightly periodicals include the cultural Tamil publications *Kumudam*, *Kalki*, *Vaarantari Rani* and *Ananda Vikatan*, the Malayalam fortnightly *Vanitha*, the English *Illustrated Weekly of India*, *India Today*, *Sunday* and the sensationalist *Blitz News Magazine*, published in English, Hindi, Marathi and Urdu. The main monthly periodicals are the *Reader's Digest* and the Hindi *Manohar Kahaniyan*.

The majority of publications in India are under individual ownership (66% in 1982), while newspapers owned by joint stock companies claim the largest part of the total circulation (50.1% in 1983). The most powerful groups own most of the large English dailies and frequently have considerable private commercial and industrial holdings. Four of the major groups are as follows:

Times of India Group (controlled by ASHOK JAIN and family): dailies: the *Times of India*, *Economic Times*, the Hindi *Navbharat Times*, the *Maharashtra Times* (Bombay); periodicals: the *Illustrated Weekly of India*, *Career and Competition Times*, *Science Today*, the Hindi weekly *Dharmayug*, the Hindi fortnightly *Dinaman*, the English fortnightlies *Femina* and *Filmfare* and Hindi pubs including *Parag* and *Sarita*.

Indian Express Group (controlled by the RAMNATH GOENKA family): publishes nine dailies including the *Indian Express*, the Marathi *Lokasatta*, the Tamil *Dinamani*, the Telugu *Andhra Prabha*, the Kannada *Kannada Prabha* and the English *Financial Express*; six periodicals including the English weeklies the *Indian Express* (Sunday edition), *Screen*, the Telugu *Andhra Prabha Illustrated Weekly* and the Tamil *Dinamani Kadir* (weekly).

Hindustan Times Group (controlled by the K. K. BIRLA family): dailies: the *Hindustan Times* (Delhi and Patna), *Pradeep* (Patna) and the Hindi *Hindustan* (Delhi); periodicals: the weeklies the *Overseas Hindustan Times*, the Hindi *Saptahik Hindustan* (Delhi) and the Hindi monthly *Nandan* and *Kadambini* (New Delhi).

Ananda Bazar Patrika Group (controlled by AVEEK SARKAR and family): dailies: the *Ananda Bazar Patrika* (Calcutta) and the English *Business Standard* and *The Telegraph*; periodicals include: the English weeklies *Sunday* and *Sportsworld*, the English fortnightly *Business World*, Bengali weekly *Desh*, Hindi weekly *Ravivar*, Bengali monthly *Anandamela*, Bengali fortnightly *Anandalok* and the Bengali monthly *Sananda*.

PRINCIPAL DAILIES

Delhi (incl. New Delhi)

Daily Milap: 8A Bahadur Shah Zafar Marg, New Delhi 110 002; tel. (11) 3317737; f. 1923; Urdu; nationalist; also publ. from Jullundur and Hyderabad; Man. Editor PUNAM SURI; Chief Editor NAVIN SURI; circ. (Delhi) 21,000.

Daily Pratap: Pratap Bhawan, 5 Bahadur Shah Zafar Marg, New Delhi 110 002; tel. (11) 3317938; f. 1919; Urdu; Editor K. NARENDRA; circ. 27,000.

The Economic Times: Bahadur Shah Zafar Marg, New Delhi 110 002; tel. (11) 3312277; telex 3161337; f. 1961; English; also publ. from Calcutta, Bangalore and Bombay; combined circ. 90,000, circ. (Delhi) 26,000.

Financial Express: Bahadur Shah Zafar Marg, New Delhi 110 002; tel. (11) 3311111; telex 3165803; f. 1961; morning; English; also publ. from Bombay and Madras; combined circ. 36,000.

Hindustan: 18/20 Kasturba Gandhi Marg, New Delhi 110 001; tel. (11) 3318201; telex 3166310; f. 1936; morning; Hindi; also publ. from Patna; Editor HARI NARAYAN NIGAM; circ. (Delhi) 119,000.

The Hindustan Times: 18/20 Kasturba Gandhi Marg, New Delhi 110 001; tel. (11) 3318201; telex 3166310; f. 1923; morning; English; also publ. from Patna; Editor H. K. DUA; circ. (Delhi) 268,000.

Indian Express: Bahadur Shah Zafar Marg, New Delhi 110 002; tel. (11) 3311111; telex 3165908; f. 1953; English; also publ. from Bombay, Chandigarh, Cochin, Bangalore, Ahmedabad, Madras, Madurai, Hyderabad, Vizianagaram and Vijayawada; Editor ARUN SHOURIE; combined circ. 646,000, circ. (Delhi and Chandigarh) 155,500.

Janasatta: 9/10 Bahadur Shah Zafar Marg, New Delhi 110 002; f. 1983; Hindi; tel. (11) 3311111; telex 3165803; also publ. from Chandigarh and Bombay; Editor-in-Chief PRABHASH JOSHI; circ. (Delhi) 90,000.

National Herald: Herald House, Bahadur Shah Zafar Marg, New Delhi 110 002; tel. (11) 3319014; telex 3162500; f. 1938; English; nationalist; also publ. from Lucknow; Editor-in-Chief A. N. DAR.

Navbharat Times: 7 Bahadur Shah Zafar Marg, New Delhi 110 002; tel. (11) 3312277; telex 3161337; f. 1947; Hindi; also publ. from Bombay, Lucknow, Jaipur and Patna; Editor RAJENDRA MATHUR; combined circ. 368,000; circ. (Delhi) 271,000.

Directory

Patriot: Link House, Bahadur Shah Zafar Marg, New Delhi 110 002; tel. (11) 3311056; f. 1963; English; Editor R. K. MISHRA; circ. 33,000.

The Statesman: Connaught Circus, New Delhi 110 001; tel. (11) 3315911; telex 3166324; f. 1875; morning; English; also publ. from Calcutta; Delhi Editor M. L. KOTRU; combined circ. 175,000.

Times of India: 7 Bahadur Shah Zafar Marg, Delhi 110 002; tel. (11) 3312277; telex 3173300; English; also publ. from Bombay, Jaipur, Bangalore, Ahmedabad, Lucknow and Patna; Editor DILEEP PADGAONKAR; circ. (Delhi) 194,000.

Andhra Pradesh

Hyderabad

Deccan Chronicle: 36 Sarojini Devi Rd, Hyderabad 500 003; tel. (0842) 72126; telex 4256644; f. 1938; English; Editor T. VENKATRAM REDDY; circ. 53,500.

Eenadu: Somajiguda, Hyderabad 500 482; tel. (0842) 223422; telex 4256521; f. 1974; Telugu; also publ. from Tirupati, Visakhapatnam and Vijayawada; Chief Editor RAMOJI RAO; combined circ. 277,000.

Newstime: 6-3-570 Somajiguda, Hyderabad 500 482; tel. (0842) 223422; telex 4256521; f. 1984; also publ. from Vijaywada and Visakhapatnam; Editor RAMOJI RAO; circ. 60,000.

Rahnuma-e-Deccan Daily: 5-3-831, Shankar Bagh, Hyderabad 500 012; tel. (0842) 43210; f. 1949; morning; Urdu; independent; Editor SYED VICARUDDIN; circ. 25,000.

Siasat Daily: Jawaharlal Nehru Rd, Hyderabad 500 001; tel. (0842) 44188; telex 4256579; f. 1949; morning; Urdu; Editor ABID ALI KHAN; circ. 40,000.

Vijayawada

Andhra Jyoti: Andhra Jyoti Bldg, POB 712, Vijayawada 520 010; tel. (866) 74532; telex 475217; f. 1960; Telugu; also publ. from Hyderabad and Tirupati; Editor NANDURI RAMAMOHANA RAO; combined circ. 157,000.

Andhra Patrika: POB 534, Gandhinagar, Vijayawada 520 003; tel. (866) 61247; f. 1914; Telugu; also publ. from Hyderabad; Editor S. RADHAKRISHNA; combined circ. 20,000.

Andhra Prabha: 16-1-28, Kolandareddy Rd, Vijayawada 520 016; tel. (866) 61351; telex 475231; f. 1935; Telugu; also publ. from Bangalore, Hyderabad and Vijianagram; Editor P. V. RAO; combined circ. 79,000.

Indian Express: George Oakes Building, Besant Rd, Vijayawada 520 003; English; also publ. from Bangalore, Madras, Cochin, Hyderabad, Vijianagram and Madurai; Editor ARUN SHOURIE; combined circ. 333,000.

Assam

Guwahati

Assam Tribune: Tribune Bldgs, Guwahati 781 003; tel. 23251; f. 1938; English; Editor R. N. BOROOAH; circ. 36,000.

Dainik Asam: Tribune Bldgs, Guwahati 781 003; tel. 23251; f. 1965; Assamese; Editor P. C. BORUA; circ. 46,000.

Bihar

Patna

Aryavarta: Mazharul Haque Path, Patna 800 001; tel. (612) 22130; telex 267; f. 1940; morning; Hindi; Chief Editor S. N. JHA; circ. 72,000.

Hindustan Times: Buddha Marg, Patna 800 001; tel. (612) 23434; f. 1918; morning; English; Editor H. K. DUA; circ. 26,000.

The Indian Nation: Mazharul Haque Path, Patna 800 001; tel. (612) 22130; telex 267; f. 1930; morning; English; Editor DEENA NATH JHA; circ. 40,000.

Pradeep: Buddha Marg, Patna 800 001; tel. (612) 23413; f. 1947; morning; Hindi; Editor PARAS NATH SINGH; circ. 34,000.

Goa

Panaji

Gomantak: Gomantak Bhavan, St Inez, Goa 403 001; tel. 3212; f. 1962; morning; Marathi; Editor NARAYAN G. ATHAWALAY; circ. 15,000.

Navhind Times: Dempo House, Campal, Goa 403 001; tel. 5684; f. 1963; morning; English; Editor V. R. PADIYAR; circ. 21,000.

Gujarat

Ahmedabad

Gujarat Samachar: Gujarat Samachar Bhavan, Khanpur, Ahmedabad 380 001; tel. (272) 22821; telex 1216642; f. 1932; morning; Gujarati; also publ. from Surat, Baroda and Bombay; Editor SHRIYANS SHAH; combined circ. 339,000.

INDIA

Indian Express: Janasatta Bldg, Mirzapur Rd, Ahmedabad; f. 1968; English; Editor ARUN SHOURIE; circ. (Ahmedabad) 17,000.

Lokasatta—Janasatta: Mirzapur Rd, POB 188, Ahmedabad 380 001; tel. (272) 26300; f. 1953; morning; Gujarati; also publ. from Rajkot and Vadodara; Editor HASMUKH GANDHI; combined circ. 92,000.

Sandesh: Sandesh Bldg, Cheekanta Rd, Ahmedabad 380 001; tel. (272) 24241; telex 121532; f. 1923; Gujarati; also publ. from Vadodara; Editor C. S. PATEL; combined circ. 230,000.

Times of India: 139 Ashram Rd, POB 4046, Ahmedabad 380 009; tel. (272) 402151; telex 121490; f. 1968; English; also publ. from Bombay, Delhi, Bangalore, Jaipur, Patna and Lucknow; Editor DILEEP PADGAONKAR; circ. (Ahmedabad) 50,000.

Western Times: Sanskar Kendra, Paldi, Ahmedabad 380 006; tel. (272) 77116; f. 1967; English and Gujarati edns; Man. Editor NIKUNJ PATEL; Editor RAMU PATEL; circ. 14,000 (English), 27,000 (Gujarati).

Rajkot

Jai Hind: POB 59, Sharda Baug, Rajkot 360 001; tel. (281) 40511; f. 1948; morning and evening (in Rajkot); Gujarati; also publ. from Ahmedabad; Man. Editor Y. N. SHAH; combined circ. 52,000.

Phulchhab: Phulchhab Bhavan, Mahatma Gandhi Rd, Rajkot 360 001; tel. (281) 44611; f. 1950; morning; Gujarati; Editor HARSUKH M. SANGHANI; circ. 91,000.

Surat

Gujaratmitra and Gujaratdarpan: Gujaratmitra Bhavan, nr Old Civil Hospital, Sonifalia, Surat 395 003; tel. (261) 23284; telex 188261; f. 1863; morning; Gujarati; Editor B. P. RESHAMWALA; circ. 80,000.

Jammu and Kashmir
Jammu

Kashmir Times: Residency Rd, Jammu 180 001; tel. 44777; f. 1955; morning; English; Editor V. BHASIN; circ. 42,000.

Srinagar

Srinagar Times: Badshah Bridge, Srinagar; f. 1969; Urdu; circ. 14,000.

Karnataka
Bangalore

Deccan Herald: 66 Mahatma Gandhi Rd, Bangalore 560 001; tel. (812) 573291; telex 845339; f. 1948; morning; English; Editor-in-Chief K. N. HARI KUMAR; circ. 137,500.

Indian Express: 1 Queen's Rd, Bangalore 560 001; tel. (812) 76894; telex 845597; f. 1965; English; also publ. from Cochin, Hyderabad, Madras, Madurai, Vijayawada and Vizianagaram; Editor ARUN SHOURIE; combined circ. 333,000.

Kannada Prabha: 1 Queen's Rd, Banglalore 560 001; tel. (812) 76893; Kannada; Editor KHADRI SHAMANNA; circ. 91,000.

Prajavani: 75 Mahatma Gandhi Rd, Bangalore 560 001; tel. (812 53291; telex 845339; f. 1948; morning; Kannada; Editor-in-Chief K. N. HARIKUMAR; Editor M. B. SINGH; circ. 200,000.

Manipal

Udayavani: Udayavani Bldg, Press Corner, Manipal 576 119; tel. 20841; f. 1970; Kannada; Editor T. S. U. PAI; circ. 78,000.

Kerala
Calicut

Deshabhimani: 11/127 Convent Rd, Calicut 673 032; tel. (495) 77286; f. 1946; morning; Malayalam; publ. by the CPI-M; also publ. from Cochin; Chief Editor S. RAMACHANDRAN PILLAI; combined circ. 74,000.

Mathrubhumi: Mathrubhumi Bldgs, Robinson Rd, Calicut 673 001; tel. (495) 63651; f. 1923; Malayalam; Chief Editor N. V. K. WARRIER; also publ. from Trivandrum and Cochin; combined circ. 440,000.

Kottayam

Deepika: POB 7, Kottayam 686 001; tel. (481) 3706; telex 888203; f. 1887; Malayalam; independent; also publ. from Trichur; Editor JOSE PANTHAPLAMTHOTTIYIL; combined circ. 54,000.

Malayala Manorama: Malayala Manorama, K. K. Road, POB 26, Kottayam 686 001; tel. (481) 3615; telex 888201; f. 1887; also publ. from Calicut, Trivandrum and Cochin; morning; Malayalam; Chief Editor K. M. MATHEW; combined circ. 632,500.

Trichur

Express: POB 15, Trichur 680 001; tel. 21830; f. 1944; Malayalam; Editor K. BALAKRISHNAN; circ. 51,000.

Trivandrum

Kerala Kaumudi: POB 77, Pettah, Trivandrum 695 024; tel. (471) 71050; telex 435214; f. 1911; Malayalam; Editor-in-Chief M. S. MANI; circ. 164,000.

Madhya Pradesh
Bhopal

Dainik Bhaskar: 6 Dwarka Sadan, Habibganj, Bhopal; tel. (755) 65163; f. 1958; morning; Hindi and English; also publ. from Indore, Jabalpur and Gwalior; Editor R. C. AGRAWAL; combined circ. 132,000.

Indore

Nai Dunia: 60/1 Babu Labhchand, Chhajlani Marg, Indore 452 009; tel. (731) 62061; telex 735342; f. 1947; morning; Hindi; also publ. from Bhopal; Man. Editor BASANTILAL SETHIA; combined circ. 103,000.

Maharashtra
Bombay

Bombay Samachar: Red House, Syed Abdulla Brelvi Rd, Fort, Bombay 400 001; tel. (22) 2045531; telex 114237; f. 1822; morning and Sunday; Gujarati; political and commercial; Editor JEHAN D. DARUWALA; circ. 136,000.

The Economic Times: Head Office, POB 213, Bombay 400 001; tel. (22) 4150271; telex 1173300; f. 1961; also publ. from New Delhi, Calcutta and Bangalore; English; Editor MANU SHROFF; combined circ. 90,000.

Financial Express: Express Towers, Nariman Point, Bombay 400 021; tel. (22) 2022627; telex 112585; f. 1961; morning; English; also publ. from New Delhi and Madras; Editor SWAMINATHAN S. AIYAR; combined circ. 36,000.

Free Press Journal: Free Press House, 215 Free Press Journal Rd, Nariman Point, Bombay 400 021; tel. (22) 2874566; telex 112570; f. 1930; English; also publ. from Indore; Editor ARUN SADHU; combined circ. 40,000.

Indian Express: Express Towers, Nariman Point, Bombay 400 021; tel. (22) 2022627; telex 112276; f. 1940; English; Editor ARUN SHOURIE; circ. 141,000.

The Indian Post: J. K. Bldg, N. M. Marg, Ballard Estate, Bombay 400 038; tel. (22) 4151415; telex 1174514; f. 1987; English; Editor-in-Chief VINOD MEHTA.

Inquilab: 156D J. Dadajee Rd, Tardeo, Bombay 400 034; tel. (22) 4942586; telex 1175624; f. 1938; Urdu; Editor RIYAZ AHMED KHAN; circ. 23,000.

Janmabhoomi: Janmabhoomi Bhavan, Ghoga St, Fort, Bombay 400 001; tel. (22) 2870831; telex 116859; f. 1934; evening; Gujarati; Propr Saurashtra Trust; Editor HARINDRA DAVE; circ. 36,000.

Lokasatta: Express Towers, Nariman Point, Bombay 400 021; tel. (22) 2022627; f. 1948; morning (except Sunday); Marathi; Editor MADHAVRAO GADKARI; circ. 267,000.

Maharashtra Times: Dr Dadabhai Naoroji Rd, POB 213, Bombay 400 001; tel. (22) 4150271; telex 1173300; f. 1962; Marathi; Editor G. S. TALWALKAR; circ. 156,000.

Mid-Day: 156D J. Dadajee Rd, Tardeo, Bombay 400 034; tel. (22) 4942586; telex 1175624; f. 1979; daily and Sunday; English; also publ. from New Delhi; Editor-in-Chief ANIL DHARKAR; circ. (Bombay) 55,000.

Mumbai Sakal: Dr N. B. Parulekar Rd, Prabhadevi, Bombay 400 025; tel. (22) 4304387; f. 1970; daily and Sunday; Marathi; also publ. from Pune and Kolhapur; combined circ. 190,000.

Navbharat Times: Dr Dadabhai Naoroji Rd, Bombay 400 001; tel. (22) 4150271; telex 1173300; f. 1950; Hindi; also publ. from New Delhi; circ. (Bombay) 95,000.

Navshakti: Free Press House, 215 Nariman Point, Bombay 400 021; tel. (22) 2874566; telex 112570; f. 1932; Marathi; Editor T. S. KOKJE; circ. 52,000.

Pravasi: Janmabhoomi Bhavan, Ghoga St, Fort, Bombay 400 001; tel. (22) 2870831; telex 116859; f. 1939; morning; Gujarati; Propr Saurashtra Trust; Editor HARINDRA DAVE; circ. 38,000.

The Times of India: Dr Dadabhai Naoroji Rd, Bombay 400 001; tel. (22) 4150271; telex 1173300; f. 1838; morning; English; also publ. from Delhi, Ahmedabad, Bangalore, Jaipur, Patna and Lucknow; Editor DILEEP PADGAONKAR; circ. (Bombay and Bangalore) 297,000.

Nagpur

Hitavada: Wardha Rd, Nagpur; tel. (712) 23155; f. 1911; morning; English; also publ. from Bhopal; Editor M. Y. BODHANKAR; combined circ. 27,000.

Maharashtra: 510 Ogale Rd, Mahal, Nagpur; f. 1941; Marathi; nationalist; Editor M. R. DANGRE; circ. 17,000.

INDIA

Nagpur Times: 37 Farmland, Ramdaspeth, Nagpur 440 010; tel. (712) 22935; telex 715235; f. 1933; English; Editor M. V. PADALKAR; circ. 15,000.

Nava Bharat: Cotton Market, Nagpur 440 018; tel. (712) 46145; telex 715453; f. 1938; morning; Hindi; also publ. from Bhopal, Jabalpur, Bilaspur, Indore and Raipur; Editor-in-Chief R. G. MAHESWARI; combined circ. 186,000.

Tarun Bharat: 28 Farmland, Ramdaspeth, Nagpur 440 010; tel. (712) 25052; f. 1944; Marathi; independent; also publ. from Pune and Belgaum; Editor L. T. JOSHI; combined circ. 93,000.

Pune

Kesari: 568 Narayan Peth, Pune 411 030; tel. (212) 449250; f. 1881; Marathi; also publ. from Solapur, Kolhapur, Ahmednagar and Sangli; Editor Dr SHARATCHANDRA GOKHALE; combined circ. 93,000.

Sakal: 595 Budhwar Peth, Pune 411 002; tel. (212) 448403; telex 145504; f. 1932; daily and Sunday; Marathi; also publ. from Bombay and Kolhapur; Editor VIJAY KUVALEKAR; Gen. Man. K. M. BHIDE; combined circ. daily 190,000.

Orissa
Cuttack

Samaj: Gopabandhu Bhawan, Buxibazar, Cuttack 753 001; tel. (671) 20994; telex 676267; f. 1919; Oriya; Editor R. N. RATH; circ. 118,000.

Punjab
Jalandhar

Ajit: Ajit Bhavan, Nehru Garden Rd, Jalandhar 144 001; f. 1955; Punjabi; tel. 75961; telex 385265; Man. Editor S. BARJINDER SINGH; circ. 124,000.

Hind Samachar: Pacca Bagh, Jalandhar 144 001; tel. 75951; telex 385221; f. 1948; morning; Urdu; Editor VIJAY KUMAR CHOPRA; circ. 63,000 (weekdays), 78,000 (Sunday).

Jag Bani: Pacca Bagh, Jalandhar 144 001; tel. 75951; telex 385221; f. 1978; morning and Sunday; Punjabi; publ. by Hind Samachar Ltd; Editor VIJAY KUMAR CHOPRA; circ. 94,000.

Punjab Kesari: Civil Lines, Jalandhar 144 001; tel. 75951; telex 385221; f. 1965; morning and Sunday; Hindi; also publ. from Delhi; Editor VIJAY KUMAR CHOPRA; combined circ. 519,000.

Chandigarh

The Tribune: 29C Chandigarh 160 020; tel. (172) 28461; telex 395285; f. 1881; English, Hindi and Punjabi; Editor-in-Chief (all edns) V. N. NARAYANAN; Editor (Hindi edn) RADHE SHYAM SHARMA; Editor (Punjabi edn) HARBHAJAN SINGH HALWARVI; circ. 146,000 (English), 34,000 (Hindi), 45,000 (Punjabi).

Rajasthan
Jaipur

Rajasthan Patrika: Kesargarh, Jawahar Lal Nehru Marg, Jaipur 302 004; tel. (141) 61321; telex 365435; f. 1956; Hindi; English; also publ. from Jodhphur, Bikaner, Udaipur and Kota; Editor VIJAY BHANDARI; combined circ. (Hindi) 207,000, (English) 4,000.

Rashtradoot: M.I. Rd, POB 30, Jaipur 302 001; tel. (141) 72634; f. 1951; Hindi; also publ. from Kota and Bikaner; Chief Editor RAJESH SHARMA; circ. (Jaipur) 104,000, (Kota) 42,000, (Bikaner) 30,000.

Tamil Nadu
Madras

Daily Thanthi: 46 E.V.K. Sampath Rd, Madras 600 007; tel. (44) 31331; telex 418101; f. 1942; Tamil; also publ. from Bangalore, Coimbatore, Cuddalore, Madurai, Salem, Tiruchi, Tirunelveli and Vellore; Editor R. THIRUVADI; combined circ. 309,500.

Dinakaran: 106/107 Kutchery Rd, Mylapore, Madras 600 004; tel. (44) 71006; telex 416065; f. 1977; Tamil; also publ. from Madurai, Trichy, Salem and Coimbatore; Editor K. KESAVAN; combined circ. 156,000.

Dinamani: Express Estates, Mount Rd, Madras 600 002; tel. (44) 810551; telex 41222; f. 1934; morning; Tamil; Editor IRAVATHAM MAHADEVAN; circ. 180,000 (Madurai and Madras).

The Hindu: 859/860 Anna Rd, Madras 600 002; tel. (44) 566567; telex 418358; f. 1878; morning; English; independent; also publ. from Bangalore, Coimbatore, Hyderabad, New Delhi and Madurai; Editor G. KASTURI; combined circ. 418,000.

Indian Express: Express Estate, Mount Rd, Madras 600 002; tel. (44) 810551; telex 41222; also publ. from Delhi, Bombay, Chandigarh, Cochin, Bangalore, Ahmedabad, Madurai, Hyderabad, Vizianagaram and Vijayawada; Editor ARUN SHOURIE; circ. 333,000 (Madras, Madurai, Bangalore, Cochin, Hyderabad, Vijayawada and Vizianagaram).

Murasoli: 93 Kodambakkam High Rd, Madras 600 034; tel. (44) 470044; f. 1960; Tamil; Editor MURASOLI MARAN; circ. 54,000.

Tripura
Agartala

Dainik Sambad: 11 Jagannath Bari Rd, Agartala 799 001; tel. 3928; f. 1966; Bengali; Editor B. C. DUTTA BHAUMIK.

Uttar Pradesh
Agra

Amar Ujala: Sikandara Rd, Agra 282 007; tel. (562) 72408; telex 565255; f. 1948; Hindi; also publ. from Bareilly and Meerut; Chief Editor ABIL K. AGARWAL; circ. 71,000 (Agra), 48,000 (Bareilly), 46,000 (Meerut).

Allahabad

Amrit Prabhat: 10 Edmonstone Rd, Allahabad 211 001; tel. (532) 52620; f. 1977; Hindi; also publ. from Lucknow; Chief Editor TUSHAR KANTI GHOSH; Editor KAMLESH BIHARI MATHUR; combined circ. 44,000.

Northern India Patrika: 10 Edmonstone Rd, Allahabad 211 001; tel. (532) 52665; f. 1959; English; also publ. from Lucknow; Chief Editor TUSHAR KANTI GHOSH; Editor S. K. BOSE; combined circ. 46,000.

Kanpur

Daily Jagran: 2 Sarvodaya Nagar, Kanpur 208 005; tel. 216161; telex 325289; f. 1942; Hindi; also publ. from Gorakhpur, Jhansi, Lucknow, Meerut, Agra and Varanasi (Allahabad); Editor NARENDRA MOHAN; combined circ. 345,000.

Vyapar Sandesh: 48/12 Lathi Mohal Lane, Kanpur, 208 001; tel. (512) 69889; f. 1958; Hindi; commercial news and economic trends; Editor HARI SHANKAR SHARMA; circ. 13,000.

Lucknow

National Herald: 1 Bisheshwar North Rd, Lucknow 226 001; f. 1938 Lucknow, 1968 Delhi; English; Editor A. N. DAR.

The Pioneer: 20 Vidhan Sabha Marg, Lucknow 226 001; tel. (522) 36516; f. 1865; English; also publ. from Varanasi; Editor SOMNATH SAPRU; combined circ. 91,000.

Swatantra Bharat: Pioneer House, 20 Vidhan Sabha Marg, Lucknow 226 001; tel. (522) 36516; f. 1947; Hindi; also publ. from Varanasi; Editor RAJ NATH SINGH; combined circ. 82,000.

Varanasi

Aj: Sant Kabir Rd, Kabirchaura, POB 1007 & 1052, Varanasi 221 001; tel. (542) 62061; telex 545213; f. 1920; Hindi; also publ. from Gorakhpur, Patna, Allahabad, Ranchi, Agra and Kanpur; Editor S. V. GUPTA; circ. 155,000 (Varanasi, Allahabad and Gorakhpur), 54,000 (Kanpur and Agra), 130,000 (Patna and Ranchi).

West Bengal
Calcutta

Aajkaal: 96 Raja Rammohan Sarani, Calcutta 700 009; tel. (33) 353671; telex 212216; f. 1981; morning; Bengali; Chief Editor PRATAP K. ROY; circ. 163,000.

Amrita Bazar Patrika: 41A Acharya J. C. Bose Rd, Calcutta 700 017; tel. (33) 296055; telex 217245; f. 1868; morning; English; nationalist; also published from Jamshedpur (Bihar); Editor T. K. GHOSH; combined circ. 128,000.

Ananda Bazar Patrika: 6 Prafulla Sarkar St, Calcutta 700 001; tel. (33) 274880; telex 215468; f. 1922; morning; Bengali; Editor AVEEK SARKAR; circ. 390,500.

Bartaman: 76A Acharya J.C. Bose Rd, Calcutta 700 014; tel. (33) 243907; telex 217380; f. 1984; Editor BARUN SENGUPTA; circ. 105,000.

Business Standard: 6 Prafulla Sarkar St, Calcutta 700 001; tel. (33) 243907; telex 215468; f. 1975; morning; English; Editor AVEEK SARKAR (acting); circ. 21,000.

Dainik Basumati: 166 Bepin Behari Ganguly St, Calcutta 700 012; tel. (33) 359462; f. 1914; Bengali; independent nationalist; Editor ASHIM SHOME; circ. 26,000.

The Economic Times: 105/7A, S. N. Banerjee Rd, Calcutta 700 014; tel. (33) 294400; telex 217580; English; also publ. from Delhi, Bangalore and Bombay; circ. (Calcutta) 17,000.

Jugantar: 41A Acharya J. C. Bose Rd, Calcutta 700 017; tel. (33) 296055; telex 217245; f. 1936; Bengali; Editor T. K. GHOSH; circ. 302,000.

Paigam: 26/1 Market St, Calcutta 700 087; tel. (33) 246040; f. 1948; Bengali; morning; Editor MARJINA TARAFDAR; circ. 28,000.

INDIA

Sanmarg: 160C Chittaranjan Ave, Calcutta 700 007; tel. (33) 315301; f. 1948; Hindi; Editor RAMAWTAR A. GUPTA; circ. 69,500.

The Statesman: Statesman House, 4 Chowringhee Sq., Calcutta 700 001; tel. (33) 271000; telex 214509; f. 1875; morning; English; independent; also publ. from New Delhi; Editor SUNANDA K. DATTA-RAY; combined circ. 175,000.

The Telegraph: 6 Prafulla Sarkar St, Calcutta 700 001; tel. (33) 278000; telex 215468; f. 1982; English; Editor M. J. AKBAR; circ. 115,000.

Vishwamitra: 74 Lenin Sarani, Calcutta 700 013; tel. (33) 249567; telex 213370; f. 1916; morning; Hindi; commercial; also publ. from Bombay; Editor PRAKASH CHANDRA AGRAWALLA; combined circ. 100,000.

SELECTED PERIODICALS
Delhi and New Delhi

Alive: Delhi Press Bldg, E-3, Jhandewala Estate, Rani Jhansi Rd, Delhi 110 055; tel. (11) 526311; f. 1940; fortnightly; English; political and cultural; Editor C. P. KHARE; circ. 20,000.

Bal Bharati: Patiala House, Publications Division, Ministry of Information and Broadcasting, Delhi; tel. (11) 387038; f. 1948; monthly; Hindi; for children; Editor P. K. BHARGAVA; circ. 30,000.

Biswin Sadi: 3583 Netaji Subash Marg, Darya Ganj, POB 7013, New Delhi 110 002; tel. (11) 271637; f. 1937; monthly; Urdu; Editor Z. REHMAN NAYYAR; circ. 35,000.

Career and Competition Times: 7 Bahadur Shah Zafar Marg, New Delhi 110 002; tel. (11) 3312277; telex 3161337; f. 1981; monthly; English; Editor Y. C. HALAN; circ. 57,000.

Careers Digest: 21 Shankar Market, Delhi 110 001; tel. (11) 44726; f. 1963; monthly; English; Editor O. P. VARMA; circ. 35,000.

Catholic India: CBCI Centre, nr Goldakkhana, New Delhi 110 001; tel. (11) 344470; telex 3161366; quarterly.

Champak: Delhi Press Bldg, E-3, Jhandewala Estate, Rani Jhansi Rd, Delhi 110 055; tel. (11) 524143; f. 1969; fortnightly; Hindi, also in English, Gujarati and Marathi; Editor VISHWA NATH; circ. 85,000.

Children's World: Nehru House, 4 Bahadur Shah Zafar Marg, New Delhi 110 002; tel. (11) 3316970; f. 1968; monthly; English; Editor K. RAMAKRISHNAN; circ. 25,000.

Competition Success Review: 604 Prabhat Kiran, Rajendra Place, Delhi 110 008; tel. (11) 5712898; monthly; English; f. 1963; Editor S. K. SACHDEVA; circ. 291,000.

The Congress: 24 Akbar Rd, New Delhi 110 011; tel. (11) 3019080; f. 1988; weekly; Hindi and English; organ of the All India Congress Committee (I); Editor-in-Chief GHULAM NABI AZAD; circ. 60,000.

Dinaman: 10 Daryaganj, New Delhi 110 002; tel. (11) 271911; f. 1965; fortnightly; Hindi; news; Editor SATISH JHA; circ. 39,000.

Employment News: Government of India, East Block IV, Level 7, R. K. Puram, New Delhi 110 066; tel. (11) 608979; f. 1976; weekly; Hindi, Urdu and English edns; Editor (all edns) N. N. SHARMA; combined circ. 360,000.

Filmi Duniya: 16 Darya Ganj, Delhi 110 002; tel. (11) 278087; telex 3166205; f. 1958; monthly; Hindi; Chief Editor NARENDRA KUMAR; circ. 121,000.

Filmi Kaliyan: 16/39 Subhash Nagar, New Delhi 110 027; tel. (11) 272080; f. 1969; monthly; English; cinema; Editor-in-Chief V. S. DEWAN; circ. 121,000.

Grih Shobha: Delhi Press Bldg, E-3 Jhandelwala Estate, Rani Jhansi Rd, Delhi 110 055; tel. (11) 526311; f. 1979; monthly; Hindi and Gujarati; Editor VISHWA NATH; circ. 292,000.

India Perspectives: Room 137, 'A' Wing, Shastri Bhavan, New Delhi 1; tel. (11) 389471; f. 1988; Chief Editor DALIP SINGH.

India Today: F 14/15, Connaught Place, New Delhi 110 001; tel. (11) 3315801; telex 3161245; f. 1975; fortnightly; English and Hindi; Editor AROON PURIE; circ. 353,000 (English), 222,000 (Hindi).

Indian Horizons: Azad Bhavan, Indraprastha Estate, New Delhi 110 002; tel. (11) 3318647; telex 314904; f. 1951; quarterly; English; publ. by the Indian Council for Cultural Relations; Editor A. SRINIVASAN; circ. 5,000.

Indian Railways: POB 467, New Delhi 110 001; tel. (11) 388598; telex 313561; f. 1956; monthly; English; publ. by the Ministry of Railways (Railway Board); Editor MANOHAR D. BANERJEE; circ. 12,000.

Intensive Agriculture: Ministry of Agriculture and Rural Development, Directorate of Extension, New Delhi 110 066; tel. (11) 600591; f. 1955; monthly; English; Editor SHUKLA HAZRA; circ. 15,000.

Jagat (Hindi) Monthly: 8/818 Ajmeri Gate, Delhi 110 006; f. 1958; Hindi; popular and family magazine; Editor PREM CHAND VERMA; circ. 18,000.

Jagat Weekly: 8/818 Ajmeri Gate, Delhi 110 006; tel. (11) 664847; f. 1956; Urdu; progressive; Editor PREM CHAND VERMA; circ. 11,000.

Journal of Industry and Trade: Ministry of Commerce and Supply, Delhi 110 011; tel. (11) 3016664; f. 1952; monthly; English; Man. Dir A. C. BANERJEE; circ. 2,000.

Kadambini: Hindustan Times House, Kasturba Gandhi Marg, New Delhi 110 001; tel. (11) 3318201; telex 3166310; f. 1960; monthly; Hindi; Editor RAJENDRA AWASTHY; circ. 71,000.

Krishak Samachar: Bharat Krishak Samaj, Dr Panjabrao Desmukh Krishak Bhavan, A-1 Nizamuddin West, New Delhi 110 013; tel. (11) 619508; f. 1957; monthly; English and Hindi edns; agriculture; Editor K. PRABHAKAR REDDY; circ. (English) 11,000, (Hindi) 28,000.

Kurukshetra: Krishi Bhavan, Delhi 110 001; monthly; English; rural development; Editor RATNA JUNEJA; circ. 13,000.

Lalita: 92 Daryaganj, Delhi 110 002; tel. (11) 272482; f. 1959; monthly; Hindi; Editor L. RANIGUPTA; circ. 20,000.

Link Indian News Magazine: Link House, Bahadurshah Zafar Marg, New Delhi 110 002; tel. (11) 3311056; telex 3162384; f. 1958; weekly; independent; Editor R. K. MISHRA; circ. 11,000.

Mayapuri: A-5, Mayapuri, New Delhi 110 064; tel. (11) 591439; telex 3176125; f. 1974; weekly; Hindi; cinema; Editor A. P. BAJAJ; circ. 153,000.

Nandan: Hindustan Times House, New Delhi 110 001; tel. (11) 3318201; telex 3166310; f. 1963; monthly; Hindi; Editor JAI PRAKASH BHARTI; circ. 215,000.

Nav Chitrapat: 92 Daryaganj, Delhi 110 002; tel. (11) 272482; f. 1932; monthly; Hindi; Editor SATYENDRA SHYAM; circ. 36,000.

New Age: 15 Kotla Rd, Delhi 110 002; tel. (11) 3310762; telex 3165982; f. 1953; main organ of the Communist Party of India; weekly; English; Editor PAULY V. PARAKAL; circ. 215,000.

Organiser: 29 Rani Jhansi Rd, Delhi 110 055; tel. (11) 529595; f. 1947; weekly; English; Editor V. P. BHATIA; circ. 66,000.

Overseas Hindustan Times: Hindustan Times House, Kasturba Gandhi Marg, Delhi 110 001; weekly; English.

Panchajanya: 29 Rani Jhansi Marg, New Delhi 110 055; tel. (11) 529595; f. 1947; weekly; Hindi; Gen. Man. and Man. Editor R. S. AGNIHOTRI; circ. 34,000.

Parag: 10 Daryaganj, New Delhi 110 002; tel. (11) 277360; f. 1958; children's monthly; Hindi; Editor HARI KRISHNA DEVSARE; circ. 60,000.

Priya: 92 Daryaganj, Delhi 110 002; f. 1960; monthly; Hindi; Editor SATYENDRA SMYAM; circ. 28,000.

Punjabi Digest: 209 Hemkunt House, 6 Rajendra Place, POB 2549, New Delhi 110 008; tel. (11) 5715225; f. 1971; literary monthly; Gurmukhi; Chief Editor Sardar J. B. SINGH; circ. 67,000.

Rangbhumi: 5A/15 Ansari Rd, Darya Ganj, Delhi 110 002; tel. (11) 274667; f. 1941; Hindi; films; Editor S. K. GUPTA; circ. 30,000.

Ruby Magazine: 3583 Netaji-Subash Marg, Darya Ganj, POB 7014, New Delhi 110 002; tel. (11) 271637; f. 1966; monthly; Urdu; Editor REHMAN NAYYAR; circ. 23,000.

Sainik Samachar: Block L-1, Church Rd, New Delhi 110 001; tel. (11) 3019668; f. 1909; pictorial weekly for India's armed forces; English, Hindi, Urdu, Tamil, Punjabi, Telugu, Marathi, Kannada, Gorkhali, Malayalam, Bengali, Assamese and Oriya edns; Editor-in-Chief BIBEKANANDA RAY; circ. 18,000.

Saptahik Hindustan: 18–20 Kasturba Gandhi Marg, Delhi 110 001; tel. (11) 3318201; telex 3166310; f. 1950; weekly; Hindi; Editor MRINAL PANDE; circ. 40,000.

Sarita: Delhi Press Bldg, E-3, Jhandewala Estate, Rani Jhansi Rd, Delhi 110 055; tel. (11) 526311; f. 1946; fortnightly; Hindi; Editor VISHWA NATH; circ. 257,000.

Shama: 13/14 Asaf Ali Rd, New Delhi 110 002; tel. (11) 732666; telex 3161601; f. 1939; monthly; Urdu; art and literature; Editors M. YUNUS DEHLVI, IDREES DEHLVI, ILYAS DEHLVI; circ. 61,000.

Sher-i-Punjab: Hemkunt House, 6 Rajendra Place, New Delhi 110 008; tel. (11) 5715225; f. 1911; weekly news magazine; Chief Editor Sardar JANG BAHADUR SINGH; circ. 15,000.

South Asia Journal: Sage Publications India (Pvt) Ltd, POB 4215, New Delhi 110 048; tel. (11) 6419884; f. 1987; quarterly; journal of the Indian Council for South Asian Co-operation (ICSAC); Chair. DINESH SINGH; Editor-in-Chief BIMAL PRASAD.

The Sun: 8B Bahadur Shah Zafar Marg, POB 7164, Delhi 110 002; tel. (11) 3319286; telex 3165931; f. 1977; weekly; English; Editor V. B. GUPTA; circ. 41,000.

Surya India: Kanchenjunga Bldg, 18 Barakhamba Rd, Delhi; tel. (11) 3310202; telex 3162399; f. 1977; monthly; English; political and social news; Editor Dr J. K. JAIN.

INDIA

Sushama: 13/14 Asaf Ali Rd, New Delhi 110 002; tel. (11) 732666; telex 3161601; f. 1959; monthly; Hindi; art and literature; Editors IDREES DEHLVI, ILYAS DEHLVI, YUNUS DEHLVI; circ. 64,000.

Vigyan Pragati: PID Bldg, Hillside Rd, New Delhi 110 012; tel. (11) 585359; f. 1952; monthly; Hindi; popular science; Editor SHYAM SUNDER SHARMA; circ. 115,000.

Woman's Era: Delhi Press Bldg, E-3, Jhandewala Estate, Rani Jhansi Rd, Delhi 110 055; tel. (11) 526311; f. 1973; fortnightly; English; Editor VISHWA NATH; circ. 104,000.

Yojana: Planning Commission, Yojana Bhavan, Parliament St, Delhi 110 001; tel. (11) 383655; f. 1957; fortnightly; English, Tamil, Bengali, Marathi, Gujarati, Assamese, Malayalam, Telugu, Kannada, Punjabi, Urdu and Hindi edns; Chief Editor S. Z. HASSAN; circ. 90,000.

Andhra Pradesh
Hyderabad

Islamic Culture: Opposite Osmania University Post Office, Hyderabad 7; f. 1927; quarterly; English; Editor Prof. SYED SIRAJUDDIN; circ. 700.

Vijayawada

Andhra Jyoti Sachitra Vara Patrika: Vijayawada 520 010; tel. (866) 74532; f. 1967; weekly; Telugu; Editor PURANAM SUBRAMANYA SARMA; circ. 83,000.

Bala Jyoti: Labbipet, Vijayawada 520 010; tel. (866) 74532; f. 1980; monthly; Telugu; Asst Editor SASIKANT SATAKARNI; circ. 43,000.

Jyoti Chitra: Labbipet, Vijayawada 520 010; tel. (866) 74532; f. 1977; weekly; Telugu; Editor T. KUTUMBA RAO; circ. 86,000.

Vanita Jyoti: Labbipet, Vijayawada 520 010; tel. (866) 74532; f. 1978; monthly; Telugu; Asst Editor J. SATYANARAYANA; circ. 28,500.

Assam
Guwahti

Asam Bani: Tribune Bldg, Guwahti 781 003; tel. 23251; f. 1955; weekly; Assamese; Editor TILAK HAZARIKA; circ. 35,000.

Bihar
Patna

Anand Digest: Govind Mitra Rd, Patna 800 004; tel. 50341; f. 1981; monthly; Hindi; family magazine; Editor Dr S. S. SINGH; circ. 61,000.

Balak: Govind Mitra Rd, POB 5, Patna 800 004; tel. 50341; f. 1926; monthly; Hindi; children's; Editor S. R. SARAN; circ. 32,000.

Jyotsana: Rajendranagar, Patna; f. 1947; monthly; Hindi; Editor S. NARAYAN; circ. 11,000.

Nar Nari: Nari Prakashan, Patna 800 004; f. 1949; monthly; Hindi; Editor V. VATSYAYAN; circ. 10,000.

Gujarat
Ahmedabad

Aaspas: nr Khanpur Gate, Khanpur, Ahmedabad 380 001; tel. (272) 391131; f. 1976; weekly; Gujarati; Editor GUNVANT C. SHAH; circ. 100,373.

Akhand Anand: Swami Akhandanand Marg, POB 50, Bhadra, Ahmedabad; tel. (272) 391798; f. 1947; monthly; Gujarati; Pres. H. M. PATEL; Editor RAMANLAL MANEKLAL BHATT; circ. 32,000.

Chitralok: Gujarat Samachar Bhavan, Khanpur, POB 254, Ahmedabad; f. 1952; weekly; Gujarati; films; Editor SHREYANS SHAH; circ. 21,000.

Sakhi: Sakhi Publications, Jai Hind Press Bldg, nr Gujarat Chamber, Ashram Rd, Navrangpura, Ahmedabad 380 009; tel. (272) 407052; f. 1984; monthly; Gujarati; women's; Editor Y. N. SHAH; circ. 14,000.

Stree: Sandesh Bhavan, Gheekanta, POB 151, Ahmedabad 380 001; tel. (272) 24243; telex 121532; f. 1962; weekly; Gujarati; Editor LILABEN PATEL; circ. 84,000.

Zagmag: Gujarat Samachar Bhavan, Khanpur, Ahmedabad 380 001; tel. (272) 22821; telex 1216642; f. 1952; weekly; Gujarati; for children; Editor BAHUBALI S. SHAH; circ. 38,000.

Rajkot

Amruta: Sharda Baug, Rajkot 360 001; tel. (281) 40513; f. 1967; weekly; Gujarati; films; Editor Y. N. SHAH; circ. 31,000.

Niranjan: Niranjan Publications, Jai Hind Press Bldg, Sharda Baug, Rajkot 360 001; tel. (281) 40513; f. 1971; fortnightly; Gujarati; children's; Editor N. R. SHAH; circ. 25,000.

Parmarth: Sharda Baug, Rajkot 360 001; tel. (281) 40511; monthly; Gujarati; philosophy and religion; Editor Y. N. SHAH; circ. 30,000.

Phulwadi: Sharda Baug, Rajkot 360 001; tel. (281) 40513; weekly; Gujarati; for children; Editor Y. N. SHAH; circ. 54,000.

Karnataka
Bangalore

Mysindia: 38A Mahatma Gandhi Rd, Bangalore; f. 1939; weekly; English; news and current affairs; Editor D. N. HOSALI; circ. 14,000.

New Leader: 93 North Rd, St Mary's Town, Bangalore 560 005; f. 1887; weekly; English; Editor Rt Rev. HERMAN D'SOUZA; circ. 10,000.

Prajamata: North Anjaneya Temple Rd, Basavangudi, Bangalore 560 004; tel. (812) 602634; f. 1931; weekly; Kannada; news and current affairs; Chief Editor G. V. ANJI; circ. 58,500.

Sudha: 66 Mahatma Gandhi Rd, Bangalore 560 001; tel. (812) 573291; telex 845339; f. 1965; weekly; Kannada; Editor-in-Chief K. N. HARIKUMAR; circ. 207,000.

Manipal

Taranga: Udayavani Bldg, Press Corner, Manipal 576 119; tel. 20841; f. 1983; weekly; Kannada; Editor S. K. GULVADI; circ. 177,000.

Kerala
Calicut

Mathrubhumi Illustrated Weekly: Mathrubhumi Bldg, K. P. Kesava Menon Rd, Calicut 673 001; tel. 63651; f. 1923; weekly; Malayalam; Editor N. V. KRISHNA WARRIOR; circ. 102,000.

Cochin

The Week: Manorama Bldgs, Panampilly Nagar, POB 2314, Cochin 682 016; tel. 366285; telex 885696; f. 1982; weekly; Chief Editor MAMMEN MATHEW; circ. 64,000.

Kottayam

Balarama: POB 226, Kottayam 686 001; tel. (481) 3721; telex 888201; f. 1972; children's fortnightly; Malayalam; Chief Editor BINA PHILIP MATHEW; circ. 211,000.

Malayala Manorama: Malayala Manorama, Kottayam 686 001; tel. (481) 3615; telex 888201; f. 1937; weekly; Malayalam; Chief Editor MAMMEN VERGHESE; circ. 667,000.

Vanitha: POB 226, Kottayam 686 001; tel.(481) 3721; telex 888201; f. 1975; women's fortnightly; Malayalam; Chief Editor K. M. MATHEW; circ. 219,500.

Madhya Pradesh

Krishak Jagat: POB 3, Bhopal 462 001; tel. (755) 73466; f. 1946; weekly; Hindi; also Marathi edn; agriculture; Chief Editor S. C. GANGRADE; Editor V. K. BONDRIYA; circ. 12,000.

Maharashtra
Bombay

Bhavan's Journal: Bharatiya Vidya Bhavan, Bombay 400 007; tel. (22) 8114462; f. 1954; fortnightly; English; literary; Man. Editor J. H. DAVE; Editor S. RAMAKRISHNAN; circ. 25,000.

Blitz News Magazine: 17/17H Cawasji Patel St, Bombay 400 001; tel. (22) 2047166; telex 116801; f. 1941; weekly; English, Hindi, Marathi and Urdu edns; Editor-in-Chief R. K. KARANJIA; combined circ. 419,000.

Bombay: 28 A&B Jolly Maker Chambers-II, Nariman Point, Bombay 400 021; tel. (22) 2026152; telex 115373; f. 1979; fortnightly; English; Editor MOHINI BHULLAR; circ. 21,000.

Business India: Nirmal, 18th Floor, Nariman Point, Bombay 400 021; tel. (22) 2024422; telex 113557; f. 1978; fortnightly; English; Publr ASHOK H. ADVANI; Editor RUSI ENGINEER; circ. 64,000.

Business World: 145 Atlanta, 209 Ceremonial Blvd, Nariman Point, Bombay 400 021; tel. (22) 240581; telex 112354; f. 1980; fortnightly; English; Editor AVEEK SARKAR (acting); circ. 59,000.

Chitralekha: 62 Vaju Kotak Marg, Fort, Bombay 400 001; tel. (22) 261526; telex 1178298; f. 1950; weekly; Gujarati; Editors Mrs M. V. KOTAK, H. MEHTA; circ. 302,000.

Cine Blitz: 17/17H Cowasji Patel St, Bombay 400 001; tel. (22) 2043546; telex 116801; f. 1974; monthly; English; films; Editor RITA K. MEHTA; circ. 81,500.

Commerce: N.K.M. International House, 178 Backbay Reclamation, Bombay 400 020; tel. (22) 2024505; telex 116915; f. 1910; weekly; English; Editor P. S. JHA; circ. 7,000.

Current Weekly: Nariman Bhavan, 15th Floor, Nariman Point, Bombay 400 021; tel. (22) 2024067; f. 1949; English; Editor AYUB SYED; circ. 80,000.

Debonair: 41A Dr E. Moses Rd, Bombay 400 018; tel. (22) 4920780; f. 1972; English; monthly; Editor DILIP THAKORE; circ. 103,000.

Dharmayug: Dr Dadabhai Naoroji Rd, Bombay 400 001; tel. (22) 4150271; telex 1173504; f. 1950; weekly; Hindi; Editor GANESH MANTRI; circ. 92,000.

Economic and Political Weekly: Hitkari House, 284 Shahid Bhagatsingh Rd, Bombay 400 038; tel. (22) 266072; f. 1966; English; Editor KRISHNA RAJ.

The Economic Scene: Orient House, Mangalore St, Ballard Estate, Bombay 400 038; tel. (22) 267621; telex 112618; f. 1976; monthly; English; Editor ACHYUT VAZE.

Eve's Weekly: J. K. Somani Bldg, Bombay Samachar Marg, Bombay 400 023; tel. (22) 271444; f. 1947; English; Editor GULSHAN EWING; circ. 40,000.

Femina: Times of India Bldg, Dr Dadabhai Naoroji Rd, Bombay 400 001; tel. (22) 4150271; telex 1173504; f. 1959; fortnightly; English and Gujarati; Editor VIMLA PATIL; circ. 69,500.

Filmfare: Times of India Bldg, Dr Dadabhai Naoroji Rd, Bombay 400 001; tel. (22) 4150271; telex 1173504; f. 1952; fortnightly; English and Hindi; Editor RAUF AHMED; circ. 63,000.

Gentleman: 920 Tulsiani Chambers, Nariman Point, Bombay 400 021; tel. (22) 2872142; f. 1980; monthly; English; Editor MINHAZ MERCHANT; circ. 81,000.

Illustrated Weekly of India: Dr Dadabhai Naoroji Rd, Bombay 400 001; tel. (22) 4150271; telex 1173504; f. 1929; weekly; English; Editor PRITISH NANDY; circ. 102,000.

Indian and Eastern Engineer: Piramal Mansion, 235 Dr Dadabhai Naoroji Rd, Bombay 400 001; tel. (22) 261322 f. 1858; monthly; English; Editor S. K. GHASWALA; circ. 7,000.

Indian PEN: Theosophy Hall, 40 New Marine Lines, Bombay 400 020; tel. (22) 292175; f. 1934; quarterly; organ of Indian Centre of the International PEN; Editor NISSIM EZEKIEL.

Janmabhoomi Pravasi: Janmabhoomi Bhavan, Ghoga St, Fort, Bombay 400 001; tel. (22) 2870831; telex 116859; f. 1939; weekly; Gujarati; Editor HARINDRA J. DAVE; circ. 99,000.

Mirror: J. K. Somani Bldg, Samachar Marg, Bombay 400 023; tel. (22) 271444; f. 1961; monthly; English; Editor PRABHA GOVIND; circ. 54,000.

Onlooker: Free Press House, 215 Free Press Journal Marg, Nariman Point, Bombay 400 021; tel. (22) 2874566; telex 112570; f. 1939; fortnightly; English; news magazine; Editor VIRENDRA KAPOOR; circ. 61,000.

Pravasi: Janmabhoomi Bhavan, Ghoga St, Fort, Bombay 400 001; tel. (22) 2870831; telex 116859; f. 1939; weekly; Gujarati; Propr Saurashtra Trust; Editor HARINDRA DAVE; circ. 96,000.

Reader's Digest: Orient House, Mangalore St, Ballard Estate, Bombay 400 038; tel. (22) 267291; telex 1173389; f. 1954; monthly; English; Man. Dir and Publr ANIL GORE; Editor ASHOK MAHADEVAN; circ. 302,000.

Savvy: Esperanca, 7th Floor, Shahid Bhagat Singh Rd, Bombay 400 039; tel. (22) 2024135; telex 112029; f. 1984; monthly; English; Editor INGRID ALBOURQUE; circ. 45,000.

Screen: Express Towers, Nariman Point, Bombay 400 021; tel. (22) 2022627; f. 1951; film weekly; English; Editor UDAYA TARA NAYAR; circ. 114,000.

Shree: 40 Cawasji Patel St, Bombay 400 023; tel. (22) 2044171; telex 1176844; f. 1967; weekly; Marathi; Editor KAMLESH D. MEHTA; circ. 73,500.

Shreewarsha: 40 Cawasji Patel St, Bombay 400 023; f. 1980; weekly; Hindi; Editor and Man. Dir R. M. BHUTTA; circ. 50,000.

Society: Esperanca, 7th Floor, Shahid Bhagat Singh Rd, Bombay 400 039; tel. (22) 2024181; telex 112029; f. 1979; monthly; English; Editor MALAVIKA KAMARAJU; circ. 60,000.

Star and Style: J. K. Somani Bldg, Bombay Samachar Marg, Bombay 400 023; tel. (22) 271444; f. 1965; fortnightly; English; film and fashion; Editor GULSHAN EWING; circ. 87,000.

Stardust: Esparanca, 7th Floor, Shahid Bhagat Singh Rd, Bombay 400 039; tel. (22) 2024181; telex 112029; f. 1971; monthly; English; Editor VANITA GHOSH; circ. 159,000.

The Sunday Observer: 127 M.G. Rd, Bombay 400 023; tel. (22) 2042590; telex 113369; f. 1981; weekly; English; also publ. from New Delhi; Editor RAHUL SINGH; circ. 64,000.

2001: Dr Dadabhai Naoroji Rd, Bombay 400 001; tel. (22) 4150271; telex 1173504; f. 1966; monthly; English; Editor MUKUL SHARMA; circ. 40,000.

Update: Botawala Bldg, 8 Horniman Circle, Bombay 400 023; tel. (22) 252695; telex 113957; f. 1983; fortnightly; English; Editor KIRON KASBEKAR; circ. 25,000.

Vyapar: Janmabhoomi Bhavan, Ghoga St, Fort, Bombay 400 001; tel. (22) 2870831; telex 116859; f. 1949; Gujarati (2 a week) and Hindi (weekly); commerce; Propr Saurashtra Trust; Editor S. J. VASANI; circ. 37,000 (Gujarati), 20,000 (Hindi).

Yuvdarhsan: c/o Warsha Publications Pvt Ltd, Warsha House, 6 Zakaria Bunder Rd, Sewri, Bombay 400 015; tel. (22) 441843; f. 1975; weekly; Gujarati; Editor and Man. Dir R. M. BHUTTA; circ. 29,000.

Nagpur

All India Reporter: AIR Ltd, Congress Nagar, POB 209, Nagpur 440 012; tel. (712) 34321; f. 1914; monthly; English; law journal; Chief Editor V. R. MANOHAR; circ. 36,000.

Pune (Poona)

Swaraj: 595 Budhawar Peth, Pune 411 002; tel. (212) 448403; f. 1936; weekly; Marathi; Gen. Man. K. M. BHIDE; circ. 44,000 (Pune).

Rajasthan
Jaipur

Rashtradoot Saptahik: HO, M.I. Rd, POB 30, Jaipur 302 001; tel. (141) 72634; f. 1983; Hindi; also publ. from Kota and Bikaner; Chief Editor RAJESH SHARMA; combined circ. 145,000.

Tamil Nadu
Madras

Ambulimama: 188 Arcot Rd, Vadapalani, Madras 600 026; f. 1947; monthly; Tamil; Editor NAGI REDDI; circ. 78,000.

Ambuli Ammavan: 188 Arcot Rd, Vadapalani, Madras 600 026; f. 1970; children's monthly; Malayalam; Editor NAGI REDDI; circ. 35,000.

Ananda Vikatan: 757 Mount Rd, Madras 600 002; tel. (44) 82074; f. 1924; weekly; Tamil; Editor S. BALASUBRAMANIAN; circ. 242,000.

Andhra Prabha Illustrated Weekly: Express Estates, Mount Rd, Madras 600 002; f. 1952; weekly; Telugu; Editor POTTURI VENKATESWARA RAO; circ. 60,000.

Chandamama: 188 Arcot Rd, Vadapalani, Madras 600 026; f. 1947; children's monthly; Hindi, Gujarati, Telugu, Kannada, English, Bengali, Punjabi, Assamese; Editor NAGI REDDI; combined circ. 462,000.

Chandoba: 188 Arcot Rd, Vadapalani, Madras 600 026; f. 1952; monthly; Marathi; Editor NAGI REDDI; circ. 114,000.

Dinamani Kadir: Express Estate, Mount Rd, Madras 600 002; weekly; Editor G. KASTURI RANGAN (acting); circ. 55,000.

Frontline: 859/860 Anna Salai, Madras 600 002; tel. (44) 566567; telex 418358; f. 1984; English; fortnightly; Editor G. KASTURI; circ. 75,000.

Jahnamamu (Oriya): 188 Arcot Rd, Vadapalani, Madras 600 026; f. 1972; children's monthly; Editor NAGI REDDI; circ. 90,000.

Kalai Magal: POB 604, Madras 600 004; tel. (44) 76011; f. 1932; monthly; Tamil; literary and cultural; Editor R. NARAYANASWAMY; circ. 31,000.

Kalkandu: 151 Purasawalkam High Rd, Madras; f. 1948; weekly; Tamil; Editor TAMIL VANAN; circ. 199,000.

Kalki: 84/1c Race Course Rd, Guindy, Madras 600 032; tel. (44) 431543; f. 1941; weekly; Tamil; literary and cultural; Editor K. RAJENDRAN; circ. 100,000.

Kumudam: 151 Purasawalkam High Rd, Madras 600 010; tel. (44) 662146; telex 41462; f. 1947; weekly; Tamil; Editor S. A. P. ANNAMALAI; circ 556,000.

Malai Mathi: Madras; f. 1958; weekly; Tamil; Editor P. S. ELANGO; circ. 92,000.

Pesum Padam: 325 Arcot Rd, Madras 600 024; tel. (44) 422064; f. 1942; monthly; Tamil; films; Man. Editor K. NATARAJAN; circ. 35,000.

Picturpost: 325 Arcot Rd, Madras 600 024; tel. (44) 422064; f. 1943; monthly; English; films; Man. Editor K. NATARAJAN; circ. 11,000.

Rani Muthu: 46c E. V. K. Sampath Rd, Madras 600 007; tel. (44) 30495; f. 1969; monthly; Tamil; Editor A. MA. SAMY; circ. 150,000.

Sportstar: Kasturi Bldgs, Madras 600 002; tel. (44) 846567; telex 41358; f. 1978; English; weekly; Editor G. KASTURI; circ. 92,000.

Thuglak: 757 Mount Rd, Madras 600 002; tel. (44) 82074; f. 1970; fortnightly; Tamil; Editor CHO S. R. RAMASWAMY; circ. 177,000.

Vaarantari Rani: 1091 Periyar E.V.R. High Rd, Madras 600 007; tel. (44) 38471; f. 1962; weekly; Tamil; Editor A. MA. SAMY; circ. 352,000.

Other Towns

Mathajothidam: 3 Arasamaram, Vellore; f. 1949; monthly; Tamil; astrology; Editor V. K. V. SUBRAMANYAM; circ. 28,000.

Uttar Pradesh
Allahabad

Alokpaat: Mitra Prakashan (Pvt) Ltd, 281 Muthiganj, Allahabad 211 003; tel. (532) 51042; telex 540280; f. 1986; Bengali; Editor ALOKE MITRA; circ. 106,000.

INDIA

Jasoosi Duniya: 5 Kolhan Tola St, Allahabad; f. 1953; monthly; Urdu and Hindi edns; Editor S. ABBAS HUSAINY; combined circ. 70,000.

Manohar Kahaniyan: Mitra Prakashan (Pvt) Ltd, 281 Muthiganj, Allahabad 211 003; tel. (532) 51042; telex 540280; f. 1940; monthly; Hindi; Editor ALOKE MITRA; circ. 375,000.

Manorama: Mitra Parkashan (Pvt) Ltd, 281 Muthiganj, Allahabad 211 003; tel. (532) 51042; telex 540280; f. 1924; fortnightly; Hindi; Editor ALOKE MITRA; circ. 195,000.

Maya: Mitra Prakashan (Pvt) Ltd, 281 Muthiganj, Allahabad 211 003; tel. (532) 51042; telex 540280; f. 1929; monthly; Hindi; Editor ALOKE MITRA; circ. 237,000.

Nutan Kahaniyan: 15 Sheocharan Lal Rd, Allahabad 211 003; tel. (532) 56612; f. 1975; Hindi; monthly; Editor N. P. SINGH; circ. 162,500.

Probe India: Mitra Prakashan (Pvt) Ltd, 281 Muthiganj, Allahabad 211 003; tel. (532) 53681; telex 540280; f. 1978; monthly; English; Editor ALOKE MITRA; circ. 45,500.

Satyakatha: Mitra Prakashan (Pvt) Ltd, 281 Muthiganj, Allahabad 211 003; tel (532) 51042; telex 540280; f. 1974; monthly; Hindi; Editor ALOKE MITRA; circ. 165,000.

Kanpur

Kanchan Prabha: Rajendra Nagar (East), Kanpur 226 004; f. 1974; Hindi; monthly; Man. Editor P. C. GUPTA; Editor Y. M. GUPTA; circ. 26,000.

Other Towns

Current Events: 15 Rajpur Rd, Dehra Dun; f. 1955; quarterly review of national and international affairs; English; Editor DEV DUTT; circ. 5,000.

West Bengal
Calcutta

All India Appointment Gazette: 7 Old Court House St, Calcutta 700 001; tel. (33) 226485; f. 1973; weekly; English; Editor S. C. TALUKDAR; circ. 156,000.

Anandalok: 6 Prafulla Sarkar St, Calcutta 700 001; tel. (33) 278000; telex 215468; f. 1975; fortnightly; Bengali; film; Editor SEVABRATA GUPTA; circ. 79,000.

Anandamela: 6 Prafulla Sarkar St, Calcutta 700 001; tel. (33) 278000; telex 215468; f. 1975; monthly; Bengali; juvenile; Editor AVEEK SARKAR, (acting); circ. 62,500.

Capital: 1/2 Old Court House Corner, POB 14, Calcutta 700 001; tel. (33) 200099; telex 217172; f. 1888; fortnightly; English; financial; Editor S. BANERJEE, (acting); circ. 8,000.

Competition Leader: 7 Old Court House St, Calcutta 700 001; f. 1977; monthly; English; Editor S. C. TALUKDAR; circ. 97,000.

Desh: 6 Prafulla Sarkar St, Calcutta 700 001; tel. (33) 274880; telex 215468; f. 1933; weekly; Bengali; literary; Editor S. GHOSH; circ. 84,500.

Engineering Times: Wachel Molla Mansion, 8 Lenin Sarani, Calcutta 700 072; f. 1955; weekly; English; Editor E. H. TIPPOO; circ. 19,000.

Khela: 96 Raja Rammohan Sarani, Calcutta 700 009; tel. (33) 355302; telex 212216; f. 1981; weekly; Bengali; sports; Editor ASOKE DASGUPTA; circ. 20,500.

Naba Kallol: 11 Jhamapookur Lane, Calcutta 700 009; tel. (33) 354294; f. 1960; monthly; Bengali; Editor P. K. MAZUMDAR; circ. 48,000.

Neetee: 4 Sukhlal Johari Lane, Calcutta; f. 1955; weekly; English; Editor M. P. PODDAR.

Ravivar: 6 Prafulla Sarkar St, Calcutta 700 001; tel. (33) 278000; telex 215468; f. 1977; weekly; Hindi; Editor UDAYAN SHARMA; circ. 36,000.

Sananda: 6 Prafulla Sarkar St, Calcutta 700 001; tel. (33) 278000; telex 215468; f. 1986; monthly; Bengali; Editor APARNA SEN; circ. 64,000.

Screen: P-5, Kalakar St, Calcutta 700 070; f. 1960; weekly; Hindi; Editor M. P. PODDAR; circ. 58,000.

Sportsworld: 6 Prafulla Sarkar St, Calcutta 700 001; tel. (33) 278000; telex 215468; weekly; English; Editor MANSUR ALI KHAN PATAUDI; circ. 33,000.

Statesman: Statesman House, 4 Chowringhee Sq., Calcutta 700 001; tel. (33) 271000; telex 215303; f. 1875; overseas weekly; English; Editor SUNANDA KUMAR DATTA-RAY.

Suktara: 11 Jhamapooker Lane, Calcutta 700 009; tel. (33) 355294; f. 1948; monthly; Bengali; juvenile; Editor M. MAJUMDAR; circ. 64,000.

Sunday: 6 Prafulla Sarkar St, Calcutta 700 001; tel. (33) 274880; telex 215468; f. 1973; weekly; English; Editor VIR SINGHVI; circ. 127,500.

NEWS AGENCIES

Press Trust of India Ltd: 357 Dr Dadabhai Naoroji Rd, Bombay 400 001; tel. (22) 252371; telex 112343; f. 1947, re-established 1978; Chair. H. R. KHANNA; Gen. Man. P. UNNIKRISHNAN.

United News of India (UNI): 9 Rafi Marg, New Delhi 110 001; tel. (11) 383845; telex 3166305; f. 1961; Indian language news; special services covering banking, business, economic affairs, agriculture, overseas news and features; brs in 90 centres in India; Chair. P. K. MAHESHWARI; Gen. Man. and Chief Editor (vacant).

Foreign Bureaux

Agence France-Presse (AFP): 204 Surya Kiran Bldgs, 19 Kasturb Gandhi Marg, New Delhi 110 001; tel. (11) 3322881; telex 3165075; Bureau Chief YVES DE SAINT-JACOB.

Agentstvo Pechati Novosti (USSR): 2/8 Shantiniketan, New Delhi 110 021; tel. (11) 674347; Correspondent ALEKSANDR V. YELEZNOV.

Agenzia Nazionale Stampa Associata (ANSA) (Italy): A-293 New Friends Colony, New Delhi 110 065; tel. (11) 634402; telex 3165381; Chief Rep. ELIO CRISCUOLI.

Allgemeiner Deutscher Nachrichtendienst (ADN) (German Democratic Republic): C-64 Anand Niketan, New Delhi 110 021; tel. (11) 671864; telex 3166860; Correspondent GÜNTER CASCHUBE.

Associated Press (AP) (USA): 6B Jorbagh Lane, New Delhi 110 003; tel. (11) 698775; telex 3165932; Bureau Chief EARLEEN FISHER.

Československá tisková kancelář (ČTK) (Czechoslovakia): C-59 Anand Niketan, New Delhi 110 021; tel. (11) 672276; telex 3172231; Correspondent JIŘÍ CHRÁST.

Deutsche Presse-Agentur (dpa) (Federal Republic of Germany): B-1/44 Amrita Sher Gill Marg, New Delhi 110 003; tel. (11) 617792; telex 3162331; Chief Rep. CHRISTIAN FÜRST.

Inter Press Service (IPS) (Italy): C-13, 1st Floor, East Nizamuddin, New Delhi 110 013; tel. (11) 615992; Correspondent M. VENUGOPALA RAO.

Islamic Republic News Agency (IRNA) (Iran): B-159 Greater Kailash-I, New Delhi 110 048; tel. (11) 6446866; telex 3166041; Bureau Chief BEHYAR M. R. BEHDANI.

Jiji Tsushin-sha (Japan): N-50 Panchshila Park, New Delhi 110 017; tel. (11) 6445296; telex 3165590; Correspondent FUMIHIKO SUGIYAMA.

Kyodo Tsushin (Japan): PTI Bldg, 1st Floor, 4 Parliament St, New Delhi 110 001; tel. (11) 381954; telex 3165016; Bureau Chief KAZUHISA INOUYE.

Magyar Tavirati Iroda (MTI) (Hungary): F-3/17 Vasant Vihar, New Delhi 110 057; tel. (11) 677397; telex 3172373; Correspondent PÉTER RÁCZ.

Novinska Agencija Tanjug (Yugoslavia): 14 Palam Marg, Vasant Vihar, New Delhi 110 057; tel. (11) 672649; Correspondent BOZIDAR FRANCUSKI.

Prensa Latina (Cuba): C-105 Anand Niketan, New Delhi 110 021; tel. (11) 675015; telex 3166532; Correspondent MANUEL N. ESCOBEDO.

Reuters (UK): 1 Kautilya Marg, Chanakyapuri, New Delhi 110 021; tel. (11) 3014043; telex 3166423; Bureau Chief HUGH PAIN.

Telegrafnoye Agentstvo Sovetskovo Soyuza (TASS) (USSR): A-10/6 Vasant Vihar, New Delhi 110 057; tel. (11) 672351; telex 3166092; Bureau Chief SERGEY A. SOLOVYOV.

United Press International (UPI) (USA): Ambassador Hotel, Suite 202–204, Sujan Singh Park, New Delhi 110 003; tel. (11) 698991; telex 3162846; Bureau Chief JONATHAN LANDAY.

Xinhua (New China) News Agency (People's Republic of China): 50D, Shanti Path, Chanakyapuri, New Delhi 110 021; tel. (11) 601392; telex 3162250; Chief TAN RENXIA.

The following agencies are also represented: Associated Press of Pakistan, Bangladesh Sangbad Sangsta, BTA (Bulgaria), PAP (Poland) and Viet-Nam News Agency.

CO-ORDINATING BODIES

Press Information Bureau: Shastri Bhavan, Dr Rajendra Prasad Rd, New Delhi 110 001; tel. (11) 383643; f. 1946 to co-ordinate press affairs for the govt; represents newspaper managements, journalists, news agencies, parliament; has power to examine journalists under oath and may censor objectionable material; Prin. Information Officer I. RAMAMOHAN RAO.

Registrar of Newspapers for India: Ministry of Information and Broadcasting, West Block 8, Wing 2, Ramakrishna Puram, New Delhi 110 066; tel. (11) 698758; f. 1956 as a statutory body to collect

INDIA

press statistics; maintains a register of all Indian newspapers; Registrar KRIPA SAGAR.

PRESS ASSOCIATIONS

All-India Newspaper Editors' Conference: 36–37 Northend Complex, Rama Krishna Ashram Marg, New Delhi 110 001; tel. (11) 344519; f. 1940; 450 mems; Pres. VISHWA BANDHU GUPTA; Sec.-Gen. R. KRISHNAMURTHY.

Editors' Guild of India: A2 First Floor, 28 Feroz Shah Rd, New Delhi 110 001; f. 1977; Pres. RAMOJI RAO; Sec.-Gen. H. K. DUA.

The Foreign Correspondents' Association of South Asia: c/o Los Angeles Times, F-160 Malcha Marg, New Delhi 110 021; tel. (11) 3011374; 143 mems; Pres. ALEXANDER JELEZNOV; Sec. S. GOPAL.

Indian Federation of Working Journalists: Flat 29, New Central Market, Connaught Circus, New Delhi 110 001; tel. (11) 3310459; f. 1950; 13,000 mems; Pres. K. VIKRAM RAO; Sec.-Gen. MANOHAR ANDHARE.

Indian Languages Newspapers' Assocn: Janmabhoomi Bhavan, Ghoga St, POB 10029, Fort, Bombay 400 001; tel. (22) 2870537; f. 1941; 300 mems; Pres. ABHAY CHHAJLANI; Gen. Secs G. W. DESHPANDE, RAJENDRA SHARMA.

Indian Newspaper Society: IENS Bldgs, Rafi Marg, New Delhi 110 001; tel. (11) 385401; telex 3166312; f. 1939; 589 mems; Pres. PRAVINCHANDRA V. GANDHI; Sec. S. BHUSHAN JAIN.

National Union of Journalists (India): 7 Jantar Mantar Rd, New Delhi 110 001; tel. (11) 3321610; f. 1972; over 5,000 mems; Pres. BALBIR K. PUNJ; Sec.-Gen. K. N. GUPTA.

Press Institute of India: Sapru House Annexe, Barakhamba Rd, New Delhi 110 001; tel. (11) 3318066; f. 1963; 30 mem. newspapers and other orgs; Chair. G. KASTURI; Dir S. PRAKASA RAO.

Publishers

Delhi and New Delhi

Affiliated East West Press (Pvt) Ltd: G-1/16 Ansari Rd, New Delhi 110 002; tel. (11) 279113; textbooks; Man. Dir K. S. PADMANABHAN.

Allied Publishers (Pvt) Ltd: 13/14 Asaf Ali Rd, New Delhi 110 002; tel. (11) 275001; telex 315153; academic and general; Man. Dir R. N. SACHDEV.

Amerind Publishing Co (Pvt) Ltd: 66 Janpath, New Delhi 110 001; tel. (11) 3324578; telex 3161990; f. 1970; offices at Calcutta, Bombay and New York; scientific and technical; Dirs G. PRIMLANI, M. PRIMLANI.

Arnold Heinemann Publishers India (Pvt) Ltd: AB/9 Safdarjung Enclave, New Delhi 110 029; tel. (11) 607806; telex 3166417; literature and general; Man. Dir G. A. VAZIRANI.

Atma Ram and Sons: Kashmere Gate, POB 1429, Delhi 110 006; tel. (11) 2523082; f. 1909; scientific, technical, humanities, medical; Dir S. PURI; Man. Dir ISH K. PURI.

B.R. Publishing Corpn: 29/9, Nangia Park, Shakti Nagar, Delhi 110 007; tel. (11) 7120113; telex 3166778; a division of D. K. Publishers Distributors (Pvt) Ltd; Dir PRAVEEN MITTAL.

Cambridge Publishing House: D-36 South Extension, Part 1, New Delhi 110 049; tel. (11) 619125; juvenile; Propr ARUN KUMAR GUPTA.

S. Chand and Co Ltd: Ram Nagar, POB 5733, New Delhi 110 055; tel. (11) 772081; telex 3161310; f. 1917; educational and general in English and Hindi; also book exports and imports; Man. Dir SHYAM LAL GUPTA.

Children's Book Trust: Nehru House, 4 Bahadur Shah Zafar Marg, New Delhi 110 002; tel. (11) 3316970; f. 1961; children's books in several languages; Exec. Trustee K. SHANKAR PILLAI; Editor K. RAMAKRISHNAN.

Concept Publishing Co: A/15-16, Commercial Block, Mohan Garden, New Delhi 110 059; tel. (11) 272187; f. 1975; geography, rural and urban development, education, sociology, economics, anthropology, information sciences, ecology; Man. Dir ASHOK KUMAR MITTAL; Man. Editor ARVIND KUMAR MITTAL.

Eurasia Publishing House (Pvt) Ltd: Ram Nagar, New Delhi 110 055; tel (11) 772080; f. 1964; educational in English and Hindi; Man. Dir S. L. GUPTA.

Heritage Publishers: 4C Ansari Rd, Darya Ganj, New Delhi 110 002; tel. (11) 266258; f. 1973; social sciences, art and architecture, economics, commerce, literature; Dir B. R. CHAWLA.

Hind Pocket Books (Pvt) Ltd: G. T. Rd, Shahadara, Delhi 110 032; tel. (11) 2282046; f. 1958; fiction and non-fiction paperbacks in English, Hindi, Punjabi and Urdu; Man. Dir DINANATH MALHOTRA; Editorial Dir MADHVI MALHOTRA.

Hindustan Publishing Corpn: 6 U.B. Jawahar Nagar, Delhi 110 007; tel. (11) 2915059; archaeology, pure and applied sciencies, sociology, anthropology, economics; Dir S. K. JAIN.

Inter-India Publications: D-17, Raja Garden Extension, New Delhi 110 015; tel. (11) 4513145; f. 1977; academic and research works; Dir MOOL CHAND MITTAL.

Lancers Books: POB 4236, New Delhi 110 048; tel. (11) 6414617; f. 1977; politics with special emphasis on north-east India; Propr S. KUMAR.

Motilal Banarsidass: 41 UA Bungalow Rd, Jawahar Nagar, Delhi 110 007; tel. (11) 2911985; telex 3166053; f. 1903; Indology, in English and Sanskrit; Dirs N. P. JAIN, J. P. JAIN, R. P. JAIN, S. L. JAIN.

Munshiram Manoharlal Publishers (Pvt) Ltd: 54 Rani Jhansi Rd, POB 5715, New Delhi 110 055; tel. (11) 771668; telex 3165233; art, architecture, archaeology, history, politics; Man. Dir DEVENDRA JAIN.

National Book Trust: A-5 Green Park, New Delhi 110 016; tel. (11) 664020; telex 3173034; f. 1967; autonomous organization established by the Ministry of Human Resources Development to produce and encourage the production of good literary works; Chair. ANAND SWARUP.

Oxford and IBH Publishing Co (Pvt) Ltd: 66 Janpath, New Delhi 110 001; tel. (11) 3324578; telex 3161990; f. 1964; science, technology and reference in English; Dirs GULAB PRIMLANI, MOHAN PRIMLANI.

Oxford University Press: YMCA Library Bldg, Jai Singh Rd, POB 43, New Delhi 110 001; tel. (11) 350490; telex 3161108; educational, scientific, medical and reference; Gen. Man. S. K. MOOKERJEE.

Penguin Books India Ltd: B/4/246 Safdarjung Enclave, New Delhi 110 029; tel. (11) 673538; telex 3162062; Indian literature; Man. Dir AVEEK SARKAR.

People's Publishing House (Pvt) Ltd: 5E Rani Jhansi Rd, Delhi 110 055; tel. (11) 529823; f. 1947; Marxism, Leninism, peasant movement; Gen. Man. P. P. G. JOSHI.

Prentice-Hall of India (Pvt) Ltd: M-97 Connaught Circus, New Delhi 110 001; tel. (11) 3351779; telex 3161808; Man. Dir A. K. GHOSH.

Rajkamal Prakashan (Pvt) Ltd: 1B Netaji Subhas Marg, New Delhi 110 002; tel. (11) 274463; f. 1946; Hindi; literary; also literary journal and monthly trade journal; Man. Dir SHEILA SANDHU.

Rajpal and Sons: 1590 Madarsa Rd, Kashmere Gate, Delhi 110 006; tel. (11) 2519104; f. 1891; humanities, social sciences, art, juvenile; Hindi; Man. Partner VISHWANATH MALHOTRA.

Rupa & Co: 3831 Pataudi House Rd, Daryaganj, New Delhi 110 002; tel. (11) 272161; f. 1936.

Sage Publications India (Pvt) Ltd: M-32 Market, Greater Kailash-1, POB 4215, New Delhi 110 048; tel. (11) 6419884; social science; Man. Dir TEJESHWAR SINGH.

Sahgal, N. D., and Sons: Dariba Kalan, Delhi; f. 1917; politics, history, general knowledge, sport, fiction and juvenile in Hindi; Man. G. SAHGAL.

Shiksha Bharati: Madrasa Rd, Kashmere Gate, Delhi 110 006; tel. (11) 2523904; f. 1955; textbooks, popular science and juvenile in Hindi and English; Man. Partner VEENA MALHOTRA.

Sterling Publishers (Pvt) Ltd: L-10 Green Park Extension, New Delhi 110 016; tel. (11) 669560; telex 3161443; f. 1965; academic books on the humanities and social sciences, paperbacks; Chair. O. P. GHAI; Man. Dir S. K. GHAI.

Tata McGraw-Hill Publishing Co Ltd: 12/4 Asaf Ali Rd, New Delhi 110 002; tel. (11) 278251; telex 3161979; f. 1970; engineering, sciences, management, humanities, social sciences; Dir N. R. SUBRAMANIAN.

Technical and Commercial Book Co: 75 Gokhale Market, Tis Hazari, Delhi 110 054; tel. (11) 228315; telex 112651; f. 1913; technical; Propr D. N. MEHRA; Man. RAMAN MEHRA.

Vikas Publishing House (Pvt) Ltd: 5 Ansari Rd, New Delhi 110 002; tel. (11) 866536; telex 31592262; medicine, sciences, engineering, textbooks, academic, fiction, women's studies; Man. Dir NARENDRA KUMAR.

Wiley Eastern Ltd: 4835/24 Ansari Rd, New Delhi 110 002; tel. (11) 276802; f. 1966; Man. Dir A. MACHWE.

Bombay

Allied Publishers (Pvt) Ltd: 15 J. N. Heredia Marg, Ballard Estate, Bombay 400 038; tel. (22) 267926; telex 1175909; f. 1934; economics, medicine, politics, history, philosophy, science, mathematics and fiction; Man. Dir S. M. SACHDEV.

Asia Publishing House (Pvt) Ltd: 18/20 K. Dubash Marg, Bombay 400 023; tel. (22) 225353; telex 1171665; f. 1981; humanities, social sciences, science, inflight magazines and general; English; Man. Dir ANANDA JAISINGH.

Bharatiya Vidya Bhavan: Munshi Sadan, Kulapati Munshi Marg, Bombay 400 007; tel. (22) 8118261; f. 1938; art, literature, culture, philosophy, religion, history of India in English, Hindi, Sanskrit and Gujarati; various periodicals; Pres. GIRDHARILAL MEHTA; Vice-Pres C. SUBRAMANIAM, PRAVINCHANDRA V. GANDHI.

Blackie and Son (Pvt) Ltd: Blackie House, 103–105 Walchand Hirachand Marg, POB 381, Bombay 400 001; tel. (22) 261410; f. 1901; educational, scientific and technical, general and juvenile; Man. Dir D. R. BHAGI.

Himalaya Publishing House: 'Ramdoot', Dr Bhalerao Marg (Kelewadi), Girgaon, Bombay 400 004; tel. (22) 360170; f. 1976; textbooks; Dir D. P. PANDEY.

India Book House (Pvt) Ltd: 412 Tulsiani Chambers, Nariman Point, Bombay 400 021; tel. (22) 240626; telex 116297; Chair. G. L. MIRCHANDANI.

International Book House (Pvt) Ltd: Indian Mercantile Mansions Extension, Madame Cama Rd, Bombay 400 039; tel. (22) 2021634; f. 1941; general, educational, scientific and law; Man. Dir S. K. GUPTA; Gen. Man. C. V. THAMBI.

Jaico Publishing House: 121 Mahatma Gandhi Rd, Bombay 400 023; tel. (22) 270621; f. 1947; general paperbacks; imports scientific, technical and educational; Man. Dir JAMAN SHAH.

Popular Prakashan (Pvt) Ltd: 35c Pandit Madan Mohan Malaviya Marg, Tardeo, Popular Press Bldg, opp. Roche, Bombay 400 034; tel. (22) 4941656; f. 1968; sociology, biographies, current affairs, medicine, history, politics and administration in English and Marathi; Jt Man. Dirs R. G. BHATKAL, S. G. BHATKAL.

Somaiya Publications (Pvt) Ltd: 172 Mumbai Marathi Grantha Sangrahalaya Marg, Dadar, Bombay 400 014; tel. (22) 4130230; telex 112723; f. 1967; economics, sociology, history, politics, mathematics, sciences, language, literature, education, psychology, religion, philosophy, logic; Chair. Dr S. K. SOMAIYA.

Taraporevala, Sons and Co (Pvt) Ltd D.B.: 210 Dr Dadabhai Naoroji Rd, Fort, Bombay 400 001; tel. (22) 2041433; f. 1864; Indian art, culture, history, sociology, scientific, technical and general in English; Pres. R. J. TARAPOREVALA.

N. M. Tripathi (Pvt) Ltd: 164 Samaldas Gandhi Marg, Bombay 400 002; tel. (22) 313651; f. 1888; law and general in English and Gujarati; Chair. D. M. TRIVEDI.

Calcutta

Academic Publishers: 12/1A Bankim Chatterjee St, POB 12341, Calcutta 700 073; tel. (33) 324697; f. 1958; textbooks; Man. Partner B. K. DHUR.

Advaita Ashrama: 5 Dehi Entally Rd, Calcutta 700 014; tel. (33) 290898; f. 1899; religion, philosophy, spiritualism, Vendanta; publication centre of Ramakrishna Math and Ramakrishna Mission; Pres. Swami SWANANDA.

Allied Book Agency: 18A Shyama Charan De St, Calcutta 700 073; tel. (33) 312594; general and academic; Dir B. SARKAR.

Ananda Publishers (Pvt) Ltd: 45 Beniatola Lane, Calcutta 700 009; tel. (33) 314352; literature, general; Dir A. SARKAR.

Assam Review Publishing Co: 29 Waterloo St, Calcutta 700 069; tel. (33) 282251; f. 1926; publrs of *Tea Plantation Directory* and *Tea News*; Partners G. L. BANERJEE, S. BANERJEE.

Book Land (Pvt) Ltd: 1 Shankar Ghosh Lane, Calcutta 700 007; economics, politics, history and general; Man. Dir J. N. BASU.

Chuckerverty, Chatterjee and Co Ltd: 15 College Sq., Calcutta 700 012; Dir BINODELAL CHAKRAVARTI.

Eastern Law House (Pvt) Ltd: 54 Ganesh Chunder Ave, Calcutta 700 013; tel. (33) 274989; f. 1918; legal, commercial and accountancy; Dir ASOK DE; br in New Delhi.

Firma KLM Private Ltd: 257B B. B. Ganguly St, Calcutta 700 012; tel. (33) 274391; f. 1950; Indology, scholarly in English, Bengali, Sanskrit and Hindi; Man. Dir R. N. MUKERJI.

Intertrade Publications (India) (Pvt) Ltd: 55 Gariahat Rd, POB 10210, Calcutta 700 019; tel. (33) 474872; f. 1954; economics, medicine, law, history and trade directories; Man. Dir Dr K. K. ROY.

A. Mukherjee and Co (Pvt) Ltd: 2 Bankim Chatterjee St, Calcutta 700 073; tel. (33) 311406; f. 1940; educational and general in Bengali and English; Man. Dirs RAJEEV NEOGI, RANJAN SENGUPTA.

Naya Prokash: 206 Bidhan Sarani, POB 11468, Calcutta 700 006; tel. (33) 316009; f. 1960; agriculture, horticulture, Indology, history, political science, defence studies; Partners BARINDRA MITRA, PARTHA SANKAR BASU.

New Era Publishing Co: 31 Gauri Bari Lane, Calcutta 700 004; f. 1944; Propr Dr P. N. MITRA; Man. S. K. MITRA.

W. Newman and Co Ltd: 3 Old Court House St, Calcutta 700 069; f. 1851; general; Man. Dir P. N. BHARGAVA.

Punthi Pustak: 136/4B Bidhan Sarani, Calcutta 700 004; tel. (33) 558473; religion, history, philosophy; Propr S. K. BHATTACHARYA.

Renaissance Publishers (Pvt) Ltd: 15 Bankim Chatterjee St, Calcutta 700 012; f. 1949; politics, philosophy, history; Man. Dir J. C. GOSWAMI.

Saraswati Library: 206 Bidhan Sarani, Calcutta 700 006; tel. (33) 345492; f. 1914; history, philosophy, religion, literature; Man. Partner B. BHATTACHARJEE.

M. C. Sarkar and Sons (Pvt) Ltd: 14 Bankim Chatterjee St, Calcutta 700 073; tel. (33) 312490; f. 1910; reference; Dirs SUPRIYA SARKAR, SAMIT SARKAR.

Thacker's Press and Directories: M.P. Works Pvt Ltd, 6B, Bentinck St, POB 2512, Calcutta 700 001; industrial pubs and directories; Chair. JUTHIKA ROY; Dirs B. B. ROY, A. BOSE.

Visva-Bharati: 6 Acharya Jagadish Bose Rd, Calcutta 700 017; tel. (33) 449868; f. 1923; literature; Dir JAGADINDRA BHOWMICK.

Madras

Higginbothams Ltd: 814 Anna Salai, POB 311, Madras 600 002; tel. (44) 831841; f. 1844; general; Gen. Man. (vacant).

B. G. Paul and Co: 4 Francis Joseph St, Madras; f. 1923; general, educational and oriental; Man. K. NILAKANTAN.

T. R. Publications: 32 II Main Rd, C.I.T. East, Madras 600 035; tel. (44) 441246; telex 416643.

Thompson and Co (Pvt) Ltd: 33 Broadway, Madras 600 001; f. 1890; directories in English, Tamil, Telugu and Malayalam; Man Dir K. M. CHERIAN.

Other Towns

Bharat Bharti Prakashan: Western Kutchery Rd, Meerut 250 001; tel. 73748; f. 1952; textbooks; Man. Dir RAJENDRA AGARWAL.

Bharati Bhawan: Govind Mitra Rd, Patna 800 004; tel. (612) 50325; f. 1942; educational and juvenile; other brs in Muzaffarpur, Ranchi, Darbhanga and Calcutta; Partners T. K. BOSE, DOLLY BOSE, SUROJIT BOSE and SANJIB BOSE.

Bishen Singh Mahendra Pal Singh: 23A Connaught Place, POB 137, Dehradun 248 001; tel. (935) 24048; f. 1957; botany; Dir GAJENDRA SINGH.

Catholic Press: Ranchi 834 001 Bihar; f. 1928; books and periodicals; Dir WILLIAM TIGGA.

Chugh Publications: 2 Strachey Rd, POB 101, Allahabad; tel. (532) 21589; sociology, economics, history, general; Propr RAMESH KUMAR.

Geetha Book House: K. R. Circle, Mysore 570 001; tel. (821) 33589; f. 1959; general; Dirs M. GOPALA KRISHNA, M. GURURAJA RAO.

Goel Publishing House: Subhash Bazar, Meerut 250 001; tel. 27843; textbooks; Dir KAMAL K. RASTOGI.

Kalyani Publishers: 1/1 Rajinder Nagar, Ludhiana, Punjab; tel. (161) 20221; textbooks; Dir RAJ KUMAR.

Kitabistan: 30 Chak, Allahabad 211 003; tel. (532) 51885; f. 1932; general, agriculture, govt pubs in Urdu, Farsi and Arabic; Partners A. U. KHAN, SULTAN ZAMAN, NASEEM FAROOQI.

The Law Book Co (Pvt) Ltd: 18c Sardar Patel Marg, Civil Lines, POB 1004, Allahabad 211 001; tel. (532) 2415; f. 1929; legal texts in English; Man. Dir L. R. BAGGA; Dirs RAJEEV R. BAGGA, DEEPAK BAGGA, ANIL BAGGA, RAKESH BAGGA.

Macmillan India Ltd: 248 Upper Palace Orchards, Bangalore 560 080; tel. (532) 53807; telex 845615; scholarly monographs in English and Hindi, textbooks and general; Pres. and Man. Dir S. G. WASANI.

Navajivan Publishing House: PO Navajivan, Ahmedabad 380 014; tel. (272) 447634; f. 1919; Gandhiana and related social science; in English, Hindi and Gujarati; Man. Trustee JITENDRA DESAI.

Nem Chand and Bros: Civil Lines, Roorkee 247 667; tel. 2258; f. 1951; engineering textbooks and journals.

Orient Longman Ltd: 5-9-41/1 Bashir Bagh, Hyderabad 500 029; tel. (842) 230343; telex 4256803; f. 1948; educational, technical, general and children's in almost all Indian languages; Chair. J. RAMESHWAR RAO.

Publication Bureau: Panjab University, Chandigarh 160 014; tel. (172) 22782; f. 1948; textbooks and general; Head of Bureau and Sec. R. K. MALHOTRA.

Ram Prasad and Sons: Hospital Rd, Agra 282 003; tel. (562) 72935; f. 1905; agricultural, arts, commerce, education, general, pure and applied science, economics, sociology; Dirs H. N., R. N., B. N. and Y. N. AGARWAL; Mans S. N. AGARWAL and R. S. TANDON.

Upper India Publishing House (Pvt) Ltd: Aminabad, Lucknow 226 018; tel. (522) 42711; f. 1921; Indian history, religion, art and science; English and Hindi; Man. Dir S. BHARGAVA.

INDIA   *Directory*

Government Publishing House

Publications Division: Ministry of Information and Broadcasting, Govt of India, Patiala House, New Delhi 110 001; tel. (11) 387321; f. 1941; culture, art, literature, planning and development, general; also 21 magazines in English and several Indian languages; Dir Dr S. S. SHASHI.

PUBLISHERS' ASSOCIATIONS

All India Booksellers' and Publishers' Association: 17L Connaught Circus, POB 328, New Delhi 110 001; tel. (11) 42166; Pres. A. N. VARMA.

Federation of Indian Publishers: Federation House, 18/1C Institutional Area, JNU Rd, New Delhi 110 067; tel. (11) 654847; 11 affiliated asscns; 189 mems; Pres. RAMDAS BHATKAL; Gen. Sec. S. BALWANT.

Federation of Publishers and Booksellers Associations in India: 4833/24 Govind Lane, 1st Floor, Ansari Rd, New Delhi 110 002; tel. (11) 272845; 17 affiliated asscns; 680 mems; Pres. N. K. MEHRA; Sec. S. C. SETHI.

Publishers' and Booksellers' Guild: 5A Bhawani Dutta Lane, Calcutta 700 073; tel. (33) 311541; 36 mems; Pres. PRABIR KUMAR MAZUMDER; Sec. KALYAN SHAH.

Radio and Television

Radio broadcasting in India began in 1927 and came under government control in 1930. A television station was established in Delhi, on an experimental basis, in 1959, and the first general service began in Delhi in 1965. In 1976 television broadcasting became independent of All India Radio, under the name Doordarshan India. Colour transmissions began in 1981. To maximize broadcasting coverage, the Government installs and maintains radio and television sets in community centres. Both radio and television carry commercial advertising.

In 1986 there were an estimated 62m. radio receivers and 12.5m. television receivers in use.

RADIO

All India Radio (AIR): Akashvani Bhavan, Parliament St, New Delhi 110 001; tel. (11) 382021; telex 313225; broadcasting is controlled by the Ministry of Information and Broadcasting and is govt-financed; operates a network of 96 broadcasting centres, covering 91% of the population and about 80% of the total area of the country; proposes to cover 97.5% of the population and 91% of the total area of the country through 198 radio stations by March 1990; Dir-Gen. A. R. SHINDE.

The News Services Division of AIR, centralized in New Delhi, is one of the largest news organizations in the world. It has 42 regional news units, which broadcast 273 bulletins daily in 24 languages and 36 dialects. Eighty-one bulletins in 19 languages are broadcast in the Home Services and 64 bulletins in 24 languages in the External Services.

Radio broadcasting stations are grouped into five zones:

East: Agartala, Aizawl, Bhagalpur, Calcutta, Cuttack, Darbhanga, Dibrugarh, Gangtok, Guwahati, Imphal, Jeypore, Kohima, Kurseong, Pasighat, Patna, Ranchi, Sambalpur, Shillong, Silchar, Siliguri, Tawang, Tezu and Tura.

North: Ajmer, Allahabad, Bikaner, Chandigarh, Delhi, Gorakhpur, Jaipur, Jodhpur, Jullundur, Kanpur, Lucknow, Mathura, Najibabad, Rampur, Rohtak, Simla, Udaipur and Varanasi.

South: Alleppey, Bangalore, Bhadravati, Coimbatore, Cuddapah, Dharwar, Gulbarga, Hyderabad, Calicut, Madras, Mangalore, Mysore, Pondicherry, Port Blair, Tiruchirapalli, Tirunelveli, Trichur, Trivandrum, Vijayawada and Vishakhapatnam.

West: Ahmedabad, Ambikapur, Aurangabad, Bhopal, Bhuj, Bombay, Chhatarpur, Gwalior, Indore, Jabalpur, Jagdalpur, Jalgaon, Nagpur, Panaji, Parbhani, Pune, Raipur, Rajkot, Ratnagiri, Rewa, Sangli, Suratgarh and Vadodara (Baroda).

Kashmir: Jammu, Leh and Srinagar.

TELEVISION

Doordarshan India (Television India): Mandi House, Doordarshan Bhavan, Copernicus Marg, New Delhi 110 001; tel. (11) 382094; telex 3166143; f. 1976; broadcasting is controlled by the Ministry of Information and Broadcasting and is govt-financed; programmes: 280 hours weekly; Dir-Gen. SHIV SHARMA.

While only 0.2% of India's 685m. inhabitants owned a television receiver in 1981, 15% (102m.) had access to television through community centres. In 1987, 47% of the country's area and 70.4% of the population were covered by the TV network. There were 282 transmitters in operation in January 1989, and, by the end of the seventh Five-Year Plan (1985–90), 82.8% of the population should be covered by the TV network through 423 transmitters.

There are 18 television stations, located at Ahmedabad, Bangalore, Bombay, Calcutta, Cuttack, Delhi, Gauhati, Gorakhpur, Hyderabad, Jaipur, Jalandhar, Lucknow, Madras, Nagpur, Rajkot, Ranchi, Srinagar and Trivandrum. There are also nine relay centres, situated at Amritsar, Asansol, Kanpur, Kodaikannal, Kurseong, Murshidabad, Mussoorie, Panaji and Pune.

Finance

(cap. = capital; p.u. = paid up; res = reserves; dep. = deposits; m. = million; brs = branches; amounts in rupees)

BANKING

State Banks

Reserve Bank of India: Central Office, Shahid Bhagat Singh Rd, Bombay 400 023; tel. (22) 2861602; telex 114222; f. 1935; nationalized 1949; sole bank of issue; cap. and res 1,550m. (1987); Gov. R. N. MALHOTRA; 11 brs.

State Bank of India: Madame Cama Rd, POB 10121, Bombay 400 021; tel. (22) 2022426; telex 112995; f. 1955; cap. and res 5,741.9m., dep. 292,224m. (1987); subsidiaries in Bikaner and Jaipur, Hyderabad, Indore, Mysore, Patila, Saurashtra and Travancore; controls 28 state co-operative banks and 349 dist. co-operative banks; 34 private-sector banks and 194 regional rural banks; rep. brs and offices world-wide; Chair. DHRUBA NARAYAN GHOSH; Man. Dir. V. ATAL; 10,976 brs.

Commercial Banks

Fourteen of India's major commercial banks were nationalized in 1969 and a further six in 1980. They are managed by 15-mem. boards of directors (two directors to be appointed by the central government, one employee director, one representing employees who are not workmen, one representing depositors, three representing farmers, workers, artisans, etc., five representing persons with special knowledge or experience, one Reserve Bank of India official and one Government of India official). The Department of Banking of the Ministry of Finance controls all banking operations.

There were 54,382 branches of public sector and other commercial banks in December 1987.

Aggregate deposits of all scheduled commercial banks amounted to Rs 1,394,398m. in December 1988.

Allahabad Bank: 2 Netaji Subhas Rd, Calcutta 700 001; tel. (33) 209258; telex 217547; f. 1865; cap. and res 339.6m., dep. 30,500m. (1987); Chair. and Man. Dir R. L. WADHWA; 1,303 brs.

Andhra Bank: Andhra Bank Bldg, Sultan Bazar, Hyderabad 500 001; tel. (842) 40141; telex 15283; f. 1923; nationalized 1980; cap. p.u. 170m., dep. 21,381m. (1987); Chair. and Man. Dir K. R. NAYAK; 933 brs.

Bank of Baroda: 3 Walchand Hirachand Marg, Ballard Pier, POB 10046, Bombay 400 038; tel. (22) 260341; telex 116345; f. 1908; cap. p.u. 680m., dep. 85,796m. (1987); Chair. and Man. Dir PREMJIT SINGH; 1,965 brs (world-wide).

Bank of India: Express Towers, Nariman Point, POB 234, Bombay 400 021; tel. (22) 2023020; telex 112281; f. 1906; cap. p.u. 840m., dep. 125,720m. (1988); Chair. and Man. Dir R. SRINIVASAN; Gen. Man. K. C. CHAKRABERTTI; 2,084 brs (world-wide).

Bank of Maharashtra: 'Lokmangal', 1501 Shivajinagar, Pune 411 005; tel. (212) 52731; telex 145207; f. 1935; cap. and res 311m., dep. 25,658m. (1987); Chair. and Man. Dir P. S. DESHPANDE; 1,000 brs.

Canara Bank: 112 Jayachamarajendra Rd, POB 6648, Bangalore 560 002; tel. (812) 76851; telex 845205; f. 1906; cap. p.u. 415m., dep. 78,784m. (1987); Chair. and Man. Dir N. D. PRABHU; 1,843 brs.

Central Bank of India: Chandermukhi, Nariman Point, Bombay 400 021; tel. (22) 2026428; telex 112909; f. 1911; cap. and res. 1,180.2m., dep. 82,430m. (1987); Chair. and Man. Dir M. N. GOIPORIA; 2,569 brs.

Corporation Bank: Mangaladevi Temple Rd, POB 88, Mangalore 575 001; tel. (824) 26416; telex 842228; f. 1906; nationalized 1980, cap. 200m., dep. 11,284m. (1987); Chair. and Man. Dir Y. S. HEGDE; Gen. Mans K. R. RAMAMOORTHY, K. R. SHENOY; 411 brs.

Dena Bank: 17 Horniman Circle, Fort, Bombay 400 023; tel. (22) 296746; telex 112511; f. 1938; cap. p.u. 220m., dep. 27,859m. (1988); Chair. and Man. Dir G. S. DAHOTRE; 1,051 brs.

Indian Bank: 31 Rajaji Salai, POB 1866, Madras 600 001; tel. (44) 514151; telex 41307; f. 1907; cap. p.u. 370m., dep. 44,586m. (1987); Chair. and Man. Dir M. GOPALAKRISHNAN; Gen. Man. K. SUBRAMANIAN; 1,106 brs.

Indian Overseas Bank: 762 Anna Salai, POB 3765, Madras 600 002; tel. (44) 82041; telex 416123; f. 1937; cap. p.u. 650m., dep.

INDIA

Directory

46,476m. (1987); Chair. and Man. Dir P. S. GOPALAKRISHNAN; 1,097 brs (world-wide).

New Bank of India: 1 Tolstoy Marg, New Delhi 110 001; tel. (11) 3311452; telex 3166920; f. 1936; nationalized 1980; cap. p.u. 170m., dep. 15,209m. (1987); Chair. and Man. Dir R. C. SUNEJA; 564 brs.

Oriental Bank of Commerce: Harsha Bhavan, E Block, Connaught Place, POB 329, New Delhi 110 001; tel. (11) 3321459; telex 3165462; f. 1943; nationalized 1980; cap. and res 180m., dep. 15,441m. (1987); Chair. and Man. Dir S. P. TALWAR; Gen. Mans K. K. SAGGAR, R. C. KAPOOR; 456 brs.

Punjab and Sind Bank: 21 Bank House, Rajendra Place, New Delhi 110 008; tel. (11) 321658; telex 313684; f. 1908; nationalized 1980; cap. 245m., dep. 17,616m. (1987); Chair. and Man. Dir M. S. CHAHAL; 638 brs.

Punjab National Bank: 7 Bhikaiji Cama Place, Africa Ave, POB 274, New Delhi 110 066; tel. (11) 602303; telex 3161906; f. 1895; cap. 1000m., dep. 83,970m. (1987); Chair. and Man. Dir J. S. VARSHNEYA; 2,773 brs (world-wide).

Syndicate Bank: POB 1, Manipal 576 119; tel. 8261; telex 82242; f. 1925; cap. 420m., dep. 52,143m. (1987); Chair. and Man. Dir P. S. V. MALLYA; 1,442 brs.

UCO Bank (United Commercial Bank): 10 Biplabi Trailokya Maharaj Sarani (Brabourne Rd), POB 2455, Calcutta 700 001; tel. (33) 260120; telex 214323; f. 1943; cap. p.u. and res 1,028m., dep. 63,587m. (1988); Chair. and Man. Dir K. MANMOHAN SHENOI; 1,747 brs.

Union Bank of India: 239 Backbay Reclamation, Nariman Point, Bombay 400 021; tel. (22) 2024647; telex 114208; f. 1919; cap. and res 591m., dep. 43,633m. (1987); Chair. and Man. Dir YUVRAJ KARAN; 1,668 brs.

United Bank of India: 16 Old Court House St, Calcutta 700 001; tel. (33) 237471; telex 217387; f. 1950; cap. p.u. 26.9m., dep. 33,678m. (1986); Chair. and Man. Dir J. V. SHETTY; 1,075 brs.

Vijaya Bank: 14 Mahatma Gandhi Rd, Bangalore 560 001; tel. (812) 573341; telex 8452428; f. 1931; nationalized 1980; cap. p.u. 189.9m., dep. 16,710m. (1987); Chair. and Man. Dir K. SADANANDA SHETTY; 682 brs.

Principal Private Banks

Bank of Madura Ltd: 758 Anna Salai, POB 5225, Madras 600 002; tel. (44) 863456; telex 417807; cap. p.u. 35m., dep. 2,547m. (1987); Chair. S. V. SHANMUGAVADIVELU; 249 brs.

Bombay Mercantile Co-operative Bank Ltd: 78 Mohamedali Rd, Bombay 400 003; tel. (22) 325961; telex 1173727; f. 1939; cap. p.u. 25m., dep. 3,334m. (June 1988); Chair. GHULAM GHOUSE; Exec. Vice-Chair. and Man. Dir ZAIN G. RANGOONWALA; 33 brs.

Karnataka Bank Ltd: POB 716, Kodialbail, Mangalore 575 003; tel. (824) 27815; telex 842280; f. 1924; cap. p.u. 10m., dep. 3,575m. (1987); Chair. P. SUNDARRAO; Gen. Man. H. M. RAMA RAO; 267 brs.

The Sangli Bank Ltd: Rajwada Chowk, POB 158, Sangli 416 416; tel. 3611; telex 193211; f. 1916; cap. p.u. 4.3m., dep. 2,265m. (1986); Chair. and CEO A. B. ARADHYE; Gen. Man. A. K. CHATTERJEE; 166 brs.

United Western Bank Ltd: 172/4 Raviwar Peth, Shivaji Circle, POB 2, Satara 415 001; tel. 2523; telex 147212; f. 1936; cap. 7.5m., dep. 3,396m. (1987); Chair. K. B. DAMLE; Jt Gen. Mans P. V. KULKARNI, S. T. MODAK; 173 brs.

Foreign Banks

There are 26 foreign banks (with 140 branches) operating in India, of which the most important are:

Abu Dhabi Commercial Ltd (UAE): Rehmat Manzil, 75 Veer Nariman Rd, Bombay; tel. (22) 223866; telex 115481; Man. EBRAHIM ABDUL RAHMAN.

Algemene Bank Nederland NV (Netherlands): 14 Veer Nariman Rd, Bombay 400 023; tel. (22) 2042331; telex 113246; Gen. Man. (India) B. FUNKE; 3 brs.

American Express International Banking Corpn (USA): Dalamal Towers, First Floor 211, Nariman Point, Bombay 400 021; tel. (22) 233230; telex 113808; Vice-Pres. (India) JOHN FILMERIDIS; 3 brs.

Banca Nazionale del Lavoro (Italy): 61 Maker Chambers VI, 6th Floor, Nariman Point, Bombay 400 021; tel. (22) 2043736; telex 114053; Rep. L. C. AGARWAL.

Bank of America National Trust and Savings Association (USA): Express Towers, Ground Fl., Nariman Point, Bombay 400 021; tel. (22) 2023431; telex 112152; Regional Vice-Pres. RICHARD WORTLEY; 4 brs.

The Bank of Bahrain and Kuwait BSC: Embassy Centre, 207 Nariman Point, Bombay 400 021; tel. (22) 2041838; telex 115101; CEO ARJAN GURBUXANI.

Bank of Credit and Commerce International (Overseas) Ltd (Cayman Islands): Marker Chambers III, Nariman Point, Bombay 400 021; tel. (22) 241091; telex 115839; Gen. Man. (India) B. N. CHOUDHURY; 1 br.

Bank of Oman Ltd: Air India Bldg, Nariman Point, Bombay 400 021; tel. (22) 2026096; telex 115936; CEO M. V. KULKARNI.

Bank of Tokyo Ltd (Japan): Jeevan Prakash, Sir P. Mehta Rd, Bombay 400 001; tel. (22) 2860564; telex 112155; Gen. Man. YOSHUKE YOSHIOKA; 3 brs.

Banque Nationale de Paris (France): French Bank Bldg, 62 Homji St, Fort, POB 45, Bombay 400 001; tel. (22) 2860943; telex 112341; Man. P. GRANDAMY; 5 brs.

Barclays Bank PLC (UK): 67 Maker Towers 'F', Cuffe Parade, Colaba, Bombay 400 005; tel. (22) 212797; telex 112073; Rep. NOEL DAVENPORT.

British Bank of the Middle East (Hong Kong): 16 Veer Nariman Rd, Fort, Bombay 400 023; tel. (22) 258203; telex 115956; Man. S. DAULET SINGH.

Citibank, N.A. (USA): Sakhar Bhavan, 230 Backbay Reclamation, Nariman Point, Bombay 400 021; tel. (22) 258792; telex 112288; Vice-Pres. J. RAO; 5 brs.

Deutsche Bank AG (Asia) (Federal Republic of Germany): Tulsiani Chambers, Nariman Point, POB 9995, Bombay 400 021; tel. (22) 223262; telex 114042; CEO HEINRICH FRESE.

Grindlays Bank (UK): 90 Mahatma Gandhi Rd, POB 725, Bombay 400 023; tel. (22) 271295; telex 114792; Gen. Man. CSHOK KAPUR; 54 brs.

Hongkong and Shanghai Banking Corpn (Hong Kong): 52/60 Mahatma Gandhi Rd, POB 128, Bombay 400 001; tel. (22) 274921; telex 112223; CEO COLIN BAMFORD; 21 brs.

Midland Bank (UK): 152 Maker Chamber No. IV, 14th Floor, 222 Nariman Point, Bombay 400 021.

Mitsui Bank Ltd (Japan): 6 Wallace St, Bombay 400 001; tel. (22) 2043931; telex 112987; Gen. Man. and CEO KEN-ICHIRO NAKANO; 1 br.

Oman International Bank (Oman): 1A Mittal Court, Nariman Point, Bombay 400 021; tel. (22) 2047444; telex 113569; CEO V. V. CHANDY.

Royal Bank of Canada: N-104 Panchshila Park, New Delhi 110 017; tel. (11) 6410785; telex 3162927; Regional Rep. COLIN D. LIPTROT.

Sanwa Bank Ltd (Japan): World Trade Centre, 5th Floor, Barakhamba Lane, New Delhi 110 001; tel. (11) 3318008; telex 3162961; Gen. Man. MOTONORI KATSUKI.

Société Générale (France): Maker Chambers IV, Ground Floor, Bajaj Marg, Nariman Point, POB 11635, Bombay 400 021; tel. (22) 2041212; telex 112635; Gen. Man. DANIEL MOLLE.

Sonali Bank (Bangladesh): 15 Park St, Calcutta 700 016; tel. (33) 297998; telex 212727; Dep. Gen. Man. MD. SANAUL HAQUE; 1 br.

Standard Chartered Bank (UK): 23-25 Mahatma Gandhi Rd, Fort, POB 558, Bombay 400 023; tel. (22) 257198; telex 112230; Chief Man. MAGNUS E. STIRLING; 24 brs.

Banking Organizations

Indian Banks' Association: Stadium House, 81-83 Veer Nariman Rd, Bombay 400 020; tel. (22) 222365; telex 115146; 85 mems; Chair. R. SRINIVASAN; Sec. N. S. PRADHAN.

Indian Institute of Bankers: 'The Arcade', World Trade Centre, 2nd Floor, East Wing, Cuffe Parade, Bombay 400 005; tel. (22) 217003; telex 113524; f. 1928; 307,849 mems; Pres. R. N. MALHOTRA; Chief Sec. R. D. PANDYA.

National Institute of Bank Management: Kondhwe Khurd, Pune 411 022; tel. (212) 669080; telex 145256; f. 1968; Dir B. K. GHOSE.

DEVELOPMENT FINANCE ORGANIZATIONS

Agricultural Finance Corpn Ltd: Dhanraj Mahal, 1st Floor, Chatrapati Shivaji Maharaj Marg, Bombay 400 039; tel. (22) 2028924; telex 115849; f. 1968; a consortium of commercial banks, set up to help member commercial banks participate in agriculture and rural development projects; provides project consultancy services to commercial banks, Union and State govts, public sector corpns, the World Bank, the ADB, FAO, the International Fund for Agricultural Development and other institutions and to individuals; undertakes techno-economic and investment surveys in agriculture and agro-industries etc.; project office in New Delhi; regional offices in Calcutta, Lucknow and Madras; brs in Ahmedabad, Bhopal, Guwahati, Hyderabad, Patna and Trivandrum; Chair. Dr. G. V. K. RAO; Man. Dir B. VENKATA RAO.

Credit Guarantee Corpn of India Ltd: Bombay; f. 1971; promoted by the Reserve Bank of India; guarantees loans and other credit facilities extended by (i) scheduled and non-scheduled commercial banks to small traders, farmers and self-employed persons and small borrowers under a differential interest rates scheme; (ii) scheduled and non-scheduled commercial banks and state financial corpns to small transport and business enterprises; (iii) scheduled commercial banks and certain state and central co-operative banks to service co-operative socs assisting their mems engaged in industrial activity; Chair. Dr R. K. HAZARI; Man. C. S. SUBRAMANIAM.

Industrial Credit and Investment Corpn of India Ltd: 163 Backbay Reclamation, Bombay 400 020; tel. (22) 2022535; telex 113062; f. 1955 to assist industrial enterprises by providing finance in both rupee and foreign currencies in the form of long- or medium-term loans or equity participation, sponsoring and underwriting new issues of shares and securities, guaranteeing loans from other private investment sources, furnishing managerial, tech. and admin. advice to industry; also offers export development capital, venture capital, technology finance, merchant banking services and equipment leasing facilities; regional offices at Calcutta, Madras and New Delhi; share cap. 801m., res 2,408m. (March 1988); Chair. and Man. Dir N. VAGHUL.

Industrial Development Bank of India (IDBI): Nariman Bhavan, 227 Vinay K. Shah Marg, Nariman Point, Bombay 400 021; tel. (22) 231199; telex 112193; f. 1964, reorg. 1976; the main financial institution for co-ordinating and supplementing the working of other financial institutions and also for promoting and financing industrial development; 5 regional offices and 20 br. offices; cap. p.u. 4,950m., res 6,580m. (Nov. 1988); Chair. and Man. Dir SURESH S. NADKARNI.

Industrial Finance Corpn of India: Bank of Baroda Bldg, 16 Sansad Marg, POB 363, New Delhi 110 001; tel. (11) 3322052; telex 3166123; f. 1948 to provide medium- and long-term finance to cos and co-operative socs in India, engaged in manufacture, preservation or processing of goods, shipping, mining, hotels and power generation and distribution; promotes industrialization of less developed areas, and sponsors training in management techniques and development banking; cap. p.u. 700m., res 2,256.2m. (June 1988); Chair. D. N. DAVAR; 8 regional offices and 11 br. offices.

National Bank for Agriculture and Rural Development: Sterling Centre, Dr Annie Besant Rd, Worli, POB 6552, Bombay 400 018; tel. (22) 4924306; telex 1173770; f. 1982 to provide credit for agricultural and rural development through commercial, co-operative and regional rural banks; cap. and res 3,276.7m. (1986); held 50% each by the cen. govt and the Reserve Bank; Chair. P. R. NAYAK; Man. Dir G. P. BHAVE; 16 regional offices and 7 sub-offices.

STOCK EXCHANGES

There are 16 stock exchanges in India, including:

Ahmedabad Share and Stock Brokers' Association: Manek Chowk, Ahmedabad 380 001; tel. (272) 347149; telex 1216789; f. 1894; 299 mems; Pres. CHANDRAKANT BAPULAL DESAI; Sec. D. M. PANCHAL.

Bangalore Stock Exchange Ltd: Unity Bldgs, 'M' Block, J.C. Rd, Bangalore 560 002; tel. (812) 237238; 108 mems; Pres. KRISHNA MURTHY S. LOKKUR; Sec. M. RAGHAVENDRA RAO.

Bombay Stock Exchange: Phiroze Jeejeebhoy Towers, 25th Floor, Dalal St, Bombay 400 001; tel. (22) 275626; telex 115925; f. 1875; 554 mems; Pres. GOVINDBHAI B. DESAI; Exec. Dir M. R. MAYYA.

Calcutta Stock Exchange Association Ltd: 7 Lyons Range, Calcutta 700 001; tel. (33) 203335; telex 217414; f. 1908; 660 mems; Pres. DILIP KHANDELWAL; Sec. D. J. BISWAS.

Delhi Stock Exchange Association Ltd: 3 & 4/4B Asaf Ali Rd, New Delhi 110 002; tel. (11) 271302; telex 3165317; 117 mems; Pres. HARISH BHASIN.

Ludhiana Stock Exchange: Lajpatrai Market, Ludhiana 141 008; tel. 38248; telex 386429; f. 1984; 220 mems; Pres. BRIJ MOHAN LALL MUNJAL.

Madras Stock Exchange Ltd: Exchange Bldg, 11 Second Line Beach, POB 183, Madras 600 001; tel. (44) 512237; telex 418059; f. 1937; 142 mems; Pres. V. K. PADMANABHAN; Sec. V. RAMESH.

The other recognized stock exchanges are: Hyderabad, Madhya Pradesh (Indore), Cochin, Kanpur, Pune, Guwahati, Jaipur, Kanara (Mangalore), and Magadh (Patna).

INSURANCE

In January 1973 all Indian and foreign insurance companies were nationalized. The general insurance business in India is now transacted by only four companies, subsidiaries of the General Insurance Corpn of India.

Deposit Insurance Corpn: Vidyut Bhavan, Pathakwadi, Bombay 400 002; insures deposits of up to Rs 10,000 in the 956 banks insured by the corpn; cap. 20m.; Chair. K. R. PURI; Man. V. S. MOHARIR.

General Insurance Corpn of India (GIC): Industrial Assurance Bldg, 4th Floor, Churchgate, Bombay 400 020; tel. (22) 220046; telex 113833; f. 1973 by the reorg. of 106 private life and non-life insurance cos as the four groups listed below: Man. Dir B. D. SHAH; subsidiaries:

National Insurance Co Ltd: 3 Middleton St, Calcutta 700 071; telex 217074; Chair. and Man. Dir G. C. BHATTACHARYA.

New India Assurance Co Ltd: New India Assurance Bldg, Mahatma Gandhi Rd, Fort, Bombay 400 023; tel. (22) 274617; telex 112423; f. 1919; Chair. and Man. Dir S. K. SETH.

The Oriental Insurance Co Ltd: Oriental House, A-25/27 Asaf Ali Rd, New Delhi 110 002; tel. (11) 279221; telex 3162583; Chair. and Man. Dir H. J. SEQUEIRA.

United India Insurance Co Ltd: 24 Whites Rd, Madras 600 014; tel. (44) 810061; telex 416141; cap. and res 966m.; Chair. and Man. Dir M. M. BHAGAT.

Life Insurance Corpn of India: Jeevan Bima Marg, Bombay 400 021; tel. (22) 2021383; telex 112327; f. 1956; controls all life insurance business; Chair. R. NARAYANAN; Man. Dirs N. K. SHINKAR, M. G. DIWAN; 1,279 brs.

Insurance Association

Indian Insurance Companies' Association: Bombay; f. 1928 to represent the interests of the insurance industry; 43 mems.

Trade and Industry

CHAMBERS OF COMMERCE

There are chambers of commerce in most commercial and industrial centres. The following are among the most important:

Associated Chambers of Commerce and Industry of India: 2nd Floor, Allahabad Bank Bldg, 17 Parliament St, New Delhi 110 001; tel. (11) 310704; telex 3161754; f. 1921; a central org. of 350 chambers of commerce and industry and industrial asscns representing more than 20,000 cos throughout India; 6 promoter chambers, 53 ordinary mems, 15 patron mems and 222 corporate mems; Pres. L. M. THAPAR; Sec.-Gen. B. P. GUNAJI.

Federation of Indian Chambers of Commerce and Industry: Federation House, Tansen Marg, New Delhi 110 001; tel. (11) 3319251; telex 3162521; f. 1927; 461 mem. bodies, 928 assoc. mems, 72 cttee mems; Pres. ROHIT C. MEHTA; Sec.-Gen. D. H. PAI PANANDIKER.

Indian National Committee of International Chambers of Commerce: Federation House, Tansen Marg, New Delhi 110 001; tel. (11) 3319251; telex 3162521; f. 1929; 46 org. mems, 180 assoc. mems, 68 cttee mems; Pres. BAHUBALI GULABCHAND; Sec.-Gen. D. H. PAI PANANDIKER.

Bengal Chamber of Commerce and Industry: 6 Netaji Subhas Rd, Calcutta 700 001; tel. (33) 208393; telex 217369; f. 1853; 221 mems; Pres. SAMIR GHOSH; Sec. PRADIP DAS GUPTA.

Bengal National Chamber of Commerce and Industry: 23 R. N. Mukherjee Rd, Calcutta 700 001; telex 212189; f. 1887; 340 mems, 30 affiliated industrial and trading asscns; Pres. SUBIMAL GHOSH; Sec. SUNIL BANIK.

Bharat Chamber of Commerce: 28 Hemanta Basu Sarani, Calcutta 700 001; tel. (33) 208286; f. 1900; 705 mems; Pres. G. D. SHAH; Sec. B. S. SARKAR.

Bihar Chamber of Commerce: Judges' Court Rd, POB 71, Patna 800 001; tel. (612) 53505; f. 1926; 800 ordinary mems, 150 asscn mems; Pres. B. P. GUPTA; Sec.-Gen. G. K. SARAFF.

Bombay Chamber of Commerce and Industry: Mackinnon Mackenzie Bldg, 4 Shoorji Vallabhdas Marg, Ballard Estate, POB 473, Bombay 400 001; tel. (22) 264681; telex 1173571; f. 1836; 670 ordinary mems, 460 asscn mems; Pres. VINOD L. DOSHI; Sec. VIVEK S. DATE.

Calcutta Chamber of Commerce: 18H Park St, Stephen Court, Calcutta 700 071; tel. (33) 290758; 425 mems; Pres. P. K. JALAN; Sec. Dr M. K. SAHARIA.

Federation of Madhya Pradesh Chambers of Commerce and Industry: Udyog Bhavan, 129A Malviya Nagar, Bhopal 462 003; tel. (755) 551472; f. 1975; 345 ordinary mems, 59 asscn mems; Pres. D. P. MANDELIA; Sec.-Gen. SURESH BHARGAVA.

Gujarat Chamber of Commerce and Industry: Gujarat Chamber Bldg, Ranchhodlal Marg, POB 4045, Ahmedabad 380 009; tel. (272) 402301; f. 1949; 5,042 mems; Pres. NAREN MADHUBHAI PATEL; Sec.-Gen. I. N. KANIA.

Indian Chamber of Commerce: India Exchange, 4 India Exchange Place, Calcutta 700 001; tel. (33) 203242; telex 217432; f. 1925; 361 ordinary mems, 64 assoc. mems; Pres. J. N. SAPRU; Sec.-Gen. B. K. AGRAWAL.

Indian Merchants' Chamber: IMC Marg, Bombay 400 020; tel. (22) 2046633; telex 115195; f. 1907; 168 asscn mems, 1,878 mem. firms; Pres. ROHIT J. PATEL; Sec.-Gen. RAMU PANDIT.

INDIA

Directory

Madras Chamber of Commerce and Industry: 41 Kasturi Ranga Rd, Alwarpet, Madras 600 018; tel. (44) 451452; telex 41536; f. 1836; 194 mem. firms, 25 assocn., 10 affiliated and 11 hon.; Chair. HARI ESWARAN; Secs N. KANNAN, N. VENKATARAMAN.

Maharashtra Chamber of Commerce: Oricon House, 6th Floor, 12 K. Dubhash Marg (Rampart Row), Fort, Bombay 400 023; tel. (22) 244548; telex 113527; f. 1927; more than 2,000 mems; Pres. ARVIND R. DOSHI; Sec.-Gen. S. S. PINGLE.

Merchants' Chamber of Uttar Pradesh: 14/76 Civil Lines, Kanpur 208 001; tel. (532) 246874; f. 1932; 200 mems; Pres. K. G. LAHOTI; Sec. B. K. PARIEK.

North India Chamber of Commerce and Industry: 9 Gandhi Rd, Dehra Dun, Uttar Pradesh; tel. (935) 23479; f. 1967; 102 ordinary mems, 29 asscn mems, 5 mem. firms, 91 assoc. mems; Pres. DEV PANDHI; Sec.-Gen. B. L. JAIN.

Oriental Chamber of Commerce: 6 Dr Rajendra Prasad Sarani (Clive Row), Calcutta 700 001; tel. (33) 203609; f. 1932; 276 ordinary mems, five assoc. mems; Pres. SHAHANSHAH JEHANGIR; Jt Sec. KAZI ABU ZOBER.

PHD Chamber of Commerce and Industry: PHD House, 4/2 Siri Institutional Area, opp. Asian Games Village, POB 130, New Delhi 110 016; tel. (11) 665425; telex 3173058; f. 1905; 1,100 mems; Pres. M. M. SABHARWAL; Sec.-Gen. M. L. NANDRAJOG.

Southern India Chamber of Commerce and Industry: Indian Chamber Bldgs, Esplanade, POB 1208, Madras 600 108; tel. (44) 562228; telex 416689; f. 1910; more than 1,000 mems; Pres. M. A. ALAGAPPAN; Sec. J. PRASAD DAVIDS.

United Chamber of Trade Associations: Amirchand Marg, Katra Rathi, Delhi 110 006; tel. (11) 238444; 80 mems; Pres. MAHESHAWR DAYAL; Gen. Sec. P. R. MITTAL.

Upper India Chamber of Commerce: 14/113 Civil Lines, POB 63, Kanpur 208 001; tel. (512) 210684; f. 1888; 131 mems; Pres. D. N. DIKSHIT; Sec. K. K. GANGADHARAN.

Uttar Pradesh Chamber of Commerce: 15/197 Civil Lines, Kanpur 208 001; tel. 62321; f. 1914; 200 mems; Pres. V. K. SRIVASTAVA; Sec. AFTAB SAMI.

FOREIGN TRADE CORPORATIONS

Cashew Corpn of India Ltd: Mahatma Gandhi Rd, POB 1019, Ernakulam, Cochin 682 011; tel. (484) 352177; telex 8856202; imports raw cashew nuts for distribution to the export-orientated sector of the cashew processing industry; also undertakes exports of cashew kernels; cap. p.u. Rs15m., res and surplus Rs104.7m. (1988); Chair. P. K. SHUNGLU.

Export Credit Guarantee Corpn of India Ltd: Express Towers, 10th Floor, Nariman Point, POB 373, Bombay 400 021; tel. (22) 2023023; telex 113231; f. 1957 to insure for risks involved in exports on credit terms and to supplement credit facilities by issuing guarantees, etc.; cap. Rs60m., res Rs249m. (1987); Chair. and Man. Dir J. G. KANGA; Gen. Man. N. M. CHORDIA.

Handicrafts and Handlooms Exports Corpn of India Ltd: Lok Kalyan Bhavan, 11A Rouse Ave Lane, New Delhi 110 002; tel. (11) 3311086; telex 3161522; f. 1958; govt undertaking dealing in export of handicrafts, handloom goods, ready-to-wear clothes, carpets and precious jewellery, while promoting exports and trade development; subsidiary of the State Trading Corpn of India Ltd; cap. p.u. Rs75m. (1988); Chair. and Man. Dir M. P. PINTO; Gen. Man. S. S. SAHNI.

Minerals and Metals Trading Corpn of India Ltd: Scope Complex, Core 1, 7 Lodi Rd, New Delhi 110 003; tel. (11) 3319448; telex 3174042; f. 1963; export of iron and manganese ore, ferromanganese, finished stainless steel products, mica, coal and other minor minerals; import of steel, non-ferrous metals, rough diamonds, fertilizers, etc. for supply to industrial units in the country; cap. p.u. Rs350m., res and surplus Rs 1,579m. (1986); 10 regional offices in India; foreign offices in Japan and Romania; Chair. and Man. Dir I. P. HAZARIKA.

Projects and Equipment Corpn of India Ltd: Hansalaya, 15 Barakhamba Rd, New Delhi 110 001; tel. (11) 3313351; telex 3165256; f. 1971; export of engineering, industrial and railway equipment; undertakes turnkey and other projects and management consultancy abroad; cap. p.u. Rs15m., res and surplus Rs129.5m. (1988); Chair. and Man. Dir B. K. SHROFF.

State Trading Corpn of India Ltd: Chandralok, 36 Janpath, New Delhi 110 001; tel. (11) 353164; telex 3165180; f. 1956; govt undertaking dealing in exports and imports; cap. p.u. Rs300m., res and surplus Rs2,376.2m. (1988); 19 regional brs and 19 offices overseas; Chair. M. Y. PRIYOLKAR.

Trade Development Authority: Bank of Baroda Bldg, 16 Parliament St, POB 767, New Delhi 110 001; tel. (11) 310214; telex 3165155; f. 1970 to promote selective development of exports of high quality products; arranges investment in export-orientated ventures undertaken by India with foreign collaboration; brs in Frankfurt, New York, Tokyo, Harare, Dubai, Los Angeles and Kuala Lumpur; Chair. A. N. VERMA.

INDUSTRIAL AND AGRICULTURAL ORGANIZATIONS

Organizations engaged in the financing of agricultural and industrial development are listed under Finance. There are also industrial development corporations in the separate states. The following are among the more important industrial and agricultural organizations.

Coal India Ltd: 10 Netaji Subhas Rd, Calcutta 700 001; tel. (33) 209101; telex 217180; cen. govt holding co with seven subsidiaries; responsible for almost total (more than 90%) planning and production of coal mines; cap. p.u. Rs30,123.1m. (1986); Chair. and Man. Dir M. P. NARAYANAN.

Cotton Corpn of India Ltd: Air India Bldg, 12th Floor, Nariman Point, Bombay 400 021; tel. (22) 2024363; telex 113463; f. 1970 as an agency in the public sector for the purchase, sale and distribution of home-produced cotton and imported cotton staple fibre; exports long staple cotton; cap. p.u. Rs230m. (1988); Chair. and Man. Dir M. B. LAL.

Fertilizer Corpn of India Ltd: Madhuban, 55 Nehru Place, New Delhi 110 019; tel. (11) 6418727; telex 315197; f. 1961; fertilizer factories at Sindri, Gorakhpur, Talcher and Ramagundam, producing nitrogenous, phosphatic and some industrial products; cap. p.u. Rs5,659.7m. (1987); Chair. and Man. Dir R. GUPTA.

Food Corpn of India: 16–20 Barakhamba Lane, New Delhi 110 001; tel. (11) 3310551; telex 312418; f. 1965 to undertake trading in food grains on a commercial scale but within the framework of an overall govt policy; to provide farmers an assured price for their produce; to supply food grains to the consumer at reasonable prices; also purchases, stores, distributes and sells food grains and other foodstuffs and arranges imports and handling of food grains and fertilizers at the ports; distributes sugar in a number of states and has set up rice mills; cap. p.u. Rs7,276.7m., res and surplus Rs204m. (1986); Chair. T. S. BROCA; Man. Dir A. MOHANDAS MOSES.

Housing and Urban Development Corpn Ltd: HUDCO House, Lodhi Rd, New Delhi 110 003; tel. (11) 699534; telex 3161037; f. 1970; to finance and undertake housing and urban development programmes including the setting-up of new or satellite towns and building material industries; auth. cap. Rs810m., res and surplus Rs 857m. (1986); six brs; Chair. and Man. Dir S. K. SHARMA.

Indian Dairy Corpn: Suraj Plaza II, Sayajigunj, Baroda 390 005; tel. (265) 66637; telex 175239; aims to promote dairying in India; to execute the IDA/EEC/Govt of India dairy development programme 'Operation Flood' which aims at covering 155 districts for dairy development to link them to major urban centres for milk marketing to enable the organized dairy sector to obtain a commanding share of these markets, to set up a nat. milk herd and a nat. milk network; cap. p.u. Rs10m., res and surplus Rs1,100m. (1986); Chair. Dr VERGHESE KURIEN; Man. Dir R. P. ANJA.

Jute Corpn of India Ltd: 1 Shakespeare Sarani, Calcutta 700 071; telex 213266; f. 1971; objects: (i) to undertake price support operations in respect of raw jute; (ii) to ensure remunerative prices to producers through efficient marketing; (iii) to operate a buffer stock to stabilize raw jute prices; (iv) to handle the import and export of raw jute; (v) to promote the export of jute goods; cap. p.u. Rs50m. (1986); Chair. and Man. Dir AMITABHA MAJUMDAR.

National Co-operative Development Corpn: 4 Siri Institutional Area, Hauz Khas, New Delhi 110 016; tel. (11) 669246; telex 3173059; f. 1962 to plan and promote country-wide programmes through co-operative societies for the production, processing, marketing, storage, export and import of agricultural produce, foodstuffs and notified commodities; also programmes for the development of poultry, dairy, fish products, coir, handlooms, distribution of consumer articles in rural areas and minor forest produce in the co-operative sector; seven regional and eight project offices; Pres. BHAJAN LAL; Man. Dir T. C. A. SRINIVASARAMANUJAN.

National Industrial Development Corpn Ltd: Chanakya Bhavan, Africa Ave, Chanakyapuri, POB 5212, New Delhi 110 021; tel. (11) 670154; telex 3162891; f. 1954; consultative engineering services to cen. and state govts, public and private sector enterprises, the UN and overseas investors; cap. p.u. Rs6m. (1986); Chair. and Man. Dir R. C. BAJPAI.

National Minerals Development Corpn Ltd: Khanÿ Bhavan, 10-3-311/A Castle Hills, Masab Tank, POB 52, Hyderabad 500 028; tel. (842) 222071; telex 1556452; f. 1958; cen. govt undertaking under the Ministry of Steel and Mines; to exploit minerals (excluding coal, atomic minerals, lignite, petroleum and natural gas) in public sector; may buy, take on lease or otherwise acquire mines for prospecting, development and exploitation; iron ore mines at Bailadila-11C, Bailadila-14 and Bailadila-5 in Madhya Pradesh, and at Donimalai in Karnataka State, and diamond mines at Panna in Madhya Pradesh; research and development laboratories and consultancy wing at Hyderabad; investigates mineral projects; iron ore production in 1986/87 was 9.2m. metric tons, diamond production 15,190 carats; cap. p.u. Rs1,130.7m., res and surplus Rs58.7m. (1986–87); Chair. and Man. Dir P. C. GUPTA.

National Productivity Council: Utpadakta Bhavan, Lodi Rd, New Delhi 110 003; tel. (11) 690331; telex 3166059; f. 1958 to increase productivity and to improve quality by improved techniques which aim at efficient and proper utilization of available resources; autonomous body representing national orgs of employers and labour, govt ministries, professional orgs, local productivity councils, small-scale industries and other interests; 75 mems; Chair. OTIMA BORDIA; Dir-Gen. Dr G. K. SURI.

National Research Development Corpn: 20–22 Zamroodpur Community Centre, Kailash Colony Extension, New Delhi 110 048; tel. (11) 6432121; telex 3171358; f. 1953 to stimulate development and commercial exploitation of new inventions with financial and technical aid; finances development projects to set up demonstration units in collaboration with industry; exports technology; cap. p.u. Rs23.7m. (1988); Man. Dir N. K. SHARMA.

National Seeds Corpn Ltd: Beej Bhavan, Pusa, New Delhi 110 012; tel. (11) 569721; telex 313705; f. 1963 to improve and develop the seed industry; cap. p.u. Rs143.2m., res and surplus Rs13m. (1986); Man. Dir Dr S. K. SENGUPTA.

The National Small Industries Corpn Ltd: Laghu Udyog Bhavan, Okhla Industrial Estate, New Delhi 110 020; tel. (11) 6837071; telex 3162376; f. 1955 to aid, advise, finance, protect and promote the interests of small industries; cap. p.u. Rs309.9m., (1987), all shares held by the govt; Chair. J. S. JUNEJA.

Rehabilitation Industries Corpn Ltd: 25 Free School St, Calcutta 700 016; tel. (33) 241181; telex 217327; f. 1959 to create employment opportunities through multi-product industries, ranging from consumer goods to engineering products and services, for refugees from Bangladesh and migrants from Pakistan, repatriates from Burma and Sri Lanka, and other immigrants of Indian extraction; cap. p.u. Rs41.1m. (1986); Chair. and Man. Dir RAJAT BARUA.

State Farms Corpn of India Ltd: Farm Bhavan, 14–15 Nehru Place, New Delhi 110 019; tel. (11) 6413125; f. 1969 to administer the central state farms; activities include the production of quality seeds of high-yielding varieties of wheat, paddy, maize, bajra and jowar; advises on soil conservation, reclamation and development of waste and forest land; consultancy services on farm mechanization; auth. cap. Rs200m. (1987); Chair. A. R. MALLU; Man. Dir P. S. G. NAIR.

Steel Authority of India Ltd: Ispat Bhavan, Lodi Rd, POB 3049, New Delhi 110 003; tel. (11) 690481; telex 3162689; f. 1973 to provide co-ordinated development of the steel industry in both the public and private sectors; steel plants at Bhilai, Bokaro, Durgapur, Rourkela; alloy steel plants at Durgapur and Salem; subsidiary Indian Iron and Steel Corpn Ltd, Burnpur; combined ingot steel capacity is 10.9m. metric tons annually; cap. p.u. Rs39,724.8m., res Rs648.7m. (1987); Chair. V. KRISHNAMURTHY.

Tea Board of India: 14 Brabourne Rd, POB 2172, Calcutta 700 001; tel. (33) 260210; telex 214527; f. to provide financial assistance to tea research stations; sponsors and finances independent research projects in universities and tech. institutions to supplement the work of tea research establishments; also promotes tea production and export; Chair. R. K. TRIPATHY.

PRINCIPAL INDUSTRIAL ASSOCIATIONS

Ahmedabad Textile Mills' Association: Ranchhodlal Marg, Navrangpura, POB 4056, Ahmedabad 380 009; tel. (272) 402273; telex 126227; f. 1891; 37 mems; Pres. Dr BIHARILAL KANAIYALAL.

All India Manufacturers' Organization (AIMO): Jeevan Sahakar, 4th Floor, Sir P.M. Rd, Fort, Bombay 400 001; tel. (22) 2861016; telex 116179; f. 1941; 1,500 mems; Pres. RAMGOPAL M. DUJODWALA.

Assocn of Indian Automobile Manufacturers: 148 M.G. Rd, Bombay 400 023; tel. (22) 242416; telex 114869; f. 1960; 28 mems; Pres. B. DE SOUZA; Sec. S. G. SHAH.

Bharat Krishak Samaj (Farmers' Forum, India): Dr Panjabrao Desmukh Krishak Bhavan, A-1 Nizamuddin West, New Delhi 110 013; tel. (11) 619508; f. 1954; national farmers' org.; Pres. (ex-officio) Minister of Agriculture and Rural Development; more than 1m. ordinary mems, 40,000 life mems; Chair. Dr BAL RAM JAKHAR; Sec.-Gen. Dr D. A. BHOLAY.

Bombay Millowners' Association: Elphinstone Bldg, 10 Veer Nariman Rd, Fort, POB 95, Bombay 400 001; tel. (22) 2040411; telex 115372; f. 1875; 37 mem. cos; Chair. SUDHIR K. THACKERSEY; Sec.-Gen. R. L. N. VIJAYANAGAR.

Bombay Motor Merchants' Association Ltd: Sukh Sagar, 3rd Floor, Sandhurst Bridge, Bombay 400 007; tel. (22) 8112769; 485 mems; Pres. S. ZORAWAR SINGH ANAND; Gen. Sec. S. TARLOCHAN SINGH ANAND.

Bombay Piece-Goods Merchants' Mahajan: 250 Shaikh Memon St, Bombay 400 002; tel. (22) 255750; f. 1881; 1,700 mems; Pres. SURENDRA TULSIDAS SAVAI; Secs PRAMOD P. NARSANA, DINESH M. MEHTA.

Calcutta Baled Jute Association: 6 Netaji Subhas Rd, Calcutta 700 001; tel. (22) 208393; telex 217369; f. 1892; 49 mems; Chair. PURANMULL KANKARIA; Sec. A. E. SCOLT.

Calcutta Flour Mills Association: 6 Netaji Subhas Rd, Calcutta 700 001; tel. (33) 208393; telex 217369; f. 1932; 22 mems; Chair. D. N. JATIA; Sec. PROSENJIT DAS GUPTA.

Calcutta Tea Traders' Association: 6 Netaji Subhas Rd, Calcutta 700 001; tel. (33) 208393; telex 217369; f. 1886; Chair. D. K. GHOSH; Sec. PROSENJIT DAS GUPTA.

Confederation of the Engineering Industry—CEI: 23–26 Institutional Area, Lodi Rd, New Delhi 110 003; tel. (11) 615115; telex 3166655; f. 1986; over 2,000 mem. companies, 35 affiliated asscns; Pres. BRIJ MOHAN LALL; Dir-Gen. TARUN DAS.

East India Cotton Association Ltd: Cotton Exchange, Marwari Bazar, Bombay 400 002; tel. (22) 314876; telex 113152; f. 1921; 350 mems; Pres. CHANDRASINH H. MIRANI; Sec. V. M. UNCHAGAONKAR.

Federation of Gujarat Mills and Industries: Federation Bldg, R. C. Dutt Rd, Baroda 390 005; tel. (265) 325101; f. 1918; 300 mems; Pres. PANKAJ KADAKIA; Sec. Dr PARESH RAVAL.

Federation of Indian Export Organizations: PHD House, 3rd Floor, Siri Institutional Area, Hauz Khas, opposite Asian Games Village, New Delhi 110 016; tel. (11) 666582; telex 3173194; f. 1965; 1,650 mems; Pres. RAMU S. DEORA; Sec.-Gen. CHANDRAKANT G. RAO.

Grain, Rice and Oilseeds Merchants' Association: Grainseeds House, 72/80 Yusef Meheralli Rd, Bombay 400 003; tel. (22) 8554021; f. 1899; 1,000 mems; Pres. RAICHAND LILADHAR SHAH; Sec. R. J. BHATT.

Indian Chemical Manufacturers' Association: India Exchange, 4 India Exchange Place, Calcutta 700 001; tel. (33) 203242; telex 217432; f. 1938; 240 mems; Pres. S. M. DATTA; Sec. B. K. AGRAWAL.

Indian Jute Mills Association: Royal Exchange, 6 Netaji Subhas Rd, Calcutta 700 001; tel. (33) 209918; telex 217369; sponsors and operates export promotion, research and product development; regulates labour relations; Chair. H. V. KANORIA.

Indian Mining Association: 6 Netaji Subhas Rd, Calcutta 700 001; tel. (33) 263861; telex 217369; f. 1892; 50 mems; Sec. K. MUKERJEE.

Indian Mining Federation: 135 Biplabi Rashbehari Basu Rd, Calcutta 700 001; tel. (33) 250484; f. 1913; 40 mems; Chair. H. S. CHOPRA; Sec. S. K. GHOSE.

Indian Motion Picture Producers' Association: Imppa House, Dr Ambedkar Rd, Bombay 400 050; tel. (22) 536344; f. 1938; 1,500 mems; Pres. RAMRAJ NAHTA; Asst Sec. E. K. MOHANDAS.

Indian National Shipowners' Association: 22 Maker Tower, F, Cuffe Parade, Bombay 400 005; tel. (22) 212103; telex 114611; f. 1929; 29 mems; Pres. K. M. SHETH; Sec. B. V. NILKUND.

Indian Paper Mills Association: India Exchange, 8th Floor, India Exchange Place, Calcutta 700 001; tel. (33) 203242; telex 217432; f. 1939; 37 mems; Pres. N. D. MOHTA; Sec. B. GHOSH.

Indian Sugar Mills Association: Sugar House, 39 Nehru Place, New Delhi 110 019; tel. (11) 6416601; telex 3162654; f. 1932; 166 mems; Pres. RAM V. TYAGRAJAN; Sec.-Gen. S. L. JAIN.

Indian Tea Association: Royal Exchange, 6 Netaji Subhas Rd, Calcutta 700 001; tel. (33) 208393; telex 217369; f. 1881; 58 mem. companies; 238 tea estates; Chair. R. N. DEOGUN; Sec. Y. K. VOHRA.

Industries and Commerce Association: ICO Association Rd, POB 70, Dhanbad 826 001; tel. (326) 2639; f. 1933; 53 mems; Pres. P. K. AGARWALLA; Asst Sec. D. D. BANERJEE.

Jute Balers' Association: 12 India Exchange Place, Calcutta 700 001; tel. (33) 201491; f. 1909; 275 mems; represents all Indian jute balers; Chair. MOHANLAL SETHIA; Sec. SUJIT CHOUDHURY.

Master Stevedores' Association: Royal Exchange, 6 Netaji Subhas Rd, Calcutta 700 001; tel. (33) 208393; telex 217369; f. 1934; 11 mems; Pres. D. S. BOSE; Sec. ALBAN E. SCOLT.

Silk and Art Silk Mills' Association Ltd: Resham Bhavan, 78 Veer Nariman Rd, Bombay 400 020; tel. (22) 2041006; telex 114685; f. 1939; 440 mems; Chair. M. H. DOSHI; Sec. K. A. SAMUEL.

Southern India Mills' Association: Racecourse, Coimbatore 641 018, Tamil Nadu; f. 1933; 200 mems; Chair. D. LAKSHMINARAYANASWAMY; Sec. T. RANGASWAMY.

INDIA
Directory

EMPLOYERS' FEDERATIONS

Council of Indian Employers: Federation House, Tansen Marg, New Delhi 110 001; tel. (11) 3319251; telex 3161768; f. 1956; Sec. R. C. PANDE; comprises:

All India Organization of Employers (AIOE): Federation House, Tansen Marg, New Delhi 110 001; tel. (11) 3319251; telex 3161768; f. 1932; mems 62 industrial asscns and 164 corporate cos; Pres. M. A. ALAGAPPAN; Sec.-Gen. D. H. PAI PANANDIKAR.

Employers' Federation of India (EFI): Army and Navy Bldg, 148 Mahatma Gandhi Rd, Bombay 400 023; tel. (22) 245070; telex 112529; f. 1933; 230 mems; Pres. KESHUB MAHINDRA; Sec. V. B. MAHATME.

Standing Conference of Public Enterprises (SCOPE): SCOPE Complex, Lodhi Rd, New Delhi 110 003; tel. (11) 360101; telex 3174057; f. 1973; representative body of all central public enterprises in India; advises the govt and public enterprises on matters of major policy and co-ordination; trade enquiries, regarding imports and exports of commodities, carried out on behalf of mems; 200 mems; Chair. S. P. WAHI; Sec.-Gen. WARIS RASHEED KIDWAI.

Employers' Association of Northern India: 14/69 Civil Lines, POB 344, Kanpur 208 001; tel. (512) 210513; f. 1937; 163 mems; Chair. P. C. JAIN; Sec.-Gen. S. C. SAXENA.

Employers' Federation of Southern India: 41 Kasturi Ranga Rd, Alwarpet, Madras 600 018; tel. (44) 451452; telex 41536; f. 1920; 245 mem. firms; Pres. E. B. UNNI; Sec. N. KANNAN.

TRADE UNIONS

In the absence of compulsory registration and the need to file returns, a precise estimate of the aggregate trades-union membership in India is not available, but in 1986 it was believed that only about 10m. workers, out of a labour force of 222.5m., belonged to unions.

Indian National Trade Union Congress (INTUC): 1B Maulana Azad Rd, New Delhi 110 011; tel. (11) 381850; f. 1947; the largest and most representative trade union org. in India; 4,503 affiliated unions with a total membership of 4,730,644; affiliated to ICFTU; 26 state brs and 29 nat. industrial feds; Pres. G. RAMANUJAM; Gen. Sec. Shri GOPESHWAR.

Centre of Indian Trade Unions: 6 Talkatora Rd, New Delhi 110 001; tel. (11) 384071; f. 1970; 1.8m. mems; 20 state brs; over 3,000 affiliated unions; Pres. B. T. RANADIVE; Gen. Sec. SAMAR MUKHERJEE.

National industrial federations:

All India Council of Atomic Energy Employees: Tel Rasayan Bhavan, Tilak Rd, Dadar, Bombay 400 014; f. 1981; 3,000 mems; Pres. RAJA KULKARNI; Gen. Sec. MARY EMMANUEL.

Indian National Cement Workers' Federation: Mazdoor Karyalaya, Congress House, Bombay 400 004; tel. (22) 351809; 90,786 mems; Pres. H. N. TRIVEDI; Gen. Sec. N. NANJAPPAN.

Indian National Chemical Workers' Federation: Tel Rasayan Bhavan, Tilak Rd, Dadar, Bombay 400 014; tel. (22) 4121742; Pres. RAJA KULKARNI; Gen. Sec. K. H. DASTOOR.

Indian National Electricity Workers' Federation: 19 Mazdoor Maidan, Power House, Jaipur 302 006; tel. (141) 76175; 124,600 mems; 17 affiliated unions; Pres. DALIP SINGH AZAD; Gen. Sec. DAMODAR MAURYA.

Indian National Metal Workers' Federation: 26 K Rd, Jamshedpur 831 001; tel. (657) 3506; Pres. V. G. GOPAL; Gen. Sec. S. GOPESHWAR.

Indian National Mineworkers' Federation: Michael John Smriti Bhawan, Rajendra Path, Dhanbad, Bihar; tel. 3506; f. 1949; 364,151 mems in 155 affiliated unions; Pres. KANTI MEHTA; Gen. Sec. S. DAS GUPTA.

Indian National Paper Mill Workers' Federation: Ballarpur, Chanda; Pres. G. SANJEEVA REDDY; Gen. Sec. P. J. NAIR.

Indian National Port and Dock Workers' Federation: POB 87, Vasco-da-Gama 403 802, Goa; f. 1954; 18 affiliated unions; 81,000 mems; Pres. MOHAN NAIR; Gen. Sec. JANAKI MUKHERJEE.

Indian National Press Workers' Federation: 162 South Ave, New Delhi 110 011; Pres. S. W. DHABE.

Indian National Sugar Mills Workers' Federation: 19 Lajpatrai Marg, Lucknow; tel. (522) 47638; 100 affiliated unions; 40,000 mems; Pres. C. SINGH; Gen. Sec. RAM YASH SINGH.

Indian National Textile Workers' Federation: Mazdoor Manzil, G. D. Ambekar Marg, Parel, Bombay 400 012; tel. (22) 4123713; f. 1948; 430 affiliated unions; 484,879 mems; Pres. P. L. SUBBIAH; Gen. Sec. H. J. NAIK.

Indian National Transport Workers' Federation: Sham Shivir, Tansen Marg, Gwalior 474 002; Pres. T. S. VIYOGI; Gen. Sec. K. S. VERMA.

National Federation of Petroleum Workers: Tel Rasayan Bhavan, Tilak Rd, Dadar, Bombay 400 014; tel. (22) 4121742; f. 1959; 22,340 mems; Pres. RAJA KULKARNI.

Assam Chah Karmachari Sangha: POB 13, Dibrugarh 786 001; tel. (33) 20870; 11,858 mems; 20 brs; Pres. BIJOY CHANDRA BHAGAVATI; Gen. Sec. A. K. BHATTACHARYA.

All India Trade Union Congress (AITUC): 24 Canning Lane, New Delhi 110 001; tel. (11) 386427; f. 1920; affiliated to WFTU; more than 3m. mems, c. 4,000 affiliated unions; 22 state brs, 10 national federations; Pres. INDRAJIT GUPTA.

Major affiliated unions:

Annamalai Plantation Workers' Union: Valparai, Via Pollachi, Tamil Nadu; over 21,000 mems.

Zilla Cha Bagan Workers' Union: Mal, Jalpaiguri, West Bengal; 15,000 mems; Pres. NEHAR MUKHERJEE; Gen. Sec. BIMAL DAS GUPTA.

United Trades Union Congress (UTUC): 249 Bepin Behari Ganguly St, Calcutta 700 012; f. 1949; 608,052 mems from 607 affiliated unions; 10 state brs; Pres. N. SRIKANTAN NAIR; Sec.-Gen. P. CHOWDHURY.

Major affiliated unions:

All India Farm Labour Union: c/o UTUC Jakkanpur New Area, Patna 800 001, Bihar; c. 35,000 mems; Pres. MAHENDRA SINGH TIKAIT.

Bengal Provincial Chatkal Mazdoor Union: Calcutta; textile workers; 28,330 mems.

Bharatiya Mazdoor Sangh: Ram Naresh Bhavan, Tilak Gali, New Delhi 110 055; tel. (11) 523644; Pres. MANHAR BHAI MEHTA; Gen. Sec. G. PRABHAKAR.

Hind Mazdoor Sabha (HMS): Nagindas Chambers, 167 P. D'Mello Rd, Bombay 400 038; tel. (22) 262185; f. 1948; affiliated to ICFTU; 2.5m. mems from 1,481 affiliated unions; 18 regional brs; Pres. KAMALA SINHA; Gen. Sec. UMRAOMAL PUROHIT.

Major affiliated unions:

Bombay Port Trust Employees' Union: Pres. Dr SHANTI PATEL; Gen. Sec. S. K. SHETYE.

Colliery Mazdoor Congress, Asansol (Coalminers' Union): Pres. MADHU DANDAVATE; Gen. Sec. JAYANTA PODDER.

Koyala Ispat Mazdoor Panchayat, Jharia (Steel Workers' Union): Gen. Sec. HIT NARAYAN SINGH.

Oil and Natural Gas Commission Employees' Mazdoor Sabha: Vododara; 4,000 mems; Pres. R. DULARE; Gen. Sec. G. G. PARADKAR.

South Central Railway Mazdoor Union: 7C, Railway Bldg, Accounts Office Compound, Secunderabad 500 025 AP; tel. (842) 77823; f. 1966; 71,600 mems; Pres. K. S. N. MURTHY; Gen. Sec. N. SUNDARESAN; 120 brs.

West Bengal Chah Mazdoor Sabha: Jalpaiguri, West Bengal; tel. 349; 45,000 mems; Pres. B. D. RAI; Gen. Sec. SAMIR ROY.

Confederation of Central Government Employees and Workers: New Delhi 110 060; tel. (11) 587804; 1.2m. mems; Pres. S. MADHUSUDAN; Sec.-Gen. S. K. VYAS.

Affiliated union:

National Federation of Post, Telephone and Telegraph Employees (NFPTTE): C-1/2 Baird Rd, New Delhi 110 001; tel. (11) 322545; f. 1954; 221,880 mems (est.); Pres. R. G. SHARMA; Gen. Sec. O. P. GUPTA.

All India Bank Employees' Association (AIBEA): 10/9 East Patel Nagar, New Delhi; Pres. D. P. CHADDA; Gen. Sec. TARAKESWAR CHAKRAVARTY.

All India Defence Employees' Federation (AIDEF): 70 Market Rd, Kirkee, Pune 411 003; tel. (212) 58761; 299 affiliated unions; 400,000 mems; Pres. SAMUEL AUGUSTINE; Gen. Sec. K. M. MATHEW.

All India Port and Dock Workers' Federation: 9 Second Line Beach, Madras 600 001; tel. (44) 25983; f. 1948; 100,000 mems in 26 affiliated unions; Pres. S. R. KULKARNI; Gen. Sec. S. C. C. ANTHONY PILLAI.

All India Railwaymen's Federation (AIRF): 4 State Entry Rd, New Delhi 110 055; tel. (11) 343493; f. 1924; 773,818 mems; 14 affiliated unions; Pres. UMRAOMAL PUROHIT; Gen. Sec. J. P. CHAUBEY.

National Federation of Indian Railwaymen (NFIR): 3 Chelmsford Rd, New Delhi 110 055; f. 1952; 15 affiliated unions; 750,000 mems; Pres. KESHAV H. KULKARNI; Gen. Sec. SASHI BHUSAN RAO.

Transport

RAILWAYS

India's railway system is the largest in Asia and the fourth largest in the world. The total length of Indian railways in March 1987 was 61,813 route-km. The Government exercises direct or indirect control over all railways through the Railway Board.

A 16.43-km underground railway for Calcutta was scheduled for completion by 1988. In 1986 the underground network covered a total of 10 km, in two sections. When completed, it is expected to carry more than 1m. people daily.

Indian Government Administration (Ministry of Railways, Railway Board): Rail Bhavan, Raisina Rd, New Delhi; tel. (11) 388931; telex 313561; Chair. RAJ KUMAR JAIN.

Zonal Railways

The railways are grouped into nine zones:

Central: Victoria Terminus, Bombay; tel. (22) 268041; Gen. Man. VIJAYA SINGH.

Eastern: 17 Netaji Subhas Rd, Calcutta 700 001; tel. (33) 226811; Gen. Man. R. D. KITSON.

North Eastern: Gorakhpur 273 012; tel. (551) 3041; Gen. Man. GAURI SHANKAR.

Northeast Frontier: Maligaon, Guwahati 781 011; tel. 88422; telex 2352336; Gen. Man. K. SUBRAHMANYAN.

Northern: Baroda House, New Delhi 110 001; tel. (11) 387227; Gen. Man. J. RAJAGOPALACHARI.

South Central: Rail Nilayam, Secunderabad 500 371; tel. (842) 74848; Gen. Man. M. A. CHERIAN.

South Eastern: Calcutta 700 043; tel. (33) 451741; Gen. Man. NIKHILESH MITRA.

Southern: Park Town, Madras 600 003; tel. (44) 564141; Gen. Man. K. V. BALAKRISHNAN.

Western: Churchgate, Bombay 400 020; tel. (22) 298016; Gen. Man. E. SRIDHARAN.

ROADS

In December 1983 there were 1,554,204 km of roads in India, 31,756 km of which were national highways. Total outlay on roads and bridges in the sixth Five-Year Plan (1980–1985) was Rs34,389.6m., and the proposed total outlay in the seventh Five-Year Plan (1985–90) was Rs52,000m.

Ministry of Surface Transport (Roads Wing): 1 Transport Bhavan, Parliament St, New Delhi 110 001; tel. (11) 385047; telex 312448; responsible for the maintenance of India's system of national highways, with a total length of 31,756 km in 1983, connecting the state capitals and major ports and linking with the highway systems of neighbouring countries. This system includes 63 highways which constitute the main trunk roads of the country.

Border Roads Development Board: f. 1960 to accelerate the economic development of the north and north-eastern border areas; it has constructed and improved 18,500 km of roads and maintains about 17,500 km (1987).

INLAND WATERWAYS

About 15,655 km of rivers are navigable by power-driven craft, and 3,490 km by large country boats. Services are mainly on the Ganga and Brahmaputra and their tributaries, the Godavari, the Mahanadi, the Narmada, the Tapi and the Krishna.

Central Inland Water Transport Corpn Ltd: 4 Fairlie Place, Calcutta 1; tel. (33) 202321; telex 212779; f. 1967; inland water transport services in Bangladesh and the north-east Indian states; also shipbuilding and repairing, general engineering, dredging, lightening of ships and barge services; Chair. and Man. Dir S. K. BHOSE.

SHIPPING

In July 1984 India was 16th on the list of principal merchant fleets of the world. In March 1987 the fleet had 374 vessels totalling 9.5m. dwt. There are some 55 shipping companies in India. The major ports are Bombay, Calcutta, Cochin, Haldia, Kandla, Madras, Mangalore, Mormugao, Paradip (Paradeep), Tuticorin and Vishakhapatnam (Visakhapatnam). An auxiliary port to Calcutta at Haldia was opened to international shipping in 1977 and has since undergone further modernization. Provision of Rs9,550m. was made in the seventh Five-Year Plan (1985–90) for development of major ports.

Bombay

Bharat Line Ltd: Bharat House, 104 Apollo St, Fort, Bombay 400 001; Chair. and Man. Dir GUNVANTRAI T. KAMDAR; brs in Calcutta, Bhavnagar and Madras.

Chowgule Steamships Ltd: Bakhtawar, 3rd Floor, Nariman Point, POB 11596, Bombay 400 021; tel. (22) 2026822; telex 112409; f. 1963; seven bulk carriers and one tanker totalling 379,565 dwt; Chair. VISHWASRAO DATTAJI CHOWGULE; Man. Dir SHIVAJIRAO DATTAJI CHOWGULE.

Great Eastern Shipping Co Ltd: Hong Kong Bank Bldg, 60 Mahatma Gandhi Rd, Bombay 400 001; tel. (22) 274869; telex 112824; f. 1948; cargo services; 28 vessels; Chair. VASANT J. SHETH; Dep. Chair. and Man. Dir K. M. SHETH; br. in New Delhi.

Scindia Steam Navigation Co Ltd: Scindia House, Narottam Morarjee Marg, Ballard Estate, Fort, Bombay 400 038; tel. (22) 268161; telex 01173519; f. 1919; cargo services; 23 vessels; Chair. N. S. PARULEKAR; Man. Dir V. M. PAREKH; brs at Calcutta, Gandhidham, Mangalore and London.

Shipping Corpn of India Ltd: Shipping House, 245 Madame Cama Rd, Bombay 400 021; tel. (22) 259900; telex 112371; f. 1961 as a govt undertaking; fleet of 146 vessels consisting of tankers, freighters, VLCCs, combination carriers, product carriers, passenger-cum-cargo ships, bulk carriers totalling 5.36m. dwt; operates 24 services; brs in Calcutta, New Delhi, Mombasa, Rameshwaram and London; Chair. Dr R. SINGH; Vice-Chair. and Man. Dir K. DEV.

South-East Asia Shipping Co Ltd: 402–406 Himalaya House, Dr Dadabhoy Naoroji Rd, Bombay 400 001; tel. (22) 269231; telex 112753; f. 1948; world-wide cargo services; five vessels totalling 61,259 dwt; Chair. N. H. DHUNJIBHOY; CEO D. P. ADENWALLA.

Calcutta

India Steamship Co Ltd: 21 Hemanta Basu Sarani, POB 2090, Calcutta 700 001; tel. (33) 281171; telex 212549; f. 1928; cargo services; 16 vessels totalling 261,189 dwt; Chair. K. K. BIRLA; Exec. Dir S. N. ROY; brs in Bombay, Delhi and London.

Ratnakar Shipping Co Ltd: 14–15 Old Court House St, Calcutta 700 001; tel. (33) 228901; telex 217659; world-wide tramping services; nine vessels totalling 331,583 dwt; Exec. Pres. Lt-Gen. (retd) P. R. PURI.

Surrendra Overseas Ltd: Apeejay House, 15 Park St, Calcutta 700 016; tel. (33) 295455; telex 213485; cargo services; eight vessels (six bulk carriers and two cargo vessels totalling 176,145 dwt); Dir JIT PAUL.

Madras

South India Shipping Corpn Ltd: Chennai House, 7 Esplanade Rd, POB 234, Madras 600 108; tel. (44) 30141; telex 41371; eight bulk carriers totalling 344,319 dwt; Chair. J. H. TARAPORE; Man. Dir F. G. DASTUR.

CIVIL AVIATION

There are four international airports in India: Bombay Airport, Calcutta Airport, Delhi Airport and Madras Airport. There are about 90 other airports.

Air India: Air India Bldg, Nariman Point, Bombay 400 021; tel. (22) 2024142; telex 112427; f. 1932 as Tata Airlines; renamed Air India in 1946; in 1953 became a state corpn responsible for international flights; services to 39 online stations in 25 countries covering five continents; Chair. RATAN TATA; Man. Dir RAJAN JETLEY; fleet of 10 Boeing 747-200B, 3 Airbus A300-B4, 6 Airbus A310-300, 1 DC-8-73F, 1 Il-76, 1 Boeing 747-200C.

Indian Airlines: Airlines House, 113 Gurudwara Rakabganj Rd, Parliament St, New Delhi 110 001; tel. (11) 388951; telex 312131; f. 1953; state corpn responsible for regional and domestic flights; services to 73 cities throughout India and in Afghanistan, Bangladesh, Maldives, Nepal, Pakistan, Singapore, Sri Lanka and Thailand; Chair. RAHUL BAJAJ; Man. Dir GERRY T. PAIS; fleet of 27 Boeing 737, 9 HS-748, 4 F-27, 13 Airbus.

Vayudoot Private Ltd: Safdarjung Airport, New Delhi 110 003; tel. (11) 693851; telex 3161052; f. 1981 to connect the smaller towns of north-eastern India; links 78 airfields with Calcutta, Delhi, Hyderabad and Bombay; jtly owned by Indian Airlines and Air India; Chair. B. K. GOSWAMY; Gen. Man. HARSH VARDHAN; fleet of 3 HAL 748, 1 F-27, 10 Dornier 228.

Tourism

The tourist attractions of India include its scenery, its historic forts, palaces and temples, and its rich variety of wild life. Tourist infrastructure has recently been expanded by the provision of more luxury hotels and improved means of transport. In 1987 there were 1,163,774 foreign visitors to India.

Department of Tourism of the Government of India: Ministry of Tourism, Transport Bhavan, Parliament St, New Delhi 110 001; tel. (11) 384111; telex 312827; formulates and administers govt policy for promotion of tourism; plans the organization and develop-

INDIA

ment of tourist facilities; operates tourist information offices in India and overseas; Dir-Gen. B. K. GOSWAMY.

India Tourism Development Corpn Ltd: Jeevan Vihar, 3 Sansad Marg, New Delhi 110 001; tel. (11) 310923; telex 3163361; f. 1966; operates hotels (largest hotel chain owner), resort accommodation, tourist transport services, duty-free shops and a travel agency and provides consultancy and management services; Chair. and Man. Dir B. K. GOSWAMY.

Atomic Energy

There are three operating nuclear power stations, at Tarapur near Bombay, at Kalpahkam (Tamil Nadu) and at Kota (Rajasthan). Four more stations are being built at Narora (Uttar Pradesh), Kakrapar (Gujarat), Kaiga (Karnataka), and Rawatbhata (Rajasthan). India has six heavy water plants in operation and two more are under construction. A nuclear fuel complex at Hyderabad (Andhra Pradesh) produces the fuel required by the nuclear power stations.

Atomic Energy Commission: Chhatrapati Shivaji Maharaj Marg, Bombay 400 039; tel. (22) 2022543; telex 112355; organizes research on the use of atomic energy for peaceful purposes; Chair. Dr M. R. SRINIVASAN; Sec. S. RAJGOPAL.

Bhabha Atomic Research Centre (BARC): Trombay, Bombay 400 085; tel. (22) 5512791; telex 1171017; f. 1957; national centre for research in and development of nuclear energy for peaceful uses; Dir Dr P. K. IYENGAR; five research reactors:

APSARA: 1 MW, research and isotope production, criticality 1956.

CIRUS: 40 MW, isotope production and material testing, criticality 1960.

ZERLINA: Zero Energy Reactor for Lattice Investigations and New Assemblies, criticality 1961, decommissioned 1983.

PURNIMA: criticality 1972, originally Plutonium Oxide fuelled fast critical facility, modified as PURNIMA II with Uranium 233 in the form of Uranyl nitrate solution as fuel, criticality 1984. Being modified as PURNIMA III to mock-up the core of the KAMINI reactor, which is under construction at Igcar, Kalpakkam.

DHRUVA: 100 MW, research, isotope production, material and reactor components testing, criticality 1985.

Other major facilities include:

ISOMED: for radiation sterilization of medical products.

MOX: fuel fabrication facility to make uranium oxide and plutonium oxide fuel.

FRP: Fuel reprocessing plant to reprocess irradiated fuel from CIRUS and DHRUVA.

Van de Graaff: 5.5-MV accelerator for studies in nuclear reactions, ion implantation etc.

INDONESIA

Introductory Survey

Location, Climate, Language, Religion, Flag, Capital

The Republic of Indonesia consists of a group of about 13,700 islands, lying between the mainland of South-East Asia and Australia. The archipelago is the largest in the world, and it stretches from the Malay peninsula to New Guinea. The principal islands are Java, Sumatra, Kalimantan (Borneo), Sulawesi (Celebes), Irian Jaya (West New Guinea), the Moluccas and Timor. Indonesia's only land frontiers are with Papua New Guinea, to the east of Irian Jaya, and with the Malaysian states of Sarawak and Sabah, which occupy northern Borneo. The climate is tropical, with an average annual temperature of 26°C (79°F) and heavy rainfall during most seasons. The official language is Bahasa Indonesia (a form of Malay) but some 25 local languages (mainly Javanese) and more than 250 dialects are also spoken. An estimated 78% of the inhabitants profess adherence to Islam. About 11% of the population are Christians, while most of the remainder are either Hindus or Buddhists. The national flag (proportions 3 by 2) has two equal horizontal stripes, of red and white. The capital is Jakarta, on the island of Java.

Recent History

Indonesia was formerly the Netherlands East Indies, except for the former Portuguese colony of East Timor (see below).

Dutch occupation began in the 17th century and gradually extended over the whole archipelago. Nationalist opposition to colonial rule began in the early 20th century. During the Second World War the territory was occupied by Japanese forces from March 1942. On 17 August 1945, three days after the Japanese surrender, a group of nationalists proclaimed the independence of Indonesia. The first President of the self-proclaimed republic was Dr Sukarno, a leader of the nationalist movement since the 1920s. The declaration of independence was not recognized by the Netherlands, which attempted to restore its pre-war control of the islands. After four years of intermittent warfare and negotiations between the Dutch authorities and the nationalists, agreement was reached on a formal transfer of power. On 27 December 1949 the United States of Indonesia became legally independent, with Dr Sukarno continuing as President. Initially, the country had a federal constitution which gave limited self-government to the 16 constituent regions. In August 1950, however, the federation was dissolved and the country became the unitary Republic of Indonesia. The 1949 independence agreement excluded West New Guinea (now Irian Jaya), which remained under Dutch control until October 1962; following a brief period of UN administration, however, it was transferred to Indonesia in May 1963.

President Sukarno followed a policy of extreme nationalism, and his regime became increasingly dictatorial. His foreign policy was sympathetic to the People's Republic of China but, under his rule, Indonesia also played a leading role in the Non-Aligned Movement (see p. 232). Inflation and widespread corruption eventually provoked opposition to Sukarno's regime; in September–October 1965 there was an abortive military coup, in which the Indonesian Communist Party (PKI) was strongly implicated. A mass slaughter of alleged PKI members and supporters ensued. In March 1966 President Sukarno was forced to transfer emergency executive powers to military commanders, led by Gen. Suharto, Chief of Staff of the Army, who outlawed the PKI, and in February 1967 President Sukarno transferred full power to Gen. Suharto. In March the People's Consultative Assembly removed Sukarno from office and named Gen. Suharto acting President. He became Prime Minister in October 1967 and, after his election by the Assembly, he was inaugurated as President in March 1968. In July 1971, in the first general election since 1955, the government-sponsored Sekretariat Bersama Golongan Karya (Joint Secretariat of Functional Groups), known as Sekber Golkar, won a majority of seats in the House of Representatives. President Suharto was re-elected in March 1973.

Under Suharto's 'New Order', real power passed from the legislature and Cabinet to a small group of army officers and to the Operation Command for the Restoration of Order and Security (Kopkamtib), the internal security organization. Left-wing movements were suppressed, and a liberal economic policy adopted. A general election in May 1977 gave Golkar a majority in the legislature, and Suharto was re-elected President (unopposed) in March 1978. Despite criticism of the Government (most notably a petition signed by 50 prominent citizens in 1980), Golkar won an increased majority in the elections in May 1982, although the campaign was marred by considerable violence. In March 1983 Suharto was re-elected, again unopposed, as President.

During 1984 Suharto's attempt to introduce legislation requiring all political, social and religious organizations to adopt Pancasila, the state philosophy (which advocates political consensus and religious tolerance), as their only ideology encountered opposition, particularly from the Petition of 50 (the signatories of the 1980 protest). Serious rioting and a series of bombings and arson attempts in and around Jakarta were allegedly instigated by Muslim opponents of the proposed legislation, and many Muslims were tried and sentenced to long terms of imprisonment. The law concerning mass organizations was enacted in June 1985, and all the political parties had accepted Pancasila by July. In 1986 and 1987 several factors gave rise to widespread criticism of Suharto and his Government within Indonesia and abroad: the publication, in an Australian newspaper, of a report accusing the Suharto family of corrupt practices; allegations of abuses of human rights in East Timor (see below); the execution of nine former PKI members (imprisoned for their alleged involvement in the 1965 coup attempt) in February 1987; and the Government's subsequent refusal to allow lawyers of the International Federation of Human Rights into the country, amid further reports of abuses of human rights. In the April 1987 general election, however, Golkar won 299 of the 500 seats in the House of Representatives. Moreover, for the first time the party achieved an overall majority of seats in each of Indonesia's 27 provinces.

In February 1988 new legislation reaffirmed the 'dual (i.e. military and socio-economic) function' of the Indonesian Armed Forces (ABRI). Shortly afterwards, Gen. Try Sutrisno (hitherto Chief of Staff of the Army) replaced Gen. L. B. Murdani as Commander-in-Chief of the Armed Forces. In March Suharto was again re-elected unopposed as President. At the subsequent vice-presidential election, in a departure from recent procedure, Suharto did not recommend a candidate, but encouraged the People's Consultative Assembly to choose one. However, Lt-Gen. (retd) Sudharmono, the Chairman of Golkar, and Dr Jailani Naro, the leader of the United Development Party (PPP), were both nominated for the post, and Suharto was obliged to indicate his preference for Sudharmono before Dr Naro withdrew his candidacy and Sudharmono was elected unopposed. During the electoral process, a senior member of ABRI, Brig.-Gen. Ibrahim Salim, suggested that the nomination procedure for the vice-presidency was unfair. He was prevented from completing his speech and subsequently lost his seat in the People's Consultative Assembly. ABRI disapproved of Sudharmono's appointment as, under his chairmanship of Golkar, there had been a shift away from military dominance in the grouping and he was suspected of having left-wing sympathies. A cabinet reshuffle took place in March, and 19 new ministers were appointed.

ABRI's influence was further eroded in September by the replacement of Kopkamtib, commanded by Gen. Murdani, by the Co-ordinating Board for the Development of National Stability (Bakorstanas), led by Gen. Sutrisno. Kopkamtib had been a military organization, whose chief responsibility was the suppression of left-wing movements, whereas Bakorstanas included representatives from the Cabinet and non-military government departments, and its main task was to expose corruption. In October Sudharmono resigned as Chairman of Golkar and was replaced by Gen. (retd) Wahono, who was acceptable both to ABRI and the developing bureaucratic elite. By January 1989 an anti-communist campaign had resulted in the expulsion of three senior officials from Golkar and the execution of two former members of the armed forces, convicted in 1968 for their involvement in the 1965 attempted coup. The lack of evidence of any genuine communist re-emergence led to the belief that the campaign was organized by ABRI to discredit Sudharmono.

In 1975 Portugal withdrew from its colony of East Timor. The territory's capital, Dili, was occupied by the forces of the left-wing Frente Revolucionário de Este Timor Independente (Fretilin), which advocated independence for East Timor. To prevent Fretilin from gaining full control, Indonesian troops intervened and set up a provisional government. In July 1976 East Timor was fully integrated as the 27th province of Indonesia. In February 1983 the UN Commission on Human Rights adopted a resolution affirming East Timor's right to independence and self-determination, and in 1988 the UN still did not recognize Indonesia's absorption of the territory. In September 1983, following a five-month cease-fire during which talks took place between Fretilin and the Government, the armed forces launched a major new offensive. During 1984 conditions in East Timor worsened, with widespread hunger, disease and repression among civilians, and continuing battles between rebels and Indonesian troops. The rebels suffered a serious set-back in August 1985, when the Australian Government recognized Indonesia's incorporation of East Timor. An estimated 10,000 Indonesian troops were deployed in East Timor in 1987. In November 1988 Suharto visited East Timor, prior to announcing that travel restrictions, in force since the annexation in 1976, were to be withdrawn. Eight of the 13 regencies in the territory were scheduled to open to Indonesians at the beginning of 1989, although foreigners would continue to require permits from the armed forces. This development may have been prompted by Indonesia's failure to gain the chairmanship of the Non-Aligned Movement in 1988; conditions in East Timor were cited by those countries who refused to support Indonesia's claim.

In May 1977 there was a rebellion in Irian Jaya, said to have been organized by the Organisasi Papua Merdeka (OPM), or Free Papua Movement, which seeks unification with Papua New Guinea. Fighting continued until December 1979, when Indonesia and Papua New Guinea finalized a new border administrative agreement. Since then, however, there have been frequent border incidents, and in early 1984 fighting broke out in Jayapura, the capital of Irian Jaya. As a result, about 10,000 refugees fled over the border into Papua New Guinea. In October 1984 Indonesia and Papua New Guinea signed a five-year agreement establishing a joint border security committee; by the end of 1985 Indonesians were continuing to cross into Papua New Guinea, but a limited number of repatriations took place in 1986. There was also concern among native Irian Jayans (who are of Melanesian origin) at the introduction of large numbers of Javanese into the province, under the Government's transmigration scheme. This was interpreted as an attempt to reduce the Melanesians to a minority and thus to stifle opposition. In 1986 it was announced that the Government intended to resettle 65m. people over 20 years, in spite of protests from human rights and conservation groups that the scheme would cause ecological damage and interfere with the rights of the native Irian Jayans. By August 1987 some 650,000 families had been resettled under the scheme. Relations with Papua New Guinea improved when the Prime Minister, Paias Wingti, visited President Suharto in January 1988. However, a series of cross-border raids by the Indonesian armed forces in October and November, in an attempt to capture Melanesian separatists operating on the border, led to renewed tension between the two countries.

Under President Suharto, Indonesia's foreign policy is one of non-alignment, although the country maintains close relations with the West. In the mid-1980s Indonesia improved its relations with the USSR, and in March 1987 Eduard Shevardnadze, the Soviet Minister of Foreign Affairs, visited Indonesia on a tour of South-East Asian States, in order to discuss the problem of Kampuchea. Indonesia is a member of the Association of South East Asian Nations (ASEAN, see p. 101) and supports that organization's opposition to Viet-Nam's military presence in Kampuchea. In July 1988 Indonesia organized preliminary negotiations for the contending Kampuchean factions: the Jakarta Informal Meeting. The discussions, which did not result in agreement, were attended not only by Viet-Nam but also by other members of ASEAN.

In July 1985 Indonesia and the People's Republic of China signed a memorandum of understanding on the resumption of direct trade links, which had been suspended since 1967. In April 1988 the Indonesian Government indicated its readiness to re-establish full diplomatic relations with the People's Republic, subject to the assurance that China would not seek to interfere in Indonesia's internal affairs; previously, Suharto had insisted that China acknowledge its alleged complicity in the 1965 attempted coup. Conflicting claims by Indonesia, Viet-Nam, China, Malaysia and the Philippines over the disputed Spratly Islands, in the South China Sea, and China's continued support of the Khmer Rouge faction in Kampuchea remain obstacles to a full Sino-Indonesian *rapprochement*.

For a limited period in September 1988, Indonesia closed the straits of Sunda and Lombok to international shipping, owing to 'live firing exercises'. The USA, Australia and the Federal Republic of Germany expressed concern at this contravention of the Law of the Sea, whereby foreign vessels are allowed 'innocent passage' through the straits. In October the Australian Minister for Foreign Affairs and Trade, Gareth Evans, visited Indonesia. Despite tensions between the two countries concerning Indonesian incursions into Papua New Guinea and the temporary closure of the straits, a joint communiqué, confirming co-operation in the formerly disputed Timor Gap area, was issued.

Government

The highest authority of the state is the People's Consultative Assembly, with 1,000 members who serve for five years. The Assembly includes 500 members of the House of Representatives, the country's legislative organ. The House has 100 appointed members and 400 directly elected representatives. The remaining 500 seats in the Assembly are allocated to regional representatives, members of the Armed Forces belonging to Golkar, and delegates of other organizations, selected in proportion to their elected seats in the House. Executive power rests with the President, elected for five years by the Assembly. He governs with the assistance of an appointed Cabinet, responsible to him.

There are 27 provinces, and local government is through a three-tier system of Provincial, Regency and Village Assemblies. Provincial Governors are appointed by the President.

Defence

Military service is selective. In June 1988 the total strength of the armed forces was 285,000 men: army 215,000, navy 43,000 and air force 27,000. There was also a paramilitary force of some 115,000. Defence expenditure for 1987/88 was budgeted at 2,188,000m. rupiahs.

Economic Affairs

Indonesia has extensive natural wealth but, with a large and rapidly increasing population, it remains a relatively poor country in terms of average income. The fertile island of Java is one of the most densely populated areas in the world, but some of the other large islands are sparsely inhabited. In 1987, according to estimates by the World Bank, Indonesia's gross national product (GNP), measured at average 1985–87 prices, was US $76,766m., equivalent to $450 per head. Between 1980 and 1987, it was estimated, GNP per head expanded, in real terms, at an average rate of 1.9% per year. The average annual increase in overall gross domestic product (GDP), measured in constant prices, was 7.9% in 1965–80, slowing to 3.4% in 1980–86.

The economy is predominantly agricultural. More than one-half of the working population are employed in agriculture, forestry and fishing, which together provided 25.8% of Indonesia's GDP in 1986. Export revenue from agricultural products in 1987 was US $1,650m., 5.6% lower than in 1986. The reduction was attributable mainly to a drought. In 1984 Indonesia became self-sufficient in its staple crop, rice. In 1987, however, production of milled rice increased by only 1.7%, to 27.5m. metric tons. Imports of rice were avoided, despite an estimated annual increase of 2.4% in consumption of rice. Oil palm, rubber, coffee, sugar cane, tea, coconuts and tobacco are among the country's principal cash crops. Indonesia is the world's second largest producer of natural rubber (after Malaysia), and production was 1,016,000 tons in 1986. Earnings from rubber exports increased from US $713.2m. in 1986 to $960.5m. in 1987. Indonesia is also one of the world's largest coffee exporters, and a member of the International Coffee Organization

INDONESIA

(ICO, see p. 223). Coffee production totalled 380,000 tons in 1986/87 and increased to 400,000 tons in 1987/88. Exports in 1987/88, however, reached only 270,580 tons, compared with 297,314 tons in 1986/87, owing to ICO policies which allegedly discriminated against the coarser robusta beans which Indonesia produces.

About two-thirds of Indonesia's land area is covered by tropical rain forests; however, since 1980 the country's exports of forest products have slumped, owing to falling demand and restrictions on exporting unprocessed timber. All log exports have been banned since January 1985, but the World Bank estimated in 1988 that deforestation was still taking place at a rate of 900,000 ha annually. In 1986 output of industrial logs was 28.2m. cu m. Export restrictions resulted in a sharp decline in earnings from timber (to only US $221m.) in 1983/84, which prompted a significant increase in the export of plywood. In 1987 revenue from plywood exports reached $2,000m., raising total forestry exports in that year to $2,330m., an increase of 64.7% compared with 1986.

Indonesia's principal mineral resource is petroleum; in 1986 proven recoverable reserves were assessed at 9,000m. barrels. In 1977 a record 615.1m. barrels were produced. Output fell sharply in the 1980s, owing to OPEC restrictions (imposed to counter the world slump in petroleum prices). Despite a reduction in output compared with 1986, export revenue in 1987 rose by 18.3%, owing to a slight increase in petroleum prices. Production declined from 479m. barrels in 1987 to 423m. barrels in 1988. New production-sharing terms were introduced in 1988 to encourage exploration, owing to a decline in the number of new wells drilled (from 157 in 1986 to only 75 in 1987). Since 1984 Indonesia has produced all its own requirements of refined petroleum products, and in the late 1980s, to compensate for low international prices, some Malaysian crude petroleum was also being processed. Indonesia is the world's leading exporter of liquefied natural gas (LNG). In 1987 Indonesia's exports of LNG increased in volume to 17.63m. metric tons, a growth of 8.5% compared with 1986, but declined by 13.5% in value, to $2,400m. In 1988 exports of LNG reached 19.1m. tons, most of which was supplied to Japan, although Indonesia also has agreements with the USA, Taiwan and the Republic of Korea. New plants for processing liquefied petroleum gas (LPG) were opened in Arun and in Badak (East Kalimantan) in the late 1980s. Indonesia has expanded its LPG production substantially, and in 1988 it was expected to export 2.45m. tons. Tin, bauxite, nickel, copper, gold and coal are also mined. Mine output of tin was 26,093 metric tons in 1987, making Indonesia the world's third largest producer (after Malaysia and Brazil). Proven reserves of coal were assessed at 1,730m. tons in 1988, although annual output had reached only about 4m. tons.

The manufacturing sector contributed only 14.4% of GDP in 1986 and employed only about 10% of the work-force. Significant investment was needed to satisfy the demands of a labour force expanding by 2.3% per annum and to compensate for declines in revenue from petroleum exports. In 1986 the Government initiated a process of economic deregulation, which continued in 1987 and 1988, with increasing effect: foreign investment was encouraged through changes in regulations governing investment and export; several state enterprises were 'privatized'; non-tariff restrictions on imports were repealed; some import monopolies were abolished, most notably plastics; industrial licensing procedures were simplified; and foreigners were permitted to trade on a new secondary market to supplement the Jakarta stock exchange. As a result of these reforms, Indonesia's manufacturing base expanded and diversified rapidly, and in 1987/88 export revenue from manufactured products totalled US $6,730m. (an increase of 46.9% compared with 1986/87, accounting for 39.3% of total exports in that year (17.2% excluding petroleum-related products).

Repelita IV (1984–89), the fourth Five-Year Plan, emphasized expansion of the industrial sector and non-oil exports, and forecast an annual GDP growth rate of 5% (at 1973 prices). In 1987/88 GDP growth was 4.2%, compared with 4.0% in 1986/87. The target for annual industrial growth in Repelita IV was 9.5%. By 1988 actual industrial growth had reached 10.2% per annum. In 1986 foreign reserves stood at $10,700m., but in 1987 they fell to $6,251m., remaining at a similar level, $6,000m., in January 1989. Indonesia's development plans have been financed largely by foreign aid. The country receives continuous aid from the Inter-Governmental Group for Indonesia (IGGI). For the fiscal year 1988/89, donor countries pledged total aid of $4,020m., in response to Indonesia's deregulation measures. Foreign investment rose sharply; in the first 11 months of 1988 the Capital Investment Co-ordinating Board approved 133 projects, worth a total of $4,170m., compared with investments of $1,466m. in the whole of 1987. In September 1986 the rupiah was devalued by 30.7% in relation to the US dollar, in order to bolster foreign exchange reserves, to maintain the balance of payments, and to mitigate the effect of the decline in petroleum revenues. The deficit on the current account of the balance of payments increased from $1,923m. in 1985 to $3,911m. in 1986, owing to a decline in export earnings from petroleum and gas and a decrease in non-petroleum exports. In 1987/88 imports remained close to 1986/87 levels, and consequently the sharp expansion in non-oil exports resulted in a decline of the current account deficit to only an estimated 2.7% of GDP. The annual rate of inflation rose from 4.3% in 1984/85 to 8.9% in 1986/87, but, despite improvements in the economy, fell only slightly, to 8.35%, in 1987/88, when food prices were increased by drought and adjustment to the 1986 devaluation of the rupiah was not complete. In March 1988 the foreign debt was estimated at $40,400m., compared with $37,300m. in March 1986. In 1987/88 the debt-service ratio was expected to reach 34.3% of GDP. The rise against other major currencies, since 1985, of the Japanese yen (in which 30% of Indonesia's total debt is denominated) has added substantially to debt-servicing costs. Since the early 1970s Indonesia has had a surplus on the balance of trade, amounting to US $5,199m. in 1987. Total exports increased from $14,805m. in 1986 to $17,570m. in 1987. Imports, however, also rose, from $10,718m. in 1986 to $12,370m. in 1987.

In the 1989/90 budget proposals, total expenditure was projected to total 36,574,900m. rupiahs, an increase of 26% compared with the estimate for 1988/89. Current budget expenditure in 1989/90 was expected to increase by 17%, to 23,000,000m. rupiahs, and development expenditure by 47%, to 13,000,000m. rupiahs; debt-servicing costs were estimated at 12,000,000m. rupiahs; aid contributions were expected to account for 31% of total revenue. The major recipients of the development budget were to be the sectors of communications, tourism and agriculture.

Indonesia's principal trading partner is Japan, accounting for 29.1% of imports and 42.1% of exports in 1987, followed by the USA and Singapore, which, respectively, accounted for 11.4% and 7.7% of imports and 19.1% and 8.2% of exports. Indonesia's main imports are machinery, fuel, chemicals and transport equipment.

Social Welfare

About 10% of the population benefit from a state insurance scheme. Benefits include life insurance and old-age pensions. In addition, there are two social insurance schemes, administered by state corporations, providing pensions and industrial accident insurance. In 1984/85 Indonesia had 1,306 hospitals (with a total of 106,035 beds), 5,453 community health centres and more than 18,000 other health centres. About one-half of the hospitals are privately administered. In 1985 there were 18,447 physicians working in the country. Expenditure on health services by the central Government in the financial year ending 31 March 1987 was about 464,000m. rupiahs (1.9% of total spending). In the 1988/89 budget, about 3.2% of proposed development expenditure (289,200m. rupiahs) was allocated to health, family planning and social welfare.

Education

Education is mainly under the control of the Ministry of Education and Culture, but the Ministry of Religion is in charge of Islamic religious schools at the primary level. Primary education, beginning at seven years of age and lasting for six years, was made compulsory in 1987. Secondary education, which is not compulsory, begins at 13 years of age and lasts for a further six years, comprising two cycles of three years each. Secondary enrolment was 53.5% of the school-age population at junior high school (age 13–15) and 34.8% at senior high school (age 16–18) in 1987/88. In 1987/88 26.6m. pupils were enrolled at 144,561 primary schools, while 8.8m. were receiving general secondary education. There were 1,297,533 students in higher education in 1987/88. In 1987/88 there were 48 state universities and teacher-training colleges, and 25 private universities. Expenditure on education by the central Government in 1986/87 was about 2,113,000m. rupiahs, representing 8.5% of total spending. In 1985, according to estimates by

INDONESIA

UNESCO, the rate of adult illiteracy was 25.9% (males 17.0%; females 34.6%).

Public Holidays

1989: 1 January (New Year's Day), 5 March (Ascension of the Prophet Muhammad), 24 March (Good Friday), 4 May (Ascension Day), 7 May (Id al-Fitr, end of Ramadan), 14 July (Id al-Adha, Feast of the Sacrifice), 4 August (Muharram, Islamic New Year), 17 August (Indonesian National Day), 13 October (Mouloud, Prophet Muhammad's Birthday), 25 December (Christmas Day).

1990: 1 January (New Year's Day), 23 February (Ascension of the Prophet Muhammad), 13 April (Good Friday), 27 April (Id al-Fitr, end of Ramadan), 24 May (Ascension Day), 4 July (Id al-Adha, Feast of the Sacrifice), 24 July (Muharram, Islamic New Year), 17 August (Indonesian National Day), 2 October (Mouloud, Prophet Muhammad's Birthday), 25 December (Christmas Day).

Weights and Measures

The metric system is in force.

Statistical Survey

Source (unless otherwise stated): Central Bureau of Statistics, 8 Jalan Dokter Sutomo, POB 3, Jakarta; tel. (021) 363366; telex 45159.

Note: Unless otherwise stated, figures for the disputed former Portuguese territory of East Timor (annexed by Indonesia in July 1976) are not included in the tables.

Area and Population

AREA, POPULATION AND DENSITY

Area (sq km)	
Indonesia	1,904,569*
East Timor	14,874†
Population (census results)	
31 October 1980	
Indonesia	146,934,948
East Timor	555,350
31 October 1985 (inter-censal survey)	
Indonesia	
Males	81,321,445
Females	82,094,867
Total	163,416,312
East Timor	
Males	322,667
Females	308,009
Total	630,676
Population (official estimates at mid-year)‡	
1985	163,393,000
1986	166,940,000
1987	170,534,000
Density (per sq km) at 31 October 1985	
Indonesia	85.8
East Timor	42.4

* 735,358 sq miles.   † 5,743 sq miles.
‡ Figures include East Timor. The estimates have not been adjusted to accord with the survey of 31 October 1985.

PRINCIPAL ISLANDS
(population at survey of 31 October 1985)

	Area (sq km)	Population	Density (per sq km)
Jawa (Java) and Madura	132,187	99,852,812	755.4
Sumatera (Sumatra)	473,606	32,604,024	68.8
Kalimantan (Borneo)	539,460	7,721,665	14.3
Sulawesi (Celebes)	189,216	11,552,917	61.1
Others	570,100	11,684,894	20.5
Indonesia	1,904,569	163,416,312	85.8
East Timor	14,874	630,676	42.4
Total	1,919,443	164,046,988	85.5

PRINCIPAL TOWNS (population)

	1980 Census	1983*
Jakarta (capital)	6,503,449	7,347,800
Surabaya	2,027,913	2,223,600
Bandung	1,462,637	1,566,700
Medan	1,378,955	1,805,500
Semarang	1,026,671	1,205,800
Palembang	787,187	873,900
Ujung Pandang (Makassar)	709,038	840,500
Malang	511,780	547,100
Padang	480,922	656,800
Surakarta	469,888	490,900
Yogyakarta	398,727	420,700
Banjarmasin	381,286	423,600
Pontianak	304,778	342,700

* Revised official estimates for 31 December.

BIRTHS AND DEATHS (UN estimates, annual averages)

	1970–75	1975–80	1980–85
Birth rate (per 1,000)	41.4	36.4	32.1
Death rate (per 1,000)	17.3	15.1	12.6

Source: UN, *World Population Prospects: Estimates and Projections as Assessed in 1984*.

ECONOMICALLY ACTIVE POPULATION (ISIC Major Divisions, survey of 31 October 1985, including East Timor)

	Males	Females	Total
Agriculture, hunting, forestry and fishing	22,074,219	12,067,590	34,141,809
Mining and quarrying	346,157	69,355	415,512
Manufacturing	3,170,142	2,625,777	5,795,919
Electricity, gas and water	64,966	4,749	69,715
Construction	2,043,370	52,207	2,095,577
Trade, restaurants and hotels	4,577,378	4,767,832	9,345,210
Transport, storage and communications	1,933,707	24,626	1,958,333
Financing, insurance, real estate and business services	201,497	48,984	250,481
Community, social and personal services	5,506,915	2,810,370	8,317,285
Activities not adequately defined	32,243	35,054	67,297
Total employed	39,950,594	22,506,544	62,457,138
Unemployed	898,057	470,420	1,368,477
Total labour force	40,848,651	22,976,964	63,825,615

INDONESIA

Agriculture

PRINCIPAL CROPS ('000 metric tons)

	1984	1985	1986
Rice (paddy)	38,136	39,033	39,275
Maize	5,288	4,330	5,767
Potatoes	372	364	350*
Sweet potatoes	2,157	2,161	2,287
Cassava (Manioc)	14,159	14,057	13,329
Other roots and tubers	311	351	300
Pulses	387	334*	354*
Soybeans	769	870	1,233
Groundnuts (in shell)†	762	754	844
Coconuts*	10,700	11,600	11,650
Copra	1,101	1,260	1,300†
Palm kernels	280.6	252.2	243.7
Vegetables	3,093	3,610	3,543*
Bananas	2,759	1,700*	1,900*
Other fruit	4,334	3,867*	3,980*
Sugar cane*	22,957	24,922	25,500
Coffee (green)	331	311	399
Tea (made)	126	132	121
Tobacco (leaves)	109	165	170
Natural rubber	1,041	1,057	1,016

* FAO estimate. † Unofficial estimate.
Source: FAO, *Production Yearbook*.

LIVESTOCK ('000 head, year ending September)

	1984	1985	1986
Cattle	6,543	6,480	6,465
Sheep	4,790	4,940	5,193
Goats	11,947	12,117	12,289
Pigs	5,112	5,371	5,643
Horses	659	696	702
Buffaloes	2,743	2,838	2,936

Chickens (million): 307 in 1984; 331 in 1985; 375 in 1986.
Ducks (million): 25 in 1984; 24 in 1985; 27 in 1986.
Source: FAO, *Production Yearbook*.

LIVESTOCK PRODUCTS ('000 metric tons)

	1984	1985	1986
Beef and veal	168	179	190
Buffalo meat	48	49	49
Mutton and lamb	35	25*	25*
Goats' meat	48	50	51
Pig meat	119	133	149
Poultry meat	233	265	280
Cows' milk	179	210	220
Hen eggs	272.3	294.1	344.3
Other poultry eggs	82.1	77.3	87.5
Cattle and buffalo hides	34.7	36.5	38.3

Note: Figures for meat refer to inspected production only, i.e. from animals slaughtered under government supervision.
* FAO estimate.
Source: FAO, *Production Yearbook*.

Forestry

ROUNDWOOD REMOVALS ('000 cubic metres, excluding bark)

	1984	1985	1986
Sawlogs, veneer logs and logs for sleepers:			
Coniferous*	384	330	351
Non-coniferous	26,958	23,500	25,000†
Pulpwood*	200	200	200
Other industrial wood*	2,535	2,585	2,631
Fuel wood*	124,895	127,356	129,587
Total	154,972	153,970	157,768

* FAO estimates. † Unofficial estimate.
Source: FAO, *Yearbook of Forest Products*.

SAWNWOOD PRODUCTION ('000 cubic metres, including boxboards)

	1984	1985	1986*
Coniferous (soft wood)*	13	14	13
Broadleaved (hard wod)	6,600	7,065	7,037
Total	6,613	7,079	7,050

* FAO estimates.
Railway sleepers (FAO estimates, '000 cubic metres): 7 per year.
Source: FAO, *Yearbook of Forest Products*.

Fishing

('000 metric tons, live weight)

	1984	1985	1986
Carps, barbels, etc.	120.4	127.9	132.3
Other freshwater fishes (incl. unspecified)	291.3	300.1	308.5
Milkfish	84.4	93.5	103.2
Other diadromous fishes	16.3	17.6	19.5
Scads	135.3	172.5	190.0
Goldstripe sardinella	109.4	108.5	109.0
Bali sardinella	79.4	54.0	77.7
'Stolephorus' anchovies	109.3	106.9	111.8
Skipjack tuna	80.7	87.4	98.5
Other tunas, bonitos, billfishes, etc.	182.3	192.8	206.6
Indian mackerels	114.3	125.0	132.0
Other marine fishes (incl. unspecified)	708.8	731.6	788.7
Total fish	2,031.7	2,118.0	2,277.7
Marine shrimps, prawns, etc.	132.9	144.1	154.0
Other crustaceans	20.2	23.6	20.6
Molluscs	64.5	47.6	59.4
Other aquatic animals	2.5	5.8	9.4
Total catch	2,251.9	2,339.1	2,521.2
Inland waters	548.2	580.3	607.0
Indian Ocean	168.7	147.6	170.1
Pacific Ocean	1,535.0	1,611.1	1,744.0

Aquatic plants ('000 metric tons): 9.1 in 1984; 6.0 in 1985; 8.6 in 1986.
Source: FAO, *Yearbook of Fishery Statistics*.

INDONESIA   *Statistical Survey*

Mining

(metric tons, unless otherwise indicated)

	1985	1986	1987
Crude petroleum ('000 barrels)	483,645	507,288	479,040
Natural gas ('000 million cu ft)	1,577,790	1,628,859	1,731,083
Bauxite	830,471	648,815	635,309
Coal	1,491,652	1,725,356	1,886,974
Nickel ore*	955,604	1,533,094	1,825,716
Copper*	233,446	251,229	258,836
Tin	22,413	24,049	26,093
Gold (kg)	234.4	202.2	138.7
Silver (kg)	2,151.8	2,428.6	3,297.2

* Figures refer to gross weight. In 1985 the metal content (in metric tons) was: Nickel 22,934; Copper 74,300.

Industry

SELECTED PRODUCTS
('000 metric tons, unless otherwise indicated)

	1984	1985	1986
Wheat flour	1,074	1,191	1,151
Refined sugar	1,573	1,677	1,874
Cotton yarn ('000 bales)*	1,281	1,395	1,553
Nitrogenous fertilizers	2,462	2,877	2,909
Cement	6,693	10,477	11,088
Cigarettes (million)	102,897	119,236	114,312
Tyres ('000)†	3,336	3,899	4,480
Kerosene ('000 barrels)	39,141.4	38,382.9	43,043.3
Jet fuel ('000 barrels)	4,923.0	3,845.3	1,561.4
Distillate fuel oils ('000 barrels)	43,934.5	50,059.9	55,846.3
Residual fuel oils ('000 barrels)	67,281.6	44,716.5	47,814.4
Aluminium	206.9	216.8	n.a.
Radio receivers ('000)	933	1,014	966
Television receivers ('000)	517	565	539
Motor vehicles—assembly ('000)	167	142	168

* Including synthetic yarn.   † For motor cars only.

Palm oil ('000 metric tons): 1,132 in 1984; 1,230 in 1985; 1,298 in 1986 (Source: FAO).

Motor spirit ('000 metric tons): 2,271 in 1984; 3,234 in 1985 (Source: UN, *Industrial Statistics Yearbook*).

Tin (primary metal, metric tons): 22,467 in 1984; 20,418 in 1985; 22,080 in 1986 (Source: International Tin Council).

Finance

CURRENCY AND EXCHANGE RATES

Monetary Units
100 sen = 1 rupiah (Rp.).

Denominations
Coins: 5, 10, 25, 50 and 100 rupiahs.
Notes: 100, 500, 1,000, 5,000 and 10,000 rupiahs.

Sterling and Dollar Equivalents (30 September 1988)
£1 sterling = 2,884.8 rupiahs;
US $1 = 1,706.0 rupiahs;
10,000 rupiahs = £3.466 = $5.862.

Average Exchange Rate (rupiahs per US $)
1985 1,110.6
1986 1,282.6
1987 1,643.8

BUDGET ESTIMATES
('000 million rupiahs, year ending 31 March)

Revenue	1986/87	1987/88	1988/89
Petroleum and natural gas	9,738.2	6,938.6	5,855.8
Other tax receipts	7,140.4	9,133.9	11,687.9
Income tax	2,880.5	3,315.9	3,762.1
Sales tax	2,143.3	3,546.0	4,787.6
Import tax and excise tax	1,634.8	1,737.6	2,399.8
Export tax	78.8	70.9	144.4
Other taxes	403.0	463.5	594.0
Non-tax receipts	953.9	1,163.6	1,259.3
Total domestic receipts	17,832.5	17,236.1	21,803.0
Foreign aid receipts	3,589.1	5,547.0	7,160.6
Programme aid	81.4	121.3	1,163.0
Project aid and export credits	3,507.7	5,425.7	5,997.6
Total	21,421.6	22,783.1	28,963.6

Expenditure	1986/87	1987/88	1988/89
Personal emoluments	4,212.6	4,316.9	4,816.3
Salaries and pensions	3,211.1	3,276.1	3,739.2
Rice allowances	482.5	482.5	482.5
Food allowances	313.3	315.0	323.2
Other remunerations	116.6	118.0	140.8
Missions abroad	89.1	125.3	130.6
Purchases of goods	1,366.5	1,175.1	1,333.2
Domestic products	1,296.7	1,086.2	1,222.0
Foreign products	69.8	88.9	111.2
Regional subsidies	2,639.7	2,649.1	2,893.0
Personal	2,374.3	2,433.7	2,656.1
Non-personal	265.4	215.4	236.9
Debt servicing	4,223.2	6,805.4	10,648.0
Domestic debts	40.0	40.0	40.0
Foreign debts	4,183.2	6,765.4	10,608.0
Others	683.6	80.0	375.0
Total ordinary budget	13,125.6	15,026.5	20,065.5
Total development budget	8,296.0	7,756.6	8,897.6
Locally financed	4,788.3	2,330.9*	2,900.0
Project aid	3,507.7	5,425.7†	5,997.6
Total	21,421.6	22,783.1	28,963.1

* Excluding rupiah project aid.
† Including Rp. 1,006,800m. in rupiah project aid.
Source: Ministry of Finance.

DEVELOPMENT EXPENDITURE
(estimates '000 million rupiahs, year ending 31 March)

	1986/87	1987/88	1988/89
Agriculture and irrigation	1,105.5	1,180.7	1,299.5
Industry	489.3	229.7	243.4
Mining and Energy	1,036.6	1,129.1	1,217.4
Tourism and transport	1,063.3	1,288.1	1,654.4
Trade and co-operatives	116.6	132.5	147.5
Manpower and transmigration	394.5	156.7	226.0
Regional, rural and urban development	938.9	873.7	1,032.2
Religious affairs	41.9	15.6	17.8
Education, culture and youth	1,145.9	1,021.5	1,075.6
Health, family planning and social welfare	311.6	207.7	289.2
Housing and sanitation	332.7	412.0	438.3
Law enforcement	40.6	14.0	21.1
National defence and security	554.0	510.0	555.0
Information and communications	41.5	24.0	31.4
Science and technology	169.6	158.6	193.6
Armed forces and civil service	127.0	45.4	71.5
Investment through banking system	202.0	191.0	207.9
Natural resources and living conditions	189.5	166.2	175.8
Total	8,296.0	7,756.5	8,897.6

Source: Ministry of Finance.

INDONESIA

Statistical Survey

INTERNATIONAL RESERVES
(US $ million at 31 December)

	1985	1986	1987
Gold*	906	1,360	1,319
IMF special drawing rights	56	43	6
Reserve position in IMF	80	89	103
Foreign exchange	4,838	3,919	5,483
Total	5,880	5,411	6,611

* Valued at market-related prices.
Source: IMF, *International Financial Statistics*.

MONEY SUPPLY ('000 million rupiahs at 31 December)

	1985	1986	1987
Currency outside banks	4,460	5,338	5,802
Demand deposits at deposit money banks	5,560	6,082	6,776

Source: IMF, *International Financial Statistics*.

COST OF LIVING (Consumer Price Index—average of monthly figures. Base: April 1977–March 1978 = 100)

	1984	1985	1986
Food	222.8	228.2	247.8
Housing	414.7	458.1	295.3
Clothing	217.8	225.0	236.4
Miscellaneous	235.0	248.4	264.8
All items	237.2	248.4	262.9

NATIONAL ACCOUNTS ('000 million rupiahs at current prices)
National Income and Product

	1984	1985	1986
Domestic factor incomes*	81,437.6	86,938.2	86,246.1
Consumption of fixed capital	4,321.6	4,690.8	4,789.9
Gross domestic product at factor cost	85,759.2	91,692.0	91,036.0
Indirect taxes, *less* subsidies	1,295.6	2,862.5	5,453.3
GDP in purchasers' values	87,054.8	94,491.5	96,489.3
Net factor income from abroad	−4,168.2	−3,932.0	−4,250.6
Gross national product	82,886.6	90,559.5	92,238.7
Less Consumption of fixed capital	4,321.6	4,690.8	4,789.9
National income in market prices	78,565.0	85,868.7	87,448.8

* Compensation of employees and the operating surplus of enterprises. The amount is obtained as a residual.

Expenditure on the Gross Domestic Product

	1984	1985	1986
Government final consumption expenditure	9,121.5	10,893.1	11,328.7
Private final consumption expenditure	51,398.9	56,857.9	61,682.4
Increase in stocks	2,551.5	5,288.6	5,250.5
Gross fixed capital formation	19,625.5	19,618.3	20,042.8
Total domestic expenditure	82,697.1	92,657.9	98,304.4
Exports of goods and services	22,984.9	21,671.1	20,041.7
Less Imports of goods and services	18,627.2	19,837.5	21,856.8
GDP in purchasers' values	87,054.8	94,491.5	96,489.3

Gross Domestic Product by Economic Activity

	1984	1985	1986
Agriculture, forestry and fishing	20,333.9	22,412.0	24,921.6
Mining and quarrying	15,985.8	15,403.6	10,740.9
Manufacturing	11,081.6	12,713.3	13,899.9
Electricity, gas and water	655.2	781.3	858.0
Construction	4,756.8	5,301.8	5,242.6
Wholesale and retail trade	13,973.5	14,561.4	16,081.2
Transport and communications	5,112.5	6,149.0	6,392.0
Finance, insurance and real estate	2,691.8	2,802.4	3,279.5
Government services	3,717.9	3,998.6	4,134.8
Ownership of dwellings	2,275.9	2,443.0	2,631.5
Public administration	6,469.9	7,925.1	8,307.3
Total	87,054.8	94,491.5	96,489.3

BALANCE OF PAYMENTS (US $ million)

	1985	1986	1987
Merchandise exports f.o.b.	18,527	14,396	17,206
Merchandise imports f.o.b.	−12,705	−11,938	−12,710
Trade balance	5,822	2,458	4,496
Exports of services	1,612	1,576	1,610
Imports of services	−9,445	−8,204	−8,484
Balance on goods and services	−2,011	−4,170	−2,378
Private unrequited transfers (net)	61	71	86
Government unrequited transfers (net)	27	188	142
Current balance	−1,923	−3,911	−2,150
Direct capital investment (net)	310	258	307
Other long-term capital (net)	1,570	2,624	2,265
Short-term capital (net)	−98	1,295	642
Net errors and omissions	651	−1,269	−435
Total (net monetary movements)	510	−1,003	629
Valuation changes (net)	58	75	248
Changes in reserves	568	−928	876

Source: IMF, *International Financial Statistics*.

FOREIGN AID (US $ million)*

	1984/85	1985/86
Concessionary loans from IGGI†	2,228.3	2,148.8
Bilateral	710.0	601.4
Belgium	—	6.0
Canada	21.7	—
France	26.2	23.3
Germany, Fed. Repub.	73.1	29.8
Italy	—	—
Japan	486.4	489.2
Netherlands	24.0	22.4
Switzerland	—	21.2
USA	78.6	9.5
Multilateral (international agencies)	1,518.3	1,547.4
IBRD	964.9	1,234.1
ADB	553.4	313.3
Semi-concessionary loans and commercial loans, including export credit for projects	1,260.7	951.7
Cash loans	705.1	1,864.2
Total	4,194.1	4,964.7

* Figures refer to agreed commitments to provide aid, rather than to actual disbursements.
† Inter-Governmental Group for Indonesia.
Source: Bank Indonesia.

INDONESIA

Statistical Survey

External Trade

PRINCIPAL COMMODITIES (US $ million)

Imports c.i.f.	1985	1986	1987
Food and live animals	556.1	610.0	623.8
Cereals and cereal preparations	296.1	308.5	306.4
Beverages and tobacco	20.9	28.1	32.6
Crude materials (inedible) except fuels	129.0	830.1	990.6
Mineral fuels, lubricants, etc.	1,287.7	1,106.9	1,144.0
Petroleum and petroleum products	1,275.5	1,086.3	1,067.9
Crude and partly refined petroleum	928.0	634.6	586.4
Crude petroleum	846.5	566.0	505.1
Petroleum products	347.6	451.8	481.5
Animal and vegetable oils, fats and waxes	35.6	17.9	96.9
Chemicals and related products	1,916.6	1,909.7	2,325.9
Chemical elements and compounds	820.9	860.5	978.9
Basic manufactures	1,717.9	1,668.3	1,784.9
Iron and steel	717.8	645.4	693.8
Universals, plates and sheets	379.2	383.9	364.1
Machinery and transport equipment	3,617.0	4,117.5	4,818.7
Non-electric machinery	2,335.6	2,446.3	3,183.7
Electrical machinery, apparatus, etc.	419.7	481.2	592.6
Transport equipment	861.6	1,190.0	1,042.4
Road motor vehicles and parts*	390.0	653.4	710.4
Lorries and trucks (incl. ambulances)	132.7	16.6	26.2
Miscellaneous manufactured articles	331.9	389.3	469.6
Other commodities and transactions	46.5	40.6	83.3
Total	10,259.1	10,718.4	12,370.3

* Excluding tyres, engines and electrical parts.

Exports f.o.b.	1985	1986	1987
Food and live animals	1,383.1	1,773.8	1,683.8
Coffee, tea, cocoa and spices	900.9	1,190.8	963.4
Coffee (incl. extracts, etc.)	561.9	821.7	538.7
Beverages and tobacco	48.7	68.7	71.9
Crude materials (inedible) except fuels	1,403.1	1,473.1	1,959.9
Crude rubber, etc.	718.4	713.2	960.5
Wood, lumber and cork	243.7	281.4	415.7
Rough or roughly squared wood	6.8	0.0	0.0
Metalliferous ores and metal scrap	266.4	306.5	308.4
Non-ferrous ores and concentrates	266.0	300.7	305.9
Mineral fuels, lubricants, etc.	12,757.3	8,309.6	8,981.9
Petroleum and petroleum products	9,083.4	5,501.0	6,156.9
Crude petroleum	8,251.3	4,593.3	5,040.4
Petroleum products	832.0	907.7	1,116.5
Residual fuel oils	424.1	671.9	765.0
Gas (natural and manufactured)	3,634.5	2,775.6	2,399.0
Animal and vegetable oils, fats and waxes	414.1	165.7	290.2
Chemicals and related products	210.0	260.3	251.0
Basic manufactures	1,804.4	1,984.4	3,267.2
Wood and cork manufactures (excl. furniture)	952.3	1,139.7	1,922.8
Non-ferrous metals	505.6	346.8	412.1
Tin	240.5	148.7	155.4

Exports f.o.b.—*continued*	1985	1986	1987
Machinery and transport equipment	98.0	62.6	57.1
Miscellaneous manufactured articles	437.0	678.1	731.8
Other commodities and transactions	30.9	28.8	274.8
Total	18,586.7	14,805.0	17,569.6

PRINCIPAL TRADING PARTNERS (US $ million)

Imports	1985	1986	1987
Australia	460.5	413.5	462.7
Canada	198.1	214.3	303.0
China, People's Republic	248.9	337.1	408.4
France	284.4	280.7	392.0
Germany, Fed. Republic	677.1	719.1	840.0
Japan	2,644.4	3,128.2	3,596.1
Korea, Republic	205.0	159.0	268.4
Netherlands	215.1	189.3	316.1
Saudi Arabia	882.4	638.7	630.5
Singapore	839.1	968.8	946.8
Taiwan	290.7	409.0	458.8
Thailand	47.9	72.2	75.4
United Kingdom	300.4	341.7	324.8
USA	1,720.9	1,482.4	1,415.1
Total (incl. others)	10,259.1	10,718.4	12,370.3

Exports	1985	1986	1987
Australia	149.2	158.6	309.8
Germany, Fed. Republic	254.9	334.2	361.1
Hong Kong	348.4	345.2	419.6
Italy	152.0	151.8	174.9
Japan	8,593.5	6,644.1	7,393.3
Korea, Republic	656.2	355.5	673.3
Netherlands	392.0	452.6	493.4
Philippines	198.6	108.3	71.4
Singapore	1,625.6	1,238.9	1,449.2
Taiwan	353.7	316.6	473.7
Trinidad and Tobago	311.5	70.3	0.0
United Kingdom	191.4	196.6	212.4
USA	4,040.2	2,901.5	3,348.7
Total (incl. others)	18,586.7	14,805.0	17,569.6

Transport

RAILWAYS (traffic)

	1984	1985	1986
Passenger-km (million)	6,379	6,774	7,327
Freight ton-km (million)	1,173	1,333	1,465

ROAD TRAFFIC (motor vehicles registered at 31 December)

	1985	1986	1987
Passenger cars	990,651	1,063,959	1,170,103
Lorries and trucks	845,338	882,331	953,694
Buses and coaches	227,304	256,574	303,378
Motor cycles	4,794,517	5,118,907	5,554,305

INDONESIA

INTERNATIONAL SEA-BORNE SHIPPING

	1983	1984	1985
Goods loaded ('000 metric tons)	88,687	97,731	91,781
Goods unloaded ('000 metric tons)	56,944	60,097	63,417
Merchant shipping fleet* ('000 grt)		1,950	1,857	n.a.

* At 30 June.

CIVIL AVIATION (traffic on scheduled services)

	1983	1984	1985
Kilometres flown (million)	129.7	142.0	120.0
Passengers carried ('000)	6,205	6,694	6,285
Passenger-km (million)	8,419	9,402	9,529
Freight ton-km (million)	167.2	169.8	146.2

Tourism

	1982	1983	1984
Visitors ('000)	592.0	638.9	683.0
Receipts (US $ million)	358.8	440.0	519.0

Source: Directorate General of Tourism.
1986: 693,447 visitors; **1987:** 1,060,347 visitors.

Communications Media

	1984	1985	1986
Television receivers (registered)	5,699,487	5,971,724	6,103,579
Telephones (registered)	788,365	717,990	784,836

Education

(1987/88)

	Schools	Teachers	Pupils and Students
Primary	144,561	1,107,100	26,649,890
General secondary	26,246	572,362	8,797,795
Technological	1,142	34,384	449,101

Source: Department of Education and Culture.

Directory

The Constitution

Indonesia had three provisional constitutions: in August 1945, February 1950 and August 1950. In July 1959 the Constitution of 1945 was re-enacted by presidential decree. The General Elections Law of 1969 supplemented the 1945 Constitution, which has been adopted permanently by the People's Consultative Assembly. The following is a summary of its main provisions:

GENERAL PRINCIPLES

The 1945 Constitution consists of 37 articles, four transitional clauses and two additional provisions, and is preceded by a preamble. The preamble contains an indictment of all forms of colonialism, an account of Indonesia's struggle for independence, the declaration of that independence and a statement of fundamental aims and principles. Indonesia's National Independence, according to the text of the preamble, has the state form of a Republic, with sovereignty residing in the People, and is based upon the *Pancasila*:

1. Belief in the One Supreme God.
2. Just and Civilized Humanity.
3. The Unity of Indonesia.
4. Democracy led by the wisdom of deliberations (*musyawarah*) among representatives.
5. Social Justice for all the people of Indonesia.

STATE ORGANS

Majelis Permusyawaratan Rakyat—MPR (People's Consultative Assembly)

Sovereignty is in the hands of the People and is exercised in full by the People's Consultative Assembly as the embodiment of the whole Indonesian People. The Consultative Assembly is the highest authority of the State, and is to be distinguished from the legislative body proper (Dewan Perwakilan Rakyat, see below) which is incorporated within the Consultative Assembly. The Consultative Assembly, with a total of 1,000 members, is composed of all members of the Dewan, augmented by delegates from the regions, members of political organizations (including members of the armed forces belonging to Golkar), and representatives of other groups. The Assembly sits at least once every five years, and its primary competence is to determine the constitution and the broad lines of the policy of the State and the Government. It also elects the President and Vice-President, who are responsible for implementing that policy. All decisions are taken unanimously in keeping with the traditions of *musyawarah*.

The President

The highest executive of the Government, the President, holds office for a term of five years and may be re-elected. As Mandatory of the MPR he must execute the policy of the State according to the Decrees determined by the MPR during its Fourth General and Special Sessions. In conducting the administration of the State, authority and responsibility are concentrated in the President. The Ministers of the State are his assistants and are responsible only to him.

Dewan Perwakilan Rakyat—DPR (House of Representatives)

The legislative branch of the State, the House of Representatives, sits at least once a year. It has 500 members: 100 nominated by the President and 400 directly elected. Every statute requires the approval of the DPR. Members of the House of Representatives have the right to submit draft bills which require ratification by the President, who has the right of veto. In times of emergency the President may enact ordinances which have the force of law, but such Ordinances must be ratified by the House of Representatives during the following session or be revoked.

Dewan Pertimbangan Agung—DPA (Supreme Advisory Council)

The DPA is an advisory body assisting the President who chooses its members from political parties, functional groups and groups of prominent persons.

Mahkamah Agung (Supreme Court)

The judicial branch of the State, the Supreme Court and the other courts of law are independent of the Executive in exercising their judicial powers.

Badan Pemeriksa Keuangan (Supreme Audit Board)

Controls the accountability of public finance, enjoys investigatory powers and is independent of the Executive. Its findings are presented to the DPR.

INDONESIA
Directory

The Government

HEAD OF STATE

President: SUHARTO (inaugurated 27 March 1968; re-elected March 1973, March 1978, March 1983 and March 1988).
Vice-President: Gen. SUDHARMONO.

CABINET
(January 1989)

Minister of Home Affairs, concurrently Chairman of the Election Committee: Gen. RUDINI.
Minister of Foreign Affairs: ALI ALATAS.
Minister of Defence and Security: Gen. L. B. MURDANI.
Minister of Justice: ISMAIL SALEH.
Minister of Information: HARMOKO.
Minister of Finance: Prof. Dr JOHANNES B. SUMARLIN.
Minister of Trade: Dr ARIFIN M. SIREGAR.
Minister of Co-operatives: BUSTANIL ARIFIN.
Minister of Agriculture: Dr WARDOYO.
Minister of Forestry: Dr HASRUL HARAHAP.
Minister of Industry: HARTARTO.
Minister of Mining and Energy: Dr GINANDJAR KARTASASMITA.
Minister of Public Works: RADINAL MOCHTAR.
Minister of Communications: AZWAR ANAS.
Minister of Tourism, Posts and Telecommunications: Gen. SUSILO SUDARMAN.
Minister of Manpower: COSMAS BATUBARA.
Minister of Transmigration: SUGIARTO.
Minister of Education and Culture: Prof. FUAD HASSAN.
Minister of Health: ADHYATMA.
Minister of Religious Affairs: Haji MUNAWIR SJADZALI.
Minister of Social Affairs: Mrs HARYATI SUBADIO.
Minister-Co-ordinator for Political Affairs and Security: Adm. SUDOMO.
Minister-Co-ordinator for the Economy, Finance, Industry and Development Supervision: RADIUS PRAWIRO.
Minister-Co-ordinator for Public Welfare: SUPARDJO RUSTAM.
Minister of State and State Secretary: Maj.-Gen. MURDIONO.
Minister of State for National Development Planning, concurrently Chairman of the National Development Planning Board: Dr SALEH AFIF.
Minister of State for Research and Technology, concurrently Chairman of the Board for the Study and Application of Technology: Prof. Dr BUCHARUDDIN JUSUF HABIBIE.
Minister of State for Population and the Environment: Prof. Dr EMIL SALIM.
Minister of State for Public Housing: SISWONO JUDO HUSODO.
Minister of State for Youth and Sports: AKBAR TANJUNG.
Minister of State for State Administrative Reforms, concurrently Vice-Chairman of the National Development Planning Board: SARWONO KUSUMAATMADJA.
Minister of State for Women's Affairs: Mrs A. SULASIKIN MURPRATOMO.
Junior Minister and Cabinet Secretary: SAADILAH MURSJID.
There are five other Junior Ministers.

Officials with the rank of Minister of State:
Attorney-General: SUKARTON MARMOSUDJONO.
Governor of Bank Indonesia: ADRIANUS MOOY.
Commander-in-Chief of the Indonesian Armed Forces: Gen. TRY SUTRISNO.

MINISTRIES

Office of the President: Istana Merdeka, Jakarta; tel. (021) 331097.
Office of the Vice-President: Jalan Merdeka Selatan 6, Jakarta; tel. (021) 363539.
Office of the Attorney-General: Jalan Sultan Hasanuddin 1, Jakarta; tel. (021) 773557.
Office of the Cabinet Secretary: Jalan Veteran 18, Jakarta Pusat; tel. (021) 348531.
Office of Co-ordinating Minister for Political Affairs and Security: Jalan Merdeka Barat 15, Jakarta; tel. (021) 376004.
Office of the Minister of State for the Role of Women: Jalan Merdeka Barat 15, Jakarta Pusat 10110; tel. (021) 3805563.
Ministry of Agriculture: Jalan Harsono Room 3, Ragunan Pasar Minggu, Jakarta Selatan; tel. (021) 783006.
Ministry of Communications: Jalan Merdeka Barat 8, Jakarta 10110; tel. (021) 366332; telex 46116.
Ministry of Co-operatives: Jalan Mohd Ikhwan Ridwan Rais 5, Jakarta; tel. (021) 357758.
Ministry of Defence and Security: Jalan Merdeka Barat 13, Jakarta Pusat; tel. (021) 374408.
Ministry of the Economy, Finance, Industry and Development Supervision: Jalan Lapangan Banteng Timur 4, Jakarta; tel. (021) 365079.
Ministry of Education and Culture: Jalan Jenderal Sudirman, Senayan, Jakarta Pusat; tel. (021) 581618.
Ministry of Finance: Jalan Lapangan Banteng Timur 4, Jakarta Pusat; tel. (021) 348938.
Ministry of Foreign Affairs: Jalan Taman Pejambon 6, Jakarta Pusat; tel. (021) 368014.
Ministry of Forestry: Gedung Pusat Kehutanan, Senayan, Jakarta Selatan; tel. (021) 581820.
Ministry of Health: Jalan Hr. Rasuna Said Blx 5, No. Kav. 49, Jakarta Pusat; tel. (021) 5201595.
Ministry of Home Affairs: Jalan Merdeka Utara 7, Jakarta Pusat; tel. (021) 373908.
Ministry of Industry: Jalan Jenderal Gatot Subroto Kav. 52-53, Jakarta; tel. (021) 511661.
Ministry of Information: Jalan Merdeka Barat 9, Jakarta Pusat; tel. (021) 377408; telex 44264.
Ministry of Justice: Jalan Hr. Rasuna Said No. Kav. 4/5, Jakarta Pusat; tel. (021) 513004.
Ministry of Manpower: Jalan Jenderal Gatot Subroto, Jakarta Pusat; tel. (021) 515717.
Ministry of Mining and Energy: Jalan Merdeka Selatan 18, Jakarta Pusat; tel. (021) 360232.
Ministry of National Development Planning: Jalan Taman Suropati 2, Jakarta Pusat; tel. (021) 336207; telex 61623.
Ministry for Population and the Environment: Jalan Medan Merdeka Barat 15, Jakarta Pusat; tel. (021) 371295; telex 46143.
Ministry of Public Housing: Jalan Kebon Sirih 31, Jakarta Pusat; tel. (021) 333649.
Ministry of Public Welfare: Jalan Merdeka Barat 3, Jakarta Pusat; tel. (021) 353055.
Ministry of Public Works: Jalan Pattimura 20, Kebayoran Baru, 12110 Jakarta Selatan; tel. (021) 717564; telex 47247.
Ministry of Religious Affairs: Jalan M. H. Thamrin 6, Jakarta Pusat; tel. (021) 320135.
Ministry of Research and Technology: Gedung Menara Patra, 3rd Floor, Jalan M. H. Thamrin 8, Jakarta Pusat; tel. (021) 324767.
Ministry of Social Affairs: Jalan Ir H. Juanda 36, Jakarta Pusat; tel. (021) 341329.
Ministry for State Administrative Reforms: Jalan Taman Suropati 2, Jakarta Pusat; tel. (021) 334811.
Office of the State Secretary: Perpustakaan, Dewan Perwakilan Rakyat-R.I., Jalan Jenderal Gatot Subroto, Senayan, Jakarta.
Ministry of Tourism, Posts and Telecommunications: Jalan Kebon Sirih 36, Jakarta; tel. (021) 346855.
Ministry of Trade: Jalan Mohd Ikhwan Ridwan Rais 5, Jakarta; tel. (021) 348667.
Ministry of Transmigration: Jalan Letjen. Haryono MT, Cikoko, Jakarta Selatan; tel. (021) 794682.
Ministry of Youth and Sports: Jalan Jenderal Sudirman, Senayan, Jakarta Pusat; tel. (021) 581986.
Directorate-General of Tourism: Jalan Kramatraya 81; tel. (021) 359001.

Legislature

MAJELIS PERMUSYAWARATAN RAKYAT—MPR
(People's Consultative Assembly)

The Assembly consists of the members of the House of Representatives, regional delegates, members of political organizations (including members of the Armed Forces belonging to Golkar), and representatives of other groups. In 1987 the membership of the Assembly was expanded to 1,000.

Chairman: KHARIS SUHUD.

INDONESIA   *Directory*

	Seats
Members of the House of Representatives	500
Regional representatives*	147
Political organizations†	253
Others	100
Total	1,000

* To be a minimum of four, and a maximum of eight, representatives from each region.
† Including members of the Armed Forces belonging to Golkar. Organizations are represented on a proportional basis, according to the composition of the House of Representatives.

Dewan Perwakilan Rakyat—DPR
(House of Representatives)

In March 1960 a presidential decree prorogued the elected Council of Representatives and replaced it by a nominated House of 283 members (increased to 460 in 1968). Subsequently, the number of appointed members was reduced to 96. The remaining 364 were directly elected. In 1987, as a result of an increase in the size of the electorate, the House of Representatives was expanded from 460 to 500 members; of these, 100 members were nominated by the President and 400 directly elected.

Speaker: KHARIS SUHUD.

General Election, 23 April 1987

	Seats
Golkar	299
Partai Persatuan Pembangunan	61
Partai Demokrasi Indonesia	40
Appointed members*	100
Total	500

*Members of the political wing of the Indonesian Armed Forces (ABRI).

Political Organizations

A presidential decree of January 1960 enables the President to dissolve any party whose membership does not cover one-quarter of Indonesia, or whose policies are at variance with the aims of the State.
The following parties and groups participated in the general election held in April 1987:

Sekretariat Bersama Golongan Karya (Sekber Golkar) (Joint Secretariat of Functional Groups): Jalan Anggrek Nelimurni, Jakarta 11480; tel. 5481618; telex 62147; f. 1964; reorg. 1971; the governing alliance of groups representing farmers, fishermen and the professions; Pres. and Chair. of Advisory Bd SUHARTO; Gen. Chair. Gen. (retd) WAHONO; Sec.-Gen. RACHMAT WITOELAR.

Partai Demokrasi Indonesia (PDI) (Indonesian Democratic Party): Jakarta; f. 1973 by the merger of five nationalist and Christian parties; Gen. Chair. SURYADI; Sec.-Gen. NICO DARYANTO.

Partai Persatuan Pembangunan (PPP) (United Development Party): Jalan Diponegoro 60, Jakarta; tel. 356381; f. 1973 by the merger of four Islamic parties (Nahdatul Ulama—NU, Sarikat Islam, Perti and Muslimin Indonesia—MI); Pres. JAILANI NARO; Sec.-Gen. MARDINSYAH.

The following groups are in conflict with the Government:

Frente Revolucionário de Este Timor Independente (Fretilin): based in East Timor; f. 1974; seeks independence for East (fmrly Portuguese) Timor; entered into alliance with the UDT in 1986; c. 13,000 mems in 1987; Sec. for International Relations JOSÉ RAMOS HORTA; Mil. Commdr JOSÉ XANANA GUSMÃO.

Organisasi Papua Merdeka (OPM) (Free Papua Movement): based in Irian Jaya; f. 1963; seeks unification with Papua New Guinea; Leader ELKY BEMEI.

União Democrática Timorense (UDT): based in Dili, East Timor; f. 1974; advocates self-determination for East Timor through a gradual process in which ties with Portugal would be maintained; allied itself with Fretilin in 1986.

Diplomatic Representation

EMBASSIES IN INDONESIA

Afghanistan: Jalan Dr Kusuma Atmaja 15, Jakarta; tel. (021) 333169; Chargé d'affaires: MUHAMMAD RAHIM ROHEEN.

Algeria: Jl. H. R. Rasuna Said Kav. 10-1, Kuningan, Jakarta; tel. 514719; Ambassador: MUHAMMAD KESSOURI.

Argentina: Jalan Panarukan 17, Jakarta 10310; tel. (021) 338088; telex 45529; Ambassador: OMAR RICARDO DEL AZAR SUAYA.

Australia: Jalan M. H. Thamrin 15, Jakarta; tel. (021) 323109; Ambassador: BILL MORRISON.

Austria: Jalan Diponegoro 44, Jakarta 10310; tel. (021) 338101; telex 46387; Ambassador: Dr ERNST ILLSINGER.

Bangladesh: Jalan Mendut 3, Jakarta; tel. (021) 324850; Ambassador: Maj.-Gen. MOINUL HUSSEIN CHOWDHURY.

Belgium: Wisma BCA, 15th Floor, Jalan Jendral Sudirman 22–23, Jakarta 12920; tel. (021) 5780510; telex 44413; Ambassador: NESTOR COCKX.

Brazil: Jalan Cik Ditiro 39, Menteng, Jakarta 10310; tel. (021) 358378; telex 45657; Ambassador: ANDRÉ GUIMARÃES.

Bulgaria: Jalan Imam Bonjol 34/36, Jakarta 10310; tel. (021) 346725; telex 45106; Ambassador: OGNYAN MITEV.

Burma: Jalan Haji Agus Salim 109, Jakarta; tel. (021) 320440; Ambassador: U THAN HLA.

Canada: Wisma Metropolitan, 5th Floor, Jalan Jendral Sudirman 29, POB 52/JKT, Jakarta; tel. (021) 510709; telex 62131; Ambassador: JACK WHITTLETON.

Chile: Bina Mulia Bldg (Revlon), 7th Floor, Jalan Rasuna Said Kav. 10, Jakarta 12950; tel. (021) 5201131; telex 62587; Ambassador: THOMAS AMENABAR VERGARA.

Czechoslovakia: Jalan Prof. Mohd Yamin 29, POB 319, Jakarta; tel. 344994; telex 45139; Ambassador: RICHARD KRAL.

Denmark: Denmark House, Jalan Abdul Muis 34, POB 2329, Jakarta Pusat; tel. (021) 346615; telex 44188; Ambassador: MICHAEL BENDIX.

Egypt: Jalan Teuku Umar 68, Jakarta; tel. (021) 331141; Ambassador: MUHAMMAD ALI KAMEL.

Finland: Bina Mulia Bldg, 10th Floor, Jalan H. R. Rasuna Said Kav. 10, Kuningan, Jakarta 12950; tel. (021) 516980; telex 62128; Ambassador: ERIK HEINRICHS.

France: Jalan M. H. Thamrin 20, Jakarta; tel. (021) 332807; Ambassador: LOÏC HENNEKINNE.

German Democratic Republic: Jalan Raden Saleh 56, POB 2252, Jakarta; tel. (021) 349547; telex 46463; Ambassador: SIEGFRIED KÜHNEL.

Germany, Federal Republic: Jalan M. H. Thamrin 1, Jakarta; tel. (021) 323908; telex 44333; Ambassador: THEODOR WALLAU.

Holy See: Jalan Merdeka Timur 18, POB 4227, Jakarta (Apostolic Nunciature); tel. (021) 341142; Apostolic Pro-Nuncio: FRANCESCO CANALINI.

Hungary: 36 Jalan Rasuna Said, Kav. X/3 Kuningan, 12950 Jakarta; tel. (021) 5781223; telex 46839; Ambassador: GYULA BARANYI.

India: Jalan H. R. Rasuna Said S-1, Kuningan, Jakarta; tel. (021) 5204150; telex 44260; Ambassador: R. S. KALHA.

Iran: Jalan Hos Cokroaminoto 110, Jakarta; tel. (021) 330623; Ambassador: ABDOLAZIM HASHEMI-NIK.

Iraq: Jalan Teuku Umar 38, Jakarta; tel. (021) 355017; telex 46280; Ambassador: ZAKI ABDULHAMID AL-HABBA.

Italy: Jalan Diponegoro 45, Jakarta; tel. (021) 337440; telex 61546; Ambassador: MICHELE MARTINEZ.

Japan: Jalan Mohammad Hoesni Thamrin 24, Jakarta; tel. (021) 324308; Ambassador: SUMIO EDAMURA.

Korea, Democratic People's Republic: Jalan Teuku Umar 72/74, Jakarta; tel. (021) 3100707; Ambassador: CHO SONG-BOM.

Korea, Republic: Jalan Jendral Gatot Subroto 57, Jakarta Selatan; tel. (021) 512309; Ambassador: YOUNG-SUP KIM.

Malaysia: Jalan Imam Bonjol 17, Jakarta 10310; tel. (021) 336438; telex 44445; Ambassador: Tuan Haji MUHAMMAD KHATIB BIN ABDUL HAMID.

Mexico: Jalan M. H. Thamrin 59, Jakarta; tel. (021) 337974; Ambassador: GUILLERMO CORONA MUÑOZ.

Netherlands: Jalan H. R. Rasuna Said, Kav. S-3, Kuningan, Jakarta 12950; tel. (021) 511515; telex 62411; Ambassador: Baron G. W. DE VOS VAN STEENWIJK.

New Zealand: Jalan Diponegoro 41, Menteng, POB 2439, Jakarta; tel. (021) 330680; telex 46109; Ambassador: GORDON PARKINSON.

Nigeria: 34 Jalan Diponegoro, Jakarta; tel. (021) 345484; telex 44580; Ambassador: (vacant).

Norway: Bina Mulia Bldg, 4th Floor, Jalan H. R. Rasuna Said Kav. 10, Jakarta 12950; tel. (021) 511990; telex 62127; Ambassador: TOROLF RAA.

Pakistan: Jalan Teuku Umar 50, Jakarta; tel. (021) 350576; Ambassador: MATAHAR HUSEIN.

INDONESIA

Papua New Guinea: Panin Bank Centre, 1 Jalan Jendral Sudirman, Jakarta; tel. (021) 711225; Ambassador: SEBULON KULU.

Philippines: Jalan Imam Bonjol 6–8, Jakarta; tel. (021) 3100334; Ambassador: Brig.-Gen. RAMON FAROLAN.

Poland: Jalan Diponegoro 65, Jakarta; tel. (021) 320509; Ambassador: PAWEL CIESLAR.

Romania: Jalan Cik Ditiro 42A, Jakarta; tel. (021) 3106240; telex 61208; Ambassador: VALERIU GEORGESCU.

Saudi Arabia: Jalan Imam Bonjol 3, Jakarta; tel. (021) 346342; Ambassador: MUHAMMAD SAID BASRAWI.

Singapore: Jalan Proklamasi 23, Jakarta; tel. (021) 348761; Ambassador: J. F. CONCEICAO.

Spain: Wisma Kosgoro 12A, Jalan M. H. Thamrin 53, Jakarta; tel. (021) 325996; telex 45667; Ambassador: JOSÉ ANTONIO ACEBAL Y MONFORT.

Sri Lanka: Jalan Diponegoro 70, Jakarta; tel. (021) 321018; Ambassador: RUDRA S. RAJASINGHAM.

Sweden: Jalan Taman Cut Mutiah 12, POB 2824, Jakarta 10001; tel. (021) 333061; telex 61452; Ambassador: KARL GÖRAN ENGSTRÖM.

Switzerland: Jalan H. R. Rasuna Said, Blok X 3/2, Kuningang, 12950 Jakarta Selatan; tel. (021) 516061; telex 44113; Ambassador: BERNARD FREYMOND.

Syria: Jalan Gondangdia Lama 38, Jakarta; tel. (021) 359261; Ambassador: NADIM DOUAY.

Thailand: Jalan Imam Bonjol 74, Jakarta; tel. (021) 343762; Ambassador: RONGPET SUBHARITIKUL.

Turkey: Jalan R. S. Kuningan Kav. I, Kuningan, Jakarta; tel. (021) 516258; Ambassador: METIN INEGOLLU.

USSR: Jalan M. H. Thamrin 13, Jakarta; tel. (021) 322162; Ambassador: STANISLAV I. SEMIVOLOS.

United Kingdom: Jalan M. H. Thamrin 75, Jakarta 10310; tel. (021) 330904; telex 61166; Ambassador: KELVIN WHITE.

USA: Jalan Merdeka Selatan 5, Jakarta; tel. (021) 360360; Ambassador: JOHN CAMERON MONJO (designate).

Venezuela: Central Plaza Bldg, 17th Floor, Jl. Sudirman, Jakarta; tel. (021) 516885; telex 62701; Ambassador: JESÚS GARCÍA CORONADO.

Viet-Nam: Jalan Teuku Umar 25, Jakarta; tel. (021) 347325; Ambassador: TRINH XUAN LANG.

Yugoslavia: Jalan Hos Cokroaminoto 109, Jakarta; tel. (021) 333593; telex 45149; Ambassador: Dr DJORDJE JAKOVLJEVIĆ.

Judicial System

There is one codified criminal law for the whole of Indonesia. Europeans are subject to the Code of Civil Law published in the State Gazette in 1847. For Indonesians the civil law is the uncodified customary law (*Hukum Adat*) which varies from region to region. Alien orientals (i.e. Arabs, Indians, etc.) and Chinese are subject to certain parts of the Code of Civil Law and the Code of Commerce. The work of codifying this law has started but in view of the great complexity and diversity of customary law it may be expected to take a considerable time to achieve.

Supreme Court: The final court of appeal.

Chief Justice: Lt-Gen. ALI SAID.

High Courts in Jakarta, Surabaya, Medan, Ujungpandang (Makassar), Banda Aceh, Padang, Palembang, Bandung, Semarang, Banjarmasin, Menado, Denpasar, Ambon and Jayapura deal with appeals from the District Courts.

District Courts deal with marriage, divorce and reconciliation.

Religion

All citizens are required to state their religion. In 1984 an estimated 78% of the population were Muslims, while 11% were Christians, 2% were Hindus and 5% professed adherence to tribal religions.

ISLAM

In 1987 there were an estimated 140m. Muslims in Indonesia, giving it the world's largest Islamic population.

Indonesian Ulama Council (MUI): Central Muslim organization; Chair. HASAN BASRI.

CHRISTIANITY

Persekutuan Gereja-Gereja di Indonesia (Communion of Churches in Indonesia): Jalan Salemba Raya 10, Jakarta 10430; tel. (021) 884321; f. 1950; 54 mem. churches; Chair. Rev. Dr SORITUA A. E. NABABAN; Gen. Sec. Rev. Dr FRIDOLIN UKUR.

The Roman Catholic Church

Indonesia (excluding East Timor) comprises seven archdiocese and 26 dioceses. At 31 December 1986 there were an estimate 4.23m. adherents in the country, representing about 2.6% of th total population.

East Timor comprises the single diocese of Dili, directly respons ible to the Holy See. At 31 December 1986 the territory ha an estimated 534,638 Roman Catholics (about 80% of the tota population).

Bishops' Conference: Konperensi Waligeraja Indonesia, Tamar Cut Mutiah 10, Jakarta 11/14; tel. (021) 336422; f. 1973; Pres. Mos Rev. JULIUS RIYADI DARMAATMADJA, Archbishop of Semarang.

Archbishop of Ende: Most Rev. DONATUS DJAGOM, Keuskupar Agung, Tromol Pos 210, Ende, Flores; tel. 176.

Archbishop of Jakarta: Most Rev. LEO SOEKOTO, Jalan Katedraa 7, Jakarta 10710; tel. (021) 362392.

Archbishop of Medan: Most Rev. ALFRED GONTI PIUS DATUBARA Jalan Imam Bonjol 39, 20152 Medan, Sumatra Utara; tel. (061 516647.

Archbishop of Merauke: Most Rev. JACOBUS DUIVENVOORDE, Keuskupan Agung, Merauke 99602, Irian Jaya; tel. (0971) 21011.

Archbishop of Pontianak: Most Rev. HIERONYMUS HERCULANUS BUMBUN, POB 120, Jalan A.R. Hakim 92A, Pontianak 78001, Kalimantan Barat; tel. (0561) 2382.

Archbishop of Semarang: Most Rev. JULIUS RIYADI DARMAATMADJA, Keuskupan Agung, Jalan Pandanaran 13, 50231 Semarang; tel. (024) 313025.

Archbishop of Ujung Pandang: Most Rev. FRANCIS VAN ROESSEL, Keuskupan Agung, Jalan Thamrin 5-7, Ujung Pandang; tel. (0411) 5744.

Other Christian Churches

Protestant Church in Indonesia (Gereja Protestan di Indonesia): Jalan Medan Merdeka Timur 10, Jakarta-Pusat; tel. 342895; merger of eight churches of Calvinist tradition; 2,287,000 mems, 2,896 congregations, 1,920 pastors (1985); Chair. Rev. D. J. LUMENTA.

Numerous other Protestant communities exist throughout Indonesia, mainly organized on a local basis. The largest of these (1985 memberships) are: the Batak Protestant Christian Church (1,875,143); the Christian Church in Central Sulawesi (100,000); the Christian Evangelical Church in Minahasa (730,000); the Christian Protestant Church in Indonesia (210,924); the East Java Christian Church (123,850); the Evangelical Christian Church in West Irian (360,000); the Evangelical Christian Church of Sangir-Talaud (190,000); the Indonesian Christian Church/Huria Kristen Indonesia (316,525); the Javanese Christian Churches (121,500); the Kalimantan Evangelical Church (182,217); the Karo Batak Protestant Church (164,288); the Nias Protestant Christian Church (250,000); the Protestant Church in the Moluccas (575,000); the Protestant Evangelical Church in Timor (700,000); the Simalungun Protestant Christian Church (155,000); and the Toraja Church (250,000).

The Press

PRINCIPAL DAILIES

Java

Berita Buana: Jalan Tanah Abang Dua 33-35, Jakarta Pusat 10110; tel. (021) 340011; telex 46472; f. 1970; Indonesian; Editor SUKARNO HADI WIBOWO; circ. 150,000.

Berita Yudha: Jalan Bangka II/2, 2nd Floor, Kebayoran Baru, Jakarta; tel. (021) 75286; f. 1971; Indonesian; Editor SUNARDI; circ. 50,000.

Harian Indonesia (Indonesia Rze Pao): Jalan Toko Tiga Seberang 21, POB 534, Jakarta Kota; f. 1966; Chinese; Editors Drs T. W. SLAMET, HADI WIBOWO; circ. 40,000.

Harian Umum AB: CTC Bldg, 2nd Floor, Kramat Raya 94, Jakarta Pusat; f. 1965; official armed forces journal; Dir GOENARSO; Editor-in-Chief N. SOEPANGAT; circ. 80,000.

The Indonesia Times: Jalan Letjen. S. Parman Kav. 72, POB 224, Slipi, Jakarta; tel. (021) 592403; telex 46968; f. 1974; English; Chief Editor R. P. HENDRO; circ. 35,000.

Indonesian Daily News: Surabaya; f. 1957; English; Editor HOS. NURYAHYA; circ. 10,000.

Indonesian Observer: Jalan A. M. Sangaji 11, 10001 Jakarta; tel. (021) 43334; f. 1955; English; independent; Editor (vacant); circ. 25,000.

INDONESIA

Jakarta Post: Jalan Palmerah Selatan 15B/C, Jakarta Pusat 10270; tel. (021) 5483948; telex 46327; f. 1983; English; Gen. Man. MOHAMED CHUDORI; Editor SABAM SIAGIAN; circ. 17,000.

Jawa Pos: Jalan Kembang Jepun 167, Surabaya; tel. (031) 22778; telex 31988; f. 1949; Indonesian; Chief Editor DAHLAN ISKAN; circ. 52,000.

Kedaulatan Rakyat: Jalan P. Mangkubumi 40-42, Yogyakarta; f. 1945; Indonesian; independent; Editor IMAN SUTRISNO; circ. 50,000.

Kompas: Jalan Palmerah Selatan 20-28, POB 615/DAK, Jakarta Pusat; tel. (021) 543008; telex 46327; f. 1965; Indonesian; Editor Drs JAKOB OETAMA; circ. 415,000.

Masa Kini: Jalan Suroto 16, Yogyakarta 55224; f. 1966; tel. 86662; Chief Editor H. DJARNAWI HADIKUSUMA; circ. 25,000.

Merdeka: Jalan A. M. Sangaji 11, Jakarta; tel. (021) 364858; f. 1945; Indonesian; independent; Dir and Chief Editor B. M. DIAH; circ. 130,000; publication suspended by govt order in Nov. 1987.

Pelita (Torch): Jalan Diponegoro 60, Jakarta; f. 1974; Indonesian; Muslim; Editor AKBAR TANJUNG; circ. 80,000.

Pewarta Surabaya: Jalan Karet 23, POB 85, Surabaya; f. 1905; Indonesian; Editor RADEN DJAROT SOEBIANTORO; circ. 10,000.

Pikiran Rakyat: Jalan Asia-Afrika 77, Bandung; f. 1950; independent; Editor ATANG ROSWITA; circ. 80,000.

Pos Kota: Jalan Gajah Mada 63, Jakarta; f. 1970; Indonesian; Editor H. SOFYAN LUBIS; circ. 250,000.

Pos Sore: Jalan Asemka 29/30, Jakarta; tel. (021) 24039; f. 1971; Indonesian; Editor S. ABIJASA; circ. 40,000.

Sinar Pagi: Jalan Letjen. Haryono MT 22, Jakarta Selatan; f. 1971; Indonesian; Editor C. T. SIAHAAN; circ. 25,000.

Suara Karya: Jalan Bangka 11/2, Kebayoran Baru, Jakarta; f. 1971; Indonesian; Editor SYAMSUL BASRI; circ. 100,000.

Suara Merdeka: Jalan Kaligawe Km 5, Semarang; tel. (024) 21480; telex 22269; f. 1950; Indonesian; Publr Ir BUDI SANTOSO; Editor SUWARNO; circ. 145,000.

Suara Pembaruan: Jakarta; f. 1987; fmrly known as Sinar Harapan (Ray of Hope); Publr ALBERT HASIBUAN; Editor SUTARNO.

Suara Pembaruan: Jalan Dewi Sartika 136/D, Jakarta 13630; tel. (021) 8091695; Dir ALBERT HASIBUAN; Chief Editor SETIADI TRYMAN.

Surabaya Post: Jalan AIS Nasution 1, Surayaba; tel. (031) 45523; telex 31158; f. 1953; independent; Publr Mrs TUTY AZIS; Editor A. AZIS; circ. 85,000.

Kalimantan

Banjarmasin Post: Jalan Pasar Baru 222, Banjarmasin; f. 1971; Indonesian; Chief Editor H. J. DJOK MENTAYA; circ. 50,000.

Gawi Manuntung: Jalan Pangeran Samudra 97B, Banjarmasin; f. 1972; Indonesian; Editor M. ALI SRI INDRADJAYA; circ. 5,000.

Sulawesi

Pedoman Rakyat: Jalan H. A. Mappanyukki 28, Ujungpandang; f. 1947; independent; Editor M. BASIR; circ. 30,000.

Sumatra

Analisa: Jalan Jend. A. Yani 37-43, Medan; tel. (061) 326655; telex 51326; f. 1972; Indonesian; Editor SOFFYAN; circ. 75,000.

Haluan: Jalan Damar 57 C/F, Padang; f. 1948; Editor-in-Chief RIVAI MARLAUT; circ. 40,000.

Mimbar Umum: Merah; tel. (061) 517807; telex 51905; f. 1947; Indonesian; independent; Editor MOHD LUD LUBIS; circ. 55,000.

Sinar Indonesia Baru: Jalan Brigjen. Katamso 54, ABCD Medan; f. 1970; Indonesian; Chief Editor G. M. PANGGABEAN; circ. 60,000.

Suara Rakyat Semesta: Jalan K. H. Ashari 52, Palembang; Indonesian; Editor DJADIL ABDULLAH; circ. 10,000.

Waspada: Jalan Soeprapto/Katamso 1, Medan; tel. 520858; telex 51347; f. 1947; Man. Editor PRABUDI SAID; circ. 60,000 (daily), 55,000 (Sunday).

PRINCIPAL PERIODICALS

Basis: POB 299 yk, Yogyakarta 55001; tel. (0274) 88283; f. 1951; monthly; cultural; Editor DICK HARTOKO; circ. 3,000.

Berita Negara: Jalan Pertjetakan Negara 21, Kotakpos 2111, Jakarta; f. 1951; 2 a week; official gazette.

Bobo: Jalan Palmerah Selatan 22, Jakarta 10270; tel. (021) 5483008; telex 46327; f. 1973; weekly; children's magazine; Editor TINEKE LATUMETEN; circ. 190,000.

Buana Minggu: Jalan Tanah Abang Dua 33, Jakarta Pusat 10110; tel. (021) 364190; telex 46472; weekly; Sunday; Indonesian; Editor WINOTO PARARTHO; circ. 193,450.

Budaja Djaja: Jalan Gajah Mada 104-110A, Jakarta Barat; f. 1968; cultural; independent; Editor AJIP ROSIDI; circ. 4,000.

Business News: Jalan H. Abdul Muis 70, Jakarta; tel. (021) 348207; f. 1956; 3 a week (Indonesian edn), 2 a week (English edn); Chief Editor SANJOTO SASTROMIHARDJO; circ. 15,000.

Depthnews Indonesia: Jalan Jatinegara Barat III/6, Jakarta Timur; tel. (021) 814994; f. 1972; weekly; publ. by Press Foundation of Indonesia; Editor SUMONO MUSTOFFA.

Dunia Wanita: Jalan Brigjen. Katamso 1, Medan; f. 1949; fortnightly; Indonesian; women's magazine; Chief Editor Mrs PRAPUDI SAID; circ. 10,000.

Economic Review: c/o BNI 1946, Jalan Lada 1, POB 1946 KB, Jakarta 11110; tel. (021) 6901217; telex 42680; f. 1947; quarterly; English.

Economics and Finance in Indonesia: Institute for Economic and Social Research, University of Indonesia, Jalan Raya Salemba 4, POB 295/JKT, Jakarta; quarterly; circ. 4,000.

Ekonomi Indonesia: Jalan Merdeka, Timur 11-12, Jakarta; tel. (021) 494458; monthly; English; economic journal; Editor Z. ACHMAD; circ. 20,000.

Femina: Jalan H. R. Rasuna Said, Blok B, Kav. 32-33, Jakarta Selatan; tel. (021) 513816; telex 62338; f. 1972; weekly; women's magazine; Publisher SOFJAN ALISJAHBANA; circ. 130,000.

Fokus: Jakarta; f. 1982; Editor H. S. WARDOYO; circ. 10,000.

Gema Jusani: Jalan Salemba Tengah 47, Jakarta Pusat; f. 1981; monthly; Indonesian; journal of Corps of Invalids; Editor H. ANWAN BEY; circ. 20,000.

Hai: Jalan Palmerah Selatan 22, Jakarta 10270; tel. 5483008; telex 41216; f. 1973; weekly; youth magazine; Editor ARSWENDO ATMOWILOTO.

Harian Pagi Umum (Bali Post): Jalan Kepudang 67A, Denpasar; f. 1948; weekly (Indonesian edn), monthly (English edn); Editor RAKA WIRATMA; circ. 5,000.

Horison: Jalan Gajah Mada 104-110A, Jakarta Barat; f. 1966; monthly; literary and cultural; independent; Editors MOCHTAR LUBIS, H. B. JASSIN, TAUFIC ISMAEL; circ. 4,000.

Hukum & Keadilan: Jalan Gajah Mada 110A, Jakarta Barat; f. 1974; fortnightly; independent law journal; Editors SUARDI TASRIF, SOENARDI, ADNAN BUYUNG NASUTION; circ. 3,000.

Indonesia Magazine: 20 Jalan Merdeka Barat, Jakarta; tel. (021) 352015; telex 46655; f. 1969; monthly; English; Chair. G. DWIPAYANA; Editor-in-Chief HADELY HASIBUAN; circ. 15,000.

Intisari (Digest): Jalan Palmerah Selatan 26-28, POB 615/DAK, Jakarta 11001; tel. (021) 5483008; telex 46327; f. 1963; monthly; investment and trading; Editors IRAWATI, Drs J. OETAMA; circ. 141,000.

Keluarga: Jalan Sangaji 11, Jakarta; fortnightly; women's and family magazine; Editor S. DAHONO.

Majalah Ekonomis: Jakarta; monthly; English; business; Chief Editor S. ARIFIN HUTABARAT; circ. 20,000.

Majalah Kedokteran Indonesia (Journal of the Indonesian Medical Asscn): Jalan Kesehatan 111/29, Jakarta 11/16; f. 1951; monthly; Indonesian, English.

Manglé: Jalan Lodaya 19-21, 40262 Bandung; tel. (022) 411438; f. 1957; weekly; Sundanese; Chief Editor Drs OEJANG DARAJATOEN; circ. 74,000.

Matra: Jakarta; f. 1986; monthly; men's magazine; general interest and current affairs; Editor-in-Chief FIKRI JUFRI; circ. 100,000.

Mimbar Kabinet Pembangunan: Jalan Merdeka-Barat 7, Jakarta; f. 1966; monthly; Indonesian; publ. by Dept of Information.

Mimbar Pembangunan: Jalan Merdeka-Barat 7, Jakarta; f. 1968; quarterly; Indonesian; publ. by Dept of Information.

Mimbar Penerangan: Jalan Merdeka-Barat 7, Jakarta; f. 1950; quarterly; Indonesian; publ. by Dept of Information.

Mutiara: Jalan Dewi Sartika 136D, Cawang, Jakarta Timur; general interest; Publr H. G. RORIMPANDEY.

Peraba: Bintaran Kidul 5, Yogyakarta; weekly; Indonesian and Javanese; Roman Catholic; Editor W. KARTOSOEHARSONO.

Pertani PT: Jalan Pasar Minggu, Kalibata, POB 247 KBY, Jakarta Selatan; tel. (021) 793108; telex 47249; f. 1974; monthly; Indonesian; agricultural; Pres. Dir Ir RUSLI YAHYA.

Rajawali: Jakarta; monthly; Indonesian; civil aviation and tourism; Dir R. A. J. LUMENTA; Man. Editor KARYONO ADHY.

Selecta: Kebon Kacang 29/4, Jakarta; fortnightly; illustrated; Editor SAMSUDIN LUBIS; circ. 80,000.

Sinar Jaya: Jalan Sultan Agung 67A, Jakarta Selatan; bi-weekly; agriculture; Chief Editor Ir SURYONO PROJOPRANOTO.

Tempo: Gedung Tempo, 8th Floor, Jl. H. R. Rasuna Said Kav. C-17, Jakarta; tel. (021) 5201022; telex 46777; f. 1971; weekly; Indonesian; current affairs; Editor GOENAWAN MOHAMAD; circ. 150,000.

INDONESIA

Topik: Jalan A. M. Sangaji 9-11, Jakarta; f. 1972; monthly; Indonesian; Editor B. M. Diah; circ. 10,000.

NEWS AGENCIES

Antara (Indonesian National News Agency): Wisma Antara, 19th and 20th Floors, 17 Jl. Merdeka Seletan, POB 257, Jakarta 10002; tel. (021) 344379; telex 44305; f. 1937; state radio, TV and 53 newspaper subscribers in 1987; 27 brs in Indonesia, three overseas brs; eight bulletins in Indonesian and seven in English; one European edn, one Asian edn; monitoring service of stock exchanges world-wide; photo service; Man. Dir/Editor-in-Chief Handjojo Nitimihardjo.

Kantorberita Nasional Indonesia (KNI News Service): Jalan Jatinegara Barat III/6, Jakarta Timur; tel. (021) 811003; f. 1966; independent national news agency; foreign and domestic news in Indonesian and English; Dir and Editor-in-Chief Drs Sumono Mustoffa; Exec. Editor Sudjarwo.

Foreign Bureaux

Agence France-Presse (AFP): Jalan Indramayu 18, Jakarta Pusat 10310; tel. (021) 334877; Chief Correspondent Alain Boebion.

Agencia EFE (Spain): J. L. Cilandak VI/37, Kebayoran Baru, Jakarta-Selantan, Jakarta; Bureau Chief Miriam Padilla.

Agenzia Nazionale Stampa Associata (ANSA) (Italy): Jalan Suwiryo 20 (Pav), Jakarta; tel. (021) 587422; Correspondent Louise Wanandar.

Associated Press (AP) (USA): Jalan Kebon Sirih 40 (Flat 30), POB 2056, Jakarta; tel. (021) 367690; telex 46439; Correspondent Ghafur Fadyl.

Inter Press Service (IPS) (Italy): Jalan Tambak 18, Jakarta 10320; tel. (021) 585-3948; Chief Correspondent Kalayanamitra.

Jiji Tsushin-sha (Japan): Jalan Maluku 28, Menteng, Jakarta; tel. (021) 353463; Correspondent Shigeki Yamashita.

Kyodo Tsushin (Japan): Skyline Bldg, 11th Floor, M. H. Thamrin 9, Jakarta Pusat; tel. (021) 345012; Correspondent Masayuki Kitamura.

Reuters (UK): 17th Floor, Wisma Antara, Jalan Medan Merdeka Selatan 17, POB 2318, Jakarta Pusat; tel. (021) 345011; telex 45373; Correspondent Jeremy Clift.

Telegrafnoye Agentstvo Sovetskovo Soyuza (TASS) (USSR): 7 Surabaya, Jakarta; Correspondent Yuri Sagajda.

United Press International (UPI) (USA): Wisma Antara, 14th Floor, Jalan Medan Merdeka Selatan 17, Jakarta; tel. (021) 341056; Bureau Chief John Hail.

PRESS ASSOCIATIONS

Persatuan Wartawan Indonesia (Indonesian Journalists' Asscn): Gedung Dewan Pers, 4th Floor, 34 Jalan Kebon Sirih, Jakarta 10110; tel. (021) 353131; f. 1946; 4,000 mems (Aug. 1984); Exec. Chair. Zulharmans; Gen. Sec. Atang Ruswita.

Serikat Penerbit Suratkabar (SPS) (Indonesian Newspaper Publishers' Asscn): Gedung Dewan Pers, Floor 6, Jalan Kebonsirih 34, Jakarta Pusat; f. 1946; tel. (021) 359671; Chair. D. M. Sunardi; Sec.-Gen. Muhammad Chudori.

Yayasan Pembina Pers Indonesia (Press Foundation of Indonesia): Jalan Jatinegara Barat III/6, Jakarta Timur; tel. (021) 8194994; f. 1967; Chair. Sugiarso Suroyo, Mochtar Lubis.

Publishers

Jakarta

Akadoma: Jalan Proklamasi 61, Jakarta Pusat; tel. (021) 882328; Dir Adam Saleh.

Aksara Baru: Kav. 46A, Jalan Jend. Sudirman, Blok B/5, Bendungan Hilir, Jakarta Pusat; tel. (021) 586640; f. 1972; general science and university texts; Man. H. Ali Amran.

Aries Lima: Komplex Maya Indah II, Blok B/2, Jalan Kramat Raya 3E, Jakarta Pusat; tel. (021) 367038; f. 1974; general and children's; Pres. Tuti Sundari Azmi.

Balai Pustaka: Jalan Dr Wahidin 1, POB 29, Jakarta; tel. (021) 361701; telex 45905; f. 1908; children's, literary, scientific pubis and periodicals; CEO/Pres. Drs Zakaria Idris.

Bhratara Karya Aksara: Jalan Rawabali II/5, Kawasan Industri Pulogadung, Jakarta Timur; tel. (021) 4890280; telex 49283; f. 1958; university and educational textbooks; Man. Dir Ahmad Jayusman.

Bina Aksara: Kav. 36A, Jalan Jend., Sudirman, Blok B/5, Bendungan Hilir, Jakarta Pusat; tel. (021) 586640; Man. H. Ali Amran.

Bulan Bintang: Jalan Kramat Kwitang 1/8, Jakarta 10420; tel. (021) 342883; f. 1954; religious, social science, natural and applied sciences, art; Pres. Amran Zamzami; Man. Dir Fauzi Amelz.

C. V. Haji Masagung: Jalan Kwitang 8, POB 145, Jakarta 10002; tel. (021) 330507; telex 44268; f. 1953; general, textbooks, science; Pres. M. O. Masagung.

Djambatan: Jalan Kramat Raya 152, Tromolpos 116, Jakarta Pusat; tel. (021) 345131; f. 1954; children's, textbooks, social sciences, fiction; Dir Roswitha Pamoentjak Singgih.

Dunia Pustaka Jaya: Jalan Kramat Raya 5K, Jakarta 10450; tel. (021) 367339; f. 1971; fiction, religion, essays, poetry, drama, criticism, art, philosophy and children's; Man. Yus Rusamsi.

Erlangga: Jalan Kramat IV/11, Jakarta Pusat; tel. (021) 356593; f. 1952; secondary school and university textbooks; Man. Dir M. Hutauruk.

Gaya Favorit Press: Jalan H. Rasuna Said, Blok B Kav. 32-33, Jakarta 12910; tel. (021) 513816; telex 62338; f. 1971; fiction, popular science and children's; Man. Dir Ny Mirta Kartohadiprodjo.

Ghalia Indonesia: Jalan Pramuka Raya 4, Jakarta Timur; tel. (021) 884814; f. 1972; children's and general science, textbooks; Man. Dir Lukman Saad.

Gramedia: Jalan Palmerah Selatan 22, Lantai IV, POB 615, Jakarta Pusat; tel. (021) 5483008; telex 46327; f. 1973; university textbooks, general non-fiction, children's and magazines; Gen. Man. Alfons Taryadi.

Gunung Mulia: Jalan Kwitang 22, Jakarta Pusat; tel. (021) 372208; f. 1951; general, children's, religious, home economics; Man. Liem Kie Djian.

Hidakarya Agung PT: Jalan Kebon Kosong F74, Kemayoran, Jakarta Pusat; tel. (021) 411074; Dir Chairi Machmud.

Ichtiar: Jalan Majapahit 6, Jakarta Pusat; tel. (021) 341226; f. 1957; textbooks, law, social sciences, economics; Dir John Semeru.

Indira PT: Jalan Borobudur 20, Jakarta Pusat; tel. (021) 882754; telex 48211; f. 1953; general science and children's; Man. Dir Wahyudi Djojoadinoto.

Kinta PT: Jalan Kemanggisan Ilir V/110, RT 005/013 Pal Merah Jakarta Barat; tel. (021) 350221; f. 1950; textbooks, social science, general; Man. Drs Mohamad Saleh.

Mutiara Sumber Widya PT: Jalan Pulokambing 9, Industrial Estate Pulogadung, Jakarta Timur; tel. (021) 4893810; telex 46709; f. 1951; textbooks, religious, social sciences, general and children's; Pres. Firdaus Oemar; Dir Fahmi Oemar.

Penerbit Universitas Indonesia: Jalan Salemba Raya 4, Jakarta; tel. (021) 335373; f. 1969; science; Man. Dr Edi Swasono.

Pradnya Paramita PT: Jalan Bunga 8-8A, Matraman, Jakarta 13140; tel. (021) 881369; f. 1973; children's, general, educational, technical and social science; Dir Soenarto Sindoepranoto.

Pustaka Antara PT: Jalan Teluk Betung 55, Jakarta Pusat 10230; tel. (021) 326510; f. 1952; textbooks, political, religious, children's and general; Man. Dir Aida Joesoef Ahmad.

Pustaka Sinar Harapan: Jalan Dewi Sartika 136D, Jakarta 13630; tel. (021) 803208; telex 48202; f. 1981; general science, fiction, comics, children's; Dir Aristides Katoppo.

Sastra Hudaya: Jalan Kalasan 1, Jakarta Pusat; tel. (021) 882321; f. 1967; religious, textbooks, children's and general; Man. Adam Saleh.

Tintamas Indonesia: Jalan Kramat Raya 60, Jakarta Pusat 10420; tel. (021) 346186; f. 1947; biography, history, modern science and culture, especially Islamic; Man. Miss Marhamah Djambek.

Widjaya: Jalan Pecenongan 48C, Jakarta Pusat; tel. (021) 363446; f. 1950; textbooks, children's, religious and general; Man. (vacant).

Yasaguna: Jalan Minangkabau 44, POB 422, Jakarta Selatan; tel. (021) 820422; f. 1964; agricultural, children's, handicrafts; Dir Hilman Madewa.

Bandung

Alma'arif: Jalan Tamblong 48-50, Bandung; tel. (022) 50708; f. 1949; textbooks, religious and general; Man. H. M. Baharthah.

Alumni: Jalan Dr. Djundjunan 190, POB 272, Bandung; tel. (022) 87672; telex 28460; f. 1968; university and school textbooks; Dir Eddy Damian.

Angkasa: Jalan Merdeka 6, POB 354, Bandung; tel. (022) 51795; telex 28530; Dir Fachri Said.

Binacipta: Jalan Ganesya 4, Bandung; tel. (022) 84319; f. 1967; textbooks, scientific and general; Dir Mrs R. Bardin.

Diponegoro Publishing House: Jalan Mohammad Toha 44-46, Bandung 40252; tel. (022) 471215; f. 1963; religious, textbooks, fiction, non-fiction, general; Man. Dra Anisah Dahlan.

Eresco PT: Jalan Hasanudin 9, Bandung 40132; tel. (022) 82311; f. 1957; scientific and general; Man. Mrs H. P. Rochmat Soemitro.

Orba Sakti: Jalan Pandu Dalam 3/67, Bandung; tel. (022) 614718; Dir H. Hasbulloh.

INDONESIA

Directory

Pelita Masa: Jalan Lodaya 25, Bandung; tel. (022) 50823; f. 1973; reference and children's; Man. ROCHDI PARTAATMADJA.

Remaja Karya: Jalan Ciateul 34–36, POB 284, Bandung 40252; tel. (022) 470287; textbooks and children's fiction; Man. ROZALI USMAN.

Rosda: Jalan Raya Cimahi-Padalarang Km 12.5, 858, Bandung; tel. (022) 56627; f. 1969; school textbooks, children's; Dir NY H. MURSYIDAH.

Tarsito: Jalan Guntur 20, Bandung; tel. (022) 421915; Dir T. SITORUS.

Tira Pustaka: Jalan Cemara Raya 1, Kav. 10D, Jaka Permai Jakasampurna, Bekasi Jawa Barat, Bandung; tel. (0219) 71276; telex 62612; Dir WILLIE KOEN.

Flores

Penerbit Nusa Indah: Jalan Katedral 5, Ende 86312, Flores; tel. 251; f. 1970; religious and general; Dir HENRI DAROS.

Kudus

Menara Kudus: Jalan Menara 2, Kudus; tel. 143527; f. 1958; religious; Man. HILMAN NAJIB.

Medan

Hasmar: Jalan Letjen Haryono M.T. 1, POB 446, Medan; tel. (061) 24181; primary school textbooks; Dir HASBULLAH LUBIS; Man. AMRAN SAID RANGKUTI.

Islamiyah: Jalan Sutomo 328–329, Kotakpos 11, Medan; tel. (061) 25426; f. 1954.

Madju: Jalan Sutomo P342, Medan; f. 1950; textbooks, children's and general; Pres. and Dir H. MOHAMED ARBIE.

Semarang

Effhar COY PT: Jalan Dorang 7, Semarang; tel. (024) 23518; f. 1974; school textbooks; Dir DARADJAT HARAHAP.

Intan: Jalan Macandan, Ketandan, Klaten, Jawa-Tengah; tel. (0272) 21641; Dir EDY WIDYANTO.

Surabaya

Airlangga University Press: Dharmahusada 47, Surabaya; tel. (031) 472719; Dir Drs SOEDHARTO.

Assegaff: Jalan Panggung 136, Surabaya; tel. (031) 22971; f. 1951; religion, languages, primary school textbooks; Man. HASSAN ASSEGAFF.

Bina Ilmu PT: Jalan Tunjungan 53E, Surabaya; tel. (031) 472214; f. 1973; school textbooks; Pres. ARIEFIN NOOR.

Bintang: Jalan Potroagung III/1A, Surabaya; tel. (031) 315941; Dir AGUS WINARNO.

Grip: Jalan Kawung 2, POB 129, Surabaya; tel. (031) 22564; f. 1958; textbooks and general; Man. Mrs SURIPTO.

Institut Dagang Muchtar: Jalan Embong Wungu 8, Surabaya; tel. (031) 42973; textbooks for business colleges; Pres. Z. A. MOECHTAR.

Jaya Baya: Jalan Embong Malang 69H, POB 250, Surabaya 60275; tel. (031) 41169; f. 1945; religion, philosophy and ethics; Man. TADJIB ERMADI.

Karunia: Jalan Peneleh 18, Surabaya; tel. (031) 44120; f. 1970; textbooks and general; Man. HASAN ABDAN.

Marfiah: Jalan Kalibutuh 131, Surabaya; reference and primary school textbooks; Man. S. WAHYUDI.

Sinar Wijaya: Komplek Terminal Jembatan Merah, Stand C33-37, Surabaya; tel. (031) 270284; Dir DULRADJAK.

Ujungpandang

Bhakti Centra Baru PT: Jalan Jend. Akhmad Yani 15, Ujungpandang 90174; tel. (0411) 5192; telex 71276; f. 1972; textbooks, religion and general; Gen. Man. MOHAMMAD ALWI HAMU.

Yogyakarta

Centhini Yayasan: Jalan Dr Sutomo 9, Yogyakarta; tel. 3010; f. 1984; Javanese Culture; Chair H. KARKONO KAMAJAYA.

Indonesia UP: Jalan Dr Sutomo 9, Yogyakarta; tel. 3010; f. 1950; general science; Dir H. KARKONO KAMAJAYA.

Kedaulatan Rakyat PT: Jalan P. Mangkubumi 40–42, Yogyakarta; tel. (0274) 2163; telex 25176; Dir DRONO HARDJUSUWONGSO.

Yayasan Kanisius: Jalan Panembahan Senopati 24, Yogyakarta; tel. (0274) 2309; telex 25143; f. 1922; textbooks, religious and general; Man. R. P. S. PADMOBUSONO.

Government Publishing House

Balai Pustaka (State Publishing and Printing House): Jalan Dr Wahadin 1, Jakarta; history, anthropology, politics, philosophy, medical, arts and literature.

PUBLISHERS' ASSOCIATION

Ikatan Penerbit Indonesia (IKAPI) (Asscn of Indonesian Book Publishers): Jalan Kalipasir 32, Jakarta 10340; tel. (021) 321907; f. 1950; 293 mems; Pres. ROZALI USMAN SH; Sec. SETIA DHARMA MADJID.

Radio and Television

In 1986 there were an estimated 32.8m. radio receivers and 4.9m. registered television receivers in use. In March 1989 Indonesia's first private commercial television station was to begin broadcasting; it was to be limited initially to Jakarta.

Directorate-General of Posts and Telecommunications: Jalan Kebon Sirih 37, Jakarta; tel. (021) 346000; telex 44407; Dir-Gen. S. ABDULRACHMAN.

RADIO

Radio Republik Indonesia (RRI): Jalan Merdeka Barat 4–5, POB 157, Jakarta; tel. (021) 349091; telex 44349; f. 1945; 49 stations; Dir ARSYAD SUBIK; Dep. Dirs JUL CHAIDIR (Overseas Service), SURYANTA SALEH (Programming), CHAIRUL ZEN (Programme Development), DJAMALUL ABIDIN ASS (Administration).

Voice of Indonesia: Medan Merdeka Barat 4–5, Jakarta; (021) 366811; foreign service; daily broadcasts in Arabic, English, French, German, Indonesian, Japanese, Bahasa Malaysia, Mandarin, Spanish and Thai.

TELEVISION

Rajawali Citra Televisi Indonesia (RCTI): Jakarta; f. 1989; first private channel; 20-year licence; Pres. Dir BAMBANG TRITIATMOJO.

Yayasan Televisi Republik Indonesia (TVRI): TVRI Senayan, Jalan Gerbang Pemuda, Jakarta; tel. (021) 582328; telex 46154; f. 1962; state-controlled; Dir Dr ISHADI.

Finance

(cap. = capital; auth. = authorized; p.u. = paid up;
res = reserves; dep. = deposits; m. = million; brs = branches;
amounts in rupiahs)

BANKING

In addition to the five state commercial banks and one state savings bank, there were 69 private national banks, one national development bank, 27 regional development banks, two private savings banks, 11 foreign banks and 13 non-bank financial institutions in 1986.

Central Bank

Bank Indonesia: Jalan M. H. Thamrin 2, Jakarta; tel. (021) 372408; telex 44164; f. 1828; nationalized 1951; central bank since 1953; cap. and res 447,000m., dep. 3,406,000m. (March 1986); Gov. ADRIANUS MOOY; Pres. T. M. ZAHIRSJAH.

State Banks

Bank Bumi Daya: Jalan Imam Bonjol 61, POB 106, Jakarta 10002; tel. (021) 333721; telex 61117; f. 1959; commercial and foreign exchange bank, specializes in credits to the plantation and forestry sectors; cap. and res 365,458m., dep. 7,408,354m. (June 1988); Pres. Dir H. SURASA; 82 brs, 17 sub-brs.

Bank Dagang Negara: Jalan M. H. Thamrin 5, POB 338/JKT, Jakarta; tel. (021) 321707; telex 61628; f. 1960; auth. foreign exchange bank; specializes in credits to the mining sector; cap. p.u. 250m., dep. 5,141,631m. (March 1986); Pres. H. M. WIDARSADIPRADJA; 127 brs.

Bank Ekspor Impor Indonesia: Jalan Lapangan Setasiun 1, POB 32, Jakarta Kota; tel. (021) 673122; telex 42702; f. 1968; commercial and foreign exchange bank; specializes in credits for manufacture and export; cap. 200m., dep. 5,276,080m. (March 1986); Pres. MOELJOTO DJOJOMARTONO; 56 brs.

Bank Negara Indonesia 1946: Jalan Lada 1, POB 1946 KB/JAK, Jakarta Kota 11110; tel. (021) 6901217; telex 42674; f. 1946; commercial bank; specializes in credits to the industrial sector; cap. and res 461,464m., dep. 11,242,726m. (Dec. 1987); Pres. A. KUKUH BASUKI; 277 domestic brs, 6 overseas brs.

Bank Rakyat Indonesia; Jalan Jenderal Sudirman Kav. 42–43, Jakarta; tel. (021) 586111; telex 44728; f. 1895, present name since 1946; commercial and foreign exchange bank; specializes in credits to co-operatives in agriculture and fisheries, in rural credit generally and international business; cap. 300m., dep. 5,276,080m. (March 1986); Pres. KARMADY ARIEF; 295 brs.

INDONESIA

Bank Tabungan Negara (State Savings Bank): Jalan Hr Rasuna Said C-17, Jakarta Selatan; tel. (021) 5781210; telex 62313; f. 1964; savings bank; cap. p.u. 100m., dep. 810,033m. (June 1986); Pres. SASONOTOMO; 14 brs.

Selected National Private Banks

PT Bank Bali: Jalan Hayam Wuruk 84–85, Jakarta 11160; tel. (021) 6498006; telex 42724; f. 1954; foreign exchange bank; cap. p.u. 7,088m., dep. 255,871m. (March 1986); Pres. G. KARYADI; Chair. P. H. SUGIRI; 5 brs, 3 sub-brs.

PT Bank Buana Indonesia: Jalan Asemka 32–35, Jakarta; tel. (021) 672901; telex 42042; f. 1956; foreign exchange bank; cap. p.u. 7,500m., dep. 370,654m. (June 1988); Pres. HENDRA SURYADI; 13 brs, 13 sub-brs.

PT Bank Central Asia: Jalan Jenderal Sudirman Kav. 22–23, Jakarta; tel. (021) 671771; telex 42860; f. 1957; cap. p.u. 32,000m., dep. 594,227m. (June 1986); Pres. A. ALI; CEO Dir MOCHTAR RIADY; 20 brs, 15 sub-brs, repr. office 1.

PT Bank Duta: Jalan Kebon Sirih 12, Jakarta 10110; tel. (021) 3800900; telex 48308; f. 1966; foreign exchange bank; cap. p.u. 10,000m., dep. 352,104m. (March 1986); Pres. ABDULGANI; Dirs BEY YOESOEF, MUCHTAR MANDALA, DICKY ISKANDAR DI NATA; 7 brs, 2 sub-brs.

PT Bank Niaga: Jalan Gajah Mada 18, Jakarta; tel. (021) 377809; telex 45894; f. 1955; foreign exchange bank; cap. p.u. 9,896m., dep. 271,515m. (March 1986); Pres. Dir ROBBY DJOHAN; Man. Dirs I. JONOSEWOJO, WIJATNO SOEPENADIE; 16 brs, 4 sub-brs.

PT Bank NISP: Jalan Taman Cibeunying Selatan 31, Bandung; tel. (022) 57926; telex 28269; f. 1941; cap. p.u. 3,257m., dep. 88,195m. (Aug. 1986); Pres. KARMAKA SURJAUDA; Man. Dirs PETER EKO SUTIOSO, ANWARY SURJAUDAJA; 3 brs.

PT Bank Pacific: Jalan K. H. Samanhudi 17–19, Jakarta; tel. (021) 376408; telex 44818; f. 1958; foreign exchange bank; cap. p.u. 12,000m., dep. 82,974m. (March 1986); Pres. M. HATTA ABDULAH; Man. Dirs OEMAR SAID, ABDUL FIRMAN, H. P. TOAR; 5 brs, 3 sub-brs.

PT Bank Perdania: Jalan Raya Mangga Besar 7–11, Jakarta; tel. (021) 621708; telex 41120; f. 1956; foreign exchange bank; Pres. ISMED SIREGAR. 1 br., 1 sub-br.

PT Bank Umum Nasional: Jalan Prapatan 50, Jakarta; tel. (021) 365563; telex 46034; f. 1952; foreign exchange bank; cap. p.u. 9,100m., dep. 295,989m. (March 1986); Pres. Dir KAHARUDIN ONGKO, S. RANTY, V. U. KULIH; Exec. Dir M. DJAILANI; 15 brs, 4 sub-brs.

PT Overseas Express Bank: Jalan Pecenongan 84, POB 471 Jakarta 10120; tel. (021) 358103; telex 46350; f. 1974; foreign exchange bank; cap. p.u. 6,000m., dep. 257,642m. (March 1988); Chair. I NYOMAN MOENA; 9 brs.

PT Pan Indonesia (Panin) Bank: Panin Bank Centre, Jalan Jen. Sudirman, Senayan, Jakarta; tel. (021) 7394545; telex 47394; f. 1971; foreign exchange bank; cap. p.u. 16,000m., dep. 437,367m. (Sept. 1988); Pres. PRIJATNA ATMADJA; 14 brs, 12 sub-brs.

PT Sejahtera Bank Umum: Jalan Tiang Bendera 15, Jakarta Barat; tel. (021) 673804; telex 42760; f. 1952; cap. p.u. 3,650m., dep. 69,446m. (June 1986); Pres. LESMANA BASUKI; Man. Dir STEPHANUS SOEARTO; 4 brs, 2 sub-brs.

PT South East Asia Bank Ltd: Jalan Asemka 16–17, Jakarta; tel. (021) 672197; telex 42731; f. 1957; cap. p.u. 4,000m., dep. 24,110m. (June 1986); Pres. Dir AGUS SALIM; Man. Dirs Drs B. SURYADI, TRISNO HARIANTO, HARIONO; 2 brs.

PT United City Bank: Jalan Hayam Wuruk 121, Jakarta; tel. (021) 6293508; telex 41165; f. 1968; cap. p.u. 18,203m., dep. 31,316m. (Dec. 1986); Pres. TJOKROPRANOLO; 3 brs, 2 sub-brs.

Development Bank

Bank Pembangunan Indonesia (BAPINDO) (Development Bank of Indonesia): Jalan Gondangdia Lama 2–4, POB 140, Jakarta 10002; tel. (021) 321908; telex 44214; f. 1960; state bank; provides medium- and long-term investment loans to new and existing business enterprises; equity financing and general banking services; and non-financial assistance, industrial research, and technical consultancy services; cap. p.u. 49,981m., total resources 1,459,900m. (Dec. 1986); Pres. SUBEKTI ISMAUN; 21 brs.

Selected Finance Corporations

PT Bahana Pembinaan Usaha Indonesia (BAHANA): Jalan Teuku Cik Ditiro 23, POB 3228, Jakarta 10350; tel. (021) 325207; telex 45332; f. 1973; cap. p.u. 6,000m.; Pres. BAHAUDDIN DARUS.

PT Inter-Pacific Financial Corpn: Jalan Jenderal Sudirman Kav. 31, Jakarta; tel. (021) 5781118; telex 46289; f. 1973; cap. p.u. 1,500m.; Pres. and Dir S. R. DWIANTO.

PT Multinational Finance Corpn (MULTICOR): Wisma BCA, 12th Floor, Jalan Jenderal Sudirman Kav. 22-23, Jakarta 12920; tel. (021) 5781450; telex 44932; f. 1974; cap. p.u. 1,000m.; Pres. and Dir K. R. WYNN.

PT Mutual International Finance Corpn: Nusantara Bldg, 17th Floor, Jalan M. H. Thamrin 59, Jakarta 10350; tel. (021) 331108; telex 61390; f. 1973; cap. p.u. 1,200m.; Pres. Dir ROCHMAT TANUSEPUTRA; Dep. Pres. Dir T. MARUYAMA.

PT Private Development Finance Co of Indonesia: Jalan Abdul Muis 60, Jakarta; tel. (021) 366608; telex 46778; f. 1973; cap. p.u. 4,539m.; Chair. and CEO SUDIARSO.

PT Usaha Pembiayaan Pembangunan Indonesia (PT Indonesian Development Finance Co): UPPINDO Bldg, Jalan Abdul Muis 28, POB 24, Jakarta 10002; tel. (021) 354621; telex 46349; f. 1972; cap. p.u. 17,220m. (Aug. 1987); Chair. HENDROBUDIYANTO; Pres. and Dir SARWONO WISHNUWARDHANA.

Foreign Banks

Algemene Bank Nederland NV (Netherlands): Jalan Ir H. Juanda 23–24, POB 2950, Jakarta 10001; tel. (021) 362309; telex 44124; Man. LEN H. STEFFEN.

Bangkok Bank Ltd (Thailand): Jalan M. H. Thamrin 3, POB 1165, Jakarta; tel. (021) 366008; telex 46193; f. 1968; Gen. Man. and Sr Vice-Pres. PHAIBUL INGKHAVAT; Br. Man. SAKSITH TEJASAKULSIN.

Bank of America NT & SA (USA): Wisma Antara, 1st Floor, Jalan Medan Merdeka Selatan 17, POB 195, Jakarta; tel. (021) 348031; telex 44374; f. 1968; Vice-Pres. and Man. Z. MISSERLIAN.

Bank of Tokyo Ltd (Japan): Nusantara Bldg, Jalan M. H. Thamrin 59, POB 2711, Jakarta 10001; tel. (021) 333409; telex 61501; Gen. Man. SHIGEYOSHI AKAIKE.

The Chase Manhattan Bank, NA (USA): Chase Plaza, Jalan Jenderal Sudirman, Kav. 21, POB 311/JKT, Jakarta; tel. (021) 5782213; telex 44369; Country Man. FRANCIS X. SHEA.

Citibank, NA (USA): Jalan Jend Sudirman 1, Jakarta 12930; tel. (021) 5782007; telex 44368; f. 1912; Vice-Pres JAMES F. HUNT, EDWIN GERUNGAN, ROBERT THORNTON.

Deutsche Bank (Asia) (Federal Republic of Germany): Jalan Imam Bonjol 80, POB 135, Jakarta 10002; tel. (021) 331092; telex 44114; Man. Dr KLAUS ZEIDLER.

Hongkong and Shanghai Banking Corpn (Hong Kong): Jalan Hayam Wuruk 8, POB 2307, Jakarta 10001; tel. (021) 377808; telex 44160; br. at Jalan Pintu Besar Selatan 109B, Jakarta; tel. 672380; Man. K. R. WHITSON.

Standard Chartered Bank (UK): Wisma Kosgoro, Jalan M. H. Thamrin 53, POB 57/JKWK, Jakarta 10350; tel. (021) 325008; telex 61179; Man. B. R. KNIGHT.

Westpac Banking Corpn (Australia): 10th Floor, Summitmas Towers Bldg, Jalan Jenderal Sudirman 61/62, Jakarta; tel. (021) 5201213; telex 46125; f. 1972; Chief Rep. JOHN W. BREWSTER.

Banking Association

Indonesian National Private Banks Association (Perhimpunan Bank-Bank Nasional Swasta—PERBANAS): Jalan Sindanglaya 1, Jakarta Pusat 10310; tel. (021) 351939; telex 41513; f. 1952; 67 mems; Chair. I. NYOMAN MOENA; Sec.-Gen. JUSUF WANTAH.

STOCK EXCHANGES

In 1987 24 companies, including 18 joint ventures, were listed on the stock exchange. In December changes in the capital market were made to encourage the participation of foreign investors.

Badan Pelaksana Bursa Komoditi (Indonesian Commodity Exchange Board—ICEB): Bursa Bldg, 2nd and 4th Floors, Jalan Medan Merdeka Selatan 14, Jakarta 10110; tel. 371918; telex 44194; trades in rubber, coffee and auction for transfer of textile quota; Chair. RUDY LENGKONG.

Badan Pelaksana Pasar Modal (BAPEPAM) (Capital Market Executive Agency): Jalan Medan Merdeka Selatan 14, Jakarta 10110; tel. (021) 365509; telex 45604; Chair. Prof Drs BARLI HALIM; Exec. Sec. JUSUF ANWAR.

INSURANCE

In accordance with Ministry of Finance regulations, all 12 non-life foreign insurance companies had merged by 1980 with one or more domestic companies to form joint ventures. In 1982 a new regulation allowed foreign companies to form joint ventures in the life insurance sector.

In 1988 there were 105 insurance companies, comprising 12 non-life joint venture companies, 58 non-life companies, 24 life companies, four reinsurance companies, five social insurance companies, and two life joint venture company.

Insurance Supervisory Authority of Indonesia: Directorate of Financial Institutions, Ministry of Finance, Jalan Lapangan Banteng Timur 2–4, Jakarta Pusat; tel. (021) 360298; telex 46415; Dir Dr BAMBANG SUBIANTO.

INDONESIA

Selected Life Insurance Companies

PT Asuransi Jiwa Buana Putra: Jalan Salemba Tengah 23, Jakarta Pusat; tel. (021) 8582481; telex 44338; f. 1974; Pres. SOEBAGYO SOETJITRO.

PT Asuransi Jiwa Central Asia Raya: Jalan Gajah Mada 3-5, Jakarta; tel. (021) 348512; telex 46414; Pres. WARDOYO, S. H.

PT Asuransi Jiwa Ikrar Abadi: Jalan Letjen. S. Parman 108, POB 3562, Jakarta 11440; tel. (021) 591335; f. 1975; Pres. Dir HARRY HARMAIN DIAH.

PT Asuransi Jiwa Iman Adi: Jalan Matraman Raya 102, Slipi, Jakarta; Man. B. W. DUMALANG.

PT Asuransi Jiwa 'Panin Putra': Jalan Pintu Besar Selatan 52A, Jakarta 11110; tel. (021) 672586; telex 42881; f. 1974; Pres. Dir SUJONO SOEPENO; Chair. NUGROHO TJOKROWIRONO.

PT Asuransi Jiwa Jiwasraya: Jalan H. Juanda 34, POB 240, Jakarta Pusat; tel. (021) 345031; telex 45601; f. 1959; Pres. RUCHIMAT BRATASASMITA.

PT Asuransi Pensiun Bumiputera 1974: Jalan HOS Cokroaminoto 85, POB 3504, Jakarta; tel. (021) 344347; telex 44494; f. 1974; Gen. Man. SUDIBYO SUTOWIBOWO.

Bumi Asih Jaya Life Insurance Co: Jatinegara Barat 144, Jakarta 13320; tel. (021) 8190408; telex 48278; f. 1967; Pres. K. M. SINAGA.

Bumiputera 1912 Mutual Life Insurance Co: Wisma Bumiputera, Floors 18-21, Jalan Jend. Sudirman Kav. 75, Jakarta 12910; tel. (021) 5782717; telex 44494; f. 1912; Pres. SUGIARTO.

PT Mahkota Jaya Abadi (Life Insurance Ltd): Jalan Sisingamangaraja 11, Jakarta Selantan; Man. WIDODO SUKARNO.

Selected Non-Life Insurance Companies

PT Asuransi Bintang: Jalan Hayam Wuruk 4CX, Jakarta Pusat; tel. (021) 372908; telex 45648; f. 1955; general insurance; Man. Dir B. MUNIR SYAMSOEDDIN; Gen. Mans. OLOAN HARAHAP, SUDIRMAN NOORDEEN.

PT Asuransi Central Asia: Jalan Gajah Mada 3, Jakarta Pusat; tel. (021) 373073; telex 46569; Pres. ANTHONY SALIM.

PT Asuransi Indrapura: Wisma Metropolitan 2, 11th Floor, Jalan Jenderal Sudirman, Jakarta 12920; tel. 5780660; telex 62641; f. 1954; Presiding Dir ROBERT TEGUH.

PT Asuransi Jasa Indonesia: Jalan Letjen. M. T. Haryono, Kav. 61, Jakarta Selatan; tel. (021) 7994508; telex 47365; Pres. IWA SEWAKA.

PT Asuransi 'Ramayana': Jalan Kebon Sirih 49, Jakarta Pusat; tel. (021) 337148; telex 61670; f. 1956; Pres. R. G. DOERIAT; Dirs SADIJONO HARJOKUSUMO, F. X. WIDIASTANTO.

PT Tugu Pratama Indonesia: Gedung Patra, 1st Floor, Jalan Gatot Subroto, Kav. 32-34, Jakarta 12950; tel. (021) 512041; telex 62800; general insurance; Pres. SONNI DWI HARSONO.

PT Asuransi Wahana Tata: Jalan Roa Malaka Selatan 6, Jakarta 11230; tel. (021) 670123; telex 42937; Pres. RUDY WANANDI.

PT Maskapai Asuransi Indonesia: Jalan Sultan Hasanuddin 53-54, Kebayoran Baru, Jakarta Selatan; tel. (021) 710708; telex 47290; Dirs P. L. KESUMA, JAN F. H. NINKEULA.

PT Perusahaan Maskapai Asuransi Murni: Jalan Roa Malaka Selatan 21-23, Jakarta Barat; tel. (021) 679968; telex 42851; f. 1953; Dirs HASAN DAY, HOED IBRAHIM, R. SOEGIATNA PROBOPINILIH.

PT Maskapai Asuransi Timur Jauh: Jalan Medan Merdeka Barat 1, Jakarta Pusat; tel. (021) 370266; telex 44828; f. 1954; Pres. Dir BUSTANIL ARIFIN; Dirs V. H. KOLONDAM, SOEBAKTI HARSONO.

Joint Ventures

PT Asuransi Jayasraya: Jl. M. H. Thamrin 9, Jakarta; tel. (021) 324207; Dirs SUPARTONO, SADAO SUZUKI.

PT Asuransi Insindo Taisho: Nusantara Bldg, 20th Floor, Jl. M. H. Thamrin 59, Jakarta 10350; tel. (021) 336101; telex 61409; Pres. Dir PUTU WIDNYANA, Vice-Pres. KOICHI NEMOTO.

PT Asuransi New Hampshire Agung: Wisma American International, Jl. KH. Hasyim Ashari 35 Jakarta; tel. (021) 356581; Pres. Dir PETER MEYER; Vice-Pres. Dir HERMAN EFFENDI.

PT Asuransi Royal Indrapura: Chase Plaza, 6th Floor, Jalan Jenderal Sudirman Kav. 21, Jakarta 12920; tel. (021) 5782364; telex 62137; Dirs F. LAMURY, R. J. BROADHURST.

Insurance Association

Dewan Asuransi Indonesia (Insurance Council of Indonesia): Jalan Majapahit 34, Blok V/29, Jakarta 10160; tel. (021) 363264; telex 44981; f. 1957; Chair. PURWANTO; Gen. Sec. SOEDJIWO; Exec. Sec. BAMBANG HADIKUSUMO.

Trade and Industry

National Development Planning Agency (Bappenas): Jalan Taman Suropati 2, Jakarta; tel. (021) 348990; formulates Indonesia's national economic development plans; Chair. Prof. Dr J. B. SUMARLIN; Vice-Chair. Dr SALEH AFIFF.

CHAMBER OF COMMERCE

Kamar Dagang dan Industri Indonesia (KADIN) (Indonesian Chamber of Commerce and Industry): Chandra Bldg, 3rd-5th Floors, Jalan M. H. Thamrin 20, Jakarta Pusat 12170; tel. (021) 32400; telex 61262; f. 1968; 27 regional offices throughout Indonesia; Pres. SUKAMDANI S. GITOSARDJONO; Sec.-Gen. SOEKAMTO SAJIDIMAN.

TRADE AND INDUSTRIAL ORGANIZATIONS

Association of State-Owned Companies: CTC Bldg, Jalan Kramat Raya 94-96, Jakarta; tel. (021) 346071; telex 44208; co-ordinates the activities of state-owned enterprises; Pres. ODANG.

Association of Indonesian Coffee Exports (AEKI): Jakarta; Chair. DHARYONO KERTOSASTRO.

Badan Koordinasi Penanaman Modal (BKPM) (Investment Co-ordinating Board): Jalan Jenderal Gatot Subroto 44, POB 3186, Jakarta; tel. (021) 512008; telex 45651; f. 1976; Chair. SANYOTO SASTROWARDOYO.

CAFI (Commercial Advisory Foundation in Indonesia): Jalan Probolinggo 5, POB 249, Jakarta 10002; tel. 324487; f. 1958; information, consultancy and translation services; Chair. Dr R. Ng. S. SOSROHADIKOESOEMO; Man. Dir BENNY SUDIBJO PONTJOSOEGITO.

Export Arbitration Board: Jalan Kramat Raya 4-6, Jakarta; Chair. Ir R. M. SOSROHADIKUSUMO; Vice-Chair. SANUSI.

Gabungan Perusahaan Ekspor Indonesia (Indonesian Exporters' Federation): Jalan Kramat Raya 4-6, Jakarta; Pres. NAAFII; Sec. A. SOFYAN MUNAF.

GINSI (Importers' Asscn of Indonesia): Jalan Kesejahteraan 98, Pintu Timur, Arena Pekan Raya, POB 2744/JKT, Jakarta Pusat 10110; tel. (021) 377008; telex 46793; f. 1956; 2,360 mems; Chair. ZAHRI ACHMAD; Sec. Gen. K. S. OETOMO.

Indonesian Palm Oil Producers' Association: Jakarta; Chair. NUKMAN NASUTION.

Indonesian Textile Association (API): Panin Bank Centre, 3rd Floor, Jalan Jend Sudirman 1, Jakarta Pusat 10270; tel. (021) 7396094; telex 47228; f. 1974; Gen. Sec. Drs H. FAHMY CHATIB.

Indonesian Tobacco Association: Jalan Kramat Raya 4-6, Jakarta; tel. (021) 31357; telex 61517; Pres. H. A. ISMAIL.

Masyarakat Perhutanan Indonesia (MPI) (Indonesian Forestry Community): Gedung Manggala Wanabakti, 9th Floor, Wing C/Blok IV, Jalan Jenderal Gatot Subroto, Jakarta Pusat 10270; tel. (021) 583010; telex 46977; f. 1974; 8 mems; Pres. M. HASAN.

National Board of Arbitration (BANI): Jalan Merdeka Timur 11, Jakarta; f. 1977; resolves company disputes; Chair. Prof. R. SUBEKTI.

Shippers' Council of Indonesia: Jalan Kramat Raya 4-6, Jakarta; Pres. R. S. PARTOKUSUMO.

STATE TRADING ORGANIZATIONS

General Management Board of the State Trading Corporations (BPU-PNN): Jakarta; f. 1961; Pres. Col SUHARDIMAN.

PT Aneka Tambang: Jalan Bungur Besar 24, POB 2513, Jakarta; tel. (021) 410108; telex 49147; f. 1968; minerals; Pres. Ir KOSIM GANDATARUNA.

PT Dharma Niaga Ltd: Jalan Abdul Muis 6/8/10, POB 2028, Jakarta; tel. (021) 349978; telex 44312; f. 1970; import, export, distribution, installation, after sales service; Pres. Drs ABU SADIKIN.

PT Indosat: Jalan Merdeka Barat 21, Jakarta 10110; tel. 3802614; telex 44383; telecommunications.

PT Nurtanio: BPP Teknologi Bldg, Jalan M. H. Thamrin 8, Jakarta; tel. (021) 322395; telex 44331; aerospace; Chair. Dr B. J. HABIBIE.

Perum Perhutani (State Forest Corpn): Gedung Manggala Wanabakti, Blok IV/Lantai 4, Jalan Gatot Subroto Senayan, POB 19/JKWB, Jakarta Pusat; tel. (021) 587090; telex 46283; f. 1973; Pres. Dir Ir HARTONO WIRJODARMODJO.

Perum Pos dan Giro: Jalan Cilaki 73, Bandung 40115; tel. (022) 431050; telex 28174; provides postal and giro services; CEO MOELJOTO.

Perum Tambang Batubara: Jalan Prof. Dr Supomo SH Nr 10, Jakarta 12870; tel. (021) 8295608; telex 48203; f. 1968; coal-mining; Pres. ACHMAD PRIJONO; Exec. Dir TIMALU SUJATMIKO.

Perusahaan Pertambangan Minyak & Gas Bumi Negara (PERTAMINA): Jalan Merdeka Timur 1A, POB 12, Jakarta; tel. (021) 3031; telex 44152; f. 1957; state-owned petroleum and natural gas mining enterprise; Pres. and Dir FAISAL ABDA'OE.

INDONESIA

Perusahaan Umum Telekomunikasi (Perumtel): Jalan Cisanggarung 2, 40114 Bandung; tel. (022) 436100; telex 28220; domestic telecommunications; CEO Ir W. MOENANDIR.

PT Tambang Timah (Persero): Jalan Jenderal Gatot Subroto, Jakarta; tel. (021) 510731; telex 62404; tin; Gen. Man. SUDJATMIKO.

PT Tjipta Niaga: Jalan Kalibesar Timur IV/1, POB 1314/JAK, Jakarta; tel. (021) 673923; telex 42747; f. 1964; import and distribution of basic goods, bulk articles, sundries, provisions and drinks, and export of Indonesian produce; Pres. Drs E. SIMANDJUNTAK.

TRADE UNION FEDERATION

All-Indonesia Union of Workers (SPSI): Jalan Tanah Abang III/21, Jakarta; tel. (021) 349197; f. 1973, renamed 1985; comprises 10 national industrial unions; Chair. IMAM SUDARWO; Vice-Chair. Drs SUKARNO; Gen. Sec. ADOLF RACHMAN.

Transport

RAILWAYS

There are railways on Java, Madura and Sumatra, totalling 6,521 km (4,049 miles) in 1987, of which 110 km (68.31 miles) were electrified. A US $31m. railway project, supported mainly by the World Bank, was under way in 1988, to improve passenger and freight train operations.

Perusahaan Jawatan Kereta Api (Indonesian State Railways): Jalan Perintis Kermedekaan 1, Bandung 40113, Java; tel. (022) 58001; telex 28263; six regional offices; controls 6,380 km of track on Java and Sumatra, of which 125 km are electrified (1986); Chief Dir Ir SUHARSO.

ROADS

There is an adequate road network on Java and Bali, but on most of the other islands traffic is by jungle track or river boat. Total length of roads in 1986 was 219,009 km, of which 12,942 km were main or national roads and 198 km were motorway. In 1986 plans for a three-island tunnel and bridge link-up between Sumatra, Java and Bali were approved. In 1987 the ADB approved a US $150m. loan for the ninth road (maintenance) sector project, which was scheduled for completion by 1991 and aimed to repair 4,000 km of roads and to replace 80 bridges in 10 provinces.

Directorate General of Highways: Ministry of Public Works, Jalan Pattimura 20, Kebayoran Baru Jakarta; tel. (021) 7203165; Dir Gen. Ir SURYATIN SASTROMIJOYO.

SHIPPING

The Ministry of Communications controls 392 ports, of which the four main ports of Tanjung Priok (near Jakarta), Tanjung Perak (near Surabaya), Belawan (near Medan) and Ujung Pandang (in South Sulawesi) have been designated gateway ports for nearly all international shipping to deal with Indonesia's exports and are supported by 15 collector ports. A six-year port modernization programme, costing US $186.5m., began in 1985. Among the ports which will be upgraded is Surabaya's Tanjung Perak, which will have expanded container facilities. Panjang Port, on Sumatra, was to be expanded between 1987 and 1989. In 1986 the total merchant fleet (inter-island and ocean-going) was 6,757 vessels, including 35 ocean-going cargo vessels and 78 bulk carriers.

Inter-island shipping is conducted by state-owned and private shipping lines, and there are numerous small craft.

Directorate General of Sea Communications: Ministry of Communications, Jalan Medan Merdeka Timur 5, Jakarta; tel. (021) 363009; telex 46117; Dir-Gen. J. E. HABIBIE.

Indonesian National Ship Owners' Association (INSA): Jalan Tanah Abang III/10, Jakarta; tel. (021) 375682; telex 46428; Pres. BOED IHAROJO SASTROHADIWIRJO.

Indonesian Oriental Lines, PT Perusahaan Pelayaran Nusantara: Jalan Raya Pelabuhan Nusantara, POB 2062, Jakarta 10001; tel. (021) 494344; telex 44233; 6 ships; Pres. Dir A. J. SINGH.

PT Jakarta Lloyd: Jalan Agus Salim 28, Jakarta Pusat 10340; tel. (021) 331301; telex 44375; f. 1950; services to USA, Europe, Japan, Australia and the Middle East; 4 semi-containers, 3 full containers, 3 general cargo vessels; Pres. Dir Capt. BAMBANG WAHYUDIONO.

PT Karana Line: Jalan Kali Besar Timur 30, POB 30, Jakarta Kota; tel. (021) 679103; telex 42727; 6 ships; Pres. Dir HAPOSAN PANGGABEAN.

PT Pelayaran Bahtera Adhiguna: Jalan Kalibesar Timur 10-12, POB 1313 Jakarta 11110; tel. (021) 676547; telex 42854; f. 1971; 8 ships; Pres. H. DJAJASUDHARMA.

PT Pelayaran Nasional Indonesia (PELNI): Jalan Angkasa 18, POB 115, Jakarta; tel. (021) 417817; telex 44301; state-owned; national shipping co; 4 passenger ships, 34 cargo vessels; Pres. Dir SOEDHARNO MUSTAFA.

PT Pengembangan Armada Niaga Nasional: Pann Bldg, Jalan Cikini IV/II, Jakarta; tel. (021) 322003; telex 46286; state-controlled; 24 ships; Pres. A. NAZAHAR.

PT Perusahaan Pelayaran Nusantara 'Nusa Tenggara': Kantor Pusat, Jalan Diponegoro 115 Atas, POB 69, Denpasar 80001, Bali; tel. (0361) 27720; telex 35210; 5 ships; Man. Dir KETUT DERESTHA.

PT Perusahaan Pelayaran Samudera Admiral Lines: Jalan Gunung Sahari 79-80, POB 476, Jakarta Pusat; tel. (021) 417908; telex 49122; 9 ships; Pres. H. SJOFJAN AFFANDIE.

PT Perusahaan Pelayaran Samudera Gesuri Lloyd: Gesuri Lloyd Bldg, Jalan Tiang Bendera 45, POB 289/JKT, Jakarta 11220; tel. (021) 675870; telex 42043; f. 1964; 7 cargo vessels, 5 charter ships; Pres. Dir ADIL NURIMBA.

PT Perusahaan Pelayaran Samudera 'Samudera Indonesia': Jalan Kali Besar Barat 43, POB 1244, Jakarta Kota; tel. (021) 671093; telex 42753; 4 ships; Pres. Dir S. SASTROSATAMO.

PT Perusahaan Pelayaran Samudera Trikora Lloyd: Jalan Malaka 1, POB 1076/JAK, Jakarta 11001; tel. (021) 671751; telex 42061; f. 1964; 5 ships; Pres. Dir B. SASTROHADIWIRYO; Man. Dir M. HARJONO KARTOHADIPRODJO.

PT Perusahaan Pertambangan Minyak dan Gas Bumi Negara (PERTAMINA): Directorate for Shipping and Telecommunications, Jalan Jos Sudarso 32-34, POB 265, Tanjung Priok, Jakarta; tel. (021) 494309; telex 42753; state-owned; tanker services; 80 tankers and 380 small vessels; Pres. and Chair. ABDUL RACHMAN RAMLY.

CIVIL AVIATION

The first stage of a new international airport, the Sukarno-Hatta Airport, at Cengkareng, near Jakarta, was opened in April 1985, to complement Halim Perdanakusuma Airport which was to handle charter and general flights only. Construction of an international passenger terminal at the Frans Kaisepo Airport, in Irian Jaya, was completed in 1988. Other international airports include Polonia Airport in Medan (North Sumatra), Ngurah Rai Airport at Denpasar (Bali), Juanda Airport, near Surabaya (East Java), Sam Ratulangi Airport, in Manado (North Sulawesi) and Hasanuddin Airport, near Ujung Pandang (South Sulawesi). Domestic air services link the major cities, and international services are provided by the state airline, PT Garuda Indonesian Airways, and by numerous foreign airlines.

Directorate General of Air Communications: Ministry of Communications, Jalan Angkasa I/2, Jakarta; tel. (021) 416321; telex 49482; Dir-Gen. SUTOYO.

PT AOA Zamrud Aviation Corpn: Denpasar; f. 1969; domestic passenger and cargo services and charter flights; Pres. UTOJO UTOMO; Dir DJOEBER AFFANDI; fleet of 3 DC-3.

PT Bali International Air Service: Jalan Angkasa 1-3, POB 2965, Jakarta; tel. (021) 6295388; telex 41247; f. 1970; private company; subsidiary of BIA; charter services; Pres. J. A. SUMENDAP; Gen. Man. G. B. RUNGKAT; fleet of 4 Trislander, 2 BN Islander, 1 Cessna 404.

PT Bouraq Indonesia Airlines (BOU): Jalan Angkasa 1-3, POB 2965, Jakarta; tel. (021) 6295364; telex 41247; f. 1970; private company; scheduled domestic passenger and cargo services linking Jakarta with points in Java, Kalimantan, Sulawesi, Bali, Timor and Tawau (Malaysia); Pres. J. A. SUMENDAP; fleet of 16 HS-748, 4 VC8, 3 NC12 Aviocar.

PT Garuda Indonesia: Jalan Medan Merdeka Selatan 13, Jakarta 10110; tel. (021) 3801901; telex 49113; f. 1950; state airline; operates domestic, regional and international services to Australia, Austria, Belgium, Egypt, France, the Federal Republic of Germany, Hawaii, Hong Kong, Italy, Japan, Malaysia, the Netherlands, New Zealand, the Philippines, Singapore, Switzerland, Thailand, Taiwan, the United Arab Emirates, the United Kingdom and the USA; Pres. Dir M. SOEPARNO; fleet of 6 Boeing 747, 34 Fokker-28, 18 DC-9, 6 DC-10, 9 Airbus A-300.

PT Mandala Airlines: Jalan Veteran I/34, POB 3706, Jakarta; tel. (021) 368107; f. 1969; privately-owned; passenger and cargo services from Jakarta to Medan, Padang, Semarang, Surabaya, Ujungpadang, Ambon, Denpasar and Menado; Pres. Dir SANTOSO; fleet of 3 Vickers Viscount, 6 Lockheed Electra.

PT Merpati Nusantara Airlines: Jalan Angkasa 2, POB 323, Jakarta 10002; tel. (021) 413608; telex 49154; f. 1962; subsidiary of PT Garuda Indonesian Airways; domestic and regional services to Australia and Malaysia; Pres. SOERATMAN; fleet of 2 Viscount 828, 15 F-27, 2 HS-748, 17 Twin Otter, 22 CASA CN-212, 2 Hercules L-10.

PT Sempati Air Transport: Jalan Medan Merdeka Timur 7, POB 2068, Jakarta; tel. (021) 343323; telex 45132; f. 1968; subsidiary of

INDONESIA

PT Tri Usaha Bhakti; passenger and cargo services throughout ASEAN countries; Pres. Capt. DOLF LATUMAHINA; fleet of 6 Fokker F-27.

Tourism

Indonesia's tourist industry is based mainly on the islands of Java, famous for its volcanic scenery and religious temples, and Bali, renowned for its traditional dancing and religious festivals. In 1987 a total of 1,060,347 tourists visited Indonesia, an increase of 28.1% over 1986 arrivals.

Direktorat Jenderal Pariwisata (Directorate General of Tourism): 81 Jalan Kramat Raya, Jakarta; tel. (021) 343150; telex 45625; f. 1957; private body to promote national and international tourism; Chair. HAMENGKU BUWONO; Vice-Chair. Sri BUDOYO; Dir-Gen. JOOP AVE.

Atomic Energy

In 1986 the Government conducted research on the construction of Indonesia's first nuclear power plant, in central Java, but a decision to build a plant was postponed, owing to the lack of available funds and to considerations of safety.

National Atomic Energy Agency (Badan Tenaga Atom Nasional—BATAN): Jalan K. H. Abdul Rachim, Kuningan Barat, Mampang Prapatan, POB 85/KBY, Jakarta Selatan; tel. (021) 511109; telex 46354; f. 1958; Dir-Gen. Ir DJALI AHIMSA.

IRAN

Introductory Survey

Location, Climate, Language, Religion, Flag, Capital

The Islamic Republic of Iran lies in western Asia, bordered by the USSR to the north, by Turkey and Iraq to the west, by the Persian (Arabian) Gulf and the Gulf of Oman to the south, and by Pakistan and Afghanistan to the east. The climate is one of great extremes. Summer temperatures of more than 55°C (131°F) have been recorded, but in the winter the great altitude of much of the country results in temperatures of −18°C (0°F) and below. The principal language is Farsi (Persian), spoken by about 50% of the population. Turkic-speaking Azerbaizhanis form about 27% of the population, and Kurds, Arabs, Baluchis and Turkomans form less than 25%. The great majority of Persians and Azerbaizhanis are Shi'i Muslims, while the other ethnic groups are mainly Sunni Muslims. There are also small minorities of Christians (mainly Armenians), Jews and Zoroastrians. The Bahá'í faith, which originated in Iran, has been severely persecuted. The national flag (proportions 3 by 1) has three horizontal stripes, of green, white and red, with the emblem of the Islamic Republic centrally positioned in red and the inscription 'Allaho Akbar' ('God is Great') repeated 22 times at the top and bottom. The capital is Teheran.

Recent History

Iran, called Persia until 1935, was formerly a monarchy, ruled by a Shah (Emperor). The country adopted its first imperial constitution in 1906, when the Qajar dynasty was in power. In 1921 Reza Khan, a Cossack officer, staged a military coup and became Minister of War. In 1923 he became Prime Minister, and in 1925 the National Assembly deposed the Shah and handed full power to Reza Khan. He was subsequently elected Shah, taking the title Reza Shah Pahlavi, and began the modernization of the country. During the Second World War Reza Shah favoured Nazi Germany. British and Soviet forces entered Iran in 1941, forcing the Shah to abdicate in favour of his son, Muhammad Reza Pahlavi.

After the war, British and US forces left Iran, although Soviet forces remained in Azerbaizhan until 1946. The Majlis (National Consultative Assembly) approved the nationalization of the petroleum industry in March 1951. The leading advocate of this measure was Dr Muhammad Mussadeq, leader of the National Front, who became Prime Minister in April 1951. After internal disturbances, Mussadeq was deposed in August 1953 in a coup supported by the USA and other Western countries. The dispute over nationalization was settled in August 1954, when an agreement was reached with foreign interests whereby concessions for petroleum drilling were granted to a consortium of eight companies. The Shah assumed total control of government in 1963, when he began an extensive redistribution of large estates to small farmers. In 1965 the Prime Minister, Hassan Ali Mansur, was assassinated, reportedly by a follower of the Ayatollah Ruhollah Khomeini, a Shi'i Muslim religious leader (exiled in 1964) who opposed the Shah's 'White Revolution' because it conflicted with traditional Islamic customs. The next Prime Minister was Amir Abbas Hoveida, who held office until 1977.

Between 1965 and 1977 Iran enjoyed political stability and considerable economic growth, based on revenue from petroleum. In March 1975 the Shah introduced a single-party system, based on the Iran National Resurgence Party (Rastakhiz). Opposition grew, however, and during 1977 and 1978 demonstrations and strikes against the Shah and his secret police (SAVAK) rose to crisis level. The most effective opposition came from the exiled religious leader, Ayatollah Khomeini, who conducted his campaign from France, where he had arrived in October 1978 after 14 years of exile in Iraq. Khomeini demanded a return to the principles of Islam, and the response to this call in Iran was so great that the Shah felt compelled to leave the country in January 1979. Khomeini arrived in Teheran shortly afterwards, and effectively took power, on 11 February. A 15-member Islamic Revolutionary Council was formed.

Iran quickly cut its ties with the Central Treaty Organization (CENTO) and aligned itself with the Arab world against Israel. Khomeini declared Iran an Islamic Republic on 1 April, and introduced a constitution which vests supreme authority in the Wali Faqih, a religious leader (initially Khomeini) appointed by the Shi'ite clergy, with no fixed term of office, while the elected President is chief executive. A presidential election in January 1980 resulted in a win for Abolhasan Bani-Sadr, who took about 75% of the votes. In February he was sworn in as President, and also became Chairman of the Revolutionary Council. Elections to the 270-seat Majlis (National Assembly) followed, and resulted in a clear win for the Islamic Republican Party (IRP), which was identified with Khomeini.

After the Majlis began its first session in May 1980, the Islamic Revolutionary Council was dissolved. It was clear that a rift was developing between President Bani-Sadr and the more extreme element in the IRP, and in June Khomeini dismissed Bani-Sadr as Commander-in-Chief of the Armed Forces and as President. Bani-Sadr fled to France, where he formed a 'National Council of Resistance' in alliance with Massoud Rajavi, the leader of the Iranian Mujaheddin Khalq (an Islamic guerrilla group), who had also fled to France. Bani-Sadr left the council in April 1984 because of his objection to Rajavi's increasing co-operation with the Iraqi Government. Rajavi himself left Paris in June 1986 for Baghdad, Iraq.

In November 1979 Iranian students seized 63 hostages in the US Embassy in Teheran. The original purpose of the seizure was to give support to a demand for the return of the Shah (then in the USA) to Iran to face trial. The problem was not resolved by the death of the Shah in Egypt in July 1980, as the Iranians made other demands, the most important of which was for a US undertaking not to interfere in the affairs of Iran. Intense diplomatic activity finally resulted in the release of the 52 remaining US hostages in January 1981.

Meanwhile, political chaos developed. A three-man Presidential Council replaced Bani-Sadr until a new presidential election in July 1981. In late June, however, a bomb exploded at the headquarters of the IRP, killing Ayatollah Beheshti (the Chief Justice of Iran and leader of the IRP), four government ministers, six deputy ministers and 20 members of the Majlis.

The presidential election in July 1981 resulted in a win for the Prime Minister, Muhammad Ali Rajai. Muhammad Javad Bahonar then became Prime Minister. A further bomb outrage occurred in late August, this time killing both the President (Rajai) and the Prime Minister (Bahonar). Ayatollah Muhammad Reza Mahdavi Kani became Prime Minister in September 1981, and another presidential election took place on 2 October. Hojatoleslam Ali Khamenei, a leading figure in the IRP, was elected President, winning more than 16m. of the 16.8m. votes cast. Later in October, Mir Hussein Moussavi, who had been Minister of Foreign Affairs since July, was appointed Prime Minister. A new Council of Experts was elected in December 1982 to choose a successor to Ayatollah Khomeini.

War broke out with Iraq in September 1980, when Iraq invaded Iran over a front of 500 km (300 miles) after a border dispute. The Gulf War, as it became known, soon degenerated into a conflict of attrition, with neither side able to launch a decisive offensive. When, beginning in October 1983, Iran staged a series of offensives across its northern border with Iraq, threatening the only remaining outlet for Iraqi exports of petroleum through the Kirkuk pipeline, Iraq intensified its attacks, with missiles and aircraft, against Iranian towns and petroleum installations. With French-built Super Etendard fighter aircraft and Exocet missiles, Iraq threatened to destroy Iran's petroleum industry, centred on Kharg Island in the Gulf. Iran countered by promising to make the Gulf impassable to all shipping if Iraqi military action destroyed its ability to export oil by that route.

In February and March 1984 a further Iranian offensive resulted in the capture of marshlands around the man-made Majnoun Islands in southern Iraq, the site of petroleum reserves estimated at 8,000m. barrels. Iraq failed to recapture the lost territory and was censured internationally for its alleged use of mustard gas in the fighting. A long hiatus ensued, and Iraq exploited the delay to construct a formidable defensive network along the southern front.

Although it had declared a maritime exclusion zone at the north-east end of the Persian Gulf, enclosing Kharg Island, in August 1982 and made spasmodic attacks against shipping (not only oil tankers but, in some cases, ships well outside the zone), Iraq refrained from attacking tankers using the Kharg terminal until May 1984. Iran retaliated by attacking Saudi Arabian and Kuwaiti tankers in the Gulf. A sporadic series of attacks on shipping by both Iran and Iraq continued, while Iraqi fighter aircraft inflicted damage on the Kharg Island oil terminal in occasional raids, dating from the end of February 1984.

Two peace formulas that were proposed in 1984 by President Mubarak of Egypt, as well as attempts at mediation by Saudi Arabia and Japan, were rejected by Iran, which refused to negotiate with the Iraqi regime of Saddam Hussain. With the success of a limited offensive in the central sector of the war front in October 1984, Iran expelled the Iraqis from all of its territory. The most serious problem associated with Iran's ethnic, religious and political minorities since the Islamic Revolution has been the demand for autonomy from the Kurds in the north-west, which has often led to open warfare in that area.

Active suppression of opposition to the Islamic regime continues. A report by the UN Human Rights Commission, published in February 1987, estimated the number of executions by the Government at a minimum of 7,000 between 1979 and 1985. The Mujaheddin-e-Khalq (the most prominent opposition guerrilla group in Iran) assess the number of executions at 70,000 since June 1981. The Iranian Communist Party (the Tudeh Party) was banned in April 1983, its leaders were arrested, and 18 Soviet diplomats were expelled from the country.

In August 1983 the resignation of the Ministers of Commerce and of Labour, followed shortly afterwards by the dismissal of three other Ministers, was the result of factional strife within the Government. The outgoing Ministers were right-wing 'bazaaris', the merchant class, who opposed, on grounds of religion and self-interest, the programme of nationalization and land reform advocated by the technocrats in the Council of Ministers. Prime Minister Moussavi nominated five replacements from the latter group but, in the case of three of them, had to make alternative choices before all the posts were filled by candidates acceptable to the predominantly conservative, clerical Majlis, which is required to approve Government appointments, and has also obstructed basic policy initiatives, particularly in the field of economic reform.

Elections to the second Majlis were held on 15 April and 17 May 1984, and a high proportion of the 1,230 or more candidates were professional people. The elections were boycotted by the Liberation Movement (the sole officially-recognized opposition party), led by Dr Mehdi Bazargan (who had been Prime Minister from February to November 1979), in protest against the allegedly undemocratic conditions prevailing in Iran. Some 60%–70% of the electorate (totalling 24m.–25m.) voted in the elections. When the second Majlis was opened on 28 May, it was estimated that more than 50% of the seats were filled by new members, and this gave rise to hopes that Prime Minister Moussavi might have greater success in implementing his economic programme. However, the Council of Guardians, which exists to determine whether legislation that has been approved by the Majlis is both constitutional and conforms to Islamic law, remained of a conservative, clerical cast and continued to be an obstacle to socialist economic reform.

Moussavi's Council of Ministers suffered a reverse in August 1984, when, under the provisions of new legislation requiring a separate vote of confidence for each Minister, five of its members failed to win the approval of the Majlis and had to be replaced.

Widespread active popular opposition to the Islamic regime was not conspicuous until 1985. Dissatisfaction with the conduct of the war with Iraq, and with austere economic conditions, precipitated demonstrations and rioting in several Iranian cities, including Teheran.

Only three candidates, including President Khamenei, contested the August 1985 presidential election. The Council of Guardians rejected the candidature of nearly 50 people who had applied to stand in the election, including Dr Mehdi Bazargan, leader of the Liberation Movement of Iran, the only legally-recognized opposition party, who opposed the continuation of the war with Iraq. Ali Khamenei was re-elected President for a second four-year term, with 85.7% of the total (14,244,630) votes being cast in his favour.

Although 99 deputies either voted against him or abstained, Hussein Moussavi was confirmed as Prime Minister by the Majlis on 13 October 1985. A dispute over the composition of Moussavi's new Council of Ministers, which President Khamenei considered to be too radical (withholding his approval from half of Moussavi's appointees), was not resolved until the intervention of Ayatollah Khomeini on Moussavi's behalf. On 28 October the Majlis approved 22 of the 24 nominations that had been submitted by Moussavi, rejecting only the candidates for the portfolios of economic affairs and finance, and mines and metals. Ministers for these posts were finally approved in January 1986.

In the continuing Gulf War Iran had ignored Iraqi terms for a cease-fire, insisting that only the removal of the regime of Saddam Hussain, the withdrawal of all Iraqi forces from Iran (which was achieved by Iranian military action) and Iraqi settlement of Iranian claims for US $350,000m. in war damages (as calculated in March 1985) could bring an end to hostilities. The UN had painstakingly engineered an agreement between Iran and Iraq in June 1984, suspending attacks on civilian targets, but, after the failure of an Iranian offensive in March 1985 (and with the war on the ground once more in a state of deadlock), Iraq declared Iranian airspace a war zone and resumed its bombardment of Iranian cities from the ground and from the air. Iraq, making full use of its superiority in the air, struck more than 30 Iranian population centres in the first half of 1985. President Saddam Hussain's stated intention was to carry the war to every part of Iran until the Iranian leadership decided to begin negotiating.

Iraqi raids on petroleum installations and on tankers carrying Iranian oil in the Gulf from May 1984 onwards reduced the level of Iran's exports, but until mid-1985 Iraqi attacks did not threaten the continuation of oil exports, and the terminal remained largely undamaged. Between August 1985 and January 1986, however, Iraq made a concentrated series of some 60 raids on Kharg Island and oil shipments from the terminal were reduced to a trickle, while the overall rate of exports of crude petroleum fell to 1.2m. b/d in February. In the latter month Iraq announced an expansion of the area of the Gulf from which it would try to exclude Iranian shipping. Previously confined to the waters around Iran's Gulf ports, the area was broadened to include the coast of Kuwait. Attacks on tankers and other commercial vessels in the Gulf were increased by both sides during 1986, and Iran intensified its practice of intercepting merchant vessels in the Gulf and confiscating goods which it believed to be destined for Iraq. Iraq was successful in damaging the alternative oil export facilities which Iran established at the islands of Sirri and Larak (in response to more concentrated Iraqi raids on Kharg Island), despite their remoteness at the mouth of the Persian Gulf (see Economic Affairs). However, despite extensive damage to the Kharg terminal, Iran was able to sustain its petroleum exports by exploiting the ample spare capacity available there, and by the transhipment of petroleum to the floating terminals at Sirri and Larak, where it is transferred to tankers for export.

The next important engagement in the land war did not occur until 1986. In February 1986 Iran began the Wal-Fajr (Dawn) 8 offensive, so called to commemorate the month of Ayatollah Khomeini's return to Iran in 1979. Massed Iranian forces crossed the Shatt al-Arab waterway and occupied the disused Iraqi port of Faw, on the Persian Gulf, and, according to Iran, about 800 sq km of the Faw peninsula. From this position, within sight of the Kuwaiti island of Bubiyan (commanding the Khawr Abdullah channel between the peninsula and the island), Iran threatened Iraq's only access to the Gulf. However, the difficulty of the terrain to the west prevented further Iranian gains, and the position on the Faw peninsula was not easily defensible, in view of the problem of maintaining supply lines across the Shatt al-Arab. To divert Iraqi forces, Iran had begun a complementary assault along the Faw–Basra road. When Iraq launched a counter-offensive on Faw in mid-February, Iran opened up a second front (the Wal-Fajr 9 offensive) in Iraqi Kurdistan, several hundred kilometres to the north. Iraq's counter-offensive failed to dislodge an estimated 30,000 Iranian troops from in and around Faw. At the end of February the UN Security Council, while urging the combatants to agree on a cease-fire, implicitly blamed Iraq for starting the war.

In May 1986 Iraq made its first armed incursions into Iran since withdrawing its forces from Iranian territory in 1982. Iranian forces counter-attacked and drove the Iraqis out of the country in July. Also in May, Iraqi aircraft raided Teheran for the first time since June 1985, initiating a new wave of reciprocal attacks on urban and industrial targets in Iran and Iraq, in particular on petroleum-related installations, which continued for the remainder of 1986 and into 1987.

In November 1986 it emerged that the USA, despite its discouragement of arms sales to Iran by other countries, had been conducting secret negotiations with the Islamic Republic since July 1985 and had made three shipments of weapons and spare parts to Iran through Israeli intermediaries, in September 1985 and July and October 1986, allegedly in exchange for Iranian assistance in releasing American hostages who had been detained by Shi'ite extremists in Lebanon, and an Iranian undertaking to abstain from involvement in international terrorism. The talks were reportedly conducted by the Speaker of the Majlis, Hojatoleslam Hashemi Rafsanjani, with Ayatollah Khomeini's consent but without the knowledge of other senior government figures.

In late 1986 and early 1987 Iranian forces mounted offensives against Basra, and, after suffering heavy casualties, advanced to within 10 km of the city. Although further offensives were launched in 1987, Iranian forces failed to capture Basra. Offensives launched at other points on the front failed to provide a decisive military end to the war.

During 1986 and 1987 the waters of the Gulf increasingly became the focus of international attention. Iran had begun to attack Kuwaiti shipping, and neutral shipping using Kuwait, because of Kuwait's support for Iraq. Kuwait then chartered Soviet tankers, and in May the USA agreed to re-register 11 Kuwaiti tankers under the US flag, entitling them to US naval protection. The USS Stark was mistakenly attacked by an Iraqi Mirage jet aircraft on 17 May 1987. The navies of the two superpowers were thus directly involved in the Gulf.

On 20 July 1987, as a response to this escalation of tension, the UN Security Council adopted Resolution 598, urging an immediate cease-fire in the Gulf War, the withdrawal of military forces to international boundaries, and the co-operation of Iran and Iraq in mediation efforts to achieve a peace settlement. By early 1988, in spite of intervention by the league of Arab States and a visit by the UN Secretary-General to Iran and Iraq, no success had been achieved in the implementation of Resolution 598. The main obstacle appeared to be Iranian insistence that the UN Security Council identify Iraq as the aggressor in the Gulf War.

Meanwhile, on 24 July 1987, the re-registered Kuwaiti tanker USS Bridgeton struck a mine while under US naval escort in the Gulf, and in August the UK and France sent minesweepers to the Gulf region, to be followed in September by vessels from the Netherlands, Belgium and Italy. Iraqi air attacks on tankers transporting Iranian oil, and Iranian reprisals against merchant shipping involved in trade with Iraq, continued to take place. The number of vessels attacked by both sides during 1987 was estimated at a minimum of 178, compared with 80 in 1986.

Relations between Iran and Saudi Arabia became increasingly strained after an incident in Mecca in July 1987, when 402 people, including 275 Iranian pilgrims, lost their lives. The Saudi Arabian Government maintained that most of the victims were trampled to death when 150,000 Iranians demonstrated in support of Ayatollah Khomeini, while the Iranians alleged that units of the Saudi Arabian police had opened fire.

In January and February 1988 the intervention of Ayatollah Khomeini, regarding two important questions of government, was believed to have strengthened the hand of socialist reformers, identified with Hashemi Rafsanjani, the Speaker of the Majlis, and Prime Minister Moussavi; and to have dealt a blow to the conservative clerical faction within the Iranian establishment. Elections to the third Majlis in April and May provided a further boost for the radicals in the Government by producing an assembly strongly representative of their views. In June Hashemi Rafsanjani was re-elected as Speaker of the Majlis and Hossein Moussavi was overwhelmingly endorsed as Prime Minister.

In March the Mujahidin Iranian National Liberation Army (NLA), supported by Iraq, mounted its first major offensive since its creation in 1987. In mid-April Iraqi forces recaptured the Faw peninsula, and in May drove Iranian forces across the Shatt al-Arab into Iran. The appointment of Hojatoleslam Hashemi Rafsanjani as acting Commander-in-Chief of the armed forces in June came too late to prevent further Iranian defeats, despite the creation of a general command headquarters to rationalize the disjointed military command structure. In mid-June Iraq recaptured Majnoun Island and the surrounding area, the site of one of the world's biggest oilfields, on the southern front.

In early July the USS Vincennes shot down an Iran Air Airbus A300B flying over the Strait of Hormuz, having mistakenly assumed it to be an attacking F-14 fighter-bomber. All 290 passengers and crew were killed. This was regarded as a set-back to Majlis Speaker Rafsanjani, who sought to end Iran's diplomatic isolation, and a boost to Iran's conservative mullahs, who were thought to favour the continuation of the Gulf War.

In July Iraqi troops crossed into Iranian territory for the first time since 1986, capturing the border town of Dehloran. In mid-July the last Iranian troops occupying territory in southern Iraq were dislodged. On 18 July, to universal surprise, Iran announced its official and unconditional acceptance of Resolution 598. The first clause of the resolution required the combatants to withdraw to international borders and to observe a cease-fire. However, due to a dispute regarding the terms of the resolution, it was not until 20 August that a cease-fire finally came into force.

Negotiations between Iran and Iraq for a comprehensive peace settlement began at foreign ministerial level in Geneva on 25 August 1988, under the aegis of the UN. However, the negotiations soon became deadlocked in disputes concerning sovereignty over the Shatt al-Arab, the right of navigation in the waterway and the Gulf, the exchange of prisoners of war, and the withdrawal of troops to within international borders. In November, in an attempt to break the deadlock, the UN sought to persuade both sides to agree to an exchange of prisoners. Iran and Iraq agreed to the repatriation of all sick and wounded prisoners, and the first exchange was reported to have occurred on 24 November. However, attempts to arrange a comprehensive exchange of prisoners of war collapsed almost immediately. In February 1989 the UN sought to persuade representatives of the Iranian and Iraqi Governments to accelerate confidence-building measures in order to break the deadlock in the negotiations.

There has been some speculation about Ayatollah Khomeini's successor as Walih Faqih. Ayatollah Montazeri's prospects of succession may have been damaged by his close association with Hojatoleslam Mehdi Hashemi, who was executed in September 1987 after he had been found guilty, among other charges, of forming a private army with the aim of overthrowing the Government. In December Khomeini altered his political testament, although its contents were not disclosed, but there was speculation that he wished the succession to pass to an elected leadership council. In October 1988 Khomeini named his son, Ahmad Khomeini, as the executor and the sole interpreter of his political legacy after his death.

The cease-fire of August 1988 stimulated new conflicts and exacerbated existing tensions within the Government. In September Ayatollah Khomeini acted to avert a rift in the leadership, regarding Iran's future political and economic direction, which focused on the extent to which ties with Western countries should be restored. The Government's claim in October that opposition parties would be allowed to operate freely, provided that they did not conspire against the country's political system, was offset by widespread reports of mass arrests and summary executions of alleged dissidents, in particular of suspected members of the People's Mujahidin Organization of Iran, since the cease-fire. There was speculation in January 1989 regarding possible changes to the country's administrative system, in particular the creation of a powerful executive presidency.

In February 1989 Khomeini ordered that a British author, Salman Rushdie, be killed for writing material offensive to Islam in his novel, *The Satanic Verses*. The confused response from Iran to Rushdie's apology was a further indication of conflicts and tensions within the Government.

Government

Legislative power is vested in the Islamic Consultative Assembly (Majlis), with 270 members. The chief executive of the administration is the President. The Majlis and the President are both elected by universal adult suffrage for a term of four years. A 12-member Council of Guardians supervises elections and ensures that legislation is in accordance with the Constitution and with Islamic precepts. The Committee to Determine the Expediency of the Islamic Order, created in February 1988, rules on legal and theological disputes between the Majlis and the Council of Guardians. The executive, legislative and judicial wings of state power are subject to the authority of the Wali Faqih. Ayatollah Hussain Ali Montazeri was chosen as eventual successor to the Wali Faqih in November 1985 by the Council of Experts, which had been appointed to determine the succession in December 1982.

Defence

In June 1988 Iran's regular armed forces totalled 604,500 (army 305,000, Revolutionary Guard Corps (Pasdaran) about 250,000, navy 14,500, air force 35,000). Including active paramilitary forces, however, the total strength could be up to 2m. There were 350,000 army reserves and more than 2.5m. in paramilitary forces, including 2.5m. in the Home Guard (Hezbollahi, 'of the party of God'). There is a 24–30-month period of military service. Defence expenditure for 1988/89 was estimated at IR 580,000m.

Economic Affairs

Before the Islamic Revolution and the Gulf War, Iran was one of the world's leading producers of petroleum, and massive government revenues from the petroleum industry stimulated the rest of the economy. Although industrial activity now predominates over agriculture in the formation of the gross national product (GNP), agriculture still occupies a major proportion of the total labour force (21.9%, according to a census carried out in late 1986). However, in spite of official claims of increases in agricultural output, imports of foodstuffs were estimated at $2,000m. in 1987. The high level of food imports is causing concern in Iran, but there are doubts that significant increases in agricultural productivity can be achieved in the short term. Agriculture has suffered massive losses of labour, and the issue of land ownership, raised by the revolution, remains unresolved. In 1988, however, the Government appeared to have obtained the necessary authority to implement radical economic reforms, and was expected to reactivate a programme of land reform. Provision of farm inputs is inadequate, and the state marketing system is ineffective. Cereals, sugar beet, fruits, nuts and vegetables are grown. Dairy produce, wool, hair and hides are also produced. There is a small fishing industry, both in the Caspian Sea, where caviar is obtained, and in the Persian Gulf. Forests cover more than 20m. ha. There are considerable deposits of copper and iron ore. A major copper complex at Sar Cheshmeh opened in May 1982.

The Islamic revolution of 1978–79 and the Gulf War, which began in 1980, have hampered the economy considerably. Petroleum remains predominant, and sales of oil accounted for about 24% of state revenue in 1986/87, compared with 74% in 1975/76 and 63% in 1983/84. However, production, which averaged about 6m. barrels per day (b/d) in 1976, fell to 5.2m. b/d in 1978 and to 3.1m. b/d in 1979. The onset of the Gulf War in September 1980 seriously affected output, and production in 1980/81 averaged only 1.5m. b/d, falling to 1.3m. b/d in 1981/82, and to 400,000 b/d in 1982/83. However, the average rate of production rose to 1.7m. b/d in 1983/84. Government revenue from petroleum fell from US $23,000m. in 1977/78 to $8,500m. in 1981/82, but recovered to $23,000m. in 1982/83 and $21,500m. in 1983/84. In 1984/85 oil exports of 1.68m. b/d were worth $17,000m., and in 1985/86 the value of oil exports declined to between $13,000m. and $15,000m. The most important buyers of Iranian oil are Japan (which accounts for about 20% of oil exports), Italy, Romania and the Federal Republic of Germany.

Potentially as great a threat to oil exports as actual damage to facilities has been the effect of the war on tanker insurance in the Gulf, which fluctuates according to the level of military activity in the area. For example, charges on vessels destined for Iran's main export terminal at Kharg Island rose to 7.5% of hull value in mid-1984 (10 times the premium at the beginning of the year), and between May and August Japan instructed its tankers not to use Kharg Island, both developments coinciding with the initiation of Iraqi attacks on tankers using the terminal there. Iran has repeatedly flouted OPEC quotas in order to maximize its earnings of foreign exchange while the Kharg Island terminal remains operational. It has also offered substantial discounts on its petroleum exports, undercutting official OPEC prices, and has undertaken to pay shipping and insurance costs, in order to attract customers who might otherwise be deterred by the risks to commercial shipping in the Gulf. In October 1984 Iran agreed to a reduction in its OPEC production quota from 2.4m. b/d to 2.3m. b/d.

In January 1985 Iran increased its oil prices, realigning them more closely with those of other OPEC producers. Prices of light crude were cut by $1.05, to $28.05, per barrel in February, when OPEC's 'marker' price for Arabian Light was reduced by $1 to $28 per barrel. By mid-1985, however, Iran was once again offering discounts on its oil. Barter deals (oil for goods) helped to increase exports of oil to more than 2.3m. b/d in April 1985, with overall production reaching about 3m. b/d. In 1984 25% of all oil exports were in the form of barter exchanges or under bilateral trade agreements.

Between August 1985 and January 1986 Iraq launched a series of some 60 attacks against the Kharg Island terminal (which was still responsible for more than 80% of Iran's oil exports). At the beginning of October, as a result of damage caused by these attacks, exports were reported to be of the order of only 750,000–800,000 b/d, compared with an average rate of about 1.5m. b/d in the months preceding the new wave of air raids. However, by dint of rapid repairs, the ample spare capacity available at Kharg, and alternative means of export, such as the shuttle to Sirri (despite Iraqi attacks on tankers shuttling oil), Iran was able to claim that exports in October finally averaged 1.7m. b/d. Average oil production in Iran at the end of 1985 was between 2.2m. and 2.5m. b/d, while exports were about 1.6m. b/d. Iraqi attacks on Kharg were reported to have reduced exports from the terminal to a trickle by January 1986, and the overall rate of export fell from about 1.5m. b/d in January to 1.2m. b/d in February. In August an Iraqi raid demonstrated that the Sirri oil-export facility was vulnerable to attack and Iran was forced to transfer more of its export operations to the floating terminal at Larak Island (250 km east of Sirri, in the Strait of Hormuz), which had been established in June. The terminal at Larak was itself attacked in November. Further Iraqi attacks on Kharg Island in September and October left only three out of 16 oil-loading berths at the terminal operational, and Iran's oil exports averaged only 800,000 b/d in the latter month. Iraq then concentrated its attacks on Iran's floating terminals and on the tanker shuttle service supplying them with oil, largely ignoring the Kharg Island terminal until June 1987. In April 1988 US warships damaged Salman, one of three oil rigs 150 km west of Sirri Island, and other installations. Offshore production may have fallen to 50,000 b/d or less after the attack. The Salman platform resumed operations in August, at 35% of its capacity, raising offshore production to 200,000 b/d.

At the end of January 1986 Iran offered to halve its oil production, and in February pressed OPEC to suspend oil exports for two weeks, in an attempt to force up international prices, which were falling more quickly than hitherto, following the decision of OPEC, in December 1985, to increase production in pursuit of a 'fair' share of an already glutted market. In July the world price of crude petroleum declined to less than $10 per barrel, and in August OPEC members, at Iranian instigation, agreed to reduce their output and to revert to earlier production quotas (imposed in October 1984) for two months from 1 September. Although Iraq refused to participate in the new agreement, Iran averred that military action in the Gulf War would effectively limit Iraqi oil production. In October, when the price of oil had risen to about $15 per barrel, OPEC members (excluding Iraq, which refused to participate in OPEC output programmes that did not allocate to it a quota commensurate with its production capacity or, at least, one the equal of Iran's) agreed to increase collective production by some 200,000 b/d. In December these OPEC members accepted a 7.25% reduction in their output for the first half of 1987, which, it was hoped, would enable the organization to support, from 1 February, a fixed price of $18 per barrel. The reduction gave Iran a production quota of 2.26m. b/d, compared with 2.32m. b/d in November and December. Iran's average output of crude oil was 2.04m. b/d during 1986, compared with 2.19m. b/d in 1985. Average production rose by 12.8% in 1987, compared with 1986, to 2.30m. b/d.

The OPEC production programme succeeded in sustaining the price of its oil at $18 per barrel during the first half of 1987. In June OPEC members agreed to retain the $18 per barrel benchmark but to increase their collective production by 800,000 b/d during the second half of the year to 16.6m. b/d. Iran's quota was raised to 2.37m. b/d. In June Iraqi aircraft attacked the Kharg Island terminal for the first time since January. It was reported that, in the interim, three oil-loading berths at Kharg had been made operational again. Iran exported at an average rate of 2.2m. b/d in August and 1.6m. b/d in September, according to oil industry sources, compared with an OPEC quota of 1.7m. b/d. By mid-October Iraqi attacks had reduced the number of tankers shuttling oil from Kharg to 20.

At the OPEC meeting which was held in December 1987, Iran demanded an increase in the central reference price of at least $2 per barrel, output reductions by members, and refused to participate in a new agreement which awarded Iraq the same quota as that given to Iran. It was finally agreed to retain the $18 per barrel reference price and the 'ceiling' of 16.6m. b/d (15.06m. b/d excluding Iraq) on collective production for a further six months from 1 January 1988. During the first half of 1988 prices remained below the OPEC reference level as member states continued to exceed their quotas. In May, however, OPEC decided to retain the 16.6m. b/d 'ceiling' and the $18 reference price for a further six months. In August, when the cease-fire in the Gulf War took effect, Iran was producing at its quota level of about 2.37m. b/d, though Iraqi attacks had meant that it had rarely been able to produce so much during the preceding six months. While Iranian representatives at OPEC meetings urged reductions in output in order to defend the $18 benchmark, Iran was allegedly so desperate for oil revenue that it was selling oil at less than $10 per barrel.

Plans for three oil pipelines were abandoned during 1986; however, it was confirmed in September 1987 that Iran was constructing a 1,100-km pipeline from its oilfields in the province of Khuzestan to Jask, outside the Persian Gulf, and well out of range of Iraqi aircraft. In early 1988 the Government revived the Moharram pipeline project, which it had abandoned in mid-1986. The project was expected to enter service in November, and, with a capacity of 600,000 b/d, to provide just over one-third of Iran's total exports (1.7m. b/d), as stipulated by OPEC. Discussions on a proposed export pipeline through Turkey, the development of which had been postponed since mid-1986, resumed in 1988. The pipeline was expected to be operative in 1992.

Iran has apparently budgeted at least $15,000m. for the expansion of the petroleum and petrochemical industries during the five years from 1984/85, the first stage of a 20-year plan, which it is hoped will make Iran self-sufficient in petrochemicals. Imports of petrochemicals cost $1,500m. in 1987. In March 1988 the Government announced investment in the petrochemical industry totalling $1,800m. during the next Five-Year Plan. There are plans for five new petroleum refineries, making a total of eleven. With the destruction of the main Abadan refinery (capacity 628,000 b/d), Iran's refining capacity fell to 555,000 b/d in 1980. The average production of Iran's refineries was 642,000 b/d in 1983/84, rising to 685,310 b/d in 1984/85, and at the end of 1985 it was reported that the refineries were operating at 31% above design capacity, giving a total output of 728,000 b/d. When the planned refineries become operational in the early 1990s, refining capacity could reach between 1m. b/d and 1.5m. b/d. Iran's own estimate of its recoverable petroleum reserves was 92,900m. barrels in January 1988, and it is preparing to exploit reserves (estimated at 8,000m. barrels) in deposits around the Majnoun Islands, captured from Iraq in February 1984. The Gulf War has made huge demands on Iran's financial resources, and for 1985/86 IR 400,000m. were allocated to basic war expenditure, with other war-related allocations set at IR 785,500m. (a total of IR 1,185,500m., or 30.6% of the proposed budget of IR 3,868,700m.). The official Iranian assessment of the cost of war damage was $350,000m. in March 1985 (including $160,000m. in the petroleum sector), while the cost of the war effort was estimated at $6,500m. for the period 1980–85. In August 1987, the Speaker of the Majlis, Ali Akbar Hashemi Rafsanjani, said that the war had cost Iran $3,000m. during the preceding 12 months alone. Owing to the cost of the war, and the effect of economic boycotts and of internal troubles since the Islamic Revolution, the Iranian economy declined in 1979/80 and 1980/81. These factors notwithstanding, according to Prime Minister Moussavi, Iran's GNP increased, in real terms, by 15.2% in 1982/83, when growth in the industrial sector was 14.8%. In the same year, Iran had a currency surplus of about $6,000m. and total foreign reserves of $9,500m. at March 1983. The National Iranian Industries Organization claimed that industrial output rose by 23% during 1983/84. However, this year was acknowledged as the most successful for the economy since the revolution. As a result of the continuing fall in the price of oil, government income was seriously reduced during 1985/86 and fell even further in 1986/87. Oil revenues declined to an estimated $6,600m., according to OPEC, compared with an estimated $13,000m.–$15,000m. in 1985/86. This downward trend was halted in early 1987, when the volume of exports of oil increased and prices rose. The value of oil exports was estimated at $9,700m. in 1987/88, and that of earnings from non-oil exports at $1,170m. The value of oil revenues in 1988/89 was forecast at $7,000m.–$8,000m. In mid-1986 reserves of foreign exchange (which fluctuate according to the level of petroleum sales) were independently estimated at $3,000m.–$4,000m., compared with government estimates of $6,000m.–$8,000m. There is evidence that economic growth declined to less than 10% in 1984/85, and may have fallen to zero in 1985/86. With oil revenues falling, a decline in real GNP (the first since 1980/81) may have been recorded in 1986/87. In 1987/88 the economy apparently grew again, however. The Government was believed to have withdrawn some $3,000m. from its reserves of foreign exchange in 1986. Reserve holdings have since steadily increased, however, and were estimated at $6,000m.–$7,000m. in mid-1988. According to official sources, Iran's foreign debt had declined to $420m. by mid-1988 (to be repaid by 1992), compared with $4,700m. in 1978. In February 1989 the Government announced its decision to resume foreign borrowing in order to finance development projects. However, such borrowing was to be strictly limited to revenue-producing projects and would not exceed $3,000m. over the next five years. With the same aim, the Government also declared its intention to resume exports of natural gas to the USSR.

Despite efforts to reduce the import bill and conserve foreign exchange, the value of imports rose from $11,845m. in 1982/83 to $24,200m. in 1983/84, although they declined to about $17,500m. in 1984/85 and to an estimated $15,000m. in 1985/86, after a tightening of import controls. Further controls were introduced in 1987, which permitted the import of only basic commodities. Non-military imports declined to $5,600m. in 1986/87. Trade with the West is now increasing steadily, and the Federal Republic of Germany remains Iran's leading supplier and a major purchaser of its non-oil exports. As a result of the suspension of US imports and the imposition of EEC and Japanese sanctions, in the years after the revolution Iran found new sources of supply in the Third World and among non-aligned countries in Western Europe. A protocol which envisages the development of economic relations between Iran and the USSR was signed in Moscow in September 1985. In October 1987 the USA placed a ban on all imports of Iranian goods and imposed tighter restrictions on US exports to Iran. It had earlier been revealed that, in July, Iran had become the second largest supplier of petroleum to the USA, and that, by October, Iranian exports to the USA (valued at some $1,000m.) were already at a higher level than in any year since the Islamic Revolution. These measures were taken by the USA as a 'direct result' of Iranian policy in the Gulf War. With the cost of the war and a burgeoning 'black market', inflation has been a persistent problem for the economy. The official rate of inflation fell from 32.5% in 1980/81 to 17% in 1983/84, and to 7.6% in 1984/85. In the first half of 1987, however, the rate was unofficially estimated at between 30% and 50%. In March 1988 the Government acknowledged an annual inflation rate of 20%.

Proposed expenditure in the budget for 1984/85 was cut by the Majlis, partly in an attempt to reduce inflation and an anticipated budget deficit of $10,000m. The budget for 1985/86 envisaged a 25% fall in the deficit, compared with the projected level for 1984/85. The plan and budget committee of the Majlis reduced budget expenditure from a proposed $42,000m. to $38,300m., with almost the entire reduction being made in current expenditure, to bring it into line with the anticipated fall in revenue from lower oil exports. The value of oil exports for 1985/86 was estimated at $19,700m. for budget purposes, but they eventually realized only $13,000m.–$15,000m. The budget for 1986/87 envisaged total expenditure of IR 4,049,700m. ($50,600m.) and provided for an increase of 12.5% in defence spending, while allocations to all other sectors were to be reduced, compared with those for 1985/86. Despite criticism of the Government's failure to allow for the rapid fall in oil prices, and the consequent decline in oil revenues, in preparing the budget, the Majlis unexpectedly increased planned expenditure for 1986/87 to IR 4,249,700m. ($53,100m.). Although projected oil revenue was revised downwards to IR 1,500,000m. ($18,600m.), even this proved to be an appreciable over-estimate, with actual revenue failing to reach one-half of that figure. In March 1987 the Majlis approved a budget of 4,000,000m. rials ($55,555m.) for 1987/88. War-related expenditure of $9,722m. was to account for 24% of current expenditure totalling $40,600m. (In recent years, however, actual spending on the war has been much greater than budget allocations.) A budget deficit of some $13,820m. was predicted, mainly as a result of the low volume of foreign exchange earnings, with oil revenues projected at $11,740m. In March 1988 the Majlis approved the budget for 1988/89, including estimated oil revenue of $9,000m., reduced from the Government's estimate of $10,000m. More funds were to be allocated to defence, agriculture, industry, health and education, but spending on services was to be reduced to $140m. Owing to the cost of the war, the budget deficit was projected at $15,000m.

The Islamic Republic's first five-year development plan was announced in August 1983. It was intended as the first step towards quadrupling the annual level of the gross domestic product over 20 years. The aims of the plan, covering 1983/84–1987/88, were stated to be the expansion of education and culture, securing the interests of the *mostazafin* (the deprived or downtrodden people), and the development of the agricultural sector. The Government's long-term objective is to secure economic independence for Iran by achieving self-sufficiency in food and by reducing dependence on the petroleum sector. (Crude oil's share of GNP was 20% in 1982/83, and oil exports accounted for 97% of all sales by value in 1983/84.) The value of non-oil exports (mainly carpets, caviar, pistachio nuts, dried fruit, hides and sulphur) rose from $283.7m. in 1982/83 to an estimated $1,170m. in 1987/88.

The Five-Year Plan was criticized for being too optimistic, and the Majlis forced its revision, cutting total expenditure by 10%. The Plan was returned to the Plan and Budget Organization again in early 1984, and in January 1985 the Majlis approved legislation that transformed the Plan and Budget Organization into a ministry. In January 1986 the Majlis approved the outline of the revised Five-Year Development Plan, which had been redrafted by the Ministry of Planning and Budget. A new five-year development plan, presented to the Majlis in October 1988, envisaged total investment of IR 22,736,000m., mainly by the private sector. In the same context, the Government planned to invest IR 5,383,000m.

Following the announcement of a cease-fire in the Gulf War in August 1988, the cost of repairing war-damage to Iran's industrial plant was estimated at $40,000m. While this, and other estimates, was highly speculative, it seemed certain that the possibilities for foreign participation in reconstruction would be numerous and the potential rewards huge.

Social Welfare

Under Article 29 of the 1979 Constitution, the Government has a duty to provide every citizen with insurance benefits covering illness, unemployment and retirement. In 1984 Iran had 589 hospital establishments, with a total of 70,000 beds. In 1983 there were 15,945 physicians working in the country.

Education

Education is officially compulsory for eight years, between six and 14 years of age, but this has not been fully implemented in rural areas. Primary education, which is provided free of charge, begins at the age of six and lasts for five years. Secondary education, from the age of 11, lasts for up to seven years: a first cycle of three years and a second of four years. As a proportion of school-age children, the total enrolment at primary and secondary schools in 1982 was 67% (boys 78%; girls 55%). There are 21 universities, including nine in Teheran, which were closed by the Government in 1980 but have been reopened gradually since 1983. According to the Statistical Centre of Iran, 146,000 students were enrolled at Iran's colleges and universities in the academic year 1984/85. In 1976 adult illiteracy averaged 63.8% (males 52.4%; females 75.7%). According to the census of October 1986, the rate of illiteracy was 38% among Iranians aged over six years, compared with 52.5% in 1976. Post-revolutionary policy has been to eliminate mixed-sex schools and to reduce instruction in art and music, while greater emphasis has been placed on agricultural and vocational programmes in higher education. According to the Government, 24,000 new schools were built between the revolution, in 1979, and 1984.

Public Holidays

The Iranian year 1368 runs from 21 March 1989 to 20 March 1990, and the year 1369 runs from 21 March 1990 to 20 March 1991.

1989: 11 February (National Day—Fall of the Shah), 5 March (Leilat al-Meiraj, ascension of Muhammad), 20 March (Oil Nationalization Day), 21–24 March (Now Ruz, the Iranian New Year), 1 April (Islamic Republic Day), 2 April (Revolution Day), 7 May (Id al-Fitr, end of Ramadan), 9 June (Birthday of Twelfth Imam), 14 July (Martyrdom of Imam Ali, and Id al-Adha, feast of the Sacrifice), 13 August (Ashoura), 13 October (Mouloud, Birth of Muhammad).

1990: 11 February (National Day—Fall of the Shah), 23 February (Leilat al-Meiraj), 20 March (Oil Nationalization Day), 21–24 March (Now Ruz, the Iranian New Year), 1 April (Islamic Republic Day), 2 April (Revolution Day), 27 April (Id al-Fitr), 9 June (Birthday of Twelfth Imam), 4 July (Id al-Adha), 14 July (Martyrdom of Imam Ali), 2 August (Ashoura), 2 October (Mouloud).

Weights and Measures

The metric system is in force, but some traditional units are still in general use.

Statistical Survey

The Iranian year runs from 21 March to 20 March.

Source (except where otherwise stated): Statistical Centre of Iran, Dr Fatemi Ave, Cnr Rahiye Moayeri, Opposite Sazeman-e-Ab, Teheran 14144; tel. 655061; telex 213233.

Area and Population

AREA, POPULATION AND DENSITY

Area (sq km)	1,648,000*
Population (census results)†	
1 November 1976	33,708,744
8 October 1986	
Males	25,491,645
Females	24,365,739
Total	49,857,384
Density (per sq km) at October 1986 census	30.3

* 636,296 sq miles.
† Excluding adjustment for underenumeration, estimated to have been 2.28% in 1976.

PRINCIPAL TOWNS (estimated population, spring 1982)

Tehran (Teheran)	6,022,029*	Abadan	294,068‡
Mashad (Meshed)	1,500,000*	Orumiyeh	262,588
Isfahan	1,000,000*	Rasht	259,638
Tabriz	852,296	Qazvin	244,265
Shiraz	800,416	Kerman	238,777
Bakhtaran		Hamadan	234,473
(Kermanshah)	531,350	Ardebil	221,970
Karaj	526,272†	Arak	209,970
Ahwaz	470,927	Yazd	193,282
Qom	424,048	Khorramshahr	140,490‡

* Population at 8 October 1986 census, including suburbs.
† Including suburbs.
‡ Population at November 1976 census.

BIRTHS AND DEATHS (UN estimates, annual averages)

	1970-75	1975-80	1980-85
Birth rate (per 1,000)	45.5	42.0	40.8
Death rate (per 1,000)	13.5	11.6	12.0

Source: UN, *World Population Prospects: Estimates and Projections as Assessed in 1984*.

1986: Registered live births 2,033,285 (birth rate 40.9 per 1,000); Registered deaths 190,061 (death rate 3.8 per 1,000).
Note: Registration is incomplete.

ECONOMICALLY ACTIVE POPULATION*
(November 1976 census)

	Males	Females	Total
Agriculture, forestry, hunting and fishing	2,763,934	227,935	2,991,869
Mining and quarrying	86,604	3,284	89,888
Manufacturing	1,032,960	639,099	1,672,059
Construction	1,180,913	7,807	1,188,720
Electricity, gas, water supply	59,716	1,917	61,633
Commerce	656,177	12,317	668,494
Transport, storage and communications	422,647	8,824	431,471
Services	1,324,586	296,011	1,620,597
Others (not adequately defined)	59,863	14,826	74,689
Total in employment	7,587,400	1,212,020	8,799,420
Unemployed	759,650	236,986	996,636
Total	8,347,050	1,449,006	9,796,056

* Including nomadic tribes and other unsettled population.

October 1986 census (employment distribution by sector): Agriculture 21.9%; Industry 25.5%; Services 42%.

Agriculture

PRINCIPAL CROPS (estimates, '000 metric tons)

	1982/83	1983/84	1984/85
Wheat	6,660	5,956	6,207
Barley	1,903	2,034	2,293
Rice (paddy)	1,605	1,215	1,474
Sugar beet	4,321	3,648	3,392
Sugar cane	1,810	2,053	2,126
Tea (green leaves)*	157	162	194
Oil seeds†	138	188	118
Cotton (lint)	358	300	351
Tobacco	25	21	22
Pulses	296	290	303
Potatoes	1,814	1,740	1,784
Onions	965	736	844
Pistachios	95	84	94

* Production of made tea is assumed to be 22.5%.
† Sunflower seeds and soybeans.

Source: Ministry of Agriculture and Rural Development.

LIVESTOCK
(FAO estimates, '000 head, year ending September)

	1984	1985	1986
Horses	316	316	316
Mules	123	123	123
Asses	1,800	1,800	1,800
Cattle	8,200	8,350	8,350
Buffaloes	230	230	230
Camels	27	27	27
Pigs	20	n.a.	n.a.
Sheep	34,000	34,500	34,500
Goats	13,600	13,600	13,600

Chickens (FAO estimates, million): 90 in 1984; 95 in 1985; 100 in 1986.

Source: FAO, *Production Yearbook*.

LIVESTOCK PRODUCTS (FAO estimates, '000 metric tons)

	1984	1985	1986
Beef and veal	165	168	168
Buffalo meat	10	10	10
Mutton and lamb	234	234	234
Goats' meat	45	45	45
Poultry meat	235	240	245
Other meat	18	18	18
Cows' milk	1,650	1,700	1,700
Buffaloes' milk	39	39	39
Sheep's milk	705	715	715
Goats' milk	223	223	223
Cheese	104.4	106.4	106.4
Butter	69.7	71.4	71.4
Hen eggs	210	220	230
Honey	6	6	6
Wool:			
greasy	16.2	16.3	16.3
clean	8.9	9.0	9.0
Cattle and buffalo hides	34.4	35.1	35.1
Sheep skins	39.0	39.0	39.0
Goat skins	9.1	9.1	9.1

Source: FAO, *Production Yearbook*.

IRAN

Statistical Survey

Forestry

ROUNDWOOD REMOVALS (FAO estimates, '000 cu metres)

	1984	1985	1986
Sawlogs, veneer logs and logs for sleepers*	369	369	369
Other industrial wood†	4,007	4,007	4,007
Fuel wood	2,357	2,369	2,381
Total	6,733	6,745	6,757

* Assumed to be unchanged since 1977.
† Assumed to be unchanged since 1974.
Source: FAO, *Yearbook of Forest Products*.

SAWNWOOD PRODUCTION ('000 cu metres)

	1975	1976	1977
Sawnwood (incl. boxboards)*	90	90	90
Railway sleepers	80	54	73
Total	170	144	163

* FAO estimate (production assumed to be unchanged since 1974).
1978–86: Annual production as in 1977 (FAO estimate).
Source: FAO, *Yearbook of Forest Products*.

Fishing

('000 metric tons, live weight)

	1984	1985	1986
Inland waters	22.1	21.4	30.3
Marine fishes	88.4	90.8	115.1
Marine crustaceans and molluscs	4.8	5.6	6.7
Total catch	115.3	117.8	152.1

Source: FAO, *Yearbook of Fishery Statistics*.

Production of caviar (metric tons, year ending 20 March): 222 in 1982/83; 170 in 1983/84; 248 in 1984/85 (Source: Iran Fishery Co).

Mining

CRUDE PETROLEUM (net production, '000 barrels per day)

	1982/83	1983/84	1984/85
Southern oilfields	2,442	2,454	2,113
Naftshahr oilfield	0	0	0
Offshore oilfields	242	255	258
Doroud-Forouzan-Abouzar-Soroush	60	63	70
Bahregansar-Nowruz	0	0	0
Salman-Rostam	160	172	168
Sirri	22	20	20
Total	2,684	2,709	2,371

Source: Ministry of Oil.

NATURAL GAS (million cu metres)

	1982/83	1983/84	1984/85
Consumption (domestic)*	18,000	15,500	21,500
Flared	12,400	12,300	9,400
Total production	30,400	27,800	30,900

* Includes gas reinjected to maintain oilfield pressure.
Source: Bank Markazi Iran, *Economic Report and Balance Sheet 1363*.

OTHER MINERALS* ('000 metric tons, year ending 20 March)

	1983/84	1984/85	1985/86
Hard coal†	800	850	900
Iron ore‡	450	450	450
Copper ore‡	65	60	60
Lead ore‡	20.0	20.0	20.4
Zinc ore‡	30	30	36
Chromium ore‡	23	23	23
Magnesite (crude)	5	5	5
Native sulphur	20	30	30
Barytes	85	91	91
Salt (unrefined)	753	753	753
Gypsum (crude)†	5,440	4,990	4,990

* Estimated production, based on data from the US Bureau of Mines.
† Figures refer to calendar years 1983, 1984 and 1985.
‡ Figures refer to the metal content of ores.
Source: UN, *Industrial Statistics Yearbook*.

Industry

PETROLEUM PRODUCTS ('000 metric tons)

	1983	1984	1985
Liquefied petroleum gas*†	1,080	1,000	1,200
Naphtha	141	136	142
Motor spirit (petrol)	3,704	4,368	4,547
Aviation gasoline	60	80	90
Kerosene	3,000	3,100	3,100
White spirit*	70	80	80
Jet fuel	300	350	350
Distillate fuel oils	9,428	10,667	11,359
Residual fuel oils	10,195	11,265	11,683
Lubricating oils*	460	460	394
Petroleum bitumen (asphalt)*	1,474	1,444	1,624

* Estimated production.
† Includes production from natural gas plants ('000 metric tons): 500 in 1983; 400 in 1984; 600 in 1985; and from petroleum refineries: 580 in 1983; 600 in 1984; 600 in 1985.
Source: UN, *Industrial Statistics Yearbook*.

OTHER PRODUCTS (year ending 20 March)

	1982/83	1983/84	1984/85
Refined sugar ('000 metric tons)	487	489	483
Cigarettes (million)	13,546	15,104	16,154
Paints ('000 metric tons)	45.2	58.9	61.5
Cement ('000 metric tons)	10,356	11,093	11,888
Refrigerators ('000)	551	693	744
Gas stoves ('000)	420	464	416
Telephone sets ('000)	237	319	329
Radios and recorders ('000)	32	176	204
Television receivers ('000)	401	551	524
Motor vehicles (assembled) ('000)	201	272	303
Footwear (million pairs)	47	50	53
Machine-made carpets ('000 sq m)	6,039	8,242	9,307

Production of Electricity (estimates, million kWh): 28,823 in 1982/83; 33,009 in 1983/84; 36,594 in 1984/85 (Source: Ministry of Energy).

IRAN

Statistical Survey

Finance

CURRENCY AND EXCHANGE RATES

Monetary Units
100 dinars = 1 Iranian rial (IR).

Denominations
Coins: 1, 2, 5, 10, 20 and 50 rials.
Notes: 100, 200, 500, 1,000, 2,000, 5,000 and 10,000 rials.

Sterling and Dollar Equivalents (30 September 1988)
£1 sterling = 120.88 rials;
US $1 = 71.48 rials;
1,000 Iranian rials = £8.273 = $13.989.

Average Exchange Rate (rials per US $)
1985   91.052
1986   78.760
1987   71.460

Note: The data on exchange rates refer to the official rate of the Central Bank, applicable to all foreign exchange transactions since December 1984, and to almost all transactions prior to that date. Since 22 May 1980 this valuation of the Iranian rial has been linked to the IMF's special drawing right (SDR) at a mid-point rate of SDR 1 = 92.30 rials. Prior to December 1984, a system of multiple exchange rates was in operation, with a preferential rate, applicable to proceeds from non-oil exports, and another rate applicable to sales of foreign exchange for tourism.

GOVERNMENT BUDGET ESTIMATES
(million rials, year ending 20 March)

Revenue	1985/86	1986/87
General revenue	3,780,400	3,574,700
Income from taxation	1,138,200	1,169,800
Oil	1,867,000	1,600,000
Sales of foreign exchange	119,000	111,000
Other	396,300	424,200
Special income	259,900	269,700
Deficit finance	354,400	475,000
Total	**4,134,800**	**4,049,700**

Expenditure	1985/86	1986/87
Expenditure	3,874,900	3,780,000
War expenditure	400,000	430,000
War reconstruction	50,000	35,000
Fixed investment	1,085,800	949,200
Repayment of foreign loans	33,800	24,500
Current expenditure	2,305,300	2,341,300
From special income	259,900	269,700
Total	**4,134,800**	**4,049,700**

CENTRAL BANK RESERVES
(US $ million at 31 December)

	1980	1981	1982
Gold*	220	247	229
IMF special drawing rights	307	339	331
Reserve position in IMF	299	165	84
Foreign exchange*	9,617	1,102	5,287
Total	**10,443**	**1,853**	**5,931**

* Figures refer to 20 December. Gold is valued at 35 SDRs per troy ounce.
Source: IMF, *International Financial Statistics*.

MONEY SUPPLY ('000 million rials at 20 December)

	1981	1982	1983
Currency outside banks	1,248.3	1,465.4	1,756.9
Official entities' deposits at Central Bank	166.5	329.1	335.0
Demand deposits at commercial banks	1,222.1	1,498.2	1,830.1
Total	**2,636.9**	**3,292.7**	**3,922.0**

Source: IMF, *International Financial Statistics*.

COST OF LIVING (Consumer Price Index; base: 1980 = 100)

	1983	1984	1985
Food	179.5	195.6	205.8
Fuel and light	140.8	146.3	151.9
Clothing	193.0	221.5	227.2
Rent	130.2	145.1	163.8
All items (incl. others)	176.6	198.6	207.4

Source: ILO, *Year Book of Labour Statistics*.

NATIONAL ACCOUNTS
('000 million rials at current prices, year ending 20 March)

National Income and Product

	1982/83	1983/84	1984/85
Domestic factor incomes*	9,913.4	12,538.4	13,641.0
Consumption of fixed capital	708.1	932.9	1,062.0
Gross domestic product (GDP) at factor cost	10,621.5	13,471.3	14,703.0
Indirect taxes	315.0	416.8	481.6
Less Subsidies	180.2	138.6	155.0
GDP in purchasers' values	10,756.3	13,749.5	15,029.6
Factor income from abroad	89.3	108.4	90.7
Less Factor income paid abroad	89.5	115.1	102.1
Gross national product (GNP)	10,756.1	13,742.8	15,018.2
Less Consumption of fixed capital	708.1	932.9	1,062.0
National income in market prices	10,048.0	12,809.9	13,956.2

* Compensation of employees and the operating surplus of enterprises.
Source: UN, *National Accounts Statistics*.

1985/86 ('000 million rials): GDP in purchasers' values 15,305.8; Net factor income from abroad −33.6; GNP 15,272.2 (Source: IMF, *International Financial Statistics*).

Expenditure on the Gross Domestic Product

	1983/84	1984/85	1985/86
Government final consumption expenditure	2,100.2	2,143.0	2,391.2
Private final consumption expenditure	7,232.7	8,129.6	8,745.8
Increase in stocks	1,991.6	1,929.0	1,843.3
Gross fixed capital formation	2,944.6	2,884.1	2,537.3
Statistical discrepancy	−554.2	29.0	−391.8
Total domestic expenditure	13,714.9	15,114.7	15,125.8
Exports of goods and services	1,885.2	1,520.1	1,215.7
Less Imports of goods and services	1,850.6	1,605.2	1,035.7
GDP in purchasers' values	13,749.5	15,029.6	15,305.8
GDP at constant 1974/75 prices	3,486.7	3,495.0	3,443.4

Source: UN, *Monthly Bulletin of Statistics*.

IRAN

Statistical Survey

Gross Domestic Product by Economic Activity (at factor cost)

	1982/83	1983/84	1984/85
Agriculture, hunting, forestry and fishing	1,912.1	2,138.5	2,493.9
Mining and quarrying	1,927.8	1,951.8	1,696.4
Manufacturing	894.4	1,072.9	1,167.3
Electricity, gas and water	98.6	90.9	107.0
Construction	685.6	1,088.6	1,115.2
Trade, restaurants and hotels	1,702.8	2,842.8	3,205.4
Transport, storage and communications	709.8	947.6	1,138.4
Finance, insurance, real estate and business services	1,253.0	1,627.5	1,867.2
Government services	1,040.5	1,175.7	1,189.8
Other services	607.8	782.0	975.1
Sub-total	10,832.4	13,718.3	14,955.7
Less Imputed bank service charge	210.9	247.0	252.7
Total	10,621.5	13,471.3	14,703.0

Source: UN, *National Accounts Statistics*.

BALANCE OF PAYMENTS (US $ million, year ending 20 March)

	1982/83	1983/84	1984/85
Merchandise exports f.o.b.	20,452	21,507	17,087
Merchandise imports f.o.b.	−12,552	−18,027	−14,729
Trade balance	7,900	3,480	2,358
Exports of services	1,121	1,335	1,069
Imports of services	−3,288	−4,457	−3,841
Current balance	5,733	358	−414
Long-term capital (net)	−1,866	−271	−421
Short-term capital (net)	19	−2,203	−2,397
Net errors and omissions	968	844	−901
Total (net monetary movements)	4,854	−1,272	−4,133
Valuation changes (net)	−900	−5	−28
Changes in reserves	3,954	−1,277	−4,161

Source: IMF, *International Financial Statistics*.

External Trade

PRINCIPAL COMMODITIES
(US $ million, year ending 20 March)

Imports c.i.f.	1982/83	1983/84	1984/85
Food and live animals	2,164	2,368	2,070
Beverages and tobacco	7	90	82
Crude materials (inedible) except fuels	461	802	522
Mineral fuels, lubricants, etc.	207	205	299
Animal and vegetable oils and fats	192	338	361
Chemicals and chemical products	1,679	2,084	1,768
Paper, textiles, iron and steel, mineral products, etc.	3,507	5,326	3,561
Machinery and motor vehicles	3,331	6,317	5,452
Miscellaneous manufactured articles	284	530	379
Other commodities	13	43	21
Total	11,845	18,103	14,494

Exports f.o.b. (excl. petroleum and gas)	1982/83	1983/84	1984/85
Agricultural and traditional goods	255.3	318.1	295.0
Carpets	67.0	88.9	89.8
Fruit (fresh and dried)	78.8	125.5	79.8
Animal skins and hides, and leather	40.6	34.6	48.7
Caviar	18.9	19.0	21.9
Casings	17.6	13.6	11.4
Others	32.4	36.5	43.4
Metal ores	7.1	12.5	38.8
Industrial manufactures	21.3	26.0	27.3
Shoes	1.7	2.8	2.6
Biscuits and pastries	—	1.3	0.3
Textile manufactures	9.6	10.0	14.3
Cements	3.4	3.1	1.1
Motor vehicles	1.5	1.4	0.2
Others	5.1	7.4	8.8
Total	283.7	356.6	361.1

PETROLEUM EXPORTS
('000 barrels per day, year ending 20 March)

	1982/83	1983/84	1984/85
Crude petroleum	1,686	2,045	1,607
Refined oil products	181	57	67

Source: Ministry of Oil.

Value of crude petroleum exports ('000 million rials, year ending 20 December; estimates): 731.5 in 1981; 1,508.3 in 1982; 1,621.0 in 1983; 1,065.9 in 1984; 1,156.7 in 1985 (Source: IMF, *International Financial Statistics*).

Total Exports ('000 million rials, year ending 20 December; estimates): 980.8 in 1981; 1,632.4 in 1982; 1,684.7 in 1983; 1,127.8 in 1984; 1,218.6 in 1985 (Source: IMF, *International Financial Statistics*).

PERCENTAGE GEOGRAPHICAL DISTRIBUTION OF CRUDE PETROLEUM EXPORTS

	1982	1983	1984
Western Europe	50.8	48.4	49.3
Japan	14.6	20.2	16.7
Asia (excluding Japan)	24.3	21.7	22.5
Africa	0.2	0.1	1.4
South America	1.0	1.8	1.2
Eastern Europe	9.1	7.8	8.9

Source: Ministry of Oil.

IRAN

Statistical Survey

PRINCIPAL TRADING PARTNERS
(US $ million, year ending 20 March)

Imports c.i.f.	1982/83	1983/84	1984/85
Argentina	152	421	382
Australia	295	292	388
Austria	194	329	265
Belgium	338	417	560
Brazil	222	425	481
France	382	291	138
Germany, Fed. Republic	1,936	3,443	2,775
Italy	552	839	643
Japan	1,250	3,022	2,064
Korea, Republic	400	503	428
Netherlands	312	404	358
New Zealand	290	304	287
Romania	463	313	168
Spain	359	384	301
Sweden	210	492	458
Switzerland	296	356	265
Turkey	774	853	523
United Arab Emirates	127	335	302
United Kingdom	709	1,087	1,211
Total (incl. others)	11,845	18,103	14,494

Exports f.o.b.*	1982/83	1983/84	1984/85
Bulgaria	—	2.4	9.1
Czechoslovakia	7.9	5.1	24.4
France	9.9	7.9	3.5
German Democratic Republic	4.4	5.8	9.9
Germany, Fed. Republic	53.3	73.4	64.2
Hungary	1.4	10.7	16.5
Italy	35.6	33.0	38.6
Japan	7.0	8.4	5.2
Korea, Republic	—	0.9	4.9
Kuwait	15.2	9.4	5.6
Lebanon	5.5	2.8	2.3
Netherlands	4.3	3.8	3.5
Saudi Arabia	9.0	4.5	4.2
Switzerland	9.8	13.2	24.1
Turkey	0.3	2.0	5.8
USSR	55.5	40.0	43.2
United Arab Emirates	18.1	50.2	33.0
United Kingdom	8.6	16.3	17.7
Total (incl. others)	283.7	356.6	361.1

* Excluding petroleum products and hydrocarbon solvents obtained from petroleum.

Transport

RAILWAYS (traffic)

	1981	1982	1983
Passenger-km (million)	2,728	4,735	5,784
Freight ton-km (million)	3,811	5,566	6,762

Source: UN, *Statistical Yearbook*.

ROAD TRAFFIC ('000 vehicles in use)

	1981	1982	1983
Cars	1,540	1,604	1,694
Buses	48	71	57
Trucks	281	293	332
Ambulances	366	425	575
Motor cycles	435	472	475

MERCHANT SHIPPING FLEET
('000 gross registered tons at 30 June)

	1982	1983	1984
Oil tankers	631	916	918
Other vessels	682	879	1,188
Total	1,313	1,795	2,106

Source: UN, *Statistical Yearbook*.

INTERNATIONAL SEA-BORNE SHIPPING
(estimated freight traffic, '000 metric tons)

	1983	1984	1985
Goods loaded	93,780	94,100	78,667
Crude petroleum and petroleum products	93,680	94,000	78,578
Goods unloaded	12,280	12,000	12,205
Petroleum products	3,280	3,000	2,557

Source: UN, *Monthly Bulletin of Statistics*.

CIVIL AVIATION (traffic on scheduled services)

	1982	1983	1984
Kilometres flown (million)	14.9	23.5	28.6
Passengers carried ('000)	2,009	3,191	4,088
Passenger-km (million)	1,852	3,021	4,089
Freight ton-km (million)	42.1	74.7	90.3

Source: UN, *Statistical Yearbook*.

Tourism

	1980	1981	1982
Visitors	156,380	185,756	62,373

1984: Total number of visitors 157,000 (estimate).
1986/87: Total number of visitors 171,837 (85,801 tourists).

Education
('000 students)

	1982/83*	1983/84*
Kindergartens	178	203
Primary schools	5,593	5,994
Junior high schools	1,717	1,818
High schools	849	867
Technical and vocational schools	127	148
Colleges and teacher training colleges	19	30
Others†	223	189
Total	8,706	9,249
Number of institutions	61,967	65,361
Number of teachers‡	425,600	432,822

* The Iranian year runs from 21 March to 20 March. The year 1982/83 corresponds to the Iranian year 1361; 1983/84 to 1362.
† Includes students at schools for exceptional children and on general adult courses.
‡ Includes kindergartens, primary, junior high, and high schools.

Source: Ministry of Education.

Directory

The Constitution

A draft constitution for the Islamic Republic of Iran was published on 18 June 1979. It was submitted to a 'Council of Experts', elected by popular vote on 3 August 1979, to debate the various clauses and to propose amendments. The amended Constitution was approved by a referendum on 2-3 December 1979.

The Constitution states that the form of government of Iran is that of an Islamic Republic, and that the spirituality and ethics of Islam are to be the basis for political, social and economic relations. Persians, Turks, Kurds, Arabs, Baluchis, Turkomans and others will enjoy completely equal rights.

The Constitution provides for a President to act as chief executive. The President is elected by universal adult suffrage for a term of four years. Legislative power is held by the Majlis (Islamic Consultative Assembly), with 270 members who are similarly elected for a four-year term. Provision is made for the representation of Zoroastrians, Jews and Christians.

All legislation passed by the Islamic Consultative Assembly must be sent to the Council for the Protection of the Constitution (Article 94), which will ensure that it is in accordance with the Constitution and Islamic legislation. The Council for the Protection of the Constitution consists of six religious lawyers appointed by the Faqih (see below) and six lawyers appointed by the High Council of the Judiciary and approved by the Islamic Consultative Assembly. Articles 19-42 deal with the basic rights of individuals, and provide for equality of men and women before the law and for equal human, political, economic, social and cultural rights for both sexes.

The press is free, except in matters that are contrary to public morality or insult religious belief. The formation of religious, political and professional parties, associations and societies is free, provided they do not negate the principles of independence, freedom, sovereignty and national unity, or the basis of Islam.

The amended Constitution contains a significant change from the earlier draft. It provides for a *Wali Faqih* (religious leader) who, in the absence of the Imam Mehdi (the hidden Twelfth Imam), carries the burden of leadership. Article 107 gives Ayatollah Khomeini these powers for the rest of his natural life. Thereafter, an elected Council of Experts will choose an individual or three or five people to form a council of leadership, and the choice must be 'approved by the nation'. According to Article 57 the executive, legislative and judicial branches of state power are under the authority of the Faqih. Among the extensive powers reserved to the Faqih is the right to appoint half the members of the Council for the Protection of the Constitution (see above). He is also Supreme Commander of the Armed Forces and can appoint the Joint Chiefs of Staff and the Head of the Revolutionary Guard. He appoints four of the seven members of the National Defence Council and, on their recommendation, appoints the senior commanders of the armed forces. He also has power to declare war and make peace on the recommendation of the National Defence Council. The first Faqih has the right to vet all candidates for the presidency (a right which was exercised by Ayatollah Khomeini). The Faqih can also dismiss the President on the basis of a Supreme Court decision or a vote of no confidence by the Islamic Consultative Assembly.

PROVINCIAL DIVISIONS

According to the state division of May 1977, Iran was divided into 23 provinces (Ostans), 472 counties (shahrestan) and 499 municipalities (bakhsh).

The Government

WALI FAQIH (RELIGIOUS LEADER)

Ayatollah SAYED RUHOLLAH MOUSSAVI KHOMEINI (formally designated in Constitution adopted by referendum on 2-3 December 1979).

HEAD OF STATE

President: Hojatoleslam SAYED ALI KHAMENEI (took office 13 October 1981; re-elected 16 August 1985).

COUNCIL OF MINISTERS
(February 1989)

Prime Minister: MIR HOSSEIN MOUSSAVI.
Deputy Prime Minister in charge of Political Affairs: ALI REZA MOAYERI.
Minister of Foreign Affairs: Dr ALI AKBAR VELAYATI.
Minister of Education and Training: MUHAMMAD ALI NAJAFI.
Minister of Islamic Guidance: Hojatoleslam Dr SAYED MUHAMMAD KHATAMI.
Minister of the Islamic Revolutionary Guard Corps: ALI SHAMKHANI.
Minister of Commerce: (vacant).
Minister of Health: Dr ALI REZA MARANDI.
Minister of Posts, Telegraphs and Telephones: Eng. SAYED MUHAMMAD GHARAZI.
Minister of Justice: Dr HASSAN HABIBI.
Minister of Defence: Col MUHAMMAD HUSSEIN JALALI.
Minister of Roads and Transport: Eng. MUHAMMAD SAYEDIKIYA.
Minister of Industries: Eng. GHOLAM REZA SHAFEI.
Minister of Heavy Industry: Eng. BEHZAD NABAVI.
Minister of Higher Education and Culture: Dr MUHAMMAD FARHADI.
Minister of Mines and Metals: MUHAMMAD REZA AYATOLLAHI.
Minister of Labour and Social Affairs: ABOLQASSEM SARHADIZADEH.
Minister of the Interior: Hojatoleslam SAYED ALI AKBAR MOHTASHAMI.
Minister of Agriculture: ISA KALANTARI.
Minister of Housing and Urban Development: Eng. SERAG ED-DIN KAZEROUNI.
Minister of Energy: NAMDAR ZANGANEH.
Minister of Oil: GHOLAMREZA AQAZADEH.
Minister of Economic Affairs and Finance: MUHAMMAD JAVAD IRAVANI.
Minister of Intelligence and Internal Security: Hojatoleslam MUHAMMAD MUHAMMADI REYSHAHRI.
Minister of Construction Jihad: GHOLAMREZA FOROUZESH.
Minister of Planning and Budget: MASSOUD ZANJANI.
Minister of State and Head of State Welfare Organization: JAVAD EZHEH'I.
Minister of State for Executive Affairs and Supervisor of Prime Minister's Office: (vacant).

MINISTRIES

Ministry of Mines and Metals: 248 Somayeh Ave, Teheran; tel. (021) 836051; telex 212718.
Ministry of Roads and Transport: 49 Taleghani Ave, Teheran; tel. (021) 646770.

All ministries are in Teheran.

President and Legislature

PRESIDENTIAL ELECTION
16 August 1985

Candidates	Votes	%
Hojatoleslam SAYED ALI KHAMENEI	12,203,870	85.7
MAHMOUD MOSTAFAVI KASHANI	1,402,416	9.8
HABIBOLLAH ASGAR-OWLADI	283,297	2.0
Invalid	355,047	2.5
Total	14,244,630	100.0

MAJLIS-E-SHURA E ISLAMI—ISLAMIC CONSULTATIVE ASSEMBLY

Elections to the third Majlis took place in two rounds, on 8 April and 13 May 1988. These were the first elections not to be contested by political parties. The Islamic Republican Party, which had won a clear majority of seats in the elections to the Majlis in 1980 and 1984 (as the larger of only two parties permitted to participate), was disbanded in June 1987. In the 1988 elections the 270 seats were contested by some 1,600 candidates, recommended by political groups and approved by local screening committees.

Speaker: Hojatoleslam ALI AKBAR HASHEMI RAFSANJANI.

IRAN
Directory

Deputy Speakers: Hojatoleslam MAHDI KARRUBI, Hojatoleslam HOSSEIN HASHEMIAN.

COUNCIL OF EXPERTS

Elections were held on 10 December 1982 to appoint a Council of Experts which was to choose an eventual successor to the Wali Faqih, Ayatollah Khomeini, after his death. The Constitution provides for a three- or five-man body to assume the leadership of the country if there is no recognized successor on the death of the Wali Faqih. The Council comprises 83 clerics. (In November 1985 it was announced that the Council had elected Ayatollah Hossein Ali Montazeri to be Ayatollah Khomeini's successor.)

Chairman: Ayatollah ALI MESHKINI.
Deputy Chairmen: Hojatoleslam ALI AKBAR HASHEMI RAFSANJANI, Ayatollah IBRAHIM AMINI.
Secretaries: Mr TAHERI, Mr KHORRAMABADI, MUHAMMAD MOMEN.

SHURA-E-NIGAHBAN—COUNCIL OF GUARDIANS

The Council of Guardians, composed of six qualified Muslim jurists and six lay Muslim lawyers, appointed by Ayatollah Khomeini and the Supreme Judicial Council, respectively, was established in 1980 to supervise elections and to examine legislation passed by the Majlis, ensuring that it accords with the Constitution and with Islamic precepts.

Chairman: Ayatollah MUHAMMAD MUHAMMADI GUILANI.

COMMITTEE TO DETERMINE THE EXPEDIENCY OF THE ISLAMIC ORDER

Formed in February 1988, by order of Ayatollah Khomeini, to arbitrate on legal and theological questions in legislation passed by the Majlis, in the event of a dispute between the latter and the supervisory Council of Guardians. The Committee comprises the six qualified religious jurists on the Council of Guardians and seven leading government officials: President Khamenei, Prime Minister Moussavi, Majlis Speaker Rafsanjani, Chief Justice Ardebili, Prosecutor-General Khoeniha, Muhammad Tavasoli (the head of Ayatollah Khomeini's office) and the minister concerned with the relevant legislation.

Chairman: Hojatoleslam SAYED ALI KHAMENEI.

Political Organizations

The Islamic Republican Party was founded in 1978 to bring about the Islamic Revolution under the leadership of Ayatollah Khomeini. After the revolution the IRP became the ruling party in what was effectively a one-party state. In June 1987 Ayatollah Khomeini officially disbanded the IRP at the request of party leaders, who said that it had achieved its purpose and might only 'provide an excuse for discord and factionalism' if it were not dissolved. Of the parties listed below, only the Nelzat-Azadi (Liberation Movement of Iran) has enjoyed official recognition and been allowed to participate in elections.

Democratic Party of Iranian Kurdistan: Mahabad; f. 1945; seeks autonomy for Kurdish area; mem. of the National Council of Resistance; 54,000 mems; Sec.-Gen. Dr ABD AR-RAHMAN QASSEMLOU.

Fedayin-e-Khalq (Warriors of the People): urban Marxist guerrillas.

Hezb-e-Komunist Iran (Communist Party of Iran): f. 1979 on grounds that Tudeh Party was Moscow-controlled; Sec.-Gen. 'AZARYUN'.

Komala: f. 1969; Kurdish wing of the Communist Party of Iran; Marxist-Leninist; Leader IBRAHIM ALIZADEH.

Mujahidin-e-Khalq (Holy Warriors of the People): Islamic guerrilla group; since June 1987 comprising the National Liberation Army; mem. of the National Council of Resistance; Leaders MASSOUD RAJAVI and MARYAM RAJAVI (in Baghdad 1986-).

Muslim People's Republican Party: Tabriz; over 3.5m. members (2.5m. in Azerbaizhan); Sec.-Gen. HOSSEIN FARSHI.

National Democratic Front: f. March 1979; Leader HEDAYATOLLAH MATINE-DAFTARI (in Paris, January 1982-).

National Front (Union of National Front Forces): comprises Iran Nationalist Party, Iranian Party, and Society of Iranian Students.

Nelzat-Azadi (Liberation Movement of Iran): f. 1961; emphasis on basic human rights as defined by Islam; Gen. Sec. Dr MEHDI BAZARGAN; Principal Officers Prof. SAHABI, Dr YAZDI, S. SADR, Dr SADR, Eng. SABAGHIAN, Eng. TAVASSOLI.

Pan-Iranist Party: extreme right-wing; calls for a Greater Persia; Leader MOHSEN PEZESHKPOUR.

Sazmane Peykar dar Rahe Azadieh Tabaqe Kargar (Organization Struggling for the Freedom of the Working Class): Marxist-Leninist.

Tudeh Party (Communist): f. 1941; declared illegal 1949; came into open 1979; banned again April 1983; pro-Moscow; First Sec. Cen. Cttee ALI KHAVARI.

The National Council of Resistance (NCR) was formed in Paris in October 1981 by former President ABOLHASAN BANI-SADR and the Council's current leader, MASSOUD RAJAVI, the leader of the Mujahiddin-e-Khalq in Iran. In 1984 the Council comprised 15 opposition groups, operating either clandestinely in Iran or from exile abroad. BANI-SADR left the Council in 1984 because of his objection to RAJAVI's growing links with the Iraqi Government. The French Government asked RAJAVI to leave Paris in June 1986 and he is now based in Baghdad, Iraq. On 20 June 1987 RAJAVI, Secretary of the NCR, announced the formation of a National Liberation Army (10,000–15,000-strong) as the military wing of the Mujahiddin-e-Khalq. There is also a National Movement of Iranian Resistance, led by a former Prime Minister, Dr SHAPOUR BAKHTIAR. Dissident members of the Tudeh Party founded the Democratic Party of the Iranian People in Paris in February 1988.

Diplomatic Representation

EMBASSIES IN IRAN

Afghanistan: Abbas Abad Ave, Pompe Benzine, Corner of 4th St, Teheran; tel. (021) 627531; Chargé d'affaires a.i.: Dr BASSIR RANJBAR.

Algeria: Vali Asr Ave, Ofogh St, No. 26, Teheran; tel. (021) 293482; telex 212393; Ambassador: (vacant).

Argentina: POB 98-164, Ave Mossadegh, Blvd Nahid, No. 35, Tajrish, Teheran; Chargé d'affaires a.i.: EDELBERTO J. LEMOS.

Australia: 123 Khaled al-Islambuli Ave, POB 15875-4334, Teheran 15138; tel. (021) 626202; telex 212459; Ambassador: MICHAEL LANDLE.

Austria: Taleghani Ave, Corner Forsat Ave No. 140, Teheran; tel. (021) 828431; telex 212872; Ambassador: HERBERT TRAXL.

Bahrain: Park Ave, 31st St, No. 16, Teheran; Ambassador: (vacant).

Bangladesh: Gandhi Ave, 5th St, Building No. 14, POB 11365-3711, Teheran; tel. (021) 682979; telex 212303; Chargé d'affaires a.i.: ASHFAQUR RAHMAN.

Belgium: Fereshteh Ave, Shabdiz Lane, 3 Babak St, POB 11365-115, Teheran 19659; tel. (021) 294574; telex 212446; Ambassador: RAYMOND SCHRIJVERS.

Brazil: Vanak Sq., Vanak Ave No. 58, Teheran 19964; tel. (021) 685175; telex 212392; Ambassador: RONALD LESLIE MORAES SMALL.

Bulgaria: Vali Asr Ave, Tavanir St, Nezami Ganjavi St No. 82, POB 11365-7451, Teheran; tel. (021) 685662; telex 212789; Ambassador: STEFAN POLENDAKOV.

Canada: Ostad Motahhari Ave, Darya-e-Nur Ave No. 50.

China, People's Republic: Pasdaran Ave, Golestan Ave 1 No. 53, Teheran; Ambassador: WANG BENZUO.

Colombia: Teheran; Ambassador: ANTONIO BAYONA.

Cuba: Africa Ave, Amir Parviz St No. 1/28, Teheran; tel. (021) 632953; Ambassador: LUIS MARISY FIGUEREDO.

Czechoslovakia: Enghelab Ave, Sarshar St No. 61, POB 1500, Teheran; tel. (021) 828168; Ambassador: MILAN MACHA.

Denmark: Intersection Africa and Modaress Expressway, Bidar St No. 40, POB 11365-158, Teheran; tel. (021) 297371; telex 212784; Ambassador: IB R. ANDREASEN.

Finland: Gandhi Ave, 19th St, No. 26, POB 15875-4334, Teheran; tel. (021) 684985; telex 212930; Ambassador: TAPANI BROTHEROUS.

France: ave de France No. 85, Teheran; Ambassador: CHRISTIAN GRAEFF.

Gabon: POB 337, Teheran; tel. (021) 823828; telex 215038; Ambassador: J. B. ESSONGUE.

German Democratic Republic: Mirza-e-Shirazi Ave, Ali Mirza Hassani St 15, Teheran; tel. (021) 627858; telex 212453; Ambassador: Dr WOLFGANG BATOR.

Germany, Federal Republic: 324 Ferdowsi Ave, POB 11365-179, Teheran; tel. 314111; telex 212488; Ambassador: Dr ARMIN FREITAG.

Ghana: Ghaem Magham Farahani Ave, Varahram St No. 12, Teheran; Chargé d'affaires a.i.: HUMPHREY OKPOTI LARSEY.

Greece: Afrigha Expressway (Ex. Jordan Ave), Niloufar St No. 20, POB 11365-8151, Teheran 19677; tel. (021) 4272384; Ambassador: DIMITRI ARGYRIADES.

IRAN

Holy See: Razi Ave, No. 97, ave de France Crossroad, POB 11365-178, Teheran (Apostolic Nunciature); tel. (021) 6403574; Apostolic Pro-Nuncio: Mgr GIOVANNI V. BULAITIS.
Hungary: Abbas Abad Park Ave, 13th St No. 18, Teheran; tel. (021) 622800; Ambassador: Dr ZSIGMOND KÁZMÉR.
India: Saba-e-Shomali Ave, No. 166, POB 11365-6573, Teheran; tel. (021) 894554; telex 212858; Ambassador: RAMISA CHANDER ARORA.
Indonesia: Ghaem Magham Farahani Ave, No. 210, POB 11365-4564, Teheran; tel. (021) 626865; telex 212049; Ambassador: MOHAMMAD SABIR.
Ireland: 8 Mirdamad Ave, North Razan St, Teheran; tel. (021) 222731; telex 213865; Chargé d'affaires: NOËL PURCELL O'BYRNE.
Italy: 81 ave de France, Teheran; tel. (021) 672107; telex 214171; Ambassador: VITTORIO AMEDEO FARINELLI.
Japan: Bucharest Ave, N.W. Corner of 5th St, POB 11365-814, Teheran; tel. (021) 623396; telex 212757; Ambassador: YUHIRO FUJIMOTO.
Korea, Democratic People's Republic: Fereshteh Ave, Sarvestan Ave, No. 11, Teheran; Ambassador: CHO KYU-IL.
Korea, Republic: 37 Bucharest Ave, Teheran; tel. (021) 621125; Chargé d'affaires a.i.: SUNG KU KANG.
Kuwait: Dehkadeh Ave, 3-38 Sazman-Ab St, Teheran; tel. (021) 636712; Ambassador: AHMAD ABD AL-AZIZ AL-JASSIM.
Lebanon: Teheran; Ambassador: JA'FAR MA'AWI.
Libya: Ostad Motahhari Ave, No. 163, Teheran; Sec.-Gen. Committee of People's Bureau: MAHDI AL-MABIRASH.
Malaysia: Bucharest Ave, No. 8, Teheran; tel. (021) 629523; Chargé d'affaires a.i.: SOPIAN BIN AHMAD.
Mauritania: (relations severed by Mauritania, June 1987).
Netherlands: Vali Asr Ave, Ostad Motahhari Ave, Sarbederan St, Jahansouz Alley No. 36, Teheran; tel. (021) 896011; telex 212788; Ambassador: Dr HURAK.
New Zealand: Mirza-e-Shirazi Ave, Kucheh Mirza Hassani, No. 29, POB 11365-436, Teheran; tel. (021) 625061; telex 212078; Ambassador: (vacant).
Nicaragua: Teheran; Ambassador: GONZALO MURILLO.
Nigeria: Jomhoori Islami Ave, 31st St, No. 9, POB 11365-7148, Teheran; tel. (021) 684934; Ambassador: A. AL-GAZALI.
Norway: Bucharest Ave, 6th St, No. 23, POB 15875-4891, Teheran 15146; tel. (021) 624644; telex 213009; Ambassador: BERNT STANGHOLM.
Oman: Pasdaran Ave, Golestan 9, No. 5 and 7, POB 41-1586, Teheran; tel. (021) 243199; telex 212835; Chargé d'affaires a.i.: RASHID BIN MUBARAK BIN RASHID AL-ODWALI.
Pakistan: Dr Fatemi Ave, Jamshidabad Shomali, Mashal St No. 1, Teheran; tel. (021) 934331; TANVIR AHMAD KHAN.
Philippines: 22 Kayhan St, Moghaddas Ardebili Ave, Zafaranieh, POB 19395-4797, Teheran; tel. (021) 295840; Ambassador SUROTANI P. USODAN.
Poland: Africa Expressway, Piruz St No. 1/3, Teheran; tel. (021) 227262; Ambassador: STEFAN SZYMCZYKIEWICZ.
Portugal: Mossadegh Ave, Tavanir Ave, Nezami Ghanjavi Ave, No. 30, Teheran; tel. (021) 681380; telex 212588; Ambassador: FERNANDO PINTO DOS SANTOS.
Qatar: Africa Expressway, Golazin Ave, Parke Davar No. 4, Teheran; tel. (021) 221255; telex 212375; Chargé d'affaires a.i.: I. MUHAMMAD AL-QAYED.
Romania: Fakhrabad Ave 22-28, Teheran; tel. (021) 759841; telex 212791; Ambassador: ILIE CASU.
Saudi Arabia: (relations severed by Saudi Arabia, April 1988).
Senegal: Vozara Ave, 4 8th St, BP 3217, Teheran; tel. (021) 624142.
Somalia: Shariati Ave, Soheyl Ave No. 20, Teheran; Chargé d'affaires a.i.: MUHAMMAD SHEIKH AHMAD.
Spain: Ghaem Magham Farahani Ave, Varahram St No. 14, Teheran; tel. (021) 624575; telex 212980; Ambassador: JOSÉ MARÍA SIERRA.
Sudan: Khaled Islambouli Ave, 23rd St, No. 10, Teheran; tel. (021) 628476; telex 213372; Ambassador: IBRAHIM AHMAD OTHMAN HAMRA.
Sweden: Taleghani Ave, Forsat Ave, Teheran; tel. (021) 828305; telex 212822; Ambassador: GORAN BUNDY.
Switzerland: 13 Boustan Ave, POB 11365-176; Teheran; tel. (021) 268227; telex 212851; Ambassador: HEINRICH REIMANN.
Syria: Bucharest Ave, 10th St, No. 42, Teheran; Ambassador: IBRAHIM YUNIS.
Thailand: Baharestan Ave, Parc Amin ed-Doleh No. 4, POB 11495-111, Teheran; tel. (021) 301433; telex 214140; Ambassador: WAIPOTE SUWANAMOLI.
Tunisia: (diplomatic relations severed by Tunisia, 26 March 1987).
Turkey: Ferdowsi Ave No. 314, Teheran; tel. (021) 315299; Ambassador: VULKAN VURAL.
USSR: Neauphle-le-Château Ave, Teheran; Ambassador: VLADIMIR GUDEV.
United Arab Emirates: Zafar Ave, No. 355-7, Teheran; tel. (021) 221333; telex 212697; Chargé d'affaires a.i.: T. AHMAD AL-HAIDAN.
United Kingdom: 143 Ferdowsi Ave, POB 11365-4474, Teheran 11344; tel. (021) 675011; telex 212493; Chargé d'affaires: NICHOLAS BROWNE (withdrawn February 1989).
Venezuela: Bucharest Ave, 9th St, No. 31, POB 15875-4354, Teheran; tel. (021) 625185; telex 213790; Ambassador: Dr JOSÉ RAFAEL ZANONI.
Yemen Arab Republic: Bucharest Ave, No. 26, Teheran; Chargé d'affaires a.i.: ABDULLAH AR-RAZI.
Yemen, People's Democratic Republic: Bucharest Ave, 10th St, No. 41, Teheran; Ambassador: KHADIR SALIH AL-HAMZAH.
Yugoslavia: Vali Asr Ave, Fereshteh Ave, Amir Teymour Alley, No. 12, Teheran; tel. (021) 294127; telex 214235; Ambassador: MIRKO ZARIĆ.
Zaire: Vali Asr Ave, Chehrazi St, No. 68, POB 11365-3167, Teheran; tel. (021) 222199; Chargé d'affaires a.i.: N'DJATE ESELE SASA.

Judicial System

In August 1982 the Supreme Court revoked all laws dating from the previous regime which did not conform with Islam. In October 1982 all courts set up prior to the Islamic Revolution were abolished. In June 1987 Ayatollah Khomeini ordered the creation of clerical courts to try members of the clergy opposed to government policy. A new system of *qisas* (retribution) is being established, where the emphasis is on speedy justice. Islamic codes of correction were introduced in 1983, including the amputation of a hand or fingers for theft, flogging for fornication and violations of the strict code of dress for women, and stoning for adultery. One hundred and nine offences may be punished by the death penalty. More than 1,000 itinerant justices have been appointed to tour the country, deciding cases in each locality and dispensing immediate punishment. The aim is to keep imprisonment to a minimum. In January 1983, however, investigative teams were formed to ensure that the judiciary did not exceed its authority. In 1984 there was a total of 2,200 judges. The new Supreme Court has 16 branches.

SUPREME COURT

Chief Justice: Ayatollah ABD AL-KARIM MOUSSAVI ARDEBILI.
Prosecutor-General: Hojatoleslam MUHAMMAD MOUSSAVI KHOENIHA.
Head of Military Revolutionary Courts and Head of Drug Offences Court: Hojatoleslam MOKHDAI.
Islamic Revolutionary Prosecutor: Hojatoleslam RAAZINI.
President of the Administrative Tribunal: Hojatoleslam MUHAMMAD YAZDI.
Head of Clerical Courts: Hojatoleslam ALI HOSSEIN FALAHIAN.
Clerical Court Prosecutor: ALI RAZINI.

Religion

According to the 1979 Constitution, the official religion is Islam of the Ja'fari sect (Shi'ite), but other Islamic sects, including Zeydi, Hanafi, Maleki, Shafe'i and Hanbali, are valid and will be respected. Zoroastrians, Jews and Christians will be recognized as official religious minorities. According to the 1976 census, there were then 310,000 Christians (mainly Armenian), 80,000 Jews and 30,000 Zoroastrians.

ISLAM

The great majority of the Iranian people are Shi'a Muslims, but there is a minority of Sunni Muslims. Persians and Azerbaizhanis are mainly Shi'i, while the other ethnic groups are mainly Sunni.

During 1978 there was a revival of the influence of the Ayatollahs (or senior Shi'ite divines). Ayatollah RUHOLLAH KHOMEINI of Qom, who had been exiled to Iraq in 1964 and moved to near Paris in October 1978, conducted a campaign of opposition to the Shah, returning to Iran in February 1979 and bringing about the downfall of the Shah's regime. Other important Ayatollahs include Ayatollah ABD AL-KARIM MOUSSAVI ARDEBILI, Ayatollah AHMAD AZARI-

QOMI, Ayatollah HOSSEIN ALI MONTAZERI of Teheran, Ayatollah ABOLGHASSEM KHOI of Najaf, Iraq, and the Ayatollahs SHAHABOLDIN MARASHI NAJAFI and MUHAMMAD REZA GOLPAYEGHANI of Qom. The three last-named, Ayatollah KHOMEINI and Ayatollah SAYED TABATABAI QOMI (who has been under house arrest in Mashad since 1985) are the only five Shi'a clergymen to bear the title Ayatollah al-Ozma (Grand Ayatollah).

CHRISTIANITY
The Roman Catholic Church

At 31 December 1986 there were an estimated 14,450 adherents in Iran, comprising 9,450 of the Chaldean Rite, 3,000 of the Armenian Rite and 2,000 of the Latin Rite.

Armenian Rite

Bishop of Isfahan: Dr VARTAN TEKEYAN, Armenian Catholic Bishopric, Khiaban Ghazzali 22, Teheran; tel. (021) 677204; diocese founded 1934.

Chaldean Rite

Archbishop of Ahwaz: HANNA ZORA, Archbishop's House, POB 61956, Zahedi St, Ahwaz; tel. (061) 24980.

Archbishop of Teheran: YOUHANNAN SEMAAN ISSAYI, Archevêché, Forsat Ave 91, Teheran 15819; tel. (021) 823549.

Archbishop of Urmia (Rezayeh) and Bishop of Salmas (Shahpour): THOMAS MERAM, Khalifagari Kaldani Katholiq, POB 338, Orumiyeh 57135; tel. (0441) 22739.

Latin Rite

Archbishop of Isfahan: (vacant), Consolata Church, POB 11365-445, Teheran; tel. (021) 673210; Apostolic Administrator Fr JEAN-BAPTISTE DARRIBAT.

The Anglican Communion

Anglicans in Iran are adherents of the Episcopal Church in Jerusalem and the Middle East, formally inaugurated in January 1976. The Rt Rev. HASSAN DEHQANI-TAFTI, the Bishop in Iran since 1961, was President-Bishop of the Church from 1976 to 1986. Following an assassination attempt against him in October 1979, the Bishop went into exile (he now resides in the United Kingdom and has been Assistant Bishop of Winchester, in the Church of England, since 1982).

Bishop in Iran: Rt Rev. HASSAN BARNABA DEHQANI-TAFTI, Bishop's House, POB 12, Isfahan; diocese founded 1912.

Presbyterian Church

Synod of the Evangelical (Presbyterian) Church in Iran: Assyrian Evangelical Church, Khiaban-i Hanifnejad, Khiaban-i Aramanch, Teheran; Moderator Rev. ADEL NAKHOSTEEN.

ZOROASTRIANS

There are about 30,000 Zoroastrians, a remnant of a once widespread sect. Their religious leader is MOUBAD.

OTHER COMMUNITIES

Communities of Armenians, and somewhat smaller numbers of Jews (an estimated 30,000 in 1986), Assyrians, Greek Orthodox Christians, Uniates and Latin Christians are also found as officially recognized faiths. The Bahá'í faith, which originated in Iran, has about 300,000 Iranian adherents, although at least 10,000 are believed to have fled since 1979 in order to escape persecution. The Government banned all Bahá'í institutions in August 1983.

The Press

Teheran dominates the press scene as many of the daily papers are published there and the bi-weekly, weekly and less frequent publications in the provinces generally depend on the major metropolitan dailies as a source of news. A press law which was announced in August 1979 required all newspapers and magazines to be licensed and imposed penalties of imprisonment for insulting senior religious figures. Offences against the Act will be tried in the criminal courts. In the Constitution which was approved in December 1979, the press is free, except in matters that are contrary to public morality, insult religious belief or slander the honour and reputation of individuals. Many of the papers which were published under the Shah's regime ceased publication after the revolution. In August 1980 Ayatollah Khomeini issued directives which indicated that censorship would be tightened up, and several papers were closed down in 1981. The radical daily *Azadegan* (Morning of the Liberated) was closed by the Prosecutor-General in June 1985 and reappeared under a different title, *Abrar* (Rightly Guided), after complaints from deputies in the Majlis of its criticism of conservative members of the assembly. Later in 1985, however, a policy of relative liberalization of the press was introduced. Ayatollah Khomeini told journalists in September and October that criticism of the government was permissible, provided that it was constructive and not designed to arouse dissent.

PRINCIPAL DAILIES

Abrar (Rightly Guided): Apadan Ave 198, Abbasabad, Teheran; tel. (021) 859971; f. 1985 after closure of *Azadegan* by order of the Prosecutor-General; morning; Farsi.

Alik: POB 11365-953, Jomhoori Islami Ave, Alik Alley, Teheran 11357; tel. (021) 676671; f. 1931; afternoon; political and literary; Armenian; Propr A. AJEMIAN.

Bahari Iran: Khayaban Khayham, Shiraz; tel. 33738.

Ettela'at (Information): Khayyam St, Teheran; tel. (021) 311071; telex 212336; f. 1925; evening; Farsi; political and literary; owned and managed by Mostazafin Foundation from October 1979 until 1 January 1987, when it was placed under the direct supervision of *Wilayat-e-Faqih* (religious jurisprudence); Editor Mr SHIRANI; circ. 250,000.

Jomhoori Islami (Islamic Republic): Teheran; was organ of the Islamic Republican Party until it was dissolved in 1987; continues to appear.

Kayhan (Universe): Ferdowsi Ave, Teheran; tel. (021) 310251; telex 212467; f. 1941; evening; Farsi; political; also publishes *Kayhan International* (f. 1959; daily and weekly; English; Editor HOSSEIN RAGHAFIE), *Kayhan Arabic* (f. 1980; daily and weekly; Arabic), *Kayhan Persian* (f. 1942; daily; Persian), *Kayhan Turkish* (f. 1984; weekly; Turkish), *Kayhan Havaie* (f. 1950; weekly for Iranians abroad; Farsi), *Kayhan Andishe* (World of Religion; f. 1985; 6 a year; Farsi), *Zan-e-Ruz* (Woman Today; weekly; Farsi), *Kayhan Varzeshi* (World of Sport; weekly; Farsi), *Kayhan Bacheha* (Children's World; weekly; Farsi), *Kayhan Farhangi* (World of Culture; f. 1984; monthly; Farsi); owned and managed by Mostazafin Foundation from October 1979 until 1 January 1987, when it was placed under the direct supervision of *Wilayat-e-Faqih* (religious jurisprudence); Chief Editor SAYED HASSAN SHAH-SHERAGI; circ. 350,000.

Khorassan: Meshed; Head Office: Khorassan Daily Newspapers, 14 Zohre St, Mobarezan Ave, Teheran; f. 1948; Propr MUHAMMAD SADEGH TEHERANIAN; circ. 40,000.

Mojahed: organ of the Mujaheddin Khalq; ceased publication June 1986.

Rahnejat: Darvazeh Dowlat, Isfahan; political and social; Propr N. RAHNEJAT.

Risala'at (The Message): Teheran; organ of right-wing group of the same name; political; Propr Ayatollah AHMAD AZARI-QOMI.

Teheran Times: No. 2 Martyr Dehqani Alley, North Iranshahr Ave, Homa St, Block 2, Teheran 15836; tel. (021) 825022; telex 213662; f. 1979; independent; English; Editor-in-Chief M. B. ANSARI.

PRINCIPAL PERIODICALS

Acta Medica Iranica: Faculty of Medicine, Enghelab Ave, Teheran Medical Sciences Univ., Teheran 14-174; tel. (021) 6112743; f. 1960; quarterly; English, French, German; under the supervision of the Educational Vice-Chancellor (M. PAZHUHI) and the Editorial Board; Propr and Editor-in-Chief PARVIZ JABAL-AMELI (Vice-Chancellor for Research); circ. 2,000.

Al-Akha: Khayyam Ave, Tehran; telex 212336; f. 1960; weekly; Arabic; Editor NAZIR FENZA.

Akhbar-e-Pezeshki: 86 Ghaem Magham Farahani Ave, Teheran; weekly; medical; Propr Dr T. FORUZIN.

Armaghan: Baghe Saba, 127 Salim Street, Teheran 16137; tel. (021) 750698; f. 1910; monthly; literary and historical; Propr Dr MUHAMMAD VAHID-DASTGERDI; circ. 3,000.

Ashur: Ostad Motahhari Ave, 11-21 Kuhe Nour Ave, Teheran; tel. (021) 622117; f. 1969; Assyrian; monthly; Founder and Editor Dr W. BET-MANSOUR; circ. 8,000.

Auditor: 77 Ferdowsi Ave North, Teheran; quarterly; financial and managerial studies.

Ayandeh: POB 19575-583, Niyavaran, Teheran; tel. (021) 283254; monthly; Iranian literary, historical and book review journal; Editor Prof. IRAJ AFSHAR.

Daneshkadeh Pezeshki: Faculty of Medicine, Teheran Medical Sciences University; tel. (021) 6112743; f. 1947; 10 a year; medical magazine; Propr Dr HASSAN AREFI; circ. 1,500.

Daneshmand: POB 15875-3649, Teheran; tel. (021) 854969; f. 1963; monthly; scientific and technical magazine; Editor ALI MIRZAEI.

Dokhtaran and Pesaran: Khayyam Ave, Teheran; f. 1947; weekly teenage magazine; Editor NADER AKHAVAN HAYDARI.

IRAN
Directory

Donaye Varzesh: Khayyam Ave, Ettela'at Bldg, Teheran; telex 212336; weekly; sport; Editor Mr SAMIMI.

Echo of Islam: POB 14155-3987, Teheran; monthly; English; published by Ministry of Islamic Guidance.

Ettela'at Banovan: 11 Khayyam St, Teheran; telex 212336; weekly; women's magazine; Editor Mrs RAHNAWARD; circ. 85,000.

Ettela'at Haftegi: 11 Khayyam St, Teheran; telex 212336; weekly; Editor Mr NAYYERI; circ. 60,000.

Farhang-e-Iran Zamin: POB 19575-583, Niyavaran, Teheran; tel. (021) 283254; annual; Iranian studies; Editor Prof. IRAJ AFSHAR.

Faza: Enghelab Ave, Teheran; aviation; Propr H. KAMALI-TAQARI.

Film va Honar: Teheran; weekly; Editor A. RAMAZANI.

Honar va Memar: Enghelab Ave No. 256, Teheran; monthly; scientific and professional; Propr A. H. ECHRAGH.

Iran Exports: Lalezarno Ave No. 105, POB 15815-3373, Teheran 11456; tel. (021) 3852113; telex 215017; f. 1987; quarterly; English; business and trade.

Iran Press Digest (Economic): Hafiz Ave, 4 Kucheh Hurtab, POB 11365-5551, Teheran; tel. (021) 668114; telex 212300; weekly; Editor J. BEHROUZ.

Iran Press Digest (Political): Hafiz Ave, 4 Kucheh Hurtab, POB 11365-5551, Teheran; tel. (021) 668114; telex 212300; weekly.

Iran Trade and Industry: POB 1228, Hafiz Ave, Teheran; monthly; English.

Iran Tribune: POB 111244, Teheran; monthly; English.

Jam: POB 1871, Jomhoori Islami Ave, Sabuhi Bldg, Teheran; monthly; arts; Propr A. VAKILI.

Jame'e Dandan-Pezeshki Iran: 2 Ex-Shahi Alley, Shahid Dr Abbaspour St, Vali Asr Ave, POB 14155-3695, Teheran; tel. (021) 686508; telex 212918; monthly; medical; organ of Iranian Dental Assen; Propr Dr HAMID ADELI-NAJAFI.

Javanan Emrooz: 11144 Khayyam Ave, POB 11335-9365, Ettela'at, Teheran; tel. (021) 311205, telex 212336; f. 1966; weekly; youth; Editor ALI AGHA MUHAMMADI.

Javaneh: POB 15875-1163, Motahhari Ave, Cnr Mofatteh St, Tajrish, Teheran; tel. (021) 839051; published by Soroush Press; quarterly.

Kayhan Bacheha (Children's World): Shahid Shahsheragi Ave, Teheran; tel. (021) 310251; telex 212467; f. 1956; weekly; Editor AMIR HOSSEIN FARDI; circ. 150,000.

Kayhan Varzeshi (World of Sport): Ferdowsi Ave, Teheran; tel. (021) 310251; telex 212467; f. 1955; weekly; Dir MAHMAD MONSETI; circ. 125,000.

Mahjubah: POB 14155-3897, Teheran; Islamic women's magazine; published by the Islamic Thought Foundation.

Majda: 2 Ex-Shahi Alley, Shahid Dr Abaspour St, Vali-Asr Ave, Teheran; tel. (021) 686508; telex 212918; f. 1963; three a year; medical; journal of the Iranian Dental Association.

Mokhtarein va Mobtakerin: Motahhari Ave, Cnr Mofatteh St, POB 15875-1163, Teheran; tel. (021) 839051; quarterly; Farsi; published by Soroush Press; Iranian technological innovations.

Music Iran: 1029 Amiriye Ave, Teheran; f. 1951; monthly; Editor BAHMAN HIRBOD; circ. 7,000.

Nameh-e-Mardom: Teheran; organ of the Tudeh Party.

Neda-e-Nationalist: W. Khayaban Hafiz (Khayaban Rish Kutcha Bostan), POB 1999, Teheran.

Negin: Vali Asr Ave, Adl St 52, Teheran; monthly; scientific and literary; Propr and Dir M. ENAYAT.

Pars: Alley Dezhban, Shiraz; f. 1941; irregular; Propr and Dir F. SHARGHI; circ. 10,000.

Pezhuhshgar: Vali Asr Ave, Teheran; scientific; Propr Dr R. OLUMI.

Salamate Fekr: M.20, Kharg St, Teheran; tel. (021) 223034; f. 1958; monthly; organ of the Mental Health Soc.; Editors Prof. E. TCHEHRAZI, ALI REZA SHAFAI.

Sepid va Siyah: Ferdowsi Ave, Teheran; monthly; popular; Editor Dr A. BEHZADI; circ. 30,000.

Setareye Esfahan: Isfahan; weekly; political; Propr A. MIHANKHAH.

Sokhan: Hafiz Ave, Zomorrod Passage, Teheran; f. 1943; Khanlari; monthly; literary and art; Propr PARVIZ NATEL-KHANLARY.

Soroush: Motahhari Ave, Corner Mofatteh St, POB 15875-1163, Teheran; tel. (021) 839051; f. 1972; weekly in Farsi, monthly in English, French and Arabic; cultural magazine.

Tarikh-e-Islam: Amiriyeh 94 Ku, Ansari, Teheran; monthly; religious; Propr A. A. TASHAYYOD.

Tebb-o-Daru: POB 3033, Inqilah Ave, Teheran; medical; Man. Dr SH. ASSADI ZADEH.

Teheran Mossavar: Lalezar Ave, Teheran; weekly; political and social.

Vahid: 55 Jomhoori Islami Ave, Jam St, Teheran; weekly; literature; Propr Dr S. VAHIDNIA.

Yaghma: 15 Khanequah Ave, Teheran; tel. (021) 305344; f. 1948; monthly; literature; Propr HABIB YAGHMAIE.

Zan-e-Ruz (Woman Today): Ferdowsi Ave, Teheran; telex 212467; f. 1964; weekly; women's; circ. over 100,000.

NEWS AGENCIES

Islamic Republic News Agency (IRNA): 873 Vali Asr Ave, POB 764, Teheran; tel. (021) 892050; telex 212827; f. 1936; Man. Dir Dr KAMAL KHARRAZI.

Foreign Bureaux

Agence France-Presse (AFP): POB 1535, Ghaen St, Teheran; tel. (021) 314190; telex 2479; Correspondent JACQUES CHARMELOT.

Agenzia Nazionale Stampa Associata (ANSA) (Italy): 7 East Africa St, Nahid Blvd, Teheran; tel. (021) 009821; telex 213629; Correspondent (vacant).

Anatolian News Agency (Turkey): Teheran.

Kyodo Tsushin (Japan): No. 23, First Floor, Couche Kargozar, Couche Sharsaz Ave, Zafar, Teheran; tel. (021) 220448; telex 214058; Correspondent MASARU IMAI.

Reuters (UK): POB 15875-1193, Teheran; tel. (021) 847700; telex 212634; (Correspondent, HUGH POPE, expelled from Iran in July 1986 for allegedly revealing military secrets).

Telegrafnoye Agentstvo Sovetskovo Soyuza (TASS) (USSR): Kehyaban Hamid, Kouche Masoud 73, Teheran; Correspondent (vacant).

Xinhua (New China) News Agency (People's Republic of China): 75 Golestan 2nd St, Pasdaran Ave, Teheran; tel. (021) 241852; telex 212399; Correspondent XU BOYUAN.

Publishers

Ali Akbar Elmi: Jomhoori Islami Ave, Teheran; Dir ALI AKBAR ELMI.

Amir Kabir: 28 Vessal Shirazi St, Teheran; f. 1950; historical, social, literary and children's books; Dir ABD AR-RAHIM JAFARI.

Boroukhim: Ferdowsi Ave, Teheran; dictionaries.

Danesh: 357 Nasser Khosrow Ave, Teheran; f. 1931 in India, transferred to Iran in 1937; literary and historical (Persian); imports and exports books; Man. Dir NOOROUAH IRANPARAST.

Ebn-e-Sina: Meydane 25 Shahrivar, Teheran; f. 1957; educational publishers and booksellers; Dir EBRAHIM RAMAZANI.

Eghbal Printing & Publishing Organization: 15 Booshehr St, Dr Shariati Ave, Teheran; tel. (021) 768113; f. 1903; Man. Dir DJAVAD EGHBAL.

Iran Chap Co: Sepah Ave, Teheran; tel. (021) 212336; telex 3281; f. 1966; newspapers, books, magazines, book binding, colour printing and engraving; Man. Dir M. DOAEI.

Kanoon Marefat: 6 Lalezar Ave, Teheran; Dir HASSAN MAREFAT.

Khayyam: Jomhoori Islami Ave, Teheran; Dir MOHAMMAD ALI TARAGHI.

Majlis Press: Ketab-Khane Majlis-e-Showraie Eslami No. 1, Baharistan Sq., Teheran 11564; tel. (021) 393257; f. 1924; Dir ABD AL-HOSSEIN HAIERI; Ketab Khane Majlis-e-Showraie Eslami No. 2, Imam Khomeini Ave, Teheran 13174; tel. (021) 662906; f. 1950; Dir ABD AL-HOSSEIN HAIERI.

Safiali Shah: Baharistan Sq., Teheran; Dir MANSOUR MOSHFEGH.

Sahab Geographic and Drafting Institute: 30 Somayeh St, Hoquqi Crossroad, Dr Ali Shariati Ave, POB 11365-617, Teheran; tel. (021) 765691; maps, atlases, and books on geography, science, history and Islamic art; Founder and Pres. ABBAS A. SAHAB.

Scientific and Cultural Publications Co: Ministry of Higher Education and Culture, POB 5433-5437, Teheran; tel. (021) 686317; f. 1974; Iranian and Islamic studies and scientific and cultural books; Pres. M. BOROUJERDI.

Taban Press: Nassir Khosrow Ave, Teheran; f. 1939; Propr A. MALEKI.

Teheran Economist: 99 Sargord Sakhaie Ave, Teheran-11.

Teheran University Press: 16 Kargar Shomali Ave, Teheran; tel. (021) 632062; f. 1944; university textbooks; Man. Dir Dr FIRUZ HARIRCHI.

Towfigh: Jomhoori Islami Ave, Teheran; publishes humorous Almanac and pocket books; distributes humorous and satirical books; Dir Dr FARIDEH TOWFIGH.

IRAN   Directory

Zawar: Jomhoori Islami Ave, Teheran; Dir Akbar Zawar.

Radio and Television

There were over 10m. radio receivers and 2.1m. television sets in use in 1986.

Islamic Republic of Iran Broadcasting (IRIB): Mossadegh Ave, Jame Jam St, POB 19395-1774, Teheran; tel. (021) 21961; telex 212431; semi-autonomous government authority; non-commercial; operates two national television and three national radio channels, as well as local provincial radio stations throughout the country; Dir-Gen. Hojatoleslam Sayed Muhammad Hashemi.

RADIO

Radio Network 1 (Voice of the Islamic Republic of Iran): there are three national radio channels: Radio Networks 1 and 2 and Radio Quran, which broadcasts recitals of the Quran (Koran) and other programmes related to it; covers whole of Iran and reaches whole of Europe, SW USSR, whole of Asia, Africa and part of USA; medium-wave regional broadcasts in local languages; Arabic, Armenian, Assyrian, Azerbaizhani, Baluchi, Bandari, Dari, Farsi, Kurdish, Mazandarani, Pashtu, Turkoman, Turkish and Urdu; external broadcasts in English, French, German, Spanish, Turkish, Arabic, Kurdish, Urdu, Pashtu, Armenian, Bengali, Russian and special overseas programme in Farsi; 53 transmitters.

TELEVISION

Television (Vision of the Islamic Republic of Iran): 625-line, System B; Secam colour; two production centres in Teheran producing for two networks and 28 local TV stations.

Finance

(cap. = capital; p.u. = paid up; dep. = deposits; res = reserves; brs = branches; m. = million; amounts in rials)

BANKING

Prior to the Islamic Revolution, the banking system comprised 36 banks. Banks were nationalized in June 1979 and a revised banking system has been introduced consisting of nine banks. Three banks were reorganized, two (Bank Tejarat and Bank Mellat) resulted from mergers of 22 existing small banks, three specialize in industry and agriculture and one, the Islamic Bank (now Islamic Economy Organization), set up in May 1979, was exempt from nationalization. A change-over to an Islamic banking system, with interest being replaced by a 4% commission on loans, began on 21 March 1984 and will take several years to complete.

Although the number of foreign banks operating in Iran has fallen dramatically since the Revolution, some 30 are still represented. Since the exclusion of French banks from the Iranian market at the end of 1983, Federal German, Swiss, Japanese and British banks have been responsible for about 30% of total trade financing.

Central Bank

Bank Markazi Jomhouri Islami Iran (Central Bank): Ferdowsi Ave, POB 1136-58551, Teheran; tel. (021) 310100; telex 212503; f. 1960; Bank Markazi Iran until Dec. 1983; central note-issuing bank of Iran, government banking; cap. p.u. 125,000m., dep. 6,839,029m., res 72,431m., total assets 7,198,215m. (March 1985); Gov. Majid Ghassemi.

Commercial Banks

Bank Keshavarzi (Agricultural Bank): 129 Patrice Lumumba Ave, Jalal al-Ahmad Expressway, POB 14155-6395, Teheran; tel. (021) 9121; telex 212058; f. 1979 as merger of the Agricultural Development Bank of Iran and the Agricultural Co-operative Bank of Iran; State-owned; cap. 132,270.6m., dep. 103,534m. (August 1986); 306 brs; Man. Dir Ali-Reza Talayi.

Bank Mellat (Nation's Bank): Park Shahr, Varzesh Ave, POB 11365-5964, Teheran; tel. (021) 891021; telex 213251; f. 1980 as merger of the following: National Bank of Iran, Bank Bimeh Iran, Bank Dariush, Distributors' Co-operative Credit Bank, Iran Arab Bank, Bank Omran, Bank Pars, Bank of Teheran, Foreign Trade Bank of Iran; State-owned; cap. p.u. 33,500m., dep. 966,390m., res 27,541m., (March 1987); 770 brs throughout Iran and 3 brs abroad; Chair. and Man. Dir Muhammad Ali Vatani.

Bank Melli Iran (The National Bank of Iran): Ferdowsi Ave, POB 11365-171, Teheran; tel. (021) 33231; telex 212890; f. 1928; State-owned; cap. 25,000m., res 10,100m., dep. 2,765,461m., total assets 3,832,300m. (March 1987); 1,614 brs throughout Iran, 24 brs abroad; Chair. and Man. Dir Kazem Najafi Elmi.

Bank Refah Kargaran: POB 111628, 125 Ayatollah Shahid Dr Moffateh Ave, Teheran; tel. (021) 825000; telex 213786; f. 1961; State-owned; cap. p.u. 10,000m., dep. 298,186m. (March 1983); 84 brs throughout Iran.

Bank Saderat Iran (The Export Bank of Iran): 124 Jomhouri Islami Ave, POB 11365-7168, Teheran; tel. (021) 670041; telex 213077; f. 1952, reorganized 1979; State-owned; cap. p.u. and res. 21,320.4m., dep. 1,470,655.3m. (March 1986); 2,200 brs in Iran, 18 foreign brs; Man. Dir Abbas Khafafi.

Bank Sepah (Army Bank): Imam Khomeini Sq, Teheran; tel. (021) 311091; telex 212462; f. 1925, reorganized 1979; State-owned; cap. p.u. 8,000m., total assets 1,031,900m. (March 1987); 666 brs throughout Iran and 5 brs abroad; Man. Dir Sassan Manuchehri.

Bank Tejarat (Commercial Bank): 130 Taleghani Ave, POB 11365-5416, Teheran; tel. (021) 890131; telex 212077; f. 1979 as merger of the following: Irano-British Bank, Bank Etebarate Iran, The Bank of Iran and the Middle East, Mercantile Bank of Iran and Holland, Bank Barzagani Iran, Bank Iranshahr, Bank Sanaye Iran, Bank Shahriar, Iranians' Bank, Bank Kar, International Bank of Iran and Japan, Bank Russo-Iran; State-owned; cap. p.u. 39,120m., dep. 702,302m., res 921m. (March 1987); 664 brs throughout Iran and brs in London and Paris; Chair. and Man. Dir Muhammad Jafar Eftekhar.

Islamic Economy Organization (formerly Islamic Bank of Iran): Ferdowsi Ave, Teheran; f. February 1980; cap. 2,000m.; provides interest-free loans and investment in small industry.

Development Bank

Bank Sanat va Madan (Bank of Industry and Mines): 593 Hafiz Ave, POB 11365/4978, Teheran; tel. (021) 893271; telex 212816; f. 1979 as merger of the following: Industrial Credit Bank (ICB), Industrial and Mining Development Bank of Iran (IMDBI), Development and Investment Bank of Iran (DIBI), Iranian Bankers Investment Company (IBICO); cap. p.u. 40,980m., res 97,953m., total assets 606,267m. (1984); Chair. and Man. Dir Morteza Aramy Parchebaf.

Housing Bank

Bank Maskan (Housing Bank): Ferdowsi Ave, Teheran; tel. (021) 675021; telex 213904; f. 1980; State-owned; cap. p.u. 42,663.8m., dep. 221,153.4m., total assets 1,313,708m. (June 1985); provides mortgage and housing finance; 187 brs; Chair. and Man. Dir Abdullah Ebtehaj.

STOCK EXCHANGE

Teheran Stock Exchange: Taghinia Bldg, 521 South Saadi Ave, Teheran 11447; tel. (021) 311149; f. 1966; Chair. of Council M. Nourbakhsh.

INSURANCE

The nationalization of insurance companies was announced on 25 June 1979.

Bimeh Iran (Iran Insurance Co): POB 11365-9153, Saadi Ave, Teheran; tel. (021) 304026; telex 212782; f. 1935; State-owned insurance company; all types of insurance; cap. p.u. 4,400m.; Man. Dir Amir Sadeghi Neshat.

Bimeh Markazi Iran (Central Insurance Co): 149 Taleghani Ave, Teheran; Pres. Ahmad Geranmayeh.

Dana Insurance Co Ltd: POB 2868, Enghelab Ave, Teheran; in association with Commercial Union Assurance Co. Ltd.

Hafez Insurance Co: Ostad Motahhari Ave, 44 Daraye Noor St, Teheran; f. 1974; most classes of insurance; Man. Dir K. Helmi.

Iran-American International Insurance Co: Ave Zohre, Teheran.

Pars, Société Anonyme d'Assurances: Avenue Saadi, Teheran; f. 1955; fire, marine, motor vehicle, third party liability, personal accident, group, life, contractor's all-risk and medical insurance.

Shirkat Sahami Bimeh Arya (Arya Insurance Co Ltd): 202 Soraya Ave, Teheran; f. 1952; nationalized 1979; cap. 300m.; Man. Dir Khalil Karimabadi.

Shirkat Sahami Bimeh Asia (Asia Insurance Co Ltd): Asia Insurance Bldg, Taleghani Ave, Teheran; tel. (021) 836040; telex 213664; f. 1960; Man. Dir Masoum Zamiri.

Shirkat Sahami Bimeh Iran and America: 8 Apartments Kavah, 20 Mitu Zohra, Mobarezan Ave, Teheran; f. 1974; cap. 1,000m.; Man. Dir Khosrow Shabai.

Shirkat Sahami Bimeh Melli (The National Insurance Co Ltd): Ayatollah Taleghani Ave, Rasekh St, POB 1786, Teheran; f. 1956; all classes of insurance; Man. Dir Reza Fatemi.

Shirkat Sahami Bimeh Omid: Boulevard Karimkhan Zand, Kheradniand Jonoubi Ave 99, Teheran; f. 1960.

Shirkati Sahami Bimeh Sakhtiman Va Kar (Construction and Labour): Apartments Bank Kar, Khayaban-e-Hafiz; f. 1964; cap. 200m.; Man. Dir SAMAD TAHERI.

Shirkat Sahami Bimeh Teheran: 43 Khayaban Khushbin Villa, Teheran; f. 1974; cap. 500m.; Man. Dir ERAJ ALI ABADI.

Shirkat-i-Sahami Bimeh Dan: 315 Enghelab Ave, Teheran; f. 1974; cap. 500m.; joint venture between Iranian interests and Commercial Union Insurance Co, London; Man. Dir MANSOOR AKHWAN.

Trade and Industry

CHAMBER OF COMMERCE

Iran Chamber of Commerce, Industries and Mines: 254 Taleghani Ave, Teheran; tel. (021) 836031; telex 213382; supervises the affiliated 20 Chambers in the provinces.

STATE ENTERPRISES

Iranian Offshore Oil Company (IOOC): 339 Dr Beheshti Ave, POB 1434, Teheran; tel. (021) 624102; telex 212707; wholly owned subsidiary of NIOC; f. 1980; development, exploitation and production of crude oil, natural gas and other hydrocarbons in all offshore areas of Iran in Persian Gulf; Chair. MUHAMMAD HADI NEJAD HOSEYNIHAN; Man. Dir M. AGHAEE.

National Iranian Drilling Co: Chair. MANSOUR PARVINIAN.

National Iranian Industries Organization (NIIO): Teheran; owns 500 factories in Iran.

National Iranian Industries Organization Export Co (NECO): No. 8, Second Alley, Bucharest Ave, POB 14335-586, Teheran; tel. (021) 6409523; telex 212429.

National Iranian Oil Company (NIOC): Taleghani Ave (POB 1863), Teheran; a State organization controlling all petroleum, petrochemical and natural gas operations in Iran; incorporated April 1951 on nationalization of oil industry to engage in all phases of oil operations; in February 1979 it was announced that in future Iran would sell oil direct to the oil companies and in September 1979 the Ministry of Oil took over control of the National Iranian Oil Company, and the Minister of Oil took over as Chairman and Managing Director; Chair. of Board and Gen. Man. Dir GHOLAMREZA AQAZADEH (Minister of Oil); Directors: EHSANOLLAH BUTORABI (Engineering), MUHAMMAD REZA KADIVAR (Refining), HEYDAR ALI ALIZADEH (Distribution and Pipelines), SAYED KAZEM VAZIRI HAMANEH (Administration), SAYED MOSTAFA ZEINEDIN (Legal Affairs), ALLAHKARAM MIRZAI (International Affairs), MORTEZA NASSIR (Corporate Planning Affairs), MOSTAFA KALMOR (Commercial Affairs), MUHAMMAD HASAN TAVALAI (Oil Production).

National Petrochemical Company (NPC): Teheran; wholly owned subsidiary of NIOC; Man. Dir MUSTAFA TAHERI.

CO-OPERATIVES

Central Organization for Co-operatives of Iran: Teheran; in October 1985 there were 4,598 labour co-operatives, with a total membership of 703,814 and capital of 2,184.5m. rials, and 9,159 urban non-labour co-operatives, with a total membership of 262,118 and capital of 4,187.5m. rials.

Central Organization for Rural Co-operatives of Iran (CORC): Teheran; Man. Dir SAYED HASSAN MOTEVALLI-ZADEH.

The CORC was founded in 1963, and the Islamic Government of Iran has pledged that it will continue its educational, technical, commercial and credit assistance to rural co-operative societies and unions. At the end of the Iranian year 1363 (1984/85) there were 3,104 Rural Co-operative Societies with a total membership of 3,925,000 and share capital of 25,900m. rials. There were 181 Rural Co-operative Unions with 3,097 members and capital of 7,890m. rials.

TRADE FAIR

Export Promotion Centre of Iran: POB 11-48, Tajrish, Teheran; tel. (021) 21911; telex 212896; international trade fairs and exhibitions; Pres. HOSSEIN KHABBAZAN.

Transport

RAILWAYS

Iranian State Railway: Rahe-Ahan Sq., Teheran; tel. (021) 555120; telex 213103; f. 1938; Pres. Eng. SADEGH AFSHAR; Vice-Pres. AKBAR SOHRABIAN (Admin. and Finance), Vice-Pres. NASSER POURMIRZA (Technical and Operations), Vice-Pres. HAMIDREZA MEHRAZMA (Planning and Technical Studies), Vice-Pres. Eng. VAHAB JAMSHIDI (Construction and Renovation).

The total length of main lines in the Iranian railway system, which is generally single-tracked, is 4,567 km (4,473 km of 1,435 mm gauge and 94 km of 1,676 mm gauge). There were plans to add 1,300 km to the system by 1989. The system includes the following main routes:

Trans-Iranian Railway runs 1,392 km from Bandar Turkman on the Caspian Sea in the north, through Teheran, and south to Bandar Imam Khomeini on the Persian Gulf.

Southern Line links Teheran to Khorramshahr via Qom, Arak, Dorood, Andimeshk and Ahwaz; 937 km.

Northern Line links Teheran to Gorgan via Garmsar, Firooz Kooh and Sari; 499 km.

Teheran–Kerman Line via Kashan, Yazd and Zarand; 1,106 km.

Teheran–Tabriz Line linking with the Azerbaizhan Railway; 736 km.

Tabriz–Djulfa Electric Line: 146 km.

Garmsar–Meshed Line connects Teheran with Meshed via Semnan, Damghan, Shahrud and Nishabur; 812 km.

Qom–Zahedan Line when completed will be an intercontinental line linking Europe and Turkey, through Iran, with India. Zahedan is situated 91.7 km west of the Baluchistan frontier, and is the end of the Pakistani broad gauge railway. The section at present links Qom to Kerman via Kashan, Sistan, Yazd, Bafq and Zarand; 1,005 km. A branch line from Sistan was opened in 1971 to Isfahan to the steel mill at Zarrin Shahr; 112 km. A broad-gauge (1,976-mm) track connects Zahedan and Mirjaveh, on the border with Pakistan; 94 km.

Zahedan-Quetta (Pakistan) Line: 685km; not yet linked to national network.

Ahwaz–Bandar Khomeini Line connects Bandar Khomeini with the Trans-Iranian railway at Ahwaz; this line is due to be double-tracked; 112 km.

Azerbaizhan Railway extends from Tabriz to Djulfa (146.5 km), meeting the Caucasian railways at the Soviet frontier. Electrification works for this section have been completed and the electrified line was opened in April 1982. A standard gauge railway line (139 km) extends from Tabriz (via Sharaf-Khaneh) to the Turkish frontier at Razi.

A 730-km line to link Bandar Abbas and Bafq has been under construction since 1982, and there are plans for it to be electrified by 1990.

Underground Railway. An agreement was signed in March 1976 between the Municipality of Teheran and French contractors for the construction of a subway. Four lines are to be built with a total length of 143 km. Construction began during 1978, but the project was suspended after the revolution in 1979, and work was not resumed until September 1986.

ROADS

In 1985 there were 490 km of motorways, 16,551 km of paved main roads, 23,025 km of paved feeder roads, 46,866 km of gravel roads and 49,440 km of earth roads. There is a paved highway (A1) from Bazargan on the Turkish border to the Afghanistan border. The A2 highway runs from the Iraqi border to Mir Javeh on the Pakistan border; 2,220 km of the A2 has been completed, and the remaining 80 km are under construction.

Ministry of Roads and Transport: 49 Taleghani Ave, Teheran; tel. (021) 646770.

INLAND WATERWAYS

Principal waterways:

Lake Rezaiyeh (Lake Urmia) 80 km west of Tabriz in North-West Iran; and River Karun flowing south through the oilfields into the River Shatt al-Arab, thence to the head of the Persian Gulf near Abadan.

Lake Rezaiyeh: From Sharafkhaneh to Golmankhaneh there is a twice-weekly service of tugs and barges for transport of passengers and goods.

River Karun: Regular cargo service is operated by the Mesopotamia-Iran Corpn Ltd. Iranian firms also operate daily motorboat services for passengers and goods.

SHIPPING

Persian Gulf: The main oil terminal is at Kharg Island. The principal commercial non-oil ports are Bandar Shahid Rajai (which was officially inaugurated in 1983 and handles 9m. of the 12m. tons of cargo passing annually through Iran's Persian Gulf ports), Bandar Khomeini, Bushehr, Bandar Abbas and Chah Bahar. A project to develop Bandar Abbas port, which pre-dates the Islamic

IRAN

Revolution and was originally to cost IR 1,900,000m., is now in progress. Khorramshahr, Iran's biggest port, was put out of action in the Gulf War, and Bushehr and Bandar Khomeini also sustained war damage, which has restricted their use. In August 1988 the Iranian news agency (IRNA) announced that Iran was to spend $200m. on the construction of six 'multi-purpose' ports on the Arabian and Caspian seas, while ports damaged in the war were to be repaired. During 1988 Iran signed a contract with the USSR for two cargo ships which will provide the basis of a new shipping line between the ports of Anzali and Noshahr, on the Caspian Sea, and Baku, in the USSR.

Caspian Sea: Principal port Bandar Anzali (formerly Bandar Pahlavi) and Bandar Nowshahr.

Iranian National Tanker Co: 67 Shahid Atefi St, Africa Ave, POB 16765-947, Teheran; tel. (021) 296041; telex 213938; fleet of 21 very and ultra-large crude oil carriers, 9 petroleum products carriers, 2 tankers of 60,000 tons, 7 tankers of 25,000–30,000 tons; support fleet of 32 tugs and supply boats; Chair. and Man. Dir MUHAMMAD SOURI.

Irano–Hind Shipping Co: No. 3, 13th St, Miremad Ave, Dr Beheshti Ave, Teheran; tel. (021) 850213; telex 215233; joint venture between the Islamic Republic of Iran and the Shipping Corpn of India; fleet of 9 vessels, including two refrigerated cargo ships; Chair. L. M. S. RAJWAR; Vice-Chair. M. H. DAJMAR; Man. Dir AHMAD MAKHMALI.

Islamic Republic of Iran Shipping Lines (IRISL): POB 15875-4646, Arya Building, 127 Ghaem Magham Farahani Ave, Teheran 15896; tel. (021) 833061; telex 212794; f. 1967; affiliated to the Ministry of Commerce Jan. 1980; fleet of 95 vessels; liner services between the Persian Gulf and Europe, the Far East and South America; Chair. and Man. Dir MUHAMMAD HOSSEIN DAJMER.

Ports and Shipping Organization: 751 Enghelab Ave, Teheran; tel. (021) 837041; telex 212271; Man. Dir Eng. MUHAMMAD MADAD.

CIVIL AVIATION

The two main international airports are Mehrabad (Teheran) and Abadan. An international airport was opened at Isfahan in July 1984 and the first international flight took place in March 1986. Work on a new international airport, 40 km south of Teheran, abandoned in 1979, was due to be resumed in the mid-1980s. An international airport is to be built near Gorgan, east of the Caspian Sea. A new runway was opened at Kerman airport in January 1986, and the terminal was to be expanded by 1987. Six airports have been added to the national network since the Islamic Revolution. In addition, airports at Ardebil, Sari and Meshed are to be expanded to take heavy aircraft.

Iran Air (Airline of the Islamic Republic of Iran): Iran Air Bldg, Mehrabad Airport, Teheran; telex 212975; f. 1962; Man. Dir MUHAMMAD REZA MAJIDI; serves Persian Gulf area, Athens, Beijing, Bombay, Damascus, Frankfurt, Geneva, Istanbul, Karachi, Larnaca, London, Paris, Rome, Tokyo, Vienna and, from 1988, Lagos, Cotonou and Accra; Man. Dir Eng. MOHAMMAD REZA MAJIDI; fleet of 2 Boeing 747-200B, 1 Boeing 747-100B, 1 Boeing 747-F, 4 Boeing 747-SP, 3 Boeing 707, 5 Airbus A300B2-203, 5 Boeing 727-200, 2 Boeing 727-100, 3 Boeing 737-200, 1 Boeing 707F.

Iran Asseman Airlines: POB 13145-1476, Mehrabad Airport, Teheran; tel. (021) 661967; telex 212575; f. after Islamic Revolution as result of merger of Air Taxi Co (f. 1958), Pars Air (f. 1969), Air Service Co (f. 1962) and Hoor Asseman; Man. Dir ALI ABEDZADEH; domestic routes and charter services; fleet of 2 Fokker F28-4000, 4 Falcon 20F, 6 Turbo Commander, 2 Aero Commander, 8 Shrike Commander, 2 Piper Chieftain, 2 Islander.

Tourism

Tourism has been adversely affected by political upheaval since the revolution. Iran's chief attraction for the tourist is its wealth of historical sites, notably Isfahan, Rasht, Tabriz, Susa and Persepolis. There were 62,373 visitors to Iran in 1982, compared with 185,756 in 1981. The total rose to an estimated 157,000 in 1984, and to 171,837 during the Iranian year 21 March 1986–20 March 1987.

Atomic Energy

Atomic Energy Organization of Iran: POB 14155-1339, Teheran; tel. (021) 61381; telex 213383; f. 1973; originally set up to produce nuclear power to provide for the base load electricity needs of the country; main aim now is the exploration and exploitation of uranium (deposits have been found in several regions of Iran in commercially viable quantities); to utilize nuclear technology in industry, agriculture and medicine; to provide research and development work and training for greater national self-sufficiency in nuclear science and technology; Bushehr nuclear power plant, a pressurized water reactor (two 1,200 MW units), which was being built by Kraftwerk Union AG of the Federal Republic of Germany, is now planned to be completed by an international consortium; Pres. REZA AMROLLAHI.

Isfahan Nuclear Technology Centre (INTC): POB 81465-1589, Isfahan 81465; tel. (031) 58081; telex 212165; f. 1979; applied engineering research in areas related to nuclear reactor technology.

Teheran University Nuclear Centre: Institute of Nuclear Science and Technology, POB 2989, Teheran; f. 1958; research in nuclear physics, electronics, nuclear chemistry, radiobiology and nuclear engineering; training and advice on nuclear science and the peaceful applications of atomic energy; a 5-MW pool-type research reactor on the new campus of Teheran University went critical in November 1967; a 3-MeV Van de Graaff-type accelerator became operational in 1972; Dir Dr J. MOGHIMI.

IRAQ

Introductory Survey

Location, Climate, Language, Religion, Flag, Capital

The Republic of Iraq is an almost land-locked state in western Asia, with a narrow outlet to the sea on the Persian (Arabian) Gulf. Its neighbours are Iran to the east, Turkey to the north, Syria and Jordan to the west, and Saudi Arabia and Kuwait to the south. The climate is extreme, with hot, dry summers, when temperatures may exceed 43°C (109°F), and cold winters, especially in the highlands. Summers are humid near the Persian Gulf. The official language is Arabic, spoken by about 80% of the population. About 15% speak Kurdish, while there is a small Turkoman-speaking minority. About 95% of the population are Muslims, of whom more than 50% belong to the Shi'i sect. However, the regime that came to power in 1968 has been dominated by members of the Sunni sect. The national flag (proportions 3 by 2) has three equal horizontal stripes, of red, white and black, with three five-pointed green stars on the central white stripe. The capital is Baghdad.

Recent History

Iraq was formerly part of Turkey's Ottoman Empire. During the First World War (1914–18), when Turkey was allied with Germany, the territory was captured by British forces. In 1920 Iraq was placed under a League of Nations mandate, administered by the United Kingdom (UK). In 1921 Amir Faisal ibn Hussain, a member of the Hashimi (Hashemite) dynasty of Arabia, was proclaimed King of Iraq, and his brother, Abdullah, was proclaimed Amir (Emir) of neighbouring Transjordan (later renamed Jordan), also administered by the UK under a League of Nations mandate. The two new monarchs were sons of Hussain (Hussein) ibn Ali, the Sharif of Mecca, who had proclaimed himself King of the Hijaz (now part of Saudi Arabia) in 1916. The British decision to nominate Hashemite princes to be rulers of Iraq and Transjordan was a reward for Hussain's co-operation in the wartime campaign against Turkey.

During its early years the new kingdom was faced by Kurdish revolts (1922–32) and by border disputes in the south. The leading personality in Iraqi political life under the monarchy was Gen. Nuri as-Said, who became Prime Minister in 1930 and held the office for seven terms, over a period of 28 years. He strongly supported Iraq's friendship with the UK and with the West in general. After prolonged negotiations, a 25-year Anglo-Iraqi Treaty of Alliance was signed in 1930. The British mandate ended on 3 October 1932, when Iraq became fully independent.

King Faisal I died in 1933 and was succeeded by his son, Ghazi. In 1939, however, King Ghazi was killed in a motor accident. The new king, Faisal II, was only three years old at the time of his accession, and his uncle, Prince Abd al-Ilah, acted as regent until 1953, when the king assumed full powers. Like Gen. Nuri, Prince Abd al-Ilah was pro-Western in outlook. An attempted pro-Nazi coup in May 1941 was thwarted by the intervention of British forces. Despite nationalist opposition, Iraq declared war on Germany and Italy in January 1943. British troops were withdrawn in October 1947, although a British air base remained until 1959. Iraqi forces participated in the Arab–Israeli war of 1948–49. The Constitutional Union Party, founded by Gen. Nuri in 1949, became the sole legal party in 1953, after all opposition groups were banned. In 1955 Iraq signed the Baghdad Pact, an agreement on collective regional security against a possible threat from the USSR.

In February 1958 Iraq and Jordan formed an Arab Federation, with King Faisal of Iraq as its Head of State. In March Gen. Nuri resigned as Iraqi Prime Minister to become Prime Minister of the new union. On 14 July, however, a military revolution overthrew the Iraqi monarchy. King Faisal, Prince Abd al-Ilah and Gen. Nuri were all killed. The victorious rebels abolished the 1925 Constitution, dissolved the legislature and proclaimed a republic, with Brig. (later Lt-Gen.) Abd al-Karim Kassem at the head of a left-wing nationalist regime. Iraq withdrew from the Baghdad Pact in March 1959. For more than four years, Kassem maintained a precarious and increasingly isolated position, opposed by Pan-Arabs, Kurds and other groups. In February 1963 the Pan-Arab element in the armed forces staged a coup in which Kassem was killed. A new government was formed under Col (later Field Marshal) Abd as-Salem Muhammad Aref, who had briefly held office as Deputy Prime Minister after the 1958 revolution. President Aref initiated a policy of closer relations with the United Arab Republic (Egypt). Martial law, in force since 1958, was ended in January 1965, and a civilian government was inaugurated in September 1965. President Aref was killed in an air accident in March 1966, and was succeeded by his brother, Major-Gen. Abd ar-Rahman Muhammad Aref. Iraq declared war on Israel at the outbreak of the Six-Day War in June 1967, but Iraqi forces were not involved in the conflict. The second President Aref was ousted by members of the Arab Socialist Renaissance (Baath) Party on 17 July 1968. Major-Gen. (later Field Marshal) Ahmad Hassan al-Bakr, a former Prime Minister, became President and Prime Minister, and supreme authority was vested in the Revolutionary Command Council (RCC), of which President al-Bakr was also Chairman. Provisional constitutions, proclaiming socialist principles, were introduced in September 1968 and July 1970. A National Charter, to be the basis of a permanent constitution, was issued in November 1971. This envisaged an elected National Assembly but, until the Assembly's formation, power remained with the RCC.

Relations with the Syrian Government deteriorated after a younger generation of Baathists seized power in Syria in 1970. A bitter rivalry has since existed between Syrian and Iraqi Baathists. Relations with Syria dramatically improved in October 1978, when President Assad of Syria visited Baghdad. Plans were announced for eventual complete political and economic union of the two countries. Economic difficulties, such as the dispute over water from the Euphrates river, were soon settled but progress on political union was slow. On 16 July 1979 the Vice-Chairman of the RCC, Saddam Hussain, who had long been the real power in Iraq, replaced Bakr as Chairman, and as President of Iraq. A few days later, an attempted coup was reported and several members of the RCC were executed for their alleged part in the plot. The suspicion of Syrian implication put an end to all further talk of political union between Iraq and Syria, but economic co-operation continued.

During 1979 the National Progressive Front, an alliance of Baathists and Communists, broke up amid accusations that the Baathists were conducting a 'reign of terror'. In February 1980 President Hussain announced his 'National Charter', reaffirming the principles of non-alignment. In June elections, the first since the 1958 revolution, were held for a 250-member, legislative National Assembly, followed in September by elections for a 50-member Kurdish Legislative Council.

Relations with Iran, precarious for many years, developed into full-scale war in September 1980. Prior to 1975, Iran had been supporting a rebellion by Kurds in northern Iraq. An agreement between Iran and Iraq, signed in 1975, defined the southern border between the two countries as a line along the middle of the Shatt al-Arab waterway, and also virtually ended the Kurdish rebellion by depriving it of Iranian support. In the years after 1975, however, Iraq grew increasingly dissatisfied with the 1975 agreement. Iraq also wanted the withdrawal of Iranian forces from Abu Musa and Tumb islands, which Iran occupied in 1971.

The Iranian revolution of 1979 exacerbated these grievances. Conflict soon developed over Arab demands for autonomy in Iran's Khuzestan region (named 'Arabistan' by Arabs), which Iran accused Iraq of encouraging. Iraq's Sunni leadership was suspicious of Shi'ite Iran, and feared that trouble might arise from its own Shi'ites, who form more than 50% of the population. Border squabbling took place between Iraq and Iran in the summer of 1980, and more extensive fighting began after Iran ignored Iraqi diplomatic efforts, demanding the withdrawal of Iranian forces from the border area of Zain ul-Qos in Diali province. Iraq maintained that this area should have been returned under the 1975 agreement, which Iraq then abrogated on 16 September 1980. Iraqi advances into Iran began on 22 September along a front of 500 km (300 miles). Fierce Iranian resistance brought about a stalemate, which lasted until the spring of 1982, when Iranian counter-offensives led to the retaking of the port of Khorramshahr in May and the withdrawal of Iraqi troops from the territory which they had taken in 1980. In July 1982 the Iranian army crossed into Iraq.

The Gulf War, as it was known, degenerated into a conflict of attrition, with Iraq holding an advantage in terms of the quantity and sophistication of its armaments, and Iran having a greater supply of manpower, without being able to stage a decisive offensive. While Iran launched a series of attacks across its northern border with Iraq in October 1983, threatening the last outlet for Iraqi exports of petroleum through the Kirkuk pipeline, Iraq intensified missile attacks and bombing raids against Iranian towns and petroleum installations. During the autumn of 1983 Iraq took delivery of five French-built Super Etendard fighter aircraft. With these and with the Exocet missiles which it already possessed, Iraq threatened to destroy Iran's oil industry, centred on Kharg Island in the Gulf. Iran, in turn, said that it would block the Gulf at the Straits of Hormuz to all traffic (including exports of one-sixth of the West's petroleum requirements) if Iraqi military action made it impossible to export its oil by that route.

In February 1984 a further Iranian offensive resulted in the capture of marshlands around the Majnoun Islands in southern Iraq, the site of rich petroleum deposits. Iraq failed to recapture all the lost territory, and a long hiatus ensued, during which Iraq constructed a formidable defensive network, including dams and a huge artificial lake, along the southern front. In 1984 the balance of military power moved in Iraq's favour, and its financial position improved as the USA and the USSR, both officially neutral in the war with Iran, provided aid. The USSR increased its military aid following a *rapprochement* in March, precipitated by Iran's anti-Soviet stance. (At the end of 1987 it was estimated that the USSR had supplied Iraq with military aid worth $10,000m. since lifting a ban on arms sales in 1982.) The USA assisted Iraq with the financing of crucial oil export pipeline projects and an increasing allocation of commodity credits, which totalled $2,500m. between 1981 and 1985. (Iraq and the USA re-established full diplomatic relations on 26 November 1984, more than 17 years after they had been broken off by Iraq following the Arab–Israeli war of 1967.) Egypt was estimated to have provided military supplies worth more than US $2,000m., and Brazil, Chile and the People's Republic of China also sold arms to Iraq. The delivery of eight French Mirage F-1 EQ5 fighter aircraft in October 1984 brought the Iranian Levan Island oil terminal within Iraq's range and underlined its superiority in the air.

Although it had declared a maritime exclusion zone at the north-east end of the Persian Gulf, enclosing Kharg Island, in August 1982 and made spasmodic attacks against shipping (not only tankers but, in some cases, ships well outside the zone), Iraq refrained from attacking tankers using the Kharg Island oil terminal until May 1984. After the first series of attacks on some dozen vessels, regardless of nationality, Iran retaliated by attacking Saudi Arabian and Kuwaiti tankers in the Gulf. A sporadic series of Iraqi attacks on Gulf tanker traffic, and on the Kharg Island terminal itself, continued, with limited success. The attacks were not sufficiently intensive or destructive to starve Iran of vital oil revenues.

Saddam Hussain retained his positions as Chairman of the RCC and Regional Secretary of the Baath Party, following its regional Congress in June 1982. In fact, a subsequent purge throughout the administration left him more firmly in control than before. Kurdish rebels became active again in northern Iraq, occasionally supporting Iranian forces. Another threat was posed by the Supreme Council of Iraqi Opposition Groups, formed in Teheran in November 1982 by the exiled Shi'ite leader, Hojatoleslam Muhammad Baqir al-Hakim.

An attempted coup was believed to have taken place in Baghdad in October 1983, led by the recently dismissed head of intelligence, Barzan Takriti (the President's half-brother), and a number of senior army officers, who were later reported to have been executed. Iraq's Shi'ite community (about 55% of the total population) was not attracted by Khomeini's brand of fundamentalism and has remained loyal to Iraq and its Sunni President, while the opposition of Iranian-backed terrorist groups (such as the Shi'ite fundamentalist Dawa group, which has repeatedly attempted to assassinate Hussain) has had no significant effect. While the cease-fire in the Gulf War of August 1988, which was precipitated by Iraqi military successes, strengthened Hussain's position, it also allowed domestic conflicts to find expression again. Hussain's regime is widely regarded as one of the most autocratic in the Arab world, and in February 1989 there were reports of a further attempt by senior army officers to stage a coup. In November 1988 Hussain announced a programme of political reforms, including the introduction of a multi-party political system, and in January 1989 he declared that these would be incorporated into a new constitution. This development was regarded as an attempt to retain the loyalty of Iraq's Shi'ite community, which sought a liberalization of Iraqi society as a reward for its role in the war against Iran.

Meanwhile, the problem of autonomy for Iraq's 2.5m.–3m. Kurds (currently in limited operation in three provinces) remained unresolved. Resources were repeatedly diverted from the war with Iran to control Kurdish rebellion in the north-east of the country. Hussain sought an accommodation with the Kurds, and a series of discussions began in December 1983, after a cease-fire had been agreed with Jalal Talibani, the leader of the main Kurdish opposition party in Iraq, the Patriotic Union of Kurdistan (PUK). These discussions did not include the other main Kurdish group, the Democratic Party of Kurdistan (DPK), led by Masoud Barzani. The breakdown of the talks in May 1984 frustrated hopes for a government of national unity, including the PUK and the Communist Party of Iraq. However, it was reported that Hussain persisted, informally, in trying to persuade the PUK to join the National Progressive Front. Negotiations on Kurdish autonomy collapsed again in January 1985. After a cease-fire lasting 14 months, fighting broke out in Kurdistan between PUK guerrillas and government troops. The PUK blamed the Government's continued persecution and execution of Kurds; its refusal to permit consideration in autonomy talks of the one-third of Kurdistan which, in Kirkuk province, contains some of Iraq's main oilfields; and an agreement with Turkey to act jointly to quell Kurdish resistance, which had been made in October 1984. Then, in February 1985, the PUK rejected the offer of an amnesty for President Hussain's political opponents, at home and abroad, and fighting has continued, with Kurdish and Iranian forces repeatedly collaborating in raids against Iraqi military and industrial targets.

Since 1987, when the Iranian military threat began to recede, Iraq had concentrated more resources in the north of the country to counter the activities of the Kurdish separatist movement, which claimed to control a 'liberated zone' of 10,000 sq km. In May 1988 the DPK and the PUK announced the formation of a coalition of six organizations to continue the struggle for Kurdish self-determination and to co-operate militarily with Iran. The introduction of a cease-fire in the Gulf War in August 1988 allowed Iraq to divert more troops and equipment to Kurdistan, and to launch a new offensive to overrun guerrilla bases near the borders with Iran and Turkey, during which chemical weapons were allegedly used, forcing Kurdish civilians and fighters to escape into Iran and Turkey. By mid-September, more than 100,000 Kurdish refugees were believed to have escaped into Turkey, while Iraqi Kurds seeking refuge in Iran joined an estimated 100,000 of their countrymen, 40,000 of whom had escaped from Halabja, after attacks with chemical weapons on the city in March.

On 26 September 1988 the UN Security Council adopted a resolution (No. 620) unanimously condemning the use of chemical weapons in the Gulf War. However, Iraq continued to deny that it was using chemical weapons against the Kurds, despite what the USA described as compelling evidence to the contrary. On 6 September, with its army effectively in control of the border with Turkey, the Iraqi Government offered a full amnesty to all Iraqi Kurds inside and outside the country, excluding only Jalal Talibani, the leader of the PUK. However, the offer was generally dismissed by Kurds as a propaganda ploy. An attempt by the US Senate to impose trade sanctions on Iraq, because of its use of chemical weapons, was defeated in October.

In June 1984 the UN had engineered an agreement between Iran and Iraq, suspending attacks on civilian targets. However, in March 1985, with the war on the ground in a state of deadlock, Iraq resorted to air raids on Iranian towns and declared Iranian airspace a war zone. Thousands of civilians were killed in attacks on more than 30 Iranian towns and cities, including Teheran, between March and May. Iran retaliated with shelling and air raids on Iraqi cities, including

Basra and Baghdad (which was struck by ground-launched missiles).

In March 1985 King Hussein of Jordan and President Mubarak of Egypt made an unexpected visit to Baghdad to demonstrate their support for Saddam Hussain, despite the fact that full diplomatic relations had not existed between Egypt and Iraq since Egypt's signing of the peace treaty with Israel in 1979.

In April 1985 the UN Secretary-General, Javier Pérez de Cuéllar, visited both Teheran and Baghdad, in an attempt to establish a basis on which peace negotiations could begin. Iraq made it clear that it was interested only in a permanent cease-fire and immediate, direct negotiations with Iran; while Iran continued to insist on the removal of Saddam Hussain, an Iraqi admission of responsibility for starting the war, and the payment of reparations.

In response to an Irano-Libyan strategic alliance which was becoming more open in character, Iraq withdrew its diplomatic mission from Tripoli in June 1985, and asked the Libyans to withdraw theirs from Baghdad. A partial *rapprochement* between Libya and Iraq took place in September 1987.

Between August 1985 and January 1986 Iraq made a concentrated series of some 60 air raids on Iran's main oil terminal at Kharg Island. Exports from the terminal were reduced to a trickle by the beginning of 1986, by which time Iraq had already turned its attention to attacks on tankers shuttling oil from Kharg to the makeshift floating terminal at Sirri Island, 450 km to the south-east, for transhipment.

In February 1986 Iraq announced an expansion of the area of the Gulf from which it would try to exclude Iranian shipping. Previously confined to the waters around Iran's Gulf ports, the area was extended to include the coast of Kuwait. Attacks on tankers and other commercial vessels in the Gulf were increased by both sides during 1986, when they numbered 80, compared with the 46 recorded in 1985. In August 1986 an Iraqi air raid demonstrated that the Sirri oil export facility was vulnerable to attack, and Iran was forced to transfer more of its export operations to the floating terminal at Larak Island (250 km east of Sirri, at the mouth of the Strait of Hormuz), which had been established in June. However, even the Larak facility proved to be within the range of Iraqi aircraft, and was itself attacked in November. Further Iraqi attacks on Kharg Island in September and October left only three out of 16 oil-loading berths at the terminal operational.

In February 1986 Iran began the Wal-Fajr (Dawn) 8 offensive. Some 85,000 Iranian troops crossed the Shatt al-Arab waterway and occupied the disused Iraqi oil port of Faw, on the Persian Gulf, and, according to Iran, about 800 sq km of the Faw peninsula. From this position, within sight of the Kuwaiti island of Bubiyan (commanding the Khor Abdullah channel between the Faw peninsula and the island), Iran threatened Iraq's only access to the Gulf and Iraq's Umm Qasr naval base, to the north-west. To divert Iraqi forces, Iran had begun a complementary assault along the Faw-Basra road. When Iraq mounted a counter-offensive on Faw in mid-February, Iran opened up a second front with the Wal-Fajr 9 offensive in Iraqi Kurdistan, several hundred kilometres to the north. At the beginning of 1988 Iran retained its foothold on the Faw peninsula.

The next major Iranian offensive (Karbala-4) was launched in December 1986 in the region of Basra, and was directed against Iraqi positions on islands in the Shatt al-Arab waterway. However, the attack was repulsed by the Iraqis, and the Iranians suffered heavy casualties. In January 1987 a two-pronged offensive, Karbala-5, was launched by Iran towards Basra. Iranian forces, attacking from the east, established a bridgehead inside Iraq, between the Shatt al-Arab and the artificial Fish Lake, and advanced gradually towards Basra, sustaining heavy casualties, while an attack from the south-east secured a group of islands in the Shatt al-Arab. By mid-February, Iranian forces from the east had advanced to within about 10 km of Basra, but, confronted by the city's main network of defensive fortifications, no further gains were made.

In July 1986 the ruling Arab Baath Socialist Party held an extraordinary regional conference, the first since June 1982. Three new members were elected to the party's Regional Command (RC), increasing its number to 17. Naim Haddad, who had been a member of the RC and of the ruling Revolutionary Command Council (RCC) since their formation in 1968, was not re-elected to the RC, and was subsequently removed from the RCC, on which he was replaced by Sa'adoun Hammadi, the Chairman, or Speaker, of the National Assembly. These changes effectively strengthened Saddam Hussain's position as leader of the party.

Iraq continued to attack tankers shuttling Iranian oil from Kharg Island to the floating terminals at Sirri and Larak Islands during 1987, while Iran intensified its attacks on Kuwaiti shipping and on neutral vessels suspected of carrying cargoes destined for Iraq, via Kuwait, or tankers carrying oil to be sold on Iraq's behalf. In April 1987 the USSR allowed Kuwait to charter three Soviet tankers, and in May the USA agreed to re-register 11 Kuwaiti tankers under the American flag, entitling them to US naval protection. The US decision followed the apparently accidental attack on the *USS Stark* by an Iraqi Mirage jet aircraft on 17 May. The USA progressively reinforced its naval presence in the Gulf during the second half of 1987, a policy which Iran considered to be provocative.

The escalation of tension in the Gulf resulted in the adoption by the UN Security Council, on 20 July 1987, of Resolution 598, urging an immediate cease-fire in the Gulf War, the withdrawal of all forces to internationally recognized boundaries, and the co-operation of Iran and Iraq in mediation efforts to achieve a peace settlement. Iraq agreed to abide by the resolution if Iran would also do so. Iran criticized the resolution for failing to identify Iraq as the aggressor in the war, and claimed that the belligerent US naval presence in the Gulf rendered it null and void, but failed to deliver a definitive response. During his visit to Teheran, the UN Secretary-General, Javier Pérez de Cuéllar, was informed by Iranian leaders that they supported the provision in Resolution 598 for the establishment of an 'impartial body' to apportion responsibility for the war, but that a report establishing Iraq's guilt would have to be published before Iran would observe a cease-fire. Iraq refused to countenance any deviation from the original terms of the resolution, and echoed the view of the Western powers on the Security Council in accusing Iran of temporizing. An extraordinary meeting of the League of Arab States in Amman, Jordan, in November unanimously condemned Iran for prolonging the Gulf War, deplored its occupation of Arab (i.e. Iraqi) territory, and urged it to implement Resolution 598.

Following the Arab League 'summit' in Amman, the Iraqi Government, in common with eight other Arab countries, re-established diplomatic relations with Egypt. Meanwhile, during the 'summit', a meeting between President Hussain and President Assad revived speculation of a *rapprochement* between Iraq and Syria, which has supported Iran in the Gulf War. President Assad, however, had obstructed the League's adoption of an Iraqi proposal that member states should sever their diplomatic links with Iran, and Syria subsequently averred that the good relations between Syria and Iran were unchanged.

On 24 July 1987 the re-registered Kuwaiti tanker *USS Bridgeton* struck a mine while under US naval escort in the Gulf. In August the UK and France sent minesweepers to the Gulf region, to be followed in September by vessels from the Netherlands, Belgium and Italy. At the end of the year the US naval force in and just outside the Gulf numbered more than 30 ships, and the Soviet fleet totalled an estimated 23 vessels. The increased presence of US and European naval forces in the Gulf failed to deter attacks on shipping, in particular oil tankers, by Iran and Iraq. In 1987 at least 178 attacks were recorded, compared with 80, the previous highest total, in 1986.

At the end of December 1987, the USSR, which had resisted attempts by the Western powers among the five permanent members of the UN Security Council to initiate discussions on the procedure for imposing an arms embargo against Iran, agreed that such discussions should proceed, on condition that they ran parallel with talks on the withdrawal of national naval forces from the Gulf and their replacement by a UN force. However, the USSR's insistence on the withdrawal of foreign navies from the Gulf, together with the USA's growing military involvement in the area in 1988, prevented the adoption of an arms embargo.

During 1987/88, for the first time in six years, owing to disorganization and a shortage of volunteers, Iran was unable to launch a major winter offensive. Iraqi forces advanced along the length of the war front, but not before Kurdish guerrillas had, in February 1988, made inroads into government-controlled territory in Iraqi Kurdistan, where Iranian forces, with Kurdish assistance, had earlier established bridgeheads. This was the largest Kurdish offensive since

1974/75, uniting forces from the DPK and the PUK. In March 1988 Iraq retaliated, using chemical weapons against the captured town of Halabja.

In mid-April 1988 Iraqi forces regained control of the Faw peninsular, and in May they recaptured the Shalamcheh area, driving the Iranians across the Shatt al-Arab. In mid-June they recaptured Majnoon Island, and at the end of the month expelled Iranian forces from Iraqi territory in Kurdistan. On 13 July Iraqi forces crossed into Iranian territory for the first time since 1986. Remaining pockets of Iranian resistance in southern Iraq had collapsed by mid-July, and on 18 July, to universal surprise, Iran officially announced its unconditional acceptance of Resolution 598. However, the implementation of a cease-fire was delayed by Iraq's demand for the initiation of direct peace talks with Iran, under UN auspices, prior to the cessation of hostilities. Iraq eventually withdrew this demand, and on 20 August a cease-fire came into force, monitored by a specially-created UN observer force of 350 officers, the UN Iran-Iraq Military Observer Group (UNIIMOG).

Negotiations between Iran and Iraq for a comprehensive peace settlement, based on the full implementation of Resolution 598, began at ministerial level in Geneva on 25 August 1988, under the aegis of the UN. However, deadlock soon arose over the question of the location of frontiers, in particular the southern border through the Shatt al-Arab waterway. This and other disputes, mostly concerning issues for which there was no provision in Resolution 598, delayed the implementation of the resolution beyond the introduction of a cease-fire. Clause Three, for example, urged the repatriation of prisoners of war. In November Iran and Iraq agreed to exchange all sick and wounded prisoners of war. The first exchanges took place in the same month, but the arrangements collapsed shortly afterwards, following a dispute over the number of prisoners involved. Resolution 598 also envisaged the creation of an impartial judicial body to determine who was responsible for starting the war. Its conclusions, when reached, seemed likely to prove to be a major obstacle to a peace settlement. While it was generally accepted that Iraq had initiated the conflict by invading Iran on 22 September 1980, Iraq maintained that the war began on 4 September with Iranian shelling of Iraqi border posts.

In February 1989 the negotiations for a peace settlement, which had been in suspension since November 1988, were renewed.

Government

Power rests with the President and a Revolutionary Command Council (RCC), which in early 1989 comprised nine members (including the Chairman and Vice-Chairman). Considerable influence is wielded by the Iraq Regional Command of the Baath Party, while the routine administration of the country is carried out by an appointed Council of Ministers. Legislative responsibility is shared between the RCC and the National Assembly, with 250 members elected by universal adult suffrage for four years. The country is divided into 15 Provinces and three Autonomous Regions. A Kurdish autonomous area has been set up, and elections to a 50-member Kurdish Legislative Council were held in September 1980 and August 1986.

Defence

Military service is compulsory for all men at the age of 18 years, and lasts between 21 months and two years, extendable in wartime. In June 1988 the armed forces totalled 1m. regular members; the army had a total strength of 955,000 (including an estimated 480,000 active reserves); the air force had a strength of 40,000, and the navy 5,000. In order to wage the Gulf War, these forces were supplemented by a 650,000-strong popular army and possibly 10,000 volunteers from Arab countries. Estimated defence expenditure in 1987 was ID 4,350m. (US $13,990m.).

Economic Affairs

Prior to the discovery of petroleum in Iraq, agriculture was the dominant sector of the economy, and dates were the most lucrative export commodity. Dates remain Iraq's second most valuable export, but petroleum is now the most important sector of the economy, providing more than 95% of the country's earnings of foreign exchange. In 1979 Iraq achieved a record annual output of 170.5m. metric tons of crude petroleum. In 1980, when the Gulf War with Iran began, production declined to 130.1m. tons, but Iraq was briefly the second largest oil producer in the Middle East, after Saudi Arabia. Thereafter, output declined sharply. As a result of the fall in production and prices of petroleum, Iraq has experienced economic decline in recent years. In 1985, according to UN estimates, the country's gross domestic product (GDP), at current prices, was US $46,774m., equivalent to $2,942 per head. Between 1980 and 1985, it was estimated, GDP declined, in real terms, at an average rate of 2.1% per year, with real GDP per head falling by 4.8% annually.

Iraq was one of the founder-members of the Organization of the Petroleum Exporting Countries (OPEC), whose first conference was held in Baghdad in 1960. Iraq officially assessed its total reserves of crude petroleum at 160,000m. barrels in 1986, placing Iraq second only to Saudi Arabia in the extent of its reserves. Discovered and proven reserves were reported to total 72,000m. barrels. An independent estimate evaluated Iraq's proven reserves at 100,000m. barrels at 1 January 1988, more than double their total one year earlier. Owing to the outbreak of the Gulf War, which caused a reduction of refinery capacity and export facilities, and to a decline in international demand for oil, production of crude petroleum in 1980 fell by 23.7%, to an average of 2.64m. barrels per day (b/d), but, as a result of a rise in prices, government revenues from the petroleum industry increased from US $21,200m. in 1979 to $26,500m. in 1980. Production of crude petroleum declined to only 43.9m. metric tons, an average of about 900,000 b/d, in 1981. Iraq's exports of petroleum reached a record 3.2m. b/d in 1980, and by July 1985 the country's production of crude oil had returned to pre-war levels of 4m. b/d. However, because of the Gulf War, Iraq could export only about 650,000 b/d in 1983 through the 980-km (610-mile) pipeline across Turkey, its only remaining normal outlet for oil exports, plus 50,000–60,000 b/d by road. Revenues were in the range $9,000m.–$11,000m. per year in 1981–85, and declined to $6,813m. in 1986.

The country's main port, Basra, was closed in 1980 because of the war, and by 1988 no attempt had been made to restore it. The 1981–85 Five-Year Development Plan had to be abandoned, although a 1986–90 Plan was instituted with the aim of improving the country's social services and infrastructure. Countries that had been eager to invest in Iraq and to bid for lucrative construction contracts even after the war with Iran had begun, when Iraq was an oil-rich country committed to an ambitious programme of development, experienced difficulty in obtaining payment. Foreign contractors have been asked to defer receipt of payments, to refinance the foreign currency portion of outstanding payments, or to accept part-payment in petroleum, owing to a shortage of convertible currency in Iraq. The country's reserves of foreign exchange, which had been about $35,000m. at the beginning of the war in 1980, declined to less than $5,000m. by mid-1983. Estimates in 1987 assessed the level of reserves as ranging between zero and $2,000m. The value of exports declined from $26,278m. in 1980 to $9,220m. in 1984, rising to $10,357m. in 1985. Exports were only $7,538m. in 1986 but reached $9,014m. in 1987. Import costs increased from $13,942m. in 1980 to $21,534m. in 1982. As a result of efforts to restrict purchases, the cost of imports was reduced to $12,166m. in 1983, and declined further in subsequent years. Imports fell from $10,190m. in 1986 to only $7,415m. in 1987.

Measured in constant prices, Iraq's GDP declined marginally in 1985, although there were substantial increases in agricultural and industrial productivity. In 1986, however, the precipitate fall in oil prices during the first half of the year and the decline in the value of the dollar frustrated hopes that the economy would make a significant recovery. Although the Government was able to reduce public spending in most sectors, severe fighting in the Gulf War necessitated an increase in expenditure on weapons and military equipment. Iraq's total foreign debt was estimated at up to $70,000m. in February 1989. Of this total, $25,000m.–$30,000m. was in the form of loans from neighbouring Gulf states; about $12,800m. was civil debt guaranteed by export credit agencies for payment during 1985–90; and a further $6,000m. owing to Western companies and not covered by export credit guarantees. Japan is the largest creditor (with more than $3,000m. in civil debt owing in mid-1988, $2,400m. of which was covered by export credits), followed by Italy, the Federal Republic of Germany, France and Turkey. Some $3,000m. per year is required merely to service the Western portion of the foreign debt. In October 1985 the Rafidain Bank raised a $500m. Euroloan. Iraq has also been forced to reschedule payments due on two $500m. Euroloans raised in 1983 and 1985 to finance foreign trade and development projects. Saudi Arabia and Kuwait loaned about $26,000m. to Iraq in the first year of the war, and, through the Arabian Oil Co (which operates in the Neutral Zone), subsequently provided some $3,000m. per year in revenues from up to 310,000 b/d of oil (250,000 b/d from the Neutral Zone and the remainder from Saudi Arabia), sold on Iraq's behalf to compensate it for lost export capacity. In mid-1987 Saudi Arabia assured Iran that it was selling a negligible amount of oil on Iraq's behalf. Kuwait continued to sell about 100,000 b/d until the end of August, when the arrangement was reportedly terminated by both countries, although sales appear to have continued.

The Euroloan that Iraq secured in 1983 was used to finance the expansion of its sole functioning oil pipeline from Kirkuk to Cayhan in Turkey. The pipeline was pumping about 1m. b/d in 1987. In addition, Iraq has two new pipeline projects under way. Construction work on a new pipeline, 980 km in length, running parallel to the existing line from Kirkuk to the Mediterranean port of Yumurtalik in Turkey was completed in mid-1987. The new pipeline has a capacity of 500,000 b/d, giving a combined capacity for the two lines of 1.5m. b/d, since it became operational at the end of July 1987. There are also plans to double the capacity of this line. In April 1987 Turkey and Iraq finalized plans to construct a third trans-Turkish pipeline. The line, with a capacity of 70,000 b/d, will run from oilfields at Ain Zalah, near Mosul, to the Batman oil refinery in Turkey, a distance of 240 km, and is expected to take one year to construct. The construction of another refinery in Turkey to process Iraqi crude oil was suspended in July 1988. A two-stage oil pipeline project, agreed with Saudi Arabia in November 1983, aimed to increase Iraq's export capacity by 1.6m. b/d by 1988. The first stage, of 640 km (398 miles), was opened in September 1985 and links Iraq's southern oilfields with the Saudi Petroline to the terminal at Yanbu. The line's capacity is 500,000 b/d, but through-put has been limited to 350,000 b/d–400,000 b/d by the Saudi Arabian Government. In March 1987, however, Saudi Arabia agreed to allow Iraq to export oil through Yanbu at the spur-line's full capacity of 500,000 b/d, on condition that it charged official OPEC prices for its crude. Work on the second stage, for which a contract was awarded in September 1987, involves the laying of a 970-km independent Iraqi pipeline parallel to the Saudi line, terminating at Yanbu, on the Red Sea, and providing a total through-put of 1.65m. b/d by September 1989. Another project, a joint venture with Jordan to build a pipeline, with a capacity of 1m. b/d, 1,650 km long, from western Iraq to Aqaba on Jordan's Red Sea coast, was suspended in 1984, as Iraq could secure no guarantee of compensation from the US Bechtel Corporation, the project's managing contractor, for Israeli sabotage of the pipeline, which would have terminated close to Jordan's border with Israel.

When the new lines across Turkey and the two phases of the trans-Saudi Arabia development are in full operation, Iraq's pipeline export capacity will total about 3.2m. b/d, making it the second largest exporter in OPEC, after Saudi Arabia. The facilities in the south, which were put out of action by the war, could provide another 3m. b/d in exports once they have been rehabilitated, and to this can be added the 100,000 b/d–250,000 b/d of petroleum products that are transported by road through Jordan and Turkey. Iraq's production quota of 1.2m. b/d, allocated to it by OPEC in March 1982, was not reduced when OPEC cut production by 1.5m. b/d in October 1984, in order to prevent a further fall in prices on the world market, which was over-supplied with oil. With new export outlets becoming available, Iraq campaigned for an increase in its OPEC production quota, although it had already consistently exceeded its allocation. Overproduction led to further falls in prices: in July 1986 the international price of crude petroleum declined to less than $10 per barrel. When, in August, at Iran's suggestion, OPEC agreed to reduce its members' aggregate production to a maximum of 16.7m. b/d for two months (effectively reverting to the quota restrictions that had been imposed in October 1984), Iraq refused to participate in the agreement. Iran asserted that Iraqi production would be curtailed by military action in the Gulf War. The effect of the two months of production restraint was to stabilize oil prices at about $15 per barrel, and in October OPEC agreed to raise production by 200,000 b/d. Iraq renewed its demand for a production quota equivalent to that allotted to Iran when OPEC met to set its members output levels for 1987 in December. Alone of the organization's 13 members, Iraq refused to accept a 7.25% reduction in its quota (a notional 1.8m. b/d) for the first half of 1987, which was intended to enable OPEC to support a fixed price of $18 per barrel during that period. Under the new arrangement, Iraq was asked to observe a quota of 1.47m. b/d, compared with 2.26m. b/d for Iran (and Iraq's actual production rate of about 1.7m. b/d in December 1986). In June 1987 Iraq declined to participate in the OPEC agreement covering production in the second half of the year, in which it was allocated a notional quota of 1.54m. b/d, compared with actual export capacity of about 2.7m. b/d in August, and the 2.37m. b/d allocated to Iran. At OPEC's meeting in December 1987 Iraq declined to participate in the agreement covering production in the first half of 1988, whereby its notional quota was unchanged. In December 1987 Iraq was producing oil at a rate of about 2.7m. b/d. In May 1988 OPEC decided to retain the existing quota and reference price for the second half of the year.

The cease-fire in the Gulf War, which took effect in August 1988, prompted preliminary attempts by OPEC to bring Iraq back into future production agreements by raising its quota to take account of increased export capacity. If Iraq were not to rejoin the OPEC quota system, Iraqi production was expected to rise to as much as 3.8m. b/d by August 1989, assuming that the cease-fire in the Gulf War could be maintained. In November 1987 Iraqi production reached 2.8m. b/d, and was maintained at the 2.5m. b/d level for several months. Production rose again in August 1988, to 2.7m. b/d, and exports to 2.3m. b/d. Iraq refused to accept an OPEC quota unless it were given parity with Iran. In November 1988, however, the OPEC quotas for both Iraq and Iran for the first half of 1989 were set at 2.64m. b/d.

Even before the re-establishment of diplomatic relations with the USA in November 1984, trade between the USA and Iraq had been increasing. The value of commodity credits granted to Iraq by the US Department of Agriculture was a record $633m. in the year to September 1984, and totalled $573m. in 1987. US exports to Iraq totalled $683.3m. in 1987, compared with $527.5m. in 1986. Total Iraqi exports to the USA rose from $39.3m. in 1982 to $526m. in 1987, when the USA resumed purchase of oil from Iraq. Trade with the USSR consists mainly of Soviet military supplies. In accordance with its political support for Iraq in the Gulf War, the USSR virtually ceased purchases of oil from Iran and approached Iraq and Saudi Arabia for its main Gulf supplies, after the signing of an accord with Iraq in April 1984 to increase co-operation in oil production. In July Iraq obtained a $2,000m. credit from the USSR for a number of development projects, including oil exploration and production, dam construction and energy use.

During 1987 extensive changes were made in the country's economic structure. Many state organizations, which were responsible for administering parts of the economy, were abolished, or merged, and more private companies were created, with the intention of reducing state control and securing greater efficiency in the industrial and agricultural sectors. Iraq has introduced more liberal import regulations to enable private companies to become more involved in foreign trade. The import programme for 1988 increased the private sector's share to 14%, compared with 6% for the co-operative sector. The campaign for economic reform also resulted in ministerial changes. In 1987 the Ministry of Light Industries was reconstituted as the Ministry of Industry, while the former Ministry of Industry and Minerals became the Ministry of Heavy Industries; and in August it was announced that four ministries (including those of Irrigation and of Agriculture) were to be merged, and others reorganized. In March 1988 the two industry ministries were merged to form the Ministry of Industry and Minerals, and the Military Industries Commission (MIC) was granted the status of a ministry. In July responsibility for civilian and military industries was united under a single ministry. The larger role which is envisaged for the private industrial sector is emphasized by the 1986–90 Development Plan, which proposes the initiation of 229 private schemes.

Social Welfare

A limited Social Security Scheme was introduced in 1957 and extended in 1976. Benefits are given for old age, sickness, unemployment, maternity, marriage and death. Health services are free. Many of the new health facilities that were scheduled under the 1981–85 Five-Year Plan have been completed in spite of the war. More than $1,500m. has been spent on building more than 30 new hospitals, which will provide about 11,500 beds. These additions meant that at the end of 1986 Iraq had 228 hospital establishments, with a total of 32,166 beds. There were reportedly 6,074 physicians working in the country at the end of 1986.

Education

Education is free, and primary education, beginning at six years of age and lasting for six years, has been made compulsory in an effort to reduce illiteracy. Enrolment at primary schools of children in the relevant age-group reached 100% in 1978, but the proportion had fallen to 86% by 1985. Secondary education begins at 12 years of age and lasts for up to six years, divided into two cycles of three years each. An estimated 43% of children in the appropriate age-group (53% of boys; 32% of girls) attended secondary schools in 1986. There are 47 teacher-training institutes, 19 technical institutes and six universities.

Public Holidays

1989: 1 January (New Year's Day), 6 January (Army Day), 8 February (14 Ramadan Revolution, anniversary of the 1963 coup), 5 March* (Leilat al-Meiraj, ascension of Muhammad), 7 May* (Id al-Fitr, end of Ramadan), 14 July (Republic Day, anniversary of the 1968 coup, and Id al-Adha*, Feast of the Sacrifice), 4 August* (Islamic New Year), 13 August* (Ashoura), 13 October* (Mouloud, Birth of Muhammad).

1990: 1 January (New Year's Day), 6 January (Army Day), 8 February (14 Ramadan Revolution, anniversary of the 1963 coup), 23 February* (Leilat al-Meiraj), 27 April* (Id al-Fitr), 4 July (Id al-Adha*), 14 July (Republic Day, anniversary of the 1968 coup), 24 July* (Islamic New Year), 2 August* (Ashoura), 2 October* (Mouloud).

* These holidays are dependent on the Islamic lunar calendar and may vary by one or two days from the dates given.

Weights and Measures

The metric system is in force. Some local measurements are also used, e.g. 1 meshara or dunum = 2,500 sq metres (0.62 acre).

Statistical Survey

Source: Central Statistical Organization, Ministry of Planning, Karradat Mariam, ash-Shawaf Sq., Baghdad; tel. 537-0071; telex 212218.

Area and Population

AREA, POPULATION AND DENSITY

Area (sq km)	438,317*
Population (census results)†	
17 October 1977	12,000,497
17 October 1987	
Males	8,364,873
Females	7,913,443
Total	16,278,316
Population (official estimates at October)†	
1984	15,077,000
1985	15,585,000
1986	16,110,000
Density (per sq km) at October 1987	37.1

* 169,235 sq miles. This figure includes 924 sq km (357 sq miles) of territorial waters but excludes the Neutral Zone, of which Iraq's share is 3,522 sq km (1,360 sq miles). The Zone lies between Iraq and Saudi Arabia, and is administered jointly by the two countries. Nomads move freely through it but there are no permanent inhabitants.
† Figures exclude Iraqis abroad, estimated at 129,000 in 1977. Estimates have not been adjusted to take account of the results of the 1987 census.

GOVERNORATES (estimated population at October 1986)

	Area* (sq km)	Population ('000)	Density (per sq km)
Nineveh	37,698	1,393	37.0
Salah ad-Din	29,004	454	15.7
At-Ta'meem	10,391	674	64.9
Diala	19,292	706	36.6
Baghdad	5,159	4,868	943.6
Al-Anbar	137,723	598	4.3
Babylon	5,258	759	144.4
Karbala	5,034	337	66.9
An-Najaf	27,844	484	17.4
Al-Qadisiya	8,507	524	61.6
Al-Muthanna	51,029	259	5.1
Thi-Qar	13,626	741	54.4
Wasit	17,308	494	28.5
Maysan	14,103	417	29.6
Basrah (Basra)	19,070	1,346	70.6
Autonomous Regions:			
D'hok	6,120	343	56.0
Arbil	14,471	774	53.5
As-Sulaimaniya	15,756	939	59.6
Total	437,393†	16,110	36.8

* Excluding territorial waters (924 sq km).
† Total area, including territorial waters: 438,317 sq km.

Population (at census of 17 October 1987): 1,507,926 in Nineveh governorate; 1,108,773 in Babylon governorate; more than 750,000 in five other governorates (Diala, al-Anbar, Thi-Qar, Basrah and as-Sulaimaniya).

PRINCIPAL TOWNS (population at 1977 census)

Baghdad (capital)	3,236,000*	Mosul	1,220,000
Basrah (Basra)	1,540,000	Kirkuk	535,000

* The population of Baghdad at the 17 October 1987 census was 3,844,608.

BIRTHS AND DEATHS

Average annual birth rate 47.4 per 1,000 in 1970–75, 47.0 per 1,000 in 1975–80; death rate 14.6 per 1,000 in 1970–75, 13.0 per 1,000 in 1975–80 (UN estimates).

IRAQ

ECONOMICALLY ACTIVE POPULATION (1977 census)

	Males	Females	Total
Agriculture, forestry and fishing	591,066	352,824	943,890
Mining and quarrying	34,716	2,119	36,835
Manufacturing	235,777	48,618	284,395
Electricity, gas and water	22,241	949	23,190
Construction	316,560	5,136	321,696
Trade, restaurants and hotels	207,949	16,155	224,104
Transport, storage and communications	172,814	4,985	177,799
Financing, insurance, real estate and business services	26,023	5,066	31,089
Community, social and personal services	871,879	86,100	957,979
Activities not adequately defined	46,258	11,979	58,237
Total employed	2,525,283	533,931	3,059,214
Unemployed	64,278	10,447	74,725
Total labour force	2,589,561	544,378	3,133,939

Agriculture

PRINCIPAL CROPS ('000 metric tons)

	1984	1985	1986
Wheat	471	1,406	1,036
Rice (paddy)	109	149	141
Barley	482	1,331	1,046
Maize	30	41	54
Potatoes	120	115*	120*
Green string beans	80	78	84
Green broad beans	101	93	152
Chick-peas	9	9	14
Lentils	3	4	3
Sunflower seed	10	10*	10
Sesame seed	6	9	9
Swiss chard	29	18	21
Olives	11†	12†	13*
Cabbages	15	11	11
Tomatoes	531	612	523
Pumpkins, etc.	69	70	75*
Cucumbers	358	411	368
Lettuce	70	60	48
Aubergines	177	233	176
Green peppers	37	39	38
Onions (dry)	97	175	157
Carrots	20	18	12
Watermelons	571	757	551
Melons	302	435	356
Grapes	425†	440†	450*
Dates	251	100	434
Sugar cane	86	84	38
Apples	116†	120†	122*
Peaches and nectarines*	30	30	32
Plums*	29	30	32
Oranges	153†	157†	160*
Tangerines, etc.*	45	46	47
Squash	69	49	54
Apricots*	31	32	33
Tobacco (leaves)	14	17	13
Seed cotton	7	7	20

* FAO estimates. † Unofficial figure.
Source: Central Statistical Organization and FAO, *Production Yearbook*.

Statistical Survey

LIVESTOCK ('000 head, year ending September)

	1984*	1985*	1986
Horses	50	50	53*
Mules	25	28	28*
Asses	400	450	450*
Cattle	1,550	1,500	1,573
Buffaloes	150	145	137
Camels	50	55	60*
Sheep	8,300	8,500	8,639
Goats	2,300	2,350	1,408

Poultry (million): 55* in 1984; 65* in 1985; 75* in 1986.
*FAO estimates. (Source: FAO, *Production Yearbook*).

LIVESTOCK PRODUCTS ('000 metric tons)

	1984	1985	1986*
Beef and veal	40*	35*	39
Buffalo meat	3*	3*	3
Mutton and lamb	55*	50*	51
Goats' meat	12*	11*	11
Poultry meat	125	150*	195
Cows' milk	336†	300*	320
Buffalo milk	25†	25*	25
Sheep's milk	165*	167*	170
Goats' milk	69*	70*	70
Cheese	33.6*	32.9*	33.7
Butter	8.3*	7.9*	8.2
Hen eggs	40.7*	61.5*	85.0
Wool:			
greasy	17†	17†	17
clean	7*	7*	7
Cattle and buffalo hides	5.8*	5.1*	5.6
Sheep skins	10.4*	9.3*	9.6
Goat skins	2.5*	2.3*	2.3

* FAO estimates. † Unofficial figure.
Source: FAO, *Production Yearbook*.

Fishing

(FAO estimates, '000 metric tons, live weight)

	1984	1985	1986
Inland waters	16.0	16.0	15.6
Indian Ocean	5.0	5.5	5.0
Total catch	21.0	21.5	20.6

Source: FAO, *Yearbook of Fishery Statistics*.

Mining

	1983	1984	1985
Crude petroleum ('000 metric tons)	46,760	58,741	69,891
Natural gas ('000 terajoules)	13	19	23

* Estimate.
Source: UN, *Industrial Statistics Yearbook*.

Crude petroleum ('000 metric tons): 82,300 in 1986; 104,700 in 1987 (Source: UN, *Monthly Bulletin of Statistics*).

Industry

SELECTED PRODUCTS
('000 metric tons, unless otherwise indicated)

	1983	1984	1985
Wheat flour	1,850	n.a.	n.a.
Cigarettes (million)	7,900	7,000	7,000
Cement*	5,600	8,000	8,000
Liquefied petroleum gas*†	260	280	400
Naphtha	300	400	500
Motor spirit (petrol)	1,500	1,600	1,650
Kerosene	570	700	750
Jet fuel	360	370	380
Distillate fuel oils	3,000	3,400	3,900
Residual fuel oils	4,600	4,900	5,100
Lubricating oils	100	100	100
Paraffin wax*	60	60	60
Petroleum bitumen (asphalt)	280	340	400
Electric energy (million kWh)	16,200	18,460	18,760

* Estimated production.
† Includes estimated production ('000 metric tons) from natural gas plants: 160 in 1983; 160 in 1984; 200 in 1985; and from petroleum refineries: 100 in 1983; 120 in 1984; 200 in 1985.

Source: UN, *Industrial Statistics Yearbook*.

Finance

CURRENCY AND EXCHANGE RATES

Monetary Units
1,000 fils = 20 dirhams = 1 Iraqi dinar (ID).

Denominations
Coins: 1, 5, 10, 25, 50 and 100 fils; 1 dinar.
Notes: 250 and 500 fils; 1, 5 and 10 dinars.

Sterling and Dollar Equivalents (30 September 1988)
£1 sterling = 525.66 fils;
US $1 = 310.86 fils;
100 Iraqi dinars = £190.24 = $321.69.

Exchange Rate
From February 1973 to October 1982 the Iraqi dinar was valued at US $3.3862. Since October 1982 it has been valued at $3.2169. The dinar's average value in 1982 was $3.3513.

BUDGET ESTIMATES (ID million)

Revenue	1981	1982
Ordinary	5,025.0	8,740.0
Economic development plan	6,742.8	7,700.0
Autonomous government agencies	7,667.8	n.a.
Total	19,434.9	n.a.

Petroleum revenues (estimates, US $ million): 9,198 in 1981; 10,250 in 1982; 9,650 in 1983; 10,000 in 1984; 11,900 in 1985; 6,813 in 1986; 11,300 in 1987.

Expenditure	1981	1982
Ordinary	5,025.0	8,740.0
Economic development plan	6,742.0	7,700.0
Autonomous government agencies	7,982.4	n.a.
Total	19,750.2	n.a.

CENTRAL BANK RESERVES
(US $ million at 31 December)

	1975	1976	1977
Gold	168.0	166.7	176.1
IMF special drawing rights	26.9	32.5	41.5
Reserve position in IMF	31.9	31.7	33.4
Foreign exchange	2,500.5	4,369.8	6,744.7
Total	2,727.3	4,600.7	6,995.7

IMF special drawing rights (million SDRs at 31 December): 113.7 in 1981; 74.2 in 1982; 8.6 in 1983; 0.1 in 1984; 5.1 in 1987.
Reserve position in IMF (million SDRs at 31 December): 111.9 in 1981; 111.9 in 1982.
Note: No figures for gold or foreign exchange have been available since 1977.
Source: IMF, *International Financial Statistics*.

CONSUMER PRICES INDEX (IFS) (1975 = 100)

	1976	1977	1978
All items	112.8	123.1	128.8

External Trade

PRINCIPAL COMMODITIES (ID million)

Imports c.i.f.	1976	1977*	1978
Food and live animals	159.6	154.0	134.5
Cereals and cereal preparations	70.0	79.9	74.9
Sugar, sugar preparations and honey	37.2	24.1	10.2
Crude materials (inedible) except fuels	33.7	20.5	25.1
Chemicals	58.5	47.4	58.7
Basic manufactures	293.3	236.7	285.2
Textile yarn, fabrics, etc.	44.3	69.4	72.7
Iron and steel	127.5	44.3	73.2
Machinery and transport equipment	557.4	625.8	667.4
Non-electric machinery	285.4	352.5	368.1
Electrical machinery, apparatus, etc.	106.9	120.2	160.5
Transport equipment	165.2	153.1	138.8
Miscellaneous manufactured articles	33.2	49.4	51.7
Total (incl. others)	1,150.9	1,151.3	1,244.1

* Provisional. Revised total is ID 1,323.2 million.

Total imports (estimates, ID million): 1,738.9 in 1979; 2,208.1 in 1980; 2,333.8 in 1981.

Exports f.o.b.*	1976	1977	1978
Mineral fuels, lubricants, etc.	2,595.6	2,557.3	3,223.1
Petroleum and petroleum products	2,595.6	2,557.3	3,222.9
Crude and partly refined petroleum	2,564.2	2,541.1	3,204.4
Petroleum products	31.4	16.2	18.5
Total (incl. others)	2,626.5	2,583.8	3,267.3

* Figures are provisional. Revised totals (ID million) are: 2,738.1 in 1976; 2,849.6 in 1977; 3,266.4 in 1978; 6,329.0 in 1979.

Total exports (estimates, ID million): 7,760.4 in 1980; 3,109.7 in 1981; 3,055.7 in 1982; 3,041.8 in 1983.
Exports of crude petroleum (estimates, ID million) were: 2,691.6 in 1976; 2,806.9 in 1977; 3,204.2 in 1978; 6,287.0 in 1979; 7,718.4 in 1980; 3,067.7 in 1981; 3,013.7 in 1982; 2,999.8 in 1983; 3,494.6 in 1984; 4,101.9 in 1985.

Source: IMF, *International Financial Statistics*.

IRAQ

PRINCIPAL TRADING PARTNERS (ID million)

Imports	1983	1984	1985
Australia	10.7	35.2	45.7
Austria	33.7	49.0	53.3
Brazil	32.7	67.0	118.9
China, People's Republic	22.1	11.5	40.5
France	118.7	117.1	112.5
Germany, Fed. Republic	323.6	236.3	211.0
Italy	162.9	116.5	128.2
Japan	369.4	258.3	352.1
Jordan	18.0	50.2	34.2
Korea, Republic	54.1	39.5	68.8
Malaysia	35.0	16.9	49.9
Netherlands	42.7	57.9	37.2
Sweden	52.0	37.7	46.2
Switzerland	55.2	26.8	36.5
Turkey	101.7	218.6	259.2
United Kingdom	118.6	118.2	109.8
USA	45.1	153.6	126.0
Yugoslavia	40.8	50.8	71.0
Total (incl. others)	2,062.8	2,080.7	2,266.0

Exports (excl. petroleum)	1983	1984	1985
China, People's Repub.	—	—	0.9
Hong Kong	—	—	0.7
India	1.7	0.8	0.6
Japan	—	0.3	0.5
Jordan	3.4	2.1	6.8
Kuwait	5.3	4.0	2.0
Saudi Arabia	1.0	0.7	0.5
Turkey	8.2	16.5	21.8
United Arab Emirates	2.5	0.4	2.3
United Kingdom	0.9	0.5	0.8
Total (incl. others)	81.8	82.7	46.9

Note: Since 1975 no official figures have been available for the destination of petroleum exports.

Transport

RAILWAYS (traffic)

	1984	1985	1986
Passenger-km (million)	1,227	1,118	1,005
Freight ton-km (million)	1,254	1,245	1,294

ROAD TRAFFIC ('000 licensed motor vehicles)

	1984	1985	1986
Passenger cars	393.5	447.5	491.8
Goods vehicles	189.4	197.9	206.5
Buses	36.6	38.7	40.2
Total	619.5	684.1	738.5

SHIPPING (movement of cargo vessels in Iraqi ports)

	1978	1979	1980
Number of vessels			
Entered	1,127	1,664	1,446
Cleared	1,136	1,124	1,485
Gross registered tons ('000)			
Entered	13,841	14,006	18,187
Cleared	13,871	n.a.	n.a.
Cargo ('000 metric tons, excl. crude petroleum)			
Entered	4,191	6,717	6,535
Cleared	897	1,335	1,097

CIVIL AVIATION (revenue traffic on scheduled services)

	1982	1983	1984
Kilometres flown (million)	13.3	15.7	13.4
Passengers carried ('000)	481	454	435
Passenger-km (million)	1,470	1,249	1,200
Freight ton-km (million)	53.7	44.3	52.0

Source: UN, *Statistical Yearbook*.

Tourism

ARRIVALS OF VISITORS BY COUNTRY OF ORIGIN ('000)

	1978	1979	1980
Egypt	109.8	190.2	229.7
Jordan	63.6	86.6	108.3
Kuwait	160.1	191.3	137.6
Saudi Arabia	102.8	142.0	105.5
Syria	26.4	207.4	248.0
Turkey	59.8	56.2	84.5
Total (incl. others)	719.8	1,168.0	1,212.8

Total arrivals ('000): 1,564 in 1981; 2,020 in 1982.

Education

(1986/87)

	Schools	Pupils	Teachers
Primary	8,210	2,917,474	122,408
Secondary (General)	2,315	1,012,426	39,261
Vocational	245	133,568	7,660
Teacher training*	43	28,164	1,443
Universities	6	110,173	6,014
Technical institutes	19	32,322	2,313

* Teacher training schools were abolished at the end of the 1985/86 academic year. Figures refer to teacher training institutes.

Directory

The Constitution

The following are the principal features of the Provisional Constitution, issued on 22 September 1968:

The Iraqi Republic is a popular democratic and sovereign state. Islam is the state religion.

The political economy of the state is founded on socialism.

The state will protect liberty of religion, freedom of speech and opinion. Public meetings are permitted under the law. All discrimination based on race, religion or language is forbidden. There shall be freedom of the Press, and the right to form societies and trade unions in conformity with the law is guaranteed.

The Iraqi people is composed of two main nationalities: Arabs and Kurds. The Constitution confirms the nationalistic rights of the Kurdish people and the legitimate rights of all other minorities within the framework of Iraqi unity.

The highest authority in the country is the Council of Command of the Revolution (or Revolutionary Command Council—RCC), which will promulgate laws until the election of a National Assembly. The Council exercises its prerogatives and powers by a two-thirds majority.

Two amendments to the Constitution were announced in November 1969. The President, already Chief of State and head of the government, also became the official Supreme Commander of the Armed Forces and President of the Command Council of the Revolution. Membership of the latter body was to increase from five to a larger number at the President's discretion.

Earlier, a Presidential decree replaced the 14 local government districts by 16 governorates, each headed by a governor with wide powers. In April 1976 Tekrit (Saladin) and Karbala became separate governorates, bringing the number of governorates to 18, although three of these are designated Autonomous Regions.

The 15-article statement which aimed to end the Kurdish war was issued on 11 March 1970. In accordance with this statement, a form of autonomy was offered to the Kurds in March 1974, but some of the Kurds rejected the offer and fresh fighting broke out. The new Provisional Constitution was announced in July 1970. Two amendments were introduced in 1973 and 1974, the 1974 amendment stating that 'the area whose majority of population is Kurdish shall enjoy autonomy in accordance with what is defined by the Law'.

The President and Vice-President are elected by a two-thirds majority of the Council. The President, Vice-President and members of the Council will be responsible to the Council. Vice-Presidents and Ministers will be responsible to the President.

In July 1973 President Bakr announced a National Charter as a first step towards establishing the Progressive National Front. A National Assembly and People's Councils are features of the Charter. A law to set up a 250-member National Assembly and a 50-member Kurdish Legislative Council was adopted on 16 March 1980, and the two Assemblies were elected in June and September 1980 respectively.

The Government

HEAD OF STATE

President: SADDAM HUSSAIN (assumed power 16 July 1979).
Vice-President: TAHA MOHI ED-DIN MARUF.

REVOLUTIONARY COMMAND COUNCIL

Chairman: SADDAM HUSSAIN.
Vice-Chairman: IZZAT IBRAHIM.
Secretary-General: KHALED ABD AL-MONEIM RASHID.
Members:
TAHA YASSIN RAMADAN
ADNAN KHAIRALLAH
SA'ADOUN SHAKER MAHMOUD
TAREQ AZIZ ISA
HASSAN ALI NASSAR AL-AMIRI
Dr SA'ADOUN HAMMADI
TAHA MOHI ED-DIN MARUF

COUNCIL OF MINISTERS
(February 1989)

President and Prime Minister: SADDAM HUSSAIN.
First Deputy Prime Minister: TAHA YASSIN RAMADAN.
Deputy Prime Minister and Minister of Foreign Affairs: TAREQ AZIZ.
Deputy Prime Minister and Minister of Defence: Gen. ADNAN KHAIRALLAH.
Minister of Transport and Communications: MUHAMMAD HAMZA AZ-ZUBAIDI.
Head of Presidency Diwan (Presidential Cabinet): AHMAD HUSSAIN AS-SAMARRAI.
Minister of the Interior: SAMIR MUHAMMAD ABD AL-WAHAB ASH-SHAYKHALI.
Minister of Education: ABD AL-QADIR IZZUDIN HAMMUDI.
Minister of Higher Education and Scientific Research: Dr MUNDHIR IBRAHIM.
Minister of Justice: AKRAM ABD AL-QADR ALI.
Minister of Finance: HIKMAT OMAR MEKHAYLEF.
Minister of Housing and Construction: TAHER MUHAMMAD HASSOUN AL-MARZOUK.
Minister of Planning: SAMAL MAJID FARAJ.
Minister of Health: (vacant).
Minister of Oil: ISAM ABD AR-RAHIM ASH-SHALABI.
Minister of Trade: MUHAMMAD MAHDI SALIH.
Minister of Agriculture and Irrigation: KARIM HASSAN REDHA.
Minister of Culture and Information: LATIF NASIF AL-JASIM.
Minister of Labour and Social Affairs: BAKR MAHMOUD RASOUL.
Minister of Awqaf (Religious Endowments) and Religious Affairs: ABDULLAH FADEL-ABBAS.
Minister of Local Government: ADNAN DAHWOUD SALMAN.
Minister of Industry and Military Production: Brig-Gen. HUSSAIN KAMEL.
Minister of State for Foreign Affairs: Dr SA'ADOUN HAMMADI.
Minister of State for Military Affairs: Gen. ABD AL-JABBAR KHALIL ASH-SHANSHAL.
Minister of State at the President's Office: HASHIM AQRAWI SUBHI.
Advisers to President (with status of Minister): SUBHI YASIN KHUDAIR, ABD AL-GHANI ABD AL-GHAFUR, SAMIR MUHAMMAD AL-WAHHAB, ABD AL-HASAN RAHI FIR'AWN, SAADI MAHDI SALIH, MAZBAN KADR HADI, KHALED ABD AL-MONEIM.
Ministers of State: HASHIM HASSAN, ABDULLAH ISMAIL AHMAD, ARSHAD AHMAD MUHAMMAD AZ-ZIBARI.

MINISTRIES

Office of the President: Presidential Palace, Karradat Mariam, Baghdad.
Office of the First Deputy Prime Minister: Karradat Mariam, Baghdad.
Ministry of Agriculture and Irrigation: Khulafa St, Khullani Sq., Baghdad; tel. 887-3251; telex 212222.
Ministry of Awqaf and Religious Affairs: North Gate, St opposite College of Engineering, Baghdad; tel. 888-9561; telex 212785.
Ministry of Culture and Information: Nr an-Nusoor Sq., fmrly Qasr as-Salaam Bldg, Baghdad; tel. 551-4333; telex 212800.
Ministry of Defence: North Gate, Baghdad; tel. 888-9071; telex 212202.
Ministry of Education: POB 258, Baghdad; tel. 886-0000; telex 2259.
Ministry of Finance: Khulafa St, Nr ar-Russafi Sq., Baghdad; tel. 887-4871; telex 212459.
Ministry of Foreign Affairs: Opposite State Org. for Roads and Bridges, Karradat Mariam, Baghdad; tel. 537-0091; telex 212201.
Ministry of Industry and Military Production: Nidhal St, Nr Sa'adoun Petrol Station, Baghdad; tel. 887-2006; telex 212205.
Ministry of Labour and Social Affairs: Khulafa St, Khullani Sq., Baghdad; tel. 887-1881; telex 212621.
Ministry of Local Government: Karradat Mariam, Baghdad; tel. 537-0031; telex 212568.
Ministry of Oil: POB 6178, al-Mansour, Baghdad; tel. 541-0031; telex 212216.
Ministry of Planning: Karradat Mariam, ash-Shawaf Sq., Baghdad; tel. 537-0071; telex 212218.

IRAQ　　Directory

Ministry of Trade: Khulafa St, Khullani Sq., Baghdad; tel. 887-2682; telex 212206.

Ministry of Transport and Communications: Nr Martyr's Monument, Karradat Dakhil, Baghdad; tel. 776-6041; telex 212020.

KURDISH AUTONOMOUS REGION

Executive Council: Acting Chair. MUHAMMAD AMIN MUHAMMAD.

Legislative Council: Chair. AHMAD ABD AL-QADIR AN-NAQSHABANDI.

Legislature

NATIONAL ASSEMBLY

No form of National Assembly existed in Iraq between the 1958 revolution, which overthrew the monarchy, and June 1980. The existing provisional constitution contains provisions for the election of an assembly at a date to be determined by the Government. The members of the Assembly are to be elected from all political, social and economic sectors of the Iraqi people. In December 1979 the RCC invited political, trade union and popular organizations to debate a draft law for setting up a 250-member National Assembly (elected from 56 constituencies) and a 50-member Kurdish Legislative Council, both to be elected by direct, free and secret ballot. Elections for the first National Assembly took place on 20 June 1980, and for the Kurdish Legislative Council on 11 September 1980 and 13 August 1986. The Assembly is dominated by members of the ruling Baath Party.

Elections for the second National Assembly were held on 20 October 1984. The total number of votes cast was 7,171,000 and Baath Party candidates won 73% (183) of the 250 seats, compared with 75% in the previous Assembly. The number of women elected rose to 33. Elections scheduled to be held in late August 1988 were postponed for six months, owing to uncertainty over the course of the Gulf War.

Chairman: Dr SA'ADOUN HAMMADI.

Chairman of the Kurdish Legislative Council: AHMAD ABD AL-QADIR AN-NAQSHABANDI.

Political Organizations

National Progressive Front: Baghdad; f. July 1973, when Arab Baath Socialist Party and Iraqi Communist Party signed a joint manifesto agreeing to establish a comprehensive progressive national and nationalistic front. In 1975 representatives of Kurdish parties and organizations and other national and independent forces joined the Front; the Iraqi Communist Party left the National Progressive Front in mid-March 1979; Sec.-Gen. NAIM HADDAD (Baath).

Arab Baath Socialist Party: POB 6012, al-Mansour, Baghdad; revolutionary Arab socialist movement founded in Damascus in 1947; has ruled Iraq since July 1968, and between July 1973 and March 1979 in alliance with the Iraqi Communist Party in the National Progressive Front; founder and Sec.-Gen. MICHAEL AFLAQ; Regional Command Sec. SADDAM HUSSEIN; Deputy Regional Command Sec. IZZAT IBRAHIM; mems. of Regional Command: TAHA YASSIN RAMADAN, HASSAN ALI AL-AMIRI, SA'ADOUN SHAKER, TAREQ AZIZ, ADNAN KHAIRALLAH, MUHAMMAD HAMZAH AZ-ZUBAYDI, ABD AL-GHANI ABD AL-GHAFUR, SAMIR MUHAMMAD ABD AL-WAHHAB, ABD AL-HASSAN RAHI FIR'AWN, SAADI MAHDI SALIH, SA'ADOUN HAMMADI MAZBAN KHADR HADI, ALI HASSAN AL-MAJID, KAMIL YASSIN RASHID and LATIF NASIF AL-JASIM; approx. 100,000 mems.

Iraqi Communist Party: Baghdad; f. 1934; became legally recognized in July 1973 on formation of National Progressive Front; left National Progressive Front March 1979; First Sec. AZIZ MUHAMMAD.

Kurdistan Democratic Party: Aqaba bin Nafi's Sq., Baghdad; f. 1946; Kurdish Party; supports the National Progressive Front; Sec.-Gen. HASHIM HASSAN AQRAWI.

Kurdistan Revolutionary Party: f. 1972; succeeded Democratic Kurdistan Party; admitted to National Progressive Front 1974; Sec.-Gen. ABD AS-SATTAR TAHER SHAREF.

There are several illegal opposition groups, including:

Ad-Da'wa al-Islamiya (Voice of Islam): f. 1968; Mem. Supreme Council of the Islamic Revolution of Iraq; guerrilla group.

Umma (Nation) Party: f. 1982; opposes Saddam Hussein's regime; Leader SAAD SALEH JABR.

There is also a Democratic Party of Kurdistan (DPK; f. 1946) in opposition to the Iraqi Government (Leader MASOUD BARZANI); a Patriotic Union of Kurdistan (PUK; f. 1975; Leader JALAL TALIBANI), a Socialist Party of Kurdistan (SPK; f. 1975; Leader RASSOUL MARMAND); a United Socialist Party of Kurdistan (USPK) (Leader MAHMOUD OSMAN), a breakaway group from the PUK; and the Kurdish Hezbollah (party of God; f. 1985; Leader Sheikh MUHAMMAD KALED) a breakaway group from the DPK and a member of the Supreme Council of the Islamic Revolution, which is based in Teheran under the leadership of the exiled Iraqi Shi'ite leader, Hojatoleslam MUHAMMAD BAQIR AL-HAKIM.

Various alliances of political groups have been formed to oppose the regime of Saddam Hussein in recent years. The most recent was formed in May 1988, comprising the DPK, the PUK, the SPK, the People's Democratic Party of Kurdistan, the USPK, and the predominantly Kurdish Iraqi Communist Party.

Diplomatic Representation

EMBASSIES IN IRAQ

Afghanistan: Maghrib St, ad-Difa'ie, 27/1/12 Waziriya, Baghdad; tel. 422-9986; Ambassador: MOHAMMAD SA'ED.

Albania: Baghdad; Ambassador: GYLANI SHEHU.

Algeria: ash-Shawaf Sq., Karradat Mariam, Baghdad; tel. 537-2181; Ambassador: LARBI SI LAHCÈNE.

Argentina: Hay al-Jamia District 915, St 24, No. 142, POB 2443, Baghdad; tel. 776-8140; telex 213500; Ambassador: GERÓNIMO CORTES-FUNES.

Australia: al-Karada ash-Sharqiya Masba 39B/35, POB 661, Baghdad; tel. 719-3423; telex 212148; Ambassador: R. STEELE.

Austria: POB 294, Hay Babel 929/2/5 Aqaba bin Nafi's Sq., Masbah, Baghdad; tel. 719-9033; telex 212383; Ambassador: Dr ERWIN MATSCH.

Bahrain: al-Mansour, Hay al-Watanabi, POB 27117, Mah. 605, Zuqaq 7, House 4/1/44, Baghdad; tel. 541-6992; telex 213364; Ambassador: ABD AR-RAHMAN AL-FADHIL.

Bangladesh: 75/17/929 Hay Babel, Baghdad; tel. 718-4143; telex 2370; Ambassador: Brig. AHM ABD AL-MOMEN.

Belgium: Hay Babel 929/27/25, Baghdad; tel. 719-8297; telex 212450; Ambassador: MARC VAN RYSSELBERGHE.

Brazil: 609/16 al-Mansour, Houses 62/62–1, Baghdad; tel. 551-1365; telex 2240; Ambassador: A. F. WERNER.

Bulgaria: Ameriya, New Diplomatic Quarter, POB 28022, Baghdad; tel. 556-8197; Ambassador: ASSEN ZLATANOV.

Canada: 47/1/7 al-Mansour, Baghdad; tel. 542-1459; telex 212486; Ambassador: A. PERCY SHERWOOD.

Central African Republic: 208/406 az-Zawra, Harthiya, Baghdad; tel. 551-6520; Ambassador: Col FRANÇOIS DIALLO.

Chad: 97/4/4 Karradat Mariam, POB 8037, Baghdad; tel. 537-6160; Ambassador: HAMID MUHAMMAD ISHAQ.

China, People's Republic: New Embassy Area, International Airport Rd, Baghdad; tel. 556-2740; telex 212195; Ambassador: ZHANG JUNHUA.

Cuba: St 7, District 929 Hay Babel, al-Masba Arrasat al-Hindi; tel. 719-5177; telex 212389; Ambassador: ARGILES PÉREZ.

Czechoslovakia: Dijlaschool St, No. 37, Mansour, Baghdad; tel. 541-7136; Ambassador: Dr MIROSLAV KOTORA.

Denmark: Zukak No. 34, Mahallat 902, Hay al-Wahda, House No. 18/1, POB 2001, Alwiyah, Baghdad; tel. 719-3058; telex 212490; Ambassador: TORBEN G. DITHMER.

Djibouti: POB 6223, al-Mansour, Baghdad; tel. 551-3805; Ambassador: ABSEIA BOOH ABDULLA.

Egypt: Baghdad; Ambassador: IBRAHIM AWF.

Finland: POB 2041, Alwiya, Baghdad; tel. 719-6174; telex 212454; Ambassador: HAAKAN KROGIUS.

France: 102/55/7 Abu Nawas, Baghdad; tel. 719-6061; telex 212160; Ambassador: MAURICE COURAGE.

German Democratic Republic: 12/10/929 Hay Babel, Baghdad; tel. 719-0071; Ambassador: OTTO BECKER.

Germany, Federal Republic: Zuqaq 2, Mahala 929, Hay Babel (Masbah Square), Baghdad; tel. 719-2037; telex 212262; Ambassador: Dr RICHARD ELLERKMANN.

Greece: 63/3/913 Hay al-Jamia, al-Jadiriya, Baghdad; tel. 776-9511; telex 212479; Ambassador: EPAMINONDAS PEYOS.

Holy See: as-Sa'adoun St 904/2/46, POB 2090, Baghdad (Apostolic Nunciature); tel. 719-5183; Apostolic Pro-Nuncio: Mgr LUIGI CONTI.

Hungary: Abu Nuwas St, az-Zuwiya, POB 2065, Baghdad; tel. 776-5000; telex 212293; Ambassador: TAMÁS VARGA.

India: Taha St, Najib Pasha, Adhamiya, Baghdad; tel. 422-2014; telex 212248; Ambassador: K. N. BAKSHI.

IRAQ
Directory

Indonesia: 906/2/77 Hay al-Wahda, Baghdad; tel. 719-8677; telex 2517; Ambassador: Abd ar-Rachman Gunadirdja.
Italy: 1 Zuqaq, 73 Mahalla, 913 Hay al-Jamia (University Circle), Jadiriya, Baghdad; tel. 776-5059; telex 212242; Ambassador: Dr Ugo Toscano.
Japan: 929/17/70 Hay Babel, Masba, Baghdad; tel. 719-3840; telex 212241; Ambassador: Keizo Kimura.
Jordan: House No. 1, St 12, District 609, al-Mansour, POB 6314, Baghdad; tel. 541-2892; telex 2805; Ambassador: Hilmi Lozi.
Kuwait: 35/5/915 Hay al-Jamia, Baghdad; tel. 776-3151; telex 212108; Ambassador: Abd ar-Razzaq al-Baijan.
Lebanon: Iwadia Askary St, House 5, Baghdad; tel. 416-8092; telex 2263; Ambassador: (vacant).
Libya: Baghdad; Head of the Libyan People's Bureau: Abbas Ahmad al-Massrati (acting).
Malaysia: 6/14/929 Hay Babel, Baghdad; tel. 719-2048; telex 2452; Ambassador: Anaitullah Karim.
Mauritania: al-Mansour, Baghdad; tel. 551-8261; Ambassador: Muhammad Yehya Walad Ahmad al-Hadi.
Mexico: 601/11/45 al-Mansour, Baghdad; tel. 719-8039; telex 2582; Chargé d'affaires: Víctor M. Delgado.
Morocco: Hay al-Mansour, POB 6039, Baghdad; tel. 552-1779; Ambassador: Aboleslam Zenined.
Netherlands: 29/35/915 Jadiriya, POB 2064, Baghdad; tel. 776-7616; telex 212276; Ambassador: C. J. Vreedenburgh.
New Zealand: 2D/19 az-Zuwiya, Jadiriya, Baghdad; POB 2350, Alwiyah, Baghdad; tel. 776-8177; telex 212433; Ambassador: (vacant).
Nigeria: 2/3/603 al-Mansour, Baghdad; tel. 5421750; Ambassador: Ali Gombe.
Norway: 20/3/609 Hay al-Mansour, Baghdad; tel. 5410097; telex 212715; Ambassador: Torolf Raa.
Oman: POB 6180, 213/36/15 al-Harthiya, Baghdad; tel. 551-8198; telex 212480; Ambassador: Bashir bin-Saleem Binfargi.
Pakistan: 14/7/609 al-Mansour, Baghdad; tel. 541-5120; Ambassador: Khalid Mahmoud.
Philippines: Hay Babel, Baghdad; tel. 719-3228; telex 3463; Ambassador: C. C. Pastores.
Poland: 30 Zuqaq 13, Mahalla 931, Hay Babel, POB 2051, Baghdad; tel. 719-0296; Ambassador: Dr Witold Jurasz.
Portugal: 66/11 al-Karada ash-Sharqiya, Hay Babel, Sector 925, St 25, No. 79, POB 2123, Alwiya, Baghdad; tel. 776-4953; telex 212716; Ambassador: Fernando Andresen Guimaraes.
Qatar: 152/406 Harthiya, Hay al-Kindi, Baghdad; tel. 551-2186; telex 2391; Ambassador: Muhammad Rashid Khalifa al-Khalifa.
Romania: Arassat al-Hindia, Hay Babel, Mahalla 929, Zukak 31, No 452/A, Baghdad; tel. 7762860; telex 2268; Ambassador: Ionel Mihail Cetateanu.
Saudi Arabia: 48A/1/7, 609 al-Mansour, Baghdad; tel. 551-3566; Ambassador: Tarad ibn Abdullah al-Harithi.
Senegal: Jadiriya 75G 31/15, POB 565, Baghdad; tel. 776-7636; Ambassador: Y. Barro.
Somalia: 603/1/5 al-Mansour, Baghdad; tel. 551-0088; Ambassador: Yasin Shire Farah.
Spain: ar-Riyad Quarter, District 908, Street No. 1, No. 21, POB 2072, Alwiya, Baghdad; tel. 719-2852; telex 212239; Ambassador: Juan López de Chicheri.
Sri Lanka: 07/80/904 Hay al-Wahda, POB 1094, Baghdad; tel. 719-3040; Ambassador: N. Navaratnarajah.
Sudan: 38/15/601 al-Imarat, Baghdad; tel. 542-4889; Ambassador: Ali Adam Muhammad Ahmad.
Sweden: 15/41/103 Hay an-Nidhal, Baghdad; tel. 719-5361; telex 212352; Ambassador: Arne Thorén.
Switzerland: Hay Babel, House No. 41/5/929, POB 2107, Baghdad; tel. 719-3091; telex 212243; Ambassador: Hans-Rudolf Hoffmann.
Thailand: 1/4/609, POB 6062, al-Mansour, Baghdad; tel. 5418798; telex 213345; Ambassador: Cheuy Suetrong.
Tunisia: Mansour 34/2/4, POB 6057, Baghdad; tel. 551-7786; Ambassador: Habib Nouira.
Turkey: 2/8 Waziriya, POB 14001, Baghdad; tel. 422-2768; telex 214145; Ambassador: Sönmez Köksal.
Uganda: 41/1/609 al-Mansour, Baghdad; tel. 551-3594; Ambassador: Swaib M. Musoke.
USSR: 4/5/605 al-Mutanabi, Baghdad; tel. 541-4749; Ambassador: Viktor J. Minin.
United Arab Emirates: al-Mansour, 50 al-Mansour Main St, Baghdad; tel. 551-7026; telex 2285; Ambassador: Muhammad Abd al-Latif Rashid.
United Kingdom: Zukak 12, Mahala 218, Hay al-Kheloud, Baghdad; tel. 537-2121; telex 213414; Ambassador: T. J. Clark.
USA: 929/7/57 Hay Babel, Masba, POB 2447, Alwiyah, Baghdad; tel. 719-6138; telex 212287; Ambassador: April C. Glaspie.
Venezuela: al-Mansour, House No. 12/79/601, Baghdad; tel. 552-0965; telex 2173; Ambassador: Freddy Rafael Alvarez Yanes.
Viet-Nam: 29/611 Hay al-Andalus, Baghdad; tel. 551-1388; Ambassador: Tran Ky Long.
Yemen Arab Republic: Jadiriya 923/28/29, Baghdad; tel. 776-0647; Ambassador: Ahmad Muhammad ar-Rawdhi.
Yemen, People's Democratic Republic: 906/16/8, Hay al-Wahda, Baghdad; tel. 719-6027; telex 213542; Ambassador: Muhammad Ahmad Salman.
Yugoslavia: 16/35/923 Hay Babel, Jadiriya, POB 2061, Baghdad; tel. 776-7887; telex 213521; Ambassador: Stojan Andov.

Judicial System

Courts in Iraq consist of the following: The Court of Cassation, Courts of Appeal, First Instance Courts, Peace Courts, Courts of Sessions, Shari'a Courts and Penal Courts.

The Court of Cassation: This is the highest judicial bench of all the Civil Courts; it sits in Baghdad, and consists of the President and a number of vice-presidents and not fewer than 15 permanent judges, delegated judges and reporters as necessity requires. There are four bodies in the Court of Cassation, these are: (*a*) the General body, (*b*) Civil and Commercial body, (*c*) Personal Status body, (*d*) the Penal body.

Courts of Appeal: The country is divided into five Districts of Appeal: Baghdad, Mosul, Basra, Hilla, and Kirkuk, each with its Court of Appeal consisting of a president, vice-presidents and not fewer than three members, who consider the objections against the decisions issued by the First Instance Courts of first grade.

Courts of First Instance: These courts are of two kinds: Limited and Unlimited in jurisdiction.

> **Limited Courts** deal with Civil and Commercial suits, the value of which is five hundred Dinars and less; and suits, the value of which cannot be defined, and which are subject to fixed fees. Limited Courts consider these suits in the final stage and they are subject to Cassation.
>
> **Unlimited Courts** consider the Civil and Commercial suits irrespective of their value, and suits the value of which exceeds five hundred Dinars with first grade subject to appeal.

First Instance Courts consist of one judge in the centre of each *Liwa*, some *Qadhas* and *Nahiyas*, as the Minister of Justice judges necessary.

Revolutionary Courts: These deal with major cases that would affect the security of the State in any sphere: political, financial or economic.

Courts of Sessions: There is in every District of Appeal a Court of Sessions which consists of three judges under the presidency of the President of the Court of Appeal or one of his vice-presidents. It considers the penal suits prescribed by Penal Proceedings Law and other laws. More than one Court of Sessions may be established in one District of Appeal by notification issued by the Minister of Justice mentioning therein its headquarters, jurisdiction and the manner of its establishment.

Shari'a Courts: A Shari'a Court is established wherever there is a First Instance Court; the Muslim judge of the First Instance Court may be a *Qadhi* to the Shari'a Court if a special *Qadhi* has not been appointed thereto. The Shari'a Court considers matters of personal status and religious matters in accordance with the provisions of the law supplement to the Civil and Commercial Proceedings Law.

Penal Courts: A Penal Court of first grade is established in every First Instance Court. The judge of the First Instance Court is considered as penal judge unless a special judge is appointed thereto. More than one Penal Court may be established to consider the suits prescribed by the Penal Proceedings Law and other laws.

One or more Investigation Court may be established in the centre of each *Liwa* and a judge is appointed thereto. They may be established in the centres of *Qadhas* and *Nahiyas* by order of the Minister of Justice. The judge carries out the investigation in accordance with the provisions of Penal Proceedings Law and the other laws.

There is in every First Instance Court a department for the execution of judgments presided over by the Judge of First

IRAQ
Instance if a special president is not appointed thereto. It carries out its duties in accordance with the provisions of Execution Law.

Religion

ISLAM

About 95% of the population are Muslims, more than 50% of whom are Shi'ite. The Arabs of northern Iraq, the Bedouins, the Kurds, the Turkomans and some of the inhabitants of Baghdad and Basra are mainly of the Sunni sect, the remaining Arabs south of the Diyali belong to the Shi'i sect.

CHRISTIANITY

There are Christian communities in all the principal towns of Iraq, but their principal villages lie mostly in the Mosul district. The Christians of Iraq fall into three groups: (a) the free Churches, including the Nestorian, Gregorian, and Jacobite; (b) the churches known as Uniate, since they are in union with the Roman Catholic Church including the Armenian Uniates, Jacobite Uniates, and Chaldeans; (c) mixed bodies of Protestant converts, New Chaldeans, and Orthodox Armenians.

Roman Catholic Church:

Latin Rite: Archbishop of Baghdad: HE Mgr PAUL DAHDAH, Archevêché Latin, Wahdah 904/8/44, POB 2090, Baghdad; tel. 719-9537; approx. 3,500 adherents.

Armenian Rite: Archbishop of Baghdad: Most Rev. PAUL COUSSA, POB 2344, Baghdad; tel. 719-2461; approx 2,000 adherents.

Chaldean Rite: Archbishop of Mosul: Most Rev. GEORGES GARMO, Archevêché Chaldéen, Mosul; tel. 762149; Patriarch of Babylon of the Chaldeans: His Beatitude PAUL II CHEIKHO Patriarcat Chaldéen Catholique, Baghdad; tel. 888-0689; with 18 archbishops and bishops in Iraq, Iran, Syria, Turkey, Egypt, USA and Lebanon; approx. 290,000 adherents.

Syrian Rite: Archbishop of Mosul: Most Rev. CYRIL EMANUEL BENNI, Archevêché Syrien Catholique, Mosul; tel. 762160; Archbishop of Baghdad: Most Rev. ATHANASE MATTI SHABA MATOKA, Archevêché Syrien Catholique, Baghdad; tel. 718-9474; approx. 22,500 adherents.

Orthodox Syrian Community: 12,000 adherents.

Armenian Orthodox (Apostolic) Community: Bishop AVAK ASADOURIAN, Primate of the Armenian Diocese of Iraq, Younis as-Saba'awi Sq., Baghdad; tel. 887-3637; nine churches (four in Baghdad); 23,000 adherents, mainly in Baghdad.

JUDAISM

Unofficial estimates put the present size of the community at 2,500, almost all living in Baghdad.

OTHERS

About 30,000 Yazidis and a smaller number of Turkomans, Sabeans and Shebeks make up the rest of the population.

Sabean Community: 20,000 adherents; Head Sheikh DAKHIL, Nasiriyah; Mandeans, mostly in Nasiriyah.

Yazidis: 30,000 adherents; Leader TASHIN BAIK, Ainsifni.

The Press

DAILIES

Al-Baath ar-Riyadhi: Baghdad; sports; Propr and Editor UDAI SADDAM HUSSAIN.

Baghdad Observer: POB 624, Karantina, Baghdad; f. 1967; English; State-sponsored; Editor-in-Chief NAJI AL-HADITHI; circ. 22,000.

Al-Iraq: POB 5717, Baghdad; f. 1976; Kurdish; formerly Al-Ta'akhi; organ of the National Progressive Front; Editor-in-Chief SALAHUDIN SAEED; circ. 30,000.

Al-Jumhuriya (The Republic): POB 491, Waziriya, Baghdad; f. 1963, re-founded 1967; Arabic; Editor-in-Chief SAMI MAHDI; circ. 220,000.

Ar-Riyadhi (Sportsman): POB 58, Jadid Hassan Pasha, Baghdad; f. 1971; Arabic; published by Ministry of Youth; circ. 30,000.

Tariq Ash-Sha'ab (People's Path): as-Sa'adoun St; Baghdad; Arabic; organ of the Iraqi Communist Party; Editor ABD AR-RAZZAK AS-SAFI.

Ath-Thawra (Revolution): Aqaba bin Nafi's Square, POB 2009, Baghdad; tel. 96161; f. 1968; Arabic; organ of Baath Party; Editor-in-Chief HAMEED SAEED; circ. 250,000.

Directory

WEEKLIES

Alif Baa (Alphabet): POB 491, Karantina, Baghdad; Arabic; Editor-in-Chief KAMIL ASH-SHARQI; circ. 150,000.

Al-Idaa'a wal-Television (Radio and Television): Iraqi Broadcasting and Television Establishment, Karradat Mariam, Baghdad; tel. 537-1161; telex 212246; radio and television programmes and articles; Arabic; Editor-in-Chief KAMIL HAMDI ASH-SHARQI; circ. 40,000.

Majallati: Children's Culture House, POB 8041, Baghdad; telex 2606; Arabic; children's newspaper; Editor-in-Chief FAROUQ SALLOUM; circ. 30,000.

Ar-Rased (The Observer): Baghdad; Arabic; general.

Sabaa Nisan: Baghdad; f. 1976; Arabic; organ of the General Union of the Youth of Iraq.

Sawt al-Fallah (Voice of the Peasant): Karradat Mariam, Baghdad; f. 1968; Arabic; organ of the General Union of Farmers Societies; circ. 40,000.

Waee ul-Ummal (The Workers' Consciousness): Headquarters of General Federation of Trade Unions in Iraq, Gialani St, Senak, POB 2307, Baghdad; Arabic; Iraq Trades Union organ; Chief Editor KHALID MAHMOUD HUSSEIN; circ. 25,000.

PERIODICALS

Afaq Arabiya (Arab Horizons): Aqaba bin Nafi's Sq., POB 2009, Baghdad; monthly; Arabic; literary and political; Editor-in-Chief Dr MOHSIN J. AL-MUSAWI.

Al-Aqlam (Pens): Adamiya, POB 4032, Baghdad; tel. 443-6044; telex 214135; f. 1964; publ. by the Ministry of Culture and Information; monthly; Arabic; literary; Editor-in-Chief Dr ALI J. AL-ALLAQ; circ. 7,000.

Bagdad: Dar al-Ma'mun for Translation and Publishing, Karradat Mariam, POB 24015, Baghdad; tel. 538-3171; telex 212984; fortnightly; French; cultural and political.

Al-Funoon al-Ida'iya (Fields of Broadcasting): Cultural Affairs House, Karradat Mariam, Baghdad; quarterly; Arabic; supervised by Broadcasting and TV Training Institute; engineering and technical; Chief Editor MUHAMMAD AL-JAZA'RI.

Gilgamesh: Dar al-Ma'mun for Translation and Publishing, Karradat Mariam, POB 24015, Baghdad; tel. 538-3171; telex 212984; quarterly; English; cultural.

Hurras al-Watan: Baghdad; Arabic.

L'Iraq Aujourd'hui: Aqaba bin Nafi's Sq, POB 2009, Baghdad; f. 1976; bi-monthly; French; cultural and political; Editor NADJI AL-HADITHI; circ. 12,000.

Iraq Oil News: al-Mansour, POB 6178, Baghdad; tel. 541-0031; telex 2216; f. 1973; monthly; English; publ. by the Information and Public Relations Div. of the Ministry of Oil.

Journal of the Faculty of Medicine, The: College of Medicine, University of Baghdad, Jadiriya, Baghdad; tel. 93091; f. 1935; quarterly; Arabic and English; medical and technical; Editor Prof. YOUSUF D. AN-NAAMAN.

Majallat al-Majma' al-'Ilmi al-'Iraqi (Iraqi Academy Journal): Iraqi Academy, Waziriyah, Baghdad; f. 1947; quarterly; Arabic; scholarly magazine on Arabic Islamic culture; Gen. Sec. Dr NURI HAMMOUDI AL-QAISI.

Majallat ath-Thawra az-Ziraia (Magazine of Iraq Agriculture): Baghdad; quarterly; Arabic; agricultural; published by the Ministry of Agriculture.

Al-Maskukat (Coins): State Organization of Antiquities and Heritage, Karkh, Salihiya St, Baghdad; tel. 537-6121; f. 1969; annually; the journal of numismatics in Iraq; Chair. of Ed. Board Dr MUAYAD SA'ID DAMERJI.

Al-Masrah wal-Cinema: Iraqi Broadcasting, Television and Cinema Establishment, Salihiya, Baghdad; monthly; Arabic; artistic, theatrical and cinema.

Al-Mawrid: Aqaba bin Nafi's Sq, POB 2009, Baghdad; f. 1971; monthly; Arabic; cultural.

Al-Mu'allem al-Jadid: Ministry of Education, al-Imam al-A'dham St, A'dhamaiya, Nr Antar Sq., Baghdad; tel. 422-5081; telex 212259; f. 1935; quarterly; Arabic; educational, social, and general; Editor KHALIL AS-SAMARRAI; circ. 105,000.

An-Naft wal-Aalam (Oil and the World): publ. by the Ministry of Oil, POB 6178, Baghdad; f. 1973; monthly; Arabic; Editor-in-Chief QASIM AHMAD TAQI AL-URAIBI (Minister of Oil).

Sawt at-Talaba (The Voice of Students): al-Maghreb St, Waziriyah, Baghdad; f. 1968; monthly; Arabic; organ of National Union of Iraqi Students; circ. 25,000.

As-Sina'a (Industry): POB 5665, Baghdad; every 2 months; Arabic and English; publ. by Ministry of Industry and Minerals; Editor-in-Chief ABD AL-QADER ABD AL-LATIF; circ. 16,000.

IRAQ

Sumer: State Organization of Antiquities and Heritage, Karkh, Salihiya St, Baghdad; tel. 537-6121; f. 1945; annually; archaeological, historical journal; Chair. of Ed. Board Dr MUAYAD SA'ID DAMERJI.

Ath-Thaquafa (Culture): Place at-Tahrir, Baghdad; f. 1970; monthly; Arabic; cultural; Editor-in-Chief SALAH KHALIS; circ. 5,000.

Ath-Thaquafa al-Jadida (The New Culture): Baghdad; f. 1969; monthly; pro-Communist; Editor-in-Chief SAFA AL-HAFIZ; circ. 3,000.

At-Turath ash-Sha'abi (Popular Heritage): Aqaba bin Nafi's Sq., POB 2009, Baghdad; monthly; Arabic; specializes in Iraqi and Arabic folklore; Editor-in-Chief LUTFI AL-KHOURI; circ. 15,000.

Al-Waqai al-Iraqiya (Official Gazette of Republic of Iraq): Ministry of Justice, Baghdad; f. 1922; Arabic and English weekly editions; circ. Arabic 13,000, English 1,000; Dir AMER HASSAN FAHD.

NEWS AGENCIES

Iraqi News Agency (INA): Zaytoon St, POB 3084, Baghdad; tel. 887-5661; telex 212267; f. 1959; Dir-Gen. TAHA YASSIN HASSAN AL-BASRI.

Foreign Bureaux

Agence France-Presse (AFP): Apt 761-91-97, POB 190, Baghdad; tel. 551-4333; Corresp. FAROUQ SHOUKRI.

Allgemeiner Deutscher Nachrichtendienst (ADN) (German Democratic Republic): Zukak 24, Mahalla 906, Hay al-Wahda, Beit 4, Baghdad; Correspondent HANS DAHNE.

Associated Press (AP) (USA): Hay al-Khadra 629, Zuqaq No. 23, Baghdad; tel. 555-9041; telex 213324; Corresp. SALAH NASRAWI.

Deutsche Presse-Agentur (dpa) (Federal Republic of Germany): POB 5699, Baghdad; Correspondent NAJHAT KOTANI.

Reuters (UK): House No. 8, Zuqaq 75, Mahalla 903, Hay al-Karada, Baghdad; tel. 719-1843; telex 213777.

Telegrafnoye Agentstvo Sovetskovo Soyuza (TASS) (USSR): 67 Street 52, Alwiya, Baghdad; Correspondent ANDREI OSTALSKY.

Xinhua (New China) News Agency (People's Republic of China): al-Mansour, Adrus District, 611 Small District, 5 Lane No. 8, Baghdad; tel. 541-8904; telex 213253; Corresp. SHEN ZHAODU.

ANSA (Italy) also has an office in Baghdad.

Publishers

National House for Publishing, Distribution and Advertising: Ministry of Culture and Information, al-Jumhuriya St, POB 624, Baghdad; tel. 425-1846; telex 212392; f. 1972; publishes books on politics, economics, education, agriculture, sociology, commerce and science in Arabic and other Middle Eastern languages; sole importer and distributor of newspapers, magazines, periodicals and books; controls all advertising activities, inside Iraq as well as outside; Dir-Gen. M. A. ASKAR.

Afaq Arabiya Publishing House: Adamiya, POB 4032, Baghdad; tel. 443-6044; telex 214135; publisher of literary monthlies, *Al-Aqlam* and *Afaq Arabiya*, periodicals, *Foreign Culture, Art, Folklore*, and cultural books; Chair. Dr MOHSIN AL-MUSAWI.

Dar al-Ma'mun for Translation and Publishing: Karradat Mariam, POB 24015, Baghdad; tel. 538-3171; telex 212984; publisher of newspapers and magazines including: *The Baghdad Observer* (daily newspaper), *Bagdad* (monthly magazine), *Gilgamesh* (quarterly magazine).

Al-Hurriyah Printing Establishment: Karantina, Sarrafia, Baghdad; tel. 69721; telex 212228; f. 1970; largest printing and publishing establishment in Iraq; State-owned; controls *Al-Jumhuriyah* (see below).

Al-Jamaheer Press House: Sarrafia, Baghdad; f. 1963; publisher of a number of newspapers and magazines, *Al-Jumhuriyah, Baghdad Observer, Alif Baa, Yord Weekly*; Pres. SAAD QASSEM HAMMOUDI.

Al-Ma'arif Ltd: Mutanabi St, Baghdad; f. 1929; publishes periodicals and books in Arabic, Kurdish, Turkish, French and English.

Al-Muthanna Library: Mutanabi St, Baghdad; f. 1936; booksellers and publishers of books in Arabic and oriental languages; Man. MUHAMMAD K. M. AR-RAJAB.

An-Nahdah: Mutanabi St, Baghdad; politics, Arab affairs.

Kurdish Culture Publishing House: Baghdad; f. 1976; attached to the Ministry of Culture and Information.

Ath-Thawra Printing and Publishing House: Aqaba bin Nafi's Sq., POB 2009, Baghdad; tel. 96161; telex 212215; f. 1970; state-owned; Chair. TARIQ AZIZ.

Thnayan Printing House: Baghdad.

Radio and Television

In 1985 there were an estimated 2.2m. radio receivers and 600,000 television receivers in use.

RADIO

State Organization for Broadcasting and Television: Broadcasting and Television Bldg, Salihiya, Karkh, Baghdad; tel. 537-1161; telex 212246.

Iraqi Broadcasting and Television Establishment: Salihiya, Baghdad; tel. 31151; telex 212446; f. 1936; radio broadcasts began 1936; home service broadcasts in Arabic, Kurdish, Syriac and Turkoman; foreign service in French, German, English, Russian, Swahili, Turkish and Urdu; there are 16 medium wave and 30 short wave transmitters; Dir-Gen. HAMID SAID; Dir-Gen. of Radio ADNAN RASHID SHUKR; Dir of Engineering and Technical Affairs MUHAMMAD FAKHRI RASHID.

Idaa'a Baghdad (Radio Baghdad): f.1936; 22 hours daily.

Idaa'a Sawt al-Jamahir: f. 1970; 24 hours.

Other stations include **Idaa'a al-Kurdia, Idaa'a al-Farisiya** (Persian).

TELEVISION

Baghdad Television: Ministry of Culture and Information, Iraqi Broadcasting and Television Establishment, Salihiya, Karkh, Baghdad; tel. 537-1161; telex 212446; f. 1956; government station operating daily on two channels for 9 hours and 8 hours respectively; Dir-Gen. Dr MAJID AHMAD AS-SAMARRIE.

Kirkuk Television: f. 1967; government station; 6 hours daily.

Mosul Television: f. 1968; government station; 6 hours daily.

Basra Television: f. 1968; government station; 6 hours daily.

Missan Television: f. 1974; government station; 6 hours daily.

Kurdish Television: f. 1974; government station; 8 hours daily.

There are 18 other TV stations operating in the Iraqi provinces.

Finance

(cap. = capital; p.u. = paid up; dep. = deposits; res = reserves; brs = branches; m. = million; amounts in Iraqi dinars)

All banks and insurance companies, including all foreign companies, were nationalized in July 1964. The assets of foreign companies were taken over by the State.

BANKING

Central Bank

Central Bank of Iraq: Rashid St, POB 64, Baghdad; tel. 887-1101; telex 212203; f. 1947 as National Bank of Iraq; name changed as above 1956; has the sole right of note issue; cap. and res 125m. (1983); Gov. HIKMAT IBRAHIM AL-AZZAWI; brs in Mosul and Basra.

Commercial Banks

In May 1988 it was announced that a second commercial bank, Rashid Bank, would be established, with capital of ID 100m., to compete with Rafidain Bank.

Rafidain Bank: New Banks' St, POB 11360 Massarif, Baghdad; tel. 888-9725; telex 212211; f. 1941; State-owned; cap. p.u. 100m., res 501m., dep. 12,856.9m., total assets 18,279.3m. (Dec. 1986); Pres. and Chair. TARIQ TALIB AT-TUKMAJI; 224 brs in Iraq.

Rashid Bank: Baghdad; f. 1988; State-owned; cap. 100m.; Dir-Gen. ABDEL MAJID AL-ANI; 3 brs.

Specialized Banks

Agricultural Co-operative Bank of Iraq: Rashid St, POB 5112, Baghdad; tel. 888-4191; f. 1936; State-owned; cap. p.u. 280.6m.; Chair. and Man. Dir FATHI ABD AR-RAZZAQ ASH-SHEIKH SAID; Gen. Man. ABD AR-RAZZAQ AL-HILALI; 21 brs.

Industrial Bank of Iraq: al-Khullani Sq., POB 5025, Baghdad; tel. 887-2181; telex 212224; f. 1940; State-owned; cap. p.u. 75m., dep. 3.3m. (Dec. 1982); Dir-Gen. ABD AS-SALAM ABD AR-RAHMAN ALAWI; 8 brs.

Real Estate Bank of Iraq: POB 14185, Baghdad; tel. 537-5165; telex 212635; f. 1949; State-owned; gives loans to assist the building industry; cap. p.u. 800m. (June 1988); acquired the Co-operative Bank in 1970; Gen. Man. KADHIM AR-RUBAI; 27 brs.

INSURANCE

Iraqi Life Insurance Co: 25/5/21 Kurd al-Pasha, al-Karada ash-Sharqiya, POB 989, Baghdad; telex 213818; f. 1959; Chair. and Gen. Man. ABD AL-KHALIQ RAUF KHALIL.

IRAQ

Iraq Reinsurance Company: Aqaba bin Nafi's Sq., Khalid bin al-Waleed St, POB 297, Baghdad; tel. 719-5131; telex 212233; f. 1960; transacts reinsurance business on the international market; total assets 76.8m. (1985); Chair. and Gen. Man. K. M. AL-MUDARIES.

National Insurance Co: al-Aman Bldg, Al-Khullani St, POB 248, Baghdad; tel. 886-0730; telex 2397; f. 1950; cap. p.u. 20m.; State monopoly for all direct non-life insurance; Chair. and Gen. Man. MOWAFAQ H. RIDHA.

STOCK EXCHANGE

Capital Market Authority: Baghdad; Chair. MUHAMMAD HASSAN FAG EN-NOUR.

Trade and Industry

CHAMBERS OF COMMERCE

Federation of Iraqi Chambers of Commerce: Mustansir St, Baghdad; tel. 888-6111; f. 1969; all Iraqi Chambers of Commerce are affiliated to the Federation; Chair. ABD AL-MOHSEN A. ABU ALKAHIL; Sec.-Gen. FUAD H. ABD AL-HADI.

EMPLOYERS' ORGANIZATION

Iraqi Federation of Industries: Iraqi Federation of Industries Bldg, al-Khullani Sq., Baghdad; f. 1956; 6,000 mems; Pres. HATAM ABD AR-RASHID.

INDUSTRIAL ORGANIZATIONS

In 1987 and 1988, as part of a programme of economic and administrative reform, to increase efficiency and productivity in industry and agriculture, many of the State organizations previously responsible for various industries were abolished or merged, and new State enterprises or mixed-sector national companies were established to replace them. For example, all the State organizations within the Ministries of Industry and of Heavy Industries were abolished and their functions and responsibilities combined in a smaller number of State enterprises; the five State organizations, grouped under the Ministry of Irrigation, were replaced by 14 national companies; and the number of State enterprises serving the farming sector was halved to six (see Agricultural Organizations). In 1987 and 1988 (up to June) 811 State organizations and departments were abolished. In August 1988 some 32 State enterprises were attached to the newly created Ministry of Industry and Military Production, in addition to 11 under the aegis of the Military Industries Commission (MIC), which is, itself, attached to the new ministry. Newly created State enterprises include the following:

Iraqi State Enterprise for Cement: f. 1987 by merger of central and southern State cement enterprises.

National Company for Chemical and Plastics Industries: Dir-Gen. RAJA BAYYATI.

The Rafidain Company for Building Dams: f. 1987 to replace the State Org. for Dams.

State Enterprise for Battery Manufacture: f. 1987; Dir-Gen. ADEL ABBOUD.

State Enterprise for Communications and Post: f. 1987 from State org. for post, telegraph and telephones, and its subsidiaries.

State Enterprise for Construction Industries: f. 1987 by merger of State orgs for gypsum, asbestos, and the plastic and concrete industries.

State Enterprise for Cotton Industries: f. 1988 by merger of State org. for cotton textiles and knitting, and the Mosul State org. for textiles.

State Enterprise for Drinks and Mineral Water: f. 1987 by merger of enterprises responsible for soft and alcoholic drinks.

State Enterprise for the Fertilizer Industries: f. by merger of Basra-based and central fertilizer enterprises.

State Enterprise for Generation and Transmission of Electricity: f. 1987 from State Org. for Major Electrical Projects.

State Enterprise for Import and Export: f. 1987 to replace the five State organizations responsible to the Ministry of Trade for productive commodities, consumer commodities, grain and food products, exports and imports.

State Enterprise for Leather Industries: f. 1987; Dir Gen. MUHAMMAD ABD AL-MAJID.

State Enterprise for Sugar Beet: f. 1987 by merger of sugar enterprises in Mosul and Sulaimaniya.

State Enterprise for Textiles: f. 1987 to replace the enterprise for textiles in Baghdad, and the enterprise for plastic sacks in Tikrit.

State Enterprise for Tobacco and Cigarettes.

State Enterprise for Woollen Industries: f. by merger of State orgs for textiles and woollen textiles and Arbil-based enterprise for woollen textiles and women's clothing.

AGRICULTURAL ORGANIZATIONS

The following bodies are responsible to the Ministry of Agriculture and Agrarian Reform:

State Agricultural Enterprise in Dujaila.

State Enterprise for Agricultural Supplies: Dir-Gen. MUHAMMAD KHAIRI.

State Enterprise for Developing Animal Wealth.

State Enterprise for Fodder.

State Enterprise for Poultry (Central and Southern Areas).

State Enterprise for Poultry (Northern Area).

State Enterprise for Sea Fisheries: POB 260, Basra; telex 7011; Baghdad office: POB 3296, Baghdad; tel. 92023; telex 212223; fleet of 3 fish factory ships, 2 fish carriers, 1 fishing boat.

TRADE UNIONS

General Federation of Trade Unions of Iraq: POB 3049, al-Waziriya, Palestine St, Baghdad; tel. 425-3854; telex 212457; f. 1959; 6 vocational trade unions and 18 local trade union federations in the governorates of Iraq. Number of workers in industry is 536,245, in agriculture 150,967 (excluding peasants) and in other services 476,621 (1986); GFTU is a member of the International Confederation of Arab Trade Unions and of the World Federation of Trade Unions; Pres. FADHIL MAHMOUD GHAREB.

Union of Teachers: Al-Mansour, Baghdad; Pres. Dr ISSA SALMAN HAMID.

Union of Palestinian Workers in Iraq: Baghdad; Sec.-Gen. SAMI ASH-SHAWISH.

There are also unions of doctors, pharmacologists, jurists, artists, and a General Federation of Iraqi Women (Chair. MANAL YOUNIS).

CO-OPERATIVES

At the end of 1986 there were 843 agricultural co-operatives, with a total of 388,153 members. At the end of 1985 there were 67 consumer co-operatives, with 256,522 members.

PEASANT SOCIETIES

General Federation of Peasant Societies: Baghdad; f. 1959; has 734 affiliated Peasant Societies.

PETROLEUM AND GAS

Ministry of Oil: POB 6178, al-Mansour City, Baghdad; tel. 551-0031; telex 212216; solely responsible for petroleum sector and activities relevant to it; the Ministry was merged with INOC in May 1987; the State organizations responsible to the ministry for oil refining and gas processing, for oil products distribution, for oil training, and for gas were simultaneously abolished, and those for northern and southern oil, for oil equipment, for oil and gas exploration, for oil tankers, and for oil projects were converted into companies, as part of a plan to streamline the oil industry and make it more efficient; Minister of Oil ISAM ABD AR-RAHIM ASH-SHALABI.

Iraq National Oil Company (INOC): al-Khullani Sq., POB 476, Baghdad; tel. 887-1115; telex 212204; f. in 1964 to operate the petroleum industry at home and abroad; when Iraq nationalized its petroleum, structural changes took place in INOC and it became solely responsible for exploration, production, transportation and marketing of Iraqi crude petroleum and petroleum products. INOC was merged with the Ministry of Oil in 1987, and the functions of some of the organizations under its control were transferred to newly created ministerial departments or to companies responsible to the ministry.

Iraqi Oil Tankers Company: POB 37, Basra; tel. 319990; telex 207007; fmrly the State Establishment for Oil Tankers; reformed as a company in 1987; responsible to the Ministry of Oil for operating a fleet of 15 oil tankers; Chair. ADNAN ABD AL-HAMID NASIR.

National Company for Distribution of Oil Products and Gas: Rashid St, POB 3, South Gate, Baghdad; tel. 888-9911; telex 212247; fmrly a State organization; reformed as a company in 1987; fleet of 6 tankers; Dir-Gen. HAZIM ALI AT-TALIB.

National Company for Manufacturing Oil Equipment: fmrly a State organization; reformed as a company in 1987.

National Company for Oil and Gas Exploration: INOC Building, POB 476, al-Khullani Sq, Baghdad; fmrly the State Establishment for Oil and Gas Exploration; reformed as a company

IRAQ

in 1987; responsible for exploration and operations in difficult terrain such as marshes, swamps, deserts, valleys and in mountainous regions; Chair. Dr HASHIM AL-KHURSAN.

National Company for Oil Projects: POB 198, as-Sa'adoun St, Baghdad; tel. 776-3250; telex 212230; fmrly the State Org. for Oil Projects; reformed as a company in 1987; responsible for construction of petroleum projects, mostly inside Iraq through direct execution, and also for design supervision of the projects and contracting with foreign enterprises, etc.; Dir-Gen. RAJIH MOHI ED-DIN.

Northern Petroleum Company (NPC): POB 1, at-Ta'meem Governorate; f. 1987 by the merger of the fmr Northern and Central petroleum organizations to carry out petroleum operations in northern Iraq; Dir-Gen. Dr SAMI SHARIF.

Southern Petroleum Company (SPC): POB 240, Basra; fmrly the Southern Petroleum Organization; reformed as the SPC in 1987 to undertake petroleum operations in southern Iraq; Dir-Gen. MOUJID ABD AZ-ZAHRA AL-UBAIDA.

State Enterprise for Oil and Gas Industrialization in the South: f. 1988 by merger of enterprises responsible for the gas industry and oil refining in the south.

State Enterprise for Petrochemical Industries.

Transport

RAILWAYS

The metre-gauge line runs from Baghdad, through Khanaqin and Kirkuk, to Arbil. The standard gauge line covers the length of the country, from Rabia, on the Syrian border, via Mosul, to Baghdad, and from Baghdad to Basra and Umm Qasr, on the Arabian Gulf. A 404-km standard gauge line linking Baghdad to Husaibah, near the Iraqi-Syrian frontier, was completed in 1983. The 550-km line from Baghdad to al-Qaim (on the Syrian border) and the 273-km Kirkuk-Baiji-Haditha line, which was designed to serve industrial projects along its route, were opened in 1986. The 150-km line linking the Akashat phosphate mines and the fertilizer complex at al-Qaim was formally opened in January 1986 but had already been in use for two years. Lines totalling some 2,400 km were planned at the beginning of the 1980s, but by 1988 only 800 km had been constructed. All standard gauge trains are now hauled by diesel-electric locomotives. There are plans to replace all existing narrow gauge (one metre) line with standard gauge (1,435 mm). As well as the internal service, there is a regular international service between Baghdad and Istanbul. A rapid transit transport system is to be established in Baghdad undertaken as part of the 1987-2001 development plan for the city but work will only commence when the Gulf War is over.

Responsibility for all railways, other than the former Iraq Republic Railways (see below), and for the design and construction of new railways, which was formerly the province of the New Railways Implementation Authority, was transferred to the newly created State Enterprise for Implementation of Transport and Communications Projects.

State Enterprise for Iraqi Railways: Baghdad Central Station Bldg, Damascus Sq., Baghdad; tel. 537-30011; telex 212272; fmrly the Iraqi Republic Railways, under the supervision of State Org. for Iraqi Railways; reformed as a State Enterprise in 1987; total length of track (1986): 2,029 km, consisting of 1,496 km of standard gauge, 533 km of one-metre gauge; Pres. T. T. ABD AR-RAZZAK; Dir-Gen. MUHAMMAD Y. AL-AHMAD.

New Railways Implementation Authority: POB 17040, al-Hurriya, Baghdad; tel. 537-0021; telex 2906; f. to design and construct railways to augment the standard-gauge network and to replace the metre-gauge network; Sec.-Gen. R. A. AL-UMARI.

ROADS

At the end of 1986, according to the Central Statistical Organization, there were 33,238 km of roads (23,872 km of new paved roads; 650 km of old paved roads; 8,716 km of earth roads or roads under construction).

The most important roads are: Baghdad-Mosul-Tel Kotchuk (Syrian border), 521 km; Baghdad-Kirkuk-Arbil-Zakho (border with Turkey), 544 km; Kirkuk-Sulaimaniya, 109 km; Baghdad-Amara-Basra-Safwan (Kuwaiti border), 595 km; Baghdad-Rutba-Syrian border (to Damascus), 555 km; Baghdad-Babylon-Diwaniya, 181 km. A 137-km section, from Tulaiha to Rutba, of a six-lane 1,200-km international Express Highway, was opened in August 1987. A 200-km section, between Rutba and the Jordanian and Syrian borders, and a section to the southern town of Soukh ash-Sheyoukh were also scheduled for completion before the end of 1987. The entire project, designed to link the Gulf states with the Mediterranean coast, is scheduled for completion in 1988. Studies have been completed for a second, 525-km Express Highway linking Baghdad and Zakho on the Turkish border. The estimated cost of the project is more than $3,000m. and is likely to preclude its implementation in the immediate future. An elaborate network of roads has been constructed behind the war front with Iran in order to facilitate the movement of troops and supplies. A new six-lane highway was completed in 1987, running from Safwan, on the Kuwaiti border, via Zubair and Nasiriyah, to Baghdad.

Iraqi Land Transport Co: Baghdad; f. 1988 to replace State Organization for Land Transport; fleet of more than 1,000 large trucks; Dir Gen. AYSAR AS-SAFI.

Joint Land Transport Co: Baghdad; joint venture between Iraq and Jordan; operates a fleet of some 750 trucks.

State Enterprise for Implementation of Expressways: f. 1987; Dir-Gen. FAIZ MUHAMMAD SAID.

State Enterprise for Roads and Bridges: Karradat Mariam, Karkh, POB 917, Baghdad; tel. 32141; telex 212282; responsible for road and bridge construction projects to the Ministry of Housing and Construction.

SHIPPING

The ports of Basra and Umm Qasr are usually the commercial gateway of Iraq. They are connected by various ocean routes with all parts of the world, and constitute the natural distributing centre for overseas supplies. The Iraqi State Enterprise for Maritime Transport maintains a regular service between Basra, the Gulf and north European ports. The port of Basra has been closed because of the Gulf War (between Iraq and Iran). There is also a port at Khor az-Zubair, which came into use during 1979, though it too has been closed, owing to the war.

At Basra there is accommodation for 12 vessels at the Maqal Wharves and accommodation for 7 vessels at the buoys. There is 1 silo berth and 2 berths for oil products at Muftia and 1 berth for fertilizer products at Abu Flus. There is room for 8 vessels at Umm Qasr. There are deep-water tanker terminals at Khor al-Amaya and Faw for 3 and 4 vessels respectively. The latter port, however, was abandoned during the early part of the Gulf War. Debris will have to be cleared from the access lanes to Iraq's Gulf ports before any of them can become fully operational once again.

For the inland waterways, which are now under the control of the State Enterprise for Iraqi Ports, there are 1,036 registered river craft, 48 motor vessels and 105 motor boats.

State Enterprise for Iraqi Ports: Maqal, Basra; tel. 413211; telex 207008; f. 1987 when State Org. for Iraqi Ports was abolished; fleet of 26 vessels (incl. 17 dredgers, 6 crane ships, 2 pilot ships and 1 cargo/training ship); Acting Pres. FALEH MAHMOUD EL-MOUSA.

State Enterprise for Iraqi Water Transport: Airport St, al-Furat Quarter, POB 23016, Baghdad; telex 212565; f. 1987 when State Org. for Iraqi Water Transport was abolished; responsible for the planning, supervision and control of six nat. water transportation enterprises incl:

State Enterprise for Maritime Transport (Iraqi Line): al-Jadiriya al-Hurriya Ave, POB 13038; Baghdad; tel. 776-3201; telex 212565; Basra office: 14 July St, POB 766, Basra; tel. 210206; telex 207052; f. 1952; fleet of 21 vessels (incl. 16 general cargo vessels, 4 barges and 1 tanker); Dir-Gen. JABER Q. HASSAN; Operations Man. M. A. ALI.

Shipping Company

Arab Bridge Maritime Navigation Co: Amman, Jordan; f. 1987; joint venture by Egypt, Iraq and Jordan to improve economic co-operation; an expansion of the company that established a ferry link between the ports of Aqaba, Jordan, and Nuweibeh, Egypt, in 1985; cap. US $6m.; Chair. SULAYMAN MUTAWALLI SULAYMAN (Egyptian Minister of Transport, Communications and Naval Transport).

CIVIL AVIATION

There are international airports near Baghdad, at Bamerni, and at Basra. A new airport, Saddam International, is under construction at Baghdad. Internal flights connect Baghdad to Basra and Mosul.

National Company for Civil Aviation Services: al-Mansour, Baghdad; tel. 551-9443; telex 212662; f. 1987 following the abolition of the State Organization for Civil Aviation; responsible for the provision of aircraft, and for airport and passenger services.

Iraqi Airways Co: Saddam International Airport, Baghdad; tel. 551-9999; telex 212297; f. 1988; Dir-Gen. NOUREDDIN AL-SAFI; formerly Iraqi Airways, prior to privatization in September 1988; regular services from Baghdad to Abu Dhabi, Algiers, Amman, Amsterdam, Athens, Bahrain, Bangkok, Basra, Beirut, Belgrade, Berlin, Bombay, Bucharest, Budapest, Cairo, Casablanca, Copenhagen, Damascus, Dhahran, Doha, Dubai, Frankfurt, Geneva, Istanbul, Jeddah, Karachi, Khartoum, Kuala Lumpur, Kuwait, London, Madrid, Moscow, Mosul, Munich, New Delhi, Paris, Prague, Rome, Sofia, Tripoli, Tunis, Vienna, Warsaw; fleet: 3 Boeing 747-200C, 2 Boeing 707-320C, 6 Boeing 727-200, 2 Boeing 737-200, 1 Boeing 747SP, 24 Ilyushin Il-76T/M, 5 Antonov An-12, 5 Antonov An-24, 6 JetStar II, 4 Falcon 50, 2 Falcon 20F, 4 Piaggio P.166.

Tourism

The Directorate-General for Tourism was abolished in August 1988 and the various bodies under it and the services run by it were offered for sale or lease to the private sector. The directorate was responsible for 21 summer resorts in the north, and for hotels and tourist villages throughout the country. These were to be offered on renewable leases of 25 years or sold off.

Atomic Energy

A French-built research reactor at Tamuz, near Baghdad, was destroyed in an Israeli air raid in June 1981. Israel claimed that the reactor was part of an Iraqi programme to construct nuclear weapons. The war with Iran delayed a French commitment to rebuild the reactor.

In March 1984 it was reported that the USSR had agreed to build a nuclear power station in Iraq.

IRELAND

Introductory Survey

Location, Climate, Language, Religion, Flag, Capital

The Republic of Ireland consists of 26 of the 32 counties which comprise the island of Ireland. The remaining six counties, in the north-east, form Northern Ireland, which is part of the United Kingdom. Ireland lies in the Atlantic Ocean, about 80 km (50 miles) west of Great Britain. The climate is mild and equable, with temperatures generally between 0°C (32°F) and 21°C (70°F). Irish is the official first language, but its use as a vernacular is now restricted to certain areas, collectively known as the Gaeltacht, mainly in the west of Ireland. English is universally spoken. Official documents are printed in English and Irish. Almost all of the inhabitants profess Christianity: about 95% are Roman Catholics and 5% Protestants. The national flag (proportions 2 by 1) consists of three equal vertical stripes, of green, white and orange. The capital is Dublin.

Recent History

The whole of Ireland was formerly part of the United Kingdom. In 1920 the island was partitioned, the six north-eastern counties remaining part of the United Kingdom, with their own government. On 6 December 1922 the 26 southern counties achieved dominion status, under the British Crown, as the Irish Free State. The dissolution of all remaining links with Great Britain culminated in the adoption, by plebiscite, of a new constitution, which gave the Irish Free State full sovereignty within the Commonwealth as from 29 December 1937. Formal ties with the Commonwealth were ended on 18 April 1949, when the 26 southern counties became a republic. The partition of Ireland remains a contentious issue, and the Provisional wing of the Irish Republican Army (IRA) has mounted a violent campaign to achieve reunification.

In the general election of February 1973, Fianna Fáil, Ireland's traditional ruling party with 44 years in office, was defeated. Jack Lynch, who had been Prime Minister since 1966, resigned, and Liam Cosgrave formed a coalition between his own party, Fine Gael, and the Labour Party. The Irish Government remained committed to power-sharing in the six counties, but resisted any British military withdrawal from Northern Ireland (see Northern Ireland, Vol. II).

Following the assassination of the British Ambassador to Ireland by the Provisional IRA in July 1976, the Irish Government introduced stronger measures against terrorism. President Carroll O'Daly resigned in October 1976, and Dr Patrick Hillery of Fianna Fáil, the only candidate nominated for the presidency, took office in December. Fianna Fáil won the general election of June 1977 and Jack Lynch again became Prime Minister, maintaining the improved relations with the British Government which had been achieved by the Cosgrave administration; he aimed at devolved government in Northern Ireland, rather than a totally united Ireland, a policy which aroused criticism from within Fianna Fáil. After the murder by the IRA in August 1979 of Admiral of the Fleet the Earl Mountbatten of Burma, a prominent British public figure, at Mullaghmore, County Sligo, and the massacre on the same day of 18 British soldiers at Warrenpoint in Northern Ireland, Lynch agreed to increase border security. In December Lynch resigned as Prime Minister and was succeeded by Charles Haughey, formerly Minister for Health, who pursued the aim of a united Ireland with a measure of autonomy for the six northern counties, provided that a power-sharing executive be maintained.

In June 1981, following an early general election, Dr Garret FitzGerald, who had been Minister for Foreign Affairs in 1973-77, became Prime Minister. He formed a coalition government between his own party, Fine Gael, and the Labour Party. However, the rejection by the Dáil of the coalition's budget proposals brought another general election in February 1982. Haughey was returned to power, with the support of three Workers' Party members and two independents. The worsening economic situation, however, made the Fianna Fáil Government increasingly unpopular, and in November Haughey lost the support of the independents over proposed public expenditure cuts. In the subsequent general election Fianna Fáil failed to gain an overall majority and Dr FitzGerald again became Prime Minister. In December he formed a coalition with the Labour Party, and included four of its members in the Cabinet. In September 1983 a controversial referendum approved a constitutional amendment to ban abortion. At elections to the European Parliament in June 1984, Fianna Fáil won eight of the 15 seats allotted to Ireland, while Fine Gael won six. The Labour Party lost all four of the seats that it had previously held.

During 1986 Dr FitzGerald's Government lost popularity, partly due to the formation, in December 1985, of a new party, the Progressive Democrats. A controversial government proposal to end a 60-year constitutional ban on divorce was defeated by national referendum in early June, and shortly afterwards, as a result of a series of defections, the Government lost its parliamentary majority. In January 1987 Labour members refused to support Fine Gael's budget proposals envisaging reductions in planned public expenditure, and the coalition collapsed. At a general election held on 17 February, Fianna Fáil, led by Charles Haughey, won 81 of the 166 seats in the Dáil, with 44% of the first-preference votes, while the Progressive Democrats, contesting their first election, won 14 seats. Fine Gael's strength declined from 68 to 51 seats. Sinn Fein (the political wing of the IRA) failed to secure any seats in the election. In November 1986 it had abandoned its policy of abstentionism from Parliament, which it had pursued since 1922. In March 1987 Charles Haughey became Prime Minister for the third time, and a Cabinet of Fianna Fáil members was announced. Haughey retained popular support, despite instituting an unprecedented austerity programme. As a minority government, the Fianna Fáil administration was dependent on opposition support to secure approval for its budget proposals. Since the policy of austerity that Haughey adopted was similar to that initially envisaged by Fine Gael, this did not present a problem. Massive reductions in public expenditure in 1987 and 1988 led to an encouraging economic recovery, so that all parties in the Dáil united in support of the 1989 budget proposals, announced in January, which increased welfare payments and eased the tax burden on low-paid workers.

Regular discussions between the British and Irish heads of government, initiated in May 1980, led to the formation in November 1981 of an Anglo-Irish Intergovernmental Council, intended to meet at ministerial and official levels. Anglo-Irish relations were damaged by Ireland's neutral stance over the Argentine invasion of the Falkland Islands in 1982, but formal discussions by the heads of government were resumed in November 1983.

In May 1983 representatives of the three main political parties in the Republic, and of the Social Democratic and Labour Party of Northern Ireland, initiated the New Ireland Forum to discuss the future of Ireland and Northern Ireland. The Forum's report was rejected by the British Government, but discussions between the United Kingdom and Ireland continued, and in November 1985 resulted in the signing of the Anglo-Irish Agreement. The Agreement provided for regular participation in Northern Ireland affairs by the Irish Government on political, legal, security and cross-border matters. The involvement of the Government of Ireland was to be through an Intergovernmental Conference. The Agreement maintained that no change in the status of Northern Ireland would be made without the assent of the majority of its population. The terms of the Agreement were approved by both the Irish and the British Parliaments, although in Northern Ireland many Protestants expressed strong disapproval.

Under the provisions of the Anglo-Irish Agreement, the Irish Government pledged co-operation in the implementation of new measures to improve cross-border security, in order to suppress IRA operations. It also promised to participate in the European Convention on the Suppression of Terrorism, which it subsequently signed in February 1986. The Convention had not been signed by the Irish Government previously, because it was thought to contravene a provision in the Constitution which prevented extradition for political offences.

IRELAND

Introductory Survey

In March 1987 the new Haughey Government pledged to honour the Anglo-Irish Agreement and to co-operate with the United Kingdom in its efforts to suppress terrorism. Relations between the two countries were strained, however, when the Irish Government repeated its requests for reform in the emergency provisions whereby some alleged offences in Northern Ireland are tried by a single judge, without a jury. In November the discovery of an illegal shipment of armaments from Libya, intended for the IRA, and the perpetration of a bombing outrage (resulting in the deaths of 11 civilians) by the IRA at Enniskillen, Northern Ireland, increased pressure on the Irish Government to approve new extradition procedures. In December the Government approved amendments to the 1965 Extradition Act, whereby the European Convention on the Suppression of Terrorism was ratified, but controversial measures were also introduced, without consulting the British Government, granting the Irish Attorney-General the right to approve or reject warrants for extradition of suspected IRA terrorists to the United Kingdom. In January 1988, however, the Irish Supreme Court ruled that members of the IRA could not be protected from extradition to Northern Ireland on the grounds that their offences were politically motivated. In May the British Government accepted the conditions imposed by the amendments. The first application for the extradition of an IRA suspect under the new agreement failed, however, because of a technical defect in the warrant. In December the Irish Attorney-General, John Murray, refused to grant the extradition of an alleged terrorist, Patrick Ryan, who was repatriated to Ireland in November, following a similar refusal by the Belgian authorities. The Irish decision was based on allegations that Ryan would not receive a fair trial in the United Kingdom because publicity had prejudiced his case. Owing to the hostility of the British reaction to this decision, Haughey cancelled a planned meeting with the British Prime Minister, Margaret Thatcher, at the EEC 'summit' conference in Rhodes, Greece, in December. The British Government was subsequently invited to invoke the 1976 Criminal Law Jurisdiction Act, whereby suspects may be tried in Ireland for alleged crimes committed elsewhere.

Relations between the Irish and British Governments were strained in 1988. Irish confidence in the impartiality of the British system of justice was severely undermined by proposed legislation to combat terrorism in Northern Ireland (see Northern Ireland, Vol. II) and by the decision, in January 1988, not to prosecute members of the Royal Ulster Constabulary (RUC) allegedly implicated in a policy of shooting terrorist suspects, without attempting to apprehend them, in Northern Ireland in 1982. Moreover, the British Government refused to publish the findings of an official inquiry into these allegations. Strained relations with the United Kingdom did not, however, present a threat to the Anglo-Irish Agreement, and the co-ordination between the Garda (Irish police force) and the RUC, established under the agreement, resulted in an unprecedentedly high level of co-operation on cross-border security in 1988.

Ireland has been a member of the EEC since 1973. In May 1987 the country affirmed its commitment to the EEC when, in a referendum, 69.9% of Irish voters supported adherence to the Single European Act, which aimed to secure closer economic and political co-operation between EEC member-states and to provide a common European foreign policy.

Government

Legislative power is vested in the bicameral National Parliament, comprising a Senate (with restricted powers) and a House of Representatives. The Senate (Seanad Éireann) has 60 members, including 11 nominated by the Prime Minister and 49 indirectly elected for five years. The House (Dáil Éireann) has 166 members, elected by universal adult suffrage for five years (subject to dissolution) by means of the single transferable vote, a form of proportional representation.

The President is a constitutional Head of State, elected by direct popular vote for seven years. Executive power is effectively held by the Cabinet, led by the Taoiseach (Prime Minister), who is appointed by the President on the nomination of the Dáil. The President appoints other Ministers on the nomination of the Prime Minister with the previous approval of the Dáil. The Cabinet is responsible to the Dáil.

Defence

In June 1988 the regular armed forces totalled 13,200. The army comprised 11,600, the navy 800 and the air force 800. There was also a reserve of 15,800. The defence budget for 1988 was estimated at I£292.0m. Military service is voluntary.

Economic Affairs

In 1987, according to estimates by the World Bank, Ireland's gross national product (GNP), measured at average 1985–87 prices, was US $21,761m., equivalent to $6,030 per head. Between 1980 and 1987, it was estimated, GNP per head decreased, in real terms, at an average rate of 1.4% per year. Between 1986 and 1987, however, real GNP per head increased by 2.5%. Agriculture has been overtaken in importance by the industrial sector; in 1987 industrial goods accounted for about 80% of total export earnings. In that year agriculture, forestry and fishing accounted for 15.2% of employment, 10.1% of gross domestic product (GDP) and 25.0% of total exports. Ireland's accession to the EEC in 1973 provided a larger market for agricultural exports, but the imposition of price reductions and quotas by the EEC restrained output.

Tourism has become an important sector of the economy. In 1987 there were 2,662,000 foreign visitors to Ireland, an increase of 8.0% compared with 1986, and revenue from tourism amounted to I£721m.

Major industrial expansion has taken place since 1960, promoted by the Industrial Development Authority (IDA), which in 1986 negotiated new investment totalling more than I£550m., expected to create 15,700 jobs. In 1987 there were about 890 foreign companies operating in the Republic, employing 40% of the total manufacturing work-force. The USA is the principal foreign investor, followed by the United Kingdom and Canada, attracted by tax relief on exports. Companies producing automotive and aerospace components, pharmaceuticals and computer software are important targets of IDA efforts. Manufacturing output increased in volume by 47% between 1980 and 1987. By 1988, however, indigenous industry had declined by 2% per annum since 1973, adversely affected by reductions in public expenditure. As one of the less-developed members of the EEC, Ireland has received substantial assistance from the Community's Regional Fund: in 1986 net EEC transfers to Ireland amounted to 4.9% of GDP. At 1987 prices, net receipts from the EEC between 1973 and 1987 totalled I£10,000m. The principal manufacturing sectors are food and beverages, metals and engineering, electronics, chemicals, textiles and tobacco. In 1987 the mining, manufacturing and construction sectors together accounted for 35.4% of GDP.

Expansion was encouraged in the financial sector in the late 1980s. Turnover at the Dublin Stock Exchange in 1987 increased by 37% compared with 1986, to I£38,000m. Construction of an international financial services centre, promoted by the IDA, began in Dublin in 1988; the total development cost was estimated at I£250m.

Ireland's principal exports are machinery, food, live animals and chemical products. In 1986 the value of Ireland's exports declined by 3.8%, while imports declined by 8.6%. In 1987, however, exports increased by 14.4% and imports by 6.2%, to an estimated I£10,723.5m. and I£9,155.2m. respectively. There was a trade surplus of I£314m. in 1985, rising to I£753m. in 1986 and I£1,568m. in 1987. In 1987 the current account was I£263m. in surplus, after 20 years in deficit. Exports were expected to reach I£12,000m. in 1988, assuring an even larger surplus on the current account. The United Kingdom remains the principal foreign trade partner, accounting for 41.7% of imports and 34.2% of exports in 1987. Since its accession to the EEC, Ireland has improved its European trade links, particularly with France and the Federal Republic of Germany. Projects, planned by the Government to facilitate trade, to improve links to air and sea ports will be eligible for 75% EEC funding.

There have been four discoveries of petroleum off shore. The largest, announced in July 1983, is off the southern coast, with a flow of approximately 10,000 barrels per day. There are substantial reserves of natural gas in the Kinsale field, and a further discovery was made in 1985. In 1987, following more than a decade of disappointing exploration in the Irish Sea, the Government offered more attractive licensing terms to companies exploring for petroleum, natural gas and other minerals. In March proposals were made to construct gas pipelines on three routes across the Irish Sea, which would give Irish consumers access to the British national grid. Gas is the principal source of energy, providing 54% of total requirements in 1984, while petroleum provided 20%, peat 18%, hydroelectric power 7% and coal 1%. A programme for further exploitation of the limited low-grade coal deposits is under way. Europe's largest lead-zinc mines are at Navan. Production began in 1983 at an alumina plant in County Limerick, processing imported bauxite. The full capacity of the plant is 800,000 metric tons per year. In 1979 the first drilling for uranium took place in County Donegal.

In 1987 GDP totalled I£17,667m., an increase in real terms of 2%, compared with 1986. In spite of the creation of jobs by the IDA, the unemployment rate rose sharply, from 7.4% of the labour force in 1979 to 19.9% in January 1988. By January 1989 unemployment was 19.0%, and more than 30,000 people, many of them graduates, were expected to emigrate in that year to seek work in the United Kingdom, the USA and Australia.

Substantial government investment resulted in a borrowing requirement amounting to 13% of GNP in 1986. In 1987 the government borrowing requirement was reduced to 10.4% of GNP. In January 1989 Ireland's national debt amounted to I£25,000m., with debt-service payments averaging I£2,000m. per year. Sufficient funds were raised in 1988 to begin net repayments on the foreign debt. The rate of inflation was reduced from a peak of 20.4% in 1981 to only 2.1% in the year to January 1989. Owing to a large influx of capital, Ireland's reserves of foreign exchange rose from US $2,143m. at the end of 1984 to $4,803m. in October 1988.

In 1979 Ireland joined the European Monetary System (EMS), ending the punt's alignment with sterling. The realignment amounted to a devaluation against the pound, which was beneficial to exporters. In 1986, however, a decline in international prices for petroleum resulted in the rapid appreciation of the punt in relation to sterling, and in August, in an attempt to increase exports, the Irish Government devalued the punt by 8% against other currencies in the EMS. A relaxation of controls on overseas investment came into effect in January 1989, as an initial move towards a 'single market' in the EEC.

Following stringent budgets in 1987 and 1988 (when public expenditure was reduced by 3% and 4.5% respectively, adversely affecting the provision of education and health services), the government borrowing requirement declined to only 3.4% of GNP in 1988, compared with a forecast of 8.2% (although this was partially due to a I£500m. revenue from a tax-amnesty programme). The 1989 budget proposals, announced in January, aimed at relieving poverty, with substantial increases in social welfare payments and reductions in the basic rate of tax. Economic growth was projected at 3% (an increase of 1.5% compared with 1988), while the annual rate of inflation was estimated to remain below 2.75%. Total estimated expenditure in 1989 was I£8,150m.

Social Welfare

Social welfare benefits in Ireland may be grouped into two broad categories: those receivable under compulsory insurance schemes by contributors and their dependants; and those receivable on a non-contributory basis by people of inadequate means. Child benefit is also paid to all households for each child.

Social Welfare Insurance is compulsory for both manual and non-manual workers. The social insurance scheme provides for widows', retirement and old-age pensions; unemployment, disability, maternity, deserted wives', invalidity, and dental and optical benefits; and death grants. The cost is shared by the employer, the employee and the state. Compulsory social insurance was extended to self-employed persons with effect from April 1988; their contributions provide funds for old-age, widows' and orphans' pensions. An occupational injuries benefit scheme is also in operation.

People of inadequate means who are not entitled to benefit under these contributory schemes may receive non-contributory pensions or other benefits from the state or other public funds. These benefits include widows' pensions, deserted wives' and unmarried mothers' allowances, old-age and blindness pensions, supplementary welfare allowance, unemployment assistance and family income supplement. Expenditure on social welfare in 1988 was estimated at I£2,600m.

Health services are provided by eight health boards, under the administration of the Department of Health. There are three categories of entitlement, with people on low incomes qualifying for the full range of health services free of charge, and people in two higher bands of income qualifying for progressively fewer free services.

Drugs and medicines are available free of charge to all people suffering from specified long-term ailments. Hospital in-patient and out-patient services are free of charge to all children under 16 years of age, suffering from specified long-term ailments. Immunization and diagnostic services, as well as hospital services, are free of charge to everyone suffering from an infectious disease. A maintenance allowance is also payable in certain cases. Government expenditure on health was estimated at I£1,044m. in 1987. In addition, there are various community welfare services for the chronically sick, the elderly, the disabled and families under stress. In 1980 Ireland had 209 hospital establishments, with a total of 33,028 beds, and in 1981 there were 4,443 physicians working in the country.

Education

Education in Ireland is compulsory for nine years between six and 15 years of age. Primary education may begin at the age of four and lasts for eight years. Most children attend a national school until the age of 12, when they transfer to a post-primary school. In 1986/87 the total enrolment at primary and secondary schools was equivalent to 94% of the school-age population. In 1987/88 there were 3,386 primary schools, with a total of 565,334 pupils.

Post-primary education takes place in four types of school and lasts for up to five years, comprising a first cycle of three years and a second of two years. Secondary schools are private institutions, administered by boards of governors or religious communities, but they are subsidized by the Department of Education. Pupils take the Intermediate Certificate at 15 or 16 years of age, and may proceed to a two-year course leading to the Leaving Certificate at 17 or 18. Enrolment at the 500 secondary schools numbered 214,485 pupils in 1987/88. The 254 vocational schools provide primary school leavers with a general course which is similar to that for pupils in secondary schools, but with a greater emphasis on non-academic subjects. Enrolment at vocational schools in 1987/88 was 85,666. There were 16 state comprehensive schools in 1987, offering academic and technical subjects, structured to the needs, abilities and interests of the pupils, and leading to examinations for the Intermediate Certificate or the Leaving Certificate. The 45 community schools offer a similar curriculum. They were originally intended to replace existing vocational and secondary schools in rural areas, but since 1985 they have also been established in new city areas. In 1986/87 an estimated 82% of children in the post-primary group were receiving post-primary education.

Six Technical Colleges in Dublin and nine Regional Technical Colleges provide a range of craft, technical, professional and other courses. The majority of courses lead to academic awards granted by the National Council for Educational Awards at Certificate, diploma, degree and postgraduate levels.

The gaining of certain successes in the Leaving Certificate examination qualifies for entrance to the two universities: the University of Dublin (Trinity College), which offers a full range of courses; and the National University of Ireland, which comprises the University Colleges of Cork, Dublin and Galway. They are both self-governing, though they receive annual state grants. The National Institutes for Higher Education, at Limerick and Dublin, offer degree courses of a largely technological nature, although the humanities are represented. The Department of Education provides grants to about one-third of students in further education.

In the 1988 budget an estimated I£1,072m. was allocated to education.

Public Holidays

1989: 2 January (for New Year), 17 March (St Patrick's Day), 24 March (Good Friday), 27 March (Easter Monday), 5 June (June Bank Holiday), 7 August (August Bank Holiday), 30 October (October Bank Holiday), 25–26 December (Christmas).
1990: 1 January (New Year), 17 March (St Patrick's Day), 13 April (Good Friday), 16 April (Easter Monday), 4 June (June Bank Holiday), 6 August (August Bank Holiday), 29 October (October Bank Holiday), 25–26 December (Christmas).

Weights and Measures

The imperial system of weights and measures is in force, but metrication is being introduced gradually.

Statistical Survey

Source (unless otherwise stated): Central Statistics Office, St Stephen's Green House, Earlsfort Terrace, Dublin 2; tel. (01) 767531.

Area and Population

AREA, POPULATION AND DENSITY

Area (sq km)	
Land	68,895
Inland waters	1,388
Total	70,283*
Population (census results)	
5 April 1981	3,443,405
13 April 1986†	
Males	1,769,690
Females	1,770,953
Total	3,540,643
Population (official estimates at 15 April)	
1987	3,543,000
1988	3,538,000
Density (per sq km) at April 1988	50.3

* 27,136 sq miles.
† Source: *Census of the Population of Ireland, 1986—Summary Population Report.*

PROVINCES (1986 census)

	Land area (sq km)	Population	Density (per sq km)
Connaught	17,122	431,409	25.2
Leinster	19,633	1,852,649	94.4
Munster	24,127	1,020,577	42.3
Ulster (part)	8,012	236,008	29.5
Total	68,895	3,540,643	51.4

PRINCIPAL TOWNS
(population, including suburbs or environs, at 1986 census)

Dublin (capital)*	920,956	Galway	47,104
Cork	173,694	Waterford	41,054
Limerick	76,557		

* Greater Dublin area, including Dún Laoghaire (population 54,715 in 1986).

BIRTHS, MARRIAGES AND DEATHS (rates per 1,000)

	Birth rate	Marriage rate	Death rate
1980	21.9	6.4	9.7
1981	21.0	6.0	9.4
1982	20.4	5.8	9.4
1983	19.1	5.6	9.3
1984	18.2	5.2	9.1
1985	17.6	5.3	9.4
1986	17.3	5.2	9.5
1987*	16.6	5.1	8.8

* Provisional figures.

ECONOMICALLY ACTIVE POPULATION
(estimates, '000 persons, excluding unemployed)

	1986	1987	1988*
Agriculture, forestry and fishing	168	164	162
Mining, quarrying and turf production	8	7	7
Manufacturing	211	208	208
Construction	72	71	70
Electricity, gas and water	15	14	14
Commerce, insurance and finance	212	213	221
Transport and communications	65	66	64
Public administration and defence	71	70	69
Other economic activities	258	267	272
Total	1,081	1,080	1,086

* Preliminary estimates.

Agriculture

PRINCIPAL CROPS ('000 metric tons)

	1985	1986	1987
Wheat	495	424	402
Oats	106	102	106
Barley	1,494	1,428	1,599
Potatoes	686	619	697
Sugar beet*	1,309	1,274	1,623

* Figures relate to quantities delivered to factories.

LIVESTOCK ('000 head)

	1985	1986	1987
Cattle	6,907	6,718	6,647
Sheep	3,989	4,234	4,575
Pigs	1,004	1,003	999

LIVESTOCK PRODUCTS ('000 metric tons)

	1985	1986	1987
Beef and veal	449.2	510.9	484.8
Mutton and lamb	48.1	46.2	49.5
Pig meat	135.6	137.1	140.6
Poultry meat	58	60	69
Edible offals	76*	77*	77*
Cows' milk†	5,683	5,478	5,390
Butter‡	160.4	153.5	134.4
Cheese‡	78.6	63.3	65.2
Dry milk	190	181	168
Hen eggs	37	37	39
Cattle hides	38.3*	38.3*	n.a.
Sheep skins	7.0*	7.4*	n.a.

* FAO estimate (Source: FAO, *Production Yearbook* and *Quarterly Bulletin of Statistics*).
† Figures refer to deliveries. Estimated production of cows' milk (in '000 metric tons) was: 6,064 in 1985; 6,209 in 1986; 6,121 in 1987.
‡ Figures refer to factory production. Total production of cheese (in '000 metric tons) was: 85 in 1985; 70 in 1986.

IRELAND

Forestry

ROUNDWOOD REMOVALS ('000 cubic metres, excluding bark)

	1985	1986	1987
Sawlogs, veneer logs and logs for sleepers	657	663	784
Pulpwood	553	609	613
Other industrial wood	27	n.a.	n.a.
Fuel wood	61	58	49
Total	1,271	1,330	1,446

SAWNWOOD PRODUCTION
('000 cubic metres, including boxboards)

	1985	1986	1987
Coniferous (soft wood)	271	271	317
Broadleaved (hard wood)*	5	7	11
Total	276	278	328

* Estimated production.

Fishing

SEA FISH (landings in metric tons)

	1984	1985	1986
Brill	110	121	98
Common sole	313	348	328
Turbot	208	178	187
Atlantic cod	5,464	6,523	5,806
Haddock	3,766	3,472	2,055
European hake	1,066	1,050	1,026
Atlantic herring	31,622	31,716	38,020
Atlantic mackerel	53,212	60,700	55,189
European plaice	2,420	3,043	2,494
Ray	2,112	2,553	1,978
Whiting	8,813	9,111	6,927
Others	31,898	45,935	55,116
Total catch	141,004	164,750	169,224

INLAND FISH (catch in metric tons)

	1984	1985	1986
Atlantic salmon	839	1,493	1,655
Sea trout	25	22	22
European eel	89	87	n.a.

Mining

('000 metric tons, unless otherwise indicated)

	1985	1986	1987
Coal	57	54	45
Natural gas (terajoules)	90,394	63,268	62,362
Lead*	34.6	36.4	33.8
Zinc*	191.6	181.7	177.0
Silver (metric tons)*	9	8	7
Peat	3,211	5,629	6,251

* Figures refer to the metal content of ores mined.

Industry

SELECTED PRODUCTS
('000 metric tons, unless otherwise indicated)

	1985	1986	1987*
Flour	174	178	178
Margarine	18.0	21	22
Cigarettes (million)	8,037	6,825	6,659
Wool yarn	8.6	8.7	8.7
Woven cotton fabrics (million sq m)	30	n.a.	n.a.
Woven woollen fabrics (million sq m)	3.3	2.5	2.2
Footwear ('000 pairs)	2,097	2,492	2,202
Nitrogenous fertilizers†	260	238	224
Phosphate fertilizers†	8.0	3.0	3.0
Motor spirit (petrol)	317	326	298
Distillate fuel oils	434	508	533
Residual fuel oils	487	582	559
Cement	1,457	1,398	1,448
Electric energy (million kWh)	11,919	12,466	12,866
Manufactured gas (terajoules)	2,293	746	106

* Provisional.
† Source: FAO, *Quarterly Bulletin of Statistics*. Figures are in terms of nitrogen or phosphoric acid, and refer to estimated production during the 12 months ending 30 June of the year stated.

Finance

CURRENCY AND EXCHANGE RATES

Monetary Units:
100 pence = 1 Irish pound (I£ or punt).

Denominations:
Coins: 1, 2, 5, 10, 20 and 50 pence.
Notes: 1, 5, 10, 20, 50 and 100 pounds.

Sterling and Dollar Equivalents (30 September 1988)
£1 sterling = I£1.1820;
US $1 = 70.03 pence;
I£100 = £84.60 sterling = $142.80.

Average Exchange Rate (US $ per Irish pound)
1985   1.0656
1986   1.3415
1987   1.4881

BUDGET (I£ million)

Revenue	1986*	1987*	1988†
Customs	81.5	88	95
Excise	1,380.3	1,391	1,412
Capital taxes	33.8	40	40
Income tax	2,388.5	2,713	2,706
Corporation tax, etc.	258.0	257	280
Motor vehicle duties	130.8	139	140
Stamp duties	158.6	169	186
Value added tax	1,527.1	1,585	1,666
Youth employment levy	91.3	97	97
EEC agricultural levies	12.9	11	13
Total (incl. others)	6,709.3	7,151	7,035

* Out-turn.   † Post-budget estimate.

IRELAND

Statistical Survey

Expenditure	1986*	1987†	1988‡
Debt service	1,989	2,118	2,173
Agriculture, fisheries and forestry	369	313	263
Defence	295	287	292
Justice (incl. police)	372	361	370
Education	956	1,064	1,072
Social welfare	1,612	1,667	1,698
Health	1,049	1,043	1,020
Housing	199	36	38
Industry and labour	248	217	215
Total (incl. others)	8,124	8,024	8,183

* Out-turn. † Provisional out-turn. ‡ Post-budget estimate.

GOLD RESERVES AND CURRENCY IN CIRCULATION
(I£ million at 31 December)

	1985	1986	1987
Official gold reserves	76.4	75.3	83.0
Coin and bank notes in circulation	1,081.0	1,127.3	1,148.4

COST OF LIVING
(Consumer Price Index; base: November 1968 = 100)

	1986	1987	1988 (August)
Food	704.7	724.0	747.2
Alcoholic drink	822.8	862.7	895.4
Tobacco	768.4	811.9	837.4
Clothing and footwear	602.6	609.3	617.9
Fuel and light	1,041.2	1,019.9	1,016.7
Housing	463.2	512.8	499.0
Durable household goods	572.1	574.4	587.2
Other goods	813.8	835.6	872.0
Transport	967.7	989.0	1,009.6
Services and related expenditure	932.0	970.0	1,009.6
All items	762.8	786.8	806.8

NATIONAL ACCOUNTS (I£ million at current prices)
National Income and Product

	1985	1986	1987
Gross domestic product at factor cost	15,818.5	16,564	17,667
Net factor income from the rest of the world*	−1,965.7	−1,957	−1,946
Gross national product at factor cost	13,882.8	14,607	15,721
Less Consumption of fixed capital	1,717.1	1,795	1,916
Net national product at factor cost	12,135.7	12,812	13,805
of which:			
Compensation of employees	9,525.8	10,139	10,630
Other domestic income	2,609.9	2,673	3,175
Indirect taxes, less subsidies	1,800.7	1,979	2,108
Net national product at market prices	13,936.4	14,791	15,913
Consumption of fixed capital	1,717.1	1,795	1,916
Gross national product at market prices	15,653.5	16,586	17,829
Less Net factor income from the rest of the world*	−1,965.7	−1,957	−1,946
Gross domestic product at market prices	17,619.2	18,543	19,775
Balance of exports and imports of goods and services*	−341.8	−488	−1,323

National Income and Product—continued

	1985	1986	1987
Available resources	17,277.4	18,055	18,452
of which:			
Private consumption expenditure	10,384.8	11,117	11,481
Government consumption expenditure	3,232.5	3,438	3,560
Gross fixed capital formation	3,457.2	3,449	3,439
Increase in stocks	202.9	51	−28

* Excludes transfers between Ireland and the rest of the world.

Gross Domestic Product by Economic Activity (at factor cost)

	1985	1986	1987
Agriculture, forestry and fishing	1,699.3	1,635	1,874
Mining, manufacturing and construction	5,936.8	6,192	6,584
Public administration and defence	1,051.6	1,126	1,185
Transport, communications and trade	2,889.3	3,054	3,250
Other services	5,051.5	5,409	5,724
Adjustment for financial services	−810.0	−852	−950
Total	15,818.5	16,564	17,667

BALANCE OF PAYMENTS (I£ million)

	1985	1986	1987
Current Receipts:			
Merchandise exports (f.o.b.)*	9,526.8	9,181	10,447
Tourism and travel	518.0	492	562
Trading and investment income	793.8	732	755
International transfers	1,319.3	1,366	1,322
Other items	707.0	691	791
Total	12,864.9	12,462	13,877
Current Expenditure:			
Merchandise imports (c.i.f.)*	9,390.2	8,746	9,137
Tourism and travel	401.7	510	547
Foreign trading and investment income	2,772.9	2,705	2,717
International transfers	345.5	409	436
Other items	604.7	604	777
Total	13,515.0	12,974	13,614
Current balance	−650.1	−513	263

* Adjusted for balance-of-payments purposes.

External Trade

PRINCIPAL COMMODITIES (distribution by SITC, I£'000)

Imports c.i.f.	1985	1986	1987†
Food and live animals	994,441	983,180	985,469
Cereals and cereal preparations	172,675	183,894	180,729
Vegetables and fruit	179,473	185,045	187,905
Animal feeding-stuff (excl. cereals)	147,902	188,193	185,307
Crude materials (inedible) except fuels	297,318	251,326	257,351

IRELAND

Statistical Survey

Imports c.i.f.—*continued*	1985	1986	1987†
Mineral fuels, lubricants, etc.	1,122,027	732,794	676,514
Petroleum, petroleum products, etc.	944,990	554,170	511,739
Crude petroleum oils, etc.	254,340	119,838	144,412
Refined petroleum products	668,465	419,159	353,315
Motor spirit (petrol) and other light oils	155,607	88,702	80,965
Motor spirit (incl. aviation spirit)	146,517	82,139	76,045
Gas oils (distillate fuels)	224,099	144,024	110,048
Other fuel oils	175,306	107,291	90,267
Chemicals and related products.	1,103,253	1,047,824	1,126,241
Organic chemicals	200,636	165,024	201,624
Medicinal and pharmaceutical products.	167,443	167,014	174,733
Manufactured fertilizers	183,087	151,178	139,172
Artificial resins and plastic materials, etc.	213,789	218,446	247,744
Products of polymerization, etc.	147,715	147,446	163,555
Basic manufactures	1,414,976	1,369,938	1,442,726
Paper, paperboard, etc.	265,205	265,699	298,763
Paper and paperboard	161,822	162,690	182,762
Textile yarn, fabrics, etc.	343,887	334,073	342,171
Non-metallic mineral manufactures	126,726	126,872	131,346
Iron and steel	170,973	150,908	155,636
Machinery and transport equipment	2,945,812	2,703,969	3,065,335
Power generating machinery and equipment	142,836	135,038	174,398
Machinery specialized for particular industries.	295,851	269,679	281,146
General industrial machinery, equipment and parts.	290,064	273,088	296,726
Office machines and automatic data processing equipment	988,047	876,052	1,006,446
Parts and accessories for office machines, etc.	756,783	664,048	716,337
Telecommunications and sound equipment	172,063	150,157	157,624
Other electrical machinery, apparatus, etc.	557,359	499,412	603,286
Road vehicles and parts (excl. tyres, engines and electrical parts)	402,886	381,056	399,417
Passenger motor cars (excl. buses)	238,260	216,534	230,596
Miscellaneous manufactured articles	1,090,596	1,121,282	1,172,788
Clothing and accessories (excl. footwear)	344,569	373,429	379,335
Total (incl. others)*	9,428,198	8,621,291	9,155,207

* Including transactions not classified by commodity (I£'000): 290,660 in 1985; 266,230 in 1986; 280,373 in 1987. These amounts include imports through Shannon Free Airport (I£'000): 111,104 in 1985; 83,676 in 1986; 87,430 in 1987. The total also includes imports of non-monetary gold (I£'000): 5,788 in 1985; 5,178 in 1986; 5,380 in 1987.
† Provisional.

Exports f.o.b.	1985	1986	1987†
Food and live animals	2,204,985	2,194,723	2,676,203
Live animals	251,525	255,393	173,893
Bovine animals	180,143	161,928	115,668
Meat and meat preparations	608,832	659,191	763,031
Fresh, chilled or frozen meat	568,604	617,839	712,764
Meat of bovine animals.	445,974	503,743	590,081
Dairy products and birds' eggs	536,224	469,963	620,227
Milk and cream	195,928	170,619	180,317
Preserved, concentrated or sweetened milk and cream	189,287	164,622	173,721
Butter	207,651	166,799	322,465
Beverages and tobacco	236,383	228,272	236,745
Beverages	197,364	192,362	205,595
Crude materials (inedible) except fuels	450,071	406,997	439,637

Exports f.o.b.—*continued*	1985	1986	1987†
Chemicals and related products.	1,406,491	1,251,001	1,307,169
Organic chemicals	742,382	620,014	582,048
Organo-inorganic and heterocyclic compounds	550,344	481,653	430,264
Heterocyclic compounds (incl. nucleic acids)	511,061	446,027	400,291
Basic manufactures	903,881	884,597	942,246
Textile yarn, fabrics, etc.	298,261	297,379	314,702
Machinery and transport equipment	2,889,431	2,850,158	3,364,528
General industrial machinery, equipment and parts.	221,671	226,746	253,337
Office machines and automatic data processing equipment	1,826,668	1,845,828	2,242,727
Automatic data processing machines and units	1,288,624	1,281,306	1,484,607
Complete digital data processing machines	965,303	1,019,337	1,220,457
Electrical machinery, apparatus, etc.	427,595	547,863	613,962
Miscellaneous manufactured articles	1,080,626	1,108,921	1,304,260
Clothing and accessories (excl. footwear)	187,407	197,626	211,233
Professional, scientific and controlling instruments and apparatus	334,085	312,741	354,228
Total (incl. others)*	9,743,038	9,374,310	10,723,498

* Including transactions not classified by commodity (I£'000): 427,807 in 1985; 361,927 in 1986; 360,885 in 1987. These amounts include exports through Shannon Free Airport (I£'000): 291,663 in 1985; 238,157 in 1986; 241,145 in 1987. The total also includes exports of non-monetary gold (I£'000): 1,655 in 1985; 1,467 in 1986; 1,202 in 1987.
† Provisional.

PRINCIPAL TRADING PARTNERS* (I£'000)

Imports c.i.f.	1985	1986	1987†
Belgium/Luxembourg	205,809	188,412	197,489
Canada	83,851	77,334	85,841
Denmark	96,743	87,561	85,158
Finland	77,229	78,676	82,958
France	456,201	428,213	401,238
Germany, Federal Republic	729,349	771,583	764,584
Italy	213,987	227,710	224,955
Japan	334,351	328,407	397,643
Netherlands	356,923	331,912	338,787
Spain	101,023	119,596	117,966
Sweden	149,138	139,836	139,532
Switzerland	94,872	85,479	68,374
United Kingdom	4,026,169	3,587,779	3,815,917
USA	1,602,174	1,365,383	1,555,414
Total (incl. others)	9,428,198	8,621,291	9,155,207

* Imports by country of origin; exports by country of final destination. The distribution excludes trade through Shannon Free Airport (see previous tables) except for Canada, the USA and the EEC.
† Provisional.

Exports f.o.b.	1985	1986	1987†
Belgium/Luxembourg	396,366	450,201	512,829
Canada	171,656	118,478	110,010
Denmark	88,535	91,505	97,650
Egypt	109,002	86,697	70,646
France	821,653	876,615	994,372
Germany, Federal Republic	985,310	1,022,089	1,202,610
Italy	363,930	334,273	392,478
Netherlands	663,722	555,712	778,271
Nigeria	105,543	33,102	41,120
Spain	111,217	137,260	164,160
Sweden	170,889	173,546	205,367
United Kingdom	3,211,097	3,201,368	3,662,630
USA	953,927	815,799	833,806
Total (incl. others)	9,743,038	9,374,310	10,723,498

Transport

RAILWAYS (traffic, '000)

	1984	1985	1986
Passengers carried	15,560	20,090	21,735
Passenger train-km	8,273	9,336	9,655
Freight tonnage	3,383	3,379	3,126
Freight train-km	4,411	4,305	4,239

ROAD TRAFFIC (licensed motor vehicles at 30 September)

	1984	1985	1986
Private cars	712,479	710,933	712,475
Goods vehicles	84,103	93,369	101,475
Public service vehicles	7,436	7,653	8,132
Motor cycles	26,305	26,025	25,735

SHIPPING (sea-borne freight traffic, '000 net registered tons)*

	1985	1986	1987
Displacement	20,455	20,915	22,557

* Figures refer to vessels engaged in both international and coastal trade.

CIVIL AVIATION

	1985/86	1986/87	1987/88
Kilometres flown ('000)	25,562	25,935	28,177
Passengers carried	2,133,089	2,279,637	2,669,671
Freight carried (tons)	37,232	35,828	38,599
Mail carried (tons)	1,895	1,590	1,892
Passenger-km ('000)	2,524,078	2,523,247	2,831,335
Freight ton-km ('000)	86,772	78,792	88,445

Tourism

FOREIGN TOURIST ARRIVALS ('000)

	1985	1986	1987
Long-stay visitors:			
Great Britain	1,119	1,127	1,242
Northern Ireland	585	586	566
France	95	90	100
Germany, Federal Republic	98	100	111
Netherlands	33	33	40
Other continental Europe	108	114	129
United States	392	309	367
Canada	30	34	31
Other areas	69	71	74
Sub-total	2,529	2,464	2,662
Day-trippers	7,413	7,329	7,368
Total	9,942	9,793	10,030

Communications Media

	1985	1986	1987
Television licences	717,024	751,955	787,501
Telephones in use	942,000	946,000	789,000
Daily newspapers	7	7	8

Radio receivers (1986): 2,060,000 in use (Source: UNESCO, *Statistical Yearbook*).

Book production (1985): 2,679 titles (including 2,051 pamphlets).

Education

(1986/87)

	Institutions	Teachers (full-time)	Students (full-time)
Primary schools	3,388	21,205	567,567
Secondary schools	503	12,112	215,618
Vocational schools	252	5,052	83,182
Comprehensive schools	15	533	8,941
Community schools	44	1,777	30,455
Teacher (primary) training colleges	6	176	1,832
Preparatory colleges	1		29
Technical colleges*	9	1,111	11,376
Technology colleges*	9	901	7,964
Universities and Institutes	7	n.a.	33,443

* Third-level pupils only.

Sources: Department of Education, Dublin 1; Higher Education Authority.

Directory

The Constitution

The original Constitution of the Irish Free State came into operation on 6 December 1922. Certain provisions which were regarded as contrary to national sentiments were gradually removed by successive amendments, with the result that by 1937 the text differed considerably from that of the original document. It was superseded by an entirely new Constitution, which was approved by Parliament on 14 June 1937, and enacted by the people by means of a plebiscite on 1 July. This new Constitution came into operation on 29 December 1937. Ireland became a republic on 18 April 1949. The following is a summary of the Constitution's main provisions:

TITLE OF THE STATE

The title of the State is Éire or, in the English language, Ireland.

NATIONAL STATUS

The Constitution declares that Ireland is a sovereign, independent, democratic State. It affirms the inalienable, indefeasible and sovereign right of the Irish nation to choose its own form of government, to determine its relations with other nations, and to develop its life, political, economic and cultural, in accordance with its own genius and traditions.

The Constitution applies to the whole of Ireland, but, pending the re-integration of the national territory, the laws enacted by the Parliament established by the Constitution have the same area and extent of application as those of the Irish Free State.

THE PRESIDENT

At the head of the State is the President, elected by direct suffrage, who holds office for a period of seven years. He, on the advice of the Government or its head, summons and dissolves Parliament, signs and promulgates laws and appoints judges; on the nomination of the Dáil he appoints the Prime Minister and, on the nomination of the Prime Minister with the previous approval of the Dáil, he appoints the other members of the Government. The supreme command of the Defence Forces is vested in him, its exercise being regulated by law.

In addition, the President has the power to refer certain Bills to the Supreme Court for decision on the question of their constitutionality; and also, at the instance of a prescribed proportion of the members of both Houses of Parliament, to refer certain Bills to the people for decision at a referendum.

The President, in the exercise and performance of certain of his constitutional powers and functions, has the aid and advice of a Council of State.

PARLIAMENT

The Oireachtas, or National Parliament, consists of the President and two Houses, viz. a House of Representatives called Dáil Éireann, and a Senate, called Seanad Éireann. The Dáil consists of 166 members, who are elected for a five-year term by adult suffrage on the system of proportional representation by means of the single, transferable vote. Of the 60 members of the Senate, 11 are nominated by the Prime Minister, six are elected by the universities, and 43 are elected from five panels of candidates established on a vocational basis, representing: national language and culture, literature, art, education and such professional interests as may be defined by law for the purpose of this panel; agriculture and allied interests, and fisheries; labour, whether organized or unorganized; industry and commerce, including banking, finance, accountancy, engineering and architecture; and public administration and social services, including voluntary social activities.

A maximum period of 90 days is afforded to the Senate for the consideration or amendment of Bills sent to that House by the Dáil, but the Senate has no power to veto legislation.

EXECUTIVE

The Executive Power of the State is exercised by the Government, which is responsible to the Dáil and consists of not fewer than seven and not more than 15 members. The head of the Government is the Prime Minister.

FUNDAMENTAL RIGHTS

The State recognizes the family as the natural, primary and fundamental unit group of Society, possessing inalienable and imprescriptible rights antecedent and superior to all positive law. It acknowledges the right to life of the unborn and guarantees in its laws to defend and vindicate that right. It acknowledges the right and duty of parents to provide for the education of their children, and, with due regard to that right, undertakes to provide free education. It pledges itself also to guard with special care the institution of marriage.

The Constitution contains special provision for the recognition and protection of the fundamental rights of citizens, such as personal liberty, free expression of opinion, peaceable assembly, and the formation of associations and unions.

Freedom of conscience and the free practice and profession of religion are, subject to public order and morality, guaranteed to every citizen. No religion may be endowed or subjected to discriminatory disability. Since December 1972, when a referendum was taken on the issue, the Catholic Church has no longer enjoyed a special, privileged position.

SOCIAL POLICY

Certain principles of social policy intended for the general guidance of Parliament, but not cognizable by the courts, are set forth in the Constitution. Among their objects are the direction of the policy of the State towards securing the distribution of property so as to subserve the common good, the regulation of credit so as to serve the welfare of the people as a whole, the establishment of families in economic security on the land, and the right to an adequate means of livelihood for all citizens.

The State pledges itself to safeguard the interests, and to contribute where necessary to the support, of the infirm, the widow, the orphan and the aged, and shall endeavour to ensure that citizens shall not be forced by economic necessity to enter occupations unsuited to their sex, age or strength.

AMENDMENT OF THE CONSTITUTION

No amendment to the Constitution can be effected except by the decision of the people given at a referendum.

The Government

(February 1989)

HEAD OF STATE

President: Dr Patrick Hillery (Pádraig Ó hIrighile) (assumed office 3 December 1976; re-elected 21 October 1983).

THE CABINET

Taoiseach (Prime Minister) and Minister for the Gaeltacht: Charles J. Haughey.

Tánaiste (Deputy Prime Minister) and Minister for Foreign Affairs: Brian Lenihan.

Minister for Industry and Commerce: Ray Burke.

Minister for the Environment: Pádraig Flynn.

Minister for Defence: Michael J. Noonan.

Minister for Tourism and Transport: John P. Wilson.

Minister for Energy and Communications: Michael Smith.

Minister for Finance and Minister for the Public Service: Albert Reynolds.

Minister for Health: Rory O'Hanlon.

Minister for Social Welfare: Dr Michael Woods.

Minister for Agriculture and Food: Michael O'Kennedy.

Minister for Justice: Gerard Collins.

Minister for Education: Mary O'Rourke.

Minister for Labour: Bertie Ahern.

Minister for the Marine: Brendan Daly.

MINISTRIES

Office of the President: Áras an Uachtaráin, Phoenix Park, Dublin 8; tel. (01) 772815.

Office of the Prime Minister: Government Bldgs, Upper Merrion St, Dublin 2; tel. (01) 689333; telex 25800.

Department of Agriculture and Food: Kildare St, Dublin 2; tel. (01) 789011; telex 93607.

Department of Defence: Parkgate, Dublin 8; tel. (01) 771881; telex 25250.

IRELAND

Department of Education: Marlborough St, Dublin 1; tel. (01) 734700; telex 31136.

Department of Energy and Communications: 25 Clare St, Dublin 2; tel. (01) 715233; telex 90335.

Department of the Environment: Custom House, Dublin 1; tel. (01) 793377; telex 31014.

Department of Finance and Department of the Public Service: Government Bldgs, Upper Merrion St, Dublin 2; tel. (01) 767571; telex 30357.

Department of Foreign Affairs: 80 St Stephen's Green, Dublin 2; tel. (01) 780822; telex 25300.

Department of the Gaeltacht: 1 Lower Grand Canal St, Dublin 2; tel. (01) 764751; telex 30782.

Department of Health: Custom House, Dublin 1; tel. (01) 735777; telex 24894.

Department of Industry and Commerce: Kildare St, Dublin 2; tel. (01) 614444; telex 93478.

Department of Justice: 72–76 St Stephen's Green, Dublin 2; tel. (01) 789711; telex 90495.

Department of Labour: Davitt House, 50-60 Mespil Rd, Dublin 4; tel. (01) 765861; telex 24534.

Department of the Marine: Leeson Lane, Dublin 2; tel. (01) 615666; telex 90253.

Department of Social Welfare: Áras Mhic Dhiarmada, Dublin 1; tel. (01) 786444; telex 32969.

Department of Tourism and Transport: Kildare St, Dublin 2; tel. (01) 789522; telex 93478.

Legislature

OIREACHTAS (PARLIAMENT)

Parliament comprises two Houses—Dáil Éireann (House of Representatives), with 166 members, and Seanad Éireann (Senate), with 60 members, of whom 11 are nominated by the Taoiseach and 49 elected (six by the universities and 43 from specially constituted panels).

Dáil Éireann

Speaker: SEAN TREACY.

General Election, 17 February 1987

Party	Votes*	% of votes*	Seats
Fianna Fáil	784,606	44.15	81
Fine Gael	481,137	27.07	51
Progressive Democrats	210,587	11.85	14
Labour Party	114,553	6.45	12
Workers' Party	67,263	3.78	4
Sinn Fein	32,933	1.85	—
Others	86,163	4.85	4
Total	1,777,242	100.00	166

* The election was conducted by means of the single transferable vote. Figures refer to first-preference votes.

Seanad Éireann

Speaker: TRAS HONAN.

Election, February 1987 (11 members nominated)

Party	Seats at election
Fianna Fáil	30
Fine Gael	16
Labour	3
Independents*	11

* Including university representatives.

Political Organizations

Comhaontas Glas (The Green Alliance): 5A Upper Fownes St, Dublin 2; tel. (01) 771436; fmrly The Ecology Party; desires a humane, ecological society, freedom of information and political decentralization; Co-ordinators PAUL O'BRIEN, PATRICIA MCKENNA, ROGER GARLAND.

Communist Party of Ireland: James Connolly House, 43 East Essex St, Dublin 2; tel. (01) 711943; f. 1933; its aim is a united, socialist, independent Ireland; Chair. MICHAEL O'RIORDAN; Gen. Sec. JAMES STEWART.

Democratic Socialist Party: POB 806, Dublin 8; tel. (01) 309892; f. 1982 following merger of Socialist Party (f. 1970) and Limerick Socialist Organization; aims to create a democratic socialist Ireland, opposes Irish nationalist claim to Northern Ireland; Pres. JAMES KEMMY; Sec. JOE HOLOHAN.

Fianna Fáil (literally, Soldiers of Destiny—The Republican Party): 13 Upper Mount St, Dublin 2; tel. (01) 761551; f. 1926; supports the peaceful reunification of Ireland; Pres. CHARLES HAUGHEY; Gen. Sec. FRANK WALL.

Fine Gael (United Ireland Party): 51 Upper Mount St, Dublin 2; tel. (01) 761573; telex 31569; f. 1933; mem. of the European People's Party (Christian Democratic Group) in the European Parliament; Leader ALAN DUKES; Nat. Exec. Chair. SEAN BARRETT; Gen. Sec. EDWARD O'REILLY.

Irish Republican Socialist Party: 34 Upper Gardiner St, Dublin 1; tel. (01) 721175; f. 1974; political wing of INLA (see Northern Ireland, Vol. II); aims to establish a united 32-county democratic socialist republic in Ireland; Chair. JIM LAINE; Gen. Sec. FRANCIS BARRY.

The Labour Party: 16 Gardiner Place, Dublin 1; tel. (01) 788411; telex 90570; originated with the addition of political functions to the Trade Union Congress in 1912; at the end of 1930 it was decided to separate the political and industrial functions of the Party, and the TUC and the Labour Party became separate bodies; Chair. MERVYN TAYLOR; Vice-Chair. EMMETT STAGG; Leader of Parl. Labour Party RICHARD SPRING; Gen. Sec. RAYMOND KAVANAGH.

Progressive Democrats: 25 South Frederick St, Dublin 2; tel. (01) 794399; f. 1985; represents a break with Fianna Fáil and Fine Gael; desires a peaceful approach to the Northern Ireland situation; tax reforms; the encouragement of private enterprise; a clear distinction between church and state; and constitutional reform, including the abolition of the Senate and a pluralist Republican Constitution; Leader DESMOND O'MALLEY; Gen. Sec. PATRICK COX.

Republican Sinn Fein: f. 1986 by disaffected members of Sinn Fein; supports military resistance to British rule in Northern Ireland; Chair. DAITHI O'CONNELL.

Sinn Fein ('Ourselves Alone'): 44 Parnell Sq., Dublin 1; tel. (01) 726932; f. 1905; advocates the complete overthrow of British rule in Ireland; seeks the reunification of Ireland by revolutionary means, and the establishment of a 32-county democratic socialist republic; Pres. GERARD ADAMS.

The Workers' Party (WP): 30 Gardiner Place, Dublin 1; tel. (01) 740716; telex 31490; f. 1905; formerly Sinn Fein The Workers' Party; aims to establish an All-Ireland Unitary Socialist State; Pres. PROINNSIAS DE ROSSA; Gen. Sec. SEAN GARLAND.

Diplomatic Representation

EMBASSIES IN IRELAND

Argentina: 15 Ailesbury Drive, Dublin 4; tel. (01) 691546; Ambassador: JUAN JOSÉ ARIAS URIBURU.

Australia: 6th Floor, Fitzwilton House, Wilton Terrace, Dublin 2; tel. (01) 761517; telex 25762; Ambassador: BRIAN BURKE.

Austria: 15 Ailesbury Court, 93 Ailesbury Rd, Dublin 4; tel. (01) 694577; telex 30366; Ambassador: Dr HELGA WINKLER-CAMPAGNA.

Belgium: 2 Shrewsbury Rd, Dublin 4; tel. (01) 692082; telex 93322; Ambassador: Baron PANGAERT D'OPDORP.

Canada: 65–68 St Stephen's Green, Dublin 2; tel. (01) 781988; telex 93803; Ambassador: DENNIS MCDERMOTT.

China, People's Republic: 40 Ailesbury Rd, Dublin 4; tel: (01) 691707; telex 30626; Ambassador: ZHOU YANG.

Denmark: 121–122 St Stephen's Green, Dublin 2; tel. (01) 756404; telex 93523; Ambassador: VAGN KORSBÆK.

Egypt: 12 Clyde Rd, Ballsbridge, Dublin 4; tel. (01) 606566; telex 33202; Ambassador: ABD EL-HAMID ABD EL-AZIZ ONSI.

France: 36 Ailesbury Rd, Dublin 4; tel. (01) 694777; Ambassador: JEAN-MAX BOUCHAUD.

Germany, Federal Republic: 31 Trimleston Ave, Booterstown, Blackrock, Co Dublin; tel. (01) 693011; telex 93809; Ambassador: Dr HELMUTH RUECKRIEGEL.

Greece: 1 Upper Pembroke St, Dublin 2; tel. (01) 767254; telex 30878; Ambassador: PANAYOTIS A. TSOUNIS.

Holy See: 183 Navan Rd, Dublin 7 (Apostolic Nunciature); tel. (01) 309344; Papal Nuncio: Most Rev. GAETANO ALIBRANDI.

IRELAND *Directory*

India: 6 Leeson Park, Dublin 6; tel. (01) 970843; telex 30670; Ambassador: PREM SHUNKER.

Iran: 72 Mount Merrion Ave, Blackrock, Co Dublin; tel. 880252; telex 90336; Ambassador: BAHRAM GHASEMI.

Italy: 63/65 Northumberland Rd, Dublin 4; tel. (01) 601744; telex 93950; Ambassador: Dr FRANCESCO CARLO GENTILE.

Japan: 22 Ailesbury Rd, Dublin 4; tel. (01) 694244; Ambassador: YOSHIFUMI ITO.

Korea, Republic: 20 Clyde Rd, Ballsbridge, Dublin 4; tel. 608800; Ambassador: KI CHOO LEE.

Netherlands: 160 Merrion Rd, Ballsbridge, Dublin 4; tel. (01) 693444; telex 24849; Ambassador: A. B. HOYTINK.

Nigeria: 56 Leeson Park, Dublin 6; tel. (01) 604366; telex 24163; Ambassador: A. D. J. BLANKSON.

Norway: Hainault House, 69/71 St Stephen's Green, Dublin 2; tel. (01) 783133; telex 90173; Ambassador: KIRSTEN OHM.

Portugal: Knocksinna House, Knocksinna, Foxrock, Dublin 18; tel. (01) 893375; telex 30777; Ambassador: PEDRO JOSÉ RIBEIRO DE MENEZES.

Spain: 17A Merlyn Park, Dublin 4; tel. (01) 691640; telex 93826; Ambassador: JOSÉ A. DE YTURRIAGA.

Sweden: Sun Alliance House, 13-17 Dawson St, Dublin 2; tel. (01) 715822; telex 93341; Ambassador: ILMAR BEKERIS.

Switzerland: 6 Ailesbury Rd, Ballsbridge, Dublin 4; tel. (01) 692515; telex 93299; Ambassador: CHARLES HUMMEL.

Turkey: 60 Merrion Rd, Ballsbridge, Dublin 4; tel. (01) 685240; telex 31563; Ambassador: HAUL DAG.

USSR: 184-186 Orwell Rd, Rathgar, Dublin 6; tel. (01) 975748; telex 33622; Ambassador: GENNADI VASILEVICH URANOV.

United Kingdom: 33 Merrion Rd, Dublin 4; tel. (01) 695211; telex 25296; Ambassador: Sir NICHOLAS FENN.

USA: 42 Elgin Rd, Ballsbridge, Dublin 4; tel. (01) 688777; telex 93684; Ambassador: MARGARET HECKLER.

Judicial System

Justice is administered in public by Judges appointed by the President on the advice of the Government. The Judges of all Courts are completely independent in the exercise of their judicial functions. The jurisdiction and organization of the Courts are dealt with in the Courts (Establishment and Constitution) Act, 1961, and the Courts (Supplemental Provisions) Acts, 1961 to 1981.

Attorney-General: JOHN MURRAY.

SUPREME COURT

The Supreme Court, consisting of the Chief Justice and five other Judges, has appellate jurisdiction from all decisions of the High Court. The President of Ireland may, after consultation with the Council of State, refer a Bill which has been passed by both Houses of the Oireachtas (other than a Money Bill or certain others), to the Supreme Court to establish whether it or any other provisions thereof are repugnant to the Constitution.

Chief Justice: THOMAS A. FINLAY.

Judges:
BRIAN WALSH.
SEAMUS HENCHY.
FRANCIS GRIFFIN.
ANTHONY HEDERMAN.
NIALL MCCARTHY.

COURT OF CRIMINAL APPEAL

The Court of Criminal Appeal, consisting of the Chief Justice or an ordinary Judge of the Supreme Court and two Judges of the High Court, deals with appeals by persons convicted on indictment, where leave to appeal has been granted. The decision of this Court is final unless the Court or Attorney-General or the Director of Public Prosecutions certifies that a point of law involved should, in the public interest, be taken to the Supreme Court.

HIGH COURT

The High Court, consisting of the President of the High Court and 15 ordinary Judges, has full original jurisdiction in, and power to determine, all matters and questions whether of law or fact, civil or criminal. The High Court on circuit acts as an appeal court from the Circuit Court. The Central Criminal Court sits as directed by the President of the High Court to try criminal cases outside the jurisdiction of the Circuit Court. The duty of acting as the Central Criminal Court is assigned, for the time being, to a Judge of the High Court.

President: LIAM HAMILTON.

Judges:
SEAN GANNON, DECLAN COSTELLO, RONAN KEANE, DONAL BARRINGTON, MELLA CARROLL, RORY O'HANLON, HENRY D. BARRON, FRANCIS D. MURPHY, KEVIN LYNCH, SEAMUS EGAN, ROBERT BARR, GERARD LARDNER, JOHN J. BLAYNEY, JOHN J. P. MACKENZIE, RICHARD JOHNSON.

CIRCUIT AND DISTRICT COURTS

The civil jurisdiction of the Circuit Court is limited to £15,000 in contract and tort and in actions founded on hire-purchase and credit-sale agreements and to a rateable value of £200 in equity, and in probate and administration, but where the parties consent the jurisdiction is unlimited. In criminal matters the Court has jurisdiction in all cases except murder, treason, piracy and allied offences. One Circuit Judge is permanently assigned to each circuit outside Dublin and five to the Dublin circuit. In addition there is one permanently unassigned Judge. The Circuit Court acts as an appeal court from the District Court, which has a summary jurisdiction in a large number of criminal cases where the offence is not of a serious nature. In civil matters the District Court has jurisdiction in contract and tort (except slander, libel, seduction, slander of title, malicious prosecution and false imprisonment) where the claim does not exceed £2,500 and in actions founded on hire-purchase and credit-sale agreements.

All criminal cases except those dealt with summarily by a Justice in the District Court are tried by a Judge and a jury of 12 members. Juries are also used in very many civil cases in the High Court. In a criminal case the jury must be unanimous in reaching a verdict but in a civil case the agreement of nine members is sufficient.

Religion

CHRISTIANITY

The organization of the churches takes no account of the partition of Ireland into two separate political entities. Thus the Republic of Ireland and Northern Ireland are subject to a unified jurisdiction for ecclesiastical purposes. The Roman Catholic Primate of All Ireland and the Church of Ireland (Protestant Episcopalian) Primate of All Ireland now have their seats in Northern Ireland, at Armagh, and the headquarters of the Presbyterian Church in Ireland is at Belfast, Northern Ireland.

At the end of 1986 the Roman Catholic population of Ireland was estimated to be 3,963,658. In 1984 people belonging to the Presbyterian Church numbered just over 347,000.

The Roman Catholic Church

Ireland (including Northern Ireland) comprises four archdioceses and 23 dioceses.

Archbishop of Armagh and Primate of All Ireland: HE Cardinal TOMÁS Ó FIAICH, Ara Coeli, Armagh, BT61 7QY, Northern Ireland; tel. (0861) 522045.

Archbishop of Cashel and Emly: Most Rev. DERMOT CLIFFORD, Archbishop's House, Thurles, Co Tipperary; tel. (0504) 21512.

Archbishop of Dublin and Primate of Ireland: Most Rev. DESMOND CONNELL, Archbishop's House, Drumcondra, Dublin 9; tel. (01) 373732.

Archbishop of Tuam: Most Rev. JOSEPH CASSIDY, St Jarlath's, Tuam, Co Galway; tel. (093) 24166.

Besides the hierarchy, the Roman Catholic Church has numerous religious orders strongly established in the country. These play an important role, particularly in the spheres of education, health and social welfare.

Church of Ireland
(The Anglican Communion)

Ireland (including Northern Ireland) comprises two archdioceses and 10 dioceses.

Central Office of the Church of Ireland: Church of Ireland House, Church Ave, Rathmines, Dublin 6; tel. (01) 978422; 379,211 mems; Chief Officer and Sec. to the Representative Church Body R. H. SHERWOOD.

Archbishop of Armagh and Primate of All Ireland: Most Rev. ROBERT HENRY ALEXANDER EAMES, The See House, Cathedral Close, Armagh, BT61 7EE, Northern Ireland; tel. (0861) 522851.

Archbishop of Dublin and Primate of Ireland: Most Rev. DONALD CAIRD, The See House, 17 Temple Rd, Milltown, Dublin 6; tel. (01) 977849.

IRELAND

Protestant Churches
Baptist Union of Ireland: 117 Lisburn Rd, Belfast, BT9 7AF; tel. (0232) 663108; Sec. Pastor J. R. GRANT.

Lutheran Church: 21 Merlyn Park, Dublin 4; tel. 692529; Rev. PAUL G. FRITZ.

Methodist Church: 3 Upper Malone Rd, Belfast, BT9 6TD; tel. (0232) 668458; Sec. Rev. CHARLES G. EYRE; Pres. Rev. T. STANLEY WHITTINGTON, 4 Strathyre Park, Belfast, BT10 0AZ; tel. (0232) 629677.

Non-Subscribing Presbyterian Church of Ireland: 102 Carrickfergus Rd, Warne, Co Antrim; tel. (0574) 72600; Clerk to Gen. Synod Rev. Dr JOHN W. NELSON.

Presbyterian Church: Church House, Fisherwick Place, Belfast, BT1 6DW; tel. (0232) 322284; Moderator Rt Rev. Dr WILLIAM FLEMING; Clerk of Assembly and Gen. Sec. Very Rev. Dr T. J. SIMPSON.

The Religious Society of Friends: Swanbrook House, Morehampton Rd, Dublin 4; tel. 683684; Registrar PEARL D. M. LAMB.

BAHÁ'Í FAITH
National Spiritual Assembly: 24 Burlington Rd, Dublin 4; tel. 683150.

JUDAISM
Chief Rabbi: Very Rev. EPHRAIM MIRVIS, Herzog House, Zion Rd, Rathgar, Dublin 6; tel. (01) 967351.

The Press

The Constitution of Ireland provides for the recognition and protection of the fundamental rights of the citizen, including free expression of opinion. Despite the powerful position of the Roman Catholic Church in Ireland there is open discussion on controversial issues. The right of a journalist's professional secrecy is not recognized by the Irish Courts.

Ireland has seven daily newspapers, five in Dublin and two in Cork, including four morning papers which are distributed nationally. There are four national Sunday papers.

DAILIES
Cork
Cork Evening Echo: 95 Patrick St, Cork; tel. (021) 963300; telex 6014; f. 1892; Editorial Dir D. CROSBIE; Editor JAMES O'SULLIVAN; circ. 36,250.

Cork Examiner: 95 Patrick St, Cork; tel. (021) 963300; telex 6014; f. 1841; national; Editor T. CREAMER; circ. 63,560.

Dublin
Evening Herald: Independent House, 90 Middle Abbey St, Dublin 1; tel. (01) 731333; f. 1891; independent national; Editor MICHAEL BROPHY; circ. 132,314.

Evening Press: Tara House, Tara St, Dublin 2; tel. (01) 713333; f. 1954; Editor SEAN WARD; circ. 129,695.

Irish Independent: Independent House, 90 Middle Abbey St, Dublin 1; tel. (01) 731666; telex 33472; f. 1905; non-party; Editor VINCENT DOYLE; circ. 174,788.

Irish Press: Tara House, Tara St, Dublin 2; tel. (01) 713333; telex 93752; f. 1931; independent; Editor H. LAMBERT; circ. 86,655.

The Irish Times: 11-15 D'Olier St, Dublin 2; tel. (01) 792022; telex 93639; f. 1859; independent national; Editor CONOR BRADY; circ. 88,739.

WEEKLY AND OTHER NEWSPAPERS
Anglo-Celt: Anglo-Celt Place, Cavan; tel. (049) 31100; f. 1846; Friday; nationalist; Editor E. T. O'HANLON; circ. 18,868 (incl. USA and Canada).

Argus: Argus Newspapers Ltd, Jocelyn St, Dundalk; tel. (042) 31500; f. 1835; Thursday; Editor KEVIN MULLIGAN; circ. 10,000.

Cavon Leader: 21 Farnham St, Cavan; tel. (049) 32777; Wednesday; Editor EUGENE MCGEE; circ. 10,500.

Clare Champion: O'Connell St, Ennis, Co Clare; tel. (065) 28105; f. 1903; Thursday; independent; Editor J. F. O'DEA; Man. Dir F. GALVIN; circ. 21,040.

Connacht Tribune: Market St, Galway; tel. (091) 67251; telex 50066; f. 1909; Friday; nationalist; Editor J. CUNNINGHAM; circ. 29,085.

Connaught Telegraph: Ellison St, Castlebar, Co Mayo; tel. (094) 21711; f. 1828; Wednesday; Man. Dir J. CONNOLLY; Editor TOM COURELL; circ. 12,000.

Directory

Derry People and Donegal News: Crossview House, High Rd, Letterkenny, Co Donegal; tel. (074) 21014; f. 1902; Saturday; nationalist; Editor T. QUIGLEY.

Donegal Democrat: Donegal Rd, Ballyshannon, Co Donegal; tel. (072) 51201; f. 1919; Friday; republican; Man. Dir CECIL J. KING; Editor JOHN BROMLEY; circ. 18,304.

Drogheda Independent: 9 Shop St, Drogheda, Co Louth; tel. (041) 38658; f. 1884; Thursday; Editor PAUL MURPHY; circ. 16,491.

Dundalk Democrat: 3 Earl St, Dundalk, Co Louth; tel. (042) 34058; f. 1849; Saturday; independent; Editor T. P. ROE; circ. 18,400.

East Cork News: 25 Michael St, Waterford; tel. (051) 74951; f. 1981; Wednesday; Editor PETER DOYLE.

Echo and South Leinster Advertiser: Mill Park Rd, Enniscorthy, Co Wexford; tel. (054) 33231; f. 1902; Wednesday; independent; Editor JAMES GAHAN; circ. 21,500.

The Guardian: The People Newspapers Ltd, 1 North Main St, Wexford; tel. (053) 22155; f. 1881; Friday; Man Dir RAY DOYLE; circ. 37,141.

Iris Oifigiuil (Dublin Gazette): Stationery Office, Dublin 8; tel. (01) 781666; f. 1922; Tuesday and Friday; official paper publ. under government authority; Editor The Controller.

Irish Catholic: 55 Lower Gardiner St, Dublin 1; tel. (01) 747538; f. 1888; Thursday; Editor NICK LUNDBERG; circ. 40,100.

The Kerryman (The Corkman): Clash Industrial Estate, Tralee, Co Kerry; tel. (066) 21666; telex 28100; f. 1904; Thursday; independent; Editor S. MCCONVILLE; circ. 41,185.

Kilkenny People: 34 High St, Kilkenny; tel. (056) 21015; f. 1892; independent nationalist weekly; Editor and Man. Dir JOHN E. KERRY KEANE; circ. 17,825.

Leinster Express: Dublin Rd, Portlaoise, Co Laois; tel. (0502) 21666; telex 60024; f. 1831; Wednesday for Saturday; Editor TEDDY FENNELLY; circ. 16,245.

Leinster Leader: 19 South Main St, Naas, Co Kildare; tel. (045) 97302; f. 1880; Saturday; nationalist; Editor S. CARROLL; circ. 14,000.

Leitrim Observer: St George's Terrace, Carrick-on-Shannon, Co Leitrim; tel. (078) 20025; f. 1889; Wednesday; national; Editor G. DUNNE; circ. 11,400.

Limerick Chronicle: 54 O'Connell St, Limerick; tel. (061) 45233; f. 1766; Tuesday; independent; Editor BRENDAN HALLIGAN; circ. 8,000.

Limerick Echo and Shannon News: 51 O'Connell St, Limerick; tel. (061) 49966; f. 1897; Thursday; independent; Editor MARTIN BYRNES; circ. 12,500.

Limerick Leader: 54 O'Connell St, Limerick; tel. (061) 315233; f. 1889; 3 a week; independent; Editor BRENDAN HALLIGAN; circ. Monday and Wednesday 3,788, Friday 33,901.

Longford Leader: Market Sq., Longford; tel. (043) 45241; telex 31901; f. 1897; Friday; independent; Editor EUGENE MCGEE; circ. 19,500.

Mayo News: The Fairgreen, Westport, Co Mayo; tel. (098) 25365; f. 1892; Wednesday; independent; Man. Editor SEAN STAUNTON; circ. 12,000.

Meath Chronicle and Cavan and Westmeath Herald: 12 Market Sq., Navan, Co Meath; tel. (046) 21442; f. 1897; Saturday; Man. Dir JOHN T. DAVIS; Editor JAMES DAVIS; circ. 17,500.

Midland Tribune: Emmet St, Birr, Co Offaly; tel. (0509) 20003; f. 1881; Wednesday; national; Editor J. I. FANNING; circ. 10,000.

The Munster Express: 37 The Quay and 1-6 Hanover St, Waterford; tel. (051) 72141; f. 1859; independent; 2 a week; Editor and Gov. Dir J. J. WALSH; circ. 19,125.

Nationalist and Leinster Times: 42 Tullow St, Carlow, Co Carlow; tel. (0503) 31731; telex 31442; f. 1883; Wednesday for Friday; independent; Man. Dir and Editor DESMOND FISHER; circ. 18,909.

Nationalist and Munster Advertiser: Nationalist Newspaper Co Ltd, Queen St, Clonmel, Tipperary; tel. (052) 22211; f. 1890; Thursday for Saturday; nationalist; Editor BRENDAN LONG; circ. 14,484.

New Ross Standard: 1 North Main St, Wexford; tel. (053) 22155; f. 1880; Friday; Proprs The People Newspapers Ltd; Man. Dir RAY DOYLE; circ. 37,141.

The Northern Standard: The Diamond, Monaghan; tel. (047) 82188; f. 1839; Friday; county newspaper of Co Monaghan; Editor P. SMYTH; circ. 13,250.

Roscommon Champion: Church St, Roscommon; tel. (0903) 25051; f. 1927; weekly; news, features and sport; Editor SEAMUS DOOLEY; circ. 10,000.

Sligo Champion: Wine St, Sligo; tel. (071) 69222; f. 1836; Wednesday; nationalist; Editor S. FINN; circ. 26,519.

IRELAND   *Directory*

Southern Star: Skibbereen, Co Cork; tel. (028) 21200; f. 1889; Saturday; non-political; Editor W. J. O'REGAN; circ. 17,408.

Sunday Independent: Independent House, 90 Middle Abbey St, Dublin; tel. (01) 731666; telex 33472; f. 1905; non-party; Editor AENGUS FANNING; circ. 222,351.

The Sunday Press: Tara House, Tara St, Dublin 2; tel. (01) 713333; telex 25353; f. 1949; independent; Editor MICHAEL KEANE; circ. 266,019.

Sunday Tribune: 15 Lower Baggot St, Dublin 2; tel. (01) 615555; telex 90995; f. 1980; Editor VINCENT BROWNE.

Sunday World: Newspaper House, 18 Rathfarnham Rd, Terenure, Dublin 6; tel. (01) 901980; telex 24886; f. 1973; Editor COLIN MCCLELLAND; circ. 366,806.

Tipperary Star: Friar St, Thurles, Co Tipperary; tel. (0504) 21122; f. 1909; Saturday; independent; Editor MICHAEL DUNDON; circ. 10,983.

Tullamore Tribune: Church St, Tullamore, Co Offaly; tel. (0506) 21152; f. 1978; Wednesday; Editor G. V. OAKLEY; circ. 5,000.

Waterford News & Star: 25 Michael St, Waterford; tel. (051) 74951; f. 1848; Thursday; Editor P. DOYLE; circ. 18,621.

Western People: Francis St, Ballina, Co Mayo; tel. (096) 21188; telex 40787; f. 1883; Tuesday; independent nationalist; Man. Editor TERENCE REILLY; Dir and Sec. P. A. MAGUIRE; circ. 28,242.

Westmeath Examiner: 19 Dominick St, Mullingar, Co Westmeath; tel. 48426; f. 1882; weekly; Man. Dir NICHOLAS J. NALLY; circ. 13,135.

Westmeath Independent and Offaly Independent: Gleeson St, Athlone, Co Westmeath; tel. (0902) 72003; telex 53005; f. 1846; Thursday; Editor MARGARET GRENNAN; circ. 12,000.

Wicklow People: Independent House, 90 Middle Abbey St, Dublin 1; tel. (01) 731666; f. 1883; Friday; Proprs The People Newspapers Ltd; Man. Dir RAY DOYLE; Editor DERMOT WALSH; circ. 36,536.

SELECTED PERIODICALS

Aspect: POB 15, New Rd, Greystones, Co Wicklow; tel. (0404) 875514; f. 1982; monthly; current affairs; Editor JOHN O'NEILL.

Business & Finance: 50 Fitzwilliam Sq., Dublin 2; tel. (01) 764587; f. 1964; weekly; Editor AILEEN O'TOOLE; Man. Editor W. AMBROSE; circ. 11,270.

Caritas (1934) Ireland: St Augustine's, Blackrock, Co Dublin; tel. (01) 885518; quarterly; publ. by The Hospitaller Brothers of St John of God; covers the Order's health services in Ireland.

Horizon: 2-6 Tara St, Dublin 2; tel. (01) 713500; bimonthly; publ. by Jude Publications Ltd; circ. 8,000.

Hot Press: 6 Wicklow St, Dublin 2; tel. (01) 795077; fortnightly; music, leisure, current affairs; Editor NIALL STOKES; circ. 21,500.

In Dublin: 15 Lower Baggot St, Dublin 2; tel. (01) 615555; f. 1976; fortnightly; listings and reviews of theatre, music, restaurants, exhibitions, news and current affairs; Editor JOHN DOYLE; circ. 15,000.

Industry and Commerce: 2-6 Tara St, Dublin 2; tel. (01) 713500; monthly; publ. by Jude Publications Ltd; circ. 10,000.

Ireland of the Welcomes: Baggot St Bridge, Dublin 2; tel. (01) 765871; telex 93755; f. 1952; every 2 months; publ. by Irish Tourist Board; Irish cultural items; Publr CHRIS KANE; Editor PETER HARBISON; circ. 125,000.

Ireland's Own: North Main St, Wexford; tel. 22155; f. 1902; weekly; stories, articles, serials, cartoons, family reading; Editor RONAN DODD; circ. 58,500.

Ireland Today: Dept of Foreign Affairs, 80 St Stephen's Green, Dublin 2; tel. (01) 780822; telex 93720; Editor BILL NOLAN; circ. 21,500.

Irish Business: 128 Lower Baggot St, Dublin 2; tel. (01) 619236; f. 1975; monthly; Editor FRANK FITZGIBBON; circ. 9,750.

Irish Catholic: 55 Lower Gardiner St, Dublin 1; tel. (01) 742795; f. 1888; weekly; Editor NICK LUNDBERG; circ. 40,100.

Irish Doctor: 2-6 Tara St, Dublin 2; tel. (01) 713500; publ. by Medical Press Ltd; circ. 6,500.

The Irish Exporter: 2-6 Tara St, Dublin 2; tel. (01) 713500; monthly; publ. by Jude Publications Ltd; circ. 8,500.

Irish Farmers' Journal: The Irish Farm Centre, Naas Rd, Dublin 12; tel. (01) 501166; telex 33338; f. 1948; weekly; Editor MATTHEW DEMPSEY; circ. 70,038.

Irish Field: POB 74, 11-15 D'Olier St, Dublin 2; tel. (01) 792022; telex 93639; f. 1870; Saturday; horse-racing, show-jumping and breeding; Proprs The Irish Times Ltd; Man. Editor V. LAMB; circ. 10,755.

Irish Journal of Medical Science: Royal Academy of Medicine in Ireland, 6 Kildare St, Dublin 2; tel. (01) 767650; f. 1832; monthly; organ of the Royal Academy of Medicine; Editor Dr JOHN F. MURPHY.

Irish Law Reports Monthly: The Round Hall Press, Kill Lane, Blackrock, Co Dublin; tel. 892922; f. 1981; Sr Editor BART DALY.

Irish Law Times: The Round Hall Press, Kill Lane, Blackrock, Co Dublin; tel. 892922; f. 1867; monthly; Editor BART DALY.

Irish Marketing Journal: 59 Upper Georges St, Dun Laoghaire, Co Dublin; tel. (01) 800692; f. 1974; monthly; Editor NORMAN BARRY; circ. 5,300.

IT-Irish Tatler: The Village Centre, Ballybrack, Co Dublin; tel. 826411; f. 1890; Editor NOELLE CAMPBELL-SHARP; circ. 27,138.

Journal of the Institute of Bankers in Ireland: Nassau House, Nassau St, Dublin 2; tel. (01) 777199; f. 1898; quarterly; Editor DERMOT FINUCANE; circ. 13,000.

Magill: 15 Lower Baggot St, Dublin 2; tel. (01) 606055; f. 1977; 14 issues a year; deals with Irish current affairs; Publr VINCENT BROWNE; Editor (vacant); circ. 20,500.

Management: Jemma Publications Ltd, 22 Brookfield Ave, Blackrock, Co Dublin; tel. (01) 886946; telex 90169; f. 1954; monthly; Editor FRANK CORR; circ. 7,500.

Motoring Life: G. P. Publications, 48 North Great George's St, Dublin 1; tel. (01) 721636; f. 1946; monthly; Editor FERGAL K. HERBERT; circ. 12,000.

The Pioneer: 27 Upper Sherrard St, Dublin 1; tel. (01) 749464; f. 1948; monthly; official organ of Pioneer Total Abstinence Association of the Sacred Heart; Editor Rev. J. C. SMYTH; circ. 20,000.

RTE Guide: Radio Telefís Éireann, Donnybrook, Dublin 4; tel. (01) 693111; weekly programme of the Irish broadcasting service; Editor (vacant); circ. 125,522.

Reality: Redemptorist Publications, 75 Orwell Rd, Rathgar, Dublin 6; tel. (01) 961488; f. 1936; Christian monthly; Editor Rev. KEVIN DONLON; circ. 30,000.

Social and Personal: The Village Centre, Ballybrack, Co. Dublin; tel. 826411; Editor NOELLE CAMPBELL-SHARP; circ. 10,500.

Strategy: 59 Upper Georges St, Dun Laoghaire, Co Dublin; tel. (01) 802787; weekly; Editor NORMAN BARRY; circ. 9,000.

Studies: 35 Lower Leeson St, Dublin 2; tel. (01) 766785; f. 1912; quarterly review of letters, history, religious and social questions; Editor BRIAN LENNON.

Success Magazine: The Village Centre, Ballybrack, Co Dublin; tel. (01) 826411; f. 1982; Man. Dir and Editor-in-Chief NOELLE CAMPBELL-SHARP; circ. 10,500.

U Magazine: 126 Lower Baggot St, Dublin 2; tel. (01) 608264; f. 1979; monthly; women's interest; Editor MARLENE LYNG; circ. 25,915.

Woman's Way: 126 Lower Baggot St, Dublin 2; tel. (01) 608264; f. 1963; weekly; Editor CELINE NAUGHTON; circ. 70,800.

NEWS AGENCIES

There is no national news agency.

Foreign Bureaux

Agenzia Nazionale Stampa Associata (ANSA) (Italy): 4 Idrone Close, Templeogue, Dublin 16; tel. 941389; Bureau Chief ENZO FARINELLA.

Reuters Ltd (UK): Elm House, Clanwilliam Court, Lower Mount St, Dublin 2; tel. (01) 603377; telex 90930; Correspondent PAUL MAJENDIE.

Telegrafnoye Agentstvo Sovetskovo Soyuza (TASS) (USSR): 59 Glenbrook Park, Dublin 14; Correspondent IGOR PONOMAREV.

PRESS ORGANIZATION

Provincial Newspapers Association of Ireland: 24 Dame St, Dublin 2; tel. (01) 793679; f. 1917; 37 mems; association of Irish provincial newspapers; Pres. W. P. O'HANLON; Sec. UNA SHERIDAN.

Publishers

Anvil Books Ltd: 45 Palmerston Rd, Dublin 6; tel (01) 973628; f. 1964; imprint: The Children's Press; biography, Irish history, folklore, sociology, children's; Man. Dir R. DARDIS.

Arlen House—The Women's Press: Kinnear Court, 16-20 South Cumberland St, Dublin 2; tel. (01) 717383; f. 1977; fiction, biography, classics, poetry and women's studies; Chief Exec. CATHERINE ROSE.

The Blackwater Press: c/o Folens & Co Ltd, Airton Rd, Tallaght, Co Dublin; tel. (01) 515311; non-fiction, history, Irish studies; Editor ANNE SENIOR.

IRELAND

Boole Press Ltd: POB 5, Dún Laoghaire, Co Dublin; tel. (01) 808025; telex 30547; f. 1979; scientific, technical, medical, scholarly; Chair M. O'REILLY.

Comhairle Bhéaloideas Éireann: University College, Belfield, Dublin 4; University College Dublin Press.

The Dolmen Press Ltd: The Lodge, Mountrath, Portlaoise; tel. (0502) 32213; f. 1951; poetry, literary; Publr LIAM MILLER.

Duffy, James & Co Ltd: 21 Shaw St, Dublin 2; f. 1830; official Catholic publications, religious books, works of Irish interest, plays; Man. Dir EOIN O'KEEFFE.

Dundalgan Press (W. Tempest) Ltd: Francis St, Dundalk; tel. (042) 34013; f. 1859; historical and biographical works; Man. Dir J. V. MCQUAID; Sec. BRIAN A. MCQUAID.

Eason & Son Ltd: 66 Middle Abbey St, Dublin 1; tel. (01) 733811; telex 32566; f. 1886; general Irish interest; Chair. W. H. CLARKE.

Educational Co of Ireland Ltd: POB 43A, Ballymount Rd, Walkinstown, Dublin 12; tel. (01) 500611; f. 1877, inc. 1910; school textbooks; Dirs F. MAGUIRE, S. O'NEILL, URSULA NÍ DHÁLAIGH.

C. J. Fallon Ltd: POB 1054, Lucan Rd, Palmerstown, Dublin 20; tel. (01) 265777; f. 1927; educational; Man. Dir H. J. MCNICHOLAS.

Folens and Co Ltd: Airton Rd, Tallaght, Co Dublin; tel. (01) 515311; educational; Man. Dir D. FOLENS.

Four Courts Press: Kill Lane, Blackrock, Co Dublin; tel. (01) 892922; f. 1977; philosophy, theology; Man. Dir MICHAEL ADAMS.

Gallery Press: Loughcrew, Oldcastle, Co Meath; tel. (049) 41779; f. 1970; poetry, plays, prose by Irish authors; Chief Exec. PETER FALLON.

Gill and Macmillan Ltd: Goldenbridge, Inchicore, Dublin 8; tel. (01) 531005; telex 92197; f. 1968; literature, biography, history, social sciences, theology, philosophy and textbooks; Man. Dir M. H. GILL.

Irish Academic Press: Kill Lane, Blackrock, Co Dublin; tel. (01) 892922; f. 1974; imprints: Irish University Press, Irish Academic Press, Ecclesia Press; history, travel, literature, bibliography; Man. Dir MICHAEL ADAMS.

Mercier Press Ltd: 4 Bridge St, POB 5, Cork; tel. (021) 504022; telex 75463; f. 1946; Irish folklore, history, law, music, bibliography, religious; Man. Dir JOHN SPILLANE.

The O'Brien Press: 20 Victoria Rd, Rathgar, Dublin 6; tel. (01) 979598; f. 1974; fiction, biography, history, general, children's; Man. Dir MICHAEL O'BRIEN; Gen. Editor IDE NÍ LAOGHAIRE.

Phoenix Publishing Co Ltd: 20 Parnell Sq., Dublin 1; tel. (01) 749215; educational; Dirs W. SHORTLAND, R. WALKER.

Poolbeg Press Ltd: Knocksedan House, Forrest Great, Swords, Co Dublin; tel. (01) 401133; telex 32895; f. 1976; fiction; Editor HILARY O'DONOGHUE.

The Round Hall Press: Kill Lane, Blackrock, Co Dublin; tel. (01) 892922; law books and journals; Man. Dir BART DALY.

Runa Press: 2 Belgrave Terrace, Monkstown, Co Dublin; tel. (01) 801869; f. 1942; belles-lettres, educational (university), essays, poetry, science, philosophy; Dir RHODA HANAGHAN.

Veritas Publications: Veritas House, 7-8 Lower Abbey St, Dublin 1; tel. (01) 788177; f. 1900; general, religion, school textbooks, audio, video tapes, multi-media education kits; Dir Rev. MARTIN TIERNEY.

Ward River Press: Knocksedan House, Forrest Great, Swords, Co Dublin; tel. (01) 401133; telex 24639; f. 1980; general; Editor HILARY O'DONOGHUE.

Wolfhound Press: 68 Mountjoy Sq., Dublin 1; tel. 740354; f. 1974; literature, biography, art, children's, fiction, history; Publr SEAMUS CASHMAN.

Government Publishing House

Stationery Office: Bishop St, Dublin 8; tel. (01) 781666.

PUBLISHERS' ASSOCIATION

Cumann Leabharfhoilsitheoirí Éireann (CLÉ) (Irish Book Publishers' Association): Book House Ireland, 65 Middle Abbey St, Dublin 1; tel. (01) 730108; f. 1970; 55 mems; Pres. STEPHEN MACDONOGH; Admin. CECILY GOLDEN.

Radio and Television

In 1986 there were an estimated 996,000 radio receivers and 918,000 television receivers in use, including 740,000 colour sets. In January 1989 new broadcasting legislation came into effect, providing for a new commercial television channel and a possible 26 commercial radio stations.

Directory

Radio Telefís Éireann (RTE): Donnybrook, Dublin 4; tel. (01) 693111; telex 93700; autonomous statutory corporation, f. 1960 under the Broadcasting Authority Act; controls and operates radio and television in the Republic; operations are financed by repayable state loans to a permitted limit of I£25m. and surpluses earned on the operating account, and the current expenditure by net licence revenue and sale of advertising time; governed by Authority of nine, appointed by the government; Chair. of Authority JAMES P. CULLITON; Dir-Gen. VINCENT FINN; Dir of Programmes (Television) BOB COLLINS; Dir of Programmes (Radio) KEVIN HEALY.

RADIO

RTE broadcasts on two channels (Radio 1 and Radio 2) approx. 262 hours a week, Cork local radio 13 hours a week and community radio 8-9 hours a week. Advertising is limited to 10% of transmission time.

Raidió na Gaeltachta: Casla, Connamara, Co Galway; tel. (091) 72235; telex 50815; f. 1972; broadcasts a minimum of 53 hours per week for Irish-speaking communities; financed by RTE; Controller BREANDÁN FEIRITÉAR; c. 60,000 listeners.

TELEVISION

Reception of both RTE-1, from seven main transmitters, and of RTE-2 is available to 98% of the population. Advertising is limited to 10% of transmission time. Regular transmissions: c. 3,400 hours yearly on RTE-1, 2,300 hours on RTE-2.

Finance

(cap. = capital; p.u. = paid up; auth. = authorized; res = reserves; dep. = deposits; m. = million; brs = branches; amounts in Irish pounds unless otherwise stated)

BANKING

Bank Ceannais na hÉireann (Central Bank of Ireland): POB 559, Dame St, Dublin 2; tel. (01) 716666; telex 31041; f. 1942; sole issuer of Irish currency in the State; cap. and res I£894.0m., dep. I£1,503.6m. (Dec. 1987); Gov. M. F. DOYLE; Gen. Man. TIMOTHY O'GRADY-WALSHE.

Principal Banks

Algemene Bank Nederland (Ireland) Ltd: 121-122 St Stephen's Green, Dublin 2; tel. (01) 717333; telex 93473; f. 1972; wholly-owned subsidiary of Algemene Bank Nederland NV, Amsterdam; cap. I£11.4m., dep. I£426.7m. (1987); Chair. D. E. WILLIAMS; Man. Dir C. V. REILLY.

Allied Irish Banks PLC: POB 452, Bankcentre, Ballsbridge, Dublin 4; tel. (01) 600311; telex 93768; f. 1966; mem. of Associated Banks; cap. issued I£53.0m., dep. I£7,767.8m. (1987); Chair. NIALL CROWLEY; Group CEO GERALD B. SCANLAN; 253 brs and sub-brs in the Republic of Ireland, 73 brs in Northern Ireland and Great Britain, 5 overseas brs and 1 rep. office.

Allied Irish Investment Bank PLC: Bankcentre, Ballsbridge, Dublin 4; tel. (01) 604733; telex 93917; f. 1966; merchant banking, corporate finance and investment management; cap. auth. I£10m., cap. p.u. I£8m., dep. I£1,524m., total assets I£1,611m. (1987); Chair. and Man. Dir PATRICK M. DOWLING; Sec. D. COVENEY.

Anglo Irish Bank Corporation PLC: 2 Lower Merriot St, Dublin 2; tel. (01) 760141; f. 1964; merchant bank concerned primarily with retail banking, instalment credit, leasing and treasury; acquired by City of Dublin Bank Group 1978; cap. auth. I£10m., issued I£7.4m., assets I£117.4m. (1987); Chair. THOMAS KENNY; CEO SEAN FITZPATRICK.

Ansbacher & Co Ltd: 52 Lower Leeson St, Dublin 2; tel. (01) 613699; telex 93241; f. 1950; dep. I£69.1m. (Dec. 1985); Chair. D. W. O'GRADY; Man. Dir G. J. MOLONEY.

Bank of America NT & SA: Russell Court, St Stephen's Green, Dublin 2; tel. (01) 781222; telex 93817.

Bank of Ireland: Head Office: Lower Baggot St, Dublin 2; tel. (01) 615933; telex 93427; 54 Donegall Place, Belfast BT1 5BX; tel. (0232) 244901; telex 74327; 2 Lombard St, London, EC3P 3EU; tel. (01) 626-2575; telex 8813504; f. 1783; cap. I£161.7m.; dep. I£7,289.3m. (1987); mem. of Associated Banks; Gov. Dr W. J. L. RYAN; CEO M. HELY HUTCHINSON; brs in Britain, Northern Ireland, Jersey, New York and Cayman Islands, rep. offices in Chicago and Frankfurt.

Banque Nationale de Paris (Ireland) Ltd: 111 St Stephen's Green West, Dublin 2; tel. (01) 712811; telex 90641; Chair. E. PHILIPPON; Gen. Man. PAUL-FRANÇOIS GAUVIN.

Barclays Bank PLC: 47/48 St Stephen's Green, Dublin 2; tel. (01) 611777; telex 30427; Gen. Man. for Ireland J. D. C. BURKE.

IRELAND

Chase Bank (Ireland) PLC: Russell Court, St Stephen's Green, Dublin 2; tel. (01) 784355; telex 93644; wholly-owned subsidiary of Chase Manhattan Overseas Banking Corpn; cap. I£2m., res I£8m., dep. I£186.5m.; Man. Dir Douglas K. Bonnar; Sec. D. White.

Cuideachta an Cháirde Thionnscail, Teoranta (Industrial Credit Corporation PLC): 32–34 Harcourt St, Dublin 2; tel. (01) 720055; telex 93220; f. 1933; state-owned; industrial and commercial financing; cap. I£34m., dep. I£354m. (Oct. 1986); Chair. J. T. Barton; Man. Dir F. A. Casey.

Guinness and Mahon Ltd: 17 College Green, Dublin 2; tel. (01) 796944; telex 93667; f. 1836; affiliated to Guinness, Mahon and Co Ltd, London; cap. auth. I£5.5m., issued I£5.5m.; Non-Exec. Dir Patrick Moorsom (Chair.); Chief Exec. Michael J. Pender.

Hill Samuel & Co (Ireland) Ltd: Hill Samuel House, Adelaide Rd, Dublin 2; tel. (01) 686566; telex 93760; f. 1964; subsidiary co of Hill Samuel Group PLC; merchant bank providing full banking services, investment portfolio management services and corporate finance services; cap. I£2.5m., res I£7.2m., dep. I£205m. (Oct. 1987); Chair. H. Donaldson; Man. Dir S. O'Shea.

Investment Bank of Ireland Ltd: 26 Fitzwilliam Place, Dublin 2; tel. (01) 616433; telex 93811; f. 1966; merchant bank; subsidiary of Bank of Ireland; auth. cap. I£10m., issued cap. I£6m., dep. I£1,345m. (March 1988); Chair. M. A. Keane.

Irish Bank of Commerce Ltd: 52/53 Harcourt St, Dublin 2; tel. (01) 756411; telex 90880; f. 1973; merchant bank; subsidiary of Crédit Commercial de France; cap. I£2m., res I£977,000, dep. I£114.5m. (1986); Chair. A. G. Murphy; CEO Gerard A. E. Watson.

Irish Intercontinental Bank Ltd: 91 Merrion Sq., Dublin 2; tel. (01) 760291; telex 33322; f. 1973; subsidiary of Krediedbank NV, Antwerp, Belgium; merchant bank; cap. issued I£7m.; dep. I£384.8m. (1986); Chair. D. McAleese; CEO Patrick McEvoy.

National Irish Bank Trust Co Ltd: 7-8 Wilton Terrace, Dublin 2; tel. (01) 785066; nominal cap. I£250,000; Chair. J. Lacey.

National Irish Investment Bank Ltd: 7 Wilton Terrace, Dublin 2; tel. (01) 785066; telex 93347; f. 1969; merchant bank; subsidiary of the National Irish Bank Ltd; cap. issued I£9.75m. (Dec. 1987); Chair. J. Lacey; Man. Dir M. K. Condell.

Smurfit Paribas Bank Ltd: 94 St Stephen's Green, Dublin 2; tel. (01) 774573; telex 90951; f. 1983; merchant bank; Chair. Ivor Kenny; CEO Patrick Miller.

Standard Chartered Bank Ireland Ltd: 18 Dawson St, Dublin 2; tel. (01) 776951; telex 93926; f. 1978; cap. I£2.5m.; Chair. J. Roche; Man. Dir H. G. MacWilliam.

Trinity Bank: 40 Dame St, Dublin 2; tel. (01) 796811; telex 93243; f. 1972; merchant bank; subsidiary of Brown Shipley and Co Ltd and asscd with the Philadelphia National Bank; cap. p.u. I£1.3m., res I£542,930 dep. I£42.3m. (March 1987); Chair. Lord Fárnham; Jt Man. Dirs Paul A. Cran, John McGilligan.

UDT Bank Ltd: 13-16 Fleet St, Dublin 2; tel. (01) 713311; telex 24146; Chair. Don C. McCrickard.

Ulster Bank Ltd: 33 College Green, Dublin 2; tel. (01) 777623; telex 25166; and 47 Donegall Place, Belfast, BT1 5AU; tel. (0232) 220222; telex 747334; subsidiary of National Westminster Bank PLC (United Kingdom); issued and p.u. cap. £4.25m., dep. £1,387m.; Chair. F. J. O'Reilly; CEO V. Chambers; 157 brs.

Ulster Investment Bank Ltd: 2 Hume St, Dublin 2; tel. (01) 613444; telex 93980; f. 1973; mem. of National Westminster Bank Group; cap. I£3m.; res I£21.1m., dep. I£684m.; Chair. Martin Rafferty; CEO Brian McConnell.

Savings Banks

Post Office Savings Bank: College House, Townsend St, Dublin 2; tel. (01) 728888; telex 33444; dep. I£1,329m. (Dec. 1987); f. 1861; Man. of Savings R. McDonnell; over 1,400 brs.

Association of Trustee Savings Banks in Ireland: Administration Centre, Douglas, Cork; tel. (021) 361301; telex 75347; f. 1817; total assets exceed I£730m.; Jt Secs M. N. Conlon, G. F. Walsh.

Banking Associations

The Institute of Bankers in Ireland: Nassau House, Nassau St, Dublin 2; tel. (01) 793311; f. 1898; Pres. Mark Hely Hutchinson; CEO and Sec. Patrick J. Rock.

Irish Bankers' Federation: Nassau House, Nassau St, Dublin 2; tel. (01) 715311; telex 93957; Dir Gen. James A. Bardon; Pres. Dr W. J. L. Ryan.

STOCK EXCHANGE

The Stock Exchange (Irish Unit): 24–28 Anglesea St, Dublin 2; tel. (01) 778808; telex 93437; f. 1799 as the Dublin Stock Exchange; merged in 1971 with the Cork Stock Exchange to form the Irish Stock Exchange; amalgamated in 1973 with the United Kingdom stock exchanges to form The Stock Exchange, centred in London; Pres. K. Beaton; Gen. Man. Tom Healy; 99 mems.

INSURANCE

Principal Companies

Abbey Life Assurance (Ireland) Ltd: Abbey Life House, Temple Rd, Blackrock, Co Dublin; tel. (01) 832377; f. 1981; Chair. P. A. C. Seymour; Gen. Man. J. L. Rennie.

Cornhill Insurance PLC: Russell Court, St Stephen's Green, Dublin 2; tel. (01) 730622; Man. S. B. Hehir.

Eagle Star Insurance Co Ltd: Shield House, 45-47 Pembroke Rd, Ballsbridge, Dublin 4; tel. (01) 683943; telex 30737.

Guardian Royal Exchange Assurance PLC: 35–38 St Stephen's Green, Dublin 2; tel. (01) 61500; f. 1968; issued cap. 34.7m. (1978); Chair. J. E. H. Collins; Man. Dir P. R. Dugdale.

Hibernian Insurance Co Ltd: Haddington Rd, Dublin 4; tel. (01) 608288; telex 30872; f. 1908; Hibernian Fire and General Insurance Co Ltd; fire and general; cap. p.u. 2m.; Chair. Patrick A. Duggan; Dir and Gen. Man. E. F. Walsh.

Irish Life Assurance PLC: Irish Life Centre, Lower Abbey St, Dublin 1; tel. (01) 720288; f. 1939; cap. p.u. 500,000; industrial and life assurance, annuity group assurance and pension schemes; Chair. John Reihill; Man. Dir T. D. Kingston; Sec. L. G. Andrews.

Irish National Insurance Co PLC: 9-10 Dawson St, Dublin 2; tel. (01) 776881; telex 30460; f. 1919; fire, engineering, third party, employers' liability, motor, general, accident, burglary, bonds, livestock, reinsurance, contractors all risks; brs in London and Paris; member of New Ireland Holdings PLC Group; Chair. Mairtin McCullough; Man. Dir A. J. Hatch.

Irish Public Bodies Mutual Insurances Ltd: 1 Westmoreland St, Dublin 2; tel. (01) 778000; telex 93290; f. 1926; fire and accident; Chair. Josephine Quinlan; Gen. Man. B. Doyle; Sec. and Asst Gen. Man. Eamon Smyth.

New Ireland Assurance Co PLC: 11-12 Dawson St, Dublin 2; tel. (01) 717077; telex 90692; f. 1924; auth. cap. I£7.6m.; Chair. Eoin Ryan; Man. Dir John F. Casey; Sec. E. O'Brien.

Norwich Union Life Insurance Society and **Norwich Union Fire Insurance Society Ltd:** 60/63 Dawson St, Dublin 2; tel. (01) 717181; telex 93426; f. 1797, in Ireland 1816; Chair. M. D. Corbett.

Phoenix Assurance PLC: Phoenix House, 7/9 South Leinster St, Dublin 2; tel. (01) 764091; f. 1782; fire, accident, motor, marine and aviation; cap. p.u. 61m.; Man. J. E. Doherty.

PMPA Insurance PLC: Wolfe Tone House, Wolfe Tone St, Dublin 1; tel. (01) 726444; telex 31003; Administrator. Kevin Kelly.

Shield Insurance Co Ltd: Shield House, 45-47 Pembroke Rd, Ballsbridge, Dublin 4; tel. (01) 683943; telex 30737; f. 1950; general, excluding life; Chair. J. G. Ronan.

Standard Life Assurance Co: 90 St Stephen's Green, Dublin 2; tel. (01) 757411; est. in Scotland 1825, operating in Ireland since 1834; life assurance and annuities; assets exceed £15,000m. (sterling); Chair. (in Edinburgh) Norman Lessels; Man. Dir A. Scott Bell.

Zurich Insurance Co: Stephen Court, 18–21 St Stephen's Green, Dublin 2; tel. (01) 764276; Man. E. O. Baily.

Insurance Associations

Insurance Institute of Ireland: Office and Library: 32 Nassau St, Dublin 2; tel. 772753; f. 1885; Pres. D. D. Ryan; Sec.-Gen. M. D. Matson; 3,271 mems.

Irish Insurance Federation: Russell House, Stephen's Green, Dublin 2; tel. (01) 782499; Sec. A. Cassells.

Trade and Industry

CHAMBERS OF COMMERCE

Association of Western Chambers of Commerce of Ireland: James St, Westport; mem. chambers: Ballina, Ballyshannon, Castlebar, Ennis, Galway, Letterkenny, Limerick, Sligo, Westport; Chair. Charles N. Rabbitt; Sec. Michael Browne.

The Chambers of Commerce of Ireland: 7 Clare St, Dublin 2; tel. (01) 612888; telex 90716; f. 1923; Pres. D. Miller; Deputy Pres. M. Quinn; Sec.-Gen. P. Skehan; 52 mems.

EMPLOYERS' ASSOCIATIONS

Confederation of Irish Industry: Confederation House, Kildare St, Dublin 2; tel. (01) 779801; telex 93502; f. 1932; 2,000 mems; Pres.

IRELAND

Dermot P. Whelan; Dir-Gen. Liam Connellan; Sec. Gerard Sheehy.

Federated Union of Employers: Baggot Bridge House, 84–86 Lower Baggot St, Dublin 2; tel. (01) 601011; telex 93806; 3,500 mems; Pres. A. G. Grogan; Dir-Gen. John Dunne; Sec. John Casey.

TRADE UNIONS

Irish Congress of Trade Unions: 19 Raglan Rd, Dublin 4; tel. (01) 680641; f. 1959; represents 666,900 workers in the Republic and Northern Ireland; Gen. Sec. Donal Nevin; 83 affiliated unions (July 1988).

Principal affiliated unions:

*These unions have their head office in the United Kingdom and the membership figure given is for the Republic of Ireland and Northern Ireland together.

*__Amalgamated Transport and General Workers' Union:__ Transport House, 102 High St, Belfast, BT1 2DL; tel. (0232) 232381; telex 747202; Irish Sec. J. Freeman; 100,000 mems.

*__Amalgamated Union of Engineering Workers—Engineering Section:__ 26–34 Antrim Rd, Belfast, BT15 2AA; tel. (0232) 743271; Sec. J. Blair; 26,812 mems (1983).

*__Amalgamated Union of Engineering Workers, Technical, Administrative and Supervisory Section:__ 26–34 Antrim Rd, Belfast, BT15 2AA; tel. (0232) 746189; Irish Rep. J. Bowers; 6,350 mems.

*__Association of Professional, Executive, Clerical and Computer Staff:__ 291 Antrim Rd, Belfast, BT15 2GZ; tel. (0232) 748678; Area Sec. P. A. McCartan; 4,000 mems.

*__Association of Scientific, Technical and Managerial Staffs:__ R. Jeary, New Forge Lane, Malone Rd, Belfast, BT9 5NW; Irish Rep. J. Tierney, 38 Lower Leeson St, Dublin 2; tel. (01) 762306; 20,000 mems.

Automobile, General Engineering and Mechanical Operatives' Union: 22 North Frederick St, Dublin 1; tel. (01) 744233; Gen. Sec. Laurence Doyle; 3,500 mems.

Bakery and Food Workers' Amalgamated Union: 12 Merrion Sq., Dublin 2; tel. (01) 619457; f. 1889; Gen. Sec. Patrick Shanley; 4,000 mems.

Building and Allied Trades' Union: Arus Hibernia, 13 Blessington St, Dublin 7; tel. (01) 301911; incorporating National Union of Woodworkers and Woodcutting Machinists and the Ancient Guild of Incorporated Brick and Stonelayers and Allied Trades' Union; Gen. Sec. Patrick O'Shaughnessy.

Civil and Public Services Staff Union: 72 Lower Leeson St, Dublin 2; tel. (01) 765394; Gen. Sec. John O'Dowd; 12,003 mems.

Communications Union of Ireland: 575–577 North Circular Rd, Dublin 1; tel. (01) 743402; f. 1922; Gen. Sec. Seamus DePaor; 9,000 mems (1985).

*__Confederation of Health Service Employees:__ 27 Ulsterville Ave, Lisburn Rd, Belfast, BT9 7AS; tel. (0232) 662994; Irish Rep. W. F. Jackson; 19,000 mems.

Electrical Trades Union: 5 Cavendish Row, Dublin 1; tel. (01) 747047; f. 1923; Gen. Pres. Gary Browne; 10,538 mems.

*__Electrical, Electronic, Telecommunication and Plumbing Union:__ AUEW House, 1a Adela St, Belfast, BT14 6AW; tel. (0232) 740244; Irish Rep. C. C. Lowry.

Electricity Supply Board Officers' Association: 43 East James's Place, Lower Baggot St, Dublin 2; tel. (01) 767444; f. 1959; Gen. Sec. John Hall; Pres. Eamon Kelly; 3,035 mems.

Federated Workers' Union of Ireland: 29/30 Parnell Sq., Dublin 1; tel. (01) 733977; f. 1924; merged with Federation of Rural Workers 1981 and with the Irish Women Workers' Union in 1984; Gen. Sec. William A. Attley; 52,000 mems.

*__Furniture, Timber and Allied Trades Union:__ 52 Peter's Hill, Belfast, BT13 2AB; tel. (0232) 243588; District Organizer J. Willey; 1,302 mems (1986).

*__General, Municipal, Boilermakers and Allied Trades Union:__ 102 Lisburn Rd, Belfast, BT9 6AG; tel. (0232) 681421; T. D. Douglas; 11,001 mems.

Ireland Association of Secondary Teachers: 36 Lower Baggot St, Dublin 2; tel. (01) 607444; f. 1909; Gen. Sec. Kieran Mulvey; 12,000 mems.

Irish Distributive and Administrative Trade Union (IDATU): O'Lehane House, 9 Cavendish Row, Dublin 1; tel. (01) 746321; f. 1901; Gen. Sec. John Mitchell; 21,000 mems.

Irish Federation of Musicians and Associated Professions: Cecilia House, 63 Lower Gardiner St, Dublin 1; tel. (01) 744645; Gen. Sec. P. Pringle; 1,000 mems.

Irish Medical Organization: 10 Fitzwilliam Place, Dublin 2; tel. (01) 767273; Sec. Gen. Michael B. McCann; Deputy Sec.-Gen. Ed Madden; 4,000 mems.

Irish Municipal Employees' Trade Union: 8 Gardiner Place, Dublin 1; tel. (01) 743362; Gen. Sec. Sean Redmond; 3,000 mems.

Irish National Painters and Decorators' Trade Union: 76 Aungier St, Dublin 2; tel. (01) 751720; Gen. Sec. Gerard Fleming; 3,010 mems.

Irish National Teachers' Organization: 35 Parnell Sq., Dublin 1; tel. (01) 722533; f. 1868; Pres. T. Honan; Sec. E. G. Quigley; 24,600 mems (1987).

Irish National Union of Vintners', Grocers' and Allied Trades Assistants: 20 Parnell Sq., Dublin 1; tel. (01) 746634; f. 1917; Gen. Sec. J. Cagney; 4,680 mems.

Irish Transport and General Workers' Union: Liberty Hall, Dublin 1; tel. (01) 749731; f. 1909; Gen. Pres. John F. Carroll; Gen. Sec. Chris Kirwan; 160,000 mems.

Local Government and Public Services Union: 9 Gardiner Place, Dublin 1; tel. (01) 728899; Gen. Sec. P. Flynn; 18,000 mems (1987).

Marine, Port and General Workers' Union: 14 Gardiner Place, Dublin 1; tel. (01) 726566; Gen. Sec. Seamus Redmond; 7,000 mems.

National Association of Transport Employees: 33 Parnell Sq., Dublin 1; tel. (01) 743971; Gen. Sec. M. Cox; 3,445 mems.

National Engineering and Electrical Trade Union: 6 Gardiner Row, Dublin 1; tel. (01) 745935; f. 1966 as result of merger between National Engineering Union, National Union of Scalemakers and Irish Engineering Industrial and Electrical Trade Union; Jt Gen. Secs K. M. P. McConnell (Financial), I. J. Moneley (Industrial); 10,000 mems.

*__National Graphical Association (1982):__ Graphic House, 107 Clonskeagh Rd, Dublin 6; tel. (01) 697788; Gen. Sec. A. D. Dubbins; Regional Officer N. S. Broughall; 4,864 mems.

*__National Union of Journalists (Irish Council):__ Liberty Hall, Dublin 1; tel. (01) 748694; Chair. Michael Foley; National Exec. mems Kieran Fagan, Barry Coughlan (Republic of Ireland), Paul McGill (Northern Ireland); 2,943 mems (1987).

*__National Union of Public Employees:__ 523 Antrim Rd, Belfast, BT15 6BS; tel. (0232) 23988; Irish Rep. Ms I. McCormack; 12,000 mems.

*__National Union of Tailors and Garment Workers:__ Irish Divisional Office, 44 Elmwood Ave, Belfast, BT9 6BB; tel. (0232) 662942; Irish Rep. Martin Dummigan; 10,200 mems.

Postal and Telecommunications Workers' Union: 53 Parnell Sq., Dublin 1; tel. (01) 726911; f. 1923; Gen. Sec. David T. Begg; 10,000 mems.

Public Service Executive Union: 30 Merrion Square, Dublin 2; tel. (01) 764315; f. 1893; Gen. Sec. D. Murphy; 4,500 mems.

Teachers' Union of Ireland: 73 Orwell Rd, Rathgar, Dublin 6; tel. (01) 961588; Gen. Sec. James Dorney; 7,000 mems.

*__Transport Salaried Staffs' Association:__ 7 Gardiner Place, Dublin 1; tel. (01) 743467; f. 1897; Sec. D. Casey; 3,025 mems.

*__Union of Construction, Allied Trades and Technicians:__ 56 Parnell Sq. West, Dublin 1; tel. (01) 731599; Republic of Ireland Rep. Noel O'Neill; 18,178 mems.

Union of Professional and Technical Civil Servants: 16 Earlsfort Terrace, Dublin 2; tel. (01) 789855; f. 1919; Gen. Sec. G. Maxwell; 6,000 mems.

*__Union of Shop, Distributive and Allied Workers:__ 1st Floor, Leicester House, 61–63 Royal Ave, Belfast, BT1 1FX; tel. (0232) 241851; Sec. Alan White; 6,905 mems.

Principal unaffiliated unions:

Institute of Journalists (Irish Region): The Lodge, Glendalough, Co Wicklow; tel. (0404) 5196; Chair. George Peche; Education Officer Valerie Cox.

Irish Bank Officials' Association: 93 St Stephen's Green, Dublin 2; tel. (01) 722255; telex 90746; f. 1917; Gen. Sec. Job M. Stott.

National Busworkers' Union: 54 Parnell Sq., Dublin 1; tel. (01) 744205; Gen. Sec. Thomas Darby.

Post Office Officials' Association: Lismullen, Navan; tel. (046) 378178; Gen. Sec. Eoghan O'Neill.

DEVELOPMENT ORGANIZATIONS

Córas Tráchtála (Irish Export Board): Merrion Hall, Strand Rd, Sandymount, Dublin 4; tel. (01) 695011; telex 93678; f.1959; promotion and development of exports and aid for Irish exporters and a comprehensive service to foreign buyers, financed by a

IRELAND

grant-in-aid; 24 overseas offices; Chair. C. McCarthy; CEO A. P. McCarthy.

Industrial Development Authority of Ireland: Wilton Park House, Wilton Place, Dublin 2; tel. (01) 686633; telex 93431; f. 1949; autonomous state-sponsored organization with national responsibility for industrial development; administers financial incentive schemes for new industrial investment; aims (i) to promote investment in manufacturing and internationally-traded services (including financial services); (ii) to develop indigenous industry; (iii) to stimulate entrepreneurial and small-scale industries; 19 overseas offices; Man. Dir Padraic White; Exec. Dir Kieran McGowan.

Irish Co-operative Organization Society Ltd: The Plunkett House, 84 Merrion Sq., Dublin 2; tel. (01) 764783; telex 30379; f. 1894 as co-ordinating body for agricultural co-operative movement; Pres. Michael Gibbons; Dir-Gen. J. C. Moloney; mems: 200 co-operatives, approx. 140,000 farmers.

Irish Goods Council: Merrion Hall, Strand Rd, Dublin 4; tel. (01) 696011; serves industry in the home market; Chair. Tom Hardiman; CEO Vivian Murray.

PRINCIPAL NATIONALIZED INDUSTRIES

An Post (The Post Office): GPO, Dublin 1; tel. (01) 728888; telex 33444; f. 1984; provides national postal, savings and agency services through 2,200 outlets; 8,951 employees; Chair. Feargal Quinn; CEO Gerard P. Harvey.

Bord Gais Eireann (BGE) (The Irish Gas Board): POB 51, Inchera, Little Island, Co Cork; tel. (021) 509199; telex 75087; 24A D'Olier St, Dublin 2; tel. (01) 797822; telex 32888; f. 1975; state gas transmission company; Chair. P. J. Dineen; CEO J. J. Lynch.

Bord na Mona (Irish Peat Board): Lower Baggot St, Dublin 2; tel. (01) 688555; telex 30206; f. 1946; develops Ireland's peat resources, produces milled peat and machine turf for electricity generation, machine turf and briquettes for general, industrial and domestic use and horticultural moss peat products for gardeners; 4,000 employees; Chair. B. Halligan; Man. Dir E. O'Connor.

Bord Solathair an Leictreachais (Electricity Supply Board): 27 Lower Fitzwilliam St, Dublin 2; tel. (01) 771821; telex 25313; f. 1927; controls 11 generating stations operating on peat, 2 oil stations, 2 oil or gas stations, 2 gas stations, 10 hydro stations and 2 coal-fired stations; 12,454 employees; Chair. Prof. C. T. G. Dillon; CEO P. J. Moriarty.

Comhlucht Groighe Naisiunta Na h-Eireann Teoranta (Irish National Stud Co Ltd): Tully, Kildare; tel. (045) 21251; telex 60706; f. 1946 primarily for the running of a stud farm for thoroughbred horses at the National Stud and in particular to provide the services of first-class stallions; advisory service to breeders; farming activities such as raising cattle, hay etc.; cap. issued I£3.4m. held by minister of finance; 54 employees; Chair. John M. Oxx; Man. John Clarke.

Irish Steel Ltd: Haulbowline, Cobh, Co Cork; tel. (021) 811731; telex 76123; 25 St Stephen's Green, Dublin; tel. (01) 600200; telex 76123; f. 1947; steelmaking, rolling and galvanized sheetmaking; auth. cap. I£125m.; 555 employees; Chair. W. Hugh O'Connor; CEO L. S. Coughlan.

Nitrigin Eireann Teoranta (NET): 60 Northumberland Rd, Dublin 4; tel. (01) 689833; telex 93977; f. 1961; production of nitrogenous fertilizers and complete fertilizers; cap. auth. I£77.5m.; 800 employees; Chair. S. MacHale; Man. Dir T. A. Jago.

Siuicre Eireann Cpt (Irish Sugar PLC): St Stephen's Green House, Dublin 2; tel. (01) 767501; telex 30662; f. 1933; processing of sugar beet grown by 7,000 Irish farmers for domestic and industrial purposes, processing of vegetables for human consumption and formulation of other food products, production of animal feedstuffs, manufacture of specialized machinery, and production and distribution of ground limestone; 2,864 employees; Chair. B. M. Cahill; Man. Dir C. K. Comerford.

   Erin Foods Ltd: St Stephen's Green House, Dublin 2; tel. (01) 767501; telex 25352; f. 1958; a division of Irish Sugar PLC; processing of vegetables, manufacture of soups and formulated products; Group Chair. James E. Fitzpatrick; Man. Dir Maurice Sheehy.

Telecom Eireann: St Stephen's Green West, Dublin 2; tel. (01) 714444; telex 91111; f. 1984; provides telecommunications services; 15,000 employees; Chair. M. W. J. Smurfit.

In addition to these there exist numerous smaller state-sponsored bodies. Among those not mentioned elsewhere in this chapter are: The Irish Livestock and Meat Board, The Voluntary Health Insurance Board, The Hospitals Trust Board and the Institute for Industrial Research and Standards.

Transport

Coras Iompair Eireann (CIE) (The Irish Transport Co): Heuston Station, Dublin 8; tel. (01) 771871; telex 25153; f. 1945; government-appointed; controls the railways, inland waterways and road transport services; Chair. and CEO G. T. Paul Conlon.

RAILWAYS

In 1985 there were 1,876 km (1,166 miles) of track, of which 37 km (23 miles) were electrified, controlled by Coras Iompair Eireann (see above). The Dublin Area Rapid Transit (DART) was built at a cost of I£113m., to provide extra passenger capacity.

INLAND WATERWAYS

The commercial canal services of CIE have been discontinued. However, the Grand Canal and the canal link into the Barrow Navigation System are maintained by the CIE for use by pleasure craft. The River Shannon is navigable for 241 km (150 miles). Other inland waterways are estimated at 188 km (117 miles).

ROADS

At 31 December 1986 there were 92,303 km (57,354 miles) of roads of which 5,255 km (3,265 miles) were main roads. About 94% of all roads were surfaced.

SHIPPING

The principal sea ports are Dublin, Dun Laoghaire, Cork, Waterford, Rosslare, Limerick, Foynes, Galway, New Ross, Drogheda, Dundalk, Fenit and Whiddy Island.

B+I Line PLC (British & Irish Steam Packet Co Ltd): Ferryport, Alexandra Rd, Dublin 1; tel. (01) 788077; telex 33303; f. 1836; drive on/drive off car ferry and roll on/roll off freight services between Dublin and Holyhead, and Rosslare and Pembroke; roll-on/roll-off freight service between Dublin and Liverpool; groupage and roll-on/roll-off from all parts of Britain to and from Ireland; unit load freight service between Dublin and Le Havre, Rotterdam and Antwerp; agents in Ireland for Sealand Inc., C.M.A. and Isle of Man Steam Packet Co; Chief Exec. J. J. Kennedy; Sec. Pem Ryan; 6 vessels and other vessels on charter.

Celtic Coasters Ltd: Beech Hill, Clonskeagh, Dublin 4; tel. (01) 694300; telex 93793; f. 1958; shipowners/ship-agents; also in Cork; associate company of Dublin Shipping Ltd; Chair. L. St J. Devlin; Gen. Man. E. Connor; 1 tanker.

Dublin Shipping Ltd: 6 Beech Hill, Clonskeagh, Dublin 4; tel. (01) 696477; telex 93793; Chair. C. Jones; Man. Dir E. Connor; 5 tankers.

Irish Shipping Ltd: Merrion Hall, Strand Rd, Dublin 4; tel. (01) 695522; telex 25126; f. 1941; world-wide tramping service; Dir and Gen. Man. W. A. O'Neill; 10 carriers.

Sealink British Ferries: Adelaide House, 7 Haddington Terrace, Dun Laoghaire, Co Dublin; tel. (01) 807777; telex 30847; services between Dun Laoghaire and Holyhead, Rosslare and Fishguard, passengers, drive-on/drive-off car ferry, roll-on/roll-off services; Dublin (North Wall) and Holyhead containers and freight.

CIVIL AVIATION

There are international airports at Shannon, Dublin, Cork and Knock, but only Shannon is used for transatlantic flights. The national airline is Aer Lingus.

Aer Rianta (Irish Airports): Dublin Airport, Dublin; tel. (01) 379900; telex 31266; responsible for the management and development of Dublin, Shannon and Cork airports; Chair. F. J. Boland; CEO Martin Dully.

Airlines

Aer Lingus PLC: POB 180, Dublin Airport, Dublin; tel. (01) 370011; telex 31404; f. 1936; incorporated Aerlinte Eireann 1947; regular services to 29 cities in Europe, the USSR and the USA; Chair. Brian A. Slowey; CEO David Kennedy; fleet of 3 Boeing 747, 8 737-200, 4 737-200C, 4 One-Eleven 200, 4 Shorts 360, 2 737-300.

Aer Turas Teoranta: Corballis Rd South, Dublin Airport, Dublin; tel. (01) 379131; telex 33393; f. 1962; world-wide cargo charter services; CEO P. J. Cousins; fleet of 1 Douglas DC8-63FQN, 1 Canadair CL-44J.

Ryanair: College Park House, Nassau St, Dublin 2; telex 91608; f. 1986; scheduled carrier; Chair. Arthur Walls; CEO Eugene O'Neill; fleet of 2 Rombac 1-11-500, 2 HS.748, 1 Bandeirante.

Tourism

Intensive marketing campaigns have been undertaken in recent years to develop new markets for Irish tourism. The country has

IRELAND

numerous beauty spots, notably the Killarney Lakes and the west coast. In 1987 a total of 2,662,000 foreign tourists (excluding excursionists) visited the Republic.

Bord Faílte Eíreann (Irish Tourist Board): Baggot St Bridge, Dublin 2; tel. (01) 765871; telex 93755; f. 1955; Chair. and Chief Exec. MARTIN DULLY; Sec. NIALL REDDY.

Dublin and Eastern Regional Tourism Organization Ltd: 1 Clarinda Park North, Dun Laoghaire, Co Dublin; tel. (01) 808571; telex 93560; Chair. T. ELMORE; Man. MATT MCNULTY.

ISRAEL

Introductory Survey

Location, Climate, Language, Religion, Flag, Capital

The State of Israel lies in western Asia, occupying a narrow strip of territory on the eastern shore of the Mediterranean Sea. The country also has a narrow outlet to the Red Sea at the northern tip of the Gulf of Aqaba. All of Israel's land frontiers are with Arab countries, the longest being with Egypt to the west and with Jordan to the east. Lebanon lies to the north, and Syria to the north-east. The climate is Mediterranean, with hot, dry summers, when the maximum temperature in Jerusalem is generally between 30°C and 35°C (86°F to 95°F), and mild, rainy winters, with a minimum temperature in Jerusalem of about 5°C (41°F). The climate is sub-tropical on the coast but more extreme in the Negev Desert, in the south, and near the shores of the Dead Sea (a lake on the Israeli-Jordanian frontier), where the summer temperature may exceed 50°C (122°F). The official language of Israel is Hebrew, spoken by about two-thirds of the population, including most Jews. About 15% of Israeli residents, including Muslim Arabs, speak Arabic (which is also the language spoken by the inhabitants of the 'occupied areas'), while many European languages are also spoken. About 82% of the population profess adherence to Judaism, the officially recognized religion of Israel, while almost 14% are Muslims. The national flag (proportions 250 by 173) has a white background, with a six-pointed blue star composed of two overlapping triangles (the 'Shield of David') between two horizontal blue stripes near the upper and lower edges. The Israeli Government has designated the city of Jerusalem (part of which is Jordanian territory annexed by Israel in 1967) as the country's capital, but this is not recognized by the United Nations, and most foreign governments maintain their embassies in Tel-Aviv.

Recent History

The Zionist movement, launched in Europe in the 19th century, aimed at the re-establishment of an autonomous community of Jews in their historic homeland of Palestine (the 'Promised Land'). The growth of Zionism was partly due to the insecurity that was felt by Jewish minorities in many European countries as a result of racial and religious hostility, known as anti-semitism, which sometimes included discrimination, persecution and even massacre.

Palestine, for long inhabited by Arabs, became a part of Turkey's Ottoman Empire in the 16th century. During the First World War (1914–18), when Turkey was allied with Germany, the Arabs under Ottoman rule rebelled. Palestine was occupied by British forces in 1917–18, when the Turks withdrew. Meanwhile, in November 1917, the British Foreign Secretary, Arthur Balfour, declared British support for the establishment of a Jewish national home in Palestine, providing that the rights of 'the existing non-Jewish communities' there were safeguarded. The Balfour Declaration, as it is known, was confirmed by the governments of other countries then at war with Turkey.

British occupation of Palestine continued after the war, when the Ottoman Empire was dissolved. In 1920 the territory was formally placed under British administration by a League of Nations mandate, which incorporated the Balfour Declaration. British rule in Palestine was hampered by the conflict between the declared obligations to the Jews and the rival claims of the indigenous Arab majority. In accordance with the mandate, Jewish settlers were admitted to Palestine (whose population in 1919 was almost entirely Arab), but only on the basis of limited annual quotas. Serious anti-Jewish rioting by Arabs occurred in 1921 and 1929. Attempts to restrict immigration led to Jewish-sponsored riots in 1933. The extreme persecution of Jews by Nazi Germany caused an increase in the flow of Jewish immigrants, both legal and illegal, but this intensified the unrest in Palestine. In 1937 a British proposal to establish separate Jewish and Arab states, while retaining a British-mandated area, was accepted by most of the Zionists but rejected by the Arabs, and by the end of that year the conflict between the two communities had developed into open warfare, which continued throughout 1938. A British offer of eventual independence for a bi-communal Palestinian state, made in 1939, led to further incidents, but the scheme was postponed because of the Second World War (1939–45). During the war the Nazis caused the deaths of an estimated 6m. Jews in central and eastern Europe, more than one-third of the world's total Jewish population. The enormity of this massacre, known to Jews as the Holocaust, greatly increased international sympathy for Jewish claims to a homeland in Palestine.

After the war, there was strong opposition by Palestinian Jews to continued British occupation. Numerous terrorist attacks were made by Jewish groups against British targets. In November 1947 the UN approved a plan for the partition of Palestine into two states, one Jewish (covering about 56% of the area) and one Arab. The plan was, however, rejected by Arab states and by the leadership of the Palestinian Arabs. Meanwhile, the conflict between the two communities in Palestine escalated into full-scale war.

On 14 May 1948 the United Kingdom (UK) terminated its Palestine mandate, and Jewish leaders immediately proclaimed the State of Israel, with David Ben-Gurion as Prime Minister. Although the new nation had no agreed frontiers, it quickly received wide international recognition. Neighbouring Arab states sent forces into Palestine in an attempt to crush Israel. Fighting continued until January 1949. The cease-fire agreements left Israel in control of 75% of Palestine, including West Jerusalem. The *de facto* territory of Israel was thus nearly one-third greater than the area that had been assigned to the Jewish state under the UN partition plan. Most of the remainder of Palestine was controlled by Jordanian forces. This area, known as the West Bank (or, to Israelis, as Judaea and Samaria), was annexed by Jordan in December 1949 and, following a referendum, fully incorporated in April 1950. No independent Arab state was established in Palestine, and the independence of Israel was not recognized by any Arab government until 1980.

When the British mandate ended, the Jewish population of Palestine was about 650,000 (or 40% of the total), compared with 56,000 in 1920. With the establishment of Israel, the new state encouraged further Jewish immigration. The Law of Return, adopted in July 1950, established a right of immigration for all Jews. The rapid influx of Jewish settlers enabled Israel to consolidate its specifically Jewish character. At the same time, many former Arab residents of Palestine had become refugees in neighbouring countries, mainly Jordan and Lebanon. About 400,000 Arabs had evacuated their homes prior to May 1948, and another 400,000 fled subsequently. In 1964 some exiled Palestinian Arabs formed the Palestine Liberation Organization (PLO), with the aim, at that time, of the overthrow of Israel.

In July 1956 the Egyptian Government announced the nationalization of the company that operated the Suez Canal. In response, Israel launched an attack on Egypt in October, occupying the Gaza Strip (part of Palestine under Egyptian occupation since 1949) and the Sinai Peninsula. After pressure from the UN and the USA, Israeli forces evacuated these areas in 1957, when a UN Emergency Force (UNEF) was established in Sinai. In May 1967 the United Arab Republic (Egypt) secured the withdrawal of UNEF from its territory. Egyptian forces immediately reoccupied the garrison at Sharm esh-Sheikh, near the southern tip of Sinai, and closed the Straits of Tiran to Israeli shipping, effectively blockading the Israeli port of Eilat, situated at the head of the Gulf of Aqaba. In retaliation, Israel attacked Egypt and other Arab countries in June. Israeli forces quickly overcame opposition and made substantial territorial gains. The Six-Day War, as it is known, left Israel in possession of all Jerusalem, the West Bank area of Jordan, the Sinai Peninsula in Egypt, the Gaza Strip and the Golan Heights in Syria. East Jerusalem was almost immediately integrated into the State of Israel, while the other conquered territories were regarded as 'occupied areas'.

Ben-Gurion resigned in June 1963 and was succeeded by Levi Eshkol. Three of the parties in the ruling coalition merged to form the Israel Labour Party in 1968. On the death of Eshkol in February 1969, Golda Meir was elected Prime Minister by the

Labour Party executive. She continued in office following the general elections of October 1969 and December 1973. A cease-fire between Egypt and Israel was arranged in August 1970, so ending the two years of war of attrition in the Suez Canal zone, but other Arab states and Palestinian Arab guerrilla, mainly PLO, groups continued their hostilities. Another war between the Arab states and Israel broke out on 6 October 1973, coinciding with Yom Kippur (the Day of Atonement), the holiest day of the Jewish year. In simultaneous attacks on Israeli-held territory, Egyptian forces crossed the Suez Canal and reoccupied part of Sinai, while Syrian troops launched an offensive on the Golan Heights. Israel made cease-fire agreements with Egypt and Syria on 24 October. A disengagement agreement with Syria was signed in May 1974. A further disengagement agreement between Israel and Egypt was signed in September 1975.

General Itzhak Rabin had succeeded Golda Meir as Prime Minister of a Labour Alignment coalition after her resignation in June 1974. In December 1976 Rabin lost the support of the National Religious Party (NRP) and subsequently resigned, continuing in office in a caretaker capacity until May 1977, when the Labour Alignment was unexpectedly defeated in a general election. The Likud (Consolidation) bloc, led by Menachem Begin of the Herut (Freedom) Party, was able to form a government in June 1977 with the support of minority parties.

In November 1977 President Anwar Sadat of Egypt visited Israel, indicating a tacit recognition by Egypt of the State of Israel. In September 1978 President Carter of the USA, President Sadat and Prime Minister Begin met at Camp David, in the USA, and drew up two agreements. The first was a 'framework for peace in the Middle East', providing for autonomy for the West Bank and the Gaza Strip after a transitional period of five years, and the second was a 'framework for the conclusion of a peace treaty between Egypt and Israel', which was subsequently signed in Washington on 26 March 1979. In February 1980 Egypt became the first Arab country to grant diplomatic recognition to Israel. Israel's phased withdrawal from Sinai was completed in April 1982. The approval in July 1980 of legislation which stated explicitly that Jerusalem should be for ever the undivided capital of Israel, and Israel's formal annexation of the Golan Heights in December 1981, subsequently inhibited prospects of agreement on Palestinian autonomy.

In June 1982 a major crisis developed when Israeli forces launched 'Operation Peace for Galilee', advanced through Lebanon and surrounded West Beirut, trapping 6,000 PLO fighters. Egypt withdrew its ambassador from Tel-Aviv in protest at the Israeli action. Intensive diplomatic efforts resulted in the evacuation of 14,000–15,000 PLO and Syrian fighters from Beirut to various Arab countries at the end of August 1982. With Israeli troops in effective control of Beirut, a horrific massacre took place in the Palestinian refugee camps of Sabra and Chatila in mid-September; Israel finally acknowledged a figure of 700–800 dead. The Israeli Government instituted an enquiry, which blamed Lebanese Phalangists for the actual killing, but concluded that Israel's political and military leaders bore indirect responsibility through their negligence. General Ariel Sharon was forced to resign as Minister of Defence.

Lengthy talks between Israel and Lebanon, begun in December 1982, culminated in the signing on 17 May 1983 of a 12-article agreement, formulated by the US Secretary of State, George Shultz, declaring an end to hostilities and calling for the withdrawal of all foreign forces from Lebanon within three months. Syria rejected the agreement, leaving some 30,000 troops and 7,000 PLO men in the north-east of Lebanon, and Israel consequently refused to withdraw from the south. In September 1983 Israel redeployed its forces south of Beirut along the Awali river.

In January 1981 Begin called an early general election for June. Begin's belligerent stance over the threat of Syrian missiles in Lebanon in June, and the efforts of a new Minister of Finance, Yoram Aridor, to curb the rise in the cost of living, resulted in an unexpected swing in his favour; and by making an agreement with the religious parties, Begin was able to form a new coalition Government in early August. When Israeli forces moved into Lebanon in June 1982, support for Begin continued until the operation escalated into a full-scale war.

By the summer of 1983, the Government's prestige had been damaged by the Beirut massacres and by a capitulation to wage demands by the country's doctors. Begin announced his resignation on 30 August 1983. Itzhak Shamir, the Minister of Foreign Affairs since 1980, succeeded him as leader of the Likud bloc and as Prime Minister, his Likud grouping having a theoretical majority of seven seats in the Knesset, with the support of minority religious parties.

Problems with the economy troubled the Government during the second half of 1983, and the Labour Party was able to force a general election in July 1984. Neither the Labour Alignment (which won 44 of the 120 seats in the Knesset) nor Likud (41 seats) could form a viable coalition government, and therefore the President, Chaim Herzog, invited the Labour leader, Shimon Peres, to form a 'Government of national unity' with Likud. An agreement was reached whereby Peres was to be Prime Minister for two years and one month from September 1984, while Itzhak Shamir was to be Deputy Prime Minister and Minister of Foreign Affairs, after which time they were to exchange their respective posts for a further two years and one month.

Israeli forces in Lebanon had withdrawn to the Awali river in September 1983. Responsibility for policing the occupied southern area fell increasingly on an Israeli-controlled militia, the so-called 'South Lebanon Army' (SLA). The Israeli 'Government of national unity' was pledged to withdraw from Lebanon, and completed a three-phased withdrawal in June 1985, leaving a 10–20 km buffer strip on the Lebanese side of the border, controlled by the SLA, in which Israel continued to have influence.

From 1984 onwards, numerous attempts were made, both by the parties immediately concerned (Israel and the Arabs), and by other powers (including the USA, the USSR, the UN and the EEC), to find a solution to the most pressing problem in the Middle East—the desire of Palestinians for an independent state. A situation of virtual deadlock had arisen because the PLO would not recognize Israel's right to exist, and Israel, convinced that the PLO was a terrorist organization, refused any direct talks with the PLO: repeated proposals by King Hussein of Jordan for an international peace conference, to be convened by the UN, were rejected by Israel on the grounds that the PLO would be represented.

Towards the end of 1988 there were signs that this deadlock might soon be broken. In December 1987, following the deaths of four Palestinians in a collision with an Israeli army truck at a military checkpoint in the Gaza Strip, demonstrations and civil disobedience against Israeli rule had intensified and soon spread to the other Occupied Territories. The uprising (intifada) probably began as a spontaneous expression of frustration at occupation and depressed living conditions, but it soon became exploited and orchestrated by an underground leadership calling itself the Unified National Council of the Uprising (UNCU), comprising elements from across the Palestinian political spectrum (the PLO, the Communist Party and Islamic Jihad). Israeli forces found themselves seriously provoked by the stone-throwing and random violence, and tried to crush the uprising with increasing severity, for which they were condemned by world opinion. By January 1989 it was estimated that more than 350 Palestinians had been killed since the uprising began in December 1987.

Against the background of escalating violence in the Occupied Territories, other developments were taking place which were creating circumstances under which Israel might be stimulated into seeking, or accepting, a solution. At the end of July 1988 King Hussein abrogated Jordan's legal and administrative responsibilities in the West Bank, cancelled the Jordanian programme of investment there (launched in 1986), and declared that he was no longer prepared to act as the representative of the Palestinians in any international conference on the Palestinian question. This undermined Israel's Palestine policy, and greatly strengthened the negotiating position of the PLO.

In November 1988, at a meeting of the Palestine National Council in Algiers, the PLO declared an independent Palestinian State (notionally on the West Bank), and endorsed UN Security Council Resolution 242, thereby implicitly granting recognition to Israel. In December, in Stockholm, Yasser Arafat stated explicitly that 'the Palestine National Council accepted two States, a Palestinian State, and a Jewish State, Israel'. Later in December, before the UN General Assembly in Geneva, Arafat presented a three-point peace initiative, including an international conference under UN auspices, a UN peace-keeping force to supervise Israeli withdrawal from the Occupied Territories, and a comprehensive settlement based on UN Security Council Resolutions 242 and 338. Although the USA refused to accept the PLO proposals, alleging ambigu-

ISRAEL

ities, the PLO's explicit rejection of violence caused the US Government to decide to open a dialogue with the PLO, thus changing the direction of US-Israeli policy over Palestine. The United Kingdom, among other countries, urged Israel to make a positive response to the change in the PLO's position.

Israel's Prime Minister, Itzhak Shamir, however, declared that he would not negotiate with the PLO, distrusting its undertaking to abandon violence. Instead, he appeared to favour the introduction of limited self-rule for the Palestinians of the West Bank and Gaza Strip, as outlined in the 1978 US-sponsored Camp David accords with Egypt. Meanwhile, intense international pressure for an international Middle East peace conference developed at the end of 1988, with both the USA and the USSR increasing diplomatic efforts to bring Israel and the PLO to negotiations.

While Yasser Arafat was so active politically in November and December 1988, Israel was hampered by the uncertainty caused by the results of the general election which had taken place on 1 November. As in 1984, neither Likud (40 seats) nor Labour (39 seats) secured enough seats to be able to form a coalition with groups of smaller parties. The religious parties won 18 seats in the election, gaining potential significance in the formation of a government either by Likud or Labour. After two changes of direction, Peres and the Labour Party eventually agreed to the formation in December of another 'Government of national unity' under the Likud leader, Itzhak Shamir, with Peres as Deputy Prime Minister and Minister of Finance. In the coalition accord, no mention was made of an international Middle East peace conference, nor were any new proposals advanced for solving the Arab–Israeli problem.

Government

Supreme authority in Israel rests with the Knesset (Assembly), with 120 members elected by universal suffrage for four years (subject to dissolution), on the basis of proportional representation. The President, a constitutional Head of State, is elected by the Knesset for five years. Executive power lies with the Cabinet, led by the Prime Minister. The Cabinet takes office after receiving a vote of confidence in the Knesset, to which it is responsible. Ministers are usually members of the Knesset, but non-members may be appointed.

The country is divided into six administrative districts. Local authorities are elected at the same time as elections to the Knesset. There are 31 municipalities (including two Arab towns), 115 local councils (46 Arab and Druze) and 49 regional councils (one Arab) comprising representatives of 700 villages.

Defence

The Israel Defence Forces consist of a small nucleus of commissioned and non-commissioned regular officers, a contingent called up for national service, and a large reserve. Men are called up for 36 months of military service, and women for 24 months. Military service is compulsory for Jews and Druzes, but voluntary for Christians and Arabs. Total regular armed forces numbered 141,000 (including 110,000 conscripts) in June 1988, and full mobilization to 645,000 can be quickly achieved with reserves of 504,000. The armed forces are divided into an army of 104,000, a navy of 9,000 and an air force of 28,000. The defence budget for 1988/89 was 8,945m. new shekels (US $5,710m.).

Economic Affairs

In 1987, according to estimates by the World Bank, Israel's gross national product (GNP) was US $29,803m., equivalent to $6,810 per head. Between 1980 and 1987, GNP per head increased, in real terms, by an annual average of 0.3%.

Of the total labour force of about 1,494,000, about 5% are employed in agriculture and about 27% in industry (manufacturing, mining and construction). Continuous immigration and an economic boycott by Arab countries obliged Israel to develop agriculture and industry on an intensive scale and to seek far afield for international trade. Citrus fruit is the main export crop and the oldest export industry. However, sales declined in both volume and value, owing to competition (particularly from Spain), adverse weather and fluctuating exchange rates. Earnings from exports of citrus fruit reached a peak of US $247m. in 1981/82. They declined to $113m. in 1983/84 but in 1986/87 they totalled about $200m., a rise of 16% compared with 1985/86, owing mainly to favourable changes in exchange rates. Agricultural exports totalled $613m. in 1987, compared with over $2,000m. for cut diamonds, Israel's largest export earner.

Introductory Survey

During 1983 a major economic crisis developed. The shekel was being supported at an artificially high level in 1982 and 1983 as part of a strategy to curb an inflation rate which exceeded 100% every year in 1980–83. Israel's gross domestic product grew in real terms, by only 1.0% in 1982, and by 1.8% in 1983. Meanwhile, Israel's foreign debt was $24,200m. in 1983, the highest per caput in the world; the cost of servicing this debt amounted to the total amount of US aid for the 1984 fiscal year—$2,400m. (Israel is the largest recipient of US military and economic aid.) The trade deficit was $3,470m. in 1983, a 17% increase compared with 1982; the deficit on trade in goods and services exceeded $5,000m. in 1983; defence expenditure, already absorbing more than one-quarter of the country's gross national product, increased as a result of commitments in Lebanon. From September 1982 the Treasury had made the reduction of inflation its priority, but found it difficult to counteract the indexation of wages to inflation.

The shekel was devalued by 7.5% in August 1983, and by 23% in October, and, in an attempt to reduce budget expenditure, subsidies on food, electricity, water and public transport were reduced.

Labour unrest grew as inflation accelerated at the end of 1983 to 190%. The total budget for 1984/85 was set at $22,700m., while cuts in departmental appropriations amounted to $800m. In response to government economies, the real value of wages fell by 25% in the year to March 1984. The shekel was allowed to depreciate in line with inflation. As a result, the annual rate of inflation rose from 150% in October 1983 to about 400% in July 1984.

The new Government which took office in September 1984 immediately requested more aid from the USA, which the US Government, in turn, refused to grant until Israel reduced spending and introduced a thoroughgoing economic austerity programme to curb inflation. The Histadrut (the General Federation of Labour in Israel) opposed a planned 'freeze' of wages and prices, and refused to accept a reduction in the cost-of-living increment. The shekel was devalued by 9% in September.

The Government's three-month economic programme was approved by employers and unions in November 1984. Prices, wages, taxes and profits were 'frozen', while the shekel was maintained at its existing value against the US dollar. In addition, one-third was cut from the cost-of-living increment, and it was decided to shed 14,000 jobs from the public sector. Inflation subsequently fell to 3.7% in December. Inflation in the year to December 1984 was 444.9%, compared with 190% in 1983. A second economic programme, designed to consolidate the success of the first, and to last for eight months, came into operation in February 1985, including further cuts in subsidies on essential goods, controlled price increases on unsubsidized goods, and cash compensation for wage-earners.

The austerity programme had been intended to clear the way for substantial reductions in government expenditure. The Cabinet agreed a budget for 1985/86, involving planned expenditure of $23,300m., somewhat more than that for 1984/85, with cuts in spending ($1,300m.) which were considerably less than the amount for which Itzhak Modai, the Minister of Finance, had argued. The inability to implement a policy of strict budgetary control did not assist Israel's cause in securing increased aid from the US Government, which repeatedly stressed the need for greater economic stringency. The US Congress approved military aid of $1,800m. for the year beginning in October 1985, compared with $1,400m. in 1984/85, but any increase in economic aid remained conditional on concerted action to reform the economy. The country's reserves of foreign exchange, which fell to $2,300m. in January 1985, continued to dwindle. In March the US Government agreed to provide economic aid of $1,200m. in 1985/86 (the same amount as in 1984/85), and in June the US House of Representatives approved additional emergency aid of $1,500m. to be spread over 1985/86 and 1986/87 to support Israel's foreign currency reserves.

A 19% rise in prices, recorded in April 1985, prompted the Government to implement a new set of austerity measures in May, including a three-month 'freeze' on wages and contracts in the public sector. The Histadrut opposed any attempt to alter the existing arrangement of wages indexation, which continued to undercut government attempts to reduce spending.

In June food subsidies were cut so that prices rose by an average of 25%, and the shekel was devalued by 18.8% to US $1 = 1,500 shekels, at which point most prices, the currency exchange rate and wages were to be 'frozen' until October. A one-day general strike took place in protest against these measures. However, a compromise agreement between the Government, the employers and the Histadrut, concluded in July, made provision to compensate salaried employees for part of the rises in prices and the wages 'freeze' and averted a prolonged general strike.

At the end of September the price 'freeze' was extended until the end of June 1986. A new shekel, worth 1,000 of the old units, was officially introduced on 1 January 1986, partly as a financial practicality (the old shekel had become unwieldy in calculation, owing to inflation) and to restore faith in the currency in the face of the widespread use of the US dollar as an alternative currency in barter and on the 'black market'. In December 1985 the Cabinet cut the budget for the fiscal year 1986/87 by $580m. to $21,200m. (30,300m. new shekels). The economic stabilization programme, launched in July 1985, reduced monthly rates of inflation, giving an overall rate for 1985 of 185.2%. Between July 1985 and the end of the year the real value of wages fell by about 25%, and in February 1986 the Histadrut called a strike of public-sector employees to protest against the continuation of stringent monetary policy in the 1986/87 budget.

The monthly rate of inflation remained below 2% in the first half of 1986. The success of the economic programme was indicated by the announcement of a surplus (the first ever) of $1,100m. on the current account of the balance of payments in fiscal 1985; an achievement that was only in part due to emergency economic aid of $750m. from the USA. Israel's reserves of foreign exchange increased by 60% between July 1985 and July 1986, to about $3,500m., and the trade deficit declined by 17% during 1985.

In June 1986 the Knesset approved an extension of the price 'freeze' until the end of the year, while the Government sought the co-operation of the Histadrut in 'freezing' public-sector wages for a further 12 months. During 1986, with lower inflation, compensation payments, and the partial indexation that was still in operation, wages rose to a level higher than that prevailing prior to the introduction of the economic austerity programme in July 1985. The success of the Government's austerity measures, however, assisted by injections of US aid into the economy, was reflected in an overall rate of inflation of 19.7% in 1986 (compared with 185.2% in 1985 and 444.9% in 1984), a surplus of $1,371m. in the current account of the balance of payments in fiscal 1986, and an increase in reserves to $4,200m. A new 10-point programme was introduced in January 1987, with the approval of the manufacturers' association and the Histadrut. To run until 31 March 1988, it included large cut-backs in spending on health, education and social welfare; a major reform of the tax system; a wages 'freeze'; a partial de-indexation of cost-of-living payments, reducing the level of compensation from 70% to 43% of rises in prices; and reductions in the public-sector work-force. In January 1987 the shekel was devalued by 10.2% in relation to a 'basket' of international currencies. (The shekel, which had formerly been aligned with the US dollar, was linked with a 'basket' of currencies in July 1986, in an attempt to prevent wide fluctuations in the exchange rate and to stabilize returns from foreign trade.) In April the Knesset approved a budget of 39,300m. new shekels ($24,600m.) for fiscal 1987/88, incorporating spending cuts of 400m. new shekels, which still left a substantial deficit of 1,400m. new shekels.

The Government's economic programme kept inflation for 1987 to 16.1%, the lowest annual rate for 15 years. Israel's reserves of foreign exchange rose to $5,700m. in November 1987, on receipt of the US economic aid grant for the fiscal year 1987/88, totalling $1,200m. In November the Government claimed that Israel's real GDP was growing at a rate of more than 4% per year, compared with only 2.2% in 1986. Unemployment, which, as a result of the shedding of thousands of public-sector jobs by the Government in a cost-saving exercise, had risen to the equivalent of 7.9% of the civilian labour force during the second quarter of 1986, declined to 5.6% during the same period of 1987, its lowest level since 1985. However, the trade deficit widened by about 50% during the first half of 1987, compared with the corresponding period in 1986, to a record $2,200m. Israel's foreign debt rose by more than $800m. to $24,800m. in 1986, largely owing to the decline in the value of the US dollar against other leading currencies.

The success that was achieved was made possible only by a continuing policy of financial stringency. According to the Bank of Israel's report for 1986, defence spending, expressed as a percentage of national income, was lower than at any time since 1967. This reflected the Minister of Finance's success in securing cuts in the defence budget, particularly through the cancellation of the expensive Lavi fighter aircraft project.

The budget for 1988/89 was approved by the Cabinet in January 1988. Total expenditure was fixed at 47,800m. new shekels ($29,900m.), incorporating cuts totalling 742m. new shekels ($463m.). Spending on defence was to be 8,945m. new shekels ($5,710m.); state subsidies on food, public transport, health and education were all reduced. Government revenue was to include $3,000m. in aid from the USA (comprising $1,200m. in civilian and $1,800m. in economic aid), the same as in 1987/88.

The cost of military operations and the disruption caused by the uprising (*intifada*) in the Occupied Territories contributed towards 1988 being a bad year for the Israeli economy. Inflation in January 1989 was running at 20% and GDP was estimated to have risen by only 1% in 1988, compared with 5% in 1987. Moreover, many Israeli companies were facing liquidity problems. The Government was compelled to introduce yet another austerity plan in January 1989. This entailed cutting 1,000m. shekels from the coming year's budget expenditure. The measures included a further reduction of subsidies on foodstuffs and fuel, higher public transport charges, higher medical charges, and a cut of 120m. shekels in the defence budget. The shekel was devalued by 12%, after an earlier devaluation of 5% in December 1988.

Social Welfare

There is a highly advanced system of social welfare. Under the National Insurance Law, the state provides retirement pensions, benefits for industrial injury and maternity, and allowances for large families. The Histadrut (General Federation of Labour), to which more than 90% of all Jewish workers in Israel belong, provides sickness benefits and medical care. The Ministry of Social Welfare provides for general assistance, relief grants, child care and other social services. In 1983 Israel had 11,895 physicians, equivalent to one for every 339 inhabitants, one of the best doctor-patient ratios in the world. In 1987 there were 153 hospitals (of which 60 were private) and 27,500 beds.

Education

Israel has European standards of literacy and educational services. Free compulsory primary education is provided for all children between five and 15 years of age. There is also secondary, vocational and agricultural education. Post-primary education is also free, and it lasts six years, of which four are compulsory. Enrolment at primary and secondary schools in 1981 was equivalent to 89% of children aged six to 17. There are six universities, one institute of technology and one institute of science (the Weizmann Institute), which incorporates a graduate school of science.

Public Holidays

The Sabbath starts at sunset on Friday and ends at nightfall on Saturday. The Jewish year 5750 begins on 30 September 1989, and the year 5751 on 20 September 1990.

1989: 21 March (Purim), 20–26 April (Passover), 10 May Independence Day), 9 June (Shavuot), 30 September (Rosh Hashanah, Jewish New Year), 9 October (Yom Kippur), 14–21 October (Succot—public holidays on first and last days of festival), 21 October (Simhat Torah).

1990: 11 March (Purim), 10–17 April (Passover), 29 April (Independence Day), 30 May (Shavuot), 20 September (Rosh Hashanah, Jewish New Year), 29 September (Yom Kippur), 4–11 October (Succot—see 1989), 12 October (Simhat Torah).

(The Jewish festivals and fast days commence in the evening of the dates given.)

Islamic holidays are observed by Muslim Arabs, and Christian holidays by the Christian Arab community.

Weights and Measures

The metric system is in force.

1 dunum = 1,000 sq metres.

ISRAEL

Statistical Survey

Source: Central Bureau of Statistics, Hakirya, Givat Ram, POB 13015, Jerusalem 91130; tel. (02) 211400.

Area and Population

AREA, POPULATION AND DENSITY

Area (sq km)	
Land	21,501
Inland water	445
Total	21,946*
Population (*de jure*; census results)†	
20 May 1972	3,147,683
4 June 1983	
Males	2,011,590
Females	2,026,030
Total	4,037,620
Population (*de jure*; official estimates at 31 December)†	
1985	4,266,200
1986	4,331,300
1987	4,406,500
Density (per sq km) at 31 December 1987 . . .	200.8

* 8,473.4 sq miles. Area includes East Jerusalem, annexed by Israel in June 1967.
† Including the population of East Jerusalem and Israeli residents in certain other areas under Israeli military occupation since June 1967. Beginning in December 1981, figures also include non-Jews in the Golan sub-district, an Israeli-occupied area of Syrian territory. Census results exclude adjustment for under-enumeration.

ADMINISTERED TERRITORIES*

	Area (sq km)	Estimated population (31 December 1987)
Golan	1,176	23,900
Judaea and Samaria . . .	5,879	860,000
Gaza Area†	378	564,100
Total	7,433	1,448,000

The area figures in this table refer to 1 October 1973. No later figures are available.
* The area and population of the Administered Territories have changed as a result of the October 1973 war.
† Not including El-Arish and Sinai which, as of April 1979 and April 1982 respectively, were returned to Egypt.

POPULATION BY RELIGION (census of 4 June 1983)

	Males	Females	Total	%
Jews	1,662,725	1,687,272	3,349,997	82.97
Muslims . . .	268,644	257,995	526,639	13.04
Christians . .	45,897	48,260	94,157	2.33
Druze . . .	33,833	32,028	65,861	1.63
Others . . .	491	475	966	0.02
Total . . .	2,011,590	2,026,030	4,037,620	100.00

PRINCIPAL TOWNS (population at 4 June 1983)

Jerusalem (capital)	428,668*	Petach-Tikva . .	123,868
Tel-Aviv—Jaffa .	327,625	Ramat Gan . .	117,072
Haifa . . .	235,775	Beersheba . .	110,813
Holon . . .	133,460	Bene Beraq . .	96,150

* Including East Jerusalem, annexed in June 1967.

BIRTHS, MARRIAGES AND DEATHS*

	Registered live births		Registered marriages		Registered deaths	
	Number	Rate (per 1,000)	Number	Rate (per 1,000)	Number	Rate (per 1,000)
1980 . .	94,321	24.3	29,592	7.6	26,364	6.8
1981 . .	93,308	23.6	29,652	7.5	26,085	6.6
1982 . .	96,695	24.0	29,555	7.4	27,780†	6.9
1983 . .	98,724	24.0	31,096	7.6	27,731	6.8
1984 . .	98,478	23.7	29,871	7.2	27,805	6.7
1985 . .	99,376	23.5	29,158	6.9	28,093	6.6
1986 . .	99,341	23.1	30,113	7.0	29,415	6.8
1987 . .	99,022	22.7	30,267	6.9	29,444	6.7

* Including East Jerusalem.
† Excluding casualties of war.
‡ Provisional.

IMMIGRATION*

	1985	1986	1987
Immigrants:			
on immigrant visas . . .	4,665	2,928	5,924
on tourist visas† . . .	802	1,014	1,231
Potential immigrants:			
on potential immigrant visas	4,240	4,330	4,682
on tourist visas† . . .	935	1,233	1,128
Total	10,642	9,505	12,965

* Excluding immigrating citizens (446 in 1984) and Israeli residents returning from abroad.
† Figures refer to tourists who changed their status to immigrants or potential immigrants.

ECONOMICALLY ACTIVE POPULATION
(annual averages, '000 persons aged 14 and over)

	1985	1986	1987
Agriculture, forestry and fishing	78.1	70.0	72.0
Mining and quarrying . . .	6.2	5.5	4.7
Manufacturing	307.4	316.9	323.7
Electricity and water . . .	11.7	12.4	13.6
Construction	72.3	61.8	67.7
Trade, restaurants and hotels	169.5	178.1	193.4
Transport, storage and communications . . .	86.4	86.7	91.6
Financing and business services	131.6	133.8	134.3
Public and community services	405.0	405.8	404.3
Personal and other services .	90.9	87.9	89.1
Activities not adequately defined	9.1	8.7	9.3
Total employed	1,368.3	1,367.9	1,403.7
Unemployed	98.5	104.0	90.3
Total civilian labour force	1,466.8	1,471.9	1,494.0

ISRAEL

Agriculture

PRINCIPAL CROPS (metric tons, year ending August)

	1984/85	1985/86	1986/87
Wheat	127,700	168,500	298,000
Barley	6,500	11,200	20,500
Cotton lint	99,000	69,000	59,200
Groundnuts	22,300	23,000	21,100
Hay	100,000	100,000	120,000
Vegetables	764,700	754,400	719,400
Potatoes	204,400	206,800	218,400
Melons and pumpkins	132,000	136,600	154,700
Citrus fruit	1,487,000	1,308,700	1,508,400
Pomegranates	117,500	123,000	124,700
Stone fruit	63,800	64,200	58,000
Grapes (table)	40,000	51,500	50,700
Grapes (wine)	40,500	30,800	37,800
Bananas	81,000	82,100	81,300
Olives	39,000	38,000	25,000
Avocados	77,200	68,000	134,700

LIVESTOCK ('000 head)

	1984/85	1985/86	1986/87
Cattle	316	326	341
Poultry	27,550	30,250	30,470
Sheep	262	291	320
Goats	126	127	131

Milk production (million litres): 788.1 in 1984/85; 845.0 in 1985/86; 880.1 in 1986/87.

Fishing

('000 metric tons, live weight)

	1984	1985	1986
Inland waters	13.4	14.5	14.8*
Mediterranean and Black Sea	4.6	4.6	5.0*
Atlantic Ocean	5.0	2.7	2.1
Indian Ocean	0.1	0.1	0.1*
Total catch	23.1	21.9	22.0

* Estimate.
Source: FAO, *Yearbook of Fishery Statistics*.

Mining

	1985	1986	1987
Crude petroleum (million litres)	10	14	17
Natural gas (million cu m)	53	40	45
Phosphate rock ('000 metric tons)	2,195	2,518	2,731
Potash	1,953	2,035	2,057

Industry

SELECTED PRODUCTS
('000 metric tons, unless otherwise stated)

	1985	1986	1987
Wheat flour	507	514	529
Refined vegetable oils (metric tons)	72,279	79,640	76,876
Margarine	32.7	33.7	32.6
Wine ('000 litres)	18,348	17,381	16,995
Beer ('000 litres)	51,066	52,281	53,638
Cigarettes (metric tons)	6,709	6,723	6,888
Cotton yarn (metric tons)	15,235	14,914	16,132
Newsprint (metric tons)	819	1,148	2,028
Writing and printing paper (metric tons)	53,845	64,930	65,119
Other paper (metric tons)	29,334	35,752	36,737
Cardboard (metric tons)	45,746	54,468	61,636
Rubber tyres ('000)	930	744	920
Ammonia (metric tons)	106,424	89,400	97,056
Ammonium sulphate (metric tons)	60,389	46,251	40,843
Sulphuric acid	178	182	143
Chlorine (metric tons)	32,944	29,844	32,901
Caustic soda (metric tons)	31,248	26,991	29,717
Polyethylene (metric tons)	73,879	76,881	90,323
Liquefied petroleum gas (metric tons)	162,627	168,261	191,867
Paints (metric tons)	33,930	40,609	43,391
Cement	1,596	1,624	2,226
Commercial vehicles (number)	1,130	1,152	971
Electricity (million kWh)	15,010	15,503	17,102

Finance

CURRENCY AND EXCHANGE RATES

Monetary Units
100 agorot (singular: agora) = 1 new shekel (sheqel).

Denominations
Notes: 5, 10, 50 and 100 new shekels.

Sterling and Dollar Equivalents (30 September 1988)
£1 sterling = 2.779 new shekels;
US $1 = 1.643 new shekels;
100 new shekels = £35.99 = $60.86.

Average Exchange Rate (new shekels per US $)
1985   1.1788
1986   1.4878
1987   1.5946

Note: The new shekel, worth 1,000 of the former units, was introduced on 1 January 1986.

ISRAEL

CENTRAL GOVERNMENT BUDGET ESTIMATES
(million new shekels, year ending 31 March)

Revenue	1986/87	1987/88
Ordinary budget	23,154.2	26,372.0
Income tax and property tax	8,071.6	8,905.8
Customs and excise	1,095.2	1,218.4
Purchase tax	1,440.2	2,101.8
Employers' tax	560.3	385.0
Value added tax	4,603.1	5,153.1
Other taxes	1,252.6	1,474.2
Interest	356.6	509.0
Transfer from development budget	4,992.0	5,749.1
Other receipts	782.6	875.6
Development budget	10,248.8	12,922.0
Foreign loans	8,194.9	7,072.2
Internal loans	7,112.7	9,865.9
Transfer to ordinary budget	−5,718.8	−6,595.4
Other receipts	660.0	2,579.2
Total	**33,403.0**	**39,294.0**

Revised budget estimates (million new shekels, year ending 31 March): 1987/88: Revenue and Expenditure 41,257; 1988/89: Revenue and Expenditure 53,088.

Expenditure*	1986/87	1987/88
Ordinary account	23,154.2	26,372.0
Ministry of finance	134.3	168.8
Ministry of defence	7,664.0	8,193.8
Ministry of health	398.3	406.1
Ministry of education and culture	1,870.9	2,352.4
Ministry of police	407.5	469.4
Ministry of labour and social welfare	2,357.1	3,003.8
Other ministries†	562.6	696.2
Interest	5,381.0	6,506.0
Pensions and compensations	541.8	680.4
Transfers to local authorities	523.3	506.3
Subsidies	1,305.9	1,326.5
Reserves	1,058.1	1,049.6
Other expenditures	949.3	1,012.7
Development budget	10,248.8	12,922.0
Agriculture	122.0	131.8
Industry, trade and tourism	613.9	536.3
Housing	397.7	399.3
Public buildings	119.9	149.9
Development of energy resources	42.0	41.4
Debt repayment	8,326.1	10,910.0
Other expenditures	627.2	753.4
Total	**33,403.0**	**39,294.0**

* Does not include the entire defence budget.
† Includes the President, Prime Minister, State Comptroller and the Knesset.

CENTRAL BANK RESERVES (US $ million at 31 December)

	1985	1986	1987
Gold*	39.1	43.5	50.5
IMF special drawing rights	0.1	—	0.1
Foreign exchange	3,680.1	4,659.6	5,876.0
Total	**3,719.3**	**4,703.1**	**5,926.6**

* Valued at 35 SDRs per troy ounce.
Source: IMF, *International Financial Statistics*.

MONEY SUPPLY (million new shekels at 31 December)

	1985	1986	1987
Currency outside banks	481	974	1,365
Demand deposits	508	1,203	1,922
Total money	**989**	**2,178**	**3,287**

Source: IMF, *International Financial Statistics*.

COST OF LIVING
(Consumer Price Index, annual averages. Base: 1980 = 100)

	1983	1984	1985
All items	1,173.5	5,560.4	22,500

(Consumer Price Index, annual averages. Base: 1985 = 100)

	1986	1987
All items	148.1	177.5

NATIONAL ACCOUNTS ('000 new shekels at current prices)
National Income and Product

	1981	1982	1983
Compensation of employees	132,090	298,755	762,718
Operating surplus	79,886	168,431	390,038
Domestic factor incomes	211,976	467,186	1,152,756
Consumption of fixed capital	34,309	77,111	187,209
Statistical discrepancy	−2,035	−12,401	−16,439
Gross domestic product at factor cost	244,250	531,896	1,323,526
Indirect taxes	28,504	64,940	176,894
Less Subsidies	23,448	39,223	86,401
GDP in purchasers' values	249,306	557,613	1,414,019
Net factor income from abroad	−7,701	−21,116	−54,325
Gross national product	241,605	536,497	1,359,694
Less Consumption of fixed capital	34,309	77,111	187,209
National income in market prices	207,296	459,386	1,172,485

Expenditure on the Gross Domestic Product

	1981	1982	1983
Government final consumption expenditure	91,419	190,553	451,286
Private final consumption expenditure	152,680	352,930	919,040
Increase in stocks	−5,223	−222	−9,852
Gross fixed capital formation	57,219	131,369	335,801
Total domestic expenditure	296,095	674,630	1,696,275
Exports of goods and services	113,517	228,302	550,097
Less Imports of goods and services	160,306	345,319	832,353
GDP in purchasers' values	249,306	557,613	1,414,019
GDP at constant 1980 prices	110,291	111,447	113,497

ISRAEL

BALANCE OF PAYMENTS (US $ million)

	1985	1986	1987
Merchandise exports f.o.b.	6,602	7,675	9,085
Merchandise imports f.o.b.	−9,107	−9,614	−12,891
Trade balance	−2,415	−1,939	−3,806
Export of services	4,283	4,026	4,695
Import of services	−5,786	−5,992	−6,711
Balance on goods and services	−3,918	−3,905	−5,822
Private unrequited transfers (net)	877	1,147	1,329
Government unrequited transfers (net)	4,197	4,225	3,496
Current balance	1,156	1,467	−997
Long-term capital (net)	116	567	387
Short-term capital (net)	−527	−1,094	739
Net errors and omissions	−346	51	519
Total (net monetary movements)	399	991	648
Valuation changes (net)	145	77	432
Changes in reserves	544	1,068	1,080

Source: IMF, *International Financial Statistics*.

External Trade

PRINCIPAL COMMODITIES (US $ '000)

Imports	1985	1986	1987
Diamonds, rough	1,098,600	1,522,000	1,837,000
Machinery and parts	1,250,800	1,413,200	1,708,100
Electrical machinery and parts	418,800	575,400	680,600
Iron and steel	268,200	297,900	318,500
Metal products n.i.e.	187,800	225,100	264,900
Vehicles	382,300	586,100	915,300
Chemicals and related products	609,500	835,100	1,040,100
Crude petroleum and petroleum products	1,352,000	786,200	1,032,700
Cereals	277,100	251,100	233,600
Textiles and textile articles	222,700	331,000	392,000
Total (incl. others)	8,319,600	9,635,200	11,916,400

Exports	1985	1986	1987
Diamonds, worked	1,432,700	1,879,400	2,301,900
Clothing	218,300	282,200	344,800
Textiles and textile articles	135,800	151,900	209,400
Fruit and vegetables	541,900	523,100	636,200
Fertilizers	159,800	158,900	184,100
Organic chemicals	238,700	266,100	307,900
Inorganic chemicals	174,500	178,800	208,000
Chemical products	564,600	489,400	n.a.
Transport equipment	318,900	242,400	291,700
Machinery and parts	661,700	766,700	882,900
Electrical machinery and parts	216,900	279,300	345,400
Metals and metal products	677,000	875,100	863,600
Total (incl. others)	6,260,400	7,154,300	8,475,400

PRINCIPAL TRADING PARTNERS (US $ '000)

Imports	1985	1986	1987
Argentina	36,500	27,100	37,600
Australia	45,500	58,100	50,000
Austria	45,200	56,400	59,800
Belgium/Luxembourg	991,000	1,258,400	1,695,600
Brazil	37,800	22,700	17,500
Canada	103,500	80,400	113,200
Denmark	36,400	48,700	60,000
Finland	44,300	56,000	70,400
France	303,200	385,600	545,900
Germany, Fed. Rep.	898,300	1,213,500	1,539,100
Greece	16,600	24,800	48,100
Hong Kong	25,200	51,800	86,700
Italy	411,000	559,800	755,200
Japan	186,200	307,400	401,000
Netherlands	221,000	301,700	381,200
Romania	20,300	28,800	30,600
South Africa	174,700	202,900	221,300
Spain	77,100	125,700	125,800
Sweden	74,300	106,800	172,000
Switzerland	545,900	774,100	879,800
United Kingdom	753,900	985,000	1,117,500
USA	1,679,000	1,788,600	1,932,400

Exports	1985	1986	1987
Australia	58,500	56,600	71,200
Austria	31,100	41,700	41,900
Belgium/Luxembourg	235,400	265,500	278,200
Brazil	31,200	44,300	47,300
Canada	65,300	78,100	85,300
France	262,500	313,100	390,600
Germany, Fed. Rep.	329,400	373,400	473,600
Greece	53,000	44,600	96,700
Hong Kong	190,100	273,300	378,900
Italy	249,100	251,700	306,900
Japan	210,000	323,300	494,600
Netherlands	276,100	309,200	384,900
Norway	24,800	27,100	27,500
Portugal	32,100	28,300	19,500
Singapore	53,600	40,100	37,000
South Africa	63,800	63,800	81,600
Spain	29,900	55,800	99,300
Sweden	34,900	43,500	51,900
Switzerland	133,300	178,900	197,600
Turkey	34,400	34,000	34,300
United Kingdom	477,000	513,300	656,600
USA	2,138,000	2,348,700	2,753,900

Transport

RAILWAYS (traffic)

	1985	1986	1987
Passengers ('000)	2,814	2,516	2,544
Freight ('000 metric tons)	6,016	6,406	6,851

ROAD TRAFFIC, 1987 (motor vehicles)

Private cars (incl. station wagons)	696,712
Trucks, trailers	131,996
Buses	8,356
Taxis	7,652
Motor cycles, motor scooters	33,814
Other vehicles	3,469
Total	881,999

ISRAEL

SHIPPING
(international sea-borne freight traffic, '000 metric tons)*

	1985	1986	1987
Goods loaded	7,088	7,336	8,052
Goods unloaded	9,206	9,712	11,324

* Excluding petroleum.

CIVIL AVIATION (El Al revenue flights only, '000)

	1985	1986	1987
Kilometres flown	40,512	42,581	45,184
Revenue passenger-km	6,608,000	6,931,000	7,558,000
Mail (tons)	1,046	1,083	1,247

Tourism

	1985	1986	1987
Tourist arrivals	1,264,367	1,101,481	1,378,742

Communications Media
(at December each year)

	1983	1984	1985
Telephones in use	1,527,000	1,625,000	1,791,450
Daily newspapers	40	n.a.	21
Periodicals	n.a.	n.a.	890

Radio receivers: an estimated 3m. in 1983.
TV receivers: 582,000 in 1983.
Telephones in use: 2,065,000 in 1987.

Education
(1987/88, provisional figures)

	Schools	Pupils	Teachers
Jewish			
Kindergarten	n.a.	265,800	n.a.
Primary schools	1,317	483,641	34,691
Intermediate schools	295	112,571	12,908
Secondary schools	528	198,870	24,031
Vocational schools	312	93,660	n.a.
Agricultural schools	26	5,020	n.a.
Teacher training colleges	n.a.	11,490	n.a.
Others (handicapped)	194	12,041	3,152
Arab			
Kindergarten	n.a.	20,800	n.a.
Primary schools	336	141,152	6,719
Intermediate schools	56	24,021	1,693
Secondary schools	81	37,488	2,347
Vocational schools	38	6,002	n.a.
Agricultural schools	2	642	n.a.
Teacher training colleges	n.a.	475	n.a.
Others (handicapped)	16	1,210	183

Directory

The Constitution

There is no written Constitution. In June 1950 the Knesset voted to adopt a State Constitution by evolution over an unspecified period. A number of laws, including the Law of Return (1950), the Nationality Law (1952), the State President (Tenure) Law (1952), the Education Law (1953) and the 'Yad-va-Shem' Memorial Law (1953), are considered as incorporated into the State Constitution. Other constitutional laws are: The Law and Administration Ordinance (1948), the Knesset Election Law (1951), the Law of Equal Rights for Women (1951), the Judges Act (1953), the National Service and National Insurance Acts (1953), and the Basic Law (The Knesset) (1958). The provisions of constitutional legislation that affect the main organs of government are summarized below:

THE PRESIDENT

The President is elected by the Knesset for a maximum of two five-year terms.

Ten or more Knesset Members may propose a candidate for the Presidency.

Voting will be by secret ballot.

The President may not leave the country without the consent of the Government.

The President may resign by submitting his resignation in writing to the Speaker.

The President may be relieved of his duties by the Knesset for misdemeanour.

The Knesset is entitled to decide by a two-thirds majority that the President is too incapacitated owing to ill health to fulfil his duties permanently.

The Speaker of the Knesset will act for the President when the President leaves the country, or when he cannot perform his duties owing to ill health.

THE KNESSET

The Knesset is the parliament of the State. There are 120 members. It is elected by general, national, direct, equal, secret and proportional elections.

Every Israeli national of 18 years or over shall have the right to vote in elections to the Knesset unless a court has deprived him of that right by virtue of any law.

Every Israeli national of 21 and over shall have the right to be elected to the Knesset unless a court has deprived him of that right by virtue of any law.

The following shall not be candidates: the President of the State; the two Chief Rabbis; a judge (shofet) in office; a judge (dayan) of a religious court; the State Comptroller; the Chief of the General Staff of the Defence Army of Israel; rabbis and ministers of other religions in office; senior State employees and senior Army officers of such ranks and in such functions as shall be determined by law.

The term of office of the Knesset shall be four years.

The elections to the Knesset shall take place on the third Tuesday of the month of Cheshven in the year in which the tenure of the outgoing Knesset ends.

Election day shall be a day of rest, but transport and other public services shall function normally.

Results of the elections shall be published within 14 days.

The Knesset shall elect from among its members a Chairman and Vice-Chairman.

The Knesset shall elect from among its members permanent committees, and may elect committees for specific matters.

The Knesset may appoint commissions of inquiry to investigate matters designated by the Knesset.

The Knesset shall hold two sessions a year; one of them shall open within four weeks after the Feast of the Tabernacles, the other

ISRAEL — Directory

within four weeks after Independence Day; the aggregate duration of the two sessions shall not be less than eight months.

The outgoing Knesset shall continue to hold office until the convening of the incoming Knesset.

The members of the Knesset shall receive a remuneration as provided by law.

THE GOVERNMENT

The Government shall tender its resignation to the President immediately after his election, but shall continue with its duties until the formation of a new government. After consultation with representatives of the parties in the Knesset, the President shall charge one of the Members with the formation of a government. The government shall be composed of a Prime Minister and a number of ministers from among the Knesset Members or from outside the Knesset. After it has been chosen, the government shall appear before the Knesset and shall be considered as formed after having received a vote of confidence. Within seven days of receiving a vote of confidence, the Prime Minister and the other ministers shall swear allegiance to the State of Israel and its Laws and undertake to carry out the decisions of the Knesset.

The Government

HEAD OF STATE

President: Gen. CHAIM HERZOG (took office 5 May 1983; re-elected 23 February 1988).

THE CABINET
(February 1989)

Prime Minister and Minister of Labour: ITZHAK SHAMIR (Likud).
Deputy Prime Minister and Minister of Finance: SHIMON PERES (Labour).
Deputy Prime Minister and Minister of Foreign Affairs: MOSHE ARENS (Likud).
Minister of Defence: ITZHAK RABIN (Labour).
Deputy Prime Minister and Minister of Education and Culture: ITZHAK NAVON (Labour).
Second Deputy Prime Minister and Minister of Housing: DAVID LEVI (Likud).
Minister of Transport: MOSHE KATZAV (Likud).
Minister of Police: CHAIM BAR-LEV (Labour).
Minister of Trade: ARIEL SHARON (Likud).
Minister of Energy: MOSHE SHAHAL (Labour).
Minister of Justice: DAN MERIDOR (Likud).
Minister of Agriculture: AVRAHAM KATZ-OZ (Labour).
Minister of Tourism: GIDEON PATT (Likud).
Minister of Health: YAACOV TSUR (Labour).
Minister of Economics and Planning: ITZHAK MODAI (Likud).
Minister of Communications: GAD YAACOBI (Labour).
Minister of Interior: ARIE DERI (Shas).
Minister of Immigration: ITZHAK PERES (Shas).
Minister of Science: EZER WEIZMAN (Labour).
Minister of Environmental Quality: RONNI MILO (Likud).
Ministers without Portfolio: MOSHE NISSIM (Likud), EHUD OLMERT (Likud), MORDECHAI GUR (Labour), RAFI EDRI (Labour).

MINISTRIES

Office of the Prime Minister: Hakirya, Ruppin St, Jerusalem.
Ministry of Agriculture: POB 7011, Hakirya, Tel-Aviv 61070; tel. 03-255473; telex 361496.
Ministry of Defence: Hakirya, Tel-Aviv.
Ministry of Education and Culture: Hakirya, 14 Klausner St, Tel-Aviv; tel. 03-414155.
Ministry of Energy and Infrastructure: Hakirya, Jerusalem.
Ministry of Finance: 1 Kaplan St., Kiryat Ben-Gurion, POB 883, Jerusalem; tel. 02-558111.
Ministry of Foreign Affairs: Hakirya, Romema, Jerusalem; tel. 02-303111; telex 25223.
Ministry of Health: 2 Ben Tabai St, Jerusalem; tel. 02-638212.
Ministry of Housing and Construction: Hakirya, 23 Hillel St, Jerusalem.
Ministry of the Interior: POB 6158, 91 061 Jerusalem; tel. 02-660151; telex 26162.
Ministry of Religious Affairs: 236 Jaffo St, Jerusalem.

Ministry of Tourism: POB 1018, 24 King George St, Jerusalem; tel. 02-237311.
Ministry of Transport: Klal Bldg, 97 Jaffa Rd, Jerusalem; tel. 02-229211.

Legislature

KNESSET

Speaker: DOV SHILANSKY.

General Election, 1 November 1988

Party	Votes	Seats
Likud	709,305	40
Labour	685,363	39
Shas	107,709	6
Ratz	97,513	5
National Religious Party	89,720	5
Agudat Israel	102,714	5
Hadash	84,032	4
Tehiya	70,370	3
United Workers Party (Mapam)	56,345	3
Shinui	39,538	2
Moledet	44,174	2
Degal Hatora	34,279	2
Tzomet	45,489	2
Arab Democratic Party	27,012	1
Progressive List for Peace	33,695	1
Others (12 parties)	55,874	—
Total	**2,283,132**	**120**

Political Organizations

Agudat Israel: Jerusalem; ultra-orthodox Jewish party; stands for strict observance of Jewish religious law; Leader AVRAHAM SHAPIRA.

Agudat Israel World Organization (AIWO): Hacherut Sq., POB 326, Jerusalem 91002; tel. 02-384357; f. 1912 at Congress of Orthodox Jewry, Kattowitz, Germany (now Katowice, Poland), to help solve the problems facing Jewish people all over the world; more than 500,000 mems in 25 countries; Pres. Rabbi Dr I. LEWIN (New York); Chair. Rabbi J. M. ABRAMOWITZ (Jerusalem), Rabbi M. SHERER (New York); Gen. Sec. ABRAHAM HIRSCH (Jerusalem).

Arab Democratic Party: Nazareth; f. 1988; aims: to unify Arab political forces so as to influence Palestinian and Israeli policy; international recognition of the Palestinian people's right to self-determination; the holding of an international peace conference in the Middle East, with the participation of all parties to the conflict, including the PLO, as sole representative of the Palestinian people, on an equal footing; the withdrawal of Israel from all territories occupied in 1967; Chair. ABD AL-WAHAB DARAWSHAH.

Centre Party (Shinui): f. 1988; as a merger of dissidents from the Labour Alignment and Likud blocs with the Shinui party, led by AMNON RUBINSTEIN, which withdrew from the coalition govt of nat. unity in May 1987; mems included MOSHE AMIRAV, expelled from Herut Central Cttee for holding indirect talks with PLO.

Council for Peace and Security: f. 1988 by four retd Israeli generals: Maj.-Gen. AHARON YARIV, Maj.-Gen. ORI ORR, Brig.-Gen. YORAM AGMON and Brig.-Gen. EPHRAIM SNEH; MOSHE AMIRAV of Centre Party a founder mem.; aims: an Israeli withdrawal from the Occupied Territories in return for a peace treaty with the Arab nations.

Degal Hatora: f. 1988 as breakaway from Agudat Israel; orthodox Western Jews.

Gush Emunim (Bloc of the Faithful): f. 1967; engaged in unauthorized establishment of Jewish settlements in the occupied territories; Leader Rabbi MOSHE LEVINGER.

Hadash (Democratic Front for Peace and Equality): POB 26205, Tel-Aviv; descended from the Socialist Workers' Party of Palestine (f. 1919); renamed Communist Party of Palestine 1921, Communist Party of Israel (Maki) 1948; pro-Soviet anti-Zionist group formed New Communist Party of Israel (Rakah) 1965; Jewish Arab membership; aims for a socialist system in Israel, a lasting peace between Israel and the Arab countries and the Palestinian Arab people, favours full implementation of UN Security Council Resolutions 242 and 338, Israeli withdrawal from all Arab territories occupied since 1967, formation of a Palestinian Arab state in the West Bank and Gaza Strip, recognition of national rights of State of Israel and Palestine people, democratic rights and defence of working class interests, and demands an end of discrimination

ISRAEL

against Arab minority in Israel and against oriental Jewish communities. Fought 1988 general election as Hadash (Democratic Front for Peace and Equality), an alliance with the Black Panther movement of Oriental Jews, winning 4 seats in the Knesset; Sec.-Gen. MEIR VILNER.

Israel Labour Party: 110 Ha'yarkon St, Tel-Aviv; tel. 03-209222; f. 1968 as a merger of the three Labour groups, Mapai, Rafi and Achdut Ha'avoda; a Zionist democratic socialist party, was in government from 1948 to 1977; with the United Workers' Party (Mapam), formed the main opposition bloc under name of Labour-Mapam Alignment until elections of July 1984; formed National Unity government with Likud in 1984 and again in 1988; Yahad (Together) (f. 1984; advocates a peace settlement with the Arab peoples and the Palestinians; Leader EZER WEIZMANN) joined the Labour bloc in Jan. 1987; Chair. of Israel Labour Party SHIMON PERES; Sec.-Gen. (vacant).

Kach (Thus): 111 Agripas St, Jerusalem; tel. 02-247202; f. 1977; right-wing religious nationalist party; advocates creation of a Torah state and expulsion of all Arabs from Israel and the Occupied Territories; not allowed to contest the 1988 general election; Leader Rabbi MEIR KAHANE.

Likud (Consolidation): Tel-Aviv; f. September 1973; is a parliamentary bloc of Herut (Freedom; f. 1948; Leader ITZHAK SHAMIR; Sec.-Gen. MOSHE ARENS), the Liberal Party of Israel (f. 1961; Chair. AVRAHAM SHARIR), Laam (For the Nation) (f. 1976; fmrly led by YIGAEL HURWITZ, who left the coalition to form his own party, Ometz, before the 1984 general election), Ahdut (a one-man faction, HILLEL SEIDEL) and Tami (f. 1981; represents the interests of Sephardic Jews; Leader AHARON UZAN), which joined Likud in June 1987; Herut and the Liberal Party formally merged in August 1988 to form the Likud-National Liberal Movement; aims: territorial integrity (advocates retention of all the territory of post-1922 mandatory Palestine); absorption of newcomers; a social order based on freedom and justice, elimination of poverty and want; development of an economy that will ensure a decent standard of living; improvement of the environment and the quality of life. Likud was the sole government party from June 1977 until September 1984 when it formed the National Unity government with Likud; a new National Unity government was formed after the 1988 election; Leader of Likud ITZHAK SHAMIR.

Moledet (Homeland): f. 1988; right-wing nationalist party; aims: the expulsion ('transfer') of the 1.5m. Palestinians living in the West Bank and Gaza Strip; Leader Gen. RECHAVAM ZE'EVI.

Morasha (Heritage): Tel-Aviv; merged with National Religious Party faction in the Knesset July 1986.

National Religious Party: 166 Ibn Gavirol St, Kastel Bldg, Tel-Aviv; f. 1956; stands for strict adherence to Jewish religion and tradition, and strives to achieve the application of religious precepts of Judaism in everyday life; it is also endeavouring to establish the Constitution of Israel on Jewish religious law (the Torah); withdrew from (Labour) government coalition in December 1976 and before the 1984 general election supported the Likud coalition; 135,000 mems; Leader Prof. AVNER SHAKI.

New Liberal Party: Tel-Aviv; f. 1987 as a merger of three groups: Shinui-Movement for Change (f. 1974 and restored 1978, when Democratic Movement for Change split into two parties; centrist; Leader AMNON RUBINSTEIN), the Centre Liberal Party (f. 1986 by members of the Liberal Party of Israel; Leader ITZHAK BERMAN), and the Independent Liberal Party (f. 1965 by 7 Liberal Party of Israel Knesset mems, after the formation of the Herut Movement and Liberal Party of Israel bloc; 20,000 mems; Chair. MOSHE KOL; Gen. Sec. NISSIM ELIAD); Leaders AMNON RUBINSTEIN, ITZHAK BERMAN and MOSHE KOL.

Poale Agudat Israel: f. 1924; working-class Orthodox Judaist party; Leader Dr KALMAN KAHANE.

Political Zionist Opposition (Ometz): f. 1982; one-man party, YIGAEL HURWITZ.

Progressive List for Peace: f. 1984; Jewish Arab; advocates recognition of the PLO and the establishment of a Palestinian state in the West Bank and the Gaza Strip; Leader MUHAMMAD MU'ARI.

Ratz (Civil Rights and Peace Movement): 21 Tchernihovsky St, Tel-Aviv 63291; tel. 03-5101847; f. 1973; concerned with human and civil rights, opposes discrimination on basis of religion, sex or ethnic identification and advocates a peace settlement with the Arab countries and the Palestinians; Leader Mrs SHULAMIT ALONI.

Religious Zionism Party (Matzad): Tel-Aviv; f. 1983; breakaway group from the National Religious Party; also known as Morasha (Heritage); Leader Rabbi HAIM DRUCKMAN.

Shas (Sephardic Torah Guardians): f. 1984 by splinter groups from Agudat Israel; ultra-orthodox Jewish party; Spiritual Leader Rabbi ELIEZER SHACH.

Tami: f. 1981; represents the interests of Sephardic Jews; Leader AHARON UZAN.

Directory

Tehiya—Zionist Revival Movement: 34 Rehov Hahalut, Jerusalem; tel. 02-244281; f. September 1979; aims: Israeli sovereignty over Judaea, Samaria, Gaza; extensive settlement programme; economic independence; uniting of religious and non-religious camps; opposes Camp David accords; Leaders YUVAL NE'EMAN, RAFAEL EITAN, GEULA COHEN, Rabbi ELIEZER WALDMAN.

Telem—State Renewal Movement: f. 1981 by the late MOSHE DAYAN; proposes the administration of a unilateral Palestinian autonomy in Judaea and Samaria, against the annexation of territories to Israel; supports Likud coalition; Leader MORDECHAI BEN-PORAT.

Tzomet Party: f. 1988; right-wing nationalist party; breakaway group from Tehiya party; Leader RAFAEL EITAN.

United Arab List: Arab party affiliated to Labour Party.

United Workers' Party (Mapam): POB 1777, Tel-Aviv 61016; tel. 03-266245; telex 33499; f. 1948; left-wing socialist-Zionist Jewish-Arab party; grouped in Labour-Mapam Alignment with Israel Labour Party from January 1969 until Sept. 1984 when it withdrew in protest over Labour's formation of a national government with Likud; 45,000 mems; Sec.-Gen. ELIAZAR GRANOT.

Yahad (Together): f. 1984; advocates a peace settlement with the Arab peoples and the Palestinians; joined the Labour Party parliamentary bloc in January 1987; Leader EZER WEIZMANN.

Diplomatic Representation

EMBASSIES IN ISRAEL

Argentina: 112 Rehov Hayarkon, 2nd Floor, Tel-Aviv; tel. 03-293411; telex 33730; Ambassador: ALBERTO E. HAM.

Australia: Beit Europa, 37 Shaul Hamelech Blvd, Tel-Aviv 64928; tel. 03-250451; telex 33777; Ambassador: J. B. CAMBELL.

Austria: 11 Rehov Herman Cohen, Tel-Aviv; tel. 03-246186; telex 33435; Ambassador: Dr OTTO PLEINERT.

Belgium: 266 Rehov Hayarkon, Tel-Aviv 63504; tel. 03-454164; telex 342211; Ambassador: (vacant).

Bolivia: 73A Rehov Nordau, Herzliya 'B'; tel. 052-582261; Ambassador: SIMÓN SEJAS TORDOYA.

Brazil: 14 Hei Beiyar, Tel-Aviv; tel. 03-219292; telex 33752; Ambassador: Dr LAMO SOUTELLO ALVES.

Burma: 19 Rehov Yona, Ramat Gan; Chargé d'affaires a.i.: U BA YIN.

Cameroon: Tel-Aviv.

Canada: 220 Rehov Hayarkon, Tel-Aviv 63405; tel. 03-228122; telex 341293; Ambassador: JAMES K. BARTLEMAN.

Chile: 54 Rehov Pinkas, Apt 45, Tel-Aviv; tel. 03-440414; telex 342189; Ambassador: SANTIAGO BENADAVA.

Colombia: 52 Rehov Pinkas, Tel-Aviv; tel. 03-449616; telex 342165; Ambassador: LAZAR GILINSKI.

Costa Rica: 13 Diskin St, Apt 1, Jerusalem; tel. 02-660674; telex 26319; Ambassador: LAUREANO ALBÁN.

Côte d'Ivoire: The Tower, 3 Rehov Daniel Frisch, POB 14371; 64371 Tel-Aviv; tel. 03-262211; telex 341143; Ambassador: JEAN-PIERRE BONI.

Denmark: 23 Rehov Bnei Moshe, POB 21080, Tel-Aviv 61210; tel. 03-440405; telex 33514; Ambassador: JAKOB RYTTER.

Dominican Republic: Sderot Shaul Hamelech 4, Apt. 81, 64733 Tel-Aviv; Ambassador: RAMÓN A. CASTILLO.

Ecuador: 'Asia House', 4 Rehov Weizman, POB 30, Tel-Aviv 64239; tel. 03-258764; telex 342179; Ambassador: LUIS ORTIZ-TERÁN.

Egypt: 54 Rehov Bezel, Tel-Aviv; telex 361289; Ambassador: MUHAMMAD BASSIOUNI.

El Salvador: 16 Kovshei Katamon, POB 4005, Jerusalem 91039; tel. 02-26144; Ambassador: ENRIQUE GUTTFREUND.

Finland: Beith Eliahu, 2 Rehov Ibn Gvirol, Tel-Aviv 64077; tel. 03-250527; telex 33552; Ambassador: OSMO VAINOLA.

France: 112 Tayelet Herbert Samuel, Tel-Aviv; tel. 03-245371; telex 33662; Ambassador: ALAIN PIERRET.

Germany, Federal Republic: 16 Rehov Soutine, Tel-Aviv 64684; telex 33621; Ambassador: WILHELM HAAS.

Greece: 65 Shderot Shaul Hamelech, Tel-Aviv; tel. 03-509704; telex 341227; Ambassador: EMMANUEL GHIKAS.

Guatemala: 1 Bernstein Cohen, 47239 Ramat Hasharon, Tel-Aviv; tel. 03-490456; Ambassador: Col RAMIRO GEREDA ASTURIAS.

Haiti: 14 Tevuot Haaretz, Shikun Dan, Tel-Aviv; tel. 03-496222; Ambassador: FRANCK M. JOSEPH.

ISRAEL

Directory

Honduras: 46 Rehov Hei Beiyar, Apt 3, Kikar Hamedina, Tel-Aviv 62093; tel. 03-218015; telex 361499; Ambassador: MOISES STARKMAN.
Hungary: (see Sweden).
Italy: 'Asia House', 4 Rehov Weizman, Tel-Aviv; tel. 03-264223; telex 342664; Ambassador: ALBERTO LEONCINI-BARTOLI.
Japan: 'Asia House', 4 Rehov Weizman, Tel-Aviv; tel. 342202; Ambassador: SHOZO KADOTA.
Liberia: 119 Shderot Rothschild, Tel-Aviv; tel. 03-203191; telex 361637; Ambassador: Maj. SAMUEL B. PEARSON, Jr.
Malawi: Tel-Aviv; Ambassador: MCLEEN WONGA MACHINJILI.
Mexico: 14 Rehov Hei Beiyar, Tel-Aviv; telex 32352; Ambassador: ROGELIO MARTÍNEZ.
Netherlands: 'Asia House', 4 Rehov Weizman, Tel-Aviv 61333; tel. 03-257377; telex 342180; Ambassador: J. H. R. D. VAN ROIJEN.
Norway: 10 Rehov Hei Beiyar, Tel-Aviv; tel. 03-295207; telex 33417; Ambassador: TORLEIV ANDA.
Panama: 28 Rehov Hei Beiyar, Kikar Hamedina, Tel-Aviv; tel. 03-256711; Ambassador: Maj. RODOLFO CASTRELLÓN.
Peru: 52 Rehov Pinkas, Apt 31, 8th Floor, Tel-Aviv 62261; tel. 03-454065; telex 371351; Ambassador: GUILLERMO FERNÁNDEZ-CORNEJO.
Philippines: 12 Rehov Hei Beiyar, Tel-Aviv; telex 32104; Ambassador: ETTA C. ENRIQUEZ.
Portugal: Tel-Aviv.
Romania: 24 Rehov Adam Hacohen, Tel-Aviv; Ambassador: IULIAN BITULEANU.
South Africa: 2 Rehov Kaplan, Tel-Aviv 64734; tel. 03-256147; telex 361208; Ambassador: JOHAN L. VILJOEN.
Spain: Tel-Aviv; Ambassador: PEDRO LÓPEZ DE AGUIRREBENGOA.
Sweden: 'Asia House', 4 Rehov Weizman, Tel-Aviv; telex 33650; Ambassador: SVEN HIRDMAN; also contains a Hungarian interests section.
Switzerland: 228 Rehov Hayarkon, Tel-Aviv; tel. 03-5464455; telex 342237; Ambassador: JEAN-PIERRE KEUSCH.
Thailand: Tel-Aviv; Ambassador: SUCHINDA YONGSUNTHON.
Togo: Tel-Aviv.
Turkey: 34 Rehov Amos, Tel-Aviv 62495; tel. 03-454155; Chargé d'affaires a.i.: EKREM ESAT GÜVENDIREN.
United Kingdom: 192 Rehov Hayarkon, Tel-Aviv 63405; tel. 03-249171; telex 33559; Ambassador: MARK ELLIOTT.
USA: 71 Rehov Hayarkon, Tel-Aviv 63903; tel. 03-654338; telex 33376; Ambassador: WILLIAM A. BROWN.
Uruguay: 52 Rehov Pinkas, Tel-Aviv; tel. 03-440411; telex 342669; Ambassador: JUAN ANDRÉS PACHECO.
Venezuela: Textile Center, 2 Rehov Kaufmann, Tel-Aviv; tel. 03-656287; telex 342172; Ambassador: NESTOR COLL BLASINI.
Zaire: 60 Hei Beiyar, Kikar Hamedina, Tel-Aviv; tel. 03-452681; telex 371239; Ambassador: Gen. ELUKI MONGA AUNDU.

The Jewish Agency for Israel

POB 92, Jerusalem 91920; tel. 02-202222; telex 25236.
Organization: The governing bodies are the Assembly which determines basic policy, the Board of Governors which sets policy for the Agency between Assembly meetings and the Executive responsible for the day to day running of the Agency.
Chairman of Executive: SIMCHA DINITZ.
Chairman of Board of Governors: MANDEL KAPLAN.
Director-General: GIDEON WITKON.
Secretary-General: HOWARD WEISBAND.
Functions: According to the Agreement of 1971, the Jewish Agency undertakes the immigration and absorption of immigrants in Israel, including absorption in agricultural settlement and immigrant housing; social welfare and health services in connection with immigrants; education, youth care and training; neighbourhood rehabilitation through project renewal.
Budget (1988/89): US $414m.

Judicial System

The law of Israel is composed of the enactments of the Knesset and, to a lesser extent, of the acts, orders-in-council and ordinances that remain from the period of the British Mandate in Palestine (1922–48). The pre-1948 law has, largely, been replaced, amended or reorganized, in the interests of codification, by Israeli legislation. This legislation generally follows a pattern which is very similar to that operating in England and the USA.
Attorney-General: JOSEPH HARISH.

CIVIL COURTS

The Supreme Court is the highest judicial instance in the State. It has jurisdiction as an Appellate Court from the District Courts in all matters, both civil and criminal (sitting as a Court of Civil Appeal or as a Court of Criminal Appeal), and as a Court of First Instance (sitting as a High Court of Justice) in matters in which it considers it necessary to grant relief in the interests of justice and which are not within the jurisdiction of any other court or tribunal. This includes applications for orders in the nature of *habeas corpus*, *mandamus*, prohibition and *certiorari*, and enables the court to review the legality of acts of administrative authorities of all kinds.
President of the Supreme Court: MEIR SHAMGAR.
Vice-President of the Supreme Court: MIRIAM BEN-PORAT.
Justices of the Supreme Court: M. EYLON, A. BARAK, M. BEJSKI, SH. LEVIN, D. LEVIN, G. BACH, S. NETANYAHU, A. HALIMA, E. GOLDBERG.
Chief Registrar: Judge S. TZUR (magistrate).
The District Courts: Jerusalem, Tel-Aviv, Jaffa, Haifa, Beersheba, Nazareth. They have unlimited jurisdiction as Courts of First Instance in all civil and criminal matters not within the jurisdiction of a Magistrates' Court, all matters not within the exclusive jurisdiction of any other tribunal, and matters within the concurrent jurisdiction of any other tribunal so long as such tribunal does not deal with them, and as an Appellate Court in appeals from judgments and decisions of Magistrates' Courts and judgments of Municipal Courts and various administrative tribunals.
Magistrates' Courts: There are 28 Magistrates' Courts, having criminal jurisdiction to try contraventions, misdemeanours and certain felonies, and civil jurisdiction to try actions concerning possession or use of immovable property, or the partition thereof whatever may be the value of the subject matter of the action, and other civil actions on a limited basis.
Labour Courts: Established in 1969. Regional Labour Courts in Jerusalem, Tel-Aviv, Haifa and Beersheba, composed of Judges and representatives of the public. A National Labour Court in Jerusalem, presided over by Judge Z. Bar-Niv. The Courts have jurisdiction over all matters arising out of the relationship between employer and employee; between parties to a collective labour agreement; matters concerning the National Insurance Law and the Labour Law and Rules.

RELIGIOUS COURTS

The Religious Courts are the Courts of the recognized religious communities. They are competent in certain defined matters of personal status concerning members of their community. Where any action of personal status involves persons of different religious communities the President of the Supreme Court will decide which Court shall have jurisdiction. Whenever a question arises as to whether or not a case is one of personal status within the exclusive jurisdiction of a Religious Court, the matter must be referred to a Special Tribunal composed of two Justices of the Supreme Court and the President of the highest court of the religious community concerned in Israel. The judgments of the Religious Courts are executed by the process and offices of the Civil Courts.
Jewish Rabbinical Courts: These Courts have exclusive jurisdiction in matters of marriage and divorce of Jews in Israel who are Israeli citizens or residents. In all other matters of personal status they have concurrent jurisdiction with the District Courts with the consent of all parties concerned.
Muslim Religious Courts: These Courts have exclusive jurisdiction in matters of marriage and divorce of Muslims who are not foreigners, or who are foreigners subject by their national law to the jurisdiction of Muslim Religious Courts in such matters. In all other matters of personal status they have concurrent jurisdiction with the District Courts with the consent of all parties concerned.
Christian Religious Courts: The Courts of the recognized Christian communities have exclusive jurisdiction in matters of marriage and divorce of members of their communities who are not foreigners. In all other matters of personal status they have concurrent jurisdiction with the District Courts with the consent of all parties concerned. But neither these Courts nor the Civil Courts have jurisdiction to dissolve the marriage of a foreign subject.
Druze Courts: These Courts, established in 1963, have exclusive jurisdiction in matters of marriage and divorce of Druze in Israel, who are Israeli citizens or residents, and concurrent jurisdiction with the District Courts in all other matters of personal status of Druze with the consent of all parties concerned.

ISRAEL

Religion

JUDAISM

Judaism, the religion of the Jews, is the faith of the majority of Israel's inhabitants. On 31 December 1987 Judaism's adherents totalled 3,612,900, equivalent to 82% of the country's population. Its basis is a belief in an ethical monotheism.

There are two main Jewish communities: the Ashkenazim and the Sephardim. The former are the Jews from Eastern, Central, or Northern Europe, while the latter originate from the Balkan countries, North Africa and the Middle East.

There is also a community of about 10,000 Falashas (Ethiopian Jews) who have been airlifted to Israel at various times since the fall of Emperor Haile Selassie in 1974.

The supreme religious authority is vested in the Chief Rabbinate, which consists of the Ashkenazi and Sephardi Chief Rabbis and the Supreme Rabbinical Council. It makes decisions on interpretation of the Jewish law, and supervises the Rabbinical Courts. There are 8 regional Rabbinical Courts, and a Rabbinical Court of Appeal presided over by the two Chief Rabbis.

According to the Rabbinical Courts Jurisdiction Law of 1953, marriage and divorce among Jews in Israel are exclusively within the jurisdiction of the Rabbinical Courts. Provided that all the parties concerned agree, other matters of personal status can also be decided by the Rabbinical Courts.

There are 195 Religious Councils, which maintain religious services and supply religious needs, and about 405 religious committees with similar functions in smaller settlements. Their expenses are borne jointly by the State and the local authorities. The Religious Councils are under the administrative control of the Ministry of Religious Affairs. In all matters of religion, the Religious Councils are subject to the authority of the Chief Rabbinate. There are 365 officially appointed rabbis. The total number of synagogues is about 7,000, most of which are organized within the framework of the Union of Israel Synagogues.

Head of the Ashkenazi Community: The Chief Rabbi AVRAHAM SHAPIRO.

Head of the Sephardic Community: Jerusalem; tel. 02-244785; The Chief Rabbi MORDECHAI ELIAHU.

Two Jewish sects still loyal to their distinctive customs are:

The Karaites, a sect which recognizes only the Jewish written law and not the oral law of the Mishna and Talmud. The community of about 12,000, many of whom live in or near Ramla, has been augmented by immigration from Egypt.

The Samaritans, an ancient sect mentioned in 2 Kings xvii, 24. They recognize only the Torah. The community in Israel numbers about 500; about half of them live in Holon, where a Samaritan synagogue has been built, and the remainder, including the High Priest, live in Nablus, near Mt Gerizim, which is sacred to the Samaritans.

ISLAM

The Muslims in Israel are mainly Sunnis, and are divided among the four rites of the Sunni sect of Islam: the Shafe'i, the Hanbali, the Hanafi and the Maliki. Before June 1967 they numbered approx. 175,000; in 1971, approx. 343,900. On 31 December 1987 the total Muslim population of Israel was 614,500.

Mufti of Jerusalem: POB 20002, Jerusalem; tel. 02-285994; Sheikh SAAD ED-DIN AL-ALAMI (also Chair. Supreme Muslim Council for Jerusalem).

There was also a total of 76,100 Druzes in Israel at 31 December 1987.

CHRISTIANITY

The total Christian population of Israel on 31 December 1987 was 103,000.

United Christian Council in Israel: POB 116, Jerusalem 91000; f. 1956; 17 mems (churches and other bodies); Pres. Dr RAY REGISTER; Gen. Sec. CHARLES KOPP.

The Roman Catholic Church

Armenian Rite

The Armenian Catholic Patriarch of Cilicia is resident in Beirut, Lebanon.

Patriarchal Vicariate of Jerusalem: Via Dolorosa, Third Station, POB 19546, Jerusalem; tel. 02-284262; f. 1856; Vicar Patriarchal Fr JOSEPH ROUBIAN.

Chaldean Rite

The Chaldean Patriarch of Babylon is resident in Baghdad, Iraq.

Patriarchal Vicariate of Jerusalem: Chaldean Patriarchal Vicariate, Saad and Said Quarter, Nablus Rd, Jerusalem; Vicar Patriarchal HENRI GOUILLON.

Latin Rite

The Patriarchate of Jerusalem covers Palestine, Jordan and Cyprus. At 31 December 1986 there were an estimated 62,811 adherents.

Bishops' Conference: Conférence des Evêques Latins dans les Régions Arabes, Patriarcat Latin, POB 14152, Jerusalem; tel. 02-282323; f. 1967; Pres. His Beatitude MICHEL SABBAH.

Patriarchate of Jerusalem: Patriarcat Latin, POB 14152, Jerusalem; tel. 02-282323; Patriarch: His Beatitude MICHEL SABBAH; Vicar General for Israel: Mgr HANNA KALDANY (Titular Bishop of Gaba), Vicariat Patriarcal Latin, Nazareth.

Maronite Rite

The Maronite community, under the jurisdiction of the Maronite Patriarch of Antioch (resident in Lebanon), has about 6,350 members.

Patriarchal Vicariate of Jerusalem: Vicariat Maronite, Maronite St 25, Jerusalem; tel. 02-282158; Vicar Patriarchal AUGUSTIN HARFOUCHE (also representing the Archbishop of Tyre, Lebanon, as Vicar General for Israel).

Melkite Rite

The Greek-Melkite Patriarch of Antioch (Maximos V Hakim) is resident in Damascus, Syria.

Patriarchal Vicariate of Jerusalem: Vicariat Patriarcal Grec-Melkite Catholique, POB 14130, 0091141 Jerusalem; tel. 02-282023; about 3,000 adherents (1984); Vicars Patriarchal Mgr HILARION CAPUCCI (Titular Archbishop of Caesarea in Palestine), Mgr LOTFI LAHAM (Titular Archbishop of Tarsus).

Archbishop of Akka (Acre): Most Rev. MAXIMOS SALLOUM, Archevêché Grec-Catholique, POB 279, Haifa; tel. 04-523114; about 42,000 adherents (1984).

Syrian Rite

The Syrian Catholic Patriarch of Antioch is resident in Beirut, Lebanon.

Patriarchal Vicariate of Jerusalem: Vicariat Patriarcal Syrien Catholique, Nablus Rd, POB 19787, Jerusalem; tel. 02-282657; about 1,000 adherents in Palestine and Jordan (Dec. 1986); Vicar Patriarchal Mgr PIERRE ABD AL-AHAD.

The Greek Orthodox Church

The Patriarchate of Jerusalem contains an estimated 260,000 adherents throughout the Middle East.

Patriarch of Jerusalem: DIODOROS I, Greek Orthodox Patriarchate St, Old City, POB 19632-633, Jerusalem; tel. 02-284917.

The Anglican Communion

Episcopal Church in Jerusalem and the Middle East: St George's Close, POB 1248, Jerusalem; President-Bishop Rt Rev. SAMIR KAFITY, Bishop in Jerusalem.

Other Christian Churches

Other denominations include the Armenian Orthodox Church (900 members), the Coptic Orthodox Church (700 members), the Russian Orthodox Church, the Ethiopian Orthodox Church, the Romanian Orthodox Church, the Lutheran Church and the Church of Scotland.

The Press

Tel-Aviv is the main publishing centre. Largely for economic reasons there has developed no local press away from these cities; hence all papers regard themselves as national. Friday editions, Sabbath eve, are increased to up to twice the normal size by special weekend supplements, and experience a considerable rise in circulation. No newspapers appear on Saturday.

Most of the daily papers are in Hebrew, and others appear in Arabic, English, French, Polish, Yiddish, Hungarian and German. The total daily circulation is 500,000–600,000 copies, or 21 papers per hundred people, although most citizens read more than one daily paper.

Most Hebrew morning dailies have strong political or religious affiliations. *Al-Hamishmar* is affiliated to Mapam, *Hatzofeh* to the National Religious Front—World Mizrahi. *Davar* is the long-established organ of the Histadrut. Most newspapers depend on subsidies from political parties, religious organizations or public funds. The limiting effect on freedom of commentary entailed by this party press system has provoked repeated criticism.

The Jerusalem Arabic daily *Al-Anba* has a small circulation (10,000) but an increasing number of Israeli Arabs are now reading Hebrew dailies. The daily, *Al-Quds*, was founded in 1968 for Arabs in Jerusalem and the West Bank; the small indigenous press of occupied Jordan has largely ceased publication or transferred

ISRAEL — Directory

operations to Amman. Two of the four Arabic newspapers which are published in occupied East Jerusalem, the daily, *Al-Mithaq*, and the weekly, *Al-Ahd*, were closed by the Israeli authorities in August 1986. It was alleged that they were financed and managed by the Popular Front for the Liberation of Palestine. The Palestinian news agency in the West Bank town of Nablus was closed for two years in October 1987. Since the Palestinian uprising in the Occupied Territories began in December 1987, further action has been taken by the Israeli authorities to curb allegedly pro-PLO press activities. In February 1988 the left-wing newspaper, *Derech Hanitzotz*, was closed by the Israelis for its alleged links with the Democratic Front for the Liberation of Palestine; in March the Palestine Press Service in East Jerusalem (the only remaining Arab news agency in the Occupied Territories) was closed by military order for six months; and in April the minor weekly magazine *Al-Awdah* (The Return) (also based in East Jerusalem) was closed, on the grounds that it was being funded by the PLO.

There are around 400 other newspapers and magazines including some 50 weekly and 150 fortnightly; over 250 of them are in Hebrew, the remainder in eleven other languages.

The most influential and respected dailies, for both quality of news coverage and commentary, are *Ha'aretz* and the trade union paper, *Davar*, which frequently has articles by government figures. These are the most widely read of the morning papers, exceeded only by the popular afternoon press, *Ma'ariv* and *Yedioth Aharonoth*. The *Jerusalem Post* gives detailed and sound news coverage in English.

The Israeli Press Council (Chair. JOSHUA ROTENSTREICH), established in 1963, deals with matters of common interest to the Press such as drafting the code of professional ethics which is binding on all journalists.

The Daily Newspaper Publishers' Association represents publishers in negotiations with official and public bodies, negotiates contracts with employees and purchases and distributes newsprint.

DAILIES

Al-Anba (The News): POB 428, 37 Hillel St, Beit Agron, Jerusalem; f. 1968; Arabic; published by Jerusalem Publications Ltd; Editor and Man. Dir OVADIA DANON; circ. 10,000.

Davar (The Word): POB 199, 45 Sheinkin St, Tel-Aviv; tel. 03-286141; telex 33807; f. 1925; morning; Hebrew; official organ of the General Federation of Labour (Histadrut); Editor HANNAH ZEMER; circ. 39,000; there are also weekly magazine editions.

Al-Fajr (The Dawn): Jerusalem; Arabic; Publr PAUL AJILOUNY; Man. Editor ABD AL-KHADER; Editor HANNAH SINIORA.

Ha'aretz (The Land): 21 Salman Schocken St, POB 233, Tel-Aviv; tel. 03-5121212; telex 33748; f. 1918; morning; Hebrew; liberal, independent; Editor GERSHOM G. SCHOCKEN; circ. 55,000 (weekdays), 75,000 (weekends).

Hadashot (The News): Tel-Aviv; late morning; Hebrew.

Al-Hamishmar (The Guardian): Al-Hamishmar House, 4 Ben Avigdor St, Tel-Aviv; tel. 03-57171; f. 1943; morning; Hebrew; organ of the United Workers' Party (Mapam); Editor MARK GEFEN; circ. 25,000.

Hamodia (The Informer): Yehuda Hamackabbi 3, POB 1306, Jerusalem; morning; Hebrew; organ of Agudat Israel; Editors M. A. DRUCK, H. M. KNOPF; circ. 15,000.

Hatzofeh (The Watchman): 66 Hamasger St, Tel-Aviv; tel. 03-336056; f. 1938; morning; Hebrew; organ of the National Religious Party; Editor M. ISHON; circ. 16,000.

Israel Nachrichten: 52 Harakevet St, Tel-Aviv; tel. 03-370011; f. 1974; morning; German; Editor S. HIMMELFARB; circ. 20,000.

Israelski Far Tribuna: 113 Givat Herzl St, Tel-Aviv; tel. 03-3700; f. 1952; Bulgarian; circ. 6,000.

Al-Ittihad (Unity): POB 104, Haifa; tel. 04-511296; f. 1944; Arabic; organ of the Israeli Communist Party (Rakkah); Chief Editor EMILE HABIBY.

The Jerusalem Post: POB 81, Romema, 91000, Jerusalem; tel. 02-551616; telex 26121; f. 1932; morning; English; independent; Editor and Man. Dir ARI RATH; Editor ERWIN FRENKEL; circ. 30,000 (weekdays), 50,000 (weekend edition); there is also a weekly international edition, circ. 60,000.

Le Journal d'Israel: 26 Agra St, POB 28330, Tel-Aviv; f. 1971; French; independent; Chief Editor J. RABIN; circ. 10,000; also overseas weekly selection; circ. 15,000.

Letzte Nyess (Late News): 52 Harakevet St, POB 28034, Tel-Aviv; f. 1949; morning; Yiddish; Editor S. HIMMELFARB; circ. 23,000.

Ma'ariv (Evening Prayer): 2 Carlebach St, Tel-Aviv 61200; tel. 03-439111; telex 33735; f. 1948; mid-morning; Hebrew; independent; published by Modiin Publishing House; Editor IDO DISSENTCHIK; circ. daily 115,000, weekend 220,000.

Mabat: 56 Wolfson St, Tel-Aviv; f. 1971; morning; economic and social; Editor S. YARKONI.

Al-Mawqif: Jerusalem; Arabic; owned by the Arab Council for Public Affairs.

Al-Mithaq (The Covenant): Jerusalem; Arabic; Editor MAHMOUD KHATIB; (closed down by Israeli authorities August 1986).

An-Nahar (Day): Jerusalem; Arabic; pro-Jordanian; Editor OTHMAN HALLAQ.

The Nation: Jerusalem; f. 1988; English; Editor and Publr HESH KESTIN.

Nowiny i Kurier: 52 Harakevet St, Tel-Aviv; f. 1952; morning; Polish; Editor S. HIMMELFARB; circ. 15,000.

Al-Quds (Jerusalem): POB 19788, Jerusalem; tel. 02-284061; telex 02-282475; f. 1968; Arabic; Publr MAHMOUD ABU ZALAF; Editor-in-Chief WALID ABU ZALAF; circ. 40,000.

Ash-Sha'ab (The People): Jerusalem; f. 1972; Arabic; circ. 15,000; Editor SALAH ZUHAIKA.

Sha'ar: 52 Harakevet St, Tel-Aviv 64284; Hebrew; economy and finance; Editor S. HIMMELFARB.

Shearim (The Gates): 64 Frishman St, Tel-Aviv; tel. 03-242126; organ of Poale Agudat Israel; Editor MAIER HALACHMI; circ. 12,000.

Uj Kelet: 52 Harakevet St, Tel-Aviv; f. 1918; morning; Hungarian; independent; Editor S. HIMMELFARB; circ. 20,000.

Viata Noastra: 52 Harakevet St, Tel-Aviv; f. 1950; morning; Romanian; Editor S. HIMMELFARB; circ. 30,000.

Yedioth Aharonoth (The Latest News): 138 Petah Tikva Rd, Tel-Aviv 61000; tel. 972-3212212; telex 33847; f. 1939; evening; independent; Editor-in-Chief DOV JUDKOWSKI; circ. 300,000, Friday 540,000.

Yom Yom: POB 1194, 34–36 Itzhak Sadeh St, Tel-Aviv; f. 1964; morning; Yiddish; economy and finance; Editor S. HIMMELFARB.

WEEKLIES AND FORTNIGHTLIES

Al-Ahd (Sunday): Jerusalem; weekly; Arabic; (closed down by Israeli authorities August 1986).

Al-Awdah (The Return): East Jerusalem; weekly; Arabic and English; Proprs IBRAHIM QARA'EEN, Mrs RAYMONDA TAWIL; circ. 10,000; (closed down by Israeli authorities April 1988).

Bama'alah: POB 303, Tel-Aviv; Hebrew; journal of the young Histadrut Movement; Editor N. ANAELY.

Bamahane: Military POB 1013, Tel-Aviv; f. 1948; military, illustrated weekly of the Israel Armed Forces; Hebrew; Editor-in-Chief YOSSEF ESHKOL; circ. 70,000.

Bitaon Heyl Ha'avir (Air Force Magazine): Doar Zwai 1560, Zahal; tel. 03-260948; f. 1948; fortnightly; Hebrew; Man. Editor D. MOLAD; Editor-in-Chief AHARON LAPIDOT; Technical Editor RAM AVRAHAMI; circ. 30,000.

Davar Hashavua: 45 Sheinkin St, Tel-Aviv; tel. 02-286141; f. 1946; weekly; Hebrew; popular illustrated; published by Histadrut, General Federation of Labour; Editor TUVIA MENDELSON; circ. 43,000.

Derech Hanitzotz/Tariq ash-Sharara (The Shining Way): East Jerusalem; twice weekly; left-wing; Hebrew and Arabic; published by Nitzotz-Ashara Organization; circ. Hebrew edition 800, Arabic edition 1,500; (closed down by Israeli authorities in February 1988).

Ethgar: 75 Einstein St, Tel-Aviv; twice weekly; Hebrew; Editor NATHAN YALIN-MOR.

Gesher (The Bridge): Jerusalem; fortnightly; Hebrew; Editor ZIAD ABU ZAYAD.

Glasul Populurui: 37 Eilath St, POB 2675, Tel-Aviv; weekly of the Communist Party of Israel; Romanian; Editor MEÏR SEMO.

Haolam Hazeh: POB 136, 3 Gordon St, Tel-Aviv; tel. 03-232262; f. 1937; weekly; independent; illustrated news magazine; Editor-in-Chief URI AVNERY.

Harefuah: 39 Shaul Hamelech Blvd, Tel-Aviv 64928; f. 1920; fortnightly journal of the Israeli Medical Association; Hebrew with English summaries; Editor I. SUM; circ. 7,500.

Hotam: Al-Hamishmar House, Choma U'Migdal St, Tel-Aviv; weekly of the United Workers' Party (Mapam); Hebrew.

Al-Hurriya (Freedom): 38 King George St, Tel-Aviv; Arabic weekly of the Herut Party.

Illustrirte Weltwoch: Tel-Aviv; f. 1956; weekly; Yiddish; Editor M. KARPINOVITZ.

Jerusalem Post International Edition: POB 81, Romema, Jerusalem 91000; tel. 02-551616; telex 26121; f. 1959; weekly; English; overseas edition of the *Jerusalem Post* (q.v.); circ. 60,000 to 95 countries.

Kol Ha'am (Voice of the People): 37 Eilath St, POB 2675, Tel-Aviv; f. 1947; Hebrew; organ of the Communist Party of Israel; Editor B. BALTI.

ISRAEL

Laisha: 35 Bnei Brak St, POB 28122, Tel-Aviv 67132; tel. 03-371464; f. 1946; Hebrew; women's magazine; Editor ZVI ELGAT.

Ma'ariv Lanoar: 2 Carlebach St, Tel-Aviv 67132; tel. 03-439111; f. 1957; weekly for youth; Hebrew; Editor AMNON BEI-RAV; circ. 100,000.

Magallati (My Magazine): Arabic Publishing House, POB 28049, Tel-Aviv; tel. 03-371438; f. 1960; young people's fortnightly; Man. JOSEPH ELIAHOU; Editor-in-Chief IBRAHIM MUSA IBRAHIM; Editors GAMIL DAHLAN, MISHEL HADDAD; circ. 7,500.

MB (Mitteilungsblatt): POB 1480, Tel-Aviv; tel. 03-664461; f. 1932; German monthly journal of the Irgun Olei Merkas Europa (Settlers from Central Europe); Editor ZEEV ESTREICHER.

Al-Mirsad (The Telescope): POB 1777, Tel-Aviv; tel. 03-266244; f. 1948; Arabic; Mapam.

Reshumot: Ministry of Justice, Jerusalem; f. 1948; Hebrew, Arabic and English; official Government gazette.

Sada at-Tarbia (The Echo of Education): published by the Histadrut and Teachers' Association, POB 2306, Rehovot; f. 1952; fortnightly; Arabic; educational; Editor TUVIA SHAMOSH.

OTHER PERIODICALS

Ariel: Cultural and Scientific Relations Division, Ministry for Foreign Affairs, Jerusalem; Publishers, Editorial and Distribution: Jerusalem Post Publications Ltd, POB 3349, Jerusalem 91002; tel. 02-381515 (editorial); f. 1962; quarterly review of the arts and letters in Israel; regular edns in English, Spanish, French and German; occasional edns in several other languages; Editor ASHER WEILL; circ. 20,000.

Avoda Urevacha Ubituach Leumi: POB 915, Jerusalem; f. 1949; monthly review of the Ministry of Labour and Social Affairs, and the National Insurance Institute, Jerusalem; Hebrew; Chief Editor AVNER MICHAELI; Editor MICHAEL KLODOVSKY; circ. 2,500.

Bakalkala Uvems'har (Economics and Trade): POB 20027, Tel-Aviv; tel. 03-288224; telex 33484; f. 1919; monthly; Hebrew; published by Federation of Israeli Chambers of Commerce; Editor Z. AMIT.

Al-Bushra (Good News): POB 6088, Haifa; f. 1935; monthly; Arabic; organ of the Ahmadiyya movement; Editor FALAHUD DIN O'DEH.

Business Diary: 37 Hanamal St, Haifa; f. 1947; weekly; English, Hebrew; shipping movements, import licences, stock exchange listings, business failures, etc.; Editor G. ALON.

Christian News from Israel: 30 Jaffa Rd, Jerusalem; f. 1949; half-yearly; English, French, Spanish; issued by the Ministry of Religious Affairs; Editor SHALOM BEN-ZAKKAI; circ. 10,000.

Di Goldene Keyt: 30 Weizmann St, Tel-Aviv; f. 1949; literary quarterly; Yiddish; published by the Histadrut; Editor A. SUTZKEVER; Co-Editor ALEXANDER SPIEGELBLATT; Man. Editor MOSHE MILLIS.

Divrei Haknesset: c/o The Knesset, Jerusalem; f. 1949; Hebrew; records of the proceedings of the Knesset; published by the Government Printer, Jerusalem; Editor LIORA SEGEV (acting); circ. 350.

Doing Business with Israel: POB 20027, Tel-Aviv; published by Federation of Israeli Chambers of Commerce; Editor ZVI SEGAL.

The Family Physician: 101 Arlosoroff St, POB 16250, Tel-Aviv 62098; tel. 03-433388; f. 1970; three times a year; Hebrew with English summaries; medical; Editor Prof. MAX R. POLLIACK; circ. 4,500.

Folk un Zion: POB 92, Tel-Aviv; tel. 02-533123; f. 1950; bi-monthly; current events relating to Israel and World Jewry; circ. 3,000; Editor MOSHE KALCHHEIM.

Frei Israel: POB 8512, Tel-Aviv; progressive monthly, published by Assen for Popular Culture; Yiddish.

Gazit: 8 Zvi Brook St, POB 4190, Tel-Aviv; f. 1932; monthly; Hebrew and English; art, literature; Publisher G. TALPHIR.

Hameshek Hahaklai: 21 Melchett St, Tel-Aviv; f. 1929; Hebrew; agricultural; Editor ISRAEL INBARI.

Al-Hamishmar (The Guardian): 4 Ben Avigdor St, Tel-Aviv; Bulgarian monthly of United Workers' Party.

Hamizrah Hehadash (The New East): Israel Oriental Society, The Hebrew University, Mount Scopus, Jerusalem 91905; tel. 02-883633; f. 1949; annual of the Israel Oriental Society; Middle Eastern, Asian and African Affairs; Hebrew with English summary; Editor AHARON LAYISH; circ. 1,500–2,000.

Hamionai (The Hotelier): POB 11586, Tel-Aviv; f. 1962; monthly of the Israel Hotel Association; Hebrew and English; Editor Z. PELTZ.

Hapraklit: 8 Wilson St, POB 14152, Tel-Aviv 61141; tel. 03-5614695; f. 1943; quarterly; Hebrew; published by the Israel Bar Association; Editor-in-Chief A. POLONSKI; Editor ARNAN GAVRIELI; circ. 9,000.

Hassadeh: 8 Shaul Hamelech Blvd, POB 40044, Tel-Aviv 61400; tel. 03-252171; f. 1920; monthly; review of settlement and agriculture; Hebrew with English summaries; Editor J. M. MARGALIT; circ. 7,000.

Hed Hagan: 8 Ben Saruk St, Tel-Aviv; f. 1935; Hebrew; educational; Editor Mrs ZIVA PEDAHZUR; circ. 6,300.

Hed Hahinukh: 8 Ben Saruk St, Tel-Aviv 62969; tel. 03-260211; f. 1926; monthly; Hebrew; educational; published by the Israeli Teachers' Union; Editor ORA GADELL; circ. 40,000.

Innovation: POB 7422, 31070 Haifa; tel. 04-255104; f. 1975; monthly; English; industrial research and development in Israel; published by A. G. Publications Ltd; Editor A. GREENFIELD.

Israel Business: POB 7422, 31070 Haifa; tel. 04-255104; f. 1961; monthly; English; business news and economic devt; published by A.G. Publications Ltd; Editor A. GREENFIELD.

Israel Economist: 6 Hazanowitz St, POB 7052, Jerusalem 91070; tel. 02-234131; f. 1945; monthly; English; independent; political and economic; Editor BEN MOLLOV; Publisher ISRAEL KELMAN; also publishes *Keeping Posted* (diplomatic magazine), *Mazel and Brucha* (jewellers' magazine); annuals: *Travel Agents' Manual, Electronics, International Conventions in Israel, Arkia, In Flight*, various hotel magazines.

Israel Environment Bulletin: Environmental Protection Service, Ministry of the Interior, POB 6158, Jerusalem 91061; tel. 02-660151; telex 26162; f. 1973; Editor SHOSHANA GABBAY; circ. 2,000.

Israel Export and Trade Journal: POB 11586, Tel-Aviv; f. 1949; monthly; English; commercial and economic; published by Israel Periodicals Co Ltd; Man. Dir ZALMAN PELTZ.

Israel Journal of Medical Sciences: POB 1435, Jerusalem 91013; tel. 02-227085; f. 1965; monthly; Editor-in-Chief Dr M. PRYWES; Man. Mrs S. TOLEDANO; circ. 5,500.

Israel Journal of Psychiatry and Related Sciences: Israel Science Publishers, POB 3115, Jerusalem 91030; f. 1963; quarterly; Editor-in-Chief E. L. EDELSTEIN.

Israel Journal of Veterinary Medicine: POB 3076, Rishon Le-Zion 75130; f. 1943; quarterly of the Israel Veterinary Medical Asscn; formerly *Refuah Veterinarith*; Editor Prof. M. TORTEN.

Israel Scene: POB 92, Jerusalem 91920; tel. 02-533123; telex 26436; f. 1980 as continuation of Israel Digest; monthly; English; published by the World Zionist Organization; news, features and analysis; circ. 20,000; Editor ASHER WEILL.

Israel-South Africa Trade Journal: POB 11587, Tel-Aviv; f. 1973; bi-monthly; English; commercial and economic; published by Israel Publications Corpn Ltd; Man. Dir Z. PELTZ.

Israel Tax Law Letter: POB 7422, Haifa 31070; tel. 04-255104; f. 1980; English; irregular; new developments in Israel tax law; Editor A. GREENFIELD.

Israels Aussenhandel: POB 11586, Tel-Aviv 61114; tel. 03-280215; telex 341118; f. 1967; monthly; German; commercial; published by Israel Periodicals Co Ltd; Editor PELTZ NOEMI; Man. Dir ZALMAN PELTZ.

Al-Jadid (The New): POB 104, Haifa; f. 1951; literary monthly; Arabic; Editor SALEM JUBRAN; circ. 5,000.

Kalkalan: 8 Akiva St, POB 7052, Jerusalem; f. 1952; monthly; independent; Hebrew commercial and economic; Editor J. KOLLEK.

Kiryat Sefer: POB 503, Jerusalem; tel. 02-585019; f. 1924; bibliographical quarterly of the Jewish National and University Library, Jerusalem; Hebrew; Editor Dr A. SHINAN.

Knowhow: POB 7422, 31070 Haifa; tel. 972 4255105; f. 1988; monthly; English; recent technological innovations and technology transfer opportunities; Editor A. GREENFIELD.

Labour in Israel: 93 Arlosorof St, POB 303, Tel-Aviv 62098; tel. 03-431111; telex 342488; quarterly; English, French, German and Spanish; bulletin of the Histadrut (General Federation of Labour in Israel); circ. 28,000.

Leshonenu: Academy of the Hebrew Language, POB 3449, Jerusalem 91034; tel. 02-632242; f. 1929; 4 a year; for the study of the Hebrew language and cognate subjects; Editor J. BLAU.

Leshonenu La'am: Academy of the Hebrew Language, POB 3449, Jerusalem 91034; tel. 02-632242; f. 1945; popular Hebrew philology; Editors E. EITAN, M. MEDAN.

Ma'arachot (Campaigns): Hakirya, 3 Mendler St, POB 7026, Tel-Aviv; tel. 03-268426; f. 1939; military and political bi-monthly; Hebrew; periodical of Israel Defence Force; Editors Col U. DROMI, Maj. R. ROJANSKI.

Melaha Vetaassiya (Trade and Industry): POB 11587, Tel-Aviv; f. 1969; bi-monthly review of the Union of Artisans and Small Manufacturers of Israel; Hebrew; Man. Dir Z. PELTZ.

Mibifnim (From Within): 3 Ta'as St, Ramath-Gan, POB 40016, Tel-Aviv 61400; tel. 03-7514938; f. 1923; quarterly of the United

ISRAEL
Directory

Kibbutz Movement (TKM); Hebrew; Editor DANI HADARI; circ. 5,000.

Molad: POB 1165, Jerusalem 91010; f. 1948; annual; Hebrew; independent political and literary periodical; published by Miph'ale Molad Ltd; Editor EPHRAIM BROIDO.

Monthly Bulletin of Statistics: Israel Central Bureau of Statistics, POB 13015, Jerusalem 91130; f. 1949.

Foreign Trade Statistics: f. 1950; Hebrew and English; appears annually, 2 vols; imports/exports.

Judea, Samaria and Gaza Area Statistics: f. 1971; Hebrew and English.

Tourism and Hotel Services Statistics Quarterly: f. 1973; Hebrew and English.

Price Statistics Monthly: f. 1959; Hebrew.

Foreign Trade Statistics Quarterly: f. 1950; Hebrew and English.

Transport Statistics Quarterly: f. 1974; Hebrew and English.

Agricultural Statistics: f. 1970; quarterly; Hebrew and English.

New Statistical Projects: quarterly.

Moznayim (Balance): POB 7098, Tel-Aviv; f. 1929; monthly; Hebrew; literature and culture; Editors CHAIM PESSAH, ASHER REICH; circ. 3,000.

Na'amat-Urim Lahorim: 93 Arlosoroff St, Tel-Aviv; tel. 03-442193; f. 1934; monthly journal of the Council of Women Workers of the Histadrut; Hebrew; Editor ZIVIA COHEN; circ. 16,500.

Nekuda: Hebrew; organ of the Jewish settlers of the West Bank and Gaza Strip.

New Outlook: 9 Gordon St, Tel-Aviv 63458; tel. 03-236496; f. 1957; monthly; Israeli and Middle Eastern Affairs; dedicated to the quest for Arab-Israeli peace; Editor-in-Chief CHAIM SHUR; Man. Editor FAYE BITTKER; circ. 10,000.

Proche-Orient Chrétien: POB 19079, Jerusalem 91190; tel. 02-283285; f. 1951; quarterly on churches and religion in the Middle East; circ. 800.

Quarterly Review of the Israel Medical Association (Mif'al Haverut Hutz—World Fellowship of the Israel Medical Association): 39 Shaul Hamelech Blvd, Tel-Aviv 61332; tel. (03) 255521; quarterly; English; also published in French; Editor-in-Chief YEHUDA SHOENFELD.

La Revue de l'A.M.I. (World Fellowship of the Israel Medical Association): 39 Shaul Hamelech Blvd, Tel-Aviv 64928; quarterly; French and English; Editors Dr S. ERDMAN, Dr S. TYANO.

Scopus: Hebrew University of Jerusalem, Mount Scopus, Jerusalem 91905; tel. 02-882837; telex 26458; f. 1946; annual; English; published by Division for Development and Public Relations, Hebrew University of Jerusalem; Editor V. LONDON; circ. 17,000.

The Sea: Hane'emanim 8, POB 33706, Haifa; tel. 04-529818; every six months; published by Israel Maritime League; review of marine problems; Pres. M. POMROCK; Sec.-Gen. ZADOK ESHEL; Chief Editor M. LITOVSKI; circ. 5,000.

Shdemot: 10 Dubnov, Tel-Aviv 64732; tel. 03-2521711; three a year; Hebrew; English edition, *Kibbutz Currents*; journal of the Kibbutz Movement; Editor SHALOM LILKER; circ. 2,500.

Shituf (Co-operation): 24 Ha'arba St, POB 7151, Tel-Aviv; f. 1948; bi-monthly; Hebrew; economic, social and co-operative problems in Israel; published by the Central Union of Industrial, Transport and Service Co-operative Societies; Editor L. LOSH; circ. 12,000.

Sillages: POB 92, Jerusalem; tel. 02-527156; f. 1980; published by Inf. Service of World Zionist Org.; literary and political; French; Editor-in-Chief KATY BISRAOR.

Sinai: POB 642, Jerusalem; tel. 02-526231; f. 1937; Hebrew; Torah science and literature; Editor Dr YITZCHAK RAPHAEL.

Sindibad: POB 28049, Tel-Aviv; f. 1970; children's monthly; Hebrew; Man. JOSEPH ELIAHOU; Editors WALID HUSSEIN, JAMIL DAHLAN; circ. 8,000.

Spectrum: Jerusalem; monthly of the Israel Labour Party; Editor DAVID TWERSKY.

At-Ta'awun (Co-operation): POB 303, Tel-Aviv; tel. 03-431836; telex 342488; f. 1961; Arabic; published by the Arab Workers' Dept of the Histadrut; co-operatives irregular; Editor MUHAMMAD GHANAYIM.

Terra Santa: POB 186, Jerusalem; tel. 02-282354; f. 1921; monthly; published by the Custody of the Holy Land (the official custodians of the Holy Shrines); Italian, Spanish, French, English and Arabic editions published in Jerusalem, by the Franciscan Printing Press, German edition in Munich, Maltese edition in Valletta.

Tmuroth: 48 Hamelech George St, POB 23076, Tel-Aviv; f. 1960; monthly; Hebrew; organ of the Liberal Labour Movement; Editor S. MEIRI.

WIZO Review: Women's International Zionist Organization, 38 Sderoth David Hamelekh, Tel-Aviv 64237; tel. 03-257321; telex 35770; f. 1947; two a month; English edition (five a year), Spanish and German editions (three a year); Editor DIANA HARRISON; circ. 20,000.

Zion: POB 4179, Jerusalem 91041; tel. 02-637171; f. 1935; quarterly; Hebrew, with English summaries; research in Jewish history; Editors H. BEINART, S. ETTINGER, M. STERN.

Zraim: 7 Dubnov St, POB 40027, Tel-Aviv; f. 1953; Hebrew; journal of the Bnei Akiva (Youth of Tora Va-avoda) Movement; Editor ELYAHU DAVID.

Zrakor: Haifa; f. 1947; monthly; Hebrew; news digest, trade, finance, economics, shipping; Editor G. ALON.

The following are all published by Weizmann Science Press of Israel, 8A Horkania St, POB 801, Jerusalem 91007; tel. 02-663203; telex 26144; Editor P. GREENBERG.

Israel Journal of Botany: f. 1951; quarterly; Editor Prof. A. HALEVI.

Israel Journal of Chemistry: f. 1951; quarterly; Editor Prof. H. LEBANON.

Israel Journal of Earth Sciences: f. 1951; quarterly; Editor Dr C. BINYAMINI.

Israel Journal of Mathematics: f. 1951; monthly, 3 vols of 4 issues per year; Editor Prof. H. M. FARKAS.

Israel Journal of Technology: f. 1951; quarterly; Editor Prof. D. ABIR.

Israel Journal of Zoology: f. 1951; quarterly; Editor Prof. Y. L. WERNER.

Journal d'Analyse Mathématique: f. 1955; one or two vols per year; Editor Prof. ZABRODSKY.

Lada'at (Science for Youth): f. 1971; Hebrew; ten issues per vol.; Editor Dr H. MEYER.

Mada (Science): f. 1955; popular scientific bi-monthly in Hebrew; Editor-in-Chief KAPAI PINES; circ. 11,000.

PRESS ASSOCIATIONS

Daily Newspaper Publishers' Association of Israel: 74 Petach Tikva Rd, POB 51202, Tel-Aviv 61200; telex 33498; safeguards professional interests and maintains standards, supplies newsprint to dailies; negotiates with trade unions, etc.; mems all daily papers; affiliated to International Federation of Newspaper Publishers; Pres. SHABTAI HIMMELFARB; Gen. Sec. BETZALEL EYAL.

Israel Press Association: Sokolov House, 4 Kaplan St, Tel-Aviv.

NEWS AGENCIES

Jewish Telegraphic Agency (JTA): Israel Bureau, Jerusalem Post Building, Romema, Jerusalem; Dir DAVID LANDAU.

ITIM, News Agency of the Associated Israel Press: 10 Tiomkin St, Tel-Aviv; f. 1950; co-operative news agency; Dir and Editor ALTER WELNER.

Palestine Press Service: Salah ad-Din St, East Jerusalem; Proprs IBRAHIM QARA'EEN, Mrs RAYMONDA TAWIL; only Arab news agency in the Occupied Territories; (closed down by Israeli authorities for six months, March 1988).

Foreign Bureaux

Agence France-Presse: 16 Hatikva Yemin Moshe St, POB 1507, Jerusalem; Correspondent PIERRE LEMOINE.

Agencia EFE (Spain): POB 3279, Avizohar 2, Apt 9, Bet Ha'Kerem, Jerusalem 91032; tel. 02-528658; telex 26446; Correspondent ELÍAS-SAMUEL SCHERBACOVSKY.

Agenzia Nazionale Stampa Associata (ANSA) (Italy): Industry House, 29 Hamered St, Tel-Aviv 68125; tel. 03-656279; telex 341704; Bureau Chief GRAZIANO MOTTA: 7 Marcus St, Jerusalem 92233; tel. 02-666098; telex 26420; Correspondent GIORGIO RACCAH.

Associated Press (AP) (USA): 30 Ibn Gavirol St, POB 20220, Tel-Aviv 61201; tel. 03-262283; telex 341411; POB 1625, 18 Shlomzion Hamalcha, Jerusalem; tel. 02-224632; telex 25258; Chief of Bureau NICHOLAS TATRO.

Deutsche Presse-Agentur (dpa) (Federal Republic of Germany): 30 Ibn Gavirol St, POB 16231, Tel-Aviv 61161; tel. 03-254268; telex 33416; Correspondents GIDEON BERLI, CHRISTIAN FÜRST.

Jiji Tsushin-Sha (Japan): 88A Herzl Ave, Jerusalem 96344; tel. (02) 532605; Correspondent HIROKAZU OIKAWA.

Kyodo News Service (Japan): 19 Lessin St, Tel-Aviv; tel. 03-258185; telex 361568; Correspondent HIDEO MIYAWAKI.

Reuters (UK): 38 Hamasger St, Tel-Aviv 67211; tel. 03-335176; telex 361567; Beit Agron, 37 Hillel St, Jerusalem 94581; tel. 02-221541; telex 26189.

ISRAEL

United Press International (UPI) (USA): 138 Petah Tikva Rd, Tel-Aviv; Bureau Man. BROOKE W. KROEGER; Bureau Man. in Jerusalem LOUIS TOSCANO.

The following are also represented: North American Newspaper Alliance and TASS (USSR).

Publishers

Achiasaf Ltd: 13 Yosef Hanassi St, POB 4810, Tel-Aviv; tel. 03-283339; f. 1933; general; Man. Dirs SCHACHNA ACHIASAF, MATAN ACHIASAF.

Am Hassefer Ltd: 9 Bialik St, Tel-Aviv; tel. 03-53040; f. 1955; Man. Dir DOV LIPETZ.

'Am Oved' Ltd: 22 Mazah St, POB 470, Tel-Aviv; tel. 03-291526; f. 1942; fiction, non-fiction, reference books, school and university textbooks, children's books, poetry, classics, science fiction; Man. Dir AHARON KRAUS.

Amichai Publishing House Ltd: 5 Yosef Hanassi St, Tel-Aviv; tel. 03-284990; f. 1948; Man. Dir YITZHAK ORON.

Arabic Publishing House: 17A Hagra St, POB 28049, Tel-Aviv; tel. 03-371438; f. 1960; established by the Histadrut (trade union) organization; periodicals and books; Dir JOSEPH ELIAHOU; Editor-in-Chief IBRAHIM M. IBRAHIM.

Carta, The Israel Map and Publishing Co Ltd: Yad Haruzim St, POB 2500, Jerusalem 91024; tel. 02-713536; telex 26587; f. 1958; the principal cartographic publisher; Pres. EMANUEL HAUSMAN; Man. Dir SHAY HAUSMAN.

Dvir Publishing Co Ltd, The: 32 Shoben St, POB 149, Tel-Aviv; tel. 03-812244; f. 1924; literature, science, art, education; Publrs O. ZMORA, A. BITAN.

Eked Publishing House: 29 Bar-Kochba St, POB 11138, Tel-Aviv; tel. 03-283648; f. 1959; poetry, belles lettres, fiction; Man. Dir MARITZA ROSMAN.

Encyclopedia Publishing Co: 29 Jabotinski St, Jerusalem; tel. 02-632310; telex 26144; f. 1947; Hebrew Encyclopedia and other encyclopaedias; Chair. ALEXANDER PELI.

Rodney Franklin Agency: 5 Karl Netter St, POB 37727, Tel-Aviv 61376; tel. 03-288948; telex 341118; exclusive representative of various British and USA publishers; Dir RODNEY FRANKLIN.

Gazit: 8 Zvi Brook St, POB 4190, Tel-Aviv; tel. 03-53730; art publishers; Editor GABRIEL TALPHIR.

Hakibbutz Hameuchad Publishing House Ltd: 15 Nehardea St, POB 40015, Tel-Aviv; tel. 03-751483; f. 1940; general; Dir UZI SHAVIT.

Israeli Music Publications Ltd: 25 Keren Hayesod St, POB 7681, Jerusalem 91076; tel. 02-241377; f. 1949; books on music and musical works; Dir STANLEY SIMMONDS.

Izre'el Publishing House Ltd: 76 Dizengoff St, Tel-Aviv; tel. 03-285350; f. 1933; Man. ALEXANDER IZRE'EL.

The Jerusalem Publishing House Ltd: 39 Tchernechovski St, POB 7147, Jerusalem 91071; tel. 02-636511; telex 26456; f. 1967; biblical research, history, encyclopaedias, archaeology, arts of the Holy Land, cookbooks, guide books, economics, politics; Dir SHLOMO S. GAFNI; Man. Editor RACHEL GILON.

Jewish History Publications (Israel 1961) Ltd: 29 Jabotinski St, Jerusalem; tel. 02-632310; telex 26144; f. 1961; encyclopaedias, World History of the Jewish People series; Chair. ALEXANDER PELI; Man. Dir IDIT REGEV; Editor-in-Chief Prof. J. PRAWER.

Karni Publishers Ltd: 32 Shoben St, POB 149, Tel-Aviv 61001; tel. 03-812244; f. 1951; children's and educational books; Publrs O. ZMORA, A. BITAN.

Keter Publishing House Jerusalem Ltd: POB 7145, Givat Shaul B, Jerusalem 91071; tel. 02-521201; telex 25275; f. 1959; original and translated works in all fields of science and humanities, published in English, French, German, other European languages and Hebrew; publishing imprints: Israel Program for Scientific Translations, Israel Universities Press, Keter Books, Encyclopedia Judaica; Man. Dir YAACOV PACHTER.

Kiryat Sefer: 15 Arlosoroff St, Jerusalem; tel. 02-521141; f. 1933; concordances, dictionaries, textbooks, maps, scientific books; Dir AVRAHAM SIVAN.

Magnes Press, The: The Hebrew University, Jerusalem; tel. 02-660341; f. 1929; biblical studies, Judaica, and all academic fields; Dir DAN BENOVICI.

Rubin Mass Ltd: 11 Marcus St, POB 990, Jerusalem 91009; tel. 02-632565; telex 26144; f. 1927; Hebraica, Judaica, export; Dir OREN MASS.

Massada Press Ltd: 29 Jabotinski St, Jerusalem; tel. 02-632310; telex 26144; f. 1961; encyclopaedias, Judaica, the arts, educational material, children's books; Chair. ALEXANDER PELI; Man. Dir NATHAN REGEV.

Ministry of Defence Publishing House: 27 David Elazar St, Hakiriya, Tel-Aviv 67673; tel. 03-217940; f. 1939; military literature, Judaism, history and geography of Israel; Dir SHALOM SERI.

M. Mizrachi Publishers: 67 Levinsky, Tel-Aviv; tel. 03-625652; f. 1960; children's books, novels; Dir MEIR MIZRACHI.

Mosad Harav Kook: POB 642, Jerusalem; tel. 02-526231; f. 1937; editions of classical works, Torah and Jewish studies; Dir Rabbi M. KATZENELENBOGEN.

Otsar Hamoreh: 8 Ben Saruk, POB 303, Tel-Aviv; tel. 03-260211; f. 1951; educational.

Alexander Peli Jerusalem Publishing Co Ltd: 29 Jabotinski St, Jerusalem; tel. 02-632310; telex 26144; f. 1977; encyclopaedias, Judaica, history, the arts, educational material; Chair. ALEXANDER PELI; Man. Dir NATHAN REGEV.

Schocken Publishing House Ltd: POB 2316, Tel-Aviv 61022; tel. 03-200127; telex 342449; f. 1938; general; Dir Mrs RACHELI EDELMAN.

Shikmona Publishing Co Ltd: Givat Shaul B, POB 7145, Jerusalem 91071; tel. 02-660188; f. 1965; Zionism, archaeology, art, fiction and non-fiction.

Sifriat-Ma'ariv Ltd: Derech Petach Tikva 72A, POB 20208, Tel-Aviv 61201; f. 1954; Man. Dir IZCHAK YACHIN; Editor-in-Chief ARIE NIR.

Sifriat Poalim Ltd: 2 Choma Umigdal St, Tel-Aviv 67771; tel. 03-376845; f. 1939; general literature; Gen. Man. NATHAN SHAHAM.

Sinai Publishing Co: 72 Allenby St, Tel-Aviv; tel. 03-663672; f. 1853; Hebrew books and religious articles; Dir MOSHE SCHLESINGER.

World Zionist Organization Torah Education Dept: POB 7044, Jerusalem; tel. 02-632584; f. 1945; education, Jewish philosophy, studies in the Bible, children's books published in Hebrew, English, French, Spanish, German, Swedish and Portuguese.

Weizmann Science Press of Israel: 8A Horkanya St, POB 801, Jerusalem 91007; tel. 02-783203; f. 1955; publishes scientific books and periodicals; Man. Dir Mrs HAVA ASPLER; Exec. Editor P. GREENBERG.

Yachdav United Publishers Co Ltd: 29 Carlebach St, POB 20123, Tel-Aviv; tel. 03-5614121; telex 341118; f. 1960; educational; Chair. EPHRAIM BEN-DOR; Exec. Dir ARIE FRIEDLER.

Yavneh Publishing House Ltd: 4 Mazeh St, Tel-Aviv 65213; tel. 03-297856; telex 35770; f. 1932; general; Dir AVSHALOM ORENSTEIN.

S. Zack and Co: 2 King George St, Jerusalem; tel. 02-227819; f. c. 1930; fiction, science, philosophy, religion, children's books, educational and reference books; Dir MICHAEL ZACK.

PUBLISHERS' ASSOCIATION

Israel Book Publishers Association: 29 Carlebach St, POB 20123, Tel-Aviv 67132; tel. 03-5614121; telex 341118; f. 1939; mems: 84 publishing firms; Chair. RACHELI EIDELMAN; Man. Dir ARIE FRIEDLER.

Radio and Television

In 1987 there were an estimated 3m. radio receivers and 900,000 TV receivers in use.

RADIO

Israel Broadcasting Authority (IBA) (Radio): POB 6387, Jerusalem; tel. 02-222121; telex 26488; f. 1948; station in Jerusalem with additional studios in Tel-Aviv and Haifa. IBA broadcasts six programmes for local and overseas listeners on medium, shortwave and VHF/FM in 16 languages; Hebrew, Arabic, English, Yiddish, Ladino, Romanian, Hungarian, Moghrabit, Persian, French, Russian, Bucharian, Georgian, Portuguese, Spanish and Ethiopian; Chair. MICHA YINON; Dir-Gen. URI PORAT; Dir of Radio (vacant); Dir External Services VICTOR GRAJEWSKY.

Galei Zahal: POB MPO 01005, Zahal; tel. 814888; f. 1951; Israeli defence forces broadcasting station, Tel-Aviv, with studios in Jerusalem; broadcasts music, news and other programmes on medium-wave and FM stereo in Hebrew; Dir R. BEN YISHAI; Dir of Engineering S. KASIF.

TELEVISION

Israel Broadcasting Authority (IBA): POB 7139, Jerusalem 91071; tel. 02-557111; telex 25301; broadcasts began in 1968; station in Jerusalem with additional studios in Tel-Aviv; one colour network (VHF with UHF available in all areas); broadcasts in Hebrew

ISRAEL

Directory

and Arabic; Dir of Television T. SA'AR; Dir of Engineering YAAKOV SVIRY.

Israel Educational Television: Ministry of Education and Culture, 14 Klausner St, Tel-Aviv; tel. 03-5434343; telex 342325; f. 1966 by Hanadiv (Rothschild Memorial Group) as Instructional Television Trust; began transmission in 1966; school programmes form an integral part of the syllabus in a wide range of subjects; also adult education; Gen. Man. YAAKOV LORBERBAUM; Dir of Engineering A. KAPLAN.

In September 1986 the Government approved the establishment of a commercial radio and television network to be run in competition with the State system.

Finance

(cap. = capital; p.u. = paid up; dep. = deposits; m. = million; res = reserves; brs = branches)

BANKING

Central Bank

Bank of Israel: Bank of Israel Bldg, Kiryat Ben Gurion, POB 780, Jerusalem 91007; tel. 02-552211; telex 25213; f. 1954 as the Central Bank of the State of Israel; cap. 320m. new shekels, dep. 15,927m. new shekels, res 5,329m. new shekels (Dec. 1987); Gov. Prof. MICHAEL BRUNO; Deputy Gov. Dr Y. PLESSNER; Mans M. FRAENKEL, S. PELED, G. MAOR, M. LAHAV, O. HEZRONI, F. WIEDER, V. MEDINA, S. BILITZKI, M. HERZBERG, I. IGRA, M. RABOY; 2 brs.

Principal Israeli Banks

American Israel Bank Ltd: 28A Rothschild Blvd, POB 1346, Tel-Aviv 61013; tel. 03-250245; telex 342247; f. 1933; subsidiary of Bank Hapoalim BM; total assets 658.3m. new shekels, cap. and res 24.7m. new shekels, dep. 624m. new shekels (Dec. 1986); Chair. M. AMIT; Man. Dir A. SCHER; 20 brs.

Bank Hapoalim BM: 50 Rothschild Blvd, POB 27, Tel-Aviv 61000; tel. 03-673333; telex 342121; f. 1921 as the Workers' Bank, name changed as above 1961; cap. and res 1,500m. new shekels, dep. 32,900m. new shekels (Dec. 1987); Chair. Bd of Man. AMIRAM SIVAN; 345 brs and offices.

Bank Leumi le-Israel BM: 24–32 Yehuda Halevi St, Tel-Aviv 65546; tel. 03-648111; telex 33586; f. 1902 as Anglo-Palestine Co; renamed Anglo-Palestine Bank 1930; name changed as above 1951; total assets 31,128.7m. new shekels, dep. 29,253.7m. new shekels (Dec. 1987); Chair. MOSHE SANBAR; Gen. Man. DAVID FRIEDMAN; 244 brs.

Finance and Trade Bank Ltd: 14 Rothschild Blvd, POB 937, Tel-Aviv 61008; tel. 03-629756; telex 33520; f. 1979; subsidiary of United Mizrahi Bank Ltd; cap. and res 26.5m. new shekels, dep. 75.5m. new shekels (June 1988); Chair. MICHAEL ZVINERI; Man. Dir AHARON HILDESHEIMER.

First International Bank of Israel Ltd: Shalom Mayer Tower, 9 Ahad Ha'am St, POB 29036, Tel-Aviv 61290; tel. 03-636111; telex 341252; f. 1972 as a result of a merger between The Foreign Trade Bank Ltd and Export Bank Ltd; total assets 5,273.4m. new shekels, dep. 4,839.2m. new shekels, res 1.2m. new shekels (Dec. 1987); Chair. YIGAL ARMON; Man. Dir SHALOM SINGER; 89 brs.

Industrial Development Bank of Israel Ltd: 2 Dafna St, Tel-Aviv 61334; tel. 03-430611; telex 033646; f. 1957; Chair. A. FRIEDMANN; Man. Dir JOSEPH SARIG.

Israel Ampal Industrial Development Bank Ltd: 111 Arlosoroff St, POB 27, Tel-Aviv 61000; f. 1956; cap. p.u. 9,752m. shekels, dep. 379m. shekels (Dec. 1986); Chair. M. OLENIK; Man. Dirs M. BACHAR, M. ARNON.

Israel Bank of Agriculture Ltd: 83 Hahashmonaim St, POB 2440, Tel-Aviv 61024; tel. (03) 285141; telex 35739; f. 1951; total assets 620.3m. new shekels, cap. p.u. 11m. new shekels, dep. 563.7m. new shekels (Dec. 1986); Chair. GIDON MAKOFF; Gen. Man. ISRAEL RAUCH.

Israel Continental Bank Ltd: 65 Rothschild Blvd, POB 37406, Tel-Aviv 61373; tel. 03-204148; telex 341447; f. 1973; capital held jointly by Bank Hapoalim BM and Bank für Gemeinwirtschaft AG; total assets 376.3m. new shekels, cap. and res 29.5m. new shekels, dep. 310.4m. new shekels (Dec. 1986); Chair. Dr WALTER HESSELBACH; Man. Dir MOSHE GOLDNER; 3 brs.

Israel Discount Bank Ltd: 27-31 Yehuda Halevi St, Tel-Aviv 65546; tel. 03-637111; telex 33724; f. 1935; cap. p.u. 920,000 new shekels, dep. 19,210m. new shekels (June 1988); Chair. JOSEF CIECHANOVER; Man. Dir GIDEON LAHAV; more than 250 brs in Israel and abroad.

Israel General Bank Ltd: 38 Rothschild Blvd, POB 677, Tel-Aviv 61006; tel. 03-645645; telex 33515; f. 1934 as Palestine Credit Utility Bank Ltd, name changed as above 1964; Chair. Baron EDMOND DE ROTHSCHILD; Man. Dir ABRAHAM BIGGER; 3 brs.

Leumi Agricultural Development Bank Ltd: 19 Rothschild Blvd, POB 2, Tel-Aviv 65121; tel. 03-632111; telex 33586; f. 1922; subsidiary of Bank Leumi le-Israel BM; cap. and res 36m. new shekels, debentures and dep. 945m. new shekels (Dec. 1987); Chair. R. PELED; Gen. Man. L. MALOWANCZYK.

Leumi Industrial Development Bank Ltd: 19 Rothschild Blvd, POB 2, Tel-Aviv 65121; tel. 03-632111; telex 33586; f. 1944; subsidiary of Bank Leumi le-Israel BM; cap. and res 16.5m. new shekels, dep. 502.3m. new shekels (Dec. 1986); Chair. R. PELED; Man. Dir L. MALOWANCZYK.

Maritime Bank of Israel Ltd: 16 Ahad ha'am St, POB 29373, Tel-Aviv 61293; f. 1962; total assets 123.9m. new shekels, dep. 104.9m. new shekels (Dec. 1986); Chair. DAVID GOLAN; Man. Dir MOSHE MEIRAV.

North American Bank Ltd: 116 Allenby St, POB 30218, Tel-Aviv 61301; f. 1978; Man. Dir. D. ZAFRIR; 4 brs.

Union Bank of Israel Ltd: 6–8 Ahuzat Bayit St, POB 2428, Tel-Aviv 65143; tel. 03-631631; telex 033493; f. 1951; subsidiary of Bank Leumi le-Israel BM; total assets 2,418.6m. new shekels, cap. p.u. 111.8m. new shekels, dep. 2,281.4m. new shekels (Dec. 1987); Chair. Dr M. HETH; Man. Dir D. FRIEDMANN; Gen. Man. S. SOROKER; 25 brs.

United Mizrahi Bank Ltd: 13 Rothschild Blvd, Tel-Aviv 65121; tel. 03-629211; telex 36125; f. 1923 as Mizrahi Bank Ltd; 1969 absorbed Hapoel Hamizrahi Bank Ltd and name changed as above; total assets 10,208.9m. new shekels, cap. p.u. 344.6m. new shekels, dep. 8,612.9m. new shekels (Dec. 1987); Chair. YZHAK JAEGER; Man. Dir MICHAEL ZVINERI; 85 brs.

Mortgage Banks

Israel Development and Mortgage Bank Ltd: 16–18 Simtat Beit Hashoeva, Tel-Aviv; tel. 03-611881; telex 32368; f. 1959; subsidiary of Israel Discount Bank Ltd; cap. p.u. 879,400 new shekels; res 21.6m. new shekels (Dec. 1986); Chair. M. B. GITTER; Jt Gen. Mans M. ELDAR, J. SHEMESH.

Leumi Mortgage Bank Ltd: 31–37 Montefiore St, POB 69, Tel-Aviv 65201; tel. 03-202444; f. 1921; subsidiary of Bank Leumi le-Israel BM; total assets 1,657.3m. new shekels (Dec. 1987); Chair. A. ZELDMAN; Gen. Man. S. TAGNER; 2 brs.

Merav Mortgage and Savings Bank Ltd: 49 Rothschild Blvd, POB 116, Tel-Aviv 61000; f. 1922; subsidiary of First International Bank of Israel Ltd; cap. and res 1,558m. shekels (Dec. 1983); Chair. A. SACHAROV; Man. Dir E. SHANOON.

Mishkan-Hapoalim Mortgage Bank Ltd: 2 Ibn Gvirol St, Tel-Aviv 64077; f. 1950; subsidiary of Bank Hapoalim BM; Chair. M. OLENIK; Man. Dir A. KROIZER.

Tefahot, Israel Mortgage Bank Ltd: 9 Heleni Hamalka St, POB 93, Jerusalem 91000; tel. 02-219111; f. 1945; subsidiary of United Mizrahi Bank Ltd; cap. and res 115m. new shekels, total assets 3,181m. new shekels (Dec. 1987); Chair. Y. YEGER; Man. Dir DAVID BLUMBERG; 23 brs.

Foreign Banks

Barclays Discount Bank Ltd: 103 Allenby Rd, POB 1292, Tel-Aviv 61012; tel. 03-643333; telex 33550; f. 1971 by Barclays Bank International Ltd and Israel Discount Bank Ltd to incorporate Israel brs of Barclays; cap. and res 94.7m. new shekels, dep. 1,224.3m. new shekels (Dec. 1987); Chair. GIDEON LAHAV; Gen. Man. MOSHE NEUDORFER; 70 brs; wholly owned subsidiary: **Mercantile Bank of Israel Ltd**, POB 512, 24 Rothschild Blvd, Tel-Aviv; f. 1924; cap. and res 7.1m. new shekels, dep. 62m. new shekels, (Dec. 1987); Chair. G. LAHAV, Man. Dir SHLOMO MAGRISO.

Four branches of the Jordan-based Cairo-Amman Bank were opened in the occupied West Bank, between November 1986 and August 1987 to provide financial services to the Palestinian community. The branches operated in both Jordanian dinars and Israeli shekels and were subject to dual Jordanian and Israeli regulatory authority. The Palestinian uprising in the Occupied Territories and Jordan's severance of legal and administrative links with the West Bank in July 1988 may cause these branches to be closed.

STOCK EXCHANGE

Tel-Aviv Stock Exchange: 54 Ahad Ha'am St, POB 29060, Tel-Aviv 65543; tel. 03-627411; telex 342112; f. 1953; Chair. HAIM STOESSEL; Gen. Man. J. NITZANI.

INSURANCE

The Israel Insurance Association lists 35 companies, a selection of which are listed below; not all companies are members of the association.

ISRAEL

Ararat Insurance Co Ltd: Ararat House, 13 Montefiore St, Tel-Aviv 65164; tel. 03-640888; telex 341484; f. 1949; cap. p.u. 9.1m. new shekels; Co-Chair. AHARON DOVRAT, PHILIP ZUCKERMAN; Gen. Man. PINCHAS COHEN.

Aryeh Insurance Co of Israel Ltd: 9 Ahad Ha'am St, Tel-Aviv 65251; tel. 03-652671; telex 342125; f. 1948; Chair. AVINOAM M. TOCATLY.

Clal Insurance Co Ltd: 42 Rothschild Blvd, POB 326, Tel-Aviv 61002; tel. 03-627711; telex 341701; f. 1962; Man. Dir R. BEN-SHAOUL.

Hassneh Insurance Co of Israel Ltd: 115 Allenby St, POB 805, Tel-Aviv 61007; f. 1924; Man. Dir EITAN AVNEYON.

Israel Phoenix Assurance Co Ltd: 30 Levontin St, Tel-Aviv 65116; tel. 03-620111; telex 341199; f. 1949; Chair. of Board DAVID J. HACKMEY; Man. Dir JOSEPH D. HACKMEY.

Israel Reinsurance Co Ltd, The: 5 Drujanov St, POB 11589, Tel-Aviv 61114; tel. 03-296141; telex 342677; f. 1951; Chair. N. MISHOR; Man. Dir S. JANNAI.

Maoz Insurance Co Ltd: Tel-Aviv; f. 1945; formerly Binyan Insurance Co Ltd; Chair. B. YEKUTIELI.

Menorah Insurance Co Ltd: Menorah House, 73 Rothschild Blvd, Tel-Aviv 65786; tel. 03-294771; telex 341433; f. 1935; Pres. DAVID HIRSCHFELD.

Migdal Insurance Co Ltd: 26 Sa'adiya Ga'on St, POB 37633, Tel-Aviv 61375; tel. 03-298129; telex 342331; part of Bank Leumi Group; f. 1934; Chair. B. YEKUTIELI; Gen. Mans U. E. LEVY, M. ZANGEN.

Palglass Palestine Plate Glass Insurance Co Ltd: 30 Achad Ha'am St, Tel-Aviv 65541; f. 1934; Gen. Man. AKIVA ZALZMAN.

Sahar Insurance Co Ltd: Sahar House, 23 Ben-Yehuda St, POB 26222, Tel-Aviv 63806; tel. 03-630311; telex 33759; f. 1949; Chair. A. SACHAROV; Man. Dir AL. SACHAROV.

Samson Insurance Co Ltd: Aviv Bldg, 5 Jabotinski Rd, Ramat-Gan 52520, POB 33678, Tel-Aviv; f. 1933; Chair. A. GOLZ; Gen. Man. D. SERR.

Sela Insurance Co Ltd: 53 Rothschild Blvd, Tel-Aviv 65124; tel. 03-61028; telex 35744; f. 1938; Man. Dir E. SHANI.

Shiloah Co Ltd: 2 Pinsker St, Tel-Aviv 63322; f. 1933; Gen. Man. Dr S. BAMIRAH; Man. Mme BAMIRAH.

Yardenia Insurance Co Ltd: 22 Maze St, Tel-Aviv 65213; f. 1948; Man. Dir H. LEBANON.

Zion Insurance Co Ltd: 120 Allenby Rd, Tel-Aviv 65128; f. 1935; Chair. A. R. TAIBER.

Trade and Industry

CHAMBERS OF COMMERCE

Federation of Israeli Chambers of Commerce: 84 Hahashmonaim St, POB 501, Tel-Aviv; tel. 03-288224; telex 33484; co-ordinates the Tel-Aviv, Jerusalem, Haifa and Beersheba Chambers of Commerce; Dir ZVI AMIT.

Jerusalem Chamber of Commerce: POB 183, 10 Hillel St, Jerusalem 91000; tel. 02-224333; f. 1908; about 300 mems; Pres. JOSEPH PERLMAN; Vice-Pres HAIM COHEN, AVRAHAM DASKAL, SHALOM P. DORON, AVNER PEREZ, GIORA MURAG, OVADIA HASSON, ADIM TALBAR; Dir-Gen. SHLOMO NAHMIAS.

Haifa Chamber of Commerce and Industry (Haifa and District): POB 33176, 53 Haatzmaut Rd, Haifa 31331; tel. 04-663471; telex 46653; f. 1921; 700 mems; Pres. GAD SASSOWER; Gen. Sec. A. MEHULAL.

Chamber of Commerce, Tel-Aviv-Jaffa: 84 Hahashmonaim St, POB 20027, Tel-Aviv 67011; tel. 03-5612444; telex 33484; f. 1919; 1,800 mems; Pres. DAN GILLERMAN; Man. Dir ZVI AMIT; Dept Dirs BARRY PINTOW, J. SHOSTAK.

Federation of Bi-National Chambers of Commerce with and in Israel: 84 Hahashmonaim St, POB 1127, Tel-Aviv; federates: Israel-America Chamber of Commerce and Industry; Israel-British Chamber of Commerce; Australia-Israel Chambers of Commerce; Chamber of Commerce and Industry Israel-Africa; Chamber of Commerce Israel-Belgique-Luxembourg; Canada-Israel Chamber of Commerce and Industry; Israel-Danish Chamber of Commerce; Chambre de Commerce Israel-France; Chamber of Commerce and Industry Israel-Germany; Camera di Commercio Israeli-Italia; Israel-Japan Chamber of Commerce; Israel-Latin America, Spain and Portugal Chamber of Commerce; Netherlands-Israel Chamber of Commerce; Israel-Norway Chamber of Commerce; Handelskammer Israel-Schweiz; Israel-South Africa Chamber of Commerce; Israel-Sweden Chamber of Commerce; also incorporates Bi-National Chamber of Commerce existing in 20 foreign countries with Israel.

Israel-British Chamber of Commerce: POB 16065, Tel-Aviv 61160; tel. 03-259732; telex 342315; f. 1951; 440 mems; Gen. Sec. FELIX KIPPER; Chair. B. GROSS.

TRADE AND INDUSTRIAL ORGANIZATIONS

Agricultural Export Co (AGREXCO): Tel-Aviv; state-owned agricultural marketing organization; Dir-Gen. AMOTZ AMIAD.

The Agricultural Union: Tchlenov 20, Tel-Aviv; consists of more than 50 agricultural settlements and is connected with marketing and supplying organizations, and Bahan Ltd, controllers and auditors.

Central Union of Artisans and Small Manufacturers: POB 4041, Tel-Aviv 61040; f. 1907; has a membership of over 40,000 divided into 70 groups according to trade; the union is led by a 17-man Presidium; Chair. JACOB FRANK; Sec. ITZHAK HASSON; 30 brs.

Citrus Marketing Board: 6 Wissotzky St, POB 21371, Tel-Aviv 61213; the growers' institution for the control of the Israel citrus industry; Board made up of representatives of the Government and the growers. Functions: control of plantations, supervision of picking and packing operations, marketing of the crop overseas and on the home markets; shipping; supply of fertilizers, insecticides, equipment for orchards and packing houses and of packing materials, technical research and extension work; long-term financial assistance to growers; Chair. REUVEN EILAND.

Cotton Production and Marketing Board: Tel-Aviv.

Export Institute: Tel-Aviv; gives advice and financial backing to Israeli exporters; Dir-Gen. YOSSI GINOSSAR.

Farmers' Union of Israel: 8 Kaplan St, POB 209, Tel-Aviv; tel. 03-252227; f. 1913; membership of 7,000 independent farmers, citrus and winegrape growers; Pres. ELIAHU IZAKSON; Chair. Council IZCHAK-ZIV-AV; Dir-Gen. SHLOMO REISMAN.

General Association of Merchants in Israel: 6 Rothschild Blvd, Tel-Aviv; the organization of retail traders; has a membership of 30,000 in 60 brs.

Israel Diamond Exchange Ltd: POB 3222, Ramat-Gan; tel. 03-214211; f. 1937; production, export, import and finance facilities; estimated exports (1987) US $2,302m.; Pres. MOSHE SCHNITZER.

Israel Fruit Production Board: Tel-Aviv; Dir-Gen. EZRA MEIR.

Israel Journalists' Association Ltd: 4 Kaplan St, Tel-Aviv; tel. 03-256141; Sec. YONA SHIMSHI.

Kibbutz Industries Association: Tel-Aviv; responsible for marketing and export of the goods produced by Israel's 268 kibbutzim (Dec. 1985).

Manufacturers' Association of Israel: 29 Hamered St, POB 50022, Tel-Aviv 61500; tel. 03-650121; telex 342651; 1,200 mem.-enterprises employing nearly 72% of industrial workers in Israel; Pres. DOV LAUTMAN; Dir-Gen. ARNON TIBERG.

The Histadrut

Hahistadrut Haklalit shel Haovdim Beeretz Israel (General Federation of Labour in Israel): 93 Arlosoroff St, Tel-Aviv 62098; tel. 03-431111; telex 342488.

The General Federation of Labour in Israel, usually known as the Histadrut, is the largest voluntary organization in Israel, and the most important economic body in the state. It is open to all workers, including members of co-operatives and of the liberal professions, who join directly as individuals. The Histadrut engages in four main fields of activity: trade union organization; economic development; social insurance based on mutual aid; and educational and cultural activities. Dues—averaging 4.5% of wages—cover all its trade union, health and social services activities. The Histadrut was founded in 1920.

Secretary-General: ISRAEL KESSAR.

ORGANIZATION

In 1988 the Histadrut had a membership of 1,600,000, including over 160,000 in collective, co-operative and private villages (kibbutzim and moshavim) affiliated through the Agricultural Workers' Union, and 360,000 wives (who have membership status); 170,000 of the members were Arabs. In addition some 110,000 young people under 18 years of age belong to the Organization of Working and Student Youth, a direct affiliate of the Histadrut. The main religious labour organizations, Histadrut Hapoel Hamizrahi and Histadrut Poalei Agudat Israel, belong to the trade union section and welfare services, which thus extend to 85% of all workers in Israel.

All members take part in elections to the Histadrut Convention (Veida), which elects the General Council (Moetsa) and the Executive Committee (Vaad Hapoel). The latter elects the 43-member Executive Bureau (Vaada Merakezet), which is responsible for day-to-day implementation of policy. The Executive Committee also elects the Secretary-General, who acts as its chairman as well as head of the organization as a whole and chairman of the Executive Bureau. Nearly all political parties are represented on the Histadrut Executive Committee. Throughout Israel there are 72 local Labour Councils.

The Executive Committee has the following departments: Trade Union, Integration of Arab Members, Mutual Security Centre, Organization, International, Finance, Legal, Employment, Vocational Training, Absorption and Development, Academic Workers, Culture and Education, Institute of Economic and Social Research, Diaspora Communities, Youth and Sport, Consumers' Authority, Industrial Democracy, Religious Affairs and Higher Education.

TRADE UNION ACTIVITIES

Collective agreements with employers fix wage scales, which are linked with the retail price index; provide for social benefits, including paid sick leave and employers' contributions to sick and pension and provident funds; and regulate dismissals. Dismissal compensation is regulated by law. The Histadrut actively promotes productivity through labour management boards and the National Productivity Institute, and supports incentive pay schemes.

There are unions for the following groups: clerical workers, building workers, teachers, engineers, agricultural workers, technicians, textile workers, printing workers, diamond workers, metal workers, food and bakery workers, wood workers, government employees, seamen, nurses, civilian employees of the armed forces, actors, musicians and variety artists, social workers, watchmen, cinema technicians, institutional and school staffs, pharmacy employees, medical laboratory workers, X-ray technicians, physiotherapists, social scientists, microbiologists, psychologists, salaried lawyers, pharmacists, physicians, occupational therapists, truck and taxi drivers, hotel and restaurant workers, workers in Histadrut-owned industry, garment, shoe and leather workers, plastic and rubber workers, editors of periodicals, painters and sculptors and industrial workers.

Director Histadrut Trades Union Department: CHAIM HABERFELD.

ECONOMIC ACTIVITIES AND SOCIAL SERVICES

These include Hevrat Haovdim (Economic Sector, literally, 'the Workers' Company', employing 260,000 workers in 1983), Kupat Holim (the Sick Fund, covering almost 77% of Israel's population), seven pension funds, and NA'AMAT (women's organization which runs nursery homes and kindergartens, organizes vocational education and promotes legislation for the protection and benefit of working women).

Other Trade Unions

General Federation of West Bank Trade Unions: Sec.-Gen. SHAHER SAAD.

Histadrut Haovdim Haleumit (National Labour Federation): 23 Sprintzak St, Tel-Aviv 64738; tel. 03-258351; f. 1934; 150,000 mems.

Histadrut Hapoel Hamizrahi (National Religious Workers' Party): 166 Even Gavirol St, Tel-Aviv; 125,000 mems in 81 settlements.

Histadrut Poale Agudat Israel (Agudat Israel Workers' Organization): 64 Frishman St, POB 11044, Tel-Aviv; tel. 03-242126; has 33,000 members in 16 settlements and 8 educational insts.

Transport

RAILWAYS

Freight traffic consists mainly of grain, phosphates, potash, containers, oil and building materials. Rail service serves Haifa and Ashdod, ports on the Mediterranean Sea, while a combined rail-road service extends to Eilat port on the Red Sea. Work is in progress on a 173-km extension of the network to Eilat. Passenger services operate between the main towns: Nahariya, Haifa, Tel-Aviv and Jerusalem. In 1986 it was announced that the State-owned system was to be sold to the private sector.

Israel State Railways: Central Station, POB 44, Haifa; tel. 04-531211; telex 46570; all lines are managed and operated from Haifa. The total length of main line is 528 km and there are 337 km of branch line; gauge 1,435 mm; Gen. Man. ELIAHU BARAK; Deputy Gen. Man. (Admin.) DAVID GUY; Deputy Gen. Man. (Tech.) LEON HEYMAN.

Underground Railway

Haifa Underground Funicular Railway: 124 Hanassi Ave, Haifa; opened 1959; 2 km in operation; Man. D. SCHARF.

ROADS

At the beginning of 1987 there were 12,823 km of paved roads, of which 3,923 km were inter-urban, out of which 284 km were motorways with four or more lanes.

Ministry of Housing and Construction: Public Works Dept, 23 Hillel St, Jerusalem.

SHIPPING

In 1987 Israel had a merchant fleet of 71 ships.

Haifa and Ashdod are the main ports in Israel. The former is a natural harbour, enclosed by two main breakwaters and dredged to 39 ft below mean sea-level. In 1965 the deep water port was completed at Ashdod which had a capacity of about 7.3m. tons in 1985.

The port of Eilat is Israel's gate to the Red Sea. It is a natural harbour, operated from a wharf. Another port, to the south of the original one, started operating in 1965. Gaza port fulfils the needs of the Gaza Strip.

The Israel Ports Authority: Maya Building, 74 Petach Tikva Rd, POB 20121, Tel-Aviv; tel. 03-338911; telex 33677; f. 1961; to plan, build, develop, administer, maintain and operate the ports. In 1985/86 investment plans amounted to US $57.8m. for the development budget in Haifa, Ashdod and Eilat ports. Cargo traffic April 1985–March 1986 amounted to 13.3m. tons (oil excluded); Chair. ZVI KEINAN; Dir-Gen. Ing. SHAUL RAZIEL.

ZIM Israel Navigation Co Ltd: 7–9 Pal-Yam Ave, POB 1723, Haifa 31000; tel. 04-652111; telex 46501; f. 1945; runs cargo and container services in the Mediterranean and to N Europe, N and S America, Far East, Africa and Australia; operates about 70 ships (including 30 general cargo ships and one oil tanker) totalling 1.8m. dwt; total cargo carried: 7.5m. metric tons in 1986; Chair. ZVI ZUR; Man. Dir MATTY MORGENSTERN.

CIVIL AVIATION

El Al Israel Airlines Ltd: POB 41, Ben Gurion Airport, Lod, Tel-Aviv; tel. 03-9716111; telex 381107; f. 1948; the Government is the major stockholder; daily services to most capitals of Europe; over 20 flights weekly to New York; services to the USA, Canada, Egypt, Kenya, South Africa and Turkey; fleet of 4 Boeing 747-200B, 2 Boeing 747-200B Combi, 1 Boeing 747-200F, 1 Boeing 747-100F, 3 Boeing 757-200, 2 Boeing 737-200, 4 Boeing 767-200; Chair. NACHMAN PEREL; Pres. RAFAEL HAR-LEV.

Arkia Israeli Airlines Ltd: Sde-Dov Airport, POB 39301, Tel-Aviv 61392; tel. 03-422777; telex 341749; f. 1980 through merger of Kanaf-Arkia Airlines and Aviation Services; scheduled passenger services linking Tel-Aviv, Jerusalem, Haifa, Eilat, Rosh Pina and Masada; cargo services to European destinations; fleet of 3 De Havilland Dash-7, 5 Navajo Chieftain, 1 Islander, 1 Aero Commander, 2 Cessna 337 (4 Boeing 707 leased from El Al); Chair. S. ZIV; Pres. JOSEPH ROSEN.

Tourism

In 1987 1,378,742 tourists visited Israel.

Ministry of Tourism: Hakirya, POB 1018, Jerusalem; tel. 02-237311; Minister of Tourism AVRAHAM SHARIR; Dir-Gen. RAFAEL FARBER.

Atomic Energy

Israel Atomic Energy Commission: 26 Rehov Hauniversita, Ramat Aviv, POB 7061, Tel-Aviv; tel. 03-422922; telex 33450; f. 1952; advises the government on long term policies and priorities in the advancement of nuclear research and development; supervises the implementation of policies approved by the government, including the licensing of nuclear power plants and the promotion of technological and industrial applications; represents Israel in its relations with scientific institutions abroad and international organizations engaged in nuclear research and development (Israel is a member of IAEA); Chair. The Prime Minister; Dir-Gen. YONA S. ETTINGER.

The Atomic Energy Commission has two research and development centres: the Nahal Soreq Nuclear Research Centre and the Negev Nuclear Research Centre near Dimona. The main fields of research are: nuclear physics and chemistry, plasma physics, solid state physics and chemistry, optics and electro-optics, reactor physics and engineering, radiation chemistry and biology, metallurgy and materials engineering, nuclear medicine and radio-pharmaceutics, non-destructive testing and environmental studies. Research and development projects and work with industrial applications include studies in isotopes, radiopharmaceuticals, medical and solid state lasers, crystal growth, high-tech. materials (including ceramics, ultra-pure electro-optical materials, infra-red glasses), mineral prospecting and the recovery of uranium from phosphates, use of intense sources of radiation in the medical, chemical and food industries, and the engineering and design of equipment for use in highly corrosive environments. The centres also provide national services: radiation protection, production and distribution of radioactive and stable isotopes, molecule and radio-pharmaceutical labelling, high vacuum engineering, training of personnel, information and documentation, etc.

Negev Nuclear Research Centre: POB 9001, Beersheba; equipped with a natural uranium-fuelled and heavy water-moderated reactor IRR-2 of 25 MW thermal; Dir GIORA AMIR.

Soreq Nuclear Research Centre: Yavne 70600; tel. 08-434211; telex 381455; f. 1954; equipped with a 'swimming pool' type research reactor IRR-1 of 5 MW thermal; Dir G. FRANK.

Weizmann Institute of Science: POB 26, Rehovot; tel. 08-483111; telex 381300; f. 1949; incorporates the Daniel Sieff Research Institute (f. 1934); includes 21 research units grouped into 5 faculties (Mathematical Sciences, Physics, Chemistry, Biophysics-Biochemistry, Biology), and a department of science teaching within the Feinberg Graduate School; 12 research centres have been established; the scientific staff numbers about 630, including 390 resident scientists, some 120 long-term visiting scientists, and 120 research assistants; there are about 500 students studying at the Feinberg Graduate School and doing research in the Institute's laboratories; the technical staff numbers 830 and there are 540 administrative and service personnel; Chair. Bd of Govs Lord SIEFF of BRIMPTON; Pres. Prof. ARYEH DVORETZKY; Chair. Scientific Council Prof. ZEEV VAGER.

ITALY

Introductory Survey

Location, Climate, Language, Religion, Flag, Capital

The Italian Republic comprises a peninsula, extending from southern Europe into the Mediterranean Sea, and a number of adjacent islands. The two principal islands are Sicily, to the south-west, and Sardinia, to the west. The Alps form a natural boundary to the north, where the bordering countries are France to the north-west, Switzerland and Austria to the north and Yugoslavia to the north-east. The climate is temperate in the north and Mediterranean in the south, with mild winters and long, dry summers. The average temperature in Rome is 7.4°C (45.3°F) in January and 25.7°C (78.3°F) in July. The principal language is Italian. German and Ladin are spoken in the Alto Adige region on the Austrian border, and French in the Valle d'Aosta region (bordering France and Switzerland), while in the Basilicata region of south-eastern Italy there is an Albanian-speaking minority. Catalan is spoken in north-western Sardinia. Almost all of the inhabitants profess Christianity: more than 90% are adherents of the Roman Catholic Church. There is freedom of expression for other Christian denominations and for non-Christian religions. The national flag (proportions 3 by 2) has three equal vertical stripes, of green, white and red. The capital is Rome.

Recent History

The Kingdom of Italy, under the House of Savoy, was proclaimed in 1861 and the country was unified in 1870. Italy subsequently acquired an overseas empire, comprising the African colonies of Eritrea (now part of Ethiopia), Italian Somaliland and Libya. Benito Mussolini, leader of the Fascist Party, became Prime Minister in October 1922 and assumed dictatorial powers in 1925-26. Relations between the Italian state and the Roman Catholic Church, a subject of bitter controversy since Italy's unification, were codified in 1929 by a series of agreements, including the Lateran Treaty, which recognized the sovereignty of the State of the Vatican City (q.v.), a small enclave within the city of Rome, under the jurisdiction of the Pope. Italian forces from Eritrea and Somaliland attacked and occupied neighbouring Ethiopia in 1935-36. Under Mussolini's rule, Italy also supported the Fascist forces in the Spanish Civil War of 1936-39, and annexed Albania in April 1939. From June 1940, Italy supported Nazi Germany in the Second World War. Italian forces from Albania attacked Greece in October 1940, but were defeated and forced to withdraw. In 1941 British forces captured Eritrea and Italian Somaliland, and ended Italy's occupation of Ethiopia, and in 1942 British and French forces occupied Libya. As forces from the allied powers invaded Italy, the Fascist regime crumbled. King Victor Emmanuel III dismissed Mussolini, and the Fascist Party was dissolved, in July 1943. With Italy's effective withdrawal from the war, German forces assumed the occupation of Albania. In Italy itself, anti-Fascist partisans joined allied forces in resisting the occupation by the remaining German troops. German forces in Italy surrendered, and Mussolini was killed, in April 1945. Italy's overseas empire was dissolved. In 1950, however, the British military administration of Italian Somaliland ended and the pre-war colony became a UN Trust Territory, with Italy returning as the administering power, until its merger with neighbouring British Somaliland, to form the independent state of Somalia, in 1960.

In May 1946 King Victor Emmanuel abdicated in favour of his son, Umberto II. However, he reigned for only one month. On 10 June, following a referendum, the monarchy was abolished and Italy became a republic. Until 1963 the Christian Democrats' monopoly of power was unchallenged; industry expanded rapidly in a liberal economic system supported by capital from the USA. By 1963, however, low wage rates and lack of social reforms had increased discontent, and in the elections of that year the Communist Party, together with other parties of the extreme right and left, made considerable gains at the expense of the Christian Democrats. The result of these losses was a rapid succession of mainly coalition governments involving the Christian Democrats and one or more of the other major parties.

Aldo Moro's coalition government of Christian Democrats and Republicans, formed in November 1974, resigned in January 1976 after the withdrawal of support by the Socialists. Moro formed a minority Christian Democratic administration in February, but this government was forced to resign in April. General elections for both Houses of Parliament were held in June, when the Communists won 34.4% of the votes for the Chamber of Deputies. Although the Christian Democrats still led the poll with 38.7% (the same as in the 1972 election), the Communists increased their strength in the 630-member Chamber from 179 to 228 seats, and continued to press for the 'historic compromise', a plan for a broad-based government with representatives from the Christian Democratic, Socialist and Communist parties, based on an alliance between Communism and Roman Catholicism. This was rejected by the Christian Democrats, who insisted on excluding the Communists from power, although they could no longer govern against Communist opposition in Parliament. In July a minority government of Christian Democrats was formed by Giulio Andreotti, a former Prime Minister, with the assurance of the abstention of the Communist deputies, and proceeded to introduce severe austerity measures to cope with the continuing economic crisis. In July 1977 the Communists, after four months of negotiations, were allowed a voice in policy-making but no direct role in the Government. The minority government was forced to resign in January 1978, owing to pressure from the Communists, who wanted a more active participation in government, but Andreotti formed a new, almost identical administration in March, with Communist support. The first crisis faced by this government was the murder in May 1978 of Aldo Moro, the former Prime Minister, by the Brigate Rosse (Red Brigades), a terrorist group. The second came in June, when the President, Giovanni Leone, resigned as a result of allegations of corruption. A series of inconclusive ballots finally ended with the inauguration in July of Alessandro Pertini, a former President of the Chamber of Deputies, as the first Socialist President of the Republic.

The Andreotti administration collapsed in January 1979, when the Communists withdrew from the official parliamentary majority, subsequently renewing their claim to posts in the Council of Ministers. A new coalition government was formed by Andreotti in March, only to be defeated within 10 days on a vote of confidence. At elections in June the Communists' share of the vote for the Chamber of Deputies declined to 30.4%, and they returned to the role of opposition in the next Parliament.

In August 1979 Francesco Cossiga, a former Minister of the Interior, formed a minority 'government of truce', composed of Christian Democrats, Liberals and Social Democrats, relying on the abstention of the Socialists. In spite of its mandate, the new government's initiatives were repeatedly thwarted by obstructionism in Parliament. Cossiga's second administration, formed in April 1980, admitted the Socialists to the Government for the first time in six years in a majority coalition with the Christian Democrats and the Republicans. The deliberate exclusion of the Communists led to an open campaign by their representatives in Parliament to bring down the new coalition. In September the Government was forced out of office in a secret ballot on its economic programme. In October 1980 Arnaldo Forlani, the chairman of the Christian Democratic party, assembled a coalition of Christian Democrats, Socialists, Republicans and Social Democrats. The new administration's integrity was damaged by a series of scandalous allegations, and it was finally forced to resign in May 1981, after it had been made known that more than 1,000 of Italy's foremost establishment figures belonged to a secret masonic lodge named P-2 ('Propaganda Due') which had extensive criminal connections, both in Italy and abroad. The lodge was linked with many political and financial scandals and even right-wing terrorism, culminating in the summer of 1982 with the collapse of one of the leading Italian banks, Banco Ambrosiano, and the death of its president, Roberto Calvi.

ITALY

In June 1981 Senator Giovanni Spadolini, leader of the small Republican party, formed a majority coalition of Socialists, Republicans, Christian Democrats, Social Democrats and Liberals, thus becoming the first non-Christian Democratic Prime Minister since 1946. This government fell in August 1982, after the defection of the Socialists, but was reconstituted later that month with the same ministers. In November Spadolini resigned, following a quarrel between Christian Democratic and Socialist ministers concerning the worsening economic situation. A new government was formed in December by Amintore Fanfani, a former Christian Democratic Prime Minister, leading a coalition of Christian Democrats, Socialists, Social Democrats and Liberals, committed to controlling the economy by increasing taxes and reducing public expenditure. This administration lasted until April 1983, when the Socialists withdrew their support and called for a general election. Parliament was dissolved in May, despite attempts by President Pertini to secure the formation of a new government. In the elections held in June, the Christian Democrats, who had rarely won less than 38% of the total vote in any poll since 1946, received only 32.9% of valid votes for the Chamber of Deputies. This loss of support meant that several of the smaller parties increased their shares of the vote. The Socialists made a small advance, taking 11.4% of the total vote. This increase, combined with the loss of support for the Christian Democrats, resulted in the accession of Bettino Craxi, the leader of the Socialist Party, as the first Socialist Prime Minister in the history of the republic. The new administration, a five-party coalition of Christian Democrats, Socialists, Republicans, Social Democrats and Liberals, took office in August, committed to cutting the budget deficit and to economic reform. Its anti-inflation measures included a government decree, imposed in February 1984, to reduce automatic index-linked wage increases (the 'scala mobile'). Despite opposition, the decree became law in June.

The repercussions of the P-2 scandals (see above) continued in 1984, when Pietro Longo, leader of the Social Democrats in the coalition government, resigned from his post as Budget Minister in July, after allegations that he was a member of the P-2 lodge. Craxi continued to consolidate his position by winning votes of confidence in the Senate and the Chamber of Deputies for his programme of economic reforms. In local and regional elections, held in May 1985, the Communists' share of the vote fell sharply, to 30.2%, while support for the Christian Democrat and Socialist parties increased. The result of a referendum, held in June and sponsored by the Communists, on the Government's decree of the previous year reducing the 'scala mobile', further vindicated the coalition's policies, when 54.3% of votes cast supported the Government.

In July 1985 Francesco Cossiga, President of the Senate and a former Christian Democratic Prime Minister, succeeded Alessandro Pertini as President of the Republic. The seizure of an Italian cruise ship, the *Achille Lauro*, in the eastern Mediterranean by Palestinian terrorists in October, and the subsequent repercussions, led to the collapse of the Government when the Republicans withdrew from the coalition, claiming that they had not been fully consulted on policy decisions. A reconciliation was achieved within a few days, and Craxi's resignation as Prime Minister was revoked. In June 1986, however, Craxi resigned, following a vote of 'no confidence' in the Chamber of Deputies, thus bringing to an end Italy's longest administration (1,060 days) since the Second World War. President Cossiga subsequently nominated the former Prime Minister Giulio Andreotti, a Christian Democrat and hitherto Minister of Foreign Affairs, to form a new government. However, the refusal of the other coalition parties to support his nomination led to Craxi's return to power in July, on condition that he would transfer the premiership to a Christian Democrat in March 1987.

Craxi duly submitted his resignation, and that of his Government, in March 1987. President Cossiga nominated Giulio Andreotti to form a new government. However, the bitter rivalry between the Christian Democrats and the Socialists led Andreotti to abandon his attempt to form a government, and Nilde Jotti, the Communist President of the Chamber of Deputies, was subsequently selected for the task by President Cossiga. Her failure to reconcile the two parties led President Cossiga to request Bettino Craxi to revive his former coalition Government for a vote of confidence. However, the Christian Democratic ministers resigned from the Government in protest against Socialist proposals to hold referendums on nuclear issues and judicial reforms. Oscar Scalfaro, the Christian Democratic Minister of the Interior, in turn failed to form a new government, and in April Amintore Fanfani, the Christian Democratic President of the Senate, was appointed as the head of a 'caretaker' government comprising 16 former Christian Democratic ministers and nine unallied members. Following a vote of 'no confidence' in the Chamber of Deputies, a general election was called for June, when the Christian Democrats obtained 34.3% of the votes and the Socialists obtained 14.3%. The Communists suffered their worst post-war electoral result, obtaining 26.6% of the votes, and thereby losing 21 seats in the Chamber of Deputies. The Green Party obtained 2.5% of the votes and entered the Chamber for the first time, occupying 13 seats. Fanfani resigned in July, when Giovanni Goria, a Christian Democrat and the former Minister of the Treasury, became Prime Minister, and reappointed a five-party coalition government. In November Goria resigned, following the withdrawal of the Liberal Party from the coalition, owing to a dispute over economic policy. Although Goria's resignation was rejected by President Cossiga, a series of strikes and other economic problems had seriously weakened the Government by the end of 1987. In February 1988, following difficulties in enacting financial legislation, Goria again announced his resignation, which was rejected by President Cossiga, who requested him to remain as 'caretaker' Prime Minister pending the approval of the 1988 budget and the formation of a new government. Despite the Senate's approval of the budget in the following month, Goria's resignation was precipitated by opposition to the Government's decision to resume construction of the Montalto di Castro nuclear power station (suspended in 1987 because of public concern over environmental risks). Ciriaco De Mita, the Secretary-General of the Christian Democrats, was requested to form a government. After five weeks of inter-party consultations, the formation of a coalition of the same five parties was agreed upon, and in April De Mita was sworn in at the head of a new government which included nine newly-appointed ministers and six ministers with changed portfolios. In October 1988 a crisis was narrowly averted when the Government secured a majority of votes in favour of abolishing the secret ballot in Parliament. The reform of parliamentary voting procedures had become a matter of priority for De Mita, who regarded the secret ballot as a source of instability in Italy's political life: henceforth, open voting was to be applied in both chambers of Parliament, except in extraordinary circumstances, such as issues of conscience.

In May 1988 local elections were held throughout the country, in which the Christian Democrats' share of the votes increased to 36.8% and the Socialists' share increased to 18.3%, while the Communists' share decreased to 21.9%, signifying their worst defeat in local polls for 35 years.

In the same month the Council of Ministers' decision to give its final approval to a regional autonomy accord for the Alto Adige resulted in a series of bombings, carried out by German-speaking extremists in the provincial capital of Bolzano. At provincial elections held in November, the neo-Fascist MSI-DN Party almost doubled its share of the votes, thereby replacing the Christian Democrats as the largest Italian-language grouping in the region.

In the late 1980s the Italian authorities intensified their efforts to combat organized crime. In December 1987 the biggest trial of Mafia suspects ever held, in which 452 defendants were tried in connection with more than 400 alleged offences (including drug smuggling, political corruption and 97 murders), ended in Palermo, Sicily, with the imprisonment of 338 defendants. After a series of attacks carried out by the Mafia on politicians, and the murder of a senior Sicilian judge in September 1988, a 'Mafia war' broke out in Sicily, with the worst bloodshed since the early 1980s. Later in the same month a new law was passed, investing the newly-appointed anti-Mafia commissioner with increased powers of investigation and co-ordination in an attempt to combat organized crime against the State. In November a 19-month trial of Mafia suspects in Turin concluded with the conviction of 130 defendants and the imposition of a record number of 26 life sentences.

Italy's foreign policy has traditionally been governed by its firm commitment to Europe, through participation in the EEC, and by its role in NATO. As a consequence of the US air raid on Libya in April 1986, Italian armed forces took control of Lampedusa island, lying south of Sicily (of which region it forms a part) and about 300 km north of Tripoli, following an unsuccessful Libyan attack on the island's US radar facilities. In May eight Libyan diplomats were expelled from Italy in response to Libya's expulsion of 25 Italian diplomats from Tripoli earlier in the month. In March 1987 Gen. Licio Giorgieri, an Italian air force officer in charge of the procurement of air and space weapons, was assassinated by the Red Brigades in what was believed to be part of a wider anti-NATO campaign, protesting against European participation in the USA's Strategic Defense Initiative. In September 1987 the Italian Government dispatched a task force of eight naval vessels to defend its merchant ships in the Persian Gulf, following reports of the alleged involvement of an Italian businessman in the supply of arms to Iran. (Italy obtains 45% of its oil requirements via the Strait of Hormuz.) In November 1988 it was announced that the task force was to return to Italy. In June 1988, despite fierce opposition from left-wing parties, the Government voted to accept the transfer to Italy of 72 American fighter aircraft which, under an agreement between the USA and Spain, were to be withdrawn from their base in Spain by 1991.

In April 1988 two car bombs exploded outside a US servicemen's club in Naples, killing five people and injuring 16. An Arab organization claimed responsibility for the attack. In the same month Prof. Roberto Ruffilli, a senator and close aide of the Prime Minister, was murdered. In July 21 people, all of whom belonged to the 'Fighting Communist Party' (PCC), a group associated with the Red Brigades, including two people suspected of Ruffilli's murder, were arrested.

Government

Under the 1948 Constitution, legislative power is held by the bicameral Parliament, elected by universal suffrage for five years (subject to dissolution) on the basis of proportional representation. The Senate has 315 elected members (seats allocated on a regional basis) and seven life Senators. The Chamber of Deputies has 630 members. The minimum voting age is 25 years for the Senate and 18 years for the Chamber. The two houses have equal power.

The President of the Republic is a constitutional Head of State elected for seven years by an electoral college comprising both Houses of Parliament and 58 regional representatives. Executive power is exercised by the Council of Ministers. The Head of State appoints the President of the Council (Prime Minister) and, on the latter's recommendation, other Ministers. The Council is responsible to Parliament.

The country is divided into 20 regions, of which five (Sicily, Sardinia, Trentino-Alto Adige, Friuli-Venezia Giulia and Valle d'Aosta) enjoy a special status. There is a large degree of regional autonomy. Each region has a regional council elected every five years by universal suffrage and a Giunta regionale responsible to the regional council. The regional council is a legislative assembly, while the Giunta holds executive power.

Defence

Italy has been a member of NATO since 1949. In June 1988 it maintained armed forces totalling 386,000 (including 270,500 conscripts): an army of 265,000, a navy of 48,000 and an air force of 73,000. Military service lasts 12 months in all the services. In 1987 defence expenditure was an estimated 16,454,000m. lire, and the defence budget for 1988 was 17,314,000m. lire.

Economic Affairs

After the Second World War, Italy experienced rapid economic development and was transformed from a mainly rural country into a modern industrial power. Between 1950 and 1980 the average income per head increased by more than 200% in real terms. Despite such gains, Italy's standard of living is generally below that of other countries in the EEC. In 1987, according to estimates by the World Bank, Italy's total GNP was US $596,995m., equivalent to $10,420 per head (at average 1985–87 prices), having increased since 1980 at an average real rate of 1.3% per year. The average annual increase in overall gross domestic product (GDP), measured in constant prices, was 3.9% in 1965–80, slowing to 1.3% in 1980–86. In 1987, according to government figures, GDP increased by 3.1%.

Although agriculture has always represented an important part of the Italian economy, a substantial advance has taken place since the war in the proportion of the GDP contributed by industrial activity, particularly in engineering and other manufacturing sectors. This change has been far more pronounced in the northern part of the country, with its proximity to the rest of Europe. The long-term economic problem, therefore, remains the integration of the southern half of Italy, where the average annual income is still substantially less than that in the north, and where employment and production lag far behind. There are several development agencies and banks that attempt to increase investment in the south, to improve infrastructure and communications and to promote the region's industrialization.

In 1983 agriculture employed only 12.2% of the working population. In 1986 agriculture provided 5% of GDP, while industry provided 39%. Plans to improve and modernize the agricultural sector have been thwarted by increased consumption and the inadaptability of many small farms to mechanization. In 1987 about 68% of farms in Italy were less than 5 ha, and only 2% were larger than 50 ha. The principal crops, by volume, in 1986 were sugar beet, wheat, maize, grapes and tomatoes. In 1986 Italy was Europe's leading producer of soybeans, with an output of more than 800,000 tons. Italy is a leading producer and exporter of wine. Italy's total catch of fish decreased to 547,600 metric tons in 1986, compared with 575,000 tons in 1985.

Tourism is an important source of income, and in 1987 tourist receipts totalled 15,782,808m. lire. There are more than 5m. Italians living abroad and their remittances form a valuable source of income. The flourishing 'submerged economy', operating outside government control, is estimated to account for as much as one-third of the national income.

Industrial growth in Italy has, in the past, concentrated on the development of heavy industry, in which the State plays an important part through the large holding companies, IRI, ENI and EFIM. However, many of these industries, such as steel and shipbuilding, are now in decline, leading to the closure of plant and redundancies among the work-force. In 1986 Finsider, part of the IRI group and the world's third-largest steel producer, incurred a financial loss of 980,400m. lire, and the loss increased to some 1,500,000m. lire in the following year. In mid-1988 Finsider went into voluntary liquidation and was subsequently reorganized and revived under the new name of Ilva. At the end of the year Italy was seeking EEC consent for its plan to remove 1.18m. tons of its capacity for production of hot-rolled steel and to eliminate 20,000 jobs by 1990, in return for permission to cancel 7,670,000m. lire of the steel industry's debts. As the result of a limited 'privatization' programme (introduced in 1983), ENI became profitable for the first time in 12 years, recording a net profit of more than 800,000m. lire in 1985, following a loss of 64,000m. lire in the previous year. The joint turnover of IRI, ENI and EFIM in 1985 was estimated to be in excess of 100,000,000m. lire, following overall losses recorded by IRI and EFIM of 6,000,000m. lire in 1983. Industrial production increased by an annual average of only 0.2% in 1980–86. However, improvements in labour costs, together with increased investment and the adoption of new technologies, have resulted in higher productivity and manufacturing output in a wide range of industries, including motor cars, textiles, clothing, electronics and consumer goods. In 1987 sales of cars reached a record 1,977,000, representing a 7.7% increase over the 1986 total. Industrial production rose by 4.1% in the year to June 1986. In the 12 months to May 1987 industrial production rose by 5.3%. The employers' association, Confindustria, predicted that industrial production would increase by 2.9% in 1988. Investment in manufacturing industry was expected to rise by 9.6% in 1987 and by 6% in the following year.

Italy depended on imported petroleum for 57.4% of its energy requirements in 1984. Imports of crude petroleum accounted for about 14% of total import costs in 1987; in that year Libya was Italy's largest supplier of crude petroleum, providing 16.1% of total domestic requirement, while Iran was its second largest supplier. In June 1983 a natural gas pipeline from Algeria came 'on stream', and was expected to supply 12,000m. cu m of methane by the mid-1980s. In May 1984 agreement was reached with the USSR whereby Italy would receive up to 6,000m. cu m of gas per year through the Siberian pipeline. Italy's nuclear power resources remain small. The country currently has three completed nuclear power stations, providing a total generating capacity of 1,273MW. In November 1987 a referendum on nuclear energy resulted in the suspension of plans for the construction of further nuclear power stations. In August 1988 the Council of Ministers adopted a new 15-year National Energy Plan, which was expected to cost 80,000,000m. lire and aimed to reduce Italy's dependence on imported energy from 81% to 75%, and to spend almost half of the planned investment on projects to conserve energy. According to the plan, the production of coal and of gas was to meet 29% and 28% of the country's energy requirements, respectively, by the year 2000.

In 1988 Italy became the first European country to ban the export of waste materials to Third World countries, following protests held at ports in the south of the country against the docking of a container vessel carrying toxic waste dumped by Italian companies in Nigeria. The Government subsequently announced plans to spend more than 10,000,000m. lire annually on the disposal of urban refuse and toxic waste.

The Italian economy relies heavily on the export of its manufactured goods to pay for essential imports of petroleum, raw materials and food. Recession in Europe and the rising cost of petroleum, coupled with high inflation and undiminished internal demand, led to annual trade deficits after 1978. Modest economic growth during 1984 caused a rapid rise in the level of imports, while exports were constrained by the overvaluation of the Italian currency within the European Monetary System (EMS). As a result, by 1984 the annual trade deficit had reached 19,163,200m. lire and in 1985 grew to a record 23,115,400m. lire. The trade deficit for 1986 fell to 3,722,000m. lire, mainly owing to the decline in international petroleum prices. A sharp rise in imports in 1987 resulted in a trade deficit of 11,138,000m. lire. In the first nine months of 1988 the trade deficit was 9,873,000m. lire. The current account of the balance of payments, which had been transformed from a deficit of US $9,964m. in 1980 to a surplus of $1,380m. in 1983, was in deficit by $2,501m. in 1984, and by $3,540m. in 1985. A surplus of $2,912m. was achieved in 1986, but there was a deficit of $1,078m. in 1987. The lira was devalued in relation to the EEC currencies within the EMS several times between 1981 and 1983. Concern over the disparity between Italy's rate of inflation and large trade and public sector deficits, and those of other member countries, prompted a further devaluation of 8% in July 1985.

From the early 1970s, increased spending on social services and industry caused high levels of government expenditure and a public sector deficit far in excess of those of Italy's European competitors. The failure of revenue and taxation to equal this growth produced a large budget deficit, financed by government borrowing, interest payments for which further fuel the public borrowing requirement. Government spending, measured as a proportion of GDP, reached 58% in 1983 and the public sector deficit rose to 16.8% of GDP. Subsequent governments tried to limit this deficit by cuts in public spending, measures against tax evasion and by increases in indirect taxation. Measures introduced by the Craxi Government succeeded in limiting the annual deficit to 95,350,000m. lire in 1984, or 15.4% of GDP. Further restraints on spending were expected to reduce the deficit to 14.8% of GDP in 1985. However, preliminary estimates suggested an acceleration in the growth of the deficit, caused by the need to pay interest on short-term government bonds used to finance the growing national debt. Accumulated government debt in 1984 totalled 93% of GDP, and interest payments represented 9.6% of GDP. In 1986 the national debt increased to the equivalent of 95.9% of annual GDP, or 684,900,000m. lire at current prices, and was expected to exceed 100% of GDP by the end of 1987.

The high public-sector deficit was one of the main causes of inflation, which averaged 16% annually in 1975–84. Reduced price rises for energy and raw materials, and the Government's success in curtailing inflation-linked wage increases, together with measures designed to cut public spending in health services and pensions, brought inflation down to an average of 8.6% in 1985, to 6.1% in 1986, and to 4.6% in 1987; in the 12 months to November 1988 the average rate was 5.3%. Plans to introduce the 'lira nuova', to be worth 1,000 of the existing unit, were postponed in late 1986, owing to conflicts between parliamentary finance and budget commissions. In February 1988 the Council of Ministers approved a draft law to introduce the 'lira nuova'. Unemployment increased gradually from an average of 8% of the labour force in 1980 to an estimated 12.6% in 1984. In December 1985 the unemployment rate reached 13.2%, the highest level since the Second World War. The average rate was 10.3% in 1986 and 11.0% in 1987. According to the OECD, 39.3% of unemployed people in 1986 were less than 25 years of age, and this proportion was expected to rise to 43% in 1988. In July 1988 the unemployment rate was 16.2% compared with a rate of 10.5% in July 1987.

During this period a growing number of women had begun to search for paid employment, thereby increasing the number of unemployed. During 1986 the Government announced plans to spend 120,000,000m. lire, over the next 10 years, on the development of industries and infrastructure in the south, where the unemployment rate was about double that of the north.

In November 1986 the Government averted a general strike by negotiating a series of concessions with the trade unions. The agreements envisaged additional social costs for employees, totalling 880,000m. lire, to be included in the 1987 budget, and the provision of an extra 1,500,000m. lire, over the next three years, to finance the implementation of a new agreement on wages for 3.5m. public-sector workers who had been adversely affected by the flat-rate indexed pay rises of recent years. A series of strikes, in particular by transport workers, throughout 1987 culminated, in November, in a general strike by public-sector employees protesting against the Government's economic policy, which aimed to decrease the public-sector deficit by reducing expenditure on social welfare, by increasing unemployment and by reducing development aid for the south. The 1987 budget deficit amounted to 113,560,000m. lire (compared with the Government's original target of 100,000,000m. lire). The projected deficit for 1988 was 122,000,000m. lire: in July the Government adopted measures to reduce this by increasing indirect taxation and by further reductions in public spending, in order to eliminate the need for new government borrowing. By the end of 1988, however, the budget deficit for the year was estimated at 125,000,000m. lire. The Government planned to restrict the 1989 budget deficit to 117,350,000m. lire (or some 10.2% of GDP, compared with 11% in 1988). During 1988 there were strikes in a number of sectors, and in December the three principal trade union groupings threatened to strike in protest at supplementary tax measures introduced by the Government, including the imposition of value-added tax on some basic foodstuffs, and an amnesty (upon payment of a fine) for those guilty of tax evasion (thought to be a considerable number). In January 1989 the Government conceded measures which would link increases in direct taxation to the rate of inflation.

Social Welfare

Italy has a comprehensive system of social benefits covering unemployment and disability as well as retirement pensions and family allowances. These benefits are all provided by the social security system (Istituto Nazionale della Previdenza Sociale). There is also an industrial injuries scheme, operated by the Istituto Nazionale per l'Assicurazione contro gli Infortuni sul Lavoro.

A comprehensive national health service, aiming to provide free medical care for all citizens, was introduced in 1980. However, minimum charges are still made for essential medicines, medical examinations and hospital treatment. All workers will be eligible for benefits under a unified national medical insurance scheme. In 1986 Italy had 1,752 hospital establishments, with a total of 450,377 beds: equivalent to one for every 79 inhabitants. In 1986 there were 84,339 registered physicians working in Italy. Expenditure by the central Government in 1985 included 45,502,000m. lire for health and 117,372,000m. lire for social security and welfare.

Education

Education is free and compulsory between the ages of six and 14 years. The curricula of all Italian schools are standardized by the Ministry of Education. After primary school, for children aged six to 11 years, the pupil enters the lower secondary school (scuola media unificata). An examination at the end of three years leads to a lower secondary school certificate, which gives access to all higher secondary schools. Pupils wishing to enter a classical lycée (liceo classico) must also pass an examination in Latin.

Higher secondary education is provided by classical, artistic and scientific lycées, training schools for elementary teachers and technical and vocational institutes (industrial, commercial, nautical, etc.). After five years at a lycée, the student sits an examination for the higher secondary school certificate (maturità), which allows automatic entry into any university faculty. Special four-year courses are provided at the teachers' training schools and the diploma obtained permits entry to a special university faculty of education, the magistero, and a few other faculties. The technical institutes provide practical courses which prepare students for a specialized university faculty.

ITALY

University courses last for a minimum of four years. Study allowances are awarded to students according to their means and merit. Expenditure on education by the central Government was 31,134,635m. lire in 1986.

Public Holidays

1989: 2 January (for New Year's Day), 6 January (Epiphany), 27 March (Easter Monday), 25 April (Liberation Day), 1 May (Labour Day), 12 May (Festival of the Tricolour), 15 August (Assumption), 1 November (All Saints' Day), 5 November (National Unity Day), 8 December (Immaculate Conception), 25 December (Christmas Day), 26 December (St Stephen).

1990: 1 January (New Year's Day), 6 January (Epiphany), 16 April (Easter Monday), 25 April (Liberation Day), 1 May (Labour Day), 12 May (Festival of the Tricolour), 15 August (Assumption), 1 November (All Saints' Day), 5 November (National Unity Day), 8 December (Immaculate Conception), 25 December (Christmas Day), 26 December (St Stephen).

There are also numerous local public holidays, held on the feast day of the patron saint of each town.

Weights and Measures

The metric system is in force.

Statistical Survey

Source (unless otherwise stated): Istituto Centrale di Statistica, Via Cesare Balbo 16, 00100 Rome; tel. (06) 4673; telex 610338.

Area and Population

AREA, POPULATION AND DENSITY

Area (sq km)	301,279*
Population (census results)	
24 October 1971	54,136,547
25 October 1981	
Males	27,506,354
Females	29,050,557
Total	56,556,911
Population (official estimates at 31 December)	
1985	57,202,345
1986	57,290,519
1987	57,399,108
Density (per sq km) at 31 December 1987	190.5

* 116,324 sq miles.

REGIONS (31 December 1987)

Region	Area ('000 hectares)	Population	Regional capital	Population of capital
Abruzzi	1,079	1,257,988	L'Aquila	66,772
Basilicata	999	621,506	Potenza	67,394
Calabria	1,508	2,146,724	Catanzaro	103,004
Campania	1,360	5,731,426	Napoli (Naples)	1,200,958
Emilia-Romagna	2,212	3,924,199	Bologna	427,240
Friuli-Venezia Giulia	785	1,210,242	Trieste	237,191
Lazio	1,720	5,137,270	Roma (Rome)	2,817,227
Liguria	542	1,749,572	Genova (Genoa)	722,026
Lombardia (Lombardy)	2,386	8,886,402	Milano (Milan)	1,478,505
Marche	969	1,428,557	Ancona	104,255
Molise	444	334,680	Campobasso	50,919
Piemonte (Piedmont)	2,540	4,377,229	Torino (Turin)	1,025,390
Puglia	1,935	4,042,996	Bari	358,906
Sardegna (Sardinia)	2,409	1,651,218	Cagliari	221,790
Sicilia (Sicily)	2,571	5,141,343	Palermo	728,843
Toscana (Tuscany)	2,299	3,568,308	Firenze (Florence)	421,299
Trentino-Alto Adige	1,362	881,986	Bolzano (Bozen)*	101,230
			Trento (Trent, Trient)*	100,677
Umbria	846	818,226	Perugia	147,602
Valle d'Aosta	326	114,325	Aosta	36,716
Veneto	1,836	4,374,911	Venezia (Venice)	327,700

* Joint regional capitals.

ITALY

Statistical Survey

PRINCIPAL TOWNS (population at 31 December 1987)

Town	Population	Town	Population
Roma (Rome, the capital)	2,817,227	Ferrara	143,046
Milano (Milan)	1,478,505	Ravenna	136,324
Napoli (Naples)	1,200,958	Rimini	130,787
Torino (Turin)	1,025,390	Pescara	130,525
Palermo	728,843	Reggio nell' Emilia	130,015
Genova (Genoa)	722,026	Siracusa (Syracuse)	123,706
Bologna	427,240	Monza	122,726
Firenze (Florence)	421,299	Sassari	120,497
Catania	372,212	Bergamo	118,655
Bari	358,906	Terni	110,704
Venezia (Venice)	327,700	Forlí	110,334
Messina	270,546	Vicenza	109,932
Verona	258,523	La Spezia	107,435
Taranto	244,845	Cosenza	105,913
Trieste	237,191	Piacenza	104,976
Padova (Padua)	223,907	Torre del Greco	104,646
Cagliari	221,790	Ancona	104,255
Brescia	198,839	Pisa	103,527
Reggio di Calabria	178,714	Catanzaro	103,004
Modena	176,556	Novara	102,961
Parma	175,301	Udine	102,021*
Livorno (Leghorn)	173,114	Lecce	101,520
Prato	164,824	Bolzano (Bozen)	101,230
Foggia	159,192	Trento (Trent, Trient)	100,677
Salerno	153,807	Alessandria	100,523
Perugia	147,602		

* Estimate for 31 December 1986.

BIRTHS, MARRIAGES AND DEATHS

	Registered live births		Registered marriages		Registered deaths	
	Number	Rate (per 1,000)	Number	Rate (per 1,000)	Number	Rate (per 1,000)
1979	670,221	11.9	323,930	5.7	538,352	9.5
1980	640,401	11.3	322,968	5.7	554,510	9.7
1981	623,103	11.0	316,953	5.6	545,291	9.7
1982	619,097	10.9	312,494	5.5	534,935	9.4
1983	601,928	10.6	303,663	5.3	564,330	9.9
1984	587,871	10.3	298,028	5.2	534,676	9.4
1985	577,345	10.1	295,990	5.2	547,436	9.6
1986*	554,845	9.7	296,539	5.2	542,127	9.5
1987*	552,329	9.6	305,328	5.3	531,739	9.3

* Provisional.

Average expectation of life (1977–79): Males 70.61 years; females 77.19 years.

EMIGRATION

Destination	1984	1985	1986
Belgium	2,891	2,402	1,996
France	4,708	4,057	3,808
Germany, Federal Repub.	27,609	21,092	19,793
Switzerland	18,892	17,091	14,021
United Kingdom	2,653	2,350	1,710
Other European Countries	3,789	3,594	3,319
Argentina	830	882	852
Brazil	475	545	502
Canada	1,432	1,818	1,391
USA	3,959	3,541	3,062
Venezuela	930	890	723
Oceania	1,282	1,243	1,053
Other Countries	7,868	7,232	5,632
Total	**77,318**	**66,737**	**57,862**

ECONOMICALLY ACTIVE POPULATION*
(annual averages, '000 persons aged 14 years and over)

	1984	1985	1986
Agriculture, forestry, hunting and fishing	2,426	2,296	2,241
Energy and water	206	209	220
Manufacturing	4,881	4,766	4,719
Construction	1,956	1,921	1,882
Trade, restaurants and hotels	4,293	4,365	4,407
Transport, storage and communications	1,069	1,091	1,120
Financing, insurance, real estate and business services	658	716	749
Community, social and personal services	5,158	5,377	5,518
Total employed	**20,647**	**20,742**	**20,856**
Persons seeking work for the first time	1,167	1,250	1,296
Other unemployed	1,223	1,222	1,315
Total labour force	**23,038**	**23,213**	**23,467**
Males	14,986	15,040	15,068
Females	8,052	8,173	8,399

* Figures exclude permanent members of institutional households (150,000 in 1986) and persons on compulsory military service (231,000 in 1986).

Agriculture

PRINCIPAL CROPS ('000 metric tons)

	1985	1986	1987
Wheat	8,460.7	9,102.1	9,359.1
Barley	1,629.5	1,543.0	1,707.9
Oats	362.8	397.3	360.8
Rice (paddy)	1,122.7	1,137.2	1,043.9
Maize	6,356.6	6,401.1	5,761.9
Dry broad beans	174.0	162.8	159.6
Green broad beans	116.8	111.9	109.2
Dry beans	60.6	59.8	55.4
Soybeans (Soya beans)	286	n.a.	n.a.
Green beans	261.7	272.2	256.3
Green peas	217.0	200.1	198.3
Potatoes	2,397.0	2,550.9	2,463.9
Onions	483.4	496.7	477.4
Carrots	270.6	346.2	374.6
Turnips	60.2	53.5	43.3
Artichokes	417.6	495.5	453.2
Fennel	333.1	337.8	350.1
Celery	104.1	137.6	137.1
Cabbages	478.2	493.4	494.4
Cauliflowers	350.3	401.8	422.7
Endives, lettuces, radishes	780.1	831.2	850.8
Spinach	80.9	96.6	101.1
Aubergines (Egg-plants)	297.4	294.6	295.9
Tomatoes	6,563.2	5,369.6	4,770.5
Pumpkins	340.8	344.8	344.4
Water melons	783.0	740.7	714.5
Melons	351.3	369.2	356.3
Sugar beet	9,567.2	14,957.8	15,483.3
Tobacco	166.5	145.7	160.3
Grapes	9,583.7	11,531.9	11,497.5
Olives	3,387.9	1,899.4	3,457.4
Oranges	2,162.1	2,217.5	1,342.9
Lemons	737.7	813.3	591.8
Apples	2,014.1	2,019.5	2,234.2
Pears	805.6	913.0	892.5
Peaches	1,424.9	1,436.2	1,513.7
Fresh figs	48.7	47.9	42.7
Dried figs	5.5	5.0	3.9
Almonds (unshelled)	105.6	122.7	121.8

ITALY

LIVESTOCK ('000 head)

	1985	1986	1987
Cattle	8,910	8,819	8,793
Buffaloes	101	102	n.a.
Sheep	11,293	11,451	11,456
Goats	1,089	1,201	1,206
Pigs	9,169	9,278	9,383
Horses	248	253	250
Mules	56	52	50
Asses	94	91	86

Chickens: (FAO estimates, million, year ending September): 111 in 1985; 111 in 1986.

LIVESTOCK PRODUCTS ('000 metric tons)

	1984	1985	1986
Beef and veal	1,182	1,205	1,180
Mutton and lamb	67	66	64
Goats' meat	4	4	3.5
Pig meat	1,218	1,187	1,172
Horse meat	52	55	54
Poultry meat	1,019	996	1,008
Other meat	197	200	203
Edible offals	213	214	210
Lard	210	224	221
Cows' milk	10,901	10,946	10,858
Buffaloes' milk	70	74	74
Sheep's milk	599	611	615
Goats' milk	126	128	128
Butter	81	83	n.a.
Cheese	661	667	n.a.
Hen eggs	603	612	584
Wool: greasy	12.7	12.9	12.0
clean	6.1	6.2	n.a.

1987 ('000 metric tons): Beef and veal 1,174; Mutton and lamb 67; Goats' meat 3.3; Pig meat 1,231; Horse meat 54.

Forestry

ROUNDWOOD REMOVALS ('000 cubic metres, excl. bark)

	1984	1985	1986
Sawlogs, veneer logs and logs for sleepers	2,333	2,460	3,203
Pulpwood	980	908	965
Other industrial wood	1,071	1,189	476
Fuel wood	4,844	4,891	4,979
Total	9,228	9,448	9,623

Source: FAO, *Yearbook of Forest Products*.

SAWNWOOD PRODUCTION ('000 cubic metres)

	1984	1985	1986
Coniferous (soft wood)	1,003	1,166	854
Broadleaved (hard wood)	1,179	1,388	1,001
Total	2,182	2,554	1,855

Railway sleepers ('000 cubic metres): 52 in 1984; 45 in 1985; 64 in 1986.

Source: FAO, *Yearbook of Forest Products*.

Fishing

('000 metric tons, live weight)

	1984	1985	1986
Trouts	35.8	33.0	35.5
European hake	29.6	33.8	24.4
Surmullets (Red mullets)	11.9	12.5	10.9
Jack and horse mackerels	10.6	11.7	10.8
European sardine (pilchard)	45.8	47.4	52.2
European anchovy	43.7	57.3	32.4
Other fishes (incl. unspecified)	195.1	183.9	181.9
Total fish	372.4	379.5	348.0
Shrimps, prawns, etc.	18.0	20.2	14.6
Other crustaceans	12.8	13.2	15.2
Mediterranean mussel	66.3	76.0	78.6
Striped venus	38.9	25.6	26.5
Cuttlefishes	13.1	14.9	15.5
Squids	12.3	14.9	17.2
Octopuses	12.9	13.2	14.3
Other molluscs	18.4	17.5	17.7
Total catch	565.0	575.0	547.6
Inland waters	43.8	41.3	43.9
Mediterranean and Black Sea	480.5	492.2	456.1
Atlantic Ocean	40.0	40.7	47.6
Indian Ocean	0.7	0.8	—

Source: FAO, *Yearbook of Fishery Statistics*.

Mining

('000 metric tons)

	1985	1986	1987
Bauxite	n.a.	2.3	15.1
Lead concentrates*	25.7	21.7	21.0
Zinc concentrates*	86.8	50.5	67.8
Barytes	127.2	112.5	82.2
Fluorspar	152.9	145.5	135.6
Pyrites	690.4	760.9	784.9
Petroleum	2,342.5	2,510.6	3,904.5
Asphalt and bituminous rock	88.7	66.9	71.0
Lignite	1,892.4	1,541.2	1,641.7
Crude sulphur	4.9	n.a.	n.a.

* Figures refer to gross weight of ores and concentrates. In 1987 the metal content (in '000 metric tons) was: Lead 12.2; Zinc 33.2.

Industry

SELECTED PRODUCTS
('000 metric tons, unless otherwise indicated)

	1985	1986	1987
Wine ('000 hectolitres)	62,577	76,987	n.a.
Pig iron	12,062.5	11,916.3	11,334.9
Steel	23,897.6	22,881.9	22,858.7
Rolled iron	20,373.6	20,096.8	20,846.5
Other iron and steel-finished manufactures	795.4	828.5	865.0
Iron alloys and *spiegel-eisen* special pig irons	281.9	260.6	238.2
Fuel oil	20,065.8	21,371.3	21,504.7
Synthetic ammonia	1,477.2	1,888.6	1,745.1
Sulphuric acid at 50° Bé	4,358.2	4,168.3	4,358.7
Synthetic organic dyes	15.0	16.2	17.5
Tanning materials	53.9	38.8	37.0
Caustic soda	1,031.1	1,042.7	1,216.2
Rayon and acetate filament yarn	30.3	30.2	n.a.
Cotton yarn	221.1	230.3	261.3

ITALY

—continued	1985	1986	1987
Natural methane gas (million cu m)	14,158.1	15,893.3	16,217.6
Sewing machines ('000)	425.3	335.3	327.2
Typewriters ('000)	482.3	443.9	383.4
Passenger motor cars ('000)	1,384.2	1,652.8	1,711.8
Lorries (Trucks) ('000)	184.5	179.0	200.4
Hydroelectric power (million kWh)*	44,056	44,001	42,076.0
Thermoelectric power (million kWh)*	132,198	138,605	148,820.0

* Net production.

Finance

CURRENCY AND EXCHANGE RATES

Monetary Units
100 centesimi = 1 Italian lira (plural: lire).

Denominations
Coins: 5, 10, 20, 50, 100, 200 and 500 lire.
Notes: 1,000, 2,000, 5,000, 10,000, 20,000, 50,000 and 100,000 lire.

Sterling and Dollar Equivalents (30 September 1988)
£1 sterling = 2,359.0 lire;
US $1 = 1,395.0 lire;
10,000 lire = £4.239 = $7.168.

Average Exchange Rate (lire per US $)
1985 1,909.4
1986 1,490.8
1987 1,296.1

STATE BUDGET (million lire—1987)

Revenue	
Property and income taxes	129,067,252
Business taxation and duties	63,838,450
Customs and frontier charges	} 24,379,299
Taxes on manufacturing and consumption	
Public lottery and sweepstakes	1,202,942
State monopolies	5,312,238
Other ordinary revenue	59,490,081
Total real revenue	283,290,262
Capital movements	585,588
General total	283,875,850

Expenditure	
Ministry of the Treasury	249,134,701
Ministry of Finance	13,053,060
Ministry of Justice	3,297,000
Ministry of Education	35,492,170
Ministry of the Interior	44,082,416
Ministry of Public Works	4,163,501
Ministry of Agriculture and Forests	2,738,989
Ministry of Defence	19,967,837
Ministry of Labour and Social Welfare	38,631,301
Other Ministries	32,404,488
General total	442,965,463

INTERNATIONAL RESERVES (US $ million at 31 December)*

	1985	1986	1987
Gold†	23,558	26,055	34,050
IMF special drawing rights	326	587	948
Reserve position in IMF	1,160	1,268	1,447
Foreign exchange	14,109	18,132	27,819
Total	39,153	46,042	64,264

* Excluding deposits made with the European Monetary Co-operation Fund.
† Valued at market-related prices.
Source: IMF, *International Financial Statistics*.

MONEY SUPPLY ('000 million lire at 31 December)

	1985	1986	1987
Currency outside banks	46,329	49,863	53,789
Demand deposits at commercial banks	250,279	281,613	302,860

Source: IMF, *International Financial Statistics*.

COST OF LIVING (Consumer Price Index; base: 1980 = 100)

	1984	1985	1986
Food	165.9	180.3	190.2
Fuel and light	201.9	219.8	205.1
Clothing	171.9	190.4	206.2
Rent	196.2	207.9	294.7
All items (incl. others)	174.3	190.3	201.5

Source: ILO, *Year Book of Labour Statistics*.

NATIONAL ACCOUNTS ('000 million lire)

	1985	1986	1987
Gross domestic product at factor cost	765,450	845,173	913,631
of which:			
Agriculture, forestry and fisheries	39,536	41,360	42,738
Industry	265,101	286,868	306,230
Other activities	391,538	443,472	478,953
Less imputed bank service charge	−34,356	−39,806	−41,387
Public administration	103,631	113,279	127,097
Net factor income from abroad	−5,378	−6,907	−6,535
Gross national product at factor cost	760,072	838,266	907,096
Indirect taxes, *less* subsidies	50,180	57,065	68,964
Gross national product in market prices	810,252	895,331	976,060
Balance of exports and imports of goods and services	3,318	−13,599	−7,384
Available resources	813,570	881,732	968,676
of which:			
Private consumption expenditure	497,991	549,081	602,014
Government consumption expenditure	135,754	147,881	166,722
Gross fixed capital formation	171,706	180,260	195,086
Increase in stocks	13,497	11,417	11,389

ITALY

BALANCE OF PAYMENTS (US $ million)

	1985	1986	1987
Merchandise exports f.o.b.	76,073	96,719	116,310
Merchandise imports f.o.b.	−82,157	−92,194	−116,215
Trade balance	−6,083	4,425	95
Exports of services	27,284	32,188	39,514
Imports of services	−25,768	−32,170	−39,666
Balance on goods and services	−4,568	4,543	−57
Private unrequited transfers (net)	1,325	1,465	1,278
Government unrequited transfers (net)	−298	−3,096	−2,300
Current balance	−3,540	2,912	−1,078
Direct capital investment (net)	−873	−2,848	1,753
Other long-term capital (net)	2,848	−1,488	519
Short-term capital (net)	−2,136	2,644	5,778
Net errors and omissions	−3,998	338	−1,571
Total (net monetary movements)	−7,699	1,558	5,401
Valuation changes (net)	2,562	2,653	3,894
Exceptional financing	262	883	34
Changes in reserves	−4,875	5,094	9,329

Source: IMF, *International Financial Statistics*.

External Trade

Note: Data refer to the trade of Italy (excluding the communes of Livigno and Campione) and San Marino, with which Italy maintains a customs union. The figures include trade in second-hand ships, and stores and bunkers for foreign ships and aircraft, but exclude manufactured gas, surplus military equipment, war reparations and repayments and gift parcels by post. Also excluded are imports of military goods and exports of fish landed abroad directly from Italian vessels. Figures include gold ingots for non-monetary uses.

PRINCIPAL COMMODITIES
(distribution by SITC, '000 million lire)

Imports c.i.f.	1985	1986	1987
Food and live animals	20,130.5	19,204.3	19,646.2
Live animals	2,253.5	2,338.2	2,261.7
Bovine cattle	1,682.1	106.7	1,643.4
Meat and meat preparations	4,281.3	4,153.0	4,167.4
Fresh, chilled or frozen meat	4,117.6	4,006.9	4,002.3
Meat of bovine cattle	2,461.2	2,281.1	2,307.5
Dairy products and eggs	3,296.5	3,091.6	3,280.4
Cereals and cereal preparations	2,638.7	2,593.8	2,500.5
Maize (unmilled)	403.6	318.8	412.6
Beverages and tobacco	1,719.8	1,572.8	1,688.1
Crude materials (inedible) except fuels	15,811.3	12,881.0	13,063.3
Wood, lumber and cork	2,088.1	1,988.7	2,259.3
Shaped or simply worked wood	1,365.1	1,324.2	1,590.4
Textile fibres and waste	3,406.0	2,501.3	2,537.2
Metalliferous ores and metal scrap	3,204.2	2,341.0	2,079.5
Mineral fuels and lubricants	46,596.0	24,039.1	22,785.8
Petroleum and petroleum products	37,015.9	17,590.7	17,463.8
Crude petroleum	25,472.0	12,439.1	11,483.5
Animal and vegetable oils and fats	1,306.9	1,065.1	1,256.3
Chemicals	16,186.1	16,406.9	17,686.3
Chemical elements and compounds	6,190.1	4,780.9	5,858.9
Organic chemicals	5,068.7	3,708.7	4,710.0
Plastic materials, etc.	4,095.5	4,272.8	4,851.1

Imports c.i.f.—continued	1985	1986	1987
Basic manufactures	22,005.3	22,467.0	25,093.3
Textile yarn, fabrics, etc.	5,235.7	5,339.7	6,121.9
Iron and steel	4,967.8	5,240.5	5,394.6
Non-ferrous metals	3,708.1	3,317.0	3,609.5
Copper and copper alloys	1,572.9	1,333.3	1,451.2
Machinery and transport equipment	34,655.6	36,778.6	43,938.0
Non-electric machinery			
Electrical machinery, apparatus, etc.	22,264.7	23,580.6	27,919.1
Transport equipment	12,390.9	13,198.0	16,018.9
Road motor vehicles and parts	10,231.4	11,364.4	14,075.5
Passenger cars (excl. buses)	6,972.5	7,527.5	9,532.9
Miscellaneous manufactured articles	9,043.0	9,901.1	11,799.2
Scientific instruments, watches, etc.	3,970.6	4,213.5	4,916.3
Other commodities and transactions	5,354.7	4,678.0	4,640.1
Total	172,809.2	148,993.9	161,596.6

Exports f.o.b.	1985	1986	1987
Food and live animals	8,522.4	7,602.9	7,659.9
Fruit and vegetables	4,254.4	3,928.7	4,025.3
Fresh fruit and nuts	2,007.3	1,879.9	1,848.8
Beverages and tobacco	2,058.1	1,638.3	1,686.2
Crude materials (inedible) except fuels	2,515.3	2,256.3	2,345.4
Mineral fuels, lubricants, etc.	7,093.5	4,154.0	3,754.6
Petroleum products	6,673.6	3,943.8	3,513.1
Animal and vegetable oils and fats	571.3	487.6	464.5
Chemicals	11,447.4	10,520.2	11,334.3
Chemical elements and compounds	3,811.7	3,125.7	3,449.7
Plastic materials, etc.	3,317.2	3,318.8	3,659.7
Basic manufactures	34,104.6	32,829.4	33,573.6
Textile yarn, fabrics, etc.	8,989.5	8,849.7	8,945.8
Textile yarn and thread	2,312.8	2,228.4	2,287.9
Woven non-cotton fabrics (excl. narrow or special fabrics)	4,709.5	4,565.8	4,479.3
Non-metallic mineral manufactures	5,226.7	5,195.1	5,549.1
Iron and steel	6,728.7	5,642.6	5,308.4
Machinery and transport equipment	47,295.0	49,278.0	52,380.6
Non-electric machinery			
Electrical machinery, apparatus, etc.	35,330.6	36,807.7	39,095.5
Domestic electrical equipment	2,461.8	2,617.8	2,805.8
Transport equipment	11,964.4	12,470.3	13,285.1
Road motor vehicles and parts	9,024.9	10,047.3	11,268.1
Passenger cars (excl. buses)	3,107.1	4,089.1	4,814.4
Miscellaneous manufactured articles	34,733.9	35,655.1	36,508.4
Clothing (excl. footwear)	10,086.9	11,162.9	11,630.1
Clothing not of fur	9,381.4	10,460.4	10,875.0
Footwear	7,106.2	7,141.5	6,825.8
Other commodities and transactions	1,382.1	909.4	746.8
Total	149,723.6	145,331.2	150,454.3

ITALY

PRINCIPAL TRADING PARTNERS* ('000 million lire)

Imports c.i.f.	1985	1986	1987
Algeria	4,787.1	2,438.4	2,306.3
Argentina	951.2	531.0	447.8
Australia	1,079.7	905.8	862.1
Austria	3,084.1	3,188.0	3,730.5
Belgium/Luxembourg	6,412.2	6,920.2	8,032.1
Brazil	2,660.6	1,707.0	1,878.8
Canada	1,003.5	855.9	1,072.4
Denmark	1,463.9	1,547.7	1,682.9
Egypt	3,057.7	1,195.1	1,307.3
France	21,546.2	21,654.4	23,592.4
Germany, Federal Republic	28,742.5	30,506.7	34,076.3
Iran	2,848.6	1,313.0	1,357.6
Iraq	2,196.8	1,134.3	1,573.5
Japan	2,827.5	3,119.6	3,457.8
Kuwait	2,724.0	1,220.0	1,242.4
Libya	6,811.3	2,962.1	3,083.5
Netherlands	8,796.0	8,771.0	9,035.3
Saudi Arabia	2,783.4	2,780.4	1,687.2
South Africa	3,510.0	2,852.7	2,313.5
Spain (excl. Canary Is)	3,335.5	3,156.2	3,599.6
Sweden	1,984.7	1,943.0	2,253.0
Switzerland	6,666.7	6,485.3	7,718.4
USSR	5,692.2	3,464.9	3,676.0
United Kingdom	8,540.1	7,596.6	8,513.8
USA	10,294.2	8,495.6	8,618.9
Yugoslavia	2,195.0	2,004.4	2,367.7
Total (incl. others)	172,809.2	148,993.9	161,596.6

Exports f.o.b.	1985	1986	1987
Algeria	1,802.2	1,430.2	1,003.1
Austria	3,293.9	3,445.7	3,793.9
Belgium/Luxembourg	4,442.6	4,842.5	5,078.5
Canada	1,867.2	1,788.2	1,749.2
Denmark	1,236.7	1,389.0	1,284.5
France	21,003.3	22,704.3	24,570.8
Germany, Federal Republic	24,172.1	26,355.3	27,958.9
Greece	2,619.8	2,141.5	2,195.0
Iran	1,156.4	973.7	655.3
Japan	1,765.4	1,966.2	2,403.9
Libya	2,401.6	1,406.3	1,441.7
Netherlands	4,630.0	4,755.3	4,640.1
Nigeria	654.4	376.0	412.1
Saudi Arabia	3,505.5	2,179.8	1,886.2
Spain (excl. Canary Is)	2,446.9	3,660.2	5,283.9
Sweden	1,647.8	1,748.1	2,039.1
Switzerland	6,070.3	6,607.2	7,082.2
Turkey	1,346.6	1,256.0	1,350.8
USSR	2,913.9	2,410.8	2,847.2
United Kingdom	10,423.8	10,299.0	11,192.9
USA	18,356.7	15,604.6	14,456.0
Venezuela	827.9	538.3	619.3
Yugoslavia	2,262.8	2,020.3	1,867.1
Total (incl. others)	149,723.6	145,331.2	150,454.3

* Imports by country of production; exports by country of consumption.

Transport

STATE RAILWAYS (traffic)

	1985	1986	1987
Passenger journeys ('000)	380,213	393,200	394,200
Passenger-km (million)	37,401	40,500	41,395
Freight ton-km (million)	17,968	17,410	18,427

Statistical Survey

ROAD TRAFFIC (licensed vehicles at 31 December)

	1984	1985	1986
Passenger motor cars	20,888,210	22,494,641	23,495,460
Buses and coaches	71,981	76,296	77,891
Goods vehicles	1,683,218	1,793,595	1,887,415
Tractors (non-agricultural)	38,227	40,249	42,767
Trailers and semi-trailers	408,810	482,063	534,101
Motorcycles and scooters	1,696,325	2,000,317	2,204,275
Mopeds	3,767,654	3,341,125	n.a.

SHIPPING

Merchant Fleet ('000 gross registered tons)

	1984	1985	1986
Total	9,117	8,003	8,060

Sea-borne Freight Traffic (international and coastwise)

	1984	1985	1986
Vessels entered ('000 n.r.t.)	304,365	310,412	323,991
Vessels cleared ('000 n.r.t.)	303,421	309,821	322,525
Goods loaded ('000 metric tons)	88,292	88,292	95,252
Goods unloaded ('000 metric tons)	248,480	249,022	256,316

CIVIL AVIATION (traffic on scheduled services)

	1984	1985	1986
Passengers carried ('000)	12,593.6	13,540.8	13,811.1
Passenger-km (million)	16,077.0	17,303.8	16,921.0
Freight ton-km (million)	689.4	755.3	844.1

Tourism

	1985	1986	1987
Foreign tourist arrivals*	53,634,408	53,314,906	52,724,941
Amount spent (million lire)	15,952,880	14,691,006	15,782,808

* Including excursionists and cruise passengers. Arrivals at accommodation establishments were 19,783,976 in 1985; 19,092,676 in 1986; 21,322,787 in 1987.

Number of hotel beds: (31 December 1986) 1,646,513.

TOURIST ARRIVALS BY COUNTRY OF ORIGIN
(including excursionists)

	1985	1986	1987
Austria	5,265,085	5,413,624	5,542,812
Belgium	795,832	1,038,993	990,069
France	8,708,159	8,570,229	9,042,482
Germany, Federal Republic	11,717,155	9,555,440	9,617,677
Netherlands	1,660,220	1,743,102	1,388,693
Switzerland	12,465,534	11,299,825	10,452,491
United Kingdom	1,770,713	2,047,774	1,999,353
USA	1,834,420	1,591,542	1,482,607
Yugoslavia	3,075,251	3,880,658	4,835,022
Total (incl. others)	53,634,408	53,314,906	52,724,941

Communications Media

	1984	1985	1986
Telephones in use	24,331,000	25,614,000	26,873,000
Radio licences	14,319,493	14,223,345	14,817,162
Television licences	13,951,161	13,915,813	14,605,448
Book titles produced*	14,312	15,545	16,297

* Excluding reprints.

Education

(1985/86)

	Schools	Teachers	Students
Pre-school	28,943	108,184	1,660,986
Primary	27,748	273,800	3,703,108
Secondary:			
Scuola Media	10,028	294,259	2,756,577
Secondaria Superiore	7,587	267,937	2,605,002
of which:			
Technical	2,679	122,355	1,195,455
Vocational	1,676	59,616	513,327
Teacher training	887	21,484	197,349
Art Licei	256	11,103	74,014
Classical, linguistic and			
scientific Licei	2,089	53,379	624,857
Higher	74	50,996	1,113,175

Directory

The Constitution

The Constitution of the Italian Republic was approved by the Constituent Assembly on 22 December 1947 and came into force on 1 January 1948. The fundamental principles are set out in Articles 1–12, as follows:

Italy is a democratic republic based on the labour of the people.

The Republic recognizes and guarantees as inviolable the rights of its citizens, either as individuals or in a community, and it expects, in return, devotion to duty and the fulfilment of political, economic and social obligations.

All citizens shall enjoy equal status and shall be regarded as equal before the law, without distinction of sex, race, language or religion, and without regard to the political opinions which they may hold or their personal or social standing.

It shall be the function of the Republic to remove the economic and social inequalities which, by restricting the liberty of the individual, impede the full development of the human personality, thereby reducing the effective participation of the citizen in the political, economic and social life of the country.

The Republic recognizes the right of all citizens to work and shall do all in its power to give effect to this right.

The Republic, while remaining one and indivisible, shall recognize and promote local autonomy, fostering the greatest possible decentralization in those services which are administered by the State, and subordinating legislative methods and principles to the exigencies of decentralized and autonomous areas.

The State and the Catholic Church shall be sovereign and independent, each in its own sphere. Their relations shall be governed by the Lateran Pact ('Patti Lateranensi'), and any modification in the pact agreed upon by both parties shall not necessitate any revision of the Constitution.

All religious denominations shall have equal liberty before the law, denominations other than the Catholic having the right to worship according to their beliefs, in so far as they do not conflict with the common law of the country.

The Republic shall do all in its power to promote the development of culture and scientific and technical research. It shall also protect and preserve the countryside and the historical and artistic monuments which are the inheritance of the nation.

The juridical system of the Italian Republic shall be in conformity with the generally recognized practice of international law. The legal rights of foreigners in the country shall be regulated by law in accordance with international practice.

Any citizen of a foreign country who is deprived of democratic liberty such as is guaranteed under the Italian Constitution, has the right of asylum within the territory of the Republic in accordance with the terms of the law, and his extradition for political offences will not be granted.

Italy repudiates war as an instrument of offence against the liberty of other nations and as a means of resolving international disputes. Italy accepts, under parity with other nations, the limitations of sovereignty necessary for the preservation of peace and justice between nations. To that end, it will support and promote international organizations.

The Constitution is further divided into Parts I and II, in which are set forth respectively the rights and responsibilities of the citizen and the administration of the Republic.

PART ONE

Civic Clauses

Section I (Articles 13–28). The liberty of the individual is inviolable and no form of detention, restriction or inspection is permitted unless it be for juridical purposes and in accordance with the provisions of the law. The domicile of a person is likewise inviolable and shall be immune from forced inspection or sequestration, except according to the provisions of the law. Furthermore, all citizens shall be free to move wheresoever they will throughout the country, and may leave it and return to it without let or hinderance. Right of public meeting, if peaceful and without arms, is guaranteed. Secret organizations of a directly or indirectly political or military nature are, however, prohibited.

Freedom in the practice of religious faith is guaranteed.

The Constitution further guarantees complete freedom of thought, speech and writing, and lays down that the Press shall be entirely free from all control or censorship. No person may be deprived of civic or legal rights on political grounds.

The death penalty is not allowed under the Constitution except in case of martial law. The accused shall be considered 'not guilty' until he is otherwise proven. All punishment shall be consistent with humanitarian practice and shall be directed towards the re-education of the criminal.

Ethical and Social Clauses

Section II (Articles 29–34). The Republic regards the family as the fundamental basis of society and considers the parents to be responsible for the maintenance, instruction and education of the children. The Republic shall provide economic assistance for the family, with special regard to large families, and shall make provision for maternity, infancy and youth, subject always to the liberty and freedom of choice of the individuals as envisaged under the law.

Education, the arts and science shall be free, the function of the State being merely to indicate the general lines of instruction. Private entities and individuals shall have the right to conduct educational institutions without assistance from the State, but such non-state institutions must ensure to their pupils liberty and instruction equal to that in the state schools. Institutions of higher culture, universities and academies shall be autonomous within the limitations prescribed by the law.

Education is available to all and is free and obligatory for at least eight years. Higher education for students of proven merit shall be aided by scholarships and other allowances made by the Republic.

Economic Clauses

Section III (Articles 35–47). The Republic shall safeguard the right to work in all its aspects, and shall promote agreement and co-

ITALY

operation with international organizations in matters pertaining to the regulation of labour and the rights of workers. The rights of Italian workers abroad shall be protected.

All workers shall be entitled to remuneration proportionate to the quantity and quality of their work, and in any case shall be ensured of sufficient to provide freedom and a dignified standard of life for themselves and their families.

The maximum working hours shall be fixed by law, and the worker shall be entitled to a weekly day of rest and an annual holiday of nine days with pay.

Women shall have the same rights and, for equal work, the same remuneration as men. Conditions of work shall be regulated by their special family requirements and the needs of mother and child. The work of minors shall be specially protected.

All citizens have the right to sickness, unemployment and disability maintenance.

Liberty to organize in trade unions is guaranteed and any union may register as a legal entity, provided it is organized on a democratic basis. The right to strike is admitted within the limitations of the relevant legislation.

Private enterprise is permitted in so far as it does not run counter to the well-being of society nor constitute a danger to security, freedom and human dignity.

Ownership of private property is permitted and guaranteed within the limitations laid down by the law regarding the acquisition, extent and enjoyment of private property. Inheritance and testamentary bequests shall be regulated by law.

Limitation is placed by law on private ownership of land and on its use, with a view to its best exploitation for the benefit of the community.

The Republic recognizes the value of mutual co-operation and the right of the workers to participate in management.

The Republic shall encourage all forms of saving, by house purchase, by co-operative ownership and by investment in the public utility undertakings of the country.

Political Clauses

Section IV (Articles 48-54). The electorate comprises all citizens, both men and women, who have attained their majority. Voting is free, equal and secret, and its exercise is a civic duty. All citizens have the right to associate freely together in political parties, and may also petition the Chambers to legislate as may be deemed necessary.

All citizens of both sexes may hold public office on equal terms.

Defence of one's country is a sacred duty of the citizen, and military service is obligatory within the limits prescribed by law. Its fulfilment shall in no way prejudice the position of the worker nor hinder the exercise of political rights. The organization of the armed forces shall be imbued with the spirit of democracy.

All citizens must contribute to the public expenditure, in proportion to their capacity.

All citizens must be loyal to the Republic and observe the terms of the law and the Constitution.

PART TWO

Sections I, II and III (Articles 55-100). These sections are devoted to a detailed exposition of the Legislature and legislative procedure of the Republic.

Parliament shall comprise two Chambers, namely the Chamber of Deputies (Camera dei Deputati) and the Senate of the Republic (Senato).

The Chamber of Deputies is elected by direct universal suffrage, the number of Deputies being 630. All voters who on the day of the elections are 25 years of age, may be elected Deputies.

Seats are apportioned by dividing the number of inhabitants of the Republic, as shown in the last general census by 630, and allocating the seats proportionally to the population of each constituency.

The Senate of the Republic is elected on regional basis, the number of eligible Senators being 315. No region shall have less than seven Senators. Valle d'Aosta has only one Senator.

Seats are allocated proportionally among the Regions in the same way as the Chamber of Deputies.

The Chamber of Deputies and the Senate of the Republic are elected for five years.

The term of each House cannot be extended except by law and only in the case of war.

Members of Parliament shall receive remuneration fixed by law.

The President of the Republic must be a citizen of at least fifty years of age and in full enjoyment of all civic and political rights. The person shall be elected for a period of seven years (Articles 84-85).

The Government shall consist of the President of the Council and the Ministers who themselves shall form the Council. The President of the Council, or Prime Minister, shall be nominated by the President of the Republic, who shall also appoint the ministers on the recommendation of the Prime Minister (Article 92).

Section IV (Articles 101-113). Sets forth the judicial system and procedure.

Section V (Articles 114-133). Deals with the division of the Republic into regions, provinces and communes, and sets forth the limits and extent of autonomy enjoyed by the regions. Under Article 131 the regions are enumerated as follows:

Piemonte (Piedmont)	Marche
Lombardia (Lombardy)	Lazio
Veneto	Abruzzi
Liguria	Molise
Emilia-Romagna	Campania
Toscana (Tuscany)	Puglia
Umbria	Basilicata
Calabria	Trentino-Alto Adige*
Sicilia (Sicily)*	Friuli-Venezia Giulia*
Sardegna (Sardinia)*	Valle d'Aosta*

*These five regions have a wider form of autonomy based on constitutional legislation specially adapted to their regional characteristics (Article 116). Each region shall be administered by a Regional Council, in which is vested the legislative power and which may make suggestions for legislation to the Chambers, and the Giunta regionale which holds the executive power (Article 121).

The final articles provide for the establishment of the Corte Costituzionale to deal with constitutional questions and any revisions which may be found necessary after the Constitution has come into operation.

The Government

(February 1989)

HEAD OF STATE

President of the Republic: Francesco Cossiga (took office 3 July 1985).

COUNCIL OF MINISTERS

A coalition of Christian Democrats (DC), Socialists (PSI), Social Democrats (PSDI), Liberals (PLI) and Republicans (PRI).

Prime Minister: Ciriaco De Mita (DC).
Deputy Prime Minister: Gianni De Michelis (PSI).
Minister of Foreign Affairs: Giulio Andreotti (DC).
Minister of the Interior: Antonio Gava (DC).
Minister of Justice: Prof. Giuliano Vassalli (PSI).
Minister of Finance: Dott. Emilio Colombo (DC).
Minister of the Budget and of Economic Planning: Amintore Fanfani (DC).
Minister of the Treasury: Giuliano Amato (PSI).
Minister of Defence: Dott. Valerio Zanone (PLI).
Minister of Education: Prof. Dott. Giovanni Galloni (DC).
Minister of Public Works: Enrico Ferri (pro PSDI).
Minister of Transport: Giorgio Santuz (DC).
Minister of Agriculture and Forests: Avv. Calogero Mannino (DC).
Minister of Posts and Telecommunications: Dott. Oscar Mammì (PRI).
Minister of Industry: Dott. Adolfo Battaglia (PRI).
Minister of Labour and Social Security: Rino Formica (PSI).
Minister of State Participation: Luigi Granelli (DC).
Minister of Foreign Trade: Dott. Renato Ruggiero (PSI).
Minister of Health: Carlo Donat Cattin (DC).
Minister of Tourism and of the Performing Arts: Dott. Franco Carraro (PSI).
Minister of Culture: Vincenzo Bono Parrino (PSDI).
Minister of the Merchant Navy: Giovanni Prandini (DC).
Minister of State Participation: Carlo Fracanzani (DC).
Minister of the Environment: Dott. Giorgio Ruffolo (PSI).
Ministers without Portfolio:
  Regional Affairs and Institutional Reforms: Dott. Antonio Maccanico (pro PRI).
  Relations with Parliament: Sergio Mattarella (DC).
  Civil Defence: Vito Lattanzio (DC).

ITALY

Public Administration: PAULO CIRINO POMICINO (DC).
EEC Affairs: Prof. ANTONIO LA PERGOLA (pro PSI/PSDI).
Scientific Research: Prof. ANTONIO RUBERTI (PSI).
Urban Areas: CARLO TOGNOLI (PSI).
Special Affairs: ROSA RUSSO JERVOLINO (DC).
Minister with responsibility for the South (Mezzogiorno): REMO GASPARI (DC).

MINISTRIES

Office of the President: Palazzo del Quirinale, 00187 Rome; tel. (06) 4699; telex 611440.

Office of the Prime Minister: Palazzo Chigi, Piazza Colonna 370, 00100 Rome; tel. (06) 6779; telex 613199.

Ministry of Agriculture and Forests: Via XX Settembre, 00187 Rome; tel. (06) 4665; telex 610148.

Ministry of the Budget and of Economic Planning: Via XX Settembre 97, 00187 Rome; tel. (06) 47611; telex 626432.

Ministry of Culture: Via del Collegio Romano 27, 00186 Rome; tel. (06) 6723; telex 621407.

Ministry of Defence: Palazzo Baracchini, Via XX Settembre, 00187 Rome; tel. (06) 4759841; telex 611438.

Ministry of the Environment: Piazza Venezia 11, 00187 Rome; tel. (06) 6797124.

Ministry of Education: Viale Trastevere 76A, 00153 Rome; tel. (06) 58491; telex 613181.

Ministry of Finance: Viale America, EUR, 00144 Rome; tel. (06) 5997; telex 614460.

Ministry of Foreign Affairs: Piazzale della Farnesina 1, 00194 Rome; tel. (06) 36911; telex 610611.

Ministry of Foreign Trade: Viale America 341, EUR, 00144 Rome; tel. (06) 5993; telex 610083.

Ministry of Health: Viale dell'Industria 20, 00144 Rome; tel. (06) 5994.

Ministry of Industry: Via Vittorio Veneto 33, 00187 Rome; tel. (06) 4705; telex 622550.

Ministry of the Interior: Piazza Viminale, Palazzo Viminale, Via Depretis, 00184 Rome; tel. (06) 46671.

Ministry of Justice: Via Arenula 70, 00186 Rome; tel. (06) 65101; telex 623072.

Ministry of Labour and Social Security: Via Flavia 6, 00187 Rome; tel. (06) 4683; telex 626144.

Ministry of the Merchant Navy: Viale Asia 18, EUR, 00144 Rome; tel. (06) 5908.

Ministry of Posts and Telecommunications: Viale America, EUR, 00187 Rome; tel. (06) 54601; telex 616082.

Ministry of Public Works: Piazza Porta Pia 1, 00198 Rome; tel. (06) 84821.

Ministry of State Participation: Via Sallustiana 53, 00187 Rome; tel. (06) 4750420; telex 614229.

Ministry of Tourism and Performing Arts: Via della Ferratella in Laterano 51, 00184 Rome; tel. (06) 77321; telex 616400.

Ministry of Transport: Piazza della Croce Rossa 1, 00161 Rome; tel. (06) 84901; telex 613111.

Ministry of the Treasury: Via XX Settembre 97, 00187 Rome; tel. (06) 47611; telex 623139.

Legislature

PARLAMENTO
(Parliament)

Senato
(Senate)

President: GIOVANNI SPADOLINI (Republican).

General Election, 14–15 June 1987

Parties	Votes	%	Seats
Christian Democrats (DC)	10,870,056	33.6	125
Communists (PCI)	9,171,180	28.3	100
Socialists (PSI)	3,531,312	10.9	36
Italian Social Movement–National Right (MSI-DN)	2,115,196	6.5	17
Republicans (PRI)	1,247,204	3.8	8
Social Democrats (PSDI)	762,670	2.4	5
Liberals (PLI)	699,980	2.2	3
Radicals (PR)	571,339	1.8	3
Greens	632,856	2.0	1
Proletarian Democracy (DP)	493,290	1.5	1
Others	n.a.	7.0	16
Total	n.a.	100.0	315

In addition to the 315 elected members, there are seven life members.

Camera dei Deputati
(Chamber of Deputies)

President: Signora NILDE JOTTI (Communist).

General Election, 14–15 June 1987

Parties	Votes	%	Seats
Christian Democrats (DC)	13,231,960	34.3	234
Communists (PCI)	10,249,690	26.6	177
Socialists (PSI)	5,501,980	14.3	94
Italian Social Movement–National Right (MSI-DN)	2,282,212	5.9	35
Republicans (PRI)	1,428,358	3.7	21
Social Democrats (PSDI)	1,140,086	3.0	17
Radicals (PR)	987,675	2.6	13
Greens	969,534	2.5	13
Liberals (PLI)	810,961	2.1	11
Proletarian Democracy (DP)	542,021	1.7	8
Others	1,428,577	3.3	7
Total	30,573,054	100.0	630

Political Organizations

Federazione Nazionale per Le Liste Verdi (Green Party): Via Magenta 5, 00185 Rome; tel. (06) 4957383; f. 1987; advocates environmentalist and anti-nuclear policies; branch of the European Green movement.

Movimento Sociale Italiano-Destra Nazionale (MSI-DN) (Italian Social Movement-National Right): Via della Scrofa 19, 00186 Rome; tel. (06) 6543014; f. 1946; neo-Fascist party; Pres. PINO ROMUALDI; Sec.-Gen. GIANFRANCO FINI; 400,000 mems.

Partito Comunista Italiano (PCI) (Communist Party): Central Office: Via delle Botteghe Oscure 4, 00186 Rome; tel. (06) 6711; f. 1921; the largest Communist Party in Western Europe; advocates far-reaching economic, social and democratic reforms, to be implemented by a broad coalition of democratic forces; programme includes development of the South, democratic planning, agrarian reform, democratic reform of the State and social services, and other policies leading to an original Italian path towards socialism; advocates an independent foreign policy for peace and international détente and co-operation; Gen. Sec. ACHILLE OCCHETTO; 1.50m. mems (1985).

Partito della Democrazia Cristiana (DC) (Christian Democrat Party): Central Office: Piazza Don Luigi Sturzo 15, EUR, 001441 Rome; tel. (06) 59011; f. 1943, the successor to the pre-Fascist Popular Party; while extending its appeal to voters of all classes, the party attempts to maintain a centre position; it is openly and militantly anti-communist; Pres. and Sec.-Gen. ARNALDO FORLANI; Admin. Sec. SEVERINO CITARISTI.

Partito Liberale Italiano (PLI) (Liberal Party): Via Frattina 89, 00187 Rome; tel. (06) 6796951; f. 1848 by Cavour, its chief aim is the realization of the principle of freedom in all public and private matters; Pres. (vacant); Sec. RENATO ALTISSIMO; 153,000 mems.

Partito Radicale (PR) (Radical Party): Via Torre Argentina 18, 00186 Rome; tel. (06) 6547771; telex 610495; campaigns on civil rights issues; Pres MARCO PANNELLA, DOMENICO MODUGNO; Sec.-Gen. SERGIO STANZANI; 5,382 mems.

Partito Repubblicano Italiano (PRI) (Republican Party): Piazza dei Caprettari 70, 00186 Rome; tel. (06) 6544641; f. 1897; followers of the principles of Mazzini (social justice in a modern free society)

ITALY — *Directory*

and modern liberalism; Pres. BRUNO VISENTINI; Political Sec. GIORGIO LA MALFA; 110,000 mems.

Partito Socialista Democratico Italiano (PSDI) (Social Democrat Party): Via Santa Maria in Via 12, 00187 Rome; tel. (06) 67271; f. 1969 after breaking away from the former United Socialist Party, of which it had been part since 1966; composed of former Social Democrats and stands to the right of the PSI; Pres. GIUSEPPE SARAGAT; Sec. ANTONIO CARIGLIA; 200,000 mems.

Partito Socialista Italiano (PSI) (Socialist Party): Via del Corso 476, 00186 Rome; tel. (06) 67781; telex 616300; f. 1892; in 1921 a group broke away to found Italian Communist Party; a further rift in 1947 led to the foundation of the Italian Social Democrat Party; in 1966 merged with the Democratic Socialist Party to form the United Socialist Party, but in 1969 the Democratic Socialists broke away; a centre-left party at the service of the workers and of the civil life of the nation, aiming to create conditions for greater prosperity, freedom and social justice in the country; it adheres to the Socialist International and believes that socialism is inseparable from democracy and individual freedom; Sec.-Gen. BETTINO CRAXI.

Südtiroler Volkspartei (SVP) (South Tyrol People's Party): Brennerstrasse 7A, 39100 Bozen/Bolzano; tel. (0471) 974484; regional party of the German and Ladin-speaking people in the South Tyrol; Pres. SILVIUS MAGNANO; Gen. Sec. Dr BRUNO HOSP.

There are also numerous small political parties, including the following: Union Valdôtaine (regional party for the French minority in the Valle d'Aosta); Partito Sardo d'Azione (Sardinian autonomy party); Democrazia Proletaria (left-wing); and Lotta Continua (left-wing).

Diplomatic Representation

EMBASSIES IN ITALY

Afghanistan: Via Carlo Fea 1, 00161 Rome; tel. (06) 8322972; Chargé d'affaires a.i.: (vacant).

Albania: Via Asmara 9, 00199 Rome; tel. (06) 8380725; telex 614169; Ambassador: DASHNOR DERVISHI.

Algeria: Via Barnaba Oriani 26, 00197; Rome; tel. (06) 804141; telex 680846; Ambassador: MOURAD BENCHEIKH.

Angola: Via Filippo Bernardini 21, 00165 Rome; tel. (06) 6374325; telex 614505; Ambassador: ARMINDO FERNANDES DO ESPIRITO SANTO VIEIRA.

Argentina: Piazza dell'Esquilino 2, 00185 Rome; tel. (06) 4742551; telex 610386; Ambassador: ALFREDO E. ALLENDE.

Australia: Via Alessandria 215, 00198 Rome; tel. (06) 832721; telex 610165; Ambassador: ARCHIBALD DUNCAN CAMPBELL.

Austria: Via G.B. Pergolesi 3, 00198 Rome; tel. (06) 868241; telex 610139; Ambassador: Dr FRIEDRICH FRÖLICHSTHAL.

Bangladesh: Via Antonio Bertoloni 14, 00197 Rome; tel. (06) 878541; telex 614615; Ambassador: WALIUR RAHMAN.

Belgium: Via dei Monti Parioli 49, 00197 Rome; tel. (06) 3609441; telex 610425; Ambassador: MARCEL VAN DE KERKCHOVE.

Bolivia: Via Toscana 30, 00198 Rome; tel. (06) 4757438; Ambassador: JULIO PANTOJA SALAMANCA.

Brazil: Palazzo Pamphil, Piazza Navona 14, 00186 Rome; tel. (06) 650841; telex 610099; Ambassador: CARLOS ALBERTO LEITE BARBOSA.

Bulgaria: Via Pietro P. Rubens 21, 00197 Rome; tel. (06) 3609640; telex 610234; Ambassador: RAYKO NIKOLOV.

Burma: Via Bellini 20, Rome; tel. (06) 859374; Ambassador: U SAN MAUNG.

Cameroon: Via di Pieta 82/A, 00186 Rome; tel. (06) 6783546; telex 611558; Ambassador: FÉLIX SABAL LECCO.

Canada: Via G. B. de Rossi 27, 00161 Rome; tel. 855341; telex 610056; Ambassador: CLAUDE CHARLAND.

Chile: Via Nazionale 54, 2nd Floor, 00184 Rome; tel. (06) 4742258; telex 611420; Ambassador: MARIANO FONTECILLA DE SANTIAGO CONCHA.

China, People's Republic: Via Bruxelles 56, 00198 Rome; tel. (06) 8448186; telex 680159; Ambassador: DU GONG.

Colombia: Via Giuseppe Pisanelli 4, 00197 Rome; tel. (06) 6799586; telex 611266; Ambassador: FREDERICO ESTRADA VÉLEZ.

Congo: Via Modena 50, 00184 Rome; tel. (06) 4746163; telex 626645; Ambassador: JOSEPH TCHICAYA.

Costa Rica: Piazza della Torretta 26, 00186 Rome; tel. (06) 6785995; Ambassador: OCTAVIO TORREALBA TORUNO.

Côte d'Ivoire: Via Lazzaro Spallanzani 4–6, 00161 Rome; tel. (06) 868040; telex 610396; Ambassador: SOULEJMANE SAKO.

Cuba: Via Licinia 7, 00153 Rome; tel. (06) 5755984; telex 610677; Ambassador: JAVIER ARDIZONES CEBALLOS.

Cyprus: Via Michele Mercati 51, 00197 Rome; tel. (06) 879837; telex 621033; Ambassador: ANDROS NICOLAIDES.

Czechoslovakia: Via Colli della Farnesina 144, 00194 Rome; tel. (06) 3278742; telex 610306; Ambassador: NORBERT ŽÍDEK.

Denmark: Via dei Monti Parioli 50, 00197 Rome; tel. (06) 3600441; telex 624696; Ambassador: IB RITIO ANDREASEN.

Dominican Republic: Via Domenico Chelini 9, 00197 Rome; tel. (06) 874665; Ambassador: GUIDO EMILIO D'ALESSANDRO TAVAREZ.

Ecuador: Via Guido d'Arezzo 14, 00198 Rome; tel. (06) 851784; telex 613256; Ambassador: ROQUE CAÑADAS PORTILLA.

Egypt: 119 Roma Villa Savoia, Via Salaria 267, 00199 Rome; tel. (06) 856193; telex 610044; Ambassador: YEHIA RIFAAT.

El Salvador: Via Castellini 13, 00197 Rome; tel. (06) 3601853; Ambassador: DAVID TREJO.

Ethiopia: Via Nicolò Tartaglia 11, 00197 Rome; tel. (06) 803057; telex 614414; Ambassador: TESFAYE ABDI.

Finland: Via Lisbona 3, 00198 Rome; tel. (06) 858329; telex 625600; Ambassador: EEVA KRISTIINA FORSMAN.

France: Piazza Farnese 67, 00186 Rome; tel. (06) 6565241; telex 610093; Ambassador: GILBERT PÉROL.

Gabon: No. 31 Largo A. Vessela, 00199 Rome; tel. (06) 3012449; telex 612264; Ambassador: EDOUARD TEALE.

German Democratic Republic: Via di Trasone 56–58, 00199 Rome; tel. (06) 8390045; telex 610353; Ambassador: Dr WOLFGANG KIESEWETTER.

Germany, Federal Republic: Via Po 25C, 00198 Rome; tel. (06) 860341; telex 610179; Ambassador: Dr FRIEDRICH RUTH.

Ghana: Via Ostriana 4, 00199 Rome; tel. (06) 8391200; telex 610270; Ambassador: (vacant).

Greece: Via Mercadente 36, 00198 Rome; tel. (06) 859630; telex 610416; Ambassador: NICOLAS ATHANASSIOU.

Guatemala: Via dei Colli della Farnesina 128, 00194 Rome; tel. (06) 3272632; Ambassador: OSCAR ERNESTO PADILLA VIDAURRE.

Guinea: Via Adelaide Ristori 9/13, 00198 Rome; tel. (06) 878989; telex 611487; Ambassador: ABD AN-NIOUMA SANDOUNO.

Haiti: Via Ruggero Fauro 59, 00197 Rome; tel. (06) 872777; Ambassador: NICHOLAS LEMITHE.

Holy See: Via Po 27–29, 00198 Rome; tel. (06) 862092; Apostolic Nuncio: Mgr LUIGI POGGI.

Honduras: Via Bafile 5/4, 00195 Rome; tel. (06) 3581453; telex 622014; Ambassador: ARTURO GUILLERMO LÓPEZ LUNA.

Hungary: Via dei Villini 14, 00161 Rome; tel. (06) 860241; Ambassador: GYÖRGY MISUR.

India: Via XX Settembre 5, 00187 Rome; tel. (06) 464642; telex 611274; Ambassador: AKBAR MIRZA KHALEELI.

Indonesia: Via Campania 55, 00187 Rome; tel. (06) 4759251; telex 610317; Ambassador: JACOB PIAY.

Iran: Via della Tamilluccia 651, 001351 Rome; tel. (06) 3284294; telex 611337; Ambassador: HAMID ABUTALEBI.

Iraq: Via della Camilluccia 355, 00135 Rome; tel. (06) 346357; telex 622678; Ambassador: HISHAM FAKHRI NAFEI AT-TABAQCHALI.

Ireland: Largo del Nazareno 3, 00187 Rome; tel. (06) 6782541; telex 626030; Ambassador: CHRISTOPHER P. FOGARTY.

Israel: Via M. Mercati 12, 00197 Rome; tel. (06) 874541; telex 610412; Ambassador: MORDECHAI DRORY.

Japan: Via Quintino Sella 60, 00187 Rome; tel. (06) 4757151; telex 610063; Ambassador: SEIYA NISHIDA.

Jordan: Via Guido d'Arezzo 5, 00198 Rome; tel. (06) 857396; telex 612573; Ambassador: TAREK K. MADI.

Kenya: Via Icilio 14, 00153 Rome; tel. (06) 7281192; Ambassador: (vacant).

Korea, Republic: Via Barnaba Oriani 30, 00197 Rome; tel. (06) 805292; telex 610182; Ambassador: NAM KI LEE.

Kuwait: Via Archimede 124, 00197 Rome; tel. (06) 874419; telex 620426; Ambassador: AHMAD GHAITH ABDULLAH.

Lebanon: Via Giacomino Carissimi 38, 00198 Rome; tel. (06) 867119; telex 611411; Ambassador: KHALIL MAKKAWI.

Lesotho: Via di Porta Pertusa 4, 00165 Rome; tel. (06) 6378183; telex 610053; Ambassador: GERARD PHIRINYANE KHOJANE.

Liberia: Viale Bruno Buozzi 64, 00197 Rome; tel. (06) 805810; telex 612569; Ambassador: GABRIEL TARR MYERS.

Libya: Via Nomentana 365, 00162 Rome; tel. (06) 830951; telex 611114; Ambassador: ABD UR-RAHMAN M. SHALGAM.

Luxembourg: Via Guerrieri 3, 00153 Rome; tel. (06) 5780456; telex 622532; Ambassador: PAUL MERTZ.

Madagascar: Via Riccardo Zandonai 84A, 00194 Rome; tel. (06) 3277797; telex 680297; Ambassador: APOLINAIRE ANDRIATSIAFAJATO.

ITALY — Directory

Malaysia: Via Nomentana 297, 00162 Rome; tel. (06) 855764; telex 611035; Ambassador: Datuk Ismail bin Budin.

Malta: Lungotevere Marzio 12, 00186 Rome; tel. (06) 6879990; telex 611205; Ambassador: Maurice Abela.

Mexico: Via Lazzaro Spallanzani 16, 00161 Rome; tel. (06) 851187; telex 625279; Ambassador: Horacio Flores de la Peña.

Monaco: Via Bertoloni 36, 00197 Rome: tel. (06) 803361; Ambassador: René Novella.

Morocco: Via Lazzaro Spallanzani 8, 00196 Rome; tel. (06) 8448653; telex 620854; Ambassador: M. M. Yahia Benslimane.

Netherlands: Via Michele Mercati 8, 00197 Rome; tel. (06) 873141; telex 610138; Ambassador: Baron W. Van Pallandt.

New Zealand: Via Zara 28, 00198 Rome; tel. (06) 4402928; telex 626615; Ambassador: Francis Anthony Small.

Nicaragua: Via Brescia 16, 00198 Rome; tel. (06) 865476; telex 626575; Ambassador: Orestes Papi.

Nigeria: Via Orazio 14–18, 00198 Rome; tel. (06) 6531048; telex 610666; Ambassador: James Kolo.

Norway: Via delle Terme Deciane 71, 00153 Rome; tel. (06) 5755833; telex 610585; Ambassador: Torbj_rn Christiansen.

Oman: Via Enrico Petrella 4, 00198 Rome; tel. (06) 8848038; telex 612524; Ambassador: Muhammad bin Taher Aideed.

Pakistan: Via della Camilluccia 682, 00135 Rome; tel. (06) 3276775; telex 622083; Ambassador: M. Afzal Qadir.

Panama: Via del Vignola 39, 00196 Rome; tel. (06) 3619587; telex 622670; Ambassador: Nelva Torrijos de Soler.

Paraguay: Via Emilio de Cavalieri 12, 00198 Rome; tel. (06) 8448236; Ambassador: Aníbal Fernández.

Peru: Via Po 22, 00198 Rome; tel. (06) 856556; telex 625589; Ambassador: Luis Solari Tudela.

Philippines: Via San Valentino 12-14, 00197 Rome; tel. (06) 803530; telex 612104; Ambassador: José M. Zaldarriaga.

Poland: Via Paolo Rubens 20, 00197 Rome; tel. (06) 3609455; telex 610325; Ambassador: Józef Wiejacz.

Portugal: Via Giacinta Pezzana 9, 00197 Rome; tel. (06) 878016; telex 612304; Ambassador: Tomas Andresen.

Romania: Via Nicolò Tartaglia 36, 00197 Rome; tel. (06) 804567; Ambassador: Constantin Tudor.

San Marino: Via Eleonora Duse 35, 00197 Rome; tel. (06) 804567; Chargé d'affaires a.i.: Dott. Savina Zafferani.

Saudi Arabia: Via G. B. Pergolesi 9, 00198 Rome; tel. (06) 868161; telex 613115; Ambassador: Khaled an-Nasser at-Turki.

Senegal: Via Lisbona 3, 00198 Rome; tel. (06) 859497; telex 612522; Ambassador: Henri Pierre Arphang Senghor.

Somalia: Via dei Villini 9-11, 00161 Rome; tel. (06) 853740; telex 613123; Ambassador: Muhammad Muhamoud Abdullah.

South Africa: Via Tanaro 14, 00198 Rome; tel. (06) 8443246; telex 621667; Ambassador: David de V. du Buisson.

Spain: Palazzo Borghese, Largo Fontenella Borghese 19, 00186 Rome; tel. (06) 6798506; telex 612435; Ambassador: Emilio Menéndez del Valle.

Sri Lanka: Via Giuseppe Cuboni 618, 00197 Rome; tel. (06) 805362; telex 612602; Ambassador: Chandra Nawaratne de Zoysa.

Sudan: Via di Porta Ardeatina 1, 00184 Rome; tel. (06) 7573344; telex 610302; Ambassador: Abd al-A'As-Sinada.

Sweden: CP 7201, 00100 Rome; Piazza Rio de Janeiro 3, 00161 Rome; tel. (06) 4402721; telex 610264; Ambassador: Sven Fredrik Hedin.

Switzerland: Via Barnaba Oriani 61; 00197 Rome; tel. (06) 803641; telex 610304; Ambassador: Gaspard Bodmer.

Syria: Piazza dell' Ara Coeli, 00186 Rome; tel. (06) 6797791; telex 613083; Ambassador: Burhan Kaial.

Tanzania: Via G.B. Vico 9, 00196 Rome; tel. (06) 3610901; telex 612286; Ambassador: Abbas Kleist Sykes.

Thailand: Via Nomentana 132, 00162 Rome; tel. (06) 837073; telex 616297; Ambassador: Suchinda Yongsunthon.

Tunisia: Via Asmara 7, 00199 Rome; tel. (06) 8390748; telex 610190; Ambassador: Noureddine Mejdoub.

Turkey: Via Palestro 28, 00185 Rome; tel. (06) 4941549; telex 612131; Ambassador: Necdet Tezel.

USSR: Via Gaeta 5, 00185 Rome; tel. (06) 4743989; telex 611286; Ambassador: Nikolai Lunkov.

United Arab Emirates: Via S. Crescenziano 25, 00199 Rome; tel. (06) 8394839; telex 622671; Ambassador: Nasser Salman al-Aboodi.

United Kingdom: Via XX Settembre 80A, 00187 Rome; tel. (06) 4755441; telex 626119; Ambassador: Sir Derek Thomas.

USA: Via Vittorio Veneto 119A, 00187 Rome; tel. (06) 4674; telex 622322; Ambassador: Peter Secchia (designate).

Uruguay: Via Vittorio Veneto 183, 00187 Rome; tel. (06) 492796; telex 611201; Ambassador: Mateo Márquez Seré.

Venezuela: Viale Bruno Buozzi 109, Apto 6, 00197 Rome; tel. (06) 872552; telex 610361; Ambassador: Luis Manuel Peñalver.

Viet-Nam: Piazza Barberini 12, 00187 Rome; tel. (06) 4754098; telex 610121; Ambassador: Huynh Cong Tam.

Yemen Arab Republic: Via Verona 3, 00161 Rome; tel. (06) 4270811; telex 621447; Ambassador: Ahmad Muhammad ash-Shijni.

Yugoslavia: Via dei Monti Parioli 20, 00197 Rome; tel. (06) 3600796; telex 616303; Ambassador: Ante Skataretiko.

Zaire: Via Annone 71/79, 00199 Rome; tel. (06) 8393665; telex 611104; Ambassador: Kitshodi Nzekele.

Zambia: Via Ennio Quirino Visconti 8, 00193 Rome; tel. (06) 310307; telex 611421; Ambassador: Mike Liswaniso.

Judicial System

The Constitutional Court was established in 1956 and is an autonomous constitutional body, standing apart from the judicial system. Its most important function is to pronounce on the constitutionality of legislation both subsequent and prior to the present Constitution of 1948. It also judges accusations brought against the President of the Republic or ministers.

At the base of the system of penal jurisdiction are the Preture (District Courts), where offences carrying a sentence of up to three years' imprisonment are tried. Above the Preture are the Tribunali (Tribunals) and the Corti di Assise presso i Tribunali (Assize Courts attached to the Tribunals), where graver offences are dealt with. From these courts appeal lies to the Corti d'Appello (Courts of Appeal) and the parallel Corti di Assise d'Appello (Assize Courts of Appeal). Final appeal may be made, on juridical grounds only, to the Corte Suprema di Cassazione.

Civil cases may be taken in the first instance to the Giudici Conciliatori (Justices of the Peace), Preture or Tribunali, according to the economic value of the case. Appeal from the Giudici Conciliatori lies to the Preture, from the Preture to the Tribunali, from the Tribunali to the Corti d'Appello, and finally, as in penal justice, to the Corte Suprema di Cassazione on juridical grounds only.

Special divisions for cases concerning labour relations or young persons are attached to civil courts. Cases concerned with the public service and its employees are tried by Tribunali Amministrativi Regionali and the Consiglio di Stato.

A new penal code was to be introduced in October 1989.

Consiglio Superiore della Magistratura (CSM): Piazza dell' Indipendenza 6, 00185 Rome; f. 1958; tel. (06) 497981; supervisory body of judicial system; 33 mems.

President: Francesco Cossiga.

Vice-President: Giancarlo de Carolis.

CONSTITUTIONAL COURT

Corte Costituzionale: Palazzo della Consulta, Piazza del Quirinale 41, 00187 Rome; tel. (06) 46981; consists of 15 judges, one-third appointed by the President of the Republic, one-third elected by Parliament in joint session, one-third by the ordinary and administrative supreme courts.

President: Livio Paladin.

Vice-President: Guglielmo Roherssen.

ADMINISTRATIVE COURTS

Consiglio di Stato: Palazzo Spada, Piazza Capo di Ferro 13, 00186 Rome; tel. (06) 650801; established in accordance with Article 10 of the Constitution; has both consultative and judicial functions.

President: Gabriele Pescatore.

Corte dei Conti: Via Baiamonti 25, Rome, and Via Barberini 38, Rome; functions as the court of public auditors for the state.

President: Silvio Pirrami Traversari.

SUPREME COURT OF APPEAL

Corte Suprema di Cassazione: Palazzo di Giustizia, 00100 Rome; tel. (06) 6568941; supreme court of civil and criminal appeal.

First President: Giuseppe Tamburrino.

Vice-President: Mario Barba.

Religion

More than 90% of the population of Italy are adherents of the Roman Catholic Church.

ITALY — *Directory*

Under the terms of the Concordat signed in 1929, Roman Catholicism was recognized as the official religion of Italy. However, a new Concordat was signed in February 1984 between the Prime Minister and Cardinal Agostino Casaroli, the Papal Secretary of State, to replace the earlier agreement. Following approval by both chambers of the Italian Parliament, the new Concordat was formally ratified in June 1985. The Concordat stated that Roman Catholicism would no longer be the state religion, abolished compulsory religious instruction in schools and reduced state financial contributions. The Vatican City's sovereign rights as an independent state, under the terms of the Lateran Treaty of 1929, were not affected.

Several Protestant churches also exist in Italy, with a total membership of about 50,000. There is a small Jewish community, and in 1987 an agreement between the state and Jewish representatives recognized certain rights for the Jewish community, including the right to observe religious festivals on Saturdays by not attending school or work.

CHRISTIANITY

The Roman Catholic Church

For ecclesiastical purposes, Italy comprises the Papal See of Rome, the Patriarchate of Venice, 59 archdioceses (including six directly responsible to the Holy See), 158 dioceses (including seven within the jurisdiction of the Pope, as Archbishop of the Roman Province, and 17 directly responsible to the Holy See), two territorial prelatures (including one directly responsible to the Holy See) and seven territorial abbacies (including four directly responsible to the Holy See). Almost all adherents follow the Latin rite, but there are two dioceses and one abbacy (all directly responsible to the Holy See) for Catholics of the Italo-Albanian (Byzantine) rite.

Bishops' Conference: Conferenza Episcopale Italiana, Circonvallazione Aurelia 50, 00165 Rome; tel. (06) 6237141; f. 1985; Pres. HE Cardinal UGO POLETTI, Vicar-General of Rome.

Primate of Italy, Archbishop and Metropolitan of the Roman Province and Bishop of Rome: His Holiness Pope JOHN PAUL II.

Patriarch of Venice: HE Cardinal MARCO CÈ.

Archbishops:
Acerenza: (vacant).
Amalfi-Cava de' Tirreni: Most Rev. FERDINANDO PALATUCCI.
Ancona-Osimo: Most Rev. CARLO MACCARI.
Bari-Bitonto: Most Rev. MARIANO ANDREA MAGRASSI.
Benevento: Most Rev. CARLO MINCHIATTI.
Bologna: HE Cardinal GIACOMO BIFFI.
Brindisi-Ostuni: Most Rev. SETTIMIO TODISCO.
Cagliari: Most Rev. OTTORINO PIETRO ALBERTI.
Camerino-San Severino Marche: Most Rev. BRUNO FRATTEGIANI.
Campobasso-Boiano: Most Rev. PIETRO SANTORO.
Capua: Most Rev. LUIGI DILIGENZA.
Catania: Most Rev. DOMENICO PICCHINENNA.
Catanzaro-Squillace: Most Rev. ANTONIO CANTISANI.
Chieti-Vasto: Most Rev. ANTONIO VALENTINI.
Cosenza-Bisignano: Most Rev. DINO TRABALZINI.
Crotone-Santa Severina: Most Rev. GIUSEPPE AGOSTINO.
Fermo: Most Rev. CLETO BELLUCCI.
Ferrara-Comacchio: Most Rev. LUIGI MAVERNA.
Florence: HE Cardinal SILVANO PIOVANELLI.
Foggia-Bovino: (vacant).
Gaeta: Most Rev. VINCENZO MARIA FARANO.
Genoa-Bobbio: Most Rev. GIOVANNI CANESTRI.
Gorizia: Most Rev. ANTONIO VITALE BOMMARCO.
Lanciano-Ortona: Most Rev. ENZIO D'ANTONIO.
L'Aquila: Most Rev. MARIO PERESSIN.
Lecce: Most Rev. MICHELE MINCUZZI.
Lucca: Most Rev. GIULIANO AGRESTI.
Manfredonia-Vieste: Most Rev. VALENTINO VAILATI.
Matera-Irsina: (vacant).
Messina-Lipari-Santa Lucia del Mela: Most Rev. IGNAZIO CANNAVÓ.
Milan: HE Cardinal CARLO MARIA MARTINI.
Modena-Nonantola: Most Rev. SANTO BARTOLOMEO QUADRI.
Monreale: Most Rev. SALVATORE CASSISA.
Naples: Most Rev. MICHELE GIORDANO.
Oristano: Most Rev. PIER GIULIANO TIDDIA.
Otranto: Most Rev. VINCENZO FRANCO.
Palermo: HE Cardinal SALVATORE PAPPALARDO.
Perugia-Città della Pieve: Most Rev. CESARE PAGANI.
Pescara-Penne: Most Rev. ANTONIO JANNUCCI.
Pisa: Most Rev. ALESSANDRO PLOTTI.
Potenza-Muro Lucano-Marsico Nuovo: Most Rev. GIUSEPPE VAIRO.
Ravenna-Cervia: Most Rev. ERSILIO TONINI.
Reggio Calabria-Bova: Most Rev. AURELIO SORRENTINO.
Rossano-Cariati: Most Rev. SERAFINO SPROVIERI.
Salerno-Campagna-Acerno: Most Rev. GUERINO GRIMALDI.
Sant' Angelo dei Lombardi-Conza-Nusco-Bisaccia: Most Rev. ANTONIO NUZZI.
Siena-Colle di Val d'Elsa-Montalcino: Most Rev. ISMAELE MARIO CASTELLANO.
Sorrento-Castellammare di Stabia: Most Rev. ANTONIO ZAMA.
Spoleto-Norcia: (vacant).
Syracuse: Most Rev. CALOGERO LAURICELLA.
Taranto: Most Rev. SALVATORE DE GIORGI.
Trani-Barletta-Bisceglie: Most Rev. GIUSEPPE CARATA.
Trento: Most Rev. GIOVANNI SARTORI.
Turin: HE Cardinal ANASTASIO ALBERTO BALLESTRERO.
Udine: Most Rev. ALFREDO BATTISTI.
Urbino-Urbania-Sant' Angelo in Vado: Most Rev. DONATO UGO BIANCHI.
Vercelli: Most Rev. ALBINO MENSA.

In addition, the Most Rev. VITO ROBERTI, the Bishop of Caserti, has been granted the personal title of Archbishop.

Azione Cattolica Italiana (ACI) (Catholic Action): Via della Conciliazione 1, 00193 Rome; tel. (06) 6568751; most of the nation-wide lay Catholic organizations in Italy are affiliated to Catholic Action, which has a total membership of one and a half million and is organized in the following divisions: Settore Adulti (Adult Section), Settore Giovani (Youth Section), Azione Cattolica Ragazzi (Children's Catholic Action), Federazione Universitaria Cattolica Italiana—FUCI (University Federation), Movimento Laureati (Graduates' Movement), Movimento Maestri (Teachers' Movement), Movimento Lavoratori (Workers' Movement) and Movimento Studenti (Students' Movement). The Presidency-National is the supreme executive body and co-ordinator of the different branches of Catholic Action. Pres. Avv. RAFFAELE CANANZI; Chaplain Mgr FIORINO TAGLIAFERRI; Sec.-Gen. Dott. IDA BOZZINI.

Protestant Churches

Federation of the Protestant Churches in Italy: Via Firenze 38, 00184 Rome; tel. (06) 4755120; the Federation was formed in 1967; total mems approx 50,000; Pres. Pastor GIORGIO BOUCHARD; includes the following organizations:

Chiesa Apostolica Italiana

Comunione delle Chiese Cristiane Libere

Comunitá Ecumenica di Ispra-Varese

Chiesa Evangelica Luterana in Italia (Lutheran Church): Via Toscana 7, 00187 Rome; tel. (06) 4757519; Via Palestrina 14, 20124 Milan; Dean JOACHIM MIETZ; 20,100 mems.

Chiesa Evangelica Metodista d'Italia (Evangelical Methodist Church of Italy): Via Firenze 38, 00184 Rome; tel. (06) 4743695; f. 1861; Pres. Pastor CLAUDIO MARTELLI; 4,000 mems.

Tavola Valdese (Waldensian Church): Via Firenze 38, 00184 Rome; tel. (06) 4745537; Moderator Pastor FRANCO GIAMPICCOLI; Sec.-Treas. ROSELLA PANZIRONI; 22,000 mems.

Unione Cristiana Evangelica Battista d'Italia (Italian Baptist Union): Piazza in Lucina 35, 00186 Rome; tel. (06) 6876124; f. 1873; Pres. Pastor PAOLO SPANU; Admin. Sec. FRANCO CLEMENTE; 5,000 mems.

Associated Organizations

Salvation Army (Esercito della Salvezza): Via dei Marrucini 40, 00185 Rome; tel. (06) 492614; Officer Commanding for Italy Lt-Col EMMANUEL MIAGLIA; 17 regional centres.

Seventh-day Adventists: Lungotevere Michelangelo 7, 00192 Rome; tel. (06) 315936; represents 88 communities in Italy; Supt ENRICO LONG; Sec. SALVATORE DALFINO.

JUDAISM

Union of Italian Jewish Communities: Lungotevere Sanzio 9, 00153 Rome; tel. (06) 5803670; f. 1930; represents 21 Jewish communities in Italy; Pres. TULLIA ZEVI; Chief Rabbi of Rome Dr ELIO TOAFF.

Rabbinical Council: Chief Rabbi Dott. ELIO R. TOAFF (Via Catalana 1A, Rome), Rabbi Dott. GIUSEPPE LARAS (Via Guastalla 19, Milan), Rabbi Dott. SERGIO SIERRA (Via San Pio V 12, Turin).

BAHÁ'Í FAITH

Assemblea Spirituale Nazionale: Via Antonio Stoppani 10, 00197 Rome; tel. (06) 879647; mems resident in 270 localities.

The Press

In view of Italy's population the number of daily newspapers is rather small (about 70 titles), with the bulk of them appearing in the industrial north. Between 1944 and 1967 no fewer than 161 newspapers ceased publication. The average total daily circulation

ITALY

in 1985 was about 8.4m., while sales totalled about 6.1m. copies per day; sales in the north and centre of the country accounted for 81% of this figure, in the south for 19%. Between 1980 and 1985, sales of daily newspapers increased by approximately 21%, and they were expected to reach 6.3m., on a daily average, at the end of 1986.

Rome and Milan are the main press centres. The most important national dailies are *Corriere della Sera* in Milan and Rome and *Il Giorno* in Milan, followed by *La Repubblica* in Rome and Turin's *La Stampa* circulating in the north and centre. The other large dailies circulate in and reflect their own region; e.g. *La Nazione* serves Florence and its region, *Il Messaggero* and *Il Tempo* Rome and the centre, *Il Secolo XIX*, based in Genova, extends throughout the Italian riviera, *Il Mattino* serves the Naples region and *La Sicilia* and *Giornale di Sicilia* serve Sicily. Although there are comparatively few small dailies, weekly papers are numerous.

The daily press has experienced economic difficulties for many years, but since 1973 rises in labour costs and the price of raw materials have created a critical situation. The dailies have become entirely dependent on financial support from large industrial companies, financial institutions, political parties or other groups with substantial capital who are prepared to stand a financial loss in return for a measure of control over an important information medium. All the political parties represented in parliament have a daily or weekly paper as party organ. The most important are the Communist *L'Unità*, the Socialist *Avanti!* and the Christian Democrat *Il Popolo*. In addition, political parties own or have a holding in papers which are not run as party organs. The Christian Democrats, for example, control seven provincial dailies. Catholic organizations have a controlling interest in several papers and *Avvenire* is owned totally by the Church.

The most important dailies in terms of circulation are: Milan's *Corriere della Sera* (468,000), Turin's *La Stampa* (433,000), Rome's *La Repubblica* (486,000) and *Il Messaggero* (330,000), *L'Unità* (Milan edition 296,000; Rome edition 300,000), Milan's *Il Giorno* (212,000), Florence's *La Nazione* (288,000), Bologna's *Il Resto del Carlino* (301,000), and the sports newspapers, Milan's *Gazzetta dello Sport* (523,000) and Rome's *Corriere dello Sport* (232,000). The five dailies accorded most prestige for the standard of their articles and news coverage are *Corriere della Sera*, *Il Giorno*, *Il Giornale*, *La Stampa* and *La Repubblica*. The leading financial paper is Milan's *Il Sole/24 Ore*.

There are some 430 non-daily newspapers and over 7,000 periodicals. The illustrated weekly papers and magazines frequently have higher sales than the average daily. Ten of the largest appear in Milan, five in Rome and one in Turin. Many tend towards sensationalism, particularly the popular *Domenica del Corriere*, which has a circulation of 225,000, and the right wing *Oggi* and *Gente*. Other weekly illustrated periodicals with a large circulation include *Epoca*, *L'Europeo* and, largest of all, the Catholic *Famiglia Cristiana* (1,109,000). Among the serious and influential magazines should be mentioned *Panorama*, *L'Espresso*, *L'Europeo*, *Epoca*, *Il Tempo*, the financial *Mondo Economico*, the small circulating political and cultural *Il Ponte*, the Communist *Rinascita* and the right-wing *Il Borghese*.

DAILIES

Ancona

Corriere Adriatico: Via Berti 20, 60100 Ancona; tel. (071) 204386; f. 1860; Dir Dott. ARNALDO GIULIANI; circ. 30,000.

Bari

La Gazzetta del Mezzogiorno: Viale Scipione l'Africano 264, 70124 Bari; tel. (080) 364122; telex 810844; f. 1887; independent; Pres. STEFANO ROMANAZZI; Man. Dir GIUSEPPE GORJUX; Dir GIUSEPPE GIACOVAZZO; circ. 74,089.

Bergamo

L'Eco di Bergamo: Viale Papa Giovanni XXIII 118, 24100 Bergamo; tel. (035) 212344; f. 1880; Catholic; Dir and Editor Mgr ANDREA SPADA; circ 45,491.

Il Giornale di Bergamo-Oggi: Via Don Luigi Palazzolo 29, 24100 Bergamo; tel. (035) 244154; f. 1981; Dirs ANDREA BARBIERI, FRANCESCO BARBIERI; circ. 12,000.

Bologna

Il Resto del Carlino: Via Enrico Mattei 106, 40138 Bologna; tel. (051) 532313; f. 1885; independent; Dir FRANCO CANGINI; circ. 300,949.

Bolzano

Alto Adige: Lungotalvera S. Quirino 26, 39100 Bolzano; tel. (0471) 46666; f. 1945; independent; Dir LUCIANO CESCHIA; circ. 47,435.

Dolomiten: Via del Vigneto 7, 39100 Bolzano; tel. (0471) 925111; telex 400161; f. 1923; independent; German language; Editor Dr JOSEF RAMPOLD; circ. 40,000.

Brescia

Bresciaoggi Nuovo: Via Malta 4, 25121 Brescia; tel. (030) 22941; telex 300838; telex 303165; f. 1974; Man. SERGIO MILANI; circ. 15,826.

Il Giornale di Brescia: Via Solferino 22, 25121 Brescia; tel. (030) 29901; telex 303 165; f. 1945; Editor GIAN BATTISTA LANZANI; Man. Dir. FRANCESCO PASSERINI GLAZEL; circ. 57,000.

Cagliari

L'Unione Sarda: Viale Regina Elena 14, 09100 Cagliari; tel. (070) 6013; f. 1889; independent; Dir GIANNI FILIPPINI; circ. 87,741.

Catania

Espresso Sera: Via S. Maria del Rosario 26, 95131 Catania; tel. (095) 333535; Dir GIUSEPPE SIMILI; circ. 4,145.

La Sicilia: Viale Odorico da Pordenone 50, 95126 Catania; tel. (095) 330544; telex 971321; f. 1945; independent; Dir Dott. MARIO CINACIO SANFILIPPO; circ. 74,961.

Como

L'Ordine: Grandate; tel. (031) 450858; f. 1879; Catholic; Dir EGIDIO MAGGIONI; circ. 8,752.

La Provincia: Via Varese 87, 22100 Como; tel. (031) 261282; f. 1892; independent; Dir SERGIO CARLESI; circ. 30,000.

Cremona

La Provincia: Via delle Industrie 2, 26100 Cremona; tel. (0372) 411221; f. 1947; independent; Pres. ANGELO DUCHI; Man. Editor VITTORIO PALOSCHI; circ. 19,341.

Florence

La Città: Via Campo di Marte 13/15, 50100 Florence; tel. (055) 663663; f. 1980; Man. Dir ELVIO BERTUCCELLI; circ. 15,144.

La Nazione: Via Ferdinando Paolieri 2, 50121 Florence; tel. (055) 24851; f. 1859; independent; Dir ROBERTO CIUNI; circ. 288,000.

Foggia

Qui Foggia: Via Bari km 1,600, 71100 Foggia; tel. (0881) 35897; Dir MICHELE CAMPANARO.

Genova

L'Avvisatore Marittimo: Via San Vincenzo 42, 16121 Genova; tel. (010) 562929; telex 213155; f. 1919; shipping and financial; Editor CARLO BELLIO; circ. 4,765.

Corriere Mercantile: Via Archimede 169, 16142 Genova; tel. (010) 53691; f. 1824; political and financial; independent; Editor MIMMO ANGELI; circ. 33,650.

Il Lavoro: Salita di Negro 7, 16123 Genova, tel. (010) 540184; f. 1903; socialist; Editor CESARE LANZA; circ. 22,476.

Il Secolo XIX: Via Varese 2, 16122 Genova; tel. (010) 53881; f. 1887; independent; Dir TOMMASO GIGLIO; circ. 150,008.

Lecce

Quotidiano di Lecce/Brindisi/Taranto: Viale degli Studenti (Palazzo Casto), 73100 Lecce; tel. (099) 44541; f. 1979; Man. Editor VITTORIO BRUNO STAMMERRA; circ. 21,788.

Livorno

Il Tirreno: Viale Alfieri 9, 57100 Livorno; tel. (0586) 401141; f. 1877; independent; Editor LUIGI BIANCHI; circ. 63,559.

Mantova

Gazzetta di Mantova: Via Fratelli Bandiera 32, 46100 Mantova; tel. (0376) 321341; f. 1964; independent; Man. Editor RINO BULBARELLI; circ. 28,088.

Messina

Gazzetta del Sud: Via Taormina 15, 98100 Messina; tel. (090) 21801; f. 1952; independent; Dir NINO CALARCO; circ. 59,745.

Milan

Avvenire: Via Mauro Macchi 61, 20124 Milan; tel. (02) 69661; telex 325096; f. 1968; Catholic; Dir GUIDO FOLLONI; circ. 117,254.

Corriere della Sera: Via Solferino 28, 20121 Milan; tel. (02) 6339; telex 31001; f. 1876; independent; contains weekly supplement, *Il Sette*; Dir UGO STILLE; circ. 468,072.

La Gazzetta dello Sport: Via Solferino 36, 20121 Milan; tel. (02) 6339; telex 321697; f. 1896; sport; Dir CANDIDO CANNAVÒ; circ. 522,801 (daily), 821,166 (Monday edition).

Il Giornale: Via Gaetano Negri 4, 20123 Milan; tel. (02) 85661; telex 333279; f. 1974; independent, controlled by staff; Man. Editor INDRO MONTANELLI; circ. 176,912.

ITALY

Il Giorno: Piazza Cavour 2, 20121 Milan; tel. (02) 77681; telex 330380; Rome office: Largo Goldoni 44; tel. (06) 6780304; f. 1965; independent; Editor LINO RIZZI; circ. 211,643.

Italia Oggi: Via Carducci 29, 20123 Milan; tel. (02) 85961; telex 321191; f. 1986; independent; financial; Editor MARCO BORSA; circ. 105,000.

La Notte: Piazza Cavour 2, 20121 Milan; tel. (02) 77391; f. 1952; evening; independent; Editor PIERO GIORGIANNI; circ. 153,888.

Il Sole/24 Ore: Via Paolo Lomazzo 52, 20154 Milan; tel. (02) 31031; telex 331325; f. 1965; financial, political, economic; Dir GIANNI LOCATELLI; Editor GIANCARLO LUNATI; circ. 170,624.

Modena

Nuova Gazzetta di Modena: Via Emilia Est 36, 41100 Modena; tel. (059) 223707; Dir CARLO ACCORSI; circ. 10,820.

Naples

Il Giornale di Napoli: Via C. Poerio 189/A, 80121 Naples.

Il Mattino: Via Chiatamone 65, 80121 Naples; tel. (081) 411422; f. 1892, reformed 1950; independent; Dir FRANCO ANGRISANI; circ. 179,626.

Roma: Via C. Colombo 45, 80133 Naples; tel. (081) 325,000; circ. 44,029.

Padova

Il Mattino di Padova: Via Pelizzo 15, 35100 Padova; tel. (049) 657933; f. 1978; Dir FABIO BARBIERI; circ. 27,437.

Palermo

Giornale di Sicilia: Via Lincoln 21, 90133 Palermo; tel. (091) 235546; telex 911088; f. 1860; independent; Dir ANTONIO ARDIZZONE; circ. 69,520.

L'Ora: Via Stabile, 90141 Palermo; tel. (091) 581733; f. 1900; independent; Dir PAOLO BRUNO CARBONE; circ. 21,613.

Parma

Gazzetta di Parma: Via Emilio Casa 5, 43100 Parma; tel. (0521) 30003; f. 1735; Pres. GIAMPAOLO PELLEGRINI; Dir N. H. BALDASSARRE MOLOSSI; circ. 47,949.

Pavia

La Provincia Pavese: Via Tasso 47, 27100 Pavia; tel. (0382) 472101; f. 1870; independent; Editor GAETANO RIZZUTO; circ. 17,106.

Piacenza

Libertà: Via Benedettine 68, 29100 Piacenza; tel. (0523) 21718; f. 1883; Dir ERNESTO PRATI; circ. 34,356.

Reggio Emilia

Gazzetta di Reggio: Via Farini 8, 42100 Reggio Emilia; tel. (0552) 30745; Dir UMBERTO BONAFINI; circ. 13,865.

Rome

Avanti!: Via Tomacelli 146, 00186 Rome, tel. (06) 6782491; f. 1896; organ of Socialist Party; Dir UGO INTINI; circ. 54,000.

Corriere dello Sport-Stadio: Piazza Indipendenza 11B, 00185 Rome, tel. (06) 4992; telex 614472; f. 1924; 13 regional editions; Editor Dr GIORGIO TOSATTI; circ. 231,719 (daily), 408,166 (Monday edition).

Il Fiorino: Via Parigi 11, 00185 Rome; tel. (06) 47490; f. 1969; business; Editor LUIGI D'AMATO; circ. 29,546.

Il Giornale d'Italia: Via Parigi 11, 00185 Rome; tel. (06) 47490; Dir LUIGI D'AMATO; Editor FRANCO SIMEONI; circ. 102,322.

International Daily News: Via Barberini 3, 00187 Rome; tel. (06) 4740673; telex 614495; f. 1976; English; Editor G. CARLO RIPOSIO.

Il Manifesto: Via Tomacelli 146, 00186 Rome; tel. (06) 6790151; telex 626158; f. 1971; splinter communist; Man. Editor RINA GAGLIARDI; circ. 58,602.

Il Messaggero: Via del Tritone 152, 00187 Rome; tel. (06) 47201; telex 624644; f. 1878; independent; Editor MARIO PENDINELLI; circ. 330,000.

Ore 12: Via Paisiello 6, 00198 Rome; tel. (06) 8442680; financial; independent; Dir ENZO CARETTI; circ. 35,000.

Paese Sera: Via del Tritone 61/62, 00187 Rome; tel. (06) 672151; f. 1949; left wing; Dir CLAUDIO FRACASSI; circ. 130,988.

Il Popolo: Corso Rinascimento 113, 00186 Rome; tel. (06) 65151; telex 613276; f. 1944; organ of Christian Democrat Party; Editor MARCELLO GILMOZZI; circ. 43,000.

Puglia: Via due Macelli 23, 00187 Rome; tel. (06) 6787751; Dir MARIO GISMONDI; circ. 6,777.

La Repubblica: Piazza Indipendenza 11b, 00185 Rome; tel. (06) 49821; telex 620660; f. 1976; left-wing; contains weekly supplement, *Affari e Finanza* and *Venerdì di Repubblica*, on Friday, *Il Trovaroma* on Saturday (in Rome edition only); Editor EUGENIO SCALFARI; circ. 486,000.

Il Tempo: Piazza Colonna 366, 00187 Rome; tel. (06) 65041; telex 614087; f. 1944; right-wing; Editor GIANNI LETTA; circ. 186,554.

L'Umanità: Via S. Maria in Via 12, 00187 Rome; tel. (06) 6727222; f. 1947; organ of the Social Democrat Party; Dir Prof. RUGGERO PULETTI; circ. 16,000.

L'Unità: Via dei Taurini 19, 00185 Rome; tel. (06) 4950351; telex 613461; f. 1924; newspaper of the Communist Party; Dir EMANUELE MACALUSO; circ. 300,000 (weekday), 800,000 (Sunday).

La Voce Repubblicana: Via Tomacelli 146, 00186 Rome; tel. (06) 6791610; f. 1919; organ of the Republican Party; circ. 12,000.

Sassari

La Nuova Sardegna: Via Porcellana 9, 07100 Sassari; tel. (079) 275858; f. 1891; independent; Editor ALBERTO STATERA; circ. 47,765.

Taranto

Corriere del Giorno: Piazza Dante 5, Zona 'Bestat', 74100 Taranto; tel. (099) 3203; f. 1947; Editor RICCARDO CATACCHIO; circ. 10,151.

Trento

L'Adige: Via Rosmini 35, 38100 Trento; tel. (0461) 8511; f. 1945; Christian Democrat; Editor-in-Chief PIERO AGOSTINI; circ. 16,759.

Treviso

La Tribuna de Treviso: Piazza Ancillotto 8, 31100 Treviso; tel. (0422) 50801; Dir PAOLO OJETTI; circ. 16,625.

Trieste

Il Piccolo (Giornale di Trieste): Via Silvio Pellico 8, 34122 Trieste; tel. (040) 77861; f. 1881; independent; Dir PAOLO FRANCIA; circ. 50,654.

Primorski Dnevnik: Via dei Montecchi 6, 34137 Trieste; tel. (040) 794672; telex 460270; f. 1945; Slovene; Man. Dir SAMSA BOGUMIL.

Turin

La Stampa and **Stampa Sera:** Via Marenco 32, 10126 Turin; tel. (011) 65681; telex 221121; f. 1867; independent; morning edition, *La Stampa;* evening edition, *Stampa Sera;* circ. 433,366 (morning), 26,006 (evening); Dirs GAETANO SCARDOCCHIA (morning), LUCA BERNARDELLI (evening).

Tuttosport: Via Villar 2, 10147 Turin; tel. (011) 26121; telex 224230; f. 1945; sport; Dir PIERO DARDANELLO; circ. 157,461.

Udine

Messaggero Veneto: Viale Palmanova 290, 33100 Udine; tel. (0432) 64941; telex 450449; f. 1946; Editor VITTORINO MELONI; circ. 45,788.

Varese

La Prealpina: Viale Tamagno 13, 21100 Varese; tel. (0332) 286177; f. 1888; Dir MARIO LODI; circ. 26,219.

Venice

Il Gazzettino: Via Torino 110, 30172 Venezia-Mestre; tel. (041) 665111; f. 1887; independent; Dir GIORGIO LAGO; circ. 112,160.

La Nuova Venezia: Salizzada S. Lio, 5620 Castello, 30122 Venice; tel. (041) 710300; Dir PAOLO OJETTI.

Verona

L'Arena: Viale del Lavoro 11, 37036 S. Martino Buon Albergo, Verona; tel. (045) 990077; telex 481815; f. 1866; independent; Dir GIUSEPPE BRUGNOLI; circ. 51,755.

Vicenza

Il Giornale di Vicenza: Viale S. Lazzaro 89, 36100 Vicenza; tel. (0444) 564533; f. 1945; Editor MINO ALLIONE; circ. 36,759.

SELECTED PERIODICALS

Fine Arts

Casabella: Via Marconi 17, 20090 Segrate, Milan; tel. (02) 2131851; f. 1928; 11 a year; architecture and interior design; Editor VITTORIO GREGOTTI; circ. 54,000.

Domus: Via A. Grandi 5/7, 20089 Rozzano, Milan; tel. (02) 824721; telex 313589; f. 1928; 11 a year; architecture, interior design and art; Editor MARIO BELLINI; circ. 60,000.

Flash Art/Heute Kunst: Via Solferino 11, 20121 Milan; tel. (02) 2364133; bi-monthly; Dir GIANCARLO POLITI.

Il Fotografo: Via Rivoltana 8, 20090 Segrate, Milan; tel. (02) 75421; monthly; photography; Dir GIORGIO COPPIN.

ITALY

Graphicus and Graphicus News: Viale Mattioli 39 (Castello del Valentino), 10125 Turin; tel. (011) 6509659; f. 1911; 20 a year; graphic arts; Dir STEFANO AJANI; Editor LUCIANO LOVERA; circ. 4,600/5,500.

L'Illustrazione Italiana: Via Gen. Biancardi 1 bis, 21052 Busto Arsizio (VA); f. 1873; quarterly; fine arts.

Interni: Via Trentacoste 7, 20134 Milan; tel. (02) 215631; telex 350523; monthly; interior decoration and design; Editor DOROTHEA BALLUFF; circ. 60,000.

Lotus International: Via Trentacoste 7, 20134 Milan; tel. (02) 23693293; telex 313123; f. 1960; quarterly; architecture, town-planning; Editor PIERLUIGI NICOLIN.

Rivista Italiana di Musicologia: Leo S. Olschki, Viuzzo del Pozzetto, 50126 Florence; tel. (055) 6530684; f. 1966; every 6 months; music; Editors A. L. BELLINA, A. COLLISANI, F. DELLA SETA, R. DI BENEDETTO, G. MORELLI, A. POMPILIO, T. WALKER.

Storia dell'Arte: Via Ernesto Codignola, 50018 Casellina di Scandicci; tel. (055) 2798; telex 573690; quarterly; art history; Dir GIULIO CARLO ARGAN.

General, Literary and Political

Archivio Storico Italiano: Leo S. Olschki, Viuzzo del Pozzetto, 50126 Florence; tel. (055) 6530684; f. 1842; quarterly; history; Editor ARNALDO D'ADDARIO.

Belfagor: POB 66, 50100 Florence; tel. (055) 6530684; f. 1946; every 2 months; historical and literary criticism; Editor CARLO FERDINANDO RUSSO; circ. 5,000.

La Bibliofilia: Leo S. Olschki, Viuzzo del Pozzetto, 50126 Florence; tel. (055) 6530684; f. 1899; every 4 months; bibliography; Editor L. BALSAMO.

Il Borghese: Viale Regina Margherita 7, 20122 Milan; tel. (02) 592966; f. 1950; weekly; extreme right-wing, political and cultural; Editor MARIO TEDESCHI.

Civitas: Via Tirso 92, 00198 Rome; tel. (06) 865651; f. 1919; monthly; magazine of political studies; Dir PAOLO EMILIO TAVIANI.

Comunità: Via Manzoni 12, 20121 Milan; tel. (02) 790957; f. 1945; quarterly; culture; Editor RENZO ZORZI; circ. 9,000.

Critica Letteraria: Via Stazio 15, 80123 Napoli; f. 1973; quarterly; literary criticism; Editor P. GIANNANTONIO; circ. 3,000.

Critica Marxista: Via dei Polacchi 41, 00186 Rome; tel. (06) 6789680; f. 1962; 6 a year; Dir ALDO ZANARDO.

Critica Sociale: Foro Buonaparte 24, 20121 Milan; tel. (02) 806319; f. 1891; monthly; Socialist; Dir CARLO TOGNOLI; circ. 25,000.

La Discussione: Piazzale Luigi Sturzo 31, 00144 Rome; tel. (06) 5901353; f. 1953; weekly; Christian Democrat; Dir PIERLUIGI MAGNASCHI; circ. 50,000.

Domenica del Corriere: Via Scarsellini 17, Milan; tel. (02) 2588; telex 310031; f. 1899; illustrated weekly review; Dir MARCELLO MINERBI; circ. 225,000.

Epoca: Arnoldo Mondadori Editore SpA, Via Marconi 27, 20090 Segrate, Milan; tel. (02) 7542; telex 310119; f. 1950; illustrated; topical weekly; Dir CARLO ROGNONI; circ. 94,000.

L'Espresso: Via Po 12, 00198 Rome; tel. (06) 84781; telex 610629; weekly; independent left; political; illustrated; Editor GIOVANNI VALENTINI; circ. 311,000.

L'Europeo: Via Civitavecchia 102, Milan; tel. (02) 2588; f. 1945; weekly; Liberal; political and news; Dir SALVATORE GIANNELLA; circ. 125,000.

Famiglia Cristiana: Via Giotto 36, 20145 Milan; tel. (02) 467071; telex 332232; f. 1931; weekly; Catholic; illustrated; Dir LEONARDO ZEGA; circ. 1,109,419.

Gazzetta del Lunedì: Via Varese 2, Genova; tel. (010) 517851; f. 1945; weekly; political; Dir MIMMO ANGELI; circ. 150,000.

Gente: Via Vitruvio 43, 20124 Milan; tel. (02) 27751; f. 1957; weekly; illustrated political, cultural and current events; Editor A. TERZI; circ. 722,000.

Giornale della Libreria: Viale Vittorio Veneto 24, 20124 Milan; tel. (02) 6597950; f. 1888; monthly; organ of the Associazione Italiana Editori; bibliographical; Editor CARLO ENRICO RIVOLTA.

Il Giornale del Mezzogiorno: Via Messina 31, 00198 Rome; tel. (06) 8443151; telex 621401; f. 1946; weekly; politics, economics; Dir VITO BLANCO.

Giorni: Via Zuretti 34, 20125 Milan; tel. (02) 6883151; left-wing weekly; Dir DAVIDE LAJOLO; circ. 180,000.

The International Spectator: Viale Mazzini 88, 00195 Rome; tel. (06) 319806; quarterly; English journal of the Istituto Affari Internazionali; Editor GIANNI BONVICINI.

Lettere Italiane: Leo S. Olschki, POB 66, 50100 Florence; tel. (055) 6530684; f. 1949; quarterly; literary; Dirs V. BRANCA, G. GETTO.

Il Mondo: Gruppo Rizzoli, Corso Garibaldi 86, 20121 Milan; tel. (02) 665941; weekly; business and commerce; circ. 62,781.

Mondo Economico: Via P. Lomazzo 47, 20154 Milan; tel. (02) 3492451; f. 1948; weekly; economics; business, finance; Editor GIANNI LOCATELLI; circ. 50,000.

Il Mulino: Strada Maggiore 37, 40125 Bologna; tel. (051) 222419; f. 1951; every 2 months; culture and politics; Editor NICOLA MATTEUCCI.

Nuovi Argomenti: Via Sicilia 136, 00187 Rome; tel. (06) 47497376; f. 1953; quarterly; Liberal; Editors ALBERTO MORAVIA, LEONARDO SCIASCIA, ENZO SICILIANO.

Oggi: Gruppo Rizzoli, Corso Garibaldi 86, 20121 Milan; tel. (02) 665941; f. 1945; weekly; topical, literary; illustrated; Dir WILLY MOLCO; circ. 533,878.

Panorama: Arnoldo Mondadori Editore SpA, Via Marconi 27, 20090 Segrate, Milan; tel. (02) 7542; f. 1962; weekly; current affairs; Editor CLAUDIO RINALDI; circ. 420,000.

Il Pensiero Politico: Leo S. Olschki, Viuzzo del Pozzetto, 50126 Florence, tel. (055) 6530684; f. 1968; every 4 months; political and social history; Editor S. MASTELLONE.

Il Ponte: Viale A. Giacomini 8, 50132 Florence; tel. (055) 473964; f. 1945; monthly; politics, art and literature; Publr VALLECCHI EDITORE SpA; Editor MARCELLO ROSSI.

Rinascita: Via dei Taurini 19, 00185 Rome; tel. (06) 4951251; f. 1944; weekly; Communist; Dir GIUSEPPE CHIARANTE; Editor LUCIANO BARCA; circ. 80,000.

Rivista Critica di Storia della Filosofia: Viale Monza 106, 20127 Milan; f. 1946; quarterly; philosophy; Publr Franco Angel Editore Srl; Editor Prof. MARIO DAL PRA.

Scuola e Didattica: Via L. Cadorna 11, 25186 Brescia; tel. (030) 29931; telex 300836; 19 a year; education.

Selezione dal Reader's Digest: Via Alserio 10, 20173 Milan; tel. (02) 69871; telex 311286; monthly; Editor-in-Chief PIETRO MARIANO BENNI.

Il Settimanale: Via Bissolati 76, 00187 Rome; tel. (06) 465588; weekly; political, economic, cultural and current events.

Storia Illustrata: Via Marconi 27, 20090 Segrate, Milan; tel. (02) 75421; f. 1957; monthly; history; Publr Mondadori Editore; circ. 105,701.

Tempo: Via S. Valeria 5, 20100 Milan; f. 1938; topical illustrated weekly; Dir CARLO GREGORETTI; circ. 230,000.

Volksbote: Via Museo 42, 39100 Bolzano; tel. (0471) 925111; organ of the Südtiroler Volkspartei; German language.

Religion

Città di Vita: Piazza Santa Croce 16, 50122 Florence; tel. (055) 242783; f. 1946; every 2 months; cultural review of religious research in theology, art and science; Dir P. M. GIUSEPPE ROSITO; circ. 2,000.

La Civiltà Cattolica: Via di Porta Pinciana 1, 00187 Rome; tel. (06) 6798351; f. 1850; fortnightly; Catholic; Editor GIAN PAOLO SALVINI.

Il Fuoco: Via Giacinto Carini 28, 00152 Rome; tel. (06) 5810969; every 2 months; art, literature, science, philosophy, psychology, theology; Dir PASQUALE MAGNI.

Humanitas: Via G. Rosa 71, 25100 Brescia; tel. (030) 46451; f. 1946; every 2 months; religion, philosophy, science, politics, history, sociology, literature, etc.; Dir STEFANO MINELLI.

Protestantesimo: Via Pietro Cossa 42, 00193 Rome; tel. (06) 631585; f. 1946; quarterly; theology and current problems, book reviews; Prof. Dr VITTORIO SUBILIA.

La Rivista del Clero Italiano: Largo Gemelli 1, 20123 Milan; tel. (02) 8856369; telex 321033; f. 1920; monthly; Dir BRUNO MAGGIONI.

Rivista di Storia della Chiesa in Italia: c/o Herder Editrice e Libreria, Piazza Montecitorio 117-120, 00186 Rome; f. 1947; 2 a year.

Rivista di Storia e Letteratura Religiosa: Biblioteca Erik Peterson, Università di Torino, Via S. Ottavio 20, 10124 Turin; tel. (011) 830556; f. 1965; every 4 months; religious history and literature; Dir FRANCO BOLGIANI.

Science and Technology

L'Automobile: Viale Regina Margherita 290, 00198 Rome; tel. (06) 4402061; f. 1945; monthly; motor mechanics, tourism; Dir CARLO LUNA; circ. 1,500,000.

Fonderia: Via Roncaglia 14, 20146 Milan; tel. (02) 4986634; telex 321655; f. 1951; every 2 months; foundry techniques; Dir ANTONIO PASSANITI; circ. 3,500.

Gazzetta Medica Italiana-Archivio per le Scienze Mediche: Corso Bramante 83-85, 10126 Turin; tel. (011) 678282; monthly; medical science; Dir ALBERTO OLIARO.

ITALY

Il Giornale dell' Officina: Via Roncaglia 14, 20146 Milan; tel. (02) 436006; telex 321655; f. 1948; monthly; mechanical industry magazine; Dir GABRIELE FAPPIANO; circ. 4,500.

L'Italia Agricola: Via Nazionale 89/A, 00184 Rome; tel. (06) 463651; f. 1864; quarterly; agriculture; Dir BORIS FISCHETTI; circ. 20,000.

Macchine: Via Roncaglia 14, 20146 Milan; tel. (02) 468280; telex 321655; f. 1948; monthly; technical review of mechanical engineering industry; Dir ANTONIO PASSANITI; circ. 10,000.

Meccanica: Piazza Leonardo da Vinci 32, 20133 Milan; tel. (02) 23994209; telex 333467; quarterly; Journal of Italian Association of Theoretical and Applied Mechanics; Dir Prof. CARLO CERCIGNANI.

Il Medico d'Italia: Piazza Cola di Rienzo 80A, 00192 Rome; tel. (06) 6874034; 2 a week; medical science; Editor Prof. EOLO PARODI.

Minerva Medica: Corso Bramante 83–85, 10126 Turin; tel. (011) 678282; monthly, medical science; Dir ALBERTO OLIARO.

Monti e Boschi: Via Emilia Levante 31/2, 40139 Bologna; tel. (051) 492211; telex 510336; f. 1949; 2 a month; ecology and forestry; Publisher EDAGRICOLE; Editor UMBERTO BAGNARESI; circ. 15,600.

Motor: Piazza Antonio Mancini 4G, 00196 Rome; tel. (06) 3965431; f. 1942; monthly; motor mechanics; Dir SERGIO FAVIA DEL CORE; circ. 120,000.

Physis: Leo S. Olschki, CP 66, 50100 Florence; Viuzzo del Pozzetto, 50126 Florence; tel. (055) 6530684; f. 1959; quarterly; history of science; Editor V. CAPPELLETTI.

La Rivista dei Combustibili: Viale De Gasperi 3, 20097 S. Donato Milanese; tel. (02) 510031; telex 321622; f. 1947; monthly; fuels review; Dir Prof. ALBERTO GIRELLI; circ. 2,000.

Rivista Geografica Italiana: Via Curtatone 1, 50123 Florence; tel. (055) 282150; f. 1894; quarterly geographical review; Editor PIERO INNOCENTI.

Utensil: Via Roncaglia 14, 20146 Milan; tel. (02) 4986634; telex 321655; f. 1978; 9 a year; technology and marketing in the tool industry; Dir ANTONIO PASSANITI; circ. 12,000.

Women's Publications

Amica: Via Scarsellini 17, 20161 Milan; tel. (02) 6339; telex 310031; f. 1962; weekly; Editor P. PIETRONI; circ. 211,000.

Annabella: Via Civitavecchia 102, Milan; tel. (02) 25843213; telex 312119; f. 1932; weekly; Editor M. VENTURI; circ. 270,000.

Confidenze: Arnoldo Mondadori Editore SpA, Via Marconi 27, 20090 Segrate, Milan; tel. (02) 75421; telex 320457; f. 1946; weekly; Dir ALDO GUSTAVO CIMARELLI; circ. 400,000.

Gioia: Via Vitruvio 43, 20124 Milan; f. 1938; weekly; Editor SILVANA GIACOBINI; circ. 351,000.

Grazia: Arnoldo Mondadori Editore SpA, Via Marconi 27, 20090 Segrate, Milan; f. 1938; weekly; Dir ANDREINA VANNI; circ. 400,000.

Intimità: Via Borgogna 5, 20122 Milan; tel. (02) 781051; weekly; published by Cino del Duca, Dir G. GALLUZZO; circ. 468,000.

Mille Idee per la Donna: Rizzoli Editore SpA, Via Angelo Rizzoli 2, 20132 Milan; tel. (02) 2588; monthly; Dir MARA SANTINI; circ. 362,800.

Vogue Italia: Piazza Castello 27, 20121 Milan; tel. (02) 85611; telex 313454; monthly; Editor FRANCA SOZZANI.

Miscellaneous

Annali della Scuola Normale Superiore di Pisa: Scuola Normale Superiore, Pisa; tel. (050) 597111; telex 590548; f. 1873; quarterly; mathematics, philosophy, philology, history, literature; Editor (Mathematics) Prof. EDOARDO VESENTINI; Editor (literature and philosophy) Prof. GIUSEPPE NENCI; circ. 1,300.

Atlante: Via Mosè Bianchi 6, 20149 Milan; tel. (02) 4694451; telex 333183; published by Istituto Geografico de Agostini (Novara); travel, art, geography, ethnology, archaeology; Dir Dott. MASSIMO MORELLO.

Comunità Mediterranea: Lungotevere Flaminio 34, 00196 Rome; quarterly; legal; Editor ENRICO NOUNÈ.

Cooperazione Educativa: La Nuova Italia, Via dei Piceni 16, 00185 Rome; tel. (06) 4940228; f. 1952; monthly; education; Dir GIORGIO TESTA.

Israel: Largo Don Morosini 1, 00195 Rome; f. 1916; weekly; cultural; Jewish; Editor C. A. VITERBO.

Il Maestro: Clivo Monte del Gallo 50, 00165 Rome; f. 1945; fortnightly; Catholic teachers' magazine; Dir RITA LUDOVICO; circ. 40,000.

Milano Finanza: Via Ptta. Bossi 4, 20121 Milan; tel. (02) 809161; f. 1986; weekly; financial; Dir PAOLO PANERAI; circ. 90,000.

Quattroruote: Via A. Grandi 5/7, 20089 Rozzano, Milan; telex 313589; f. 1956; motoring; monthly; Editor RAFFAELE MASTROSTEFANO; circ. 600,000.

Qui Touring: Touring Club Italiano, Corso Italia 10, 20122 Milan; tel. (02) 85261; telex 321160; f. 1971; monthly; travel, art, geography; Editor TCI; circ. 510,000.

Radiocorriere-TV: Via Arsenale 41, 10121 Turin; tel. (011) 5710; weekly; RAI official guide to radio and television programmes; Dir GINO NEBIOLO.

NEWS AGENCIES

Agenzia Giornalistica Italia (AGI): Via Nomentana 92, 00161 Rome; tel. (06) 84361; telex 610512; Editor GIANNA NACCARELLI.

Agenzia Nazionale Stampa Associata (ANSA): Via della Dataria 94, 00187 Rome; tel. (06) 67741; telex 610242; f. 1945; 18 regional offices in Italy and 89 branches all over the world; service in Italian, Spanish, French, English; Pres. GIOVANNI GIOVANNINI; Man. Dir and Gen. Man. PAOLO DE PALMA; Chief Editor SERGIO LEPRI.

Inter Press Service (IPS): Via Panisperna 207, 00184 Rome; tel. (06) 485692; telex 610574; f. 1964; Editor-in-Chief PABLO PIACENTINI.

Foreign Bureaux

Agencia EFE (Spain): Via dei Canestrari 5, 00186 Rome; tel. (06) 6548802; telex 612323; Bureau Chief JORGE DEL CORRAL Y DIEZ DEL CORRAL.

Agence France-Presse (AFP): Piazza Santi-Apostoli 66, 00187 Rome; tel. (06) 6793623; Bureau Chief YVES GACON.

Allgemeiner Deutscher Nachrichtendienst (ADN) (German Democratic Republic): Via Prato della Signora 22/23, 00199 Rome; Bureau Chief Dr HEINZ SIMON.

Associated Press (AP) (USA): Piazza Grazioli 5, 00186 Rome; tel. (06) 6789936; telex 610196; Bureau Chief DENNIS F. REDMONT.

Československá tisková kancelář (ČTK) (Czechoslovakia): Via Bevagna 11417, 00191 Rome; tel. (06) 3270777; telex 610135.

Deutsche Presse-Agentur (dpa) (Federal Republic of Germany): Via della Mercede 55, Int. 15, 00187 Rome; tel. (06) 6789810; telex 610046; Bureau Chief FRANK RAFALSKI.

Kyodo Tsushin (Japan): Via Panama 110, 00198 Rome, tel. (06) 8440709; telex 680840; Bureau Chief KATSUO UEDA.

Magyar Távirati Iroda (MTI) (Hungary): Via Topino 29, 00199 Rome; Correspondent FERENC GARZO.

Reuters (UK): Via della Cordonata 7, 00187 Rome; tel. (06) 6782501; telex 621065.

Telegrafnoye Agentstvo Sovetskovo Soyuza (TASS) (USSR): Viale dell'Umanesimo 172, 00144 Rome; tel. (06) 5915883; telex 610034; Correspondent NIKOLAJ TETERIN.

United Press International (UPI) (USA): Via della Mercede 55, 00187 Rome; tel. (06) 6795747; telex 624580; Manager for Italy PEGGY POLK.

Xinhua (New China) News Agency (People's Republic of China): Via Bruxelles 59, 00198 Rome; tel. (06) 865028; telex 612208; Bureau Chief WANG YANLIN.

The following are also represented: CNA (Taiwan) and Jiji Tsushin-Sha (Japan).

PRESS ASSOCIATIONS

Associazione della Stampa Estera in Italia: Via della Mercede 55, 00187 Rome; tel. (06) 6786005; foreign correspondents' asscn; Pres. DENNIS REDMONT; Sec. SANTIAGO FERNÁNDEZ ARDANAZ.

Federazione Italiana Editori Giornali (FIEG): Via Piemonte 64, 00187 Rome; tel. (06) 461683; telex 625361; f. 1950; association of newspaper proprietors; Pres. GIOVANNI GIOVANNINI; Dir-Gen. SEBASTIANO SORTINO; 276 mems.

Federazione Nazionale della Stampa Italiana: Corso Vittorio Emanuele 349, 00186 Rome; tel. (06) 6547741; f. 1877; 17 affiliated unions; Pres. GUIDO GUIDI; Nat. Sec. GIULIANA DEL BUFALO; 16,000 mems.

Unione Stampa Periodica Italiana (USPI): Via Nazionale 163, 00184 Rome; tel. (06) 6783117; Pres. Avv. VITTORIO CIAMPI; Sec.-Gen. GIAN DOMENICO ZUCCALÀ; 4,000 mems.

Publishers

There are over 300 major publishing houses and many smaller ones.

Bologna

Edizioni Calderini: Via Emilia Levante 31/2, 40139 Bologna; tel. (051) 492211; telex 510336; f. 1954; art, sport, electronics, mechanics, university and school textbooks, travel guides, nursing, architecture; Man. Dir SERGIO PERDISA.

ITALY

Capitol Dischi CEB: Via Minghetti 17/19, 40010 Cadriano di Granarolo, Bologna; tel. (051) 766612; telex 511039; f. 1956; children's fiction, textbooks, reference, medicine, art, biography, educational films and records; Chair. MAURIZIO MALIPIERO; Gen. Man. RAFFAELE MALIPIERO.

Nuova Casa Editrice Licinio Cappelli SpA: Via Marsili 9, 40124 Bologna; tel. (051) 330411; f. 1948; medical science, history, politics, literature, textbooks; Chair. and Man. Dir NICOLA MILANO; Gen. Man. MARIO MUSSO.

Edagricole: Via Emilia Levante 31, 40139 Bologna; tel. (051) 492211; telex 510336; f. 1936; agriculture, veterinary science, gardening, biology, textbooks, directories; Man. Dir SERGIO PERDISA; Editor LUISA MANZONI.

Malipiero Editore SpA: Via Liguria 8–10, CP 788, 40100 Bologna; tel. (051) 792111; telex 510260; f. 1969; albums and books for children and young people, dictionaries, pocket dictionaries, stamp albums, etc.; Chair. GIUSEPPE MALIPIERO; Man. Dir. PIERPAOLO MALIPIERO.

Società Editrice Il Mulino: Via S. Stefano 6, 40125 Bologna; tel. (051) 233415; f. 1954; politics, history, philosophy, social sciences, linguistics, literary criticism, law, music, theatre, psychology, economics, journals; Gen. Man. GIOVANNI EVANGELISTI.

Nicola Zanichelli Editore: Via Irnerio 34, 40126 Bologna; tel. (051) 293111; telex 214885; f. 1859; educational, history, literature, philosophy, science, technical books, law, psychology, architecture, earth sciences, linguistics, medicine and economics; Chair. and Gen. Man. FREDERICO ENRIQUES; Vice-Chair. and Man. Dir LORENZO ENRIQUES.

Brescia

Editrice La Scuola SpA: Via Cadorna 11, Brescia; tel. (030) 29931; telex 300836; f. 1904; educational magazines, educational textbooks, audiovisual aids and toys; Chair. Dr Ing. LUCIANO SILVERI; Man. Dir Dr Ing. ADOLFO LOMBARDI.

Busto Arsizio

Bramante Editrice: Via Biancardi 1 bis, 21052 Busto Arsizio; tel. (0331) 620324; f. 1958; art, history, encyclopaedias, natural sciences, interior decoration, arms and armour, music; Chair. Dr GUIDO CERIOTTI.

Florence

Casa Editrice Bonechi: Via dei Cairoli 18B, 50131 Florence; tel. (055) 576841; telex 571323; f. 1973; art, travel, reference, Man. Dir GIAMPAOLO BONECHI; Gen. Man. MARCO BANTI.

Cremonese: Borgo Santa Croce 17, 50122 Florence; tel. (055) 2476371; f. 1929; history, reference, engineering, science, textbooks, architecture, mathematics, aviation; Chair. ALBERTO STIANTI.

Giunti Barbera Editore; Via Vincenzo Gioberti 34, 50121 Florence; tel. (055) 670451; telex 571438; f. 1854; art, psychology, literature, science, law; Dir Dott. SERGIO GIUNTI.

Le Monnier: Via A. Meucci 2, 50015 Grassina, Florence; tel. (055) 6813801; f. 1836; academic and cultural books, textbooks, dictionaries; Man. Dirs Dott. MARCO PAOLETTI, Dott. VANNI PAOLETTI, Dott. ENRICO PAOLETTI.

La Nuova Italia Editrice SpA: Via Ernesto Codignola 1, 50018 Florence; tel. (055) 572798; f. 1926; biography, psychology, philosophy, philology, education, history, politics, belles-lettres, art, music and science; Man. Dirs MARIO CASALINI, FEDERICO CODIGNOLA, MARIO ERMINI, SERGIO PICCIONI.

Casa Editrice Leo S. Olschki: POB 66, 50100 Florence; tel. (055) 6530681; f. 1886; reference, periodicals, textbooks, humanities; Man. ALESSANDRO OLSCHKI.

Adriano Salani Editore SpA: Via del Giglio 15, 50123 Florence; tel. (055) 263288; f. 1987; art, classics, history, children's books; Editor MARIO SPAGNOL.

Edizioni Remo Sandron: Via L.C. Farini 10, 50121 Florence; f. 1839; textbooks; Pres. E. MULINACCI.

RCS Sansoni Editore SpA: Via Benedetto Varchi 47, 50132 Florence; tel. (055) 243334; telex 57466; f. 1976; art, archaeology, literature, philology, philosophy, essays, science, social sciences, natural sciences, history, law, teach-yourself books, magazines; Chair. and Man. Dir SANDRO ALFIERI.

Vallecchi Editore SpA: Viale Giovanni Milton 7, 50129 Florence; tel. (055) 473964; telex 573084; f. 1918; art, fiction, classics; Chair. ENRICO VALLECCHI; Man. Dir ATTILIO VALLECCHI.

Genova

Casa Editrice Marietti SpA: Via Palestro 10/8, 16122 Genova; tel. (010) 882419; telex 271596; f. 1820; liturgy, theology, fiction, history, politics, literature, philosophy, art, children's books; Editor ANTONIO BALLETTO.

Libreria degli Studi (formerly LUPA): Via Balbi 42, Genova; f. 1943; textbooks, fine arts; Dir MARIO BOZZI.

Milan

Adelphi Edizioni SpA: Via S. Giovanni sul Muro 14, 20121 Milan; tel. (02) 871266; f. 1962; classics, philosophy, biography, music, art, psychology, religion and fiction; Man. Dir GIUSEPPE LUCIANO FOÀ; Editor ROBERTO CALASSO.

Editrice Àncora: Via G. B. Niccolini 8, 20154 Milan; tel. (02) 3189941; f. 1934; religious, educational; Dir SEVERINO MEDICI.

Franco Angeli Libri Srl: Viale Monza 106, CP 17130, 20127, Milan; tel. (02) 2827651; f. 1956; general; Man. Dir FRANCO ANGELI.

Carisch SpA: Via General Fara 39, 20124 Milan; tel. (02) 66981814; telex 326397; f. 1884; music and musicology; records; educational musical instruments; Pres. PIETRO MERAVIGLIA MANTEGAZZA.

Casa Editrice Ciancimino: Via Fontana 16, Milan; f. 1936; encyclopaedias and technical books for mechanical, electrical and radio industries; Dir MICHELE CIANCIMINO.

Gruppo Editoriale Fabbri SpA: Via Mecenate 91, 20138 Milan; tel. (02) 50951; telex 311321; f. 1980; juveniles, education, textbooks, reference, literature, maps and encyclopaedia series, art books; Chair. GIOVANNI GIOVANNINI; Man. Dir MARIO SPERANZA.

Bompiani: Via Mecenate 91, 20138 Milan; tel. (02) 50951; telex 311321; f. 1929; modern literature, biographies, theatre, science, art, history, classics, dictionaries, pocket books; Dir MARIO ANDREOSE.

Sonzogno: Via Mecenate 91, 20138 Milan; tel (02) 50951; telex 311321; f. 1861; fiction, non-fiction, illustrated, guides; Dir MARIO ANDREOSE.

Feltrinelli SpA: Via Andegari 6, 20121 Milan; tel. (02) 808346; f. 1954; fiction, juvenile, science, technology, textbooks, poetry, art, music, history, literature, political science, philosophy, reprint editions of periodicals; Chair. INGE FELTRINELLI; Man. Dir GIUSEPPE ANTONINI.

Garzanti Editore: Via Senato 25, 20121 Milan; tel. (02) 77871; telex 325218; f. 1938; literature, poetry, science, art, history, politics, encyclopaedias, dictionaries, scholastic and children's books; Chair. GUGLIELMO MAGATTI; Man. Dirs PIO FOLCIA, FRANCO RAMPINI.

Antonio Vallardi: Via Senato 25, 20121 Milan; tel. (02) 77871; telex 325218; f. 1822; art, literature, travel, reference, dictionaries, children's books, teach-yourself books; Editor VANNA MASSAROTTI.

Ghisetti e Corvi Editori SpA: Corso Concordia 7, 20129 Milan; tel. (02) 706232; f. 1937; educational textbooks.

Casa Editrice Libraria Ulrico Hoepli: Via Hoepli 5, 20121 Milan; tel. (02) 865446; telex 313395; f. 1870; grammars, art, technical, scientific and school books, encyclopaedias; Chair. ULRICO HOEPLI; Man. Dir GIANNI HOEPLI.

Edizioni Labor: Viale Beatrice d'Este 34, 20122 Milan; f. 1934; encyclopaedias, art, history, children's books, religion; Gen. Mans ERCOLE ERCOLI, Dott. GIANCARLO AGAZZI.

Longanesi e C.: Via T. Salvini 3, 20122 Milan; tel. (02) 782551; telex 353273; f. 1946; religion, music, art, history, philosophy, fiction; Pres. S. PASSIGLI; Man. Dir M. SPAGNOL.

Massimo: Corso di Porta Romana 122, 20122 Milan; tel. (02) 5454104; f. 1955; fiction, biography, history, social science, philosophy, pedagogy, theology, school texts; Chair. CESARE CRESPI.

Arnoldo Mondadori Editore: Via Marconi 27, 20090 Segrate, Milan; tel. (02) 75421; telex 320457; f. 1907; literature, fiction, politics, science, music, art, religion, philosophy, children's books, magazines; Man. Dir SERGIO POLILLO.

Ugo Mursia Editore SpA: Via Tadino 29, 20124, Milan; tel. (02) 29403030; telex 325294; f. 1922; general fiction and non-fiction, textbooks, reference, art, history, philosophy, biography, sports, children's books; Gen. Man. Dott. GIANCARLA MURSIA.

Nuova Accademia Editrice: Via Cavalcabò 9, 20146 Milan; tel. (02) 464884; f. 1946; books on general culture; Pres. LUIGI PINELLI.

Editore dall'Oglio: Via Santa Croce 20/2, 20122 Milan; tel. (02) 8351575; f. 1925; general literature, biography, history, fiction; Gen. Man. BRUNO ROMANO.

Edizioni Paoline: Piazza Soncino 5, 20092 Cinisello Balsamo—Milan; tel. (02) 6600621; telex 325183; f. 1914; religious; Gen. Man. ANTONIO TARZIA.

Etas Periodici SpA: Via Mecenate 86/7, 20138 Milan; tel. (02) 5075; telex 331342; technical periodicals; Man. Dir Dott. EUGENIO DE ROSA.

Editrice Piccoli Srl: Via Santa Sofia 10, 20122 Milan; tel. (02) 861847; f. 1944; children's books; Chair. AURELIO PICCO.

Rcs Editore SpA: Via Angelo Rizzoli 2, 20132 Milan; f. 1929; newspapers, magazines and books; Chair. ANTONIO COPPI; Man. Dir GIORGIO FATTORI.

ITALY

Riccardo Ricciardi Editore SpA: Via Alessandro Manzoni 10, 20121 Milan; f. 1907; classics, philology, history, literature; Gen. Man. Dott. MAURIZIO MATTIOLI.

G. and C. Ricordi SpA: Via Berchet 2, 20121 Milan; tel. (02) 88811; telex 310177; f. 1808; academic, art, music; Chair. GIANNI BABINI; Man. Dir GUIDO RIGNANO.

Rusconi Libri SpA: Via Livraghi 1B, 20126 Milan; tel. (02) 2574141; telex 312233; f. 1969; books; Pres. EDILIO RUSCONI; Gen. Man. FERRUCCIO VIVIANI.

Libri Scheiwiller: Via Sacchi 3, 20121 Milan; f. 1977; art, literature and archaeology; Chair. GIANCARLO LUNATI; Man. Dir VANNI SCHEIWILLER.

L'Editrice Scientifica: Via Ariberto 20, 20123 Milan; tel. (02) 8390274; f. 1949; university publications in chemistry and medicine; Dirs Dotts. LEONARDA and GUIDO GUADAGNI.

Edizioni Scolastiche Bruno Mondadori: Via Archimede 23, 20129 Milan; tel. (02) 5456036; f. 1946; textbooks and educational books; Chair. and Man. Dir ROBERTA MONDADORI; Man. Dir ROBERTO GULLI; Gen. Man. MARIO CANDIANI.

Selezione dal Reader's Digest SpA: Via Alserio 10, 20159 Milan; tel. (02) 69871; telex 330378; f. 1948; educational, reference, general interest; Man. Dir EDOARDO LUCHESCHI.

Carlo Signorelli SpA: Via Siusi 7, 20132 Milan; children's and textbooks, dictionaries.

La Sorgente: Via Garofalo 44, 20133 Milan; tel. (02) 230720; f. 1936; children's books; Man. Dir Dr GIORGIO VIGNATI.

Sugarco Edizioni: Viale Tunisia 41, 20124 Milan; tel. (02) 652192; f. 1957; fiction, biography, history, philosophy, guidebooks; Chair. PAOLO PILLITTERI; Gen. Man. VINCENZO NAGARI.

Casa Editrice Luigi Trevisini: Via Tito Livio 12, Milan; tel. (02) 5450704; f. 1849; school textbooks; Dirs ENRICO TREVISINI, LUIGI TREVISINI.

Il Vaglio Cultura Arte: Via Vitruvio 39, 20124 Milan; tel. (02) 2846903; f. 1985; art and architecture; *Arte Lombarda nuova serie* (4 a year); Man. Prof. MARIA LUISA GATTI PERER.

Vita e Pensiero: Largo A. Gemelli 1, 20123 Milan; tel. (02) 8856335; telex 321033; f. 1918; publisher to the Catholic University of the Sacred Heart; cultural, scientific books and magazines.

Naples

Casa Editrice Libraria Idelson: Via Alcide De Gasperi 55, 80133 Naples; tel. (081) 5524733; f. 1908; medicine, psychology, biology; CEO GUIDO GNOCCHI.

Liguori Editore: Via Mezzocannone 19, 80134 Naples; tel. (081) 206077; f. 1949; linguistics, mathematics, engineering, economics, law, history, philosophy, sociology; Man. Dir Dott. ROLANDO LIGUORI.

Gaetano Macchiaroli Editore: Via Michetti 11, 80127, Naples; tel. (081) 5780568; archaeology, classical studies, history, philosophy, political science.

Società Editrice Napoletana: Corso Umberto I 34, 80138 Naples; tel. (081) 206602; f. 1973; art, poetry, literature, history; Dir A. DE DOMINICIS.

Novara

Instituto Geografico De Agostini-Novara: Via Giovanni da Verrazano 15, 28100 Novara; tel. (0321) 4241; telex 200290; geography, maps, encyclopaedias, dictionaries, art, literature, textbooks, science; Chair. ADOLFO BOROLI; Man. Dirs MARCO BOROLI, MARCO DRAGO.

Padova

CEDAM—Casa Editrice Dr A. Milani: Via Jappelli 5/6, 35121 Padova; tel. (049) 656677; f. 1902; law, economics, political and social sciences, engineering, science, medicine, literature, philosophy, textbooks; Dirs ANTONIO MILANI, CARLO PORTA.

Libreria Editrice Gregoriana: Via Roma 82, 35122 Padova; tel. (049) 661033; f. 1922; *Lexicon Totius Latinitatis*, religion, philosophy, psychology, social studies; Dir DON GIANCARLO MINOZZI.

Libreria Editrice Internazionale Zannoni e Figlio: Corso Garibaldi 14, 35122 Padova; tel. (049) 44170; f. 1919; medicine, technical books, scholastic books, miscellaneous; Dir GIULIANA ZANNONI.

Liviana Editrice: Via L. Dottesio 1, 35138 Padova; tel. (049) 8710099; f. 1948; secondary-school and university textbooks, journals and essays; Pres. LUIGI VECCHIA; Gen. Man. Dott. GIORGIO RACCIS.

Piccin Nuova Libraria SpA: Via Altinate 107, 35100 Padova; tel. (049) 655566; telex 432074; f. 1980; scientific textbooks and journals; Man. Dir Dr MASSIMO PICCIN.

Valmartina Editore: Via L. Dottesio 1, 35138 Padova; tel. (049) 8710195; foreign languages, guide books.

Rome

Armando Armando Editore Srl: Piazza Sidney Sonnino 13, 00153 Rome; tel. (06) 5806620; philosophy, psychology, social sciences, languages, ecology, education; Man. Dir ENRICO JACOMETTI.

Edizioni Borla Srl: Via delle Fornaci 50, 00165 Rome; tel. (06) 6381618; f. 1863; religion, philosophy, psychoanalysis, ethnology, literature, novels for teenagers; Man. Dir VINCENZO D'AGOSTINO.

Edizioni d'Arte di Carlo E. Bestetti & C. Sas: Via di San Giacomo 18, 00187 Rome; tel. (06) 6790174; f. 1947; art, architecture, industry; Man. Dir CARLO BESTETTI.

Ausonia: Viale dei Primati Sportivi 27, EUR, 00144 Rome; tel. (06) 595959; f. 1919; textbooks; Pres. E. LUCCHINI; Gen. Man. G. LUCCHINI.

AVE (Anonima Veritas Editrice): Via Aurelia 481, 00165 Rome; tel. (06) 6233041; f. 1935; theology, sociology, pedagogy, psychology, essays, learned journals, religious textbooks; Man. Dir ANTONIO SANTANGELO.

Vito Bianco Editore: Via Messina 31, 00198 Rome; tel. (06) 8443151; telex 621401; various, especially marine publications; Chair. Dott. VITO BIANCO.

Bulzoni Editore—Le edizioni universitarie d'Italia: Via dei Liburni 14, 00185 Rome; tel. (06) 4455207; f. 1969; science, arts, fiction, textbooks; Man. Dir MARIO BULZONI.

E. Calzono: Via del Collegio Romano 9, Rome; f. 1872; art, archaeology, philosophy, science, religion, economics; Dir Dr RICCARDO GAMBERINI MONGENET.

Editrice Ciranna: Via Capograssa 115, 04010 Borgo San Michele-Latina, Rome; tel. (0773) 250746; f. 1940; school textbooks; Man. Dir LIDIA FABIANO.

Armando Curcio Editore SpA: Via Arno 64, 00198 Rome; tel. (06) 84871; telex 614666; f. 1954; encyclopaedias, classics, history, science, reference, geography, art; Chair. Dr ALDO STACCHI; Man. Dir SILVIO ROTUNNO.

Editrice Dante Alighieri (Albrighi, Segati & C.): Via Timavo 3, 00195 Rome; tel. (06) 383491; f. 1928; school textbooks, science and general culture; Pres. SALVATORE SPINELLI; Man. Dir SILVANO SPINELLI.

Edizioni Europa: Via G.B. Martini 6, 00198 Rome; tel. (06) 8449124; f. 1944; essays, literature, art, history, politics, music, economics; Chair. Prof. PIER FAUSTO PALUMBO.

Hermes Edizioni Srl: Via Flaminia 158, 00196 Rome; tel. (06) 3601656; f. 1979; alternative medicine, astrology, nature, dietetics; Gen. Man. GIOVANNI CANONICO.

Giuseppe Laterza e Figli SpA: Via di Villa Sacchetti 17, 00197 Rome; tel. (06) 803693; f. 1885; belles lettres, biography, reference, religion, art, classics, history, economics, philosophy, social science; Man. Dir VITO LATERZA; Editorial Dir ENRICO MISTRETTA.

Le Edizioni del Lavoro: Via Boncompagni 19, 00187 Rome; tel. (06) 4746420; f. 1979; history, politics, economics, philology, sociology, periodicals; Chair. and Man. Dir LUCA BORGOMEO.

Guida Monaci SpA: Via Vitorchiano 107, 00189 Rome; tel. (06) 3288805; telex 623234; f. 1870; commercial and industrial, financial, administrative and medical directories; publishes *Annuario Generale Italiano, Annuario Amministrativo Italiano, Chi Sono Nelle Attività Italiane, Chi Sono Nelle Attività Amministrative, Chi Sono Nelle Attività Sanitarie, Annuario Sanitarie, Agenda* Ediz. Nazionale e Regionali (yearly); Dir ALBERTO ZAPPONINI.

Fratelli Palombi Srl: Via dei Gracchi 181-185, 00192 Rome; tel. (06) 354960; f. 1914; history, art, etc. of Rome; Man. Dir Dott. MARIO PALOMBI.

Jandi Sapi Editori Srl: Via Crescenzio 62, 00193 Rome; tel. (06) 6545515; f. 1941; industrial and legal publications; Dir Dr FRANCO VOLPINI.

Angelo Signorelli: Via Falconieri 84, 00152 Rome; tel. (06) 539954; f. 1912; science, general literature, textbooks; Man. Dirs GIORGIO SIGNORELLI, GILBERTA ALPA.

Edizioni Studium: Via Cassiodoro 14, 00193 Rome; tel. (06) 6875456; f. 1927; philosophy, literature, sociology, pedagogy, religion, economics, law, science, history, psychology; periodical *Studium*.

Stresa

Libraria Editoriale Sodalitas Sas: Centro Internazionale Studi Rosminiani, Corso Umberto 15, 28049 Stresa; tel. (0323) 31623; f. 1925; philosophy, theology, *Rivista Rosminiana* (quarterly); Dir Prof. PIER PAOLO OTTONELLO.

Trento

G.B. Monauni: Trento; tel. (0461) 21445; f. 1725; art, archaeology, ethnology, folklore, science, history; Man. Dir Dott. G. B. MONAUNI.

ITALY

Turin

Editrice L'Artist Modern: Via Garibaldi 59, 10121 Turin; tel. (011) 541371; f. 1901; art; Dir. F. NELVA.

Bollati Boringhieri Editore SpA: Corso Vittorio Emanuele II 86, 10121 Turin; f. 1957; psychology, social and human sciences, fiction and classical literature; Chair. ROMILDA BOLLATI; Man. Dir GIULIO BOLLATI.

Giulio Einaudi Editore SpA; Via Umberto Biancamano 1, CP 245, 10121 Turin; tel. (011) 533653; telex 220344; f. 1933; fiction, classics, general; Gen. Man. GIULIO EINAUDI.

Giorgio Giappichelli Editore Sas: Via Po 21, 10124 Turin; tel. (011) 8397019; f. 1921; university publications on literature, law, economics, politics and sociology.

Lattes S. e C. Editori: Via Confienza 6, 10121 Turin; f. 1893; technical, textbooks; Pres. MARIO LATTES.

Levrotto e Bella, Libreria Editrice Universitaria: Corso Vittorio Emanuele II 26, 10123 Turin; tel. (011) 832535; f. 1942; university textbooks; Man. Dir TERENZIO GUALINI.

Loescher: Via Vittorio Amedeo II 18, 10121 Turin; tel. (011) 549333; f. 1867; school textbooks, general literature, academic books; Chair. MAURIZIO PAVIA.

Edizioni Minerva Medica: Corso Bramante 83–85, 10126 Turin; tel. (011) 678282; medical books and journals; Dir PAOLO OLIARO.

Petrini: Corso Trapani 48, 10139 Turin; tel. (011) 3358641; f. 1872; school textbooks; Dir VITTORIO GALLEA.

Rosenberg & Sellier: Via Andrea Doria 14, 10123 Turin; tel. (011) 532150; telex 224202; f. 1979; philology, social sciences, literature, philosophy; Chair. UGO GIANNI ROSENBERG; Man. Dir KATIE ROGGERO.

Società Editrice Internazionale SpA (SEI): Corso Regina Margherita 176, 10152 Turin; tel. (011) 5211441; telex 216216; f. 1908; textbooks, fiction, art, literature, philosophy, children's books, etc.; Man. Dir Dr GIAN NICOLA PIVANO.

Unione Tipografico-Editrice Torinese (UTET): Corso Raffaello 28, 10125 Turin; tel. (011) 6502184; f. 1795; university and specialized editions on history, geography, art, literature, economics, law, sciences, encyclopaedias, dictionaries, etc.; Pres. Dott. GIANNI MERLINI.

Venice

Alfieri Edizioni d'Arte: San Marco 1991, Cannaregio 6099, 30124 Venice; tel. (041) 5223323; f. 1939; modern art, Venetian art, architecture, periodicals; Chair. GIORGIO FANTONI; Gen. Man. MASSIMO VITTA ZELMAN.

Marsilio Editori: S. Croce 518A, Fondamenta S. Chiara, 30135 Venice; tel. (041) 5207188; f. 1961; literature, arts, fiction, history, music, cinema, philosophy, social sciences; Man. Dirs Dott. EMANUELA BASSETTI, Dott. PAOLO LENARDA, Dott. MARIA CONCETIA FOZZER.

Verona

Bertani Editore Srl: Via S. Salvatore Corte Regia 4, 37121 Verona; tel. (045) 32686; f. 1973; politics, literature, anthropology, sociology, theatre, cinema, geography, humanities, history of Verona, psychology, cultural journals; Man. Dir MARIO QUARANTA; Editorial Dir GIORGIO BERTANI.

Arnoldo Mondadori Editore: Via Arnoldo Mondadori 15, 37131 Verona; tel. (045) 934602; telex 480071; f. 1946; children's books; Man. Editor ALESSANDRO DALAI; Man. Ed. MARGHERITA FORESTAN.

Vicenza

Neri Pozza Editore: Contrà Oratorio dei Servi 19–21, 36100 Vicenza; tel. (0444) 320787; f. 1946; art, fiction, history, politics; Man. Dir NERI POZZA.

Government Publishing House

Istituto Poligrafico e Zecca dello Stato: Piazza Verdi 10, 00198 Rome; tel. (06) 85081; f. 1928; State publishing house (Italian State Stationery Office); art books and reproductions; Chair. GIUSEPPE LA LOGGIA; Gen. Dir ALFREDO MAGGI.

PUBLISHERS' ASSOCIATION

Associazione Italiana Editori: Via Delle Erbe 2, 20121 Milan; tel. (02) 8059244; telex 335550; f. 1869; Via Crescenzio 19, 00193 Rome; tel. (06) 6540298; Pres. CARLO ENRICO RIVOLTA; Sec.-Gen. ACHILLE ORMEZZANO.

Radio and Television

In 1986 there were an estimated 14,817,162 radio receivers and 14,605,448 television receivers in use.

In April 1975 a law was passed designed to guarantee the political independence of the RAI and the objectivity of its news coverage. Notably, the new law sought to increase the autonomy of the two existing television channels and to reinforce parliamentary supervision of programme planning. Since the state monopoly on broadcasting was abolished in 1976, approximately 450 local private commercial television stations have been set up all over Italy. Although electronically-transmitted national networks in competition to RAI are technically illegal, seven stations in particular are national networks. A thousand private local radio stations have also begun broadcasting since a court case in 1975 established the right of every citizen to free local information. In 1987 the Italian Constitutional Court granted private radio stations permission to launch commercial international stations.

Radiotelevisione Italiana (RAI-TV): Viale Mazzini 14, 00195 Rome; tel. (06) 3878; telex 61142; f. 1924; a public share capital company; a permanent parliamentary commission of senators and deputies from all political groups formulates and oversees general guidelines for programmes; the board of directors nominates the President and Vice-President from within its members and appoints the Director-General; Pres. ENRICO MANCA; Vice-Pres. Prof. GIAMPIERO ORSELLO; Dir-Gen. Dr BIAGIO AGNES.

RADIO

Programmes comprise the National Programme (general), Second Programme (recreational), Third Programme (educational); there are also regional programmes in Italian and in the languages of ethnic minorities. The Foreign and Overseas Service (Radio Roma) broadcasts in 27 languages to Africa, the Americas, Australia, Europe, Japan, the Near East and South Asia.

TELEVISION

There are three RAI television channels, RAI Uno, RAI Due and RAI Tre. There are local programmes in Italian and also in German for the Alto Adige. Seven private stations (Canale 5, Dee Jay TV, Video Music, Euro TV, Italia Uno, Rete A and Rete Quattro) have nationwide networks.

Canale 5: Palazzo dei Cigni, Milano 2, 20090 Segrate, Milan; tel. (02) 21621; telex 316197; f. 1979.

Italia Uno: Via F. Testi 7, 200090 Milan; tel. 6073881.

Rete Quattro: Via Marconi 27, 20090 Segrate, Milan; tel. 216001.

Finance

(cap. = capital; p.u. = paid up; res = reserves; dep. = deposits; m. = million; brs = branches; amounts in lire)

There are more than 1,000 banks in Italy, with a total of over 13,000 branches. Many of them are state controlled, including the majority of the large banks. There are more than 100 private banks, and a large number of co-operative and savings banks (*banche popolari, casse di risparmio, casse rurali*) of widely ranging size and importance. In addition, there are 90 specialized credit institutions which provide medium- and long-term finance, and other services outside the scope of the banks. In early 1987 reforms giving the Central Bank the right to authorize commercial banks to establish merchant banking subsidiaries were announced.

BANKING
Central Bank

Banca d'Italia: Via Nazionale 91, 00184 Rome; tel. (06) 47921; telex 610021; f. 1893; cap. 300m., res 2,664,879m. (Dec. 1986); since 1926 the Bank has had the sole right to issue notes in Italy; Gov. Dott. CARLO AZEGLIO CIAMPI; Gen. Man. Dott. LAMBERTO DINI; 98 brs.

Major Commercial Banks

Banca Agricola Mantovana SpA: Corso Vittorio Emanuele 30, 46100 Mantova; tel. (0376) 3311; telex 300435; f. 1870; cap. 2,823m., res 662,861m., dep. 3,309,163m. (Dec. 1987); Pres. PIERMARIA PACCHIONI; Gen. Man. MARCELLO MELANI; 95 brs.

Banca Agricola Milanese SpA: Via Mazzini 9–11, 20123 Milan; tel. (02) 88091; telex 310608; f. 1874; cap. 34,500m., res 332,841m., dep. 2,443,033m. (Dec. 1986); Pres. FRANCESCO CESARINI; Gen. Man. ADRIANO PINCHERLE; 46 brs.

Banca d'America e d'Italia SpA (BAI): Via Borgogna 8, 20122 Milan; tel. (02) 77951; telex 311350; f. 1918; cap. 46,246m., res 802,704m. (1987); Chair. VINCENZO POLLI; Man. Dir GIANEMILIO OSCULATI; 98 brs.

Banca Antoniana di Padova e Trieste: Via 8 Febbraio 5, 35100 Padova; tel. (049) 839111; telex 430252; f. 1893; cap. 5,937m., res

ITALY

519,901m., dep. 4,670,932m. (Dec. 1987); Pres. Dr DINO MARCHIORELLO; Gen. Man. ANICETO VITTORIO RANIERI; 48 brs.

Banca Cattolica del Veneto SpA: Via dell'Industria, 36040 Torri di Quartesolo, Vicenza; tel. (0444) 519111; telex 434240; f. 1892; dep. 5,586,542m., total assets 10,034,739m. (June 1988); Chair. FELICIANO BENVENUTI; CEO and Man. Dir DOMENICO SPEDALE; Gen. Man. CARLO EMANUELE GALLONE; 204 brs.

Banca Commerciale Italiana SpA (COMIT): Piazza della Scala 6, 20121 Milan; tel. (02) 88501; telex 310080; f. 1894; cap. 630,000m., res 3,327,000m., dep. 59,043,000m. (Dec. 1986); Chair. Dott. FRANCESCO CINGANO; Gen. Mans M. ARCARI, E. BENEDULE, F. BONICALZA, C. CAMMILLI, L. FAUSTI; 455 brs, including many overseas brs.

Banca Credito Agrario Bresciano SpA: Via Trieste 8, 25175 Brescia; tel. (030) 22931; telex 301558; f. 1883; cap. 75,000m., res 139,945m., dep. 3,683,888m. (Dec. 1987); Chair. DOMENICO BIANCHI; Man. Dir CORRADO FAISSOLA; Gen. Man. VOLFANGO SOMMAZZI; 77 brs.

Banca del Friuli SpA: Via Vittorio Veneto 20, 33100 Udine; tel. (0432) 4921; telex 450152; f. 1872; cap. 24,000m.; res 416,598m.; dep. 3,664,034m. (Dec. 1987); Pres. Dott. PAOLO MALIGNANI; Gen. Man. LORENZO SCARPIS; 81 brs.

Banca Nazionale dell'Agricoltura SpA: Via Salaria 231, 00199 Rome; tel. (06) 85881; telex 612121; f. 1921; total assets 31,579,500m. (Dec. 1986); Chair. Count Dott. GIOVANNI AULETTA ARMENISE; Man. Dirs Prof. FREDERICO PEPE, ULPIANO QUARANTA; 209 brs including brs abroad.

Banca Nazionale delle Comunicazioni: Via S. Martino della Battaglia 4, 00185 Rome; tel. (06) 46761; telex 625593; f. 1927; cap. 9,549m., res 148,128m., dep. 2,507,239m. (Dec. 1985); Pres. Dr GIUSEPPE CADARIO; Gen. Man. GIORGIO QUATTRINI; 17 brs.

Banca Nazionale del Lavoro: Via Vittorio Veneto 119, 00187 Rome; tel. (06) 47021; telex 610116; f. 1913; total assets 98,727,000m. (1986); Chair. of the Board Dott. NERIO NESI; Man. Dir and Chief Gen. Man. Prof. FRANCESCO BIGNARDI; 414 brs incl. 11 overseas brs.

Banca Popolare Commercio e Industria Srl: Via della Moscova 33, 20121 Milan; tel. (02) 62751; telex 310276; f. 1888; cap. 10,426m., res 345,927m., dep. 3,544,023m. (Dec. 1987); Chair. ENRICO GIANZINI; Gen. Man. GIUSEPPE VIGORELLI; 20 brs.

Banca Popolare dell' Emilia Srl: Via San Carlo 8/20, 41100 Modena; tel. (059) 202111; telex 511392; f. 1867; cap. 2,528m., res 503,985m., dep. 3,314,238m. (Dec. 1987); Chair. Avv. PIER LUIGI COLIZZI; Gen. Man. Avv. FAUSTO BATTINI; 80 brs.

Banca Popolare di Bergamo Srl: Piazza Vittorio Veneto 8, 24100 Bergamo; tel. (035) 392111; telex 300410; f. 1869; co-operative bank; cap. 28,145m., res 1,250,816m., dep. 8,836,706m. (Dec. 1987); Chair. E. ZANETTI; Gen. Man. GIUSEPPE A. BANFI; 126 brs.

Banca Popolare di Cremona Srl: Via Cesare Battisti 14, 26100 Cremona; tel. (0372) 4041; telex 321099; f. 1865; cap. 7,545m., res 179,839m., dep. 1,084,101m. (Dec. 1986); Pres. Dott. ANGELO DUCHI; Gen. Man. Dott. FRANCO CARNIGLIA; 28 brs.

Banca Popolare di Lecco SpA: Piazza Garibaldi 12, 22053 Lecco; tel. (0341) 480111; telex 380003; f. 1872; cap. 64,444m., res 302,691m., dep. 3,840,479m. (Dec. 1987); Pres. Dott. GIANCARLO BELLEMO; Gen. Man. Rag. B. BRUMANA; 60 brs.

Banca Popolare di Milano Srl: Piazza F. Meda 4, 20121 Milan; tel. (02) 77001; telex 310202; f. 1865; cap. 34,038m., res 1,279,124m., dep. 16,823,109m. (Dec. 1985); Pres. PIERO SCHLESINGER; Gen. Man. ALDO COVA; 20 brs.

Banca Popolare di Novara Srl: Via Carlo Negroni 12, 28100 Novara; tel. (0321) 4451; telex 200371; f. 1871; co-operative bank; cap. 47,128m., res 2,022,034m., dep. 20,128,781m. (Dec. 1987); Chair. ROBERTO DI TIERI; Man. Dirs PIERO BONGIANINO, CARLO PIANTANIDA; 382 brs and agencies.

Banca Popolare Veneta Srl: Piazza Salvemini 18, 35131 Padova; tel. (049) 843111; telex 430868; f. 1866; cap. 13,465m., res 333,486m., dep. 3,240,194m. (Dec. 1986); Chair. Dott. GIORGIO DE BENEDETTI; Gen. Man. Dott. ANTONIO CEOLA; 83 brs and agencies.

Banca Popolare di Verona Srl: Piazza Nogara 2, 37100 Verona; tel. (045) 930111; telex 480009; f. 1867; cap. 7,699m., res 1,044,926m., dep. 5,078,916m. (Dec. 1987); Pres. Prof. GIORGIO ZANOTTO; Gen. Man. GIANFRANCO DEL NERO; 89 brs and agencies.

Banca Provinciale Lombarda SpA: Via Gennaro Sora 4, 24100 Bergamo; tel. (035) 394111; telex 300140; f. 1932; cap. 120,000m., res 482,007m., dep. 7,370,239m. (Dec. 1987); Chair. CARLO GAY; Man. Dir GIUSEPPE MAZZARELLO; 144 brs.

Banca San Paolo-Brescia SpA: POB 346, Corso Martiri della Libertà 13, 25100 Brescia; tel. (030) 29921; telex 300010; f. 1888; cap. 70,000m., res 333,685m., dep. 4,739,220m. (Dec. 1986); Pres. Dott. Ing. ADOLFO LOMBARDI; Gen. Man. Dott. ALBERTO VALDEMBRI; 78 brs.

Banca Toscana SpA: Via del Corso 6, 50122 Florence; tel. (055) 43911; telex 570507; f. 1904; total assets 12,983,000m. (Dec. 1986); Pres. GIUSEPPE BARTOLOMEI; Man. Dir. FABIO TAITI; 182 brs.

Banca Popolare Vicentina Srl (fmrly Banca Popolare di Vicenza): Via Battaglione Framarin 18, 36100 Vicenza; tel. (0444) 991111; telex 480092; cap. 3,993m., res 386,630m., dep. 2,401,475m. (Dec. 1987); Pres. GIUSEPPE NARDINI; Gen. Man. CARLO PAVESI.

Banco Lariano SpA: Piazza Cavour 15, 22100 Como; tel. (031) 271356; telex 380018; f. 1908; cap. 250,000m., res 628,409m., dep. 7,785,156m. (Dec. 1986); Chair. Dr ROBERTO ARDIGÀ; Gen. Man. Dott. ANTONIO ROMANO; 125 brs.

Banco di Napoli: Via Toledo 177-178, 80132 Naples; tel. (081) 7911111; telex 710570; f. 1539; chartered public institution with no shareholders; total assets 60,430,000m. (Dec. 1986); Chair. Prof. LUIGI COCCIOLI; CEO Prof. FERDINANDO VENTRIGLIA; 500 brs.

Banco di Roma SpA: Viale U. Tupini 180, 00144 Rome; tel. (06) 54451; telex 616184; f. 1880; total assets 67,849,700m. (Dec. 1986); Chair. ANTONIO ZURZULO; Man. Dirs Dott. ERCOLE CECCATELLI, Dott. MARCELLO TACCI; 333 brs including agencies and overseas brs.

Banco San Geminiano e San Prospero SpA: Via dei Servi 22, 41100 Modena; tel. (059) 200111; telex 510603; f. 1897; cap. 24,000m., res 554,623m., dep. 3,808,170m. (Dec. 1986); Chair. GUSTAVO VIGNOCCHI; Gen. Man. FRANCO FRANCESCHINI; 80 brs.

Banco di Santo Spirito SpA: Largo A. Fochetti 16, 00154 Rome; tel. (06) 51721; telex 610162; f. 1605; cap. 1,034,100m., total assets 53,199,600m. (Dec. 1986); Chair. RODOLFO RINALDI; Man. Dir ELIO TARTAGLIA; 238 brs.

Banco di Sardegna: Viale Umberto 36, 07100 Sassari; tel. (079) 279111; telex 790049; f. 1953; public credit institution; cap. 139,000m., res 395,888m., dep. 5,674,804m. (1986); Pres. and Chair. Dr ANGELO SOLINAS; Gen. Man. Dr ANGELO GIAGU DE MARTINI; 76 brs.

Banco di Sicilia: Via Generale Magliocco 1, 90141 Palermo; tel. (091) 274111; telex 910050; f. 1860; public credit institution; total assets 35,133,016m. (Dec. 1987); Chair. Prof. GIANNINO PARRAVICINI; Gen. Man. and CEO Dr OTTAVIO SALAMONE; 348 brs.

Cassa Centrale di Risparmio VE per le Province Siciliane: Piazza Cassa di Risparmio 4, 90133 Palermo; tel. (091) 273111; telex 910029; f. 1861; savings bank; cap. and res 320,161m., dep. 4,787,365m. (Dec. 1985); Pres. Dott. GIOVANNI FERRARO; Gen. Man. Dott. AGOSTINO MULÈ; 230 brs.

Cassa di Risparmi e Depositi di Prato: Via degli Alberti 2, 50047 Prato; tel. (0574) 4921; telex 572382; f. 1830; savings bank; cap. 160,040m., res 222,635m., dep. 3,501,060m. (Dec. 1986); Pres. Avv. MAURO GIOVANNELLI; Gen. Man. Dott. VITTORIO POSTIGLIONE; 22 brs.

Cassa di Risparmio di Firenze: Via Bufalini 4/6, 50122 Florence; tel. (055) 27801; telex 572391; f. 1829; commercial bank; res 802,951m., dep. 7,151,126m. (Dec. 1987); Chair. and Pres. LAPO MAZZEI; Gen. Man. LUIGI TINTI; 170 brs.

Cassa di Risparmio di Genova e Imperia: Via Cassa di Risparmio 15, 16123 Genova; tel. (010) 20911; telex 270089; f. 1846; res 862,336m., dep. 6,038,088m. (Dec. 1987); Pres. Avv. GIOVANNI DAGNINO; Gen. Man. Dott. GIOVAN BATTISTA VILLA; 132 brs.

Cassa di Risparmio della Provincia di Bolzano—Südtiroler Landessparkasse: Via Cassa di Risparmio 12B, 39100 Bolzano; tel. (0471) 901111; telex 400090; f. 1854; cap. 14,086m., res 167,708m., dep. 2,147,052m. (Dec. 1985); Pres. Avv. JOSEF BRANDSTÄTTER; Gen. Man. Dott. FRANZ OBERMAIR; 49 brs.

Cassa di Risparmio delle Provincie Lombarde (CARIPLO): Via Monte di Pietà 8, 20100 Milan; tel. (02) 88661; telex 313010; f. 1823; savings bank; total assets 57,044,800m., (Dec. 1986); Chair. ROBERTO MAZZOTTA; Man. Dir SANDRO MOLINARI; 439 brs and agencies.

Cassa di Risparmio di Roma: Via del Corso 320, 00186 Rome; tel. (06) 67071; telex 613541; f. 1836; savings bank; cap. 115,000m., res 212,014m., dep. 16,787,931m. (Dec. 1986); Chair. Prof. PELLEGRINO CAPALDO; Gen. Man. CESARE GERONZI; 157 brs.

Cassa di Risparmio di Torino: Via XX Settembre 31, 10121 Turin; tel. (011) 57661; telex 212278; f. 1827; savings bank; res 1,698,602m., dep. 15,936,685m. (Dec. 1987); Chair. Prof. ENRICO FILIPPI; Man. Dirs ALESSANDRO CONFORTI, GIANFRANCO PENONE, NATALE MONZEGLIO; 222 brs.

Cassa di Risparmio di Venezia: San Marco 4216, 30124 Venice; tel. (041) 5207644; telex 410049; cap. and res 575,254m., dep. 3,136,259m. (Dec. 1987); Pres. Prof. GIULIANO SEGRE; Gen. Man. Rag. PAOLO BORTOLUZZI; 70 brs.

Cassa di Risparmio di Verona, Vicenza e Belluno: Via G. Garibaldi 1, 37121 Verona; tel. (045) 936111; telex 480056; f. 1825; res 739,828m., dep. 7,645,801m. (Dec. 1986); Pres. Avv. ALBERTO PAVESI; Gen. Man. Rag. ANTONIO FINOTTI; 147 brs.

ITALY

Credito Commerciale SpA: Via Armorari 4, 20123 Milan; tel. (02) 88241; telex 321573; f. 1907; subsidiary of Monte dei Paschi de Siena; total assets 14,971,168m. (Dec. 1986); Pres. CESARE PANIZZA; Gen. Man. Rag. GIOVANNI DELLA ROSA; 68 brs.

Credito Emiliano: Via Emilia S. Pietro 4, 42100 Reggio-Emilia; tel. (0522) 4651; telex 530305; f. 1910; cap. 27.9m., res 267,825m., dep. 2,906,887m. (Dec. 1986); Pres. GIORGIO FERRARI; Gen. Man. FRANCO BIZZOCHI; 52 brs.

Credito Italiano SpA: Piazza Cordusio 2, 20123 Milan; tel. (02) 88621; telex 312401; f. 1870; cap. and res 3,083,219m., dep. 51,442,140m. (Dec. 1987); Chair. Prof. NATALINO IRTI; Man. Dirs LUCIO RONDELLI, PIER CARLO MARENGO; 496 brs including six overseas.

Credito Lombardo SpA: Via San Pietro all'Orto 24, 20121 Milan; tel. (02) 77361; telex 334889; f. 1924; cap. 4,000m., res 164,413m., dep. 1,769,064m. (Dec. 1985); Pres. Dr VIRGILIO DAGNINO; Gen. Man. ENRICO C. MASSONE; 8 brs.

Credito Romagnolo SpA: POB 775, Via Zamboni 20, 40126 Bologna; tel. (051) 338111; telex 510131; f. 1896; cap. 60,927m., res 1,287,917m., dep. 11,622,256m. (Dec. 1986); Pres. Dr LUIGI DESERTI; Gen. Man. MARIO FANTINI; 193 brs.

Credito Varesino SpA: Via Vittorio Veneto 2, 21100 Varese; tel. (0332) 253111; telex 326695; f. 1898; cap. 60,000m., res 376,968m., dep. 4,696,837m. (Dec. 1987); Chair. RINALDO OSSOLA; Chief Gen. Man. PIERO FORTI; 66 brs.

Istituto Bancario Italiano SpA (IBI): Via Manzoni 3, 20121 Milan; tel. (02) 88901; telex 321434; f. 1918; cap. 150,000m., res 169,922m., dep. 6,456,000m. (Dec. 1986); Chair. GIAMPIERO CANTONI; Gen. Man. CARLO GILTRI; 69 brs.

Istituto Bancario San Paolo di Torino: Piazza San Carlo 156, 10121 Turin; tel. (011) 5551; telex 212040; Public Law Bank; f. 1563; cap. 2,000,000m., res 3,628,491m., dep. 65,226,279m. (Dec. 1987); Chair. Prof. GIOVANNI ZANDANO; Chief Gen. Man. Prof. ZEFFERINO FRANCO; 411 brs including overseas brs.

Monte dei Paschi di Siena: Piazza Salimbeni 3, 53100 Siena; tel. (0577) 294111; telex 572346; f. 1472; public law credit institution; total assets 73,042,168m. (Dec. 1987); Chair. PIERO BARUCCI; CEO and Chief Gen. Man. CARLO ZINI; Exec. Vice-Pres. and Gen. Man. (international) ATTILIO BORDOGNA; 469 brs in Italy; rep. offices in London, Cairo, Frankfurt, New York, São Paulo and Singapore.

Nuovo Banco Ambrosiano SpA (NBA): Piazza Paolo Ferrari 10, 20121 Milan; tel. (02) 85941; telex 335687; f. 1982 (formerly Banco Ambrosiano, f. 1896); 65% owned by a consortium of 8 banks, 13% owned by one financial company and 35% owned by 50,000 private shareholders; total assets 10,083,904m. (June 1987); Chair. GIOVANNI BAZOLI; CEO and Gen. Man. GINO TROMBI; 132 brs.

FINANCIAL INSTITUTIONS

CENTROBANCA (Banca Centrale di Credito Popolare) SpA: Corso Europa 20, 20122 Milan; tel. (02) 77811; telex 320387; f. 1946; cap. 150,000m., res 479,738m., dep. 7,002,135m. (Dec. 1986); central organization for medium- and long-term operations of Banche Popolari (co-operative banks) throughout Italy; Chair. LINO VENINI; Gen. Man. GIAN GIACONO FAVERIO; 234 brs.

Consorzio di Credito per le Opere Pubbliche (CREDIOP): Via Quintino Sella 2, 00187 Rome; tel. (06) 47711; telex 611020; f. 1919; cap. and res 1,045,275m.; provides loans to industrial, commercial and service companies, medium- and long-term loans to public authorities and their agencies, and export credits; Pres. and Chair. Ing. PAOLO BARATTA; Gen. Man. Dr GIORGIO CIGLIANA.

INTERBANCA (Banca per Finanziamenti a Medio e Lungo Termine SpA): Corso Venezia 56, 20121 Milan; tel. (02) 77311; telex 312649; cap. 45,644m., res 112,806m. (May 1985); Pres. GIORGIO CAPPON; Gen. Man. GASTONE TESTA.

Istituto Mobiliare Italiano (IMI): Viale dell'Arte 25, 00144 Rome; tel. (06) 54501; telex 610256; f. 1931; public-law credit institute; specializes in medium- and long-term finance for industry and public utilities, merchant banking, personal financial services and asset management. These facilities are also available to foreign concerns willing to make productive investment in Italy or to import Italian-made capital goods; cap. p.u. 1,650,000m.; legal res 1,249,000m.; outstanding loans 27,864,000m. (March 1987); Pres. Dr LUIGI ARCUTI; Dir-Gen. RAINER MASERA; 10 regional offices in Italy.

Istituto per l'Assistenza allo Sviluppo del Mezzogiorno (IASM) (Institute for assistance in the development of southern Italy): Viale Pilsudski 124, 00197 Rome; tel. (06) 84721; telex 680232; f. 1962; aids investment to promote economic development in the South; Pres. Dr NINO NOVACCO.

Istituto Regionale per il Finanziamento alle Industrie in Sicilia (IRFIS): Via Giovanni Bonanno 47, 90143 Palermo; tel. (091) 266200; telex 910332; f. 1950; provides credit facilities for business ventures in Sicily, credit for domestic and export trade and for developing tourist facilities; Pres. Prof. ANTONIO MUCCIOLI; Dir-Gen. GIUSEPPE BIONDO.

Istituto per lo Sviluppo Economico dell'Italia Meridionale (ISVEIMER): Via A. De Gasperi 71, 80133 Naples; tel. (081) 7853111; telex 711020; public credit institution granting medium-term loans in mainland southern Italy; cap. and res 457,800m.; Pres. GIUSEPPE DI VAGNO; Dir-Gen. Dott. ANTONIO MERCUSA; 8 brs.

Mediobanca SpA, Banca di Credito Finanziario: Via Filodrammatici 10, 20121 Milan; tel. (02) 88291; telex 311093; f. 1946; deals in all medium- and long-term credit transactions; accepts medium-term time deposits either direct or through all the branches (approx. 1,100) of Banca Commerciale Italiana, Credito Italiano and Banco di Roma, and their subsidiaries. It grants advances of any type, provided they have a duration of from one to 20 years. It also promotes and manages syndicates to underwrite and/or place bond issues and syndicates to underwrite capital increases; cap. 170,000m. listed on the Italian Stock Exchanges; total res 906,495m. (June 1986); 'privatization' authorized in 1988. Chair. FRANCESCO CINGANO; Gen. Man. SILVIO SALTERI.

BANKERS' ORGANIZATIONS

Associazione Bancaria Italiana: Piazza del Gesú 49, 00186 Rome; tel. (06) 67671; telex 622107; Via della Posta 3, 20123 Milan; tel. (02) 806689; telex 324195; f. 1919; Pres. Prof. PIERO BARUCCI; Gen. Man. Dr FELICE GIANANI; membership (1,110 mems) is comprised of the following institutions: public credit institutions; banks of national interest (big commercial banks); private banks and bankers; co-operative banks; saving banks; rural banks; agricultural credit institutions; mortgage banks; industrial credit institutions; leasing and factoring; finance houses.

Associazione fra le Casse di Risparmio Italiane: Viale di Villa Grazioli 23, 00198 Rome; tel. (06) 866253; telex 622033; f. 1912; Pres. CAMILLO FERRARI; Gen. Man. Dott. EDOARDO FATTORINI.

Associazione Nazionale Aziende Ordinarie di Credito (ASSBANK): Via Brennero 1, 20123 Milan; tel. (02) 4988235; telex 334355; Piazza di Spagna 20, Rome; Pres. Dott. Prof. TANCREDI BIANCHI; Dir-Gen. Dott. GIOVANNI LA SCALA.

Associazione Nazionale fra gli Istituti de Credito Agrario (ANICA): Via Bertoloni 3, 00197 Rome; tel. (06) 877506; telex 620311; Pres. Prof. GIUSEPPE GUERRIERI; Sec.-Gen. Dr ERNESTO DE MEDIO.

Associazione Nazionale L. Luzzatti fra le Banche Popolari: Via Montevideo 18, 00198 Rome; tel. (06) 852051; Pres. Prof. FRANCESCO PARRILLO; Dir-Gen. Prof. GIUSEPPE MURÈ.

Associazione Sindacale fra le Aziende del Credito (ASSICREDITO): Via G. Paisiello 5, 00198 Rome; tel. (06) 858041; Via della Posta 7, 20123 Milan; Pres. Dott. CARMELO PETYX; Dir Dott. PERUSINO PERUSINI.

Associazione Tecnica delle Banche Popolari Italiane: Via Nazionale 230, 00184 Rome; tel. (06) 4742214; Pres. LINO VENINI; Dir-Gen. Dott. ARTURO FANTECHI.

THE STOCK EXCHANGE

Commissione Nazionale per le Società e la Borsa (CONSOB) (Commission for Companies and the Stock Exchange): Via Isonzo 19, 00198 Rome; tel. (06) 84771; telex 612434; f. 1974 to have regulatory control over companies quoted on stock exchanges, convertible bonds, unlisted securities, insider trading. A law passed in April 1983 extended its powers to all forms of public saving except bank deposits and mutual funds; Chair. FRANCO PIGA; Governors BRUNO PAZZI, ALDO POLINETTI, MARIO BESSONE, VINCENZO MATTURI. There are 10 stock exchanges, of which the following are the most important:

Genova: Borsa Valori, Via G. Boccardo 1; tel. (010) 2094400; Pres. Dott. GIORGIO ANCONA.

Milan: Borsa Valori, Piazza Affari 6; tel. (02) 85341; telex 321430: Foreign Relations Dept, tel. (02) 8057674; Pres. (vacant).

Naples: Borsa Valori, Palazzo Borsa, Piazza Bovio; tel. (081) 323232; Pres. GIORGIO FOCAS.

Rome: Borsa Valori, Via dei Burro 147, 00186; tel. (06) 6794541; f. 1821; Pres. Dott. FRANCO BALLARINI.

Turin: Borsa Valori, Via San Francesco da Paola 28; tel. (011) 547743; telex 220614; Pres. Dott. SIDNEY CALVI.

INSURANCE

L'Abeille SpA: Via Leopardi 15, 20123 Milan; tel. (02) 85891; telex 316029; f. 1956; cap. 8,211m. (July 1986); Chair. Dott. ANTONIO SOZZANI; Man. Dir Dott. PIERRE MERCIER.

Alleanza Assicurazioni SpA: Viale Luigi Sturzo 37, 20154 Milan; tel. (02) 62961; telex 331303; f. 1898; cap. 144,000m.; Chair. Prof.

ITALY

Dott. LIBERO LENTI; Vice-Chair. Avv. ENRICO RANDONE; Gen. Mans Dott. ALBERTO GIORGETTI, Dott. DANTE LAMPERTI.

Allianz Pace, Assicurazioni e Riassicurazioni SpA: Piazza Cavour 5, 20121 Milan; tel. (02) 62421; telex 311636; f. 1919; cap. 15,000m.; Chair. Dott. RAFFAELE DURANTE; Man. Dir CARLO CARLIN.

Assicuratrice Edile SpA: Via A. De Togni 2, 20123 Milan; tel. (02) 88411; telex 334697; f. 1960; cap. 8,000m. (June 1987); Chair. Dott. GIAN CARLO BORINI; Vice-Pres. Dott. CLAUDIO REICHLIN; Man. Dir Rag. GIAMPIERO SVEVO.

Assicurazioni Generali SpA: Central Head Office: Piazza Duca degli Abruzzi 2, 34132 Trieste; tel. (040) 6711; telex 460190; Head offices: Piazza San Marco 105, 30124 Venice; Via Tiziano 32, 20145 Milan; f. 1831; cap. 1,060,000m. (1988); Chair. and Man. Dir Avv. ENRICO RANDONE; Vice-Chair. Dott. CAMILLO DE BENEDETTI, Dott. MARIO LUZZATTO, ANDRÉ ROSA; Man. Dirs Dott. EUGENIO COPPOLA DI CANZANO, Dott. ALFONSO DESIATA.

Le Assicurazioni d'Italia (ASSITALIA) SpA: Corso d'Italia 33, 00198 Rome; tel. (06) 84831; telex 611051; f. 1923; cap. 150,000m. (June 1987); Pres. Avv. PIER LUIGI CASSIETTI; Man. Dir Prof. Avv. VINCENZO MUNGARI.

Aurora Assicurazioni SpA: Via R. Montecuccoli 20, 20147 Milan; tel. (02) 41441; telex 312562; f. 1947; cap. 50,000m. (July 1987); Chair. Avv. EMILIO DUSI; Vice-Chair. Dott. CAMILLO GIUSSANI; Man. Dir AUGUSTO TRAINA.

Ausonia Assicurazioni SpA: Palazzo Ausonia, Milanofiori, 20089 Rozzano, Milan; tel. (02) 824731; telex 321225; f. 1907; cap. 175,000m. (May 1987); Chair. Dott. GAETANO LAZZATI; Vice-Chair. Dott. ANTONIO CORTI; Man. Dir SILLA GIULIO GRAZIOLI.

Compagnia Assicuratrice Unipol SpA: Via Stalingrado 45, 40128 Bologna; tel. (051) 507111; telex 510674; f. 1962; cap. 80,672m. (June 1987); Chair. Dott. ENEA MAZZOLI; Vice-Chair. and Man. Dir CINZIO ZAMBELLI.

Compagnia Italiana di Assicurazioni (COMITAS) SpA: Via Martin Piaggio 13/A, 16122 Genova; tel. (010) 55261; telex 270543; f. 1948; cap. 12,000m. (June 1987); Chair. Avv. GIOVANNI BONELLI; Vice-Chair. BRUNO SCACCHI; Man. Dir Dott. FERDINANDO MENCONI.

Compagnia Latina di Assicurazioni SpA: Viale Regina Giovanna 27, 20129 Milan; tel. (02) 20571; telex 310083; f. 1958; cap. 55,000m. (April 1987); Chair. Prof. Avv. UGUCCIONI CALTABIANO; Man. Dir SILLA GIULIO GRAZIOLI.

Compagnia Tirrena: Via Massimi 158, 00136 Rome; tel. (06) 33071; telex 621394; f. 1945; cap. 45,000m. (June 1986); Chair. and Gen. Man. Dott. GIOVANNI AMABILE.

Compagnie Riunite di Assicurazione (CRA): Via Consolata 3, 10122 Turin; tel. (011) 57741; telex 212597; f. 1935; cap. 40,000m. (June 1987); Chair. Ing. ETIENNE BENEZECH; Man. Dir Dott. GIUSEPPE BIANCO.

L'Edera SpA: Piazzale de Matthaeis 41, 03100 Frosinone; tel. (0775) 872579; telex 626152; f. 1960; cap. 1,000m. (March 1986); Pres. Avv. GIUSEPPE TODINI; Man. Dir FRANCO ZEPPIERI.

FATA (Fondo Assicurativo Tra Agricoltori) SpA: Via Urbana 169/A, 00184 Rome; tel. (06) 47651; telex 620838; f. 1927; cap. 20,000m. (June 1987); Chair. ARCANGELO LOBIANCO; Man. Dir LUIGI SCOTTI; Gen. Man. FRANCO RIZZI.

La Fenice Ri.—Compagnia di Riassicurazioni SpA: Via Assarotti 5, 16122 Genova; tel. (010) 870293; telex 271297; cap. 50,000m. (March 1986); Chair. Dott. CARLO GALEAZZI; Man. Dir Dott. SERGIO CHIOSTRI; Gen. Man. EDOARDO DANTI.

La Fiduciaria: Via A. Finelli 8, 40126 Bologna; tel. (051) 240901; telex 511491; f. 1970; cap. 6,390m. (April 1987); Chair. Prof. ANTONIO BINNI; Vice-Chair. Rag. CESARE BIANCO; Man. Dir Ing. GIANFRANCO POGGI.

Firs Italiana di Assicurazioni SpA: Via Adelmo Niccolai 24, 00155 Rome; tel. (06) 40691; telex 620185; f. 1965; cap. 12,600m. (March 1987); Chair. Avv. FRANCESCO AURITI; Man. Dir Dott. ANDREA GOTTI LEGA.

La Fondiaria Assicurazioni SpA: Via Lorenzo il Magnifico 1, 50129 Florence; tel. (055) 47941; telex 570430; cap. 69,600m. (June 1986); Chair. Dott. RAUL GARDINI; Vice-Chair. Dott. ALBERTO PECCI; Man. Dir ALFONSO SCARPA.

Intercontinentale Assicurazioni SpA: Via di Priscilla 101, 00199 Rome; tel. (06) 8300; telex 611155; f. 1961; cap. 90,000m. (May 1988); Chair. BENEDETTO SALAROLI; Man. Dir Dott. ENNIO BAIOCCHI.

Istituto Nazionale delle Assicurazioni (INA): Via Sallustiana 51, 00187 Rome; tel. (06) 47221; telex 610336; f. 1912; National Insurance Institute; a state institute with an autonomous management; Chair. Prof. ANTONIO LONGO; Gen. Man. Dott. MARIO FORNARI.

Italia Assicurazioni SpA: Via Fieschi 9, 16121 Genova; tel. (010) 53801; telex 270136; f. 1872; cap. 40,000m.; Chair. ALFONSO SCARPA; Vice-Chair. Dott. CARLO GALEAZZI; Man. Dir Dott. BRUNO MONDINI.

ITAS, Istituto Trentino-Alto Adige per Assicurazioni: Via Mantova 67, 38100 Trento; tel. (0461) 982112; telex 400884; f. 1821; cap. 25,000m. (March 1987); Chair. Dott. EDO BENEDETTI; Dir-Gen. Dott. ETTORE LOMBARDO.

Latina Renana Assicurazioni SpA: Via Nazario Sauro 26, 40121 Bologna; tel. (051) 266567; telex 214661; f. 1959; cap. 16,500m. (May 1986); Chair. Prof. Avv. ALBERTO CALTABIANO; Man. Dir SILLA GIULIO GRAZIOLI.

Lavoro e Sicurtà SpA: Piazza Erculea 13–15, 20122 Milan; tel. (02) 85751; telex 320038; f. 1963; cap. 5,000m. (June 1986); Chair. Rag. FRANCESCO GETTULI; Vice-Chair. and Man. Dir ENZO ZENI.

Lloyd Adriatico SpA: Largo Ugo Irneri 1, 34123 Trieste; tel. (040) 77811; telex 460350; f. 1936; cap. 40,000m. (June 1986); Chair. Avv. GIORGIO IRNERI; Man. Dir Dott. ANTONIO SODARO.

Lloyd Internazionale SpA: Via Massimi 158, 00136 Rome; tel. (06) 33071; telex 621394; f. 1959; cap. 16,000m. (May 1986); Chair. Prof. ROBERTO TANA; Gen. Man. Dott. LUIGI APUZZO.

Lloyd Italico (Divisione dell'Italia Assicurazioni): Via Fieschi 9, 16121 Genova; tel. (010) 53801; telex 270136; f. 1917; cap. 30,000m.; Chair. ALFONSO SCARPA; Man. Dir Dott. CLAUDIO REICHLIN.

MAA Assicurazioni Auto e Rischi Diversi SpA: Via Tonale 26, 20125 Milan; tel. (02) 69791; telex 334397; f. 1952; cap. 30,000m.; Pres. Dott. Ing. ENRICO BONZANO; Vice-Chair. and Man. Dir GIANCARLO GORRINI; Dirs-Gen. Rag. CARLO GIUSSANI, Dott. RAFFAELE PELLINO.

La Minerva: Via Milano 2, 20090 Segrate, Milan; tel. (02) 216081; telex 321284; f. 1943; cap. 8,000m. (March 1986); Chair. Dott. CHARLES WYNIGER; Man. Dirs Dott. GIUSEPPE PICCIOLA, Dott. GIAN PIERO PORTIGLIA.

La Nationale Assicurazioni SpA: Piazza del Porto di Ripetta 1, 00186 Rome; tel. (06) 67701; telex 611032; f. 1962; cap. 20,000m. (June 1987); Chair. Dott. FAUSTO PANZERI; Man. Dir LUCIANO CITTADINI.

Norditalia Assicurazioni SpA: Viale Certosa 222, 20156 Milan; tel. (02) 30761; telex 331345; f. 1963; cap. 55,250m. (March 1986); Chair. Prof. RENZO COSTI (acting):

La Previdente Assicurazioni SpA: Via Copernico 38, 20125 Milan; tel. (02) 69561; telex 330488; f. 1917; cap. 25,000m. (June 1986); Chair. Ing. GIUSEPPE GAROFANO; Man. Dir Dott. ROBERTO PONTREMOLI.

RAS-Riunione Adriatica di Sicurtà: Corso Italia 23, 20122 Milan; tel. (02) 88441; telex 320065; and Piazza della Repubblica 1, 34122 Trieste; tel. (040) 7692; telex 460006; f. 1838; cap. 155,000m., res 905,500m. (Dec. 1987); Chair. and Man. Dir Dott. UMBERTO ZANNI.

SAI—Società Assicuratrice Industriale SpA: Corso Galileo Galilei 12, 10126 Turin; tel. (011) 65621; telex 212080; f. 1921; cap. 165,000m. (June 1987); Chair. Dr Ing. SALVATORE LIGRESTI; Man. Dir Dott. GIORGIO BRINATTI.

SAPA (Security and Property Assurance) SpA: Via Riva Villasanta 3, 20145 Milan; tel. (02) 38841; telex 312061; f. 1965; cap. 11,880m. (June 1987); Chair. BENEDETTO SALAROLI; Man. Dir ALDO COSMI.

SARA assicurazioni SpA: Via Po 20, 00198 Rome; tel. (06) 84751; telex 614526; f. 1924; official insurer for Automobile Club d'Italia; cap. 18,000m. (March 1986); Chair. FILIPPO CARPI DE RESMINI; Gen. Mans ENZO BOIANI, MARCO ROCCA.

Savoia: Via S. Vigilio 1, 20142 Milan; tel. (02) 84421; telex 311270; cap. 24,000m. (Sept. 1986); Chair. Avv. GIOVANNI BONELLI; Dir-Gen. VINCENZO POLLANI.

Società Cattolica di Assicurazione: Lungadige Cangrande 16, 37126 Verona; tel. (045) 938711; telex 480482; f. 1896; cap. 9,073m. (Dec. 1987); Chair. Dott. ALFREDO BERZANTI; Gen. Man. Ing. GIULIO BISOFFI.

Società Italiana di Assicurazioni, SpA (SIDA): Via Massimi 158, 00136 Rome; tel. (06) 33071; telex 621394; f. 1914; cap. 12,000m.; Chair. ALBERTO PUGLIESE; Gen. Man. Dott. GIOVANNI AMABILE.

Società Italiana Assicurazioni e Riassicurazioni (SIAT): Via B. Bosco 15, 16121 Genova; tel. (010) 55461; telex 270307; f. 1967; cap. 9,975m. (June 1987); Chair. Dott. GIORGIO BUDA; Gen. Man. Dott. GIANCARLO CAMERA.

Società Italiana Cauzioni (SIC): Via Crescenzio 12, 00193 Rome; tel. (06) 6530848; telex 611050; f. 1948; cap. 10,000m. (March 1986); Chair. Avv. Conte CARLO D'AMELIO; Man. Dir GIANLUIGI BOCCIA.

Società Reale Mutua di Assicurazioni: Via Corte d'Appello 11, 10122 Turin; tel. (011) 55961; telex 215105; f. 1828; res 745,742m. (1985); Chair. PIER CARLO ROMAGNOLI; Gen. Mans ITI MIHALICH and GIUSEPPE SOLINAS.

Toro Assicurazioni SpA: Via Arcivescovado 16, 10121 Turin; tel. (011) 57331; telex 221567; f. 1833; cap. 110,000m. (April 1986); Chair. Dott. UMBERTO AGNELLI; Man. Dir Rag. FRANCESCO TORRI.

ITALY
Directory

Unione Italiana di Riassicurazione SpA: Via dei Giuochi Istmici 40, 00194 Rome; tel. (06) 365931; telex 610348; f. 1922; cap. 100,000m. (Nov. 1987); Chair. Dott. MARIO LUZZATTO; Man. Dir ARRIGO BIANCHI DI LAVAGNA.

Unione Subalpina di Assicurazioni SpA: Via Alfieri 22, 10121 Turin; tel. (011) 55121; telex 221201; f. 1928; cap. 9,187.5m. (June 1986); Chair. Avv. VITTORIO BADINI CONFALONIERI; Man. Dir Dott. Rag. ADOLFO CELLINI.

Unipol: Via Stalingrado 45, Bologna; tel. (051) 507111; telex 510674; Pres. ENEA MAZZOLI.

Universo Assicurazioni SpA: Strada Maggiore 53, 40125 Bologna; tel. (051) 587511; telex 511170; f. 1972; cap. 22,500m. (April 1988); Chair. and Man. Dir Rag. SERGIO GETICI; Gen. Man. Dott. GIORGIO DI GIANSANTE.

Veneta Assicurazioni SpA: Via Enrico degli Scrovegni, 35131 Padova; tel. (049) 848111; telex 430482; f. 1961; cap. 18,000m. (May 1988); Chair. BENEDETTO SALAROLI; Man. Dirs Dott. JEAN PAUL FESTEAU, Dott. GASPARE MASARACCHIA.

Vittoria Assicurazioni SpA: Piazza San Babila 3, 20122 Milan; tel. (02) 77901; telex 331030; cap. 12,000m. (June 1988); Chair. Prof. LUIGI GUATRI; Man. Dir Dott. GIUSEPPE DE'CHIARA.

INSURANCE ASSOCIATIONS

Associazione Nazionale fra le Imprese Assicuratrici (ANIA): Head Office: Piazza S. Babila 1, 20122 Milan; tel. (02) 77641; telex 333288; Deputation: Via della Frezza 70, 00186 Rome; tel. (06) 6782941; telex 613621; f. 1944; Chair. Avv. EMILIO DUSI; Cons. Del. Dott. ENRICO TONELLI; 185 mems.

Trade and Industry

CHAMBERS OF COMMERCE

Unione Italiana delle Camere di Commercio, Industria, Artigianato e Agricoltura (Italian Union of Chambers of Commerce, Industry, Crafts and Agriculture): Piazza Sallustio 21, 00187 Rome; tel. (06) 47041; telex 622327; f. 1954 to promote the development of chambers of commerce, industry, trade and agriculture; Pres. PIERO BASSETTI; Sec.-Gen. Dott. GIUSEPPE CERRONI; 765 mems.

EXPORT INSTITUTE

Istituto Nazionale per il Commercio Estero (ICE) (National Institute for Foreign Trade): Via Liszt 21, EUR, 00100 Rome; tel. (06) 59921; telex 610160; f. 1919; government agency for the promotion of foreign trade; Pres. Dott. GIUSEPPE RATTI; Dir-Gen. Dott. MASSIMO MANCINI.

EMPLOYERS' ASSOCIATION

Confederazione Generale dell'Industria Italiana (CONFINDUSTRIA) (General Confederation of Italian Industry): Viale dell'Astronomia 30, EUR, 00144 Rome; tel. (06) 59031; telex 611393; f. 1919, re-established 1944; mems: 106 territorial asscns and 98 branch asscns, totalling 100,000 firms and 3,000,000 employers; office in Brussels; Pres. Dott. SERGIO PININFARINA; Dir-Gen. Dott. PAOLO ANNIBALDI.

Principal Affiliated Industrial Organizations

Associazione degli Industriali della Birra e del Malto (Brewers): Via Savoia 29, 00198 Rome; tel. (06) 865161; telex 614486; Pres. Ing. ALDO BASSETTI; Pres. Del. CESARE MARTIN.

Associazione Industrie Aerospaziali (AIA) (Aerospace Industry): Via Nazionale 200, 00184 Rome; tel. (06) 460247; telex 622250; f. 1946; Pres. Ing. GIAN CARLO BOFFETTA; Gen. Sec. Dott. SERGIO LIBERI.

Associazione Industrie Siderurgiche Italiane (ASSIDER) (Iron and Steel Industries): Via XX Settembre 1, 00187 Rome; tel. (06) 463867; f. 1946; Pres. Ing. ADAMO ADAMI; Dir Gen. Dr GIANCARLO LONGHI; 140 mems.

Associazione Italiana degli Industriali dell' Abbigliamento (Clothing Manufacturers): Foro Buonaparte 70, 20121 Milan; tel. (02) 809016; telex 333594; f. 1945; Pres. TINO COSMA; Sec.-Gen. Dott. ADRIANO BENVENUTO; 650 mems.

Associazione Italiana Industriali Prodotti Alimentari (AIIPA) (Food Manufacturers): Via Pietro Verri 8, 20121 Milan; tel. (02) 708660; telex 330881; Viale Umberto·Tupini 103, 00144 Rome; (06) 5924449; f. 1946; Pres. Dott. DEMETRIO CORNO; Dir Dott. GIOVANNI FRANCO CRIPPA; 300 mems.

Associazione Italiana Tecnico Economica del Cemento (AITEC) (Cement): Via di S. Teresa 23, 00198 Rome; tel. (06) 864714; Via Borgonuovo 12, 20121 Milan; tel. (02) 6571861; f. 1959; Pres. Dott. Ing. MARIO FEDERICI; Dir Dott. ANTONIO TRIFOGLI.

Associazione Mineraria Italiana (Mining): Via Cola di Rienzo 297, 00192 Rome; tel. (06) 352261; telex 622264; f. 1144; Pres. VITO GUARRASI; Dir Dott. FRANCESCO SAVERIO GUIDI; 150 mems.

Associazione Nazionale Calzaturifici Italiani (ANCI) (Footwear Manufacturers): Via Dogana 1, 20123 Milan; tel. (02) 809721; telex 320018; f. 1945; Pres. NATALINO PANCALDI; Dir LEONARDO SOANA.

Associazione Nazionale Costruttori Edili (ANCE) (Builders): Via Guattani 16, 00161 Rome; tel. (06) 84881; telex 626846; f. 1946; Pres. RICCARDO PISA; Man. Dir CARLO FERRONI; mems: 19,000 firms in 99 provincial and 20 regional asscns.

Associazione Nazionale delle Fonderie (ASSOFOND) (Foundries): Via F. Rismondo 78, 27100 Pavia; tel. (0382) 308403; telex 326344; f. 1948; Pres. Dott. Ing. GIAMPIERO BECCARIA; Dir Dott. GIUSEPPE MAZZONE.

Associazione Nazionale dell'Industria Farmaceutica (FARMINDUSTRIA) (Pharmaceutical Industry): Piazza di Pietra 34, 00196 Rome; tel. (06) 650981; telex 614281; f. 1978; Pres. Dott. ALBERTO ALEOTTI; Dir Dott. DOMENICO MUSCOLO; 265 mem. firms.

Associazione Nazionale fra Industrie Automobilistiche (ANFIA) (Motor Vehicle Industries): Corso Galileo Ferraris 61, 10128 Turin; tel. (011) 57611; telex 221334; f. 1912; Pres. Dott. GREGORIO RAMPA; Dir-Gen. Dott. EMILIO DI CAMILLO; 220 mems.

Associazione Nazionale Industria Meccanica Varia ed Affine (ANIMA) (Engineering and Allied Industries): Piazza Diaz 2, 20123 Milan; tel. (02) 809006; telex 310392; f. 1945; Pres. LUIGI CAZZANIGA; Sec.-Gen. Dott. Ing. ENRICO MALCOVATI; 1,100 mems.

Associazione Nazionale Industrie Elettrotecniche ed Elettroniche (ANIE) (Electrotechnic and Electronic Industries): Via Algardi 2, 20148 Milan; tel. (02) 32641; telex 321616; Pres. ALESSANDRO SIGNORINI; Sec.-Gen. LORENZO TRINGALI-CASANUOVA.

Associazione Nazionale Italiana Industrie Grafiche, Cartotecniche e Trasformatrici (Printing, Paper-Making and Processing Industries): Piazza Conciliazione 1, 20123 Milan; tel. (02) 4981051; telex 331674; f. 1946; Pres. Dott. PIERFRANCO GIUNCAIOLI; Sec.-Gen. Dott. FELICE SCIOMACHEN; 1,052 mems.

Federazione Italiana delle Industrie delle Acque Minerali, delle Terme e delle Bevande Analcooliche (Mineral Water and Non-Alcoholic Beverage Industries): Via Sicilia 186, 00187 Rome; tel. (06) 4557251; telex 626063; f. 1919; Pres. Dr CARLO VIOLATI; Dir Dr CARMELO CALLIPO.

Federazione Italiana Industriali Produttori Esportatori ed Importatori di Vini, Acquaviti, Liquori, Sciroppi, Aceti ed Affini (FEDERVINI) (Producers, Importers and Exporters of Wines, Liqueurs and Allied Products): Via Mentana 2B, 00185 Rome; tel. (06) 4740700; telex 612506; f. 1921; Pres. Conte ALBERTO MARONE CINZANO; Dir FRANCESCO ARTALE.

Federazione Nazionale dell'Industria Chimica (FEDERCHIMICA) (Chemical Industry): Via Accademia 33, 20131 Milan; tel. (02) 63621; telex 332488; Via Tomacelli 132, 00186 Rome; tel. (06) 6878683; telex 612504; f. 1945; Pres. GIORGIO PORTA; Dir-Gen. Dott. GUIDO VENTURINI.

Unione Industriali Pastai Italiani (UNIPI) (Pasta Manufacturers): Via Po 102, 00198 Rome; tel. (06) 853291; telex 611540; Pres. Ing. GIANFRANCO CARLONE; Dir Dr GIUSEPPE MENCONI.

Unione Nazionale Cantieri e Industrie Nautiche ed Affini (UCINA) (Shipyard and Nautical Industries): Via G. Giardino 4, 20123 Milan; Via Vincenzo Renieri 23, 00143 Rome; tel. (06) 5919744; telex 611585; Pres. GIORGIO ADREANI.

Unione Petrolifera (Petroleum Industries): Viale Civiltà del Lavoro 38, 00144 Rome; tel. (06) 5914841; telex 611455; f. 1948; Pres. Dott. GIAN MARCO MORATTI; Dir-Gen. Ing. BRUNO DATTILO; 38 mems.

Other Employers' and Industrial Organizations

Associazione Nazionale Comuni Italiani (ANCI): Via dei Prefetti 46, 00186 Rome; tel. (06) 6793601; Pres. Sen. RICCARDO TRIGLIA; Sec.-Gen. GIOVANNI SANTO.

Associazione Nazionale Esattori e Ricevitori delle Imposte Dirette e dei Tesorieri degli Enti Locali (ANERT) (Local Government Tax Administrators): Via Parigi 11, 00185 Rome; tel. (06) 485764; Pres. Prof. ANGELO SENIN; Sec.-Gen. RAFFAELE FORNARIO.

Associazione Sindacale Intersind: Via Cristoforo Colombo 98, 00147 Rome; tel. (06) 51751; f. 1960; represents state-controlled firms; Pres. Dr AGOSTINO PACI; Dir-Gen. Dr GIUSEPPE CAPO.

Associazione Sindacale per le Aziende Petrochimiche e Collegate a Partecipazione Statale (State-controlled Petrochemical Companies): Via Due Macelli 66, 00187 Rome; tel. (06) 67341; Pres. Avv. GUIDO FANTONI; Vice-Pres. and Dir-Gen. Dott. MODESTINO FUSCO.

Associazione fra le Società Italiane per Azioni (ASSONIME) (Limited Companies): Piazza Venezia 11, 00187 Rome; tel. (06)

ITALY

6784413; telex 613381; f. 1936; Pres. Dott. EMANUELE DUBINI; Dir-Gen. ALFONSO DE TOMMASI.

Confederazione Generale della Agricoltura Italiana (General Agricultural): Corso Vittorio Emanuele 101, 00186 Rome; tel. (06) 65121; telex 612533; f. 1945; Pres. STEFANO WALLNER; Dir-Gen. GIUSEPPE PRICOLO; Sec.-Gen. ARCANGELO MAFRICI.

Confederazione Generale Italiana del Commercio e del Turismo (CONFCOMMERCIO) (Commerce and Tourism): Piazza G.G. Belli 2, 00153 Rome; tel. (06) 58661; telex 614217; f. 1946; Pres. Dott. FRANCESCO COLUCCI; Sec.-Gen. Dott. PIETRO ALFONSI; 125 national and 97 territorial asscns affiliated.

Confederazione Italiana della Piccola e Media Industria (CONFAPI) (Small and Medium Industry): Via Colonna Antonina 52, 00186 Rome; tel. (06) 6782441; f. 1947; Pres. Dr GIUSEPPE SPINELLA; Sec.-Gen. CARLO BAGNI; 20,000 mems.

Confederazione Italiana della Proprietà Edilizia (CONFEDILIZIA) (Property and Building): Via Pisanelli 25, 00196 Rome; tel. (06) 3606764; Pres. Dott. Ing. ATTILIO VIZIANO; Man. Dir Dott. Ing. ADRIANO PASTA.

Delegazione Sindacale Industriale Autonoma della Valle d'Aosta (Autonomous Industrial Delegation of the Valle d'Aosta): Via G. Elter 6, 11100 Aosta; Pres. Dr ETTORE FORTUNA; Sec. Dr ROBERTO ANSALDO.

Federazione Associazioni Industriali (Industrial Asscns): Via Petitti 16, 20149 Milan; tel. (02) 324846; telex 331098; Pres. BRUNO CREMONA; Dir Dott. UMBERTO MALTAGLIATI.

Federazione delle Associazioni Italiane Alberghi e Turismo (FAIAT) (Hotels and Tourism): Via Toscana 1, 00187 Rome; tel. (06) 4741151; telex 613116; f. 1950; Pres. GIOVANNI COLOMBO; Gen. Man. ALESSANDRO CIANELLA; 25,000 mems.

Federazione Italiana della Pubblicità (FIP) (Advertisers): Via Maurizio Gonzaga 4, 20123 Milan; tel. (02) 865262; Pres. GIANFRANCO MAI; Sec.-Gen. MARIO CORNELIO.

Federazione Nazionale Imprese Trasporti (FENIT) (Transport Undertakings): Via Parigi 11, 00185 Rome; tel. (06) 4741043; f. 1946; Pres. ANGELO MARIA SANZA; Gen. Man. Dr CARLO GIZZI; 234 mems.

Unione Nazionale Aziende Autoproduttrici e Consumatrici di Energia Elettrica (UNAPACE) (Concerns producing and consuming their own Electrical Power): Via Paraguay 2, 00198 Rome; tel. (06) 864602; telex 616387; f. 1946; Pres. Dr Ing. LODOVICO PRIORI; Dir Dr Ing. ALDO BUSCAGLIONE.

TRADE UNIONS

There are three main federations of Italian trade unions, CGIL, CISL and UIL, all of which have close ties with political parties. The CGIL is dominated by the Communists, the CISL has links with the Christian Democrats and the UIL is associated with the Socialists. In 1972 all the confederations formally agreed that union leadership and holding party political office were not compatible with independence from party line and a united front between the confederations was seen as crucial to the success of the unions.

National Federations

Confederazione Autonomi Sindacati Artigiani (CASA): V. A. Bargoni 8, 00153 Rome; tel. (06) 5892275; f. 1958; federation of artisans' unions and regional and provincial associations; Pres. GIUSEPPE GUARINO; Sec.-Gen. GIACOMO BASSO.

Confederazione Generale Italiana dell' Artigianato (Artisans): Piazza Venezia 11, 00187 Rome; telex 616261; f. 1945; independent; 157 mem. unions; 600,000 associate enterprises; Pres. MANLIO GERMOZZI.

Confederazione Generale Italiana dei Professionisti e Artisti (CIPA) (Artists and Professional People): Via S. Nicola da Tolentino 21, 00187 Rome; tel. (06) 461849; federation of 19 unions; Pres. Prof. Ing. G. B. ORMEA.

Confederazione Generale Italiana del Lavoro (CGIL) (General Union of Italian Workers): Corso d'Italia 25, 00198 Rome; tel. (06) 84761; telex 623083; f. 1944; Communist and Socialist; federation of 17 unions; Gen. Sec. BRUNO TRENTIN; 4,556,000 mems.

Confederazione Italiana Dirigenti di Azienda (CIDA): Via Nazionale 75, 00184 Rome; tel. (06) 4818551; federation of six managers' unions; Pres. Dott. FAUSTO D'ELIA; Sec.-Gen. RAFFAELE CIABATTINI.

Confederazione Italiana dei Sindacati Autonomi Lavoratori (CISAL): Via Cavour 310, 00184 Rome; tel. (06) 6785402; f. 1957; no international affiliations; federation of 67 unions; Gen. Sec. Dr GUSSONI GERMANO; 1,423,000 mems.

Confederazione Italiana dei Sindacati Lavoratori (CISL): Via Po 21, 00198 Rome; tel. (06) 84731; telex 614045; f. 1950; affiliated to the International Confederation of Free Trade Unions and the European Trade Union Confederation; federation of 17 unions; Sec.-Gen. FRANCO MARINI; Dep. Secs-Gen. ERALDO CREA, MARIO COLOMBO; 2,953,000 mems.

Confederazione Italiana Sindacati Nazionali dei Lavoratori (CISNAL): Via P. Amedeo 42, 00185 Rome; tel. (06) 4817919; f. 1950; upholds traditions of national syndicalism; federation of 64 unions, 90 provincial unions; Gen. Sec. IVO LAGHI; 1,969,635 mems.

Confederazione Nazionale dell' Artigianato (CNA): Via di S. Prassede 24, 00187 Rome; tel. (06) 4757441; telex 622543; provincial associations; Pres. BRUNO MARIANI; Gen. Sec. Dr MAURO TOGNONI.

Federazione fra le Associazioni e i Sindacati Nazionali dei Quadri Direttivi dell'amministrazione dello Stato (DIRSTAT): Via Plinio 21 00193 Rome; tel. (06) 6874285; f. 1948; federation of 33 unions and associations of civil service executives and officers; Sec.-Gen. Dott. GIANCARLO TRENTANI; Treas. Dr V. DONATO.

Unione Italiana del Lavoro (UIL): Via Lucullo 6, 00187 Rome; tel. (06) 49731; telex 622425; f. 1950; Socialist, Social Democrat and Republican; affiliated to the International Confederation of Free Trade Unions and European Trade Union Confederation; 35 national trade union federations and 95 provincial union councils; Gen. Sec. GIORGIO BENVENUTO; 1,351,398 mems.

Principal Unions

Banking and Insurance

Federazione Autonoma Bancari Italiana (FABI) (Bank Workers): Via Tevere 46, Rome; tel. (06) 855751; f. 1948; independent; Sec. LUIGI MARMIROLI; 56,000 mems.

Federazione Autonoma Lavoratori Casse di Risparmio Italiane (FALCRI) (Savings Banks Workers): Via Mercato 5, Milan; Via Carducci 4, Rome.

Federazione Italiana Bancari e Assicuratori (FIBA): Via Modena 5, 00184 Rome; tel. (06) 4741245; affiliated to the CISL; Gen. Sec. SERGIO AMMANNATI; 58,980 mems.

Federazione Italiana Sindacale Lavoratori Assicurazioni Credito (Employees of Credit Institutions): Via Vicenza 5A, 00184 Rome; tel. (06) 4958261; affiliated to the CGIL; Sec. NICOLETTA ROCCHI; 60,000 mems.

Federazione Nazionale Assicuratori (FISAC) (Insurance Workers): Via Vincenzo Monti 25, Milan; Via Val d'Ossola 100, Rome; independent; Pres. GIUSEPPE PAGANI; Sec.-Gen. EZIO MARTONE.

Unione Italiana Lavoratori Assicurazioni (UILAS) (Assurance Co Workers): Via Piemonte 39/A, Rome; affiliated to the UIL; National Sec. GUGLIELMO BRONZI; 13,000 mems.

Building and Building Materials

Federazione Autonoma Italiana Lavoratori Cemento, Legno, Edilizia ed Affini (FAILCLEA) (Workers in Cement, Wood, Construction and Related Industries): Piazza E. Duse 3, Milan; affiliated to the CISAL; Sec. ENZO BOZZI.

Federazione Lavoratori delle Costruzioni (FLC): includes the following three organizations:

Federazione Italiana Lavoratori delle Costruzioni a Affini (FILCA) (Building Industries' Workers): Via dei Mille 23, Rome; tel. (06) 497801; f. 1955; affiliated to the CISL; Sec.-Gen. CARLO MITRA; 194,493 mems.

Federazione Nazionale Lavoratori Edili Affini e del Legno (FeNEAL) (Builders and Woodworkers): Via dei Mille 23, Rome; affiliated to the UIL and the FLC; Sec.-Gen. GIANCARLO SERAFINI; 135,000 mems.

Federazione Italiana Lavoratori del Legno, Edili ed Affini (FILLEA) (Wood-workers, Construction Workers and Allied Trades): Via dei Mille 23, 00184 Rome; tel. (06) 497801; affiliated to the CGIL; Sec. ANNIO BRESCHI; 434,154 mems.

Chemical, Mining and Allied Industries

Federazione Unitaria Lavoratori Chimici (FULC) (Chemical and Allied Workers): Via Bolzano 16, Rome; affiliated to the CGIL, CISL and UIL; Secs.-Gen. FAUSTO VIGEVANI, DANILO BERETTA, ERNESTO CORNELLI; 450,000 mems.

Unione Italiana Lavoratori Miniere e Cave (Mine Workers): Rome; independent; National Sec. BACCI LUCIANO; 16,000 mems.

Clothing and Textiles

Federazione Italiana Lavoratori Tessili Abbigliamento, Calzaturieri (FILTEA) (Textile and Clothing Workers and Shoe Manufacturers): Via Leopoldo Serra 31, 00153 Rome; tel. (06) 55431; f. 1966; affiliated to the CGIL; Gen. Sec. ALDO AMORETTI; 180,000 mems.

Federazione Italiana dei Lavoratori Tessili e Abbigliamento (FILTA-CISL): Via Goito 39, 00185 Rome; tel. (06) 4270041; affiliated to the CISL; Gen. Sec. AUGUSTA RESTELLI; 125,084 mems.

ITALY

Directory

Engineering and Metallurgy

Confederazione Sindacale Italiana Libere Professioni (CONSILP) (Liberal Professions): Via Leopoldo Traversi 40, 00154 Rome; Sec.-Gen. Dott. UBALDO PROCACCINI.

Federazione Architetti (FEDERARCHITETTI) (Architects): Piazza Sallustio 24, 00187 Rome; Pres. Dott. Arch. GIANCARLO CAMPIOLI; Sec.-Gen. Dott. Arch. NICOLA D'ERRICO.

Federazione Impiegati Operai Metallurgici (FIOM–CGIL) (Metalworkers): Corso Trieste 36, 00198 Rome; tel. (06) 8471; f. 1902; affiliated to the CGIL; Sec. SERGIO GARAVINI; 450,000 mems.

Federazione Italiana Metalmeccanici (FIM) (Metal Mechanic Workers): Corso Trieste 36, 00198 Rome; tel. (06) 8471; affiliated to the CISL; Sec. Gen. RAFFAELE MORESE; 277,789 mems.

Sindacato Nazionale Ingegneri Liberi Professionisti Italiana (SNILPI) (Liberal Professionals-Engineers): Via Salaria 292, 00199 Rome; Pres. Dott. Ing. LUIGI LUCHERINI; Sec.-Gen. Dott. Ing. GIUSEPPE MILONE.

Unione Italiana Lavoratori Metallurgici (UILM) (Metalworkers): Corso Trieste 36, 00198 Rome; tel. (06) 8442757; f. 1950; affiliated to the UIL; Sec. FRANCO LOTITO; 139,000 mems.

Food and Agriculture

Confederazione Generale dell' Agricoltura Italiana (CONFAGRICOLTURA) (Farmers): Corso Vittorio Emanuele 101, 00186 Rome; tel. (06) 65121; telex 612533; Pres. Dr STEFANO WALLNER.

Confederazione Italiana Coltivatori (Farmers): Via Mariano Fortuny 20, 00196 Rome; tel. (06) 3969931; independent; Pres. GIUSEPPE AVOLIO; Vice-Pres. MASSIMO BELLOTTI.

Confederazione Nazionale Coltivatori Diretti (CONACOLTIVATORI) (Small-holders): Via XXIV Maggio 43, 00187 Rome; tel. (06) 46821; telex 6751055; independent; Pres. On. ARCANGELO LOBIANCO; Sec.-Gen. PIETRO GNISCI.

Federazione Italiana Salariati Braccianti Agricoli e Maestranze Specializzate (FISBA) (Permanent Unskilled and Skilled Agricultural Workers): Via Tevere 20, 00198 Rome; tel. (06) 855455; f. 1950; Sec. CIRINO BRANCATO; 347,265 mems.

Federazione Lavoratori dell' Agroindustria (Workers in the Agricultural Industry): Via Leopoldo Serra 31, 00153 Rome; tel. (06) 5543531; f. 1988; affiliated to the CGIL; Sec.-Gen. ANGELO LANA; 438,000 mems.

Federazione Nazionale Braccianti, Salariati, Tecnici, (FEDERBRACCIANTI) (Agricultural Workers): Rome; tel. (06) 461760; affiliated to the CGIL; Sec. ANDREA GIANFAGNA; 600,000 mems.

Federazione Unitaria Lavoratori Prodotti Industrie Alimentari (Workers in the Manufactured Food Industry): Rome; affiliated to the CISL and the IUF; Sec. Dr E. CREA; 40,000 mems.

Unione Coltivatori Italiana (UCI) (Farmers): Via in Lucina 10, 00186 Rome.

Unione Generale Coltivatori (UGC): Via Tevere 20, 00198 Rome; tel. (06) 862857; affiliated to the CISL; Pres. SANTE RICCI; 131,562 mems.

Unione Italiana Lavoratori Industrie Alimentari Saccariferi (UILIAS) (Food Workers): Via del Viminale 43, 00184 Rome; tel. (06) 463486; affiliated to the UIL; Sec. LIVIO CAUDURO.

Unione Italiana Mezzadri e Coltivatori Diretti (UIMEC) (Land Workers): Via XX Settembre 118, 00187 Rome; tel. (06) 4750911; affiliated to the UIL; Sec. FURIO VENARUCCI; 100,000 mems.

Medical

Federazione Italiana Sindacati Ospedalieri (FISOS) (Hospital Workers' Unions): Via Salaria 89, 00198 Rome; tel. (06) 854815; affiliated to the CISL; Sec. Gen. MORENO GORI; 150,501 mems.

Sindacato Nazionale Medici (SNM) (Doctors): Via S. Nicola da Tolentino 21, 00184 Rome; affiliated to the CISNAL; Sec. VINCENZO AGAMENNONE.

Papermaking, Printing and Publishing

Federazione Italiana Lavoratori del Libro (FEDERLIBRO): Via Fabio Massimo 57, 00192 Rome; tel. (06) 318202; affiliated to the CISL; Gen. Sec. GIUSEPPE SURRENTI; 35,000 mems.

Federazione Italiana Lavoratori Poligrafici e Cartai (Printing Workers and Papermakers): Via Piemonte 39, 00186 Rome; affiliated to the CGIL; Sec.-Gen. GIORGIO COLZI; 80,000 mems.

Public Services

Federazione Autonoma Italiana Lavoratori Elettrici (FAILE) (Electrical Workers): Via Cavour 310, Rome; affiliated to CISAL; Sec. ANGELO ISERNIA.

Federazione della Funzione Pubblica (FP): Via Rovereto 11, 00198 Rome; tel. (06) 869578; affiliated to the CISL; Sec. Gen. DARIO PAPPUCIA; 244,835 mems.

Federazione Italiana Dipendenti Aziende Elettriche (FIDAE) (Electrical Undertakings): Via Piemonte 32, Rome; affiliated to the CGIL; f. 1920; Gen. Sec. GIORGIO BUCCI; 57,000 mems.

Federazione Italiana Dipendenti Enti Locali (Local Government Employees): Via XX Settembre 40, Rome; tel. (06) 4759295; f. 1951; affiliated to the CISL; Sec. CRISTOFORO MELINELLI; 150,000 mems.

Federazione Italiana Lavoratori Esattoriali (Tax Collectors): Via A. Poliziano 80, 00184 Rome; tel. (06) 732246; affiliated to the UIL; Sec. LUCIANO PARODI.

Federazione Italiana Lavoratori Statali (State Employees): Via Livenza 7, 00198 Rome; affiliated to the CISL; Gen. Sec. MARZIO BASTIANONI; 60,605 mems.

Federazione Lavoratori Aziende Elettriche Italiane (FLAEI) (Workers in Italian Electrical Undertakings): Via Salaria 83, 00198 Rome; tel. (06) 862352; f. 1948; affiliated to the CISL; Sec. FIORINDO FUMAGALLI; 41,210 mems.

Federazione Nazionale Dipendenti Enti Locali (Employers of Local Authorities): Via Principe Amadeo 42, 00185 Rome; tel. (06) 4750202; affiliated to the CISNAL; Sec. Dott. ARMANDO LA ROCCA.

Federazione Nazionale Dipendenti Enti Pubblici (UILDEP) (Public Employees): Via Lucullo 6, Rome; f. 1962; affiliated to the UIL; Gen. Sec. GIAMPIETRO SESTINI; 30,000 mems.

Federazione Nazionale Lavoratori Funzione Pubblica: Via Leopoldo Serra 31, 00153 Rome; tel. (06) 55431; affiliated to the CGIL and Public Services International; Sec.-Gen. ALDO GIUNTI.

Federazione Nazionale Lavoratori Energia (Employees of Gas Undertakings): Via Piemonte 32, 00187 Rome; tel. (06) 484526; affiliated to the CGIL; Sec. GIORGIO BUCCI; 72,000 mems (gas, water and electricity workers).

Unione Italiana Lavoratori Pubblico Impiego (UIIPI) (Public Office Workers): Via Lucullo 6, 00187 Rome; affiliated to the UIL; Sec. BRUNO BUGLI; 238,000 mems.

Unione Italiana Lavoratori Servizi Pubblici (Public Services Workers): Via Nizza 33, 00198 Rome; tel. (06) 865303; f. 1958; affiliated to the UIL; Sec. GIUSEPPE AUGIERI; 15,500 mems.

Unione Nazionale Dipendenti Enti Locali (UNDEL) (Local Authority Employees): Via Po 162, 00198 Rome; tel. (06) 852340; affiliated to the UIL; Gen. Sec. FABRIZIO LUCARINI; 85,000 mems.

Teachers

Federazione Italiana Scuola Università e Ricerca (University Teachers): Via S. Croce in Gerusalemme 107, 00185 Rome; tel. (06) 757941; affiliated to the CISL; Gen. Secs GIORGIO ALESSANDRINI, PIETRO TALAMO; 184,235 mems.

Sindacato Nazionale Autonomo Lavoratori della Scuola (SNALS): Via Leopoldo Serra 5, 00153 Rome; tel. (06) 5898741; f. 1976; grouping of all independent teachers' unions; National Sec. NINO GALLOTTA.

Sindacato Nazionale Scuola Elementare (Elementary School Teachers): Via Santa Croce in Gerusalemme 91, 00185 Rome; tel. (06) 7574856; f. 1944; affiliated to the CISL; Sec.-Gen. LUIGI PICCINATO; 124,000 mems.

Tourism and Entertainments

Federazione Informazione e Spettacolo (FIS) (Actors, Artists and Media Workers): Via Boncompagni 19, 00187 Rome; tel. (06) 4957842; affiliated to the CISL; Gen. Sec. GIUSEPPE SURRENTI; 43,388 mems.

Federazione Italiana Lavoratori Commercio Albergo Mensa e Servizi (FILCAMS) (Hotel and Catering Workers): Rome; tel. (06) 4750300; f. 1960; affiliated to the CGIL; Sec.-Gen. GILBERTO PASCUCCI; 189,000 mems.

Federazione Italiana Lavoratori Informazione Spettacolo (FILIS) (Theatre Workers): Via E. Manfredi 10A, 00197 Rome; tel. (06) 877532; affiliated to the CGIL; Gen. Sec. GUGLIELMO EPIFANI.

Federazione Italiana Personale Aviazione Civile (Aviation Employees): Via Ostiense 224, Rome; affiliated to the CGIL; Sec. PIERRO TORINO.

Federazione Italiana Sindacati Addetti Servizi Commerciali Affini e del Turismo (Commercial and Tourist Unions): Via Livenza 7, 00198 Rome; tel. (06) 851042; affiliated to the CISL; Sec.-Gen. RENATO DI MARCO; 99,860 mems.

Unione Italiana Lavoratori Turismo Commercio e Servizi (UIL-TuCS): Via Nizza 59, 00198 Rome; tel. (06) 8844947; f. 1977; affiliated to the UIL; Gen. Sec. RAFFAELE VANNI; 140,000 mems.

Transport and Telecommunications

Federazione Italiana Dipendenti Aziende Telecomunicazioni (FIDAT) (Employees of Telecommunications Undertakings): Via

ITALY

Po 102, 00198 Rome; tel. (06) 855651; affiliated to the CGIL; Sec. GIANFRANCO TESTI; 12,000 mems.

Federazione Italiana Lavoratori Trasporti e Ausiliari del Traffico (FILTAT) (Transport and Associated Workers): Via Nizza 45, Rome; tel. (06) 8448640; affiliated to the CISL; Sec. PIETRO LOMBARDI; 60,000 mems.

Federazione Italiana dei Postelegrafonici (Postal, Telegraph and Telephone Workers): Via Cavour 185, 00187 Rome; tel. (06) 461321; affiliated to the CGIL; Sec. GIUSEPPE MASTRACCHI; 35,000 mems.

Federazione Italiana Trasporti Settore Marittimi (Italian Maritime): Via Boncompagni 19, 00187 Rome; tel. (06) 497881; telex 622005; affiliated to the International Transport Workers' Federation; Nat. Sec. MARIO GUIDI.

Federazione Nazionale Autoferrotranvieri Internavigatori (FNAI) (Bus, Railway and Tram Workers): Rome; tel. (06) 483783; affiliated to the UIL; Sec. BRUNO MONOSILIO.

Federazione Italiana Sindacati dei Trasporti (FILT): Via G. B. Morgagni 27, 00198 Rome; tel. (06) 89961; affiliated to the CGIL; Sec. LUCIO DE CARLINI.

Federazione Italiana Trasporti (FIT): Via Livenza 7, 00198 Rome; tel. (06) 866742; affiliated to the CISL; Sec.-Gen. GAETANO ARCONTI; 152,085 mems.

Federazione Nazionale Lavoratori Auto-Ferrotramvieri e Internavigatori (FENLAI): Via Isonzo 20, Rome; affiliated to the CISL; Gen. Sec. LAURO MORRA; 28,091 mems.

Federazione Poste e Telecomunicazioni (FPT): Via dell'Esquilino 38, 00185 Rome; tel. (06) 4820264; f. 1981; affiliated to the CISL; Sec.-Gen. ERMINIO CHIOFFI; 133,696 mems.

Federazione dei Sindacati Dipendenti Aziende di Navigazione (FEDERSINDAN): Via Tevere 48, Rome; independent; Sec.-Gen. Dott. GIUSEPPE AURICCHIO.

Sindacato Autonomo Unificato Ferrovieri Italiani (Railway Workers): Via Anamari 20, 00185 Rome; tel. (06) 4955251; f. 1950; affiliated to the CISL; National Sec. SILVIO SATURNO; 40,000 mems.

Sindacato Italiano Lavoratori Uffici Locali ed Agenzie Postelegrafoniche (Post and Telegraph Workers): Via Esquilino 38, 00185 Rome; affiliated to the CISL; Gen. Sec. GIOVANNI MARIA NIEDDU; 62,268 mems.

UILTRASPORTI: Via Gaeta 15, 00185 Rome; tel. (06) 479911; affiliated to the UIL; Sec. RAFFAELE LIGUORI.

Unione Italiana Lavoratori Trasporti Ausiliari Traffico e Portuali (UILTATEP) (Transport and Associated Workers): Via Palestro 78, 00185 Rome; tel. (06) 4950698; f. 1950; affiliated to the UIL; Sec.-Gen. RAFFAELE LIGOURI; 134,280 mems.

Unione Italiana Marittimi (UIM) (Seamen): Rome; tel. (06) 422800; affiliated to the UIL; National Sec. GIORGIO MARANGONI; 12,500 mems.

Miscellaneous

Federazione Italiana Agenti Rappresentanti Viaggia-tori-Piazzisti 'Fiarvep' (Commercial Travellers and Representatives): Corso Porta Vittoria 43, Milan; affiliated to the CGIL; Sec. LIONELLO GIANNINI.

Federazione Nazionale Pensionati (FNP) (Pensioners): Via Alessandria 26, 00198 Rome; tel. (06) 861218; f. 1952; affiliated to the CISL; Sec. GIANFRANCO CHIAPELLA; 800,000 mems.

Sindacato Nazionale Musicisti (Musicians): Rome; tel. (06) 490467; independent; National Sec. Maestro SALVATORE ALLEGRA.

Sindacato Pensionati Italiani (Pensioners): Via Morgagni 27, Rome; affiliated to the CGIL; Gen. Sec. ARVEDO FORNI; 1,800,000 mems.

Co-operative Unions

Confederazione Cooperative Italiane (CONFCOOPERATIVE): Borgo S. Spirito 78, 00193 Rome; tel. (06) 650861; telex 622465; f. 1945; federation of co-operative unions; Pres. DARIO MENGOZZI; Sec.-Gen. VINCENZO MANNINO.

Associazione Generale delle Cooperative Italiane (AGCI): Viale Somalia 164, 00199 Rome; tel. (06) 8313753; telex 622285; f. 1952; Pres. RENATO ASCARI RACCAGNI; Sec.-Gen. GINO MARINONI.

Federazione Italiana dei Consorzi Agari (FEDERCONCORZI) (Landowners' Consortia): Via Curtatone 3, 00185 Rome; tel. (06) 46641; telex 610010; Pres. FERNANDINO TRUZZI; Dir-Gen. LUIGI SCOTTI.

Federazione Nazionale della Cooperazione Agricola (Agricultural Co-operatives): Via Nazionale 69, 00184 Rome; tel. (06) 483824; Pres. CARLO FORCELLA; Dir Dr SANRO ROSSI.

Lega Nazionale delle Cooperative e Mutue (National League of Co-operative and Friendly Societies): Via Guattani 9, 00161 Rome;

tel. (06) 841371; telex 611346; 10 affiliated unions; Pres. ONELIO PRANDINI.

STATE HOLDINGS AND NATIONALIZED BODIES

Ente Nazionale Idrocarburi (ENI): Piazzale Enrico Mattei 1, 00144 Rome; tel. (06) 59001; telex 610082; state-owned energy corporation with subsidiaries including AGIP, AGIP Petroli, SNAM and AGIP Carbone operating in the energy sector; Enimont in chemicals; SAMIM in mining and metallurgy; SNAMPROGETTI and SAIPEM in engineering and services; Nuovo Pignone in machines and instruments; SOFID and ENI International Holding SA in the financial sector; Chair. FRANCO REVIGLIO.

Ente Nazionale per l'Energia Elettrica (ENEL): Via Giovanni Battista Martini 3, 00198 Rome; tel. (06) 85091; f. 1962 to generate and distribute electrical power throughout various areas of the country and to work in conjunction with the Ministry of Industry and Trade; Chair. FRANCO VIEZZOLI.

Ente Partecipazioni e Finanziamento Industria Manifatturiera (EFIM): Via XXIV Maggio 43/45, 00187 Rome; tel. (06) 47101; telex 621381; f. 1962 as a state law agency, managing three holding companies and more than 100 companies. Its main fields of activity are on-land transports, aeronautics, armaments and defence systems, glass, aluminium and plant engineering; Pres. ROLANDO VALIANI.

Istituto per la Ricostruzione Industriale (IRI): Via Vittorio Veneto 89, 00187 Rome; tel. (06) 47271; f. 1933 as an autonomous agency controlling banking and industrial undertakings, IRI is responsible for many of the companies in which the State participates, including the national airline Alitalia, the road company ANAS, the RAI television service, the SIP telephone network, the three main commercial banks, the iron and steel producer Ilva, the shipping company Italmare and the holding company SPA; Chair. Prof. ROMANO PRODI.

Società Italiana per l'esercizio telefonico SpA (SIP): Via San Dalmazzo 15, 10122 Turin; tel. (011) 5771; telex 610467; cap. 880,000m. (1980); operates, under government licence, the telephone system over the entire country except for intertoll system; 21.7m. telephones (1983).

Transport

Direzione Generale della Motorizzazione Civile e del Trasporti in Concessione: Viale del Policlinico 2, 00100 Rome; tel. (06) 859271; telex 616041; controls road transport and traffic, and public transport services (railways operated by private companies, motorbuses, trolley-buses, funicular railways and inland waterways); Dir-Gen. Ing. GAETANO DANESE.

RAILWAYS

The majority of Italian lines are in the hands of the State. The first railway line (Naples–Portici) was opened in 1835. The present-day Italian State Railways comprise an amalgamation, begun in 1905 and completed in 1907, of three private companies. In 1988 the total length of the network was 15,983 km, 57% of which is electrified. Apart from the state railway system there are 27 local and municipal railway companies, many of whose lines are narrow gauge. There are metro systems in Rome, Milan and Naples; and a metro system is planned for Turin. A high-speed service with tilting trains is in operation between Rome and Milan.

Ente Ferrovie dello Stato: Piazza della Croce Rossa 1, 00161 Rome; tel. (06) 84901; telex 610089; a public enterprise which administers the State Railways, headed by an Administrative Board; Special Commissioner MARIO SCHIMBERNI; Dir-Gen. Prof. GIOVANNI COLETTI.

ROADS

In 1984 there were 301,307 km of road in Italy, including 45,618 km of major roads, 108,082 km of secondary roads and 5,941 km of motorway. All the *autostrade* (motorways) are toll roads except for the one between Salerno and Reggio Calabria and motorways in Sicily. By law ANAS is responsible for the planning, construction and management of the motorway network. The 13-km Mount Frejus highway tunnel, linking Italy and France through the Alps, opened in 1980.

Azienda Nazionale Autonoma delle Strade Statali (ANAS) (National Autonomous Road Corporation): Via Monzambano 10, 00185 Rome; tel. (06) 4957641; f. 1928, reorganized 1946; responsible for the administration of state roads and their improvement and extension; the president is the Minister of Public Works.

SHIPPING

In 1984 the merchant fleet had a displacement of 9.1m. gross tons.

ITALY

Genova

Costa Armatori SpA (Linea C): Via Gabriele D'Annunzio 2, 16100 Genova; tel. (010) 54831; telex 270068; passenger and cargo service; Mediterranean–North, Central and South America; Caribbean cruises; Chair. NICOLA COSTA.

Franconia Srl: POB 607, Via XX Settembre 37-11, 16121 Genova; tel. (010) 818851; telex 270017; Chair. FRIGERIO BRUNO; Man. Dir EMANUELE RAVANO.

'Garibaldi' Società Cooperativa di Navigazione Srl: Piazza Dante 8, 16121 Genova; tel. (010) 581635; telex 270548; f. 1918; tanker and cargo services; Pres. GIAN FRANCO VIALE; Man. Dir MARIO DI LELLA.

Industriale Marittima SpA: Via Porta d'Archi 10/21, 16121 Genova; tramp; Man. Dir A. PORTA FIGARI.

'Italia di Navigazione' SpA: Torre WTC, Via de Marini 1, Genova; tel. (010) 24021; telex 270032; f. 1932; freight services to Mediterranean, North, South and Central America and South Pacific; Chair. LUCIO DE GIACOMO; Man. Dir ROBERTO COLONNELLO.

Messina, Ignazio and C. SpA: Via G. d'Annunzio 91, 16121 Genova; tel. (010) 53961; tel. 270450; services to Arabian Gulf, Nigeria, North, East and West Africa, Libya and Near East, Red Sea, Malta, Europe; Chair. I. MESSINA; Man. Dirs GINAFRANCO MESSINA, GIORGIO MESSINA, P. MESSINA.

Navigazione Alta Italia, SpA: Via Corsica 19, 16128 Genova; tel. (010) 56331; telex 270181; f. 1906; worldwide dry and bulk cargo; Chair. and Man. Dir SEBASTIANO CAMELI; Gen. Man. ROMANO GUGLIELMINI.

Sidermar di Navigazione SpA: Via XX Settembre 41, Genova; tel. (010) 56341; telex 270412; f. 1956; cargo; Chair. Dott. DARIO DEL BUONO; Man. Dir Dott. CARLO CIONI.

Naples

Garolla Fratelli SpA: Pontile Falvio Giola 45, 80133 Naples; tel. (081) 5534477; telex 710256; Chair. R. GAROLLA; Dirs F. GAROLLA, C. GAROLLA.

Fratelli Grimaldi Armatori: Via M. Campodisola 13, 80133 Naples; tel. (081) 205466; telex 710058; passenger, cargo, containers and tramp to Europe, Middle East, South, Central and North America; Dirs M. GRIMALDI, G. GRIMALDI, A. GRIMALDI, U. GRIMALDI.

Tirrenia di Navigazione SpA: Head Office: Palazzo Sirignano, Rione Sirignano 2, 80121 Naples; tel. (081) 7201111; telex 710028; Pres. GUIDO DE VITA; Dir Gen. PIETRO FERRIGNO.

Palermo

D'Amico Società di Navigazione SpA: Via Siracusa 27, 90141 Palermo; tel. (091) 298737; telex 610157; tramp and liner; Mans CIRO D'AMICO, ANTONIO D'AMICO.

Sicilia Regionale Marittima SpA (SIREMAR): Via Francesco Crispi 120, 90139 Palermo; tel. (091) 582688; telex 910135; ferry services; Pres. DOMENICO CANGIALOSI; Man. Dir LUIGI FIORENTINO.

Sicula Oceanicas SA (SIOSA): Via Mariano Stabile 179, 90139 Palermo; tel. (091) 217939; telex 910098; f. 1941; cruises, passenger and cargo; Italy to North Europe, South, Central, North America; Dir G. GRIMALDI.

Rome

D'Amico Fratelli, Armatori, SpA: Via Liguria 36, 00187 Rome; tel. (06) 4671; telex 614545; dry cargo, tankers and fruit transport; Dirs GIUSEPPE D'AMICO, VITTORIO D'AMICO.

Linee Marittime dell'Adriatico SpA: Via del Nuoto 11, 00194 Rome; tel. (06) 3272312; telex 611034.

Trieste

Fratelli Cosulich, SpA: Piazza S. Antonio 4, 34122 Trieste; tel. (040) 61583; telex 460018; f. 1854; shipowners and shipping agents; cargo to Near East, Red Sea, Far East and South America; brs in Catania, Genoa, Hong Kong, Livorno, Messina, Naples, Palermo, Salerno, Turin, Zürich; Chair. and Man. Dir GEROLIMICH COSULICH.

Lloyd Triestino di Navigazione SpA: Palazzo del Lloyd Triestino, Piazza Unità d'Italia 1, 34121 Trieste; tel. (040) 7364; telex 460321; f. 1836; cargo services by container, roll on/roll off and conventional vessels to Africa, Australasia and Far East; Pres. Dott. Ing. VITTORIO FANFANI; Dir-Gen. Ing. TOMMASO RICCI.

Other Towns

Adriatica di Navigazione SpA: Zattere 1411, CP 705, 30123 Venice; tel. (041) 781611; telex 410045; f. 1937; passenger and freight services from Italy to Eastern Mediterranean, Egypt, Greece, Yugoslavia; Pres. Dott. ROBERTO FIORENTINI; Man. Dir CLAUDIO BONICIOLLI.

Snam SpA: Piazza Vanoni 1, San Donato Milanese, POB 12060, 20097 Milan; tel. (02) 5201; telex 310246; f. 1941; purchase, transport and sale of natural gas, transport of crude oil and petroleum products by means of pipeline and tanker fleet; Pres. Ing. PIO PIGORINI; Vice-Pres. and Man. Dir Ing. LUIGI MEANTI; Man. Dirs Ing. VITTORIO MEAZZINI, Dr ANGELO FERRARI.

SHIPPING ASSOCIATIONS

Associazione Italiana dell' Armamento di Linea (FEDARLINEA): Via Ferdinando di Savoia 8, 00196 Rome; tel. (06) 3603447; f. 1967; Pres. Dr MARIO BONACCHI; Dir Dr GIUSEPPE RAVERA.

Confederazione Italiana degli Armatori (CONFITARMA): Via dei Sabini 7, 00187 Rome; tel. (06) 6787541; telex 626135; f. 1901; Pres. EGIDIO ORTONA; Dir GIUSEPPE PERASSO; 300 mems.

CIVIL AVIATION

National Airline

Alitalia (Linee Aeree Italiane): Palazzo Alitalia, Piazzale Giulio Pastore, 00144 Rome; tel. (06) 54441; telex 626211; f. 1946; state-owned airline; international services throughout Europe and to Africa, North and South America, the Middle East, the Far East and Australia; Chair. Dr CARLO VERRI; Dep. Chair. VITTORIO VACCARI; Man. Dirs MAURIZIO MASPES, LUCIANO SARTORETTI; fleet of 5 Boeing 747-200B Combi, 6 Boeing 747-200B, one Boeing 747-200F, 8 Airbus A300B4, 8 ATR-42, 34 DC-9-580, 21 DC-9-32, 22 DC-9-30, 4 Piaggio P166-DL3 and 5 SIAI Marchetti SF-260.

Other Airlines

Aero Trasporti Italiani SpA (ATI): Aeroporto Capodichino, 80144 Naples; tel. (081) 7091111; telex 711005; f. 1963; subsidiary of Alitalia; operates scheduled domestic services and services and charter flights to the Middle East, North Africa and Canary Islands and within Europe; Chair. Prof. CARLO BERNINI; Man. Dir Dr MARIO FRANCHI; fleet of 22 Douglas DC-9-32, 6 ATR 42, 12 MD-80.

Alisarda SpA: 193 Corso Umberto, 07026 Olbia, Sardinia; tel. (0789) 52600; telex 790043; f. 1963; scheduled services between Olbia and Milan, Rome, Pisa, Bologna, Catania, Verona and Cagliari, seasonal services between Olbia, Turin, Genova, Bergamo, Verona, Venice, Monaco, Nice, Paris, Geneva, Zürich, Frankfurt and Munich; Pres. Avv. SERGIO PERALDA; Man. Dir FRANCO TRIVI; Commercial Man. ALFREDO PICCINATO; fleet of 4 MD-82, 1 Bell 412 and 3 DC-9-51.

Tourism

A great number of tourists are attracted to Italy by its Alpine and Mediterranean scenery, sunny climate, Roman buildings, medieval and Baroque churches, Renaissance towns and palaces, paintings and sculpture and famous opera houses. Each of the 91 Provinces has a Board of Tourism; there are also about 300 Aziende Autonome di Cura, Soggiorno e Turismo, with information about tourist accommodation and health treatment, and about 2,000 Pro Loco Associations concerned with local amenities. In 1987 more than 52.7m. foreign visitors (including excursionists) arrived in Italy. There are about 4m. tourist beds.

Ministero del Turismo e dello Spettacolo: Via della Ferratella in Laterano 51, 00100 Rome; tel. (06) 7732; the government department for tourism; Dirs-Gen. Dott. MARIO DE PAULIS (Tourism and Sport), Dott. ROCCO MOCCIA (Performing Arts).

Ente Nazionale Italiano per il Turismo (ENIT) (National Tourist Board): Via Marghera 2, 00185 Rome; tel. (06) 49711; telex 621314; f. 1919; Pres. Avv. GABRIELLO MORETTI; Dir-Gen. GIAMPIERO GALLIAN.

Atomic Energy

Italy has only two completed nuclear power stations, with a total generating capacity of 1,120 MW. Three more plants in Piedmont, Lombardy and Puglia were planned. Each plant was to consist of two 1,000 MW pressurized water reactors. A nuclear-related referendum held in November 1987, in which national plans for atomic energy were opposed, led to the suspension of the construction of the planned nuclear power stations, and to the reformulation of the Five-Year National Energy Plan. Nuclear power provided 0.1% of total electricity in 1987.

ENEA—Comitato Nazionale per la Ricerca e per lo Sviluppo dell'Energia Nucleare e delle Energie Alternative: Via Regina Margherita 125, 00198 Rome; tel. (06) 85281; telex 610183; f. 1960; supervises pure and applied research into nuclear power plants, provides technical and economic evaluations and supervision of

ITALY

health and environmental protection; promotes energy saving and the use of renewable energy sources; Chair. UMBERTO COLOMBO; Vice-Pres. Prof. LUIGI NOÈ; Dir-Gen. Dr FABIO PISTELLA.

Ente Nazionale per l'Energia Elettrica (ENEL): Via G.B. Martini 3 (Piazza Verdi), 00198 Rome; tel. (06) 85091; state electricity authority; has nuclear power stations in operation in the following areas: Caorso: a 860 MWe plant; Latina: a 210 MWe (MAGNOX) plant; Garigliano: a 160 MWe (BWR) plant; Trino Vercellese: a 256 MWe (PWR) plant; Pres. Dr FRANCO VIEZZOLI; Dir-Gen. Ing. ALBERTO NEGRONI.

JAMAICA

Introductory Survey

Location, Climate, Language, Religion, Flag, Capital

Jamaica is the third largest island in the Caribbean Sea, lying 145 km (90 miles) to the south of Cuba and 160 km (100 miles) to the south-west of Haiti. The climate varies with altitude, being tropical at sea-level and temperate in the mountain areas. The average annual temperature is 27°C (80°F) and mean annual rainfall is 198 cm (78 inches). The official language is English, although a local patois is widely spoken. The majority of the population belong to Christian churches, of which the Anglican Communion is the strongest. There is also a large community of Rastafarians. The national flag (proportions 2 by 1) consists of a diagonal gold cross on a background of black (left and right) and green (above and below). The capital is Kingston.

Recent History

Jamaica became a British colony in 1655. Plans for independence were made in the 1940s. Internal self-government was achieved in 1959, and full independence, within the Commonwealth, on 6 August 1962. In 1958 Jamaica joined with Trinidad, Barbados, the Leeward Islands and the Windward Islands to form the West Indies Federation. Jamaica seceded in 1961, following a referendum, and the Federation broke up.

The two dominant political figures after the Second World War were the late Sir Alexander Bustamante, leader of the Jamaica Labour Party (JLP), who retired as Prime Minister in 1967, and Norman Manley, a former Premier and leader of the People's National Party (PNP), who died in 1969. The JLP won the elections of 1962 and 1967 but, under the premiership of Hugh Shearer, it lost the elections of February 1972 to the PNP, led by Michael Manley, the son of Norman Manley. Michael Manley was an advocate of democratic socialism and his government put great emphasis on social reform and economic independence.

The early 1970s were marked by escalating street violence and crime, with gang warfare rife in the slum areas of Kingston. Between January and June 1976 162 people were killed, and in June the Government declared a state of public emergency. Despite the unrest, high unemployment and severe economic stagnation, the PNP was returned to power in December 1976 with an increased majority. The state of emergency was lifted in June 1977. By January 1979, however, there was again widespread political unrest, and violent demonstrations signalled growing discontent with the Manley Government.

In February 1980, with a worsening economic crisis, Manley rejected the IMF's conditions for further loans to Jamaica and called a general election to seek support for his economic policies and his decision to end dependence on the IMF. The electoral campaign was one of the most violent in Jamaica's history, although the level of violence dropped after a joint plea by Manley and Edward Seaga, leader of the opposition JLP, to their supporters for an end to the bloodshed. In the October election, in contrast to the close result predicted, the JLP had a decisive victory, receiving about 57% of the total votes and winning 51 of the 60 seats in the House of Representatives. Seaga was thus given a convincing mandate to implement his policies for a return to close political and economic links with the USA and the promotion of free enterprise. Diplomatic relations with Cuba were severed in October 1981, and Jamaica was seen to be moving nearer to the USA, with whose financial support the Seaga administration was giving a credible economic performance. The PNP, wishing to regain support, dissociated itself from the communist Workers' Party of Jamaica (WPJ) in an attempt to regain the support of more moderate voters. In February 1981 Manley offered to resign as PNP leader, and agreed to continue only upon the expulsion of extreme left-wing members from the party. Electoral reforms were also proposed, and a new electoral roll was to be completed before the next general election, due in 1985.

In November 1983, when only 70% of this work was complete, the JLP called an early election, to be held on 15 December. Only four days were allowed for the nomination of candidates. The PNP, unable to present candidates at such short notice, refused to take part and declared the elections void. The JLP, opposed by minor independent candidates in only six constituencies, won all 60 seats in the House of Representatives and formed a one-party legislature. Manley announced that the PNP would undertake extraparliamentary opposition to the JLP Government. At the inauguration of the new Parliament in January 1984, there were violent demonstrations by about 7,000 PNP supporters, led by Michael Manley.

Devaluations of the Jamaican dollar, and the withdrawal of food subsidies, provoked demonstrations and sporadic violence as the prices of foodstuffs and energy increased by between 50% and 100%. In order to offset the effects of economic austerity measures, imposed at the instigation of the IMF, the Government extended its programme of food stamps to cover more than one-half of the population. Unemployment, and the consequences of illicit trading in drugs, contributed to a rise in the incidence of crime and violence, especially in Kingston. The Government increased its powers to combat political and violent crime, although the measures were criticized as autocratic by the PNP. The PNP warned of social instability as a result of Seaga's economic policies, and argued for the need to hold fresh elections after the completion of the new electoral roll, while opinion polls highlighted the unpopularity of the Seaga administration. In January 1985 violent demonstrations erupted again in Kingston after a further rise in the price of petrol. Widespread opposition by government employees to redundancies, price rises and wage restraint led to a virtual general strike in June, organized by six major trade unions. Seaga remained unmoved and stressed the necessity for further austerity.

In May 1986, however, Seaga defied recommendations by the IMF, the World Bank and the US Agency for International Development (USAID) for a continuation of restrictive policies, and, instead, introduced an expansionary budget for 1986/87, in an attempt to stimulate economic growth (see Economic Affairs). This move, however, was criticized by opposition parties. Municipal elections, originally scheduled for June 1984, were held in July 1986, having been postponed three times. The PNP obtained control of 11 of the 13 municipalities in which polling took place, winning 57% of the total votes. In the light of these results, Manley appealed again for an early general election (constitutionally due by April 1989) but this demand was ignored by Seaga. Further criticisms of government economic policies were expressed when large debt arrears to the IMF led to the suspension, in September, of the Fund's loan agreement. (A 15-month stand-by arrangement was agreed in January 1987.) During 1987 several members of the JLP left the party, and the Government received severe criticism from the PNP, following the launch of its 'debt-for-equity' scheme in July (see Economic Affairs). A serious outbreak of drug-related violence began in the same month. In October the Government presented a plan intended to combat crime, which included proposals for the imposition of harsher punishments for those convicted of drug trafficking and the provision of improved equipment for the Jamaica Defence Force.

In August 1988 Seaga and Manley signed a non-violence pact, aimed at preventing a repetition of the level of casualties experienced during the 1980 general election campaign. There were also fears about the effect on the tourist industry and about the likelihood of securing fair polls in some areas. An ombudsman was appointed to supervise political activities during the approach to the general election. Prime Minister Seaga prepared for the election campaign in the budget of April 1988, when he announced plans to increase expenditure on health, social services and education, all of which had been seriously affected by the austerity of the previous years. The date of the general election, however, remained uncertain and a cause of controversy. The Constitution required Parliament to be dissolved by 10 Janauary 1989 (five years after its first meeting), but it allowed elections at any time in a three-month 'grace period' after this date. The PNP objected to the use of this period without reasonable justification.

JAMAICA

In September 1988, however, Jamaica was struck by Hurricane Gilbert, the worst in the country's recorded history. More than 100,000 homes were destroyed, while the economy, particularly agriculture, was severely disrupted (see Economic Affairs). Seaga's successful efforts to secure international aid won him some initial support, but this soon disappeared, particularly following controversy over the alleged preferential allocation of relief resources to JLP supporters. After a brief, and relatively peaceful, campaign, the general election was held on 9 February 1989. The PNP received about 57% of the votes cast and won 44 of the 60 seats in the House of Representatives. Michael Manley, who had developed a more moderate image during his years in opposition, again became Prime Minister.

In October 1983 Jamaica contributed troops to the US-led invasion of Grenada and led the Caribbean force which remained, after the removal of the majority of the American forces, to keep the peace and to assist in training the new Grenadian police force.

Prior to his re-election as Prime Minister in February 1989, Michael Manley announced his intention of maintaining good relations with the USA. He also declared that he would re-establish formal diplomatic relations with Cuba and seek greater co-operation within CARICOM, of which Jamaica is a founder-member (see p. 106).

Government

The Head of State is the British monarch, who is represented locally by a Governor-General, appointed on the recommendation of the Prime Minister. The Governor-General acts, in almost all matters, on the advice of the Cabinet.

Legislative power is vested in the bicameral Parliament: a Senate, with 21 appointed members, and a House of Representatives, with 60 elected members. Thirteen members of the Senate are appointed by the Governor-General on the advice of the Prime Minister and eight on the advice of the Leader of the Opposition. Members of the House are elected by universal adult suffrage for five years (subject to dissolution). Executive power lies with the Cabinet. The Governor-General appoints the Prime Minister and, on the latter's recommendation, other Ministers. The Cabinet is responsible to Parliament.

Defence

In June 1988 the Jamaica Defence Force consisted of 2,500 men, including an army of 2,200, a coastguard of 150 and an air force of 150 men. There are reserves of some 750 (50 coastguards, 700 in the army). Defence expenditure in 1987/88 was estimated to be US $5.49m.

Economic Affairs

In 1987, according to estimates by the World Bank, Jamaica's gross national product (GNP), measured at average 1985–87 prices, was US $2,256m., equivalent to US $960 per head. Between 1980 and 1987 GNP per head was estimated to have fallen, in real terms, by an average of 2.5% per year. In 1988 the economy, based mainly on tourism, bauxite and sugar, was severely disrupted by Hurricane Gilbert. Agriculture was particularly badly affected.

The traditional major crops of the agricultural sector are sugar cane, bananas, coffee and cocoa. A wide range of citrus and tropical fruits and vegetables are also grown. In 1986 agricultural production accounted for 6% of Jamaica's gross domestic product (GDP). Along with forestry and fishing, the sector employed 25% of the work-force in 1987. Sugar production has been affected by the recent low level of international prices and by poor crops. Jamaica's annual output of raw sugar declined from 290,000 metric tons in 1978 to 192,820 tons in 1984. In 1985, however, production rose by 12.2%, to 206,707 tons, owing to favourable weather conditions and more efficient factory operations, and export earnings increased from J$ 226.2m. in 1984 to J$ 273.2m. The Government has closed all but two of the state-run sugar factories, in an attempt to restructure the industry, and in June 1986 announced plans for a six-year scheme to improve efficiency. This was to include the rehabilitation of two factories, the improvement of irrigation systems and an increase in research. The scheme aimed to achieve production of 245,000 tons of raw sugar per year, to cover EEC and US quotas and domestic demands. (The Sugar Industry Authority later protested that the production target was unattainable.) In 1986 sugar production declined slightly, to 200,287 metric tons, but export earnings increased to J$ 347.5m. Production continued to decline during 1987, to a total of 187,966 tons. Export earnings from sugar in that year were about US $70m., while domestic sales earned some J $128m. In 1988 Hurricane Gilbert cost the industry some J $150m. in damage, and, although export quotas were fulfilled, sugar had to be imported for domestic consumption. Production, however, had risen to about 220,000 tons, and a slight increase was forecast for 1989.

Jamaica's banana plantations were damaged by Hurricane Allen in 1980, and the country's annual exports fell from the usual level of 70,000 metric tons to 19,000 tons in 1981, rising to only 34,231 tons by 1987. The recovery in the industry was strong, however, in 1987, when exports earned US $20.3m. Hurricane Gilbert affected all the banana plantations and reduced exports to about 28,500 tons (50,000 tons had been expected). However, the industry hoped to export between 40,000 and 45,000 tons in 1989, with shipments expected to resume by April. Cocoa production in 1983 reached 2,782 tons, the highest output for 20 years. Coffee is being developed with aid from Japan, the principal market for Jamaica's Blue Mountain coffee. The hurricane in 1988 was expected to reduce anticipated production of about 2,180 metric tons by two-thirds. More than 1,000 ha needed replanting, and storm damage was estimated at J $210m. Local rice production is being increased in order to reduce Jamaica's imports (up to 53,000 tons per year) by more than one-half. Production in 1985 reached 13,500 tons, an increase of 237% on the 1984 total. Since 1980 the Government has encouraged the diversification of crops, the improvement of techniques and the cultivation of under-used land, in order to reduce the country's growing demand for imported food. During 1986, however, several government agricultural projects experienced difficulties, and by mid-1987 four major vegetable projects had collapsed. Severe flooding during June 1986 was estimated to have caused agricultural losses of J $124m. Non-traditional agricultural exports earned US $15.1m. in 1986, export volumes having grown by 127% between 1983 and 1986. Over the same period, the annual level of domestic food production increased by 35%, to 473,000 metric tons. The immediate consequences of the 1988 hurricane were probably most serious in this sector because of the ensuing food shortages, although recovery was likely to be relatively rapid. It was estimated that some 150,000 subsistence farmers, with their dependants, account for up to one-third of the total population of Jamaica. This group constituted the main welfare problem in the aftermath of the hurricane, which caused them damage costing about J $750m. Further problems of food supply resulted from the loss of the poultry industry, at a cost of more than J $400m.

Jamaica is one of the world's largest producers of bauxite and alumina, and production levies make the industry an important source of government revenue. Until 1980, exports of bauxite and alumina contributed some 75% of total foreign exchange earnings. Owing to a reduction in demand on the international aluminium market, total bauxite production has fallen substantially, from 12.1m. metric tons in 1980 to only 6.2m. tons by 1985, when export earnings were US $145m. In that year two alumina refineries were closed, although the Government subsequently reopened the plant at Clarendon. The Government was determined that the domestic economy should not be adversely affected by the decisions of multi-national companies, but it became involved in a long dispute with its partner at Clarendon, the Aluminium Company of America (Alcoa). Production of alumina declined, and exports fell to 730,707 tons in 1985. Total bauxite production rose to 7.0m. tons in 1986 and to 7.7m. tons in 1987. Exports of crude bauxite increased substantially by 1987, to 3.7m. tons, earning US $113.4m. Alumina production increased only moderately, and exports earned US $200.9m. in 1987. The hurricane in 1988 had a marginal affect on the bauxite industry. Total bauxite output declined by 3.3%, crude bauxite exports decreased slightly (to 3.5m. tons) and alumina production was below target, although maintaining its 1987 level. During 1988, however, the Government had resolved its dispute with Alcoa. The Clarendon refinery, now equally owned, was to increase its production capacity from 750,000 tons per year to 1m. tons, while the Government reduced the bauxite levy for 1989. Furthermore, in March 1989 the Alpart refinery (closed in 1985) was due to be reopened.

Tourism has become Jamaica's major source of foreign exchange. In 1982 tourist arrivals reached a record 650,000.

Tourist arrivals increased by a further 21% in 1983, and also rose during 1984, to reach 843,775. There was an increase of 13.2% in the number of cruiseship passenger arrivals during 1985, but the number of stop-over visitors fell by 5.3% and tourist arrivals totalled 833,221. In 1986 the total number of arrivals was 941,493, and several schemes for the expansion of tourist accommodation were in progress. Gross earnings from tourism rose to US $435m. in 1984, from $399m. in 1983, but fell to $406.8m. in 1985. In 1986, however, earnings totalled some US $500m., and in 1987 they reached US $595m. In that year tourist arrivals exceeded 1m. for the first time, reaching 1,037,634. Hurricane Gilbert had some impact, but there was confidence in the industry's ability to effect a quick recovery. Despite concern about political violence, the 1989 general election campaign passed without an incident serious enough to affect tourist arrivals.

Manufacturing is an expanding sector, and includes the production of cement, textiles, tobacco and a number of consumer goods. 'Free zones' were established at Kingston and Montego Bay, and a wide range of manufacturing and assembly industries were encouraged by the Government, but during 1988 the zones experienced industrial unrest over pay and conditions. Between 1981 and 1987, however, Jamaica attracted more than 800 new investments, worth in excess of US $300m., and more than 63,000 new jobs were created. Despite criticisms of the US Government's Caribbean Basin Initiative (CBI), the development scheme has been of particular help to the Jamaican garment industry. This expanded rapidly when the quota of Jamaican garments that could be exported to the USA was increased by 108% for 1987. There was another increase in 1988, of 37%. Furthermore, under the so-called '807 scheme', garments made in Jamaica from cloth cut in the USA could then be sent back in a separate quota. This was increased by about 40% for 1988 and by 8% for 1989. In 1987 garment exports earned US $185.6m., an increase of almost 90% since the previous year. Trade is chiefly with the USA, Canada and the United Kingdom. A joint consortium of US and Italian companies failed to find commercially exploitable offshore deposits of petroleum to ease Jamaica's high import bill for petroleum. Government policy has been redirected towards energy conservation and the development of alternative energy sources. There are some peat deposits, and it was hoped that, by 1995, a series of hydroelectricity schemes could provide up to 25% of Jamaica's current energy needs. Expansion in the bauxite industry, however, could mean that requirements will increase by that proportion between 1988 and 1992.

The decline in production of Jamaica's traditional export crops and industries, and low international prices, have been compounded by the rising level of imports. As a result, the current deficit on the balance of payments grew from US $42.1m. in 1977 to $408.6m. in 1982. The dramatic devaluations of the Jamaica dollar in 1983 and 1984 (see below), while assisting the competitiveness of Jamaican export industries, increased the cost of imports, especially of petroleum and foodstuffs, which comprise about 50% of total imports. The price of staple foods rose sharply in 1984. Petrol prices increased by 50% in January 1984, and by a further 21% in 1985. However, the merchandise trade deficit was reduced from US $441.5m. in 1982 to $334.7m. in 1984. Although imports were reduced in 1985, a fall of 20% in the value of exports increased the trade deficit to US $435.6m. A fall in the world price of crude petroleum during 1986 enabled the Government to reduce the cost of oil purchases by 45%, and there was a reduction in the merchandise trade deficit, to $247.9m., but in 1987 the deficit increased to $358.2m. In the first eight months of 1988 the trade deficit increased by 27%, compared with the corresponding period in the previous year. Hurricane Gilbert's effects were expected to exacerbate this tendency considerably. There has also been a problem with the volume of emigration from the country, although this can provide an important source of foreign exchange with receipts from emigrants. More than 14,500 migrant farm workers in North America earned J $380m. in 1987. In that year, however, 31,000 people emigrated from Jamaica, the highest number since 1971 (it had fallen to 4,315 in 1983).

The Jamaican economy suffered from a prolonged recession during the 1970s, and by 1980 was in a state of crisis. The JLP Government, on coming to power in 1980, prepared a three-year economic recovery plan which envisaged a considerable injection of foreign investment into the private sector. In 1980 the PNP Government had rejected the terms of an IMF support programme, but the JLP Government reopened negotiations and secured a three-year agreement on assistance totalling US $650m. The restoration of Jamaica's credit with the IMF encouraged aid from Western countries. The full potential of foreign investment in export manufacturing industries, however, was not realized, and in September 1983 the economy failed to meet the IMF's conditions for further payments. An IMF stand-by agreement for US $143m. was finalized in April 1984. The conditions for the agreement included a reduction of the budget deficit by half, from an equivalent of 15.4% of GDP, within a year. Although the Jamaican economy failed to meet all the IMF requirements in the September test period, the Fund granted a technical waiver to allow further payments to be made.

Another agreement was reached for facilities of US $115m. over a 22-month period, commencing in July 1985, subject to continued restraints on government spending. In September 1985 the economy again failed the quarterly performance test, and payments were temporarily suspended. However, a waiver of the IMF-imposed conditions was granted. The economy passed the December test, postponed until January 1986, satisfying the condition that a positive balance of payments of US $60m. should be shown for the financial year 1985/86. In addition, the budget deficit was reduced to 5.7% of GDP. Despite recommendations by officials of the IMF, the World Bank and the US Agency for International Development (USAID) for continued economic austerity, the Government introduced an expansionary budget for 1986/87, claiming that it could produce an annual growth rate of 5% in real GDP. By September 1986, however, Jamaica had incurred debt arrears of US $70m. in its payments to the IMF, making the withdrawal of new payments and the servicing of external debts virtually impossible, although an agreement was signed in October for US $60m. to be paid in two loans by the World Bank. In March 1987 Jamaica's gross external debt was estimated at US $3,500m., causing a heavy burden of servicing payments, equivalent to about 45% of export earnings for the financial year 1986/87. In July 1987 the Government launched a 'debt-for-equity' programme, which aimed to convert some US $200m. of the foreign debt into investments in the country.

The overvaluation of the Jamaican dollar, in relation to the US dollar, led to the creation in January 1983 of a 'parallel market' in exchange rates in order to attract foreign exchange earnings back into Jamaica's banks. By November, however, the exchange rate had not stabilized and, to comply with IMF requirements, the official and 'parallel' exchange rates were unified. As a result, the Jamaican dollar was effectively devalued by 43%. Further smaller devaluations continued during 1984 and 1985, reducing the exchange rate for one US dollar from J $1.78 in November 1983 to J $5.76 by July 1985. After a rapid decline in the Jamaican dollar's value in October, the Government intervened to stabilize the exchange rate at US $1 = J $5.50, which it pledged to maintain during the financial year 1986/87. Negotiations with the IMF, to discuss the renewal of the suspended loan agreement, eventually secured a 15-month stand-by agreement with the IMF, from March 1987, giving access to credits of US $132.8m. In June the World Bank announced loans to Jamaica totalling US $104m., and in December the Caribbean Group for Co-operation in Economic Development agreed to provide the Government with an annual US $180m. for three years to support its programme for economic growth. In September 1988 the IMF authorized a new stand-by agreement, the requirements for the previous arrangement having been satisfied. It gave access to credits of US $105.9m., over 14 months, and sanctioned government efforts to rebuild social services. Following Hurricane Gilbert, the IMF agreed to allow more time to complete economic performance tests.

GDP, measured in constant prices, contracted by 5.8% in 1980, but grew by 2.5% in 1981, and by 1.0% in 1982. After growth of 2.0% in 1983, GDP contracted by 0.4% during 1984 and by 4.6% in 1985, owing to the recession in the bauxite industry. However, growth of 2.3% was achieved in 1986 and 5% in 1987. A similar rate of growth had been expected in 1988, and, despite the hurricane in that year, growth of about 3% was achieved. Inflation, which had been running at 30% in 1980, fell to 6.5% in 1982. However, the depreciation of the currency, and the rise in prices, caused increases in the rate of inflation, which rose to 11.6% in 1983, and to an average of 27.8% in 1984. In 1985, however, inflation fell to an average of 25.7% and in 1986 it fell still further, to an average rate of

JAMAICA

15.1%. By July 1987 the rate of inflation had been reduced to 6.6%, meeting the IMF's stipulations. Inflation in 1988 averaged 8.8%, a lower rate than expected. In spite of government incentives to create jobs, unemployment affected 20.8% of the labour force in October 1987, although this represented a slight decline on the previous year's level.

The cultivation of hemp (marijuana), and the use of Jamaica as a transit centre for the movement of illegal drugs, has posed a serious problem for the Government. It has been estimated that marijuana worth US $750m. is exported to the USA annually, making it unofficially the country's largest export earner. In 1984 1,091 acres (442 ha) of cultivated marijuana were destroyed by the authorities, 450,000 lb (204 metric tons) of cured marijuana were seized, and 4,451 people were arrested for drug-related offences. Between 1985 and 1987 the US Government spent more than US $2.6m. on a programme to eradicate the trading of marijuana in Jamaica.

Jamaica is a member of the Organization of American States (see p. 190), the Caribbean Common Market (CARICOM, p. 107) and the International Bauxite Association (p. 223).

Social Welfare

Social welfare is undertaken by the Government. The Social Development Commission arranges and co-ordinates social welfare in the villages. Contributory national insurance and housing trust schemes are run by the Government. In 1979 Jamaica had 30 government-controlled hospitals, with a total of 7,648 beds, and there were 759 physicians working in the country. In the 1988/89 budget, projected expenditure on health was increased by 123%, to J $128.9m. In 1988, however, Hurricane Gilbert destroyed three hospitals.

Education

Primary education is compulsory in certain districts, and free education is ensured. The education system consists of a primary cycle of six years, followed by two secondary cycles of three and four years respectively. In 1983 more than 90% of children between six and 11 years of age were enrolled at primary schools, while 58% of those aged 12 to 18 attended secondary schools. In 1981 only 2% of the adult population had received no schooling. Higher education is provided by technical colleges and by the University of the West Indies, which has five faculties situated at its Mona campus in Kingston. In 1986 the Government announced that students were to be charged higher education fees, covering up to 30% of tuition costs. The new fees were to be introduced progressively, over two years at the technical colleges and over three years at the University. Expenditure on education by the central Government in the financial year 1988/89 was estimated to be J $133.6m., an increase of 67% on the level of the previous year.

Public Holidays

1989: 2 January (for New Year's Day), 8 February (Ash Wednesday), 24-27 March (Easter), 23 May (Labour Day), 7 August (for Independence Day), 16 October (for National Heroes' Day), 25-26 December (Christmas).

1990: 1 January (New Year's Day), 28 February (Ash Wednesday), 13-16 April (Easter), 21 May (Labour Day), 6 August (Independence Day), 15 October (National Heroes' Day), 25-26 December (Christmas).

Weights and Measures

Both the imperial and the metric systems are in use.

Statistical Survey

Sources (unless otherwise stated): Department of Statistics, 9 Swallowfield Rd, Kingston 5, Jamaica; tel. 926-2175; Jamaica Information Service, Jamaica High Commission, St James's St, London, SW1A 1JS, United Kingdom; tel. (01) 499-8600.

Area and Population

AREA, POPULATION AND DENSITY

Area (sq km)	10,991*
Population (census results)	
7 April 1970	1,848,512
8 June 1982	2,190,357
Population (official estimates at 31 December)	
1984	2,190,000
1986	2,346,900
1987	2,355,400
Density (per sq km) at 31 December 1987	214.3

* 4,243.6 sq miles.

PARISHES

	Area (sq miles)	Population (31 Dec. 1986)
Kingston	8.406	641,500
St Andrew	186.308	
St Thomas	286.800	85,300
Portland	314.347	77,100
St Mary	235.745	111,600
St Ann	468.213	147,100
Trelawny	337.651	73,200
St James	229.728	149,500
Hanover	173.855	65,200
Westmorland	311.604	126,600
St Elizabeth	468.085	144,400
Manchester	320.482	157,800
Clarendon	461.864	214,400
St Catherine	460.396	353,200
Total	**4,263.484***	**2,346,900**

* Other sources give the total area of the country as 4,243.6 square miles.

Capital: Kingston (population 104,000 at 1980 census).

Other towns (1970 census): Montego Bay (42,800); Spanish Town (41,600).

JAMAICA   Statistical Survey

BIRTHS, AND DEATHS*

	Registered live births		Registered deaths	
	Number	Rate (per 1,000)	Number	Rate (per 1,000)
1982	61,500	27.9	14,500	6.6
1983	61,400	27.4	12,600	5.6
1984	57,500	25.2	13,400	5.9
1985	56,200	24.3	13,900	6.0
1986	54,100	23.2	13,300	5.7
1987	52,300	22.2	12,400	5.3

Registered marriages: 10,536 in 1987.

* Data are tabulated by year of registration rather than by year of occurrence.

CIVILIAN LABOUR FORCE (at October)

	1985	1986	1987
Agriculture, forestry and fishing	278,900	267,200	269,300
Mining, quarrying and refining	6,000	6,300	5,300
Manufacturing	100,600	115,300	138,200
Construction and installation	34,800	35,400	38,600
Transport, communications and public utilities	34,700	38,300	42,100
Commerce	115,300	125,100	128,100
Public administration	81,100	79,900	72,800
Other services	127,200	150,100	158,600
Activities not adequately defined	2,400	3,000	2,000
Total employed	781,000	820,600	855,000
Unemployed	268,800	234,900	224,200
Total labour force	1,049,800	1,055,500	1,079,200

Agriculture

PRINCIPAL CROPS ('000 metric tons)

	1984	1985	1986
Sweet potatoes	36	32	32*
Cassava	20	18	18*
Other roots and tubers	192	202	200*
Coconuts*	120	120	120
Vegetables and melons	147	124	126
Sugar cane	2,422	2,270	2,083*
Oranges*	32	33	33
Lemons and limes*	23	24	24
Grapefruit and pomelo*	21	22	22
Bananas*	150	160	160
Coffee (green)*	2	2	2

* FAO estimates.
Source: FAO, *Production Yearbook*.

LIVESTOCK
(FAO estimates, '000 head, year ending September)

	1984	1985	1986
Horses	4	4	4
Mules	10	10	10
Asses	24	23	23
Cattle	290	280	290
Pigs	240	245	245
Sheep	5	5	6
Goats	420	430	430
Poultry	5,000	5,000	5,000

Source: FAO, *Production Yearbook*.

LIVESTOCK PRODUCTS ('000 metric tons)

	1984	1985	1986*
Beef and veal	12	11	11
Goats' meat*	2	2	2
Pig meat	6	6	6
Poultry meat	30	23	23
Cows' milk	49	50*	50
Hen eggs*	17.4	17.5	17.5

* FAO estimates.
Source: FAO, *Production Yearbook*.

Forestry

ROUNDWOOD REMOVALS ('000 cubic metres, excl. bark)

	1982	1983	1984
Total	43	84	93

1985–86: Annual output as in 1984 (FAO estimate).
Source: FAO, *Yearbook of Forest Products*.

Fishing

('000 metric tons, live weight)

	1984	1985	1986
Total catch	9.6	10.2	10.5

Source: FAO, *Yearbook of Fishery Statistics*.

Mining

('000 metric tons)

	1985	1986	1987
Bauxite*	6,119.4	5,522.4	7,802.1
Alumina	1,461.7	1,314.8	1,613.0

* Dried equivalent of crude ore.

JAMAICA

Industry

SELECTED PRODUCTS
('000 metric tons, unless otherwise indicated)

	1983	1984	1985
Margarine and lard	8.4	9.0	8.9
Crude vegetable oil ('000 kilolitres)	13	12	15
Wheat flour	62	86	132
Other flour	24	n.a.	n.a.
Raw sugar	198	188	225
Animal foodstuffs	217	216	165
Rum and gin ('000 hectolitres)	147	173	148
Beer ('000 hectolitres)	604	517	568
Soft drinks ('000 hectolitres)	393	371	372
Cigars (million)	19	22	21
Cigarettes (million)	1,359	1,270	1,314
Woven cotton fabrics ('000 metres)	4	n.a.	n.a.
Footwear ('000 pairs)	600*	n.a.	n.a.
Jet fuels	45	40	42
Motor gasoline—Petrol	160	150	155
Kerosene	75	70	72
Distillate fuel oils	201	200	210
Residual fuel oils	504	400	410
Lubricating oils	25	28	30
Bitumen—Asphalt	13	15	15
Liquefied petroleum gas	18	19*	20*
Rubber tyres ('000)	196	209	210
Quicklime	122	115*	115*
Cement	278	259	241
Electric energy (million kWh)	2,399	2,400	2,400

* Estimates.
Source: UN, *Industrial Statistics Yearbook*.
1987 (million): Cigars 18.6; Cigarettes 1,272.8.

Finance

CURRENCY AND EXCHANGE RATES

Monetary Units
100 cents = 1 Jamaican dollar (J $).

Denominations
Coins: 1, 5, 10, 20, 25 and 50 cents.
Notes: 50 cents; 1, 2, 5, 10, 20 and 100 dollars.

Sterling and US Dollar Equivalents (30 September 1988)
£1 sterling = J $9.267;
US $1 = J $5.480;
J $100 = £10.791 = US $18.248.

Average Exchange Rate (J $ per US $)
1985 5.5586
1986 5.4778
1987 5.4867

Note: Since November 1983, when the previous official and 'parallel' market rates were unified, the exchange rate has been determined by the commercial banks in an auction market.

BUDGET (J $ million, year ending 31 March)

Revenue	1986/87
Recurrent Revenue:	
Customs	231.5
Excise duties	31.0
Income tax	1,514.6
Land and property tax	26.2
Stamp duties	522.8
Motor vehicle licences	62.6
Consumption duty	858.0
Betting and gaming tax	32.8
Retail sales tax	49.4
Other taxes and duties	166.4
Sub-total	**3,495.1**
Non-tax receipts	83.4
Transfer from Capital Development Fund	20.0
Total	**3,598.7**

Expenditure	1986/87
Recurrent Expenditure:	
Interest on public debt	1,078.6
General administration	437.3
Public order and safety	395.2
Agriculture	55.9
Education and social welfare	691.8
Public health	313.6
Trade and industry	26.9
Public utilities and transport	66.0
Housing	58.6
Other	28.2
Sub-total	**3,152.1**
Capital Expenditure:	
General administration	316.5
Agriculture	67.5
Education and social welfare	28.5
Housing	248.4
Health	16.5
Public utilities and transport	64.7
Financing of public enterprises	50.8
Public debt	1,043.7
Sub-total	**1,836.6**
Total	**4,988.7**

COST OF LIVING (Consumer Price Index; end of December. Base: January 1975 = 100)

	1985	1986	1987*
Food and drink	729.6	818.4	839.9
Fuel and household supplies	863.2	915.0	925.4
Housing	423.1	458.6	476.3
Household furnishings and furniture	761.6	835.8	885.7
Personal clothing and accessories	541.3	639.5	659.2
Personal expenses	728.4	806.4	844.0
Transport	575.4	579.5	578.7
Miscellaneous expenses	523.8	542.8	549.9
All items	**670.7**	**742.5**	**762.9**

* Preliminary.

JAMAICA

Statistical Survey

NATIONAL ACCOUNTS (J $ million at current prices)
Expenditure on the Gross Domestic Product

	1986	1987*
Government final consumption expenditure	2,063.6	2,294.7
Private final consumption expenditure	8,719.4	9,819.8
Increase in stocks	167.5	136.5
Gross fixed capital formation	2,410.9	3,421.9
Total domestic expenditure	**13,361.4**	**15,672.9**
Exports of goods and services	7,016.2	8,618.1
Less Imports of goods and services	7,049.6	8,573.5
GDP in purchasers' values	**13,328.0**	**15,717.5**

* Preliminary.

BALANCE OF PAYMENTS (US $ million)

	1985	1986	1987
Merchandise exports f.o.b.	568.6	589.5	708.4
Merchandise imports f.o.b.	−1,004.2	−837.4	−1,066.6
Trade balance	**−435.6**	**−247.9**	**−358.2**
Exports of services	697.6	821.5	932.3
Imports of services	−784.8	−760.1	−849.7
Balance on goods and services	**−522.8**	**−186.5**	**−275.6**
Private unrequited transfers (net)	153.2	111.6	116.0
Government unrequited transfers (net)	65.2	34.8	62.5
Current balance	**−304.4**	**−40.1**	**−97.1**
Direct capital investment (net)	−9.05	−4.6	163.4
Other long-term capital (net)	117.9	−188.1	
Short-term capital (net)	121.7	88.2	18.1
Net errors and omissions	17.0	80.0	212.9
Total (net monetary movements)	**−56.8**	**−64.6**	**297.3**
Valuation changes (net)	−33.5	−143.7	−229.0
Exceptional financing	96.8	179.7	5.9
Official financing (net)	−10.8	−12.4	—
Changes in reserves	**−4.2**	**−40.9**	**74.2**

Source: IMF, *International Financial Statistics*.

External Trade

COMMODITY GROUPS (US $'000)

Imports	1986	1987
Food and live animals	166,180	181,923
Beverages and tobacco	9,865	12,028
Crude materials (inedible) except fuels	30,150	37,008
Mineral fuels, lubricants, etc.	202,666	219,524
Animal and vegetable oils and fats	10,583	15,475
Chemicals	107,765	119,424
Basic manufactures	168,871	n.a.
Machinery and transport equipment	174,583	245,822
Miscellaneous manufactured articles	87,237	135,527
Other commodities and transactions	18,498	22,223
Total	**976,398**	**1,216,067**

Exports	1986	1987
Food and live animals	122,907	150,596
Beverages and tobacco	29,637	33,855
Crude materials (inedible) except fuels	314,732	333,387
Mineral fuels, lubricants, etc.	18,273	14,111
Animal and vegetable oils and fats	71	303
Chemicals	18,558	20,830
Basic manufactures	8,634	n.a.
Machinery and transport equipment	19,249	11,159
Miscellaneous manufactured articles	65,483	15,038
Other commodities and transactions	32	—
Total	**597,576**	**696,057**

PRINCIPAL TRADING PARTNERS (J $'000)

Imports c.i.f.	1984	1985	1986
Canada	246,344	223,000	282,492
Ecuador	30,131	45,847	148,284
Germany, Federal Republic	73,549	66,321	78,754
Japan	130,276	433,552	196,829
Mexico	49,091	277,044	82,991
Netherlands	42,056	84,793	76,621
Netherlands Dependencies	604,546	507,506	74,367
Trinidad and Tobago	89,852	181,356	103,751
United Kingdom	244,989	326,951	362,584
USA	2,036,052	2,545,619	2,675,854
Total (incl. others)	**4,509,548**	**6,146,681**	**5,322,277**

Exports f.o.b.*	1984	1985	1986
Barbados	38,949	65,665	62,063
Canada	409,085	511,792	500,208
Ghana	—	92,244	36,154
Guyana	12,288	20,978	23,143
Japan	—	46,537	34,632
Netherlands	171	72,480	232,492
Norway	33,036	72,767	92,649
Sweden	101,708	17,720	22,573
Trinidad and Tobago	124,298	85,910	86,755
USSR	145,099	157,082	137,270
United Kingdom	369,089	525,690	609,688
USA	1,375,586	1,022,644	1,052,768
Total (incl. others)	**2,675,758**	**2,958,815**	**3,089,238**

* Excluding re-exports.

Transport

RAILWAYS
(1985): 1.01m. passengers carried; 24.9m. passenger-miles.

ROAD TRAFFIC
(vehicles in use at 31 December 1986)

Passenger Cars	42,888
Buses and coaches	
Goods vehicles	26,486
Tractors (non-agricultural)	
Motocycles and scooters	5,605

JAMAICA

SHIPPING

International Sea-borne Freight Traffic
(estimates, '000 metric tons)

	1983	1984	1985
Goods loaded	6,278	7,894	5,485
Goods unloaded	3,166	3,625	3,672

Source: UN, *Monthly Bulletin of Statistics*.

CIVIL AVIATION (traffic on scheduled services)

	1982	1983	1984
Kilometres flown (million)	14.5	9.8	10.4
Passengers carried ('000)	873	716	747
Passenger-km (million)	1,230	1,079	1,303
Freight ton-km (million)	11.6	16.6	19.5

Source: UN, *Statistical Yearbook*.

Tourism

Total number of visitors (1987): 1,037,634.

Communications Media

RADIO RECEIVERS
(1987): 1,448,122 in use.

TELEVISION RECEIVERS
(1987): 462,055 in use.

TELEPHONES
(1986): 152,295 in use.

DAILY NEWSPAPERS
(1988): 3.

Education

(1984/85)

	Institutions	Teachers	Students
Basic schools	269	n.a.	10,903
Primary	792	9,695	335,218
Secondary	141	7,936	125,000
Tertiary	14	n.a.	7,544
University	1	399	5,354

Directory

The Constitution

The Constitution came into force at the independence of Jamaica on 6 August 1962.

HEAD OF STATE

The Head of State is the British monarch, who is locally represented by a Governor-General, appointed on the recommendation of the Jamaican Prime Minister.

THE LEGISLATURE

The Senate or Upper House consists of 21 Senators of whom 13 will be appointed by the Governor-General on the advice of the Prime Minister and eight by the Governor-General on the advice of the Leader of the Opposition.

The House of Representatives consists of 60 elected members called Members of Parliament.

A person is qualified for appointment to the Senate or for election to the House of Representatives if he or she is a citizen of Jamaica or other Commonwealth country, of the age of 21 or more and has been ordinarily resident in Jamaica for the immediately preceding 12 months.

THE PRIVY COUNCIL

The Privy Council consists of six members appointed by the Governor-General after consultation with the Prime Minister, of whom at least two are persons who hold or who have held public office. The functions of the Council are to advise the Governor-General on the exercise of the Royal Prerogative of Mercy and on appeals on disciplinary matters from the three Service Commissions.

THE EXECUTIVE

The Prime Minister is appointed from the House of Representatives by the Governor-General as the person who, in the Governor-General's judgement, is best able to command the support of the majority of the members of that House.

The Leader of the Opposition is appointed by the Governor-General as the member of the House of Representatives who, in the Governor-General's judgement, is best able to command the support of the majority of those members of the House who do not support the Government.

The Cabinet consists of the Prime Minister and not fewer than 11 other Ministers, not more than four of whom may sit in the Senate. The members of the Cabinet are appointed by the Governor-General on the advice of the Prime Minister.

THE JUDICATURE

The Judicature consists of a Supreme Court, a Court of Appeal and minor courts. Judicial matters, notably advice to the Governor-General on appointments, are considered by a Judicial Service Commission, the Chairman of which is the Chief Justice, members being the President of the Court of Appeal, the Chairman of the Public Service Commission and three others.

CITIZENSHIP

All persons born in Jamaica after independence automatically acquire Jamaican citizenship and there is also provision for the acquisition of citizenship by persons born outside Jamaica of Jamaican parents. Persons born in Jamaica (or persons born outside Jamaica of Jamaican parents) before independence who immediately prior to independence were citizens of the United Kingdom and colonies also automatically become citizens of Jamaica.

Appropriate provision is made which permits persons who do not automatically become citizens of Jamaica to be registered as such.

FUNDAMENTAL RIGHTS AND FREEDOMS

The Constitution includes provisions safeguarding the fundamental freedoms of the individual, irrespective of race, place of origin, political opinions, colour, creed or sex, subject only to respect for the rights and freedoms of others and for the public interest. The fundamental freedoms include the rights of life, liberty, security of the person and protection from arbitrary arrest or restriction of movement, the enjoyment of property and the protection of the law, freedom of conscience, of expression and of peaceful assembly and association, and respect for private and family life.

The Government

Head of State: HM Queen ELIZABETH II.

Governor-General: Sir FLORIZEL AUGUSTUS GLASSPOLE (took office 27 June 1973).

PRIVY COUNCIL OF JAMAICA

L. E. ASHENHEIM, Dr VERNON LINDO, EWART FORREST, G. OWEN, W. H. SWABY, Dr DOUGLAS FLETCHER.

JAMAICA

THE CABINET
(February 1989)

Prime Minister and Minister of Defence and Information: MICHAEL MANLEY.
Deputy Prime Minister and Minister of Production, Development and Planning: PERCIVAL J. PATTERSON.
Attorney-General and Minister of Justice: KARL RATTRAY.
Minister of Foreign Affairs and Foreign Trade: Senator DAVID COORE.
Minister of Finance and the Public Service: SEYMOUR MULLINGS.
Minister of National Security: K. D. KNIGHT.
Minister of Agriculture: HORACE CLARKE.
Minister of Construction: O. D. RAMTALLIE.
Minister of Education: Senator CARLYLE DUNKLEY.
Minister of Health: EASTON DOUGLAS.
Minister of Industry and Commerce: CLAUDE CLARKE.
Minister of Labour, Welfare and Sports: PORTIA SIMPSON.
Minister of Local Government: RALPH BROWN.
Minister of Mining and Energy: HUGH SMALL.
Minister of Public Utilities and Transport: ROBERT PICKERSGILL.
Minister of Tourism: Senator FRANK PRINGLE.
Minister of Youth, Culture and Community Development: Dr DOUGLAS MANLEY.
Minister without Portfolio (Parliamentary Affairs) and Leader of the House of Representatives: Dr KEN MCNEIL.
Minister without Portfolio (Office of the Prime Minister): Senator PAUL ROBERTSON.

MINISTRIES

Office of the Prime Minister: 1 Devon Rd, POB 272, Kingston 6; tel. 927-9941; telex 2398.
Ministry of Agriculture: Hope Gardens, Kingston 6; tel. 927-9831.
Ministry of Construction: 2 Hagley Park Rd, Kingston 10; tel. 926-1590.
Ministry of Education: 2 National Heroes Circle, Kingston 4; tel. 922-1400.
Ministry of Finance and Planning: 30 National Heroes Circle, Kingston 4; tel. 922-8600; telex 2447.
Ministry of Foreign Affairs, Foreign Trade and Industry: 85 Knutsford Blvd, Kingston 5; tel. 926-4220; telex 2114.
Ministry of Health: 10 Caledonia Ave, Kingston 5; tel. 926-9220.
Ministry of Justice: 12 Ocean Blvd, Kingston; tel. 922-0080.
Ministry of Labour: 1F North St, Kingston; tel. 922-9500.
Ministry of Local Government: Ocean Blvd, Kingston; tel. 922-1670.
Ministry of Mining, Energy and Tourism: 36 Trafalgar Rd, Kingston 10; tel. 926-9176.
Ministry of National Security: 12 Ocean Blvd, Kingston; tel. 922-0080.
Ministry of the Public Service: Citibank Bldg, 63–67 Knutsford Blvd, Kingston 5; tel. 926-3235.
Ministry of Public Utilities and Transport: POB 9000, 2 St Lucia Ave, Kingston 5; tel. 926-8130.
Ministry of Youth, Culture and Community Development: POB 503, 12 Ocean Blvd, 5th Floor, Kingston; tel. 922-1710.

Legislature

PARLIAMENT

Senate

President: HOWARD COOKE.
The Senate has 20 other members.

House of Representatives

Speaker: HEADLEY CUNNINGHAM.

General Election, 9 February 1989

	Seats
People's National Party (PNP)	44
Jamaica Labour Party (JLP)	16
Total	**60**

Directory

Political Organizations

Jamaica American Party: Kingston; f. 1986; advocates US statehood for Jamaica; Leader JAMES CHISHOLM.
Jamaica Labour Party (JLP): 20 Belmont Rd, Kingston 5; f. 1943 by Sir Alexander Bustamante as political wing of the Bustamante Industrial Trade Union; supports free enterprise in a mixed economy and close co-operation with the USA; Leader EDWARD SEAGA; Chair. BRUCE GOLDING; Gen. Sec. RYAN PERALTO.
People's National Party (PNP): 89 Old Hope Rd, Kingston 5; f. 1938 by Norman Manley on socialist principles, with national independence as its goal; advocates social and economic change and nationalization of public utilities; foreign policy of non-alignment, although acknowledging a special relationship with third world countries; affiliated with the National Workers' Union; Pres. MICHAEL MANLEY; Chair. P. J. PATTERSON; Gen. Sec. Dr PAUL ROBERTSON.
Workers' Party of Jamaica (WPJ): f. 1978 out of the Workers Liberation League; pro-Soviet Communist party; Gen. Sec. Dr TREVOR MUNROE.

Diplomatic Representation

EMBASSIES AND HIGH COMMISSIONS IN JAMAICA

Argentina: 40 Knutsford Blvd, Kingston 5; tel. 926-5588; telex 2107; Ambassador: PAULINO MUSSACCHIO.
Australia: First Life Bldg, 64 Knutsford Blvd, Kingston 5; tel. 926-3550; telex 2355; High Commissioner: MICHAEL LANDALE.
Belgium: 6 Oxford Rd, Kingston 5; tel. 926-4295; telex 2430; Ambassador: FRANS CRAENINCKX.
Brazil: First Life Bldg, 64 Knutsford Blvd, Kingston 5; tel. 929-8607; telex 2221; Ambassador: EDMUNDO RADWANSKI.
Canada: Mutual Security Bank Bldg, 30 Knutsford Blvd, POB 1500, Kingston 10; tel. 926-1500; telex 2130; High Commissioner: KATHRYN MCCALLION.
China, People's Republic: 8 Seaview Ave, Kingston 10; tel. 927-0850; telex 2202; Chargé d'affaires: HUANG DONGBI.
Colombia: 53 Knutsford Blvd, Kingston 5; tel. 929-1701; telex 2200; Ambassador: Dr VICTOR ALCIDES RAMIREZ PERDOMO.
Costa Rica: 21 John Wesley Ave, Kingston 6; tel. 927-4493; Ambassador: Dr ROGER CHURNSIDE.
France: 13 Hillcrest Ave, Kingston 6; tel. 927-9811; telex 2367; Ambassador: MICHEL REUILARD.
Germany, Federal Republic: 10 Waterloo Rd, Kingston 10; tel. 926-5665; telex 2146; Ambassador: ROLF ENDERS.
Haiti: 2 Monroe Rd, Kingston; tel. 927-7595; Chargé d'affaires: ANDRÉ A. RAMEAU.
India: 4 Retreat Ave, POB 446, Kingston 6; tel. 927-0486; High Commissioner: KHIANGTE C. LALVUNGA.
Israel: Pan Jamaican Bldg, 60 Knutsford Blvd, Kingston 5; tel. 926-8768; telex 2466; Ambassador: URI PROSOR.
Japan: 'The Atrium', 3rd Floor, 32 Trafalgar Rd, Kingston 5; tel. 929-3338; telex 2304; Chargé d'affaires a.i.: TATSUO NOGUCHI.
Korea, Democratic People's Republic: 18 New Haven Ave, Kingston 6; tel. 927-7087; telex 2491; Ambassador: SHIN MYONG HO.
Korea, Republic: Pan Jamaican Bldg, 2nd Floor, 60 Knutsford Blvd, Kingston 5; tel. 929-3035; Ambassador: KIE YUL MOON.
Mexico: PCJ Bldg, 36 Trafalgar Rd, Kingston 10; tel. 926-4242; telex 2255; Ambassador: GUSTAVO EVARISTO IRUEGAS.
Netherlands: Xerox Bldg, 53 Knutsford Blvd, Kingston 5; tel. 926-1247; telex 2177; Chargé d'affaires a.i.: HANS VAN DEN DOOL.
Nigeria: 5 Waterloo Rd, Kingston 10; tel. 926-6400; telex 2443; High Commissioner: Prof. ADE ADEFUYE.
Panama: 7 Trafalgar Rd, Kingston 5; tel. 927-6970; Ambassador: JACINTA DE BAYARD.
Peru: Oxford House, 2nd Floor, 6 Oxford Rd, Kingston 5; tel. 926-1151; telex 3597; Ambassador: VICTOR FERNÁNDEZ-DÁVILA.
Spain: Xerox Bldg (3rd Floor), 53 Knutsford Blvd, Kingston 5; tel. 929-6710; telex 2364; Ambassador: IGNACIO MASFERRER.
Trinidad and Tobago: 60 Knutsford Blvd, Kingston 5; tel. 926-5730; telex 2387; High Commissioner: KNOWLSON W. GIFT.
USSR: 22 Norbrook Drive, Kingston 8; tel. 924-1048; telex 2216; Ambassador: VLADIMIR ALEKSANDROVICH ROMANCHENKO.
United Kingdom: Trafalgar Rd, POB 575, Kingston 10; tel. 926-9050; telex 2110; High Commissioner: ALAN JEFFREY PAYNE.
USA: Mutual Life Centre, 2 Oxford Rd, Kingston 5; tel. 929-4850; Ambassador: MICHAEL SOTIRHOS.

JAMAICA

Venezuela: Royal Bank Bldg, 5th Floor, 30–36 Knutsford Blvd, Kingston 5; tel. 926-5510; telex 2179; Chargé d'affaires: CARLOS GRISANTI.

Judicial System

The Judicial System is based on English common law and practice. Final appeal is to the Judicial Committee of the Privy Council in the United Kingdom.

Justice is administered by the Privy Council, Court of Appeal, Supreme Court (which includes the Revenue Court and the Gun Court), Resident Magistrates' Court (which includes the Traffic Court), two Family Courts and the Courts of Petty Sessions.

THE SUPREME COURT

POB 491, Kingston.
Chief Justice: EDWARD ZACCA.
Senior Puisne Judge: C. F. B. ORR.
Puisne Judges: W. D. MARSH, V. O. MALCOLM, T. N. TIBBLES, P. O. BINGHAMS, U. D. GORDON, C. A. PATTERSON, Miss A. E. MCKAIN, L. H. WOLFE, C. W. WALKER, L. B. ELLIS, T. T. HARRISON, S. R. PANTON, A. B. EDWARDS, C. D. R. E. LANGRIN, S. A. SMITH, N. ST E. CLARKE.
Master: Mrs L. E. VANDERPUMP.
Registrars: Mrs H. HARRIS, M.K.S. HARRISON (acting).
Deputy Registrars: Mrs C. MORGAN-GREAVES, Mrs M. BAILEY, Mrs HOWARD (acting).

COURT OF APPEAL

President: B. H. CAREY (acting).
Judges: B. H. CAREY, I. X. FORTE, Miss M. MORGAN, U. D. GORDON, H. E. DOWNER, M. L. WRIGHT, U. V. CAMPBELL.
Registrar: Mrs A. G. HENDRICKS.

JUDICIAL SERVICE COMMISSION

Chairman: Chief Justice.
Members: President of the Court of Appeal, Chairman of the Public Service Commission and three others.

Religion

There are over 100 Christian denominations. The Anglican Church is the largest religious body, and had 317,600 adherents according to a 1970 estimate. Presbyterians number about 92,000. Other religious bodies include the Methodist, Baptist and Congregational Churches, the Ethiopian Orthodox Church, the Disciples of Christ, the Moravian Church, the Salvation Army, the Society of Friends and the Seventh-day Adventist Church. Rastafarianism, a cult derived from belief in the divinity of Ras (Prince) Tafari Makonnen (later Emperor Haile Selassie) of Ethiopia, is growing in importance.

CHRISTIANITY

Jamaica Council of Churches: 14 South Ave, POB 30, Kingston 10; tel. 092-60974; f. 1941; 11 member churches and seven agencies; Pres. Rev. OLIVER DALEY; Gen. Sec. Mrs CYNTHIA CLAIR.

The Anglican Communion

Anglicans in Jamaica are adherents of the Church in the Province of the West Indies, comprising eight dioceses. The Archbishop of the Province is the Bishop of the North East Caribbean and Aruba. The Bishop of Jamaica, whose jurisdiction also includes Grand Cayman (in the Cayman Islands), is assisted by two suffragan Bishops (of Mandeville and Montego Bay).
Bishop of Jamaica: Rt Rev. NEVILLE WORDSWORTH DESOUZA, Church House, 2 Caledonia Ave, Kingston 5; tel. 926-6609.

The Roman Catholic Church

Jamaica comprises the archdiocese of Kingston in Jamaica (also including the Cayman Islands) and the diocese of Montego Bay. At 31 December 1984 the estimated total of adherents in Jamaica and the Cayman Islands was 151,000, representing about 7% of the total population.
Bishops' Conference: Antilles Episcopal Conference, 21 Hopefield Ave, POB 43, Kingston 6; tel. 927-9915; f. 1975; 17 mems from the Caribbean region and Bermuda; Pres. Most Rev. SAMUEL EMMANUEL CARTER, Archbishop of Kingston in Jamaica.

Archbishop of Kingston in Jamaica: Most Rev. SAMUEL EMMANUEL CARTER, Archbishop's Residence, 21 Hopefield Ave, POB 43, Kingston 6; tel. 927-9915.

Other Christian Churches

Assembly of God: Evangel Temple, 3 Friendship Park Rd, Kingston 3; tel. 928-2728; 191,200 mems; Pastor WILSON.
Baptist Union: 6 Hope Rd, Kingston 10; tel. 926-1395; Pres. Rev. BURCHELL TAYLOR; Gen. Sec. Rev. CAWLEY BOLT.
First Church of Christ, Scientist: 17 National Heroes Circle, Kingston.
Methodist: 143 Constant Spring Rd, POB 892, Kingston 8; tel. 925-6768; f. 1789; 18,508 mems; Chair. Rev. C. EVANS BAILEY; Synod Sec. Rev. GILBERT G. BOWEN.
Moravian: 3 Hector St, Kingston 5; tel. 928-1861; 25,000 mems; Pres. Rev. ROBERT G. FOSTER.
Seventh-day Adventist: 56 James St, Kingston; tel. 922-7440; f. 1901; 6,125 mems; Pastor Rev. E. H. THOMAS.
United Church of Jamaica and Grand Cayman: 12 Carlton Cres, POB 359, Kingston 10; tel. 926-8734; 13,450 mems; Gen. Sec. Rev. SAM H. SMELLIE.

BAHÁ'Í FAITH

National Spiritual Assembly: 208 Mountain View Ave, Kingston 6; tel. 927-7051; 6,300 mems resident in 320 localities.

JUDAISM

United Congregation of Israelites: 92 Duke St, Kingston; tel. 922-5931; f. 1655; c. 250 mems; Spiritual Leader and Sec. ERNEST H. DE SOUZA; Pres. LLOYD ALBERGA.

The Press

DAILIES

Daily Gleaner: 7 North St, POB 40, Kingston; tel. 922-3400; telex 2319; f. 1834; morning; independent; Chair. and Man. Dir OLIVER CLARKE; Editor Dr DUDLEY STOKES; circ. 45,000.
The Jamaica Record: 7-11 West St, Kingston; tel. 922-3952; Man. Dir and Exec. Editor MARK RICKETTS.
Star: 7 North St, POB 40, Kingston; tel. 922-3400; evening; Editor J. C. PROUTE; circ. 58,000.

PERIODICALS

Caribbean Challenge: 55 Church St, POB 186, Kingston; tel. 922-5636; f. 1957; monthly; Editor JOHN KEANE; circ. 24,000.
Caribbean Shipping: Creative Communications Inc, POB 105, Kingston 10; quarterly.
Catholic Opinion: 11 Duke St, Kingston; monthly; religious.
Children's Own: 7 North St, POB 40, Kingston; weekly; distributed during term time; circ. 99,443.
The Enquirer: 7-11 West St, Kingston; tel. 922-3952; weekly; Man. Dir and Exec. Editor MARK RICKETTS.
Government Gazette: POB 487, Kingston; f. 1868; Government Printer EARL BROWN; circ. 4,817.
Jamaica Chamber of Commerce Journal: 7-8 East Parade, Kingston; 6 a year; circ. 2,000.
Jamaica Churchman: 2 Caledonia Ave, Kingston 5; monthly; Editor Rev. LAURENCE SMALL; circ. 6,000.
Jamaican Housewife: Kingston; weekly.
Jamaica Journal: 12-16 East St, Kingston; tel. 922-0620; f. 1967; quarterly; literary, historical and cultural review.
Jamaica Manufacturer: 85A Duke St, Kingston; quarterly; circ. 3,000.
Jamaica Weekly Gleaner: 7 North St, POB 40, Kingston; tel. 922-3400; weekly; overseas; Chair. and Man. Dir OLIVER CLARKE; circ. 13,599.
Public Opinion: 2 Torrington Rd, Kingston; weekly.
Sports Life: 18 East St, Kingston; weekly.
Sunday Gleaner: 7 North St, POB 40, Kingston; tel. 922-3400; weekly; circ. 91,800.
Swing: 102 East St, Kingston; f. 1968; monthly; entertainment and culture; Editor ANDELL FORGIE; circ. 12,000.
The Vacationer: POB 614, Montego Bay; tel. 952-0997; f. 1987; weekly; Pres. and Gen. Man. EVELYN L. ROBINSON; circ. 8,000.
The Western Mirror: POB 1258, Westgate Plaza, Montego Bay; tel. 952-5253; f. 1980; 2 a week; Gen. Man. and Editor LLOYD B. SMITH; circ. 12,000.

JAMAICA   *Directory*

Weekend Star: 7 North St, POB 40, Kingston; tel. 922-3400; weekly; Editor LLOYD WILLIAMS; circ. 92,000.

West Indian Medical Journal: Faculty of Medical Sciences, University of the West Indies, Kingston 7; tel. 927-1214; f. 1951; quarterly; Editor Dr VASIL PERSAUD; Asst Editor BRIDGET WILLIAMS; circ. 2,000.

West Indian Sportsman: 75 Church St, Kingston; quarterly; circ. 7,000.

PRESS ASSOCIATION

Press Association of Jamaica (PAJ): 2B Ruthven Rd, Kingston 10; tel. 926-2434; f. 1943; 220 mems; Pres. FRANKLYN MCKNIGHT; Sec. CLAIRE FORRESTER.

NEWS AGENCIES

Jampress: 3 Chelsea Ave, Kingston 10; tel. 926-3740; telex 3552; f. 1984; government news agency; Editor-in-Chief GLORIA MARAGH.

Foreign Bureaux

Inter Press Service (IPS) (Italy): 2 Balmoral Ave, Kingston 10; tel. 929-2973; Correspondent FITZROY NATION.

Associated Press (USA), CANA (Caribbean News Agency) and Reuters (UK) are also represented in Jamaica.

Publishers

Caribbean Publishing Co Ltd: 18 East Kings House Rd, Kingston 6; tel. 927-0810.

Caribbean Universities Press Jamaica Ltd: POB 83, Kingston 7; tel. 926-2628; academic; Man. Dir VIVALYN LATTY-SCOTT.

Hallmark Publishers Ltd: 10 Hagley Park Plaza, Kingston 10; tel. 929-4823.

Jamaica Publishing House Ltd: 97 Church St, Kingston; tel. 922-1385; f. 1969; wholly-owned subsidiary of Jamaica Teachers' Asscn; educational, English language and literature, mathematics, history, geography, social sciences, music; Chair. ELLORINE WALKER; Man. LEO A. OAKLEY.

Kingston Publishers Ltd: 1A Norwood Ave, Kingston 5; tel. 926-0091; telex 2293; f. 1970; educational textbooks, general, travel, atlases; Chair. MICHAEL HENRY.

Unique Publications Ltd: 18 East Kings House Rd, Kingston 6; tel. 927-0810.

Government Publishing House

Government Printing Office: 77 Duke St, Kingston; tel. 922-5950; law; Government Printer EARL BROWN.

Radio and Television

In 1987 there were an estimated 1,448,122 radio receivers and 462,055 television receivers in use.

Jamaica Broadcasting Corpn (JBC): 5 South Odeon Ave, POB 100, Kingston 10; tel. 926-5620; telex 2218; f. 1959; a publicly-owned statutory corporation; semi-commercial radio and television; 2 radio stations; Chair. FRANK PHIPPS; Gen. Man. ULRIC SIMMONDS.

Educational Broadcasting Service: Multi-Media Centre, 37 Arnold Road, Kingston 4; tel. 922-9370; f. 1964; radio broadcasts during school term; Pres. OUIDA HYLTON-TOMLINSON.

Radio Jamaica Ltd (RJR): Broadcasting House, 32 Lyndhurst Rd, POB 23, Kingston 5; tel. 926-1100; telex 3661; f. 1950; island-wide commercial and public service AM and FM radio broadcasting 24 hrs a day; Man. Dir J. A. LESTER SPAULDING; Programme Dir DONALD TOPPING (Supreme Sound service); Programme Man. NORMA BELL (FAME-FM service).

Finance

(cap. = capital; p.u. = paid up; res = reserves; dep. = deposits; m. = million; amounts in Jamaican dollars; brs = branches)

BANKING

Central Bank

Bank of Jamaica: Nethersole Place, POB 621, Kingston; tel. 922-0750; telex 2165; f. 1960; cap. p.u. 4m., res 4.9m. (Dec. 1984), dep. 1,896.6m. (1988); Gov. Dr HEADLEY BROWN.

Commercial Banks

The Bank of Nova Scotia Jamaica Ltd: Scotiabank Centre Bldg, Duke and Port Royal Sts, POB 709, Kingston; tel. 922-1000; telex 2433; f. 1967; cap. p.u. 50.8m., dep. 1,868.4m. (Oct. 1986); Gen. Man. A. B. LINDO; 43 brs.

CIBC: 1 King St, POB 762, Kingston; tel. 922-6120; telex 2169; cap. p.u. 8.0m., dep. 397.3m. (Aug. 1986); Man. Dir G. S. NIESEN.

First Jamaica National Bank Ltd: 88 Harbour St, POB 115, Kingston; tel. 922-0110; telex 3515; cap. p.u. 5.0m., res 0.4m., dep. 3.5m. (1986); Man. Dir L. F. REYNOLDS; 1 br.

Jamaica Citizens Bank Ltd: 4 King St, POB 483, Kingston 1; tel. 922-5850; telex 2129; f. 1976; cap. p.u. 8.0m., res 4.2m., dep. 295.3m. (1986); Gen. Man. ELON BECKFORD.

Mutual Security Bank: 30–36 Knutsford Blvd, POB 612, Kingston 5; tel. 929-8950; telex 2306; fmrly Royal Bank Jamaica Ltd; cap. p.u. 19.2m., res 13.8m., dep. 750.6m. (1986); Chair. RICHARD ASENHEIM; Man. Dir DOUGLAS FOLKES.

National Commercial Bank Jamaica Ltd: 'The Atrium', 32 Trafalgar Rd, POB 88, Kingston; tel. 929-9053; telex 2139; f. 1977; cap. 60m., dep. 2,241m. (Sept. 1986); Chair. Dr KEITH S. PANTON; Man. Dir D. A. BANKS; 40 brs and agencies.

National Export-Import Bank of Jamaica: 48 Duke St, POB 3, Kingston; tel. 922-9690; telex 2165; replaces Jamaica Export Credit Insurance Corpn.

Workers Savings and Loan Bank: 134 Tower St, POB 270, Kingston; tel. 922-8650; telex 2226; f. 1973; cap. p.u. 14.7m., res 4.5m., dep. 413.7m. (1986); Gen. Man. EVERETTE PALMER (acting); 10 brs.

Development Banks

Jamaica Mortgage Bank: 33 Tobago Ave, POB 950, Kingston 5; tel. 929-6350; f. 1971; became a statutory organization wholly owned by the Government in June 1973; established by the Government and the United States Agency for International Development to function primarily as a secondary market facility for home mortgages and to mobilize long-term funds for housing developments in Jamaica; also insures home mortgage loans made by approved financial institutions, thus transferring risk of default on a loan to the Government.

National Development Bank: 15 Oxford Rd, Kingston 5; tel. 929-6124; telex 2381; replaced Jamaica Development Bank, f. 1969; Chair. DONALD RAINFORD; Man. Dir Dr NOEL A. LYON.

Banking Association

Bankers' Association of Jamaica: Kingston; Pres. ELON BECKFORD.

STOCK EXCHANGE

Jamaica Stock Exchange Ltd: POB 621, Bank of Jamaica Tower, Nethersole Place, Kingston; tel. 922-0806; f. 1968; Chair. DONALD BANKS; Gen. Man. WAIN ITON.

INSURANCE

Government Supervisory Authority: Office of the Superintendent of Insurance, 51 St Lucia Ave, POB 800, Kingston 5; tel. 926-1790; Superintendent E. W. TAYLOR.

Jamaica Insurance Advisory Council: NEM House, 2nd Floor, 9 King St, Kingston; tel. 922-8710; Man. DENISE Y. COLE.

British Caribbean Insurance Co Ltd: 36 Duke St, POB 170, Kingston; tel. 922-1260.

Dyoll Insurance Co Ltd: 40–46 Knutsford Blvd, POB 313, Kingston 5; tel. 926-4711; telex 2208; f. 1965; Pres. PETER J. C. THWAITES; Vice-Pres. PAUL BIGNELL.

Globe Insurance Co of the West Indies Ltd: 60 Knutsford Blvd, Kingston 10; tel. 926-3720; telex 2150.

Insurance Co of the West Indies Ltd (ICWI): ICWI Building, 2 St Lucia Ave, POB 306, Kingston 5; tel. 926-9182; telex 2246; Gen. Man. JENNIFER COX.

Jamaica General Insurance Co Ltd: 9 Duke St, POB 408, Kingston; tel. 922-6420.

Jamaica Mutual Life Assurance Society: 2 Oxford Rd, POB 430, Kingston 5; tel. 926-9024; f. 1844; Pres. A. TENNYSON PALMER.

Life of Jamaica Ltd: 17 Dominica Drive, Kingston 5; tel. 929-8920; f. 1970; life insurance; Pres. R. DANNY WILLIAMS; Exec. Vice-Pres. H. A. HALL.

National Employers' Mutual General Insurance Association Ltd: 9 King St, Kingston; tel. 922-1460.

Trade and Industry

CHAMBERS OF COMMERCE

Associated Chambers of Commerce of Jamaica: 7-8 East Parade, POB 172, Kingston; tel. 922-0150; f. 1974; 10 associated Chambers of Commerce; Pres. WINSTON MEEKS.

Jamaica Chamber of Commerce: 7-8 East Parade, POB 172, Kingston; tel. 922-0150; f. 1779; 10 associated Chambers of Commerce; 720 mems; Pres. SAMEER YOUNIS.

ASSOCIATIONS

All-Island Banana Growers' Association Ltd: Banana Industry Bldg, 10 South Ave, Kingston 4; tel. 922-5492; f. 1946; 5,089 mems (1986); Chair. BOBBY POTTINGER; Sec. I. CHANG.

All-Island Jamaica Cane Farmers' Association: 4 North Ave, Kingston 4; tel. 922-3010; f. 1941; registered cane farmers; 22,895 mems; Chair. TREVOR G. MIGNOTT; Man. D. D. MCCALLA.

Banana Export Co (BECO): 10 South Ave, Kingston 4; tel. 922-5490; telex 2148; f. 1985 to replace Banana Co of Jamaica; oversees the development of the banana industry; Chair. MARSHALL HALL.

Citrus Growers' Association Ltd: 1A North Ave, Kingston Gdns, POB 159, Kingston; tel. 922-8230; telex 2315; f. 1944; 16,000 mems; Chair. IVAN H. TOMLINSON.

Jamaica Banana Producers' Association Ltd: 6A Oxford Rd, POB 237, Kingston; tel. 922-5490; telex 2278; f. 1927; Chair. C. H. JOHNSTON; Man. Dir Dr MARSHALL HALL.

Jamaica Exporters' Association (JEA): 13 Dominica Drive, POB 9, Kingston 5; tel. 929-1292; telex 2421; Pres. PRAKESH VASWANI.

Jamaica Livestock Association: Newport East, POB 36, Kingston; f. 1941; tel. 922-7130; telex 2382; 7,316 mems; Chair. Brig. DAVID SMITH; Man. Dir HENRY J. RAINFORD.

Jamaica Manufacturers' Association Ltd: 85A Duke St, Kingston; tel. 922-8880; f. 1947; 640 mems; Pres. ANTHONY BARNES.

Jamaican Association of Sugar Technologists: c/o Sugar Industry Research Institute, Mandeville; tel. 962-2241; f. 1936; 264 mems; Pres. C. GORDON; Hon. Sec. H. M. THOMPSON.

Private Sector Organization of Jamaica (PSOJ): 39 Hope Rd, Kingston 10; tel. 927-6238; telex 2421; federative body of private business individuals, companies and associations; Pres. PETER J. C. THWAITES.

Small Business Association: 2 Trafalgar Rd, Kingston 10; tel. 927-7071; Pres. ERROL DUNKLEY.

Sugar Manufacturing Corpn of Jamaica Ltd: 5 Trevennion Park Rd, Kingston 5; tel. 926-5930; telex 2113; 8 mems; established to represent the sugar manufacturers in Jamaica; deals with all aspects of the sugar industry and its by-products; provides liaison between the Government, the Sugar Industry Authority and the All-Island Jamaica Cane Farmers' Asscn; Chair. Sen. CHRISTOPHER BOVELL; Gen. Man. Lt-Col DELROY C. M. ORMSBY.

GOVERNMENT ORGANIZATIONS

Agricultural Development Corpn: 46 Trinidad Terrace, Kingston; tel. 926-9160; f. 1952; Chair. Dr C. L. BENT; Sec. D. FORRESTER.

Cocoa Industry Board: Marcus Garvey Drive, POB 68, Kingston 15; tel. 923-6411; telex 3658; f. 1957; has statutory powers to regulate and develop the industry; owns and operates four central fermentaries; Chair. L. O. MINOTT; Man. FITZ. D. SHAW.

Coconut Industry Board: 18 Waterloo Rd, Half Way Tree, Kingston 10; tel. 926-1770; 9 mems; Chair. P. D. MCCONNELL; Gen. Man. R. A. WILLIAMS.

Coffee Industry Board: Marcus Garvey Drive, POB 508, Kingston; tel. 923-7211; telex 3578; f. 1950; 9 mems; has wide statutory powers to regulate and develop the industry; Chair. CECIL LANGFORD; Man. JOHN PICKERSGILL.

Coffee Industry Development Co: Marcus Garvey Drive, Kingston; tel. 923-7211; f. 1981; to implement a coffee expansion programme financed by the Commonwealth Development Corporation.

Jamaica Bauxite Institute: Hope Gdns, POB 355, Kingston 6; tel. 927-2073; telex 2309; f. 1975; adviser to the Government in the negotiation of agreements, consultancy services to clients in the bauxite/alumina and related industries, laboratory services for mineral and soil-related services, Pilot Plant services for materials and equipment testing, research and development; Exec. Dir Dr CARLTON DAVIS.

Jamaica Commodity Trading Co Ltd: 8 Ocean Blvd, POB 1021, Kingston; tel. 922-0971; telex 2318; f. 1981 as successor to State Trading Corpn; oversees all importing on behalf of state; Chair. DAVID GAYNAIR; Man. Dir Mrs ANDREE NEMBHARD.

Jamaica Promotions (JAMPRO) Ltd: 35 Trafalgar Rd, Kingston 10; tel. 929-9450; telex 2222; f. 1988; economic development agency; formed by merger of Jamaica Industrial Development Corpn, Jamaica National Export Corpn and Jamaica National Investment Promotion Ltd; Pres. V. CORINNE MCLARTY; Chair. CARLTON ALEXANDER.

National Development Agency Ltd: 12 Ocean Blvd, Kingston; tel. 922-5445; telex 2444.

Petroleum Corpn of Jamaica (PCJ): 36 Trafalgar Rd, POB 597, Kingston 10; tel. 929-5380; telex 2356; state oil company; owns and operates petroleum refinery; holds exploration and exploitation rights to local petroleum and gas reserves; Chair. RICHARD ASHENHEIM; Man. Dir WILLIAM SAUNDERS.

Sugar Industry Authority: 5 Trevennion Park Rd, Kingston 5; tel. 926-5930; telex 2113; Chair. FRANK G. DOWNIE.

Urban Development Corpn: 12 Ocean Blvd, 8th Floor, Kingston; tel. 922-8310; telex 2281; f. 1968; responsibility for urban renewal and development within designated areas; Chair. ARTHUR ZAIDIE; Gen. Man. GLORIA KNIGHT.

TRADE UNIONS

Bustamante Industrial Trade Union (BITU): 98 Duke St, Kingston; tel. 922-2443; f. 1938; Pres. HUGH SHEARER; Gen. Sec. GEORGE FYFFE; 100,459 mems.

National Workers' Union of Jamaica (NWU): 130-132 East St, Kingston 16; tel. 922-1150; f. 1952; affiliated to ICFTU, ORIT, etc.; Pres. MICHAEL MANLEY; Gen. Sec. LLOYD GOODLEIGH; 102,000 mems.

Trades Union Congress of Jamaica: POB 19, 25 Sutton St, Kingston; tel. 922-5313; affiliated to CCL and ICFTU; Pres. E. SMITH; 20,000 mems.

Principal Independent Unions

Dockers' and Marine Workers' Union: 48 East St, Kingston; tel. 922-6067; Pres. MILTON A. SCOTT.

Independent Portworkers' Union: Kingston.

Industrial Trade Union Action Council: 2 Wildman St, Kingston; Pres. RODERICK FRANCIS.

Jamaica Federation of Musicians' Union and Affiliated Artistes: POB 1125, Montego Bay 1; tel. 926-8029; f. 1958; Pres. HEDLEY H. G. JONES; Sec. CARL AYTON; 1,700 mems.

Jamaica Local Government Officers' Union: c/o Public Service Commission, Knutsford Blvd, Kingston; Pres. E. LLOYD TAYLOR.

Jamaica Teachers' Association: 97 Church St, Kingston; tel. 922-1385; Pres. E. DOWNIE.

Master Printers' Association of Jamaica: Kingston 11; f. 1943; 44 mems; Pres. HERMON SPOERRI; Sec. RALPH GORDON.

National Union of Democratic Teachers (NUDT): 69 Church St, Kingston; tel. 922-3902; f. 1978; Pres. PAULETTE CHEVANNES; Gen. Sec. JOHN HAUGHTON.

Union of School and Agricultural Workers (USAW): 2 Wildman St, Kingston; tel. 922-1483; f. 1978; Pres. DUNSTON WHITTINGHAM; Gen. Sec. KEITH COMRIE.

United Portworkers' and Seamen's Union: 20 West St, Kingston.

University and Allied Workers' Union (UAWU): Students' Union, University of West Indies, Mona; affiliated to the WPJ; Gen. Sec. Dr TREVOR MUNROE.

There are also 17 employers' associations registered as trade unions.

CO-OPERATIVES

The Jamaica Social Welfare Commission promotes Co-operative Societies in the following categories: Consumer, Co-operative Farming, Credit, Credit and Marketing, Fishermen's Irrigation, Land Lease, Land Purchase, Marketing, Supplies Co-ops, Thrift, Transport and Tillage.

Transport

RAILWAYS

There are 294 km (182 miles) of standard-gauge railway operated by the Jamaica Railway Corporation. The main lines are from Kingston to Montego Bay and Spanish Town to Port Antonio. The railway is subsidized by the Government. There are also two railways for the transport of bauxite.

Jamaica Railway Corporation (JRC): POB 489, Kingston; tel. 922-6621; telex 3509; f. 1845 as earliest British colonial railway; transferred to JRC in 1960; autonomous; govt-owned; Chair. G. MARTIN; Gen. Man. K. FOSTER.

Kaiser Jamaica Bauxite Co Railway: Discovery Bay; industrial.

JAMAICA

ROADS

Jamaica has a good network of tar-surfaced and metalled motoring roads. At the end of 1984 there were 16,638 km (10,332 miles) of roads, of which about 4,991 km (3,099 miles) were paved. This included 786 km (488 miles) of main roads and 689 km (428 miles) of secondary roads.

SHIPPING

The principal ports are Kingston and Montego Bay. The port at Kingston has four container berths, and is a major transhipment terminal for the Caribbean area. Jamaica has interests in the multinational shipping line WISCO (West Indies Shipping Corporation). Services are also provided by a number of foreign lines.

Jamaica Freight and Shipping Co Ltd (JFS): 80–82 Second St, Port Bustamante, POB 167, Kingston 13; tel. 923-9271; telex 2260; cargo services to and from the USA, Caribbean, Central and South America, the United Kingdom, Japan and Canada; Exec. Chair. CHARLES JOHNSTON; Man. Dir GRANTLEY STEPHENSON.

Jamaica Merchant Marine (JMM): 7th floor, Dyoll Bldg, 40/46 Knutsford Blvd, Kingston 5; tel. 922-0290; telex 2483; f. 1975; carries grain from USA and general cargo from UK; Chair. NOEL A. HYLTON.

Port Authority of Jamaica: 15–17 Duke St, Kingston; tel. 922-0290; telex 2386; Gen. Man. LUCIEN RATTRAY.

Shipping Association of Jamaica: 5–7 King St, POB 40, Kingston 15; tel. 922-8220; telex 2431; f. 1939; 35 mems; Pres. FRANCIS X. KENNEDY; Gen. Man. ALVIN C. HENRY.

CIVIL AVIATION

There are two international airports linking Jamaica with North America, Europe, and other Caribbean islands. The Norman Manley International Airport is situated 22.5 km (14 miles) outside Kingston. The Donald Sangster International Airport is 5 km (3 miles) from Montego Bay.

Air Jamaica Ltd: 72–76 Harbour St, Kingston; tel. 922-3460; telex 2389; f. 1968; government-owned; services to Canada, the Cayman Islands, Haiti, Puerto Rico, the USA and, in co-operation with British Airways, the UK; Chair. TONY HART; Pres./Man. Dir NOEL A. HYLTON; fleet of 2 Airbus A300B4 (further 2 on order), 4 Boeing 727-200.

Trans-Jamaican Airlines: POB 218, Montego Bay; tel. 952-5401; internal services to Kingston, Negril, Ocho Rios and Port Antonio; government corporation; Chair. LOTSE HARVEY; Admin. Dir B. G. OSBORNE.

Tourism

Tourists, mainly from the USA, visit Jamaica for its beaches, mountains and historic buildings. In 1987 there were 1,037,634 visitors and tourist receipts were estimated to be US $595m.

Jamaica Tourist Board (JTB): 21 Dominica Drive, POB 360, Kingston 5; tel. 929-9200; telex 2140; f. 1955; a statutory body set up by the Government to develop all aspects of the tourist industry of Jamaica through marketing, promotional and advertising efforts; Chair. JOHN ISSA; Dir of Tourism CARROLE BRADY.

Jamaica Hotel and Tourist Association: 2 Ardenne Rd, Kingston 10; tel. 926-3635; telex 2426; Pres. PETER ROUSSEAU; Gen. Man. CAMILLE NEEDHAM.

JAPAN

Introductory Survey

Location, Climate, Language, Religion, Flag, Capital

Japan lies in eastern Asia and comprises a curved chain of more than 3,000 islands. Four large islands, named (from north to south) Hokkaido, Honshu, Shikoku and Kyushu, account for about 98% of the land area. Hokkaido lies just to the south of Sakhalin, a large Soviet island, and about 1,300 km (800 miles) east of the USSR's mainland port of Vladivostok. Southern Japan is about 150 km (93 miles) east of Korea. Although summers are temperate everywhere, the climate in winter varies sharply from cold in the north to mild in the south. Temperatures in Tokyo are generally between −6°C (21°F) and 30°C (86°F). Typhoons and heavy rains are common in summer. The language is Japanese. The major religions are Shintoism and Buddhism, and there is a minority of Christians. The national flag (proportions usually 3 by 2) is white, with a red disc (a sun without rays) in the centre. The capital is Tokyo.

Recent History

Following Japan's defeat in the Second World War, Japanese forces surrendered in August 1945. Japan signed an armistice in September 1945, agreeing to cede control over many of its outer islands, and the country was placed under US military occupation. A new democratic constitution, which took effect from May 1947, renounced war and abandoned the doctrine of the Emperor's divinity. Following the peace treaty of September 1951, Japan regained its sovereignty on 28 April 1952. The Tokara Archipelago and the Amami Islands (parts of the Ryukyu group) were restored to Japanese sovereignty in December 1951 and December 1953 respectively. Rival conservative political groups merged in November 1955 to form the Liberal-Democratic Party (LDP), which has held power ever since. The Bonin Islands and the remainder of the Ryukyu Islands (including Okinawa), administered by the USA from 1945, were returned to Japan in June 1968 and May 1972 respectively.

Nobusuke Kishi became Prime Minister in February 1957 and held office until July 1960, when he was succeeded by Hayato Ikeda. In November 1964 Ikeda resigned, owing to ill health, and was replaced by Eisaku Sato, who was to become the longest-serving Prime Minister in Japanese history. Sato remained in office until July 1972, when he was succeeded by Kakuei Tanaka, hitherto the Minister of International Trade and Industry. Tanaka visited Beijing in September 1972, when he agreed to Japan's recognition of the People's Republic of China and a consequent severance of Japanese diplomatic (though not commercial) relations with Taiwan. After some electoral set-backs, Tanaka resigned as Prime Minister in December 1974. He was succeeded by Takeo Miki, a former Deputy Prime Minister.

During his premiership, Tanaka allegedly accepted bribes, totalling 500m. yen, from the Marubeni Corporation, a representative in Japan of the Lockheed Aircraft Corporation (a leading US aerospace company), in return for using his influence to promote the purchase of Lockheed TriStar airliners by All Nippon Airways, Japan's principal domestic airline. In July 1976 Tanaka was arrested, on charges of accepting bribes, and resigned from the LDP. In December a general election for the House of Representatives (the Lower House of the Diet) resulted in a major set-back for the LDP, which lost its overall majority for the first time. Miki resigned as Prime Minister, and was succeeded by Takeo Fukuda, who had resigned in November as Deputy Prime Minister.

The LDP suffered another reverse in July 1977, at elections for one-half of the seats in the House of Councillors (the Upper House of the Diet), and in November Fukuda carried out a major reshuffle of the Cabinet, giving ministerial office to some economic experts. In the LDP presidential election of November 1978 Fukuda was unexpectedly defeated by Masayoshi Ohira, the LDP Secretary-General. Ohira became Prime Minister in December, and a new cabinet was formed. Lacking an overall majority in the Lower House and facing increasing opposition to proposed tax increases, the Government's legislative programme was seriously hindered.

At elections to the Lower House in October 1979 the LDP again failed to win an overall majority, and significant gains were made by the Communists. Ohira survived a challenge to his leadership of the LDP, but in May 1980 the Government was defeated in a motion of 'no confidence', proposed by the Japan Socialist Party (JSP), and Ohira dissolved the Lower House. Ohira died before the elections in June, when the LDP won 284 of the 511 seats, although obtaining only a minority of the votes cast. In July Zenko Suzuki, a relatively little-known compromise candidate, was elected President of the LDP and subsequently appointed Prime Minister. He faced a series of crises during 1981, including a set-back in relations with the USA and criticism from the opposition over Japan's defence policy. In November 1981 Suzuki reshuffled the Cabinet, distributing major posts among the five feuding LDP factions. The growing factionalism of the LDP and the worsening economic crisis led to the resignation of Suzuki as Prime Minister and LDP President in October 1982.

Suzuki's successor was Yasuhiro Nakasone, who was supported by the Suzuki and Tanaka factions of the LDP. In his former post, as Minister of State and Director-General of the Administrative Management Agency, Nakasone had been responsible for implementing the Suzuki Government's expenditure cuts. At elections in June 1983 for one-half of the seats in the Upper House, a new electoral system was used. Of the 126 contested seats, 50 were filled on the basis of proportional representation. As a result, two small parties entered the House for the first time. Nevertheless, the LDP increased its strength from 134 to 137 members in the 252-seat chamber. This result was seen as an endorsement of Nakasone's policies of increased spending on defence, closer ties with the USA and greater Japanese involvement in international affairs.

In October 1983, after judicial proceedings lasting nearly seven years, a Tokyo court found Kakuei Tanaka, the former Prime Minister, guilty of accepting bribes. In September 1985 he began appeal proceedings against the conviction and the sentence (a heavy fine and four years' imprisonment), and he continued to be an 'independent' member of the Diet. Despite resigning from the LDP, Tanaka remained a major influence on the party, and members of the Tanaka faction held important positions in Nakasone's Cabinet. Tanaka's refusal to resign his legislative seat led to a boycott of the Diet by the opposition, which forced Nakasone to dissolve the House of Representatives in preparation for a premature general election in December 1983. The election campaign was dominated by the issues of political ethics and Nakasone's forthright style of leadership. The LDP suffered the worst defeat in its history, losing 36 seats (and its majority) in the Lower House. Nakasone came second (behind Takeo Fukuda) in his district, whereas Tanaka was returned with an overwhelming majority. The Komeito (Clean Government Party), the Democratic Socialist Party (DSP) and the JSP gained seats, while the Communists and the New Liberal Club (NLC) lost seats. The LDP formed a coalition with the NLC (which had split from the LDP over the Tanaka affair in 1976) and several independents, and Nakasone remained as President of the LDP by promising to reduce Tanaka's influence. Six members of Tanaka's faction held posts in Nakasone's new Cabinet, including that of Minister of Finance.

Following the trial of Tanaka, a series of reforms was introduced, whereby Cabinet members were required to disclose the extent of their personal assets. However, these reforms were regarded by some as superficial. Nakasone's domestic policy was based on the 'Three Reforms': administrative reforms, particularly of government-run enterprises such as the railways; fiscal reforms, to enable the Government to balance its budget after many years of persistent deficit; and educational reforms, to liberalize the rigid examination-dominated system. In March 1984 Nakasone introduced Japan's most austere budget since 1955.

In November 1984 Nakasone was re-elected as President of the LDP, guaranteeing him two further years in office as Prime Minister, the first to serve a second term since Eisaku Sato (1964–72). The unexpected late challenge to his leadership by part of the Tanaka faction (headed by Susumu Nikaido, Vice-President of the LDP) was indicative of the widespread disaffection with Nakasone's assertive style of leadership. The continued importance of the Tanaka faction was emphasized when six members were awarded portfolios in the new Cabinet. (However, Tanaka suffered a cerebral haemorrhage in February 1985, and was too ill to contest the general election in July 1986.)

In December 1985 Nakasone reshuffled his Cabinet, preserving a balance among the five major factions. In March 1986 plans to denationalize the Japanese National Railways in 1987 were approved by the Cabinet but strongly opposed by the JSP (the transfer to the private sector was implemented smoothly in April 1987). In June 1986 Nakasone secured approval for the dissolution of the Diet in spite of objections from the opposition parties. This enabled the Prime Minister to announce the holding of a premature general election for the House of Representatives (18 months ahead of schedule) to coincide with the triennial election for one-half of the seats in the House of Councillors on 6 July. The Government hoped to benefit from the higher level of participation expected to arise from the holding of both polls on the same day. The polling resulted in decisive victories for the LDP. In the election to the House of Representatives, the LDP obtained 49.4% of the votes, its highest level of electoral support since 1963, and won a record 304 of the 512 seats. The increased LDP majority was achieved largely at the expense of the JSP and the DSP. Of the main opposition parties, only the Komeito and the Communists maintained their strength in the House of Representatives. The LDP, therefore, was able to dispense with its coalition partner, the NLC (which disbanded in August and rejoined the LDP). The new Cabinet was composed entirely of LDP members. In September the leaders of the LDP agreed to alter bylaws to allow party presidents one-year extensions beyond the normal limit of two terms of two years each, and then applied this provision to Nakasone. Nakasone could thus retain the posts of President of the LDP and Prime Minister of Japan until 30 October 1987. In December 1986 the tax committee of the LDP issued proposals for a new programme of tax reforms, including the introduction of 5% value-added tax (VAT) and the abolition of tax-free savings schemes. Because of widespread opposition, however, the VAT proposal was withdrawn from the programme before it was approved as legislation by the Diet in September 1987. In 1986 a record trade surplus was registered. In an attempt to correct this imbalance, to reflate the domestic economy and to stabilize the Japanese currency, Nakasone relaxed his policy of domestic fiscal austerity in May 1987.

In July 1987 the Secretary-General of the LDP, Noboru Takeshita, left the Tanaka faction, with 113 other members, and announced the formation of a major new faction in the ruling party, the Takeshita faction. Susumu Nikaido, a former Vice-President of the LDP and the second most powerful man in the Tanaka faction, retained only about 20 supporters. The remainder of the Tanaka faction comprised a small group of independents who were uncommitted to either side. In the same month, Tanaka's political standing was weakened even further when the Tokyo high court upheld the decision, taken in 1983, which found him guilty of accepting bribes.

In October 1987 three senior politicians presented themselves as candidates to succeed Nakasone when he resigned from his post as President of the LDP: Takeshita, the Secretary-General of the LDP; Kiichi Miyazawa, the Minister of Finance; and Shintaro Abe, the Chairman of the Executive Council of the LDP and a former Minister of Foreign Affairs. After negotiations with the three candidates, Nakasone nominated Takeshita as his successor. It was widely believed that Nakasone had chosen this nomination procedure, rather than putting the selection of the new President to the vote of the LDP Diet members, because he feared that the latter procedure might cause further splits in the ruling party. On 6 November the Diet was convened and Takeshita was formally elected as Prime Minister. In the new Cabinet, Takeshita carefully maintained a balance among the five major factions of the LDP. He retained only two members of Nakasone's previous Cabinet, but appointed four members of the Nakasone faction to senior ministerial posts (including Nakasone's staunch ally, Sosuke Uno, to the post of Minister of Foreign Affairs). At the request of Nakasone, Kiichi Miyazawa was appointed Deputy Prime Minister and Minister of Finance, and Shintaro Abe was assigned the important post of Secretary-General of the LDP. Takeshita claimed that he would work to continue Nakasone's domestic and foreign policies, with particular emphasis on correcting the external trade imbalance and further liberalizing the financial market.

The implementation of a programme of tax reform, which Nakasone had failed to achieve, was one of the most important issues confronting Takeshita's Government. In June 1988 the LDP's tax deliberation council proposed the introduction of a new indirect tax (a general consumption tax or a type of VAT), which was to be levied at a rate of 3%. This proposal, however, encountered widespread opposition. In the same month, the Prime Minister and the LDP suffered a serious set-back when several leading figures in the party, including Nakasone, Shintaro Abe, Kiichi Miyazawa and Takeshita himself, were alleged to have been indirectly involved, through secretaries and political aides, in share-trading irregularities with the Recruit Cosmos Company. Despite strenuous denials by these politicians of any knowledge or involvement in such transactions, the Recruit scandal enabled the opposition parties to postpone consideration by the Diet of the tax reform proposals (which also included the reduction of income taxes). As the situation became increasingly serious, the opposition began to demand the resignation of the alleged participants and a full parliamentary investigation into the alleged share transactions. In November, shortly after the LDP had agreed to establish a 50-member committee to investigate the affair, the House of Representatives approved the tax reform measures (which constituted the most wide-ranging revision of the tax system for 40 years) and sent the legislation to the House of Councillors, where it was approved in the following month. Although Takeshita carried out a cabinet reshuffle (in December), which was widely viewed as an attempt to restore public confidence in the Government, three Ministers were forced to resign from their posts in December 1988 and January 1989, owing to their alleged involvement in the Recruit scandal. The three politicians were: Kiichi Miyazawa, the Deputy Prime Minister and Minister of Finance; Takashi Hasegawa, the Minister of Justice (who resigned after only three days in office); and Ken Harada, Minister of State and Director-General of the Economic Planning Agency. The LDP's loss of an important by-election for a seat in the House of Councillors in February 1989 was widely interpreted as an indication of the political damage that the party had suffered as a result of the impending introduction of the unpopular consumption tax and the continuing shares scandal. In the same month, the Chairman of the DSP, Saburo Tsukamoto, was forced to resign, as a result of his implication in the Recruit affair.

The Showa era came to an end when, after a long illness, Emperor Hirohito, who had reigned since 1926, died in January 1989. He was succeeded by his son, Akihito, and the new era was named Heisei ('achievement of universal peace').

Nakasone was committed to raising Japan's international status by fostering friendly relations with other world leaders. Throughout his term in office, he and his Minister of Foreign Affairs made many successful tours to numerous countries, to promote political and social links. Takeshita vowed to continue this emphasis on improving Japan's international relations, and he and his Minister of Foreign Affairs undertook a considerable number of official visits, notably to Western Europe and South-East Asia, during 1988. However, there is continued concern in the EEC over trade protectionism in Japan, and in the USA over the steadily worsening imbalance of bilateral trade. Partial deregulation of the financial markets has been introduced in an attempt to alleviate the problem, and several measures to stimulate imports were introduced in 1986–88. Relations between Japan and the USA deteriorated in April 1987, when it was discovered that the Toshiba Machine Company had illegally exported sophisticated submarine equipment to the USSR between 1982 and 1984. The USA claimed that these sales had endangered the security of both countries. In February 1989, however, Takeshita was the first foreign leader to hold an official meeting with the new US President, George Bush, following the latter's inauguration in January. Relations between the two countries had improved to some extent, owing partly to Japan's continued efforts to correct the trade imbalances and to the increase in expenditure by the Japanese Government on defence and foreign aid.

JAPAN

Japan continues to receive military support from the USA. Since 1982 Japan has been under continued pressure from the USA to increase its defence spending (which was equivalent to about 0.9% of the country's gross national product in 1983-85) and to assume greater responsibility for security in the Western Pacific area. In 1986 the Japanese Government decided to exceed the self-imposed limit on defence expenditure of 1% of the gross national product (GNP), set in 1976. The Government proposed defence spending equivalent to 1.004% of the forecast GNP in 1987/88, and also announced that it would maintain defence expenditure at around this level until 1991. This increase was welcomed by the USA but Nakasone stressed that Japan would not become a major military power. The JSP, however, accused the Nakasone Government of seeking to revive the nationalism of the pre-1945 militarist era. Japan's increasing defence commitment was evident in 1988, under the leadership of Takeshita, when defence expenditure of 3,700,300m. yen (equivalent to 1.013% of projected GNP) was budgeted for 1988/89.

Stability in South-East Asia is a vital consideration in Japanese foreign policy, since Japan depends on Asia for about one-third of its foreign trade, including imports of vital raw materials. In 1978 a treaty of peace and friendship was signed with the People's Republic of China. A meeting between Chinese and Japanese leaders, held in Beijing in June 1986, ended with a pledge by both sides to reduce China's large trade deficit with Japan. This pledge was reiterated when the Japanese Prime Minister visited China in November. In 1987, however, China expressed growing concern about Japan's increased expenditure on defence and its more assertive military stance. In August 1988 Takeshita undertook an official visit to China, which was aimed at further improving relations between the two countries. During the visit, the Japanese Prime Minister announced that Japan would advance 810,000m. yen in loans to China between 1990 and 1995.

Japan has demanded from the USSR the return of four small islands (the 'Northern Territories') lying a few kilometres from Hokkaido, which were annexed in 1945 by the USSR. Japan claims sovereignty over the islands under the provisions of an 1855 treaty between Japan and Russia. The Soviet claims are based on possession and on the 1945 Yalta agreement, in which the USA and the United Kingdom agreed that the Kurile Islands would be occupied by the USSR. Japan, supported since the early 1950s by the USA, argues that the islands are not part of the Kuriles. There has been no substantial progress in the matter since 1956, when Japan and the USSR resumed diplomatic relations. Consequently, the two countries have still not signed a peace treaty formally ending the Second World War. Following a visit to Tokyo by the Soviet Minister of Foreign Affairs in December 1988, however, Japan and the USSR agreed to establish a high-level joint working group to negotiate the future of the disputed territory and the conclusion of a peace treaty.

There was a noticeable improvement in relations between Japan and the USSR in 1986. In January the Soviet Minister of Foreign Affairs, Eduard Shevardnadze, visited Japan (the first visit of a Soviet Foreign Minister to Japan for 10 years). The two countries agreed to improve economic and trade relations, and to resume regular ministerial consultations. Japan and the USSR signed a new cultural agreement in June, when the Japanese Foreign Minister, Shintaro Abe, visited Moscow. In January 1987 Nakasone began a tour of Eastern Europe, the first such tour by a Japanese Prime Minister.

Government

Under the Constitution of 1947, the Emperor is Head of State but has no governing power. Legislative power is vested in the bicameral Diet, consisting of the House of Representatives or Lower House (512 seats), whose members are elected for a four-year term, and the House of Councillors or Upper House (252 seats), members of which are elected for six years, one-half being elected every three years. At the Upper House election of June 1983, an element of proportional representation was introduced, when 50 national seats were determined according to the number of votes for each party. There is universal suffrage for all adults from 20 years of age. Executive power is vested in the Cabinet. The Prime Minister is appointed by the Emperor (on designation by the Diet) and himself appoints the other Ministers. The Cabinet is responsible to the Diet.

Japan has 47 prefectures, each administered by an elected Governor.

Defence

Although the Constitution renounces war and the use of force, the right of self-defence is not excluded. Japan maintains ground, maritime and air self-defence forces. Military service is voluntary. The USA provides equipment and training staff and also maintains bases. The total strength of the self-defence forces in June 1988 was 245,000, comprising: army 156,000, navy 44,000 and air force 45,000. Proposed expenditure on defence for 1989/90 was 3,920,000m. yen.

Economic Affairs

Japan is not well endowed with natural resources, and about 67% of the total land area is forested. The country is self-sufficient in rice but has to import about 50% of its requirements of other cereals and fodder crops. Mineral resources are meagre, except for limestone and sulphur, and Japanese industry is heavily dependent on imported raw materials and fuels. In 1986 the Japanese Government decided that nearly 40% of Japanese coal production was to cease by 1991 (closing about one-half of its 11 coal-mines). Apart from its high cost, the coal industry has suffered from the rising importance of nuclear power. In 1986 Japan was the world's third largest consumer of petroleum, and, because the country produces virtually none of its own, petroleum accounted for 27% of Japan's import costs in 1985. In 1986 and 1987, however, the cost of petroleum imports fell sharply, to 15% and 14%, respectively, of total import costs, owing mainly to the decline in international petroleum prices. The Government has authorized the construction of three nuclear and eight coal-fired power stations as part of a programme to reduce the country's dependence on imported petroleum. Nuclear energy accounted for 26.3% of Japan's electricity output in 1986, compared with 25% contributed by petroleum-fired power stations. Petroleum was previously the largest source of electricity in Japan. Japan relies on imports for 91% of its total energy requirements. Since 1969 concessions have been granted for offshore petroleum exploration in the Korean Straits, the Sea of Japan and off Hokkaido Island. Drilling began in 1971. The Japan National Oil Company (JNOC) was established in 1978.

Based on the promotion of manufacturing industries for the export market, Japan achieved and maintained a very high rate of economic growth after 1945. Gross national product (GNP) expanded, in real terms, at an average annual rate of 10.3% between 1962 and 1972, and in 1971 Japan's GNP became the second largest in the world, ranking behind only the USA (Soviet bloc countries excluded). In 1987, according to estimates by the World Bank, Japan's GNP, measured at average 1985-87 prices, was US $1,925,614m., equivalent to $15,770 per head, a level comparable to that of industrialized countries in Western Europe. Between 1980 and 1987 the average annual increase in Japan's GNP per head was 3.1% in real terms. Overall, Japan's gross domestic product (GDP), measured in constant prices, increased at an average rate of 6.3% per year in 1965-80, but the rise slowed to 3.7% per year in 1980-86. The growth rate of GNP, in real terms, was 4.3% in the financial year 1985/86, but fell to 2.6% in 1986/87, owing mainly to the effect on exports of the rapid appreciation of the yen in relation to the US dollar. However, because of the strength of recovery of the Japanese economy and its ability to readjust to the situation of the strong yen (notably through domestic reflation), real GNP increased by 4.9% in 1987/88. According to government projections, the rate of real GNP growth in 1988/89 was expected to be 3.8%, a target which was likely to be an under-estimate by about 1%.

Between 1982 and 1987 the Japanese Government pursued an austere policy concerning government spending, in an attempt to reduce the budget deficit. In the 1985/86 budget the cost of servicing government bonds became the largest item of expenditure for the first time. A five-year 'freeze' on general expenditure was introduced, to enable the Government to cease issuing deficit-financing bonds to make up the 30% of government spending not covered by tax revenues. The Nakasone Government was unable to introduce value-added tax (VAT) in 1987 because of almost universal opposition, and the proportion of government spending that is covered by tax revenue is far lower than in any other advanced nation.

In September 1986 the Japanese Cabinet, reacting to pressure from US and domestic business leaders, proposed a supplementary budget for 1986/87 (involving additional spending of US $23,500m.) in an attempt to stimulate domestic growth. Priority was given to public works and new housing construction, which were allocated $20,000m. The budget proposals for 1987/88, however, projected the smallest increase in spending for 32 years. The proposals envisaged total expenditure of 54,101,000m. yen, representing an increase of only 0.02% over the corresponding total in the 1986/87 budget. Only spending on defence (increased by 5.2%) and overseas development aid (up by 5.3%) were allowed to rise significantly. An important development was the decision by the Government to exceed the self-imposed limit (set in 1976) of 1% of GNP on defence expenditure. The proposed spending on defence for 1987/88 was 3,517,400m. yen, which was equivalent to 1.004% of the forecast GNP in that financial year.

In May 1987, however, in an attempt to reflate the domestic economy (in response to continuing US protests about Japan's growing trade surplus with the USA), the Japanese Prime Minister relaxed his policy of domestic fiscal austerity substantially, when he introduced a supplementary budget, involving proposed additional spending of 6,000,000m. yen. A considerable reduction in income taxes, which constituted a part of the tax-reform programme that the Diet approved in October, was also expected to stimulate personal consumption and to contribute to domestic demand through the lessening of the tax burden. This move towards a more positive fiscal policy was continued into early 1988. The proposed 1988/89 budget, which was adopted by the Diet in January 1988, was the most expansionary budget for six years. Total projected expenditure was set at 56,699,700m. yen, which represented a 4.8% increase over the spending level of 1987/88. The rise in expenditure was partly due to greatly improved tax revenues and to the acquisition of capital revenue through the sale of the Government's shares in the Nippon Telegraph and Telephone Corporation (NTT). Defence spending was to increase by 5.2%, to 3,700,300m. yen (equivalent to 1.013% of the projected GNP), while foreign aid was to rise by 6.5%, to about 701,000m. yen, and spending on public works was to grow by 19.9%. In December 1988 the House of Councillors approved tax legislation, including the controversial general consumption tax, which was to be levied at a rate of 3%. The move towards a more positive fiscal policy was continued in 1989. In January the Government introduced a supplementary budget (financed largely by an increase in tax revenues), which increased total projected 1988/89 expenditure to 61,851,700m. Total projected expenditure in the proposed budget for 1989/90 was set at 60,414,200m. yen. Defence spending was to rise by 5.9%, to 3,920,000m. yen (equivalent to 1.006% of the projected GNP), while foreign aid was to increase by 7.8%, to 755,700m. yen.

In 1986 Japan was one of the world's three biggest donors of development aid, and planned to double its aid budget by 1992. In May 1987 the Japanese Government pledged to recycle $20,000m. of its huge trade surpluses to indebted developing countries (notably in Latin America, but also in Asia). This was in addition to $10,000m. of aid and credits already promised by Japan. In December the Japanese Prime Minister announced plans to establish a low-interest development fund of $2,000m., linking Japan with the Association of South East Asian Nations (ASEAN). The Government also pledged to double, to $50,000m., its official development aid, over the five years 1988–92, to developing countries. In 1988, according to government figures, Japan surpassed the USA as the world's largest donor of development aid on a disbursement basis.

In 1986 the level of unemployment began to cause concern in Japan, as the high value of the yen forced manufacturers to transfer production overseas. The unemployment rate rose to 2.9% of the labour force in 1985, the highest level since records began in 1953, and remained at a similar level throughout 1986. The unemployment rate rose to a record 3.1% in mid-1987, but had dropped to about 2.5% by mid-1988. The average annual increase in consumer prices was 2.0% in 1985 and 0.6% in 1986. By December 1986 inflation had been eliminated, with the consumer price index at the same level as 12 months previously. In 1987 average consumer prices increased by only 0.1%, the lowest annual rise for 29 years, but in 1988 the inflation rate rose slightly, to reach 0.7%.

In the 1980s Japan's economy was characterized by large trade surpluses. There was a massive surplus of $82,743m. in 1986, with exports increasing by 19.1% and imports declining by 2.4% (despite the huge appreciation of the yen against the US dollar). In 1987 imports were expected to increase as the strength of the yen lowered import prices, consumer spending grew and the Government's 'Action Programme' (including reductions in tariffs and the simplification of import procedures), which was introduced at the beginning of 1986, promoted imports of manufactured goods (especially from Western Europe and newly-industrialized South Asian countries). Imports did, in fact, increase by more than 18% in 1987, to reach a total of $149,515m., but exports rose by 10%, to $229,221m., resulting in a trade surplus of $79,706m. Since 1984 there has been continual criticism from the USA concerning the strength and extent of trade protectionism in Japan. In March 1987 the US Government imposed $300m. in punitive tariffs on a range of Japanese electronic goods; however, about one-half of this total had been removed by the end of the year. In 1986, as exports from Japan to Europe continued to rise, a further dispute between Japan and the EEC appeared likely. EEC officials claimed that Japanese exporters were actively transferring sales to Europe, where the appreciation of the yen in relation to local currencies had not been as marked as its appreciation against the US dollar. In 1987 the Republic of Korea became Japan's second largest export market (after the USA), while exports to the People's Republic of China, the United Kingdom, the Federal Republic of Germany, Taiwan and Hong Kong were also considerable. In 1987 the surplus on the current account of Japan's balance of payments reached a record $90,684m., which was 5.6% larger than the previous year's surplus. The surplus declined in 1988 to $79,500m., owing mainly to a large increase in expenditure by Japanese tourists abroad. The strength of the yen has not immediately reduced Japan's trade surplus (as initially expected), because the adverse affect on exports was offset by the fall in petroleum prices in 1986 and by reductions in the cost of raw materials and other imports. The increase in the value of the yen led to a shift in the emphasis of the Japanese economy from exports to expansion of domestic demand. In 1985 Japan became the world's largest exporter of manufactured goods, surpassing the USA and the Federal Republic of Germany. In 1986, however, the combined output of mining and manufacturing declined for the first time since 1975. After a year of very low growth in 1986/87, however, industrial production rose by 5.8% in 1987/88 and was projected to increase by 7.9% in 1988/89. This recovery in Japanese industry could be attributed to the strength of domestic demand, the fall in the cost of imports of raw materials and the increase in the transference of Japanese manufacturing companies abroad.

Farming in Japan is labour-intensive, but the proportion of the working population employed in agriculture, forestry and fishing fell from 19% in 1970 to 8.3% in 1987. Japan's agricultural labour force totalled 4.5m. in 1987. Japan produces about 70% of its total food requirements. The principal staple food crops are rice (which contributed 34% to total agricultural output in 1986), wheat, barley and potatoes. Japan is a leading fishing nation, both in coastal and deep-sea waters. Since 1976, however, the fishing industry has been seriously affected by the establishment of exclusive fishing zones by many countries. In 1986, yielding to US pressure, Japan agreed to end all commercial whaling in 1988. The killing of whales for 'scientific purposes', however, continued.

Industrial activity (mining, manufacturing and construction) employed 33% of the labour force in 1987, compared with 44% in 1970. Heavy industries predominate in the manufacturing sector, particularly motor vehicles, steel, machinery, electrical equipment and chemicals. In 1985 Japan was the world's largest producer of ships and the second largest producer of passenger cars, paper, synthetic fibres, cement, synthetic resins and steel. In recent years, however, the shipbuilding market has contracted sharply, and in 1985 the world's largest operator of oil tankers, Sanko Steamship, became the biggest company in Japan ever to file for bankruptcy. In 1986/87 Japanese exports of steel declined by 15%, to 25.7m. tons (the lowest annual total since 1973), owing to the rise in the value of the yen and to the increase in competition from developing countries, such as the Republic of Korea and Taiwan (which were also increasingly competitive with their expanding shipbuilding industries). Japan's electronics industry is expanding rapidly, however, and Japanese electronic goods are now extremely competitive on the world market. Between 1980 and early 1986 there was a 120% rise in the output of electrical machinery in Japan. As a whole, Japan ranks second in the world (after the USA) in industrial production. Japan's estimated investment in technology in 1984/85 was $28,800m., which was surpassed only by the USA.

Japan has been under pressure to revalue its currency in view of the favourable conditions of Japanese exports on the world market. In September 1985, following the agreement of the Group of Five (comprising the USA, Japan, the Federal Republic of Germany, the United Kingdom and France) to curb the continued increase in the value of the US dollar, the yen appreciated in value. The exchange rate was US $1 = 152 yen in September 1986, compared with $1 = 240 yen in September 1985. Initially, this rapid appreciation of the yen resulted in trading difficulties for Japan's export industries. In October 1986, therefore, Japan and the USA agreed on the desirability of maintaining the exchange rate at around $1 = 160 yen. At 31 December 1987, however, the rate stood at $1 = 121.35 yen: the US dollar's lowest level in relation to the Japanese currency since the Second World War. The US dollar recovered to 136.5 yen at 31 August 1988, but declined to a new post-war 'low' of 120.9 yen in November.

As part of a major privatization scheme, Japanese National Railways were denationalized in 1987, and the Government sold its shares in NTT and in Japan Air Lines.

Social Welfare

Almost all of the population are insured under the various schemes covering health, welfare annuities, unemployment and industrial accidents. Workers normally retire at 55 years of age, with the average pension being about 40% of salary. In 1982 Japan had 9,403 hospital establishments, with a total of 1,401,999 beds (equivalent to one for every 84 inhabitants), and there were 161,260 physicians working in the country.

Education

A kindergarten system provides education for children aged between three and five years of age, although the majority of kindergartens are privately controlled. At the age of six, children are required to attend elementary schools (shogakko), from which they proceed, after six years, to lower secondary schools (chugakko) for a further three years. Education is compulsory to the age of 15, and there are plans to increase the age limit to 18. In 1986 all children aged six to 11 were enrolled at primary schools, while 96% of those aged 12 to 17 received secondary education. Upper secondary schools provide a three-year course in general topics or a vocational course in subjects such as agriculture, commerce, fine art and technical studies. Higher education is divided into three types of institution. Universities (daigaku) offer a four-year degree course, as well as post-graduate courses. Japan has more than 400 universities, both public and private. Junior colleges (tanki-daigaku) provide less specialized two- to three-year courses. Both universities and junior colleges provide facilities for teacher-training. Technical colleges (tokushu-kyoiku-gakko) offer a five-year specialized training for technicians in many fields of engineering.

Public Holidays

1989: 1 January (New Year's Day), 15 January (Adults' Day), 11 February (National Foundation Day), 21 March (Vernal Equinox Day), 29 April (Emperor's Birthday), 3 May (Constitution Memorial Day), 5 May (Children's Day), 15 September (Respect for the Aged Day), 23 September (Autumnal Equinox), 10 October (Sports Day), 3 November (Culture Day), 23 November (Labour Thanksgiving Day).

1990: 1 January (New Year's Day), 15 January (Adults' Day), 11 February (National Foundation Day), 21 March (Vernal Equinox Day), 29 April (Emperor's Birthday), 3 May (Constitution Memorial Day), 5 May (Children's Day), 15 September (Respect for the Aged Day), 23 September (Autumnal Equinox), 10 October (Sports Day), 3 November (Culture Day), 23 November (Labour Thanksgiving Day).

Weights and Measures

The metric system is in force.

Statistical Survey

Source (unless otherwise stated): Statistics Bureau, Management and Co-ordination Agency, 19-1 Wakamatsucho, Shinjuku-ku, Tokyo 162, tel. (3) 202-1111, *Monthly Statistics of Japan, Japan Statistical Yearbook.*

Area and Population

AREA, POPULATION AND DENSITY

Area (sq km)	377,815*
Population (census results)†	
1 October 1980	117,060,396
1 October 1985	
Males	59,497,316
Females	61,551,607
Total	121,048,923
Population (official estimates at 1 October)†	
1984	120,235,358
1986	121,672,326
1987	122,264,000
Density (per sq km) at 1 October 1987	323.6

* 145,875 sq miles.
† Excluding foreign military and diplomatic personnel and their dependants.

PRINCIPAL CITIES* (population at 31 March 1988)

City	Pop.	City	Pop.
Tokyo (capital)†	8,155,781	Oita	392,566
Yokohama	3,121,601	Urawa	391,530
Osaka	2,543,520	Hirakata	385,739
Nagoya	2,099,564	Omiya	383,720
Sapporo	1,582,073	Fukuyama	363,123
Kobe	1,426,838	Asahikawa	362,523
Kyoto	1,419,390	Iwaki	357,056
Fukuoka	1,157,111	Takatsuki	353,940
Kawasaki	1,114,173	Suita	341,590
Hiroshima	1,042,629	Nagano	341,074
Kitakyushu	1,035,053	Nara	338,842
Sendai	865,630	Fujisawa	336,892
Sakai	807,680	Machida	335,347
Chiba	800,620	Takamatsu	327,538
Okayama	575,837	Toyohashi	325,862
Kumamoto	554,904	Toyama	316,061
Kagoshima	527,979	Toyoda	314,996
Hamamatsu	522,299	Kochi	311,710
Funabashi	515,295	Hakodate	311,591
Higashiosaka	502,893	Naha	309,641
Sagamihara	498,995	Koriyama	303,418
Amagasaki	497,212	Akita	294,536
Shizuoka	469,782	Okazaki	292,302
Niigata	469,521	Aomori	292,264
Himeji	450,374	Kawagoe	290,828
Nagasaki	445,814	Kashiwa	290,762
Matsudo	439,106	Tokorozawa	288,747
Matsuyama	433,886	Miyazaki	281,990
Hachioji	432,731	Maebashi	280,639
Yokosuka	430,656	Fukushima	271,226
Kanazawa	422,751	Koshigaya	270,854
Kawaguchi	418,880	Yao	269,439
Kurashiki	415,780	Yokkaichi	267,850
Utsunomiya	415,695	Akashi	261,035
Nishinomiya	412,267	Shimonoseki	260,219
Ichikawa	412,214	Kasugai	259,393
Gifu	407,827	Ichinomiya	258,584
Toyonaka	405,859	Tokushima	257,531
Wakayama	401,194	Neyagawa	256,168

* Except for Tokyo, the data for each city refer to an urban county (*shi*), an administrative division which may include some scattered or rural population as well as an urban centre.
† The figure refers to the 23 wards (*ku*) of Tokyo. The population of Tokyo-to (Tokyo Prefecture) was 11,680,282.

BIRTHS, MARRIAGES AND DEATHS*

	Registered live births		Registered marriages†		Registered deaths	
	Number	Rate (per '000)	Number	Rate (per '000)	Number	Rate (per '000)
1979	1,642,580	14.2	788,505	6.8	689,664	6.0
1980	1,576,889	13.6	774,702	6.7	722,801	6.2
1981	1,529,455	13.0	776,531	6.6	720,262	6.1
1982	1,515,392	12.8	781,252	6.6	711,883	6.0
1983	1,508,687	12.7	762,552	6.4	740,038	6.2
1984	1,489,780	12.5	739,991	6.2	740,247	6.2
1985	1,431,577	11.9	735,850	6.1	752,283	6.3
1986	1,382,946	11.4	710,962	5.9	750,620	6.2

* Figures relate only to Japanese nationals in Japan.
† Data are tabulated by year of registration rather than by year of occurrence.

ECONOMICALLY ACTIVE POPULATION*
(annual averages, '000 persons aged 15 and over)

	1985	1986	1987
Agriculture and forestry	4,640	4,500	4,460
Fishing and aquatic culture	450	450	430
Mining and quarrying	90	80	80
Manufacturing	14,530	14,440	14,250
Electricity, gas and water	330	320	310
Construction	5,300	5,340	5,330
Trade and restaurants	13,180	13,390	13,660
Transport, storage and communications	3,430	3,530	3,480
Financing, insurance, real estate and business services	3,920	4,150	
Community, social and personal services (incl. hotels)	11,970	12,120	17,110
Activities not adequately defined	230	210	
Total employed	58,070	58,530	59,110
Unemployed	1,560	1,670	1,730
Total labour force	59,630	60,200	60,840
Males	35,960	36,260	n.a.
Females	23,670	34,940	n.a.

* All figures are rounded, so totals may not always be the sum of their component parts.

JAPAN   Statistical Survey

Agriculture

PRINCIPAL CROPS ('000 metric tons)*

	1985	1986	1987
Wheat	874	876	864
Rice (brown)†	11,662	11,647	10,627
Barley	378	344	353
Potatoes	3,649	3,980	3,880
Sweet potatoes	1,527	1,507	1,423
Yams	168	n.a.	n.a.
Taro (Coco yam)	375	n.a.	n.a.
Dry beans	141	128	n.a.
Soybeans (Soya beans)	228	245	287
Groundnuts (in shell)	51	47	46
Cabbages	3,067	n.a.	n.a.
Tomatoes	802	816	833
Cauliflowers	129	n.a.	n.a.
Pumpkins, squash and gourds	273	n.a.	n.a.
Cucumbers and gherkins	1,033	1,040	1,020
Aubergines (Eggplants)	599	594	604
Chillies and peppers (green)	172	n.a.	n.a.
Onions (dry)	1,326	1,252	1,294
Carrots	663	671	656
Watermelons	820	840	852
Melons	366	n.a.	n.a.
Grapes	311	302	308
Sugar cane	2,638	2,240	2,374
Sugar beets	3,921	3,862	3,827
Apples	910	986	998
Pears	470	489	n.a.
Peaches and nectarines	205	219	212
Oranges	331	317	n.a.
Tangerines, mandarins, clementines and satsumas	2,491	2,168	2,518
Other citrus fruit	379	n.a.	n.a.
Strawberries	196	n.a.	n.a.
Tea (green)	96	94	96
Tobacco (leaves)	116	117	104

* Data at harvest time.
† To obtain the equivalent in paddy rice, the conversion factor is 150 kg of brown rice equals 186.6 kg of paddy.

LIVESTOCK ('000 head)

	1985	1986	1987
Cattle	4,698	4,742	4,694
Sheep	24	26	27
Goats	51	48	48
Horses	23	23	22
Pigs	10,718	11,061	11,354
Chickens	316,925	325,849	331,952

LIVESTOCK PRODUCTS (metric tons)

	1985	1986	1987
Beef and veal	555,257	558,592	565,472
Pig meat	1,531,727	1,551,651	1,580,662
Poultry meat	1,750,005	1,788,546	1,861,750
Cows' milk	7,380,369	7,456,940	7,334,900
Butter*	88,933	87,718	68,935
Cheese*	68,367	73,042	76,595
Hen eggs	2,152,356	2,230,968	2,373,727
Honey	7,225	n.a.	n.a.
Raw silk	9,592	8,341	7,864
Cattle hides (fresh)†	31,500	32,100	n.a.

* Industrial production only (i.e. butter and cheese manufactured at milk plants), excluding farm production.
† FAO estimates (Source: FAO, *Production Yearbook*).

Forestry

INDUSTRIAL ROUNDWOOD ('000 cubic metres)

	1983	1984	1985
Sawn timber	19,392	18,946	18,814
Pulp	1,894	1,748	1,789
Veneer sheets and plywood	442	457	433
Others	10,262	11,360	11,908
Total	**31,990**	**32,511**	**32,944**

Source: Ministry of Agriculture, Forestry and Fisheries, *Report on Demand and Supply of Lumber*.
Fuel wood ('000 cubic metres): 524 in 1984; 521 in 1985.
Sawn timber ('000 cubic metres): 18,397 in 1986; 18,774 in 1987.

SAWNWOOD PRODUCTION ('000 cubic metres)

	1984	1985	1986*
Coniferous (soft wood)	23,788	23,869	24,113
Broadleaved (hard wood)	4,810	4,534	4,580
Total	**28,598**	**28,403**	**28,693**

* Estimates.
Source: FAO, *Yearbook of Forest Products*.

Fishing

('000 metric tons, live weight)

	1984	1985	1986*
Freshwater fishes	63.7	63.6	89.0
Chum salmon (Keta or Dog salmon)	136.4	178.7	151.5
Flounders, halibuts, soles, etc.	260.7	215.2	167.1
Pacific cod	114.0	117.6	100.5
Alaska pollack	1,604.9	1,533.2	1,421.8
Pacific sandlance	164.4	122.5	141.3
Pacific saury (Skipper)	210.0	245.9	217.2
Japanese jack mackerel	139.4	158.1	114.6
Japanese scad	98.2	71.7	70.7
Japanese amberjack	152.5	151.0	145.9
Japanese pilchard (sardine)	4,179.4	3,866.9	4,209.5
Japanese anchovy	224.1	205.8	210.6
Skipjack tuna (Oceanic skipjack)	446.2	314.7	412.1
Yellowfin tuna	119.4	98.3	123.8
Bigeye tuna	127.9	156.2	164.1
Other tuna-like fishes	190.6	186.5	173.2
Chub mackerel	813.5	771.9	944.8
Other fishes (incl. unspecified)	1,344.8	1,343.2	1,502.2
Total fish	**10,390.0**	**9,800.8**	**10,360.0**
Marine crabs	98.7	99.6	94.8
Other crustaceans	117.7	99.2	114.3
Pacific cupped oyster	257.1	251.2	251.6
Japanese scallop	209.2	226.8	249.6
Japanese (Manila) clam	128.3	131.7	120.5
Other marine clams	98.1	95.9	103.4
Japanese flying squid	173.7	132.5	90.4
Other squids and cuttlefishes	352.2	395.4	372.9
Other molluscs	83.3	82.4	86.9
Other sea creatures†	112.7	93.3	122.5
Total catch†	**12,021.0**	**11,408.9**	**11,966.8**
Inland waters	202.6	205.2	198.7
Atlantic Ocean‡	206.0	203.6	273.3
Indian Ocean	54.1	58.8	47.4
Pacific Ocean	11,558.2	10,941.3	11,447.4

* Provisional.
† Excluding aquatic mammals (including whales, see below).
‡ Including the Mediterranean and Black Sea.
Source: FAO, *Yearbook of Fishery Statistics*.

JAPAN

WHALING*

	1984	1985	1986
Number of whales caught	4,313	3,025	2,883

* Figures include whales caught during the Antarctic summer season beginning in the year prior to the year stated.

Aquatic plants ('000 metric tons): 762.5 in 1984; 707.5 in 1985; 780.2 in 1986.

Source: FAO, *Yearbook of Fishery Statistics*.

Mining

('000 metric tons, unless otherwise indicated)

	1985	1986	1987
Coal	16,383	16,012	13,049
Zinc ore	253	222	166
Iron	338	291	266
Manganese	21	6	n.a.
Silica stone	14,357	13,637	14,291
Limestone	164,156	162,358	165,957
Chromite (metric tons)	11,920	10,642	11,815
Copper ore (metric tons)	43,208	34,978	23,817
Lead (metric tons)	49,951	40,327	27,870
Gold ore (kg)	5,309	10,280	8,590
Crude petroleum (million litres)	623	736	707
Natural gas ('000 cu m)	2,224,640	2,105,385	2,167,746

Source: Ministry of International Trade and Industry.

Industry

SELECTED PRODUCTS
('000 metric tons, unless otherwise indicated)

	1984	1985	1986
Wheat flour[1]	4,227	4,243	4,231
Sugar*	2,147.2	2,079.2	2,057.9
Distilled alcoholic beverages ('000 hectolitres)	9,030	9,260	8,955†
Beer ('000 hectolitres)[1]	45,819	48,511	49,966†
Cigarettes (million)[1]	306,867	308,500	292,000
Cotton yarn—pure (metric tons)	390,709	392,526	399,156
Cotton yarn—mixed (metric tons)	46,031	44,505	45,527
Woven cotton fabrics—pure and mixed (million sq m)	2,089.8	2,060.9	1,974.2
Flax, ramie and hemp yarn (metric tons)	6,404	6,293	8,848
Jute yarn (metric tons)	8,794	6,577	5,669
Linen fabrics ('000 sq m)	24,786	25,274	34,229
Jute fabrics ('000 sq m)	612	481	327
Woven silk fabrics—pure and mixed ('000 sq m)	115,116	114,538	108,221
Wool yarn—pure and mixed (metric tons)	120,930	123,427	112,109
Woven woollen fabrics—pure and mixed ('000 sq m)[2]	327,134	325,601	312,964
Rayon continuous filaments (metric tons)	79,714	76,381	75,787
Acetate continuous filaments (metric tons)	31,107	28,213	26,986
Rayon discontinuous fibres (metric tons)	266,562	244,910	217,210
Acetate discontinuous fibres (metric tons)[3]	41,140	38,427	36,972
Woven rayon fabrics—pure and mixed (million sq m)[2]	632.2	656.3	638.8
Woven acetate fabrics—pure and mixed (million sq m)[2]	64.6	63.0	61.5
Non-cellulosic continuous filaments (metric tons)	648,114	653,638	615,571
Non-cellulosic discontinuous fibres (metric tons)	767,037	792,287	787,240
Woven synthetic fabrics (million sq m)[2,4]	3,296.8	3,067.6	2,859.4
Leather footwear ('000 pairs)[5]	55,708	53,387	51,975
Mechanical wood pulp	9,127.3	9,278.9	9,240.0
Chemical wood pulp[6]			
Newsprint	2,553.4	2,592.1	2,640.6
Other printing and writing paper	4,551.1	4,746.4	4,949.5
Other paper	4,324.7	4,451.5	4,681.9
Paperboard	7,915.4	8,678.9	8,789.9
Synthetic rubber	1,160.5	1,158.0	1,153.4
Motor vehicle tyres ('000)	143,311	149,513	147,517
Rubber footwear ('000 pairs)	64,998	62,367	58,064
Ethylene—Ethene	4,385.7	4,226.9	4,291.4
Propylene—Propene	2,980.7	3,057.1	3,166.9
Benzene—Benzol	2,217.6	2,279.4	2,260.9
Toluene—Toluol	811.2	829.3	830.3
Xylenes—Xylol	1,400.9	1,523.5	1,570.2
Methyl alcohol—Methanol	280.1	254.3	220.8
Ethyl alcohol—95% (kilolitres)	167,627	179,197	168,782
Sulphuric acid—100%	6,451.4	6,580.0	6,562.4
Caustic soda—Sodium hydroxide	3,085.3	3,074.1	3,076.4
Soda ash—Sodium carbonate	1,036.2	1,057.1	1,020.8
Ammonium sulphate	1,829.4	1,837.0	1,783.4
Nitrogenous fertilizers (a)[7]	1,075	1,210	953
Phosphate fertilizers (b)[7]	647	641	464
Liquefied petroleum gas	8,139	8,354	7,831
Naphtha (million litres)	11,672	10,348	9,672
Motor spirit—Gasoline (million litres)[8]	36,383	36,453	34,332
Kerosene (million litres)	26,841	24,248	24,089
Jet fuel (million litres)	3,737	4,327	4,020
Gas oil (million litres)	24,782	25,468	26,123
Heavy fuel oil (million litres)	76,441	65,117	61,589
Lubricating oil (million litres)	2,228	2,256	2,233
Petroleum bitumen—Asphalt	5,137	5,001	5,573
Coke-oven coke	51,275	51,742	48,139
Cement	78,851	72,847	71,264
Pig-iron	80,403	80,569	74,651
Ferro-alloys[9]	1,418	1,389	1,105
Crude steel	105,588	105,279	98,275
Aluminium—unwrought: primary	286.7	226.5	140.2
secondary[10]	840.3	866	865
Electrolytic copper	935.1	936.0	943.0
Refined lead—unwrought (metric tons)	278,494	285,372	283,142
Electrolytic, distilled and rectified zinc—unwrought (metric tons)	754,445	739,624	708,032
Calculating machines ('000)	83,713	86,031	64,211
Radio receivers ('000)	13,589	12,995	13,911
Television receivers ('000)	15,512	17,727	13,863
Merchant vessels launched ('000 g.r.t.)	9,395	9,354	7,750

JAPAN

—continued	1984	1985	1986
Passenger motor cars ('000)	7,073.2	7,646.8	7,809.8
Lorries and trucks ('000)	4,319.5	4,544.7	4,407.6
Motorcycles, scooters and mopeds ('000)	4,026.3	4,536.3	3,396.6
Cameras: photographic ('000)	15,338	17,040	17,383
cinematographic ('000)	79.1	51.1	7.8
Watches and clocks ('000)	221,907	257,354	281,703
Construction: new dwellings started ('000)[11]	1,187.2	1,236.1	1,364.6
Electric energy (million kWh)[1]	648.572	671,952	676,359
Town gas (teracalories)	121,840	124,515	130,673

* Twelve months ending September.
† Provisional.
[1] Twelve months beginning 1 April of the year stated.
[2] Including finished fabrics.
[3] Including cigarette filtration tow.
[4] Including blankets made of synthetic fibres.
[5] Sales.
[6] Including pulp prepared by semi-chemical processes.
[7] Figures refer to the 12 months ending 30 June of the year stated and are in terms of (a) nitrogen, 100%, and (b) phosphoric acid, 100%.
[8] Including aviation gasoline. [9] Including silico-chromium.
[10] Including alloys.
[11] Including buildings and dwelling units created by conversion.

1987: Leather footwear ('000 pairs) 51,984; Chemicals ('000 metric tons): Xylenes (Xylol) 1,767.3, Soda ash (Sodium carbonate) 1,098.0, Ammonium sulphate 1,803.0; Petroleum products (million litres): Naphtha 8,733, Motor spirit (Gasoline) 24,520, Kerosene 20,054, Jet fuel 4,038, Gas oil 25,236, Heavy fuel oil 60,344, Lubricating oil 2,284; Coke-oven coke ('000 metric tons) 46,431; Cement ('000 metric tons) 71,550; Radio receivers ('000) 8,396; Passenger motor cars ('000) 7,891.1; Motorcycles, scooters and mopeds ('000) 2,630.6; Town gas (teracalories) 132,992.

Sources: Ministry of Agriculture, Forestry and Fisheries, Ministry of International Trade and Industry, Ministry of Finance and Ministry of Construction.

Finance

CURRENCY AND EXCHANGE RATES

Monetary Units
1,000 rin = 100 sen = 1 yen.

Denominations
Coins: 1, 5, 10, 50 and 100 yen.
Notes: 500, 1,000, 5,000 and 10,000 yen.

Sterling and Dollar Equivalents (30 September 1988)
£1 sterling = 226.5 yen;
US $1 = 133.9 yen;
1,000 yen = £4.415 = $7.468.

Average Exchange Rate (yen per US $)
1985 238.54
1986 168.52
1987 144.64

GENERAL BUDGET ESTIMATES
('000 million yen, year ending 31 March)

Revenue	1986/87	1987/88	1988/89
Taxes and stamps	40,560	41,194	45,090
Public bonds	10,946	10,501	8,841
Others	2,583	2,406	2,769
Total	54,089	54,101	56,700

Expenditure	1986/87	1987/88	1988/89
Social security	9,835	10,090	10,385
Education and science	4,845	4,850	4,858
Government bond servicing	11,320	11,334	11,512
Defence	3,344	3,517	3,700
Public works	6,223	6,082	7,382
Local finance	10,185	10,184	10,906
Pensions	1,850	1,896	1,880
Total (incl. others)	54,089	54,101	55,700

INTERNATIONAL RESERVES
(US $ million at 31 December)

	1985	1986	1987
Gold*	931	1,037	1,203
IMF special drawing rights	2,116	2,218	2,463
Reserve position in IMF	2,275	2,382	2,853
Foreign exchange	22,328	37,657	75,657
Total	27,650	43,294	82,176

* Valued at 35 SDRs per troy ounce.
Source: IMF, *International Financial Statistics*.

MONEY SUPPLY ('000 million yen at 31 December)

	1985	1986	1987
Currency outside banks	23,406.8	26,198.0	28,582.6
Demand deposits at deposit money banks	65,572.7	72,016.4	74,390.1
Total money	88,979.5	98,214.4	102,972.7

COST OF LIVING (Consumer Price Index; average of monthly figures. Base: 1985 = 100)

	1984	1986	1987
Food (incl. beverages)	98.3	100.2	99.3
Housing	97.5	102.5	105.4
Rent	97.4	102.6	105.8
Fuel, light and water charges	100.4	95.0	88.0
Clothing and footwear	96.7	102.2	103.3
Miscellaneous	98.7	102.0	103.2
All items	98.0	100.6	100.7

Source: Management and Co-ordination Agency, *Annual Report on the Consumer Price Index*.

JAPAN

Statistical Survey

NATIONAL ACCOUNTS ('000 million yen at current prices)

	1984	1985	1986
Government final consumption expenditure	29,448.8	30,685.3	32,571.1
Private final consumption expenditure	175,984.3	184,764	191,651.4
Increase in stocks	1,137.8	2,253.8	1,293.4
Gross fixed capital formation	83,176.0	87,825	91,301.7
Total domestic expenditure	289,746.9	305,528.1	316,817.6
Exports of goods and services	45,066.0	46,307.1	38,089.9
Less Imports of goods and services	36,865.5	35,531.6	24,791.1
Gross domestic product (GDP)	297,947.5	316,303.7	330,116.3
Factor income received from abroad	4,953.4	5,768.4	5,337.5
Less Factor income paid abroad	4,448.2	4,631.1	4,108.3
Gross national product (GNP)	298,452.7	317,441.0	331,345.5
Less Consumption of fixed capital	40,715.4	43,478.3	46,106.0
Statistical discrepancy	−1,278.8	−1,479.2	−1,488.1
National income in market prices	256,458.6	272,483.5	283,751.4

1987 ('000 million yen): GNP 344,888.

Gross Domestic Product by Economic Activity

	1984	1985	1986
Agriculture, forestry and fishing	9,625.6	9,798.2	9,481.0
Mining and quarrying	1,207.6	1,208.0	1,235.7
Manufacturing	88,845.0	94,160.0	96,651.6
Electricity, gas and water	9,658.1	10,449.2	11,860.3
Construction	22,437.0	23,433.0	24,672.2
Wholesale and retail trade	42,288.6	43,218.9	43,512.6
Transport, storage and communications	18,716.3	19,531.6	20,322.7
Finance and insurance	16,540.5	17,840.8	18,316.7
Real estate	29,204.8	30,997.7	32,895.8
Public administration	13,765.3	14,395.2	15,149.0
Other services	56,853.5	93,297.3	67,511.5
Sub-total	309,142.3	328,329.9	341,615.1
Import duties	1,337.3	1,268.1	942.4
Less Imputed bank service charge	13,810.9	14,773.5	13,929.2
Total	296,668.7	314,824.5	328,628.3
Statistical discrepancy	1,278.7	1,479.2	1,488.1
Gross domestic product	297,947.5	316,303.7	330,116.3

BALANCE OF PAYMENTS (US $ million)

	1986			1987		
	Credit	Debit	Balance	Credit	Debit	Balance
Goods and services:						
Merchandise f.o.b.	205,591	112,764	92,827	224,605	128,219	96,386
Freight	6,699	3,950	2,749	7,538	6,868	670
Insurance on merchandise	239	446	−207			
Non-merchandise insurance	−77	400	477	5,416	12,192	−6,776
Other transportation	4,378	9,457	−5,079			
Tourists						
Other travel	1,463	7,229	−5,766	2,097	10,760	−8,663
Investment income	29,086	19,613	9,473	49,245	32,575	16,670
Military transactions	2,101	—	2,101	1,856	—	1,856
Other government services	904	453	451	871	441	430
Other private services	8,907	17,084	−8,177	12,617	22,506	−9,889
Total	259,291	171,396	87,895	304,245	213,561	90,684
Unrequited transfers:						
Private transfer payments	354	939	−585	546	1,518	−972
Reparations	—	—	—	—	—	—
Other government transfers	65	1,530	−1,465	87	2,784	−2,697
Total	419	2,469	−2,050	633	4,302	−3,669
Total current account	259,710	173,865	85,845	304,245	213,561	90,684
Capital flows:						
Long-term capital:						
Direct investments	226	14,480	−14,254	1,165	19,519	−18,354
Trade credits (net)	−40	1,836	−1,876	−1	535	−536
Loans (net)	−34	9,281	−9,315	−119	16,190	−16,309
Securities (net)	545	101,977	−101,432	−6,081	87,757	−93,838
Others (net)	−63	4,521	−4,584	1,334	8,829	−7,495
Balance	634	132,095	−131,461	−3,702	132,830	−136,532
Short-term capital:						
Trade credits (net)	—	1,464	−1,464	—	235	−235
Others (net)	—	145	−145	24,100	—	24,100
Balance on capital account	634	133,704	−133,070	20,398	133,065	−112,667
Net errors and omissions	4,897	—	4,897	—	4,857	−4,857
Overall balance (net monetary movements)			−44,767			−29,545
of which:						
Gold and foreign exchange reserves			15,729			39,240
Others			−60,496			−68,785
of which: commercial banks			−58,506			−71,801

Source: Bank of Japan, *Balance of Payments, Monthly.*

JAPAN

JAPANESE DEVELOPMENT ASSISTANCE (US $ million)

	1985	1986	1987
Official:			
Bilateral grants:			
Donations	1,185	1,703	2,221
Reparations	636	855	1,154
Technical assistance	549	849	1,067
Direct loans	1,372	2,143	3,027
Total	2,557	3,846	5,248
Capital subscriptions or grants to international agencies	1,240	1,788	2,207
Total	3,797	5,634	7,454
Other Government capital:			
Export credits	−152	−858	−2,047
Direct investment capital	−1	332	287
Loans to international agencies	−148	−198	−47
Total	−302	−724	−1,808
Total official	3,495	4,910	5,646
Private:			
Export credits	−994	273	1,081
Direct investments	1,046	2,902	7,421
Other bilateral security investments	5,138	5,315	4,357
Loans to international agencies	2,832	1,326	1,865
Donations to non-profit organizations	101	82	92
Total private	8,123	9,898	14,816
Grand total	11,618	14,809	20,462

Source: Ministry of International Trade and Industry.

External Trade

PRINCIPAL COMMODITIES (US $ million)

Imports c.i.f.	1985	1986	1987
Food and live animals	14,787.4	18,245.9	20,752.0
Meat and meat preparations	1,926.6	2,586.9	3,338.4
Fresh, chilled or frozen meat	1,844.0	2,477.7	n.a.
Fish and fish preparations*	4,610.0	6,426.4	7,992.2
Crustacea and molluscs (fresh and simply preserved)	2,284.7	3,196.5	n.a.
Cereals and cereal preparations	3,950.7	3,485.2	3,160.4
Wheat and meslin (unmilled)	973.8	885.5	784.8
Maize (unmilled) for feeding	1,362.7	1,158.1	1,100.5
Fruit and vegetables	1,828.1	2,363.8	2,832.4
Sugar, sugar preparations and honey	344.2	452.8	477.0
Raw sugar	209.6	278.9	289.6
Coffee, tea, cocoa and spices	1,138.7	1,593.1	1,359.4
Beverages and tobacco	760.0	940.5	1,643.2
Crude materials (inedible) except fuels	17,715.0	17,292.0	21,751.1
Oil-seeds, oil nuts and oil kernels	1,875.2	1,567.7	1,616.7
Soya beans (excl. flour)	1,206.1	1,072.4	1,086.5
Wood, lumber and cork	3,720.4	4,044.4	6,245.6
Rough or roughly squared wood	3,699.6	2,922.8	4,347.9
Textile fibres and waste	2,155.1	1,863.3	2,702.0
Cotton	1,048.7	818.4	1,136.7
Raw cotton (excl. linters)	1,021.3	797.1	1,114.4
Metalliferous ores and metal scrap	6,232.1	5,763.4	6,120.1
Iron ore and concentrates	3,044.9	2,759.3	2,618.4
Non-ferrous ores and concentrates	2,229.0	2,080.0	772.9
Copper ores and concentrates (excl. matte)	1,209.3	1,227.5	1,475.7

Imports c.i.f.—continued	1985	1986	1987
Mineral fuels, lubricants, etc.	55,799.2	36,903.8	39,136.8
Coal, coke and briquettes	5,209.3	4,943.9	4,669.7
Coal (excl. briquettes)	5,196.5	4,926.5	4,633.5
Petroleum and petroleum products	40,574.9	24,116.6	27,445.3
Crude and partly refined petroleum	34,599.4	19,480.8	20,663.4
Petroleum products	5,975.5	4,635.8	6,781.9
Residual fuel oils	2,019.5	1,093.2	1,476.8
Gas (natural and manufactured)	10,006.1	7,843.3	7,021.8
Animal and vegetable oils and fats	328.9	244.7	270.8
Chemicals	8,072.7	9,733.1	11,844.9
Chemical elements and compounds	4,142.4	4,566.0	5,470.3
Organic chemicals	2,410.6	2,849.0	3,494.0
Inorganic chemicals	742.1	766.6	868.6
Medicinal and pharmaceutical products	1,291.9	1,724.4	2,110.0
Basic manufactures	10,885.5	12,389.5	18,055.2
Textile yarn, fabrics, etc.	1,891.1	2,173.9	2,974.9
Non-metallic mineral manufactures	1,264.3	1,927.9	2,847.4
Iron and steel	1,479.5	1,761.8	2,483.8
Non-ferrous metals	4,041.5	3,654.7	5,644.0
Aluminium and aluminium alloys	1,861.3	1,641.0	2,669.4
Machinery and transport equipment	11,106.3	13,283.1	17,263.5
Non-electric machinery	4,727.9	5,317.8	6,745.5
Electrical machinery, apparatus, etc.	3,795.2	4,506.1	5,893.8
Transport equipment	2,583.1	3,459.2	4,624.3
Aircraft and parts†	1,483.6	1,776.8	1,742.0
Miscellaneous manufactured articles	6,349.2	8,633.4	13,396.0
Clothing (excl. footwear)	1,995.1	2,852.7	4,649.4
Other commodities and transactions	3,743.5	8,741.7	5,401.7
Re-imports	1,568.9	1,544.5	1,736.5
Non-monetary gold	2,026.7	6,983.9	3,467.1
Total	129,538.7	126,407.8	149,515.1

* Including crustacea and molluscs.
† Excluding tyres, engines and electrical parts.

Exports f.o.b.	1985	1986	1987
Food and live animals	1,202.0	1,365.9	1,424.2
Beverages and tobacco	113.7	110.4	121.3
Crude materials (inedible) except fuels	1,240.2	1,414.1	1,489.5
Mineral fuels, lubricants, etc.	589.9	588.1	782.2
Animal and vegetable oils and fats	111.4	90.5	85.1
Chemicals	7,697.7	9,483.8	11,662.3
Chemical elements and compounds	3,242.9	3,953.4	4,998.7
Organic chemicals	2,511.8	3,141.3	4,017.3
Plastic materials, etc.	2,260.6	2,842.6	3,405.5
Basic manufactures	28,835.8	29,600.0	30,126.1
Rubber manufactures	1,894.7	2,040.3	2,240.0
Rubber tyres and tubes	1,544.6	1,642.2	1,807.2
Textile yarn, fabrics, etc.	4,900.1	5,444.8	5,544.7
Woven textile fabrics (excl. narrow or special fabrics)	3,360.6	3,706.4	3,741.5
Fabrics of synthetic (excl. regenerated) fibres	2,033.5	2,133.3	2,003.6
Non-metallic mineral manufactures	2,147.5	2,362.3	2,522.5

JAPAN

Statistical Survey

Exports f.o.b.—*continued*	1985	1986	1987
Iron and steel	13,565.8	12,706.2	12,610.0
Bars, rods, angles, shapes, etc.	1,777.4	1,437.1	1,058.6
Universals, plates and sheets	5,209.2	5,249.9	6,077.7
Thin plates and sheets (uncoated)	2,420.9	2,581.2	3,027.5
Tubes, pipes and fittings	3,659.5	3,398.7	2,567.5
Non-ferrous metals	1,466.9	1,563.7	1,771.9
Other metal manufactures	3,458.4	3,912.8	3,635.7
Machinery and transport equipment	108,387.4	133,325.6	149,562.7
Non-electric machinery	29,537.2	38,380.7	44,754.7
Power generating machinery	3,788.9	4,939.0	5,904.0
Internal combustion engines (non-aircraft)	2,884.7	3,841.8	4,876.0
Office machines	7,785.2	11,305.4	14,391.9
Metalworking machinery	2,599.2	3,636.9	3,475.1
Heating and cooling equipment	1,588.0	1,793.1	2,031.8
Electrical machinery, apparatus, etc.	29,700.9	35,518.5	40,883.1
Electric power machinery	2,057.8	2,453.2	2,724.0
Telecommunications apparatus	12,242.1	13,643.6	15,071.3
Television receivers	2,624.8	1,727.2	1,422.3
Radio receivers	2,654.4	2,755.5	2,463.5
Thermionic valves, tubes, etc.	4,953.4	6,342.4	8,312.3
Transport equipment	49,149.4	59,426.4	63,925.0
Road motor vehicles and parts*	n.a.	50,929.4	44,942.2
Passenger cars (excl. buses)	25,402.2	32,945.2	35,693.2
Lorries and trucks (incl. ambulances)	7,396.0	8,021.8	7,324.2
Parts for cars, buses, etc.*	5,227.7	8,253.3	10,713.8
Motor cycles and parts	2,625.9	2,686.3	2,628.3
Motor cycles	2,092.4	2,064.1	1,884.4
Ships and boats	5,929.4	4,878.5	4,359.7
Miscellaneous manufactured articles	25,751.9	31,125.0	31,599.2
Scientific instruments, watches, etc.	10,046.1	12,407.8	13,722.6
Scientific instruments and photographic equipment	6,830.9	8,509.3	9,447.9
Watches, clocks and parts	1,730.2	1,963.4	1,980.8
Musical instruments, sound recorders, etc.	14,537.4	17,559.7	16,828.9
Sound recorders, phonographs and parts	9,230.4	11,228.6	10,085.2
Sound recorders and phonographs	n.a.	9,909.6	8,406.0
Other commodities and transactions	1,758.6	2,047.8	2,368.6
Re-exports	1,712.6	1,975.0	2,198.9
Total	175,637.8	209,151.2	229,221.2

* Excluding tyres, engines and electrical parts.

PRINCIPAL TRADING PARTNERS* (US $ million)

Imports c.i.f.	1985	1986	1987
Australia	7,452.2	6,980.3	7,869.3
Brazil	1,840.2	1,874.6	2,032.4
Brunei	1,892.2	1,285.2	1,300.5
Canada	4,772.9	4,895.4	6,072.9
China, People's Republic	6,482.7	5,652.4	7,401.4
France	1,323.7	1,855.1	2,871.3
Germany, Federal Republic	2,928.0	4,297.8	6,150.3
Hong Kong	763.4	1,065.8	n.a.
India	1,188.6	1,297.0	1,530.1
Indonesia	10,119.0	7,310.9	8,427.3
Iran	2,505.8	1,383.3	1,555.6
Italy	1,049.8	1,495.4	2,134.8
Korea, Republic	4,091.9	5,292.0	8,075.5
Kuwait	1,162.3	1,156.6	1,795.8
Malaysia	4,330.1	3,845.6	4,771.9
Mexico	1,869.9	1,439.0	1,625.2
Oman	3,065.9	1,615.7	1,555.6
Philippines	1,243.1	1,220.7	1,352.9
Qatar	2,185.1	1,126.5	979.0
Saudi Arabia	10,244.7	5,204.8	7,311.1
Singapore	1,593.9	1,463.3	2,047.6
South Africa	1,843.9	2,228.7	2,259.2
Switzerland	1,758.1	2,571.2	3,101.4
Taiwan	3,385.5	4,690.5	7,128.1
Thailand	1,026.9	1,390.9	1,796.0
USSR	1,429.3	1,972.0	2,351.9
United Arab Emirates	8,916.3	5,947.2	5,926.3
United Kingdom	1,816.8	3,573.4	3,057.0
USA	25,093.0	29,054.4	31,499.5
Total (incl. others)	129,538.7	126,407.8	149,515.1

Exports f.o.b.	1985	1986	1987
Australia	5,379.0	5,226.8	5,146.2
Belgium and Luxembourg	1,492.9	2,221.1	n.a.
Canada	4,520.2	5,526.1	5,610.9
China, People's Republic	12,477.4	9,856.2	8,249.8
France	2,083.1	3,151.7	4,014.4
Germany, Federal Republic	6,937.8	10,477.3	12,832.6
Hong Kong	6,509.2	7,160.6	8,872.0
India	1,596.4	2,099.4	1,957.3
Indonesia	2,172.5	2,661.6	2,990.0
Iran	1,347.7	1,144.5	1,043.2
Iraq	1,305.6	1,210.2	390.7
Italy	1,116.7	1,723.2	2,102.7
Korea, Republic	7,097.2	10,474.5	13,229.3
Kuwait	1,536.1	1,219.0	857.0
Malaysia	2,168.2	1,708.4	2,167.8
Mexico	994.0	1,032.0	1,388.9
Netherlands	2,071.1	3,261.0	4,070.9
New Zealand	1,072.4	1,102.5	1,127.5
Norway	639.1	1,169.0	n.a.
Panama	3,326.1	3,196.8	2,416.4
Philippines	936.6	1,088.1	1,414.7
Saudi Arabia	3,890.0	2,761.7	3,239.4
Singapore	3,860.5	4,576.6	6,008.1
South Africa	1,019.9	1,355.2	1,863.3
Spain	751.0	1,270.3	n.a.
Sweden	1,094.2	1,438.3	1,931.3
Switzerland	1,160.8	1,886.8	2,266.1
Taiwan	5,025.5	7,851.8	11,346.3
Thailand	2,030.4	2,029.7	2,953.3
USSR	2,750.6	3,149.5	2,563.3
United Arab Emirates	1,164.4	1,032.5	n.a.
United Kingdom	4,722.8	6,646.8	8,400.3
USA	65,277.6	80,455.6	83,580.0
Total (incl. others)	175,637.8	209,151.2	229,221.2

* Imports by country of production; exports by country of last consignment.

Source: Ministry of Finance, *The Summary Report, Trade of Japan*.

JAPAN

Transport

RAILWAYS (traffic, year ending 31 March)

	1983/84	1984/85	1985/86
National railways			
Passengers (million)	6,797	6,884	6,941
Freight ton-km (million)	27,086	22,721	21,625
Private railways			
Passengers (million)	11,741	11,869	12,048
Freight ton-km (million)	560	513	509

ROAD TRAFFIC
('000 licensed vehicles, year ending 31 March)

	1983/84	1984/85	1985/86
Cars	25,028	25,848	25,828
Buses	230	231	231
Lorries	8,382	8,306	8,418
Special purpose vehicles	912	944	942
Total	34,551	35,328	35,420

Source: Ministry of Transport.

SHIPPING

Merchant Fleet (registered at 30 June)

	1984	1985	1986
Vessels	10,425	10,288	10,011
Displacement ('000 gt)	40,358	39,940	38,487

Source: *Lloyd's Register of Shipping*.

International Sea-borne Traffic

	1984	1985	1986
Vessels entered:			
Number	38,980	39,856	40,129
Displacement ('000 net tons)	347,907	352,589	345,284
Goods ('000 metric tons):			
Loaded	94,800	94,307	88,123
Unloaded	603,159	603,684	598,908

Source: Ministry of Finance.

Statistical Survey, Directory

CIVIL AVIATION (domestic and international services)

	1984	1985	1986
Passengers carried ('000)	51,018	50,337	53,640
Passenger/km (million)	64,601	65,529	70,934
Freight ton/km* ('000)	2,699,260	3,089,530	3,589,650

* Including excess baggage.
Original Source: Ministry of Transport.

Tourism

	1984	1985	1986
Foreign visitors	2,110,346	2,327,047	2,061,526
Money received (US $ million)	970	1,137	1,379

Communications Media

('000)

	1984	1985	1986
Television subscribers*	31,062	31,509	31,955
Daily newspaper circulation†	48,232	48,232	48,569

* At 31 March.   † In October.

Education

(1987)

	Institutions	Teachers	Students
Primary schools	24,933	448,977	10,226,323
Lower secondary schools	11,230	292,057	6,081,330
High schools	5,508	274,913	5,375,107
Technological colleges	62	5,955	50,078
Junior colleges	561	48,762	437,641
Graduate schools and universities	474	197,034	1,934,483

Directory

The Constitution

The Constitution of Japan was promulgated on 3 November 1946 and came into force on 3 May 1947. The following is a summary of its major provisions:

THE EMPEROR

Articles 1–8. The Emperor derives his position from the will of the people. In the performance of any state act as defined in the Constitution, he must seek the advice and approval of the Cabinet though he may delegate the exercise of his functions, which include: (i) the appointment of the Prime Minister and the Chief Justice of the Supreme Court; (ii) promulgation of laws, cabinet orders, treaties and constitutional amendments; (iii) the convocation of the Diet, dissolution of the House of Representatives and proclamation of elections to the Diet; (iv) the appointment and dismissal of Ministers of State and as well as the granting of amnesties, reprieves and pardons and the ratification of treaties, conventions or protocols; (v) the awarding of honours and performance of ceremonial functions.

RENUNCIATION OF WAR

Article 9. Japan renounces for ever the use of war as a means of settling international disputes.

Articles 10–40 refer to the legal and human rights of individuals guaranteed by the Constitution.

-THE DIET

Articles 41–64. The Diet is convened once a year, is the highest organ of state power and has exclusive legislative authority. It comprises the House of Representatives (511 seats) and the House of Councillors (252 seats). The members of the former are elected for four years whilst those of the latter are elected for six years and election for half the members takes place every three years. If the House of Representatives is dissolved, a general election must take place within 40 days and the Diet must be convoked within 30 days of the date of the election. Extraordinary sessions of the Diet may be convened by the Cabinet when one quarter or more of the members of either House request it. Emergency sessions of the House of Councillors may also be held. A quorum

JAPAN

of at least one third of the Diet members is needed to carry on Parliamentary business. Any decision arising therefrom must be passed by a majority vote of those present. A bill becomes law having passed both Houses except as provided by the Constitution. If the House of Councillors either vetoes or fails to take action within 60 days upon a bill already passed by the House of Representatives, the bill becomes law when passed a second time by the House of Representatives, by at least a two-thirds majority of those members present.

The Budget must first be submitted to the House of Representatives. If, when it is approved by the House of Representatives, the House of Councillors votes against it or fails to take action on it within 30 days, or failing agreement being reached by a joint committee of both Houses, a decision of the House of Representatives shall be the decision of the Diet. The above procedure also applies in respect of the conclusion of treaties.

THE EXECUTIVE

Articles 65–75. Executive power is vested in the cabinet consisting of a Prime Minister and such other Ministers as may be appointed. The Cabinet is collectively responsible to the Diet. The Prime Minister is designated from among members of the Diet by a resolution thereof.

If the House of Representatives and the House of Councillors disagree on the designation of the Prime Minister, and if no agreement can be reached even through a joint committee of both Houses, provided for by law, or if the House of Councillors fails to make designation within 10 days, exclusive of the period of recess, after the House of Representatives has made designation, the decision of the House of Representatives shall be the decision of the Diet.

The Prime Minister appoints and may remove other Ministers, a majority of whom must be from the Diet. If the House of Representatives passes a no-confidence motion or rejects a confidence motion, the whole Cabinet resigns unless the House of Representatives is dissolved within 10 days. When there is a vacancy in the post of Prime Minister, or upon the first convocation of the Diet after a general election of members of the House of Representatives, the whole Cabinet resigns.

The Prime Minister submits bills, reports on national affairs and foreign relations to the Diet. He exercises control and supervision over various administrative branches of the Government. The Cabinet's primary functions (in addition to administrative ones) are to: (a) administer the law faithfully; (b) conduct State affairs; (c) conclude treaties subject to prior (or subsequent) Diet approval; (d) administer the civil service in accordance with law; (e) prepare and present the budget to the Diet; (f) enact Cabinet orders in order to make effective legal and constitutional provisions; (g) decide on amnesties, reprieves or pardons. All laws and Cabinet orders are signed by the competent Minister of State and countersigned by the Prime Minister. The Ministers of State, during their tenure of office, are not subject to legal action without the consent of the Prime Minister. However, the right to take that action is not impaired.

Articles 76–95. Relate to the Judiciary, Finance and Local Government.

AMENDMENTS

Article 96. Amendments to the Constitution are initiated by the Diet, through a concurring vote of two-thirds or more of all the members of each House and are submitted to the people for ratification, which requires the affirmative vote of a majority of all votes cast at a special referendum or at such election as the Diet may specify.

Amendments when so ratified must immediately be promulgated by the Emperor in the name of the people, as an integral part of the Constitution.

Articles 97–99 outline the Supreme Law, while Articles 100–103 consist of Supplementary Provisions.

The Government

HEAD OF STATE

His Imperial Majesty AKIHITO, Emperor of Japan (succeeded to the throne 7 January 1989).

THE CABINET
(February 1989)

Prime Minister: NOBORU TAKESHITA.
Minister of Finance: TATSUO MURAYAMA.
Minister of Justice: MASAMI TAKATSUJI.
Minister of Foreign Affairs: SOSUKE UNO.
Minister of Education: TAKEO NISHIOKA.
Minister of Health and Welfare: JUNICHIRO KOIZUMI.
Minister of Agriculture, Forestry and Fisheries: TSUTOMU HATA.
Minister of International Trade and Industry: HIROSHI MITSUZUKA.
Minister of Transport: SHINJI SATO.
Minister of Posts and Telecommunications: SEIICHI KATAOKA.
Minister of Labour: HYOSUKE NIWA.
Minister of Construction: HIKOSABURO OKONOGI.
Minister of Home Affairs and Chairman of the Public Safety Commission: SHIGENOBU SAKANO.
Minister of State and Chief Cabinet Secretary: KEIZO OBUCHI.
Minister of State and Director-General of the Management and Co-ordination Agency: SABURO KANEMARU.
Minister of State and Director-General of the Hokkaido Development and Okinawa Development Agencies: CHIKAO SAKAMOTO.
Minister of State and Director-General of the Defence Agency: KICHIRO TAZAWA.
Minister of State and Director-General of the Economic Planning Agency: KOICHIRO AINO.
Minister of State, Director-General of the Science and Technology Agency and Chairman of the Atomic Energy Commission: MOICHI MIYAZAKI.
Minister of State and Director-General of the Environment Agency: MASAHISA AOKI.
Minister of State and Director-General of the National Land Agency: HIDEO UTSUMI.
Director of the Cabinet Legislative Bureau: OSAMU MIMURA.

MINISTRIES

Imperial Household Agency: 1-1, Chiyoda, Chiyoda-ku, Tokyo; tel. (3) 213-1111.
Prime Minister's Office: 1-6, Nagata-cho, Chiyoda-ku, Tokyo; tel. (3) 581-2361.
Ministry of Agriculture, Forestry and Fisheries: 1-2, Kasumigaseki, Chiyoda-ku, Tokyo; tel.(3) 502-8111.
Ministry of Construction: 2-1, Kasumigaseki, Chiyoda-ku, Tokyo; tel. (3) 580-4311.
Ministry of Education: 3-2, Kasumigaseki, Chiyoda-ku, Tokyo; tel. (3) 581-4211.
Ministry of Finance: 3-1-1, Kasumigaseki, Chiyoda-ku, Tokyo; tel. (3) 581-4111; telex 24980.
Ministry of Foreign Affairs: 2-2, Kasumigaseki, Chiyoda-ku, Tokyo; tel. (3) 580-3311; telex 22350.
Ministry of Health and Welfare: 1-2-2, Kasumigaseki, Chiyoda-ku, Tokyo 100; tel. (3) 503-1711.
Ministry of Home Affairs: 2-1, Kasumigaseki, Chiyoda-ku, Tokyo; tel. (3) 581-5311.
Ministry of International Trade and Industry: 1-3, Kasumigaseki, Chiyoda-ku, Tokyo; tel. (3) 501-1511; telex 22916.
Ministry of Justice: 1-1-1, Kasumigaseki, Chiyoda-ku, Tokyo 100; tel. (3) 580-4111.
Ministry of Labour: 2-2, Kasumigaseki 1-chome, Chiyoda-ku, Tokyo; tel. (3) 593-1211.
Ministry of Posts and Telecommunications: 1-3, Kasumigaseki, Chiyoda-ku, Tokyo; tel. (3) 504-4798; telex 2225234.
Ministry of Transport: 2-1, Kasumigaseki, Chiyoda-ku, Tokyo; tel. (3) 580-3111.
Cabinet Legislation Bureau: Tokyo; tel. (3) 581-7271.
Defence Agency: 9-7, Akasaka, Minato-ku, Tokyo; tel. (3) 408-5211.
Economic Planning Agency: 3-1, Kasumigaseki, Chiyoda-ku, Tokyo; tel. (3) 581-0261.
Environment Agency: 1-2-2, Kasumigaseki, Chiyoda-ku, Tokyo; tel. (3) 581-3351; telex 33855.
Hokkaido Development Agency: 3-1-1, Kasumigaseki, Chiyoda-ku, Tokyo 100; tel. (3) 581-9111.
Management and Co-ordination Agency: 3-1-1, Kasumigaseki, Chiyoda-ku, Tokyo; tel. (3) 581-6361.
National Land Agency: 1-2-2, Kasumigaseki, Chiyoda-ku, Tokyo 100; tel. (3) 593-3311.
Okinawa Development Agency: 1-6, Nagata-cho, Chiyoda-ku, Tokyo; tel. (3) 581-2361.
Science and Technology Agency: 2-2, Kasumigaseki, Chiyoda-ku, Tokyo; tel. (3) 581-5271.

Legislature

KOKKAI
(Diet)

The Diet consists of two Chambers: the House of Councillors (Upper House) and the House of Representatives. The 512 members of the House of Representatives are elected for a period of four years (subject to dissolution). For the House of Councillors, which has 252 members, the term of office is six years, with one-half of the members elected every three years.

House of Councillors

Speaker: YOSHIHIKO TSUCHIYA.

Party	Seats after elections* 26 June 1983	6 July 1986
Liberal-Democratic Party†	137	142
Japan Socialist Party	44	41
Komeito	26	25
Japanese Communist Party	14	16
Democratic Socialist Party	11	12
New Liberal Club†	2	2
Second Chamber Club	2	3
Salaried Workers' Party	—	3
Tax Party	—	2
Social Democratic Federation	—	1
Independents	—	4
Others	13	—
Vacant	3	1

* One-half of the 252 seats are renewable every three years. At each election, 50 of the 126 seats were allocated on the basis of proportional representation.
† In August 1986 the New Liberal Club rejoined the Liberal-Democratic Party, from which it had separated in 1976.

House of Representatives

Speaker: KENZABURO HARA.

General Election, 6 July 1986

Party	Votes	% of votes	Seats
Liberal-Democratic Party*	29,875,496	49.42	304
Japan Socialist Party	10,412,583	17.23	86
Komeito	5,701,277	9.43	57
Japanese Communist Party	5,313,246	8.79	27
Democratic Socialist Party	3,895,927	6.45	26
New Liberal Club*	1,114,800	1.84	6
Social Democratic Federation	499,670	0.83	4
Other parties	120,627	0.20	—
Independents	3,515,042	5.81	2
Total	60,448,668	100.00	512

* In August 1986 the New Liberal Club rejoined the Liberal-Democratic Party, from which it had separated in 1976.

Political Organizations

The Political Funds Regulation Law provides that any organization which wishes to support a candidate for an elective public office must be registered as a political party. There are over 10,000 registered parties in the country, mostly of local or regional significance. The conservative Liberal-Democratic Party has the support of big business and the rural population and is also by far the richest of the political parties. The proportion of votes for the two socialist parties increased slowly at each election after 1952. The split between the two parties reflects a long-standing division between supporters of a mass popular party (now represented by the DSP) and those seeking a class party on Socialist lines. The Communist Party of Japan split in 1964, the official party being independent and supporting neither the USSR nor the People's Republic of China.

Democratic Socialist Party—DSP (Minshato): 2-3-13, Toranomon, Minato-ku, Tokyo; tel. (03) 501-5111; f. 1960 by a right-wing breakaway faction of the Socialist Party of Japan; advocates an independent foreign policy; 72,000 mems (1983); Chair. (vacant); Sec.-Gen. KEIGO OUCHI.

Japan Socialist Party—JSP (Nippon Shakaito): 1-8-1, Nagata-cho, Chiyoda-ku, Tokyo; tel. (03) 580-1171; f. 1945; seeks the establishment of collective non-agression and a mutual security system, including Japan, the USA, the USSR and the People's Republic of China; 55,000 mems (1983); Chair. TAKAKO DOI; Sec.-Gen. TSURUO YAMAGUCHI.

Japanese Commmunist Party—JCP: 4-26-7 Sendagaya, Shibuya-ku, Tokyo; tel. (03) 403-6111; f. 1922; 490,000 mems (1988); Chair. Cen. Cttee KENJI MIYAMOTO; Chair. of the Presidium HIROMU MURAKAMI; Head of Secr. MITSUHIRO KANEKO.

Komeito (Clean Government Party): 17, Minamimoto-machi, Shinjuku-ku, Tokyo; tel. (03) 353-0111; f. 1964; advocates political moderation, humanitarian socialism, and policies respecting 'dignity of human life'; 183,000 mems (1986); Founder DAISAKU IKEDA; Chair. JUNYA YANO; Sec.-Gen. NAOHIKO OKUBO.

Liberal-Democratic Party—LDP (Jiyu-Minshuto): 1-11-23, Nagata-cho, Chiyoda-ku, Tokyo 100; tel. (03) 581-0111; f. 1955; advocates the establishment of a welfare state, the promotion of industrial development, the improvement of educational and cultural facilities and constitutional reform as needed; follows a foreign policy of alignment with the USA; 5,776,956m. mems (Aug. 1988); Pres. NOBORU TAKESHITA; Sec.-Gen. SHINTARO ABE; Chair. of Gen. Council MASAYOSHI ITO.

Progressive Party: Shinpoto, 2-2-1, Marunouchi, Chiyoda-ku, Tokyo; tel. (03) 213-5550; f. 1987 by breakaway group from the New Liberal Club (a breakaway group of the LDP, which rejoined the LDP in Aug. 1986); Leader SEIICHI TAGAWA.

Salaried Workers' Party (Salaryman Shinto): 1-15-8, Kyoda, Setagaya-ku, Tokyo; tel. (03) 234-8669; advocates reform of the tax system; Leader SHIGERU AOKI.

Second Chamber Club (Ni-In Club): c/o House of Councillors, 1-7-1, Nagata-cho, Chiyoda-ku, Tokyo; tel. (03) 581-3111; successor to the Green Wind Club (Ryukufukai), which originated in the House of Councillors in 1946–47; Sec. YUKIO AOSHIMA.

Social Democratic Federation—SDF (Shaminren): 1-1-7, Motoakasaka, Minato-ku, Tokyo; tel. (03) 405-5644; f. 1977 as the Socialist Citizens' League; Leader SATSUKI EDA.

Tax Party (Zeikinto): c/o House of Councillors, 1-7-1, Nagata-cho, Chiyoda-ku, Tokyo; tel. (03) 581-3111; Sec. CHINPEI NOZUE.

Diplomatic Representation

EMBASSIES IN JAPAN

Algeria: 10–67, Mita 2-chome, Meguro-ku, Tokyo 153; tel. (03) 711-2661; telex 23260; Ambassador: ABDELMOU' NAAM AHRIZ.

Argentina: Chiyoda House, 17–8, Nagata-cho 2-chome, Chiyoda-ku, Tokyo 100; tel. (03) 592-0321; telex 22489; Ambassador: ENRIQUE J. ROS.

Australia: 1-12, Shiba Koen 1-chome, Minato-ku, Tokyo 108; tel. (03) 453-0971; telex 22298; Ambassador: GEOFFREY MILLER.

Austria: 1-20, Moto Azabu 1-chome, Minato-ku, Tokyo 106; tel. (03) 451-8281; telex 26361; Ambassador: Dr MICHAEL FITZ.

Bangladesh: 7-45, Shirogane 2-chome, Minato-ku, Tokyo 108; tel. (03) 442-1501; telex 28826; Ambassador: A. K. M. HEDAYETUL.

Belgium: 5, Niban-cho, Chiyoda-ku, Tokyo 102; tel. (03) 262-0191; telex 24979; Ambassador: (vacant).

Bolivia: Kowa Bldg, No. 38, Room 804, 8th Floor, 12-24, Nishi-Azabu 4-chome, Minato-ku, Tokyo 106; tel. (03) 499-5441; telex 32177; Ambassador: Dr ARNOLD HOFMAN-BANG SOLETO.

Brazil: 11-12, Kita Aoyama 2-chome, Minato-ku, Tokyo 107; tel. (03) 404-5211; telex 22590; Ambassador: CARLOS A. B. BUENO.

Bulgaria: 36-3A, Yoyogi 5-chome, Shibuya-ku, Tokyo 151; tel. (03) 465-1021; Ambassador: PETAR BASHIKAROV.

Burma: 8-26, Kita Shinagawa 4-chome, Shinagawa-ku, Tokyo 140; tel. (03) 441-9291; Ambassador: U BA THWIN.

Cameroon: 9-12, Minami Nanpeidai-cho, Shibuya-ku, Tokyo 150; tel. (03) 496-1125; telex 2428032; Ambassador: ETIENNE NTSAMA.

Canada: 3-38, Akasaka 7-chome, Minato-ku, Tokyo 107; tel. (03) 408-2101; telex 22218; Ambassador: BARRY CONNELL STEERS.

Central African Republic: 32-2, Ohyama-cho, Shibuya-ku, Tokyo 151; tel. (03) 460-8341; telex 24793; Ambassador: NOEL EREGANI.

Chile: Nihon Seimei Akabanebashi Bldg, 8th Floor, 3-1-14, Shiba, Minato-ku, Tokyo 105; tel. (03) 452-7561; telex 24585; Ambassador: GUSTAVO PONCE LEROU.

China, People's Republic: 3-4-33, Moto Azabu, Minato-ku, Tokyo 106; tel. (03) 403-3380; telex 28705; Ambassador: YANG ZHENYA.

Colombia: 10-53, Kami Osaki 3-chome, Shinagawa-ku, Tokyo 141; tel. (03) 440-6491; Ambassador: FIDEL DUQUE RAMÍREZ.

JAPAN   *Directory*

Costa Rica: Kowa Bldg, No. 38, Room 901, 12–24, Nishi Azabu 4-chome, Minato-ku, Tokyo 106; tel. (03) 486-1812; Chargé d'affaires (a.i.): ANA LUCÍA NASSAR SOTO.

Côte d'Ivoire: Kowa Bldg, No. 38, Room 701, 12–24, Nishi Azabu 4-chome, Minato-ku, Tokyo 106; tel. (03) 499-7021; telex 26631; Ambassador: PIERRE NELSON COFFI.

Cuba: 2-51 Minami Azabu 4-chome, Minato-ku, Tokyo 106; tel. (03) 449-7511; telex 22369; Ambassador: AMADEO BLANCO VALDÉS-FAULY.

Czechoslovakia: 16-14, Hiroo 2-chome, Shibuya-ku, Tokyo 150; tel. (03) 400-8122; telex 24595; Ambassador: Ing. RUDOLF JAKUBIK.

Denmark: 29–6, Sarugaku-cho, Shibuya-ku, Tokyo 150; tel.(03) 496-3001; telex 24417; Ambassador: W. THUNE ANDERSEN.

Dominican Republic: Kowa Bldg, No. 38, Room 904, 12–24, Nishi Azabu 4-chome, Minato-ku, Tokyo 106; tel. (03) 499-6020; telex 33701; Ambassador: ALFONSO CANTO DINZEY.

Ecuador: Kowa Bldg, No. 38, Room 806, 12–24, Nishi Azabu 4-chome, Minato-ku, Tokyo 106; tel. (03) 499-2800; telex 25880; Ambassador: Dr MARCO TULIO CORDERO.

Egypt: 5–4, Aobadai 1-chome, Meguro-ku, Tokyo 153; tel. (03) 770-8021; telex 23240; Chargé d'affaires a.i.: ABDEL FATTAH M. EZZELDIN.

El Salvador: Kowa Bldg, No. 38, 8th Floor, 12–24, Nishi Azabu 4-chome, Minato-ku, Tokyo 106; tel. (03) 499-4461; telex 25829; Ambassador: Dr ERNESTO ARRIETA PERALTA.

Ethiopia: Roppongi Hilltop House, B-1, 4-25, Roppongi 3-chome, Minato-ku, Tokyo 106; tel. (03) 585-3151; telex 28402; Ambassador: WORKU MOGES.

Fiji: Noa Bldg, 10th Floor, 3–5, Azabudai 2-chome, Minato-ku, Tokyo 106; tel. (03) 587-2038; telex 32150; Ambassador: MUHAMMAD HAROON SHAKUR.

Finland: 3-5-39, Minami Azabu, Minato-ku, Tokyo 106; tel. (03) 442-2231; telex 26277; Ambassador: PAULI OPAS.

France: 11–44, Minami Azabu 4-chome, Minato-ku, Tokyo 106; tel. (03) 473-0171; Ambassador: BERNARD DORIN.

Gabon: 12-11, Higashi Gotanda 3-chome, Shinagawa-ku, Tokyo 141; tel. (03) 448-9540; telex 24812; Ambassador: PATRICE MAKIKA.

German Democratic Republic: Akasaka Mansion, 5–16, Akasaka 7-chome, Minato-ku, Tokyo 107; tel. (03) 585-5404; telex 28283; Ambassador: MANFRED SCHMIDT.

Germany, Federal Republic: 5–10, Minami Azabu 4-chome, Minato-ku, Tokyo 106; tel. (03) 473-0151; telex 22292; Ambassador: Dr HANS-JOACHIM HALLIER.

Ghana: Mori Bldg, No. 28, 11th Floor, 16–13, Nishi Azabu 4-chome, Minato-ku, Tokyo 106; tel. (03) 409-3861; telex 22487; Ambassador: JAMES LESLIE MAYNE AMISSAH.

Greece: 16–30, Nishi Azabu 3-chome, Minato-ku, Tokyo 106; tel. (03) 403-0871; Ambassador: Dr GEORGE LIANIS.

Guatemala: 38 Kowa Bldg, Room 905, 4-12-24, Nishi Azabu, Minato-ku, Tokyo 106; tel. (03) 400-1830; Chargé d'affaires (a.i.): MANUEL E. PALOMO PERALTA.

Guinea: 12-6, Minami Azabu 1-chome, Minato-ku, Tokyo 106; tel. (03) 769-0451; Ambassador: BOUBACAR BARRY.

Haiti: Kowa Bldg, No. 38, Room 906, 12–24, Nishi Azabu 4-chome, Minato-ku, Tokyo 106; tel. (03) 486-7070; telex 29601; Chargé d'affaires a.i.: FRITZNEL LAFONTANT.

Holy See: Apostolic Nunciature, 9-2, Sanban-cho, Chiyoda-ku, Tokyo 102; tel. (03) 263-6851; Apostolic Pro-Nuncio: Archbishop WILLIAM AQUIN CAREW.

Honduras: Kowa Bldg, No. 38, Room 802, 8th Floor, 12–24, Nishi Azabu 4-chome, Minato-ku, Tokyo 106; tel. (03) 409-1150; telex 28591; Ambassador: ANÍBAL ENRIQUE QUIÑÓNEZ ABARCA.

Hungary: 3-1, Aobadai 2-chome, Meguro-ku, Tokyo 153; tel. (03) 476-6061; telex 22688; Ambassador: ANDRÁS FORGÁCS.

India: 2-11, Kudan Minami 2-chome, Chiyoda-ku, Tokyo 102; tel. (03) 262-2391; Ambassador: ARJUN GOBINDRAM ASRANI.

Indonesia: 2-9, Higashi Gotanda 5-chome, Shinagawa-ku, Tokyo 141; tel. (03) 441-4201; telex 22920; Ambassador: Lt-Gen. (retd) YOGI SUPARDI.

Iran: 10-32, Minami Azabu 3-chome, Minato-ku, Tokyo 106; tel. (03) 446-8011; telex 22753; Ambassador: SEYED MUHAMMAD HOSSEIN ADELI.

Iraq: 4-7, Akasaka 8-chome, Minato-ku, Tokyo 107; tel. (03) 423-1727; telex 28825; Ambassador: Dr RASHID M. S. AL-RISAI.

Ireland: Kowa Bldg, No. 25, 8-7, Sanban-cho, Chiyoda-ku, Tokyo 102; tel. (03) 263-0695; telex 23926; Ambassador: SEÁN G. RONAN.

Israel: 3, Niban-cho, Chiyoda-ku, Tokyo 102; tel. (03) 264-0911; telex 22636; Ambassador: NAHUM ESCHOL.

Italy: 5–4, Mita 2-chome, Minato-ku, Tokyo 108; tel. (03) 453-5291; telex 22433; Ambassador: BARTOLOMEO ATTOLICO.

Jordan: 4A, B, Chiyoda House, 4th Floor, 17–8, Nagata-cho 2-chome, Chiyoda-ku, Tokyo 100; tel. (03) 580-5856; telex 23708; Ambassador: KHALED MADADHA.

Kenya: 24-20, Nishi Azabu 3-chome, Minato-ku, Tokyo 106; tel. (03) 479-4006; telex 2422378; Chargé d'affaires a.i.: JOHN D. ODEDE.

Korea, Republic: 2-5, Minami Azabu 1-chome, Minato-ku, Tokyo 106; tel. (03) 452-7611; telex 22045; Ambassador: WONKYUNG LEE.

Kuwait: 13-12, Mita 4-chome, Minato-ku, Tokyo 108; tel. (03) 455-0361; telex 25501; Ambassador: ABDUL-AZIZ ABDULLATIF AL-SHAREKH.

Laos: 3-3-21, Nishi Azabu, Minato-ku, Tokyo 106; tel. (03) 408-1166; Ambassador: SOUPHANTHAHEUANGSI SISALEUMSAK.

Lebanon: Chiyoda House, 5th Floor, 17–8, Nagata-cho 2-chome, Chiyoda-ku, Tokyo 100; tel. (03) 580-1227; telex 25356; Ambassador: SAMIR EL-KHOURY.

Liberia: Odakyu Fudosan Minami Aoyama Bldg, 6th Floor, 8-1, Minami Aoyama 7-chome, Minato-ku, Tokyo 107; tel. (03) 499-2451; Ambassador: STEPHEN J. KOFFA, Sr.

Libya: 10-14, Daikanyama-cho, Shibuya-ku, Tokyo 150; tel. (03) 477-0701; telex 22181; Secretary of the People's Bureau: WANIS M. ABURWELA.

Madagascar: 3-23, Moto Azabu 2-chome, Minato-ku, Tokyo 106; tel. (03) 446-7252; telex 25941; Ambassador: HUBERT M. RAJAOBELINA.

Malaysia: 20–16, Nanpeidai, Shibuya-ku, Tokyo 150; tel. (03) 770-9331; telex 24221; Ambassador: Dato' J. A. KAMIL.

Mexico: 15-1, Nagata-cho 2-chome, Chiyoda-ku, Tokyo 100; tel. (03) 581-1131; telex 26875; Ambassador: Dr SERGIO GONZÁLEZ GÁLVEZ.

Mongolia: Pine Crest Mansion, 21-4, Shoto, Kamiyama-cho, Shibuya-ku, Tokyo 150; tel. (03) 469-2088; Ambassador: BUYANTYN DASHTSEREN.

Morocco: Silva Kingdom Bldg, 5th and 6th Floors, 16–3, Sendagaya 3-chome, Shibuya-ku, Tokyo 151; tel. (03) 478-3271; telex 23451; Ambassador: ABDELAZIZ BENJELLOUN.

Nepal: 14-9, Todoroki 7-chome, Setagaya-ku, Tokyo 158; tel. (03) 705-5558; telex 23936; Ambassador: NARAYAN PRASAD ARJAL.

Netherlands: 6-3, Shiba Koen 3-chome, Minato-ku, Tokyo 105; tel. (03) 431-5126; telex 22855; Ambassador: HERMAN C. POSTHUMUS MEYJES.

New Zealand: 20–40, Kamiyama-cho, Shibuya-ku, Tokyo 150; tel. (03) 467-2271; telex 22462; Ambassador: RODNEY J. GATES.

Nicaragua: Kowa Bldg, No. 38, Room 903, 9th Floor, 12–24, Nishi Azabu 4-chome, Minato-ku, Tokyo 106; tel. (03) 499-0400; telex 28119; Ambassador: JORGE HUEZO CASTRILLO.

Nigeria: 2-19-7, Uehara, Shibuya-ku, Tokyo 151; tel. (03) 468-5531; telex 24397; Ambassador: MAI-BUKAR GARBA DOGON-YARO.

Norway: 12-2, Minami Azabu 5-chome, Minato-ku, Tokyo 106; tel. (03) 440-2611; telex 26440; Ambassador: H. W. FREIHOW.

Oman: Silva Kingdom Bldg, 3rd Floor, 16–3, Sendagaya 3-chome, Shibuya-ku, Tokyo 151; tel. (03) 402-0877; telex 29544; Chargé d'affaires a.i.: MOHAMED SAID RAJAD AL-AJEEL.

Pakistan: 14-9, Moto Azabu 2-chome, Minato-ku, Tokyo 106; tel. (03) 454-4861; Ambassador: MANSOOR AHMED.

Panama: Kowa Bldg, No. 38, Room 902, 12–24, Nishi Azabu 4-chome, Minato-ku, Tokyo 106; tel. (03) 499-3741; telex 22157; Ambassador: Dr ALBERTO A. CALVO PONCE.

Papua New Guinea: Mita Kokusai Bldg, Room 313, 3rd Floor, 1-4-28, Mita, Minato-ku, Tokyo 108; tel. (03) 454-7801; telex 25488; Ambassador: JOSEPH KAAL NOMBRI.

Paraguay: Asahi Kami Osaki Bldg, 5th Floor, 5-8, Kami Osaki 3-chome, Shinagawa-ku, Tokyo 141; tel. (03) 447-7496; telex 27496; Ambassador: JUAN CARLOS A. HRASE VON BARGEN.

Peru: 4-27, Higashi 4-chome, Shibuya-ku, Tokyo 150; tel. (03) 406-4240; telex 26435; Ambassador: LUIS MACCHIAVELLO AMOROS.

Philippines: 11-24, Nampeidai-machi, Shibuya-ku, Tokyo 150; tel. (03) 496-2731; telex 22694; Ambassador: RAMON V. DEL ROSARIO.

Poland: 13-5, Mita 2-chome, Meguro-ku, Tokyo 153; tel. (03) 711-5224; Ambassador: RYSZARD FRACKIEWICZ.

Portugal: Olympia Annex, Apt 304–306, 31-21, Jingumae 6-chome, Shibuya-ku, Tokyo 150; tel. (03) 400-7907; Ambassador: Dr JOSÉ EDUARDO MELLO GOUVEIA.

Qatar: 16-22, Shirogane 6-chome, Minato-ku, Tokyo 108; tel. (03) 446-7561; telex 24877; Ambassador: MOHAMED ALI AL-ANSARI.

Romania: 16-19, Nishi Azabu 3-chome, Minato-ku, Tokyo 106; tel. (03) 479-0311; telex 22664; Ambassador: Prof. Dr CONSTANTIN VLAD.

JAPAN — Directory

Rwanda: Kowa Bldg, No. 38, Room 702, 12–24, Nishi Azabu 4-chome, Minato-ku, Tokyo 106; tel. (03) 486-7800; telex 27701; Ambassador: Joseph Nizeyimana.

Saudi Arabia: 1–53, Azabu Nagasaka-cho, Minato-ku, Tokyo 106; tel. (03) 589-5241; telex 25731; Ambassador: Fawzi bin Abdul Majeed Shobokshi.

Senegal: 3–4, Aobadai 1-chome, Meguro-ku, Tokyo 153; tel. (03) 464-8451; telex 25493; Ambassador: Kéba Birane Cissé.

Singapore: 12–3, Roppongi 5-chome, Minato-ku, Tokyo 106; tel. (03) 586-9111; telex 22404; Ambassador: Lee Khoon Choy.

Somalia: 9–10, Shiroganedai 5-chome, Minato-ku, Tokyo 108; tel. (03) 442-7138; telex 33160; Ambassador: Hassan Abshir Farah.

Spain: 3–29, Roppongi 1-chome, Minato-ku, Tokyo 106; tel. (03) 583-8531; telex 22471; Ambassador: Camilo Barcia García-Villamil.

Sri Lanka: 14–1, Akasaka 1-chome, Minato-ku, Tokyo 107; tel. (03) 585-7431; telex 24524; Ambassador: Karunasena Kodituwakku.

Sudan: Yada Mansion, 6–20, Minami-Aoyama 6-chome, Minato-ku, Tokyo 107; tel. (03) 406-0811; telex 23876; Ambassador: Mohammed Abdel Dayim Basheer.

Sweden: Mori Bldg, No. 25, 24th Floor, 4–30, Roppongi 1-chome, Minato-ku, Tokyo 106; tel. (03) 582-6981; telex 24586; Ambassador: Ove F. Heyman.

Switzerland: 9–12, Minami Azabu 5-chome, Minato-ku, Tokyo 106; tel. (03) 473-0121; telex 24282; Ambassador: Dr Roger Bär.

Syria: 15–45, Akasaka 6-chome, Minato-ku, Tokyo 107; tel. (03) 586-8977; telex 29405; Chargé d'affaires a.i.: Jalal al-Baroudi.

Tanzania: 21–9, Kami Yoga 4-chome, Setagaya-ku, Tokyo 158; tel. (03) 425-4531; telex 22121; Ambassador: Raphael Haji Lukindo.

Thailand: 14–6, Kami Osaki 3-chome, Shinagawa-ku, Tokyo 141; tel. (03) 441-7352; Ambassador: M. L. Birabhongge Kasemsri.

Tunisia: 1–18–8, Wakaba-cho, Shinjuku-ku, Tokyo 160; tel. (03) 353-4111; telex 27146; Chargé d'affaires a.i.: Mannoubi Fassatoui.

Turkey: 33–6, Jingumae 2-chome, Shibuya-ku, Tokyo 150; tel. (03) 470-5131; telex 22856; Ambassador: Umut Arik.

USSR: 2–1–1, Azabudai, Minato-ku, Tokyo 106; tel. (03) 583-4224; Ambassador: Nikolai Nikolayevich Solovev.

United Arab Emirates: Kotsu Anzen Kyoiku Centre Bldg, 7th Floor, 24–20, Nishi Azabu 3-chome, Minato-ku, Tokyo 106; tel. (03) 478-0650; telex 23552; Ambassador: Hamad Salem al-Makami.

United Kingdom: 1, Ichiban-cho, Chiyoda-ku, Tokyo 102; tel. (03) 265-5511; telex 22755; Ambassador: Sir John Whitehead.

USA: 10–5, Akasaka 1-chome, Minato-ku, Tokyo 107; tel. (03) 583-7141; telex 22118; Ambassador: Michael H. Armacost (designate).

Uruguay: Kowa Bldg, No. 38, Room 908, 12–24, Nishi Azabu 4-chome, Minato-ku, Tokyo 106; tel. (03) 486-1888; telex 2422843; Ambassador: Alfredo Giró Pintos.

Venezuela: Kowa Bldg, No. 38, 7th Floor, 12–24, Nishi Azabu 4-chome, Minato-ku, Tokyo 106; tel. (03) 409-1501; telex 25255; Ambassador: Fernando Báez-Duarte.

Viet-Nam: 50–11, Moto Yoyogi-cho, Shibuya-ku, Tokyo 151; tel. (03) 466-3311; Ambassador: Vo Van Sung.

Yemen Arab Republic: Kowa Bldg, No. 38, Room 807, 12–24, Nishi Azabu 4-chome, Minato-ku, Tokyo 106; tel. (03) 499-7151; telex 32431; Ambassador: Muhammad Abdul Koddos Alwazir.

Yugoslavia: 7–24, Kita Shinagawa 4-chome, Shinagawa-ku, Tokyo 140; tel. (03) 447-3571; telex 22360; Ambassador: Tarik Ajanović.

Zaire: Harajuku Green Heights, Room 701, 53–17, Sendagaya 3-chome, Shibuya-ku, Tokyo 151; tel. (03) 423-3981; telex 24211; Ambassador: Murairi Mitima Kaneno.

Zambia: 3-9-19, Ebisu, Shibuya-ku, Tokyo 150; tel. (03) 445-1043; telex 25210; Ambassador: Boniface Salimu Zulu.

Zimbabwe: 3–11–23, Minami Azabu, Minato-ku, Tokyo 152; tel. (03) 473-0266; telex 32975; Chargé d'affaires a.i. Robert Masango.

Judicial System

The basic principles of the legal system are set forth in the Constitution, which lays down that the whole judicial power is vested in a Supreme Court and in such inferior courts as are established by law, and enunciates the principle that no organ or agency of the Executive shall be given final judicial power. Judges are to be independent in the exercise of their conscience, and may not be removed except by public impeachment, unless judicially declared mentally or physically incompetent to perform official duties. The justices of the Supreme Court are appointed by the Cabinet, the sole exception being the Chief Justice, who is appointed by the Emperor after designation by the Cabinet.

The Court Organization Law, which came into force on 3 May 1947, decreed the constitution of the Supreme Court and the establishment of four types of inferior court—High, District, Family (established 1 January 1949), and Summary Courts. The constitution and functions of the courts are as follows:

THE SUPREME COURT

This court is the highest legal authority in the land, and consists of a Chief Justice and 14 associate justices. It has jurisdiction over Jokoku (appeals) and Kokoku (complaints), prescribed specially in codes of procedure. It conducts its hearings and renders decisions through a Grand Bench or three Petty Benches. Both are collegiate bodies, the former consisting of all justices of the Court, and the latter of five justices. A Supreme Court Rule prescribes which cases are to be handled by the respective Benches. It is, however, laid down by law that the Petty Bench cannot make decisions as to the constitutionality of a statute, ordinance, regulation, or disposition, or as to cases in which an opinion concerning the interpretation and application of the Constitution or of any laws or ordinances is at variance with a previous decision of the Supreme Court.

Chief Justice: Koichi Yaguchi.

INFERIOR COURTS

High Court

A High Court conducts its hearings and renders decisions through a collegiate body, consisting of three judges, though for cases of insurrection the number of judges must be five. The Court has jurisdiction over the following matters:

Koso appeals from judgments in the first instance rendered by District Courts, from judgments rendered by Family Courts, and from judgments concerning criminal cases rendered by Summary Courts.

Kokoku complaints against rulings and orders rendered by District Courts and Family Courts, and against rulings and orders concerning criminal cases rendered by Summary Courts, except those coming within the jurisdiction of the Supreme Court.

Jokoku appeals from judgments in the second instance rendered by District Courts and from judgments rendered by Summary Courts, except those concerning criminal cases.

Actions in the first instance relating to cases of insurrection.

District Court

A District Court conducts hearings and renders decisions through a single judge or, for certain types of cases, through a collegiate body of three judges. It has jurisdiction over the following matters:

Actions in the first instance, except offences relating to insurrection, claims where the subject matter of the action does not exceed 900,000 yen, and offences liable to a fine or lesser penalty.

Koso appeals from judgments rendered by Summary Courts, except those concerning criminal cases.

Kokoku complaints against rulings and orders rendered by Summary Courts, except those coming within the jurisdiction of the Supreme Court and High Courts.

Family Court

A Family Court handles cases through a single judge in case of rendering judgments or decisions. However, in accordance with the provisions of other statutes it conducts its hearings and renders decisions through a collegiate body of three judges. A conciliation is effected through a collegiate body consisting of a judge and two or more members of the conciliation committee selected from among citizens.

It has jurisdiction over the following matters:

Judgment and conciliation with regard to cases relating to family as provided for by the Law for Adjudgment of Domestic Relations.

Judgment with regard to the matters of protection of juveniles as provided for by the Juvenile Law.

Actions in the first instance relating to adult criminal cases of violation of the Labour Standard Law, the Law for Prohibiting Liquors to Minors, or other laws especially enacted for protection of juveniles.

Summary Court

A Summary Court handles cases through a single judge, and has jurisdiction in the first instance over the following matters:

Claims where the value of the subject matter does not exceed 900,000 yen (excluding claims for cancellation or change of administrative dispositions).

JAPAN

Actions which relate to offences liable to fine or lesser penalty, offences liable to a fine as an optional penalty, and certain specified offences such as habitual gambling and larceny.

A Summary Court cannot impose imprisonment or a graver penalty. When it deems proper the imposition of a sentence of imprisonment or a graver penalty, it must transfer such cases to a District Court, but it can impose imprisonment with hard labour not exceeding three years for certain specified offences.

A Procurator's Office, with its complement of procurators, is established for each of these courts. The procurators conduct searches, institute prosecutions and supervise the execution of judgments in criminal cases, and act as representatives of the public interests in civil cases of public concern.

Religion

The traditional religions of Japan are Shintoism and Buddhism. Neither is exclusive, and many Japanese subscribe at least nominally to both. Since 1945 a number of new religions (Shinko Shukyo) have evolved, based on a fusion of Shinto, Buddhist, Daoist, Confucian and Christian beliefs.

SHINTOISM

Shintoism is an indigenous religious system embracing the worship of ancestors and of nature. It is divided into two cults: national Shintoism, which is represented by the shrines; and sectarian Shintoism, which developed during the second half of the 19th century. In 1868, Shinto was designated a national religion, and all Shinto shrines acquired the privileged status of a national institution. Complete freedom of religion was introduced in 1947, and state support of Shinto was banned. There are an estimated 81,000 shrines, 101,000 priests and c. 90m. adherents.

BUDDHISM

World Buddhist Fellowship: Rev. FUJI NAKAYAMA, Hozenji Buddhist Temple, 3-24-2 Akabane-dai, Kita-ku, Tokyo.

CHRISTIANITY

In 1988 the Christian population was estimated at 1,081,387.
National Christian Council in Japan: Japan Christian Centre, 2-3-18-24, Nishi Waseda, Shinjuku-ku, Tokyo 160; tel. (03) 203-0372; telex 27890; f. 1923; 14 mems (churches and other bodies), 20 assoc. mems; Chair. Rev. KENTARO TAKEUCHI; Gen. Sec. Rev. MUNETOSHI MAEJIMA.

The Anglican Communion
Anglican Church in Japan (Nippon Sei Ko Kai): 4-21, Higashi 1-chome, Shibuya-ku, Tokyo 150; tel. (03) 400-2314; f. 1887; 11 dioceses; Primate of Japan Most Rev. CHRISTOPHER ICHIRO KIKAWADA, Bishop of Osaka; Gen. Sec. Rev. JINTARO UEDA; 57,457 mems (1987).

The Orthodox Church
Japanese Orthodox Church (Nippon Haristosu Seikyoukai): Holy Resurrection Cathedral (Nicolai-Do), 1-3, 4-chome, Surugadai Kanda, Chiyoda-ku, Tokyo 101; tel. (03) 291-1885; three dioceses; Archbishop of Tokyo, Primate and Metropolitan of All Japan Most Rev. THEODOSIUS; 24,783 mems.

Protestant Church
United Church of Christ in Japan (Nihon Kirisuto Kyodan): Japan Christian Center, Room 31, 3-18, Nishi Waseda 2-chome, Shinjuku-ku, Tokyo 160; tel. (03) 202-0541; f. 1941; union of 34 Congregational, Methodist, Presbyterian, Reformed and other Protestant denominations; Moderator Rev. TSUJI NOBUMICHI; Gen. Sec Rev. JOHN M. NAKAJIMA; 200,519 mems (March 1988).

The Roman Catholic Church
Japan comprises three archdioceses and 13 dioceses. There were 445,884 adherents in 1987.
Roman Catholic Bishops' Conference of Japan (Chuo Kyogikai): 10-1, Rokubancho, Chiyoda-ku, Tokyo 102; tel. (03) 262-3691; telex 32624; f. 1973; Pres. Most Rev. PETER SEICHI SHIRAYANAGI, Archbishop of Tokyo; Gen. Sec. PETER JUNICHI IWAHASHI.
Archbishop of Nagasaki: Cardinal JOSEPH ASAJIRO SATOWAKI, Catholic Center, 10-34, Uenomachi, Nagasaki-shi 852; tel. (0958) 46-4246.
Archbishop of Osaka: Most Rev. PAUL HISAO YASUDA, Archbishop's House, Koyoen Nishiyama-cho 1-55, Nishinomiya-shi 662, Hyogo-ken; tel. (0798) 73-0921.
Archbishop of Tokyo: Most Rev. PETER SEIICHI SHIRAYANAGI, Archbishop's House, 16-15, Sekiguchi 3-chome, Bunkyo-ku, Tokyo 112; tel. (03) 943-2301.

Other Christian Churches
Among other denominations active in the country are the Christian Catholic Church, the German Evangelical Church, the Japan Baptist Convention, the Japan Baptist Union, the Japan Evangelical Lutheran Church, the Korean Christian Church in Japan (10,000 mems) and the Tokyo Union Church.

OTHER COMMUNITIES

Bahá'í Faith
The National Spiritual Assembly of the Bahá'ís of Japan: 2-13, 7-chome, Shinjuku Shinjuku-ku, Tokyo 160; tel. (03) 209-7521.

Islam
Islam has been active in Japan since the late 19th century. There is a small Japanese and foreign Muslim community, maintaining a mosque at Kobe and an Islamic centre in Tokyo.
Islamic Center, Japan: 1-16-11, Ohara, Setagaya-ku, Tokyo 156; tel. (03) 460-6169; telex 2425329; f. 1965; Dir A. R. SIDDIQI.

The New Religions
Many new cults have emerged in Japan since the end of the Second World War. Collectively these are known as the New Religions (Shinko Shukyo), of which the following are the most important:
Rissho Kosei-kai: 2-11-1, Wada Suginami-ku, Tokyo 166; tel. (03) 383-1111; telex 2322455; f. 1938; Buddhist lay organization based on the teaching of the Lotus Sutra, active inter-faith co-operation towards peace; Pres. Rev. Dr NIKKYO NIWANO; 6.2m. mems with 236 brs world-wide (1988).
Soka Gakkai: 32, Shinano-machi, Shinjuku-ku, Tokyo 160; tel. (03) 353-0616; telex 33145; f. 1930; the lay society of Nichiren Shoshu (Orthodox Nichiren Buddhism); membership of 7.95m. households (1987); Buddhist groups promoting education, international cultural exchange and world peace; Hon. Pres. DAISAKU IKEDA; Pres. EINOSUKE AKIYA.

The Press

The average circulation of Japanese daily newspapers is the highest in the world after the USSR and the USA, and the circulation per head of population is highest at about 565 copies per 1,000 inhabitants (1984). The large number of weekly news journals is a notable feature of the Japanese press. In 1984 a total of 2,700 magazines were published by 1,200 magazine publishing companies. Technically the Japanese press is highly advanced, and the major newspapers are issued in simultaneous editions in the main centres.

The two newspapers with the largest circulations are the *Asahi Shimbun* and *Yomiuri Shimbun*. Other influential papers include *Mainichi Shimbun*, *Nihon Keizai Shimbun*, *Chunichi Shimbun* and *Sankei Shimbun*.

PRINCIPAL DAILIES

Tokyo
Asahi Evening News: 8-5, Tsukiji 7-chome, Chuo-ku, Tokyo 104; tel. (03) 546-7111; f. 1954; evening; English; Editor-in-Chief TENUO KUNUGI; circ. 29,000.
Asahi Shimbun: 3-2, Tsukiji 5-chome, Chuo-ku, Tokyo 104; tel. (03) 545-0131; telex 22226; f. 1879; Man. Dir (Editorial Affairs) T. NAKAE; circ. morning 7.9m., evening 4.7m.
Daily Sports: 1-1-17, Higashi-Shimbashi, Minato-ku, Tokyo 105; tel. (03) 571-6681; f. 1948; morning; Man. Editor TAKASHI KONDO; circ. 410,000.
The Daily Yomiuri: 7-1, 1-chome, Ohtemachi, Chiyoda-ku, Tokyo 100-55; tel. (03) 242-1111; f. 1955; morning; English; Editor TAKEMOTO IINUMA; circ. 45,000.
Dempa Shimbun: 11-15, Higashi Gotanda 1-chome, Shinagawa-ku, Tokyo 141; tel. (03) 445-6111; telex 2424461; f. 1950; morning; Man. Editor HAJIME NINOMIYA; circ. 285,000.
Hochi Shimbun: 1-1, 2-chome, Hirakawa-cho, Chiyoda-ku, Tokyo 102; tel. (03) 265-2311; f. 1872; morning; Man. Editor TOKUTEI ENDO; circ. 654,000.
The Japan Times: 5-4, 4-chome, Shibaura, Minato-ku, Tokyo 108; tel. (03) 453-5312; telex 2422319; f. 1897; morning; English; Chair. TOSHIAKI OGASAWARA; Pres. J. SUZUKI; circ. 57,000.
Komei Shimbun: 17, Minami-motomachi, Shinjuku-ku, Tokyo; tel. (03) 353-0111; organ of the Komeito political party; circ. 800,000, Sunday edn 1.4m.
The Mainichi Daily News: 1-1-1, Hitotsubashi, Chiyoda-ku, Tokyo 100; tel. (03) 212-0321; f. 1922; morning; English; also publ. from Osaka; Man. Editor TAKAHARU YOSHIZAWA; combined circ. 40,000.

JAPAN

Mainichi Shimbun: 1-1, 1-chome, Hitotsubashi, Chiyoda-ku, Tokyo 100; tel. (03) 212-0321; telex 22324; f. 1872; Gen. Man. and Editor KEN KONDO; circ. morning 4.2m., evening 2.2m.

Naigai Times: 14-14, 7-chome, Ginza, Chuo-ku, Tokyo 104; tel. (03) 543-1061; f. 1949; evening; Editor-in-Chief KENICHI TOUYA; circ. 296,000.

Nihon Keizai Shimbun: 9-5, 1-chome, Ohtemachi, Chiyoda-ku, Tokyo 100; tel. (03) 270-0251; telex 22308; f. 1876; morning, evening and weekly (English edn: *The Japan Economic Journal*); economic news; Man. Editor T. OHTA; circ. morning 1.37m., evening 1.36m.

Nihon Kogyo Shimbun: 7-2, 1-chome, Ohtemachi, Chiyoda-ku, Tokyo 100; tel. (03) 231-7111; f. 1933; morning; business and financial; Pres. TERUMI NAGATA; Man. Editor HIROSHI KONDO; circ. 409,000.

Nihon Nogyo Shimbun (Agriculture): 2-3, Akihabara, Taito-ku, Tokyo 110; tel. (03) 255-5211; f. 1928; morning; Man. Editor MASAO OKU; circ. 503,000.

Nikkan Kogyo Shimbun (Industrial Daily News): 8-10, 1-chome, Kudan-kita, Chiyoda-ku, Tokyo 102; tel. (03) 263-2311; f. 1917; morning; Man. Editor NAGARU SHIBUYA; circ. 545,000.

Nikkan Sports: 5-10, 3-chome, Tsukiji, Chuo-ku, Tokyo 104; tel. (03) 542-2111; f. 1946; morning; Editor FUMIKI OKAZAKI; circ. 728,000.

Nikkan Suisan Keizai Shimbun (Fisheries): 6-8-19, Roppongi, Minato-ku, Tokyo 106; tel. (03) 404-6531; f. 1948; morning; Man. Editor SADAYOSI SASAGO; circ. 58,000.

Sankei Shimbun: 7-2, 1-chome, Ohtemachi, Chiyoda-ku, Tokyo 100; tel. (03) 231-7111; f. 1950; Man. Editor Y. HOSOYA; circ. morning 802,000, evening 355,000.

Sankei Sports: 7-2, 1-chome, Ohtemachi, Chiyoda-ku, Tokyo 100; tel. (03) 231-7111; f. 1963; morning; Man. Editor SHUNICHIRO KONDO; circ. 649,000.

Seikyo Shimbun: 18, Shinano-machi, Shinjuku-ku, Tokyo 160; tel. (03) 353-6111; telex 33145; f. 1951; organ of Soka Gakkai religious movement; Prin. Officer EINOSUKE AKIYA; circ. 4.7m.

Shipping and Trade News: Tokyo News Service Ltd, Tsukiji Hamarikyu Bldg, 3-3, Tsukiji 5-chome, Chuo-ku, Tokyo 104; tel. (03) 542-6511; telex 2523285; f. 1949; English; Man. Editor K. TADA; Editor M. NAKAJIMA; circ. 15,000.

Sports Nippon: Palace Side Bldg, 1-1, 1-chome, Hitotsubashi, Chiyoda-ku, Tokyo 100; tel. (03) 213-3351; f. 1949; morning; Man. Editor JANSUKE EGUMA; circ. 785,000.

Tokyo Shimbun: 3-13, 2-chome, Konan, Minato-ku, Tokyo 108; tel. (03) 471-2211; f. 1942; Man. Editor TSUYOSHI SATO; circ. morning 803,181, evening 590,000.

Tokyo Sports: 5-10, 3-chome, Tsukiji, Chuo-ku, Tokyo 104; tel. (03) 543-6760; f. 1959; evening; Man. Editor MASAAKI WAKITA; circ. 872,000.

Tokyo Times: 1-16, 1-chome, Higashi-Shimbashi, Minato-ku, Tokyo 105; tel. (03) 571-4831; f. 1946; morning; Man. Editor YOSHIHARU TAKEUCHI; circ. 199,000.

Yomiuri Shimbun: 7-1, 1-chome, Ohtemachi, Chiyoda-ku, Tokyo 100; tel. (03) 242-1111; f. 1874; Pres. YOSOJI KOBAYASHI; Man. Editor KENYA MIZUKAMI; circ. morning 5.43m., evening 3.12m.

Yukan Fuji: 7-2, 1-chome, Ohtemachi, Chiyoda-ku, Tokyo 100; tel. (03) 231-7111; f. 1969; evening; Editor T. MAMIZUKA; circ. 1.2m.

Osaka District

Asahi Shimbun: 2-4, 3-chome, Nakano-shima, Kita-ku, Osaka 530; tel. (06) 231-0131; f. 1879; Man. Editor T. SHIBATA; circ. morning 2.18m., evening 1.37m.

Daily Sports: 1-18-11, Edobori, Nishi-ku, Osaka 550; tel. (06) 443-0421; f. 1948; morning; Editor SABURO NAKAZATO; circ. 585,000.

Hochi Shimbun: 2-22-17, Honjo-Nishi, Oyodo-ku, Osaka 531; tel. (06) 374-2311; f. 1964; morning; Man. Editor S. SUZUKI; circ. 336,000.

The Mainichi Daily News: 1-6-20, Dojima, Kita-ku, Osaka; tel. (06) 343-1121; f. 1922; morning; English; Man. Editor YOSHIO HIDACHI; circ. 30,000.

Mainichi Shimbun: 1-6-20, Dojima, Kita-ku, Osaka 530; tel. (06) 343-1121; f. 1882; Man. Editor FUTOSHI SAKOTA; circ. morning 1.61m., evening 932,000.

Nihon Keizai Shimbun: 1-1, Kyobashi-maeno-cho, Higashi-ku, Osaka 540; tel. (06) 943-7111; f. 1950; Man. Editor KEIJI SAMEJIMA; circ. morning 596,000, evening 387,000.

Nikkan Sports: 92-1, 5-chome, Hattori-kotubuki-cho, Toyonaka City 561; tel. (06) 862-1011; f. 1950; morning; Editor YOUJI KUGAI; circ. 452,000.

Osaka Nichi-nichi Shimbun: 1-5-13, Kitadori, Edobori, Nishi-ku, Osaka 550; tel. (06) 441-5551; f. 1946; Man. Editor MITSUKE KISHIMOTO; circ. 89,000.

Osaka Shimbun: 2-4-9, Umeda, Kita-ku, Osaka 530; tel. (06) 343-1221; f. 1922; evening; Man. Editor TERUKAZU HIGASHIYAMA; circ. 163,000.

Osaka Sports: 4th Floor, Osaka-ekimae Daiichi Bldg, 1-3-1-400, Umeda, Kita-ku, Osaka 530; tel. (06) 345-7657; f. 1968; evening; Editor SEN ASANO; circ. 510,000.

Sankei Shimbun: 2-4-9, Umeda, Kita-ku, Osaka 530; tel. (06) 343-1221; f. 1933; Man. Editor A. SAWA; circ. morning 1.19m., evening 708,000.

Sankei Sports: 2-4-9, Umeda, Kita-ku, Osaka 530; tel. (06) 343-1221; f. 1955; morning; Editor HIROSHI TANAKA; circ. 500,000.

Sports Nippon: 3-2-25, Oyodo-minami, Oyodo-ku, Osaka 531; tel. (06) 458-5981; f. 1949; morning; Man. Editor JIRO TANAKA; circ. 555,000.

Yomiuri Shimbun: 8-10, Nozaki-cho, Kita-ku, Osaka 530; tel. (06) 361-1111; f. 1952; Pres. G. SAKATA; Man. Editor KOUTARO FURUSAWA; circ. morning 2.21m., evening 1.4m.

Kanto District

Chiba Nippo (Chiba Daily News): 4-14-10, Chuo, Chiba City 280; tel. (0472) 22-9211; f. 1957; morning; Man. Editor MASAKI ISHIBASHI; circ. 129,000.

Ibaraki: 2-15, Kitami-machi, Mito City 310; tel. (0292) 21-3121; f. 1891; morning; Man. Editor ISAMU MUROFUSHI; circ. 122,000.

Jyomo Shimbun: 1-50-21, Furuichi-machi, Maebashi City 371; tel. (0272) 51-4341; f. 1887; morning; Man. Editor TOSHIO HIGUCHI; circ. 199,000.

Kanagawa Shimbun: 23, 2-chome, Ohtemachi, Naka-ku, Yokohama City 231; tel. (045) 201-0831; f. 1942; morning; Man. Editor RIKUO UCHIYAMA; circ. 211,000.

Shimotsuke Shimbun: 1-8-11, Showa, Utsunomiya City 320; tel. (0286) 25-1111; f. 1884; morning; Man. Editor MICHIYOSHI YASUNAGA; circ. 235,000.

Tochigi Shimbun: 45, Shimo-tomatsuri 1-chome, Utsunomiya City 320; tel. (0286) 22-5291; f. 1950; morning; Man. Editor TADASHI TOYOSAKA; circ. 76,000.

Tohoku District
(North-east Honshu)

Akita Sakigake Shimpo: 2-6, 1-chome, Ohtemachi, Akita 010; tel. (0188) 62-1231; f. 1874; Man. Editor SABURO WASHIO; circ. morning and evening each 231,000.

Daily Tohoku: 1-3-12, Jyoka, Hachinohe 031; tel. (0178) 44-5111; f. 1945; morning; Editor HIROAKI NIIYAMA; circ. 84,000.

Fukushima Mimpo: 13-17, Ohtemachi, Fukushima City 960; tel. (0245) 31-4111; f. 1892; Man. Editor SHIGEO TAKAHASHI; circ. morning 248,000, evening 12,000.

Fukushima Minyu: 9-9, Naka-machi, Fukushima City 960; tel. (0245) 23-1191; f. 1895; Man. Editor TERUO ABE; circ. morning 168,000, evening 9,000.

Iwate Nippo: 3-2, Uchimaru, Morioka City 020; tel. (0196) 53-4111; f. 1938; Man. Editor GEN-ICHIRO MURATA; circ. morning and evening each 210,000.

Kahoku Shimpo: 2-28, 1-chome, Itsutsubashi, Sendai City 980, tel. (0222) 22-6121; f. 1897; Man. Editor T. SUZUKI; circ. morning 450,000, evening 175,000.

Too Nippoh: 2-11, 2-chome, Shin-machi, Aomori City 030; tel. (0177) 73-1111; f. 1888; Man. Editor KOUJI YAMADA; circ. morning 241,000, evening 236,000.

Yamagata Shimbun: 5-12, 2-chome, Hatago-cho, Yamagata City 990; tel. (0236) 22-5271; f. 1876; Man. Editor KENICHI SOHMA; circ. morning and evening each 216,000.

Chubu District
(Central Honshu)

Asahi Shimbun: 3-3, 1-chome, Sakae, Naka-ku, Nagoya City 460; tel. (052) 231-8131; telex 22226; f. 1935; Editor YOUICHI HOSOKAWA; circ. morning 485,000, evening 247,000.

Chubu Keizai Shimbun: 4-4-12, Meieki, Nakamura-ku, Nagoya City 450; tel. (052) 561-5211; f. 1946; morning; Man. Editor TADANORI KATO; circ. 96,000.

Chukyo Sports: Chukei Bldg, 4-4-12, Meieki, Nakamura-ku, Nagoya City 450; tel. (052) 582-4076; f. 1968; evening; Man. Editor RYOTARO MOTOYAMA; circ. 299,000.

Chunichi Shimbun: 6-1, 1-chome, Sannomaru, Naka-ku, Nagoya City 460; tel. (052) 201-8811; f. 1942; Man. Editor TADASHI YAMAGUCHI; circ. morning 1.98m., evening 830,000.

Chunichi Sports: 6-1, 1-chome, Sannomaru, Naka-ku, Nagoya City 460; tel. (052) 201-8811; f. 1954; evening; Dir YASUO MIZUTANI; circ. 579,000.

JAPAN

Gifu Nichi-nichi Shimbun: 9, Imakomachi, Gifu City 500; tel. (0582) 64-1151; f. 1879; Pres. MIKIO SUGIYAMA; Man. Editor KIMINORI MUTO; circ. morning 123,000, evening 31,000.

Mainichi Shimbun: 4-7-35, Meieki, Nakamura-ku, Nagoya City 450; tel. (052) 561-2211; f. 1935; Man. Editor AKIRA HORIKOSHI; circ. morning 221,000, evening 101,000.

Nagoya Times: 3-10, 1-chome, Marunouchi, Naka-ku, Nagoya City 460; tel. (052) 231-1331; f. 1946; evening; Man. Editor ISAO KIMI; circ. 143,000.

Shinano Mainichi Shimbun: 657, Minamiagata-cho, Nagano City 380; tel. (0262) 36-3111; telex 3322444; f. 1873; Man. Editor K. TAGA; circ. morning 417,000, evening 61,000.

Shizuoka Shimbun: 3-1-1, Toro, Shizuoka City 422; tel. (0542) 82-1111; f. 1941; Man. Editor KAKUJI OISHI; circ. morning 621,000, evening 621,000.

Yamanashi Nichi-Nichi Shimbun: 6-10, 2-chome, Kitaguchi, Kofu City 400, tel. (0552) 31-3000; f. 1872; morning; Man. Editor TAKEHISA NAKAGOMI; circ. 158,000.

Hokuriku District
(North Coastal Honshu)

Fukui Shimbun: 1-14, 1-chome, Haruyama, Fukui City 910; tel. (0776) 23-5111; f. 1899; morning; Man. Editor MAKOTO TSUCHIDA; circ. 150,000.

Hokkoku Shimbun: 5-1, 2-chome, Korinbo, Kanazawa City 920; tel. (0762) 63-2111; f. 1893; Man. Editor S. ARAI; circ. morning 244,000, evening 84,000.

Hokuriku Chunichi Shimbun: 7-15, 2-chome, Korinbo, Kanazawa City 920; f. 1960; Editor K. OYAIZU; circ. morning 120,000, evening 20,000.

Kita Nihon Shimbun: 2-14, Yasuzumi-cho, Toyama City 930; tel. (0763) 32-1111; f. 1940; Man. Editor RUUZO UENO; circ. morning 197,000, evening 32,000.

Niigata Nippo: 274-1, Niban-cho, Higashinaka-dori, Niigata City 951; tel. (0252) 29-2211; f. 1942; Man. Editor SACHIO IGARASHI; circ. morning 418,000, evening 98,000.

Yomiuri Shimbun: 4-5, Shimonoseki-machi, Takaoka City 933; tel. (0766) 23-1234; f. 1961; Editor M. NAGAHARA; circ. morning 146,000, evening 11,000.

Kinki District
(West Central Honshu)

Ise Shimbun: 34-6, Hon-cho, Tsu City 514; tel. (0592) 24-0003; f. 1878; morning; Man. Editor MASAO KOBAYASHI; circ. 97,000.

Kobe Shimbun: 1-1, 7-chome, Kumoidori, Chuo-ku, Kobe City 651; tel. (078) 221-4121; f. 1898; Man. Editor TADAO TANAKA; circ. morning 473,000, evening 277,000.

Kyoto Shimbun: 239, Shoshoi-machi Ebisugawa-kitairu, Karasuma-dori, Nakakyo-ku, Kyoto 604; tel. (075) 222-2111; f. 1879; Man. Editor T. ADACHI; circ. morning 467,000, evening 355,000.

Nara Shimbun: 606, Sanjo-machi, Nara City 630; tel. (0742) 26-1331; f. 1946; morning; Man. Editor YOSHIKATA HIROSHIBA; circ. 87,000.

Chugoku District
(Western Honshu)

Chugoku Shimbun: 7-1, Dobashi-cho, Naka-ku, Hiroshima City 733; tel. (082) 291-2111; f. 1892; Pres. AKIRA YAMAMOTO; Man. Editor YUKIO OGATA; circ. morning 622,000, evening 113,000.

Oka-Nichi: 6-30, Hon-cho, Okayama 700; tel. (0862) 31-4211; f. 1946; evening; Man. Editor KEIJI FUKUHARA; circ. 40,000.

San-In Chuo Shimpo: 383, Tono-machi, Matsue 690; tel. (0852) 21-4491; f. 1882; morning; Man. Editor TADASHI SUGITANI; circ. 150,000.

Sanyo Shimbun: 1-23, 2-chome, Yanagi-cho, Okayama 700; tel. (0862) 31-2211; f. 1879; Man. Editor HITOSHI KAWAI; circ. morning 396,000, evening 83,000.

Yamaguchi Shimbun: 1-1-7, Higashi-Yamato-cho, Shimo-noseki 750; tel. (0832) 66-3211; f. 1946; morning; Pres. KAZUYUGI OGAWA; Editor ATSUMU YOSHIKURA; circ. 58,000.

Shikoku Island

Ehime Shimbun: 12-1, 1-chome, Ohtemachi, Matsuyama, 790; tel. (0899) 41-8111; f. 1941; Man. Editor AKIRA YAMADA; circ. morning 213,000, evening 24,000.

Kochi Shimbun: 2-15, 3-chome, Honcho, Kochi City 780; tel. (0888) 22-2111; f. 1904; Man. Editor SHOROKU HASHII; circ. morning 212,000, evening 127,000.

Shikoku Shimbun: 15-1, Nakano-machi, Takamatsu 760; tel. (0878) 33-1111; f. 1889; Man. Editor TASUO MURAI; circ. morning 179,000, evening 20,000.

Tokushima Shimbun: 6, 1-chome, Saiwai-cho, Tokushima 770; tel. (0886) 23-2121; f. 1941; Editor-in-Chief YOSHIMI IBATA; circ. morning 212,000, evening 39,000.

Hokkaido Island

Asahi Shimbun: 1-1, 1-chome, Nishi, Kita Nijo, Chuo-ku, Sapporo 060; tel. (011) 281-2131; f. 1959; Editor A. ISHIZUKA; circ. morning 178,000, evening 117,000.

Hokkai Times: 6, 10-chome, Nishi Minami-Ichijo, Chuo-ku, Sapporo 060; tel. (011) 231-0131; f. 1946; Man. Editor KIICHI SHIOGUCHI; circ. morning 167,000, evening 40,000.

Hokkaido Shimbun: 6, 3-chome, Odori-Nishi, Chuo-ku, Sapporo 060; tel. (011) 221-2111; f. 1942; Editor K. SAKUTA; circ. morning 1.1m, evening 800,000.

Mainichi Shimbun: 1, Nishi 6, Kita-yojo, Chuo-ku, Sapporo 060; tel. (011) 221-4141; f. 1959; Rep. ISAO MIYASIMA; circ. morning 101,000, evening 47,000.

Nikkan Sports: Times Bldg, 10-6, Nishi, Minami-Ichijo, Chuo-ku, Sapporo 060; tel. (011) 231-5110; f. 1962; morning; Man. Editor AKIRA ABE; circ. 148,000.

Yomiuri Shimbun: 1, 4-chome, Kita-yojo, Chuo-ku, Sapporo 060; tel. (011) 231-7611; f. 1959; Editor A. SHIDARA; circ. morning 260,000, evening 133,000.

Kyushu Island

Asahi Shimbun: 12-1, 1-chome, Sunatsu, Kokura Kita-ku, Kita-Kyushu City 802; tel. (093) 531-1131; f. 1935; Man. Editor TOMONORI MATSUMOTO; circ. morning 824,000, evening 223,000.

Fukunichi: 2-1, 1-chome, Imaizumi, Chuo-ku, Fukuoka 810; tel. (092) 711-2520; f. 1946; morning; Man. Editor TAKAAKI SATANI; circ. 135,000.

Kagoshima Shimpo: 7-28, Jonan-cho, Kagoshima 892; tel. (0992) 26-2100; f. 1959; morning; Man. Editor MOTOYOSH HAGIWARA; circ. 57,000.

Kumamoto Nichi-nichi Shimbun: 2-33, Kamidori-machi, Kumamoto 860; tel. (096) 326-1111; f. 1942; Editor KEISUKE HISANO; circ. morning 332,000, evening 107,000.

Kyushu Sports: Fukuoka Tenjin Centre Bldg, 2-14-8, Tenjin-cho, Chuo-ku, Fukuoka 810; tel. (092) 781-7452; f. 1966; morning; Man. Editor T. OKAMIYA; circ. 262,000.

Mainichi Shimbun: 13-1, Konya-machi, Kokura Kita-ku, Kitakyushu 802; tel. (093) 541-3131; f. 1935; Man. Editor HARUJI SHINOHARA; circ. morning 652,000, evening 166,000.

Minami Nihon Shinbun: 1-2, Yasui-cho, Kagoshima-shi, Kagoshima 892; tel. (0992) 26-4111; f. 1881; Man. Editor SHINOBU FUKUISHI; circ. morning 344,000, evening 34,000.

Miyazaki Nichi-nichi Shimbun: 1-33, 1-chome, Takachihodori, Miyazaki 880; tel. (0985) 25-2371; f. 1940; Man. Editor RYOJI TANAKA; morning; circ. 200,000.

Nagasaki Shimbun: 3-1, Mori-machi, Nagasaki 852; tel. (0958) 44-2111; f. 1889; Man. Editor HISASHI IWANAGA; circ. morning 167,000, evening 54,000.

Nihon Keizai Shimbun: 3-1, 2-chome, Sumiyoshi, Hakata-ku, Fukuoka City; tel. (092) 281-4931; f. 1964; Editor TAKESHI INOUE; circ. morning 157,000, evening 62,000.

Nishi Nippon Shimbun: 4-1, 1-chome, Tenjin, Chuo-ku, Fukuoka 810; tel. (092) 711-5555; f. 1877; Man. Editor TSUNEO TAKIGUCHI; circ. morning 771,000, evening 217,000.

Oita Godo Shimbun: 9-15, 3-chome, Fudai-cho, Oita 870; tel. (0975) 36-2121; f. 1886; Man. Editor MOTOO ASAKUNO; circ. morning 202,000, evening 202,000.

Okinawa Times: 2-2-2, Kumoji, Naha City, 900; tel. (0988) 67-3111; f. 1948; Man. Editor TAKAO MIYAGI; circ. morning 245,000, evening 244,000.

Ryukyu Shimpo: 1-10-3, Izumizaki, Naha City, Okinawa 900; tel. (0988) 65-5111; f. 1893; Editor-in-Chief TATSUHIRO HIGA; circ. morning 173,000, evening 173,000.

Saga Shimbun: 3-18, 1-chome, Matsubara, Saga City 840; tel. (0952) 25-4811; f. 1884; morning; Man. Editor YOSHINO NORICHIKA; circ. 118,000.

Sports Nippon: 4-1, 1-chome, Kiyotaki, Moji-ku, Kita-kyushu 801; tel. (093) 321-4001; f. 1955; morning; Man. Editor T. DOI; circ. 230,000.

Yomiuri Shimbun: 1-11, Meiwa-machi, Kokurakita-ku, Kitakyushu 802; tel. (093) 531-5131; f. 1964; Man. Editor MAKOTO WATARAI; circ. morning 887,000, evening 156,000.

WEEKLIES

Asahi Graphic: Asahi Shimbun Publishing Co, 5-3-2, Tsukiji, Chuo-ku, Tokyo 104; tel. (03) 545-0131; telex 22226; f. 1923; pictorial review; Editor TOSHIAKI FUJII; circ. 200,000.

JAPAN

Asahi Journal: Asahi Shimbun Publications Dept, 5-3-2, Tsukiji, Chuo-ku, Tokyo 104; tel. (03) 545-0131; telex 22226; f. 1959; review; Editor TETSUYA TSUKUSHI.

Economist: Mainichi Newspapers Publishing Dept, 1-1-1, Hitotsubashi, Chiyoda-ku, Tokyo; tel. (03) 212-0321; telex 24851; f. 1923; Editorial Chief EISUKE TODA; circ. 117,000.

Shukan Asahi: Asahi Shimbun Publishing Co, 5-3-2, Tsukiji, Chuo-ku, Tokyo 104; tel. (03) 545-0131; telex 22226; f. 1922; general interest; Editor YOSHITAKA NAGAYAMA; circ. 600,000.

Shukan Bunshun: Bungei-Shunju Ltd., 3-23, Kioicho, Chiyoda-ku, Tokyo 102; tel. (03) 265-1211; f. 1959; general interest; Editor MASARU SHIRAISHI; circ. 491,000.

Shukan Daiyamondo: Diamond Inc, 1-4-2, Kasumi-gaseki, Chiyoda-ku, Tokyo; tel. (03) 504-6517; telex 2424461; f. 1913; economics; Editor MASATO OGUMA.

Shukan Gendai: Kodansha Co Ltd, 2-12-21, Otowa, Bunkyo-ku, Tokyo; tel. (03) 945-1111; f. 1959; general; Editor AKIYA SUGIMOTO.

Shukan Post: Shogakukan Publishing Co Ltd, 2-3-1, Hitotsubashi, Chiyoda-ku, Tokyo; tel. (03) 230-5211; telex 2322192; f. 1969; general; Editor SUSUMU SEKINE.

Shukan Sankei: Sankei Publishing Ltd, 6-1-25, Kojimanchi, Chiyoda-ku, Tokyo; tel. (03) 234-0301; f. 1952; general interest; Editor OSAMU SASAKI.

Shukan Shincho: Shinchosha, 71, Yarai-cho, Shinjuku-ku, Tokyo 162; tel. (03) 266-5311; f. 1956; general interest; Editor HIKOYA YAMADA; circ. 800,000.

Shukan Toyo Keizai: Tokyo Keizai Shinpo Sha, 1-4, Hongkoku-cho, Nihonbashi, Chuo-ku, Tokyo; tel. (03) 246-5401; f. 1895; business and economics; Editor HISAYOSHI KATSUMATA; circ. 60,000.

Shukan Yomiuri: Yomiuri Shimbun Publications Dept, 1-7-1, Ohtemachi, Chiyoda-ku, Tokyo 100; tel. (03) 242-1111; telex 22228; f. 1938; general interest; Editor AKIRA NAKAHO.

Student Times: Japan Times Inc, 4-5-4, Shibaura, Minato-ku, Tokyo; tel. (03) 453-5311; f. 1951; English and Japanese; Editor YUKIO KAKUCHI.

Sunday Mainichi: Mainichi Newspapers Publications Dept, 1-1-1, Hitotsubashi, Chiyoda-ku, Tokyo; tel. (03) 212-0321; telex 22324; f. 1922; general interest; Editor IWAMI TAKAO; circ. 322,000.

Tenji Mainichi: Mainichi Newspapers Publications Dept, 1-1-1, Hitotsubashi, Chiyoda-ku, Tokyo; tel. (03) 212-0321; telex 22324; f. 1922; in Japanese braille; Editor MICHITOSHI ZENIMOTO; circ. 12,000.

PERIODICALS

Airview: Kantosha Co Ltd, 601 Kojun Bldg, 6-8-7, Ginza, Chuo-ku, Tokyo 104; tel. (03) 572-3421; f. 1951; monthly; aviation engineering; Editor YASUYUKI TAKASAWA; circ. 50,000.

All Yomimono: Bungei-Shunju Ltd, 3-23, Kioicho, Chiyoda-ku, Tokyo 102; tel. (03) 265-1211; f. 1930; monthly; popular fiction; Editor KENICHI FUJINO; circ. 150,000.

Asahi Camera: Asahi Shimbun Publications Dept, 5-3-2, Tsukiji, Chuo-ku, Tokyo 104; tel. (03) 545-0131; telex 22226; f. 1926; monthly; photography; Editor YASUSHI SATO; circ. 65,000.

Bijutsu Techô: Bijutsu Shuppan-sha, Inaoka Bldg, 2-36, Kanda, Jinbo-cho, Chiyoda-ku, Tokyo 101; tel. (03) 234-2151; f. 1948; monthly; fine arts; Editor NORIO OHASHI; circ. 60,000.

Bungaku (Literature): Iwanami Shoten, 2-5-5, Hitotsubashi, Chiyoda-ku, Tokyo 101; tel. (03) 265-4111; telex 29495; f. 1933; monthly; Editor KOICHIRO HOSHINO; circ. 26,000.

Bungei-Shunju: Bungei-Shunju Ltd, 3-23, Kioicho, Chiyoda-ku, Tokyo 102; tel. (03) 265-1211; f. 1923; monthly; general; Editor TAKASHI TSUTSUMI; circ. 565,000.

Business JAPAN: Nihon Kogyo Shimbun Co, Sankei Bldg, 1-7-2, Ohtemachi, Chiyoda-ku, Tokyo 100; tel. (03) 231-7111; f. 1955; monthly; Pres. H. FUKAYA; Editor JANICHI KIKUCHI; circ. 63,000.

Business Tokyo: Keizaikai Corporated Inc, 2-13-18, Minami Aoyama, Minato-ku, Tokyo 107; tel. (03) 475-6181; telex 32707; monthly; Chair. SEICHU SATO; Editor ANTHONY PAUL; circ. 150,000.

Chuokoron: Chuokoron-Sha Inc, 2-8-7, Kyobashi, Chuo-ku, Tokyo 104; tel. (03) 563-1261; f. 1887; monthly; general interest; Chief Editor TAKASHI HIRABAYASHI; circ. 180,000.

Fujinkoron: Chuokoron-Sha Inc, 2-8-7, Kyobashi, Chuo-ku, Tokyo 104; tel. (03) 563-1261; f. 1916; women's literary monthly; Editor KAZUO MATSUMURA; circ. 268,000.

Gakujin (Alpinist): Tokyo Shimbun Publications Dept, 2-3-13, Konan, Minato-ku, Tokyo 108; f. 1947; monthly; Editor T. NISHIYAMA; circ. 150,000.

Geijutsu Shincho: Shinchosha, 71, Yaraicho, Shinjuku-ku, Tokyo 162; tel. (03) 266-5111; telex 27433; f. 1950; monthly; fine arts, music, architecture, drama and design; Editor-in-Chief MIDORI YAMAKAWA; circ. 150,000.

Gendai: Kodansha Co Ltd, 2-12-21, Otowa, Bunkyo-ku, Tokyo 112; tel. (03) 945-1111; telex 2722570; f. 1966; monthly; cultural and political; Editor AKINARI SUGIMOTO; circ. 300,000.

Gunzo: Kodansha Co Ltd, 2-12-21, Otowa, Bunkyo-ku, Tokyo 112; tel. (03) 945-1111; telex 345509; f. 1946; literary monthly; Editor KEIKO AMANO; circ. 30,000.

Horitsu Jiho: Nippon Hyoron Sha Co Ltd, Nihon Seimei Minamiotsuka Bldg, 3-10-10, Minamiotsuka, Toshima-ku, Tokyo 170; tel. (03) 987-8611; f. 1929; monthly; law journal; Editor YOSHIO KAGO; circ. 25,000.

Ie-no-Hikari (Light of Home): Ie-no-Hikari Asscn, 11, Ichigaya Funagawara-cho, Shinjuku-ku, Tokyo 160; tel. (03) 260-3151; telex 2322367; f. 1925; monthly; rural and general interest; Pres. YASUO OGUSHI; Editor KENJI YOKOYAMA; circ. 1.2m.

Iwa-To-Yuki (Rock and Snow): Yama-kei Publrs Co, 1-1-33, Shiba-Daimon, Minato-ku, Tokyo 105; tel. (03) 436-4026; f. 1958; every 2 months; mountaineering; Editor TSUNEMICHI IKEDA; circ. 50,000.

Japan Company Handbook: Toyo Keizai Shinposha, 1-2-1, Nihonbashi Hongoku-cho, Chuo-ku, Tokyo 103; tel. (03) 246-5621; f. 1974; quarterly; English; Editor TAKASHI YAMAZAKI; circ. 50,000.

Japan Quarterly: Asahi Shimbun, 5-3-2, Tsukiji, Chuo-ku, Tokyo 104; tel. (03) 545-0131; f. 1954; English; political, economic and cultural; Editor WADA TAKASHI; circ. 6,000.

Jitsugyo No Nihon: Jitsugyo No Nihon Sha Ltd, 1-3-9, Ginza, Chuo-ku, Tokyo 104; tel. (03) 562-1021; f. 1897; every 2 months; economics and business; Editor MASABUMI NOJI; circ. 48,000.

Journal of Electronic Engineering: Dempa Publications Inc, 1-11-15, Higashi Gotanda, Shinagawa-ku, Tokyo 141; tel. (03) 445-6111; telex 2424461; f. 1964; monthly; Editor HIDEO HIRAYAMA; circ. 51,000.

Journal of the Electronics Industry: Dempa Publications Inc, 1-11-15, Higashi Gotanda, Shingawa-ku, Tokyo 141; tel. (03) 445-6111; telex 2424461; f. 1953; monthly; Editor HIDEO HIRAYAMA; circ. 108,000.

Kagaku (Science): Iwanami Shoten Publishers, 2-5-5, Hitotsubashi, Chiyoda-ku, Tokyo 101; tel. (03) 265-4111; telex 29495; f. 1931; Editor SHIGEKI KOBAYASHI; circ. 29,000.

Kagaku Asahi: Asahi Shimbun Publications Dept, 5-3-2, Tsukiji, Chuo-ku, Tokyo 104; tel. (03) 545-0131; telex 22226; f. 1941; monthly; scientific; Editor TADASHI NISHIOKA; circ. 95,000.

Kagakushi-Kenkyu: (History of Science Society of Japan), Iwanami Shoten, 2-5-5, Hitotsubashi, Chiyoda-ku, Tokyo 101; tel. (03) 265-4111; telex 29495; f. 1941; quarterly journal; Editor ICHIRO YABE; circ. 4,000.

Kaisha Shikiho: Toyo Keizai Shinpo Sha, 1-2-1, Nihonbashi Hongoku-cho, Chuo-ku, Tokyo 103; tel. (03) 246-5470; f. 1936; quarterly; corporate data and information; Editor SEISHI SHIBOOTA; circ. 1.1m.

Keizai Hyoron: Nippon Hyoron Sha Co Ltd, Nihon Seimei Minamiotsuka Bldg, 3-10-10, Minamiotsuka, Toshima-ku, Tokyo 170; tel. (03) 987-8611; f. 1946; monthly; economic review; Editor TOSHIRO TANAKA; circ. 25,000.

Keizaijin: Kansai Economic Federation, Nakanoshima Center Bldg, 6-2-27, Nakanoshima, Kita-ku, Osaka 530; tel. (06) 441-0102; telex 5248208; f. 1947; monthly; economics; Editor K. KOJIMA; circ. 3,000.

Kokka: Asahi Shimbun Publications Dept, Tsukiji Hamarikyu Bldg, 7th Floor, 5-3-3, Tsukiji, Chuo-ku, Tokyo 104; tel. (03) 542-6722; f. 1889; monthly; Far Eastern art; Chief Editor YOSHIHO YONEZAWA; circ. 1,000.

Liberal Star: 1-11-23, Nagata-cho, Chiyoda-ku, Tokyo 100; tel. (03) 581-6211; f. 1972; monthly; publ. by the LDP; Editor KOICHI YAMAGUCHI; circ. 18,000.

Mizue: Bijutsu Shuppan-sha, Inaoka Bldg, 2-36, Kanda, Jimbo-cho, Chiyoda-ku, Tokyo 101; tel. (03) 234-2151; f. 1905; quarterly; fine arts; Editor RYOHEI KUMONO; circ. 30,000.

Ongaku No Tomo (Friends of Music): Ongaku No Tomo Sha Corpn, 6-30, Kagurazaka, Shinjuku-ku, Tokyo 162; tel. (03) 235-2211; telex 23718; f. 1941; monthly; classical music; Editor MIYAKO HORIUCHI; circ. 120,000.

Sekai: Iwanami Shoten, 2-5-5, Hitotsubashi, Tokyo 101; tel. (03) 265-4111; telex 29495; f. 1946; monthly; review of world and domestic affairs; Editor AKIO YAMAGUCHI; circ. 120,000.

Shinkenchiku: 2-31-2, Yushima, Bunkyo-ku, Tokyo 113; f. 1925; monthly; architecture; Editor SHOZO BABA; circ. 87,000.

Shiso (Thought): Iwanami Shoten, 2-5-5, Hitotsubashi, Chiyoda-ku, Tokyo 101; tel. (03) 265-4111; telex 29495; f. 1921; monthly; philosophy, social sciences and humanities; Editor ATSUSHI AIBA; circ. 34,000.

JAPAN

Shosetsu Shincho: Shincho-sha, 71, Yaraicho, Shinjuku-ku, Tokyo 162; tel. (03) 266-5111; f. 1947; monthly; literature; Chief Editor REIKO KAWANO; circ. 300,000.

Shukan FM: Ongaku No Tomo Sha Corpn, 6-30, Kagurazaka, Shinjuku-ku, Tokyo 162; tel. (03) 235-2111; telex 2352129; f. 1971; fortnightly; guide to music broadcasts; Editor AKIO MIZUSHIMA; circ. 145,000.

Sincho: Shinchosha, 71, Yaraicho, Shinjuku-ku, Tokyo 162; tel. (03) 266-5111; f. 1904; monthly; literary; Editor TADAO SAKAMOTO; circ. 40,000.

So-en: Bunka Publishing Bureau, 3-22-1, Yoyogi, Shibuya-ku, Tokyo 151; tel. (03) 370-3111; telex 232475; f. 1936; fashion monthly; Editor TAMAE EJIMA; circ. 230,000.

Statistics Monthly: Toyo Keizai Shinpo Sha, 1-2-1, Nihonbashi Hongoku-cho, Chuo-ku, Tokyo 103; tel. (03) 246-5470; f. 1939; monthly; Editor KODEN WATANABE; circ. 14,000.

Stereo: Ongaku No Tomo Sha Corpn, 6-30, Kagurazaka, Shinjuku-ku, Tokyo 162; tel. (03) 235-2111; telex 2352129; f. 1963; monthly; records and audio; Editor SEIZABURO MOGAMI; circ. 150,000.

Sûgaku (Mathematics): Mathematical Society of Japan, 4-25-9-203, Hongo, Bunkyo-ku, Tokyo 113; tel. (03) 816-5961; f. 1947; quarterly; circ. 7,000.

Tokyo Business Today: Toyo Keizai Shinpo Sha, 1-2-1, Nihonbashi Hongoku-cho, Chuo-ku, Tokyo 103; tel. (03) 246-5470; f. 1934; monthly; English; business and finance; Editor NOZOMU NAKAOKA; circ. 30,000.

The-Yama-To-Keikoku (Mountain and Valley): Yama-Kei Publishers Co, 1-1-33, Shiba-Daimon, Minato-ku, Tokyo 105; tel. (03) 436-4023; f. 1930; monthly; mountaineering; Editor AKIRA YAMAGUCHI; circ. 230,000.

NEWS AGENCIES

Jiji Tsushin-Sha (Jiji Press): Shisei Kaikan, 1-3, Hibiya Park, Chiyoda-ku, Tokyo 100; tel. (03) 591-1111; f. 1945; Pres. KAZUO HARANO.

Kyodo Tsushin (Kyodo News Service): 2-2-5, Toranomon, Minato-ku, Tokyo 105; tel. (03) 584-4111; telex 22207; f. 1945; Pres. SHINJI SAKAI; Man. Dir YASUHIKO INUKAI; Man. Editor ASAHI KAMIYAMA.

Radiopress Inc: Fuji TV Bldg, 3-1, Kawada-cho, Shinjuku-ku, Tokyo 162; tel. (03) 353-1621; f. 1945; provides news from China, the USSR, Democratic People's Repub. of Korea, Viet-Nam and elsewhere to the press and govt offices; Pres. SHOTARO TAKAHASHI.

Sun Telephoto: Palaceside Bldg, 1-1, 1-chome, Hitotsubashi, Chiyoda-ku, Tokyo 100; tel. (03) 213-6771; f. 1952; Pres. KEN-ICHIRO MATSUOKA; Man. Editor YU YAMAMOTO.

Foreign Bureaux

Agence France-Presse (AFP): Asahi Shimbun Bldg, 11th Floor, 5-3-2, Tsukiji, Chuo-ku, Tokyo 104; tel. (03) 545-3061; telex 22368; Bureau Chief RENÉ FLIPO.

Agencia EFE (Spain): Kyodo Tsushin Kaikan, 9th Floor, 2-2-5, Toranomon, Minato-ku, Tokyo 105; tel. (03) 585-8940; telex 34502; Bureau Chief JOSEP BOSCH.

Agentstvo Pechati Novosti (APN) (USSR): 3-9-13, Higashigotanda, Shinagawa-ku, Tokyo 141; tel. (03) 447-3536; telex 822958; Bureau Chief ALEXEI K. PANTELEYEV.

Agenzia Nazionale Stampa Associata (ANSA) (Italy): Kyodo Tsushin Kaikan, 2-2-5, Toranomon, Minato-ku, Tokyo 105; tel. (03) 584-6667; telex 7228286; Correspondent ROBERTO MAGGI.

Allgemeiner Deutscher Nachrichtendienst (ADN) (German Democratic Republic): 4-9-9, Jingumae, Shibuya-ku, Tokyo 150; tel. (03) 478-3842; Correspondent RAINER KÖHLER.

Antara (Indonesia): Kyodo Tsushin Bldg, 9th Floor, 2-2-5, Toranomon, Minato-ku, Tokyo 107; tel. (03) 584-4234; Correspondent PIDWAN SURYANTHO.

Associated Press (AP) (USA): Asahi Shimbun Bldg, 11th Floor, 5-3-2, Tsukiji, Chuo-ku, Tokyo 104; tel. (03) 545-5901; telex 22260; Bureau Chief THOMAS J. DYGARD.

Bulgarska Telegrafna Agentsia (BTA): Daiichi Aoyama Mansion, Room 802, 1-10, 5-chome, Minami Aoyama, Minato-ku, Tokyo 107; tel. (03) 407-6926; Correspondent IVAN A. GAYTANDJIEV.

Central News Agency (Taiwan): Kyowa Bldg, Room 503, 1-5-6, Iidabashi, Chiyoda-ku, Tokyo; tel. (03) 264-4717; Bureau Chief CHIEM CHAO HUNG.

Deutsche Presse-Agentur (dpa) (Federal Republic of Germany): Shisei Kaikan, Room 202, 1-3, Hibiya Koen, Chiyoda-ku, CPOB 1512, Tokyo 100; tel. (03) 580-6629; telex 22533; Bureau Chief HELMUT RÄTHER.

Keystone Press Agency (UK): Kaneda Bldg, 3-17-2, Shibuya, Shibuya-ku, Tokyo 150; tel. (03) 407-0375; Pres. JUNZO SUZUKI.

Directory

Magyar Távirati Iroda (MTI) (Hungary): 22-1, Minami-Aoyama 4-chome, Minato-ku, Tokyo 107; tel. (03) 405-7087; telex 28446; Bureau Chief: Dr ANDRÁS TROM.

Prensa Latina (Cuba): 36-6, 3-chome, Nozawa Setagoya-ku, Tokyo; tel. (03) 421-9455; telex 29962; Correspondent JOSÉ AGUILAR.

Reuters (UK): Shuwa Kamiyacho Bldg, 3rd Floor, 4-3-13, Toranomon, Minato-ku, Tokyo 105; tel. (03) 432-4141; telex 22349; Man. Dir MICHAEL SALAMON.

Telegrafnoye Agentstvo Sovetskovo Soyuza (TASS) (USSR): 5-1, 1-chome, Hon-cho, Shibuya-ku, Tokyo 151; tel. (03) 377-0380; Correspondent VIKTOR ZATSEPIN.

United Press International (UPI) (USA): Palaceside Bldg, 1-1, Hitsubashi 1-chome, Chiyoda-ku, Tokyo 100; tel. (03) 212-7911; telex 22364; Bureau Chief STEWART SLAVIN.

Xinhua (New China) News Agency (People's Republic of China): 3-35-23, Ebisu, Shibuya-ku, Tokyo 150; tel. (03) 441-3766; Correspondent LIU WENYU.

Yonhap (United) News Agency (Republic of Korea): Kyodo Tsushin Bldg, 2-2-5, Toranomon, Minato-ku, Tokyo 105; tel. (03) 584-4681; f. 1945; Bureau Chief JUNG KIL.

PRESS ASSOCIATIONS

Foreign Press Center: Nippon Press Centre Bldg, 6th Floor, 2-2-1, Uchisaiwai-cho, Chiyoda-ku, Tokyo 100; tel. (03) 501-3401; f. 1976; est. by Japan Newspaper Publrs' and Editors' Asscn and the Japan Fed. of Economic Orgs; provides services to the foreign press; Pres. TERUJI AKIYAMA; Man. Dir FUMIO KITAMURA.

Foreign Press in Japan: 20F Yurakucho Denki Bldg, 1-7-1, Yurakucho, Chiyoda-ku, Tokyo; tel. (03) 211-3161; f. 1960; 140 companies; Pres. WILLIAM HORSLEY; Man. HAJIME HORIKAWA.

Nihon Shinbun Kyokai (Japan Newspaper Publishers' and Editors' Asscn): Nippon Press Center Bldg, 2-1, Uchisaiwai-cho 2-chome, Chiyoda-ku, Tokyo 100; tel. (03) 591-4401; telex 27504; f. 1946; mems include 166 companies, including 114 daily newspapers, 4 news agencies and 48 radio and TV companies; Pres. YOSOJI KOBAYASHI; Man. Dir and Sec.-Gen. TOSHIE YAMADA.

Nihon Zasshi Kyokai (Japan Magazine Publishers' Asscn): 1-7, Kanda Surugadai, Chiyoda-ku, Tokyo; tel. (03) 291-0775; f. 1956; 68 mems; Pres. GENZO CHIBA; Sec. JUN TANAKA.

Publishers

Akane Shobo Co Ltd: 3-2-1, Nishikanda, Chiyoda-ku, Tokyo; tel. (03) 363-0641; f. 1949; juvenile; Pres. MASAHARU OKAMOTO.

Akita Publishing Shoten Co Ltd: 2-10-8, Iidabashi, Chiyoda-ku, Tokyo 102; tel. (03) 264-7011; f. 1948; social sciences, history, juvenile; Chair. SADAO AKITA; Man. Dir SADAMI AKITA.

Asahi Shimbun Publications Dept: 5-3-2, Tsukiji, Chuo-ku, Tokyo; tel. (03) 545-0131; telex 22226; f. 1879; general; Pres. TOICHIRO HITOTSUYANAGI; Man. Dir TADASHI KOJIMA.

Baifukan Co Ltd: 3-12, Kudan Minami 4-chome, Chiyoda-ku, Tokyo 102; tel. (03) 262-5256; f. 1924; engineering, natural and social sciences, psychology; Pres. ITARU YAMAMOTO.

Bijutsu Shuppan-Sha: Inaoka Bldg, 6th Floor, 2-36, Kanda Jimbocho, Chiyoda-ku, Tokyo 101; tel. (03) 234-2151; f. 1905; art and architecture; Pres. ATSUSHI OSHITA.

Chikuma Shobo Publishing Co Ltd: 2-8, Kanda Ogawamachi, Chiyoda-ku, Tokyo 101-91; tel. (03) 294-6711; f. 1940; general fiction and non-fiction; Rep. HIDESATO SEKINE.

Chuokoron-Sha Inc: 2-8-7, Kyobashi, Chuo-ku, Tokyo; tel. (03) 563-1261; telex 32505; f. 1887; philosophy, history, economic, political and natural science, literature, fine arts; Pres. HOJI SHIMANAKA; Man. Dir SHIGERU TAKANASHI.

Froebel-Kan Co Ltd: 3-1, Kanda Ogawa-machi, Chiyoda-ku, Tokyo 101; tel. (03) 292-7786; telex 24907; f. 1907; juvenile, educational, music; Pres. YUUJI OKAYASU; Dir HARRY IDICHI.

Fukuinkan Shoten: 6-6-3, Honkomagome, Bunkyo-ku, Tokyo 113; tel. (03) 942-0032; telex 33597; f. 1950; juvenile; Pres. KATSUMI SATO; Man. Dir TADASHI MATSUI.

Gakken Co Ltd: 4-40-5, Kamiikedai, Ohta-ku, Tokyo 145; tel. (03) 726-8131; telex 26389; f. 1946; fiction, juvenile, educational, art, history, reference, encyclopaedias, dictionaries, languages; Pres. HIROSHI FURUOKA; Chair. HIDETO FURUOKA.

Hakusui-Sha: 3-24, Kanda Ogawa-machi, Chiyoda-ku, Tokyo; tel. (03) 291-7811; f. 1915; general literature, science and languages; Pres. TAKASHI TAKAHASHI.

Heibonsha Ltd Publishers: 5, Sanbancho, Chiyoda-ku, Tokyo 102; tel. (03) 265-0451; f. 1914; encyclopaedias, art, history, geography, Japanese and Chinese literature; Pres. NAOYA SHIMONAKA.

JAPAN — Directory

Hirokawa Publishing Co: 3-27-14, Hongo, Bunkyo-ku, Tokyo; tel. (03) 815-3651; f. 1926; natural sciences, medicine, textbooks; Pres. SETSUO HIROKAWA.

The Hokuseido Press: 32-4, Honkomagome 3-chome, Bunkyo-ku, Tokyo 113; tel. (03) 827-0511; f. 1914; regional non-fiction, textbooks; Pres. MASAZO YAMAMOTO.

Ie-No-Hikari Association: 11, Funagawara-cho, Ichigaya, Shinjuku-ku, Tokyo 162; tel. (03) 266-9000; telex 2322367; f. 1925; social science, agriculture; Pres. SHIGENORI TOKONABE; Man. Dir AKIRA SUZUKI.

Iwanami Shoten Publishers: 2-5-5, Hitotsubashi, Chiyoda-ku, Tokyo 101; tel. (03) 265-4111; telex 29495; f. 1913; natural and social sciences, literature, history, geography; Chair. YUJIRO IWANAMI; Pres. TORU MIDORIKAWA.

Jimbun Shoin: Takakura-Nishi-iru, Bukkoji-dori, Shimogyo-ku, Kyoto; tel. (075) 351-3343; f. 1922; literary, philosophy, history, fine arts; Pres. MUTSUHISA WATANABE.

Kanehara & Co Ltd: 31-14, Yushima 2-chome, Bunkyo-ku, Tokyo; tel. (03) 811-7161; f. 1875; medical, agricultural, engineering and scientific; Pres. HIDEO KANEHARA.

Kodansha Ltd: 12-21, Otowa 2-chome, Bunkyo-ku, Tokyo 112; tel. (03) 945-1111; telex 34509; f. 1909; art, educational, illustrated children's, fiction, cookery, encyclopaedias, natural science, paperbacks, magazines; Pres. SAWAKO NOMA; Chair. TOSHIYUKI HATTORI.

Kyoritsu Shuppan Co Ltd: 4-6-19, Kobinata 4-chome, Bunkyo-ku, Tokyo 112; tel. (03) 947-2511; f. 1926; scientific and technical; Pres. MASAO NANJO; Gen. Man. Publishing Division MITSUAKI NANJO.

Maruzen Co Ltd: 3-10, Nihonbashi 2-chome, Chuo-ku, Tokyo 103; tel. (03) 272-7211; telex 26516; f. 1869; general; Pres. KUMAO EBIHARA; Chair. SHINGO IIZUMI.

Minerva Shobo Co Ltd: 1, Tsutsumidani-cho, Hinooka, Yamashina-ku, Kyoto 607; tel. (075) 581-5191; f. 1948; general non-fiction and reference; Pres. NOBUO SUGITA.

Misuzu Shobo Publishing Co: 3-17-15, Hongo, Bunkyo-ku, Tokyo; tel. (03) 815-9181; f. 1947; general, philosophy, history, literature, science, art; Pres. TAMIO KITANO; Man. Dir TOSHITO OBI.

Nanzando Co Ltd: 4-1-11, Yushima, Bunkyo-ku, Tokyo; tel. (03) 814-3681; medical reference, paperbacks; Man. Dir KIMIO SUZUKI.

Obunsha Co Ltd: 55, Yokodera-cho, Shinjuku-ku, Tokyo; tel. (03) 266-6000; f. 1931; textbooks, reference, general science and fiction, magazines, encyclopaedias, dictionaries; software; audio-visual aids; Pres. KAZUO AKAO; Man. Dir S. SATO.

Ohmsha Ltd: 3-1, Kanda Nishiki-cho, Chiyoda-ku, Tokyo 101; tel. (03) 233-0641; telex 2223125; f. 1914; engineering, technical and scientific; Pres. N. TANEDA; Man. Dir S. SATO.

Ongaku No Tomo Sha Corpn (ONT): 6-30, Kagurazaka, Shinjuku-ku, Tokyo 162; tel. (03) 235-2111; telex 23718; f. 1941; folios, concert hall, music magazines; Pres. SUNAO ASAKA.

Sankei Shimbun Shuppankyoku Co: 3-15, Ohtemachi, Chiyoda-ku, Tokyo; tel. (03) 231-7111; f. 1950; history, social sciences, politics, juvenile; Man. Dir SHINYA UEDA.

Sanseido Co Ltd: 2-22-14, Misakicho, Chiyoda-ku, Tokyo 101; tel. (03) 230-9411; f. 1881; dictionaries, educational, languages, social and natural science; Chair. HISANORI UENO; Pres. MASAAKI MORIYA.

Seibundo-Shinkosha Publishing Co Ltd: 1-5-5, Kanda Nishiki-cho, Chiyoda-ku, Tokyo; tel. (03) 292-1211; f. 1912; technical, scientific, general non-fiction; Pres. and Man. Dir SHIGEO OGAWA.

Shinkenchiku-Sha Ltd: 31-2, Yushima 2-chome, Bunkyo-ku, Tokyo; tel. (03) 811-7101; f. 1925; architecture; Editor SHOZO BABA; Publr YOSHIO YOSHIDA.

Shogakukan Inc.: 2-3-1, Hitotsubashi, Chiyoda-ku, Tokyo 101; tel. (03) 230-5655; telex 2322192; f. 1922; juvenile, education, geography, history, encyclopaedias, dictionaries; Pres. TETSUO OHGA.

Shokokusha Publishing Co Ltd: 25, Saka-machi, Shinjuku-ku, Tokyo 160; tel. (03) 359-3231; f. 1932; architectural, technical and fine arts; Chair. and Pres. TAISHIRO YAMAMOTO.

Shufunotomo Co Ltd: 9, Kanda Surugadai 2-chome, Chiyoda-ku, Tokyo 101; tel. (03) 294-1118; telex 26925; f. 1916; domestic science, fine arts, gardening, handicraft, cookery and magazines; Pres. HARUHIKO ISHIKAWA.

Shunju-Sha Co Ltd: 2-18-6, Soto-kanda, Chiyoda-ku, Tokyo; tel. (03) 255-9611; f. 1918; philosophy, religion, literary, economics, music; Pres. AKIRA KANDA; Man. YOSHIKAZU SAWAHTA.

Taishukan Shoten: 3-24, Kanda Nishiki-cho, Chiyoda-ku, Tokyo 101; tel. (03) 294-2221; f. 1918; reference, Japanese and foreign languages, sports, dictionaries, audio-visual aids; Man. Dir SHIGEO SUZUKI.

Tokyo News Service Ltd: Tsukiji Hamarikyu Bldg, 10th Floor, 3-3, Tsukiji 5-chome, Chuo-ku, Tokyo 104; tel. (03) 542-6511; telex 2523285; f. 1947; shipping, trade and shipbuilding; Pres. T. OKUYAMA.

University of Tokyo Press: 7-3-1, Hongo, Bunkyo-ku, Tokyo 113; tel. (03) 811-0964; f. 1951; natural and social sciences, humanities; Japanese and English; Man. Dir NORIHIRO SAITO.

Yama-kei Publishing Co Ltd: 1-1-33, Shiba-Daimon, Minato-ku, Tokyo 105; tel. (03) 436-4021; f. 1930; natural science, geography, mountaineering; Pres. YOSHIMITSU KAWASAKI.

Yuhikaku Publishing Co Ltd: 2-17, Kanda Jimbo-cho, Chiyoda-ku, Tokyo; tel. (03) 264-1311; f. 1877; social sciences, law, economics; Chair. SHIRO EGUSA; Pres. TADATAKA EGUSA.

Zoshindo Juken Kenkyusha: 2-19-15, Shinmachi, Nishi-ku, Osaka 550; tel. (06) 532-1581; f. 1890; educational, juvenile; Pres. SHIGETOSHI OKAMOTO.

Government Publishing House

Government Publications' Service Centre: 2-1, 1-chome, Kasumigaseki, Chiyoda-ku, Tokyo 100; tel. (03) 504-3885.

PUBLISHERS' ASSOCIATIONS

Japan Book Publishers' Association: 6, Fukuro-machi, Shinjuku-ku, Tokyo 162; tel. (03) 268-1301; Pres. TOSHIYUKI HATTORI; Exec. Dir TOSHIKAZU GOMI.

Publishers Association for Cultural Exchange: 2-1, Sarugaku-cho 1-chome, Chiyoda-ku, Tokyo 101; tel. (03) 291-5685; f. 1953; 135 mems; Pres. Dr TATSURO MATSUMAE; Dir YASUKO KORENAGA.

Radio and Television

There were an estimated 94.5m. radio receivers and 31.9m. television licences in 1986.

Nippon Hoso Kyokai, NHK (Japan Broadcasting Corporation): Broadcasting Centre, NHK Hoso Centre, 2-2-1, Jinnan, Shibuya-ku, Tokyo 150; tel. (03) 465-1111; telex 22377; f. 1925; non-commercial public corpn; operates five (two TV and three radio) networks and 2 DBS TV services; TV channels equally divided between general and educational networks; central stations at Tokyo, Osaka, Nagoya, Hiroshima, Kumamoto, Sendai, Sapporo and Matsuyama, and over 6,000 local stations; overseas service in 21 languages; Chair. Board of Govs ICHIRO ISODA; Pres. MASATO KAWAHARA.

National Association of Commercial Broadcasters in Japan (MINPOREN): Bungei Shunju Bldg, 3, Kioi-cho, Chiyoda-ku, Tokyo 102; tel. (03) 265-7481; telex 29889; Pres. SUNAO NAKAGAWA; Sec.-Gen. SEIGO NAGATAKE; asscn of 137 companies (103 TV cos, 34 radio cos). Among the TV cos, 36 operate radio and TV, with 307 radio stations and 6,284 TV stations. These include:

Asahi Hoso—Asahi Broadcasting Corpn: 2-2-48, Oyodo-Minami, Oyodo-ku, Osaka 531; tel. (06) 458-5321; Chair. TSUNEJIRO HIRAI; Chair. KIYOSHI HARA.

Bunka Hoso—Nippon Cultural Broadcasting, Inc: 1-5, Wakaba, Shinjuku-ku, Tokyo 160; tel. (03) 357-1111; telex 2322941; f. 1952; Chair. MASATOSHI IWAMOTO; Pres. MASAMI KOBAYASHI.

Nihon Tampa Hoso—Nihon Short-Wave Broadcasting Co: 9-15, Akasaka 1-chome, Minato-ku, Tokyo 107; tel. (03) 583-8151; f. 1954; Pres. KINYA SEKIGUCHI.

Nippon Hoso—Nippon Broadcasting System, Inc: 1-9-3, Yuraku-cho, Chiyoda-ku, Tokyo 100; tel. (03) 287-1111; f. 1954; Chair. N. SHIKANAI; Pres. S. HIRAYAMA.

Okinawa Televi Hoso—Okinawa Television Broadcasting Co Ltd: 2-32-1, Kume, Naha 900, Okinawa; f. 1959; Pres. Y. YAMASHIRO.

Ryukyu Hoso—Ryukyus Broadcasting Co: 2-3-1, Kumoji, Naha 900, Okinawa; tel. (0988) 67-2151; f. 1954; Pres. KUNIO OROKU.

Tokyo Hoso—Tokyo Broadcasting System, Inc: 5-3-6, Akasaka, Minato-ku, Tokyo 107; tel. (03) 584-3111; telex 24883; f. 1951; Chair. HIROSHI SUWA; Pres. KOZO HAMAGUCHI.

There are also 92 commercial television stations operated by Asahi Broadcasting Co, Nippon TV Network Co, Fuji Telecasting Co and others, including:

Televi Asahi—Asahi National Broadcasting Co Ltd: 4-10, Roppongi 6-chome, Minato-ku, Tokyo 106; tel. (03) 405-3211; f. 1959; Chair. YOSHIO AKAO; Pres. KIKUO TASHIRO.

Yomiuri Televi Hoso—Yomiuri Telecasting Corporation: 1-8-11, Higashi-Tenma, Kita-ku, Osaka 530; tel. (06) 356-3500; f. 1958; 20 hrs colour broadcasting daily; Chair. MITSUO MUTAI; Pres. IKUO AOYAMA.

JAPAN

Television News Agencies

Asahi Video Projects Ltd: 6-4-10, Roppongi, Minato-ku, Tokyo; tel. (03) 405-3211; f. 1958; Pres. K. SAMEJIMA.

Kyodo Television Ltd: 28, Sanbancho, Chiyoda-ku, Tokyo 102; tel. (03) 263-4161; telex 2322906; f. 1958; Pres. TOSHIKANE BOJO.

Finance

(cap. = capital; p.u. = paid up; res = reserves; dep. = deposits; m. = million; brs = branches; amounts in yen)

BANKING

Japan's central bank and bank of issue is the Bank of Japan. More than half the credit business of the country is handled by 87 private commercial banks, seven trust banks and three long-term credit banks, collectively designated 'All Banks'.

Of the latter category, the most important are the city banks, some of which have a long and distinguished history, originating in the time of the *zaibatsu*, the private entrepreneurial organizations on which Japan's capital wealth was built up before the Second World War. Although the *zaibatsu* were abolished as integral industrial and commercial enterprises during the Allied Occupation, the several businesses and industries which bear the former *zaibatsu* names, such as Mitsubishi, Mitsui and Sumitomo, continue to flourish and to give each other mutual assistance through their respective banks and trust corporations.

Among the commercial banks, the Bank of Tokyo, specializes in foreign exchange business, while the Industrial Bank of Japan provides a large proportion of the finance for capital investment by industry. The Long-Term Credit Bank of Japan and Nippon Credit Bank Ltd also specialize in industrial finance; the work of these three privately-owned banks is supplemented by the government-controlled Japan Development Bank.

The government has established a number of other specialized organs to supply essential services not performed by the private banks. Thus the Japan Export-Import Bank advances credits for exports of heavy industrial products and imports of raw materials in bulk. A Housing Loan Corporation assists firms building housing for their employees, while the Agriculture, Forestry and Fisheries Finance Corporation provides loans to the named industries for equipment purchases. Similar services are provided for small businesses by the Small Business Finance Corporation.

An important financial role is played by co-operatives and by the many small enterprise institutions. Each prefecture has its own federation of co-operatives, with the Central Co-operative Bank of Agriculture and Forestry as the common central financial institution. This bank also acts as an agent for the government-controlled Agriculture, Forestry and Fisheries Finance Corporation.

There are also three types of private financial institutions for small business. The 68 Sogo Banks (mutual loan and savings banks) are now similar to commercial banks. There are 446 Credit Associations and 455 Shinkin Banks (credit associations), which lend only to members. The latter also receive deposits.

The commonest form of savings is through the government-operated Postal Savings System, which collects small savings from the public by means of the post office network. Total deposits stood at 110,715,200m. yen in April 1987. The funds thus made available are used as loan funds by government financial institutions, through the Ministry of Finance's Trust Fund Bureau.

Clearing houses operate in each major city of Japan, and total 184 institutions. The largest are those of Tokyo and Osaka.

Central Bank

Nippon Ginko (Bank of Japan): 2-1-1, Hongoku-cho, Nihonbashi, Chuo-ku, Tokyo 103; tel. (03) 279-1111; telex 22763; f. 1882; cap. and res 874,242m., dep. 1,530,530.8m. (Sept. 1986); Gov. M. SATOSHI SUMITA.

Principal Commercial Banks

Bank of Tokyo Ltd: 3-2, Hongoku-cho 1-chome, Nihonbashi, Chuo-ku, Tokyo 103; tel. (03) 245-1111; telex 22220; f. 1946; specializes in foreign exchange business; cap. p.u. 118,744m., dep. 12,039,268m. (March 1988); Chair. YUSUKE KASHIWAGI; Pres. MINORU INOUYE; about 250 brs.

Bank of Yokohama Ltd: 47, Honcho 5-chome, Naka-ku, Yokohama Kanagawa 231; tel. (045) 201-4991; telex 24945; f. 1920; cap. p.u. 47,376m., dep. 7,641,854m. (March 1988); Chair. JIRO YOSHIKUNI; Pres. MASATAKA OKURA; 199 brs.

Dai-Ichi Kangyo Bank Ltd: 1-5, Uchisaiwai-cho 1-chome, Chiyoda-ku, Tokyo 100; tel. (03) 596-1111; telex 22315; f. 1971; cap. p.u. 203,785m., dep. 33,833,260m. (Sep. 1987); Chair. ICHIRO NAKAMURA; Pres. KUNIJI MIYAZAKI; 361 brs.

Directory

Daiwa Bank Ltd: 56, Bingomachi 2-chome, Higashi-ku, Osaka 541; tel. (06) 271-1221; telex 63977; f. 1918; cap. 93,058m., dep. 14,531,448m. (March 1987); Chair. SUSUMU FURUKAWA; Pres. SUMIO ABEKAWA; 198 brs.

Fuji Bank Ltd: 5-5, Ohtemachi 1-chome, Chiyoda-ku, Tokyo 100; tel. (03) 216-2211; telex 22367; f. 1880; cap. 133,900m., dep. 26,806,734m. (March 1987); Chair. YOSHIRO ARAKI; Pres. TAIZO HASHIDA; 295 brs.

Hokkaido Takushoku Bank Ltd: 7, Nishi 3-chome, Odori, Chuo-ku, Sapporo 060; tel. (011) 271-2111; telex 932533; f. 1900; cap. 39,200m., dep. 6,819,170m. (March 1987); Chair. AKIRA GOMI; Pres. SHIGERU SUZUKI; 206 brs.

Kyowa Bank Ltd: 1-2, Ohtemachi 1-chome, Chiyoda-ku, Tokyo 100; tel. (03) 287-2111; telex 24275; f. 1948; cap. 52,500m., dep. 9,811,628m. (March 1987); Chair. TETSUO YAMANAKA; Pres. KOSUKE YOKOTE; 238 brs.

Mitsubishi Bank Ltd: 7-1, Marunouchi, 2-chome, Chiyoda-ku, Tokyo 100; tel. (03) 240-1111; telex 22358; f. 1919; cap. 133,261m., dep. 25,120,500m. (March 1987); Chair. HAJIME YAMADA; Pres. KAZUO IBUKI; 271 brs.

Mitsui Bank Ltd: 1-2, Yuraku-cho 1-chome, Chiyoda-ku, Tokyo 100; tel. (03) 501-1111; telex 22378; f. 1876; cap. p.u. 99,512m., dep. 17,593,458m. (March 1987); Chair. KENICHI KAMIYA; Pres. KENICHI SUEMATSU; 229 brs.

Saitama Bank Ltd: 4-1, Tokiwa 7-chome, Urawa City, Saitama Prefecture 336; tel. (488) 24-2411; telex 22811; f. 1943; cap. 50,000m., dep. 8,571,716m. (March 1987); Chair. SHIGETAKE IJICHI; 200 brs.

Sanwa Bank Ltd: 4-10, Fushimimachi, Higashi-ku, Osaka 541; tel. (06) 202-2281; telex 63234; f. 1933; cap. 131,422m., dep. 25,051,712m. (March 1987); Chair. KENJI KAWAKATSU; Pres. HIROSHI WATANABE; 287 brs.

Sumitomo Bank Ltd: 22, Kitahama 5-chome, Higashi-ku, Osaka 541; tel. (06) 227-2111; telex 63266; f. 1895; cap. 129,839m., dep. 27,783,445m. (March 1987); Chair. ICHIRO ISODA; Pres. SOTOO TATSUMI; 371 brs.

Taiyo Kobe Bank Ltd: 56, Naniwa-cho, Chuo-ku, Kobe 650; tel. (078) 331-8101; telex 78823; f. 1973; cap. p.u. 88,306m., dep. 15,283,608m. (March 1987); Chair. TERUYUKI OKUMURA; Pres. YASUO MATSUSHITA; 364 brs.

Tokai Bank Ltd: 21-24, Nishiki, 3-chome, Naka-ku, Nagoya 460; tel. (052) 211-1111; telex 59612; f. 1941; cap. p.u. 102,733m., dep. 18,511,513m. (March 1987); Chair. RYUICHI KATO; Pres. KIICHIRO ITOH; 277 brs.

Principal Trust Banks

Chuo Trust and Banking Co Ltd: 7-1, Kyobashi 1-chome, Chuo-ku, Tokyo 104; tel. (03) 567-1451; telex 33368; f. 1962; cap. and res 141,477m., dep. 1,842,442m. (March 1988); Chair. TAKESHI SEKIGUCHI; Pres. KEI SAKANOUE; 53 brs.

Mitsubishi Trust and Banking Corporation: 4-5, Marunouchi 1-chome, Chiyoda-ku, Tokyo 100; tel. (03) 212-1211; telex 24259; f. 1927; cap. 59,934m., dep. 19,920,953m. (March 1987); Pres. TAKUJI SHIDACHI; 62 brs.

Mitsui Trust and Banking Co Ltd: 1-1, Nihonbashi-Muromachi 2-chome, Chuo-ku, Tokyo 103; tel. (03) 270-9511; telex 26397; f. 1924; cap. 81,011m., dep. 18,782,886m. (March 1988); Chair. SEIICHI KAWASAKI; Pres. TAKESHI NAKAJIMA; 56 brs in Japan, 6 brs overseas.

Sumitomo Trust and Banking Co Ltd: 15, Kitahama 5-chome, Higashi-ku, Osaka 541; tel. (06) 220-2121; telex 63775; f. 1925; cap. 60,431m., dep. 18,696,104m. (March 1987); Chair. TAKESHI TASHIRO; Pres. OSAMU SAKURAI; 59 brs.

Toyo Trust and Banking Co Ltd: 4-3, Marunouchi 1-chome, Chiyoda-ku, Tokyo 100; tel. (03) 287-2211; telex 22123; f. 1959; cap. p.u. 46,816m., dep. 12,588,577m. (March 1987); Chair. CHIGAZO MORITA; Pres. MITSUO IMOSE; 63 brs.

Yasuda Trust and Banking Co Ltd: 2-1, Yaesu 1-chome, Chuo-ku, Tokyo 103; tel. (03) 278-8111; telex 23720; f. 1925; cap. 48,476m., dep. 14,573,947m. (March 1987); Pres. FUJIO TAKAYAMA; 61 brs.

Long-Term Credit Banks

The Long-Term Credit Bank of Japan Ltd: 2-4, Ohtemachi 1-chome, Chiyoda-ku, Tokyo 100; tel. (03) 211-5111; telex 24308; f. 1952; cap. 140,225.4m., dep. and debentures 17,162,820m. (Sep. 1987); Chair. BINSUKE SUGIURA; Pres. MAMORU SAKAI; 27 brs.

The Nippon Credit Bank Ltd: 13-10, Kudan-kita 1-chome, Chiyoda-ku, Tokyo 102; tel. (03) 263-1111; telex 26921; f. 1957; cap. 96,365m., dep. and debentures 11,430,618m. (March 1988); Chair. SHIRO EGAWA; Pres. SEISHI MATSUOKA; 23 brs.

Nippon Kogyo Ginko (The Industrial Bank of Japan, Ltd): 3-3, Marunouchi 1-chome, Chiyoda-ku, Tokyo 100; tel. (03) 214-1111; telex 22325; f. 1902; medium- and long-term financing; cap. p.u.

JAPAN

212,578m., dep. and debentures 26,032,977m., loans and discounts 17,354,273m. (March 1988); Chair. KISABURO IKEURA; Pres. KANEO NAKAMURA; 32 brs.

Principal Government Credit Institutions

Agriculture, Forestry and Fisheries Finance Corporation: Koko Bldg, 9-3, Ohtemachi 1-chome, Chiyoda-ku, Tokyo 100; tel. (03) 270-2261; f. 1953; finances plant and equipment investment; cap. 168,233m. (March 1987); Pres. SAKUE MATSUMOTO; Vice-Pres. YASUTAKA MIYAMOTO.

The Export-Import Bank of Japan: 4-1, Ohtemachi 1-chome, Chiyoda-ku, Tokyo 100; tel. (03) 287-1221; telex 2223728; f. 1950 to supplement and encourage the financing of exports, imports and overseas investment by ordinary financial institutions; cap. p.u. 967,300m. (March 1987); Pres. TAKASHI TANAKA; 1 br.

Housing Loan Corporation: 4-10, Koraku 1-chome, Bunkyo-ku, Tokyo 112; tel. (03) 812-1111; f. 1950 to provide long-term capital for the construction of housing at low interest rates; cap. 97,200m. (March 1987); Pres. SHOZO KONO; Vice-Pres. RYOICHI FUKUSHIMA.

The Japan Development Bank: 9-1, Ohtemachi 1-chome, Chiyoda-ku, Tokyo 100; tel. (03) 270-3211; telex 24343; f. 1951; provides long-term loans; subscribes for corporate bonds; guarantees corporate obligations; invests in specific projects; borrows funds from govt and abroad; issues external bonds and notes; cap. 233,971m.; loans outstanding 80,314,000m. (March 1988); Gov. Gen. TAKAHASHI; Dep. Gov. SHIJURO OGATA; 7 brs.

National Finance Corporation: Koko Bldg, 9-3, Ohtemachi 1-chome, Chiyoda-ku, Tokyo 100; tel. (03) 270-1361; f. 1949 to provide business funds, particularly to very small enterprises unable to obtain loans from banks and other private financial institutions; cap. 26,000m. (March 1987); Gov. HIROSHI YOSHIMOT; Dep. Gov. TETSUEI TOKUGOUA.

Norinchukin Bank (Central Co-operative Bank for Agriculture, Forestry and Fisheries) 8-3, Ohtemachi 1-chome, Chiyoda-ku, Tokyo 100; tel. (03) 279-0111; telex 23918; f. 1923; main banker to agricultural, forestry and fisheries co-operatives; receives deposits from individual co-operatives, federations and agricultural enterprises; extends loans to these and to local govt authorities and public corpns; adjusts excess and shortage of funds within co-operative system; issues debentures, invests funds and engages in other regular banking business; cap. 45,000m., dep. and debentures 24,019,000m. (Aug. 1987); Pres. OSAMU MORIMOTO; Vice-Pres. SHOSI AKABANE; 40 brs.

The Overseas Economic Co-operation Fund: 4-1, Ohtemachi 1-chome, Chiyoda-ku, Tokyo 100; tel. (03) 215-1311; telex 28790; f. 1961 to provide long-term loans or investments for projects in developing countries; cap. 1,412,244m. (1984); Chair. MITSUHIDE YAMAGUCHI; Pres. SHOUICHI TANIMURA.

Shoko Chukin Bank (Central Co-operative Bank for Commerce and Industry): 10-17, 2-chome, Yaesu, Chuo-ku, Tokyo 104; tel. (03) 272-6111; telex 25388; f. 1936 to provide general banking services to facilitate finance for smaller enterprise co-operatives and other organizations formed mainly by small- and medium-sized enterprises; issues debentures; cap. 214,400m.; dep. and debentures 10,436,700m. (Aug. 1987); Pres. SATOSHI SASAKI; Dep. Pres. HIROSHI YONESATO; 98 brs.

Small Business Finance Corporation: Koko Bldg, 9-3, Ohtemachi 1-chome, Chiyoda-ku, Tokyo 100; tel. (03) 270-1261; f. 1953 to lend plant and equipment funds and long-term operating funds to small businesses (capital not more than 100m., or not more than 300 employees) which are not easily secured from other financial institutions; cap. p.u. 41,910m. (May 1988) wholly subscribed by govt; Gov. KIICHI WATANABE; Vice-Gov. MINORU HARADA.

Principal Foreign Banks

In 1987 there were 79 foreign banks operating in Japan.

Algemene Bank Nederland NV (Netherlands): Fuji Bldg, 2-3, Marunouchi 3-chome, Chiyoda-ku, Tokyo 100, CPOB 374; tel. (03) 211-1767; brs in Kobe, Osaka, Fukuoka; Man. W. A. J. KORTEKAAS.

American Express Bank Ltd (USA): Toranomon Mitsui Bldg, 8-1, Kasumigaseki 3-chome, Chiyoda-ku, Tokyo 100; tel. (03) 595-4571; telex 24880; brs in Naha, Okinawa; Sr Rep. (Japan) and Sr Vice-Pres. RYUSUKE PAUL FUKUDA.

Amro Bank (Netherlands): Yurakucho Denki Bldg, 7-1, Yuraku-cho 1-chome, Chiyoda-ku, Tokyo 100; tel. (03) 284-0701; telex 25830.

Bangkok Bank Ltd (Thailand): Bangkok Bank Bldg, 8-10, Nishishinbashi 2-chome, Minato-ku, Tokyo 105; tel. (03) 503-3333; telex 24373; 1 br.

Bank of America NT & SA: Ark Mori Bldg, 12-32, Akasaka 1-chome, Minato-ku, Tokyo 107; tel. (03) 587-3111; telex 22272; br in Osaka; Sr Vice-Pres. and Area Gen. Man. LARRY GREENBERG.

Bank of India: Mitsubishi Denki Bldg, 2-3, Marunouchi 2-chome, Chiyoda-ku, Tokyo 100; tel. (03) 212-0911; Chief Man. P. K. MUKERJI; br. in Osaka.

Bank Indonesia: Hibiya Park Bldg 310, 8-1, Yuraku-cho 1-chome, Chiyoda-ku, Tokyo 100; tel. (03) 271-3415.

Bank Negara Indonesia 1946: Kokusai Bldg, 1-1, Marunouchi 3-chome, Chiyoda-ku, Tokyo 100; tel. (03) 214-5621; telex 26249; Gen. Man. HERMANSJAH DJAMALUDIN.

Bankers Trust Co (USA): Kishimoto Bldg, 2-1, Marunouchi 2-chome, Chiyoda-ku, Tokyo 100; tel. (03) 286-0720; Man. Dir and Gen. Man. MASAYUKI YASUOKA.

Banque Indosuez (France): Banque Indosuez Bldg, 1-2, Akasaka 1-chome, Minato-ku, Tokyo 107; tel. (03) 582-0271; telex 24309; Gen. Man. BERNARD DELAGE; br. in Osaka and Nagoya.

Banque Nationale de Paris (France): Yusen Bldg, 3-2, Marunouchi 2-chome, Chiyoda-ku, Tokyo 100; tel. (03) 214-2881; telex 24825; Gen. Man. ANDRÉ JULLIEN.

Banque Paribas (France): Yurakucho Denki Bldg, 7-1, Yuraku-cho 1-chome, Chiyoda-ku, Tokyo 100; tel. (03) 214-5881; Gen. Man. DENIS ANTOINE.

Barclays Bank (UK): Mitsubishi Bldg, 5-2, Marunouchi 2-chome, Chiyoda-ku, Tokyo 100; (CPOB 466); tel. (03) 214-3611; telex 24968; Gen. Man. MICHAEL H. TOMALIN.

Bayerische Vereinsbank AG (Federal Republic of Germany): Togin Bldg, 4-2, Marunouchi 1-chome, Chiyoda-ku, Tokyo 100; tel. (03) 284-1341; telex 26351; Gen. Man. Dr PETER BARON.

Chase Manhattan Bank, NA (USA): New Tokio Kaijo Bldg, 1-2, Marunouchi 1-chome, Chiyoda-ku, Tokyo 100; tel. (03) 287-4000; telex 22294; Sr Vice-Pres. and Gen. Man. ROBERT H. BINNEY; br. in Osaka.

Chemical Bank (USA): Mitsubishi Shoji Bldg, Annex, 3-1, Marunouchi 2-chome, Chiyoda-ku, Tokyo 100; tel. (03) 214-1351; Vice-Pres. and Gen. Man. PETER C. HALEY.

Citibank NA (USA): 2-1, Ohtemachi 2-chome, Chiyoda-ku, Tokyo 100; tel. (03) 279-5411; brs in Kobe, Osaka, Yokohama, Nagoya; Divisional Exec. JAMES J. COLLINS.

Commerzbank AG (Federal Republic of Germany): Nippon Press Center Bldg, 2-1, Uchisaiwai-cho 2-chome, Chiyoda-ku, Tokyo 100; tel. (03) 502-4371; Gen. Mans FOLKER STREIB, HANS DIETER BRAMMER.

Continental Illinois National Bank and Trust Co of Chicago (USA): Mitsui Seimei Bldge, 2-3, Ohtemachi 1-chome, Chiyoda-ku, Tokyo 100; tel. (03) 216-1661; telex 2222265; Vice-Pres. and Gen. Man. PETER EBERHARD; 1 br.

Deutsche Bank AG (Federal Republic of Germany): ARK Mori Bldg, 12-32, Akasaka 1-chome, Minato-ku, Tokyo 107; tel. (03) 588-1971; telex 24814; Gen. Mans Dr H. J. BECK, R. DEITERT, Dr H. D. LAUMEYER, T. KAWAHARA.

Dresdner Bank AG (Federal Republic of Germany): Nihonbashi-Muromachi Center Bldg, 8th Floor, 3-2-15, Nihonbashi-Muromachi, Chuo-ku, Tokyo 103; tel. (03) 241-6411; telex 2225295; Chief Gen. Man. Dr PETER-JÖRG KLEIN.

First National Bank of Chicago (USA): Hibiya Central Bldg, 7th Floor, 2-9, Nishishimbashi 1-chome, Minato-ku, Tokyo 105; tel. (03) 502-4961; telex 2224977; Vice-Pres. and Gen. Man. THOMAS H. HODGES.

The Hongkong and Shanghai Banking Corpn (Hong Kong): 1-2, Marunouchi 2-chome, Chiyoda-ku, CPOB 336, Tokyo 100; tel. (03) 211-6461; telex 22372; CEO C. J. CROOK; 4 brs.

International Commercial Bank of China (Taiwan): Togin Bldg, 4-2, Marunouchi 1-chome, Chiyoda-ku, Tokyo 100; tel. (03) 211-2501; telex 22317; Sr Vice-Pres. and Gen. Man. LARRY Y. CHANG; 2 brs.

Korea Exchange Bank (Republic of Korea): Shin Kokusai Bldg, 4-1, Marunouchi 3-chome, Chiyoda-ku, Tokyo 100; tel. (03) 216-3561; telex 24243; f. 1967; Regional Dir and Exec. Vice-Pres. SEUNG-CHUL CHA; 3 brs.

Lloyds Bank PLC (UK): Ote Center Bldg, 5th Floor, 1-3, Ohtemachi 1-chome, Chiyoda-ku, CPOB 464, Tokyo 100; tel. (03) 214-6771; telex 23521; Man. GRAHAM M. HARRIS.

Manufacturers Hanover Trust Co (USA): Asahi Tokai Bldg, 21st Floor, 6-1, Ohtemachi 2-chome, Chiyoda-ku, Tokyo 100; tel. (03) 242-6511; telex 22687; Vice-Pres. and Gen. Man. JAMES R. BOARDMAN.

Midland Bank PLC (UK): AIU Bldg, 1-3, Marunouchi 1-chome, Chiyoda-ku, Tokyo 100; tel. (03) 284-1861; telex 26137; Regional Dir for Japan RAY SOUDAH; Chief Man. WALTER HULATT.

Morgan Guaranty Trust Co (USA): Shin Yurakucho Bldg, 12-1, Yurakucho 1-chome, Chiyoda-ku, Tokyo 100; tel. (03) 282-0230; Sr Vice-Pres. and Gen. Man. WILLIAM R. BARRETT, Jr.

National Bank of Pakistan: 20 Mori Bldg, 7-4, Nishi Shinbashi 2-chome, Minato-ku, Tokyo 105; tel. (03) 502-0331; f. 1949; Man. HAFIZ M. IQBAL.

JAPAN
Directory

National Westminster Bank PLC (UK): AIU Bldg, 1-3, Marunouchi 1-chome, Chiyoda-ku, Tokyo 100; tel. (03) 216-5301; telex 28292; Chief Man. (Japan) A. G. W. Hodge.

Oversea-Chinese Banking Corpn (Singapore): 128 Shin Tokyo Bldg, 3-1, Marunouchi 3-chome, Chiyoda-ku, Tokyo 100; tel. (03) 214-2841; telex 26186; Man. Chua Chian Seng.

Security Pacific National Bank (USA): Ark Mori Bldg, 12-32, Akasaka 1-chome, Minato-ku, POB 524, Tokyo 107; tel. (03) 587-4800; telex 24981; Sr Vice-Pres. S. Lachlan Hough.

Société Générale (France): Hibiya Central Bldg, 1-2-9, Nishi-Shinbashi, Minato-ku, Tokyo 105; tel. (03) 503-9781; telex 28611; Gen. Man. Gilles Piard; Resident Br. Man. Kazuhide Kitanosono.

Standard Chartered Bank (UK): Fuji Bldg, 2-3, Marunouchi 3-chome, Tokyo 100; tel. (03) 213-6541; telex 22484; brs in Kobe and Osaka; Man. C. D. Harrison.

State Bank of India: South Tower 352, Yurakucho Denki Bldg, 1-7-1, Yurakucho, Chiyoda-ku, Tokyo 100; tel. (03) 284-0085; telex 27377; Chief Man. A. K. Sen.

Swiss Bank Corpn: Furukawa Sogo Bldg, 6-1, Marunouchi 2-chome, Chiyoda-ku, Tokyo 100; tel. (03) 214-1731; Sr Vice-Pres. and Man. Eric Tschirren.

Union Bank of Switzerland: Yamato Seimei Bldg, 1-7, Uchisaiwai-cho 1-chome, Chiyoda-ku, Tokyo 100; tel. (03) 595-0121; telex 5950117; Man. Peter Brutsche.

Union de Banques Arabes et Françaises (UBAF) (France): Fukoku Seimei Bldg, 10F, 2-2-2 Uchisaiwai-cho, Chiyoda-ku, Tokyo 100; tel. (03) 595-0801; Man. Maxime Roche.

Westdeutsche Landesbank Girozentrale (Federal Republic of Germany): Kokusai Bldg, 1-1, Marunouchi 3-chome, Chiyoda-ku, Tokyo 100; tel. (03) 216-0581; telex 23859; Gen. Mans Klaus R. Pesch, Ulrich Zierke.

Bankers' Associations

Federation of Bankers' Associations of Japan: 3-1, Marunouchi 1-chome, Chiyoda-ku, Tokyo 100; tel. (03) 216-3761; telex 26830; f. 1945; 72 mem. asscns; Chair. Kazuo Ibuki; Man. Dir Takashi Okada.

  Tokyo Bankers' Association Inc: 3-1, Marunouchi 1-chome, Chiyoda-ku, Tokyo 100; tel. (03) 216-3761; telex 26830; f. 1945; 87 mem. banks; conducts the above Federation's administrative business; Chair. Kazuo Ibuki; Vice-Chair. Kuniji Miyazaki, Mamoru Sakai, Chiaki Kurahara.

Regional Banks Association of Japan: 3-1-2, Uchikanda, Chiyoda-ku, Tokyo 101; tel. (03) 252-5171; f. 1936; 64 mem. banks; Chair. Masataka Okura.

STOCK EXCHANGES

Fukuoka Stock Exchange: 2-14-12, Tenjin, Chuo-ku, Fukuoka 810.

Hiroshima Stock Exchange: 14-18, Kanayama-cho, Hiroshima 730; f. 1949; 20 mems; Prin. Officer Fubito Shimomura.

Nagoya Stock Exchange: 3-17, Sakae-Sanchome, Naka-ku, Nagoya 460; tel. (052) 241-1521; f. 1949; Pres. Junichiro Kumada; Man. Dir Ichiro Kawai.

Osaka Securities Exchange: 2-1, Kitahama, Higashi-ku, Osaka 541; tel. (06) 229-8643; telex 5222215; f. 1949; 94 regular mems, one Nakadachi mem. and three special mems; Chair. Munekazu Yano; Pres. Hiroshi Yamanouchi.

Sapporo Stock Exchange: 5-14-1, Nishi, Minami Ichijo, Chuo-ku, Sapporo.

Tokyo Stock Exchange: 2-1, Nihonbashi-Kabuto-cho, Chuo-ku, Tokyo 103; tel. (03) 666-0141; telex 2522759; f. 1949; 114 mems (incl. 22 foreign mems); Pres. Minoru Nagaoka; Man. Dir Mitsuo Sato.

There are also Stock Exchanges at Kyoto and Niigata.

INSURANCE
Principal Life Companies

Asahi Mutual Life Insurance Co: 7-3, Nishishinjuku 1-chome, Shinjuku-ku, Tokyo 163; tel. (03) 342-3111; telex 2323229; f. 1888; Pres. Yasuyuki Wakahara.

Chiyoda Mutual Life Insurance Co: 19-18, 2-chome, Kamimeguro Meguro, Tokyo 153; tel. (03) 719-5111; telex 2466725; f. 1904; Pres. Yasutaro Kanzaki.

Daido Mutual Life Insurance Co: 1-23-101, Esaka, Suita, Osaka 564; tel. (06) 385-1130; telex 5233311; f. 1902; Chair. Eiji Fukumoto; Pres. Kinichi Yoshizawa.

Daihyaku Mutual Life Insurance Co: 34-1, Kokuryo-cho 4-chome, Chofu-shi, Tokyo 182; tel. (0424) 85-8111; telex 2423063; f. 1914; Chair. Minoru Kawasaki; Pres. Katsuo Fukuchi.

Dai-ichi Mutual Life Insurance Co: 13-1, Yurakucho 1-chome, Chiyoda-ku, Tokyo 100; tel. (03) 216-1211; telex 29848; f. 1902; Chair. Shin-ichi Nishio; Pres. Takahide Sakurai.

Equitable Life Insurance Co Ltd: Togin Kurita Bldg, 3-26 Kanda Nishiki-cho, Chiyoda-ku, Tokyo 101; tel. (03) 233-3911; f. 1986; Chair. and CEO Donald J. Mooney.

Fukoku Mutual Life Insurance Co: 2-2, Uchisaiwaicho 2-chome, Chiyoda-ku, Tokyo 100; tel. (03) 508-1101; f. 1923; Pres. Tetsuo Furuya.

Heiwa Life Insurance Co Ltd: 2-16, Ginza 3-chome, Chuo-ku, Tokyo 104; tel. (03) 562-0351; f. 1907; Pres. Yutaka Takemoto.

INA Life Insurance Co Ltd: Shinjuku Center Bldg, 48F, 1-25-1, Nishi-Shinjuku, Shinjuku-ku, Tokyo 163; tel. (03) 348-7011; telex 32471; f. 1981; Pres. Noboru Oka; 7 brs.

Kyoei Life Insurance Co Ltd: 4-4-1, Hongokucho, Nihonbashi, Chuo-ku, Tokyo 103; tel. (03) 270-8511; telex 2226826; f. 1947; Chair. Masayuki Kitoku; Pres. Yoshio Tayama.

Meiji Mutual Life Insurance Co: 1-1, Marunouchi 2-chome, Chiyoda-ku, Tokyo 100; tel. (03) 283-8111; telex 2224861; f. 1881; Chair. Hiroshi Yamanaka; Pres. Terumichi Tsuchida.

Mitsui Mutual Life Insurance Co: 2-3, Ohtemachi 1-chome, Chiyoda-ku, Tokyo 100; tel. (03) 211-6111; telex 2223261; f. 1927; Chair. Masami Onizawa; Pres. Koshiro Sakata.

Nippon Dantai Life Insurance Co Ltd: 1-2-19, Higashi, Shibuyku, Tokyo 150; tel. (03) 407-6211; telex 2423342; f. 1934; Chair. Sakae Sawabe; Pres. Hajime Odaka.

Nippon Life Insurance Co (Nissei): 7, Imabashi 4-chome, Higashi-ku, Osaka 541; tel. (06) 209-4500; telex 5228783; f. 1889; Chair. Gen. Hirose; Pres. Gentaro Kawase.

Nissan Mutual Life Insurance Co: 6-30, Aobadai 3-chome, Meguro-ku, Tokyo 153; tel. (03) 463-1101; f. 1909; Pres. Ichirozaemon Sakamoto.

Prudential Life Insurance Co Ltd: 1-7, Kojimachi, Chiyoda-ku, Tokyo 102, tel. (03) 221-0961; f. 1987; Pres. Kiyofumi Sakaguchi.

Seibu Allstate Insurance Co Ltd: Sunshine Sixty Bldg, 37th–39th Floors, 1-1, Higashi Ikebukuro 3-chome, Toshima-ku, Tokyo 170; tel. (03) 983-6666; f. 1975; Chair. Seiji Tsutsumi; Pres. Shigeo Ikuno.

Sony Pruco Life Insurance Co Ltd: 1-1, Minamiaoyama 1-chome, Minato-ku, Tokyo 107; tel. (03) 475-8811; Pres. Tamotsu Iba.

Sumitomo Life Insurance Co: 2-2, Nakanoshima 5-chome, Kita-ku, Osaka 530; tel. (06) 231-8401; telex 5222584; f. 1926; Chair. Kenji Chishiro; Pres. Yasuhiko Ueyama.

Taisho Life Insurance Co Ltd: 9-1, Yurakucho 1-chome, Chiyoda-ku, Tokyo 100; tel. (03) 281-7651; f. 1913; Pres. Toshiyuki Koyama.

Taiyo Mutual Life Insurance Co: 11-2, Nihonbashi 2-chome, Chuo-ku, Tokyo 103; tel. (03) 272-6211; Chair. Magodayu Daibu; Pres. Kyojiro Nishiwaki.

Toho Mutual Life Insurance Co: 15-1, Shibuya 2-chome, Shibuya-ku, Tokyo 150; tel. (03) 499-1111; telex 2428069; f. 1898; Chair. Makoto Yasui; Pres. and CEO Seizo Ota.

Tokyo Mutual Life Insurance Co: 5-2, Uchisaiwai-cho 1-chome, Chiyoda-ku, Tokyo 100; tel. (03) 504-2211; telex 2228517; f. 1895; Pres. Masakazu Yogai.

Yamato Mutual Life Insurance Co: 1-7, Uchisaiwai-cho 1-chome, Chiyoda-ku, Tokyo 100; tel. (03) 508-3111; f. 1911; Pres. Yoshio Kohara.

Yasuda Mutual Life Insurance Co: 9-1, Nishishinjuku 1-chome, Shinjuku-ku, Tokyo 160; tel. (03) 342-7111; telex 2322790; f. 1880; Chair. Hajime Yasuda; Pres. Norikazu Okamoto.

Principal Non-Life Companies

Allstate Automobile and Fire Insurance Co Ltd: Sunshine Sixty Bldg, 1-1, Higashi Ikebukuro 3-chome, Toshima-ku, Tokyo 170; tel. (03) 988-2711; telex 2722056; Chair. Richard J. Haayen; Pres. Teru Khono.

Asahi Fire and Marine Insurance Co Ltd: 6-2, Kajicho 2-chome, Chiyoda-ku, Tokyo 101; tel. (03) 254-2211; telex 26974; f. 1951; Pres. Kazuo Ochi.

Chiyoda Fire and Marine Insurance Co Ltd: Kyobashi Chiyoda Bldg, 1-9, Kyobashi 2-chome, Chuo-ku, Tokyo 104; tel. (03) 281-3311; telex 24975; f. 1897; Pres. Takashi Toyabe.

Daido Fire and Marine Insurance Co Ltd: 12-1, 1-chome, Kumoji, Naha-shi, Okinawa; tel. (0988) 67-1161; f. 1971; Pres. Yusho Uezu.

Daiichi Mutual Fire and Marine Insurance Co: 5-1, Niban-cho, Chiyoda-ku, Tokyo 102; tel. (03) 239-0011; telex 26554; f. 1949; Chair. Saburo Kaneko; Pres. Fujio Matsumuro.

Dai-Tokyo Fire and Marine Insurance Co Ltd: 1-6, Nihonbashi 3-chome, Chuo-ku, Tokyo; tel. (03) 272-8811; telex 26968; f. 1918; Chair. Seiichi Sorimachi; Pres. Isao Kosaka.

JAPAN   Directory

Dowa Fire and Marine Insurance Co Ltd: 15-10, 4-chome, Nishitenman, Kita-ku, Osaka; tel. (06) 363-1121; telex 5237305; f. 1944; Pres. Masao Okazaki.

Fuji Fire and Marine Insurance Co Ltd: 11-9, Minamisenba 1-chome, Minami-ku, Osaka; tel. (06) 271-2741; telex 5532326; f. 1918; Chair. Isamu Watanabe; Pres. Hiroshi Kuzuhara.

Japan Earthquake Reinsurance Co Ltd: 6-5, 3-chome, Kanda Surugadai, Chiyoda-ku, Tokyo; tel. (03) 253-3171; f. 1966; Pres. Kenji Atsumi.

Koa Fire and Marine Insurance Co Ltd: 7-3, 3-chome, Kasumigaseki, Chiyoda-ku, Tokyo; tel. (03) 593-3111; telex 2223467; f. 1944; Pres. Minoru Hokari.

Kyoei Mutual Fire and Marine Insurance Co: 18-6, 1-chome, Shimbashi, Minato-ku, Tokyo; tel. (03) 504-0131; telex 22977; f. 1942; Chair. Hideyuki Takagi; Pres. Katsumi Gyotoku.

Nichido Fire and Marine Insurance Co Ltd: 3-16, 5-chome, Ginza, Chuo-ku, Tokyo; tel. (03) 571-5141; telex 26920; f. 1914; Chair. Yoshikazu Sato; Pres. Ikuo Egashira.

Nippon Fire and Marine Insurance Co Ltd: 2-10, Nihonbashi 2-chome, Chuo-ku, Tokyo 103; tel. (03) 272-8111; telex 24214; f. 1892; Chair. Shichisaburo Kawasaki; Pres. Masaji Shinagawa.

Nissan Fire and Marine Insurance Co Ltd: 9-5, 2-chome, Kita-Aoyama, Minato-ku, Tokyo; tel. (03) 404-4111; telex 24983; f. 1911; Pres. Seiichi Honda.

Nisshin Fire and Marine Insurance Co Ltd: Shiba Tokio Kaijo Bldg, 3-3, Shiba 2-chome, Minato-ku, Tokyo 105; tel. (03) 769-2311; telex 2224037; f. 1908; Pres. Hajime Matsumuro.

Sumitomo Marine and Fire Insurance Co Ltd: 27-2, Shinkawa 2-chome, Chuo-ku, Tokyo 104; tel. (03) 297-1111; telex 2223051; f. 1944; Pres. Sumao Tokumasu.

Taisei Fire and Marine Insurance Co Ltd: 2-1, 4-chome, Kudankita, Chiyoda-ku, Tokyo; tel. (03) 234-3111; telex 28351; f. 1950; Chair. Yutaka Shibaike; Pres. Fumio Sato.

Taisho Marine and Fire Insurance Co Ltd: 9, Kanda Surugadai 3-chome, Chiyoda-ku, Tokyo; tel. (03) 259-3111; telex 24670; f. 1918; Pres. Takeru Ishikawa.

Taiyo Fire and Marine Insurance Co Ltd: 18, Kand Nishikicho 3-chome, Chiyoda-ku, Tokyo 101; tel. (03) 293-6511; telex 2225379; f. 1951; Chair. Tamotsu Yokota; Pres. Kiyoshi Endo.

Toa Fire and Marine Reinsurance Co Ltd: 6-5, 3-chome, Kanda Surugadai, Chiyoda-ku, Tokyo; tel. (03) 253-3171; telex 24384; f. 1940; Chair. Mokuji Kashiwagi; Pres. Sumiyoshi Kusakabe.

Tokio Marine and Fire Insurance Co Ltd (Tokio Kaijo): 2-1, Marunouchi 1-chome, Chiyoda-ku, Tokyo 100; tel. (03) 212-6211; telex 24858; f. 1879; Chair. (vacant); Pres. Haruo Takeda.

Toyo Fire and Marine Insurance Co Ltd: 9-15, 1-chome, Nihonbashi-honcho, Chuo-ku, Tokyo 103; tel. (03) 245-1411; telex 2226334; f. 1950; Chair. Tsunekazu Sakano; Pres. Eizo Takao.

Yasuda Fire and Marine Insurance Co Ltd: 26-1, Nishi-shinjuku 1-chome, Shinjuku-ku, Tokyo 160; tel. (03) 349-3111; telex 2322790; f. 1887; Pres. Yasuo Goto.

The Post Office also operates life insurance and annuity plans.

Insurance Associations

Fire and Marine Insurance Rating Association of Japan: Non-Life Insurance Bldg, 9, Kanda Awajicho 2-chome, Chiyoda-ku, Tokyo 101; tel. (03) 255-1211; f. 1948; Chair. Masaji Shinagawa; Pres. Kenjiro Yamazaki.

Life Insurance Association of Japan (Seimei Hoken Kyokai): New Kokusai Bldg, 4-1, Marunouchi 3-chome, Chiyoda-ku, Tokyo 100; tel. (03) 286-2734; f. 1908; 24 mem. cos; Chair. Yoshihiko Ueyama; Exec. Dir Yoshikata Nakaouji.

Marine and Fire Insurance Association of Japan Inc: Non-Life Insurance Bldg, 9, Kanda Awajicho 2-chome, Chiyoda-ku, Tokyo 101; tel. (03) 255-1211; telex 2224829; f. 1971; 23 mems; Pres. Takeru Ishikawa; Vice-Pres. and Exec. Dir Yoshikazu Hanawa.

Trade and Industry

CHAMBERS OF COMMERCE AND INDUSTRY

The Japan Chamber of Commerce and Industry (Nippon Shoko Kaigi-sho): 2-2, 3-chome, Marunouchi, Chiyoda-ku, Tokyo; tel. (03) 283-7851; f. 1922; the cen. org. of all chambers of commerce and industry in Japan; mems 489 local chambers of commerce and industry; Chair. Rokuro Ishikawa.

Principal chambers include:

Kobe Chamber of Commerce and Industry: Kobe CIT Center Bldg, 1-14, Hamabe-dori 5-chome, Chuo-ku, Kobe 651; tel. (078) 251-1001; f. 1878; 10,268 mems; Chair. Shinichi Ishino; Pres. Takuji Ishihara.

Kyoto Chamber of Commerce and Industry: 240, Shoshoicho, Ebisugawa-agaru, Karasumadori, Nakakyo-ku, Kyoto 604; tel. (075) 231-0181; telex 5422222; f. 1882; 9,942 mems; Pres. Koichi Tsukamoto; Sr Man. Dir Hiroshi Uno.

Nagoya Chamber of Commerce and Industry: 10-19, Sakae 2-chome, Naka-ku, Nagoya, Aichi 460; tel. (052) 221-7211; telex 4424836; f. 1881; 10,235 mems; Pres. Kotaro Takeda; Sr Man. Dir Yoshihisa Harada.

Naha Chamber of Commerce and Industry: 2-2-4, Kume Naha, Okinawa; tel. 68-3758; f. 1950; 2,856 mems; Pres. Kotaro Kokuba.

Osaka Chamber of Commerce and Industry: 58-7, Uchihonmachi Hashizume-cho, Higashi-ku, Osaka; tel. (06) 944-6215; f. 1878; 25,850 mems; Pres. Susumu Furukawa; Sr Man. Dir Hironari Masago.

Tokyo Chamber of Commerce and Industry: 2-2, Marunouchi 3-chome, Chiyoda-ku, Tokyo; tel. (03) 283-7500; telex 2224920; f. 1878; 60,000 mems; Pres. Rokuro Ishikawa; Man. Dir Hiroshi Ikawa.

Yokohama Chamber of Commerce and Industry: 2, Yamashita-cho, Naka-ku, Yokohama; tel. 671-7400; f. 1880; 13,185 mems; Pres. Yutaka Uyeno; Sr Man. Dir Hirochika Kobayashi.

FOREIGN TRADE ORGANIZATIONS

The Association for the Promotion of International Trade, Japan (JAPIT): Nippon Bldg, 5th Floor, 2-6-2, Ohtemachi, Chiyoda-ku, Tokyo; tel. (03) 245-1561; telex 2228471; f. 1954 to promote trade with the People's Repub. of China; Chair. Takamaru Morita; Pres. Y. Sakurauchi.

Council of All-Japan Exporters' Association: Kikai Shinko Kaikan Bldg, 5-8, Shibakoen 3-chome, Minato-ku, Tokyo; tel. (03) 431-9507.

Japan External Trade Organization (JETRO): 2-5, Toranomon 2-chome, Minato-ku, Tokyo 105; tel. (03) 582-5522; telex 24378; f. 1958; information for foreign firms, investigation of foreign markets, exhbns of Japanese commodities abroad, import promotion, etc.; Chair. Shoichi Akazawa; Pres. Masuo Shibata.

Nihon Boeki-Kai (Japan Foreign Trade Council, Inc): 6th Floor, World Trade Center Bldg, 4-1, 2-chome, Hamamatsu-cho, Minato-ku, Tokyo 105; tel. (03) 435-5952; f. 1947; 307 mems; Pres. Yohei Mimura; Man. Dir Toshinori Hayashi.

TRADE ASSOCIATIONS

Japan Canned Foods Exporters' Association: Fuji Bldg, 6th Floor, 5-3, Yaesu 1-chome, Chuo-ku, Tokyo; tel. (03) 281-5341.

Japan General Merchandise Exporters' Association: 4-1, Hamamatsu-cho 2-chome, Minato-ku, Tokyo; tel. (03) 435-3471; f. 1953; 320 mems; Pres. Hiroshi Toyama.

Japan Hardwood Exporters' Association: Matsuda Bldg 9-1, 1-chome, Ironai, Otaru, Hokkaido 047; tel. 23-8411; telex 952701.

Japan Iron and Steel Exporters' Association: 3-2-10, Nihonbashi-Kayabacho, Chuo-ku, Tokyo; tel. (03) 669-4811.

Japan Lumber Importers' Association: Yushi Kogyo Bldg, 13-11, Nihonbashi 3-chome, Chuo-ku, Tokyo 103; tel. (03) 271-0926; f. 1950; 118 mems; Pres. S. Otsubo.

Japan Machinery Exporters' Association: Kikai Shinko Kaikan Bldg, 5-8, Shiba-Koen 3-chome, Minato-ku, Tokyo 105; tel. (03) 431-9507; telex 24744; Pres. Taiichiro Matsuo.

Japan Machinery Importers' Association: Koyo Bldg, 8th Floor, 2-11, Toranomon 1-chome, Minato-ku, Tokyo; tel. (03) 503-9736; f. 1957; 122 mems; Pres. Taiichiro Matsuo.

Japan Paper Exporters' Association: Kami Parupu Bldg, 9-11, Ginza 3-chome, Chuo-ku, Tokyo; tel. (03) 541-8108; f. 1959; 67 mems; Chair. Shigeru Uchimura.

Japan Paper Importers' Association: Kami Parupu Bldg, 9-11, Ginza 3-chome, Chuo-ku, Tokyo; tel. (03) 541-8109; f. 1981; 55 mems; Chair. Takaharu Matsui.

Japan Pearl Exporters' Association: 122 Higashi-machi, Chuo-ku, Kobe; Tokyo branch: 6-15, 3-chome, Kyobashi, Chuo-ku; tel. (03) 561-7807; f. 1954; Pres. Hiro Otsuki.

Japan Pharmaceutical, Medical and Dental Supply Exporters' Association: 7-1, Nihonbashi-Honcho 4-chome, Chuo-ku, Tokyo 103; tel. (03) 241-2106; f. 1953; 180 mem. firms; Pres. Tomio Fujiwara; Man. Dir Kuniichiro Ohno.

Japan Ship Exporters' Association: Senpaku-Shinko Bldg, 1-15-16, Toranomon, Minato-ku, Tokyo 105; tel. (03) 502-2094; telex 26421; Sr Man. Dir Yuichi Watanabe.

Japan Sugar Import and Export Council: Ginza Gas-Hall, 9-15, 7-chome, Ginza, Chuo-ku, Tokyo; tel. (03) 571-2362.

Japan Tea Exporters' Association: 81-1, Kitaban-cho, Shizuoka, Shizuoka Prefecture 420; tel. (0542) 71-3428; telex 520331.

JAPAN

TRADE FAIR

Tokyo International Trade Fair Commission: 7-24, Harumi 4-chome, Chuo-ku, CPOB 1201, Tokyo 104; tel. (03) 531-3371; telex 2523935.

PRINCIPAL INDUSTRIAL ORGANIZATIONS

General

Industry Club of Japan: 4-6, Marunouchi 1-chome, Chiyoda-ku, Tokyo; tel. (03) 281-1711; f. 1917 to develop closer relations between industrialists at home and abroad and promote expansion of Japanese business activities; c. 1,600 mems; Pres. BUNPEI OTSUKI; Exec. Dir TAKASHI DAI.

Japan Association of Corporate Executives (Keizai Doyukai): Nippon Kogyo Club Bldg, 1-4-6, Marunouchi, Chiyoda-ku, Tokyo 100; tel. (03) 211-1271; telex 32531; f. 1946; mems: business groups concerned with national and international economic and social policies; Chair. TAKASHI ISHIHARA.

Japan Commercial Arbitration Association: Izumi Shibakoen Bldg, 6-8, Shibakoen 1-chome, Minato-ku, Tokyo 105; tel. (03) 435-0710; f. 1950; 1,104 mems; provides facilities for mediation, conciliation and arbitration in international trade disputes; Pres. ROKURO ISHIKAWA.

Japan Federation of Economic Organizations (KEIDANREN) (Keizaidantai Rengo-Kai): 9-4, Ohtemachi 1-chome, Chiyoda-ku, Tokyo, 100; tel. (03) 279-1411; telex 2223188; f. 1946; private non-profit assen studying domestic and international economic problems; mems 121 industrial orgs, 877 corpns (1986); Chair. EISHIRO SAITO; Exec. Vice-Chair. NIHACHIRO HANAMURA.

Japan Federation of Employers' Associations (NIKKEIREN) (Nihon Keieisha Dantai Renmei): 4-6, Marunouchi 1-chome, Chiyoda-ku, Tokyo 100; tel. (03) 213-4463; telex 2223244; f. 1948; 100 mem. asscns; Dir-Gen. YASUICHI OGAWA; Sec.-Gen. HIROSHI KITAMURA.

Japan Federation of Smaller Enterprise Organizations (JFSEO): 2-8-4 Nihonbashi, Kayabacho, Chuo-ku, Tokyo 103; tel. (03) 668-2481; f. 1948; 18 mems and c. 1,000 co-operative socs; Pres. MASATAKA TOYODA; Chair. of Int. Affairs SEIICHI ONO.

Japan Productivity Centre (Nihon Seisansei Honbu): 3-1-1 Shibuya, Shibuya-ku, Tokyo 150; tel. (03) 409-1111; telex 23296; f. 1955; 10,000 mems; concerned with management problems; Chair. TOMITARO HIRATA; Pres. JINNOSUKE MIYAI.

Chemicals

Federation of Pharmaceutical Manufacturers' Associations of Japan: 9, 2-chome, Nihonbashi Hon-chu, Chuo-ku, Tokyo; tel. (03) 270-0581.

Japan Perfumery and Flavouring Association: Nitta Bldg, 2-1, Ginza 8-chome, Chuo-ku, Tokyo 104; tel. (03) 571-3855; f. 1947; Chair. EIICHI TOGASHI.

Japan Chemical Industry Association: Tokyo Club Bldg, 2-6, 3-chome, Kasumigaseki, Chiyoda-ku, Tokyo 100; tel. (03) 580-0751; telex 23557; f. 1948; 248 mems; Pres. SEIJI SUZUKI.

Japan Cosmetic Industry Association: Hatsumei Bldg, 9-14, Toranomon 2-chome, Minato-ku, Tokyo 105; tel. (03) 502-0576; f. 1959; 487 mem. cos; Chair. YOSHIO OHNO; Man. Dir KAORU MIYAZAWA.

Japan Gas Association: 15-12, Toranomon 1-chome, Minato-ku, Tokyo 105; tel. (03) 502-0111; telex 2222374; f. 1952; Pres. MASAFUMI OHNISHI; Vice-Pres. YOSHIMITSU SHIBASAKI.

Japan Inorganic Chemical Industry Association: Sanko Bldg, 1-13-1, Ginza Chuo-ku, Tokyo; tel. (03) 563-1326; f. 1948; Pres. KAN-ICHI TANAHASHI.

Photo-Sensitized Materials Manufacturers' Association: Kyodo Bldg, 2, 2-chome, Kanda Nishikicho, Chiyoda-ku, Tokyo 101; tel. (03) 291-6626; f. 1948; Pres. MINORU OHNISHI.

Fishing and Pearl Cultivation

Japan Fisheries Association (Dai-nippon Suisan Kai): Sankaido Bldg, 9-13, Akasaka 1, Minato-ku, Tokyo; tel. (03) 585-6683; Pres. YOSHIHIDE UCHIMURA.

Japan Pearl Export and Processing Co-operative Association: 7, 3-chome, Kyobashi, Chuo-ko, Tokyo; f. 1951; 130 mems.

National Federation of Medium Trawlers: Toranomon Chuo Bldg, 1-16, Toranomon 1, Minato-ku, Tokyo; tel. (03) 508-0361; telex 2225404; f. 1948.

Paper and Printing

Japan Federation of Printing Industries: 1-16-8, Shintomi, Chuo-ku, Tokyo; tel. (03) 553-6051; Pres. YOSHITOSHI KITAJIMA.

Japan Paper Association: Kami-Parupu Kaikan Bldg, Ginza 3-chome, 9-11 Chuo-ku, Tokyo; tel. (03) 543-2411; telex 2522907; f. 1946; 62 mems; Chair. A. SUHARA; Pres. S. HOSHINO.

Japan Paper Products Manufacturers' Association: 2-6, Kotobuki 4-chome, Taito-ku, Tokyo; tel. (03) 543-2411; f. 1949; Exec. Dir KIYOSHI SATOH.

Mining and Petroleum

Asbestos Cement Products Association: Takahashi Bldg, 10-8, 7-chome, Ginza, Chuo-ku, Tokyo; tel. (03) 571-1359; f. 1937; Chair. KOSHIRO SHIMIZU.

Cement Association of Japan: Hattori Bldg, 10-3, Kyobashi 1-chome, Chuo-ku, Tokyo 104; tel. (03) 561-8631; f. 1948; 22 mem. cos; Chair. H. KOBAYASHI; Exec. Man. Dir H. KUROSAWA.

Japan Coal Association: Hibiya Park Bldg, 1-8, Yuraku-cho 1-chome, Chiyoda-ku, Tokyo; tel. (03) 271-3484.

Japan Mining Industry Association: Shin-hibiya Bldg, 3-6, Uchisaiwai-cho 1-chome, Chiyoda-ku, Tokyo 100; tel. (03) 502-7451; f. 1948; 59 mem. cos; Pres. S. NIRATANI; Dir-Gen. T. ISHIKAWA.

Japan Petroleum Industry Association: Keidanren Kaikan, 9-4, 1-chome, Ohtemachi, Chiyoda-ku, Tokyo; tel. (03) 279-5841; telex 29400; f. 1961; Chair. JUN'NOSUKE HIDAKA; Pres. YASUOKI TAKEUCHI.

Metals

Japan Brass Makers' Association: 12-22, 1-chome, Tsukiji, Chuo-ku, Tokyo; f. 1948; 30 mems; Pres. K. TAKAHASHI; Man. Dir K. ABE.

Japan Iron and Steel Federation: Keidanren Kaikan, 1-9-4, Ohtemachi, Chiyoda-ku, Tokyo; tel. (03) 279-3611; telex 2224210; f. 1948; Chair. Y. TAKEDA.

Japan Light Metal Association: Nihonbashi Asahiseimei Bldg, 1-3, Nihonbashi 2-chome, Chuo-ku, Tokyo 103; tel. (03) 273-3041; f. 1947; 175 mems.

Japan Stainless Steel Association: Tekko Kaikan Bldg, 2-10, Nihonbashi Kayaba-cho 3-chome, Chuo-ku, Tokyo 103; tel. (03) 669-4431; Pres. MITSUNOBU KURITA; Exec. Dir KENICHIRO AOKI.

The Kozai Club: c/o Tekko Kaikan, 3-2-10, Nihonbashi Kayabacho, Chuo-ku, Tokyo; tel. (03) 669-4811; telex 2523607; f. 1947; mems 34 mfrs, 85 dealers; Chair. HIROSHI SAITO.

Steel Castings and Forgings Association of Japan (JSCFA): Tekko Bldg, 8-2, 1-chome, Marunouchi, Chiyoda-ku, Tokyo 100; tel. (03) 201-0461; f. 1972; mems 54 cos, 61 plants; Exec. Dir ATSUO NAKAJIMA.

Machinery and Precision Equipment

Electronic Industries Association of Japan: Tosho Bldg, 2-2, 3-chome, Marunouchi, Chiyoda-ku, Tokyo; tel. (03) 211-2765; f. 1948; mems 580 firms; Pres. KATSUSHIGE MITA.

Japan Camera Industry Association: Mori Bldg, No 9, 2-2, Atago 1-chome, Minato-ku, Tokyo 105; tel. (03) 434-2631; f. 1954; Pres. SHIGETADA FUKUOKA.

Japan Clock and Watch Association: Nomura Bldg, 2-1-1, Ohtemachi, Chiyoda-ku, Tokyo 100; tel. (03) 241-4300.

Japan Electric Association: 1-7-1, Yurakucho, Chiyoda-ku, Tokyo 100; tel. (03) 216-0551; f. 1921; 4,385 mems; Pres. SEIZO YOSHIMURA.

Japan Electric Measuring Instruments Manufacturers' Association: 1-9-10, Toranomon, Minato-ku, Tokyo 105; tel. (03) 502-0601.

Japan Electrical Manufacturers' Association: 4-15, 2-chome, Nagata-cho, Chiyoda-ku, Tokyo 100; tel. (03) 581-4844; telex 2222619; f. 1948; mems 245 firms; Chair. KATSUSHIGE MITA.

Japan Machine Tool Builders' Association: Kikai Shinko Bldg, 3-5-8, Shiba-Koen, Minato-ku, Tokyo 105; tel. (03) 434-3961; telex 22943; f. 1951; 113 mems; Exec. Dir S. ABE.

Japan Machinery Federation: Kikai Shinko Bldg, 5-8-3, Shiba-Koen, Minato-ku, Tokyo 105; tel. (03) 434-5381; f. 1952; Exec. Vice-Pres. SHINICHI NAKANISHI.

Japan Microscope Manufacturers' Association: c/o Olympus Optical Co Ltd, 43-2, Hatagaya 2-chome, Shibuya-ku, Tokyo 151; tel. (03) 377-2139; f. 1954; 25 mem. firms; Chair. S. KITAMURA.

Japan Motion Picture Equipment Industrial Association: Kikai-Shinko Bldg, 5-8, Shiba-Koen 3-chome, Minato-ku, Tokyo 105; tel. (03) 434-3911; Pres. MASAO SHIKATA; Gen. Sec. TERUHIRO KATO.

Japan Optical Industry Association: Kikai-Shinko Bldg, 3-5-8, Shiba-Koen, Minato-ku, Tokyo 105; tel. (03) 431-7073; f. 1946; 200 mems; Exec. Dir M. SUZUKI.

Japan Power Association: Uchisaiwai Bldg, 1-4-2, Uchisaiwai-cho, Chiyoda-ku, Tokyo 100; tel. (03) 501-3988; telex 28599; f. 1950; 112 mems; Pres. ICHIRO HORI; Exec. Dir FUJIO SAKAGAMI.

Japan Society of Industrial Machinery Manufacturers: Kikai Shinko Bldg, 3-5-8, Shiba-koen, Minato-ku, Tokyo 105; tel. (03) 434-6821; f. 1948; 263 mems; Chair. GAKUJI MORIYA.

JAPAN   Directory

Japan Textile Machinery Association: Kikai Shinko Kaikan, Room 310, 3-5-8, Shibakoen, Minato-ku, Tokyo 105; tel. (03) 434-3821; f. 1951; Pres. YOSHITOSHI TOYODA.

Textiles

Central Raw Silk Association of Japan: 7, 1-chome, Yuraku-cho, Chiyoda-ku, Tokyo.

Japan Chemical Fibres Association: 1-20, Nihonbashi-Muromachi, 3-chome, Chuo-ku, Tokyo 103; tel. (03) 241-2311; telex 2222304; f. 1948; 55 mems, 17 assoc. mems; Pres. YOSHIKAZU ITO; Dir-Gen. RYOHEI SUZUKI.

Japan Cotton and Staple Fibre Weavers' Association: 8-7, Nishi-Azabu 1-chome, Minato-ku, Tokyo; tel. (03) 403-9671.

Japan Silk and Rayon Weavers' Association: 15-12, Kudankita 1-chome, Chiyoda-ku, Tokyo; tel. (03) 262-4101.

Japan Silk Spinners' Association: Mengyo Kaikan Bldg, 8, 3-chome, Bingo Machi, Higashi-ku, Osaka; tel. (06) 232-3886; f. 1948; 95 mem. firms; Chair. ICHIJI OHTANI.

Japan Wool Spinners' Association: Sen-i-Kaikan Ueno DK Bldg, 4-15, Ueno 1-chome, Taitoh-ku, Tokyo; tel. (03) 837-7916; f. 1948; Chair. Y. NISHIMURA.

Japan Worsted and Woollen Weavers' Association: Sen-i-Kaikan 9, 3-chome, Nihonbashi Honcho, Chuo-ku, Tokyo; f. 1948; Chair. S. OGAWA; Man. Dir K. OHTANI.

Transport Machinery

Japan Association of Rolling Stock Industries: Daiichi Tekko Bldg, 8-2, Marunouchi 1-chome, Chiyoda-ku, Tokyo; tel. (03) 201-1911.

Japan Auto Parts Industries Association: 1-16-15, Takanawa, Minato-ku, Tokyo 108; tel. (03) 445-4211; telex 242-2829; f. 1948; 390 mem. firms; Chair. Y. NOBUMOTO; Exec. Dir Y. NAKAMURA.

Japan Automobile Manufacturers' Association, Inc: Ohtemachi Bldg, 6-1, Ohtemachi 1-chome, Chiyoda-ku, Tokyo; tel. (03) 216-5771; telex 2223410; f. 1967; 13 mem. firms; Pres. S. TOYODA; Exec. Man. Dir TAKAO TOMINAGA.

Japan Bicycle Manufacturers' Association: 9-3, Akasaka 1-chome, Minato-ku, Tokyo 107; tel. (03) 583-3123; f. 1955.

Japanese Shipowners' Association: Kaiun Bldg, 6-4, Hirakawacho 2-chome, Chiyoda-ku, Tokyo; tel. (03) 264-7171; telex 2322148.

Shipbuilders' Association of Japan: Senpaku Shinko Bldg, 1-15-16, Toranomon, Minato-ku, Tokyo 105; tel. (03) 502-2010; telex 2227056; f. 1947; 50 mems; Chair. KENKO HASEGAWA; Exec. Man. Dir TAKUJI SHINDO.

Ship-Machinery Manufacturers' Association of Japan: Senpaku-Shinko Bldg, 1-15-16, Toranomon, Minato-ku, Tokyo 105; tel. (03) 502-2041; f. 1956; 246 mems; Pres. HIDEO WASHIO.

Society of Japanese Aerospace Companies Inc (SJAC): Hibiya Park Bldg, Suite 518, 8-1, Yurakucho 1-chome, Chiyoda-ku, Tokyo 100; tel. (03) 211-5678; f. 1952; reorg. 1974; 143 mems, 34 assoc. mems; Chair. KENKO HASEGAWA; Exec. Dir YASUICHI ARAO.

Miscellaneous

Communications Industry Association of Japan (CIA-J): Sankei Bldg (annex), 1-7-2, Ohtemachi, Chiyoda-ku, Tokyo 100; tel. (03) 231-3156; f. 1948; non-profit org. of telecommunications equipment mfrs; Chair. KATSUSHIGE MITA; Pres. HARUO OZAWA; 240 mems.

Japan Canners' Association: Marunouchi Bldg, 4-1, Marunouchi 2-chome, Chiyoda-ku, Tokyo; tel. (03) 213-4751.

Japan Fur Association: Ginza-Toshin Bldg, 3-11-15, Ginza, Chuo-ku, Tokyo; tel. (03) 541-6987; f. 1950; Chair. KIYOJI NAKAMURA; Sec. NORIHIDE SATOH.

Japan Plastics Industry Association: Tokyo Club Bldg, 2-6, Kasumigaseki 3-chome, Chiyoda-ku, Tokyo; tel. (03) 580-0771.

Japan Plywood Manufacturers' Association: Meisan Bldg, 18-17, 1-chome, Nishishinbashi, Minato-ku, Tokyo; tel. (03) 591-9246; f. 1965; 149 mems; Pres. AKIO FUJINAKA.

Japan Pottery Manufacturers' Federation: Toto Bldg, 1-28, Toranomon 1-chome, Minato-ku, Tokyo; tel. (03) 503-6761.

The Japan Rubber Manufacturers' Association: Tobu Bldg, 1-5-26, Moto Akasaka, Minato-ku, Tokyo 107; tel. (03) 408-7101; f. 1950; 161 mems; Pres. HISAAKI SUZUKI.

Japan Spirits and Liquors Makers' Association: Koura Dai-ichi Bldg, 7th Floor, 1-6, Nihonbashi-Kayabacho 1-chome, Chuo-ku, Tokyo 103; tel. (03) 668-4621.

Japan Sugar Refiners' Association: 5-7, Sanbancho, Chiyoda-ku, Tokyo 102; tel. (03) 262-0176; f. 1949; 18 mems; Sr Man. Dir EIICHI FUJITA.

Motion Picture Producers' Association of Japan: Sankei Bldg, 7-2, 1-chome, Ohtemachi, Chiyoda-ku, Tokyo 100; tel. (03) 231-6417; Pres. SHIGERU OKADA.

Tokyo Toy Manufacturers' Association: 4-16-3, Higashi-Komagata Sumida-ku, Tokyo 130; tel. (03) 624-0461.

TRADE UNIONS

A feature of Japan's trade union movement is that the unions are in general based on single enterprises, embracing workers of different occupations in that enterprise. In 1986 union membership stood at 12.4m. workers (28.9% of the total labour force). In November 1987 the major private trade union federations (DOMEI, CHURITSUROREN and SHINSAMBETSU—see below) agreed to merge into a confederation, RENGO (National Federation of Private Sector Trade Unions; Pres. TOSHIFUMI TATEYAMA; Sec.-Gen. SEIGO YAMADA; 5.5m. mems).

Principal Federations

General Council of Trade Unions of Japan (SOHYO) (Nihon Rodo Kumiai Sohyogikai): Sohyo Kaikan Bldg, 2-11, Kanda Surugadai 3-chome, Chiyoda-ku, Tokyo; tel. (03) 251-0311; f. 1950; c. 4.3m. mems; Pres. TAKESHI KUROKAWA; Sec.-Gen. EIKICHI MAGARA.

Major affiliated unions:

All-Japan Express Workers' Union (Zennitsu): Zennitsu Kasumigaseki Bldg, 3-3-3 Kasumigaseki, Chiyoda-ku, Tokyo; tel. (03) 581-2261; 45,100 mems; Pres. M. OHNISHI.

Federation of Telecommunications Electronic Information and Allied Workers (Dentsuroren): 2-19, Soto Kanda 2-chome, Chiyoda-ku, Tokyo; tel. (03) 253-3214; 331,897 mems; Pres. AKIRA YAMAGISHI.

General Federation of Private Railway and Bus Workers' Unions (Shitetsusoren): Shitetsu Kaikan Bldg, 3-5, Takanawa 4-chome, Minato-ku, Tokyo; tel. (03) 473-0166; 200,000 mems; Pres. TAKESHI KUROKAWA.

Japan Postal Workers' Union (Zentei): Zentei Kaikan Bldg, 2-7, Koraku 1-chome, Bunkyo-ku, Tokyo; tel. (03) 812-4261; 186,170 mems; Pres. M. MORIHARA.

Japan Teachers' Union (Nikkyoso): Kyoiku Kaikan Bldg, 6-2, Hitotsubashi 2-chome, Chiyoda-ku, Tokyo; tel. (03) 262-8901; 677,300 mems; Chair. TARAOSHI FUKADA; Pres. I. TANAKA.

Japanese Federation of Steel Workers' Unions (Tekko Roren): 1-23-4, Shinkawa, Chuo-ku, Tokyo 104; tel. (03) 555-0401; 211,886 mems; Pres. K. NIINUMA.

National Council of Local and Municipal Government Workers' Unions (Jichiro): Jichiro Kaikan Bldg, 1 Rokubancho, Chiyoda-ku, Tokyo; tel. (03) 263-0261; f. 1951; 1.3m. mems; Pres. Y. MARUYAMA; Gen. Sec. NOBORU CHIBA.

National Federation of Chemical and Synthetic Chemical Industry Workers' Unions (Gokaroren): Senbai Bldg, 26-30, Shiba 5-chome, Minato-ku, Tokyo; tel. (03) 452-5591; 125,292 mems; Pres. T. MIYAUCHI.

National Metal and Engineering Workers Union (Zenkoku Kinzoku): 15-11, Sakuragaoka, Shibuya-ku, Tokyo; tel. (03) 463-4231; f. 1950; 157,159 mems; Pres. YOSHIO HASHIMURA.

National Railway Workers' Union (Kokuro): Kokuro Kaikan Bldg, 11-4, Marunouchi 1-chome, Chiyoda-ku, Tokyo; tel. (03) 212-0580; 45,000 mems; Pres. T. ROPPONGI.

National Union of General Workers, Sohyo (Zenkoku Ippan): 5-6, Misakicho 3-chome, Chiyoda-ku, Tokyo; tel. (03) 230-4071; 123,000 mems; Pres. S. MORISHITA.

Japanese Confederation of Labour (DOMEI*) (Zen Nihon Rodo Sodomei): 20-12, Shiba 2-chome, Minato-ku, Tokyo; tel. (03) 453-5371; telex 25908; f. 1964; c. 2.1m. mems; affiliated to ICFTU; Pres. TADANOBU USAMI; Gen. Sec. YOSHIKAZU TANAKA.

Major affiliated unions:

All-Japan Postal Labour Union (Zenyusei): 20-6, Sandagaya 1-chome, Shibuya-ku, Tokyo 151; tel. (03) 478-7101; 60,962 mems; Pres. HIDEMASA FUKUI; Gen. Sec. KENJI HACHISU.

All-Japan Seamen's Union (Kaiin Kumiai): 15-26, Roppongi 7-chome, Minato-ku, Tokyo; tel. (03) 403-6261; telex 2425112; 124,000 mems; Pres. KAZUKIYO DOI.

Federation of All Nissan and General Workers' Unions (Nissan Roren): 4-26, Kaigan 1-chome, Minato-ku, Tokyo 105; tel. (03) 434-4721; telex 2422385; 220,000 mems; Pres. HARUKI SHIMIZU; Gen. Sec. KATSUNARI AKITA.

Federation of Electric Power Workers' Unions of Japan (Denryokuroren): 7-15, Mita 2-chome, Minato-ku, Tokyo 108; tel. (03) 454-0231; 136,704 mems; Pres. OSAMU SUZUKI; Gen. Sec. SEIJI NODA.

Japan Confederation of Shipbuilding and Engineering Workers' Unions (Zosenjukiroren): 2-20-12, Shiba, Minato-ku, Tokyo 105; tel. (03) 451-6783; 120,941 mems; Pres. TOSHINORI ARIMURA; Gen. Sec. SUKESADA ITOH.

Japan Federation of Transport Workers' Unions (Kotsuroren): 2-20-12, Shiba, Minato-ku, Tokyo 105; tel. (03) 451-7243; 101,388 mems; Pres. HIROO MITSUOKA; Gen. Sec. BUNICHI TAMURA.

Japan Railway Workers' Union (Tetsuro): 2-20-12, Shiba, Minato-ku, Tokyo; tel. (03) 453-9081; 46,247 mems; Pres. SHIGEYUKI TSUJIMOTO; Gen. Sec. YOSHITATSU SHIMA.

Japanese Federation of Chemical and General Trade Unions (Zenkadomei): 2-20-12, Shiba, Minato-ku, Tokyo 105; tel. (03) 453-3801; f. 1951; 115,000 mems; Pres. HIROICHI HONDA; Gen. Sec. YOSHIKAZU UENO.

Japanese Federation of Textile, Garment, Chemical, Mercantile and Allied Industry Workers' Unions (Zensen): 8-16, Kudan Minami 4-chome, Chiyoda-ku, Tokyo 102; tel. (03) 265-7521; f. 1946; 1,497 affiliates; 515,029 mems; Pres. USAMI TADANOBU; Gen. Sec. JINNOSUKE ASHIDA.

Japanese Metal Industrial Workers' Union (Zenkin Domei): 2-20-12, Shiba, Minato-ku, Tokyo 105; tel. (03) 451-2141; f. 1951; 300,000 mems; Pres. IWAO FUJIWARA; Gen. Sec. AKIRA IMAIZUMI.

National Federation of General Workers' Unions (Ippan Domei): 2-20-12, Shiba, Minato-ku, Tokyo 105; tel. (03) 453-5869; 110,938 mems; Pres. KAZUO MAEKAWA; Gen. Sec. TSUTAE SATOH.

Federation of Independent Unions of Japan (CHURITSURO-REN*) (Churitsu Rodo Kumiai Renraku Kaigil): Denkiroren Kaikan Bldg, 3rd Floor, 10-3, 1-chome, Mita, Minato-ku, Tokyo; tel. (03) 455-6801; f. 1956; 1,512,352 mems; Pres. MITSUHARU WARASHINA; Gen. Sec. MANABU TAGUCHI.

Major affiliated unions:

Japanese Federation of Electrical Machine Workers' Unions (Denki Roren): Denkiroren Kaikan Bldg, 10-3, 1-chome, Mita, Minato-ku, Tokyo; tel. (03) 455-6911; f. 1953; 609,197 mems; Pres. MITSUHARU WARASHINA.

Japanese Federation of Food and Allied Workers' Unions (Shokuhin Roren): Hiroo Office Bldg, 3-18, Hiroo 1-chome, Shibuya-ku, Tokyo; tel. (03) 446-2082; f. 1965; 68,979 mems; Pres. KENICHI TAMURA; Gen. Sec. EIJI TAKADA.

National Federation of Construction Workers' Unions (Zenkensoren): 7-15, Takadanobaba 2-chome, Shinjuku-ku, Tokyo; tel. (03) 200-6221; f. 1960; 338,255 mems; Pres. RISAKU EGUCHI.

National Federation of Life Insurance Workers' Unions (Seiho Roren): Hiroo Office Bldg, 3-18, Hiroo 1-chome, Shibuya-ku, Tokyo; tel. (03) 446-2031; 359,440 mems; Pres. SHIRO YAMANOBE.

National Federation of Industrial Organizations (SHINSAMBETSU*) (Zenkoku Sangyobetsu Rodo Kumiai Rengo): Takahashi Bldg, 9-7, Nishi-Shimbashi 3-chome, Minato-ku, Tokyo; tel. (03) 433-3461; 57,769 mems; Pres. AKIHIRO KAWAI.

Major affiliated unions:

Kyoto-Shiga-block Workers' Federation (Keijichiren): Kyoto Rodosha Sogokaikan Bldg, 30-2, Mibusennen-cho, Nakagyo-ku, Kyoto-shi, Tokyo; 10,615 mems; Pres. MEIWA IKEDA.

National Machinery and Metal Workers' Union (Zenkikin): Takahashi Bldg, 9-7, Nishi Shinbashi 3-chome, Minato-ku, Tokyo; tel. (03) 434-3084; 33,935 mems; Pres. TETSUZO OGATA.

National Organization of All Chemical Workers (Shinkagaku): 9-7, Nishi Shinbashi 3-chome, Minato-ku, Tokyo; tel. (03) 433-6486; 11,430 mems; Pres. AKIHIRO KAWAI.

Major Non-Affiliated Unions

All-Japan Federation of Transport Workers' Unions (Unyu Roren): 3-3-3, Kasumigaseki, Chiyoda-ku, Tokyo 100; tel. (03) 503-2171; f. 1968; 124,481 mems; Pres. JIRO TAI.

Confederation of Japan Automobile Workers' Unions (JAW—Jidoshasoren): Kokuryu Shibakoen Bldg, 6-15, Shiba-Koen 2-chome, Minato-ku, Tokyo; tel. (03) 434-7641; f. 1972; 680,000 mems; Pres. TERUHITO TOKUMOTO.

Federation of City Bank Employees' Unions (Shiginren): Ida Bldg, 3-8, Yaesu 1-chome, Chuo-ku, Tokyo; tel. (03) 274-5611; 174,135 mems; Pres. Y. OKUMOTO.

Japan Council of Construction Industry Employees' Unions (Nikkenkyo): Dai-7 Daikyo Bldg, 30-8, Sendagaya 1-chome, Shibuya-ku, Tokyo; tel. (03) 403-7976; f. 1954; 65,479 mems; Pres. MASANORI OKAMURA.

Japan Federation of Commercial Workers' Unions (Shogyororen): 2-23-1, Yoyogi, Shibuya-ku, Tokyo; tel. (03) 370-4121; telex 29575; 140,000 mems; Pres. KENSHO SUZUKI.

National Federation of Agricultural Mutual Aid Societies Employees' Unions (Zennokyororen): Shinkuku Nokyo Kaikan Bldg, 5-5, Yoyogi 2-chome, Shibuya-ku, Tokyo; tel. (03) 370-8327; 93,382 mems; Pres. HIDEO GOTO.

National Councils

Co-ordinating bodies for unions whose members are in the same industry or have the same employer.

Council of National Enterprise Workers' Unions (Korokyo): Sohyo Kaikan, 2-11, Kanda Surugadai 3-chome, Chiyoda-ku, Tokyo; tel. (03) 251-7471; 211,000 mems; Gen. Sec. S. KAWASHUZAKI.

Council of SOHYO-affiliated Federations in the Private Sector (Sohyo Minkan Tansan Kaigi): Sohyo Kaikan, 2-11, Kanda Surugadai 3-chome, Chiyoda-ku, Tokyo; tel. (03) 251-0311; 1,479,942 mems; Gen. Sec. SIZUO MISHIMA.

FIET Japanese Liaison Council (FIET-JLC): 2-23-1, Yoyogi, Shibuya-ku, Tokyo 151; tel. (03) 370-4121; telex 29575; f. 1981; 319,000 mems; Gen. Sec. TADASHI MIURA.

Japan Council of Metalworkers' Unions (Zen Nihon Kinzoku Sangyo Rodokumiai Kyogikai): Santoku Yaesu Bldg, 6-21, Yaesu 2-chome, Chuo-ku, Tokyo 104; tel. (03) 274-2461; telex 2222534; f. 1964; 2,120,100 mems; Pres. TAKUHIKO NAKAMURA; Gen. Sec. ICHIRO SETO.

Japan Council of Public Service Workers' Unions (Nihon Komuin Rodo Kumiai Kyoto Kaigi): Sohyo Kaikan, 2-11, Kanda Surugadai 3-chome, Chiyoda-ku, Tokyo; tel. (03) 251-6263; 2,303,107 mems; Gen. Sec. YASUO MARUYAMA.

Trade Union Council for Policy Promotion (Seisaku Suishin Roso Kaigi): c/o Denryokuroren, 7-15, Mita 2-chome, Minato-ku, Tokyo 108; 5m. mems; Gen. Secs KOICHIRO HASHIMOTO, TOSHIFUMI TATEYAMA.

Trade Union Council for Multinational Companies (Takokuseki-Kigyo Taisaku Rodo Kumiai Kaigi): c/o IMF-JC, Santoku Yaesu Bldg, 6-21, Yaesu 2-chome, Chuo-ku, Tokyo 104; tel. (03) 274-2288; telex 2222534; 3.2m. mems; Chair. TAKUHIKO NAKAMURA.

CO-OPERATIVE ORGANIZATION

National Federation of Agricultural Co-operative Associations (ZEN-NOH): 8-3, Ohtemachi 1-chome, Chiyoda-ku, Tokyo; tel. (03) 245-0746; telex 2223686; purchasers of agricultural materials and marketers of agricultural products.

Transport

RAILWAYS

Japan Railways Group: 6-5, Marunouchi 1-chome, Chiyoda-ku, Tokyo 100; tel. (03) 215-9649; telex 24873; fmrly the state-controlled Japanese National Railways (JNR); reorg. and transferred to private-sector control in 1987, and divided into six passenger railway cos, one freight railway co, and five other organizations (see list below); very high-speed Tokaido-Sanyo Shinkansen line (1,069 km) links Tokyo with Shin-Yokohama, Nagoya, Kyoto, Shin-Osaka, Okayama, Hiroshima and Hakata. Tohoku Shinkansen (493 km) links Ueno in Tokyo with Omiya, Koriyama, Fukushima, Sendai and Morioka. Joetsu Shinkansen (297 km) links Ueno (Tokyo) with Omiya, Takasaki, Nagaoka and Niigata. A section between Ueno (Tokyo) and Omiya (27 km) was opened in March 1985. The 4-km link between Ueno and Tokyo stations was under construction in late-1988. In 1987 the total railway route length was about 21,206 km, of which 11,649 km was electrified. Work began in 1971 on a new 'super express' railway network, linking all the major cities. To be completed by the end of the century, it will total 7,000 km in length.

Hokkaido Railway Co: Nishi 4-chome, Kita 5-joh, Chuo-ku, Sapporo 060; Chair. TAKEI TOJOH; Pres. YOSHIHIRO OHMORI.

East Japan Railway Co: 6-5, Marunouchi 1-chome, Chiyoda-ku, Tokyo 100; tel. (03) 215-9649; telex 24873; f. 1987; Chair. ISAMU YAMASHITA; Pres. SHOJI SUMITA.

Central Japan Railway Co: 1-4, Meieki 1-chome, Nakamura-ku, Nagoya 450; Chair. SHIGEMITSU MIYAKE; Pres. HIROSHI SUDA.

West Japan Railway Co: 1-1, Ofuka-cho, Kita-ku, Osaka 530; tel. (06) 375-8917; f. 1987; Chair. TSUTOMU MURAI; Pres. TATSUO TSUNODA.

Shikoku Railway Co: 1-10, Hamano-cho, Takamatsu, Kagawa 760; tel. (0878) 51-1880; telex 2266; Pres. HIROATSU ITO.

Kyushu Railway Co: 1-1, Chuogai, Hakataeki, Hakata-ku, Fukuoka 812; tel. (092) 474-2501; Chair. MASASUKE NAKAGAWA; Pres. YOSHITAKA ISHII.

Japan Freight Railway Co: 6-5, Marunouchi 1-chome, Chiyoda-ku, Tokyo 100; Chair. SUNAO MACHIDA; Pres. MASASHI HASHIMOTO.

---

* See note at beginning of Trade Union section.

JAPAN   *Directory*

Shinkansen Holding Corpn: 6-5, Marunouchi 1-chome, Chiyoda-ku, Tokyo 100; Pres. SHOJI ISHIZUKI.

Railway Telecommunication Co Ltd: 6-5, Marunouchi 1-chome, Chiyoda-ku, Tokyo 100; tel. (03) 240-9686; f. 1986; Pres. KOICHI SAKATA.

Railway Information Systems Co Ltd: 6-5, Marunouchi 1-chome, Chiyoda-ku, Tokyo 100; tel. (03) 240-9686; f. 1986; Pres. RYOSUKE MUTO.

Railway Technical Research Institute: 8-38, Hikaricho 2-chome, Kokubunji, Tokyo 185; Chair. MASARU IBUKA; Pres. MASANORI OZEKI.

JNR Settlement Corpn: 6-5, Marunouchi 1-chome, Chiyoda-ku, Tokyo 100; Pres. TAKAYA SUGIURA.

Other Principal Private Companies

Hankyu Corporation: 8-8, Kakuta-cho, Kita-ku, Osaka 530; tel. (06) 373-5092; f. 1907; links Osaka, Kyoto, Kobe and Takarazuka; Pres. KOUHEI KOBAYASHI.

Hanshin Electric Railway Co Ltd: 3-19, Umeda 2-chome, Kita-ku, Osaka 530; tel. (06) 347-6035; f. 1899; Pres. SHUNJIRO KUMA.

Keihan Electric Railway Co Ltd: 7-24, Ohtemae 1-chome, Chuo-ku, Osaka 540; tel. (06) 944-2521; f. 1906; Chair. SEITARO AOKI; Pres. HIROSHI SUMITA.

Keihin Electric Express Railway Co Ltd: 20-20, Takanawa 2-chome, Minato-ku, Tokyo 140; tel. (03) 443-5111; Pres. MICHIO IIDA.

Keio Teito Electric Railway Co Ltd: 3-1-24, Shinjuku, Shinjuku-ku, Tokyo 160; tel. (03) 356-3111; Pres. MADOKA MINOWA.

Keisei Electric Railway Co Ltd: 10-3, 1-chome, Oshiage, Sumida-ku, Tokyo 131; tel. (03) 621-2231; f. 1909; Pres. M. SATO.

Kinki Nippon Railway Co Ltd: 1-55, 6-chome, Uehommachi, Tennoji-ku, Osaka 543; tel. (06) 771-3331; f. 1910; Pres. YOSHINORI UEYAMA.

Nagoya Railroad Co Ltd: 2-4, 1-chome, Meieki, Nakamura-ku, Nagoya-shi 450; tel. (0571) 2111; Chair. KENICHI KAJII; Pres. KENICHI KAJII.

Nankai Electric Railway Co Ltd: 1-60, Nanba 5-chome, Minami-ku, Osaka 542; tel. (06) 631-1151; Pres. S. YOSHIMURA; Vice-Pres. K. KUBO.

Nishi-Nippon Railroad Co Ltd: 1-11-17, Tenjin-cho, Chuo-ku, Fukuoka; tel. (092) 761-6631; serves northern Kyushu; Chair. H. YOSHIMOTO; Pres. GENKEI KIMOTO.

Odakyu Electric Railway Co Ltd: 8-3, 1-chome, Nishi Shinjuku, Shinjuku-ku, Tokyo 160; tel. (03) 349-2301; f. 1948; Chair. S. HIROTA; Pres. TATSUZO TOSHIMITSU.

Seibu Railway Co Ltd: 16-15, 1-chome, Minami-Ikebukuro, Toshima-ku, Tokyo 171; tel. (03) 989-2035; f. 1912; Pres. YOSHIAKI TSUTSUMI.

Tobu Railway Co Ltd: 1-2, 1-chome, Oshiage, Sumida-ku, Tokyo 131; tel. (03) 621-5057; Pres. KAICHIRO NEZU.

Tokyu Corporation: 26-20, Sakuragaoka-cho, Shibuya-ku, Tokyo 150; tel. (03) 477-6075; telex 2423395; f. 1922; Chair. and Pres. NOBORU GOTOH.

Subways, Monorails and Tunnels

Subway service is available in Tokyo, Osaka, Kobe, Nagoya, Sapporo, Yokohama, Kyoto and Fukuoka with a combined network of about 420 km. Most new subway lines are directly linked with existing private railway terminals which connect the cities with suburban areas.

Japan started its first monorail system on a commercial scale in 1964 with straddle-type cars between central Tokyo and Tokyo International Airport, a distance of 13 km. In 1984 the total length of monorail was 22.2 km.

In 1985 the 54-km Seikan Tunnel (the world's longest undersea tunnel), linking the islands of Honshu and Hokkaido, was completed at an estimated cost of 690,000m. yen. Electric rail services through the tunnel began operating in March 1988.

Kobe Municipal Rapid Transit: 6-5-1, Kanocho Chuoku, Kobe; Dir TOSHIRO YAMANAKA; 10 km open; 13.2 km under construction.

Nagoya Underground Railway: Nagoya Municipal Transportation Bureau, City Hall Annexe, 1-1, Sannomaru 3-chome, Naka-ku, Nagoya 460; tel. (052) 961-1111; 60.2 km open (1988); Gen. Man. KOSUKE TOMATSU.

Osaka Underground Railway: Osaka Municipal Transportation Bureau, 11-53, 1-chome, Kujo Minami, Nishi-ku, Osaka; tel. (06) 582-1101; f. 1933; 99.1 km open in 1987 and the 6.6 km computer-controlled 'New Tram' service began between Suminoekoen and Nakafuto in 1984; Gen. Man. EIICHI SAKAGUCHI.

Sapporo Rapid Transit: Municipal Transportation Bureau, Sapporo, Hokkaido 004; tel. (011) 892-1133; 31.6 km open; 9 km under construction; Dir T. AKIYAMA.

Tokyo Underground Railway: Teito Rapid Transit Authority, 19-6, Higashi Ueno 3-chome, Taito-ku, Tokyo 110; tel. (03) 832-2111; f. 1941; Pres. SHIRO NAKAMURA; 150.2 km open; and Transportation Bureau of Tokyo Metropolitan Govt, 2-10-1, Yuraku-cho, Chiyoda-ku, Tokyo 100; f. 1960; tel. (03) 216-1411; Dir-Gen. TSUNEHARU OCHI; 61.5 km open; combined length of underground system 205.8 km (1988).

Yokohama Rapid Transit: Municipal Transportation Bureau, 231, Minato-machi, Naka-ku, Yokohama; 2 lines of 11.5 km; Dir-Gen. M. OGURA.

ROADS

In December 1987 Japan's road network extended to 1,098,931 km, including 3,910 km of motorways. Plans have been made to cover the country with a trunk automobile highway network with a total length of 7,600 km, of which 4,330 km were expected to be completed by 1989. In mid-1988 work was completed on the world's longest suspension bridge, a 9.4-km multi-section structure spanning the Seto inland sea between Honshu and Shikoku.

There is a national omnibus service, 60 publicly operated services and 298 privately operated services.

SHIPPING

Shipping in Japan is subject to the supervision of the Ministry of Transport. At 30 June 1986 the Japanese merchant fleet had a total displacement of 38,487,000 gross tons. The main ports are Yokohama, Nagoya and Kobe.

Principal Companies

Daiichi Chuo Kisen Kaisha: Dowa Bldg, 5-15, Nihonbashi 3-chome, Chuo-ku, Tokyo 103; tel. (03) 278-6800; telex 22224322; f. 1960; fleet of 13 vessels; liner and tramp services; Chair. K. YAMADA; Pres. K. MORITA.

Iino Kaiun KK: 1-1, 2-chome, Uchisaiwai-cho, Chiyoda-ku, Tokyo 100; tel. (03) 506-3066; telex 22238; f. 1918; fleet of 10 vessels; cargo and tanker services; Chair. K. MATANO; Pres. F. OKAMURA.

Japan Line Ltd: Kokusai Bldg, 1-1, Marunouchi 3-chome, Chiyoda-ku, Tokyo 100; tel. (03) 286-6599; telex 22209; f. 1964; fleet of 22 vessels; container ship, tanker, liner, tramp and specialized carrier services; Chair. (vacant); Pres. SEISHIRO KATAOKA.

Kansai Kisen KK: Osaka Bldg, 6-32, 3-chome, Nakanoshima, Kita-ku, Osaka 552; tel. (06) 574-9171; telex 5237284; f. 1942; fleet of 9 vessels; domestic passenger services; Pres. M. OKI.

Kawasaki Kisen Kaisha Ltd (K Line): 2-9, Nishi-Shinbashi 1-chome, Minato-ku, Tokyo 105; tel. (03) 595-5000; telex 22361; f. 1919; fleet of 37 vessels; containers, cars, LNG, LPG and oil tankers, bulk ore-carrying; Chair. K. ITOH; Pres. H. MATSUNARI.

Mitsui OSK Lines Ltd: 1-1, Toranomon 2-chome, Minato-ku, Tokyo 105; tel. (03) 587-7015; telex 22266; f. 1942; 59 vessels; world-wide container, liner, tramp and specialized carrier and tanker services; Chair. S. KONDOH; Pres. KIICHIRO AIURA.

Nippon Yusen Kaisha Line (NYK): CPOB 1250, 3-2, Marunouchi 2-chome, Chiyoda-ku, Tokyo 100; tel. (03) 284-5151; telex 22236; f. 1885; 115 vessels; world-wide container, cargo, and bulk carrying services; Chair. SUSUMU ONO; Pres. KIMIO MIYAOKA.

Nissho Shipping Co Ltd: 7th Floor, 33 Mori Bldg, 8-21, Toranomon 3-chome, Minato-ku, Tokyo 105; tel. (03) 438-3511; telex 22573; f. 1943; fleet of 11 vessels; Chair. AKIRA HIRANO; Pres. MINORU IKEDA.

Ryukyu Kaiun KK: POB 98, 1-1, 4-chome, Nishihon-machi, Naha, Okinawa 900; tel. (0988) 688161; telex 795217; fleet of 6 vessels; cargo and passenger services on domestic routes; Pres. CHICHIO IJI; Man. THUTOMU OSHIRO.

Sankyo Kaiun Kabushiki Kaisha: Miki Bldg, 12-1, 3-chome, Nihonbashi, Chuo-ku, Tokyo 103; tel. (03) 273-1811; telex 2222109; f. 1959; fleet of 22 vessels; liner and tramp services; Pres. K. IKEMURA; Dir G. KUNISHIGE.

Shinwa Kaiun Kaisha Ltd: Fukoku Seimei Bldg, 2-2, 2-chome, Uchisaiwai-cho, Chiyoda-ku, Tokyo 100; tel. (03) 597-6076; telex 22348; f. 1950; fleet of 17 vessels; ore carriers, dry cargo and tankers; Pres. MICHIO HAKKAKU.

Showa Line Ltd: Hibiya Kokusai Bldg, 2-3, 2-chome, Uchisaiwai-cho, Chiyoda-ku, Tokyo 100; tel. (03) 581-8535; telex 22310; f. 1944; fleet of 11 vessels; cargo, tanker, tramping and container services world-wide; Chair. and Pres. DAIJIRO ISHII; Man. Dir AKIRA YAMADA.

Taiheiyo Kaiun KK: Room 316, Marunouchi Bldg, 4-1, 2-chome, Chiyoda-ku, Tokyo 100; tel. (03) 2012166; telex 2223434; f. 1951; fleet of 3 vessels; cargo and tanker services; Pres. H. CHIBA.

Yamashita-Shinnihon Steamship Co Ltd: Palaceside Bldg, 1-1, Hitotsu-bashi 1-chome, Chiyoda-ku, Tokyo 101; tel. (03) 282-7500;

JAPAN

telex 22345; f. 1917; fleet of 30 vessels; liner, tramp and tanker services world-wide; Pres. T. KAIJI.

CIVIL AVIATION

There are international airports at Tokyo, Osaka and Narita. In July 1986 construction of the world's first offshore international airport (to be called New Kansai International Airport) began in Osaka Bay. This airport is due to be opened in March 1993.

All Nippon Airways—ANA: Kasumigaseki Bldg, 2-5, Kasumigaseki 3-chome, Chiyoda-ku, Tokyo 100; tel. (03) 592-3385; telex 33670; f. 1952; operates domestic passenger and freight services; scheduled international services to Guam, Beijing, Hong Kong, Los Angeles and Washington, DC; charter services world-wide; Chair. TOKUJI WAKASA; Pres. AKIO KONDO; fleet of 6 Boeing 727, 14 Boeing 737, 21 Boeing 747, 29 Boeing 767, 11 TriStar 1, 19 YS-11A.

Japan Air Lines—JAL (Nihon Koku Kabushiki Kaisha): Tokyo Bldg, 7-3, Marunouchi 2-chome, Chiyoda-ku, Tokyo 100; tel. (03) 284-2543; telex 32653; f. 1951; fully transferred to private-sector control in 1987; domestic and international services, from Tokyo to Australia, Bahrain, Brazil, Canada, People's Republic of China, Denmark, Egypt, Fiji, France, Federal Republic of Germany, Greece, Hong Kong, India, Indonesia, Italy, the Republic of Korea, Kuwait, Malaysia, Mexico, Netherlands, New Zealand, Pakistan, the Philippines, Saudi Arabia, Singapore, Spain, Switzerland, Thailand, USSR, United Arab Emirates, the UK and the USA; Chair. FUMIO WATANABE; Pres. SUSUMU YAMAJI; fleet of 2 Boeing 727, 58 Boeing 747, 11 Boeing 767, 6 DC-8, 18 DC-10.

Japan Asia Airways Co: South Wing, Yurakucho Denki Bldg, 7-1, Yurakucho 1-chome, Chiyoda-ku, Tokyo 100; tel. (03) 284-2672; f. 1975; wholly-owned subsidiary of JAL; international services from Tokyo, Osaka and Okinawa to Hong Kong, Guam, Saipan and Taiwan; Chair. TOSHIO ITAKURA; Pres. TAKESHI TSUNOGAE; fleet of 2 Boeing 747, 1 DC-8, 3 DC-10.

Nihon Kinkyori Airways Co (Nihon Kinkyori Koku KK): Dai-2, Akiyama Bldg, 3-6-2, Toranomon, Minato-ku, Tokyo 105; telex 2422124; f. 1974; domestic services; Pres. KANICHI MARUI; fleet of 9 YS-11, 1 Boeing 737, 2 Twin Otter.

Nippon Airlines System: 18 Mori Bldg, 3-13, Toranomon 2-chome, Minato-ku, Tokyo 105; tel. (03) 507-8027; telex 2225182; f. 1971; domestic services and international charter flights; Chair. ISAMU TANAKA; Pres. TOSHIYASU OHTA; fleet of 11 Airbus A-300, 14 DC-9-40, 33 YS-11, 3 Bell 214B, 3 Bell 47G, 3 Bell 204B, 15 MD-81, 1 Sikorsky S-76A, 1 Ecureuil, 3 Hughes 359 HS, 1 MBB BK. 117.

Southwest Air Lines Co Ltd (Nansei Koku KK): 3-1, Yamashita-cho, Naha City, Okinawa 900; tel. 572112; telex 795477; f. 1967; subsidiary of JAL; inter-island service in Okinawa; Chair. KAMAKICHI OSHIRO; Pres. MICHIHISA IHARA; fleet of 6 YS-11, 4 Twin Otter, 7 Boeing 737-200.

Tourism

The ancient capital of Kyoto, pagodas and temples, forests and mountains, traditional festivals and the classical Kabuki theatre are some of the many tourist attractions of Japan. In 1986 there were 2,061,526 foreign visitors to Japan, and receipts from tourism totalled US $1,379m.

Department of Tourism: 2-1-3, Kasumigaseki, Chiyoda-ku, Tokyo 100; f. 1946; a dept of the Ministry of Transport; Dir-Gen. HIROKUNI TSUJI.

Japan National Tourist Organization: Tokyo Kotsu Kaikan Bldg, 2-10-1, Yuraku-cho, Chiyoda-ku, Tokyo; tel. (03) 216-1901; telex 24132; Pres. SHUNICHI SUMITA.

Japan Travel Bureau Inc: 1-13-1, Nihombashi, Chuo-ku, Tokyo 103; tel. (03) 276-7811; telex 24418; f. 1912; c. 11,000 mems; Chair. T. NAGASE; Pres. H. ISHIDA.

Atomic Energy

Thirty-six nuclear power stations were in operation by May 1988, with a combined capacity of 26,877 MW, and 13 more are expected to become operational by 1997, with a combined capacity of 40,314 MW. Projected generating capacity: 53,500 MW by 2000. In 1987, 29.1% of Japan's electricity was nuclear-generated.

Atomic Energy Bureau (AEB): Science and Technology Agency, 2-2-1, Kasumigaseki, Chiyoda-ku, Tokyo 100; tel. (03) 581-5271; f. 1956; administers and controls research and development; Dir TAKASHI MATSUI.

Japan Atomic Energy Commission (JAEC): 2-2-1, Kasumigaseki, Chiyoda-ku, Tokyo 100; tel. (03) 581-5271; f. 1955; policy board for research, development and peaceful uses of atomic energy; Chair. MOICHI MIYAZAKI.

Japan Atomic Energy Research Institute (JAERI): Fuko-kuse-imei Bldg, 2-2-2, Uchisaiwai-cho, Chiyoda-ku, Tokyo; tel. (03) 503-6111; telex 24596; f. 1956; all aspects of nuclear research: water reactor safety, fusion, development of nuclear-powered maritime vessels, HTR and utilization of radiation; Pres. TSUNEO FUJINAMI.

Japan Atomic Industrial Forum Inc (JAIF): Toshin Bldg, 1-13, Shimbashi 1-chome, Minato-ku, Tokyo 105; tel. (03) 508-2411; telex 2226623; f. 1956; non-profit org. representing c. 820 orgs involved in atomic energy development in Japan; also c. 120 overseas mems; aims to promote the peaceful use of atomic energy and the acceptance of nuclear power among the public; carries out related field surveys; Chair. JIRO ENJOJI (acting); Exec. Man. Dir KAZUHISA MORI.

Japan Nuclear Safety Commission (JNSC): 2-2-1, Kasumigaseki, Chiyoda-ku, Tokyo; tel. (03) 581-1880; f. 1978; responsible for all matters relating to safety regulations; Chair. KEISUKE MISONO.

Nuclear Safety Bureau (NSB): Science and Technology Agency, 2-2-1, Kasumigaseki, Chiyoda-ku, Tokyo; tel. (03) 581-5271; telex 2226720; f. 1976; admin. agency for nuclear safety and regulatory matters; Dir TOSHIYASU SASAKI.

Power Reactor and Nuclear Fuel Development Corporation (PNC): 1-9-13, Akasaka, Minato-ku, Tokyo; tel. (03) 586-3311; telex 26462; f. 1967; research and development of FBR, ATR and fuel cycle technologies; Pres. MINORU YOSHIDA.

JORDAN

Introductory Survey

Location, Climate, Language, Religion, Flag, Capital

The Hashemite Kingdom of Jordan is an almost land-locked state in western Asia. It is bordered by Israel to the west, by Syria to the north, by Iraq to the east and by Saudi Arabia to the south. The port of Aqaba, in the far south, gives Jordan a narrow outlet to the Red Sea. The climate is hot and dry. The average annual temperature is about 15°C (60°F) but there are wide diurnal variations. Temperatures in Amman are generally between −1°C (30°F) and 32°C (90°F). More extreme conditions are found in the valley of the River Jordan and on the shores of the Dead Sea (a lake on the Israeli-Jordanian frontier), where the temperature may exceed 50°C (122°F) in summer. The official language is Arabic. More than 90% of the population are Sunni Muslims, while there are small communities of Christians and Shi'i Muslims. The national flag (proportions 2 by 1) has three equal horizontal stripes, of black, white and green, with a red triangle, containing a seven-pointed white star, at the hoist. The capital is Amman.

Recent History

Palestine (including the present-day West Bank of Jordan) and Transjordan (the East Bank) were formerly parts of Turkey's Ottoman Empire. During the First World War (1914–18), when Turkey was allied with Germany, the Arabs under Ottoman rule rebelled. British forces, with Arab support, occupied Palestine and Transjordan in 1917–18, when the Turks withdrew.

British occupation continued after the war, when the Ottoman Empire was dissolved. In 1920 Palestine and Transjordan were formally placed under British administration by a League of Nations mandate. In 1921 Abdullah ibn Hussein, a member of the Hashimi (Hashemite) dynasty of Arabia, was proclaimed Amir (Emir) of Transjordan. In the same year, his brother, Faisal, became King of neighbouring Iraq (also administered by the United Kingdom (UK) under a League of Nations mandate). The two new monarchs were sons of Hussein ibn Ali, the Sharif of Mecca, who had proclaimed himself King of the Hejaz (now part of Saudi Arabia) in 1916. The British decision to nominate Hashemite princes to be rulers of Iraq and Transjordan was a reward for Hussein's co-operation in the wartime campaign against Turkey.

During the period of the British mandate, Transjordan (formally separated from Palestine in 1923) gained increasing autonomy. In 1928 the UK acknowledged the nominal independence of Transjordan, although retaining certain financial and military powers. Amir Abdullah followed a generally pro-British policy and supported the Allied cause in the Second World War (1939–45). The mandate was terminated on 22 March 1946, when Transjordan attained full independence. On 25 May Abdullah was proclaimed King, and a new constitution took effect.

When the British Government terminated its mandate in Palestine in May 1948, Jewish leaders in the area proclaimed the State of Israel, but Palestinian Arabs, supported by the armies of Arab states, opposed Israeli claims and hostilities continued until July. Transjordan's forces occupied about 5,900 sq km of Palestine, including East Jerusalem, and this was confirmed by the armistice with Israel in April 1949. In June 1949 the country was renamed Jordan, and in April 1950, following a referendum, King Abdullah formally annexed the West Bank territory, which contained many Arab refugees from Israeli-held areas.

In July 1951 King Abdullah was assassinated in Jerusalem by a Palestinian Arab belonging to an extremist Islamic organization. The murdered king was succeeded by his eldest son, Talal ibn Abdullah, hitherto Crown Prince. Because of Talal's mental illness, however, a joint session of the National Assembly proclaimed him unfit to reign, and deposed him, in August 1952. The crown passed to his son, Hussein ibn Talal, then 16 years of age. King Hussein formally took power in May 1953.

In March 1956, responding to Arab nationalist sentiment, King Hussein dismissed Lieut-Gen. John Glubb ('Glubb Pasha'), the British army officer who had been Chief of Staff of the Arab Legion (the Jordanian armed forces) since 1939. The Legion, with about 20,000 men, had been created in 1920 by the UK and was financed and equipped by the British Government. However, Jordan's treaty relationship with the UK was ended in March 1957. British troops completed their withdrawal from Jordan in July.

The refugee camps in the West Bank became centres of Palestinian Arab nationalism, with the aim of recovering the homeland from which Arabs had been dispossessed (about 400,000 Arab residents of Palestine evacuated their homes prior to May 1948, when the British mandate ended and Israel was established, and a further 400,000 fled subsequently). In the 1950s there were numerous attacks on Israeli territory by groups of Palestinian *fedayeen* ('martyrs'), which developed into guerrilla movements. The principal Palestinian guerrilla organization was the Palestine National Liberation Movement, known as Al-Fatah ('Conquest'), originally based in the Gaza Strip (then under Egyptian administration). In September 1963 the creation of a unified 'Palestinian entity' was approved by the Council of the League of Arab States (the Arab League, see p. 171), despite opposition from the Jordanian Government, which regarded the proposal as a threat to Jordan's sovereignty over the West Bank. The first congress of Palestinian Arab groups was held in the Jordanian sector of Jerusalem in May–June 1964, when the participants unanimously agreed to form the Palestine Liberation Organization (PLO) as 'the only legitimate spokesman for all matters concerning the Palestinian people'. The PLO was to be financed by the Arab League and was to recruit military units, from among refugees, to constitute a Palestine Liberation Army (PLA). From the outset, King Hussein refused to allow the PLA to train forces in Jordan or the PLO to levy taxes from Palestinian refugees in his country.

Despite political upheavals in Jordan and elsewhere in the Middle East, King Hussein has vigorously maintained his personal rule and has survived attempted assassination and revolt. In April 1965 Hussein nominated his brother, Hassan ibn Talal, to be Crown Prince, so excluding the King's own children from succession to the throne.

Jordan and Israel each have a small strip of coastline on the Gulf of Aqaba, providing access to the Red Sea. In May 1967 the United Arab Republic (Egypt) barred Israeli shipping from entering the Red Sea. In retaliation, Israel launched attacks on its Arab neighbours in June 1967, quickly overcoming opposition and making substantial territorial gains. The Six-Day War, as it is known, left Israel in possession of all Jordanian territory on the West Bank. The Old City of Jerusalem was incorporated into Israel, while the remainder of the conquered area has the status of an Israeli 'administered territory'. Many refugees are still housed in camps on the East Bank. Jordan was formerly a base for several Palestinian Arab guerrilla groups, mainly forces of the PLO, which made armed raids on the administered territories. The strength of these organizations frequently constituted a challenge to the Jordanian Government and, after a civil war lasting from September 1970 to July 1971, King Hussein expelled the guerrilla groups. Since then, Hussein has not allowed guerrilla activity from Jordan, but by 1979 he was again on good terms with the PLO.

In September 1971 King Hussein announced the formation of the Jordanian National Union, to be the country's sole permitted political organization. In March 1972 it was renamed the Arab National Union (ANU), but in April 1974 Hussein dissolved its executive committee. The ANU was abolished in February 1976, and since then Jordan has had no formal political parties.

In March 1972 King Hussein presented a plan for a United Arab Kingdom in which a Palestinian region (capital Jerusalem) would be federated with the Jordanian region, whose capital, Amman, would be the federal capital. Israel, the PLO and Egypt reacted unfavourably, and Egypt broke off diplomatic relations, which were not restored until September 1973.

In October 1973 Egypt and Syria launched simultaneous attacks on Israeli-held territory. Units of the Jordanian army were sent to support the Syrian offensive on the Golan Heights. Aid to Jordan from Kuwait and other wealthy Arab states, which had been suspended following the Jordanian action against Palestinian commandos, was restored after the 1973 war.

During early 1974 King Hussein became increasingly estranged from the governments of other Arab states when it became clear that they considered the PLO, rather than Jordan, to be the legitimate representative of the Palestinian Arabs. At an Arab summit meeting in Rabat, Morocco, in October 1974, King Hussein acknowledged this view, and supported a unanimous resolution which gave the PLO the right to establish an independent national authority on any piece of Palestinian land to be liberated.

The summit meeting at Rabat adopted a resolution which recognized the PLO as 'the sole legitimate representative of the Palestinian people'. In November 1974, as a response to this resolution, both chambers of the Jordanian National Assembly (which had equal representation for the East and West Banks) approved constitutional amendments which empowered the King to dissolve the Assembly and to postpone elections for up to 12 months. The Assembly was dissolved later that month, although it was briefly reconvened in February 1976, when it approved a constitutional amendment which gave the King power to postpone elections indefinitely and to convene the Assembly as required. A royal decree of April 1978 provided for the creation of a National Consultative Council, with 60 members appointed for a two-year term by the King, on the Prime Minister's recommendation, to debate proposed legislation. The Council was dissolved, and the National Assembly reconvened, in January 1984 (see below).

After the Israeli invasion of Lebanon in June 1982, President Ronald Reagan of the USA proposed the creation of an autonomous Palestinian authority on the West Bank, in association with Jordan. However, following talks with Hussein, Yasser Arafat, the Chairman of the PLO, rejected the plan. Jordan subsequently gave diplomatic support to Arafat when a Syrian-backed revolt erupted in May 1983 against his leadership of Al-Fatah, the major guerrilla group within the PLO. During the last three months of the year, Jordanian diplomats in several European countries, and targets in Amman, came under attack from terrorists who were thought to be members of a radical Arab group, based in Syria, which was angered by Jordan's backing for Arafat, by its call for Egypt to be readmitted to the community of Arab states and by the possibility of a revival of the Reagan plan.

King Hussein dissolved the National Consultative Council in January 1984 and recalled the National Assembly for its first session since 1967. He thereby created the kind of Palestinian forum (60% of Jordan's population of 2.4m. are Palestinian and there are 1.3m. Palestinians living in the West Bank) which was called for in the Reagan plan, and effectively infringed the Rabat resolution of 1974, which recognized the PLO as the sole representative of the Palestinian people. Israel allowed the surviving West Bank deputies to attend the Assembly, which approved constitutional amendments enabling elections to be held in the East Bank alone, and West Bank deputies to be chosen by the Assembly itself. Also in January, the Jordanian Council of Ministers resigned, and a new one, containing a higher proportion of Palestinians, took office. King Hussein embarked on a series of talks with Yasser Arafat in January 1984. There was strong opposition to the Reagan plan among Jordanian Palestinians, while Hussein and Arafat stood by the resolution which had been adopted at the Arab summit meeting of 1974, recognizing the PLO as 'the sole legitimate representative of the Palestinian people'.

These developments revealed a split in the Arab world between a moderate body of opinion (formed by Jordan, Egypt and Arafat's wing of the PLO) on one side, and a more radical group, including Syria, Libya and the rebel wing of the PLO, on the other. In February 1984 the Jordanian Embassy in Tripoli, Libya, was burnt down during a demonstration, and Jordan responded by severing diplomatic relations with Libya. Attacks by militant Arab groups on Jordanian diplomats around the world took place throughout 1984 and during 1985.

In 1984 the US Government renewed its efforts to gain Congressional support for an 8,000-strong Jordanian strike force, equipped by the USA, which would respond to requests for military assistance from Arab governments within a 2,400-km (1,500-mile) radius of Jordan. King Hussein tried to distance Jordan from any interest or involvement in the creation of such a force. Then, in March, the planned sale to Jordan of 1,613 Stinger anti-aircraft missiles was cancelled by President Reagan, partly owing to pro-Israeli opposition to the plan in the US Congress, but also owing to King Hussein's recent harsh criticism of US policy in the Middle East. In June the Reagan administration abandoned its plans for a Jordanian strike force. Jordan consequently purchased an air defence system from the USSR in January 1985, having already made an agreement to buy French anti-aircraft missiles in September 1984.

Jordan received $136m. in US aid in 1984. In 1985 US President Reagan advocated the sale of arms worth $500m.–$570m. to Jordan, but there was considerable opposition to the proposal. Instead, in June, King Hussein was offered economic aid of $250m., to be spread over 15 months in 1985 and 1986, in addition to the sums ($111.7m. and $117m., respectively) already allocated for those years. The US Senate authorized the aid but ordered it to be spread over 27 months. In February 1986 the US administration indefinitely postponed a proposed sale to Jordan of military equipment worth $1,500m., when it became clear that the proposal would not be approved by the Senate. In 1987 the level of US aid to Jordan declined to $55.7m.

In September 1984 Jordan re-established diplomatic relations with Egypt, which had been broken off after the Egypt-Israel peace treaty of 1979. President Mubarak of Egypt has since given his support to King Hussein's proposals for Middle East peace negotiations. Hussein rejected the Israeli offer of direct negotiations, excluding the PLO, in October, calling instead for a conference of all the concerned parties in the Middle East, including the PLO.

The Palestine National Council (PNC), which finally met in Amman in November 1984, replied non-committally to King Hussein's offer of a joint Jordanian-Palestinian peace initiative, with the UN Security Council's Resolution 242, adopted in November 1967, as the basis for negotiations. Until November 1988 the PLO refused to recognize the resolution because it made mention only of a Palestinian 'refugee problem' and not of the right of Palestinians to self-determination.

In February 1985 King Hussein and Yasser Arafat announced the terms of a joint Jordanian-Palestinian agreement, proposing a confederated state of Jordan and Palestine. Both this agreement and King Hussein's quadripartite plan, announced in May, foundered on Israel's refusal to negotiate with the PLO and Israel's rejection of proposals for an international peace conference. The US Government, meanwhile, refused to meet members of the PLO or its nominees until the PLO recognized Israel's right to exist, renounced terrorism and, in essence, accepted Resolution 242.

In July 1985 Israel independently rejected a list of seven Palestinians, five of whom were members of the PLO or had links with the PNC, whom King Hussein had presented to the USA as candidates for a joint Jordanian-Palestinian delegation to preliminary peace talks.

An extraordinary meeting of the Arab states in August 1985 (which was boycotted by Syria, Libya, Lebanon, the PDRY and Algeria) neither condemned nor endorsed the Hussein/Arafat peace initiative but reaffirmed Arab allegiance to the Fez plan of September 1982.

Further progress was hampered by a series of terrorist incidents in which the PLO was implicated. These incidents gave Israel further cause to reject the PLO as a credible partner in peace negotiations. King Hussein was under increasing pressure to advance the peace process, if necessary without the participation of the PLO. In September President Reagan revived the plan to sell military equipment, valued at $1,900m., to Jordan. The proposal was approved by Congress on the condition that Jordan enter into direct talks with Israel before 1 March 1986. However, a *rapprochement* developed between Jordan and Syria. Among other differences, Jordan supported Iraq in the Gulf War, while Syria supported Iran. Nevertheless, both countries support a Middle East peace settlement through an international conference, and at talks in Riyadh in October 1985 they rejected 'partial and unilateral' solutions and affirmed their adherence to the Fez plan omitting any mention of the Jordanian-Palestinian initiative. Through a reconciliation with Syria, which is opposed to Yasser Arafat's leadership of the PLO, King Hussein may have hoped to exert pressure on Arafat to take the initiative in the peace process and signal PLO acceptance of Resolution 242.

Although he remained opposed to the concept of preliminary negotiations, Peres intimated, in a speech at the UN in October 1985, that he would not rule out the possibility of an international conference. Rumours of secret meetings between the two leaders were followed, at the end of October, by the unofficial disclosure to the Israeli press of a document drawn up by the Israeli Prime Minister's office, which purported to summarize the state of negotiations between Israel and Jordan, listing points of agreement and dispute in peace proposals, should formal talks commence. The document suggested the establishment of an interim Israeli-Jordanian condominium in the West Bank, granting a form of Palestinian autonomy, and recorded mutual agreement on the desirability of an international forum for peace talks, with Israel consenting to the participation of the USSR (provided that it re-established diplomatic relations with Israel) and Syria but not of the PLO, on whose involvement King Hussein still insisted.

The Jordanian Prime Minister, Ahmad Ubeidat, resigned in April 1985. A new Cabinet was sworn in under the premiership of Zaid ar-Rifai, who had been Prime Minister during the 1970s.

Frustrated by the lack of co-operation from Yasser Arafat in advancing the aims of the Jordanian-PLO peace initiative, King Hussein publicly severed political links with the PLO on 19 February 1986. In January, according to King Hussein, the USA had undertaken to invite the PLO to an international peace conference (whereas, before, it had agreed only to consider talks with the PLO) if it would officially acknowledge UN Security Council Resolutions 242 and 338 as the basis for negotiations. Arafat refused to make such a commitment without prior acknowledgement by the USA of the Palestinian right to self-determination.

Following King Hussein's announcement, Arafat was ordered to close his main PLO offices in Jordan by 1 April 1986. The activities of the PLO were henceforth to be restricted to an even greater extent than before, and a number of Fatah officers loyal to Arafat were expelled. King Hussein urged the PLO either to change its policies or its leadership. In July Jordan closed all 25 Fatah offices in Amman, so that only 12 belonging to the PLO remained.

Since the termination of political co-ordination with the PLO, Jordan has continued to reject Israeli requests for direct peace talks which exclude a form of PLO representation. However, Jordan's subsequent efforts to strengthen its influence in the Israeli-occupied territories and to foster a Palestinian constituency there, independent of Arafat's PLO, have coincided with Israeli measures to grant a limited autonomy to the Palestinian community in the West Bank (for example, by appointing Arab mayors in four towns in place of Israeli military governors). In March 1986 the Jordanian House of Representatives approved a draft law increasing the number of seats in the House from 60 to 142 (71 seats each for the East and West Banks), thereby providing for greater representation for West Bank Palestinians in the National Assembly. Then, in August, with Israeli support, a five-year development plan for the West Bank and the Gaza Strip, involving projected expenditure of US $1,300m., was announced in Amman. The plan was condemned by Yasser Arafat and West Bank Palestinians as representing a normalization of relations with Israel. There is considerable support for Arafat among Palestinians in the Occupied Territories and in Jordan, and this was consolidated when he re-established himself at the head of a reunified PLO at the 18th session of the Palestine National Council in April 1987 (when the Jordan-PLO accord of 1985 was formally abrogated).

In May 1987, following several secret meetings with King Hussein, Shimon Peres (who was now the Israeli Minister of Foreign Affairs) claimed to have made significant progress on the crucial issue of Palestinian representation at a Middle East peace conference, and to have the consent of Egypt, Jordan and the USA to convene an international conference, including the five permanent members of the UN Security Council and a delegation of Palestinians who 'reject terrorism and violence' and accept Security Council Resolutions 242 and 338 as the basis for negotiations. The Jordanian Prime Minister, Zaid ar-Rifai, confirmed Jordan's willingness to participate in a conference in a joint Jordanian-Palestinian delegation, including the PLO, provided that it complied with the stated conditions. King Hussein appeared to have accepted that a conference would have no power to impose a peace settlement and would be only a preliminary to direct negotiations between the main protagonists. However, Peres failed to secure the support of a majority of the Israeli Cabinet for his proposals. The Israeli Prime Minister, Itzhak Shamir, was opposed in principle to an international peace conference and reiterated his alternative proposal of direct regional talks, excluding the PLO.

During 1987 King Hussein pursued his efforts, begun in 1986, to reconcile Syria and Iraq, with the wider aim of securing Arab unity. He was instrumental in arranging the first full 'summit' meeting of the Arab League for eight years, which took place in Amman in November, principally to discuss the Gulf War. In September Jordan had restored diplomatic relations with Libya, which had modified its support for Iran in the Gulf War and urged a cease-fire. The Arab 'summit' unanimously adopted a resolution of solidarity with Iraq, which condemned Iran for its occupation of Arab territory and for prolonging the Gulf War (although Syria obstructed the adoption of diplomatic or other sanctions). King Hussein's appeal for Egypt to be restored to membership of the League was successfully resisted by Syria and Libya, but nine Arab states re-established diplomatic relations with Egypt soon after the 'summit', and these were followed by Tunisia in January 1988 and by the People's Democratic Republic of Yemen in February. President Hussain of Iraq and President Assad of Syria held two sessions of talks at the summit, and the resumption of co-operation between Jordan and the PLO was announced.

In December 1987 a violent Palestinian uprising (*intifada*) began in the West Bank and the Gaza Strip, in protest against the continuing Israeli occupation of those territories. Security measures were increased in Jordan to prevent pro-Palestinian demonstrations. In April 1988, however, Black September, a Palestinian terrorist group, claimed responsibility for a series of bomb attacks in Amman.

In February 1988 the intensity of the *intifada*, which Israel was unable to suppress, and world-wide condemnation of Israeli tactics prompted renewed peace initiatives, led by George Shultz, the US Secretary of State. The Shultz Plan envisaged the convening of an international peace conference involving all parties in the Arab–Israeli conflict and the five permanent members of the UN Security Council, with the Palestinians being represented by a joint Jordanian-Palestinian delegation containing no representatives of the PLO. However, the exclusion of the PLO, as well as the plan's failure to consider the Palestinians' right to self-determination and to the establishment of an independent Palestinian state in the West Bank, made it unacceptable to the Arab nations.

In June 1988, at an extraordinary 'summit' meeting of the Arab League, King Hussein gave his unconditional support to the *intifada* and disclaimed any ambition to restore Jordanian rule in the West Bank. He also insisted that the PLO must represent the Palestinians at any future peace conference and repeatedly stressed the PLO's status as 'the sole legitimate representative of the Palestinian people'. The 'summit' rejected the Shultz Plan and gave support to the *intifada* and the Palestinians, insisting on PLO participation in any future peace negotiations.

The *intifada* increased international support for the PLO and Palestinian national rights, as well as heightening Palestinian aspirations to statehood. Jordan could no longer present itself as a viable alternative to the PLO. At the end of July 1988, King Hussein cancelled the West Bank development plan, announced in 1986, and severed Jordan's legal and administrative links with the region, in accordance with the agreements reached at the recent Arab League 'summit' meeting, whereby he was to transfer administrative responsibility for the West Bank to the PLO. However, the abruptness of his actions aroused Palestinian opposition, which King Hussein attempted to suppress, especially by means of press censorship. Jordan's disengagement from the West bank effectively rendered the Shultz Plan redundant.

In August 1988 there was a limited cabinet reshuffle, in which the Ministry of Occupied Territories Affairs was downgraded to the status of an independent department attached to the Ministry of Foreign Affairs, to be known as the Palestinian Affairs Department. King Hussein also dissolved the lower house of the National Assembly, the House of Representatives, where one-half of the seats were held by representatives of the West Bank, and in October postponed legislative elections, pending the revision of electoral laws. Elections were not expected to take place for another two years.

On 15 November 1988 the PLO proclaimed the establishment of an independent state of Palestine and, for the first time, endorsed the UN Security Council's Resolution 242 as a basis for a Middle East peace settlement, thus implicitly recognizing Israel. Jordan and 60 other countries recognized the new state. In December Yasser Arafat addressed a special session of the UN General Assembly in Geneva, where he renounced violence on behalf of the PLO. Subsequently, the USA opened a dialogue with the PLO, and it appeared that Israel would have to negotiate directly with the PLO if it wished to seek a solution to the Palestinian question, and that Jordan's future participation in the peace process was likely to be of less significance.

In December 1988 King Hussein again reshuffled his Cabinet. Marwan al-Qassim became Minister of Foreign Affairs, replacing Taher al-Masri, who had been the principal opponent of King Hussein's decision to withdraw from the West Bank and also of the severe economic measures that the Prime Minister, Zaid ar-Rifai, had introduced.

Government

Jordan is a constitutional monarchy. Legislative power is vested in a bicameral National Assembly. The Senate (House of Notables) has 30 members, appointed by the King for eight years (one-half of the members retiring every four years), while the House of Representatives (House of Deputies) has 60 members, including 50 Muslims and 10 Christians, elected by universal adult suffrage for four years (subject to dissolution). In each House there is equal representation for the East Bank and the (occupied) West Bank. In March 1986 the House of Representatives approved a draft law to increase its membership from 60 to 142. Executive power is vested in the King, who governs with the assistance of an appointed Council of Ministers, responsible to the Assembly. In July 1988, following the disengagement from the West Bank, King Hussein dissolved the House of Representatives, and in October 1988 he postponed elections, pending a revision of electoral laws.

There are eight administrative provinces, of which three have been occupied by Israel since June 1967.

Defence

The total strength of the Jordanian armed forces in June 1988 was 82,250. The army had 74,000 men, the air force 11,000 and the navy (coastguard) 250. Reserves number 35,000 (30,000 in the army). There are paramilitary forces of more than 19,000 men: a Civil Militia of more than 15,000 and a Public Security Force of 4,000. Military service is voluntary. The Government has announced plans to establish a 200,000-strong force to defend the border with Israel. The estimated defence budget in 1988 was 256m. dinars.

Economic Affairs

In 1987, according to estimates by the World Bank, the gross national product (GNP) of the East Bank region of Jordan, measured at average 1985–87 prices, totalled US $4,370m., equivalent to $1,540 per head. Between 1980 and 1987, it was estimated, GNP per head in this region decreased, in real terms, at an average rate of 0.8% per year. Between 1980 and 1986, the East Bank region's gross domestic product (GDP) expanded, in real terms, at an average annual rate of 5.1%.

In 1986 approximately 7% of the labour force were employed in agriculture, compared with 28% in 1970. The agricultural sector contributed 8% of GDP in 1986. Israeli occupation of the West Bank in 1967 resulted in the loss of 80% of the fruit-growing area and 45% of the area under vegetables, and had a serious effect on cereal production. Only about 6% of Jordan's land is arable. The principal crops are tomatoes, citrus fruit, cucumbers, watermelons, aubergines and wheat. In 1984 the Government established the Agricultural Marketing and Processing Co, with the aim of increasing agricultural exports. The Jordan Valley Authority has made great progress with irrigation schemes in the valley of the River Jordan.

With its economy underpinned by foreign aid and by remittances from Jordanian workers abroad (some 310,000 in 1983), Jordan enjoyed sustained economic growth from the mid-1970s. The increased economic activity of Amman, owing to the disturbances in Beirut, and of Aqaba, owing to the Gulf War which closed Basra to the Iraqis, have also benefited the Jordanian economy. Real GDP increased by 17.6% in 1980, but thereafter the growth rate declined, reaching only 0.8% in 1984, before rising to 3.1% in 1987. The current deficit on the balance of payments declined from US $260.5m. in 1985 to only $39.8m. in 1986, before rising again, to $351.8m., in 1987. Transfer payments (including receipts of workers' remittances) partly offset the chronic deficit on merchandise trade. The trade deficit was JD 819.1m. in 1985. It declined to JD 624.6m. in 1986, but rose to JD 666.8m. in 1987. Recurring deficits led the Government to seek new loans. In 1984 and 1985 it obtained Euroloans of $200.8m. and $215m., respectively, both with eight years' credit, and in 1987 one of $150m., with seven years' credit. Consequently, the external public debt rose from JD 870.3m. in 1983 to JD 1,261.6m. in 1987, the debt-service ratio increasing from 7.4% to 17.5%. The 1989 budget envisaged debt-service payments of JD 209.7m., compared with a projected JD 178m. in 1988. The budget for 1989 proposed total expenditure of JD 1,035.4m. (a decrease of 3.7% compared with expenditure of JD 1,075.3m. in the 1988 budget). The budget deficit was projected at JD 122.3m., an increase of 82.8% compared with the 1988 figure of JD 66.9m. The annual rate of inflation averaged 3.2% in 1980–86, but there was zero inflation in 1986 and prices fell slightly in 1987.

The targets of the 1981–85 Development Plan were not attained. Under the 1986–90 Five-Year Development Plan, expenditure was projected at JD 3,115m., 33% of which was to be provided by foreign borrowing. The Plan aimed for real growth in GDP of 5% per year, and, with 39% of total investment to be allocated to the services sector (compared with less than 30% in the previous Plan), it was hoped that as many as 100,000 jobs would be created during its term. The phosphate and potash industries and other important export industries were to be developed with a view to increasing the value of exports by an annual rate of 8.3%. Industrial exports (including potash and phosphates), were worth JD 131.4m. ($385m.) in 1987, nearly 1% more than in 1986. The industrial sector provided 28% of the East Bank's GDP in 1986.

The major part of Jordan's foreign aid comes from oil-rich Arab states and, as a 'front-line state' in the Arab-Israeli conflict, the country was pledged annual aid of $1,250m. for 10 years by the Arab League at its 1978 summit meeting in Baghdad. This figure was never achieved. Jordan's stance on the split within the PLO, relations with Egypt, the Gulf War and the search for a settlement of the Palestinian question led to the failure of certain Arab countries (notably Libya and Syria) to fulfil their aid obligations. Only Saudi Arabia, of the seven original Arab donor countries, made its payments in full. Total Arab aid under the Baghdad agreement reached only $455m. in 1987.

The amount of aid that Jordan receives is also dependent on the condition of the Middle East's petroleum industry. The falling price of petroleum in the mid-1980s meant that less money was available for the oil-based economies to give in aid. For similar reasons, there were fewer jobs and lower wages for expatriate Jordanian workers, 276,000 of whom worked in the Gulf states in 1986. Between 10,000 and 18,000 Jordanian workers returned to Jordan from the Gulf in 1984 and 1985, contributing to an unemployment rate which was estimated at 8% (or 42,864) of the labour force in 1986. In September 1987 the rate was unofficially estimated at 17%. Workers' remittances are Jordan's principal source of foreign exchange. Their value declined by 17%, to $1,204m., in 1985, but recovered to $1,237m. in 1986, before falling to $934m. in 1987. In June 1988 Jordan's reserves of foreign exchange declined to only $18.7m., sufficient to maintain the purchase of imports for only one week. In early November 1988 the combination of a shortage of foreign currency reserves, a decline in the value of the dinar (of more than 30% since mid-October), and the deteriorating balance-of-payments position prompted the Government to introduce various austerity measures. Bans were imposed on the import of several luxury items. These restrictions were to remain in force until the end of 1989. Customs duties on non-essential items, airport tax and fees payable for work permits were also increased. The Government hoped to save at least US $350m. by these measures. In February 1989, amid increasing pressure on the currency, the Government cancelled all licences for money-changers.

A further set-back to Jordan's economy was the decline in trade with Iraq (nevertheless its major export market and principal supplier of imports in 1987), which was reduced to buying only goods essential to its war effort. In August 1988 Iraq promised to try to settle its outstanding debts to Jordan within two years, thus ending a four-month trade dispute. The Iraqi Government also agreed to use the Jordanian port of Aqaba for exports of heavy industrial goods upon completion of a US $25m. multi-berth expansion programme. The other principal recipients of Jordan's exports in 1987 were Saudi Arabia and India, while the USA remained the second largest source of imports. Jordan's trade with Egypt has revived, in tandem with the recently improved diplomatic relations between the two countries, exports to Egypt increasing from JD 3m. in 1985 to JD 13m. in 1987.

In a country that is short of natural resources, phosphates predominate. In 1985 Jordan was the world's fifth largest producer of phosphate rock. In 1987 phosphates were the country's second largest export commodity (after chemicals), accounting for 24.5% of total export earnings. The Ruseifa mine was closed in July 1985, owing to a decline in international demand for low-grade phosphate. Jordan's output of phosphates totalled 6.2m. tons (gross weight) in 1986, and exports were 5.2m. tons. Output rose to 6.8m. tons in 1987. Development plans centre on the Jordan Phosphate Mines Company's three existing sites. In the longer term, however, the industry will probably focus on a major new mine at Shidiyah, in the south-east, which has proven phosphate reserves of 1,200m. tons and was expected to start producing at an annual rate of between 800,000 and 1m. tons in 1989, rising to 3m. tons by 1991. Allied industries form an important part of Jordan's industrial development programme. A potash project on the Dead Sea, developed by the Arab Potash Company, began production in September 1982, and a phosphate fertilizer complex opened at Aqaba in December. Several other industrial projects were also under consideration in 1988, including plans to construct a series of plants to extract salt from the Dead Sea, a phosphate rock dedusting project, and a plant to produce dicalcium phosphate mix (which can be added to livestock feed). The chemical industry is of increasing significance. Earnings from the export of chemicals reached JD 69.9m. (28.1% of total exports) in 1987, compared with JD 54.5m. in 1986.

Jordan possesses 45,000m. tons of oil-bearing shale, but the exploitation of this resource is in its infancy and the country is almost wholly dependent on imported petroleum for its energy needs. The imported crude petroleum is refined at Jordan's only refinery, at Zarqa. The annual capacity of the refinery was increased to about 4.5m. tons in 1984, and output rose to 2.6m. tons in 1985. Of this total, 1.8m. tons came from Saudi Arabia, 698,600 tons from Iraq, and 2,800 tons from Jordan's Hamzah oilfield (output 146,809 barrels in 1987). In December 1984 the Government announced a plan to double investment in oil exploration, following promising discoveries in Azraq, and to restrict oil consumption by reducing oil subsidies and by increasing the prices of electricity and petroleum-based products. The aim was to reduce the annual increase in oil consumption to zero in 1986. The level of oil subsidies was reduced from $92m. in 1984 to $14m. (JD 5m.) in 1986. Overall energy consumption increased by only 3%–4% in 1984, compared with the previous annual average rise of 17%. The cost of crude petroleum imports declined from JD 192.6m. in 1985 to JD 92.8m. in 1986, before rising to JD 118.6m. in 1987. A Ministry of Energy and Mineral Resources, created in 1984, is exploring alternative energy sources, including solar and wind power. A 'wind farm' has been established at Al-Ibrahammiyeh. Following the abandonment in 1985 of plans to construct a pipeline to carry crude petroleum from Iraq to Aqaba, an agreement to receive Saudi Arabian crude petroleum via the Trans-Arabian Pipeline (Tapline), at the Zarqa refinery, was renewed.

A five-year development plan for the Occupied Territories (1986–90) was announced by the Jordanian Government in November 1986. Jordan intended to contribute $120m., over four years, towards the plan's total required investment of JD 461.5m. ($1,292.3m.) for projects in the West Bank and the Gaza Strip, with the aim of creating 20,000 jobs and allowing the 1.3m. Palestinians living in these areas to achieve a greater degree of economic independence. However, by January 1988 the target for foreign investment in the plan had not been attained. The USA had contributed $4.5m. and had promised an additional $14m., to be paid in 1988. In July 1988, as part of his policy of disengagement from the West Bank, King Hussein cancelled the development plan. However, Jordan is continuing to contribute its share of the cost for projects already under way.

In February 1989 the Heads of State of Jordan, Egypt, Iraq and the Yemen Arab Republic signed an agreement to establish a new economic community, the Arab Co-operation Council (ACC), whose permanent secretariat was to be in Amman. This initiative, however, is unlikely to provide an immediate solution to Jordan's economic problems.

Social Welfare

There is no comprehensive welfare scheme but the Government administers medical and health services. In 1985 the East Bank region had 44 hospital establishments, with 3,578 beds, and 2,576 physicians. A new Social Security Law, providing security for both employers and employees, was put into effect in 1978 and extended in 1981. Of total expenditure by the central Government in 1985, JD 27.0m. (4.0%) was for health services, and a further JD 54.9m. (8.1%) for social security and welfare. In June 1987 there were 845,542 refugees registered with UNRWA in Jordan and a further 373,586 in the West Bank.

Education

Primary education is free and, where possible, compulsory. It starts at the age of five years and eight months and lasts for six years. A further three-year period, known as the preparatory cycle, is also compulsory. The preparatory cycle is followed by the three-year secondary cycle. UNRWA provides schooling for Palestinian Arab refugees. In 1984/85 there were 3,065 primary and secondary schools, of which more than 2,000 were state-run, with 863,892 pupils and 34,119 teachers. In 1983 an estimated 88% of East Bank children aged six to 11 years attended primary schools. In 1982 about 71% of those aged 12 to 17 years received secondary education. There are nine universities in Jordan. Expenditure on education by the central Government in 1985 was JD 86.6m. (12.7% of total spending).

Public Holidays

1989: 15 January (Arbor Day), 5 March (Leilat al-Meiraj, Ascension of the Prophet), 22 March (Arab League Day), 7 May (Id al-Fitr, end of Ramadan), 25 May (Independence Day), 14 July (Id al-Adha), 11 August (King Hussein's Accession), 4 August (Islamic New Year), 13 October (Mouloud, Birth of the Prophet), 14 November (King Hussein's Birthday).

1990: 15 January (Arbor Day), 23 February (Leilat al-Meiraj), 22 March (Arab League Day), 27 April (Id al-Fitr), 25 May (Independence Day), 4 July (Id al-Adha), 24 July (Islamic New Year), 11 August (King Hussein's Accession), 2 October (Mouloud), 14 November (King Hussein's Birthday).

Weights and Measures

The metric system is in force. In Jordan the dunum is 1,000 sq m (0.247 acre).

Statistical Survey

Source: Department of Statistics, Jabal Amman, 1st Circle, POB 2015, Amman; tel. 24313.

Area and Population

AREA, POPULATION AND DENSITY
(East and West Banks)

Area (sq km)	97,740*
Population (UN estimates at mid-year)†	
1985	3,515,000
1986	3,656,000
1987	3,804,000
Density (per sq km) at mid-1987	38.9

* 37,738 sq miles.

† Source: UN, *World Population Prospects: Estimates and Projections as Assessed in 1984*. In its 1988 assessment, the UN estimated the mid-1987 population at 3,790,000.

East Bank: Area 89,206 sq km; population 2,132,997 (males 1,115,841; females 1,017,156) at census of 10 November 1979; estimated population 2,796,100 at 31 December 1986.

GOVERNORATES
(East Bank only; estimated population at 31 December 1986)

Amman	1,160,000
Irbid	680,200
Zarqa	404,500
Balqa	193,800
Karak	120,100
Mafraq	98,600
Ma'an	97,500
Tafiela	41,400
Total	**2,796,100**

PRINCIPAL TOWNS (including suburbs)

Population in December 1986: Amman (capital) 972,000; Zarqa 392,220; Irbid 271,000; Salt 134,100.

BIRTHS, MARRIAGES AND DEATHS (East Bank only)*

	Live Births	Marriages	Deaths
1981	95,628	15,325	7,162
1982	97,974	17,488	7,741
1983	98,398	17,055	7,860
1984	102,521	18,189	8,303
1985	102,712	20,152	8,731
1986	112,451	19,397	8,853

* Data are tabulated by year of registration rather than by year of occurrence. Figures exclude foreigners, but include registered Palestinian refugees.

ECONOMICALLY ACTIVE POPULATION
(Jordanians only)

	1984	1985	1986
Agriculture	34,850	36,833	37,436
Mining and manufacturing	47,414	49,869	52,706
Electricity and water	4,585	5,195	5,418
Construction	52,733	51,947	54,183
Trade	46,487	47,225	49,258
Transport and communications	41,178	44,391	46,302
Financial and insurance services	14,444	16,104	16,748
Social and administrative services	216,848	220,635	230,525
Total employed	**458,539**	**472,199**	**492,576**
Unemployed	n.a.	n.a.	42,864
Total civilian labour force	n.a.	n.a.	535,440

Agriculture

PRINCIPAL CROPS (East Bank only; '000 metric tons)

	1985	1986	1987*
Barley	19.7	9.0	33.1
Wheat	62.8	30.8	79.8
Squash	49.5	36.9	n.a.
Citrus fruits	81.3	87.4	121.7
Bananas	10.4	13.4	12.8
Grapes	26.2	23.2	18.6
Olives	19.7	31.8	20.4
Tomatoes	251.1	220.6	236.8
Eggplants (Aubergines)	57.3	50.6	56.6
Cauliflowers	35.4	24.6	34.2
Cabbages	28.9	16.4	
Watermelons	36.9	51.3	91.3
Melons		15.2	
Potatoes	26.2	22.5	n.a.
String beans	20.5	12.4	n.a.
Cucumbers	69.0	64.3	67.2

* Preliminary figures.

LIVESTOCK
(East Bank only; '000 head, year ending September)

	1984	1985	1986*
Horses	12	12	3
Mules	3	3	3
Asses	19*	19*	19
Cattle	37	35	35
Camels	15	14	14
Sheep	960	1,121	1,100
Goats	394	515	500
Poultry	32,000*	33,000*	34,000

* FAO estimates.

Source: FAO, *Production Yearbook*.

JORDAN

Forestry

ROUNDWOOD REMOVALS
(FAO estimates, '000 cubic metres)

	1980	1981	1982
Industrial wood	4	4	4
Fuel wood	4	4	5
Total	8	8	9

1983–86: Annual output as in 1982 (FAO estimates).
Source: FAO, *Yearbook of Forest Products*.

Fishing

(metric tons, live weight)

	1984	1985	1986
Total catch	20*	40*	65

* FAO estimate.
Source: FAO, *Yearbook of Fishery Statistics*.

Mining and Industry

(East Bank only; '000 metric tons, unless otherwise indicated)

	1985	1986	1987
Phosphates	6,067.1	6,249.2	6,845.4
Potash	908.2	1,102.0	1,203.2
Salt	32.2	33.7	n.a.
Petroleum products	2,423.9	2,257.1	2,404.5
Chemical acids	1,007.6	1,024.8	1,103.2
Fertilizers	510.5	551.1	604.0
Cement	2,022.9	1,794.7	2,371.6
Iron	198.4	209.6	217.0
Alcoholic drinks ('000 litres)	5,547.2	5,457.2	5,320.0
Cigarettes (million)	3,538.1	3,327.7	4,000.4
Electricity (million kWh)	2,154.4	2,646.8	3,123.8

1985: Crude petroleum 1,882 metric tons.

Finance

CURRENCY AND EXCHANGE RATES

Monetary Units
 1,000 fils = 1 Jordanian dinar (JD).

Denominations
 Coins: 1, 5, 10, 20, 25, 50, 100 and 250 fils.
 Notes: 500 fils; 1, 5, 10 and 20 dinars.

Sterling and Dollar Equivalents (30 September 1988)
 £1 sterling = 639.7 fils;
 US $1 = 378.3 fils;
 100 JD = £156.32 = $264.34.

Average Exchange Rates (US $ per JD)
 1985 2.5379
 1986 2.8583
 1987 2.9522

Note: Since 1975 the value of the Jordanian dinar has been linked to the IMF's special drawing right, with a mid-point exchange rate of JD 1 = SDR 2.579.

BUDGET ESTIMATES (East Bank only; JD '000)

Revenue	1988*	1989
Local revenues (taxes, etc.)	610,900	547,500
Grants and loans	225,000	225,000
Loans for development projects	146,300	103,000
Loan repayments	26,300	37,600
Total	1,008,500	913,100

Expenditure	1988*	1989
Capital and development expenditure	451,500	346,500
Recurrent expenditure	623,800	688,900
Defence	256,000	251,500
Total	1,075,300	1,035,400

* Subsequently revised.

CENTRAL BANK RESERVES
(US $ million at 31 December)

	1985	1986	1987
Gold*	189.8	203.5	200.1
IMF special drawing rights	24.1	23.9	12.1
Foreign exchange	398.7	413.2	412.6
Total	612.6	640.6	624.8

* National valuation.
Source: IMF, *International Financial Statistics*.

MONEY SUPPLY (JD million at 31 December)

	1985	1986	1987
Currency outside banks	531.79	583.87	655.78
Demand deposits at commercial banks	308.45	310.74	322.81

Source: IMF, *International Financial Statistics*.

COST OF LIVING
(Consumer Price Index; base: 1980 = 100)

	1984	1985	1986
Food	118.4	121.0	122.9
Fuel and light	123.9	128.5	124.8
Clothing	138.7	138.5	125.1
Rent	130.4	138.1	135.8
All items (incl. others)	126.2	130.0	130.0

1987: Food 119.5; All items 129.6.
Source: ILO, mainly *Year Book of Labour Statistics*.

NATIONAL ACCOUNTS
(East Bank only; JD million at current prices)
Expenditure on the Gross Domestic Product

	1985	1986	1987
Government final consumption expenditure	405.2	449.9	459.8
Private final consumption expenditure	1,401.7	1,238.4	1,281.7
Increase in stocks	16.8	25.3	446.0
Gross fixed capital formation	473.1	459.7	
Total domestic expenditure	2,296.8	2,173.3	2,187.5
Exports of goods and services	778.1	630.3	753.6
Less Imports of goods and services	1,469.0	1,163.7	1,254.8
GDP in purchasers' values	1,605.9	1,639.9	1,686.3
GDP at constant 1980 prices	1,235.3	1,261.5	1,301.2

Source: IMF, *International Financial Statistics*.

JORDAN

BALANCE OF PAYMENTS (US $ million)

	1985	1986	1987
Merchandise exports f.o.b.	788.9	732.0	933.1
Merchandise imports	−2,426.7	−2,158.4	−2,400.1
Trade balance	−1,637.9	−1,426.4	−1,467.0
Exports of services	1,268.2	1,158.9	1,350.0
Imports of services	−1,476.6	−1,390.9	−1,576.9
Balance on goods and services	−1,846.3	−1,658.4	−1,693.9
Private unrequited transfers (net)	846.2	984.4	742.9
Government unrequited transfers (net)	739.6	634.2	599.1
Current balance	−260.5	−39.8	−351.8
Direct capital investment (net)	25.7	18.8	38.3
Other long-term capital (net)	277.4	127.8	188.2
Short-term capital (net)	−54.9	−47.1	238.7
Net errors and omissions	−29.6	−17.2	27.9
Total (net monetary movements)	−41.9	42.5	141.3
Monetization of gold (net)	0.3	0.6	−12.5
Valuation changes (net)	141.5	146.5	316.7
Changes in reserves	99.9	189.7	445.5

Source: IMF, *International Financial Statistics*.

External Trade

PRINCIPAL COMMODITIES (JD '000)

Imports	1985	1986	1987
Food and live animals	175,784	165,568	155,719
Beverages and tobacco	4,036	6,672	7,999
Crude materials (inedible) except fuels	33,070	28,646	28,528
Mineral fuels, lubricants, etc.	223,270	116,480	156,138
Crude petroleum	192,640	92,832	118,590
Animal and vegetable oils and fats	10,152	9,417	8,018
Chemicals	67,639	74,865	91,671
Basic manufactures	169,597	140,947	169,391
Machinery and transport equipment	207,385	176,604	186,290
Miscellaneous manufactured articles	105,165	79,863	87,734
Other commodities and transactions	78,347	51,137	24,057
Total	1,074,445	850,199	915,545

Exports	1985	1986	1987
Phosphates	66,084	64,805	61,002
Potash	30,887	31,396	28,003
Chemicals	50,959	54,455	69,932
Cement	7,132	3,975	10,482
Vegetables, fruit and nuts	24,086	21,852	20,010
Cigarettes	1,716	1,297	3,017
Basic manufactures	32,586	15,647	26,861
Machinery and transport equipment	2,104	1,408	2,464
Miscellaneous manufactured articles	18,513	7,320	9,877
Total (incl. others)	255,346	225,615	248,773

PRINCIPAL TRADING PARTNERS (JD '000)

Imports	1985	1986	1987
Belgium	21,621	24,356	22,819
China, People's Republic	13,582	11,243	14,363
France	33,938	33,175	34,222
Germany, Fed. Republic	65,638	65,114	70,504
Italy	73,427	50,220	46,647
Iraq	72,951	80,274	99,401
Japan	67,813	66,642	55,664
Korea Republic	8,170	10,293	13,818
Kuwait	2,892	2,404	16,966
Netherlands	26,006	27,383	27,907
Romania	14,667	14,672	21,191
Saudi Arabia	159,058	49,670	76,761
Spain	15,926	11,692	11,251
Switzerland	58,889	11,173	10,068
Taiwan	20,856	18,040	16,794
Turkey	28,583	27,467	35,021
United Kingdom	63,276	68,786	58,303
USA	128,045	75,529	93,389

Exports	1985	1986	1987
China, People's Republic	2,278	7,570	10,044
Egypt	3,033	3,979	13,448
France	5,252	7,070	5,187
India	45,310	34,126	22,034
Indonesia	9,081	7,606	7,993
Iraq	65,850	42,458	59,865
Italy	3,655	7,099	9,266
Japan	5,815	5,690	7,435
Kuwait	7,738	8,813	8,614
Pakistan	5,941	3,456	10,253
Poland	3,287	3,721	7,068
Romania	10,015	7,524	6,418
Saudi Arabia	39,083	27,817	26,204
Syria	3,901	4,570	7,201
United Arab Emirates	805	845	4,861
Yugoslavia	3,069	7,689	6,923

Transport

RAILWAYS (traffic; East Bank only)

	1984	1985	1986
Passengers carried	30,196	34,247	31,304
Freight carried (tons)	3,152,663	2,582,702	2,789,524

ROAD TRAFFIC (motor vehicles registered, East Bank only)

	1984	1985	1986
Cars (private)	118,497	121,502	126,540
Taxis	12,439	12,699	13,208
Buses	3,346	3,513	3,783
Motorcycles	6,377	6,439	6,503
Others*	70,998	77,301	82,327
Total	211,657	221,454	232,361

* Trucks, vans, tankers, agricultural, construction and government vehicles.

SHIPPING (East Bank only; Aqaba port)

	1985	1986	1987
Number of vessels calling	2,671	2,677	2,555
Freight loaded ('000 tons)	8,177.6	9,696.5	11,271.6
Freight unloaded ('000 tons)	6,370.1	7,153.2	8,743.8

JORDAN

CIVIL AVIATION (East Bank only)

	1984	1985	1986
Passengers (number)	1,346,800	1,290,300	1,132,000
Freight (tons)	37,879	43,095	43,301

Tourism

(East Bank only)

	1984	1985	1986
Arabs	1,254,895	1,549,885	1,622,212
Europeans	102,351	108,443	88,805
Asians	133,467	132,795	112,803
Americans	65,215	54,677	31,139
Others	32,267	44,107	57,079
Total	1,588,195	1,889,907	1,912,038

Communications Media

(East Bank only)

	1984	1985	1986
Telephones in use	113,666	147,873	177,894

Radio receivers (1986): 850,000 in use.
Television receivers (1986): 250,000 in use.

Education

(East Bank)

	Schools*	Teachers	Pupils
1983/84	3,000	31,476	856,262
1984/85	3,065	34,119	863,892
1985/86	3,205	37,516	894,695

* Excluding schools for the handicapped.

Directory

The Constitution

The revised Constitution was approved by King Talal I on 1 January 1952.

The Hashemite Kingdom of Jordan is an independent, indivisible sovereign state. Its official religion is Islam; its official language Arabic.

RIGHTS OF THE INDIVIDUAL

There is to be no discrimination between Jordanians on account of race, religion or language. Work, education and equal opportunities shall be afforded to all as far as is possible. The freedom of the individual is guaranteed, as are his dwelling and property. No Jordanian shall be exiled. Labour shall be made compulsory only in a national emergency, or as a result of a conviction; conditions, hours worked and allowances are under the protection of the State.

The Press, and all opinions, are free, except under martial law. Societies can be formed, within the law. Schools may be established freely, but they must follow a recognized curriculum and educational policy. Elementary education is free and compulsory. All religions are tolerated. Every Jordanian is eligible for public office, and choices are to be made by merit only. Power belongs to the people.

THE LEGISLATIVE POWER

Legislative power is vested in the National Assembly and the King. The National Assembly consists of two houses: the Senate and the House of Representatives.

THE SENATE

The number of Senators is one-half of the number of members of the House of Representatives. Senators must be unrelated to the King, over 40, and are chosen from present and past Prime Ministers and Ministers, past Ambassadors or Ministers Plenipotentiary, past Presidents of the House of Representatives, past Presidents and members of the Court of Cassation and of the Civil and Shari'a Courts of Appeal, retired officers of the rank of General and above, former members of the House of Representatives who have been elected twice to that House, etc. . . . They may not hold public office. Senators are appointed for four years. They may be reappointed. The President of the Senate is appointed for two years.

THE HOUSE OF REPRESENTATIVES

The members of the House of Representatives are elected by secret ballot in a general direct election and retain their mandate for four years. General elections take place during the four months preceding the end of the term. The President of the House is elected by secret ballot each year by the Representatives. Representatives must be Jordanians of over 30, they must have a clean record, no active business interests, and are debarred from public office. Close relatives of the King are not eligible. If the House of Representatives is dissolved, the new House shall assemble in extraordinary session not more than four months after the date of dissolution. The new House cannot be dissolved for the same reason as the last. (The House was dissolved by Royal Decree in July 1988, pending revision of the electoral laws.)

GENERAL PROVISIONS FOR THE NATIONAL ASSEMBLY

The King summons the National Assembly to its ordinary session on 1 November each year. This date can be postponed by the King for two months, or he can dissolve the Assembly before the end of its three months' session. Alternatively, he can extend the session up to a total period of six months. Each session is opened by a speech from the throne.

Decisions in the House of Representatives and the Senate are made by a majority vote. The quorum is two-thirds of the total number of members in each House. When the voting concerns the Constitution, or confidence in the Council of Ministers, 'the votes shall be taken by calling the members by name in a loud voice'. Sessions are public, though secret sessions can be held at the request of the Government or of five members. Complete freedom of speech, within the rules of either House, is allowed.

The Prime Minister places proposals before the House of Representatives; if accepted there, they are referred to the Senate and finally sent to the King for confirmation. If one house rejects a law while the other accepts it, a joint session of the House of Representatives and the Senate is called, and a decision made by a two-thirds majority. If the King withholds his approval from a law, he returns it to the Assembly within six months with the reasons for his dissent; a joint session of the Houses then makes a decision, and if the law is accepted by this decision it is promulgated. The Budget is submitted to the National Assembly one month before the beginning of the financial year.

THE KING

The throne of the Hashemite Kingdom devolves by male descent in the dynasty of King Abdullah Ibn al Hussein. The King attains his majority on his eighteenth lunar year; if the throne is inherited by a minor, the powers of the King are exercised by a Regent or a Council of Regency. If the King, through illness or absence, cannot perform his duties, his powers are given to a Deputy, or to a Council of the Throne. This Deputy, or Council, may be appointed by Iradas (decrees) by the King, or, if he is incapable, by the Council of Ministers.

On his accession, the King takes the oath to respect and observe the provisions of the Constitution and to be loyal to the nation.

JORDAN

Directory

As head of the State he is immune from all liability or responsibility. He approves laws and promulgates them. He declares war, concludes peace and signs treaties; treaties, however, must be approved by the National Assembly. The King is Commander-in-Chief of the Navy, the Army and the Air Force. He orders the holding of elections; convenes, inaugurates, adjourns and prorogues the House of Representatives. The Prime Minister is appointed by him, as are the President and members of the Senate. Military and civil ranks are also granted, or withdrawn, by the King. No death sentence is carried out until he has confirmed it.

MINISTERS

The Council of Ministers consists of the Prime Minister, President of the Council, and of his Ministers. Ministers are forbidden to become members of any company, to receive a salary from any company, or to participate in any financial act of trade. The Council of Ministers is entrusted with the conduct of all affairs of State, internal and external.

The Council of Ministers is responsible to the House of Representatives for matters of general policy. Ministers may speak in either House, and, if they are members of one House, they may also vote in that House. Votes of confidence in the Council are cast in the House of Representatives, and decided by a two-thirds majority. If a vote of 'no confidence' is returned, the Ministers are bound to resign. Every newly-formed Council of Ministers must present its programme to the House of Representatives and ask for a vote of confidence. The House of Representatives can impeach Ministers, as it impeaches its own members.

AMENDMENTS

Two amendments were passed in November 1974 giving the King the right to dissolve the Senate or to take away membership from any of its members, and to postpone general elections for a period not to exceed a year, if there are circumstances in which the Council of Ministers feels that it is impossible to hold elections. A further amendment in February 1976 enabled the King to postpone elections indefinitely. In January 1984 two amendments were passed, allowing elections 'in any part of the country where it is possible to hold them' (effectively, only the East Bank) and empowering the National Assembly to elect deputies from the Israeli-held West Bank.

The Government

HEAD OF STATE

King HUSSEIN IBN TALAL (proclaimed King on 11 August 1952; crowned on 2 May 1953).

CABINET
(February 1989)

Prime Minister and Minister of Defence: ZAID AR-RIFAI.
Deputy Prime Minister and Minister of Foreign Affairs: MARWAN AL-QASSIM.
Deputy Prime Minister and Minister of Education: DHOUQAN AL-HINDAWI.
Minister of Finance and Customs: Dr HANNA AWDAH.
Minister of Information: Dr HANI AL-KHASAWNEH.
Minister of Youth: Dr AWAD KHULAYFAT.
Minister of Justice: RIYADH ASH-SHAKAA.
Minister of Agriculture: YOUSUF HAMDAN.
Minister of Water and Irrigation: AHMAD DAHQAN.
Minister of Energy and Mineral Resources: Dr HISHAM AL-KHATIB.
Minister of Awqaf (Religious Endowments) and Islamic Affairs: ABD AL-AZIZ AL-KHAYAT.
Minister of Trade and Industry: HAMDI AT-TABBAH.
Minister of Supply: FAYEZ AL-TARAWNEH.
Minister of Transport and Communications: KHALID AL-HAJ HASSAN.
Minister of Higher Education: NASR AD-DIN AL-ASAD.
Minister of Culture and National Heritage: Dr MUHAMMAD AL-HAMMOURI.
Minister of Health: ZUHEIR MALHAS.
Minister of Labour: MARWAN DOUDIN.
Minister of Social Development: Dr FAWAZ TOUQAN.
Minister of the Interior: RAJAI AD-DAJANI.
Minister of Planning: TAHER KANAAN.
Minister of Public Works and Housing: SHAFIQ AZ-ZAWAYDAH.
Minister of Tourism: YANAL HIKMAT.
Minister of Municipal, Rural and Environmental Affairs: MARWAN AL-HAMOUD.
Ministers of State for Prime Ministerial Affairs: ZUHEIR AJLOUNI, AMER KHAMMASH.
Minister of State, Chief of the Royal Court, Adviser to King Hussein on Armed Forces Affairs: SHARIF ZAID IBN SHAKER.
Ministers of State, Advisers to King Hussein at the Royal Court: ADNAN ABU AWDAH, AMER KHAMMASH.

MINISTRIES

Office of the Prime Minister: POB 80, 35216, Amman; tel. 641211; telex 21444.
Ministry of Agriculture: POB 2099, Amman; tel. 639391; telex 24176.
Ministry of Awqaf (Religious Endowments) and Islamic Affairs: POB 659, Amman; tel. 666141; telex 21559.
Ministry of Communications: POB 71, Amman; tel. 624301; telex 21666.
Ministry of Culture and Information: POB 1794, Amman; tel. 661147; telex 21749.
Ministry of Defence: POB 1577, Amman; tel. 644361; telex 21200.
Ministry of Education: POB 1646, Amman; tel. 669181; telex 21396.
Ministry of Finance: POB 85, Amman; tel. 636321; telex 23634.
Ministry of Foreign Affairs: POB 1577, Amman; tel. 644361; telex 21255.
Ministry of Health: POB 86, Amman; tel. 665131; telex 21595.
Ministry of the Interior: POB 100, Amman; tel. 663111; telex 23162.
Ministry of Justice: POB 6040, Amman; tel. 663101.
Ministry of Labour: POB 9052, Amman; tel. 630343.
Ministry of Municipal, Rural and Environmental Affairs: POB 1799, Amman; tel. 641393.
Ministry of Public Works: POB 1220, Amman; tel. 624191; telex 21944.
Ministry of Social Development: POB 6720, Amman; tel. 643838.
Ministry of Supply: POB 830, Amman; tel. 630371; telex 21278.
Ministry of Tourism: POB 224, Amman; tel. 642311; telex 21741.
Ministry of Trade and Industry: POB 2019, Amman; tel. 663191; telex 21163.
Ministry of Transport: POB 1929, 35214 Amman; tel. 641461; telex 21541.

Legislature

MAJLIS AL-UMMA
(National Assembly)

Senate

The Senate (House of Notables) consists of 30 members, appointed by the King. A new Senate was appointed by the King on 12 January 1984.

President: AHMAD AL-LOUZI.

House of Representatives

Elections to the then 60-seat House of Representatives (30 from both the East and West Banks) took place in April 1967. There were no political parties. The House was dissolved by Royal Decree on 23 November 1974, but reconvened briefly on 15 February 1976. Elections were postponed indefinitely.

In April 1978 a National Consultative Council was formed by Royal Decree. It consisted of 60 members appointed by the King, and served terms of two years. The third term began on 20 April 1982. The King, by his constitutional right, dissolved the Council on 7 January 1984 and reconvened the House of Representatives. Eight members from the East Bank had died since the House was last convened and by-elections to fill their seats took place on 12 March 1984. The seven vacant seats of members from the Israeli-occupied West Bank, where elections could not take place, were filled by a vote of the members of the House in accordance with a constitutional amendment unanimously approved on 9 January 1984.

In March 1986 the House of Representatives approved a draft electoral law providing for the number of seats in the House to be increased from 60 to 142 (71 from the East Bank and 71 from the West Bank, including 11 from the refugee camps in the East Bank) at the next election. In October 1987, while opening a new session of the National Assembly, King Hussein announced that

JORDAN

elections to the House of Representatives were to be postponed for two years. On 30 July 1988 King Hussein dissolved the House of Representatives, (one-half of whose 60 seats were held by deputies for the West Bank) and on 31 July he severed Jordan's legal and administrative links with the West Bank. (Theoretically, the Senate cannot legislate without the House of Representatives.) Legislative elections were postponed in October 1988, pending a revision of the 1986 electoral laws.

Speaker: AKEF AL-FAYEZ.

Political Organizations

Political parties were banned before the elections of July 1963. In September 1971 King Hussein announced the formation of a Jordanian National Union. This was the only political organization allowed. Communists, Marxists and 'other advocates of imported ideologies' were ineligible for membership. In March 1972 the organization was renamed the Arab National Union. In April 1974 King Hussein dissolved the executive committee of the Arab National Union, and accepted the resignation of the Secretary-General. In February 1976 the Cabinet approved a law abolishing the Union. Membership was estimated at about 100,000.

Diplomatic Representation

EMBASSIES IN JORDAN

Algeria: 3rd Circle, Jabal Amman; tel. 641271; Ambassador: ABDERRAHMAN SHRAYYET.
Australia: POB 35201, 4th Circle, Jabal Amman; tel. 673246; telex 21743; Ambassador: TERENCE GOGGIN.
Austria: POB 815368, Amman; tel. 644635; telex 22484; Ambassador: Dr ARNOLD MOEBIUS.
Bahrain: Amman; tel. 664148; Ambassador: IBRAHIM ALI IBRAHIM.
Belgium: Amman; tel. 675683; telex 22340; Ambassador: GUIDO VANSINA.
Brazil: POB 5497, Amman; tel. 642183; telex 23827; Ambassador: FELIX BAPTISTA DE FARIA.
Bulgaria: POB 950578, Um Uzaina al-Janoubi, Amman; tel. 818151; telex 22247; Ambassador: YANTCHO DEMIREV.
Canada: POB 815403, Pearl of Shmeisani Bldg, Shmeisani, Amman; tel. 666124; telex 23080; Ambassador: MICHAEL D. BELL.
Chile: Shmeisani, Amman; tel. 661336; telex 21696; Chargé d'affaires a.i.: ALBERTO YOACHAM.
China, People's Republic: Shmeisani, Amman; tel. 666139; telex 21770; Ambassador: ZHANG ZHEN.
Czechoslovakia: POB 2213, Amman; tel. 665105; Ambassador: KAREL FISER.
Egypt: POB 35178, Zahran St, 3rd Circle, Jabal Amman; tel. 641375; Ambassador: IHAB SEID WAHBA.
France: POB 374, Jabal Amman; tel. 641273; telex 21219; Ambassador: PATRICK LECLERCQ.
German Democratic Republic: Amman.
Germany, Federal Republic: 31 Benghazi St, POB 183, Jabal Amman; tel. 689351; telex 1235; Ambassador: Dr HERWIG BARTELS.
Greece: POB 35069, Jabal Amman; tel. 672331; telex 21566; Ambassador: HANNIBAL VELLIADIS.
Hungary: POB 3441, Amman; tel. 674916; telex 21815; Ambassador: Dr EGYED ANDOR.
India: POB 2168, 1st Circle, Jabal Amman; tel. 637262; telex 21068; Ambassador: GURCHARAN SINGH.
Iran: POB 173, Jabal Amman; tel. 641281 telex 21218.
Iraq: POB 2025, 1st Circle, Jabal Amman; tel. 639331; telex 21277; Ambassador: (vacant).
Italy: POB 9800, Jabal Luweibdeh, Amman; tel. 638185; telex 21143; Ambassador: LUIGI AMADUZZI.
Japan: POB 2835, Jabal Amman; tel. 672486; telex 21518; Ambassador: AKIRA NAKAYAMA.
Korea, Democratic People's Republic: Amman; tel. 666349; Chargé d'affaires: KIM YONG HO.
Korea, Republic: 3rd Circle, Jabal Amman, Abu Tamman St, POB 3060, Amman; tel. 642268; telex 29457; Ambassador: DONGSOON PARK.
Kuwait: POB 2107, Jabal Amman; tel. 641235; telex 21377; Ambassador: (vacant).
Lebanon: 2nd Circle, Jabal Amman; tel. 641381; Ambassador: PIERRE ZIADÉ.
Morocco: Jabal Amman; tel. 641451; telex 21661; Chargé d'affaires: SALEM FANKHAR ASH-SHANFARI.
Oman: Amman; tel. 661131; telex 21550; Ambassador: KHAMIS BIN HAMAD AL-BATASHI.
Pakistan: Amman; tel. 622787; Ambassador: Prof. EHSAN RASHID.
Philippines: POB 925207, Abbas Aqad St, 2nd Circle, Jabal, Amman; tel. 645161; telex 23321; Ambassador: JUAN V. SAEZ.
Poland: POB 2124, 1st Circle, Jabal Amman; tel. 637153; telex 21119; Ambassador: LUDWIK JANCZYSZYN.
Qatar: Amman; tel. 644331; telex 21248; Ambassador: Sheikh HAMAD BIN MUHAMMAD BIN JABER ATH-THANI.
Romania: Amman; tel. 663161; Ambassador: TEODOR COMAN.
Saudi Arabia: POB 2133, 5th Circle, Jabal Amman; tel. 644154; Ambassador: Sheikh IBRAHIM MUHAMMAD AS-SULTAN.
Spain: Jabal Amman; tel. 622140; telex 21224; Ambassador: (vacant).
Sudan: Jabal Amman; tel. 624145; telex 21778; Ambassador: AHMAD DIAB.
Sweden: POB 927117, Shmeisani, Amman; tel. 669177; telex 22039; Ambassador: LARS LÖNNBACK.
Switzerland: Jabal Amman; tel. 644416; telex 21237; Ambassador: HARALD BORNER.
Syria: POB 1377, 4th Circle, Jabal Amman; tel. 641935; Chargé d'affaires: MAJID ABOU SALEH.
Tunisia: Jabal Amman; tel. 674307; telex 21849; Ambassador: SAID BEN MUSTAPHA.
Turkey: POB 2062, Queen Zain ash-Sharaf St, 2nd Circle, Jabal Amman; tel. 641251; telex 23005; Ambassador: SEMIH BELEN.
USSR: Amman; tel. 641158; Ambassador: ALEKSANDR IVANOVICH ZINCHUK.
United Arab Emirates: Jabal Amman; tel. 644369; telex 21832; Ambassador: ABDULLAH ALI ASH-SHURAFA.
United Kingdom: POB 87, Abdoun, Amman; tel. 823100; telex 22209; Ambassador: ANTHONY REEVE.
USA: POB 354, Jabal Amman; tel. 644371; telex 21510; Ambassador: ROSCOE S. SUDDARTH.
Yemen Arab Republic: Amman; tel. 642381; telex 23526; Ambassador: ALI ABDULLAH ABU LUHOUM.
Yugoslavia: POB 5227, Amman; tel. 665107; telex 21505; Ambassador: ZORAN S. POPOVIĆ.

Judicial System

With the exception of matters of purely personal nature concerning members of non-Muslim communities, the law of Jordan was based on Islamic Law for both civil and criminal matters. During the days of the Ottoman Empire, certain aspects of Continental law, especially French commercial law and civil and criminal procedure, were introduced. Due to British occupation of Palestine and Transjordan from 1917 to 1948, the Palestine territory has adopted, either by statute or case law, much of the English common law. Since the annexation of the non-occupied part of Palestine and the formation of the Hashemite Kingdom of Jordan, there has been a continuous effort to unify the law.

Court of Cassation. The Court of Cassation consists of seven judges, who sit in full panel for exceptionally important cases. In most appeals, however, only five members sit to hear the case. All cases involving amounts of more than JD100 may be reviewed by this Court, as well as cases involving lesser amounts and cases which cannot be monetarily valued. However, for the latter types of cases, review is available only by leave of the Court of Appeal, or, upon refusal by the Court of Appeal, by leave of the President of the Court of Cassation. In addition to these functions as final and Supreme Court of Appeal, the Court of Cassation also sits as High Court of Justice to hear applications in the nature of habeas corpus, mandamus and certiorari dealing with complaints of a citizen against abuse of governmental authority.

Courts of Appeal. There are two Courts of Appeal, each of which is composed of three judges, whether for hearing of appeals or for dealing with Magistrates Courts' judgments in chambers. Jurisdiction of the two Courts is geographical, with the Court for the Western Region sitting in Jerusalem (which has not sat since June 1967) and the Court for the Eastern Region sitting in Amman. The regions are separated by the River Jordan. Appellate review of the Courts of Appeal extends to judgments rendered in the Courts of First Instance, the Magistrates' Courts, and Religious Courts.

Courts of First Instance. The Courts of First Instance are courts of general jurisdiction in all matters civil and criminal except those

JORDAN

specifically allocated to the Magistrates' Courts. Three judges sit in all felony trials, while only two judges sit for misdemeanour and civil cases. Each of the seven Courts of First Instance also exercises appellate jurisdiction in cases involving judgments of less than JD20 and fines of less than JD10, rendered by the Magistrates' Courts.

Magistrates' Courts. There are 14 Magistrates' Courts, which exercise jurisdiction in civil cases involving no more than JD250 and in criminal cases involving maximum fines of JD100 or maximum imprisonment of one year.

Religious Courts. There are two types of religious court: The Shari'a Courts (Muslims): and the Ecclesiastical Courts (Eastern Orthodox, Greek Melkite, Roman Catholic and Protestant). Jurisdiction extends to personal (family) matters, such as marriage, divorce, alimony, inheritance, guardianship, wills, interdiction and, for the Muslim community, the constitution of Waqfs (Religious Endowments). When a dispute involves persons of different religious communities, the Civil Courts have jurisdiction in the matter unless the parties agree to submit to the jurisdiction of one or the other of the Religious Courts involved.

Each Shari'a (Muslim) Court consists of one judge (Qadi), while most of the Ecclesiastical (Christian) Courts are normally composed of three judges, who are usually clerics. Shari'a Courts apply the doctrines of Islamic Law, based on the Koran and the Hadith (Precepts of Muhammad), while the Ecclesiastical Courts base their law on various aspects of Canon Law. In the event of conflict between any two Religious Courts or between a Religious Court and a Civil Court, a Special Tribunal of three judges is appointed by the President of the Court of Cassation, to decide which court shall have jurisdiction. Upon the advice of experts on the law of the various communities, this Special Tribunal decides on the venue for the case at hand.

Religion

Over 80% of the population are Sunni Muslims, and the King can trace unbroken descent from the Prophet Muhammad. There is a Christian minority, living mainly in the towns, and there are smaller numbers of non-Sunni Muslims.

ISLAM

Chief Justice and President of the Supreme Muslim Secular Council: Sheikh MUHAMMAD MHELAN.

Director of Shari'a Courts: Sheikh SUBHI AL-MUWQQAT.

Mufti of the Hashemite Kingdom of Jordan: Sheikh MUHAMMAD ABDO HASHEM.

CHRISTIANITY

The Roman Catholic Church

Latin Rite

Jordan forms part of the Patriarchate of Jerusalem (see chapter on Israel).

Vicar-General for Transjordan: Mgr SELIM SAYEGH (Titular Bishop of Aquae in Proconsulari), Latin Vicariate, POB 1317, Amman.

Melkite Rite

The Greek-Melkite archdiocese of Petra (Wadi Musa) and Philadelphia (Amman) contained an estimated 19,962 adherents at 31 December 1986.

Archbishop of Petra and Philadelphia: Most Rev. SABA YOUAKIM, Archevêché Grec-Melkite Catholique, POB 2435, Jabal Amman; tel. 624757.

Syrian Rite

The Syrian Catholic Patriarch of Antioch is resident in Beirut, Lebanon.

Patriarchal Vicariate of Jerusalem: Mont Achrafieh, Rue Barto, POB 10041, Amman; Vicar Patriarchal Mgr PIERRE ABD AL-AHAD.

The Anglican Communion

Within the Episcopal Church in Jerusalem and the Middle East, Jordan forms part of the diocese of Jerusalem. The President Bishop of the Church is the Bishop in Jerusalem (see the chapter on Israel).

Assistant Bishop in Amman: Rt Rev. ELIA KHOURY, POB 598, Amman.

Other Christian Churches

The Coptic Orthodox Church, the Greek Orthodox Church (Patriarchate of Jerusalem) and the Evangelical Lutheran Church in Jordan are also active.

The Press

Jordan Press Association: Amman; Pres. RAKAN AL-MAJALI.

DAILIES

Al-Akhbar (News): POB 62420, Amman; f. 1976; Arabic; publ. by the Arab Press Co; Editor RACAN EL-MAJALI; circ. 15,000.

Ad-Dustour (The Constitution): POB 591, Amman; tel. 664153; telex 21392; f. 1967; Arabic; publ. by the Jordan Press and Publishing Co; owns commercial printing facilities; Chair. OSAMA M. ASH-SHERIF; Gen. Man. KAMEL ASH-SHERIF; circ. 60,000.

Ar-Rai (Opinion): POB 6710, Amman; tel. 667171; telex 21497; f. 1971; Arabic; independent; published by Jordan Press Establishment; Gen. Man. MUHAMMAD AMAD; Editor-in-Chief MAHMOUD AL-KAYED; circ. 80,000.

The Jordan Times: POB 6710, Amman; tel. 661242; telex 21497; f. 1975; English; published by Jordan Press Establishment; Responsible Editor RAKAN MAJALI; Editor-in-Chief RAMI G. KHOURI; circ. 15,000.

Sawt ash-Shaab (Voice of the People): Amman; f. 1983; Arabic; circ. 30,000.

PERIODICALS

Akhbar al-Usbou (News of the Week): POB 605, Amman; tel. 677881; telex 21644; f. 1959; weekly; Arabic; economic, social, political; Chief Editor and Publr ABD AL-HAFIZ MUHAMMAD; circ. 100,000.

Al-Aqsa (The Ultimate): POB 1957, Amman; weekly; Arabic; armed forces magazines.

Al-Fajr al-Iqtisadi (Economic Dawn): Amman; f. 1982; weekly; economic; owned by Al-Fajr for Press, Publication and Distribution; Dir-Gen. and Editor-in-Chief YOUSUF ABU-LAIL.

Huda El-Islam (The Right Way of Islam): POB 659, Amman; tel. 666141; telex 21559; f. 1956; monthly; Arabic; scientific and literary; published by the Ministry of Awqaf and Islamic Affairs; Editor Dr AHMAD MUHAMMAD HULAYYEL.

The Jerusalem Star: POB 591, Amman; tel. 664153; telex 21392; f. 1982; weekly; English; publ. by Jordan Press and Publishing Co; Dir SAIF ASH-SHARIF; Editor-in-Chief OSAMA M. ASH-SHERIF; circ. 15,000.

Jordan: POB 224, Amman; telex 21497; f. 1969; published quarterly by Jordan Information Bureau, Washington; circ. 100,000.

Al-Liwa' (The Standard): Amman; f. 1972; weekly; Arabic; Chief Editor HASSAN ATTEL.

Military Magazine: Army Headquarters, Amman; f. 1955; quarterly; dealing with military and literary subjects; published by Armed Forces.

As-Sabah (The Morning): POB 2396, Amman; weekly; Arabic; circ. 6,000.

Shari'a: POB 585, Amman; f. 1959; fortnightly; Islamic affairs; published by Shari'a College; circ. 5,000.

Shehan: Al-Karak; Editor REYAD AL-HROUB.

NEWS AGENCIES

Jordan News Agency (PETRA): POB 6845, Amman; tel. 644455; telex 21220; f. 1965; government-controlled; Dir-Gen. ALI SAFADI.

Foreign News Bureaux

Agence France-Presse (AFP): POB 3340, Amman; tel. 642976; telex 21469; Bureau Man. Mrs RANDA HABIB.

Agenzia Nazionale Stampa Associata (ANSA) (Italy): POB 35111, Amman; tel. 642936; telex 21207; Correspondent JOHN HALABI.

Associated Press (AP) (USA): POB 35111, Amman; tel. 644097; telex 23514; Correspondent JOHN RICE.

Deutsche Presse Agentur (dpa) (Federal Republic of Germany): POB 35111, Amman; tel. 623907; telex 21207; Correspondent JOHN HALABI.

Reuters (UK): POB 667, Amman; tel. 623776; telex 21414.

Telegrafnoye Agentstvo Sovetskovo Soyuza (TASS) (USSR): Jabal Amman, Nabich Faris St, Block 111/83 124, Amman; Correspondent NIKOLAI LEBEDINSKY.

Central News Agency (Taiwan), Iraqi News Agency, Middle East News Agency (Egypt), Qatar News Agency, Saudi Press Agency and UPI (USA) also maintain bureaux in Amman.

Publishers

Jordan Press and Publishing Co Ltd: Amman; tel. 664153; telex 21392; f. 1967 by *Al-Manar* and *Falastin* dailies; publishes *Ad-*

JORDAN

Dustour (daily), and *The Jerusalem Star* (English weekly); Chair. MAHMOUD ASH-SHARIF; Gen. Man. KAMEL ASH-SHARIF; Editor-in-Chief ABD AS-SALAM TARAWNEH.

Jordan Press Establishment: POB 6710, Amman; publishes *Ar-Rai* (daily) and the *Jordan Times* (daily); Chair. MAHMOUD KHAYED.

Other publishers in Amman include: Dairat al-Ihsaat al-Amman, George N. Kawar, Al-Matbaat al-Hashmiya and The National Press.

Radio and Television

The number of radio receivers in 1988 was an estimated 1,100,000; the number of TV receivers in 1988 was 250,000 (incl. 130,000 colour) (East Bank only).

Jordan Radio and Television Corporation (JRTV): POB 909, Amman; tel. 638760; telex 21285; f. 1968; government TV station broadcasts for 90 hours weekly in Arabic and English; in colour; advertising accepted; Dir-Gen. ISAM ARIDA; Dir of Programmes (Arabic) S. MASHINI; Dir of Programmes (English) J. ZADA; Dir (Eng.) RADI ALKHAS.

Finance

(cap. = capital; p.u. = paid up; dep. = deposits; m. = million; res = reserves; brs = branches; JD = Jordanian dinars)

BANKING

Central Bank

Central Bank of Jordan: POB 37, King Hussein St, Amman; tel. 630301; telex 21250; f. 1964; cap. p.u. JD6m., dep. JD171.8m., res JD12m., total assets JD820m. (Dec. 1986); 2 brs; Gov. HUSSAIN AL-QASSIM.

National Banks

Arab Bank Ltd: POB 950545, King Faisal St, Amman; tel. 660131; telex 23091; f. 1930; cap. p.u. JD22m., dep. JD3,092m., res JD139m., total assets JD3,897m. (Dec. 1987); 26 brs in Jordan, 43 brs abroad; Chair. ABD AL-MAJID SHOMAN.

Bank of Jordan Ltd: POB 2140, 3rd Circle, Jabal Amman; tel. 644327; telex 22033; f. 1960; cap. p.u. JD5.25m., dep. JD92m. total assets JD121.7m. (Dec. 1987); 26 brs; Chair. TAWFIK SHAKER FAKHOURI; Gen. Man. Dr MICHEL MARTO.

Cairo Amman Bank: POB 715, Shabsough St, Amman; tel. 639321; telex 21240; f. 1960; cap. p.u. JD5m., dep. JD117.6m., res JD9.6m., total assets JD190.7m. (Dec. 1986); associated with Banque du Caire, Cairo, which has a 12% share in the bank, and succeeded their Amman Branch; remaining 88% is owned by local interests; 19 brs; Chair. and Gen. Man. JAWDAT SHASHA'A.

Jordan-Gulf Bank SA: POB 9989, Shmeisani, al-Burj Area, Amman; tel. 603931; telex 21959; f. 1977; cap. p.u. JD6m., dep. JD120.5m., total assets JD102.6m. (Dec. 1987); 60% Jordanian-owned and 40% by Gulf businessmen; 22 brs; Chair. HE MUHAMMAD NAZZAL AL-ARMOUTI; Gen. Man. ADNAN DARWAZA.

Jordan Islamic Bank for Finance and Investment: POB 926225, Amman; tel. 677377; telex 21125; f. 1978; cap. p.u. JD6m., dep. JD158.5m., res JD3.9m., total assets JD197.4m. (Dec. 1987); 13 brs; Chair. Sheikh SALEH A. KAMEL; Gen. Man. MUSA A. SHIHADEH.

Jordan Kuwait Bank: POB 9776, Amman; tel. 662125; telex 21994; f. 1976; cap. p.u. JD5m., dep. JD129m. (Dec. 1987); 14 brs; Chair. Sheikh NASSER AS-SABAH; Deputy Chair. and Gen. Man. SUFIAN IBRAHIM YASSIN SARTAWI.

Jordan National Bank SA: POB 1578, Amman; tel. 642391; telex 21820; f. 1956; cap. p.u. JD9.2m., dep. JD140.1m., res JD12.9m. total assets JD162.2 (Dec. 1987); 30 brs in Jordan, 4 brs in Lebanon, 1 br in Cyprus; Chair. HE ABD AL-KADER TASH; Deputy Chair. YOUSUF I. MOU'ASHER.

Petra Bank: POB 6854, Wadi Sagra St, Amman; tel. 627311; telex 21868; f. 1977; cap. p.u. JD5m., dep. JD225.2m., res JD7.4m., total assets JD308.8m. (Dec. 1985); 60% owned by Jordanians and 40% by other Arab interests; 23 brs in Jordan; Chair. and Gen. Man. Dr AHMAD CHALABI.

Syrian Jordanian Bank: POB 926636, King Hussein St, Amman; tel. 661138; telex 22102; f. 1979; cap. p.u. JD1m., dep. 7.1m., total assets JD11.9m. (1987); 1 br; Chair. Management Cttee Dr MAHER G. SHUKRI; Gen. Man. HISHAM J. SAFADI.

Foreign Banks

Arab Land Bank (Egypt): POB 6729, Amir Muhammad St, Amman; tel. 628357; telex 21208; wholly-owned subsidiary of the Central Bank of Egypt; cap. JD5m., dep. JD27.2m., res JD1.8m., total assets JD41.8m. (Dec. 1986); 3 brs in Amman; Chair. HASSOUNEH HASID; Gen. Man. OMAR LOTFI.

Bank of Credit and Commerce International SA: POB 7943, King Hussein St, Amman; tel. 621367; telex 21455; 3 brs; Gen. Man. ABRAR HUSSAIN ZAIDI.

The British Bank of the Middle East (Hong Kong): POB 925286, Amman; tel. 669121; telex 22338; f. 1889; cap. p.u. JD5m., dep. JD66m., total assets JD78m. (Dec. 1987); 5 brs; Chair. W. PURVES; Area Man. D. M. TAIT.

Citibank NA: Jordan Insurance Bldg, 3rd Circle, Jabal Amman; tel. 644065; telex 21314; Gen. Man. GHADA DABBAS.

Grindlays Bank: POB 9997, Shmeisani, Amman; tel. 660301; telex 21980; cap. p.u. JD5m., dep. JD45m. (Dec. 1987); mem. of the Australia-New Zealand Banking Group Ltd; brs in Amman (7 brs), Aqaba, Irbid (sub-branch in Northern Shouneh), Zerka and Kerak; Gen. Man. in Jordan ALAN JOHN COOPER.

Rafidain Bank (Iraq): POB 1194, Amman; tel. 624365; telex 1334; f. 1941; cap. p.u. JD3m., res JD548,263, dep. JD10.2m. (Dec. 1983); 4 brs; Gen. Man. ADNAN AL-AZAWI.

Bank Al-Mashrek (Lebanon) also has a branch in Amman.

Specialized Credit Institutions

Agricultural Credit Corporation: POB 77, Amman; tel. 661105; f. 1959; cap. p.u. JD8.7m., dep. JD182,992, res JD3.5m., total assets JD29.5m. (Dec. 1986); 18 brs; Chair. and Man. Dir Dr SAMI SUNA'A.

The Arab Jordan Investment Bank: POB 8797, Amman; tel. 664126; telex 21719; f. 1978; cap. p.u. JD5m., dep. JD96.1m., res JD5.3m., total assets JD113m. (Dec. 1986); 2 brs; Chair. and Gen. Man. ABD AL-KADER AL-QADI.

Cities and Villages Development Bank: POB 1572, Amman; tel. 668151; telex 22476; f. 1979; cap. p.u. JD11.5m., gen. res JD6.6m., total assets JD49.4m. (Dec. 1986); Gen. Man. MUHAMMAD SALEH HOURANI.

Housing Bank: Police College St, Abdali, POB 7693, Amman; tel. 667126; telex 21693; f. 1973; cap. p.u. JD12m., dep. JD338.5m., total assets JD473.6m. (Dec. 1987); 81 brs; Chair. and Dir-Gen. ZUHAIR KHOURI.

Industrial Development Bank: POB 1982, Jabal Amman, Zahran St, Amman; tel. 642216; telex 21349; f. 1965; cap. p.u. JD5.7m., total assets JD61.8m. (Dec. 1987); Chair. ROUHI EL-KHATIB; Gen. Man. ZIYAD ANNAB.

Jordan Co-operative Organization: POB 1343, Amman; tel. 665171; telex 21835; f. 1968; cap. p.u. JD1m., dep. JD8.8m., res JD632,325, total assets JD21.6m. (Dec. 1986); Chair. MORAIWID AT-TEL.

Jordan Securities Corporation: POB 926691, Amman; tel. 664183; telex 22258; f. 1979; cap. p.u. JD4m., dep. JD21.1m., total assets JD32.5m. (Dec. 1986); Chair. ZUHAIR KHOURI; Gen. Mans SALEM MASA'DEH, ABD AL-QADIR DWEEK; (scheduled to merge with Arab Finance Corpn to form a full commercial bank).

Social Security Corporation: POB 926031, Amman; telex 22287; f. 1978; Dir-Gen. Dr M. MAHDI EL-FARHAN.

STOCK EXCHANGE

Amman Financial Market: POB 8802, Amman; tel. 663170; telex 21711; f. 1978; Chair. and Gen. Man. Dr HASHIM SABAGH.

INSURANCE

Al-Ahlia Insurance Co (Jordan) Ltd: POB 2938, UTG. Bldg, Shmeisani, opposite Syndicates Bldg, Sharif Abd al-Hamid Sharaf St, Amman; tel. 677689; telex 23503; merged with the National Insurance Co, Dec. 1985.

Jordan Insurance Co Ltd: POB 279, Companies Bldg, 3rd Circle, Jabal Amman, Amman; tel. 634161; telex 21486; f. 1951; cap. p.u. JD1,100m.; Chair. and Man. Dir JAWDAT SHASHA'A; 10 brs (4 in Saudi Arabia, 4 in the United Arab Emirates, 1 in Kuwait, 1 in Lebanon).

Middle East Insurance Co Ltd: POB 1802, Shmeisani, Yaquob Sarrouf St, Amman; tel. 605144; telex 21420; f. 1963; cap. p.u. JD2m.; Man. Dir SAMI I. GAMMOH.

United Insurance Co Ltd: POB 7521, United Bldg, Shmeisani, Yaqoub Sarrouf St, Amman; tel. 625828; telex 21323; f. 1972; merged with the Arab Belgium Insurance Co Jan. 1986; merged with Ash-Sharq Insurance (Jordan Agency) and New India Insurance (Jordan Agency) February 1988; all types of insurance; cap. JD1.5m.; Chair. RAOUF SA'AD ABUJABER; Mans MICHEL S. SUSU, NAZEH K. AZAR.

There are 31 local and 11 foreign insurance companies operating in Jordan. The first reinsurance company in the country was registered on 1 January 1987.

Trade and Industry

CHAMBERS OF COMMERCE AND INDUSTRY

Amman Chamber of Commerce: POB 287, Amman; tel. 666151; telex 21543; f. 1923; Pres. Muhammad Asfour; Dir Muhammad Tijani.

Amman Chamber of Industry: POB 1800, Amman; tel. 641648; telex 22079; f. 1962; 4,344 industrial companies registered (1987); Pres. Isam Bdeir; Exec. Dir Muhammad S. Jaber.

PUBLIC CORPORATIONS

Jordan Valley Authority: POB 2769, Amman; tel. 642472; telex 21692; projects in Stage I of the Jordan Valley Development Plan were completed in 1979. In 1988 about 26,000 ha was under intensive cultivation. Infrastructure projects also completed include 1,100 km of roads, 2,100 housing units, 100 schools, 15 health centres, 14 administration buildings, 4 marketing centres, 2 community centres, 2 vocational training centres. Electricity is now provided to all the towns and villages in the valley from the national network and domestic water is supplied to them from tube wells. Contributions to the cost of development came through loans from Kuwait Fund, Abu Dhabi Fund, Saudi Fund, Arab Fund, USAID, Fed. Germany, World Bank, EEC, Italy, Netherlands, UK, Japan and OPEC Special Fund. Many of the Stage II irrigation projects are now completed or under implementation. Projects under way include the construction of the Wadi al-Arab dam, the raising of the King Talal dam and the 14.5-km extension of the 98-km East Ghor main canal. Stage II will include the irrigation of 4,700 ha in the southern Ghor. The target for the Plan is to irrigate 43,000 ha of land in the Jordan Valley. Future development in irrigation will include the construction of the Maqarin dam and the Wadi Malaha storage dam; Pres. Muhammad Bani Hani.

Agricultural Marketing and Processing Co of Jordan: POB 7314, Amman; tel. 819161; telex 23796; f. 1984; govt-owned; Chair. and Gen. Man. Ghazi Abu Hassan.

PHOSPHATES

Jordan Phosphate Mines Co Ltd (JPMC): POB 30, Amman; tel. 660141; telex 21223; f. 1930; engaged in production and export of rock phosphate; Chair. Ali Khrais; Dir-Gen. Wasef Azar; Marketing and Sales Man. Makram Zorekat; three mines in operation; production 6.5m. tons (1988); exports 5.5m. tons (1988).

Jordan Fertilizer Industries Co (JFIC): Amman; engaged in production and export of phosphate fertilizer and aluminium fluoride; acquired by JPMC in 1986; cap. 55m.; Man. Dir Mahmoud Mardi.

TRADE UNIONS

The General Federation of Jordanian Trade Unions: Wadi as-Sir Rd, POB 1065, Amman; f. 1954; 33,000 mems; member of Arab Trade Unions Confederation; Chair. Sami Hassan Mansour; Gen. Sec. Abd ar-Razzaq Hamad.

There are also a number of independent unions, including:

Drivers' Union: POB 846, Amman; Sec.-Gen. Sami Hassan Mansour.

Engineers' Association: Amman; Sec.-Gen. Leith Shubellat.

Union of Petroleum Workers and Employees: POB 1346, Amman; Sec.-Gen. Brahim Hadi.

Transport

RAILWAYS

Aqaba Railway Corporation: POB 50, Ma'an; tel. 332234; telex 64003; f. 1975; length of track 292 km (1,050-mm gauge); Dir-Gen. Mardi Qatamin.

Formerly a division of the Hedjaz-Jordan Railway (see below), the Aqaba Railway was established as a separate entity in 1979; it retains close links with the Hedjaz but there is no regular through traffic between Aqaba and Amman. It comprises the 169-km line south of Menzil (leased from the Hedjaz-Jordan Railway) and the 115-km extension to Aqaba, opened in October 1975, which serves phosphate mines at el-Hasa and Wadi el-Abyad. A development programme is being implemented to increase the transport capacity of the line to 4m. tons of phosphate per year. Plans for connecting the new phosphate mine at Shidiya to the railway system by 1990/91 are under consideration.

Hedjaz-Jordan Railway (administered by the Ministry of Transport): POB 582, Amman; tel. 6895413; telex 21541; f. 1902; length of track 496 km (1,050-mm gauge); Dir-Gen. A. H. ad-Djazi.

This was formerly a section of the Hedjaz Railway (Damascus to Medina) for Muslim pilgrims to Medina and Mecca. It crosses the Syrian border and enters Jordanian territory south of Dera'a, and runs for approximately 366 km to Naqb Ishtar, passing through Zarka, Amman, Qatrana and Ma'an. Some 844 km of the line, from Ma'an to Medina in Saudi Arabia, were abandoned for over sixty years. Reconstruction of the Medina line, begun in 1965, was scheduled to be completed in 1971 at a cost of £15m., divided equally between Jordan, Saudi Arabia and Syria. However, the reconstruction work was suspended at the request of the Arab States concerned, pending further studies on costs. The line between Ma'an and Saudi Arabia (114 km) is now completed, as well as 15 km in Saudi Arabia as far as Halet Ammar Station. A new 115-km extension to Aqaba (owned by the Aqaba Railway Corporation (see above) was opened in 1975. In 1987 a study conducted by Dorsch Consult (Federal Republic of Germany) into the feasibility of reconstructing the Hedjaz Railway to high international specifications to connect Saudi Arabia, Jordan and Syria, concluded that the reopening of the Hedjaz line would be viable only if it were to be connected with European rail networks.

ROADS

Amman is linked by road with all parts of the kingdom and with neighbouring countries. All cities and most towns are connected by a two-lane paved road system. In addition, several thousand km of tracks make all villages accessible to motor transport. In 1987, the latest inventory showed the East Bank of Jordan to have 2,603 km of main roads, 1,519 km of secondary roads (both types asphalted) and 1,503 km of other roads. Road-building schemes valued at JD108m. were to be carried out in the 1986-90 Five-Year Plan. In November 1985 Jordan, Egypt and Iraq signed an agreement providing for the operation of an overland route between Cairo, Amman and Baghdad.

Joint Land Transport Co: Amman; joint venture of govts of Jordan and Iraq; operates about 750 trucks.

Jordan-Syria Land Transport Co: Amman; f. 1981; transports goods between ports in Jordan and Syria; operates 366 trucks and lorries.

SHIPPING

The port of Aqaba is Jordan's only outlet to the sea and has two general berths of 340 m and 215 m, with seven main transit sheds, covered storage area of 4,150 sq m, an open area of 50,600 sq m and a phosphate berth 210 m long and 10 m deep. Ten new berths and storage facilities are being built, and a separate potash berth, a container terminal, and a fertilizer jetty are planned. An oil terminal became operational at Aqaba port in 1985. A ferry link between Aqaba and the Egyptian port of Nuweibeh was opened in April 1985 and is expected to increase tourism and trade between the two countries.

Arab Bridge Maritime Navigation Co: Amman; f. 1987; joint venture by Egypt, Iraq and Jordan to improve economic co-operation; an extension of the company that established a ferry link between Aqaba and the Egyptian port of Nuweibeh in 1985; cap. US $6m.; Chair. Sulayman Mutawalli Sulayman (Egyptian Minister of Transport, Communications and Naval Transport).

T. Gargour & Fils: POB 419, Amman; tel. 622307; telex 21213; f. 1928; shipping agents and owners; Chair. John Gargour.

Jordan Maritime Navigation Co: Amman; privately owned.

Jordan National Shipping Lines Ltd: POB 5406, Shmeisani, Amman; tel. 666214; telex 21730; POB 657 Aqaba; tel. 315342; telex 62276; owned 75% by the government; service from Antwerp, Zeebrugge, Bremen and Sheerness to Aqaba; daily passenger ferry service from Aqaba to Nuweibeh (Egypt); land transportation to destinations in Iraq and elsewhere in the region; two bulk carriers; Chair. Wasif Azar; Gen. Man. Y. et-Tal.

Jordanian Shipping Transport Co: Amman; f. 1984; two cargo vessels.

Kawar, Amin & Sons Co (Pvt) Ltd: POB 222, Majali Bldg, Abd al-Hamid Sharaf St, Shmeisani, Amman; tel. 622324; telex 21212; chartering and shipping agents; operates three general cargo ships; Chair. Tawfiq A. Kawar; Gen. Man. Ghassoub F. Kawar; Shipping Man. Abd al-Aziz Kasaji.

Petra Navigation and International Trading Co Ltd: POB 8362, White Star Bldg, Amman; tel. 662421; telex 21755; two ro/ro cargo vessels; Man. Dir A. H. Armoush; Gen. Man. G. Baconi.

Syrian-Jordanian Shipping Co: rue Port Said, BP 148, Latakia, Syria; tel. 316356; telex 451002; operates two general cargo ships; transported 48,000 metric tons of goods in 1987; Chair. Osman Lebbadi.

PIPELINES

Two oil pipelines cross Jordan. The former Iraq Petroleum Company pipeline, carrying petroleum from the oilfields in Iraq to

JORDAN

Haifa, has not operated since 1967. The 1,717-km (1,067-mile) pipeline, known as the Trans-Arabian Pipeline (Tapline), carries petroleum from the oilfields of Dhahran in Saudi Arabia to Sidon on the Mediterranean seaboard in Lebanon. Tapline traverses Jordan for a distance of 177 km (110 miles) and has frequently been cut by hostile action. Tapline stopped pumping to Syria and Lebanon at the end of 1983, when it was first due to close. It was later scheduled to close in 1985, but in September 1984 Jordan renewed an agreement to receive Saudi Arabian crude oil through Tapline. The agreement can be cancelled by either party at two years' notice.

CIVIL AVIATION

There are international airports at Amman and Aqaba. The new Queen Alia International Airport at Zizya, 40 km south of Amman, was opened in May 1983.

Civil Aviation Authority: Amman; Dir-Gen. AMIN HUSSEINI.

Royal Jordanian Airline: Head Office: Housing Bank Commercial Centre, Shmeisani, POB 302, Amman; tel. 672872; telex 21501; f. 1963; government-owned but undergoing privatization 1987–; services to Middle East, North Africa, Europe, USA and Far East; fleet of one Boeing 747-200B, three Boeing 707-320C, four Boeing 727-200A, eight Lockheed L-1011-500, three Airbus A310-300; Chair. and CEO ALI GHANDOUR.

Arab Wings Co Ltd: POB 341018, Amman; tel. 891994; telex 21608; f. 1975; subsidiary of Royal Jordanian; executive jet charter service, air ambulances, priority cargo; Chair. ALI GHANDOUR; Man. Dir HE SHARIF GHAZI RAKAN NASSER.

Tourism

The ancient cities of Jerash and Petra, and Jordan's proximity to biblical sites, have encouraged tourism. In 1986 there were 1,912,038 foreign visitors to Jordan. Earnings from tourism in 1987 were US $600m.

Ministry of Tourism: Tourism Authority, POB 224, Amman; tel. 642311; telex 21741; f. 1952; Minister of Tourism YANAL HIKMAT; Dir-Gen. Jordan Tourism Authority NASRI ATALLAH.

INDEX OF INTERNATIONAL ORGANIZATIONS

(Main reference only)

A

ABEDA, 93
Academy of Arab Music, 172
Acuerdo de Cartagena, 90
Aerospace Medical Association, 239
AFESD, 95
Africa Reinsurance Corporation—Africa-Re, 89
African Adult Education Association, 227
— Airlines Association, 270
— Association for Literacy and Adult Education, 227
— — — Public Administration and Management, 230
— — of Cartography, 262
— Bureau for Educational Sciences, 188
— Centre for Applied Research and Training in Social Development, 30
— — — Monetary Studies, 225
— Civil Aviation Commission—AFCAC, 188
— Commission on Agricultural Statistics (FAO), 54
— Development Bank—ADB, 88
— — Fund—ADF, 88
— Forestry Commission (FAO), 54
— Groundnut Council, 223
— Institute for Higher Technical Training and Research, 31
— Monetary Fund, 31
— Organization of Cartography and Remote Sensing, 262
— Petroleum Producers' Association, 223
— Posts and Telecommunications Union, 243
— Regional Centre for Engineering Design and Manufacturing, 30
— — — — Solar Energy, 30
— — — — Technology, 262
— — Organization for Standardization, 266
— Timber Organization, 215
— Training and Research Centre in Administration for Development—CAFRAD, 218
Afro-Asian Housing Organization, 218
— People's Solidarity Organization, 230
— Rural Reconstruction Organization, 218
AFROLIT Society (for the Promotion of Adult Literacy in Africa), 227
Agence de coopération culturelle et technique, 218
Agency for the Prohibition of Nuclear Weapons in Latin America, 230
AGFUND, 218
Agudath Israel World Organisation, 245
Aid to Displaced Persons and its European Villages, 257
ALADI, 170
ALECSO, 172
All Africa Conference of Churches, 245
Alliance Internationale de Tourisme, 265
— Israélite Universelle, 245
Al-Quds Committee (OIC), 194
Amnesty International, 257
Andean Development Corporation, 90
— Group, 90
— Judicial Tribunal, 90
— Parliament, 90
— Reserve Fund, 90
Anti-Slavery Society for the Protection of Human Rights, 257
ANZUS, 92
Arab Academy of Maritime Transport, 172
— Air Carriers' Organization, 270
— Authority for Agricultural Investment and Development, 218
— Bank for Economic Development in Africa—BADEA, 93
— Bankers Association, 225
— Bureau for Narcotics, 172
— — — Prevention of Crime, 172
— — of Criminal Police, 172
— Centre for the Study of Arid Zones and Dry Lands, 172
— Civil Aviation Council, 172
— Common Market, 126
— Company for Drug Industries and Medical Appliances, 126
— — — Industrial Investment, 126
— — — Livestock Development, 126
— Co-operative Federation, 126
— Drilling and Workover Company, 193
— Engineering Company (OAPEC), 193
— Federation for Cement and Building Materials, 126
— — — of Chemical Fertilizers Producers, 126
— — — Engineering Industries, 126
— — — Leather Industries, 126
— — — Paper Industries, 126
— — — Petroleum, Mining and Chemicals Workers, 233
— — — Shipping Industries, 127
— — — Textile Industries, 127
— Fund for Economic and Social Development—AFESD, 95
— — — Technical Assistance to African and Arab Countries, 172
— Geophysical Exploration Services Company, 193
— Gulf Programme for the United Nations Development Organizations—AGFUND, 218
— Industrial Development Organization, 172
— Iron and Steel Union, 266
— Labour Organization, 172
— League, 171
— — Educational, Cultural and Scientific Organization—ALECSO, 172
— Logging Company, 193
— Maritime Petroleum Transport Company, 193
— Mining Company, 126
— Monetary Fund, 96
— Organization for Agricultural Development, 172
— — — Standardization and Metrology, 172
— — of Administrative Sciences, 172
— Petroleum Investments Corporation—APICORP, 193
— — Services Company, 193
— — Training Institute, 193
— Postal Union, 172
— Satellite Communication Organization, 172
— Seaports Federation, 127
— Shipbuilding and Repair Yard Company, 193
— Sports Confederation, 260
— States Broadcasting Union, 172
— Sugar Federation, 127
— Telecommunications Union, 172
— Tourism Organization, 265
— Towns Organization, 255
— Union of Fish Producers, 127
— — — Food Industries, 127
— — — Land Transport, 127
— — — Pharmaceutical Manufacturers and Medical Appliance Manufacturers, 127
— — — Railways, 270
ASEAN, 101
— Finance Corporation, 102
— Reinsurance Corporation, 102
Asia and Pacific Commission on Agricultural Statistics (FAO), 54
— — — Plant Protection Commission (FAO), 54
— Pacific Academy of Ophthalmology, 238
ASIAFEDOP, 209
Asian and Pacific Centre for Transfer of Technology, 26
— — — Coconut Community, 223
— Clearing Union—ACU, 225
— Development Bank—ADB, 98
— — Fund—ADF, 98
— Highway Network Project, 27
— Productivity Organization, 266
— Reinsurance Corporation, 225
— Students' Association, 272
— Vegetable Research and Development Center, 215
Asia-Pacific Broadcasting Union, 244
— Forestry Commission (FAO), 54
— Telecommunity, 243
Asian-African Legal Consultative Committee, 235
Asian-Pacific Dental Federation, 239
— Postal Union, 243
Asistencia Recíproca Petrolera Estatal Latinoamericana, 225
Asociación de Empresas Estatales de Telecomunicaciones, 91
— del Congreso Panamericano de Ferrocarriles, 272
— Interamericana de Bibliotecarios y Documentalistas Agrícolas, 215
— Latinoamericana de Instituciones Financieros de Desarrollo, 219
— — — Integración—ALADI, 170
— Médica Panamericana, 243
Associated Country Women of the World, 257

INDEX

Association des universités partiellement ou entièrement de langue française, 227
— for Childhood Education International, 227
— — Paediatric Education in Europe, 238
— — Systems Management, 233
— — the Advancement of Agricultural Science in Africa, 215
— — — Promotion of the International Circulation of the Press, 244
— — — Study of the World Refugee Problem, 255
— — — Taxonomic Study of the Flora of Tropical Africa, 249
— internationale de la Mutualité, 257
— of African Central Banks, 225
— — — Development Finance Institutions, 89
— — — Geological Surveys, 249
— — — Tax Administrators, 225
— — — Trade Promotion Organizations, 266
— — — Universities, 227
— — Arab Universities, 227
— — Caribbean Universities and Research Institutes, 227
— — Commonwealth Universities, 115
— — Development Financing Institutions in Asia and the Pacific, 218
— — European Airlines, 270
— — — Atomic Forums—FORATOM, 249
— — — Chambers of Commerce, 266
— — — Institutes of Economic Research, 225
— — — Journalists, 244
— — French-Language Television Services, 244
— — Geoscientists for International Development, 249
— — Institutes for European Studies, 227
— — International Bond Dealers, 225
— — Iron Ore Exporting Countries, 223
— — National European and Mediterranean Societies of Gastro-enterology, 239
— — Natural Rubber Producing Countries, 223
— — Partially or Wholly French-Language Universities, 227
— — Secretaries General of Parliaments, 230
— — Social Work Education in Africa, 257
— — South Pacific Airlines, 204
— — South-east Asian Institutions of Higher Learning, 227
— — — Nations—ASEAN, 101
— — Tin Producing Countries, 223
Assofoto (CMEA), 125
Atlantic Treaty Association, 230
Autorité du bassin du Niger, 219
Aviation sans frontières, 257

B

BADEA, 93
Bahá'í International Community, 246
Balkan Medical Union, 239
Baltic and International Maritime Council, 270
BAM International, 218
Banco Centroamericano de Integración Económica—BCIE, 108
Bangkok Declaration (ASEAN), 101
Bank for International Settlements—BIS, 104
Banque arabe pour le Développement économique en Afrique—BADEA, 93
— centrale des états de l'Afrique de l'ouest—BCEAO, 154
— de développement des états de l'Afrique centrale, 154
— des Etats de l'Afrique centrale, 154
— ouest-africaine de développement—BOAD, 154
Baptist World Alliance, 246
Benelux Economic Union, 225
Berne Union, 84
Biometric Society, 249
BIS, 104
British Commonwealth Ex-services League, 116
Broadcasting Organizations of Non-aligned Countries, 244
Bureau international de la récupération, 262
Business Co-operation Centre (EEC), 145

C

CAB International (Commonwealth), 114
CABI Bureau of Agricultural Economics, 114
— — — Animal Breeding and Genetics, 114
— — — Crop Protection, 114
— — — Dairy Science and Technology, 114
— — — Horticulture and Plantation Crops, 114
— — — Nutrition, 114
— — — Pastures and Field Crops, 114
— — — Plant Breeding and Genetics, 114
— — — Soils, 114
— Forestry Bureau, 114
— Institute of Biological Control, 114
— — — Entomology, 114
— — — Parasitology, 114
— Mycological Institute, 114
CACM, 108
Cadmium Association, 223
CAFRAD, 218
Caisse centrale de coopération économique (Franc Zone), 155
Caribbean Agricultural Research and Development Institute, 107
— Community and Common Market—CARICOM, 106
— Conference of Churches, 246
— Congress of Labour, 233
— Development Bank, 107
— Examinations Council, 107
— Food and Nutrition Institute, 215
— Free Trade Association, 106
— Meteorological Institute, 107
— Plant Protection Commission (FAO), 54
— Tourism Association, 265
CARICOM, 106
CARIFTA, 106
Caritas Internationalis, 218
Cartagena Agreement (Andean Group), 90
Catholic International Education Office, 227
— — Federation for Physical and Sports Education, 227
— — Union for Social Service, 257
CEAO, 119
CEEAC, 218
Celtic League, 230
Central American Air Navigation Service Corporation, 109
— — Bank for Economic Integration, 108
— — Common Market—CACM, 108
— — Institute for Business Administration, 109
— — — of Public Administration, 109
— — Monetary Council, 108
— — Union, 108
— — Research Institute for Industry, 109
— — University Confederation, 109
— Commission for the Navigation of the Rhine, 270
— Control Administration of the United Power Grids of European CMEA Members, 125
— Office for International Carriage by Rail, 270
Centre africain de formation et de recherches administratives pour le développement—CAFRAD, 218
— de Recherches sur les Méningites et les Schistosomiases (OCCGE), 242
— for Educational Research and Innovation (OECD), 182
— — Latin American Monetary Studies, 225
— — Research and Documentation on International Language Problems, 227
— Muraz (OCCGE), 242
Centro de Estudios Monetarios Latinoamericanos, 225
— Interamericano de Investigación y Documentación sobre Formación Profesional, 228
— Internacional de Agricultura Tropical, 216
— Regional de Educación de Adultos y Alfabetización Funcional para América Latina, 230
CERN, 250
Charles Darwin Foundation for the Galapagos Isles, 249
Chicago Convention (ICAO), 66
Christian Conference of Asia, 246
— Democrat International, 231
— Medical Commission (WCC), 210
— Peace Conference, 246
CILSS, 220
CIOMS, 237
CLASEP, 209
CLTC, 209
Club of Dakar, 218
— — the Sahel, 218
CMEA, 124
Cocoa Producers' Alliance, 223
COCOM, 266
Codex Alimentarius Commission (FAO/WHO), 55
Collaborative International Pesticides Analytical Council Ltd, 215
Colombo Plan for Co-operative Economic and Social Development in Asia and the Pacific, 110
COMECON, 124
Comisión Técnica de las Telecomunicaciones de Centroamérica—COMTELCA, 109
Commission for Inland Fisheries of Latin America (FO), 55
— of the Churches in International Affairs (WCC), 210
— — European Communities, 139
— on African Animal Trypanosomiasis (FAO), 55
— — Fertilizers (FAO), 55
— — Inter-Church Aid, Refugee and World Service (WCC), 210

INDEX *International Organizations*

— — Plant Genetic Resources (FAO), 55
— — the Churches' Participation in Development (WCC), 210
Commissions for Controlling the Desert Locust (FAO), 54
Committee for European Construction Equipment, 266
— of European Foundry Associations, 266
Common Organization for the Control of Desert Locust and Bird Pests, 215
Commonwealth, 111
— Advisory Aeronautical Research Council, 116
— Agricultural Bureaux, 114
— Air Transport Council, 115
— Association of Architects, 116
— — — Science, Technology and Mathematics Educators—CASTME, 115
— Broadcasting Association, 115
— Council for Educational Administration, 115
— Countries League, 116
— Engineers' Council, 116
— Forestry Association, 115
— Foundation, 116
— Fund for Technical Co-operation, 113
— Games Federation, 116
— Geological Surveys Consultative Group, 116
— Institute, London, 115
— — (Scotland), Edinburgh, 115
— Journalists' Association, 115
— Lawyers' Association, 116
— Legal Advisory Service, 116
— — Education Association, 116
— Magistrates' Association, 116
— Medical Association, 115
— Parliamentary Association, 116
— Pharmaceutical Association, 115
— Press Union, 115
— Secretariat, 111
— Society for the Deaf, 115
— Telecommunications Organization, 115
— Trade Union Council, 116
— War Graves Commission, 116
— Youth Exchange Council, 116
Communauté des radios publiques de langue française, 244
— — télévisions francophones, 244
— économique de l'Afrique de l'Ouest—CEAO, 119
— — des Etats de l'Afrique Centrale, 218
— — — pays des Grands Lacs, 226
— — du bétail et de la viande du Conseil de l'Entente, 121
Community of French-Language Radio Broadcasters, 244
Comparative Education Society in Europe, 227
Computers (CMEA), 125
Confederación Interamericana de Educación Católica, 228
— Latinoamericana de Asociaciones Cristianas de Jóvenes, 273
— Universitaria Centroamericana, 109
Confederation of ASEAN Journalists, 244
— — Asia-Pacific Chambers of Commerce and Industry, 266
— — European Soft Drinks Associations, 266
— — International Contractors' Associations, 266
— — Socialist Parties of the European Community, 231
Conference of European Churches, 246
— — International Catholic Organizations, 246
— — Regions in North-West Europe, 219
Conférence permanente des Recteurs, Présidents et Vice-chanceliers des Universités européennes, 230
Conseil de l'Entente, 121
— international des radios-télévisions d'expression française, 244
Consejo de Fundaciones Americanas de Desarrollo, 219
— Interamericano de Música, 220
— Latinoamericano de Iglesias, 247
— Monetario Centroamericano, 108
Consultative Committee of the Bars and Law Societies of the European Community, 235
— Council for Postal Studies (UPU), 80
— — of Jewish Organizations, 246
— Group for International Agricultural Research—CGIAR (IBRD), 62
Contadora Group, 231
Convention on International Trade in Endangered Species, 40
Co-operation Council for the Arab States of the Gulf, 122
Co-ordinating Committee for International Voluntary Service, 257
— — Multilateral Export Controls—COCOM, 266
— — — the Liberation Movements of Africa (OAU), 187
Corporación Andina de Fomento, 90
— Centroamericana de Servicios de Navegación Aérea, 109
Council for International Organisations of Medical Sciences, 237
— — Mutual Economic Assistance—CMEA (COMECON), 124
— — the Development of Economic and Social Research in Africa, 255
— — International Congresses of Entomology, 249
— of American Development Foundations, 219
— — Arab Economic Unity, 126
— — Europe, 128
— — European National Youth Committees, 272
— — on International Educational Exchange, 272
Court of Auditors of the European Communities, 141
— — Justice of the European Communities, 141
Customs Co-operation Council, 266

D

Dairy Society International, 215
Danube Commission, 270
Desert Locust Control Organization for Eastern Africa, 215
Duke of Edinburgh's Award Scheme, 116

E

East Asia Travel Association, 265
Eastern and Southern African Management Institute, 31
— — — — Mineral Resources Development Centre, 30
— Regional Organisation for Planning and Housing, 254
— — — — Public Administration, 231
ECA, 28
ECE, 24
ECLAC, 27
Eco-Bank, 133
Econometric Society, 226
Economic and Social Commission for Asia and the Pacific—ESCAP (UN), 25
— — — — Western Asia—ESCWA, 31
— — Commission for Africa—ECA (UN), 28
— — — Europe—ECE (UN), 24
— — — Latin America and the Caribbean—ECLAC (UN), 27
— Community of Central African States, 218
— — — the Great Lakes Countries, 226
— — — West African States—ECOWAS, 132
— Co-operation Organization—ECO, 219
— Development Institute (IBRD), 62
— Research Committee of the Gas Industry, 266
ECOSOC, 12, 19
ECOWAS, 132
ECSC, 145
EEC, 134
EFTA, 152
EIB, 142
EIRENE—International Christian Service for Peace, 257
EMS, 147
English-speaking Union of the Commonwealth, 255
Entente Council, 121
Entraide Ouvrière Internationale, 259
ESCAP, 25
ESCAP/WMO Typhoon Committee, 26
ESCWA, 31
Euratom, 144
EUROCONTROL, 270
EUROFEDOP, 209
Eurofinas, 226
Euronet DIANE, 144
Europa Nostra, 220
European Agricultural Guidance and Guarantee Fund, 143
— Air Navigation Planning Group (ICAO), 67
— Aluminium Association, 223
— and Mediterranean Plant Protection Organization, 215
— Alliance of Press Agencies, 244
— Association for Animal Production, 215
— — — Cancer Research, 239
— — — Health Education and Libraries, 239
— — — Personnel Management, 233
— — — Population Studies, 255
— — — Research on Plant Breeding, 215
— — — the Study of Diabetes, 239
— — — Trade in Jute Products, 223
— — of Advertising Agencies, 266
— — — Conservatoires, Music Academies and Music High Schools, 220
— — — Exploration Geophysicists, 250
— — — Internal Medicine, 239
— — — Manufacturers of Radiators, 267
— — — Music Festivals, 222
— — — National Productivity Centres, 267
— — — Radiology, 239
— — — Social Medicine, 239
— — — Teachers, 227
— — — Veterinary Anatomists, 250

1516

INDEX

- Atomic Energy Community—Euratom, 144
- — — Society, 250
- Baptist Federation, 246
- Brain and Behaviour Society, 239
- Brewery Convention, 267
- Broadcasting Union, 244
- Builders of Internal Combustion Engines and Electric Locomotives, 262
- Bureau of Adult Education, 227
- Ceramic Association, 267
- Civil Aviation Conference, 270
- — — Service Federation, 233
- Coal and Steel Community—ECSC, 145
- Commission for the Control of Foot-and-Mouth Disease (FAO), 55
- — — of Human Rights, 128
- — — on Agriculture (FAO), 55
- Committee for Standardization, 267
- — — — the Protection of the Population against the Hazards of Chronic Toxicity, 239
- — — of Associations of Manufacturers of Agricultural Machinery, 267
- — — — Paint, Printing Ink and Artists' Colours Manufacturers' Associations, 267
- — — — Sugar Manufacturers, 223
- — — — Textile Machinery Manufacturers, 267
- — — on Crime Problems, 129
- — — — Legal Co-operation, 129
- — Communities, 134
- — — Commission, 139
- — — Council of Ministers, 140
- — — Court of Auditors, 141
- — — — Justice, 141
- — — Joint Research Centre, 145
- Computer Manufacturers Association, 262
- Confederation of Agriculture, 215
- — — — Iron and Steel Industries, 267
- — — — Woodworking Industries, 267
- Conference of Ministers of Transport, 270
- — — — Postal and Telecommunications Administrations, 243
- Convention for Constructional Steelwork, 263
- — — — the Protection of Human Rights, 128
- — — on Social Security, 129
- Co-ordination Centre for Research and Documentation in Social Sciences, 255
- Council, 140
- — — of Chemical Manufacturers' Federations, 267
- Court of Human Rights, 128
- Cultural Centre, 220
- — — Foundation, 227
- Currency Unit, 149
- Economic Community—EEC, 134
- Federation for Catholic Adult Education, 227
- — — — the Welfare of the Elderly, 257
- — — of Associations of Insulation Enterprises, 267
- — — — — Particle Board Manufacturers, 267
- — — — Chemical Engineering, 263
- — — — Conference Towns, 233
- — — — Corrosion, 263
- — — — Financial Analysts' Societies, 226
- — — — Handling Industries, 267
- — — — Management Consultants' Associations, 267
- — — — National Associations of Engineers, 263
- — — — Plywood Industry, 267
- — — — Productivity Services, 267
- — — — Tile and Brick Manufacturers, 267
- Financial Management and Marketing Association, 226
- Forestry Commission (FAO), 55
- Foundation for Management Development, 228
- Free Trade Association—EFTA, 152
- Furniture Manufacturers Federation, 267
- General Galvanizers Association, 267
- Glass Container Manufacturers' Committee, 267
- Grassland Federation, 215
- Healthcare Management Association, 239
- Industrial Research Management Association, 233
- Inland Fisheries Advisory Commission (FAO), 55
- Insurance Committee, 226
- Investment Bank, 142
- League Against Rheumatism, 239
- Livestock and Meat Trade Union, 215
- Molecular Biology Organization, 250
- Monetary Co-operation Fund, 147
- — System, 147
- Motel Federation, 265
- Movement, 231

- Organisation for the Safety of Air Navigation, 270
- Organization for Caries Research, 239
- — — Civil Aviation Electronics, 263
- — — Nuclear Research, 250
- — — Quality, 267
- Orthodontic Society, 239
- Packaging Federation, 268
- Parliament, 141
- Passenger Train Time-Table Conference, 271
- Patent Office, 268
- Railway Wagon Pool, 271
- Regional Development Fund, 143
- Social Charter, 129
- — Fund, 143
- Society for Comparative Endocrinology, 239
- — — Opinion and Marketing Research, 268
- — — Rural Sociology, 255
- — — of Culture, 220
- Space Agency, 250
- Strategic Research Programme in Information Technology—ESPRIT, 144
- Telecommunications Satellite Organization—EUTELSAT, 243
- Trade Union Confederation, 234
- Travel Commission, 265
- Union of Arabic and Islamic Scholars, 228
- — — Coachbuilders, 268
- — — Medical Specialists, 240
- — — Women, 231
- Unit of Account, 147
- University Institute, 146
- Venture Capital Association, 226
- Young Christian Democrats, 231
- Youth Centre, 130
- — Foundation, 130
European-Mediterranean Seismological Centre, 250
Eurospace, 263
Eurotransplant Foundation, 240
EUTELSAT, 243
Evangelical Alliance, 246
Experiment in International Living, 255

F

FAO, 53
Federación Campesina Latinoamericana, 234
- de Cámaras de Comercio del Istmo Centroamericano, 109
- — — y Asociaciones Industriales Centroamericanas, 109
- Latinoamericana de Bancos, 226
Federation of Arab Scientific Research Councils, 250
- — Asian Scientific Academies and Societies, 250
- — — Women's Associations, 257
- — Central American Chambers of Commerce, 109
- — European Biochemical Societies, 250
- — French-Language Obstetricians and Gynaecologists, 240
- — Industrial Chambers and Associations in Central America, 109
- — International Civil Servants' Associations, 234
- — Technical and Scientific Organizations of the Socialist Countries, 263
- — the European Dental Industry, 240
- — World Health Foundations, 240
Fédération Aéronautique Internationale, 260
- des gynécologues et obstétriciens de langue française, 240
FEOGA, 143
Fondo Andino de Reservas, 90
- Latinoamericano de Reservas, 90
Fonds d'aide et de coopération (Franc Zone), 155
- d'Entraide et de Garantie des Emprunts (Conseil de l'Entente), 121
Food Aid Committee, 219
- and Agriculture Organization—FAO, 53
Foundation for International Scientific Co-ordination, 250
Franc Zone, 154
Frères des Hommes, 218
Friends (Quakers) World Committee for Consultation, 246
Fund for Co-operation, Compensation and Development (ECOWAS), 132

G

Gambia River Basin Development Organization, 219
General Agreement on Tariffs and Trade—GATT, 56
- Anthroposophical Society, 246
- Association of International Sports Federations, 260
- — — Municipal Health and Technical Experts, 240
- Fisheries Council for the Mediterranean—GFCM (FAO), 55

INDEX

— Union of Chambers of Commerce, Industry and Agriculture for Arab Countries, 268
Generalized System of Preferences, 37
Geneva Conventions (Red Cross), 166
Graduate Institute of International Studies, 228
Graphical International Federation, 234
Group of Eight, 231
— — Latin American and Caribbean Sugar Exporting Countries, 223
Grupo Andino, 90
Gulf Co-operation Council, 122
— Investment Corporation, 123
— Organization for Industrial Consulting, 268

H

Habitat, 35
Hague Conference on Private International Law, 235
Hansard Society for Parliamentary Government, 231

I

IAEA, 58
IATA, 271
IBEC, 159
IBRD, 60
ICAO, 66
ICC, 160
ICCROM, 221
ICFTU, 162
ICPHS, 254
ICSU, 248
IDA, 64
IDB, 156
IFAD, 68
IFC, 65
ILO, 69
IMCO, 71
IMF, 72
— Institute, 74
IMO, 71
Inca-Fiej Research Association, 244
Indian Ocean Commission, 219
— — Fishery Commission (FAO), 55
Indo-Pacific Fishery Commission (FAO), 55
INMARSAT, 243
Institut d'émission des départements d'outre-mer (Franc Zone), 154
— de formation et de recherche démographique, 29
— de Léprologie E. Marchoux (OCCGE), 242
— d'Ophtalmologie tropicale africaine (OCCGE), 242
— Pierre Richet, 242
— universitaire de hautes études internationales, 228
Institute for International Sociological Research, 255
— — Latin American Integration, 157
— of Air Transport, 271
— — Commonwealth Studies, London, 115
— — International Business Law and Practice (ICC), 161
— — Law, 235
— — Nutrition of Central America and Panama, 109
Instituto Andino de Estudios Sociales, 209
— Centroamericano de Administración de Empresas, 109
— — — Pública, 109
— — — Estudios Sociales, 209
— — — Investigación y Tecnología Industrial, 109
— de Formación del Caribe, 209
— de Nutrición de Centro América y Panamá, 109
— del Cono Sur, 209
— para la Integración de América Latina—INTAL, 157
INTELSAT, 243
Inter-African Bureau for Animal Resources, Nairobi, 188
— — — Soils, 188
— Coffee Organization, 223
— Committee for Hydraulic Studies, 263
— Phytosanitary Commission, 188
— Socialists and Democrats, 231
Inter-American Association of Agricultural Librarians and Documentalists, 215
— — — Sanitary and Environmental Engineering, 240
— Bar Association, 235
— Centre for Research and Documentation on Vocational Training, 228
— Children's Institute, 192
— Commercial Arbitration Commission, 268
— Commission of Women, 192
— — on Human Rights, 190
— Confederation for Catholic Education, 228
— Conference on Social Security, 257
— Council for Education, Science and Culture, 190
— Court of Human Rights, 190
— Defense Board, 192
— Development Bank—IDB, 156
— Economic and Social Council, 190
— Indian Institute, 192
— Institute for Co-operation on Agriculture, 192
— — of Capital Markets, 226
— Investment Corporation, 157
— Juridical Committee, 190
— Music Council, 220
— Nuclear Energy Commission, 192
— Planning Society, 219
— Press Association, 244
— Regional Organization of Workers—ORIT, 162
— Society of Cardiology, 240
— Tropical Tuna Commission, 216
Inter-Arab Investment Guarantee Corporation, 172
Interatomenergo (CMEA), 125
Interatominstrument (CMEA), 125
Interchim (CMEA), 125
Interchimvolokno (CMEA), 125
Interelektro (CMEA), 125
Interetalonpribor (CMEA), 125
Interfilm, 221
Intergovernmental Authority on Drought and Development—IGADD, 219
— Bureau for Informatics, 263
— Committee for Migration, 158
— — — Physical Education and Sport, 79
— Copyright Committee, 235
— Council of Copper Exporting Countries, 223
— Maritime Consultative Organization—IMCO, 71
— Oceanographic Commission, 250
— Programme for the Development of Communication (UNESCO), 79
Interkosmos (CMEA), 125
Intermetall (CMEA), 125
International Abolitionist Federation, 257
— Academic Union, 254
— Academy of Astronautics, 250
— — — Aviation and Space Medicine, 240
— — — Cytology, 240
— — — Legal and Social Medicine, 237
— — — Tourism, 265
— Accounting Standards Committee, 226
— Advertising Association Inc., 268
— Aeronautical Federation, 260
— African Institute, 255
— Agency for Research on Cancer, 83
— — — the Prevention of Blindness, 237
— Air Transport Association, 271
— Alliance of Distribution by Cable, 244
— — — Women, 231
— Amateur Athletic Federation, 260
— — Boxing Association, 260
— — Radio Union, 260
— — Swimming Federation, 260
— — Wrestling Federation, 260
— Anatomical Congress, 240
— Association against Noise, 257
— — for Bridge and Structural Engineering, 263
— — — Business Research and Corporate Development, 268
— — — Cereal Science and Technology, 216
— — — Child and Adolescent Psychiatry and Allied Professions, 240
— — — Children's International Summer Villages, 257
— — — Cybernetics, 263
— — — Dental Research, 240
— — — Earthquake Engineering, 250
— — — Ecology, 250
— — — Education to a Life without Drugs, 258
— — — Educational and Vocational Guidance, 228
— — — — Information, 228
— — — Hydraulic Research, 261
— — — Mass Communication Research, 255
— — — Mathematical Geology, 250
— — — Mathematics and Computers in Simulation, 250
— — — Mutual Benefit Societies, 257
— — — Plant Physiology, 251
— — — — Taxonomy, 251
— — — Religious Freedom, 246
— — — Research in Income and Wealth, 226

INDEX

— — — Suicide Prevention, 257
— — — the Development of Documentation, Libraries and Archives in Africa, 228
— — — — Exchange of Students for Technical Experience, 272
— — — — History of Religions, 254
— — — — Physical Sciences of the Ocean, 250
— — — — Protection of Industrial Property, 235
— — — — Rhine Vessels Register, 271
— — — — Study of the Liver, 237
— — — Vegetation Science, 216
— — — of Agricultural Economists, 216
— — — — Librarians and Documentalists, 216
— — — — Medicine and Rural Health, 240
— — — Allergology and Clinical Immunology, 237
— — — Applied Linguistics, 255
— — — — Psychology, 240
— — — Art Critics, 221
— — — — (Painting-Sculpture-Graphic Art), 221
— — — Asthmology, 240
— — — Bibliophiles, 221
— — — Biological Standardization, 251
— — — Botanic Gardens, 251
— — — Broadcasting, 244
— — — Buddhist Studies, 246
— — — Buying Groups, 268
— — — Catholic Health Care Institutions, 240
— — — Chain Stores, 268
— — — Colleges of Physical Education, 228
— — — Conference Interpreters, 234
— — — — Translators, 234
— — — Congress Centres, 268
— — — Crafts and Small and Medium-Sized Enterprises, 234
— — — Democratic Lawyers, 235
— — — Dental Students, 272
— — — Department Stores, 268
— — — Documentalists and Information Officers, 255
— — — Educators for World Peace, 231
— — — Electrical Contractors, 268
— — — Geodesy, 251
— — — Geomagnetism and Aeronomy, 251
— — — Gerontology, 237
— — — Group Psychotherapy, 240
— — — Horticultural Producers, 216
— — — Hydatid Disease, 239
— — — Hydrological Sciences, 251
— — — Insurance and Reinsurance Intermediaries, 268
— — — Islamic Banks, 226
— — — Juvenile and Family Court Magistrates, 235
— — — Law Libraries, 235
— — — Legal Sciences, 235
— — — Lighthouse Authorities, 261
— — — Literary Critics, 221
— — — Logopedics and Phoniatrics, 240
— — — Medical Laboratory Technologists, 234
— — — Medicine and Biology of the Environment, 239
— — — Meteorology and Atmospheric Physics, 251
— — — Metropolitan City Libraries, 255
— — — Museums of Arms and Military History, 221
— — — Music Libraries, Archives and Documentation Centres, 222
— — — Mutual Insurance Companies, 234
— — — Oral and Maxillofacial Surgeons, 240
— — — Papyrologists, 228
— — — Penal Law, 235
— — — Photobiology, 251
— — — Ports and Harbors, 271
— — — Rolling Stock Builders, 263
— — — Scholarly Publishers, 268
— — — Schools of Social Work, 258
— — — Scientific Experts in Tourism, 265
— — — Sedimentologists, 251
— — — Sound Archives, 244
— — — Students in Economics and Management, 272
— — — Technological University Libraries, 263
— — — Textile Dyers and Printers, 268
— — — Theoretical and Applied Limnology, 251
— — — Universities, 228
— — — University Professors and Lecturers, 228
— — — Volcanology and Chemistry of the Earth's Interior, 251
— — — Wood Anatomists, 251
— — — Workers for Troubled Children and Youth, 258
— — on Water Pollution Research and Control, 251
— Astronautical Federation, 251
— Astronomical Union, 248
— Atomic Energy Agency—IAEA, 58
— Automobile Federation, 271

— Baccalaureate Office, 228
— Bank for Economic Co-operation—IBEC, 159
— — — Reconstruction and Development—IBRD (World Bank), 60
— Bar Association, 235
— Bauxite Association, 223
— Bee Research Association, 216
— Bible Reading Association, 246
— Board on Books for Young People, 221
— Booksellers Federation, 268
— Botanical Congress, 251
— Brain Research Organization, 240
— Bridge, Tunnel and Turnpike Association, 261
— Broncoesophagological Society, 240
— Bureau for Epilepsy, 240
— — — the Standardization of Man-Made Fibres, 268
— — of Chambers of Commerce (ICC), 161
— — — Education—IBE, 79
— — — Fiscal Documentation, 226
— — — Weights and Measures, 251
— Cargo Handling Co-ordination Association, 263
— Cartographic Association, 251
— Catholic Migration Commission, 258
— — Union of the Press, 244
— Cell Research Organization, 240
— Centre for Advanced Mediterranean Agronomic Studies, 216
— — — Technical and Vocational Training (ILO), 70
— — — Genetic Engineering and Biotechnology, 80
— — — Local Credit, 226
— — — Scientific and Technological Information (CMEA), 125
— — — Settlement of Investment Disputes (IBRD), 62
— — — Technical Expertise (ICC), 160
— — — the Study of the Preservation and Restoration of Cultural Property—ICCROM, 221
— — — Theoretical Physics (IAEA), 59
— — — Tropical Agriculture, 216
— — of Films for Children and Young People, 221
— — — Insect Physiology and Ecology, 251
— Chamber of Commerce—ICC, 160
— — — Shipping, 271
— Children's Centre, 258
— Chiropractors Association, 241
— Christian Federation for the Prevention of Alcoholism and Drug Addiction, 258
— — Service for Peace, 257
— Civil Airports Association, 271
— — Aviation Organization—ICAO, 66
— — Defence Organization, 258
— Cocoa Organization, 223
— Coffee Organization, 223
— College of Surgeons, 237
— Colour Association, 263
— Commission for Agricultural and Food Industries, 216
— — — Optics, 241
— — — Physics Education, 252
— — — Plant-Bee Relationships, 252
— — — the Conservation of Atlantic Tunas, 216
— — — — History of Representative and Parliamentary Institutions, 231
— — — — Islamic Heritage, 195
— — — — Prevention of Alcoholism and Drug Dependence, 257
— — — — Protection of the Rhine against Pollution, 257
— — — — Scientific Exploration of the Mediterranean Sea, 252
— — — — Southeast Atlantic Fisheries, 216
— — — of Agricultural Engineering, 262
— — — Jurists, 235
— — — Sugar Technology, 216
— — on Civil Status, 235
— — — Glass, 252
— — — Illumination, 263
— — — Irrigation and Drainage, 262
— — — Large Dams, 262
— — — Occupational Health, 241
— — — Radiation Units and Measurements, 252
— — — Radiological Protection, 241
— — — Zoological Nomenclature, 252
— Committee for Historical Sciences, 254
— — — Recording the Productivity of Milk Animals, 216
— — — Social Sciences Information and Documentation, 255
— — — the Diffusion of Arts and Literature through the Cinema, 221
— — of Catholic Nurses, 241
— — — Foundry Technical Associations, 262
— — — Military Medicine and Pharmacy, 239
— — — the Red Cross—ICRC, 166
— — on Aeronautical Fatigue, 263

INDEX

— — — the History of Art, 254
— Comparative Literature Association, 221
— Confederation for Printing and Allied Industries, 268
— — of Art Dealers, 268
— — — Catholic Organizations for Charitable and Social Action, 218
— — — European Sugar Beet Growers, 223
— — — Executive and Professional Staffs, 234
— — — Free Trade Unions—ICFTU, 162
— — — Societies of Authors and Composers, 221
— — — the Butchers' and Delicatessen Trade, 268
— Conference on Assistance to Refugees in Africa, 43
— — — Large High-Voltage Electric Systems, 263
— Congress and Convention Association, 265
— — of African Studies, 228
— — on Tropical Medicine and Malaria, 239
— Container Bureau, 271
— Co-operation for Development and Solidarity, 219
— Co-operative Alliance, 268
— Copper Research Association, Inc., 263
— Copyright Society, 235
— Cotton Advisory Committee, 223
— Council for Adult Education, 228
— — — Bird Preservation, 252
— — — Building Research, Studies and Documentation, 263
— — — Distance Education, 228
— — — Health, Physical Education and Recreation, 260
— — — Laboratory Animal Science, 239
— — — Philosophy and Humanistic Studies—ICPHS, 254
— — — Physical Fitness Research, 241
— — — Scientific and Technical Information, 252
— — — the Exploration of the Sea, 252
— — — Traditional Music, 222
— — — Christians and Jews, 246
— — — Environmental Law, 236
— — — French-speaking Radio and Television Organizations, 244
— — — Graphic Design Associations, 221
— — — Jewish Women, 246
— — — Museums, 221
— — — Nurses, 241
— — — Psychologists, 252
— — — Scientific Unions, 248
— — — Shopping Centres, 269
— — — Societies of Industrial Design, 269
— — — Tanners, 269
— — — the Aeronautical Sciences, 252
— — — Voluntary Agencies, 258
— — — Women, 258
— — on Alcohol and Addictions, 258
— — — Archives, 255
— — — Disability, 258
— — — Jewish Social and Welfare Services, 258
— — — Monuments and Sites, 221
— — — Social Welfare, 258
— Court of Justice, 14, 20
— Cricket Conference, 260
— Criminal Police Organization, 236
— Crops Research Institute for the Semi-Arid Tropics, 216
— Customs Tariffs Bureau, 236
— Cycling Union, 261
— Cystic Fibrosis (Mucoviscidosis) Association, 241
— Dachau Committee, 258
— Dairy Federation, 216
— Democrat Union, 231
— Dental Federation, 237
— Development Association—IDA, 64
— — Law Institute, 236
— Diabetes Federation, 237
— Earth Rotation Service, 252
— Economic Association, 226
— Electrotechnical Commission, 263
— Emergency Food Reserve, 49
— Energy Agency (OECD), 184
— Epidemiological Association, 237
— Ergonomics Association, 255
— European Construction Federation, 234
— Exhibitions Bureau, 269
— Falcon Movement, 232
— Federation for European Law, 236
— — — Household Maintenance Products, 269
— — — Housing and Planning, 256
— — — Hygiene, Preventive Medicine and Social Medicine, 241
— — — Information and Documentation, 264
— — — — Processing, 264
— — — Medical and Biological Engineering, 241
— — — — Psychotherapy, 241

— — — Parent Education, 228
— — — the Theory of Machines and Mechanisms, 262
— — — Theatre Research, 221
— — of Accountants, 226
— — — Actors, 234
— — — Agricultural Producers, 216
— — — Air Line Pilots' Associations, 234
— — — Airworthiness, 264
— — — Association Football, 261
— — — Associations of Specialists in Occupational Safety and Hygiene, 269
— — — — Textile Chemists and Colourists, 269
— — — Automatic Control, 262
— — — Automotive Engineering Societies, 264
— — — Beekeepers' Associations, 216
— — — Blue Cross Societies, 258
— — — Building and Woodworkers, 162
— — — Business and Professional Women, 234
— — — Catholic Universities, 228
— — — Cell Biology, 252
— — — Chemical, Energy and General Workers' Unions, 162
— — — Clinical Chemistry, 239
— — — Commercial, Clerical, Professional and Technical Employees—FIET, 162
— — — Consulting Engineers, 264
— — — Disabled Workers and Civilian Handicapped, 258
— — — 'Ecole Moderne' Movements, 228
— — — Educative Communities, 258
— — — Fertility Societies, 241
— — — Film Archives, 221
— — — — Producers' Associations, 221
— — — Free Teachers' Unions, 162
— — — Freight Forwarders' Associations, 271
— — — Grocers' Associations, 269
— — — Gynecology and Obstetrics, 241
— — — Hospital Engineering, 264
— — — Human Rights, 259
— — — Industrial Energy Consumers, 262
— — — Institutes for Socio-religious Research, 256
— — — 'Jeunesses Musicales', 222
— — — Journalists, 163
— — — Library Associations and Institutions, 228
— — — Medical Students Associations, 272
— — — Modern Languages and Literatures, 254
— — — Multiple Sclerosis Societies, 241
— — — Musicians, 222
— — — Newspaper Publishers, 244
— — — Operational Research Societies, 252
— — — Ophthalmological Societies, 241
— — — Organisations for School Correspondence and Exchange, 228
— — — Oto-Rhino-Laryngological Societies, 237
— — — Park and Recreation Administration, 261
— — — Pharmaceutical Manufacturers Associations, 241
— — — Philosophical Societies, 254
— — — Phonogram and Videogram Producers, 269
— — — Physical Education, 229
— — — — Medicine and Rehabilitation, 237
— — — Plantation, Agricultural and Allied Workers, 163
— — — Popular Travel Organizations, 265
— — — Press Cutting Agencies, 244
— — — Resistance Movements, 231
— — — Scientific Editors' Associations, 252
— — — Secondary Teachers, 229
— — — Senior Police Officers, 236
— — — Social Science Organizations, 256
— — — — Workers, 259
— — — Societies for Electroencephalography and Clinical Neurophysiology, 237
— — — — — Electron Microscopy, 252
— — — — — of Classical Studies, 254
— — — Stock Exchanges, 226
— — — Surgical Colleges, 241
— — — Teachers' Associations, 229
— — — — of Modern Languages, 229
— — — Textile and Clothing Workers, 209
— — — the Cinematographic Press, 244
— — — — Periodical Press, 245
— — — — Socialist and Democratic Press, 245
— — — Thermalism and Climatism, 241
— — — Tourist Centres, 265
— — — Trade Unions of Employees in Public Service, 209
— — — — — Transport Workers, 209
— — — University Women, 229
— — — Vexillological Associations, 256
— — — Workers' Educational Associations, 229

INDEX   *International Organizations*

- Fellowship of Former Scouts and Guides, 259
- — — Reconciliation, 246
- Fertilizer Industry Association, 262
- Film and Television Council, 245
- Finance Corporation—IFC, 65
- Fiscal Association, 226
- Food Information Service, 252
- Foundation of the High-Altitude Research Stations Jungfraujoch and Gornergrat, 252
- Fragrance Association, 269
- Frequency Registration Board (ITU), 76
- Fund for Agricultural Development—IFAD, 68
- Fur Trade Federation, 269
- Gas Union, 262
- Geographical Union, 248
- Glaciological Society, 252
- Graphical Federation, 163
- Group of National Associations of Manufacturers of Agro-chemical Products, 269
- — — — Scientific, Technical and Medical Publishers, 252
- Guild of Dispensing Opticians, 241
- Gymnastic Federation, 261
- Hibernation Society, 252
- Ho-Re-Ca, 265
- Hockey Federation, 261
- Hop Growers' Convention, 216
- Hospital Federation, 241
- Hotel Association, 265
- Humanist and Ethical Union, 246
- Hydrographic Organization, 253
- Industrial Relations Association, 234
- Information Management Congress, 264
- Institute for Adult Literacy Methods, 229
- — — — Children's Literature and Reading Research, 221
- — — — Comparative Music Studies and Documentation, 222
- — — — Conservation of Historic and Artistic Works, 222
- — — — Cotton, 224
- — — — Educational Planning (UNESCO), 79
- — — — Labour Studies (ILO), 70
- — — — Ligurian Studies, 256
- — — — Peace, 231
- — — — Strategic Studies, 231
- — — — Sugar Beet Research, 217
- — — — the Unification of Private Law, 236
- — — of Administrative Sciences, 256
- — — — Communications, 245
- — — — Iberoamerican Literature, 222
- — — — Philosophy, 229
- — — — Public Administration, 229
- — — — — Finance, 226
- — — — Refrigeration, 253
- — — — Seismology and Earthquake Engineering, 264
- — — — Sociology, 256
- — — — Space Law, 236
- — — — Tropical Agriculture, 217
- — — — Welding, 262
- Institution for Production Engineering Research, 262
- Interchurch Film Centre, 221
- Investment Bank, 164
- Iron and Steel Institute, 264
- Islamic Law Commission, 195
- — News Agency, 195
- Jazz Federation, 222
- Judo Federation, 261
- Juridical Institute, 236
- Jute Organization, 224
- Laboratory for Research on Animal Diseases, 217
- — — of Marine Radioactivity, 58
- Labour Conference (ILO), 69
- — Office (ILO), 69
- — Organisation—ILO, 69
- Law Association, 236
- — Commission, 18
- Lead and Zinc Study Group, 224
- League against Epilepsy, 241
- — — Rheumatism, 237
- — — for Human Rights, 231
- — — of Societies for Persons with Mental Handicap, 259
- Leprosy Association, 237
- Liaison Centre for Cinema and Television Schools, 222
- Lifeboat Federation, 259
- Livestock Centre for Africa, 217
- Maize and Wheat Improvement Center, 217
- Maritime Arbitration Organization (ICC), 160
- — — Bureau (ICC), 161
- — — Committee, 236
- — — Organization—IMO, 71
- — — Radio Committee, 245
- — — Satellite Organization, 243
- Mathematical Union, 248
- Measurement Confederation, 262
- Medical Association for the Study of Living Conditions and Health, 241
- — — Society of Paraplegia, 239
- Metalworkers' Federation, 163
- Mineralogical Association, 253
- Monetary Fund—IMF, 72
- Montessori Association, 229
- Movement of Catholic Students, 247
- Music Centre, 222
- — Council, 222
- Narcotics Control Board, 242
- Natural Rubber Organization, 224
- North Pacific Fisheries Commission, 217
- Nuclear Information System—INIS, 59
- — Law Association, 236
- — Safety Advisory Group, 59
- Numismatic Commission, 256
- Olive Oil Council, 224
- Olympic Committee, 165
- Optometric and Optical League, 242
- Organisation of Legal Metrology, 253
- Organization for Biological Control of Noxious Animals and Plants, 217
- — — — Medical Physics, 242
- — — — Motor Trades and Repairs, 269
- — — — Standardization, 264
- — — — the Study of the Old Testament, 246
- — — of Citrus Virologists, 217
- — — — Consumers' Unions, 269
- — — — Employers, 234
- — — — Experts, 234
- — — — Journalists, 245
- — — — Motor Manufacturers, 269
- — — — the Flavour Industry, 269
- — Palaeontological Association, 253
- — Patent Documentation Centre, 84
- — Peace Academy, 256
- — — Bureau, 231
- — — Research Association, 256
- — Peat Society, 253
- — Pediatric Association, 237
- — PEN, 222
- — Penal and Penitentiary Foundation, 236
- — Pepper Community, 224
- — Pharmaceutical Federation, 242
- — — Students' Federation, 272
- — Philatelic Federation, 261
- — Phonetic Association, 253
- — Phycological Society, 253
- — Planned Parenthood Federation, 259
- — Polar Motion Service, 252
- — Police Association, 236
- — Political Science Association, 231
- — Poplar Commission (FAO), 55
- — Press Institute, 245
- — — Telecommunications Council, 245
- — Primatological Society, 253
- — Prisoners' Aid Association, 259
- — Psycho-Analytical Association, 242
- — Public Relations Association, 234
- — Publishers' Association, 269
- — Radiation Protection Association, 253
- — Radio and Television Organization, 245
- — — Consultative Committee (ITU), 76
- — Rail Transport Committee, 271
- — Railway Congress Association, 271
- — Rayon and Synthetic Fibres Committee, 269
- — Reading Association, 229
- — Red Cross, 166
- — — Locust Control Organization for Central and Southern Africa, 217
- — Regional Organization of Plant Protection and Animal Health, 217
- — Rehabilitation Medicine Association, 242
- — Research Group on Wood Preservation, 264
- — Rhinologic Society, 238
- — Rice Commission (FAO), 55
- — — Research Institute, 217
- — Road Federation, 271
- — — Safety, 271
- — — Transport Union, 271

1521

INDEX — International Organizations

- — Rowing Federation, 261
- — Rubber Research and Development Board, 264
- — — Study Group, 224
- — Savings Banks Institute, 226
- — Schools Association, 229
- — Scientific Council for Trypanosomiasis Research and Control, 188
- — Sea-Bed Authority, 33
- — Secretariat for Arts, Mass Media and Entertainment Trade Unions, 163
- — Seed Testing Association, 217
- — Sericultural Commission, 217
- — Service for National Agricultural Research, 217
- — Shipowners' Association (CMEA), 125
- — Shipping Federation Ltd, 271
- — Shooting Union, 261
- — Shopfitting Organisation, 269
- — Silk Association, 224
- — Skating Union, 261
- — Ski Federation, 261
- — Social Science Council, 256
- — — Security Association, 259
- — — Service, 259
- — Society and Federation of Cardiology, 238
- — — for Business Education, 229
- — — — Cardiovascular Surgery, 242
- — — — Contemporary Music, 222
- — — — Education through Art, 229
- — — — General Semantics, 253
- — — — Horticultural Science, 217
- — — — Human and Animal Mycology, 253
- — — — Labour Law and Social Security, 236
- — — — Mental Imagery Techniques, 242
- — — — Music Education, 229
- — — — Photogrammetry and Remote Sensing, 264
- — — — Research on Civilization Diseases and Environment, 242
- — — — Rock Mechanics, 253
- — — — Soil Mechanics and Foundation Engineering, 262
- — — — Soilless Culture, 217
- — — — Stereology, 253
- — — — the Study of Medieval Philosophy, 229
- — — — Tropical Ecology, 253
- — — of Art and Psychopathology, 242
- — — — Audiology, 238
- — — — Biometeorology, 253
- — — — Blood Transfusion, 242
- — — — City and Regional Planners, 234
- — — — Criminology, 238
- — — — Developmental Biologists, 242
- — — — Geographical Pathology, 238
- — — — Internal Medicine, 238
- — — — Lymphology, 242
- — — — Neuropathology, 239
- — — — Orthopaedic Surgery and Traumatology, 242
- — — — Psychosomatic Obstetrics and Gynaecology, 238
- — — — Radiology, 242
- — — — Social Defence, 256
- — — — Soil Science, 217
- — — — Surgery, 242
- — — — Urology, 242
- — Sociological Association, 256
- — Solar Energy Society, 264
- — Solid Wastes and Public Cleansing Association, 262
- — Special Committee on Radio Interference, 264
- — Statistical Institute, 256
- — Studies Association, 256
- — Sugar Organization, 224
- — Table Tennis Federation, 261
- — Tea Committee, 224
- — — Promotion Organization, 224
- — Telecommunication Union—ITU, 76
- — Telecommunications Satellite Organization, 243
- — Telegraph and Telephone Consultative Committee (ITU), 76
- — Tennis Federation, 261
- — Textile, Garment and Leather Workers' Federation, 163
- — — Manufacturers Federation, 269
- — Theatre Institute, 222
- — Tin Council, 224
- — — Research Institute, 264
- — Trade Centre (GATT/UNCTAD), 56
- — Translations Centre, 253
- — Transport Workers' Federation, 163
- — Tropical Timber Organization, 224
- — Tungsten Industry Association, 224
- — Typographic Association, 222
- — Union against Cancer, 238
- — — — Tuberculosis and Lung Disease, 238
- — — for Conservation of Nature and Natural Resources, 253
- — — — Electro-heat, 262
- — — — Health Education, 238
- — — — Inland Navigation, 271
- — — — Oriental and Asian Studies, 254
- — — — Pure and Applied Biophysics, 248
- — — — Quaternary Research, 254
- — — — the Protection of Industrial Property (Paris Convention), 84
- — — — — — Literary and Artistic Works (Berne Union), 84
- — — — — Scientific Study of Population, 256
- — — — Vacuum Science, Technique and Applications, 264
- — — of Air Pollution Prevention Associations, 262
- — — — Anthropological and Ethnological Sciences, 255
- — — — Architects, 234
- — — — Biochemistry, 248
- — — — Biological Sciences, 248
- — — — Building Societies and Savings Associations, 226
- — — — Crystallography, 248
- — — — Family Organisations, 259
- — — — Food and Allied Workers' Associations, 163
- — — — — Science and Technology, 254
- — — — Forestry Research Organizations, 217
- — — — Geodesy and Geophysics, 248
- — — — Geological Sciences, 248
- — — — Heat Distributors, 264
- — — — Immunological Societies, 249
- — — — Latin Notaries, 236
- — — — Lawyers, 236
- — — — Local Authorities, 232
- — — — Marine Insurance, 269
- — — — Metal, 264
- — — — Microbiological Societies, 249
- — — — Nutritional Sciences, 249
- — — — Pharmacology, 249
- — — — Physiological Sciences, 249
- — — — Prehistoric and Protohistoric Sciences, 255
- — — — Producers and Distributors of Electrical Energy, 262
- — — — Psychological Science, 249
- — — — Public Transport, 271
- — — — Pure and Applied Biophysics, 249
- — — — — — Chemistry, 249
- — — — — — Physics, 249
- — — — Radio Science, 249
- — — — Railways, 272
- — — — Socialist Youth, 233
- — — — Societies for the Aid of Mental Health, 259
- — — — Students, 272
- — — — Tenants, 259
- — — — Testing and Research Laboratories for Materials and Structures, 262
- — — — the History and Philosophy of Science, 249
- — — — Theoretical and Applied Mechanics, 249
- — — — Therapeutics, 238
- — — — Young Christian Democrats, 232
- — Universities Bureau, 228
- — Veterinary Association for Animal Production, 217
- — Vine and Wine Office, 224
- — Water Resources Association, 265
- — — Supply Association, 265
- — Waterfowl and Wetlands Research Bureau, 254
- — Weightlifting Federation, 261
- — Whaling Commission, 269
- — Wheat Council, 224
- — Wool Secretariat, 224
- — — Study Group, 225
- — — Textile Organisation, 269
- — Workers' Aid, 259
- — Wrought Copper Council, 270
- — Yacht Racing Union, 261
- — Young Christian Workers, 272
- — Youth and Student Movement for the United Nations, 273
- — — Hostel Federation, 273
- — — Library, 229
- Interoceanmetall (CMEA), 125
- Inter-Parliamentary Union, 232
- INTERPOL, 236
- Interport (CMEA), 125
- Interrobot (CMEA), 125
- Intertextilmash (CMEA), 125
- Inter-University European Institute on Social Welfare, 259
- Inuit Circumpolar Conference, 232
- Islamic Capitals Organization, 195
- — Centre for Technical and Vocational Training and Research, 195

INDEX

– – – the Development of Trade, 195
– Chamber of Commerce, Industry and Commodity Exchange, 195
– Commission for Economic, Cultural and Social Affairs (OIC), 194
– – – the International Crescent, 195
– Conference, 194
– Council of Europe, 246
– Court of Justice, 195
– Development Bank, 168
– Educational, Scientific and Cultural Organization, 195
– Foundation for Science, Technology and Development, 195
– Jurisprudence Academy, 195
– Research and Training Institute, 169
– Solidarity Fund, 195
– States Broadcasting Organization, 195
ITU, 76

J

Jaycees International, 273
Jewish Agency for Israel, 232
Joint Commonwealth Societies' Council, 116
– Conference of African Planners, Statisticians and Demographers (ECA), 29
– European Torus–JET, 145
– Institute for Nuclear Research, 254

K

Kagera River Basin Organization, 220

L

LAFTA, 170
Lagos Plan of Action, 29
LAIA, 170
Lake Chad Basin Commission, 219
Latin American and Caribbean Institute for Economic and Social Planning, 28
– – Association of Development Financing Institutions, 219
– – – National Academies of Medicine, 238
– – Banking Federation, 226
– – Catholic Press Union, 245
– – Commission for Science and Technology, 219
– – Confederation of Tourist Organizations, 266
– – – – Workers (WCL), 209
– – – – Young Men's Christian Associations, 273
– – Council of Churches, 247
– – Demographic Centre, 28
– – Economic System–SELA, 219
– – Energy Organization–OLADE, 265
– – Episcopal Council, 247
– – Farmworkers Federation, 234
– – Features Agency, 219
– – Fisheries Development Organization, 219
– – Forestry Commission (FAO), 55
– – Free Trade Association–LAFTA, 170
– – Housing and Human Settlements Development Organization, 219
– – Integration Association–ALADI, 170
– – Iron and Steel Institute, 265
– – Multinational Fertilizer Marketing Enterprise, 219
– – Parliament, 232
– – Shipping Organization, 219
– – Tourism Training Institute, 219
Law Association for Asia and the Pacific, 236
– of the Sea Convention, 33
Lead Development Association, 225
League for the Exchange of Commonwealth Teachers, 115
– of Arab States, 171
– – European Research Libraries, 229
– – Red Cross and Red Crescent Societies–LORCS, 167
Liaison Organization of the European Engineering Industries, 270
Liberal International, 232
Lions Clubs International, 259
Liptako-Gourma Integrated Development Authority, 219
Lomé Convention, 149
Lutheran World Federation, 247

M

Malacological Union, 254
Mano River Union, 219

Marine Environment Protection Committee (IMO), 71
Maritime Safety Committee (IMO), 71
Médecins sans frontières, 259
Medical Women's International Association, 238
Mensa International, 257
Mercado Común Centroamericano, 108
Middle East Council of Churches, 247
– – Neurosurgical Society, 242
Miners' International Federation, 163
Moral Re-Armament, 247
Multi-fibre Arrangement, 57
Multilateral Investment Guarantee Agency, 66
Muslim World League, 247
Mutual Aid and Loan Guarantee Fund (Conseil de l'Entente), 121
– Assistance of the Latin-American Government Oil Companies, 225

N

NATO, 179
Near East Forestry Commission (FAO), 55
– – Regional Commission on Agriculture (FAO), 55
– – – Economic and Social Policy Commission (FAO), 55
New World Information and Communication Order–NWICO, 79
Niger Basin Authority, 219
Nigeria Trust Fund (ADB), 89
Non-aligned Movement, 232
NORDEL, 177
Nordic Council, 176
– – of Ministers, 177
– Cultural Fund, 178
– Economic Research Council, 177
– Federation of Factory Workers' Unions, 234
– Industrial Fund, 177
– Investment Bank, 177
– Project Fund, 177
– Society for Cell Biology, 254
NORDTEST, 177
North American Forestry Commission (FAO), 55
– Atlantic Assembly, 232
– – Council, 179
– – Treaty Organisation–NATO, 179
Northern Shipowners' Defence Club, 272
Northwest Atlantic Fisheries Organization, 217
Nuclear Energy Agency (OECD), 184

O

OAPEC, 193
OAS, 190
OAU, 186
ODECA, 232
OECD, 182
OECS, 107
Office de Recherches sur l'Alimentation et la Nutrition africaine (OCCGE), 242
– of the United Nations Disaster Relief Co-ordinator–UNDRO, 34
OIC, 194
OMVG, 219
OMVS, 219
OPEC, 196
– Fund for International Development, 199
– News Agency, 196
Open Door International, 232
Opus Dei, 247
OPW (CMEA), 125
Organisation de mise en valeur du fleuve Gambie–OMVG, 219
– for Economic Co-operation and Development–OECD, 182
– – the Collaboration of Railways, 272
– of Eastern Caribbean States–OECS, 107
– pour la Mise en Valeur du Fleuve Sénégal–OMVS, 219
– – l'aménagement et le développement du bassin de la rivière Kagera, 220
Organismo Internacional Regional de Sanidad Agropecuaria, 217
– para la Proscripción de las Armas Nucleares en la América Latina, 230
Organización de Estados Centroamericanas–ODECA, 232
– – Iberoamericanos para la Educación, la Ciencia y la Cultura, 229
– – las cooperativas de América, 232
– – Solidaridad de los Pueblos de Africa, Asia y América Latina, 232
– – Universidades Católicas de América Latina, 230
– Latinoamericana de Energía, 265
– Regional Interamericana de Trabajadores–ORIT, 162

INDEX   *International Organizations*

Organization for Co-operation in the Roller-Bearings Industry (CMEA), 125
– – Co-ordination and Co-operation in the Fight against Endemic Diseases, 242
– – – in the Fight against Endemic Diseases in Central Africa, 242
– – Museums, Monuments and Sites in Africa, 229
– – the Development of the Senegal River, 219
– – – Management and Development of the Kagera River Basin, 220
– of African Unity—OAU, 186
– – – Trade Union Unity—OATUU, 188
– – American States—OAS, 190
– – Arab Petroleum Exporting Countries—OAPEC, 193
– – Asia-Pacific News Agencies, 245
– – Central American States, 232
– – Ibero-American States for Education, Science and Culture, 229
– – Solidarity of the Peoples of Africa, Asia and Latin America, 232
– – the Catholic Universities of Latin America, 230
– – – Cooperatives of America, 232
– – – Islamic Conference, 194
– – – Petroleum Exporting Countries—OPEC, 196
– – Trade Unions of West Africa, 133
Orient Airlines Association, 272
ORIT, 162

P

Pacific Asia Travel Association, 266
– Basin Economic Council, 219
– Conference of Churches, 247
– Economic Co-operation Conference, 227
– Forum Line, 204
– Science Association, 254
– Telecommunications Council, 244
Pan-African Documentation and Information Service, 30
– Institute for Development, 220
– News Agency, 188
– Postal Union, 188
– Telecommunications Union, 188
– Youth Movement, 273
Pan American Development Foundation, 220
– – Health Organization, 192
– – Railway Congress Association, 272
Pan-American Association of Ophthalmology, 243
– Institute of Geography and History, 192
– Medical Association, 243
Pan-Pacific and South East Asia Women's Association, 259
– Surgical Association, 243
Paris Convention, 84
Parlamento Andino, 90
– Latinoamericano, 232
Parliamentary Association for Euro-Arab Co-operation, 232
Pax Romana International Catholic Movement for Intellectual and Cultural Affairs, 247
Permanent Court of Arbitration, 236
– International Association of Navigation Congresses, 262
– – – – Road Congresses, 262
– – Committee of Linguists, 255
– Inter-State Committee on Drought Control in the Sahel, 220
Population Council, 220
– Information Network for Africa, 29
Postal, Telegraph and Telephone International, 163
– Union of the Americas and Spain, 244
Preferential Trade Area for Eastern and Southern African States, 220
Press Foundation of Asia, 245
Primary Tungsten Association, 224
Public Services International, 163
Pugwash Conferences on Science and World Affairs, 254

R

Rabitat al-Alam al-Islami, 247
Red Cross, 166
Regional Animal Production and Health Commission for Asia, the Far East and the South-West Pacific (FAO), 55
– Centre for Consulting Engineering and Management (ECA), 30
– – – Engineering Design and Manufacturing (ECA), 30
– – – Adult Education and Functional Literacy in Latin America, 230
– – – Services in Surveying, Mapping and Remote Sensing, 265
– – – Training in Aerial Surveys, 265
– Commission on Farm Management for Asia and the Far East (FAO), 55

– – – Food Security for Asia and the Pacific (FAO), 55
– – – Land and Water Use in the Near East (FAO), 55
– Co-ordination Centre for Research and Development of Coarse Grains, Pulses, Roots and Tuber Crops (ESCAP), 26
– Fisheries Advisory Commission for the Southwest Atlantic (FAO), 55
– Food and Nutrition Commission for Africa (FAO/WHO/OAU), 55
– Institute for Population Studies (ECA), 29
– Network for Agricultural Machinery (ESCAP), 26
Rehabilitation International, 243
Research Centre for Islamic History, Art and Culture, 195
Rotary International, 259
Royal Asiatic Society of Great Britain and Ireland, 222
– Commonwealth Society, 116
– – – for the Blind, 115
– Over-Seas League, 117

S

SAARC, 220
SADCC, 205
Salvation Army, 247
Scientific, Technical and Research Commission (OAU), 188
SELA, 219
Service Civil International, 260
Shelter-Afrique, 89
Ship-chartering Co-ordination Bureau (CMEA), 125
SIFIDA, 89
Sistema Económica Latinoamericano—SELA, 219
Socialist Educational International, 232
– International, 232
– – Women, 233
Sociedad Interamericana de Cardiología, 240
– – – Planificación, 219
– – – Prensa, 244
Société de neuro-chirurgie de langue française, 243
– internationale financière pour les investissements et le développement en Afrique (ADB), 89
Society for International Development, 220
– of African Culture, 222
– – Comparative Legislation, 236
– – French-Speaking Neuro-Surgeons, 243
– – Saint Vincent de Paul, 260
SOLIDARIOS, 219
Soroptimist International, 247
South Asian Association for Regional Co-operation—SAARC, 220
– Pacific Bureau for Economic Cooperation—SPEC, 203
– – Commission, 201
– – Conference, 201
– – Forum, 203
– – – Fisheries Agency, 204
– – Regional Environment Programme, 201
– – Trade Commission, 204
South-East Asian Ministers of Education Organization, 230
Southern African Centre for Cooperation in Agricultural Research, 206
– – Development Co-ordination Conference—SADCC, 205
– – Transport and Communications Commission (SADCC), 205
SPEC, 203
Special Arab Assistance Fund for Africa (BADEA), 93
– Bureau for Boycotting Israel (Arab League), 172
Standing Committee on Commonwealth Forestry, 115
– Conference of Rectors, Presidents and Vice-Chancellors of the European Universities, 230
Statistical, Economic and Social Research and Training Centre for the Islamic Countries, 195
– Institute for Asia and the Pacific, 26
Stockholm International Peace Research Institute, 233
Sugar Association of the Caribbean, Inc., 225
Supreme Council for Sports in Africa, 189

T

Technical Commission for Telecommunications in Central America, 109
Theosophical Society, 247
Third World Forum, 257
Trade Unions International of Agricultural, Forestry and Plantation Workers, 211
– – – – Chemical, Oil and Allied Workers, 211
– – – – Food, Tobacco, Hotel and Allied Industries Workers, 211
– – – – Metal Workers, 211
– – – – Public and Allied Employees, 211

INDEX

– – – – Textile, Clothing, Leather and Fur Workers, 211
– – – – Transport Workers, 211
– – – – Workers in Commerce, 211
– – – – – Energy, 211
– – – – – of the Building, Wood and Building Materials Industries, 211
Transnational Association of Acupuncture and Taoist Medicine, 243
Transplantation Society, 239
Treaty for the Prohibition of Nuclear Weapons in Latin America (Tlatelolco Treaty), 59
– of Brussels (WEU), 208
– – Lagos (ECOWAS), 132
– – Montevideo (ALADI), 170
– – Rome (EEC), 136
– on the Non-Proliferation of Nuclear Weapons—NPT, 59
Tribunal de Justicia del Acuerdo de Cartagena, 90
Trilateral Commission, 233
Trusteeship Council (United Nations), 14, 20

U

UATI, 261
UDEAC, 154
UMOA, 154
UNCHS, 35
UNCTAD, 37
UNDOF, 45
UNDP, 38
UNDRO, 34
UNEP, 40
UNESCO, 77
UNFICYP, 45
UNFPA, 46
UNHCR, 42
UNICEF, 36
UNIDO, 79
UNIFIL, 45
Union douanière et économique de l'Afrique centrale—UDEAC, 154
– mondiale des voix françaises, 222
– monétaire ouest-africaine—UMOA, 154
– of African Railways, 189
– – Arab Jurists, 236
– – Banana Exporting Countries, 225
– – European Railway Industries, 272
– – – – Road Services, 272
– – Industrial and Employers' Confederations of Europe, 270
– – International Associations, 237
– – – Fairs, 270
– – – Technical Associations, 261
– – Latin American Universities, 230
– – National Radio and Television Organizations of Africa, 245
Unión de Universidades de América Latina, 230
– Internacional del Notariado Latino, 236
– Postal de las Américas y España, 244
UNITAR, 22
Unitas Malacologica, 254
United Bible Societies, 247
– Lodge of Theosophists, 247
– Nations, 3
– – Budget, 7
– – Capital Development Fund, 39
– – Centre for Human Settlements—UNCHS (Habitat), 35
– – Charter, 9
– – Children's Fund—UNICEF, 36
– – Commission on Human Settlements, 35
– – Conference on the Law of the Sea—UNCLOS, 33
– – – – Trade and Development—UNCTAD, 37
– – Conferences, 17
– – Department of Technical Co-operation for Development, 38
– – Development Fund for Women, 39
– – – Programme—UNDP, 38
– – Disaster Relief Co-ordinator's Office—UNDRO, 34
– – Disengagement Observer Force—UNDOF, 45
– – Economic and Social Commission for Asia and the Pacific—ESCAP, 25
– – – – – – Western Asia—ESCWA, 31
– – – – – Council—ECOSOC, 12, 19
– – – – – Commission for Africa—ECA, 28
– – – – – Europe—ECE, 24
– – – – – Latin America and the Caribbean—ECLAC, 27
– – Educational, Scientific and Cultural Organization—UNESCO, 77
– – Environment Programme—UNEP, 40
– – Fund for Population Activities—UNFPA, 46

International Organizations

– – – – Science and Technology for Development, 39
– – General Assembly, 9, 18
– – Good Offices Mission in Afghanistan and Pakistan—UNGOMAP, 45
– – High Commissioner for Refugees—UNHCR, 42
– – Industrial Development Fund, 80
– – – – Organization—UNIDO, 79
– – Information Centres, 6
– – Institute for Disarmament Research, 22
– – – – Training and Research—UNITAR, 22
– – Interim Force in Lebanon—UNIFIL, 45
– – International Research and Training Institute for the Advancement of Women, 22
– – Iran-Iraq Military Observer Group—UNIIMOG, 45
– – Observer Missions and Peace-Keeping Forces, 44
– – Observers, 6
– – Peace-Keeping Force in Cyprus—UNFICYP, 45
– – Population Fund—UNFPA, 46
– – Relief and Works Agency for Palestine Refugees in the Near East—UNRWA, 47
– – Research Institute for Social Development—UNRISD, 22
– – Revolving Fund for Natural Resources Exploration, 39
– – Secretariat, 15, 17
– – Security Council, 10, 19
– – Sudano-Sahelian Office, 39
– – Transport and Communications Decade in Africa, 29
– – Truce Supervision Organization—UNTSO, 44
– – Trusteeship Council, 14, 20
– – University, 23
– – Volunteers, 39
– Towns Organization, 222
Universal Alliance of Diamond Workers, 163
– Esperanto Association, 230
– Federation of Travel Agents' Associations, 266
– Postal Union—UPU, 80
Universidad de Trabajadores de América Latina, 209
University for Peace, 23
UNRISD, 22
UNRWA, 47
UNTSO, 44
UPU, 80

V

Victoria League for Commonwealth Friendship, 117
Vienna Institute for Development, 220

W

War Resisters' International, 233
Warsaw Treaty of Friendship, Co-operation and Mutual Assistance—Warsaw Pact, 207
Watch Tower Bible and Tract Society, 247
WCC, 210
WCL, 209
West Africa Rice Development Association, 225
– – Women's Association, 133
– African Clearing House, 227
– – Development Bank, 154
– – Economic Community—CEAO, 119
– – Monetary Union, 154
– – Universities' Association, 133
– – Youth Association, 133
– Indian Sea Island Cotton Association Inc., 225
– Indies Shipping Corporation, 107
Western Central Atlantic Fishery Commission (FAO), 55
– European Union—WEU, 208
WFC, 48
WFP, 49
WFTU, 211
WHO, 81
WIPO, 84
WMO, 85
WMO/ESCAP Panel on Tropical Cyclones, 26
Women's International Democratic Federation, 233
World Administrative Radio Conference (ITU), 76
– Airlines Clubs Association, 272
– Alliance of Reformed Churches (Presbyterian and Congregational), 247
– – – Young Men's Christian Associations, 273
– Association for Animal Production, 217
– – – Christian Communication, 245
– – – Educational Research, 230
– – – Public Opinion Research, 257
– – – World Federation, 233
– – of Girl Guides and Girl Scouts, 273

– – – Industrial and Technological Research Organizations, 265
– – – Judges, 237
– – – Law Professors, 237
– – – Lawyers, 237
– – – Societies of (Anatomic and Clinical) Pathology, 238
– – – Travel Agencies, 266
– – – Veterinary Food-Hygienists, 218
– – – – Microbiologists, Immunologists and Specialists in Infectious Diseases, 218
– Bank—IBRD, 60
– Blind Union, 260
– Bridge Federation, 261
– Bureau of Metal Statistics, 265
– Chess Federation, 261
– Confederation for Physical Therapy, 243
– – of Labour—WCL, 209
– – – Organizations of the Teaching Profession, 230
– – – Teachers, 209
– Conference on Religion and Peace, 247
– Congress of Authors and Composers, 221
– – – Faiths, 247
– Council of Churches, 210
– – – Credit Unions, 227
– – – Indigenous Peoples, 233
– – – Management, 270
– – – Young Men's Service Clubs, 273
– Crafts Council, 221
– Disarmament Campaign, 233
– Education Fellowship, 230
– Employment Programme, 70
– Energy Conference, 262
– Federation for Medical Education, 243
– – – Mental Health, 243
– – of Advertisers, 270
– – – Agriculture and Food Workers, 209
– – – Associations of Clinical Toxicology Centres and Poison Control Centres, 238
– – – – – Paediatric Surgeons, 238
– – – Building and Woodworkers Unions, 209
– – – Christian Life Communities, 247
– – – Clerical Workers, 209
– – – Democratic Youth, 273
– – – Diamond Bourses, 225
– – – Engineering Organizations, 265
– – – Industry Workers, 209
– – – International Music Competitions, 222
– – – Neurology, 238
– – – Neurosurgical Societies, 243
– – – Occupational Therapists, 243
– – – Public Health Associations, 243
– – – Scientific Workers, 235
– – – Societies of Anaesthesiologists, 238
– – – Teachers' Unions, 211
– – – the Deaf, 260
– – – Trade Unions—WFTU, 211

– – – United Nations Associations, 233
– Fellowship of Buddhists, 247
– Food Council, 48
– – Programme—WFP, 49
– Gold Council, 225
– Health Organization—WHO, 81
– Intellectual Property Organization—WIPO, 84
– Jewish Congress, 247
– Medical Association, 238
– Meteorological Organization—WMO, 85
– Methodist Council, 248
– Movement of Christian Workers, 235
– Organization of Gastroenterology, 238
– – – Systems and Cybernetics, 254
– – – the Scout Movement, 273
– ORT Union, 260
– Packaging Organisation, 270
– Peace Council, 233
– – through Law Center, 237
– Petroleum Congresses, 265
– Ploughing Organization, 218
– Poultry Science Association, 218
– Psychiatric Association, 238
– Sephardi Federation, 248
– Society for the Protection of Animals, 260
– – of Ekistics, 257
– Student Christian Federation, 248
– Tourism Organization, 266
– Trade Centers Association, 270
– – Union Congress, 211
– Underwater Federation, 261
– Union for Progressive Judaism, 248
– – of Catholic Philosophical Societies, 257
– – – – Teachers, 230
– – – – Women's Organisations, 248
– – – French Speakers, 222
– – – Jewish Students, 273
– – – Liberal Professions, 235
– University Service, 220
– Veterans Federation, 260
– Veterinary Association, 218
– Wide Fund for Nature, 254
– Wildlife Fund, 254
– Young Women's Christian Association, 273

Y

Youth for Development and Co-operation, 273

Z

Zinc Development Association, 225
Zone Franc, 154
Zonta International, 260